All Music Guide to Rock

The best CDs, albums & tapes

Rock, Pop, Soul, R&B, and Rap

Edited by Michael Erlewine,
Vladimir Bogdanov, and
Chris Woodstra

with Stephen Thomas Erlewine,
Richie Unterberger, and
William Ruhlmann

Miller Freeman Books

San Francisco

Published by Miller Freeman Books
600 Harrison Street, San Francisco, CA 94107
Publishers of *Guitar Player, Bass Player* and *Keyboard* magazines

un Miller Freeman
A United News & Media company

Distributed to the book trade in the U.S. and Canada by
Publishers Group West, P.O. Box 8843, Emeryville, CA 94662

Distributed to the music trade in the U.S. and Canada by
Hal Leonard Publishing, P.O. Box 13819, Milwaukee, WI 53213

Library of Congress Cataloging-in-Publication Data:
All music guide to rock : the best CDs, albums & tapes : rock, pop, soul, R&B and rap / edited by
     Michael Erlewine, Vladimir Bogdanov, and Chris Woodstra.
          p.   cm. — (AMG all music guide series)
     Includes index.
     ISBN 0-87930-376-X (trade paper)
     1. Sound recordings—Reviews. 2. Music—Discography.
     I. Erlewine, Michael. II. Bogdanov, Vladimir, 1965-. III. Woodstra, Chris. IV. Series.
ML156.9.A39 1995
016.78164'0266—dc20   95-40238
                                                 MN

Cover Design: Tom Erlewine
Production Editor: Dorothy Cox
Proofreading and Production: Carolyn Keating, Beverly Zegarski, Ellyn Hament, Colleen Wilder,
     Jim Hicks, and Wendy Davis

Printed in the United States of America
   96 97 98 99   5 4 3 2

CONTENTS

FOREWORD

Music is an essential part of my life and I am not alone in this. Tracking down the very best music is very time consuming–a fine art. Each hour of music listened to takes an hour of life; there is no such thing as an abridged recording. A guide can be a great help. There is something wonderful about the discovery of a new genre, artist, or a really great piece of music by one of our favorite artists. That is what this book is all about–a concise guide to the very best in rock music.

AMG editors Chris Woodstra, Stephen Thomas Erlewine, Richie Unterberger, and William Ruhlmann have done an outstanding job in compiling this book and in coordinating their work with that of eighty-five additional free-lance writers.

Special thanks to Vladimir Bogdanov and Ludmilla Lobenko (and to all the AMG staff) for their unceasing efforts with the database and many other aspects of this project. I would also like to thank my wife Margaret for her support. There was a lot of midnight oil burned to put this book into your hands and the spirit of the editing team, from the outset, was first rate.

—Michael Erlewine
Managing Editor, All Music Guides

ALL MUSIC GUIDE DATABASE

The *All Music Guide* is more than this book. It is an ongoing database project, the largest collection of substantive album ratings and reviews ever assembled. In fact, the 15,000+ albums listed in this book represent a rather small subset (albeit the most important one) of a very much larger collection of over 300,000 albums and reviews. The *All Music Guide* is also available in the following formats:

Books:
All Music Guide, (1400 pages, 2nd Edition, Miller Freeman Books, 1994)
All Music Guide to Jazz (Miller Freeman Books, 1994)
All Music Guide to World Music (Miller Freeman Books, available Spring 1996)
VideoHound & All-Movie Guide Stargazer (Visible Ink, 1995)

Electronic Formats:
All Music Guide CD-ROM (Selectware/Compton's)
MusicRoms (music and data) for Blues, Jazz, R&B, Latin, etc. (Selectware/Compton's)
All Music Guide (hard disk version) (Great Bear Technology)
World Beat CD-ROM (Medio)
All Movie Guide CD-ROM (Corel, 1995)

In-store Kiosks:
Musicland's SoundSite
Sam Goody's
Phonolog's The Source

Online:
Compuserve (GO ALLMUSIC)
CompuServe (GO ALLMOVIE)
Internet: ALLMUSIC.COM
            ALLMOVIE.COM
            Compact Disc Connection (BBS 408-730-9015)
            CDNow! (CDNOW.COM)
            Entertainment Connection (ECONNECTION.COM, BBS 914-426-2285)
            Music Boulevard (www.MusicBlvd.com)
Dimple Records
Reason Ware
Apple's E-World: Hollywood Online
The Microsoft Network: New Age Forum: New Age Music
The New Age (our web site) (TheNewAge.com)

We welcome your feedback. Perhaps we have left out some of your favorite albums, and/or included ones that you don't consider essential. Let us know about it. We welcome criticism, suggestions, additions, and/or deletions. The All Music Guide is a continuing project. Perhaps you are expert on the complete output of a particular artist or group and would like to participate in future editions of this book and/or our larger computer database. We would be glad to hear from you. Call or write:

ALL MUSIC GUIDE
315 Marion Avenue
Big Rapids, MI 49307
(616) 796-3437
FAX (616) 796-3060
A division of Matrix Software

ABOUT THE EDITORS

All Music Guide editor **Michael Erlewine** helped form the Prime Movers Blues Band in Ann Arbor, Michigan in 1965. He was the lead singer and played amplified harmonica in this pace-setting band (the first of its kind). The original band included a number of now well-known musicians including Iggy Pop (drums), "Blue" Gene Tyranny (piano; now a well-known avant-garde classical composer); Jack Dawson (bass; became bass player for Siegel-Schwall Blues Band); and Michael's brother Dan Erlewine (lead guitar; now monthly columnist for *Guitar Player* magazine). Michael has extensively interviewed blues performers, both in video and audio, and, along with his band, helped to shape the first few Ann Arbor Blues festivals. Today Michael is a systems programmer and director of Matrix Software. Aside from the company's work in music and film data, Matrix is the largest center for astrological programming and research in North America. Michael has been a practicing astrologer for more than 30 years and has an international reputation in that field.

Michael is also very active in Tibetan Buddhism and serves as the director of the Heart Center Karma Thegsum Choling, one of the main centers in North America for the translation, transcription, and publication of psychological texts and teachings of the Karma Kagyu Lineage of Tibetan Buddhism. Michael has been married for 23 years, and he and his wife Margaret live in Big Rapids, Michigan. They have four children.

Russian mathematician and programmer **Vladimir Bogdanov** has been involved in the design and development of *All Music Guide* databases since 1991. Having experience in many different fields such as nuclear physics, psychology, social studies and ancient chronology he now applies his knowledge to the construction of unique music reference tools utilizing the latest computer technologies. His personal interest lies in applying artificial intelligence and other mathematical methods to areas with complex semantic structures, like music, film, literature. Vladimir's ultimate goal is to provide people with the means to find what they need, even if they don't know what they are looking for.

Chris Woodstra has had a lifelong obsession with music and is an avid record collector. He has worked many years in music retail, he was a DJ, hosting programs in every genre of music, and has been a contributing editor for several local arts and entertainment magazines. Working as an editor for the *All Music Guide* database has given him the opportunity to combine his technical skills, a B.S. in Physics and Mathematics, and his love of music for the first time in his life. Being a perfectionist by nature, Chris makes sure that any information going into the database has been carefully researched and verified.

Stephen Thomas Erlewine is the associate editor of the *All Music Guide*. He studied English at the University of Michigan and was the arts editor of the school's newspaper, *The Michigan Daily*. In addition to editing the *All Music Guide,* Erlewine is a freelance writer and musician.

Richie Unterberger is a writer and editor who lives in San Francisco. He was the editor of the travel and music sections of *The Millennium Whole Earth Catalog* (Harper Collins, 1994). Between 1985 and 1991, he was the editor of *Option* magazine, the national publication devoted to coverage of all types of alternative and independently produced music. In his professional work, he is dedicated to enhancing the appreciation of the arts, culture, and history in as educational, entertaining, and affordable a fashion as possible, in both multimedia technologies and more traditional print mediums. Since watching *A Hard Day's Night* at the age of four, his favorite group has been the Beatles.

William Ruhlmann is a freelance journalist and critic covering the performing arts with a special emphasis on popular music. He is the author of a series of illustrated biographies of major popular music artists, the most recent of which is *Barbra Streisand;* his next book, *Bruce Springsteen,* will be published in the spring of 1996. Mr Ruhlmann is a regular contributor to *Goldmine* magazine, and he has written liner notes for retrospective albums by a wide range of performers including box sets by Chicago and by Tommy Dorsey and His Orchestra featuring Frank Sinatra.

ARTIST NAME (Alternate name in parentheses). ———

VITAL STATISTICS For indivdual performers, date and place of birth and death, if known.

STYLE One or more styles of music associated with each performer or group.

BIOGRAPHY A quick view of the artist's life and musical career. For major performers, proportionately longer biographies are provided.

ALBUM REVIEWS These are the 15,000+ albums selected by our editors and contributors.

KEY TO SYMBOLS ○ ● ☆ ★

☆ **ESSENTIAL RECORDINGS** Albums marked with a star should be part of any good collection of the genre. Often, these are also a good first purchase (filled star). By hearing these albums, you can get a good overview of the entire genre. These are must-hear and must-have recordings. You can't go wrong with them.

●★ **FIRST PURCHASE** Albums marked with either a filled circle or a filled star should be your first purchase. This is where to begin to find out if you like this particular artist. These albums are representative of the best this artist has to offer. If you don't like these picks, chances are this artist is not for you. In the case of an artist who has a number of distinct periods, you will find an essential pick marked for each period. Albums are listed chronologically when possible.

○ **LANDMARK RECORDINGS** Albums marked with an open circle are singled out as landmark or career turning points for the particular artist. These are classic albums—prime stuff. A land-mark recording is either a pivotal recording that marked a change in their career or a high point in their recording output.

ALBUM RATINGS: ✦ TO ✦✦✦✦✦

In addition to the stars and circles used to distinguish exceptional noteworthy albums, as explained above, all albums are rated on a scale from one to five diamonds.

ALBUM TITLE The name of the album is listed in bold as it appears on the original when possible. Very long titles have been abbreviated, or repeated in full as part of the comment, where needed.

DATE The year of an album's first release, if known. ——

RECORD LABEL Record labels indicate the current (or most recent) release of this recording. Label numbers are not included because they change frequently.

REVIEWERS The name of each review's author are given at the end of the review. "AMG" indicates a review written by the *All Music Guide* staff.

BOOKS For selected performers, reviews of relevant books are included after the album reviews. The publisher and date of publication are included in parentheses after the author. Books are also rated on a one to five scale.

David Bowie (David Robert Jones)

b. Jan. 8, 1947, Brixton, England

Dance-Pop, Hard Rock, Art-Rock/Progressive-Rock, Pop/Rock

Although he succeeded as a singer, musician, songwriter, and film and stage actor, David Bowie's chief artistic accomplishment may have been his astute manipulation of his own image as a star. When he achieved international fame in the early '70s, Bowie brought a new, highly conscious approach to stardom that involved the frequent creation of new personae. No wonder that when he made his film acting debut in 1976, he seemed so good at it: acting was what a large part of his career was about. Born in Brixton, South London, as David Jones, the singer was already playing in bands by his late teens. He changed his name to avoid confusion with Davy Jones of the Monkees. His early-'60s work was rock and blues oriented, then he turned to an Anthony Newley-style expressive show-music approach. But his breakthrough British hit "Space Oddity" (1969) was a folkie ballad about an astronaut who doesn't come home. By the time of *Hunky Dory* (1971), Bowie had turned again more toward rock, using the first of many strong collaborators, guitarist Mick Ronson.

It was Bowie's concept album *The Rise and Fall of Ziggy Stardust and the Spiders from Mars* (1972) that made him a giant star in England, where he adopted the image of his fantasy rocker, with bright red hair and futuristic stage suits. In America, "Space Oddity" became a belated hit in 1973, the year Bowie "retired" from stage work only to return in 1974 with an even more elaborate stage show. More an established star than a real record-seller in the U.S., Bowie finally hit #1 with "Fame" (cowritten by John Lennon and Carlos Alomar) in 1975. The late '70s found him collaborating with electronics whiz Brian Eno. He made a major commercial comeback in 1983 with *Let's Dance*, produced by ex-Chic coleader Nile Rodgers. . . .

After releasing two unsuccessful albums with Tin Machine, Bowie returned to his solo career in 1993, with his first solo album since 1987, *Black Tie White Noise;* although it received favorable reviews, it fell off the charts quickly. —*William Ruhlmann*

☆ **The Rise & Fall of Ziggy Stardust** / 1972 / Rykodisc ✦✦✦✦

Regarded by many to be Bowie's best album, Bowie took the melodicism developed on *Hunky Dory* and beefed it up with a punchy, rigid, freeze-dried "rock" setting. It's a perfect setting for Bowie's concept of a plastic rock star, Ziggy Stardust. *The Rise and Fall of Ziggy Stardust and the Spiders from Mars,* without a doubt, was an important defining effort for the glam rock movement. —*Rick Clark*

○ **Sound + Vision** / 1989 / Rykodisc ✦✦✦✦

An extravagantly produced three-disc-plus-CDV (video minidisc) boxed set, it digs deeper than *Changesbowie.* This features much previously unavailable stuff but comes up short on certain primary radio tracks. It's a good complement to *Changesbowie,* in spite of a little track duplication. —*Rick Clark*

★ **Changesbowie** / 1990 / Rykodisc ✦✦✦✦✦

Except for the substitution of a "Fame '90" remix over the original #1 hit, this is a great sampling of big cuts from all of Bowie's many phases, from "Space Oddity" to "Ashes to Ashes." While Bowie has had some classic albums, the uninitiated should start here. —*Rick Clark*

BOOKS

✦✦✦ **Bowie: An Illustrated Record**, by Roy Carr & Charles Shaar Murray (Avon, 1981). The best book (actually, one of the few) to focus on Bowie's music, rather than his public persona. Includes detailed analysis, often entertainingly biting, of every one of Bowie's albums and singles, even dating back to the many obscure nonhits he released in the '60s before finding stardom with "Space Oddity." Tons of good photos and press clippings, as well as a couple of overview essays and a lengthy discography, including bootlegs. —*Richie Unterberger*

ACKNOWLEDGMENTS

This book would not have been possible without the guidance of Andrew Gun McIver and Ven. Khenpo Kathar Rinpoche.

Special thanks to John Dougan and Bruce Eder. Thanks to Brad Balfour, Bruce Bastin, Carl Bierling, Dave Datta, John DeBlasio, Doug Henkle, Pat Higgins, the staff of Holland Compact Disc, Terry Housome, Matt Kelsey, Bob Koester, Archie Patterson, Neal Umphred, and Panther White.

To our production staff...

Special thanks to Karen Barto, Nancy Lee Beilfuss, John Bush, Julie Clark, Mark Donkers, Steve Huey, Deborah Kirby, Ludmila Lobenko, Angie Pullen, and Sara Sytsma.

and to all the Matrix Staff...

Kyle Alexander, Irene Baldwin, Richard Batchelder, Sandra Brennan, Stephanie Clement, Walt Crocket, Teresa Swift-Eckert, Brandy Ellison, Iotis Erlewine, Margaret Erlewine, Phillip Erlewine, Stephen Erlewine, Tom Erlewine, Kevin Fowler, Jeff Jawer, Mary King, Madeline Koperski, Jennifer Page, John Pattee, Forest Ray, Tom Roberts, Robert Walker.

All Music Guide to Rock

Editors:
Michael Erlewine
Vladimir Boganov
Chris Woodstra
Stephen Thomas Erlewine
Richie Unterberger
William Ruhlmann

Contributors:
Steve Aldrich
Ashley S. Battel
George Bedard
Vladimir Bogdanov
Myles Boisen
John Book
Rob Bowman
Rick A. Bueche
Scott Bultman
John Bush
Matt Carlson
Bil Carpenter
Kenneth M. Cassidy
Jim Chrispell
Rick Clark
Bill Dahl
Hank Davis
Michael P. Dawson
Robert DeFreitas
Donna DiChario
Jim Dorsch
John Dougan
Bruce Eder

Iotis Erlewine
Meredith Erlewine
Michael Erlewine
Michael Anne Erlewine
Stephen Thomas Erlewine
Colin Escott
John Floyd
Niles J. Frantz
Michael Freedberg
Robert Gordon
Tom Graves
Will Grega
Jeff Hannusch
Dan Heilman
Larry Hoffman
Steve Huey
Eddie Huffman
Mark A. Humphrey
David Jehnzen
Julian Katz
Michael Katz
Kit Kiefer
Cub Koda
Linda Kohanov
Paul Kohler
Larry Lapka
Kip Lornell
Dennis MacDonald
Brian Mansfield
Richard Meyer
David A. Milberg
Gary Mollica

Michael G. Nastos
Jim O'Neal
Jas Obrecht
Christine Ohlman
Richard Pack
Roch Parisien
Archie Patterson
Heather Phares
Matthew Plichta
J. Poet
Bob Porter
Laura Post
Jim Powers
Bruce Boyd Raeburn
Chip Renner
William Ruhlmann
Ali Sinclair
Richard Skelly
Sara Sytsma
David Szatmary
Jeff Tamarkin
Bob Tarte
"Blue" Gene Tyranny
Neal Umphred
Richie Unterberger
David Vinopal
Stephen Winick
Chris Woodstra
Jim Worbois
Ron Wynn

INTRODUCTION

by Stephen Thomas Erlewine and Chris Woodstra

Rock & roll is entering its fifth decade of existence. In that time, stacks of worthwhile recordings have piled up. And while live rock and roll is electrifying, the history of the music is for better or worse passed on through recordings. *The All Music Guide to Rock* doesn't attempt to tell the history of rock & roll, it offers a guide to performers and their recordings. Like the previous books in the *All Music* series, *The All Music Guide to Rock* features contributions from several well-known writers. The intent is not to draw comparisons between the artists, but to provide a guide to the artists themselves; to find out the best recordings from Pat Boone to Michael Bolton, from Elvis Presley to Madonna, judging each artist's music on its own terms.

Given our space limitations, certain artists had to be excluded, yet we included a broad range of musicians reflecting the wide range of stylistic variations rock & roll has taken over the years. Rock & roll encompasses blues, R&B, country, traditional pop, folk, vaudeville, British music hall, electronic music—nearly every form of music finds its way into rock & roll, and every subgenre of rock & roll has found its way into *The All Music Guide to Rock.* That doesn't mean every rockabilly or doo wop singer, or every heavy metal or punk band has been included. Nevertheless, you'll find scores of rockabilly, doo wop, metal, and punk records in here, along with psychedelia, garage rock, British Invasion, pub rock, low-fi, post-punk, techno, house, Brill Building pop, Southern rock...the vast variety of styles that make popular music so intriguing.

What makes rock & roll so interesting is the sheer amount of variety it offers. It's been a long road from Chuck Berry and Elvis Presley to Dr. Dre and Pavement, and all the side roads have something interesting to offer. It may be the songcraft of Neil Diamond or it could be the trance-inducing electronics of the Orb. It could be the direct rock & roll of Bob Seger and John Mellencamp or the minimalistic approaches of the Ramones, AC/DC and Unrest, who all take simplicity in different sonic directions. Is it all rock and roll? No, in the conventional three-chord sense it's not, but it is all popular music that owes its existence to rock & roll. There's not an obvious link between Sonic Youth and Chuck Berry, yet there are links between Chuck Berry and the Velvet Underground, and the Velvet Underground and Sonic Youth.

The All Music Guide to Rock tries to explain Sonic Youth to Chuck Berry fans and, just as importantly, Chuck Berry to Sonic Youth fans. In the meantime, the book explores unheralded subgenres like garage and surf rock that rarely get space in conventional rock books. It also spotlights cult figures from the Celibate Rifles to Scott Walker that may have never gotten popular recognition, yet they had a small impact in shaping popular music—or they simply made intriguing, interesting music. *The All Music Guide to Rock* may not explore every genre of rock & roll in depth, yet it helps make sense of the ever-changing entity that is rock & roll. If the book does anything, it should open you up to some terrific music you may not have heard before.

As the decades have passed, the music has changed and so have the recording formats. For the past decade, the compact disc has been the dominant medium, replacing the long-playing album. However, in the early years of rock & roll, the single was the primary method of recording. Artists like Elvis Presley, Chuck Berry, Fats Domino, Buddy Holly, the Everly Brothers, and Jerry Lee Lewis didn't think in terms of making cohesive full-length albums— they were making their next hit single. Around 1966, long-playing albums became the dominant musical format in rock & roll, with British Invasion bands like the Beatles and the Kinks making records that were tied together by both lyrical and musical themes. Soon, artists were putting more thought into making cohesive albums. Initially, this meant "concept albums"— records like The Who's *Tommy,* The Kinks' *Arthur,* or the Moody Blues' *Days of Future Passed* —that told specific stories with their songs. Concept albums gave way to a wave of progressive rock bands that wrote music that could only be told over the course of a full-length album, as well as psychedelic bands like the Grateful Dead and Jefferson Airplane and hard rock bands like Led Zeppelin that didn't have hit singles, they had hit albums. Ever since the late '60s, bands have been concentrating their creative efforts on full-length albums, and have had long, successful careers without the benefit of hit singles. Consequently, albums were more important to the careers of '70s rockers like David Bowie and Queen than they were to the careers of Duane Eddy or the Ventures. That explains why Bowie and Queen have more albums listed than Eddy or the Ventures—it's not a critical judgment about which band is more important, it's a reflection of their particular era.

Within the text are biographies and reviews of 2,500 artists. The goal of *The All Music Guide* is not to draw comparisons between Carpenters and Mötley Crüe albums, or pit the Beatles against the Clash. Rather, the intent of *The All Music Guide to Rock* is to provide a guide to the recordings of a particular artist, offering a biography and description of the music, as well as capsule reviews of their albums. If the description of a musician intrigues you, the book also provides a starting point for each artist, in the form of a filled-in circle or star. Each entry in the book has a filled-in circle, with the possible exception of artists with only one album. *The All Music Guide to Rock* also highlights each artist's best or most important records with an empty circle. Within each entry, to the right of the album's title, is a rating for the album itself, on a scale from one to five. These ratings are based on the artist themselves, not of their overall worth (for instance, a four-diamond Whitney Houston album is not necessarily the same as a four-diamond Black Sabbath album). The only global rating in the book is a star, which signals an album that is the best of its genre—in other words, it's essential listening.

Many of the artists included in *The All Music Guide to Rock* have a fairly complete discography, but some of the records were not reviewed because of space constraints. Similarly, some artists have selected listings, particularly acts that only had a handful of hits. On the other hand, musicians like James Brown and Elvis Presley have simply released too many albums for each album to be reviewed. In this case, all of their major records have been included, along with some interesting minor albums that help to showcase the depth of their artistry. Overall, even when records haven't been reviewed, they have been rated, providing a guideline, if not a description.

The All Music Guide to Rock has been culled from a much larger database that is available in several electronic formats as listed in the front of the book. *The All Music Guide* is constantly updated and corrected, so if you spot any mistakes or inconsistencies, please contact us.

A

Aaliyah

Urban

Detroit-born contemporary R&B singer Aaliyah (born Aaliyah Haughton) became an overnight sensation in 1994 with her debut album, *Age Ain't Nothing but a Number* and its two hit singles, "Back & Forth" and "At Your Best (You Are Love)." Aaliyah was only 15 years old when her debut record was released in 1994. Her age became controversial when news of her marriage to her producer, R. Kelly, was leaked out at the end of the year. *—Stephen Thomas Erlewine*

○ **Age Ain't Nothing But a Number** / 1994 / Blackground ♦♦♦♦

Aaliyah has a pleasant voice, but the real reason the teenager's debut album, *Age Ain't Nothing But A Number,* was a hit is the radio-ready production courtesy of R. Kelly, her husband. Kelly wraps Aaliyah's voice in layers of lush synths and deep grooves, while adding songs that are frequently better than the ones on his own album, *12 Play. Age* may have its share of filler, but its singles are slyly seductive. *—Stephen Thomas Erlewine*

ABBA

Group, Dance-Pop, Pop

During the '70s, ABBA's slick light Euro-pop made them one of the world's most successful acts, particularly outside America. Each of the four members—Benny Andersson, Bjorn Ulvaeus, Anni-Frid (Frida) Lyngstad, and Agnetha Faltskog—had already enjoyed some professional success previous to the band's formation. The spirited single "Waterloo" earned ABBA much recognition when they won the 1974 Eurovision Song Contest. From there, ABBA scored a seemingly endless string of predominantly bouncy pop hits, featuring well-crafted catchy melodies (some quite good) and the band's distinctive (but occasionally shrill) multilayered female vocals. The string ran out when ABBA disbanded in 1982, with Lyngstad and Faltskog going solo and Andersson and Ulvaeus writing for the musical theater. Of the 14 American Top 40 pop hits, "Dancing Queen" was ABBA's biggest, hitting #1 in 1976. In Great Britain, ABBA hit the Top 40 25 times between 1974 and 1983, scoring nine #1 hits. ABBA's influence can be heard in such U.K. groups as Erasure (who recorded a tribute EP, *Abba-esque*) as well as in the Swedish groups Roxette and Ace of Base. *—Rick Clark and William Ruhlmann*

Ring Ring / 1973 / Polar ♦♦

This, the first album by the group later called ABBA (they were called Bjorn, Benny, Agnetha & Anni-Frid at the time), originally was released only in Sweden; England and America didn't show any interest until the group won the Eurovision Song Contest with "Waterloo" the following year, although "Ring Ring" had been a hit in several other countries. It's clear that this team has spent a lot of time listening to albums like *Abbey Road* and *Honky Chateau,* not to mention *Sweet Baby James.* But they've also been absorbing a broad range of the pop charts of the late '60s and early '70s. At the same time, they haven't put together the ABBA sound yet. For one thing, the men sing almost as much as the women, and for another, Benny Andersson and Bjorn Ulvaeus have underproduced the recordings, even as they have overarranged the music. (Eventually released in Europe, *Ring Ring* has not been released officially in the U.S., although import copies are readily available.) *—William Ruhlmann*

Waterloo / 1974 / Atlantic ♦♦

ABBA's second (and U.S. debut) album contains the title track, an American Top Ten hit and U.K. chart-topper, as well as "Honey, Honey," a minor U.S. hit, and "Ring Ring," a minor British hit co-written by the ABBA team of Benny Andersson, Stig Anderson, and Bjorn Ulvaeus with Neil Sedaka and Phil Cody. It is, however, an uneven collection ranging from reggae to near-hard rock, demonstrating that ABBA had not yet gotten its pop assembly line fully into operation. *—William Ruhlmann*

Abba / 1975 / Atlantic ♦♦♦

ABBA appears on the cover of this album sitting in the back of a limousine and drinking champagne, which may have been intended as an ironic comment on their one-hit wonder status at the time but became an apt reflection of their status after this record's success. The lead-off track is the irresistible "Mamma Mia," their second U.K. chart topper and a U.S. Top 40 hit, and also included are the equally catchy "SOS" (Top Ten in Britain, Top 40 in America) and the minor U.K. hit "I Do, I Do, I Do, I Do, I Do," which actually did better in the U.S. *—William Ruhlmann*

○ **Arrival** / Jan. 1977 / Atlantic ♦♦♦♦

ABBA's appropriately titled fourth album of new material appeared after the group had "arrived" as major stars. It featured "Dancing Queen," a tame disco number that went to #1 in both the U.S. and U.K., as well as "Knowing Me, Knowing You" (another U.K. #1 that hit the Top 40 in the U.S.) and a third single, "Money, Money, Money." *—William Ruhlmann*

○ **The Album** / Feb. 1978 / Atlantic ♦♦♦♦

ABBA's fifth new studio album continued their phenomenal international success, featuring the U.K. #1s "The Name Of The Game" and "Take A Chance On Me," and achieving ABBA's highest ever showing in the U.S. LP charts: it reached the Top 20 and sold a million copies in six months. It was also musically ambitious, featuring "The Girl With The Golden Hair," described as "3 scenes from a mini-musical," which anticipated the theatrical ambitions Andersson and Ulvaeus would fulfill with *Chess* six years later. *— William Ruhlmann*

Voulez-Vous / Jun. 1979 / RCA ♦♦

Internationally, it was business as usual for ABBA on its sixth studio album, which included the hits "Voulez Vous," "I Have A Dream," "Angeleyes," "Does Your Mother Know," and "Chiquitita," all of which made the U.K. Top Five. But America had begun to lose interest: the album stopped at gold (500,000 copies), with only "Chiquitita" getting into the Top 40. *—William Ruhlmann*

Super Trouper / Dec. 1980 / Atlantic ♦♦

Always pop-savvy, ABBA took account of the passing of disco with this release and moved back toward the pop-rock sound more typical of their early albums with this, their seventh. They were rewarded with their last big U.S. hit, "The Winner Takes It All," plus two more American chart entries and an uptick in album sales. In the U.K., they continued to roll along, with the title track becoming their final #1 single. *—William Ruhlmann*

The Visitors / 1981 / Atlantic ♦♦♦

ABBA's swan song was also perhaps their most musically sophisticated album. Although it was short on big hits ("The Visitors" and "When All Is Said And Done" charted in the U.S., "One Of Us" and "Head Over Heels" in the U.K., with only "One Of Us" making the Top 10), it was a consistent record imbued with a sense of the pressures that were splitting the group (the title track was subtitled "Crackin' Up"). *—William Ruhlmann*

○ **The Singles: The First Ten Years** / 1982 / Atlantic ✦✦✦✦
This 23-track double LP contains 16 of ABBA's 20 U.S. chart entries and 22 of their 25 U.K. hits. Especially notable are the group's final new single, "Under Attack," and the terrific ballad "The Day Before You Came," which had previously appeared in the U.S. only as a non-LP B-side. This collection supersedes the previous *Greatest Hits* albums, and, since ABBA was a singles band, captures their essence. — *William Ruhlmann*

Abba Live / 1986 / Atlantic ✦✦
ABBA turns in close copies of their studio hits in these live performances recorded between 1977 and 1981. For completists only. — *William Ruhlmann*

★ **Gold: Greatest Hits** / 1993 / Polydor ✦✦✦✦✦
A 19-track, 77-minute CD collection released in Europe in 1992 and in the U.S. the following year to cash in on the resurgence of interest in ABBA, this is an excellent single-disc hits package, and, given that the group's catalog was sold to PolyGram in 1989, the only one that's available in the U.S., where the earlier *Greatest Hits*, *Greatest Hits, Vol. 2*, and *The Singles: The First Ten Years* (all originally released on LP by Atlantic) are out of print. — *William Ruhlmann*

○ **More Abba Gold** / Jun. 1, 1993 / Polydor ✦✦✦✦
All of the singles and important album tracks that aren't featured on *Gold* are available on *More ABBA Gold*. — *Stephen Thomas Erlewine*

○ **Thank You For The Music [Box]** / Apr. 18, 1995 / Polydor ✦✦✦✦
Released in Europe in October 1994 and in the U.S. six months later, *Thank You For The Music* is the ABBA box set retrospective, tracing their ten years of record making, 1972-1982, including 52 previously released tracks on the first three discs, plus a fourth disc of rarities. Listening to all the singles, plus scattered album tracks and B-sides, provides a clear picture of the group's development. Early on, there is considerable stylistic experimentation, as these pop dabblers ape everything from Phil Spector's "Wall of Sound" rock to big-band swing. But after "Dancing Queen," they find their niche in disco, and the second disc is loaded with hit songs anchored to the familiar bass-heavy walking beat and swooping synths-meant-to-sound-like-strings that defined that most '70s of genres. On the third disc, covering their last years, ABBA returns to the more propulsive pop/rock of early classics like "SOS" and "Mamma Mia," revving up the tempo in acknowledgment of the arrival of new wave. Wracked by romantic discord, they also achieve somewhat more meaningful lyrics before calling it a day. In the album's liner notes, the band members register mild protest at the inclusion of unreleased material on the fourth disc—what they finished and liked, they released, they note. Fair warning. Most prominent in a collection of alternate takes, miscellaneous B-sides, foreign language recordings, and TV soundtracks is the 23½-minute "ABBA Undeleted," a medley of 15 song fragments and Swedish studio chatter that suggests ABBA had a few more hits in them if they had found the time to finish them off. Nevertheless, this remains "fan only" material. (This album is not to be confused with the 1983 compilation of the same title released by Epic Records in the U.K.) — *William Ruhlmann*

Gregory Abbott

Soul, Urban
Gregory Abbott is a soul singer from New York. He studied psychology at Boston and Stanford universities and taught English at the University of California at Berkeley before launching his singing career in 1986. He scored a #1 hit on both the pop and R&B charts with "Shake You Down" (1986) and reached the R&B Top Ten with "I Got the Feelin' (It's Over)" (1987) and "I'll Prove It to You" (1988). — *William Ruhlmann*

● **Shake You Down** / 1986 / Columbia ✦✦✦✦
Great soul can come from the most unlikely of places. Abbott was a Wall Street researcher with the same silky croon as Marvin Gaye. He and some friends set up a home studio and produced the huge 1987 hit, "Shake You Down," the best thing from his debut. — *John Floyd*

I'll Prove It to You / 1988 / Columbia ✦✦✦

ABC

Group, Dance-Pop, New Wave, Pop/Rock
One of the more popular new wave bands of the early '80s, the British group ABC built upon the detached, synthesized R&B-pop of David Bowie and Roxy Music, adding a self-conscious, campy

sense of theatrics and style. Under the direction of vocalist Martin Fry, the group scored several catchy, synth-driven dance-pop hits in the early '80s, including "Poison Arrow," "Look of Love," and "Be Near Me." During the late '70s, Fry ran his own fanzine, *Modern Drugs*, while he attended Sheffield University; like many fanzines, *Modern Drugs* concentrated on local bands, as well as fashion.

ABC formed in 1980, after Fry interviewed the Vice Versa members Mark White (guitar) and Stephen Singleton (saxophone) for his fanzine. The two musicians asked Fry to join their band as a vocalist, and he soon became part of the group; the lineup also featured drummer David Robinson and bassist Mark Lickley. Soon, Fry had taken control of the electronic band, steering them in a more pop-oriented direction and the group was renamed ABC. By the fall of 1981, the band had signed a record contract with Phonogram Records, which agreed to distribute ABC's own label, Neutron. ABC released their first single, "Tears Are Not Enough," in November; it peaked at number 19 on the U.K. charts. Before they recorded their second single, Robinson left the band and was replaced by David Palmer in early 1982. Two singles, "Poison Arrow" and "The Look of Love," became British Top Ten hits in the spring, paving the way for their debut album, *The Lexicon of Love*, to enter the charts at number one. "All of My Heart" also became a Top Ten hit in the fall of 1982.

Toward the end of 1982, the group began concentrating on the United States. Their American success was helped greatly by the fledgling MTV network, which aired videos for "The Look of Love" and "Poison Arrow" frequently, making both singles Top 25 hits in the spring of 1983. Palmer left the band in the summer of 1983, as ABC was recording their second album. Featuring a harder, more rock sound driven by guitars, not keyboards, *Beauty Stab* was released late in 1983. Supported by the number 18 single "That Was Then but This Is Now," the album didn't perform as well as the debut, peaking at number 12; the record also was a commercial disappointment in the U.S., peaking at number 69, with the single only reaching number 89. Late in 1984, ABC—now consisting solely of Fry and White, augmented by various session musicians—released "(How to Be A) Millionaire," which failed to put a halt to their commercial slide. Following its release, the duo moved to New York, where they added David Yarritu and Eden to the group; neither member could play or sing—they were added for the visual effect.

Released at the beginning of 1985, the light, catchy "Be Near Me" became a hit single in Britain, climbing to number 26. Due to the single's success, *How to Be A Zillionaire* became a Top 30 hit in both the U.K. and U.S. "Be Near Me" was released as a U.S. single toward the end of 1985 and it became the group's first Top Ten hit. Even though they had a fair amount of success in 1985, ABC wasn't able to capitalize on their fortunes in 1986, as the subsequent singles stalled on the charts. Fry was also ill for most of the latter half of the year; he recovered in 1987 and began writing and recording with White. In the summer of 1987, ABC released "When Smokey Sings," a tribute to Smokey Robinson; the single was a major hit, reaching number five in the U.S. and number 11 in the U.K. *Alphabet City* followed that fall, peaking at number seven in the U.K. and number 48 in the U.S. Two years later, they released *Up*, which only charted in the U.K. *Absolutely*, a greatest hits collection, made it into the British Top Ten upon its release in 1990. — *Stephen Thomas Erlewine*

○ **The Lexicon of Love** / 1982 / Mercury ✦✦✦✦
ABC's stylish debut successfuly melded the cool detachment of Bryan Ferry and David Bowie with a more pop-oriented production than either Roxy Music or Bowie. Even if the songs tended to blend together over the course of the album, the record was successful, scoring two hits with "The Look of Love" and "Poison Arrow." — *Stephen Thomas Erlewine*

Beauty Stab / 1983 / Mercury ✦✦✦
For their second album, ABC toned down the synths and turned up the guitars, making an inconsistent set of rocking, Roxy-styled pop that does have its impressive moments, particularly the single "That Was Then but This Is Now." — *Stephen Thomas Erlewine*

How to Be a . . . Zillionaire! / 1985 / Mercury ✦✦✦
Darkly humorous dance grooves incorporate some hip-hop. The album contains the hit "Be Near Me." — *Rick Clark*

Alphabet City / 1987 / Mercury ✦✦✦
Possibly ABC's best album effort—soulful, sleek, modern dance music. — *Rick Clark*

Up / 1989 / Mercury ♦♦
ABC's formula started to sound tired on their fifth album, which completed their contract with PolyGram, and unlike their first four, missed the charts in the U.S., while managing only one week in the U.K. charts. The singles "One Better World" and "The Real Thing" were likewise only minor hits in England and nonentities in America. —*William Ruhlmann*

● **Absolutely ABC: The Best of ABC** / 1990 / Mercury ♦♦♦♦
Singer/songwriter Martin Fry's Bowie/Roxy vocal affectations and sweeping productions (aided by Mark White) are showcased to great effect on this fine anthology, which contains all of this act's essential dance-pop hits. —*Rick Clark*

Abracadabra / 1991 / MCA ♦♦
The production and dance grooves are more atmospheric, while borrowing from the mid-'70s Philly soul arrangements. —*Rick Clark*

Paula Abdul

b. Jun. 19, 1962, Los Angeles, CA
Dance-Pop, Urban, Pop
In the wake of Madonna's success, many dance-pop divas filled the charts, but out of them all, Paula Abdul was the only one that sustained a career. The former L.A. Lakers cheerleader and choreographer began to make inroads in pop music when she was hired as an assistant dance director on the Jacksons' "Victory" tour, which led to a job choreographing Janet Jackson's videos for *Control*. Abdul's work on Jackson's videos helped make the album a hit, making her a sought-after choreographer. After working on *The Tracy Ullman Show* and videos for ZZ Top, Duran Duran, and the Pointer Sisters, Abdul began a recording career, releasing her debut album, *Forever Your Girl*, in 1988. The first two singles drawn from the record were moderate hits, but the release of "Straight Up" at the end of the year made her a superstar. Staying at the top of the charts for three weeks, "Straight Up" began a string of six #1 singles (with "The Way That You Love Me" recharting at number three in 1989) that ran through the summer of 1991.

Abdul's singles were hits not because her singing was exceptional—her voice is thin and transparent—but because she worked with savvy producers that had a knack for picking songs with solid pop and dance hooks. Abdul's spectacular big-budget videos helped push the sales of *Forever Your Girl* past seven million in the U.S. alone. While her second album, 1991's *Spellbound*, wasn't as successful, it still sold over three million copies and spent two weeks at number one.

After *Spellbound*, Abdul took a few years off. During that time, she successfully fought a lawsuit filed by a former backup singer that alleged it was she, not Abdul, that had sung on *Forever Your Girl*. Abdul released her third album, *Head over Heels*, in the summer of 1995. —*Stephen Thomas Erlewine*

● **Forever Your Girl** / Jun. 1988 / Virgin ♦♦♦♦
Choreographer-turned-diva Abdul debuts with this upbeat collection of dance-pop that yielded a string of Top 40 hits, including four #1 smashes—"Straight Up," "Cold Hearted," "Opposites Attract," and "Forever Your Girl." —*Donna DiChario*

Shut up & Dance: Dance Mixes / 1990 / Virgin ♦♦
Abdul makes a valiant effort to translate her extremely popular dance hits into a mix that would make them even more comfortable in a dance club setting. However, the overuse of numerous sound effects turn some songs such as "Straight Up" into nothing more than a continual stream of background noise. Perhaps it would have been best if Abdul were to have left these popular hits in their original form. —*Ashley S. Battel*

Spellbound / 1991 / Captive/Virgin ♦♦♦
This fine sophomore set includes sweet pop-soul balladry ("Rush, Rush") and the usual dance tunes ("The Promise of a New Day"). —*Bil Carpenter*

Head Over Heels / 1995 / Captive/Virgin ♦♦
Four years after the release of *Spellbound*, Paula Abdul returned with the sleek *Head over Heels*. *Head over Heels* doesn't sound all that different from her previous album; it incorporates a couple of current dance trends without ever letting the beats dominate the accessible pop melodies of the songs. Unfortunately, the songs are more well-constructed than well-written—all of the arrangements hide the fact that the songs usually lack strong hooks. That weakness is accentuated by the length of the album. Approaching

nearly 70 minutes, *Head over Heels* spends too much time with lesser songs. Abdul remains an engaging presence, even with her limited vocal talents, and the record's best songs—the slinky "My Love Is for Real," for instance—are more mature and seductive than her earlier works, showing that she may grow old gracefully. —*Stephen Thomas Erlewine*

The A-Bones

Group, Rock & Roll
Hailing from Brooklyn, NY, the A-Bones play sloppy and greasy rock with a maniacal intensity. Named after a song by the Trashmen and fronted by vocalist Billy Miller and drummer Miriam Linna, the A-Bones started life as an offshoot to their earlier, rockabilly-tinged combo, the Zantees. Their love for the awesomely arcane is reflected in the choice of material they cover ("Go, Go, Go for Louie's Place") and the original songs they've added to the underbelly of rock's history. They were most recently seen rocking their brains out in the science-fiction cult movie, *I Was a Teenage Mummy*. No two ways about it, the A-Bones are definitely a noise combo to be reckoned with. —*Cub Koda*

Free Beer for Life! / 1988 / Norton ♦♦♦
A six-song mini-LP featuring sloppiness and stupidity galore. "Musical" highlights include "Devil Dance," "Spinning My Wheels," "Mumbo Jumbo," and a righteous cover of Mike Fern's immortal "A-Bomb Bop." —*Cub Koda*

● **The Life of Riley** / 1991 / Norton ♦♦♦♦
An album chock-full of stupid, greasy, stompin', wack-oid rock & roll by America's premier grease-pit combo. Atonal highlights include "El Kabong," "Go Go Go for Louie's Place," and drummer Miriam Linna's lyrical scream-fest, "Go Betty Go." —*Cub Koda*

I Was a Teenage Mummy / 1992 / Norton ♦♦♦
Music from the original motion-picture soundtrack of this black & white sci-fi cult-classic for the '90s. Titles include "Mark of the Squealer," "Little Egypt," "The Fez Man Walks," and "Mum's the Word." —*Cub Koda*

Music Minus Five / 1993 / Norton ♦♦♦
New York's A-Bones continue their vendetta against melody with this 14-track album. Featuring sloppy jalopy renditions of "Bonomo Twine Time," "What the Heck," and "Little Bo Pete," it's obvious from listening that they didn't spend their previous royalties on music lessons. —*Cub Koda*

Above the Law

Group, Rap
The Los Angeles rap crew Above The Law consists of the Cold 187um (Gregory Hutchinson), KM.G the Illustrator (Kevin Dulley), Go Mack (Authur Goodman), and Total K-oss (Anthony Stewart). On their records, Above The Law mix hard-hitting tales of urban violence with explicit sex talk and/or commentary. The group released their first album, *Livin' like Hustlers*, in 1990. —*Ron Wynn*

Livin' Like Hustlers / 1990 / Ruthless ♦♦♦
Prototype gangsta rap. —*Ron Wynn*

○ **Vocally Pimpin' EP** / 1991 / Epic ♦♦♦♦
Improved production and studio techniques, and sharper quips. —*Ron Wynn*

● **Black Mafia Life** / 1993 / Warner Brothers ♦♦♦♦
While the controversy rages on regarding "gangsta" rap, such groups as Above The Law keep issuing sordid, offensive collections chronicling their misadventures. As usual, their narratives are heavily obscene, sprinkled with violent, often sexist imagery. But unlike some others, there's no humor or absurdist logic operating as a counterbalance to the constant refrain of guns and "ho's." You could argue that groups like Above The Law aren't glamorizing the brutal, ugly lifestyle depicted in "Never Missin' A Beat" or "Pimpology 101" but relating it; the cold, callous tone and complete disrespect for life expressed speak far more effectively about the urgency of the situation than tons of strident anti-"gangsta" rhetoric. —*Ron Wynn*

Uncle Sam's Curse / 1994 / Ruthless ♦♦♦

Colonel Abrams

Urban
Detroit-born vocalist Colonel Abrams (his actual name) enjoyed moderate success in the late '80s, singing in a harsh, terse soul style while fitting his voice into a dance, rather than R&B or ur-

ban, setting. Abrams was in the group Conservative Manor with his brother Morris in the late '60s, then sang lead vocals for 94 East in 1976. Their roster included Prince on guitar. Abrams later joined Surprise Package, a New Jersey group. He scored a mild hit in 1984 with the ballad "Leave the Message Behind the Door" for New York's Streetwise Records. The follow-up, "Music Is the Answer," was an international dance hit and earned him a deal with MCA in 1985. He had more success with the singles "Trapped," "I'm Not Gonna Let You," and "How Soon We Forget" in the late '80s, and also recorded a pair of LPs. Abrams' single "Bad Timing" was produced by Cameo's Larry Blackmon for the independent Horrus label in 1990. — *Ron Wynn*

● **Colonel Abrams** / 1986 / MCA ✦✦✦✦
Colonel Abrams straddled the category of love man and disco dancer on his debut album (with a touch of the preacher thrown in), and he was rewarded with four R&B chart hits: "Trapped" (#20), "The Truth" (#78), "I'm Not Gonna Let" (#7), and "Over And Over" (#68). All found the beat heavy and Abrams confidently emoting in a manly style borrowed from the young Teddy Pendergrass. — *William Ruhlmann*

About Romance / 1992 / RCA ✦✦✦

You and Me Equals Us / MCA ✦✦

AC/DC

Group, Hard Rock, Heavy Metal
AC/DC's mammoth power chord roar became one of the most influential hard rock sounds of the '70s. In its own way, it was a reaction against the pompous art-rock and lumbering stadium rock of the early '70s. AC/DC's rock was minimalist—no matter how huge and bludgeoning the guitar chords were, there was a clear sense of space and restraint. Combined with Bon Scott's larynx-shredding vocals, the band spawned countless imitators over the next two decades.

AC/DC was formed in 1973 by guitarist Malcolm Young after his band, the Velvet Underground, collapsed (Young's band has no relation to the seminal American group). With his younger brother Angus as lead guitarist, the band played some gigs around Sydney. Angus was only 15 years old at the time and his sister suggested that he should wear his school uniform on stage; the look became the band's visual trademark. While still in Sydney, the original lineup (featuring singer Dave Evans) cut a single called "Can I Sit Next to You," with ex-Easybeats Harry Vanda and George Young (Malcolm and Angus's older brother) producing.

The band moved to Melbourne the following year, where drummer Phil Rudd and bassist Mark Evans joined the band. The band's chauffeur, Bon Scott, became their lead vocalist when their singer, Dave Evans, refused to go on stage.

Previously, Scott had been a drummer for the Australian pop bands Fraternity and the Valentines. More importantly, he helped cement the group's image as brutes—he had several convictions on minor criminal offenses and was rejected by the Australian army for being "socially maladjusted." And AC/DC *was* socially maladjusted. Throughout their career they favored crude double entendres and violent imagery, all spiked with a mischievous sense of fun.

The group released two albums—*High Voltage* and *TNT*—in Australia in 1974 and 1975. Material from the two records comprised the 1976 release *High Voltage* in the U.S. and U.K.; the group also toured both countries. *Dirty Deeds Done Dirt Cheap* followed at the end of the year. Evans left the band at the beginning of 1977, with Cliff Williams taking his place. In the fall of 1977, AC/DC released *Let There Be Rock*, which became their first album to chart in the U.S.

Powerage, released in the spring of 1978, expanded their audience even further, thanks in no small part to their dynamic live shows (which were captured on 1978's live *If You Want Blood, You've Got It*). What really broke the doors down for the band was the following year's *Highway to Hell*, which hit number 17 in the U.S. and number eight in the U.K., becoming the group's first million-seller.

AC/DC's train was derailed when Bon Scott died on February 20, 1980. The official coroner's report stated he had "drunk himself to death." In March, the band replaced Scott with Brian Johnson. The following month, the band recorded *Back in Black*, which would prove to be their biggest album, selling over ten million copies in the U.S. alone. For the next few years, the band was one of the largest rock bands in the world, with *For Those About to*

Rock (We Salute You) topping the charts in the U.S. In 1982, Rudd left the band; he was replaced by Simon Wright.

After 1983's *Flick of the Switch*, the band's commercial standing began to slip; they were able to reverse their slide with 1990's *The Razor's Edge*, which spawned the hit "Thunderstruck." While they haven't proved to be the commercial powerhouse they were during the late '70s and early '80s, the '90s have seen them maintain their status as a top international concert draw, as well as one of the most enduring hard rock bands in the world. — *Stephen Thomas Erlewine*

○ **High Voltage** / Oct. 1976 / Atco ✦✦✦
AC/DC kicked things off properly by blowing away the girders with their concussion bomb skronk. Raw, raunchy, and fun-o-plenty, its songs include "The Jack," guaranteed to offend every woman in listening radius. — *Tom Graves*

○ **Let There Be Rock** / Jun. 1977 / Atco ✦✦✦✦
A great follow-up, it proved these Aussies would be a nasty itch for a long time. There's great meltdown boogie on songs like "Let There Be Rock," "Problem Child," and "Whole Lotta Rosie." — *Tom Graves*

Powerage / May 1978 / Atco ✦✦✦

If You Want Blood You've Got It / Dec. 1978 / Atco ✦✦✦
Although the sound engineering lacks, rock & roll still ain't much more in your face than this. Fans had known what a great live band AC/DC was, and this was the album that proved it to everyone else. This collects the best tracks from the early years and spits them back louder than bejeezus. — *Tom Graves*

☆ **Highway to Hell** / Aug. 1979 / Atco ✦✦✦✦✦
This is a classic of hard rock/heavy metal noise-grunge-skronk-pillage-and-burn. Earlier AC/DC albums had great riffs and killer chords, but *Highway to Hell* proved the boys could write too. Not a clinker on this thudfest, and songs like "Highway to Hell" and "Girls Got Rhythm" have appropriately become rock staples. — *Tom Graves*

★ **Back in Black** / Aug. 1980 / Atco ✦✦✦✦✦
Following Bon Scott's death, AC/DC came back with reinforcements and released another truly great hard-rock album. Brian Johnson ups the ante with his own tough-as-tacks vocals. Robert "Mutt" Lange's production on *Back in Black* remains one of the most powerful in all of hard rock. All in all, this is great diamond-hard, full-throttle rock & roll. — *Tom Graves*

Dirty Deeds Done Dirt Cheap / Apr. 1981 / Atco ✦✦✦
An odds-'n'-sods collection of earlier Bon Scott-era tracks, it's worth it alone for the unforgettable title track. — *Tom Graves*

For Those About to Rock We Salute You / Nov. 1981 / Atco ✦✦✦
For Those About to Rock We Salute You is another masterwork from the Brian Johnson period. The title song has become the group's signature track and is featured in AC/DC concerts with pyrotechnics galore. It's a must for those who don't mind staring into the face of deafness. — *Tom Graves*

Flick of the Switch / Aug. 1983 / Atco ✦✦

74 Jailbreak / 1984 / Atco ✦✦✦
Actually an EP of Bon Scott-period material, it's nonetheless some of AC/DC's best and most blistering blues. In particular the title song and an incendiary "Baby, Please Don't Go" are worth the admission. — *Tom Graves*

Fly on the Wall / Jul. 1985 / Atco ✦✦

Who Made Who / May 1986 / Atco ✦✦✦
On paper, *Who Made Who* is just a cheap soundtrack to a cheap movie (Stephen King's disastrous *Maximum Overdrive*), but it's actually much more than that. It serves as a ripping AC/DC retrospective, tearing through such classics as "You Shook Me All Night Long" and "For Those About to Rock," adding the pounding title track to their canon, and rescuing overlooked songs like "Sink the Pink" from otherwise mediocre albums. It's not a perfect retrospective—there's no "Back in Black," "Highway to Hell," or "Dirty Deeds Done Dirt Cheap"—but what is here is terrific. — *Stephen Thomas Erlewine*

Blow up Your Video / Feb. 1988 / Atco ✦✦✦
Blow up Your Video shows signs of the band breaking out of their mid-'80s slump. Angus Young's guitar lurches and growls throughout the album, coming to a blistering head on "This Means War" and "Heatseeker." Any record with moments this smashingly visceral deserves at least one listen. — *Stephen Thomas Erlewine*

The Razor's Edge / 1990 / Atco ✦✦✦
The band unarguably slipped a few notches in the late '80s, but *The Razor's Edge* brought them back into the '90s with a vengeance. Great hooks, great sound, and a great single, "Money Talks." Whoever said they sold out? — *Tom Graves*

AC/DC Live / 1992 / Atco ✦✦
Most of AC/DC's casual fans will be happy with the shorter, single-disc version, which includes all of the hits and eliminates all of the ten-minute-plus excesses that are proudly featured on the double-disc set. Hardcore fans will need the double-disc set. — *Stephen Thomas Erlewine*

Accept

Group, Heavy Metal
With their brutal, simple riffs and aggressive, fast tempos, the German heavy metal band Accept was one of the top metal bands of the early '80s. While their sheer speed had a calculable effect on the evolution of thrash and speed metal, it was Wolf Hoffman and Jan Kommet's thick guitars and vocalist Udo Dirkschneider's Bon Scott-styled shrieking that helped earn them a large following in Europe, if not in America. Nevertheless, bassist Peter Baltes and drummer Stefan Kaufmann's manic rhythms are what distinguished the band's early albums from the rest. When the band decided to add some melody to their approach on 1985's *Metal Heart* and 1986's *Russian Roulette*, Dirkschneider jumped ship and formed his own band, Udo, in 1987. Accept went through three new vocalists, settling on David Reece, and churned out three more albums before finally calling it quits in 1989. The group reunited in the mid-'90s, releasing *Death Row* in 1995. — *Stephen Thomas Erlewine*

Breaker / 1981 / Polydor ✦✦✦
○ **Restless and Wild** / 1983 / Portrait ✦✦✦✦
Accept created what would eventually become speed-metal with "Fast as a Shark." Very influential. — *John Book*
○ **Balls to the Wall** / 1984 / Portrait ✦✦✦✦
This is another strong album. — *John Book*
○ **Metal Heart** / 1985 / Portrait ✦✦✦✦
With *Metal Heart*, Accept made a move toward a more accessible, melodic brand of heavy metal, which proved nearly as successful as their previous relentlessly speedy attack. — *David Jehnzen*
● **Accept [compilation]** / 1986 / Portrait ✦✦✦
Bringing together one song from *Balls to the Wall* and the majority of *Restless & Wild*, *Accept* features the best material from Accept's early records, when they were at their heaviest and most influential. — *David Jehnzen*
Russian Roulette / 1986 / Portrait ✦✦✦
Although *Russian Roulette* has a harder attack than *Metal Heart*, it is still dominated by hooks. The combination of intense sonic fury and melody made it their last great album; not coincidentally, it was their last with original singer Udo Dirkschneider. — *David Jehnzen*

The Accused

Group, Hardcore, Thrash, Heavy Metal
Accused is a band from Seattle that combines punk and hardcore with slight metal influences. Ex-Fartz vocalist Blaine Cook assembled the band after his previous group fell apart. In 1984, the Accused independently released their debut EP. For the next few years, they worked on their blend of hardcore, punk, and metal. In 1987, they released their first full-length record, *More Fun than an Open Casket Funeral*, on Combat Records. After one more album, Combat Records dropped the band, causing the members to go their separate ways; only guitarist Tommy Niemeyer, who helped form Gruntruck with Skin Yard vocalist Ben McMillan, did anything of national interest. When the new decade came around the band re-formed, recording an album for Nastymix, the Seattle rap label known for Sir Mix-A-Lot. The record, *Grinning Like an Undertaker*, was released in 1990 with great results. — *John Book*

Return of Martha Splatterhead / 1986 / Combat ✦✦
A very good album, it includes songs from their very rare debut EP. — *John Book*
● **More Fun Than an Open Casket Funeral** / 1987 / Combat ✦✦✦✦
More Fun Than an Open Casket Funeral is the best album the band has ever done, and the best of punk and metal combined. It's an essential album for those getting into the Seattle music scene for the first time. — *John Book*

Grinning Like an Undertaker / 1990 / Nastymix ✦✦✦
Produced by well-known producer/engineer Jack Endino, it features magnificent drumming by Josh Sinder. — *John Book*
Straight Razor / 1991 / Nastymix ✦✦✦
Everything that *Grinning...* wasn't, *Straight Razor* is. It was the last recording to feature Josh Sinder. — *John Book*
Martha Splatterhead's Maddest / Combat ✦✦
The band gets diverse by taking on different styles while still holding on to their "trashcore" edge. It features guest appearances by Metal Church's Kurdt Vanderhoof and rapper Sir Mix-A-Lot. — *John Book*

Ace

Group, Pop/Rock
Ace was a British pub rock band formed in December 1972 by Paul Carrack (keyboards, vocals), Alan "Bam" King (guitar, vocals), Phil Harris (guitar, vocals), Terry "Tex" Comer (bass), and Steve Witherington (drums) (replaced before the first album by Fran Byrne). They debuted on record with *Five-A-Side* (1974), which contained their hit "How Long," prominently featuring Carrack. They were never able to top that success, however, and they split up in July 1977. Carrack has gone on to be a member of Squeeze and Mike + the Mechanics as well as maintaining a solo career. — *William Ruhlmann*

○ **Five-A-Side** / 1974 / Anchor ✦✦✦✦
Five-A-Side, Ace's debut album, is notable for introducing the world to the soulful singing talent of Paul Carrack, especially on the hit "How Long," which went to #1 on some charts in 1975. The band has a low-key style, frequently dominated by Carrack's piano and organ work, that is sometimes suggestive of Traffic and of the Tulsa country-rock sound of J.J. Cale, Delaney & Bonnie, and Leon Russell, although they never work up quite as much of a sweat as the last two. Already road-weary when they made this album, Ace, especially in Carrack's lyrics, comments extensively on the travails of being in a struggling rock & roll band. Even "How Long," which sounds like the lament of a lover betrayed, is really about somebody quitting the group. All of which makes the irony of the song's being their sole hit all the more acute. — *William Ruhlmann*

Time for Another / Dec. 1975 / Anchor ✦✦
Although Ace emphasized its Englishness and pub-rock origins by posing on the album cover in a pub, complete with dartboard and pints of beer in hand, their second album continued to bear the musical influence of America, specifically the Southwestern America of Tulsa's soulful Shelter Records label and people like Leon Russell and J.J. Cale. Theirs was a low-key, percolating approach that would be taken to mass success a few years down the line by Dire Straits. But *Time For Another* lacked the chief ingredient that had made its predecessor, *Five-A-Side*, successful: a hit on the order of "How Long." Keyboard player and vocalist Paul Carrack made a couple of valiant attempts, notably on the side-openers "I Think It's Gonna Last" and "No Future In Your Eyes." But Ace was a group of equals in creative participation, if not in talent, and much of the album was given over to the undistinguished contributions of other band members. With this album, the band was on its way to being a one-hit wonder. — *William Ruhlmann*

No Strings / Jan. 1977 / Anchor ✦✦
Six Aside / 1982 / Polydor ✦✦✦
● **Best of Ace** / 1988 / See For Miles ✦✦✦✦

Ace of Base

Group, Dance-Pop
Comprised of vocalists Jenny and Linn Berggren, Jonas "Joker" Berggren (keyboards), and Ulf "Buddha" Ekberg (keyboards), the Swedish quartet Ace of Base became an internationally popular act with their 1993 debut album, *The Sign*. Ace of Base's simple, melodic Euro-disco was equally popular on radio and in the clubs, earning the quartet three U.S. Top ten singles—"All That She Wants," "Don't Turn Around," and "The Sign," which spent six weeks at number one. — *Stephen Thomas Erlewine*

The Sign / 1993 / Arista ✦✦✦
Ace of Base's strong point is not versatility—all of their hit singles have exactly the same beat. But that doesn't matter. On their debut album, *The Sign*, they managed to create a piece of melodic Euro-disco that was a huge hit all over the world, appealing to both dance clubs and pop radio. And with singles like "All That She

Wants," "The Sign," and "Don't Turn Around," it's easy to see why they were hits—the beat is relentless and the hooks are incessantly catchy. —*Stephen Thomas Erlewine*

Johnny Ace (John Alexander)

b. Jun. 9, 1929, Memphis, TN, **d.** Dec. 25, 1954
R&B
One of the more tragic '50s R&B heroes, Johnny Ace (born John Alexander) was a fixture on the Memphis Beale Street blues scene, playing with Bobby Bland and Roscoe Gordon in the fabled Beale Streeters. He struck out solo in the early '50s, recording the gorgeous, stark ballad "Pledging My Love" in 1954, and died playing Russian roulette on Christmas Eve 1954. —*John Floyd*

● **Johnny Ace Memorial Album** / 1974 / MCA ✦✦✦✦
The greatest hits from this ill-fated Memphis blues pianist includes the posthumous smash "Pledging My Love." —*Bill Dahl*

David Ackles

b. Feb. 27, 1937
Singer-Songwriter
David Ackles is a critically claimed but commerically ignored singer/songwriter who made four albums between 1968 and 1973, the most prominent of which was 1972's *American Gothic*, which was produced by lyricist Bernie Taupin, who is a big Ackles fan. Despite his obscurity, Ackles has exerted an influence on subsequent singer/songwriters, as acknowledged by Elvis Costello. —*William Ruhlmann*

The Road to Cairo / 1968 / Elektra ✦✦
David Ackles / 1968 / Elektra ✦✦
Subway to the Country / 1970 / Elektra ✦✦✦
● **American Gothic** / 1972 / Elektra ✦✦✦✦
The years have only been kind to the album considered David Ackles's masterpiece when it was released. Ackles combined an early '70s singer-songwriter sensibility with a theater music background that placed him as much in the tradition of Brecht-Weill and Jacques Brel as Bob Dylan. Not only are his songs fully realized, dramatic statements, but Ackles proves himself a warm, accomplished singer. When this album got no higher than #167 in the charts, Ackles's fans were heartbroken. Decades later, *American Gothic* remains one of those great albums that never found its audience. It waits to be rediscovered. —*William Ruhlmann*

Five & Dime / 1973 / Columbia ✦✦✦
American Gothic, the predecessor to *Five & Dime*, was David Ackles' ambitious portrait of American life, in its broad scope and geography and diversity of style. *Five & Dime* is more a collection of miniatures, still drawn with Ackles' customary eye for detail and sung in his rich, knowing voice. Its pleasures are more subtle than those in the expansive *American Gothic*, but no less real. (And "Surf's Down," complete with harmonies by Dean Torrance of Jan & Dean, is the wickedest beach music parody since "Back In The U.S.S.R.") This is music of wit, feeling, and sophistication that should be heard by fans of American songcraft from Stephen Foster and Irving Berlin to Randy Newman. Criminally, it was also David Ackles's last album. —*William Ruhlmann*

Barbara Acklin

b. Feb. 28, 1944, Chicago, IL
Soul, R&B
Acklin began singing background vocals at Chess in the mid-'60s. Signing with Chicago's Brunswick label (where she was a receptionist), Acklin debuted on the R&B charts in 1968 as Gene Chandler's duet partner before stepping out on her own later that year with the brassy "Love Makes a Woman," her biggest R&B and pop hit. Acklin was also a prolific composer at Brunswick, writing or co-writing hits for Jackie Wilson and the Chi-Lites. —*Bill Dahl*

● **Love Makes a Woman** / 1968 / Brunswick ✦✦✦✦
Unrepresented on CD as yet, this is '60s Chicago soul songstress Acklin's debut album, with her irresistible title-track smash. —*Bill Dahl*

○ **Seven Days of Night** / 1969 / Brunswick ✦✦✦✦
More excellent late-'60s soul from Brunswick's top female artist, this album includes "Just Ain't No Love" and "Am I the Same Girl," both R&B hits. —*Bill Dahl*

The Action

Group, British Invasion
In the mid-'60s, the Action had a strong grass-roots following among British mods. But despite the production services of George Martin, they never managed anything close to a hit record. The Action were the most soul-oriented of the mod groups, favoring guitar-oriented covers of Motown tunes and standard R&B dance numbers of the day like "Harlem Shuffle."

Martin's production put the emphasis on Reggie King's rich blue-eyed soul vocals and the group's high vocal harmonies, with occasional horns. Their later original material shows an increased sophistication in both songwriting and production. The Action were akin to a more soul-oriented Small Faces, though they didn't match the Faces' energy or songwriting. —*Richie Unterberger*

● **The Ultimate Action** / 1981 / Edsel ✦✦✦✦
The Ultimate Action is indeed the ultimate compilation of this cult band. The 17 cuts (three were added to the CD reissue) include both sides of all five of their Parlophone singles, plus a batch of unreleased songs and obscure Continental-only singles. This respectable collection has its moments, especially their riveting cover of the Marvelettes' "I'll Keep on Holding On" (a great lost hit-single-that-never-was) and the brooding mod lament "Wasn't It You." —*Richie Unterberger*

Bryan Adams

b. Nov. 5, 1959, Kingston, Ontario, Canada
Pop/Rock
Bryan Adams was one of the most popular mainstream rock & rollers to emerge in the '80s, producing a series of platinum albums and Top Ten hits. Adams wasn't an innovator on the level of Bruce Springsteen, or even John Cougar Mellencamp. He followed in their footsteps, smoothing out their rougher edges while retaining a down-to-earth earnestness in both his straightforward rock & roll and his husky voice. At the beginning of his career, he relied more on rock than pop, but as his career progressed, he became known for his ballads. But both his rockers and his slow numbers were the result of his craftsmanship, both as a writer and a performer—Adams never let anything obscure a good hook.

Born in Canada, Adams began his career as a songwriting partner of Jim Vallence, a former member of Prism. Vallence and Adams wrote songs for several Canadian rockers, including Loverboy and Bachman-Turner Overdrive, as well as Bonnie Tyler and Kiss. Adams landed a solo record contract with A&M Records in 1981, releasing an eponymous album by the end of year; it failed to make the charts. The following year, he released *You Want It You Got It*, which managed to reach the U.S. charts. For most of 1982, he toured the country, opening for the Kinks, Loverboy, and Foreigner.

Bryan Adams's commercial breakthrough came in 1983 with *Cuts like a Knife.* "Straight from the Heart," a ballad taken from the record, reached the Top Ten before the album was released. The album also made it into the Top Ten, while the title track peaked at number 15; a third single, "This Time," reached number 24.

Late in 1984, Adams returned with the surging, mid-tempo "Run to You," which became his second Top Ten single; it also became his first British hit, peaking at number 11. *Reckless*, also released in late 1984, became a blockbuster success, spending two weeks at the top of the U.S. album charts and selling over five million copies. Besides "Run to You," *Reckless* featured five other Top 15 singles, including the number-one "Heaven," "Summer of '69," "Somebody," "One Night Love Affair," and "It's Only Love," a duet with Tina Turner.

Released in 1987, *Into the Fire* proved to be a considerable commercial disappointment, spending 33 weeks on the charts, selling one million copies, and spawning only one Top Ten hit, "Heat of the Night." Four years later, Adams returned with "(Everything I Do) I Do It for You," the theme song for *Robin Hood: Prince of Thieves.* The song became a huge hit, spending seven weeks at number one in the U.S.; in Britain, it was at the top of the charts for an astonishing 16 weeks, which was the longest stay at number one since Frankie Laine's "I Believe" in 1953. The success of "(Everything I Do) I Do It for You" re-established Adams as a mainstream rock commerical powerhouse, setting the stage for the triple-platinum *Waking up the Neighbours*, released in the fall of 1991. *Waking up the Neighbours* launched the #2 hit "Can't Stop This Thing We Started," the minor hit "There Will Never Be

Another Tonight," and two Top 15 singles, "Thought I'd Died and Gone to Heaven" and "Do I Have to Say the Words?"

The following year, Bryan Adams released a greatest hits collection, *So Far, So Good*, which featured a new track, "Please Forgive Me." The ballad became another Top Ten success, as did the similar-sounding "All for Love"—a collaboration with Rod Stewart and Sting taken from *The Three Musketeers*—which reached number one. In 1995, Adams released a live album, appropriately titled *Live! Live! Live!*; the record fell off the charts quickly. In the summer of 1995, Adams had his fourth number one single, "Have You Ever Really Loved a Woman?," taken from the *Don Juan DeMarco* soundtrack; the single spent five weeks at number one. —*Stephen Thomas Erlewine*

Bryan Adams / 1980 / A&M ✦✦
You Want It You Got It / 1981 / A&M ✦✦✦
With its crystal-clear production, courtesy of Bob Clearmountain, *You Want It You Got It* is state-of-the art nouveau rock & roll of the post-Springsteen era: the guitars rev up, the bass drum is deeper than a well, the vocals are nasal and punky. The songs don't have the craft or commitment of Adams's peers/competitors—Springsteen, Petty, Mellencamp, et al.—but you may not know it for the first few spins, just because the sound is so hot and infectious, and by then it may not matter. Actually, this is a much more enjoyable record in many respects than the rock & roll assembly-line products Adams constructed once he hit the arenas. As it was, with this one, he was on his way. All he did later was take this approach and make it slicker. —*William Ruhlmann*

○ **Cuts Like a Knife** / Jan. 1983 / A&M ✦✦✦✦
A Top Ten breakthrough album in America for this Canadian rocker, it was carried by the strength of "Straight from the Heart." —*Donna DiChario*

○ **Reckless** / 1984 / A&M ✦✦✦✦
Radio-friendly pop-rock driven by Adams's trademark gravelly vocals that spawned three Top Ten hits, including "Heaven," "Run to You," as well as a duet with Tina Turner on "It's Only Love." —*Donna DiChario*

Into the Fire / Mar. 1987 / A&M ✦✦
Adams keeps the fire burning with the Top Ten "Heat of the Night." —*Donna DiChario*

Waking up the Neighbours / 1991 / A&M ✦✦✦
After the disappointing *Into the Fire*, Adams returned to the top of the charts with *Waking Up the Neighbours*, thanks to the massive success of "(Everything I Do) I Do It for You." —*Stephen Thomas Erlewine*

● **So Far So Good** / Nov. 2, 1993 / A&M ✦✦✦✦
Eliminating the filler that tends to clutter his albums, *So Far, So Good* simply gathers all of Adams's big hits (including a new one, "Please Forgive Me") in one concise package, making it the one essential Bryan Adams album and the only one that can be listened to straight through from start to finish. —*Stephen Thomas Erlewine*

Live! Live! Live! / 1995 / A&M ✦✦

Faye Adams

R&B
This heavily gospel-influenced chanteuse scored three chart-topping R&B hits in 1953-1954. From Newark, NJ, Adams joined Joe Morris's band in 1952 as featured singer. A year later, she was a star, thanks to her moving ballad "Shake a Hand" on Al Silver's New York-based Herald label. The song has proven an R&B standard, covered by the likes of Little Richard and Ruth Brown. Two more #1 R&B hits followed in rapid succession: "I'll Be True" (covered by Bill Haley and the Comets) and "Hurts Me to My Heart." She later moved to Imperial, and stirred up some action with "Keeper of My Heart" in 1957, before returning to the church. —*Bill Dahl*

● **Golden Classics: Shake a Hand** / 1990 / Collectables ✦✦✦✦
This gospel-influenced vocalist's '50s hits package includes the powerful "Shake a Hand." —*Bill Dahl*

Oleta Adams

Seattle, WA
Soul, Urban
The youngest daughter of a minister, Oleta's first musical experi-

ence was in the choir of her father's church. Discovered by Tears for Fears while performing solo in a Hyatt Regency lounge in Kansas City, MO, she was featured prominently on their *Seeds of Love* album. Tears for Fears member Roland Orzabal produced her 1990 debut album, *Circle of One*, featuring the hit "Get Here." She was a 1991 Grammy nominee. —*Scott Bultman*

● **Circle of One** / 1990 / Fontana ✦✦✦✦
The former backing vocalist for Tears for Fears performs very well on her debut album, establishing her as a singer to watch. She has soothing and deep vocals with a heavy gospel influence, featuring the hits "Get Here" and the relaxing "Rhythm of Life." —*John Book*

Evolution / 1993 / Mercury ✦✦✦
After the success of her debut, Adams doesn't change the formula for her second album. Which isn't a bad thing—the stylish love ballads she sings are some of the best adult contemporary pop of the early '90s. —*Stephen Thomas Erlewine*

Barry Adamson

b. 1958
Urban, Alternative Pop/Rock
Adamson's work as a bassist for Magazine and Nick Cave's Bad Seeds gave little indication of the complex, cinematic works he has composed as a solo artist. After leaving the Bad Seeds in 1987, Adamson decided to follow the path of film composers like John Barry, Ennio Morricone, and Bernard Herrmann, whose work had intrigued him since childhood. His first full-length album, 1989's *Moss Side Story* (he had released one previous EP in 1988), was a tour de force blending post-punk, industrial, spy guitar, and various classic movie composer quotes into a seamless 54-minute soundtrack to an ominous film noir that didn't exist. This recording led to Adamson's work on soundtracks for actual films in the early '90s, including *Delusion, Gas Food Lodging*, and *Shuttle Cock*. Adamson has also continued to compose quasi-cinematic recordings for imaginary films, although none has matched the sustained excitement of *Moss Side Story*. —*Richie Unterberger*

● **Moss Side Story** / 1989 / Mute ✦✦✦✦
Adamson's first full-length album is still unequivocally his best. Elements of rock, voices from news reports, blood-curdling wordless female vocals (courtesy of experimental/punk diva Diamanda Galas), lounge keyboards, and swirling funereal ambient music are interwoven on this taut and compelling, almost continuous imaginary "soundtrack." The result is a sinister and edgy soundscape that's as gripping as any black-and-white thriller. The CD adds three bonus cuts, including Adamson's updates of "The Man With The Golden Arm" and "Alfred Hitchcock Presents." —*Richie Unterberger*

Delusion / 1991 / Mute ✦✦
It's perhaps unsurprising that Adamson's eclectic compositional talent doesn't work nearly as well when he has to wed his vision to an actual film. This soundtrack for an obscure 1991 movie contains plenty of interesting bits, elements, and pieces—somber Spanish guitar, haunting orchestral passages, *Phantom of the Opera* organ phrases, manic Latin music, and a too-brief, ominous update of the 1963 British instrumental hit "Diamonds." The problem is that it doesn't ebb and flow into a sum greater than its parts. In fact, the jarring bits of dialogue (which are meaningless without the context of the film) are often downright annoying, and make the sum substantially less than whatever whole it may have formed. —*Richie Unterberger*

Soul Murder / 1992 / Mute ✦✦✦
Equally as ambitious as *Moss Side Story*, this album doesn't come off nearly as well. Apparently constructed to evoke similar underworld soundscapes, too much of this is built around simple, sparse (sometimes electronic) riffs. The production lacks force and density, and the pieces don't flow into each other with the cohesion that Adamson has demonstrated in other work. Nifty bits of haunting orchestral ambience and lounge jazz keyboards remain, and it does hit a groove at times, especially with the goofy French pop song (with childish vocals) "Un Petit Miracle" and the brutal ska treatment of the James Bond theme. —*Richie Unterberger*

The Negro Inside / 1993 / Mute ✦✦
Something of a holding pattern. On this six-song EP, Adamson extrapolates from contemporary black dance beats, samples his American publicist's answering machine message and Jane Birkin's hit "Je T'Aime," and throws in lounge jazz piano bits and more. The pieces aren't that striking, and one gets the sense that

he's tossing out some ideas to play with in the interim between full-length scores/albums. —*Richie Unterberger*

Hasil Adkins

b. 1936, Madison, WV
Rockabilly
A crazed rockabilly one-man band, Adkins has been recording in a tarpaper shack in the hills of West Virginia since the mid-'50s. The absolutely crudest and wildest of all rock & rollers, Adkins's lyrics stray as far from the standard '50s clichés as you can get. Songs about eating peanut butter on the moon, chopping girls' heads off and mounting them on his wall, and doing something called the "hunch" are typical lyrical fare for Adkins. Combining a three-octave voice that can go from sub-glottal Elvis moans to blood-curdling screams with an over-amplified guitar that sounds like a gigantic rubber band, there is nothing in pop music that sounds like Hasil Adkins, a true rock & roll primitive. —*Cub Koda*

● **Out to Hunch** / 1986 / Norton ✦✦✦✦
All the lunatic classics: "She Said," "Chicken Walk," "No More Hot Dogs," "The Hunch," "We Got a Date" and the mind-boggling arrangements of "Memphis" and "High School Confidential." Not for the faint of heart. —*Cub Koda*

○ **Chicken Walk** / 1986 / Buffalo Bop ✦✦✦✦
More crazed '50s and early-'60s sides. (Import) —*Cub Koda*

The Wild Man / 1987 / Norton ✦✦✦
His '80s recordings, just as crazy. —*Cub Koda*

Peanut Butter Rock and Roll / 1990 / Norton ✦✦

Moon Over Madison / 1990 / Norton ✦✦

Live in Chicago / Nov. 1992 / Bughouse ✦✦

Look at That Caveman Go!! / 1993 / Norton ✦✦✦
Seventeen careening, out-of-control live recordings by America's favorite rockabilly legend-lunatic. "She Goes like This" and "Devonna Rock" may be two of his wildest recordings ever, but the true highlight is a rockin' in the insane asylum version of George Jones's country classic "Today I Started Loving You Again." File under retro-alternative if the record store happens to be on the planet Mars. —*Cub Koda*

Achy Breaky Ha Ha Ha / 1994 / Norton ✦✦✦
The West Virginia wildman shows the other side of his talent, tackling a batch of early country standards and quirky originals in his usual one-man-band style. As far removed from modern country as you can get, Adkins originals like "Gonna Have Me a Yard Sale," "Song of Death," "Of Course Not," "Leaves of Autumn" and "Tomorrow I'll Still Be Loving You" sit alongside Bill Monroe's "I Hear a Sweet Voice Calling," Hank Williams's "You Win Again" and Johnny Cash's "I Still Miss Someone" for a roughcut set that's rife with high and lonesome charm. —*Cub Koda*

Adolescents

Group, Punk, Hardcore
A wild Los Angeles hardcore band, the Adolescents were fronted by guitarist Rikk Agnew. The band released its first album in 1981, disbanded and re-formed in 1986 with Agnew, singer Tony Montana, and bassist Steve Soto. The group again disbanded in 1989. —*David Szatmary*

● **Adolescents** / 1981 / Frontier ✦✦✦✦
Guitarist Rikk Agnew led this seminal '80s West Coast punk outfit. —*David Szatmary*

Brats in Battalions / 1987 / Triple X ✦✦

Balboa Funzone / 1988 / Triple X ✦✦✦
Hard-hitting, wild hardcore by the re-formed group. —*David Szatmary*

Live 1981 and 1986 / 1989 / Triple X ✦✦✦
An excellent live record, it samples both periods of the California mosh masters. —*David Szatmary*

Adverts

Group, Punk
With their raw, enthusiastic immaturity, the Adverts were a bright, but short-lived light of the punk era, distinguished by the fact that their bassist, Gayle Advert, was one of the first female stars of punk rock. After they (barely) mastered one chord, the Adverts began playing at London's Roxy Club in 1976, where they quickly came to the attention of the Damned's guitarist Brian James.

James offered the band an opening spot on the Damned's tour and directed them toward Stiff Records. Stiff released their self-deprecating debut single, "One Chord Wonders," in 1977, when the band could still barely play, but when they released their second single, the disturbingly funny "Gary Gilmore's Eyes," the group rocketed into the U.K. Top 20 in a storm of controversy. The Adverts' first album, *Crossing the Red Sea with the Adverts*, fulfilled the single's promise, but the second, 1979's *Cast of Thousands*, sounded like they poured all of their musical ideas into their first album; the group broke up the following year. —*Stephen Thomas Erlewine*

● **Crossing the Red Sea with the Adverts** / 1978 / Bright ✦✦✦✦
Some will argue eloquently that the Adverts' debut is the great overlooked U.K. punk record of the late-'70s. I think it's X-Ray Spex's *Germ Free Adolescents*, but I'm willing to give the Adverts second place. From the moment they released their first single ("One Chord Wonders") up to and including the release of this album, the Adverts recorded great, arty, fast and loud punk clamor rooted in anomie ("Bored Teenagers"), class consciousness ("Safety in Numbers") and comic book horror ("Gary Gilmore's Eyes"). Led by the Rotten/Strummer-isms of frontman T.V. Smith, *Crossing the Red Sea* sounds as snotty, defiant and liberating as it did 17 years ago. In fact, it sounds surprisingly relevant and more intelligent than I remember. An ignored masterpiece. —*John Dougan*

Cast of Thousands / 1979 / RCA ✦✦

Aerosmith

Group, Hard Rock, Heavy Metal
Aerosmith was one of the most popular hard rock bands of the '70s, setting the style and sound of hard rock and heavy metal for the next two decades with their raunchy, bluesy swagger. The Boston-based quintet found the middle ground between the menace of the Rolling Stones and the campy, sleazy flamboyance of the New York Dolls, developing a lean, dirty riff-oriented boogie that was loose and swinging and as hard as a diamond. In the meantime, they developed a prototype for power-ballads with "Dream On," a piano ballad that was orchestrated with strings and distorted guitars. Aerosmith's ability to pull off both ballads and rock & roll made them extremely popular during the mid-'70s, when they had a string of gold and platinum albums. By the early '80s, the group's audience had declined as the band fell prey to drug and alcohol abuse. However, their career was far from over—in the late '80s, Aerosmith pulled off one of the most remarkable comebacks in rock history, returning to the top of the charts with a group of albums that equalled, if not surpassed, the popularity of their '70s albums.

In 1970, the first incarnation of Aerosmith formed when vocalist Steven Tyler met guitarist Joe Perry while working at a Sunapee, NH, ice cream parlor. Tyler, who originally was a drummer, and Perry decided to form a power trio with bassist Tom Hamilton. The group soon expanded to quartet, adding a second guitarist called Ray Tabano; he was quickly replaced by Brad Whitford, a former member of Earth Inc. With the addition of drummer Joey Kramer, Tyler became the full-time lead singer by the end of year. Aerosmith relocated to Boston at the end of 1970.

After playing clubs in the Massachusetts and New York areas for two years, the group landed a record contract with Columbia Records in 1972. Aerosmith's self-titled debut album was released in the fall of 1973, climbing to number 166. "Dream On" was released as the first single and it was a minor hit, reaching number 59. For the next year, the band built a fan base by touring America, supporting groups as diverse as the Kinks, Mahavishnu Orchestra, Sha Na Na, and Mott the Hoople. The performance of *Get Your Wings* (1974), the group's second album and first produced by Jack Douglas, benefitted from their constant touring, spending a total of 86 weeks on the chart.

Aerosmith's third record, 1975's *Toys in the Attic*, was a success both commercially and artistically. By the time the album was recorded, the band's sound had developed into a sleek, hard-driving hard rock powered by simple, almost brutal, blues-based riffs. Many critics at the time labeled the group as punk rockers, and it's easy to see why—instead of adhering to the world-music pretentions of Led Zeppelin or the prolonged gloomy mysticism of Black Sabbath, Aerosmith stripped heavy metal to its basic core, spitting out spare riffs that not only rocked, but rolled. Steven Tyler's lyrics were filled with double entendres and clever jokes and the entire band had a street-wise charisma that separated them from the heavy, lumbering arena rockers of the era. *Toys in the Attic* captured the essence of the newly invigorated Aerosmith.

"Sweet Emotion," the slyly funky first single from *Toys in the Attic*, broke into the Top 40 in the summer of 1975, with the album reaching number 11 shortly afterward. Its success prompted the re-release of the power ballad "Dream On," which shot into the Top Ten in early 1976. Both *Aerosmith* and *Get Your Wings* climbed back up the charts in the wake of *Toys in the Attic*, peaking at number 21 and 74 respectively. "Walk This Way," the final single from *Toys in the Attic*, was released around the time of the group's new 1976 album, *Rocks*. Although it didn't feature a Top Ten hit like "Walk This Way," *Rocks* went platinum quickly, peaking at number three.

In early 1977, Aerosmith took a break and prepared material for their fifth album. Released late in 1977, *Draw the Line* was another hit, climbing to number 11 on the U.S. charts, but the band was showing signs of exhaustion. In addition to another tour in 1978, the band appeared in the movie *Sgt. Pepper's Lonely Hearts Club Band*, performing "Come Together," which eventually became a #23 hit. *Live! Bootleg* appeared late in 1978 and became another success, reaching number 13. Aerosmith recorded *Night in the Ruts* in 1979, releasing the record at the end of the year. By the time of its release, Joe Perry had left the band to form the Joe Perry Project with vocalist Ralph Morman, bassist David Hull, and drummer Ronnie Stewart. *Night in the Ruts* performed respectably, climbing to number 14 and going gold, yet it was the least successful Aerosmith record to date. Brad Whitford left the group in early 1980, forming the Whitsford-St. Holmes Band with former Ted Nugent guitarist Derek St. Holmes.

As Aerosmith regrouped with new guitarists Jimmy Crespo and Rick Dufay, the band released *Aerosmith's Greatest Hits* in late 1980; the record would eventually sell over six million copies. The new lineup of Aerosmith released *Rock in a Hard Place* in 1982. Peaking at number 32, it failed to match the performance of *Night in the Ruts* and showed that the band was out of ideas. Perry and Whitford returned to the band in 1984 and the group began a reunion tour dubbed "Back in the Saddle." Early in the tour, Tyler collapsed on stage, offering proof that the band hadn't conquered their notorious drug and alcohol addictions. The following year, Aerosmith released *Done with Mirrors*, the original lineup's first record since 1979 and their first for Geffen Records. Although it didn't perform as well as *Rock in a Hard Place*, the album showed that the band was revitalized.

After the release of *Done with Mirrors*, Tyler and Perry completed a rehabilitation program. In 1986, the pair appeared on Run D.M.C.'s cover of "Walk This Way," along with appearing in the video. "Walk This Way" became a hit, reaching number four and receiving saturation airplay in MTV. "Walk This Way" set the stage for the band's full-scale comeback effort, the Bruce Fairburn-produced *Permanent Vacation* (1987). Tyler and Perry collaborated with professional hard rock songwriters like Holly Knight and Desmond Child, resulting in the hits "Dude (Looks like a Lady)," "Rag Doll" and "Angel." *Permanent Vacation* peaked at number 11 and sold over three million copies.

Pump, released in 1989, continued the band's winning streak, reaching number five, selling over four million copies, and spawning the Top Ten singles "Love in an Elevator," "Janie's Got a Gun," and "What It Takes." Aerosmith released *Get a Grip* In 1993, like *Permanent Vacation* and *Pump*, *Get a Grip* was produced by Bruce Fairburn and featured significant contributions by professional songwriters. The album was as successful as the band's previous two records, featuring the hit singles "Livin' on the Edge," "Cryin'," and "Amazing." In 1994, Aerosmith released *Big Ones*, a compilation of hits from their Geffen years; it went double platinum shortly after its release. —*Stephen Thomas Erlewine*

Aerosmith / Jan. 1973 / Columbia ✦✦✦
The debut from this Boston band shows a sensitive side with their best-known ballad, "Dream On." But the focus remains on the raw, aggressive garage-rock style amply displayed on "Mama Kin," "One Way Street," and "Make It." —*Donna DiChario*

○ **Get Your Wings** / Mar. 1974 / Columbia ✦✦✦✦
Aerosmith took the Yardbirds classic "Train Kept a Rollin' " and made it their own with Steven Tyler's blistering vocals and Joe Perry's ace guitar work. —*Donna DiChario*

☆ **Toys in the Attic** / Apr. 1975 / Columbia ✦✦✦✦✦
A solid slice of classic '70s raunch and roll, Aerosmith defined grunge-rock with their best and now-classic "Sweet Emotion" and "Walk this Way." —*Donna DiChario*

☆ **Rocks** / May 1976 / Columbia ✦✦✦✦✦
Although the hits ("Back in the Saddle" and "Last Child") weren't as big as "Sweet Emotion" and "Walk This Way," *Rocks* remains Aerosmith's finest moment, full of relentlessly sleazy rock powered by some of the dirtiest guitar riffs ever committed to tape. —*Stephen Thomas Erlewine*

Draw the Line / Dec. 1977 / Columbia ✦✦✦
Where the decadent celebration of *Rocks* was glorious, *Draw the Line* collapses in its own hedonism, mainly because the band didn't write enough songs that match even the worst of *Rocks* and *Toys in the Attic*. Only the title track and the pseudo-pomp rock of "Kings and Queens" stand out among the murk. —*Stephen Thomas Erlewine*

Live Bootleg / Oct. 1978 / Columbia ✦✦
While it has its moments, *Live Bootleg* is surprisingly devoid of energy, giving a false impression of the group in concert. —*Stephen Thomas Erlewine*

Night in the Ruts / Nov. 1979 / Columbia ✦
Night In The Ruts is the sound of Aerosmith near the bottom. They go through the hard rock motions, but there's no spark in the performances and no distinctiveness to the songwriting. The album's single was an anemic remake of the Shangri-Las' "Remember (Walking In The Sand)" that crept to number 67. The album itself, although a Top 20 gold-seller, was Aerosmith's least successful to this point. Bad as things were, they proceeded to get worse: lead guitarist Joe Perry decamped after the recording of this album, and rhythm guitarist Brad Whitford soon followed. —*William Ruhlmann*

★ **Greatest Hits** / Oct. 1980 / Columbia ✦✦✦✦✦
A solid collection of hits, it includes their stellar Beatles remake "Come Together." All hits, no misses. —*Donna DiChario*

Rock in a Hard Place / Aug. 1982 / Columbia ✦
The only album that Aerosmith made in a six-year period between 1979 and 1985, *Rock In A Hard Place* is the work of original members Steven Tyler, Tom Hamilton, and Joey Kramer, with replacement guitarists Jimmy Crespo and Rick Dufay standing in for the departed Joe Perry and Brad Whitford. It has a more punk-oriented, less hard rock approach than typical Aerosmith, but is far below their usual standard. When it proved a commercial disaster, Aerosmith parted company with Columbia Records and looked to be on its last legs. —*William Ruhlmann*

○ **Done with Mirrors** / Nov. 1985 / Geffen ✦✦✦✦
Joe Perry returned to the fold in 1985, and the band turned out their finest record since *Rocks*. Unlike the records that preceded it, *Done With Mirrors* was powered by the same smart-assed lyrics and filthy guitars that formed the core of Aerosmith's best songs. It didn't receive the commercial or critical attention that *Permanent Vacation* did two years later, but *Done With Mirrors* is the better album; it marks the beginning of their remarkable comeback. —*Stephen Thomas Erlewine*

Classics Live / Apr. 1986 / Columbia ✦✦
With Aerosmith on the way back up, Columbia Records assembled this album of live recordings from 1977 to 1983 in order to cash in. Both the original band and the interim edition with guitarists Jimmy Crespo and Rick Dufay are represented, some of the band's better known material is featured, and the result is a second-rate redundancy. Stick to *Live Bootleg* for live Aerosmith recordings. —*William Ruhlmann*

Classics Live 2 / Jun. 1987 / Columbia ✦✦✦
A rare case where the sequel surpasses the original release, *Classics Live 2* is the leanest, toughest, and best live album Aerosmith has released. —*Stephen Thomas Erlewine*

Permanent Vacation / Aug. 1987 / Geffen ✦✦✦
Apart from the strong singles—"Dude (Looks like a Lady)," "Angel," and "Rag Doll"—*Permanent Vacation* isn't as consistent or rocking a record as *Done with Mirrors*; too often, it relies on slick, horn-spiked production instead of genuine grit, making the moments when Joe Perry's guitar does kick into overdrive all the more splendid. —*Stephen Thomas Erlewine*

○ **Gems** / 1988 / Columbia ✦✦✦✦
Gems is not a greatest hits album. Instead, it's a collection of album tracks and AOR staples ("Mama Kin," "Lord of the Thighs," "Chip Away the Stone," "Rats in the Cellar") that may not make sense as a retrospective, but rocks harder, stronger and longer than most albums they released during the 1970s. —*Stephen Thomas Erlewine*

● **Pump** / Sep. 1989 / Geffen ✦✦✦✦
Where *Permanent Vacation* seemed a little overwhelmed by its
pop concessions, *Pump* revels in them without ever losing sight of
Aerosmith's dirty hard-rock core. Which doesn't mean the record is
a sellout—"What It Takes" has more emotion and grit than any of
their other power ballads; "Janie's Got a Gun" tackles more complex territory than most previous songs; and "The Other Side" and
"Love in an Elevator" rock relentlessly, no matter how many horns
and synths fight with the guitars. Such ambition and successful
musical eclecticism make *Pump* rank with *Rocks* and *Toys in the
Attic. —Stephen Thomas Erlewine*

Pandora's Box / 1991 / Columbia ✦✦
A bare-bones three-CD box set concentrating on Aerosmith's glory
days at Columbia during the 1970s, *Pandora's Box* has plenty of
fine music but ultimately fails as a retrospective. All the hits are
available in better singles collections (or more consistent original
albums), and the rarities and the packaging are nothing special.
Because of licensing restrictions, the set isn't able to cover their
startling 1980s comeback, so it's not comprehensive, either; it's for
die-hard fans only. —*Stephen Thomas Erlewine*

Get a Grip / 1993 / Geffen ✦✦✦
Coming on the heels of the commercially and artistically successful *Pump*, the fitfully entertaining *Get A Grip* pales against its predecessor's musical diversity. But it's not for lack of trying. In fact,
Aerosmith tries too hard, making a stab at social commentary
("Livin' On the Edge") while keeping adolescent fans in their corner with their trademark raunch-rock ("Get a Grip" and "Eat the
Rich"), as well as having radio-ready hit ballads ("Cryin'," "Amazing," and "Crazy"). The problem is, it's a studied performance—it
sounds like what an Aerosmith album *should* sound like. Most of
the album *sounds* good; it's just that there isn't much beneath the
surface. —*Stephen Thomas Erlewine*

● **Big Ones** / 1994 / Geffen ✦✦✦✦
Big Ones serves up the hits and nothing but the hits; Aerosmith's
excellent debut for Geffen, *Done With Mirrors*, is conveniently
overlooked. So what's left is some of the finest mainstream hard
rock of the late '80s and early '90s—the fruits of one of the most
remarkable comebacks in rock & roll history. Unfortunately,
there's precious little of the classic Aerosmith raunch; in fact, the
two new tracks are the hardest, slinkiest tracks here. Otherwise,
the uptempo tracks bog down in overproduction ("Love in An Elevator") and the frequently embarrassingly overwrought power ballads ("Angel" and "Crazy") dominate too much of the album. So
what's left? The band's best stab at social commentary ("Janie's
Got a Gun"), a sublime slinky throwaway ("Deuces Are Wild"), deliciously sleazy blues-rockers ("Rag Doll," "(Dude) Looks like a
Lady") and their best ballads ("What It Takes" and "Cryin' "). —
Stephen Thomas Erlewine

Afghan Whigs

Group, Alternative Pop/Rock
With their 1988 debut, *Big Top Halloween*, the Cleveland-based
Afghan Whigs sounded like a more ambitious (and pretentious)
Replacements underneath the roar of their guitars. Switching
record labels to Sub Pop in 1990 (becoming one of the first non-
Seattle bands on their roster in the process), the band increased
their volume while lead singer/songwriter Greg Dulli deepened
his lyrical word play. With their second Sub Pop album, *Congregation*, and their final independent release, *Uptown Avondale*, the
Whigs developed a soul music fixation that added a new dimension to their punky guitar roar. This infatuation came to fruition
on their major-label debut, 1993's *Gentlemen*, their strongest,
most consistent record to date; it confirmed their status as critics'
darlings while substantially increasing their cult following. —
Stephen Thomas Erlewine

Big Top Halloween / 1988 / Ultrasuede ✦✦

Up in It / 1990 / Sub Pop ✦✦✦
More pop than you'd expect from a Sub Pop release, this is still
loud, hard riff-raunch with a thick, unyielding sound. —*John
Dougan*

○ **Congregation** / Aug. 1991 / Sub Pop ✦✦✦✦
Dulli's songwriting continues to improve on their last full-length
independent album, while the band itself sounds tougher and able
to keep up with the twists in the songwriting. —*Stephen Thomas
Erlewine*

Uptown Avondale / 1992 / Sub Pop ✦✦✦
The Whigs' final independent release was a scorching EP of soul
and R&B covers, and is arguably their finest moment. —*Stephen
Thomas Erlewine*

● **Gentlemen** / 1993 / Elektra ✦✦✦✦
With their major label debut, *Gentlemen*, the Afghan Whigs have
finally come into their own. Throughout *Gentlemen*, the Whigs act
as if they were Minneapolis punks ripping through the Stax songbook as written by Paul Westerberg. It's a riveting, original album,
uncompromising in its honesty and punk/soul roots—in short,
with this album, the Afghan Whigs have fulfilled the promise of
their earlier, independent records. —*Stephen Thomas Erlewine*

Afros

Group, Rap
A trio with a penchant for sight gags linked to huge bushy hair-
styles from the same decade (two members, Hurricane and Koot
Tee, were clean shaven, while DJ Kippy-O had an extensive Afro).
The group also has a good pedigree, with Hurricane being a DJ for
the Beastie Boys and a rapper for Davy D. Their material is more
in a mode of parody/satire than confrontation, with a couple of po-
litical-consciousness and cultural-awareness cuts added to spice
the menu. —*Ron Wynn*

○ **Kickin' Afrolistics** / 1990 / Ral ✦✦✦✦
A wacky trio combine a love for '70s blaxploitation films and comedy with occasional inspired political commentary and witty
repartee. —*Ron Wynn*

After 7

Group, Urban
After 7 emerged in the '90s as a solid contemporary ensemble able
to perform creditably in either vintage soul or modern New Jack
and urban styles. The Indianapolis trio includes brothers Melvin
and Kevin Edmonds (the brothers of producer/performer Babyface) and Keith Mitchell (cousin of Babyface's long-time partner
L.A. Reid). They signed with Virgin in 1989 and had immediate
success with their LP *After 7.* Such songs as "Can't Stop" and "Heat
of the Moment" were major winners on the urban and Quiet
Storm circuit, and a remix of "Can't Stop" also attracted sizable
dance attention. They recorded with Johnny Gill, then enjoyed another hit release in 1992, *Takin' My Time.* It included a sterling remake of the Originals' "Baby, I'm for Real." —*Ron Wynn*

● **After 7** / 1989 / Virgin ✦✦✦✦
The debut release from this offspring of R&B-producing whiz
Babyface Reid. Some good singing, but the production dominates.
—*Ron Wynn*

Takin' My Time / 1992 / Virgin ✦✦✦
An excellent vocal trio that combines state-of-the-art, uptempo
New Jack Swing tunes with classic romantic ballads. After 7 had
several chart hits culled from this release, doing particularly well
with a remake of the Originals' "Baby, I'm For Real." The lead vocalist is a relative of producer and vocalist Babyface. —*Ron Wynn*

After the Fire

Group, Pop/Rock
After The Fire was formed by guitarist Peter Banks after he left
Yes in 1972. Other members included guitarist John Russell,
bassist Andy Piercy, and drummer Ivor Twidell. They struggled,
but hit the U.K. Top 40 in 1979 with "One Rule for You." Then, in
1983, they covered Falco's hit "Der Kommissar," and outdid his
success with it in the U.S., where it went to number 5. —*William
Ruhlmann*

● **ATF** / 1982 / Epic ✦✦✦✦
ATF is a compilation album released by Epic Records in the U.S. in
the wake of After The Fire's success with "Der Kommissar," but
containing material that dates back to 1979, including the U.K. hits
"One Rule For You" and "Laser Love." "Dancing In The Shadows"
also became a U.S. chart entry at #85, but After The Fire really
was a one-hit wonder. Still, the album makes for pleasant, if dated,
techno power pop of the late '70s/early '80s. —*William Ruhlmann*

Agnostic Front

Group, Punk, Hardcore
At the beginning of the '80s, Agnostic Front was on the forefront of
New York's hardcore punk scene, playing their music as one re-
lentless blur. By their second album, they added some metal ele-

ments—thicker guitar riffs and a deep drum sound—to their music, making the group one of the first bands to bridge the gap between metal and punk. —*Stephen Thomas Erlewine*

Victim in Pain / 1984 / Combat ✦✦✦
It continues to be an influence for many hardcore and punk bands. —*John Book*

○ **Cause for Alarm** / 1986 / Combat ✦✦✦✦
An album that presented hardcore to many metal listeners for the first time. Politically aware and frighteningly true, they're not a metal band but they demonstrated the kinds of things metal lacked back then. —*John Book*

Liberty & Justice For . . . / 1987 / Combat ✦✦✦
The album contained a slight influence from metal, and thus sold quite well within the metal community. —*John Book*

Live at CBGB / 1989 / Combat ✦✦✦
This is Agnostic Front the way they should be enjoyed, in concert, with full support from the crowd. It's the band's last album before their temporary hiatus. —*John Book*

One Voice / 1992 / Combat ✦✦

Last Warning / Jun. 15, 1993 / Combat ✦✦

● **The Best of Agnostic Front** / Combat ✦✦✦✦
While it isn't as cohesive as some of their proper albums, Agnostic Front's best moments are featured on this best-of collection. —*Stephen Thomas Erlewine*

a-ha

Group, Techno-Pop/Dance, Pop/Rock
For a short time in the summer of 1985, a-ha were superstars. Thanks to their groundbreaking video for "Take on Me"—a clever clip that combined pencil sketches with live-action footage of the attractive band members—the band had a huge hit single. Their pleasantly catchy brand of synthesized pop in the vein of Duran Duran wasn't what made the song hit; it was the video. Consequently, the band wasn't able to score another big hit after "Take on Me," even though they tried valiantly several times ("The Sun Always Shines on T.V." made a small dent on the charts in the beginning of 1986). a-ha turned toward a more moody, synth-based adult-contemporary pop with their 1988 album, *Stay on These Roads*; they have pursued the same musical direction ever since. —*Stephen Thomas Erlewine*

● **Hunting High and Low** / Jun. 1985 / Warner Brothers ✦✦✦✦
This is friendly synthesizer pop, fronted by the emotive, sometimes falsetto vocals of Morten Harket. But it was Harket's looks, as exhibited in the semi-animated video, that sent "Take on Me" to number one in the summer of 1985. The album also contains the follow-up, "The Sun Always Shines on T.V." (number 20). But so far, this million-selling debut is the beginning and end of a-ha as legitimate record makers in the U.S. (In the U.K., in contrast, the album spawned four Top Ten hits, including the title track and "Train of Thought.") —*William Ruhlmann*

Scoundrel Days / 1986 / Warner Brothers ✦✦
In the U.S., this close copy of a-ha's debut album was a considerable disappointment, with only "Cry Wolf" getting as high as number 50. But in England, it was a different story, as *Scoundrel Days* became a-ha's second straight album to peak at number two and there were three Top 20 hits in "I've Been Losing You," "Cry Wolf," and "Manhattan Skyline." —*William Ruhlmann*

Stay on These Roads / 1988 / Warner Brothers ✦✦
a-ha's recording career hit the skids in America with its third release. But in the U.K., the album became the group's third straight to peak at number two, though it charted for a shorter period than the first two albums, and there were four Top 25 hits—the title track, "The Blood That Moves the Body," "Touchy!," and "You Are the One." (Also included was a-ha's 1987 theme from the James Bond movie *The Living Daylights*, a U.K. number five that missed the U.S. charts.) Even in a country with a demonstrated affection for Scandinavians, however (remember ABBA?), that was a falloff, if the decline was more gradual, and three albums in, a-ha wasn't demonstrating any development from its first hit, just more of the same and a little less distinctive. —*William Ruhlmann*

East of the Sun, West of The Moon / 1990 / Warner Brothers ✦
Prime evidence of a career out of gas: a-ha leads off their fourth album with a remake of the Everly Brothers hit "Crying in the Rain." It gave them a #13 hit in the U.K. (the album went to number 12),

but this is really the sound of a band working out their record contract. —*William Ruhlmann*

Memorial Beach / Apr. 1992 / Warner Brothers ✦
For its fifth album, a-ha varies its style somewhat, trying for a U2 approach on lead-off track "Dark Is the Night for All." This is a long way from the peppy appeal of "Take on Me," but just as far from an improvement. —*William Ruhlmann*

A House

Group, Alternative Pop/Rock
A House is a quartet from Dublin, formed in April 1985 from the remains of Last Chance and featuring singer/guitarist Dave Couse, guitarist Fergal Bunbury, bassist Martin Nealy, and drummer Dermot Wylie. They released their first single, "Kick Me Again, Jesus," on their own Hip Records label in 1987. —*William Ruhlmann*

● **On Our Big Fat Merry-Go-Round** / 1988 / Sire ✦✦✦✦
On its debut album, A House reveals a taste for driving, catchy guitar rock somewhat in the style of U2, although the lyrics are full of attitude (attacks on journalists ["That's Not The Truth"] and production team Stock-Aitken-Waterman ["Stone The Crows"]) and violent imagery—song titles include "I Want To Kill Something," "Watch Out You're Dead," and "Violent Love." The album contains the raving "Call Me Blue," which hit number 9 on Billboard's Modern Rock Tracks chart in December 1988. —*William Ruhlmann*

I Want Too Much / 1990 / Sire ✦✦✦

I Am the Greatest / 1992 / Radioactive ✦✦✦
I Am The Greatest is the unusual but intriguing new album from Dublin, Ireland's A House. In places, melodious with a bent twist; in others, dissonant with an arresting groove. Picture the Velvet Underground nursed on Celtic roots. Highlights: the title track's dissection of the price of fame and "Endless Art," essentially a roll call of dead, influential artists. —*Roch Parisien*

Air Supply

Group, Pop
With their heavily orchestrated, sweet ballads, the Australian soft-rock group Air Supply became a staple of early-'80s radio, scoring a string of seven straight Top Five singles. Air Supply, for most intents and purposes, was the duo of vocalists Russell Hitchcock and Graham Russell; other members came through the group over the years, yet they only functioned as backing musicians and added little to the group's sound. Hitchcock and Russell met while performing in a Sydney, Australia, production of *Jesus Christ Superstar* in 1976. The two singers formed a partnership and with the addition of four supporting musicians—keyboardist Frank Esler-Smith, guitarist David Moyse, bassist David Green, and drummer Ralph Cooper—Air Supply was born.

For several years, the group gained no attention outside of Australia, earning one significant hit single, "Love and Other Bruises." Their first international exposure came in the late '70s, when Rod Stewart had them as his opening act on a North American tour. Air Supply signed a record contract with Arista in 1980, releasing their first album by the end of the year. *Lost in Love*, their debut, was a major success in the U.S., selling over two million copies and spawning the hit singles "Lost in Love," "All Out of Love," and "Every Woman in the World." The following year they released their second album, *The One That You Love*. The title track became their only #1 hit and it also featured two other Top Ten hits, "Here I Am (Just When I Thought I Was Over You)" and "Sweet Dreams." With their third album, 1982's *Now and Forever*, their popularity dipped slightly—it only had one Top 10 hit, "Even the Nights Are Better," and the other two singles, "Young Love" and "Two Less Lonely People in the World," scraped the bottom of the Top 40. Air Supply released a *Greatest Hits* collection in 1983, featuring a new single, "Making Love Out of Nothing At All." The single spent two weeks at number two while the album peaked at number seven and eventually sold over four million copies.

Two years later, they released *Air Supply*, their fourth album. It featured the #19 single "Just As I Am," but it was clear that their audience was shrinking—the album was their first not to go platinum. *Hearts in Motion* (1986) was even less successful, peaking at number 84 and spending only nine weeks on the charts. After its disappointing performance, Air Supply broke up. Hitchcock and Russell reunited in 1991, releasing *Earth Is . . .*,but the album failed to make the charts as did 1993's *Vanishing Race* and 1995's *News From Nowhere.* —*Stephen Thomas Erlewine*

○ **Lost in Love** / 1980 / Arista ✦✦✦✦

○ **The One That You Love** / 1981 / Arista ✦✦✦✦

Now & Forever / 1982 / Arista ✦✦✦

Air Supply / 1985 / Arista ✦✦✦

Hearts in Motion / 1986 / Arista ✦✦

● **Greatest Hits** / 1988 / Arista ✦✦✦✦

This self-explanatory collection includes "Lost in Love" (number one), "The One That You Love" (number one), "Every Woman in the World" (number five), "All Out of Love" (number two), "Sweet Dreams" (number five), "Making Love Out of Nothing at All" (number two), "Even the Nights Are Better" (number five), and many more soft pop hits. —*Rick Clark*

The Earth Is . . . / Jul. 23, 1991 / Giant ✦✦

The return of Air Supply was greeted by overwhelming indifference when this album appeared in the summer of 1991. The only track that attracted any attention at all was a remake of Nilsson's cover of Badfinger's "Without You," which hobbled to number 48 on Billboard's Adult Contemporary chart, an especially galling failure given that Mariah Carey took the same song to number three on the pop charts in 1994. —*William Ruhlmann*

The Vanishing Race / 1993 / Giant ✦✦

News From Nowhere / 1995 / Giant ✦✦

The Alarm

Group, Alternative Pop/Rock

An English foursome, the Alarm (inspired by U2's lofty dispatches) initially generated a rock-heavy acoustic guitar-based rock, loaded with anthemic melodies and issue-oriented lyrics. Later the band switched to electric guitars and developed a more mainstream/alternative sound that earned them an audience among the MTV set. Even though the Alarm has been quite popular in England, they've only had one pop chart hit stateside with the #77 "Presence of Love." —*Rick Clark*

The Alarm / 1983 / IRS ✦✦✦

This is a five-song EP that introduced the Alarm in the U.S. It is led off by "The Stand," a forceful anthem that established the band's powerful, vaguely political message. Actually, they were always more stance than stand, more notable for their fury than their sense. It made for stirring listening, though. —*William Ruhlmann*

Declaration / 1984 / IRS ✦✦✦

The Alarm's first full-length album was, to a certain extent, a collection of the singles they had been releasing since October 1982: "Marching On," "The Stand," "Sixty-Eight Guns" (number 17 U.K., number 106 U.S.), "Where Were You Hiding When the Storm Broke?" (number 22 U.K.) and "The Deceiver" (number 51 U.K., number 104 U.S.). As such, it had a strident, immediate appeal that was also somewhat relentless: the Alarm seemed to play every song as if it was the climax of their set. In the short term, that excited listeners, however; *Declaration* was a number six hit in England and broke through to the Top 50 in the U.S. In retrospect, it's more smoke than fire. —*William Ruhlmann*

○ **Strength** / 1985 / IRS ✦✦✦✦

In addition to an improved sense of musicality and dynamics, *Strength* featured the Alarm's finest group of songs, making it their single best studio album. —*Stephen Thomas Erlewine*

Eye of the Hurricane / 1987 / IRS ✦✦✦

This should have been the album that put the Alarm on the path to major stardom; instead, it marked the limits of their appeal. From the early fervor of their punk/acoustic debut, the group had evolved into more of a mainstream rock act without ever getting out from under the shadow of their mentors, U2. In fact, here they sounded more like U2 than ever, and now that that group had ascended to superstardom, the comparison only hurt them. The signal hit here was "Rain In The Summertime," an overproduced leadoff track followed by "Rescue Me" and "Presence Of Love." All three tracks got AOR radio play in the U.S., so you couldn't say the Alarm wasn't getting exposure, especially when they were touring with Bob Dylan. However, they weren't getting through. —*William Ruhlmann*

Electric Folklore: Live / 1988 / IRS ✦✦

The Alarm chose to address the career crisis precipitated by their declining record sales by emphasizing their live act in the form of this six-song EP, recorded in concert at the Wang Center for the Performing Arts in Boston on April 26, 1988. Lead singer Mike Peters took the opportunity to criticize American radio and quote

Woody Guthrie. The set effectively demonstrated that the group was a powerhouse live, but did not in itself reverse their fortunes, getting to number 62 in the U.K., and, in the U.S., where nobody's ever understood what EPs are for, only number 167. What they really needed was a hit, and it was getting hard to understand why a band that seemed to want to write an anthem every time out couldn't get one. —*William Ruhlmann*

Change / 1989 / IRS ✦✦✦

Clearly, change was called for in the Alarm's career, and on their fourth album, the group achieved a tighter hard rock sound by turning to producer Tony Visconti. Their extensive roadwork and promotional efforts had opened doors for them at AOR and college radio, which played "Sold Me Down The River," "Devolution Workin' Man Blues," and "Love Don't Come Easy." "River" even became the Alarm's biggest U.S. hit single, peaking at number 50. But the album sold about the same as *Eye Of The Hurricane*, indicating that all the hard work had only enabled them to run in place. The problem remained the same: the Alarm had calmed down from its early martial style and turned into a competent mainstream rock band, but they still sounded too much like U2, and the rock riffs and throaty vocals still didn't add up to memorable songs. —*William Ruhlmann*

Newid / 1989 / IRS ✦✦

● **Standards** / 1990 / IRS ✦✦✦✦

This solid anthology covers everything from early aggressive topical folk-rock anthems ("Marching On," "The Stand") to more mainstream rock hits like "Strength" and "Sold Me down The River." —*Rick Clark*

Raw / 1991 / IRS ✦✦

It's hard to avoid the conclusion that the Alarm's fifth new studio album, *Raw*, released six months after the career-summarizing hits collection *Standards*, was a contractual obligation record. Lacking promotion, it crept into the pop chart for a single week at number 161, while the title track earned some AOR and college radio play. Despite that title, this was another competent mainstream rock collection, its unnecessary highlight a cover of Neil Young's "Rockin' in the Free World." "Moments in Time" presented a ballad-tempo history of the band, always a sure sign of an impending breakup (cf. "Creeque Alley," "The Ballad of Mott," etc.): "Somewhere we got lost along the way," sings Mike Peters. Sad, but true. —*William Ruhlmann*

Arthur Alexander

b. 1942, Florence, AL, **d.** Jun. 9, 1993

Soul, R&B

Alexander was one of the first true singing, songwriting stars of "country-soul," a genre that wed Southern Black R&B singers to songs written in a country format and played basically by White musicians. Alexander's "You Better Move On" (#24-1962), was the first hit to come out of Rick Hall's fledgling Muscle Shoals studio. Alexander's work was immediately appreciated by his peers in the business; those who have covered his tunes (self-penned or otherwise) read like a Who's Who from both sides of the Atlantic—"Anna" (Beatles); "Soldiers of Love" (Beatles and Marshall Crenshaw); "Burning Love" (Elvis Presley); "Set Me Free" (Joe Tex, Esther Phillips, Percy Sledge). The Rolling Stones' cover of "You Better Move On" led to valuable contacts for Rick Hall, and the resulting business enabled him to build the new FAME studio. It was the start of the whole Muscle Shoals sound, and Alexander's career was one of its cornerstones. He went on, after a brief retirement, to record for both Warner Brothers and Buddah.

"Anna (Go to Him)," one of Alexander's best-known tunes, epitomizes the anguished, haunting tone of his music. From the onset, the heavily echoed piano and tortured vocal set a mood that is soulful, mysterious, a little spooky, and totally mesmerizing. His work is essential to any country-soul collection.

Warner Bros. issued an Arthur Alexander retrospective anthology in 1994 featuring the early '70s LP he recorded for them, plus some unissued tracks.

As Alexander began a comeback in 1993, he died of a heart attack. However, the album he completed before his death, *Lonely Like Me*, is a gentle record that is a fine way to end his career. —*Christine Ohlman*

Soldier of Love / 1987 / Ace ✦✦✦

14 tracks from the '60s, half previously unissued, a few from his rare Dot LP, a couple of tracks from obscure 45s, and a fine, more sparsely produced alternate version of the title track. Although

this isn't as exceptional as his best stuff, it's fairly solid, and while the material isn't top-notch, Alexander's oddly reserved and affecting vocals are uniformly strong. —*Richie Unterberger*

○ **Lonely Just Like Me** / 1993 / Elektra/Nonesuch ✦✦✦✦
The final album from soul/country vocalist Arthur Alexander. It was like all his work—simple, unsophisticated, and sung with an earthy, direct intensity. This was part of the American Explorers series on Elektra/Nonesuch, and Alexander got some critical attention with his probing, often searing vocals. Unfortunately, he died just as this album was gaining some attention. —*Ron Wynn*

★ **The Ultimate Arthur Alexander** / 1993 / Razor & Tie ✦✦✦✦✦
Alexander's songs are better known in versions by the Beatles, Elvis Presley and the Rolling Stones, but no one recorded better versions than Arthur Alexander himself. *The Ultimate Arthur Alexander* truly lives up to its title, gathering together the best songs (including "Anna [Go To Him]," "You Better Move On," and "Soldiers of Love") from Alexander's remarkably influential and underrated career. Absolutely essential for any R&B and soul collection. — *Stephen Thomas Erlewine*

○ **Rainbow Road** / 1994 / Warner Archives ✦✦✦✦
Songwriter and vocalist Arthur Alexander was sorely neglected during his lifetime, despite possessing a stark, compelling voice and being among pop and soul's greatest storytellers. He remained on the outside, coming close but never attaining stardom. This CD features 15 fantastic songs, most from the great 1972 Warner Bros. album recorded in Memphis that Alexander thought would finally earn him that elusive smash. There are also some singles cut in Nashville as companion records to the Memphis session. The 15 tracks range from the hypnotic title cut and "In The Middle Of It All" to the uptempo burners "You Got Me Knockin' " and "Burning Love." There's also a moving gospel number, "Thank God He Came." This disc is a wonderful tribute to an unjustly ignored artist. —*Ron Wynn*

Alice in Chains

Group, Alternative Pop/Rock, Heavy Metal
Out of all the Seattle grunge bands of the early '90s, Alice in Chains had the strongest ties with heavy metal. Soundgarden also approximated the mammoth, heavy riffs of Black Sabbath, yet they leavened their attack with humor. On record, Alice In Chains rarely alleviates the gloom. Their music wallows in death, despair, and drugs. With guitarist Jerry Cantrell's lean, lethal riffs, drummer Sean Kinney's subtly menacing rhythms and Layne Staley's flat, emotionless vocals, the band is relentlessly heavy. What keeps Alice in Chains from being a standard-issue metal band is Cantrell's subtly crafted songs, which rely on shifting textures and dynamics for their impact. Staley's lyrics never celebrate the darkness that he writes about; instead, they intensify the already oppressively gloomy atmosphere, making their music frighteningly claustrophobic.

Although their debut, *Facelift*, was popular in metal circles—particularly "We Die Young" and "Man in the Box"—Alice in Chains' fan base began to build in early 1992 with their acoustic *Sap* EP. Their second full-length album, *Dirt*, expanded their audience dramatically, selling over two million copies and earning them a headlining slot on Lollapalooza 93. Before the tour began, bassist Mike Starr left the group and was replaced by Mike Inez. At the beginning of 1994, Alice in Chains released their second EP, *Jar of Flies*, which became the first EP to debut at number one on the *Billboard* album charts. — *Stephen Thomas Erlewine*

Facelift / 1990 / Columbia ✦✦✦
Alice In Chains' first album earned them a strong following with its crunching, foreboding rock, including the singles "Man in the Box" and "We Die Young." *Facelift* might not have the grand thematic sweep of *Dirt*, but makes up for it with sheer energy and muscular riffs. —*Stephen Thomas Erlewine*

○ **Sap** / Feb. 1992 / Columbia ✦✦✦✦
Before Alice In Chains delivered their second album, they released *Sap*, a five-song EP featuring acoustic-oriented material. For anyone who pigeonholed them as mere gloom-mongers after their debut, *Sap* was a shock; it showed that they were capable of playing quieter, more intricate music without losing any intensity. — *Stephen Thomas Erlewine*

● **Dirt** / Oct. 1992 / Columbia ✦✦✦✦
To say that *Dirt* is a dark album is something of an understatement. Alice In Chains convey a stark, stoic beauty to the pain of their protagonists. The violence and disturbing elements (both

musical and lyrical) are offset by a mantra-like feel of inner strength and acceptance. Musically, Alice In Chains' rhythm section lays down a heavy, doom-struck base over which twin guitars and double-tracked vocals slash appealingly. There are lots of interesting tempo and time signature changes, the band veering into progressive rock territory on occasion. —*Roch Parisien*

Jar of Flies / 1994 / Columbia ✦✦✦
Like *Sap* before it, *Jar of Flies* is a quieter, acoustic-oriented experimental EP released between full-length albums, but it also works well as a coda to the epochal *Dirt*. Although the songs are calmer, they are by no means gentle, providing harrowing examinations of loss. Thankfully, musical stretches like the instrumental "Whale & Wasp" and the swing-blues of "Swing On This" are successful, and the best material here ("I Stay Away" and "No Excuses") rivals the best tracks on *Dirt*. —*Stephen Thomas Erlewine*

All About Eve

Group, Alternative Pop/Rock
All About Eve is a British "gothic rock" group formed in the late '80s with a lineup including singer/bassist Julianne Regan, guitarist Tim Bricheno, bassist Andy Cousin, and drummer Mark Price. They hit the U.K. charts with "In The Clouds" in 1987 and the Top Ten album *All About Eve* in 1988. Bricheno left the group in 1990 and was replaced on a temporary basis by Marty Willson-Piper of The Church. — *William Ruhlmann*

● **All About Eve** / 1988 / Mercury ✦✦✦
'60s British folk-rock meets '80s goth; oddly, it works! —*Steve Aldrich*

Scarlet and Other Stories / 1989 / Mercury ✦✦✦

Touched by Jesus / 1991 / Vertigo ✦✦✦
Lineup features the Church guitarist, Marty Willson-Piper. (Import) —*Steve Aldrich*

Ultraviolet / 1994 / MCA ✦✦

All-4-One

Group, Urban
Comprising Tony Borowiak, Jamie Jones, Delious Kennedy, and Alfred Nevarez, the Californian contemporary R&B vocal quartet All-4-One's 1994 debut album sailed into the Top Ten thanks to the enormous hit single "I Swear," which stayed at number one for eleven weeks. —*Stephen Thomas Erlewine*

● **All-4-One** / 1994 / Blitzz/Atlantic ✦✦✦✦

And The Music Speaks / 1995 / Blitzz/Atlantic ✦✦✦

Davie Allan

Instrumental Rock, Psychedelic
Providing the soundtrack to numerous biker and teen exploitation movies in the mid and late '60s, Davie Allan & the Arrows bridged the surf and psychedelic eras. Their driving, basic instrumentals featured loads and loads of fuzz guitar, as well as generous dollops of tremelo bar waggling and wah-wah. The guitarist and his band first made their mark with the minor hit "Apache '65," a version of the Shadows/Jorgen Ingmann instrumental classic "Apache." Hooking up with notorious exploitation movie producer Mike Curb, the Arrows provided the soundtracks to numerous B-movies on the Tower and Sidewalk labels; their greatest success, "Blues Theme" (from *The Wild Angels*, starring Peter Fonda), made the Top 40 in 1967. When Curb abandoned racy movies for the Osmonds and purged MGM Records of its psychedelic acts, the Arrows' flight was over. —*Richie Unterberger*

Loud Loose And Savage / 1994 / ✦✦✦
Allan, best known for creating the fuzz-guitar instrumental hit "Blue's Theme" in the biker movie *The Wild Angels*, pops up again with a little-known soundtrack he did back in the '80s for another drive-in classic built on the same chassis. The accent here is on fuzz ("Hogg Heaven"), fuzz ("Grungy") and more fuzz ("Blue Shift"), with Allan churning out true-blue '60s biker music as if nothing had changed since the last time he saw the charts nearly 30 years ago. —*Cub Koda*

● **King Fuzz** / Fuzzwalk ✦✦✦✦
The only compilation of Allan's numerous '60s recordings, condensing the highlights of his 1965-67 soundtracks, albums, and B-sides into 15 songs. For all but specialists, "Blues Theme" is all you need. The guitar pyrotechnics are occasionally impressive, but the repetitive fuzz-psychedelic riffs are numbing over the course of an entire LP. —*Richie Unterberger*

Lee Allen

b. Jul. 2, 1926, **d.** Oct. 18, 1994

R&B

The blasting tenor saxophone of Lee Allen was every bit as integral a factor in the sizzling sound of the '50s New Orleans R&B as were the well-documented contributions of Fats Domino, Lloyd Price, and Little Richard. As a key member of the studio band at Cosimo's, Allen played searing solos that sparked hundreds of Crescent City classics. Allen's wallpaper-peeling sax solos are instantly identifiable—check out Richard's "Slippin' and Slidin' " and "Tutti Frutti" for irrefutably exciting evidence.

But despite his sax mastery, Allen failed to sustain a brief solo career. Signing with Al Silver's New York-based Ember label, he managed one decent-sized hit in 1958, the rocking instrumental "Walkin' with Mr. Lee," while the second-line scorcher "Boppin' at the Hop" inexplicably never received any national airplay.

When the New Orleans sound shifted to a funkier beat, Allen's muscular sound fell out of favor on the local recording scene. Nevertheless, Allen remained active until his death in 1994, touring extensively with Domino, as well as working with a variety of young rockers (including the Blasters) who revered his blistering sound. —*Bill Dahl*

● **Walkin' with Mr. Lee** / 1958 / Collectables ✦✦✦✦
New Orleans' leading tenor sax man during the '50s, this, his only solo album, has some hot-rockin' instrumentals. —*Bill Dahl*

Richie Allen

Surf

One of the unheralded architects of the Southern Californian surf sound, Allen (real name Richie Podolor) played a lot of session guitar on surf and hot rod records in the early '60s, particularly for producer Gary Usher. He also played guitar for drummer Sandy Nelson on the classic "Teen Beat" and other instrumentals, and recorded quite a few surf instrumentals under his own name, although these were rather placid and routine when stacked up against the best of the genre. Reverting to his real name, Podolor racked up production credits with Iron Butterfly, Steppenwolf, and Three Dog Night in the late '60s, and remains active behind the boards today. —*Richie Unterberger*

● **Surfer's Slide** / 1963 / Imperial ✦✦✦✦
No less than 34 tracks on this retrospective of Allen/Podolor's early-'60s work, almost all original instrumentals. Compared to much vintage surf, it's disappointingly sedate, the emphasis on ballad-tempo mood pieces with plenty of tremolo and cowboy movie theme influences. His best guitar work, on the obscure but smoking Sandy Nelson instrumental "Casbah," can be found on the compilation *Wax 'Em Down! —Richie Unterberger*

G.G. Allin

Punk, Hardcore

For years, G.G. Allin promised to leave this world with a suicide on stage, preferably on Halloween. Instead, Allin died a traditional rock & roll death—cocaine and heroin in the veins—which is the only traditional thing he ever did.

In the strictest sense, Allin was not a musician, he was a performance artist with an insatiable desire to shock. Allin was notorious for performing in the nude, defecating and urinating on stage, smearing excrement all over himself and the audience, attacking the audience, mutilating himself, and ending the show quickly; his last concert lasted under ten minutes and ended in a riot. His music was the aural equivalent of his stage show—an amateurish, barely competent series of short blasts of loud violence on albums called *Eat My Fuc, Freaks, Faggots, Drunks & Junkies*, and the aptly titled *America's Most Hated*.

Eventually, the consequences of Allin's onstage antics caught up to him and he spent several years in jail. Upon his release in 1993, Allin began touring again, but only for a couple of months; he died on June 28, 1993, in New York, leaving behind a recorded legacy that can only be called vile and repulsive. —*Stephen Thomas Erlewine*

Always Was, Is, and Always Shall Be / 1980 / Orange ✦✦

Eat My Fuc / 1984 / Blood ✦✦

Live Fast, Die Fast / 1984 / Black & Blue ✦✦

You Give Love a Bad Name / 1987 / Awareness ✦✦

Hated in the Nation / 1987 / ROIR ✦✦✦
Compilation of live performances from various points in G.G.'s career. Of course, it's missing a great deal of relevant information, and the recording quality is crude. This is probably the best place

to be introduced to the demented moron who made obscenity a political statement, as G.G. was still possessed of an intelligible voice on these recordings. He can even carry a tune on the earlier tracks, unthinkable to those familiar only with his later work. His between-song banter with the audience is hilariously stupid. Features guest appearances from Dinosaur Jr.'s J. Mascis and the MC5's Wayne Kramer and Dennis Thompson. Most of G.G.'s earlier recordings are out of print, so if you're a fan, find this. —*Steve Huey*

● **Freaks, Faggots, Drunks & Junkies** / 1988 / Awareness ✦✦✦✦
Allin is at his scatological best/worst here. —*Dan Heilman*

Suicide Sessions / 1989 / Awareness ✦✦✦

Banned in Boston / 1989 / Black & Blue ✦✦

Doctrine of Mayhem / 1990 / Black & Blue ✦✦

○ **Hated (Original Soundtrack)** / 1993 / Performance ✦✦✦✦
Soundtrack to the must-see documentary film on Allin of the same title. The liner notes contain quotes from the film from G.G. and associates, which, together with several of Allin's signature songs and other material, offer about as understandable a portrait of him as one can get. The sound (and musical) quality of most of these selections, whether live or studio recordings, is wretched, but somehow they make more sense that way. ("Suck My Ass It Smells," in particular, must be heard for one to believe that somebody bothered to record it.) Cover art by John Wayne Gacy. —*Steve Huey*

Anti-Social Personality Disorder: Live / 1993 / Evergreen ✦
Bad even for G.G., this is an album of live performances culled from Allin's 1989 tour, which ended with his conviction for felonious assault. As the liner notes say, "during the majority of the tour, G.G. did not know or care where he was." Besides the prerequisite awful sound quality, he has a major problem singing into the mike. For that matter, he has a major problem singing in general, preferring a drunken, guttural, sometimes-understandable growl that often resembles vomiting. Any suspicions that Allin is just acting should be allayed by the psychotic rambling on "Jesus and Mother's Cunt." He also has some unsavory comments about TV host Morton Downey Jr. stemming from a confrontational appearance on Downey's show. —*Steve Huey*

Brutality & Bloodshed For All / 1993 / Alive ✦✦✦
The last album before G.G.'s death, and his last opus of stale, uninspired punk riffs, egomania, violence, depravity, and universal hatred. All of the lyrics were written during Allin's term in Jackson State Prison. The production is actually somewhat clear, but this unfortunately makes G.G. sound like a deranged Muppet on many tracks. Still, this is a must for fans, as the package includes remembrances of G.G., copies of his birth and death certificates, and a photo of the Murder Junkies posing around Allin's open coffin. —*Steve Huey*

The Allman Brothers Band

Group, Blues Rock, Southern Rock

The Allman Brothers Band was the major instigator of the Southern-rock genre of the '70s and one of the major rock acts of the first half of that decade; it continues to be popular today. In its original configuration, the group consisted of Duane Allman (b. Nov 20, 1946–d.Oct 29, 1971) on guitar; Gregg Allman (b. Dec 8, 1947) on organ and vocals; Dickey Betts (b. Dec 12, 1943) on guitar and vocals; Berry Oakley (b. Apr 4, 1948–d. Nov 11, 1971) on bass; and Butch Trucks and Jaimo (born John Lee Johnson, Jul 8, 1944) on drums. This sextet was a showcase for the twin-guitar work of Duane Allman and Dickey Betts and for the bluesy singing of Gregg Allman. They cut three albums between 1969 and 1971. *Live at the Fillmore East*, the Allmans' breakthrough third album, went gold four days before bandleader Duane Allman was killed in a motorcycle accident. The group continued as a quintet, finishing its fourth album, *Eat a Peach* (1972), which was a major success. After bassist Oakley was also killed in a motorcycle accident, the group was augmented with bassist Lamar Williams (b. 1947–d. Jan 1983) and pianist Chuck Leavell to complete its fifth album, *Brothers and Sisters*, which topped the charts and spawned the #2 single "Ramblin' Man." But the group split up in acrimony after the release of *Win, Lose or Draw* in 1975.

The Allmans re-formed in 1978, this time returning to the sextet format, with Allman, Betts, Trucks, and Jaimo being joined by guitarist Dan Toler and bassist David Goldflies for the gold-selling *Enlightened Rogues* (1979). Two more albums, *Reach for the Sky* and *Brothers of the Road* (for which David Toler replaced Jaimo and Mike Lawler was added on piano), were released before the band split again.

Following the release of a boxed set retrospective, *Dreams*, in 1989, the Allmans again re-formed, with Warren Haynes on second lead guitar and Allen Woody on bass, and to date they have released four more albums and toured extensively. *—William Ruhlmann*

○ **The Allman Brothers Band** / 1969 / Polydor ✦✦✦✦

The Allmans' aggressive synthesis of blues, rock, jazz, and gospel made an impressive entrance on this 1969 debut, with soon-to-be-standards like "Whipping Post" and the dynamic moody "Dreams." Highlights like "Don't Want You No More," "It's Not My Cross to Bear," "Black Hearted Woman," and "Trouble No More" are further reasons why this was one of the greatest bands to ever emerge from the American South. *—Rick Clark*

○ **Idlewild South** / 1970 / Polydor ✦✦✦✦

The Allmans' second effort may not have been quite as strong as their powerful debut, but *Idlewild South* had more than a handful of gems with songs like the celebratory "Revival," the earthy "Midnight Rider," and the instrumental "In Memory of Elizabeth Reed," with its soaring twin-guitar counterpuntal melodies. *—Rick Clark*

☆ **At Fillmore East** / 1971 / Polydor ✦✦✦✦✦

The double-disc *Allman Brothers Band at Fillmore East* is one of rock's greatest live albums, featuring amazing interplay within highly dynamic arrangements. Most of the tracks exceed ten minutes, yet the Allmans never stumble. "Hot 'Lanta," "In Memory of Elizabeth Reed," and "Statesboro Blues" are highlights. Contrary to claims that these are untouched performances, *Fillmore East* actually was a skillfully edited document (courtesy of producer Tom Dowd) taken from a run of shows at Bill Graham's Fillmore. (Mobile Fidelity offers an audiophile version in a mock-road-case style package, complete with photos and notes from Tom Dowd.) *—Rick Clark*

★ **Eat a Peach** / 1972 / Polydor ✦✦✦✦✦

Half of *Eat a Peach* consists of more fiery improvisations from the *Live at Fillmore* dates, in the form of the "Mountain Jam." Even though this was released after Duane Allman's fatal motorcycle accident, the studio sides include some tracks showcasing his soaring lead work. Creatively, the band was in peak form with great tracks like "Ain't Wastin' Time No More" (number 77), "Melissa" (number 86), "One Way Out" (number 86), "Stand Back," "Blue Sky," and the delicate acoustic guitar instrumental "Little Martha." (Also available on Mobile Fidelity) *—Rick Clark*

Duane & Gregg / 1972 / Polydor ✦✦✦

Juvenilia. These are recordings made by the Allman Brothers prior to the formation of the Allman Brothers Band. Gregg is in fine voice and Duane is a remarkable guitarist, but this is embryonic compared to their mature work. Contains an early version of "Melissa." *—William Ruhlmann*

○ **Brothers and Sisters** / 1973 / Polydor ✦✦✦✦

In spite of the inclusion of Dickey Betts's "Ramblin' Man" (#2) and "Jessica," *Brothers and Sisters* is a noticeable comedown from the previous four albums. Muddy production doesn't help matters either. *—Rick Clark*

○ **Beginnings** / 1973 / Polydor ✦✦✦✦

Beginnings is nothing more than the first two albums on a single disc. Since its release, Polygram has done a markedly improved remastering job, releasing each album separately. *—Rick Clark*

Win, Lose or Draw / 1975 / Polydor ✦✦

The Allman Brothers' sixth album was their final new studio effort before their first breakup in 1976. It featured the minor hit singles "Nevertheless" and "Louisiana Lou And Three Card Monty John" and was a Top Five, gold-selling release, but that was just on momentum. In fact, it's a tired effort by a highly competent band that's going through the motions and repeating itself. *—William Ruhlmann*

The Road Goes on Forever / 1975 / Polydor ✦✦

A two-LP set compiled from the Allmans' first five albums and rushed out for the 1975 Christmas season when *Win Lose Or Draw* took a quick nosedive on the charts. It features a lot of good music, but the Allmans aren't a singles band, so compilations don't really do them justice unless, like *Dreams*, they have a lot of time to do so. *—William Ruhlmann*

Gregg & Duane Allman / 1975 / Springboard ✦✦

Wipe the Windows, Check The Oil, Dollar Gas / 1976 / Polydor ✦✦✦

By the time this, the Allmans' second live album, was released in the fall of 1976, the band had suffered what appeared to be an irrevocable split, which cast a pall over the record and made it their lowest charting since their debut. In retrospect, it's an appealing effort, chronicling the version of the band that existed from the death of Berry Oakley to the first breakup (a one-guitar, two-keyboards lineup) and featuring concert versions of some of the better material from *Eat a Peach* and *Brothers and Sisters*. *—William Ruhlmann*

Enlightened Rogues / 1979 / Polydor ✦✦✦

After six years of spotty albums, the Allmans made a strong comeback with this Tom Dowd-produced effort. Gregg Allman is in fine voice, and the band kicks up some sparks throughout. Some of the material is a little weak, but "Crazy Love," a duet by Bonnie Bramlett and Dickie Betts, is a highlight. *—Rick Clark*

Reach for the Sky / 1980 / Arista ✦✦

The second album from *Allmans Mach Two* shows them holding their own, wearing their influences (especially gospel) a bit more on their sleeves, and even coming up with a minor single in "Angeline." *—William Ruhlmann*

Brothers of the Road / 1981 / Arista ✦✦

"Straight From The Heart" (#39), written by Dickey Betts and Johnny Cobb and sung by Gregg Allman, is one of the group's better accommodations to pop music, and on the whole, this is an accessible version of their trademark sound: call it Allmans Lite. The ruling influence here may be Arista president Clive Davis, who also oversaw the pop-oriented Grateful Dead albums of the same period. But the main duty of pop music is to sell, and when this album petered out at #44, the Allmans called it quits for the second time. *—William Ruhlmann*

○ **Dreams** / 1989 / Polydor ✦✦✦✦

This is a thoughtfully compiled boxed set, containing highlights throughout the Allman Brothers' entire career, as well as solo projects and early pre-Allman recordings. A booklet, with generous annotation and photos, is provided. The remastering is a noticeable improvement over initial CD releases of the Allman catalog. If you've got the bucks for a boxed set, this is a worthwhile acquisition for completists and those looking for a comprehensive introduction. *—Rick Clark*

○ **Seven Turns** / Oct. 1990 / Epic ✦✦✦✦

After a nine-year absence, the Allmans return with a vengeance on *Seven Turns*, with tracks like the hard-swinging opener, "Good Clean Fun" and the powerful blues-rock work-out "Gambler's Roll." The Dickey Betts-penned title track, a mystical take on life, is the album's spiritual highlight, while "True Gravity" is the musical peak, ranking with "In Memory of Elizabeth Reed" as one of the band's best instrumentals. Overall, *Seven Turns* is their strongest album since 1972's *Eat a Peach*. *—Rick Clark*

Decade of Hits 1969-1979 / 1991 / Polydor ✦✦✦

○ **Live at Ludlow Garage: 1970** / 1991 / Polydor ✦✦✦✦

It's no *Fillmore East*, of course, but this archival release does present the classic lineup of the Allmans at their near-peak, and fans especially will be pleased to have more Duane on disc. *—William Ruhlmann*

Shades of Two Worlds / 1991 / Epic ✦✦✦

Weaker than *Seven Turns*, *Shades of Two Worlds* still has its moments, particularly the extended rave-up "Kind of Bird." "Bad Rain" and "Nobody Knows" are two other highlights. *—Rick Clark*

○ **The Fillmore Concerts** / 1992 / Polydor ✦✦✦✦

Fillmore Concerts is an expanded version of the classic *At Fillmore East*, featuring several songs that didn't make the original album, re-edited tracks that now run at their original length, and sterling remastered sound; for hardcore fans, it's the ultimate version of this landmark set. *—Stephen Thomas Erlewine*

Evening with the Allman Brothers Band / Mar. 1992 / Epic ✦✦

Given that they scored their big breakthrough with *Fillmore East* and that their career has been based on concert work, it's surprising that the Allmans have released so few live albums. This one finds them in vintage form, playing extended versions of both recent tunes and old favorites. A second-set album was intended, but presumably was cancelled after this record sold poorly. *—William Ruhlmann*

Where It All Begins / 1994 / Epic ✦✦✦
Twenty-five years after their debut album, the Allman Brothers continue to make records in the same basic style, alternating Gregg Allman's bluesy (and increasingly craggy) vocals against Dickey Betts's more country-tinged ones and relying on extended song structures that leave plenty of room for high-pitched, melodic guitar runs by Betts and his current partner, Warren Haynes. There are no classics here, but this is a respectable recreation of the Allmans' standard fare (much of it sounds familiar the first time you listen), which is why it is selling to their fan base and no one else. — *William Ruhlmann*

Duane Allman

b. Nov. 20, 1946, **d.** Oct. 29, 1971
Blues Rock, Southern Rock
During his brief career, the late Duane Allman managed to become one of rock's greatest guitarists, with his liquid, yet visceral electric lead and slide guitar playing. Allman's consistently high caliber of recorded work as a session sideman (particularly at Rick Hall's Fame Studio in Muscle Shoals) for artists like Wilson Pickett, King Curtis, and Clarence Carter, and in his role in the groundbreaking Allman Brothers Band and Derek & the Dominos, has understandably inspired thousands of guitarists.

Allman's star was still rising when his life was tragically cut short by a motorcycle accident in October of 1971. He was just 24 years old. — *Rick Clark*

● **Anthology** / 1972 / Polydor ✦✦✦✦
A superb collection of Duane's work with the Allmans, it also includes many great session gigs. — *Dan Heilman*

○ **Anthology, Vol. 2** / 1974 / Polydor ✦✦✦✦
This features more great guitar work in tandem with Aretha Franklin, Wilson Pickett, and others. — *Dan Heilman*

Gregg Allman Band

Group, Blues Rock, Southern Rock
Gregg Allman is the lead vocalist and keyboardist of the Allman Brothers Band. Fans of the Allman Brothers should find this solo work generally satisfying. — *Rick Clark*

● **Laid Back** / 1973 / Polydor ✦✦✦✦
His debut solo album showcases Allman's soulful, earthy keyboard work and leathery drawl to good effect. "These Days" and the reworked Allman Brothers Band standard "Midnight Rider" are exceptional. — *Rick Clark*

The Gregg Allman Tour / Mar. 1975 / Polydor ✦✦
In the wake of his debut solo album, *Laid Back*, Gregg Allman assembled a backup band and went on tour, resulting in this two-LP live album, which combines his interests in rock, blues, gospel, and country music and finds him backed by a 24-piece orchestra. But there isn't enough original material to establish the star's identity, and the idea of including tracks by opening act Cowboy smacks of filler and record company manipulation. Given that Allman's reputation was based on live work and the Allman Brothers Band's *At Fillmore East* album, this was especially disappointing. (The lead-off track, a cover of the 1965 Fontella Bass and Bobby McClure hit "Don't Mess Up A Good Thing," hit #106.) — *William Ruhlmann*

○ **Playin' up a Storm** / 1977 / Razor & Tie ✦✦✦✦
There's weaker material here, but the playing and singing more than compensate. — *Rick Clark*

I'm No Angel / 1986 / Epic ✦✦✦
The title track was a comeback hit. Allman's voice is distanced in the mix by a little too much reverb. The band tracks are particularly hot. — *Rick Clark*

Just Before the Bullets Fly / 1988 / Epic ✦✦
"Demons" is a highlight on this, another solid journeyman outing. As on *I'm No Angel*, the release suffers from overly wet mixes. — *Rick Clark*

Marc Almond

b. Jul. 9, 1959, Southport, Lancashire, England
Dance-Pop, New Wave
After disbanding Soft Cell, vocalist Marc Almond pursued a solo career that followed the same vaguely sleazy, electronic dance-pop his former group had made popular. Almond's strength was never his personality—his voice tends to waver around the notes instead of hitting them—it was the atmosphere he created with the synths

and drum machines. Underneath all of the electronics and disco rhythms, Almond harkened back to the days of cabaret singers, updating it with his tongue-in-cheek for dance clubs of the '80s.

Before he properly started a solo career, Marc Almond formed Marc and the Mambas, a loose congregation that featured Matt Johnson of The The and Annie Hogan. "*Untitled*" (1983), the group's first album, featured covers of Lou Reed, Syd Barrett, and Jacques Brel; throughout his career, Almond would cover the songs of Brel, which he had learned from the records of Scott Walker. Like Walker, Almond used Brel's heavily orchestrated compositions and social ruminations as a starting point, both musically and lyrically—Almond added a self-conscious element of camp with his Euro-disco and occasionally sleazy lyrics. *Torment and Toreros* (1983), Marc and the Mambas' second album, explored this path in more detail than "*Untitled*," only to an orchestral background. After its release, the group broke up.

Almond formed the backing group the Willing Sinners in 1984, releasing *Vermin in Ermine* in 1984. He began to hit his stride with this album, which fulfilled most of his campy cabaret fantasies. *Stories of Johnny*, released the following year, was more cohesive, spawning a British hit with the title song. Even though he maintained a cult following in England and various parts of Europe, his records were not being released in the U.S.

In 1987, Almond released *Mother Fist...and Her Five Daughters*, his first proper solo album and his bleakest work to date; a compilation, *Singles 1984-1987*, appeared the same year. *The Stars We Are*, released the following year, was a brighter, more welcoming album that revived his commercial career. In addition to a duet with Nico on "Your Kisses Burn," Almond duetted with Gene Pitney on Pitney's own "Something's Gotten Hold of My Heart," which became a number one single. *The Stars We Are* also became his first album released in the U.S. since Soft Cell.

Almond followed the success of *The Stars We Are* in 1990 with the pet project *Jacques*, a collection of Brel songs. That same year, he released *Enchanted*, which was more successful than *Jacques*, yet it didn't reach the heights of *The Stars We Are*. In 1991, he released *The Tenement Symphony* and in 1993, a compilation entitled *Twelve Years of Tears* appeared. — *Stephen Thomas Erlewine*

Untitled / 1983 / Some Bizarre ✦✦

Torment and Toreros / 1983 / Some Bizarre ✦✦

Vermin in Ermine / 1984 / Some Bizarre ✦✦

Mother Fist and Her Five Daughters / 1987 / Some Bizarre ✦✦

● **Singles: 1984–1987** / 1987 / Some Bizarre ✦✦✦✦
This is a compilation of Almond's solo work. — *Steve Aldrich*

○ **Stars We Are** / 1988 / Capitol ✦✦✦✦
Accessible "big-pop" is a fine introduction to Almond. — *Steve Aldrich*

Jacques / 1989 / Some Bizarre ✦✦✦
Almond sings Jacques Brel. — *Steve Aldrich*

Enchanted / 1990 / Capitol ✦✦

Memorabilia / 1991 / Mercury ✦✦✦
A compilation of solo material and Soft Cell sides. — *Steve Aldrich*

Tenement Symphony / Oct. 29, 1991 / Sire ✦✦
Only a few of Marc Almond's post-Soft Cell albums have been released in the U.S. This one, his debut on Sire after two releases on Capitol, is a characteristic effort, mixing lightly danceable synthesizer tracks with Almond's somewhat melodramatic singing. (Americans can reference Depeche Mode and Erasure for an essentially similar approach.) The last six tracks are grouped together as "Tenement Symphony" and call upon Almond's longtime favorite, Jacques Brel ("Jackie"), as well as tossing in some Debussy for good measure. Pretentious, but good-natured. — *William Ruhlmann*

Twelve Years of Tears / May 25, 1993 / Sire ✦✦✦

12 Years of Tears / May 25, 1993 / Warner Brothers ✦✦✦
Contrary to what the title may lead you to believe, *12 Years of Tears* is not a compilation but rather an album of a September 1992 concert at Royal Albert Hall. Almond samples material from throughout his career (from "Tainted Love" to "Jacky"), in a strong performance that is only slightly marred by occasionally weak vocals. — *AMG*

Herb Alpert

b. Mar. 31, 1935, Los Angeles, CA
Pop

Trumpeter Herb Alpert started in rock & roll, working with Jan & Dean and others. He took a $200 demo of the instrumental "Twinkle Star," overdubbed bullfight crowd noises, and retitled it "The Lonely Bull." It became his first hit record. Shortly thereafter Alpert formed A&M Records with Jerry Moss as well as a studio group named the Tijuana Brass. The TJB scored consistently on both the single and album charts over the next ten years, with five albums going to #1. Alpert's laidback vocal style later found mega-success with the smash "This Guy's in Love with You," trading his original Latin-flavored style for straight MOR. —*Cub Koda*

The Lonely Bull / Dec. 1962 / A&M ✦✦✦
The early breakthrough sound of the TJB featuring the title track and the cream of Los Angeles session players. —*Cub Koda*

○ **Whipped Cream & Other Delights** / Apr. 1965 / A&M ✦✦✦✦
Whipped Cream & Other Delights is usually celebrated for its cover, but the music here shouldn't be ignored. It's the first time that Alpert recorded an album full of tunes with crossover potential; it makes perfect sense that it topped the album charts for eight weeks. —*Stephen Thomas Erlewine*

Greatest Hits / Mar. 1970 / A&M ✦✦✦
Herb Alpert & The Tijuana Brass's well-timed *Greatest Hits* album appeared at the start of the 1970s, just as the group's star was fading. It may be that Alpert already had in mind a second volume, since several of the album's tracks were not among its successful singles and several of those singles were missing. But the LP did include the Top 10 hits "The Lonely Bull" and "A Taste Of Honey," the Top 40 hits "Spanish Flea," "Tijuana Taxi," and "Zorba The Greek," and the chart singles "Mexican Shuffle" and "Whipped Cream," providing a good sampler of what made the Brass such fun in the 1960s. —*William Ruhlmann*

Four Sider / Nov. 1973 / A&M ✦✦
When Herb Alpert wound down activity with the Tijuana Brass at the end of the 1960s and the beginning of the 1970s, his record label, A&M, began releasing hits collections and compilations culled from the group's catalog. First came *Greatest Hits*, then *Solid Brass*, then *Greatest Hits, Volume 2*, and then this 21-track album, originally released as a double-LP (hence the title). Twelve of Alpert's 27 pop chart hits up to this point were included (which was twice as many as you would find on *Greatest Hits*), among them the Top Tens "The Lonely Bull" and "A Taste of Honey," and the chart-topping "This Guy's in Love with You." But most of these songs had turned up on one of the earlier compilations already, not to mention the original albums on which they were featured. The major exception was Alpert's most recent hit at the time, a minor chart entry with Gato Barbieri's theme from the movie *Last Tango In Paris*, which was making its first LP appearance. The music was, as always, pleasant, but the repeated cannibalization of Alpert's catalog was beginning to become a consumer concern. —*William Ruhlmann*

○ **Rise** / Sep. 1979 / A&M ✦✦✦✦
On *Rise*, Alpert experimented with a jazz/funk fusion, which resulted in one of his finest albums. On the strength of the hit title track, the album sold over a million copies, making it his most popular record. —*Stephen Thomas Erlewine*

● **Classics, Vol. 1** / Jan. 1987 / A&M ✦✦✦✦
All the high points from the ten-year dominance of Alpert and the Tijuana Brass; includes "A Taste of Honey," "Spanish Flea," and others. —*Cub Koda*

● **Classics, Vol. 20** / Feb. 1987 / A&M ✦✦✦✦
This set features Alpert's solo hits from "This Guy's in Love with You" to "Rise." —*Cub Koda*

Alpha Band

Group, Pop/Rock
The Alpha Band was a folk-rock trio formed from the group assembled by Bob Dylan for his Rolling Thunder Revue of 1975-76. It came together in July 1976, featuring guitarist/vocalist Steven Soles, guitarist/mandolin player/singer David Mansfield, and guitarist/vocalist T-Bone Burnett. The Alpha Band released three albums and then broke up in 1979. —*William Ruhlmann*

Alpha Band / 1976 / Arista ✦✦✦
Steven Soles provides a country-pop influence, T-Bone Burnett adds some absurdist lyrics, and David Mansfield picks his way through the instrumental thicket (while Bob Neuwirth lingers in the shadows) on the Alpha Band's promising debut. They aren't

quite a band at this point, but they are heading off in several interesting directions all at the same time. —*William Ruhlmann*

● **Spark in the Dark** / 1977 / Pathe ✦✦✦✦
On the Alpha Band's second album, T-Bone Burnett began to seem like the focus of the group, his songs and performances giving definition to an otherwise disparate, if engaging, collection of songs. Which is to say that the group was becoming a dry run for Burnett's solo career. There is a nod to the Alphas' mentor, Bob Dylan, on his "You Angel You," and Ringo Starr guests on drums on that track and on "Born In Captivity." —*William Ruhlmann*

Statue Makers of Hollywood / 1978 / Arista ✦✦
The last is the least for the Alpha Band, if only because T-Bone Burnett finally comes out of the closet as a born-again Christian and starts preaching in an unseemly, self-righteous way, and his bandmates don't do anything to stop him. Burnett would learn to cloak the preaching in his subsequent solo career, and so return to critical favor. —*William Ruhlmann*

Gerald Alston

b. Nov. 8, 1942
Urban
Gerald Alston inherited some big soul shoes and filled them admirably for 17 years. The nephew of gospel great Johnny Fields and Shirley Alston of the Shirelles, the North Carolina-born singer learned his trade in the church. As a teen he formed the New Imperials, a group that did both secular and religious music, calling themselves Gospel Jubilee when they appeared in churches. During a local appearance the Manhattans borrowed some audio equipment from Alston's band. When they came to pick it up they heard him rehearsing with his band. They asked the 17-year-old to join them, and Alston took over as their lead singer in 1971. Alston remained until 1988, and the group enjoyed enormous success in the '70s and '80s. Their 1976 single "Kiss and Say Goodbye" was both a #1 R&B and pop hit, the first (and only one) the band ever earned. They won a Grammy in 1980 for "Shining Star." Alston sang a duet with fledgling vocalist Regina Belle in 1986, "Where Did We Go Wrong." The Bobby Womack-produced tune was Belle's debut. Alston signed with Motown in 1988. He hasn't had much commercial luck as a solo act, though the releases *Gerald Alston* and *Open Invitation* were well produced and wonderfully sung. The 1992 date *Always in the Mood* was his most recent. —*Ron Wynn*

● **Gerald Alston** / 1988 / Motown ✦✦✦✦
Top-flight R&B ballads and excellent singing. —*Ron Wynn*

Open Invitation / 1990 / Motown ✦✦✦
The follow-up album that made him a star in sentimental circles. —*Ron Wynn*

○ **Always in the Mood** / 1992 / Motown ✦✦✦✦
Former Manhattans lead vocalist Gerald Alston has emerged as one of the 1990s' best soul and love singers. His passionate, intense leads never lose their steam or conviction, and he wisely avoids doing songs with rappers and doesn't let production gimmicks and studio trappings overwhelm his vocals. —*Ron Wynn*

Altered Images

Group, New Wave, Power Pop/Anglo-Pop
Altered Images was a British power-pop group formed in 1979 and led by film actress Claire Grogan. The group lasted until 1984, their biggest success coming with the U.K. Top Three hit "Happy Birthday" in 1981. —*William Ruhlmann*

● **Happy Birthday** / 1981 / Portrait ✦✦✦✦
Their debut album contains their first U.K. hit, the title track, produced by Martin Rushent of Joy Division fame. —*William Ruhlmann*

Pinky Blue / 1982 / Portrait ✦✦
The band's follow-up is a slicker though less interesting affair. "I Could Be Happy" and "See Those Eyes" show that they can still pull off a couple of catchy singles but a cover of Neil Diamond's "Song Sung Blue" is certainly a mistake. —*Chris Woodstra*

Bite / 1983 / Portrait ✦✦
Hopelessly out-of-touch and past her prime, Grogan takes on a more mature and sophisticated pose (as revealed on the album cover) and takes a stab at dance-pop. The results, of course, are uninteresting with the exception of the single "Don't Talk to Me About Love," a U.K. Top Ten. —*Chris Woodstra*

○ **Collected Images** / 1984 / Epic ✦✦✦✦
○ **Best of** / 1994 / Pinnacle ✦✦✦✦
A greatest hits collection, containing tracks from all three of their albums, that succinctly summarizes their career. —*Stephen Thomas Erlewine*

Alternative TV

Group, Punk, New Wave
Although a part (albeit a small part) of the early English punk-rock scene, Alternative TV is probably best known for the scabrous fanzine (*Sniffin' Glue*) published by lead singer Mark Perry (aka Mark P). Perry's 'zine embodied punk's tear-it-down ethos with a wonderfully petulant and sarcastic attitude, a fact that makes his transition to punk musician such a profound disappointment. Ironically, Perry's band turned out to be far less interesting than his mimeographed fanzine. Daringly attempting to add the space-rock influences of Can and the satirical art-rock damage of Frank Zappa to the, primarily, faster and louder punk zeitgeist, Perry fell from grace with a resounding thud. The music meandered, the lyrics sounded painfully overwritten and narcissistic, and Perry's tuneless "singing" didn't help at all. Oddly enough, Alternative TV did produce some worthwhile music and had a long career for a band so conspicuously lacking in talent (Perry led a version of this band until 1990). From 1979-1980, Perry led an equally mediocre band called the Good Missionaries, who had the good sense to call it a career after one record. —*John Dougan*

○ **The Image Has Cracked** / 1978 / Deptford ✦✦✦✦
What You See Is What You Are / 1978 / Deptford ✦✦✦
Vibing up the Senile Man / 1979 / Deptford ✦✦
Live at the Rat Club '77 / 1979 / Crystal ✦✦
Action Time Vision / 1980 / Deptford ✦✦✦
○ **Strange Kicks** / 1981 / IRS ✦✦✦✦
Peep Show / 1987 / Anagram ✦✦✦
● **Splitting In 2** / 1989 / Anagram ✦✦✦✦
A handful of tracks from the first album and some outtakes and unreleased stuff makes up the only consistently listenable album in the surprisingly large Alternative TV library. It's not that the irritating mannerisms aren't here, it's simply that they're more bearable, and some of the songs are, surprise, actually good. —*John Dougan*

Dragon Love / 1990 / Chapter 22 ✦✦

Dave Alvin

Roots-Rock
Most neo-rockabilly artists merely mimic the music without expanding its vocabulary or its creative horizons. Dave Alvin is the exception that proves the rule. From his teeth-cutting days with the now-defunct Blasters (which featured Dave's brother Phil on vocals) up to his current solo career, Alvin has used rockabilly and country as a springboard (as opposed to sole inspiration) for his sympathetic and precise songwriting, which tackles some of the same issues as John Mellencamp's. He's also one hell of an axe slinger. —*John Floyd*

● **Romeo's Escape** / Dec. 1987 / Razor & Tie ✦✦✦✦
The former guitarist/songwriter of the Blasters has his solo debut, singing his own songs. As with the Blasters, it's the songs that impress most, notably here "Fourth of July" and "Border Radio." —*William Ruhlmann*

Blue Blvd / 1991 / Hightone ✦✦✦
Highlighted by an appearance by the legendary R&B saxophonist Lee Allen, Alvin's second solo album offers more of his revved-up mix of rockabilly, blues, and rock & roll. —*Stephen Thomas Erlewine*

Museum of the Heart / 1993 / Hightone ✦✦✦
Dave Alvin's third album contains more thoughtful story songs of hard living and romantic loss, set to rockabilly beats and overlaid with melodic guitar playing. If there's any criticism to be made of his approach, it's that he sometimes seems too satisfied with his obvious gifts to really push himself, which makes you think that there's a spark missing that would vault him into the big time. Maybe, maybe not. —*William Ruhlmann*

King of California / 1994 / Hightone ✦✦✦
Dave Alvin makes an "unplugged" album, reprising many of his familiar tunes, "Fourth of July," "Every Night About This Time," and "Border Radio" among them, in an acoustic setting that wouldn't be foreign to Woody Guthrie. Neither would the lower class portraits of struggle that are Alvin's metier. The songs stand up well in this relatively unadorned, becalmed setting; in fact, some are even more poignant. —*William Ruhlmann*

Phil Alvin

Roots-Rock
Phil Alvin was the lead singer of the Blasters in the early '80s. He released an eclectic solo album, *Un "Sung" Stories*, in 1986, with backing from the Dirty Dozen Brass Band and Sun Ra and the Arkestra. —*William Ruhlmann*

● **Un "Sung" Stories** / 1986 / Slash ✦✦✦✦
Leaving the Blasters, lead singer Phil Alvin moved back in time from that band's rockabilly approach to jazz and jump-blues styles, employing the Dirty Dozen Brass Band and Sun Ra & His Arkestra on songs by Cab Calloway and others. —*William Ruhlmann*

County Fair 2000 / Oct. 25, 1994 / Hightone ✦✦✦

Amazing Blondel

Group, Art-Rock/Progressive-Rock
One of England's most unusual rock outfits of the 1970s, Amazing Blondel was a trio whose members played instruments dating from medieval to Elizabethan times, and songs styled to those periods. Named for Richard the Lionhearted's legendary favorite minstrel, Amazing Blondel consisted of three musicians from Scunthorpe, England—John David Gladwin (lute, oboe, cittern, double bass), Terry Wincott (pipe organ, harmonium, cittern, recorders, flute, crumhorn, tabor pipe, ocarina, guitar), and Edward Baird (guitar, guitern, percussion). Gladwin and Wincott founded the group as a duo following the break-up of the band Methuselah, of which both had been members. They'd wearied of playing shows where the instruments were so loud it was impossible to hear themselves singing, and, as their acoustic set had gone over well with audiences, the duo moved in that direction.

In 1970, with help from several musicians, including legendary British guitarist Big Jim Sullivan, they recorded an album entitled *Amazing Blondel*. By that time, Baird had joined Gladwin and Wincott to make a trio. Their first album was a collection of soft acoustic rock numbers that included one medieval-styled number that seemed to go over better than anything else, and that was the direction they aimed for in their future releases. Soon after, they were signed to Island Records, and began refining their sound, both on stage and in the studio.

The trio became known for playing upwards of 40 instruments on stage, though without backup musicians—each song was simply planned for no more than three instruments at any one time. Although Gladwin and company were the first to admit that they were no virtuosos on their chosen instruments, their work sounded credible to modern ears, and their shows were fun despite the delicacy of the array of instruments, which required as much as five hours to get into tune—and unlike most rock acts of the era, if they couldn't get them into tune, the group didn't perform.

Despite their reliance on acoustic instruments, the trio wasn't adverse to composing extended suites that ran up to 25 minutes, and while some of the music had a repetitive quality, the best of it played off of achingly beautiful melodies. *England*, released in 1972, was the high point for the trio, and got them their heaviest airplay to date in America if only modest sales. Gladwin left soon after its release, however, and the Amazing Blondel were reduced to a duo for their follow-up, *Blondel* (1973). It marked the last of their "period" style material. On subsequent albums, beginning with *Mulgrave Street*, the group—supported by various rock musicians, including Mick Ralphs, Paul Rogers, and Steve Winwood—would aim for a harder, more contemporary sound vaguely resembling Steeleye Span. None of the records would succeed much outside of England, though they ultimately did record a live album in Japan. —*Bruce Eder*

Amazing Blondel / 1970 / Bell ✦✦
The group's debut album shows them still finding their way, with more of a mainstream rock sound and a host of session people (including British studio veteran Big Jim Sullivan on guitar) sur-

rounding them. The folky tracks came off sounding the best, and pointed the way to the group's future. —*Bruce Eder*

Evensong / 1970 / Island ✦✦✦
A self-consciously archaic album, built around medieval balladry and madrigals and performed on period instruments. The group doesn't sound entirely at ease yet working in this style, but the music has a crisp, folk-like feel and the timbre and singing have great charm. —*Bruce Eder*

Fantasia Lindum / 1971 / Island ✦✦✦
The concept album rears its head, and rears back about five centuries—while other progressive rock outfits were doing album-side-length suites about apocalypse, Amazing Blondel adapted this form to songs about idealized love between men and women, mankind and God, and mankind and nature. The whole thing plays sort of like the Strawbs without the sardonic edge, or the way a rock suite by John Bunyan might've sounded. —*Bruce Eder*

○ **England 72** / 1972 / Island ✦✦✦✦
A staggeringly beautiful collection of love songs and odes to nature, all have a distinctly pre-20th-century (indeed, pre-19th-century) feel. Exquisitely sung and played. —*Bruce Eder*

● **England** / 1973 / Island ✦✦✦✦
The best record ever made by the trio, a lyrical, gentle, yet ambitious expansion of their sound into a richer vein, with a wider range of instrumentation, some eerie mixes of medieval instruments and psychedelic effects, and a compelling beauty that makes this record linger long in the memory. The sound is very elegant, but this time out the group has timed and edited everything perfectly, so none of it overstays its welcome. Sort of the way the Moody Blues might've sounded circa the year 1500. —*Bruce Eder*

Blondel / 1973 / Island ✦✦✦
The group—reduced to a duo—in its swan song for Island Records. The album lacks the panache of their previous albums, although it also has a smoothness that makes each track a very easy listen, and the antique sensibilities are beginning to give away to more modern songwriting techniques. —*Bruce Eder*

Mulgrave Street / 1974 / DJM ✦✦
Their first album for Beatles publisher Dick James's DJM Records shows Blondel, as they were now known, moving into more of a modern electric folk-rock idiom, with help from Paul Kossof, Mick Ralphs, Paul Rodgers, Eddie Jobson, Simon Kirke, and other British rock alumni of the early-to-middle '70s. More contemporary than their earlier work, but nowhere near as distinctive. —*Bruce Eder*

Inspiration / 1975 / DJM ✦✦✦
A further effort at rocking up the folky sound, and so successful at it that one had to wonder why stick with the name or the image at all? —*Bruce Eder*

Bad Dreams / 1976 / DJM ✦✦
Live in Tokyo / 1977 / DJM ✦✦

The Amazing Rhythm Aces

Group, R&B, Country-Rock
One of the first and best Southern country-rock bands, the Aces were formed out of Jesse Winchester's backup band in 1974 and produced six albums bristling with rock, bluegrass, hardcore honky-tonk country, Western swing, and R&B. They scored their biggest hit with "Third Rate Romance;" supplied country singer Mel McDaniel with his hits "Big Old Brew" and "Anger and Tears;" and had minor hits with "The End Is Not in Sight (The Cowboy Song)" and "Burning the Ballroom Down." After three albums, they disbanded in 1981. Lead singer and songwriter Russell Smith pursued a solo career. —*Kit Kiefer*

● **Stacked Deck** / 1975 / ABC ✦✦✦✦
"Amazing" is certainly the word. In addition to "Third Rate Romance," which has been covered by artists as diverse as Earl Scruggs and Elvis Costello (and was a hit once again on the country chart in the mid-'90s), this album features a collection of amazing tunes by an incredibly hot band that sound fresh 20 years after they were recorded. Look for the single of "Third Rate Romance" which features the non-LP "Mystery Train" on the flip side. —*Jim Worbois*

Too Stuffed to Jump / 1976 / ABC ✦✦✦
Although *Too Stuffed to Jump* isn't quite as strong a record as the debut, the album features enough good material to recommend it. Some different influences come into play on this one, like the

jazzy shuffle of "Same Ole Me." And who could not hear Leon Russell in "Typical American Boy"? —*Jim Worbois*

Toucan Do It Too / 1977 / ABC ✦✦
Compared to the first album, *Toucan Do It Too* just doesn't have life or joy. Still, it's a pleasant record from the Aces and the title track is particularly memorable. —*Jim Worbois*

Burning the Ballroom Down / 1978 / ABC ✦✦
This record is a bit more focused than the last and, for that reason, stands up a bit better over time. With the song "I Pity the Mother and Father," Smith explores territory not often examined in popular music; it will speak to anyone with kids who are growing up way too fast. — *Jim Worbois*

The Amazing Rhythm Aces / 1978 / Columbia ✦✦✦
By 1979, the Aces' recording career was winding down and their longtime label folded. As a result, this record was released on both ABC and Columbia with the only difference being the picture on the back cover. This album also saw the departure of guitarist/producer Barry Burton. Whatever the causes, this is their strongest album in some time. —*Jim Worbois*

How the Hell Do You Spell Rhythum? / 1980 / Warner Brothers ✦✦
The band goes out in tighter-than-tight style, covering "Futher on Down the Road," Delbert McClinton's "Object of My Affection," and Van Morrison's "Wild Night" and introducing the original version of "Big Ole Brew." —*Kit Kiefer*

Full House: Aces High / 1981 / MSS ✦✦
4 You 4 Ever: Best of Amazing Rhythm Aces / 1982 / M&R ✦✦✦

Eric Ambel

Roots-Rock
Singer/guitarist Eric Ambel, a former member of Joan Jett's Blackhearts, joined the roots-rock band the Del Lords in 1981. — *William Ruhlmann*

○ **Roscoe's Gang** / 1988 / Enigma ✦✦✦✦
On his debut solo album, Del Lord Eric Ambel cuts songs by buddies like Scott Kempner and Peter Holsapple, not to mention fave raves like Bob Dylan's "If You Gotta Go, Go Now," Swamp Dogg's "Total Destruction To Your Mind," and Neil Young's "Vampire Blues." "Recorded absolutely live in the studio. No overdubs, second takes or rehearsal," warns the record jacket, but that only contributes to the party atmosphere. Ambel is an authoritative singer, aided and abetted by Syd Straw, and he plays a vicious lead guitar, too. A worthy addition to the '80s roots rock library. —*William Ruhlmann*

Loud & Lonesome / 1995 / East Side Digital ✦✦✦

Ambitious Lovers

Group, Alternative Pop/Rock
A surprisingly accessible rock group led by "no wave" guitarist Arto Lindsay (b. May 28, 1953) and Peter Scherer that still manages to express Lindsay's odd combination of Brazilian, pop, and avant-garde styles. —*William Ruhlmann*

Envy / 1984 / EG ✦✦✦
Despite its smooth rhythms and concessions to pop, *Envy* more or less picks up where *DNA* left off. Arto's guitar wanders in and out of noiseland, producing some ear-shattering effects, but mostly this begins his musical odyssey with the sounds of his youth—that is, Brazilian music. In fact, Lindsay occasionally sings in Portuguese. Which begs another point: Lindsay is not the greatest singer in the world, but the twists and turns that make this album uniquely wonderful help smooth over any problems one may have with his vocals. A startling and very successful debut. —*John Dougan*

● **Greed** / 1988 / Virgin ✦✦✦✦
Switching labels and making keyboardist Peter Scherer a prominent member now that the Ambitious Lovers are a duo, *Greed* is great. Loaded with smooth effortless pop, this is an astounding conflation of Lindsay's (and Scherer's) arty proclivities with the sensual sounds of Brazilian music as played by Caetano Veloso, Gilberto Gil and Milton Nascimento. Plenty of all-star cameos (Vernon Reid, John Zorn, Bill Frisell, and John Lurie) make this a remarkably intense and satisfying record, proving that the Ambitious Lovers are a formidable proposition and make music like few other bands. —*John Dougan*

○ **Lust** / 1991 / Elektra ✦✦✦✦
Bouncing around from label to label is not the best way to encourage band stability, but that fact hasn't hurt the Ambitious Lovers one bit. If *Greed* blew you away, then *Lust* makes a perfect companion. The pop moves here are even more pronounced, making it safe to assume that hardcore noise addicts have ditched Lindsay at this point. But what beautiful music they are missing: the sensuous rhythms of "Ponta de Lanca Africano," the blissful "E Preciso Perdoar" and "Tuck It In." A big plus is an appearance by Brazil's most brilliant (my opinion) singer/songwriter, Caetano Veloso, who contributes to the darkly poetic "Villain." *—John Dougan*

Ambrosia

Group, Art-Rock/Progressive-Rock, Pop/Rock
Ambrosia, a '70s Los Angeles group, synthesized art-rock with a relatively slick West Coast pop sound, especially toward the end of their career. They produced a few multiformat hits with "Biggest Part of Me" (#3), "How Much I Feel" (#3), "Holding on to Yesterday" (#17), and "You're the Only Woman" (#13). *—Rick Clark*

● **Ambrosia** / 1975 / 20th Century ✦✦✦✦
A wonderful debut album, it was engineered by Alan Parsons. Top-notch mid-'70s art-rock, with great musicianship, it features "Holdin' on to Yesterday" and "Nice, Nice, Very Nice." *—Scott Bultman*

Somewhere I've Never Travelled / 1976 / Warner Brothers ✦✦✦
Their second album is more in the symphonic realm but just as good as their debut. *—Scott Bultman*

Life Beyond L.A. / 1978 / Warner Brothers ✦✦
One Eighty / 1980 / Warner Brothers ✦✦✦
It contains their biggest pop hits, "Biggest Part of Me" and "You're the Only Woman." *—Scott Bultman*

Road Island / 1982 / Warner Brothers ✦✦

America

Group, Pop/Rock
America was a light folk-rock act of the early '70s who had several Top Ten hits, including the number ones "A Horse with No Name" and "Sister Golden Hair." Vocalists/guitarists Dewey Bunnell, Dan Peak, and Gerry Beckley met while they were still in high school in the late '60s; all three members were sons of U.S. Air Force officers who were stationed in the U.K. After they completed school in 1970, they formed an acoustic folk-rock quartet called Daze in London, which was soon pared down to the trio of Bunnell, Peak, and Beckley. Adopting the name America, the group landed a contract with Jeff Dexter, a promoter for the Roundhouse concert venue. Dexter had America open for several major artists and the group soon signed with Warner Bros. Records. By the fall of 1970, the group was recording their debut album in London, with producers Ian Samwell and Jeff Dexter.

"A Horse with No Name," America's debut single, was released at the end of 1971. In January of 1972, the song—which strongly recalled the acoustic numbers of Neil Young—became a number three hit in the U.K. The group's self-titled debut album followed the same stylistic pattern and became a hit as well, peaking at number 14. Following their British success, America returned to North America, beginning a supporting tour for the Everly Brothers. "A Horse with No Name" was released in the U.S. that spring, where it soon became a #1 single, pushing Neil Young's "Heart of Gold" off the top of the charts; *America* followed the single to the top of the charts. "I Need You" became another Top Ten hit that summer, and the group began work on its second album with the Beatles' producer George Martin. "Ventura Highway," the first single released from this collaboration, became their third straight Top Ten hit in December of 1972. In the beginning of 1973, America won the Grammy award for Best New Artist of 1972.

Homecoming was released in January of 1973, becoming a Top Ten hit in the U.S. and peaking at number 21 in the U.K. Under Martin's direction, America's essential sound didn't change, it just became more polished. However, the hits stopped coming fairly soon—they had only one minor Top 40 hit in 1973. *Hat Trick*, the group's third album, was released toward the end of 1973; it failed to make it past number 28 on the American charts. Released in the late fall of 1974, *Holiday* was the third record the group made with George Martin. *Holiday* returned America to the top of the charts, peaking at number three and launching the hit singles "Tin

Man" and "Lonely People." "Sister Golden Hair," pulled from 1975's *Hearts*, became their #1 single. That same year, the group released *History / America's Greatest Hits*, which would eventually sell over four million copies.

Although America's 1976 effort *Hideaway* went gold and peaked at number 11, the group's audience was beginning to decline. At the end of 1976, Dan Peek left the group, deciding to become a Contemporary Christian recording artist. The group continued as a duo, releasing *Harbor* to a lukewarm reception. America's last Martin-produced record, *Silent Letter*, was released in 1979 to little attention. America returned to the Top Ten in 1982 with "You Can Do Magic," an adult contemporary pop number that featured synthesizers along with their trademark harmonies. "The Border" became their last Top 40 hit in 1983, peaking at number 33. America released their last album, *America in Concert*, in the summer of 1985, yet the group has continued to tour successfully into the '90s. *—Stephen Thomas Erlewine*

● **History: Greatest Hits** / 1975 / Warner Brothers ✦✦✦✦
A nice roundup of their peak years (1971-1975), it includes tracks like "A Horse with No Name" (#1), "I Need You" (#9), "Ventura Highway" (#8), "Tin Man" (#4), "Lonely People" (#5), "Sister Golden Hair" (#1), and more. *—Dan Heilman*

○ **Encore: More Greatest Hits** / 1991 / Rhino ✦✦✦✦
This followup to their *Greatest Hits* contains "The Border" (#33), "Right Before Your Eyes" (#45), "Today's the Day" (#23), and "You Can Do Magic" (#8). The rest of the tracks are album sides or previously unreleased material. *—AMG*

American Breed

Group, Pop/Rock
The American Breed was a 1960s rock quartet from Cicero, IL, led by Gary Loizzo. They scored a gold Top Ten hit in early 1968 with "Bend Me, Shape Me." Later, drummer Andre Fischer and keyboard player Kevin Murphy were members of Rufus. *—William Ruhlmann*

● **Bend Me, Shape Me [compilation]** / 1994 / Varese Sarabande ✦✦✦✦
Out of the American Breed's three Top 40 hits, only "Bend Me, Shape Me" has become a staple of oldies radio. Similarly, it's the most memorable thing on *Bend Me, Shape Me*, an extensive single-disc compilation of the group's career. Even though the rest of the material is a bit weak, the band was able to exploit their slightly polished and psychedelized garage-rock sound, making several enjoyable songs, including the hits "Step out of Your Mind" and "Green Light." *—Stephen Thomas Erlewine*

American Flyer

Group, Country-Rock, Pop/Rock
American Flyer was a 1970s folk-rock quartet made up of former members of other groups: Craig Fuller was from Pure Prairie League, Eric Kaz had been a member of Blues Magoos, Steve Katz was in Blood, Sweat & Tears, and Doug Yule had drummed in the Velvet Underground. Together they charted with two albums on United Artists in the mid-'70s. *—William Ruhlmann*

● **American Flyer** / 1976 / United Artists ✦✦✦✦
American Flyer deserved better. Eric Kaz had written great love songs for Linda Ronstadt and Bonnie Raitt, and Craig Fuller was coming off his Top 40 hit "Amie" with Pure Prairie League. As it happened, Steve Katz's "Back In '57" turned out to be one of the album's highlights, but "Let Me Down Easy," by Kaz and Fuller, was a minor hit, and there was also Kaz's classic co-composition, "Love Has No Pride." But those were just the cream of an excellent set produced by George Martin. Add it all up, and it should have meant more than a chart peak in the lower reaches of the Top 100, an early indication that, for whatever reasons, American Flyer was not destined to become the next Crosby, Stills, Nash & Young. *—William Ruhlmann*

Spirit of a Woman / 1977 / United Artists ✦✦
Maybe there was only room for one really successful country-folk-rock group with good songs and strong harmonies in the mid-'70s, and the job had already been taken by the Eagles. Who knows? American Flyer's second and final album didn't have as many great songs as the debut, and some of them were swamped by strings, but it was a pleasant work, notably featuring a version of Eric Kaz's "I'm Blowin' Away," which Bonnie Raitt had covered a couple of years earlier. *—William Ruhlmann*

American Music Club

Group, Alternative Pop/Rock
A traditional-sounding rock band in these postmodern times? Well, American Music Club, led by Mark Eitzel, may be an anomaly, but it's a pretty engaging proposition on record. Eitzel's songwriting is very straightforward: good people living through hard times, and he's very much the agreeable populist. His bandmates add to this mix by playing no-nonsense, bare-bones rock & roll that, if slightly derivative of blues-rock structures, is also loaded with enough panache. Smart and direct, a fine American band.

American Music Club formed in the mid-'80s when guitarist Vudi saw the Naked Skinnies, one of Eitzel's early bands, perform. The Naked Skinnies had recently moved to San Francisco from Ohio, with hopes of making it big in California. Instead, the group wound up being banned from clubs. Vudi had seen one of those performances and asked Eitzel if he wanted to work together; soon the pair had formed American Music Club, adding bassist/vocalist Dan Pearson as a permanent member.

Initially, the band's music drew equally from post-punk bands like Joy Division and singer/songwriters like Nick Drake and Van Morrison, adding flourishes of experimental art rock. The band's first album, 1986's *The Restless Stranger*, followed this pattern in particular. After its release, the group's drummer left and their record producer, Tom Mallon, played percussion and guitars on 1987's *Engine*, which featured a more pronounced folk-rock influence. With their third album, 1988's *California*, the band began to build a cult following, thanks to positive reviews in underground and alternative magazines. For *California*, American Music Club was stripped down to a four-piece, with Mallon playing drums. Mallon left the band after its release; he was replaced by Mike Simms. AMC also added a multi-instrumentalist, Bruce Kaphan, in time for their next record.

American Music Club's fourth album, 1991's *Everclear*, was their breakthrough, incorporating elements of rock & roll, folk, country, jazz, and schmaltzy, crooning pop into a languid, atmospheric web of sound. *Everclear* earned the band some mainstream attention, as *Rolling Stone* named it one of the best albums of the year and voted Eitzel the best songwriter. All of the attention led to a major label contract with Reprise. Before they recorded their first album for Reprise, Simms left the band and was replaced by Tim Mooney. *Mercury*, released in the spring of 1993, continued AMC's string of rave reviews and small record sales, even if it sold slightly better than their indie releases.

San Francisco, the group's sixth album, was released in the fall of 1995. Like the band's previous albums, it was critically well-received but it had little exposure on radio and MTV. —*John Dougan & Stephen Thomas Erlewine*

The Restless Stranger / 1986 / Grifter ♦♦

Engine / 1987 / Frontier ♦♦♦

○ **California** / 1988 / Frontier ♦♦♦♦
Stark-sounding, highly personal songs, they cemented the reputation of bandleader Mark Eitzel. —*Steve Aldrich*

United Kingdom / 1990 / Demon ♦♦♦
This import CD of studio and live tracks also includes the entire *California* album. —*Steve Aldrich*

○ **Everclear** / 1991 / Alias ♦♦♦♦
With more expansive production and arrangements that don't water down the quality of Eitzel's material, this is a brilliant album. —*Steve Aldrich*

● **Mercury** / 1993 / Reprise ♦♦♦♦
On their major-label debut, American Music Club continues to mine despair from Mark Eitzel's heart and the results are captivating. Mitchell Froom's production polishes some of their rougher edges, but *Mercury* is by no means an easy listen. Eitzel's songs are beautifully sad, etched with grace and elegant suffering, as well as an often overlooked self-deprecating humor. —*Stephen Thomas Erlewine*

San Francisco / 1994 / Reprise ♦♦♦
No one could accuse Mark Eitzel of lightening up on American Music Club's second major-label album, but the band has loosened up a bit. Where *Mercury* gracefully sulked in its own gorgeous melancholy, *San Francisco* features more colors and emotions—everything from the weeping ballad "Wish the World Away" and the measured attack of "It's Your Birthday" to the almost joyful "Hello Amsterdam." *San Francisco* proves that AMC is indeed a band, not just Eitzel's project. The finest moments on the record

come from the interplay between the musicians, which is what raises *San Francisco* from being merely a collection of good songs to an excellent record. —*Stephen Thomas Erlewine*

Hello Amsterdam [EP] / 1995 / Reprise ♦♦
A six-song EP formed around the poppiest song on *San Francisco*, *Hello Amsterdam* doesn't break any new ground for either American Music Club or Mark Eitzel. It's a pleasant diversion for fans, though it gives credence to the rumours that AMC is near the end of their career. —*Stephen Thomas Erlewine*

AMG

Group, Rap
Select recording artist AMG has thus far not made much hip-hop impact. His tough-talking, prototype gangsta-rap was featured on two discs for Select in 1991. *Bitch Betta Have My Money* charted, peaking at 63 on the pop album charts. —*Ron Wynn*

Give a Dog Bone / 1991 / Select ♦♦♦
Sullen, cold and occasionally provocative commentary from AMG that doesn't shed much light on any situation, social, political or romantic. The production is acceptable, and the rapping and rhymes are mildly amusing, but there's little here that's inspirational, compelling or worth hearing more than once. —*Ron Wynn*

● **Bitch Betta Have My Money** / 1992 / Select ♦♦♦♦
The 1990s furor over sexist language was triggered by a flood of recordings similar to this one. It's debatable as to whether the tone and sentiments expressed by AMG are tongue-in-cheek, but the steady stream of vulgarities and the message that women's roles are exclusively those of a sexual surrogate and cash cow will certainly strike many as indefensible. The rap style is fluid enough, although the rhymes are more repetitious than clever. —*Ron Wynn*

Ballin' Out Of Control / 1995 / Select ♦♦♦

Amon Duul

Group, Art-Rock/Progressive-Rock
Amon Duul was a progressive art-rock group that emerged from a commune outside Munich in 1968 and promptly split into two parts, Amon Duul I and Amon Duul II. Amon Duul I made only one album, *Phallus Dei*, while Amon Duul II, whose principal members included Renate Knaup-Kroetenschwanz (vocals), John Weinzierl (guitar, vocals), and Chris Karrer (guitar), made a series of records throughout the 1970s. —*William Ruhlmann*

○ **Yeti** / 1970 / Repertoire ♦♦♦♦

● **Dance of the Lemmings** / 1971 / Mantra ♦♦♦♦
These two double albums (*Yeti* and *Dance of the Lemmings*) define the term "space rock." Amon Duul II was the musical component of the original sun tribe of Amon collective. *Yeti* is a full-throttle voyage into the realms of supersonic guitars and keyboards that fuses psychedelic and progressive to mind blowing perfection. *Tanz Der Lemminge* travels further out into space with its extended sci-fi lyrical concepts. More elaborate and sophisticated musically, the layers of electric and acoustic guitars blend with mellotron and electronics to achieve celestial free flight. —*Archie Patterson*

Tori Amos

North Carolina
Singer-Songwriter, Alternative Pop/Rock
Tori Amos (b. Myra Ellen Amos) was one of several female singer/songwriters who combined the stark lyrical attack of alternative rock with a distinctly '70s musical approach. Her music falls between the orchestrated meditations of Kate Bush and the stripped-down poetics of Joni Mitchell. In addition to reviving the singer/songwriter traditions of the '70s, Amos revived the piano as a rock & roll instrument. With her 1992 album *Little Earthquakes*, Amos built a dedicated following that continued to expand with her second album, *Under the Pink.*

Born in North Carolina but raised in Maryland, Tori Amos was the daughter of a methodist preacher. By the age of four, she was singing and playing piano in the church choir; she began writing her own songs shortly afterward. Amos won a scholarship to Baltimore's Peabody Conservatory based on her instrumental prowess. While she was studying at Peabody, she became infatuated by rock & roll, particularly the music of Led Zeppelin. She began writing pop ballads and performing in local bars. Amos moved to Los Angeles in her late teens to become a pop singer.

Atlantic Records signed her in 1987, recording an uninspired pop-metal album called *Y Kant Tori Read* the following year. The record was a complete failure, attracting no attention from radio or press and selling very few copies; nevertheless, she didn't lose her record contract. By 1990, Amos had adopted a new approach, singing spare, haunting semi-confessional piano ballads that were arranged like Kate Bush but had the melodies and lyrical approach of Joni Mitchell. Atlantic sponsored a trip to England in 1991, where she played a series of concerts in support of an EP, *Me and A Gun*.

The harrowing "Me and A Gun" was an autobiographical song, telling the tale of a rape. It gained positive reviews throughout the media and both the EP and the concerts sold well. *Little Earthquakes*, Amos' first album as a singer/songwriter, was released in late 1991 and sold well in both the U.S. and the U.K. In 1992, she released the *Crucify* EP, which featured three covers, including Nirvana's "Smells Like Teen Spirit" and Led Zeppelin's "Thank You." Delivered in early 1994, *Under the Pink*, the full-length follow-up to *Little Earthquakes*, was a bigger hit, selling over a million copies and launching the minor hit singles "God" and "Cornflake Girl." —*Stephen Thomas Erlewine*

Y Kant Tori Read / 1988 / Atlantic ✦
● **Little Earthquakes** / 1991 / Atlantic ✦✦✦✦
The album just screams Kate Bush, from the cover shot on in. But once past that, we discover plenty of rewards. Amos engages us like few ever attempted. Her lyrical directness and the sparce production draw us almost uncomfortably close to the artist. An album as challenging as it is beautiful, *Little Earthquakes* stands as a major work. —*Steve Aldrich*

Crucify / 1992 / Atlantic ✦✦✦
Crucify is a five-song EP that builds upon the success of *Little Earthquakes*. Most notable among the songs is her voice/piano reading of Nirvana's "Smells Like Teen Spirit," showing what a fine songwriter Kurt Cobain is; the title song (a different mix than the version on *Earthquakes*) and her versions of the Rolling Stones' "Angie" and Led Zeppelin's "Thank You" are equally noteworthy. —*Stephen Thomas Erlewine*
○ **Under the Pink** / 1994 / Atlantic ✦✦✦✦
More difficult and ambitious than her critically acclaimed debut, the core of *Under The Pink* reveals the strong, stark presence of a compelling singer-songwriter at her piano. —*Roch Parisien*

Anderson-Bruford-Wakeman-Howe

Group, Art-Rock/Progressive-Rock
The group Yes has had a long and complicated history. By 1989, there were two different factions, one led by bassist Chris Squires that owned the rights to the name "Yes" and this one, featuring singer Jon Anderson, drummer Bill Bruford, keyboard player Rick Wakeman, and guitarist Steve Howe. This quartet made an album, titled *Anderson, Bruford, Wakeman, Howe*, and went on the road playing what it called "An Evening of Yes Music, Plus," which occasioned a lawsuit. Finally, all was resolved, and the next version of Yes was a mega-edition featuring eight members, who made the album *Union*. —*William Ruhlmann*

Anderson-Bruford-Wakeman-Howe / 1989 / Arista ✦✦✦
File under "Yes." When this version of the band couldn't obtain rights to the name, they put their album out under their combined names, but it's still Yes by any other name. Jon Anderson's tenor wails through spacey lyrics, Rick Wakeman constructs cathedrals of synthesized sound, Steve Howe rips high-pitched guitar leads, and Bill Bruford makes his drums sound like tympani. For all that, it's a pedestrian effort for these veterans, not as bombastic as some of their stuff, not as inspired as others, but it definitely has the "Yes" sound. ("She Gives Me Love" even refers to "Long Distance Runaround.") —*William Ruhlmann*

Al Anderson

b. 1947
Roots-Rock
Anderson started with a local Connecticut band, the Wildweeds, in the late '60s, scoring with the hit "No Good to Cry." He joined NRBQ in 1971. In addition to work with the band, he has released the odd solo album over the years, most strongly connected to his love and mastery of country music.

After NRBQ released *Message for the Mess-Age* in early 1994,

Anderson announced he was leaving the band to concentrate on his songwriting and country music in particular. —*Cub Koda*
Al Anderson / 1972 / Vanguard ✦✦✦
● **Party Favors** / 1988 / Twin/Tone ✦✦✦✦
NRBQ's brilliant guitarist and vocalist steps out on his solo debut, a lively, if somewhat disappointing, effort from one of rock's undiscovered greats. —*Jeff Tamarkin*

Jon Anderson

b. Oct. 25, 1944, Accrington, Lancashire, England
Art-Rock/Progressive-Rock
Jon Anderson's cherubic tenor voice is one of English art-rock band Yes' most distinctive elements. As a lyricist, Anderson has generally been mystically obscure, at times seeming more fascinated with the sound of the words than with their actual thematic coherence. Nevertheless, he was one of art-rock's most aggressive conceptualizers. Aside from Yes, Anderson has engaged in numerous side projects, including several successful outings with synthwhiz Vangelis. —*Rick Clark*

Olias of Sunhillow / Jul. 1976 / Atlantic ✦✦✦
This Yes vocalist's debut solo album is his most pleasing. A near-impressionist piece of music, it has elements of mysticism and science fiction interwoven like a lost *Tale from Topographic Oceans*. —*Bruce Eder*

Song of Seven / Nov. 1980 / Atlantic ✦✦
Jon Anderson records naturally sound like Yes records, and not only because of his high, frequently double-tracked tenor. Anderson, who wrote, arranged, and produced this, his second solo album, fills his overstuffed arrangements with dense keyboard textures and sparkling acoustic guitar strumming, just like the music of his band. (Since Yes had disbanded when Anderson made this album, he had little incentive to stray too far from the group's sound if he was to woo its fans to his now full-time solo career.) For parts of this album, he evokes touches of early rock & roll and seems to be singing of romance, but by late in the second side, amid sound effects of birds and children, his keening vocals, in melodies seemingly borrowed from Anglican hymnals, are going on about the strength of dreams and stairways of love. Restraint is not one of Anderson's characteristics. —*William Ruhlmann*

Animation / Jun. 1982 / Atlantic ✦✦
Greatest Hits / 1984 / Warner Brothers ✦✦✦
Three Ships / Dec. 1985 / Elektra ✦✦
3 Ships is the Jon Anderson Christmas album, and it ought to be better than it is. You'd think with the choirboy earnestness of his voice, Anderson would be ideally suited to put some new life into the seasonal format. But he has brought his synthesizer with him (as well as several choruses), and he manages to overproduce both his original tunes and the traditional material, swamping them with sound effects and overly loud percussion tracks as though he were making a dance record. —*William Ruhlmann*

In the City of Angels / 1988 / Columbia ✦✦
In 1988, Anderson quit Yes for the second time and released his first regular solo album in six years, *In The City Of Angels*. Stewart Levine, best known for his work with Culture Club, was brought in to produce; Anderson worked with a team of L.A. session stars and wrote a couple of songs with ex-Motown ace Lamont Dozier. All of this seemed to portend a more commercial-sounding, straightahead pop effort from the usually ethereal Anderson. The result is about half and half: when writing with Dozier, Anderson expresses conventional romantic sentiments, for which he doesn't really have a feel. His tenor is so chaste and angelic, it's hard for him to be believable on earthly love songs. And soon enough, especially on later tracks, Anderson is once again in spiritual outer space, where he seems most comfortable. The compromise, however, did not appeal to fans, who avoided this album. —*William Ruhlmann*

Laurie Anderson (Laura Phillips Anderson)

b. 1947, Chicago, IL
Experimental
With a background as a sculptor and a spoken-word performance artist who had worked with literary mavericks John Girono and William Burroughs and Fluxus-inspired avant-garde artists and musicians, Laurie Anderson, at first blush, seemed too arty and too much of a cult figure to have a high-profile career as a pop/rock performer. Still, in the world of popular music, stranger

things have happened. Her 1981 debut single, the sensational avant-garde pop song "O Superman" (originally released on the One Ten label, re-released on Warner Bros.), enthralled some critics, but clocking in at 11 mostly repetitive minutes with barely a hint of melody, it alienated many others. A hit in England, "O Superman," along with Anderson's considerable reputation as a force in the Lower East Side arts scene and the enthusiastic, early support she received from the New York music press, secured her a long, successful career as an interdisciplinary performer.

Since "O Superman" catapulted her into the "rock scene," Anderson has been as exciting and intriguing a performer as rock & roll (or at least her permutation of it) has ever seen. Funny, challenging, haunting and often mesmerizing, Anderson's unique talents wipe away the notion that avant-garde proclivities have no place in pop music or are so intellectually rigorous as to be beyond the grasp of their audience. Not a musician in the traditional sense (another fact that raised the ire of her detractors), Anderson artfully and intelligently combines music, video, spoken word, and dance, creating both complex performance pieces and simple, unabashed pop songs, often in collaboration with such formidable musicians as Peter Gabriel, Bill Laswell, Adrian Belew, Lou Reed and Nile Rodgers. Not as prolific a performer as her fans would like, she remains a continually fascinating and provocative artist, who has since broadened her reach by successes in film (*Home of the Brave*) and publishing (*The Nerve Bible*). —*John Dougan*

● **Big Science** / 1982 / Warner Brothers ✦✦✦✦
Big Science is essentially a chunk of the more elaborate and difficult four-part multimedia performance piece *United States*. But, that said, *Big Science* never sounds like a portion, it is in fact a meal in itself. The music is moody and minimalistic, and Anderson's wry observations are perspicacious, smartalecky and, at times, laugh-out-loud funny. There have been numerous artists attempting work like this since *Big Science*; few, however, equal Anderson's panache. Not your average pop record. Oh yeah, "O Superman" is here in all its glory. —*John Dougan*

United States Live / 1984 / Warner Brothers ✦✦✦
Once her popularity seemed assured, Warner Bros. felt safe releasing this five-record set (since reissued on four CDs) comprising *United States*' entire four-and-a-half hours. It's not the first place I'd recommend going to hear Anderson's work, but for those so inclined it's well worth the effort. Although live performances of *United States* included film segments that ran during some of her monologues, *United States* is about communication and how we interpret and use language. It's a bit pretentious, a tad long-winded, and its size makes it unwieldy to listen to in one sitting, but this is an important work loaded with enough insight, wit and humanity to make relistening and re-evaluating worthwhile. — *John Dougan*

Mister Heartbreak / 1984 / Warner Brothers ✦✦✦
A more pop-oriented record (there are songs here and musicians like Adrian Belew and Peter Gabriel), Anderson displays a functional singing voice here that graces such wonderful songs as "Sharkey's Day" and "Excellent Birds" (a duet with Gabriel). More accessible than *Big Science*, but in some ways a record that indicates that while she may not be a musician herself, Anderson certainly knows how to pick them, work with them, and challenge them. A thoroughly wonderful record. —*John Dougan*

Home of the Brave / 1986 / Warner Brothers ✦✦✦
○ **Strange Angels** / 1989 / Warner Brothers ✦✦✦✦
Purists may disagree, but I think *Strange Angels* is Anderson's most stunning work. It may be due to its nearly giddy selection of pop songs (including the supremely ecstatic "Babydoll"), but here Anderson sounds supremely confident—as a pop singer/songwriter. Rather than weighing down her songs with avant-gardisms, *Strange Angels* positively luxuriates in this conflation of the avant-garde and the popular. Hence, there is a relentless joyfulness that imbues this record, but never sacrifices intelligence one iota. A brilliantly conceived record, *Strange Angels* offers the best of both worlds to the benighted and aficionados. —*John Dougan*

Bright Red / 1994 / Warner Brothers ✦✦✦
Almost six years after *Strange Angels*, Anderson's follow-up was the dark and foreboding *Bright Red*. A slight disappointment, Brian Eno's production heightens the almost amorphous quality of the material, which succeeds in fits and starts. Still, there are moments like "Speechless" and "Poison" that are as gripping as any-

thing she's ever recorded. As with any artist this interesting, Anderson's prodigious talents are on display; you'll simply have to dig a little deeper for them to be revealed. —*John Dougan*

○ **The Ugly One With The Jewels And Other Stories** / 1995 / Warner Brothers ✦✦✦✦
On her later albums, Laurie Anderson had moved from her earlier spoken word-plus-effects style to a more overtly musical approach, with less effective results. *The Ugly One With The Jewels*, a recording of a live performance of readings from her book *Stories From The Nerve Bible*, returned her to speaking instead of singing, and it was her best album since *Big Science*. The 18 stories reflected Anderson's extensive travels, including forays into the Third World and to convents, although she made Los Angeles and Houston sound just as exotic. In fact, telling her stories over sounds from birds to guitars to electronic beeps, she seemed an anthropologist from another world, always finding the natives friendly but strange. And she didn't fail to recognize that she could appear just as odd to them: "The Ugly One With The Jewels" was a name used by one of her subjects to describe her. —*William Ruhlmann*

Lee Andrews & the Hearts

Group, R&B, Doo-Wop
Specializing in smooth ballads, this Philadelphia R&B vocal quintet notched three hits in 1957-1958. Andrews formed the Hearts in 1953, and they debuted the next year on the Rainbow label. Chess picked up their first big seller, "Long Lonely Nights," from the tiny Mainline label in 1957. Mainline also originally issued their biggest hit for Chess, "Teardrops." Moving to United Artists, the group charted for the last time in 1958 with the typically polished "Try the Impossible." Andrews and a shifting lineup of Hearts continued to record through the '60s. —*Bill Dahl*

● **Biggest Hits** / 1981 / Collectables ✦✦✦✦
Classy '50s doo-wop, heavy on dreamy ballads. —*Bill Dahl*

The Angels

Group, Girl-Group
One of the leading girl-groups of the early '60s, thanks to the #1 hit "My Boyfriend's Back." With Linda Jansen as lead and sisters Jiggs and Barbara Allbut providing harmony, the Orange, NJ, trio signed with Caprice Records in 1961 and hit with "Til." Jansen was replaced by Peggy Santiglia (b. May 4, 1944) and the trio signed with Mercury's Smash subsidiary in 1963, cutting the bouncy "My Boyfriend's Back" at the height of the girl-group craze. "I Adore Him" proved mildly successful later that year. —*Bill Dahl*

And the Angels Sing / 1962 / Caprice ✦✦✦
Nice compilation of their earlier, pre-hit material. —*Cub Koda*

● **My Boyfriend's Back** / 1963 / Collectables ✦✦✦✦
Their major hit and 11 other solid girl group performances, including the quirky "Love Me Now." In and out of print. —*Cub Koda*

The Animals

Group, British Invasion, Psychedelic
One of the most important bands originating from England's R&B scene during the early 1960s, the Animals were second only to the Rolling Stones in influence among R&B-based bands in the first wave of the British Invasion. The Animals had their origins in a Newcastle-based group called the Kansas City Five, whose membership included pianist Alan Price, drummer John Steel, and vocalist Eric Burdon. Price exited to join the Kontours in 1962, while Burdon went off to London. The Kontours, whose membership included Bryan "Chas" Chandler, eventually were transmuted into the Alan Price R&B Combo, with John Steel joining on drums. Burdon's return to Newcastle in early 1963 heralded his return to the lineup. The final member of the combo, guitarist Hilton Valentine, joined just in time for the recording of a self-produced EP under the band's new name, the Animals. That record alerted Graham Bond to the Animals; he was likely responsible for pointing impresario Giorgio Gomelsky to the group.

Gomelsky booked the band into his Crawdaddy Club in London, and they were subsequently signed by Mickie Most, an independent producer who secured a contract with EMI's Columbia imprint. A studio session in February 1964 yielded their Columbia debut single, "Baby Let Me Take You Home" (adapted from "Baby Let Me Follow You Down") which rose to number 21 on the British charts. For years, it has been rumored incorrectly that the

Animals got their next single, "House of the Rising Sun," from Bob Dylan's first album, but more recently it has been revealed that, like "Baby Let Me Take You Home," the song came to them courtesy of Josh White. In any event, the song—given a new guitar riff by Valentine and a soulful organ accompaniment devised by Price—shot to the top of the U.K. and U.S. charts early that summer. This success led to a follow-up session that summer, yielding their first long-playing record, *The Animals*. Their third single, "I'm Crying," rose to number eight on the British charts. The group compiled an enviable record of Top Ten successes, including "Don't Let Me Be Misunderstood," and "We've Gotta Get Out of This Place," along with a second album, *Animal Tracks*.

In May of 1965, immediately after recording "We've Gotta Get Out of This Place," Alan Price left the band, citing fear of flying as the reason; subsequent biographies of the band have indicated that the reasons were less psychological. When "House of the Rising Sun" was recorded, using what was essentially a group arrangement, the management persuaded the band to put one person's name down as arranger. Price came up the lucky one, supposedly with the intention that the money from the arranger credit would be divided later on. The money was never divided, however, and as soon as it began rolling in, Price suddenly developed his fear of flying and exited the band. Others cite the increasing contentiousness between Burdon and Price over leadership of the group as the latter's reason for leaving the band. In any case, a replacement was recruited in the guise of Dave Rowberry.

In the meantime, the group was growing increasingly unhappy with the material they were being given to record by manager Mickie Most. Not only were the majority of these songs much too commercial for their taste, but they represented a false image of the band, even if many were successful. "It's My Life," a number 7 British hit and a similar smash in America, caused the Animals to terminate their association with Most and with EMI Records. They moved over to Decca/London Records and came up with a more forceful, powerful sound on their first album for the new label, *Animalisms*. The lineup shifts continued, however—Steel exited in 1966, after recording *Animalisms*, and he was replaced by Barry Jenkins, formerly of the Nashville Teens. Chandler left in mid-1966 after recording "Don't Bring Me Down" and Valentine remained until the end of 1966, but essentially "Don't Bring Me Down" marked the end of the original Animals.

Burdon reformed the group under the aegis of Eric Burdon and the New Animals, with Jenkins on drums, John Weider on guitar and violin, Danny McCulloch on bass, and Vic Briggs on guitar. He remained officially a solo act for a time, releasing a collection of material called *Eric Is Here* in 1967. As soon as the contract with English Decca was up, Burdon signed with MGM directly for worldwide distribution, and the new lineup made their debut in mid-1967. Eric Burdon and the New Animals embraced psychedelia to the hilt amid the full bloom of the Summer of Love. By the end of 1968, Briggs and McCulloch were gone, to be replaced by Burdon's old friend keyboard player/vocalist Zoot Money and his longtime stablemate guitarist Andy Summers, while Weider switched to bass. Finally, in 1969, Burdon pulled the plug on what was left of the Animals. He hooked up with a Los Angeles-based group called War, and started a subsequent solo career that continues to this day.

The original Animals reunited in 1976 for a superb album called *Before We Were So Rudely Interrupted*, which picked up right where *Animalisms* had left off a decade earlier, and which was well received critically but failed to capture the public's attention. In 1983, a somewhat longer lasting reunion came about between the original members, augmented by the presence of Zoot Money on keyboards. The resulting album, *Ark*, consisting of entirely new material, was well received by critics and charted surprisingly high, and a world tour followed. By the end of the year and the heavy touring schedule, however, it was clear that this reunion was not going to be a lasting event. The quintet split up again, having finally let the other shoe drop on their careers and history, and walked away with some financial rewards, along with memories of two generations of rock fans cheering their every note. — *Bruce Eder*

The Animals [US] / 1964 / MGM ✦✦✦
Early blues-oriented material rounded out by a few more commercial tracks—this album is stronger than the British version, as it includes several more commercial tracks off of their singles. — *Bruce Eder*

Animals [UK] / 1964 / Columbia ✦✦
The group's British debut long-player in England is a somewhat dry collection of blues and R&B covers, showing the group still trying to gain some confidence within the studio. Note: All material from this album appears on EMI's *Complete Animals* double-CD set. — *Bruce Eder*

The Animals on Tour / 1965 / MGM ✦✦
Lest anyone think this is a live album, don't be fooled by the title—MGM Records used the "On Tour" moniker for an album by Herman's Hermits as well, but that wasn't a live one either. The tracks are good ones, though, showing a lot more flash than their first long-player. — *Bruce Eder*

○ **Animal Tracks [UK]** / 1965 / Columbia ✦✦✦✦
The band's second British album displays far more energy and dexterity than its predecessor. Originals such as "For Miss Caulker" are paired up with excellent covers like "Bright Lights Big City," "I Ain't Got You," and "Roadrunner," along with Ray Charles's "Hallelujah I Love Her So" and "I Believe to My Soul." Note: All tracks appearing on this album are available on EMI's *Complete Animals* double CD. — *Bruce Eder*

○ **Animalization** / 1966 / PolyGram ✦✦✦✦
The best of the group's early albums, mostly sophisticated blues-based rock which, for the first time on an LP, managed to capture the spontaneity of their live sound while also allowing them a chance to really stretch out in the studio. Around this time in the band's history, however, the albums get confusing—*Animalization*, released in September of 1966 by MGM in America, was simply the British *Animalisms* with three tracks missing, and four other songs ("Don't Bring Me Down," "Cheating," "Inside Looking Out," and "See See Rider") added. But MGM's *Animalism*, released two months later, consisted of tracks recorded in America during the original group's final U.S. tour that never saw the light of day in England. — *Bruce Eder*

Animalism [US] / 1966 / MGM ✦✦✦
The last gasp of the original Animals, albeit with Barry Jenkins on the drums in place of John Steel and Dave Rowberry on the ivories in lieu of Alan Price. A superb collection of rock numbers, as advanced from the band's early classics as the Stones' *Aftermath* repertory was from "It's All Over Now." Loud, intense, well-focused, hard-rocking blues. — *Bruce Eder*

○ **Animalisms** / 1966 / Decca ✦✦✦✦
Very similar in line-up to the American *Animalization*, this is probably the group's best non-compilation album, with a finely developed R&B sound throughout and excellent playing, all yielding an incomparable collection of good, solid, bluesy, ballsy rock numbers, highlighted by "Gin House Blues" and "Don't Bring Me Down." — *Bruce Eder*

Winds of Change / 1967 / MGM ✦✦✦
Recently reissued on compact disc by One Way Records, this album marked the debut of Eric Burdon & the Animals, a decidedly looser, more psychedelic outfit than any the blues-singing idol had previously been associated with. "San Franciscan Nights," "Paint It Black," and "Yes I'm Experienced" (Burdon's answer to Jimi Hendrix's "Are You Experienced?") were moody and pulsating, and also fiercely experimental—one can get a glimpse of this band at work in the D.A. Pennebaker movie *Monterey Pop*, doing "Paint It Black" on stage. It was a logical extension of the later work of the original Animals into the Summer of Love. — *Bruce Eder*

Eric Is Here / 1967 / One Way ✦✦
During the months after Eric Burdon and the remaining members of the original Animals split, the singer cut this album backed by an orchestra and doing songs by Randy Newman, Barry Mann and Cynthia Weill, and other pop-music fixtures—quite a turnaround for the blues purist Burdon, and also very effective as mainstream pop music, including the U.S. hit "Help Me Girl." To add to the general confusion surrounding this material, some of it seems to have been recorded with the original Animals, or at sessions conducted while they were still together. Several songs, including "Help Me Girl," show up on Sequel Records' *Inside Looking Out*. — *Bruce Eder*

Every One of Us / 1968 / MGM ✦✦
A rather spare and disappointing album, recorded amid the splintering of the original New Animals. Keyboard player Zoot Money arrived to flesh out the lineup even as guitarist Vic Briggs and bassist Danny McCullough prepared to leave. — *Bruce Eder*

The Twain Shall Meet / 1968 / MGM ◆◆◆

Also part of One Way's reissue program, *Twain Shall Meet* was a more lopsidedly experimental album—even its major hit, "Sky Pilot," a venture into anti-war politicking on an epic level, marked a new level of sophistication for the band, which played hard and became well known for their ability to jam on stage. —*Bruce Eder*

Love Is / 1968 / MGM ◆◆

One can get an idea of the confusion that fans must have felt by virtue of the fact that *Love Is* was the third album by Eric Burdon and the Animals to be issued in 1968, even with a major lineup change taking place. Future Police-man Andy Somers (aka Summers) arrived on guitar to join his longtime stablemate Zoot Money, while John Weider moved over to bass. This album marked the end of the Animals as a continuously operating music unit, and betrays an understandable lack of direction and enthusiasm. —*Bruce Eder*

Before We Were So Rudely Interrupted / 1976 / Jet ◆◆◆

The title says it all—returning to the studio a decade after their break up, the original group lineup with Alan Price picks up right where *Animalization* and *Animalism* left off, with superb musicianship and a good if unspectacular selection of material. —*Bruce Eder*

Ark / 1983 / IRS ◆◆

The group's formal reunion, complete with a new repertory and a well- financed recording. The album has its dark, moody moments, and sometimes bogs down in the sheer heaviness of the sound and sensibilities, but where Burdon is on target as a singer, which is 70 percent of the time, the group sounds amazingly good. —*Bruce Eder*

Rip It to Shreds: Their Greatest Hits Live / 1984 / IRS ◆◆

A document of the group's 1983 reunion tour. They played better shows along this tour than the one they actually taped—some of the balances (especially on the guitars) are a little off, and the band's sound and overall performance are somewhat creaky and anemic at times, but it is a fair representation of a largely successful attempt at recapturing past glories. —*Bruce Eder*

The Animals with Sonny Boy Williamson / 1988 / Charly ◆◆

Another repackaging of the group's early live recording with American blues great Sonny Boy Williamson, in moderately good sound—the group's set sounds better on Sundazed's *In the Beginning.* —*Bruce Eder*

★ **The Best of the Animals** / 1988 / ABKCO ◆◆◆◆◆

The original Animals' American hits, including "House of the Rising Sun," "Don't Let Me Be Misunderstood," "It's My Life," and "We Gotta Get Out of This Place," in a compilation originally released in 1965. The lineup of songs is strong but the sound is indifferent—the *British Complete Animals* covers the same territory and a lot more to much greater effect, at only twice the cost with three times the music and infinitely superior sound and notes. —*Bruce Eder*

○ **Inside Looking Out: The 1965-1966 Sessions** / 1990 / Sequel ◆◆◆◆

Together with the double-CD *The Complete Animals, Inside Looking Out* forms a complete retrospective of the great British Invasion band. This 22-song compilation features all of the essential recordings cut by the group in 1965 and 1966 after they broke with their original producer Mickie Most, and before Eric Burdon dissolved the core of the original lineup to pursue solo stardom with an Animals group featuring entirely different musicians. These tracks were perhaps more soul-oriented than their previous recordings, but the group still burns on the hits "Inside Looking Out" and "Don't Bring Me Down." Despite the absence of original keyboardist Alan Price, the group continued to showcase Burdon's passionate vocals and burning, vibrant organ (by Price's replacement Dave Rowberry) on both renowned and obscure R&B tunes, with an occasional original thrown in. Besides the entirety of their final British LP "Animalisms" (from 1966) and the above-mentioned singles, the CD includes the hits "Help Me Girl" and "See See Rider" (credited to "Eric Burdon and the Animals," these were possibly Burdon solo records). The four tracks from their first release, an independently released 1963 EP featuring primitive R&B standards, are small but noteworthy bonus cuts that close this collection. —*Richie Unterberger*

★ **The Complete Animals** / Jul. 1990 / EMI ◆◆◆◆◆

The title is a bit of a misnomer; this double CD does include the complete sessions that the Animals recorded with producer Mickie Most in 1964 and 1965. The 40 songs capture the band at their peak, including most of their best and biggest hits: "House Of The Rising Sun," "Don't Let Me Be Misunderstood," "We Gotta Get Out of This Place," "I'm Crying," "It's My Life," and "Boom Boom." Most of the rest of the tunes don't match the excellence of these smashes, though they're solid. The great majority of them are covers of vintage R&B/rock tunes by Chuck Berry, Fats Domino, and the like, which aren't quite as durable as reinterpretations from the same era by the Stones and Yardbirds. When they hit the mark, though, the Animals produced some great album tracks that have been mostly forgotten by time, such as "I'm Mad Again" (originally by John Lee Hooker), "Worried Life Blues," and "Bury My Body." After leaving Most, the group would maintain their peak for another year or so (this period is represented on the fine import collection *Inside Looking Out*) despite the departure of one of rock's all-time finest organists, Alan Price. This compilation has everything that Price recorded with the group, including four previously unreleased cuts and the non-LP Eric Burdon original on the B-side of "It's My Life," "I'm Gonna Change The World." —*Richie Unterberger*

The Best of Eric Burdon & The Animals, 1966-68 / 1991 / Polydor ◆◆◆

The best attempt so far to sort out the post-1966 Animals tracks, drawing from their English Decca and American MGM sides. The material is the best of their work from the post-British invasion era, remastered superbly and carefully organized, with informative and entertaining notes. —*Bruce Eder*

○ **Best of Eric Burdon & The Animals, Vol. 2** / 1991 / Polydor ◆◆◆◆

The Best of Eric Burdon & the Animals—Vol. 2 is a surprisingly hard-rocking collection from this group's psychedelic period. Excellent songs. —*Bruce Eder*

In the Beginning / 1994 / Sundazed ◆◆◆

Recorded in December of 1963 at a live concert, this CD captures the Animals at their rawest and most animated on record, ripping ferociously through a bunch of standards (by Chuck Berry, James B. Odom et al.), playing the crowd and making snide comments about their London rivals the Rolling Stones, all with Sonny Boy Williamson II hanging somewhere around the stage. Sundazed has actually found the original master to this oft-bootlegged piece of rock/blues history. —*Bruce Eder*

BOOK

◆◆◆ **Wild Animals**, by Andy Blackford (Sidgwick & Jackson, UK, 1986). The Animals' peak as a truly important group in the mid-'60s was brief, and accordingly, this biography is on the slim side. Appropriately, it focuses almost entirely on the original lineup, before Eric Burdon took the Animals name in 1966 and fronted a variety of psychedelic and hard rock bands for the next few years. For Animals and British Invasion fans, there are a fair number of interesting stories here, including the conception of their classic "House of the Rising Sun," the group's dislike of their more pop-oriented (though excellent) hit singles, and the conflicts between them and producer Mickey Most, and manager Mike Jeffries. There are lots of quotes from members of the band, but in some important respects, it's disappointing. Some of their great singles are barely discussed, and Blackford isn't a top-notch writer, occasionally wandering from the subject into tangents about the era's pop culture. —*Richie Unterberger*

Animotion

Group, Dance-Pop

Riding the wave of MTV-friendly synth-pop of the mid-'80s, Animotion took the coldly catchy "Obsession" to the Top Ten in the beginning of 1985. After that, success was elusive—the follow-up, "Let Him Go," barely cracked the Top 40 just four months later. In 1988, over half of the band left the lineup, including the leaders Bill Wadhams and Astrid Plane; actress Cynthia Rhodes and former Device member Paul Engemann became the lead vocalists. (Fortunately, the personnel changes apparently didn't cause any animosity—Plane married Charles Ottavio, Animotion's bassist and one of the founding members of the group.) The new lineup was lucky enough to score a Top Ten hit with "Room to Move," a lightweight song from a Dan Ackroyd movie that was even more lightweight (*My Stepmother Is an Alien*). After that brief flash of success, Animotion disappeared from the picture. —*Stephen Thomas Erlewine*

Animotion / 1985 / Polydor ✦✦✦
Strange Behavior / 1986 / Casablanca ✦✦

Paul Anka

b. Jul. 30, 1941, Ottawa, Ontario, Canada
Pop, Teen Idol
Hugely successful vocalist from 1957 into the '80s, as well as writer of several venerable pop music standards. The young native of Ottawa, Canada, took the U.S. by storm in 1957 with his rock-slanted ballad "Diana," a #1 smash on ABC-Paramount Records. Dramatic renditions of "You Are My Destiny," "Lonely Boy," "Put Your Head on My Shoulder," and "Puppy Love" elevated the youth to teen-idol status over the next three years. Moving to RCA in 1962, the maturing Anka continued to chart regularly, although some of his most notable '60s copyrights were bequeathed to others—he wrote "My Way" for Frank Sinatra as well as the theme for TV's "Tonight Show." Anka returned to the top pop slot in 1974 with the controversial million-seller "(You're) Having My Baby," cut in Muscle Shoals and issued on United Artists, and he enjoyed several follow-up smashes, many featuring vocalist Odia Coates. —*Bill Dahl*

My Way / Aug. 1974 / Camden ✦✦
This is a British compilation of Paul Anka's Buddah Records recordings of the early 1970s. The first side is drawn from his May 1972 album *Jubilation* and leads off with that album's title song, a gospel-influenced chart single. The second side consolidates the December 1971 *Paul Anka* album and features Anka's version of "My Way," the song he adapted from the French tune "Comme d'Habitude" and gave to Frank Sinatra, as well as "She's A Lady," an Anka composition that was a gold-selling hit for Tom Jones. Anka was making a small comeback with this contemporary-sounding material, but it was not until he moved to United Artists in 1974 that he would become a really successful record-maker again. —*William Ruhlmann*

● **30th Anniversary Collection** / 1989 / Rhino ✦✦✦✦
The best package of Anka's early teen-idol hits, featuring "Diana," "Puppy Love," "Put Your Head on My Shoulder," and "You Are My Destiny," as well as his '70s easy listening hits ("My Way," "(You're) Having My Baby"). —*Cub Koda*

Another Bad Creation

Group, Urban
Michael Bivins, a founding member of New Edition and now currently part of the trio Bell Biv Devoe, struck commercial gold as the manager/producer of this Atlanta pre-teen quintet. Chris Sellers, Dave Shelton, Romell Chapman, and brothers Marliss and Demetrius Pugh landed a platinum release with *Coolin' at the Playground Ya' Know!* for Motown in 1991. Both "Iesha" and "Playground" were Top Ten pop and R&B singles. —*Ron Wynn*

● **Coolin' at the Playground Ya Know** / 1991 / Motown ✦✦✦✦
This bit of kiddie R&B did well with its intended audience. Motown has reviled itself in the 1990s through more concentrated marketing strategies and smarter, streetwise production. While ithasn't been able to do as well with this group as Boyz II Men, Motown scored some points by recycling some Jackson 5 material and aiming at the audience forfeited by Bell Biv Devoe's move into adult territory. —*Ron Wynn*

It Ain't What U Wear It's How U Play It / Sep. 21, 1993 / Motown ✦✦✦

Adam Ant

b. Nov. 3, 1954
New Wave
One of the seminal figures of new wave, Adam Ant (b. Stuart Leslie Goddard) had several distinct phases to his career. Initially, he explored a jagged, guitar-oriented post-punk with his group Adam and the Ants before giving way to a more pop-oriented, glam-tinged musical direction that brought him to the top of the charts. After that had run its course, he refashioned himself as a mainstream singer, which enabled him to stretch his career out for a couple of years. Once it seemed like his musical career had evaporated, he made an unexpected comeback in the early '90s as an adult alternative artist. During all this time, he recorded several

great pop singles and had a surprisingly large impact on alternative rock.

Adam Ant formed Adam and the Ants with guitarist Lester Square, bassist Andy Warren, and drummer Paul Flanagan in London in 1977. The group's approach was more theatrical than most punk groups, incorporating sado-masochastic imagry into their concerts. During this time, the group's lineup was fairly unstable, with Square being replaced by Mark Gaumont. The band released their debut, *Dirk Wears White Socks*, on the independent label Do It in 1979. *Dirk* was an ambitious and somewhat dark album, filled with jerky rhythms, angular guitar riffs, and elements of glam rock crept in Adam's vocals; Adam reacquired the rights to the record in 1983, reissuing it in a resequenced and remixed form, with the tracks "Catholic Day" and "Day I Met God" replaced by "Zerox" and "Kick," as well as including a new version of "Cartrouble."

At the time of its release, *Dirk Wears White Sox* wasn't a critical or commercial success, and the band felt the need to rework their image. Ant hired Malcolm McLaren, the manager of the Sex Pistols, to help redefine their image. McLaren dressed the band in pirate outfits and suggested a more accessible and pop-oriented, rhythmic variation on punk. Adam and the Ants followed his advice, preparing material for a new album. However, McLaren persuaded all of the Ants to leave Adam, using them as the core members of Bow Wow Wow. Adam Ant immediately formed a new version of the Ants, adding guitarist Marco Pirroni, bassist Kevin Mooney, and drummers Terry Lee Miall and Merrick (b. Chris Hughes). Pirroni, in particular, became very important in the band's musical direction, co-writing the majority of the songs with Adam, thus beginning a collaboration between the duo that would continue into the '90s.

Driven by an relentless, driving beat and chanting melodies, the new band's first album, 1980's *Kings of the Wild Frontier*, became an enormous hit in the U.K., launching three Top 10 hit singles, including the number two "Antmusic." The band' success was helped by a series of visually enticing videos, prominently featuring the skinny, handsome Adam Ant decked out in pirate gear. *Prince Charming*, released the following year, retained the same formula as *Kings of the Wild Frontier*, spawning two number one singles, "Stand and Deliver" and "Prince Charming." Even though the album was a commercial success, the formula was beginning to wear thin.

After *Prince Charming*, Adam Ant ditched the Ants for a solo career, retaining Marco Pirroni as a songwriting collaborator and a supporting musician. Adam's first solo album, *Friend or Foe*, was released in 1982 and featured the number one single "Goody Two Shoes," and the Top 10 title track. Although his next album, 1983's *Strip*, had some highlights and hit singles, it marked the end of his reign as Britain's top pop star.

Released in 1985, the Tony Visconti-produced *Vive le Rock* had some fun moments, but the performance was too studied and the record didn't earn any hit singles, so Adam Ant pursued a surprisingly successful career in acting. In 1990, Ant made a comeback with the catchy hit single "Room at the Top" from the *Manners & Physique* record, but the album failed to produce another hit single. For the next five years, Ant concentrated on acting.

By the time Adam Ant returned to recording in 1995, echoes of his music could be heard in the spiky singles of Elastica, the neo-goth industrial rock of Nine Inch Nails, and the psuedo-glam of Suede. Instead of capitalizing on the burgeoning new wave revival, Adam Ant's 1995 comeback *Wonderful* had little to do with the stylish, intensely rhythmic music he made in the early '80s. Instead, the album repositioned him as a more mature pop-rocker, crafting songs that featured acoustic guitars as prominently as electrics. The album was a moderate hit in the U.S and the U.K., as was the single "Wonderful." —*Stephen Thomas Erlewine*

○ **Dirk Wears White Sox** / 1979 / Epic ✦✦✦✦
The debut album (originally released on Do-it Records in 1979) finds a young Adam Ant exploring the sometimes awkward fusion of punk and glam. While the somewhat pretentious lyrics and inexperienced playing are a drawback, the raw energy can stand up against later releases. A remixed version of the album was reissued in 1983 and is now available on compact disc. —*Chris Woodstra*

○ **Kings of the Wild Frontier** / 1980 / Epic ✦✦✦✦
Combining pounding tom-toms (from two drummers and drum kits) and a guitar style adapted from Ennio Morricone movie soundtracks with a visual motif borrowed from pirates and Native

Americans, this second album was their apex, featuring the signature tune "Antmusic." — *William Ruhlmann*

Prince Charming / 1981 / Epic ♦♦♦
The final album with the Ants is bland in comparison to the brilliant *Kings of the Wild Frontier*. While "Stand and Deliver" is one of the high points of the band's career, "Ant Rap" is certainly the low point. The essential tracks can all be found on *Antics in the Forbidden Zone*. — *Chris Woodstra*

Friend or Foe / 1982 / Epic ♦♦♦
As a solo artist Adam Ant struck gold in the U.S. with this album, which adopts the same musical style as that of the Ants and features the hit "Goody Two Shoes" and a version of the Doors' "Hello, I Love You." — *William Ruhlmann*

Strip / Nov. 1983 / Epic ♦♦
With this album, Adam Ant's musical career began to hit the skids. He was still popular enough in the U.K. to squeeze out one more Top Ten hit with "Puss 'N Boots," but the album stopped at #20 after three straight Top Five hits. In the U.S., where Ant had peaked with his solo debut, *Friend Or Foe*, the year before, this one got only to a disastrous #65. And no wonder—the mixture of driving, danceable rock with humor that had made *Kings Of The Wild Frontier*, *Prince Charming*, and even some of *Friend Or Foe* enjoyable had given way to a lighter pop approach and outright camp, especially on the title track, a minor singles chart entry produced by Phil Collins. Somehow, Ant had lost his appeal, and fast. — *William Ruhlmann*

Vive Le Rock / 1985 / Epic ♦

● **Antics in the Forbidden Zone** / 1990 / Epic ♦♦♦♦
The most comprehensive overview of the band. In 22 tracks, all of the hits are represented as well as key album cuts and a rare B-side, "Beat My Guest." An essential part of any new wave collection. — *Chris Woodstra*

Manners & Physique / Feb. 1990 / MCA ♦♦
For his comeback album and first new release in five years, Adam Ant turned to old Prince crony Andre Cymone, who transformed him into a dance music singer, producing and playing all the instruments on contemporary dance tracks, over which Ant's long time partner Marco Pirroni played lead guitar and Ant himself contributed appropriately rhythmic vocals. Some of the lyrics had his old flair for mockery, but, like most dance music singers, he came off as only a part of the production, rather than its focus. Nevertheless, the makeover was good for a U.K./U.S. Top 20 hit in "Room At The Top" and respectable chart peaks of #19 (England) and #57 (America), a big improvement over 1985, when he looked washed up. — *William Ruhlmann*

Peel Sessions / 1991 / Dutch East India ♦♦♦
A nice collection of recordings made for John Peel's radio show from 1978 to 1979. This is probably the best documentation of the early days of the band, combining tracks from *Dirk Wears White Sox*, early singles, and previously unreleased material. Essential for hardcore fans. — *Chris Woodstra*

B-side Babies! / Sep. 27, 1994 / Epic/Legacy ♦♦♦
Since Adam Ant once had a group called the B-Sides, it makes sense that his singles, both as lead singer of Adam and the Ants and as a solo, would have non-LP B-sides. And since Ant was a hit in the U.K. before he made it in America, and always bigger in Britain, many of those B-sides appeared only on English singles. This is a collection of them, songs recorded between 1980 and 1985 that gave Ant a chance to try novelty approaches while the A-sides relentlessly beat out his trademark "Antmusic." In fact, songs like "Making History" do have that characteristic yodel and the Burundi-style drumming of Terry Miall and Merrick. But elsewhere, Ant tries different things, frequently light, slight things like "Juanito The Bandito." But fun was always one of his qualities, and it's here in abundance. — *William Ruhlmann*

Wonderful / 1995 / Capitol ♦♦♦
Adam Ant recorded his first album in five years (and second in ten years) at Abbey Road Studio No. 2, where the Beatles recorded, and a Beatle sound wore off on the songs, which sounded like Beatle music of 1966-67, from the rhythmic cadences to the strummed acoustic guitars and backwards tape sounds. Ant was always better at image than music, whether he was mixing Native American and pirate gear or employing African-style drumming more for the look than the sound back in the Antmusic days. Since then, he hasn't had any musical compass, although he posed as a dance music frontman on 1990's *Manners & Physique*. Here he

borrowed Madonna's photographer, Anton Corbijn, and her basic theme—sex-as-amusement/nourishment/salvation. He succeeded in sounding horny, but that didn't make him seductive. — *William Ruhlmann*

Anthrax

Group, Thrash, Heavy Metal
Nearly as much as Metallica or Megadeth, Anthrax has been responsible for the emergence of speed and thrash metal. Combining the speed and fury of hardcore punk with the prominent guitars and vocals of heavy metal, Anthrax helped create a new sub-genre of heavy metal on their early albums. Guitarists Scott Ian and Dan Spitz are a formidable pair, spitting out lightning-fast riffs and solos that never seem masturbatory. Unlike Metallica or Megadeth, they had the good sense to temper their often serious music with a healthy dose of humor and realism.

After their first album, *Fistful of Metal*, singer Joey Belladonna and bassist Frank Bello joined the lineup. Belladonna helped take the band further away from conventional metal clichés and over the next five albums (with the exception of 1988's *State of Euphoria*, where the band sounded like they were in a creative straightjacket) Anthrax arguably became the leaders of speed metal.

As the '80s became the '90s, Anthrax began to increase their experiments with hip-hop, culminating in a tour with Public Enemy in 1991 and a joint re-recording of PE's classic "Don't Believe the Hype."

After their peak period of the late '80s, Anthrax kicked Belladonna out of the band in 1992 and replaced him with ex-Armored Saint vocalist John Bush—a singer that was gruffer and deeper, fitting most metal conventions perfectly. Subsequently, their sound became less unique and their audience shrank slightly as a consequence, but it would be foolish to count Anthrax out—these guys are too clever to fade away. — *Stephen Thomas Erlewine*

Fistful of Metal / 1984 / Megaforce ♦♦♦
The band's debut album featured bassist Dan Lilker, who left and formed Nuclear Assault. It's not as fast or hard as their later albums. — *John Book*

Armed and Dangerous / 1985 / Megaforce ♦♦♦
This EP featured the debut of vocalist Joey Belladonna (vocals) and Frank Bello (bass). — *John Book*

○ **Spreading the Disease** / 1985 / Megaforce ♦♦♦♦
Spreading the Disease demonstrates that a speed-metal band can still have a knack for creating a song accessible for pop audiences. This is an essential Anthrax album. — *John Book*

● **Among the Living** / 1987 / Megaforce ♦♦♦♦
"The" Anthrax album to have is a high point in speed-metal history. Harsh, powerful, and strong, it's flawless from beginning to end. — *John Book*

○ **I'm the Man** / 1987 / Megaforce ♦♦♦♦
This EP consists of a few non-album tracks and some live material. The title track pokes fun at rap, the Beastie Boys, Metallica, the Mentors, and themselves. Anthrax was the first heavy metal band to experiment with rap. — *John Book*

State of Euphoria / 1988 / Megaforce ♦♦♦
Free-spirited, it's a showcase for vocalist Joey Belladonna's talent. — *John Book*

○ **Persistence of Time** / 1990 / Megaforce ♦♦♦♦
Second best to *Among the Living*, the band makes strong political statements without sounding preachy. — *John Book*

○ **Attack of the Killer B's** / 1991 / Island ♦♦♦♦
The band gets loose on this compilation of B-sides, covers, and rejects. It shows a lighter side of Anthrax. — *John Book*

○ **Sound of White Noise** / 1993 / Elektra ♦♦♦♦
On their first album with vocalist John Bush, Anthrax emphasized their rhythm section, creating a ballsy, pulsating groove. Bush's aggressive vocals effortlessly meshed with the lean, snarling guitar riffs, making *Sound of White Noise* one of the group's finest. — *Stephen Thomas Erlewine*

Live—the Island Years / Apr. 5, 1994 / Island ♦♦♦
This 70-minute concert recording from October 1991, issued after Anthrax had switched record labels, provides a good overview of the band's first seven years, including songs from the albums

Spreading the Disease, Among the Living, State Of Euphoria, Persistence of Time, and *Attack of the Killer B's*. Public Enemy joins them for "Bring the Noise," and there are two tracks, the otherwise unavailable "Metal Thrashing Mad" and "In My World," recorded live in the studio in January 1992. — *William Ruhlmann*

The Anti-Nowhere League

Group, Punk, Alternative Pop/Rock
There is an old expression about a blind pig finding a chestnut now and again, and that certainly rings true when addressing the overnight phenomenon known as the Anti-Nowhere League. Fronted by a codpiece-wearing goon of a lead singer with questionable personal hygiene who went by the name Animal, the League somehow managed to release one vulgar, loud, stupid, funny, thoroughly great EP, but hung around like a bunch of talentless louts who never got the message to clear off. Playing standard, raunchy, Sex Pistol-influenced punk rock, Animal cranked up the disgust factor either by uttering a string of obscenities or boasting about his indiscriminate taste in partners (including animals) in sexual intercourse. A punk parody worthy of Nick Lowe, the League actually got a lot of press when it looked as though their record was going to be banned in England and, or so it was whispered at the time, the U.S. Fortunately, it wasn't, and the grubby glory of this group of shameless yobs became ours to cherish. They did record a few full-length albums (including a live one recorded in Yugoslavia), and all are worthless. — *John Dougan*

● **We Are . . . the League** / 1982 / WXYZ ♦♦♦♦
Featuring a thrash-and-bash version of Ralph McTell's "Streets of London" and the disgusting "So What," this is a refreshing blast of ignorance that revels in its own tastelessness the way pigs roll around in the mud. Lead singer Animal growls and tells of mighty sexual exploits, while guitarist Magoo coughs up hairball after hairball of distortion. Special treat is the hilariously dumb "I Hate . . . People." — *John Dougan*

Live in Yugoslavia / 1983 / ID ♦♦♦

R I P / 1985 / Dojo ♦♦

Long Live the League / 1985 / ABC ♦♦

Perfect Crime / 1987 / GWR ♦♦
In the five years it took them to make a second studio album, the Anti-Nowhere League evolved from its obscenity-laced, power chord punk sound to something more like such mainstream U.K. rock bands as the Stranglers and Big Country. This just made them more pretentious and less amusing, however. — *William Ruhlmann*

Live & Loud!! / 1990 / Link ♦♦♦

○ **Best of the Anti-Nowhere League** / 1993 / Cleopatra ♦♦♦♦
The League were loud, obnoxious, hostile, vulgar, and, above all, stupid. Anything you'll ever need by this band is here, including their first five singles and the original, uncensored version of their ode to corruption and bestiality "So What," which was brought to the attention of heavy metal fans when Metallica covered it on the B-side of their "Sad But True" single. — *Steve Huey*

Any Trouble

Group, Rock & Roll, New Wave
Led by Clive Gregson, Any Trouble was an underappreciated bright spot on Stiff Records, which had no shortage of talented artists. Gregson's appearance and hardened love songs might have led to (somewhat accurate) comparisons with Elvis Costello, but his songs were not as vicious and his band rocked with enthusiasm, not abandon. Any Trouble's records were overlooked when they were released in the early '80s, yet they hold up and contain their fair share of engaging rock and pop. — *Stephen Thomas Erlewine*

● **Where Are All the Nice Girls?** / 1980 / Stiff ♦♦♦♦
The first album is a pure pub/pop rock delight. Leading off with the infectious "Second Choice" (one of the great "should have been hits") and ending up with the unlikely ABBA cover "Name of the Game," Gregson and company run though 12 tunes, almost all obsessed with love gone wrong. A cult favorite. — *Chris Woodstra*

Wheels in Motion / 1981 / Stiff ♦♦♦
The playing on their sophomore effort is more sophisticated and the production is cleaner but it lacks some of the bite of the first album. Gregson's now standard obsession makes an appearance on the album's highlight, "Trouble with Love." — *Chris Woodstra*

○ **Live at the Venue** / 1981 / Teldec ♦♦♦♦
Originally released as a promo for radio, this live show from 1980 finds the band in its natural setting. Playing with higher energy than in the studio, this provides the best picture of the band at its peak. This is their only album still available. — *Chris Woodstra*

Any Trouble / 1983 / EMI ♦♦♦
The band's move from the Stiff label to EMI marked an attempt to crack the U.S. market with a mainstream radio-ready album and a new lineup. Unfortunately overlooked at the time, material from this album continued to be a part of Gregson's solo sets in the '90s. — *Chris Woodstra*

Wrong End of the Race / 1984 / EMI ♦♦♦
Issued as a double LP in England and a single LP in the U.S., *Wrong End of the Race* compiles unnecessary rerecordings of previously released songs, some new tracks, and a few interesting covers. Their weakest set and final attempt before Gregson left to pursue a more successful solo career. — *Chris Woodstra*

Aphex Twin

Techno
Richard D. James, known as the Aphex Twin, began his musical career in rural Cornwall, making instruments with old Radio Shack gadgetry. The result of his experimentations from 1985 through 1992 is *Selected Ambient Works, Vol. 1*. Eager to cash in on the ambient-house craze, the German techno label R&S Records released *Selected Ambient Works, Vol. 1*, even though James's main work was full-throttle, nose-bleed techno. The LP caused an underground sensation, making many critics' top tens for 1993.

James's first stateside release, under the Polygon Window moniker, was *Surfing On Sine Waves*. Amidst a great deal of hype, James released the quadruple LP, *Selected Ambient Works, Vol. 2*, to mixed reviews in the spring of 1994. In 1995, James released *I Care Because You Do,* a schizophrenic ride of an album that unites the work on the two volumes of *Selected Ambient Works* with his distorted brand of techno. — *John Bush*

○ **Selected Ambient Recordings 85-92** / 1993 / R&S ♦♦♦♦
A collection of electronic soundscapes by Richard James (aka Aphex Twin), arguably the leader in the ambient techno movement, *Selected Ambient Recordings 85-92* is nothing short of stunning. Musically, much of this brings to mind Brian Eno or Kraftwerk, whom he never heard until after he recorded this material. — *Stephen Thomas Erlewine*

Selected Ambient Works, Vol. 2 / Apr. 1994 / Sire ♦♦♦
Selected Ambient Works, Vol. 2 is a more difficult and challenging album than the Aphex Twin's previous collection. The music is all texture; there are only the faintest traces of beats and forward movement. Instead, all of these untitled tracks are long, unsettling electronic soundscapes, alternately quiet and confrontational; although most of the music is rather subdued, it is never easy listening. While some listeners may find this double-disc album dull (both discs run over 70 minutes), many listeners will be intrigued and fascinated by the intricately detailed music of the Aphex Twin. — *Stephen Thomas Erlewine*

● **I Care Because You Do** / 1995 / Sire ♦♦♦♦
James's most consistent work, *I Care* fuses his earlier hardcore techno days with the smooth rhythms and atmospherics of his ambient work, often on the same song. "Ventolin" is one of the harshest singles ever recorded; closer "Next Heap With"'s orchestration makes it the highlight of the album. — *John Bush*

A.R. Kane

Group, Alternative Pop/Rock
A.R. Kane is the British dance music duo of Londoners Alex Ayuli and Rudy Tambala, who debuted with the single "When You're Sad" on One Little Indian Records in the U.K. in 1986. They followed with an EP, *Lolita*, on 4AD Records, in 1987, and the same year teamed up with Martyn and Steve Young of Colourbox and DJ David Dorrell under the name M/A/R/R/S to create the dance track "Pump Up the Volume," which hit #1 in Great Britain and #13 in the U.S., where it went gold. As A.R. Kane, they released *69* in 1988 and *i* in 1989 on Rough Trade Records, then disbanded. In 1991, the group was picked up by David Byrne's Luaka Bop label for U.S. distribution, causing them to re-form, and *Americana*, a compilation of earlier work, was issued in the U.S. in 1992. In 1994, A.R. Kane issued its first new album in five years, *New Clear Child*. — *William Ruhlmann*

69 / 1988 / Rough Trade ♦♦

"I" / 1989 / Rough Trade ♦♦♦

Remixes / 1990 / Rough Trade ♦♦♦

● **Americana** / Jan. 28, 1992 / Luaka Bop ♦♦♦♦
This dance music duo is liable to sound like nearly anything, from pop balladry to ambient sound to U2-like guitar rock to disco/techno, especially on their U.S. debut, which is culled from their U.K. albums and EPs, plus one newly recorded track, "Water." — *William Ruhlmann*

New Clear Child / 1994 / ♦♦
On its first new album in five years, A.R. Kane has settled down into a light dance pop sound dominated by throaty vocals. The approach is more focused, but still ethereal, and also reminiscent of cocktail jazz. — *William Ruhlmann*

Arabian Prince

Group, Rap
A founding member of the Compton, CA, rap group Niggaz With Attitudes (N.W.A.), The Arabian Prince found the going tough when he departed the group for a solo career in 1988. His debut *Brother Arab* on Orpheus barely scraped the bottom of the R&B and pop charts in 1989. — *Ron Wynn*

Brother Arab / Sep. 1989 / Orpheus ♦♦♦
Hard-hitting hip-hop with an unrepentant gangsta tone. Arabian Prince angered some in the middle class community with this unrelenting condemnation of inner city life. It was vicious and vulgar, but delivered with the kind of cold, harsh slant that made it convincing. — *Ron Wynn*

● **Tha Underworld** / 1992 / EMI America ♦♦♦♦
Arabian Prince doesn't discuss anything that hasn't been talked about numerous times by other gangsta types. But his commentaries on drugs, violence, sex, and such are done in such a deadpan, yet defiant and angry manner, that you're hooked even while being disgusted by a litany of hopelessness and injustice. — *Ron Wynn*

The Arc Angels

Group, Blues Rock
The Arc Angels are an Austin, TX, rock quartet formed by the late Stevie Ray Vaughan's rhythm section, Tommy Shannon (bass) and Chris Layton (drums) after the guitarist's death in 1990. The group is filled out by two lead vocalist/lead guitarists, Doyle Bramhall II and Charlie Sexton. Sexton had a Top 40 single in "Beat's So Lonely" at the age of 17 in 1986. The Arc Angels released their self-titled debut album in January 1992. — *William Ruhlmann*

Arc Angels / 1992 / Geffen ♦♦♦
Arc Angels is a supergroup in the making. Backstopped by Chris Layton and Tommy Shannon (the late Stevie Ray Vaughan's former rhythm section) the Austin-based combo is fronted by two young yet veteran guitarist-vocalists in Charlie Sexton and Doyle Bramhall II. Sexton and Bramhall alternate lead vocal duties depending on who wrote the song, and trade-off vocals on co-written tracks. Either way, the former's guttural rasp blends smoothly—like a well-aged Scotch—with the latter's velvet-coated blues. It would have been really easy to over-sweeten this stuff in the studio for the benefit of mainstream radio but, to the group's credit, Arc Angels maintains a credible balance between muscle and accessibility. — *Roch Parisien*

Arcade

Group, Hard Rock
Arcade is a hard rock quintet formed by singer Stephen Pearcy after he left Ratt. It includes guitarists Donny Syracuse and Frankie Wilsex, bassist Michael Andrews, and drummer Fred Coury. Arcade released its debut album on Epic Records in 1993. — *William Ruhlmann*

Arcade / Apr. 1993 / Epic ♦♦♦
Stephen Pearcy has a distinctive whine that cuts through the hard rock, and his new band straddles the line approaching heavy metal while retaining a melodic restraint. When this is done right (Guns N' Roses), it means megabucks, but it often takes persistence in the form of audience building and then the luck of a radio hit with a power ballad. Pearcy carries a certain cachet from Ratt, and that got him into the lower reaches of the chart and the attention of AOR radio programmers, who gave a few spins to "Nothin'

To Lose" and "Cry No More." But that makes this no more than a promising beginning in the hard rock sweepstakes, and it would help if Pearcy and Co. had something more to offer than musical and lyrical clichés. — *William Ruhlmann*

A/2 / 1994 / Epic ♦♦

Arcadia

Group, Dance-Pop, Pop/Rock
During a short hiatus in late 1984 and early 1985, three Duran Duran members—lead singer Simon LeBon, keyboardist Nick Rhodes, and drummer Roger Taylor—formed Arcadia, a short-lived splinter group which offered an artier version of Duran Duran's new wave synth-pop. Arcadia released their only album, *So Red the Rose*, in 1985, just after Duran Duran's popularity reached a peak. Consequently, the album became a hit based on name recognition alone, as did the single "Election Day," which sailed into the American and British Top Ten. After their brief moment of success, the members of Arcadia reformed Duran Duran without guitarist Andy Taylor. — *Stephen Thomas Erlewine*

So Red the Rose / 1985 / Capitol ♦♦♦
This album was recorded by three-fifths of Duran Duran: Simon LeBon, Nick Rhodes, and Roger Taylor. It's a must for Duran Duran fans and includes "Election Day" with Grace Jones. — *Kenneth M. Cassidy*

Tasmin Archer

Urban, Pop/Rock
British soul singer Tasmin Archer's silky voice on her debut album *Great Expectations* and hit single "Sleeping Satellite" helped propel her toward massive media exposure in the U.K. and respectable success in the U.S. in 1993. Archer's music echoes the highly textured and polished dance-pop of Seal, yet it leans more toward straightforward pop, as evidenced by her 1994 collection of Elvis Costello covers, *Shipbuilding*. — *Stephen Thomas Erlewine*

● **Great Expectations** / 1993 / Capitol ♦♦♦♦
Brit vocalist Tasmin Archer maps out some interesting terrain somewhere between Seal and Tracy Chapman on her debut *Great Expectations*—a layered, well-produced mix of acoustic and synthetic instrumentation overlaid with committed, soulful vocals. Lead track "Sleeping Satellite" was a hit in several parts of Europe, and it's a hypnotic, fashionably retro-psych-soul beauty. That track is backstopped by several more solid contenders, including a sombre-yet-vibrant "In Your Care," an emotionally honest "Ripped Inside," and the uncharacteristically forceful "Somebody's Daughter." While perhaps not living up to the album title, there are enough good ones (and one great one) here to make *Great Expectations* well worth investigating. — *Roch Parisien*

Shipbuilding / Mar. 8, 1994 / SBK ♦♦♦
Shipbuilding is an EP of Elvis Costello covers demonstrating Archer's superb interpretive skills. — *Stephen Thomas Erlewine*

Archers Of Loaf

Group, Alternative Pop/Rock
Formed in the early '90s, the indie-rock quartet Archers Of Loaf specialize in an off-kilter, noisy and surprisingly tuneful brand of alternative rock. The Archers begin with Pavement's warped guitar-pop sensibilities, adding more sheets of pure white noise and more cryptic lyrics, and play with an often invigorating, reckless sense of fun. The band became a college/underground sensation when the single "Web in Front" became a hit on alternative and college radio in the summer of 1993. They followed it with the acclaimed debut *Icky Mettle* later in the year; it also received a sizable amount of airplay on college radio. In 1994, the band released two EPs and worked on their second record, *Vee Vee*, which was released in early 1995; like its predecessor, *Vee Vee* was a college radio hit, securing the Archers of Loaf's place as one of the hippest indie-rock bands of the mid-'90s. — *Stephen Thomas Erlewine*

● **Icky Mettle** / 1994 / Alias ♦♦♦♦
Icky Mettle, the Archers Of Loaf's debut album, is filled with jagged guitars playing broken riffs, yet they have enough melodic sense to tie it all together into memorable songs, as evidenced by the alternative rock hit "Web in Front." As that song's lyrics suggest ("All I ever wanted was to be your spine"), the group cherishes the obscure, but they are never weird for weirdness' sake—their fragmented poetry fits the cut-and-paste of the noisy music. — *Stephen Thomas Erlewine*

Vee Vee / Mar. 1995 / Alias ✦✦✦

Icky Mettle, the Archers' debut album, became just enough of an underground hit to scare the band away from most of their pop instincts. Filled with unexpected, jarring shards of noise and melodies that never quite manage to be catchy, *Vee Vee* relies more on attitude and energy than their previous records. It's an approach that works—for all their oblique song structures and overt noise, Archers of Loaf is a band that can rock hard. With the harder rhythms and jerky guitars, the group can usually obscure the elliptical hooks by just rocking out, which means the album is a bracing listen, yet not an engaging one. *—Stephen Thomas Erlewine*

Archies

Group, Bubblegum

Not satisfied with his success with the Monkees, bubblegum pop manufacturer Don Kirshner formed this studio group based on the comic books and animated television show of the same name in the late '60s. Hiring an array of seasoned session musicians to support lead vocalists Ron Dante, Jeff Barry, and Ellie Greenwich, the Archies managed to produce several hits in the late '60s under the direction of Jeff Barry, including the massive hit single, "Sugar, Sugar." After a short spark of success, the group promptly vanished, leaving only nostalgic memories. *—Stephen Thomas Erlewine*

● **20 Greatest Hits** / Onyx Classix ✦✦✦✦

Argent

Group, Art-Rock/Progressive-Rock, Pop/Rock

Ex-Zombies keyboardist Rod Argent (b. June 14, 1945) formed Argent in 1969. Like the Zombies, Argent was capable of some excellent melodies even when indulging in more extended art-rock forays. Rod Argent had as many chops as Keith Emerson, was able to pull out all the stops when needed, but he seemed to have a greater understanding of the value of economy in note selection. Guitarist Russ Ballard (b. Oct 31, 1947) was equally tasty, and Argent's rhythm section, bassist Jim Rodford (b. July 7, 1945) and drummer Rob Henrit (b. May 2, 1945), delivered all the right fire and dynamics. Their self-titled debut and sophomore effort, *Ring of Hands*, are standouts.

Argent's one huge hit, "Hold Your Head Up," went to #1. After Argent's demise, Ballard went on to a moderately successful solo career. Both Ballard and Argent became successful producers. Henrit and Rodford went on to join the Kinks. *—Rick Clark*

● **Anthology: The Best of Argent** / 1976 / Epic ✦✦✦✦

"Hold Your Head Up" is included, as well as other well-crafted rockers. *—Dan Heilman*

Joan Armatrading

b. Dec. 9, 1950, St. Kitts, West Indies

Singer-Songwriter

Born on the island of St. Kitts in the West Indies, Joan Armatrading moved to England in 1958. In 1969, she met Pam Nestor, with whom she wrote the songs that appeared on her first album, *Whatever's for Us* in 1972. She broke through to pop success in England in 1976 with her Top Ten single "Love And Affection" and self-titled third album, which also was her U.S. chart debut. *Show Some Emotion* (1977) and *To the Limit* (1978) confirmed her status as an important singer/songwriter. In the '80s, Armatrading's music took on more of a rock and new wave sound, resulting in her most popular albums, *Me Myself I* (1980), *Walk Under Ladders* (1981), and *The Key* (1983), all of which made the U.K. Top Ten and the U.S. Top 100. Armatrading continues to record and tour regularly. *—William Ruhlmann*

Whatever's for Us / 1972 / A&M ✦✦

Joan Armatrading's debut album is all but co-credited to Pam Nestor, who co-wrote 11 of the 14 songs and whose picture and bio appear on the album jacket. (She doesn't perform on the record, however.) Since Armatrading dispensed with the collaboration on later albums, a comparison is instructive. On these relatively short songs (averaging about 2:45), Armatrading is more outward-looking than on her later songs. Much of her work is done in close-ups, but many of the songs on *Whatever's For Us* pull back from the "I-you" focus of subsequent efforts to take in the family, especially, and the world at large. Granted, neither is viewed positively, at least in the formal sense. For the album, Ar-

matrading used some of Elton John's brain trust, and especially when she plays piano, the resulting sound is not unlike an early John album such as *Tumbleweed Connection*. *Whatever's For Us* is a promising debut that, nevertheless, does not include any material that has proven to be memorable. *—William Ruhlmann*

Back to the Night / 1975 / A&M ✦✦✦

Even this early on, Armatrading's basic theme—the conflict between the need for romantic attachment and the need for independence—is in place in all its paradoxical glory. She revels in the joys of love and is repelled by the threat love represents to her identity. On this release, the message overwhelms the medium, however; Armatrading hasn't yet developed the musical structures to make her lyrical concerns memorable. *—William Ruhlmann*

○ **Joan Armatrading** / Sep. 1976 / A&M ✦✦✦✦

Her third album was the one most people fell in love with, attracted by her Caribbean-flavored singing of articulate romantic lyrics and Glyn Johns's tasteful folk/rock production, especially on "Love and Affection." *—William Ruhlmann*

Show Some Emotion / Oct. 1977 / A&M ✦✦✦

A companion piece to *Joan Armatrading*, this lovely album contains the title track, "Warm Love," and "Willow." *—William Ruhlmann*

To the Limit / Oct. 1978 / A&M ✦✦✦

She began to up the musical ante with a more rock-oriented approach, and her songs also took a more argumentative tone, especially in the critical "Barefoot and Pregnant." *—William Ruhlmann*

Steppin' Out / 1979 / A&M ✦✦✦

In 1979, Armatrading's following in the U.S. was not big enough to justify the release of this concert album, although it was recorded in North America. It demonstrates her rapport with her fans and her effectiveness as a live performer and includes such favorites as "Love And Affection" and "You Rope You Tie Me." *—William Ruhlmann*

How Cruel / Nov. 1979 / A&M ✦✦✦

How Cruel is a four-song, one-sided, 12-inch EP released, according to the blurb on the cover, because the tunes were "so good they couldn't wait for an album!!!" (The title track had already appeared, albeit not in the U.S., on the live *Steppin' Out* album.) In fact, the songs are good, although the decision to release them probably had more to do with having something in the marketplace between the autumn 1978 release of *To The Limit* and the spring 1980 release of *Me Myself I*. The best track is "How Cruel," a complaint about her career ("I had somebody say once I was way too black/And someone answers she's not black enough for me") with a terrific sax solo by Lon Price, although "He Wants Her," with a lazy reggae beat, also impresses. *—William Ruhlmann*

○ **Me Myself, I** / May 1980 / A&M ✦✦✦✦

On the trio of albums that made her reputation in 1976-78, *Joan Armatrading*, *Show Some Emotion*, and *To The Limit*, Armatrading relied on the pristine production of Glyn Johns to underscore the sensitivity of her folk-based confessional songs. Here, on her first full-length album in two years, she turned to rock producer Richard Gottehrer and a session band that included Anton Fig, Chris Spedding, and members of the E Street Band, making her case for being a mainstream rocker. The songs were less serious, too, notably the title track, a U.K. hit. (The album's other British chart single was the ballad "All The Way From America," which was more in the style of her earlier work.) The result was the best-selling album Armatrading has ever had in either the U.S. or U.K. *—William Ruhlmann*

Walk under Ladders / Sep. 1981 / A&M ✦✦✦

Dominant keyboard lines and the characteristic fat percussion approach of producer Steve Lillywhite completed Armatrading's transformation from folkie to new wave diva on this album. Still, it was songs like "The Weakness In Me" to which old fans responded, although the U.K. hits were "I'm Lucky" and "No Love." Another British Top 10, the album was less successful in the U.S., consolidating Armatrading's expanded following without propelling her to major stardom. *—William Ruhlmann*

○ **The Key** / Mar. 1983 / A&M ✦✦✦✦

The best of Armatrading's later albums, which took on a much harder rock edge. Steve Lillywhite produced, and Armatrading provided some good uptempo material, including "Drop the Pilot" and "(I Love It When You) Call Me Names." *—William Ruhlmann*

○ **Track Record** / Nov. 1983 / A&M ♦♦♦♦
A reasonable best-of that samples Armatrading's first decade of recording. — *William Ruhlmann*

Secret Secrets / Feb. 1985 / A&M ♦♦♦
Mike Howlett, known for the dance-friendly keyboard-dominated pop sheen of his productions for groups like A Flock Of Seagulls and Berlin, gives a similar sound to Armatrading here (lots of echo on the vocals, lots of shimmering, horn-like synthesizer parts). It isn't really a good fit, though the record sold respectably and produced a minor U.K. chart hit in "Temptation." — *William Ruhlmann*

Sleight of Hand / May 1986 / A&M ♦♦
Armatrading becomes her own producer here (with Steve Lillywhite returning as mixer), and does herself no favors, continuing to overwhelm her songs with effects. By now, her cult was beginning to become disaffected, and she had failed to break through to the pop mainstream; meaning that, at least at this point, she seemed destined to keep playing concerts to fans who would call out for "Love And Affection" while selling fewer and fewer records. — *William Ruhlmann*

The Shouting Stage / Jul. 1988 / A&M ♦♦
The good news is that, after several albums of flirting with rock and overproduction, Joan Armatrading has developed a spare sound once again focusing on her songs and singing, backed by such tasteful accompanists as Dire Straits members Mark Knopfler and Alan Clark. The not-so-good news is that, lyrically, Armatrading seems trapped in a romantic cul-de-sac—when she doesn't have the object of her affections, she longs for him, but when she does have him, she argues with him and suspects him of infidelity, not to mention emotional abuse. There is a traditional sense of relationships mixed in with hints of the nascent "men just don't get it" flavor of '90s feminism. One is tempted to say that you can't have it both ways, but then Armatrading's emotional outpourings have always had more to do with contemporaneous honesty than long-term consistency. — *William Ruhlmann*

● **Classics, Vol. 21** / 1989 / A&M ♦♦♦♦
Featuring some of her best songs and covering a bit more ground than *Track Record, Classics* is a good introduction to the rich and varied career of Joan Armatrading. — *Stephen Thomas Erlewine*

Hearts and Flowers / Jun. 1990 / A&M ♦♦
For much of her 12th new studio album, Joan Armatrading sounds like she is ending a bad relationship, but by the last two songs she sounds like she's beginning a good one. Still, she pledges herself to someone she worries may not have the same commitment she does. Thus, perhaps the album's signal song (and Armatrading's first UK chart single in five years) is "More Than One Kind Of Love," in which she touts the value of friendship over romance: "Good friendships seldom die," she sings, and we are painfully aware that, especially in Armatrading's world, even good love affairs seldom live. Still, this is less a revelation than an incremental development in the artist's work, and *Hearts And Flowers* doesn't contain any songs that rank among her best. — *William Ruhlmann*

The Very Best of Joan Armatrading / 1991 / A&M ♦♦♦

Square the Circle / Jun. 23, 1992 / A&M ♦♦♦
Joan Armatrading, who has spent the better part of her career demanding greater commitment and fidelity from men than they seem willing to give her, turns the tables on her 13th album, abandoning herself to lust for "the wrong guy" and unfaithfulness to her beloved. The equation produces interesting, if not always successful results, such as the characterstically convoluted "Can't Get Over (How I Broke Your Heart)," but makes a poor lead-in to the philosophical "If Women Ruled The World," which proves that sexism sounds just as lame-brained coming from a woman as it does coming from a man. "Not all men kill babies," Armatrading admits, which is certainly a relief to hear. But if women ruled the world there would be "no more war, no more hate…no more sons dying young." This from a woman who lived under the Margaret Thatcher regime during the Falklands War. — *William Ruhlmann*

Armored Saint

Group, Heavy Metal
Possibly one of the most underrated heavy metal bands of the '80s, Armored Saint began playing in the garages of Los Angeles in 1982. Their first record label pretty much ignored them, despite incredible success on stage in the U.S. and Europe. The death of gui-

tarist Dave Prichard in 1990 almost closed the book on the Armored Saint story, but the band rebounded into an upsurge of sales after re-signing to Metal Blade Records. — *John Book*

March of the Saint / 1984 / Chrysalis ♦♦♦
This is the band's debut album. — *John Book*

Delirious Nomad / 1985 / Chrysalis ♦♦♦
A powerful set of songs, *Delirious Nomad* was able to get a few underground hits on the radio. — *John Book*

Raising Fear / 1987 / Chrysalis ♦♦♦
This album made them the most underrated band in America, and was the last album to feature guitarist David Prichard. — *John Book*

Saints Will Conquer / 1988 / Restless ♦♦
● **Symbol of Salvation** / Mar. 1991 / Metal Blade ♦♦♦♦
Their latest album following the death of guitarist David Prichard consists of awesome American heavy metal, tighter than before and already considered to be the band's best. — *John Book*

Army of Lovers

Group, Alternative Pop/Rock
Army of Lovers is a European disco collective masterminded by producer Anders Wollbeck and synth programmer/vocalist Alexander Bard. On their self-titled debut album, they used a variety of lead singers and relied heavily on the work of producer/mixer Emil Hellman. With 1992's *Massive Luxury Overdose*, Bard, Jean-Pierre Barda (vocals, drums), and De La Cour (vocals, keyboards) were the featured musicians. — *Stephen Thomas Erlewine*

Army of Lovers / Aug. 13, 1991 / Giant ♦♦♦
● **Massive Luxury Overdose** / 1992 / Giant ♦♦♦♦
Superior production, with multi-tracked vocals and intercut rhythms, are the best things about this release. The lyrics and vocals are typical dance; exuberantly delivered, but more generic than distinctive and designed to support the beat rather than work off it. — *Ron Wynn*

P.P. Arnold

b. 1946, Los Angeles, CA
Soul
A soul vocalist who came from a family of gospel singers, Pat (P.P.) Arnold began singing as a four-year-old. She got her start backing Bobby Day before being invited to join the Ikettes, backing Ike and Tina Turner. Arnold toured with them in the '60s, including one stint with the Rolling Stones. Mick Jagger persuaded her to remain in London, and she later recorded for the Immediate label (then run by the Stones' manager Andrew Loog-Oldham). Loog-Oldham, Jagger, and Mike Hurst produced Arnold's debut LP, *The First Lady of Immediate*, in 1967, which included the single "The First Cut Is the Deepest," which was written by Cat Stevens and later popularized by Rod Stewart. Arnold also had moderate success with the singles "The Time Has Come," "(If You Think) You're Groovy," and "Angel in the Morning" in the late '60s, though they were hits in England and Europe rather than America. Arnold was part of the cast for the play *Catch My Soul* in 1969, and subsequently acted in the television shows *Fame* and *Knots Landing*, plus Andrew Lloyd Webber's *Starlight Express*. Arnold re-entered the music world in the mid-'80s. She sang lead on a Boy George song for the film *Electric Dreams* in 1984 while on 10 Records. She worked with Dexter Wansel and Loose Ends on the single "A Little Pain," which she recorded as Pat Arnold. She then had another English hit with the single "Burn It Up" on the Rhythm King label. The Beatmasters later produced her "Dynamite." — *Ron Wynn*

● **P. P. Arnold Collection** / 1991 / Sony ♦♦♦♦
Transplanted American R&B singer hits it big with achingly soulful ballads. A '60s curio and more, especially "The First Cut Is the Deepest." — *Bruce Eder*

Arrested Development

Group, Rap, Urban
An innovative conglomeration from Brownsville, TN, fusing blues and Southern soul with the hip-hop innovations of De La Soul and PM Dawn. With group leader Speech's intelligent, insightful lyrics and laidback delivery, as well as the clever turntable techniques and creative self-production of their debut, *3 Years, 5 Months & 2*

Days in the Life of…, Arrested Development became the hip-hop success story of 1992, sweeping year-end critical polls and going multi-platinum.

Two years later, after gangsta rap had re-emerged as the dominent commercial force in rap, Arrested Development released *Zingalamaduni*, its second album; it received favorable reviews but bombed commercially. —*John Floyd & Stephen Thomas Erlewine*

● **Three Years, Five Months & Two Days in the Life of…** / 1992 / Chrysalis ◆◆◆◆
A crew that became one of 1992's sensations by infusing hip-hop with blues sensibility on their debut, *Three Years, Five Months & Two Days in the Life of…*, especially on the single "Tennessee." —*Ron Wynn*

Unplugged / 1993 / Chrysalis ◆◆
Basically a live rerecording of *3 Years, 5 Months, & 2 Days in the Life of…* (minus their breakthrough hit, "Tennessee"), *Unplugged* breaks no new ground for Arrested Development. Eight of the eleven songs on the album are from their debut, and the three new tracks are slight. The album is filled out with remixes of seven tracks, which are the instrumental tracks with the vocals turned down (they are still slightly audible). Despite the fact that it doesn't offer anything not on *3 Years*, the album is an enjoyable listen. —*Stephen Thomas Erlewine*

Zingalamaduni / 1994 / Chrysalis ◆◆◆
Arrested Development's proper follow-up to their smash debut doesn't stray too far from the rootsy Southern hip-hop that made *3 Years* a hit, but it doesn't ignite as frequently as its predecessor. While its best tracks, like "Mister Landlord" and "Prasin' U," are the equal of "Mr. Wendal" or "People Everyday," there is no statement of purpose on the level of "Tennessee." The album is too unfocused to be as impressive as the debut, yet *Zingalamundi* shows that the group is more than a one-hit wonder. —*Stephen Thomas Erlewine*

Steve Arrington
Soul
Drummer Steve Arrington got his start playing with the Young Mystics. After they disbanded, he moved from his native Ohio to San Francisco. The group Slave emerged from a union of two former Ohio bands, the Young Mystics and Black Satin Soul. Arrington joined them in 1978, starting as a background singer but becoming lead vocalist on such hits as "Just a Touch of Love," "Watching You," and "Wait for Me." Arrington left Slave in 1983, forming a new band, Steve Arrington's Hall of Fame. He recorded for both Kongflather and Atlantic, enjoying his greatest success with the 1985 LP *Dancin' in the Key of Life.* It included a Top Ten R&B hit in the title track and Top 20 single with "Feel So Real." Arrington experienced a religious conversion in 1986, and began using his shows as forums for these beliefs in 1986 and 1987. He subsequently left pop music, and is now a minister at his own Amazing Love Full Gospel Church in Kettering, OH, a suburb of Dayton. —*Ron Wynn*

Steve Arrington's Hall of Fame: I / 1983 / Atlantic ◆◆◆

Positive Power / 1984 / Atlantic ◆◆
On his second album with his Hall of Fame, Steve Arrington hewed to his love-man-with-the-funk stance, promising "15 rounds of lovin', kissin', and a-huggin' " as the second single, "15 Rounds," put it. The first single was called "Hump To The Bump." You get the idea. —*William Ruhlmann*

● **Dancin' in the Key of Life** / 1985 / Atlantic ◆◆◆◆

Jam Packed / 1987 / Manhattan ◆◆
Former Slave drummer and vocalist Steve Arrington enjoyed some success in the 1980s with a group that mirrored the Slave style—uptempo funk with a steady, driving backbeat and earnestly sung lead vocals. Arrington had pretty much exhausted his creativity by the time they issued *Jam Packed*; the arrangements sound stagnant and his vocals lack the energy and punch of earlier sessions. Only a couple of decent funk tracks keep this from being a total disaster. —*Ron Wynn*

Art Bears
Group, Art-Rock/Progressive-Rock, New Wave
A warm and wonderful avant-garde band consisting of Fred Frith, Chris Cutler and vocalist extraordinaire Dagmar Krause. Frith and Cutler were longtime members of the seminal English radical political avant garde art-rock band Henry Cow, while Krause sang primarily with the fine German band Slapp Happy and in Henry Cow's latter years. The Art Bears was intended as a short-term project, but, even so, their three-year existence resulted in three excellent albums that relied on shorter, more traditional, almost pop-oriented song forms than huge, complex musical and lyrical extrapolations. The political tinge of the Henry Cow years never went away, and it was unsurprising that Marxist rhetoric and anti-capitalist diatribes formed much of band's lyrical firmament. Frith, as he proved in Cow, was (and is) a guitarist of astonishing ability, combining a searing, complex technique reminiscent of the free music improvisations of seminal British guitarist Derek Bailey with a boyhood love of blues and early British rock & roll. Cutler, a pop music theorist as well as drummer, skittishly plays his trap kit, providing a propulsive rhythmic base upon which Frith can dazzle. Admittedly, Dagmar Krause's quasi-operatic, very German singing style can take some getting used to, but she is a daring singer, unafraid to bend and twist her voice into knots or screech with uncontrolled passion and exuberance. Their life was fleeting, but the Art Bears wrote and recorded bold, challenging, idiosyncratic music that, despite its occasional difficulty, is ultimately very rewarding. —*John Dougan*

○ **Hopes and Fears** / 1978 / Cuneiform ◆◆◆◆
Good luck locating this long out-of-print gem, but if you do, and you've liked the other two Art Bears records, then by any means necessary, make it yours. It isn't exactly an upbeat, life-affirming record (songs like "The Song of Investment Capital Overseas" is a hint); still, Frith's playing is exceptional and the passion put forth is undeniable. If there is an art-rock heaven, this is the music played there. —*John Dougan*

Winter Songs / 1979 / Ralph ◆◆◆

The World As It Is Today / 1981 / Recommended ◆◆◆

● **Winter Songs/The World as It Is Today** / 1987 / Recommended ◆◆◆◆
Two of the Art Bears' three recordings reissued on one CD released by Chris Cutler on his specialty label Recommended. *Winter Songs* is the stronger of the two; the songs tend to be less confrontational, almost pastoral. But having both recordings in one place (trust me, Art Bears stuff was not widely available) makes it the most important single purchase by this band you can make. All three are in extremely good form, especially Krause, whose singing never fails to be compelling. —*John Dougan*

Art of Noise
Group, Techno-Pop/Dance
Anne Dudley, Gary Lanagan, and J. J. Jeczalik were members of producer Trevor Horn's in-house studio band in the early '80s before they formed Art of Noise, a techno-pop group whose music was an amalgam of studio gimmickry, tape splicing, and synthesized beats. The Art of Noise took material from a variety of sources—hip-hop, rock, jazz, R&B, traditional pop, found sounds, and noise all worked their way into the group's distinctly postmodern soundscapes.

Dudley was the center of the group, having arranged and produced material for Frankie Goes to Hollywood, ABC, and Paul McCartney before forming the Art of Noise. The trio signed with Trevor Horn's ZTT label, releasing their first EP, *Into Battle with the Art of Noise*, in 1983. The following year, the group released the full-length *(Who's Afraid Of?) The Art of Noise!*, which featured the hit single "Close (To the Edit)."

After "Close (To the Edit)," the group parted ways with Horn and ZTT, releasing *In Visible Silence* in 1986; the album included the U.K. Top 10 hit "Peter Gunn," which featured Duane Eddy on guitar. *Re-works of Art of Noise*, an album of remixes and live tracks, was released that same year. *In No Sense? Nonsense!*, released in 1987, saw the band experimenting with orchestras and choirs, as well as horns and rock bands. The next year, the Art of Noise released a greatest hits collection, *The Best of the Art of Noise*, which featured their collaboration with Tom Jones on Prince's "Kiss."

Below the Waste (1990) captured the band experimenting with world music; it received a lukewarm critical and commercial reception. The following year, a low-key remix album directed by Killing Joke's Youth called *The Ambient Collection* appeared. Later in the year, the Art of Noise broke up; Dudley eventually worked with Killing Joke's Jaz Coleman and Phil Collins. —*Stephen Thomas Erlewine*

Art of Noise / 1983 / ZTT/Island ✦✦✦
The Art of Noise debuted with this long (ten-track, or ten-title, anyway) EP (also called *Into Battle with the Art of Noise*), dominated by tracks like "Beat Box" (#1 Dance/Disco), a collage of steady bass drum beats and sound effects. No use looking for embedded meaning; this was surface sound all the way. If you wanted, you could dance to it, but its real function may have been as a new kind of background music. — *William Ruhlmann*

Into Battle with the Art of Noise / 1983 / ZTT/Island ✦✦✦

○ **(Who's Afraid Of?) The Art of Noise!** / 1984 / ZTT/Island ✦✦✦✦
The Art of Noise's first full-length album washes much of their debut EP. But it also contains the single "Close (To The Edit)" (#8 U.K./#102 U.S. Pop/#23 R&B/#4 Dance/Disco), the best evocation of the group's sound-effects-and-tape-loops-plus-beat esthetic. — *William Ruhlmann*

Re-Works of the Art of Noise / 1986 / China ✦✦✦

In No Sense? Nonsense! / 1987 / China ✦✦✦

● **The Best of the Art of Noise** / 1988 / China ✦✦✦✦
All of the Art of Noise's best tracks are here, including "Close (To the Edit)," "Legacy," and a cover of Prince's "Kiss" with Tom Jones on lead vocals. — *Stephen Thomas Erlewine*

Below the Waste / 1989 / China ✦✦✦

Ambient Collection / 1990 / China ✦✦✦

Art Zoyd
Group, Art-Rock/Progressive-Rock
One of the longest-lived French experimental ensembles, Art Zoyd combines free jazz with chamber music to create their own particular neo-classical style. — *Archie Patterson*

Symphonie Pour Le Jour Ou Bruleront Les Cites / 1976 / Art Zoyd
This original recording of their *Symphonie...* features some of the most adventurous arrangements and virtuoso playing to ever grace a jazz-rock album. Loose threads of strings, percussion, bass, winds and guitar feverishly intertwine to create an elaborately arranged work full of musical twists and turns. — *Archie Patterson*

The Artwoods
Group, British Invasion
Falling somewhere between the Animals and John Mayall, the Artwoods were one of the rootsier first-wave British R&B bands. While they maintained reasonable popularity as a club act, the group's success on record was minimal, although they cut seven singles and an album between 1964 and 1967. The group's chief flaws were the rather limited abilities of its lead singer, Art Wood (brother of Ron Wood), and its limited songwriting talent (virtually all of their material was U.S. soul/blues/R&B covers). Those who favor the tougher side of the British Invasion will enjoy their energetic, organ-based sound, however. Organist Jon Lord went on to join Deep Purple, and drummer Keef Hartley played with John Mayall for a while in the late '60s. — *Richie Unterberger*

● **100 Oxford St** / 1983 / Edsel ✦✦✦✦
A fine 16-track package, including most of their mid-'60s singles and seven songs from their 1966 LP *Art Gallery*. The material varies from traditional blues numbers ("Sweet Mary") to contemporary Memphis and Motown soul covers. The highlights are "Don't Cry No More," an all-out soul stomper, and the haunting, rocking R&B/pop ballad "Oh My Love," which could have well been a hit if enough people had heard it. Comes with a four-page booklet of photos and liner notes written by Art Wood himself. — *Richie Unterberger*

Daniel Ash
Alternative Pop/Rock
British guitarist Daniel Ash was a founding member of the new wave band Bauhaus in 1978 and continued with members David Jay and Kevin Haskins as Love and Rockets after splitting from lead singer Peter Murphy in 1983. In 1991, Ash began a solo career while maintaining his participation in Love and Rockets. — *William Ruhlmann*

Deluxe Coming Down / 1991 / Beggars Banquet ✦✦

Coming Down / Feb. 1991 / Beggars Banquet ✦✦
Daniel Ash of Love and Rockets turns in a wildly eclectic mixture of sounds on his debut, from the wispy "Blue Moon" that opens the record to "Walk This Way," which borrows the music from San-

tana's "Oye Como Va," and even a cover of the Beatles' "Day Tripper." It's a busman's holiday of a record. Not bad, but no evidence that he's ready to strike out on his own. — *William Ruhlmann*

● **Foolish Thing Desire** / Nov. 17, 1992 / Beggars Banquet ✦✦✦✦
Daniel Ash takes a more straightforward approach on his second solo album, writing or co-writing all the songs himself and giving the record a stylistic consistency unlike his debut, *Coming Down*. The pace is slow, the guitars are distorted, the vocals are whispery and echoed—we're talking Velvet Underground, T. Rex, Jesus and Mary Chain, all of it diffused by co-producer John A. Rivers' keyboard washes. Occasionally, as on "Get Out Of Control," Ash and Rivers goose things up to rock & roll velocity, but much of the time they just bliss out. — *William Ruhlmann*

Get out of Control / 1993 / Beggars Banquet ✦✦✦

Ashford & Simpson
Group, Soul, Disco, R&B, Urban
Nickolas Ashford (b. May 4, 1942, Fairfield, SC) and Valerie Simpson (b. Aug 26, 1946, New York City) have two careers, as songwriters and as performers, with the former seemingly more important than the latter until the mid '80s. The two met in 1964 and scored their first songwriting hit in 1966 with Ray Charles's recording of their "Let's Go Get Stoned." After a period at Scepter Records, they moved to Motown, where they wrote hits for the duo of Marvin Gaye and Tammi Terrell ("Ain't Nothing Like the Real Thing," "You're All I Need to Get By"). When Diana Ross left the Supremes for a solo career, Ashford and Simpson wrote "Reach out and Touch Somebody's Hand" for her.
Their own performing career was launched in 1973 with *Keep It Comin'* on Motown and *Gimme Something Real* on Warner Bros. Their first success came in 1977 with the gold-selling *Send It*, which contained the Top Ten R&B hit "Don't Cost You Nothing." *Is It Still Good to Ya*, a second gold album, contained the #2 R&B hit "It Seems to Hang On" in 1978. *Stay Free*, their third straight gold album, contained "Found a Cure," another R&B smash that also made the Top 40 on the pop chart. *A Musical Affair*, 1980, featured the hit "Love Don't Make It Right," but was not as successful as previous efforts.
Meanwhile, A&S continued to work with other artists, scoring successes with Ross, Chaka Khan ("I'm Every Woman"), and Gladys Knight. Their own career saw a resurgence in 1984 with *Solid*, which went gold and produced the R&B #1 "Solid" (#12 on the pop charts), "Outta the World," and "Babies." — *William Ruhlmann*

Keep It Comin' / 1973 / Motown ✦✦✦

Gimme Something Real / Oct. 1973 / Warner Brothers ✦✦
This album launched the soul duo Ashford and Simpson on a run of successful Warner Bros. albums. The title track and several other singles utilized the patented formula of gospel-tinged vocals, slick, polished backing, and alternately sentimental or earnest lyrics. — *Ron Wynn*

I Wanna Be Selfish / Jul. 1974 / Warner Brothers ✦✦✦
Ashford and Simpson were in the midst here of their hit string of Warner Bros. albums. They included bits and pieces of gospel-tinged R&B, disco, funk, and sophisticated pop, linking everything through their own energetic vocals and harmonies, plus skillful production and a good group of songs. — *Ron Wynn*

○ **Come As You Are** / Apr. 1976 / Warner Brothers ✦✦✦✦
One of Ashford and Simpson's best Warner Bros. albums, especially from a production standpoint. The mix between uptempo and slow, love songs and dance tunes, was perfect, and their interaction had been honed to the point where each anticipated the other. Simpson's soaring vocals and Ashford's less impressive but still strong support, plus their outstanding harmonizing, was at its peak. — *Ron Wynn*

So So Satisfied / Jan. 1977 / Warner Brothers ✦✦✦
The Ashford/Simpson sound has always been lush, sentimental, and soulful, yet subdued. That's the case on this '77 release. The title cut was a moderate hit, and, as always, the sweeping strings, lyrics, and production were first-rate. Ashford/Simpson albums can get extremely sappy, and at times this one did as well. But they're also usually superbly performed and constructed, and this was no exception. — *Ron Wynn*

○ **Send It** / Sep. 1977 / Warner Brothers ✦✦✦✦
Exuberant lead vocals, great teamwork, and excellent production made this '77 set a top entry in the Ashford and Simpson sweepstakes. They were at the top of their production and performance games in the late '70s, cranking out their own hits and also producing everyone in the R&B/soul world from Gladys Knight to themselves. —*Ron Wynn*

○ **Is It Still Good to Ya** / Aug. 1978 / Warner Brothers ✦✦✦✦
The disco arrangements are a little dated, but this is still Ashford & Simpson's best '70s album, as their two similar voices intertwine on a collection of songs about devoted love, among them the title track and "It Seems to Hang On." —*William Ruhlmann*

Stay Free / Aug. 1979 / Warner Brothers ✦✦✦
The title track was spectacular, and the rest of the album was expertly produced, performed, and arranged. Ashford & Simpson dominated the '70s as few couples ever have in any era; they were the textbook blend of classic R&B energy and urban contemporary class and sophistication. Their best material was neither so generic that it lacked soul, nor so soulful that it couldn't attract a crossover audience. —*Ron Wynn*

A Musical Affair / Aug. 1980 / Warner Brothers ✦✦
The Ashford & Simpson machine was beginning to slow down a little as the '80s began, mainly due to overwork. They'd done so many outside sessions for Chaka Khan, Gladys Knight, etc., plus their own albums and tours, that they just began to run dry. The material on this '80s release was more gimmicky and clichéd than on any of their great '70s dates. There were still some marvelous moments; there just weren't as many of them. —*Ron Wynn*

Performance / Sep. 1981 / Warner Brothers ✦✦✦

Street Opera / May 1982 / Capitol ✦✦
Ashford & Simpson came up with an intriguing tack for this early '80s session: take a contemporary situation and use a quasi-operatic format to illuminate it. The only problem came in the execution; the songs weren't up to the concept, although most weren't terrible. They were just good, faceless urban contemporary dance and love tunes, hardly the kind of transcendent things needed to make this worthy of operatic pretensions. —*Ron Wynn*

High-Rise / Aug. 1983 / Capitol ✦✦
Ashford & Simpson had come close to exhausting their creative quotient by the mid-'80s. Simpson still sang effectively, and Ashford harmonized and contrasted her nicely, but they'd stated and restated both their own situations and any variations on it four albums before. As a result, the feeling that you've heard it all once too often permeates this album. Not that their fans wouldn't want to listen once more, nor that what they had to say wasn't at times compelling; it's just that it no longer was special. —*Ron Wynn*

● **Solid** / Oct. 1984 / Warner Brothers ✦✦✦✦
Ashford & Simpson have always been the prime representatives in R&B of the joys of wedded bliss, and this extended valentine is their most consistent set as well as their biggest hit ever. —*William Ruhlmann*

Real Love / Aug. 1986 / Capitol ✦✦✦
Although not as successful as their mid-'70s dates, *Real Love* did include some emphatic harmonies and above-average compositions, as well as consistently exciting vocals. What hurt it was the lack of interest in classic R&B arrangements during the late '80s, and the failure of any one single to emerge as a major hit. —*Ron Wynn*

Solid Plus Seven / Jan. 13, 1987 / Capitol ✦✦✦
This wasn't one of their finest, although it adhered to the usual high production standards. But it lacked the kind of resolute love songs, knockout rhythm tracks, or humorous slice-of-life pieces that separate great Ashford & Simpson material from good or merely competent cuts. There's not enough of the former and too much of the latter on this release. —*Ron Wynn*

Love or Physical / Feb. 1989 / Capitol ✦✦✦

● **Capitol Gold: The Best of Ashford & Simpson** / Jun. 21, 1993 / Capitol ✦✦✦✦
Ashford & Simpson scored 33 entries on the R&B singles charts between 1973 and 1990, all but one of them on Warner Bros. or Capitol. This compilation licenses the two biggest hits from the duo's tenure at Warner, "It Seems to Hang On" and "Found a Cure," both of which hit the Top 10, and features the eight Capitol titles that made the R&B Top 40—"Street Corner," "Love It Away," "High-Rise," "Solid," "Outta the World," "Babies," "Count Your

Blessings," and "I'll Be There tor You." There are also six tracks culled from the five Capitol albums, bringing the disc's time to over 71 minutes. In other words, this is about as comprehensive an overview of A&S's career as could be managed by one label on one disc. There are good biographical liner notes by compiler David Nathan. —*William Ruhlmann*

Asia

Group, Art-Rock/Progressive-Rock, Pop/Rock
When they appeared in the early '80s, Asia seemed to be a holdover from the '70s, when super-groups and self-important progressive rockers reigned supreme. Featuring members of such seminal art-rock bands as King Crimson (John Wetton), Emerson, Lake & Palmer (Carl Palmer), and Yes (Steve Howe), as well as Geoff Downes from the Buggles, Asia did feature stretches of indulgent instrumentals on their records. However, they also could be surprisingly poppy and that is what brought them to the top of the charts with their debut album, *Asia*, and its hit single, "Heat of the Moment." *Alpha*, their second album, also had a couple of hits ("Don't Cry" and "The Smile Has Left Your Eyes") but its follow-up, *Astra*, was a flop. The group disbanded in 1985, only to reunite in 1990 without John Wetton; Pat Thrall took his place. After churning out a couple of new songs for a greatest hits collection, the band hit the road, including two sold-out dates in front of 20,000 fans in Moscow, of all places. Since then, they have toured sporadically. —*Stephen Thomas Erlewine*

○ **Asia** / 1982 / Geffen ✦✦✦✦
The debut release for this supergroup (featuring Steve Howe [Yes], John Wetton [King Crimson], Carl Palmer [ELP] and Geoff Downes [the Buggles]) showcases their classy pop/rock, with several hits. —*Paul Kohler*

Alpha / 1983 / Geffen ✦✦✦
The follow-up album has the same lineup as the first. —*Paul Kohler*

Astra / Nov. 1985 / Geffen ✦✦
Asia was always a bland, derivative excuse for a dinosaur rock band, but when their debut album came out in 1982 and sold three million copies, they seemed like a repudiation of the new wave movement, the pop music equivalent of the Reagan revolution in politics. Like Ronnie, however, Asia ran out of gas around mid-decade. True, they were still constructing keyboard-dominated, heroic-voiced arena pop, but suddenly nobody cared anymore, or at least not enough customers to vault them into the Top Ten, and for this kind of band, it's platinum or don't bother. So, first, guitarist Steve Howe took his marbles and went home to Yes, and then the rest of the band packed it in, too. They'd be back, of course, when the money was right. —*William Ruhlmann*

● **Then & Now** / 1990 / Geffen ✦✦✦✦
This compilation includes all of their Top 40 hits—"Heat of the Moment" (#4), "Only Time Will Tell" (#17), "Don't Cry" (#10), and the #34 "The Smile Has Left Your Eyes"—as well as some unreleased tracks. —*AMG*

Live in Moscow / Nov. 1990 / Rhino ✦

Aqua / 1992 / JRS ✦✦
Their latest release for a new label is noticeably missing the vocal work of former bassist John Wetton. Carl Palmer, Steve Howe, and Geoff Downes are still on hand, producing more of their brand of slick, smooth rock. It's reminiscent of the revamped Bad Company. —*Scott Bultman*

Aria / 1994 / ✦✦

The Association

Group, Pop/Rock
Between 1966 and 1969, the Association was one of the most successful practitioners of romantic light pop. The band's smooth Lettermen-like harmonies helped make songs like "Cherish" (#1 pop), "Never My Love" (#2 pop), and "Everything That Touches You" (#10 pop) staples of adult easy-listening formats and elevators throughout the planet. Before the Association, founding-member Terry Kirkman had actually performed coffeehouses with Frank Zappa for several years.

Their first hit, the upbeat "Along Comes Mary" (#7 pop), met with resistance from radio programmers, afraid that the song was about marijuana. The exuberant "Windy," on the other hand, easily sailed all the way to #1, becoming the band's biggest seller. Interestingly, "Windy" (which knocked Aretha Franklin's "Respect" out of the top slot) was originally written as a waltz. Attempts to infuse a more progressive "rock" sound with "Six Man Band" (#47 pop) were met with indifference from the public. That was to be their last hit.

The Association ground on until 1972, when the death of bassist Brian Cole, plus the poor commercial response to their Columbia Records debut, *Waterbeds in Trinidad*, provided impetus for the band's dissolution. The band has managed a few reunions, most notably the 1980 HBO reunion special, and a moderate hit "Dreamer" (#66) on Elektra. *—Rick Clark*

○ **Association's Greatest Hits** / 1968 / Warner Brothers ✦✦✦✦
At only 13 songs, this is concise but not definitive. *—Jeff Tamarkin*

Stop Your Motor / Jul. 1971 / Warner Brothers ✦✦
The Association was three years beyond their last Top 40 hit when they made this, their final album for Warner Bros. Records, in 1971. There they are on the cover in '70s regalia, all sporting fashionable facial hair, none but Jim Yester attempting a smile. But the lush pop music inside, dominated by their choral sound, is strictly 1967, and the times, as they will, had changed. The only thing that's unfortunate about the failure of this album is that it contained a wonderful version of Jimmy Webb's "P.F. Sloan," a song in which a great pop songwriter in decline ponders the fate of another great pop songwriter who has disappeared entirely (as of '71, that is), sung by a great pop group facing its own disappearance. Irony upon irony, and a good tune, too. *—William Ruhlmann*

● **Songs That Made Them Famous** / 1986 / Pair ✦✦✦✦
Beyond the hits, all of which are included here ("Windy," "Cherish," "Along Comes Mary"), the Association made stunning orchestral folk-pop that still makes the listener feel good. *—Jeff Tamarkin*

The Association's Golden Heebie-jeebies / 1987 / Edsel ✦✦
The liner notes make a game effort at presenting the Association as a band that could be meaningfully psychedelic when it wanted to be. Accordingly, this 15-song compilation draws from the trippier efforts of their first three albums (originally issued in 1966 and 1967). The fact of the matter is, though, that these guys offered about as much of a genuine psychedelic experience as smoking a banana peel. Being a pop-rock band in Southern California during this period, they couldn't help but reflect the era's wilder ethos in some modestly adventurous arrangements and slightly ambitious lyrics. Still, more often than not, this collection sounds like nothing so much as a psychedelic Four Freshmen, dominated by frothy harmonies that are as reliable an indication of substance as the whipped cream on a lemon meringue pie. The material is not downright obnoxious—it's somewhat pleasant—but with three exceptions, the songs pass from one ear to the other as easily as whipped cream goes through the digestive system. Two of those three exceptions, "Along Comes Mary" and "Windy," are available on any greatest hits collection; the other, the haunting raga-rocker (and minor hit single) "Pandora's Golden Heebie Jeebies," was reissued in much stronger company on Rhino's *Nuggets Volume 5*. *—Richie Unterberger*

Rick Astley

b. Feb. 6, 1966, Warrington, England
Dance-Pop
With his rich, deep voice Rick Astley became an overnight sensation in the late '80s with his well-crafted dance-pop. Astley was discovered by the producer Pete Waterman in 1985 singing in the English soul band, FBI. After that, Waterman's production team—Stock, Aitken, and Waterman—took Astley under their wing, writing and producing such impeccably crafted pop singles as "Never Gonna Give You Up" and "Together Forever." After two hugely successful albums in the U.S. and the U.K., Astley grew tired of being labeled Stock, Aitken, and Waterman's "puppet" and severed his connections with the team; he resurfaced in 1991 with the soul-injected *Free*, which contained the Top Ten hit, "Cry for Help." *—Stephen Thomas Erlewine*

● **Whenever You Need Somebody** / 1987 / RCA ✦✦✦✦
There's a retro-disco sound on this album, which includes the hits "Together Forever" and "Never Gonna Give You Up." *—Kenneth M. Cassidy*

Hold Me in Your Arms / 1988 / RCA ✦✦✦
Apart from "She Wants to Dance With Me," Astley's second album didn't have songs as strong as those on his debut. Most of the album was pleasant dance-pop filler, showing the weaknesses of the Stock-Aitken-Waterman production team. *—Stephen Thomas Erlewine*

Free / 1991 / RCA ✦✦✦
On his third album, Astley takes more control, for a streamlined sound. It includes "Cry for Help." *—Kenneth M. Cassidy*

Body & Soul / Sep. 1993 / RCA ✦✦
The bottom fell out of Rick Astley's recording career with this, his fourth album, which peaked at #185 during its sole week in the *Billboard 200*. The single "Hopelessly" managed an anemic #28 in the Hot 100, while climbing to #4 in the Adult Contemporary chart. But easy listening is not where a boy toy like Astley (who fills his CD booklet with cheesecake shots) wants to be. He wants to be in the buzz bin on MTV, and no wonder—he has nowhere to go otherwise but to start working his way up as a lounge act in Vegas, an evil fate to contemplate when you're only 27 and you've been on bedroom walls all over the Western world for five years. That's show biz. *—William Ruhlmann*

Virginia Astley

Alternative Pop/Rock
Astley is more widely known for the people she's played with than her own records. A classically trained British pianist and flutist who also happens to be Pete Townshend's sister-in-law, she contributed piano to Townshend's "Slit Skirts," and has played sessions for Siouxsie and the Banshees. Her late-'70s band, the Ravishing Beauties, also included future Dream Academy singer Kate St. John and Nicky Holland, who would work with Tears for Fears and Ryuichi Sakamoto. Astley's sparse body of work combines ambient, even experimental textures and song structures with her pretty soprano vocals. Producing three albums (only the last of which was released in the U.S.) and a handful of single and EP tracks, she remains virtually unknown to American audiences. Her records are recommended to listeners looking for intriguing ambient British pop who find the Cocteau Twins and the 4AD stable too wimpy and pretentious. *—Richie Unterberger*

From Gardens Where We Feel Secure / 1983 / Happy Valley ✦✦✦

Promise Nothing / 1983 / Les Disques du Crepuscule ✦✦✦

● **Hope in a Darkened Heart** / 1986 / David Geffen Co. ✦✦✦✦
Tuneful, delicate, often charming, occasionally cutesy songs, mostly produced by Ryuichi Sakamoto (who also plays keyboards). The swirling synthesizers and spare classical touches paint a dreamy canvas at their best, making one regret that Astley has not had a chance to build upon this effort in the nearly ten years that have passed without a follow-up. *—Richie Unterberger*

The Astronauts

Group, Surf
Along with Minnesota's Trashmen, the Astronauts (from Colorado) were the premier landlocked, Midwestern surf group of the 1960s. They recorded numerous singles and albums and achieved vast regional popularity, but only scored one modest national hit, "Baja." With little material of their own, they judiciously tapped heavyweights like Lee Hazelwood (who wrote "Baja"), Roger Christian, and Gary Usher, as well as covering tunes by Dick Dale and Henry Mancini. The group shone brightest on the instrumentals, which used mounds of Fender reverb and two rhythm guitars; when they sang, the results were much less successful. *—Richie Unterberger*

● **Surf Party** / 1988 / RCA ✦✦✦✦
This compilation of 20 songs from their 1963-64 heyday features the best of their sleek instrumentals and raucous R&B-influenced numbers. "Competition Coupe" (written by surf scenesters Christian and Usher) stands up well to early numbers in the same vein by the Beach Boys and Jan & Dean, but covers of classics like "Around And Around," "Twist And Shout," and "Susie-Q" are leadfooted. And the group original "You Gotta Let Me Go" is a transparent ripoff of the Beatles' "I'll Be Back." The instrumentals on this collection have a gloriously supple power, though. Besides "Baja," highlights include the instrumental themes to the obscure films *Surf Party* and *Ride The Wild Surf*, the latter of which was written by Roger Christian, Brian Wilson, and Jan Berry. *—Richie Unterberger*

Live / 1989 / Bear Family
This CD combines their two live albums from the early '60s ("Everything Is A-OK" and "Astronauts Orbit Kampus") onto one disc. As a premier American teen combo of the pre-Beatle era, this makes for unbelievably exciting, greasy, shake 'em on down rock 'n' roll from beginning to end. (Import) *—Cub Koda*

Rarities / 1991 / Bear Family

Atlanta Rhythm Section

Group, Southern Rock
The Atlanta Rhythm Section was formed out of remnants of Roy Orbison's Candymen backup group and the smooth rockers the Classics IV around 1970. Manager/producer Buddy Buie (who had also handled Classics IV) gave the group a glossy production sheen, while nonstop touring helped to build their following. Slicker and more melodic than most Southern rock bands of the genre, they scored consistently on both the album and singles charts during their decade together. —*Cub Koda*

Back Up Against the Wall / 1973 / Decca ♦♦
○ **Third Annual Pipe Dream** / 1974 / Polydor ♦♦♦♦
Dog Days / 1975 / Polydor ♦♦♦
Atlanta Rhythm Section / 1976 / Decca ♦♦♦
○ **Red Tape** / 1976 / Polydor ♦♦♦♦
○ **Rock 'n' Roll Alternative** / Dec. 1976 / Polydor ♦♦♦♦
A Rock And Roll Alternative was the Atlanta Rhythm Section's breakthrough record. After five albums and four years of trying, they hadn't gotten higher than #74 in the LP lists, but this time their mixture of country and rock finally found its audience, largely due to the single "So Into You" (#7 pop, #11 easy listening), so that the album soared to #11 and went gold. It was only fair: the ARS had perfected a sound that was lighter and more accessible than the Allmans/Lynyrd Skynyrd school of Southern rock, but no less accomplished, and *A Rock And Roll Alternative* was the embodiment of it. —*William Ruhlmann*

Champagne Jam / 1978 / Polydor ♦♦♦
Underdog / 1979 / Polydor ♦♦
Are You Ready / 1979 / Polydor ♦
The Boys from Doraville / 1980 / Polydor ♦♦
Quinella / 1981 / Columbia ♦♦♦
● **The Best of Atlanta Rhythm Section** / 1982 / Polydor ♦♦♦♦
This well-compiled anthology not only covers ARS's biggest radio hits, but it does a good job of highlighting key album tracks that showcase their sophisticated style of Southern rock. Included are "Spooky" (number 17), "Imaginary Lover" (number seven), "So into You" (number seven), "Georgia Rhythm" (number 68), "Jukin'" (number 82), "Do It Or Die" (number 19), "Angel (What in the World's Come over Us)" (number 79), "Doraville" (number 35), and more. —*Rick Clark*

Atlantic Starr

Group, Soul, Disco, Urban
New York-based Atlantic Starr began in 1976. Brothers David (guitar, vocals), Jonathan (trombone), and Wayne (keyboards) Lewis started a funk and soul band, adding lead vocalist Sharon Bryant, bassist Clifford Archer, drummer Porter Carroll, saxophonist Koran Daniels, percussionist/flutist Joseph Phillips, and trumpeter William Sudderth. They signed with A&M a couple of years later, staying through 1987 and landing several hits, among them "Gimme Your Lovin'," "Circles," "When Love Calls," "Stand Up," "Silver Shadow," "One Love," and the crossover hit "Secret Lovers." Their albums *Brillance* and *As the Band Turns* were also Top 20 pop hits, their most successful A&M LPs. They switched to Warner Bros. in 1987, and their first release, *All in the Name of Love*, included another pop smash, "Always," the group's sole number one pop and R&B hit. They enjoyed more R&B successes with Warner through the '80s. Sharon Bryant left in 1989 for Polydor; she was replaced by Barbara Weathers, who later left for a solo career as well. *Love Crazy*, in 1991, was their most recent release. —*Ron Wynn*

Atlantic Starr / 1978 / A&M ♦♦
Atlantic Starr basically introduced their mixture of sleek ballads, uptempo urban contemporary tunes, and light pop on this '78 set. They were still establishing boundaries and finding a style, but they did score one moderate hit with the song "Gimme Your Lovin'." —*Ron Wynn*

Straight to the Point / 1979 / A&M ♦♦
Their A&M album included another mild hit, the song "Losin' You," but was otherwise more important as a continuation project rather than a finished product. The Lewis brothers were still polishing their sound, and Sharon Bryant had yet to emerge as a

dominant lead vocalist. Producer Bobby Eli wisely just chose to keep developing the group, rather than running them through heavy paces. —*Ron Wynn*

Radiance / 1981 / A&M ♦♦
Atlantic Starr began finding their audience with their third album. The song "When Love Calls" was Sharon Bryant's breakout number, signaling that she had a strong, assertive voice and star quality in her delivery. It also indicated that they would be more successful accenting slick, polished material rather than chunky '70s funk. —*Ron Wynn*

○ **Brilliance** / 1982 / A&M ♦♦♦♦
This was the album that came closest to making them superstars. It had two hit singles in "Circles" and "Love Me Down," and they now had the cohesive, smooth urban contemporary group sound down cold. Bryant was confident and assured, the arrangements and production were equally perfected, and everything was geared for them to reach the pinnacle they'd achieve later in the decade. —*Ron Wynn*

Yours Forever / 1983 / A&M ♦♦♦
This was their biggest album to date, although it actually didn't have as many good songs as its predecessor. But "Touch A Four Leaf Clover" was strong enough to assure Sharon Bryant that it was time to leave, and she departed after this album. The backings, compositions, production, and arrangements are tight and expertly designed. —*Ron Wynn*

○ **As the Band Turns** / 1986 / A&M ♦♦♦♦
Their biggest hit album came in 1986, with new singer Barbara Weathers proving the perfect replacement for Bryant. In fact, her lighter, less assured, but more sensual sound proved ideal on the duets "Secret Lovers" and "If Your Heart Isn't In It." The Lewis brothers and Joseph Phillips added just enough musical support and the group's early funk history was now merely a memory. They'd made the transition to urban (and urbane) balladeers. —*Ron Wynn*

● **Secret Lovers: The Best of Atlantic Starr** / 1986 / A&M ♦♦♦♦
A nice anthology, although it emphasizes the ballad smashes and doesn't convey much of their earlier, harder flavor. Atlantic Starr moved to Warner Bros. in the late '80s, so their former label cranked out a greatest hits LP to take advantage of their hit status. These songs were staples of '80s urban contemporary radio, and the ballads are still carried in the '90s on many Quiet Storm playlists. —*Ron Wynn*

My First Love / 1986 / Warner Brothers ♦♦♦
Best of Atlantic Starr / 1986 / A&M ♦♦♦
○ **Classics, Vol. 10** / 1987 / A&M ♦♦♦♦
This collection gathers their A&M hits, which also include "Freak-A-Ristic," "Secret Lovers" and "If Your Heart Isn't In It." But the group scored its biggest smash after moving to Warner Bros., the R&B and pop chart-topping "Always." —*Ron Wynn*

All In the Name of Love / 1987 / Warner Brothers ♦♦♦
A judicious combo of modern R&B and pop, this includes their hit "Always." —*Bil Carpenter*

We're Movin' Up / 1988 / Warner Brothers ♦♦♦
Prototype classy love ballads, dance-pop, urban contemporary production/arrangements, and one or two above-average leads. Atlantic Starr has shuttled personnel often but never tampered much with their basic formula. They do it well, and there's little here that's disturbing, poorly performed, or routinely performed. Porscha Martin made a good replacement for Barbara Weathers, who was a good replacement for Sharon Bryant, and, well, you get the idea. —*Ron Wynn*

Love Crazy / 1992 / Reprise ♦♦♦
Lush ballads, especially "Masterpiece." —*Bil Carpenter*
Time / 1994 / Arista

The Atlantics

Group, Surf
One of the greatest instrumental surf groups did not even hail from America. The Atlantics, despite their name, were an Australian combo that not only emulated the sound of California surf music, but ranked among its very best practitioners. Featuring a reverb-heavy, extremely "wet" sound, the Atlantics attacked original material, standards, and movie themes with a nervy blend of precision and over-the-top intensity. As in Dick Dale's music, touches of Middle Eastern influences can be detected in the

rhythms of melodies (some members of the group claimed Greek and Egyptian heritage). Their second single, "Bombora," went to the top of the Australian charts in 1963, and the follow-up "The Crusher" was also a big hit. But Beatlemania spelled commercial death for the Atlantics, as it did for U.S. surf combos, in 1964 and 1965. After several albums and a few more equally fine instrumental singles, the Atlantics became a vocal group in the last half of the '60s, but are most renowned for their instrumental recordings. Still regarded with respect in Australia and New Zealand, they remain virtually unknown elsewhere, except to fanatical surf music specialists. —*Richie Unterberger*

● **The CBS Singles Collection 1963-1965** / Canetoad ◆◆◆◆
Both sides of their first nine singles. Includes "Bombora," "The Crusher," strong originals, and hard-boiled overhauls of "Goldfinger" and "Peter Gunn." As essential as Dick Dale, though much more obscure. —*Richie Unterberger*

The Au Pairs
Group, New Wave
Blasting into the post-punk consciousness with a tremendous debut album, the Au Pairs, fronted by lesbian feminist Lesley Woods, played brittle, dissonant, guitar-based rock that shared political and musical kinship with the Mekons and (especially) the Gang of Four. The music was danceable, imbued with an almost petulant irony, and for a while, very hip and well-liked by critics. Unlike many bands of the moment, however, the Au Pairs (at least initially) music was backed up with searing, confrontational songs celebrating sexuality from a woman's perspective. Also, they took swipes at the conservative political climate sweeping England after Margaret Thatcher's election as Prime Minister. Occasionally, Wood's commitments to sexual and social politics made her sound inflexible, doctrinaire and hectoring (especially on their OK second album), but at first blush, the Au Pairs were a mighty intimidating proposition, able to take on so much and deliver great music in the process. After a desultory live album in 1983 (*Au Pairs Live in Berlin*), the band split up, and Woods and her bandmates have maintained a low profile. —*John Dougan*

● **Playing with a Different Sex** / 1981 / Human ◆◆◆◆
Opening with the tongue-in-cheek "We're So Cool," the Au Pairs' debut record is a stunner, from Lesley Wood's scratchy guitar and declamatory vocals to lead guitarist Paul Foad's brittle soloing. This is an uncompromising, defiant record that asks no quarter: gender roles are turned upside down, hetero- and homosexual relationships put under a microscope, and theories about sex and sexuality turned upside down. Similarly, the tense political situation in Northern Ireland is harrowingly addressed in "Armagh," which details Tory-sanctioned torture and sexual abuse of wrongly imprisoned Irish women. An unflinching look at the world, *Playing With a Different Sex* is one of the great, and perhaps forgotten, post-punk records. —*John Dougan*

Sense & Sensuality / 1982 / Kamera ◆◆◆
Live in Berlin / 1983 / AKA ◆◆◆

Brian Auger
b. 1939, London
Art-Rock/Progressive-Rock, Pop/Rock
Brian Auger is a British jazz-rock organist. In 1962, he was leading the Brian Auger Trio, which evolved by 1964 into the five-piece Brian Auger Trinity, and then into Steampacket. In 1966, Auger organized a new Trinity with a rhythm section of Dave Ambrose (bass) and Clive Thacker (drums), which also appeared with singer Julie Driscoll. It was this group that scored a #5 U.K. (#106 U.S.) single hit with a cover of Bob Dylan and Rick Danko's "This Wheel's on Fire" and a #11 chart album with *Open* in 1968. The group charted two albums, *Jools & Brian* and *Streetnoise* in the U.S. in 1969. Minus Driscoll, the Trinity had a #100 U.S. singles chart entry with "Listen Here" and an LP listing with *Befour* in 1970. By 1972, Auger had organized a new group, the Oblivion Express, which charted eight LPs in the U.S. through 1977. —*William Ruhlmann*

● **Streetnoise** / 1969 / Atco ◆◆◆◆
Prototype album from the period when the British jazz-rock movement was emerging. Although it's more rock than jazz, especially in the rhythms and instrumentation, the songs were long enough to allow some degree of solo space, and Auger is an entertaining, energetic player despite his limits (he wasn't among the more ambitious or progressive keyboard players). —*Ron Wynn*

Best of Brian Auger & The Trinity / 1970 / Polydor ◆◆◆
○ **A Better Land** / 1971 / RCA ◆◆◆◆

Patti Austin
b. Aug. 10, 1948, California
Urban
A professional since the age of five, Patti Austin was a protégé of Dinah Washington and Sammy Davis, Jr. A 1969 single for United Artists titled "Family Tree" cracked the R&B top 50. Austin cut her debut LP, *End of a Rainbow*, for Creed Taylor's CTI label in 1976, followed by *Havana Candy* in 1977 and *Body Language* in 1980. She sang lead vocals for Japanese koto player Yutaka Yokokura on "Love Light" in 1978, did a duet with Michael Jackson on "It's the Falling in Love" for *Off the Wall*, and sang "The Closer I Get to You" on Tom Browne's album in 1979. Austin dueted with George Benson on "Moody's Mood for Love" in 1980. She sang backgrounds for sessions by Houston Person, Noel Pointer, Ralph McDonald, Angela Bofill, and Roberta Flack. Austin did vocals on Quincy Jones's *The Dude* LP in 1981, and was featured on the hit "Razzamatazz." She inked a solo deal on Jones's Qwest label, and her 1982 LP *Every Home Should Have One* included the #1 pop hit (#9 R&B) "Baby, Come to Me," which got widespread exposure via the ABC soap opera *General Hospital*. The follow-up single, "How Do You Keep the Music Playing," was the theme for the film *Best Friends*. Both songs paired Austin with James Ingram. She continued recording for Jones's Qwest label through the '80s, but couldn't recapture her pop or R&B success, despite working with several top producers, including Jam/Lewis in 1985. Austin switched to GRP in 1990, and recorded *Love Is Gonna Getcha*, with the singles "Through the Test of Time" and "Good in Love." She subsequently recorded *Carry On* and *Live, with Shelton Becton* in 1991 and 1992. —*Ron Wynn*

End of a Rainbow / Feb. 1976 / CTI ◆◆◆
Havana Candy / Nov. 1977 / CTI ◆◆
CTI was having its troubles financially at the time. They recycled arrangements for all their artists and limited their budgets. Austin sang this undistinguished material with as much conviction as she could muster, but the general pallid air lingering over the production also affected her vocals. —*Ron Wynn*

Live at the Bottom Line / 1979 / Epic ◆◆◆
Patti Austin came closest on this late '70s live set to transferring onto vinyl the qualities that make her an outstanding vocalist outside the studio. There's more spontaneity, emotion, and charisma in the vocals on this album than on almost all her other releases combined; perhaps the nightclub setting inspired her, or, more likely, Austin was free to sing without any agendas, marketing strategies, or producers' visions being factored into the process. —*Ron Wynn*

Body Language / Jul. 1980 / CTI ◆◆
The fourth album Patti Austin cut for the CTI label wasn't much different from the previous three. It was a patchwork quilt: a little fusion, a little quasi-jazz, some urban contemporary material, and even a standard or two. She sang them all with ease and grace, although things were so smooth they were almost comatose at times. Austin would later go on to score much bigger hits working with Quincy Jones, who at least injected enough hooks and tricks into his urban contemporary stuff to grab someone's attention. —*Ron Wynn*

○ **Every Home Should Have One** / Sep. 1981 / Qwest ◆◆◆◆
Quincy Jones-produced pop album featuring "Baby, Come to Me," which became a belated hit when it was featured on *General Hospital*, two years after the album came out. —*William Ruhlmann*

In My Life / Jun. 1983 / CTI ◆◆◆
Patti Austin / Mar. 1984 / Qwest ◆◆◆
Patti Austin enjoyed good chart action and radio airplay with this mid-'80s release. A pair of singles, "Hot! In the Flames Of Love" and "Star Struck," got both R&B and dance attention, while the album had some other competent uptempo material and a couple of good ballads. It wasn't her best on Qwest, but it was far from her worst. —*Ron Wynn*

Getting Away with Murder / Oct. 1985 / Qwest ◆◆◆
Patti Austin's third Qwest album was a reasonable success, making the Top 50 on the R&B chart and throwing off three R&B chart singles, "Honey For The Bees," "The Heat Of Heat," and the title track. But you could tell it was supposed to do a lot better on the

pop chart: five heavyweight producers (Russ Titelman, Tommy LiPuma, Monte Moir, and Jimmy Jam and Terry Lewis), plus 14 songwriters, contributed to what was doubtless a big-budget production, and that means label head Quincy Jones was looking for a lot more in the way of crossover than a low chart ranking for "The Heat Of Heat." In retrospect, the fault lies with all that high-priced help, while Austin gives her all in any guise they confound for her—sultry balladeer, disco diva, pop princess. — *William Ruhlmann*

● **The Real Me** / Aug. 1988 / Qwest ✦✦✦✦
And how! Austin tackles standards such as "Smoke Gets in Your Eyes" and "They Can't Take That Away from Me," and succeeds brilliantly. Her version of Comden, Green, and Bernstein's "I Can Cook, Too" is enough by itself to make this a pick. — *William Ruhlmann*

Love Is Gonna Getcha / Mar. 1990 / GRP ✦✦
Her debut for GRP included the somewhat cutesy but nicely done title track, a decent mix of fusion, light jazz, show biz, and pre-rock pop. Patti Austin can really sing anything, and unfortunately, on most of her albums, that's what happens; she gets any- and everything shoved her way. The album did land her two mild hits, "Through The Test of Time" and "Good in Love." — *Ron Wynn*

Carry on / Nov. 30, 1991 / GRP ✦
Patti Austin, a gifted singer when she gets good material, works in murky waters on this '91 release. There are so many different things offered, from fusion and pop to more mainstream jazz and soul, that the album has no main course or personality. On the other hand, Austin does sing everything well, and GRP has enlisted enough of their session pros to ensure that the musical support is excellent. It's well-played, superbly sung filler. — *Ron Wynn*

Live / Mar. 1992 / GRP ✦✦✦
● **Best of** / 1994 / Columbia ✦✦✦✦
That Secret Place / Apr. 1994 / GRP ✦✦
This is virtually a duet album between Patti Austin and guitarist Lee Ritenour, who produced, bringing with him a Who's Who of New York fusion players. It's a tasteful, well-constructed, consistently dull and lifeless effort. Here a reggae beat, there an actual duet with El DeBarge, and all devoid of any real fire. The closest anyone comes to life is when they cover Aretha Franklin's "Rock Steady" and Austin sneaks in elements of impersonation. But if during Austin's Qwest days they were trying to turn her into a soul-pop singer along the lines of Janet Jackson, now GRP is trying to make another Anita Baker out of her, and the fit is no better. — *William Ruhlmann*

Auteurs

Group, Alternative Pop/Rock
When the Auteurs released their debut album in 1993, the British press linked them with the massively popular Suede as part of a "glam revival." While the band can blast out guitar-drenched rockers like Suede, the Auteurs come to life when they draw from the quiet side of such distinctively English guitar-pop bands as the Kinks, the Smiths, and George Harrison. Luke Haines, the group's guitarist, vocalist, and songwriter, writes highly melodic pop songs that combine the airy melodicism of Harrison with the cutting social observations of Davies; they're sharp, intelligent songs, full of humor and gorgeous melancholy, even when they're loud rockers. With their two albums, *New Wave* and *Now I'm a Cowboy*, they've earned a devoted cult in the U.K., without gathering much support in the United States. — *Stephen Thomas Erlewine*

● **New Wave** / 1993 / Plan 9/Caroline ✦✦✦✦
The debut from this underrated group hearkens back to the golden years of British pop. The auteur of the Auteurs, Luke Haines, is as acerbic and insightful about modern British life as Ray Davies, singing about marrying showgirls and the upper classes. Songs like "Junk Shop Clothes" and "Bailed Out" have a Merseybeat quality, while "Early Years" points the way to the group's angrier, harder sound. More than just pastiche artists, *New Wave* presents the Auteurs as a group with both wit and heart. — *Heather Phares*

Now I'm a Cowboy / 1994 / Capitol ✦✦✦
On the Auteurs' second album, the tunes are tighter, and the hooks and wit are even sharper than on "New Wave." The band even rocks out (in a refined way, of course) on songs like "Lenny Valentino." Haines continues to write about the scheming rich and shabbily genteel, wrapping his words in loud guitars and sighing

cellos. "New French Girlfriend" and "Chinese Bakery" are just two of the gems on *Now I'm a Cowboy,* proving that the Auteurs have plenty to say and a catchy way to say it. — *Heather Phares*

Autosalvage

Group, Psychedelic
One of the relatively few New York psychedelic groups to achieve national recognition, Autosalvage's time in the limelight was fairly dim and brief. The band included bassist Skip Boone, the brother of Lovin' Spoonful bassist Steve Boone, and Rick Turner, who contributed guitar to most of the tracks on Ian & Sylvia's 1966 album, *Play One More.* Autosalvage's self-titled 1968 album revealed a fairly large palette, with touches of folk, blues, and strings. The group's cheerful harmonies owed a bit to the Lovin' Spoonful, and Frank Zappa (perhaps impressed by their sometimes disjointed and improvisational material) was a fan, but their material was not strong enough to forge a distinctive identity. Boone and drummer Darius Davenport also appear on the obscure 1968 album by Bear, but otherwise the Autosalvage's debut was also their curtain call. — *Richie Unterberger*

Autosalvage / 1968 / RCA ✦✦✦
Cuts like the opening track (titled, confusingly enough, "Auto Salvage") show the band at their best—strong melody, airy harmonies, a churning psychedelic arrangement. They didn't live up to that potential often on their only album, which is saddled by a fair amount of mediocre and rambling material. The British reissue adds informative historical liner notes. — *Richie Unterberger*

Frankie Avalon (Francis Avallone)

b. Sep. 18, 1939, Philadelphia
Pop, Teen Idol
At the end of the '50s and beginning of the '60s, Frankie Avalon was one of the biggest teen idols around, hitting the top of the charts consistently from 1958 until the end of 1960. Avalon didn't possess a terrific voice, but he did have material that was tailor-made for a receptive teen audience. At the height of his popularity, he had five Top Ten hits in 1959 including "Dede Dinah," "Ginger Bread," "Why," and "Venus." When the '60s began in earnest, Avalon embarked on an acting career; he starred in a hugely successful series of beach movies with Annette Funicello. After he began acting, Avalon didn't return to music for the rest of the decade. In the '70s, Avalon began making occasional film and television appearances while he worked the nostalgia and club circuits; he continues to sing and act in the '90s. — *Stephen Thomas Erlewine*

● **The Best of Frankie Avalon** / 1995 / Varese Sarabande ✦✦✦✦
The definitive compilation: the original versions of 18 songs from 1958-62, all but one of them a chart hit of some sort. Has all the Top Ten smashes and a bunch of minor post-1959 singles that found him swinging towards pop crooner material that had barely any relation to rock & roll whatsoever. — *Richie Unterberger*

The Avengers

Group, Punk
The Avengers were a San Francisco-based hardcore punk rock group formed in 1977, featuring Penelope Houston (vocals), Greg Westermark (guitar), Jofnathan Postal (bass), and Danny Furioso (drums). They had broken up by the time their only full-length album was released in 1983. — *William Ruhlmann*

● **Avengers** / 1983 / CD Presents ✦✦✦✦
Although it was released in 1983, this collection represents just about everything San Francisco's late, great Avengers recorded from 1977-78. By contemporary standards, it's by-the-book punk thrash: Greg Ingraham's guitar spews up hairball after hairball of distortion, while Penelope Houston snarls in her best impression of Johnny Rotten. However, contemporary standards diminish what great music this was and what a great band the Avengers were. Dozens of bands came in their wake, but few could recapture the excitement and ferocity of their sound. Houston, who reemerged years later as a folk-rocker, is in full fury on these 14 tracks, especially the youth culture solidarity anthem "We Are The One" and the tale of desperation "Thin White Line." A few spins of this and you'll hear how the Avengers influenced everyone from Black Flag to X. Yes, they were that good. A forgotten classic. — *John Dougan*

Average White Band

Group, Soul, Funk
The Average White Band had their name jokingly bestowed on

them by Bonnie Bramlett of Delanie & Bonnie; during their prime, AWB's solid grooves and overall chemistry were anything but average. But the name did reflect their paradoxical position: they were an American-style soul band made up of native Scots. The group was formed in Glasgow, Scotland, in early 1972 by Alan Gorrie (b. Jul 19, 1946, Perth, Scotland) (bass/vocals), Michael Rosen (soon replaced by Hamish Stuart [b. Oct 8, 1949, Glasgow, Scotland] [guitar/vocals]), Onnie McIntyre (b. Sep 25, 1945, Lennox Town, Scotland) (vocals/guitar), Robbie McIntosh b. 1950, Scotland—d. Sep 23, 1974, Los Angeles), Roger Ball (b. Jun 4, 1944, Dundee, Scotland) (keyboards/saxophone), and Malcolm Duncan (b. Aug 24, 1945, Montrose, Scotland) (saxophone). After their 1973 debut album, *Show Your Hand,* went unnoticed, they hooked up with producer Arif Mardin to record *Average White Band* (frequently called *AWB* because of the initials on the cover). Released in August 1974, the album topped the charts and spawned the near-instrumental dance hit "Pick up the Pieces," which also went to #1. Meanwhile, tragedy struck the band, when drummer Robbie McIntosh died of a drug overdose; he was replaced by Steve Ferrone (b. Apr 25, 1950, Brighton, England). AWB nearly replicated its success with the third album, *Cut the Cake,* and its title single, both of which reached the Top Ten. But the sameness of the group's approach and such side projects as an album with Ben E. King broke its momentum. Also, the rise of disco left its funky soul style sounding dated. AWB managed a couple more gold albums in *Person to Person* (January 1977) and *Warmer Communications* (March 1978), and its popularity lasted longer in the U.K. than in the U.S., but by the start of the '80s the band was permanently out of fashion. The band members have worked as session sidemen for artists ranging from Chaka Khan to Paul McCartney and Badfinger. —*Rick Clark & William Ruhlmann*

Show Your Hand / 1973 / MCA ✦✦✦
○ **AWB** / Aug. 1974 / Atlantic ✦✦✦✦
Average White Band's self-titled second album was also their best. It contained their biggest and best hit, "Pick up the Pieces," as well as "Keepin' It to Myself." —*Dan Heilman*

Put It Where You Want It / Mar. 1975 / MCA ✦✦✦
Put It Where You Want It is a retitled reissue of the Average White Band's first album, *Show Your Hand* (1973). —*William Ruhlmann*

Cut the Cake / Jun. 1975 / Atlantic ✦✦✦
Scotland's Average White Band revived blue-eyed soul and took it into the funk era during the '70s, making several acclaimed and successful albums that paid tribute to the Rascals/Righteous Brothers sound, but were more uptempo and groove-dominated. One such album was 1975's *Cut the Cake,* which included the hit title track, the nice "School Boy Crush," and two of the group's best ballads, "Cloudy" and "If I Ever Lose This Heaven." By this time, Stephen Ferrone had taken over on drums, giving them a looser bottom sound, while special guest Ray Barretto added some Afro-Latin spice on two cuts, and regulars Hamish Stuart, Onnie McIntyre, Roger Ball, Alan Gorrie, and Malcolm Duncan continued their patented playing and singing. —*Ron Wynn*

Soul Searching / Jul. 1976 / Atlantic ✦✦
The funk era was peaking when the Average White Band issued *Soul Searching* in 1976. Disco changed the rhythm rules, and now string orchestrations, lengthy suites, and more subdued Afro-Latin percussion were becoming the dominant sound. Although they got a gold album and did some clever experimenting with jazz and Latin beats, this wasn't among their biggest releases. The title cut attracted some attention, and there were a couple of R&B hits. *Soul Searching* stands as a monument to past success and a model of overall creativity. —*Ron Wynn*

Person to Person / Jan. 1977 / Atlantic ✦✦✦
The Average White Band gave those who'd never experienced their brand of blue-eyed soul/funk live a treat in 1977 with the release of the two-album set *Person to Person,* a concert album with many hits done at various concert stops. This has now been made into a two-disc set, and while the discs are a bit short, the music sounds just as fresh and exuberant. The opening disc's highlights are the energetic "If I Ever Lose This Heaven," "Cloudy," and the closing "T.L.C." The second disc contains a sparkling rendition of "Pick Up The Pieces," the song that made them a hit act, plus "School Boy Crush" and a great version of "I Heard It Through The Grapevine" to wrap things up. —*Ron Wynn*

Benny & Us / Jul. 1977 / Atlantic ✦✦✦
Warmer Communications / Mar. 1978 / Atlantic ✦✦
Feel No Fret / Mar. 1979 / RCA ✦✦
Average White Band, Vol. 8 / 1980 / Atlantic ✦✦✦
Shine / May 1980 / Arista ✦✦
Cupids in Fashion / 1982 / RCA ✦
Best of Average White Band / 1984 / RCA ✦✦✦
Aftershock / 1989 / Track Record ✦
The Average White Band was down to a trio consisting of singer/bassist Alan Gorrie, guitarist/singer Onnie McIntyre, and saxophonist Roger Ball on *Aftershock,* the band's first new album in six years and last new album so far. The threesome brought in a lot of session players, however, starting with Alex Ligertwood, who sang on three songs, and Eliot Lewis, who handled keyboards and programming, and including such friends as Chaka Khan and the Ohio Players. Producer John Robie, known for his mechanistic dance tracks, emphasized AWB's traditional funk sound without finding an effective way to update it, resulting in an album that was faithful to the band's heyday but did not address its career decline. —*William Ruhlmann*

● **Pickin' up the Pieces: The Best of Average White Band (1974-1980)** / 1992 / Rhino ✦✦✦✦
All of the Average White Band's biggest hits, as well as important album tracks, are featured on this definitive 18-track collection. —*Stephen Thomas Erlewine*

Kevin Ayers

Group, Singer-Songwriter, Art-Rock/Progressive-Rock
Born in Kent, England, Kevin Ayers was one of the founders of the art-rock band Soft Machine in 1966, though he left the band in December 1968. He released his first solo album, *Joy of a Toy,* in November 1969, then formed a short-lived band called the Whole World in March 1970, but otherwise has maintained a part-time solo career, playing to a cult following that has never gotten large enough to get him into the charts. —*William Ruhlmann*

Joy of a Toy / Nov. 1969 / Beat Goes On ✦✦✦
As the Soft Machine's first bassist and original principal songwriter, Kevin Ayers was an overlooked force behind the group's groundbreaking recordings in 1967 and 1968. This, his solo debut, is so tossed-off and nonchalant that one gets the impression he wanted to take it easy after helping pilot the manic innovations of the Softs. Laissez-faire sloth has always been part of Ayers's persona, and this record's intermittent lazy charm helped establish it. That doesn't get around the fact, however, that this set of early progressive rock does not feature extremely strong material. Ayers's command of an assortment of instruments is impressive, and his deep bass vocals and playful, almost goofy song-sketches are affecting, but they don't really stick with the listener. It's no accident that some of the tracks recall the early Soft Machine; Robert Wyatt drums on most of the songs, and "Song For Insane Times" is virtually a bonafide Soft Machine performance, featuring actual backing from the group itself. A likable but slight album that is at its best when Ayers is at his folkiest. —*Richie Unterberger*

Shooting at the Moon / Mar. 1970 / Beat Goes On ✦✦
Ayers put together a progressive rock supergroup of sorts for his second album, including Lol Coxhill on sax, David Bedford on keyboards, and a 17-year-old Mike Oldfield on bass; all three musicians would go on to notable solo careers in progressive rock and experimental music. The success of this haphazard affair depends on your appetite for disjointed art rock. There's a not inconsiderable amount of challenging jams that owe a lot to avant-garde jazz and electronics. Ayers is better off when he sticks to his greatest strength: the sweet, folky ballads intoned in his unique bass voice, like "May I" and "The Oyster And The Flying Fish," though these eventually segue into discordant instrumental riffing. The title track is an update of an old song from the original Soft Machine's repertoire that was performed more straightforwardly (and much more successfully) as "Jet-Propelled Photograph" on their 1967 demos (which have been reissued on numerous packages). —*Richie Unterberger*

○ **Whatevershebringswesing** / Jan. 1971 / Beat Goes On ✦✦✦✦
This album of songs about melancholy and solitude may, at first, seem like a disparate collection. After listening a few times the essence of the song cycle becomes clear. The near-hit "Stranger in Blue Suede Shoes" and "Song from the Bottom of a Well" are among the standout tracks. —*Jim Powers*

Bananamour / May 1973 / Beat Goes On ✦✦✦
A solid, enjoyable collection of songs written from the point of view of Kevin Ayers's own particular brand of existentialism—self-conscious individualism sustained by plenty of wine. The American version of this album contains the near-hit "Caribbean Moon," as well as the Syd Barrett tribute "Oh Wot a Dream." —*Jim Powers*

June 1st 1974 / 1974 / Island ✦✦✦
Kevin Ayers's guests take over Side A, with Eno turning in a powerful "Baby's On Fire," John Cale a harrowing "Heartbreak Hotel," and Nico an endless "The End." Ayers runs the show on Side B, playing an engaging set of melodic folk-rock topped by his sturdy baritone. —*William Ruhlmann*

Confessions of Doctor Dream / May 1974 / Beat Goes On ✦✦
Kevin Ayers's fifth album, *The Confessions Of Doctor Dream And Other Stories*, is typical of his work. He sings in his distinctive deep voice with his cultured English accent (sounds a lot like John Cale) on songs set in a variety of pop styles, from hard rock to a kind of music hall approach. He is frequently playful and engaging, although his songs don't ultimately add up to much. The album's second side contains an 18-minute song called "The Confessions Of Doctor Dream," featuring a cameo by Nico, that exemplifies Ayers's amiable, if unfocused appeal. —*William Ruhlmann*

Sweet Deceiver / Mar. 1975 / Beat Goes On

● **Odd Ditties** / 1976 / Harvest ✦✦✦✦
It is indeed an oddity that, for all the considerable ambition of his albums, this collection of singles and unreleased outtakes may be Ayers's most satisfying LP. Why? Perhaps because when he's constrained within the 45 format, he taps his strongest and most endearing qualities—easygoing, sing-along melodies, droll, nonchalant (even non sequitur) lyrics, good-natured sotto voce vocals, and even female backup harmonies. There's little trace of the inaccessible, difficult (usually instrumental) passages that occupy much of the space on his early albums. Spanning 1969 to 1973, this includes eight tracks that wound up on flop singles, as well as six outtakes from the albums he recorded during this period, though there were no obvious reasons for their exclusion (too pop-oriented, perhaps?). These are, indeed, "odd ditties": catchy, with occasional Caribbean rhythms and French lyrics, but way too goofball to be taken to heart by a mass audience, at times sounding like a more together Syd Barrett. Needless to say, none of these nifty tunes were anything close to hits. But if they had been, the world would have been a better place. —*Richie Unterberger*

Yes We Have No Mananas / Jul. 1976 / Beat Goes On ✦✦✦
Although the slick, nearly AOR-style production threatens to swamp the music on this album, the solid songwriting wins out in the end. Ayers has written several songs about achieving stardom; the pithy "Star" is a highlight. A cover of Marlene Dietrich's "Falling in Love with You" is this album's near-hit. —*Jim Powers*

Rainbow Takeaway / Apr. 1978 / Beat Goes On

Diamond Jack and the Queen of Pain / 1983 / Charly ✦✦

● **Kevin Ayers Collection** / 1983 / See For Miles ✦✦✦✦
This hour-long chronological sampling of Ayers's Harvest and Island discs features several rare single sides (like "Puis-Je?," the French language version of "May I?") in addition to some of his best album cuts. With an extensive biographical essay in the liner notes, this is the ideal place to get acquainted with Ayers's work. —*Jim Powers*

Aztec Camera

Group, Alternative Pop/Rock
For most intents and purposes, Aztec Camera is Roddy Frame, a Scottish guitarist/vocalist/songwriter. Several other musicians have passed through the band over the years—including founding members Campbell Owens (bass) and Dave Mulholland (drums)—but the one constant has been Frame. Throughout his career, he has created a sophisticated, lush and nearly jazzy acoustic-ori-

ented guitar pop, relying on gentle melodies and clever wordplay inspired by Elvis Costello.
Aztec Camera released their debut album, *High Land, Hard Rain*, in 1983. Before its release, Owens and Mulholland had left the group, leaving Frame to assemble the record himself. Upon its release, the album won significant amounts of critical praise for its well-crafted, multilayered pop. After releasing a stop-gap EP, *Oblivious*, the group's second full-length record, *Knife*, appeared in 1984. Produced by Mark Knopfler, the album was more polished and immediate than the debut, featuring horn arrangements and a slight R&B influence. Three years later, Roddy Frame returned with *Love*, which featured musical support from several studio musicians. *Love* was a synthesized stab at pop-R&B, resulting in his greatest commercial success—the album launched four hit singles, including the Top Ten "Somewhere in My Heart."
Two years later, Aztec Camera returned to a more guitar-oriented sound with *Stray*. It wasn't as commercially successful as *Love*, yet it was a hit with fans that missed the chiming hooks of Frame's early work. *Dreamland*, released in 1993, followed the same pattern as *Stray* and achieved about the same amount of commercial and critical success. —*Stephen Thomas Erlewine*

● **High Land, Hard Rain** / Jun. 1983 / Sire ✦✦✦✦
This intelligent and detailed, if somewhat overambitious, debut showcases vocalist/songwriter Roddy Frame's catchy and wordy acoustic-based pop songs. Imagine a folky version of Elvis Costello, with better guitar chops, and you've got the picture here. None of the Camera's other albums have come close to matching this release. —*John Floyd*

Knife / Sep. 1984 / Sire ✦✦✦
Aztec Camera's second album cuts back the ethereal atmosphere, revealing a stripped-down, vaguely R&B-influenced pop sense. —*Stephen Thomas Erlewine*

Aztec Camera / Mar. 1985 / Sire ✦✦
This is a five-song EP, four of whose songs were recorded live at the Dominion Theatre in London on October 16, 1984. The fifth track is a cover of Van Halen's "Jump," which sounds like an unlikely choice, except when you consider that, at heart, Aztec Camera is a pop band, whatever its other pretensions may be. Roddy Frame turns out to be a good, if wispy frontman, and much of this set is a folkie showcase of his songwriting. —*William Ruhlmann*

Backwards and Forwards / Mar. 1985 / Sire ✦✦

Love / Nov. 1987 / Sire ✦✦
Roddy Frame dispensed with the previous members of Aztec Camera and turned to a group of American session musicians and high-powered producers (Russ Titelman, Tommy LiPuma) for his third full-length album, on which he also abandoned his singer/songwriter, folk-rock approach in favor of an American R&B style. It's a distinct step down from the ingenuity of his first couple of records, and was met with indifference in the U.S., which seemed to be its intended target. In the U.K., the album belatedly took off after its second single, "Somewhere In My Heart," went to #3, and became Aztec Camera's only Top 10 LP. (Other U.K. chart singles were "How Men Are" [#25] and "Working In A Goldmine" [#31].) —*William Ruhlmann*

○ **Stray** / Jun. 1990 / Sire ✦✦✦✦
After a lukewarm stab at soul (*Love*), Roddy Frame returns to a brilliantly textured guitar pop on *Stray*, covering rock, soul, and jazzy pop in the space of one album. It's all tied together by Frame's intelligent, sometimes precious, lyrics and melodic pop sense—it's one of Aztec Camera's finest albums. —*Stephen Thomas Erlewine*

○ **Dreamland** / May 25, 1993 / Sire ✦✦✦✦
Aztec Camera's first album since 1990's *Stray* continues singer/songwriter Roddy Frame's return to form. Highlighted by the gorgeous Motown-Byrds hybrid single "Dream Sweet Dreams" and the lush, warm ballads "Valium Summer" and "Let Your Love Decide," *Dreamland* is Aztec Camera's best effort since their debut. —*Stephen Thomas Erlewine*

B

The B-52's
Group, Dance-Pop, Alternative Pop/Rock, New Wave

Athens, GA, has been a hotbed of alternative talent for quite a while, but the town's rise to cutting-edge musical prominence was aided in no small part by the 1976 formation of the B-52's, a wildly unorthodox party band that featured a guitarist with a five-string Mosrite electric and two mini-skirted, go-go-booted female singers who sported extremely bouffant hairdos. (The complete original lineup was: Fred Schneider (b. Jul 1, 1951, Newark, Georgia) (vocals), Kate Pierson (b. Apr 27, 1948, Weehawken, New Jersey) (vocals/organ); Cindy Wilson (b. Feb 28, 1957, Athens, Georgia) (vocals); Cindy's brother Ricky Wilson (b. Mar 19, 1953, Athens, Georgia—d. Oct 12, 1985) (guitar); and Keith Strickland (b. Oct 26, 1953, Athens, Georgia) (drums).

The recklessly exuberant self-titled Warner debut was a left-field success, selling tons of copies with little radio support. The followup, *Wild Planet*, picks up where the B-52's left off, with mixed results; nevertheless, it also enjoyed success.

A dance-mix EP (*Party Mix!*), a mini-album (*Mesopotamia*), and a belated full-length third album (*Whammy!*) provided further variations on the band's sound, but the "fun" seemed increasingly forced.

Ricky Wilson passed away in 1985 from AIDS before the release of the uneven *Bouncing off the Satellites*. With Keith Strickland taking over guitar duties, the B-52's returned from an extended break and put out the hugely successful *Cosmic Thing*. Produced by Don Was and Nile Rodgers, *Cosmic Thing* successfully synthesized the band's wacky energy with just the right amount of streamlining. Its follow-up, *Good Stuff*, preceded by the departure of Cindy Wilson, was to *Cosmic Thing* what *Wild Planet* was to *The B-52's*, more of the same, but less effective and less popular. —*Rick Clark & William Ruhlmann*

★ **The B-52's** / Jul. 1979 / Warner Brothers ✦✦✦✦✦
It's all here on the debut album: the "Secret Agent Man" drum/guitar tracks that compel the feet to dance, topped by shrill female vocals and the brash speak-singing of Fred Schneider, giving forth with some of the strangest non sequiturs like an overexcited carnival barker. Includes "Planet Claire" and the hit "Rock Lobster." —*William Ruhlmann*

Wild Planet / Sep. 1980 / Warner Brothers ✦✦✦
Wild Planet is more of the same, as the B-52's celebrate the joys of living in your own "Private Idaho" and the wonders of quiche lorraine. —*William Ruhlmann*

Party Mix! / Jul. 1981 / Warner Brothers ✦✦
Party Mix! is a six-track mini-album that selects three tracks each from the B-52's' first two albums, *The B-52's* and *Wild Planet*, and presents them in dance mixes. Since the group's bouncy songs are already dance-ready, this makes for alternatives rather than real improvements, even from a dance floor perspective. —*William Ruhlmann*

Mesopotamia / Jan. 1982 / Warner Brothers ✦✦
After setting dance floors alight and funny bones aquiver with their first two albums, *The B-52's* and *Wild Planet* in 1979-1980, the B-52's seemed to run out of gas soon after, issuing a stop-gap remix mini-album, *Party Mix*, in 1981, and then turning in *another* stop-gap mini in this lackluster set, produced by David Byrne, who must have seemed like a good choice, although his sense of humor is less zany, if just as weird, as the B's. *Mesopotamia* is the sound of a band that once sounded like it was on a steady path now losing its footing. —*William Ruhlmann*

Whammy! / Apr. 1983 / Warner Brothers ✦✦✦
After the still-born *Mesopotamia, Whammy!* is a pleasing return to the classic fun-loving wackiness of the first album, even if some of the songs sound a little forced and self-conscious. —*Stephen Thomas Erlewine*

Bouncing off the Satellites / Sep. 1986 / Warner Brothers ✦✦
Released about a year after the death of guitarist Ricky Wilson, *Bouncing Off the Satellites* is a disjointed, uneven record that starts off strong but collapses into a mess of studio slickness by the end of the album. —*Stephen Thomas Erlewine*

○ **Cosmic Thing** / Jun. 1989 / Reprise ✦✦✦✦
Belatedly, and despite the death of their musical leader Ricky Wilson, the B-52's found enormous commercial success with this album, which effectively recapitulates their zany virtues, especially on the two Top 10 hits "Love Shack" and "Roam." —*William Ruhlmann*

○ **Best of the B-52's: Dance This Mess Around** / 1990 / WEA ✦✦✦✦

Good Stuff / Jun. 23, 1992 / Reprise ✦✦✦
If *Cosmic Thing* found them returned to most-favored party band status, this follow-up gamely soldiers on in similar fashion. Without Cindy Wilson, *Good Stuff* becomes Kate Pierson's showcase, while even Fred Schneider turns in his most purely musical performance to date. If the B-52's hit some dead ends while trying to stretch out a bit, be assured there are enough classic bits to make this one worthwhile. —*Steve Aldrich*

Babble
Group, Alternative Pop/Rock

Babble is the duo of New Zealand native Alannah Currie (b. Sept. 28, 1957) and Englishman Tom Bailey (b. Jan. 18, 1956), who formerly made up the Thompson Twins, a dance-rock band that charted with seven albums in the U.S. between 1982 and 1989, the most successful of which was the million-selling Top Ten hit *Into The Gap* (1984), which featured their biggest single, "Hold Me Now" (#3). They reorganized as a six-piece band with Indian and new age influences and released their first album as Babble, *The Stone*, in 1994. —*William Ruhlmann*

The Stone / Mar. 8, 1994 / Reprise ✦✦
Babble would have you believe that they changed their name from the Thompson Twins because they have adopted a radically different musical approach that necessitated a new identity. Actually, the change probably had more to do with the poor sales of their last album under the old moniker, the unfortunately titled *Queer* (1991), which didn't make the charts, culminating a gradual decline in their fortunes since *Into The Gap* was a Top 10 million seller in 1984. In fact, *The Stone* sounds a lot like a Thompson Twins record, especially when Tom Bailey is singing, although the group has brought in some ambient sounds, borrowed some cheesy Indian restaurant music, and stolen the main riff from "I Am The Walrus." It has also hired a rapper named Q. Tee. These are not improvements. By whatever name they choose, Bailey and Currie have not returned to form. —*William Ruhlmann*

Babes in Toyland
Group, Alternative Pop/Rock

Babes in Toyland are about as harsh as rock music gets—guitarist Kat Bjelland screams and thrashes her guitar to the gut-pounding, throttling beat of bassist Maureen Herman and drummer Lorie

Barbero. Over their two albums and two EPs, the all-female trio offer no escape from their strongly female-oriented, but not necessarily feminist, rock.

Bjelland formed Babes in Toyland in 1987 in Minneapolis, after playing around San Francisco for several years in various bands which featured, at various times, Jennifer Finch of L7 and Courtney Love of Hole. After releasing a single on Sub Pop's singles club, Babes in Toyland came to the attention of Sonic Youth, who took them on a tour of Europe. Soon, they recorded their abrasive debut, *Spanking Machine*, with producer Jack Endino; one more independent EP followed before they signed to Reprise. In between labels, original bassist Michelle Leon left the group.

Sonic Youth's Lee Ranaldo produced their second album, *Fontanelle*, which showed no signs of concession to a major label. In early 1993, the band broke up for several days before re-forming to record the *Painkillers* EP and hitting the road with Lollapalooza 93.

Even though Lollapalooza offered the group a boost in public exposure, they chose not to capitalize on it; instead, it took them nearly two years before they released a new record, *Nemesisters*, in April of 1995. —*Stephen Thomas Erlewine*

○ **Spanking Machine** / 1990 / Twin/Tone ✦✦✦✦
A great one the first time out of the blocks. Kat Bjelland's guitar is a rampaging string machine, while her vocals pin you to the wall. Not for the weak or fainthearted. —*John Dougan*

To Mother / 1991 / Twin/Tone ✦✦✦
An EP follow-up that's strong but not life-changing. —*John Dougan*

● **Fontanelle** / 1992 / Reprise ✦✦✦✦
Fontanelle, Babes in Toyland's major-label debut, is stronger than *Spanking Machine*. The band has grown tighter and more vicious, making their anger sting even more. Not to be missed is Kat Bjelland's attack on Courtney Love, "Bruise Violet," one of the harshest songs ever recorded. —*Stephen Thomas Erlewine*

Painkiller / Jun. 22, 1993 / Warner Brothers ✦✦✦
Painkiller features four solid new tracks, one re-recording, and one track that is a brutal, 35-minute live performance of the *Fontanelle* album. It's a good introduction to the intense, loud punk rock of Babes in Toyland. —*AMG*

Nemesisters / 1995 / Reprise ✦✦
On *Nemesisters*, Babes in Toyland becomes a full-fledged heavy metal band. Most of the raw, slashing guitars of their early records are gone, replaced by a pulsing, plodding grind that never catches fire. Gone are the inspired, angry jokes, replaced by jokes that just aren't that funny—the opener "Hello," the cheap puns of "Sweet 69," and the deconstructionist covers of "All By Myself" and "Deep Song," which are too obvious to be humorous. "Sweet 69" does have a pummelling heavy groove that makes its jokes forgivable, yet the majority of the album is simply dull, recycled riffs and rhythms, and that is hard to forgive. —*Stephen Thomas Erlewine*

Babyface (Kenny Edmonds)

Group, Urban
With his friend Antonio Reid, Babyface formed a Cincinnati-based band, the Deele, in the early '80s. They were introduced by members of Midnight Star to Solar Records executive Dick Griffey, who put them to work producing music for Carrie Lucas, the Whispers, and Dynasty. Since then, they've produced hits for Sheena Easton, Pebbles, Paula Abdul, and others.

During the '90s Babyface's dominance has extended beyond the production arena and into the performing circle. A series of hit releases depicting him simultaneously as a vulnerable romantic and accomplished lover turned Babyface into arguably this decade's biggest Urban male vocalist. The string actually began in the mid '80s with the underrated *Lovers*, but picked up steam with *Tender Lover* in 1989. *Tender Lover* crossed him over into pop territory and eventually sold more than two million copies, ending any doubts that Babyface would be a major solo star. The singles "Whip Appeal" and "It's No Crime" were Top Ten R&B and pop hits, and remain staples on Urban radio. He followed that with *A Closer Look* in 1991, and his most recent LP, *For the Cool in You*, earned another platinum certification and ranked among 1993's biggest Urban/R&B albums. —*Bil Carpenter*

Lovers / 1989 / Solar ✦✦✦
An '89 session that's been reissued to take advantage of the fact that Babyface is the hottest entity on the current R&B market. He sings with just enough earnestness to be soulful and just enough

sophistication and slickness to avoid sounding too much like a throwback. —*Ron Wynn*

● **Tender Lover** / Jul. 1989 / Solar ✦✦✦✦
Babyface's second solo album yielded the first number one R&B hit of the 1990s while establishing Edmonds as a major personality and performer. He wrote or co-wrote much of the material and even played several instruments. It is a combination of slick production and nicely sung sentimental tributes and heartache ballads. —*Ron Wynn*

○ **A Closer Look** / Nov. 19, 1991 / Solar ✦✦✦✦
Babyface has established himself as both a performing and production star in the '90s. His alternately innocent, hurt, and disillusioned vocals are this decade's equivalent of the soul/love songs of the '70s and '80s. He can sing sentimental material, tender tunes, or seem angry and confused. His lyrics get overly coy, but they've struck many responsive chords among women in particular. It's not soul, but its what many who never heard Sam Cooke think it is. —*Ron Wynn*

For the Cool in You / Aug. 1993 / Epic ✦✦✦
Babyface has supplanted Luther Vandross as the reigning prince of vocal romanticism in black popular music among the affluent crowd. His ability to sound poignant, vulnerable and appealing, as well as write and produce catchy songs replete with hooks, have won him widespread popularity and consistent commercial success. Such tracks as "For The Cool In You," "A Bit Old-Fashioned," and "I'll Always Love You" demonstrate his mastery of an ideal formula. Babyface sings with the right blend of authority, conviction, earnestness, and innocence, and if he's hardly a compelling pure singer, he's the right vocalist for the current era. —*Ron Wynn*

When Can I See You Again / 1994 / Epic ✦✦✦

The Babys

Group, Pop/Rock
The Babys (formed 1976) were a moderately successful mainstream pop/rock outfit from England. Their debut failed to live up to advance hype concerning their visual appeal and Raspberries-meets-Free concept.

Their hits included "If You've Got the Time" (#88), "Isn't It Time" (#13), "Every Time I Think of You" (#13), "Back on My Feet Again" (#33), and "Turn and Walk Away" (#51).

The Babys disbanded in 1981. Lead singer John Waite (b. Jul 4, 1954) later enjoyed one of the biggest hits of 1984 with the #1 "Missing You." Lead guitarist Wally Stocker (b. Mar 17, 1954) joined Air Supply's road band, and keyboardist Jonathan Cain went to work with Journey. —*Rick Clark*

● **Anthology** / Oct. 1981 / Chrysalis ✦✦✦✦
This album is a good collection of the group's efficient mainstream pop-rock. —*Dan Heilman*

Bachman-Turner Overdrive

Group, Rock & Roll, Pop/Rock
Bachman-Turner Overdrive was formed by Randy Bachman and C. F. Turner, two expatriates of Canada's the Guess Who. They specialized in no-nonsense blue-collar rock & roll; in fact, part of the band's name came from the trucking industry magazine *Overdrive*. This isn't to say that BTO was without musical sophistication, certainly evidenced in the jazzy "Lookin' Out For No. 1." The band's initial demos were rejected by over two dozen record labels before Mercury picked them up.

Several of the band's radio tracks became substantial hits, particularly "Takin' Care of Business" (#12 pop) and the #1 hit "You Ain't Seen Nothing Yet," which had a stuttering vocal hook inspired by the speech impediment of the band's first manager, Gary Bachman.

After the Top Ten success of the band's fourth album, *Four Wheel Drive* (1975), BTO's fortunes began to decline. Randy Bachman left in 1977, although the group continued without him with Jim Clench. The group officially changed its name to BTO in 1978, but by that time not many people were paying attention. After releasing *Rock N' Roll Nights* in 1979, the band called it quits.

In 1984, the group re-formed with Randy Bachman and recorded another self-titled album, which was released without much notice. Although they didn't make another album, BTO continued to tour into the '90s. —*Rick Clark*

Bachman-Turner Overdrive / May 1973 / Mercury ✦✦
This is their debut. —*Larry Lapka*

Bachman-Turner Overdrive II / Dec. 1973 / Mercury ✦✦✦
This is excellent hard rock. —*Larry Lapka*

○ **Not Fragile** / Aug. 1974 / Mercury ✦✦✦✦
Featuring the #1 "You Ain't Seen Nothing Yet," this is the band's best noncompilation album. —*Donna DiChario*

Bachman-Turner-Bachman As Brave Belt / Feb. 1975 / Reprise ✦✦✦

As Brave Belt / Feb. 1975 / Warner Brothers ✦✦✦
This is a reissue of Brave Belt's 1972 second album *Brave Belt II*, put out in the wake of the success of the former Brave Belt members under the name Bachman-Turner Overdrive. —*William Ruhlmann*

Four Wheel Drive / May 1975 / Mercury ✦✦✦
Excellent hard rock. —*Larry Lapka*

Head on / Dec. 1975 / Mercury ✦✦✦
This is really the end of the Bachman-Turner Overdrive story, the group's last album to feature Randy Bachman. Bachman's dominance of the group is apparent—his face alone fills the front cover, he produced the record, and he wrote or co-wrote five of the nine songs. His unhappiness is apparent, too: listen to him sing, "I feel there's no use in hanging around" on the lead-off track, "Find Out About Love," and plead, "I'm an average man, but my name is in lights" in "Average Man." By the time you get to the cocktail jazz ballad "Lookin' Out For #1" (BTO's sole entry on the easy listening chart), you can tell he's not including the group. By the time of BTO's next album, Bachman was gone, and their hit-making days were behind them. —*William Ruhlmann*

● **The Best of B.T.O. (So Far)** / Jul. 1976 / Mercury ✦✦✦✦
Everything you need to hear, this no-frills hard-driving '70s rock showcases the band at the height of their popularity. —*Donna DiChario*

Freeways / Feb. 1977 / Mercury ✦✦✦
This is the last album under the Bachman-Turner name, after which Randy Bachman left the group for a solo career. —*Larry Lapka*

Street Action / Feb. 1978 / Mercury ✦✦
After Randy Bachman's departure, it was recorded under the B.T.O. name. —*Larry Lapka*

Rock N' Roll Nights / Mar. 1979 / Mercury ✦✦

● **Greatest Hits** / 1981 / Mercury ✦✦✦✦
All the essential hits are here on this good-sounding set. The lack of liner notes keeps this from being an informative place to start, but if you are looking for just the music, the high points are here. —*Rick Clark*

B T O / Sep. 1984 / Compleat ✦✦
This is a reunion album imbued with the usual BTO pop melodies, hard rock guitar, and working class sentiments, notably on the lead-off track, "For The Weekend." But by 1984, the band was a '70s nostalgia act, and there really was no audience for their new music. —*William Ruhlmann*

○ **The Anthology** / Jul. 20, 1993 / PolyGram 3145 ✦✦✦✦
This double-disc set features fine remastering from the original masters, plus extensive liner notes. This is an ideal choice for the *true* fan who is just converting to CD, and is looking for more than the basic hits package. Hit seekers will still find *BTO's Greatest Hits* more than adequate. —*Rick Clark*

Bad Brains

Group, Alternative Pop/Rock, Hardcore
Along with Black Flag and Minor Threat, the Bad Brains were the leaders of Washington, D.C.'s hardcore punk movement in the early '80s, although they didn't sound like either band. The Bad Brains tempered their ferocious hardcore with a good dose of dub and reggae without deviating from the "hard fast loud" rules that were vital to the scene. Led by vocalist H.R. and the blistering guitarist Dr. Know, the Bad Brains were notorious for their exhilarating live show, which had a raw, vital energy that they rarely captured in the studio. As the years passed, the band's reggae elements became more pronounced and—like most other punk bands—their punk elements lost some of their edge, turning into an honest, brutal version of heavy metal. Throughout their career, H.R. left and rejoined the group frequently.

Fifteen years after they formed, the Bad Brains released their first major-label album, *Rise*, in 1993. In between those years, their eclectic, intelligent approach to punk affected a generation of

rockers who enthusiastically embrace these ideas in their music. —*Stephen Thomas Erlewine*

Bad Brains / 1982 / ROIR ✦✦✦
On their debut album, Bad Brains established their explosive mix of reggae and hardcore. At this stage, the mix was still tentative, with the band able to pull off the punk better than the reggae, but the band's sheer energy made the album successful. —*Stephen Thomas Erlewine*

○ **Rock for Light** / 1983 / Plan 9/Caroline ✦✦✦✦
On their Ric Ocasek-produced second album, Bad Brains were able to balance the hardcore and reggae elements more skillfully than they had on their debut, but *Rock for Light* suffers from a lack of cohesiveness. Even if it is a little inconsistent, the unique power of their vision makes the album worthwhile. —*Stephen Thomas Erlewine*

● **I Against I** / 1986 / SST ✦✦✦✦
Slick production helped the Brains make the most satisfying metal/reggae record of their career. Dr. Know's guitar is pushed way up front in the mix, and the funkier backbeat (replacing the hardcore speed blur) kicks every track (especially "Return to Heaven") into high gear. —*John Dougan*

Live / 1988 / SST ✦✦✦
Compiled from a series of 1987 concerts, *Live* captures the Bad Brains at the height of their onstage prowess, yet it is necessary listening for hardcore fans. —*Stephen Thomas Erlewine*

Attitude: The ROIR Session / 1989 / Ineffect ✦✦

Quickness / 1989 / Plan 9/Caroline ✦✦
Quickness was the Bad Brains' most metal-oriented record to date, with the band eliminating most of the reggae numbers and concentrating on thick, driving rhythms accentuated by metallic, jazz-tinged leads by Dr. Know. —*Stephen Thomas Erlewine*

Youth Are Getting Restless: Live in Amsterdam / 1990 / Plan 9/Caroline ✦✦✦
The Youth Are Getting Restless repeats some of the same material from *Live*, albeit in different versions. The album was culled from the same tour as *Live*, but it captures a blistering concert from Amsterdam instead of compiling various performances. Consequently, it's a tighter and more exciting album, their best live record. —*Stephen Thomas Erlewine*

Spirit Electricity / 1991 / SST ✦✦✦

Rise / 1993 / Epic ✦✦
Bad Brains took longer than most bands do to reach the majors (that is, among those who ever do), and by now they are very different from the group that made their debut with a self-titled cassette on ROIR in 1982. As heard on *Rise*, they are basically a thrash metal band with elements of rap and reggae. In other words, they're fairly trendy. Meanwhile, of course, they're now playing in a bigger league, and their competition includes everyone from Metallica to Public Enemy, against whom they come off as reasonable competition, but no more. Hope they got a big advance and didn't spend it all in one place. —*William Ruhlmann*

God of Love / 1995 / Maverick ✦✦
For *God of Love*, the Bad Brains' first album for Madonna's label Maverick, the original lineup of the group reunited. Presumably, this was for the reported multi-million dollar record contracted—which was offered after the success of Green Day and the Beastie Boys—and not because the band had any great love for each other; during the supporting tour, HR slugged their manager and left the group, only to return within a week. Ric Ocasek, the producer of their breakthrough *Rock for Light*, also returned to produce the record. However, just because all the original participants returned, it didn't mean the sound or the inspiration returned. *God of Love* was flat and unenergetic. It failed to have an impact and faded from view soon after its release. —*Stephen Thomas Erlewine*

Bad Company

Group, Hard Rock
Supergroups usually don't enjoy lengthy fruitful careers, but Bad Company was a highly successful exception, producing a string of hit records from 1974 to 1982. Paul Rodgers and Simon Kirke of Free, Boz Burrell from King Crimson, and Mott the Hoople's Mick Ralphs delivered Bad Company's sparse, crunchy hard rock.

Their self-titled debut, recorded in ten days, exuded an appealing unpolished sound at a time when a lot of rock seemed to be trading its visceral essence for arty pretension. After their second album (*Straight Shooter*), Bad Company began to lose some of its freshness, opting for a more processed sound.

Bad Company broke up in 1983, but by the late '80s, a new lineup with Kirke and Ralphs emerged. Brian Howe filled Rodgers's slot. Even though this lineup produced some substantial rock hits, the band's sound is disappointingly interchangeable with a load of other professional radio rock acts. —*Rick Clark*

○ **Bad Company** / Jun. 1974 / Swan Song ♦♦♦♦
This powerhouse debut includes "Can't Get Enough," "Ready for Love," and the title track. —*Dan Heilman*

Straight Shooter / Apr. 1975 / Swan Song ♦♦♦
Their hot streak continues on this fine follow-up, with "Feel Like Makin' Love." —*Dan Heilman*

Run with the Pack / Jan. 1976 / Swan Song ♦♦
By this, their third album, it was becoming increasingly clear that Bad Company's music was a formula, and an unusually restrictive one. (They did try adding strings on the title track, which is one of the rewrites of the song "Bad Company.") With the band touring the world and momentum on their side, *Run With The Pack* shot up the charts, too, but it didn't get quite as high or stay quite as long as its predecessors, mostly because of the lack of really memorable material—the biggest single was a cover of the Coasters' hit "Young Blood." —*William Ruhlmann*

Burnin' Sky / Mar. 1977 / Swan Song ♦♦♦
The string finally ran out for Bad Company with its fourth album. Their approach was so simple that it almost inevitably became formulaic, and although Mick Ralphs continued to screech with his sparse guitar leads and Paul Rodgers continued to present his lust in a soulful voice—well, we had heard it several times. By its fourth album, Bad Company was getting sloppy around the edges, but the real reason this was the first Bad Company to miss the Top Ten in the U.S. and the U.K. is that there was no hit single. Clearly, it was time to try something new. —*William Ruhlmann*

Desolation Angels / Mar. 1979 / Swan Song ♦♦♦
After a couple of mediocre efforts, *Desolation Angels* marked a return to form for Bad Company. It was also the band's last consistent album, powered by "Rock N' Roll Fantasy" and "Gone, Gone, Gone." —*Stephen Thomas Erlewine*

Rough Diamonds / Aug. 1982 / Swan Song ♦♦
Instead of capitalizing on their "Rock 'N' Roll Fantasy" resurgence, Bad Company disappeared for another three years before trying it again with *Rough Diamonds*. Remember, it was not yet common in the music business for major groups to stay away from the marketplace that long. In Bad Company's case, the results were disastrous: the album didn't even make the Top 25 in the U.S. or go gold, much less platinum, and the music was softer and less distinctive than on their earlier records. —*William Ruhlmann*

● **10 from 6** / Dec. 1985 / Swan Song ♦♦♦♦
This concise collection of hits is perhaps overly brief. —*Dan Heilman*

Fame & Fortune / Oct. 1986 / Atlantic ♦♦

Dangerous Age / Aug. 1988 / Atco ♦♦♦

Holy Water / Jun. 1990 / Atco ♦♦♦

Here Comes Trouble / Sep. 1992 / Atco ♦♦♦
Down to a trio of Mick Ralphs, Simon Kirke, and Brian Howe, the-band-that-calls-itself-Bad-Company relied on studio musicians to fill out the sound and producer Terry Thomas to write most of the material on this anonymous-sounding fourth album by the second edition of the group. Even those willing to tolerate Ralphs/Simon/Howe calling itself "Bad Company" didn't show much interest, so that they fell off from the platinum showing of 1990's *Holy Water* to much more modest sales this time around, despite the chart singles "How About That" (#38) and "This Could Be The One" (#87). —*William Ruhlmann*

The Best of Bad Company Live . . . What You Hear Is What You Get / 1993 / Atlantic ♦
With only its original guitarist and drummer intact, Bad Company flails away at all of its trademark rockers, winding up sounding like a distasteful parody of the real thing. —*Stephen Thomas Erlewine*

Bad English

Group, Hard Rock
In the late '80s, ex-Journey guitarist Neal Schon teamed up with ex-Babys vocalist John Waite and other arena rock veterans to form Bad English. One of the last supergroups of the decade, they made power ballads like there was no tomorrow, and they did it better than most because Waite could carry a tune and Schon created the power ballad prototype during his years in Journey. In late 1989/early 1990, the group scored two huge hit singles—"When I See You Smile" and "Price of Love"—and were big draws in concert. However, the follow-up album, *Backlash*, experienced one of massive proportions, failing to have even one Top Forty hit. The band called it quits soon after its release. —*Stephen Thomas Erlewine*

● **Bad English** / Jun. 1989 / Epic ♦♦♦♦
Amid some tailor-made power ballads lurks some decent hard rock. —*Dan Heilman*

Backlash / Aug. 1991 / Epic ♦♦
The best laid plans. . . . Bad English may have been an artificial construction, as are all supergroups, but it had worked the first time around and there didn't seem to be any reason to think in wouldn't again. Nevertheless, *Backlash* was a major disappointment: after scoring three Top 40 hits with their debut, the group managed only a paltry #42 for this album's sole singles chart entry, "Straight To Your Heart," a Journey-like arena rock number. With that, the LP topped out at #72 and didn't even go gold, and these boys weren't accustomed to that, so they bailed. Which says something about the band's musical necessity (or lack thereof) that is only confirmed by listening to the soulless, mechanical rock-by-the-numbers that fills this record. —*William Ruhlmann*

Bad Manners

Group, Ska-Revival
Bad Manners, composed of vocalist Buster Bloodvessel (born Douglas Trendle), Louis Cook (guitar), Davis Farren (bass), Martin Stewart (keyboards), Brian Tuitti (drums), Gus Herman (trumpet), Chris Kane (saxophone), and Andrew Marson (saxophone), was one of the many bands to take its inspiration from the Specials and the ska revival movement in England in the late '70s. They quickly became the novelty favorites of the fad through their bald, enormous-bodied frontman's silly onstage antics, earning early exposure through 2-Tone Records package tours and an appearance in the live documentary *Dance Craze*. In the early '80s, they managed several U.K. hits including "Ne-Ne Na-Na Na-Na Nu-Nu," "Lip Up Fatty," "Special Brew" and "Can Can." By the mid-'80s, the ska craze was over and the band retired temporarily only to return in 1989 with *Return of the Ugly*, remaining a live attraction despite a lack of recent hits. —*Chris Woodstra*

Ska 'n' B / 1980 / Magnet ♦♦♦
Comprised mainly of goodtime party covers like "Monster Mash," the band's debut takes the "nutty sound" of Madness one step further toward all-out silliness. —*Chris Woodstra*

Loonee Tunes! / 1980 / Magnet ♦♦♦
Their second album (released only in the U.K.) continues in the mindless-fun direction of the *Ska'n'B*. —*Chris Woodstra*

○ **Bad Manners** / 1981 / MCA ♦♦♦♦
Their first American LP combines the highlights from their first U.K. release, *Ska'n'B*, and the second, *Loonee Tunes*. Juvenile fun and pure entertainment from the peak of the ska-revival. —*Chris Woodstra*

Gosh It's . . . Bad Manners / 1981 / Magnet ♦♦

Forging Ahead / 1982 / Magnet ♦♦♦
Forging Ahead shows the band in peak form for the last time as the ska-revival was losing momentum. Includes the hit cover of Millie's (retitled) classic "My Girl Lollipop." —*Chris Woodstra*

● **Klass** / 1983 / MCA ♦♦♦♦
This is the most representative collection of the band's fun version of ska/bluebeat. All of their British hits are covered including the endlessly catchy "Ne-Ne Na-Na Na-Na Nu-Nu." —*Chris Woodstra*

The Height of Bad Manners / 1983 / Telstar ♦♦♦
A fine import-only collection covering the band's peak in popularity and energy. —*Chris Woodstra*

Mental Notes / 1985 / Portrait ♦♦♦
An attempt at a more serious album after the novelty wore off, *Mental Notes* fails to capture the magic and fun of the early releases. The album moves from mind-numbing mediocrity to downright awful (as in their cover of Todd Rundgren's "Bang the Drum All Day"). —*Chris Woodstra*

Return of the Ugly / 1989 / Combat ✦✦✦
Return of the Ugly is an unexpected return to form after a long absence. Every bit as enjoyable as their early efforts but a commercial failure nearly a decade after the ska-revival peak. Worth seeking out. —*Chris Woodstra*

Fat Sound / 1993 / Triple X ✦✦✦

Bad Religion

Group, Alternative Pop/Rock
Out of all of the Southern Californian hardcore punk bands of the early '80s, Bad Religion stayed around the longest. For over a decade, they retained their underground credibility without turning out a series of indistinguishable records that all sound the same. Instead, the band refined their attack, adding inflections of psychedelia, heavy metal, and hard rock along the way, as well as a considerable dose of melody. Between their 1982 debut and their first major-label record, 1993's *Recipe for Hate*, Bad Religion stayed vital in the hardcore community by tightening their musical execution and keeping their lyrics complex and righteously angry.

Bad Religion formed in the northern suburbs of Los Angeles in 1980, comprising guitarist Brett Gurewitz, vocalist Greg Graffin, bassist Jay Bentley, and drummer Jay Lishrout. Gurewitz established his own record company, Epitaph, to release the band's records. Between their self-titled EP and their first full-length record, Pete Finestone replaced Lishrout as the group's drummer. *How Could Hell Be Any Worse?*, their debut album, was released in 1982 and it gained them some attention on the national U.S. hardcore scene. After its release, the group's lineup changed, as bassist Paul Dedona and drummer Davy Goldman joined the group. *Into the Unknown,* the group's second album, appeared in 1983. Featuring a vaguely psychedelized sound and several keyboards, the album was musically impressive, yet it made many of their fans angry and the band's following decreased dramatically.

In the meantime, the band's lineup was undergoing some more shakeups. Gurewitz had to take 1984 off to recover from various substance abuse problems, leaving Graffin as the band's only original member. In addition to Graffin, the 1984 incarnation of the band featured former Circle Jerks guitarist Greg Hetson, bassist Tim Gallegos, and returning drummer Pete Finestone. Bad Religion's next release, the harder, punkier *Back to the Known* EP restored faith among the group's devoted fans. After its release, the group went on hiatus for three years.

When Bad Religion returned in 1987, the band featured Gurewitz, Graffin, Lishrout, Hetson, and Finestone. They released *Suffer* the following year, a record that re-established the group as prominent players in the U.S. underground punk/hardcore scene. *No Control* (1989) and *Against the Grain* (1990). By the time of their 1993 album, *Recipe for Hate*, alternative rock had become popular with the mainstream; in addition, the band's following was quite large. These two factors contributed to Bad Religion signing a major-label contract with Atlantic Records. *Recipe for Hate* was originally released on Epitaph but it was soon re-released with the support of Atlantic. The group's first proper major-label album was 1994's *Stranger Than Fiction;* it was also Gurewitz's last album with the group. Before the release of *Stranger Than Fiction,* Epitaph had an unexpected hit with the Offspring's *Smash*, causing Gurewitz to spend more time at the label; reports also indicated that he was unpleased with Bad Religion's major label contract. The group replaced Gurewitz for their supporting tour, which proved to be their most successful to date. —*Stephen Thomas Erlewine*

How Can Hell Be Any Worse (1980-1985) / 1982 / Epitaph ✦✦✦
Durable standard Southern California post-punk hardcore with brains. —*John Dougan*

○ **Into the Unknown** / 1983 / Epitaph ✦✦✦✦
Slightly spacy but more direct and hard-hitting. (Mini-album) —*John Dougan*

Back to the Known / 1984 / Epitaph ✦✦
Apparently, Bad Religion felt they had departed from their hardcore roots too much on *Into the Unknown*, so they returned immediately with the aptly titled EP, *Back to the Known*. As the title suggests, the band eliminated all the hints of psychedelia and keyboards that flowed throughout the previous album, concentrating on relentless punk rock. While it's a stylistic retreat, the band's strength is blistering hardcore punk, which is something *Back to the Known* delivers in spades. —*Stephen Thomas Erlewine*

○ **Suffer** / 1988 / Epitaph ✦✦✦✦
Featuring a reunited version of the original band, *Suffer* is a fast, stripped-down, blazing record that relentlessly tears through its songs. In terms of sheer sonic intensity, *Suffer* is their best record yet, even if it is lacking in musical diversity. —*Stephen Thomas Erlewine*

● **No Control** / 1989 / Epitaph ✦✦✦✦
No Control is even more uncompromising than *Suffer*, except that this time, Bad Religion concentrated more on songwriting and melody, making the album their most impressive straight hardcore effort. —*Stephen Thomas Erlewine*

Against the Grain / 1990 / Epitaph ✦✦✦
Against the Grain continues the raging attack of *No Control,* and benefits from a clearer production, which makes the music sound even more threatening. In addition, Greg Graffin's lyrics have become more direct, which makes his social commentary all the more effective. —*Stephen Thomas Erlewine*

Recipe for Hate / 1993 / Atlantic ✦✦✦
Although it doesn't sound all that different from what X was doing ten years ago (and fairly close to the music they were making, too), the seminal L.A. punk rockers gained a larger audience with *Recipe for Hate.* Featuring guest spots from Eddie Vedder and Johnette Napolitano from Concrete Blonde, *Recipe for Hate* features a smoother version of punk. All of the trademark anger and guitars are still present, but some of the melodies, harmonies and riffs lean toward mainstream rock & roll. Fortunately, this all works in Bad Religion's favor—their music is more accessible, but it doesn't lack integrity. —*Stephen Thomas Erlewine*

Stranger Than Fiction / 1994 / Atlantic ✦✦
As if to prove that signing to a major label hasn't affected their sound at all, Bad Religion turns in one of their hardest records to date with *Stranger Than Fiction.* Despite several fine moments, including the galvanizing re-recorded single "20th Century Digital Boy," the album sounds more like a retreat than a step forward. Bad Religion have been making this music for nearly 15 years and often with more imagination than this; *Stranger Than Fiction* may rock, but it never stretches boundaries. —*Stephen Thomas Erlewine*

The Bad Seeds

Group, Garage Rock
Corpus Christi, TX, was one of the most notable fountains of garage rock in the 1960s, and the Bad Seeds were the first group of note on the scene. They released three singles on the local J-Beck label, which went on to record Zakary Thaks, whose 45s are esteemed by collectors as among the very best garage music of the '60s, even though they remain virtually unknown to all but the most avid historians. The Bad Seeds were not as good as Zakary Thaks, and released a few respectable singles in the raunchy, heavily Stones-influenced garage style that was a trademark of Texas rock groups in the mid-'60s. Lead singer Mike Taylor released a few singles on his own in a folk-pop style after the Bad Seeds split. —*Richie Unterberger*

J Beck Story / 1984 / Eva ✦✦✦
A compilation of all three of the Bad Seeds' singles, as well as six tunes cut by Mike Taylor as a solo act. Most of the Bad Seeds' material is respectable '60s Texas punk (one of the singles was a surfish instrumental). Taylor's singles, which aren't at all similar to the Bad Seeds, are pop-folk in the P.F. Sloan vein, ranging from pleasant to disposable. —*Richie Unterberger*

Badfinger

Group, Power Pop/Anglo-Pop, Pop/Rock
Rarely has a recorded group had so much apparent opportunity and so much bad luck as Badfinger. Paul McCartney discovered Badfinger's demo and signed them to the Beatles' Apple label. McCartney penned their first hit, "Come and Get It," which was featured (along with a couple of their other songs) in the movie *The Magic Christian,* and their debut, *Magic Christian Music.* With their follow-up, *No Dice,* Badfinger's image as a poor man's Beatles began to evaporate, due to the new sophistication found in the writing skills of all the band members. George Harrison and Todd Rundgren took turns producing their third album, *Straight Up,* which had two more international hits with "Baby Blue" and "Day After Day." Poised to take advantage of this great success,

Badfinger lost momentum as Apple Records began to crumble under mismanagement and confusion.

In November 1973, Badfinger released *Ass*–a good album, but one that was a little rough around the edges. Only months later, Badfinger released their self-titled debut for Warners, who were eager to try to regain the momentum from *Straight Up*. The album was an improvement over *Ass*, but it still suffered from the hasty release. Determined to get it right, Badfinger went into the studio with Chris Thomas and produced some of their very best music in *Wish You Were Here*.

Upon discovering a questionable disappearance of monies from Badfinger's publishing escrow account, Warners pulled the record weeks after its release, in spite of glowing reviews. Undaunted but terribly upset by the situation, the band cut another album, *Head First*, which Warners also barred from release.

Depressed by personal and professional problems, Pete Ham (guitar/vocal/keys) hung himself in his garage on April 23, 1975. After a five year break, Tom Evans (bass/vocals) and Joey Molland (guitar/vocals) regrouped and released the spotty *Airwaves* on Elektra; the subsequent *Say No More* was even weaker. In 1983, Evans (bass/vocals), frustrated over not receiving proper royalty compensation and other endless band business problems, took his life. Molland sporadically continued with Badfinger during the rest of the '80s and '90s, hiring different sidemen for each tour, while also pursuing a solo career. —*Rick Clark*

Magic Christian Music / Feb. 16, 1970 / Capitol ✦✦✦
Magic Christian Music is Badfinger's uneven debut. The band hadn't found their *sound* yet. Nevertheless, tracks like "Come and Get It" and "Maybe Tomorrow" gave power-pop fans a good taste of this band's potential. —*Rick Clark*

○ **No Dice** / Nov. 9, 1970 / Capitol ✦✦✦✦
Badfinger's distinctive melodic abilities, great vocals, and solid ensemble work on *No Dice*, was a strong case that this quartet could stand on its own, apart from Apple's shadow. "I Can't Take It," "Midnight Caller," the beautifully romantic "We're for the Dark," and "No Matter What," (one of the greatest pop singles ever), are among *No Dice*'s many highlights. —*Rick Clark*

○ **Straight Up** / Dec. 13, 1971 / Capitol ✦✦✦✦
George Harrison and Todd Rundgren took turns producing Badfinger's third album, *Straight Up*, which produced two international hits with the gorgeous "Day After Day" and the wall-of-sound pop/rock masterpiece "Baby Blue." Badfinger forges a unique sound with their sweeping, strained high harmonies, thick, edgy rhythm-guitar parts, and a drumming style that featured an exaggerated hi-hat attack on the backbeat. Check out "Take It All," "Sometimes," and the powerful "It's Over" for examples. —*Rick Clark*

Ass / Nov. 26, 1973 / Apple ✦✦✦
A step down from Badfinger's two previous classics, *Ass* was the final kiss-off on the Beatles' rapidly deteriorating Apple Record label. In spite of some fairly inconsequential tracks, "Apple of My Eye" (the single), "Icicles," "I Can Love You," and the first half of the "I Want You/She's So Heavy" rip, "Timeless," more than redeem this release. —*Rick Clark*

Badfinger / Feb. 1974 / Warner Brothers ✦✦
Tentatively titled *For Love or Money*, this was an unfortunate rush job that, in spite of it all, generated a handful of fine songs. Produced by Chris Thomas (Beatles, Roxy Music, Pink Floyd), Joey Molland's darkly meditative "Give It Up," "Andy Norris," and "Island" are fine contributions. "Lonely You," "Shine On," and "Song for a Lost Friend" showcase Pete Ham's emotive lower tenor and his considerable melodic skills. On the down side, "Matted Spam" is a horrible attempt at marrying soul with their sound, and "I Miss You" has enough sugar on it to put Paul McCartney into a coma. Regardless of that, fans of the band will be glad to know that an import CD can be obtained. —*Rick Clark*

Wish You Were Here / Nov. 1974 / Warner Brothers ✦✦✦
After many professional and personal distractions, Badfinger refocused their creative energies and, with producer Chris Thomas, created one of their finest albums. The urgent fanfare of the opening track, "Just a Chance," sets the make-it-or-break-it undercurrent here. This features two impressive medleys, "In the Meantime/Some Other Time" and "Meanwhile Back at the Ranch/Should I Smoke," which features stately horn backing by the Average White Band. (Import) —*Rick Clark*

Airwaves / Mar. 1979 / Elektra ✦✦
Using the magic of overdubbing and a complement of star studio musicians, Tom Evans and Joey Molland take a respectable shot at recreating the three-part harmonies and pop sheen of the early '70s Badfinger. "I want to get back," Evans sings on the title track, and you would, too, if you had been reduced to manual labor after hobnobbing with the Beatles. Like early Badfinger, much of this evokes their old mentors, especially "Love Is Gonna Come At Last" (#69), their first singles chart hit in seven years. Often, however, the material is only pedestrian, and although this album actually did a little better commercially than the group's two Warner Bros. albums of 1974, it didn't make for a real comeback. —*William Ruhlmann*

Say No More / 1981 / Radio ✦✦
Badfinger lists itself as a quintet on this album, including longtime members Joey Molland and Tom Evans, plus keyboard player Tony Kaye, drummer Richard Bryans, and guitar player Glenn Sherba. Certainly, they sound more like a band on this record than they did on its predecessor, *Airwaves*, which was basically a Molland-Evans duo album, but that is not an improvement. They tend to rock out more here, downplaying the more folkish and melodic pop tendencies in their music. Sometimes, as on "Because I Love You," they sound like the Raspberries trying to sound like the Beatles. The hit, such as it was, was "Hold On" (#56), a shadow of former glories, and although this album charted briefly, it only confirmed that Badfinger was no longer a record seller. —*William Ruhlmann*

○ **The Best of Badfinger, Vol. 2** / 1989 / Rhino ✦✦✦✦
A decent attempt at chronicling the last half of their career, which included one of the great lost pop/rock albums of the '70s, *Wish You Were Here*. With the exception of important tracks like Joey Molland's "Love Time" and Pete Ham's "Dennis," *Wish…* is well represented. Key tracks from the self-titled Warner debut are included, as well as several sides from the never-released *Head First*. Also included are the only two tracks worth having from their 1979 album *Airwaves*. Until the Warner albums get released on CD stateside (which is doubtful), this is the only place you can get these fine tracks. —*Rick Clark*

Day After Day: Live / Sep. 24, 1990 / Rykodisc ✦✦
A live set from 1974, it was recorded in Cleveland. —*Dan Heilman*

● **Come and Get It: The Best of Badfinger** / 1995 / Apple ✦✦✦✦
A well-chosen 21-track best-of, wisely emphasizing their melodic, tender side rather than their oft-pedestrian hard rockers, *Come and Get It* draws from all four of their late-'60s and early-'70s Apple albums, although the absence of "We're For The Dark" from *No Dice* is a signficant omission. —*Richie Unterberger*

Badlands

Group, Hard Rock
After spending some time in the coveted role as Ozzy Osbourne's guitarist in the mid-'80s, Jake E. Lee decided to form his own band after he left Ozzy's band. Formed in 1988, Badlands kicked out a rougher, bluesier brand of metal than what Lee played during his years with Osbourne. While earning respect in the metal world, Badlands weren't able to cross over to a wider audience. —*Stephen Thomas Erlewine*

● **Badlands** / Jun. 1989 / Atlantic ✦✦✦✦
Great blues-influenced metal by the band, featuring Jake E. Lee, formerly the guitarist for Ozzy Osbourne. —*John Book*

Voodoo Highway / Jun. 1991 / Atlantic ✦✦✦
A more blues-rock oriented album than the debut featuring the single "The Last Time." —*Robert DeFreitas*

David Baerwald

Singer-Songwriter, Pop/Rock
After the quick dissolution of David & David in the mid-'80s, David Baerwald began a solo career, releasing his solo debut, *Bedtime Stories*, in 1990. As with David & David's sole album, it was an album of deceptively laidback pop; the calm production and subtle, memorable melodies hid the fact that Baerwald's characters were either inflicting or suffering from emotional pain. It was a triumph, winning raves from critics, but it sold very few copies. With his second album, 1993's *Triage*, Baerwald decided to have the music match the message, creating soundscapes that recalled a subdued, more pop-friendly Tom Waits. Again, the critical praise was substantial but the record sold even less than the first. —*Stephen Thomas Erlewine*

● **Bedtime Stories** / May 1990 / A&M ◆◆◆◆
Sparse arrangements lay the foundation for Baerwald's thought-provoking musings and solid vocals. —*Donna DiChario*

Triage / Oct. 6, 1992 / A&M ◆◆◆
Like *Bedtime Stories, Triage* focuses on deceit and corruption, but this time the political and social is mixed in with the personal. Baerwald's music fits his themes, with dark guitars and synthesizers covering the clanking percussion. It's a remarkably accomplished record, even if its pretensions sometimes overwhelm its accomplishments. —*Stephen Thomas Erlewine*

Joan Baez

b. Jan. 9, 1941, Staten Island, NY
Folk
The most accomplished interpretive folksinger of the '60s, Joan Baez has influenced nearly every aspect of popular music in a career still going strong after more than 30 years. Baez is possessed of a once-in-a-lifetime soprano, which, since the late '50s, she has put in the service of folk and pop music as well as a variety of political causes. Starting out in Boston, Baez first gained recognition at the 1959 Newport Folk Festival, then cut her debut album, *Joan Baez*, released in December 1960. The record was made up of 13 traditional songs, some of them Child ballads, given near-definitive treatment. A moderate success on release, the album took off after the breakthrough of *Joan Baez—Vol. 2*, released a year later, and both albums became huge hits, as did Baez's third album, *Joan Baez in Concert*. Each album went gold and stayed in the bestseller charts more than two years.

From 1962 to 1964, Baez was the popular face of folk music, headlining festivals and concert tours and singing at a variety of political rallies, including the August 1963 March on Washington led by Dr. Martin Luther King, Jr. During this period, she began to champion the work of folk songwriter Bob Dylan, and gradually her repertoire moved from traditional material toward the socially conscious work of the emerging generation of '60s artists like him.

In the late '60s and early '70s, Baez moved toward country and rock music and also began to write her own songs, culminating in the gold-selling *Diamonds & Rust* in 1975. Since then, while her recording career has gradually declined, she has maintained her status on the concert circuit and her commitment to social issues. —*William Ruhlmann*

☆ **Joan Baez** / 1960 / Vanguard ◆◆◆◆◆
Revelatory first album features Baez singing traditional folk songs. —*William Ruhlmann*

Joan Baez in Concert, Part 2 / 1963 / Vanguard ◆◆◆
A superb follow-up to *Part 1*, with some more interesting material. —*Bruce Eder*

5 / 1964 / Vanguard ◆◆◆
A good folk set, from a variety of sources. —*Bruce Eder*

Farewell, Angelina / 1965 / Vanguard ◆◆◆
Baez moves toward contemporary work, with songs by Donovan and Woody Guthrie. She sings four songs by Bob Dylan, including the title track. —*William Ruhlmann*

○ **Noel** / 1966 / Vanguard ◆◆◆◆
An album of stately beauty, Baez's pure, soaring soprano is accompanied by a consort of recorders and viols, lute, harpsichord, baroque organ, winds, strings, and percussion. Her rendition of the "Coventry Carol" is stirring, and Baez pours her heart into "The Carol of the Birds." Considering Baez's politics, one would never know she recorded this album in the Vietnam War era. —*Decibel Dennis MacDonald*

Joan / 1967 / Vanguard ◆◆◆
Ornate, heavily orchestrated versions of other people's songs. Over-produced, but quite beautiful. —*Bruce Eder*

Any Day Now / 1968 / Vanguard ◆◆◆
All-Dylan album includes definitive performance of "Love Is Just a Four-Letter Word." —*William Ruhlmann*

● **The First Ten Years** / 1970 / Vanguard ◆◆◆◆
A nearly perfect cross-section of her most enduring work, both traditional and contemporary. —*Bruce Eder*

Come from the Shadows / 1972 / A&M ◆◆◆
After recording for the folk label Vanguard for more than a decade, Baez moved to A&M. On this label debut, she maintained her interest in country music, recording in Nashville with some of the city's session aces. She also continued to dedicate herself to

radical politics, from her set opener "Prison Trilogy," which pledged, "We're gonna raze the prisons to the ground," to the closer, John Lennon's "Imagine." In between were her call on Bob Dylan to return to protest music ("To Bobby") and her sister Mimi Farina's touching tribute to Janis Joplin, "In the Quiet Morning." —*William Ruhlmann*

Hits the Greatest & Others / 1973 / Vanguard ◆◆◆
An alternate cross-section of Baez's Vanguard music, including her monster hit "The Night They Drove Old Dixie Down." —*Bruce Eder*

Where Are You Now, My Son? / 1973 / A&M ◆◆◆
This isn't only *not* the place to start listening to Joan Baez, it's the album that separates the true fans from the, um, fellow travelers. Side 2 is taken up by the title song, a musical account of Baez's trip to Hanoi over Christmas of 1972, complete with the sound of U.S. bombs falling on the city. Side 1, on the other hand, contains one of Baez's best original songs, "A Young Gypsy," and two by her sister, "Mary Call" and "Best of Friends." —*William Ruhlmann*

★ **Diamonds and Rust** / 1975 / A&M ◆◆◆◆◆
Baez's peak as a songwriter (title track) and folk/rock interpreter, singing songs of Jackson Browne, John Prine, and Bob Dylan. —*William Ruhlmann*

Joan Baez in Concert / 1976 / Vanguard ◆◆◆
A vibrant concert recording with a radiant sound, humor, and topicality. —*Bruce Eder*

○ **The Best of Joan Baez** / 1977 / A&M ◆◆◆◆
Emotionally charged songs from her '70s albums on A&M. Not early Baez, this album of touching songs is probably too commercial for diehard folk fans. Excellent. —*Michael Erlewine*

Honest Lullaby / 1979 / Portrait ◆◆◆
On her second album for CBS's Portrait label (and her last new album issued in the U.S. for eight years), Baez was given a full-scale pop-rock production by veteran Barry Beckett and the studio band in Muscle Shoals, AL. The result, on songs that range from "Let Your Love Flow" to "Before the Deluge," is accessible but not particularly memorable '70s-style pop. If you always wanted to know what the words to "No Woman, No Cry" are, however, this is the place to find out. —*William Ruhlmann*

Very Early Joan Baez / 1983 / Vanguard ◆◆◆
A masterful raid on the vault, recapturing the purity and simplicity of her debut recording. —*Bruce Eder*

○ **Live Europe 83: Children of the Eighties** / 1983 / Ariola ◆◆◆◆
While Baez declined to record again in the U.S. unless she could get on a major label, she did make several live albums in Europe in the interim. This is the best of them, mixing old favorites like "Farewell, Angelina" with new originals like her heartfelt "For the Children of the Eighties." (Import) —*William Ruhlmann*

○ **Recently** / 1988 / Gold Castle ◆◆◆◆
Baez returned to U.S. record shops with a vengeance here, delivering her interpretations of songs by Dire Straits, Johnny Clegg, U2, and Peter Gabriel, performers whose political consciousness had been formed by listening to old Joan Baez albums. And on the title track, a stunning original, she boldly answered ex-husband David Harris's downbeat memoir of the '60s, "Dreams Die Hard," as well as other '80s revisionists. —*William Ruhlmann*

○ **Rare, Live & Classic** / Sep. 1993 / Vanguard ◆◆◆◆
Spanning three discs, the box set *Rare, Live & Classic* is an odd mix of Baez's best-known songs and rarities. For the hardcore collector, there are plenty of interesting items here, including previously unreleased duets with Bob Dylan, Donovan, Bill Wood, and Jeffrey Shurtleff, but for the casual fan, there's too much material; they would be better off with her original albums or single-disc compilations. —*Stephen Thomas Erlewine*

Philip Bailey

b. May 8, 1951, Denver, CO
Soul, Urban
The falsetto-singing co-lead vocalist in Earth, Wind & Fire, Philip Bailey, launched a solo career during the band's hiatus, resulting in his hit duet with Phil Collins, "Easy Lover," in 1985. He also makes gospel records.

Bailey has continued the juggling act between Urban Contemporary material and gospel through the '80s and '90s. A greatest hits collection of his gospel singles was issued by Word/Epic in 1991, and his LP *Family Affair* was also reissued that year. —*William Ruhlmann and Ron Wynn*

Continuation / 1983 / CBS ♦♦
Philip Bailey's debut solo album. — *William Ruhlmann*

The Wonders of His Love / 1985 / Word ♦♦
Philip Bailey's debut gospel album. — *William Ruhlmann*

● **Chinese Wall** / 1985 / Columbia ♦♦♦♦
At the time Philip Bailey persuaded Phil Collins to produce his second solo album, *Chinese Wall*, Collins was among the hottest pop stars in the world. The advantage to that, of course, is the exposure it affords, and after the merely modest success of his debut solo album, *Continuation*, Bailey needed the reflected glory. On the other band, it's hard to shine yourself in such a glare, and although Bailey's name was on the gold-selling hit single "Easy Lover," a duet with Collins that helped the album take off, it's Collins' singing and drumming that one remembers. Elsewhere, tunes like "Photogenic Memory" and "Walking On The Chinese Wall" better represent Bailey's ability to handle a variety of material from ballads to techno dance tracks with his elastic falsetto. Still, *Chinese Wall* was a gold-selling standoff that made Bailey a solo hitmaker without really establishing him on his own. — *William Ruhlmann*

Triumph / 1986 / Word ♦♦
Philip Bailey's second gospel album. — *William Ruhlmann*

Family Affair / 1989 / Word ♦♦
Philip Bailey's third gospel album. — *William Ruhlmann*

Inside Out / 1990 / CBS ♦♦
Philip Bailey turned to Nile Rodgers to produce *Inside Out*, his followup to *Chinese Wall*, and though Rodgers didn't turn it into a dance record on the order of his old band Chic (the sort of thing he did do to other clients), the result is no more than pedestrian Black pop, which is why Bailey's secular solo career ran out of gas at this point and he willingly re-upped with the new edition of Earth, Wind & Fire. He didn't make another secular solo album for eight years. — *William Ruhlmann*

Philip Bailey / Mar. 29, 1994 / Zoo

○ **The Best of Philip Bailey: A Gospel Collection** / Word ♦♦♦♦
This is a compilation album culled from Philip Bailey's three gospel albums, *The Wonders Of His Love, Triumph*, and *Family Affair*. Bailey brings the same creamy pop production and warm falsetto singing to his inspirational work that he does to his solo albums and to Earth, Wind & Fire, although he is far gentler here (except when he's being religiously righteous on "Call To War"). Note that this is listed as the pick among his gospel albums, not his entire solo catalog. — *William Ruhlmann*

Bailter Space

Group, Alternative Pop/Rock
From the ashes of New Zealand's punk guitar experimentalists the Gordons several years after the group disbanded, their former guitarists formed Bailter Space in 1987. Not quite as assaultive as the Gordons, Bailter Space did retain a good portion of their previous band's sonic attack, although now it was applied to more fully formed pop songs which occasionally even featured keyboards. — *Stephen Thomas Erlewine*

○ **Tanker** / 1988 / Flying Nun ♦♦♦♦
Thermos / 1990 / Flying Nun ♦♦♦
● **Aim** / Matador ♦♦♦♦
Robot World / Matador ♦♦♦

Dan Baird

b. Dec. 12, 1953
Rock & Roll
After the Georgia Satellites disbanded at the end of the '80s, their lead singer/songwriter Dan Baird embarked on his own solo career in 1992. Not surprisingly, it sounded a lot like the Satellites' energetic, straightforward rock & roll. — *Stephen Thomas Erlewine*

○ **Love Songs for the Hearing Impaired** / Oct. 1991 / Def American ♦♦♦♦
Love Songs for the Hearing Impaired is straight, raw rock & roll that only *seems* shallow; it's hard work to write something as irresistibly stupid as "I Love You Period" and something as touching as "Julie." Baird's songwriting maintains that peak throughout the album, while he and his band never stop rocking for a second. — *Stephen Thomas Erlewine*

Anita Baker

b. Dec. 20, 1957, Detroit, MI
Soul, Urban, Pop
Anita Baker's strong, sensual alto helped her break the doors down in the middle of the '80s. More than any other singer, she defined quiet storm—smooth, romantic soul for adults. Baker's music is sophisticated without being cold, romantic without being saccharine; besides soul, her singing has roots in jazz and classic pop, bringing a refined romanticism to her music. Although her 1983 debut, *The Songstress*, disappeared upon its release, her 1986 album, *Rapture*, was a modern classic that ushered in a new era of urban contemporary and modern pop singing. None of her following records were quite as good, but her singing remains impressive on each album and she remained one of the most popular urban/adult contemporary singers of the '80s and '90s. — *Stephen Thomas Erlewine*

○ **The Songstress** / Jun. 1983 / Elektra ♦♦♦♦
Not too many people heard it at the time of its release, but this album contains Baker's characteristically tasteful arrangements and remarkably evocative singing. Reissued by Elektra. — *William Ruhlmann*

● **Rapture** / Mar. 1986 / Elektra ♦♦♦♦
Baker invented a new musical genre, "quiet storm," with this gorgeous album of love ballads sung in her compelling voice. Contains "Caught Up In the Rapture" and the Top Ten hit "Sweet Love." — *William Ruhlmann*

Giving You the Best That I Got / Oct. 1988 / Elektra ♦♦♦
Baker topped the charts with this worthy follow-up to *Rapture*, which contains the hit title song and "Just Because." — *William Ruhlmann*

Compositions / Jun. 1990 / Elektra ♦♦♦
As a singer, Baker has more in common with Sarah Vaughan and Nancy Wilson than with most of her contemporaries. *Compositions*, for which Baker co-wrote seven of the tunes, evokes a lush, romantic atmosphere like its predecessors, and Baker recorded her vocals live with the rhythm section. — *Brian Mansfield*

Rhythm of Love / 1994 / Elektra ♦♦♦
Baker has been making solid, if unspectacular, records for several years now, trying to recapture the grace of *Rapture*. Despite several good songs and uniformly strong vocals, *Rhythm of Love* doesn't have enough flair to win back a mass audience. — *Stephen Thomas Erlewine*

Ginger Baker

b. Aug. 19, 1939, Lewisham, London, England
Fusion, Art-Rock/Progressive-Rock
Peter "Ginger" Baker is one of the most prominent drummers in popular music. He was born in Lewisham, London, and joined Alexis Korner's Blues, Incorporated in mid-1962, then moved on to the Graham Bond Trio (later the Graham Bond Organization) in February 1963, where he played with bassist Jack Bruce. The two then joined guitarist Eric Clapton in the summer of 1966 to form Cream, one of the most successful and influential British blues-rock groups of the late '60s. Cream broke up in November 1968 and was succeeded by Blind Faith, featuring Baker, Clapton, Steve Winwood, and Rick Grech, which lasted for one album and tour in 1969. In January 1970, Baker formed the loosely organized Ginger Baker's Air Force, which recorded two albums. He formed the Baker Gurvitz Army with Adrian and Paul Gurvitz in late 1974, and they made three albums. At the end of the decade, he had such groups as Energy and Ginger Baker's Nutters and played with Hawkwind and Atomic Rooster, before retiring to play polo. In 1982, he moved to an olive farm in Italy. But he was wooed back to music by producer Bill Laswell and made a number of instrumental albums before reuniting with Jack Bruce in BBM in 1994. — *William Ruhlmann*

○ **Ginger Baker's Air Force** / May 1970 / Polydor ♦♦♦♦
Early 70s all-star rock band. — *Michael G. Nastos*

○ **Horses & Trees** / 1986 / Celluloid ♦♦♦♦
This instrumental percussion album mixes rock with various world musics, especially African influences, creating a stimulating soundscape. An impressive return from one of popular music's most distinctive drummers. — *William Ruhlmann*

● **Middle Passage** / 1990 / Axiom ✦✦✦✦
With producer Bill Laswell, mixing African drummers (Ayib Di-eng, Mar Gueye, Magette Fall) with fusioneers (Bernie Worrell, Jonas Hellborg, Nicky Skopelitis) and bassists (Jah Wohble and Laswell) to land in a "middle passage" of worldbeat. Not bad at all. —*Michael G. Nastos*

Unseen Rain / 1992 / Dayight ✦✦✦
This is an instrumental trio album with drummer Ginger Baker as leader and also featuring bassist Jonas Hellborg and pianist Jens Johansson. Baker is characteristically busy at the drum kit, but the three play off each other well, creating what is in essence a free-form jazz date. —*William Ruhlmann*

LaVern Baker

b. Nov. 11, 1929, Chicago, IL
R&B
Baker began working Chicago clubs as Little Miss Sharecropper in 1946 and made recordings under that name for National in 1950. She also recorded with the Todd Rhodes band for King, but came to Atlantic in 1953 and quickly emerged as a bright star of rhythm and blues with twenty R&B chart hits between 1955 and 1965. The biggest were "Play It Fair," "Jim Dandy," and "I Cried a Tear". These and other hits are available on *Soul On Fire* (Atlantic). A versatile performer, she also recorded blues (*LaVern Baker Sings Bessie Smith*) and gospel for Atlantic. After a hiatus, she appeared in the Broadway show *Black and Blue*. A recent recording of her live nightclub act, *Live in Hollywood 91* (Rhino), is available. —*Bob Porter*

○ **Sings Bessie Smith** / Jan. 27, 1958 / Atlantic ✦✦✦✦
One of the best tribute albums ever, these Bessie Smith classics are updated just enough to suit Baker's style. She gets a rare opportunity to really show what she can do as a singer. Highly recommended. —*George Bedard*

Blues Ballads / 1959 / Atlantic ✦✦✦
Before she became a successful rock & roll vocalist, LaVern Baker did straight jazz and gutbucket blues, and that's what she's singing here. These tunes didn't have any crossover appeal, but they're gritty, unpolished, and sung with the intensity and energy that made Baker's later material so memorable. —*Ron Wynn*

Precious Memories / 1959 / Atlantic ✦✦✦
LaVern Baker sang gospel with passion, exuberance, and reverence on this '59 session. She was backed by a small combo with the Alex Bradford singers and sounded more magnificent and moving than at any time she had done jazz, blues or R&B. This one is very hard to find and has not as of yet been reissued on CD. —*Ron Wynn*

Saved / 1961 / Atlantic ✦✦✦
Early '60s jazz and blues material by LaVern Baker. She returned in the '60s to the songs she had cut prior to her rock and roll success. There was an interesting crew of guest stars on these sessions, among them Phil Spector on guitar, Sticks Evans on bass drums, and Taft Jordan on trumpet. Baker had a hit with a single from some earlier sessions, "You're the Boss with Jimmy Ricks." This song was issued on a single, but there's no listing for any album. —*Ron Wynn*

See See Rider / 1963 / Atlantic ✦✦✦
An excellent early '60s single by LaVern Baker, done in first-rate stomping, hollering fashion. It was similar in tone and style to the material that she cut for Atlantic in the '50s, although she didn't enjoy the same results. This song was included on a Charly anthology, *Real Gone Gal*, but was otherwise issued only as a single. —*Ron Wynn*

Let Me Belong to You / 1970 / Brunswick ✦

Real Gone Gal / 1984 / Charly ✦✦

★ **Soul on Fire: The Best of LaVern Baker** / 1991 / Rhino ✦✦✦✦✦
This well-annotated collection rounds up every important hit Baker had with Atlantic, and a few choice rarities as well. —*John Floyd*

LaVern Baker Live in Hollywood '91 / 1992 / Rhino ✦✦✦
Recent recordings show Baker can still belt out a song. She's returned to the jazz and jazzy blues sound of her youth. —*Ron Wynn*

Woke up This Mornin' / Apr. 1992 / DRG ✦✦

Mickey Baker

b. Oct. 15, 1925, Louisville, KY
R&B
Of all the guitarists who helped transform rhythm and blues into rock & roll, Mickey Baker is one of the very most important, ranking almost on the level of Chuck Berry and Bo Diddley. The reason he isn't nearly as well known as those legends is that a great deal of his work wasn't issued under his own name, but as a backing guitarist for many R&B and rock & roll musicians. Baker originally aspired to be a jazz musician, but turned to calypso, mambo, and then R&B, where the most work could be found. In the early and mid-'50s, he did countless sessions for Atlantic, King, RCA, Decca, and OKeh, playing on such classics as the Drifters' "Money Honey" and "Such a Night," Joe Turner's "Shake Rattle & Roll," Ruth Brown's "Mama, He Treats Your Daughter Mean," and Big Maybelle's "Whole Lot of Shakin' Going On." He also released a few singles under his own name, and made a Latin jazz-tinged solo album, *Guitar Mambo*. Baker's best work, though, was recorded as half of the duo Mickey & Sylvia. Their hit "Love Is Strange," as well as several other unknown but nearly equally strong tracks, featured Mickey's keening, bluesy guitar riffs, which were gutsier and more piercing than most anything else around in the late '50s. Mickey & Sylvia split in the late '50s (though they recorded off and on until the middle of the next decade), and Baker recorded his best solo album, the all-instrumental *The Wildest Guitar*, around 1960. In 1961, he took the male spoken part (usually assumed to be Ike Turner) on Ike & Tina Turner's first hit, "It's Gonna Work out Fine." Shortly afterwards he moved to France, making a few hard-to-find solo records and working with a lot of French pop and rock performers, including Ronnie Bird, the best '60s French rock singer. He's recorded only sporadically since the mid-'60s. —*Richie Unterberger*

Rock with a Sock / 1952-1957 / Bear Family ✦✦✦
This 28-cut single disc covers several early and mid-'50s tracks with Baker finding creative ways to perform on period-piece rock and R&B/novelty material. His playing is uniformly impressive, even when fitting into less-than-outstanding productions and compositions. There are five Mickey and Sylvia tracks that conclude the session; they range from the interesting "Hello Stranger" to the odd "Woe, Woe Is Me," but really take away from the disc's purpose—to showcase Mickey Baker the player and demonstrate why he has such a sterling reputation among guitar fans and musicians. —*Ron Wynn*

● **Wildest Guitar** / 1959 / Atlantic ✦✦✦✦
Despite Baker's well-deserved reputation as one of the most influential guitar players of early rock & roll, *The Wildest Guitar* was one of the few chances he really got to strut his stuff as a solo artist. This entirely instrumental set features keening, sharp bluesy riffs in much the same distinctive style that gained him fame on "Love Is Strange" and other tunes with Mickey & Sylvia. The choice of material, though, is a bit surprising, favoring some surprisingly cornball standards: "Third Man Theme," "Autumn Leaves," "Lullaby Of The Leaves," and Cole Porter's "Night And Day." Baker (who also arranged the album) manages to invest all of these with a snazzy R&B feel and biting solos. And he does actually write four of the twelve tunes himself, on which he fashions the kind of straightforward R&B that one would be more likely to expect. This is a pretty good showcase to hear Baker's unadorned virtuosity. But he's really better appreciated within the context of stronger material, either as half of Mickey & Sylvia or on the innumerable '50s R&B cuts (many on Atlantic) that feature his session work. —*Richie Unterberger*

Marty Balin

b. Jan. 30, 1942, Cincinnati, OH
Pop/Rock
The lead singer and cofounder of Jefferson Airplane, Marty Balin's aching tenor was the centerpiece of some of their most reflective recordings as well as a few hits, including his self-penned "Miracles," which went #3 for Jefferson Starship. In 1978, Balin left for a solo career that leaned more toward MOR pop than rock. His singles included "Hearts" (#8), "Atlanta Lady (Something About Your Love)" (#28), and "What Love Is." —*Rick Clark*

Balin Top Tracks / 1981 / EMI America ✦

Balin / May 1981 / EMI America ✦✦
Nearly 40, Marty Balin returned to his long-interrupted solo career in 1981 after spending 16 years founding and leading Jefferson Airplane and guiding Jefferson Starship to new heights. The

aching tenor was in place and the pop sensibility was as strong as ever (there were two hits, "Hearts" [#8] and "Atlanta Lady [Something About Your Love]" [#27]), but the album was a disappointment to fans who had waited so long for Balin to make his move. He leaned on his friend Jesse Barish for material, contributing to only one of the songs as co-composer, and although his voice conveyed erotic longing as strongly as it had on Starship hits like "Miracles," as a solo artist he seemed to lack the rock edge the group had provided. —*William Ruhlmann*

Lucky / Feb. 1983 / EMI America ✦✦

Having established himself as a solo artist with his debut album, *Balin*, Marty Balin did not address the shortcomings of that record (mediocre playing and writing) on its follow-up. Instead, he was put in the hands of producer Val Garay, who constructed a contemporary pop-rock album around him without much attention to his strengths as a singer or writer. (Again, Balin's pen was nearly absent.) The singles were the love songs "What Love Is" (#63) and "Do It For Love" (#102), but they didn't match earlier efforts in the same style, and radio and record company lost sight of the album shortly after its release, scuttling Balin's major label solo career. —*William Ruhlmann*

● **Balince: A Collection** / 1990 / Rhino ✦✦✦✦

Drawing from his days as a lead vocalist for both Jefferson Airplane and Starship and from his solo recordings, this best-of also includes five unreleased tracks. —*Jeff Tamarkin*

Better Generation / Dec. 1991 / GWE ✦✦✦

His smooth-as-silk voice as inviting as ever, Balin showcases new material and remakes a couple of Airplane favorites on this 1991 recording. —*Jeff Tamarkin*

Hearts & Other Classics / 1992 / CEMA ✦✦

B.A.L.L.

Group, Alternative Pop/Rock
More infatuated with the image of pop music than its sound, B.A.L.L. set out to satirize bloated '70s rock in all of its glory. And it wasn't *Dark Side of the Moon* that was their target; it was George Harrison's *Concert for Bangladesh*, as well as T. Rex and Bob Dylan. The cover of their second album, *Bird*, lampooned the Beatles' "butcher cover" for *Yesterday and Today*.

Not surprisingly, B.A.L.L. featured two superstars of the American indie underground—ex-Shockabilly guitarist Kramer, and former Half Japanese and Velvet Monkeys guitarist Don Fleming. Along with their two drummers, David Licht (also of Shockabilly) and Jay Spiegel (also of Half Japanese), the band cranked out four albums of driving guitars soaking in distortion with a relentless beat. After their final album in 1990, the group split with Kramer, pursuing production work for his Shimmy Disc record label among other side projects like Bongwater; Fleming became a highly regarded record producer (Sonic Youth, the Posies, Alice Cooper) and formed another band, Gumball. —*Stephen Thomas Erlewine*

Period / 1987 / Shimmy Disc ✦✦✦

B.A.L.L.'s first album was a stab at post-modern musical satire, with the grungy quartet deconstructing rock classics and writing songs that ridiculed the self-absorbed obsessions of the '70s. In theory, it's a clever idea, yet *Period* only was partially successful because the band had neither written enough hooks to make their originals memorable, nor had they developed a distinctive sound. Nevertheless, there are enough isolated moments of infectious audacity to make *Period* worthwhile. —*Stephen Thomas Erlewine*

○ **Bird** / 1988 / Shimmy Disc ✦✦✦✦

With their second album, *Bird*, B.A.L.L. managed to perfect the jokey pop culture satire they sketched out on their debut album. From the parody of the Beatles' "butcher cover" to the disembowlments of T. Rex's "Buick Mackane" and Ringo Starr's "It Don't Come Easy," the record revels in its hipper-than-thou pretentions, yet B.A.L.L. has developed a dirty guitar grind that keeps them from falling into their own cleverness. —*Stephen Thomas Erlewine*

Trouble Doll / 1989 / Shimmy Disc ✦✦

Trouble Doll combines a mediocre side of live *Bird* material with a side of original songs that collapse in their own self-conscious, grungy incoherence. —*Stephen Thomas Erlewine*

● **Four (Hardball)** / 1990 / Shimmy Disc ✦✦✦✦

Lots of chops, plenty of fun. Their most well-thought-out record. —*John Dougan*

Hank Ballard & the Midnighters

b. Nov. 18, 1936, AL
R&B
Though born in Alabama, Ballard moved to Detroit at an early age, forming a doo-wop group called the Royals by age 16. He signed to the King label in early 1953. Mid-size chart hits followed, and the group's name was changed to the Midnighters to avoid confusion with labelmates the Five Royales when "Work with Me Annie" became a national hit. Banned because of "explicit" lyrics, the song spawned a flurry of answer records (some by Ballard himself), most of them hitting the R&B charts as well. The hits kept coming throughout the early '60s, but the flipside of one of them became a national hit when Chubby Checker rerecorded "The Twist," spawning a national craze. Ballard's best records are informed by gospel-style harmonies and gritty guitar work, usually played by Alonzo Tucker. —*Cub Koda*

○ **Singin' & Swingin'** / Jun. 1959 / King ✦✦✦✦

Vintage red-hot R&B, shouting vocals, and frenzied instrumentals. Hank Ballard led one of the finest R&B orchestras on the '50s circuit, and his King albums are masterpieces. His singing was usually steamy, his lyrics laden with innuendo, and he kept up a furious pace throughout each album. This is one of about 10 Ballard albums that have been reissued on CD, and is certainly well worth getting in any configuration. —*Ron Wynn*

★ **Sexy Ways: The Best of Hank Ballard & The Midnighters** / 1993 / Rhino ✦✦✦✦✦

Hank Ballard & the Midnighters were the 2 Live Crew of the early '50s, burning up the airwaves and black jukeboxes with lascivious-for-the-time period tunes like "Work with Me Annie," "Annie Had a Baby" and the title track. Although Ballard would go on to write dance hits including the original version of "The Twist," the Midnighters at their best ("Open Up the Back Door") were Black doo-wop at the end of a dark alley. Forget all previous compilations on these guys, this is the one you want. —*Cub Koda*

Afrika Bambaataa

Rap, Urban
Some call him the godfather of rap; others put him in the category of genre creator. Bronx disc jockey Afrika Bambaataa's record "Planet Rock," co-written by John Robie and produced by Arthur Baker, was the seminal presentation of scratching, electronic additions, high-tech beats, cutting rhythms, and highly processed vocals. The single, and its followers like "Looking for the Perfect Beat" and "Renegades of Funk" opened the door for the '80s electro-funk movement. Later, his collaboration with James Brown on "Unity" and his joint vocals with John Lydon on "World Destruction" furthered the link between hip-hop, funk, soul, and rock. He's also done other work as a member of the group Shango, but it's as a producer, compositional force, rapper, and father figure that Afrika Bambaataa rules within the hip-hop nation. —*Ron Wynn*

☆ **Looking for the Perfect Beat** / 1982 / Tommy Boy ✦✦✦✦✦

Producer Arthur Baker proved the real star on this seminal 1982 album, adding what were then state-of-the art studio effects and mixing gimmicks to balance often repetitive rhythms. This was a milestone record, despite what sound like limited rap skills by 1990s standards. —*Ron Wynn*

○ **Unity** / 1984 / Tommy Boy ✦✦✦✦

★ **Planet Rock** / 1986 / Tommy Boy ✦✦✦✦✦

All the important early 12-inchers from 1982-1984 are here, including "Planet Rock" and "Looking for the Perfect Beat," plus three previously unreleased tracks. (Recorded with Soulsonic Force) —*John Floyd*

○ **Beware (The Funk Is Everywhere)** / 1986 / Tommy Boy ✦✦✦✦

Another stunning assortment of singles are included, with heavier beats, thicker rhythms, and a blistering cover of the MC5's "Kick Out the Jams." —*John Floyd*

Death Mix Throwdown / 1987 / Blatant ✦✦

The Light / 1988 / EMI America ✦✦

Diverse personalities and styles are the hook for this 1988 album, which isn't a Bambaataa project, but a group effort with some Bambaataa involvement. The guest list ranges from Boy George to

George Clinton, Yellowman, UB40 and Bootsy Collins, with Bambaataa offering a brief, rather formulaic rap on UB40's "Reckless" and "Shout It Out." This was a mildly entertaining effort, but so varied that there was no cohesion or unified focus. *—Ron Wynn*

1990-2000: The Decade of Darkness / Jun. 1991 / EMI America
♦♦♦

After several lackluster albums, Bambaataa came back with a record that explored modern-day dance trends without losing his signature sound. Fueled by righteous social commentary throughout the songs, the record showed that he wasn't creatively spent. It wasn't as innovative as his groundbreaking singles from the early '80s, but it was far from being an embarrassment. *—Stephen Thomas Erlewine*

Don't Stop . . . Planet Rock [The Remix Ep] / 1992 / Tommy Boy
♦♦

An updated EP takes the by-now-ancient "Planet Rock" beat and runs it through the 1990s hip-hop production machine. The results aren't all that successful, even though the sound is now contemporary. But its hook was old-school, as was its charm. The newer version lacks bite. *—Ron Wynn*

Bananarama

Group, Dance-Pop, Pop/Rock
This British female dance-pop vocal trio, consisting of Sarah Dallin, Keren Woodward, and Siobhan Fahey, came on the scene just as MTV was becoming an influential force in the early '80s. Some of Bananarama's early recordings were with English artists Fun Boy Three. Their slight, airy vocals and strong grooves earned them a number of hits on both sides of the Atlantic. In the U.K., their biggest singles were "He Was Really Sayin' Somethin'" (with the Fun Boy Three), "Shy Boy," "Na Na Hey Hey Kiss Him Goodbye" (a remake of the hit by Steam), "Cruel Summer," "Robert De Niro's Waiting," "Venus" (a remake of the Shocking Blue hit), "Love in the First Degree," "I Want You Back," and "Help" (the Beatles hit), all Top Ten hits, while in the U.S. they reached the Top Ten with "Cruel Summer," "Venus" (#1), and "I Heard a Rumour." Fahey, who married Dave Stewart of Eurythmics in August 1987, retired from the group in December (later to form Shakespear's Sister) and was replaced by Jacqui Sullivan, who quit in mid-1991, leaving Bananarama a duo. *—Rick Clark*

○ **Deep Sea Skiving** / Mar. 1983 / London ♦♦♦♦
Although this was not their American breakthrough, it was their biggest U.K. success, hitting the Top Ten and featuring the hits "He Was Really Sayin' Somethin'," "Shy Boy," and "Na Na Hey Hey Kiss Him Goodbye." It establishes the formula for the group's success, with its untrained unison trio singing and pop exuberance. The amateurishness of the singers was what made them so appealing. *— William Ruhlmann*

Bananarama / May 1984 / London ♦♦♦
The group adopted a more glamorous fashion style for this album, which finally brought them U.S. success with the Top Ten "Cruel Summer." Also included "Robert De Niro's Waiting." *— William Ruhlmann*

True Confessions / Jul. 1986 / Razor & Tie ♦♦♦
Bananarama scored its biggest U.S. hit with this third album, earning gold sales due to the #1 single "Venus." *—William Ruhlmann*

Wow / Sep. 1987 / London ♦♦♦

● **Greatest Hits Collection** / Nov. 1988 / London ♦♦♦♦
All of Bananarama's irresistible hit singles are collected on this infectious disc. *—Stephen Thomas Erlewine*

Pop Life / 1991 / London ♦♦

The Band

Group, Rock & Roll
Composed of four Canadians and one American, the Band first came together in Toronto in the early '60s as Ronnie Hawkins's backup group. Hawkins recorded nine 45s for Roulette between 1959 and 1963. Drummer Levon Helm plays on all nine, guitarist Robbie Robertson and bass player Rick Danko can be heard on the last three, pianist Richard Manuel on the last two, and organist Garth Hudson plays on the final outing only. Leaving Hawkins collectively in early 1964, they called themselves the Levon Helm

Sextet, Levon and the Hawks, and (for a brief spell) the Canadian Squires, releasing two singles before becoming Bob Dylan's backup ensemble for his crazed electric tour of North America, Australia, and Europe in the fall of 1965 through the spring of 1966. (After a couple of gigs, Levon headed back to Arkansas.)

Playing with Dylan had a profound influence on the Band. Woodshedding for two years in Woodstock, NY, they released their debut album, *Music from Big Pink*, in summer 1968. Over the succeeding eight years, the Band stood completely apart from everything else happening in rock & roll. There was no precedent for what they did and there have been no antecedents. Ironically, given that they were four-fifths Canadian, their music embodied an essence of Americana that no one else in rock & roll has approached. Chief writer, Torontonian Robbie Robertson, wrote about the South, the land, rural America, tradition, and the value and richness of heritage and blood ties. The settings for his songs took place in cornfields, during the Civil War, and at carnivals at the edge of town. He was most concerned with displaced people and the passing of a way of life. Sonically, the Band was equally unique. Hudson played accordion, sax, and organ; drummer Levon Helm doubled on mandolin and guitar; pianist Manuel drummed whenever Helm was out front; bassist Rick Danko played fiddle when they needed a rural or "old-timey" feel; guitarist Robbie Robertson had a pinched, economical style that kept one teetering on the edge of tension. As a unit, they quite consciously avoided any of the current trends. They didn't want their voices to blend, because that is what everyone else was doing; they wanted their piano to sound like a funky old upright, not like a brand spanking new Yamaha Grand; and so on. In the process they created some of the most ethereal and evocative music imaginable. *—Rob Bowman*

☆ **Music from Big Pink** / Jul. 1, 1968 / Capitol ♦♦♦♦♦
Everything about the Band's debut album, *Music from Big Pink*, flew in the face of the current ethos of rock & roll in 1968. For example, the disc opens in an unusual fashion, with a ballad, the Richard Manuel/Bob Dylan composition "Tears of Rage." There is not a guitar solo on the album, and this was a time when Jeff Beck, Eric Clapton, and Jimi Hendrix ruled the world. There was a lot of harmony singing that was deliberately ragged: together but not together—community, where the people that made up the community could be individuals. And then there were the songs, enigmatic tales such as "The Weight," "Chest Fever," and the first released version of Bob Dylan's "I Shall Be Released." An unbelievably strong debut. (Also available as a Mobile Fidelity Ultradisc) *—Rob Bowman*

★ **The Band** / Sep. 22, 1969 / Capitol ♦♦♦♦♦
Big Pink had been a fine, even superior debut; *The Band* was their masterpiece. Robbie Robertson's songwriting had grown by leaps and bounds. As players, all five musicians had reached a completely new level of ensemble cohesion. The sum was very much greater than the parts, and the parts were as good as any that existed. The album's single, "Up on Cripple Creek," became the Band's first and only Top 30 release. It was one of several songs on the album that had an "old-timey" feel. Other highlights on this masterpiece include "Rag Mama Rag," "The Night They Drove Old Dixie Down," and "King Harvest." *—Rob Bowman*

Stage Fright / Aug. 17, 1970 / Capitol ♦♦♦
Stage Fright was a reaction to a level of adulation that the Band members were unprepared for. It was conceived as a lighter, less serious, more rock & roll type of album. The final product ended up somewhat darker, as the Band themselves were going through a number of changes. "The Shape I'm In" and "Stage Fright" tell the story well. Some of the original feeling manifests itself in romps such as "Strawberry Wine" and "W.S. Walcott Medicine Show." *—Rob Bowman*

Cahoots / Sep. 15, 1971 / Capitol ♦♦
Cahoots was the first album recorded at Albert Grossman's Bearsville Studios in Woodstock. The sessions were difficult, as the studio was still having the bugs worked out and the Band was experiencing internal problems. Robertson's songs had become much more difficult; the structures, chord changes, and arrangements were increasingly complex. Despite these factors, the album has a number of gems, including "Life Is a Carnival" with its great Allen Toussaint horn arrangement, Dylan's "When I Paint My Masterpiece," a duet between Richard Manuel and Van Morrison entitled "4% Pantomime," "The River Hymn," and "Where Do We Go from Here?" *—Rob Bowman*

○ **Rock of Ages** / Aug. 15, 1972 / Capitol ✦✦✦✦
Recorded on New Year's Eve 1971/72, this was the Band's last gig for a year and a half. Allen Toussaint was brought in again to write horn arrangements for many of the Band's classics. The results were inspired. Highlights are many, but of particular note are a cover of Marvin Gaye's "Baby Don't Do It" and a live recording of a track that had earlier been relegated to B-side status only, "Get up Jake." —*Rob Bowman*

Moondog Matinee / Oct. 15, 1973 / Capitol ✦✦
The Band essentially went back to being the Hawks of the late 1950s and early '60s on this album of cover tunes. They demonstrated considerable expertise on their versions of rock & roll and R&B standards like Clarence "Frogman" Henry's "Ain't Got No Home," Chuck Berry's "The Promised Land," and Fats Domino's "I'm Ready," but of course that didn't do much to satisfy the audience that they had established with their original material and that, two years after the disappointing *Cahoots*, was waiting for something in the same league with their first three albums. —*William Ruhlmann*

○ **Northern Lights Southern Cross** / Nov. 1, 1975 / Capitol ✦✦✦✦
The first studio album of Band originals in four years, in many respects *Northern Lights—Southern Cross* was viewed as a comeback. It also can be seen as a swan song. The album was the Band's finest since their self-titled sophomore effort. Totaling eight songs in all, on this album the Band explores new timbres, utilizing for the first time 24 tracks and what was (then) new synthesizer technology. "Acadian Driftwood" stands out as one of Robertson's finest compositions, the equal to anything else the Band ever recorded. —*Rob Bowman*

○ **The Best of the Band** / 1976 / Capitol ✦✦✦✦
With this album, Capitol Records began the inevitable process of repackaging the music of the Band, which the company would do at increasing length without solving the fundamental problem that the Band, despite the quality of their individual songs, was not a singles act and was hard to summarize in a compilation. That said, for the real neophyte, this single-disc, 11-song album may be as good as anything. It contains the Band's two most famous songs, "The Weight" and "The Night They Drove Old Dixie Down," as well as the group's only Top 30 hit, "Up On Cripple Creek," and such songs as "Tears Of Rage" and "Stage Fright" that they probably played at nearly every show they performed. It's true that if you really want to understand the Band, you have to hear all of *Music From Big Pink* and *The Band.* But if you just want a snapshot, here it is. —*William Ruhlmann*

Islands / 1977 / Capitol ✦✦
Theoretically, even though the Band had given up touring as of Thanksgiving 1976, they were going to keep making records, and *Islands* was the first album released in the new era. Only, it wasn't; it was the album they scraped together to complete their 10-LP contract with Capitol Records and the last new full-length album the original five members ever made. The playing, as ever, was impeccable, and the record had its moments, notably a Richard Manuel vocal on the chestnut "Georgia On My Mind" that had been released as a single in 1976 to boost Georgia Governor Jimmy Carter's successful run for the Presidency. But the songwriting quality was mediocre, and the Band had set such a standard for itself in that department that *Islands* couldn't help suffering enormously in comparison. —*William Ruhlmann*

Anthology / 1978 / Capitol ✦✦✦
Deciding 1976's *The Best Of The Band* wasn't enough (or wanting to have a product out to compete with *The Last Waltz*), Capitol released the two-LP *Anthology*, a skimpy 20-track, two-LP set with liner notes by rock critic Robert Palmer. It's more complete than *The Best Of The Band*, but shares the same problem—that the Band is best appreciated on their full-length albums rather than on any compilation. —*William Ruhlmann*

○ **The Last Waltz** / Apr. 1978 / Warner Brothers ✦✦✦✦
The Band's farewell gig was held at Winterland in San Francisco on Thanksgiving 1976. Guests from all periods of their career were invited to participate. The luminaries included Bob Dylan, Van Morrison, Neil Young, Joni Mitchell, Muddy Waters, Eric Clapton, and Paul Butterfield. The four-hour concert was one of the most spectacular in rock history. Two hours of it were released on this three-LP (now two-CD) set. Utilizing horns one more time, this was the gig of the Band's life and one of the greatest in rock history. We are privileged that it exists in a form where we can hear it as often as we want. —*Rob Bowman*

● **To Kingdom Come** / 1989 / Capitol ✦✦✦✦
If (and only if) you have it in your budget for just *one* Band set, *To Kingdom Come (The Definitive Collection)* provides a good collection of their best songs, presented in remastered form. Even though the sequencing is chronological, experiencing these songs out of the context of their original albums may be disconcerting for some. In other words, the best way to *hear* this great group is to start with their first two albums, then move on to *Rock of Ages*, and so on. Nevertheless, this is an exceptionally solid overview. —*Rick Clark*

Jericho / 1993 / Rhino ✦✦✦
A full seventeen years after *The Last Waltz*, the Band reformed without Robbie Robertson or the late Richard Manuel and recorded *Jericho*. Far from being an embarrassment, *Jericho* is their strongest record since *Northern Lights, Southern Cross* and arguably their best since *Stage Fright*. Without Robertson, the Band relies on a variety of sources for their material (including Bob Dylan, Bruce Springsteen and Jules Shear) and prove that they can interpret nearly any song well. Musically, the Band can still juggle rock, folk, blues, and country effortlessly, producing a rootsy sound distinctly their own. It sounds like the heyday of the group, which is more than can be said of either of Robertson's solo albums. —*Stephen Thomas Erlewine*

Across the Great Divide / 1994 / Capitol ✦✦✦
Capitol's 1989 compilation *To Kingdom Come* was subtitled "The Definitive Collection," so what is this? Well, the other one was only a two-disc set, and this is a three-disc set. As the CD reissue/box set boom goes on, record companies have taken to redoing acts they've already done once, so even though the Band has one classy CD anthology (and a few tacky ones), Capitol gives us another. In this case, they've divided it into two discs' worth of the greatest hits, followed by a disc of rarities (some not so rare) and unreleased tracks that includes pre-Band recordings by the Hawks, collaborations with Bob Dylan, live tracks from the Woodstock and Watkins Glen festivals, and the like. All of which pushes this set up a price point or two from the earlier one without adding anything substantial to the story. —*William Ruhlmann*

Band of Susans

Group, Alternative Pop/Rock
An often-changing lineup does not interfere with this New York City band's love of guitars. Often loud and brash, their triple-guitar attack has a solid rock & roll base, nowhere near as pretentious as Glenn Branca or as discordant as Sonic Youth. —*Bruce Eder*

● **Hope Against Hope** / 1988 / Blast First ✦✦✦✦
○ **Love Agenda** / 1989 / Blast First ✦✦✦✦
Their cover of the Rolling Stones' "Child of the Moon" is a must-hear. —*Robert Gordon*

Word & The Flesh / 1991 / Restless ✦✦✦
Triple-guitar attack—a sea of six-strings. —*Robert Gordon*

Veil / 1993 / Restless ✦✦✦
Now / Restless ✦✦

The Bangles

Group, Pop/Rock
The Bangles combined the chiming riffs and catchy melodies of British Invasion guitar-pop with a hint of the energy of new wave. In the process, they became one of the handful of all-female bands of the '80s to win both critical and commercial success. The critical success came first—with their self-titled debut EP and full-length album, *All Over the Place*—and popular success arrived once they polished their sound, adding some synthesizers and deviating slightly from their trademark jangling guitar hooks. Once they were selling at the platinum level, the Bangles didn't stay together long, but they left behind them several pop gems.

In 1981, the original version of the group formed when guitarist/vocalist Vicki Peterson and drummer/vocalist Debbi Peterson responded to an advertisement guitarist/vocalist Susanna Hoffs placed in a local Los Angeles paper, *The Recycler*. Taking the name the Bangs, the trio added bassist Annette Zilinskas and released an EP, *Getting out of Hand*, on their own independent label, Downkiddie. In early 1982, the band had to change their name to the Bangles, since there was already a New York–based group called the Bangs recording. After an appearance on a *Rodney on the ROQ* compilation and a series of local concerts, Miles Copeland signed the band to the IRS subsidiary Faulty Products and landed them an opening spot for the English Beat. That summer, the Bangles released a self-titled EP on Faulty Products.

In early 1983, the Bangles signed with CBS Records and Zilinskas left the band to join Blood on the Saddle. She was replaced by bassist/vocalist Michael Steele, a former member of the proto-punk hard rock group the Runaways. The group released their first full-length album, *All Over the Place*, in the summer of 1984. While it didn't feature any charting singles, the record managed to climb to number 80 on the American charts, on the strength of support from college radio and MTV, as well as strong reviews. In particular, a cover of Katrina and the Waves' "Goin' Down to Liverpool" and the original "Hero Takes a Fall" received heavy airplay on college stations.

The Bangles released their second album, *Different Light*, in the spring of 1986. It was preceded by the colorful, neo-psychedelic single "Manic Monday," which was written by Prince under the pseudonym Christopher. "Manic Monday" became a number two hit in both America and Britain, sending *Different Light* into the Top Five as well. A cover of Jules Shear's "If She Knew What She Wants" was a relative commercial disappointment, stalling at number 29 on the U.S. charts, but the third single from *Different Light*, "Walk Like an Egyptian," was a major hit, spending four weeks at number one in America; it peaked at number three in Britain. After the Bangles completed a summer tour, Hoffs starred in the movie *The Allnighter*, which was directed by her mother Tamara; the film was released in the summer of 1987. "Walking Down Your Street," the final single pulled from *Different Light*, was released in early 1987 and peaked at number 11.

Later in 1987, the Bangles recorded a hard-rocking version of Paul Simon's "Hazy Shade of Winter" for the soundtrack of *Less Than Zero*; the single peaked at number two in early 1988. *Everything*, the band's third album, was released in the fall of 1988. *Everything* was a slicker affair than either of their previous albums, yet it didn't perform quite as well as *Different Light*. "In Your Room," the first single taken from the album, made it to number five and the ballad "Eternal Flame" became the group's second number one single in early 1989, but the record ran out of steam shortly after the release of the third single, "Be With You," which never made it past number 30. After a brief summer tour, the group disbanded and Hoffs began a solo career. Hoffs released her debut solo album, *When You're a Boy*, in 1991; it never made it past number 83 and the single, "My Side of the Bed," stalled at number 30. — *Stephen Thomas Erlewine*

Bangles / Jun. 1982 / Faulty ♦♦♦
On this, their debut long-playing record, a five-song EP, the Bangles have already established their chiming guitars and 1966-era Beatles sound, although they are a little rougher (and more energetic) than they would be on their big-selling Columbia albums. This record featured bass player Annette Zilinskas, later replaced by Michael Steele. — *William Ruhlmann*

○ **All Over The Place A** / May 1984 / Columbia ♦♦♦♦
Featuring the Bangles' rich harmonies and slightly ragged folk/pop-rock ensemble work, *All Over the Place* is an absolute gem. Highlights like "Hero Takes a Fall," "Dover Beach," "James," "Tell Me," "Live," and "Going Down to Liverpool" easily make this their best album. — *Rick Clark*

Different Light / Jan. 1986 / Columbia ♦♦♦
The Bangles' most successful album, *Different Light* presented the band with a more polished sheen, depending on a lot more outside material from professional songsmiths. Prince penned the slight (but tuneful) "Manic Monday," which became their first big hit. That was followed by the novelty-ish "Walk like an Egyptian," their first number one hit. The highlights, however, went to an inspired reading of Jules Shears's "If She Knew What She Wants" (a number 29 hit) and a bouncy version of Big Star's "September Gurls." — *Rick Clark*

Everything / Oct. 1988 / Columbia ♦♦♦
With two fine albums under their belt, the Bangles stumbled on this inappropriately titled effort. Aside from the inspired pop-psychedelic tease of "In Your Room," much of *Everything* suffers from lightweight songwriting. Nevertheless, one of the album's low points, the treacly ballad "Eternal Flame," soared to number one. — *Rick Clark*

● **Greatest Hits** / May 1990 / Columbia ♦♦♦♦
Greatest Hits is just that, including a great version of Simon & Garfunkel's "Hazy Shade of Winter," a hit from the *Less Than Zero* soundtrack that's not found on their other albums. Another previously unreleased track is a workmanlike reading of the Grassroots chestnut "Where Were You When I Needed You." The highlights from their weakest album, *Everything*, are provided, rendering that album inconsequential. It would've been nice if Sony had utilized the space available on CD to include more essential album tracks from their first two albums, like "September Gurls," "Live," and "James." As collections go, this is a logical place to start, but *All Over the Place* is their most appealing album. — *Rick Clark*

Peter Banks

b. Apr. 8, 1947
Art-Rock/Progressive-Rock
The original Yes lead guitarist, who departed after their second album, Banks's angular guitar style was the model for the sound later perfected by his replacement in Yes, Steve Howe. Banks's later appearances have been few but notable, leading a short-lived Yes-like band called Flash, recording one solo album, and playing lead guitar on a '70s Lonnie Donegan skiffle comeback album. — *Bruce Eder*

Peter Banks & Jan Akkerman / 1972 / Sovereign ♦♦♦
Peter Banks / 1973 / Sovereign ♦♦
● **The Two Sides of Peter Banks** / Aug. 1973 / One Way ♦♦♦♦
One of the most listenable progressive electric-guitar solo albums of the early '70s, it consists of strange, moody extended instrumentals and skiffle-like jams, and features supporting players from Genesis and Focus. — *Dan Heilman*

Instinct / 1994 / ♦♦
Self-Contained / 1995 / One Way ♦♦♦

The Bar-Kays

Group, Soul, Funk
Even though four group founders were killed in a 1967 plane crash along with Otis Redding, the Bar-Kays came back to reign as one of the top R&B outfits of the 70s. The original Bar-Kays were a Memphis instrumental combo that scored an R&B hit in 1967 on Volt with the rousing "Soul Finger." Guitarist Jimmy King, organist Ronnie Caldwell, drummer Carl Cunningham, and saxist Phalon Jones perished with Redding, leaving trumpeter Ben Cauley and bassist James Alexander to re-form the group. After honing their chops with session work at Stax, the new Bar-Kays kicked off a long string of R&B smashes in 1976 with "Shake Your Rump to the Funk" on Mercury. — *Bill Dahl*

○ **Soul Finger** / 1967 / Rhino ♦♦♦♦
The Bar-Kays were being trained as a second generation Booker T and the M.G.'s, largely by MG drummer Al Jackson. *Soul Finger* was their first album, coming off the success of the their debut single, the group-written title cut. The album is in the classic Memphis soul instrumental vein; sparse arrangements, accentuated low-end, walloping snare drum, and slightly delayed backbeat with horns taking the place of vocals. *Soul Finger* was the only album made by this particular version of the group. — *Rob Bowman*

Gotta Groove / 1969 / Stax ♦♦♦
After the plane crash in December 1967, trumpeter Ben Cauley and bass player James Alexander regrouped, forming a second edition of the Bar-Kays. *Gotta Groove* was the new group's first release. Modelled on earlier Bar-Kays work, the album is totally instrumental, including covers of the Mar-Key's "Grab This Thing" and the Beatles' "Yesterday" and "Hey Jude." No standout cuts but plenty of fine, hard-driving slices of Memphis instrumental soul. — *Rob Bowman*

Black Rock / Feb. 1971 / Volt ♦♦♦
As the title implies, the Bar-Kays were redefining both their image and their sound. Adding vocals for the first time, the group produced hard rock covers of Aretha Franklin's "Baby I Love You," Sam and Dave's "You Don't Know Like I Know," and Sly's "Dance to the Music." The recording is an odd melange of Vanilla Fudge, Chicago, and Funkadelic. Appended to the end is an instrumental version of "Montego Bay" that was cut as a single between *Gotta Groove* and this album. Certainly dated, *Black Rock* will not be to everybody's taste. — *Rob Bowman*

Do You See What I See? / 1972 / Polydor ♦♦
Some vigorous funk and an occasional soulful ballad by the Bar-Kays, who were re-establishing their funk credentials and rebuilding after recovering from the '67 plane crash. This album included the title track and several other short, peppy vocal and instrumen-

tal numbers, although it wasn't as well-produced as some later '70s and '80s efforts. —*Ron Wynn*

Coldblooded / 1974 / Stax ✦✦✦
One of the albums that the Bar-Kays cut for Stax in the early '70s after they revamped the group following the disastrous late '60s plane crash that killed all but two of the originals. The new lineup featured guitarist Lloyd Smith, drummer Michael Beard, vocalist John Colbert, trumpeter Charles Allen, saxophonist Havery Henderson, and others. This was classic Southern funk, with gospel-tinged vocals, energetic horn tracks, and lyrics that ranged from downhome musings to urban admonitions. —*Ron Wynn*

○ **Too Hot to Stop** / Oct. 1976 / Mercury ✦✦✦✦
One of their best '70s dates, the Bar-Kays were in overdrive throughout this one. The title track was a huge hit, and the other uptempo tunes were equally fast-paced and tightly played. The few slow songs provided enough changes of pace to keep things varied. The horn charts, production, and arrangements were funk personified, although they were starting to add synthesized elements in anticipation of changes on the urban front. —*Ron Wynn*

Flying High on Your Love / Nov. 1977 / Mercury ✦✦✦
The Bar-Kays were riding the crest as the top funk band in the South. This album didn't have any one standout track, but had several solid ones that got wide regional airplay and even a little national attention. They were beginning to modify their sound as well, peeling back the horns a bit and putting the bass/synthesizer underplay more to the front. —*Ron Wynn*

Money Talks / Oct. 1978 / Stax ✦✦✦
Prototype Southern funk and hot R&B licks. —*Ron Wynn*

Light of Life / Dec. 1978 / Mercury ✦✦
The second of two Bar-Kays albums that were issued in 1978, this one utilized similar horn charts and upbeat, fast-paced funk rhythms that the group had made popular. It didn't have as many slow numbers either, and was more animated and exuberant than its predecessor. —*Ron Wynn*

Injoy / Oct. 1979 / Mercury ✦✦
The Bar-Kays debuted on Mercury at the end of the '70s and gradually altered their style. Horn funk was dying out in 1980, and while they weren't yet ready to disband their horn section, they were steadily reducing their role. They kept the same collective, half-sung, half-yelled vocals, but now the bass/drum/synthesizer interplay was at the center, with the horns in the background. —*Ron Wynn*

○ **As One** / Nov. 1980 / Mercury ✦✦✦✦
This was arguably their best Mercury album. It included "Move Your Boogie Body," plus their finest inspirational tune, "Deliver Us," and the title cut was a solid winner as well. They had found the ideal mix of horns, electronics, funk backbeats, and R&B/gospel vocals, and everything clicked on every selection. —*Ron Wynn*

Nightcruising / Nov. 1981 / Mercury ✦✦✦
Another fine early '80s album, with one of their biggest hits in the decade, the single "Hit and Run." The Bar-Kays were for a time the dominant funk band around, and were one of the few that had been able to survive into the '80s. The horns were still there, although they'd soon be purged from the arrangements. —*Ron Wynn*

Propositions / Nov. 1982 / Mercury ✦✦
Signs of decline begin to emerge with this album. They were now moving squarely away from the driving, horn-centered funk that had made their reputation, and trying to cope with a slimmer backbeat and more groove-oriented sound. They adapted the slinky, synthesized formula patented by Cameo and had some success, but weren't singing with the same aggressiveness and confidence. —*Ron Wynn*

Dangerous / Apr. 1984 / Mercury ✦✦
The title cut did moderately well, and everything else was decently produced, but the Bar-Kays' heyday had passed by the time this was issued. Groups were now doing either New Jack Swing-styled material with rap inserts or returning to more intra-group harmonizing. They had pretty much dispatched the horn charts, but the group's production, arrangements, and content were too old-school for many '80s fans. —*Ron Wynn*

Banging the Wall / Sep. 1985 / Mercury ✦✦
Pro forma stuff from the revamped Bar-Kays. They cut the group's personnel, completely moved away from their classic sound, and were now doing tightly syncopated, groove-centered material.

Only the vocal arrangements sounded familiar, and while they maintained their energy, they didn't get the necessary material to have any hits from this session. —*Ron Wynn*

Contagious / Oct. 1987 / Mercury ✦✦
Things were basically a lost cause for the Bar-Kays by the time they issued this album in 1987. Audiences were now solidly into rap, New Jack Swing-styled R&B or smoother, more sophisticated urban contemporary material, and the Bar-Kays weren't able to cover any of those bases. Plus, their new songs didn't sound enough like their hits to score any points with the older audiences that enjoyed them. This is among the last albums they did for a major label. —*Ron Wynn*

Animal / 1988 / Mercury ✦✦✦
One of their top-selling releases. —*Ron Wynn*

● **Best of [Stax]** / 1988 / Stax ✦✦✦✦
A nice overview of this major Stax band in their second incarnation. —*Ron Wynn*

○ **The Best of [Mercury]** / May 18, 1993 / Mercury ✦✦✦✦
A solid overview of the Bar-Kays' years as a trailblazing funk outfit. —*Stephen Thomas Erlewine*

The Barbarians

Group, Garage Rock, Pop/Rock
With their appearances on the *Nuggets* compilation and the *T.A.M.I. Show*, the Barbarians are one of the best-remembered garage bands of the '60s. Not that it's easy to forget the sight of a one-handed drummer, complete with hook, driving his band through a garage-punk number in the company of the day's biggest British Invasion, soul, and surf stars. Moulty was hardly self-conscious about his handicap; on the tiny hit single immortalized on *Nuggets* (titled, logically enough, "Moulty"), he tells the story of the triumph over his loss in no uncertain melodramatic terms. The band also managed a somewhat bigger hit single, the British Invasion-inspired novelty "Are You a Boy or Are You a Girl." —*Richie Unterberger*

Are You a Boy or Are You a Girl? / 1966 / One Way ✦✦✦
While the Barbarians live up to a lot of people's vision of the classic garage band image-wise, their album is disappointing and thin-sounding—the material is average and doesn't even rock terribly hard. "Are You A Boy Or Are You A Girl" and "Moulty" are both here, but much of the rest of the songs are overdone standards ("House Of The Rising Sun" is especially lame). "What The New Breed Say" is an okay anthem of rebellion, and "I'll Keep On Seeing You" a modestly touching ballad, but as songwriters the Barbarians were light-years behind their principal New England rivals, the Remains. Disappointingly, the LP doesn't include their best song, "Hey Little Bird" (which they performed on the *T.A.M.I. Show*). Die-hards are advised to track down the cut on the obscure garage band compilation reissue *The New England Teen Scene Vol. II*, although the studio version isn't as ferocious as their rendition on film. —*Richie Unterberger*

Barenaked Ladies

Group, Alternative Pop/Rock
Barenaked Ladies is a pop quintet from Toronto founded by Ed Robertson (guitar, vocals) and Steven Page (guitar, vocals) in 1988. Completing the band are Tyler Stewart (drums) and brothers Jim (bass) and Andrew Creeggan (keyboards). They released a successful independent EP in 1990 and their debut album, *Gordon*, was a substantial hit in Canada in 1992. Their second album, *Maybe You Should Drive*, was released in 1994. —*William Ruhlmann*

● **Gordon** / Mar. 1992 / Sire ✦✦✦✦
Gordon contains re-recordings of key tracks from their Indy cassette that outsold many a "big star" major-label release in Canada, and that cemented BNL's witty, gosh-darn reputation: "Brian Wilson," "If I Had A Million Dollars," and "Be My Yoko Ono." New numbers "Box Set"—poking fun at music industry excess—and "New Kid (On The Block)"—poking fun at different music industry excess—carry on the tradition. But... surprise surprise ...the group has decided it doesn't want to be typecast as a cute, cuddly, novelty-tune act. *Gordon* also contains several serious moments, notably "The Flag"'s metaphor for abusive relationships, and the poignant, "it's tough growing up in a complicated world" ballad "What A Good Boy." —*Roch Parisien*

Maybe You Should Drive / 1994 / Sire ✦✦✦
Barenaked Ladies are a little less interested in the quirky and comic on their second album, perhaps recognizing that They Might Be Giants have that niche covered. Instead, though, they are

showing their sensitive folk-pop roots, which makes them winning, if a little wet. (XTC, anyone?) But one thing they aren't is "alternative," a matter dealt with in the chorus of the song "Alternative Girlfriend," when they sing, "There's nothing left that won't cross over." Well put, and present company included. — *William Ruhlmann*

Lou Barlow

Alternative Pop/Rock
In many ways, Sebadoh leader Lou Barlow is the key figure of the '90s low-fi movement. On both his band and his solo recordings, Barlow alternately turns in full-formed pop songs and sketchy sonic experiments. Sonically, there's not much difference between his Sebadoh tracks and his solo work—it's fuzzy, distorted, with chiming guitars floating through the murk every once in a while. However, Barlow's solo recordings are looser and more off-the-cuff, ranging from a cover of Bryan Adams' "Run to You" to one-joke noise rockers like "Puffin' on a Pot Pipe." Barlow's solo recordings are only for hardcore fans—he doesn't edit, he apparently includes everything he records on his discs—yet for his fans, everything he records is worth hearing. — *Stephen Thomas Erlewine*

○ **Collection of Home Recordings** / 1994 / Smells Like ✦✦✦✦
Lou Barlow's first *Collection of Home Recordings* is a looser affair than his albums with Sebadoh and his folkier side project, Sentridoh. Instead, it's a collection of musings that backfires as often as it connects, yet it remains intriguing and fascinating throughout its brief running time. — *Stephen Thomas Erlewine*

● **Lou Barlow and Friends: Another Collection of Home Recordings** / 1995 / Mint ✦✦✦✦
Another Collection of Home Recordings isn't all that different from Lou Barlow's first collection—it's still him composing songs that are either slight or significant on his portastudio, with the occasional help of some friends and family members. However, *Another Collection* serves as a more effective introduction to Barlow's insular world since it has more flashes of humor than the previous record. — *Stephen Thomas Erlewine*

Richard Barone

Alternative Pop/Rock
In the early '80s, Richard Barone was the lead singer/songwriter and guitarist of the Bongos, a New Jersey-based pop-rock band that garnered critical acclaim but ran into record company problems. He launched a solo career in 1987 with the release of *Cool Blue Halo*. — *William Ruhlmann*

Nuts & Bolts / 1983 / Passport ✦✦✦
Soon after guitarist James Mastro joined the Bongos, he and Bongos leader Richard Barone made this album, a duo record in which Barone writes and sings lead on all the songs on Side 1, and Mastro takes the lead on Side 2. That means the first side is a bit more like the usual Bongos neo-'60s pop-rock sound, tuneful and terrific, and the second side doesn't even seem to be neo-. Mastro's songs sound like they were lifted unchanged from some mid-'60s American rock band. (Not surprisingly, there's a cover of Tommy Roe's "Dizzy"). — *William Ruhlmann*

● **Cool Blue Halo** / 1987 / Line ✦✦✦✦
Former Bongos leader Richard Barone writes and sings wonderful pop songs in a mid-'60s, Beatlesque manner. On this live album, he assembled an unusual backup band (featuring cellist Jane Scarpantoni) to play some new songs, Bongos favorites, and logical covers like "Cry Baby Cry." — *William Ruhlmann*

Primal Dream / 1990 / Paradox/MCA ✦✦✦
Barone's first full-fledged studio solo album is long on stirring and beautifully arranged rockers, with some striking guitar work. The touchstone is still *Beatles '65*, but Barone updates it, and his tunes are irresistible. — *William Ruhlmann*

Clouds Over Eden / 1993 / Mesa ✦✦✦
With his lush productions and craftsmanlike songs, Richard Barone is entering the same retro territory as Chris Isaak, an alternative (in the old sense) pop universe that wipes out the 1970s and draws a straight line through Buddy Holly and Duane Eddy to the Hollies and the Beatles. The guitars chime, the melodies are singable, the beat is steady, the sound is sweetened by the occasional use of strings, and Barone sings in a controlled, eager-to-please tenor. Only the lyrics, which speak of darkness, loneliness, and rejection, betray the modernist sensibility and turn the songs into moody meditations rather than pop confections. — *William Ruhlmann*

Baroques

Group, Psychedelic
A minor psychedelic band with a mixture of interesting and generic material, the Baroques recorded one LP for Chess in 1967, when the blues/R&B/soul-oriented label was considering breaking into the rock market. Popular only on a regional level, the Milwaukee group was dominated by the morose compositions and low, odd vocal range of singer/lead guitarist Jay Borkenhagen. With a slight garage feel, their unusual, occasionally oddball material was built around electric (sometimes "baroque") keyboards and fuzz guitar riffs, with occasional detours into uplifting folk-rock and freak-out jamming. Disbanding in 1968, they won't appeal to many listeners besides psychedelic specialists, but recorded some idiosyncratically worthwhile stuff, most of which has been reissued on small collector labels. — *Richie Unterberger*

The Baroques / 1967 / Chess ✦✦✦

Baroque Demos / 1990 / Baroque ✦✦
Poorly packaged collection of 1967-68 demos, rendered largely unnecessary by the recent *Purple Day* compilation, which includes almost everything here. — *Richie Unterberger*

● **Purple Day** / 1995 / Baroque ✦✦✦✦
22-track compilation has virtually everything you'd want to hear by the band: most of the 1967 LP and a dozen demos from 1967-68, some of which are different versions of songs from the album, others of original material they didn't release at the time. — *Richie Unterberger*

Syd Barrett

b. Jan. 6, 1946, Cambridge, England
Psychedelic
Like a supernova, Roger "Syd" Barrett burned briefly and brightly, leaving an indelible mark upon psychedelic and progressive rock as the founder and original singer, songwriter, and lead guitarist of Pink Floyd. Barrett was responsible for most of their brilliant first album, 1967's *The Piper at the Gates of Dawn*, but left and/or was fired from the band in early 1968 after his erratic behavior had made him too difficult to deal with (he appears on a couple tracks on their second album, *A Saucerful of Secrets*). Such was his stature within the original lineup that few observers thought the band could survive his departure; in fact, the original group's management decided to keep Syd on and leave the rest of the band to their own devices. Pink Floyd never recaptured the playful humor and mad energy of their work with Barrett.

After a period of hibernation, Barrett re-emerged in 1970 with a pair of albums, *The Madcap Laughs* and *Barrett*, which featured considerable support from his former bandmates (especially his replacement, David Gilmour, who produced most of the sessions). Members of the Soft Machine also play on these records, which have a ragged, unfinished, and folky feel. Barrett's eccentric humor, sly wordplay, and infectious melodies range from brilliant to chaotic on his solo work. Lacking the taut power of his recordings with the Floyd in 1967, they nevertheless remain fascinating and moving glimpses into a creative psyche gone awry after (it is theorized) too much fame and too many drugs too early. With increasing psychological problems, Syd withdrew into near-total reclusion after these albums. He never released any more material, and these days rarely appears in public, let alone plays music.

Although they attracted little attention upon their release, his albums also attracted a cult audience. Barrett's music and mystique achieved a lasting influence that continues to grow over two decades later. Latter-day new wave psychedelic acts like Julian Cope, the Television Personalities, and (especially) Robyn Hitchcock acknowledge Barrett's tremendous influence on their work. The Barrett cult became large enough to warrant the release of an entire album of previously unreleased material and outtakes, *Opel*, in the late '80s, as well as his sessions for the BBC. — *Richie Unterberger*

● **The Madcap Laughs** / Jan. 1970 / Capitol ✦✦✦✦
While this collection bears similarities to the songs found on *The Piper at the Gates of Dawn*, the only Pink Floyd album Barrett contributed to significantly, it nevertheless comes across more as a session of run-throughs and demos than as a finished record. Its very roughness is its charm, undercutting the whimsy of the songs with Barrett's ultimate strangeness. — *William Ruhlmann*

Barrett / Nov. 1970 / Capitol ✦✦✦
On his second solo album, Barrett was joined by Humble Pie drummer Jerry Shirley and Pink Floyd members Rick Wright (organ) and Dave Gilmour (guitar). Gilmour and Wright acted as producers as well. Instrumentally, the result is a bit fuller and smoother than the first album, although it's since been revealed that Gilmour and Wright embellished these songs as best they could without much involvement from Barrett, who was often unable or unwilling to perfect his performance. The songs, however, are just as fractured as on his debut, if not more so. "Baby Lemonade," "Gigolo Aunt," and the nursery rhyming "Effervescing Elephant" rank among his peppiest and best-loved tunes. Elsewhere, the tone is darker and more meandering. It was regarded as something of a charming but unfocused throwaway at the time of its release, but Barrett's singularly whimsical and unsettling vision holds up well. —*Richie Unterberger*

Peel Sessions / 1987 / Dutch East India ✦✦
In February 1970, Syd Barrett performed five songs for John Peel's show on the BBC, accompanied by Jerry Shirley on drums and Dave Gilmour on guitar. Besides reprising "Terrapin" from his first album, the session featured three of the strongest tunes from his second LP, "Gigolo Aunt," "Baby Lemonade," and (a very brief) "Effervescing Elephant." This five-song EP also includes the bouncy, easygoing "Two Of A Kind," which doesn't appear on any other release; it's since been claimed that this was actually a composition by Pink Floyd organist Rick Wright. The rest of the songs don't differ much from the officially released versions; they're somewhat sparer and looser. A decent if not absolutely essential relic for the Barrett/Floyd fan, with excellent sound. —*Richie Unterberger*

Opel / Apr. 1989 / Capitol ✦✦✦
For several years, the existence of "lost" material by Barrett had been speculated on by the singer's vociferous cult, fueled by numerous patchy bootlegs of intriguing outtakes. The release of *Opel* lived up to, and perhaps exceeded, fans' expectations. With 14 tracks spanning 1968-1970, including six alternate takes and eight songs that had never been officially released in any form, it is equally as essential as his two 1970 LPs. The tone is very much in keeping with his pair of solo albums; ragged, predominantly acoustic, melodic, and teetering on the edge of dementia. At the same time, it's charming and lyrically pungent, with Barrett's inimitable sense of childlike whimsy. The production is generally more minimal than on his other albums, even bare-bones at times, but if anything, this adds to the music's stark power. Highlights are the lengthy brooding title track, the multi-layered swirl of "Swan Lee," the alternate take of "Dark Globe" (with much better, more restrained vocals than the previous version), and the exuberant, infectious "Milky Way." Meticulous liner notes and excellent sound complete this lovingly archival package. —*Richie Unterberger*

Octopus: The Best of Syd Barrett / May 29, 1992 / Cleopatra ✦✦✦
A well-chosen 14-track, single-disc compilation of Barrett's solo work, presumably discount-priced and aimed at the casual listener. But Barrett is such a specialized taste and has such a small body of work that one wonders why Cema Special Markets (a division of EMI) would bother. —*William Ruhlmann*

○ **Crazy Diamond** / Apr. 19, 1994 / EMI ✦✦✦✦
A three-CD box set which enshrines Barrett's complete recorded legacy as a solo artist. Besides including his two 1970 albums, this collection includes the 1989 compilation of unreleased material, *Opel*. The chief attraction of this set for Barrett fans is no less than 19 previously unreleased alternate takes from throughout his quite brief solo career. All of those alternate takes, it's important to note, are alternate versions of songs that appear on the three previously available albums; no entirely unheard compositions were unearthed. Nonetheless, these alternate takes are more interesting listening than you might expect, for a couple of reasons. First, Barrett was so mercurial (and occasionally unfocused) in the studio that it was difficult to get him to play a song the same way twice. Second, the alternate takes are usually starker and more acoustic in nature than the official versions; they're not better, but have interesting different slants. With some of the songs repeated two, three, or even four times, this is definitely for the hardcore fan. But it's a beautifully produced document, with a meticulously detailed booklet, of a uniquely primitive visionary, with many moments of charming and chilling power. It includes everything salvageable

that he produced, with the exception of *The Peel Sessions*. It doesn't match his work with the original Pink Floyd, but the music continues to influence and be emulated (most notably by Robyn Hitchcock), though never equaled. —*Richie Unterberger*

BOOK

✦✦✦ **Crazy Diamond: Syd Barrett & The Dawn of Pink Floyd**, by Mike Watkinson & Pete Anderson. (Omnibus, 1991). Syd Barrett is one of rock's most haunted and mysterious figures, disappearing into the ether after dominating Pink Floyd's brilliant 1967 debut and managing a couple of erratic but worthwhile solo records. More sensational rumors have circulated about Barrett than virtually any other '60s legend, as befits a major talent who seemingly went mad almost immediately from a combination of drugs and the pressures of stardom, seldom appearing in public after 1970, and exhibiting memorably (sometimes ghoulishly) eccentric behavior on those rare occasions. The authors of this fine bio approach their subject with a great deal of sympathy and respect, resisting the temptation to poke easy mirth at the disturbed genius' clownish and aberrant actions. And there are plenty of those: former friends and associates, all of whom are in a huge awe of his talent, recount numerous fascinating (if often tragicomic) tales of his charisma and instability, which would find him refusing to give keys or lyrics to his sessionmen, or perform in smelly rags without bothering to open his mouth or play his instrument during his last days with Pink Floyd. This complements the early sections of Nicholas Schaffner's fine Floyd bio *Saucerful of Secrets* well, adding lots of new information and stories without a lot of repetition, and focusing more on his solo career and subsequent vociferous cult than the group bio does. —*Richie Unterberger*

Barry & the Remains

Group, Pop/Rock
The Remains, fronted by Barry Tashian, were a blistering, shake 'em down rock & roll teen combo, probably the finest Boston had to offer in the mid '60s; they seemed poised for national stardom after signing to Epic for their debut album. Success eluded them, however, and they fell victim to the label's massive "Bosstown sound" promo campaign, which backfired for all groups signed to Epic at that time. The Remains became cult favorites with '60s collectors, with varied compilations appearing on foreign labels over the years. —*Cub Koda*

● **The Remains** / 1966 / Epic/Legacy ✦✦✦✦
A fabulous reissue that shows the group as one of the finest, and possibly *the* finest, British Invasion-inspired American garage band of the mid-'60s. The Remains had it all, except success: their first-rate original material combined tight harmonies and tuneful melodies with brash energy. This 21-track disc repackages their entire 1966 LP and adds a wealth of bonus cuts, including all their non-LP singles and some excellent unreleased songs. —*Richie Unterberger*

Live in Boston / 1984 / Eva ✦✦
This live-in-the-studio demo was accorded raves by the few collectors who managed to hear it before its appearance on this LP. Although Remains leader Barry Tashian had said that it captures the band's prowess better than their studio material, in the event it's a disappointment. Six of the seven songs are cover versions of very well-known rock hits—"Johnny B.Goode," "I'm A Man," "All Day And All Of The Night," "Hang On Sloopy," "Like A Rolling Stone"—competently done, but hardly revelatory, as the Remains' chief strength was their excellent songwriting. The version of the original tune "Why Do I Cry" is indeed fine and powerful, but the Remains' legacy is best heard on the excellent, nearly all-original *Barry & The Remains* collection on Epic. —*Richie Unterberger*

Dave Bartholomew

b. Dec. 24, 1920, Edgard, LA
New Orleans R&B
A major contributor to New Orleans R&B, Dave Bartholomew was a pivotal figure as a writer, arranger, producer, and A&R man for Imperial. It was Bartholomew's productions that helped make Fats Domino a major player in R&B and rock and roll, and he assembled the great house band that backed Domino, Little Richard, Lloyd Price, Smiley Lewis, and several other Crescent City greats. This band included pianist Allen Toussaint, bassist Frank Fields, saxophonists Lee Allen, Alvin "Red" Tyler, and Herb Hardesty, and

drummer Earl Palmer. Bartholomew recorded as a solo artist for King and others prior to taking over at Imperial, but his fame came from that stint. Bartholomew greatly reduced his activities after Domino left Imperial in the early '60s, but occasionally resurfaced to conduct his band. —*Ron Wynn*

★ **Spirit of New Orleans** / 1993 / EMI ✦✦✦✦✦
A two-disc set featuring fifty tracks and several different artists (including Fats Domino, Smiley Lewis, T-Bone Walker, Shirley and Lee, and Earl King), *Spirit of New Orleans* effectively conveys Bartholomew's groundbreaking achievements in R&B and rock & roll. —*Stephen Thomas Erlewine*

Dave Bartholomew and the Maryland Jazz Band / 1995 / GHB

Rob Base

Rap
A New York-based DJ who caused a stir with his clipped cadences and straight-ahead raps contrasted by choruses lifted from classic soul songs, notably Frankie Beverly and Maze's "Joy and Pain," which he neglected to credit. He had a partner, DJ E-Z Rock, on his first release *It Takes Two*. He did the second on his own, and continued the practice, this time using as his base (no pun intended) music from Edwin Starr, Marvin Gaye & Tammi Terrell, and Native-American rockers Redbone. —*Ron Wynn*

● **It Takes Two** / 1988 / Profile ✦✦✦✦
A wildly successful debut album from 1988 contains the excellent title cut and "Joy and Pain," which lifts from the Maze hit of the same name. Base is joined by DJ E-Z Rock. —*John Floyd*

The Incredible Base / 1989 / Profile ✦✦✦
On this good follow-up to his hit debut release, Base makes first-rate party raps and utilizes surging samples, rhythms, and grooves. He also makes a good plea for a resolution of rap rivalries on a reworking of the Edwin Starr/Temptations classic "War." —*Ron Wynn*

Basehead

Group, Alternative Pop/Rock
Basehead is the creation of Michael Ivey, a middle-class suburban kid from Maryland. Ivey recorded the bulk of Basehead's 1992 debut, *Plays with Toys*, on a four-track at home with various friends. Combining laidback, stoned hip-hop rhythm tracks, pop hooks, drawled raps, and pseudo-folky guitar, the record received glowing reviews in alternative publications and was played frequently on college radio. Ivey assembled a touring band and used them on parts of Basehead's 1993 follow-up, *Not in Kansas Anymore*. The critical reception was mixed and the record didn't receive much airplay or sales. The following year Ivey assembled the alternative hip-hop collection *B.Y.O.B.*, which featured several of his own contributions. —*Stephen Thomas Erlewine*

● **Play with Toys** / 1992 / Imago ✦✦✦✦

Not in Kansas Anymore / 1993 / Imago ✦✦✦

The Basement Wall

Group, Garage Rock
One of the more pop-oriented '60s garage bands, this Baton Rouge, LA, group had a big regional hit with "Never Existed" in 1967. Their sound contained elements of Texas punk, the bouncing Farfisa organ style of the Five Americans, and British Invasion harmonies. Likeable if not terribly significant, they disbanded in 1968, and much of their unreleased material was issued in the mid-'80s. —*Richie Unterberger*

Incredible Sound Of . . . / 1985 / Cicadelic ✦✦✦
The documentation on this album is sketchy, but apparently much, maybe most, of these 14 songs were previously unissued. This competent punk-pop material spans 1966–1968. Ronnie Weiss of the fine Texas band Mouse & The Traps (whose "A Public Execution" was included on *Nuggets*) plays lead guitar on "Never Existed." —*Richie Unterberger*

Bash & Pop

Group, Alternative Pop/Rock
After the Replacements quietly dissolved in 1991, their bassist Tommy Stinson formed his own band, Bash & Pop, in the following year. As their 1993 debut *Friday Night Is Killing Me* shows, the name accurately describes their rough, sloppy rock & roll. It suffered the same fate as many Replacements albums—it barely sold any copies. —*Stephen Thomas Erlewine*

Friday Night Is Killing Me / Jan. 1993 / Warner Brothers ✦✦✦
On his first album away from the Replacements, Tommy Stinson proves that Paul Westerberg wasn't the only gifted songwriter in the band. Stinson's songs aren't as incisive as Westerberg's, but they are solid rock & roll numbers, performed by a tight yet loose band. Although it's obvious that Bash & Pop have listened to their fair share of the Rolling Stones and the Faces, they don't recycle riffs; their sound is clearly good old-fashioned rock & roll, but the playing, songwriting, and Stinson's enthusiastic, ragged voice make the album sound fresh. —*Stephen Thomas Erlewine*

Basia (Basia Trzetrzelewska)

b. Sep. 30, 1959, Jaworzno, Poland
Pop
Vocalist Basia Trzetrzelewska spent a couple of years in the pop band Matt Bianco, an offshoot of Blue Rondo A La Turk, before she launched a solo career in 1987. With the musical assistance of Matt Bianco's Danny White, Basia developed a subtle cocktail-jazz-pop which was first showcased on her 1987 debut album, *Time and Tide*. Supported by the singles "New Day for You" and "Time and Tide," the record became a hit in Europe and America, where the album went platinum. Her second record, 1990's *London Warsaw New York*, was just as successful, but her third album, 1994's *Sweetest Illusion*, failed to find an audience. —*Stephen Thomas Erlewine*

Time and Tide / Aug. 1987 / Epic ✦✦✦
This 1987 mix of pop-soul has Brazilian overtones on "Astrud," a tribute to Astrud Gilberto. —*Bil Carpenter*

● **London Warsaw New York** / Feb. 1990 / Epic ✦✦✦✦
Melodic pop-jazz, it includes "Cruising for Bruising" and "Baby You're Mine." —*Kenneth M. Cassidy*

Sweetest Illusion / 1994 / Epic ✦✦
Taking four years between albums (with the intercession of the 1991 EP *Brave New Hope*), Basia returned in 1994 to discover that the appeal of her English-as-a-second-language cocktail jazz style had waned; after two straight platinum sellers, this one didn't even go gold. The wonder may be that she got as far as she did with an approach to music that confused awkwardness with sophistication. —*William Ruhlmann*

Fontella Bass

b. Jul. 3, 1940, St. Louis, MO
Soul
An explosive gospel and soul singer, Fontella Bass is the daughter of the great vocalist Martha Bass and sister of David Peaston, as well as ex-wife of Art Ensemble of Chicago trumpeter Lester Bowie. But none of that family history means as much as her own skills, which include a tremendous voice, great range, and distinctive delivery. Bass, who is also a fine pianist and organist, sang in several church choirs, as her mother was a member of Clara Ward's gospel troupe. She later moved into R&B, singing in Oliver Sain's band and working with Little Milton in the early '60s. Bass teamed with Bobby McClure for two duets on Checker in 1965. "Don't Mess up a Good Thing" reached number five on the R&B charts and inched into the pop Top 30, while "You'll Miss Me When I'm Gone" got into the R&B Top 30. Bass's debut single as a solo act was her greatest; "Rescue Me" topped the R&B charts for a month, peaked at number four on the pop charts, and was among the era's finest soul singles. The follow-up, "Recovery," was better than it has been credited, and reached number 13. Bass never again attained solo stardom, but has remained busy in the ensuing years. She later sang with Bowie's group, the Art Ensemble of Chicago, and was featured on the LP *Les Stances a Sophie*. She has also been part of the gospel group From the Root to the Source, and has reunited with Bowie on occasional projects. —*Ron Wynn*

● **Rescued: The Best of Fontella Bass** / 1992 / Chess ✦✦✦✦
"Rescue Me" might have been her only big hit, but Fontella Bass was a terrific gospel-influenced soul vocalist who cut several great sides for Checker/Chess Records in the mid-'60s. They might not have gotten the attention they deserved when they were released, but they have held up very well over the years. *Rescued: The Best of Fontella Bass* collects sixteen of her finest tracks, including "Rescue Me," three duets with Bobby McClure and a previously unreleased song; it makes a convincing case that she should have had more hit singles than she did. —*Stephen Thomas Erlewine*

Stiv Bators

d. Jun. 4, 1990
Punk, Power Pop/Anglo-Pop
With the Dead Boys, Stiv Bators was a ferocious post-Iggy Pop punk rocker, full of bleak, energetic nihilism and violence. When the group fell apart in the early '80s, Bators cut an album that departed from his group's sonic attack—it actually approaches power-pop at times—without losing his dynamic punk persona. It was the only full-length solo album he ever completed; after the release of *Disconnected*, he formed the Wanderers, which had a short life before he formed Lords of the New Church. In 1987, Bators joined the re-formed Dead Boys for a single; in 1988 he sang on a Lyres single. In 1990, Bators died from injuries sustained in an automobile accident in Paris. —*Stephen Thomas Erlewine*

● **Disconnected** / 1980 / Bomp! ✦✦✦✦
The Church and the New Creatures / 1983 / Lolita ✦✦

Bats

Group, Alternative Pop/Rock
One of the shining stars of the fertile Flying Nun record label in New Zealand, the Bats were formed in 1982 in Christchurch by guitarist/vocalist Robert Scott from the Clean, bassist Paul Kean (ex-Toy Love), drummer Malcolm Grant (ex-Builders), and vocalist/multi-instrumentalist Kaye Woodward. With their fresh take on garagey folk-rock that flirts with power-pop, the band quickly became critics' favorites in the late '80s. After two generally overlooked (except by critics and specialists) albums for Communion Records, they signed to Mammoth Records in 1991, gaining only slightly more mainstream exposure. The band remains active with Robert Scott occasionally stepping out for reunions with the Clean. —*Chris Woodstra*

○ **Compiletely Bats** / 1987 / Flying Nun ✦✦✦✦
Collection of non-LP tracks. —*Steve Aldrich*

● **Daddy's Highway** / 1988 / Communion ✦✦✦✦
The Bats' full-length debut immediately endears itself with the band's offbeat, at times frantic, version of jangly folk-rock with charmingly off-kilter harmonies. Robert Scott's effortless melodies and catchy hooks give an overall upbeat feeling despite a decidedly melancholy subject matter. —*Chris Woodstra*

The Law of Things / 1990 / Communion ✦✦✦
Law of Things is essentially *Daddy's Highway, Part 2*, displaying their update on '60s pop sensibility in full force. The production is slightly slicker but the songs continue in the same tradition that made the first album endlessly enjoyable. —*Chris Woodstra*

Fear of God / 1991 / Mammoth ✦✦✦
Though a bit redundant after the first two albums, *Fear of God* finds Robert Scott continuing his craftsmanlike songwriting without fail. The songs are perfect slices of pop even if they aren't particularly memorable this time out. —*Chris Woodstra*

Silverbeet / Dec. 1992 / Mammoth ✦✦✦
"Courage", "Sighting The Sound", "No Time For Your Kind", "Half Way To Nowhere"—all heady songs delivered at power-pop pace with such overwhelming resolve so to leave the listener almost woozy...like OD'ing on midway rides after downing too much cotton candy. The Bats offer an occasional change of pace, such as the hypnotizing "Stay Away" and doleful "Valley Floor." Soaring and somber, moody and frenetic, *Silverbeet* is not your usual confectionary. But let this stuff seep in for a few listens and you may find yourself readily converted. —*Roch Parisien*

Spill The Beans / 1994 / Mammoth ✦✦

Bauhaus

Group, Alternative Pop/Rock
Bauhaus are the founding fathers of goth-rock, creating a minimalistic, overbearingly gloomy style of post-punk rock driven by jagged guitar chords and cold, distant synthesizers. Throughout their brief career, the band explored all the variations on their bleak musical ideas, adding elements of glam rock, experimental electronic rock, funk, and heavy metal. While their following has never expanded beyond a cult, they have kept their cult alive well into the '90s, a full decade after they disbanded.

The group formed in 1978 in Northampton, England. Guitarist/vocalist Daniel Ash, bassist/vocalist David Jay (born David Jay Haskins), and drummer Kevin Haskins had played together as a trio called the Craze before forming Bauhaus with vocalist Peter Murphy. Originally, the band was called Bauhaus 1919 after the German art movement; by 1979, they had dropped the 1919 from their name.

In August of 1979, the group released their debut single, "Bela Lugosi's Dead" on the independent record label Small Wonder Records. Although it did not make the pop charts, it became the de facto goth-rock anthem, staying in the U.K. independent charts for years. Three months later, the group signed with Beggars Banquet's subsidiary label, 4AD. The group's second single, "Dark Entries," was a remake of the B-side of "Bel Lugosi's Dead" and was released in January 1980. Following their first European tour, Bauhaus released their third single, "Terror Couple Kill Colonel," in the summer of that year, becoming a hit on the indie charts. After touring America for the first time in September, the group released a version of T. Rex's "Telegram Sam;" like their other singles, it was a major indie success. In October, they released their debut album, *In the Flat Field*, which reached number one on the independent charts and number 72 on the pop charts. The success of the album led to their first hits on the pop charts—both "Kick in the Eye" and "The Passions of Lovers" made the U.K. Top 60 in 1981. In October, they released their second album, *Mask*, which revealed a more ambitious musical direction; the new direction, which featured elements of metal and electronic sonic textures, made the music lighter and more accessible without abandoning the dark, foreboding core of their music. *Mask* was a commercial success, peaking at number 30 on the U.K. charts.

Early in 1982, Bauhaus filmed a cameo for the David Bowie/Catherine Deneuve film *The Hunger*, performing "Bel Lugosi's Dead" in a London nightclub. In March, the group released the EP *Searching for Satori*, which reached number 45 on the U.K. charts; another successful single, "Spirit," followed in the summer. That fall, the group had a number 15 hit with their version of David Bowie's "Ziggy Stardust." The success of the single propelled their third album, *The Sky's Gone Out*, to number four on the album charts. Not coincidentally, *The Sky's Gone Out* was their most musically accessible and brightest album to date.

Peter Murphy contracted pneumonia at the beginning of 1983, which prevented him from participating in the recording sessions for Bauhaus' fourth album, *Burning from the Inside*. Consequently, the record featured substantial contributions from David Ash and David Jay, who both pursued more personal and atmospheric directions. After Murphy recovered, the band toured Japan and then returned to the U.K. to promote the summer release of *Burning from the Inside*. The album was another hit, peaking at number 13. In July, Bauhaus performed their final concert in London, playing a series of encores, which included farewells from the group. A press release issued shortly afterward confirmed that the band had broken up.

After Bauhaus' breakup, Murphy formed Dali's Car with Japan's Mick Karn and then pursued a solo career; while he had the occasional hit, including 1990's "Cuts You Up," he never became more than a cult favorite. Ash continued with Tones on Tail, a project he began in 1981; Kevin Haskins also joined the band after Bauhaus' split. David Jay did made some solo records and joined the Jazz Butcher briefly. Ash, Haskins, and Jay formed Love and Rockets in 1985 after a proposed Bauhaus reunion fell apart because Peter Murphy wasn't interested in the project. Love and Rockets were one of the more popular alternative acts of the late '80s, scoring a crossover number three hit single in 1989 with "So Alive." —*Stephen Thomas Erlewine*

In the Flat Field / Nov. 1980 / Nesak ✦✦✦
It captures the brooding bleakness of early Bauhaus. —*David Szatmary*

Mask / Oct. 1981 / Beggars Banquet ✦✦✦
In this follow-up to *In the Flat Field*, Bauhaus matures by creating an album that stands on its own rather than a collection of scattered hits strung together with not-so-strong fillers. Feedback-driven looped guitars, fuzz bass, and Peter Murphy's ever-haunting, commanding vocals help to create their best album. More raw than their later material, yet nicely refined next to their first, it includes "The Passion of Lovers" and "Kick in the Eye." —*Julian Katz*

Press the Eject & Give Me the Tape / 1982 / Beggars Banquet ✦✦
The Sky's Gone Out / Oct. 1982 / A&M ✦✦✦
An upbeat, commercially successful Bauhaus album (#4 in the UK), it includes a remake of Bowie's "Ziggy Stardust" and a three-part mini-opera, "The Three Shadows." —*David Szatmary*

○ **Burning from the Inside** / Jul. 1983 / A&M ◆◆◆◆
During the recording sessions for Bauhaus's final album, *Burning from the Inside*, Peter Murphy suffered from pneumonia, leaving David J and Daniel Ash to complete most of the record themselves. The result is the band's most pop-oriented album; it's also their best, even if it is slightly incohesive. —*Stephen Thomas Erlewine*

Singles: 1981-1983 / Oct. 1983 / Beggars Banquet ◆◆◆
● **Singles: 1979-1983** / Nov. 1985 / Beggars Banquet ◆◆◆◆
Essentially, Bauhaus was a singles band—all of their best moments were individual songs, not entire albums. And the double-disc *The Singles 1979-1983* collects them all, including some B-sides and album tracks, making it the one essential Bauhaus purchase. —*Stephen Thomas Erlewine*

Swing the Heartache: The BBC Sessions / Jul. 1989 / Beggars Banquet ◆◆◆
This is a posthumous collection of five sessions on English BBC, some from John Peel's famous show, on which Bauhaus abandoned hits such as "Bela Lugosi" and "Dark Entries" to experiment with different songs and revamp certain prereleased material. The loose, live-recorded format suits this group, whose creative and skilled musicianship is highlighted on this recording. "God in an Alcove" and "Swing the Heartache" are rendered much better here. It's a better greatest-hits album than the double set *1979-1983*. —*Julian Katz*

Bay City Rollers

Group, Pop/Rock
The Bay City Rollers were a Scottish pop/rock band of the '70s with a strong following among teenage girls. The origins of the group go back to the formation of the duo the Longmuir Brothers in the late '60s, consisting of drummer Derek Longmuir (b. Mar. 19, 1952, Edinburgh, Scotland) and his bass-playing brother Alan (b. June 20, 1953, Edinburgh, Scotland). They eventually changed their name to Saxon, adding singer Nobby Clarke and John Devine. Then they changed their name again by pointing at random to a spot on a map of the United States: Bay City, Michigan. Their first hit was a cover of the Gentrys' "Keep on Dancing," which reached #9 in the U.K. in September 1971. In June 1972, guitarist Eric Faulkner (b. Oct. 21, 1954, Edinburgh, Scotland) joined. In January 1973, singer Leslie McKeown (b.Nov. 12, 1955, Edinburgh, Scotland) and guitarist Stuart Wood (b. Feb/ 25. 1957, Edinburgh, Scotland) replaced Clarke and Devine, stabilizing the quintet's lineup.

After flopping with three singles, they finally hit the Top Ten again in February 1974 with a cover of the Shangri-Las' "Remember (Walking in the Sand)." At this point, the Rollers became a teen sensation in Great Britain, with their good looks and tartan knickers, and they scored a series of Top Ten U.K. hits over the next two-and-a-half years: "Shang-A-Lang," "Summerlove Sensation," "All of Me Loves All of You," "Bye Bye Baby" (a cover of the Four Seasons hit that went to #1), "Give a Little Love" (another #1), "Money Honey," "Love Me Like I Love You," and "I Only Wanna Be with You" (a cover of the Dusty Springfield hit). Their albums *Rollin'*, *Once Upon a Star*, *Wouldn't You Like It*, and *Dedication* were also Top Ten successes, with *Rollin'* and *Once Upon a Star* getting to #1. They scored their first U.S. hit with "Saturday Night," which was released in September 1975 and hit #1 in January 1976. It was followed by the Top Ten hits "Money Honey" and "You Made Me Believe in Magic." The Rollers also had five straight gold albums in the U.S.: *Bay City Rollers, Rock N' Roll Love Letter, Dedication, It's a Game,* and *Greatest Hits.*

Alan Longmuir left the band in June 1976 and was replaced by Ian Mitchell (b. Aug. 22, 1958, Downpatrick, County Down, Northern Ireland) who was in turn replaced by Pat McGlynn (b. Mar. 31, 1958, Edinburgh, Scotland) in June 1977. Longmuir returned in 1978, the same year that McKeown was replaced by Duncan Faure and Faulkner quit to go solo. But by then the Bay City Rollers had scored their last hits. —*William Ruhlmann*

Rollin' / Oct. 1974 / Bell ◆◆
While the single "Saturday Night" put them on the charts, it sealed their fate as well—forever after, they would be known as a bubblegum band. However, a listen to *Rollin'* shows that there was a bit more to these boys, as not every song fits neatly into the bubblegum mould. In fact, "Angel Angel," written by band members Faulkner & Wood, is a nice stab at a pop song. —*Jim Worbois*

Once upon a Star / May 1975 / Bell ◆◆
Bay City Rollers / Sep. 1975 / Arista ◆◆
This is the American version of the *Rollin'* album but without the diversity of the other record. Featuring a slightly different track lineup, the LP is definitely targeted at the bubblegum audience. —*Jim Worbois*

Wouldn't You Like It / Dec. 1975 / Bell ◆◆
Rock N' Roll Love Letter / Mar. 1976 / Arista ◆◆◆
Are they bubblegum? Are they pop? Or maybe disco? Unfortunately, this album does nothing to answer that question. The single, a fairly respectable cover of Tim Moore's "Rock n' Roll Love Letter," was a nice step in the pop direction. —*Jim Worbois*

Dedication / Sep. 1976 / Bell ◆◆
From the opening notes of "Let's Pretend," it sounds like producer Jimmy Ienner was trying to refashion the Bay City Rollers as Eric Carmen-lite. Unfortunately for the band, Carmen had beaten them to the punch and Shaun Cassidy would soon prove he could do it better than Carmen. Still, they managed to get three tracks from this album in the Top 60—"Dedication," "I Only Want to Be with You," and "Yesterday's Hero." —*Jim Worbois*

It's a Game / Jul. 1977 / Arista ◆◆
● **Greatest Hits** / Nov. 1977 / Arista ◆◆◆◆
Strangers in the Wind / 1978 / Arista ◆◆
Elevator / Arista ◆◆◆
Unfortunately for the band, by the time they dropped Bay City from their name, it was too late to resurrect their career. Too bad because this is the record they were meant to make. It also makes one wonder whether, under the right circumstances, they could have been making records this strong all along?! —*Jim Worbois*

Be Bop Deluxe

Group, Art-Rock/Progressive-Rock
Be-Bop Deluxe was a 1970s British rock group led by guitarist Bill Nelson (b. Dec 18, 1948, Wakefield, Yorkshire, England) that veered between glam-rock, pop, and heavy metal, with lots of demonstrations of Nelson's guitar prowess. After recording with Gentle Revolution and on his own, Nelson put together the first lineup of Be-Bop Deluxe in 1972: Ian Parkin (guitar); Robert Bryan (drums); and Nicholas Chatterton-Dew (drums). But after the release of the first album, *Axe Victim*, Nelson sacked the band. The second album, *Futurama*, featured Nelson with a rhythm section of bassist Charles Tumahai and drummer Simon Fox. Keyboard player Andrew Clark joined for the third album, *Sunburst Finish*, which contained the U.K. chart single "Ships in the Night." Be-Bop Deluxe released a fourth album, *Modern Music*, a concert recording, *Live! In the Air Age*, that became their only U.K. Top Ten hit, and a fifth studio album, *Drastic Plastic*, before Nelson folded the enterprise, briefly tried another group, Red Noise, and went solo again in 1979. Since then he has recorded prolifically, if experimentally, and handled occasional production jobs. —*William Ruhlmann*

Axe Victim / 1974 / Harvest ◆◆◆
When Be-Bop Deluxe's first album was released during the glam-rock wave in 1974, and the band (then comprising Bill Nelson and Ian Parkin on guitars, Robert Bryan on bass, and Nicholas Chatterton-Dew on drums) turned up on the back of the record cover in heavy makeup, it was viewed as being in the David Bowie mold, which certainly took in Nelson's thin but confident tenor vocals and the uptempo rock approach, and even ballads like "Adventures In A Yorkshire Landscape" that sounded a lot like Bowie's "Rock 'N' Roll Suicide." But it was already obvious that Nelson was an unusually lyrical guitarslinger, and in fact the tunes often took a backseat to his sometimes jazzy, sometimes metallish excursions. He was, as he sang, "an axe victim," but at the same time, Be-Bop Deluxe's musical identity was uncertain. —*William Ruhlmann*

Futurama / Jul. 1975 / Harvest ◆◆
Bill Nelson sacked the rest of Be-Bop Deluxe after the release of *Axe Victim* and hired bassist Charles Tumahai and drummer Simon Fox to make *Futurama*. The back cover shows Nelson, decked out in a fool's costume, chained and restrained by his new bandmates. But on the record, he lets his guitar playing free to dominate the proceedings even more than it did on Be-Bop's debut and constructs sometimes overly elaborate arrangements that overwhelm whatever substance the songs might otherwise have. —*William Ruhlmann*

○ **Sunburst Finish** / Jan. 1976 / Harvest ✦✦✦✦
Adding keyboard player Andrew Clark to make Be-Bop Deluxe a quartet, Bill Nelson finally found a balance between his virtuosic guitar playing and the demands of pop songwriting. The arrangements were still busy, but the humor of Nelson's music was on display as never before, and the songs frequently were catchy. For the first time, it began to seem that the group had a future beyond serving as a foundation for Nelson's splashy guitar work, as Be-Bop Deluxe charted in the U.S. and the U.K. and even scored a Top 25 British hit with "Ships In The Night." —*William Ruhlmann*

Modern Music / Sep. 1976 / Harvest ✦✦✦
Things had changed for Be-Bop Deluxe by the time of its fourth album. The band that turned up in glam-rock regalia on its 1974 debut, *Axe Victim*, was in suit and tie on the cover of *Modern Music* in 1976. Inside, the band's transformation into a sophisticated pop group seemed complete. Arrangements were still ornate, but the songs were dominated by their highly imagistic lyrics, and as often as not, Nelson was borrowing ideas from the Beatles. It didn't quite work, despite pleasant numbers such as "Orphans Of Babylon" and "Kiss Of Light," perhaps because a true pop sensibility requires a gift for simplicity that Nelson has never exhibited. The album charted high in England and made the Top 100 in the U.S., but it was Be-Bop's peak, not its breakthrough. —*William Ruhlmann*

Live! in the Air Age / Aug. 1977 / Harvest ✦✦✦

Drastic Plastic / Feb. 1978 / Harvest ✦✦✦

The Best of & The Rest / 1979 / Harvest ✦✦✦

○ **Singles A's & B's** / 1981 / Harvest ✦✦✦✦

Electrical Language / 1983 / Cocteau ✦✦✦

● **Raiding the Divine Archive: The Best of Be Bop Deluxe** / Aug. 1990 / Capitol ✦✦✦✦
The release is a smartly assembled overview of the arty-sci-fi-rock outfit (heavier on the rock), led by Bill Nelson, one of the most powerfully elegant lead guitarists of the '70s. The band was an early experimenter of techno-rock. Dense clinical production (sometimes recalling mid-period Roxy Music), further underscored by Nelson's cold detached vocals, occasionally does a poor job of drawing the listener into appreciating the band's real musical strengths. —*Rick Clark*

The Beach Boys
Group, Surf, Pop/Rock
The Beach Boys are the most successful and important American band of the rock music era. They were formed in 1961 in Hawthorne, CA, around the three Wilson brothers: Brian (b. Jun 20, 1942) (bass, piano, vocals), Dennis (b. Dec 4, 1944—d. Dec 28, 1983) (drums, vocals), and Carl (b. Dec 21, 1946) (guitar, vocals). Additional members were Mike Love (b. Mar 15, 1941) (vocals), the Wilsons' cousin, and Al Jardine (b. Sep 3, 1942) (guitar, vocals). From the start, the focus of the group's music was Brian Wilson, who combined a fascination with vocal harmony in the Four Freshmen mold with a love of Chuck Berry-derived rock & roll. Added to that was the subject matter of middle-class teenage life in Southern California—surfing, cars, and girls.

The result was massive popular success for the group during the first half of the 1960s, starting with their first chart entry, "Surfin'" in 1962. "Surfin'" was released on a local record label. Subsequently, the group signed to the major label Capitol Records, where they stayed for the rest of the '60s. But their early recordings have continued to turn up on one discount label after another ever since. To date, the most complete and best quality version of the material is to be found on the 1991 DCC album *Lost and Found!* (1961–62).

The Beach Boys' first Capitol single, "Surfin' Safari," was released in June 1962 and became their first Top 40 hit. It was followed in October by a debut album of the same name. Similarly, in March 1963, Capitol released the single "Surfin' U.S.A.," which became the group's first Top Ten hit, and the *Surfin' U.S.A.* album, which went gold. They followed in July with "Surfer Girl," another Top Ten, and in September with a gold-selling *Surfer Girl* LP.

By this point, Brian Wilson, who was composing nearly all of the material (with lyrics by himself, Love, and others), had taken over production of the group's records as well. Given the accelerated recording schedule of the day, it was an awesome task when coupled with his onstage performing duties. This is illustrated by the release of the Beach Boys' fourth album, the million-selling

Little Deuce Coupe, less than a month after *Surfer Girl*. The album featured a version of their latest Top Ten hit, "Be True to Your School."

The Beach Boys dominated the pop music of 1963, but in early 1964, the Beatles arrived in the U.S., followed by the rest of the British Invasion, and the Beach Boys felt the competition keenly. Unlike most American recording artists, however, the group did not suffer a drop-off in popularity. In fact, 1964 was another banner year for the Beach Boys, with the Top Ten singles "Fun, Fun, Fun," "When I Grow Up (To Be a Man)," and "Dance, Dance, Dance," as well as their first #1 single, the gold-selling "I Get Around," and three more gold albums, *Shut Down, Vol. 2* (*Vol. 1* had been a various artists album), *All Summer Long*, and their first #1 LP, *Beach Boys Concert*. (There was also a Beach Boys' *Christmas Album*.)

The strain of all that work caught up with Brian Wilson, however, and at the end of 1964, he retired from onstage work with the Beach Boys, retaining his composing and producing duties. The group eventually settled on Bruce Johnston (b. Jun 24, 1944) as his replacement.

The first product of this arrangement was the March 1965 album *The Beach Boys Today!*, which contained a version of their next #1 single, "Help Me, Rhonda," followed four months later by the group's eighth straight gold album, *Summer Days (And Summer Nights!!)* and its single, the Top Ten "California Girls." Such recordings gave evidence of the expansion of Brian Wilson's musical imagination, which found him taking longer to make records that were more ambitious than the group's early teen anthems.

While Wilson prepared his next opus, Capitol's release schedule was satisfied by the *Beach Boys' Party* album, released in September, featuring a hit cover of "Barbara Ann." In March 1966, Wilson released "Caroline, No," which was billed as a solo single and made the Top 40. But he did not launch a full-fledged solo career at this time, instead completing the group's *Pet Sounds* (May 1966), which featured the Top Ten hits "Sloop John B" and "Wouldn't It Be Nice" and was universally hailed as one of the greatest rock albums of all time, though it did not sell as well as Beach Boys albums usually did.

Wilson trumped it with the #1 gold single "Good Vibrations," released in October. By this point, he was being hailed as a genius in the media, as he prepared a new album tentatively titled *Smile*. The album never appeared, however. A single, "Heroes and Villains" (July 1967), offered tantalizing clues to what would become a legendary unheard, unfinished masterpiece. But then Brian Wilson, whether because of the pressure to top himself and compete with the Beatles and others, internal disagreements within the group, psychological problems, or drug abuse, ceded leadership of the Beach Boys, and their next album, *Smiley Smile* (September 1967), was produced by the group as a whole.

At the same time, the Beach Boys suffered a commercial decline, and though they continued to release new albums—*Wild Honey* (December 1967), *Friends* (June 1968), *20/20* (February 1969)—and singles through the end of the decade, they ceased to be an important force in popular music. In 1970, the group switched to the Reprise subsidiary of Warner Bros. Records for a series of albums that sometimes drew critical approval without restoring their commercial appeal—*Sunflower* (August 1970), *Surf's Up* (August 1971), *Carl and the Passions/So Tough* (May 1972) (initially packaged with a reissue of *Pet Sounds*), and *Holland* (January 1973).

The Beach Boys returned to prominence in the mid-'70s on a wave of nostalgia and a potent concert act that focused on their early hits. Capitol Records had repackaged their catalogue repeatedly, but *Endless Summer*, a June 1974 double LP compiling their early-'60s work, amazingly topped the charts, becoming their first gold album in seven years. In July 1976, the Beach Boys released *15 Big Ones*, their first new studio album in more than three years and their first album in a decade to credit Brian Wilson as producer. The album spawned a Top Ten hit in a cover of Chuck Berry's "Rock and Roll Music," but the group's commercial appeal, at least as far as new recordings, was temporary. Subsequent albums *The Beach Boys Love You* (April 1977) and *M.I.U. Album* (September 1978) sold less well. Brian Wilson's "comeback" also proved elusive after 1977.

The Beach Boys moved to their third major label with the release of *L.A. (Light Album)* on the Caribou subsidiary of CBS Records in March 1979. But neither that album nor its follow-up, *Keepin' the Summer Alive* (March 1980) did anything to change the group's commercial status. In December 1983, Dennis Wilson drowned. In June 1985, the group returned with *The Beach Boys*, their first new album in five years, which marked the end of their Caribou contract.

The Beach Boys recorded sporadically thereafter. In 1987, they scored a surprising hit cover of "Wipeout," co-billed with rap act the Fat Boys. In 1988, minus Brian Wilson, who finally launched a solo career, they returned to #1 with "Kokomo," from the hit film *Cocktail*. In 1992, they released their first new album in seven years, *Summer in Paradise*.

Especially with the dawn of the CD era, the extensive repackagings of Beach Boys material have continued apace. 1993 finally brought a five-CD boxed set retrospective, *Good Vibrations: Thirty Years of the Beach Boys*. In 1995, after the resolution of various legal issues, lead singer Mike Love and Brian Wilson were working together again and there were plans for an archival release of the legendary *Smile* sessions. *— William Ruhlmann*

Surfin' Safari / Oct. 29, 1962 / Capitol ◆◆
The Beach Boys' debut album contains the Top 40 title track and the chart entries "Ten Little Indians" and "409," as well as a version of "Summertime Blues." It has a youthful exuberance but is not as accomplished as the group's albums would become shortly. *— William Ruhlmann*

Surfin' U.S.A. / Mar. 25, 1963 / Capitol ◆◆
The title track, which was really the music from Chuck Berry's "Sweet Little Sixteen" with new lyrics (he now gets the writing credit), was the Beach Boys' breakthrough hit, and the album, a gold-selling Top 10 hit, also featured the Top 40 "Shut Down" and a lovely Brian Wilson falsetto lead on "Farmer's Daughter." But the rest was filler. *— William Ruhlmann*

Shut Down / Jun. 1963 / Capitol ◆◆

Surfer Girl / Sep. 23, 1963 / Capitol ◆◆
The Beach Boys' third album features the Top 10 title song, "Little Deuce Coupe," the paean to cocooning, "In My Room," and "Catch A Wave." It is also the first Beach Boys album to be produced by Brian Wilson. But there's still a little too much filler to merit a higher grade. *— William Ruhlmann*

Little Deuce Coupe / Oct. 21, 1963 / Capitol ◆◆
The fourth album was also the Beach Boys' fourth to be released within one year, so let's not blame them for the repetitions. Moving the group from the beach to the race track, it features the second LP appearances of the title track, "Shut Down," and "409," as well as a version of "Be True To Your School" that differs from the concurrently released single (which featured the Honeys on cheerleading backup vocals). *— William Ruhlmann*

Shut Down, Vol. 2 / Mar. 23, 1964 / Capitol ◆◆
Given a confusing title and released by Capitol while the label was still trying to keep up with the Beatles' initial onslaught of popularity, this LP climbed to only #13, but it included the brilliant "Fun, Fun, Fun," the lovely "Don't Worry, Baby" and "The Warmth Of The Sun," along with the usual filler. *— William Ruhlmann*

All Summer Long / Jul. 13, 1964 / Capitol ◆◆
The Beach Boys rebounded from the British Invasion with their first #1 single, "I Get Around" and this summer '64 release, which also includes such lesser but still good tracks as "Little Honda," "Wendy," and "Don't Back Down." *— William Ruhlmann*

The Beach Boys Concert / Oct. 19, 1964 / Capitol ◆
This album actually topped the charts for four weeks; today, it's a historical artifact, with its waves of screaming fans competing with the band. Not one of the best live albums ever made, but certainly filled with energy. *— William Ruhlmann*

○ **The Beach Boys Today!** / Mar. 8, 1965 / Capitol ◆◆◆◆
The first album to be released after Brian Wilson's retirement from the stage includes a raft of hits: "When I Grow Up To Be A Man," "Dance, Dance, Dance," "Do You Wanna Dance?," and an alternate version of the Beach Boys' second #1, "Help Me, Rhonda." Even the filler, including "Don't Hurt My Little Sister," was improving. *— William Ruhlmann*

○ **Summer Days (And Summer Nights!!)** / Jul. 5, 1965 / Capitol ◆◆◆◆
The summer album for 1965 contains "California Girls" and the single version of "Help Me, Rhonda." Those are the only hits, but the album also contains several examples of Brian Wilson's increasing musical sophistication and eccentricity, among them "Let Him Run Wild," "You're So Good To Me," "Summer Means New

Love," and the bizarre "I'm Bugged At My Old Man." *— William Ruhlmann*

The Beach Boys Party! / Nov. 8, 1965 / Capitol ◆◆◆
Far more than the throwaway it seemed at the time, this contrived party-in-the-studio album finds the Beach Boys commenting on the folk boom and the British Invasion and turning in fun versions of rock & roll favorites and their own hits. Contains the hit "Barbara Ann," which is actually sung by Dean Torrence of Jan and Dean. *— William Ruhlmann*

☆ **Pet Sounds** / May 16, 1966 / Capitol ◆◆◆◆◆
The group's most well-realized, ambitious, and well-produced album. A wistful, bittersweet, achingly beautiful foray into postteenage angst ("God Only Knows," "Wouldn't It Be Nice," "That's Not Me") and uncertainty ("Don't Talk") augmented with one hit rock single ("Sloop John B"). The most serious record this band ever did, teens confronting time and aging. *— Bruce Eder*

Smiley Smile / Sep. 18, 1967 / Capitol ◆◆◆
Smiley Smile has long been underrated because of what it is not, namely Brian Wilson's unfinished masterpiece, *Smile*. What it is is an exploratory album containing Wilson's two magnificent singles, "Good Vibrations" and "Heroes And Villains," plus much of the eccentric material intended for *Smile*, albeit as patched together by the other Beach Boys. It remains a curiosity, but nevertheless, some of the '60s' most imaginative music is found here. *— William Ruhlmann*

Wild Honey / Dec. 18, 1967 / Capitol ◆◆◆
Remembered as the album on which the other Beach Boys really took over, *Wild Honey* actually features a lot of Brian Wilson, who has co-writing credits on nine of its 11 tracks, including the Top 40 title track and the Top 20 "Darlin'." Also included is the original version of "Here Comes The Night," later redone as a disco tune. *— William Ruhlmann*

Friends / Jun. 24, 1968 / Capitol ◆◆
Brian Wilson's participation is reduced here, but he still contributes the delightful curiosity "Busy Doin' Nothin'," and the album also contains the Top 50 title track and the Wilson-Jardine collaboration "Wake The World." *— William Ruhlmann*

Stack O Tracks / Aug. 1968 / Capitol ◆◆
Considering that the Beach Boys are known for their singing, it's odd they'd think to release an album consisting of the instrumental tracks to many of their familiar songs. Call it the first karaoke album. *— William Ruhlmann*

20/20 / Feb. 3, 1969 / Capitol ◆◆
This was a contractual obligation album marking the end of the Beach Boys' tenure at Capitol Records, but it is an interesting set nevertheless, containing the singles "Do It Again," "Bluebirds Over The Mountain," and "I Can Hear Music," as well as the *Smile* outtake "Cabinessence" and Dennis Wilson's collaboration with mass murderer Charles Manson, "Never Learn Not to Love." *— William Ruhlmann*

Sunflower / Aug. 31, 1970 / Caribou ◆◆◆
The group's first new '70s album, and a highpoint for all concerned, from the transcendental doo-wop music of "This Whole World" to the simple pleasantries of "Add Some Music." *— Bruce Eder*

○ **Surf's Up [Caribou]** / Aug. 30, 1971 / Caribou ◆◆◆◆
Its title notwithstanding, this album has less to do with surfing than with the band coming to terms with aging and with changing audiences—environmentalism shares space alongside the title track, a poignant, serious masterpiece of modern pop music. *— Bruce Eder*

Carl and the Passions: So Tough / May 15, 1972 / Caribou ◆◆
For reasons best known to themselves, the Beach Boys chose to package their new 1972 album as a twofer with their 1966 masterpiece *Pet Sounds*. The new album inevitably suffered in comparison, but the Brian Wilson tunes "You Need A Mess Of Help To Stand Alone" and "Marcella" are stand-outs. *— William Ruhlmann*

Holland / Jan. 8, 1973 / Caribou ◆◆◆
The California sun mixed with mysticisms and some outrageous sound experiments (all with a great beat). A failed effort to renew the group's sound with a change of venue (to Holland) that is salvaged largely by the presence of one great rock number ("Sail on Sailor") and a conceptual piece ("California Saga") that has a phenomenal middle section. *— Bruce Eder*

The Beach Boys in Concert / Nov. 19, 1973 / Caribou ✦✦✦
With virtually no audience presence on this live album, it's a good deal less exciting than either of their Capitol live recordings. But some of the concert renditions ("Don't Worry Baby") are superior to the studio originals, and the record as a whole is consistently rewarding. A farewell to the band's third golden era, with a big sound and an excellent cross-section of songs. —*Bruce Eder*

○ **Endless Summer** / Jun. 24, 1974 / Capitol ✦✦✦✦
A notable collection, as the record that sparked the commercial revival of the band's fortunes during the '70s, although all of the material on it has been remastered in superior form on other Capitol CDs. —*Bruce Eder*

Spirit of America / Apr. 14, 1975 / Capitol ✦✦✦
A follow-up to *Endless Summer*, much weaker in content (except for the inclusion of "Breakaway"), but its near-repeat success helped put the group back in the spotlight. —*Bruce Eder*

Good Vibrations: Best of the Beach Boys / Jun. 23, 1975 / Brother ✦✦✦
A well-chosen compilation of Beach Boys songs recorded between 1966 and 1973, this album makes a good followup to the *Endless Summer* and *Spirit Of America* collections. —*William Ruhlmann*

15 Big Ones / Jul. 5, 1976 / Caribou ✦✦
A return to simplicity and the group's roots, complete with a hit Chuck Berry cover ("Rock and Roll Music") and a lot of songs about beaches, babes, and amusement parks. It was a hit too. —*Bruce Eder*

Love You / Apr. 11, 1977 / Caribou ✦✦✦
The Beach Boys had hailed the return of Brian Wilson with their 1976 album *15 Big Ones*, but it was on this follow-up, produced by Wilson, who also wrote almost all of it as well, that he was heard in all his demented glory, singing with childlike wonder about Johnny Carson, among other topics. Strange, but fascinating, especially for longtime Wilson watchers. —*William Ruhlmann*

M.I.U. Album / Sep. 25, 1978 / Caribou ✦✦✦
The group's last halfway-good album, sparked by pleasant singing, some unexpected rock cover versions, and funny wordplay by Brian Wilson. —*Bruce Eder*

L.A. (Light Album) / Mar. 16, 1979 / Caribou ✦✦
The Beach Boys went into their outtakes archive for this cobbled-together collection, which nevertheless features the lovely Brian and Carl Wilson collaboration "Good Timin'." Much of it is mediocre, however, and the nearly 11-minute disco version of "Here Comes The Night" is an embarrassment. —*William Ruhlmann*

Keepin' the Summer Alive / Mar. 17, 1980 / Caribou ✦
A low point. Bruce Johnston produces a Beach Boys soundalike album using the actual group, plus 22 other credited musicians, while Carl Wilson collaborates with Randy Bachman of Bachman-Turner Overdrive. —*William Ruhlmann*

Ten Years of Harmony / Dec. 1981 / Caribou ✦✦✦
An adequate collection of their best 1970-1980 period music, but missing some tracks. —*Bruce Eder*

Beach Boys Rarities / 1983 / Capitol ✦✦✦
Alternate takes, surprising cover versions, and different mixes of familiar songs make this a delight for collectors and hard-core fans. To anyone else, it's pleasant but non-essential. —*William Ruhlmann*

The Beach Boys / Jun. 1985 / Caribou ✦✦
The Beach Boys' first all-new studio album in five years (and last for seven years) is a concerted attempt to regain old glories, which it did to an extent, selling better than any record since *15 Big Ones* (1976) and spinning off the Top 40 single "Getcha Back" and the chart entry "It's Gettin' Late." But despite the production sheen provided by Steve Levine (of Culture Club fame), this is another competent but uninspired effort. —*William Ruhlmann*

Still Cruisin' / Aug. 1989 / Capitol ✦✦
The Beach Boys' success with soundtracks, notably their #1 1988 hit with "Kokomo" from *Cocktail*, provides the rationale for this hodgepodge of oldies and one-off singles. Their new savior, producer Terry Melcher, helps them sound like a professional '60s cover band. Meanwhile, Brian Wilson has quietly disappeared. —*William Ruhlmann*

Lost and Found! (1961-62) / 1991 / DCC ✦✦
Before securing a deal with Capitol, the Beach Boys made their first inroads into the music business with recordings for several tiny L.A. labels in 1961 and 1962. This CD presents no less than 16 takes from these sessions, along with sundry studio chatter. Only a few of these cuts were issued at the time: their debut single "Surfin'" and a single issued under the pseudonym Kenny and the Cadets. This compilation is definitely for the serious fan; the sound is very basic and thin in comparison to their famous recordings, and there are multiple takes of most of the songs that can make for trying listening. That said, it is also at times a fascinating glimpse into history, showing the Beach Boys polishing their already impressive harmonies on early versions of "Surfer Girl" and "Surfin' Safari." Much of the rest of the material is a bit maudlin in nature, owing more to doo-wop and teen idol balladry than the driving surf music that would make the group superstars in 1963. This compilation of mostly previously unissued material features songs from their very first recording session in October of 1961, and includes exhaustive liner notes. —*Richie Unterberger*

★ **The Absolute Best, Vol. 1** / 1991 / Capitol ✦✦✦✦✦
The early hits and their best-known songs ("Surfin' USA," "Fun, Fun, Fun," etc.), and a good anthology from that standpoint—but none of all the really interesting stuff from the albums and B-sides. It's also a little too predictable, making it okay for the unadventurous. —*Bruce Eder*

☆ **Absolute Best, Vol. 2** / 1991 / Capitol ✦✦✦✦✦
The second half of this collection is much more interesting than the first, containing as it does some of their most offbeat celebrated tracks. —*Bruce Eder*

Summer in Paradise / 1992 / Brother ✦
What would the Beach Boys be like if Brian Wilson were banned and lead singer Mike Love ruled the roost? Like this—writing bad new songs, recording bad covers of old songs—a pointless parody of themselves. —*William Ruhlmann*

☆ **Good Vibrations: Thirty Years of the Beach Boys** / Jun. 21, 1993 / Capitol ✦✦✦✦✦
A 5-CD box set, containing a whopping 142 tracks and covering the group's entire career, that manages to feel like too much and not enough at the same time. True, all of the key hits and most of their finest album tracks are here. The group's decline after 1966—and very sharp decline after 1970—is inescapable, and even though most of the material here is from the 1960s, the fourth disc especially (spanning the early 1970s to the late 1980s) is very rough sailing indeed. It's true that about 50 of these tracks are previously unreleased, but be warned that many of them are demos, backing tracks, and alternate versions of well-known songs that aren't a great deal different from the officially released versions. Also, some of the unreleased "tracks" are radio spots. That's not to say that these rare items aren't interesting for the fan; they are. It's just that it's too overwhelming a package for the non-fanatic, and a rather expensive, spotty one for the devoted fan (who will undoubtedly already have at least half the contents). By far, the most interesting unreleased tracks date from the legendary *Smile* sessions (nearly an album's worth). Never actually completed, they aren't quite the masterpiece that some have claimed, but are extremely interesting, often beautiful excursions into psychedelic production and songwriting that often resemble sound paintings more than songs. Comes with a 60-page booklet by Beach Boy historian David Leaf. —*Richie Unterberger*

Lei'd In Hawaii Rehearsal [Bootleg] / 1994 / Vigotone ✦✦✦
Live Beach Boys bootlegs pale in comparison with the ones from studio sources, but this may be the most interesting, presenting a perfect-quality rehearsal tape from August, 1967 (with Brian very much present). Spare, fragile versions of several of their '60s hits (one of these takes, "Surfer Girl," closed the official *Good Vibrations* box set, if you need a preview); Mike Love ruins "Heroes And Villains" with a corny narration. Also includes a couple of interesting '60s outtakes ("We're Together Again," from 1968, and "Sherry She Needs Me," from 1965, although the vocals weren't added until 1976), and a good quality radio broadcast of four songs from a November 1963 show at the Hollywood Bowl. —*Richie Unterberger*

20 Good Vibrations—The Greatest Hits / Apr. 4, 1995 / Capitol ✦✦✦
Amazingly, given the number of Beach Boys compilations, there has yet to be a one-disc anthology presenting their biggest singles from "Surfin' Safari," which hit the Top Ten on some charts in

1962, to "Kokomo," a #1 hit in 1988. This album attempts to fill that gap. It includes those two, as well as such chart-toppers as "Surfin' U.S.A.," "I Get Around," "Barbara Ann," and "Good Vibrations." But it fails in its mission in a number of respects. For one thing, it's only 49 minutes long—another 25 minutes of hits could have been included. For another, the choices are somewhat idiosyncratic. "Catch a Wave" was never a single, much less a hit, but it's here, while "When I Grow Up (To Be a Man)," a Top Ten single, is not. All the tracks except "Kokomo" are Capitol recordings from 1962-1966, which means later hits on other labels, notably the Top Ten "Rock and Roll Music" (1976), are missing. And in a couple of instances, the hit versions are not included: "Be True to Your School" and "Help Me, Rhonda" are significantly different album tracks, not the original singles. Finally, the sequencing is not chronological, which make the group's stylistic changes confusing. All in all, this is not the ideal hits collection, and unless you're a big fan of "Kokomo" who happens not to own the *Cocktail* soundtrack, you'd be better off sticking to one or both of the *Absolute Best* collections or *Endless Summer*. —*William Ruhlmann*

Smile / Bootleg ♦♦♦
In 1966, Brian Wilson began work on the *Smile* LP, which was intended as the ultimate pop/progressive/psychedelic record. Many vocal and instrumental tracks were recorded, but the project was abandoned in 1967 due to accumulated pressures from Wilson's family, fellow Beach Boys, and the record company, combined with Brian's own fragile and sensitive ego. In the ensuing years, *Smile* was accorded status as the most legendary unreleased album of all time, although the record was in fact never close to being finished. Many, though by no means all, of the tracks in progress were bootlegged in the 1980s; many, though by no means all, of these, in turn, finally surfaced on Capitol's *Good Vibrations* box set. Several bootlegs of the *Smile* sessions are still easily available, most featuring tracks which still haven't been officially released, or alternate takes and mixes of ones that did surface. A lot of these are interesting, to say the least, including the "Fire" part of the legendary "Elements" suite, the downright avant-garde "George Fell Into His French Horn," and extended snippets of "Good Vibrations" and "Heroes In Villains" as works in progress. There are numerous exquisitely beautiful passages, great ensemble singing, and brilliant orchestral pop instrumentation to be found on these outtakes, but the fact is that Wilson somehow lacked the discipline needed to combine them into a pop masterpiece that was both brilliant and commercial. Search for the double-CD compilation versions of these outtakes, which, though expensive, are more thorough than the various single-disc versions available. —*Richie Unterberger*

Time To Get Alone / Bootleg
An expensive double CD of unreleased '60s material. The first disc puts their much-vaunted family psychodrama on display more nakedly than anywhere else, opening with a 40-minute (!) reel of rehearsals for "Help Me Rhonda" which finds dad Murry Wilson sitting in on the sessions. Perhaps drunk, Murry harps and hectors his sons' band on how to sing their lines, accusing them of bigheadedness when the results aren't to his satisfaction; the boys put up with it as best they can. Disc one also has a half hour of outtakes and rehearsals from the *Party!* album, including a few songs ("Laugh At Me," "Ticket To Ride," "California Girls," "Little Deuce Coupe") that didn't make it onto the finished product. Disc two has marginally different versions and alternate mixes of songs from their *Today*, *Summer Days*, and *Pet Sounds* albums, along with reels of outtakes from the "Good Vibrations" and "Heroes And Villains" singles (themselves usually packaged with *Smile* bootlegs). Certainly *Time To Get Alone* is for fanatics only, but those fanatics will find it interesting and occasionally fascinating. —*Richie Unterberger*

Pet Sounds Rehearsals / Bootleg ♦♦♦
Almost an hour of rehearsal takes and backing tracks for some of *Pet Sounds*' best tracks. Like the Beatles *Get Back* bootlegs, these are fascinating artifacts for scholars of the group, but pretty low on entertainment value. The piano practices for "You Still Believe In Me" verge on low comedy at times with the constant grating mistakes, reminiscent of that Monty Python sketch where John Cleese, playing Beethoven, couldn't get the intro right to his Fifth Symphony. We also get to hear how many overzealous bicycle bells and horns were stripped from the final take, as well as a work-in-progress document of "I Just Wasn't Made For These Times" and basic tracks for "Wouldn't It Be Nice" and "I'm Waiting For The Day." —*Richie Unterberger*

BOOKS

♦♦♦♦ **The Beach Boys**, by David Leaf (Courage, 1978). The extremely dark and troubled history of the Beach Boys is well-known by now. This is the book that blew the lid off their clean-cut image, and remains by far the best and most honest history of both their music and lives. The group's genius, expressed so well in their love of surf, hot rods, girls, and good times, hid explosive conflicts, most notably an abusive father, dissension within the group over leader Brian Wilson's increasingly experimental and bizarre material, drummer Dennis Wilson's involvement with the Charles Manson cult, poor label and management relations, an inability to maintain their popularity after it crested with "Good Vibrations" in 1966, and, most of all, the disintegration of Brian Wilson's psyche after the mid-'60s. Leaf probes the minefield with painful but sensitive honesty, also analyzing their recordings extensively, and Brian Wilson's innovative songwriting and production methods particularly. The only criticisms to offer are that Leaf's praise for Brian Wilson, and mourning of his victimization at the hands of family and friends, can be excessive; also, some of the classic, pre-*Pet Sounds* records are glanced over, although Leaf himself provided extensive details about them in his excellent liner notes to the Beach Boys' CD reissues. Littered with fine photos; look for the 1985 edition, which includes a lengthy update. —*Richie Unterberger*

♦♦♦ **Look! Listen! Vibrate! Smile!**, by Dominic Priore (Dominic Priore, 1988). The Beach Boys' *Smile* is the most famous unreleased album of all time (although a lot of the music, or tracks-in-progress, have turned up on official CD releases in recent years). This, believe it or not, is a 250-page book devoted to the work. More like a book-length fanzine, actually, consisting mainly of reprints of contemporary press clips that were published in 1966 and 1967, around the time the album was in production, at least theoretically. Some of these are quite interesting; more often, they're fairly superficial. Better are the essays contributed specifically for the book, including a lengthy piece on the album by Beach Boys biographer David Leaf, and a long song-by-song description of the known *Smile* sessions. *Smile* was eventually aborted by a maze of artistic, family, and business complications, and this is a useful record of its conception and destruction, though its appeal will be limited to fanatics and specialists, and the gushing appraisals of Wilson's talents in the newly written pieces can go overboard. An update with much new material is planned soon. —*Richie Unterberger*

The Bears

Group, Alternative Pop/Rock
In 1987, guitarist Adrian Belew (whose previous credits included Frank Zappa, Talking Heads, and King Crimson) formed the Bears with a few friends he'd known before he became a hot hired gun for alternative music stars. The Bears' quirky Anglo-pop/rock (similar to XTC's unorthodox song constructions and changes) fused seamlessly with Belew's bizarre tonal washes and occasionally dissonant leads.

After the second album, *Rise and Shine*, Belew returned to his own solo work, which has since reflected the tunefulness of the Bears as opposed to his more jarring earlier work; the remaining Bears continue as a trio called the Psychodots. —*Rick Clark*

● **The Bears** / 1987 / Primitive Man ♦♦♦♦
Fans of XTC/Squeeze-style oddball pop/rock will love this debut. The band's punchy arrangements and vocals and Belew's peculiar guitar gymnastics shine on super-melodic tracks like "Figure It Out," "None of the Above," and "Honey Bee." —*Rick Clark*

Rise and Shine / Apr. 1988 / Primitive Man ♦♦♦
The songs aren't as strong as those on their debut, but *Rise & Shine* is still a good showcase for fans of Belew's playing. —*Rick Clark*

Beastie Boys

Group, Rap
When they were terrorizing America in 1987 with *Licensed to Ill*, nobody imagined that seven years later the Beastie Boys would still be recording, let alone be respected and release a series of consistently creative albums. But that is what happened. The Beasties have managed to tie together the two largest underground musical movements of the '80s—hip-hop and punk/post-

punk—into one wildly eclectic mix, borrowing from any genre they can get their hands on.

Originally, the Beastie Boys were a hardcore New York punk band in the early '80s, releasing a couple of weak EPs before becoming infatuated with the burgeoning rap underground. By that time, the Beastie Boys were three—Adam Yauch (MCA), Mike Diamond (Mike D), and Adam Horovitz (Ad-Rock). The trio hooked up with Rick Rubin, one of the cofounders of Def Jam Records, who produced the group's first full-length album, *Licensed to Ill*, which was released in late 1986. A brutal and hysterical amalgam of hard rock, hip-hop, and satiric macho posturing, *Licensed to Ill* followed the footsteps of Run-DMC's groundbreaking commercial breakthrough *Raising Hell*, becoming the first rap album to reach number one; it eventually sold over four million copies and scored a number seven single with "(You Gotta) Fight for Your Right (To Party)."

After a tour that wallowed in its own decadence, the group became embroiled in a vicious fight with Def Jam which prevented them from releasing new material for a couple of years. In 1989, the Beastie Boys reappeared on Capitol Records with *Paul's Boutique*, an album that was radically different from their debut. Although it was a commercial failure, it was a surreal, brilliantly inventive record that foreshadowed many hip trends of the early '90s.

After another three-year absence, the Beastie Boys emerged with *Check Your Head* in 1992. For the album, the Beastie Boys returned to playing live instruments, creating a sloppy, inspired album that featured equal doses of Stax soul, hardcore punk, '70s funk, reggae, and '90s hip-hop beats. It was as bold of a departure from *Paul's Boutique* as that album was from *Licensed to Ill*, except this time, it sold. The Beastie Boys emerged as cultural icons for the new alternative audience, which continued with their follow-up, 1994's *Ill Communication*, a record that refined the innovations of *Check Your Head*. —*Stephen Thomas Erlewine*

☆ **Licensed to Ill** / 1986 / Def Jam ✦✦✦✦✦
The impact of this album in 1987 was about as subtle as a brick through a window. It was the first #1 hip-hop album, selling four million copies, and the first album from a White rap group. From the opening kick of John Bonham's drums (taken from "When the Levee Breaks"), the Beasties proceed to steal from every record they can get their hands on and rhyme about an absurd array of macho fantasies. Sure, it's obnoxious—but it's an act, and an insanely humorous one at that; no other rappers brag about being thrown out of White Castle, drinking Budweiser, or having "more rhymes than Phyllis Diller." Even if some of it sounds dated today, the sheer force of the music and the whiny rhymes still make this worth hearing. —*Stephen Thomas Erlewine*

★ **Paul's Boutique** / 1989 / Capitol ✦✦✦✦✦
Endlessly complex and relentlessly innovative, *Paul's Boutique* is the Beastie Boys' masterpiece. It's very dense, with samples from nearly every genre of music and clever, literate, absurd lyrics dropping references from Jack Kerouac to *Dragnet; Paul's Boutique* is a virtual catalog of pop culture, deeply rooted in the 1970s. As rappers, the Beasties have grown immeasurably, writing lyrics that are both smart-assed and smart. Musically, the album is much richer than *Ill*, covering everything from funk and pop to country and hip-hop, with several layers of samples and beats on each track. *Paul's Boutique* is a brilliant, visionary album, and hasn't aged a day since its release. —*Stephen Thomas Erlewine*

☆ **Check Your Head** / 1992 / Capitol ✦✦✦✦✦
Check Your Head returned the Beastie Boys to the spotlight, although in the most unlikely manner possible. Refashioning themselves as a loose and gritty groove band, the Beasties picked up their instruments again and made an album of dirty Stax and New Orleans funk, tripped-out reggae, hard hip-hop, blistering hardcore punk, and scores of pop culture references and jokes. In its own way, *Check Your Head* is as trailblazing as *Paul's Boutique,* with its inspired amateurishness, it acknowledges no boundaries or limitations, creating a post-post-punk world where Eddie Harris, Bob Dylan, Cheap Trick, Groove Holmes, Spoonie Gee, and Biz Markie exist together as one music. And, strange as it may sound, it works. —*Stephen Thomas Erlewine*

Some Old Bullshit / 1994 / Capitol ✦✦
Sadly, the title is accurate. Even for die-hard Beastie fans, the early hardcore punk of "Pollywog Stew" wears thin quickly, and "Cooky Puss," while fairly interesting, only hints at their future inventive-

ness, leaving *Some Old Bullshit* for completists only. —*Stephen Thomas Erlewine*

○ **Ill Communication** / May 23, 1994 / Grand Royal ✦✦✦✦
More of a refinement and restatement of *Check Your Head* than a bold departure, *Ill Communication* still finds the Beastie Boys in prime form, adding more elements of jazz to their dense, surrealistic sound. From the scores of wah-wah guitars to the short hardcore punk songs, *Ill Communication* is firmly entrenched in '70s worship without ever once sounding like it's recycled. It may offer the same thing as *Check Your Head*, but *Ill Communication* never sounds formulaic or tired. —*Stephen Thomas Erlewine*

Root Down EP / 1995 / Grand Royal ✦✦
Released as the Beastie Boys were beginning a U.S. arena tour in spring 1995, the *Root Down* EP features a handful of rote remixes and tepid live tracks that are only of interest to die-hard fans. —*Stephen Thomas Erlewine*

The Beat

Group, Power Pop/Anglo-Pop
A Los Angeles-based power-pop outfit formed by Paul Collins (ex-Nerves), the Beat recorded its self-titled debut LP after signing to Columbia Records in 1979. Despite good reviews and some regional success, the album failed to make much impact. A second attempt, 1982's *The Kid's Are the Same* (this time credited to Paul Collins' Beat), also failed and effectively broke up the band. However, Collins returned the following year with a harder rocking line-up including Patti Smith Group drummer Jay Dee Daugherty. Their EP, *To Beat or Not to Beat*, was again ignored; it proved to be the band's last recording. While it seemed that the Beat's only claim to fame would be forcing the (English) Beat to change its name in the U.S., their albums are now seen as classic examples of power-pop and have been reissued on CD in the '90s. —*Chris Woodstra*

● **Beat** / 1979 / Columbia ✦✦✦✦
The Beat's great self-titled debut was produced by Bruce Botnick (the Doors), is a must-own for lovers of melodic guitar-driven pop'n'roll. Check out "Different Kind of Girl," "Don't Wait Up for Me" and "Walking out on Love." Great tunes! —*Rick Clark*

The Kids Are the Same / 1982 / Columbia ✦✦✦

Beat Happening

Group, Alternative Pop/Rock
One of the hardest tricks to pull off in rock & roll is to make minimal, primitive music without seeming pretentious. Beat Happening pulls it off with grace. Based in Olympia, WA, the group's three members switch instruments constantly, providing a spare base for Heather and Calvin's lead vocals. Heather's voice is soft, calm and feminine; Calvin sounds like Johnny Cash. Beat Happening's Velvet Underground and folk hybrid has gained numerous fans in the underground. At times, their unassuming folk-rock and occasional loud guitar workouts sound sloppy and careless, not simple and pure, but at their best, Beat Happening is entirely original and rewarding pleasure.

Beat Happening leader Calvin Johnson has also gained fame in the underground as the leader of K Records, a resolutely independent record label that has been the home to the Kill Rock Stars compilations, various riot grrrl groups, and other bands that reflect the trends of the American underground in the '90s. —*Stephen Thomas Erlewine*

Beat Happening / 1985 / K ✦✦✦
○ **Jamboree** / 1988 / Sub Pop ✦✦✦✦
As much fun as the title indicates, just screwier. —*John Dougan*

Black Candy / 1989 / Sub Pop ✦✦
Spirited bashing, slightly more cohesive than earlier efforts. —*John Dougan*

○ **1983-85** / 1990 / K ✦✦✦✦
● **Dreamy** / 1991 / Sub Pop ✦✦✦✦
Their most consistent work, *Dreamy* barely lasts thirty minutes. Over those ten songs, however, the band weave their graceful way through jilted love songs such as "Left Behind," "I've Lost You," and "Cry For A Shadow." Too beautiful to be depressing, Heather's clear vocals and Calvin's endearing, off-key baritone produce an honest, straightforward album. —*John Bush*

You Turn Me on / Oct. 2, 1992 / Sub Pop ✦✦✦
You Turn Me On's songs are the best Beat Happening has written. "Godsend" is nine minutes of slowly-building bliss; "Noise" and "Sleepyhead" are indie-pop at its best. However, the consistency and flowing grace of 1991's *Dreamy* is sacrificed, perhaps due to the band's using both Steve Fisk and Stuart Moxbam as producers. A flawed but beautiful album. —*John Bush*

Beat Rodeo

Group, Alternative Pop/Rock, Roots-Rock
'80s pop/rock quartet led by singer/songwriter/guitarist Steve Almaas from Minneapolis (who had previously played bass in the Suicide Commandos) and featuring guitarist/singer Bill Schunk, bassist/vocalist Dan Prater, and drummer Mike Osborn. That lineup made the debut album, *Staying Out Late with Beat Rodeo*, first released on Zensor Records in Germany in July 1984, then picked up for U.S. distribution by I.R.S. Records in 1985. By the time of the second album, *Home in the Heart of the Beat*, Lewis King had replaced Osborn and George Usher had been added on keyboards. — *William Ruhlmann*

Staying out Late with . . . Beat Rodeo / Jul. 1984 / IRS ✦✦
Steve Almaas's Beat Rodeo proves to be a pleasant but rather weightless pop/rock band of the mid-'80s, neo-mid-'60s mode. A couple of decades have gone by, and so they faithfully recreate the earnest vocals, the bouncy beats, the bright, quickly strummed guitars. They are abetted by producers Don Dixon (it's his metier) and Richard Gottehrer, who gets a typically sharp sound on the two tracks he handled (added to the domestically released I.R.S. Records version of the album). All of this sounded hipper in 1985, when the Blasters, Green On Red, and many others were playing "roots" or "retro" rock, but by now it sounds like an amusing curiosity. (Originally released, minus the Gottehrer tracks, on Zensor Records in Germany in July 1984.) — *William Ruhlmann*

Home in the Heart of the Beat / 1986 / IRS ✦✦✦
Less overtly retro than *Staying Up Late*, Beat Rodeo's second album, produced by Scott Litt (R.E.M., etc.) rocked a little harder and at the same time, with the addition of keyboards (plus guest sax by Lenny Pickett and guest vocals by Syd Straw), was somewhat smoother as well. More important, Steve Almaas's songs were more substantial—musically more ambitious, lyrically more personal and direct. Beat Rodeo still didn't catch on, but *Home in the Heart of the Beat* demonstrated that they were a band with potential. — *William Ruhlmann*

The Beatles

Group, Rock & Roll, British Invasion, Psychedelic, Pop/Rock
The most successful and significant rock group in history, the Beatles were formed in Liverpool, England, in the late '50s by John Lennon (b. Oct 9, 1940—d. Dec 8, 1980) (guitar, vocals), Paul McCartney (b. Jun 18, 1942) (bass, vocals), and George Harrison (b. Feb 25, 1943) (guitar, vocals). Ringo Starr (born Richard Starkey, Jul. 7, 1940) (drums, vocals) joined the group in 1962 in time for their first formal recordings.

The Beatles ingested every popular music style of their day—the raucous rock & roll of Jerry Lee Lewis and Little Richard, the more sophisticated pop/rock of Buddy Holly, the soul of Motown and the Phil Spector-produced girl groups, the pop/R&B of the Isley Brothers and Larry Williams, the country-rockabilly of Carl Perkins, the pop-schmaltz of Broadway show tunes—and synthesized them into a style of their own, both in their cover versions and in the original songs written by Lennon and McCartney. And that was only the beginning. By a year or so into their recording career, the Beatles had begun to throw off their influences and forge new directions in popular music, meanwhile picking up elements of classical music, Indian music, and electronic music, among other forms.

The Beatles' earliest extant recordings date from June 1961, when, while performing at a nightclub in Germany, they were hired to be the backup band for singer Tony Sheridan and cut six songs with him, plus two—"Ain't She Sweet" and an original instrumental called "Cry for a Shadow"—on their own. After they achieved fame, these recordings frequently were reissued. The best version of them is found on the Polydor CD *The Early Tapes of the Beatles*. Another early set of recordings comes from a clandestine tape of the group's club set made on New Year's Eve 1962 and released without their authorization on various albums starting in 1977.

Prior to that, the Beatles had signed to the Parlophone subsidiary of EMI Records in the U.K. and released "Love Me Do" in October 1962. It was the first of 22 singles Parlophone would release through 1970, of which 21 would hit the Top Ten (all but "Love Me Do") and 17 would hit #1. The first of those Top Ten hits, "Please Please Me," was released in January 1963. In March came an album of the same name, the first of 11 studio LPs of new material the Beatles would release in the U.K. through 1970, all of which would hit #1.

The Beatles' success in Britain was not at first duplicated in the U.S., which was not surprising at the time. Until the Beatles, few British recording artists found sustained popularity in America. Capitol Records, the U.S. subsidiary of EMI, even declined to release Beatles records in the U.S., and they were licensed to other small labels. For example, Vee Jay Records released "Please Please Me" in February 1963, followed by the Beatles' third single, "From Me to You," in May and a modified version of the *Please Please Me* album, retitled *Introducing the Beatles*, in July. None of these recordings scored at the time, nor at first did the Beatles' fourth single, "She Loves You," issued by Swan Records in September. (In Britain, "She Loves You" became the best-selling single in history; later, it would top the American charts, too.)

The Beatles released their second U.K. album, *With the Beatles*, in November, along with their fifth single, "I Want to Hold Your Hand." These works finally convinced Capitol Records to take them on in the U.S., and in January 1964 the label released the single along with a modified version of *With the Beatles* retitled *Meet the Beatles!*

(A word on the "modified" versions of Beatles albums in the U.S. In the 1960s, standard practice for album releases in the U.K. differed from that in the U.S. in two important respects. First, U.K. albums tended to have more songs—The Beatles' early albums had up to 14 selections on them, while American policy was to have 11 or 12. Second, U.K. albums tended not to contain songs also released as singles, while American albums usually were built around a hit single. Since Capitol had discretion about the form in which it could release Beatles records in the U.S., it frequently reconfigured the U.K. versions, deleting tracks, adding a current single, and choosing a different title. Gathered up, the extra tracks might later turn up on an album that had no U.K. counterpart.)

With "I Want to Hold Your Hand" and *Meet the Beatles!*, both of which topped the charts, Beatlemania hit the U.S. Over the next six years, the Beatles reached the American album charts with 26 albums, 13 of which hit #1, 18 of which went gold, 11 of which sold at least a million copies, and nine of which sold at least two million copies. They included newly recorded studio albums, movie soundtracks, reissues of earlier recordings, and interview and documentary albums chronicling the pheonomenon of their success.

On the U.S. singles chart, the Beatles scored 64 times through 1970, including 45 Top 40 hits, 32 of which reached the Top Ten, and 20 of which hit #1. 21 singles went gold. In addition to regular A-side releases, the chart singles included B-sides, reissues, EPs, and even a German language version of "She Loves You." In one astonishing string, every new Beatles single released on Capitol between July 1965 and March 1970—16 records—went gold and hit the Top Ten; all but four hit #1.

The group's unprecedented commercial success, which redefined the record industry, was matched by their artistic accomplishments and cultural impact. Sticking to their album releases as they occurred in the U.K. (the format the U.S. catalogue would be brought into line with in the CD reissue era), their third album was *A Hard Day's Night* (July 1964), half of whose songs were heard in their feature film debut of the same name. Writing all 13 songs, Lennon and McCartney began to reveal an unexpected depth on such tracks as the hesitant romantic ballad "If I Fell" and the vengeful "I'll Cry Instead," alongside the automatic crowd pleasers such as the title track and "Can't Buy Me Love."

The fourth album, *Beatles for Sale* (December 1964) (material from which turned up in the U.S. on *Beatles '65* and *Beatles VI*) further demonstrated the group's evolution, notably on such tracks as "No Reply" and "I'm a Loser," although the unusually large number of cover songs—six of 14—suggested that the pace of writing new material was beginning to show. (Not that you could tell from their singles, as "I Feel Fine"/"She's a Woman," released concurrently—their sixth straight U.K. #1 and their sixth U.S. #1 of 1964 alone—was as strong as any of their releases so far.)

Help! (August 1965), containing many of the songs from their second movie, showed them moving more toward a country-rock style (the influence of Buddy Holly is pervasive), though it also includes "Yesterday," a ballad on which McCartney is accompanied by a string quartet that became the most popular song standard of the decade. The folkish and country influences were also heard on the Beatles' sixth album, *Rubber Soul* (December 1965).

1966 found the Beatles taking greater time with their recordings and stretching the releases out more. After undertaking world tours in 1964, 1965, and 1966, they retired from live performing. In the course of the year, they released only one new album, *Revolver* (August) and a separate single, "Paperback Writer"/"Rain" (May). (A second single, "Yellow Submarine"/"Eleanor Rigby," was culled from the LP.) The records showed extraordinary studio experimentation and musical growth.

They were dwarfed, however, by the Beatles' next record releases, "Penny Lane"/"Strawberry Fields Forever" (February 1967) and *Sgt. Pepper's Lonely Hearts Club Band* (June 1967), recordings that for decades continued to top critics' polls of the greatest pop records ever made and that succeeded in bringing the public along in their inventiveness—*Sgt. Pepper* topped the charts for months and sold eight million copies in the U.S. alone.

This may have been the Beatles' peak, though they continued to make valuable and popular music for another two years. In August 1967, their manager, Brian Epstein, died, and subsequently they suffered various reversals. Their *Magical Mystery Tour* TV film (shown in the U.K. in December 1967) was panned, though the accompanying music was typically successful; they launched a record company, Apple, that eventually drained their income; and there were other dubious business deals.

Meanwhile, they were working on a sprawling two-record set, *The Beatles* (November 1968), immediately dubbed "the white album" because of its blank cover, that revealed a breakdown in musical unity, with a single member dominating each track, sometimes to the point of bringing in his own sidemen in addition to the other Beatles. This was followed by an abortive film and recording project, initially called *Get Back* and abandoned after work on it in January 1969.

The Beatles reconvened for a final album project, *Abbey Road* (September 1969), then broke up, with the *Get Back* project, much altered, turning up in record stores and movie theaters in May 1970 under the title *Let It Be*. All four band members launched solo careers, and all four topped the charts at one time or another, though Paul McCartney proved the most consistently popular. John Lennon was assassinated in December 1980.

Beatle music has proven perennially popular, starting with hits compilations and reissues released in the 1970s and continuing with CD reissues in the 1980s. When Capitol released a set of radio performances in December 1994, *Live at the BBC*, it sold five million copies. Meanwhile, the three surviving Beatles, having resolved various financial and personal disputes, began some recording together in connection with a video documentary project promised for the near future. — *William Ruhlmann*

☆ **Please Please Me** / Mar. 22, 1963 / Capitol ♦♦♦♦♦
Nearly 30 years after its release, the Beatles' first album still stands not only as a blueprint for what the group itself would accomplish in the next three years, but for what a large part of popular music would sound like from then on. Listening now, one revels anew in the songwriting of John Lennon and Paul McCartney (songs include "I Saw Her Standing There"), their remarkable harmonies and solo singing, and the encyclopedia of pop and rock they offer from other sources—especially light pop and hard R&B (like the show-stopping closer, Lennon's take on the Isley Brothers' "Twist and Shout"). The CD reissue is in the original mono, but Mobile Fidelity has issued the album in stereo. — *William Ruhlmann*

Introducing the Beatles / Jul. 22, 1963 / Vee-Jay ♦♦♦
The first Beatles album released in the U.S., *Introducing The Beatles* is a slightly abridged version of *Please Please Me*, which had been released in the U.K. four months earlier. It includes two fewer tracks than its British counterpart, deleting "Please Please Me" and "Ask Me Why." Today, of course, there's no reason to prefer it to *Please Please Me*, which was released in the U.S. in 1987, but from 1963 to 1965, when Capitol Records belatedly released the material on *The Early Beatles*, this (plus some inferior Vee Jay repackagings) was the only American album containing most of the Beatles' initial recordings. — *William Ruhlmann*

☆ **With the Beatles** / Nov. 22, 1963 / Capitol ♦♦♦♦♦
In only a few months, and despite a torrid schedule, the Beatles demonstrated enormous growth on their second album (growth and change would be constants throughout their remarkable career). From the forceful "It Won't Be Long" to the bouncy "All My Loving," their original songs have made a leap, especially in ensemble playing, and the covers again offer a broad range, from Broadway show music ("Till There Was You" from *The Music Man*) to two great Motown songs ("You Really Got a Hold on Me" and "Money"). The CD reissue is in mono, while Mobile Fidelity has issued it in stereo. — *William Ruhlmann*

Meet the Beatles / Jan. 20, 1964 / Capitol ♦♦♦
When the U.S. subsidiary of their U.K. label, Capitol Records, finally decided to issue a Beatles album, they took both sides of the group's current single "I Want to Hold Your Hand," pulled "I Saw Her Standing There" from *Please Please Me*, and culled nine of the 14 tracks from *With the Beatles* for this release. They also performed some studio gimmickry, supposedly to make the music sound more pleasing to American ears. The album is great anyway. — *William Ruhlmann*

The Beatles' Second Album / Apr. 10, 1964 / Capitol ♦♦♦
The other five tracks from *With the Beatles*, the B-sides of three singles, "She Loves You," and two newly recorded songs (one a raucous version of Little Richard's "Long Tall Sally") make up the cobbled-together contents of Capitol's second U.S. Beatles album. The shuffling doesn't matter a bit, since the overall quality of the Beatles' output is so high. — *William Ruhlmann*

Hard Day's Night [U.S.] / Jun. 26, 1964 / United Artists ♦♦♦
The difference between this album and the U.K. Parlophone album of the same name is that the U.K. record is the Beatles' third regular album release (following *Please Please Me* and *With The Beatles*), while this album is a soundtrack recording from their motion picture. The U.K. album contains 14 new songs, some of which are heard in the movie, but the U.S. one contains eight Beatles songs, all from the film, plus four instrumental tracks (courtesy of Beatle producer George Martin) used as movie scoring. All those wonderful tunes you remember from the movie are here, from the title track and "Can't Buy Me Love" to "And I Love Her." Missing are non-movie tracks that Capitol Records parceled out on subsequent U.S. Beatles albums. Obviously, the album to buy is the U.K. version, and if you are a CD buyer, there's no problem: it's the only one available. Both the U.K. and U.S. versions are available on cassette, however, so be careful. The U.S. version notes that it is a soundtrack on the spine of the tape box. — *William Ruhlmann*

☆ **A Hard Day's Night [U.K.]** / Jul. 10, 1964 / Capitol ♦♦♦♦♦
Maybe it was all the success of the previous year, but on their third (U.K.) album, the Beatles sound positively triumphant, roaring through exciting songs like the title tune, "Can't Buy Me Love," and "Any Time at All." On their first album to be entirely self-written, it's the material (produced under incredible pressure) that continues to impress. "I Should Have Known Better," "If I Fell," "And I Love Her"—these are songs a generation can sing word-for-word decades later. At the same time, one can hear around the edges the beginnings of Lennon's darker side and individual voice, as more than once he refers to something he can't stand. "I'll Cry Instead" is almost bitter. *A Hard Day's Night*'s freshness has not dated an hour. — *William Ruhlmann*

Something New / Jul. 20, 1964 / Capitol ♦♦♦
Capitol Records initially did not have the rights to *A Hard Day's Night*, issued in the U.S. as a soundtrack by United Artists, the company that released the film. Instead, Capitol cobbled together a competing record containing eight of the 14 songs from the U.K. version, two songs from a U.K. EP, and a German-language version of "I Want to Hold Your Hand." — *William Ruhlmann*

☆ **Beatles for Sale** / Dec. 4, 1964 / Capitol ♦♦♦♦♦
In a sense, this fourth U.K. album is a step back for the Beatles as they return to the eight-originals-with-six-covers formula of their first two albums. Fatigue is clearly setting in. But some of the originals are gems, especially Lennon's "No Reply" and "I'm a Loser," songs confirming his sense of anguish. The covers of Chuck Berry, Carl Perkins, and Little Richard are, once again, inspired recastings of formative material for the group. — *William Ruhlmann*

Beatles VI / Dec. 15, 1964 / Capitol ♦♦♦
Capitol strikes again, using the remaining six tracks from *Beatles for Sale*, four newly recorded songs (two of them covers of Larry Williams hits), and the B-side of a single, to create another

"new" Beatles album. —*William Ruhlmann*

Beatles '65 / Jun. 14, 1965 / Capitol ✦✦✦

Dave Dexter, Jr. (a name which will live in infamy) "assisted" the Beatles by pulling eight tracks from *Beatles for Sale*, one from *A Hard Day's Night*, and both sides of the latest Beatles single ("I Feel Fine"/"She's a Woman") for the creation of this album. —*William Ruhlmann*

☆ **Help! [U.K.]** / Aug. 6, 1965 / Capitol ✦✦✦✦✦
The Beatles' fifth U.K. album contained seven songs used in their film plus seven other songs and marked a move to a softer, more reflective style. The lyrics are more prominent and thoughtful, and the sound more often features slow tempos, acoustic guitars, and other instruments. Here Lennon continued to cry for "Help!" and bitterly declared "You've Got to Hide Your Love Away" over a strummed acoustic. Here McCartney took a bluegrass/country turn in "I've Just Seen a Face" and achieved his biggest ballad with "Yesterday" (singing before a string quartet). Once again, the Beatles had exhibited remarkable growth and pointed the way for all of pop music to follow. —*William Ruhlmann*

Help! Original Soundtrack [U.S.] / Aug. 13, 1965 / Capitol ✦✦✦
Things got even more confusing (if possible) on the American release front when Capitol began to adopt similar titles for its albums while still monkeying with the contents. Capitol's *Help!* is a true soundtrack, as it includes only the seven Beatles tracks actually heard in the film, and the album is filled out with music from the film score by Ken Thorne. —*William Ruhlmann*

☆ **Rubber Soul [U.K.]** / Dec. 3, 1965 / Capitol ✦✦✦✦✦
Although the Beatles' sixth (U.K.) album is less consistent than some of their other releases, it has its share of memorable songs, among them Lennon's "Norwegian Wood," "Nowhere Man," and "In My Life" and McCartney's "Michelle." Again, the sound is softer and more sophisticated than any of the group's 1964 material. —*William Ruhlmann*

Rubber Soul [U.S.] / Dec. 6, 1965 / Capitol ✦✦✦
In its by-now-familiar style, Capitol Records took the U.K. *Rubber Soul*, cut four songs, added two culled from Side 2 of the U.K. *Help!*, and emerged with a 12-track U.S. version. —*William Ruhlmann*

"Yesterday" . . . and Today/ Jun. 20, 1966 / Capitol ✦✦✦
Those of you keeping score will note that some tracks are still unaccounted for, and here they are on a "new" Capitol album, *"Yesterday"...and Today*. Its 11 tracks contain those four lost *Rubber Soul* tracks, two more from the second side of *Help!*, both sides of the 1965 single "We Can Work It Out"/"Day Tripper," and three new songs taken from the next U.K. Beatles album (being recorded at that time). —*William Ruhlmann*

☆ **Revolver [U.K.]** / Aug. 5, 1966 / Capitol ✦✦✦✦✦
Those three songs swiped for *"Yesterday"...and Today* were the least of another astonishing leap in songwriting and production that introduced "Eleanor Rigby," "Yellow Submarine," "She Said, She Said," "Good Day Sunshine," "For No One," "Got to Get You into My Life," and "Tomorrow Never Knows." If McCartney was becoming a consummate pop craftsman with a command of horns and strings, Lennon was delving into a drugged psyche while experimenting with tape loops and strange sounds. And George Harrison, whose unprecedented three songs were led by "Taxman," was finally flowering into a first-rate songwriter. —*William Ruhlmann*

Revolver [U.S.] / Aug. 8, 1966 / Capitol ✦✦✦
In preparing *Revolver* for U.S. release, Bill Miller simply cut the three songs already used on *Yesterday...and Today*, resulting in an 11-song version. —*William Ruhlmann*

○ **Collection of Beatle Oldies** / Dec. 10, 1966 / Parlophone ✦✦✦✦
In the U.K., where singles frequently did not appear on albums, this album culled 16 popular Beatles tunes from 1963 to 1966. The Beatles' first greatest-hits album. —*William Ruhlmann*

☆ **Sgt. Pepper's Lonely Hearts Club Band** / Jun. 1, 1967 / Capitol ✦✦✦✦✦
The Beatles' finest album is a song cycle full of childlike whimsy and irresistibly catchy songs. Its playfulness belies an amazingly fluid arrangement of melodies, lyrics, and sounds that flow together into a whole, creating its own magical world. An openended embrace of light pop, hard-rock, Indian music, swing, classical music, and blues, the album makes the case for musical unity-in-diversity, seemingly gathering all that came before it into

surprising yet perfect combinations. The Beatles only occasionally approached this achievement in isolated moments afterwards, and nobody else came even close, then or since. —*William Ruhlmann*

☆ **Magical Mystery Tour** / Nov. 27, 1967 / Capitol ✦✦✦✦✦
Six songs from the group's TV film *Magical Mystery Tour*, plus their three 1967 singles. Especially notable among them is "Penny Lane"/"Strawberry Fields Forever," perhaps the most impressive two-sided hit ever recorded. And with songs like "All You Need Is Love," "Hello Goodbye," "The Fool on the Hill," and the title track, the rest of the album isn't too shabby, either. —*William Ruhlmann*

☆ **The Beatles (White Album)** / Nov. 22, 1968 / Capitol ✦✦✦✦✦
In their later recordings, the Beatles largely eschewed the elaborate arrangements and instrumentation of 1967 in favor of returning to the simpler sound of the four-piece band. They did not, however, return to the ensemble style of 1964, rather serving as backup to one of four leaders, depending on who wrote the song. On this sprawling double album, already apparent individual styles gain ascendency; likewise, musical styles are not so much combined as separated out in pastiche form—the Beach Boys pop of "Back in the USSR," the blues of "Yer Blues," the folk of "Rocky Raccoon," the hard rock of "Birthday," the schmaltzy pop of "Good Night." The musical facility is amazing but also seems near-parodic. —*William Ruhlmann*

Yellow Submarine / Jan. 13, 1969 / Capitol ✦✦✦
There are really only four new songs here, and even they predate the material on *The Beatles*, but this is a pleasant enough soundtrack album, dominated by the musical score written by Beatles producer George Martin. —*William Ruhlmann*

☆ **Abbey Road** / Sep. 26, 1969 / Capitol ✦✦✦✦✦
The Beatles' last unified statement finds them going out at a peak of musical achievement, from Lennon's "Come Together" to Harrison's "Something," with McCartney dominating the Side 2 medley in which the group rocks out in fine style. *Abbey Road* is the best-selling Beatles album ever. —*William Ruhlmann*

Hey Jude (Or the Beatles Again) / Feb. 26, 1970 / Capitol ✦✦✦
The first U.S. Beatles compilation album, this gathers singles and stray tracks dating back to 1964 and features the first LP (and thus stereo) releases of such songs as "Paperback Writer," "Lady Madonna," and "Hey Jude." —*William Ruhlmann*

In the Beginning: Early Tapes (Circa 1960) / May 4, 1970 / Polydor ✦✦
Before beginning their recording career, the Beatles recorded a few tracks in Hamburg in 1961 as the backing group for British singer Tony Sheridan. Reissued in countless different packages around the globe after the Beatles became famous, this should in no way be considered their first album; not only were their skills rudimentary, but Sheridan takes all but one of the lead vocals on this set of fairly tame covers of popular and early rock standards. Several tracks are of interest: "Ain't She Sweet," with a lead vocal by John Lennon, was a small American hit single in 1964; the driving instrumental "Cry For A Shadow" was written by Lennon and George Harrison; and "My Bonnie," with Paul McCartney's shouts clearly audible in the background, was responsible for bringing the group to the attention of Brian Epstein. —*Richie Unterberger*

☆ **Let It Be** / May 8, 1970 / Capitol ✦✦✦✦
Flawed, botched, and overproduced by Phil Spector, the final new Beatles album to be released (most of it was recorded prior to *Abbey Road*) nevertheless included the title song, "The Long and Winding Road," an abbreviated version of "Get Back," and such lovely tunes as "Two of Us," which, for one last time, presented Paul McCartney and John Lennon and their acoustic guitars, harmonizing together. —*William Ruhlmann*

The Beatles Christmas Album [Record Club] / Dec. 18, 1970 / Apple ✦✦✦
Between 1963 and 1969, the Beatles recorded seven special Christmas singles for their fan club. These were not formal musical efforts, but closer to off-the-cuff comedy. Early on, they tend to be cheery and thankful for their success, and later on the recordings are more esoteric. (Reflecting their breakup, the 1969 recording is four separate pieces.) The result is an interesting curiosity for fans, although not necessarily the sort of thing you'd want to put on while trimming the tree. This album, compiling the Christmas singles, was available from the fan club between 1970 and 1972. It has never been released commercially, and most extant copies are bootlegs. —*William Ruhlmann*

● **1962-1966** / Apr. 2, 1973 / Capitol ◆◆◆◆
A 26-track double-album of the Beatles' greatest hits up through
1966. Although it is primarily devoted to singles, the collection
also includes a few key album tracks. Released on CD Oct. 5,
1993.— *William Ruhlmann*

● **1967-1970** / Apr. 2, 1973 / Capitol ◆◆◆◆
Twenty-eight songs from the second half of the Beatles' career, focusing on the hits but also including key album tracks. Released
on CD Oct. 5, 1993. — *William Ruhlmann*

Rock & Roll Music / Jun. 7, 1976 / Capitol ◆◆◆
A double-pocket compilation emphasizing the Beatles' more uptempo material (and hence, their earlier work). All tracks are previously released, though "I'm Down" makes its first appearance on
LP. (Later released as two single albums.) — *William Ruhlmann*

Live at the Hollywood Bowl / May 4, 1977 / Capitol ◆◆◆
Previously unreleased live performances culled from shows at the
Hollywood Bowl in 1964 and 1965. The screaming never stops,
but the group's musical talent and personal charm shine through.
— *William Ruhlmann*

Live! at the Star-Club in Hamburg, Germany / Jun. 13, 1977 /
  Lingasong ◆◆
The historical interest of this album is considerable: the Beatles,
on the precipice of fame, playing their last Hamburg club show on
December 31, 1962 (contrary to the 1961 date given on some liner
notes). The problem, from a latter-day perspective, was that the
Beatles didn't play all that well, and, more importantly, the sound
is not up to par in the least, as it was captured on a primitive
portable recorder. That said, it's interesting to hear the Beatles as
they were in their club days, with a set list (almost exclusively covers) of early rock & roll tunes, several of which never made their
way onto any official Beatle release. Their primal energy does
come through, despite the missed notes and faint vocals. The U.S.
and European versions of this double album differ slightly, and
the album has been reissued, in its entirety and in piecemeal excerpts, numerous times since it first appeared. — *Richie Unterberger*

Love Songs / Oct. 21, 1977 / Capitol ◆◆◆
Two albums of Beatles ballads, starting with "Yesterday," and including some of the best romantic music of the '60s. All tracks previously released. — *William Ruhlmann*

Beatles Rarities [U.K.] / Oct. 19, 1979 / Parlophone ◆◆◆
In 1978, Parlophone Records in the U.K. released *The Beatles Collection*, a boxed set containing the Beatles' 12 original U.K. albums. Since the British tendency in the 1960s was not to include
singles on albums, this meant that the box did not contain more
than 30 tracks that had only appeared in Britain on singles and
EPs. To make up for that to some extent, Parlophone added to the
box a *Rarities* album containing 17 of those stray tracks (in the
U.S., the box was released in a limited edition with a slightly different *Rarities* album, not to be confused with the *Rarities* album
released in the U.S. in 1980, which is completely different). The
idea was to include the least easily available of the lost tracks, so
hits like "Hey Jude" weren't included. In 1979, Parlophone issued
the *Rarities* album separate from the box, and heard on its own it
comes across as a miscellaneous collection which demonstrates
that even Beatles B-sides could be enjoyable performances. —
William Ruhlmann

Rarities [U.S.] / Mar. 4, 1980 / Capitol ◆◆
A disappointment even to hardcore fans when it was released, this
gathered a few stray non-LP tracks and alternate mixes/versions
that were slightly different from commonly available takes. Most
of the rare tracks have been reissued on the *Past Masters* or *Please
Please Me* CDs; the only reason to seek this out is if you're determined to track down the marginally different versions of a half-
dozen songs like "Help!," "Don't Pass Me By," "Penny Lane," and
"I'm Only Sleeping." — *Richie Unterberger*

Reel Music / Mar. 22, 1982 / Capitol ◆◆
A 14-track selection of previously released songs used in various
Beatles movies. — *William Ruhlmann*

The 20 Greatest Hits / Oct. 11, 1982 / Capitol ◆◆◆
The Beatles reached the #1 position on the *Billboard* magazine
singles chart 20 times. Here are those songs. — *William
Ruhlmann*

☆ **Past Masters, Vol. 1** / Mar. 7, 1988 / Capitol ◆◆◆◆◆
When EMI and Capitol released the Beatles' recordings on compact disc, it was decided to issue the albums in their original
British formats in both the U.K. and the U.S. The British albums
frequently did not contain singles released by the Beatles at the
same time, and there were other odd tracks not included on albums. Thus two discs were necessary to gather the stray material
(some of which included their biggest hits). This first volume, for
example, running from 1962 to 1965, contains "She Loves You," "I
Want to Hold Your Hand," and "I Feel Fine." — *William Ruhlmann*

☆ **Past Masters, Vol. 2** / Mar. 7, 1988 / Capitol ◆◆◆◆◆
Completing the CD release of the Beatles' complete EMI/Capitol
catalog, this disc contains "We Can Work It Out," "Paperback
Writer," "Lady Madonna," "Hey Jude," "Get Back," "Let It Be," and
other later Beatles songs. — *William Ruhlmann*

○ **Live at the BBC** / 1994 / Apple/Capitol ◆◆◆◆
From 1962 to 1965, the Beatles made 52 appearances on the BBC,
recording live-in-the-studio performances of both their official releases and several dozen songs that they never issued on disc. This
magnificent two-disc compilation features 56 of these tracks, including 29 covers of early rock, R&B, soul, and pop tunes that
never appeared on their official releases, as well as the Lennon-
McCartney original "I'll Be On My Way," which they gave away in
1963 to Billy J. Kramer rather than record it themselves. These
performances are nothing less than electrifying, especially the previously unavailable covers, which feature quite a few versions of
classics by Chuck Berry, Little Richard, Carl Perkins, and Elvis
Presley. There are also off-the-beaten-path tunes by the Everly
Brothers and Buddy Holly, on down to obscurities by the Jodi-
mars, Chan Romero (a marvelous "Hippy Hippy Shake"), Eddie
Fontaine, and Ann-Margret. The greatest gem is probably their
fabulous version of Arthur Alexander's "Soldier Of Love," which
(like several of the tracks) would have easily qualified as a highlight of their early releases if they had issued it officially. Restored
from existing tapes of various quality, the sound is mostly very
good, and never less than listenable. Unfortunately, they weren't
able to include every single rarity that the Beatles recorded for the
BBC; the absence of Carl Perkins' "Lend Me Your Comb," which
has circulated on bootlegs in a high-fidelity version, is especially
mystifying. Minor quibbles aside, these performances, available
on bootlegs for years, compose the major missing chapter in the
Beatles' legacy, and it's great to have them easily obtainable in a
first-rate package. — *Richie Unterberger*

○ **Unsurpassed Demos** / Yellow Dog [Bootleg] ◆◆◆◆
In May 1968, the Beatles assembled at George Harrison's home to
demo material for their upcoming *White Album* sessions. The results have been frequently bootlegged; this is the most comprehensive single-disc collection, including 24 tunes in all. Predominantly acoustic in arrangement, with minimal percussion (if Ringo
is present, it's not immediately evident), this has a great informal,
almost campfire spirit, despite the tensions so widely reported of
the group in the subsequent studio sessions. Many of the songs are
extremely close in arrangement to the final studio versions, but it's
great to hear them approach their ultimate shape with a camaraderie and light, joyful tone that unavoidably got muted when
they were ironed out in the control room. John's songs are the
most interesting (great versions of "Revolution," "Julia," "I'm So
Tired," and "Sexy Sadie" especially), with occasional added half-se-
rious lyrics; there are good versions of "Back In The U.S.S.R." and
"Blackbird" as well. Also interesting are a bunch of songs that did-
n't make it onto the album: Lennon's "Child Of Nature" (changed
into "Jealous Guy" for *Imagine*), McCartney's "Singalong Junk"
(which would surface on his first solo LP), and Harrison's "Sour
Milk Sea" (given to Jackie Lomax), "Not Guilty," and "Circles"
(both of which he'd eventually release on solo albums). — *Richie
Unterberger*

Sessions / Chthonian [Bootleg] ◆◆◆
This compilation of 13 studio outtakes, spanning 1962-69, was actually slated for release by EMI in the mid-'80s, but pulled at the
eleventh hour, and has been frequently bootlegged ever since.
That's really a shame; the Beatles didn't record a great deal of unreleased songs, but this collection boils down their vault material
to the very most essential items (though one could argue for the
addition of two or three of the brilliant alternate takes that surfaced on later bootlegs like *Ultra Rare Trax*). Highlights include
"Besame Mucho," from their mid-'62 audition for EMI; "How Do
You Do It?," which George Martin wanted them to release as their

first single (and which was later a big hit for Gerry & the Pace-makers); the scorching 1964 R&B cover "Leave My Kitten Alone," with a great Lennon vocal; the tuneful ballad "That Means A Lot," given to P.J. Proby (the Beatles' version is vastly better); "Come And Get It," given by Paul to Badfinger (who recorded a version almost identical to this demo); and Harrison's hard-rock *White Album* outtake "Not Guilty," which was easily worthy of inclusion on that record. There are also outstanding, significantly different alternate takes of "I'm Looking Through You," "One After 909" (a 1963 version, re-recorded six years later), and "While My Guitar Gently Weeps," an acoustic version that may rank as the Beatles' finest unreleased outtake. *Sessions* is necessary for the serious Beatle fan. —*Richie Unterberger*

Decca Tapes / Yellow Dog [Bootleg] ♦♦
On January 1, 1962, nearly a full year before the release of their debut single, the Beatles unsuccessfully auditioned for Decca Records. The complete, 15-song tape of the session—including a dozen covers and three Lennon-McCartney originals—has been much bootlegged since the 1970s, and has periodically appeared on piecemeal semi-legal releases (always missing the Lennon/Mc-Cartney tunes), but is easily available in its entirety on several different packages. The historical significance of this tape is vast; it illustrates where the Beatles were at this crucial juncture of their career. Less flatteringly, it illustrates how vastly they improved between the time of this audition and their first official album release, *Please Please Me*, 15 months later. In comparison, the sound here is thin and awkward, rife with tentative guitar phrases, nervous lead vocals, and stiff drumming (by Pete Best, who was still in the band at this point). Keeping in mind that this was never intended for public release, in hindsight one finds a great deal of potential and charm, as well as outlines of their great harmonies. The group ended up reprising a lot of the covers, like "Money" and "Till There Was You," on their early albums and BBC broadcasts in much better versions; they also covered some odd popular standards ("September In The Rain," "Sheik Of Araby") that appear nowhere else. Especially fascinating are the three Lennon/McCartney tunes, "Hello Little Girl," "Love Of The Loved," and "Like Dreamers Do," which they never released on EMI, but ended up giving to the Fourmost, Cilla Black, and the Applejacks respectively; the Beatles' versions are much more rock-oriented and much better. —*Richie Unterberger*

Ultra Rare Trax/Back-Track/Unsurpassed Masters / Bootleg ♦♦♦
The release of the 13-song *Sessions* bootleg was followed a few years later by a veritable flood of EMI outtakes on the multi-volume series *Ultra Rare Trax*, which has appeared with further embellishments on the *Back-Track* and *Unsurpassed Masters* series. Besides reprising material from *Sessions*, these unearthed dozens of alternate takes of classic Beatles material spanning their entire career, ranging from nearly identical alternate mixes to radically different arrangements and versions. The latter are the most interesting, standouts being the vastly different, folkier (and great) earlier versions of "Strawberry Fields Forever" and a much different version of "Norwegian Wood." There are also considerably different takes of "She's A Woman," "From Me To You," "Can't Buy Me Love," "The Fool On The Hill," "I Saw Her Standing There," "A Hard Day's Night," and "Flying," as well as rehearsals and backing tracks which provide intimate glimpses of works-in-progress like "Help." The fidelity on these are usually outstanding, easily up to official standards, making these outtakes essential for serious Beatle scholars and many general Beatle fans. —*Richie Unterberger*

Live In Tokyo / Bootleg ♦♦♦
When the Beatles performed in Tokyo in 1966, they were filmed by Japanese television, resulting in one of the finest quality live tapes of the group from the Beatlemania era. The problem lies in the performances; by this time, they had tired of touring and were to a large degree going through the motions. So, despite the release-quality fidelity of this set, listeners may be taken aback by the fair number of flubbed notes, off-key harmonies, and indifferent vocals (on Harrison's "If I Needed Someone" in particular). All things considered, it could have been much worse; the group was struggling with jet-decibel-level screaming fans and primitive sound systems, after all, and they largely do manage to sing and play with reasonable conviction, especially McCartney, always the most committed onstage performer of the four. Includes many of their hits from the late-'64 to mid-'66 era; especially interesting is the stringless band version of "Yesterday," as none of the Beatles except Paul played on the studio recording. —*Richie Unterberger*

Get Back Sessions / Bootleg ♦♦♦
Get Back was the original title of the *Let It Be* album, but the album was shelved for a year before it finally gained official release. Because the Beatles were filmed for hundreds of hours during the course of the sessions, more unreleased material dates from this juncture of their career than any other. Unfortunately, the bulk of this ranks among their worst unreleased stuff, consisting mostly of sloppy rehearsals and chaotic covers of dozens of rock & roll oldies. An unbelievable number of different bootlegs have issued this material in varying configurations since 1969, and although the recent CDs feature vastly improved sound quality, not much can be done to salvage the performances, which after all were never intended for circulation. However, there are some excellent cuts to be found, particularly in several alternate takes of songs from *Let It Be* (especially the stringless "Long And Winding Road"), and even the lousy stuff serves as a fascinating illustration of the group's vast array of influences, their working methods in the studio, and, at worst, the roots of the band's disintegration. It's impossible to recommend specific collections, as there are hundreds of different titles floating around, even some box sets, and they're always uncovering more outtakes. The non-completist should look for the *Get Back* album as it was originally mastered and sequenced (featuring nearly the same content as *Let It Be*, but adding a couple of different songs and containing much different, less elaborate, un-Spectorized mixes) and/or the rooftop session from the film's final sequence, which is an inspired live performance of most of the material from *Let It Be*. —*Richie Unterberger*

BOOKS

More books have been written about the Beatles, by a wide margin, than any other rock performers; some are excellent, many are unduly repetitive and sensational. The following is a selection of the best and most essential.

♦♦♦♦♦ **The Beatles Recording Sessions**, by Mark Lewisohn (Harmony, 1988). If you had to pick one Beatles book for your permanent library, this would be the winner, over some top-flight competition. Lewisohn, probably the world's leading Beatle authority, was granted access to most of the session tapes recorded by the group (usually at Abbey Road Studios) for EMI between 1962 and 1970—hundreds of hours worth of rehearsals, alternate takes, unreleased material, and finished product. The result is presented as a diary that takes you through every single session the group recorded, giving you a fly-on-the-wall insight into the crafting and perfection of every song they released (and a few that remained in the can). It's much more than a studio log, however; Lewisohn combines scholarship with acute critical observation, leading the reader through the act of the creative process in the manner of a storyteller, not a mere scorekeeper. Interspersed throughout are fascinating quotes and recollections from many session musicians and EMI engineers and technicians, as well as lots of rare photos. It's absorbing to learn of the existence of substantially different versions of "Norwegian Wood," "Strawberry Fields Forever," "Helter Skelter," and "And I Love Her," to single out just a few examples; it's also instructive to learn the specifics of the large role producer (and frequent sessionman) George Martin played in refining and shaping their sound for record. An excellent interview with Paul McCartney tops off a reference work that you'll be returning to again and again. —*Richie Unterberger*

♦♦♦ **The Beatles: The Authorized Biography**, by Hunter Davies (McGraw-Hill, 1968). The first reasonable attempt to tell the Beatles story in a comprehensive fashion for the adult market remains one of the best. As an authorized biographer, Davies was to some extent required to sanitize some dirty laundry; there's nothing about Brian Epstein's homosexuality or the wilder aspects of their Hamburg days and Beatlemania tours. On the other hand, he was granted access to their homes and recording sessions, giving what seems to be a reasonable picture of where the group's heads were at circa 1967. Periodically reissued with new forwards by the author, packed with first-hand material from the Beatles and their closest associates, it remains a good source of information, though many of the gaps, sensational and otherwise, have been filled in the intervening decades. —*Richie Unterberger*

♦♦♦♦ **Shout!: The Beatles In Their Generation**, by Philip Norman (Simon & Schuster, 1981). This covers much of the same ground as the Hunter Davies biography, but its franker viewpoint gives it the edge as the best general interest account of their lives and music. Unencumbered by obligations to censor facts and subdue conflicts, Norman wasn't granted access to the Fab Four themselves, but interviewed a great many of their associates, with a resulting account that takes us through Liverpool, Hamburg, Beatlemania, and their fractious dissolution with exacting detail. The good times and the artistic triumphs aren't neglected, but you also get a complete perspective that takes heed of their business entanglements, occasionally ferocious in-fighting, and the ruthlessness that could be required from the group and their advisors to claw to the top and remain there. Unlike the Davies book, it takes the tale all the way to its sorry end in early 1970, and is especially strong in its coverage of the ill-fated Apple empire. Norman is occasionally too cynical for his own good, but this is required reading for rock fans. — *Richie Unterberger*

✦✦✦✦ The Beatles Forever, by Nicholas Schaffner (McGraw-Hill, 1977). Somewhat overlooked in surveys of the best Beatle books, this is probably the best introductory volume to the group, gracefully weaving together biographical information, critical descriptions of their recordings, and a general account of how the Beatles affected and fit into the zeitgeist of their time. There's no first-hand interview material, but Schaffner's thorough research uncovered a great deal of quotes, from the Beatles and from contemporary reviews and critics, that aren't printed in most Beatle bios. The last third of the book covers their '70s solo years, which remain the source of their most interesting solo work, in equal depth. Out-of-print, but easy to find used. — *Richie Unterberger*

✦✦✦ The Complete Beatles Chronicle, by Mark Lewisohn (Harmony, 1992). Having documented the Beatles' studio work to near-perfection in *Recording Sessions*, Lewisohn went a step further with this volume, which details all of the professional activities of their career—every live performance, recording session, radio broadcast, concert, film, and TV appearance, from 1957 to 1970. Unlike *Sessions*, it's really more for the fanatic than the fan—there's a fair amount of repetition with *Sessions*, and there's too much minutiae for the general reader. That said, it's still filled with fascinating detail, much of which clarifies hazy rumors and myths about the group—you can check this out to ascertain, for instance, exactly when and under what circumstances Stuart Sutcliffe left the group, or read for yourself how chaotic the filming of *Magical Mystery Tour* was. Packed with good photos, and the exhaustive supplement listing every song the Beatles ever played live (and their sources) is a valuable bonus. — *Richie Unterberger*

✦✦ The Beatles: An Illustrated Record, by Roy Carr & Tony Tyler (Harmony, 1975). To a large degree, this lavishly illustrated and gorgeously designed volume—the first comprehensive critical retrospective of the Beatles' work—has been surpassed by more thoroughly researched and written books in the past two decades. Still, it's a passionate overview of the Beatles' oeuvre by two leading British *New Musical Express* scribes who aren't afraid to call it as they see it; they have little patience for McCartney's most sentimental side, or Harrison's religious diatribes, in particular. Some great humor and wit (with some occasional wrongheadedness) in these pithy assessments, with coverage of the members' early '70s solo recordings as well. — *Richie Unterberger*

✦✦✦✦ Lennon Remembers, by Jann Wenner (Straight Arrow, 1971). In late 1970, just after the release of his first proper solo album, and less than a year after the official breakup of the Beatles, Lennon granted an interview of mammoth length to *Rolling Stone* publisher Wenner. The result, 25 years later, still stands as the most famous and fascinating rock interview of all time. Lennon, fresh from primal scream therapy and still nursing wounds over the Beatles' demise, lashed out at a lot of targets in these conversations, not the least of which was his former partner and soulmate, Paul McCartney. Forever exploding the Fab Four's happy-go-lucky image, Lennon detailed the seamier side of their success with an eagerness that, one suspects, he regretted slightly in the ensuing years, criticizing mass adulation, George Martin's production, and the Beatles' films with succinct venom. It's not all cathartic rage; there are plenty of fascinating stories of the composition of Beatle classics, detailed insights into his musical and artistic influences, and extremely personal anecdotes about his relationship with Yoko

Ono, the other Beatles, and the experiences that triggered the *Plastic Ono Band* album.—Richie Unterberger

✦✦✦ The Playboy Interviews With John Lennon & Yoko Ono, by David Sheff (edited by G. Barry Golson) (Playboy Press, 1981). When Lennon emerged from a five-year hiatus in late 1980, he gave another book-length interview to *Playboy* to coincide with the release of his and Yoko's *Double Fantasy* album. In the decade since the Rolling Stone interviews, he'd mellowed (not much) and harbored a more mature perspective about his fame and his past. A good deal of this focuses on the *Double Fantasy* sessions and the relationship between John and Yoko, and while plenty interesting, is not as essential as *Lennon Remembers*. For Beatle fans, though, this contains an essential segment in which John gives his impressions and memories of virtually every song the Beatles ever recorded, as well as many from his solo albums. A lot of this material wasn't published in *Playboy* itself, and this book-length compendium of what turned out to be his final lengthy interview is quite worthwhile. —*Richie Unterberger*

✦✦✦ A Hard Day's Write, by Steve Turner (HarperPerennial, 1994). There's not much original material in this volume, but it's a first-rate assemblage of facts and anecdotes, from an extremely wide variety of sources, that illustrate the stories, circumstances, and characters that inspired every single Beatle song. Especially in their later years, when their compositions became increasingly lyrically sophisticated, these can be quite fascinating. There's a good two pages on the characters and incidents that inspired "Polythene Pam," for instance, and quotes from the real-life women that inspired "She's Leaving Home" and "Lucy in the Sky with Diamonds." Turner wasn't able to talk to the composers themselves for comments, and the book's chief flaw—not one the author could have done much about—is that the description of Lennon's songs benefit from far more personal and insightful comments from the author than McCartney's or Harrison's, as John was always by the far the frankest interview subject of the group when asked about his work. Still, it's a well-written book that manages to uncover yet more fascinating stories about the group and their creative process, embellished by many rarely seen photos. —*Richie Unterberger*

✦✦✦ Apple to the Core, by Peter McCabe and Robert D. Schonfeld (Pocket, 1972). The collapse of Apple Records mirrored the collapse of the Beatles and, if one stretches a bit, the collapse of a lot of the '60s highest ideals. Begun as a utopian business venture, Apple quickly turned into the albatross that broke the camel's back; the financial and business pressures of the company were one of the chief factors in the Beatles' split. This meticulous look into the dissolution of the Apple empire is painful for Beatlemaniacs, not because it's poorly done, but because it's done all too well. The disputes over publishing and management, as well as the intergroup and interwife sniping, may be fairly common within successful bands, but they've rarely played out with such tragic drama. Some of McCabe and Schonfeld's research and conclusions were fleshed out and expounded upon by subsequent bios, and a few inaccuracies pop up, but this is a biting inside look at the wheelings, dealings, and treachery of the music business, where money comes before art. The authors also deserve credit for their tough, unsentimental, and fair portrayals of the Beatles as real, flawed human beings like you or me, resisting the full or partial deification employed by most of their other biographers. —*Richie Unterberger*

✦✦✦✦ A Day in the Life: The Music and Artistry of the Beatles, by Mark Hertsgaard (Delacorte Press, 1994). There are several books that focus on analysis of the Beatles' music, *Twilight of the Gods* (by Wilfrid Mellers), *Tell Me Why* (by Tim Riley), and *Revolution in the Head* (by Ian MacDonald) being the most well known. This more recent effort is recommended above those because it is a far more interesting and accessible read, and places the Beatles' recordings in the context of their professional lives and impact upon the greater music community and society. Hertsgaard draws heavily (though quite selectively) from the best of the previous books about the Beatles, so although the information is assembled and presented well, it's much more highly recommended as an overview for those who haven't read widely about the group than to Beatlemaniacs, who will be familiar with most of the material here. The most distinctive bonus of the volume is the extensive discussion of unreleased studio outtakes and alternate versions to illuminate these critiques, as this material has rarely been discussed at length in print, with the exception of Mark Lewisohn's *The Beatles Recording Sessions.* —*Richie Unterberger*

The Beau Brummels

Group, Folk-Rock, Pop/Rock
The Beau Brummels (original 1964 lineup: Sal Valentino [b. Salvatore Willard Spanpinato, Sep. 8, 1942, San Francisco] [vocals], Ron Elliott [b. Oct 21, 1943, Healdsburgh, California] [guitar/vocals], Declan Mulligan [b. County Tipperary, Ireland] [guitar], Ron Meagher [b. Oct 2, 1941, Oakland, California] [bass], Ron Petersen [b. Jan 8, 1942, Rudyard, Michigan] [drums]), from San Francisco, enjoyed a brief run on the Top 40 pop charts in 1965 with a bracing blend of Brit Invasion pop and West Coast folk-rock.

Sylvester Stone (later of Sly & the Family Stone) produced the band's first two albums, as well as their biggest hits, "Laugh Laugh" (#15) and "Just a Little" (#9). The fatalistic "You Tell Me Why," the band's last Top 40 hit, and the aggressive Byrds-like rocker "Don't Talk to Strangers" (#52) revealed the Beau Brummels to be a group possessing much depth. Unfortunately, the band's label (Autumn) folded at the end of 1965.

Two subsequent albums on Warner, *Triangle* and *Bradley's Barn*, are out of print but worth seeking out. In 1973, Leo Kottke recorded a fine version of "You Tell Me Why" (minus the bridge) for his album *Ice Water.* In 1975 the Beau Brummels re-formed for an impressive reunion on Warner, then called it quits. —*Rick Clark*

The Beau Brummels, Vol. 2 / 1965 / Sundazed ♦♦♦
No big hits on this album, but it's the best LP by the Brummels' first album. The twelve original songs feature several fine Ron Elliott harmony folk-rockers that stand up well to the Byrds' material from the same era, including "I Want You," "You Tell Me Why," "Sad Little Girl," and the Byrds imitation "Don't Talk To Strangers." The CD reissue adds bonus alternate versions of "Woman" and "When It Comes To Your Love." —*Richie Unterberger*

○ **Introducing the Beau Brummels** / Apr. 1965 / Sundazed ♦♦♦♦
A much stronger debut than the norm for the era. Ten of the twelve cuts are Ron Elliott originals, including the hits "Laugh Laugh," "Still In Love With You Baby," and "Just A Little." The hard-rocking numbers are the weakest, but "Stick Like Glue" and "I Would Be Happy" are fine Beatlesque numbers, and "They'll Make You Cry" is a first-rate moody folk-rocker. The CD reissue adds two bonus tracks, a demo of "Just A Little" and the single "Good Time Music." —*Richie Unterberger*

Beau Brummels '66 / Jul. 1966 / Warner Brothers ♦♦♦
○ **Triangle** / Jul. 1967 / Warner Brothers ♦♦♦♦
A beautiful venture by the surviving trio into a more authentic form of folk and country-rock, with a repertoire that recalls the more famous Everly Brothers classic, *Roots.* —*Bruce Eder*

Bradley's Barn / Oct. 1968 / Edsel ♦♦♦
● **The Best of the Beau Brummels: Golden Archive Series** / 1987 / Rhino ♦♦♦♦
Probably the best (and best-sounding) anthology covering their golden years, although it lacks their brilliant, later country-based work at its best. —*Bruce Eder*

Autumn of Their Years / 1994 / Big Beat ♦♦♦
These underrated '60s folk-rock pioneers cut a great number of unreleased outtakes/demos during their mid-'60s prime that didn't make it onto the albums they released for the tiny Autumn label during that period. 14 of those songs were released in the early 1980s by Rhino on the fine *From The Vaults* album. *Autumn Of Their Years* reprises ten of those tunes and adds sixteen previously unreleased cuts for a grand total of 26, all of which are group originals. There are a lot of fine moments here, but it's actually a bit much for all but hardcore fans. First off, the best cuts—ones like "She Sends Me," "Dream On," and "Love Is Just A Game," which display their supremely haunting folk-rock melodicism and minor-key harmonies—were already available on *From The Vaults.* The sixteen newly found demos aren't as good, production-wise (several are acoustic sketches) or material-wise. Earlier demos of their hits "Laugh Laugh," "Just A Little," and "Still In Love With You Baby" are interesting in comparison to the originals, but not as good. And some strong cuts from *From The Vaults* are inexplicably omitted. Of the new vault finds, the highlight is "Tomorrow Is

Another Day," an acoustic ballad showcasing Sal Valentino's rich and moving vocals. —*Richie Unterberger*

The Beautiful South

Group, Alternative Pop/Rock
A British group formed by singer Paul Heaton (b. May 9, 1962, Birkenhead, Merseyside) after the demise of the Housemartins in 1988, characterized by melodic songs with sweet, jazz-pop arrangements that belie their witty, caustic lyrics. Other band members include Briana Corrigan (vocals), David Rotheray (guitar), Sean Welch (bass), David Hemmingway (drums/vocals), and David Stead (drums). They scored two U.K. Top Ten singles with "Song For Whoever" and "You Keep It All In" in 1989 and topped the charts with "A Little Time" in 1990. Their first two albums, *Welcome to the Beautiful South* (1989 #10) and *Choke* (1990 #11) also hit the U.K. Top Ten. There was a third album, *Miaow,* in 1994, and their greatest hits album, *Carry on up the Charts,* was the biggest U.K. hit of the 1994 Christmas season. —*William Ruhlmann*

○ **Welcome to the Beautiful South** / Oct. 1989 / Go! Discs ♦♦♦♦
The difference between the catchy light pop that constitutes the Beautiful South's music and the bitter, pessimistic lyrics innocently sung by Paul Heaton is so great it constitutes a kind of malevolent seduction. But that's the point. Released in the U.S. in January 1990. —*William Ruhlmann*

Choke / Nov. 1990 / Go! Discs ♦♦♦
The Beautiful South's second album conceals its bitter, mean cynicism in layers of lush, jazz-tinged pop, making all of the bile go down easily. —*Stephen Thomas Erlewine*

0898 / Apr. 1992 / Go! Discs ♦♦♦
There are no big poses or walls of crunchy guitars on *0898.* Instead, the group—which includes three lead vocalists—deals in fragile melodies and harmonies, soulful but low-key instrumentation, and lyrics full of subtle social commentary and humor. In North America, where mainstream audiences have been well trained to salivate to very obvious musical bells, the Beautiful South may be too clever for its own good. At times, the group even couches itself in the guise of a smooth lounge act, rebelling against current trends by having something to say while not making a racket about it. Producer John Kelly (Peter Gabriel) has contributed an incisive and full-bodied production to *0898,* a great improvement over the rather thin sound of the group's previous *Choke.* —*Roch Parisien*

Miaow / 1994 / Go! Discs ♦♦♦
● **Carry on Up the Charts: The Best of** / 1994 / Go! Discs ♦♦♦♦
Carry on up the Charts: The Best of the Beautiful South was the surprise British hit of 1994, going quintuple platinum five times between its late fall release and the summer of 1995. The success was surprising because while the band had been modestly popular, their last few albums were sliding down the charts. However, their hits collection, *Carry on up the Charts,* flew to number one and stayed there for weeks. It's nothing more than all their singles, yet compiled together they make the most convincing case for the Beautiful South's sly, cynical sophisticated pop. *Carry on up the Charts* was finally released in the United States in the fall of 1995, with less tracks. —*Stephen Thomas Erlewine*

Beck

Alternative Pop/Rock
With his portastudio, keyboard, drum machine, and guitar, singer/songwriter Beck (b. Beck Hansen) created music that celebrated the junk culture of the '90s. Beck's music drew from hip-hop, folk, experimental rock, psychedelia, pop, and rock & roll, recycling everything into a colorful, messy and willfully diverse brand of post-modern rock, filled with warped, satiric imagery and clumsy poetry. With all of his rootless eclecticism, Beck is distinctly a product of the '90s; all of his influences were processed through television and records, not real life experiences. But that trashy, disposable quality is what makes his music unique.

Beck came to national attention in early 1994, when his folky hip-hop single "Loser" began to receive airplay on alternative rock stations across America. "Loser" was originally released independently on a Californian label in late 1993. The single became a club hit and quickly spread to underground and alternative radio stations. Beck became the center of a major-label bidding war; he eventually signed with DGC Records. Beck released his debut album, *Mellow Gold*, in early 1994. *Mellow Gold* received rave reviews and became a gold record as "Loser" climbed into the Top 10. Beck's contract with DGC allows him to release records that he and the company deem as uncommercial on indie records. Consequently, the singer/songwriter released two new records by the summer of 1994, which were both recorded roughly around the same time as *Mellow Gold*. *Stereopathetic Soul Manure* was a noisy, more experimental album than his debut and was released on Flipside Records. *One Foot in the Grave* accentuated his folk roots and was released on K Records. Neither album sold on the level of *Mellow Gold*, but they sold respectably.

As he prepared his second album for DGC, Beck toured with Lollapalooza Five in the summer of 1995. — *Stephen Thomas Erlewine*

● **Mellow Gold** / 1994 / DGC ✦✦✦✦
Beck's debut album became a hit, thanks to the lazy folk/hip-hop fusion of "Loser," but the remainder of *Mellow Gold* proves he's not a one-hit wonder. From the warped TV-folk of "Pay No Mind (Snoozer)" and the pounding rhythms of "Beercan" to the trashy garage-rock of "F—-in With My Head" and "Soul Suckin' Jerk," Beck turns his fascination with pop culture into exciting music that refuses to acknowledge any boundaries. — *Stephen Thomas Erlewine*

One Foot in the Grave / 1994 / K ✦✦✦
One Foot in the Grave appeared in the summer of 1994, after the Top Ten "Loser" had made Beck into a crossover sensation. Recorded for the staunchly independent Washington-based record label K, *One Foot in the Grave* didn't follow the surrealistic rock/hip-hop fusion that formed the core of *Mellow Gold*, nor did it continue the noisy experimentations of his second record, *Stereopathetic Soul Manure*. Instead, the album accentuated Beck's folk roots, which were apparent throughout *Mellow Gold*. The record is a quiet affair, showcasing Beck's talents for bizarre, postmodern wordplay and slyly melodic songwriting. — *Stephen Thomas Erlewine*

Stereopathetic Soul Manure / 1994 / Flipside ✦✦
Released almost immediately after Beck's first album *Mellow Gold*, *Stereopathetic Soul Manure* is a noisier record than his debut, flaunting the experimental rock influences that *Mellow Gold* only hinted at. For the most part, the record is a non-stop attack of noise and fragmented songs, recalling the mid-'80s records of Sonic Youth and Pussy Galore, yet the occasional pop and folk-oriented song creeps in, though none of them are as well-constructed as those on the debut or his third album *One Foot in the Grave*, which followed a few months later. — *Stephen Thomas Erlewine*

Beck Bogert & Appice

Group, Hard Rock
This early-'70s hard rock trio comprised ex-Yardbird guitarist Jeff Beck (b. Jun. 24, 1944, Wallington, Surrey, England) and two former Vanilla Fudge members in drummer Carmine Appice (b. Dec. 15, 1946, New York City) and bassist Tim Bogert (b. Aug. 27, 1944, Richfield, New Jersey).

Beck, Bogert & Appice pushed Cream's concept of free-for-all interplay into new realms of lumbering excessiveness. They released only one album stateside, but there was a much-sought-after live-in-Japan effort, which has finally been included (in part) on Beck's *Beckology* boxed set. — *Rick Clark*

Beck Bogert & Appice / 1973 / Epic ✦✦✦
Guitar virtuoso Beck toys with hard rock, supported by bassist Tim Bogert and drummer Carmine Appice. Included is a cover of Stevie Wonder's "Superstition." — *Donna DiChario*

Live in Japan / 1974 / Epic ✦✦

Jeff Beck

b. Jun. 24, 1944, Wallington, Surrey, England
Rock & Roll, Hard Rock, Fusion
Utterly distinctive and certainly one of the most important electric lead guitarists in rock history, Jeff Beck was the wildcard element that gave the post-Clapton Yardbirds work its futuristic quality. His pioneering experiments with feedback and various effects, particularly on the classic "Shapes of Things," influenced thousands of musicians.

After leaving the Yardbirds, Beck went on to a highly successful solo career that produced an excellent debut (*Truth*), featuring Rod Stewart on vocals, Ron Wood (bass), Nicky Hopkins (keys), and

Mickey Waller (drums). The next few albums contained fine moments with Stewart and replacement vocalist Bobby Tench, but during the mid-'70s Beck switched gears and released the instrumental jazz-rock fusion *Blow by Blow*, generating his greatest commercial success. Further efforts to delve into that style were less notable, but even when the material wasn't up to par, Beck's liquid, yet impulsive style has been generally amazing. — *Rick Clark*

★ **Truth** / Aug. 1968 / Epic ✦✦✦✦✦
Along with Led Zeppelin's self-titled first album, Jeff Beck's *Truth* is considered the primo primer for what came to be known as heavy metal. Fusing the thunderous rhythm section of Ron Wood on bass and Mickey Waller on drums with his paint-blistering lead guitar and Rod Stewart's gravel-and-whiskey vocals, Beck's visionary approach to blues and rock & roll influenced practically every rock band that followed on both sides of the Atlantic. Although Beck could be unpredictable and eclectic (witness his straightforward, acoustic reading of "Greensleeves"), *Truth* features the smoking "Beck's Bolero," "Rock My Plimsoul," and the wah-wah pièce de resistance, "I Ain't Superstitious." — *Tom Graves*

Beck-Ola / Jun. 1969 / Epic ✦✦✦
A year after Jeff Beck recorded *Truth*, he came back with the even heavier *Beck-Ola*. Although the songwriting seems diluted, and the addition of Nicky Hopkins on piano added spice in all the wrong places, *Beck-Ola* is still a gut-slamming good time. Notable tracks include "Spanish Boots" and "Plynth (Water Down the Drain)." — *Tom Graves*

Rough & Ready / Oct. 1971 / Epic ✦✦✦
After Jeff Beck nearly died in a car crash, he came back in 1971 with a new group and a new sound, reflecting his more introspective state of mind. Although the firepower and guitar blasts are still there, he burns cooler. With the help of the jazzy Max Middleton on piano, Beck created one of rock's most haunting set pieces, "Raynes Park Blues." Other highlights include the dynamic ballad "Jody" and the hard grinding rock groove of "I've Been Used." — *Tom Graves & Rick Clark*

Jeff Beck Group / Apr. 1972 / Epic ✦✦✦
Continuing with the same group lineup as on *Rough and Ready*, *Jeff Beck Group* was slagged off by critics for Steve Cropper's admittedly lazy production. However, several of the songs hold up masterfully, including the skronky "Ice Cream Cakes," the superlative redo of Don Nix's "Going Down," and the beautifully sad and wistful instrumental, "Definitely Maybe." Beware of early, poor-sounding versions. — *Tom Graves*

● **Blow by Blow** / Mar. 1975 / Epic ✦✦✦✦
When Jeff Beck announced that he was working on an all-instrumental album, few but his legion of guitar fans could have predicted the far-reaching impact of this pivotal jazz-rock fusion album. Teamed with the Beatles' ex-producer George Martin, Beck singlehandedly created a new subtext for rock & roll. With his virtuosity and taste at an all-time peak, Beck let loose with unforgettable tracks such as the Roy Buchanan-inspired "Cause We've Ended As Lovers" and the percolating "Freeway Jam." This is one of rock's great instrumental works. — *Tom Graves*

○ **Wired** / May 1976 / Epic ✦✦✦✦
Nearly *Blow by Blow*'s equal, although Beck doesn't venture any further musically. Charles Mingus's "Goodbye Pork Pie Hat" is worth the price alone. (Available on Mobile Fidelity's Ultradisc) — *Tom Graves*

Live . . . With the Jan Hammer Group / Mar. 1977 / Epic ✦✦
Jeff Beck toured to promote *Wired*, backed by a jazz-fusion group led by synthesizer player Jan Hammer. This straightforward live souvenir combines songs from *Blow By Blow* and *Wired*, plus a few other things, and while it features typically fiery playing from Beck, the backup is a bit too heavy-handed and the occasional vocals (by Hammer and drummer Tony Smith) are embarrassing. — *William Ruhlmann*

There and Back / Jun. 1980 / Epic ✦✦✦
Jeff Beck's first new studio album in four years found him moving from old keyboard partner Jan Hammer (three tracks) to new one Tony Hymas (five), which turned out to be the difference between competition and support. Hence, the second side of this instrumental album is more engaging and less of a funk-fusion extravaganza than most of the first. If it were anybody else, you'd say that this was a transitional album, but this was the only studio album Beck released between 1976 and 1985, which makes it more like

an unexpected Christmas letter from an old friend: "Everything's fine, still playing guitar." — *William Ruhlmann*

Flash / Jul. 1985 / Epic ♦♦
Produced by Nile Rodgers and Arthur Baker, *Flash* is Beck's surprisingly successful stab at a pop album, featuring a fine performance with Rod Stewart on "People Get Ready." — *Stephen Thomas Erlewine*

○ **Jeff Beck's Guitar Shop** / Oct. 1989 / Epic ♦♦♦♦
A guitar hero in his prime, he's full of fury and finesse, with topnotch support from Terry Bozzio and Tony Hymas. — *Jas Obrecht*

○ **Beckology** / 1991 / Epic ♦♦♦♦
Covering everything from his earliest (and terrific) tracks with the Tridents through his spot-on interpretation of Santo & Johnny's "Sleep Walk," *Beckology* features great remastering, smart packaging (resembling a vintage Fender tweed guitar case), and the essential Yardbirds and solo years material. The set (55 tracks in all) also collects the best material from weaker albums such as *Flash* and *There and Back*. A definitive overview of Beck's career would have included his work as a sideman with artists like Stevie Wonder, Rod Stewart, and Donovan; nevertheless, *Beckology* is as comprehensive a collection as one will find on this innovative guitarist. — *Tom Graves & Rick Clark*

Frankie's House / Jan. 5, 1992 / Epic ♦♦
Beck fans will find his playing here mesmerizing, surpassing the technical mastery of *Guitar Shop*. Apart from a sizzling instrumental version of "High Heeled Sneakers," less devoted listeners will find *Frankie's House* as captivating as most other incidental film music. — *Stephen Thomas Erlewine*

Crazy Legs / Jun. 29, 1993 / Epic ♦♦
Jeff Beck has made many strange albums, but none were ever quite as strange as this. With the Big Town Playboys offering support, Beck rips through 15 Gene Vincent numbers (not "Be-Bop-A-Lula," however), paying tribute to Vincent's guitarist, Cliff Gallup. Beck sounds terrific as he reconstructs Gallup's parts, but he doesn't add anything to the originals. Still, *Crazy Legs* is a fun listen and offers many insights into Beck's playing, if not Gallup's. — *Stephen Thomas Erlewine*

● **Best of Beck** / 1995 / Epic ♦♦♦♦
Beck's career has been so stylistically varied, it's hard to compile one disc that does it justice. *Best of Beck* isn't that disc—it doesn't feature much of the Jeff Beck Group, for starters. Nevertheless, it offers a taste of his capabilities, making it an effective introduction to one of the greatest guitarists in rock & roll. — *Stephen Thomas Erlewine*

Walter Becker

b. Feb. 20, 1950
Pop/Rock
Guitarist/bassist/songwriter/producer Walter Becker hooked up with his partner Donald Fagen when both were attending Bard College in upstate New York in the late '60s. They became members of Jay and the Americans, then signed a songwriting contract with ABC Records in the early '70s. At ABC, they formed the group Steely Dan, which gradually dwindled down to just the two of them while they sold millions of records during the '70s. They split up in 1981, with Becker turning to a part-time producing career (China Crisis, Rickie Lee Jones) and moving to Hawaii. Becker produced Fagen's *Kamakiriad* album in 1993, and the duo toured as Steely Dan again in 1993 and 1994. Becker belatedly launched a solo career with the release of his debut album, *11 Tracks of Whack*, in 1994. — *William Ruhlmann*

○ **11 Tracks of Whack** / Sep. 27, 1994 / Giant ♦♦♦♦
It's not surprising that Steely Dan cofounder Walter Becker's debut solo album sounds like a Steely Dan record. What is a little surprising, though, is that, in his lead singing debut, he sounds so much like his erstwhile partner Donald Fagen. Not that you'd mistake the two (Fagen projects more and is slightly grittier), but they sing in the same register with the same sly phrasing and the same accent. Other differences from the Dan are equally subtle: Becker adopts a sparer musical approach, for one thing, the missing element being the prominence of Fagen's keyboards (although Fagen does play on the record and co-produced it). Nothing gets in the way of Becker's voice, and he proves to be a less ornate lyricist than Fagen, restricting himself largely to tales of romantic dislocation. On the whole, this album sounds like what you'd expect—one half of Steely Dan. — *William Ruhlmann*

George Bedard

Group, Rock & Roll, Blues Rock, Rockabilly
While other youngsters in the '60s were listening to British invasion bands and wishing they were on the Ed Sullivan show, a young George Bedard was in his basement teaching himself guitar, playing along with records by blues legends Howlin' Wolf, B. B. King, and Muddy Waters. By the early '70s Bedard teamed up with blues harpist/guitarist Steve Nardella to form the Silvertones, one of the finest Ann Arbor, MI, blues/rockabilly bands of the '70s. Combining genres is a path Bedard has pursued relentlessly, working in groups both as soloist and sideman, covering a wide range of styles from country to jazz to rockabilly and back to his first love, the blues. There's not much Bedard can't play extremely well in any of these idioms, his style always informed by taste and economy. Though his solo recordings have been few, George Bedard remains a guitar hero's guitar hero. — *Cub Koda*

○ **Upside** / 1992 / Schoolkids ♦♦♦♦
Bedard's debut album features great originals and a rollicking textbook approach to everything from rockabilly to T-Bone Walker-style blues. Worth it just for the explosive solo on "What a Shame." — *Cub Koda*

The Bee Gees

Group, Disco, Pop/Rock
One of the most successful pop groups of the 1960s and '70s, the Bee Gees have had two distinct careers and at present are embarked on a third. The name is an acronym for "Brothers Gibb," and the nucleus of the group has always been the brothers Barry (b. Sept. 1, 1946, Douglas, Isle of Man), Robin, and Maurice Gibb (the last two are twins, b. Dec. 22, 1949, Manchester, England), though in their first successful manifestation the group also featured guitarist Vince Melouney (b. Aug. 19, 1945, Australia) and drummer Colin Petersen (b. Mar. 24, 1946, Melbourne, Australia).

The Gibb brothers were the sons of band leader Hugh Gibb, and were performing in Manchester, England, when they were still children. The family migrated to Brisbane, Australia in 1958, which is where the Bee Gees were organized as a pop group. After achieving some success there, they moved back to England in January 1967, where they hooked up with manager Robert Stigwood (an Australian who was an associate of Beatles manager Brian Epstein). Their first British and American single, the vibrato-laden ballad "New York Mining Disaster 1941," appearing during the *Sgt. Pepper* Summer of Love of 1967, was in keeping with the eclectic pop scene of the time and became a Top 15 hit in both the U.K. and the U.S. It also led to charges that they were copying the Beatles. (The Bee Gees would never earn approval from rock critics.)

They enjoyed a series of hit singles and albums over the next couple of years (due to their enormous chart success, only Top Tens will be noted)— *Bee Gees' First* (U.S. #7/U.K. #8, 1967); "Massachusetts" (U.K. #1, 1967; "World" (U.K. #9, 1967); "Words" (U.K. #8, 1968); "I've Gotta Get a Message to You" (U.K. #1/U.S. #8, 1968); *Idea* (U.K. #4, 1968); "First of May" (U.K. #6, 1969); "I Started a Joke" (U.S. #6, 1969); and their answer to *Sgt. Pepper*, the red-felt-covered double-LP *Odessa* (U.K. #10, 1969) (they also wrote the Marbles' "Only One Woman" [U.K. #5, 1968])—after which they were rent by dissension. Melouney quit in December 1968. Robin Gibb left for a solo career in the spring of 1969. He had a solo hit with "Saved by the Bell" (U.K. #2) in July, but follow-ups were less successful. Petersen was fired in August, just as the Bee Gees' "Don't Forget to Remember" (U.K. #2) was hitting the charts. In September, *Best of the Bee Gees* made U.K. #7/U.S. #9. Barry and Maurice Gibb carried on as the Bee Gees, releasing *Cucumber Castle* (April 1970), the soundtrack from a film in which they appeared. Each one also made a flop solo single.

The trio reformed in December 1970 and scored two reunion hits, "Lonely Days" (U.S. #3, 1971) and "How Can You Mend a Broken Heart" (U.S. #1, 1971). In the U.K., they had "Run to Me" (#9, 1972). The rest of the early '70s were a rough time for them, but in April 1975 they organized a new backup group (Alan Kendall on guitar, Dennis Byron on drums, Blue Weaver on keyboards) and returned to the top of the U.S. charts with a disco beat, falsetto vocals, and a song called "Jive Talkin' " (U.K. #5). It was followed by "Nights on Broadway" (U.S. #7, 1975), "You Should Be Dancing" (U.S. #1/U.K. #5, 1976), and "Love So Right" (U.S. #3, 1977), while

Children of the World (1976) and the live album *Here...At Last* (1977) each went to U.S. #8.

In 1977, they were engaged by Stigwood to write songs for the movie *Saturday Night Fever,* and their contributions helped make the resulting double soundtrack album one of the best-selling records of all time, moving a reported 30 million copies worldwide. (As of 1993, it was certified by the Record Association of America for sales of 11 million copies in the U.S., making it the seventh biggest selling LP in history.) It spawned three U.S. #1 Bee Gees hits, "Stayin' Alive" (U.K. #4), "Night Fever" (U.K. #1), and "How Deep Is Your Love" (U.K. #3). The soundtrack also featured hits written by the Bee Gees for others: "If I Can't Have You," by Yvonne Elliman (U.S. #1/U.K. #4) and Tavares' "More Than a Woman" (U.K. #7). In the late '70s, the Bee Gees wrote and produced hits for Samantha Sang ("Emotion," U.S. #3, 1977), Frankie Valli ("Grease," U.S. #1/U.K. #3, 1978), and Andy Gibb (the youngest Gibb brother, b. Mar. 5, 1958, Manchester, England—d. Mar. 10, 1988, Oxford, England) ("I Just Want to Be Your Everything," U.S. #1, 1977; "Love Is Thicker than Water," U.S. #1, 1978; "Shadow Dancing," U.S. #1 1978; "An Everlasting Love," U.S. #5, 1978; "[Our Love] Don't Throw It All Away," U.S. #9, 1978).

At one point, five of the Top Ten singles on the *Billboard* Hot 100 had been written, produced, and/or performed by the Bee Gees. They also appeared in the film and on the soundtrack of *Sgt. Pepper's Lonely Hearts Club Band* (U.S. #5, 1978), a fiasco. But *Spirits Having Flown* (1979) (U.K./U.S. #1) contained three more #1 hits in the U.S.: "Too Much Heaven" (U.K. #3), "Tragedy" (U.K. #1), and "Love You Inside Out." They also released *Bee Gees Greatest* (U.S. #1/U.K. #4, 1979).

In 1980, Barry Gibb wrote and produced Barbra Streisand's *Guilty* album (U.S. #1), another multi-million-selling success that contained "Woman in Love" (U.S./U.K. #1) and their duets on the title track (U.S. #3) and "What Kind of Fool" (U.S. #10). The Bee Gees themselves, however, suffered from the backlash against disco in the 1980s and sustained a second career slump, even though they reverted to their pre-disco sound with 1981's *Living Eyes. Staying Alive,* their soundtrack to the sequel to *Saturday Night Fever,* was a U.S. #6 in 1983. The same year, Barry Gibb produced Kenny Rogers's *Eyes that See in the Dark* (U.S. #6) and wrote Rogers's hit duet with Dolly Parton, "Islands in the Stream" (U.S. #1/U.K. #7). In 1982, Barry Gibb worked with Dionne Warwick, resulting in "Heartbreaker" (U.K. #2/U.S. #10) and "All the Love in the World" (U.K. #10). In 1985, the Gibb brothers wrote and produced for Diana Ross, scoring with "Chain Reaction" (U.K. #1). (Robin and Barry Gibb also made solo records during this period.) *E.S.P.,* the Bee Gees' first new non-soundtrack studio album in six years, which reunited them with producer Arif Mardin, was released in 1987 and became a substantial hit in the U.K. (#5), along with the single "You Win Again" (#1), but flopped in the U.S. Follow-ups have seen moderate British success, while in America the single "One" (#7) returned them to commercial favor in 1989. Their records have sold poorly since, however. — *William Ruhlmann*

The Bee Gee's First / Jul. 1967 / Polydor ♦♦♦
Though this is their first album, by 1967 the Brothers Gibb were already seasoned performers with a couple with records to their credit and 11 years of performing together. Originally slagged as being Beatles' plagiarists (presumably because they were both from the north of England) there is no solid basis for the comparison. This is a fine record by anyone's standard and holds up well nearly 30 years later. —*Jim Worbois*

Horizontal / Jan. 1968 / Polydor ♦♦♦
This album is a little more moody than *1st* with its use of minor chords and song structure. At the same time, the Bee Gees continue to grow as songwriters and there is no shortage of good songs. The hit, "Massachusetts" pretty much sets the tone for the album; if you like that one, you're sure to like the rest of the album as well. —*Jim Worbois*

Idea / Aug. 1968 / Polydor ♦♦
On *Idea* the Bee Gees stretch out somewhat and, in addition to their usual fare, have a go at a Hollies-type song ("Kitty Can") and a jazzy number ("Kilburn Towers"). Not everything on the record works, but at least they weren't afraid to try something different. —*Jim Worbois*

○ **Odessa** / Jan. 1969 / Polydor ♦♦♦♦
Odessa is the Bee Gees' finest moment of the '60s. —*AMG*

● **The Best of the Bee Gees, Vol. 1** / Jun. 1969 / Polydor ♦♦♦♦
Best of Bee Gees collects their greatest pop hits from the '60s. —*AMG*

Cucumber Castle / Apr. 1970 / Polydor ♦♦

○ **Two Years On** / Jan. 1971 / Atco ♦♦♦♦
After a turbulent period in the late '60s, the Bee Gees temporarily packed it in. When they regrouped, the band consisted solely of the three brothers. What resulted was their largest commercial success to date. In addition to featuring "Lonely Days," the Bee Gees' highest-charting single to date and their first gold record, this is a fine record in its own right. It's as strong as any Bee Gees album from their early years and worth looking for. —*Jim Worbois*

Trafalgar / Sep. 1971 / Polydor ♦♦♦
Trafalgar's "How Can You Mend A Broken Heart?" was the Bee Gees' first number one single. Despite this chart success, this record doesn't rate as highly as some of their other albums of this period due to somewhat lackluster material. —*Jim Worbois*

To Whom It May Cancern / 1972 / Polydor ♦♦

Life in a Tin Can / Jan. 1973 / Polydor ♦♦
The Bee Gees were now recording in the U.S. (Los Angeles, to be exact) and, if anything, that proved to be a detriment. For the most part, this is a record of "sensitive" ballads, much like everything else coming out of Southern California at the time and, for that reason, doesn't stand up against much of their earlier work. —*Jim Worbois*

○ **The Best of the Bee Gees, Vol. 2** / Jul. 1973 / Polydor ♦♦♦♦
Best of the Bee Gees, Volume 2 gathers together the group's biggest and best hits from the early '70s. —*AMG*

Mr. Natural / May 1974 / Polydor ♦

○ **Main Course** / May 1975 / Polydor ♦♦♦♦
On *Main Course* the Bee Gees began incorporating soul into their well-constructed sound, inching the group closer to their watershed disco years. Like most Bee Gees' albums, the material is fairly inconsistent, yet the strongest moments—including the hit singles "Jive Talkin'" and "Nights on Broadway"—rank with the group's best work. —*Stephen Thomas Erlewine*

Children of the World / Sep. 1976 / Polydor ♦♦

● **Bee Gees Gold, Vol. 1** / Oct. 1976 / Polydor ♦♦♦♦
Some of the best post-Beatles pop comes from the Bee Gees' first fertile era. —*Dan Heilman*

☆ **Saturday Night Fever** / Nov. 1977 / RSO ♦♦♦♦♦
One of the biggest-selling albums of all time, this double-disc soundtrack features the Bee Gees hits "Stayin' Alive," "Night Fever," and "How Deep Is Your Love," Yvonne Elliman's "If I Can't Have You," and a selection of popular disco hits by Tavares, K.C. & the Sunshine Band, and others. This wasn't only the soundtrack to a film, it was the soundtrack to an era. That era is over, but it's evoked by the music. —*William Ruhlmann*

○ **1963-1966: Birth of Brilliance** / 1978 / Festival ♦♦♦♦
32-song double CD presents much of the best material from the domestic Excelsior compilations of their early years, as well as some songs (some of which are pretty good) that don't appear on those sets. Because of its better sound, this collection has the edge as the best compilation of their early work, though it's hard to find. —*Richie Unterberger*

○ **Spirits Having Flown** / Jan. 1979 / RSO ♦♦♦♦

● **Greatest** / Oct. 1979 / RSO ♦♦♦♦
This is the cream of their stunning string of late-'70s hits. —*Dan Heilman*

○ **Early Years, Vol. 1** / 1980 / Excelsior ♦♦♦♦
Before moving to England in 1967 to successfully earn their fortune, the Bee Gees were one of Australia's most popular beat groups. They actually recorded quite a bit of material in the mid-'60s that ranks among their most rock-oriented, strongly recalling the Hollies and the lighter early Beatles with their strong melodies, harmonies, rhythm guitars, and cheery enthusiasm. The packaging on this budget double album leaves something to be desired, but it's the best American compilation of material from the group's most obscure and, in some ways, best era. Barry Gibb, though only a teenager, composed most of the songs here, many of them strong. "Wine And Women" and, especially, the driving "I Want Home" compare favorably to the best mid-'60s Hollies hits; "Peace Of Mind" and "All Of My Life" rank among the best early Beatle ripoffs; "I Was A Lover, A Leader Of Men" shows unusual

(and, as it turns out, mostly undeveloped) lyrical sophistication; and the Robin Gibb-penned "I Am The World" is a strange melodrama worthy of Roy Orbison. Any fan of British Invasion pop will enjoy this set, and shouldn't let any preconceptions from either the band's more orchestrated late-'60s work or their disco hits keep them from checking this out. —*Richie Unterberger*

Early Years, Vol. 2 / 1980 / Excelsior ✦✦✦
Another flimsily packaged double-album compilation of mid-'60s Australian-era Bee Gees. It's weaker than *Volume One*; the material isn't as strong, and more of it dates from their mawkish, pre-Beatle-influenced period, where they sounded like an MOR kiddie version of the Everly Brothers. Still... "Claustrophobia," "Could It Be I'm In Love With You," and "To Be Or Not To Be" are more great lost early Beatle ripoffs, and songs like "Big Chance" and "I Don't Know Why I Bother With Myself" are quite affecting, lyrically introspective numbers that argue the case of the Bee Gees as one of rock's premier cases of arrested development. As on the first volume, most of the material was penned by Barry Gibb, with occasional contributions by Robin and covers. —*Richie Unterberger*

Living Eyes / 1981 / RSO ✦✦

Staying Alive / Jun. 1983 / RSO ✦✦✦
This sequel to *Saturday Night Fever* lacked the box office clout of the original, and the soundtrack album was likewise a disappointing seller, but it actually contains some of the better Bee Gees work of the '80s, notably the sad ballad "Someone Belonging To Someone." —*William Ruhlmann*

E.S.P. / Sep. 1987 / Warner Brothers ✦✦

One / Jul. 25, 1989 / Warner Brothers ✦✦✦
The Bee Gees made a commercial comeback outside the U.S. with 1987's *E.S.P.* and its single, "You Win Again." *One*, on the other hand, had an improved chart showing in the U.S., while sales fell off elsewhere. The Bee Gees are remarkable pop craftsmen—"It's My Neighborhood" is a canny, if blatant, rewrite of Michael Jackson's "Beat It," for example, and it only reminds you that Jackson's falsetto whoops owe something to Barry Gibb. And, say what you will, "One" and "House Of Shame" are convincing pop music. ("One" was a Top Ten comeback hit that topped soft-rock radio playlists.) This stuff works as pop for the same reason "I've Gotta Get A Message To You" and "You Should Be Dancing" did: the melodies are catchy, the hooks are deathless, and the vocals convey emotion over meaning. It may be weightless, but it's polished. —*William Ruhlmann*

Tales from the Brothers Gibb / 1990 / Polydor ✦✦✦
This exhaustive 4-disc boxed set contains too much for anyone but hardcore fans. —*Dan Heilman*

High Civilization / Apr. 1991 / Warner Brothers ✦✦
A misstep. The Bee Gees seem to have felt that, their comeback completed by the Top 10 success of "One," it was time to go really contemporary and take on, oh, say, Prince. Wrong. The techno-rock sounds silly with those near-Chipmunk harmonies, and it's all overdone. You can't really blame a band that has had recurring success by faithfully following contemporary pop trends for trying it, but you can blame them for failing. —*William Ruhlmann*

Size Isn't Everything / Nov. 1993 / Polydor ✦✦✦
These guys are persistent and they work hard for the money, carefully cloning current fashion. You can just hear them saying, "We did disco, we can do hip-hop," and you can hear them try on "Paying The Price Of Love," with its heavy percussion track. But it wasn't their approximation of the Compton beat that got them (just barely) back in the pop charts, it was the hook, which wasn't all that different from "Massachusetts." —*William Ruhlmann*

Bel Canto

Group, Alternative Pop/Rock
This chamber-rock trio from Norway offers an authentic medieval sound based almost exclusively on the modern techniques of synthesis, with original music that expresses a stream of loss and sorrow from the past. Almost all their songs are built on a specific type of energy: female power, or the power of the earth, sometimes both destructive and hysterical. Bel Canto has an elaborate orchestration, utilizing a wide range of instruments. —*Vladimir Bogdanov*

White-Out Conditions / 1987 / Nettwerk ✦✦✦
Bel Canto's first album is refreshing and intriguing. Although it's uneven, it is definitely more than just a search for a new style. —*Vladimir Bogdanov*

● **Birds of Passage** / 1989 / Nettwerk ✦✦✦✦
Completely professional material, well composed and performed. —*Vladimir Bogdanov*

○ **Shimmering, Warm & Bright** / 1992 / Dali ✦✦✦✦
The famous warm "medieval electronic" sound of Bel Canto reaches the point of elaborate purity on this mature album. —*Vladimir Bogdanov*

The Bel-Airs

Group, Surf
One of the very first instrumental surf combos, this Southern Californian group recorded one of the first big regional surf hits, "Mr. Moto." Its heavily reverbed guitar lines, distinct Mexican melodic influence, and honking sax helped set the prototype for hundreds of songs that would be recorded in the next two or three years. None of the other material the group recorded in the early '60s was as successful or memorable; guitarist Paul Johnson has been active for the last several decades, often playing surf-style music. —*Richie Unterberger*

Origins of Surf Music 1960-1963 / 1987 / Iloki ✦✦
Compilation of rare sides, including early home demos featuring nothing more than two guitars, and later sessions cut at L.A.'s famed Gold Star Studios in 1963. Interesting as a document of some of the very first surf recordings, but not terribly interesting in and of itself—"Mr. Moto" (two versions included here) towers over everything else. Comes with an extensively annotated booklet by founding member Paul Johnson. —*Richie Unterberger*

Adrian Belew

Alternative Pop/Rock, Art-Rock/Progressive-Rock
This avant-garde guitar slinger cut his teeth with Frank Zappa and became a critical darling during his stint in the '80s with Talking Heads and the re-formed King Crimson. He has released albums both as a solo artist and with the late-'80s band, the Bears. —*John Floyd*

○ **Lone Rhino** / Jul. 1982 / Island ✦✦✦✦
Lone Rhino, Belew's finest album of straight playing, features the guitarist stretching out over arty rock and funk backdrops, creating a spellbinding array of textures. —*Stephen Thomas Erlewine*

Twang Bar King / Sep. 1983 / Island ✦✦
Adrian Belew is an inventive guitarist and a versatile songwriter, but on his second album, as on his first, that doesn't quite add up to being a major artist. He really hasn't escaped his influences, chief among them David Byrne and Talking Heads, with whom he served as sideman. (His strained tenor vocals are virtually identical to Byrne's.) While he has a welcome sense of humor and his imagination gives the record a sense of constant surprise, those are one-time effects, and Belew needs to write material that bears repeated listenings. —*William Ruhlmann*

Desire Caught by the Tail / 1986 / Island ✦✦

Mr. Music Head / Apr. 1989 / Atlantic ✦✦✦
Former King Crimson member Belew shines on his own, with aggressive guitar work framing a set of thoughtful alternative rockers. —*Donna DiChario*

○ **Young Lions** / May 1990 / Atlantic ✦✦✦✦
Guitar-propelled modern rock, included is a duet with David Bowie on "Pretty Pink Rose." —*Donna DiChario*

Desire of the Rhino King / 1991 / Island ✦✦✦
Desire of the Rhino King, a scattershot compilation of his earlier, more experimental records for Island, offers some of his best playing, but the music lacks cohesion out of the context of the original recordings. —*Stephen Thomas Erlewine*

● **Inner Revolution** / Feb. 1992 / Atlantic ✦✦✦✦
Belew uses his well-developed one-man-band and state-of-the-studio abilities to produce a Beatle pastiche that ranks with the best of such Fab Four idolators as Todd Rundgren, the Raspberries, and ELO, and that's no mean feat. He can sing (almost) like John Lennon and play guitar like George Harrison. His sturdy songwriting makes this much more than just a successful genre exercise. —*William Ruhlmann*

Here / 1994 / Plan 9/Caroline ✦✦✦

Belfast Gypsies

Group, British Invasion
When Van Morrison left Them in 1966, the group splintered into

two factions. One, led by Alan Henderson, retained the name, relocated to America, and released four undistinguished albums. The other, built around organist Jackie McAuley and his brother Pat on drums, was much truer to Them's tough R&B roots. The group somehow hooked up with producer Kim Fowley, who was temporarily based in London, to release a couple of unsuccessful singles; they then followed Fowley to Scandinavia, where they released their one album in August, 1967. A bit of an anachronistic throwback to the R&B/beat boom sound of a couple years earlier, the LP is a successful approximation of Them's sound, the major drawback being the absence of Van Morrison. Splitting shortly afterwards, Jackie McAuley briefly resurfaced in the late '60s with the folk-rock group Trader Horne, which also featured ex-Fairport Convention singer Judy Dyble. —*Richie Unterberger*

Them Belfast Gypsies / 1978 / Sonet ◆◆◆
A reissue of their 1967 self-titled Scandinavian album, with informative liner notes by British rock scholar Brian Hogg. Kim Fowley gives this rough-hewn R&B a manic, freaky edge on cuts like "People, Let's Freak Out," "Suicide Song," and "Secret Police." The (unidentified) lead singer is obviously trying to emulate Van Morrison's vocals ("Gloria's Dream") is a blatant cop of "Gloria"), but is not nearly in his league. Still, it's quite a solid effort, Jackie McAuley's organ pacing the band's brittle rock/R&B. Includes some decent originals and a diverse assortment of imaginative covers, ranging from Donovan to traditional folk to a tongue-in-cheek classical instrumental. Their tense version of "It's All Over Now, Baby Blue" is one of the greatest obscure Dylan covers, and the magnificent harmonica on "Midnight Train" is a highlight. —*Richie Unterberger*

Bell Biv Devoe

Group, Urban
Former members of New Edition Ricky Bell, Michael Bivins, and Ronnie DeVoe struck pay dirt with their 1990 debut, which crossed over into the White pop charts in addition to dominating the R&B world. Their outside production efforts have resulted in hit debuts by the R&B groups Another Bad Creation and Boyz II Men. Bell Biv Devoe's follow-up arrived three years later; by that time, their audience had moved on to other artists, leaving the group behind with a solid, but unappreciated, album. —*John Floyd*

● **Poison** / Mar. 1990 / MCA ◆◆◆◆
BBD describe their style as "R&B on the smooth tip with a hip-hop feel," and that's just what you'll find on this hugely successful debut. Equally adept at sumptuous ballads and big-beat dance thumpers, BBD have taken Teddy Riley's new-jack innovations to both a wider audience and a new creative plateau. —*John Floyd*

Wbbd-Bootcity! [Remix Album] / 1991 / MCA ◆◆
With Bell Biv DeVoe's debut album *Poison* having run its course by the summer of 1991, and without a follow-up in the pipeline, MCA assembled this stopgap album (in the form of a radio show, complete with a Bell Biv DeVoe interview) consisting of remixed versions of hits like "Do Me!," "She's Dope!," "When Will I See You Smile Again?," and "Poison." The group's commercial potency was demonstrated when it became a solid-selling Top 20 hit, but it's for dancers and hard-core fans only. —*William Ruhlmann*

Hootie Mack / 1993 / MCA ◆◆◆
Hootie Mack not only keeps the same energetic vibe that made *Poison* a hit, but expands upon that base, adding a more street-oriented production that, at its best, is more sexy and funky than their debut. Unfortunately, the high points on this album aren't as numerous as those on *Poison*; not only that, but the good songs didn't receive much airplay, causing the album to drop off the charts quickly. —*Stephen Thomas Erlewine*

Archie Bell & the Drells

b. Sep. 1, 1944, Henderson, TX
Soul, Disco
Few groups offered good-time soul music as enjoyable, danceable, and high-spirited as Archie Bell & the Drells. The singer (from Houston, as he was eager to proclaim in the middle of some of his uptempo hits) had a left-field number one smash with the limb-loosening "Tighten Up," which took off right after Archie was drafted. In 1968, Archie (who was able to fit in some recording and performing duties until his stint in the army was over) teamed with emerging Philadelphia soul mavens Kenneth Gamble and Leon Huff, who produced and wrote Bell's material over the next couple years. With sophisticated arrangements and punchy horn

charts, dance hits like "I Can't Stop Dancing," "(There's Gonna Be A) Showdown," and "Do the Choo Choo" were instrumental in establishing the sound of Philadelphia as an artistic force. After a fallow period in the early '70s, Bell reunited with Gamble & Huff on the Philadelphia International for a run of successful, discofied dance soul in the mid-'70s. —*Richie Unterberger*

● **Tightening It Up: the Best of Archie Bell & the Drells** / 1994 / Rhino ◆◆◆◆
20 of the group's big and small hits, charting their course from Southern-fried soul through the sound of Philadelphia and disco. —*Richie Unterberger*

Chris Bell

Power Pop/Anglo-Pop
Memphis singer/songwriter Chris Bell cofounded the influential power-pop quartet Big Star in 1971, with Alex Chilton. Bell left the group before the release of their second album, *Radio City*, to pursue a solo career. He died in an automobile accident on Dec 27, 1978. It wasn't until 1992 that Bell's work was released in an album form. —*Rick Clark*

○ **I Am the Cosmos** / 1992 / Rykodisc ◆◆◆◆
A collection of the late Chris Bell's solo work, it includes mostly demos. The title track is a brilliant downer (Big Star and Badfinger at half-speed) that opens the album. "You and Your Sister" is a gorgeous heartbreaker, rendered with delicate acoustic guitars and Mellotron and guest vocalist Alex Chilton. Not everything Bell undertakes is so fragile. "I Don't Know" (and its later, inferior incarnation "Get Away"), "Make a Scene," and "Fight at the Table" are relentless rockers. Bell's voice may be an acquired taste for some, as it occasionally gets a little whiney. When it does connect with the music, the results can be quite affecting, particularly on "You and Your Sister," "Speed of Sound," and the title track. Ryko has done a great job remastering these tapes, and the packaging is a first-rate labor of love. —*Rick Clark*

William Bell (William Yarborough)

b. Jul. 16, 1937, Memphis, TN
Soul
William Bell was one of the first artists signed to the Stax label during its fledgling years in Memphis, and he greatly influenced the "Stax sound" as both a performer and writer. His self-penned "You Don't Miss Your Water" (1961) almost defined the genre known as country-soul, with the unmistakable gospel feel of Bell's elegant, lilting vocal over a country-church piano figure. It was this perfect marriage of styles that became Bell's trademark at Stax and opened the door for others—most notably Otis Redding (who initially mined the same country-soul vein)—to follow. With the ascent of Redding, Bell's star began to fade somewhat. He continued to record (the beautiful, string-laden "I Forgot to Be Your Lover" in 1968) and, most importantly, to write—(his own "Tribute to a King," written after Redding's death, and Albert King's "Born under a Bad Sign," both co-written with Booker T. Jones). After Stax's collapse in 1975, Bell moved to Mercury, where he scored his first-ever million-seller with "Tryin' to Love Two." Bell continues to live and work in Memphis. —*Christine Ohlman*

● **The Soul of a Bell** / 1967 / Stax ◆◆◆◆
The 1967 debut album of Stax's resident balladeer is loaded with Memphis soul ballads and an occasional raver. —*Bill Dahl*

Bound to Happen / 1969 / Stax ◆◆◆
Wow William Bell / 1971 / Stax ◆◆◆

○ **The Best of William Bell** / 1988 / Stax ◆◆◆◆
Post-Atlantic work from the late '60s and early '70s, it includes Bell's playful duets with Judy Clay. —*Bill Dahl*

On a Roll / 1989 / Wilbe ◆◆
William Bell, one of the classic Southern soul singers, tried to update his production and surroundings in the '80s while retaining his traditional sound. His albums for his own Wilbe label, particularly this late effort, were only partially successful. His singing was mostly solid, his material mostly undistinguished. —*Ron Wynn*

A Little Something Extra / 1992 / Stax ◆◆◆
A fine collection of Stax outtakes from the 1960s, *Little Something Extra* features several tracks, including his smoldering version of "Will You Love Me Tomorrow?," that rival his original singles. —*Stephen Thomas Erlewine*

Regina Belle

Soul, R&B

Regina Belle has emerged as a prolific, consistently engaging vocalist on the urban contemporary scene. Born in New Jersey, Belle's early experience was in gospel, though she was also attracted to R&B during her childhood. She studied trombone, tuba, and steel drums, and at 12 won a school contest singing the Emotions' "Don't Ask My Neighbors." Belle sang in a New Jersey vocal group, and studied opera and jazz in college. New York disc jockey Vaughn Harper introduced her to the Manhattans, and she began working as their opening act. Belle recorded a duet with them, "Where Did We Go Wrong," that was produced by Bobby Womack in 1986. She earned a solo Columbia contract in 1987, and the single "Please Be Mine" earned both praise and a number two R&B hit. A follow-up single, "So Many Tears," also made the R&B Top 20, and the hit "Without You," pairing her with Peabo Bryson, was the only memorable thing about the film *Leonard Pt. 6.* Her second LP, *Stay with Me,* secured her success, and she has gone on to earn more acclaim. Her most recent LP was *Passion* in 1993. — *Ron Wynn*

All by Myself / Jun. 1987 / Columbia ✦✦✦
Her debut album of soft soul and dance music. — *Bil Carpenter*

● **Stay with Me** / Aug. 1989 / Columbia ✦✦✦✦
A romantic interlude of smooth soul numbers. — *Bil Carpenter*

Passion / Feb. 1993 / Columbia ✦✦
There's no doubting Regina Belle's skills; on *Passion* she was a majestic, soaring singer, hitting high notes with ease and displaying remarkable vocal technique. Even when singing at low volume or tackling clichéd material, Belle made it palatable with her gorgeous tone, fine articulation and excellent delivery. There was no wasted effort, loss of power or cracking voice on any number. Unfortunately, she didn't get enough worthwhile material to adequately frame her talents. Like too many urban contemporary albums, there was plenty of production gloss but little substance. When you peeled away the layers of background vocalists and strings, you were left with lyrics that said little and meant less, salvaged only by Belle's singing. — *Ron Wynn*

Belly

Group, Alternative Pop/Rock

Belly's debut album, 1993's *Star,* was one of the major alternative rock hits of the year, managing to crossover into the mainstream with the minor hit "Feed the Tree." Led by vocalist/guitarist Tanya Donelly, a former member of the Throwing Muses and the Breeders, Belly's music is more straightforward and pop-oriented than her previous bands. The group's melodies are ethereal yet catchy, supported by lush, interweaving guitar hooks. The layered, swirling guitars conceal some dark lyrical undercurrents that save the group from being too precious.

Donelly formed Belly in 1992 with former Muses bassist Fred Abong, adding brothers Tom and Chris Gorman (guitar and drums, respectively) before the group went into the studio to record their debut album. Belly released a series of British singles in 1992 that earned the band a following in both the U.K. and the U.S. Abong left the group after the recording of the album; the band recorded some a handful of B-sides with various bassists before replacing him with Gail Greenwood in early 1993, after the release of their debut.

Star, the band's debut album, was released in early 1993 and immediately became an alternative hit, selling more than all of the previous Muses and Breeders releases combined. "Feed the Tree," the first single from the album became a hit and the group embarked on a successful tour that ran throughout 1993. Several other alternative radio hits followed, including "Slow Dog" and "Gepetto."

Belly returned in 1995 with *King,* their first album recorded with Greenwood. *King* failed to meet the high expectations raised by *Star.* "Now They'll Sleep" became a moderate hit on alternative radio, as did "Superconnected," but the album didn't sell in numbers comparable to *Star,* slipping out of the charts two months after its release. — *Stephen Thomas Erlewine*

● **Star** / Jan. 1993 / Sire/Reprise ✦✦✦✦
Driven by four superb singles—"Gepetto," "Feed the Tree," "Slow Dog," and "Dusted"—Belly's debut album is a terrific set of effortlessly melodic guitar-pop, alternating between bright pop songs and atmospheric ballads. Even with her sweetest melodies, lead singer/guitarist Tanya Donelly has enough realism and dark fantasies in her songs to keep *Star* from being cloying or saccharine. In fact, her songs are so good that it's a wonder she didn't start her own band sooner. — *Stephen Thomas Erlewine*

King / 1995 / Sire/Reprise ✦✦✦
On "Red," the third song on *King,* Belly shifted gears between three different tempos and lyrical moods, abruptly jumping from one to the other. Not every song was quite so jarring, but the overall effect of Belly's second album was disquieting in an appropriately "alternative" way—the guitar chords were familiar, but loosely played and never stayed for long in a single pattern; Tanya Donelly's singing could coo or declaim, repeating lines that never quite added up to choruses; and her lyrics, despite what often seemed like promising beginnings, always wandered off into, well, navel-gazing. There were all the elements of stirring music and compelling songs in this material, but it seemed to have been deliberately skewed toward the vague and impressionistic and away from clarity and coherence. — *William Ruhlmann*

The Belmonts

Group, Doo-Wop

Bronx-based vocal group that enjoyed a string of national hits from 1958 to 1960 with Dion DiMucci as lead singer, under the name Dion and the Belmonts. After Dion went solo, the Belmonts carried on as a trio and managed six more chart entries in the early '60s. Carlo Mastrangelo (b. Oct. 5, 1938, Bronx, NY) sang lead on the group's first and biggest post-Dion hit in 1961 on the Sabrina label, "Tell Me Why" (#18). The group also included Angelo D'Aleo (b. Feb. 3, 1940, Bronx, NY) and Freddie Milano (b. Aug. 22, 1939, Bronx, NY). Mastrangelo was replaced by Frank Lyndon in May 1962. The Belmonts staged reunions with Dion in 1967, 1972, and 1973. The Belmonts returned to the charts in the company of Freddy Cannon in 1981 with "Let's Put the Fun Back in Rock N Roll." — *William Ruhlmann*

● **The Belmonts' Carnival of Hits** / Oct. 1962 / Sabrina ✦✦✦✦

Summer Love / 1969 / Dot ✦✦✦

Cigars, Acappella, Candy / 1972 / Elektra ✦✦✦
These are new recordings of New York City street-corner doo-wop. — *Hank Davis*

Cheek to Cheek / 1978 / Strawberry ✦✦

Jesse Belvin

b. Dec. 15, 1933, San Antonio, TX, **d.** Feb. 6, 1960
R&B

An influential, silky-voiced R&B crooner and songwriter from the '50s, Belvin is best known for his 1956 hit "Goodnight My Love" and for writing the Penguins' hit "Earth Angel." — *John Floyd*

Just Jesse Belvin / 1959 / RCA ✦✦✦
The next-to-last album made by R&B crooner/balladeer Jesse Belvin. It's part slick pop, part soulful R&B, although his sound has more Nat "King" Cole influence than gospel. Belvin's work merged the smooth, sophisticated West Coast sound with the more earthy Southern approach. — *Ron Wynn*

○ **Mr. Easy** / Dec. 8, 1959 / RCA ✦✦✦✦
The album that Belvin was working on when he was killed in a car crash in 1960. It would have been a nice transitional work, as he was aiming for a harder, more gospel-tinged style, although he still liked doing sophisticated, slick ballads. These songs show that Belvin had enormous potential as a '60s crossover act. — *Ron Wynn*

○ **Jesse Belvin's Best** / 1966 / Camden ✦✦✦✦
A good collection of '50s tracks by West Coast balladeer and light R&B vocalist Jesse Belvin. He had a silky, smooth style and was a top crooner. Belvin had a huge hit in 1956, "Goodnight My Love," and another pop success in 1958, "Guess Who." He worked in the same territory as Brook Benton, and was a bit removed from Billy Eckstine and Herb Jeffries, who were more jazz-oriented. — *Ron Wynn*

…But Not Forgotten / United ✦✦✦
Terrible sound quality, but this old LP features the balladeer's best-known mid-'50s work for Modern Records. — *Bill Dahl*

○ **Yesterdays** / 1975 / RCA ✦✦✦✦

● **Blues Balladeer** / 1990 / Specialty ✦✦✦✦
Loaded with previously unissued gems, Belvin's introspective, subdued vocals are delightful. — *Bill Dahl*

○ **Goodnight My Love** / 1991 / Capitol ✦✦✦✦
My Last Goodbye / RCA ✦✦✦
Sentimental love songs, ballads, and some uptempo R&B from the great crooner Jesse Belvin, who was killed in a 1960 car crash in Arkansas. He was the ultimate romantic vocalist, and might have made similar inroads as Sam Cooke had he lived into the '60s. This is an overview of his material. —*Ron Wynn*

Pat Benatar (Pat Andrzejewski)

b. Jan. 10, 1953, Brooklyn, NY
Pop/Rock
Pat Benatar's polished mainstream pop/rock made her one of the more popular female vocalists of the early '80s. Although she came on like an arena rocker with her power chords, tough sexuality and powerful vocals, her music was straight pop/rock underneath all the bluster.

Benatar began singing in New York in the late '70s; eventually she was discovered by Rick Newman at his "Catch a Rising Star" club in 1979. Under the management of Newman, Benatar signed with Chrysalis Records, releasing her debut album, *In the Heat of the Night,* that same year. The record launched her string of hit singles with the number 23 "Heartbreaker." Featuring the Top Ten hit "Hit Me with Your Best Shot," Benatar's second album, 1980's *Crimes of Passion* was a greater success, selling over four million copies and winning the Grammy for Best Female Rock Vocal Performance. Her third album, *Precious Time* (1981), reached number one on the album charts; a single from the album called "Fire and Ice" won Benatar another Grammy. She married her producer/guitarist Neil Geraldo in 1982, the same year the platinum *Get Nervous* was released. Benatar released a live album, *Live from Earth,* the following year; it contained one of her biggest hits, "Love Is a Battlefield." Although 1984's *Tropico* contained her biggest hit "We Belong" (number five), the album was her lowest-charting to date.

"Invincible" (1985), taken from *The Legend of Billie Jean* soundtrack, was her last Top Ten hit. Even though it included the single "Sex as a Weapon," Benatar's *Seven the Hard Way* (1985) became her first album to not go platinum—it didn't even go gold. She took a couple of years off before returning with *Wide Awake in Dreamland* in 1988; it didn't chart as high as *Seven the Hard Way,* yet it earned a gold record, as did *Best Shots,* a greatest hits collection released the following year.

Benatar didn't record a new album until 1991, when she released the blues record, *True Love.* It proved a critical and commercial disaster, prompting her to return to her mainstream rock on 1993's *Gravity's Rainbow;* nevertheless, the reversal in musical direction didn't return her to the top of the charts. —*Stephen Thomas Erlewine*

○ **In the Heat of the Night** / Sep. 1979 / Chrysalis ✦✦✦✦
This debut album features her trademark power-pop song "Heartbreaker." —*Donna DiChario*

○ **Crimes of Passion** / Aug. 1980 / Chrysalis ✦✦✦✦
She won the Grammy Award for Best Rock Vocal Performance—Female for this album. —*Donna DiChario*

Precious Time / Jul. 1981 / Chrysalis ✦✦✦
Pat Benatar's third album *Precious Time* was her only number one record, yet it wasn't as consistent as her previous two albums. While it follows the same polished arena rock formula of *In the Heat of the Night* and *Crimes of Passion, Precious Time* only takes off on the singles "Fire and Ice" and "Promises in the Dark," which exploit Benatar's powerful voice and her band's sleek variation on hard rock. —*Stephen Thomas Erlewine*

Get Nervous / Nov. 1982 / Chrysalis ✦✦
Get Nervous was Pat Benatar's fourth platinum album in a row and it showed a few signs that her trademark hard rocking pop was wearing thin. *Precious Time* also was weaker than her prior records, yet *Get Nervous* failed to have a hit single as well-crafted as "Fire and Ice." Instead, the record was an attempt at replicating the sound of "Heartbreaker," "Hit Me With Your Best Shot," and "Fire and Ice," that never quite made the mark. —*Stephen Thomas Erlewine*

Live from Earth / Oct. 1983 / Chrysalis ✦✦
As the title suggests, the bulk of *Live from Earth* is compiled from various concerts, where Benatar faithfully recreates the sound of her albums. The remaining two songs were new studio, including

the single "Love Is a Battlefield," her best song since "Fire and Ice." Unfortunately, she didn't write it, nor did any of her band members. —*Stephen Thomas Erlewine*

Tropico / Nov. 1984 / Chrysalis ✦✦✦
On *Tropico,* Pat Benatar began refashioning her sound, moving toward a more middle-of-the-road sound as evidenced by the hit single "We Belong." The change in direction revitalized the singer, resulting in her best album since *Precious Time.* —*Stephen Thomas Erlewine*

Seven the Hard Way / Nov. 1985 / Chrysalis ✦✦✦
Seven the Hard Way continues the slick pop approach of *Tropico* and is benefitted by a wealth of songs written by professional songwriters. At this point, Benatar and her band weren't coming up with material as catchy or memorable as "Invincible" and "Sex as a Weapon," so the presence of the pro songwriting was a blessing, not a curse. —*Stephen Thomas Erlewine*

Wide Awake in Dreamland / Jun. 1988 / Chrysalis ✦✦
While *Wide Awake in Dreamland* was more successful on the charts than *Seven the Hard Way,* it didn't feature as many hit songs. Only "All Fired Up" cracked the Top 40, a sign that her sound was losing its commercial appeal. Aft the release of *Wide Awake,* Benatar took some time off of recording, returning to recording in 1991 with a blues album called *True Love.* —*Stephen Thomas Erlewine*

● **Best Shots** / Nov. 1989 / Chrysalis ✦✦✦✦
Multi-Grammy winner Benatar has vocal range to spare on this hits collection, including her rockers "Heartbreaker," "Fire and Ice," and "Hell Is for Children." —*Donna DiChario*

True Love / Apr. 1991 / Chrysalis ✦
Benatar's stab at the blues mixes traditional standards with three new songs, none suited to her power-pop style. Still, this gives diehard fans a chance to hear Benatar's vocals in a different context. —*Donna DiChario*

Gravity's Rainbow / Jun. 1, 1993 / Chrysalis ✦✦
Gravity's Rainbow marked Pat Benatar's return to arena rock after the dismal failure of her blues album *True Love.* While it is well-produced and carefully constructed, the album failed to capture an audience. Although she had returned to the sound that made her famous, both radio and the record-buying public had lost interest and the album slipped off the charts shortly after its release. —*Stephen Thomas Erlewine*

○ **Very Best Of: All Fired Up** / 1994 / Chrysalis ✦✦✦✦
A double-disc collection featuring all of her hits and popular album tracks, *All Fired Up: The Very Best of Pat Benatar* is the definitive collection of the popular mainstream rocker. It trims away the fat from her spotty albums, leaving the best material she recorded throughout her career. Nevertheless, it features too much material for most listeners and is only worthwhile to dedicated fans. —*Stephen Thomas Erlewine*

Brook Benton (Benjamin Franklin Peay)

b. Sep. 19, 1931, Camden, SC, **d.** Apr. 9, 1988
R&B
Silky smooth: that was Brook Benton's byword from his first record to his very last, as the singer parlayed his rich baritone pipes into seven #1 R&B hits and eight Top Ten items. Stints on the gospel circuit preceded Benton's first secular session for Okeh in 1953, but his career didn't begin to take off until he teamed with writer/producer Clyde Otis. Benton cowrote and sang hundreds of demos for other artists before frequent collaborator Otis signed his friend to Mercury; together they pioneered a lush, violin-studded variation on the standard R&B sound, which beautifully showcased Benton's intimate vocals.

Benton crashed the top spot on the R&B charts in early 1959 with his moving "It's Just a Matter of Time," then rapidly encored with three more R&B chart-toppers—"Thank You Pretty Baby," "So Many Ways," and "Kiddio." Pairing with Mercury labelmate Dinah Washington, their delightful repartee on "Baby (You've Got What It Takes)" and "A Rockin' Good Way" paced the R&B lists in 1960.

The early '60s were a prolific period for Benton, but he left Mercury a few years later and bounced between labels before reemerging with the atmospheric Tony Joe White ballad "Rainy Night in Georgia" on Cotillion in 1970. Benton later made a half-hearted attempt to cash in on the disco craze, but his hitmaking reign was at an end long before his death in 1988. —*Bill Dahl*

The Satin Sound / SMI
● **Anthology** / 1986 / Rhino ♦♦♦♦
This is a slightly more modest version than the *40 Greatest.* —
Hank Davis
○ **40 Greatest Hits** / 1989 / Mercury ♦♦♦♦
Everything you need to know about Benton's bluesy, sexy pop music is included here, with the duets with Dinah Washington. —
Hank Davis
This Is Brook Benton / RCA ♦♦♦
Brook Benton recorded almost all of his hits for Mercury Records
between 1959 and 1964. He then signed to RCA Victor, apparently
with the intention of moving from the singles charts to the LP
charts and becoming what they used to call an "all-around entertainer." At least, that's the impression you get from this 20-track,
55-minute compilation of Benton's 1965-1966 recordings for RCA.
Backed by a full orchestra, Benton essays a set of pop standards—
"Call Me Irresponsible," "A Nightingale Sang In Berkeley Square,"
"Unforgettable"—in what seems to be his bid to join the ranks of
Nat "King" Cole and Billy Eckstine. (He really pulls out the stops
trying to top Cole's definitive reading of "Unforgettable.") Benton
acquits himself adequately, but his R&B material is preferable.
This set contains only one song from the Benton-Clyde Otis songwriting partnership, the countryish "Mother Nature, Father Time,"
and, not coincidentally, that's the only singles chart entry to be
found here, too. — *William Ruhlmann*

Berlin
Group, Pop/Rock
This Los Angeles-based synth-pop group, founded by bassist John
Crawford, singer Terri Nunn, and keyboard player David Diamond, made its first national impression with the provocative single "Sex (I'm A…)" from the gold-selling debut EP *Pleasure Victim* in 1983. The group was filled out by guitarist Ric Olsen, keyboard player Matt Reid, and drummer Rob Brill. Berlin's first
full-length LP was the gold *Love Life* in 1984. In 1985, the group
was pared down to a trio of Crawford, Nunn, and Brill. Berlin
topped the charts in 1986 with the single "Take My Breath Away,"
the love theme from the Tom Cruise movie *Top Gun.* Nunn left for
a solo career in 1987, and Crawford and Brill teamed up in the Big
F. — *William Ruhlmann*
○ **Pleasure Victim** / 1982 / Geffen ♦♦♦♦
Berlin pulled three dance-pop hits from this seven-track, 29-
minute debut EP, which successfully combined synth-beats with
the sexy vocals of Terri Nunn, especially on the uninhibited "Sex
(I'm A…)." (*Pleasure Victim* was released by Enigma in Septem-
ber 1982 and reissued by Geffen in January 1983. An extra track
was added when it was released on CD.) — *William Ruhlmann*
Love Life / 1984 / Geffen ♦♦♦
Berlin consolidated its position as synth-pop sex merchant (and
thus the successor to Blondie) with this, its first full-length album.
Mike (A Flock Of Seagulls) Howlett produced most of the record,
although disco impresario Giorgio Moroder and his partner Richie
Zito worked on two tracks, among them the Top 25 single "No
More Words." The result was a gold-selling, Top 30 album of
danceable pop. But this was Berlin's high-water mark: reduced to
a trio in 1985, they again teamed with Moroder for the ballad
"Take My Breath Away" in 1986, but were history by 1987, as the
sex/dance crown passed to Madonna. — *William Ruhlmann*
Count Three and Pray / 1986 / Geffen ♦♦♦
Berlin's third and last new recording before breaking up contains
its #1 hit, the ballad "Take My Breath Away," which was featured
in the film *Top Gun.* — *William Ruhlmann*
● **The Best of Berlin 1979-1988** / 1989 / Geffen ♦♦♦♦
All of Berlin's greatest hits and best material are included on this
fine single-disc collection. — *Stephen Thomas Erlewine*

Chuck Berry (Charles Edward Anderson Berry)
b. Oct. 18, 1926, St. Louis, MO
Rock & Roll
It's impossible to give the reader a suitable description of Chuck
Berry's rock & roll, and you really don't need one: the innovations
he brought to the music, his dazzling, lucid lyrics, a guitar lick that
everyone who's ever picked up a guitar has attempted to duplicate,
vocals that place you dead-center into his detailed vignettes, can
be heard everywhere. They are ingrained in rock's collective conscience, from the '60s shimmy of the Beatles up to the latest heavy

metal raving. The St. Louis-born Berry brought his unique stylings
to pianist Johnnie Johnson's jump-blues boogie trio in 1953; he
quickly became the band's leader and began filtering Johnson's
tinkly, omnipresent piano runs into his guitar style. In 1955
Muddy Waters suggested that Berry pass a demo tape to Chess-la-
bel head Leonard Chess. Chess jumped on a Berry original called
"Ida May" (based on an age-old country tune), changed the name
to "Maybellene" and gave Berry his first hit in 1955. The song's
choogling guitar sound, flowing lyrics, and tight, driving rhythm
laid the groundwork for an amazing string of hits that have inspired generations. "Johnny B. Goode," "Too Much Monkey Business," "Little Queenie," "Carol," "Sweet Little Sixteen," "Back in the
USA," "Roll over Beethoven," and dozens more just like them
dealt with everything from tragicomic social drama and teen love
and heartbreak to urban protest, all the while giving rock & roll a
good deal of its language and most of its style. A list of rock &
rollers who've used Berry's hits for their own jump bands reads like
a Who's Who: the Rolling Stones, the Beatles, the Beach Boys, the
Yardbirds, Bob Dylan, Bruce Springsteen; the list is endless. Chuck
Berry hasn't made a worthwhile record in decades and slops
through concerts with only a paycheck on his mind. But if it
weren't for Berry's legacy, books like the one you're reading would
be considerably smaller. — *John Floyd*
○ **After School Session** / Chess ♦♦♦♦
While Chuck Berry's first album, *After School Session,* featured
only one hit single, the Top Ten "School Day," several of the songs
became rock & roll standards, including "Too Much Monkey Business," "No Money Down," and "Brown Eyed Handsome Man." *After School Session* also featured a couple of stylistic variations, including the calypso-flavored "Havana Moon" and the straight
blues of "Wee, Wee Hours." — *Stephen Thomas Erlewine*
○ **One Dozen Berrys** / 1958 / Chess ♦♦♦♦
The core of *One Dozen Berrys,* Chuck Berry's second album, was
formed by the hit single "Sweet Little Sixteen," "Oh, Baby Doll,"
and "Rock and Roll Music." Besides "Reelin' and Rockin'," which
failed as a single, not many of the album tracks became rock &
roll standards, yet the overall quality of the record is quite high,
with "It Don't Take but a Few Minutes" and "Low Feeling" being
particularly strong. — *Stephen Thomas Erlewine*
○ **Is on Top** / 1959 / Chess ♦♦♦♦
Berry's best '50s Chess album (his third) features many of his
biggest hits, plus atmospheric instrumentals like "Blues for
Hawaiians." — *Cub Koda*
Rockin' at the Hops / 1960 / Chess ♦♦♦
Chuck Berry opens this, his fourth album, with "Bye Bye Johnny,"
a sequel to "Johnny B. Goode," and closes it with "Let It Rock,"
which makes for two classics out of 12 songs in less than 28 minutes. There are also two good minor songs, "Too Pooped To Pop"
and "Betty Jean." The filler includes instrumentals, blues workouts,
covers, the usual. The classics are available elsewhere. — *William
Ruhlmann*
New Juke Box Hits / 1961 / Chess ♦♦♦
Chuck Berry's fifth Chess Records album, *New Juke Box Hits,* was
recorded and released in the midst of the legal difficulties that
would put him in jail the following year. That distraction seems to
have kept him from composing top-flight material, while the at-
tendant publicity adversely affected his record sales, such that the
album contained no hits. The included single was "I'm Talking
About You," later successfully recorded by the Rolling Stones, and
the album also contained "Thirteen Question Method" and "Don't
You Lie To Me," worthy minor entries in the Berry canon. Elsewhere, Berry filled out the record covering others' hits—Nat "King"
Cole's "Route 66," B.B. King's "Sweet Sixteen," Little Richard's "Rip
It Up." The result is a good rock & roll set, but not in the same
league with Berry's earlier albums. — *William Ruhlmann*
Chuck Berry on Stage / 1963 / Chess ♦♦
Supposedly recorded live at the Tivoli Theater in Chicago, this al-
bum sounds suspiciously like studio recordings with lots of ap-
plause and screaming added, the whole suffering from inferior
sound due to the overdubbing. The Chuck Berry hits are better
heard in their original studio versions. — *William Ruhlmann*
○ **More Chuck Berry** / 1963 / Chess ♦♦♦♦
Most of his best Chess recordings are here with no clinkers. In-
cludes "Maybellene," "Roll Over Beethoven," "Around and
Around," "Thirty Days," "Johnny B. Goode," and "Rock and Roll
Music." — *George Bedard*

☆ **St. Louis to Liverpool** / 1964 / Chess ✦✦✦✦✦
This album, recorded and issued after Berry's 1964 prison release, is one of the decade's finest albums, a concise shot of brilliance that includes such career-defining statements as "You Never Can Tell," "No Particular Place to Go," and "Nadine." —*John Floyd*

○ **Chuck Berry's Golden Decade** / 1967 / Chess ✦✦✦✦
It is out of print, and it has been superseded by *The Great Twenty-Eight* and *The Chess Box*, but when *Chuck Berry's Golden Decade* was released as a two-disc, 24-track LP in 1967, it was a rock & roll motherlode, the first time that a substantial chunk of Berry's classics had been put together on one album. These songs, released between 1955 and 1964 (that's the decade), constitute as good a definition of rock & roll as anybody has come up with. —*William Ruhlmann*

The London Sessions / 1972 / Chess ✦✦✦
One-half of this album is a studio recording featuring Ian McLagan and Kenny Jones of the Faces. The other half is a live recording from the Lancaster Arts Festival in Coventry, England, featuring performances of "My Ding-A-Ling" and "Reelin' And Rockin'" that, in edited form, became the first hit singles for Chuck Berry in many years. ("My Ding-A-Ling" went gold and hit #1.) This goldselling, Top 10 album represents Berry's commercial, if not artistic, peak. —*William Ruhlmann*

○ **Chuck Berry's Golden Decade, Vol. 2** / 1973 / Chess ✦✦✦✦
Spurred by the success of "My Ding-A-Ling" and *The London Chuck Berry Sessions*, Chess not only reissued the 1967 compilation *Chuck Berry's Golden Decade*, but also assembled this second volume, which contains another 24 Berry songs from the late 1950s to the mid-1960s on two LPs. Of course, the first album gathered the best-known and biggest hits, but there was plenty of memorable material left over, and this album contains the Top 40 hits "Carol" and "You Never Can Tell," the chart entries "Sweet Little Rock And Roller," "Jo Jo Gunne," "Run Rudolph Run," "Merry Christmas Baby," "Let It Rock," "Jaguar And Thunderbird," "Little Queenie," and "Promised Land," the R&B hit "No Money Down," and such hits-for-others as "Come On" (the Rolling Stones' first U.K. single). That's more than enough to earn the album a "best" rating, although it is now out of print and has been superseded by *The Chess Box*. —*William Ruhlmann*

Bio / 1973 / Chess ✦✦✦
Chuck Berry's 15th new studio album and his follow-up to *The London Chuck Berry Sessions* demonstrated the fluke nature of its predecessor by missing the charts. Berry told his autobiography in song in the title track and the brief LP's other six tracks recycled his familiar themes and riffs. The result is an adequate, but inessential collection. —*William Ruhlmann*

Chuck Berry's Golden Decade, Vol. 3 / 1974 / Chess ✦✦✦
Chess Records had just about exhausted its catalog of Chuck Berry hits with *Vol. 2* of this series of 24-track double-LPs. Only "Beautiful Delilah" and "Little Marie" were singles chart entries that hadn't yet been used. But among the non-hits were such notable recordings as "House Of Blue Lights" and "Go Bobby Soxer," the former one of five previously unreleased selections. There are also generous helpings of Berry's blues performances and instrumentals. This is not an album to get if you are looking for the hits, but it helps fill out the portrait of an extraordinary artist. (Out of print.) —*William Ruhlmann*

Rockit / 1979 / Atco ✦✦✦
Rockit was Chuck Berry's 17th and last new studio album. By the time he made it, Berry was a decade and a half from the end of his "golden decade" of unequaled rock & roll creativity, and more than half a dozen years beyond his commercial peak. His final new material didn't threaten either of those high points, but it didn't hurt his reputation, either. Still in place were the tight guitar parts, the rolling piano of Johnny Johnson, the clearly enunciated, clever and slangy lyrics, the bouncing beat. Berry didn't sound as exuberant as he once had, and the songs were largely retreads of past triumphs, but this was an enjoyable, consistent effort, a modest capper to a great career. —*William Ruhlmann*

★ **The Great Twenty-Eight** / 1982 / Chess ✦✦✦✦✦
A single-disc compilation of Berry's original Chess greats, every one a gem: "Maybellene," "Johnny B. Goode," "Roll over Beethoven," "Sweet Little Sixteen," and "Little Queenie" are the music the Beatles and others cut their teeth on. Beyond essential. —*Cub Koda*

○ **Rock 'n' Roll Rarities** / 1986 / Chess ✦✦✦✦
On this follow-up to *The Great Twenty-Eight*, the songs are familiar, but the versions are not. Delving into the Chess Records archives, producer Steve Hoffman has come up with 20 tracks, many in unreleased or unusual versions. Some are demos, some are stereo recordings of songs usually heard in mono. Hoffman has remixed many of them, bringing up the '50s and '60s sound quality to near-'80s standard. Start with *The Great Twenty-Eight*, but come to this collection for interesting new ways to hear the old Berry favorites. —*William Ruhlmann*

More Rock 'n Roll Rarities from the Golden Era of Chess Records / Aug. 1986 / Chess ✦✦✦
This second volume of producer Steve Hoffman's discoveries in the Chess Records vaults features some less prominent Chuck Berry tunes, again in the form of demos, unreleased alternate takes, and stereo remixes. We are getting into collector territory here, but there are still some enjoyable examples of the Berry repertoire. —*William Ruhlmann*

Hail! Hail! Rock 'n' Roll / 1987 / MCA ✦✦✦
This is the soundtrack to a documentary film chronicling a concert held to celebrate Chuck Berry's 60th birthday. The band was led by Keith Richards and featured Berry's regular pianist, Johnnie Johnson, Richards's regular pianist, Chuck Leavell, Rolling Stones sax player Bobby Keys, bassist Joey Spampinato from NRBQ, and drummer Steve Jordan from Richards's solo band. The guests included Robert Cray, Linda Ronstadt, Eric Clapton, Julian Lennon, and Etta James. Berry was ragged-voiced but enthusiastic, the band had spirit, and the guests, even if they were sometimes unlikely, were sincere. The best way to hear Berry's music is to obtain the original recordings, of course, but as a souvenir of the Taylor Hackford film, this is an enjoyable romp through the catalog. —*William Ruhlmann*

☆ **The Chess Box** / 1988 / Chess ✦✦✦✦✦
A 3-CD box of Berry's career at Chess, from '50s classics to mid-'70s chart entries, and all the high spots in between. —*Cub Koda*

Missing Berries / 1990 / Chess ✦✦✦
The third and final collection of Chuck Berry rarities from the Chess Records vaults, *Missing Berries* concentrates on Berry's blues recordings which were never quite as captivating as his rock & roll, yet they're fascinating for devoted fans. —*Stephen Thomas Erlewine*

BOOK

✦✦✦ **Chuck Berry: The Autobiography**, by Chuck Berry (Harmony, 1987). Berry, as he makes a point of noting, wrote every word of this volume, which covers his professional career and personal life in detail. It could have benefited from some editing, actually. Not for the style of his prose, which is clear if a bit oddly meticulous, detached, and exacting, but for length; you learn a lot, perhaps more than you need to know, about his many romantic and sexual affairs, and his troubles with the law. Still, by and large it's very interesting, with an authentic flavor missing from the standard, semi-ghostwritten "as told to" rock bio format. He offers a lot of tour stories, often digressing into explanations/justifications for his famed idiosyncrasies (like usually performing with pick-up bands), and comments about the injustices of music business artistic and financial practices at length. The most interesting section is an entire chapter devoted to his songwriting, with specific comments about the genesis and meaning of many of his classics. —*Richie Unterberger*

Dave Berry (David Holgate Grundy)

b. Feb. 6, 1941, Woodhouse, Sheffield, Yorkshire, England
British Invasion
Briefly a big star in Britain in the mid-'60s, Dave Berry faced the same dilemma as several other British teen idols of the era: R&B was obviously nearest and dearest to his heart, but he needed to record blatantly pop material to make the hit parade. It was also obvious that Berry was in fact much more suited toward pop ballads than rough 'n' tumble R&B, regardless of his personal preferences. At his peak, his output was divided between hard R&B/rockers and straight pop. Help from ace session players like Jimmy Page and John Paul Jones notwithstanding, his smooth voice was frankly ill-equipped to deliver the goods with anything close to the same panache as Mick Jagger or Eric Burdon on the bluesier items. He made a rather good go of it, on the other hand,

with romantic pop/rock ballads, hitting the British Top Ten with "The Crying Game" (1964), Bobby Goldsboro's "Little Things" (1965), and the excruciatingly sentimental "Mama" (1966). "This Strange Effect," written by Ray Davies (though not released by the Kinks), was a huge European hit for him in 1965 as well.

Berry's voice was not exactly teeming with character, and he never made the slightest impression on the U.S. market, but the best of his material is quite pleasant period fare. He remains well regarded in his homeland, where the Sex Pistols unexpectedly covered his toughest track, "Don't Gimme No Lip Child." Even more unexpectedly, "The Crying Game" brought Berry's voice to his biggest international audience ever in 1992, when it was used as the theme song for one of the year's most successful films. — *Richie Unterberger*

● **This Strange Effect** / 1986 / See For Miles ◆◆◆◆
All the Dave Berry you need, with all but one of the 20 tracks dating from his 1964-66 heyday. Sensibly divided into a 10-song R&B side and a 10-song pop side, it includes all his hit singles—"The Crying Game," "Little Things," "Memphis," the unfortunate "Mama"—as well as "This Strange Effect" and "Don't Gimme No Lip Child." Some of the R&B tracks are mediocre; others (especially "Gimme No Lip") growl along neatly. Some of the lesser-known pop numbers are pretty nifty as well, the highlight being "I'm Gonna Take You There," which was penned by Graham Gouldman (who also wrote hits for the Yardbirds and the Hollies in the mid-'60s). — *Richie Unterberger*

Heidi Berry

Folk-Rock
Heidi Berry is an American folk-rock singer/songwriter who has lived in England since she was a child. She debuted with the mini-album *Firefly* in 1987, and performed with This Mortal Coil. Her full-length debut album, *Below the Waves,* was released by 4AD Records in 1989 and was followed by *Love* in 1991 and *Heidi Berry* in 1993. — *William Ruhlmann*

Love / 1991 / 4AD ◆◆◆

● **Heidi Berry** / Jan. 1993 / Warner Brothers ◆◆◆◆
Heidi Berry is an art-rock singer-songwriter with a vocal style akin to that of the late Sandy Denny, which is to say that she has a sonorous alto and emphasizes its hypnotic, droning qualities over its phrasing. The song settings are often stately and classical, with elaborate string parts and swirling synthesizers, although Berry kicks up her heels with a folk-rock exuberance at times and covers Anna McGarrigle's "Heart Like A Wheel" to let you know her antecedents. — *William Ruhlmann*

Richard Berry

b. Apr. 11, 1935, Extension, LA
R&B
If for no other reason than that he was the original writer and performer of "Louie Louie" (itself based on "El Loca Cha Cha," by Rene Touzet), Richard Berry holds a permanent place of honor in the history of rock & roll. Beyond that, though, Berry was an important if secondary figure of the early- and mid-'50s Los Angeles R&B scene. As a teenager, with the Flairs and as a solo act, Berry recorded quite a few singles that demonstrated his versatilty with ballads, novelty songs, and even Little Richard-styled numbers. His facility with deep-voiced, comic material was a clear forerunner of the Coasters, and in fact he was the uncredited lead singer on Leiber & Stoller's "Riot in Cell Block #9," recorded by the Robins, later to mutate into the Coasters. He took another uncredited vocal as Etta James' deep-voiced sparring partner on "Roll with Me, Henry," one of the biggest R&B hits of the mid-'50s. Berry originally recorded "Louie Louie" in 1956; the record was a regional hit in several West Coast cities, but no more than that.

Berry's recording career petered out in the late '50s, though he remained an active performer. In the early '60s, several Northwest bands seized upon "Louie Louie" as cover material, scoring sizable regional hits; finally, in 1963, the Kingsmen broke the song nationally, reaching number two. In the decades since then, "Louie Louie" became one of the most oft-covered rock standards of all time; there are probably well over 1000 versions by now. The song was investigated by the FBI, and inspired parades and campaigns to adopt it as the official song of the State of Washington. The original version, ironically, remains extremely difficult to find, appearing only on obscure compilations (the Berry version on Rhino's *Louie Louie* anthology is a re-recording). For Berry, there was a

happy ending; in the late '80s, he regained the rights to his song that he had lost many years ago. — *Richie Unterberger*

● **Get out of the Car** / 1982 / Flair ◆◆◆◆
Twenty songs from the mid-'50s, both solo and with the Flairs. Berry wrote or co-wrote most of the tunes, which are solid if somewhat generic R&B on the verge of rock & roll, occasionally treading into doo-wop territory. He's most memorable on the uptempo, comic jiving numbers, with a sardonic and sassy tone that pointed the way for the Coasters. This doesn't have "Louie Louie" or any of the late-'50s material he recorded for the Flip label, which is available on the hard-to-find Swedish import *Louie Louie.* — *Richie Unterberger*

Better Than Ezra

Group, Alternative Pop/Rock
New Orleans trio Better than Ezra began their life as a Dinosaur Jr.-influenced combo in the late '80s, yet they were sidetracked by the accidental death of their lead guitarist. Deciding to continue life as a trio, the band eventually released their first album in 1994 on their own label. It was picked up the following year by Elektra. After MTV and alternative radio picked up the single "Good," *Deluxe* became a national hit. — *Stephen Thomas Erlewine*

○ **Deluxe** / 1995 / Elektra ◆◆◆◆
Despite the distorted guitars of "Good," Better Than Ezra is primarily a folk-rock band; after the first two songs, all the pseudo-Dinosaur Jr. growl leaves their amplifiers and the band concentrates on the jangling sensitive stuff, which is too bad, since they do the louder stuff better. "Good" gets by on the stop-start grunge guitars, which disguise the minimal melody. The remainder of *Deluxe* follows the same song structures as "Good," only without the loud guitars the faults become clearer—namely, a lack of hooks. — *Stephen Thomas Erlewine*

Bettie Serveert

Group, Alternative Pop/Rock
Comprised of vocalist/guitarist Carol van Dijk, guitarist Peter Visser, bassist Herman Bunskoeke, and drummer Berend Dubbe, the Dutch guitar-pop quartet Bettie Serveert released their debut album, *Palomine,* in 1992. Bettie Serveert has jangly hooks and sweet melodies to spare, yet the group can rock as hard as the Pretenders. Featuring the radio hits "Kid's Allright" and "Tom Boy," *Palomine* made the band alternative rock stars. The group's second album, *Lamprey,* was released in 1995 to favorable reviews. — *Stephen Thomas Erlewine*

● **Palomine** / 1993 / Matador ◆◆◆◆
What makes *Palomine,* Bettie Serveert's debut album, such a wonderful record is the way the band balances the sweet guitar-pop of "Tom Boy" with yearning ballads like "Palomine" and gutsy garage-rockers like "The Kid's Alright" without ever sounding forced or clichéd. Instead, all of the band's music is tied together by their weaving guitars, pulsing rhythms, and especially Carol van Dijk's voice, which conveys more genuine emotion and grit than most vocalists in alternative rock. — *Stephen Thomas Erlewine*

Lamprey / 1995 / Matador ◆◆◆
Lamprey, Bettie Serveert's second album, is a reprise of *Palomine,* down to the way Carol van Diijk's voice catches in her throat as she goes into the chorus of "Ray Ray Rain"—just as it did on "Palomine." If anything, *Lamprey* lacks the hooks of *Palomine,* substituting the winding guitar licks that enhanced the melodies of the first album for the melodies themselves. Though the group turns in a couple of affecting songs—"Ray Ray Rain" and "Crutches"—the album is essentially a rewrite of the first, only without the charm or the benefit of hard-rockers like "The Kid's Alright." — *Stephen Thomas Erlewine*

Dickey Betts

b. Dec. 12, 1943, Jacksonvile, FL
Southern Rock
Dickey Betts joined The Allman Brothers Band as second lead guitarist and singer in the late '60s. In addition to matching band leader Duane Allman lick for lick, Betts also wrote such memorable songs as "Revival" (#92, 1971) and the instrumental tour de force "In Memory of Elizabeth Reed." After Duane Allman was

killed in a road accident in 1971, Betts and Allman's brother Gregg shared leadership of the band, with Betts writing and singing the group's biggest hit, "Ramblin' Man" (#2, 1973). Members of the band began solo careers in 1973, and Betts released his first solo album *Highway Call*, in 1974. The Allmans split up in 1976, and Betts formed Dickey Betts and Great Southern. The Allmans reformed in 1978, with Betts contributing "Crazy Love" (#29, 1979), "Angeline" (#58, 1980) and "Straight from the Heart" (#39, 1981). But they split again, and both Betts and the Allmans were inactive for several years. Betts returned with the Dickey Betts Band and *Pattern Disruptive* in 1988, and in 1989 he and a couple of members of his backup band joined a second, more permanent reformation of the Allmans. — *William Ruhlmann*

● **Highway Call** / Nov. 1974 / PolyGram ✦✦✦✦
Betts has made occasional solo albums, starting with this one, which picks up from the country-rock style of his Allmans hit "Ramblin' Man." There's a lot of tasty guitar set in ensemble arrangements also featuring steel guitar and the prominent fiddle of Vassar Clements. — *William Ruhlmann*

Dickey Betts & Great Southern / 1977 / Arista ✦✦✦
Dickey Betts's first solo album, *Highway Call* (1974), was something of a lark between Allman Brothers albums, but with the Allmans' split in 1976, he formed a backup band, Great Southern, and released this, an attempt to launch a full-fledged solo career. Betts exactly recreated the original instrumentation of the Allmans in Great Southern—two lead guitars ("Dangerous Dan" Toler joined him), keyboards, bass, and two drummers. And the sound bore a notable resemblance to the Allmans songs Betts had contributed. But the band doesn't quite catch fire like the Allmans did, and there aren't any classic tunes on the order of "Ramblin' Man" or "In Memory Of Elizabeth Reed," so what you're left with is an Allmans soundalike record, without Gregg Allman to alternate the lead vocals. — *William Ruhlmann*

Atlanta's Burning Down / 1978 / Arista ✦✦
Dickey Betts took a slightly poppier approach on his second Great Southern album, perhaps in an attempt to distinguish the band's sound from that of the Allman Brothers Band. The title track was even a string-filled ballad. But the result was more updated Western swing than contemporary pop-rock, and the album was a commercial disaster. Betts then broke up Great Southern and took bandmates Dan Toler and David Goldflies with him into a reunion of the Allmans. — *William Ruhlmann*

Pattern Disruptive / 1988 / Epic ✦✦✦
After a long layoff, Betts cut this blistering guitar rock album in a style strongly reminiscent of the Allman Brothers Band. In fact, his band contains pianist Johnny Neel and second guitarist Warren Haynes, both of whom would join the next edition of the Allmans when they re-formed; Allmans drummer Butch Trucks guests. — *William Ruhlmann*

Between

Group, Art-Rock/Progressive-Rock
Between was Peter Michael Hamel's cross-cultural experimental rock group that recorded in Germany in the 1970s. Composed of musicians from Germany, Argentina and the USA, Between composed six albums. — *Archie Patterson*

● **Dharana** / 1978 / Wergo ✦✦✦✦
Dharana is the standout album in Between's ouevre. The music is a fusion of Hamel's warm, mantric keyboard melodies, Roberto Detree's classical acoustic guitar, Robert Eliscu's oboe, and the multi-percussive colorations of Cotch Black. It is one of the finest "world fusion" albums ever done. — *Archie Patterson*

Bevis Frond

Group, Rock & Roll, Art-Rock/Progressive-Rock, Psychedelic
Bevis Frond is not a group, it's guitarist Nick Saloman. The bulk of Bevis Frond's albums are long, trippy, psychedelic guitar workouts. Saloman recorded his first album, *Miasma*, after receiving an award for damages after being gravely hurt in a motorcycle accident. *Miasma* set a precedent almost all of his other albums follow—long passages of Hendrix/Cream psychedelia, occasionally interrupted by fragments of pop melody. Unlike most of what passes for psychedelia in the late '80s and '90s, the Bevis Frond is genuinely strange and truly psychedelic; it is music that you haven't heard before. — *Stephen Thomas Erlewine*

Inner Marshland / 1987 / Reckless ✦✦✦

Miasma / 1987 / Reckless ✦✦✦

Bevis through the Looking Glass / 1988 / Reckless ✦✦✦

○ **Any Gas Faster** / 1990 / Reckless ✦✦✦✦

● **A Gathering of Fronds** / 1992 / Reckless ✦✦✦✦
Frond's 1991 double LP *New River Head* could not fit on a single CD. Those remaining six tracks are the bulk of this disc, which also features Frond's contributions to some compilation albums as well as songs only available on flexi-discs and singles included with magazines. Among the "pleasant refrains till now unavailable on compact disc" (taken from the disc's subtitle) are cover versions of Iron Butterfly's "Possession" and Muddy Waters's "Express Man", two songs which Frond makes over in his own style but which shows the influence of each artist on his music. The rest of the songs are in the classic Bevis Frond tradition: some quick power-poppers, some guitar freakouts, and some psychedelic "Solar Marmalade," as well as a track he recorded for his mum at age 14 in 1967. — *Jim Powers*

Big Audio Dynamite

Group, Alternative Pop/Rock
After British guitarist/singer Mick Jones (b. Jun. 26, 1955, Brixton, London, England) was fired from the punk rock group the Clash in 1983, he formed Big Audio Dynamite (B.A.D.) in 1984 with video artist Don Letts (effects and vocals), Greg Roberts (drums), Dan Donovan (keyboards), and Leo 'E-Zee Kill' Williams (bass). B.A.D. debuted on record with the single "The Bottom Line" in September 1985. The group followed the more experimental funk elements of the Clash's *Combat Rock*, adding samplers, dance tracks, and found sounds to Jones's concise pop songwriting. Jones suffered from a near-fatal bout of pneumonia in 1988, but bounced back with 1989's *Megatop Phoenix*. After that record, the band split apart at the end of 1989. Jones added Gary Stonadge (bass/vocals), Chris Kavanagh (drums/vocals), and Nick Hawkins (guitar/vocals) to form Big Audio Dynamite II, while Letts, Williams, and Roberts formed Screaming Target and Donovan joined the Sisters of Mercy. Releasing *The Globe*, the first full-length album with the new lineup, in 1991, B.A.D. II experienced their greatest success yet with the American Top 40 hit single "Rush." In 1994, the band's name was truncated to Big Audio, and the album *Higher Power* was released.

After *Higher Power*, Big Audio parted ways with Epic Records, signing with Radioactive in early 1995. On *Punk* (1995), their first album for Radioactive, the group was renamed Big Audio Dynamite. — *Stephen Thomas Erlewine and William Ruhlmann*

This Is Big Audio Dynamite / Oct. 1985 / Columbia ✦✦✦
Since Mick Jones was the more melodic, pop force in the Clash, it was a surprise that the band he formed after being kicked out of that group was such an unusual mix of synthesized drumming and spoken-word tape inserts, although beneath all the gimmicky sounds (and perhaps accentuated by them) were Jones's often winning songs, among which were the U.K. Top 40 hits "EMC2" and "Medicine Show." — *William Ruhlmann*

● **No. 10, Upping St.** / Oct. 1986 / Columbia ✦✦✦✦
Temporarily reuniting with his former Clash partner Joe Strummer (who co-produced this album and co-wrote five songs), Mick Jones expands on the formula of the debut with Big Audio Dynamite's second album. *No. 10 Upping Street* features better songs that meld samples, found sounds, dance rhythms, and elements of hip-hop more completely and effectively than those on the first record. "C'mon Every Beatbox" and "V. Thirteen" made the U.K. singles chart. "Badrock City," added to the album after its initial release, made the U.S. R&B singles chart. — *Stephen Thomas Erlewine and William Ruhlmann*

Tighten Up, Vol. '88 / Jun. 1988 / Columbia ✦✦
Mick Jones tightens the rather free-form structures of the previous B.A.D. albums on *Tighten Up, Vol. '88*. While he was aiming for a greater commercial success, the result was only partially successful; the best tracks didn't work as singles, and the singles didn't have the creative spark that marks the best of B.A.D.'s music. "Just Play Music!" made the U.K. singles chart.— *Stephen Thomas Erlewine*

Megatop Phoenix / Sep. 1989 / Columbia ✦✦✦
On *Megatop Phoenix*, Jones delves even further into a dance-influenced, cut-and-paste approach to pop music that manages to capture all of the inventiveness of late-'80s dance music without

losing sight of the melodies that have always been his strength. —*Stephen Thomas Erlewine*

○ **The Globe** / Aug. 1991 / Columbia ✦✦✦✦
Although the second incarnation of Big Audio Dynamite doesn't sound all that different from the first, Mick Jones's songwriting and concepts are reinvigorated on *The Globe*, making it one of the best B.A.D. albums. It also ranked as their most commercially successful in the U.S., where "Rush" hit the Top 40, with the title track also charting. —*Stephen Thomas Erlewine*

Higher Power / Nov. 8, 1994 / Columbia ✦✦
Nine years and six albums on, Big Audio's formula of Mick Jones-penned pop tunes, hip-hop beats, and odd found sounds was beginning to sound worn. As indicated on such tracks as "Looking For A Song" and "Harrow Road," carrying on seemed to have become something of a burden for Jones, who increasingly turned to '60s-derived guitar riffs and simple pop melodies. The rhythm section remained too far down in the mix to induce dancing, and the tape inserts—well, Jones was still no Pink Floyd. Obviously, by whatever name they chose, Big Audio needed to rethink their approach. —*William Ruhlmann*

Punk / 1995 / Radioactive ✦✦
For his first album for Radioactive, Mick Jones changed the name of his group back to Big Audio Dynamite and delivered *Punk*. While the name was a retreat back to the BAD's most creative and exciting days of the '80s, the music on *Punk* simply reiterated all of the ideas of their last few albums—which means that it restated the same themes as all of their previous records. Far from being "punk," with all its classic rock references and allusions to the glory days of 1977, the album sounds tied to the past. —*Stephen Thomas Erlewine*

Big Black

Group, Alternative Pop/Rock
Proudly and self-consciously abrasive, Big Black's music is polarizing; either you think that Steve Albini's relentlessly thin, metallic, emotionless guitar grind and distorted vocals is an uncompromising work of art or you think it's self-indulgent crap. The band's clinical noise and grotesque, often misogynist, lyrics easily made them the most extreme, nihilistic band in the American underground in the mid-'80s. After recording three EPs with an unstable lineup, Big Black recorded its first full album with Albini and Santiago Durango on guitar, Dave Lovering on bass, and a drum machine. None of their recordings show much of a musical progression; instead, the band gets harder, noisier, and nastier on each subsequent record. Before the band recorded their final and best album, 1987's *Songs About Fucking*, Durango left the group to study law; Albini pulled the plug on the band shortly afterward.

Although Big Black's life-span was short, Albini's influence on the American independent music scene of the late '80s and '90s has been substantial. After Big Black's breakup he formed the equally uncompromising Rapeman, but Albini's real influence has been through his numerous productions. Over the years he has produced literally hundreds of bands; most of the bands he has produced are justifiably unknown, but some are quite famous—including the Pixies, the Breeders, Urge Overkill, PJ Harvey, and Nirvana. Albini's simple production functions as a type of photograph, capturing the band in an aural black and white; his production shows all of the band's strengths, as well as all of their faults. He frequently cuts the bass levels to a minimum, leaving only a harsh guitar grind, which makes his records a bit wearing to listen to. Many young bands of the '90s have embraced his signature guitar grind, as well as his strident punk-rock ethics, as a reaction to alternative music's move into the mainstream. —*Stephen Thomas Erlewine*

○ **Atomizer** / 1986 / Homestead ✦✦✦✦

Hammer Party / 1986 / Homestead ✦✦✦
Combining Big Black's first two EPs, *Lungs* and *Bulldozer*, on one disc, *Hammer Party* shows the band evolving from Steve Albini's one-man guitar and drum machine aggro-fest to the fleshed-out, but no less insular, attack of the bass-less trio. It's the band's sparest work, but also some of its most abrasive. For CD release, a third EP, *Racer-X*, was added to *The Hammer Party*. —*Stephen Thomas Erlewine*

○ **The Rich Man's Eight-Track** / 1987 / Touch & Go ✦✦✦✦
Rich Man's Eight-Track combines the *Headache* EP and *Atomizer* album on one disc. *Atomizer*, the band's first full-length album, is a self-consciously aggressive and noxious onslaught of guitars and

drums, wallowing in its own depravity; for the first time, Albini and company achieve the sound they were aiming for. *Headache* isn't as good; it's a retread of *Atomizer* without any of the surprise. —*Stephen Thomas Erlewine*

● **Songs About Fucking** / 1987 / Touch & Go ✦✦✦✦
Easily the best album Big Black ever recorded, the bleak noise of *Songs About Fucking* matches the empty nihilism of Albini's ranting lyrics; for once, the sheer force of their music actually makes the band seem threatening, scary, and dangerous. —*Stephen Thomas Erlewine*

Big Bopper (Jiles Perry Richardson)

Group, Rock & Roll
Legendary as one of the three rock greats to die in the tragic 1959 Clear Lake, IA, plane crash that also claimed the lives of Buddy Holly and Ritchie Valens, the Big Bopper (born Jiles Perry Richardson) had just established himself as a rock hitmaker with the rollicking "Chantilly Lace." Born in the heart of Texas, Richardson grew up in Beaumont and changed his first name to J.P. He broke into show biz as a DJ over KTRM radio, where he coined the nickname "The Big Bopper." He began recording for Mercury in 1957, his animated baritone scaling pop playlists the next year with "Chantilly Lace"—easily his top seller—and the equally raucous novelty "Big Bopper's Wedding." Richardson wrote "White Lightning," a huge country hit for George Jones, and Johnny Preston's #1 one smash "Running Bear." —*Bill Dahl*

● **Hellooo Baby!: Best of Big Bopper, 1954-59** / 1989 / Rhino ✦✦✦✦
Hellooo Baby! The Best of the Big Bopper, 1954-1959 is a single-CD compilation of the Bopper's finest, including "Chantilly Lace," "Little Red Riding Hood," and "The Big Bopper's Wedding." It's wild and fun. —*Cub Koda*

Big Boys

Group, Punk
Coming out of the then-overlooked Austin, TX punk scene of the early '80s, the Big Boys combined two irresistible rock styles into one feverish mix: raging, speedy guitars and fat, funky backbeats. And although they went on to make a few so-so recordings, never really living up to their early promise, it's difficult not to be supportive of what the Big Boys tried to do in the start of the hardcore era, wherein the sexiness of a funky rhythm section disappeared amongst the ultra-fast tempos and sexless pummeling. On their wonderful EP *Fun, Fun, Fun*, the Boys tore up Kool & the Gang's "Hollywood's Swinging" like it was their birthright, and the transition from speedcore ranting to danceable funk and roll was rarely more eloquently rendered. In 1984, never reaching beyond a loyal but small audience, the Boys split up and provided musicians for a seemingly endless number of early alternative-rock bands like Rapeman, Scratch Acid, and Poison 13. Guitarist Tim Kerr relocated to Portland, OR and began his wonderful, eponymously named record label. Chris Gates, however, hooked up with ex-Minor Threat/Dag Nasty guitarist Brian Baker and formed Junkyard, proof positive that even hardcore purists were capable of egregious attempts at selling out. —*John Dougan*

Recorded Live at Raul's Club / 1980 / Rat Race ✦✦

Where's My Towel / 1981 / Wasted Talent ✦✦✦

● **Fun, Fun, Fun . . .** / 1982 / Moment ✦✦✦✦
This is the most succinct and totally wonderful record the Boys ever made. With lots of anthemic choruses, raging guitars and soulful backbeats, the enthusiasm and warmth of this record never lets up. Great guitar playing by Tim Kerr, and vocalist Randy Turner bellows with authority. Perhaps not the most important overlooked record of its time, *Fun* is clearly a neglected gem. —*John Dougan*

Lullabies Help The Brain Grow / 1983 / Enigma ✦✦

No Matter How Long the Line Is at the Cafeteria, . . . / 1984 / Enigma ✦✦✦

○ **Wreck Collection** / 1988 / Unseen Hand ✦✦✦✦
If you disagree with me and are of the opinion that the Big Boys could do no wrong, than this anthology (compiled by celebrated hardcore producer Spot) runs the gamut from grubby-sounding demos to slick selected outtakes. Fairly coherent, this set does little to elevate the Boys' reputation, but is as strong an historical overview as is likely to ever be released. Caveat emptor: this is very difficult to find. —*John Dougan*

The Fat Elvis / 1993 / Touch & Go ✦✦✦
The Skinny Elvis / 1993 / Touch & Go ✦✦✦

Big Brother & The Holding Company

Group, Blues Rock, Psychedelic
Big Brother and the Holding Company was a psychedelic blues-rock group formed in San Francisco in September 1965. It consisted of guitarist Sam Andrew (b. Dec 18, 1941), guitarist James Gurly, bassist Peter Albin (b. Jun 6, 1944), and drummer David Getz (b. 1938). The group's formal debut was at the Trips Festival in January 1966. In June, singer Janis Joplin (b. Jan 19, 1943–d. Oct 4, 1970) joined. Big Brother signed to the independent Mainstream label in 1966 and recorded *Big Brother & the Holding Company*. But after their spectacular appearance at the Monterey Pop Festival in May 1967, they switched to major label Columbia, which released the chart-topping, million-selling *Cheap Thrills* in August 1968. Joplin went solo in November, and Big Brother broke up, but it re-formed to make *Be a Brother* (1970) and *How Hard It Is* (1971). Big Brother broke up again in 1972. It re-formed in 1987 with singer Michelle Bastian. — *William Ruhlmann*

Big Brother & The Holding Company / 1967 / Columbia ✦✦✦
Big Brother's debut LP was a low-budget quickie, but it included a Joplin classic in Top 50 hit "Down On Me" and was a good example of San Francisco psychedelia. — *William Ruhlmann*

★ Cheap Thrills / Aug. 1968 / Columbia ✦✦✦✦✦
Cheap Thrills, the major-label debut of Janis Joplin, was one of the most eagerly anticipated, and one of the most successful, albums of 1968. Joplin and Big Brother had earned extensive press notice ever since they played the Monterey Pop Festival in June 1967, but their only recorded work was a poorly produced, self-titled Mainstream album, and they spent a year getting out of their contract with Mainstream in order to sign with Columbia while demand built. When *Cheap Thrills* appeared in August 1968, it shot into the charts, reaching #1 and going gold within a couple of months, while "Piece Of My Heart" became a Top 40 hit. Joplin, with her ear- (and vocal cord-) shredding voice, was the obvious standout. Nobody had ever heard singing as emotional, as desperate, as determined, as loud as Joplin's, and *Cheap Thrills* was her greatest moment. Big Brother's backup, typical of the guitar-dominated sound of San Francisco psychedelia, made up in enthusiasm what it lacked in precision. But everybody knew who the real star was, and Joplin played her last gig with Big Brother while the album was still on top of the charts. Neither she nor the band would ever equal it. Heard today, *Cheap Thrills* is a musical time capsule and remains a showcase for one of rock's most distinctive singers. — *William Ruhlmann*

Be a Brother / Oct. 1970 / Columbia ✦✦
Big Brother comes back as a sextet with the additions of guitarist David Schallock and singer/songwriter/producer Nick Gravenites. Of course, it's a different band without Janis Joplin, but that psychedelic sound is still in place, albeit with a Chicago blues edge courtesy of Gravenites. There's also an amusing reply to Merle Haggard's "Okie From Muskogee," "I'll Change Your Flat Tire, Merle." — *William Ruhlmann*

How Hard It Is / 1971 / Columbia ✦✦

Cheaper Thrills / 1984 / Made To Last ✦✦
Recorded on July 28, 1966, before the band had cut any studio material, this performance was one of Janis Joplin's first gigs with Big Brother. The sound is decent, with several famous staples of their repertoire already in place—"Down On Me," "Coo-Coo," "Ball And Chain." Yet in comparison with their best studio and live recordings from 1967 and 1968, this is a bit limp. Big Brother were never noted for their polish, but made up for that with reckless bravado; however, that's largely missing at this juncture in their development, where they sound somewhat tentative in their adaptation of R&B and garage-band ethos to heavy guitar arrangements. Big Brother were never noted for their songwriting ability either, and this set is pretty reliant on R&B staples like "Let The Good Times Roll" and "I Know You Rider"; the unabashedly psychedelic workout "Gutra's Garden" hasn't aged well at all. Joplin's vocals are fairly strong, but these early versions of "Down On Me" and, especially, "Ball And Chain" don't hold a candle to her performances of the same tunes at the 1967 Monterey Pop Festival. Other members of the band take the lead vocal on a few numbers, emphatically proving—as they always did when given a chance—that Janis was necessary to put them on the map. This recording is an interesting

glimpse into the group's formative days, though, and features eight songs not on their late-'60s albums. — *Richie Unterberger*

Live / 1984 / Rhino ✦✦
This album is culled from a July 28, 1966, show at California Hall in San Francisco and chronicles the sound of Big Brother only a month after Janis Joplin joined. They're still getting themselves together, but Joplin already sounds powerful and much of the material from the first album is heard here in development. (This album also was released by Made To Last Records under the title *Cheaper Thrills.*) — *William Ruhlmann*

Big Chief

Group, Alternative Pop/Rock, Hardcore
Formed in 1989 and composed of Matt O'Brien (bass), Phil Durr (guitar), Mark Dancey (guitar), Barry Henssler (vocals), and Mike Danner (drums), Big Chief is the only major band to come out of Ann Arbor, MI, in years. The group explosively combines hardcore punk with '70s funk. One member did the artwork for Soundgarden's *Badmotorfinger*, and the members are involved with *Motorbooty*, a fanzine edited by Dancey. After several years with independent labels, Big Chief signed to Capitol Records and made its major label debut with *Platinum Jive* in 1994. — *Stephen Thomas Erlewine*

Drive It Off / 1991 / Get Hip ✦✦✦
● Face / Jul. 1991 / Sub Pop ✦✦✦✦
Mack Avenue Skull Game Original Sound / Sep. 7, 1993 / Sub Pop ✦✦✦
○ Platinum Jive / Oct. 11, 1994 / Capitol ✦✦✦✦
In the title and packaging of its major label debut album, Big Chief faithfully impersonates a hits compilation, including, for example, a photograph of guitarist Phil Durr's supposed solo album *A Fly's Dick From Freedom* and their own fictional 1973 album *We Gotta Impeach Nixon* on 8-track! It's a cute joke, and makes you wish that sense of humor and imaginativeness were found on the record itself. Instead, Big Chief turns out to be a hard rock/funk group in the Red Hot Chili Peppers/Jane's Addiction tradition, trendy but unremarkable. The only unusual hints are a little flute and sax playing and a riff from "Pearly Queen" in "Takeover Baby," suggesting somebody in the band is a fan of Traffic. — *William Ruhlmann*

Big Country

Group, Pop/Rock
Scottish group Big Country burst onto the 1982 rock scene with a uniquely expansive twin-guitar sound (made by Stuart Adamson [b. Apr. 11, 1958, Manchester, England], formerly of the Skids, and Bruce Watson [b. Mar. 11, 1961, Timmins, Ontario, Canada]) that at times recalled bagpipes. Bassist Tony Butler (b. Feb. 13, 1957, London, England) (whose credits included the Pretenders and Pete Townshend) and drummer Mark Brzezicki (b. Jun. 21, 1957, Slough, Buckinghamshire, England) (also Townshend) provided an aggressively supple rhythmic foundation.

The Chris Thomas-produced debut effort "Harvest Home" didn't chart, but *The Crossing*, cinematically produced by the innovative Steve Lillywhite, captured the band's sonic vision perfectly. It contains the band's first (and only significant stateside) hit, "In a Big Country."

Big Country followed *The Crossing* with an EP containing the fine "Wonderland," which basically echoed the spirit of "In a Big Country." In England, meanwhile, Big Country scored a brief string of hits, gaining enough popularity to sell out two nights at London's Wembley Stadium in December of 1984. This was further aided by the release of the album *Steeltown*, which entered the British charts at #1. After a 20-month layoff, Big Country released *The Seer.* "Look Away" was a 1986 British hit, but only received moderate attention on U.S. rock radio. The rather generic *Peace in Our Time*, released in 1988 on a new label (Reprise), was a misguided redirection of their sound, ditching most of the qualities that made the band so appealing.

Big Country and Reprise then parted ways, and 1991's *No Place Like Home* was released only in the U.K. Big Country resurfaced on Fox/RCA in 1993 with *The Buffalo Skinners*, which failed to chart in the U.S. — *Rick Clark*

○ The Crossing / Aug. 1983 / Mercury ✦✦✦✦
One of the most unusual and exciting debut rock releases of the early '80s, the album contains expansive hits, including "In a Big Country" and "Fields of Fire." Producer Steve Lillywhite (U2, Sim-

ple Minds) aided in the band's larger-than-life sound and grand themes. Other highlights are "Chance" and "Harvest Home." (*The Crossing* went gold in the U.S. in January 1984.) —*Rick Clark*

Wonderland [EP] / Apr. 1984 / Mercury ♦♦♦
Big Country followed up its debut album, *The Crossing*, with this four-song EP, which contained the characteristically anthemic title track, a U.S. chart single and U.K. Top 10 hit. Also included were "All Fall Together" and two U.K. B-sides, "Angle Park" and "The Crossing." None of these tracks turned up on a Big Country album in the U.S. until 1994, when *The Best Of Big Country* featured "Wonderland." Although out of print, this record provides an effective sampler of the Big Country sound. —*William Ruhlmann*

Steeltown / Nov. 1984 / Mercury ♦♦♦
Big Country came out of one of the less dominant parts of the United Kingdom with an anthemic sound and vaguely revolutionary-sounding lyrics to captivate the British listening public and at least interest Americans. Big Country continued its winning ways at home with this, its second album, which topped the charts and produced three Top 40 hits—"East Of Eden," "Where The Rose Is Sown," and "Just A Shadow." But in the U.S., the album was perceived as proving that the band's sound, guitars-as-bagpipes, courtesy of the E-bow, was a one-time novelty, while Stuart Adamson's lyrics, full of British socialist working-class fervor, seemed jingoistic and pretentious. Nevertheless, much of the music, as on the first album, made for stirring rock & roll. —*William Ruhlmann*

The Seer / Jul. 1986 / Mercury ♦♦♦
Continuing their trademark sound to a fine effect, it contains the hits "Look Away," "The Teacher," "One Great Thing," and "Hold the Heart." —*Rick Clark*

Peace in Our Time / Sep. 1988 / Reprise ♦♦
For its fourth album, Big Country made two changes seemingly intended to bolster its fortunes in America—switching from Mercury Records to Reprise and enlisting hot producer Peter Wolf. The bagpipe guitar sound was de-emphasized, along with the political lyrics, and Wolf treated singer Stuart Adamson as he had Starship singer Mickey Thomas, adding echo and backup harmonies to beef him up. On songs like the lead-off single "King Of Emotion" (Top 20 in Britain, non-charting in the U.S.), Wolf sought to retain Big Country's heroic quality while adding the widescreen dramatic style and cheerleader choral approach of Starship's "We Built This City." It was a brave try, but didn't really suit the group, making *Peace in Our Time* Big Country's least representative and least interesting album. (Nevertheless, the title track made the U.K. Top 40, and "Broken Heart [Thirteen Valleys]" also charted.) —*William Ruhlmann*

No Place Like Home / Sep. 1991 / ♦♦

The Buffalo Skinners / Sep. 14, 1993 / Fox ♦♦♦
Scotland's Big Country were never able to surpass the expectations set by their 1983 debut *The Crossing* and its fistful of rousing rock anthems like "In A Big Country" and "Fields Of Fire." *The Buffalo Skinners*—the group's most recent attempt to recapture lost ground in North America—succeeds because it doesn't waste all of its energy trying to top the past. One can sense a conscious effort here to restrain those elements that had become Big Country formula—guitars that sound like bagpipes, vocals dripping with drama, and the shouted "Hah's" that would seem to punctuate every BC chorus— without the complete abandonment found on 1988's misguided *Peace in Our Time*. There's no fluff, bluff or bluster on *Buffalo Skinners*—just a solid serving of earthy rock with integrity. —*Roch Parisien*

● **The Best of Big Country** / Feb. 22, 1994 / Mercury ♦♦♦♦
All the British chart hits are here, including the fine, otherwise unavailable (except for 12" vinyl EP) 1984 single "Wonderland" and the 1990 singles "Save Me" (from the British compilation *Through a Big Country*) and "Heart of the World," plus "Republican Party Reptile," the only track from Big Country's U.K.-only 1991 album *No Place Like Home* to be released in the U.S. It includes good liner notes and release info. —*Rick Clark*

Big Head Todd & the Monsters

Group, Rock & Roll
During the late '80s and early '90s, Big Head Todd & the Monsters (the Colorado-based trio of guitarist/keyboard player Todd Park Mohr, bassist Rob Squires, and drummer Brian Nevin) built their audience through constant touring, playing college towns across the country. With these tours, they built a solid fan base before

they had even signed to a major label. Although they have released several records, they haven't been able to completely transfer the live appeal of their laidback, slightly jazzy, blues-based pop to tape. Nevertheless, their records contain many fine moments, and 1993's *Sister Sweetly*, which went gold and stayed in the charts over a year, showed that they were continuing to improve their songwriting as well as their playing. It was followed by their second major label album, *Strategem*, in 1994. —*Stephen Thomas Erlewine*

Another Mayberry / 1989 / Big ♦♦♦
That big head of Todd Park Mohr's is full of country and folk guitar licks (played on electric guitar a la '60s folk-rock) that give his music a relentlessly familiar feel, even if he got his riffs secondhand off of R.E.M. albums. Similarly, his husky voice and slightly slurred enunciation evoke generations of rock singers. So, his band's debut album, while pleasantly recognizable on first listen, also has trouble distinguishing itself. After a while, though, the subtlety of his lyrics becomes more apparent, and while the result isn't as impressive as, say, the Smiths, Mohr proves to have an individual world view beyond the chiming guitar chords. (Originally released in 1989 on the group's own Big Records label, *Another Mayberry* was reissued by Giant Records in 1994.) —*William Ruhlmann*

Midnight Radio / 1991 / Big ♦♦♦

● **Sister Sweetly** / Feb. 1993 / Giant ♦♦♦♦
There was a reason that *Sister Sweetly* expanded Big Head Todd's cult—it's their most consistent and satisfying album yet, full of acoustic charm, relaxed funk, and breezy blues. —*Stephen Thomas Erlewine*

Strategem / Sep. 27, 1994 / Giant ♦♦
The sleeper success of *Sister Sweetly*, which went gold without ever breaking the Top 100, held promise for this, Big Head Todd's second major label release. So far, the group had sold to its fan base and to a sympathetic wider audience that responded to its neo-'70s sound. Singer/songwriter/guitarist Todd Park Mohr is a near soundalike for the late Quicksilver Messenger Service leader Dino Valenti, and his band follows the cadences and blues-folk guitar lines of the San Francisco psychedelic bands and the Southern rock bands, especially Lynyrd Skynyrd. What *Strategem* needed was songwriting that could distinguish the group, consolidate its following, and advance its career. Instead, the album seems a step back, its songs ponderous, its performances too clipped and restrained. As a result, the album was on and off the charts in two months, and the band suddenly had to make up lost ground. —*William Ruhlmann*

Big Star

Group, Power Pop/Anglo-Pop, Pop/Rock
Next to the Velvet Underground, Memphis's Big Star is the grandaddy of all cult groups. The crisp, succinct pop found on their first two albums was ignored upon release in the early '70s, but by the '80s, Big Star's sound was everywhere. Everyone from the dB's, R.E.M., and the Replacements to Tommy Keene, Matthew Sweet, Teenage Fanclub, and Primal Scream has integrated Big Star's formula into their own styles, and this has turned Big Star-cofounder Alex Chilton (b. Dec. 28, 1950, Memphis, TN) into a cult icon. The group was formed by Chris Bell (b. Jan. 12, 1951, Memphis, TN, d. Dec. 27, 1978, Memphis, TN) in 1971 and, in addition to singer/guitarists Chilton and Bell, featured bassist Andy Hummell (b. Jan 26, 1951, Memphis, TN) and drummer Jody Stephens (b. Oct. 4, 1952). Although Bell was living in the home of the blues and soul, it was the Anglo-pop stylings of the Beatles and the Kinks that rang his bell. Alex Chilton, former vocalist for the Box Tops, shared Bell's affection for Brit-pop and joined the group, rechristened Big Star after a local supermarket chain.

With producer Terry Manning, the group recorded *#1 Record* in 1972, released on the studio's in-house Ardent label at a time when rock had become tediously pompous and self-indulgent. It was well-received in the press, and seemed like a radio natural, but poor distribution squelched whatever hit potential it had.

Chris Bell, disappointed with the poor reception of his band's debut, struck out on his own in 1972. Bell, who shared vocal and writing credits on the first album, died in a car wreck before he was able to release his solo work. His sound was equally idiosyncratic, remaining distinctly flavored by the British sound. Most of his work has since been released on a Rykodisc collection called *I Am the Cosmos*.

Chilton was left to mastermind the blistering *Radio City*. The lush charm of *#1 Record* was replaced by Chilton's slashing, skewered guitar runs and his mangy, stray-cat vocals. The album was loaded with would-be classics ("September Gurls," "Back of a Car," "You Get What You Deserve") but again, the album was poorly distributed and fell between the cracks.

Disenchanted with the politics of the music business, and suffering from drug and alcohol abuse, Chilton hooked up with Memphis producer Jim Dickinson and vented his spleen on *3rd/Sister Lovers*, recorded in 1974 but shelved until 1978. More a Chilton solo project than a group effort, the album was an erratic but sometimes brilliant emotional outcry which balanced the beautiful ("Stroke It Noel," "Blue Light") with the horrific ("Holocaust," "Kangaroo").

With the demise of Big Star, lead singer Alex Chilton pursued a renegade solo career that has taken him full circle from untamed reckless garage rock to his earthy mid-southern musical R&B roots.

The effervescent, near-perfect guitar pop found on *#1 Record* and *Radio City* have maintained their vitality, making them legitimate rock classics that deserve more than their cult status. It is fair to say that, in spite of almost nonexistent commercial success, Big Star has been an important influence on many of the post-punk/power-pop bands since the late '70s. Among those bands who owe a debt to Big Star are R.E.M., the Replacements, the Posies, Game Theory, the Bangles, Teenage Fanclub, and Primal Scream. —*Rick Clark*

○ **#1 Record** / 1972 / Ardent ♦♦♦♦
The problem with coming in late on an artwork lauded as "influential" is that you've probably encountered the work it influenced first, and so its truly innovative qualities are lost. Thus, if you are hearing Big Star's debut album for the first time decades after its release (as, inevitably, most people must), you may be reminded of Tom Petty and the Heartbreakers or R.E.M., who came after, that is, if you don't think of the Byrds and the Beatles, circa 1965. What was remarkable about *#1 Record* in 1972 was that nobody except Big Star (and maybe Badfinger and the Raspberries) wanted to sound like this—simple, light pop with sweet harmonies and jangly guitars. Since then, dozens of bands have rediscovered those pleasures. But in a way, that's an advantage because, whatever freshness is lost across the years, Big Star's craft is only confirmed. These are sturdy songs, feelingly performed, and once you get beyond the style to the content, you'll still be impressed. —*William Ruhlmann*

○ **Radio City** / 1974 / Ardent ♦♦♦♦
Largely lacking co-leader Chris Bell, Big Star's second album also lacked something of the pop sweetness (especially the harmonies) of *#1 Record*. What it possessed was Alex Chilton's urgency (sometimes desperation) on songs that made his case as a genuine rock & roll eccentric. If *#1 Record* had a certain pop perfection that brought everything together, *Radio City* was the sound of everything falling apart, which proved at least as compelling. —*William Ruhlmann*

☆ **Third/Sister Lovers** / 1978 / Rykodisc ♦♦♦♦♦
Basically an Alex Chilton solo project, it is aided by remaining bandmate Jody Stephens (drums) and a slew of Memphis players. Chilton, frustrated at the music biz and career let-downs, enlisted producer Jim Dickinson to aid in this creative tightrope-walk without a net. The result is a listening experience that's as uncompromisingly harrowing as Neil Young's *Tonight's the Night*. Not for the casual listener, it's still essential in any serious rock listener's collection.

Never really finished, the album has been released several times under different titles and with different tracks since it first appeared under the name *3rd* on PVC Records (7903) in 1978. The version currently in print, Rykodisc RCD-10220, was released February 21, 1992; it resequences the material and features more of it than any earlier version, including two previously unreleased tracks. —*Rick Clark and William Ruhlmann*

★ **#1 Record/Radio City** / 1992 / Stax ♦♦♦♦♦
Their first two albums (1972, 1974) were loaded with amazing songs and performances. Mid-period Beatles, Kinks, and Byrds turned inside out and regurgitated into a unique sound. A must-own for any lover of Anglo-pop/rock. —*Rick Clark*

Big Star Live / Feb. 21, 1992 / Rykodisc ♦♦♦
A weak performance from a live radio special, it may be of interest to hardcore fans but it certainly is no place to start discovering Big Star. —*Rick Clark*

Columbia: Live at Missouri University / Sep. 14, 1993 / Zoo ♦♦
This "reunion" of sorts features original Big Star-members Alex Chilton and Jody Stephens, augmented by Ken Stringfellow and Jonathan Auer, the two frontmen for the Posies. The performances are ragged but, for the most part, right. Once Chilton gets down to business, he delivers strong performances on "September Gurls" and Todd Rundgren's "Slut." Auer and Stringfellow particularly shine on Chris Bell's "I Am the Cosmos" and "Back of a Car." —*Rick Clark*

Big Three [U.K.]

Group, British Invasion
Around the time the Beatles started recording, the Big Three were one of their biggest Liverpool rivals. Their then-novel power trio attack was anchored by drummer Johnny "Hutch" Hutchinson, who actually filled the drum set for the Beatles as an emergency replacement on a few gigs. Managed by Brian Epstein as well, the Big Three were renowned locally as a tough, R&B-inflected outfit, but were made to cover pop material more suited for Gerry & the Pacemakers on most of their singles. The group only managed to cut four singles in 1963 and 1964, as well as a *Live at the Cavern* EP that remains the only official release recorded at one of the most legendary rock clubs of all time. A couple of these singles dented the British Top 40 briefly, but the original lineup broke up in late 1963; bassist Johnny Gustafson went on to join the Merseybeats for a time, and played on three albums by Roxy Music in the 1970s. While eyewitness accounts affirm that the Big Three were a powerful live outfit, they were unsuccessful at translating this energy to record, and had no songwriting ability to speak of, dooming their status to a footnote of the British Invasion. —*Richie Unterberger*

● **Cavern Stomp** / 1982 / Edsel ♦♦♦♦
All 13 of the tracks released by the Big Three—their four singles, the *Live at the Cavern* EP, and a live track from a compilation. "Some Other Guy" (#37) and "By The Way" (#22) were minor British hits in the early days of Merseybeat, although the Beatles recorded much better versions of "Some Other Guy" (an obscure American R&B number by Richie Barrett) on several BBC broadcasts. Passable, energetic Merseybeat, leaning more toward R&B than most of their peers, but not terribly memorable. Comes with a detailed four-page history of the group, much of which is devoted to drummer Johnny Hutchinson griping about the group's bad luck: manager Brian Epstein neglected them and spent most of his time on the Beatles, the Big Three didn't get enough time to record in the studio, other groups covered R&B songs for British hits before they could release their own versions, etc. All of which comes off as so much sour grapes. It's clear enough from the recorded evidence that the group's own limitations as songwriters and performers were the chief reasons that they never approached the success of the Beatles and the other major Liverpool groups. —*Richie Unterberger*

Bikini Kill

Group, Alternative Pop/Rock
The premier riot grrrl band. Feminist punks found an angry and literate leader in Kathleen Hanna, who along with fronting Bikini Kill is also a writer and has been a stripper. The Olympia, WA, band formed in the early '90s, along with the riot grrrl movement, which proved that hardcore punk was not the sole territory of angry boys. The band made their own record label, Kill Rock Stars, on which like-minded bands also put out material. —*Heather Phares*

Bikini Kill / 1992 / Kill Rock Stars ♦♦♦
The group's scabrous debut LP. Hanna's lyrics and singing are equally caustic, creating explosive songs like "Feels Blind" and the amusingly titled "Suck My Left One." This group has anger and intelligence on its side. —*Heather Phares*

● **Pussywhipped** / 1994 / Kill Rock Stars ♦♦♦♦
A more experimental follow-up from these punk rock furies. While there's still lots of vitriol, the songs are more varied and even catchy. "Rebel Girl" is a manifesto just waiting to be discovered, and the rest of the album sees the band occasionally adding fun to their recipe for punk chaos. A good starting point. —*Heather Phares*

Ronnie Bird

b. 1946
Pop/Rock
During the mid-'60s, Ronnie Bird was the only French artist to successfully emulate the sounds of the British Invasion across the channel. Bird was one of the few French singers—past or present—with a facility for singing rock & roll, in French, without sounding strained or embarrassing. His first few discs were crafted with the help of expatriate guitarist Mickey Baker, the same Mickey Baker who was half of Mickey & Sylvia, and responsible for great session work on numerous rock and R&B songs in the '50s. Baker played on Bird's discs and actually wrote a few tracks with Ronnie, although most of Bird's records were French covers of songs by British giants like the Stones, Who, Pretty Things, and Hollies. For a time, Bird's band included guitarist Mick Jones, who'd go on to fame with Foreigner in the '70s.

Although extremely derivative of the tougher side of the British Invasion, Bird's covers and originals were respectably hard-driving and well-executed. Dabbling in soul and psychedelia at times as the '60s progressed, Bird eased out of the music business and immigrated to New York in the '70s. He was unquestionably the best French rocker of the '60s. —*Richie Unterberger*

En Public / 1984 / Big Beat ✦✦✦
Although it purports to be a live recording, these are obviously studio tracks with overdubbed screams. If you can ignore that, these are decent performances from his mid-'60s heyday. Eight of the fourteen songs are available sans audience in their original undubbed form on the 1965 LP. —*Richie Unterberger*

● **1965** / 1987 / Big Beat ✦✦✦✦
1965 is a compilation of Bird's first four EPs, released on French Decca in 1964 and 1965. Divided about evenly between covers and originals (three co-written with Mickey Baker), these 16 songs represent his best and hardest-rocking output. —*Richie Unterberger*

The Birds

Group, British Invasion
If they're remembered at all, the Birds are remembered for two, and only two, things: 1) They were Ron Wood's first group; 2) As part of a misbegotten publicity stunt, they served the American Byrds (with a y) with a writ for improperly using their name when the folk-rockers deplaned for their first British tour in 1965. The Byrds kept their name, and the Birds—with an i—quickly lapsed into obscurity, Wood excepted. They did manage to issue four singles in 1964 and 1965 in a respectably tough rock/R&B vein. —*Richie Unterberger*

● **These Birds Are Dangerous** / 1985 / Edsel/Nest ✦✦✦✦
A six-song, 12-inch EP that gathers both sides of their first three singles (the fourth single couldn't be licensed). Echoes of the Stones, Pretty Things, and Who abound on these tracks, which rock out but don't establish an identifiable or original style. Includes three Ron Wood originals, as well as covers of Eddie Holland's "Leaving Here" (also part of the Who's repertoire at the time), Marvin Gaye's "No Good Without You," and Bo Diddley's "You Don't Love Me." The excellent liner notes refer, frustratingly, to several other unissued sides that could not be obtained for release on this collection. Their fourth single, an unexceptional effort released under the name Bird's Birds, can be found on the obscure compilation reissue *Nowhere Men*. —*Richie Unterberger*

Birdsongs of the Mesozoic

Group, Alternative Pop/Rock, Experimental
Birdsongs of the Mesozoic began as a side project by Roger Miller and Martin Swope, who were members of the Boston band Mission of Burma. They were joined by Rick Scott and Erik Lindgren for their debut recording, a self-titled EP, in 1983. With Mission of Burma dissolving at about this time, Birdsongs of the Mesozoic became a full-time band. The group released the LP *Magnetic Flip* in 1985 and an EP, *Beat of the Mesozoic*, in 1986.

Miller left the group in 1988 and was replaced by Ken Field on saxophone, keyboards, and percussion. The new lineup released *Faultline* and *Pyroclastics*. Swope left the group and was replaced by guitarist Michael Bierylo. The most recent lineup released the CD *Dancing on A'A* on Cuneiform.

Birdsongs of the Mesozoic plays a unique mix of rock, punk, classical, minimalism and free-form music. Instrumentation is pi-

ano, two synthesizers, guitar, saxophone, and electronic and acoustic percussion.

Previously unreleased music by the band's original formation is presented in *The Fossil Record 1980-1987* (Cuneiform). This CD includes music the band composed for *To A Random*, a film by Boston filmmaker Michael Burlingame. The band has collaborated with New York City's "Wooster Group" and composed music for the *Nova* and *Sesame Street* series on PBS. In 1994 members of the group were invited to be Artists-In-Residence at Dartmouth College, Massachusetts College of Art and Emory University. —*Jim Dorsch*

● **Sonic Geology** / 1987 / Rykodisc ✦✦✦✦
A collection of early work from this Boston-based quartet includes versions of Stravinsky's "The Rite of Spring" and "Theme from Rocky & Bullwinkle." —*Michael P. Dawson*

Birthday Party

Group, Alternative Pop/Rock
The Birthday Party was one of the darkest and most challenging post-punk groups to emerge in the early '80s, creating bleak and noisy soundscapes that provided the perfect setting for vocalist Nick Cave's difficult, disturbing stories of religion, violence, and perversity. Under the direction of Cave and guitarist Rowland S. Howard, the band tore through reams of blues and rockabilly licks, spitting out hellacious feedback and noise at an unrelenting pace. As the band's career progressed, Cave's vision got darker and their songs alternated between dirges and blistering sonic assaults.

Originally, the Australian band was called the Boys Next Door, comprising Cave, Howard, Mick Harvey (guitar, drums, organ, piano), bassist Tracy Pew, and drummer Phil Calvert. After the album *Door Door* and EP *Hee Haw* under that name, the band moved to London and switched their name to the deceptively benign Birthday Party. Once they arrived in Britain, the group's demented, knotty post-punk began to gel. They released their first international album *Prayers on Fire* in 1981, earning critical praise in the U.K. and U.S. While the band was preparing to record the follow-up, Pew was jailed for drunk driving; former Magazine member Barry Adamson, Harry Howard, and Chris Walsh filled in for the absent Pew on 1982's *Junkyard*.

After the release of *Junkyard*, the band fired Calvert and moved to Germany, where they began collaborating with experimental post-punk acts like Lydia Lunch and Einstürzende Neubauten. Harvey left the Birthday Party in the summer of 1983. The group briefly continued with drummer Des Heffner, but they soon disbanded after a final concert in Melbourne, Australia. Cave had the most successful solo career, recording a series of albums in the '80s and '90s that maintained his status as a popular cult figure; Harvey joined Cave's backing band, the Bad Seeds. Howard joined Crime and the City Solution, which also featured his brother Harry. —*Stephen Thomas Erlewine*

○ **Prayers on Fire** / 1981 / Nesak ✦✦✦✦
Howling, hellacious mangled art-noise. Surefire. —*John Dougan*

Junkyard / 1982 / Nesak ✦✦✦
Slightly less confrontational but no less disturbing. —*John Dougan*

Drunk on the Pope's Blood / 1982 / 4AD ✦✦✦
An extremely harrowing live EP, with Lydia Lunch. —*John Dougan*

○ **A Collection** / 1985 / Missing Link ✦✦✦✦
A Collection draws from the Birthday Party's *Junkyard* and *Prayers on Fire* albums, adding a few tracks from the *Hee Haw* EP and some alternate takes. The compilation has also been issued under the title *The Best and the Rarest* and provides an effective introduction to the band. —*Stephen Thomas Erlewine*

Hee Haw / 1989 / 4AD ✦✦✦

● **Hits** / 1992 / 4AD ✦✦✦✦
As an album title, *Hits* is an intentionally ironic misnomer for one of Australia's most influential rock bands of the late-'70s and early-'80s. Having "hits" was the farthest thing from The Birthday Party's collective mind over the course of five tumultuous years that followed the group's move to England from Down Under; the members reviled anything that hinted at mainstream acceptance. Ten years on, the intensity of this music is still frightening. It's a dense, mutant hybrid that evolved from punk, progressive rock, funk, and improvisational jazz, without directly owning up to any of these base materials. Vocalist Nick Cave (who has gone on to an

equally creative solo career) didn't just sing about society's dark, depraved underbelly, he lived the experience right there on disc and on stage. — *Roch Parisien*

Elvin Bishop

b. Oct. 21, 1942, Glendale, CA
Blues Rock, Southern Rock
Elvin Bishop was already playing blues guitar when he left Tulsa, OK, to go to the University of Chicago in 1960. There he hooked up with harmonica player Paul Butterfield, and they founded the Paul Butterfield Blues Band, for which Bishop served as guitarist from 1965 to 1968. Going off on his own, he was signed to promoter Bill Graham's Fillmore label. In 1974, he moved to Phil Walden's Capricorn Records, home of the Southern rock movement of the early '70s. In 1976, he scored a gold-selling Top Ten pop hit with "Fooled Around and Fell in Love." He spent most of the '80s out of the limelight, but then was signed to Bruce Iglauer's independent blues label, Alligator, for which he recorded into the '90s. — *William Ruhlmann*

The Elvin Bishop Group / Oct. 1969 / Fillmore ♦♦

Feel It! / Oct. 1970 / Fillmore ♦♦♦

Rock My Soul / Sep. 1972 / Epic ♦♦♦

○ **Let It Flow** / May 1974 / Capricorn ♦♦♦♦
For his fourth album, Elvin Bishop organized a new backup group and switched to Capricorn Records. Capricorn was known as the standard bearer of the Southern rock movement—the Allman Brothers Land, The Marshall Tucker Band, etc.—and Bishop was able to emphasize the country/blues aspects of his persona and his music in the move from Marin County, California, to Macon, Georgia. The guest artists included the Allmans' Dickey Betts, Marshall Tucker's Toy Caldwell, Charlie Daniels, and Sly Stone, and Bishop turned in one of his best sets of songs, including "Travelin' Shoes" (with its Allmans-like twin lead guitar work), which became his first charting single, just as the album was his first to make the Top 100. — *William Ruhlmann*

Juke Joint Jump / Apr. 1975 / Capricorn ♦♦♦
Elvin Bishop's Macon Takeover continued on his second Capricorn album, which had a slightly less country feel than *Let It Flow* but continued to be dominated by twin guitar playing (courtesy of Bishop and Johnny "V" Vernazza) and honky tonk piano playing (from Phil Aaberg). The song quality wasn't quite as consistent this time, but "Sure Feels Good" became Bishop's second singles chart entry. — *William Ruhlmann*

Struttin' My Stuff / Dec. 1975 / Capricorn ♦♦♦
Features the hit single "Fooled Around and Fell in Love," sung by Mickey Thomas. — *William Ruhlmann*

Hometown Boy Makes Good! / Oct. 1976 / Capricorn ♦♦
Elvin Bishop broke the bank with the success of "Fooled Around and Fell in Love" in the spring of 1976, so when he returned with this album in the fall, be turned up on the cover holding bags of money. The question, of course, was whether the hit would turn out to be a breakthrough or a fluke. The nearest thing to a follow-up to "Fooled Around" was "Spend Some Time," a ballad on which Mickey Thomas again sang soulfully. But it barely scraped into the charts, and the rest was typical Bishop good-time boogie (along with trendy tastes of disco and reggae), the relatively thin songwriting reflecting a rushed recording schedule—this was Bishop's fourth new album in just over two-and-a-half years. — *William Ruhlmann*

Raisin' Hell / 1977 / Capricorn ♦♦♦

Hog Heaven / 1978 / Capricorn ♦♦♦
Capricorn Records, having switched distribution from Warner Brothers to Phondisc, was on its way out by the time it released this, its sixth Elvin Bishop album, which may help explain why, only two years after he was in the Top 10 with "Fooled Around And Fell In Love," he didn't even reach the charts with this album. It's also true that lead singer Mickey Thomas had decamped to join Jefferson Starship, leaving Bishop to reestablish his country blues boy persona. But Maria Muldaur had signed on (she sings lead on "True Love"), and with two years between studio albums, Bishop had found the time to write some good vehicles for his guitar work and Southern rock backup band. — *William Ruhlmann*

Big Fun / 1988 / Alligator ♦♦♦
In the 10 years between the release of *Hog Heaven* and this comeback record, Elvin Bishop was represented in record stores by a *Best Of* on Capricorn and an album released only in Germany (*Is*

You Is Or Is You Ain't My Baby? on Line Records). Then he signed with Bruce Iglauer's independent blues label Alligator and made this record, which, naturally, emphasizes his more blues-oriented guitar playing, although without sacrificing his country boy identity. Dr. John tickles some of the ivories, and harmonica player Norton Buffalo (of Commander Cody and His Lost Planet Airmen) also guests. — *William Ruhlmann*

○ **Don't Let the Bossman Get You Down!** / 1991 / Alligator ♦♦♦♦
On *Don't Let the Bossman Get You Down*, Bishop projects a good-natured, humorous persona in the extended spoken-word sections of his songs, but still finds time to play a lot of tasty blues guitar. — *William Ruhlmann*

○ **Sure Feels Good: The Best of Elvin Bishop** / 1992 / PolyGram ♦♦♦♦
A fine collection of the blues-rock guitarist's best moments, which covers more material than the earlier compilation, *Best of Elvin Bishop/Crabshaw Rising.* — *Stephen Thomas Erlewine*

Back to Back / 1992 / K-Tel ♦♦

Best of Elvin Bishop: Tulsa Shuffle / May 10, 1994 / Epic/Legacy ♦♦♦
In his first manifestation as a band leader (1969-1972), Elvin Bishop lived in Marin County, California, and performed under the auspices of promoter Bill Graham. Not surprisingly, the three albums he cut in that period fit into the soul-blues-rock style of post-psychedelic San Francisco, even to the point of featuring an extended instrumental, "Hogbottom," on which Bishop takes Carlos Santana's place fronting the Santana percussion section. This 18-track compilation selects from the albums *The Elvin Bishop Group*, *Feel It!*, and *Rock My Soul*, effectively summarizing this phase in Bishop's career. The only thing wrong with it is that it would be easy to make the mistake of thinking that it covers all of his solo career rather than only the first four years, especially because there have now been four different albums released with the title *The Best of Elvin Bishop*. — *William Ruhlmann*

Stephen Bishop

b. Nov. 14, 1951, San Diego, CA
Pop
In the '70s and '80s, Stephen Bishop made a career out of light MOR pop songs that ranged from romantic to humorously quirky. A number of his songs were used on movie soundtracks: *National Lampoon's Animal House* (in which he also appeared), *Summer Lovers*, *Unfaithfully Yours*, and *Tootsie*. His Top 40 pop hits include "Save It for a Rainy Day" (which has a guitar solo by Eric Clapton), "On and On," "Everybody Needs Love," and "It Might Be You." He wrote the 1986 Phil Collins/Marilyn Martin hit "Separate Lives," the love theme from the film *White Nights*. — *Rick Clark*

● **Best of Bish** / 1988 / Rhino ♦♦♦♦
This album contains "On and On," "Save It for a Rainy Day," and other lesser hits. — *Dan Heilman*

Bjork

Alternative Pop/Rock
When the Sugarcubes dissolved after a string of unsuccessful albums in the early '90s, lead singer Bjork Gudmundsottir rejected the band's arty guitar rock pretentions, pursuing a dance-oriented solo career. With producer Nellee Hooper, Bjork released the innovative *Debut* in 1993. Featuring the singles "Human Behaviour," "Venus As A Boy," and "Big Time Sensuality," the record became an international hit as well as establishing her as a major creative force in dance music. As she was recording the follow-up to *Debut*, Bjork co-wrote the title track to Madonna's 1994 album, *Bedtime Stories*. Bjork released her second album, *Post*, in the summer of 1995; it was a hit upon its release, debuting in the American Top 40 and the British Top 10, as well as reaching the Top 10 in several European countries. — *Stephen Thomas Erlewine*

● **Debut** / Jul. 1993 / Elektra ♦♦♦♦
Bjork's first album since the breakup of the Sugarcubes outshines any of her old group's albums. Covering everything from dance-pop and club music to jazzy torch songs, *Debut* reveals Bjork as a fine songwriter, capable of writing wrenching ("Like Someone In Love") and intoxicating pop songs ("There's More To Life Than This"). Throughout the record, Bjork's thin voice shows a surprising amount of versatility. *Debut* is one of the strongest, most musically varied and consistent dance records of the '90s. — *Stephen Thomas Erlewine*

○ **Post** / 1995 / Elektra ✦✦✦✦
Debut was a worldwide success, raising the expectations for Bjork's second album, *Post*. Bjork doesn't depart from the innovations of *Debut*, she refines them; pushing the jazz/dance fusions into different territories, like the big-band explosions of "It's Oh So Quiet" and the trancey "Possibly Maybe." While it's more subtle and not quite as infectious as *Debut*, the album is more accomplished and varied, switching from the menacing "Army of Me" to the graceful "Isobel" without seeming incoherent. *—Stephen Thomas Erlewine*

Black (Colin Vearncombe)

b. May 26, 1951, Liverpool, England
Alternative Pop/Rock
Black is British singer/guitarist/keyboardist Colin Vearncomb from Liverpool (b. May 26, 1951), who gained notice on the independent label scene in England in the mid-'80s with the singles "Wonderful Life" and "Everything's Coming Up Roses," songs that matched uplifting, melodic music to dark lyrics. *—William Ruhlmann*

● **Wonderful Life** / Sep. 1987 / A&M ✦✦✦✦
This smoky-voiced singer/songwriter, whose sophisticated jazz-pop songs and dramatic vocal delivery place him somewhere between Bryan Ferry and Morrissey, hits his peak with the driving "Everything's Coming Up Roses" (not the Jule Styne song). *— William Ruhlmann*

Comedy / Oct. 1988 / A&M ✦✦✦
Seeking a U.S. breakthrough, A&M Records held Black's second album, *Comedy*, back from release until a re-recorded 1989 version of his U.K. hit "Wonderful Life" could be added as the leadoff track. There is also a remixed version of the U.K. hit "Sweetest Smile," which, like "Wonderful Life," previously appeared on Black's debut album, *Wonderful Life*. Also included were the more recent U.K. chart singles "The Big One" and "Now You're Gone." All of which means that, in its U.S. version at least, *Comedy* was almost that of a hits compilation than a formal second album. That, however, lent it a certain consistency, and in its newer songs, the album showed Black moving away from the cocktail jazz and doomy lyrics of his debut and toward a more eclectic sound, as well as lighter, more romantic sentiments. *—William Ruhlmann*

Black / Jun. 1991 / A&M ✦✦✦

Black Box

Group, Dance-Pop
Black Box is an Italian "house" dance music group made up of Daniele Davoli, Mirko Limoni, and Valeric Semplici, plus video model Katrin Quinol, that scored five U.K. Top 40 hits in 1989 and '90, including the chart-topping "Ride on Time" (sampled vocal by disco diva Loleatta Holloway) and the Top Tens "I Don't Know Anybody Else" and "Fantasy." Their 1990 album *Dreamland* made the U.K. Top 40 and went gold in the U.S., the same year that "Everybody Everybody" (vocal by disco diva Martha Wash) became their first U.S. Top Ten. "I Don't Know Anybody Else" made the U.S. Top 40 and "Strike It Up" hit the U.S. Top Ten in 1991. *— William Ruhlmann*

● **Dreamland** / May 1990 / RCA ✦✦✦✦
Black Box's only real album (*Mixedup!* is a record of remixes) features its hits "Ride On Time" (a U.K. #1), "I Don't Know Anybody Else," "Everybody Everybody," and "Fantasy." The sound is contemporary uptempo dance pop with bravura vocals by Martha Wash (who had to sue to get credit when the videos made it appear that model Katrin Quinol was singing). *—William Ruhlmann*

Mixedup! / Oct. 1991 / RCA ✦✦

The Black Crowes

Group, Rock & Roll
At the time of their 1990 debut, the kind of rock & roll the Black Crowes specialize in was out of style. Only Guns N' Roses came close to approximating a vintage Stones-style raunch, but they were too angry and jagged to pull it off completely. The Black Crowes replicated that Stonesy swagger and Faces boogie perfectly. Vocalist Chris Robinson appropriated the sound and style of vintage Rod Stewart while guitarist Rich Robinson fused Keith Richards's lean attack with Ron Wood's messy rhythmic sense. At their best, the Black Crowes echo classic rock without slavishly imitating their influences.

The Robinson brothers originally formed the Black Crowes in Georgia in 1984. By the time of their 1990 debut, *Shake Your Money Maker*, the group comprised Chris Robinson (vocals), Rich Robinson (guitar), Johnny Colt (bass), Jeff Cease (guitar), and Steve Gorman (drums). "Jealous Again," the first single from *Shake Your Money Maker*, was a moderate hit but it was the band's cover of Otis Redding's "Hard to Handle" that made the group a multi-platinum success. "Hard to Handle" climbed its way into the Top 40, propelling the album into the Top 10. The acoustic ballad "She Talks to Angels" became the band's second Top 40 hit in the spring of 1991. *Shake Your Money Maker* would eventually sell over three million copies.

The Black Crowes delivered their second album, *The Southern Harmony and Musical Companion*, in the spring of 1992. It entered the charts at number one, but it didn't have as many hit singles as the debut; none of the singles cracked the Top 40 and only "Remedy" and "Thorn in My Pride" made the Top 100. Nevertheless, the band established themselves as a popular concert attraction that summer, selling out theaters across America. During 1992, the band added keyboardist Eddie Hersch as a permanent member. The Black Crowes' third album, *Amorica*, arrived in late 1994. *Amorica* debuted in the Top 10, but none of the singles from the album made the charts; even though the record went gold, it slipped off the charts in early 1995. *—Stephen Thomas Erlewine*

○ **Shake Your Money Maker** / 1990 / Def American ✦✦✦✦
The best ideas on the Crowes' debut are all about 20 years old, but when those ideas are replicas of vintage Stones and Faces, timelessness is not an issue. The mix of throttling rockers and acoustic ballads doesn't flow with the grace of *Beggar's Banquet*, but the best songs here—"Twice as Hard," "She Talks to Angels," "Could I've Been So Blind"—act as anchors for a strikingly confident debut. *—John Floyd*

● **The Southern Harmony and Musical Companion** / 1992 / Def American ✦✦✦✦
On *The Southern Harmony & Musical Companion* the Crowes avoid the sophomore slump by taking the best elements of their debut and fleshing them out (and giving the rhythm section and keyboards more room to breathe). The Stones/Faces/Humble Pie comparisons are still relevant, but the band's own identity flourishes on such songs as "Remedy," "Black Moon Creeping," and "Sting Me." *—John Floyd*

Amorica / 1994 / American ✦✦✦
On *Amorica*, the Black Crowes finally come into their own, taking their cue from the most relaxed, groove-oriented tracks on their previous album. While the album contains no immediately obvious singles, the songs are the best the band has ever written, stretching out into a hard, jam-oriented, funky blues-rock. The Black Crowes' influences are still discernable—no band celebrates the glory days of rock culture quite as enthusiastically—but they use the music of the Stones, the Faces, and Little Feat much the same way the Stones used the music of Chuck Berry: it's a starting point that leads the band into a new direction, incorporating different musical genres and making the music original. That sense of reinterpretation is what keeps *Amorica* fresh. *—Stephen Thomas Erlewine*

Black Dog

Group, Alternative Pop/Rock
The three figures who formed the collective Black Dog Productions first saw the light of the States when their *Bytes* album appeared on TVT Records, a distributor of the influential U.K. label, Warp. Their second album remains unreleased in the U.S., but third effort *Spanners* (1995) did get a domestic release. *—John Bush*

● **Bytes** / 1993 / Warp ✦✦✦✦
The album has a curious sound that almost contradicts itself, merging sometimes cheesy-sounding drum machines with gorgous, emotional synth. The formula works throughout, creating haunting tracks that stand with Aphex Twin and Global Communication as the best music in the genre. *—John Bush*

Spanners / 1995 / East West ✦✦✦
Most tracks are good, but some are marred by that same faux-sounding drum machine. *—John Bush*

Black Flag

Group, Punk, Hardcore
Black Flag was one of the leading bands in the Los Angeles hard-

core punk rock movement of the early '80s. Its founding and only permanent member was Greg Ginn (b. Jun. 8, 1954, Phoenix, AZ) (guitar). Other members included Chuck Dukowski (b.Feb. 1, 1954, Los Angeles) (bass) (replaced in 1984 by Kira Roessler [b. Aug. 13, 1962, New Haven, CT]), Keith Morris (vocals) (replaced in 1981 by Henry Rollins [b. Feb. 13, 1961, Washington, D.C.]), and Brian Migdol (drums) (replaced by Robo in 1981, who was replaced by Bill Stevenson (b. Sept. 10, 1963, Torrance, CA], who was replaced by Anthony Martinez in 1985). Black Flag released its first album, *Damaged,* on SST Records, an independent label founded by Ginn. After releasing many other records, Black Flag broke up in 1987. — *William Ruhlmann*

★ **Damaged I** / 1981 / SST ✦✦✦✦✦
Perhaps the best album to emerge from the quagmire that was early-'80s California hardcore punk, the visceral, intensely physical presence of this record has yet to be equaled, although many bands have tried. Although Black Flag had been recording for three years prior to this release, the fact that Henry Rollins was now their lead singer made all the difference. His furious bellow and barely contained ferocity was the missing piece the band needed to become great. Also, guitarist/mastermind Greg Ginn wrote a slew of great songs for this record that, while suffused with the usual punk conceits (alienation, boredom, disenfranchisement), were capable of making one laugh out loud, especially the proto-slacker satire "TV Party." Extremely controversial when it was released, *Damaged* endured the slings and arrows of outrageous criticism (some reacted as though this record alone would cause the fall of America's youth) to become and remain an important document of its time. — *John Dougan*

Everything Went Black / 1983 / SST ✦✦✦

Family Man / 1984 / SST ✦✦✦

The First Four Years / 1984 / SST ✦✦✦
The best collection of pre-Rollins era Black Flag. Much of *The First Four Years* finds the band in developmental mode, but the sonic anarchy and political vituperation met head-on more than once, creating a ferociously good time. Not simply for completists, this is an important recording of the then-burgeoning L.A. hardcore scene. — *John Dougan*

Live '84 / 1984 / SST ✦✦

My War / 1984 / SST ✦✦

Slip It In / 1984 / SST ✦✦✦

○ **In My Head** / 1985 / SST ✦✦✦✦
After a rancorous three-year legal battle with their label Unicorn, which prevented them from releasing any new material, Black Flag binged in the mid-'80s, releasing a flurry of records that had even the most devoted fans scrambling to keep up. They did, however, start this period somewhat inauspiciously with *My War,* a pretentious mess of a record with a totally worthless second side. Featuring three tracks of slower-than-Black Sabbath muck with Rollins howling like a caged animal, it was self-indulgence masquerading as inspiration and about as much fun as wading through a tarpit. Side One, however, was quite good, with the title tracks especially intimidating. *Slip It In* followed almost immediately, and while a bit better (fewer mega-volume angst drones), the band still wanders a bit, experimenting with expanding the breadth of hardcore into a newer hard rock/punk sound. This is especially true of Greg Ginn's guitar playing, which was becoming increasingly avant-garde and exciting. Rather than simply coughing up one clichéd solo after another, he wandered harmolodically up and down the fretboard as a jazz player like Blood Ulmer would, making the material more interesting than what most Black Flag-influenced bands were playing. Keeping up with this furious pace came *Live '84,* a cassette-only release of a standard (for them anyway) Black Flag gig. Opening up with an eight-and-a-half minute hardcore/punk/jazz instrumental "The Process of Weeding Out" (which came from an earlier Black Flag instrumental EP of the same title), it was abundantly clear that Black Flag was no longer just another punk band; as much as they loved to kick out the jams, they also loved destroying the audience's preconceived notions of how punk bands were supposed to behave. Running at 70 minutes, this is a terrific live recording of Black Flag at their performing peak. Hot on the heels of the live record came *Loose Nut* and *In My Head,* which showed significant improvement over *My War* and *Slip It In.* Rollins and Ginn were exploring by-now standard lyrical themes: hate, paranoia, loneliness, anomie, and violence, but framing them around music that was

demanding, powerful and exciting. *In My Head* is the slightly better of the two, primarily because it's a little edgier and uncontrolled, but at this juncture, Black Flag was making some of the best contemporary rock music extant. — *John Dougan*

○ **Loose Nut** / 1985 / SST ✦✦✦✦

○ **Who's Got the 10 1/2?** / 1986 / SST ✦✦✦✦
Despite being on top of their game, Black Flag called it a career in 1986, but did so in fine style. The live record *Who's Got The 10 1/2?* was recorded at a barn-burner of a gig with the band (especially Ginn) sounding as though they could take on the world. Extra points for a great version of the cautionary "Drinking and Driving." The cassette and CD contain an extra 30 minutes. — *John Dougan*

○ **Wasted . . . Again** / 1987 / SST ✦✦✦✦
Wasted . . . Again is a posthumous release that is an essential career summation. For those hearing the ear-searing sounds of early-'80s SoCal hardcore punk for the first time, *Wasted . . . Again* is an essential purchase. — *John Dougan*

Black Flames

Group, Urban
This late-'80s vocal quartet took a then-novel approach, combining hip-hop fashion with a sweet sound that took its cues from such '70s groups as the Stylistics and the Chi-Lites; they even had a hit with a cover of the Chi-Lites' "Are You My Woman?" This approach was slicked up and turned to gold by such 1991 phenomenons as Boyz II Men and Another Bad Creation. — *Dan Heilman*

○ **Black Flames** / 1988 / Original Black ✦✦✦✦
It contains a good remake of "Are You My Woman?" by the Chi-Lites. — *Dan Heilman*

Black 47

Group, Pop/Rock
Black 47 (a name deriving from the year 1847, the blackest year of the Irish potato famine) is a New York-based band made up of Irish expatriates and led by songwriter/playwright Larry Kirwan. In addition to Kirwan (vocals, guitar), the band consists of Chris Byrne (uilleann pipes, tin whistle, vocals), Fred Parcells (trombone, tin whistle, vocals), Jeff Blythe (saxophone), Thomas Hamlin (percussion), and David Conrad (bass). Black 47 plays a mixture of traditional Celtic folk music, rock & roll, rap, and reggae, all topped by the idiosyncratic songwriting and persona of Kirwan. While playing a residency at the Irish pub Paddy Reilly's in Manhattan, the group released its debut album, *Black 47* on its own BLK label in 1992, and then was signed to SBK/EMI, which issued a five-song EP, also called *Black 47,* in November 1992, and a critically acclaimed debut album in March 1993. Black 47 toured extensively in 1993 and 1994 and released its second album, *Home of the Brave,* in October 1994. — *William Ruhlmann*

○ **Black 47** / Feb. 21, 1992 / BLK ✦✦✦✦

Black 47 [EP] / Nov. 17, 1992 / SBK ✦✦✦
SBK/EMI chose to herald their signing of this highly touted band by releasing a five-song EP, four of whose songs turned up on the full-length album *Fire Of Freedom* only four months later. (The exception, completists note, is "Our Lady Of The Bronx.") But that was enough to let those who hadn't yet heard the news discover that songwriter Larry Kirwan had a unique lyrical perspective embracing his Irish expatriate past with self-deprecatory humor as well as political fervor. (In "Funky Ceili," he winningly sang to a woman he had impregnated and abandoned, inviting her to come live in the Bronx and make more babies! And then there are the working class anthems that would have drawn a smile from Woody Guthrie.) The music was a surprisingly workable blend of traditional Irish folk with rock, reggae, and rap, plus a horn section. — *William Ruhlmann*

● **Fire of Freedom** / Mar. 1993 / SBK ✦✦✦✦
Street-wise, horn-driven New Jersey rock meets ethnic Irish pop. — *Roch Parisien*

Home of the Brave / Oct. 10, 1994 / SBK ✦✦✦
Larry Kirwan devotes himself to a strange mixture of Irish nationalism, American civil rights advocacy, and working-class infidelity on New York's Lower East Side. He sings with equal passion about 1920s Irish patriots and lovers' triangles, and when he loses his girlfriends to better-employed sanitation workers and dentists, he buries his misery in six-packs. It's a worldview of sorts, especially because Kirwan sees it in such heroic terms and because he

adopts music that reinforces those terms: an earnest, if slightly self-mocking singer emotes over martial rhythms, traditional Celtic folk instruments, a horn section, and dabs of rock guitar. If all of this works a little less effectively than on Black 47's debut, it's in part because Kirwan's sense of humor isn't as apparent and in part because this album really doesn't do much more than repeat the fresh approach of the first, making it begin to seem like formula. —*William Ruhlmann*

Black Oak Arkansas

Group, Hard Rock, Southern Rock
1970s Southern rock perennials from (where else?) Black Oak, AR. Founded in 1970 by Jim 'Dandy' Mangrum (b. Mar. 30, 1948, Black Oak, AR) (vocals), Harvey Jeff (guitar) (replaced in 1974 by James Henderson [b. May 20, 1954, Jackson, MS]), Stanley Knight (b. Feb. 12, 1949, Little Rock, AR) (guitar, fiddle, saxophone), Pat Daugherty (b. Nov. 11, 1947, Jonesboro, AR) (bass), Ricky Reynolds (b. Oct. 29, 1948, Manilan, AR) (guitar), and Wayne Evans (drums) (replaced in 1975 by Thomas Aldrich [b. Aug. 15, 1950, Jackson, MS], the group is best known for wildman vocalist Jim Dandy Mangrum, who predated the posturing of David Lee Roth. After recording an album under the name Knowbody Else for Stax in 1969, the band relocated to Los Angeles, changed its name, and signed to Atlantic. They built a following by touring extensively and scored a hit with a remake of Lavern Baker's "Jim Dandy." They won gold records for their albums *Black Oak Arkansas* (1971), *Raunch 'N' Roll/Live* (1973), and *High on the Hog* (1973). In July 1975, they moved to MCA Records. They suffered extensive personnel changes from 1976 on, and by the time they switched to Capricorn Records in 1977, Mangrum was the only original member. They split in 1980 after he suffered a heart attack, but in 1984 he dropped the Black Oak name and toured as Jim Dandy. —*John Floyd and William Ruhlmann*

○ **Raunch & Roll / Live** / Mar. 1973 / Atco ✦✦✦✦
A mildly chaotic live set, it was perhaps their finest hour. —*Dan Heilman*

● **Hot & Nasty: The Best of Black Oak Arkansas** / 1993 / Rhino ✦✦✦✦
Hot & Nasty: The Best of Black Oak Arkansas cherry-picks from all of the group's hit-and-miss albums, taking their two hit singles "Jim Dandy" and "Strong Enough to Be Gentle" and most of their AOR favorites. —*Stephen Thomas Erlewine*

Black Sabbath

Group, Hard Rock, Heavy Metal
No other band has come closer to embodying heavy metal than Black Sabbath. Over the years, their lineup may have changed but their music hasn't—it has remained the same loud, methodical guitar-based heavy rock that it was in the early '70s. Their slow, sludgey attack was part design and part accident. Because of an accident that cut the tips off his fingers, Tony Iommi tuned his guitar down a half-step because he couldn't play comfortably unless the strings were slightly slack; the lower tuning made his mammoth riffs sound heavier. Bassist Geezer Butler's lyrics reveled in black magic, fantasy, drugs, mental illness, and the occult, but never sex; Ozzy Osbourne sang them in a flat, almost tuneless, banshee wail. Butler and drummer Bill Ward never had any flair for playing around with the rhythm, preferring to let the beat plod on and on. Their songwriting never strayed from one riff, a chorus, another riff, and a guitar solo, but that is part of their appeal. Taken together, the primitive musicianship, bad poetry, obsessive fantasy world, crawling tempos and overpowering volume simultaneously represents everything good and bad about heavy metal.

Critics detested them when they were at the peak of their powers in the early '70s, and they still do. But critical acclaim was never essential to the band's success. Black Sabbath was, in many ways, an underground band—parents hated them, hippies hated them, self-respecting rockers hated them. Everybody hated them except the teenagers. And those were the teenagers that grew up and formed bands, from Metallica to Soundgarden to Henry Rollins. Everybody from the heaviest of metal bands to the sludgiest of grunge bands listened to Black Sabbath when they were teenagers.

Of course, after Black Sabbath hit their peak, they stuck around way too long. Some of their first six albums were great, some of them merely had good tracks, but all of them had something to recommend them. Osbourne hung around for two more records

before jumping ship for good. Former Rainbow lead vocalist Ronnie James Dio replaced him in 1979; the new lineup released their first record, *Heaven and Hell*, in 1980. It was a far cry from their best, but it sounded like *Paranoid* compared to what they would later release. Throughout the '80s, the band members kept shifting, with Iommi being the only member to remain in all of the lineups. At the end of the decade, he was the only original member left in the band. Not only was Black Sabbath suffering musically, but their credibility was in question by their devoted fans as well. In 1991, Iommi persuaded Butler to rejoin and, for a brief time, Dio. Black Sabbath continues to lurch forward in the '90s, oblivious to the criticism and declining record sales, but their early records continue to inspire—as well as infuriate—whole new generations of listeners. —*Stephen Thomas Erlewine*

○ **Black Sabbath** / May 1970 / Warner Brothers ✦✦✦✦
Their debut album set the tone with the title cut, "The Wizard," "Wasp," and "Warning." —*Cub Koda*

★ **Paranoid** / Jan. 1971 / Warner Brothers ✦✦✦✦✦
Paranoid, released in the U.K. in September 1970 and held back from U.S. release until January 1971 to avoid cutting off sales of the still-selling debut LP, became Black Sabbath's best-selling album ever. "Paranoid" and "Iron Man" (the latter released as a single a full year after the album) became Black Sabbath's only U.S. singles chart entries, and the album became their only U.K. chart-topper. Although the album was deplored by critics at the time, the reasons for its success are easy to hear now. Subtle, it ain't (listen to the way Ozzy Osbourne sings note-for-note the same simple melodies Tony Iommi plays), but that's the point. In songs like "Paranoid" and "Iron Man," generations of teenagers heard their own insecurities writ large. —*William Ruhlmann*

☆ **Masters of Reality** / Aug. 1971 / Warner Brothers ✦✦✦✦✦
Sabbath's third album, no less potent than the first two. It includes "Into the Void," "Children of the Grave," and "Lord of This World." —*Cub Koda*

○ **Black Sabbath, Vol. 4** / Sep. 1972 / Warner Brothers ✦✦✦✦
This is a surprisingly song-oriented set of cynical boogie. —*John Floyd*

○ **Sabbath, Bloody Sabbath** / Dec. 1973 / Warner Brothers ✦✦✦✦
Sabbath adds some synths to their sludge and comes up with a surprisingly solid album, which manages to expand on their patented slow, gloomy sound. —*Stephen Thomas Erlewine*

○ **Sabotage** / Aug. 1975 / Warner Brothers ✦✦✦✦
On *Sabotage*, the band was at their artiest, adding synths and found sounds which accentuated Iommi's tight solos and riffs. It may not be their best or most influential record, but *Sabotage* is certainly one of their most interesting. In fact, it was the last consistently impressive album they ever recorded. —*Stephen Thomas Erlewine*

○ **We Sold Our Soul for Rock And Roll** / Feb. 1976 / Warner Brothers ✦✦✦✦
Running over 70 minutes, *We Sold Our Soul for Rock and Roll* is a solid 16-track sampler from the band's first six albums, what you might call Sabbath's glory days. —*John Floyd & Cub Koda*

Technical Ecstasy / Oct. 1976 / Warner Brothers ✦✦
Never Say Die! / Oct. 1978 / Warner Brothers ✦✦
Never Say Die! was the last album Ozzy Osbourne recorded with Sabbath and it's easy to see why he left the group. Once, the band's plodding, gloomy riffs had a stately majesty to them—on *Never Say Die!* they simply sound lethargic. Osbourne doesn't sound like he cares much about the material, delivering his lines in a lazy, affected manner; he sings as if he had already left the group. —*Stephen Thomas Erlewine*

Heaven & Hell / May 1980 / Warner Brothers ✦✦✦
Black Sabbath's first album without Ozzy Osbourne curiously revitalized the band. The band's return to form had something to do with their new vocalist Ronnie James Dio, yet it was mostly due to the fact the band had written a set of riffs that were fairly memorable. The result was their best record since *Sabotage*, and the only good record the group recorded in the '80s. —*Stephen Thomas Erlewine*

The Mob Rules / Nov. 1981 / Warner Brothers ✦✦
Mob Rules, Black Sabbath's second album with Ronnie James Dio, went gold, but that was a testament to the strength of the previous *Heaven and Hell*, not the merits of the new record. While it essentially reiterated the formula of *Heaven and Hell*, *Mob Rules*

lacked the blunt, powerful riffs that made the former record a platinum success. — *Stephen Thomas Erlewine*

Live Evil / Dec. 1982 / Warner Brothers ✦✦
The lackluster *Live Evil* documents Sabbath's 1982 tour. While the band wasn't terrible, they weren't very captivating and the bland performances on the album reflect their mediocrity. — *Stephen Thomas Erlewine*

Born Again / Oct. 1983 / Warner Brothers ✦✦

Seventh Star / Jan. 1986 / Warner Brothers ✦
Seventh Star, Black Sabbath's 12th new studio album, actually was credited to "Black Sabbath Featuring Tony Iommi," and guitarist and sole remaining founding member Iommi was pictured alone on the front and back covers. Iommi had hired a new Sab lineup—Glenn Hughes (vocals), Eric Singer (drums), Dave "The Beast" Spitz (bass), and long-time Sab backup keyboard player Geoff Nichols, now credited as a full-fledged member—but since the band remained anonymous even after you'd heard them (especially generic singer Hughes), it was Iommi's guitar playing and rudimentary songs which dominated an album that wasn't even an echo of Black Sabbath's glory days. — *William Ruhlmann*

The Eternal Idol / Dec. 1987 / Warner Brothers ✦

Headless Cross / Apr. 1989 / IRS ✦
Black Sabbath's 14th new studio album in 19 years, *Headless Cross* featured a lineup of founder/guitarist Tony Iommi, drummer Cozy Powell, singer Tony Martin, keyboard player Geoff Nicholls (whose name gets spelled differently on different Black Sabbath album jackets), and bassist Laurence Cottle. Powell, a driving drummer, co-produced, and he gave the songs faster tempos than usual for Black Sabbath. But otherwise, this was standard issue—big guitar riffs, lyrics about death and the occult, howling vocals—of the brand of heavy metal Black Sabbath invented, although by now the band sounded like an also-ran. — *William Ruhlmann*

T Y R / 1990 / IRS ✦

Dehumanizer / Jun. 1992 / Warner Brothers ✦✦
From the group many credit with creating metal, guitarist Tony Iommi resurrected an earlier lineup of Black Sabbath for *Dehumanizer*. As is their wont, the Sabs show concern for humanity's future. Lead track "Computer God" tackles mankind's capitulation at the altar of technology. "After All" evokes the morbid/mystical themes and sonic plod of earliest Sabbath. *Dehumanizer* breaks little new ground. But with hundreds of other groups expropriating the sound these days, it's comforting to find that, 22 years on, there's still no one who can churn out those sinister, almost orchestral three chords quite as effectively as Iommi and Butler. — *Roch Parisien*

Cross Purposes / Feb. 8, 1994 / IRS ✦✦

Black Sheep

Group, Rap
Bronx rapper Andre "Dres" Titus and William "Mista Lawnge" McLean scored a big hit with the debut *A Wolf in Sheep's Clothing* for Mercury in 1991. The disc went gold, with the single "The Choice Is Yours" scoring on the R&B charts and getting extensive pop exposure as well. The follow-up, *Non-Fiction*, had less of an impact. — *Ron Wynn*

● **A Wolf in Sheep's Clothing** / 1990 / Mercury ✦✦✦✦
Bronx rappers Black Sheep scored with the single "Choice Is Yours," a song featuring the catch phrase "you can get with this or you can get with that." But while this hit and "Strobelite Honey" were more satirical, the album also included the biting "Black With N.V. (No Vision)" and "To Whom It May Concern," message tracks that harshly criticized successful blacks who turned their backs on the inner city. — *Ron Wynn*

Non-Fiction / 1994 / Mercury ✦✦✦
The follow-up to 1992's massive debut, *Non-Fiction* is a troubled sophomore album; it has a few good moments, but it can't compare to the raw immediacy of *A Wolf in Sheep's Clothing*. Dres's raps are just as solid, but the mostly R&B-influenced backing is flat and unexciting. "Without A Doubt," however, is as house-rockin' a cut as any on the debut. — *John Bush*

Cilla Black (Priscilla Maria Veronica White)

b. May 27, 1943, Liverpool, England
Pop, British Invasion

Cilla Black (born Priscilla Maria Veronica White, Liverpool, England) was the hat check girl at the Cavern, the club in Liverpool where the Beatles played in their early days. Like them, she was signed to a management contract by Brian Epstein. Parlophone, the Beatles' label, released her first single, "Love of the Loved" (written by the Beatles' John Lennon and Paul McCartney), in September 1963. It was a Top 40 U.K. hit and was followed by the chart-topping "Anyone Who Had a Heart," a dramatic ballad by Burt Bacharach and Hal David that had been a U.S. hit for Dionne Warwick and that set the pattern for Black's later recordings. Black's third single, "You're My World," was another U.K. #1 and a Top 40 hit in the U.S. in July 1964. In the U.S., Black scored only four more chart entries, "It's for You" (1964) (also by Lennon-McCartney), "He Won't Ask Me" (1964), "Alfie" (1966), and "Step Inside Love" (1968) (by McCartney). But she was much more popular in the U.K., where her Top Ten hits included "It's For You," "You've Lost That Lovin' Feelin'" (1965), "Love's Just a Broken Heart" (1966), "Alfie," "Don't Answer Me" (1966), "Step Inside Love," "Surround Yourself With Sorrow" (1969), "Conversations" (1969), and "Something Tells Me (Something's Gonna Happen Tonight)" (1971), and she also made the Top 40 with "I've Been Wrong Before" (1965) (by Randy Newman), "A Fool I Am" (1966), "What Good Am I" (1967), "I Only Live to Love" (1967), "Where Is Tomorrow" (1968), "If I Thought You'd Ever Change Your Mind" (1970), and "Baby We Can't Go Wrong" (1974). On the LP chart, *Cilla* (1965), *Cilla Sings a Rainbow* (1966), and *Sher-oo* (1968) all made the Top Ten and *The Best of Cilla Black* (1968) and *The Very Best of Cilla Black* (1983) the Top 40. In 1968, she launched a television series on the BBC and went on to become a popular British TV entertainer in the 1970s. — *William Ruhlmann*

● **Best of Cilla** / Nov. 1968 / Parlophone ✦✦✦✦
By the fall of 1968, Cilla Black had scored 14 chart entries in the U.K., of which eight had hit the Top Ten and two had gone to number one. This 14-track British compilation contains 11 of those songs, including all but one of the Top Tens. Her singles began with "Love Of The Loved," a Beatles cast-off in their Merseybeat style, but she really hit her stride copying Dionne Warwick on "Anyone Who Had A Heart," and went on to score all her hits in a melodramatic ballad style, with lots of strings and heartbreak. She is thus in a category with contemporaries like Dusty Springfield and Lulu, but unlike them, she never showed much taste for rock or blues, moving instead unerringly to the middle of the road. As a result, today she seems not much more than a footnote in the history of the Beatles. — *William Ruhlmann*

Frank Black

Alternative Pop/Rock
Inverting his stage name from Black Francis to Frank Black, the former Pixies lead singer/songwriter embarked on a solo career after he broke up the band in early 1993; actually, he began recording his solo album *before* he told the band the news. Working with former Pere Ubu member Eric Drew Feldman, Black occasionally heads into the ferocious post-punk guitar territory that marked such landmark albums as *Surfer Rosa* and *Doolittle*, but more frequently he plays up his considerably underrated melodic side. His self-titled 1993 debut album was an adventurous sketchbook of pop styles ranging from surf rock to heavy metal, from Beatlesque pop to new wave. Black's second album, 1994's *Teenager of the Year*, was a sprawling and diverse album that amplified all the best points of *Frank Black*. Although it received favorable reviews and had an alternative radio hit with "Headache," it slipped off the charts two weeks after its release. Black parted ways with Elektra and 4AD in early 1995, signing a new record contract with American. — *Stephen Thomas Erlewine*

○ **Frank Black** / 1993 / Elektra ✦✦✦✦
On *Frank Black*, Charles Thompson (formerly Black Francis of the Pixies) brings the pop undercurrents that have always floated through his music to the forefront. The sonic onslaught of the Pixies is here in small doses (portions of "Los Angeles" and "Parry the Wind High, Low," "Czar," and the Iggy Pop tribute "Ten Percenter"), but there are more Lennon, Bowie, Brian Wilson, and surf-rock influences than Iggy; even the Ramones tribute is a lovely pop number. "Los Angeles" encapsulates all of the album into one track; it begins with an acoustic folk section, slams into a punkish verse, and ends with a gorgeous Beatlesque coda. That Thompson can pull it off all in one song *and* make it work says volumes for his talents. — *Stephen Thomas Erlewine*

● **Teenager of the Year** / 1994 / Elektra ✦✦✦✦
Frank Black's second album is a wildly ambitious and eclectic piece of guitar-pop, ranging from the full-throttle roar of "Whatever Happened to Pong?" and "Thalassocracy" to the pure pop of "Headache" and the gorgeous, winding melodies of "Speedy Marie." It might be a little long, but *Teenager of the Year* is packed with thrilling, innovative pop. —*Stephen Thomas Erlewine*

Ritchie Blackmore

b. Apr. 14, 1945, Weston-Super-Mare, Avon, England
Hard Rock, Heavy Metal
British guitarist Ritchie Blackmore started out as a session player and then was a cofounder of the hard rock group Deep Purple in 1968. With Deep Purple, he made the albums *Shades of Deep Purple* (1968), *The Book of Taliesyn* (1969), *Deep Purple* (1969), *Deep Purple the Royal-Philharmonic Orchestra "Concerto for Group and Orchestra"* (1970), *Purple In Rock, Fireball* (1971), *Machine Head* (1972), *Purple Passages* (1972), *Made In Japan* (1973), *Who Do We Think We Are?* (1973), *Burn* (1974), and *Stormbringer* (1974) before leaving the group in April 1975. In Los Angeles in 1975, he took over the New York band Elf, replaced the guitarist, and renamed the resulting heavy metal quintet Ritchie Blackmore's Rainbow. Personnel would change frequently during the band's existence. The first edition featured Ronnie James Dio (born Ronald Padavona, Sept. 10, 1949, Cortland, NY) (vocals), Gary Driscoll (drums), Craig Gruber (bass), and Mickey Lee Soule (keyboards). They made the first album, *Ritchie Blackmore's Rainbow*. Driscoll, Gruber, and Soule then departed and were replaced by Jim Bain (bass), Tony Carey (keyboards), and former Jeff Beck Group drummer Cozy Powell (b. Dec. 29, 1947, Cirencester, England) for the second album, *Rainbow Rising* (1976), and the third, *On Stage*, which made the U.K. Top Ten. (From the third album on, the band was credited only as "Rainbow.") Carey and Bain then left and were replaced by David Stone (keyboards) and Bob Daisley (bass) for the fourth album, *Long Live Rock 'N' Roll* (1978), another Top Ten U.K. hit, after which, Daisley and Stone left. In 1979, Blackmore, Dio, and Powell added former Deep Purple bassist Roger Glover (b. Nov. 30, 1945, Brecon, South Wales) and Don Airey (keyboards), and started to make the fifth album, the U.K. Top Ten *Down to Earth*, but Dio left during the recording sessions and was replaced by Graham Bonnet. The album included two U.K. Top Ten singles, "Since You've Been Gone" and "All Night Long." Powell and Bonnet left in 1980 and were replaced by Bob Rondinelli (drums) and Joe Lynn Turner (vocals), and the lineup of Blackmore, Glover, Airey, Rondinelli, and Turner made the sixth album and fourth U.K. Top Ten LP *Difficult to Cure*, in 1981. The album produced the U.K. Top Ten single "I Surrender." Then Airey left and was replaced by David Rosenthal. In 1982, Blackmore, Glover, Rondinelli, Turner, and Rosenthal made their seventh album and fifth U.K. Top Ten, *Straight Between the Eyes*. The eighth album, *Bent out of Shape*, was released in 1983 and featured the band's first U.S. Top 40 hit, "Stone Cold." In 1984, Blackmore disbanded Rainbow and joined a reformed version of Deep Purple, participating in the albums *Perfect Strangers* (1984), *The House of Blue Light* (1987), *Nobody's Perfect* (1988), *Slaves and Masters* (1990), and *The Battle Rages On* (1993). —*William Ruhlmann*

● **Take It!** / 1994 / RPM ✦✦✦✦
Long before reaching superstardom with Deep Purple, Ritchie Blackmore, along with Jimmy Page, was one of the hottest session guitarists of the British Invasion. Blackmore didn't play on nearly as many hits as Page, but his vicious, lightning R&B runs during this time were, arguably, just as exciting and accomplished. Blackmore saw most of his duty as a member of the predominantly instrumental combo the Outlaws (who have CD reissue compilations of their own in the U.K.), and on sessions produced by legendary eccentric Joe Meek. Most of the material on this 24-track disc is compiled from excruciatingly rare 45s bearing Meek's credit. The material, it must be said, is dire, more often than not. Meek favored no-talent teen idols, and while Blackmore's leads often gave the sessions a lift, they're usually pretty brief. When he's given a free hand to unleash some solos, the results can be pretty thrilling, as on the Outlaws' "Shake With Me" (with a solo that ranks among the most devastating of the mid-'60s), Heinz's "I Get Up In The Morning," and his menacing instrumental version of Grieg's "Hall Of The Mountain King" classical theme (recorded with the Lancasters). There are also a couple of radio broadcasts of the Outlaws backing Gene Vincent—decent performances, lousy

fidelity. With thorough, loving liner notes, this has its moments, but its appeal is undoubtedly limited to a pretty specialized niche. —*Richie Unterberger*

Otis Blackwell

b. 1931, Brooklyn, NY
R&B, Rock & Roll
One of the true songwriting geniuses of the rocking 1950s (he wrote Elvis Presley's "Don't Be Cruel" and "All Shook Up," "Great Balls Of Fire" for Jerry Lee Lewis, and Little Willie John's "Fever"), Otis Blackwell also recorded as a vocalist (his 1953 rendition of "Daddy Rollin' Stone" for Joe Davis was later revived by the Who). A debilitating stroke has greatly limited Blackwell's activities of late. —*Bill Dahl*

● **Otis Blackwell 1953-55** / Flyright ✦✦✦✦
Nice selection of the R&B songsmith's own early output for the labels of Joe Davis. —*Bill Dahl*

The Blasters

Group, Roots-Rock
Among the rock bands that emerged from the Los Angeles scene in the early '80s, the Blasters were the most roots-conscious, producing a sound akin to '50s rockabilly and other 25-year-old musical styles. The group was led by the Alvin brothers (Phil [b. Downey, California], who sang and played rhythm guitar, and Dave [b. 1955, Los Angeles, California], who played lead guitar and wrote songs) and included John Bazz (bass), Bill Bateman (drums), and Gene Taylor (b. Forth Worth, Texas) (piano).
The group issued the album *American Music* (1980) on the local Rollin' Rock label, then switched to Slash for *The Blasters* (1981), which then was included in a licensing/distribution deal with Warner Bros. Records. The Blasters drew national attention in 1982, when the album reached the Top 40. They released a live EP of rock & roll covers later that year, then returned in 1983 with *Non Fiction*, which was dominated by Dave Alvin's songs. Those songs, steeped in rock, country, and blues traditions, also commented trenchantly on the current state of the American dream in much the same way Bruce Springsteen was doing at the time. They earned the Blasters greater critical respect, though sales did not expand. After *Hard Line* (1985) also proved to be a sales disappointment, Dave Alvin decamped in 1986 to join X. Phil Alvin kept the band going by hiring another guitarist, Hollywood Fats (born Michael Mann, 1954—d. Dec. 8, 1986), who died a few months later. Dave Alvin returned for a few gigs, then former X guitarist Billy Zoom took his place, but the Blasters had ceased to be a full-time entity. Both Dave and Phil Alvin have released solo albums. —*William Ruhlmann*

○ **American Music** / 1980 / Rollin' Rock ✦✦✦✦
○ **The Blasters** / 1981 / Slash ✦✦✦✦
You might have thought the Blasters had been in suspended animation for 25 years when their major label debut turned up in late 1981 sounding for all the world like something cut in the Sun Studios in Memphis in 1956. Dave Alvin knew all the licks and his brother Phil had the country/R&B wail down. Best of all, you couldn't tell the oldies from Dave's newly written classics. Welcome to the birth of rock & roll, all over again. —*William Ruhlmann*

Over There [Live] / Oct. 1982 / Slash ✦✦✦
On this six-song EP, recorded May 22, 1982, at the Venue in London, the Blasters take on such '50s rock 'n' roll classics as Jerry Lee Lewis's "High School Confidential" and Little Richard's "Keep A-Knockin'." The band's fidelity to their influences does not dampen their enthusiasm—they may be looking back, but they're bringing the old sound back alive. Maybe the best way to experience this band was live, not on record, at least in their early days, and this recording catches them at a fiery peak. —*William Ruhlmann*

Non Fiction / 1983 / Slash ✦✦✦
Time to start fulfilling all that potential, and the Blasters here explicitly become the mouthpiece for Dave Alvin's neo-rockabilly vision. But the problem is, how do you move beyond your roots while taking them with you? —*William Ruhlmann*

Hard Line / 1985 / Slash ✦✦
Somehow, the Blasters could never make up their minds whether they were neo or retro, whether they wanted to expand beyond their influences or just copy them. By the end of this confused, if earnest collection, they've covered John Mellencamp and declared

"Rock And Roll Will Stand." It did, but the Blasters did not. — *William Ruhlmann*

● **The Blasters Collection** / 1991 / Slash ◆◆◆◆
One of the leading American "roots" bands of the '80s, this group's anthemic no-frills rock music sounds purer and more real than ever in the post-Milli Vanilli age. — *Jeff Tamarkin*

Mary J. Blige

b. 1971, Atlanta, GA
Urban
Crowned the new "Queen of Hip-Hop Soul," Mary J. Blige enjoyed a breakout year in 1992 with *What's the 411?* Such singles as "Reminisce" and "Real Love" thrust the Atlanta-born singer into the spotlight at age 21. She was raised in Yonkers and performed in local groups before making her debut for the Uptown label. The album went platinum and a remixed version was later issued. The single "Reminisce" had a second life when it was reworked and re-done in a rap version by the duo of Pete Rock and C.L. Smooth. — *Ron Wynn*

● **What's the 411?** / 1992 / Uptown/MCA ◆◆◆◆
○ **My Life** / 1994 / Uptown/MCA ◆◆◆◆

Blind Faith

Group, Rock & Roll, Art-Rock/Progressive-Rock
The calculated grafting of ex-Cream members Eric Clapton (b.Mar 30, 1945, Ripley, Surrey, England) (guitar, vocal) and Ginger Baker (b.Aug 19, 1939, Lewisham, England) (percussion) to ex-Traffic member Steve Winwood (b.May 12, 1948, Birmingham, England) (keyboards, guitar, vocal) and bassist/violinist Rick Grech (b.Nov 1, 1945, Bordeaux, France, d.Mar 17, 1990) of the popular British group Family brought the term "supergroup" to new levels of hype. The talent involved in this amalgamation was quite impressive, but the cynical marketing minds behind this appropriately named fabrication failed to consider natural group chemistry. The volatile personalities in the lineup helped ensure that Blind Faith would be nothing more than an interesting one-off. Blind Faith debuted with a free concert before 100,000 people in London's Hyde Park on June 7, 1969. The band made an auspicious live U.S. debut, selling out Madison Square Garden on July 12. But things soured quickly, with the members going their separate ways at the conclusion of their 20-concert, six-week US tour on August 24, and Blind Faith became yet another historical footnote in the ongoing marriage of commerce and artistic expression. In spite of unrealistic pressure to live up to fan expectations, Blind Faith delivered a single, self-titled album in July 1969 that at times almost made good on its perceived potential. It still holds up today as a listening experience, thanks to Clapton's inspiring "Presence of the Lord," Winwood's reading of Buddy Holly's "Well All Right," and his own plaintive "Can't Find My Way Home." — *Rick Clark*

● **Blind Faith** / Jul. 1969 / RSO ◆◆◆◆
More than a quarter century after the release of Blind Faith's first and last album, all the stories of hype and manipulation pall before the album's enduring appeal. Steve Winwood is especially impressive, contributing three compositions, "Had To Cry Today," "Can't Find My Way Home," and "Sea Of Joy," that continue to rank among his best, and singing with his usual soulfulness. Eric Clapton's "Presence Of The Lord" is also a perennial in his repertoire, and his guitar playing throughout the record is distinctive and impressive. If Ginger Baker overplays somewhat for contemporary tastes (especially on his 15-minute showcase, "Do What You Like"), late-'60s tastes were more accommodating, and Baker nevertheless demonstrates why he is among the handful of great drummers in rock. And whatever you think of the hype, the album was a notable success. — *William Ruhlmann*

Blind Melon

Group, Rock & Roll
Although they may vehemently disagree, Blind Melon (comprising singer Shannon Hoon, Roger Stevens [guitar], Christopher Thorn [guitar], Brad Smith [bass], and Glen Graham [drums]) fits neatly into the new-hippie movement of the early '90s. While their music is not psychedelic like the Grateful Dead's, Jefferson Airplane's, or even Phish's, it has the same vibe, the same feeling—a call for love, peace, understanding, and good, rocking times. Blind Melon has a harder, guitar-based edge than most hippies, which explains why Axl Rose championed them and featured their lead

singer, Shannon Hoon, in Guns N' Roses' single and video, "Don't Cry." If anything, Blind Melon's 1993 breakthrough hit single, the breezy "No Rain," is deceiving; it may capture their spirit faithfully, but the rest of their music favors louder, more meandering guitar jams like the follow-up single, "Tones of Home." Blind Melon released their second album, *Soup*, late in the summer of 1995. — *Stephen Thomas Erlewine*

Blind Melon / Sep. 14, 1992 / Capitol ◆◆◆

Blondie

Group, Dance-Pop, New Wave, Pop/Rock
Blondie was the most commercially successful band to emerge from the much vaunted punk/new wave movement of the late '70s. The group was formed in New York City in August 1974 by singer Deborah Harry (b. Jul. 1, 1945, Miami) (formerly of Wind in the Willows) and guitarist Chris Stein (b. Jan. 5, 1950, Brooklyn) out of the remnants of Harry's previous group, the Stilettos. The lineup fluctuated over the next year. Drummer Clement Burke (b. Nov. 24, 1955, New York) joined in May 1975. Bassist Gary Valentine joined in August. In October, keyboard player James Destri (b. Apr. 13, 1954) joined, to complete the initial permanent lineup. They released their first album, *Blondie*, on Private Stock Records in December 1976. In July 1977, Valentine was replaced by Frank Infante.

In August, Chrysalis Records bought their contract from Private Stock and in October reissued *Blondie* and released the second album, *Plastic Letters*. Blondie expanded to a sextet in November with the addition of bassist Nigel Harrison (born Princes Risborough, Buckinghamshire, England), as Infante switched to guitar. Blondie broke commercially in the U.K. in March 1978, when their cover of Randy and the Rainbows' 1963 hit "Denise," renamed "Denis," became a U.K. Top Ten hit, as did *Plastic Letters*, followed by a second U.K. Top Ten, "(I'm Always Touched by Your) Presence, Dear." Blondie turned to U.K. producer/songwriter Mike Chapman for their third album, *Parallel Lines*, which was released in September 1978 and eventually broke them worldwide. "Picture This" became a U.K. Top 40 hit, and "Hanging on the Telephone" made the U.K. Top Ten, but it was the album's third single, the disco-influenced "Heart of Glass," that took Blondie to #1 in both the U.K. and the U.S. "Sunday Girl" hit #1 in the U.K. in May, and "One Way or Another" hit the U.S. Top 40 in August. Blondie followed with their fourth album, *Eat to the Beat*. Its first single, "Dreaming," went Top Ten in the U.K., Top 40 in the U.S. The second U.K. single, "Union City Blue," went Top 40. In March 1980, the third U.K. single from *Eat to the Beat*, "Atomic," became the group's third British #1. (It later made the U.S. Top 40.)

Meanwhile, Harry was collaborating with German disco producer Giorgio Moroder on "Call Me," the theme from the movie *American Gigolo*. It became Blondie's second transatlantic chart topper. Blondie's fifth album, *Autoamerican*, was released in November 1980, and its first single was the reggaeish tune "The Tide Is High," which went to #1 in the U.S. and U.K. The second single was the rap-oriented "Rapture," which topped the U.S. pop charts and went Top Ten in the U.K. But the band's eclectic style reflected a diminished participation by its members—Infante sued, charging that he wasn't being used on the records, though he settled and stayed in the lineup. But in 1981, the members of Blondie worked on individual projects, notably Harry's gold-selling solo album, *KooKoo*. *The Best of Blondie* was released in the fall of the year. *The Hunter*, Blondie's sixth and last new album, was released in July 1982, preceded by the single "Island of Lost Souls," a Top 40 hit in the U.S. and U.K. "War Child" also became a Top 40 hit in the U.K., but *The Hunter* was a commercial disappointment. At the same time, Stein became seriously ill with the genetic disease pemphigus. As a result, Blondie broke up in October 1982, with Deborah Harry launching a part-time solo career while caring for Stein, who eventually recovered. — *William Ruhlmann*

○ **Blondie** / Dec. 1976 / Chrysalis ◆◆◆◆
If new wave was about reconfiguring and recontextualizing simple pop/rock forms of the '50s and '60s in new, ironic, and aggressive ways, then Blondie, which took the girl-group style of the early and mid-'60s and added a '70s archness, fit right in. True punksters may have deplored the group early on (they never had the hip cachet of Talking Heads or even the Ramones), but Blondie's secret weapon, which was deployed increasingly over their career, was a canny pop straddle—they sent the music up and celebrated it at the same time. So, for instance, songs like "X Of-

fender" (their first single) and "In The Flesh" (their first hit, in Australia) had the tough-girl-with-a-tender-heart tone of the Shangri-Las (Brill Building songwriter Ellie Greenwich even sang backup on the latter), while going one step too far into hard-edged decadence—that is, if you chose to see that. The whole point was that you could take Blondie either way. —*William Ruhlmann*

○ **Plastic Letters** / Oct. 1977 / Chrysalis ✦✦✦
Blondie's second album was a less distinctive version of its first, matching the first record's bright, sharp production (courtesy of Richard Gottehrer), but marking a fall-off in songwriting. The two best tracks—both UK hits—were "Denis," a remake of an oldie, and "(I'm Always Touched By Your) Presence, Dear," written by departed bass player Gary Valentine, and that didn't bode well. Nevertheless, those songs were enough to assure the album's British success and to make some noise in the U.S. But Blondie would take a distinctly different approach next time out. —*William Ruhlmann*

☆ **Parallel Lines** / Sep. 1978 / Chrysalis ✦✦✦✦✦
Blondie turned to British pop producer Mike Chapman for their third album, on which they abandoned any pretensions to new wave legitimacy (just in time, given the decline of the new wave) and emerged as a pure pop band. But it wasn't just Chapman that made *Parallel Lines* Blondie's best album; it was the band's own songwriting, including Deborah Harry, Chris Stein, and James Destri's "Picture This," Harry and Stein's "Heart Of Glass," and Harry and new bass player Nigel Harrison's "One Way Or Another," plus two contributions from non-band-member Jack Lee, "Will Anything Happen?" and "Hanging On The Telephone." That was enough to give Blondie a #1 on both sides of the Atlantic with "Heart Of Glass" and three more U.K. hits, but what impresses is the album's depth and consistency—album tracks like "Fade Away And Radiate" and "Just Go Away" are as impressive as the songs pulled for singles. The result is state-of-the-art pop-rock circa 1978, with Harry's tough girl glamour setting the pattern that would be exploited over the next decade by a host of successors led by Madonna. —*William Ruhlmann*

○ **Eat to the Beat** / Oct. 1979 / Chrysalis ✦✦✦
Just as Blondie's second album, *Plastic Letters*, was a pale imitation of their debut, *Blondie*, *Eat To The Beat*, their fourth album, was a second-hand version of their breakthrough third album, *Parallel Lines*: one step forward, half a step back. There was an attempt, on such songs as "The Hardest Part" and "Atomic," to recreate the rock-disco fusion of the group's one major U.S. hit, "Heart Of Glass," without similar success, and elsewhere, the band just tried to cover too many stylistic bases. The British, who had long since been converted, made *Eat To The Beat* another chart-topper, but in the U.S., which still saw Blondie as a slightly comic one-hit wonder, the album was greeted for what it was—slick corporate rock without the tangy flavor that had made *Parallel Lines* such ear candy. —*William Ruhlmann*

Autoamerican / Nov. 1980 / Chrysalis ✦✦✦
The basic Blondie sextet was augmented, or replaced, by a dozen session musicians for the group's fifth album, *Autoamerican*, on which they continued to expand their stylistic range, with greater success, at least on certain tracks, than they had on *Eat To The Beat*. The rap pastiche "Rapture" and the Caribbean-flavored "The Tide Is High" both went to #1 on the singles charts, but they are the only memorable tracks on an album that leads off with a string-filled instrumental and also finds Deborah Harry crooning ersatz '20s pop on "Here's Looking At You" and tackling Broadway show music in a cover of "Follow Me" from *Camelot*. What a mess. —*William Ruhlmann*

★ **The Best of Blondie** / 1981 / Chrysalis ✦✦✦✦✦
All of the hits, and that's the best way to hear this creative singles band. —*Jeff Tamarkin*

The Hunter / Jul. 1982 / Chrysalis ✦✦
Autoamerican was Blondie's last real album, after which the band collapsed in legal problems and solo aspirations. *The Hunter* was only made because they still owed Chrysalis an album on their contract, and it sounds like the obligatory record it was. "Island Of Lost Souls" (the album's only U.S. singles chart entry) was a try at remaking "The Tide Is High," and "The Beast" tried to recreate at least the rap section of "Rapture." Elsewhere, Deborah Harry and Co. scraped the bottom of their songwriting barrel for an incomprehensible science fiction epic ("Dragonfly") and other second-rate material. —*William Ruhlmann*

Live! / 1988 / MCA ✦
Once More into the Bleach / 1988 / Chrysalis
Blonde & Beyond / Nov. 16, 1993 / Chrysalis ✦✦✦
Although it is a collection of rarities, outtakes, B-sides, and forgotten singles, *Blonde & Beyond* contains enough great music to make the disc enjoyable even to casual Blondie fans. —*Stephen Thomas Erlewine*

● **Platinum Collection** / Nov. 1, 1994 / EMI ✦✦✦✦
A double-CD, 47-track collection built around Blondie's singles, including every one of their U.S. and U.K. A-sides and B-sides. Not a definitive best-of, as it excludes album tracks from consideration, but pretty close. Serious fans will be most interested in five 1975 demos, recorded before the band's first LP. Bootlegged in the past, these include "Once I Had a Love," an early version of "Heart Of Glass," and a cover of the Shangri-La's' "Out In The Streets." Also of interest to fanatics are the extensive liner notes, including a detailed family tree and lengthy comments from everyone in the band except Harry and Stein. —*Richie Unterberger*

The Remix Project / 1995 / Chrysalis

Blood, Sweat & Tears

Group, Pop/Rock
For a brief period at the end of the '60s and the start of the '70s, Blood, Sweat & Tears, which fused a rock & roll rhythm section to a horn section, held out the promise of a jazz-rock fusion that could storm the pop charts. The band was organized in New York in 1967 out of the remnants of the Blues Project by keyboard player/singer Al Kooper (b. Feb. 5, 1944, Brooklyn, NY) and guitarist Steve Katz (b. May 9, 1945, Brooklyn, NY) of that group and saxophonist Fred Lipsius (b. Nov. 19, 1944, New York, NY). The rhythm section consisted of bassist Jim Fielder (b. Oct. 4, 1947, Denton, TX) and drummer Bobby Colomby (b. Dec. 20, 1944, New York, NY), and the horn section was filled out by trumpeters Randy Brecker (b. Nov. 27, 1945, Philadelphia, PA) and Jerry Weiss (b. May 1, 1946, New York) and trombonist Dick Halligan (b. Aug. 29, 1943, Troy, NY). This eight-piece band signed to Columbia Records and recorded BS&T's debut album, *Child Is Father To The Man*, which was released in February 1968. Cofounder Kooper then departed, and the group was reorganized. Singer David Clayton-Thomas (b. David Thomsett, Sept. 13, 1941, Surrey, England) was added, Halligan moved to the keyboards, and trumpeters Chuck Winfield (b. Feb. 5, 1943, Monessen, PA) and Lew Soloff (b. Feb. 20, 1944, Brooklyn, NY) replaced Brecker and Weiss, with Jerry Hyman (b. May 19, 1947, Brooklyn, NY) being added on trombone. This nine-piece unit, working with producer James William Guercio, made BS&T's self-titled second album, released in January 1969. It was a runaway hit, spawning three gold-selling Top Ten singles, "You've Made Me So Very Happy," "Spinning Wheel," and "And When I Die," selling three million copies and winning the Grammy Award for Album of the Year. It was also BS&T's highwater mark. Guercio left to work on a similar concept with Chicago Transit Authority, and BS&T increasingly became a backup group for Clayton-Thomas. Nevertheless, the third album, *Blood, Sweat & Tears 3* (1970), and the fourth, *Blood, Sweat & Tears 4* (1971), were substantial hits. Clayton-Thomas went solo in early 1972, but returned in 1974. Numerous other personnel changes took place, as the group's commercial fortunes gradually declined. BS&T left Columbia after the release of its ninth album, *More Than Ever* in 1976 and signed to ABC Records, for which it made *Brand New Day* (1977). From the late '70s on, BS&T existed largely as a group name for the concert activities of Clayton-Thomas and Colomby, who retained rights to the name. —*William Ruhlmann*

○ **Child Is Father to the Man** / Feb. 1968 / Columbia ✦✦✦✦
This is keyboard player/singer/arranger Al Kooper's finest work, an album on which he moves the folk-blues-rock amalgamation of the Blues Project into even wider pastures, taking in classical and jazz elements (including strings and horns), all without losing the pop essence that makes the hybrid work. This is one of the great albums of the eclectic post-*Sgt. Pepper* era of the late '60s, a time when you could borrow styles from Greenwich Village contemporary folk to San Francisco acid-rock and mix them into what seemed to have the potential to become a new American musical form. It's Kooper's bluesy songs, such as "I Love You More Than You'll Ever Know" and "I Can't Quit Her," and his singing, that are the primary focus, but the album is an aural delight. This is the sound of a group of virtuosos enjoying themselves in the newly

open possibilities of pop music. Maybe it couldn't have lasted; anyway, it didn't. — *William Ruhlmann*

○ **Blood, Sweat & Tears** / Jan. 1969 / Columbia ✦✦✦✦
Arguably, the BS&T that made this self-titled second album, consisting of five of the eight original members and four newcomers, including singer David Clayton-Thomas, was really a different group from the one that made the debut album, *Child Is Father To The Man*, largely under the direction of singer/songwriter/keyboard player/arranger Al Kooper. BS&T Mach II had certain similarities to the original: the musical mixture of classical, jazz, and rock elements was still apparent, and the interplay between the horns and the keyboards was still occurring, even if those instruments were being played by different people. Kooper was even still present as an arranger on two tracks, notably the initial hit "You've Made Me So Very Happy." But the second BS&T, under the aegis of producer James William Guercio, was a less adventurous unit, and, as fronted by Clayton-Thomas, a far more commercial one. Not only did the album contain three songs that neared the top of the charts as singles—"Happy," "Spinning Wheel," and "And When I Die"—but the whole album, including an arrangement of "God Bless The Child" and the radical rewrite of Traffic's "Smiling Phases," was wonderfully accessible. It was a repertoire to build a career on, and BS&T did exactly that, although they never came close to equalling this album. — *William Ruhlmann*

Blood, Sweat & Tears 3 / Jun. 1970 / Columbia ✦✦✦
Blood, Sweat & Tears had a hard act to follow in recording their third album. Nevertheless, BS&T constructed a convincing, if not quite as impressive, companion to their previous hit. David Clayton-Thomas remained an enthusiastic blues shouter, and the band still managed to put together lively arrangements, especially on the Top 40 hits "Hi-De-Ho" and "Lucretia Mac Evil." Elsewhere, they recreated the previous album's jazzing up of Laura Nyro ("He's A Runner") and Traffic ("40,000 Headmen"), although their pretentiousness, on the extended "Symphony/Sympathy For The Devil," and their tendency to borrow other artists' better-known material (James Taylor's "Fire And Rain") rather than generating more of their own, were warning signs for the future. In the meantime, *BS&T 3* was another chart-topping gold hit. — *William Ruhlmann*

Blood, Sweat & Tears 4 / Jun. 1971 / Columbia ✦✦
Having relied largely on outside songwriting for its last two wildly successful albums, Blood, Sweat & Tears decided (as many groups had before) to bring some of that song publishing income into the family by writing their own material. Singer David Clayton-Thomas contributed the Top 40 hit "Go Down Gamblin'," and he and keyboard player Dick Halligan collaborated on another chart entry, "Lisa, Listen To Me." Ex-bandleader Al Kooper even contributed a track, "John The Baptist (Holy John)." But Side Two was given over largely to songs by guitarist Steve Katz that were substandard, and the band's cohesion seemed to be disintegrating. Although the album scraped the Top 10 briefly and went gold, it marked the end of BS&T's period of wide commercial success on records. By the next outing, Clayton-Thomas had quit and the band's heyday was behind it. — *William Ruhlmann*

● **Blood, Sweat & Tears' Greatest Hits** / Feb. 1972 / Columbia ✦✦✦✦
Sometimes, a greatest hits set is timed perfectly to gather together a recording artist's most successful and familiar performances just at the point when that artist has passed the point of his maximum exposure to the public, but before the public memory has had a chance to fade. That was the case when Columbia Records assembled this compilation for release in early 1972. At that point, Blood, Sweat & Tears had released four albums and scored six Top 40 hits, each of which is heard here. But lead singer David Clayton-Thomas had just quit the group, so that the unit which recorded songs like "You've Made Me So Very Happy" was not working together anymore. And even when Clayton-Thomas returned, the band would continue to decline commercially. As such, BS&T's *Greatest Hits* captures the band's peak in 11 selections—seven singles chart entries, plus two album tracks from the celebrated debut album when Al Kooper helmed the group, and two more from the Grammy-winning multi-platinum second album. Using the short single edits of songs like "And When I Die" emphasizes their radio-ready punch over the more extended suite-like arrangements on the albums, but this selection gains in focus what it lacks in ambition. For the millions who learned to love

BS&T in 1969 when they were all over AM radio, this is the ideal selection of their most accessible material. — *William Ruhlmann*

New Blood / Oct. 1972 / Columbia ✦✦
No Sweat / Aug. 1973 / Columbia ✦
Mirror Image / Aug. 1974 / Columbia ✦
New City / May 1975 / Columbia ✦✦
More Than Ever / Jul. 1976 / Columbia ✦✦
Brand New Day / 1977 / ABC ✦✦
Nuclear Blues / 1980 / LAX ✦✦

Live & Improvised / May 7, 1991 / Columbia/Legacy ✦✦
A two-disc live set of Blood, Sweat & Tears recorded in 1975, when the band was in commercial eclipse and the lineup was full of replacements for the original members. At least David Clayton-Thomas was back in the fold, so that the run-throughs of hits like "Spinning Wheel" and "You've Made Me So Very Happy" sounded authentic. But by the mid-'70s, BS&T clearly considered itself a full-fledged jazz band that happened to have a pop music repertoire, and the performances are padded with pointless, showboating solos. So, what possible purpose was there in 1991 in releasing two CDs worth of second-rate BS&T 16 years after it was recorded? (Presumably, this is the same material issued in 1976 in Holland and Japan as a two-LP set called *In Concert*, although the present package includes no reference to the earlier album.) — *William Ruhlmann*

Bloodstone

Group, Soul, R&B
Bloodstone is a pop/R&B band founded as an a cappella singing group called the Sinceres in 1962 in Kansas City, MO. The lineup was: Willis Draffen, Jr. (b. Kansas City, MO), Charles Love, Charles McCormick, Harry Williams (b. Tupelo, MS), and Roger Lee Durham (b. 1946–d. Oct. 1973). The group played in Las Vegas for a year in 1968, then relocated to Los Angeles, where they took up playing instruments (Draffen and Love, guitars; McCormick, bass; Williams and Durham, percussion) and changed their name to Bloodstone. They then moved to England and hooked up with producer Mike Vernon, best known for his work with British blues acts like Ten Years After. With him, they signed to the British Decca Records label, which released their self-titled debut album in England in 1972. British Decca's U.S. subsidiary, London Records, released their second album, *Natural High*, in the U.S. in 1973, and its title track became a gold Top Ten pop hit. "Outside Woman," from the followup album *Unreal*, made the pop Top 40, and the group's R&B Top Ten hits of the period, in addition to those two, included "Never Let You Go" (1973) and "My Little Lady" (1975). Durham died in 1973. Bloodstone released its fourth and fifth albums, *I Need Time* and *Riddle of the Sphinx*, in 1974. In 1975, Bloodstone appeared in and recorded the soundtrack for the movie *Train Ride to Hollywood*. The albums *Lullaby Broadway* and *Do You Wanna Do a Thing* followed in 1976. Bloodstone switched to Motown Records and released *Don't Stop* in 1979. In 1981, McCormick left the band, which recruited Ron Wilson (b. Los Angeles) on keyboards and vocals and Ronald Bell (b. California) on percussion and vocals. This lineup then signed to the Isley Brothers' T-Neck Records (distributed by CBS Records) for the 1982 release *We Go a Long Way Back*, which produced their final R&B Top Ten hit in the title track. — *William Ruhlmann*

Bloodstone / 1972 / Decca ✦✦✦
Natural High / 1973 / Decca ✦✦✦
Bloodstone's finest song was the title cut, a triumphant bit of wailing soul that remains a favorite among ballad fans. It momentarily put the Kansas City-cum-Los Angeles group Bloodstone into the spotlight. The remainder of the early '70s album was decent, but it didn't really matter since no one played anything except the single anyhow. — *Ron Wynn*

I Need Time / 1974 / London ✦✦
Some above-average funk and soul, propelled by drummer Steve Ferone, who was later recruited by the Average White Band. Bloodstone were among the best harmonizers on the '70s soul/R&B circuit, and their production utilized the falsetto lead against two background voices in an exceptional manner. — *Ron Wynn*

Unreal / 1974 / London ✦✦✦
The title cut boasted some intriguing lyrics, and Bloodstone did well on the soul/R&B circuit with this early '70s work. The slow tunes were sung with passion, while the uptempo numbers were

expertly produced and right in step with '70s funk arrangements. *—Ron Wynn*

Riddle of the Sphinx / 1975 / London ♦♦
The final album before Steve Ferrone left to join the Average White Band, and also the last charting album for Bloodstone for seven years. The title cut was straightforward R&B/funk, while the rest of the album blended their usual emphatic ballads with upbeat, hard-edged funk and soul. *—Ron Wynn*

Lullaby of Broadway / 1976 / Decca ♦♦

Train Ride to Hollywood / 1976 / London ♦♦♦

Do You Wanna Do a Thing / 1976 / London ♦♦

Don't Stop / 1979 / Motown ♦♦

We Go a Long Way Back / 1982 / T Neck ♦♦
Bloodstone came back from a lengthy period off the charts with this early '80s work. The title track was one of their finest slow tunes in several years, while the other cuts, especially the uptempo ones, were produced and arranged well enough to get Bloodstone back on urban radio. *—Ron Wynn*

Bloodstone's Greatest Hits / 1985 / Columbia ♦♦♦
One of the finest soul ensembles in the '70s and '80s. Bloodstone was among the few bands of its era able to survive the changes in fan interest among R&B audiences. They were never immensely popular, but enjoyed a consistent string of successful singles. Their '80s albums weren't as solidly in the soul bag as their '70s ones, but such songs as "We Go a Long Way Back" and "Go On and Cry" were about as traditional as any vocal group got in the early '80s. Both are included on this mid-'80s anthology focusing on their cuts for the Isley Brothers' I-Neck label, distributed by Columbia. *—Ron Wynn*

Luka Bloom (Barry Moore)

b. Ireland
Singer-Songwriter
Before making his American debut, Barry Moore recorded three albums in Ireland. Perhaps because his brother is the revered Irish singer Christy Moore, he changed his name to Luka Bloom—Luka is taken from Suzanne Vega's song, Bloom from James Joyce's *Ulysses*. With his literate, melodic original songs and impassioned live performances, Bloom earned a devoted following in the New York area, which led to his record contract with Reprise. While he can occasionally suffer from over-worked lyrics and a cloying cuteness, Bloom is one of the best post-punk folk performers and songwriters. *—Stephen Thomas Erlewine*

● **Riverside** / Feb. 1990 / Reprise ♦♦♦♦
Expatriate Irishman Luka Bloom cloaks his Celtic folk songs in furious strumming on his "electro-acoustic" guitar, added instrumentation, and echo effects on everything, but he is still a folkie, blowing up his feelings to heroic proportions, whether it's the autobiography of "The Man Is Alive" or the romantic fantasy of "An Irishman In Chinatown." But the content is less convincing than the expression, which is more a characteristic of rock than folk. It isn't that Bloom has much to say, it's that he's so passionate about saying it: he's more Bono than Bob Dylan. Maybe it's an Irish thing. *—William Ruhlmann*

The Acoustic Motorbike / Jan. 1992 / Reprise ♦♦♦
Having made his mark in America and moved back home to Ireland, Luka Bloom attempted to incorporate some of the spirit of the country where he spent four years into his Irish folk-rock, covering LL Cool J's "I Need Love" and the Elvis Presley hit "Can't Help Falling In Love." But in his own songs, he didn't go much beyond such surface aspects of the U.S. as Elvis and rap, preferring to devote himself to vague, clichéd lyrics of love and longing (some of them not so much rapped as recited), once again set for the most part against his aggressive guitar strumming, various acoustic instruments, and a bottom provided by an Irish bodhran, sometimes played by his brother, Christy Moore. While Bloom's second album expanded somewhat on his first record's stylistic range and maintained its urgency, it lacked the debut's exuberance—Bloom was getting more serious when what he needed to do was to get more substantive. *—William Ruhlmann*

Turf / Jun. 14, 1994 / Reprise ♦♦♦
A portrait of the Irishman as an American neo-folkie. Having experimented with extra instrumentation on his first two albums, Luka Bloom made a man-with-guitar record his third time out, the better to emphasize his songs, which combined a strong folk tra-

ditionalism (one was called "Black Is The Colour [of my true love's hair]," another described an encounter with a mermaid) with an Amer-Irish social concern ("Freedom Song" mixed the stories of political activists from each country, "Background Noise" was a tale of violence applicable anywhere, even if it referred to the Irish Troubles). All of this made for a more focused record than Bloom's second album, although his debut remained his most satisfying effort. *—William Ruhlmann*

Michael Bloomfield

b. Jul. 28, 1944, **d.** Feb. 15, 1981
Blues Rock
Bloomfield was one of the first White players who got right into the Chicago blues scene and could actually play the music. As lead guitar for the Butterfield Blues Band, he exerted a powerful influence with far-reaching effects on young rock guitarists. He almost single-handedly pioneered the extended guitar solo, and introduced many Western ears to the sounds of the Far East with his sitar-inspired solos. The Butterfield Blues Band album *East-West* (and the lovely title cut) broke new ground in the progressive rock scene—psychedelic rock was born. Bloomfield also backed Bob Dylan in his move into electric-land on *Highway 61 Revisited*, one of the landmarks of modern rock music. He went on to record albums with his own band, the Electric Flag, and with others (*Super Session* w/Al Kooper). These later efforts saw only limited success. He was best at blues, and those first two Butterfield albums mark a high point. Part of Bloomfield's enormous influence on younger rock guitar players was due to his very outgoing and generous spirit. Bloomfield was one of those rare performers who cared as much for sharing his vision with others as he did for the music he loved. *—Michael Erlewine*

● **Super Session** / 1968 / Columbia ♦♦♦♦
Al Kooper was the mastermind behind this appropriately named album, one side of which features his "spontaneous" studio collaboration with Mike Bloomfield and the other a session with Stephen Stills. The recordings have an off-the-cuff energy that displays the inventiveness of the two guitarists to best advantage. The best-selling recording of Bloomfield's career, it inspired the follow-up *The Live Adventures of Mike Bloomfield and Al Kooper*. *—Jeff Tamarkin*

○ **It's Not Killing Me** / 1969 / CBS ♦♦♦♦

The Live Adventures of Mike Bloomfield and Al Kooper / 1969 / Columbia ♦♦

Triumverate / 1973 / Columbia ♦♦♦
The late guitarist Mike Bloomfield, blues master John Hammond, and the timeless New Orleans funk of Dr. John blend well on this one-time-only outing. *—Jeff Tamarkin*

Try It Before You Buy It / 1975 / One Way ♦♦

Mill Valley Session / 1976 / Polydor ♦♦♦

If You Love Those Blues, Play 'Em As You Please / 1977 / Guitar Player ♦♦♦

Analine / 1977 / Takoma ♦♦

Michael Bloomfield / 1978 / Takoma ♦♦♦

Between the Hard Place and the Ground / 1979 / Takoma ♦♦

Living in the Fast Lane / 1980 / AJK ♦♦♦
Michael Bloomfield was a pioneer in blues-rock, one of the performers who found a way to maintain his own sound while paying tribute to the blues greats that created the music he idolized. The 10 tracks presented on *Living In The Fast Lane* weren't as vital as his earlier material, but were done with the same intensity and passion that marked all his numbers. They were backed on several cuts by Duke Tito and the Marin Country Playboys, while on "When I Get Home," the Singers of The Church of God In Christ joined lead vocalist Roger Troy for a rousing, spirit-filled performance that was the album's high point. *—Ron Wynn*

○ **Cruisin' for a Bruisin'** / 1981 / Takoma ♦♦♦♦

○ **Bloomfield: a Retrospective** / 1984 / CBS ♦♦♦♦

Don't Say That I Ain't Your Man / 1994 / Sony ♦♦♦
15 tracks covering the pioneering blues-rock guitarist's '60s work, which was by far his best and most influential. Bloomfield worked with a bunch of bands during the decade, and the compilation flits rather hurriedly from his contributions to the Paul Butterfield Blues Band and Electric Flag to his collaborations with Al Kooper and some late-'60s solo tracks (none of his groundbreaking mid-

'60s work with Dylan is here). Collectors will be interested in the first five songs, which date from previously unreleased sessions produced by John Hammond in late 1964 and early 1965. Featuring Charlie Musselwhite on harmonica, this pre-Butterfield Blues Band outfit plays convincingly, but the material is standard-issue, and Bloomfield's vocals are thin and weak (they didn't improve much over time). As befits Bloomfield's considerable but erratic talent, this is an interesting but erratic compilation; seek out the first two Paul Butterfield albums for a more cohesive showcase of his skills. —*Richie Unterberger*

Blossom Toes

Group, Psychedelic

They never had any commercial success in the U.K. or the U.S., but Blossom Toes were one of the more interesting British psychedelic groups of the late '60s. Starting as the Ingoes, just another of thousands of British R&B/beat bands of the mid-'60s, the group hooked up with legendary impresario Giorgio Gomelsky (early mentor of the Stones and manager of the Yardbirds and Soft Machine, among others) in 1966. Gomelsky changed their name and put them on his Marmalade label. Their 1967 debut LP was miles away from R&B, reflecting an extremely British whimsy and skilled, idiosyncratic songwriting more in line with Ray Davies. After some personnel changes, the group released their second (and final) album a couple years later. Another extremely accomplished work, it was markedly different in character than their first effort, showing a far more sober tone and heavier, guitar-oriented approach. The group broke up at the end of the decade; members Brian Godding and Brian Belshaw formed the equally obscure B.B. Blunder, and Godding is still active on the fringes of the British experimental rock scene. —*Richie Unterberger*

○ **We Are Ever So Clean** / 1967 / Marmalade ◆◆◆◆
Imagine the late-'60s Kinks crossed with a touch of the absurdist British wit of the Bonzo Dog Band, and you have an idea of the droll charm of Blossom Toes' debut album. Songwriters Brian Godding and Jim Cregan were the chief architects of the Toes' whimsical and melodic vision, which conjured images of a sun-drenched Summer of Love, London style. With its references to royal parks, tea time, watchmakers, intrepid balloon makers, "Mrs. Murphy's Budgerigar," and the like, it's a distinctly British brand of whimsy. It has since been revealed that session men performed a lot of these orchestral arrangements, which embellished the band's sparkling harmonies and (semi-buried) guitars. But the cello, brass, flute, and tinkling piano have a delicate beauty that serves as an effective counterpoint. The group sings and plays as though they have wide grins on their faces, and the result is one of the happiest, most underappreciated relics of British psychedelia. —*Richie Unterberger*

○ **If Only for a Moment** / 1969 / Marmalade ◆◆◆◆
Brian Godding and Jim Cregan were still Blossom Toes' chief songwriters on their second album, but the LP stands in bold contrast to their debut in sound and attitude. Having scuttled the orchestras and developed their chops in the two-year interlude, the record bears the influence of heavy California psychedelia and Captain Beefheart with its intricate, interwoven guitar lines and occasional gruff dissonance. The more serious instrumental approach spills over to the lyrics, which are somber and at times even gloomy, occasionally reflecting the social turbulence of the late '60s, with their uncertain tenor and references to ominous "peace loving men" and "love bombs." Far less uplifting than their debut, the weighty approach is leavened by the close harmonies and sparkling guitar interplay. While not as memorable as the first album, it's above-average late-'60s psychedelia that almost acts as the downer flipside to the stoned, happy-face ambience of their early work. —*Richie Unterberger*

● **Collection** / 1988 / Decal ◆◆◆◆
The definitive anthology, packaging most of *We Are Ever So Clean* and the entirety of *If Only For A Moment*. Unfortunately, a couple minor tracks from the first LP were omitted for space reasons, but as compensation it includes the non-LP 1968 single "Postcard"/"Everyone's Leaving Me Now," which is quite similar in mood to the *Ever So Clean* songs. The double album includes an exhaustive history of the group by John Platt. —*Richie Unterberger*

Kurtis Blow

b. Aug. 9, 1959, New York, NY
Rap

Arguably rap's first crossover star, at least from a chart standpoint, New Yorker Blow emerged in the early '80s. He began doing both social protest/Afrocentric material and boasting and posturing material, though not to the degree that has since become commonplace. His landmark recording, "The Breaks," was an eye-opener for its time in terms of pace, verbal dexterity, and its rhythm track. Blow was also a big-time producer at one point, using the likes of Bob Dylan and George Clinton in guest stints and incorporating bits from television shows and cartoons in his production. Blow was finally overhauled by New School producers and rappers in the late '80s, and his early work now sounds quite dated by comparison. —*Ron Wynn*

○ **Kurtis Blow** / 1980 / Mercury ◆◆◆◆
Kurtis Blow exploded onto the fledgling rap scene with "The Breaks," still one of the rawest, most hypnotic bits of rhythm and oral narrative ever issued. Blow's defiant, posturing rap, punctuated by drums that seemed to signify an invading army, surprised, shocked and amazed listeners totally unprepared for anything so stark in 1980. An edited version only got mild pop response, but the complete single was a huge hit among black and club audiences. The song was so definitive that it rendered everything else on the LP irrelevant, even the good second single "Hard Times." —*Ron Wynn*

○ **Deuce** / 1981 / Mercury ◆◆◆◆
Things cooled quickly for Kurtis Blow following the success of "The Breaks" in 1980. He was unable to get any single from this record on the charts, even though "Rockin'" and "It's Gettin' Hot" were well produced and competently delivered. But rap was still far from being a mainstream phenomenon, and this album did very poorly commercially. —*Ron Wynn*

Tough / 1982 / Mercury ◆◆

○ **Party Time?** / 1983 / Mercury ◆◆◆◆
An ahead-of-its time collaboration between Kurtis Blow and EU, which was really a five-song EP rather than a full-length album. Rap met go-go in a rousing, nicely performed set that deserved more attention, but didn't generate much action. —*Ron Wynn*

Ego Trip / 1984 / Mercury ◆◆◆
Kurtis Blow briefly returned to the spotlight with the single "Basketball" from this LP. His brand of sparse, electro-funk rap was fading, and it was clear that Blow's skills were in production rather than performance. "Eight Million Stories" was a decent cut inspired by the old *Naked City* television series, while "Fallin' In Love Again" was among his better romantic efforts, but Blow's albums were always erratic propositions, and this one proved no different. —*Ron Wynn*

Rapper in Town / 1984 / Mercury ◆◆

America / 1985 / Mercury ◆◆◆
Consistent rap beats with poignant social commentary. —*Bil Carpenter*

Kingdom Blow / 1986 / Mercury ◆◆
Kurtis Blow's sixth Mercury LP wasn't a pretty thing to behold. He tried everything from autobiographical material ("The Bronx") to b-boy narratives ("I'm Chillin'") and novelty cuts ("Magilla Gorilla"), but nothing clicked, either commercially or aesthetically. —*Ron Wynn*

Back by Popular Demand / 1988 / Mercury ◆
The well was exhausted by the time Blowfly issued this album. His rap style, while still attractive for its clipped, brusque cadence, was wasted on forgettable material and his productions were routine. —*Ron Wynn*

★ **Best of Kurtis Blow** / 1994 / Mercury ◆◆◆◆◆
While he made many groundbreaking singles, Kurtis Blow was never a consistent album artist, making this best-of collection his definitive artistic statement. Throughout the early '80s, Blow helped define what rap could do, and these tracks confirm his status as one of hip-hop's legendary acts. —*Stephen Thomas Erlewine*

The Blue Aeroplanes

Group, Alternative Pop/Rock

The Blue Aeroplanes are an art-rock group from Bristol, England, who have drawn comparisons to critically acclaimed rock bands like the Velvet Underground because of their eclectic style and the songwriting sensibility of group leader Gerard Langley. The original core of the band included Langley's brother John on drums, Nick Jacobs on guitar, and multi-instrumentalist Dave Chapman, but personnel other than Langley has varied, and, both on records and in performances, they have always been augmented by a large cast of semi-regular sidemen. (By the time of their 1991 album *Beatsongs*, the Aeroplanes' lineup included guitarist Angelo Bruschini, guitarist Rodney Allen, bassist Andy McCreeth, drummer Paul Mulreany, and guitarist/keyboard player Alex Lee, with another eight musicians listed in the credits.) The group released *Bop Art* on the Abstract Records label in April 1984, then signed to Fire Records, for which they recorded their second album, *Tolerance* (Oct. 1986), and their third, *Spitting out Miracles* (1987), plus several EPs. *Spitting out Miracles* was their first U.S. release, followed by the compilation album *Friendloverplane* (1988) a double-LP on Fire in the U.K., reduced to a single LP on Restless in the U.S. The Blue Aeroplanes then signed to the Ensign division of Chrysalis Records and charted in the U.K. with two 1989 singles, "Jacket Hangs" and "...And Stones," as well as their 1990 and 1991 albums, *Swagger* and *Beatsongs. — William Ruhlmann*

○ **Bop Art** / 1984 / Abstract ✦✦✦✦

Lover and Confidante and Other Stories of Travel, Religion / Mar. 1986 / Fire ✦✦

Tolerance / Oct. 1986 / Fire ✦✦✦

Spitting out Miracles / 1987 / Restless ✦✦✦

● **Friendloverplane** / 1988 / Restless ✦✦✦✦
Even on this compilation of stray tracks (truncated from the double-LP version on the British Fire Records label), it's easy to hear what fans and rock critics have been raving about with regard to the Blue Aeroplanes. With their guitar-dominated pop tunes and the half-spoken, extensively enjambed lyrics of Gerard Langley, they are solidly in the tradition of electric-Bob Dylan/Velvet Underground and all that came after, serious rock with all the pretensions. In a sense, this underproduced, inconsistent collection of minor tracks is a good place to start with them, the place where they are heard in their most idiosyncratic glory, borrowing riffs from the Who, doing a letter-perfect cover of Greenwich Village folk/rocker Willie Nile's "Old Men Sleeping On The Bowery," and succeeding (when they do) more on nerve than deliberation. — *William Ruhlmann*

World View Blue / 1990 / Chrysalis ✦✦✦
Featuring eight tracks and running almost 29 minutes, this interim release is substantial enough to have been called a full-fledged album in the days before the CD, although today it's just an especially meaty EP. There are a couple of live tracks, an acoustic version of the title track, which was featured on *Swagger* (the last full-fledged album), and covers of songs by such obvious Blue Aeroplanes influences as Bob Dylan, Lou Reed, and Richard Thompson. In the original songs, one also hears less obvious influences, like British faux-punk group the Stranglers on "Razor Walk," so that this sampler has the effect of a set of sources of the Blue Aeroplanes' style. — *William Ruhlmann*

○ **Swagger** / Feb. 1990 / Chrysalis ✦✦✦✦
An excellent example of the clear-headed pop produced by the group. Guest artists include Michael Stipe of R.E.M. — *David Szatmary*

Beatsongs / 1991 / Chrysalis ✦✦✦

Life Model / 1994 / Beggars Banquet ✦✦

Blue Angel

Group, Pop/Rock
Blue Angel was a New York-based pop/rock quintet consisting of Cyndi Lauper (b. Jun. 20, 1953, Queens, NY) (vocals), Arthur Neilson (guitar), Lee Brovitz (bass), John Turi (keyboards, saxophone), and Johnny Morelli (drums). They released one self-titled album on Polydor Records in 1980. Lauper later launched a successful solo career. — *William Ruhlmann*

Blue Angel / 1980 / Polydor ✦✦✦
Blue Angel was an early showcase for Cyndi Lauper, who dominated its only album, co-writing nine of 12 tracks. Like Lauper's subsequent solo work, the music was imbued with an early-'60s girl group sound, complete with the Phil Spector/"Be My Baby" beat on "I Had A Love" and Lauper's Ronnie Spector-like vocals. Producer/engineer Roy Halee (a longtime associate of Paul Simon) recreated the sound efficiently. But unlike new-wave competitors Blondie and the Shirts, Blue Angel did nothing to update or comment on the style; they were retro and proud of it. That may have been what kept them from breaking out at the time. Three years

later, when Lauper was singing "Girls Just Want To Have Fun," she had acquired a comic sensibility and a visual style that set her apart. (Lauper re-recorded the album's leadoff track, "Maybe He'll Know," on her second solo album, *True Colors.*) — *William Ruhlmann*

Blue Cheer

Group, Hard Rock, Psychedelic, Heavy Metal
San Francisco-based Blue Cheer was what, in the late '60s, they used to call a "power trio": Dickie Peterson (b. 1948, Grand Forks, ND) (bass, vocals), Paul Whaley (drums), and Leigh Stephens (guitar). They played what later was called heavy metal, and when they debuted in January 1968 with the album *Vincebus Eruptum* and a Top 40 cover of Eddie Cochran's hit "Summertime Blues," they sounded louder and more extreme than anything that had come before them. As it turned out, they were a precursor of much that would come after. Unfortunately, Blue Cheer itself didn't get much chance to profit from its prescience. Shortly after its breakthrough, the group was wracked by personnel changes. Leigh Stephens was replaced by Randy Holden after the release of the second album, *Outsideinside* (August 1968). Holden left during the recording of the third album, and Bruce Stephens (b. 1946) (vocals, guitar), and Ralph Burns Kellogg (keyboards) joined to finish *New! Improved! Blue Cheer* (March 1969). Then Whaley quit and was replaced by Norman Mayell (b. 1942, Chicago), leaving Peterson as the only original member. Bruce Stephens quit during the recording of the fourth album, *Blue Cheer* (December 1969), and Gary L. Yoder joined to complete it. Peterson, Kellogg, Mayell, and Yoder then made *The Original Human Being* (September 1970), and *Oh! Pleasant Hope* (April 1971) before Blue Cheer broke up. Dickie Peterson reorganized a new version of the group in 1979, and in 1985, he, Whaley, and guitarist Tony Ranier released a new Blue Cheer album, *The Beast Is Back...— William Ruhlmann*

○ **Vincebus Eruptum** / Jan. 1968 / Philips ✦✦✦✦
Blue Cheer's debut psychedelic sludgefest features their explosive reworking of Eddie Cochran's "Summertime Blues." — *Rick Clark*

○ **Outsideinside** / Aug. 1968 / Philips ✦✦✦✦
Outsideinside may not have this Frisco trio's death-blast version of Eddie Cochran's classic "Summertime Blues," but there's more than enough tape-saturated hard psychedelic sludge here ("Just a Little Bit" [#92], and "The Hunter"). — *Rick Clark*

New! Improved! Blue Cheer / Mar. 1969 / Philips ✦✦✦

Blue Cheer / Dec. 1969 / Philips ✦✦

The Original Human Being / Sep. 1970 / Philips ✦✦

Oh! Pleasant Hope / Apr. 1971 / Philips ✦✦

○ **Louder Than God: Best of Blue Cheer** / 1986 / Rhino ✦✦✦✦
The fact that this collection is only available on vinyl may be a drawback for some folks, but (on one level) Blue Cheer, in all its grungy glory, makes even more sense on 8-track than on CD, so what's the complaint? After all, this one has "Just a Little Bit," and the Mercury disc doesn't. If you can find their first two albums, *Vincebus Eruptum* and *Outsideinside*, then you will have all the Blue Cheer you'll ever need. — *Rick Clark*

Blitzkrieg over Nuremberg / 1989 / Magnum ✦

● **Good Times Are So Hard to Find** / 1990 / Mercury ✦✦✦✦
This overview spans Blue Cheer's entire catalog. If only their first two albums of over-the-top psychedelic distorto-blare had been represented a little more. — *Rick Clark*

Blue Magic

Group, Soul
Blue Magic, an R&B vocal quintet whose members were Theodore Mills, Vernon Sawyer, Wendell Sawyer, Keith Beaton, and Richard Pratt, was formed in Philadelphia and signed to Atlantic Records in 1973. They hit the Top 40 of the R&B singles chart with their first three 45s before breaking through and crossing over with "Sideshow," released in April 1974, which went gold, topped the R&B charts and became a Top Ten pop hit. "Three Ring Circus," their next single, made the R&B Top Ten and the pop Top 40. Blue Magic had two more R&B chart singles in 1975 and four in 1976 before suffering a career slump, but they returned with R&B chart singles in 1981 and 1983 and made a comeback album, *From out of the Blue*, in 1989. — *William Ruhlmann*

Blue Magic / Feb. 1974 / Atco ✦✦✦
The superb debut album that launched the careers of Blue Magic. They were among the premier "sweet" soul groups, although Ted "Wizzard" Mills didn't get the buildup or hype given to the Del-

fonics' William Hart or the Stylistics' Russell Tompkins, Jr. But he could hit the same high notes and sound the same ethereal, anguished tone, which he did to perfection on the hit single "Sideshow." —*Ron Wynn*

13 Blue Magic Lane / Sep. 1975 / Atco ◆◆◆
Another superb Blue Magic album, this one included the hits "Chasin' Rainbows" and "I Like You." Ted Mills and company were keeping pace with their competitors the Delfonics, Stylistics, Spinners, and Moments, and at this point were even slightly ahead. —*Ron Wynn*

Mystic Dragons / Sep. 1976 / Atco ◆◆◆
More fine "sweet" soul, plus some red-hot dance grooves from Blue Magic, who were completing a great hit string on the WMOT label. Mills was again soaring on the ballads and perfectly in step on the uptempo cuts. Unfortunately, the coming of disco was about to pull the wheels off the soul cart. —*Ron Wynn*

Message / 1978 / Atco ◆◆◆

● **The Magic of the Blue: Greatest Hits** / 1986 / Atco ◆◆◆◆
Classy, clear Norman Harris arrangements from this Philadelphia vocal group of the '70s. Bobby Eli produced this warm love music, done at Sigma Sound and featuring "Sideshow." —*Bil Carpenter*

From out of the Blue / 1989 / Columbia ◆◆◆

Blue Nile

Group, Techno-Pop/Dance, Alternative Pop/Rock
Unlike most acts during the '80s, who depended on synthesizers and drum machines for their sound, the Blue Nile managed to create a sound that was haunting, steely cool, romantic, and melancholy. Sonically, their albums are the stuff audiophiles like. The group, founded in Glasgow, Scotland, in the early '80s, consists of singer Paul Buchanan, Robert Bell, and Paul Moore. They released their first single, "I Love This Life," on their own Peppermint Records label and saw it picked up by RSO for British distribution. Their debut album, *A Walk Across the Rooftops,* was released by Linn Products, an electronics company, in May 1984 and picked up for distribution by Virgin in the U.K., earning critical acclaim that was repeated when A&M issued it in the U.S. in June 1985. They then took four years to craft a follow-up, releasing the equally acclaimed *Hats* in October 1989 in the U.K. and January 1990 in the U.S. —*Rick Clark and William Ruhlmann*

● **A Walk Across the Rooftops** / May 1984 / A&M ◆◆◆◆
This Scottish trio's 1984 debut, originally on Linn Records, is a beautifully atmospheric collection of synth-heavy songscapes. The dichotomy between the cool synthesized musical washes (with periodic percolating drum machine parts) and the yearning, passionate (yet strangely disconnected) vocals is engaging. This album could have been the soundtrack to Jonathan Pryce's lonely quenchless dreams in the Terry Gilliam movie, *Brazil.* The Linn version sounds superior to the A&M release. —*Rick Clark*

Hats / Oct. 1989 / A&M ◆◆◆
The follow-up to *A Walk...* was five years in the making. The songs aren't as memorable, but the results are still coolly haunting. "The Downtown Lights" and "Headlights on Parade" are among the standout tracks. —*Rick Clark*

Blue Öyster Cult

Group, Hard Rock, Heavy Metal
Blue Öyster Cult was the thinking man's heavy metal group. Put together on a college campus by a couple of rock critics, it maintained a close relationship with a series of literary figures (often in the fields of science fiction and horror) including Eric Von Lustbader, Patti Smith, Michael Moorcock, and Stephen King, while turning out some of the more listenable metal music of the early and mid '70s. The band that became Blue Öyster Cult was organized in 1967 at Stony Brook College on Long Island by students (and later rock critics) Sandy Pearlman and Richard Meltzer as Soft White Underbelly and consisted of Andy Winters (bass), Donald "Buck Dharma" Roeser (guitar), John Wiesenthal (quickly replaced by Alan Lanier) (keyboards), and Albert Bouchard (drums), with Pearlman managing and Pearlman and Meltzer writing songs. Initially without a lead singer, they added Les Bronstein on vocals. This quintet signed to Elektra Records and recorded an album that was never released. They then dropped Bronstein and replaced him with their road manager, Eric Bloom, as the band's

name was changed to Oaxaca. A second Elektra album also went unreleased, though a single was issued under the name the Stalk-Forrest Group.

Cut loose by Elektra, they changed their name again, to Blue Öyster Cult, and signed to Columbia Records in late 1971, by which time Winters had been replaced by Albert Bouchard's brother Joe. *Blue Öyster Cult,* their debut album, was released in January 1972 and made the lower reaches of the charts. Columbia sent a promotional EP, *Live Bootleg,* to radio stations in October, and followed with BOC's second album, *Tyranny and Mutation,* in February 1973. Their third album, *Secret Treaties,* was released in April 1974 and became their first to break into the top 100 best-sellers. (It eventually went gold.) BOC released a live double album, *On Your Feet or on Your Knees,* in February 1975. In May 1976, came their fourth studio album, *Agents of Fortune,* including the Top 40 (Top Ten on some charts) hit single "(Don't Fear) the Reaper" (featured in the classic John Carpenter horror film *Halloween*), which became their first gold and then platinum album. (*On Your Feet* went gold shortly after.) BOC's sixth overall album, *Spectres,* was released in October 1977 and went gold in January 1978. In September 1978 came a second live album, *Some Enchanted Evening,* which eventually would become BOC's second million-seller, followed by the studio album *Mirrors* in June 1979. A year later, BOC released its ninth album, *Cultosaurus Erectus,* with the gold *Fire of Unknown Origin,* containing the Top 40 hit "Burnin' for You," following in June 1981.

In the summer of 1981, drummer Albert Bouchard was replaced by the band's tour manager and lighting designer, Rick Downey. BOC's third live album, *Extraterrestrial Live,* was released in April 1982, followed by the studio album *The Revolution by Night* in October 1983. Downey left in 1984 and was replaced in '85 by Jimmy Wilcox. The same year, Lanier left and was replaced by Tommy Zvonchek. BOC released its 13th album, *Club Ninja,* in January 1986. Bassist Joe Bouchard left in 1986 and was replaced by Jon Rogers. In 1987, Lanier returned to the group, and Ron Riddle replaced Wilcox on drums. BOC's 14th album, the concept recording *Imaginos,* became their final new album on Columbia Records in July 1988. BOC scored the movie *Bad Channels* in 1992, by which time Chuck Burgi had replaced Ron Riddle on drums. In 1994, Blue Öyster Cult released *Cult Classic,* an album of rerecorded favorites, in connection with the use of their music in the TV mini-series of horror novelist Stephen King's *The Stand.* —*William Ruhlmann*

○ **Blue Öyster Cult** / Jan. 1972 / Columbia ◆◆◆◆
Blue Öyster Cult's debut album provided the missing link between the heavy, blues-based rock of the late '60s and the bombastic heavy metal of the '70s and beyond. You could hear major influences like Steppenwolf, with its melodic/aggressive rock, the Rolling Stones (post-'65), and even boogie bands like Canned Heat in their sound. But BOC streamlined the approach, picked up the tempo, overlaid the guitars, brought the rhythm section up in the mix, and de-emphasized the blues, giving the music a machinelike propulsion. Manager/co-producer Sandy Pearlman (who co-wrote five songs) and lyricist Richard Meltzer (who co-wrote two) may have seen the group as a vehicle for their "clever" (in fact, pretentious) lyrics, but in fact lead vocalist Eric Bloom was the weakest element in the band, and you couldn't make out much of what he had to say over guitarist Donald "Buck Dharma" Roeser's furious power chording. What you could seemed to express some sort of mythology—or demonology; future metal bands would fill their songs with just such half-baked philosophies. *Blue Öyster Cult* was not quite full-fledged heavy metal: the production was too compressed, the playing too light and energetic. But it was the sound of something new and different in the world of hard rock. —*William Ruhlmann*

○ **Tyranny & Mutation** / Feb. 1973 / Columbia ◆◆◆◆
Co-producers Murray Krugman and Sandy Pearlman achieved a far sharper, more spacious production on Blue Öyster Cult's second album than they had in the cramped sound of its first, twinning, for instance, the high, ringing tone of Donald Roeser's lead guitar to Albert Bouchard's cymbals or Alan Lanier's keyboards and adding echo to give presence to Eric Bloom's still barely (or not quite) discernable vocals. In a sense, it's remarkable that albums like this have been categorized as heavy metal: despite the fullness of the aural attack, the fast tempos and raunchy sound give it much more the feel of old rockabilly or punk-rock-to-come. —*William Ruhlmann*

Secret Treaties / Apr. 1974 / Columbia ✦✦
If Blue Öyster Cult's first two albums had established its particular brand of high-energy hard rock and murky, if melodramatic, lyrical world view, *Secret Treaties* took a generic approach to that persona. The riffs (many recycled) ruled, and the same sort of imagery—titles like "Career Of Evil," "Flaming Telepaths," and "Astronomy"—suggested that BOC was rocking in place rather than moving forward. Maybe all that suggested a consistency of theme, especially in Sandy Pearlman and Richard Meltzer's mythology for the group, but it sounded dangerously like repetition; they'd said and done these things better on their debut. BOC would take more than two years to make their next studio album. — *William Ruhlmann*

On Your Feet or on Your Knees / Feb. 1975 / Columbia ✦✦
Blue Öyster Cult's first live album was also its first to peak inside the Top 40, which is more of an indication of the audience the group was building up through extensive touring than of its quality. Songs that had a tight, concentrated impact on studio albums got elongated here, and that impact was dissipated. And the song selection left a great deal to be desired if this was to be a fitting summation of the band's career so far. By its 1974 tour, BOC had dropped some classics from its first album, and the less impressive material from the third album was no substitute. — *William Ruhlmann*

● **Agents of Fortune** / May 1976 / Columbia ✦✦✦✦
Nothing Blue Öyster Cult had produced previously prepared listeners for its infectious midtempo hit, "(Don't Fear) The Reaper," which propelled it into a higher commercial orbit and caused (or reflected) a change in the balance of power in the group. The song was written by guitarist Donald "Buck Dharma" Roeser and was an indication that the band was now largely doing its own songwriting; coproducer Sandy Pearlman earned only one co-writing credit on the record, while drummer Albert Bouchard had five. Poetess Patti Smith, meanwhile, not only co-wrote two tracks, but also performed on one, "The Revenge of Vera Gemini." The result was a record much more in a pop-rock vein than the vaunted metal of the first three albums and BOC's biggest hit ever. — *William Ruhlmann*

Spectres / Oct. 1977 / Columbia ✦✦✦
On the all-important follow-up to its commercial breakthrough with *Agents of Fortune*, Blue Öyster Cult introduced some enjoyable additions to its repertoire in "Godzilla" and "R.U. Ready 2 Rock," but did not come up with a song as memorable as "(Don't Fear) the Reaper," despite trying the same formula with "Fireworks" and "Nosferatu." Instead of consolidating its success, the group seemed to be, as some of the better songs had it, "Goin' Through the Motions," seemingly unable to follow through on the pop aspirations of the previous album and unwilling to retreat to the metal pretensions of its early records. Talk about being caught between a rock and a hard place—just when Blue Öyster Cult should have been conquering, they seemed ready to retreat. — *William Ruhlmann*

Some Enchanted Evening / Sep. 1978 / Columbia ✦✦
Blue Öyster Cult marks time with a second live album on which they turn out good, if redundant, concert versions of recent favorites like "(Don't Fear) the Reaper" and "Godzilla" and add to their repertoire of live covers such oldies as the MC5's "Kick out the Jams" and the Animals' "We Gotta Get out of This Place." A perfectly acceptable, completely unnecessary souvenir record from a hard-touring band of the '70s. (It should perhaps be noted that the mid- to late '70s was a period when more live albums than usual were being released, especially in the wake of Peter Frampton's massively successful 1976 LP *Frampton Comes Alive.*) — *William Ruhlmann*

Mirrors / Jun. 1979 / Columbia ✦✦✦
Blue Öyster Cult tried a new producer on *Mirrors*, replacing long-time mentor Sandy Pearlman with Tom Werman, a CBS staffer who had worked with Cheap Trick and Ted Nugent. The result is an album that tried to straddle pop and hard rock just as those acts did, emphasizing choral vocals (plus female backup) and a sharp, trebly sound. But this approach appeared to displease long-time metal-oriented fans without attracting new ones: "In Thee" became a minor singles chart entry, but the album broke BOC's string of five gold or platinum albums in a row. The real reason simply may have been that the songs weren't distinctive enough. Much of this was generic hard rock that could have been made by any one of a dozen '70s arena bands. — *William Ruhlmann*

Cultosauraus Erectus / Jun. 1980 / Columbia ✦✦✦
Signing on with Deep Purple/Black Sabbath producer Martin Birch, Blue Öyster Cult made more of a guitar-heavy hard rock album in *Cultosaurus Erectus*, after flirting with pop ever since the success of *Agents of Fortune*. (They also promoted this album by going out on a co-headlining tour with Sabbath.) Gone are the female backup singers, the pop hooks, the songs based on keyboard structures, and they are replaced by lots of guitar solos and a beefed-up rhythm section. But the band still was not generating strong enough material to compete with their concert repertoire, so they found themselves in the bind of being a strong touring act unable to translate that success into record sales. — *William Ruhlmann*

Fire of Unknown Origin / Jun. 1981 / Columbia ✦✦✦
Just when Blue Öyster Cult was nearly written off after a series of mediocre albums, the band came roaring back with *Fire Of Unknown Origin*, their best record in five years, on which they found the appropriate mixture of metal, rock and pop that had eluded them since "(Don't Fear) The Reaper." With Sandy Pearlman, Richard Meltzer, and Patti Smith, among others, back in the writing credits, the Cult sounded like they'd been listening hard to their first two albums and *Agents of Fortune* for inspiration. Images of fire, darkness, and war were everywhere, the guitar riffs were inventive, and the melodies compelling. There was a new hit single in the Top 40 "Burnin' For You," but the overall song quality was unusually high. Somehow, BOC had recaptured the trashy gothic appeal of its best work, and the result was a gold-selling album that seemed to put the band's career back on track. — *William Ruhlmann*

Extraterrestrial Live / Apr. 1982 / Columbia ✦✦✦
Of Blue Öyster Cult's three live albums, this is the one to own. The two-record set, partially recorded on BOC's home base of Long Island, contains the band's biggest hits, "(Don't Fear) The Reaper" (making its second live appearance) and "Burnin' For You," as well as longtime concert favorites like "Cities On Flame," "The Red And The Black," and "Godzilla." But it isn't just the superior song selection that gives this album the nod over *On Your Feet or on Your Knees* and *Some Enchanted Evening*; BOC had regained its momentum in 1982 with *Fire of Unknown Origin*, and this album demonstrated their renewed spirit in the forum in which they were most comfortable—live work. In the absence of a good compilation of studio work, *Extraterrestrial Live* is the best overview of BOC available. — *William Ruhlmann*

The Revolution by Night / Oct. 1983 / Columbia ✦✦
Blue Öyster Cult seemed to regain its direction with *Fire of Unknown Origin*, but simultaneously, the band was starting to fragment, with founding member and notable songwriter Albert Bouchard departing. On *The Revolution by Night*, BOC brought in various hired guns, such as Aldo Nova and former Alice Cooper band member Neal Smith, and turned to Loverboy's producer, Bruce Fairbairn, who gave them a similar radio-ready rock sound. But though the album brought BOC its fourth (and final) singles chart entry in "Shooting Shark," it lacked a distinctive identity. You could close your eyes and not know whether you were listening to Loverboy or Foreigner or any one of several other arena rock bands. No wonder it became the band's lowest charting album in a decade. — *William Ruhlmann*

Club Ninja / Jan. 1986 / Columbia ✦✦
Blue Öyster Cult's gradual disintegration continued with *Club Ninja*, on which original member Allen Lanier was replaced by keyboard player Tommy Zvoncheck and several compositions from outside the band were featured, notably the Leggatt Brothers' "White Flags" and a couple of generic metal exercises by Bob Halligan, who had contributed much the same sort of material to Judas Priest. On what should have been the positive side, Sandy Pearlman was back in the producer's chair. But he did nothing to arrest BOC's decline into musical anonymity. — *William Ruhlmann*

Imaginos / Jul. 1988 / Columbia ✦✦✦
Blue Öyster Cult went out with a bang as a major-label recording act on their 14th and last new Columbia album, *Imaginos*. Sandy Pearlman seems to have had the idea for this concept album as early as *Secret Treaties*, on which some of its music appeared, and the recording took place over a six-year period. (As a result, album credits give the erroneous impression that the original band had reformed.) The storyline, which is easier to appreciate in the liner notes than on the record, concerns a mysterious, protean 19th cen-

tury figure who has a talent for turning up at key moments in history and influencing them for the worse. This is perhaps BOC's most consistent album, certainly its most uncompromising (none of its usual nods to pop accessibility), and also the closest thing to a real heavy metal statement from a band that never quite fit that description. Unfortunately, this ambitious work came out as BOC was dropping out of the frontline of the music business, so the album that comes closest to defining Blue Öyster Cult turned into its creative swan song. — *William Ruhlmann*

Career of Evil: The Metal Years / Feb. 1990 / Columbia ♦♦
Columbia Records' single-disc compilation of Blue Öyster Cult's 14-album catalog with the label leaves a great deal to be desired. Eight of its 13 tracks are concert recordings culled from BOC's three live albums, including the version of its biggest hit, "(Don't Fear) The Reaper"; its second biggest hit, "Burnin' for You," is not included, nor are several other significant album tracks. Taken together, the album does not present Blue Öyster Cult at its best, and as of early 1995, there is no good BOC greatest hits album on the market. — *William Ruhlmann*

Cult Classic / Jun. 14, 1994 / Herald ♦♦
Perhaps recognizing Columbia Records' failure to release a proper greatest hits album, Blue Öyster Cult re-recorded its best-known material on this collection, which was tied into the broadcast of a TV mini-series version of Stephen King's *The Stand*, a horror novel that had mentioned BOC's hit "(Don't Fear) The Reaper." The selection of songs here is good, and the current edition of BOC (original members Eric Bloom, Allen Lanier, and Donald "Buck Dharma" Roeser, plus replacement members Chuck Burgi and Jon Rogers) recreates the original recordings closely. But they are re-recordings. (The album contains 12 tracks, plus extra performances of "[Don't Fear] The Reaper" and "Godzilla" in so-called "TV mixes"—i.e., without vocals). — *William Ruhlmann*

Blue Ridge Rangers
Group, Roots-Rock
The Blue Ridge Rangers were never a band. In fact, it was never more than one person: Creedence Clearwater Revival heart and soul John Fogerty. With acrimony over the breakup of Creedence (or more to the point, the jettisoning of rhythm players Stu Cook and Doug Clifford) still fresh, Fogerty released what is ostensibly his first solo album, notable for being an all-covers country/gospel record and for Fogerty's impression of Todd Rundgren by playing all the instruments, overdubbing all the vocals, producing—everything but selling it door-to-door. The point(s) of submerging his identity (Fogerty's face is nowhere on the jacket cover) was to put some distance between himself and the Creedence legacy he wore like an albatross, pay homage to the American vernacular music he loved, and, rather inconspicuously (except for that distinctive voice), announce himself as a solo performer. Oddly enough, life as a solo artist (compounded by lengthy litigation against former Fantasy Records chair Saul Zaentz) didn't seem to agree with Fogerty, and his extremely limited production (a total of four records in 22 years), while not helping him in terms of sales, did, ironically, cement his reputation as an American rock icon. — *John Dougan*

The Blue Ridge Rangers / 1973 / Fantasy ♦♦♦
With wonderfully chosen songs like "Hearts of Stone" and George Jones's classic country weeper "She Thinks I Still Care," Fogerty's solo debut has held up well over the last two decades. It isn't the most supple or technically proficient one-man recording of all time, but it's a wonderfully engaging record; upbeat, unpretentious and loaded with good songs. Fogerty's rigid, no-frills drumming took a lot of heat for being mechanical, but no one has ever explained to my satisfaction how Fogerty's abilities on the trap kit are significantly different from Creedence's Doug Clifford. In retrospect, this was a tremendously risky record to make; country music in the early '70s was regarded as the domain of right-wing, rock & roll-hating Nashville traditionalists, and it was reasonable to assume that fans (even staunch ones) wouldn't take kindly to this genre switch. While it wasn't a huge success, it was in no way a disaster, and perhaps more importantly, served as a much-needed rock & roll history lesson. — *John Dougan*

Blue Rodeo
Group, Rock & Roll, Folk-Rock
Canadian artists Blue Rodeo (Jim Cuddy [vocals/guitar], Bazil Donovan [bass], Greg Keelor [vocals/guitar], Glenn Milchem [drums], and Bob Wiseman [keyboards/harmonica/accordion]) in-

corporate elements of the Band, mid-period Beatles, Buffalo Springfield, and Bob Dylan to fine effect. They're worth seeking out for those who share those influences. — *Rick Clark*

Outskirts / 1987 / Atlantic ♦♦♦
This highly likeable debut is a collection of mid-tempo country rockers. By adding an organ into the arrangements, they were able to distinguish themselves from the hordes of other Gram Parsons devotees in the mid-'80s. — *Chris Woodstra*

Diamond Mine / 1989 / Atlantic ♦♦♦
Diamond Mine is a considerably more quiet affair. Beginning with the very Dylanesque "God and Country," a darker, introverted mood is set by their minimalistic approach and slow tempos. — *Chris Woodstra*

● **Casino** / 1991 / East West ♦♦♦♦
Casino is a more pop-oriented album. They seem to have finally established their fine blend of harmonies and laid-back country-rock a la The Band and Bob Dylan. Produced by Pete Anderson (Dwight Yoakam, Michelle Shocked). — *Chris Woodstra*

○ **Lost Together** / 1992 / Atlantic ♦♦♦♦
Lost Together is easily the best Blue Rodeo album to date. Hit the random button on the disc player and no matter where the laser touches down, you're assured a worthwhile listening experience. Blue Rodeo have built a fortress on the foundation of their previous three outings. The straight pop song "Flying" and ballads "Already Gone" and the epic title track offer added depth and maturity without rehashing previous successes. "Willin' Fool" and "Angels" tackle the progressive elements of Blue Rodeo's second album *Diamond Mine* and sharpen them to a manic, cutting edge. "Fools Like You" spits out a defense of native rights, Greg Keelor doing his best outraged-Bob Dylan impression. — *Roch Parisien*

Five Days in July / 1994 / Musicraft ♦♦♦
Each new Blue Rodeo album seems like the best one yet and *Five Days in July* is no exception. Even the one cover (Rodney Crowell's "Til I Gain Control Again") ends up sounding like a Blue Rodeo original. Also, if you've been slow to embrace her as an artist, Sarah McLachlan's vocal contributions to songs like "What Is This Love" will totally captivate you. — *Jim Worbois*

Blue Things
Group, Folk-Rock, Pop/Rock
Along with the Remains, the Blue Things are serious contenders for the title of the Great Lost Mid-'60s American Band. The Kansas group was extremely popular in the Midwest and Texas, but remained unknown on a national level, despite a deal with RCA. Piloted by the excellent songwriting of singer and guitarist Val Stocklein, the group often sounded like a cross between the Byrds and the Beau Brummels with its melodic, energetic, guitar-oriented folk-rock and haunting harmonies. The group's sole album (*Listen & See*, 1966) and several singles chart a rapid growth from British Invasion-like material with a heavy Searchers and Buddy Holly influence to full-blown psychedelic efforts with careening guitars, organ, and backwards effects. Quite innovative for the time, these 1966 psychedelic singles met with no more than regional success. The group's impetus was derailed by the departure of Stocklein at the end of 1966, although they struggled on for a bit. Stocklein went to California and recorded a disappointing MOR-folk album for Dot in the late '60s that reprised some of his Blue Things songs. — *Richie Unterberger*

○ **Listen & See** / 1966 / RCA ♦♦♦♦
One of the most underappreciated albums of the '60s. Composed of Val Stocklein originals and well-chosen covers, the group synthesized the Beatles and Dylanesque folk-rock with a skill similar to the Byrds. Ringing 12-string and acoustic guitars, melodic harmonies, passionate vocals, and strong material abound on this nearly forgotten near-classic. — *Richie Unterberger*

The Blue Things Story, Vol. 1 (1964-65) / 1987 / Cicadelic ♦♦♦
This collection of 1964 and 1965 demos, coupled with some rare early singles, shows the band at its most British Invasion-influenced. It has quite a few fine Beatlesque harmony rockers by Stocklein, along with some nifty covers. There's a marked difference between the 1964 and 1965 demos, which show the band shifting from British Invasion emulation to a more mature and far more folk-rock-influenced direction. — *Richie Unterberger*

● **The Blue Things Story, Vol. 2 (1965-66)** / 1987 / Cicadelic ♦♦♦♦
Basically a repackage of *Listen & See*, with a couple of the less impressive cover songs deleted. In their place are four fine previously unreleased demos, two of which feature the entire band, two of

which are performed by Stocklein alone on acoustic guitar. The epic ballad "Desert Wind" is a special standout among the previously unreleased cuts. —*Richie Unterberger*

The Blue Things Story, Vol. 3 (1966) / 1987 / Cicadelic ✦✦✦
Wraps up their legacy with all of their groundbreaking, non-LP 1966 single sides—"The Orange Rooftop Of Your Mind," "One Hour Cleaners," and "You Can Live In Our Tree." It also has half a dozen 1966 demos (several acoustic), some of which are early versions of songs that ended up on *Listen & See*. The package is rounded out by a few impressive 1967 cuts from the post-Stocklein lineup, consisting of a couple of unreleased originals by other band members and their astounding psychedelic fuzz-guitar re-arrangement of "Twist And Shout." —*Richie Unterberger*

David Blue (S. David Cohen)

b. 1941, Providence, RI, d. Dec. 2, 1982
Singer-Songwriter, Folk-Rock
Born in Providence, RI, as S. David Cohen (a name he returned to for one of his albums), David Blue was a member of the folk singer/songwriter community of Greenwich Village in the '60s and a close friend of Bob Dylan's (he recounts this period of his life in Dylan's movie *Renaldo & Clara*). Blue made several albums for Elektra, Reprise, and Asylum in the '60s and '70s, and is best remembered for his songs "I Like to Sleep Late in the Morning" and "Wanted Man" (recorded by the Eagles). —*William Ruhlmann*

● **David Blue** / 1966 / Asylum ✦✦✦✦
Blue's debut album features the first recording of his remarkable "Grand Hotel" and other well-written folk/rock songs. —*William Ruhlmann*

These 23 Days in September / 1968 / Reprise ✦✦✦
Me / 1970 / Reprise ✦✦
Stories / 1972 / Asylum ✦✦✦
○ **Nice Baby and the Angel** / 1973 / Asylum ✦✦✦✦
Blue is joined by an all-star California cast (Dave Mason, Graham Nash, David Lindley, and Glenn Frey) for this excellent '70s singer-songwriter collection, which includes his "Outlaw Man." —*William Ruhlmann*
○ **Com'n Back for More** / 1975 / Asylum ✦✦✦✦
Blue takes a more jazz/rock approach here, using members of the crony group the Los Angeles Express, whose employer, Joni Mitchell, makes an appearance, as does Blue's old crony, Bob Dylan. —*William Ruhlmann*
Cupid's Arrow / 1976 / Asylum ✦✦

Bluebells

Group, Soul
During their brief time together in the early '80s, the Bluebells (songwriter Robert [Bobby Bluebell] Hodgens [b. Jun. 6, 1959] [guitar], Kenneth McClusky [b. Feb. 8, 1962] [vocals/harmonica], Dave McCluskey [b. Jan. 13, 1964] [drums], Russell Irvin [guitar] [replaced by Craig Gannon (b. Jul. 30, 1966), and Lawrence Donegan [bass] [replaced by Neil Baldwin]) made a small amount of music—several singles, most of which showed up on one EP—but that is not proportional to the quality of their music. Like fellow Scots Aztec Camera, the Bluebells crafted impeccable, jangly guitar-pop, only with better melodies and stronger hooks. Two of their singles ('I'm Falling' and "Young at Heart") hovered around the lower reaches of the U.K. Top Ten in 1984, but they soon broke up, leaving a small, but impressive, body of work. David McCluskey and his brother Ken formed a folk duo. Robert Hodgens formed Up. Craig Gannon briefly filled in for bassist Andy Rourke in the Smiths on tour, then stayed as a second live guitarist; he joined Adult Net after being fired from the Smiths in 1986. —*Stephen Thomas Erlewine*

Bluebells / 1983 / Sire ✦✦✦
The Bluebells' critically acclaimed five-song debut EP established their chiming guitar-pop quite effectively. —*Stephen Thomas Erlewine*

● **Sisters** / 1984 / London ✦✦✦✦
Sisters, the Bluebells' first full-length album, shared some songs with their debut EP, yet the repetition doesn't matter, since the record is so carefully constructed. The group's ringing, hook-laden folk-pop is consistently infectious throughout the course of the album. —*Stephen Thomas Erlewine*

Second / 1992 / ✦✦
Second is a collection of unreleased early Bluebells recordings that is worthwhile for dedicated fans. —*Stephen Thomas Erlewine*

The Blues Brothers

Group, Soul, Pop/Rock
During the late '70s, comedians Dan Aykroyd (b. Jul. 1, 1952, Ottawa) and John Belushi (b. Jan. 24, 1949, Chicago, d. Mar. 5, 1982, Los Angeles) of the television variety show *Saturday Night Live* appeared as the fictional "Blues Brothers," Elwood and Joliet Jake Blues, and employed the services of former Stax Records rhythm section players Steve Cropper and Duck Dunn, as well as keyboard player Paul Shaffer, leader of the band on David Letterman's talk show, for a run-through of soul classics. As a TV skit, this was fun, and it expanded into a chart-topping album and a successful feature film. Despite Belushi's death in 1982, the "Blues Brothers" concept has turned out to have a perennial appeal: There are performing "Blues Brothers" at the Universal Studio theme park in Orlando, Florida; the Blues Brothers' cover of "Everybody Needs Somebody to Love" charted in the U.K. Top 40 in 1990, a decade after it appeared on *The Blues Brothers* movie soundtrack; there was a *Blues Brothers* theatrical production in London's West End in 1991; and in 1992 members of the backup group recorded under the name "The Blues Brothers Band." But musically, the best thing that can be said about the Blues Brothers is that they inspired a new audience to look for the real thing. —*Rick Clark*

○ **Briefcase Full of Blues** / Dec. 1978 / Atlantic ✦✦✦✦
"The Blues Brothers" began as an affectionate joke-cum-tribute to R&B music, and taken in that spirit it retained its entertainment value, even after this live album topped the charts, sold two million copies, and produced hit singles in "Rubber Biscuit" and "Soul Man." The guardians of popular music have always been entirely too reverent and humorless, however, and it wasn't long before they were leveling charges of rip-off against the Brothers and complaining that John Belushi couldn't sing as well as Otis Redding. So what? No one seems to have noticed that Belushi was as obsessive about citing his sources as Frank Sinatra is about naming his arrangers—you'd have thought those critics would have appreciated the footnotes. The beneficiaries of Belushi's encomiums didn't mind the increased exposure or the renewed royalty checks ("I suggest you buy as many blues albums as you can," Belushi told the audience), and even today, what comes across in these performances is the sincerity of feeling—that and some tasty playing from a top-notch band. —*William Ruhlmann*

Blues Brothers [O.S.T.] / Jun. 1980 / Atlantic ✦✦✦
Made in America / Dec. 1980 / Atlantic ✦✦
The Best of the Blues Brothers / Dec. 1981 / Atlantic ✦✦✦
A solid collection, this includes the hits "Rubber Biscuit" (#37), "Soul Man" (#14), and "Gimme Some Lovin'" (#18), plus music from *The Blues Brothers* soundtrack. —*AMG*
Red, White & Blues / 1992 / Turnstyle ✦✦
Steve Cropper, Donald "Duck" Dunn, Matt "Guitar" Murphy, "Blue Lou" Marini, and Alan "Mr. Fabulous" Rubin were all members of the all-star band that backed John Belushi and Dan Aykroyd in their "Blues Brothers" incarnation between 1978 and 1980. Here, they reorganized with a few more players, notably singer Larry "T" Thurston, as the Blues Brothers Band. The music (mostly new songs) was in the BB's familiar uptempo R&B style, Elwood Blues made a cameo appearance, and the playing was sessionman-hot, but of course it just wasn't the same without Joliet Jake, who had gone to that great roadhouse in the sky 10 years before. —*William Ruhlmann*
● **The Definitive Collection** / 1992 / Atlantic ✦✦✦✦
The Definitive Collection is indeed the definitive Blues Brothers disc, containing all of their hits and signature songs. —*Stephen Thomas Erlewine*

The Blues Image

Group, Pop/Rock
The Blues Image was a one-hit wonder Latin-tinged pop/rock band, that one hit being "Ride Captain Ride," which made the Top Ten and sold a million copies in 1970. The group was formed in Tampa, FL, in 1966 by Michael Pinera (b. Sept. 29, 1948, Tampa, FL) (guitar, vocals), Manuel Bertematti (b. 1946, Tampa, FL) (percussion), and Joe Lala (b. Tampa, FL) (drums). Malcolm Jones

(b. Cardiff, Wales) (bass) joined in 1966, followed in 1968 by Frank "Skip" Konte (b. Canyon City, OK) (keyboards). The band moved to New York City in 1968 and managed a club called the Image. Then they moved to Los Angeles, where they signed to Atlantic Records' Atco division in February 1969 and released their self-titled debut album. This was followed by *Open* (1970), which featured "Ride Captain Ride." But the Blues Image never followed their hit. Pinera left, replaced by Kent Henry (guitar) and Dennis Correll (vocals). Then, the Blues Image broke up. A third album, *Red White & Blues Image*, was compiled from outtakes. Skip Konte joined Three Dog Night, while some other band members reformed as Manna. Pinera later was a member of Iron Butterfly, then Ramatam, and, with Bertematti, the New Cactus Band. He also formed a band called Thee Image and worked as a solo artist. Lala became a Los Angeles session player and worked with Joe Walsh and the various manifestations of Crosby, Stills, Nash & Young, among others. — *William Ruhlmann*

Blues Image / Jul. 1969 / Atco ✦✦✦

Red White & Blues Image / 1970 / Atco ✦✦

● **Open** / Apr. 1970 / Atco ✦✦✦✦

Blues Magoos

Group, Psychedelic
A Bronx-based quintet, denizens of the Greenwich Village club scene, and originally known by the *tres*-psychedelic moniker The Bloos Magoos (yikes!), the Blues Magoos made their mark in 1967 with a rousing, full-throttle, sub-literate, psychedelic garage rock single, "(We Ain't Got) Nothin' Yet." It wasn't a spacy, pretentious song, nor did it contain vague attempts at hippie-era mysticism, but was rather the kind of simple, direct, infectious rock & roll you could imagine five guys from the Bronx making. With a snotty lead vocal from keyboardist Ralph Scala and some wild-eyed guitar playing courtesy of then-16-year-old Emil "Peppy" Theilheim, America made the Magoos' debut single a Top Ten hit, sending it to number 5 in January 1967. With this impetus, the band used all the trappings of marketable psychedelia to promote their second album, *Psychedelic Lollipop*, which, despite the title's obvious pandering, was a fairly cool chunk of psych-garage rock: trebly, crappy-sounding guitars, a whiny Farfisa organ, yelled vocals, and a rhythm section that shelved nuance for thudding simplicity. But as the psychedelic era gave way to the hippie era's extended raga-rock proclivities, by 1969, the Magoos seemed anachronistic. Amazingly, they released a third album, with an equally idiotic title, *Electric Comic Book*, that wasn't nearly as bad as it sounds. The original Magoos split up in 1969, but Theilheim couldn't resist beating a dead horse and led a mediocre blues-rock version of the band into 1972. — *John Dougan*

● **Kaleidescopic Compendium: Best of the Blues Magoos** / 1992 / PolyGram/Mercury ✦✦✦✦
The Blues Magoos were one of the most underrated U.S. bands of the late '60s, known almost exclusively for their one irresistible hit "(We Ain't Got) Nothing Yet," which charted at #5 in July, 1967. *Kaleidescopic Compendium: The Best Of The Blues Magoos* confirms the group's depth. The disc compiles a generous 23 tracks from their first three albums and a brace of single sides. The group's psychedelia holds up better than most from the period. Andy Sandoval's four-page history of the group is concise, complete and entertaining. — *Roch Parisien*

The Blues Project

Group, Blues Rock, Folk-Rock
The Blues Project was New York's first "underground" group. In 1965, guitarist Danny Kalb, who was well established as a player on various Elektra Records folk and early folk-rock and blues albums, played on an Elektra Records sampler called *The Blues Project*. Soon after, he hooked up with Steve Katz (b. Sept. 1945, Brooklyn) (a guitarist with Elektra's Even Dozen Jug Band), Andy Kulberg (b. 1944, Buffalo, New York) (a flutist and bassist), Roy Blumenfeld (drums), and Tommy Flanders (singer and harmonica player). Al Kooper (b. Feb. 5, 1944, Brooklyn) was the final addition on keyboards, guitar, and vocals, joining after he sat in on the band's Columbia Records audition. (They eventually signed to the Verve division of MGM, now part of PolyGram.) This sextet quickly built up a reputation for its mix of rock, jazz, classical, and electric blues on numbers such as "No Time Is the Right Time" (the band's only chart single), "Flute Thing" (which became popular on progressive FM radio stations), and "Catch The Wind." Flan-

ders left after the first album, *Live at the Cafe Au Go Go* (May 1966), for a solo career. Kooper exited the band before the release of the third album, *Live at Town Hall* (September 1967) (though he appeared on it) and went on to form the more jazz-oriented Blood, Sweat & Tears, into which Katz quickly followed. The Blues Project also lost Kalb (to ill health), and remaining members Blumenfeld and Kulberg added Don Kretmar (saxophone/bass), Richard Greene (violin), and John Gregory (guitar/vocals) to make the fourth album, *Planned Obsolescence*, but then renamed the band Seatrain. Kalb, Blumenfeld, and Kretmar got back together under the Blues Project name in 1971 for the fifth album, *Lazarus*. Then Flanders returned, and David Cohen (piano) and Bill Lussended (guitar) were added for the sixth album, *Blues Project*, but this version of the group disbanded in 1972. A 1973 Central Park reunion album recorded by five of the six original members (Flanders was not included) attracted a lot of press attention but generated little musical excitement. The three original Verve albums and Rhino's best-of are the records that count. — *Bruce Eder*

Live at the Cafe Au-Go-Go / May 1966 / Verve/Forecast ✦✦✦
Arguably the first artistically successful live rock album of the mid '60s. A fine showcase for the band's many talents. — *Bruce Eder*

○ **Projections** / Nov. 1966 / Verve/Forecast ✦✦✦✦
The band's only full-length studio recording displayed an outfit that was probably more versatile than any other American group of the time, handling electric blues-rock, folk-rock, and even a bit of jazz with aplomb on both short, concise numbers and lengthy rave-up jams. The jazz instrumental "Flute Thing," the rabble-rousing "I Can't Keep From Crying," and the folk-rockish "Steve's Song," "Fly Away," and "Cheryl's Going Home" all rank among their best songs. — *Richie Unterberger*

Live at Town Hall / Sep. 1967 / Verve/Forecast ✦✦✦
Released just after Al Kooper left the band, one imagines that neither he nor the other members of the group were pleased with this LP. According to Kooper, it was a pastiche of studio outtakes and a few live performances, and only one of the songs was actually recorded at New York City's Town Hall. Anyway, this has a meandering, 10-minute "Flute Thing" and decent live versions of "Wake Me Shake Me" and "I Can't Keep From Crying" which, despite a somewhat rawer feel, are not necessary supplements to the fine studio takes. "Where There's Smoke, There's Fire" and the great "No Time Like The Right Time" had already been released as singles; to hear them without canned applause, you only need to turn to Rhino's first-rate *Best Of The Blues Project* instead. That compilation also contains the other cut of note on this album, an outtake-sounding cover of Patrick Sky's "Love Will Endure." — *Richie Unterberger*

Planned Obsolescence / Dec. 1968 / Verve/Forecast ✦✦✦

Lazarus / 1971 / Capitol ✦✦✦

The Blues Project / 1972 / Capitol ✦✦✦

Reunion in Central Park / 1973 / MGM ✦✦✦

Best of the Blues Project [Forecast] / 1989 / Verve/Forecast ✦✦✦
No Time Like the Right Time—The Best of the Blues Project is the best anthology of the band ever likely to be done. It encompasses their wealth of high points in better sound than ever. — *Bruce Eder*

● **The Best of the Blues Project [Rhino]** / 1989 / Rhino ✦✦✦✦
Excellent 16-track anthology includes the highlights of the first three albums, as well as a few non-LP singles, most notably the title track, a great hit-that-never-was that was probably their best performance. The live 1973 version of "Flute Thing" is unnecessary and should have been replaced by "Cheryl's Going Home," an excellent cut from the *Projections* album. — *Richie Unterberger*

Projections from the Past / 1989 / Hablabel ✦✦✦
A double album of dubious legality, but fairly easy availability. This captures the Blues Project's best lineup—Kooper, Katz, Kalb, Kulberg, and Blumenfeld—live at the Matrix club in San Francisco on September 1, 1966. If there's any revelation to be had from these fair-quality tapes, it's that there's not much of a revelation at all. The group performs a lot of the stronger material from their first and second albums in versions very close to the records. They shine brightest on the more adventurous material with jazz and folk tangents, like "Steve's Song," "Flute Thing," "Catch The Wind," and "Cheryl's Going Home." Most of the rest is competent but not especially brilliant white-boy blues renditions of numbers like "Hoochie Coochie Man," "You Can't Catch Me," and "You Can't Judge A Book By The Cover"; the swaggering "Shake That Baby"

is about the best of these. Essential only for serious collectors. Be warned that there are a few (not many) clumsy edits, and that the entire fourth side is simply tracks lifted from their *Live At Town Hall* LP. —*Richie Unterberger*

Blues Traveler
Group, Rock & Roll

A New York-based blues-rock quartet formed in 1988 by singer/harmonica player John Popper, guitarist Chan Kinchla, bassist Bobby Sheehan, and drummer Brendan Hill, Blues Traveler was part of a revival of the extended jamming style of '60s and '70s groups like the Grateful Dead and Led Zeppelin. Signed to A&M, they released their first album, *Blues Traveler*, in May 1990 and followed it with *Travelers & Thieves* in September 1991. Popper was in a serious car accident in 1992, leaving him unable to perform for a number of months. Fortunately, he recovered, yet he still had to perform in a wheelchair for a period of time. In April 1993, Blues Traveler released its third album, *Save His Soul*, which became its first to make the Top 100. Blues Traveler's aptly named fourth album, *Four*, released in September 1994, at first looked like a sales disappointment, but it rebounded in 1995 when "Run-Around," a single taken from it, became the group's first chart hit. —*William Ruhlmann*

● **Blues Traveler** / May 1990 / A&M ✦✦✦✦
Blues Traveler's loose jam structures on basic blues riffs mark them as a band in the tradition of such predecessors as the Grateful Dead. Unlike that communal effort, however, this group has a distinct focal point in virtuoso harmonica player and vocalist John Popper, who keeps things from meandering too much. —*William Ruhlmann*

○ **Travelers & Thieves** / Sep. 1991 / A&M ✦✦✦✦
"I have my moments," John Popper declares, and many of them, as harmonica player, singer, and lyricist are here, on an album that finds Blues Traveler stretching out much as they do onstage. Popper is a man with a lot on his mind, but when he reaches "The Best Part," his verbosity approaches a Walt Whitman-like exuberance, and guitarist Chan Kinchla is right with him, contributing sweet fills here, Pete Townshend-style strumming there. And as for the rhythm work of bassist Bobby Sheehan and drummer Brendan Hill, as Popper says, "It's all in the groove." —*William Ruhlmann*

Save His Soul / Apr. 1993 / A&M ✦✦✦
Led by the guttural vocals and incisive harmonica of imposing frontman John Popper, *Save His Soul* is a savory package that dresses obvious influences in a fresh suit of clothes. While 6 and 12 strings rule, the true inspiration here is Popper's delivery on harmonica and other wind instruments, either spitting in machine-gun rapid fire or carrying a piercing, emotive melody line with equal ease. Having restrained themselves for most of *Save His Soul*, Blues Traveler close with the seven-minute opus "Fledgling," flowing from epic, orchestral ballad mode to angst-ridden wall-of-noise. —*Roch Parisien*

Four / 1994 / A&M ✦✦✦
Lacking the rootsier edge of *Save His Soul*, *Four* finds Blues Traveler retreating to their standard blues-boogie formula, with mixed results. Of course, there are some fine songs here—including their breakthrough hit single "Run-Around"— but too often the band sounds like they're coasting. *Four* is a solid record, but it shows signs that the band's formula may be wearing thin. —*Stephen Thomas Erlewine*

The Bluesbusters
Group, Blues Rock

The Bluesbusters were a blues-rock quintet made up of guitarist/singer Paul Barrere (formerly of Little Feat), keyboardist T Lavitz (formerly of the Dixie Dregs), Freebo (longtime bass player with Bonnie Raitt), guitarist/singer Catfish Hodge, and drummer Larry Zack. A promising outfit, they folded as Barrere and Lavitz returned to reformed versions of their old groups. —*William Ruhlmann*

This Time / 1981 / Landslide ✦✦
Merry Christmas / 1984 / Tower ✦✦
● **Accept No Substitutes** / 1986 / Landslide ✦✦✦✦
Paul Barrere's bluesy vocals will be familiar to Little Feat fans, and to a lesser extent T Lavitz's keyboard textures and Freebo's propulsive bass playing will strike chords with fans of the Dixie Dregs

and Bonnie Raitt. Catfish Hodge is a less familiar vocal presence, but he has the same sort of whisky voice, and when you add in Larry Zack's drums, you have a band very much in the Southern/New Orleans tradition of the members' antecedents. There's no Lowell George (Little Feat) to write brilliant songs, and no Steve Morse (Dixie Dregs) to provide pyrotechnics on guitar, but the playing is solid and the songs are celebrations of "cookin'" and "fishin'" and "movin' to the country" on the "dixie highway" so you can live "down on the farm." —*William Ruhlmann*

Colin Blunstone
b. Jun. 24, 1945, Hatfield, Hertfordshire, UK
Pop/Rock

As the lead singer of the Zombies, Blunstone was one of the greatest '60s rock vocalists, pacing the group's minor-key masterpieces with his inimitable choked and breathy vocals. After retiring from the business briefly in the late '60s (to work in the insurance industry, of all things), he went solo in the early '70s with a string of interesting pop/rock albums that were more of an extension of the late Zombies sound than the more well-known work of Argent, the other Zombies spin-off act. The Zombies connection is hardly incidental; chief Zombie songwriters Rod Argent and Chris White gave Blunstone some songs, as did Argent member Russ Ballard, though Blunstone penned much of his material himself. With their moody melodies and baroque touches of muted keyboards, classical guitars, and inventive string arrangements, his early-'70s albums sometimes sounded like a mellower take on the direction the Zombies pursued with their pop-psychedelic masterwork *Odessey and Oracle*. Blunstone managed some small British hits with "How Could We Dare Be Wrong," "I Don't Believe in Miracles," and the Top 20 single "Say You Don't Mind," a cover of a tune written and recorded by Denny Laine after he left the Moody Blues and before he joined Wings. Blunstone's first album, *One Year* (1971), was his best, though the follow-ups *Ennismore* and *Journey* also had their moments. —*Richie Unterberger*

One Year / Nov. 1971 / Epic ✦✦✦
Ennismore / Nov. 1972 / Epic ✦✦✦
Journey / 1974 / Epic ✦✦
● **Some Years: It's the Time of Colin Blunstone** / 1995 / Legacy/Epic ✦✦✦✦
Well-chosen 17-track retrospective of his early-'70s work, including all the British hit singles and tracks from his first three solo LPs. Although it's not up to the level of the Zombies' classic records, Zombies fans should like this stuff a lot, especially "Say You Don't Mind," "Andorra," "Though You Are Far Away," and his cover of Tim Hardin's "Misty Roses." —*Richie Unterberger*

Blur
Group, Alternative Pop/Rock

Initially, Blur were one of the multitude of British bands that appeared in the wake of the Stone Roses, mining the same swirling, pseudo-psychedelic guitar-pop, only with louder guitars. Following an image makeover in the mid-'90s, the group emerged as the most popular band in the U.K., establishing themselves as the heir to the Brit-pop tradition of the Kinks, the Small Faces, the Who, the Jam, Madness, and the Smiths.

Originally called Seymour, the group was formed in London in 1989 by vocalist/keyboardist Damon Albarn, guitarist Graham Coxon, and bassist Alex James, with drummer Dave Rowntree joining the lineup shortly afterward. After performing a handful of gigs and recording a demo tape, the band signed to Food Records, a subsidiary of EMI run by journalist Andy Ross and former Teardrop Explodes keyboardist Dave Balfe. Balfe and Ross suggested that the band change their name, submitting a list of alternate names for the group's approval. From that list, the group took the name Blur.

"She's So High," the group's first single, made it into the Top 50 while the follow-up "There's No Other Way" went Top 10. Both singles were included on their 1991 Stephen Street-produced debut album, *Leisure*. Although it received favorable reviews, the album fit neatly into the dying Manchester pop scene, causing some journalists to dismiss the band as manufactured teen idols. For the next two years, Blur struggled to distance themselves from the scene associated with the sound of their first album.

Released in 1992, the snarling "Pop Scene" was Blur's first attempt at changing their musical direction. A brash, spiteful rocker driven by horns, the neo-mod single was punkier than anything the band had previously recorded and its hooks were more immediate and catchy. Despite Blur's clear artistic growth, "Pop Scene" didn't fit into the climate of British pop and American grunge in 1992 and failed to make an impression on the U.K. charts. Following the single's commercial failure, the group began work on their second album, *Modern Life Is Rubbish*, a process that would take nearly a year and a half.

XTC's Andy Partridge was originally slated to produce *Modern Life Is Rubbish*, but the relationship between Blur and Partridge quickly soured and Street was again brought in to produce the band. After spending nearly a year in the studio, the band delivered the album to Food. The record company rejected the album, declaring that it needed a hit single. Blur went back into the studio and recorded Albarn's "For Tomorrow," which would turn out to be a British hit. Food was ready to release the record but the group's U.S. record company, SBK, believed there was no American hit single on the record and asked them to return to the studio. Blur complied and recorded "Chemical World," which pleased SBK for a short while; the song would become a minor alternative hit in the U.S. and charted at number 28 in the U.K. *Modern Life Is Rubbish* was set for release in the spring of 1993 when SBK asked Blur to re-record the album with producer Butch Vig (Nirvana, Sonic Youth). The band refused and the record was released in May in Britain; it appeared in the United States that fall. *Modern Life Is Rubbish* received good reviews in Britain, peaking at number 15 on the charts, yet it failed to make much of an impression in the U.S.

Modern Life Is Rubbish turned out to be a dry run for Blur's breakthrough album, *Parklife*. Released in April 1994, *Parklife* entered the charts at number one and catapulted the band to stardom in Britain. The stylized new wave dance-pop single "Girls and Boys," entered the charts at number five; the single managed to spend 15 weeks in the U.S. charts, peaking at number 52, but the album never cracked the top of the charts. It was a completely different story in England, as Blur had a string of hit singles including the ballad "To the End" and the mod anthem "Parklife," which featured narration by Phil Daniels, the star of the film version of the Who's *Quadrophenia*.

With the success of *Parklife*, Blur opened the door for a flood of British indie-guitar bands that dominated British pop culture in the mid-'90s. Oasis, Elastica, Pulp, the Boo Radleys, Supergrass, Gene, Echobelly, Menswear, and numerous other bands all benefited from the band's success. By the beginning of 1995, *Parklife* had gone triple platinum and the band had become superstars. The group spent the first half of 1995 recording their fourth album and playing various one-off concerts, including a sold-out stadium show. Blur released "Country House," the first single from their new album, in August. *The Great Escape*, Blur's follow-up to *Parklife*, was released in September of 1995. —*Stephen Thomas Erlewine*

Leisure / Sep. 1991 / Capitol ✦✦✦
Blur is loosely lumped in with Britain's Manchester Sound; a kind of '60s-psychedelia-meets-dance-music scene. Unlike others in the genre, however, Blur parks most of the disco influences at the door in favor of hard-edged pop. *Leisure's* most accessible moments, like the singles "She's So High" and "There's No Other Way," blend captivating, fluid melodies with hypnotic, psyched-up instrumentation. More experimental moments like "Repetition" and "Bad Day" are reminiscent of early, Syd Barrett-led Pink Floyd; the dreamy atmospheres firmly anchored by sparse, chunky guitar riffs. Blur will appeal to those who don't mind having their fond recollections of the '60s fused to modern, guitar-driven pop. — *Roch Parisien*

○ **Modern Life Is Rubbish** / 1993 / SBK ✦✦✦✦
On their second album, Blur explores their influences, particularly the Kinks, David Bowie, the Smiths, and the Who. The result is an album filled with enjoyable but derivative guitar-pop singles that never manage to capture the spark of Blur's idols or create their own identity. —*Stephen Thomas Erlewine*

● **Parklife** / 1994 / Capitol ✦✦✦✦
An audacious fusion of early-'80s new wave with the timeless guitar pop of the Kinks and the Smiths, *Parklife* is Blur's most ambitious album to date, as well as their best. For once, their songwriting has enough satisfying original hooks to make the entire record consistently enjoyable. —*Stephen Thomas Erlewine*

Bob & Earl

Group, Soul, R&B
Los Angeles soul duo Bobby Relf and Earl Nelson. Their only major hit, "Harlem Shuffle" (1963) also hit the U.K. Top 10 in 1969 and was revived by the Rolling Stones in 1986. Both Relf and Nelson were heavily involved in the '50s Los Angeles doo-wop scene—Relf led a group called the Laurels, while Nelson sang with the Hollywood Flames (notably taking the lead on their 1957 hit "Buzz-Buzz-Buzz") and with Bobby Day as Bob and Earl before he and Relf joined forces. Nelson later used the name Jackie Lee (his wife's name was Jackie, his middle name was Lee) for another popular R&B dance cut in in 1965, "The Duck." —*Bill Dahl*

● **Harlem Shuffle** / 1966 / Sue ✦✦✦✦
Bobby Relf replaced Earl Nelson's former partner Bobby Byrd, who worked with him in James Brown's Famous Flames. That duo cut songs for various labels, but hadn't clicked as an act. The new Bob and Earl struck gold with this single, which made it to the Top 50 when it was issued in 1963. —*Ron Wynn*

Bobby & Laurie

Group, Pop/Rock
Sort of a mish-mash of the Beatles, Peter & Gordon, and the Everly Brothers, Bobby & Laurie were one of Australia's first, and best, responses to the British Invasion. Comprised of Bobby Bright and Laurie Allan (who were both guys), they released no less than eight singles and three albums in Australia in 1965 and 1966. Writing much of their own material, they were quite popular in their day down under, although they made no impact whatsover on the international scene. Featuring close harmonies in the Beatle style, they were actually one of the better British Invasion-inspired acts, outclassing many U.K. groups following in the Fab Four's footsteps. Leaning toward the tougher rather than the wimpier side of Merseybeat, they also roamed fairly far afield for their cover material, choosing relatively obscure U.S. R&B numbers and British beat B-sides and flops. They pursued an increasingly C&W-oriented direction before splitting at the end of 1966. —*Richie Unterberger*

● **Jump Back** / 1983 / Raven ✦✦✦✦
A 16-song compilation including most of their A-sides, as well as some interesting B-sides and tracks from their three albums. Cuts like "I Belong With You," "No Next Time," and "Judy Green" are first-rate originals that will appeal to British Invasion fans; there are also reasonably successful covers of songs by P.J. Proby, the Mojos, the Crickets, and Carter-Lewis. —*Richie Unterberger*

Bobby & The Midnites

Group, Rock & Roll
Bobby & The Midnites was a Grateful Dead spin-off group led by the Dead's guitarist/singer Bob Weir during the first half of the '80s. Its initial lineup, in addition to Weir, was: Bobby Cochran (guitar, vocals), the Dead's Brent Mydland (keyboards, vocals), Tim Bogert (bass), noted jazz-fusion drummer Billy Cobham, and Matt Kelly (harmonica, guitar, congas), who had been in Weir's '70s spin-off group, Kingfish. This sextet played its first gig at Golden Bear in Huntington Beach, CA, on June 30, 1980. Bobby & The Midnites signed to the Dead's label, Arista Records, and released their self-titled debut album in November 1981, by which time Alphonso Johnson had replaced Bogert on bass. The album charted for a couple of months, but was not a big seller. The band, having dropped Kelly and replaced Mydland with keyboard player Dave Garland, toured extensively in 1982, 1983, and 1984. In March 1983, Ken Gradney replaced Johnson on bass. In August 1984, Columbia Records released Bobby & The Midnites' second album, *Where the Beat Meets the Street*, which again was not commercially successful, though it charted briefly. Bobby & The Midnites played their final show on September 30, 1984, at Rio in Valley Stream, NY, after which Weir, while continuing with the Grateful Dead, rejoined Kingfish and did solo performances. He later performed with such groups as Nightfood and Go Ahead, and starting in 1988 began to tour regularly in a duo with bassist Rob Wasserman. —*William Ruhlmann*

Bobby & The Midnites / Nov. 1981 / Arista ✦✦✦
Bobby & The Midnites seemed to offer Grateful Dead guitarist Bob Weir an opportunity to pursue the more conventionally accessible pop-rock style he had first demonstrated a taste for in his '70s solo albums *Ace* and especially *Heaven Help The Fool*. With the

exception of a couple of reggae numbers, the Midnites' debut album found Weir playing straight-ahead guitar rock songs with mostly lovelorn lyrics, the only real ringer in the bunch being jazz drummer Billy Cobham, who seemed capable of hitting as many drums per bar as Keith Moon, and with far more control. But Weir's earnest, husky voice and off-center guitar playing did not make for a slick pop approach, and the album came off as a collection of half-baked wannabe-hits from someone who had spent his career finding success by avoiding just such a style. — *William Ruhlmann*

Where the Beat Meets The Street / Aug. 1984 / Columbia ✦✦
Where The Beat Meets the Street, the Midnites' second and final album, saw the group going for mid-'80s radio acceptance with a vengeance. As he had in his '70s group, Kingfish, Bob Weir began to take a backseat in his own band, leaving most of the singing up to Bobby Cochran and bringing in a host of outside songwriters. What you got was, as one song put it, "Rock in the '80s," a set of frisky toe-tappers that concerned themselves mostly with the magical world of rock & roll. What can Deadheads have made of this? Actually, probably only a few of them (or anyone else) got to hear this album, which sank without a trace after four weeks at the bottom of the charts, followed by the demise of the group itself. — *William Ruhlmann*

Bodacious D.F.

Group, Pop/Rock
Bodacious D.F. was the second group that singer Marty Balin became involved with after leaving Jefferson Airplane in 1970. First, he directed the activities of Grootna, with whom he did not perform, on their sole album. Then, he became involved with Bay Area band Bodacious D.F.—Mark Ryan (bass, vocals), Dewey Dagreaze (drums, vocals), Vic Smith (guitar, vocals), and Charlie Hickox (keyboards, vocals). Bodacious D.F. recorded one self-titled album in 1973, which represented Balin's first LP appearance since Jefferson Airplane's 1969 *Volunteers* album. But in 1974 Balin rejoined some of his old Jefferson Airplane cohorts in Jefferson Starship, leaving Bodacious D.F. a one-shot effort. — *William Ruhlmann*

Bodacious D. F. / 1973 / RCA ✦✦✦
Marty Balin didn't bring together the hottest band or the best set of songs for what amounted to his comeback album, but it was still inspiring to hear his emotive tenor, one of the most distinctive elements of the '60s San Francisco rock scene, rising again. The album's loose, groove-oriented arrangements pointed the way to the kind of thing Balin would do more effectively in Jefferson Starship: listen to "Drivin' Me Crazy" for hints of the transfixing style of the Starship's "Caroline" and "Miracles." Nevertheless, *Bodacious D.F.* must go down as a footnote in the career of a major artist. (A footnote well worth reissuing on CD, though, if anybody at RCA is paying attention.) — *William Ruhlmann*

BoDeans

Group, Roots-Rock
The BoDeans are a rock & roll band formed in Waukesha, WI, by singer/songwriters/guitarists Sammy Llanas and Kurt Neumann, who have played together since junior high school, along with a rhythm section of bassist Bob Griffin and drummer Guy Hoffman. The quartet signed to Slash Records (manufactured and distributed by Warner Bros.) and released its first album, the critically well-accepted *Love & Hope & Sex & Dreams* (the title comes from a line in the Rolling Stones song "Shattered") in 1986. *Outside Looking In* (1987), produced by Talking Head and Wisconsin native Jerry Harrison, saw the band reduced to a trio with the departure of Hoffman. It broke into the Top 100 best-sellers, as the BoDeans toured with U2, appeared on Robbie Robertson's self-titled debut solo album, and were named "Best New Band" in *Rolling Stone* magazine. By the time of the release of the third album, *Home* (1989), Michael Ramos (keyboards) and Danny Gayol (drums) had joined. This lineup stayed intact for the release of *Black and White* (1991), but the BoDeans were drummerless again as of the release of *Go Slow Down* (1993). — *William Ruhlmann*

● **Love & Hope & Sex & Dreams** / May 1986 / Slash ✦✦✦✦
When the BoDeans appeared with their first album, *Love & Hope & Sex & Dreams*, in 1986, they immediately were filed under "roots rock" (a popular term of the day) because of the Western twang in their guitars, their bouncy beat, and their simple, neo-

rockabilly approach to songwriting, not to mention the production of T-Bone Burnett. They led off the album with "She's A Runaway," a song of spousal abuse and revenge that indicated a higher social consciousness than much of the rest of the album, which was typified by "Misery," in which the singer laments that his girlfriend sleeps around. At their best, on "She's A Runaway," "Fadeaway," and "Angels," the BoDeans came up with infectious riffs and made maximum use of the sweet-and-sour vocal interaction between the conventional voice of Kurt Neumann and Sammy Llanas's distinctive nasal whine. Much of the album was slight, but there was enough of an individual sound to the better material to think of the BoDeans as a band of considerable promise. — *William Ruhlmann*

Outside Looking In / Sep. 1987 / Slash ✦✦
Having established themselves as contenders with their debut album, the BoDeans looked to move on to the next level in commercial and artistic terms on their second release, bringing in producer Jerry Harrison of Talking Heads and expanding beyond their "roots rock" style, to the extent of occasionally singing in falsetto, adding female backup vocals and recording near-soul pop numbers like "Runaway Love." But the songwriting wasn't as impressive, and the de-emphasis on such signature sounds as Sammy Llanas's nasal voice inclined the album toward anonymity. (Sequencing didn't help either: why bury the album's best song, the Byrds-like "What It Feels Like," as the eighth track? In fact, the album improved generally in its second half, when it sounded more like the first album.) Although they broke into the top 100 best-sellers, they failed to break a chart or radio single, which clouded their future. — *William Ruhlmann*

Home / Jul. 27, 1989 / Slash ✦✦✦
The BoDeans toured as opening act to U2 while promoting their second album, and their third album, *Home*, contained at least four songs with guitar work that seemed to have been copied from the fingers of U2's The Edge. Elsewhere, the BoDeans seemed to be seeking to escape their "roots rock" tag by turning out one genre exercise after another—country & western on "Beaujolais," '60s Motown R&B on "When The Love Is Good," '50s rock & roll on "Good Work" and "Sylvia." The only times when the band sounded like itself were when Sammy Llanas got to do one of his story songs, such as "No One" or "Far Far Away From My Heart," but those sounded more like Llanas solo efforts than group works. Things had changed for this band over three albums: initially, they sounded so style-bound that you wondered if any growth was possible, but with this album they were charging off in half a dozen directions at once. — *William Ruhlmann*

Black and White / Apr. 26, 1991 / Slash ✦✦✦
After moderate sales on their first three albums threatened to forever classify them as an alternative band, BoDeans started tackling bigger themes on *Black and White*, produced by Prince-sideman David Z. The band hardly sounds like the roots-oriented band of their previous efforts, Sam Llanas and Kurt Neumann sound more ambitious as songwriters. So "Black, White and Blood Red" is about more than race, the same way the anthemic "Naked" is about more than sex, the same way the hooky "Good Things" is about more than some guy who can't meet a girl. *Black and White* is about using individual problems as analogies to social ones. It's also about loneliness and hardship. It also didn't sell that much better (if any) than the first albums. — *Brian Mansfield*

○ **Go Slow Down** / Oct. 12, 1993 / Slash ✦✦✦✦
The BoDeans made their best album since their debut by returning to the basic folk and rock elements that had always worked best for them. On their most acoustic outing they also rediscovered themselves as songwriters, pursuing subjects unusually close at hand, whether sex, suicide or the frustrations of the music business. No matter what the topic, they sounded like they meant it, and for once their eclecticism worked for them, providing them with a bagful of styles to evoke without overdoing it. *Go Slow Down* may have been the statement of a band that had been through a lot and reached a point of emotional exhaustion, but the BoDeans used this experience to craft their most deeply felt and satisfying music. — *William Ruhlmann*

Body Count

Group, Hard Rock, Heavy Metal
Maybe no one saw the humor or maybe they were distracted by the barely competent heavy metal of the album, but rapper Ice-T's heavy metal group launched a hurricane of publicity with their

self-titled debut album, *Body Count*. Ice-T's music had been hard as heavy metal for a number of years and on 1991's landmark *OG Original Gangster*, he recorded the speed metal/hip-hop fusion "Body Count," with his band of the same name. Body Count's lineup included Ernie-C (guitar), D-Roe (guitar), Mooseman (bass), and Beatmaster V (drums), all of whom attended Crenshaw High School in South Central Los Angeles. On the 1991 Lollapalooza tour, Ice-T performed with Body Count and earned a substantial amount of fans and praise. "Body Count" was a highlight of *OG* and, not coincidentally, it was the most serious and best song on their 1992 album. For the rest of *Body Count*, the band engages in a bunch of heavy metal clichés and silly lyrics that are often cringe-inducing; if it isn't a parody, Ice-T's faith has been sorely misplaced.

After it was out for a couple of months, a fury over one of their serious songs, "Cop Killer," made the album a symbol for everything that was wrong with popular culture. After several months of constant bad publicity, Warner Brothers and Ice-T pulled the song from the album; several months later, he parted ways with the record company.

Body Count released their second album, *Born Dead*, on Ice-T's new record label Priority in 1994. The record failed to generate either controversy or sales and disappeared shortly after its fall release. —*Stephen Thomas Erlewine*

● **Body Count** / 1992 / Sire ✦✦✦✦
Divorced from the controversy that surrounded its release, Body Count's self-titled debut is a surprisingly tepid affair. Apart from the previously released "Body Count" (which appeared on Ice-T's 1991 album *O.G. Original Gangster*), the record is devoid of serious commentary, trading intelligence for a lurid comic book depiction of sex, violence and "Voodoo." All of Ice-T's half-sung/half-shouted lyrics fall far short of the standard he established on his hip-hop albums. The controversial "Cop Killer"—which is nothing more than a standard thrash-metal chant—stands out because it is one of the few tracks that doesn't rely on garish, cartoonish imagery. There's the saga of "Evil Dick," which tells Ice-T to not "sleep alone." There's "KKK Bitch," where he crashes a Ku Klux Klan meeting and screws the grand dragon's daughter. There's "Voodoo," where a witch doctor cripples our hero with a voodoo doll. There's "Mama's Gotta Die Tonight," where Ice-T offs his mother 'cause she's a racist. By the time the band works around to the power ballad "The Winner Loses" and Ice-T is crooning "My friend's addicted to cocaine," it's unclear whether the record is a parody or a horribly flawed stab at arena metal. It would help if the band wrote riffs that were memorable or if they conveyed a sense of kinetic energy instead of tossing out their riffs in a work-man-like fashion. Perhaps *Body Count* was intentionally humorous—although the group's follow-up, *Born Dead*, suggests that it wasn't—but in any case, the record was simply embarrassing. After "Cop Killer" was pulled from the album, it was replaced with a bland version of Ice-T's rap classic "The Iceberg" recorded with Jello Biafra. —*Stephen Thomas Erlewine*

Born Dead / 1994 / Capitol ✦✦
All of the controversy over "Cop Killer" and Body Count's debut album obscured one important fact—they're not a very good band. *Born Dead* makes that clear by replicating all of *Body Count*—all of the plodding riffs, embarrassing singing, obvious attempts at social commentary, and the relentless "Body Count, Body Count, Body Count, BC, BC, BC" chants. All that's missing is humor. Not even the worst material on *Body Count* is unintentionally funny; it's just embarrassing. Ice-T can pull this material off live; on record, his band just sounds like a heavy metal relic from the late '80s. —*Stephen Thomas Erlewine*

Angela Bofill

b. 1954, West Bronx, NY
Urban
This Bronx native sang with Ricardo Morero & the Group and the Dance Theater of Harlem chorus before her 1978 debut. With her strong, distinctive alto, she has carved a niche as an outstanding interpreter of soul ballads. Between 1978 and 1984, Bofill had consistent success on the R&B charts, with six albums making the Top 40 (five of which made the Top 100 on the pop charts as well), including two, *Angel of the Night* (1979) and *Too Tough* (1983), that made the Top Ten. During this period, she also placed seven singles in the R&B Top 40, with "Too Tough" making the Top Ten. Bofill's career cooled off after 1984, but she returned to the R&B

charts with *Intuition* (1988) and *I Wanna Love Somebody* (1993). —*Bil Carpenter*

Angie / 1978 / GRP ✦✦✦
Angela Bofill temporarily became the hot Latin pop singer in the late '70s with her debut for GRP. It was a smart blend of glossy urban contemporary, light jazz, and fusion; Bofill's voice had enough sophistication to sound sleek and enough Flora Purim influence to attract interest from jazz, Latin, and urban contemporary audiences. It scored three mild hits and got the then-fledging GRP label some vital sales. —*Ron Wynn*

Angel of the Night / Oct. 1979 / GRP ✦✦✦
The second Angela Bofill album for GRP was her last for them. She continued mixing light jazz, fusion, some Afro-Latin, and pop, and the title tune got wide airplay and was a moderate hit. The album did well enough to get Bofill a deal with Arista, which at the time was distributing GRP. —*Ron Wynn*

○ **Something About You** / Nov. 1981 / Arista ✦✦✦✦
Angela Bofill moved away from light jazz, fusion, and Latin, and into urban contemporary productions and quasi-R&B/soul when she signed with Arista. This was the first of several projects she did with Narada Michael Walden. He landed her a hit with the song "Tropical Love," and she also adopted a tougher, more assertive tone and sound. —*Ron Wynn*

○ **Too Tough** / Jan. 1983 / Arista ✦✦✦✦
Bofill scored one of her biggest dance and R&B hits with the title track. It had a great hook, excellent production, and good arrangement, and her vocal was the ideal mix of aggressive, enticing, and defiant. There were also two good songs done in an opposite fashion, "Is This a Dream" and "I Can See It in Your Eyes." This was arguably the best Bofill production done by Narada Michael Walden. —*Ron Wynn*

Teaser / Nov. 1983 / Arista ✦✦✦
Angela Bofill explored dance-tinged pop and R&B heavily in the mid-'80s. The System were now producing her records, adding a heavy dose of synthesized backbeats and textures. Bofill's voice didn't sound as sensual or demure as on her earlier tracks, and the light jazz/fusion/Latin background were gone. The title cut was a mild dance hit, and there were some other songs that got a little urban contemporary interest, but Bofill's voice was now secondary to the beat. —*Ron Wynn*

Let Me Be the One / Nov. 1984 / Arista ✦✦
The first of the albums produced for Bofill by the System, who introduced a more overt dance sound into her work. Bofill didn't do as many ballads and struck a more animated tone in her vocals. This strategy wasn't immediately successful, but did eventually produce some hits. —*Ron Wynn*

Tell Me Tomorrow / Oct. 1985 / Arista ✦✦

● **The Best of Angela Bofill** / Aug. 1986 / Arista ✦✦✦✦
Lazy, jazz-styled soft soul from the '70s and '80s. —*Bil Carpenter*

Intuition / Nov. 1988 / Capitol ✦✦
Angela Bofill tried to find a middle ground between the light jazz, fusion, and Latin music she did earlier in her career and the glossy urban contemporary and dance-tinged R&B and pop that had been her '80s mode. The results were mixed; much of this sounds tentative and generic, with Bofill struggling to find a comfortable way to express the lyrics and get used to the production style. —*Ron Wynn*

Love Is in Your Eyes / 1991 / Capitol ✦✦
Angela Bofill tried a little of everything on this early '90s date. There's some pop, some urban contemporary, some light fusion, and even a little Latin. None of it did very well, but it showed her versatility. Her voice had a deeper, richer, more experienced quality than when she debuted in the late '70s. Unfortunately, she found that the new generation wasn't aware of her past hits or that attuned to the fresh material. —*Ron Wynn*

I Wanna Love Somebody / Feb. 1993 / Jive ✦✦

Tommy Bolin

b. 1951, Sioux City, IA, d. Dec. 4, 1976, Miami
Hard Rock, Heavy Metal
Tommy Bolin achieved his greatest notoriety in Deep Purple, filling the position of founding member, lead-guitarist Ritchie Blackmore, who had left the band to form Rainbow. Previously Bolin had worked with Zephyr, Billy Cobham, and James Gang. After Deep Purple folded in 1976, Bolin went solo, releasing two al-

bums. Of particular note was Bolin's slide work. He passed away in Miami in 1976. —*Rick Clark*

○ **Teaser** / 1975 / Columbia ♦♦♦♦
A scattershot collection, but Bolin's forceful slide work on "The Grind" is worth the hunt. —*Rick Clark*

● **Private Eyes** / 1976 / Columbia ♦♦♦♦
It's a solid showcase for Bolin's no-nonsense lead work in a focused package. —*Rick Clark*

The Ultimate: The Best of Tommy Bolin / 1989 / David Geffen Co. ♦♦♦
An overkill boxed set, it memorializes this late guitarist. Completists will be disappointed that some of *Teaser*'s best moments are not included. —*Rick Clark*

Michael Bolton (Michael Bolotin)

b. Feb. 26, 1954, New Haven, CT
Pop/Rock
Singer/songwriter Michael Bolton had an extensive, though not very successful career under his real name, Michael Bolotin, before emerging in the mid-'80s as a major soft-rock balladeer. He turned up on RCA Records in the mid-'70s singing in a gruff, Joe Cocker-like voice both his own blue-eyed soul songs and cover tunes. Neither record buyers nor critics were much interested by the result. He then became the lead singer in Blackjack, a heavy metal band that made two albums for Polydor at the end of the '70s and the start of the '80s. In 1983, he changed his name to Michael Bolton, signed to Columbia Records as a solo act, and relaunched his career.

Michael Bolton was released in April 1983 and made the Top 100 best-sellers, as did its single, "Fools Game." At the same time, "How Am I Supposed to Live Without You," which Bolton had co-written, became a Top 40 hit for Laura Branigan. Nevertheless, Bolton's second Columbia album, *Everybody's Crazy* (1985) was a commercial flop. His breakthrough came with his third album, *The Hunger*, released in September 1987. On this album, Bolton abandoned the more hard rock aspects of his style to concentrate on blue-eyed soul singing, both on his own songs, such as "That's What Love Is All About" and on covers like Otis Redding's "(Sittin' On) The Dock of the Bay." Those two songs became Top 40 hits.

Soul Provider, released in July 1989, turned Bolton into a superstar, reaching the Top Ten, selling four million copies, and spawning five Top 40 singles, including Bolton's #1 version of "How Am I Supposed to Live Without You" and the Top Ten hits "How Can We Be Lovers" and "When I'm Back on My Feet Again." "How Am I Supposed to Live Without You" won Bolton a Grammy Award for Best Pop Vocal Performance, Male. *Time, Love & Tenderness*, released in April 1991, was even more successful, hitting #1, selling six million copies, and featuring four Top 40 hits, including the chart-topping cover of Percy Sledge's "When a Man Loves a Woman" and the Top Ten hits "Love Is a Wonderful Thing" (later the subject of a successful plagiarism suit brought against Bolton by the Isley Brothers) and "Time, Love and Tenderness."

Bolton won another Grammy Award for Best Pop Vocal Performance, Male, for "When a Man Loves a Woman," but he had to put up with abuse from two camps of detractors at the February 1992 ceremony. Just after Bolton had sung, pre-rock songwriter Irving Gordon won the Song of the Year award for "Unforgettable" and pointedly attacked songs that "scream, yell, and have a nervous breakdown" and singers who "have a hernia" when they sing. Then, backstage, Bolton faced a hostile press corps of critics unhappy with his tendency to copy great soul singers like Redding, Ray Charles, and Sledge. Bolton suggested they apply their lips to a certain part of his anatomy. He further responded with *Timeless (The Classics)* in September 1992, an album made up entirely of cover songs. It went to #1, sold three million copies, and featured a Top 40 hit in Bolton's version of the Bee Gees' "To Love Somebody." Bolton's next album of original material, *The One Thing*, came in November 1993. It hit the Top Ten, sold three million copies, and featured the Top Ten hit "Said I Loved You…But I Lied." —*William Ruhlmann*

Michael Bolton / Apr. 1983 / Columbia ♦♦♦
The former Michael Bolotin changed his name but not his style on his initial effort for Columbia Records. Bolton had essayed hard-edged arena rock with his band Blackjack, and here he did much the same thing, shout-singing in his emotive whiskey bellow over slashing guitar power chords (frequently courtesy of Blackjack's

Bruce Kulick and his brother Bob), icy keyboard fills, angelic backup choirs, and thundering rhythm sections, all intended to fill the hockey auditoriums of America alongside Journey and Foreigner. For all the clichés, Bolton was an undeniably involving singer, and songs like "Fools Game," the lead-off track and chart single, were satisfying pop efforts that suggested he might offer some competition to emerging mainstream rockers like Bryan Adams. As things would turn out, of course, the true key track was the cover of the Supremes' "Back In My Arms Again." —*William Ruhlmann*

The Hunger / Sep. 1987 / Columbia ♦♦♦
Given a third chance to resurrect his third career, Bolton made drastic changes. He decided to stop trying to be Lou Gramm of Foreigner and decided that he really wanted to be—Otis Redding? Well, that's what you'd think from his note-for-note copy of Redding's "(Sittin' On) The Dock Of The Bay," which brought him close to the Top Ten. Even more notable, though, was "That's What Love Is All About," an original ballad cowritten by Eric ("Love Has No Pride") Kaz that repositioned Bolton from heavy metal hunk to tough guy with a tender heart. There had been prior hints that Bolton could sell a big ballad, but they were always buried album tracks. This time, the ballad was issued as a single in advance of the album, and it did the trick. For the rest, Bolton employed a new set of collaborators, including members of Journey and pop songwriting queen Diane Warren. The result was platinum sales and a firm place in the middle of the road. —*William Ruhlmann*

● **Soul Provider** / Jul. 1989 / Columbia ♦♦♦♦
Michael Bolton is no fool, and when he broke through to platinum sales with *The Hunger*, nobody had to tell him to record a follow-up devoted to more of the same. Bolton produced most of the record himself, and he teamed with the cream of the era's romantic rock ballad writers, people like Diane Warren (who got five co-credits here) and Desmond Child, while the R&B copy this time was Ray Charles' version of "Georgia On My Mind." He also reclaimed "How Am I Supposed To Live Without You" from Laura Branigan. The result was five Top 40 hits and millions of albums sold. Maybe Bolton wasn't the king of the hockey rinks, but his voice was now stoking the romantic fires in bedrooms across America, which is nice work if you can get it. —*William Ruhlmann*

Early Years / 1991 / RCA ♦

○ **Time, Love & Tenderness** / Apr. 1991 / Columbia ♦♦♦♦
Michael Bolton cloned his approach from *Soul Provider* on its follow-up, *Time Love & Tenderness*, and sold as many records for his trouble. (That's six million copies.) His key collaborator once again was Diane Warren, who applied her gold-plated gift for writing contemporary love songs to six tunes, among them the hits "Time, Love And Tenderness" and "Missing You Now" (which featured saxmeister Kenny G). The obligatory R&B carbon copy was Percy Sledge's "When A Man Loves A Woman," which hit number one. The only unusual songs came at the beginning and the end. The album led off with "Love Is A Wonderful Thing" (a Top Ten hit), a song in standard '60s R&B mode that would be the subject of a plagiarism suit from the Isley Brothers, and it concluded with "Steel Bars," co-written by Bolton and…*Bob Dylan*? That's what it said, and if the song wasn't one of Bob's best, it at least indicated that Bolton might have possibilities that had so far gone unnoticed. —*William Ruhlmann*

Timeless (The Classics) / Sep. 1992 / Columbia ♦♦♦
It's hard to resist the notion that Michael Bolton, who took considerable flak in the press for storming the charts with copycat reproductions of '60s soul hits felt "suddenly compelled," as he put it here in a sleeve note, to devote an entire album to cover songs after publicly confronting his critics at the Grammy Awards ceremony in February 1992. There's not much you can do with "Yesterday" or "White Christmas" at this point. On the other hand, as with his previous R&B appropriations, versions of songs like the Four Tops' "Reach Out I'll Be There" and Sam and Dave's "Hold On, I'm Comin'" only succeeded in confirming Bolton's inferiority to his predecessors. —*William Ruhlmann*

The Artistry of Michael Bolotin / 1993 / RCA ♦♦
A ten-track compilation of Michael Bolton's early recordings of such classic rock staples as Joe Walsh's "Rocky Mountain Way" and the Guess Who's "These Eyes." Since Bolton was still trying to find his style, most of these songs fall flat, but it's interesting to hear his emotive vocals develop. —*Stephen Thomas Erlewine*

The One Thing / Nov. 1993 / Columbia ✦✦✦
You could hardly call an album that neared the top of the charts, stayed in them for ten months, and sold three million copies a flop, but when it's following two straight #1's, and the artist's last album of new material stayed in the charts twice as long and sold twice as many copies, you can call it a disappointment. Maybe it was just that this was the fourth (or fifth, if you count the covers album *Timeless [The Classics]*) time around for Bolton's successful formula, but *The One Thing* sounded pro forma even for him. That didn't keep "Said I Loved You ... But I Lied" from becoming a massive hit on soft-rock radio, but none of the other tunes really connected with his usually adoring public. It would not be wise, however, to count out a pop star as persistent as Michael Bolton. — *William Ruhlmann*

Bon Jovi

Group, Hard Rock, Pop/Rock
Bon Jovi is a hard rock quintet from New Jersey led by singer/guitarist Jon Bon Jovi (born John Bongiovi, Mar. 2, 1962, Perth Amboy, NJ) and featuring Richie Sambora (b. Jul. 11, 1959) (guitar), David Bryan (born David Rashbaum, Feb. 7, 1962, NJ) (keyboards), Alec John Such (b. Nov. 14, 1956) (bass), and Tico Torres (b. Oct. 7, 1953) (drums) that became one of the most popular rock acts of the late '80s and early '90s. The band was formed in Sayreville, NJ, in March 1983 and signed to Mercury Records, releasing its self-titled debut album in January 1984. The album reached the Top 100 and was followed by *7800 Degrees Fahrenheit* (March 1985), which went gold. Bon Jovi achieved mass success with its third album, *Slippery When Wet* (August 1986), which topped the charts and sold nine million copies. The album featured the #1 singles "You Give Love a Bad Name" and "Livin' on a Prayer" and the Top Ten hit "Wanted Dead or Alive." Bon Jovi's fifth album was *New Jersey* (September 1988), another chart-topper that sold five million copies and spawned five Top Ten hit singles including the #1's "Bad Medicine" and "I'll Be There for You." The group then went on hiatus while Jon Bon Jovi and Richie Sambora made solo albums. It returned to action with *Keep the Faith* in November 1992, which hit the Top Ten, sold a million copies, and featured the Top Ten single "Bed of Roses." *Cross Road*, a greatest hits collection, was released on October 4, 1994. It sold two million copies, reached the Top Ten, and included the Top Ten gold single "Always." — *William Ruhlmann*

Bon Jovi / Jan. 1984 / Mercury ✦✦✦
The band's debut, while lacking much of the focus found on subsequent releases, sets the blueprint for future greatness. In a superslick package, they offer a fine balance between hard rock and a strong sense of melody. — *David Jehnzen*

7800 Degrees Fahrenheit / Apr. 1985 / Mercury ✦✦✦
The band's 1985 sophomore effort was slammed by critics upon release, but showed a considerable growth in songwriting and playing. It was their first gold record and their last album before entering super-stardom with the follow-up, *Slippery When Wet*. Highlights include "In and Out of Love" and "Hardest Part of the Night." — *David Jehnzen*

● **Slippery When Wet** / Aug. 1986 / Mercury ✦✦✦✦
It is probably true that Bon Jovi's breakthrough success with *Slippery When Wet*, their third album, had more to do with lead singer Jon Bon Jovi's mop of curls and winning smile than with anything in the grooves of the record. Nevertheless, the album contained competent contemporary pop/rock, from its Eddie Van Halen-inspired guitar solos to the singer's enthusiastic, husky wail (which owed a lot to Bruce Springsteen). Jon Bon Jovi, guitarist Richie Sambora, and songwriter-for-hire Desmond Child had little more on their minds than girls and rock-as-mythology (even the working-class anthem "Livin' On A Prayer" featured a character who was forced to hock his "six string"), but that may only mean they had identified their audience—young white adolescent males—and were targeting it accurately. — *William Ruhlmann*

○ **New Jersey** / Sep. 1988 / Mercury ✦✦✦✦
Bon Jovi had perfected a formula for hard pop/rock by the time of this album, concentrating on sing-along choruses sung over and over again, frequently by a rough, extensively overdubbed chorus, producing an effect not unlike what these songs sounded like in the arenas and stadiums where they were most often heard. The lyrics had that typical pop twist—although they nominally expressed romantic commitment, sentiments such as "Lay Your Hands On Me" and "I'll Be There For You" worked equally well as

a means for the band and its audience to reaffirm their affection for each other. The only thing that marred the perfection of this communion was Jon Bon Jovi's continuing obsession with a certain predecessor from his home state; at times, he seemed to be trying to recreate *Born To Run* using cheaper materials. — *William Ruhlmann*

Keep the Faith / Nov. 1992 / Mercury ✦✦✦
After being missing in action for nearly four years, Bon Jovi returns with *Keep the Faith*, an update on their trademark pop-metal sound. Because the rules had changed since *New Jersey*, the band knew they had to shake things up a bit. Bon Jovi wants to be taken seriously this time around—hence, epics like the ten-minute "Dry County" and stabs at significance like "Fear" (plus the new short haircuts). Most of these grand statements fall flat, but there are songs here ("Bed of Roses," "Keep the Faith") that nearly match the glory days. — *Stephen Thomas Erlewine*

Keep the Faith: Spanish Version / Aug. 17, 1993 / Mercury ✦✦✦

● **Cross Road** / 1994 / Mercury ✦✦✦✦
While Bon Jovi always managed to stick a couple of killer album tracks on their records, their main strength has always been singles. *Cross Road* collects all of their biggest hits, adding a couple of new songs and Jon Bon Jovi's solo hit, "Blaze of Glory," for good measure. Even the band's detractors may not be able to resist the constant flow of big guitars, big hooks, and sweet melodies that pour out on *Cross Road*. After all, this is what state-of-the-art mainstream hard rock was all about in the late '80s. — *Stephen Thomas Erlewine*

These Days / 1995 / Mercury

Jon Bon Jovi (John Bongiovi)

b. Mar. 2, 1962, Perth Amboy, NJ
Hard Rock, Pop/Rock
Jon Bon Jovi spent the years from 1983 to 1988 establishing his hard rock band Bon Jovi as one of the most popular in the Western world with multi-platinum albums such as *Slippery When Wet* and *New Jersey*. He then put the band on hold and made a solo album, *Blaze of Glory* (July 1990), whose songs were inspired by the motion picture *Young Guns II*. Bon Jovi the band was reactivated with *Keep the Faith* in 1992. — *William Ruhlmann*

Young Guns II: "Blaze of Glory" (Music from & Inspired by the Film) / Jul. 1990 / PolyGram ✦✦✦
Abandoning his rough-and-ready rock & roll band, Jon Bon Jovi took a stab at respectability with this non-soundtrack to the film *Young Guns II*. Given his cowboy songs on Bon Jovi albums, it made sense that he'd be "inspired" by the Western, and he filled these songs (written without the help of bandmate Richie Sambora or Desmond Child) with references to shoot-'em-ups. Mainstream rock producer Danny Kortchmar put together the studio band, along with guest stars Jeff Beck, Elton John, and Little Richard, and the sound had more space and less drive than the lite-metal of Bon Jovi. Unfortunately, that kind of approach puts the spotlight squarely on the singer-songwriter, and Jon Bon Jovi wasn't quite up to the scrutiny. The New Jersey cowboy tried to howl his way through, and his still-faithful fans dutifully bought the record, but Jon Bon Jovi isn't really ready to carry off a starring role without his usual supporting cast. — *William Ruhlmann*

The Graham Bond Organization (Graham John Clifton Bond)

b. Oct. 28, 1937, Romford, Essex, England, **d.** May 8, 1974, London, England
Blues Rock, British Invasion
An important, underappreciated figure of early British R&B, Graham Bond is known in the U.S., if at all, for heading the group that Jack Bruce and Ginger Baker played in before they joined Cream. Originally an alto sax player—in fact, he was voted "Britain's New Jazz Star" in 1961—he met Bruce and Baker in 1962 after joining Alexis Korner's Blues Incorporated, the finishing school for numerous British rock and blues musicians. By the time he, Bruce, and Baker split to form their own band in 1963, Bond was mostly playing the Hammond organ, as well as handling the lion's share of the vocals. John McLaughlin was a member of the Graham Bond Organisation in the early days for a few months, and some live material that he recorded with the group was eventually issued after most of its members had achieved stardom in other contexts. Saxophonist Dick Heckstall-Smith completed Bond's

most stable lineup, which cut a couple of decent albums and a few singles in the mid-'60s.

In its prime, the Graham Bond Organisation played rhythm and blues with a strong jazzy flavor, emphasizing Bond's demonic organ and gruff vocals. The band arguably would have been better served to feature Bruce as its lead singer—he is featured surprisingly rarely on their recordings. Nevertheless, their best records were admirably tough British R&B-rock-jazz-soul, and though Bond has sometimes been labeled as a pioneer of jazz-rock, in reality it was much closer to rock than jazz. The band performed imaginative covers and fairly strong original material, and Bond was also perhaps the very first rock musician to record with the Mellotron synthesizer. Hit singles, though, were necessary for British bands to thrive in the mid-'60s, and Bond's group began to fall apart in 1966, when Bruce and Baker joined forces with Eric Clapton to form Cream. Graham attempted to carry on with the Organisation for a while with Heckstall-Smith and drummer Jon Hiseman, both of whom went on to John Mayall's Bluesbreakers and Colosseum.

Bond never recaptured the heights of his work with the Organisation. In the late '60s, he moved to the U.S., recording albums with musicians including Harvey Brooks, Harvey Mandel, and Hal Blaine. Moving back to Britain, he worked with Ginger Baker's Airforce, the Jack Bruce Band, and Cream lyricist Pete Brown, as well as forming the band Holy Magick, who recorded a couple albums. Bond's demise was more tragic than most: he developed serious drug and alcohol problems and an obsession with the occult, and it has even been posthumously speculated (in the British Bond biography *Mighty Shadow*) that he sexually abused his stepdaughter. He committed suicide by throwing himself into the path of a London Underground train in 1974. —*Richie Unterberger*

● **The Sound of 65** / Mar. 1965 / Edsel ✦✦✦
Although the Organization's first album was recorded a mere year or two before Cream's debut, it bears little resemblance to Cream's pioneering hard blues-rock. Instead, it's taut British R&B with a considerable jazz influence. That influence comes not so much from the rhythm section as saxophonist Dick Heckstall-Smith and lead singer/organist Bond himself. This LP is not as exciting or rock-oriented as contemporaries like the Rolling Stones or John Mayall, but it is respectably gritty, mostly original material, with an occasionally nasty edge. There are some obscure treasures of the British R&B explosion to be found here, including the original version of "Train Time" (later perfected by Cream), the thrilling bass runs on "Baby Be Good To Me," and the group's hard-boiled rearrangements of such traditional standards as "Wade In The Water" and "Early In The Morning." Even their blatant stab at commerciality (the ballad "Tammy") has its charm. —*Richie Unterberger*

○ **There's a Bond Between Us** / Nov. 1965 / Columbia ✦✦✦✦
Bond's second album stakes out similar territory as his debut in a more polished but slightly less exciting fashion. Some of the covers are a bit routine and hackneyed, and the original material isn't quite as strong (or frequent) as on the first effort. On a few tunes, the group expands from raveups to mellower, jazzier ballads that retain an R&B base. Highlights include the early Jack Bruce composition "Hear Me Calling Your Name" (to which he also contributes a fine lead vocal) and the excellent Bond tune "Walkin' In The Park," which holds up to the best early British R&B numbers. The album is also notable for being one of the very first rock LPs to feature the Mellotron, which Bond uses subtly and well. —*Richie Unterberger*

Solid Bond / May 1970 / Warner Brothers ✦✦✦

Graham Bond Organisation / 1984 / Charly ✦✦
This live 1964 gig is one of Giorgio Gomelsky's innumerable tapes of British club acts of the period, several of which should be released many years later in attempts to cash in on some big names who were present. These historical documents, never intended for release, ranged from superb to wretched. This LP (which, like most of these Gomelsky projects, has been reissued under numerous different covers and titles) falls about right in the middle of this scale. Bond led an erratic, interesting group that incorporated elements of jazz and improvisation into its blend of blues, R&B, and rock. Future Cream members Jack Bruce and Ginger Baker were his rhythm section in his prime, and Dick Heckstall-Smith handled horns; this is the lineup featured on this set. But it's not deathless stuff. The fidelity, for one, is muddy, especially the bottom,

Bruce's bass suffering the most. The better tunes—"Wade In The Water," "Early In The Morning," "Train Time," and "Spanish Blues"—are available in better performances and much clearer fidelity on the group's first studio album, *The Sound of 65*. The rest is routine, even below average in spots, early British R&B.The Organisation may have been among the most accomplished players on the scene, but they couldn't hold a candle to the Stones or Yardbirds in terms of imagination and excitement. A better introduction to the sound of this lineup is the fine Edsel reissue of *The Sound of 65* and *There's A Bond Between Us*, which have been combined into one package. —*Richie Unterberger*

Gary "U.S." Bonds (Gary Anderson)

b. Jun. 6, 1939, Jacksonville, FL
R&B, Rock & Roll
After moving to the Norfolk, VA, area in the mid '50s, young Gary Anderson began plying his vocal wares, first in church, later with a local group called the Turks. When he was not yet 21, he was approached by local record producer Frank Guida to join his tiny Legrand label. Guida changed Anderson's name to U.S. Bonds, hoping the first release would get extra airplay by disc jockeys mistaking it for a public service announcement. The result was the classic "New Orleans," combining rock-combo raunch with impassioned, scorched soul-singing that set the stage for all that would follow. Guida double- and triple-tracked Bonds's voice, and the resulting murky production gave all the hits (including "Quarter to Three," "School Is Out," and "Dear Lady Twist") a party-in-outer-space quality all their own. Though he has kept recording, making a couple of excellent solo albums in the early '80s with the help of Bruce Springsteen, Bonds is best seen today dotting the landscape of oldies shows the world over, singing the songs that made him famous. —*Cub Koda*

○ **Dance 'til Quarter to Three** / 1961 / Legrand ✦✦✦✦

Twist up Calypso / 1962 / Legrand ✦✦✦

Dedication / Apr. 1981 / Razor & Tie ✦✦✦
Bruce Springsteen played guitar, sang a duet, wrote three songs, and co-produced and co-arranged four songs on Gary U.S. Bonds' comeback album, recorded 20 years after his heyday. Springsteen also lent his backup group, the E Street Band, while E Street guitarist Miami Steve (Van Zandt) also contributed a song and produced the bulk of the record. The result, naturally, sounds like a Bruce Springsteen and the E Street Band album with lead vocals by Gary U.S. Bonds. Bonds's elastic tenor, in much greater clarity than it ever was in his early years, has just enough grit to be soulful, and he puts across the pop-soul tunes Springsteen and Van Zandt have constructed for him effectively. He also tackles the Beatles' "It's Only Love" and Bob Dylan's "From A Buick 6," and sings Jackson Browne's "The Pretender" as if the lyric was devoid of irony. It's an enjoyable album that does nothing to change the notion that Bonds as a recording artist essentially conforms himself to the intentions of his producer, whether that's Frank Guida, Jerry Williams, Jr., or Bruce Springsteen. —*William Ruhlmann*

Certified Soul / 1982 / Rhino ✦✦
In the wake of Gary U.S. Bonds' early '80s comeback, Rhino Records released this compilation of singles he made between 1968 and 1970 for producer Jerry Williams, Jr. Williams cast Bonds in the late '60s soul style of Wilson Pickett and Otis Redding, which meant his voice was often a harsh bark and the music had a Memphis-style funkiness, complete with horns. Bonds handled the material well, but the music still doesn't compare either to his early '60s hits or his early '80s comeback material. —*William Ruhlmann*

On the Line / Jun. 1982 / Razor & Tie ✦✦✦
On The Line, Gary U.S. Bonds' second comeback album under the sponsorship of Bruce Springsteen, was even more of a Springsteen record than its predecessor. This time, Springsteen wrote seven of the 11 songs, co-produced all of them with Miami Steve (Van Zandt) and again lent the E Street Band for the sessions. While there were no Springsteen masterpieces here, the rock & roll revival style of the material, similar to that on *Dedication*, made it, in effect, the follow-up to Springsteen's *The River* album, albeit with a different vocalist. And that vocalist was, if anything, more expressive than the author—on a song like "Out Of Work," one of Springsteen's blue-collar anthems, Bonds sang with the conviction of a journeyman who knows what work is and what it's like not to have it. —*William Ruhlmann*

Standing in the Line of Fire / 1984 / Phoenix ♦♦

For the album's title track, Gary U.S. Bonds turned to Little Steven (Van Zandt), who wrote, arranged, played lead guitar, and produced it, some of the same tasks he had undertaken for Bonds' previous two albums. As a result, the performance had much of the drive of the anthemic songs on Little Steven's solo albums. For the rest, on which he was co-billed with his backup band, the American Men, Bonds was for the first time his own boss, and he proved he could come up with sturdy rock & roll songs, although nothing to match his early hits or the songs Bruce Springsteen wrote for him in the early '80s. — *William Ruhlmann*

Warning: For Health's Sake Restrict Play Three Times Daily / 198? / ♦♦♦

Warning For Health's Sake Restrict Play Three Times Daily is a compilation of Gary U.S. Bonds' early material on producer Frank Guida's Legrand label. There has been some remixing, and some tracks are presented in stereo, but songs like "Quarter To Three," "School Is Out," "School Is In," and "Seven Day Weekend" sound much as they did on singles in the early '60s. Those are the only hits among the 13 tracks, although Bonds and Guida retain a party atmosphere throughout and one gets a greater sense of their overall style than a singles collection would provide. (Although the album does not bear a copyright date, it appears to have been released circa 1983, if only because Little Walter, who wrote the liner notes, recalls working on the tracks with Guida during Thanksgiving week 1982.) — *William Ruhlmann*

● The School of Rock 'N' Roll: Best of Gary U.S. Bonds / 1990 / Rhino ♦♦♦♦

Gary U.S. Bonds' biggest hits—"New Orleans," "Twist, Twist Senora," and especially "Quarter To Three"—were unquestionably among the best rock & roll of the early '60s. Beyond that, the going runs a bit thin. This 18-cut compilation includes all of the above hits, as well as others from his blitz of Top 40 singles in 1961 and 1962—"School Is Out," the response record "School Is In" (guess which one did worse), "Dear Lady Twist," and "Seven Day Weekend." The rest of the CD features B-sides, flop singles, and unissued material from his stay at the Legrand label in the early '60s. Most of them feature the dense production, party atmosphere, and West Indian-influenced beats that made his hits so instantly identifiable. It was nonetheless a formula, and wears thin over the course of an entire album. Two of the more interesting cuts are the original 1961 version of "Not Me," which would become a big hit for the Orlons in 1963 in a slightly sanitized version, and both parts of the 1963 single "Perdido," which works up as manic a party atmosphere as Bonds ever managed. — *Richie Unterberger*

Bone Thugs N Harmony

Group, Rap

The Cleveland-based hardcore rap collective Bone Thugs N Harmony was one of Eazy-E's last production efforts before his death in March 1995. Featuring Krayzie Bone, Layzie Bone, Bizzy Bone, Wish Bone, and Flesh-N-Bone, the group released their first EP, *Creepin on Ah Come Up*, in June of 1994. It sold over three million copies and had a crossover hit single with "Thuggish-Ruggish-Bone." — *Stephen Thomas Erlewine*

○ Creepin On Ah Come Up / 1994 / Ruthless ♦♦♦♦

Bone Thugs N Harmony came out of nowhere and scored a double-platinum hit with the *Creepin On Ah Come Up* EP, which is more notable for the group's hard-edged gangsta stance than the music, which is fairly standard hardcore hip-hop. — *Stephen Thomas Erlewine*

Boney M

Group, Disco

Although they never had much success in America, the Euro-disco group Boney M was a European phenomenon during the '70s. After German record producer Frank Farian (b. 1942) recorded the single 'Baby Do You Wanna Bump?' (which was successful in Holland and Belgium), he created Boney M to support the song, bringing in four West Indian vocalists who had been working as session singers in Germany—Marcia Barrett (b. Oct. 14, 1948, St. Catherines, Jamaica), Liz Mitchell (b. Jul. 12, 1952, Clarendon, Jamaica), Maizie Williams (b. Mar. 25, 1951, Monserrat, West Indies), and Bobby Farrell (b. Oct. 6, 1949, Aruba, West Indies). "Daddy Cool" reached the U.K. Top Ten in February 1977, followed in April by a remake of Bobby Hebb's "Sunny." In July, "Ma Baker" just missed

the U.K. number one spot, and "Belfast" hit the Top Ten in December. In 1978, Boney M was at the height of its popularity with "Rivers of Babylon"/"Brown Girl in the Ring," which became the second-biggest selling single in U.K. chart history. "Rivers of Babylon" also was Boney M's only U.S. Top 40 hit. Boney M's album *Nightflight to Venus* also topped the U.K. charts. In October 1978, "Rasputin" became another U.K. Top Ten hit, followed by the seasonal chart-topper "Mary's Boy Child"/"Oh My Lord," which became the fifth-biggest selling single in U.K. history. In March 1979, "Painter Man" hit the U.K. Top Ten, followed in May by "Hooray! Hooray! It's a Holi-Holiday." In September, the album *Oceans of Fantasy* hit number one. The group was disbanded in 1980; their music continues to sell well in Europe, with a compilation hitting the U.K. Top Ten recently. Farian went on to create the late-'80s dance sensation Milli Vanilli. — *Stephen Thomas Erlewine*

● Magic of Boney M [20 Hits] / 1980 / Atlantic/Hansa ♦♦♦♦

Boney M's top Euro-disco creations—songs that ruled the continent for a while in the mid-'70s—are compiled on this singularly pleasing singles collection. — *Stephen Thomas Erlewine*

Bongos

Group, Power Pop/Anglo-Pop

Hoboken's Bongos—founded as a trio consisting of Richard Barone (guitar, vocals), Rob Norris (bass), and Frank Giannini (drums, vocals)—made no pretense of being anything other than a pop band; fortunately, they were a good pop band, covering guitar pop from the Byrds to T. Rex, all of it pulled together by Barone's original songs. Although he was the focal point, the other members were by no means peripheral; after their first full-length album, *Drums Along the Hudson* (1982), James Mastro joined and contributed some stellar hooks. After releasing a series of singles and an EP on tiny Fetish Records in 1980 and 1981, the Bongos signed to independent PVC Records. *Drums Along the Hudson* compiled all their previously released tracks. They then moved up to major label RCA and released the five-song *Numbers with Wings EP* (1983) and the album *Beat Hotel* (1985), before leaving RCA and splitting up. (Later, *Drums Along the Hudson* and a two-fer of *Numbers with Wings* and *Beat Hotel* were reissued on CD by Razor & Tie.) At their best, the Bongos made some irresistible guitar pop. — *William Ruhlmann*

Drums Along the Hudson / 1982 / Razor & Tie ♦♦♦

Richard Barone's brief lyrics frequently lack clarity, but he sings them earnestly, and the trio plays irresistibly catchy, guitar-based pop music. Heard from the perspective of the following decade, both the playing and the lyrics sound remarkably prescient (this band could clean up in the alternative market today), although at the time they sounded noticeably retro. (*Drums Along The Hudson* compiles all the tracks on the U.K. EP *Time And The River*, along with the Bongos' previously released singles.) — *William Ruhlmann*

○ Numbers With Wings / 1983 / RCA ♦♦♦♦

This five-song EP (now available, along with *Beat Hotel*, on a single CD) marks several upgrades in the Bongos' career. They have added second guitarist James Mastro, moved up to RCA Records, and brought in producer Richard Gottehrer. Gottehrer, who has a sharp sense of rock & roll dynamics (listen to his work on the Angels' "My Boyfriend's Back"), is a felicitous choice, and the added instrumentation (and no doubt better-budgeted recording and mixing) allows the Bongos to better realize their pop sound. As a result, songs like "Numbers With Wings," with its echoed vocals and full sound, have the kind of epic sweep Richard Barone's compositions have always suggested without achieving before. Not that the band has become overblown—just fulfilled. — *William Ruhlmann*

Beat Hotel / 1985 / RCA ♦♦♦

Beat Hotel is, in a sense, the Bongos' only "real" album; *Drums Along The Hudson*, its predecessor, was a compilation of previously released single and EP tracks. As such, *Beat Hotel* is a more unified effort than the earlier LP, but lacks the urgent immediacy that all those singles tracks gave it. Richard Barone makes extensive use of a guitar synthesizer to fill out the band's sound, although it's still the normal guitar licks that dominate the music. Barone also sings engagingly, filling his songs with catchy hooks, even though on the lyric sheet it's hard to figure out what he's talking about. It's a shame that *Beat Hotel*, which seems like a transitional album, proved to be the Bongos' final effort—they remain a promising group that never had a chance to reach their potential. —*William Ruhlmann*

● **Beat Hotel/Numbers with Wings** / Jul. 24, 1992 / Razor & Tie ◆◆◆◆
This is a two-fer of the Bongos' last EP and albums. "Barbarella" and the title cut from the Richard Gottehrer-produced *Numbers with Wings* (1983) are the highlights on that set. *Beat Hotel* (1985) is their best-sounding effort, though the songwriting quality isn't as consistent. —*Rick Clark*

Karla Bonoff

b. Dec. 27, 1952, Los Angeles, CA
Singer-Songwriter
Singer/songwriter Karla Bonoff grew up in Los Angeles and briefly attended UCLA. Emerging from the Monday night hootenanny scene at the Troubadour nightclub, she was a member of Bryndle, a folk-rock group also featuring Wendy Waldman, Andrew Gold, and Kenny Edwards that formed in 1969, signed to A&M, and cut an album that was never released. Edwards, a former member of the Stone Poneys, a band featuring Linda Ronstadt, and Gold later were part of Ronstadt's backing band, and they brought Bonoff to her attention. Ronstadt recorded three of Bonoff's songs on her 1976 album, *Hasten Down the Wind*, leading to a recording contract for Bonoff and the release of three albums on Columbia Records, the last of which, *Wild Heart of the Young* (1982) featured the Top 40 hit "Personally." Bonoff worked on movie soundtracks during the '80s, notably on *Footloose* (1984) and *About Last Night* (1986). She released her fourth album, *New World*, in 1988. —*William Ruhlmann*

● **Karla Bonoff** / Sep. 1977 / Columbia ◆◆◆◆
If Karla Bonoff's debut album sounded like the sort of record that Linda Ronstadt or James Taylor were making at the same time, that shouldn't have been a surprise: the rhythm section of Leland Sklar and Russell Kunkel was the same, the tasteful chicken-scratching of guitarist Waddy Wachtel was present, and so was a cheering section including Ronstadt, Eagle Don Henley, Eagle associate J.D. Souther, and other charter members of the SoCal country/folk/rock club of the '70s. Also, Ronstadt had cut three of the songs on her last album and Bonnie Raitt had done one. All of this meant that, despite Bonoff's competent singing, which actually better accentuated the lyrics of her songs than Ronstadt's, it was hard for her to get out from under the shadow of the members of her peer group who had preceded her. Nevertheless, heard today, the album's ten songs paint an effective picture of the ups and downs of love, circa the mid-'70s. —*William Ruhlmann*

Restless Nights / Sep. 1979 / Columbia ◆◆◆
Karla Bonoff seems to have had some trouble coming up with material for her second album, which may explain why it took two years (a long time in the '70s) and contained covers of "When You Walk In The Room" and "The Water Is Wide," and also why the originals weren't as uniformly excellent as those on her first album. True, leadoff track "Trouble Again" was a gem (as Linda Ronstadt proved when she recorded it on her *Cry Like A Rainstorm—Howl Like The Wind* album in 1989), but some of the other material was only pedestrian. As usual, half of L.A. was playing and singing on the record, which meant that you got people like Don Henley and James Taylor for your money. But *Restless Nights* did not represent the leap in quality that would have been required to vault Bonoff into the ranks of her star friends (it didn't have a big hit single, either), and so, instead of providing a consolidation of her reputation, it caused a rethinking of career direction reflected on her third album. —*William Ruhlmann*

Wild Heart of the Young / Mar. 1982 / Columbia ◆◆
After two modest-selling albums, Karla Bonoff tried a new approach with her third, posing for a cover photo in a lace dress with a male model, cutting a specially chosen cover song for a hit single, and making an MTV video. And it worked, sort of. Paul Kelly's "Personally," a coy and catchy pop song utterly uncharacteristic of Bonoff's other work, did make it into the Top 40. But that didn't stimulate the album's sales enough to keep Columbia Records from dropping Bonoff. Beyond the commercial considerations, though, Bonoff's original songs, which made up the bulk of the album, simply were not up to the standard set by her debut, and *Wild Heart Of The Young* was the weakest of her three Columbia Records albums. —*William Ruhlmann*

New World / 1988 / Gold Castle ◆◆◆
Karla Bonoff returned to the album racks after six years with *New World*, on which she once again demonstrated her talent for plaintive romantic ballads. If there was nothing to match her best material, there were a couple of tunes that once again provided interpretative opportunities for Linda Ronstadt, especially "All My Life," which Ronstadt and Aaron Neville turned into a pop standard the year after this album was released, and a couple yet to be discovered, especially "Still Be Getting Over You." —*William Ruhlmann*

The Bonzo Dog Band

Group, Psychedelic, Pop/Rock
Besides, perhaps, the Mothers of Invention (with whom they were sometimes compared), the Bonzo Dog Band was the most successful group to combine rock music and comedy. Starting off as the Bonzo Dog Dada Band, then becoming the Bonzo Dog Doo-Dah Band, and then finally just the Bonzo Dog Band, the group was started by British art college students in the mid-'60s. Initially they were inclined toward trad jazz and vaudevillian routines, but by the time of their 1967 debut album, they were leaning further in pop and rock directions. A brief appearance in the Beatles' *Magical Mystery Tour* film bolstered their visibility, and Paul McCartney (under the pseudonym Apollo C. Vermouth) produced their single "I'm the Urban Spaceman," which reached the British Top Five in 1968. The Bonzos really hit their stride with their second and third albums, which found them adding elements of psychedelia to their already absurdist mix of pop, cabaret, and Dada. The Bonzos could be side-splitting, but their records also held up well because they were also capable musicians and songwriters, paced by Neil Innes and Viv Stanshall (both of whom wrote the lion's share of their best material). The group attempted to move into more serious and musical realms with their 1969 LP *Keynsham*, which unsurprisingly was acclaimed as their weakest effort. They broke up shortly afterwards; Viv Stanshall made some obscure solo recordings (he was also the grandstanding narrator on Mike Oldfield's "Tubular Bells"). Neil Innes collaborated with members of Monty Python, upon whom the Bonzos were a large influence, as well as writing the songs for and performing in the brilliant Beatles documentary spoof, *The Rutles*. —*Richie Unterberger*

Gorilla / Oct. 1967 / One Way ◆◆◆
Gorilla was the 1967 debut album by the Bonzo Dog Doo-Dah Band, who would thereafter drop the Doo-Dah from their name and establish themselves as the greatest satirical British pop band of all time. Their first effort is far more tentative and tamer than their second and third albums, when they hit their stride by expanding their musical and topical recklessness. The Bonzos, after all, did not begin as a rock band, or even a pop band, but as a somewhat vaudevillian comedy outfit that owed a great deal to British music hall traditions. This album may be low-key, but that's not to say it doesn't retain a good deal of charm. The humor is extremely dry, subtle, and British, leaning more toward their trad jazz roots than the churning London pop-rock scene. It nonetheless includes a few great moments: the deadpan jazz vamp "The Intro And The Outro" (wherein a smarmy MC introduces a bevy of historical figures in a show band, including Adolf Hitler on vibes), the film-noir satire "Mickey's Son And Daughter," and their vicious send-up of "The Sound Of Music." It's not recommended as a starting point, but those who already appreciate these wonderful British eccentrics will find this an enjoyable document of the band's more restrained roots. —*Richie Unterberger*

○ **Doughnuts in Grannys Greenhouse** / Dec. 1968 / Edsel ◆◆◆◆
Taking the "Doo Dah" out of their name for this 1968 LP, the Bonzos' second album was probably their best. Although they were hardly a rock or pop group in the traditional sense, the Bonzos couldn't help absorbing some of the vibes of British psychedelia, and the heady ambience of the era is reflected in the recklessly diverse and outrageous material. Almost all of the songs were penned by the two top Dogs, Viv Stanshall and Neil Innes, who deflate British blues, psychedelia, and other pop, jazz, and music hall styles with priceless wit. Star tracks on this saxophone-heavy album include the doo-wop ode to a spacegirl ("Beautiful Zelda"), "Trouser Press" (which gave the late American underground rock magazine its name), the droll series of poker-faced spoken sketches on "Rhinocratic Oaths" (certainly an influence on Monty Python), and the boozy "My Pink Half Of The Drainpipe," which ranks as one of the most ridiculous and hysterical songs released by a pop group of any era. —*Richie Unterberger*

Tadpoles / Aug. 1, 1969 / One Way ✦✦✦
The Bonzos' third album is a bit of a retreat from the cosmic any-thing-goes atmosphere of their second LP (*Doughnuts in Granny's Greenhouse*), slanted much more heavily toward their vaudevil-lian trad-jazz roots. Perhaps that's because Viv Stanshall and Neil Innes, who dominated the second album, contribute only three tunes here. Still, it's never less than entertaining and has some stellar moments, like the psychedelic African safari of "Ali Baba's Camel," the skit "Shirt" (another clear forerunner of Monty Python), and the British hit single "I'm The Urban Spaceman," pro-duced by Paul McCartney. —*Richie Unterberger*

Lets Make up & Be Friendly / Apr. 1972 / One Way ✦✦

○ **History of the Bonzos** / May 24, 1974 / United Artists ✦✦✦✦
Necessarily, the pick among Bonzos albums is Rhino's 1990 col-lection *The Best Of The Bonzo Dog Band*, but only because that one's in print. This compilation was released as a double-LP set in 1974 and, although out of print, is the best Bonzos compilation (and there have been quite a few). Running an hour and 42 min-utes and containing 35 tracks that span the Bonzos' five albums and some of their solo work, the album effectively presents their offbeat humor and diverse musical styles, from the 1920s music hall pop and jazz of their early period to the more rock-oriented material they made later on. The humor is absurd and whimsical rather than laugh-out-loud funny—maybe a video compilation would be the best way to appreciate them—but you can definitely hear the makings of British comedy in the Monty Python mold here. —*William Ruhlmann*

● **The Best of the Bonzo Dog Band** / 1990 / Rhino ✦✦✦✦
This is a well-chosen overview of the playful late-'60s British ab-surdists' work. Fans of Monty Python should check out this pre-cursor. —*Rick Clark*

Boo Radleys

Group, Alternative Pop/Rock
Formed in Liverpool in 1988, the English guitar-pop group the Boo Radleys developed a dedicated cult following in the early-'90s before crossing over into the mainstream in the middle of the decade. Originally, the group were one of the lesser lights of the loud, noisy My Bloody Valentine-inspired psychedelic trance-pop bands labelled "shoegazers" by the British weekly music press. By the mid-'90s the Boo Radleys had developed into a more straight-forward pop band that didn't use noise and extended guitar work-outs as a way of fleshing out their songs instead of as the basis of their music.

The Boo Radleys originally consisted of guitarist/songwriter Martin Carr, vocalist/guitarist Sice, bassist Timothy Brown, and drummer Steve Hewitt. The band released their first album, *Icha-bod and I*, on a local independent record label in 1990; Hewitt was replaced by Rob Cieka after the release of the record. With the sup-port of influential British disc jockey John Peel, the band signed with Rough Trade Records. The group released the EP *Every Heaven* in 1991; the record made it into the lower regions of the U.K. charts.

Rough Trade folded shortly after the release of *Every Heaven* and the Boo Radleys moved to Creation Records, releasing *Every-thing's Alright Forever* in 1992. *Everything's Alright Forever* was released in the U.S. through Creation's association with Columbia Records, but it didn't gain much attention in America. In England, it received favorable reviews and the group began to build a fan base. Topping several Best-of-the-Year lists, including *Melody Maker*'s, 1993's *Giant Steps* was a critical success in England and sold respectably. In America, the record launched the minor alter-native rock hit "Lazarus" and led to a second-stage spot on Lolla-palooza '94.

Released in England in the spring of 1995, the more pop-ori-ented *Wake Up!* was the band's commercial breakthrough, debut-ing at number one. The bright, horn-driven single "Wake Up Boo" entered the Top 10 and stayed on the charts until the early sum-mer, preventing the follow-up single "Find the Answer Within" from charting higher than the Top 30. *Wake Up!* was released in America in the fall of 1995. —*Stephen Thomas Erlewine*

Everything's Alright Forever / Aug. 1992 / Columbia ✦✦✦
On their second album, the Boo Radleys begin to refine their mix of grinding guitars and pop melodies. Although their songwriting isn't always impressive, the record shows a great deal of promise. —*Stephen Thomas Erlewine*

○ **Giant Steps** / 1993 / Columbia ✦✦✦✦
Giant Steps is a pastiche of every genre of pop-rock from the British Invasion on. It's an incredibly ambitious and pretentious concept, but the Boo Radley's sense of songcraft has improved enough to make the album work. *Giant Steps* has swirling, noisy guitars, Beach Boys harmonies, the arrangements of Love and Beatlesque melodies, forming a remarkably original record, rich in detail and ultimately very rewarding. —*Stephen Thomas Er-lewine*

● **Wake Up!** / 1995 / Creation ✦✦✦✦
With their third album, the Boo Radleys abandoned the overt noise that obscured the pop sensibilities of their early work and scaled back the ambitions of *Giant Steps*. The result is *Wake Up!*, a glorious, brightly-colored gem of a pop record. From the Beach Boy harmonies and trumpet fanfares of the opening "Wake Up Boo!" to the closing epic McCartney-styled ballad "Wilder," the group winds through many styles of British pop. Much of the darkness—both musically and lyrically—of their previous music has been lifted; in its place is a sterling piece of pure pop, with all the big choruses, bright melodies and simple hooks that pop implies. *Giant Steps* had elements of this grand pop, yet it tried too hard. *Wake Up!* doesn't try for as much and in doing so, it achieves more, both musically and commercially—upon the release of the album and "Wake Up Boo!" single, the Boos became genuine Top Ten pop stars in England. The Boo Radleys were always a band with ambitions. The only difference with *Wake Up!* is that they fi-nally fulfilled them. —*Stephen Thomas Erlewine*

Betty Boo (Alison Moira Clarkson)

b. Mar. 6, 1970, Kensington, London, England
Dance-Pop
British singer Betty Boo came up performing rap with the trio the She-Rockers and the duo Hit 'N' Run. She was initially billed as Betty Boop until she got a cease-and-desist order from the owners of the cartoon. Boo scored Top Ten U.K. hits with the singles "Doin' the Do" and "Where Are You Baby" and her debut album *Booma-nia* in 1990. —*William Ruhlmann*

Boomania / Oct. 23, 1990 / Rhythm King ✦✦✦
Dance pop, light hip-hop, and some sounds in between are the for-mula for Betty Boo on this '90 effort. The songs are mostly either silly novelty tunes or entertaining bits of fluff with vocal noodling around a hook and intricate production edits, snippets and beats. This is sometimes enjoyable and other times irritating. —*Ron Wynn*

● **Grrr! It's Betty Boo** / Nov. 10, 1992 / Sire ✦✦✦✦
British rapper Betty Boo doesn't have much on her mind other than man troubles, which she describes in adequate rhymes over John Coxon's standard-issue hip-hop dance tracks, borrowing (with credit given) from the Beatles and the Four Tops, but mostly from superior American rap predecessors. Boo raps through the verses and sings the choruses (with extensive backup vocals and echo, suggesting she's not much of a singer) in an engaging enough manner, but she never threatens to be more than a car-toon. —*William Ruhlmann*

Boogie Down Productions

Group, Rap, Soul
Formed in 1986 by Laurence Krisna Parker and Scott Sterling, Boogie Down Productions quickly became one of the most influ-ential and important hip-hop groups. Parker adopted the name KRS-One (an acronym for Knowledge Reigns Supreme Over Al-most Every One) and Sterling became DJ Scott LaRock, and they released an independent single, "Crack Attack," in 1986. BDP's groundbreaking 1987 debut, *Criminal Minded*, full of blunt, mat-ter-of-fact tales of life on the mean streets, was a prototype for gangsta-rap. As the album was building to a massive underground success, LaRock was shot to death in the South Bronx as he tried to settle an argument. Instead of calling it quits, KRS-One contin-ued BDP with his brother Kenny Parker and D-Nice as DJs and re-leased *By All Means Necessary* the following year. KRS-One began calling himself "the Teacher," promoting self-awareness and edu-cation in his rhymes. KRS-One began touring colleges on the lec-ture circuit around 1989, and some of his writings appeared in the *New York Times*. It became evident that KRS-One had taken his role as the Teacher too far on 1990's *Edutainment*, where most tracks were lectures pasted over lackluster beats.

KRS-One obliterated all concerns that he sold out on 1992's *Sex and Violence,* where he sounds angrier and stronger than he has in years. However, the album wasn't the commercial blockbuster it could have been. The following year, KRS-One released his first solo album, *Return of the Boom Bap,* which was even better; many hip-hop critics equated with the seminal *By All Means Necessary.* But by early 1994, it had already dropped off the R&B and hip-hop charts. —*Stephen Thomas Erlewine*

★ **Criminal Minded** / 1987 / Sugar Hill ✦✦✦✦✦

Classic early "gangsta" rap work. *Criminal Minded* was the only time the contributions of DJ Scott LaRock (Scott Sterling) were featured on a Boogie Down Productions recording, as he was murdered shortly after this was issued. The toughest, hardest-hitting BDP effort. —*Ron Wynn*

☆ **By All Means Necessary** / 1988 / Jive ✦✦✦✦✦

Boogie Down Productions' first album since the death of Scott LaRock finds KRS-One keeping his hardcore, proto-gangsta stance and strengthening it with socially conscious rhymes. All the while, the beats and samples are richer than the first record, creating a dense urban landscape for KRS-One's fiercely intelligent raps. —*Stephen Thomas Erlewine*

○ **Ghetto Music: The Blueprint of Hip Hop** / 1989 / Jive ✦✦✦✦

On BDP's third album, KRS-One strips the beat down to the basics, concentrating his efforts on his rhymes. KRS-One has called himself the Teacher, and teach he does on *Ghetto Music.* From hip-hop to heritage, there isn't a single subject that slips by him. Sadly, *Ghetto Music* would prove to be the last time he would be able to completely capture the imagination of the hip-hop audience; it remains one of BDP's finest efforts. —*Stephen Thomas Erlewine*

Edutainment / 1990 / Jive ✦✦✦

Some speculated Kris Parker (KRS-One) might be getting a bit soft with this one, despite the lengthy expositions on the impact of poverty, drugs, and violence on his life. Parker emphasized a "humanist" tone on most of the material. —*Ron Wynn*

Live Hardcore Worldwide / 1991 / Jive ✦✦✦

The Teacher sounds explosive on stage, tearing into BDP's greatest tracks and the myth that live hip-hop is bland and unnecessary. In fact, the pure energy of this album can be offputting at first—the group jumps around their catalog, playing fragments of their classics and complete tracks from *Edutainment,* and the audience sings along with almost every track. *Live Hardcore Worldwide— Paris, London & NYC!* may not be the first live hip-hop album (2 Live Crew released one a couple of months before BDP), but it is certainly the best. —*Stephen Thomas Erlewine*

○ **Sex and Violence** / 1992 / Jive ✦✦✦✦

KRS-One demolishes any idea he's losing his clout or anger. *Sex and Violence* is his most chilling, slashing, and effective overall statement since *Criminal Minded.* —*Ron Wynn*

Book of Love

Group, Alternative Pop/Rock

Book of Love was a synth-dance music quartet from New York featuring the breathy vocals of Susan Ottaviano. (The group was filled out by keyboard players Lauren Roselli, Jade Lee, and Ted Ottaviano, who is no relation to Susan.) They got their start with the club hit "Boy" in 1985 and released three albums on Sire Records—*Book of Love* (1986), *Lullaby* (1988), and *Candy Carol* (1991). —*William Ruhlmann*

● **Book of Love** / Apr. 1986 / Sire ✦✦✦✦

Book of Love plays synthesizer-based dance-pop with an edge. The music is sweeter and lighter than much of this genre, and vocalist Susan Ottaviano has a matter-of-fact phrasing style that keeps it all from getting too sweet (not unlike Deborah Harry's work with Blondie). On this debut album, songs like "You Make Me Feel So Good" have an effervescent early '60s girl group bounce, while others suggest what the early Velvet Underground & Nico might have sounded like with synthesizers. The album features the group's club hits "Boy," "Book Of Love," and "I Touch Roses." —*William Ruhlmann*

Lullaby / Jul. 1988 / Sire ✦✦✦

Book of Love's Ted Ottaviano was credited with playing "tubular bells" on the band's self-titled debut album. On its second album, *Book of Love* opened the proceedings with their own danceable version of the 1973 Michael Oldfield instrumental hit as a way of

launching into a somewhat harder-edged album. Producer Flood (of Depeche Mode fame) brought his ominous, beat-heavy approach to the group's already street-smart disco persona, with the result that tracks like "Pretty Boys And Pretty Girls" had an urgency lacking on the more pop-oriented debut. This was not, however, the way to break *Book of Love* beyond the dance clubs, and *Lullaby* did little to advance their career. —*William Ruhlmann*

Candy Carol / Apr. 1991 / Sire ✦✦✦

With song titles like "Orange Flip," *Book of Love's* third album is an aural trip to the candy shop. The arrangements, especially on "Turn the World" and "Quiver," sound like some sort of electro-pop Christmas album. These pop confectioners have always used sweetness and innocence in their recipe, but never has it sounded so sugary. —*Brian Mansfield*

Lovebubble / Sep. 1992 / Sire ✦✦

Booker T. & the MGs

Group, Soul, R&B

Booker T. & the MGs were the primary house rhythm section behind many of the great hits that came out of Stax Records in Memphis, Tennessee, in the '60s. Otis Redding, Carla Thomas, Sam and Dave, Albert King, Wilson Pickett, Eddie Floyd, and a host of others benefitted from their lean, tight sound.

Booker T. Jones (b. Dec. 11, 1944, Memphis, Tennessee), who was the keyboardist with the MGs (stands for Memphis Group), began working for Stax in 1960 as a saxophone player. There he met Mar-Keys guitarist Steve Cropper (b. Oct. 21, 1941, Willow Springs, Missouri). The two brought in bassist Lewis Steinberg (replaced in 1964 by Ex-Mar-Key Donald "Duck" Dunn [b. Nov. 24, 1941, Memphis, Tennessee]) and Al Jackson, Jr. (b. Nov. 27, 1934, Memphis, Tennessee, d. Oct. 1, 1975, Memphis, Tennessee) on drums.

On their own, the MGs released a series of classic hit instrumentals, starting with the gold Top Ten hit "Green Onions" (1962). They hit the Top Ten of the R&B charts with "Boot-Leg" (1965), "Hip Hug-Her" (1967), "Groovin'" (1967), "Soul-Limbo" (1968), and "Time Is Tight" (1969). "Hang 'Em High" and "Time Is Tight" both hit the Top Ten of the pop charts in 1969.

The group split in 1972, but was reorganized as the MGs in 1973 by Jackson and Dunn. Jackson was murdered in 1975. In 1977, Jones, Cropper, and Dunn reformed with Willie Hall (b. Aug. 8, 1950) as a replacement and made *Universal Language.* The group members worked together occasionally thereafter. In 1994, they reunited to make another album, *That's the Way It Should Be.* —*Rick Clark*

○ **Green Onions** / Oct. 1962 / Atlantic ✦✦✦✦

The title track was the signature song for Booker T. & The MGs, arguably the finest Southern soul rhythm section of all time. This early '60s album now sells in three figures for good condition copies and higher than that for sealed, mint edition. It established the immediate greatness of the organ/guitar/bass/drums lineup and demonstrated that Booker T. Jones and Steve Cropper in particular were geniuses on organ and guitar, respectively. This has been reissued on CD. —*Ron Wynn*

Soul Dressing / 1965 / Atlantic ✦✦✦

Assembled mostly from (non-hit) 1963-65 singles, this is solid stuff, but a notch below their peak collections. The best tracks ("Soul Dressing," "Tic-Tac-Toe," "Can't Be Still") are usually included on their best-of anthologies, but "Plum Nellie," featuring some ferocious, cutting-edge solos by Cropper and Jones, is an overlooked highlight. —*Richie Unterberger*

And Now, Booker T. & the MGs / 1966 / Rhino ✦✦✦

○ **Hip Hug-Her** / Jun. 1967 / Rhino ✦✦✦✦

A great album cover and songs like "Groovin'," "Soul Sanction," "Double or Nothing," and the classic title track are just the beginning of the wealth of terrific Memphis soul available on this album. —*Stephen Thomas Erlewine*

○ **Back to Back** / Aug. 1967 / Atlantic ✦✦✦✦

Recorded live in Paris in 1967, when the Stax-Volt Revue was touring Europe. This is just about exactly what you'd expect: solid, straight-ahead live versions of the instrumental group's best-known tunes, of good sound. Booker T. & the MGs take seven of the album's ten tracks, including their hits "Green Onions" and "Hip Hug-Her"; the Mar-Keys do "Last Night" and a couple of other numbers. —*Richie Unterberger*

Doin' Our Thing / Apr. 1968 / Rhino ✦✦✦
Rhino once again put together a classy reissue from the vaults of Atlantic Records. Highlights from this solid album include the title track, "Let's Go Get Stoned," and "You Keep Me Hanging On." — *Stephen Thomas Erlewine*

Soul Limbo / Oct. 1968 / Stax ✦✦✦

★ **The Best of Booker T. & The MGs** / Nov. 1968 / Atlantic ✦✦✦✦✦
The Stax Records catalog ended up partially in the hands of Atlantic Records and partially with Fantasy Records, and the dividing point is 1968. That's why there are two Booker T. & the MGs hits compilations. This one, *The Best-Of*, presents the material owned by Atlantic. There are 12 tracks, covering the group's popular instrumental hits from "Green Onions" in the summer of 1962 to "Groovin'" in the summer of 1967. Booker T. & the MGs scored some of their biggest hits, including "Hang 'Em High" and "Time Is Tight," in 1968-1969, and for those you will have to look to the Stax/Fantasy *Greatest Hits*, originally released in October 1970. Just to be confusing, in 1991 Fantasy released an album called *The Best Of* that again contains only the later material. (Rhino's *The Very Best Of* finally combined the two eras.) — *William Ruhlmann*

Uptight / Dec. 1968 / Stax ✦✦✦

The Booker T. Set / May 1969 / Stax ✦✦✦
A fine collection featuring the great soul quartet putting their spin on classic numbers, ranging from Cliff Nobles's "The Horse" to Motown, Beatles, Isley Brothers, and even some in-house songs like Eddie Floyd's "I've Never Found A Girl (To Love Me Like You Do)." The original lineup is in fine form, particularly drummer Al Jackson, Jr. This was reissued on CD in 1989. — *Ron Wynn*

○ **McLemore Avenue** / 1970 / Stax ✦✦✦✦
An instrumental reconstruction of *Abbey Road*, the title is derived from the street where Stax was located. The cover art is a better Beatles parody than anything on *The Rutles*. — *John Floyd*

○ **Melting Pot** / Jan. 1971 / Stax ✦✦✦✦

Best Of / 1986 / Fantasy ✦✦✦
Somewhat confusingly, this disc is titled identically to a CD on Atlantic which concentrates on their earlier material. This 17-cut disc draws from 1967-71, and includes three of their four Top 20 pop hits: "Soul Limbo," "Hang 'Em High," and "Time Is Tight." This perhaps lacks a bit of the edge of their mid-'60s recordings, concentrating on loping, relaxed grooves more than biting, incisive chops. The standard remains pretty high, though, with the interplay between Steve Cropper's guitar, Booker T. Joness' organ, and the rhythm section never less than telepathic. Most of the material is original, but even on the covers of period pop hits—including unlikely versions of "Something," "Eleanor Rigby," and "Mrs. Robinson"—the group is soulful and tight. This is perhaps better music for background and party listening than anything else, but within those confines it's quite good. — *Richie Unterberger*

○ **Very Best of** / 1994 / Rhino ✦✦✦✦
Contains 15 of Booker T. and the MGs pop chart hits, spanning both the 1962-67 era (now controlled by Atlantic Records) and the 1968-1971 era (now controlled by Fantasy Records). Not to be confused with either *Best Of* (81281) or the Fantasy *Best Of* (60004). — *William Ruhlmann*

That's the Way It Should Be / May 24, 1994 / Sony ✦✦✦
Booker T. and the MGs do what they do very well. What they do is present a spare, funky sound in which each instrument, drums (here played by Steve Jordan or James Gadson), bass, guitar, and organ, is heard distinctly playing medium tempo melodies with slight variations. Precision is a key, and the result, while impressive, is anything but showy. Seventeen years since their last outing, the group exhibits the same qualities and the same limitations it did in its heyday. — *William Ruhlmann*

Chuckii Booker

b. 1966
Urban
A very capable musician, Chuckii Booker has been prominent on the urban contemporary front as an instrumentalist, bandleader, songwriter, and performer. Born in Los Angeles, he was proficient on guitar and drums by age 14, but for a while preferred graphic art to music. His godfather, Barry White, signed him to a deal with White's production company in 1984, but Booker left after White failed to issue an LP he recorded. He joined Tease, and played keyboards with them for three years. Booker began to earn his repu-

tation as a producer after this, working with C.J. Anthony, White, Geoffrey Williams, and Lalah Hathaway. He also recorded as an instrumentalist with Vanessa Williams, Troop, and Kool & the Gang, and toured with Janet Jackson as her musical director on the *Rhythm Nation* tour. Booker has also recorded as a solo act for Atlantic; his most recent release was *Nice 'n Wild* in 1992. — *Ron Wynn*

Chuckii / May 1989 / Atlantic ✦✦✦
Some nice soul, synthesized R&B, and urban contemporary ballads, with just the right blend of hip-hop flavored snippets, samples, and production. The former keyboardist for Tease, Chuckii Booker also proved a solid vocalist, not overly gifted but able to effectively deliver the slow songs and punctuate the uptempo tunes. — *Ron Wynn*

● **Niice 'n Wiild** / Sep. 1992 / Atlantic ✦✦✦✦
Chuckii Booker is chasing Black lovermen such as Luther Vandross and Michael Jackson, putting major emphasis on the bass drum (well, it would be a bass drum if everything weren't programmed) and singing in an emotive tenor. Dance floors and boudoirs are given equal emphasis in the tempos. An experienced session man, Booker knows most Black styles of the last 25 years and presents them efficiently (in the album's second half, he even throws in some George Clinton-like funk and a copy of James Brown, complete with shouts of "JB's!"), the exception being rap/hip-hop, which he ignores. In those long stretches when his predecessors are between albums, there is plenty of room for him to sneak in with an acceptable substitute like the #1 hit "Games." But nothing about his second album suggests he would be any real competition head to head. — *William Ruhlmann*

The Boomtown Rats

Group, New Wave, Pop/Rock
The Boomtown Rats were an Irish rock band that scored a series of British hits between 1977 and 1980 and were led by singer Bob Geldof, who organized the Ethiopian relief efforts Band Aid and Live Aid.

The Rats were formed in Dun Laoghaire, near Dublin, Ireland, in 1975 by Geldof (born Robert Frederick Zenon Geldof, Oct. 5, 1954, Dun Laoghaire, Ireland), a former journalist, Johnnie Fingers (b.Ireland) (keyboards), Gerry Cott (b.Ireland) (guitar), Garry Roberts (b.Ireland) (guitar), Pete Briquette (b.Ireland) (bass), and Simon Crowe (b.Ireland) (drums). They took their name from Woody Guthrie's novel *Bound for Glory*. The group moved to London in October 1976 and became associated with the punk rock movement. Signing to Ensign Records, they released their debut single, "Lookin' After No. 1," in August 1977. It was the first of nine straight singles to make the U.K. Top 15.

Their debut album, *The Boomtown Rats*, was released in September 1977, on Ensign in the U.K. and on Mercury in the U.S. Their second album, *A Tonic for the Troops*, appeared in June 1978 in the U.K., along with their first U.K. Top Ten hit, "Like Clockwork." In the fall, "Rat Trap" from the album hit #1. *A Tonic for the Troops* was released in the U.S. on Columbia Records in February 1979 with two tracks from *The Boomtown Rats* substituted for tracks on the U.K. version.

The Boomtown Rats' second straight U.K. #1 came in the summer of 1979 with "I Don't Like Mondays," a song inspired by a California teenager who had gone on a killing spree and glibly justified her action with the title line. It was contained on the Rats' third album, *The Fine Art of Surfacing*, released in October 1979, and subsequently became the band's only U.S. singles chart entry. The album also contained their next U.K. Top Ten hit, "Someone's Looking at You."

The Boomtown Rats released their final U.K. Top Ten hit, "Banana Republic," in November 1980, followed by their fourth album, *Mondo Bon* in January 1981. At this point, guitarist Gerry Cott left the group, and they continued as a quintet. Their fifth album *V Deep* was released in the U.K. in February 1982. In the U.S., Columbia initially released only a four-song EP drawn from the album *The Boomtown Rats*, finally releasing the full LP in September, when it failed to chart. Also in '82, Geldof starred in the movie *Pink Floyd: The Wall*.

Columbia released the six-song compilation *Ratrospective* in March 1983, but rejected the band's newly recorded sixth album, *In the Long Grass*, which was released by Ensign in England. In 1984, Geldof and Midge Ure wrote "Do They Know It's Christmas?" and organized the star-studded Band Aid group to record it for Ethiopian relief, resulting in the biggest selling single in U.K. history. Geldof then went on to organize the two Live Aid concerts, held on July 13, 1985, in London and Philadelphia. Geldof's increased visibility led to the belated U.S. release of *In the Long Grass*, but when it failed to chart the Boomtown Rats were left without a record label. The group folded in 1986, and Geldof launched a solo career. — *William Ruhlmann*

The Boomtown Rats / Sep. 1977 / Mercury ✦✦✦

Anyone who heard the Boomtown Rats' debut single, "Lookin' After No. 1," with its rapid drum beat, slashing guitars, and aggressive singing about impatience with the dole queue, would think of the group as a particularly tight, standard punk rock band on the London scene in 1977. The Rats' debut album also featured the leering "Mary Of The Fourth Form," their second single, but the rest of the album revealed more traditional rock influences. "Joey's On The Street Again" sounded like the sort of street opera Bruce Springsteen was aiming for on *The Wild, The Innocent & The E Street Shuffle*. "I Can Make It If You Can" was the sort of ballad the Rolling Stones favored in the mid-'70s. Overall, there were enough power chords and snotty sentiments to justify the punk tag, but it was already clear that the Rats aspired to the mainstream. — *William Ruhlmann*

Tonic for the Troops / Jun. 1978 / Columbia ✦✦✦

Bob Geldof had revealed a taste for the seamy side of things in his lyrics for the Boomtown Rats' first album. On their second record, he fantasized about being Hitler in the person of the Leader of the Pack ("I Never Loved Eva Braun"), romanticized tropical suicide ("Living In An Island"), and identified with a certain wealthy recluse ("Me And Howard Hughes"). The band retained a punk energy on the album's U.K. hit singles, "Like Clockwork," "She's So Modern," and "Rat Trap" (another of Geldof's Springsteen homages), but musical identity was still a song-by-song affair. (In the U.S., Columbia replaced "Can't Stop" and "[Watch Out For] The Normal People" with "Mary Of The 4th Form" and "Joey's On The Street Again" from the first album.) — *William Ruhlmann*

The Fine Art of Surfacing / Oct. 1979 / Columbia ✦✦✦

The Boomtown Rats had achieved a peak of band interplay by their third album, leading inevitably to such developments as the use of strings, while lyricist/singer Bob Geldof had taken on an acerbic social consciousness about the pressures of modern life as his major subject. But this didn't always add up to strong songwriting. When it did, on the singles "Someone's Looking At You" and especially "I Don't Like Mondays," the Boomtown Rats could be compelling—Geldof's lyrics seemed acute instead of obvious, the band arrangements seemed crisp and clever rather than gimmicky. But that didn't happen often enough to make *The Fine Art Of Surfacing* a consistent success. — *William Ruhlmann*

Mondo Bongo / Jan. 1981 / Columbia ✦✦

On their fourth album, the Boomtown Rats submitted to ambitiousness, with singer Bob Geldof attempting to assume the mantle of Bob Dylan, the Beatles, and the Rolling Stones, while the band tried to keep up with musical fashions in Britain. The combination led to such oddities as a ska-beat rewrite of the Stones' "Under My Thumb" and a couple of side-opening mambos. The band was at its best when it returned to the pop music that was its core on such songs as the Buddy Holly-ish "Don't Talk To Me" and especially the danceable "Up All Night," but they were buried on the second side of an uneven collection that made the Rats' sense of direction seem uncertain. — *William Ruhlmann*

V Deep / Apr. 1982 / Columbia ✦✦

On their fifth album and reduced to a quintet, the Boomtown Rats moved closer to Caribbean rhythms, employing a percussionist and upping the bass guitar in the mix. They even had Dennis Bovell do a dub mix of "House On Fire" and included it at the end of the album. Meanwhile, Bob Geldof's lyrics indicated an increasingly embattled sensibility; he noted in a song called "The Bitter End," "It isn't too far." Unfortunately, nothing here matched the catchy, daring work on the Rats' first three albums, and even in England their star was beginning to fade. In America, Columbia Records at first declined to release the album, opting for a four-track EP, then allowed it to escape in September 1982, when it failed to chart. — *William Ruhlmann*

Retrospective [EP] / Mar. 1983 / Columbia

Retrospective was a six-song "best of" EP containing the Boomtown Rats' only U.S. singles chart entry, "I Don't Like Mondays," "Rat Trap," which had been a U.K. chart topper, and other fa-

vorites. It was intended as a summing up of the group for the U.S.; Columbia Records rejected the Rats' next album, *In The Long Grass*, and only released it in the wake of lead singer Bob Geldof's Live Aid celebrity. In 1987, Columbia added four tracks to *Retrospective*, to produce *Greatest Hits*. — *William Ruhlmann*

In the Long Grass / May 1985 / Columbia ✦✦✦

The Boomtown Rats' sixth album was very much a return to the pop/rock style of their first two albums—4/4 beats, prominent rock guitar lines, urgent vocals. But as the desperate lyrics (titles include "Drag Me Down" and "Hard Times") implied, the record was more a last hurrah than a new beginning. Upon its 1984 release on Mercury Records in the U.K., it did spawn a couple of minor British chart singles, but it missed the LP chart, a major decline for a band that had enjoyed Top Ten success at its height. In America, Columbia Records rejected the album, and only released it a year later to try to cash in on Bob Geldof's fame in connection with his organization of Live Aid. — *William Ruhlmann*

● The Greatest Hits / 1987 / Columbia ✦✦✦✦

Same six songs as on *Retrospective*, plus four tracks. — *William Ruhlmann*

Pat Boone (Charles Eugene Patrick Boone)

b. Jun. 1, 1934, Jacksonville, FL
Pop, Teen Idol

He was clean-cut, polite to his elders, and glorified the nutritional value of milk. To folks who hated everything the new music stood for, Pat Boone was the perfect '50s rock & roller. But no matter how music historians judge the career of Pat Boone, nobody can dispute his enormous sales figures. The well-scrubbed crooner in the white buckskin shoes sold many millions of copies of his sanitized R&B covers during the '50s, helping to facilitate acceptance of rock & roll in the pop marketplace.

Boone's family ties are impressive—he's related to frontier legend Daniel Boone through bloodlines and to country great Red Foley through marriage to his daughter. After debuting on the small Republic imprint in 1954, Boone signed with Dot and took the pop world by storm over the next couple of years with covers of R&B items by Fats Domino, Little Richard, the El Dorados, the Flamingos, Ivory Joe Hunter, and too many others to list here.

With his college-boy good looks and an affinity for smooth ballads, Boone crossed over into TV and films, scoring #1 hits in 1957 with "Love Letters in the Sand," from the movie *Bernadine*, and the theme from the movie *April Love*, both of which he starred in.

"Moody River" marked Boone's last chart-topper in 1961, although he gamely tackled everything from novelty rockers ("Speedy Gonzales") to surf songs ("Beach Girl") to sustain his success. These days, you're most likely to encounter Boone and his family (which includes Debby Boone of "You Light Up My Life" fame) on the contemporary Christian circuit or doing work for charitable organizations, the white bucks and crewcut long since retired. — *Bill Dahl*

○ Jivin' Pat / Feb. 1986 / Bear Family ✦✦✦✦

All of Boone's rockers—cover versions of Fats Domino, Little Richard, et al—are included with a revealing set of liner notes. You won't find these elsewhere unless you have an enormous singles collection. — *Hank Davis*

● Greatest Hits / 1993 / MCA ✦✦✦✦

Including 18 of his highest charting hits for the Dot label in the '50s and early '60s, this is easily the best basic Boone collection. It doesn't include his hit covers of "At My Front Door" and Little Richard's "Long Tall Sally" and "Tutti Frutti," which is perhaps just as well for all concerned. — *Richie Unterberger*

More Greatest Hits / 1994 / Varese Sarabande

Contains 17 of Pat Boone's later and lesser chart hits. — *William Ruhlmann*

Boredoms

Group, Alternative Pop/Rock, Experimental

With the support of Sonic Youth and Nirvana behind them, the Boredoms released a major label album in 1993, which may be the most impressive thing about this almost unlistenable band. For several years, the Boredoms have been the leaders of Japans wave of noise bands inspired by Sonic Youth's early records and other artists from that scene. What separates the Boredoms from early Sonic Youth is songs—the Boredoms don't have any. And they don't care if they do, either. Instead, they get by on sheer willpower and stacks of effects pedals and amplifiers. Unless you have an extreme amount of patience or enjoy listening to the soothing sounds of heavy machinery, chances are you won't be able to tolerate the Boredoms. Which is exactly what they want, by the way. —*Stephen Thomas Erlewine*

○ **Soul Discharge** / 1990 / Shimmy Disc ✦✦✦✦
Creative hardcore, it's brash, noisy, insane, and good. Play it loud to guarantee an eviction notice. —*Myles Boisen*

Wow 2 / Oct. 1992 / Avant ✦✦✦

● **Pop Tatari** / 1993 / Reprise ✦✦✦✦
The Boredoms' first major label release is their most accessible record, even if it isn't close to what's generally considered listenable. —*Stephen Thomas Erlewine*

Chocolate Synthesizer / 1994 / Reprise

Super Roots / 1994 / Reprise

Earl Bostic

b. Apr. 25, 1913, Tulsa, OK, **d.** Oct. 28, 1965, Rochester, NY
R&B
Bostic began as a jazz player in the big-band era of the '20s and '30s. In the early '40s he worked with Cab Calloway, Lionel Hampton, and others. He pioneered the hard-driving R&B sax sound of the early '40s. Bostic's band was a training ground for many great artists, including John Coltrane, Stanley Turrentine, Bill Doggett, Mickey Baker, and others. Jazz great Art Blakey says, "Nobody knew more about the saxophone than Bostic, I mean technically, and that includes Bird." Bostic had a #1 R&B hit with "Flamingo." This is hard-rockin', raunchy R&B saxophone at its best. —*Michael Erlewine*

● **The Best of Earl Bostic** / 1956 / Deluxe ✦✦✦✦
A nice cross-section of this fiery alto-saxist's '50s output, it includes his hits "Sleep" and "Flamingo." —*Bill Dahl*

○ **Showcase of Swinging Dance Hits** / 1958 / King ✦✦✦✦
Perhaps his best rocking and uptempo instrumental pop and R&B material. This album was aimed at the jukebox market and weighted toward the hottest, most furiously played cuts in the Bostic repertoire. Bostic was as technically accomplished as any alto saxophonist in his era, but he wasn't able to show that while on King. This album was one of the few times that he was able to really show his skills on uptempo material. —*Ron Wynn*

Boston

Group, Hard Rock, Pop/Rock
During the late '70s, Boston dominated AOR (album-oriented rock) FM with their dense multilayered guitars and vocals. The self-titled debut effort, which was basically constructed from band leader Tom Scholz's basement demos, eventually sold over six-and-a-half million copies. "More than a Feeling," their first single, is a perfect encapsulation of Boston's sound. After a two-year wait, Boston's follow-up, *Don't Look Back*, basically replicated the debut's formula. By then, Scholz was gaining a reputation as an obsessive perfectionist, further underscored by the seven-year wait for the group's third album, *Third Stage*.

During this time, Scholz applied his previous background as a senior product designer for Polaroid and started Scholz Research & Development, which marketed popular professional-musician outboard gear, like the Rockman.

After another long delay—eight years—Boston returned in 1994 with a new album, *Walk On*. —*Rick Clark*

● **Boston** / 1976 / Epic ✦✦✦✦
The album that virtually defined '70s FM rock sold over six million copies and featured the smash hits "More than a Feeling," "Peace of Mind," and "Let Me Take You Home Tonight." —*Donna DiChario*

Don't Look Back / 1978 / Epic ✦✦✦
Continued success with their rock formula is highlighted by the hit title track. —*Donna DiChario*

Third Stage / 1986 / MCA ✦✦✦
This chart-topping comeback appeared after a seven-year hiatus and a lineup reshuffling that left only singer Brad Delp and guitarist/producer Tom Scholz from the original band. The hits include "Amanda" and "We're Ready." —*Donna DiChario*

Walk On / 1994 / MCA ✦✦

Bow Wow Wow

Group, New Wave
Bow Wow Wow was a quartet organized by U.K. manager Malcolm McLaren (best known as the mastermind behind the Sex Pistols) at the start of the '80s. McLaren matched the trio of musicians who had constituted Adam Ant's Ants (Matthew Ashman, b. 1962, guitar; Leigh Gorman, b. 1961, bass; and David Barbarossa, b. 1961, drums) with teenage singer Annabella Lwin (b. Oct 31, 1965), retaining the earlier group's African-derived drum sound. In 1983, Lwin quit the group for a solo career, and the remaining three changed their name to the Chiefs of Relief. Both Lwin and the Chiefs issued their own albums. —*William Ruhlmann*

See Jungle! See Jungle! Go Join Your Gang, Yeah, City All Over! Go Ape Crazy! / 1981 / RCA ✦✦

● **I Want Candy** / 1982 / RCA ✦✦✦✦
This album largely recompiles Bow Wow Wow's first album, plus its *Last of the Mohicans* EP. As such, it includes the hits "Go Wild in the Country," "I Want Candy," and "Louis Quatorze" and presents the band's urgent, rhythmic sound at its most consistent. —*William Ruhlmann*

The Last of the Mohicans / 1982 / RCA ✦✦✦

When the Going Gets Tough The Tough Get Going / 1983 / Great Expectations ✦✦

Best Of / 1989 / Receiver

○ **Girl Bites Dog** / 1993 / EMI ✦✦✦✦
A CD reissue of their first cassette-only release. Featuring a 15-year-old Annabella Lwin singing songs with sex-obsessed themes backed by a driving tribal beat, *Girl Bites Dog* gives a representative view of a band with limited scope. Though it sounds a bit dated today, new wave fanatics will find this newly expanded version essential, especially for the unreleased rarities, B-sides, and extensive discography information. —*Chris Woodstra*

David Bowie (David Robert Jones)

b. Jan. 8, 1947, Brixton, England
Dance-Pop, Hard Rock, Art-Rock/Progressive-Rock, Pop/Rock
Although he succeeded as a singer, musician, songwriter, and film and stage actor, David Bowie's chief artistic accomplishment may have been his astute manipulation of his own image as a star. When he achieved international fame in the early '70s, Bowie brought a new, highly conscious approach to stardom that involved the frequent creation of new personae. No wonder that when he made his film acting debut in 1976, he seemed so good at it: acting was what a large part of his career was about. Born in Brixton, South London, as David Jones, the singer was already playing in bands by his late teens. He changed his name to avoid confusion with Davy Jones of the Monkees. His early-'60s work was rock and blues oriented, then he turned to an Anthony Newley-style expressive show-music approach. But his breakthrough British hit "Space Oddity" (1969) was a folkie ballad about an astronaut who doesn't come home. By the time of *Hunky Dory* (1971), Bowie had turned again more toward rock, using the first of many strong collaborators, guitarist Mick Ronson.

It was Bowie's concept album *The Rise and Fall of Ziggy Stardust and the Spiders from Mars* (1972) that made him a giant star in England, where he adopted the image of his fantasy rocker, with bright red hair and futuristic stage suits. In America, "Space Oddity" became a belated hit in 1973, the year Bowie "retired" from stage work only to return in 1974 with an even more elaborate stage show. More an established star than a real record-seller in the U.S., Bowie finally hit #1 with "Fame" (cowritten by John Lennon and Carlos Alomar) in 1975. The late '70s found him collaborating with electronics whiz Brian Eno. He made a major commercial comeback in 1983 with *Let's Dance*, produced by ex-Chic coleader Nile Rodgers. Bowie's work in the '80s was inconsistent, but as late as 1990 he was still able to tour the US, playing football stadiums. This was supposedly his farewell tour (again) before he turned full attention to a group project, Tin Machine.

After releasing two unsuccessful albums with Tin Machine, Bowie returned to his solo career in 1993 with his first solo album since 1987, *Black Tie White Noise;* although it received favorable reviews, it fell off the charts quickly. —*William Ruhlmann*

Space Oddity / 1969 / Rykodisc ✦✦✦
Originally titled *Man of Words Man of Music*, this release was a transitional effort from Bowie's earlier Anthony Newley affectations on Decca. Tracks range from the Bob Dylan-influenced fu-

ture-shock epic "Cygnet Committee" to lightweight rockers like "Janine." This includes "Space Oddity," Bowie's first major single and the highlight of this album. —*Rick Clark*

○ **The Man Who Sold the World** / 1970 / Rykodisc ✦✦✦✦
After the theatrical acoustic leanings of *Space Oddity*, Bowie undertook a dark foray into British hard rock that at times attempted Cream-style free-for-alls, particularly "She Shook Me Cold." The strangely dense, bass-heavy production (courtesy of Tony Visconti), coupled with Bowie's disturbing imagery, provided some powerful moments. Musically, Tin Machine's discordant roots can be found here, on one of Bowie's better efforts. —*Rick Clark*

☆ **Hunky Dory** / 1972 / Rykodisc ✦✦✦✦✦
This follow-up to *The Man Who Sold the World* found Bowie lightening his sound considerably. Some of his most memorable songs are found on this classic: the catchy pop classic "Changes" (a theme song of sorts), the beautifully expansive "Life on Mars," the moody dynamics of "Quicksand," "The Bewlay Brothers," and "Oh, You Pretty Things." —*Rick Clark*

☆ **The Rise & Fall of Ziggy Stardust** / 1972 / Rykodisc ✦✦✦✦✦
Regarded by many to be Bowie's best album, Bowie took the melodicism developed on *Hunky Dory* and beefed it up with a punchy, rigid, freeze-dried "rock" setting. It's a perfect setting for Bowie's concept of a plastic rock star, Ziggy Stardust. *The Rise and Fall of Ziggy Stardust and the Spiders from Mars*, without a doubt, was an important defining effort for the glam rock movement. —*Rick Clark*

○ **Aladdin Sane** / 1973 / Rykodisc ✦✦✦✦
It rocks harder than *Ziggy Stardust*... but flirts pretty closely at times with cabaret death (courtesy of pianist Mike Garson). "Watch That Man" is a fine rocker that manages to draw inspiration from the Stones' *Exile on Main Street*, while not totally abandoning the tight-assed rhythmic stiffness inherent in the glam sound. Other highlights include "Jean Genie," "Cracked Actor," and "Panic in Detroit." —*Rick Clark*

Images 1966-1967 / 1973 / London ✦✦✦
This double album is becoming hard to find, which is unfortunate, as it's easily the most comprehensive collection of Bowie's 1966-67 work for Deram. The 21 tracks include the entirety of his 1967 debut album, plus seven stray songs from singles and sessions that were unreleased at the time. Possibly because it wasn't heard by many listeners until it was reissued in the early '70s during Bowie's ascent to stardom, this material has been unfairly maligned. Critics and fans of *Ziggy Stardust* were shocked to discover an all-around entertainer seemingly bent upon becoming the new Anthony Newley. Indeed, much of his work from this era was overbearingly cloying and saccharine, both in the West End matinee aspirations of the lyrics and the unabashedly theatrical orchestration, which bore hardly any resemblance to good old rock & roll whatsoever. One of these, "Laughing Gnome" (featuring Chipmunk-like backup vocals), would cause Bowie considerable embarrassment when it was reissued—and became a hit—in Britain in 1973. The less idiotically cheerful efforts, though, show definite signs of an idiosyncratic talent: the odd character sketches, the fleeting references to transvestites and mysticism, even the occasional London swinging pop number ("Let Me Sleep Beside You"). The best track, "London Boys" (a 1966 single), is a neglected classic look at the downer side of the mod experience, and is the best of his many obscure pre-"Space Oddity" recordings. —*Richie Unterberger*

Pin-Ups / 1973 / Rykodisc ✦✦✦
Bowie covers a selection of personal favorite songs from the '60s by the Yardbirds, the Kinks, the Who, Pink Floyd, and more. It's an affectionate tribute that makes more of a case for Bowie's excellent taste than for his ability to transcend the original versions. It contains the hit, "Sorrow." —*Rick Clark*

David Live / 1974 / Rykodisc ✦

Diamond Dogs / 1974 / Rykodisc ✦✦
An ambitious smudge of an album, it nevertheless contains some standouts in the lean, riff-heavy hit "Rebel Rebel," the fatalistic futurism of "1984" (an early discoish harbinger of his Thin White Duke era), and the title track. —*Rick Clark*

Young Americans / 1975 / Rykodisc ✦✦✦
Bowie affects Philly Soul and a hodgepodge of other things. Ace sidemen can't save this spotty album, but the title track and "Fame" (co-written by John Lennon) became worldwide hits. —*Rick Clark*

○ **Station to Station** / 1976 / Rykodisc ✦✦✦
A transitional effort, it bridges Bowie's clinical pop-disco persona to the icy psychosis and dissonance of this next phase, working with Brian Eno. Almost as ill formed as *Diamond Dogs* (particularly the title track), but the Top Ten hit "Golden Years" and "TVC15" are highlights. —*Rick Clark*

☆ **Low** / Jan. 1977 / Rykodisc ✦✦✦✦✦
The first of several efforts with ex-Roxy Music sound painter Brian Eno, *Low* is a willful departure from Bowie's pop persona. Short songs make their point and get out of the way on the first half, followed by four dense synth-instrumental soundscapes. —*Rick Clark*

☆ **Heroes** / Feb. 1977 / Rykodisc ✦✦✦✦✦
With echoes of *Low*'s half-sung/half-instrumental approach, this one has longer songs (given a maniacal musical accompaniment by King Crimson's Robert Fripp) and chillingly desolate soundscapes. The brilliant title track features one of Bowie's most passionate performances. Those who like discordant rock should be in heaven with "Beauty and the Beast," "Joe the Lion," and "Blackout." —*Rick Clark*

Stage / 1978 / Rykodisc ✦✦✦
A great double-disc live document of Bowie's *Heroes* tour, disc one focuses on *Ziggy Stardust* and *Station to Station* material, while disc two features *Low* and *Heroes* —Rick Clark

○ **Lodger** / 1979 / Rykodisc ✦✦✦✦
The third installment with Eno returns Bowie to a more conventional (but not necessarily more commercial) song structure. Production isn't sharp sounding as *Heroes*, but it has many engaging moments, particularly the hopeful "Fantastic Voyage" and the goofy "D.J.," plus "Boys Keep Swinging," and the hyperdrive of "Look Back in Anger." —*Rick Clark*

○ **Scary Monsters (And Super Creeps)** / 1980 / Rykodisc ✦✦✦✦
One of the better post-*Low* efforts, it contains the hits "Fashion" and "Ashes to Ashes," and the dissonant rocker "It's No Game (Part 1)." Robert Fripp provides a wonderfully jarring racket on "It's No Game (Part 1)," the Tom Verlaine-penned "Kingdom Come," and several others. Pete Townshend guests on "Because You're Young." The CD includes four bonus tracks: a nice version of Kurt Weill and Bert Brecht's "Alabama Song," an instrumental that could've come off of *Low*, and 1979 re-recordings of "Space Oddity" and "Panic in Detroit," of interest only to hardcore fans —*Rick Clark*

Let's Dance / 1983 / EMI America ✦✦✦
Bowie guns for big pop success and gets it on this outing, somehow deftly side-stepping appearances of being a sell-out. The title track, "China Girl," and "Modern Love" achieved international chart success. This album also includes a nice reworking of Metro's "Criminal World." —*Rick Clark*

Love You Til Tuesday / 1984 / PolyGram ✦✦
The bulk of this reissue comes from the soundtrack to Bowie's little-seen short film of the same name. Completed in early 1969, it was shelved until its re-release on video in 1984. While several of the songs had already been released by Bowie in the U.K. on Deram, this LP has some slightly different versions. The title track and "When I Live My Dream" are represented by their 45 single takes, not the more familiar album ones; "Sell Me A Coat" has added vocals by John Hutchinson and Hermoine Farthingale, who played with Bowie in his short-lived group Feathers. The previously unreleased "Ching-A-Ling" and "When I'm Five" are in keeping with the fey, fairy-tale, childlike ambience of much of his 1967 material. The version of "Space Oddity" also features Hutchinson and Farthingale, and is faster and less effective than the eventual hit single version. Rounding out the collection are some of the more well-known numbers from his Anthony Newley period (especially the notorious "Laughing Gnome"), and his 1964 debut single "Liza Jane," an out-and-out R&B number in the Stones/Pretty Things style. A scattershot anthology that is pretty much for collectors only, focusing on his uncharacteristically showtune-like 1967 period; that era is more definitively documented on the double album *Images*. —*Richie Unterberger*

Tonight / 1984 / EMI America ✦✦
On the basis of *Tonight*, it appears that David Bowie didn't have a clear idea of how to follow the platinum success of *Let's Dance*. Instead of breaking away from the stylized pop of "Let's Dance" and "China Girl," Bowie delivers another record in the same style. Apart from the single "Blue Jean," none of the material equals the songs on *Let's Dance*, but that didn't stop *Tonight* from becoming

another platinum success. Nevertheless, the record stands as one of the weakest albums Bowie ever recorded. *—Stephen Thomas Erlewine*

Never Let Me Down / 1987 / EMI America ♦♦
Bowie broke away from the mainstream pop of *Tonight* with 1987's *Never Let Me Down*, turning a jumbled mix of loud guitar rockers and art-rock experiments, like the failed "Glass Spider." While it's not as consistent as *Tonight*, it's far more interesting, with the John Lennon homage of the title track being one of his most underrated songs. *—Stephen Thomas Erlewine*

○ **Sound + Vision** / 1989 / Rykodisc ♦♦♦♦
An extravagantly produced three-disc-plus-CDV (video mini-disc) boxed set, it digs deeper than *Changesbowie*. This features much previously unavailable stuff but comes up short on certain primary radio tracks. It's a good complement to *Changesbowie*, in spite of a little track duplication. *—Rick Clark*

★ **Changesbowie** / 1990 / Rykodisc ♦♦♦♦♦
Except for the substitution of a "Fame '90" remix over the original #1 hit, this is a wide sampling of big cuts from all of Bowie's many phases, from "Space Oddity" to "Ashes to Ashes." While Bowie has had some classic albums, the uninitiated should start here. *—Rick Clark*

Early On (1964-1966) / 1991 / Rhino ♦♦
Before landing his first commercial success with 1969's "Space Oddity," David Bowie released a number of flop records in a variety of styles. He first emerged in the mid-1960s as a mod following the paths of the Who, Kinks, and Rolling Stones. The 17-cut CD *Early On (1964-66)* is by far the most comprehensive anthology of his first works, gathering all six of his first singles and adding five previously unreleased demos from 1965. Fans of Bowie's famous work may be nonplussed by this material, in which the singer shifts from sub-Stones R&B to Who/Kinkish power chords to trendy Swinging London pop in search of his own style. He didn't establish his own identity on these fairly derivative recordings, but that's not to say they aren't without their enjoyable aspects. The 1965 single "You've Got A Habit Of Leaving" has some fierce Who-styled feedback, "Can't Help Thinking About Me" is an uneasily introspective number that foreshadows his later lyrics, and the acoustic demos find him groping closer toward a more familiar and distinctive vocal style. Several of the tunes on this collection were produced by the legendary Shel Talmy, who also handled sessions for the Who and Kinks in the mid-'60s. *—Richie Unterberger*

Black Tie White Noise / 1993 / Savage ♦♦
A fitfully successful comeback effort by Bowie, *Black Tie White Noise* works best when he subtly tries to update his sound. When he duets with Al B.Sure! on the title track and does a tepid remake of Cream's "I Feel Free," the modernization of soul and glam sounds forced, which never happens on the house beats of "Jump They Say" or the moving reworking of Morrissey's "I Know It's Gonna Happen Someday." Unfortunately, the good songs—and the best material here is easily his best since *Scary Monsters*—are obscured by the filler and ill-conceived dance experimentations. Had it been trimmed by five or six songs, the album could indeed have brought him back to the top of the charts. *—Stephen Thomas Erlewine*

★ **Singles 1969-1993** / 1993 / Rykodisc ♦♦♦♦♦
Taking *Changesbowie* one step further, *Singles 1969-1993* collects all of David Bowie's biggest hits while picking up such overlooked gems as "Drive-In Saturday" and "Loving the Alien." The comprehensiveness and quality of the songs make *Singles* the best Bowie compilation available; fans will be pleased with the inclusion of the complete lyrics to all of the songs on this two-disc set. *—Stephen Thomas Erlewine*

BOOKS

♦♦♦♦ **Bowie: An Illustrated Record**, by Roy Carr & Charles Shaar Murray (Avon, 1981). The best book (actually, one of the few) to focus on Bowie's music, rather than his public persona. Includes detailed analysis, often entertainingly biting, of every one of Bowie's albums and singles, even dating to back to the many obscure nonhits he released in the '60s before finding stardom with "Space Oddity." Tons of good photos and press clippings, as well as a couple of overview essays and a lengthy discography, including bootlegs. *—Richie Unterberger*

♦♦ **David Bowie: The Pitt Report**, by Kenneth Pitt (Omnibus

Press, 1985). Pitt, Bowie's manager in the late '60s, has been characterized by some rock critics as a stuffy square who would have steered Bowie toward a career in cabaret and all-around entertainment if the young man had stood for it. Pitt's inclinations were probably too mainstream to establish a permanent managerial relationship, but in fact he deserves substantial credit for helping to sustain Bowie's career and vision during a time when his commercial and critical recognition was almost nil. This is his version of Bowie's early career, days for which he retains a good deal of pride and affection. Somewhat drily written, relying a great deal upon quotes from contemporary reviewers and business correspondence, it nonetheless has a lot of information about one of the least-documented phases of Bowie's career. It also reveals a much more human side of the musician, one who had not yet developed his obsessions with presenting chameleon-like, impenetrable public personas. *—Richie Unterberger*

♦♦♦♦ **Alias David Bowie**, by Peter & Leni Gillman (New English Library, 1986). More than most superstars with big egos, Bowie has taken delight in being an evasive target for biographers, granting infrequent and contradictory interviews, and rarely reflecting upon his life and achievements with depth and seriousness. This didn't get much attention in the United States, but it's certainly the best of the several Bowie bios floating around. Running over 600 pages, it treats all phases of the chameleon's career with equal attention, exploring family background and early, pre-stardom days with as much detail as possible. The authors also offer reasonable, intelligent analysis of his recorded work—not just the famous '70s glam and concept albums, but the obscure '60s singles and the overlooked *The Man Who Sold the World*. They didn't have access to Bowie himself—not many people do, writers or otherwise—but they interviewed a lot of subjects who have worked with or known him for years, including such key figures as Mick Ronson, Tony Visconti, Ian Hunter, and Kenneth Pitt. *—Richie Unterberger*

The Box Tops

Group, Soul, Pop/Rock
If you forget about the Rascals and the Righteous Brothers, the Memphis-based Box Tops are the finest blue-eyed soul group. Lead singer (and former Big Star honcho) Alex Chilton had a tough, swaggering voice that belied his teenage years, sounding at times as if he were in a cutting match with the young Steve Winwood. Producers Chips Moman and Dan Penn surrounded Chilton with a crack American studio band, giving the music more muscle and deep funk than you'll ever find in "Mary Mary."

Instead of knocking off pimply, lightweight teen-fodder, the Box Tops managed to add another link in the Memphis soul chain, mixing blues, Beatlesque pop, and the sound of Stax, Hi, and Goldwax. And unlike the Monkees, the Box Tops benefited from top-notch material: Dan Penn and Spooner Oldham's "Cry Like a Baby" and "I Met Her in Church"; Wayne Thompson's "The Letter" and "Soul Deep"; and the occasional Chilton-penned nugget, such as "I Must Be the Devil." The group's heyday was brief—two years, tops—but their music remains a staple on oldies stations and has retained its vitality for over two decades. *—John Floyd*

● **The Ultimate Box Tops** / 1988 / Warner Brothers ♦♦♦♦
Included is everything you need by this blue-eyed soul combo, such as "The Letter," "Cry Like a Baby," and "Soul Deep." *—John Floyd*

Boy George (George Alan O'Dowd)

b. Jun. 14, 1961, Bexleybeath, Eltham, Kent, England
Pop/Rock
British singer Boy George combined a strong, soulful singing voice with a provocative sense of fashion, both of which were first brought to the attention of English and American audiences in the group Culture Club, for which he served as lead singer from 1982 to 1986. The group wrote and played impeccable pop music, and Boy George's androgynous persona—heavy makeup, outrageous costumes—gave the group a distinct video image in the dawn of MTV. That very distinctiveness, however, made the group date quickly, and at the same time Boy George encountered highly publicized personal difficulties. He re-emerged as a solo singer in 1987 with *Sold*, which contained a UK #1 cover of Bread's "Everything I Own," but was unable to duplicate this success in the U.S. Boy George enjoyed four British singles chart entries in 1987 and

another three in 1988. His second album, *Tense Nervous Headache* (1988) was not picked up for release in the U.S.; his third, *Boyfriend* (1989) was a Europe-only release, though Virgin Records cobbled the second and third albums together to present a second U.S. album, *High Hat* (1989). In 1991 came *The Martyr Mantras*, another patchwork album largely made up of previously non-LP dance singles. In the U.K., it was credited to a new group, Jesus Loves You, and released on Boy George's own More Protein record label, though Virgin in the U.S. billed it as a Boy George album. By 1992, Boy George had faded at home, and in the U.S. his solo career had never taken off. Then he was brought in to sing a version of the '60s chestnut "The Crying Game," in a production by the Pet Shop Boys, as the title song for a movie that became the sleeper hit of the winter of 1992-1993, resulting in his first substantial U.S. hit as a solo artist. —*William Ruhlmann*

Sold / 1987 / Virgin ♦♦♦
Boy George teamed up with Lamont Dozier to write many of the songs on his debut album, much of which has a harder dance pop edge than his work with Culture Club. But it's still that bouncy, vulnerable voice, notably on the reggae-tinged hit "Everything I Own," that remains his trademark. —*William Ruhlmann*

High Hat / 1989 / Virgin ♦♦
If Culture Club, Boy George's old group, scored surprising across-the-board success with a wild new fashion sense and old-fashioned pop-soul music, as a solo artist Boy George seems determined to address a much smaller, more targeted audience. "I'm here to tell you that the boy's back in town," he declares in "Whether They Like It Or Not," but that song title seems to express his take-it-or-leave-it attitude. Wonder about his scandalous history of addiction and homosexuality? Fine—he gives you songs with titles like "You Are My Heroin" and "You Found Another Guy." Now and then, he returns to the soulfulness of old, notably on the ballad "I'm Not Sleeping Anymore," reminding us that the voice that carried "Do You Really Want To Hurt Me" is still there. But for the most part the Boy wants to engage in thinly veiled confessions set to new jack swing percussion tracks into which he nearly disappears. Was his future on the dance floor? This album's lack of success suggested not. —*William Ruhlmann*

The Martyr Mantras / 1991 / Virgin ♦♦

Boyz II Men

Group, Urban
Under the guidance of Michael Bivins of Bell Biv Devoe, the five-man vocal group Boyz II Men became a pop sensation in 1992. Although they call their music "hip-hop doo-wop," there's very little traditional doo-wop in their music. Instead, they bring the sound of '60s and early '70s R&B vocal groups into the '90s, adding a little new jack swing to that timeless sound. Their 1991 debut, *Cooleyhighharmony*, featured a massive hit single, "Motownphilly" which exemplifies the best of their dance work. Their second single, a ballad called "It's So Hard to Say Goodbye," was an even bigger hit; its success paved the way for "The End of the Road" (taken from the *Boomerang* soundtrack), the group's follow-up single which broke Elvis Presley's record for the most weeks spent at number one. After releasing a Christmas album in 1993, Boyz II Men went to work on their second album, which appeared in the fall of 1994. *II* proved to be even more successful than its predecessor, selling over seven million copies by summer of 1995 and spawning the record-breaking hit "I'll Make Love to You." —*Stephen Thomas Erlewine*

● **Cooleyhighharmony** / 1991 / Motown ♦♦♦♦
Boyz II Men's retro sound dominated the 1991 pop and R&B marketplaces, with their singles "It's So Hard To Say Goodbye To Yesterday" and "Motownphilly" hitting the Top Ten on both charts. The album eventually sold over five million copies and put Boyz II Men at the forefront of a movement returning the emphasis on Black popular music to vocal harmonies and a cappella interaction. —*Ron Wynn*

○ **II** / 1994 / Motown ♦♦♦♦
With their second album, Boyz II Men assured their place at the top of the charts, as well as in history. "I'll Make Love to You," the album's first single, stayed on the top of the charts for over two months, only to be unseated by "On Bended Knee," the album's second single. Not surprisingly, *II* is a carefully constructed crowd pleaser, accentuating all of the finest moments from their hit debut. While there are some high-energy dance tracks, the album's

main strength is its slower numbers, where the group's vocals soar. —*Stephen Thomas Erlewine*

Brad

Group, Alternative Pop/Rock
Guitarist Stone Gossard formed Brad as a side project after his main band, Pearl Jam, became superstars in 1992. The band released their first (and to date, only) album, *Shame*, in the summer of 1993 to mixed reviews and lukewarm sales. —*Stephen Thomas Erlewine*

Shame / Apr. 27, 1993 / Epic ♦♦♦
Brad, Stone Gossard's side project from Pearl Jam, is a looser, more groove-oriented band than his regular band, which means that *Shame* can meander at times, but still makes for some enjoyable listening. Anyone expecting a *Ten—Volume 2* will undoubtedly be disappointed, but those looking for something a bit more experimental might be pleasantly surprised. —*Stephen Thomas Erlewine*

Billy Bragg

b. Dec. 20, 1957, Barking, Essex, England
Singer-Songwriter, Alternative Pop/Rock, Folk-Rock
Finding inspiration in the righteous anger of punk rock and the socially conscious folk tradition of Woody Guthrie and Bob Dylan, Billy Bragg was the leading figure of the anti-folk movement of the '80s. For most of the decade, Bragg bashed out songs alone on his electric guitar, singing about politics and love. While his lyrics were bitingly intelligent and clever, they were also warm and humane, filled with detail and wit. Even though his lyrics were carefully considered, Bragg never neglected to write melodies for songs that were strong and memorable. Throughout the '80s, he managed to chart consistently in Britain, yet he only gathered a cult following in America, which could be due to the fact he sang about distinctly British subject matter, both politically and socially.

Bragg began performing in the late '70s with the punk group Riff Raff, which lasted only a matter of months. He then joined the British Army, yet he quickly bought himself out of his sojourn with 175 pounds. After leaving the Army, he began working at a record store; while he was working, he was writing songs that were firmly in the folk and punk protest tradition. Bragg began a British tour, playing whenever he had the chance to perform. Frequently he would open for bands with only a moment's notice; soon, he had built a sizable following, as evidenced by his first EP, *Life's a Riot with Spy Vs. Spy* (1983), hitting number 30 on the U.K. independent charts. *Brewing Up with Billy Bragg* (1984), his first full-length album, climbed to number 16 in the charts.

During 1984, Bragg became a minor celebrity in Britian, as he appeared at leftist political rallies, strikes, and benefits across the country; he also helped form the "Red Wedge," a socialist musicians collective that also featured Paul Weller. In 1985, Kirsty MacColl took his songs, "New England," to number seven on the British singles chart. Featuring some subtle instrumental additions of piano and horns, 1986's *Talking to the Taxman About Poetry* reached the U.K. Top Ten.

Bragg's version of the Beatles' "She's Leaving Home," taken from the *Sgt. Pepper Knew My Father* tribute album, became his only number one single in 1988—as the double-A side with Wet Wet Wet's "With a Little Help from My Friends." That year, he also released the EP *Help Save the Youth of America* and the full-length *Workers Playtime*, which was produced by Joe Boyd (Fairport Convention, Nick Drake, R.E.M.). Boyd helped expand Bragg's sound, as the singer recorded with a full band for the first time. The following year, Bragg restarted the Utility record label as a way of featuring non-commercial new artists. *The Internationale*, released in 1990, was a collection of left-wing anthems, including a handful of Bragg originals. On 1991's *Don't Try This at Home*, he again worked with a full band, recording his most pop-oriented and accessible set of songs; the album featured the hit single, "Sexuality." Bragg hasn't released an album since *Don't Try This at Home*, choosing to concentrate on fatherhood, yet he remains a respected figure in British music. —*Stephen Thomas Erlewine*

○ **Life's a Riot with Spy Vs Spy** / 1983 / Utility ♦♦♦♦
○ **Brewing Up** / 1984 / Go! Discs ♦♦♦♦
○ **Talking with the Taxman About Poetry** / 1986 / Go! Discs ♦♦♦♦
Bragg's one-man approach is fleshed out on *Talking with the Taxman About Poetry*, his second LP. "Levi Stubb's Tears" and "The Marriage" include subtle percussion and horn flourishes; "Greet-

ings to the New Brunette" is cushioned in layers of overdubbed acoustic guitars. That makes it Bragg's most satisfying album musically, but the witty, plaintive songs listed above—in addition to "Ideology" and "The Warmest Room"—make it a stirring and evocative lyrical statement as well. —*John Floyd*

● **Back to Basics** / 1987 / Go! Discs ◆◆◆◆
This disc brings together Bragg's first three releases (*Life's a Riot with Spy vs. Spy, Brewing Up with Billy Bragg*, and the *Between the Wars* EP) and offers the best introduction to his confessional songwriting and uncompromising politics. Highlights include "A New England," "The Busy Girl Buys Beauty," and "A Lover Sings." —*John Floyd*

Help Save the Youth of America E.P.: Live & Dubious / 1988 / Go! Discs ◆◆◆
An exceptional album. —*Chip Renner*

Workers Playtime / 1988 / Go! Discs ◆◆◆
Bragg's first attempt at working with a full band could be better—most of the songs are mopey and depressing, and some of his socialist manifestos are tiresome and dogmatic. Still, cuts like "She's Got a New Spell," "Must I Paint You a Picture," and "Little Time Bomb" are excellent, and "Waiting for the Great Leap Forward" is a humble and humorous explanation of Bragg's motives and intentions, both political and emotional. —*John Floyd*

The Internationale / 1990 / Utility ◆◆

○ **Don't Try This at Home** / 1991 / Go! Discs ◆◆◆◆
With full-blown production by the likes of Johnny Marr, and with musical assistance from R.E.M., this would seem like a blatant stab at the post-modern marketplace. Maybe so, but the thrust of his band turns "Accident Waiting to Happen" and "North Sea Bubble" into throttling rockers and makes "Sexuality" his best single. There are also several gorgeous ballads, "Tank Park Salute" and "Wish You Were Here" among them. —*John Floyd*

The Peel Sessions Album / May 1992 / Dutch East India ◆◆◆
Because Bragg started his career as a solo act, these live-in-the-studio radio transcriptions don't offer anything you can't find on *Back to Basics*. But fanatics will enjoy the occasional lyric deviations, and "A13 Trunk Road to the Sea" (a rewrite of "Route 66" with British directions) is a keeper. —*John Floyd*

Brand New Heavies

Group, Urban
Another of the "acid-jazz" groups who have emerged during the '80s and '90s, the Brand New Heavies have attracted substantial attention on both sides of the Atlantic for their sometimes clever, sometimes cool mix of quasi-sophisticated vocals, jazz backing, and samples. The London band began in the mid-'80s with drummer/keyboardist Jan Kincaid, percussionist/guitarist Lascelles, guitarist Simon Bartholomew, bassist/keyboardist Andrew Levy, saxophonist Mike Smith, trumpeter Paul Dias, saxophonist/keyboardist Jim Wellman, and vocalist Jay Ella Ruth. They were active on what was then called the "rare groove" circuit, playing funk and soul. They became the Brand New Heavies in the late '80s, cutting the single "Got to Give" for the Cooltempo label. They switched to the Acid Jazz label and style in 1990. Their 1991 debut for Delicious Vinyl/Island did moderately well, but they gained even more exposure (despite generating lackluster sales) with *Heavy Rhyme Experience: Vol 1*, a 1992 record that paired them with several hip-hop groups and big-name rappers. The guest list included Main Source, Gang Starr, Grand Puba, Master Ace, Kool G. Rap, Black Sheep, Ed O.G., Tiger, The Pharcyde, and Jamalski. Vocalist N'Dea Davenport was a contributor to *Jazzmatazz*, a similar all-star jazz/hip-hop set produced by Gang Starr's Guru. Brand New Heavies released their third album, *Brother Sister,* in 1994. —*Ron Wynn*

The Brand New Heavies / 1991 / Delicious Vinyl ◆◆◆
Brand New Heavies' debut album finds them trying to weld classic soul vocals and instrumentals, as well as jazz, to contemporary hip-hop. While it isn't entirely successful, the moments that it does work make the album worth listening to. —*Stephen Thomas Erlewine*

● **Heavy Rhyme Experience, Vol. 1** / 1992 / Atlantic ◆◆◆◆
Between their debut and full-fledged second album, Brand New Heavies released an album of collaborations with some of the brightest stars in hip-hop, such as Gang Starr, Grand Puba, and Main Source. *Heavy Rhyme Experience: Vol. 1* actually works better than their debut, since the rappers bring a gritty street credi-

bility to the group's lush R&B; at its best, the album stands as a splendid fusion of jazz, soul, and hip-hop. —*Stephen Thomas Erlewine*

Brother Sister / 1994 / Delicious Vinyl ◆◆◆

Brand Nubian

Group, Rap
One of the better Islam-oriented groups that popped up in the early part of the '90s, Brand Nubian released their debut album, *One for All* in 1991. Their religious fervor never dissipated into ranting, exclusionary dogma, and the beats are seriously funky. After their debut, Brand Nubian underwent some changes, the most notable being the departure of dynamic lead rapper Grand Puba. Their 1992 album *In God We Trust* didn't receive the same glowing reviews of *One for All*, yet it sold well. —*John Floyd*

● **One for All** / 1990 / Elektra ◆◆◆◆
These post-De La Soul, daisy-age rappers are here to wrap their Islamic-slanted lyrics around challenging, clever, and hard-hitting beats and samples. —*John Floyd*

○ **In God We Trust** / 1993 / Elektra ◆◆◆◆

Brandy

Urban
Vocalist/actress Brandy Norwood was 15 years old when her debut single "I Wanna Be Down" rocketed into the Top Ten in late 1994. Thanks to her strong vocals and production, her self-titled debut album proved to be a major R&B and pop hit. In addition to her musical career, Brandy is a featured actress on television's "Thea." —*Stephen Thomas Erlewine*

○ **Brandy** / Atlantic/AG ◆◆◆◆
This teenage R&B singer hit the Top 10 late in 1994 with "I Wanna Be Down," a representative track from her solid debut album. Brandy knows her way around a hip-hop beat, layering tender-tough vocals over spare arrangements like a lower-key Janet Jackson or a more stripped-down Mary J. Blige. Good songs and crisp production make Brandy a moody, moving success. —*Eddie Huffman*

Laura Branigan

b. Jul. 3, 1957, Brewster, NY
Pop/Rock
Laura Branigan is a singer and, increasingly, an actress from Brewster, NY, who first gained notice when she became a backup singer for Leonard Cohen in 1977. Branigan achieved considerable popular success in the early '80s by applying her big, powerful voice to translated versions of Eurodisco hits. She was less successful with subsequent recordings in the second half of the '80s, though by then she had begun to appear on television and in films. —*William Ruhlmann*

○ **Branigan** / Mar. 1982 / Atlantic ◆◆◆◆
Branigan's big, expressive voice is the draw here, placed in dramatic musical settings that show it off to best advantage, especially on "Gloria," her breakthrough hit and stirring pop performance. —*William Ruhlmann*

Branigan 2 / Mar. 1983 / Atlantic ◆◆◆
"Solitaire" is the inevitable "Gloria" followup, but the album also shows unusual range, including a version of the Who's "Squeeze Box" and the dramatic ballad "How Am I Supposed to Live without You," which was a minor hit for Branigan and a much bigger hit a few years later for Michael Bolton. —*William Ruhlmann*

Self Control / Apr. 1984 / Atlantic ◆◆◆
R&B/dance overtones, including the title track. —*Bil Carpenter*

Hold Me / Jul. 1985 / Atlantic ◆◆◆
Laura Branigan began to falter in her quest to be the White, '80s Donna Summer with her fourth album, which failed to scale the sales heights of her first three, despite another clutch of dramatic, heavily produced Eurodisco tracks, three of which found their way onto the singles charts. The closest thing to a hit was "Spanish Eddie" (this album's remake of her first smash, "Gloria"), a song with an odd street-life lyric that made reference to Bob Dylan's "Desolation Row." Indeed, the ghost of Bob seemed to be haunting this album, which featured yet another song called "Forever Young." Elsewhere, Branigan again turned to songwriter Michael Bolton for "I Found Someone," and as she had with "How Am I Supposed to Live Without You," did it much better than its author, for what

it's worth. But on the whole, *Hold Me* found the Branigan formula growing stale. — *William Ruhlmann*

Touch / Jul. 1987 / Atlantic ♦♦

Laura Branigan / Apr. 1990 / Atlantic ♦♦
Short on ideas even with a three-year layoff (they couldn't even think of an album title!), the Laura Branigan brain trust, led by executive producer (and now Warner Music-U.S. chairman/CEO) Doug Morris put its faith in drum programs to carry a collection of mediocre originals, a lame cover of Vicki Sue Robinson's dance classic "Turn The Beat Around," and a Bryan Adams castoff. Branigan sang with her usual gusto, but even slick producers like Richard Perry and Peter Wolf couldn't animate the material. Lead-off track "Moonlight On Water" saw a little singles chart action, but Laura Branigan's sixth album was her least successful effort so far, failing to break into the top 100 best-sellers. — *William Ruhlmann*

Over My Heart / 1993 / Atlantic ♦♦
Laura Branigan had greater creative participation in the making of her seventh album, earning credits for songwriting, arrangements, and production. Industry vet Phil Ramone was the main producer, however, and the result was a move away from the disco diva approach of Branigan's earlier records and a move toward the pop-rock mainstream. Given that Branigan's albums had shown a downward sales pattern, it was a fair attempt at repositioning, but these undistinguished romantic ballads, whether by Branigan herself, Michael Bolton, Gloria Estefan, or others, failed to offer the singer an opportunity to steady herself in the middle of the road. As a result, *Over My Heart* came in under the pop radar screen: It didn't reach the charts and disappeared quickly after release. — *William Ruhlmann*

It's Been Hard Enough / 1994 / Atlantic ♦♦

● **The Best of Laura Branigan** / 1995 / Atlantic ♦♦♦♦

Brass Construction

Group, Soul, Funk, R&B
Vocalist/instrumentalist Randy Muller was at the helm of two pivotal East Coast funk and disco aggregations in the '70s and '80s. One was Brass Construction; the other was Skyy. Muller, a vocalist and instrumentalist who doubled on keyboards and flute, organized the band with drummer Larry Payton, trumpeters Wayne Parris and Morris Price, lead guitarist Joe Arthur, vocalist/conga player Sandy Billups, saxophonists Michael Grudge and Jesse Ward, and bassist Wade Williamson. Their 1975 debut, produced by Jeff Lane, went platinum and contained two dancefloor anthems in "Moving" and "Changin." *Brass Construction II, III, IV,* and *V* mined the same territory, though only the single "Ha Cha Cha (Funktion)" in 1977 and "L-O-V-E-U" in 1978 came close to attaining similiar commercial heights. They recorded for United Artists until 1980, then moved to Liberty and recorded for them until 1983. Muller became their producer in the early '80s, and he shifted their emphasis into a heavily synthesized direction. They continued on Capitol from 1983 to 1985, but couldn't regain their past momentum. The group's vintage hits were remixed and reissued internationally by EMI's Syncopate label in the late '80s, and Brass Construction reappeared on England's charts in 1988. — *Ron Wynn*

● **Brass Construction** / Apr. 1976 / United Artists ♦♦♦♦
One of the classic disco albums and by far the finest thing Brass Construction ever did. They came out of the chute roaring in 1975. This album went platinum, and the sounds of "Movin" and "Changin" were roaring on the streets and in the clubs throughout the year. — *Ron Wynn*

Brass Construction II / 1976 / United Artists ♦♦♦
Although the overall quality dipped considerably, the group stayed on track with the single "Ha Cha Cha." It wasn't realistic to expect them to equal their great debut, and they didn't, but this one contained enough decent singles to keep them in the mid-'70s dance and funk forefront. — *Ron Wynn*

Brass Construction III / 1977 / United Artists ♦♦♦
The danger signs were already in view. They had no standout single on their third release, and they were beginning to recycle the funk tracks and arrangements. The band members maintained their high standards, but not even their playing could completely salvage the album. Brass Construction's condition echoed disco's. — *Ron Wynn*

Brass Construction IV / 1978 / United Artists ♦♦
They kept making albums and vainly trying to recapture the heights of their first release. Brass Construction's fourth album wasn't all bad; the uptempo tunes were pretty good. But by now, they'd said all they could in the horn/funk/dance mode. — *Ron Wynn*

Brass Construction V / 1979 / United Artists ♦♦
They did manage to get one more hit, although "Music Makes You Feel Like Dancin'" was about as pro forma late '70s disco as possible. But both the genre and the group were on their last legs. The fast songs were their poorest to that point, and the few ballads were completely disposable. — *Ron Wynn*

Brass Construction VI / 1980 / United Artists ♦♦
Arguably their least interesting album. Brass Construction was due for an overhaul and clearly showed it throughout this release. The production and some of the arrangements were still acceptable, but there was no energy in the playing and even less in the lyrics or vocals. — *Ron Wynn*

Attitudes / 1982 / Liberty ♦♦
Some needed changes were evident on this release. Producer Randy Muller moved Brass Construction away from horn-driven disco/funk and toward the synthesizer-dominated, heavily syncopated sound that was now ruling R&B and dance music. He restored a little lost luster, as the single "Can You See The Light" got some urban and dance radio airplay, and the band was no longer missing in action. — *Ron Wynn*

Conversations / 1983 / Capitol ♦♦♦
Brass Construction continued to avoid the scrap heap, turning out another better than expected album. There were two more good singles in "Walkin' The Line" and "We Can Work It Out," and the production, arrangements, instrumental support, and vocals were all more inspired than they had been in the past. — *Ron Wynn*

Renegades / 1984 / Capitol ♦♦
Brass Construction kept issuing albums, even though many of their contemporaries had called it quits by the mid-'80s. This album once more spawned two minor hits in "Partyline" and "International," and also made Brass Construction one of the few hit disco acts from the '70s that had made it to the middle of the '80s. — *Ron Wynn*

Conquest / 1985 / Capitol ♦

● **The Best of Brass Construction: Movin' & Changin'** / Nov. 2, 1993 / EMI America ♦♦♦♦

○ **Golden Classics** / Collectables ♦♦♦♦
A blueprint of '70s disco, funk, and horn arrangements. — *Ron Wynn*

Toni Braxton

Urban
Toni Braxton made her vocal debut with the single "Love Shoulda Brought You Home" from the *Boomerang* soundtrack. She issued her first full session in 1993, and it soared to the top of both the pop and R&B charts. Braxton eventually earned two Grammy and two Soul Train awards, saw her self-titled release go platinum, and also reaped both critical and commercial plaudits for such singles as "Love Shoulda Brought You Home" and "Just Another Sad Love Song." — *Ron Wynn*

● **Toni Braxton** / 1993 / La Face ♦♦♦♦
Toni Braxton is both an elegant and earthy songstress, nicely balancing those seemingly divergent sentiments on her self-titled debut disc. Braxton's husky, enticing voice sounds hypnotic on "Breathe Again," dismayed on "Another Sad Love Song" and disillusioned on "Love Shoulda Brought You Home." But she's never out of control, indignant or so anguished that she fails to retain her dignity. It's a sign of how great the Babyface/L.A. Reid production team was that they didn't settle for a defining mood; they presented Braxton with enough diverse emotional settings to hold the interest of urban contemporary males and females. — *Ron Wynn*

Bread

Group, Pop/Rock
Bread was one of the most popular pop groups of the early '70s, earning a string of well-crafted, melodic soft rock singles, all of which were written by keyboardist/vocalist David Gates. A session musician and producer, Gates met guitarist/vocalist James Griffin in 1968, who had already released a solo album called

Summer Holiday. Griffin hired Gates to produce a new album, yet the pair soon became a group, adding guitarist/vocalist Robb Royer from the band Pleasure Faire, whom Gates had produced early in their career. The trio soon signed with Elektra Records, becoming one of the label's first pop bands. Naming themselves Bread, the group released their self-titled debut album in late 1968. Although it was filled with accessible, melodic soft rock that became the band's signature sound, the record had no hit singles.

With their second album *On the Waters,* Bread established themselves as hit-makers. "Make It with You," the first single released from the album, became a number one hit, which led to "It Don't Matter to Me," a song taken from *Bread,* becoming a Top Ten hit. With *On the Waters* becoming a gold record, the group embarked on a tour, adding a full-time drummer, Mike Botts, to the lineup. *Manna,* released in the spring of 1971, wasn't as big a hit as the previous record, yet it launched another Top Ten hit with "If." Royer left the group after the album and was replaced by Larry Knechtel, a Los Angeles session musician who played on records by the Byrds, the Beach Boys, Simon & Garfunkel, the Monkees, and Johnny Rivers, among others. The new lineup released their first single, "Mother Freedom," in the summer of 1971; the single was a minor hit, scraping the Top 40 at number 37. Bread's next single, "Baby I'm-a Want You," became a number three hit at the end of the year. After "Everything I Own" reached number 5 in January of 1972, an album called *Baby I'm-A Want You* was released. Peaking at number three, the record became the group's most successful album. The group's fifth album, *Guitar Man,* followed in the fall of 1972. Although it wasn't quite as successful on the pop charts, the album was a massive hit on the Adult Contemporary charts, as were Bread's previous records.

At the beginning of 1973, Bread disbanded after a dispute between Gates and Griffin. Griffin claimed that when the group was conceived, the pair agreed that the singles would be divided equally between the two songwriters; Gates wrote most Bread's hits and wanted to continue to compose the singles. The two parted ways, with each of the musicians pursuing solo careers. Bread reunited in 1976, releasing *Lost Without Your Love* in early 1977. The title track became their last Top Ten hit, peaking at number nine. In the fall of 1977, the hits collection *The Sound of Bread* knocked the Sex Pistols' *Never Mind the Bollocks—Here's the Sex Pistols* off the top of the British charts. The success could not keep the group together, as tensions between Gates and Griffin began to escalate again. After Griffin split from the group, Gates assembled a new version of the band and toured under the name Bread. Griffin sued Gates for using the name Bread, which the duo co-owned. A judge ordered the group not to perform, record, or collect royalty payments until the case was resolved; it wasn't resolved until 1984. In the meantime, Gates and Griffin pursued solo careers. Of the two musicians, Gates was more successful, scoring a number 15 hit in 1978 with the title theme to *Goodbye Girl.* However, his career declined in the '80s; by the '90s, he was running a California ranch. Griffin relocated to Nashville, forming Dreamer with Rand Meisner in the early '90s; after Dreamer's breakup, he formed Black Tie with Billy Swan and the duo had a country hit with a version of Buddy Holly's "Learning the Game." Knechtel released a new age album called *Mountain Moods* and briefly played with Elvis Costello; Botts became a session musician, writing jingles and performing on children's albums. — *Stephen Thomas Erlewine*

○ **Bread** / 1969 / Elektra ✦✦✦✦

On the Waters / 1970 / Elektra ✦✦✦
The David Gates-penned singles were some of the most romantic music around in the early '70s and this album features their only number one single, "Make It with You." In fact, the singles were often reason enough to buy Bread's albums. But Bread was no one-dimensional band. Griffin & Royer were strong writers in their own right and that diversity has helped the Bread records hold up over the years. — *Jim Worbois*

○ **Manna** / 1971 / Elektra ✦✦✦✦
Bread's third effort builds strongly on the foundation laid down on their first two records. More great singles (including a rocky "Let Your Love Go" which didn't do quite as well as the ballads on the charts) and more great album tracks were included. — *Jim Worbois*

○ **Baby I'm-A Want You** / 1972 / Elektra ✦✦✦✦
By Bread's fourth record, Royer was gone (though his presence is felt due to a couple of tracks he co-wrote with Griffin), replaced by the versatile Larry Knechtel. This slight realignment makes this

one of Bread's strongest records. If you only own the hits packages, you owe it to yourself to track this one down as well. — *Jim Worbois*

Guitar Man / 1972 / Elektra ✦✦✦

Lost without Your Love / 1977 / Elektra ✦✦

Sound of Bread / 1977 / Elektra ✦✦

● **Anthology** / 1985 / Elektra ✦✦✦✦
This album includes "Make It with You," "If," "Baby I'm-a Want You," and many other fine-tuned pop gems. — *Dan Heilman*

Breeders

Group, Alternative Pop/Rock
Initially, the Breeders were conceived as a way for Pixies' bassist Kim Deal and Throwing Muses' guitarist Tanya Donelly to let out some suppressed creative energy. Deal and Donelly both played guitar, leaving bass for Josephine Wiggs of Perfect Disaster. Taking their name from the group Deal led with her twin sister, Kelly, in their teens, the Breeders combined the spareness of Throwing Muses with the shifting dynamics and warped pop sensibilities of the Pixies. *Pod,* their critically acclaimed debut album, was released in 1990. Two years later, the group delivered *Safari,* a four-song EP that found the band getting more muscular and melodic. Soon after its recording, Donelly left the Breeders to form her own group, Belly. Kim Deal brought in her sister, Kelly, as her replacement. By this time, their permanent drummer was Jim MacPherson, who was billed as "Mike Hunt" on *Safari.*

As the Breeders were working on their new album in the beginning of 1993, the Pixies split, leaving Kim Deal able to pursue the Breeders full-time. Released late in the summer of 1993, *Last Splash* was a hazier, more disjointed continuation of the hard pop of *Safari.* With the sonic collage of "Cannonball," the Breeders had a crossover hit that catapulted the group into stardom; within a year, the album had gone platinum and the band had a prime spot on 1994's Lollapalooza tour. — *Stephen Thomas Erlewine*

● **Pod** / 1990 / 4AD/Elektra ✦✦✦✦
At the time *Pod* was released, the Breeders were just a side project for Kim Deal and Tanya Donelly, but the album was much richer than most one-shot records. Taking a little from both the Pixies and Throwing Muses, the Breeders invent an indie-rock style of their own—a sparse, dreamy, elliptical take on guitar pop. While *Pod* may rely on the sheer uniqueness of the band's spare, raw sound, the album wouldn't be nearly as successful if it wasn't for the band's exceptional songwriting. From the wonderful, slow guitar grind of "Glorious" and "Iris" to the stripped-down pop of "Doe" and "Iris," *Pod* is full of original guitar-pop pleasures. — *Stephen Thomas Erlewine*

Safari / 1992 / 4AD/Elektra ✦✦✦
There are only four songs, but the Breeders continue to improve, growing more muscular and melodic. All of the songs here, especially "Do You Love Me Now" and a cover of the Who's "So Sad About Us," rival the best on *Pod.* — *Stephen Thomas Erlewine*

○ **Last Splash** / 1993 / Elektra ✦✦✦✦
Falling halfway between the adventurous *Pod* and the magnificent heavy guitar-pop of *Safari,* *Last Splash* is ultimately a disappointing second album from the Breeders. Nearly half of *Last Splash* is filled with song fragments and incomplete songs that sound unfinished; the songs do not sound like vital, messy garage rock from inspired amateurs—they sound lazy. However, there's no denying that when *Last Splash* is good, it's splendid. From the thrilling sonic collage of "Cannonball" to the more traditional pop melodies of "Invisible Man," "I Just Wanna Get Along," "Divine Hammer," and "Drivin' On 9," the best moments on the album are truly terrific, making the underdeveloped "No Aloha," "Hag," "Mad Lucas," "Roi," and the inferior rerecording of "Do You Love Me Now?" all the more infuriating. — *Stephen Thomas Erlewine*

Brick

Group, Funk
Brick was an Atlanta band that created a successful merger of funk and jazz in the '70s they called "dazz." Brick's roster included lead vocalist/ saxophonist/ flutist Jimmy Brown, guitarist/ bassist/ vocalist Regi Hargis Hickman, lead singer Ray Ransom, who doubled as a bassist/ keyboardist/ percussionist, and Eddie Irons, who did lead vocals and played drums and keyboards. They recorded "Music Matic" for Main Street in 1976, before signing to the CBS-distributed label Bang. Their first Bang single, "Dazz," topped the

R&B charts and was a number three pop hit in 1976, and they continued on Bang until 1982. Brick scored two more huge hits in 1977, "Dusic" and "Ain't Gonna' Hurt Nobody," each with a chunky, propulsive beat and catchy, light pop-jazz refrain. Their last Top Ten R&B hit was "Sweat (Til You Get Wet)" in 1981. —*Ron Wynn*

● **Good High** / 1976 / Bang ✦✦✦✦
○ **Brick** / 1978 / Bang ✦✦✦✦

Edie Brickell & New Bohemians

Folk-Rock, Pop/Rock

Edie Brickell was born around 1966 in the Oak Cliff section of Dallas. She attended Southern Methodist University for a year and a half before drinking up enough courage in a bar one night in 1985 to get up on stage with a local band, the New Bohemians. She joined the band and wrote songs over the next year as the band changed and evolved. They finally settled on the personnel of Brad Houser (bass), Kenny Withrow (guitar), and Matt Chamberlain (drums), before taking off for Rockfield Studios in Wales to record their debut album.

That album, *Shooting Rubberbands at the Stars*, revealed Brickell to be a songwriter with a unique perspective and a singer with an intimate, conversational style. The album was hailed by critics and became a massive hit, selling over a million copies and producing the Top Ten hit "What I Am."

After the disappointing performance of their follow-up album, *Ghost of a Dog*, the New Bohemians disbanded. Brickell married Paul Simon and the couple had a child. After several years of remaining artistically quiet, Brickell released her first solo album in late summer 1994. —*William Ruhlmann*

● **Shooting Rubber Bands at the Stars** / 1989 / David Geffen Co. ✦✦✦✦

Lead singer Brickell is charmingly unique on this album of light pop with thoughtful lyrics. It features the hit "What I Am." —*Donna DiChario*

Ghost of a Dog / 1990 / David Geffen Co. ✦✦✦

An overlooked follow-up, it found Brickell expanding on her offbeat vocals. —*Donna DiChario*

Picture Perfect Morning / 1994 / David Geffen Co. ✦✦

Martin Briley

British backup musician and songwriter Martin Briley was a member of Ian Hunter's band. He moved to New York in 1977 and made three solo albums for Mercury in the first half of the '80s, the second of which featured his 1983 Top 40 single "The Salt in My Tears." —*William Ruhlmann*

Fear of the Unknown / 1981 / Mercury ✦✦✦

Martin Briley proved to be a slightly wordy pop tunesmith on his debut album, taking his musical cues (especially for those twin guitar runs) from '70s British pop acts like ELO and Queen while adopting a persona full of doubt and soured romance. The album's best song was the atypical "I Feel Like A Milkshake," in which a revved-up Dave Edmunds-like rockabilly production was at the service of one of the more clever "food=sex" metaphorical statements. More often, Briley was fending off attachment with one hand and delivering world-weary sentiments with the other, such that the album didn't so much express fear of the unknown as dissatisfaction with the known-too-well. —*William Ruhlmann*

● **One Night with a Stranger** / 1983 / Mercury ✦✦✦✦

Perhaps feeling the influence of the new wave, Martin Briley simplified the guitar lines and speeded up the tempos on his second album. He also simplified his lyrics, which may have helped him get his first and only Top 40 hit with the lead-off track, a characteristic put-down song called "The Salt In My Tears" (as in "you're not worth...") Still complaining about love gone wrong, Briley was more often casting his tales of romantic wrongdoing in the third person and increasing the humor content on songs like "She's So Flexible" and "Dumb Love," which recount unusual, if not unlikely encounters, as well as the story song "One Night With A Stranger," which revealed the dangers of one-night stands. Briley still wasn't creating a distinctive musical persona—sometimes he sounded like Sting, sometimes like Phil Collins—but his writing showed enough promise that you hoped he would yet do so. And the surprise hit seemed to give him the opportunity. —*William Ruhlmann*

Dangerous Moments / 1985 / Mercury ✦✦

Having scored a fluke hit with "Salt In My Tears" on his last album, Martin Briley went for the gold ring on his third album, hiring top pop producer Phil Ramone and studio ringers like Anton Fig and G.E. Smith. He then spent all of Side One looking for another hit, to the point of writing clichés instead of twisting them, as he had in the past, with the help of such co-writers as Nick ("Hot Child In The City") Gilder. The effort was in vain. On Side Two, he presented more of his typically clever pop-rock songs, especially "Before The Party Ends," in which he noted, "Everybody knows where I come from/I've been living in the shadow of the Beatles and the bomb." But the question, after this album disappeared from the charts, wasn't where Martin Briley had come from; it was where he was going. —*William Ruhlmann*

Brinsley Schwarz

Group, Rock & Roll

Although they were one of England's best and most important bands of the early '70s, Brinsley Schwarz was forever haunted by a well-intentioned, but disastrous, publicity stunt. In order to promote their first album, the band flew nearly all of the British press, as well as many other journalists, to New York to witness their bottom-of-the-bill showcase gig at the Fillmore East. The problems began when three members of the band were denied work visas until the day of the show. On their way to New York, the reporters were grounded for four hours. Once the press got to the Fillmore, their seats had been taken; some journalists stayed, some got kicked out after they complained, some went back to the hotel. In any case, they were more than happy to pan Brinsley Schwarz in print once they got back home. Consequently, their first album was a commercial failure.

The band decided to regroup by renting a house outside of London and rehearsing for 18 months straight. It was here that the band developed their Byrds-fixated sound into a distinctive, laid-back country-rock, that derived equally from country, R&B and rock. Bassist/vocalist Nick Lowe became a first-rate songwriter, capable of gorgeous ballads and witty, melodic pop songs. After finding an American band playing a pub called Tally Ho in the summer of 1972, the band decided that pubs provided the perfect, relaxed atmosphere for their music. Brinsley Schwarz became regulars at Tally Ho and persuaded many other pub owners to open their doors for their band.

Brinsley Schwarz soon gained a devoted following; within a year they were opening for Wings' first U.K. tour. Numerous other bands, including Dr. Feelgood, began playing the same pub circuit as the Brinsleys; these were the same venues where punk rock was born several years later. Without Brinsley Schwarz, the punk movement would have been very different. At a time when rock & roll was overwhelmingly pompous, the Brinsleys were modest and unpretentious; they played relaxed, rootsy music and they proved to English pub owners that it was profitable to book left-of-center acts. Without this precedent, the punks would have had nowhere to play.

After releasing six albums, Brinsley Schwarz split up in 1975. Guitarist Brinsley Schwarz and keyboardist Bob Andrews became members of Graham Parker's backing band, the Rumour; Lowe became a successful solo artist and producer in his own right. Over 20 years later, the band's music still sounds splendid and it is still underappreciated. —*Stephen Thomas Erlewine*

Brinsley Schwarz / 1970 / Capitol ✦✦✦

A fine country-rock debut that was unfairly panned upon its release, *Brinsley Schwarz* still sounds fresh today. —*Stephen Thomas Erlewine*

Despite It All / 1970 / Liberty ✦✦✦

Brinsley Schwarz's second album shows substantial growth, in both the band's playing and Nick Lowe's songwriting. —*Stephen Thomas Erlewine*

○ **Silver Pistol** / 1972 / Edsel ✦✦✦✦

Silver Pistol, the band's first consistently entertaining record, is filled with brilliant reconstructions of American country, folk, and rock & roll, featuring excellent songs by both Nick Lowe and Ian Gomm, as well as two covers of Jim Ford songs—"Niki Hoeke Speedway" and "Ju Ju Man." —*Stephen Thomas Erlewine*

○ **Nervous on the Road** / 1972 / United Artists ✦✦✦✦

An even better collection than *Silver Pistol, Nervous on the Road* is an expertly played and superbly written set of country-rock and laidback rock & roll. On the surface, it seems all pleasant and gentle, but dig a little deeper and you'll find Nick Lowe slyly subverting the conventions of the genre with his sharp sense of humor. —*Stephen Thomas Erlewine*

○ **Please Don't Ever Change** / 1973 / Edsel ◆◆◆◆
Brinsley Schwarz's fifth album is another fine set of exceptional originals and clever covers, all superbly played by the well-seasoned band. —*Stephen Thomas Erlewine*

○ **New Favourites** / 1974 / United Artists ◆◆◆◆
With their final album, Brinsley Schwarz turn in their most pop-oriented record, filled with infectious gems like "The Ugly Things," "Trying to Live My Life Without You," and "(What's So Funny 'Bout) Peace, Love and Understanding." Lowe's songs were the best he had ever written and show that his ambitions were beginning to conflict with those of the rest of the band. Nevertheless, there isn't a weak song or uninspired performance on *New Favourites*, making it an excellent farewell album. —*Stephen Thomas Erlewine*

Original Golden Greats / 1974 / United Artists ◆◆◆
15 Thoughts of Brinsley Schwarz / 1978 / United Artists ◆◆◆
★ **Surrender to the Rhythm** / 1991 / EMI ◆◆◆◆◆
A terrific sampler of many of Brinsley Schwarz's finest tracks, *Surrender to the Rhythm* is the perfect introduction to this highly underrated band. —*Stephen Thomas Erlewine*

Bronski Beat

Group, New Wave
A synth-pop trio from London, everything that made Bronski Beat interesting, and at times compelling, came primarily from the larynx of Glasgow-born vocalist Jimmy Somerville. Possessing a soaring tenor voice that frequently exploded into falsetto, Somerville was a rare singer, capable of imbuing even the most rote dance songs with near-palpable heartache and layers of emotional turmoil. Openly gay, Somerville and the Bronskis, despite the rock world's implicit homophobia, became cover darlings of the British music press in 1984 after the U.K. success of their first two singles, "Why" and "Smalltown Boy" (the latter producing one of the best music videos of all time). From that point on, Bronski Beat seemed poised to rule the pop world (at least in England), releasing a superb cover of the Donna Summer disco hit "I Feel Love" and a remarkable debut album, 1984's *Age of Consent*. It was only a year later that Somerville announced he was leaving Bronski Beat to form the more explicitly left-wing Communards (with pianist Richard Coles). Bronski Beat took his departure in stride, and the lead vocal slot went to a fairly anonymous singer named John Jon. There were more Bronski Beat recordings, but even fanatics would agree that the band lost everything when it lost Somerville. Ironically, the Communards got off to a fast start with a great cover of Thelma Houston's "Don't Leave Me This Way," but all in all, Somerville's work with them was far less interesting than anything he did in Bronski Beat. By 1989, Somerville was a solo act, his magnificent voice still intact and the quality of the material still in question. —*John Dougan*

● **The Age of Consent** / 1984 / London ◆◆◆◆
To say this is a great album of dance-oriented synth-pop music is to sell it extremely short; this is simply a great album, period. Somerville's soaring tenor may take some getting used to, but the songs, many of them dealing with homophobia and alienation (none more eloquently than "Smalltown Boy") and compelling vignettes about the vagaries of life as a gay man. Cynics predisposed to dismissing entire genres of music based on trendiness or a limited appeal ("dance music is for dancing, not listening") miss the point in lumping this in with more mindless forays into techno or neo-disco. As the Pet Shop Boys (the world's greatest disco band) proved a few years later, you can have substantive content and wrap it up in a compelling, visceral, dance-oriented package. Few bands understood this better, or earlier, than Bronski Beat. —*John Dougan*

Hundreds & Thousands / 1985 / London ◆◆◆
Truthdare Doubledare / 1986 / London ◆◆◆

Gary Brooker

b. May 29, 1949, Essex, England
Singer/songwriter/keyboardist Gary Brooker is best known as the leader of Procol Harum. Brooker's first group was the Paramounts, all of whose members turned up in the later group. Procol Harum

was launched in 1967 with its biggest hit, the U.K. #1/U.S. Top Ten "A Whiter Shade of Pale," which featured Brooker singing the lyrics of Keith Reid over an adaptation of a Bach cantata. Procol Harum went on to release ten albums through 1977, then broke up. Brooker launched a solo career with *No More Fear of Flying* in 1979, followed by *Lead Me to the Water* (1982), and *Echoes in the Night* (1985). He also played in Eric Clapton's backup band. Procol Harum reformed for a new album, *The Prodigal Stranger*, in 1991. —*William Ruhlmann*

No More Fear of Flying / 1979 / Chrysalis ◆◆◆
After 10 albums with Procol Harum, lead singer, composer, and keyboard player Gary Brooker launched his solo career with this album. Of course, there were Brooker's familiar characteristics—the steady piano work, the butterscotch soul voice. But he switched lyric partners for this set (except for the title track), trading longtime Procol wordsmith Keith Reid for Pete Sinfield, who had performed the same function for Procol contemporaries King Crimson and Emerson, Lake and Palmer. Brooker also tried a couple of tunes by Stiff Records pub-rocker Mickey Jupp (Jupp's versions are better) and Murray Head's "Say It Ain't So, Joe" (Roger Daltrey's version is better). The result was a varied set that succeeded in sounding like something other than Procol Harum's 11th album, although it did not demonstrate that Gary Brooker solo was going to be an improvement over the group. —*William Ruhlmann*

Lead Me to the Water / 1982 / Mercury ◆◆◆
Gary Brooker wrote music and lyrics for all the songs on his second album and acted as his own producer, resulting in perhaps his most personal statement as an artist. Unlike *No More Fear of Flying*, on which he sometimes just seemed to be the singer on his own record, here Brooker delivered his songs with feeling, enabling him to overcome the star power of his backup musicians, who included Eric Clapton, George Harrison, and Phil Collins. This was partly because Brooker no longer felt the need to separate himself from the Procol Harum sound that was so much a part of his natural musical identity. Brooker's lyrics weren't as philosophical as longtime writing partner Keith Reid's, but they could be just as intriguingly oblique. —*William Ruhlmann*

● **Echoes in the Night** / 1985 / Mercury ◆◆◆◆
Echoes In The Night was the album for all those fans who had been waiting eight years for a Procol Harum reunion. In addition to Gary Brooker's singing and keyboard work, it featured Procol organist Matthew Fisher, lyricist Keith Reid, and drummer B.J. Wilson. They didn't appear on every track, but when they got together, notably on the title song (which also featured Eric Clapton), "Saw The Fire," and especially the ambitious "Ghost Train," Procol Harum was back. Even when Fisher and Reid weren't collaborating, as on "Mr. Blue Day," Brooker aspired to a Procol approach, adding the National Philharmonic Orchestra for that old art-rock flavor. Like Brooker's other solo albums, this one didn't get much attention, but for anyone who was paying attention, *Echoes In The Night* was a welcome reminder of what the band could do. —*William Ruhlmann*

The Brothers Johnson

Group, Soul, Funk, Pop/Rock
Guitarist/vocalist George Johnson and bassist/vocalist Louis Johnson formed the band Johnson Three Plus One with older brother Tommy and their cousin Alex Weir while attending school in Los Angeles. When they became professionals, the band backed such touring R&B acts as Bobby Womack and the Supremes. George and Louis Johnson later joined Billy Preston's band, and wrote "Music in My Life" and "The Kids and Me" for him before leaving his group in 1973.

Quincy Jones hired them to play on his LP *Mellow Madness*, and recorded four of their songs, including "Is It Love that We're Missing?" and "Just a Taste of Me." Jones took them on a Japanese tour, then produced their debut LP, *Look out for Number 1*, after they signed with A&M, which was also his label at the time (1976). They scored a number-one R&B and number-three pop hit with "I'll Be Good to You," and enjoyed R&B chart toppers in 1977 and 1980 respectively with "Strawberry Letter 23" and "Stomp!," while sustaining a consistent hit presence via such songs as "Get the Funk Out Ma Face" and "Runnin' for Your Lovin.'" Jones remade "I'll Be Good to You" in 1989 with Ray Charles and Chaka Khan on his *Back on the Block* release.

The Brothers earned platinum records for *Look out for Number*

1 and *Right on Time*. Jones produced both of these, along with their third and fourth LPs, *Blam* and *Light up the Night*. The group produced its single "The Real Thing" in 1981. It reached number 11 on the R&B charts, and the Brothers had another hit with "Welcome to the Club" in 1982. They started doing separate ventures; Louis Johnson played bass on Michael Jackson's *Thriller* LP and recorded a gospel album, while George Johnson worked with Steve Arrington. Leon Sylvers produced their mid-'80s return LP *Out of Control;* it didn't equal their past success, but got them another R&B hit with "You Keep Coming Back" in 1984. They recorded *Kickin* in 1988, and co-wrote "Tomorrow" with Siedah Garrett for Jones's *Back on the Block* in 1989. —*Ron Wynn*

○ **Look out for #1** / 1976 / A&M ◆◆◆◆
Quincy Jones produced and essentially helped introduce the guitar/bass duo George and Louis Johnson to the public at large in 1976. They had done session work for Bobby Womack, the Supremes, and Billy Preston, plus Jones, prior to this album. While their vocal style was more collective than anything else, Jones's production magic and the general caliber of their playing helped make the songs "I'll Be Good to You" and "Get the Funk Out Ma Face" huge hits, and turned the album into a platinum smash. —*Ron Wynn*

○ **Right on Time** / 1977 / A&M ◆◆◆◆
The Brothers Johnson's second album was pre-sold on the strength of their debut. It went gold three days after it was issued, and the single "Strawberry Letter 23," was an international hit, while the instrumental "Q" proved a solid album cut and got widespread light jazz airplay. —*Ron Wynn*

Blam!! / 1978 / A&M ◆◆◆
The Jones/Johnson combine kept rolling with the brothers' third album. "Ain't We Funkin' Now" and "Ride-O-Rocket" were both solid hits, and the instrumental "Streetwave" was both a fusion and an urban success. —*Ron Wynn*

Light up the Night / 1980 / A&M ◆◆◆
While the album as a whole wasn't up to past standards, the Brothers Johnson did land one huge single from their fourth album. "Stomp" scored in dance clubs, on urban radio, and even had some pop crossover action. It was the last big hit for the Brothers Johnson for a while and signaled the beginning of Quincy Jones's move into other arenas besides album production. —*Ron Wynn*

Winners / 1981 / A&M ◆◆
The Brothers Johnson got socked in the face by reality with their fifth album. They didn't have Jones's production muscle or the ready-made entry onto urban radio his name provided. There was no huge single from the previous album to ease the way for this one either, and while this release was actually musically superior to *Blam!,* it didn't fare nearly as well. —*Ron Wynn*

Blast!: The Latest and the Greatest / 1983 / A&M ◆◆◆◆
The Brothers Johnson marked time with this greatest hits album and inserted four new singles for the anthology, none of which generated any attention or sales action. But they were both busy doing other things anyway, with Louis playing on *Thriller* and cutting a gospel album, and George working with Steve Arrington. —*Ron Wynn*

Out of Control / 1984 / A&M ◆◆
The Brothers Johnson attempted to reclaim their late '70s and early '80s glory with a new producer and slightly revamped sound. Leon Sylvers tried to turn them in a more pop direction, although their vocal style wasn't really suited for it. "You Keep Me Coming Back" got some airplay but didn't chart high enough to make this a successful album. —*Ron Wynn*

● **Classics, Vol. 11** / 1987 / A&M ◆◆◆◆
George and Louis Johnson's 1976 debut *Look Out For #1* launched a string of hit albums and singles that continued through 1980. That's the period covered by this anthology, which includes such hits as "I'll Be Good To You," "Stomp" and "Get The Funk Out Ma Face." They were never more than functional singers, but their direct funk and party music made its mark. —*Ron Wynn*

Kickin' / 1988 / A&M ◆◆
The Brothers Johnson again made a bid to recapture past glory when they produced this '88 session. Again, they had a single that just missed being a hit in "Kick It To The Curb." But the market was now totally different, with their brand of bass/guitar dance/funk completely out of date. —*Ron Wynn*

The Crazy World of Arthur Brown

Group, Psychedelic
One of the most electrifying one-shot artists of the '60s, British singer Brown briefly set the charts alight in 1968, as well as thrilling audiences with his theatrical performances, which saw him wearing helmets of fire and outlandish costumes. His debut album was surely one of the most left-field commercial successes of the late '60s, if not of rock history. Besides topping the British charts (and reaching number two in the U.S.) with his brilliantly demonic single "Fire," the self-proclaimed god of hellfire actually scored a Top Ten LP with his 1968 debut. Unveiling Arthur's demented, fire-obsessed lyrical visions and swooping, theatrical vocals, it showcased his band's manic, agitated psychedelic sound, which was anchored by incendiary drumming, Pete Townshend's production, and an organist who could be best described as Jimmy Smith on acid. Brown's original band broke up in early 1969; in the early '70s, he released several albums with Kingdom Come which saw him pursuing a maddeningly obscure, and less exciting, brand of arty rock. He's recorded off and on since, but his last flash of fame was his role as a priest in the film version of *Tommy.* —*Richie Unterberger*

● **Crazy World of Arthur Brown** / 1968 / Polydor ◆◆◆◆
Though a bit over-the-top, this album was still powerful and surprisingly melodic, and managed to be quite bluesy and soulful even as the band overhauled chestnuts by James Brown and Screamin' Jay Hawkins. "Spontaneous Apple Creation" is a willfully histrionic, atonal song that gives Captain Beefheart a run for his money. Though this one-shot was not (and perhaps could not ever) be repeated, it remains an exhilaratingly reckless slice of psychedelia. The CD reissue includes both mono and stereo versions of five of the songs. Although the mono mixes lack the full-bodied power of the stereo ones, they're marked by some interesting differences, especially in the brief spoken and instrumental links between tracks. —*Richie Unterberger*

Bobby Brown

b. Feb. 5, 1969
Dance-Pop, Urban
At the end of the '80s, former New Edition member Bobby Brown made the album that made new jack swing a dominant force not only on the urban charts, but on the pop charts as well. Brown's first album, *King of the Stage,* wasn't that remarkable but 1988's *Don't Be Cruel* is the definitive new jack album, thanks to the L.A. Reid and Babyface's massive production and songs, including the hits "Don't Be Cruel," "Every Little Step," and "Roni." While recording the follow-up album, Brown married pop star Whitney Houston and they had a child; their marriage has been plagued with tabloid-fueled rumors. In 1992, Brown released *Bobby,* a follow-up record that didn't have the commercial success of *Don't Be Cruel,* mainly because it lacked the focused songs and production that made that album such a huge success. —*Stephen Thomas Erlewine*

King of Stage / 1987 / MCA ◆◆
The first solo album from New Edition charter member Bobby Brown. It was decently produced and performed, but was so generic and tame that absolutely no one had any idea that Brown was about to vault to the top of the R&B lineup. —*Ron Wynn*

★ **Don't Be Cruel** / 1988 / MCA ◆◆◆◆◆
Ex-New Edition vocalist Brown released a dud debut in 1987, but his follow-up *Don't Be Cruel,* produced by new-jack kingpin Teddy Riley, was a monster hit and a brilliant statement of Brown's creative purpose. The title cut brought a level of sensitivity into new jack, and "My Prerogative" is one of the greatest dance-groove anthems produced in the late '80s. And the man can smoke on the ballads. —*John Floyd*

Dance!... Ya Know It! / 1990 / MCA ◆◆
Extended dance versions of the hits from Bobby Brown's second smash record were the lure for this '90s release. They were superbly produced, but by this point everyone had been worn out by hearing "Roni" and "My Prerogative" a zillion times and seeing the videos another zillion. —*Ron Wynn*

Bobby / 1992 / MCA ◆◆◆
Brown's follow-up to the groundbreaking *Don't Be Cruel* isn't as innovative or consistent as his previous album, but that doesn't mean it's without any charms; the singles "Humpin' Around," "Good Enough," and "Get Away" are strong and memorable,

which almost makes the abundance of filler forgivable. —*Stephen Thomas Erlewine*

Chuck Brown & Soul Searchers

Group, Soul, R&B

Washington, D.C., bandleader, performer, and songwriter Chuck Brown has been a prominent figure on the city's go-go scene since the late '70s. Brown and the Soul Searchers have also been one of the rare go-go acts to gain national attention, even though it was short-lived. The Soul Searchers included trombonist/keyboardist John "JB" Buchanan, trumpeter Donald Tillery, saxophonist/flutist Leroy Fleming, bassist Jerry Wilder, percussionist Gregory Gerran, organist Curtis Johnson, keyboardist Skip Fennell, drummer Ricardo Wellman, and guitarist LeRon Young. They vaulted into the spotlight with "Busting Loose," the top R&B single for four consecutive weeks at the end of 1978. Its fabulous arrangement, exuberant horn work, and arresting, terse vocals made the band momentary celebrities. But the follow-up, "Game Seven," flopped, and they were soon back on the go-go circuit. They had one more flirtation with the spotlight in 1984, as the single "We Need Some Money (Bout Money)" reached number 26 amid predictions that go-go was ready to explode into the mainstream. It didn't happen, but Brown remained active. He tried again in 1991 with *'90s Goin' Hard* for Goff. —*Ron Wynn*

● **Bustin' Loose** / 1979 / Valley Vue ✦✦✦✦

○ **Any Other Way to Go?** / 1987 / Rhythm Attack ✦✦✦✦
An interesting presentation by this Washington, D.C. go-go ensemble. —*Ron Wynn*

James Brown

b. May 3, 1928, Macon, GA
Soul, Funk, R&B

James Brown is probably the most influential African-American singer of recent times. Certainly, he is preeminent in terms of chart placings, and his impact on today's Black music is beyond question—it's literally in the grooves, thanks to the magic of sampling.

Brown's career stretches across 40 years—35 or more as a recording artist—so it makes no sense to talk about his style, because it inevitably evolved. He knew something different from the beginning back in Augusta, GA, where he grew up, though. ("Please, Please, Please," his first Top Ten R&B hit, was not an ordinary record, circa 1956.) The difference was urgency; he went back beyond the gospel progressions of Ray Charles to primordial rhythms and wordless vocals. It was African-American music in the purest sense.

Brown topped the R&B charts and made the pop charts with "Try Me" in 1959; in 1960 there was "Think," another R&B Top Ten that was his first pop Top 40 hit. These were followed in 1961 by "Bewildered," "I Don't Mind," and "Baby, You're Right," and in 1962 by "Lost Someone" and the instrumental "Night Train," all of which made the R&B Top Ten and the upper half of the pop Top 100. (Though Brown was known primarily for his singles, his *Live at the Apollo* album, recorded October 24, 1962, and released in 1963, was an enormous hit, staying in the charts more than a year.)

By 1965, with hits like "Papa's Got a Brand New Bag" and "I Got You (I Feel Good)," Brown had ceased fooling with conventional R&B and trying to cross over into the pop market (as he had with "Prisoner of Love," his first Top 20 pop hit in 1963), though those songs did hit the pop Top Ten. He found his groove and he turned it loose. The result was an outpouring of major dancefloor hits and socially conscious anthems over the next eight years, including the R&B chart-toppers "It's a Man's Man's Man's World," "Cold Sweat," "I Got the Feelin'," "Say It Loud—I'm Black and I'm Proud," "Give It Up or Turnit 'a Loose," "Mother Popcorn," "Super Bad," "Hot Pants," "Make It Funky," "Talking Loud and Saying Nothing," "Get on the Good Foot," "The Payback," "My Thang," and "Papa Don't Take No Mess." (Brown's initial recordings were on the Federal and King labels; later he recorded for the Polydor imprint of Poly-Gram, which now owns the earlier part of his catalog as well.)

The creative juices began to get a little watered down as the disco era dawned, but between the mid-'60s and the mid-'70s, James Brown was a force unto himself. Musically and politically, he was the dominant Black musician of the day, an importance that subsequent developments have only served to heighten.

The going has been uneven for James Brown in the '80s and

'90s. He left Polydor and cut "Rapp Payback" for TK Records in 1980, and he made other recordings for the Augusta South and Tommy Boy labels, among them the critically heralded "Unity," which paired him with Afrika Bambaataa, but failed commercially. Brown is arguably the most sampled performer by the hip-hop/rap generation, with his yells, shouts, screams, cries, and grunts incorporated on countless rap cuts. "Living in America" (December 1985) was on the soundtrack for *Rocky IV* and put Brown back into the spotlight, giving him a Top Ten R&B and pop hit. The LP *Gravity* (September 1986) produced hits in the title track and "How Do You Stop," and "I'm Real" (April 1988), from the Full Force-produced LP of the same name, nearly topped the R&B charts. But after recording a duet with Aretha Franklin, "Gimme Your Love," for her *Through the Storm* LP, Brown ended up in jail on a reckless driving charge that escalated into something more serious in 1989. He was released a year later. His most recent CDs are *Love Overdue* (1991) and *Universal James* (1992). —*Colin Escott & William Ruhlmann*

Please, Please, Please / 1959 / King ✦✦✦
Though James Brown and His Famous Flames had scored an R&B Top 10 hit in 1956 with "Please, Please, Please," Brown's next nine singles for Federal Records flopped until "Try Me," his third single of 1958, scored. That was when King Records (Federal's parent label) assembled this, Brown's debut album, out of some of those singles sessions. You can hear the sound of a group and its enthusiastic singer looking for a hit, sometimes in the rock & roll on "Chonnie-On-Chon" (1957) or the 1956 B-side "I Feel That Old Feeling Coming On," sometimes by remaking "Please, Please, Please" under another name, such as "I Don't Know" (1956), sometimes by tackling Coasters-like novelty material such as "That Dood It" (1958), sometimes by aping the smooth Sam Cooke, as on the 1958 B-side "That's When I Lost My Heart," and once by rewriting "My Bonnie (Lies Over The Ocean)" as the 1958 B-side "Baby Cries Over The Ocean." Only the two hits were really memorable, but the album presented the sound of a major star-to-be in search of his sound. —*William Ruhlmann*

Try Me! / 1959 / King ✦✦✦
When James Brown and His Famous Flames finally scored a second hit with their 11th single, "Try Me," King Records constructed this 16-track LP, including the hit along with both sides of three of its follow-ups, "I Want You So Bad"/"There Must Be A Reason," "I've Got To Change"/"It Hurts To Tell You," and "Got To Cry"/"It Was You," the B-side of a fourth follow-up, "Don't Let It Happen To Me," the 1957 single "Can't Be The Same"/"Gonna Try," the 1957 B-sides "I Won't Plead No More" and "Messing With The Blues," the B-side of Brown's first hit ("Please Please Please"), "Why Do You Do Me," and three other stray tracks. The earliest work especially sounded more like that of a doo-wop group than that of a gritty R&B solo singer. None of it measured up to "Try Me," but you could see what Brown had been aiming at, and if the set list comprised what were in effect James Brown's greatest flops, circa 1959, it demonstrated that he possessed as much promise as fervor. (*Try Me!* was reissued in 1964 under the title *The Unbeatable James Brown—16 Hits.*) —*William Ruhlmann*

Shout & Shimmy / 1962 / King ✦✦✦
On an album named after the R&B Top 40 title hit and featuring the 1961 R&B hit "I Don't Mind," James Brown and His Famous Flames can be heard making music in the variety of styles—blues, Little Richard-style rock, doo-wop—out of which they eventually would develop the James Brown funk sound of the mid-'60s. (Actually, the music is older than the copyright date, since King cobbled the LP together from non-charting singles and B-sides dating back to 1958.) It's a more primitive sound than they would later achieve, but remains infectious. (*Shout And Shimmy* was reissued in 1963 under the title *Excitement—Mr. Dynamite.*) —*William Ruhlmann*

★ **Live at the Apollo** / Jan. 1963 / Polydor ✦✦✦✦✦
An astonishing record of James and the Flames tearing the roof off the sucker at the mecca of R&B theatres, New York's Apollo. When King Records owner Syd Nathan refused to fund the recording, thinking it commercial folly, Brown single-mindedly proceeded anyway, paying for it out of his own pocket. He had been out on the road night after night for a while, and he knew that the magic that was part and parcel of a James Brown show was something no record had ever caught. Hit follows hit without a pause—"I'll Go Crazy," "Try Me," "Think," "Please Please Please," "I Don't Mind," "Night Train," and more. The affirmative screams and cries

of the audience are something you've never experienced unless you've seen the Brown Revue in a Black theatre. If you have, I need not say more; if you haven't, suffice to say that this should be one of the very first records you ever own. —*Rob Bowman*

Prisoner of Love / Sep. 1963 / King ✦✦✦
In the wake of James Brown's first substantial pop hit, "Prisoner Of Love," King rushed out this LP, as usual drawing upon old singles ("Try Me," "Lost Someone," "Bewildered"), B-sides ("Waiting In Vain," the organ instrumental "[Can You] Feel It [Part 1]"), and Brown's then-current single, "Signed, Sealed, And Delivered" (not the Stevie Wonder song). The idea seemed to be to put together a collection in the medium-tempo, string-filled, lovelorn style of the hit, so there was a lot of pleading on this record. Brown would always be more interested in the dance floor than the bedroom, but he was a convincing romantic beggar, so the album's loose concept held together. —*William Ruhlmann*

○ **Pure Dynamite! Live at the Royal** / Feb. 1964 / King ✦✦✦✦
It has only eight songs, it's less than half an hour long, and two of the songs are studio tracks with overdubbed audience noise. It's not nearly as well known as his live '60s albums recorded at the Apollo, but *Pure Dynamite!*, recorded live at Baltimore's Royal Theater in 1963, is nearly as good. This is decidedly more raucous than his 1962 *Live At The Apollo*, with the balance leaning toward uptempo ravers like "Shout And Shimmy," "Signed, Sealed, And Delivered," and the set-closing "Good Good Lovin'," all of which are positively kinetic. To break up the pace, there are some R&B torch ballads, including the song without which no J.B. show was complete, "Please, Please, Please." It's also fair to say that the recording quality is primitive, even more so than on his 1962 Apollo gig; the vocals are a bit hollow, and the audience occasionally overwhelms the music with its noisy enthusiasm. Somehow, it doesn't matter much. The performances are so energetic that you can't help getting caught up in the excitement. —*Richie Unterberger*

Papa's Got a Brand New Bag / Aug. 1965 / King ✦✦✦
Papa may have had a brand new bag, but when King Records wanted an LP to go with James Brown's first pop Top 10 hit, he didn't have a brand new set of songs to go with it. So this record leads off with both sides of the single, "Pt. 1" and "Pt. 2," and then fills up the remaining 25 minutes with previously released tracks, many with a dance theme in keeping with the hit, such as "Mashed Potatoes, U.S.A." and "Doin' The Limbo." The result is a miscellaneous compilation, much of which is set at quick tempos. —*William Ruhlmann*

I Got You (I Feel Good) / Jan. 1966 / King ✦✦✦
At the start of 1966, James Brown was at his peak as a crossover star, having hit the pop Top 10 twice in a row in the last six months, first with "Papa's Got A Brand New Bag," and then with his biggest ever pop success, "I Got You (I Feel Good)." But Brown was a singles artist almost exclusively; for him, LPs simply constituted a different configuration in which to re-sell his singles. So, his '60s LPs consisted of his current hit plus previously released singles tracks. The *I Got You (I Feel Good)* LP was no exception: Leading off with the title track, it included songs that dated back to 1959's "Good, Good Loving." Of course, some of these tracks, such as "Lost Someone," "Night Train," and "Think," were among Brown's classics, so the collection on the whole is appealing, even if arbitrary. —*William Ruhlmann*

It's a Man's Man's Man's World / Aug. 1966 / King ✦✦✦
In the early '60s, James Brown tended to release two vocal albums a year, one in the summer and one in the winter. Each album was keyed to Brown's latest hit single, with the remainder of the record made up of previous Brown recordings; Brown did not record LPs as such. As late as mid-1966, this was still the case, and this album differed only in that it featured not only the title track, an R&B #1/pop Top 10 hit, and its B-side, "Is It Yes Or Is It No?," but also an earlier 1966 single, "Ain't That A Groove (Part 1 and Part 2)," along with eight oldies, such as "Bewildered" and "I Don't Mind" (two 1961 singles). As such, there was slightly more contemporary material here than usual, but at the same time, Brown's evolution into his funk period was beginning to make the juxtapositions of new and old material more jarring. —*William Ruhlmann*

○ **Cold Sweat** / Aug. 1967 / King ✦✦✦✦
If "Cold Sweat" was a revolutionary single in 1967, clearly pointing the way to funk music, the *Cold Sweat* LP at least promised to be something new in James Brown's catalog as well. Where Brown's

albums had been collections containing his current single and miscellaneous older tracks, this one proclaimed on its cover, "All New," "Great Songs," "Never In An Album." This was not quite true. While half of the tracks had been recorded during the first half of 1967, the other half (though previously unreleased) dated from 1964. That wasn't the main problem with the album, though. Having taken a giant step forward with "Cold Sweat," Brown spent the rest of the album stepping back, covering standards such as "Nature Boy" and "Mona Lisa" (associated with Nat "King" Cole), "Fever" (Little Willie John), "Stagger Lee" (Lloyd Price), and other oddities, including "I Loves You Porgy" from *Porgy And Bess*. Brown was never anybody's idea of a smooth ballad singer, and this material was all the more incongruous when packaged with his most remarkable slab of funk yet. —*William Ruhlmann*

○ **Live at the Apollo, Vol. 2** / Aug. 1968 / Rhino ✦✦✦✦
As a whole, this double album is pretty erratic—there are a bunch of torchy R&B ballads that were somewhat anachronistic in light of the explosive funk innovations Brown was unleashing in the studio during this time, and some of those funk hits are reprised here in super-brief versions that seem to cut off before they have a chance to get started. On the other hand, some of it is as essential as anything else Brown ever recorded. In particular, the 20-minute medley of "Let Yourself Go/There Was A Time/I Feel All Right/Cold Sweat" is a magnificent, seamless ball of energy, a landmark performance in the evolution of soul and funk. Other highlights are "Bring It Up" and an 11-minute "It's A Man's, Man's, Man's World." —*Richie Unterberger*

○ **Sex Machine** / Aug. 1970 / Polydor ✦✦✦✦
Live early-'70s relentless funk groove. —*George Bedard*

Hot Pants / Aug. 1971 / Polydor ✦✦✦

○ **There It Is** / Jun. 1972 / Polydor ✦✦✦✦

Get on the Good Foot / Nov. 1972 / Polydor ✦✦✦

Black Caesar / Feb. 1973 / Polydor ✦✦
A classic early '70s soundtrack by James Brown. The film *Black Caesar* was prototype "blaxploitation" fodder, but Brown's soundtrack both defined the urban nightmare the film was trying to depict and garnered him a hit single in "Down and Out in New York City." —*Ron Wynn*

Slaughter's Big Rip-Off / Jul. 1973 / Polydor ✦✦

○ **The Payback** / Dec. 1973 / Polydor ✦✦✦✦
A superb funk album by James Brown, one of his '70s masterpieces. The title cut, with its jutting horn charts, lyric hooks, repeated phrases, and striding bass line was extremely influential, while Brown's trademark screams on the breaks, and the breaks themselves, were later sampled ad infinitum by various hip-hop groups. —*Ron Wynn*

○ **Hell** / Jul. 1974 / Polydor ✦✦✦✦
Everybody's Doin' the Hustle & Dead on The Double Bump / Sep. 1975 / Polydor ✦✦
Despite its ludicrous title, *Everybody's Doin' The Hustle & Dead On The Double Bump* found James Brown making more of an effort to connect with current musical trends and create coherent song structures than he had on the previous *Sex Machine Today*. The album in essence consisted of Brown's two moderately successful R&B singles of the period, "Hustle!!! (Dead On It)" and "Superbad, Superslick," filled out with remakes—"Papa got a *new* brand new bag," Brown noted at one point. But the reliance on keyboard textures was new for Brown, and he sounded more enthusiastic, especially in interplay with saxophonist Maceo Parker, than in recent efforts. This wasn't great Brown, by any means, but it suggested he wasn't quite through yet. —*William Ruhlmann*

Bodyheat / Dec. 1976 / Polydor ✦✦
Bodyheat is a low-key effort filled with ballads and female backup vocals. "Woman," set to the tune of "It's A Man's Man's Man's World," recasts that song's message. "Got a new kiss," Brown says in the seductive "Kiss In 77," and he also covers "What The World Needs Now Is Love," extending the romantic tone. "James Brown—A New Sound," reads the album jacket, and in his liner notes, Brown signs himself ("With the feeling of a new beginning...A New Sound.") The heat, clearly, is supposed to generate a Phoenix-like rebirth for Brown, which it didn't quite succeed in doing, perhaps because the New Sound turned out to be suspiciously close to that of Earth, Wind & Fire. —*William Ruhlmann*

○ **Solid Gold: 30 Golden Hits** / 1977 / Polydor ✦✦✦✦

At a time when James Brown's career was in commercial and artistic eclipse, when his entire 1960s catalog was out of print in the U.S., and when his work had been anthologized only in the inconsistent *Soul Classics* series, Polydor U.K. assembled the ideal two-LP hits compilation covering the first two decades of his work, from 1956's "Please, Please, Please" to 1976's "Get Up Offa That Thing." "30 Golden Hits," proclaimed the cover, "21 Golden Years." On the inside of the foldout cover, Polydor listed the release dates and (U.S.) chart figures for each song, along with an essay by Cliff White. As a result, *Solid Gold* stood not only as a model for the many Brown compilations that would follow in later years, but also for the compilation boom in general; it was thorough, respectful, and focused. Like the best compilations, it forced a reassessment of its subject by concentrating on his best work and following it through the years. If there was ever any doubt that James Brown was the major figure of R&B in the '60s, it was erased here. At the same time, of course, by implication it closed the door on Brown as an innovator: Cliff White looked forward to 1998, when another 21 years in Brown's career would have gone by, but the appearance of this set was an acknowledgement that Brown's real accomplishments were behind him. *Solid Gold* finally was released in the U.S., on CD, in 1986. It has since been superseded by the 1991 4-disc *Star Time* boxed set, but it nevertheless stands as a state-of-the-art compilation for its time, and if you want the essence of James Brown, it's here. — *William Ruhlmann*

○ **Roots of a Revolution** / 1984 / Polydor ✦✦✦✦

A double-CD retrospective that charts Brown's progress from doo-wop and Little Richard-influenced R&B to the verge of his groundbreaking mid-'60s funk. It doesn't include his biggest hits of the era (which are found on *Star Time*), but these are by and large equally exciting. Many fine overlooked R&B hits and B-sides like "Shout and Shimmy," "I've Got Money," the gospel-influenced "Oh Baby Don't You Weep," and "Maybe the Last Time," which inspired the Rolling Stones' "The Last Time" are featured here. — *Richie Unterberger*

○ **The CD of JB** / 1985 / Polydor ✦✦✦✦

Polydor Records put a tentative toe into the emerging CD stream in 1985 and enjoyed surprising commercial success with this 56-minute, 18-song James Brown sampler. Rather than taking the standard "greatest hits" approach, compiler Cliff White mixed familiar hits with rarities and even unreleased material, a shortened version of the later boxed set formula. So, along with #1 R&B hits like "Papa's Got A Brand New Bag," "Super Bad," and "Mother Popcorn," one heard a previously unreleased version of "It's A Man's World," two years older than the better known one, and "I Got You," an early version of "I Got You (I Feel Good)," culled from the withdrawn *Out Of Sight* LP. The effect, especially for a first-time listener, was to whet the appetite for more, though *The CD Of JB* was more a highlights disc than a thorough anthology. — *William Ruhlmann*

○ **In the Jungle Groove** / 1986 / Polydor ✦✦✦✦

An interesting anthology of leftover funk selections and items from the vast James Brown catalog. Several of these packages have been supplanted by recent Brown CD anthologies. But this one includes some good extended instrumental and vocal funk numbers that aren't on any of the boxed sets. — *Ron Wynn*

○ **James Brown's Funky People** / 1986 / Polydor ✦✦✦

Technically speaking, this is not a James Brown album; it is a various artists compilation culled from the People Records label, which Brown ran during the early '70s. But the songs were all produced, arranged, and written by Brown (sometimes in collaboration with others), and the artists represented—the JBs, Lyn Collins, Fred Wesley, and Maceo and the Macks—all were members of Brown's backup band. In fact, Brown also performs on several of the tracks. Hence, the material is not far removed from the funk music Brown was recording under his own name at the same time. A number of the songs were R&B hits, and though they constitute a minor part of the Brown catalog, they remain enjoyable. — *William Ruhlmann*

○ **The CD of JB II** / 1987 / Polydor ✦✦✦✦

An excellent follow-up package that includes various James Brown hits from both the soul and funk eras, beginning with "Cold Sweat" and continuing into the '70s. It's also not as vital since the issue of the '91 boxed set, but contains several fine songs. — *Ron Wynn*

○ **James Brown's Funky People, Pt. 2** / Feb. 1988 / Polydor ✦✦✦✦

More of the above, including Bobby Byrd's 1971 hits "I Know You Got Soul" and "Hot Pants—I'm Coming, Coming, I'm Coming." Delves into some more obscure tracks, such as Hank Ballard's "From the Love Side." — *Rob Bowman*

Messing with the Blues / 1991 / Polydor ✦✦✦

Although he is most famous for his innovations in soul and funk music, James Brown never lost sight of his blues and R&B roots. His albums often placed surprisingly rootsy covers of old chestnuts alongside his groundbreaking polyrhythmic workouts. This double CD compiles thirty of the bluesiest items from his vast recorded legacy. Cut between 1957 and 1985, most of the tracks actually date from the '60s; many of these, in turn, were laid down in the early part of the decade, when J.B. was gradually evolving from his more conventional beginnings. The artists whose songs are covered here read like a Who's Who of R&B pioneers: Louis Jordan, Roy Brown, Memphis Slim, Ivory Joe Hunter, Fats Domino, Chuck Willis, Little Willie John, Billy Ward, Guitar Slim, and Bobby Bland. It's quite an instructive insight into Brown's not-always-visible roots. It would be fair to say that this does not rank among his most exciting material, finding him in a smoother and more conventional style than his most innovative work. It is nonetheless always entertaining and accomplished, with Brown's love for this material shining through strongly in his committed interpretations. Especially intriguing are an 11-minute cover of Chuck Willis's "Don't Deceive Me" and a two-part, blues-based rap vamp from the early '70s, "Like It Is, Like It Was (The Blues)." The disc includes several unreleased cuts, alternate takes, and unedited versions of previously released songs. — *Richie Unterberger*

☆ **Star Time** / Jun. 1991 / Polydor ✦✦✦✦✦

One of the great boxed sets of all time; over four CDs, Brown's recorded legacy is traced from "Please Please Please" in 1956 through his 1984 duet with Afrika Bambaataa, "Unity Pt. 1." With 71 tracks in all, the set places the #1 R&B artist ever in his proper perspective as the prime progenitor of funk, one of the architects of soul, and the Godfather of Rap. To have done any one of these things would have been a bid for immortality; having done all three makes him a god. Four CDs at once is virtually too rich for one sitting. The well-written liner notes provide three different perspectives on Brown's career. A cornerstone of any great collection. — *Rob Bowman*

Love Over-Due / Jul. 1991 / Scotti Brothers ✦✦✦

Some recent James Brown, much of it delivered with fire and fury but little substance. Brown hasn't had a major hit since "I'm Real" in 1988, and there's nothing on this collection that seems like it will end the cold streak. — *Ron Wynn*

★ **20 All-Time Greatest Hits!** / Oct. 1991 / Polydor ✦✦✦✦✦

A first-rate greatest hits package that covers the essential soul singles and some of the funk-period material as well. While the finest James Brown package is the boxed set, if you're not going to get that, you wouldn't be far wrong getting this one instead. — *Ron Wynn*

○ **Love Power Peace** / 1992 / Polydor ✦✦✦✦

James Brown with the then newly formed JB's—the maestro's second great band, including Bootsy Collins, Phelps Collins, Jabo Starks, Bobby Byrd, and Fred Wesley. *Live at the Apollo* had caught James Brown, the '50s gospel/rhythm and blues singer; *Love Power Peace* captures James the funkster. In the early '70s Brown turned up the funk, recording such litanies for Black America as "Ain't It Funky Now," "Sex Machine," "Give It Up or Turn It Loose," "Super Bad," "Get Up, Get Into It, Get Involved," and "Soul Power." They're all here, along with revved-up, white-hot versions of the early- and middle-period classics. Brown had planned to release this as a triple album in 1971. When several band members left shortly after it was recorded, Brown switched from King to Polydor Records, leading him to scrap it and record a new studio album instead. In 1992, Polygram decided to make the recording available for the first time. — *Rob Bowman*

The Greatest Hits of the Fourth Decade / 1992 / Scotti Brothers ✦✦✦

Collecting Brown's 1980s hits that didn't make it onto *Star Time*, *Greatest Hits of the Fourth Decade* shows that the period was not among his most creatively fertile, even with the monster hit "Living in America." Still, the disc does pick the best tracks from a dry spell, making it a nice supplement to the box set. — *Stephen Thomas Erlewine*

○ **Soul Pride: The Instrumentals (1960-69)** / 1993 / PolyGram
◆◆◆◆

Everyone knows how hot James Brown's bands were, but not everyone's aware that he and his sidemen recorded lots of instrumental sides in the '60s. Originally scattered haphazardly over many out-of-print singles and albums, *Soul Pride* brings together the best of this work into one cohesive and chronological package. These cuts are nearly equal in power to J.B.'s vocal performances. Not only does the band cook on most of these insinuating vamps, but you can also hear the evolution of the man's sound from gritty R&B to tight-as-a-drum soul to free-form funk. Soul Brother #1 himself plays organ and adds unpredictable shouts and screams on most of these tracks. But the chief stars are sidemen like Maceo Parker, Fred Wesley, and Pee Wee Ellis, who broke new ground with their compulsive counterpoint riffs. This fiery two-disc, 36-track box set contains over two hours of music, as well as a few non-LP B-sides and previously unreleased tracks. —*Richie Unterberger*

BOOKS

◆◆◆ **Living In America: The Soul Saga Of James Brown**, by Cynthia Rose (Serpent's Tail, 1990). This is not a biography, but rather an extensive critical essay, in which Rose examines Brown's stylistic development, and his impact upon music and culture. It's not as dry as that might imply; the commentary is pretty insightful and accessible, viewing Brown's work as a strand that connects such seemingly disparate African-American idioms as gospel and rap. By far the most valuable features are the many quotes from key sidemen like Maceo Parker, Fred Wesley, Bobby Byrd, and Pee Wee Ellis, musicians who haven't often had the chance to tell their part of the James Brown story in print. —*Richie Unterberger*

◆◆◆◆ **James Brown**, by James Brown with Bruce Tucker (Thunder's Mouth Press, 1986). Probably the best biography of a soul giant. Brown discusses a lot here—his struggle with poverty and prison as a youth, the long hard climb to the top, his determination to break new ground both vocally and instrumentally in several R&B eras, his sometimes contentious relationship with King Records, his interaction with notable public figures (including U.S. presidents and presidential candidates). He does not talk a great deal about innovative sidemen such as Fred Wesley, Maceo Parker, and Bootsy Collins, though these gaps are filled in to some extent by the critical volume *Living in America*. The narrator comes off as a thoughtful, at times humble, rational, super-determined man: a contrast to his recent image, in light of his imprisonment and personal turmoil during the last decade. The 1990 version includes updates on his sobering troubles of the late 1980s. —*Richie Unterberger*

Joe Brown

b. May 13, 1941, Lincolnshire, England
Rock & Roll

Cockney Joe Brown was one of England's top guitar talents of the early '60s. He made his name playing lead on records like Billy Fury's *The Sound of Fury* before striking out on his own with his band, the Bruvvers. Joe Brown and the Bruvvers were a loud, dexterous topflight band whose main problem was repertoire—when they weren't doing great songs like "Picture of You" (a fave of the young Paul McCartney), they wasted their time on silly novelty tunes. Brown recorded well into the '70s but has been most successful as a stage actor. —*Bruce Eder*

● **Hits 'n' Pieces** / Oct. 1988 / PRT ◆◆◆◆
A somewhat regrettable collection, with "Picture of You" and three or four other worthwhile tracks surrounded by tuneless Cockney novelty dross. Still, it is the only collection of Brown's work, but more of his live recordings would've been better. See also the collection, *Roots of British Rock*. —*Bruce Eder*

Maxine Brown

b. Kingstree, SC
Soul, R&B

An underrated '60s R&B chanteuse from New York responsible for the original "Oh No Not My Baby." With an early gospel background, Brown waxed her first secular hit, "All in My Mind," for the tiny Nomar label in 1960, and quickly encored with "Funny." Switching to Wand Records, Brown recorded some fine uptown-style R&B, including the charming and often-covered "Oh No Not

My Baby" in 1964. Teamed with labelmate Chuck Jackson, Brown scored another hit the following year with a duet revival of Chris Kenner's "Something You Got." Brown later recorded for a variety of firms into the early '70s. —*Bill Dahl*

○ **The Fabulous Sound of Maxine Brown** / 1962 / Wand ◆◆◆
Some sizzling, sensual laments, ballads, and love songs from Maxine Brown, who was emerging as a secular vocalist in the early '60s after being a star in gospel. The album contained two hits in "All in My Mind" and "Funny," although it was more a collection of Scepter/Wand singles than a unified project. —*Ron Wynn*

Spotlight on Maxine Brown / 1964 / Wand ◆◆◆
Maxine Brown had her biggest hit in 1964, the epic "Oh No, Not My Baby," which was co-written by the Goffin/King team. She mixed laments, heartbreak tunes, and disillusioned stanzas, along with an occasional romantic ballad and some duets with fellow label member Chuck Jackson. —*Ron Wynn*

Maxine Brown's Greatest Hits / 1964 / Wand ◆◆◆
Maxine Brown had a handful of hits, most of them either laments or teary-eyed ballads, in the early '60s. They're all included on this release. Brown's timing at Scepter/Wand was unfortunate; the label was allocating most of its resources and promotional muscle to breaking Dionne Warwick in the pop market. Both she and Chuck Jackson didn't get the push they needed or deserved. —*Ron Wynn*

Blue Ribbon Country, Vol. 1 / 1975 / ◆◆
Maxine Brown, Bobby Womack, Tina Turner, and many others tried to follow Ray Charles's lead and cut soulful versions of country songs. In almost every case, the effort was superior to the final result. —*Ron Wynn*

● **Oh No Not My Baby: The Best of Maxine Brown** / 1990 / Kent (UK) ◆◆◆◆
This 28-song CD is undoubtedly the best compilation of this underrated soul singer's work, featuring many of her '60s singles and several tunes from the era that were unreleased until the '80s. This disc draws from her recordings for the Wand label between 1963 and 1967, when Brown was at her artistic peak. Of course the hit title track is a highlight, but there are no clunkers in this excellent collection of overlooked '60s pop-soul, featuring the New York "uptown" production that also graced the records of fellow Wand/Scepter artists like Dionne Warwick and Chuck Jackson. Brown was one of the most versatile soul divas of the '60s, showing the influence of Brill Building pop, girl groups, Motown, and even Stax soul and supper club ballads. As with a similar artist like Betty Everett, this versatility has worked against her in some ways. Neither full-fledged pop nor unabashedly soul, her work cannot be easily pigeonholed into a certain soul genre, and has cost her the respect that some purists reserve for "deep" soul singers. But her work holds up well. Collectors should be aware that this disc doesn't include any of the records she cut in the early '60s before joining Wand; the version of her 1961 Top 20 hit "All In My Mind" here is from a live 1964 release, not the original single. —*Richie Unterberger*

● **Greatest Hits** / 1995 / Tomato ◆◆◆◆
This 23-track best-of has a lot of overlap with the British import *Oh No Not My Baby*; both cover her mid-'60s period with Wand, and each has some songs not on the other. There's not a crucial difference between the pair, but the nod probably goes to the import, which has more songs and better sound. In its favor, this compilation includes five of her duets with Chuck Jackson, none of which are on the other CD (although the duets don't rank among her best material). It also has a studio version of "All In My Mind," rather than the live one on the British anthology. —*Richie Unterberger*

Roy Brown

b. Sep. 10, 1925, New Orleans, LA, d. May 25, 1981, San Fernando, CA
R&B, Rock & Roll

One of the premier shouters of the jump blues era, Brown has been called "the first singer of soul" (in John Broven's *Walking to New Orleans*), "one of the great blues lyricists of all time" (in Jeff Hannusch's *I Hear You Knockin'*), and the artist responsible for the breakthrough of New Orleans rhythm & blues. An acknowledged and obvious influence on Bobby Bland, B.B. King, Junior Parker, Little Milton, James Brown, and Jackie Wilson in the blues and R&B fields, Brown also had followers on the rock & roll side such as Elvis Presley and Buddy Holly. He was a trendsetter both in his use of fervent gospel-style singing in Black secular music and in the infectious rhythms that helped pave the way for rock & roll in songs such as "Good Rockin' Tonight" and "Rockin' at Midnight." Though never again as commercially successful as he was in 1948-1951, when he had 15 records on the charts, Brown continued to perform and record now and again in later years, still boasting the magnificent voice that enthralled and inspired listeners when he was "the mighty, mighty man" of rhythm & blues. — *Jim O'Neal*

★ **Good Rocking Tonight: The Best of Roy Brown** / 1994 / Rhino ✦✦✦✦✦

Roy Brown had a swaggering, commanding sound and striking delivery; his phrasing, sweeping treatments and huge voice could overwhelm even the hottest New Orleans orchestra. The 18 selections featured on this anthology cover 1940s and '50s numbers, including his trademark tune "Good Rocking Tonight," the hilarious "Butcher Pete, Pts. 1 & 2," and "Let The Four Winds Blow," which Fats Domino later enjoyed more success covering. Brown was the prototype R&B shouter/belter, but he could also do midtempo and creditable ballads, although nothing suited him better than a roaring uptempo number. A great single-disc introduction for novices, and a nice set for the hardcore as well. — *Ron Wynn*

Ruth Brown

b. Jan. 30, 1928, Portsmouth, VA
R&B

Jazz/R&B vocalist Ruth Brown was one of the early hitmakers for Atlantic, netting a slew of Black chart hits in the early '50s: "Teardrops from My Eyes," "5-10-15 Hours," and "Mama He Treats Your Daughter Mean." She has recorded prolifically over the years and enjoyed a comeback in the late '80s thanks to a successful Broadway show.

Ruth Brown is enjoying newfound visibility these days. She's finally been elected to the Rock and Roll Hall of Fame, and also to the Rhythm and Blues Hall of Fame. She's currently the host of National Public Radio's weekly "Bluesstage" program, heard nationwide. Her most recent recording was *Fine And Mellow* in 1991, and the excellent *Fine Brown Frame*, with such backing musicians as Thad Jones, Mel Lewis, Eddie Daniels, and Sir Roland Hanna, was reissued by Blue Note in 1993. Brown escaped serious injury during the Los Angeles earthquake in 1994, but her home was among many destroyed. — *John Floyd*

Ruth Brown Sings Favorites / 1956 / Atlantic ✦✦✦

Ruth Brown had extensive gospel and jazz roots, which Atlantic honed to perfection, turning her into an R&B queen. These songs aren't quite the same, but they show her full stylistic range and also how powerful and strong her voice was in the '50s. — *Ron Wynn*

Ruth Brown / 1957 / Atlantic ✦✦✦

Ruth Brown at her stinging, assertive, bawdy best, doing the sizzling, innuendo-laden R&B that helped make Atlantic the nation's prime independent during the early days of rock & roll. There's also plenty of equally fiery, hot musical accompaniment, with then-husband Willis Jackson sometimes featured on tenor sax. — *Ron Wynn*

Late Date with Ruth Brown / Jan. 27, 1959+Feb. 2, 1959 / Atlantic ✦✦✦

Good after-hours, smoky blues and R&B session featuring Ruth Brown in prime form. Nobody, male or female, sang with more spirit, sass, and vigor than Brown during the '50s, and this session reminded those who had forgotten that Brown could also hold her own with sophisticated material as well as sexy stuff. — *Ron Wynn*

Along Comes Ruth / 1962 / Philips ✦✦✦

Good, but not essential, early '60s session showing that both Ruth Brown and her brain trust were about to run dry. She still had the powerhouse vocals, but there are fewer inspiring songs, and by the end of side two, Brown is getting by on energy alone. — *Ron Wynn*

The Best of Ruth Brown / 1963 / Atlantic ✦✦✦

Another good anthology compiling Ruth Brown's major hits. This isn't as inclusive or comprehensive and is really geared toward fans who want only chart items. It's a good buy for the cost-conscious, and even better for someone who wants a reasonable, if not exhaustive, Brown package. — *Ron Wynn*

Ruth Brown '65 / Dec. 1964 / Mainstream ✦✦✦

Underrated, nicely produced mid-'60s album putting Ruth Brown more in the blues and interpretative mode that she moved away from during the hit years. She can still belt out numbers, but also

shows some wit and some flourishes that were sacrificed for impact when she was doing rock & roll. — *Ron Wynn*

○ **Sweet Baby of Mine (1949-1956)** / 1987 / Route 66 ✦✦✦✦

Excellent collection covering blues and R&B songs Brown did prior to becoming a huge hit artist for Atlantic in the late '50s. These were R&B gems, but such artists as Patti Page and Georgia Gibbs were covering them for the white market and Brown was locked out until 1957. But she enjoyed 11 Top 10 R&B hits, which are contained on this anthology. — *Ron Wynn*

Have a Good Time / May 10, 1988–May 11, 1988 / Fantasy ✦✦✦

Nice recent material, with Brown showing she's still got some power. — *Ron Wynn*

★ **Miss Rhythm** / 1989 / Rhino ✦✦✦✦✦

For those who don't have the funds or live near a big record store that gets imports, here's the definitive domestic anthology of her best sides. — *Ron Wynn*

○ **Blues on Broadway** / Jun. 12, 1989–Jun. 13, 1989 / Fantasy ✦✦✦✦

A great mix of show business panache with a bluesy undergirding. — *Ron Wynn*

Fine and Mellow / 1991 / Fantasy ✦✦✦

A very good recent album, heavy on the blues side of her personality. — *Ron Wynn*

Songs of My Life / 1993 / Fantasy ✦✦✦

Before Ruth Brown became an R&B and rock legend in the '50s, she was a jazz, blues, and gospel stylist. She shows that aspect of her talent on *The Songs of My Life*, a fine set produced by guitarist Rodney Jones, who also did the arrangements and conducted the backing band. While she displays her timing, interpretative skills, and still-impressive delivery and enunciation throughout, Brown also demonstrates on her rendition of Eric Clapton's "Tears in Heaven" that she retains an interest in and awareness of contemporary songs that fit her style. Ruth Brown proves that it's not the song or the lyric but the singer who makes a tune work. — *Ron Wynn*

Shirley Brown

b. Jan. 6, 1947, West Memphis, AR
Soul, R&B

Shirley Brown was a gospel singer in West Memphis, AR, before turning to soul in her teens. Her family had moved to St. Louis, and Brown started working in local clubs. Oliver Sain produced her early recordings for Abet, like "I Ain't Gonna Tell" and "Love Is Built on a Strong Foundation." Albert King helped Brown get signed to Stax, and got Al Jackson to be her producer for the seminal single "Woman to Woman." The searing confessional was turned into a country hit by Barbara Mandrell, became Brown's signature song, and topped the R&B/soul charts in 1975. She continued recording for Stax until the label folded, then moved to Arista. Her 1977 LP *Shirley Brown* contained some urgently sung material, but didn't yield any hits. Brown languished until 1984, when she issued *Intimate Storm* for Sound Town. It included several songs co-written and produced by Homer Banks, but was far too raw and soulful for the urban contemporary market. She recorded "If This Is Goodbye" for Black Diamond in 1986, then joined Malaco in 1989. Brown remains on their label. — *Ron Wynn*

● **Woman to Woman** / 1974 / Stax ✦✦✦✦

Shirley Brown created a seminal confessional and confrontational soul masterpiece with the title track. It was a chart-topping R&B song and pop hit, and was later turned into a country smash by Barbara Mandrell. The album wasn't quite as consistently insightful or memorable, but still had some other love tunes and heartache numbers. — *Ron Wynn*

Shirley Brown / 1977 / Arista ✦✦✦

For the Real Feeling / 1979 / United Artists ✦✦✦

Intimate Storm / 1985 / 4th & Broadway ✦✦

Timeless / 1990 / Malaco ✦✦✦

Shirley Brown's Malaco material has been erratic, although her vocals are still among the strongest and most soulful of the '70s R&B generation still active. The material provided by such veterans as George Jackson was decent, and the production tried to balance classic soul values with more up-to-date instrumentation and arrangements, but there was simply no definitive or ear-catching track. — *Ron Wynn*

Jackson Browne

b. Oct. 9, 1948, Heidelberg, Germany

Singer-Songwriter

As one of the guiding lights from the sensitive '70s singer/songwriter school of pop, Jackson Browne (along with Joni Mitchell) gave the word "introspection" new meaning with his earnest musical epistles from the inside. Like Mitchell and James Taylor (somewhat), Browne provided a weighty soundtrack for scores of apprehensive '60s kids trying to come to grips with growing up and finding their place in the world. Without a doubt, his first four albums are loaded with gems, even if his melodies tend to have a sameness. Browne has always attracted stellar sidemen for his records, many of whom can also be found on records by Linda Ronstadt and James Taylor.During his career, Browne has proven himself to be a very capable producer for Warren Zevon and Greg Copeland.

Hardcore Browne fanatics will claim their hero ceased to perform to their expectations after his million-selling 1976 opus *The Pretender*, but, his greatest commercial success took place from that album on. Granted, his highest-charting single, the lightweight "Somebody's Baby," was quite a departure from his previous work, but maybe Browne needed a breather.In 1982 Browne's California pop/rock phase ended and he returned with the more topical *Lawyers in Love*, which produced a hit with the title track. Subsequent albums have increasingly addressed global issues over the self-absorbed ruminations of his earlier work. Browne returned to a more introspective style of songwriting with his 1993 album, *I'm Alive*. — *Rick Clark*

☆ **Jackson Browne** / Jan. 1972 / Asylum ✦✦✦✦✦

One of the reasons that Jackson Browne's first album is among the most auspicious debuts in pop music history is that it doesn't sound like an album. Although only 23, Browne had kicked around the music business for several years, writing and performing as a member of the Nitty Gritty Dirt Band and as Nico's backup guitarist, among other gigs, while many artists recorded his material. So, if this doesn't sound like someone's first batch of songs, it's not. Browne had developed an unusual use of language, casual yet full of striking imagery, and a post-apocalyptic viewpoint to go with it. He sang with a calm certainty over spare, discretely placed backup—piano, acoustic guitar, bass, drums, congas, violin, harmony vocals—that highlighted the songs and always seemed about to disappear. In song after song, Browne described the world as a desert in need of moisture, and this wet/dry dichotomy carried over into much of the imagery. In "Doctor My Eyes," the album's most propulsive song and a Top 10 hit, he sang, "Doctor, my eyes/Cannot see the sky/Is this the prize/For having learned how not to cry?" If Browne's outlook was cautious, its expression was original. His conditional optimism seemed to reflect hard experience, and in the early '70s, the aftermath of the '60s, a lot of his listeners shared that perspective. Like any great artist, Browne articulated the tenor of his times. But the album has long since come to seem a timeless collection of reflective ballads touching on still-difficult subjects—suicide (explicitly), depression and drug use (probably), spiritual uncertainty and desperate hope—all in calm, reasoned tones, and all with an amazingly eloquent sense of language. *Jackson Browne's* greater triumph is that, having perfectly expressed his times, it transcended those times as well. (The album features a cover depicting Browne's face on a water bag—an appropriate reference to its desert/water imagery—containing the words "saturate before using." Inevitably, many people began to refer to the self-titled album by that phrase, and when it was released on CD, it became official—both the disc and the spine of the jewel box read *Saturate Before Using*.) — *William Ruhlmann*

○ **For Everyman** / Oct. 1973 / Asylum ✦✦✦✦

Jackson Browne faced the nearly insurmountable task of following a masterpiece in making his second album. Having cherry-picked years of songwriting the first time around, he turned to some of his secondary older material, which was still better than most people's best and, ironically, more accessible—notably such songs as "These Days," which had been covered six times already, dating back to Nico's *Chelsea Girl* album in 1967, and "Take It Easy," a co-composition with the Eagles' Glenn Frey, which had been a Top 40 hit for the group in 1972. Browne unsuccessfully looked for another hit single with the uptempo "Red Neck Friend," reminisced about meeting his wife and starting a family in the coy "Ready Or Not," and, at the end, finally came up with a new song to rank with those on the first album in the philosophical title

track, which reportedly was his more positive reply to Crosby, Stills, Nash & Young's "Wooden Ships." (David Crosby sang harmony.) Musically, the album was still restrained, but not as austere as *Jackson Browne*, as the singer had hooked up with multi-instrumentalist David Lindley, who would introduce interesting textures to his music on a variety of stringed instruments for the next several years. All of which is to say that *For Everyman* was a less consistent collection than Browne's debut album. But Browne's songwriting ability remained impressive. — *William Ruhlmann*

★ **Late for the Sky** / Sep. 1974 / Asylum ✦✦✦✦✦

On his third album, Jackson Browne returned to the themes of his debut record (love, loss, identity, apocalypse), and, amazingly, delved even deeper into them. "For A Dancer," a meditation on death like the first album's "Song For Adam," is a more eloquent eulogy; "Farther On" extends the "moving on" point of "Looking Into You"; "Before The Deluge" is a glimpse beyond the apocalypse evoked on "My Opening Farewell" and the second album's "For Everyman." If Browne had seemed to question everything in his first records, here he even questioned himself. "For me some words come easy, but I know that they don't mean that much," he sang on the opening track, "Late For The Sky," and added in "Farther On," "I'm not sure what I'm trying to say." Yet his seeming uncertainty and self-doubt reflected the size and complexity of the problems he was addressing in these songs, and few had ever explored such territory, much less mapped it so well. "The Late Show," the album's thematic center, doubted but ultimately affirmed the nature of relationships, while by the end, "After The Deluge," if "only a few survived," the human race continued nonetheless. It was a lot to put into a pop music album, but Browne stretched the limits of what could be found in what he called "the beauty in songs," just as Bob Dylan had a decade before. (In 1993, DCC Compact Classics licensed *Late For The Sky* from Elektra Entertainment and reissued it as a 24 karat gold compact disc [GZS-1036]. The DCC version, unlike the Asylum package, contained a lyric sheet.) — *William Ruhlmann*

The Pretender / Nov. 1976 / Asylum ✦✦✦

On *The Pretender*, Jackson Browne took a step back from the precipice so well defined on his first three albums, but doing so didn't seem to make him feel any better. Employing a real producer, Jon Landau (who worked with and managed Bruce Springsteen), for the first time, Browne made a record that sounded like a real contemporary rock record—the drums boomed, the vocals had attractive, echoed presence, the songs were tightly arranged, the instrumental licks were L.A.-tasty—but this made his songs less effective. Where the uptempo drive of "Doctor My Eyes" on the first album had emphasized the disillusioned lyric tone, here the ersatz Mexican arrangement of "Linda Paloma" and the bouncy second half of "Daddy's Tune," with its horn charts and guitar solo, undercut the lyrics. But the main problem was that the man who had delved so deeply into life's abyss on his earlier albums was in search of escape this time around, whether by crying ("Here Come Those Tears Again"), sleeping ("Sleep's Dark And Silent Gate"), or making peace with estranged love ones ("The Only Child," "Daddy's Tune"). None of it worked, however, and when Browne came to the final track—traditionally the place on his albums where he summed up his current philosophical stance—he delivered "The Pretender," a cynical, sarcastic treatise on moneygrubbing and the shallow life of the suburbs. The song was primarily inner directed; the pretender was the singer, and it would be hard to find a lyric as self-hating (or as self-pitying). In a sense, the song's defeatist tone demands rejection, but it is also a quintessential statement of its time, the post-Watergate '70s. Once again, Browne had accurately described the world around him by defining his own place in it, dire as that might be, and you had to admire that kind of honesty, even as it made you wince. — *William Ruhlmann*

Running on Empty / 1977 / Asylum ✦✦✦

Having acknowledged a certain creative desperation on *The Pretender*, Jackson Browne lowered his sights (and raised his commercial appeal) considerably with *Running On Empty*, which was more a concept album about the road than an actual live album, even though its songs were sometimes recorded on stage (and sometimes on the bus or in the hotel). Although unlike most live albums, it consisted of previously unrecorded songs, Browne had less creative participation on this album than on any he ever made, solely composing only two songs, co-writing four others, and covering another four. And he had less to say—the title song and leadoff track neatly conjoined his artistic and escapist themes. Figuratively and creatively, he was out of gas, but like "the pretender," still had to make a living. The songs covered all aspects of touring, from Danny O'Keefe's "The Road," which detailed romantic encounters, and "Rosie" (co-written by Browne and his manager Donald Miller), in which a soundman pays tribute to auto-eroticism, to, well, "Cocaine," to the travails of being a roadie ("The Load-Out"). Audience noises, humorous asides, loose playing— they were all part of a rough-around-the-edges musical evocation of the rock 'n' roll touring life. It was not what fans had come to expect from Browne, of course, but the disaffected were more than outnumbered by the newly converted. (It didn't hurt that "Running On Empty" and "The Load-Out"/"Stay" both became Top 40 hits.) As a result, Jackson Browne's least ambitious, but perhaps most accessible, album ironically became his biggest seller. But it is not characteristic of his other work: for many, it will be the only Browne album they will want to own, just as others will always regard it disdainfully as *Jackson Browne Lite. — William Ruhlmann*

Hold Out / 1980 / Asylum ◆◆
If Jackson Browne had convincingly lowered the bar set by his first three albums on his fourth and fifth ones, his sixth, *Hold Out*, found him once again seeking some measure of satisfaction, albeit in reduced circumstances. His songs were less philosophical, but they were also more personal. In "Of Missing Persons," he once again took on a eulogy as his subject, but unlike "Song To Adam" or "For A Dancer," here the song was directed to his late friend's daughter and encouraged her recovery: it was more a song for the living than for the dead. Newly aware of the world around him ("Boulevard"), he was also newly sensitive to others, notably on the mutual dependency song "Call It A Loan." But the personal tone sometimes made him less sure-footed as a performer; "Hold On Hold Out," the traditional big, long, last song on the album, was awkwardly, not winningly intimate, just as the attention-grabbing lead-off track, "Disco Apocalypse," was merely foolish instead of whatever it may have been intended to be (satire? drama?). If Browne was still trying to write himself out of the cul-de-sac he had created for himself early on, *Hold Out* represented an earnest attempt that nevertheless fell short. — *William Ruhlmann*

Lawyers in Love / 1983 / Asylum ◆◆
Jackson Browne's messages had always seemed so important that one tended to overlook the sheer songwriting craft that went into his work, craft that was apparent, for example, on his 1982 single "Somebody's Baby," which became his biggest hit ever (and which appears on none of his albums, only being available on the soundtrack to *Fast Times At Ridgemont High*), and on songs like "Downtown," a street-life portrait on his seventh album, *Lawyers In Love*. The craft seemed all the more important because Browne was so intent on turning his back on the conundrums that had obsessed him in the past. On "Cut It Away," he sang of his desire to remove his "desperate heart" (a phrase he had used before), to rid himself of "this crazy longing for something more/This question that I don't have the answer for." In place of such ambitions, Browne substituted the beginnings of social concern ("Say It Isn't True") and, most imaginatively, a humorous look at contemporary trash culture in the title track, one of the more exhilaratingly silly moments in Browne's generally dour catalog. But the craft, and the familiar tightness of Browne's veteran studio/live band, couldn't hide the essentially retread nature of much of this material. — *William Ruhlmann*

Lives in the Balance / 1986 / Asylum ◆◆◆
Usually among the most introspective of songwriters, Jackson Browne cast his gaze on the world outside on *Lives In The Balance* and did not like what he saw. Beginning with "For America," he lamented his previous indifference to social issues—"I went on speaking of the future/While other people fought and bled"—but immediately tried to make up for lost time. The album's context, of course, was five years of Ronald Reagan's presidency, with what the Left saw as an indifference to the plight of the poor at home and a dangerously aggressive policy against insurgent movements in the Central American countries of El Salvador and Nicaragua they feared would lead to a Vietnam-like war. Without naming those places, Browne wrote and sang passionately against poverty in the songs "Soldier Of Plenty" and "Lawless Avenues" and against war in "For America," "Lives In The Balance," and "Till I Go Down." Elsewhere, his more familiar themes of romantic ("In The Shape Of A Heart") and philosophical ("Black And White") disillusionment also made appearances. But, from its hard rock

sound and forceful singing to its frankly agitprop lyrics, *For America* remained primarily a political statement, and if Browne sounded more involved in his music than he had in some time, the specificity of its approach inevitably limited its appeal and its long-term significance. — *William Ruhlmann*

World in Motion / 1989 / Elektra ◆◆
Jackson Browne continued amassing a repertoire best suited to an Amnesty International benefit on his second highly politicized album, *World In Motion*. War, homelessness, and Oliver North (though not by name) were condemned; freedom, truth, and Nelson Mandela were praised. Now and then, Browne drew parallels between the personal and the political, notably in the double-edged "Anything Can Happen," but for the most part he sermonized, frequently adopting the generalized terms and reasoning that sermons usually employ. Except for the gloomy viewpoint, it was hard to recognize the Jackson Browne of his first few albums amid all the commentary, and even if you agreed with his overall political stance, that was disappointing. — *William Ruhlmann*

I'm Alive / Oct. 1993 / Elektra ◆◆◆
Jackson Browne abandoned politics for the war between the sexes on *I'm Alive*. "I have no problem with this crooked world," he sang. "...My problem is you." The album detailed the ups and downs of a relationship, starting with the defiant post-breakup title track and then doubling back to describe irritation ("My Problem Is You"), devotion ("Everywhere I Go," "I'll Do Anything"), increasing tension ("Miles Away," "Too Many Angels"), separation ("Take This Rain," "Two Of Me, Two Of You"), forgiveness ("Sky Blue and Black"), and finally acceptance ("All Good Things"). Long time fans welcomed the album as a return in style to the days of *Late For The Sky*, but a closer model might have been *Hold Out*, a complementary album concerned with the flowering of an affair rather than the withering of one, since Browne eschewed the greater philosophical implications of romance and, falling back on stock imagery (angels, rain), failed to achieve an originality of expression. Just as, in *Hold Out*, one wasn't so much inspired as informed that Browne had found love, on *I'm Alive*, one wasn't so much moved as told that he'd lost it. While it was good news that he wasn't tilting at windmills anymore, Browne did not make a full comeback with the album, despite a couple of well-constructed songs. — *William Ruhlmann*

Brownsville Station

Group, Rock & Roll
A Detroit-area rock & roll band formed in 1969 by guitarist Cub Koda. Original members also included Mike Lutz (guitar), T. J. Cronley (drums), and Tony Driggins (bass). Initially influenced by Chuck Berry, Bo Diddley, Jerry Lee Lewis, and other '50s rockers, their early albums included inspired covers and genre-faithful originals, all presented in Marshall stack, double-bass-drum bigness. Far more effective as a live act (with Koda's onstage banter influencing everyone from J. Geils's Peter Wolf to Alice Cooper), the group finally hit paydirt in late 1973 with their number three hit, the Koda-penned "Smokin' in the Boy's Room." After disbanding the group in 1979, Koda went on to a career as a solo recording artist and as a journalist for several music magazines. — *Stephen Thomas Erlewine*

○ **No B.S.** / 1970 / Warner Brothers ◆◆◆◆
Their debut album, featuring pedal-to-the-metal renditions of "Road Runner," "Rumble," and "Be Bop Confidential." — *Stephen Thomas Erlewine*

Brownsville Station / 1977 / Private Stock ◆◆◆
Their next-to-last album, featuring the cult favorite "The Martian Boogie." — *Stephen Thomas Erlewine*

● **Smoking in the Boy's Room: The Best of Brownsville Station** / 1993 / Rhino ◆◆◆◆
A roaring romp through the Brownsville Station's back pages compiled by Cub Koda himself, *Smokin' In the Boys' Room* makes a convincing case that these Ann Arbor, Michigan garage punks were one of the most underrated rock & roll bands of the '70s. — *Stephen Thomas Erlewine*

Jack Bruce (John Symon Asher Bruce)

b. May 14, 1943, Glasgow, Scotland
Art-Rock/Progressive-Rock
In the pantheon of great rock bassists, Jack Bruce certainly stands tall. His forceful yet elastic technique and his trademark wide

tonality and phrasing are utterly unique. Bruce incorporated a jazz sensibility by giving the bass freedom to voice itself beyond merely holding down the pulse with the drummer.

Along with Eric Clapton (guitar, vocals) and Ginger Baker (percussion), Bruce pioneered the hard rock trio concept, complete with extended free-for-all jams. Bruce has also done exemplary work with the Tony Williams Lifetime, Alexis Korner, the Graham Bond Organization, John Mayall's Bluesbreakers, Carla Bley, Robin Trower, Frank Zappa, West, Bruce & Laing, the Golden Palominos, and BBM.

Bruce (with co-writer Pete Brown) penned most of Cream's biggest numbers. As a solo singer/songwriter, Bruce integrated an eclectic sampling of music, ranging from folk to classical overtones to jazz-rock fusion, all focused through a rather impenetrable arty filter. —*Rick Clark*

○ **Songs for a Tailor** / 1969 / Atco ◆◆◆◆
There's not a weak song on this first and most accessible solo album. "Theme for an Imaginary Western" (also made popular by Mountain) is one of the finest songs Bruce has ever recorded. Musically, this is more subdued and keyboard-oriented than Bruce's work with Cream. —*Rick Clark*

Things We Like / 1970 / Atco ◆◆

Harmony Row / 1971 / Atco ◆◆◆
Bruce's third effort is a much more challenging listen, possessing more complicated arrangements and impenetrable lyrics than *Songs for a Tailor*. Among the album's many highlights are the aggressive multi-time-signature rock of "You Burned the Tables on Me" and the haunting "Victoria Sage." —*Rick Clark*

At His Best / 1972 / RSO ◆◆◆

Out of the Storm / 1974 / RSO ◆◆◆

How's Tricks / 1977 / RSO ◆◆◆

I've Always Wanted to Do This / 1980 / Epic ◆◆◆

Greatest Hits / 1980 / Polydor ◆◆◆

Bruce Lordan Trower (B.L.T) / 1981 / Chrysalis ◆◆◆

Truce / 1982 / Chrysalis ◆◆◆

● **Willpower: A Twenty-Year Retrospective** / 1989 / Atco ◆◆◆◆
Willpower is a well-compiled overview of Bruce's entire solo output, with choice unreleased tracks. This is the place to start if you are budgeting one disc of his music for your collection. Otherwise, get *Songs for a Tailor*. —*Rick Clark*

A Question of Time / 1990 / Epic ◆◆◆

○ **Somethin' Else** / 1993 / CMP ◆◆◆◆
Reunited with long-time collaborator Pete Brown, Jack Bruce turns in one of the finest albums of his solo career, with songs that come close to matching the splendor of his work with Cream. —*Stephen Thomas Erlewine*

Cities Of The Heart / 1994 / CMP

Tyrone Brunson

Urban
Washington, D.C., bassist and vocalist Tyrone Brunson played and sang in area bands through the '70s. He was signed to the Columbia-distributed Believe In A Dream label after some demos he'd submitted impressed CBS executives in 1982. His first single, the instrumental "The Smurf," tapped into what was then a New York dance craze, and the song won international club recognition. But when the smurf trend cooled, so did Brunson. While "The Smurf" reached number 14 on the R&B charts in 1982, the follow-up, "Sticky Situation," stalled at #25. Brunson made a slight comeback in 1984 with "Fresh," which reached #22. But neither of his LPs, *Sticky Situation* or *Fresh*, managed consistent sales. Brunson moved to MCA in 1987. Mtume produced *Love Triangle*, but it flopped. Brunson later did background vocals for Levert. —*Ron Wynn*

● **Sticky Situation** / 1984 / Epic ◆◆◆◆

Fresh / 1984 / Epic ◆◆

Love Triangle / 1987 / MCA ◆◆◆

Peabo Bryson

b. Apr. 13, 1951, Greenville, SC
Urban
Vocalist Peabo Bryson was among the premier silky-voiced soul artists who emerged as the softer, more sophisticated urban-contemporary sound became dominant in the '70s and '80s. Bryson, who was born in Greenville, SC, sang with Al Freeman & the Upsetters in 1965, and was in the group Moses Dillard & the Tex-Town Display from 1968 to 1973. He was a producer and composer for Atlanta's Bang Records in the early '70s, and sang in Michael Zager's Moon Band. His self-titled debut LP and several singles were recorded for Bang's subsidiary company Bullet, among them "Do It with Feeling," "Underground Music," "It's Just a Matter of Time," "Just Another Day," and "I Can Make It Better." All were moderate R&B hits. Bryson moved to Capitol in 1978, where his first album, *Reaching for the Sky*, went gold, and the title track was a number six R&B hit. He remained in the Moon Band until 1979, departing after "I'm So Into You" spent two weeks as the nation's number two R&B hit in 1978. Bryson has continued a prolific career as both lead act and duet participant. He has made hit duets with Natalie Cole, Roberta Flack, Melissa Manchester, and Regina Belle. Bryson recorded for Capitol until 1984, when he switched to Elektra, and enjoyed more success with "If Ever You're in My Arms Again." He moved to Columbia in 1991, issuing *Can You Stop the Rain*. He's also enjoyed more acclaim making duets with Belle. —*Ron Wynn*

○ **Reaching for the Sky** / Jan. 1978 / Capitol ◆◆◆◆
Peabo Bryson's first great album, and the vehicle that established him as a favorite of urban contemporary audiences. He was still officially working with Michael Zager's Moon Band. This was his Capitol debut, and the title track became Bryson's first R&B Top 10 hit. The album also went gold and signaled that it was only a matter of time before Bryson would split from the Zager band. —*Ron Wynn*

○ **Crosswinds** / Nov. 1978 / Capitol ◆◆◆◆
A great album, one of Peabo Bryson's first smash efforts. His vocals were at their most expressive and soulful point, and the production didn't subordinate his singing to the orchestrations or arrangements. The title track was an R&B Top 40 hit, and the album yielded a second solid song in "She's a Woman." —*Ron Wynn*

We're the Best of Friends / Nov. 1979 / Capitol ◆◆◆
Another hit album for Bryson, and one of his many successful collaborations with female vocalists. Natalie Cole's career had hit a dry spell, and she piggybacked on Bryson's hit status. But the two proved to be quite effective partners, although he was in much better vocal shape than she was at the time. His soaring leads often nearly evaporated her complementary lines, but the album still worked. It also got the pair two hits in the songs "Gimme Some Time" and a cover of Bobby Caldwell's "What You Won't Do For Love." —*Ron Wynn*

Paradise / Apr. 1980 / Capitol ◆◆
This album was one of two he issued in 1980, and it wasn't anywhere near the level of past Capitol projects. But Bryson was so hot at the time that it did get widespread airplay and didn't torpedo the momentum he'd generated in the late '70s. —*Ron Wynn*

Live & More / Dec. 1980 / Atlantic ◆◆◆
A double live album by Roberta Flack and Peabo Bryson. —*Ron Wynn*

Turn the Hands of Time / Feb. 1981 / Capitol ◆◆
Another moderately productive album for Peabo Bryson, who was beginning to slip from his pedestal in the early '80s. There was one strong number, "Let The Feeling Flow," which even got some pop airplay. Bryson's voice didn't sound as silky or inviting; most ballads lacked their customary sparkle and the uptempo tunes were faceless. —*Ron Wynn*

I Am Love / Nov. 1981 / Capitol ◆◆◆

Don't Play with Fire / Nov. 1982 / Capitol ◆◆◆
Peabo Bryson got three chart singles from this album and stayed high atop the urban contemporary and R&B charts. He still wasn't hitting the peaks he routinely climbed in the late '70s, but was maintaining his status as a hit act and romantic idol. —*Ron Wynn*

Born to Love / Jul. 1983 / Capitol ◆◆◆
Bryson hit his '80s peak with this hugely successful duet album with Roberta Flack. It did the same thing for her that his album with Natalie Cole had done in the late '70s; Flack was revived as an urban stylist. The single "Tonight I Celebrate My Love" was all over the airwaves and even used on a soap opera. It made it into the pop Top 20 and reached the number five spot on the R&B charts. —*Ron Wynn*

○ **Straight from the Heart** / May 1984 / Elektra ✦✦✦✦
Good mix of slow and uptempo tunes, including the definitive Bryson ballad, "If Ever You're in My Arms Again." — *William Ruhlmann*

● **Collection** / Jun. 1984 / Capitol ✦✦✦✦
A best-of covering Bryson's Capitol years, 1978-1983, much of it given over to his collaboration with Roberta Flack, including the hits "Tonight, I Celebrate My Love" and "You're Lookin' Like Love to Me." — *William Ruhlmann*

Take No Prisoners / Jun. 1985 / Elektra ✦✦✦
In the wake of his ascension into the pop Top Ten with the ballad "If Ever You're In My Arms Again," Peabo Bryson might have been expected to try to consolidate that success with his follow-up record. And indeed, *Take No Prisoners*, produced by such crossover veterans as Arif Mardin and Tommy LiPuma and featuring such pop songwriters as Barry Mann, Cynthia Weil, and Tom Snow, may have seemed like a try for that. But Elektra led off its singles releases with the light, uptempo title track, and followed with another, "There's Nothin' Out There," apparently in a move to solidify Bryson's R&B base. Neither of those songs found much success, however, and the potential crossover ballads, such as "Love Always Finds A Way" and "She's Over Me," never got off Side Two and onto the airwaves. As a result, the album represented a missed opportunity for Bryson, even though be sang with his usual assurance, the material was of good quality, and the production was sympathetic. — *William Ruhlmann*

Quiet Storm / Oct. 1986 / Elektra ✦✦
A prototype album for late '80s urban contemporary music. Bryson made some overproduced, effectively sung ballads and a few decent uptempo tracks, and the results were disappointing but mildly successful. The album did get extensive publicity and support, but there were no hits. — *Ron Wynn*

Positive / Jan. 1988 / Elektra ✦✦✦
Peabo Bryson's final album for Elektra was largely undistinguished, although he sang with more conviction and got better material and production than on most of his other Elektra albums. He scored another hit with a familiar weapon: the duet. This time his partner was Regina Belle, with whom he would enjoy more success on another soundtrack project. Their single "Without You" wasn't an instant hit, but eventually proved the best thing about the flop film *Leonard, Pt. 6*. — *Ron Wynn*

All My Love / May 1989 / Capitol ✦✦✦
Peabo Bryson switched labels in 1989, returning to Capitol, the place where he'd enjoyed his greatest success in the late '70s and early '80s. The results were both immediate and satisfying. This album was not only one of his strongest in many years, but such songs as "Show and Tell" and "Palm Of Your Hand" got widespread urban contemporary airplay, and D'Atra Hicks got a career boost from doing a duet with Bryson on the album. — *Ron Wynn*

Can You Stop the Rain / Jun. 1991 / Columbia ✦✦✦
Having returned to Capitol Records for 1989's *All My Love* and enjoyed a career uptick, Peabo Bryson moved again to Columbia Records, where he completed his comeback to the commercial status he had enjoyed in the early 1980s. Bryson seemed to have reconciled himself to the public's view of him as primarily a balladeer, and he delivered the goods, especially on the title track, a #1 R&B hit, and on the Cynthia Weil/Barry Mann tune "Closer Than Close," which also hit the R&B Top 10. (Bryson helped his own cause considerably by involving himself in the writing and production of five of the 11 songs.) The album topped the R&B charts, and although Bryson still had trouble crossing over to the pop charts, it was his biggest seller in seven years. The album's success, however, was quickly overshadowed by Bryson's soundtrack work, as he placed hits from the *Beauty And The Beast* and *Aladdin* scores in the charts later in 1991 and 1992. — *William Ruhlmann*

B.T. Express

Group, Funk, Disco
This funk-disco group was formed by Jeff Lane in Brooklyn during the '70s. They started in 1972 as the King Davis House Rockers, and later were called the Brooklyn Trucking Express. The roster consisted of saxophonist and vocalist Bill Risbrook, percussionist Dennis Rowe, guitarist Rick Thompson, saxophonist and flutist Carlos Ward, keyboardist Michael Jones (Kashif), lead guitarist and vocalist Wesley Hall, drummer Leslie Ming, bassist, organist

and vocalist Louis Risbrook, and vocalist Barbara Joyce Lomas. Their debut LP *Do It Till You're Satisfied* had two number one R&B and Top Ten pop hits in the title cut and "Express." Subsequent LPs yielded two more R&B Top Ten singles, "Give It What You Got/Peace Pipe" in 1975 and "Can't Stop Groovin' Now, Wanna Do It Some More" in 1976. After 1977's "Shout It Out," which cracked the R&B Top 20 (number 12), the group slumped with the album *Shout!* They were off the charts until 1980. They made a slight comeback that year with *B.T. Express 1980*, though only the single "Give Up the Funk (Let's Dance)" made it into the Top 30 (number 24). They later recorded for Record Shack, Earthtone, and King Davis, but couldn't duplicate their earlier success. Kashif scored hits as a producer, performer, and composer in the '80s. — *Ron Wynn*

○ **Do It ('til You're Satisfied)** / Nov. 1974 / Roadshow ✦✦✦✦
The title song was their best contribution to music. — *Bil Carpenter*

Non-Stop / Jul. 1975 / Roadshow ✦✦✦
The second B.T. Express album featured two smash hits in "Give It What You Got" and "Peace Pipe." They were at their funk-disco peak, cutting songs that maintained their energy long enough to air in discos, and had enough backbeat and edge to hook the R&B and funk audience. — *Ron Wynn*

Energy to Burn / May 1976 / Columbia ✦✦
Things began to decline for B.T. Express when they switched to Columbia, although funk was steadily declining in the late '70s anyway, soon to be followed by disco. They play their familiar uptempo dance and funk numbers with the same assurance and exuberance of the past, but they didn't have the same punch or appeal. — *Ron Wynn*

Function at the Junction / May 1977 / Columbia ✦✦✦
B.T. Express made a brief comeback from a slump with their fourth album. The title track was a return to the shuffle funk and disco of their first two albums, and the other songs had a light, humorous quality and celebratory edge that was an improvement from the calculated feel of the first Columbia session. — *Ron Wynn*

Shout! / Feb. 1978 / Columbia ✦✦
The last great B.T. Express album served as sort of a finale to the funk and disco era. As the '70s ended, urban contemporary was obsessed with crossover, and things that were deemed too ethnic were being discouraged. B.T. Express's heavy backbeat and lengthy tracks were falling out of favor with both radio and pop fans, although the core crowd in the discos and inner cities still enjoyed them. — *Ron Wynn*

Greatest Hits / 1980 / CBS ✦✦✦

B.T. Express 1980 / May 1980 / Excalibre ✦✦
They landed one more hit, "Does It Feel Good," but things were pretty much over for B.T. Express, at least in terms of them being a hit act. Funk and the kind of disco they'd done was virtually dead by 1980. House, Hi-NRG, and other styles that required more production than their brand of galvanizing, attacking music were in vogue. They continued on until the mid-'80s, but they never regained their position on the R&B or pop charts. — *Ron Wynn*

Old Gold, Future Gold / 1981 / Excalibre ✦✦

● **Golden Classics** / Collectables ✦✦✦✦
B.T. Express exploded on the funk-disco scene in the mid-'70s with back-to-back number-one R&B hits, "Do It ('Til You're Satisfied)" and "Express," both of which also cracked the pop Top 10. "Give It What You Got/Peace Pipe" was another big hit, but the group had peaked by the late '70s. This collection includes these three smashes, plus other respectable numbers. They were never great singers, but were a good funk ensemble. — *Ron Wynn*

Roy Buchanan

b. Sep. 23, 1939, Ozark, Alabama, **d.** Aug. 14, 1988
Blues Rock
Buchanan's reputation as a hot-shot guitarist extends back to the beginnings of rock & roll itself. On the road and recording with Dale Hawkins by his teens, Buchanan became the scat of the land around the Washington, D.C., area by the mid-to-late '60s. His use of the Fender Telecaster, using high harmonic squeals in place of feedback and distortion, was part and parcel of rock guitar's vocabulary by the early '70s. A reluctant superstar, Buchanan later became more unfocused as his career waned, but his unique stylings remain etched into his best records.

Sadly, when Buchanan seemed on the verge of a comeback in 1986, he hung himself in a police cell, after he was arrested on a drunk-driving charge. He left behind a number of records which testify that he was a consummate guitarist, capable of tones and techniques that other guitarists only dream of. —*Cub Koda*

○ **Roy Buchanan** / Aug. 1972 / Polydor ✦✦✦✦
His debut album, with a skunk-hot stage band. Buchanan's guitar sizzles on tracks like "Haunted House," "Sweet Dreams," and "The Messiah Will Come Again." —*Cub Koda*

Second Album / 1973 / Polydor ✦✦✦
More blues-based than his debut, with great stretched-out jams showcasing some of his best playing. —*Cub Koda*

That's What I Am Here For / Feb. 1974 / Polydor ✦✦✦
Excellent blues-rock guitar, it includes the riveting Hendrix tribute "Hey Joe." —*David Szatmary*

In the Beginning / Dec. 1974 / Polydor ✦

Rescue Me / 1975 / Polydor ✦✦

○ **Live Stock** / Aug. 1975 / Polydor ✦✦✦✦
Brilliant live blues-rock guitar by the legend who turned down a spot in the Rolling Stones. A must for guitar-hero fans. —*David Szatmary*

A Street Called Straight / Apr. 1976 / Atlantic ✦✦

Loading Zone / May 1977 / Atlantic ✦✦

You're Not Alone / Apr. 1978 / Atlantic ✦✦✦
Piercing guitar solos explode in a spacey atmosphere. —*David Szatmary*

My Babe / 1981 / AJK ✦✦
Buchanan was a terrific guitarist, but *My Babe* is not the place to hear him in his glory. Too often, the album is dragged down by slick production and Paul Jacobs's overbearing vocals. Buchanan's playing is fairly good, but he sounds a little uninspired, which is understandable, considering his surroundings. —*Stephen Thomas Erlewine*

When a Guitar Plays the Blues / Jul. 1985 / Alligator ✦✦✦
This is an excellent example of the blues-rock guitar virtuoso's recent work. —*David Szatmary*

Dancing on the Edge / Jun. 1986 / Alligator ✦✦✦

Hot Wires / 1987 / Alligator ✦✦✦
Another stinging effort. —*David Szatmary*

The Early Years / Oct. 1989 / Krazy Kat ✦✦✦

● **Sweet Dreams: The Anthology** / 1992 / Polydor ✦✦✦✦
Over two CDs, *Sweet Dreams* collects the finest moments from Buchanan's '70s albums, including nine unreleased tracks; as a career retrospective, it's the finest collection available. —*Stephen Thomas Erlewine*

Guitar on Fire: Atlantic Sessions / 1993 / Rhino ✦✦✦

Lindsey Buckingham

b. Oct. 3, 1948, Palo Alto, CA
Pop/Rock
Before he joined Fleetwood Mac, Lindsey Buckingham was sketching out his brand of Brian Wilson-influenced pop with Stevie Nicks in the folkie duo Buckingham/Nicks. Mick Fleetwood invited the duo to join his band in late 1974. After Buckingham joined, the band's pop tendencies flowered under his direction. Not only did he provide the group with some brilliant, surprisingly dark pop songs, he sharpened the other members' songs with his production, arrangements, and breathtaking guitar-playing. Buckingham left the band after their 1987 album, *Tango in the Night*, to concentrate on his solo work.
While Buckingham's solo albums are deceptively simple and calm on the surface, there are complex arrangements and emotions beneath the smooth production. None of them have sold anything approaching the level of *Rumours*—or even *Tango in the Night*—yet they are rich, layered pop albums; his first solo record, *Law & Order*, had a hit single with "Trouble." —*Stephen Thomas Erlewine*

Buckingham Nicks / 1973 / Polydor ✦✦✦
Buckingham Nicks, the duo album made by Lindsey Buckingham and Stevie Nicks in 1973, which served in effect as an audition tape for their entry into Fleetwood Mac in 1974, is hard not to hear as a dry run for works like *Fleetwood Mac* and *Rumours*. Many of the musical characteristics associated with those albums are here,

from Nicks's torn voice and mysterious, romantic lyrics to Buckingham's fluid acoustic and electric guitar playing and his inventive arranging. One song, "Crystal," even turned up rerecorded on *Fleetwood Mac*, and the rest are consistent with the style of the later hits. *Buckingham Nicks* lacks some of the polish of the Fleetwood Mac records, its songwriting is not as consistent overall, but it is of a piece with some of the most popular music of the 1970s. (After achieving fame with Fleetwood Mac, Buckingham and Nicks acquired *Buckingham Nicks* from Polydor, but as of the spring of 1995 they still had not released it on CD.) —*William Ruhlmann*

○ **Law and Order** / Oct. 1981 / Asylum ✦✦✦✦
Lindsey Buckingham's talents as guitarist, arranger, and producer were particularly well suited to Fleetwood Mac, a band in which he was only one among three songwriters whose material complemented each other's. As a solo artist, Buckingham retains his strengths, but he encounters a form-over-substance problem. The seven songs he wrote for his debut album come across as sketches, musical pieces for which he has constructed interesting guitar riffs and the occasional sonic effect, plus a lyric tag—"Trouble," "That's How We Do It In L.A." But they have not been fleshed out into full-fledged songs, perhaps because Buckingham hasn't much interest in lyrics, or because he declines to use more than one or two of his ideas per tune. On the eclectic choice of covers ("September Song," "A Satisfied Mind"), Buckingham at least has fully composed and written pieces to work with, but he embalms them in his production techniques. As such, *Law And Order* comes off as a high-quality demo of largely unfinished material. (Nevertheless, "Trouble" became a Top 10 single.) —*William Ruhlmann*

Go Insane / Jul. 1984 / Asylum ✦✦✦
Lindsey Buckingham's second album, like his first, *Law And Order*, was a triumph of studio wizardry over songwriting craft. Buckingham's work was ear-catching, but once he'd gotten your attention with some gimmicky sound effect or busy arrangement, he had very little to tell you. The exception was the album's most ambitious piece, the closing track, "D.W. Suite," on which Buckingham, always strongly influenced by the Beach Boys, took on what sounded like an elaborate tribute to Beach Boy Dennis Wilson, who died while the album was being made. The title track, which also had massed choral sounds (all made by Buckingham) reminiscent of a Fleetwood Mac track, became a Top 40 hit, but the album lacked the accessibility to make it more than a moderate seller, and at least at this point it appeared that Buckingham's solo albums were going to serve as laboratory experiments in which he tried out new musical ideas before bringing them to greater popular attention through Fleetwood Mac. —*William Ruhlmann*

● **Out of the Cradle** / Jun. 16, 1992 / Reprise ✦✦✦✦
Lindsey Buckingham quit Fleetwood Mac after the release of their *Tango in the Night* album in 1987 and spent the subsequent five years working on his first post-Mac solo album, *Out of the Cradle*. Perhaps because he was now focused on his solo career, Buckingham reined in the experimental style of his first two albums, producing more conventional, accessible material, much of it similar to his later work with Fleetwood Mac. The inventiveness this time was heard largely in Buckingham's electro-acoustic guitar style, which combined the power of a rock guitarist with the delicacy and precision of a classical nylon-string player. Perhaps the biggest difference from his previous solo work, however, was that Buckingham actually wrote a group of songs that were about something, not just riffs full of aural tricks. Unfortunately, Buckingham had never fully established himself in the public mind as a separate entity apart from Fleetwood Mac, so taking eight years between solo albums made *Out of the Cradle* a tough sell. Which means that, although this is his most listenable solo album, not many people heard it. —*William Ruhlmann*

The Buckinghams

Group, Pop/Rock
If everyone on the northwest side of Chicago who claims to have hung out with the Buckinghams during their heyday had faithfully bought all their releases, the rock group might have sold more records than the Beatles.
Popular attractions while still in high school, the quintet changed its name from the Pulsations to the Buckinghams to reflect the British Invasion craze and signed with Chicago's USA Records in 1966. Backing Dennis Tufano's buoyant lead vocals with prominent harmonies and punchy soul-styled brass, the

group came across the wistful "Kind of a Drag," and in short order, the Buckinghams had a million-selling pop chart-topper on their hands. They quickly graduated to recording for Columbia.

As long as songwriter Jim Holvay supplied more material of the same high quality as "Kind of a Drag," the Buckinghams were sitting pretty. Holvay cowrote "Don't You Care," "Hey Baby (They're Playing Our Song)," and the pseudo-psychedelic "Susan," and they all proved to be major hits for the band. The group's R&B roots surfaced on a vocal adaptation of Cannonball Adderley's jazz standard "Mercy, Mercy, Mercy," their second-biggest hit.

But the Buckinghams' fortunes soon changed drastically—one of the top-selling rock groups of 1967, they managed only one hit after early 1968, and by 1970 the group was kaput. Two original members, guitarist Carl Giammarese and bassist Nick Fortuna, have since revived the Buckinghams for oldies tours. —*Bill Dahl*

● **Mercy Mercy Mercy (A Collection)** / 1991 / Columbia ◆◆◆◆
These mid-'60s hitmakers from Chicago hold up well with their neat blend of pop and soul. All of their hits and more can be found on this 18-song anthology. —*Jeff Tamarkin*

Jeff Buckley

Singer-Songwriter, Folk-Rock
Since he is the son of cult songwriter Tim Buckley, Jeff Buckley faced more expectations and pre-conceived notions than most singer/songwriters. Perhaps it wasn't surprising that Jeff Buckley's music was related to his father's by only the thinnest of margins. Buckley's voice is grand and sweeping, which fits with the mock-operatic grandeur of his Van Morrison-meets-Led Zeppelin music.

Buckley began playing as a high school student in New York. Eventually, he moved to Los Angeles to study music; while he was there, he performed with several jazz and funk bands, as well as playing with Shinehead, a leader in the dancehall reggae movement. A few years later, he moved back to New York, forming Gods & Monsters with the experimental guitarist Gary Lucas. The band became a hip name, yet their life-span was short. Buckley began a solo career playing clubs and coffeehouses, building up a considerable following. Soon, he signed a record deal with Columbia Records, releasing the *Live at Sin-e* EP in November of 1993. It received good reviews, yet they didn't compare to the raves Buckley's full-length debut, 1994's *Grace*, received. Unlike the EP, the album was recorded with a full band, which gave the record textures that surprised some of his long time New York followers. Nevertheless, it made several year-end "Best of 1994" lists and earned him a belated alternative hit, "Last Goodbye," in the spring of 1995. —*Stephen Thomas Erlewine*

Live at Sin-e / 1993 / Columbia ◆◆◆
These five songs, recorded in concert, serve as a good introduction. —*Richard Meyer*

● **Grace** / 1994 / Columbia ◆◆◆◆
Jeff Buckley is many things, but humble isn't one of them. *Grace* is an audacious debut album, filled with sweeping choruses, bombastic arrangements, searching lyrics and, above all, the richly textured voice of Buckley himself, which resembles a cross between Robert Plant, Van Morrison, and his father Tim. And that's a fair starting point for his music: *Grace* sounds like a Led Zeppelin album written by an ambitious folkie with a fondness for lounge jazz. At his best—the soaring title track, "Last Goodbye," and the mournful "Lover, You Should've Come Over"—Buckley's grasp meets his reach with startling results; at its worst, *Grace* is merely promising. —*Stephen Thomas Erlewine*

Tim Buckley

b. Feb. 14, 1947, Washington, DC, **d.** Jun. 29, 1975
Singer-Songwriter, Folk-Rock
Tim Buckley's mournful wail, his synthesis of folk and jazz, and his haunting melodies seemed decidedly out of step with much of the music that was popular at the end of the '60s. Discovered by Frank Zappa-manager Herb Cohen, Buckley was signed to Elektra, where he cut several albums. Two of his best from that period, *Goodbye and Hello* and *Happy Sad*, were produced by ex-Lovin' Spoonful Jerry Yester. In 1970 Buckley moved to Cohen's Straight Records and released *Blue Afternoon*, an album that lived up to its title.

Buckley dropped out after 1971's *Starsailor* and became a taxi driver and chauffeur for a while. He returned with a new direction on *Greetings from L. A.*, which featured a down-and-dirty collection of funk rock. In 1975 Buckley died of an accidental drug over-

dose, mistaking a mix of heroin and morphine for cocaine. —*Rick Clark*

○ **Tim Buckley** / 1966 / Asylum ◆◆◆◆
Buckley's 1966 debut was the most straightforward and folk-rock-oriented of his albums. The material has a lyrical and melodic sophistication that was astounding for a 19-year-old. The pretty, almost precious songs are complemented by appropriately baroque, psychedelic-tinged production. If there was a record that exemplified the '60s Elektra folk-rock sound, this may have been it, featuring production by Elektra owner Jac Holzman and Doors producer Paul Rothchild, Love and Doors engineer Bruce Botnick, and string arrangements by Jack Nitzsche. That's not to diminish the contributions of the band, which included his longtime lead guitarist Lee Underwood and Van Dyke Parks on keyboards. Buckley was still firmly in the singer-songwriter camp on this album, showing only brief flashes of the experimental vocal flights, angst-ridden lyrics, and soul influences that would characterize much of his later work. It's not his most adventurous outing, but it's one of his most accessible, and retains a fragile beauty. —*Richie Unterberger*

○ **Goodbye & Hello** / 1967 / Asylum ◆◆◆◆
With his second album, Buckley began exploring different sonic territory, adding exotic instruments and a distinct, winding jazz influence to his increasingly complex lyrics. —*Stephen Thomas Erlewine*

○ **Dream Letter: Live in London** / Jul. 1968 / Rhino/Bizarre ◆◆◆◆
This live double-disc set captures Buckley's jazzy folk and passionate mega-octave vocal in fine form. Lee Underwood (guitar), David Friedman (vibes), and Danny Thompson (bass) provide empathetic support. —*Rick Clark*

○ **Blue Afternoon** / 1969 / Rhino/Bizarre ◆◆◆◆
Buckley's atmospheric melancholy folk-jazz shines on the first four tracks, "Happy Time," "Chase the Blues Away," "I Must Have Been Blind," and "The River." Those tracks alone make this worth having. —*Rick Clark*

○ **Happy Sad** / 1969 / Asylum ◆◆◆◆
Buckley began to turn toward softer, more introspective, and slightly jazzy tunes on his third record. This album of six lengthy compositions features some of his loveliest songs, including "Strange Feelin'," "Sing a Song for You," and the exuberant, 12-minute "Gypsy Woman." —*Richie Unterberger*

Lorca / 1970 / Asylum ◆◆◆
Tim stunned and, to a rare degree, alienated fans with the dissonant, at times wearying, avant-garde exercises in vocal gymnastics that took up the entire first side of this LP. Side Two was far more accessible, though Buckley's fusion of folk instrumentation with jazzy improvisation on extended compositions continued to take him further away from his folk-rock roots. —*Richie Unterberger*

○ **Starsailor** / 1970 / Rhino/Bizarre ◆◆◆◆
After his beginnings as a gentle, melodic baroque-folk-rocker, Buckley gradually evolved into a downright experimental singer-songwriter who explored both jazz and avant-garde territory. *Starsailor* is the culmination of his experimentation, and alienated far more listeners than it exhilarated upon its release in 1970. Buckley had already begun to delve into jazz fusion on late-'60s records like *Happy Sad*, and explored some fairly "out" acrobatic, quasi-operatic vocals on his final Elektra LP, *Lorca*. With former Mother of Invention Bunk Gardner augmenting Buckley's group on sax and alto flute, Tim applies vocal gymnastics to a set of material that's as avant-garde in its songwriting as its execution. At his most anguished (which is often on this album), he sounds as if his liver is being torn out—slowly. Almost as if to prove he can still deliver a mellow buzz, he throws in a couple of pleasant jazz-pop cuts, including the odd, jaunty French tune "Moulin Rouge." Surrealistic lyrics, heavy on landscape imagery like rivers, skies, suns, and jungle fires, top off a record that isn't for everybody, or even for every Buckley fan, but endures as one of the most uncompromising statements ever made by a singer-songwriter. —*Richie Unterberger*

Greetings from L.A. / 1972 / Rhino/Bizarre ◆◆◆
A grittier rock approach supports Buckley's plunge into eroticism. Buckley's uncaged wailing, plus his lyrical urgency, conveys a great deal of sexual tension and an absence of inner peace. Intense stuff, it's considered by many to be his best. —*Rick Clark*

Sefronia / 1973 / Rhino/Bizarre ♦♦

Look at the Fool / 1974 / Rhino/Bizarre ♦

Best of Tim Buckley / 1983 / Rhino/Bizarre ♦♦♦

Peel Sessions / 1991 / Strange Fruit/Dutch East ♦♦

Recorded in April 1968 for the BBC, these five songs—a short album, or long EP's, worth—show Buckley at his most melodic and intimate. As on his posthumously issued 1968 concert recording *Dream Letter,* the instrumentation is sparser than his Elektra albums. On these sessions, he was backed only by longtime guitarist Lee Underwood and Carter Collins on percussion. This set features songs from his second and third albums, as well as a couple of cuts that didn't make it onto record in the '60s. Highlighted by a 10-minute medley of "Hallucinations" and "Troubadour," it's a worthwhile addition to the Buckley canon. —*Richie Unterberger*

Live At The Troubadour 1969 / 1994 / Rhino/Bizarre ♦♦♦

A previously unreleased, recently unearthed recording that catches Buckley at the time he began to incorporate jazz-influenced vocal improvisation and dense, impressionistic lyrics into his recordings. Backed by a small combo, it features loose numbers with bloodcurdling vocal scatting and instrumental jamming. The nine tracks on this 78-minute disc are mostly drawn from his *Lorca* and *Blue Afternoon* albums and include two previously unavailable songs. —*Richie Unterberger*

Buffalo Springfield

Group, Rock & Roll, Country-Rock, Folk-Rock

Few American groups have produced a wealth of talent like that of Buffalo Springfield. The group's formation is the stuff of legend: driving on Sunset Boulevard in Los Angeles, Stephen Stills and Richie Furay spotted a hearse that Stills was sure belonged to Neil Young, a Canadian he had crossed paths with earlier. Indeed it was, and with the addition of fellow hearse passenger and Canadian Bruce Palmer on bass and ex-Dillard Dewey Martin on drums, the cluster of ex-folkies determined, as the Byrds had just done, to become a rock & roll band.

Over a 19-month period, during 1967 and 1968, Buffalo Springfield released three impressive albums. Their debut, including their sole big hit (Stills' "For What It's Worth"), established them as the best folk-rock band in the land bar the Byrds, though the Springfield were a bit more folk and country-oriented. The second, *Again,* is their masterpiece, as the group expanded their folk-rock base into tough hard rock and psychedelic orchestration. Possessing three strong songwriters with distinctly different yet complementary styles—Stills, Young, and Furay (the last of whom didn't begin writing until the second LP)—they also had strong and often conflicting egos, particularly Stills and Young. The group, which held almost infinite promise, rearranged their lineup several times, Young leaving the group for periods and Palmer fighting deportation, until disbanding in 1968. Their final album, although it contained some excellent material, clearly shows the group fragmenting into solo directions.

Even more than the Byrds, Buffalo Springfield's sound was undeniably American, drawing from rock, folk, and country. The intense clash of creative energies, however, finally caused the demise of the band in May of 1968. Stephen Stills went on to Crosby, Stills & Nash. Neil Young joined that group briefly for *Déjà Vu,* then went on to pursue an erratic solo career with periods of great success and brilliant music. After Springfield, Jim Messina and Richie Furay founded the country-rock group Poco. After Poco, Messina recorded a string of hits during the '70s with Kenny Loggins, as Loggins & Messina. —*Rick Clark & Richie Unterberger*

Buffalo Springfield / 1967 / Atco ♦♦♦

Their strong debut contains the Stephen Stills classic "For What It's Worth" and Neil Young's "Nowadays Clancy Can't Even Sing." "Sit Down I Think I Love You" and "Go and Say Goodbye" are also highlights. —*Rick Clark*

☆ **Buffalo Springfield Again** / 1967 / Atco ♦♦♦♦♦

On what is by far their best effort, Stills, Furay, and Young each contribute some great songs: the hits "Bluebird," "Mr. Soul," and "Rock & Roll Woman," plus standouts like "A Child's Claim to Fame," "Hung Upside Down," "Broken Arrow," "Everydays," and "Expecting to Fly." Essential stuff for any good rock & roll collection. —*Rick Clark*

Last Time Around / 1968 / Atco ♦♦♦

Their last album showcases a couple of gems in Furay's "Kind Woman" and Young's "On the Way Home." —*Rick Clark*

● **Best of Buffalo Springfield . . . Retrospective** / 1969 / Atco ♦♦♦♦

This is a decent sampler for the uninitiated. It contains all their hits and some key album tracks but isn't comprehensive enough to be essential. —*Rick Clark*

● **Buffalo Springfield [Collection]** / 1973 / Atco ♦♦♦♦

Not to be confused with their self-titled debut album, this double LP, which can still be found without too much hassle, is clearly the best Springfield compilation, at least until the overdue day when a box set appears that includes everything recorded by this superb band. It does miss some good songs, especially from the first album, but zeroes in on their very best work, and includes a nine-minute version of "Bluebird" available nowhere else, as well as excellent liner notes. —*Richie Unterberger*

★ **Buffalo Springfield / Neil Young** / Atco ♦♦♦♦♦

Stampede / Bootleg ♦♦♦

The group were nearly set to release a record of this name as their second LP, going as far as to take a cover photo. Despite rumors to the contrary, it seems as though the album was never finished, and that some of the material originally intended for it did actually appear on their later LPs. But the myth of an entire lost Springfield record inspired several bootlegs of the same name, containing outtakes from their early sessions. These outtakes, mostly written by Stills, may not constitute an actual lost album, but they're by and large superb nonetheless. "Neighbor, Don't You Worry," "We'll See," "My Kind Of Love," and "Baby Don't Scold Me" (the last of which briefly appeared on early pressings of the first Springfield LP) are all first-rate, charging folk-rock that would have fit in well on the group's debut album. There are also considerably different alternate takes of Young's "Do I Have To Come Right Out And Say It" and "Down To The Wire"; one version of the latter did appear on Neil's *Decade* collection. This studio material is usually packaged with interesting acoustic, solo Stills and Young demos from the early Springfield era, as well as live material from an early 1967 high school show—marginal fidelity, excellent performances. Not a lost grail, the *Stampede* collection is nonetheless necessary for Springfield fans and highly enjoyable on its own merits. —*Richie Unterberger*

Buffalo Tom

Group, Alternative Pop/Rock

When they released their first album in 1989, the Boston-based trio Buffalo Tom was written off as Dinosaur Jr. junior. Admittedly, their debut was in debt to J Mascis's thundering guitar and folk-tinged songs and it didn't help that Mascis produced the record, either. Over time, Buffalo Tom stripped away their grungier influences and developed into a straight-ahead rock group of the early '90s, capable of throttling rockers and beautiful ballads.

Composed of guitarist/vocalist Bill Janovitz, bassist/vocalist Chris Colbourn, and drummer Tom Maginnis, Buffalo Tom began to develop their own style with their second album, 1990's *Birdbrain,* which featured a noticeable improvement in songwriting. In 1992, Buffalo Tom released *Let Me Come Over,* a gritty set of driving rock and achingly melancholy ballads; several of its tracks became alternative radio staples, including the gorgeous ballad "Taillights Fade." Despite an increased amount of critical praise and some radio airplay, the album didn't sell. The follow-up, 1993's *Big Red Letter Day,* featured a more polished, radio-ready production, but the album received only a small push from radio and MTV. "Soda Jerk," the first single from the album, became a minor alternative radio and MTV hit. After a year-long tour, the group returned in the summer of 1995 with *Sleepy-Eyed,* a return to the more direct sound of *Let Me Come Over.* —*Stephen Thomas Erlewine*

Buffalo Tom / 1989 / SST ♦♦♦

Birdbrain / 1990 / Beggars Banquet ♦♦♦

This well-produced, eccentric batch of underground rock featured "Sunflower Suit." —*Dan Heilman*

● **Let Me Come Over** / 1992 / Beggars Banquet ♦♦♦♦

With *Let Me Come Over,* Buffalo Tom comes into its own, producing a remarkably strong album filled with exceptional songwriting. The Dinosaur Jr. comparisons are no longer accurate; now, the band sounds slightly like R.E.M. crossed with the Replacements, but that's just a starting point—the band has carved out their own brand of guitar-heavy rock & roll, somewhere between college-rock and traditional, classic rock. Buffalo Tom proves equally adept at pulling off the driving "Staples" and "Mountains of Your

Head," the majestic folk-rock of "Mineral," the ballads "Larry," "Frozen Lake," and the gorgeous "Taillights Fade," which is a masterpiece. *Let Me Come Over* is the breakthrough album from one of America's best rock & roll bands of the 1990s. —*Stephen Thomas Erlewine*

○ **Big Red Letter Day** / 1993 / Beggars Banquet ✦✦✦✦
Following the excellent *Let Me Come Over, Big Red Letter Day* features a slightly more polished production, but it doesn't diminish the band's increasingly powerful songwriting and forceful rock & roll. Buffalo Tom is America's best mainstream rock band, but is still undeservedly stuck on its fringes, as *Big Red Letter Day* proves. —*Stephen Thomas Erlewine*

Sleepy Eyed / 1995 / East West ✦✦✦
Retreating from the slick studio production of *Big Red Letter Day*, Buffalo Tom's last shot at the big-time is a stripped-down, driving folk-rock record. By now, the group has removed most of its noisier tendencies, preferring to rock with the beat instead of against it. The simplicity of the sonics makes a good background for the lyrics, which are some of the group's best to date. "Summer" and "Tangerine" prove that the group not only has more graceful lyrics than Soul Asylum, their hooks are stronger and their playing is tighter—in short, it rocks harder. —*Stephen Thomas Erlewine*

Jimmy Buffett

b. Dec. 25, 1946, Pascagoula, MS
Country-Rock, Singer-Songwriter, Pop/Rock
Singer/songwriter Jimmy Buffett has translated his easy going Gulf Coast persona into more than just a successful recording career—he has expanded into clothing, nightclubs, and literature. But the basis of the business empire that keeps him on the *Fortune* magazine list of highest-earning entertainers is his music.

Buffett moved to Nashville to try to make it in country music in the late '60s. Signed to Barnaby, he released one album, *Down to Earth* (1970), the single from which, a socially conscious song called, "The Christian?," suggested he might be more at home protesting in Greenwich Village. (Barnaby "lost" his second album, *High Cumberland Jubilee*, though they would find it and release it after he became successful.) Instead, he moved to Key West, FL, where he gradually evolved the beach bum character and tropical folk-rock style that would endear him to millions.

Signing to ABC-Dunhill Records (later absorbed by MCA), Buffett achieved notoriety but not much else with his second (released) album, *White Sport Coat and a Pink Crustacean* (1973), which featured a song called, "Why Don't We Get Drunk" ("...and screw?," goes the chorus). Buffett revealed a more thoughtful side on *Living and Dying in 3/4 Time* (1974), with its song of marital separation "Come Monday," his first singles chart entry. But it took the Top Ten song "Margaritaville" and the album in which it was featured, *Changes in Latitudes, Changes in Attitudes* (1977), to capture Buffett's tropical worldview and, for a while, turn him into a pop star.

By the start of the '80s, Buffett's yearly albums had stopped going gold, and he briefly tried the country market again. But by the middle of the decade, it was his yearly summer tours that were filling his bank account, as a steadily growing core of Sun Belt fans he dubbed "Parrotheads" made his concerts into Mardi Gras-like affairs. Buffett launched his Margaritaville line of clothes and opened the first of his Margaritaville clubs in Key West. He also turned to fiction writing, landing on the best-seller lists.

His recording career, meanwhile, languished, though a hits compilation sold millions, a 1990 live album, *Feeding Frenzy*, went gold, and a 1992 boxed set retrospective, *Boats Beaches Bars & Ballads*, became one of the best-selling boxed sets ever. Buffett finally got around to making a new album in 1994, when *Fruitcakes* became one of his fastest-selling records. It was followed in 1995 by *Barometer Soup*. —*William Ruhlmann*

Down to Earth / 1970 / Barnaby ✦✦
On his debut album, Buffett lands squarely in the Kris Kristofferson school of thoughtful Nashville singer-songwriters, notably challenging religious zealots and right-wingers in "The Christian?" One of his earliest story songs, "The Captain And The Kid," is also included. —*William Ruhlmann*

A White Sport Coat & a Pink Crustacean / Jun. 1973 / MCA ✦✦✦
Buffett was beginning to put in place his folk/rock/country sound and his laid-back, humorous, hedonistic persona with this album, which features later concert favorites like "Why Don't We Get Drunk [and screw]" and "Grapefruit—Juicy Fruit." —*William Ruhlmann*

Living & Dying in 3/4 Time / Feb. 1974 / MCA ✦✦✦
Jimmy Buffett was already on the second edition of his Coral Reefer Band by the time his third album rolled around. He had also firmly established his Gulf Coast beach-bum/poet persona, but he hadn't written a classic song until "Come Monday," which put him, and the album, on the map. —*William Ruhlmann*

A-1-A / Dec. 1974 / MCA ✦✦✦
A little hardworking for a beachcomber, Buffett released a second album in 1974. It was his most perfect evocation of noncareerist hedonism yet, even if its most telling song, "A Pirate Looks at Forty," was unusually thoughtful for a party animal. —*William Ruhlmann*

Rancho Deluxe / 1975 / United Artists ✦✦✦
This is the soundtrack to a movie written by Buffett's brother-in-law, novelist Thomas McGuane. Buffett appeared in the movie and sang "Livingston Saturday Night" with slightly more risque lyrics than he would later in his career. —*William Ruhlmann*

High Cumberland Jubilee (1972) / 1976 / Barnaby ✦✦
When Buffett's first album, *Down To Earth*, stiffed, Barnaby let him record this follow-up, then "lost" it. It was finally released after his career started to take off in 1976, but is still a minor effort. —*William Ruhlmann*

○ **Havana Daydreamin'** / Jan. 1976 / MCA ✦✦✦✦
Buffett's best overall collection of songs yet bears the influence of Steve Goodman, who wrote "This Hotel Room" and cowrote "Woman Goin' Crazy on Caroline Street." But a personal favorite is Buffett's own "My Head Hurts, My Feet Stink, and I Don't Love Jesus." —*William Ruhlmann*

○ **Changes in Latitudes, Changes In Attitudes** / Jan. 1977 / MCA ✦✦✦✦
Buffett's biggest selling regular release contains his biggest hit single, "Margaritaville." It's also a peak in terms of songwriting, both for the artist himself and in his covers of the work of Steve Goodman and Jesse Winchester, among others. Funny, wistful, and celebratory, the album is the definitive statement of Buffett's world view. —*William Ruhlmann*

○ **Son of a Son of A Sailor** / Mar. 1978 / MCA ✦✦✦✦
If this album was a slight step down from its predecessor, it was almost equally successful commercially, and it contained its share of terrific material, notably the uptempo hit "Cheeseburger in Paradise" and one of Buffett's older songs, "Livingston Saturday Night." —*William Ruhlmann*

You Had to Be There / Oct. 1978 / MCA ✦✦
Buffett has made most of his considerable fortune out of the following he's developed through his concerts, and this double-record live set recorded before an enthusiastic crowd at the Fox in Atlanta serves notice of what's to come. It also serves as a consistent best-of for the artist, most of whose albums are uneven. —*William Ruhlmann*

Volcano / Aug. 1979 / MCA ✦✦
The album that should have consolidated Buffett's status as a major star after his last two hits instead started him down the road to cult status, largely because songs like "Fins" and the title track, which are entertaining enough in concert, aren't really strong material, and they're the best things here. —*William Ruhlmann*

Coconut Telegraph / Feb. 1981 / MCA ✦✦
More Caribbean rhythms and weak jokes—"The Weather Is Here, Wish You Were Beautiful"—plus, in Mac McAnally's "It's My Job," a whiff of the elitism always implied in Buffett's stance. —*William Ruhlmann*

Somewhere over China / Jan. 1982 / MCA ✦✦
Perhaps inevitably, Buffett begins to descend from self-satisfaction to self-pity on tracks like "Where's The Party" and "I Heard I Was In Town." Here and on such tracks as "If I Could Just Get It On Paper," it's apparent that the fast life is losing its charm for the singer. —*William Ruhlmann*

One Particular Harbour / Sep. 1983 / MCA ✦✦
Another collection for the cult, including the humorous "We Are The People Our Parents Warned Us About" and a cover of Van Morrison's "Brown Eyed Girl." —*William Ruhlmann*

Riddles in the Sand / Sep. 1984 / MCA ✦✦
Buffett, who never cared for country music, hires Nashville insider Jimmy Bowen as his producer, goes to Fan Fair, puts on a cowboy hat on his album cover, and scores country hits with cheating songs like "Who's The Blonde Stranger?" Actually, things haven't

changed that much, it's just a marketing move. — *William Ruhlmann*

Last Mango in Paris / Jun. 1985 / MCA ✦✦✦
Buffett's rapid recording schedule tended to outrun his muse in the late '70s and early '80s, resulting in some uneven albums with occasional good songs. This time he came up with a far more consistent collection, including three entries on the country charts: "Gypsies in the Palace," "If the Phone Doesn't Ring, It's Me," and "Please Bypass This Heart." — *William Ruhlmann*

● **Songs You Know by Heart** / Oct. 1985 / MCA ✦✦✦✦
If anybody ever needed a compilation, it is Jimmy Buffett, who by this time had put out 14 new studio albums in 15 years but only managed to accumulate a handful of memorable songs among them. And just about all of them are here. Unless you're a Parrothead, this will be all you'll need of Jimmy Buffett. — *William Ruhlmann*

Floridays / Jun. 1986 / MCA ✦✦
If *Mango* suggested a new interest in recording and a new care in songwriting, *Floridays* marked a scuttling of such efforts. The lead-off track, "I Love The Now," was co-written by Buffett and Carrie Fisher, which just goes to show that good novelists don't necessarily write good songs together. — *William Ruhlmann*

Hot Water / Jun. 1988 / MCA ✦✦
The best song is Jesse Winchester's oldie "L'Air De La Louisiane." "Smart Woman (In A Real Short Skirt)" did not restore Buffett to the favor of feminists. And you don't get on the radio by complaining that they don't play your "Homemade Music" because there's something wrong with them. — *William Ruhlmann*

Off to See the Lizard / Jun. 1989 / MCA ✦✦
By this point, record making was starting to become just a small part of Jimmy Buffett, Inc., and this is a piece of musical product, efficiently produced and highly consumable, but not very nourishing. Not surprisingly, Buffett didn't bother to make another studio album for five years. — *William Ruhlmann*

Feeding Frenzy / Oct. 1990 / MCA ✦✦
Buffett's real business is summer touring, and this second live outing was overdue. It also makes a good sampler of his work since his last one, but unfortunately even carefully selected, the later work is inferior to the early work. — *William Ruhlmann*

○ **Boats, Beaches, Bars & Ballads** / May 1992 / MCA ✦✦✦✦
This four-disc, 72-track anthology is essential for "Parrotheads" (Buffett fans) who don't miss his concerts but aren't so hardcore that they have to own every single thing Buffett ever released. Each disc revolves around a theme (Boats, Beaches, Bars, Ballads). All of his hits and popular album tracks are here, as well as some previously unreleased material. The box includes the Parrothead Handbook, a 64-page booklet that provides a well-assembled collection of photos, reflections from Buffett, and explanations of his songs. The sound on this set is first-rate. — *Rick Clark*

Before the Beach / May 25, 1993 / MCA ✦✦
Yet another reissue of Buffett's first two Barnaby albums, this time released on his own record label, on one CD, and minus the controversial "The Christian?" — *William Ruhlmann*

Fruitcakes / May 24, 1994 / MCA ✦✦
On his first new studio album in five years, Buffett starts out talking about an investment banker, an appropriate concern for this sun-bleached entrepreneur. Soon enough, the sprung calypso rhythms kick in, and you can imagine the Parrotheads swaying and chuckling along, especially when Buffett indulges in the kind of comic raps common to his stage shows. He also covers the Grateful Dead's "Uncle John's Band," one more appropriation in his careful observation of that band's marketing plan. There's also a cover of the Kinks' "Sunny Afternoon," a wealthy man's lament, which is uncomfortably on target. But even with half a decade to come up with original material, Buffett hasn't gotten much to add to his usual sun-and-sand philosophy, and for all his millions he remains a pleasant, but distinctly minor, singer-songwriter. — *William Ruhlmann*

Jimmy Buffett's Margaritaville Cafe-New Orleans / 1995 / Margaritaville

The Buggles
Group, New Wave
The short-lived synth-pop duo Buggles (formed 1979) earned the distinction of having the first video ever played on MTV, the international hit "Video Killed the Radio Star" (#40). Made up of Geoff Downes and Trevor Horn (b. Jul. 15, 1949), Buggles joined up with Yes in 1980 and released *Drama*. Horn became a very successful techno-pop producer (*Frankie Goes to Hollywood*, *Seal*), while Downes joined the art-pop supergroup Asia. — *Rick Clark*

● **The Age of Plastic** / 1980 / Island ✦✦✦✦
A debut techno-pop effort for *Drama*-era Yes members Trevor Horn and Geoff Downes, it includes "Video Killed the Radio Star," which MTV appropriately used to christen its channel. — *Rick Clark*

Adventures in Modern Recording / 1982 / EMI ✦✦

Sandy Bull
b. 1941, New York, NY
Folk, Folk-Rock
Long before Ry Cooder, Leo Kottke, Richard Thompson, and others were impressing us with their ability to hop from genre to genre, Sandy Bull glided from classical and jazz to ethnic music and rock & roll with grace and verve on his first two albums. Accompanied on his first two albums by renowned jazz drummer Billy Higgins, Bull produced some of the first extended instrumental compositions for guitar that incorporated elements of folk, jazz, and Indian and Arabic-influenced dronish modes. Not "rock" by any stretch of the imagination, it's nevertheless easy to see that it could have had an influence on the rock musicians who began incorporating eclectic and Middle Eastern sensibilities into their music a few years later. After his debut, Bull expanded his arsenal from the acoustic guitar and banjo to include oud, bass, and electric guitar. After his second album, however, his recordings were less focused and less impressive. In the '70s, he dropped out of music altogether due to drug problems, although he began recording again in the late '80s. — *Richie Unterberger*

Fantasias for Guitar & Banjo / Aug. 1963 / Vanguard ✦✦✦
Bull's debut is most notable for the side-long cut "Blend," a 22-minute track on a folk (more or less) album in the days when that just wasn't done outside of classical and jazz records. The second side features imaginative interpretations of traditional gospel and Southern mountain tunes, as well as a work by German composer Carl Orff. — *Richie Unterberger*

● **Inventions for Guitar & Banjo** / 1965 / Vanguard ✦✦✦✦
On his second and best album, Bull added more instruments and a bit of electricity. The centerpiece of the record is "Blend II"; like "Blend" from his first album, it is a melange (somewhat more electric in tone) of folk, jazz, and Middle Eastern music, this time 24 minutes' worth. Also included on this 54-minute LP are two versions (electric and acoustic) of a Bach passage, a composition from the 14th century (Guillaume de Machaut's "Triple Ballade"), and Luiz Bonfa's "Manha de Carnival." A heavily reverbed (with drums), extended version of Chuck Berry's "Memphis, Tennessee" closes the set with an unexpected blast of rock & roll. — *Richie Unterberger*

E Pluribus Unum / 1967 / Vanguard ✦✦

Demolition Derby / 1972 / Vanguard ✦✦✦

Cindy Bullens
b. 1953
Pop/Rock
A rock singer/songwriter who appeared in *Grease* and sang backup with Elton John before cutting three albums of her own. — *William Ruhlmann*

● **Desire Wire** / 1978 / United Artists ✦✦✦✦
One of the great lost rock albums of the '70s, Bullens' debut release is full of tough, passionate, incredibly catchy rock & roll played to the hilt and sung with fire. Bullens followed it up with *Steal the Night* in 1979. Ten years later, she made *Cindy Bullens*, and it's almost as good, although no one noticed. So life is unfair. Search those used-record stores for any of them. — *William Ruhlmann*

Steal the Night / Dec. 1979 / Casablanca ✦✦✦
Cindy Bullens exhibited an unfortunate talent for hooking up with record companies that were on the way out, starting with United Artists and continuing with the classic '70s boom-and-bust label, Casablanca, a year later. Which is to say that Bullens's second album, *Steal the Night*, got lost at the end of 1979. Though not quite as impressive as her debut, it was another record full of high-energy guitar-based pop-rock, some of which, given the time of re-

lease, could have passed for new wave or power-pop; however, Bullens was a mainstream rocker at heart, and her main points of reference were the early-'60s girl groups and the British Invasion. Here was a performer who had a good, punchy voice, played guitar as well as anybody, and wrote serviceable pop songs with hooks; it's a shame she didn't make it. — *William Ruhlmann*

Cindy Bullens / 1989 / MCA ✦✦
Cindy Bullens returned after 10 years with her third shot at stardom, supported by some high-quality help: Bob Clearmountain, perhaps the top rock & roll producer/mixer of the day, was behind the board and multi-instrumentalist David Mansfield (of the Rolling Thunder Revue and the Alpha Band) was leading the musicians. Bullens herself had matured. Now a full-bodied, if less appealingly frantic singer, she conveyed more passion (and a little less excitement) than she had 10 years before, and she still knew how to rock. If *Cindy Bullens* was her least impressive effort, despite boasting powerful playing and state-of-the-art sound, it was because Bullens's songs had a few too many borrowings in the riffs, a few too many clichés in the lyrics. Nevertheless, Bullens remained an appealing rocker who shoulda been a contender. — *William Ruhlmann*

Bulletboys

Group, Hard Rock, Heavy Metal
Led by former Ratt vocalist Marq Torien, this L.A. metal band also included ex-King Kobra guitarist Mick Sweda, bassist Lonnie Vincent, and drummer Jimmy D'Anda. Their style was strongly influenced by bands such as AC/DC and Van Halen, later going in a bluesier direction. Torien's personality often drew comparisons to David Lee Roth. The group had a couple of MTV hits off their self-titled debut but faded away after their second album. Song titles like "Do Me Raw," "Hard As a Rock," and "Kissin' Kitty" give a fairly accurate impression of the band's worldview. — *Steve Huey*

● **Bulletboys** / 1988 / Warner Brothers ✦✦✦✦
Fine, fine hard rock with a little sleaze, LA-style, this debut album that put them on the heavy metal map features a great cover of "For the Love of Money," by the O'Jays. — *John Book*

Freakshow / 1991 / Warner Brothers ✦✦✦
Heavy metal that brings back the old style of Van Halen, it has some bluesy material and great guitar work. A bit more serious than the debut, and musically a lot tighter, there's lots of good songs on this one, including the single "Saint Christopher." — *John Book*

Za-Za / 1993 / Warner Brothers ✦✦

Sonny Burgess

b. 1931
Rockabilly
Sonny Burgess is one of the wildest rockers to record for the legendary Sun label in Memphis. He and his band the Pacers came out of Newport, AR, with a hard-rocking style that, unlike that of most rockabillies, owed little to nothing in the way of a stylistic debt to country music. With his red-dyed hair, matching stage suit and guitar, and wild stage performances, Burgess and the Pacers made mincemeat of the competition on many of the early-'50s rock & roll package tours. Though his Sun releases never brought him much in the way of commercial success, Sonny's recordings nonetheless remain landmarks of the early rockabilly style. Currently touring and recording with other Memphis alumni in the Sun Rhythm Section, the rockin' flame that is Sonny Burgess refuses to be snuffed out. — *Cub Koda*

○ **We Wanna Boogie** / 1990 / Rounder ✦✦✦✦
If you want a fairly definitive compilation of the Sun material by this minor rockabilly figure, but don't want to go the whole nine yards for the expensive import double CD on Bear Family, this domestic anthology is a recommended alternative. The 13 tracks contain six sides from his '50s singles (including the most noted, "Red Headed Woman" and "My Bucket's Got A Hole In It"), and seven other cuts from the '50s that were unissued at the time. — *Richie Unterberger*

● **The Classic Recordings 1956-1959** / Jul. 1991 / Bear Family ✦✦✦✦
Sonny's complete output for Sun spread over two CDs. Wild and crazed, featuring Burgess's spitfire guitar and booming vocals, and the relentless drive of the Pacers in support. — *Cub Koda*

Solomon Burke

b. 1936, Philadelphia, PA
Soul
Musically and corporeally imposing, Burke was almost as important as he says he was. His account of how he invented soul music is entertaining if fanciful, but even when SB's BS count is lowered, there is no doubt he was present at the creation of '60s soul music—and at least partially responsible for it.

Starting as "Solomon the Boy Wonder Preacher" in Philadelphia, he had been recording for six years when he finally broke through with "Just out of Reach" in 1961. Burke's best recordings probably date from the early '60s, when he was working with producer Bert Berns. Songs like "Cry to Me," "I'm Hanging up My Heart for You," "Goodbye Baby," and "The Price" collectively formed the keynote address for soul music. Some of the arrangements sound unnecessarily ornamented today, but the passion Burke brought to those recordings was that of the Boy Wonder Preacher. Live, he's still impressive, as recent recordings attest. — *Colin Escott*

Solomon Burke / 1962 / Kenwood ✦✦✦
The early hits that made Solomon Burke a new force on the soul scene. His quavering delivery, robust sound, and huge presence had both the emphatic earnestness of gospel and the celebratory spirit of soul. Burke strained, roared, sighed, and exploded on his early hits, telling masterful stories and making each song a total experience. — *Ron Wynn*

Solomon Burke's Greatest Hits / 1962 / Atlantic ✦✦✦
Solomon Burke's booming, magnificent vocals and dramatic approach were particularly effective on a string of great early '60s tracks. The lyrics, production, and setting blended soul and country elements, and Burke was the ideal singer to convey the two genres' similarities. This includes the epic tracks "Everybody Needs Somebody To Love" and "Just Out Of Reach (Of My Empty Arms)." — *Ron Wynn*

○ **The Best of Solomon Burke** / 1965 / Atlantic ✦✦✦✦
This impassioned and gritty soul man's best work from the '60s is here, including "Everybody Needs Somebody to Love" and "Cry to Me." Otis Redding fans especially should own this. — *John Floyd*

Lord We Need a Miracle / 1979 / Savoy ✦✦✦
One-time boy preacher Solomon Burke returned to his gospel roots on this earth-shaking date. There's nothing secular about anything here, from the lyrics to Burke's impassioned, heartfelt cries, shouts, and roars. The only problem was that he'd been away from gospel so long that many in the church community didn't take this album seriously. — *Ron Wynn*

○ **Let Your Love Flow** / Shanachie ✦✦✦✦
Jerry Williams (Swamp Dogg) produced an excellent late-'70s soul session for the legendary Solomon Burke on the tiny Infinity records label. Williams mixed upbeat numbers with a pronounced Afro-Latin beat and confessional country/soul tunes emphasizing Burke's trademark song sermons. The music was much too raw and rural for the pseudo-sophisticated big city radio set, but Southern soul loyalists treasured it. Shanachie's CD reissue includes two bonus cuts, and its digital sound displays the strength, clarity and power of Burke's voice. Shanachie gets high praises for reissuing the album but low marks for the horrendous misspelling of Burke's name all over the CD. — *Ron Wynn*

○ **A Change Is Gonna Come** / 1986 / Rounder ✦✦✦✦
While he wasn't scoring chart hits anymore, Burke hadn't lost any of his prowess by the mid-'80s. He cut one of the decade's great soul statements for Rounder in 1985. It's available on CD, and should be a revelation for anyone unaware of Burke's singing and performing zeal. His oral narratives were as smashing and memorable as his vocals, and the assembled band included a super three-piece horn section led by alto, tenor and baritone saxophonist Foots Samuel. This was no nostalgia trip, but a contemporary soul journey that retains its appeal years after its initial release. — *Ron Wynn*

○ **You Can Run But You Can't Hide** / 1987 / Mr. R&B ✦✦✦✦
You Can Run But You Can't Hide collects twenty tracks from Burke's formative years at Apollo, recorded between 1955-59. The material tends to be more pop-oriented than his classic Atlantic sides, but his singing is nearly as impressive as it is on his hits. — *Stephen Thomas Erlewine*

○ **The Bishop Rides South** / 1988 / Charly ✦✦✦✦
When Burke left Atlantic, he signed with New York City's Bell Records. Bell wisely sent Solomon down to Muscle Shoals. Two 1969 hits, covers of "Uptight Good Woman" and "Proud Mary," resulted, along with a slew of classic Southern soul covers. —*Rob Bowman*

● **Home in Your Heart** / 1992 / Rhino ✦✦✦✦
Home in Your Heart—The Best of Solomon Burke is a 41-track two-disc set that covers Burke's Atlantic recordings from 1961 to 1968. Seventeen of those tracks charted. All are superior examples of country-soul and gospel-soul. —*Rob Bowman*

T-Bone Burnette

b. 1945, Fort Worth, TX
Singer-Songwriter, Roots-Rock, Folk-Rock
T-Bone Burnett may not be a household name, but he has managed to attain a kind of creative freedom that many more successful artists never see. A virtual Renaissance man, Burnette has produced some great albums for Bruce Cockburn, Los Lobos, Elvis Costello, and Marshall Crenshaw. As a singer/songwriter, he has released a number of albums that have made him somewhat of a critic's darling.

Burnett first gained notoriety with the Alpha Band (after a stint in Bob Dylan's Rolling Thunder Revue) during the middle and late '70s. Among their three albums, *Spark in the Dark* most successfully sidestepped the band's tendency for heavy-handed Christian moralizing. That preachy quality has surfaced periodically in Burnett's solo work; nevertheless, it is Burnett's intelligent spiritual grounding that has also informed his artistry's many strengths.

Stylistically, Burnett has primarily drawn from folk, country, and roots-rock, but he has infused other elements, creating some provocative combinations of music. —*Rick Clark*

○ **Truth Decay** / 1980 / Takoma ✦✦✦✦
The first album after his stint with the Alpha Band was a great mix of Texas roadhouse R&B/blues-based rock, with hard-folk acoustic instrumental augmentation. Thematically, *Truth Decay* was a refreshing departure from some of the Alpha Band's relentless moralizing. Burnette still took some heavy-handed shots on songs like "Madison Ave" and "House of Mirrors," but the presence of tracks like the gritty rocker "Boomerang," "Talk Talk Talk Talk," and "Love at First Sight" makes this a must-own for lovers of Dylanish rock. —*Rick Clark*

Trap Door [EP] / 1982 / Warner Brothers ✦✦✦
From his clever reading of the Marilyn Monroe standard "Diamonds Are a Girl's Best Friend," to stunning folk-rock originals like "Hold on Tight" and "I Wish You Could Have Seen Her Dance," to the thoughtful closer "Trap Door," this EP is Burnette's most consistently satisfying release. Too bad it wasn't a full-length album. Too bad it's not out on CD yet. —*Rick Clark*

Proof through the Night / 1983 / Demon ✦✦✦
Truth Decay and *Trap Door* had earned Burnette loads of critical praise, but this follow-up featured strong performances (by an all-star lineup) and impressive production, although tracks like "Hefner and Disney" and "The Sixties" were smug, overreaching concept pieces (recalling the Alpha Band's later work) that undermined the overall strength of this release. —*Rick Clark*

○ **Behind the Trap Door** / 1984 / Demon ✦✦✦✦
T-Bone Burnett / 1986 / Dot ✦✦✦
Recorded digitally, straight to two-track, Burnette's self-titled Dot Records release is a heartfelt, low-key affair, featuring flawless country-folk musicianship and a strong collection of originals and covers. Among the highlights are "River of Love," "Shake Yourself Loose," and a version of Tom Waits's "Time." —*Rick Clark*

Talking Animals / 1988 / Columbia ✦✦
● **The Criminal under My Own Hat** / 1992 / Columbia ✦✦✦✦
On his first album in four years, Burnette adopts a spare instrumentation dominated by Marc Ribot's angular guitar work to complement a set of close-to-the-bone lyrics that strip love of sentimentality, castigate politicians and evangelists, and, as the album title (echoed in the song "Criminals") attests, do not spare the songwriter himself. The result is a gripping record in the best tradition of Burnette's mentor, Bob Dylan. —*William Ruhlmann*

Johnny Burnette

b. Mar. 28, 1934, Memphis, TN, **d.** Aug. 14, 1964, Clear Lake, CA
Rockabilly, Pop/Rock

A contemporary of Elvis Presley in the Memphis scene of the mid-'50s, Burnette played a similar brand of fiery, spare wildman rockabilly. With his brother Dorsey (on bass) and guitarist Paul Burlison forming his Rock 'N Roll Trio, he recorded a clutch of singles for Decca in 1956 and 1957 that achieved nothing more than regional success. Featuring the groundbreaking fuzzy tone of Burlison's guitar, Johnny's energetic vocals, and Dorsey's slapping bass, these recordings—highlighted by the first rock & roll version of "Train Kept A-Rollin' "—compare well to the classic Sun rockabilly of the same era. The trio disbanded in 1957, and Johnny found pop success as a teen idol in the early '60s with hits like "You're Sixteen" and "Dreamin.'" Burnette died in a boating accident in 1964. His brother, Dorsey, achieved modest success as a solo act in the early '60s, and Burlison recently resurfaced as a member of the Sun Rhythm Section. —*Richie Unterberger*

○ **Tear It Up** / 1978 / Solid Smoke ✦✦✦✦
Seventeen of their purest rockabilly cuts from their 1956-57 prime. Highlights include "Train Kept A-Rollin'," "Rock Therapy," and "Honey Hush." —*Richie Unterberger*

○ **The Best of Johnny Burnette: You're Sixteen** / 1992 / Capitol ✦✦✦✦
Burnette's best pop-oriented recordings are featured on this collection, including the classic "You're Sixteen." —*Stephen Thomas Erlewine*

● **Rockabilly Boogie** / Bear Family ✦✦✦✦
All of the Johnny Burnette Trio's primal rockabilly records, including the blazing "Train Kept A-Rollin," are collected on this single-disc compilation. The alternate takes might border on overkill, but the original takes remain powerful years after they were recorded. —*Stephen Thomas Erlewine*

Bush

Group, Alternative Pop/Rock
Led by guitarist/vocalist Gavin Rossdale, Bush became the first post-Nirvana British band to hit it big in America. Of course, they became a hit by playing by the grunge rules—they had loud guitars, guttural vocals, stop-start rhythms, and extreme dynamics. Formed in late 1992 by Rossdale, Bush landed an American record deal before they had a British label. *Sixteen Stone*, their debut album produced by Clive Langer and Alan Winstanley (producers of early-'80s hits by Madness and Elvis Costello, among others), was released in late 1994 by Interscope Records. By the end of December, Bush's "Everything Zen" video had landed in MTV's Buzz Bin and the album began to take off; by spring of 1995, the record had gone gold, despite a stack of bad reviews. By that time, the band was successful enough in the U.S. to land a British record deal, although they weren't able to match their American success in the U.K. —*Stephen Thomas Erlewine*

○ **Sixteen Stone** / 1995 / Trauma/Interscope ✦✦✦✦
Bush's grunge-by-the-numbers is certainly well produced. Under the guidance of Clive Langer and Alan Winstanley—the kings of early-'80s British pop—Bush turns in an album that follows all the rules and sounds of American hard rock, specifically Nirvana and Pearl Jam. Their songwriting isn't original, nor is it particularly catchy. What makes "Everything Zen" and "Little Things" memorable is the exact reproduction of all of Nirvana's trademarks, only with a more professional execution—in other words, all the guitars keep rhythm perfectly and Gavin doesn't shred his throat when he sings, he projects from his diaphragm. As far as pop craftsmanship goes, it's actually quite impressive. It would be even more so if they had songs to accompany their sounds. —*Stephen Thomas Erlewine*

Kate Bush

b. Jul. 30, 1958, Plumstead, England
Art-Rock/Progressive-Rock, Pop/Rock
One of the most successful and popular solo female acts of the past 20 years to come out of England, Kate Bush is also one of the most unusual, with her keening vocals and unusually literate and complex body of songs. As a girl, Catherine Bush (b. July 30, 1958 in Bexleyheath, Kent) amused herself playing an organ in the barn behind her parents' house. By the time she was a teenager, Bush was writing songs of her own. A family friend, Ricky Hopper, heard her music and arranged for a demo to be recorded, which brought Bush to the attention of Pink Floyd lead guitarist David Gilmour. By the time Bush was 16, she had been signed to EMI Records, though the company made the decision to bring her

along slowly. She studied dance (with Lindsay Kemp, who also taught David Bowie), mime (with Adam Darius), and voice, and continued writing. By 1977, she was ready to enter the recording studio and begin her formal career, which she did with an original song, "Wuthering Heights," based on material from Emily Brönte's novel.

"Wuthering Heights" rose to number one on the British charts. Bush became an overnight sensation at the age of 17, and was obligated to turn in an accompanying album in short order. This she did with *The Kick Inside*, a collection of material she had written over the previous three years; the album reached the British number three position and sold over a million copies in the United Kingdom. Bush's second album, *Lionheart*, reached number six but didn't achieve anything like the sales totals or critical acclaim of its predecessor. In England during the spring of 1979, Bush embarked on what proved to be the only concert tour of her career to date, playing a series of shows highlighted by 17 costume changes, lots of dancing, and complex lighting. The tour proved both exhausting and financially disastrous and Bush has avoided any but the most limited live concert appearances since, primarily in support of certain charitable causes.

By this time, Bush was established as one of the most challenging and eccentric artists ever to have achieved success in rock music, with a range of sounds and interests that constantly challenged listeners. "Babooshka" (1980) became her first top five single since "Wuthering Heights," and her subsequent album *Never For Ever* entered the British charts at number one in September of 1980. During this period, Bush began co-producing her own work, a decisive step toward refining her sound and also establishing her independence from her record company. Although 1982's *The Dreaming* reached number three, the single "There Goes A Tenner" failed to reach the charts, and most observers felt that Bush had lost her audience. Bush was unfazed by the criticism, and even began taking steps to make herself more independent from her record company by establishing a home studio.

After two years' absence, Bush re-emerged in August of 1985 with "Running Up That Hill," which reached number three on the English charts and became her second biggest-selling single. The accompanying album, *Hounds of Love*, the first record made at her 48-track home studio, debuted on the British charts at the number one position in September of 1985 and remained there for a full month, and soon after "Running Up That Hill" gave Bush her long-awaited American breakthrough, reaching number 30 on *Billboard*'s charts. The changes in her sound and her development as a writer/performer were showcased in the January 1987 best-of collection *The Whole Story*. That same year, Bush won the Best British Female Artist award at the sixth annual BRIT Awards in London. In October of 1989, Bush's first new album in almost four years, *The Sensual World*, reached the British number 2 spot. Bush's next album, *The Red Shoes* (1993), debuted in the American top 30, the first time one of her albums had ever charted that high, and the accompanying singles attracted much attention from the public. —*Bruce Eder*

○ **The Kick Inside** / 1978 / EMI America ✦✦✦✦
Bush's first album is her most unabashedly romantic, the sound of an impressionable and highly precocious teenage singer/songwriter spreading her wings for the first time. "Wuthering Heights" was a monster hit everywhere in the world except America, and it's still an impressive debut nearly 20 years later, but Bush would do better work than this. —*Bruce Eder*

Lionheart / 1978 / EMI America ✦✦✦
Bush's second album was something of a disappointment, lacking the depth and certainty of direction of her debut. The title track is an enigmatic paean to her mother country, "Wow" is a strong vocal workout but somewhat on the obscure side, and the rest is enjoyable and teasing but nowhere near what Bush is capable of. —*Bruce Eder*

Never for Ever / 1980 / EMI America ✦✦✦
Kate Bush returned to form on her third album, which is steeped in images of violence and anger ("Babooshka," "The Wedding List") but also includes fascinating references to classical music ("Delius"). Very finely produced as well. —*Bruce Eder*

The Dreaming / 1982 / EMI America ✦✦
Bush's most daring album is regarded as a failure by most fans, steeped as it is in mystical imagery. On a production level, the album is beautifully made, but the songwriting is only accessible to a relatively small circle of listeners. —*Bruce Eder*

○ **Hounds of Love** / 1985 / EMI America ✦✦✦✦
Bush's strongest album to date marked her breakthrough into the American charts, and yielded a set of dazzling videos. The material ranges from the sensual ("Hounds of Love," "Running Up That Hill"—the latter one of the most sensual recordings ever made) to the mystical ("Hello Earth," "The Morning Fog"). This was also the first album produced by Bush entirely at her own home studio, and the results are spellbinding, the layered instruments recalling the Beatles at the most ornate, but also displaying an exquisite timbral range, bringing out the richness of the individual instruments. Note: The British edition of this and Bush's earlier albums all have significantly better sound than their American editions, and are worth finding as imports. —*Bruce Eder*

● **The Whole Story** / 1986 / EMI America ✦✦✦✦
Bush's first best-of is an excellent compilation/overview, encompassing all her best-known songs (including "Wuthering Heights" with an improved, rerecorded vocal track) up through the major tracks off of *Hounds of Love* and her follow-up single, the haunting and dramatic "Experiment IV." —*Bruce Eder*

○ **The Sensual World** / 1989 / Columbia ✦✦✦✦
The follow-up to *Hounds of Love* is almost its match, a collection of material devoted to Bush's perceptions of love and sensuality. The best track, however, is "This Woman's Work," from a now-forgotten feature film, a beautiful and poignant look at the female psyche at its most gentle and giving. —*Bruce Eder*

○ **This Woman's Work (1978-1990)** / 1990 / EMI ✦✦✦✦
Excellent box collecting all of Bush's work, including obscure B-sides, odd mixes, and other rarities in one place. The notes are skimpy, and some people who already own some of her individual CDs will be unhappy having to duplicate their purchases, but the rarities are fascinating, and because this set is from England, it uses the superior British masters on the 1978-85 albums. (British import) —*Bruce Eder*

The Red Shoes / 1993 / Columbia ✦✦
Something of a step backward for Bush, with not much new ground covered. The beat throughout is pretty strong and catchy, her voice is in excellent form, and if one can ignore an obvious lift from the Spinners ("Rubberband Girl"), the record is enjoyable, although the title song is a little obscure. —*Bruce Eder*

Bushwick Bill

Rap
A one-time member of Houston's the Geto Boys, Bushwick Bill created a stir with his 1992 release *Little Big Man*. It was an unvarnished, sometimes frightening release, with details about the shooting incident that cost him an eye, along with the customary sexism, violent imagery, and outlandish inner city narratives that have long been the group's stock-in-trade. —*Ron Wynn*

Little Big Man / 1992 / Priority ✦✦✦
Bushwick Bill went solo and made an effective debut album, chronicling the shooting incident which cost him an eye in graphic detail. While the Geto Boys were more disgusting than incisive, he actually turned in some coherent message tracks, notably "Letter From KKK" and "Stop Lying." Of course, it wouldn't have been a Bushwick Bill disc without some disgusting tracks, and "Ever So Clear" and "Call Me Crazy" certainly fit that description. —*Ron Wynn*

Billy Butler

b. Philadelphia, PA
Soul
The younger brother of Jerry Butler, Billy Butler wasn't nearly as well known as his sibling, but recorded some fine Chicago soul in the 1960s. Recording for OKeh under producer Carl Davis, Butler's mid-'60s singles were quite similar to labelmates Major Lance and (less obviously) Curtis Mayfield as stellar examples of the finest features of the Chicago sound. Similar to Motown in its full, brassy production, the Chicago brand was earthier, with stronger tinges of gospel, doo-wop, and Latin influences. Nor was Billy terribly similar to his brother Jerry, with a punchier, more uptempo sound. With the backing group the Enchanters, Billy recorded consistently fine singles for OKeh from 1963 to 1966, scoring R&B hits with "I Can't Work No Longer" (1965) and "Right Track" (1966). Butler left OKeh after 1966 and recorded for a variety of labels, denting the R&B charts with the singles "Get on the Chase" (1969) and "Free Yourself" (1971). A songwriter of note, he con-

tributed material to fellow Chi-town soul greats Major Lance, Gene Chandler, and his brother Jerry. —*Richie Unterberger*

● **Right Track** / 1985 / Edsel ◆◆◆◆

Sixteen of the sides Butler cut for the Okeh label during 1963-66; most of them were written by himself or Curtis Mayfield. While not quite in the same league as Mayfield, this is near-classic soul: strong material, production, and backup harmonies on this mix of uptempo numbers and ballads, paced by Billy's fluid vocals. —*Richie Unterberger*

Jerry Butler

b. Dec. 8, 1939, Sunflower County, MS
Soul, R&B

It would be safer to talk about Jerry Butler's careers than about his career. Up from Mississippi, he joined Curtis Mayfield in the Impressions around 1957. They began recording the following year and broke through with *For Your Precious Love*, touted by some as the first soul record. Inevitably, he went solo and fell—or was pushed—into the pop mainstream. Reunited with Mayfield (the latter as a writer), Butler announced his return with *He Will Break Your Heart* in 1960. His subsequent recordings for Vee-Jay trod the turf where pop and R&B meet and are variable; the best are excellent.

After Vee-Jay went broke in 1966, Butler signed with Mercury and was soon placed with the team of Gamble and Huff, who produced him in Philadelphia. Jerry Butler's mellow baritone and the sweet Philly sound were a winning combination, as attested by pop and R&B hits like "Only the Strong Survive" and "Hey, Western Union Man." After the Gamble and Huff deal dissolved in 1970, Butler's career went slowly downhill. Deals with Motown and even Gamble and Huff's Philadelphia International label couldn't deliver the goods. There's something for everyone in Butler's prolificacy, but unfortunately little of it is available to sample.

Jerry Butler has made musical and political noise during the '80s and '90s. He won election to Cook County's Board of Supervisors in the late '80s. Butler also issued recordings on his own Fountain label, but they were hampered by poor distribution. He recorded *Time & Faith* for Urgent, a label distributed by Ichiban, in 1992. Butler has retained his soothing, dynamic sound and ability to sound simultaneously cool and soulful, even if his voice has lost some range and sheen. Mercury released *Iceman: The Mercury Years Anthology* in 1992, the definitive collection of his Polygram tracks, while his earlier work for Vee Jay has also been reissued. Rhino released *The Best of Jerry Butler, 1958–1969* in 1987. —*Colin Escott*

Jerry Butler Esquire / 1959 / Abner ◆◆◆

An early but impressive Jerry Butler album showing his skill at sophisticated R&B, supper club, cabaret, and even pre-rock show tunes. The velvety-smooth, cool, expressive Butler tenor was at its best on these sentimental, sometimes sappy ballads and glided along on the faster tunes, never losing its steam or pace. —*Ron Wynn*

He Will Break Your Heart / 1960 / Chameleon ◆◆◆

A hits package, it focuses on his Vee-Jay recordings, both with and without the Impressions. —*John Floyd*

Folk Songs / 1963 / Vee-Jay ◆◆◆

An interesting concept, and some liberties are being taken with the term "folk." Butler, normally a supper club/sophisticated soul vocalist, tackles some earthier, simpler material and does a reasonably good job. Still, it's clear on many numbers that these aren't his type of songs. —*Ron Wynn*

○ **Ice on Ice** / 1970 / Mercury ◆◆◆

The second of two spectacular albums that were collaborations between Jerry Butler and the Gamble/Huff production combine. It resulted in two more super hits, "Moody Woman" and "What's The Use Of Breaking Up," and was a high water mark for Butler, showing that his smooth, lush sound could work on upbeat and midtempo tunes as easily as on ballads. —*Ron Wynn*

● **The Best of Jerry Butler [Rhino]** / 1987 / Rhino ◆◆◆◆

This excellent 18-song overview of his solo hits and his first recordings with the Impressions could use a few more of his later hits. —*John Floyd*

● **The Best of Jerry Butler [Vee-Jay]** / 1987 / Vee-Jay ◆◆◆◆

Almost the same thing can be said for this one as for many other Jerry Butler hit sets, except that it's probably still available and has been issued on CD. The usual hits are here, and it's a good starting point. —*Ron Wynn*

★ **Iceman: The Mercury Years** / 1992 / PolyGram ◆◆◆◆◆

A glorious 44-song double-disc set, it collects Butler's best Mercury sides, with several previously unreleased songs and alternate mixes. The liner notes are crummy, though. —*John Floyd*

○ **Ice Man** / 1992 / Vee-Jay ◆◆◆◆

Featuring 25 of his Vee-Jay singles, including three hits with the Impressions, *The Ice Man* is the best retrospective of Butler's early years available. —*Stephen Thomas Erlewine*

○ **The Ice Man Cometh** / 1993 / Vee-Jay ◆◆◆◆

Ice on Ice and *The Ice Man Cometh* are two of his best late-'60s albums, produced by the Gamble/Huff team. They've been out of print for years, but snap them up if you can find them. —*John Floyd*

Greatest Hits / 1993 / Pilz

Great Phil. Hits / PolyGram ◆◆◆

Jerry Butler's Mercury career was uneven, hitting his peak period from the late '60s until 1970, when he worked with Gamble and Huff. The hits, plus some other tunes Butler did with Gene Chandler and Brenda Lee Eager, were included on this anthology. —*Ron Wynn*

Paul Butterfield Blues Band

Blues Rock

Chicago born Paul Butterfield (b. Dec. 17, 1942, d. May 4, 1987) started out on classical flute before switching to amplified harmonica. He hung out and jammed with Chicago South Side blues players, starting his own band in 1963. The first Butterfield album (1965) had an enormous impact on young rock players who were used to getting their blues via groups like the Rolling Stones. This album was no deferential imitation of Black music by shy Whites, but a hard-driving blues album that rocked. It was a signal to White players to stop making respectful tributes to Black music and just play it. In a flash, the image of blues as old-time music was gone, and modern Chicago-style urban blues was out of the closet and introduced to mainstream White audiences.

The first two Butterfield Blues albums are essential from a historical perspective. While *East-West*, the second album, set the tone for psychedelic rockers with its Eastern influence and extended solos, it was that incredible first album (*The Paul Butterfield Blues Band*) that put the music scene on alert to what was coming. Later Butterfield material somehow misses the mark. Butterfield was one of the only White harmonica players to develop his own style—one respected by Black players (another is the brilliant William Clarke). Butterfield has no credible imitators. His harp playing was always understated, concise, and serious—only Big Walter Horton has a better sense of note selection. —*Michael Erlewine*

☆ **Paul Butterfield Blues Band** / 1965 / Elektra ◆◆◆◆◆

Butterfield's unique amplified harmonica style is already present on his classic first album—a wakeup call for a generation of young White players wondering if they, too, could play the blues. Great guitar from Michael Bloomfield and Elvin Bishop. With Mark Naftalin (organ), Jerome Arnold (bass), and Sam Lay (drums). —*Michael Erlewine*

★ **East-West** / 1966 / Elektra ◆◆◆◆◆

These Chicago-based musicians took blues to a whole new level on this, their second album, paving the way for the experimentations that are still being explored today. —*Jeff Tamarkin*

With John Mayall / 1967 / Decca ◆◆

○ **The Resurrection of Pigboy Crabshaw** / 1968 / Elektra ◆◆◆◆

A new direction was tried on this third album, stressing horn arrangements over guitar-fueled improvisations. —*Jeff Tamarkin*

○ **The Original Lost Elektra Sessions** / 1995 / Rhino ◆◆◆◆

All but one of these 19 tracks were recorded in December, 1964, as Butterfield's projected first LP; the results were scrapped and replaced by their official self-titled debut, cut a few months later. With both Bloomfield and Bishop already in tow, these sessions rank among the earliest blues-rock ever laid down. Extremely similar in feel to the first album, it's perhaps a bit rawer in production and performance, but not appreciably worse or different than what ended up on the actual debut LP. Dedicated primarily to electric Chicago blues standards, Butterfield fans will find this well worth acquiring, as most of the selections were never officially recorded by the first lineup (although different renditions of five tracks showed up on the first album and the *What's Shakin'* compilation). — *Richie Unterberger*

The Butthole Surfers

Group, Alternative Pop/Rock
There was a time magazines couldn't print their name and radios couldn't say their name. Then there was a time, about ten years later, that they were in heavy rotation on MTV and starring in Nintendo commercials. Throughout it all, the Butthole Surfers haven't changed all that much; they remain the same gleefully gross noise terrorists that they were when their first record was released on Alternative Tentacles in 1983.

Although some critics may say all of their albums sound the same, the only thing that unites the Butthole Surfers' albums is their bracing vulgarity and offensiveness. Unlike many bands whose disgusting lyrics and abrasive music are calculatingly revolting, the Buttholes revel in the filth—they're not making some social commentary with their music, they simply *enjoy* the grotesque. Beneath all of the squalor, the Buttholes remain artpunks; their albums are never just hardcore noise, they have touches of psychedelia, country, classic rock, rockabilly, techno— anything that comes their way, really. As they get older, their songs rely more on the underpinning guitar grunge of Paul Leary, yet vocalist Gibby Haynes remains a deranged lunatic, giving the band the fuel for their gleeful nightmares. — *Stephen Thomas Erlewine*

○ **Butthole Surfers** / 1983 / Alternative Tentacles ✦✦✦✦
Their best album, randy and wild. Smart, stupid, and outrageous all at the same time. It may be out of print. — *John Dougan*

Live PCPPEP / 1984 / Alternative Tentacles ✦✦✦

Psychic . . . Powerless . . . Another Man's Sac / 1985 / Touch & Go ✦✦✦
New-age drug music on *Psychic...Powerless...Another Man's Sac.* —*John Dougan*

Cream Corn from the Socket of Davis / 1985 / Touch & Go ✦✦✦

Rembrandt Pussyhorse / 1986 / Touch & Go ✦✦✦
Chunky, cranky, out-of-control pop. —*John Dougan*

● **Locust Abortion Technician** / 1987 / Touch & Go ✦✦✦✦
Good songs, real ugly execution. —*John Dougan*

○ **Hairway to Steven** / 1988 / Touch & Go ✦✦✦✦
Actually getting manic here! —*John Dougan*

Double Live / 1989 / Touch & Go ✦✦

Pioughd / 1991 / Capitol ✦✦
Pioughd was the Buttholes' first album of original material in three years, and considering the time it took to make the record, it's a bit of a disappointment. Not that it's bad; in fact, some of it is their best. But it's rather uninspired and restates many of their old ideas in a more streamlined, accessible fashion. —*Stephen Thomas Erlewine*

○ **Independent Worm Saloon** / 1993 / Capitol ✦✦✦✦
Something has definitely changed in the music industry when the Butthole Surfers are recording for a major label, with none other than Led Zeppelin's John Paul Jones producing. And they still haven't sold out. *Independent Worm Saloon* follows the course of their past few albums—a hard '70s punk-metal bottom with lots of avant-noise noodlings and wacked-out vocals on top. The safest it gets is the heavy riff-rocker "Who Was in My Room Last Night?" (which MTV aired during the daytime); the Buttholes still include gross-outs like the heaves that begin "Clean It Up" or "The Annoying Song," which is exactly what it says it is. *Independent Worm Saloon* may run a bit long, but the times that the Butthole Surfers' shock-rock hits the mark excuses most of the indulgences. — *Stephen Thomas Erlewine*

The Buzzcocks

Group, Punk
With their crisp melodies, driving guitars, and guitarist Pete Shelley's biting lyrics, the Buzzcocks were one of the best, most influential punk bands. The Buzzcocks were inspired by the Sex Pistols' energy, yet they didn't copy the Pistols' angry political stance.

Instead, the Buzzcocks brought that intense, brilliant energy to the three-minute pop song. Shelly's alternately funny and anguished lyrics about adolescence and love were some of the best and smartest of his era; similarly, the Buzzcocks' melodies and hooks were always concise and memorable. Over the years, their powerful punk-pop has proven enormously influential, with echoes of their music being apparent in everyone from Hüsker Dü to Nirvana.

The Buzzcocks reunited in 1989, releasing their first new studio album since 1979 in 1993; although they were no longer as breathtakingly energetic, they were one of the few reunited bands that didn't embarrass themselves. —*Stephen Thomas Erlewine*

Spiral Scratch / 1977 / New Hormones ✦✦✦

Another Music in Different Kitchen / 1978 / United Artists ✦✦✦

Love Bites / 1978 / United Artists ✦✦✦

A Different Kind of Tension / 1979 / IRS ✦✦✦

★ **Singles Going Steady** / 1979 / IRS ✦✦✦✦✦
This is a magnificent collection of their first eight British singles, both A- and B-sides. Infectious melodies and buzzsaw guitars carry Shelley's finest set of broken-hearted rockers. —*John Floyd*

Buzzcocks, Pts. 1-3 / 1984 / IRS ✦✦

○ **Product** / 1989 / Restless ✦✦✦✦
One of the first rock & roll box sets, as well as one of the finest, *Product* collects nearly every studio record the Buzzcocks ever released, with the exception of their debut EP, *Spiral Scratch.* —*Stephen Thomas Erlewine*

Live at the Roxy Club: April '77 / 1989 / Trojan ✦✦

○ **Operator's Manual: The Buzzcocks Best** / 1991 / IRS ✦✦✦✦
A 25-song set, it duplicates 11 songs from the *Singles* album. It also contains the best of their three albums, only one of which was released in the U.S., and showcases a different side of the band. —*John Floyd*

Entertaining Friends / 1992 / IRS ✦✦✦

○ **Different Kind of Tension / Buzzcocks, Pts. 1-3** / 1993 / IRS ✦✦✦✦
Even at the end of their career, the Buzzcocks were recording an amazing array of ferocious pop songs. Their last album, *A Different Kind of Tension,* featured some of Pete Shelley's best songs, including some of the most personal material he has ever written. *Parts One, Two, Three* collect the band's last three singles, which are all quite impressive. —*Stephen Thomas Erlewine*

Trade Test Transmission / Jun. 2, 1993 / Caroline ✦✦✦
While it doesn't have the tight, repressed energy of their earliest records, *Trade Test Transmissions* is a surprisingly effective comeback album from the Buzzcocks, showing that the band can still turn out some terrific punk-pop. —*Stephen Thomas Erlewine*

○ **Love Bites/Another Music in a Different Kitchen** / Feb. 22, 1994 / IRS ✦✦✦✦
While the Buzzcocks' singles captured the band's energetic, tightly wound pop style perfectly, the band experimented a bit more with song structures on their full-length albums. Many of the album tracks were in the vein of their classic singles, but the band also played some twisted, draining instrumental sections than were almost as impressive as their concise pop songs. Of their first two albums, the debut *Another Music in a Different Kitchen* is the stronger record, but *Love Bites* is only a shade weaker. —*Stephen Thomas Erlewine*

By All Means

Group, Soul
The Los Angeles trio By All Means began recording for 4th and Broadway in 1988. The group featured lead vocalist, trumpeter, and trombonist James Varner, vocalist Lynn Roderick, and guitarist Billy Shepherd. Roderick was previously an actress who had appeared on *Moonlighting* and *Cagney and Lacey,* among other shows, while Shepherd had been in the Skool Boyz. Varner and Roderick met while touring with Bill Withers in 1985. Producer Stan Sheppard suggested that they form a band with his brother Billy after seeing them in performance. Their debut LP was called *By All Means,* and they had a modest hit with "I Surrender to Your Love." Their second LP was *Beyond a Dream* in 1989. They also produced tracks on Gerald Alston's solo LPs for Motown. Their most recent release was *It's Real* for Motown in 1992. —*Ron Wynn*

● **By All Means** / 1988 / Island ✦✦✦✦
A better than average debut for a trio from Los Angeles. By All Means featured vocalist Lynn Roderick, a former actress, plus vocalist and brass musician James Varner and guitarist Billy Shepherd. A pair of singles, "I Surrender" and "You Decided to Go," plus a Marvin Gaye medley, attracted some airplay and interest, as did their videos. —*Ron Wynn*

Beyond a Dream / 1989 / Island ✦✦✦
The second album from the trio By All Means. It was well produced and had some good vocals from Lynn Roderick and some decent arrangements and compositions. What it didn't have was a breakout single or a standout album cut, and didn't enable the trio to continue building from the good buzz that their debut had gotten. —*Ron Wynn*

It's Real / 1992 / Motown ✦✦

Joe Byrd & the Field Hippies
Group, Psychedelic
Emerging from a background of serious composition and multimedia happenings, multi-instrumentalist Joseph Byrd was the mastermind behind the United States of America, who released a groundbreaking album in 1968 that injected psychedelic rock with electronic arrangements and avant-garde sensibilities. After the U.S.A. broke up following their debut album, Byrd put together the Field Hippies for a similar but much less successful 1969 LP. —*Richie Unterberger*

The American Metaphysical Circus / 1969 / Columbia ✦✦✦
As a "conductor" and organ/electronic synthesizer player, Byrd is very much the leader of this circus. With a couple of drummers, a half dozen horn players (including a young Tom Scott), three female vocalists, and a half dozen or so other musicians popping up over the course of the album, there are a lot more people involved in this project than there were in the (relatively) stable lineup of the United States of the America. Despite the ambition of this LP, it ultimately serves to illustrate just how much Byrd benefited from the unique synergy provided by the other members of the U.S.A. There are all kinds of adventurous electronics and eclectic ideas bouncing back and forth, but the songwriting is simply not nearly as strong as Byrd's previous group. The best songs are the ones which most strongly recall the U.S.A. in their spacy melodicism ("Moonsong: Pelog") and driving psychedelic pulse ("You Can't Ever Come Down"). Unfortunately, the female singers on these tracks are no match for the U.S.A.'s Dorothy Moscowitz, although they seem to be aspiring to the same dreamy, icy quality. Byrd himself is quite a mediocre singer, as his attempts at taking the lead on straightforward rock material prove. Otherwise, there are some bad takeoffs on gospel and old-time music, haphazard primitive early synthesizer, and dated social commentary/satire. As ambitious in its scope as Byrd's first rock project, this album is not nearly as successful. —*Richie Unterberger*

The Byrds
Group, Country-Rock, Psychedelic, Folk-Rock
Outside of the Beatles and the Rolling Stones, there hasn't been a group from the '60s whose sound has been so widely influential. Their trademark bell-like jangle of 12-string electric guitar and rich harmonies has been internalized by artists like Tom Petty, R.E.M., Big Star, Fairport Convention, the Church, the Bangles, and the Eagles, as well as much of today's country music.
Before the advent of the British Invasion, Jim (later Roger) McGuinn, Chris Hillman, David Crosby, and Gene Clark were active in the Los Angeles folk scene. By fusing the energy of the Beatles and the weightier lyrical concepts developed by Bob Dylan, the Byrds were conceived, and folk-rock was born.
Over the course of their existence, the Byrds pioneered many musical frontiers, breaking ground in futuristic space-rock and country-rock.
Through all their endeavors, the only constant in their many lineup changes was Roger McGuinn. After the band's demise in 1973, McGuinn released a series of solo efforts.
Like Buffalo Springfield, many of the Byrds members went on to even-greater success. David Crosby helped form Crosby, Stills & Nash. Chris Hillman, along with Gram Parsons, formed the Flying Burrito Brothers. Hillman also has continued to have much success in the country field with the Desert Rose Band. Parsons managed two fine albums on Warner before dying in 1973 of a drug overdose. Gene Clark, one of the band's finest songwriters, had a

sporadic solo career; *Echoes* is a dignified compilation of his highlights. Clark died in 1991. —*Rick Clark*

☆ **Mr. Tambourine Man** / 1965 / Columbia ✦✦✦✦✦
An incredibly focused debut, it features a smart blend of well-chosen song covers and originals, plus the band's trademark 12-string electric sound and transcendent harmonies. The title track and Gene Clark's "I'll Feel a Whole Lot Better," as well as "All I Really Want to Do," are hits. Two highlights, "I Knew I'd Want You" and "Here Without You," reveal Clark as the most mature songwriter in the band at this point. —*Rick Clark*

○ **Turn! Turn! Turn!** / 1966 / Columbia ✦✦✦✦
Continuing in the vein of their debut, this has lots of electrified folk-song covers (Dylan, Seeger, traditional) and Gene Clark shines on "Set You Free This Time" (curiously omitted from their box set), "If You're Gone," and the expansive "The World Turns All Around Her." —*Rick Clark*

○ **Fifth Dimension** / Feb. 1966 / Columbia ✦✦✦✦
Clark left during the recording of this, but David Crosby and Jim McGuinn more than fill the void. The 12-string sound is much more experimental, with McGuinn and Crosby drawing inspiration from jazz and Indian music. Though this album isn't as strong as *Turn! Turn! Turn!* and *Mr. Tambourine Man*, some of their greatest moments are found here in the powerful, hymnlike "5 D," the breathtakingly beautiful psychedelia of "Eight Miles High," or the playful hit "Mr. Spaceman." Other tracks of note are the psychedelic "I See You" (later cut by Yes on their debut), "What's Happening?!?!," and the orchestrated folky "Wild Mountain Thyme." —*Rick Clark*

☆ **Younger Than Yesterday** / 1967 / Columbia ✦✦✦✦✦
Overall, it's a stronger album than *Fifth Dimension*, even though some of the psychedelia lacks much sustaining impact ("C.T.A.-102," "Mind Gardens"). Chris Hillman makes strong contributions, writing or co-writing five of the 11 tracks. Among them are the tongue-in-cheek hit "So You Want to Be a Rock'N'Roll Star" and the spirited "Have You Seen Her Face?" It also includes the hit version of Dylan's "My Back Pages." —*Rick Clark*

★ **The Byrds' Greatest Hits** / 1967 / Columbia ✦✦✦✦✦
Even though this collection only covers the first half of their career, it contains more primo stuff than *20 Essential Tracks* (see below). The mastering here isn't quite as good as that on the boxed set. —*Rick Clark*

○ **The Notorious Byrd Brothers** / Jan. 1968 / Columbia ✦✦✦✦
A classic psychedelic opus, it draws from the space-rock of *Younger*…and *Fifth*…while hinting at the country-rock to come with cuts like "Change Is Now" and "Old John Robertson." The 12-string electrics are downplayed. Production techniques like phasing, vari-speeded vocals, sound effects, and baroque string and horn arrangements play a bigger role, while the melodies and vocal execution are much spacier. Highlights include Carole King's yearning "Goin' Back," "Draft Morning," "Dolphins Smile," and "Wasn't Born to Follow" (featured in the movie *Easy Rider*). —*Rick Clark*

☆ **Sweetheart of the Rodeo** / Aug. 1968 / Columbia ✦✦✦✦✦
The Byrds made this groundbreaking country-rock classic with the songwriting aid of new member Gram Parsons. "One Hundred Years from Now" features some incredibly fine guitar and pedal-steel work from Clarence White and Lloyd Green, respectively. Versions of Dylan's "Nothing Was Delivered" and "You Ain't Going Nowhere" are pure magic, and renditions of the Louvin Brothers' "The Christian Life" and William Bell's "You Don't Miss Your Water" are standouts too. —*Rick Clark*

Preflyte / 1969 / Bumble ✦✦✦

Dr Byrd & Mr Hyde / 1969 / Columbia ✦✦
Not one of their best, this still contains two notable tracks, "This Wheel's on Fire" and "King Apathy III." There is a continued country influence but rock still predominates. —*Rick Clark*

○ **The Ballad of Easy Rider** / Feb. 1969 / Columbia ✦✦✦✦
This is another beautiful gem with hardly a weak cut. "Gunga Din," with its delicate arpeggios, is one of the finest moments by a later incarnation of the Byrds. By this time, their characteristic 12-string sound was all but gone. —*Rick Clark*

Untitled / 1970 / Columbia ✦✦✦
Originally a double-record set (one live LP/one studio) and now on single CD, this contains their last hit of any substance, "Chestnut Mare." The studio tracks are uneven, but tracks like the reflec-

tive "Just a Season," "Truck Stop Girl," "All the Things" and much of the live stuff make this set worth having, if only for Clarence White's remarkable guitar playing. —*Rick Clark*

Byrdmaniax / 1971 / Columbia ✦✦

The Best of the Byrds: Greatest Hits, Vol. 2 / 1972 / Columbia ✦✦

In the Beginning / 1988 / Rhino ✦✦✦
Before signing to Columbia Records, the Byrds made hours of rehearsal and demo tapes as they perfected their blend of folk and rock. The *Preflyte* album, released in the late '60s, presented nearly a dozen of those cuts. This CD takes the bulk of that LP and embellishes it with alternate takes and previously unreleased tracks. Discography-wise, this 17-song disc is a real tongue-twister. Five of the eleven *Preflyte* tracks reappear in the exact same version, along with six alternate takes of *Preflyte* cuts. There are also alternate takes of both sides of their 1964 Elektra single (released as the Beefeaters), the primitive acoustic demo "The Only Girl I Adore" (previously available only on an obscure Elektra compilation), a previously unissued early version of "It's No Use" (later on their first LP), and the previously totally unreleased original "Tomorrow Is a Long Ways Away," in both electric and acoustic versions. Amidst the collector details, one shouldn't lose sight of the fact that the music is excellent, though more tentative and less polished than their "official" Columbia work. The harmonies are angelic and the melodies beautiful. Though this is more derivative of the early Beatles than their later Dylan-influenced folk-rock, one can hear the group's unsurpassed crystalline blend of guitars and voices approaching full bloom. With the exception of an early version of "Mr. Tambourine Man," all the cuts are originals, most of which are fine and never appeared on their later albums; there are many good, otherwise unavailable Gene Clark songs in particular. Minor complaint: some of the alternate takes here are inferior to those on the original *Preflyte* album. —*Richie Unterberger*

Never Before / 1989 / Murray Hill ✦✦✦
This 17-song compilation of alternate takes, unreleased songs, and assorted oddities from the Byrds' mid-'60s prime is a necessary purchase for their many fanatics, but a bit choppy and insubstantial in places. The highlights are many: a rough but endearing previously unreleased cover of Dylan's "It's All Over Now, Baby Blue"; an alternate take of "Eight Miles High" which is quite different (though not as good) as the hit version; a couple pretty David Crosby ballads (including "Triad," later covered by the Jefferson Airplane); a cover of the traditional folk tune "I Know You Rider" with scintillating twelve-string guitar solos from Roger McGuinn; "Why," the raga-rock B-side of "Eight Miles High" (both the original 45 version and an alternate take are included); and the non-LP B-side of "Turn, Turn, Turn," and "She Don't Care About Time" (written by Gene Clark). A couple of instrumental jams show McGuinn at his most recklessly experimental; "Flight 713" is a taut, almost jazzy piece, while the synthesizer burps of "Moog Raga" give an insight into the electronic direction the group might have pursued if Gram Parsons hadn't joined the band. On the down side, some of the outtakes were clearly throwaways, and the stereo version of their first single was hardly a coveted item. The 1968 B-side "Lady Friend," one of Crosby's best compositions, is ruined by a ham-fisted drum track overdubbed in the 1980s (it was restored to its original version on the box set). A ragtag collection, yes, but there are plenty of stellar moments, and this CD (together with *In The Beginning*) rounds up virtually everything from the group's classic period that didn't appear on their first five albums. —*Richie Unterberger*

☆ **The Byrds** / 1990 / Columbia ✦✦✦✦✦
This thoughtfully compiled four-disc boxed set features great sound from remastered and remixed tracks. The remixes generally manage to maintain the essential integrity of the original tracks, but there are some that entirely miss the spirit, like "Just a Season" and a toothless "Why" (which, by the way, is *not* the sought-after version found on the B-side of "Eight Miles High"). Regardless, it's a must-own for anyone interested in finding out about one of America's greatest groups. —*Rick Clark*

20 Essential Tracks from the Boxed Set: 1965-90 / 1991 / Columbia ✦✦✦
That may have been the case for the first sixteen cuts, but why include the four 1990 reunion tracks, when there's much better material left on the box? An okay choice for the budget-minded, that's about it. —*Rick Clark*

In The Studio / Bootleg ✦✦✦
Comprised of alternate versions, false starts, and backing tracks of songs from the Byrds' first three LPs, you're not going to turn to this for casual listening. But as academic documents of major groups go, this is first-rate, with 70 minutes of music, sparkling sound, and a chance to hear the group polishing their material in the studio. No radically different takes or arrangements surface, but aficionados will be especially interested in the appearance of the backing track to "Stranger In A Strange Land," a long-rumored Byrds original that had never even appeared on bootleg before. —*Richie Unterberger*

BOOK

✦✦✦✦ **Timeless Flight: The Definitive Biography of the Byrds**, by Johnny Rogan (Square One, 1990, UK). Considering how enormously influential the Byrds were and are, it's surprising that only one serious attempt has been made to write their story, and that it has never been issued in the U.S. It's hard to imagine that anyone will come up with a more thorough bio than this one, which covers the band from their earliest days in 1964, when they couldn't afford instruments for all the members, up through their various reunions (the solo careers, as well as the stories of groups such as Crosby, Stills & Nash and the Flying Burritos, which featured exByrds, are not examined). As is usual for Rogan's books, there's a wealth of quotes from both archival and first-hand interviews, and intense scrutiny of the makings of virtually every one of their tracks. The first half of the book will rivet Byrds fans, covering their unlikely beginnings as ex-folkies who barely knew their way around electric instruments through the end of 1968. Rogan treats the rest of their career in equal detail, which unfortunately is not merited by the generally uninteresting quality of their post-1968 work. The huge discography tells you everything you could want to know about their released and unreleased work. —*Richie Unterberger*

David Byrne

b. May 14, 1952, Dumbarton, Scotland
Alternative Pop/Rock, Experimental
The former lead singer/songwriter and guitarist of Talking Heads, David Byrne has written theatre and film scores (Academy Award winner for *The Last Emperor*), acted and directed (*True Stories*), compiled a series of samplers of South American music, and launched a solo career with *Rei Momo* in 1989. —*William Ruhlmann*

The Catherine Wheel / Dec. 1981 / Luaka Bop ✦✦✦
This is Byrne's score for a Broadway dance production choreographed and directed by Twyla Tharp. Its sound—with herky-jerky rhythms and unusual sounds, along with Byrne's own vocals and odd lyrics on many songs—will be familiar to Talking Heads fans. As originally released, only the cassette version contained the full 73-minute score, although an abridged songs-from LP was also issued. —*William Ruhlmann*

Music for "The Knee Plays" / May 1985 / ECM ✦✦✦
This music was composed for use in segments of Robert Wilson's opera *The Civil Wars*. Byrne uses a variety of stately horn charts and recites impressionistic lyrics between and over them. The album concludes with the hilariously absurd "In the Future." —*William Ruhlmann*

Sounds from True Stories / 1986 / Luaka Bop ✦✦✦
Stylistically all over the map, this set of songs for Byrne's film (not to be confused with the Talking Heads album *True Stories*) ranges from the cowboy hoedown of "Cocktail Desperado" to a short piece for reeds written by Meredith Monk. Members of the Heads turn up, as does the Kronos Quartet. —*William Ruhlmann*

● **Rei Momo** / Oct. 1989 / Luaka Bop ✦✦✦✦
On his first full-fledged solo album, Byrne indulges his fascination with Latin and South American musical styles, employing a variety of native musicians but mixing up the sounds to suit his own distinctly non-purist vision and singing over the tracks the same kind of witty, oddball lyrics found on Talking Heads albums. (When released, the cassette version contained three more tracks than the LP.) —*William Ruhlmann*

The Forest / Jun. 1991 / Luaka Bop ✦✦
In 1988, David Byrne collaborated with Robert Wilson on a "theatre piece" called *The Forest* that premiered in Berlin. (Byrne previously had worked with Wilson on *The Civil Wars*, resulting in

his album *Music For The Knee Plays.*) Byrne's orchestral score served as the basis for this more extended version, released three years later on his Luaka Bop label. The music is stately, near-classical, and like none of his other recordings except his Academy Award-winning music for *The Last Emperor.* Byrne always was an eclectic, and in a purely musical environment (there are a few stray lyrics, but nothing to speak of), he is free to move from the European classical tradition to those of Japan and the Middle East, among other places. Depending upon your point of view, the result is either a pleasant travelogue or a mess. Or maybe both. — *William Ruhlmann*

Uh-Oh / Mar. 1992 / Luaka Bop ✦✦✦
Uh-Oh was only David Byrne's second pop-oriented solo album and his first to be released after the formal end of Talking Heads. Though informed by his various investigations into world music, the album was a natural successor to the Talking Heads records, relying on involved percussion tracks topped by Byrne's quirky singing and lyrics. By this point, disaffected fans may have grown accustomed to the idea that a David Byrne solo album could contain anything from an extended flirtation with Latin styles (*Rei*

Momo) to an eclectic instrumental score (*The Forest*), to name only his most recent solo projects. Maybe Byrne and his record label failed to get out the message that he was back to making Heads-style pop-rock (he didn't organize a tour until the album had come and gone on the charts), but *Uh-Oh* never reached its potential audience. Talking Heads fans should give it a listen. — *William Ruhlmann*

David Byrne / May 24, 1994 / Luaka Bop ✦✦
David Byrne took a spare, direct approach on his third song-based solo album, which lent his work an intimacy but did little to restore his commercial prospects, despite a first single, "Angels," that was a ringer for the Talking Heads song "Once in a Lifetime." In fact, the limited instrumentation and focus on Byrne's voice tended to create difficulties with his typically quirky lyrics—with the words in close-up, one wanted them to make some kind of sense. In a denser musical structure, such as the mbaqanga-flavored "You & Eye," one might share his enjoyment, but on other tracks with less to offer aurally, the disturbing question "What is he talking about?" became inescapable. — *William Ruhlmann*

C

C & C Music Factory / Clivilles & Cole

Group, Dance-Pop

C & C Music Factory isn't really a group—it's the product of Robert Clivilles and David Cole, two pop-savvy dance producers. In 1990, Clivilles and Cole hired all the singers and created all the tracks for *Gonna Make You Sweat*, C & C Music Factory's first album. While it was prepackaged, it wasn't necessarily faceless; in Freedom Williams, the producers had a solid, if not original or distinctive, rapper. What was really important to the success of the album was how Clivilles and Cole assembled the tracks, blending hip-hop and club sensibilities to mindlessly catchy pop songs. The three hit singles—"Gonna Make You Sweat (Everybody Dance Now)," "Here We Go," "Things That Make You Go Hmmmm...,"—were very good pop singles, and all of them were massive hits in early 1991.

After their moment in the sun, Williams left for an unsuccessful solo career and Clivilles and Cole released *Greatest Remixes, Vol. 1*, a collection of their work with C & C Music Factory as well as other artists; the album had a hit single with their re-recording of U2's "Pride."

C & C Music Factory released their second album, *Anything Goes!*, in the summer of 1994; it was a moderate hit, spending nine weeks on the charts. Unfortunately, it was the last album the duo ever made—David Cole died of spinal meningitis in early 1995. —*Stephen Thomas Erlewine*

● **Gonna Make You Sweat** / 1990 / Columbia ✦✦✦✦
All their hit hip-hop-pop singles are all here—"Gonna Make You Sweat (Everybody Dance Now)," "Here We Go," and "Things That Make You Go Hmmm..." —*Bil Carpenter*

Anything Goes! / 1994 / Columbia ✦✦✦
C&C Music Factory's first album was an enormous hit, filled with infectious bubblegum dance-pop singles. It was music of the moment, and by the time *Anything Goes* was released, the moment had passed. Clivilles and Cole's production was just as skilled, and several of the hooks on *Anything Goes* were strong, but the music was too dated to fit into the pop landscape of the mid-'90s. —*Stephen Thomas Erlewine*

The C.A. Quintet

Group, Psychedelic

Virtually no one outside Minneapolis heard of the C.A. Quintet during their late '60s heyday. It was their fortune, or curse, to actually reach a considerably bigger international audience when their album was reissued in the 1980s. Starting as a rather conventional pop/soul/garage band, their one and only album, *Trip Thru Hell* (1968), was a worthy slice of dark psychedelia. With spooky organ and the occasional trumpet of singer and songwriter Ken Erwin, the group's murky and macabre vision—dotted with trips through hell, cold spiders, sleepy hollow lanes, Colorado mornings, and the like—was genuinely original and chilling. *Trip Thru Hell* only sold 700-800 copies when it was first issued, but after gaining status among hardcore '60s psychedelic collectors, it was reissued in 1983. The group also released a few non-LP singles in 1967 and 1968, most in a much poppier vein. —*Richie Unterberger*

● **Trip Thru Hell** / 1968 / Sundazed ✦✦✦✦
There's not much to compare this album to, even in the weird musical climate of 1968—there are echoes of Country Joe & the Fish and the Doors, perhaps, in the mysterioso organ and morbid imagery. Not that Ken Erwin was in the same league as Jim Morrison, or even Country Joe, as a songwriter. But (with the exception of the brassy good-time cut "Underground Music"), psychedelia was very rarely this demently gloomy. Occasional pealing bells and curdling screams (to say nothing of the Boschlike cover art) add to the foggy underworld menace. Reissued without authorization in Europe in the 1980s, the 1995 domestic CD is a first-class job: the 12 bonus cuts gather some rare non-LP singles, alternate takes, and previously unreleased songs, and the liner notes feature extensive interviews with Ken Erwin and engineer Steve Longman. —*Richie Unterberger*

Cabaret Voltaire

Group, Electronic, Experimental

Cabaret Voltaire's story is that of a common cult band: they never sold many records and they were never critics' darlings, yet their influence was great. Their effect on techno, industrial, and electronic music is immense. Taking the electronic experiments of Brian Eno and the avant-garde bent of Can, Cabaret Voltaire added a hypnotic, almost trance-like beat, along with television and record sound bites. All of these techniques became popular during the early '90s, when groups like the techno conglomeration Front 242 and the hard, industrial Ministry expanded on these ideas. What sounded avant-garde in the late '70s and early '80s has become the standard in clubs and raves around the world.

Since 1979, Cabaret Voltaire have recorded a staggering amount of albums. Some are impressive, others are almost inaccessible. As they've grown older, their electronics have become more danceable; in 1991, they fit comfortably into the acid house, although their music was darker than most of that style. For much of their music, sound is the primary concern, not songs or compositions. Consequently, their albums can be dense, difficult listening that require patience. Even so, it is impossible to deny the importance of Cabaret Voltaire, no matter how inaccessible their music may be at times. —*Stephen Thomas Erlewine*

Mix-Up / 1979 / Mute ✦✦

Three Mantras / 1980 / Mute ✦✦✦

The Voice of America / 1980 / Mute ✦✦

○ **Red Mecca** / 1981 / Mute ✦✦✦✦
Cabaret Voltaire's first consistent record, *Red Mecca* offers a highly stylized revision of Mancini's score for *Touch of Evil* set to a dark, dense electronic landscape. —*Stephen Thomas Erlewine*

○ **2 X 45** / 1982 / Mute ✦✦✦✦

Johnny YesNo / 1983 / Mute ✦✦

○ **The Crackdown** / 1983 / Some Bizarre ✦✦✦✦
One of Cabaret Voltaire's strongest albums, *The Crackdown* features the band working a number of menacing electronic textures into a basic dance/funk rhythm; the result is one of their most distinctive, challenging records. —*Stephen Thomas Erlewine*

Micro-Phonies / 1984 / Virgin ✦✦✦

Drinking Gasoline / 1985 / Caroline ✦✦✦

The Covenant, the Sword & the Arm / 1985 / Some Bizarre ✦✦✦

Code / 1987 / Manhattan ✦✦✦

○ **The Golden Moments of Cabaret Voltaire** / 1987 / Rough Trade ✦✦✦✦
A solid collection of Cabaret Voltaire's earliest recordings, which features some of the noisiest and bleakest music they have ever recorded. —*Stephen Thomas Erlewine*

Eight Crepuscule Tracks / 1988 / Positive ✦✦✦

○ **Listen up with Cabaret Voltaire** / 1990 / Mute ✦✦✦✦
It may be a collection of rarities and outtakes, but *Listen Up With Cabaret Voltaire* is one of their strongest albums, giving listeners a good sense of the band's accomplishments. —*Stephen Thomas Erlewine*

● **The Living Legends** / 1990 / Mute ✦✦✦✦
Collecting both sides of a number of singles the band made for Rough Trade, *The Living Legends* offers the best introduction to Cabaret Voltaire's influential electronic soundscapes. —*Stephen Thomas Erlewine*

Groovy, Laidback & Nasty / 1990 / Capitol ✦✦✦

Colours / 1991 / Mute ✦✦✦

Plasticity / 1993 / Instinct ✦✦✦

International Language / 1994 / Instinct ✦✦

Cadets

Group, R&B, Doo-Wop
This West Coast group used two names for recording sessions. They called themselves "The Jacks" when doing dates for Modern and "The Cadets" on RPM. They began as a gospel group during the late '40s in Los Angeles. Ted Taylor, Aaron Collins, Lloyd Mc-Craw, and Will Jones were the original lineup, and the Cadets were among the more popular bands doing R&B covers. The Cadets' lone hit was "Stranded in the Jungle," which they recorded for Modern as The Jacks in 1956. It peaked at number eight R&B and number 15 pop. Davis and Collins would later join The Flares in 1961, while Taylor would enjoy solo success as a blues, soul, and gospel vocalist. Jones joined The Coasters in 1958 and remained there for over a decade. Collins' sisters, Betty and Rose, also recorded for Modern/RPM as "The Teen Queens." —*Ron Wynn*

● **The Cadets Greatest Hits** / Relic ✦✦✦✦

The Cadillacs

Group, Doo-Wop
Equally adept at polished ballads or torrid rockers, the Cadillacs were one of New York's top doo-wop groups. The Harlem quintet signed with Josie in 1954 and debuted with the beautiful "Gloria," but with Earl Carroll's (b. Nov 2, 1937) prominent energetic lead vocals, the Cadillacs became known for humorous jump material and hot choreography after "Speedoo" hit big for them in 1956. Tapping into the novelty R&B market pioneered by the Coasters, the Cadillacs cut a load of great rockers during the late '50s, such as "Peek-A-Boo" and "Please, Mr. Johnson," and performed in the quickie flick *Go, Johnny, Go!* in 1959. Carroll left to join the Coasters in 1958 but the group persevered, eventually signing with Mercury. Carroll has re-formed the Cadillacs in recent years. —*Bill Dahl*

○ **Meet the Orioles** / 1961 / Collectables ✦✦✦✦
A classic doo-wop album featuring one group well known for novelty tracks and another that was among the earliest creators of the genre. Some wonderful jump tunes, silly songs, and romantic ballads. —*Ron Wynn*

★ **The Best of the Cadillacs** / 1990 / Rhino ✦✦✦✦✦
One of the top novelty R&B groups of the mid '50s, these sizzling rockers also had a handful of doo-wop ballads. —*Bill Dahl*

The Complete Josie Sessions [box] / 1995 / Bear Family

○ **For Collectors Only** / Collectables ✦✦✦✦
A 60-track, three-disc collection that will delight hardcore fans of the seminal doo-wop group; most fans will be content with the single-disc collection. —*Stephen Thomas Erlewine*

John Cafferty & the Beaver Brown Band

Group, Rock & Roll
Arguably the quintessential one-shot band of all time, Cafferty and Co. (who, back in the early '70s, were simply a hack New England bar band) had their 15 minutes of fame courtesy of a ridiculously overwrought 1983 film called *Eddie and the Cruisers* (starring the ridiculously overwrought Michael Pare), which dealt with the suspicious death of a fictional singer-songwriter, modeled on a conflation of Bob Dylan and Bruce Springsteen, who had made the transition from smart rock & roller to serious artist. Seems as though Eddie had recorded a "brilliant" but unreleased album that

fused Chuck Berry-style rock & roll with French Symbolist poetry (all this in 1963!). A record way ahead of its time, the master tapes of *The Dark Side* (ooh, now that's a heavy title) went missing, right around the time of Eddie's "death." Needing a band to supply music for the film, the producers used the Springsteenish-sounding Cafferty and his clock-punching backup band. With the Springsteenish single "On the Dark Side" leading the way, Cafferty led, arguably, the most anonymous band with a hit record in the history of rock & roll. With the movie doing reasonably well in theaters and extremely well on video, sales of Cafferty's album (which, ironically, had been out for months before the band's involvement with the film and barely caused a murmur) skyrocketed. But, as the movie faded from the public consciousness, so did Cafferty's lousy, cynical imitation of Springsteen. —*John Dougan*

○ **Eddie & the Cruisers [O.S.T.]** / 1983 / RCA ✦✦✦✦
There was a year's delay before this film, which concerns the mysterious death of a fictional '60s rock star, took off via video and cable TV; but when it did, the soundtrack album, featuring such songs as "On the Dark Side" and "Tender Years," by John Cafferty & the Beaver Brown Band, took off with it. To most, the music sounded like more Bruce Springsteen clones, but it was appealing nonetheless. —*William Ruhlmann*

Tough All Over / 1985 / Scotti Brothers ✦✦✦
On the strength of the double platinum soundtrack to *Eddie and the Cruisers*, John Cafferty and the Beaver Brown Band were able to record *Tough All Over*, an album of their original songs, and release it under their own name. Released in the summer of 1985 at the tail-end of Eddie-mania, the record managed to spawn hard-rocking Top 40 hits, "C-I-T-Y" and "Tough All Over," which strongly recalled Springsteen, much like the rest of Cafferty's songs. Besides the two hits, *Tough All Over* lacked material that ranked with the best of the *Eddie and the Cruisers* soundtrack. Nevertheless, the album stayed on the charts for an impressive 32 weeks. —*Stephen Thomas Erlewine*

Roadhouse / 1988 / Scotti Brothers ✦✦
Released in 1988, after *Eddie and the Cruisers* had faded away from public consciousness, *Roadhouse* repeated the formula John Cafferty & the Beaver Brown Band established on the *Eddie* soundtrack—a simple, three-chord rock & roll in the vein of Bruce Springsteen. In terms of quality, *Roadhouse* wasn't much worse than *Tough All Over*, yet the band's moment had passed and the album failed to chart. After its release, the group returned to recording under the name Eddie & the Cruisers. —*Stephen Thomas Erlewine*

Eddie & the Cruisers 2: Eddie Lives / 1989 / RCA ✦✦

Eddie & The Cruisers: The Unreleased Tapes / 1991/ Scotti Brothers ✦

Eddie & the Cruisers: Live and in Concert / 1992 / RCA ✦

J.J. Cale

b. Dec. 5, 1938, Oklahoma City, OK
Blues Rock, Singer-Songwriter, Pop/Rock
Oklahoma-born songwriter and guitarist known for his laidback style. He wrote several songsincluding"After Midnight," and "Cocaine"—recorded by Eric Clapton. —*William Ruhlmann*

Naturally / Dec. 1971 / Mercury ✦✦✦

Really / Dec. 1972 / Mercury ✦✦✦
Cale's guitar work manages to be both understated and intense here. The same is true of his seemingly offhand singing, which finds him drawling lines like "You get your gun, I'll get mine" with disarming casualness. But he has trouble coming up with original material as strong as that on his debut, and for some, his approach will be too casual; there are many times, when the band is percolating along and Cale is muttering into the microphone, that the music seems to be all background and no foreground. You may find yourself waiting for a pay-off that never comes. —*William Ruhlmann*

Okie / May 1974 / Mercury ✦✦✦
Cale moves toward country and gospel on some songs here, but since those are two of his primary influences, the movement is slight. And longtime producer Audie Ashworth attempts to place more emphasis on Cale's vocals on some songs by double-tracking them and pushing them up in the mix. But much of this is still low-key and bluesy in what was becoming Cale's patented style. —*William Ruhlmann*

○ **Troubadour** / Sep. 1976 / Mercury ✦✦✦✦
Producer Audie Ashworth introduced some different instruments, notably vibes and what sound like horns (although none are credited), for a slightly altered sound here. But Cale's albums are so steeped in his introspective style that they become interchangeable. If you like one of them, chances are you'll want to have them all. This one is notable for introducing "Cocaine," which Eric Clapton covered on his *Slowhand* album a year later. —*William Ruhlmann*

5 / Aug. 1979 / Mercury ✦✦
As Cale's influence on others expanded, he just continued to turn out the occasional album of bluesy, minor-key tunes. This one was even sparer than usual, with the artist handling bass as well as guitar on many tracks. Listened to today, it sounds so much like a Dire Straits album, it's scary. (Mark Knopfler & Co. had appeared in 1978, seven years after Cale.) —*William Ruhlmann*

Shades / Feb. 1981 / Mercury ✦✦

Grasshopper / Mar. 1982 / Mercury ✦✦
J.J. Cale drifts toward a more pop approach on this album, starting with the lead-off track, "City Girls," which could almost but not quite be a hit single. The usual blues and country shuffle approach is in effect, but Audie Ashworth's production is unusually sharp, the playing has more bite than usual, and Cale, whose vocals are for the most part up in the mix, sounds more engaged. It's not clear, however, that this is an improvement over his usual laid-back approach, and, in any case, it shouldn't be over-emphasized— this is still a J.J. Cale album, with its cantering tempos and single-note guitar runs. It's just that, when you have a style as defined as Cale's, little movements in style loom larger. —*William Ruhlmann*

8 / 1983 / Mercury ✦✦
Twelve years and eight albums into his recording career, Cale's approach has changed little, and here is another collection of groove tunes that act as platforms for the artist's intricate guitar playing. He is sometimes accompanied by a female vocalist, co-writer Christine Lakeland. —*William Ruhlmann*

● **Special Edition** / 1984 / Mercury ✦✦✦✦
Sinuous rhythms, conversational singing, and, most of all, intricate, bluesy guitar playing characterize Cale's performances of his own songs. This compilation, covering 11 years of recording, includes the songs Eric Clapton–who borrowed heavily from Cale's style in his 1970s solo work–made famous: "After Midnight" and "Cocaine." —*William Ruhlmann*

○ **Travel Log** / Feb. 1990 / Silvertone ✦✦✦✦
Cale's first album in six years finds him taking a more aggressive stance in terms of tempos and playing, although he remains a man with a profound sense of the groove and, especially as a singer, a minimalist. But as he says, "Shuffle or die." —*William Ruhlmann*

10 / 1992 / Silvertone ✦✦✦
There are no major surprises on Cale's tenth outing; fans get the same dependable, unassuming, comfy results, like a well-worn but form-fitting pair of slippers. Subtle licks percolate and resonate from the front-porch jam session on "Jailer" and "Low Rider." "Lonesome Train" and "Shady Grove" choogle along, as amiable as they are hypnotic. The closest thing to a twist comes with the phased vocals and spiralling guitar runs of "Digital Blues."
It would be easy to imagine *Number 10* getting completely buried behind a wash of '90s white noise, but for those prepared to kick off their boots and sit a spell, Cale's latest offers up some seductive rewards. —*Roch Parisien*

Closer to You / Aug. 23, 1994 / Virgin ✦✦

John Cale

b. Dec. 3, 1940, Wales
Rock & Roll, Art-Rock/Progressive-Rock, Experimental
A former member of the Velvet Underground (for whom he played viola), Cale has moved between the worlds of rock and avant-garde classical music since launching a solo career in 1969. He also worked as producer for a variety of punk and new wave artists. —*William Ruhlmann*

Vintage Violence / Mar. 25, 1970 / Columbia ✦✦✦
Given that Cale supposedly wielded the strongest avant-garde/dissonant sensibilities on the first Velvet Underground albums, it's surprising that his first solo LP has a light, playful, cheerful feel. With its rollicking piano, acoustic guitars, and occasional pedal steel and mournful violin, as well as the obtuse, narrative/reflective lyrics, there's a comfortable, meditative lilt to these tunes, as well as a nonchalant charm not far removed from the early work of former cohort Lou Reed. Cale lets his darker undertones come to the fore on the stark ballad "Amsterdam" and the swirling, truly ominous "Ghost Story." —*Richie Unterberger*

Church of Anthrax / Feb. 10, 1971 / Columbia ✦✦✦
Cale and Terry Riley produce a dense instrumental sound equal parts jazz, rock, and contemporary classical on this album. (There is also one vocal track, sung by Adam Miller.) A bit too busy to be called "minimalist," a bit too intense to be called "ambient," it is sometimes reminiscent of the fusion style later pioneered by the likes of Miles Davis and Frank Zappa. Not easy listening by any means, but rewarding. —*William Ruhlmann*

The Academy in Paril / Jul. 19, 1972 / Reprise ✦✦✦
Cale moved to Warner Bros.' Reprise label in 1972 for his second solo album, an all-instrumental collection on which he made greater use of his classical and avant-garde training, employing the Royal Philharmonic Orchestra for two cuts and naming tunes after Brahms and John Milton. The result is an imaginative, though unfocused, album that expanded Cale's musical horizons, if not his audience. (Reissued on CD in 1993.) —*William Ruhlmann*

○ **Paris 1919** / Mar. 1973 / Reprise ✦✦✦✦
John Cale's third solo album possessed a rare beauty, demonstrating that the classically trained avant-garde rock & roll viola player could, when he wished, make melodic pop music with a lush elegance. (Reissued on CD in 1993.) —*William Ruhlmann*

○ **Fear** / Oct. 1, 1974 / Island ✦✦✦✦
Moving to Island Records for his fourth solo album (and third try at a pop vocal approach), Cale brought in Roxy Music guitarist Phil Manzanera and turned to a harder rocking style on the title track and "Gun." But "You Know More Than I Know" and other songs showed he retained the melodic qualities and talent for thoughtful ballads displayed on *Paris 1919*. —*William Ruhlmann*

Slow Dazzle / Mar. 25, 1975 / Island ✦✦✦
On the second installment of a trilogy made for Island in the mid-'70s, Cale played (as one song title had it) "Dirtyass Rock 'N' Roll," anticipating the coming punk movement. *Slow Dazzle* includes Cale's drastic reconstruction of "Heartbreak Hotel." —*William Ruhlmann*

Helen of Troy / Nov. 14, 1975 / Island ✦✦✦
Island Records declined to release this, the third of its John Cale albums, in the U.S., which meant fans had to scramble for the import copy of a record that featured guitarist Chris Spedding and a song selection highlighted by the Cale classic "I Keep A Close Watch" and his version of Jonathan Richman's "Pablo Picasso," which he had produced earlier for the Modern Lovers. —*William Ruhlmann*

○ **Guts** / 1977 / Island ✦✦✦✦
Guts is a compilation album selecting the best from Cale's three Island releases of 1974-1975: *Fear*, *Slow Dazzle*, and *Helen Of Troy*. —*William Ruhlmann*

Animal Justice / Sep. 1977 / Illegal ✦✦
This is a three-song, 45 r.p.m., 12-inch import EP featuring the hard rock track "Chicken Shit," a cover of Chuck Berry's "Memphis," and another of Cale's literary musicalizations, "Hedda Gabler." It has some of the same extreme rock venom of the second Velvet Underground album. —*William Ruhlmann*

Sabotage/Live / Dec. 1979 / Spy ✦✦✦
By 1979, Cale was leading a hard rock band (and wearing a hard-hat onstage), and this live album, recorded in June at New York club CBGB, finds him angrily churning out songs like "Mercenaries (Ready For War)" and the title track, in which he declares, "Military intelligence isn't what it used to be." Was it ever? —*William Ruhlmann*

Honi Soit / Mar. 10, 1981 / A&M ✦✦✦
Cale's first "new" studio album in six years was an excellent pop-rock collection paced by its leadoff track, "Dead or Alive." —*William Ruhlmann*

● **Music for a New Society** / Aug. 1982 / Island ✦✦✦✦
Cale's calmest collection of music since *Paris, 1919* contains an excellent version of "Close Watch," as well as the haunting "Chinese Envoy." —*William Ruhlmann*

Caribbean Sunset / Jan. 1984 / ZE ♦♦
With a rock band backing him up and Brian Eno on A.M.S. pitch changer, Cale makes another straightforward pop-rock collection. Talk about first takes—on "Experimental Number I," Cale calls out chord changes to the band as it plays the song! — *William Ruhlmann*

Comes Alive / Sep. 1984 / Mango ♦♦
Employing the same trio that backed him on *Caribbean Sunset*, Cale turns in a set of familiar favorites on this album, culled from a show at the London Lyceum in February 1984. Some of his best later songs, such as "Dead Or Alive" and "Chinese Envoy," are included. Also contains Cale's cover of the Velvet Underground favorite "Waiting For The Man." — *William Ruhlmann*

Artificial Intelligence / Sep. 6, 1985 / Beggars Banquet ♦♦
Guitarist David Young is the only holdover on this album of run-of-the-mill songs co-written with rock journalist Larry Sloman, the best of which is the ballad "Dying On The Vine." But Cale's and James Young's keyboards form the basis of the sound. — *William Ruhlmann*

Words for the Dying / Sep. 1989 / Opal ♦♦♦
○ **Songs for Drella** / 1990 / Sire ♦♦♦♦
Lou Reed and John Cale's tribute to Andy Warhol brings out the best in both of them. It's a spare collection, the only instruments being Reed's guitar and Cale's keyboards and viola. The songs trace Warhol's life in a witty, conversational way that evokes his spirit far better than any biographical work of the artist yet attempted. — *William Ruhlmann*

○ **Wrong Way Up** / Oct. 16, 1990 / Opal ♦♦♦♦
Both Eno and John Cale have always flirted with conventional pop music throughout their careers, while reserving the right to go off on less accessible experiments, which means they've always held out the promise that they would make something as attractive as this collection, on which Eno comes as close to the mainstream as he has since *Another Green World* and Cale is as catchy as he's been since *Honi Soit*. The result is one of the best albums either one has ever made. — *William Ruhlmann*

Even Cowgirls Get the Blues / 1991 / ROIR ♦♦
An archival release of live performances at CBGB in December 1978 and December 1979 finds Cale in a caustic hard rock mode, not unlike the *Sabotage/Live* album recorded in between. Patti Smith's rhythm section, Ivan Kraal and Jay Dee Dougherty, accompany Cale, and Judy Nylon, sounding a lot like Smith, takes occasional vocals. — *William Ruhlmann*

○ **Fragments of a Rainy Season** / Sep. 25, 1992 / Hannibal ♦♦♦♦
It's hard to imagine John Cale on MTV, but if he appeared on *Unplugged*, the result probably would sound like this. Alone, Cale accompanies himself on acoustic piano and guitar, playing a retrospective set of some of his best and most accessible music. The emphasis is on his more contemplative material, such as the early *Paris 1919* album, his later *Words for the Dying*, which features the poetry of Dylan Thomas set to music, and other notable Cale ballads. He does throw in some rock & roll fervor and some of his noisy *avant-garde* effects on numbers like "Guts," but for the most part this is a John Cale who, while intense, is quiet and dignified. — *William Ruhlmann*

● **Seducing Down the Door** / Jul. 5, 1994 / Rhino ♦♦♦♦
The range of John Cale's work can be shocking: It's hard to believe that the piano duets with minimalist composer Terry Riley on *Church of Anthrax*, the lush orchestral pop of *Paris 1919*, and the raucous, dissonant guitar rock of "Gun" and the rest of *Fear* are all the work of the same man, much less that they were all released within a four-year span. This well-chosen 38-track, two half-hour double-CD/cassette anthology does nothing to reconcile the apparent musical contradictions in Cale's classical-to-punk sensibility, but it does bring coherence and consolidation to a recording career that, spread across a multitude of labels and plagued by popular indifference, has been difficult to grasp as a whole. — *William Ruhlmannn*

Randy California (Randy Wolfe)

b. Feb. 20, 1951, Los Angeles, CA
Hard Rock, Psychedelic
Guitarist/singer/songwriter Randy California is best known as the leader of Spirit, although he occasionally has made solo albums. A guitar prodigy, California played in Jimi Hendrix's pre-Experience group the Blue Flames in New York's Greenwich Village in the

summer of 1966. It was Hendrix who named him Randy "California." Spirit, an eclectic band with rock, jazz, and folk tendencies, was formed in Los Angeles in 1967. After four albums, the original quintet split up in 1971. California suffered a serious riding accident and after his recovery made a solo album, *Kapt. Kopter and the (Fabulous) Twirly Birds* (1972), which featured uncredited appearances by Hendrix's Experience rhythm section of Noel Redding and Mitch Mitchell. He rejoined Spirit in 1974 and has led the band ever since. (Spirit charted with ten albums between 1968 and 1976.) Several subsequent Randy California solo albums have been released in Europe. — *William Ruhlmann*

Kapt. Kopter and The (Fabulous) Twirly Birds / 1972 / Edsel ♦♦♦
Kapt. Kopter and the (Fabulous) Twirly Birds was Randy California's debut solo album after leaving Spirit, and thus, expectations were high. California, still only 21, opted to return to the influence of his early mentor, Jimi Hendrix, who had died in 1970. California wailed through a series of tunes in a style more reminiscent of the extended arrangements of *Electric Ladyland* than the tight psychedelic pop singles on *Are You Experienced?* Beatles songs like "Day Tripper" and "Rain" became almost unrecognizable frames for California's improvisations. At least the covers were actual songs, which was more than you could say for the originals. *Kapt. Kopter* ended up proving that California was not ready to be promoted from a group guitarist who sang and wrote occasionally. — *William Ruhlmann*

Euro-American / 1982 / Beggars Banquet ♦♦
Randy California turned in his second solo album ten years after his first, and it reflected his experiences in the interim. California had spent the decade leading various lineups of Spirit, including one full-fledged reunion of the original band, and the album featured all of them, albeit not all on the same track. Spirit had built up a considerable following in Europe (the album did not see a U.S. release), and California's bi-continental focus was expressed on the LP's two sides: the "American" one was given over mostly to guitar-dominated hard rock, while the "European" side was more varied, some of it featuring light pop, along with a cover of "Wild Thing." — *William Ruhlmann*

Shattered Dreams / 1987 / Line ♦♦
This is a grab-bag of songs California has played for some time, though they are presented here in new recordings. There is "Downer," which first appeared on California's debut solo album, *Kapt. Kopter and the (Fabulous) Twirly Birds;* "Shattered Dreams" and "Hand Guns" were on his second solo album, *Euro-American;* and "Hey Joe" and "All Along the Watchtower" are covers closely associated with California's mentor, Jimi Hendrix. California hews to a guitar-drenched rock sound, and the only distinction between his solo work and the music he credits to Spirit is the backup personnel. Even that is violated here, as original Spirit drummer Ed Cassidy appears on the first two tracks, and original Spirit keyboard man John Locke and replacement Spirit bassist Larry Knight are on the second. By whatever name, California remains a talented Hendrix-steeped guitarist who has never quite succeeded as a frontman. — *William Ruhlmann*

The Call

Group, Rock & Roll, Alternative Pop/Rock
The Call, a California-based quartet featuring the passionate singing and writing of Michael Been, incorporated the fire of the Clash and the organic earthy soul of the Band to deliver their spiritually rooted, socially aware themes. —*Rick Clark*

The Call / 1982 / Mercury ♦♦
Modern Romans / 1983 / Mercury ♦♦♦
Scene Beyond Dreams / 1984 / Mercury ♦♦♦
○ **Reconciled** / 1986 / Elektra ♦♦♦♦
One of their best efforts, it features the hit "Everywhere I Go"—Christian mysticism with a nervy edge. —*Rick Clark*

Into the Woods / 1987 / Elektra ♦♦♦
○ **Let the Day Begin** / 1989 / MCA ♦♦♦♦
The title cut was a major rock hit in spite of poor retail distribution. Other highlights include the rude rough-and-tumble rock of "Same Ol' Story." —*Rick Clark*

○ **Red Moon** / 1990 / MCA ♦♦♦♦
Pressured for new product, Been rose to the occasion, creating some of his most affectingly passionate music, particularly the stirring title cut, as well as "What's Happened to You?" (reminiscent of

the Band), "Like You've Never Been Loved," "This Is Your Life," and "Floating Back." The organic style of production works beautifully with the music. —*Rick Clark*

● **The Walls Came Down: Best of the Mecury Years** / 1991 / Mercury ✦✦✦✦
This great collection of the band's early career contains the fiery debut single "The Walls Came Down." It was compiled by Been. —*Rick Clark*

Camel
Group, Art-Rock/Progressive-Rock
The British art-rock band Camel features reflective melodies within the context of extended instrumental workouts. Guitarist Andrew Latimer has been Camel's creative mainstay throughout their many incarnations, which have included keyboardists Pete Bardens and Kit Watkins. —*AMG*

Camel / 1973 / MCA ✦✦

Mirage / 1974 / Janus ✦✦

The Snow Goose / 1975 / Janus ✦✦✦

Moonmadness / 1976 / Janus ✦✦✦

○ **Rain Dances** / 1977 / Deram ✦✦✦✦
Rain Dances, Camel's fifth release, offers the most consistent and representative package in their saga. This is the band at its best. The addition of Caravan-cofounder Richard Sinclair proves profitable, as do a few colorist touches by Brian Eno on "Elke." Mel Collins's woodwinds are among the highlights, especially on *Tell Me* and the title track. From beginning to end, this project flows gracefully. —*Matthew Plichta*

○ **Breathless** / 1978 / Arista ✦✦✦✦
While it might not be as consistent as *Rain Dances*, *Breathless* nevertheless contains several fine tracks and remains one of their better efforts. —*Stephen Thomas Erlewine*

● **I Can See Your House from Here** / 1979 / Deram ✦✦✦
Although not an honest representation of the band's character, this is undoubtedly their most popular work. The one-time addition of American Kit Watkins produces some fine keyboard lead work. Rupert Hines's resourceful production and appearances by Phil Collins and Mel Collins round out this strong import release. "Survival" and "Who We Are" feature some fine orchestrations, and guitarist Latimer delivers some exceptional lead work on the album's closer, "Ice." —*Matthew Plichta*

○ **Nude** / 1981 / Decca ✦✦✦✦

The Single Factor / 1982 / Passport ✦✦

Stationary Traveller / 1984 / Decca ✦✦✦

The Collection / 1986 / Castle ✦✦✦

○ **Dust and Dreams** / 1991 / Camel ✦✦✦✦
As with *Nude* and *The Snow Goose*, Camel continues refining their concept album approach, here based on Steinbeck's *The Grapes of Wrath*. Latimer maintains a symphonylike coherence throughout, with subtle character-based themes. Guest vocalist Mae McKenna has a hand in "Rose of Sharon," a gem of lyrical and musical depth. This recent album was produced and packaged by Latimer himself and may be harder to find than their others. (Available from Camel Productions, PO Box 4876, Mt. View, CA 94040.) —*Matthew Plichta*

● **Echoes: the Retrospective** / Jul. 20, 1993 / PolyGram ✦✦✦✦
There might be a song or two that die-hard fans will miss, but this double-disc set is the place to go for anyone looking for that one essential CD purchase of Camel's music. Featured are solid remastering and great liner notes and track annotation. —*Rick Clark*

○ **Compact Compilation** / Rhino ✦✦✦✦
This is an excellent selection of tracks from four of Camel's best albums. —*Michael P. Dawson*

Cameo
Group, Funk, Urban
Over the years, Cameo has reflected the numerous changes in the world of funk. When they started in 1974, they frequently toured with Parliament and Funkadelic, which is a clue to how their sound was styled. Even though they were in the hard funk vein of George Clinton's classic outfits, they were not copycats. As the '70s became the '80s, they started to play around with their sound slightly. In 1984, they found a successful style—the synth-powered title track to their album, *She's Strange*. But that only hinted at

what was to come. With 1986's *Word Up*, Cameo recorded a funk classic—bass-driven and synth heavy, the album was the sound of the mid-'80s. "Word Up" was also the song that broke them into the mainstream, reaching the Top Ten on the pop charts; thankfully, the album didn't have just one good song, it had a whole album's worth. Unfortunately, *Word Up* was the pinnacle of Cameo's career, with their synthesizers taking precedent over the melody and songs in their later records and the funk not being quite as strong as their earlier albums. —*Stephen Thomas Erlewine*

Cardiac Arrest / 1977 / Chocolate City ✦✦✦
The first major album for Cameo, who were then doing straight funk. The album scored three hits, among them the definitive "We All Know Who We Are" and the infectious "Rigor Mortis." They were still using horns and had 13 members in the group. —*Ron Wynn*

Ugly Ego / 1978 / Casablanca ✦✦✦
Another great funk treatise, with the first-rate uptempo tune "Insane" and a decent romantic song, "Give Love A Chance." They were slowly moving toward a new sound, although the influence of classic horn-driven funk bands like the Ohio Players and Bar-Kays is still prominent. —*Ron Wynn*

We All Know Who We Are / 1978 / Casablanca ✦✦✦

○ **Secret Omen** / 1979 / Casablanca ✦✦✦✦
Cameo leaped over their rivals with this 1979 release. "I Just Want To Be" was their finest single to that point, and "Sparkle" made a good album cut and counter-tune. It was the band's biggest hit album as well, starting them on a string of five gold records. —*Ron Wynn*

Cameosis / 1980 / Casablanca ✦✦✦
When Cameo released this 1980 LP, Larry Blackmon was still heading a large band that relied on horn-driven funk reflecting the influence of second-generation Bar-Kays. There were signs of stagnation throughout *Cameosis*; however, including the neglected single "Why Have I Lost You" from the *We All Know Who We Are* album was a stroke of genius. They landed a Top 10 R&B hit with "Shake Your Pants," but this wasn't among their best funk LPs. —*Ron Wynn*

○ **Feel Me** / 1980 / Casablanca ✦✦✦✦
One of two great funk albums Cameo issued in 1980. This one had another tremendous single, "Your Love Takes Me Out," a good second uptempo tune, "Keep It Hot," and was among the few '70s-style productions that was still viable at that point. The group hadn't yet streamlined its roster or changed its sound. —*Ron Wynn*

○ **Knights of the Sound Table** / 1981 / Casablanca ✦✦✦✦
Things were still rolling for Cameo with this '81 date. It was their first album to also be issued in England, and it scored more hits for them, with "Freaky Dancin'" reaching the number three spot on the R&B charts. Changes were coming soon, but they still retained the familiar horn-dominated sound. —*Ron Wynn*

Alligator Woman / 1982 / Casablanca ✦✦✦
The final '70s-oriented funk release by Cameo was another smash in 1982. They got three hits from this album, with "Flirt" making the Top 10 and "Just Be Yourself" and the title cut also doing well. The surging horn charts would soon be a memory, but *Alligator Woman* provided a fitting conclusion to Cameo's first phase. —*Ron Wynn*

Style / 1983 / Atlanta Artists ✦✦✦
A key transitional album for Cameo. The group had pared its lineup down to four core members, revamped its instrumental and production focus, and was now incorporating more electronics and sophisticated studio techniques. They also established their own label and relocated to Atlanta. This album laid the groundwork for the highly successful albums of the late '80s, and was their declaration of independence from the Ohio Players/Bar-Kays sound they had used to build their reputation. —*Ron Wynn*

○ **She's Strange** / 1984 / Casablanca ✦✦✦✦
This was the final large-group Cameo album. Blackmon realized that horn-driven funk was finished as a commercial entity in R&B production, and he stripped the group down to a core trio the next year. However, the title track was the group's biggest R&B hit ever; it stayed atop the charts for four weeks, longer than the superior tunes "Word Up" or "Candy." "Talkin' Out the Side of Your Neck" was a good message track; Blackmon showed his savvy by mak-

ing the change in direction even as he was still reaping commercial dividends from the old style. —*Ron Wynn*

Single Life / 1985 / Casablanca ✦✦✦
This was a transitional album for Cameo, the first with a core trio and a refocused production and creative emphasis. They were now a synth-dominated band with a snaking bass sound, rather than a horn-oriented group playing elaborate arrangements and using multiple vocalists. Blackmon's through-the-nose Sly Stone imitation and a tighter style yielded immediate results; both the title track and "Attack Me With Your Love" were Top 10 R&B hits. Cameo was now right in the urban contemporary flow. —*Ron Wynn*

○ **Word Up** / 1985 / Casablanca ✦✦✦✦
Cameo's definitive album came as a surprise to those who classed them a good journeyman band. The title track became a national catch phrase in the African-American community, and "Word" remains a linguistic staple in hip-hop circles. It was also a first-rate song, with a hypnotic rhythm track and arrangement and Blackmon's best lead vocal. The follow-up singles "Candy" and "Back And Forth" were also excellent. Cameo eventually scored its only platinum album, and "Word Up" was their lone Top 10 pop hit. —*Ron Wynn*

Machismo / 1988 / Atlanta Artists ✦✦✦
Up and down, but some fiery music. —*Ron Wynn*

Real Men Wear Black / 1990 / Casablanca ✦✦✦
A disappointment, the group lacks momentum. —*Ron Wynn*

Emotional Violence / Aug. 1991 / Reprise ✦✦

● **The Best of Cameo** / May 18, 1993 / Casablanca ✦✦✦✦
Larry Blackmon and his Cameo mates ruled funk's domain for over a decade. Cameo evolved from its origins as a horn-based and -dominated ensemble into a synthesizer-oriented group that still featured sturdy bass lines and exuberant vocals, but was in tune with urban and Black America's new sensibility. These 14 selections range from the formative cuts "Rigor Mortis," "Shake Your Pants," and "It's Over" to the definitive "Word Up," "Candy," and "Back & Forth." Blackmon's alternately sneering, defiant, and aggressive vocals were the constant from Cameo's beginnings in the 1970s to their emergence as funk's reigning champions in the 1980s. —*Ron Wynn*

Luther Campbell

Hip Hop
The founder/creator of 2 Live Crew, owner of Luke Records and former concert promoter, Luther Campbell at one time was arguably the nation's most controversial hip-hop figure. Campbell formed the Miami-based quartet in 1987 and they were the centerpiece of a national campaign against allegedly obscene lyrics. He was embroiled in a volatile trial pitting him against then-Florida attorney general Jack Thompson. Campbell later became a solo artist, issuing his own discs as Luke featuring 2 Live Crew. He released *Banned in the U.S.A.,* a parody of Bruce Springsteen's "Born in the U.S.A.," and *I've Got S—T On My Mind.* Campbell also published an autobiography and revamped 2 Live Crew, adding some fresh members. They issued *Back at Your Ass for the Nine-4,* which peaked at number nine on the R&B chart in 1994. Campbell also won a Supreme Court decision which ruled that his parody of Roy Orbison's "Oh, Pretty Woman" didn't violate the copyright held by Acuff-Rose. Campbell launched the career of R&B vocalists H-Town, issuing their debut LP on Luke Records. —*Ron Wynn*

● **Banned in the U.S.A.** / 1990 / Luke ✦✦✦✦
A decent parody of Bruce Springsteen's "Born in the U.S.A." helped turn the debut by 2 Live Crew founder Luther Campbell into a mini-event. Campbell didn't show any great rapping or rhyming skills on the microphone, but did speak frankly about those he considered fake "gangstas" in between the constant sexual innuendos, invitations, admonitions and declarations. —*Ron Wynn*

I Got Shit on My Mind / 1992 / Luke ✦✦
Luther Campbell, 2 Live Crew founder, impresario and overlord, took the microphone for a second session of his impressions on various subjects, mostly sexual and occasionally political. But where his debut had the novelty factor of hearing the Crew's head man out front, the second time around was much less entertaining and a lot more tiresome. —*Ron Wynn*

Freak for Life 6996 / 1994 / Luke ✦✦

Tevin Campbell

Urban
There's some dispute over who actually discovered Texas child sensation Tevin Campbell. Some accounts credit flutist Bobbi Humphrey, while much of the publicity material credits Quincy Jones. Campbell was in the 1988 television show *Wally & the Valentines,* and also appeared in Prince's film *Graffiti Bridge.* He made a splashy impression on Jones' *Back on the Block* LP, singing lead on "Tomorrow." He was 14 at the time. Campbell made such an impact that he earned a solo deal with Jones' Qwest label. His 1991 LP *T.E.V.I.N.* included two big R&B and pop hits, "Round and Round" and "Tell Me What You Want Me to Do." His second release, *I'm Ready,* was issued in 1993. —*Ron Wynn*

● **T.E.V.I.N.** / Nov. 19, 1991 / Warner Brothers ✦✦✦✦
If *T.E.V.I.N.* had been recorded by an adult instead of a teenager, the album would still be impressive, but the fact that Tevin Campbell was only fourteen years old when this was made makes it all the more amazing. Campbell's voice is remarkably expressive, able to handle both ballads and uptempo dance tracks without losing confidence. When he has the right material—like the hit single, Prince's "Round and Round"—the results are flawless; if the material is weak, he's merely enjoyable. —*Stephen Thomas Erlewine*

I'm Ready / 1993 / Warner Brothers ✦✦✦
Teen star Tevin Campbell's *I'm Ready* signaled a compositional and performance maturity reminiscent of Stevie Wonder's coming-of-age material in the late '60s. His voice, though still youthful, was stronger, warmer, and more distinctive, and he made the romantic lyrics of such tunes as "Don't Say Goodbye Girl," "The Halls of Desire" and the title track plausible, if somewhat overdone. He also demonstrated a willingness to tackle social concerns, although "Uncle Sam" seemed a bit dated, with references to Vietnam and Birmingham. He was most effective on ballads, notably "Always In My Heart." Those who expected Campbell to have fallen by the wayside or thought he was just another prodigy whose career wouldn't evolve have already been proven wrong. —*Ron Wynn*

Camper Van Beethoven

Group, Alternative Pop/Rock
Of all of their considerable strengths, perhaps Camper Van Beethoven's strongest was the fact that, given all their ambitions and weirdness, they never were inaccessible or pretentious. It was because they never played anything as just a joke; there was always a genuine love for the music that they were playing. Whether it was country or Mideastern music, a Ringo Starr cover or a Black Flag song, Camper Van Beethoven's humor came out of a love of the music; it was not a bunch of in-jokes from a pack of hipper-than-thou, over-educated college wise-asses. For such a rough, young band, their first album, 1986's *Telephone Free Landslide Victory,* was amazingly inventive and spirited. Over the next four years, Camper Van Beethoven never lost that garagey edge to their music, no matter how arty they were (their collaborations with experimental guitarist Eugene Chadbourne) or how simple (their numerous covers, as well as originals like "Take the Skinheads Bowling" or "Eye of Fatima"). In 1990, they parted amicably, with several members making their side project, the Monks of Doom, full time; lead singer/guitarist David Lowery formed Cracker, a more straightforward band which experienced a greater commercial success in the 1990s. Camper Van Beethoven's records have not lost any charm over the years; if anything, their music sounds better a decade later than it did while they were recording. —*Stephen Thomas Erlewine*

● **Telephone Free Landslide Victory** / 1985 / IRS ✦✦✦✦
"Quirky," "eccentric," "eclectic"—all those words were used often to describe this marvelous debut by Camper Van Beethoven. The Middle East meets C&W, and skinheads go bowling. A howl. —*Jeff Tamarkin*

II & III / Jan. 1986 / IRS ✦✦✦
Similar to the debut—well played but not so humorous or sharp. —*Jeff Tamarkin*

○ **Camper Van Beethoven** / Aug. 1986 / IRS ✦✦✦✦
Their third album is the apex of their creativity—stunning musicianship, witty lyrics, and a musical melting pot. Alternative rock at its most alternative. (The CD includes their 1987 EP *Vampire Can Mating Oven*). —*Jeff Tamarkin*

Vampire Can Mating Oven EP / 1987 / Pitch A Tent ✦✦✦
Camper Van Chadbourne / 1988 / Fundamental ✦✦
○ **Our Beloved Revolutionary Sweeheart** / 1988 / Virgin ✦✦✦✦

Camper Van Beethoven moved to a major label and lost none of their wildly eclectic and tuneful spark. In fact, *Our Beloved Revolutionary* contains some of their finest, most accessible songs. — *Stephen Thomas Erlewine*

Key Lime Pie / 1989 / Virgin ✦✦✦

Camper Van Beethoven's final record is the darkest album they ever recorded, but within its gloomy grooves lurk some terrific, fractured pop songs that rank among their best material. — *Stephen Thomas Erlewine*

Camper Vantiquities / 1993 / IRS ✦✦✦

All of Camper Van Beethoven's odds and ends (ranging from singles and B-sides, songs from tribute albums, and the entire *Vampire Can Mating Oven EP*) gathered together in one place. Far from being just a way to soak collectors for all they're worth, *Camper Vantiquities* contains some of the band's finest work, making it equally appealing for fans and the curious. — *Stephen Thomas Erlewine*

Ray Campi

Rock & Roll, Rockabilly
Campi recorded a handful of classic sides in Texas during the late '50s and later staged a comeback via Ronny Weiser's Rollin' Rock revivalist label. Born in New York, Campi relocated to Austin and cut his debut single for TNT in 1956, "Caterpillar"/"Play It Cool." He cut "Ballad of Donna & Peggy Sue" for Dot before moving to Los Angeles in 1959 and signing with Colpix. After a long layoff when he became a junior high school teacher in Los Angeles, Campi's 1980 return to vinyl on Rollin' Rock, "Rockin' at the Ritz," kicked off a series of releases that celebrate the timeless charm of savage rockabilly rhythms. — *Bill Dahl*

● **Gone Gone Gone!** / Oct. 1986 / Rounder ✦✦✦✦

Latter-day, retro-rockabilly from a performer active at the genre's beginnings. — *Bill Dahl*

Can

Group, Electronic, Art-Rock/Progressive-Rock, Experimental
Always at least three steps ahead of contemporary popular music, Can was the leading avant-garde rock group of the '70s. From their very beginning, their music didn't conform to any commonly held notions about rock & roll—not even those of the counter-cultures. Inspired more by 20th century classical music than Chuck Berry, their closest contemporaries were Frank Zappa or possibly the Velvet Underground. Yet their music was more serious and inaccessible than either of those artists. Instead of recording tight pop songs or satire, Can experimented with noise, synthesizers, non-traditional music, cut-and-paste techniques, and, most importantly, electronic music; each album marked a significant step forward from the previous album, investigating new territories that other rock bands weren't interested in exploring.

Throughout their career, Can's line-up was fluid, featuring several different vocalists over the years; the core band members remained keyboardist Irmin Schmidt, drummer Jaki Liebezeit, guitarist Michael Karoli, and keyboardist Holger Czukay. During the '70s, they were extremely prolific, recording as many as three albums a year at the height of their career. Apart from a surprise U.K. Top 30 hit in 1976—"I Want More"—they were never much more than a cult band; even critics had a hard time appreciating their music. When the band split in 1978, it left behind a body of work that has proven surprisingly groundbreaking; echoes of Can's music can be heard in Public Image Limited, the Fall, and Einstürzende Neubauten, among others. As with much aggressive and challenging experimental music, Can's music can be difficult to appreciate, yet their albums offer some of the best experimental rock ever recorded. — *Stephen Thomas Erlewine*

○ **Monster Movie** / 1969 / Spoon ✦✦✦✦

Monster Movie is an avant-rock extraordinaire, the Velvet Underground, with a sharper edge and harder beat. It features the stream of consciousness poetics of African-American vocalist Malcolm Mooney, underpinned by searing guitar/keyboard excursions and relentless percussive energy. — *Archie Patterson*

Soundtracks / 1970 / Restless ✦✦✦

These psychedelic jams come from five late-'60s movie soundtracks. Some are inspired, some dated. — *Myles Boisen*

○ **Tago Mago** / 1971 / Restless ✦✦✦✦

Tago Mago is a double album that adds Stockhausen to the mix. It blends layers of keyboards, sound collages, scatter-gun guitar and a primal rhythm section with new vocalist Damo Suzuki's sensual vocal incantations. — *Archie Patterson*

○ **Ege Bamyasi** / 1972 / Restless ✦✦✦✦

Funky, urgent, and experimental at their 1972 peak, this documents a band that is still ahead of our time. — *Myles Boisen*

● **Future Days** / 1973 / Spoon ✦✦✦✦

Long, jazzy excursions with few vocal moments, it's uncharacteristic but engaging. — *Myles Boisen*

Soon over Babaluma / 1974 / Enigma ✦✦✦

The band, at its most stripped-down potency, has a new sound without Damo. — *Myles Boisen*

Limited Edition / 1974 / United Artists ✦✦

Landed / 1975 / Mute ✦✦

Another erratic waxing features some great guitar and Babaluma-style grooves, but is unfocused on the whole. — *Myles Boisen*

Flow Motion / 1976 / Mute ✦✦

More pop aspirations and overt use of ethnic textures yield mixed results, as was typical of the band's later years. — *Myles Boisen*

Unlimited Edition / 1976 / Mute ✦✦✦

These studio outtakes, from Can's history up to 1975, are fascinating electronic and ethnic musical excursions. — *Myles Boisen*

Opener / 1976 / Sunset ✦✦✦

Saw Delight / 1977 / Mute ✦✦✦

This effort is a nice mix of trance/groove instrumentals, ethnic sampling, and silly vocals in English. — *Myles Boisen*

Out of Reach / 1978 / Harvest ✦✦

Cannibalisms / 1978 / United Artists ✦✦✦

Can / 1979 / Mute ✦✦

This one suffers without bassist Holger Czukay, and from overblown pop keyboards. — *Myles Boisen*

● **Cannibalism 1** / 1980 / Spoon ✦✦✦✦

A sampler of early tracks up to 1974, it features many of their most focused grooves and stylistic extremes. — *Myles Boisen*

Delay . . . 1968 / 1981 / Spoon ✦✦✦

Their first recordings, these went unreleased for years. — *Myles Boisen*

Incandescence / 1981 / Virgin ✦✦✦

Time Rite / 1989 / Fink & Star

○ **Cannibalism 2** / 1990 / Mute ✦✦✦✦

Cannibalism 3 / 1990 / Mute ✦✦✦

Candlebox

Group, Hard Rock
Rock band featuring vocalist Kevin Martin, guitarist Peter Klett, drummer Scott Mercado, and bassist Bardi Martin. Candlebox came out of the Seattle scene, but their influences lie more toward bluesy classic rock than the grungy sound of other Seattle bands, which make them more commercially viable. The band has been derided because they were not originally from Seattle, firing perhaps legitimate criticism that they simply moved there to be discovered and signed. They were initially marketed as part of the alternative scene, but their sound is really quite mainstream. Rock audiences didn't seem to care either way, and the group's debut album went Top Ten and sold over three million copies on the strength of the hit single "You" and "Far Behind." — *Steve Huey*

Candlebox / Jul. 20, 1993 / Warner Brothers ✦✦✦

Candlebox rode the alternative bandwagon to the top of the charts with their self-titled debut album. Taking the heaviest moments of Soundgarden and Alice In Chains and adding both the confinements of a pop song and the attitude of album rock, Candlebox managed to sell over two million copies of their first album. Nothing on *Candlebox* is particularly catchy—the singles "You" and "Far Behind" are the closest they come to memorable melodies—but there is enough sheer riff power to satisfy fans of their singles. — *Stephen Thomas Erlewine*

Candyman

Rap

Los Angeles rapper Candyman was featured backing Tone-Loc before he earned his own solo stint. His 1990 debut *Ain't No Shame in My Game* scored a Top Ten pop hit with "Knockin' Boots." The following year, he followed that with another less successful LP for Epic, *Playtime Is Over*. His most recent release was *I Thought U Knew* for I.R.S. in 1993, which also failed to click. *—Ron Wynn*

● **Ain't No Shame in My Game** / 1990 / Epic ✦✦✦
Although this scored a huge crossover hit with "I Got a Man," the rest of the record didn't prove if the single was a fluke or not; jury was still out. *—Ron Wynn & Stephen Thomas Erlewine*

Playtime Is Over / 1991 / Epic ✦✦✦
A decent follow-up, but it lines up in the pop/gimmick camp despite occasionally interesting raps and production. *—Ron Wynn*

I Thought U Knew / Jun. 29, 1993 / IRS ✦✦
The third Candyman CD, his first for I.R.S., lacked either the pop charm of his debut or the leering insolence of the follow-up. *—Ron Wynn*

Canned Heat

Group, Blues Rock

A hard-luck blues band of the '60s, Canned Heat was founded by Al Wilson and Bob Hite. They seemed to be on the right track and played all the right festivals (including Monterey and Woodstock, making it very prominently into the documentaries about both) but somehow never found a lasting audience. Wilson died under mysterious (probably drug-related causes) circumstances in 1970, and Hite carried on with various reconstituted versions of the band until his death in 1981, from a heart seizure just before a show. *—Bruce Eder*

● **The Best of Canned Heat** / 1972 / EMI America ✦✦✦
All of Canned Heat's best tracks and biggest hits ("Goin' Up the Country," "On the Road Again") are included on this single-disc collection. *—Stephen Thomas Erlewine*

○ **Uncanned! The Best of Canned Heat** / May 17, 1994 / EMI America ✦✦✦
Uncanned! The Best of Canned Heat is exactly what it claims to be—the definitive portrait of the blues-soaked hippie boogie band. Spreading 41 tracks (including numerous rarities, alternate takes, and Levi commercials) over two CDs, the set is perfect for the hardcore Canned Heat collector. For casual fans, the collection simply contains too much music; they would be better served by the single-disc collection, *The Best of Canned Heat*. *—Stephen Thomas Erlewine*

The Capitols

Group, Soul

The energetic Detroit-based Capitols capitalized on mid-'60s R&B dance fever with one of the most memorable entries of the genre, "Cool Jerk." Successful local producer Ollie McLaughlin signed the trio—lead singer Sam George, Donald Norman (who wrote most of the group's material under his real surname of Storball), and Richard Mitchell—to his Karen logo, and the irresistible "Cool Jerk" made them an overnight sensation. After a couple more chart entries later that year, the trio faded quickly. George was murdered on March 17, 1982. *—Bill Dahl*

● **Golden Classics** / Collectables ✦✦✦✦
Dance-oriented mid-'60s Detroit soul, this features the notable classic "Cool Jerk." *—Bill Dahl*

The Capris

Group, Doo-Wop

The only major Capris hit, the romantic "There's a Moon Out Tonight," is a New York street-corner harmony classic. Doo-wop was back in fashion by 1961, and it was no longer limited to R&B aggregations. Led by Nick Santo (born Nick Santamaria in 1941), the Capris named themselves after the Isle of Capri in Italy. The Queens, NY, natives originally cut "There's a Moon Out Tonight" for the obscure Planet imprint in 1958, but when the song was reissued on Lost Nite (and eventually on Old Town) it became a national smash its second time around in early 1961. After many moons out of the spotlight, the Capris came back triumphantly in 1981 with an album on Ambient Sound and an appearance on the PBS-TV series *Soundstage*. *—Bill Dahl*

There's a Moon out Again! / 1982 / Ambient Sound ✦✦✦
Recorded in 1982, live to two-track, here's a perfect example of what a great modern-day doo-wop album should be. *—Cub Koda*

● **There's a Moon out Tonight** / Collectables ✦✦✦✦
Nick Santo's anguished, innocent-sounding lead on "There's A Moon Out Tonight" became a hit some three years after the song was originally issued. By this time, they had disbanded, but regrouped in a hurry trying to milk the hit. This album collects ten tunes they cut for Planet, most of them superior to "There's A Moon Out Tonight," but none of them able to duplicate that song's success. *—Ron Wynn*

Captain & Tennille

Group, Pop

Vibrant, relentlessly upbeat harmonies made Captain (born Daryl Dragon, Aug 27, 1942) & Tennille (born Toni Tennille, May 8, 1943) stars during the latter half of the 70s. Dragon, dubbed the "Captain" because of his distinctive headgear, had played keyboards with the Beach Boys prior to teaming with his wife. Their first hit on A&M, the buoyant "Love Will Keep Us Together," was a million-selling chart-topper in 1975, and a reissue of their 1974 single "The Way I Want to Touch You" also went gold. The couple hung three more gold records in their den in 1976—"Lonely Night (Angel Face)," "Shop Around," and Willis Alan Ramsey's "Muskrat Love"—and that was enough for ABC-TV to install them as hosts of their own variety program. "Do That to Me One More Time" was the last #1 item for the pair in 1979. *—Bill Dahl*

● **Captain & Tennille's Greatest Hits** / 1977 / A&M ✦✦✦✦
A solid collection of all of their mid-'70s hits. *—Stephen Thomas Erlewine*

Captain Beefheart

b. Jan. 15, 1941, Glendale, California

Rock & Roll, Art-Rock/Progressive-Rock, Psychedelic, Experimental

Drawing from gut-bucket Delta blues, free jazz, bare-boned rock, and the dissonance of 20th-century avant-garde chamber music, Captain Beefheart (born Don Van Vliet) and the Magic Band never sold many records, but they influenced many alternative artists, including Devo, XTC, Pere Ubu, and Sonic Youth.

Beefheart, an accomplished multi-instrumentalist, exhibited a vocal range that (some claim) spanned seven-and-a-half octaves, at times sounding like an utterly crazed incarnation of Howlin' Wolf. The first lineup of the Magic Band included Ry Cooder, and some of their first recordings on A&M were actually produced by future Bread founder David Gates.

Longtime friend and occasional musical cohort Frank Zappa signed Beefheart to his Straight label, allowing them complete artistic freedom. The result was the groundbreaking *Trout Mask Replica*.

Since then, Beefheart has put out a dozen albums, either with the Magic Band, with Zappa, or solo. Among those highlights are *Clear Spot*, *Bat Chain Puller*, *Doc at the Radar Station*, and *Ice Cream for Crow*. *—Rick Clark*

○ **Safe As Milk** / 1967 / Buddah ✦✦✦
Beefheart's first proper studio album is a much more accessible, pop-inflected brand of blues-rock than the efforts that followed in the late '60s—which isn't to say that it's exactly normal and straightforward. Featuring Ry Cooder on guitar, this is blues rock gone slightly askew, with jagged, fractured rhythms, soulful, twisting vocals from Van Vliet, and more doo-wop, soul, straight blues, and folk-rock influences than he would employ on his more avant-garde outings. "Zig Zag Wanderer," "Call On Me," and "Yellow Brick Road" are some of his most enduring and riff-driven songs, although there's plenty of weirdness on tracks like "Electricity" and "Abba Zaba." *—Richie Unterberger*

Strictly Personal / 1968 / Blue Thumb ✦✦

★ **Trout Mask Replica** / 1969 / Reprise ✦✦✦✦
Originally released and produced by Frank Zappa as a double album on his Bizarre/Straight label, *Trout Mask Replica* is the definitive Captain Beefheart album. To some, it is just plain weird, perhaps even anti-music. To others, it is blues with a warp or rock & roll at the absolute cutting edge. Deeply rooted in blues and jazz, the Captain taught each member of the Magic Band their extremely complex individual parts over the course of a year. Playful and challenging at the same time, rhythmically kinetic, poetically beautiful, it is an absolute masterpiece. *—Rob Bowman*

○ **Lick My Decals Off, Baby** / 1970 / Bizarre ✦✦✦✦
The bookend release to *Trout Mask Replica*, this time produced by the Captain himself. Sample title "The Smithsonian Institute Blues (The Big Dig)" should give you a sense that this is not an ordinary rock & roll record. Just a shade less essential than *Trout Mask Replica*. —*Rob Bowman*

Mirror Man / 1970 / One Way ✦✦✦
An early version of the Captain's Magic Band, recorded live in Los Angeles probably in 1968 (the cover says 1965, but that is undoubtedly erroneous). Stunning extended versions of four Beefheart originals, including his Robert Johnson-inspired "Tarotplane." —*Rob Bowman*

The Spotlight Kid / Clear Spot / 1972 / Reprise ✦✦✦
The Spotlight Kid (1972) and *Clear Spot* (1973) have been released on one CD. The Captain became slightly more accessible on these two early-'70s releases, accenting the rock & roll ingredients. Slide guitar abounds on some of the most asymmetrical riffs imaginable throughout *The Spotlight Kid*. The lyrics are just as playful. *Clear Spot* is the Captain at his most balanced—accessible without deserting the avant-garde. "Big-Eyed Beans from Venus" became one of his all-time classics. —*Rob Bowman*

Captain Beefheart & The Magic Band / 1972 / Reprise

Bluejeans & Moonbeams / 1974 / Blue Plate ✦✦

Unconditionally Guaranteed / 1974 / Blue Plate ✦✦

○ **Shiny Beast (Bat Chain Puller)** / Jan. 1978 / Bizarre ✦✦✦✦
The Captain's comeback album, with the second edition of the Magic Band. As good as *Clear Spot* or *The Spotlight Kid*, with a slightly different temperament and a touch of synthesizer. —*Rob Bowman*

○ **Doc at the Radar Station** / 1980 / Blue Plate ✦✦✦✦
The masterpiece of the Captain's late-'70s/early-'80s resurrection. This time, the new Magic Band had coalesced into an ensemble of frightening power. Cross-rhythms abut each other in some of the most hyperkinetic settings imaginable. There's not a weak song or performance to be found. Buy this. —*Rob Bowman*

○ **Ice Cream for Crow** / 1982 / Blue Plate ✦✦✦✦
The Captain's last album as of this writing, with no sign that he'll ever return. A couple of changes in the Magic Band and the Captain perhaps losing a bit of steam make this album undistinguished. There is nothing poor here; if you are into the Captain, you will want to own this. However, everything else listed is recommended first. —*Rob Bowman*

Legendary A&M Sessions / 1984 / A&M ✦✦✦
Before gaining a cult with his avant-garde excursions in the late '60s, Captain Beefheart wielded a much more traditional sort of blues-rock. That's not to say that these his two obscure mid-'60s A&M singles (packaged together on this 5-song EP, which adds a previously unreleased track from the same era) aren't well worth hearing. The Captain's Howlin' Wolf-like growl led a tough outfit that ranked among the best early American blues-rock groups, and among the few that could reasonably emulate the Rolling Stones' toughness. Produced, unbelievably enough, by future Bread leader David Gates, this reissue includes their regional hit cover of Bo Diddley's "Diddy Wah Diddy." The best track, though, is "Moonchild," their shameless derivation of Howlin' Wolf's "Smokestack Lightning." Featuring wailing harmonica, stomping riffs and adventurous, quasi-psychedelic production, it was actually written by Gates himself. To think that the same man was also responsible for "If" and "Baby I'm-a Want You" blows the mind. —*Richie Unterberger*

Irene Cara

b. Mar. 18, 1959, New York, NY
Pop/Rock
Irene Cara is best known as a singer of movie themes, though she has worked as an actress since her childhood. Raised in New York City, she appeared on Broadway in 1967 in the musical *Maggie Flynn* at age eight. She can be heard on the cast album for the show *The Me Nobody Knows*. From the age of 16, she was turning up on television and in films, including a part in the TV mini-series *Roots 2* in 1979. In 1980, she was catapulted into stardom and a singing career by her appearance in the film *Fame*, for which she sang the title song, an Oscar-winning Top Ten hit. Also from the film was her Top 40 hit "Out Here on My Own." In 1983, she topped the charts with "Flashdance...What a Feelin'," from the

movie *Flashdance*, a song she co-wrote that won another Oscar, while Cara also won a couple of Grammys for her contributions to the soundtrack. Her *What a Feelin'* album included the hits "Why Me?" and "Breakdance," and she also made the Top 40 with a third movie theme, "The Dream (Hold On to Your Dream)," from *DC Cab*. —*William Ruhlmann*

Anyone Can See / Jan. 1982 / Epic ✦✦✦

● **What a Feelin'** / Nov. 1983 / Geffen ✦✦✦✦
As a general rule, you would expect that an album featuring a gold-selling #1 hit, a Top Ten hit, and two Top 40 follow-ups would itself be a considerable success, but Irene Cara's second album had trouble staying among the 100 best-sellers. Why? That chart-topper, "Flashdance...What a Feeling," had come the previous spring, and most people who wanted to own it had purchased it either as a single or on the multi-platinum soundtrack album. Plus, Cara never established a base beyond her individual hits. This wasn't surprising, really, since, despite her participation as singer and co-lyricist, Cara essentially was the mouthpiece of Eurodisco producer Giorgio Moroder on these recordings. Thus, although Irene Cara was all over the airwaves in 1983-84, and although this album contained all five of her chart entries from the period, Cara herself failed to benefit over the long term, and as a glut for this kind of material set in, she was left behind. —*William Ruhlmann*

Carasmatic / 1987 / Elektra ✦✦

Caravan

Group, Art-Rock/Progressive-Rock
Of all of the progressive rock bands that came from England in the late '60s, Caravan was certainly one of the most interesting. Instead of indulging in the classical pomp of most of the other groups of that era, Caravan was gentle where others were overbearing, melodic where others were ponderous. That doesn't mean they weren't spontaneous; some of their best moments came when the band launched into extended, intricate improvisations. Caravan's music was based more in traditional English folk and medieval instrumentation; it was not unusual to hear lush strings and woodwinds on their albums. Although its line-up changed slightly over the '70s, the band kept releasing records until 1983; that year's *Back to Front* marked the reunion of the original quartet—guitarist/vocalist Pye Hastings, keyboardist David Sinclair, bassist/vocalist Richard Sinclair, and drummer Richard Coughlan. —*Rick Clark*

Caravan / 1968 / Verve ✦✦

If I Could Do It All over Again I'd Do / 1970 / London ✦✦✦

○ **In the Land of The Grey & Pink** / 1971 / London ✦✦✦✦

Waterloo Lily / 1972 / London ✦✦✦
Waterloo Lily follows Caravan's first personnel changes, resulting in a spotty and unfocused album, though not without merits. Keyboardist Steve Miller plays electric piano in a bluesier style than his predecessor Dave Sinclair, an organist. The band competently executes the jazzier, extended material which comprises about half the disc; the sloppy fade in/fade out of the extended suites "Nothing at All" and "It's Coming Soon" make the music seem almost inconsequential. Pye Hastings's shorter songs carry the album, especially the marvellous "The World Is Yours." —*Jim Powers*

○ **For Girls Who Grow Plump in the Night** / 1973 / London ✦✦✦✦

Caravan & The New Symphonia / 1974 / London ✦

Cunning Stunts / 1975 / BTM ✦✦✦

Blind Dog at St Dunstans / 1976 / Arista ✦✦

Better by Far / 1977 / Arista ✦

Show of Our Lives / 1981 / Decca ✦✦✦

The Album / 1983 / Kingdom ✦✦

Back to Front / 1983 / Kingdom ✦✦

The Collection / 1984 / Kindom ✦✦✦

Best of Caravan / 1987 / London ✦✦✦
A fine single-disc collection of some of their best moments, but the double-disc *Canterbury Tales* offers a better portrait of the group. —*Stephen Thomas Erlewine*

● **Canterbury Tales: The Best of Caravan** / 1994 / Decca ✦✦✦✦
Canterbury Tales is a generous two-disc helping of this great progressive rock band's first seven albums. The compilation draws most heavily from the albums *If I Could Do It All Over Again...,*

In the Land of Grey and Pink, For Girls Who Grow Plump in the Night, and *Caravan and the New Symphonia.* There are also selections from *Cunning Stunts, Waterloo Lily,* and *Caravan.* A good balance is struck between Caravan's shorter single-length pop songs and its more extended suites. The liner notes feature an informative biographical and discographical essay and lots of photographs and credits. The remastering is excellent. —*Jim Powers*

Carcass

Group, Hard Rock, Thrash, Heavy Metal
England's Carcass assisted in a revival of the death-metal genre while introducing the new grindcore style. —*John Book*

Reek of Putrefaction / 1988 / Earache ✦✦✦
Carcass was one of the original members of the grindcore movement. Bassist/vocalist Jeff Walker was a biology and anatomy student, and all members were vegetarians. All of their lyrics were lifted from some of Walker's medical textbooks, and Walker professes to be fascinated with the digestive system; the results demand to be heard by anyone with a strong stomach and a weird sense of humor. —*Steve Huey*

● **Symphonies of Sickness** / 1989 / Earache ✦✦✦✦
This hi-tech grindcore is very fast and very wicked, not for the squeamish. It makes for a good introduction to grindcore. —*John Book*

Necroticism-Descanti / 1991 / Earache ✦✦
Any hint of melody or breathing space is strictly verboten here. I have to offer grudging respect for stuff so totally non-compromising... just don't ask me to listen to it again. You have been warned. —*Roch Parisien*

Tools of the Trade / Jun. 23, 1992 / Earache ✦✦

● **Heartwork** / 1994 / Earache ✦✦✦✦
Most death-metal albums suffer from an overabundance of riffs and not enough songs, but Carcass avoids that trap with *Heartwork,* their breakthrough release. Carcass doesn't lose their shattering intensity for a split second, but are able to incorporate real song structures and actual melodies to their bludgeoning riffs and rhythms, helping *Heartwork* pave the way for death metal in the '90s. —*Stephen Thomas Erlewine*

Mariah Carey

b. Mar. 22, 1970, New York, NY
Dance-Pop, Urban, Pop/Rock
Mariah Carey has a remarkable multi-octave voice, an astonishing instrument that can reach heights only rivaled by Whitney Houston. Like Houston, Carey works the same pop-soul ballad territory, occasionally spiked by some catchy dance-oriented pop. Fortunately, Carey hasn't had a shortage of good material, either; all of her three albums feature impeccably crafted singles, designed for continuous radio play.

While she was an overnight sensation with her first single, 1990's "Vision of Love," it wasn't until 1992 that she won over many skeptical critics with her unadorned "MTV Unplugged" performance. Not that negative criticism has hurt her career any—her three albums and one EP have all sold several million copies and she has dominated the singles chart since her first album. It's a track record that very few artists can match. —*Stephen Thomas Erlewine*

○ **Mariah Carey** / 1990 / Columbia ✦✦✦✦
This extremely impressive debut is replete with smooth-sounding ballads and uplifting dance/R&B cuts. Carey convincingly seizes many opportunities to display her incredible vocal range on such memorable tracks as the popular "Vision Of Love" (featured during her television debut on *The Arsenio Hall Show,* an appearance noted by many as her formal introduction to stardom), the energetic "Someday," and the moody sounds of the hidden treasure "Vanishing." With this collection of songs acting as a springboard for future successes, Carey establishes a strong standard of comparison for other breakthrough artists of this genre. —*Ashley S. Battel*

Emotions / 1991 / Columbia ✦✦✦
A strong follow-up to Carey's self-titled debut album, *Emotions* puts to rest any concern of a "sophomore jinx." The same mix of dance/R&B/ballads which gave Carey's debut such tremendous auditory appeal can be found with equal strength on this release, indicating that placing firm belief in the notion of "Why fool with success?" may, in fact, have its merits. Most notably, the gospel in-

fluences of "If It's Over" (with music co-written by Carole King), the yearning cries for a lost love in "Can't Let Go," and the catchy, upbeat title track, all serve to send the listener on a musical journey filled with varying emotions. However, the one emotion which prevails upon completion of the album is definitely a positive one—satisfaction! —*Ashley S. Battel*

○ **MTV Unplugged Ep** / Mar. 1992 / Columbia ✦✦✦
Although Mariah Carey doesn't come close to following the traditional *Unplugged* format of only a voice and a guitar (she brought in strings and backup vocalists), her *MTV Unplugged EP* (which includes her hit version of the Jackson 5's "I'll Be There") is her best record to date, proving that her talents as a vocalist are considerable. —*Stephen Thomas Erlewine*

● **Music Box** / 1993 / Columbia ✦✦✦✦
Mariah Carey has been stung by critical charges that she's all vocal bombast and no subtlety, soul or shading. Her solution was to make an album in which her celebrated octave-leaping voice would be downplayed and she could demonstrate her ability to sing softly and coolly. Well, she was partly successful; she trimmed the volume on *Music Box.* Unfortunately, she also cut the energy level; Carey sounds detached on several selections. She scored a couple of huge hits, "Hero" and "Dreamlover," where she did inject some personality and intensity into the leads. Most other times, Carey blended into the background and let the tracks guide her, instead of pushing and exploding through them. It was wise for Carey to display other elements of her approach, but sometimes excessive spirit is preferable to an absence of passion. —*Ron Wynn*

Belinda Carlisle

b. Aug. 16, 1958, Hollywood, CA
Pop/Rock
Belinda Carlisle pursued a solo career after leaving the Go-Go's in 1984. As her solo career progressed, Carlisle removed any of the rough edges remaining in her style, transforming from a new wave rocker to a polished adult contemporary pop singer. The change was evident on her first album, 1986's *Belinda.* Featuring the number three hit single "Mad About You," the record went gold and established her as a viable hitmaker.

The following year, Carlisle released *Heaven on Earth,* her greatest solo success. Continuing the immaculately produced mainstream pop of *Belinda,* the record featured the #1 title track, the #2 single "I Get Weak" and the Top Ten ballad "Circle in the Sand." *Runaway Horses,* released in 1989, was another successful album, spawning the hit singles "Leave a Light On" and "Summer Rain," yet it showed signs that her audience was shrinking. That suspicion was confirmed by the dismal performance of 1991's *Live Your Life Be Free,* which failed to make the charts. *Real,* released in 1993, didn't revive Carlisle's career and she subsequently joined the re-formed Go-Go's in 1994. —*Stephen Thomas Erlewine*

Belinda / 1986 / IRS ✦✦✦
Belinda Carlisle's first solo record was a distinct departure from the Go-Go's energetic, catchy new wave pop. Carlisle refashioned herself as an unoffensive mainstream pop singer and the makeover worked commercially, as well as artistically. The pop on *Belinda* may not be as infectious as the Go-Go's finest singles, yet it fit in well with the slick formats of mid-'80s radio and managed to be more memorable than many of the mainstream hits of the time, as the ingratiating hit "Mad About You" proves. —*Stephen Thomas Erlewine*

○ **Heaven on Earth** / 1987 / MCA ✦✦✦✦
Her commercial peak contains "I Get Weak," "Circle in the Sand," and the title track. —*Dan Heilman*

Runaway Horses / 1989 / MCA ✦✦
Runaway Horses replicated the strengths of *Heaven on Earth,* featuring a wealth of catchy, polished mid-tempo pop songs that sounded better on the radio than they did on record. Apart from the singles "Leave a Light On," "Summer Rain," and "(We Want) The Same Thing," the album suffered from a lack of memorable material, yet that didn't distract from the overall pleasantness of the record. —*Stephen Thomas Erlewine*

Live Your Life Be Free / 1991 / MCA ✦

● **Her Greatest Hits** / 1992 / MCA ✦✦✦✦
All of Belinda Carlisle's late-'80s pop hits, including "Heaven is a Place on Earth," "Mad About You," and "I Get Weak," available on one disc. —*Stephen Thomas Erlewine*

Real / Oct. 5, 1993 / Virgin

Like *Live Your Life Be Free*, *Real* was a well-crafted and produced album alternating between ballads and light dance-pop. Like its predecessor, *Real* also suffered from a lack of memorable songs. While the record sounded good, it had nothing to support the state-of-the-art production. —*Stephen Thomas Erlewine*

Eric Carmen

b. Aug. 11, 1949, Cleveland, OH
Pop/Rock
Eric Carmen was the lead vocalist and songwriter of the Raspberries, an early-'70s band heavily influenced by mid-'60s pop, especially the Beatles. For his 1975 self-titled debut album, Carmen looked even farther into the past, to the early 20th century. His two hit singles, the heavily produced ballads "All by Myself" and "Never Gonna Fall in Love Again," were based on pieces by Russian classical composer Serge Rachmaninoff. The rest of the album and Carmen's subsequent, less commercially successful albums were a pastiche of classic pop styles. Carmen didn't enjoy a big commercial success again until 1987's "Hungry Eyes," from the *Dirty Dancing* concert tour. —*Kenneth M. Cassidy*

Eric Carmen / 1975 / Rhino ✦✦✦
Carmen achieved far greater success with his debut solo album than he ever had with his old group, the Raspberries. In part this was because, freed from the restrictions of leading a rock band, he could indulge his taste in big, lush ballads. That's what he did here, especially on the album's three Top 40 hits, one of which, "All by Myself," was a gold-selling #2 hit. —*William Ruhlmann*

All by Myself / 1977 / Arista ✦✦
Boats Against the Current / 1977 / Arista ✦✦
Change of Heart / 1978 / Arista ✦✦
Tonight You're Mine / 1980 / Arista ✦✦
● **The Best of Eric Carmen** / 1988 / Arista ✦✦✦✦
This album lacks Carmen's 1988 hit "Make Me Lose Control," but it does sample six of the eight singles-chart entries he enjoyed from 1975 to 1980, plus interesting album cuts such as "Hey Deanie," the Shaun Cassidy hit written by Carmen, and, of course, his comeback hit, "Hungry Eyes," from the *Dirty Dancing* soundtrack. —*William Ruhlmann*

Kim Carnes

b. Jul. 20, 1945, Los Angeles, CA
Pop/Rock
The raspy-voiced singer's atmospheric #1 smash, "Bette Davis Eyes," was cowritten by Jackie DeShannon. Carnes was once a member of the New Christy Minstrels with Kenny Rogers, who gave her welcome exposure in 1980 with their duet "Don't Fall in Love with a Dreamer." Later that year, a Carnes cover of the Miracles' "More Love" was a smash. She scored numerous pop hits throughout the decade and experimented with country in 1988. —*Bill Dahl*

Rest on Me / 1972 / Amos ✦✦
Kim Carnes / 1975 / A&M ✦✦
○ **Sailin'** / 1976 / A&M ✦✦✦✦
St Vincent's Court / 1979 / EMI America ✦✦✦
Romance Dance / Jun. 1980 / EMI America ✦✦✦
Soulful pop, including a cover of the Miracles' hit "More Love." —*Bil Carpenter*
○ **Mistaken Identity** / Apr. 1981 / EMI America ✦✦✦✦
A successful pop-rock album, it features the smash "Bette Davis Eyes," which held the top position on the pop charts for nine weeks. —*Bil Carpenter*
Voyeur / Sep. 1982 / EMI America ✦✦
Voyeur was Kim Carnes's all-important follow-up to *Mistaken Identity*, an album that had topped the charts and spawned the #1 hit "Bette Davis Eyes." But though Carnes and her producer, Val Garay, faithfully reproduced the exaggerated vocal phrasing and synthesizer-dance music arrangement of their hit on several tracks and were rewarded with Top 40 placings for the title track and "Does It Make You Remember," *Voyeur* only succeeded in proving that "Bette Davis Eyes" was a one-time phenomenon, not a career-making breakthrough. —*William Ruhlmann*

Cafe Racers / Nov. 1983 / EMI America ✦✦
When Kim Carnes delivered *Cafe Racers*, the second follow-up to her platinum, chart-topping 1981 album *Mistaken Identity*, radio programmers were still up for searching out a potential hit on the order of "Bette Davis Eyes," and the tracks "Invisible Hands," "You Make My Heart Beat Faster (And That's All That Matters)," "I Pretend," and "Hurricane" were all given a chance at Top 40, Adult Contemporary, and/or dance stations. But working with producer Keith Olsen, Carnes had largely eviscerated her trademark throaty vocal quality, burying it beneath slick production techniques and synth sounds, and neither she nor the songwriters drafted in could come up with anything as compelling or identifiable as her big hit. This was record-making by committee, the last thing an artist looking to consolidate earlier success needs. —*William Ruhlmann*
View from the House / Jul. 25, 1988 / MCA ✦✦✦
A folk/country set. —*Bil Carpenter*
● **Gypsy Honeymoon: Best of Kim Carnes** / 1993 / EMI America ✦✦✦✦
Don't mistake this set as a definitive collection of hits. While it contains her three biggest Top Ten numbers ("Bette Davis Eyes," "More Love," and "Don't Fall in Love with a Dreamer," a duet with Kenny Rogers), six Top Forty hits are missing. Nevertheless, the material that exists here is a good representation of Carnes's considerable singing and songwriting capabilities. —*Rick Clark*

The Carpenters

Group, Pop
With their light, airy melodies and meticulously crafted, clean arrangements, the Carpenters stood in direct contrast with the excessive, gaudy pop/rock of the '70s, yet they became one of the most popular artists of the decade, scoring 12 Top Ten hits, including three number one singles. Karen Carpenter's calm, pretty voice was the most distinctive element of their music, settling in perfectly amidst the precise, lush arrangements provided by her brother Richard. The duo's sound drew more from pre-rock pop than rock & roll, but that didn't prevent the Carpenters from appealing to a variety of audiences, particularly Top 40, easy listening and adult contemporary. While their popularity declined during the latter half of the '70s, they remained one of the most distinctive and recognizable acts the decade produced.

The Carpenters formed in the late '60s in Downey, CA, after their family moved from their native New Haven, CT. Richard had played piano with a cocktail jazz trio in a handful of local Connecticut nightclubs and bars. Once the family had moved to California, he began to study piano while he supported Karen in a trio that featured Wes Jacobs (tuba/bass). With Jacobs and Richard forming her backup band, Karen was signed to the local Californian record label Magic Lamp, who released two unsuccessful singles by the singer. The trio won a Battle of the Bands contest at the Hollywood Bowl in 1967, which led to a record contract with RCA. Signing under the name the Richard Carpenter Trio, the group cut four songs that were never released. Jacobs left the band at the beginning of 1968.

Following Jacobs' departure, the siblings formed Spectrum with Richard's college friend John Bettis. Spectrum fell apart by the end of the year, but the Carpenters continued performing as a duo. The pair recorded some demos at the house of Los Angeles session musician Joe Osborn; the tape was directed toward Herb Alpert, the head of A&M Records, who signed the duo to his record label in early 1969.

Offering, the Carpenters' first album, was released in November 1969. Neither *Offering* or the accompanying single, a cover of the Beatles' "Ticket to Ride," made a big impression—the album failed to chart and the single peaked at number 54. However, the Carpenters' fortunes changed with their second single, a version of Burt Bacharach and Hal David's "(They Long to Be) Close to You." Taken from the album *Close to You*, the single became the group's first number one, spending four weeks on the top of the U.S. charts. "Close to You" became an international hit, beginning a five year period where the duo was one of the most popular recording acts in the world. During that period the Carpenters won two Grammy Awards, including Best New Artist of 1970, and had an impressive string of Top Ten hits, including "For All We Know," "Rainy Days and Mondays," "Superstar," "Hurting Each Other," "Goodbye to Love," "Sing," "Yesterday Once More," "Top of the World," and "Please Mr. Postman."

After 1975's number four hit "Only Yesterday," the group's popularity began to decline. For the latter half of the '70s, the duo were plagued by personal problems. Richard had become addicted to prescription drugs; in 1978, he entered a recovery clinic, kicking his habit. Karen, meanwhile, became afflicted with anorexia nervosa, a disease she suffered from for the rest of her life. On top of their health problems, the group's singles had stopped reaching the Top Ten and by 1978, they weren't even reaching the Top 40. Consequently, Karen decided to pursue a solo career, recording a solo album in 1979 with Phil Ramone; the record was never completed or released and she returned to the Carpenters later that year. The reunited duo released their last album of new material, *Made in America*, in 1981. The album marked a commercial comeback, as "Touch Me When We're Dancing" made it to number 16 on the charts. However, Karen's health continued to decline, forcing the duo out of the spotlight. On February 4, 1983, Karen was found unconscious at her parents' home in New Haven; she died in the hospital that morning from a cardiac arrest, which was caused by her anorexia.

After Karen's death, Richard Carpenter concentrated on production work and assembling various compilations of the Carpenters' recorded work. In 1987, he released a solo album called *Time*, which featured guest appearances by Dusty Springfield and Dionne Warwick. Although they were scorned by critics and many rock fans during their career, the Carpenters experienced a revival in the early '90s, culminating in the 1994 release of the tribute album, *If I Were a Carpenter*. —*Stephen Thomas Erlewine*

Offering [Ticket to Ride] / 1969 / A&M ✦✦✦

○ **Close to You** / Aug. 1970 / A&M ✦✦✦✦
This was the Carpenters' breakthrough album. Its title track was their first major hit, and it spawned the follow-up "We've Only Just Begun," which has been used in countless weddings since. The album also contained various pop covers of '60s hits like "Help!" and "Baby It's You," reinforcing the group's implied ties to rock while fostering the birth of a new generation of easy listening music. This album won the Carpenters a Best New Artist Grammy for 1970. —*William Ruhlmann*

The Carpenters / May 1971 / A&M ✦✦✦

A Song for You / Jun. 1972 / A&M ✦✦✦

Now & Then / May 1973 / A&M ✦✦✦

Horizon / Jun. 1975 / A&M ✦✦

A Kind of Hush / Jun. 1976 / A&M ✦✦✦

Passage / Oct. 1977 / A&M ✦✦✦

○ **Singles 1974-1978** / 1978 / A&M ✦✦✦✦

Made in America / Jun. 1981 / A&M ✦✦✦
The last album released while Karen was alive, this smooth adult contemporary set includes "Touch Me When We're Dancing." —*Bil Carpenter*

Voice of the Heart / Nov. 1983 / A&M ✦✦✦
Consisting of previously unreleased masters for a solo album by Karen, this album was compiled by Richard. —*Bil Carpenter*

Lovelines / 1985 / A&M ✦✦
A mixed bag of unreleased Carpenters material. —*Bil Carpenter*

○ **Yesterday Once More** / May 1985 / A&M ✦✦✦✦
A 2-CD set with 27 songs, this includes mostly their big hits, like "We've Only Just Begun" and "Mr. Postman," but there are a few sleeper cuts too. —*Bil Carpenter*

Interpretations: A 25th Anniversary Celebration / 1995 / A&M ✦✦✦

Classics, Vol. 2 / A&M ✦✦✦

James Carr

b. Jun. 13, 1942, Memphis, TN
Soul
Considered to be among the very greatest of "deep" Southern male soul singers, James Carr's succession of R&B hits on the Memphis Goldwax label were all gems of "country" soul, that wonderful '60s marriage of Southern Black R&B vocalists with songs written in a country format and played mostly by White musicians. Carr's dark, gospel-inflected style, marked by a subtle, rich voice that is almost frightening in its intensity and range, has been compared to that of Otis Redding and Percy Sledge; many reviewers would class him above even these formidable peers. "At the Dark End of the Street," the first songwriting collaboration between Dan Penn and Chips Moman, is Carr's undisputed mater-

piece. Also recorded by Aretha Franklin, Clarence Carter, Linda Ronstadt, and Ry Cooder, it is the quintessential country-soul take on adulterous love.

Carr's career initially was short; Goldwax ceased operation in 1969, and Carr cut only one other single for Atlantic in 1971; however, he has recently emerged from retirement with a new album on Goldwax. His work stands at the apex of '60s soul—with Aretha, Otis, Percy, and Wilson—essential stuff! —*Christine Ohlman*

○ **You Got My Mind Messed Up** / 1966 / Vivid Sound ✦✦✦✦
A somewhat-pricey Japanese import, with its companion *A Man Needs a Woman*, of all the great Goldwax gems. Includes the classic "At the Dark End of the Street," the achingly beautiful "These Ain't Raindrops," plus 19 more. —*Christine Ohlman*

A Man Needs a Woman / 1968 / Vivid Sound ✦✦✦
Companion Japanese import to *You Got My Mind Messed Up*, this completes the Goldwax sides. Two selections from Carr's first album, plus nine more—includes the great "Pouring Water on a Drowning Man." No duplication of titles with *You Got My Mind Messed Up*. Pricey but essential. —*Christine Ohlman*

Take Me to the Limit / 1991 / Goldwax ✦✦✦
Carr's comeback, on a resurrected Goldwax label. Doesn't quite live up to his '60s stuff—maybe nothing could—but it is good contemporary Southern soul in the classic vein, and it's great to have him back! —*Christine Ohlman*

● **Essential James Carr** / 1995 / Razor & Tie ✦✦✦✦
The Essential James Carr is the first American CD collection of the soul singer's '60s singles for Goldwax Records. Featuring 20 songs—including the hits "You've Got My Mind Messed Up," "I'm a Fool for You," "The Dark End of the Street," "A Man Needs a Woman," and "Pouring Water on a Drowning Man"—the disc has all of Carr's essential tracks. —*Stephen Thomas Erlewine*

Paul Carrack

b. Apr. 22, 1951, Sheffield, England
Pop/Rock
Despite his distinctive, soulful singing style, British keyboardist Paul Carrack's most popular work has not been done under his own name. He is the voice on Ace's "How Long," Squeeze's "Tempted," and Mike & the Mechanics' "The Living Years." Carrack finally began to score his own hits in the late '80s. —*William Ruhlmann*

The Nightbird / 1980 / Vertigo ✦✦✦

Suburban Voodoo / Aug. 1982 / Epic ✦✦✦
With Suburban Voodoo, Paul Carrack re-launched his solo career following a successful stint with Squeeze that produced a hit with his lead vocal on "Tempted." By this point, Carrack was playing with Nick Lowe, who produced *Suburban Voodoo*, and the album sounds very much like a Lowe album with Carrack singing. That's all to the good, though, since Carrack's supple voice is well suited to Lowe's updated '60s rock & roll style. Carrack scored his first solo Top 40 hit with "I Need You," but that was one of the slighter tracks on an unusually tuneful album. —*William Ruhlmann*

When You Walk in the Room / 1987 / Chrysalis ✦✦

Ace Mechanic / 1987 / Demon ✦✦✦

○ **One Good Reason** / Nov. 1987 / Chrysalis ✦✦✦✦
The third of Carrack's four solo albums of the '80s is the best-realized showcase for his soulful vocals. It produced four singles-chart entries, the most successful of which was the Top Ten hit "Don't Shed a Tear," Carrack's first big hit under his own name. —*William Ruhlmann*

Groove Approved / Oct. 1989 / Chrysalis ✦✦✦
After pulling four singles off 1987's *One Good Reason*, Paul Carrack looked to be on the verge of finally establishing himself as a solo star. Instead, he stumbled with the follow-up, *Groove Approved*, a solid, workman-like collection that featured only one Top 40 number in "I Live By The Groove." One suspects that this had less to do with the album's real commercial potential than with upheavals in the record company, which was being sold by its founders to EMI during this period. Yet, afterward, Carrack went back to working with Squeeze and Mike + the Mechanics, putting his solo career on hold. —*William Ruhlmann*

● **Collection: Twenty-One Good Reasons** / 1994 / Chrysalis ✦✦✦✦
Containing not only his solo hits, but also the ones that he sang for Ace ("How Long"), Squeeze ("Tempted"), and Mike and the Mechanics ("Silent Running" and "The Living Years"), as well as two

songs with Carlene Carter, *Twenty-One Good Reasons: The Paul Carrack Collection* is the one Carrack disc to own. *—Stephen Thomas Erlewine*

Joe "King" Carrasco & the Crowns (Joseph Teutsch)

Tex-Mex, New Wave
Texas-native Joe "King" Carrasco has devoted his career to re-creating the Tex-Mex, Farfisa organ rock & roll sound of such '60s groups as the Sir Douglas Quintet and Sam the Sham and the Pharaohs. After playing in a succession of bands around Texas in the late '60s and early '70s, Carrasco founded his band El Molino in 1976 and recorded *Tex-Mex Rock-Roll* in 1978. (The album was reissued by ROIR in 1989.) By 1979 he had formed the Crowns and was calling his music "nuevo wavo," playing especially in New York, where he appeared on stage in a cape and crown. He was signed to the U.K. Stiff label and Joe Boyd's Hannibal label in the U.S., and released *Joe "King" Carrasco and the Crowns* in 1980. By 1982 he had moved up to major label MCA for *Synapse Gap*, followed by *Party Weekend* (1983). These missed the charts, however, and although Carrasco has recorded since, turning increasingly political meanwhile, his work has been harder to find. *Bandido Rock* (1987) on Rounder was credited to Joe King Carrasco Y Las Coronas. *— William Ruhlmann*

Joe "King" Carrasco and El Molino / 1978 / Big Beat ✦✦✦
This UK release is a reissue of *Joe "King" Carrasco and El Molino*, originally released in a limited edition by Texas label Lisa Records in 1978. The album was reissued in the U.S. under the title *Tex-Mex Rock-Roll* by ROIR in 1989. *— William Ruhlmann*

Joe "King" Carrasco and the Crowns / Nov. 1980 / Hannibal ✦✦✦
At a time when the New York club scene was dominated by the remnants of punk and quirky power-pop of Devo and the B-52's, Joe "King" Carrasco, whose music complemented those styles, constituted comic relief. He would sweep on in his crown and cape and play Farfisa organ-based mid-'60s-style Tex-Mex rock & roll. Carrasco was a delightful club act, but inevitably, that didn't translate adequately to vinyl. Nevertheless, this, his first national release, made a brave attempt, and even if you couldn't have Joe jumping on your table at home, a song like "Caca De Vaca" was bound to raise a smile. (This album was released originally by Stiff Records in the U.K. with a slightly different track listing.) *— William Ruhlmann*

○ **Synapse Gap** / 1982 / MCA ✦✦✦✦
Joe "King" Carrasco's Crowns boasted a beefed-up sound on their major label debut, which leaned more toward guitar rock with a loud rhythm section than earlier, cheesier Tex-Mex efforts. That did not constitute an improvement necessarily, though it probably was intended to broaden Carrasco's appeal. For the most part, this didn't lessen the band's effervescence, though the reggae tune was a bit trendy (it even featured harmonies by Michael Jackson!) and the overall impression was of an artist closer to the mainstream than the border. *— William Ruhlmann*

Party Weekend / 1983 / MCA ✦✦✦

Tales from the Crypt / 1984 / ROIR ✦✦

Bordertown / 1984 / Big Beat ✦✦

Bandido Rock / Aug. 1987 / Rounder ✦✦

Tex-Mex Rock-Roll / 1989 / ROIR ✦✦✦
Tex-Mex Rock-Roll is a reissue of *Joe "King" Carrasco and El Molino*, which originally was released in a limited edition by Texas label Lisa Records in 1978. The ROIR version contains liner notes by Carrasco's manager, Joe Nick Patoski. *— William Ruhlmann*

Royal, Loyal & Live / 1990 / Rio Royal ✦✦✦

● **Anthology** / 1995 / One Way ✦✦✦✦
This is an 18-track compilation drawn from Joe "King" Carrasco's two MCA albums *Synapse Gap (Mundo Total)* (1982) and *Party Weekend* (1983). *— William Ruhlmann*

Jim Carroll

b. 1950, New York, NY
New Wave
New York poet and rock & roll frontman Carroll published *The Basketball Diaries*, an influential book of poetry, and recorded during the early '80s, bringing his cryptic, junkie-framed lyrics to jagged, Big Apple punk. "People Who Died" was his only hit. Car-

roll's work experienced a revival in 1995, when *The Basketball Diaries* was made into a motion picture. *—John Floyd*

○ **Catholic Boy** / 1980 / Atco ✦✦✦✦
Inspired by beat poets, basketball, and the New York street hustle, Carroll took his tales from the printed pages to the punk rock stage. *—Jeff Tamarkin*

Dry Dreams / 1982 / Atco ✦✦
○ **I Write Your Name** / 1983 / Atlantic ✦✦✦✦
Disappointing follow-up, although some lyrics are worth investigating. *—Jeff Tamarkin*

Praying Mantis / 1991 / Giant ✦✦✦
● **World without Gravity: the Best of the Jim Carroll Band** / 1993 / Rhino ✦✦✦✦
This fine collection includes all of the highlights from Carroll's varied career. *—AMG*

The Cars

Group, New Wave, Pop/Rock
The Cars were one of the most popular rock bands in America between 1978 and 1985. Formed in Boston in 1976, the quintet was Rick Ocasek (guitar and vocals), Ben Orr (bass and vocals), Greg Hawkes (keyboards), Elliot Easton (guitar), and David Robinson (drums). Their 1978 debut album *The Cars*, which typified their sleek sound—new-wave energy matched to tight rhythms, disembodied vocals by Ocasek and Orr, and an affection for the sound of '60s bubblegum music—was an immediate success, spawning the singles "Just What I Needed" and "My Best Friend's Girl."

After turning out million-selling albums in 1979 (*Candy-O*), 1980 (*Panorama*), and 1981 (*Shake It Up*), the group members took a breather for solo albums before returning for their biggest album yet. *Heartbreak City* (featuring the hits "You Might Think," "Magic," and "Drive") in 1984. *Door to Door* (1987) marked a falloff in the band's popularity, and they split soon after, with Ocasek so far the most prominent solo star. *— William Ruhlmann*

○ **The Cars** / May 1978 / Elektra ✦✦✦✦
On the heels of the new wave, the Cars' debut album was a mechanized rock delight, its music spare and precise, yet undeniably catchy, with sly references to the Beatles and Tommy James and the Shondells. Vocalists Rick Ocasek and Ben Orr sounded oddly dispassionate, as if they were singing in a foreign language. But that didn't stop "Just What I Needed," "My Best Friend's Girl," and "Good Times Roll" from becoming modest hits. *— William Ruhlmann*

Candy-O / Jun. 1979 / Elektra ✦✦✦
The Cars' debut album was still charting more than a year after its release when its carbon-copy follow-up, *Candy-O*, appeared sporting a cover drawing by Vargas, noted for his *Playboy* illustrations of voluptuous women. *Candy-O* duplicated its predecessor's success, in fact outpacing the first album as the single "Let's Go" (the Cars' biggest hit so far) became one of the summer songs of the year. "It's All I Can Do" hit as well. *— William Ruhlmann*

Panorama / Aug. 1980 / Elektra ✦✦
Although it sprinted up the charts and sold the expected million copies, The Cars' third album was a disappointment, with only the single "Touch and Go" scraping into the Top 40 and the rest unmemorable. *— William Ruhlmann*

Shake It Up / Nov. 1981 / Elektra ✦✦✦
Making extensive use of video promotion, the Cars rebounded sharply with their fourth album, whose title track was actually their first Top 10 single. The album also featured the underrated "Since You're Gone." *— William Ruhlmann*

○ **Heartbeat City** / Mar. 1984 / Elektra ✦✦✦✦
A break of three years gave the Cars plenty of time to write strong material. At the same time, Michael Jackson's *Thriller* had expanded the number of singles that could be pulled from one album, good news for the radio-friendly Cars, who scored five hits off this album, including the Top 10s "You Might Think" and "Drive." As a result, the album became the Cars' all-time bestseller. *— William Ruhlmann*

● **Greatest Hits** / Oct. 1985 / Elektra ✦✦✦✦
Ultimately, the Cars were a singles band. Here are those singles, including the biggest ones, "Drive," "Shake It Up," "You Might Think," and "Tonight She Comes." *—William Ruhlmann*

Door to Door / Aug. 1987 / Elektra ✦
A major disappointment, presaging the band's 1988 split, *Door To Door* still managed to feature the hit "You Are The Girl." But guitarist/singer Rick Ocasek, who produced, was more interested in his solo career by this time. — *William Ruhlmann*

Carter the Unstoppable Sex Machine

Group, Dance-Pop, Alternative Pop/Rock
Equally revered and despised in their native England, Carter the Unstoppable Sex Machine has been on the cutting edge of the U.K.'s dance-pop scene since their first hit single in 1989. Instead of following the disco-derived pop songs of the Pet Shop Boys, Carter relies more on the underground dance club scene, bringing such techniques as spoken word samples, drum and riff samples, and a relentless beat to tuneful, hook-oriented pop songwriting. In addition, their attitude is inspired by punk rock's mentality, manifesting itself in their satiric lyrics and slash-and-burn approach to ravaging pop's past and present. Their second single, "Sheriff Fatman," is arguably the finest example of their style and it was the song that established them as a force in the U.K. Perhaps it was coincidence, but after settling a copyright infringement lawsuit with lawyers representing the Rolling Stones in 1991, Carter began to open up their sound slightly; although they were still heavily dance-oriented, they cut back on their recognizable sound bites though not at the expense of their pop sensibilities. The pop audience was not as receptive to Carter as it was just a couple of years earlier, however, and they still couldn't earn anything larger than a cult following in the U.S. Ironically, the group hasn't declined creatively and are continuing to record some of the most interesting records in the alternative dance-pop world. — *Stephen Thomas Erlewine*

○ **101 Damnations** / 1990 / Chrysalis ✦✦✦
Great crafty pop from England, it's danceable as well as thought-provoking, using synthesizers as well as real instruments. Unpredictable, yet never disappointing. — *John Book*

30 Something / 1991 / Chrysalis ✦✦
● **1992: the Love Album** / 1992 / Chrysalis ✦✦✦
With its seamless mix of samples, beats, melody, and social consciousness, Carter the Unstoppable Sex Machine's third album is their best, most fully realized record to date. — *Stephen Thomas Erlewine*

○ **Post Historic Monsters** / Jan. 25, 1994 / IRS ✦✦✦
While it didn't receive much critical or commercial attention, Carter's fourth album ranks as one of their finest, filled with inventive fusions of dance and pop. — *Stephen Thomas Erlewine*

Clarence Carter

b. Jan. 14, 1936, Montgomery, AL
Soul, R&B
A blind soul singer whose numerous hits of the late '60s and early '70s epitomized the Muscle Shoals rhythm & blues sound, Carter hit the big time with his Atlantic single "Patches" (1970) and won a lasting place in the annals of Southern soul with others like "Slip Away" and "Too Weak to Fight." In 1981 Carter broke out of a dry spell with the Venture album *Let's Burn*, featuring a track called "Workin' (On a Love Building)" which set the theme for much of what was to follow: robust, lascivious lovemaking boasts. More recent tracks such as his salacious reworking of Tampa Red's "Love Me with a Feeling" and the jukebox favorite "Strokin'" (too risque for some radio stations) further solidified the carnal Carter image. Still primarily a soul/R&B singer, Carter has incorporated more hard blues elements in his music recently than in the Muscle Shoals days, despite his new and unblues-minded penchant for playing and programming all the instruments on his albums. — *Jim O'Neal*

○ **This Is Clarence Carter** / 1968 / Atlantic ✦✦✦
Fine country-soul, blues, and humorous/novelty tracks by Clarence Carter, then at his peak both artistically and musically. He didn't score any big hits from this album, but played with the exuberance and earthy charisma that marked his biggest Atlantic hits. — *Ron Wynn*

○ **The Dynamic Clarence Carter** / 1969 / Atlantic ✦✦✦✦
Clarence Carter was churning out classic Southern soul in the late '60s. Everything, from soap opera-ish tales of deprivation to sexually suggestive boasts, country/soul ballads, and uptempo wailers, clicked. This isn't so much an album as a string of great singles, all of them sung with fire, conviction, and passion. — *Ron Wynn*

Let's Burn / 1977 / Venture ✦✦✦
Fine Southern soul, light blues, and humorous, bawdy cuts from Clarence Carter. The single "Working On a Love Building" got some national attention, as did the title cut. The production was minimal, but Carter's gritty, earnest vocals were consistently effective. — *Ron Wynn*

Touch of Blues / 1989 / Ichiban ✦✦✦
More bluesy than most of his Ichiban albums, Clarence Carter does both slow, intense 12-bar tunes and contemporary, soul-tinged numbers, but doesn't spare either the down-home philosophy or the sexually suggestive commentary on this late '80s release. It's strictly for the Southern/regional audience, but also appealed to his older fans. — *Ron Wynn*

○ **The Dr.'s Greatest Prescriptions: The Best of Clarence Carter** / Ichiban ✦✦✦✦
A selection of Carter's lascivious recent output on Ichiban Records. Classic late-'60s Muscle Shoals-soul by this deep-voiced singer, including "Slip Away" and "Patches." — *Bill Dahl*

● **Snatchin' It Back** / 1992 / Rhino ✦✦✦✦
Snatchin' It Back—The Best of Clarence Carter is a great compilation, spotlighting Carter's stellar guitar work and trademark vocals on classics like "Slip Away," "Too Weak to Fight," and "Lookin' for a Fox." His great "Tell Daddy" (covered by Etta James as "Tell Mama") is included. Dave Marsh contributes the liner notes. Soul music at its funky best, and *the* compilation to own if you're a Carter fan. — *Christine Ohlman*

Carter-Lewis

Group, British Invasion, Pop/Rock
Though they scored few hits and leaned toward the wimpish end of the British Invasion spectrum, John Carter and Ken Lewis gave '60s rock too many intriguing footnotes to be dismissed. In the dark days of pre-Beatle British rock & roll, the duo, which started recording in 1961, was among the few U.K. performers to tread an unabashedly rock path and write their own material. As hard as it is to believe, Jimmy Page was briefly a member, adding his nascent guitar to a couple of their singles in 1963. The pair sang backup harmonies on a few of the Who's early recordings, rang up hits as members of the Ivy League, and hit the Top Ten as leaders of the Flowerpot Men with their borderline hippie satire "Let's Go to San Francisco." And they wrote "A Little Bit of Soul," a huge punk/bubblegum hit for the Music Explosion in 1967. — *Richie Unterberger*

● **Carter-Lewis Story** / 1993 / Sequel ✦✦✦✦
This 26-song compilation features material recorded from 1961-71 by half a dozen acts that featured the duo as their front, most notably the Ivy League, the Flowerpot Men, and just simply Carter-Lewis, which was their moniker on their first seven singles. These 14 songs, cut between 1961-64 (all included on this CD), are arguably the most appealing of this set. At times unbearably cloying (as on their U.K. Top 30 hit "Your Momma's Out Of Town"), at their most formidable, as on "Easy To Cry" and "Sweet And Tender Romance," the duo managed some respectable, gutsy Merseybeat. And yes, the two cuts graced by Jimmy Page's presence are present. — *Richie Unterberger*

Peter Case

Singer-Songwriter, Folk-Rock
After the breakup of the early '80s power-pop band the Plimsouls, Peter Case followed a different musical path in his solo career. Instead of the concise, rocking pop songs that were the Plimsouls' speciality, Case turned to the folkie territory of a singer/songwriter, making a string of underappreciated albums since 1986, all of them distinguished by a reliance on sharp, clever lyrics supported by a fluid melodicism and spare, stripped-down rock. — *Stephen Thomas Erlewine*

Peter Case / 1986 / Geffen ✦✦✦
Case's debut suffers from diverse stylistic jumps, but its best songs (seven, by my count) are compassionate, intelligent, and intriguing. — *John Floyd*

○ **The Man with the Blue Post Modern Fragmented Neo-Traditionalist Guitar** / Apr. 11, 1989 / Geffen ✦✦✦✦
On *The Man with the Blue Postmodern Fragmented Neo-Traditionalist Guitar*, Case sticks to one style, a Mellencampish rocker oozing with compassion. This beats the debut through the range of Case's lyrical concerns and his intense vocals. — *John Floyd*

● **Six-Pack of Love** / Mar. 1992 / Geffen ✦✦✦✦
Peter Case's most folk-oriented album to date is also his most inconsistent, but there are enough solid songs to make it worthwhile for his fans. —*Stephen Thomas Erlewine*

Sings Like Hell / Apr. 5, 1994 / Vanguard ✦✦✦
On his fourth solo album and debut for Vanguard Records, Peter Case followed the recent example of Bob Dylan's *Good As I Been to You* and *World Gone Wrong* albums, recording a set of traditional and cover songs in a folk-blues style, accompanied mostly by just his own guitar, piano, and harmonica playing. Case wasn't quite as traditional as Dylan, mixing in tunes by Jesse Winchester and Roy Orbison as well as one of his own, but he achieved the same rough-hewn style with songs oriented toward poverty, street-life, and murder. It may have been more the sort of thing you'd expect to hear from a busker on the corner, but Case succeeded in showing that such music was just as worthy of recording as more polished efforts. —*William Ruhlmann*

Torn Again / Apr. 25, 1995 / Vanguard ✦✦✦
Peter Case likes to tell stories that don't make sense. When he takes on a small-time crime drama ("Workin' For The Enemy"), it isn't clear who betrayed who; when he goes back to the Civil War ("Wilderness"), he has Robert E. Lee radio in an air strike; in "Baltimore," he gets beaten up, over the course of a few verses, interrupting his narrative to tell the listener, "I want you so"; in the midst of the journey in "Airplane," his companion turns into a man. Despite these anomalies (which are really the point of his twisted tales), Case's songs, sometimes co-written with experts like Fred Koller and Tom Russell, are well-constructed. And after stripping down to the folk-blues sound of *Peter Case Sings Like Hell*, Case is confident enough about his singing and playing to add only occasional other instrumentation. If you like your songs straight, Case will frustrate you, but if you're looking for imaginative, surprising songwriting, look no further. —*William Ruhlmann*

Cashman & West

Group, Singer-Songwriter
Beginning in the '60s, Terry (Dennis Minogue) Cashman and Tommy (Picardo) West enjoyed success penning hits for Spanky & Our Gang, Mama Cass, the Partridge Family and Al Martino. Under various one- and two-hit wonder monikers (Buchanan Brothers, Morning Mist, Cashman & West), the twosome forged a reputation as a kind of Simon & Garfunkellite for the singer/songwriter movement that was making inroads to Top 40. As producers, Cashman & West worked with Jim Croce, Steve Goodman, Dion, Dean Friedman, Eric Anderson, Gail Davies, Henry Gross and others. Many of them were signed to the duo's Lifesong Record label, which was formed in 1975. —*Rick Clark*

The AM FM Blues (Their Very Best) / 1993 / Razor & Tie
This covers everything from first singles, like the Buchanan Brothers' chugging "Medicine Man" to "American City Suite," one of their best known tracks as Cashman & West. Featured are good liner notes and sound. —*Rick Clark*

Shaun Cassidy

b. Sep. 27, 1958, Los Angeles, CA
Pop/Rock, Bubblegum, Teen Idol
Actor/singer Shaun Cassidy is best known as a teenage heartthrob of the second half of the '70s. He comes from a show business family: His father, Jack Cassidy, and his mother, Shirley Jones, were both actors, as was his brother David, who preceded him in teen idol status in the early '70s. Shaun Cassidy first gained notice as a singer in Europe in 1975 and Australia in 1976, crossing over to his native country as the co-star of the 1977 television series *The Hardy Boys*, which led to the release of his first U.S. single, a remake of the Crystals' "Da Doo Ron Ron," in the spring of 1977. This was followed by the hits "That's Rock 'N' Roll," "Hey Deanie," and "Do You Believe in Magic?" over the next year. Like all teen phenomena, Cassidy only stayed hot for a couple of years, fading after an attempt to make adult rock with *Wasp* (1980). In the '90s, he appeared on stage with his brother David in a Broadway production of the musical *Blood Brothers*. —*William Ruhlmann*

Shaun Cassidy / Jun. 1977 / Warner Brothers ✦✦✦
Born Late / Oct. 1977 / Warner Brothers ✦✦✦
Given that it didn't really matter what Shaun Cassidy *sounded* like, it is to his credit that he could make as creditable a record as his second album, *Born Late*. Well aware of his position, Cassidy,

who had just turned 18 when this album was released, conjured up the elegant pop of his childhood with covers of songs like the Lovin' Spoonful's "Do You Believe in Magic" (which gave him a Top 40 hit) and the Rascals' "A Girl Like You." Best of all, though, was Cassidy's Top Ten recording of Eric Carmen's "Hey Deanie." Not that any of this mattered in the long term: although an instant platinum hit, *Born Late* was less of a success than its four-month-old predecessor, and Cassidy's reign as a teen dream was already more than half over. —*William Ruhlmann*

Under Wraps / Jul. 1978 / Warner Brothers ✦✦
Room Service / Jul. 1979 / Warner Brothers ✦✦
Wasp / Sep. 1980 / Warner Brothers ✦✦
● **Greatest Hits** / May 1993 / Curb ✦✦✦✦

The Castelles

Group, Doo-Wop
Sporting the high tenor lead of George Grant, the Philadelphia-based Castelles cut a series of beautiful doo-wop items during the mid '50s. The group was formed in 1949 and signed with Grand Records in 1953, debuting with "My Girl Awaits Me." Specializing in ballads such as "This Silver Ring" (written by '60s soul producer Jerry Ragovoy) and "Heavenly Father," the Castelles briefly moved to Atco in 1956 before calling it quits. —*Bill Dahl*

● **Sweet Sounds of the Castelles** / 1987 / Collectables ✦✦✦✦
Dreamy mid-'50s Philly doo-wop. —*Bill Dahl*

Jimmy Castor

Funk
A master of novelty/disco funk, saxophonist Jimmy Castor started as a doo-wop singer in New York. He wrote and recorded "I Promise to Remember" for Wing with the Juniors in 1956, a group whose roster included Al Casey, Jr., Orton Graves, and Johnny Williams. Castor replaced Frankie Lymon in the Teenagers in 1957 before switching to sax in 1960. He appeared on several soul-jazz and Afro-Latin sessions and had a solo hit with "Hey Leroy, Your Mama's Callin' You" on Smash in 1966. Castor also played sax on Dave "Baby" Cortez's hit "Rinky Dink." He formed the Jimmy Castor Bunch in 1972 and signed with RCA. Their first release, *It's Just Begun*, launched Castor's next phase with the song "Troglodyte (Cave Man)." It was a Top Ten R&B and pop smash. Castor continued the trend in 1975 with "The Bertha Butt Boogie" and later recorded "E-Man Boogie," "King Kong," "Bom Bom," and "Amazon." The Castor band included keyboardist/trumpeter Gerry Thomas, bassist Doug Gibson, guitarist Harry Jensen, conga player Lenny Fridle, Jr., and drummer Bobby Manigault. Thomas left the band to join the Fatback band. Castor recorded as a solo performer from 1976 until 1988. He had one of his bigger hits in many years with a 1988 revival of "Love Makes a Woman," which paired him with disco diva Joyce Sims. Castor had his own label, Long Distance, in the '80s. —*Ron Wynn*

○ **Hey Leroy** / 1967 / Smash ✦✦✦✦
Long before Jimmy Castor became a successful humorist and funkmeister, he scored a Latin hit with "Hey Leroy, Your Mama's Callin' You," a smoothly performed bit of samba with jazz touches by Castor. It was such a hit that he issued an entire album of similar tunes, none of which did anywhere near as well as the single, which cracked the R&B Top 20 (#16) and pop Top 40 (#31). —*Ron Wynn*

● **Best of the Jimmy Castor Bunch** / 1976 / RCA ✦✦✦✦
This album collected saxophonist/humorist Jimmy Castor's biggest novelty smashes from his mid-'70s days on Atlantic. Castor's "Bertha Butt Boogie" was an R&B and pop hit, and he mined the novelty field again with "E-Man Boogie" and "E-Man Groovin'," plus "King Kong." —*Ron Wynn*

Catherine Wheel

Group, Alternative Pop/Rock
Like many other British guitar bands of the early '90s, Catherine Wheel relied heavily on distortion as a way of creating texture and using their airy vocals as atmosphere. While their melodies are actually quite straight-forward, they are submerged in layers of guitar effects and droning chords. Like Lush and Ride, Catherine Wheel's blend of hooks and white noise are pop songs, not free-form explorations with a floating melody. It is that quality that created a buzz in Britain around their first EP, *She's My Friend*, in 1991. Their subsequent two albums, 1992's *Ferment* and 1993's

Chrome, earned them a solid fan base in England. The heavy rock attack of 1995's *Happy Days* increased their following in America. *—Stephen Thomas Erlewine*

Ferment / 1992 / Fontana ✦✦✦

● **Chrome** / Jul. 20, 1993 / PolyGram 3145 ✦✦✦✦
Despite his obvious inflection toward the Teardrop Explode's Julian Cope, Rob Dickinson's lead vocals serve well; breathy and wistful on numbers like "Crank," but capable of stronger angst when called upon. His palette is restricted to a certain quality of expression however—there is little place on *Chrome* for such colorful concepts as joy or playfulness. Ultimately, this somewhat claustrophobic musical and emotional range boxes in Catherine Wheel and restricts *Chrome* to being a very good (rather than great) listening experience despite its loftier ambitions. *—Roch Parisien*

○ **Happy Days** / 1995 / Fontana/Mercury ✦✦✦✦
After releasing two records that faithfully followed the noisy, swirling trance-like psychedelia of My Bloody Valentine, Catherine Wheel trims out all of their excesses on *Happy Days.* What is left is a throttling, pounding heavy metal band that accentuates the rhythm, not the texture. The change in direction is surprisingly effective and accessible—none of their previous work has been as immediate as "Way Down" or as bracing as "God Inside My Head," nor has it been as melodic as "Judy's Staring at the Sky," a duet with Tanya Don
elly. Perhaps the switch to a heavier attack shouldn't be surprising— *Chrome* was filled with harder guitars—but the fact it has produced the band's best music is a pleasant shock. *—Stephen Thomas Erlewine*

Felix Cavaliere
b. Nov. 29, 1944, Pelham, NY
Art-Rock/Progressive-Rock
Felix Cavaliere was the organist and one of the lead singers in the Young Rascals (later the Rascals), a successful pop/rock group of the mid-'60s. Since the group's demise, he has pursued a solo career. Cavaliere studied classical piano as a child and joined the Stereos in his hometown of Pelham, NY, before attending Syracuse University, where he formed the Escorts. He then moved to New York City and got his professional start as a backup musician for Sandy Scott and later Joey Dee and the Starlighters. Other future members of the Young Rascals also were in the Starlighters, and the group was launched with performances in the New York metropolitan area during 1965. They were signed to Atlantic Records and began releasing records by the end of the year. From then through 1969, the Rascals were one of the biggest groups in the country, their hits including the Cavaliere-sung "Good Lovin'," "Groovin'," "A Girl Like You," "A Beautiful Morning," and "People Got to Be Free," as they evolved from blue-eyed soul (a term coined to describe them) to pop psychedelia and jazz fusion. Their fortunes declined thereafter, and they disbanded in 1972. Cavaliere then went solo and has since released several solo albums without matching the group's commercial appeal. He also has participated in oldies shows and Rascals reunions and produced other artists. *—William Ruhlmann*

● **Felix Cavaliere** / 1974 / Bearsville ✦✦✦✦
Two years after the Rascals broke up, leader Felix Cavaliere launched his solo career with this self-titled debut. The good news was that it was a major effort: Cavaliere co-wrote all the songs, and the record was co-produced by Todd Rundgren. Cavaliere had an eclectic ability to mix rock with Latin and soul elements and to sing his songs in a compellingly soulful voice that could be stirring or smooth. The bad news was that the Rascals had been in commercial decline since their popular heyday of 1966-68, which meant that Cavaliere had the appearance of a has-been. He was unable to overcome this disadvantage, and *Felix Cavaliere* failed to establish him as a solo star. *—William Ruhlmann*

Destiny / 1975 / Bearsville ✦✦

Castles in the Air / 1979 / Epic ✦✦

Dreams in Motion / Jul. 19, 1994 / Karambolage/MCA ✦✦
Felix Cavaliere made his first album in 15 years under the auspices of co-producer Don Was and his new MCA-distributed Karambolage label. Was had resurrected the career of Bonnie Raitt and produced such '60s legends as Bob Dylan, so he must have seemed like the perfect vehicle to arrange the comeback of the former Rascals lead singer-songwriter/organist. Unfortunately, Cava-

liere and his co-writers only had a series of bland romantic tunes up their sleeves, and Was, in contrast to many of his other productions, seemed overly concerned with updating Cavaliere's sound (unless, of course, it was Cavaliere who insisted on the modernizing). Cavaliere remained in good voice as he pushed 50, but he was singing greeting-card sentiments against a slick electronic background. *—William Ruhlmann*

Nick Cave
Alternative Pop/Rock
After the Birthday Party called it quits in 1983, singer/songwriter Nick Cave assembled the Bad Seeds, a post-punk supergroup featuring former Birthday Party guitarist Mick Harvey on drums, ex-Magazine bassist Barry Adamson, and Einstürzende Neubauten's guitarist Blixa Bargeld. With the Bad Seeds, Cave continued to explore his obsessions with religion, death, love, America, and violence with a bizarre hybrid of blues, gospel, rock, and arty post-punk, although in a more subdued fashion than his work with the Birthday Party. On his albums with the Bad Seeds, his literary aspirations come to the forefront; the lyrics are narrative prose, heavy on literary allusions and myth-making. Often, Cave's gloomy lyrics, dark musical arrangements, and deep baritone voice recall the albums of Scott Walker, who also obsessed over death and love with a frightening passion. However, Cave brings a hefty amount of post-punk experimentalism to Walker's epic dark pop. By melding the grandeur of Walker to the spareness of the blues, as well as adding the self-conscious eclecticism of post-punk and his own literate lyrics, Cave has emerged as one of the most distinctive and respected figures of alternative rock. *—Stephen Thomas Erlewine*

● **From Her to Eternity** / 1984 / Mute ✦✦✦✦
Desperate and ominous, this is a chilling love letter. *—John Dougan*

○ **The Firstborn Is Dead** / 1985 / Mute ✦✦✦✦
Recorded with the Bad Seeds, this album contains angst directly influenced by early American folk-blues. *—John Dougan*

○ **Kicking Against the Pricks** / 1986 / Homestead ✦✦✦✦
All covers, all unique, all recorded with the Bad Seeds. More rock from your worst nightmare. *—John Dougan*

Your Funeral . . . My Trial / 1986 / Homestead ✦✦✦
A double EP, less focused but still good. *—John Dougan*

Tender Prey / 1988 / Mute ✦✦✦

The Good Son / 1990 / Elektra ✦✦
Slightly Brazilian-influenced, still worthwhile, but his least essential. *—John Dougan*

Henry's Dream / 1992 / Mute ✦✦✦
Henry's Dream, Nick Cave's apocalyptic, post-modern reading of gospel and the blues, is one of Cave's strongest albums. *—AMG*

Live Seeds / 1993 / Mute/Elektra ✦✦

Let Love In / 1994 / Elektra ✦✦✦
Let Love In is a darker, more brooding album than *Henry's Dream,* making it one of Nick Cave's most harrowing records. *—David Jehnzen*

Celibate Rifles
Group, Alternative Pop/Rock
Quick, who's Australia's best rock band? If you guessed Midnight Oil, you probably have the most supporters. But for my money, there's never been an Australian rock & roll band better (or more consistent) than Sydney's Celibate Rifles. Playing stripped-down, loud and fast, Ramones-inspired guitar rock, the Celibate Rifles were one of the earliest punk bands to emerge during the post-Radio Birdman/Saints era. Taking their cues from these Aussie bands, along with American hard rock of the Stooges, MC5 and Blue Oyster Cult, the Rifles, led by the twin guitar attack of Kent Steedman and Dave Morris and the deadpan baritone of vocalist Damien Lovelock, exploded out of the gates in 1982 with a series of records (released in Australia only) fueled by high-speed guitars, wah-wah-strangulated solos, and cartoonish, tongue-in-cheek lyrics. Playing initially for crowds of hard-rock-loving surfers, it didn't take long for the Rifles to develop a following. Outside of the continent, however, they were virtually unknown. That changed in 1985 with the release of *Quintessentially Yours,* a lengthy EP that was a collection of tracks from earlier albums. Although the Rifles didn't receive the attention of many lesser Amer-

ican and English bands, the releases kept coming, and they were all excellent. What didn't help was a seeming disinterest the band had in touring America. But when you're an Australian band, it's easy to see why: it's expensive, it takes forever to get here, and why bother when the records aren't getting the kind of reception they deserve? As a result, the Rifles last toured America in 1987, which is too bad, because their great live album (*Kiss, Kiss, Bang, Bang*) recorded at CBGB's on that tour, proves them to be a white-hot live band. As they continued recording and maturing, the Rifles were unafraid to take risks with their tried and true loud-and-fast sound. Soon, acoustic guitars entered the mix, tempos slowed, pianos tinkled in the background, and vocal harmonies were added. None of this increased technical skill and studio experimentation diluted the band's strengths (i.e., feral power); in fact, it may well have made them a better and more interesting band. Another development was the increased politicization and social consciousness of their material. No longer were they simply sarcastic, funny boys; rather, they were addressing serious political, environmental and social issues, thanks to Lovelock's sharp, insightful lyrics, all without any condescension or simplistic rhetoric. In 1989, Rifles albums were suddenly no longer available in domestic release, a fact that didn't help the band in their quest to develop an American following. As a result, their great album *Blind Ear* was available (when you could find it) only as a high-priced Aussie import. Also, there were signs that the Rifles were nearing the end: Steedman and Morris were playing around Sydney with other musicians and producing new bands, Lovelock released a solo album (*It's a Wig, Wig, Wig, World*) with members of the Church, and the time between Rifles releases seemed to grow longer. Another dispiriting sign was the 1992 release of *Heaven On A Stick*, which despite a wonderful title, sounded tired and tossed off. Fortunately, all this speculation turned out to be wrong, and in late 1994, the Rifles stormed back with *Spaceman in a Satin Suit*, an exhilarating return to form. A non-stop barrage of power, volume, and sharp songwriting, it shreds virtually every effort by the current generation of guitar-based alternarock careerists, and is easily the band's best record since *Blind Ear*. They may be a grizzled bunch of punk rockers, but there's nothing the Celibate Rifles couldn't teach young rock bands. Precious few of the soon-to-be-trivia-question groups currently glutting alternative rock will have careers this impressive 15 years down the road. —*John Dougan*

Sideroxylon / 1983 / Hot ✦✦✦

The Celibate Rifles / 1984 / Hot ✦✦✦

Quintessentially Yours / 1985 / What Goes On ✦✦✦

○ **The Turgid Miasma of Existence** / 1986 / Hot ✦✦✦✦
The first recording of new Celibate Rifles material to be released in America. Now fully incorporating acoustic guitars, cellos, zithers, and bass clarinets (!) into the mix, this record is more eclectic than your average Rifles release, but amazingly, there are no false moments, bad songs, or failed experiments. From the opening salvo of "Bill Bonney Regrets" through the hair-raising "Conflict of Instinct" to the sarcastically funny closing track "New Mistakes," this is a simply wonderful record that will sound refreshingly direct and engaging another 15 years from now. Lovelock's lyrics are especially wonderful, running the gamut from terse imagism to comedic tomfoolery to polemical broadsides. The album is dedicated to James Darroch, the original Rifles bass player who left in 1984 to form the great, little-known Eastern Dark (one very good EP, *Long Live the New Flesh*). Darroch died in a car accident while *Miasma* was being recorded. —*John Dougan*

Mina Mina Mina / 1986 / What Goes On ✦✦✦
Much of the earliest material recorded by the Rifles (covering the years 1982-84) is difficult to find in its original form, but these two records do an excellent job of anthologizing those heady post-Birdman/Saints days. Mostly speedy (guitars, guitars and more guitars!!) and poppy, there are some hilarious songs ("Let's Get Married"), some that show a strong '70s influence ("God Squad"), and some that indicate the band's growing maturity ("Back in the Red"). Although they would make better records, the exuberance and excitement of this music, as well as its power, hasn't diminished a bit since the day it was recorded. —*John Dougan*

Kiss Kiss Bang Bang / 1987 / What Goes On ✦✦✦
Live, loud and fast. Turn it up to 11. Added bonus: the definitive version of Radio Birdman's supercharged Aussie punk anthem, "Burn My Eye." —*John Dougan*

● **Roman Beach Party** / 1987 / What Goes On ✦✦✦✦
Around the time of this record's release I was proclaiming to anyone within the sound of my very loud voice that this was going to be the LP that broke the Rifles with the college radio crowd (pre-alternative rock) in America. It was more direct and hard-hitting than *Miasma*, but it didn't sacrifice smarts, nor did it pander to a punk-rock crowd that was evolving into a neo-heavy metal crowd. It was around the time of this LP that MTV's early alternative-rock show *The Cutting Edge* (hosted by Fleshtones lead singer Peter Zaremba) had the Rifles play live. Of course they were last, and that meant staying up until the wee hours of the morning, but if you did, you saw a ripsnorting version of *Roman Beach Party's* opening track, the anti-televangelism ode "Jesus On T.V." Unfortunately, this appearance didn't translate into huge record sales, and those who missed out on *Roman Beach Party* ignored one of the classiest hard-rock records of the '80s. —*John Dougan*

○ **Blind Ear** / 1989 / True Tone-EMI ✦✦✦✦
The best Celibate Rifles recording? Yes, but only on the days I don't think it's *Roman Beach Party*, or maybe *Mina, Mina, Mina*. Along with being the only album in Australian rock history to contain two songs about the troubles in Northern Ireland ("Sean O'Farrell" and "Belfast"), *Blind Ear* continues the Rifles' maturation process from snarling young punks to snarling adult punks. Sounding at times like the Stones (and I mean that as a compliment), the Rifles—now nearly a decade into their career—are recording some of their best songs. For proof, listen to the two aforementioned, along with their critique of yuppiedom ("Wonderful Life") and the closing track, "O Salvation." Another record that should have been huge. —*John Dougan*

○ **Platters du Jour** / 1990 / Hot ✦✦✦✦

Sofa / 1993 / Hot ✦✦✦

○ **Spaceman in a Satin Suit** / 1994 / Hot ✦✦✦✦
Starting off with one of the hardest, fastest, ecstatic bursts of rock they've ever recorded ("Spirits"), *Spaceman* is a resounding assertion that this band's career is far from over. In fact, this record wipes the floor with nearly ever note issued by the endless succession of post-Nirvana, MTV-approved alternative rock bands. Like the Ramones (and perhaps Motorhead), the Rifles seem to get better with age, and for all of us punks way past 30, that's life-affirming news. —*John Dougan*

The Cellos

Group, Doo-Wop
This five-man group formed in 1955 in Manhattan, influenced by local high school stars (the Kodoks, the Crests, the Schoolboys, and the Keynotes). After-school harmonizing led to the Cellos making a $4 demo, which in true Hollywood movie tradition got them a recording contract! Though their moment in the spotlight was relatively brief, hitting the charts with their first single—"Rang Tang Ding Dong (I Am the Japanese Sandman)"—their street-corner sound nonetheless exemplifies New York doo-wop in its earliest stages. —*Cub Koda*

● **Rang Tang Ding Dong** / 1992 / Relic ✦✦✦✦
An excellent CD compilation of all their best Apollo sides, including unreleased material. Contains the title cut, plus "Juicy Crocodile," "The Be Bop Mouse," and "You Took My Love." —*Cub Koda*

○ **The Best of on Apollo** / Relic ✦✦✦✦

Exene Cervenka (Christine Cervenka)

Roots-Rock, Folk-Rock
Exene (Christine) Cervenka was the co-lead singer and songwriter of the Los Angeles punk group X for most of the '80s. When the band took a hiatus in 1987, Cervenka turned to a solo career. She has thus far released two albums in more of a folk-rock style on Rhino. Cervenka rejoined X in 1993 for the album *Hey Zeus!* and a national tour. —*William Ruhlmann*

Twin Sisters / 1985 / Freeway ✦✦
Twin Sisters is the recorded evidence of a joint poetry reading held at McCabe's in Los Angeles on February 1, 1985, by Wanda Coleman and Exene Cervenka, each of whom get one side of the LP. Coleman's dramatically spoken and sometimes sung lyrics are personal reflections on African-American street life from an observer suffering from a self-described "triple whammy"—to be female, black, and intelligent. Cervenka's observations are somewhat more upscale, relating to the rock & roll lifestyle, including

diary notes from life on the road with X. She also reads some of the poetry of her late sister Mary. — *William Ruhlmann*

● **Old Wives' Tales** / 1989 / Rhino ♦♦♦♦
Exene Cervenka's first solo album after the breakup of X is closer in spirit to the folkie-country album she and some friends made as the Knitters than to the punk-rock throttle of her former band. Acoustic guitars and calm singing of highly poetic lyrics are the order of the day, and Cervenka makes a smooth transition to singer/songwriter. — *William Ruhlmann*

Running Sacred / 1990 / Rhino ♦♦♦

Peter Cetera

b. Sep. 13, 1944, Chicago, IL
Pop
Cetera was a vocalist, bassist, and songwriter with Chicago from 1967 to 1985, singing lead on many of the group's major ballad hits. He then launched a solo career that has resulted in more hits in the same style. — *William Ruhlmann*

Peter Cetera / Dec. 1981 / Full Moon ♦♦

Solitude / Solitaire / Jun. 1986 / Warner Brothers ♦♦♦

● **One More Story** / Aug. 1988 / Warner Brothers ♦♦♦♦
Cetera launched his solo career playing music very close to the soaring ballads of his days with Chicago. He switched gears on this album, working with Madonna producer Patrick Leonard on a more uptempo approach that lost none of his usual melodic feel for its dance rhythms. — *William Ruhlmann*

World Falling Down / Jun. 16, 1992 / Warner Brothers ♦♦
Cetera collaborated with Andy Hill on *World Falling Down* for an album that maintained his usual production sheen but moved more toward a melodic rock & roll feel. Cetera's airy tenor didn't really have enough grit to carry such an approach off, and Warner Bros. may have worried that he had veered too far from his traditional power-ballad base, since there are two added tracks produced by old partner David Foster that are more in keeping with Cetera's old hits. The record company also was careful to release only ballads as the album's singles, with the perhaps predictable result that "Restless Heart," "Feels Like Heaven" (a duet with Chaka Khan), and "Even a Fool Can See" were all over adult contemporary radio. However, the album was a commercial failure. — *William Ruhlmann*

Chad & Jeremy

Group, British Invasion, Pop/Rock
The American success of the folkish duo of Chad Stuart (b. Dec 10, 1943, Durham, England) and Jeremy Clyde (b. Mar 22, 1944, Buckinghamshire, England) pointed up the impact of the British invasion led by the Beatles in February 1964. Chad & Jeremy charted only once in their native country, but their single "Yesterday's Gone," released in May 1964, was the first of 11 U.S. chart hits they achieved through 1966. The biggest of these, and their only Top Ten, was "A Summer Song" (July 1964). Adopting a lighter approach than many of their Mersey Beat contemporaries, Chad & Jeremy focused on pop revivals such as "Willow, Weep for Me" and songs from Broadway shows, such as "I Have Dreamed" from *Carousel*, both Top 40 hits for them. Having moved to Hollywood, they were frequent television guests, both on music shows such as *Hullabaloo* and series like *Batman*. Their commercial progress was complicated after 1965, when they signed to Columbia Records, while Capitol Records continued to issue their earlier recordings (previously issued on the World Artists label), such that they were forced to compete with themselves. They recorded the musically ambitious *Of Cabbages and Kings* (September 1967) in the wake of the Beatles' *Sgt. Pepper's Lonely Hearts Club Band*. They broke up after the commercial failure of its equally ambitious follow-up, *The Ark* (September 1968). Jeremy Clyde established himself as a British stage actor. The duo reunited for a new album in 1983. — *William Ruhlmann*

○ **Painted Dayglow Smile** / Jul. 14, 1992 / Columbia/Legacy ♦♦♦♦
Chad & Jeremy signed to Columbia Records in March 1965, after spending a year on composer John Barry's Ember Records. During their three and a half years on Columbia, the duo made five albums and a couple of stray singles, as their music became increasingly ambitious and their sales declined to practically nothing. Hence, this compilation contains their last few Top 40 hits, "Before and After," "I Don't Wanna Lose You Baby," and "Distant Shores," plus a selection of album tracks, flop singles, and rarities.

The album is part of Sony's "Rock Artifacts" series, and that's a fitting subtitle. These are certainly interesting curiosities; just don't mistake this for a Chad & Jeremy greatest hits album. — *William Ruhlmann*

Yesterday's Gone [Greatest Hits] / 1994 / Drive Archive ♦♦♦
This discount-priced compilation contains 14 of the 29 tracks Chad and Jeremy recorded for Ember Records (UK)/World Artists Records (US) in 1964-1965. All seven of the duo's World Artists singles are included, among them the hits "A Summer Song," "Willow Weep for Me," "Yesterday's Gone," and "If I Loved You." An attempt to clean up the sound has been made, and there are brief, informative liner notes by Mark Humphrey. Thus, at a reduced price, this is a reasonable bare-bones presentation of Chad and Jeremy's best-known early hits. — *William Ruhlmann*

Eugene Chadbourne

b. Jan. 4, 1954, Mount Vernon, NY
Alternative Pop/Rock, Art-Rock/Progressive-Rock, Experimental
Not strictly (or some would say at all) a jazz musician, Eugene Chadbourne is certainly an improviser. His sprawling, skittering, bursting guitar forays are among modern music's most anthemic delights. He combines the wildness of the freest jazz with the unpredictable energy of manic rock, and adds his own convoluted lyrics and vocals/comments. Chadbourne began playing guitar at age 11. He moved from bottleneck blues to bebop and free jazz, then met England's Derek Bailey. Chadbourne's debut included a nod to Anthony Braxton. He began working with Frank Lowe and Billy Bang in the late '70s, then teamed with John Zorn and Tom Cora. Chadbourne's group Shockabilly mixed country, rock, free-jazz and just plain noise in an inspired, if at times completely chaotic, frenetic manner. He recorded with Camper Van Beethoven in the '80s. Chadbourne's material is considered too noncommercial for rock and too outrageous for even most free-jazz fans. — *Ron Wynn*

Country Protest / 1986 / Fundamental ♦♦♦
The warped guitarist/vocalist/deconstructionist puts original political tunes and covers of several '60s staples through his horror-show wringer. Experimental to the max. — *Jeff Tamarkin*

Corpses of Foreign War / Jun. 1986 / Fundamental ♦♦♦
Radical protest tunes radically rendered, with members of the Violent Femmes helping out. — *Jeff Tamarkin*

○ **Vermin of the Blues** / 1987 / Fundamental ♦♦♦♦
With backing from frantic Austin rockers Evan Johns & the H-Bombs, and originals like "Fried Chicken for Richard Speck" meeting covers of Count Basie and the Count 5, this is Eugene at his most perverse. — *Jeff Tamarkin*

● **LSD C&W** / 1987 / Fundamental ♦♦♦♦
The ultimate Chadbourne, featuring medleys of the Beatles, Roger Miller, and Burl Ives, plus much more insanity filtered through post-avant-garde brilliance. — *Jeff Tamarkin*

○ **Dear Eugene** / 1987 / Placebo ♦♦♦♦
Dear Eugene, What You Did Was Not Very Nice, So I Am Going to Kill… is live, solo, extremely cool. Who else would construct a Bacharach/Manson tune? — *Jeff Tamarkin*

○ **There'll Be No Tears Tonight** / Jan. 1987 / Fundamental ♦♦♦
Country fans expecting straight, faithful versions of these covers of Roger Miller, Hank Williams, and Merle Haggard will be in shock. Imagine honky tonk as free jazz, and that's what you'll get. — *Jeff Tamarkin*

The Eddie Chatterbox Double Trio Love Album / 1988 / Fundamental ♦♦♦
One of a few collaborations with the equally fried Camper Van Beethoven, this isn't as exciting as it could have been. — *Jeff Tamarkin*

Chairmen of the Board

Group, Soul
One of the most dynamic acts to emerge on Holland/Dozier/Holland's Invictus label after the legendary songwriters exited Motown. Lead Norman "General" Johnson had previously fronted the Showmen, who hit in 1961 with "It Will Stand," cut in New Orleans. Johnson's pinched, intense vocal delivery powered the pleading "Give Me Just a Little More Time," the first smash for the Chairmen in late 1969, although Danny Woods handled lead duty on the group's biggest R&B seller, "Pay to the Piper." Johnson, who wrote "Patches" for the group's first album only to see Clarence

Carter score the hit, departed in 1974 to start a solo career. —*Bill Dahl*

● **Greatest Hits** / Jan. 9, 1992 / HDH ◆◆◆◆
Driving Detroit soul of the late '60s/early '70s. General Johnson's pungent lead vocals give this quartet a unique sound. Their notable hit was 1970's "Give Me Just a Little More Time." —*Bill Dahl*

The Challengers

Group, Surf
One of the most popular of the early Southern Californian surf bands, the Challengers were formed by drummer Richard Belvy after he left the Belairs, who had recorded one of the very first surf singles, "Mr. Moto." Their debut LP, *Surfbeat* (early 1963), was one of the very first all-instrumental surf albums, and sold 200,000 copies, an astronomical number for a regional act. Recording several albums over the next couple of years, most of their repertoire consisted of covers of popular rock and surf tunes; undeniably exciting at the time, their lack of originality can make their work generic to wade through several decades later. The moody "K-39," also available on surf compilations, is their best and most famous cut. —*Richie Unterberger*

○ **Surfbeat** / 1963 / Vault ◆◆◆◆
Certainly their most popular and influential LP, devoted mostly to competent and elegantly executed covers of early rock and surf standards, with a couple original tunes. Like all of the Challengers Sundazed reissues, it adds a few bonus cuts. —*Richie Unterberger*

Surfing with the Challengers / 1963 / Vault ◆◆
Their second album stuck to the same formula as the first, with a bit more routine results, though "Tidal Wave" is a standout. —*Richie Unterberger*

Challengers on the Move / 1963 / Sundazed ◆◆◆
Perhaps the most pop-oriented and calmest of the early Challengers LPs (though not by much) in terms of material selection. Collectors will be interested in one of the four CD bonus cuts, "Lead Foot," an early version of "K-39." —*Richie Unterberger*

● **K-39** / 1964 / Vault ◆◆◆◆
Their first four LPs are quite similar to each other overall, but if you have to choose one, the nod would go to the last of the quartet. Featuring the title track (their most famous performance), it also has hot versions of "Telstar" and "Mark Of Zorro," and three bonus cuts of their competent forays into vocal hot rod music. —*Richie Unterberger*

○ **Best of the Challengers** / 1982 / Rhino ◆◆◆◆

The Chambers Brothers

Group, Soul, R&B, Psychedelic
Originally an African-American gospel group from Mississippi, the Chambers Brothers—Lester (b. Apr 13, 1940, Flora, MS) (vocals), Willie (b. Mar 2, 1938, Flora, MS) (guitar/vocals), Joe (b. Aug 22, 1942, Scott County, MS) (guitar/vocals), and George (b. Sep 22, 1931, Flora MS) (bass), plus drummer Brian Keenan (b. Jan 28, 1944, New York City)—first made their mark in the New York discotheque scene in 1965, then packed up and moved to Los Angeles. Their biggest success was the 11-minute psychedelic epic "Time Has Come Today," edited down to a four-and-three-quarter-minute Top 40 pop hit in 1968. In spite of their gospel roots and their tendency to cover soulful standards like "I Can't Turn You Loose" and "People Get Ready," the Chambers Brothers gravitated more toward a spirited, raw rock approach than toward R&B.—*Rick Clark*

● **Greatest Hits** / Oct. 1971 / Columbia ◆◆◆◆
It contains only two hits, the endless 1968 psychedelic garage-grunge hit "Time Has Come Today" plus "I Can't Turn You Loose," which doesn't touch Otis Redding's fiery version. Most of this doesn't hold up too well, but it is the best sampler available. —*Rick Clark*

Chameleons

Group, Alternative Pop/Rock
A Manchester, U.K., intellectual pop outfit that was slightly ahead of its time. Writing stylish, moody guitar-swirled pop, the Chameleons set the stage for numerous U.K. bands to come, never really reaping the benefits of their (often much better) music. Formed in 1981, the group featured vocalist/bassist Mark Burgess, guitarist Reg Smithies, guitarist Dave Fielding, and drummer Brian Schofield. A series of BBC sessions led to a record contract

with Epic, who released the single "In Shreds." "In Shreds" failed to gain an audience and the Chameleons were dropped from the label; they signed with the independent label Statik. Statik released their first two albums, *Script of the Bridge* (1983) and *What Does Anything Mean Basically?* (1985), which earned good reviews and a cult audience. In 1986, the band signed with Geffen Records and released *Strange Times*, another critically acclaimed album. Shortly after its release, the band's manager Tony Fletcher died, sending the Chameleons into a state of disarray which caused them to disband. Burgess formed the Sun and the Moon soon after the Chameleons' breakup, yet the band didn't stay together long; after they dissolved, Burgess pursued a solo career. —*John Dougan & Stephen Thomas Erlewine*

● **Script for the Bridge** / 1983 / Statik ◆◆◆◆
With dark, dense but heavily melodic songs equaling the strength of Echo & the Bunnymen and Joy Division, this is a largely undiscovered '80s classic. —*Steve Aldrich*

○ **What Does Anything Mean? Basically?** / 1985 / Statik ◆◆◆◆
Their second studio album solidly sustains the *Script* formula. —*Steve Aldrich*

○ **Strange Times** / 1986 / Geffen ◆◆◆◆
U.S. vinyl LP copies of the third album came with a bonus 12-inch E.P. —*Steve Aldrich*

The Fan & The Bellows / 1989 / Caroline ◆◆◆
Collection of singles and pre-debut album material. —*Steve Aldrich*

Tripping Dogs / 1990 / Glass Pyramid ◆◆◆
Recorded during rehearsals in 1985. —*Steve Aldrich*

Tony Fletcher Walked on Water / 1990 / Glass Pyramid

Champaign

Group, Soul, Urban
Champaign took its name from its home city of Champaign, IL. The group was an interracial septet comprising singers Pauli Carman and Rena Jones, guitarist Howard Reeder, keyboardists Michael Day and Dana Walden, bassist Michael Reed, and percussionist Rocky Maffitt. They hit a commercial peak with their 1981 debut album, *How 'Bout Us*, whose title track was a hit single (Top Five in the U.K. and on the U.S. R&B chart). Follow-ups included *Modern Heart* (1983) (which includes the Top Ten R&B hit "Try Again") and *Woman in Flames* (1984), featuring the R&B Top Ten hit "Off and On Love." —*William Ruhlmann*

Champaign / 1981 / Columbia ◆◆◆

● **How 'Bout Us** / Jan. 1981 / Columbia ◆◆◆◆
Smooth, well-crafted pop-R&B topped by the creamy vocals of Pauli Carman and Rena Jones. This debut is a pop hybrid that sounds very promising, although the group never followed through adequately. —*William Ruhlmann*

Modern Heart / Mar. 1983 / Columbia ◆◆
Champaign, a soul vocal group who downplayed the fact that they were among the rare early '80s interracial acts, had scored a big hit in 1981 with the single "How 'Bout Us." But for some reason, they didn't get a second album out fast enough to keep things moving, in part because of intra-group problems. By the time their second album came around, people had forgotten about the band and soul was again struggling, as the early '80s revival had begun petering out. This wasn't a bad album, but it was almost completely ignored. —*Ron Wynn*

Woman in Flames / Oct. 1984 / Columbia ◆◆
The interracial soul group Champaign staged a comeback of sorts with this self-produced '84 album. They got their third R&B Top Ten hit with the song "Off and On Love," and lead vocalist Pauli Carmen got enough mileage from the hit single to leave for a short-lived solo career. —*Ron Wynn*

Champaign IV / 1991 / Malaco ◆◆
Champaign's lead singer Pauli Carmen, who had been featured on their best singles, returned to the band for their '91 debut on Malaco. Unfortunately, neither he nor Malaco were able to revive the group's hit status. This was a competent bit of well-produced Southern soul that was completely bypassed by urban contemporary stations now plugged into New Jack Swing. —*Ron Wynn*

The Champs

Group, Rock & Roll, Instrumental Rock
An instrumental quintet formed in Los Angeles in 1957, the

Champs comprised Challenge Records executive Dave Burgess (born Lancaster, CA) (guitar) and session players Buddy Bruce (guitar), Chuck Rio (born Daniel Flores, Rankin, TX) (saxophone), Cliff Hills (bass), and Gene Alden (born Cisco, TX) (drums). This lineup recorded Rio's "Tequila" as a B-side to Burgess's "Train to Nowhere." "Tequila" topped the charts in 1958. The Champs essentially were a one-hit wonder, though they recorded a few more singles in the same Latin dance style and kept going until the mid-'60s. The group's lineup was fluid, and later members included Glen Campbell as well as Jimmy Seals and Dash Crofts, who formed the successful '70s duo Seals & Crofts. — *William Ruhlmann*

○ **Wing Ding** / 1993 / Ace ✦✦✦✦
Although best known for their number one instrumental "Tequila," The Champs existed into the mid-'60s and left a great many sides either unreleased or buried on albums and failed singles. This CD unearths 28 of those sides, some in true stereo, making for delightful listening all the way. The enclosed booklet features the first comprehensive history of the group, whose members included future superstars Seals & Crofts, Glen Campbell, and Los Angeles session-guitar whiz Jerry Cole. (British import) — *Cub Koda*

● **Tequila: The Champs Greatest Hits** / Apr. 19, 1994 / Capitol/Curb ✦✦✦

Gene Chandler

b. Jul. 6, 1937, Chicago, IL
Soul, R&B
Chandler is remembered by the rock & roll audience almost solely for the classic novelty and doo-wop-tinged soul ballad "Duke of Earl"; the unforgettable opening chant of the title leading the way, the song was a number one hit in 1962. He's esteemed by soul fans as one of the leading exponents of the '60s Chicago soul scene, along with Curtis Mayfield and Jerry Butler. Born Eugene Dixon, he was a member of the doo-wop group the Dukays, and "Duke of Earl" was actually a Dukays recording; Dixon was renamed Gene Chandler, and the single bore his credit as a solo singer. Chandler never approached the massive pop success of that chart-topper (although he occasionally entered the Top 20), but he was a big star with the R&B audience with straightforward mid-tempo and ballad soul numbers in the mid-'60s, many of which were written by Curtis Mayfield, and produced by Carl Davis. Chandler's success became more fitful after Mayfield stopped penning material for him, although he enjoyed some late '60s hits, and had a monster pop and soul smash in 1970 with "Groovy Situation." His last successes were the far less distinguished disco and dance-influenced R&B hits "Get Down" (1978) and "Does She Have a Friend?" (1980). — *Richie Unterberger*

○ **The Gene Chandler Situation** / 1970 / MER ✦✦✦✦
Slick Chicago soul from 1970, it includes the smash "Groovy Situation." — *Bill Dahl*

○ **The Duke of Earl** / 1993 / Vee-Jay ✦✦✦✦
Gene Chandler exploded on the '60s soul scene with "Duke of Earl," a brilliant piece of novelty/love song material. His hit singles could be formulaic, but Chandler's expressive, haunting voice never failed to lift a trite lyric or punctuate a great one. This 23-cut set contains many songs previously available only as singles, and mixes the requisite hits with nicely done obscurities like "London Town," "Day to Day," and "Baby, That's Love." This isn't the complete Gene Chandler output, but it's certainly not most of his prime early numbers and lots of smashes. — *Ron Wynn*

● **Nothing Can Stop Me: Gene Chandler's Greatest Hits** / 1994 / Varese Sarabande ✦✦✦✦
This 20-track CD is the only collection that has all of his most popular recordings, from "Duke Of Earl" through his soul hits for Constellation, Vee Jay, Checker, Mercury, and Chi-Sound, spanning 1962 to 1980 (all but three tracks were released before 1968). Some fans might prefer *The Duke Of Earl*, which focuses on his Vee Jay years, but this has a much wider breadth, and includes "Groovy Situation." Curtis Mayfield wrote eight of the songs, although they frankly don't fully measure up to the Chicago soul he was writing for his own group, the Impressions, at the time. — *Richie Unterberger*

Change

Group, Urban
Change was a studio group formed by Italian producer Jacques

Fred Petrus containing European and American musicians, including leaders Paolo Granolio (guitar) and David Romani (bass). The group is most notable for featuring Luther Vandross on lead vocals on their first two albums. Later, the group based itself in New York with singers James Robinson and Deborah "Crab" Cooper, the latter going on to join C&C Music Factory. — *Steve Huey*

● **The Glow of Love** / 1980 / Warner Brothers ✦✦✦✦
Elegant dance-music arrangements with feathery leads from Luther Vandross. Includes Change's only Top 40 hit, "A Lover's Holiday." — *Ron Wynn*

Miracles / 1981 / Atlantic ✦✦
James Robinson proved a fine replacement for Luther Vandross as Change's lead singer on a pair of early '80s albums. "Miracles" was a Top 10 hit and "Hold Tight" a good follow-up. They perfectly blended sophisticated soul leads, orchestrated backgrounds, and multi-layered production. — *Ron Wynn*

Sharing Your Love / 1982 / London ✦✦✦
The second and final album that featured lead vocalist James Robinson. Change continued scoring hits with "The Very Best In You," while the uptempo tunes clicked in the clubs and the slow songs got urban contemporary airplay. The group had toured successfully in 1981 and that momentum continued into '82. — *Ron Wynn*

This Is Your Time / 1983 / Atlantic ✦✦

Change of Heart / 1984 / Atlantic ✦✦
Change switched producers on this release, hiring the team of Jam and Lewis. Their brand of driving, synthesizer-dominated R&B worked well, getting the group back on the charts after a year's absence. The title cut made it to number seven, and the follow-up "It Burns Me Up," which didn't do as well, was just as solid a tune. This was the only album they did with Jam and Lewis at the production controls. — *Ron Wynn*

Turn on Your Radio / 1985 / Atlantic ✦
The once dominant disco group Change enjoyed its final hit with this '85 album. The lineup had changed radically from the days when Luther Vandross or James Robinson were providing exciting, soulful leads. The leads throughout this session, even on the lone successful single "Let's Go Together," were more efficient than distinctive. The group's founder, Jacques Fred Petrus, returned to the production helm and recycled the arrangements that once made them a major act. — *Ron Wynn*

Channels

Group, Doo-Wop
While never having a run of hits, the Channels were among the most popular East Coast doo-wop ensembles. Larry Hampden, Billy Morris, and Edward Dolphin were charter members of the Channels, who formed in 1955. They started with two part-time members, but then absorbed lead vocalist Earl Michael Lewis and Clifton Wright from The Lotharios. Lewis became their principal songwriter and he penned their best-known hit, "The Closer You Are." The Channels also brought a fresh style to doo-wop singing with their practice of opening a verse in five-part harmony, then having Lewis sing lead in the bridge. Later releases like "The Gleam in Your Eye" and "I Really Love You" were superbly performed, but never got the push needed for national recognition. They later recorded for Gone, Fury, Port, Hit, Enjoy, and Groove with numerous personnel changes. — *Ron Wynn*

● **Greatest Hits** / 1990 / Relic ✦✦✦✦
This velvety '50s New York doo-wop is led by the distinctive falsetto of Earl Lewis. — *Bill Dahl*

Chantays

Group, Surf
In 1963, this teenage group from Santa Ana, CA, had one of the biggest and best instrumental surf hits, "Pipeline." Competent players who went heavy on the rumbling bass, ghostly reverb, and electric keyboards, they were very much a one-shot act; their repertoire was crowded with rock & roll covers and "Pipeline" soundalikes, and none of their follow-up singles charted. — *Richie Unterberger*

● **Pipeline** / 1963 / Varese Sarabande ✦✦✦✦
A CD reissue of their 1963 debut album, with the addition of "Pipeline"'s B-side and both sides of the non-LP flop follow-up single. Mostly it's lesser variations of the "Pipeline" formula, including one instrumental penned by Tony Asher, Brian Wilson's writ-

ing partner for much of the *Pet Sounds* album. It doesn't include the single "Beyond," which can be found on the surf volume of Rhino/*Guitar Player*'s *Legends of Guitar* series. —*Richie Unterberger*

The Chantels

Group, R&B, Doo-Wop, Girl-Group
An early female R&B quartet, the Chantels were led by powerhouse vocalist Arlene Smith, whose vocals on their 1957 hit "Maybe" remain some of the most moving ever recorded. —*John Floyd*

● **The Best of the Chantels** / 1990 / Rhino ✦✦✦✦
One of the leading girl groups of the late '50s, they were distinguished by Arlene Smith's impassioned leads. —*Bill Dahl*

Harry Chapin

b. Dec. 7, 1942, New York, NY, d. Jul. 16, 1981, Jericho, NY
Singer-Songwriter
Harry Chapin's career as a popular singer/songwriter was cut short by an auto accident in 1981, yet he left behind a series of recordings that his fans continue to treasure well over a decade after his death. Chapin was never a critically acclaimed singer/songwriter. Critics accused him of over-sentimentalizing his subjects and attaching heavy-handed morals to his socially aware storysongs; the heavily orchestrated arrangements that accompanied many of his songs didn't help his case with the critics, either. Nevertheless, Chapin earned a devoted audience during the '70s, through his music and his charity work as a social activist.

Chapin began performing while he was in high school, singing in the Brooklyn Heights Boys' Choir and forming a band with his brothers Tom and Stephen. During college, he decided to pursue a career as a documentary filmmaker; in 1968, he directed the Oscar-nominated *Legendary Champions*. In 1971, he switched his careers, concentrating on a musical career. Chapin recruited a backing band through an ad in the *Village Voice*; the respondents included bassist John Wallace, guitarist Ron Palmer, and cellist Tim Scott. The group began performing in various clubs around New York and the singer/sognwriter was soon signed to Elektra records.

Heads & Tails, Chapin's first album, was released in the summer of 1972 and became a success thanks to the hit single "Taxi," which soon became the songwriter's signature tune. Later that year, he released his second album, *Sniper and Other Love Songs,* which didn't fare quite as well as his debut. *Short Stories,* Chapin's third album, appeared in the spring of 1973; it spent 23 weeks on the chart due to the success of the single "W.O.L.D.," a story about the life of a disc jockey. After recording his fourth album, *Verities & Balderdash,* Chapin disbanded his backing band and began work on his musical *The Night that Made America Famous*; both Wallace and Masters worked on the show, along with guitarist Doug Walker, drummer Howie Fields, and Chapin's brothers Tom, Steve, and Jim. While he was working on the musical, *Verities & Balderdash* became his biggest hit, peaking at number four on the U.S. charts and becoming a gold record. The album's success was benefited by the single "Cat's in the Cradle," a song about an inconsiderate, career-oriented father that was based on a poem written by Chapin's wife.

The Night that Made America Famous opened on February 26, 1975. It closed on April 6, after 75 performances; the show would earn two Tony nominations. Chapin won an Emmy award that spring for his contributions to ABC television's children's series *Make a Wish*, which was hosted by his brother Tom. That spring, the singer/songwriter co-founded World Hunger Year, a charity designed to raise money to fight international famine; the organization earned over $350,000 in its first year. In the fall of 1975, Chapin delivered *Portrait Gallery*, his follow-up to *Verities & Balderdash*. While the album performed respectably, peaking at number 53, it failed to recapture the mass audience of his previous album.

Greatest Stories—Live, a double album released in the spring of 1976, became the singer/songwriter's second gold album, peaking at number 48. Chapin was becoming more politically active throughout 1976, as evidenced by his role as a delegate at that summer's Democratic Convention. Late in 1976, he released *On the Road to Kingdom Come*, which spent a mere six weeks on the charts. The 1977 double-album *Dance Band on the Titanic* was on the charts for a few more weeks, yet it didn't spawn a hit single.

The following year, Chapin met with President Jimmy Carter, discussing the need for a Presidential Commission on Hunger; he also released *Living Room Suite* that summer, which peaked at number 133.

Chapin released a second live album, *Legends of the Lost and Found—New Greatest Stories Live*, in the fall of 1979; it was his least successful album, spending only three weeks on the charts. In 1980, he signed with Boardwalk records, releasing *Sequel* that fall; the title track of the album was a sequel to his first hit single, "Taxi," and became his last Top 40 hit.

On July 16, 1981, Chapin was driving to a business meeting on the Long Island Expressway near Jericho, NY, when his car was rear-ended by a tractor-trailer. The accident caused his gas tank to explode, killing the singer/songwriter in the process. A memorial fund was established in his name following his death, with Elektra Records providing the initial donation of $10,000. Over the years, the fund has raised an estimated $5 million, which has gone to a variety of social causes that were close to Chapin's heart. —*Stephen Thomas Erlewine*

○ **Heads & Tales** / Mar. 1972 / Elektra ✦✦✦✦
Chapin's breakthrough album included "Taxi." —*Dan Heilman*

Sniper & Other Love Songs / Oct. 1972 / Elektra ✦✦✦

Short Stories / 1974 / Elektra ✦✦✦

○ **Verities & Balderdash** / 1974 / Elektra ✦✦✦✦

Portrait Gallery / 1975 / Elektra ✦✦

○ **Greatest Stories: Live** / 1976 / Elektra ✦✦✦✦

On the Road to Kingdom Come / 1976 / Elektra ✦✦

Dance Band on the Titanic / 1977 / Elektra ✦

Living Room Suite / 1978 / Elektra ✦✦

Legends of the Lost & Found / 1979 / Elektra ✦✦

Sequel / 1980 / Boardwalk ✦✦

● **Anthology of Harry Chapin** / 1985 / Elektra ✦✦✦✦
A fine summing-up, it features "Cat's in the Cradle," "Taxi," and others. —*Dan Heilman*

Tracy Chapman

b. 1964, Cleveland, OH
Singer-Songwriter
Tracy Chapman was the most successful folk-based performer to emerge in the '80s. Born in Cleveland, she won a scholarship to the Wooster School in Connecticut, then attended Tufts University. She began singing on street corners and in coffeehouses in the Boston area, then she signed with Elektra Records after graduating from college.

Chapman cut her debut album, prominently featuring her throaty alto and acoustic guitar, with minimal added instrumentation. Her songs were closely observed tales of lower-class life (the hit "Fast Car") and political rhetoric ("Talkin' 'Bout a Revolution"), sung compellingly. Released on April 1, 1988, *Tracy Chapman* became a #1 international hit, selling three million copies in the U.S. and a reported six-and-a-half million more overseas. Chapman toured extensively behind it, including a series of Amnesty International benefits around the world. She won three 1988 Grammy Awards, including Best New Artist. *Crossroads*, her second album, was released in 1989 and was also a million-seller. Her third album, *Matters of the Heart*, was released in 1992. —*William Ruhlmann*

● **Tracy Chapman** / 1988 / Elektra ✦✦✦✦
With her choked voice and acoustic guitar, Tracy Chapman reawakened social awareness and demonstrated the power of folk music on her debut album, singing of homelessness and desperation and "Talkin' 'Bout a Revolution." Contains the Top Ten hit "Fast Car." —*William Ruhlmann*

Crossroads / 1989 / Elektra ✦✦✦
Coming after her remarkably accomplished debut, the slightly subdued follow-up *Crossroads* is a mild disappointment, but after a few plays, songs like "Bridges" and "Crossroads" reveal themselves as some of her finer work. —*Stephen Thomas Erlewine*

Matters of the Heart / 1992 / Elektra ✦✦✦
Less bold and angry than her previous work, Chapman paces *Matters of The Heart* over an acoustic course that touches equally on personal vignettes and social commentary. With her fluid, rapid-fire delivery, Chapman takes aim at society and lands several direct hits devoid of self-righteousness: songs about the down-

trodden ("Bang Bang Bang"), feminism ("Woman's Work"), and freedom ("I Used To Be a Sailor"). The album's centerpiece is "If These Are The Things," a subtle, passionate masterpiece about coming to grips with innocence lost. A couple of songs suffer from too much sweetening in the studio, diluting the impact of Chapman's potent lyrics. The extraneous bells and whistles dressing up "Dreaming On A World" provide the most obvious example of a trend Chapman would do well to avoid in the future. —*Roch Parisien*

The Charlatans

Group, Psychedelic, Folk-Rock
No relation to the British alternative rock band, the Charlatans, this San Francisco group has been widely credited as starting the Haight/Ashbury psychedelic scene. In retrospect, their contribution was more of a social one, planting seeds of a rock counterculture with their unconventional, at times outrageous dress and attitudes. While they occasionally delved into guitar distortion and fractured, stoned songwriting, the Charlatans' music was rooted in good-time jugband blues, not psychedelic freakouts. That's not to say their records didn't have a low-key, easygoing charm, although they didn't match the innovations of the Jefferson Airplane and other peers. Cutting demos for a couple of labels in 1966, most of the material they recorded at this time was unissued, and the commercial explosion of San Francisco rock passed them by. The band eventually did release a nationally distributed album in the late '60s, by which time personnel changes had diluted some of the crazy energy of the original lineup, although the LP has its engaging moments. —*Richie Unterberger*

The Charlatans / 1969 / Groucho ✦✦✦
The word is that this album failed to capture the group's essence, but it has its share of good stuff. Their good-timey sound is balanced by an engaging sincerity and folky, melodic compositions reminiscent of very early Jefferson Airplane, although there are a couple ho-hum jugband tunes. But the production and performances are too complacent and tame, lacking the spaced-out recklessness of the San Francisco scene which groups like the Airplane captured so well on record. —*Richie Unterberger*

● **Alabama Bound** / 198? / Eva ✦✦✦✦
Mid-1966 demos, recorded by Lovin' Spoonful producer Erik Jacobsen. Featuring blues, good-time music, and tentative psychedelia, it doesn't sound as crazy as one might have thought, but remains the only glimpse into the band at their most original during their early days. Also includes a live, ten-minute 1969 recording of the title track. —*Richie Unterberger*

Charlatans UK

Group, Alternative Pop/Rock
Along with the Happy Mondays, the Charlatans (U.K.) were one of the two leading bands of England's Manchester bands in the late '80s and early '90s. More pop-oriented than either the Happy Mondays or the Inspiral Carpets, the Charlatans brought '60s melodies and hooks—complete with prominent Hammond organs and swirling guitar lines—together with a pulsating dance beat, creating a new psychedelia for the '90s clubgoer. Although they weren't as inventive as the Stone Roses, when the Charlatans were at the top of their form in the early, pre-grunge '90s, they made some irresistible singles that were hits in the U.K. ("Then" and "The Only One I Know"); they weren't able to duplicate their success in America, where they were forced to tack "U.K." to the end of their name because they shared it with a San Franciscan garage rock band from the '60s.

As their career progressed, the Charlatans' sound became more streamlined, losing some of the neo-psychedelic club-oriented rhythm tracks that pigeonholed them as part of the Manchester scene, as the 1994 single "Can't Get Out of Bed" demonstrates. All the while, they haven't lost their flair for good pop singles and each of their albums have a few gems scattered among the tracks. —*Stephen Thomas Erlewine*

● **Some Friendly** / 1990 / Beggars Banquet ✦✦✦✦
This British album combines '60s psychedelia with a '90s mentality, creating a strong retro-groove. —*Donna DiChario*

Between 10th & 11th / Apr. 14, 1992 / Beggars Banquet ✦✦✦
The Charlatans' sophomore effort is surprisingly more successful than the group's debut. While lacking the knockout punch of anything as strong as "The Only One I Know," this set steers clear of the underdeveloped material that marred much of the previous al-

bum without deviating from the basic formula. It's proof positive that the Charlatans can succeed without the hype that surrounded their arrival. —*Steve Aldrich*

Up to Our Hips / 1994 / Beggars Banquet ✦✦✦
As the Manchester craze fades further into the past, the Charlatans continue to streamline their vaguely psychedelic pop approach. On *Up to Our Hips*, the band refashions '60s British Invasion pop for the 1990s, removing most of the dance tendencies lying beneath the surface of their previous albums. As "Can't Get Out of Bed" shows, their songwriting skills have continued to improve, ranking the album alongside their earlier, more popular releases. —*Stephen Thomas Erlewine*

Ray Charles (Ray Charles Robinson)
b. Sep. 23, 1930, Albany, GA
Soul, R&B
The seminal 1950s Atlantic Records recordings of Ray Charles virtually defined the very essence of soul, and his radical early '60s R&B/country synthesis helped immeasurably to bridge the gap between the two idioms. If he isn't a certifiable genius, as is often claimed, Ray Charles is certainly one of the most influential musical figures of the 20th century.

Completely blind by age seven, Charles mastered the piano in his teens and, by 1948, was already recording in a Nat Cole/Charles Brown-derived style. But Charles hit upon a daring concept of combining joyous gospel rhythms with secular lyrics just about the time he signed with Atlantic, turning the musical world on its collective ear in the process.

With his jazz combo in place, Brother Ray sat down at the 88s and began racking up the hits during the mid '50s—the #1 R&B singles included "I've Got A Woman" (January 1955), "A Fool For You" (June 1955), and "Drown In My Own Tears" (February 1956), and in June 1959, the wondrous "What'd I Say" (his first Top Ten pop hit), combining the call-and-response structure of the church with the sexually charged message of the blues. It also showcased Charles's pioneering use of the electric piano.

When Charles signed with ABC/Paramount in 1960, he shifted gears entirely, delving deep into pop and country in his own inimitable style on such #1 pop hits as "Georgia On My Mind" (September 1960), "Hit The Road Jack" (August 1961), and "I Can't Stop Loving You" (April 1962) and on the massively successful albums *Modern Sounds In Country And Western Music (Volumes One and Two)* (January and October 1962), *Ingredients In A Recipe For Soul* (August 1963), and *Sweet & Sour Tears* (March 1964). Charles's commercial success gradually declined through the early '70s. In the early '80s, he signed to Columbia Records and aimed at the country market, culminating in "Seven Spanish Angels," a duet with Willie Nelson that topped the country charts in early 1985. In the '90s, signed to Warner Bros., he was back to making pop/R&B, notably on the chart album *My World* (April 1993). And then there are those ubiquitous Diet Pepsi TV ads. —*Bill Dahl & William Ruhlmann*

The Great Ray Charles / 1956 / Atlantic ✦✦✦
A superb late '50s instrumental album showcasing the jazz side of Ray Charles. Quincy Jones provided the arrangements, and the Charles band included Fathead Newman and Hank Crawford. The CD version includes six marvelous bonus cuts, among them a remarkable cover of Fats Waller's "Ain't Misbehavin'." —*Ron Wynn*

The Great Ray Charles / 1957 / Atlantic ✦✦✦
A classic Ray Charles album. He displayed his jazz side, working with a group that included Hank Crawford and Fathead Newman. Charles played piano, organ, and alto sax. Quincy Jones provided top arrangements. This has been reissued on CD with six bonus tracks. —*Ron Wynn*

Ray Charles / Jul. 1957 / Atlantic ✦✦✦
These are animated soul and R&B recordings, although the rock and roll links are pretty obvious as well. The songs, vocals, arrangements, and production are great; only the sound quality falters. But they can also be obtained on many other anthologies with far superior sound. —*Ron Wynn*

Soul Brothers / 1958 / Atlantic ✦✦✦
An early glimpse of the jazz side of Charles, it features vibist Milt Jackson. —*Hank Davis*

○ **Ray Charles at Newport** / Oct. 1958 / Atlantic ✦✦✦✦
For his appearance at the Newport Jazz Festival on July 5, 1958, Charles pulled out all the stops, performing raucous versions of "The Right Time," "I Got A Woman," and "Talkin' 'Bout You." (This album was reissued in 1973 as a two-record set, packaged with

Ray Charles In Person under the title *Ray Charles Live* [Atlantic SD 2-503].) — *William Ruhlmann* ◆◆◆

What'd I Say / Sep. 1959 / Atlantic ◆◆◆
At a concert held at Herndon Stadium in Atlanta on May 28, 1959, Ray Charles turns in a blistering version of "What'd I Say" and takes on the big band era with versions of Tommy Dorsey's "Yes Indeed!" and Artie Shaw's "Frenesi," not to mention performances of "The Right Time" and "Tell the Truth." (This album was reissued in 1960 under the title *Ray Charles in Person* and again in 1973 as a part of a two-record set, packaged with *Ray Charles at Newport* under the title *Ray Charles Live* (Atlantic 503). — *William Ruhlmann*

○ **The Genius of Ray Charles** / 1960 / Atlantic ◆◆◆◆
Another instrumental pop, blues, and jazz masterpiece from Ray Charles. Quincy Jones again did the arrangements, and Charles covered everything from "Alexander's Ragtime Band" to "Come Rain or Come Shine." This was the first Charles album to hit the charts, although it certainly wouldn't be his last. — *Ron Wynn*

The Genius Hits the Road / Jul. 1960 / ABC/Paramount ◆◆◆
Great blues, soul, and jazzy pop from Ray Charles, then in the midst of perhaps his most creative streak as a performer. Charles's vocals were animated, urgent, and spectacular, while the arrangements, production, material, and instrumental backing were equally splendid. — *Ron Wynn*

○ **The Genius After Hours** / 1961 / Rhino ◆◆◆◆
A great all-instrumental album, with Charles playing straight jazz, pop tunes, blues, and combinations of all those forms and more. Some equally fine solos from Fathead Newman, Hank Crawford, and Charles on keyboards and alto sax. — *Ron Wynn*

○ **Genius + Soul= Jazz** / Mar. 1961 / DCC ◆◆◆◆
A memorable big band session, it produced the instrumental hit "One Mint Julep." — *Hank Davis*

Ray Charles & Betty Carter / Jul. 1961 / DCC ◆◆◆
One of the more intriguing and controversial albums in Ray Charles's distinguished career. He and Betty Carter toured together in the early '60s, cutting this session for ABC-Paramount in 1961. She has since slammed the album; Charles hasn't commented on it. You can hear the differences in style and approach, and at times Carter's jazzy touches don't mesh with Charles's soulful delivery. But there are also plenty of electric moments, and the album has worn well over the years. It's been reissued on CD. — *Ron Wynn*

○ **The Genius Sings the Blues** / Oct. 1961 / Atlantic ◆◆◆◆
Down-home, anguished laments and moody ballads were turned into triumphs by Ray Charles. He sang these songs with the same conviction, passion, and energy that made his country and soul vocals so majestic. This has not as of yet turned up in the reissue bins, but is probably headed in that direction. — *Ron Wynn*

☆ **Modern Sounds in Country & Western Music** / Jan. 1962 / Rhino ◆◆◆◆◆
Modern Sounds in Country & Western Music is historically important, and considered by most critics to be a classic, but some have mixed feelings about it. Charles's interpretations of songs previously recorded by Hank Williams, Eddy Arnold, Floyd Tillman, and Don Gibson are superb, but so often the arrangements by Marty Paich, Gerald Wilson, and Gil Fuller threaten to drown him in a sea of lachrymose bric-a-brac. "I Can't Stop Loving You" and "You Don't Know Me" were Top Ten pop and R&B. — *Rob Bowman*

☆ **Modern Sounds in Country & Western, Vol. 2** / Oct. 1962 / Rhino ◆◆◆◆◆
Charles' second installment of *Modern Sounds in Country & Western Music* is every bit as essential as the first, containing stellar interpretations of "Your Cheatin' Heart" and "You Are My Sunshine." — *Stephen Thomas Erlewine*

○ **Ingredients in a Recipe for Soul** / Jul. 1963 / DCC ◆◆◆◆
A first-rate set of soulfully sung pop, with some blues and R&B added for good measure. Charles was in another extremely productive period for ABC-Paramount and had the creative freedom to sing whatever he wanted. At this point, he also exercised more rigorous standards and got better compositions than he's gotten in the '80s and '90s. — *Ron Wynn*

Country & Western Meets Rhythm & Blues / Aug. 1965 / ABC/Paramount ◆◆◆
A partially successful revisiting by Charles of his country sessions of the early '60s. These songs weren't quite as transcendent as those on the prior dates, but he showed once again that the lines

between country, R&B, and soul weren't as rigid as many in the various camps thought. — *Ron Wynn*

○ **Ray Charles Live** / May 1973 / Atlantic ◆◆◆◆
A repackaging of *Ray Charles In Newport* and *Ray Charles In Person* presents concerts from 1958 and 1959 that found Charles in peak form, performing some of his best-known R&B hits. — *William Ruhlmann*

Porgy & Bess / Oct. 1976 / RCA Victor ◆◆◆
Charles and Cleo Laine duet on the songs from George Gershwin's opera, in a version arranged and conducted by Frank DeVol (who provides extra instrumentals) and produced by Norman Granz. The material is perfect for the performers, and they give it an effective, if unstudied, treatment. — *William Ruhlmann*

Ain't It So / Sep. 1979 / Atlantic ◆◆◆
One of the better albums from Charles's second sojourn at Atlantic in the '70s. Here, he gives us an uptempo version of Irving Berlin's "What'll I Do," and similarly revamps such standards as "Some Enchanted Evening" and "Blues In The Night." — *William Ruhlmann*

A Life in Music / Oct. 1982 / Atlantic ◆◆◆
A comprehensive five-volume Charles package; the ultimate anthology if you're seeking a complete portrait. It isn't as concise in focus as the R&B boxed set and was quite expensive when issued in the early '80s. But as a full Charles portrait, it's essential. — *Ron Wynn*

Wish You Were Here Tonight / 1983 / Columbia ◆◆◆
One of Columbia's "Best Of Times" specials, this features Ray Charles doing nice, sometimes above average, country pop and countrypolitan, plus some nondescript filler. This isn't one of his better releases, or the label's. — *Ron Wynn*

Do I Ever Cross Your Mind? / Apr. 1984 / Columbia ◆◆◆
A fairly typical example of Charles's '80s period doing country music in Nashville, which is to say respectable performances that aren't a patch on his '60s country crossover material. The title track was a minor country hit single and the album made the lower reaches of the country LP chart. But Charles remains an eclectic; some of the material fits better into the pop and R&B categories than it does country. — *William Ruhlmann*

Friendship / Aug. 1984 / Columbia ◆◆
Ray Charles was cutting decent-to-competent light country material in Nashville during the mid-'80s. His still gripping voice and masterful timing and delivery kept things from getting too disturbing, but these songs were a far cry from either his magnificent soul/R&B or his groundbreaking early '60s country. They were mostly polite, sedate, occasionally humorous duets with such country stars as George Jones, Mickey Gilley, Merle Haggard, Janie Fricke, and Hank Williams, Jr. — *Ron Wynn*

☆ **Greatest Country Western Hits** / 1988 / DCC ◆◆◆◆◆
Collecting the highlights from Charles's two *Modern Sounds in Country & Western Music* albums, *Greatest Country Western Hits* features some of the most essential country-soul material ever recorded. — *Stephen Thomas Erlewine*

☆ **Greatest Hits, Vol. 1** / 1988 / DCC ◆◆◆◆◆
The first of two volumes devoted to the hits Ray Charles did after leaving Atlantic. He turned to everything from novelty tunes to drinking songs, country, Beatles covers, and soulful pop. First-rate. — *Ron Wynn*

★ **Greatest Hits, Vol. 2** / 1988 / DCC ◆◆◆◆◆
The second volume covers more post-Atlantic Charles material, including his signature song, "Georgia On My Mind." There are also lots of other good covers, more Beatles tunes, and his versions of "Your Cheatin' Heart" and "America The Beautiful." — *Ron Wynn*

○ **Anthology** / 1989 / Rhino ◆◆◆◆
Perhaps the best single CD collection of Ray Charles' '60s and '70s ABC-Paramount material. They've also been issued on two separate anthologies, but for someone who only wants the essential items, this disc has them all over its 20 tracks. — *Ron Wynn*

Seven Spanish Angels & Other Hits / 1989 / Columbia ◆◆
A collection of what the label considered Charles's best cuts from his mid-'80s countrypolitan and country pop sessions, none of which were that great. The title track was a mildly entertaining duet between Charles and Willie Nelson. — *Ron Wynn*

○ **Soul Brothers/Soul Meeting** / 1989 / Atlantic ◆◆◆◆
A great two-disc package that combined the pivotal Ray Charles sessions with Milt Jackson. The special release even had some bonus tracks, while the remastering and annotation were mar-

velous. There was no question about the quality of the tracks; Charles and Jackson were instantly compatible, with Jackson getting to display blues elements he normally suppressed when playing with the Modern Jazz Quartet, and Charles getting space to present his jazz and improvising skills. —*Ron Wynn*

★ **The Birth of Soul** / 1991 / Rhino ♦♦♦♦♦
On three CDs, *The Birth of Soul* contains every R&B recording Ray Charles waxed while at Atlantic between 1952 and 1959. The early recordings are in the Charles Brown/Nat "King" Cole "Sepia Sinatra" vein. The later recordings go a long way toward defining the birth of soul. Robert Palmer has contributed a superb set of liner notes, contextualizing both Charles and the recordings. The sound is state of the art. This is essential seminal American music. —*Rob Bowman*

Blues & Jazz / 1994 / Rhino/Atlantic ♦♦♦
Rhino has released another Ray Charles concept set, a two-disc collection that spotlights blues vocals and jazz instrumentals culled from various sessions. The material ranges from an early Swingtime date to seminal Atlantic material featuring Charles as a leader and in collaboration with vibist Milt Jackson, David "Fathead" Newman and Edgar Blanchard. The first disc offers blues, the second jazz pieces. There's nothing wrong with these tracks; it's just hard to believe there are that many people around, especially Ray Charles fans, who don't already own them in either their original form or on one of several previously issued Atlantic packages. —*Ron Wynn*

★ **Best of Atlantic** / 1994 / Rhino ♦♦♦♦♦
For fans who don't want to invest in the three-disc box set, this is a good single-disc collection of Charles's ground-breaking Atlantic singles. —*AMG*

Genius After Hours/Great Ray / Atlantic ♦♦♦
A pair of Ray Charles masterpieces. These spotlight his instrumental and jazz side. They were recorded in the late '50s, and Charles's band at the time included Hank Crawford, Fathead Newman, and Buster Cooper, with Charles doubling on keyboards and alto sax. Quincy Jones was providing the arrangements as well. Some spectacular combo material, showing the links between blues and jazz. —*Ron Wynn*

The Early Years / Legacy ♦♦♦

Charms

Group, R&B

A Cincinnati vocal group who landed a number-one R&B hit for almost ten weeks in 1954 with "Hearts of Stone," a song that remains among the most enduring doo-wop anthems. Otis Williams, Richard Parker, Donald Peak, Joe Penn, and Rolland Bradley first recorded for Rockin' in 1953, but did "Hearts of Stone" for Deluxe the next year. They had several other hits, among them "Ling, Ting, Tong," "Two Hearts," "Ivory Tower," and "United," all of which made the Top Ten on the R&B charts between 1955 and 1957. Their songs were issued as Otis Williams and His Charms in 1956 and 1957. Williams later tried his hand at country. —*Ron Wynn*

● **The Charms Sing Their All Time Hits** / 1959 / Deluxe ♦♦♦♦

The Charts

Group, R&B, Doo-Wop

Despite never cracking *Billboard*'s R&B charts, "Deserie" by the Charts endures as a doo-wop classic. Formed in 1956, the group's manager, musician Les Cooper, got the Harlem quintet a contract with Danny Robinson's Everlast imprint. Fronted by Joseph Grier, the Charts released the mellow "Deserie" in 1957, backed with the rocking "Zoop." After a few more 45s for Everlast, the Charts disbanded in 1958. —*Bill Dahl*

● **Greatest Hits** / 1981 / Collectables ♦♦♦♦
Late-'50s harmonies from this talented Harlem doo-wop group. —*Bill Dahl*

Cheap Trick

Group, Power Pop/Anglo-Pop, Pop/Rock

Combining a love for British guitar-pop songcraft with crunching power chords and a flair for the absurd, Cheap Trick provided the necessary links between '60s pop, heavy metal, and punk. Led by guitarist Rick Nielsen, the band's early albums were filled with highly melodic, well-written songs that drew equally from the crafted pop of the Beatles, the sonic assault of the Who, and the

tongue-in-cheek musical eclecticism and humor of the Move. Their sound provided a blueprint for both power-pop and arena rock; it also had a surprisingly long-lived effect on both alternative and heavy metal bands of the '80s and '90s, who also relied on the combination of loud riffs and catchy melodies.

One of the keys to Cheap Trick's initial success in the late '70s was the fact that the band never took themselves or their music too seriously. Their songs were filled with off-hand musical references and flat-out jokes, which managed to convey both the excitement and horror of adolescence. In "Surrender," a teenage boy finds his parents making out to his Kiss records, an incident that sums up the sensibility of Cheap Trick—it's a twisted celebration of the trashiest parts of pop culture, yet one that never loses its sense of humanity. Visually, the group accentuated their sense of humor, with the heavy-set drummer, Bun E. Carlos, and the geeky Nielsen supporting the pin-up good looks of vocalist/guitarist Robin Zander and bassist Tom Petersson. The group realized the dichotomy between their members and placed the singer and the bassist on the front of their album covers, leaving the guitarist and drummer hidden on the back. Over the years, the group lost most of their flair for crunching, clever pop, turning into a standard-issue arena rock act, but for a few years, they epitomized everything that was good about pop music.

Cheap Trick's roots lie in Fuse, a late-'60s Rockford, IL, band formed by Rick Nielsen and bassist Tom Petersson, which released an unsuccessful album on Epic in 1969. After the record failed to gain any attention, the band relocated to Philadelphia and changed their name to Sick Man of Europe. The group toured Europe unsuccessfully in 1972, returning to Illinois in 1973. Upon their return to Rockford, Nielsen and Petersson changed their band's name to Cheap Trick, adding drummer Bun E. Carlos and vocalist Randy "Xeno" Hogan. Hogan was fired the following year and ex-folk singer Robin Zander joined the group.

Between 1974 and the band's first album in 1977, Cheap Trick toured constantly, playing over 200 concerts a year, including opening slots for the Kinks, Kiss, Santana, Journey, and Boston. During this time, the band built up a solid catalog of original songs that would eventually comprise their first three albums; they also perfected their kinetic live show.

Cheap Trick signed with Epic Records in 1976, releasing their self-titled debut in early 1977. The record sold well in America, yet it failed to chart. However, the group became a massive success in Japan, going gold upon release. Later that year, the band released their second album, *In Color. In Color* backed away from the harder-rocking *Cheap Trick*, featuring a slicker production and quieter arrangements that spotlighted the band's melodic skills. Due to their constant touring, the record made it into the U.S. charts, peaking at number 73; in Japan it became another goldseller.

The band realized that they were virtual superstars in Japan when they toured the country in early 1978. Their concerts were selling out within two hours and they packed Budokan Arena. Cheap Trick's concerts at Budokan Arena were recorded for release—the record appeared after their third album, 1978's *Heaven Tonight*. *Heaven Tonight* captured both the loud, raucous energy of their debut and the hook-laden songcraft of *In Color*, leading to their first Top 100 single, "Surrender," which peaked at number 62. However, the live performances on *At Budokan* (1979) captured the band's energetic, infectious live show, resulting in their commercial breakthrough in the U.S. The album stayed on the charts for over a year, peaking at number four and eventually selling over three million copies; a live version of "I Want You to Want Me" pulled from the album became their first Top Ten hit. Later that year, the group released their fourth studio album, *Dream Police*, which followed the same stylistic approach of *Heaven Tonight*. It also followed *At Budokan* into the Top Ten, selling over a million copies and launching the Top 40 hit singles "Voices" and "Dream Police." In the summer of 1980, the group released an EP of tracks recorded between 1976-79 called *Found All the Parts*.

Petersson left the group in the summer of 1980 to form a group with his wife Dagmar; he was replaced by Jon Brant. The first album recorded with Brant was the George Martin-produced *All Shook Up*, released toward the end of 1980. The album performed respectably, peaking at number 24 and going gold, yet the single "Stop This Game" failed to crack the Top 40. Epic rejected an album the group recorded in early 1981, forcing the band back into the studio to record an entirely new record. *One on One*, the group's seventh album, appeared in 1982. Although it peaked at number 39, the record was more successful than *All Shook Up*, eventually going platinum. Nevertheless, the group was entering a downhill commercial slide. *Next Position Please*, released in 1983, failed to launch a hit single and spent only 11 weeks on the charts. *Standing on the Edge* (1985) and *The Doctor* (1986) suffered similar fates, as the group was slowly losing its creative sparks.

Petersson rejoined the band in 1988 and the group began working on a new record with the help of several professional songwriters. The resulting record, *Lap of Luxury*, was a platinum Top 20 hit, featuring the number one power ballad "The Flame" and a Top Ten version of Elvis Presley's "Don't Be Cruel." *Busted*, released in 1990, wasn't as successful as *Lap of Luxury*, peaking at number 48 and effectively putting an end to the group's comeback. Cheap Trick signed with Warner Brothers in 1994, releasing *Wake Up with a Monster;* the record spent two weeks on the chart, peaking at 123. That same year, Epic Records released a sequel to *At Budokan, Budokan II.* Compiled from the same shows as *At Budokan*, the record provided an effective reminder of why the group was so popular in the late '70s, as well as proving that the band shaped the musical climate of the '90s, even if they were no longer selling millions of records. —*Stephen Thomas Erlewine*

○ **Cheap Trick** / 1977 / Epic ✦✦✦✦
Loaded with brain-crunching rude noises and attitude, this raucous debut plunders all the right stuff (Beatles, Who, the Move). All this supports some primo rockers like "Hot Love," "He's a Whore," "Taxman, Mr. Thief," and "Oh Candy," which ranks as one of the great lost rock singles of the '70s. Subsequent albums sound tame next to this one. Without a doubt, it's one of their best. —*Rick Clark*

○ **In Color** / 1977 / Epic ✦✦✦✦
Their second album ditches boisterous performances in favor of super-tight pop/rock, with hooks galore. All the same influences are there; it's just more mannered. The lightweight "I Want You to Want Me" became their first hit. Also check out "Big Eyes," "Clock Strikes Ten," and "You're All Talk." —*Rick Clark*

☆ **Heaven Tonight** / 1978 / Epic ✦✦✦✦✦
Since Cheap Trick had dispensed with the straight medicine after an excellent debut, this third album recalibrates the band's pop smarts with an impressive handful of tunes. "Surrender," in particular, is a classic. The band wears its good taste well, with a fine cover of the Move's "California Man." —*Rick Clark*

★ **Live at Budokan** / Feb. 1979 / Epic ✦✦✦✦✦
While their records were entertaining and full of skillful pop, it wasn't until *Live at Budokan* that Cheap Trick's vision truly gelled. Many of these songs, like "I Want You To Want Me" and "Big Eyes," were pleasant in their original form, but seemed more like sketches compared to the roaring versions on this album. With their ear-shatteringly loud guitars and sweet melodies, Cheap Trick unwittingly paved the way for much of the hard-rock of the next decade, as well as a surprising amount of alternative rock of the 1990s, and it was *Live at Budokan* that captured the band in all of its power. —*Stephen Thomas Erlewine*

○ **Dream Police** / Oct. 1979 / Epic ✦✦✦✦
With the big time upon them, Cheap Trick went for bigger-production sounds. Fortunately, it worked most of the time. The paranoid title cut is an effective, highly orchestrated rocker. Other notable tracks are the appealingly melodic (albeit wimpy) "Voices" and the no-frills rock of "I Know What I Want," complete with a great chorus you can shout to. In spite of its strengths, *Dream Police* marks the beginning of the band's creative decline. —*Rick Clark*

All Shook Up / 1980 / Epic ✦✦
Found All the Parts / 1980 / Epic ✦✦✦
One on One / 1982 / Epic ✦✦✦
Next Position Please / 1983 / Epic ✦✦✦
This release, produced by Todd Rundgren, is Trick's last decent album, opening with a great Robin Zander original "I Can't Take It." "Borderline," "Next Position Please," and "Younger Girls" are all strong, but the Rundgren-penned "Heaven's Falling" is magnificent. —*Rick Clark*

Standing on the Edge / 1985 / Epic ✦✦
The Doctor / 1986 / Epic ✦
Lap of Luxury / 1988 / Epic ✦✦✦
Despite its formulaic approach, *Lap of Luxury* scored a major hit with "The Flame," which briefly returned Cheap Trick to the top of the charts. The rest of the album featured either similar power bal-

lads or half-hearted hard-rockers, like their cover of "Don't Be Cruel." —*Stephen Thomas Erlewine*

Busted / 1990 / Epic ✦✦
○ **Greatest Hits** / 1992 / Epic ✦✦✦✦
Hardly a passable collection, it's certainly not definitive by any standard. Nevertheless, it'll be good for those who prefer the band's more recent cookie-cutter hits, like "The Flame" and "Can't Stop Falling in Love." —*Rick Clark*

Woke up with a Monster / 1994 / Warner Brothers ✦✦✦
Cheap Trick's Warners debut, produced by Ted Templeman (Van Halen, Little Feat) is their best album in years, certainly since 1983's *Next Position Please*; it's easily an equal to *Dream Police*. In spite of some uneven spots, there is more fire in their sound here and, when they go for the kind of big rock ballads that became their metier in recent years, there is enough attitude to counteract most of the tendency towards sappiness. Highlights are "You're All I Wanna Do," "Let Her Go," "My Gang," and the title cut. —*Rick Clark*

☆ **Budokan II** / Feb. 1994 / Epic ✦✦✦✦✦
Recorded in Japan over 1978 and 1979, this concert set amply displays everything that made Cheap Trick the great band it was—great songs set to a wall of guitars and bass, great over-the-top singing and crash and bash drumming. It's hard to pick highlights, but they absolutely make the Move's "California Man" their own. Either this album or *Live at Budokan* make a perfect introduction. —*Rick Clark*

Chubby Checker

b. Oct. 3, 1941, SC
R&B, Rock & Roll
He taught America how to twist. Not just the kids, who always learned the latest steps, but everyone—from society matrons and jetsetters to the proverbial man in the street.

Rock & roll was becoming complacent when Chubby Checker came along in 1960 with his note-for-note remake of Hank Ballard and the Midnighters' "The Twist" and got it moving again. The husky Philadelphia lad, known as Ernest Evans until Dick Clark's wife decided he resembled Fats Domino, had already waxed a few 45s for the local Parkway label, including a novelty called "The Class" that found him imitating Fats, Elvis, and even the Chipmunks. But it was "The Twist," a #1 hit not once but twice (in 1960 and 1961), that made him an international celebrity.

Checker quickly became the nation's leading dance specialist, introducing "The Hucklebuck," "The Fly," "Pony Time," and "Limbo Rock" to the gyrating masses and successfully recycling his initial routine into "Let's Twist Again" and "Slow Twistin'." While racking up monster sales figures for Parkway, Checker starred in a couple of quickie exploitation films, *Twist around the Clock* and *Don't Knock the Twist*, later trying his hand at folk songs when the twist fad finally began to fade.

The British Invasion led to some lean years for Checker although he got a little revenge by charting with a cover of the Beatles tune "Back in the U.S.S.R." in 1969. But he continued to put on a high-energy show that inevitably led to that classic million-seller—and Chubby Checker proved every time out that he was still the king of the Twist. —*Bill Dahl*

● **Chubby Checker's Greatest Hits** / Nov. 1972 / ABKCO ✦✦✦✦
In 1972, when nostalgia for late-'50s and early-'60s rock & roll was bringing Chuck Berry and others back into the charts, Allen Klein's ABKCO Records obtained the rights to reissue Chubby Checker's Cameo-Parkway singles on this 15-track mini-LP. Checker actually had many more hits than just "The Twist" and "Let's Twist Again," and this LP presents both his other dance tunes—"Pony Time," "The Fly," "Limbo Rock"—and several of his later, less successful singles when he was trying to branch out into a sort of Harry Belafonte-style folk approach. But the heart of the collection is still the early-'60s dance tunes, which demonstrate that, while Checker was not a great rocker, he still, like Freddy Cannon and Gary U.S. Bonds, was one of the people keeping the flame of rock & roll flickering between the time Buddy Holly's plane went down in Iowa and the day the Beatles flew in from London. (Released on LP, this album is long out of print, and it is listed as Checker's "pick" album because, as of 1995, there is no in-print album containing his original hits.) —*William Ruhlmann*

Cher

b. May 20, 1946, El Centro, CA
Pop/Rock

After untying the knot with Sonny Bono in 1974, Cher developed into a pop icon of a magnitude many times brighter than during her '60s duet days with her husband. Even while married to Sonny, Cher was hitting the charts as a solo act with "Bang Bang (My Baby Shot Me Down)" in 1966 and "You Better Sit Down Kids" in 1967, both on Imperial, and her output on Kapp included the 1971 #1 hit "Gypsiess, Tramps & Thieves." The gold records continued with "Half-Breed" in 1973 and "Dark Lady" in 1974, both chart-toppers on MCA. 1979's "Take Me Home" was Cher's last smash for eight years, but she wasn't idle, starring in the acclaimed motion pictures *Silkwood* and *The Witches of Eastwick* and winning the 1987 Best Actress Oscar for her role in *Moonstruck.* Cher roared back in 1989 with "After All," a duet with Peter Cetera, and the anthemic solo outing "If I Could Turn Back Time," both on Geffen. Whether she's hawking memberships for a health-club chain or tearing up a concert stage, Cher endures as one of the nation's premier celebrities. —*Bill Dahl*

● **Greatest Hits** / 1974 / MCA ✦✦✦
Cher's early-'70s hits, including "Gypsies, Tramps and Thieves," "Half-Breed," and "Dark Lady," are compiled on this collection. — *Stephen Thomas Erlewine*

I Paralyze / 1982 / Columbia ✦✦✦
This strong set has a hardy rhythm section and good range of soft-rock and pop ballads well suited for Cher's vocals. It also brought her out of an outdated style into modern music using the production skills of Olivia Newton-John's producer, John Farrar. The girl-group-styled "Rudy" and piano ballad "When the Love Is Gone" stand out. —*Bil Carpenter*

○ **Cher [Geffen]** / 1987 / Geffen ✦✦✦
Cher's late-'80s musical comeback was fueled by her success as an actress, not her songs, but her first album of the 1980s was a surprisingly consistent set of slick contemporary pop, including the hit "We All Sleep Alone." —*Stephen Thomas Erlewine*

● **Heart of Stone** / 1989 / Geffen ✦✦✦
One of the most mature albums of Cher's career, this focuses on relationships from a 40-year-old's perspective rather than a teenager's. Cuts include "If I Could Turn Back Time," "Just Like Jesse James," and a duet with Peter Cetera, "After All." —*Bil Carpenter*

● **Bang Bang, My Baby Shot Me Down: The Best of Cher** / 1991 / EMI America ✦✦✦
Bang Bang, My Baby Shot Me Down—The Best of Cher collects more than twenty of Cher's '60s solo cuts on the Imperial label. There is the Motown-styled "Dream Baby," but it's mostly folk-pop including little-known gems like the pensive "She's Not Better Than Me." —*Bil Carpenter*

Love Hurts / 1991 / Geffen ✦✦✦
Although it isn't quite as varied as its predecessor, *Love Hurts* features many of the same elements of *Heart of Stone* without winding up a retread; the approach resulted in the hits "Love and Understanding" and "Save Up All Your Tears." —*Stephen Thomas Erlewine*

Neneh Cherry

b. Mar. 10, 1964, Stockholm, Sweden
Dance-Pop

A one-time member of Rip Rig + Panic and of the punk group the Slits, she had a massive 1989 hit with "Buffalo Stance," which masterfully balanced hip-hop sensibilities with the crisp, accessible bounce of high-tech R&B.Cherry is also the stepdaughter of jazz trumpeter Don Cherry.

After several years of inactivity, Cherry returned in 1992 with the critically acclaimed *Home Brew;* although it failed to capture the same sales as her debut, it proved that she remained artistically innovative.—*John Floyd*

○ **Raw Like Sushi** / 1989 / Virgin ✦✦✦
Cherry's wonderful debut, produced by British dance master Bomb the Bass, offers a brash, sassy portrait of a contemporary feminist, unwilling to take shit from a lip-flapping homeboy and confident enough to tackle thorny issues, both political and sexual. —*John Floyd*

● **Homebrew** / 1992 / Virgin ✦✦✦
Despite the absence of a knockout single like "Buffalo Stance," *Homebrew* is a stronger album than *Raw Like Sushi.* On *Homebrew,* Cherry's melding of hip-hop and R&B is so complete that no seams show; it doesn't belong to either genre, but stands on its own. It takes a couple of plays before it starts to sink in, but after some time, even Michael Stipe's rap on "Trout" seems completely natural. —*Stephen Thomas Erlewine*

The Chi-Lites

Group, Soul

Ultra-smooth ballads were the specialty of the Chi-Lites, and they were one of the Windy City's hottest soul exports throughout most of the '70s. Changing their name from the Hi-Lites, the quartet recorded for a number of local firms before hitting in 1969 on Brunswick with "Give It Away." Lead singer Eugene Record's (b. Dec 23, 1940) floating tenor caressed the R&B chart-toppers "Have You Seen Her?" in 1971 and "Oh Girl" the next year, and the group scaled the soul playlists regularly through 1976, when Record went solo. Founding member Marshall Thompson keeps the group active today. —*Bill Dahl*

○ **Give More Power to the People** / 1970 / Brunswick ✦✦✦
The first hit album for the Chi-Lites, one of the great Chicago soul groups. Lead vocalist Eugene Record began to attain some stature with his soaring falsetto and urgent delivery, while the title track sounded a socio-political note and also sported a great dance beat. The album also had their finest ballad, "Have You Seen Her." — *Ron Wynn*

○ **A Lonely Man** / 1972 / Brunswick ✦✦✦
Their greatest album, this release contained the epic number one hit "Oh, Girl" and the superb title track. The album landed in the pop Top 10, reaching the number five spot. They had four singles reach the R&B charts, and it vaulted them to the head of the class among soft and sweet soul groups. —*Ron Wynn*

The Chi-Lites / 1973 / Brunswick ✦✦✦
Another super album, although it didn't have as much pop success as its predecessor. The song "A Letter to Myself" was another top R&B seller, and they got three other singles on the charts from the set. But it also marked the beginning of intra-group tensions, as Record reportedly wasn't pleased at the album's lack of crossover appeal. —*Ron Wynn*

Heavenly Body / 1980 / 20th Century ✦✦
The Chi-Lites made a comeback in 1980, signing with Carl Davis's Chi-Sound label. Eugene Record returned, and this debut album under that contract got them some renewed attention for the first time in years. The single "Heavenly Body" got some airplay and chart action, and they appeared on *Soul Train* that year. —*Ron Wynn*

Bottom's Up / 1983 / Larc ✦✦
The Chi-Lites were down to a trio, and sounded far less appealing doing three-member harmonies for this mid-'80s collection. Record's leads were still effective, but they seemed out of steam and lacked good songs as well. However, the title cut made it into the R&B Top 10, and the follow-up, "Bad Motor Scooter," reached the charts despite being one of their sillier efforts. —*Ron Wynn*

★ **Greatest Hits** / 1992 / Rhino ✦✦✦✦✦
This outstanding collection containing everything you need, including the hits "Oh Girl" and "Have You Seen Her?" —*John Floyd*

Chic

Group, Funk, Disco

Chic was the best and most influential disco band of the latter half of the '70s, earning hits with both their own records and the outside productions of co-leaders Nile Rodgers and Bernard Edwards. Beginning their career as the Big Apple Band, the group changed their name to Chic in 1977 after Walter Murphy & the Big Apple Band had a number one hit with "A Fifth of Beethoven." Along with the change in name came a change in music, from fusion to disco. Edwards (bass), Rodgers (guitar), and Tony Thompson (drums) hired Norma Jean Wright and Alfa Anderson to sing, and they recorded a demo of "Dance Dance Dance." Atlantic picked it up in late 1977 after a series of rejections from other record labels; the single sold a million copies in one month, catapulting Chic into the forefront of the disco scene. After Wright left for a solo career, Luci Martin joined the band. Chic's biggest hits—"Le Freak" (number one), "I Want Your Love" (number seven), and the "Good

Times" (number one)—came in 1978-1979, and as disco started to fade, so did the group's popularity. Still, Chic's influence was apparent throughout the '80s; "Good Times" alone spawned Queen's hit "Another One Bites the Dust" (a complete rip-off), and Sugarhill Gang used the record as the foundation for "Rapper's Delight," arguably the first rap single. Nile Rodgers was one of the most successful producers of the early '80s, scoring hits with David Bowie's *Let's Dance*, Madonna's *Like a Virgin*, and Mick Jagger's solo debut, *She's the Boss*. Edwards's solo productions weren't as consistent as Rodgers's, but the Power Station's album (which featured Tony Thompson on drums) was a hit. Chic reformed in 1992, but failed to recapture the fire of its glory days. — *Stephen Thomas Erlewine*

★ **Dance Dance Dance: Best of Chic** / 1991 / Atlantic ✦✦✦✦✦
You think disco was nothing more than assembly-line funk and freeze-dried beats? Then you need to step into the crisp grooves and walloping boogie found on this stunning collection of Chic's '70s recordings. Such hits as "Good Times," "Dance Dance Dance," and "Le Freak" used the stylistic innovations of James Brown and Sly Stone as a blueprint for a new era of funk. Bernard Edwards's basslines are so provocative they seem to talk, while Nile Rodgers's skeletal guitar runs hark back to Steve Cropper's slashing style. Sure, the songs don't say much. Sure, the dance mixes collected here ramble on after about six minutes. But once you step into these grooves—grooves that influenced an entire generation of artists from David Byrne to Prince—you will realize that these were indeed good times. —*John Floyd*

○ **The Best of Chic, Vol. 2** / 1992 / Rhino ✦✦✦✦
Filling out the gaps left by the first volume, *Best of Chic—Vol. 2* proves with its collection of album tracks and singles that Chic was not merely a great disco band, but was a great band, period. — *Stephen Thomas Erlewine*

Chicago (Chicago Transit Authority)

Group, Pop/Rock
Chicago is second only to the Beach Boys as the most successful American rock band of all time. The group formed officially on February 15, 1967, in the city from which it eventually would take its name. The band members intended to launch a rock group with a fully integrated horn section (a novel idea at the time), so the original lineup was a sextet consisting of Walter Parazaider (b. Mar 14, 1945) on saxophone and woodwinds, Lee Loughnane (b. Oct 21, 1946) on trumpet, Terry Kath (b. Jan 31, 1946–d. Jan 23, 1978) on guitar and vocals, Danny Seraphine (b. Aug 28, 1948) on drums, James Pankow (b. Aug 20, 1947) on trombone, and Robert Lamm (b. Oct 13, 1944) on organ and vocals. Initially, the group did without a bass player. But in December 1967, bassist/vocalist Peter Cetera (b. Sep 13, 1944) joined from rival band the Exceptions. Under the guidance of manager/producer James William Guercio, who initially named them Chicago Transit Authority (the name was shortened after the real C.T.A. objected), the group moved to Los Angeles and signed to Columbia Records, recording its debut album, *Chicago Transit Authority*, in January 1969. It sold over two million copies and spawned four chart singles, beginning a string of massive hits that lasted to the end of the decade, with each album cover sporting a variation on the Chicago logo and a sequential title with a roman numeral: *Chicago II, Chicago III,* etc. (Later, ordinary numbers were used.) Chicago's music was a mixture of styles, from hard rock to light pop, incorporating elements of jazz and classical, but after Cetera's "If You Leave Me Now" became a gold-selling #1 hit in 1976, the group became more identified with romantic ballads than anything else. Chicago went into decline after a split with Guercio in 1977 and the accidental death of Kath in 1978. But it rebounded in 1982 with "Hard to Say I'm Sorry" and the million-selling *Chicago 16* and was able to sustain its renewed popularity despite Cetera's departure for a solo career in 1985. — *William Ruhlmann*

○ **Chicago Transit Authority** / Apr. 1969 / Chicago ✦✦✦✦
The first rock & roll band to integrate a horn section into its sound successfully, Chicago Transit Authority (later Chicago), fresh from years on the Midwest bar circuit, demonstrated a wide versatility on its debut album. The band seemed capable of playing everything from lounge music to hard rock, and here it mixed ballad material with gritty funk and psychedelic guitar, often on the same song. This time capsule of the varying strands of popular music in the late '60s features the hits "Does Anybody Really Know What Time It Is?," "Beginnings," and "Questions 67 and 68." — *William Ruhlmann*

○ **Chicago II** / Jan. 1970 / Chicago ✦✦✦✦
With its second double album (now on one CD), Chicago became even more ambitious and even more successful, mounting the extended "Suite for a Girl in Buchannon," from which were excerpted the hit singles "Make Me Smile" and "Colour My World." "25 or 6 to 4" is also featured on this album. — *William Ruhlmann*

Chicago III / Jan. 1971 / Chicago ✦✦
With this album, Chicago had released three double-record sets within two years, which glutted the market and drained the band members' creativity. The result was a fall-off in quality and in sales, although *Chicago III* did manage to stay on the charts over a year, selling a million copies. There were only two Top 40 hits, "Free" and "Lowdown," neither of which is among the group's best. — *William Ruhlmann*

At Carnegie Hall, Vols. 1-4 / Oct. 1971 / Chicago ✦
Carnegie Hall may be prestigious, but it has never been a good rock venue, and Chicago seems intimidated on this four-LP (three-CD) set, recreating material from its first three albums. Completists should note the inclusion of the anti-Nixon "A Song For Richard And His Friends," not previously available. — *William Ruhlmann*

Chicago V / Jul. 1972 / Chicago ✦✦✦
The group's avant-garde roots are explored on the set-opening "A Hit by Varsse," while the album also includes the autobiographical "Alma Mater" and the hits "Saturday in the Park" and "Dialogue." — *William Ruhlmann*

Chicago VI / Jun. 1973 / Chicago ✦✦✦
Chicago demonstrates all its strength here, turning in one of its great ballads in "Just You 'N' Me" and one of its great rockers in "Feelin' Stronger Every Day." Elsewhere, the group takes on its negative reviews in "Critics' Choice" and acknowledges the impact of L.A. stardom on a bunch of Midwestern kids in "Something In This City Changes People." — *William Ruhlmann*

Chicago VII / Mar. 1974 / Chicago ✦✦
Originally intended as a jazz-oriented record, Chicago's first double studio album since *Chicago III* (now on one CD) is an ambitious but ultimately uneven affair, buttressed by the hit singles "(I've Been) Searchin' So Long," "Call On Me," and "Wishing You Were Here." — *William Ruhlmann*

Live in Japan 1972 / 1975 / CBS ✦✦✦
It's unfortunate that this album is available only in Japan because it's a tremendous improvement over *Carnegie Hall,* the concert recording Chicago was capable of making. But with a four-LP live set already in release, Columbia wasn't about to put out another one, and nobody has thought to release it domestically since. — *William Ruhlmann*

Chicago VIII / Mar. 1975 / Chicago ✦✦
Chicago keyboardist Robert Lamm had been the band's main songwriter to this point, and although he contributed four of the 10 songs here, only his "Harry Truman" was memorable. The album's biggest hit was James Pankow's "Old Days," but little else stands out. — *William Ruhlmann*

● **Greatest Hits** / Nov. 1975 / Chicago ✦✦✦✦
The biggest hits of Chicago's first five years of recording, including "Just You 'N' Me," "Feelin' Stronger Every Day," "Wishing You Were Here," "Call On Me," and "(I've Been) Searchin' So Long." — *William Ruhlmann*

Chicago X / Jun. 1976 / Chicago ✦✦
It was here that Chicago began to turn toward "power" ballads, but only because it was scoring only modest hits with such more eclectic material as Robert Lamm's "Another Rainy Day In New York City" and John Pankow's "You Are On My Mind," while Peter Cetera's "If You Leave Me Now" topped the charts, went gold, and won Grammy Awards for arrangement and vocal performance. — *William Ruhlmann*

Chicago XI / Sep. 1977 / Chicago ✦✦
On its last album to be produced by James William Guercio and to feature guitarist Terry Kath, Chicago turns in another competent but unremarkable effort. Peter Cetera's "Baby, What a Big Surprise" is his follow-up to "If You Leave Me Now," Robert Lamm continues to wax political on "Policeman" and "Vote For Me," and "Take Me Back To Chicago" accurately expresses an exhausted band's sentiments at this point. — *William Ruhlmann*

Chicago Transit Authority/Live in Concert / 1978 / Magnum ✦
Chicago sued to prevent the release of this album, which is taken from the same 1969 festival at which John Lennon recorded *Live Peace in Toronto*, but they lost. It sucks. Don't buy it. And watch out for other versions of it, too. — *William Ruhlmann*

Hot Streets / Sep. 1978 / Columbia ✦✦
Chicago had a new producer in Phil Ramone, a new guitarist in Donnie Dacus, a real album title, and their picture on the cover here, all of which seemed to spell a new beginning for the group. But despite two Top 15 hits with "Alive Again" and "No Tell Lover," this was Chicago's first album to miss the Top 10; it did not mark the rejuvenation Chicago and its fans hoped it would. The album remains the black sheep in Chicago's catalog. When CDs came in, the group declined to have it issued in the new medium, so it went out of print. When Chicago acquired the rights to its Columbia Records albums in 1995 and reissued them on its own Chicago Records imprint, it again skipped *Hot Streets*, though it did leave a catalog number (12) available, in case it changed its mind. — *William Ruhlmann*

Chicago 13 / Aug. 1979 / Chicago ✦
Disaster strikes. Chicago tries to go disco with "Street Player"; new guitarist Donnie Dacus gets his own single with "Must Have Been Crazy" (it flopped); there are no big ballads. In fact, there's nothing more worth mentioning. — *William Ruhlmann*

Chicago XIV / Jul. 1980 / Chicago ✦
Peter Cetera's "Song For You" has charm, and Robert Lamm's "Manipulation" has a certain punk edge. At another time, on another album, either might have worked, if they were redone properly. The rest is dross, and the best you can say is that at least Chicago had touched bottom. — *William Ruhlmann*

Chicago's Greatest Hits, Vol. 2 / 1981 / Chicago ✦✦✦
This album chronicles Chicago's gradual transformation in the second half of the '70s into a group that produced big ballads, usually sung by Peter Cetera. And here they are, starting with "If You Leave Me Now" and continuing with "Baby, What a Big Surprise" and the nostalgic "Old Days." — *William Ruhlmann*

If You Leave Me Now / 1982 / Columbia ✦✦
This is how the music business works: You drop an act that was once successful and has hit the skids. Then the act has a comeback with another company. What do you do? Release a compilation of previously released tracks that are still available on various other albums. At least a few people will mistake it for new product and take it home. — *William Ruhlmann*

Chicago 16 / Jun. 1982 / Full Moon ✦✦
With its back to the wall, Chicago switched record labels, dropped Donnie Dacus in favor of Bill Champlin (of the Sons of Champlin), brought in producer David Foster as new Svengali, and went back to power ballads. And it all worked, at least commercially. "Hard To Say I'm Sorry" was the summer ballad of 1982, the album went Top 10, and Chicago was back in business, albeit with far more limited musical goals than it had had at the beginning. — *William Ruhlmann*

Chicago 17 / May 1984 / Full Moon ✦✦
With sales of four million, this is the biggest-selling regular studio album Chicago has made. That's what happens when you really go for the ballads: "Stay the Night," "Hard Habit to Break," "You're The Inspiration," and "Along Comes A Woman" all fit into that category; all featured Peter Cetera, and all made the Top 40. Not surprisingly, Cetera decamped soon after. — *William Ruhlmann*

Chicago 18 / Sep. 1986 / Full Moon ✦✦
It is an article of faith in corporate lore that everyone is expendable, and Chicago Music, Inc. responded to the departure of Peter Cetera by hiring another blond, bass-playing tenor with sex appeal in the person of Jason Scheff. Some people were fooled, especially by the power ballad "Will You Still Love Me?," but others weren't (the album stopped at gold), and longtime fans were dismayed at the re-recording of "25 or 6 to 4." — *William Ruhlmann*

Chicago 19 / Jun. 1988 / Full Moon ✦
This album contained four Top 10 hits, "I Don't Wanna Live Without Your Love," "Look Away" (which hit #1), "You're Not Alone," and "What Kind Of Man Would I Be?," yet did not reach the Top 10 on the album list, definite proof that Chicago was reaching an easy-listening (or "Adult Contemporary") radio audience but missing the rock audience. It paid the bills, though. — *William Ruhlmann*

Greatest Hits: 1982-1989 / Nov. 1989 / Full Moon ✦✦✦
Chicago returned from a career dip in 1982 with "Hard to Say I'm Sorry" and continued to hit with power ballads, among them "Hard Habit to Break" and "You're the Inspiration," all sung by Peter Cetera. But the streak continued after Cetera departed in 1985, as Jason Scheff stepped in and Chicago went on to score hits like "Will You Still Love Me?," "I Don't Wanna Live without Your Love," and "Look Away," which are all heard here. — *William Ruhlmann*

○ **Group Portrait** / 1991 / Columbia ✦✦✦✦
If the two *Greatest Hits* collections don't look like adequate places to go, yet you want to have some Chicago in your collection, then *Group Portrait* is an extremely comprehensive boxed set that chronicles all the hits and important album tracks. You'll probably never find a more complete history on the band than that provided in the set's booklet. — *Rick Clark*

Twenty 1 / Jan. 1991 / Full Moon ✦✦
The '90s found Chicago's lineup minus drummer Danny Seraphine, but with guitarist DeWayne Bailey, who had been a sideman, a full-fledged member. It also found the group at its closest thing to a career crisis in a decade. This album sold poorly and spun off only one Top 40 hit, "Chasin' The Wind," despite containing some typical, if not outstanding, material in tunes like "You Come To My Senses" (which belatedly scaled the AC chart) and "Explain It To My Heart." Clearly, a new approach was in order. — *William Ruhlmann*

Night & Day: Big-Band / May 23, 1995 / Giant ✦✦✦
Generally, when contemporary performers have taken on retro projects like this one, they have tended to emphasize their fidelity to the sources—consider Linda Ronstadt hiring arranger/conductor Nelson Riddle to recreate his string backgrounds for albums like *What's New*. Chicago takes a different approach to the swing band classics it tackles here—it Chicago-izes them. The arrangements are by trombonist James Pankow, who manages to make everything from Duke Ellington's "Caravan" to Glenn Miller's theme "Moonlight Serenade" sound like a lost Chicago track. Those familiar with the originals, many of which were instrumental hits, may be surprised to hear the lyrics to songs like "Sing, Sing, Sing." Clearly, the group is aiming more at pleasing contemporary fans than evoking nostalgia, and it succeeds in re-inventing some well-established standards, even if older fans may find some of these versions radically altered. — *William Ruhlmann*

The Chiffons

Group, Girl-Group
One of the best early-'60s New York girl groups, combining sassiness and innocence on several of the style's greatest classics. The Chiffons had some singles under their belt when they reached number one with "He's So Fine," whose classic "doo-lang, doo-lang" riff was appropriated by George Harrison in 1970 for his own chart-topper, "My Sweet Lord" (Harrison was subsequently ordered to pay substantial damages to the original publishers, though he always claimed the resemblance was unintentional). Their follow-up, Goffin-King's "One Fine Day," was just as good, featuring killer piano riffs from King herself. Actually cut as a Little Eva track, the Chiffons' vocal was substituted, resulting in a Top Five hit. There were a couple other memorable hits, "I Have a Boyfriend" and the Motown-influenced "Sweet Talkin' Guy," and interesting misfires like the Martha & the Vandellas-inspired "The Real Thing," as well as some singles issued under an alter ego, the Four Pennies. The group recorded quite a bit of material during the '60s, much of it derivative; the hits are their best tracks by far. — *Richie Unterberger*

○ **Greatest Recordings** / 1990 / Ace ✦✦✦✦
A generous collection that not only features their greatest hits, but many forgotten songs that are surprisingly good. — *Stephen Thomas Erlewine*

○ **Golden Classics** / Collectables ✦✦✦✦

● **The Best of the Chiffons** / Laurie ✦✦✦✦
Everything you need by this delicious ensemble is here, including some undeservedly obscure gems. — *John Floyd*

Billy Childish

Group, Alternative Pop/Rock
Few performers in rock history have been as ferociously prolific as Billy Childish. In fact, a complete discography of his work as a solo performer and with his various bands would take up quite a few

pages in this book. A singer, songwriter, artist, poet, critic, fanzine editor, and guitarist who suffers from severe dyslexia, he's a punk-inspired Renaissance man. However, you may have never heard of him, or heard one of the over 50 recordings he's made either solo or with one of his many bands (Pop Rivets, the Milkshakes, Thee Mighty Caesars, the Delmonas, Thee Headcoats and the Natural Born Lovers), *or* read his over 40 books of poetry and assorted scribblings. Surprisingly, Childish has been recording since 1979, playing a rough-and-tumble, punk-inspired approximation of what is normally called garage rock. Not one for elaborate production techniques, the consistent element of Childish's music is that all of it sounds as though it was recorded and mixed in about an hour. He values immediacy and intensity and frequently seems itching to move on to the next song, or, more specifically, the next band. A truly primitive talent (due to his learning disability, he has had little formal education) who, a la Jad and David Fair of Half Japanese, eschews technical ability for pure emotion, Childish occupies an artistic role somewhere between mad genius and bratty goofball. Unfailingly sure of himself and his vision, his music is as honest and emotionally direct as one is likely to hear. Unfortunately, he also lacks the discipline of self-editing, and as a result, some of his lesser work rambles incoherently or simply sounds so similar as to be uninteresting. Fifteen years after his first single, "Fun in the U.K." (a tongue-in-cheek send-up of the Sex Pistols' "Anarchy in the U.K."), Childish is still producing material at an amazing rate, epitomizing the endurance and drive of an artist who in many ways is the archetypal rock outsider. —*John Dougan*

● **I Am the Billy Child** / 1991 / Sub Pop ✦✦✦✦
There is simply too much Billy Childish music available (good, bad and indifferent) to examine here in great detail. Fortunately, America's super-hip indie label Sub Pop released this superb Two-CD anthology that gets to the heart of Childish's aesthetic, offering an extremely strong selection of material that covers a nearly 14-year period. Subtitled *50 songs from 50 Records,* you will get a taste of nearly all of Childish's bands and hear "Fun in the U.K.," which he recorded with his short-lived Pop Rivets. Fans of idiosyncratic singer/songwriters like Kevin Coyne and Jonathan Richman may find themselves immediately enamored of Childish's defiantly different approach to rock & roll. If that's the case, the liner information in this set provides a solid discographical overview of Childish's work from the late '70s up to the early '90s. Buyer alert: this set was originally limited to 1,500 copies; it's a mystery as to how many are still for sale. —*John Dougan*

Toni Childs

b. Orange, CA
Singer-Songwriter
Born in Orange, CA, Toni Childs grew up in a variety of locations around the U.S. and lived in London for four years, where she had a song-publishing deal with Island Music. She then moved to Los Angeles, where she became involved with David Ricketts (of David + David) and collaborated on the soundtrack for the film *Echo Park* (1986). Her debut album, *Union,* was recorded in London, Paris, Los Angeles, and Africa, and reflected an interest in the music of Zimbabwe as well as more conventional singer/songwriter styles. It earned her an opening spot on a Bob Dylan tour and a Grammy nomination for Best Female Rock Vocal, as well as reaching the charts. Childs's follow-up, *House of Hope,* was released in 1991. Her third album, *The Woman's Boat,* appeared in 1994. —*William Ruhlmann*

● **Union** / Jun. 1988 / A&M ✦✦✦✦
Making her presence felt in the new wave of female singer/songwriters, Childs contrasts her vulnerable, dreamlike lyrics with a powerhouse booming alto voice. It includes the single "Don't Walk Away." —*Donna DiChario*

○ **House of Hope** / Jun. 1991 / A&M ✦✦✦✦
Even those who felt *Union's* power couldn't have been prepared for Child's second album, which dealt with clinging to hope in the face of death, abuse and indifference. Childs details these experiences not just in her words, but in a pain-ravaged voice that reaches into the darkest recesses of the soul. —*Brian Mansfield*

The Woman's Boat / May 24, 1994 / DGC ✦✦✦

Chill Rob G

Rap
Queens-native Chill Rob G (born Rob Frazier) is an excellent rapper whose version of "The Power" was unfortunately obliterated

by the hit rendition done by the duo Snap over the same music. Chill Rob G's original rap was done on a song called "Let the Words Flow." German producers Benito Benites and John Garrett, II, had taken it and added new musical trappings, renaming it "The Power." G's fine album *Ride the Rhythm* likewise didn't enjoy the commercial success it merited. —*Ron Wynn*

○ **Ride the Rhythm** / 1990 / Capitol ✦✦✦✦
Powerful raps with underrated percussion, production, and rhythm tracks. —*Ron Wynn*

Chilli Willi & the Red Hot Peppers

Group, Rock & Roll
Chilli Willi & the Red Hot Peppers were one of the main British pub rock groups of the early '70s, playing a laid-back yet rocking mixture of rock & roll, R&B, country and folk. The band has its origins in a folk-rock duo formed by ex-Junior's Blues Band members, Martin Stone (vocals, guitar, mandolin) and Phil "Snakefinger" Lithman (vocals, guitar, piano, lap steel, fiddle). Lithman moved to San Francisco in the late '60s, leaving Stone to play with Savoy Brown and Mighty Baby. The duo reunited in the early '70s, recording *Kings of Robot Rhythm* with vocalist Jo-Ann Kelly and various members of Brinsley Schwarz. *Kings* was released in 1972; that same year, the duo expanded to a band, adding Paul "Dice Man" Bailey (guitar, banjo, saxophone), Paul Riley (bass), and drummer Pete Thomas. During the next two years, Chilli Willi & the Red Hot Peppers became a popular live act in Britain. The full band released *Bongos Over Balham* in 1974, yet the record sold poorly and the band split in February 1975. Thomas became the drummer for Elvis Costello's backing band, the Attractions, Riley played with Graham Parker, Bailey formed Bontemps Roulez, and Stone played with the Pink Fairies before quitting the music business. Lithman moved back to San Francisco where he began to work with his former associates, the Residents, under the name Snakefinger. —*Stephen Thomas Erlewine*

● **Kings of the Robot Rhythm** / 1972 / Revelations ✦✦✦✦
Bongos over Balham / 1974 / Mooncrest ✦✦✦

The Chills

Group, Alternative Pop/Rock
The Chills were one of New Zealand's best and most popular bands of the '80s, making a small but consistent series of chiming, hook-laden guitar-pop. Both the songs and the arrangements were constructed, with interweaving guitar hooks and vocal harmonies creating a pretty, almost lush, sound that never falls into cloying sentimentality. Throughout their existence, the band's personnel changed frequently—there were more than ten different lineups—with the only constant member being guitarist Martin Phillips, the band's founder.

Phillips began playing music with the New Zealand punk band the Same in 1978. Following in the footsteps of the Clean and the Enemy, the Same played mostly covers, creating a raw fusion of British Invasion and garage rock. However, the group never recorded. Phillips applied the same approach for the Chills, the band he formed in 1980 with his sister Rachel and Jane Dodd (bass) after the Same fell apart.

In 1982, the Chills signed with Flying Nun, the influential New Zealand independent record label, and released several singles that never were widely distributed in America and Europe. During this time, the group went through an enormous amount of members: future Great Unwashed member Peter Gutteridge was a member, as was the Clean's David Kilgour, keyboardist Faser Batts, bassist Terry Moore, guitarist Martin Kean, keyboardist Peter Allison, drummer Martyn Bull, and drummer Alan Haig. While these incarnations of the Chills recorded plenty of singles, they never made an album. Released on the U.K. record label Creation, the group's first album, *Kaleidoscope World* (1986), was a collection of their early singles; it was later released in the U.S. on Homestead.

With the lineup of Phillips, bassist Justin Harwood, keyboardist Andrew Todd, and drummer Caroline Easther—the group's tenth lineup—the Chills recorded their first proper album, *Brave Worlds,* in 1987. Produced by Mayo Thompson, the leading figure of the cult band the Red Crayola and a former member of Pere Ubu, the band wasn't satisfied with the final result, claiming it was too loose and underproduced. The group, particularly Phillips, were more satisfied with their second full-length album, 1990's *Submarine Bells,* their first record released on an American major label.

Submarine Bells was recorded with yet another version of the band, with Jimmy Stephenson replacing Easther, who was suffering from tinnitus. The album was well-received by critics and college radio, yet it failed to break the band into the mainstream in either America or Britain. Two years later, they released *Soft Bomb*, which suffered the same fate as *Submarine Bells*. The following year, Martin Phillips broke up the Chills for the last time. *—Stephen Thomas Erlewine*

● **Kaleidoscope World** / 1986 / Homestead ✦✦✦✦

Brave Words / 1987 / Homestead ✦✦✦

○ **Submarine Bells** / 1990 / Slash ✦✦✦✦

Soft Bomb / 1992 / Slash ✦✦✦

New Zealand's The Chills turn in their hard-as-diamond pop style for something a little more whimsical and relaxed on *Soft Bomb*. The group is as efficient and generous as usual, however, delivering a filling 17 slices of jangly guitar confectionary. *—Roch Parisien*

Alex Chilton

b. Dec. 28, 1950, Memphis, TN
Rock & Roll, Alternative Pop/Rock
Over the course of the last 25 years, Alex Chilton's artistic career has run the gamut from singing on classic Top Ten hit records with the Memphis, TN, group the Box Tops ("The Letter," #1; "Cry Like a Baby," #2) to creating willfully chaotic solo outings with very limited commercial appeal. During the early '70s, Chilton helped form Big Star (with singer/songwriter Chris Bell). In spite of nonexistent sales, Big Star received much critical acclaim, influencing a generation of the post-punk/power-pop movement. Chilton's later solo efforts ranged from ramshackle garage rock to tight Memphis-style R&B.*—Rick Clark*

Like Flies on Sherbert / 1979 / Aura ✦✦

Bach's Bottom / 1981 / Razor & Tie ✦✦✦
Recorded during one of Chilton's more chaotic periods, *Bach's Bottom* is an interesting document of misguided talent. It's not so much the music as it is the sense of what is going on around the music that makes this 1975 outing fascinating. Chilton's dismemberment of "Free Again," "Take Me Home and Make Me Like It," the Beatles' "I'm So Tired," and "Jesus Christ" are pretty funny, while his great self-productions of "Bangkok" and the Seeds' "Can't Seem to Make You Mine" reveal his penchant for making something special happen at times when everything seems to be falling apart. *—AMG*

● **19 Years: A Collection** / 1991 / Rhino ✦✦✦✦
While it draws heavily on Big Star's disturbing third album (five tracks), *19 Years* offers a surprisingly coherent and listenable overview of Chilton's wildly inconsistent solo career, collecting some of the finest songs he has written since Big Star, as well as several exuberant covers ("Can't Seem to Make You Mine," "With a Girl like You," and "Volare"). *—AMG*

○ **Feudalist Tarts/No Sex** / 1994 / Razor & Tie ✦✦✦✦
By the mid-'80s, Chilton had located to New Orleans and recorded *Feudalist Tarts*, his first album in six years. Unlike its predecessor, *Like Flies on Sherbert*, *Feudalist Tarts* marked a return to a more ordered sound that reflected Chilton's love for R&B and blues. Among the highlights are versions of Slim Harpo's "Tee Ni Nee Ni Noo," Carla Thomas's "B-A-B-Y," and his own "Lost My Job." *Feudalist Tarts* was followed by the *No Sex* EP, which is included on this disc. "Underclass" and the title track are among Chilton's finer compositions—rich in rude rootsy sounds and sarcastic deadpan humor. *—Rick Clark*

High Priest/Black List / 1994 / Razor & Tie ✦✦✦
High Priest displays a more playful Chilton with versions of Dean Martin's "Volare," Bill Black's "Raunchy," and Charlie Rich's Sun classic "Lonely Weekends." His originals "Dalai Lama" and "Thing for You" are equally fine. *Black List*, which followed *High Priest*, opens with a great send-up of the hot rod anthem "Little GTO" and Walter Lewis's bluesy "I Will Turn Your Money Green" is the high point. Chilton plays all the instruments on both of those cuts. "Magnetic Field" and "Jailbait" are solid originals. *—Rick Clark*

Cliches / 1994 / Ardent ✦✦
With just an acoustic guitar and voice, Alex Chilton delivers a low-key not-too-perfectly-performed collection of standards, like "All of You," "Save Your Love for Me," "Let's Get Lost," and even Mel Torme's "The Christmas Song." It's Chilton's subtlest work yet, and one of his best albums. *—Rick Clark*

Man Called Destruction / 1995 / Ardent ✦✦
Since the mid-'80s, all Alex Chilton albums are basically interchangeable. Chilton and his bar band get together, knock off a handful of mediocre new songs and several (mostly obscure) R&B and rock & roll oldies. Now that Chilton is more or less sober, his pitch is a bit better, yet there isn't anything particularly special about *A Man Called Destruction*, other than the delightfully corny "What's Your Sign?" where Alex sings about the horoscope in an attempt to pick up some girl. It's the best thing here and he didn't write it. *—Stephen Thomas Erlewine*

The Chocolate Watch Band

Group, Psychedelic, Garage Rock
The Chocolate Watchband never charted a record nationally. Indeed, ask most casual 1960s rock fans about them, and you'll probably get little more than a blank stare. Most will probably remember their AVI Records labelmates the Standells more clearly, because they actually managed to chart a few singles. Alas, the Watchband had the disadvantage of being a punkier band than the Standells, and also being essentially two bands as a recording unit.

The group had its start in Los Altos, California in 1965, where guitarist Mark Loomis joined Ned Torney (guitar) in a fledgling band that later included Danny Phay (vocals), Rich Young (bass), Jo Kemling (organ), and Gary Andrijasevich (drums). This early incarnation of the Watchband found great, albeit short-lived, popularity on the local band scene, but never recorded. Phay, Torney, and Kemling were later inducted into a rival band, the Otherside, which was formed out of a band called the Topsiders, and Young was drafted into the U.S. Army. Loomis recruited Andrijasevich, Topsider guitarist, Sean Tolby, bassist Bill Flores, and vocalist David Aguilar; this unit, also named the Chocolate Watchband, made its debut in San Francisco and the surrounding area in the spring of 1966.

The quintet was a mod-outfitted garage punk unit par excellence, their sound founded on English-style R&B with a special fixation on the Rolling Stones at their most sneering. They eventually got a recording/management contract with Ed Cobb, a former member of the 1950s vocal ensemble the Four Preps. The group's first single was a cover of Davie Allan's "Blues Theme"; the single was a great showcase for the band, except for the fact that it was released under the alias of "The Hogs." Ironically, the band's first album, *No Way Out* featured much tampering by the producers. By the time the record came out in June of 1967, the group had already begun breaking up. A new incarnation of the Watchband was born in the guise of Flores and Tolby, with Tim Abbott on lead guitar, Mark Whittaker on drums, and Chris Finders on lead vocals. This line-up only lasted through the end of 1967, when Abbott and Flinders exited. Tolby moved over to lead guitar, and Aguilar returned for a few shows, but essentially the Watchband's existence as a viable performing unit were over.

The group's producers had other ideas, however. Another album, *The Inner Mystique*, was released in February of 1968, sporting the band's name but not too much else associated with the group. Cobb would have one more go at keeping the Watchband alive with *One Step Beyond*. By the time the record was made in the summer of 1968, all of the band had moved on to other projects, but Flores was persuaded to rejoin Tolby, Andrisevich, Loomis (later replaced by Phil Scoma), and Phay and have one more chance in the studio.

That would probably have been the end of the group's story, but in the early 1980s, a curious thing happened—record buyers and, more particularly, young musicians in America and Europe, discovered the Watchband. Their albums had always been collectors' items, but now the prices began escalating; a set of Australian reissues of the group's albums quickly found a market in America and Europe. More people heard the Chocolate Watchband's music and saw their movie appearances in the 1980s than did in the 1960s. Thus, it was no surprise then in 1994, Sundazed Records reissued the complete Watchband catalog on compact disc. *—Bruce Eder*

No Way Out / 1967 / Tower ✦✦✦
Possibly the best garage-punk album ever to make it out the door from a major label in the '60s, despite the presence of some non-Watchband tracks. "Are You Gonna Be There (At the Love-In)" is worth the price of admission, and "Let's Talk About Girls" makes an unforgettable opening track. Reissued on Sundazed for CD, and worth owning in that form, as an original on vinyl might set you back $100 or more. *—Bruce Eder*

The Inner Mystique / 1968 / Tower ✦✦✦
The group's second album, like its first, features too many tracks that really aren't the Watchband, but this time some of it even works. Side One of the original long-player consisted mostly of a bunch of psychedelic studio noodling courtesy of musicians hired by the producer, but even among these, "In the Past" is a bejeweled psychedelic treasure that ought to be in any collection. The rest is pure garage-punk, raw and undiluted, including savage covers of the Kinks' "I'm Not Like Everybody Else" and Bob Dylan's "It's All Over Now, Baby Blue," and "Medication," rendered here in a version superior in its lustful decadence to the original by their labelmates the Standells. Reissued in unbelievably good sound, with bonus tracks, on Sundazed Records in the '90s. —*Bruce Eder*

One Step Beyond / 1969 / Tower ✦✦✦
A last-gasp effort at milking some money out of the band's name is a fairly weak album, seldom above fair-to-mediocre musically, except for lead singer David Aguilar's "Don't Need Your Lovin'," rounded out by some killer bonus tracks ("Sitting There Standing," etc.) and the notes are a brilliant finish to the Watchband saga, tying up a pile of loose ends. —*Bruce Eder*

● **The Best of the Chocolate Watch Band** / 1983 / Rhino ✦✦✦✦
The first CD-era collection of this hard-luck band's work was also the best compilation of the band's work, but it was a good idea done a little too early. The sound is deficient compared with Rhino's usual standard, and the notes were later outdone by Sundazed Records' reissue of the band's complete catalog. It's still a good starter, however, if one can find it. —*Bruce Eder*

The Choir

Group, Power Pop/Anglo-Pop, Garage Rock
Stars in their Cleveland hometown, unknown elsewhere (except for the minor national hit "It's Cold Outside"), the Choir played an accomplished, if a bit anachronistic, British Invasion-influenced pop/rock in the late '60s. The Mersey-mod hybrid "It's Cold Outside" went to number one in Cleveland in 1967. The group was then picked up by Roulette, but a couple of subsequent singles were subject to inappropriate material and over-production, and stiffed. Obscure and unissued material by the Choir is beginning to appear on CD, and reveals them branching out from power-pop to encompass progressive sounds as they changed personnel in the late '60s. Members of the group later played in the Raspberries, and the Choir is still fondly remembered in Cleveland for their strong and melodic original material. —*Richie Unterberger*

● **Choir Practice** / 1994 / Sundazed ✦✦✦✦
This 18-song CD is the first official compilation of their work that covers their entire career, from 1966 to 1969. As the group cut only a few singles during their lifetime, most of this is previously unissued, culled from their generous vault of demos. Much anticipated by 1960s collectors, it's frankly a bit of a disappointment, despite a fair number of highlights. The Americanized mod-Merseybeat of "It's Cold Outside" is delightful; other originals like "I'd Rather You Leave Me" and "Don't Change Your Mind" show similarly irresistible harmony vocals, crafting a catchy '60s pop-rock sound that avoids sappiness. The final tracks, cut in 1969 after several personnel changes, have slightly updated progressive rock influences, though, are a bit weak, particularly the soul-rockish ones from 1968. Most crucially, though, it fails to include a number of fine previously available tracks, like the version of the beautiful ballad "Treeberry" that was briefly available on a Bomp EP (the sketchy acoustic demo here pales by comparison), and several moody numbers from the 1969 lineup (also available for a time on a cassette-only reissue in the 1980s). The crunchy Stonesish B-side of "It's Cold Outside," "I'm Going Home," is also inexplicably missing. Perhaps this is because the compilers made every effort to include material from the original master tapes and couldn't locate the masters for those tracks. It's still not a bad compilation for '60s collectors, but it could have been better. —*Richie Unterberger*

Chords

Group, Power Pop/Anglo-Pop
A highly derivative mod-revival band featuring Brett Ascott, Billy Hassett, Martin Mason, Chris Pope, and Mick Talbot (also of Merton Parkas and a future Style Council member). After a string of minor hit singles, including the brilliant "Maybe Tomorrow," and a

top 30 U.K. album, *So Far Away*, the band faded with the fad. —*Chris Woodstra*

● **So Far Away** / 1980 / Polydor ✦✦✦✦
The short-lived mod-revival produced many unmemorable albums—*So Far Away* falls into this category. While it certainly is a close approximation of the Jam's sound, the album failed to fulfill the promise of the classic single "Maybe Tomorrow," the album's only highlight. —*Chris Woodstra*

Neil Christian & the Crusaders

Group, British Invasion
There's no doubting Christian's contributions to the formative days of British rock. His groups included, at various times, Jimmy Page, Ritchie Blackmore, Nicky Hopkins, Albert Lee, and Mick Abrahams. As a singer and recording artist, though, he was distinctly lacking. He tried his hand at teen idol tunes, Merseybeatish numbers, British R&B, and bloated MOR pop, but could not overcome his fundamental lack of talent and material. Indeed, one wonders how his thin, nervous, and restrained delivery attracted such soon-to-be-virtuosos of '60s rock. His earliest numbers (some produced by the legendary Joe Meek) do have a slight British Beat period charm. File with that peculiar British Invasion subgenre of meagerly talented solo singers like P.J. Proby and Dave Berry, though Christian doesn't even measure up to their slight standards. —*Richie Unterberger*

● **1962-1973** / 1992 / See For Miles ✦✦✦✦
Virtually all of this 28-song anthology covers the years 1962-68, during which Christian ran through numerous lineups and achieved only one small British hit, the vaudevillian "That's Nice." Jimmy Page's guitar graces the 1963 single "Get A Load Of This," probably Christian's best stab at Merseybeat, and "I Like It" boasts some storming (uncredited) British R&B guitar. —*Richie Unterberger*

Lou Christie (Lugee Alfredo Giovanni Sacco)

b. Feb. 19, 1943, Glen Willard, PA
Pop/Rock
Lou Christie's shrieking, falsetto-soaked vocals led to prolonged pop stardom through the '60s. Born Lugee Sacco, Christie began recording in 1960 in Pittsburgh. "The Gypsy Cried," cut in 1962, was released on the local C&C logo and leased to Roulette, where it proved to be Christie's first sizable hit. After encoring for Roulette the next year with "Two Faces Have I," Christie moved to MGM and scored a million-seller in 1966 with the ambitious chart-topper "Lightnin' Strikes." The daring "Rhapsody in the Rain" was another major hit the same year. Christie returned to the Top Ten for the last time in 1969, with "I'm Gonna Make You Mine," on the bubblegum-oriented Buddah label. He remains a dynamic attraction on the oldies circuit. —*Bill Dahl*

● **Enlightnin'ment: The Best of Lou Christie** / 1991 / Rhino ✦✦✦✦
This solid collection contains "Lightnin' Strikes," "Two Faces Have I," and others. —*Dan Heilman*

Chubb Rock

Rap, Urban
Weighing in at 250 pounds, Chubb Rock (born Richard Simpson) often evokes images of a hip-hop Barry White (whom he dueted with on *And the Winner Is…*).Chubb Rock had a group while he was a teenager in New York but started his career in earnest after he dropped out of college. After three singles from his first album went nowhere, his second album *And the Winner Is…*was released to greater commercial and critical acclaim, thanks to a remixed single version of "Caught Up" that was released prior to the album. —*Stephen Thomas Erlewine*

Chubb Rock / 1988 / Champ ✦✦✦

Featuring Hitman Howie Tee / 1988 / Select ✦✦✦
Interesting, entertaining raps, witty quips, and good samples from disco and funk works. —*Ron Wynn*

● **And the Winner Is…** / 1989 / Select ✦✦✦✦
Sharp humor with first-rate samples and production, plus insightful commentary on ghetto violence and the ignorance of the National Academy of Recording Arts and Sciences. —*Ron Wynn*

The One / 1991 / Select ✦✦✦
Rock still raps hard, but uneven production and mixes sometime slow the momentum. —*Ron Wynn*

I Gotta Get Mine Yo / 1992 / Select ✦✦

The Church

Group, Alternative Pop/Rock, Psychedelic

At their best, the Church spins out highly textured guitar psychedelia so atmospheric that the melodies work on a subconscious level or they make a guitar-pop so melodic and hook-laden that it could be straight out of the Byrds and Beatles songbooks as interpreted by David Bowie. At their worst, they're ponderous and pretentious, with only their sonic textures to recommend them. Fortunately, for most of their nearly-fifteen year career, they have been at their best, making some of the finest psychedelic-tinged guitar pop of the '80s.

Although they were always fairly popular in their native Australia, it wasn't until 1988 that they had their first (and only) hit in America, the gorgeous "Under the Milky Way." Before they had that hit single, they had recorded several albums of rougher pop and psychedelia, indebted to the Beatles and Syd Barrett. 1988's *Starfish* was their most polished record, but it also marked the culmination of the band's pop savviness. Since that record, not only has the line-up dwindled to two members, but the music has become more concerned with texture and atmosphere, not hooks and melody. Nevertheless, they remain one of the leading guitar-driven psychedelic bands of their time. —*Stephen Thomas Erlewine*

○ **Of Skin and Heart** / 1981 / Arista ✦✦✦✦

The band's first album (now on CD with several extra tracks) is their most straight forward rock effort and one of their finest moments for this reason. "The Unguarded Moment" stands out as one of the great singles of the '80s. Issued in the U.S. in 1982 as *The Church* with a slightly modified track listing. —*Chris Woodstra*

The Blurred Crusade / 1982 / Arista ✦✦✦

The band defined their now trademark sound on their sophomore effort. Shimmering 12-stringed guitar work from Marty Willson-Piper more than hints at a Byrds influence. Steve Kilby adds to the lush backdrop with his dreamy, oblique lyric delivery. —*Chris Woodstra*

Seance / 1983 / Arista ✦✦✦

While it's often seen as one of their more excessive works, this neo-psychedelic masterpiece is actually the culmination of the band's (especially Kilbey's) mystical obsessions. While the songs are drawn out to nearly epic length, their pop sensibilty is not forgotten. —*Chris Woodstra*

○ **Remote Luxury** / 1984 / Arista ✦✦✦✦

A combination of two fine EPs, *Remote Luxury* continues to build on the sound of *Blurred Crusade*. This one takes on an even more meditative and melancholy mood. —*Chris Woodstra*

○ **Heyday** / 1986 / Arista ✦✦✦✦

The band returns to a harder, more straight-ahead rock album with *Heyday*. The more ambitious arrangements, adding horns for the first time, help to flesh out their now standard jangly retro-'60s sound. —*Chris Woodstra*

Conception / 1988 / Carrere ✦✦✦

● **Starfish** / 1988 / Arista ✦✦✦✦

Engaging alternative rock, appealing to a wider range of listeners than their previous output. This album crystallizes the intensely atmospheric layers of bassist Steve Kilbey's lead vocals with swirling guitar work from Peter Koppes and Marty Wilson-Piper, yielding a Top 40 U.S. hit with "Under the Milky Way." —*Donna DiChario*

Hindsight / 1988 / EMI ✦✦✦

This Australian-only double CD collects rare B-sides and EPs. Though this is obviously targeted for completists and collectors, it actually gives a good picture of the band's diversity. —*Chris Woodstra*

Gold Afternoon Fix / 1990 / Arista ✦✦✦

The dreamlike essence prevails again as a hypnotic backdrop for the band's cryptic lyrics. —*Donna DiChario*

Priest = Aura / 1992 / Arista ✦✦

The Australian quartet returns to their earlier sound with less structured alternative rock tracks. —*Donna DiChario*

Sometime Anywhere / May 24, 1994 / Arista ✦✦✦

Now essentially reduced to a duo, Steve Kilbey and Marty Wilson-Piper, produce a solid, though unexceptional album. Trapped by their own formula, *Sometime Anywhere* failed to make either a critical or commercial impact, leaving the band's fate up in the air. —*Chris Woodstra*

Cinderella

Group, Hard Rock, Heavy Metal

When Cinderella released their debut album, *Night Songs*, in 1986, they were packaged like a second-rate Bon Jovi imitation, which isn't surprising since Jon Bon Jovi was responsible for bringing the band to Mercury Records. Although the record isn't bad, it was standard lite-metal without much distinction, apart from lead guitarist/vocalist Tom Keifer's exaggerated Steven Tyler howl. With their second album, 1988's *Long Cold Winter,* they began to open up their sound slightly, bringing more blues and Rolling Stones influences to their hard rock. That approach reached its apex with their third album, 1990's *Heartbreak Station,* which swaggers defiantly, appropriating Stones and Aerosmith licks as if they had thought of the whole thing first. It didn't sell as well as *Long Cold Winter* did, which might be the reason why the band kept a low profile until late 1994. Either that or the drastically changed hard rock marketplace of the early '90s is what kept the band from releasing their fourth album until then. When *Still Climbing* did come out, the band was met with disinterest and resistance on MTV and radio. —*Stephen Thomas Erlewine*

Night Songs / 1986 / Mercury ✦✦✦

Jon Bon Jovi discovered this Pennsylvania band, whose album is filled with the kind of catchy pop-metal his own band plays. Produced by Andy Johns. —*Stephen Thomas Erlewine*

○ **Long Cold Winter** / 1988 / Mercury ✦✦✦✦

A commercial breakthrough for Cinderella, producing three Top 40 singles in "Don't Know What You Got (Till It's Gone)," "The Last Mile," and "Coming Home." Cinderella's sound has grown bluesier, more like Led Zeppelin than Bon Jovi, and the songs are better. —*Stephen Thomas Erlewine*

● **Heartbreak Station** / 1990 / Mercury ✦✦✦✦

After successful albums that effectively followed contemporary hard-rock trends, Cinderella reached back into the Stones and Aerosmith songbooks and created a sneering, raunchy hard-rock album that was artistically their finest moment, even if it didn't reach the same commercial heights as its predecessors. But the sales figures don't matter (it *only* sold a million copies); *Heartbreak Station* shows that Cinderella has more genuine rock & roll grit than most of the metal bands of the late '80s. —*Stephen Thomas Erlewine*

○ **Still Climbing** / 1994 / Mercury ✦✦✦✦

Cinderella returned from their self-imposed exile in late 1994 with *Still Climbing,* a gritty record that shows them building upon the bluesy hard rock of *Gypsy Road.* Arguably, it boasts a more consistent song selection and tougher sound than *Gypsy,* yet radio and MTV were resistant to the band's classical good-times-and-hard-rockin' attitude and the record disappeared soon after its release. —*Stephen Thomas Erlewine*

Circle Jerks

Group, Hardcore, Heavy Metal

The Circle Jerks were one of the first West Coast hardcore bands. Smartass ex-Black Flag vocalist Keith Morris was one of the genre's funnier mouthpieces, when his homophobia didn't get in the way. —*John Floyd*

○ **Group Sex** / 1980 / Frontier ✦✦✦✦

This fast and loud debut by the early California thrash combo offers the best intro to their pungent social commentary and bad jokes. —*John Floyd*

Wild in the Streets / 1982 / Frontier ✦✦✦

● **Golden Shower of Hits** / 1983 / Rhino ✦✦✦✦

Another batch of gleeful vulgarity, *Golden Shower of Hits* features the notorious "Jerks on 45," along with their trademark wise-assed punk. The band tempers their attack just slightly throughout, making it their most listenable album. —*Stephen Thomas Erlewine*

Wonderful / 1985 / Combat ✦
VI / 1987 / Combat ✦✦✦
Oddities, Abnormalities and Curiosities / 1995 / Mercury ✦✦✦

Eric Clapton (Eric Patrick Clapp)
....
b. Mar. 30, 1945, Ripley, England
Rock & Roll, Blues Rock, Pop/Rock

By the time Eric Clapton launched his solo career with the release of his self-titled debut album in August 1970, he was long established as one of the world's major rock stars due to his group affiliations—the Yardbirds, John Mayall's Bluesbreakers, Cream, and Blind Faith—affiliations that had demonstrated his claim to being the best rock guitarist of his generation. That it took Clapton so long to go out on his own, however, was evidence of a degree of reticence unusual for one of his stature. And his debut album, though it spawned the Top 40 hit "After Midnight," was typical of his self-effacing approach: It was, in effect, an album by the group he had lately been featured in, Delaney & Bonnie & Friends.

Not surprisingly, before his solo debut had even been released, Clapton had retreated from his solo stance, assembling from the D&B&F ranks the personnel for a group, Derek and the Dominos, with which he played for most of 1970. Clapton was largely inactive in 1971 and 1972, due to heroin addiction, but he performed a comeback concert at the Rainbow Theatre in London on January 13, 1973, resulting in the album *Eric Clapton's Rainbow Concert* (September 1973).

But Clapton did not launch a sustained solo career until July 1974, when he released *461 Ocean Boulevard*, which topped the charts and spawned the #1 single "I Shot the Sheriff."

The persona Clapton established over the next decade was less that of guitar hero than arena rock star with a weakness for ballads. The follow-ups to *461 Ocean Boulevard, There's One in Every Crowd* (April 1975), the live *E.C. Was Here* (August 1975), and *No Reason to Cry* (August 1976), were less successful. But *Slowhand* (November 1977), which featured both the powerful "Cocaine" (written by J.J. Cale, who had also written "After Midnight") and the hit singles "Lay Down Sally" and "Wonderful Tonight," was a million seller, and its follow-ups, *Backless* (November 1978), featuring the Top Ten hit "Promises," the live *Just One Night* (May 1980), and *Another Ticket* (April 1981), featuring the Top Ten hit "I Can't Stand It," were all big sellers.

Clapton's popularity waned somewhat in the first half of the '80s, as the albums *Money and Cigarettes* (February 1983), *Behind the Sun* (March 1985), and *August* (November 1986) indicated a certain career stasis. But he was buoyed up by the release of the boxed set retrospective *Crossroads* (April 1988), which seemed to remind his fans of how great he was. *Journeyman* (November 1989) was a return to form.

It would be his last new studio album for nearly five years, though in the interim he would suffer greatly and enjoy surprising triumph. On March 20, 1991, Clapton's four-year-old son was killed in a fall. While he mourned, he released a live album, *24 Nights* (October 1991), culled from his annual concert series at the Royal Albert Hall in London, and prepared a movie soundtrack, *Rush* (January 1992). The soundtrack featured a song written for his son, "Tears in Heaven," that became a massive hit single.

In March 1992, Clapton recorded a concert for *MTV Unplugged* that, when released on an album in August, became his biggest selling record ever. Two years later, Clapton returned with a blues album, *From the Cradle*. —*William Ruhlmann*

○ **Eric Clapton** / Jul. 1970 / Polydor ✦✦✦✦
The band of Delaney & Bonnie backed Clapton on his first solo outing. Naturally, the results are much closer to their style than to Cream. Although Clapton sings about "Blues Power," the heart of this album is in rock & roll. —*Stephen Thomas Erlewine*

Eric Clapton's Rainbow Concert / Sep. 1973 / Polydor ✦✦✦
By January 1973, Eric Clapton's career was going great guns as the result of compilations like *History of Eric Clapton;* the only problem was that Clapton himself was nursing a heroin addiction and hadn't been heard from since his August 1971 appearance at the concert for Bangladesh. The Who's Pete Townshend enticed Clapton out for another one-off concert appearance (in fact, there were two shows) at the Rainbow Theatre in London on January 13, 1973, and organized an all-star band to back him. It was an ensemble effort, as much a showcase for Steve Winwood—who sang lead vocals on "Presence of the Lord" and Traffic's "Pearly Queen"—as for the nominal star. But it demonstrated that the reclusive Clapton could still play, and that was welcome news. Today, the album is an adequate live document, though one can find better performances of the songs on other records. (At presstime, Polydor Records planned to reissue *Eric Clapton's Rainbow Concert* on July 25, 1995, in an expanded version running 74 minutes and containing eight additional tracks.) —*William Ruhlmann*

○ **461 Ocean Boulevard** / Jul. 1974 / Polydor ✦✦✦✦
Clapton returned from a break in recording to do the best solo album he ever made. *461 Ocean Boulevard* is laidback, but never boring, because Clapton sings and solos equally well. Clapton kept trying to remake this album, but he never recaptured its charming ambience. —*Stephen Thomas Erlewine*

There's One in Every Crowd / Mar. 1975 / Polydor ✦✦
Having stayed out of the recording studio for four years prior to making his comeback album, *461 Ocean Boulevard*, Eric Clapton returned to recording only a few months later to make its follow-up, *There's One in Every Crowd*. Perhaps he hadn't had time to write or gather sufficient material to make a similarly effective album, since the result is a scattershot mixture of styles, leading off with two gospel tunes, one a reggae version of "Swing Low, Sweet Chariot." Clapton and his second guitarist, George Terry, had written a sequel to "I Shot The Sheriff," "Don't Blame Me," which Clapton sang in his best impersonation of Bob Marley's voice. The album's best track, naturally, was the blues cover, Clapton's take on Elmore James's "The Sky Is Crying." But *There's One in Every Crowd* was a disappointing follow-up to *461 Ocean Boulevard*, and fans let Clapton know it: while the former album had topped the charts and gone gold, the latter didn't even make the Top Ten. —*William Ruhlmann*

E.C. Was Here / Aug. 1975 / Polydor ✦✦✦
Since Eric Clapton and his longtime fans have always thought of him primarily as a bluesman, it is curious that this live album, which is devoted to extended guitar solos on blues standards like "Have You Ever Loved a Woman," "Rambling On My Mind," and "Further On Up the Road," didn't become a massive hit. Maybe it was that the once reclusive Clapton was now spitting out new albums every six months, but *E.C. Was Here* did not achieve the renown it deserved upon release, and Clapton, who had been reluctant to put out a straight blues album to begin with, didn't try anything similar again for almost 20 years, instead making sure to keep his records within a pop framework that usually diluted their effectiveness. In its CD reissue, with "Drifting Blues" extended out to its full 11 1/2 minutes, the album is even more impressive. —*William Ruhlmann*

No Reason to Cry / Aug. 1976 / Polydor ✦✦✦
When he gave a speech inducting the Band into the Rock & Roll Hall of Fame, Eric Clapton said that after he heard their debut album, *Music From Big Pink*, he wanted to join the group, the fact that they already had a guitarist in Robbie Robertson notwithstanding. In the winter of 1975-1976, when he cut *No Reason to Cry* at the Band's Shangri-la Studio in Malibu, CA, he came as close as he ever would to realizing that desire. Clapton is a musical chameleon; though some of *No Reason to Cry* is identifiable as the kind of pop/rock Clapton had been making since the start of his solo career (the best of it being "Hello Old Friend," which became his first Top 40 single in two years), the most memorable music on the album occurs when he is collaborating with members of the Band and other guests. He duets with Band bassist Rick Danko on Danko's "All Our Past Times," and with Bob Dylan on Dylan's "Sign Language," as Robertson's distinctive lead guitar is heard rather than Clapton's. As a result, the album is a good purchase for fans of Bob Dylan and the Band, but not necessarily for those of Eric Clapton. (The CD reissue adds a bonus track, "Last Night," which is a traditional 12-bar blues song credited to Clapton.) —*William Ruhlmann*

○ **Slowhand** / Nov. 1977 / Polydor ✦✦✦✦
After a spell of tepid albums, Clapton made a comeback with a recording that strongly recalls *461 Ocean Boulevard*. Certain influences became more pronounced (a country feel on "Lay Down Sally" and the cover of J.J. Cale's "Cocaine"), the blues sound heartfelt, and the guitar sounds as if it had taken a shot of adrenaline. One of his best efforts. —*Stephen Thomas Erlewine*

Backless / Nov. 1978 / Polydor ✦✦✦
Having made his best album since *461 Ocean Boulevard* with *Slowhand*, Eric Clapton followed with *Backless*, which took the same authoritative, no-nonsense approach. If it wasn't quite the

masterpiece, or the sales monster, that *Slowhand* had been, this probably was because of that usual Clapton problem—material. Once again, he returned to those Oklahoma hills for another song from J.J. Cale, but "I'll Make Love to You Anytime" wasn't quite up to "Cocaine" or "After Midnight." Bob Dylan contributed two songs, but you could see why he hadn't saved them for his own album, and Clapton's own writing contributions were mediocre. Clapton did earn a Top Ten hit with Richard Feldman and Roger Linn's understated pop shuffle "Promises," but it was not one of his more memorable recordings. Of course, Clapton's blues playing on the lone obligatory blues cut, "Early in the Morning" (presented in its full eight-minute version on the CD reissue), was stellar. (*Backless* was his last album to feature the backup group that had been with him since 1974.) —*William Ruhlmann*

○ **Just One Night** / Apr. 1980 / Polydor ✦✦✦✦
For once, Clapton's backing band (including guitarist Albert Lee) pushes him into recording an interesting, listenable album. Worth the extra expense of a double set. —*Stephen Thomas Erlewine*

Another Ticket / Feb. 1981 / Polydor ✦✦✦
Now, here's a star-crossed album. Polydor rejected the first version of it, produced by Glyn Johns, and Eric Clapton was forced to cut it all over again with Tom Dowd. Then, a few dates into a U.S. promotional tour coinciding with its release, Clapton collapsed and was found to be near death from ulcers due to his alcoholism. Finally, it turned out to be the final record of his 15-year association with Polydor, which therefore had no reason to promote it. Nevertheless, the album made the Top 10, went gold, and spawned a Top 10 single in "I Can't Stand It." And the rest of it wasn't too shabby, either. The first and last Clapton studio album to feature his all-British band of the early '80s, it gave considerable prominence to second guitarist Albert Lee and especially to keyboard player/singer Gary Brooker (former leader of Procol Harum), and they gave it more of a blues-rock feel than the country-funk brewed up by the Tulsa shuffle crew Clapton had used throughout the 1970s. Best of all, Clapton had taken the time to write some songs—he's credited on six of the nine selections—and tunes such as the title track and "I Can't Stand It" held up well. This wasn't great Clapton, but it was good, and it deserved more recognition that conditions allowed it at the time. —*William Ruhlmann*

● **Time Pieces: Best of Eric Clapton** / May 1982 / Polydor ✦✦✦✦
A fine single-disc retrospective of some, but not all, of Clapton's best singles from the 1970s. —*Stephen Thomas Erlewine*

○ **Money and Cigarettes** / Feb. 1983 / Reprise ✦✦✦✦
Recorded with some old friends—including Ry Cooder, Duck Dunn, and Albert Lee—*Money and Cigarettes* is one of Clapton's finest albums. Instead of being an empty exercise in studio professionalism, the record is an appealing, low-key effort featuring some of the smoothest blues Clapton has ever played. —*Stephen Thomas Erlewine*

Time Pieces II/Live in the '70s / 1985 / Polydor ✦✦✦

Behind the Sun / Mar. 1985 / Reprise ✦✦✦
Clapton's career was in decline in the early '80s when he switched record labels from Polydor to Warner Bros. and his debut Warner album, *Money and Cigarettes*, became his first to fall below gold-record status in more than six years. As a result, Warner looked critically at his follow-up, the Phil Collins-produced *Behind the Sun*, in the fall of 1984 and rejected the first version submitted, insisting that he record several new songs written by Jerry Williams, backed by Los Angeles session players under the auspices of company producers Lenny Waronker and Ted Templeman. Warner then emphasized the new tracks, releasing two of them, "Forever Man" (which reached the Top 40) and "See What Love Can Do," as singles. The resulting album, not surprisingly, was somewhat schizophrenic, though the company may have been correct in thinking that the album as a whole was competent without being very exciting. The added tracks were not bad, but they were not the surefire hits they were supposed to be. As usual, there was some effective guitar soloing (notably on "Same Old Blues"), but despite the tinkering, *Behind the Sun* was not one of Clapton's better albums. (It went gold after nearly two years in release.) —*William Ruhlmann*

August / Nov. 1986 / Reprise ✦✦
Eric Clapton adopted a new, tougher, hard R&B approach on *August*, employing a stripped-down band featuring keyboard player Greg Phillinganes, bassist Nathan East, and drummer/producer Phil Collins, plus, on several tracks, a horn section and, on a couple of tracks, backup vocals by Tina Turner, and performing songs written by old Motown hand Lamont Dozier, among others. The excellent, but incongruous, leadoff track, however, was "It's in the Way That You Use It," which Clapton and Robbie Robertson had written for Robertson's score to the film *The Color of Money*. Elsewhere, Clapton sang and played fiercely on songs like "Tearing Us Apart," "Run," and "Miss You," all of which earned AOR radio play. That radio support may have helped the album to achieve gold status in less than six months, Clapton's best commercial showing since 1981's *Another Ticket*, despite the album's failure to generate a hit single. The title commemorates the birth in August 1986 of Clapton's son Conor. (The CD version of the album contains the bonus track "Grand Illusion.") —*William Ruhlmann*

☆ **Crossroads** / Apr. 1988 / Polydor ✦✦✦✦✦
A 4-CD box set that follows Clapton from his Yardbird days to peddling Michelob on slick TV commercials. Following every different musical path Clapton traveled in his career, the box is a musical autobiography, detailing both his strengths and weaknesses and revealing many insights. There are plenty of unreleased songs on *Crossroads*, including tracks from an aborted second Derek & the Dominos album. A truly remarkable set. —*Stephen Thomas Erlewine*

Homeboy / Sep. 1989 / Virgin ✦✦✦
Eric Clapton's score to the Mickey Rourke film *Homeboy* consists largely of bluesy instrumental pieces performed by Clapton, keyboard player Michael Kamen, bassist Nathan East, and drummer Steve Ferrone. Clapton's solo electric guitar version of "Dixie" owes much to Jimi Hendrix's version of "The Star-Spangled Banner." There are also a few blues numbers by Magic Sam and J.B.Hutto. The playing is accomplished, of course, but like most soundtracks this one seems to be missing something without the film images. —*William Ruhlmann*

○ **Journeyman** / Nov. 1989 / Reprise ✦✦✦✦
While the songs are not always first-rate, Clapton's playing was his best since the early '70s. This was his best album of the 1980s. —*Stephen Thomas Erlewine*

24 Nights / Oct. 8, 1991 / Reprise ✦✦
Eric Clapton, who had not released a live album since 1980, had several good reasons to release one in the early '90s. For one thing, his spare backup band of keyboardist Greg Phillinganes, bassist Nathan East, and drummer Steve Ferrone, was his best live unit ever, and its powerful live versions of Cream classics like "White Room" and "Sunshine Of Your Love" deserved to be documented. For another, since 1987, Clapton had been playing an annual series of concerts at the Royal Albert Hall in London, putting together various special shows—blues nights, orchestral nights, etc. *24 Nights*, a double album, was culled from two years of such shows, 1990 and 1991, and it demonstrated the breadth of Clapton's work, from his hot regular band to assemblages of bluesmen like Buddy Guy and Robert Cray to examples of his soundtrack work with an orchestra led by Michael Kamen. The result was an album that came across as a lavishly constructed retrospective and a testament to Clapton's musical stature. But it made little impact upon release (though it quickly went gold), perhaps because events overcame it—three months later, Clapton's elegy for his baby son, "Tears In Heaven," was all over the radio, and a few months after that he was redefining himself on *MTV Unplugged*—a live show as austere as *24 Nights* was grand. Still, it would be hard to find a more thorough demonstration of Clapton's abilities than the one presented here. —*William Ruhlmann*

○ **Unplugged** / Aug. 18, 1992 / Reprise ✦✦✦✦
Clapton's *Unplugged* was responsible for making acoustic-based music, and *Unplugged* albums in particular, a hot trend in the early '90s. Clapton's concert was not only one of the finest *Unplugged* episodes, but was also some of the finest music he had recorded in years. Instead of the slick productions that tainted his '80s albums, the music was straightforward and direct, alternating between his pop numbers and traditional blues songs. The result was some of the most genuine, heartfelt music the guitarist has ever committed to tape. And some of his most popular—the album sold over seven million copies in the U.S. and won several Grammies. —*Stephen Thomas Erlewine*

○ **From the Cradle** / Sep. 13, 1994 / Reprise ✦✦✦✦
For years, fans craved an all-blues album from Clapton; he waited until 1994 to deliver *From the Cradle*. The album manages to recreate the ambience of post-war electric blues, right down to the

bottomless thump of the rhythm section. If it wasn't for Clapton's labored vocals, everything would be perfect. As long as he plays his guitar, he can't fail—his solos are white-hot and evocative, original and captivating. When he sings, Clapton loses that sense of originality, choosing to mimic the vocals of the original recordings. At times, his overemotive singing is painful; he doesn't have the strength to pull off Howlin' Wolf's growl or the confidence to replicate Muddy Waters's assured phrasing. Yet, whenever he plays, it's easier to forget his vocal shortcomings. Even with its faults, *From the Cradle* is one of Clapton's finest moments. — *Stephen Thomas Erlewine*

○ **The Cream Of Clapton** / Mar. 7, 1995 / Polydor ✦✦✦✦
Eric Clapton was contracted to Polydor Records from 1966 to 1981, first as a member of Cream, then Blind Faith, and later as a solo artist and as the leader of Derek and the Dominos. This 19-track, 79-minute disc surveys his career, presenting an excellent selection from the period, including the Cream hits "Sunshine Of Your Love," "White Room," and "Crossroads"; "Presence Of The Lord," Clapton's finest moment with Blind Faith; "Bell Bottom Blues" and "Layla" from Derek and the Dominos; and 11 songs from Clapton's solo work, among them the hits "I Shot The Sheriff," "Promises," and "I Can't Stand It." The selection is thus broader and better than that found on 1982's *Time Pieces* collection, and with excellent sound and liner notes by Clapton biographer Ray Coleman, *The Cream Of Clapton* stands as the single-disc best-of to own for Clapton's greatest recordings. (Not to be confused with the popular 1987 Polydor [U.K.] compilation *The Cream Of Eric Clapton*, which has since been retitled *The Best Of Eric Clapton*.) — *William Ruhlmann*

BOOKS

✦✦✦✦ **Eric Clapton: Lost in the Blues**, by Harry Shapiro (Da Capo, 1992). There are a few Clapton bios available, and while this one does not have a great deal of first-hand interview material, it does a very good straightforward job of following his musical progression through the Yardbirds and John Mayall to Cream, Blind Faith, Derek & the Dominos, and his lengthy solo career. Every album, as a soloist or group member, is discussed in considerable detail. The author draws upon dozens of previous interviews and press clippings, spanning the mid-'60s to the early '90s, and sheds some light on the several rather mysterious lulls and metamorphoses in the mercurial guitarist's career, especially the decisions to leave all of his groups just when they were peaking or about to launch to stardom, and his years as a secluded heroin addict in the early '70s. Includes meticulous discography, "groupography," and a review of the various guitars Clapton's used over the years. -Richie Unterberger

Dave Clark Five

Group, British Invasion
For a very brief time in 1964, it seemed that the biggest challenger to the Beatles phenomenon was the Dave Clark Five. From the Tottenham area of London, the quintet had the fortune to knock "I Want to Hold Your Hand" off the top of the British charts with "Glad All Over," and were championed (for about 15 minutes) by the British press as the Beatles' most serious threat. They were the first British Invasion band to break in a big way in the States after the Beatles, though the Rolling Stones and others quickly supplanted the DC5 as the Fab Four's most serious rivals. The Dave Clark Five reached the Top 40 seventeen times between 1964 and 1967 with memorable hits like "Glad All Over," "Bits and Pieces," "Because," and a remake of Bobby Day's "Over and Over," as well as making more appearances on the *Ed Sullivan Show* than any other English act. The DC5 were distinguished from their British contemporaries by their larger-than-life production, Clark's loud stomping drum sound, and Mike Smith's leathery vocals. Though accused by detractors of lacking finesse and hipness, they had a solid ear for melodies and harmonies, and wrote much of their early material, the best of which has endured quite well, although their albums were fairly weak. Interestingly, and unusually for that era, bandleader Dave Clark managed and produced the band himself, negotiating a much higher royalty rate than artists of that period usually received. After a couple years of superstardom, the group proved unable to either keep up with the changing times or maintain a high standard of original compositions, and called it quits in 1970. — *Rick Clark & Richie Unterberger*

● **History of the Dave Clark Five** / 1993 / Hollywood ✦✦✦✦
For many years, the Dave Clark Five were one of the few major groups of the 1960s whose work was unavailable on compact disc. This two-disc, 50-track reissue not only rectifies that situation, but arguably includes more than all but devoted fans will want to hear. All of the band's mammoth mid-'60s hits —"Glad All Over," "Bits And Pieces," "Because," "Catch Us If You Can," "Any Way You Want It," and others—are included, and while they don't rival the work of British Invasion heavyweights like the Beatles, Stones, and Kinks, they still burst with exuberant melodies, harmonies, and dense production. This compilation also features worthy lesser-known hits like "Try Too Hard" and "Everybody Knows," as well as obscure but commendable beat ballads and raveups from their B-sides and albums. Nonetheless, there is a fair amount of filler, and their post-1966 work is undistinguished by either artistic growth or the hooks and heavy beat of their early material. But at their peak, the DC5 captured the *joie de vivre* of the British Invasion with a lasting power that cannot be dismissed. This reissue includes a comprehensive booklet featuring recollections from Dave Clark himself. —*Richie Unterberger*

Dave Clark Five/The Washington D.C.'s / 1993 / Repertoire ✦✦✦
A rather strange reissue, this compiles both sides of all three of the rare singles that the DC5 put out in the U.K. in 1961-1963 on the small Ember label before joining Columbia. Much less impressive than their British Invasion hits, they display the group as a run-of-the-mill band without an identity, casting about with weak pop, country, and instrumental material, although one of the songs ("I Knew It All The Time") was actually a small hit in America in early 1964. "Chaquita" was a cool instrumental ripoff of "Tequila" on the first DC5 album, but the early version here isn't nearly as good. On this CD, these tracks are combined with 17 songs by the unknown British band the Washington D.C.'s, who happened to share an album with the Dave Clark Five on an exploitative Ember reissue after "Glad All Over" became a hit. —*Richie Unterberger*

Dee Clark (Delecta Clark)

b. Nov. 7, 1938, Blytheville, AR, **d.** Dec. 7, 1990
Soul, R&B
Dee Clark was a solid R&B vocalist who had some huge hits in the late '50s and early '60s. The Arkansas-born singer moved to Chicago as a child and was in the Hambone Kids with Sammy Mc-Grier and Ronny Strong. They recorded for Okeh in 1952; the next year Clark sang with the Goldentones. This group later became the Kool Gents, then recorded as the Delegates for Vee-Jay in 1956. Clark went solo in 1957 and in 1958 enjoyed his first smash with "Nobody for You," an Abner release that reached number three R&B and just missed the Top 20 on the pop charts. He continued a string of R&B winners with "Just Keep It Up," "Hey Little Girl," and "How About That" for Abner in 1959 and 1960. Clark teamed with guitarist Phil Upchurch to write "Raindrops" in 1961, his signature tune. The song peaked at number three R&B and number two pop, and was his last major hit. Clark continued performing through the '60s, '70s, and '80s, but never again was a factor, though "Raindrops" remains a staple on oldies radio. —*Ron Wynn*

● **Rain Drops [Vee-Jay]** / 1994 / Vee-Jay ✦✦✦✦
Dee Clark was one of the most adaptable R&B vocalists of the '50s and early '60s, as this 25-song reissue shows. He did songs in a Little Richard mode, an Afro-Latin setting, and also performed ballads, novelty tunes ("Kangaroo Hop"), and covers ("Cupid"). Clark's gem was "Raindrops," a song with enough drama, hooks, and appeal to nearly top both the pop and R&B charts. It was his biggest hit, but not his only fine number. There are many cuts, such as "Nobody But You," "What Kind of Fool," and the newly issued "Bring Back My Heart," that equal or even top the tune that made him famous. —*Ron Wynn*

Gene Clark

b. Nov. 17, 1941, Tipton, MO, **d.** May 24, 1991
Country-Rock, Folk-Rock
As a founding member of the Byrds, Clark was inducted into the Rock & Roll Hall of Fame in 1991, a few months before his death. Born in Tipton, MO, into a musical family, Clark was surrounded by bluegrass and country but joined the clean-cut folk boomers, the New Christy Minstrels at 18. After hearing the Beatles, Clark quit the Minstrels and went to Los Angeles, where a fortuitous meeting with Roger McGuinn led to the forming of the Byrds.

Clark wrote some of the best early Byrds songs, one of which, "Feel a Whole Lot Better," Tom Petty recorded in 1990. Clark was the first Byrd to fly in 1966, and his subsequent solo career flickered with moments of brilliance—he was one of the seminal figures of folk-rock and country-rock. —*Mark A. Humphrey*

● **Echoes** / 1967 / Columbia ✦✦✦✦
Basically this is a CD reissue of his 1967 debut album, *Gene Clark & The Gosdin Brothers*. The Byrds comparison is really unavoidable: it's both Clark's best solo work, and not coincidentally, the one which resembles the Byrds most strongly. Indeed, this could easily pass for a somewhat less-than-average vintage Byrds album, with actual Byrds Chris Hillman and Michael Clarke forming the rhythm section, and Vern and Rex Gosdin on guitar (hence the LP title). To be brutal, it doesn't measure up to Clark's best songs from his Byrds days, but it's fairly strong, melodic '60s folk-rock nonetheless, perhaps with a bit of a more countrified, laidback, generic feel. "So You Say You Lost Your Baby," "Echoes," and especially "Tried So Hard" are standouts. The CD adds three interesting previously unreleased outtakes from the era, as well as six of the best early Byrds songs graced by Clark's songwriting and vocals. —*Richie Unterberger*

Fantastic Expedition / 1969 / A&M ✦✦✦

White Light / 1972 / A&M ✦✦✦
With good Dylanesque songs and nice subtle production by Jesse Ed Davis, this album is low-key and lyrical. —*Kenneth M. Cassidy*

○ **Roadmaster** / 1972 / Edsel ✦✦✦✦
It includes two songs from the early-'70s original Byrds that are much better than anything on the ill-fated Byrds reunion album of 1973. It's a must for fans of Clark-era Byrds. (British Import) —*Kenneth M. Cassidy*

No Other / 1974 / Line ✦✦✦
It's a slightly overproduced but interesting album. (German Import) —*Kenneth M. Cassidy*

Two Sides to Every Story / 1977 / RSO ✦✦

Firebyrd / 1984 / Takoma ✦✦

So Rebellious a Lover / 1987 / Razor & Tie ✦✦✦
This reissue features three extra cuts, but that's not what is best about it. The combination of Carla Olson and Clark's voices is great. They come together on "The Drifter," "Deportee," and "Don't It Make You Want to Go Home." The CD has a real country-folk sound. Let's hope for more gems from the archives. —*Chip Renner*

Gene Clark with the Gosdin Brothers / 1991 / Columbia ✦✦✦
Clark's solo debut was recorded with the Gosdin Brothers. —*Kenneth M. Cassidy*

Silhouetted in Light / 1992 / Edsel ✦✦✦
A very good 15-track live CD featuring Gene Clark and Carla Olson at their best. The sound is good and the song selection impressive. Pick up this import—highly recommended. —*Chip Renner*

Petula Clark

b. Nov. 15, 1932, Epsom, Surrey, England
Pop
By the time Petula Clark made her debut on American pop charts in 1964, she had already developed quite a career as an actress and singer throughout Europe, appearing in over 20 films and selling several million records. "Downtown" is the song that broke her stateside and placed her firmly in the #1 spot, displacing the Beatles' "I Feel Fine." Not only was she the first female artist from England to land that chart position, but her second record, "I Know a Place," went to #3. Only Cyndi Lauper has equaled that impressive an entry on her first two singles. Despite the competition, "Downtown" won the Grammy for Best Rock & Roll Recording in 1965. Over the next three years, Clark scored fifteen Top 40 pop hits.
Even though Clark's English origins helped her ride in on the first wave of the British Invasion, her music was definitely geared more toward the adult market. —*Rick Clark*

● **Greatest Hits of Petula Clark** / 1986 / GNP ✦✦✦✦
This import collection is much crisper and more vibrant-sounding than the domestic releases. All the major U.S. hits are here, plus some British and European chart successes never heard in the U.S.. —*Bruce Eder*

The Clash

Group, Punk, Pop/Rock
The Clash, 1976-1986, was the most accomplished band to come out of the British punk rock scene of the '70s. The group was formed by guitarist and singer Joe Strummer (b. Jan 25, 1955), guitarist and singer Mick Jones (b. Jun 26, 1955), bassist Paul Simonon (b. Dec 15, 1955), and drummer Terry Chimes—replaced in 1977 by Topper Headon (b. May 30, 1955). They first gained national recognition opening for the Sex Pistols, the other major punk band. But unlike the Pistols, the Clash had a straightforward earnestness to go with their punk anger. Their music was similarly simple, loud, and abrasive.
In December 1979, the Clash released *London Calling,* a critically acclaimed double album that found them expanding their musical style from punk to a more eclectic approach. The album spawned a single in the title song, which became their biggest U.K. single during their existence, getting to #11, while the album hit #9 in the U.K. and was their first real U.S. success at #27. "Train in Vain (Stand by Me)" from the album was the Clash's first U.S. chart single, reaching #23.
Sandinista!, a triple-LP set released in December 1980 took their eclecticism to new lengths. The album got to a disappointing #19 in the U.K. but was a surprisingly strong #24 in the U.S. The Clash again grazed the Top 40 in the U.K. with the album's "The Magnificent Seven" in May 1981.
Their next, *Combat Rock* (1982), was a straightforward rock collection that was their last album with the original personnel and their most popular. It hit #2 in the U.K. and #7 in the U.S. (where it sold a million copies), and its singles "Should I Stay or Should I Go?" and "Rock the Casbah" were hits on both sides of the Atlantic. Meanwhile, Headon left the band in July 1982, and Jones was fired by Strummer and Simonon in September 1983. He formed Big Audio Dynamite. Strummer and Simonon reorganized and added new members, releasing *Cut the Crap* in the fall of 1985, but by the start of 1986, the Clash was no more. —*William Ruhlmann*

☆ **The Clash** / 1977 / Epic ✦✦✦✦✦
The revised U.S. version of the Clash's first album, containing most of the vital punk anthems of that record, plus such later tunes as "White Man in Hammersmith Palais" and "I Fought the Law." This and the sole Sex Pistols album, *Never Mind the Bollocks, Here's the Sex Pistols,* tell the story of English '70s punk rock. —*William Ruhlmann*

○ **Give 'em Enough Rope** / 1978 / Epic ✦✦✦✦
In retrospect, Sandy Pearlman's production brings a welcome coherence to the Clash's sound, though they sound as aggressive as ever on such songs as "Safe European Home," "English Civil War," and "Tommy Gun." The most moving song is Mick Jones's "Stay Free," however, which may say more about the punk aesthetic than any of Joe Strummer's angry rants. —*William Ruhlmann*

★ **London Calling** / 1979 / Epic ✦✦✦✦✦
"What are we gonna do now?" asks Joe Strummer at the start of "Clampdown," one of this album's songs. But by the time you get to that track, it's already clear that the Clash have solved that problem by taking a giant step toward making craftsmanlike rock without sacrificing the urgency that made them punk leaders. From the title track through the reggae, rock, and pop tracks that follow, this is one of the premier albums of its time. —*William Ruhlmann*

Black Market Clash / 1980 / Epic ✦✦✦

Sandinista! / 1980 / Epic ✦✦
Believe it or not, amidst this messy triple-record (2-CD) set, there are some brilliant songs—the trouble is finding them among the dub experiments, half-finished songs, and overlong jams; listening to all this filler, it's hard to believe that the Clash made a double album the year before with absolutely no weak tracks. Patient listeners will be rewarded by "The Magnificent Seven," "Charlie Don't Surf," and "Police On My Back," and a couple of other tracks that are among the band's best work; however, most will be happy to hear the highlights on Clash compilations. —*Stephen Thomas Erlewine*

Combat Rock / 1982 / Epic ✦✦✦
The Clash are still a little too individual to be as straight-ahead a rock group as much of this album implies they are, but you can't fault a collection that contains the rock energy of "Should I Stay or

Should I Go?" and the absurdist danceability of "Rock the Casbah."
— *William Ruhlmann*

Cut the Crap / 1985 / Epic ✦✦

○ **Story of the Clash, Vol. 1** / 1988 / Epic ✦✦✦✦
A 2-disc, 28-track compilation that ranges over the Clash catalog
somewhat haphazardly. Still, this is some of their essential music.
— *William Ruhlmann*

○ **Clash on Broadway** / 1991 / Epic ✦✦✦✦
A 3-disc, 63-track compilation that treats the catalog coherently
and chronologically, with all the major songs included. It's a pricey
boxed set, but if you want one album that covers the Clash's career, this is it. — *William Ruhlmann*

○ **Super Black Market Clash** / 1994 / Epic ✦✦✦✦
An expanded version of the *Black Market Clash* EP, *Super Black
Market Clash* adds assorted singles and remixes to the original
recording. A couple of tracks aren't that interesting, but the major-
ity of the disc is splendid, featuring some of the band's best, but
unfortunately overlooked tracks, including "Armagideon Time,"
"The Prisoner," "Gates of the West," and "Capital Radio One." —
Stephen Thomas Erlewine

Classics IV

Group, Pop/Rock
This Atlanta-based group had a brief (but impressive) run on the
Billboard charts during the late '60s with their easygoing soft-pop
style. Million-sellers like "Spooky" (#3), "Traces" (#2), and
"Stormy" (#5), along with "Everyday with You Girl" (#19), have
continued to rotate endlessly on adult- and contemporary-radio
formats and oldies stations. Guitarist J. R. Cobb and producer
Bobby Buie co-wrote most of the band's material. They later
formed the Atlanta Rhythm Section, which also landed a hit with
a redone version of "Spooky" (#17) in 1979. — *Rick Clark*

● **The Very Best of the Classics IV** / 1988 / EMI America ✦✦✦✦
Here's everything you need to know about these MOR performers,
who wrote the book on the mellower side of rock before adult-
contemporary became a true category. The various members either played with Roy Orbison or went on to form the Atlanta
Rhythm Section. — *Larry Lapka*

Judy Clay

Soul
A talented journeywoman soul singer, Judy Clay (born Judy Lee)
joined the Drinkard Singers gospel group (which also included
Cissy Houston) in the late '50s. Like many singers who started
with gospel, she moved to soul in the '60s, releasing a string of
non-hit singles for the Ember and Scepter labels which are esteemed by British "Northern Soul" fans today; she also sang
backup vocals for soul singers like Wilson Pickett and Solomon
Burke. In the late '60s, she briefly teamed with Billy Vera to form
what may have been the first interracial recording duo (see separate entry), recording an album and a couple minor hit singles,
"Storybook Children" and "Country Girl-City Man (Just Across
The Line)." Her other recordings with Stax and Atlantic in the late
'60s (which include a '69 session at Muscle Shoals Sound) produced a hit R&B duet with William Bell, "Private Number," and a
minor hit solo single, "Greatest Love." She continued to work as a
backup vocalist in the '70s, with Aretha Franklin and Ray Charles
among others. Struck with a brain tumor in 1979, she returned to
gospel music shortly after her recovery. — *Richie Unterberger*

● **Featuring Storybook Children & Greatest Love** / 1995 /
Ichiban/Soul Classics ✦✦✦✦
11 of these 19 tracks are actually taken from her duet recordings
with Billy Vera, including "Storybook Children" and "Country
Girl-City Man (Just Across The Line)," most of the 1968 *Storybook
Children* LP, and the 1969 non-LP single "Reaching For The
Moon"/"Tell It Like It Is." The CD also has eight songs that Clay
recorded on her own for Atlantic and Stax in the late '60s (most at
the Muscle Shoals Sound Studio) which are generally more impressive than her duets with Vera, sporting a much earthier soul
sound. Six of those solo tracks are from singles never available on
album; two were previously unreleased. — *Richie Unterberger*

Otis Clay

b. Feb. 11, 1942, Waxhaw, MS
Soul, R&B
Otis Clay made most of his best-known records in Memphis dur-

ing the early 70s, but he's still universally hailed as Chicago's deep-
soul king. In a city filled to overflowing with legendary blues
artists, Clay has become the proud standard-bearer for Chicago's
enduring soul tradition.

Like so many of his contemporaries, Clay's intense vocal style
reflects a gospel background. He made the secular jump in 1965,
signing with Chicago's One-derful Records and issuing a series of
gospel-tinged soul records that were a lot grittier than the customary Windy City soul sound. Clay inaugurated Atlantic's Cotillion
subsidiary in 1968 with a supercharged cover of the Sir Douglas
Quintet's "She's About a Mover," produced by Rick Hall in Muscle
Shoals shortly before the singer joined forces with Hi Records
boss Willie Mitchell. With the relentlessly driving Hi Rhythm Section in tow, Clay waxed his biggest seller in 1972, "Trying to Live
My Life without You," later covered very successfully by Bob
Seger.

Although Clay's tenure on Hi may have been his most commercially potent, he's steadily recorded and gigged ever since. He is a
genuine hero in Japan, where he's recorded two sizzling live albums filled with the churning grooves, punchy horns, and searing
vocals that inevitably characterize the best deep soul—no matter
where it's recorded. — *Bill Dahl*

Trying to Live My Life without You / 1972 / Hi ✦✦✦
This UK import of Hi tracks, includes the title track, the original
version of the Bob Seger hit. — *Richard Pack*

Got to Find a Way / 1979 / P-Vine ✦✦✦
A Japanese import, it features nineteen early Chicago tracks from
1965-1967. — *Richard Pack*

○ **Soul Man Live in Japan** / 1984 / Bullseye Blues ✦✦✦✦
The greatest live soul performer, backed by the Hi rhythm section.
— *Richard Pack*

The Gospel Truth / 1994 / Blind Pig ✦✦✦
Otis Clay demonstrates how secular roots music can walk hand in
hand with fervent gospel on *The Gospel Truth*. While the sentiment and lyrics are purely devotional, Clay doesn't cast off his
blues and soul background, which steeps this material in gritty, instrumental truth. — *Roch Parisien*

● **That's How It Is** / Hi ✦✦✦✦
Twenty-one of the finest tracks Clay recorded for Hi during the
1970s are collected on this outstanding compilation. — *Stephen
Thomas Erlewine*

The Clean

Group, Alternative Pop/Rock
The Clean were one of the most influential New Zealand bands of
the post-punk era. The band formed in the town of Dunedin in
1978, when Hamish Kilgour (drums) and his brother David (guitar) recruited David's school friend, guitarist Peter Gutteridge.
Soon afterward, they opened for New Zealand punk rockers, Enemy.

The Clean were one of the first bands in the country to play
original material. They carved out a distinctive, noisy but melodic
sound, distinguished by David's screeching, distorted guitar. When
the Kilgour brothers decided in 1979 to relocate the band to Auckland (the country's largest city), Gutteridge had already left the
lineup. The Clean played with a rotating bassist before David quit
the band and moved back to Dunedin. Once he was back home, he
was introduced to bassist Robert Scott and the two started playing
together; news of his brother's new musical relationship prompted
Hamish to move back to Dunedin and begin the Clean again.

In early 1980, the group began playing around town in earnest,
playing locations that normally didn't book live music because
most clubs didn't like to feature bands that played original music.
In early 1981, a fan called Roger Shepherd began Flying Nun
Records to release a single by the Clean, "Tally Ho!". With its
jagged guitar, sweet melody and persistent organ, "Tally Ho!"
reached number 19 on the charts.

As they prepared to record their first album, they discovered the
small amount of New Zealand engineers didn't care for the band's
material, mainly because it was uncommercial. The Clean didn't
fight—they backed down, deciding to record on a four-track under
the guidance of Chris Knox and Doug Hood. In November, the
Boodle Boodle Boodle EP was released; it surprised every observer by climbing to number four on the New Zealand charts.

Boodle and the 1982 EP *Great Sounds Great* captured the
quirky sides of the Clean's sound, since they did not have the technology to replicate the band's huge, roaring live sound. Later in

1980, the group released their loudest single yet, "Getting Older." Soon after its release, David Kilgour exited the band, moving back to Dunedin. Robert Scott left after David's departure, forming a band of his own, the Bats. Hamish Kilgour moved to Christchurch—where Flying Nun Records was located—and bought his own four-track. After Hamish had begun writing and recording, David came up to Christchurch to help finish up the solo tracks, as well as to record some Clean songs that were never captured on tape. The resulting music, released under the name the Great Unwashed, was collected on the album *Clean out of Our Minds*. The music was a departure from the Clean's punk-injected sound; instead, it was folkier and more acoustic.

To promote the record, the Kilgours reunited with Peter Gutteridge while still using the name the Great Unwashed. On the ensuing tour, the band concentrated on Gutteridge's backlog of material; at the beginning of 1984, they recorded an EP called *Singles*. *Singles* earned quite a bit of airplay and sales, including a showing of their video on national television. Bassist Ross Humphries was added so David Kilgour and Gutteridge could both play guitar, yet the Great Unwashed broke up within a year. Hamish Kilgour formed Bailter Space with guitarist Alister Parker, Gutteridge began developing a new band called Snapper, and David stopped playing for a few years.

The Clean—the lineup featuring Robert Scott—reunited in 1988 for two concerts in London; a five-song EP culled from the shows a year later. The members of the band were encouraged by the results and decided to embark on a world tour. During the tour, the band wrote over a dozen songs. After the tour ended, the band record a new album, which was more straightforward and pop-oriented than their previous material. The record, *Vehicle*, was released in the spring of 1990 and the band supported its release with a world tour. After the tour's completion, the band split again. David Kilgour formed Stephen, Scott returned to the Bats, and Hamish Kilgour was inactive; the group reunited in 1994 to record a new album. —*Stephen Thomas Erlewine*

● **Compilation** / 1986 / Homestead ✦✦✦✦
This is a near complete collection of material pre-dating the mid-'80s split. —*Steve Aldrich*

Vehicle / 1990 / Rough Trade ✦✦✦
The reunion effort is this group's only proper full-length LP. —*Steve Aldrich*

Oddities / Flying Nun ✦✦

Clear Light

Group, Psychedelic
One of the better-remembered psychedelic one-shots of the '60s, Clear Light recorded one album on Elektra before splitting up. Their California psychedelia was very much in the mold of fellow Elektra artists Love, Tim Buckley, and especially the Doors, which is hardly a coincidence; like all of those artists, Clear Light worked with producer Paul Rothchild and engineer Bruce Botnick. Several of the members went on to notable careers: Douglas Lubahn played bass on several Doors albums, Dallas Taylor drummed for Crosby, Stills, & Nash, keyboardist Ralph Schuckett became a prolific session musician, and Cliff De Young became a prolific TV movie actor. —*Richie Unterberger*

Clear Light / 1967 / Elektra

● **Black Roses** / 1987 / Edsel ✦✦✦✦
All of the hallmarks of 1967 California psychedelia are here: fuzz guitars, airy melodies and harmonies, baroque arrangements. The two-drummer lineup was also novel, although you wouldn't especially notice it when listening to the album. This is a pleasant period piece, but the group doesn't have much of an identity, especially in comparison with the other Elektra Southern Californian acts to which they bore some similarity. They do manage to wreak serious havoc on their psychedelic freakout rearrangement of Tom Paxton's "Mr. Blue." The British reissue adds the non-LP B-side "She's Ready To Be Free." —*Richie Unterberger*

The Cleftones

Group, Doo-Wop
Formed in Queens, NY, in 1955, the Cleftones consisted of five friends from Jamaica High School—Herb Cox (lead), Warren Corbin (bass), Charlie James (first tenor), William McClain (baritone), and Berman Patterson (second tenor). Originally signed to Gee, the group released its first single, "You Baby You," late in 1955; an up-tempo doo-wop song, the record became a regional hit. "Little Girl of Mine," the Cleftones' second single, broke na-

tionally, charting at number eight R&B and number 57 pop in 1956; two other similar singles, "Can't We Be Sweethearts" and "String Around My Heart," were released the same year, yet they failed to attract national attention. "See You Next Year," a ballad the group recorded in 1957, did not earn the group an audience outside of New York. Two years later, McClain left the group and was replaced by Gene Pearson from the Rivileers. Patricia Spann was also added to the Cleftones' lineup that year, which helped nudge the band away from traditional group-oriented doo-wop harmonies and toward a vocal sound that was dominated by the lead vocals. In 1961, the Cleftones realized the potential of the sound with their smash hit version of the standard "Heart and Soul"; it became the group's biggest hit, reaching number 18 on both pop and R&B charts. Later that year, the group had another hit with "For Sentimental Reasons," but the band had reached a peak with "Heart and Soul" and were never able to reach those heights again. The Cleftones broke up in 1964, three years after their greatest success. —*Stephen Thomas Erlewine*

● **The Best of the Cleftones** / 1991 / Rhino ✦✦✦✦
The careening "Heart and Soul" was their only hit (1961), but doo-wop nuts will love this entire set. —*John Floyd*

George Clinton

b. Jul. 22, 1940, Kannapolis, NC
Soul, Funk
George Clinton scored a few solo hits on Capitol in the early '80s, but as the president of Parliament, P. Funk, Funkadelic, and other outfits, Clinton set a new agenda for Black music during the '70s. He combined theater, sci-fi, and funk glossolalia into something that was uniquely his own. On record he loses some of his impact, but it's still the ultimate boom-box music. That Motown passed on him says much for the stripe of Clinton's music. —*Colin Escott*

● **Computer Games** / Nov. 5, 1982 / Capitol ✦✦✦✦
Former Parliament and Funkadelic leader George Clinton made a major comeback under his own name with this album, whose irresistible grooves, vocal choruses, and absurd humor were essentially identical to the music of Funkadelic's salad days. Were you wondering where that "woof-woof" cheer heard on Arsenio Hall and at Black concerts came from? Check out "Atomic Dog." —*William Ruhlmann*

You Shouldn't-Nuf Bit Fish / Dec. 1983 / Capitol ✦✦✦
While it kept the funk percolating, George Clinton's follow-up to his post-Parliament-Funkadelic solo debut *Computer Games* didn't boast any tracks as compelling (or as nutty) as "Atomic Dog," though "Nubian Nut" and "Last Dance," which made the R&B Top 40, were fun. Most of the second side was funk without form, a common failing of Clinton's approach. —*William Ruhlmann*

Some of My Best Jokes Are Friends / Jul. 1985 / Capitol ✦✦
A wildly uneven, but at times first-rate Clinton session. The title cut was fine, and as usual, Clinton's studio sophistication, arrangements, and production were frequently incredible. But much of the humor was forced rather than clever, and Clinton seemed to strain more than usual to find the right mix of synthesized funk and bizarre quips. —*Ron Wynn*

Best of George Clinton / 1986 / Capitol ✦✦✦
This focuses on the best early Clinton material outside of the Parliament/Funkadelic arena. Most of the tracks aren't as humorously spectacular as "Atomic Dog," but there are a couple of clever ones from other albums included besides that masterpiece, such as "Loopzilla." —*Ron Wynn*

Mothership Connection (Live from the Summit, Houston, Texas) / 1986 / Capitol ✦✦
Credited to George Clinton Parliament Funkadelic, *The Mothership Connection (Live From The Summit, Houston, Texas)* is a discount-priced, six-track mini-LP consisting of one side devoted to a 24-minute soundtrack to a video of the same name, backed with three previously released Clinton studio tracks. A sprawling, often impressive concert recording featuring the immense Mothership Connection organization under George Clinton's reign. This set was perhaps the only time any album conveyed the sense of spectacle, chaos, wild humor, and musical mayhem that were routinely on display during their live shows. —*Ron Wynn*

R&B Skeletons in the Closet / Apr. 1986 / Capitol ✦✦✦
Clinton's second and third solo albums had their moments, but he didn't reach the peak of danceable madness of which he is truly capable again until this record, which contains the strange but

wonderful "Do Fries Go with That Shake?" Despite its title, it's not a collection of oldies. — *William Ruhlmann*

The Cinderella Theory / Aug. 1989 / Paisley Park ♦♦♦
On his first album for Prince's Paisley Park record label, George Clinton's willingness to experiment with samplers and hip-hop (including guest appearances by such artists as Chuck D and Flavor Flav of Public Enemy) resulted in a slightly inconsistent record, but it has more than enough truly fine songs to make *The Cinderella Theory* rank among his best solo albums. — *Stephen Thomas Erlewine*

○ **Hey Man, Smell My Finger** / Oct. 1993 / Paisley Park ♦♦♦♦
Hey Man, Smell My Finger is everything a great George Clinton album should be—conceptually disjointed, overlong, silly, sloppy, and funky as hell. Thankfully, the music here is his best since *Computer Games*, and the album proves just how responsible he is for much of the music of the 1990s, as the irresistible single "Paint the White House Black" illustrates with its numerous cameos. — *Stephen Thomas Erlewine*

Clover

Group, Rock & Roll
Clover is one of those bands that is remembered for its illustrious associations rather than its actual accomplishments. It was a country-rock band formed in Mill Valley, CA, in July 1967 by Johnny Ciambotti (bass), John McFee (guitar, vocals), Alex Call (guitar, vocals), and Mitch Howie (drums). This lineup made two albums for nearby Fantasy Records in the early '70s, after which Howie left and the group was expanded to a sextet with the addition of Huey Lewis (harmonica, vocals), Sean Hopper (keyboards, vocals), and Mickey Shine (drums). Clover moved to England in 1976 at the behest of Nick Lowe, where they made two more albums and served as the backup group on Elvis Costello's debut album, *My Aim Is True*. They returned to the U.S. in 1978 and broke up, with McFee going on to the Doobie Brothers and Lewis and Hopper forming the nucleus of Huey Lewis and the News. — *William Ruhlmann*

Clover / 1970 / Fantasy ♦♦♦

Forty-Niner / 1971 / Fantasy ♦♦♦

Unavailable / 1977 / Vertigo ♦♦♦

Love on the Wire / 1977 / Mercury ♦♦♦
Not surprisingly, Clover's fourth and final album, the second of its British sojourn, had a harder rock edge than its predecessors. Clover had come over to England as a California country rock outfit, only to land in the middle of the punk-rock revolt. Its first British album, *Clover* (or *Unavailable*, as it was called in the U.K.) retained the country sound, but by the end of 1977, the band was all uptempo rock and twin guitar leads, courtesy of Alex Call and John McFee. The music wasn't punk, exactly, but it was more aggressive. Still, Clover remained an essentially good-natured musicians' band, as the loose acappella version of Leiber and Stoller's "Keep On Rolling" demonstrated. In another time and place, maybe that would have mattered. — *William Ruhlmann*

● **Clover [Mercury]** / 1977 / Mercury ♦♦♦♦
In 1976, Clover relocated from Mill Valley, CA, to London, England, where the group hooked up with managers/record company executives Jake Riviera and Dave Robinson and signed to PolyGram Records, which, in early 1977, released this, their third album. In the U.K., the LP appeared on PolyGram's Vertigo label and was called *Unavailable;* in the U.S., PolyGram's Mercury label felt that title was a bit uncommercial and opted instead for the generic *Clover*, which as it happened had already been used for their Fantasy Records debut album in 1970. In any case, it was apparent that Riviera and Robinson felt that they'd hit upon a more authentic, American version of Brinsley Schwarz—country-rock with an edge. In fact, the band was all over the map stylistically. There were two lead singers, the smooth-voiced Alex Call and the gruffer Huey Lewis, and they sounded too different to be in the same band much less on the same song. Multi-instrumentalist John McPhee kept introducing touches of steel guitar and violin into what otherwise were rock tracks, while Lewis's harmonica was full of blues. It might have made for an interesting mixture if the result was a distinct musical identity, but either because of the songwriting or the arranging, it wasn't. And while the move across the Atlantic had earned the group a Dew recording contract, it also landed them in an emerging punk-rock scene with which they had nothing in common. "I come so far from San Francisco to walk

these streets alone," sang Call, and despite the group's talent, it was easy to see why. — *William Ruhlmann*

Chronicle / 1979 / Fantasy ♦♦♦

The Clovers

Group, R&B, Doo-Wop
One of the earliest doo-wop vocal groups, formed in the late '40s in Washington, DC. Original members were Buddy Bailey, Matthew McQuater, Hal Lucas Jr, and Harold Winley. Bobby Mitchell replaced Bailey by the time the group was signed to the fledgling Atlantic label in 1950. The Clovers racked up 13 Top Ten R&B hits between 1951 to 1954, all showcasing their solid harmonies and unerring rhythmic verve.

Before the early '50s, most non-gospel Black vocal groups were in the smooth pop vein of the Inkspots and Mills Brothers. Then the Clovers burst on the scene in 1951 with "Don't You Know I Love You," and things would never be the same.

Under the influence of Atlantic Records' Ahmet Ertegun (who wrote and produced most of their early songs), the Clovers combined quartet harmony, the big dance beat of the R&B jump bands, and the rawer sounds of urban blues into an exciting new blend that caught on with the young Black audience and put them consistently at the top of the R&B charts in the early '50s.

Going beyond this, just as their contemporary B.B.King was doing for blues, lead singers Buddy Bailey and later Charlie White brought a gospel influence to Ertegun's bluesy R&B songs—helping to lay the foundation for the soul music to come. — *George Bedard & Cub Koda*

○ **Their Greatest Recordings (The Early Years)** / 1971 / Atco ♦♦♦♦
Includes influential recordings from the early '50s of this bluesiest of doo-wop vocal groups. — *George Bedard*

○ **Love Potion No. 9 /The Best of the Clovers** / 1991 / EMI America ♦♦♦♦
The Best of the Clovers—Love Potion No. 9 features their later sides for United Artists including the classic title track. — *Cub Koda*

★ **Down in the Alley: The Best of The Clovers** / 1991 / Rhino ♦♦♦♦♦
Down in the Alley—Best of the Clovers is an excellent compilation of their best and earliest sides, including "Nip Sip," "Don't You Know I Love You," and "One Mint Julep." — *Cub Koda*

Club Nouveau

Group, Soul, Dance-Pop, Disco
Club Nouveau formed in Sacramento in 1986, including Jay King, Denzil Foster, Thomas McElroy, Samuelle Pratter, and Valerie Watson. King was the creative force behind the hit "Rumours" by the Timex Social Club in 1986, and formed King Jay Records for Club Nouveau. They made some good disco-flavored and funk tunes, and had four consecutive hits in 1986 and 1987—"Jealousy," "Situation #9," a cover of Bill Withers' "Lean on Me," and "Why You Treat Me So Bad." The last two both reached the number two spot on the R&B charts. But, in 1988, at the height of their popularity, McElroy, Prater, and Foster left the group, and were replaced by David Agent and Kevin Irving. Their final recordings for Tommy Boy/Warner Bros. didn't sustain the momentum, and they subsequently disbanded. — *Ron Wynn*

Under a Nouveau Groove / 1986 / Warner Brothers ♦♦♦
Some entertaining, if very derivative, urban contemporary dance-pop, R&B, and ballads. Club Nouveau had only hit, a cover of Bill Withers' "Lean On Me," and, by the time of this album, had virtually exhausted an already lightweight bag of tricks. This album was more interesting as a barometer of late '80s production trends than for the songs or performances. — *Ron Wynn*

● **Life Love & Pain** / 1986 / Warner Brothers ♦♦♦♦
An ultra noveau turn on old Bill Withers cut, "Lean on Me." — *Bil Carpenter*

Listen to the Message / 1988 / Warner Brothers ♦♦♦

Heavy on My Mind / Tommy Boy ♦♦♦

A New Beginning / Quality ♦♦

The Coasters

Group, R&B, Rock & Roll, Doo-Wop
Possibly the most popular doo-wop group of the '50s, the Coasters started on the West Coast as the Robins, scoring hits under the

writing-and-production helm of Jerry Lieber and Mike Stoller. When Atlantic signed Lieber and Stoller as a production team, the group split into two factions; the core of the group became the Coasters and moved to New York to record, while the Robins continued on the West Coast to diminishing acclaim. The Coasters' hits, some of the most finely crafted, well-written, and hilarious in the genre, continued throughout the rest of the decade. Carl Gardner's sly leads and Bobby Nunn's bass singing defined their sound through numerous personnel changes. When their time on the charts came to an end a number of "Coasters" groups suddenly proliferated (much like the Drifters), many of them still dotting the landscape of a million oldies shows and still singing those classic songs. —*Cub Koda*

☆ **50 Coastin' Classics: Anthology** / 1992 / Rhino ♦♦♦♦♦
Although it may well be too much for the casual fan, this double CD is easily the best Coasters retrospective ever assembled. Besides featuring every one of their hits, it also contains nine strong tunes cut in the mid-'50s by the Robins, who evolved into the Coasters after some personnel changes. As for the enticing obscurities, "Three Cool Cats" and "Besame Mucho" were cut by the Beatles on unreleased recordings in the early '60s, and "Ain't That Just Like Me" would be a small hit for the Searchers. "Down In Mexico" and "Brazil" are cool R&B/Latin melodramas, and "Shoppin' For Clothes," "What About Us," and "That Is Rock & Roll" are half-forgotten vignettes of youthful independence that stack up against the best songs of Jerry Leiber and Mike Stoller, who wrote most of the group's material. Indeed, there's little difference in quality between the hits and the B-sides on this comp, either in the group's matchless ensemble R&B/comedy vocals or Leiber/Stoller's witty songwriting. The accompanying booklet features comments on most of the tracks by Leiber and Stoller themselves. —*Richie Unterberger*

★ **The Very Best of the Coasters** / 1993 / Rhino ♦♦♦♦♦
The Coasters were the 1950s' (and early rock's) dominant novelty/comic R&B ensemble, benefiting from Jerry Lieber and Mike Stoller's lyrical wit and inspired production. They weren't simply proficient clowns; the Coasters were a skilled vocal unit whose talents were utilized on slice-of-life narratives, prophetic youth manifestos, and even an occasional teen anthem, as well as the prototype humorous vehicles "Yakety Yak" and "Poison Ivy." Although Rhino has already given them the deluxe two-disc treatment, consumers who either don't want that much Coasters material or prefer only the hits are nicely served by this 18-track anthology. It contains every major release, plus valuable lesser-known selections such as "Shoppin' For Clothes" and "What About Us." —*Ron Wynn*

Eddie Cochran

b. Oct. 3, 1938, Oklahoma City, OK, **d.** Apr. 17, 1960, Wiltshire, England
Rock & Roll, Rockabilly
As with his friend and contemporary Buddy Holly, Cochran's star has continued to shine ever more brightly since his untimely death. Partially this is because of his image—the brash, flamboyantly dressed, hot-guitar-picking, teenage smart-aleck rebel—but the substance is there too. A fine guitarist (I cite the guitar breaks on "Twenty Flight Rock" and "Jeannie Jeannie Jeannie," just to name a couple) and fine songwriter (especially in collaboration with his friend and producer Jerry Capehart), Cochran's best work captured the spirit of its time (the late '50s) so perfectly it can never seem dated: cars, girls, teenage rebellion, and angst distilled into two-and-a-half minute gems of ringing guitars, throbbing bass (his were among the first rock & roll records to exploit the electric bass's distinctive character), and growling, drawling vocals. Especially influential in Britain (where he was on tour when he was killed), echoes of Cochran's work (and sometimes his songs) have surfaced in the records of the Who, Rod Stewart, the Clash, Neil Diamond, the Stray Cats, and many, many others. —*George Bedard*

Box Set / 1988 / Liberty ♦♦♦
This six-LP import—which still, somehow, manages not to include every track Cochran recorded—is excessive for the non-fanatic. Nevertheless, it does include quite a few obscure, interesting prefame performances from the mid-'50s (some as part of the Cochran Brothers). Other bonuses include a live 1960 British TV broadcast, an album's worth of sessions and his work as a producer, and entire sides of instrumentals and stereo versions, as well as a 32-page booklet. —*Richie Unterberger*

★ **Legendary Masters** / 1990 / EMI America ♦♦♦♦♦
The definitive single-disc collection of Cochran's best: "Summertime Blues," "Cut Across Shorty," "Something Else," "Come on Everybody," and "Twenty Flight Rock." All the hits; all the feeling. —*Cub Koda*

○ **Singin' to My Baby/Never to Be Forgotten** / Feb. 23, 1993 / Capitol ♦♦♦♦
Two original albums on one compact disc, with only two hits between the two—"Sittin' in the Balcony" and "Twenty Flight Rock." But for devoted fans of Eddie Cochran, this lovingly packaged CD is worth their time, even if some of the material is slightly weak. *Singin' to My Baby* concentrates on ballad material; the posthumously released *Never To Be Forgotten* has more rockers. —*Stephen Thomas Erlewine*

Bruce Cockburn

b. May 27, 1945, Ottawa, Canada
Singer-Songwriter
Over the course of his lengthy career, Bruce Cockburn has gone from plaintive singer/songwriter folk to aggressive world beat, rock, and even some jazz. Thematically, Cockburn has gone from deeply introspective musings to human rights activism, all filtered through a distinctly mystical Christian point of view. Cockburn's poetic lyrics are consistently many cuts above those of most artists who choose to tackle this kind of weighty subject matter.
In his native Canada, Cockburn has won many Juno Awards (the equivalent to the Grammys). Overseas, he has quite a following, but stateside Cockburn has only managed two significant forays onto the radio playlists, 1980's "Wondering Where the Lions Are" (#21) and "If I Had a Rocket Launcher," his 1984 response to injustices he witnessed while in Central America. Most recently, Cockburn has signed with Sony, releasing the fine T-Bone Burnette-produced *Nothing but a Burning Light*, which recalls his earlier folkie style. —*Rick Clark*

High Winds White Sky / 1971 / Columbia ♦♦

Bruce Cockburn / 1971 / Epic ♦♦

Sunwheel Dance / 1972 / Columbia ♦♦

Night Vision / 1973 / Columbia ♦♦

Salt, Sun and Time / 1974 / True North ♦♦♦

Joy Will Find a Way / 1975 / Columbia ♦♦♦
Each of his early efforts hold up well to repeated plays, but this is one of the best from that period. Cockburn's wonderfully delicate acoustic guitar sounds great here, tastefully aided with spare sympathetic accompaniment. "Burn" and the title cut were popular tracks in Canada, but "A Long-Time Love Story" and "A Life Story" project a quiet strength that's entrancing. —*Rick Clark*

○ **In the Falling Dark** / 1976 / Columbia ♦♦♦
The follow-up to *Joy Will Find a Way* possesses some Cockburn standards in "Festival of Friends," the propulsive folk-jazz of "Silver Wheels," the meditative "Lord of the Starfields," and the title cut. The lyrics involve increasingly complex mystical Christian metaphors. Cockburn's exceptional guitar technique is showcased on the instrumental "Water into Wine." —*Rick Clark*

Circles in the Stream / 1977 / Island ♦♦♦

Further Adventures of Bruce Cockburn / 1978 / East Side Digital ♦♦♦
Included is more electric guitar and diverse instrumental backup. Some of the material tends to drag, but "Prenons La Mer" and "Can I Go with You?" sparkle with Cockburn's stunning guitar interplay and strong melodies. "Laughter" and "Rainfall" are standouts, too. —*Rick Clark*

○ **Dancing in the Dragon's Jaws** / 1979 / Columbia ♦♦♦♦
Cockburn's first stateside success produced a # 21 pop hit with "Wondering Where the Lions Are," but there is much better material to be found here on one of his best albums. The lyrics tend to be spacier, and, musically, Cockburn begins to aggressively synthesize Third World rhythms with his singer/songwriter-style folk. —*Rick Clark*

Selected Hits from 1980 Tour / 1980 / Millennium ♦♦♦

○ **Humans** / Nov. 1980 / Columbia ♦♦♦♦
This follow-up isn't as accessible as *Dancing in the Dragon's Jaws*, but it's possibly Cockburn's most brilliant artistic statement, where the struggles of the general human condition and (more personally) a divorce cause this Christian mystic to dig deep and grapple

with more down-to-earth issues. With some of his most powerfully poetic lyrics he maintains a fine balance between lofty intentions and grave disappointments. Musically, it is a heady dose of world-beat folk. —*Rick Clark*

Inner City Front / 1981 / Columbia ✦✦✦
This transitional self-produced effort featured more musical diversity, from the techno-dirge of "The Strong One" to the reggaelike "Justice." "Loner" provides a dramatic highlight. Cockburn's human rights concerns and his left-of-center politics dominate over more mystical fascinations for the first time. —*Rick Clark*

○ **The Trouble with Normal** / 1983 / Columbia ✦✦✦✦
On this, another consistently strong effort, Cockburn's brainy lyrics occasionally border on the didactic, but the imagery is usually brilliant. "Waiting for the Moon" is one of his most beautiful songs. The title cut is released in two totally different versions; the True North rendition is preferable. —*Rick Clark*

Stealing Fire / 1984 / Columbia ✦✦✦
It features a more streamlined, sophisticated rock sound. "If I Had a Rocket Launcher" became a powerful left-field AOR hit in 1984. "Lovers in a Dangerous Time" and "Nicaragua" are highlights. "Maybe the Poet" is a low point, being the highbrow artistic equivalent to Barry Mann's hideous, self-congratulatory ode to the value of pop-song craftsmen, "Who Put the Bomp (In the Bomp, Bomp, Bomp)." But it's a fine album overall. —*Rick Clark*

World of Wonders / 1986 / Columbia ✦✦✦
Cockburn's noble agenda to enlighten the planet about human oppression (with numerous on-the-money observations), sometimes makes the listener feel a little bludgeoned in the process. Nevertheless, it has more than enough highlights to make this well worth seeking out, particularly "Berlin Tonight," "Call It Democracy," "Lily of the Midnight Sky," and the title cut. —*Rick Clark*

Rumours of Glory / 1986 / Plane ✦✦✦
This well-compiled 1985 anthology is heavy on Cockburn's middle period. In spite of some duplication, it's a nice complement to the *Waiting for a Miracle* double-disc. (Import) —*Rick Clark*

○ **Waiting for a Miracle** / Jan. 1987 / Gold Castle ✦✦✦✦
This double-disc best-of collection is geared around Cockburn's Canadian singles—an odd approach, considering that much of his strongest material never enjoyed radio airplay. Because of that, *Waiting for a Miracle (Singles 1970-1987)* isn't definitive, but it is a very good collection (mainly because Cockburn is practically incapable of writing a bad song). Nevertheless, Cockburn has yet to receive the kind of treatment he deserves for a collection. *Waiting for a Miracle* is the best overview of Cockburn's music, by default. (Canadian Import) —*Rick Clark*

Big Circumstance / 1989 / Columbia ✦✦✦
Cockburn tries to balance the edge-rock approach of recent work with more reflective earlier sounds. He's most successful at illuminating big issues when he's focusing on his personal backyard (on "Understanding Nothing," "Don't Feel Your Touch") rather than the "Tibetan Side of Town." Surprise element: Cockburn displays rare flashes of humor. —*Rick Clark*

Live / 1990 / Gold Castle ✦✦✦
Stripped-down-combo reworkings of favorite Cockburn tracks are included, plus "Always Look on the Bright Side of Life," a death-humor take from the crucifixion scene in Monty Python's *Life of Brian*. —*Rick Clark*

Nothing But a Burning Light / 1991 / Columbia ✦✦✦
This T-Bone Burnett-produced effort finds Cockburn returning to the more introspective quiet spirit of his earlier work, including his most open Christian expressions in years, particularly "Cry of a Tiny Babe," a Cockburn-style Christmas story, and "Somebody Touched Me." "One of the Best Ones" is classic reflective Cockburn. Although not one of his best albums, it's a nice breather from the relentless heaviness of his last few efforts. —*Rick Clark*

Dart to the Heart / 1994 / Columbia ✦✦✦
With the exception of a few revved-up numbers (some with slide guitar and horns), this is a fairly subdued affair, featuring Cockburn's exquisite guitar work and insightful lyricism that is simultaneously grounded and mystical. It's a typically fine album for this consummate artist. —*Rick Clark*

Joe Cocker (John Robert Cocker)

b. May 20, 1944, Sheffield, England
Pop/Rock

After starting out as an unsuccessful pop singer (working under the name Vance Arnold), Joe Cocker found his niche singing rock and soul in the pubs of England with his superb backing group, the Grease Band. He hit #1 in the UK in November 1968 with his version of the Beatles' "A Little Help from My Friends." His career really took off after he sang that song at the Woodstock festival in August 1969. A second British hit came with a version of Leon Russell's "Delta Lady" in the fall of 1969 (by then, Russell was Cocker's musical director) and both of his albums, *With A Little Help from My Friends* (April 1969) and *Joe Cocker!* (November 1969), went gold in America. In 1970, his cover of the Box Tops' hit "The Letter" became his first U.S. Top Ten. Cocker's first peak of success came when Russell organized the "Mad Dogs & English-men" tour of 1970, featuring Cocker and over 40 others, and resulting in a third gold album and a concert film. Subsequent efforts were less popular, and problems with alcohol (both on stage and off) reduced Cocker's once-powerful voice to a croaking rasp. But he returned to the U.S. Top Ten with the romantic ballad "You Are So Beautiful" in 1975 and topped the charts in a duet with Jennifer Warnes on "Up Where We Belong," the theme from the 1982 film *An Officer and a Gentleman*. He has survived, still charting into the '90s. It's unlikely we've heard the last of him, since the man still seems capable of making any song his own. —*Cub Koda & William Ruhlmann*

○ **With a Little Help from My Friends** / Apr. 1969 / A&M ✦✦✦✦
The album that foisted Joe Cocker on an unsuspecting public is full of tasteful, raucous covers, Cocker's trademark hysterical vocals, and outstanding studio backing by pros like Jimmy Page and Steve Winwood. —*Tom Graves*

○ **Joe Cocker!** / Oct. 1969 / A&M ✦✦✦✦
The rare sophomore effort that was an improvement over the first, it features great tracks (and vocals) like "Delta Lady" and "She Came in Through the Bathroom Window." Arguably, it's Cocker's most soulful album. —*Tom Graves*

○ **Mad Dogs & Englishmen** / Aug. 1970 / A&M ✦✦✦✦
A superb document of Cocker's high-energy 1970 tour, it included about a zillion musicians and hangers-on. All the goods are here, and many consider this Cocker's last great moment. —*Tom Graves*

I Can Stand a Little Rain / Aug. 1974 / A&M ✦✦✦

Jamaica Say You Will / Aug. 1975 / A&M ✦✦
The comeback that Joe Cocker had achieved with 1974's *I Can Stand A Little Rain* and its hit single, "You Are So Beautiful" was not sustained by the follow-up, *Jamaica Say You Will*. The reason was simple: that bane of the interpretive singer, a lack of strong material. When there were exceptions, they tended not to be handled well. Randy Newman's "I Think It's Going To Rain Today" was sped up and overarranged, and although the Jackson Browne title track was a strong piece of material, it worked originally because of its restraint, not in the overwrought way Cocker treated it. —*William Ruhlmann*

Stingray / Apr. 1976 / A&M ✦✦✦

○ **Joe Cocker's Greatest Hits** / Nov. 1977 / A&M ✦✦✦✦
Greatest Hits features most, but not all (no "She Came In Through the Bathroom Window" or "It's a Sin When You Love Somebody"), of his biggest hits from the early '70s. Nevertheless, there's plenty of fine music here, making the record a solid compilation. —*Stephen Thomas Erlewine*

Luxury You Can Afford / Aug. 1978 / Asylum ✦✦✦

Space Captain / 1982 / Cube ✦✦✦

Sheffield Steel / Jun. 1982 / Island ✦✦✦

Civilized Man / May 1984 / Capitol ✦✦

● **Classics, Vol. 4** / 1987 / A&M ✦✦✦✦
A solid collection from his 1967-1976 peak, it includes "Feeling Alright," "You Are So Beautiful," and "With a Little Help from My Friends." —*Dan Heilman*

Unchain My Heart / Oct. 1987 / Capitol ✦✦

One Night of Sin / Aug. 1989 / Capitol ✦✦

Live! / May 1990 / Capitol ✦✦✦
This is a solid, R&B-heavy live concert. —*Dan Heilman*

Night Calls / Jul. 6, 1992 / Capitol ✦✦✦
Cocker's rep has always been as a superb interpreter of other people's material. For *Night Calls*, the Sheffield native peaks with the opening track—a memory-engraving rendition of the Brian Adams/Diane Warren-penned "Feels Like Forever." It's the higher

profile songs that ultimately disappoint on *Night Calls*. Cocker eventually works up a lather toward the end of "You've Got To Hide Your Love Away," but it never reaches the standard of other Beatles classics in his repertoire ("With A Little Help From My Friends," "She Came In Through The Bathroom Window"). The biggest let-down is the lack of commitment projected on Elton John's "Don't Let The Sun Go Down On Me." Still, even slumming Cocker sounds more real and soulful than, say, Michael Bolton in his wildest dreams. —*Roch Parisien*

○ **The Best of Joe Cocker** / Mar. 16, 1993 / Capitol ✦✦✦✦
Although Cocker's Capitol material wasn't as consistent as his A&M work, this compilation successfully distills the highlights, including the splendid "When the Night Comes," onto a single CD. —*Stephen Thomas Erlewine*

Have a Little Faith / Sep. 8, 1994 / 550 Music/Epic ✦✦✦
After eight years and five studio albums (plus a live album and a best-of album) with Capitol Records, Joe Cocker moved to 550 Music, a new Sony Music imprint, for *Have A Little Faith*. Produced by Chris Lord-Alge and his manager, Roger Davies, Cocker turned in a label debut full of well-chosen songs sung with authority. The title track, John Hiatt's "Have A Little Faith In Me," was a good choice for Cocker, as it contained that mixture of tenderness and toughness the singer has always brought out so well. Unfortunately, the new label affiliation did nothing for Cocker; *Have A Little Faith* flopped. —*William Ruhlmann*

Cocteau Twins

Group, Alternative Pop/Rock
One of the most innovative, distinctive bands of the '80s was the Cocteau Twins, an ethereal, prolific Scottish trio. Over the course of the decade, they became a major force in alternative music, although there isn't much that is forceful about their music. Instead, their music is a series of soundscapes, created with guitars, studio effects, drum machines, and Elizabeth Fraser's expansive vocals; she sings words according to their sound, not their meaning. With their atmospheric records and lush album covers, the band was the embodiment of England's arty 4AD record label during the '80s. As their career progressed, the Cocteau Twins began to harness their sound into more concrete songs, culminating in 1990's *Heaven or Las Vegas*. After one more album on 4AD, the band switched labels; with the new record company, their music started to veer slightly into new age territory, a genre that was in debt to the Cocteau's previous records. —*Stephen Thomas Erlewine*

Garlands / 1982 / 4AD ✦✦
○ **Head over Heels** / 1983 / 4AD ✦✦✦✦
Where the Cocteau Twins' first album relied more on texture than songs, *Head Over Heels* melds their dreamy, hazy soundscapes to actual songs. —*Stephen Thomas Erlewine*

○ **Treasure** / 1984 / 4AD ✦✦✦✦
On *Treasure*, the Cocteau Twins' rich, gauzy layers of sound are positively entrancing. It doesn't matter what Elizabeth Fraser is singing; her voice is only another element in the endless sonic textures. —*Stephen Thomas Erlewine*

Tiny Dynamine / 1985 / 4AD ✦✦
Moon & the Melodies / 1986 / 4AD ✦✦
Love's Easy Tears / 1986 / 4AD ✦✦✦
Victorialand / 1986 / 4AD ✦✦✦
While nearly all of the instrumental support on *Victorialand* is acoustic guitar, the essential structure of the Cocteau Twins' music hasn't changed at all, making the album a bit of a retread, no matter how enjoyable it is. —*Stephen Thomas Erlewine*

● **Pink Opaque** / 1986 / 4AD ✦✦✦✦
A compilation of the Cocteau Twins' first records, *Pink Opaque* offers a good introduction to their music. —*Stephen Thomas Erlewine*

● **Blue Bell Knoll** / 1988 / 4AD ✦✦✦✦
This, the first Cocteau Twins regular studio album to be released in the U.S., is typical of their earlier U.K. output: keyboards and guitars swirl together into sonic landscapes, over which (or rather, buried within which) Elizabeth Fraser sings in a high, ethereal voice reminiscent of Kate Bush and Jane Siberry, the difference be-

ing that the lyrics are utterly unintelligible. The result is classy mood music that might appeal to the new crop of Enya fans. —*William Ruhlmann*

Heaven or Las Vegas / 1990 / 4AD ✦✦✦
The song structures are more discernible, as are the lyrics, which perhaps makes this a little less mysterious than most Cocteau Twins albums, and a little more accessible, if also less characteristic. —*William Ruhlmann*

Four-Calendar Cafe / Sep. 27, 1993 / Capitol ✦✦✦
The Cocteau Twins' first effort outside of 4AD continues in the vein of *Heaven or Las Vegas*, with more recognizable song structures and clear phrasing from Elizabeth Frasier. Unfortunately, the songs are not as interesting as the ones on *Heaven or Las Vegas* or as intriguing as the sonic explorations of their earlier releases. —*Stephen Thomas Erlewine*

Bluebeard / 1994 / Capitol

Leonard Cohen

b. Sep. 21, 1934, Montreal, Canada
Singer-Songwriter
Although he played music during his college years, Canadian poet, novelist, and singer/songwriter Leonard Cohen did not turn professional until he was in his 30s. A graduate of McGill University, he published several books of poetry starting in the '50s and two novels, *The Favorite Game* and *Beautiful Losers*, in the '60s. After his songs had been recorded by Judy Collins, Cohen turned to singing and released his debut album, *Songs of Leonard Cohen*, in 1968. It contained such typical material as the highly poetic "Suzanne," which had been a singles hit for Noel Harrison. Cohen continued to write and record albums (though less and less frequently) throughout the '70s and '80s, all of them featuring his deepening voice and lyrics that were by turns depressing, comic, and erotic. His 1977 album, *Death of a Ladies Man*, was a collaborative effort with eccentric producer Phil Spector. By the '80s, Cohen's music was being celebrated by the school of doom-rock performers led by Nick Cave and others (resulting in the tribute album *I'm Your Fan*, 1991), but Jennifer Warnes's all-Cohen album *Famous Blue Raincoat* (1987) was a more accessible sampler. The artist himself made one of the best albums of 1988 in *I'm Your Man*. —*William Ruhlmann*

★ **The Songs of Leonard Cohen** / 1968 / Columbia ✦✦✦✦✦
His debut album features such standards as "Suzanne," "Sisters of Mercy," and "So Long Marianne." Many of these were featured in the 1971 Warren Beatty film, *McCabe and Mrs. Miller*. —*William Ruhlmann*

○ **Songs from a Room** / 1969 / Columbia ✦✦✦✦
Includes his versions of his classics, "Bird on a Wire" and "Story of Isaac." —*William Ruhlmann*

○ **Songs of Love and Hate** / 1971 / Columbia ✦✦✦✦
"Famous Blue Raincoat," "Joan of Arc," and more great Cohen songs. —*William Ruhlmann*

Leonard Cohen: Live Songs / 1973 / Columbia ✦✦
New Skin for Old Ceremony / 1974 / Columbia ✦✦✦
○ **The Best of Leonard Cohen** / 1975 / Columbia ✦✦✦✦
While it isn't a definitive collection, *Best of Leonard Cohen* is a fine cross-section of some of Cohen's best songs. —*Stephen Thomas Erlewine*

Death of a Ladies Man / 1977 / Columbia ✦✦
Recent Songs / 1979 / Columbia ✦✦✦
Various Positions / 1985 / Passport ✦✦✦
○ **I'm Your Man** / 1988 / Columbia ✦✦✦✦
Pessimism, humor, and poetry add up to a profound world view in Cohen's most recent collection. —*William Ruhlmann*

○ **The Future** / Nov. 10, 1992 / Columbia ✦✦✦✦
On his latest recording, Canada's poet-musician laureate has glimpsed *The Future*, and it's not a pretty sight. Cohen's apocalyptic vision takes us through a morbid roll-call that includes torture, environmental destruction, drug abuse, abortion, sexual abuse, murder, Stalin, Charles Manson, Hiroshima, and (shudder) lousy poets. And that's just the title track.
  Instrumental backings focus mostly on unobtrusive textures—synths, strings, female backing vocals, and the occasional flavor of pedal steel guitar, mandolin, fiddle, and horns. —*Roch Parisien*

Live / 1994 / Columbia ✦✦

Coldcut
....
Group, House Music
Coldcut, a London-based duo consisting of the DJs Matt Black and Jonathan More, were major figures in Britain's acid house scene, helping lay the foundation for that dance movement with their late '80s remixes and singles. Starting their career by making illegal remixes of popular dance hits, they first made their mark with their official remix of Eric B.& Rakim's "Paid in Full," which featured Ofra Haza; with its combination of hip-hop, house, and Mideastern music, the remix became a dance classic. For their only album, 1989's *What's That Noise?*, Coldcut recruited a number of vocalists—including the Fall's Mark E. Smith, Queen Latifah, Junior Reid, and Lisa Stansfield—for the record. Although they haven't released anything since the record, it remains a good document of the influential dance production team and their groundbreaking style. — *Stephen Thomas Erlewine*

Out to Lunch with Ahead of Our Time / 1988 / AheadOfOur-Time ✦✦✦

Stop the Crazy Thing / 1988 / AheadOfOurTime ✦✦✦

● **What's That Noise?** / 1989 / Tommy Boy ✦✦✦✦
Many good, dense dance tracks are included, plus a cameo by Lisa Stansfield. — *Dan Heilman*

Jude Cole
....
Pop/Rock
Jude Cole joined the British power-pop band the Records in 1980, after their first album was released; he stayed with them for one album. After a few years, Cole re-emerged with his own solo record, 1987's *Jude Cole*, which was a much slicker, mainstream-oriented affair than any of the Records' records, yet it did have its charm; unfortunately, it was ignored. That was not the case with his second album, 1990's *A View from 3rd Street*, which had a bonafide hit single with the sweet, yearning "Baby, It's Tonight." Another single from the album went Top 40, as Cole enjoyed a surprise success. Although he wasn't able to repeat his success with the follow-up, it was another solid album of mainstream pop/rock, full of shiny hooks and sleek, memorable melodies. — *Stephen Thomas Erlewine*

○ **Jude Cole** / 1987 / Reprise ✦✦✦✦

● **A View from 3rd Street** / Mar. 27, 1990 / Reprise ✦✦✦✦

Start the Car / 1992 / Reprise ✦✦✦

Lloyd Cole & the Commotions
....
Group, Alternative Pop/Rock
Scottish singer/songwriter Lloyd Cole formed the Commotions, who served as his backup band, in Glasgow in 1983. The group featured guitarist Nick Clark, bassist Lawrence Donegan, keyboard player Blair Cowan, and drummer Steven Irvine. Heavily influenced by Bob Dylan and the Band, Cole and the Commotions developed a familiar-sounding but distinctive folk-rock sound, highlighted by Cole's literate lyrics. The group signed to Polydor in 1984, and scored a series of U.K. hits, including "Perfect Skin." In 1989, he split the band and moved to New York, where he recorded *Lloyd Cole*, his debut solo album, with New York session players such as Voidoid and Lou Reed guitarist Robert Quine. Cole has garnered considerable critical acclaim, but so far has failed to make a commercial impact in the US. — *William Ruhlmann*

○ **Rattlesnakes** / Oct. 1984 / Capitol ✦✦✦✦
Cole's debut album reflects his Glasgow surroundings in its observations but also incorporates a Dylanish attitude toward them, while the Commotions prove to be a cohesive backup unit. Originally released in the U.K. by Polydor Records in September 1984, *Rattlesnakes* was released in the U.S. in 1985 by Geffen and reissued by Capitol in October 1988. — *William Ruhlmann*

Easy Pieces / Nov. 1985 / Capitol ✦✦✦
Producers Clive Langer and Alan Winstanley, as is their wont, created a shimmering pop surface for Lloyd Cole and the Commotions' second album, sweetening the tracks with string and brass counter-melodies and emphasizing the chiming highs of the guitar and keyboards for an attractive sound that echoed the earnestness of British bands like the Hollies and Herman's Hermits, circa 1966. It was, of course, like sugar-coating cyanide capsules, given Lloyd Cole's pleasantly sung lyrics, which detailed philosophical

disillusionment, romantic discord, and, yes, at least attempted suicide. In the U.K., *Easy Pieces* was a Top Ten hit. But although the album saw something like a proper release in the U.S. and the Commotions toured extensively, no American breakthrough materialized. (*Easy Pieces* was reissued by Capitol in October 1988.) — *William Ruhlmann*

Mainstream / Sep. 1987 / Capitol ✦✦
If Lloyd Cole was less worried about depressing his listeners on his third album, he also seemed determined to stir them up, adopting various personae in his songs, from the lover who loses interest shortly after the wedding ceremony in "Jennifer She Said" (a U.K. Top 40 hit) to Sean Penn. There were a few song narrators who seemed close to the singer himself, and they sounded just as discontented. There was little to alleviate the vitriol in the music, which was unusually muted, and long before the end Cole had begun to sound like a crank. The album's saving grace was "Hey Rusty," a song with a Springsteen-like theme and a U2-like musical track. If there were more songs this coherent, specific, and moving, *Mainstream* might have ranked with Cole's first two albums. — *William Ruhlmann*

● **1984–1989** / Jun. 1989 / Capitol ✦✦✦✦
The compilation *1984-1989* features nearly all of the best moments from Lloyd Cole and the Commotions' three albums, making it the perfect introduction to his music. — *Stephen Thomas Erlewine*

Lloyd Cole / Feb. 1990 / Capitol ✦✦✦
In the two and a half years following the release of *Mainstream*, Lloyd Cole signed to Capitol Records for the U.S., split from the Commotions, and moved to New York. For his first solo album, he assembled a team consisting of two New York band veterans—drummer/co-producer Fred Maher and guitarist Robert Quine, both of whom had played in Richard Hell's Voidoids and Lou Reed's backup group, plus bassist Matthew Sweet and Commotions keyboard player Blair Cowan. As a result, *Lloyd Cole* boasts a tougher, harder sound than the Commotions records. Cole's vocals, meanwhile, have become more direct and less stylized. His lyrics are also less adorned, and he has lightened up somewhat. Much of *Lloyd Cole* is musically astringent in a way Cole hasn't managed previously, even if the album is far less ambitious than his first two records. — *William Ruhlmann*

Don't Get Weird on Me Babe / Sep. 16, 1991 / Capitol ✦✦✦
While it's not exactly sunny, *Don't Get Weird on Me Babe* is Cole's most accessible and pop-oriented album to date, filled with fine understated pop/rockers like "She's a Girl and I'm a Man." — *Stephen Thomas Erlewine*

Bad Vibes / Oct. 1993 / Rykodisc ✦✦✦
Bad Vibes, Lloyd Cole's sixth new studio album, marks a big change in terms of sound. Producer Adam Peters and mixer Bob Clearmountain have tried to recreate the experimental days of the mid-'60s, employing a wide variety of studio gimmicks. But if *Bad Vibes* is Lloyd Cole's most produced record, it also is his earthiest. The singer's voice is recorded (sometimes with echo or double-tracking) especially high in the mix, and his singing is as stylized as it was on his first two albums, though in a different way. Here, he affects a sardonic, disengaged tone. All of this makes *Bad Vibes* Cole's most varied and most ambitious album, but far from his best. The odd sound stage and attitude are anything but accessible, and Cole himself has rarely been as vitriolic. (The U.S. Rykodisc version contains two bonus tracks, "For The Pleasure Of Your Company" and "4 M.B.," not contained on the Fantana version.) — *William Ruhlmann*

Natalie Cole
....
b. Feb. 6, 1950, Los Angeles, CA
Soul, Urban, Pop
The daughter of jazz and pop legend Nat "King" Cole, Natalie Cole has forged a successful career in two phases, doing R&B/urban contemporary and then jazz-based pop. She made her stage debut at age 11 and sang in college. Cole met the writing and producing team of Chuck Jackson and Marvin Yancey in 1973. The next year they collaborated on some sessions that were recorded at Curtis Mayfield's Curtom studios in Chicago. These helped her land a deal with Capitol, and she teamed with Jackson/Yancey for a string of hit albums and singles from 1975 until 1983. Such LPs as *Inseparable, Natalie, Thankful, Unpredictable,* and *I Love You So*

yielded five number one R&B hits between 1975 and 1977. These included "This Will Be, "Inseparable," "Our Love," and "I've Got Love on My Mind." She stayed on Capitol until 1983, then switched to Epic for her final album with the Jackson/Yancey tandem. Cole made duets with Peabo Bryson in 1979 and 1980 and Ray Parker, Jr., in 1987. She scored more hits with "Jump Start," "I Live for Your Love," and "Over You" in 1987, and "Pink Cadillac," a cover of a Bruce Springsteen tune, in 1988, and then made her stylistic shift. Cole eased into the transition with "When I Fall in Love," a number her father recorded in 1957. It was included on her 1987 LP, *Everlasting*. She fully embraced the move with the 1991 LP *Unforgettable with Love*, earning Grammy awards and landing a number-one pop album that eventually sold over five million copies. The title track featured her doing a duet with her father via electronic elaboration. She continued the jazzy trend with *Take a Look* in 1993, and has toured and done television specials working with a large orchestra conducted by Nelson Riddle. Cole was among several African-American artists who teamed with country stars on the 1994 LP *Rhythm, Country and Blues*. It proved a smash on the R&B, country, and pop charts. —*Ron Wynn*

Inseparable / 1975 / Capitol ✦✦✦
Natalie Cole scored her initial fame as a soul singer with a pronounced Aretha Franklin influence. This was her first hit album, and Cole soared to the top of the R&B charts as both "This Will Be" and "Inseparable" were number one R&B singles ("This Will Be" also was a Top Ten pop song). Nineteen years later, this album still stands as arguably her finest; it contains more earnest, aggressive and honest material than most of her other albums. —*Ron Wynn*

Natalie / 1976 / Capitol ✦✦✦
Her second early '70s album, when people were actually comparing Cole with Aretha Franklin. Those comparisons were later shown to be both premature and inaccurate, as she was never really a soul vocalist. But this album did quite well, with "Mr. Melody" becoming her fourth straight R&B Top 10 hit, and the only one of her first five singles that didn't top the R&B charts. Cole returned in the '90s to the style she perfected on these early albums. —*Ron Wynn*

Unpredictable / 1977 / Capitol ✦✦✦
Natalie Cole continued a strong run of hit albums and singles with her third '70s release. This was her second album in 1977 and earned her another hit with "Be Mine Tonight." Cole's career and personal life were going smoothly at this point, and Marvin Yancey, her husband at the time, was co-producing her material. —*Ron Wynn*

Thankful / 1977 / Capitol ✦✦✦
Her finest hour, encompassing jazz and soul. —*Bil Carpenter*

Natalie Live! / 1978 / Capitol ✦✦✦
Natalie Cole's first live record had some pleasant and a few boisterous versions of previous studio hits. It followed two consecutive platinum releases and was released during her peak period as a straight soul singer. Such singles as "Mr. Melody," "I've Got Love On My Mind" and "Sophisticated Lady (She's A Different Lady)" were an early clue that Cole was not only capable of cutting jazz-based pop, but that she was quite good at it. —*Ron Wynn*

I Love You So / 1979 / Capitol ✦✦
Cole's final '70s album seemed her most self-satisfied. Such songs as "Happy Love" and "Don't Look Back" had a serene quality and peaceful air, and she wasn't yet being overwhelmed by the problems of the '80s. Cole had gotten her career back on track with a hugely successful duet album with Peabo Bryson, and landed two moderate chart hits with this one as well. —*Ron Wynn*

We're the Best of Friends / 1979 / Capitol ✦✦
Cole's pairing with Peabo Bryson proved inspired. This was among the year's biggest R&B albums, and it put Cole and Bryson on the charts twice, reviving Cole's career and energizing Bryson's even more. He dominated Cole throughout the album, but she was smart enough to glide along beside him and reap the rewards. —*Ron Wynn*

Don't Look Back / 1980 / Capitol ✦✦
Cole's last album for Capitol wasn't as eventful as the others, even though it was squarely in the same style. She sounded less convincing on the ballads and less confident on the uptempo tracks. A couple of cuts did reach the charts, making the album something of a success commercially, but it was an indication that Cole and her production team were running out of ideas. —*Ron Wynn*

Happy Love / 1981 / Capitol ✦✦
I'm Ready / 1983 / Epic ✦✦
Dangerous / 1985 / Modern ✦✦✦
Everlasting / 1987 / Elektra ✦✦✦
Fine '80s Top 40 and light-jazz music. —*Bil Carpenter*

○ **The Collection** / 1988 / Capitol ✦✦✦✦
This contains the finest soul and sophisticated pre-rock pop tracks from Cole's days at Capitol (1975-1981). Cole made some superb singles in her early days, especially "This Will Be" and "Inseparable." At the same time, she laid the foundation for the early-'90s change that would surprise those who slept on "Mr. Melody" or "I've Got Love On My Mind." Her voice was actually more suited for these songs than the soul numbers, which were as much production and arranging triumphs as vocal victories. —*Ron Wynn*

Good to Be Back / 1989 / Elektra ✦✦✦
Natalie Cole overcame drug and emotional problems during the late '80s. This album marked her return and netted her two hits with "Miss You Like Crazy" and "Gonna Make You Mine." It also was the start of her turn toward softer, sophisticated, jazz-based pop that culminated in the '91 monster hit "Unforgettable". —*Ron Wynn*

● **Unforgettable** / 1991 / Elektra ✦✦✦✦
Natalie Cole found new glory with pre-rock pop in 1991. She earned commercial and critical success with an electronically manipulated duet with her father Nat on "Unforgettable." The subsequent album also contained some fine vocals by Natalie, doing decent renditions of such songs as "Avalon" and "Lush Life," but it was the title cut that recreated her as a diva in the Anita Baker mode. The album sold over five million copies. —*Ron Wynn*

○ **Take a Look** / 1993 / Elektra ✦✦✦✦
Those who questioned whether Natalie Cole had either the will or skill to succeed with another session of pre-rock popular music need wonder no more. There are another 18 jazz-tinged and early pop numbers, with some unexpected pleasures ("Calypso Blues," "It's Sand Man") and spectacular triumphs ("Cry Me A River," "Fiesta In Blue," "I'm Beginning To See The Light"). Cole is now completely comfortable with the pacing, flow and sensibility of pre-rock material; she has no problems with articulation or delivery, either. —*Ron Wynn*

Collective Soul

Group, Rock & Roll
This Atlanta rock band blends mainstream rock radio appeal with the young Modern Rock sound. Their hit, "Shine" from *Hints, Allegations and Things Left Unsaid* (which was essentially a demo assembled by guitarist Ed Roland), was a runaway radio hit in 1994. Released the following year, Collective Soul's self-titled second album was recorded with the full band—guitarist/vocalist Ed Roland, Dean Roland, Ross Childress, Will Turpin, and Shane Evans—and contained a minor hit with "Gel" and a major crossover hit with "December." —*Rick Clark*

Hints, Allegations and Things Left Unsaid / 1994 / Atlantic ✦✦✦
The big hit "Shine" was the necessary bridge between modern rock radio and mainstream classic rock. The sound is fashionably grungy during the verses, but the choruses are pure late-'70s rock. The production on this album is rather uneven. —*Rick Clark*

● **Collective Soul** / 1995 / Atlantic ✦✦✦✦
Recorded with a full band, Collective Soul's self-titled second album betters their debut both in songwriting and sound, since they can actually make a track like "Gel" rock. —*Stephen Thomas Erlewine*

Collins Kids

Group, Rockabilly
By the time Lawrence (b. 1944) and Lawrencine (b. 1942) Collins were eleven and thirteen, respectively, they were already tearing it up on country package shows, recording for Columbia Records, and performing on national TV almost weekly. Older sister Lorrie held up the cowgirl fringe-rustling-against-nylons teenage-sensuality department; kid brother Larry was a bundle of hyperkinetic energy, bopping all over the place while laying down exciting, twangy guitar breaks learned firsthand from the "King of Double-necked Mosrite," Joe Maphis. The Collins's recordings as time went on veered from mawkish brother/sister country-style duets to white-hot rockabilly, and they were just reaching their peak

when Lorrie eloped, effectively breaking up the act. Revered by rockabilly collectors the world over, their filmed television appearances and recordings are testimony to the fact that the Collins Kids weren't just "good for their age," they were just plain good, period. —*Cub Koda*

Introducing Larry and Lorrie / 1958 / Columbia Special Products ✦✦✦

For those who don't want to spring for the lengthy and expensive Bear Family box, this is an excellent distillation of twelve of their best late-'50s rockabilly sides. "Hoy Hoy," "Whistle Bait," "Mercy," "Just Because," and "Party" rank among the most smokin' rockabilly sides ever waxed. —*Richie Unterberger*

● **Hop Skip & Jump** / Aug. 1991 / Bear Family ✦✦✦✦
A 2-CD boxed set covering the Kids' entire career. —*Cub Koda*

Bootsy Collins

b. Oct. 26, 1951, Cincinnati, OH
Funk, Disco
Bootsy (born William Collins, Oct. 26, 1951, Cincinnati, OH) is a funk/R&B bassist/singer/bandleader. He formed his first group, the Pacesetters, in 1968, featuring Phelps "Catfish" Collins (his brother) (guitar), Frankie "Kash" Waddy (drums), and Philippe Wynne. From 1969 to 1971, the group functioned as James Brown's backup band and was dubbed the JB's. In 1972, Bootsy joined George Clinton's Parliament/Funkadelic. He launched Bootsy's Rubber Band as a spin-off of P-Funk in 1976, the band including his brother Phelps, Waddy, Joel "Razor Sharp" Johnson (keyboards), Gary "Mudd-Bone" Cooper (drums), and Robert "P-Nut" Johnson (vocals), along with "the Horny Horns." (He was sometimes billed alone as Bootsy, and sometimes as William "Bootsy" Collins.)

Signing to Warner Bros. Records, he enjoyed the first of his 15 R&B singles chart entries in 1976 with "Stretchin' Out (In a Rubber Band)." His most successful singles were "The Pinocchio Theory" (1977) and the chart-topping "Bootzilla" (1978). He also released six albums on Warners through 1982, including the gold-sellers *Ahh...The Name Is Bootsy Baby!* (1977) and *Bootsy? Player of the Year* (1978), then took a six-year recording hiatus and returned on Columbia in 1988 with the appropriately named *What's Bootsy Doin'?* In 1989, Bootsy was a member of the Bootzilla Orchestra on Malcolm McLaren's album *Waltz Darling.* In 1990, Bootsy was a featured guitarist and bassist with the dance music trio Deee-Lite. Bootsy's New Rubber Band released *Blasters of the Universe* on August 2, 1994. —*William Ruhlmann*

○ **Stretchin' out in Bootsy's Rubber Band** / 1976 / Warner Brothers ✦✦✦✦

The debut album that launched the solo career of bassist Bootsy Collins, after years of playing with everyone from James Brown to George Clinton (with whom he continued working and recording with for years). The title cut and several others established Collins's viability outside the Parliament/Funkadelic empire and contained some excellent uptempo jams. —*Ron Wynne*

○ **Ahh ... The Name Is Bootsy, Baby!** / 1977 / Warner Brothers ✦✦✦✦

His second album is a fine introduction into Bootsy's bizarre and throbbing funky fairy-tale world. —*John Floyd*

Bootsy? Player of the Year / Feb. 1978 / Warner Brothers ✦✦✦
"I've got a cartoon mind," Bootsy declares, and his goofy outlook colors this funk excursion, which maintains his fat bass lines while incorporating everything from "America The Beautiful" to "Buffalo Gals." If Bootsy is not above using a TV commercial theme as the basis for a song ("Roto-Rooter"), he is as influential as he is inclusive—betcha Ray Parker, Jr. heard that cut before he wrote "Ghostbusters," with its similar "Who ya gonna call?" tag line. But best of all is Bootsy's #1 R&B hit "Bootzilla," an engaging cacophony of beat, chant, and bluster. Bootsy was always the cartoon face of the P-Funk mob, and *Player Of The Year* was his bootsiest album yet. —*William Ruhlmann*

This Boot Is Made for Fonk-N / Jul. 1979 / Warner Brothers ✦✦✦
Good, but frequently repetitive funk and comic material from bassist Bootsy Collins. His snappy, looping bass lines and presence were beginning to sag a bit, and the material wasn't consistently creative or clever enough to overcome some severe weaknesses. But when it was good, Collins and company still made some memorable funk. —*Ron Wynne*

Ultra Wave / Nov. 1980 / Warner Brothers ✦✦
The Rubber Band doesn't seem to have been functioning at this point, so *Ultra Wave* is a "solo" Bootsy album, not that the sound is distinguishable. In fact, the problem here is not that there's too much Bootsy, it's that there's not enough. All albums that emerge from the P-Funk Mothership deliver the funk by definition, but what separates the good and great ones from the merely okay ones is an individual vision, whether it's P-Funk leader George Clinton's or Bootsy's. On *Ultra Wave*, there are tracks that could fit easily not only on any other P-Funk album, but also on those of P-Funk's more diluted competitors, the Ohio Players, say, or even Earth, Wind and Fire. "Is That My Song?" asks one title, and it's a fair question. —*William Ruhlmann*

The One Giveth, the Court Taketh Away / May 1982 / Warner Brothers ✦✦✦
One of the final albums before Bootsy Collins took a break from bandleading and returned to doing mostly session work. There were more entertaining numbers than dreary ones, and Collins and company had their final chart singles during 1982. —*Ron Wynne*

○ **What's Bootsy Doin'?** / 1988 / Columbia ✦✦✦✦
This pounding set is Collins's best work, with plenty of grooves for the brain and the booty. —*John Floyd*

Jungle Bass / 1990 / 4th & Broadway ✦✦✦
A comeback/return album for outstanding funk bassist Bootsy Collins. He signed with 4th & Broadway in 1990 and issued his first album as a leader in nearly 10 years, although he had played with Trouble Funk, L.J. Reynolds, and a number of other artists. Although it didn't have the inspired comic masterpieces or first-rate funk jams of his past albums, it was at least a decent vehicle for Collins's bass lines and rhythms. —*Ron Wynne*

● **Back in the Day: The Best of Bootsy** / 1994 / Warner Brothers ✦✦✦✦
Most of Bootsy's albums are dense with funk, spending a great deal of time concentrating on the all-mighty groove. With such a reliance on extended runs, it might seem that a compilation wouldn't make sense, yet *Back in the Day* cuts away the excesses of his albums and offers a concise distillation of what Collins is about. —*Stephen Thomas Erlewine*

Blasters of the Universe / 1994 / Rykodisc ✦✦

Glenda Collins

British Invasion
One of the many girl-group type solo singers who had a hard time making it in Britain in the early and mid-'60s, let alone the United States, Collins released 11 singles—all flops—between 1960 and 1966. Any interest she's been able to attract from collectors is due to her association with legendary British producer Joe Meek, who was at the helm of eight of the 45s. There's no question that Meek did his level best for his protégé, writing most of the singles himself and investing many of them with his immediately identifiable eccentric production values—tons of echo, manic speeded-up tapes, weedy organs, and over-the-top orchestras. The stinging session guitar of Ritchie Blackmore graces a few of these singles, some of which were recorded with British instrumental groups the Tornados (of "Telstar" fame) and the Outlaws. Collins herself had a fairly good, belting voice, though she didn't show a particularly deep feeling for rock and roll. The problem, ultimately, is fairly simple—her material wasn't very good, and in fact quite vapid more often than not. Collins never recorded again after Meek's death in early 1967. —*Richie Unterberger*

Been Invited to a Party: The Singles 1963-1966 / 1990 / Connoisseur ✦✦✦
All eight of the singles Collins recorded under Meek's auspices. Idiosyncratic production and energetic, cheery vocals, but there's not much of substance for either Meek or the performer to work with. For Meek scholars, this collection is an admirable public service, and the very dated early-'60s pop and general in-your-face innocence (as well as the occasional sparkling Ritchie Blackmore guitar lick) make this fun, in a limited way. But if you're looking for some interesting wall-of-compression Joe Meek productions, you're much better advised to begin with a number of other artists, including the Honeycombs, Heinz, the Tornados, and Screaming Lord Sutch, for starters. Best tunes: the affecting ballad "Something I Got To Tell You" (covered in a superior version by the Honeycombs) and the brassy "Baby It Hurts." —*Richie Unterberger*

Judy Collins

b. May 1, 1939, Seattle, WA
Folk, Singer-Songwriter, Folk-Rock

Judy Collins was one of the major interpretive folksingers of the '60s. A child prodigy at classical piano, she turned to folk music at the age of 15 and released her first album, *A Maid of Constant Sorrow*, in 1961 when she was 22. That album and its follow-up, *The Golden Apples of the Sun*, consisted of traditional folk material, with Collins's pure, sweet soprano accompanied by her acoustic guitar playing. By the time of *Judy Collins #3*, she had begun to turn to contemporary material and to add other musicians. (Jim (Roger) McGuinn tried out his first arrangements of "The Bells of Rhymney" and "Turn, Turn, Turn" on this album, before using them with the Byrds.)

Collins's musical horizons were expanded further by 1966 and the release of *In My Life*, which added theater music to her repertoire and introduced her audience to the writing of Leonard Cohen; it was one of her six albums to go gold. Her first gold-seller, however, was 1967's *Wildflowers*, which contained her hit version of "Both Sides Now" by the then-little-known songwriter Joni Mitchell.

By the '70s, Collins had come to be identified as much as an art song singer as a folksinger and had also begun to make a mark with her original compositions. Her best-known performances cover a wide stylistic range: the traditional gospel song "Amazing Grace," the Stephen Sondheim Broadway ballad "Send in the Clowns," and such songs of her own as "My Father" and "Born to the Breed."

Collins recorded less frequently after the end of her 23-year association with Elektra Records in 1984, though she made two albums for Gold Castle. In 1990, she signed to Columbia Records and released *Fires of Eden*, her 23rd album. —*William Ruhlmann*

Maid of Constant Sorrow / 1961 / Elektra ✦✦✦
Collins's talent is to sing these traditional chestnuts, even at the time, without the prissiness of so many female folk singers. Her phrasing has enough strength to stand up to the "Prickile Bush" and give in to "Wild Mountain Thyme." —*Richard Meyer*

Golden Apples of the Sun / 1962 / Elektra ✦✦✦
Collins takes on such diverse repertoire as Gary Davis's "Twelve Gates to the City," "Crow on the Cradle" and her setting of "Golden Apples of the Sun." —*Richard Meyer*

3rd Album / 1963 / Elektra ✦✦✦
Having established herself as one of the foremost interpreters of traditional material, Collins did the same for contemporary folk songwriters on this album, which mixed standards with pristine covers of compositions by Dylan, Bob Gibson, Pete Seeger, Ewan MacColl, and Shel Silverstein. With Jim McGuinn arranging and playing second guitar and banjo, this album, which included a fine version of Seeger's "Turn! Turn! Turn!," had a clear (if overlooked) influence on the folk-rock he pioneered with the Byrds a couple years later. —*Richie Unterberger*

Judy Collins' Concert / 1964 / Elektra ✦✦✦
On this live set recorded at Town Hall in New York in 1964, Collins stirs up the audience with a rich mixture of traditional and contemporary covers, including Billy Ed Wheeler's "Coal Tattoo" and Paxton's "Ramblin' Boy." —*Richard Meyer*

○ **5th Album** / 1965 / Elektra ✦✦✦✦
Collins took a major stride forward with this fine, consistent album, tailoring both her material and arrangements to reflect contemporary changes shaking folk and folk-rock. Features stellar interpretations of songs by several major '60s songwriters (Dylan, Eric Andersen, Phil Ochs, Gordon Lightfoot, Malvina Reynolds, Richard Farina), and first-rate accompaniment by some of the day's finest folk and folk-rock musicians, including Eric Weissberg, Bill Lee, Danny Kalb, John Sebastian, and Richard Farina (although no drums are present). —*Richie Unterberger*

○ **In My Life** / 1966 / Elektra ✦✦✦✦
Collins, who by this point has moved from the acoustic renderings of traditional folk ballads to more extensive instrumentation and the work of contemporary folk writers, takes another step here, turning to tasteful string arrangements by Joshua Rifkin and adding theater music from *Threepenny Opera* and *Marat/Sade* to the Bob Dylan covers. She also starts covering Leonard Cohen ("Suzanne," "Dress Rehearsal Rag"). —*William Ruhlmann*

Wildflowers / 1967 / Elektra ✦✦✦
Passionate and filled with memorable passages. Includes her hit "Both Sides Now" and her first major original composition "Since You Asked." Leonard Cohen's "Priests" has not appeared elsewhere. —*Bruce Eder and William Ruhlmann*

Who Knows Where the Time Goes / 1968 / Elektra ✦✦✦
Rock and country leanings are found on this album featuring guitarists James Burton and Stephen Stills. Includes the hit "Someday Soon" and Collins's own brilliant "My Father." —*William Ruhlmann*

○ **Recollections** / 1969 / Elektra ✦✦✦✦
Collins sings "Tomorrow Is a Long Time," "Early Mornin' Rain" and "Winter Sky." This is a best-of compilation. —*Richard Meyer*

Whales & Nightingales / 1970 / Elektra ✦✦✦

Living / 1971 / Elektra ✦✦✦

● **Colors of the Day: Best of Judy Collins** / 1972 / Elektra ✦✦✦✦
The biggest hits of her early career, well chosen. —*Bruce Eder*

True Stories and Other Dreams / 1973 / Elektra ✦✦✦
Collins at her most political, saluting Che Guevara, among others. Elaborately produced and well sung. —*Bruce Eder*

Judith / 1975 / Elektra ✦✦✦
A soaring collection of songs from the Depression, '70s Broadway ("Send in the Clowns"), and modern C&W. —*Bruce Eder & William Ruhlmann*

Bread and Roses / 1976 / Elektra

☆ **So Early in the Spring . . .** / 1977 / Elektra ✦✦✦✦✦
So Early in the Spring, the First 15 Years. Double-album best-of covering the years 1961 to 1976; the place to start and also some of the best singing in contemporary folk music. —*William Ruhlmann*

Hard Times for Lovers / 1979 / Elektra

Most Beautiful Songs of / 1979 / Elektra

○ **Fires of Eden** / 1990 / CBS ✦✦✦✦
A graceful, personal, and finely crafted work that crosses between art song and folk music. —*Bruce Eder*

Live at Newport / 1994 / Vanguard ✦✦✦
A 13-song compilation of material recorded at the 1959, 1963, 1964, and 1966 Newport Folk Festivals; it would have been nice if they'd been able to document what year each song was recorded. In any case, it does reflect Collins's artistic growth during this period, from an interpreter of strictly traditional fare to more contemporary material by Bob Dylan, Richard Farina, and others. Highlights include her versions of "Turn, Turn, Turn," "Blowin' In The Wind," "Hey, Nelly Nelly," "Get Together," "Hard Lovin' Loser," and "The Great Silkie," which has the same melody the Byrds used for "I Come And Stand At Every Door" on their *Fifth Dimension* album. All of the songs are previously unreleased, except "The Greenland Whale Fisheries," a duet with Theodore Bikel; on some tracks, Collins is accompanied on upright bass by Bill Lee, and on second guitar by Steve Mandell or Eric Weissberg. With good sound, a nice if not essential addition to the Collins catalog. —*Richie Unterberger*

Larry Collins

b. 1944
Rockabilly

With his sister Lorrie, guitarist and singer Larry Collins was part of the brother-sister duo the Collins Kids, who cut some of the best rockabilly of the 1950s. Playing a doubleneck guitar, Larry Collins was a brilliant guitar prodigy, and took time to cut some hot instrumental duets with mentor Joe Maphis, a country guitarist twenty years his senior. The Collins Kids broke up when Lorrie married, and Larry cut some undistinguished diluted rockabilly-pop before drifting back, like so many early rockabilly singers, to country music. As a songwriter, his most famous credit is co-penning "Delta Dawn." —*Richie Unterberger*

Rockin Rollin / 1983 / Bear Family ✦✦✦
In the mid-'50s, country picker Joe Maphis and early rockabilly guitarist Larry Collins (one-half of the Collins Kids) were both members of the *Town Hall Party*, a barn dance show broadcast from the Los Angeles area. This LP gathers odds and ends from both artists, starting with the four songs the guitarists recorded together on a rare 1957 EP. Both Maphis and Collins (then just 13) smoke on their respective double-necked axes on these instru-

mentals, which bisect country boogie and rockabilly. Side One closes with four instrumentals Maphis cut on his own between 1955 and 1957; more country-oriented than his sides with Collins, they are respectable country boogie, the standout being "Flying Fingers," which features some of the most blindingly fast guitar work recorded in any genre. The eight songs on Side Two are entirely given over to solo numbers that Collins cut in the early '60s, a few previously unreleased, a few from rare Columbia singles. Mostly soft rockabilly pop with unexceptional lead vocals (by Collins) and female harmonies, it totally lacks the fire of Larry's '50s work; even the two concluding instrumentals are insubstantial, one a Duane Eddy ripoff, one slightly anticipating the sound of surf music. Side One has some pretty hot country-cum-rockabilly, but the flip weighs this production down into "collectors only" territory. —*Richie Unterberger*

Phil Collins

b. Jan. 31, 1951, London, England
Pop/Rock
Phil Collins's ascent to the status of one of the most successful pop and adult-contemporary singers of the '80s and beyond was probably as much of a surprise to him as it was to many others. Balding and diminutive, Collins was almost 30 years old when his first solo single, "In the Air Tonight," became a #2 hit in his native U.K. (the song was a Top 20 hit in the U.S.). Between 1984 and 1990, Collins had a string of 13 straight U.S. Top Ten hits.

Long before any of that happened, however, Collins was a child actor/singer who appeared as the Artful Dodger in the London production of *Oliver!* in 1964. (He also has a cameo in *A Hard Day's Night*, among other films.) He got his first break in music at the end of his teens, when he was chosen to be a replacement drummer in the British art-rock band Genesis in 1970. (Collins maintained a separate jazz career with the band Brand X, as well.) Genesis was fronted by singer Peter Gabriel. They had achieved a moderate level of success in the U.K. and the U.S., with elaborate concept albums, before Gabriel abruptly left in 1974. Genesis auditioned 400 singers without success, then decided to let Collins have a go.

The result was a gradual simplifying of Genesis' sound and an increasing focus on Collins's expressive, throaty voice. *And Then There Were Three...* went gold in 1978, and *Duke* was even more successful. Collins made his debut solo album *Face Value* in 1981, which turned out to be a bigger hit than any Genesis album. It concentrated on Collins's voice, often in stark, haunting contexts such as the piano-and-drum dirge "In the Air Tonight," which sounded like something from John Lennon's debut solo album, *John Lennon/Plastic Ono Band.*

Collins's continuing solo work has not meant the end of Genesis. In fact, he balances group and solo careers with enormous success. In 1992, Genesis released *We Can't Dance* and began an extensive tour, and it seems likely that Collins's double success will continue. —*William Ruhlmann*

○ **Face Value** / 1981 / Atlantic ✦✦✦✦
Collins proves himself a passionate singer (and distinctive drummer) with a gift for both deeply felt ballads and snarling rockers. His debut album transformed him from the frontman of Genesis to a solo star who happened to be in Genesis too. Contains "In the Air Tonight" and "I Missed Again." —*William Ruhlmann*

Hello, I Must Be Going / 1982 / Atlantic ✦✦✦
As his hit cover of "You Can't Hurry Love" demonstrates, Collins began to inject his highly melodic pop songwriting with more soul and R&B influences on his second solo album. While some of the material was successful, much of it showed that he was still coming to grips with how to incorporate R&B techniques into his style; in retrospect, *Hello, I Must Be Going* laid the groundwork for his breakthrough album, *No Jacket Required*. —*Stephen Thomas Erlewine*

● **No Jacket Required** / 1985 / Atlantic ✦✦✦✦
From ballads like the #1 "One More Night" to uptempo funk like the #1 "Sussudio," another tour de force in what was by now one of the most identifiable styles in pop music. The 1985 Grammy winner for Album of the Year. —*William Ruhlmann*

But Seriously / 1989 / Atlantic ✦✦✦
This chart-topping fourth album contains "Another Day in Paradise," "I Wish It Would Rain Down," "Do You Remember?," and "Something Happened on the Way to Heaven," all Top Five hits. —*William Ruhlmann*

Serious Hits ... Live!/ 1990 / Atlantic ✦✦
Phil Collins runs through his hits with surprising energy on *Serious Hits... Live!,* yet the record remains an artifact for dedicated fans, not casual listeners. —*Stephen Thomas Erlewine*

Both Sides / 1993 / Atlantic ✦✦✦
Returning to the stark, melancholy sounds of *Face Value*, Phil Collins delivers a personal album with *Both Sides* in more than one sense of the word. Collins played all of the instruments on *Both Sides* and the songs are troubled, haunting tales of regret, romance, and society. Although Collins has not lost his flair for melody, the songs are edgier than most of his recent work. Some fans might not go along with Collins on this dark ride, but *Both Sides* is one of his most artistically satisfying albums. —*Stephen Thomas Erlewine*

Color Me Badd

Group, Urban
This New York-based group formed as high school students in Oklahoma City. They proved adept at both churning dance tunes and sincere, if sometimes lyrically awkward, ballads. Their 1991 debut, *C.M.B.,* was a huge hit, selling over three million copies and reaching number three on the album chart. They scored two number one pop hits with "All 4 Love" and "I Adore (Mi Amor)," with "I Wanna Sex You Up" reaching number two and both "Slow Motion" and "Thinkin' Back" making the Top 20. The LP was on the charts for 77 weeks. Their second full release, *Time & Chance,* was released in late 1993; it fell off the charts quickly. —*Ron Wynn*

● **C.M.B.** / 1991 / Giant ✦✦✦
Their debut album includes the hit "I Wanna Sex You Up," which is innovative from an instrumental perspective. —*Bil Carpenter*

Young, Gifted & Badd / 1992 / Giant ✦✦

Time & Chance / 1993 / Giant ✦✦✦

Colour Field

Group, Alternative Pop/Rock
An English group led by Terry Hall, formerly of the Specials and Fun Boy Three, Colourfield released a series of pop albums between 1985 and 1989. Hall co-wrote "Our Lips Are Sealed" with Jane Wiedlin of the Go-Go's. —*Kenneth M. Cassidy*

● **Virgins & Philistines** / 1985 / Chrysalis ✦✦✦✦
A good mix of folk and rock comes from this band led by Terry Hall (ex-Specials, Fun Boy Three). Hall is an interesting if somewhat gloomy writer. —*Kenneth M. Cassidy*

The Colour Field / 1986 / Chrysalis ✦✦✦

Deception / 1987 / Chrysalis ✦✦✦

Ray Columbus and The Invaders

Group, Pop/Rock
One of the best New Zealand groups of the '60s, and the first to successfully react to the changes wrought by the British Invasion. Starting out as a fairly accomplished outfit in the mold of Cliff Richard and the Shadows, though rawer, the group hit the top of the charts in both New Zealand and Australia with "She's a Mod" in 1964. A cover of an obscure British beat single by the equally obscure Senators, it took obvious inspiration from "She Loves You" with its yeah-yeah chorus, but it was a strong harmony rocker that was one of the biggest singles of the '60s in Australasia. Although their biggest hit was quite Beatlesque, most of the group's repertoire (much of it self-penned) was in a decidedly more pronounced R&B direction. The Invaders would have most likely ground ashore had they actually made a determined effort to invade the U.S. or U.K. markets, but they were a decent outfit that stood way above most other Kiwi acts in 1964. The group managed a few more New Zealand hits, but couldn't crack Australia in as big a way again, before splitting in 1966. Ray Columbus actually tried to crack the States as a solo artist for a year or two, recording the collectable psychedelic "Kick Me" single with a California group, the Art Collection. —*Richie Unterberger*

● **Anthology** / 1981 / Epic ✦✦✦✦
16-track compilation includes all of their key singles: "She's A Mod" and the N.Z. hits "C'Mon And Swim," "Now You Shake," "Till We Kissed," and "Yo Yo." According to the liner notes, the Yardbirds' management considered having the band cover the moody, bluesy "Now You Shake" as a single in early 1966. Also includes a live version of "She's A Mod" and their 1963 take on "I Wanna Be

Your Man," which was one of the first overseas Beatle covers. — *Richie Unterberger*

Shawn Colvin

b. Jan. 10, 1958
Singer-Songwriter

Singer and songwriter Shawn Colvin was born in South Dakota and has lived in London (Ontario) and in Carbondale, IL, where she graduated from high school. She dropped out of Southern Illinois University to join a hard rock group, later playing with the Dixie Diesels, a Western swing band in Austin. After a sojourn in San Francisco, she moved to New York City in 1980 and gradually worked her way up the folk circuit, also appearing in such off-Broadway shows as *Pump Boys and Dinettes, Diamond Studs,* and *Lie of the Mind.* Her work appeared in *The Fast Folk Musical Magazine,* and she got her first real break in 1987, singing backup on a Suzanne Vega tour. Recruited by Vega's management, she signed to Columbia Records in 1988 and released her debut album, *Steady On,* in 1989. — *William Ruhlmann*

● **Steady On** / Oct. 1989 / Columbia ✦✦✦✦
Sharp production, surprising arrangements, and Shawn Colvin's alternately breathy and ringing vocals give the best possible forum to her astute reflections on life and love. The album's roots go into rock and country as well as folk. — *William Ruhlmann*

Fat City / Oct. 1992 / Columbia ✦✦✦
Produced by bassist Larry Klein, Colvin's second album is looser than the first with a great cover of Warren Zevon's "Tenderness on the Block," and her own "Another Round of Blues." Various singles have been issued with non-CD tracks. — *Richard Meyer*

Cover Girl / Aug. 23, 1994 / Columbia ✦✦✦
When Shawn Colvin first turned up playing Greenwich Village folk clubs in the early 1980s, she used to perform a variety of cover songs, often taking rock recordings and re-imagining them for her girl-with-guitar format. When Colvin began recording in the late '80s, however, she concentrated on her own original material. *Cover Girl* brings her interpretive abilities back into focus. Songs like the Police's "Every Little Thing [He] Does Is Magic" and Talking Heads' "This Must Be The Place (Naive Melody)" are the most radical reworkings here, but not the best, perhaps because they depend on their original productions. Colvin is more successful in choosing classic but not well-known songs already in the folk idiom—Greg Brown's "One Cool Remove," Willis Alan Ramsey's "Satin Sheets," and Rolly Solley's "Killing The Blues." A fan from the old Village days can only lament that she didn't choose to include her version of Dire Straits' "Romeo And Juliet." — *William Ruhlmann*

Combustible Edison

Group, Alternative Pop/Rock

What to do if you've been slogging away in the rock underground for a decade to slight critical acclaim without making any appreciable artistic or commercial headway? In the mold of David Johansen/Buster Poindexter, the band Christmas decided to retool themselves as lounge lizards. On their debut album, the Providence, Rhode Island group plays cocktail jazz, exotica, torch ballads, and B-movie spy/guitar themes. To complete their transformation, the band has adopted ice cream-colored tuxedoes in their live performances; one member of the group has adopted the pseudonym "The Millionaire," and former Christmas singer Liz Cox calls herself "Miss Lily Banquette" as she croons languid jazz-pop tunes. — *Richie Unterberger*

I, Swinger / Mar. 1994 / Sub Pop ✦✦✦
Combustible Edison's goofy and irreverent mix owes a lot more to the music of the 1950s and early '60s than to new wave; they sound as if they've stumbled on a treasure trove of dime-store albums in their aunt's attic and can't quite get over the experience. Their immaculate recreation of late-'50s/early-'60s cheese is fun … to a point. Treading the line between self-conscious irony and the ridiculous, it probably won't prove to be more durable than those old Christmas (the band, not the season) albums. But then, nobody could have predicted the Martin Denny revival, either. — *Richie Unterberger*

Come

Group, Alternative Pop/Rock

Former Live Skull member Thalia Zadek leads Come, a slow, yet frighteningly intense, post-punk blues band. Although their music is based in the blues, it is in an ugly, mutated form with squalling guitars and lethargic vocals. Come's 1992 debut, *Eleven:Eleven,* was harrowing and powerful; it received a sizable amount of critical acclaim, particularly in Britain. — *Stephen Thomas Erlewine*

Eleven : Eleven / 1992 / Matador ✦✦✦
Come's debut album, *Eleven : Eleven* is a thoroughly impressive fusion of punk, Stones-style rock and roll, and blues. All the songs are slow and churning, ground out by post-punk/blues guitars with weary, scarred vocals that grab your attention. *Eleven : Eleven* is genuinely harrowing and disturbing, easy to admire but not necessarily easy to listen to; for those who make an attempt to meet Come halfway, *Eleven : Eleven* rewards their effort in full. (The CD includes a superb version of the Rolling Stones' "I Got the Blues.") — *Stephen Thomas Erlewine*

● **Don't Ask Don't Tell** / 1994 / Matador ✦✦✦✦
Come open up the dense, heavy psycho-blues of their debut album *Eleven:Eleven* without losing their harrowing intensity on their impressive follow-up *Don't Ask Don't Tell.* Even with the more expansive production, Thalia Zadek's wrenching vocals and bruising guitar aren't any easier to take; there's no way her brutal songs could be casual listening. However, that doesn't mean it isn't rewarding listening. — *Stephen Thomas Erlewine*

Commander Cody

Group, Country-Rock

Commander Cody & His Lost Planet Airmen were equally adept at stripped-down basic rock & roll, R&B, and gritty country-rock. Commander Cody's country-rock rocked harder than the Eagles or Poco—essentially, the group was a bar band. Much like English pub rock bands like Brinsley Schwarz and Ducks Deluxe, Commander Cody resisted the over-blown and bombastic trends of early-'70s rock, preferring a basic, no-frills approach. Commander Cody & His Lost Planet Airmen never had the impact of the British pub rockers, yet their straightforward energy gave their records a distinguishing drive; they could play country, western swing, rockabilly, and R&B, and it all sounded convincing.

The group originally formed in 1967 in Ann Arbor, MI; Commander Cody (born George Frayne, IV; piano), John Tichy (lead guitar), Steve Schwartz (guitar), Don Davis (bass), Don Bolton (aka the West Virginia Creeper; pedal steel guitar), and Ralph Mallory (drums) formed the original lineup. When the group relocated to San Francisco the following year, only Frayne, Bolton, and Tichy made the move; the group's membership included Billy C. Farlowe (vocals, harp), Andy Stein (fiddle, saxophone), guitarist Billy Kirchen, bassist "Buffalo" Bruce Barlow, and drummer Lance Dickerson at the time of their 1971 debut album, *Lost in the Ozone.* The following year the group scored a fluke Top Ten hit with "Hot Rod Lincoln," taken from their second album, *Hot Licks, Cold Steel and Trucker's Favourites.* Commander Cody was never able to capitalize on the single's success, partially because their albums never completely captured their live energy. They continued to release albums until Tichy left the band in 1976. Commander Cody released his first solo album, *Midnight Man,* in 1977, then he re-formed the group as the Commander Cody Band. The group recorded three albums between 1977 and 1980. — *Stephen Thomas Erlewine*

Lost in the Ozone / 1971 / MCA ✦✦✦
Their remarkable debut album went from gospel to the Andrews Sisters to Eddie Cochran, and was a hoot from top to bottom. — *Jeff Tamarkin*

Hot Licks, Cold Steel & Truckers' Favorites / 1972 / MCA ✦✦✦

Country Casanova / 1973 / MCA ✦✦✦
A studio effort, this didn't reflect their live prowess but was still a good time. — *Jeff Tamarkin*

○ **Live Deep in the Heart of Texas** / 1974 / Paramount ✦✦✦✦

Commander Cody & His Lost Planet Airmen / 1975 / Warner Brothers ✦✦

Tales from the Ozone / 1975 / Warner Brothers ✦

We've Got a Live One Here / 1976 / Warner Brothers ✦✦

Midnight Man [Cody Solo] / 1977 / Arista

Rock 'n Roll Again / 1977 / Arista ✦✦

Flying Dreams / 1978 / Arista

Lose It Tonight / 1980 / Line

Let's Rock / 1986 / Blind Pig ✦✦

Very Best of ... Plus / 1986 / See For Miles ✦✦✦
More tracks than their US best-of and costlier, but this collection provides a grand overview of one of the saving graces of '70s rock. (Import) —*Jeff Tamarkin*

Returns from Outer Space / 1987 / Edsel

Sleazy Roadside Stories / 1988 / Relix ✦✦
Cut live in 1973, the Cody septet cooks on this Texas jam. —*Jeff Tamarkin*

Aces High / 1990 / Relix ✦✦✦
The Commander and his current band in various late-'80s recordings. Not as sharp as the original stuff, but still fairly deranged. —*Jeff Tamarkin*

● **Too Much Fun: Best of Commander Cody** / 1990 / MCA ✦✦✦✦
Not only could they play the hell out of their instruments, but C.C. & His Lost Planet Airmen were a virtual melting pot of American music—country, R&B, rockabilly, Western swing. And always too much fun. —*Jeff Tamarkin*

Deep in the Heart of Texas / 1991 / MCA ✦✦✦
The Airmen were at their best onstage, and this 1973 set caught them at the peak of their game. —*Jeff Tamarkin*

The Commodores

Group, Soul, Funk, Pop
The Commodores got their start by being the opening act for the Jackson 5. Largely through the prolific lyrics of Lionel Richie, the band broke out nationally in the mid '70s. Their initial success was mainly with dance tunes, but in the late '70s Richie began turning out love ballads such as "Easy," "Still," and "Three Times a Lady." His departure for solo stardom crippled the band, but not before they had one more huge success with "Nightshift" in 1985. Today the group plays state fairs and oldies venues. Members included Lionel Richie (replaced in 1984 by J. D. Nicholas), Thomas McClary (who left in 1984), Ronald LaPread, William King, Walter Orange, and Milan Williams. —*Rick A. Bueche*

○ **Machine Gun** / Jul. 1974 / Motown ✦✦✦✦
The album that introduced the Alabama-based Commodores. It's still in the Southern funk genre, with slithering beats, exploding synthesizer lines, and great arrangements and riffs. The title tune was played at parties all over the country, and the follow-up single "The Zoo (Human Zoo)" was great as well. —*Ron Wynn*

○ **Caught in the Act** / Feb. 1975 / Motown ✦✦✦✦
A spectacular second album by the Southern funksters, arguably their best overall. It had both powerhouse uptempo tunes and hit ballads, and the group's energy, spontaneity, and drive were still building. It's also the studio album that comes closest to duplicating the quality of their live performances during that era. —*Ron Wynn*

Movin' on / Oct. 1975 / Motown ✦✦
The second great album the Commodores released in 1975. They hadn't yet made the crossover connection, but were among the top R&B, funk, and disco draws of the mid- and late '70s, churning out both excellent uptempo party tunes and good, if sometimes maudlin, ballads. —*Ron Wynn*

Hot on the Tracks / Jun. 1976 / Motown ✦✦✦
Another great mid-'70s album, although it had more punch with the slower cuts than the uptempo ones. The Commodores were now established stars, and they continued to dominate both the R&B charts and the touring circuit. They were also close to making the move to pop, which came with their next album. "Just To Be Close To You" and "Sweet Love" are two of their best ballads, and they've held up much better than some songs that sold far more copies. —*Ron Wynn*

Zoom / 1977 / Motown ✦✦✦

Commodores / Mar. 1977 / Motown ✦✦✦
The Commodores' early years were spent on the Southern funk circuit, where their energetic, catchy tunes and keyboard-oriented funk made them both a college and a radio staple. They scored seminal hits with "Brick House" and "Slippery When Wet," although it became apparent quite early that lead vocalist Lionel Richie also had a bright future as a solo balladeer, with such tunes as "Easy" signaling his future on adult contemporary and Quiet Storm/urban contemporary radio. This collection highlights early uptempo and ballad hits. —*Ron Wynn*

Live! / Oct. 1977 / Motown ✦✦✦
Live R&B albums seldom sell well outside their market, but this one certainly did. It made the Top 10 on the pop charts and was a testament to how hot the Commodores were in the late '70s. It's a good release, and conveys some of the excitement of their stage shows. The company, in its wisdom, currently doesn't have it available on CD. —*Ron Wynn*

Natural High / May 1978 / Motown ✦✦✦
Another huge hit album for the Commodores, still riding the crest of both R&B and pop waves in the late '70s. "Three Times A Lady" was the group and Lionel Richie's first number one pop hit and their fifth R&B chart topper. It began an unfortunate obsession with sappy themes that eventually would redirect both his and the group's focus away from the great funk and uptempo dance tunes that had initially made them famous. —*Ron Wynn*

○ **Greatest Hits** / Oct. 1978 / Motown ✦✦✦✦
A very representative anthology gathering the Commodores' prime uptempo and ballad material. It shows that they were quite versatile in their heyday, capable of being humorous or romantic with equal ease. They never topped "Brick House" for explosiveness, while "Easy" was arguably their finest slow song. The Commodores dominated the R&B charts in the late '70s and early '80s, earning four number one and three other Top 10 R&B singles, plus two number ones and three other Top 10 pop hits. —*Ron Wynn*

Midnight Magic / Jul. 1979 / Motown ✦✦✦
The Commodores closed out the '70s in great style, dominating the pop and R&B charts with this album. It reached the number three spot, and the song "Still" was their second number one pop hit and yet another R&B winner, one of three smash songs they had on those charts in 1979. Richie was then balancing things between being their lead singer, penning sappy love songs, and doing songwriting for others. —*Ron Wynn*

Heroes / Jun. 1980 / Motown ✦✦✦
The Commodores opened the '80s in great shape. This album once more put them in the pop and R&B Top 10, and they scored more big hits with the title track, "Old Fashion Love," and even some quasi-gospel, "Jesus Is Love." This was one of their last powerhouse albums, but no one suspected at the time that they wouldn't dominate the '80s as they had the '70s. —*Ron Wynn*

Love Songs / 1981 / Motown ✦✦✦

In the Pocket / Jun. 1981 / Motown ✦✦✦
The last album with both Lionel Richie and Thomas McClary, and their final statement as the group that had been the South's most commercially potent since the early '70s. Neither "Oh No" nor "Lady, You Bring Me Up" topped either chart though both were huge R&B and pop hits. Richie had been making noises about leaving and would be gone within a year, followed by McClary a year later. —*Ron Wynn*

● **All the Greatest Hits** / Nov. 1982 / Motown ✦✦✦✦
While there are many Commodores greatest hits packages available, *All the Greatest Hits* offers most of their biggest hits, making it ideal for the casual fan. —*Stephen Thomas Erlewine*

○ **Commodores Anthology** / Apr. 1983 / Motown ✦✦✦✦
The anthology series was Motown's best greatest hits line until they issued the two boxed-set *Hitsville* packages in '93. They compiled not just the hits but the important singles onto the Commodores anthology, and the sound quality was better than on either *Command Performances* or the two-in-one line. —*Ron Wynn*

Commodores 13 / Sep. 1983 / Motown ✦✦✦
This wasn't a memorable release for the Commodores, and in some ways was a painful one for longtime fans. The group was in disarray with Richie gone and McClary about to go, and didn't get good songs, production, or arrangements. Their playing and singing wasn't any better either, and the results were quite forgettable. —*Ron Wynn*

Compact Command Performances / 1984 / Motown ✦✦✦
14 songs covering the biggest Commodores material with Lionel Richie. It's a good single-disc package, although most of Motown's CDs in the late '70s and early '80s had very uneven sound. There's also a Commodores greatest hits album that came out in 1981 and a 14 greatest hits album that came out overseas a year after this one. —*Ron Wynn*

All the Great Love Songs / 1985 / Motown ✦✦✦
Included are all of Lionel Richie's love songs. —*Rick A. Bueche*

Nightshift / Jan. 1985 / Motown ✦✦✦
The Commodores made one final stab at regaining R&B glory when Lionel Richie and producer/arranger James Anthony Carmichael both left in the mid-'80s. J.D. Nicholas became their lead singer, and Dennis Lambert assumed production duties. They rebounded temporarily when "Nightshift" leaped out of an otherwise ordinary album to become a Grammy-winning R&B and pop smash. It stayed atop the R&B charts for a month and peaked at #3 pop. Unfortunately, it was also the end for Thomas McClary, who left the group once the album had run its course. It was their next-to-last hit and basically the end for the band, although they continued for a couple more years. —*Ron Wynn*

Composer: Great Love Songs Written by Lionel Richie / Jul. 1985 / Motown ✦✦
If you enjoyed the run of sentimental weepers that Lionel Richie made famous in the '70s and early '80s, they're all here on this anthology. "Easy" and "Zoom" weren't bad slow tunes, but then Richie began to overdo the maudlin lyrics and the results became predictable and pretentious, and he certainly didn't have any problems landing chart hits for a long run. It's interesting in the '90s to rediscover these songs and have the fact that Richie wasn't really a classic (or memorable) ballad vocalist decisively reaffirmed. —*Ron Wynn*

United / Oct. 1986 / Polydor ✦✦✦
The Commodores scored one last chart hit with this album, and it serves as their goodbye, even though they issued another album after it. "Nightshift" had already come and gone, and the song "Goin' to the Bank" was a far cry from the glory days, although it did go all the way to the number two position. The reconfigured lineup simply couldn't match the original band's intensity, versatility, or distinctiveness. —*Ron Wynn*

Rock Solid / 1988 / Polydor ✦✦✦
Things were pretty bleak for the Commodores by the time this late '80s set was issued. Lionel Richie and Thomas McClary were both long gone, and the recovery/momentum they'd generated from the single "Nightshift" had also dissipated. They didn't regenerate much interest through this one, mainly due to limp material and less than arresting vocals. —*Ron Wynn*

Compton's Most Wanted

Group, Rap
Interracial quartet who walk the same turf as 'hood mates N.W.A. and Ice Cube with similarly tough, swaggering grooves. Intricate production makes their best work stand out among the gangsta-rap pack. —*John Floyd*

It's a Compton Thang / 1990 / Orpheus ✦✦✦
More tense, defiant, and obscene gangsta commentary. (Also available in a censored version.) —*Ron Wynn*

○ **Straight Checkn 'em** / 1991 / Orpheus ✦✦✦✦
Compton's Most Wanted's second CD got more sullen, combative and sexist in its language and themes than the debut. Where "Duck Sick" and "It's A Compton Thang" at least had some swagger and a taste of humor to offset the posturing, "Can I Kill It?" and "Compton's Lynchin'" were more surly, while "Gangsta Shot Out" and "Growin' Up In The Hood" were fatalistic and "Raised In Compton" despairing rather than informative. Only "Mike T's Funky Scratch" sounded a lighter note, and that was due to its being a declaration of rap prowess rather than street superiority. —*Ron Wynn*

● **Music to Driveby** / Jun. 1992 / Orpheus ✦✦✦✦
The third and commercially most successful album by Los Angeles rappers Compton's Most Wanted contained such terse narratives as "Dead Men Tell No Lies" and "Hit The Floor." If there hadn't been such an abundance of similar material in the early '90s, these tales might have triggered intense scrutiny and analysis. Instead, the most common response is that M.C. Eiht's raps aren't quite as loose or expressive as those of Spice-1, Ice Cube, Nas or many others telling identical stories. —*Ron Wynn*

Con Funk Shun

Group, Funk
This Memphis-based group was among the premier funk and soul ensembles of the '70s and '80s. Lead vocalist and guitarist Michael Cooper and drummer Louis McCall formed Project Soul as California high school students. They became Con Funk Shun in 1972, when Cooper and McCall moved to Memphis. They added

bassist/keyboardist Cedric Martin, keyboardist Danny Thomas, saxophonist Karl Fuller, keyboardist/vocalist Melvin Carter, and saxophonist/percussionist Zebulon Paulle Harrel. Con Funk Shun began as an in-house band at Stax, backing various acts, while recording their own material. Some of this was later issued on Fretone, a Memphis label. They signed with Mercury in 1976, and had a long run with them until the mid-'80s. "Ffun" topped the R&B charts in 1977, and through 1986, Con Funk Shun had eight Top Ten R&B hits overall on Mercury, although they never scored a single Top Ten or Top 20 pop hit. Their sound and appeal was completely tailored to funk, soul, and later urban contemporary audiences. They did danceable ditties, comic pieces, and competent love songs and ballads, especially "Baby, I'm Hooked (Right into Your Love)." Deodato and Leon Ware were two of their producers at various times. Cooper became a star in his own right after Con Funk Shun disbanded in the late '80s. —*Ron Wynn*

● **The Best of Con Funk Shun** / 1992 / PolyGram ✦✦✦✦
This is a solid compilation of Con Funk Shun's influential late '70s and early '80s funk. —*AMG*

Concrete Blonde

Group, Alternative Pop/Rock
Built around the throaty lead vocals and spare pulsing bass work of Johnette Napolitano and the crunchy guitar execution of former Sparks member Jim Mankey, Concrete Blonde occasionally displayed some of the raw fire of the early Pretenders. Their more recent efforts have enjoyed some significant alternative-radio exposure.

After releasing two records that gained some attention in the press and college radio, Concrete Blonde released 1990's *Bloodletting*, which was significantly more accomplished than their previous work. Although the album received good reviews, it took a couple of months for the record to start climbing the charts, thanks to the surprise hit single, "Joey." Despite two impressive follow-ups, they were never able to match the success of *Bloodletting*. After the modest commercial success of 1993's *Mexican Moon*, the group quietly disbanded. Napolitano reappeared with a new band called Pretty Twisted in 1995. —*Rick Clark*

Concrete Blonde / 1987 / IRS ✦✦
With the addition of a new drummer, Jim Mankey and Johnette Napolitano's Dream 6 became Concrete Blonde, but the changes did nothing to bring musical focus to the partnership. When this debut album was released, IRS Records emphasized the track "Still In Hollywood," financing a video and promoting it to radio. The song borders on punk rock, as Mankey repeats the same riff over and over and Napolitano spits out the angry lyric like Exene Cervenka (except, of course, she is careful to stay on key). But the song's message is confused: Most aspiring stars try to *get to* Hollywood, no? Even more confused is the multiplicity of musical styles that demonstrated that Concrete Blonde's main characteristic was ambition, not talent. Napolitano didn't much care if she became the next Chrissie Hynde or the next Pat Benatar, as long as she became the next *something.* —*William Ruhlmann*

Free / Apr. 1989 / IRS ✦✦
This sophomore effort is an improvement over their slapdash-sounding debut, with punchier arrangements supporting Johnette Napolitano's throaty dramatics. Highlights include the forceful "God Is a Bullet" and the poppish "Happy Birthday." —*Rick Clark*

● **Bloodletting** / May 1990 / IRS ✦✦✦✦
Moodier than *Free,* it includes "Joey," the band's first hit. —*Rick Clark*

Walking in London / Mar. 1992 / IRS ✦✦✦
Continuing in a vein similar to that on *Bloodletting,* it contains "Ghost of a Texas Ladies' Man." —*Rick Clark*

Mexican Moon / Oct. 19, 1993 / IRS ✦✦✦
Reportedly their farewell album, *Mexican Moon* finds Johnette Napolitano exploring her fascination with Mexican and Hispanic culture, resulting in an album that can be varied and fascinating and, at times, ponderous and tedious. Even with the slight indulgences, the album is among Concrete Blonde's best and is a fine, elegant way to wrap up their rich career. —*Stephen Thomas Erlewine*

Arthur Conley

b. Jan. 4, 1946, Atlanta, GA
Soul

A protégé of Otis Redding and, like Redding, a musical disciple of Sam Cooke, Conley co-wrote (with Redding) and sang "Sweet Soul Music," one of the true anthems of the '60s. Based on Cooke's "Yeah, Man," the record was sweet and hot at the same time, with a readily identifiable horn intro and lyrics that immortalized the soul stars of the day. Conley, although signed to Atco, toured overseas with the Stax/Volt Revue and later joined the Soul Clan with Atlantic label-mates Wilson Pickett, Solomon Burke, Don Covay, Ben E. King, and Joe Tex. He has lived in France for a number of years. —*Christine Ohlman*

● **Sweet Soul Music** / 1967 / Atco ◆◆◆◆
The title track is a real killer! Conley sounds young but assured, and the Otis Redding production is solid throughout. Includes "Let Nothing Separate Us" and "I Can't Stop." —*Christine Ohlman*

○ **More Sweet Soul** / 1969 / Atco ◆◆◆◆
This wasn't an album in the classic sense but a collection of singles, as were many soul LPs in the '60s. But Conley's exuberance and spirit are so infectious that it overcomes the fact that much of this is second-level soul at best and clichéd filler at worst. —*Ron Wynn*

The Soul Clan / Atco ◆◆◆
Conley with Covay, Burke, King, and Tex. Includes "Soul Meeting" with Bobby Womack on guitar. —*Christine Ohlman*

The Connells

Group, Alternative Pop/Rock
This North Carolinian rock quartet, led by brothers Mike and David Connell, has a jangly guitar sound. Their debut album, *Darker Days*, was released on Black Park in 1986. —*William Ruhlmann*

Darker Days / 1986 / TVT ◆◆◆
The band's first album suffers from lack of direction and inexperience. They show a great deal of promise but fail to distinguish themselves much from the hordes of other Southern folk-pop bands. —*Chris Woodstra*

● **Boylan Heights** / 1987 / TVT ◆◆◆◆
Their second album shows a great improvement over its predecessor. With help from producer Mitch Easter, the band effectively combines Southern jangly guitars with Celtic influences. One of the more distinctive college rock albums of the '80s. —*Chris Woodstra*

Fun & Games / 1989 / TVT ◆◆
Fun & Games marks a slight dip in quality. The songwriting is still top notch but, at times covered by their new heavier sound. —*Chris Woodstra*

○ **One Simple Word** / 1990 / TVT ◆◆◆◆
In the course of four albums, the Connells have evolved their own style within the jangling guitar-rock sound so prevalent in alternative bands of the '80s. Mainly it's been a matter of writing more distinctive songs and having them sung by guitarist George Huntley so they sink in. This is their first album to cross over from the category of "promising" to the beginnings of a fulfillment of that promise. —*William Ruhlmann*

Ring / 1994 / TVT ◆◆◆

Consolidated

Group, Techno-Pop/Dance, Alternative Pop/Rock
With their confrontational, stridently politically correct dance music, Consolidated became a small sensation in the early '90s. Not only was the group openly socialist, but the group incorporated all of their messages into their music; their records are unapologetically political and sometimes antagonizingly so. And it was the politics, not their hip-hop/industrial mix, that earned them attention. After a couple of quiet years, Consolidated re-emerged with a new album in the summer of 1994. —*Stephen Thomas Erlewine*

The Myth of Rock / 1985 / Nettwerk ◆◆◆

● **Friendly Fascism** / Nettwerk ◆◆◆◆
While Consolidated's political consciousness is commendable, they have apparently spent more time on their lyrics than music. Too frequently, the rhythms are nothing but relentlessly simple, headache-inducing pounding, not subtly textured assaults like Public Enemy. But when their backing tracks do match the fury of their lyrics, the results are quite powerful; too bad that only happens on a third of the album. —*Stephen Thomas Erlewine*

Play More Music / 1992 / Nettwerk ◆◆◆
Consolidated play industrial music for those who want more than a night of dancing in blissed-out ecstasy, in a hip-hop style that can appeal to rockers who don't normally like rap/hip-hop. This group presents a serious challenge to those who look the other way hoping that social ills will just disappear on their own. They are, therefore, important. You won't agree with everything you hear on *Play More Music*, but you will be provoked to think about why. —*Roch Parisien*

Business of Punishment / 1994 / PolyGram ◆◆◆

The Contours

Group, Soul, R&B, Motown
One of Berry Gordy's earliest discoveries at Motown, the hard-rocking Contours cultivated a new generation of fans when their "Do You Love Me" was featured in the 1987 hit movie *Dirty Dancing*. Led by gravelly-voiced Billy Gordon, the quintet scored an R&B chart-topper in 1962 with the rollicking "Do You Love Me" on Gordy's label, then smoothed out their sound just a bit for the mid-'60s soul classics "First I Look at the Purse" and "Just a Little Misunderstanding." Dennis Edwards, who joined the group well after "Do You Love Me," was recruited to replace David Ruffin as lead of the Temptations in 1968. —*Bill Dahl*

● **Do You Love Me** / 1962 / Motown ◆◆◆◆
This rough-edged, early-'60s Motown group deserves more than its enduring one-hit status for "Do You Love Me?" —*Bill Dahl*

Ry Cooder

b. Mar. 15, 1947, Los Angeles, CA
Blues Rock, Country-Rock, Ethnic Fusion, Roots-Rock
Since his self-titled 1970 debut, Ry Cooder has drawn deeply from rich North American colloquial music and pre-rock genres like Tex-Mex, Hawaiian, gospel, vaudeville, country, ragtime, Caribbean, and blues. His passion for dignifying these sounds, plus his earthy emotive guitar technique and choice of stellar sidemen (particularly drummer Jim Keltner), have made for some great albums, especially 1974's *Paradise and Lunch*. Cooder has a knack for inventive song selections, juxtaposing old material with new in a fashion that sometimes illuminates both. It is his understanding of these earlier musical genres that informs Cooder's rock sensibilities with a unique sound, particularly on slide guitar. Besides his solo efforts, Cooder has worked with the Rolling Stones, Taj Mahal, Gordon Lightfoot, Captain Beefheart, John Hiatt, Randy Newman, and Little Feat, and produced the solid R&B Rounder debut of his backup singers Bobby King and Terry Evans. Cooder has also done extensive soundtrack work (some with Jim Dickinson) for movies, some of which are *The Long Riders, Goin' South, Southern Comfort, Crossroads,* and *Paris, Texas*. More recently, Cooder has worked with John Hiatt, Jim Keltner, and Nick Lowe under the moniker of Little Village. —*Rick Clark*

Ry Cooder / 1970 / Reprise ◆◆◆
His debut serves as a neat prototype, with its Sleepy John Estes and Woody Guthrie covers. It also introduces a most talented musician in its leader. But it's still a prototype; the best was yet to come. —*Jeff Tamarkin*

○ **Into the Purple Valley** / Jan. 1971 / Reprise ◆◆◆◆
Cooder perfects his snaky slide guitar technique and introduces exotic ethnic elements on his second album. An American traditional music celebration. —*Jeff Tamarkin*

● **Boomer's Story** / Feb. 1972 / Reprise ◆◆◆◆
Largely laidback and bluesy, this album features a number of paeans to an America long lost. —*Jeff Tamarkin*

● **Paradise & Lunch** / 1974 / Reprise ◆◆◆◆
Working with an intriguing collection of veteran musicians, the master musician and archivist turns in a stunning set of timeless remakes and new compositions. —*Jeff Tamarkin*

○ **Chicken Skin Music** / 1976 / Reprise ◆◆◆◆
Hawaiian traditional music meets Leadbelly and Ben E. King on Cooder's gospelization of rock & soul. —*Jeff Tamarkin*

Show Time / 1976 / Reprise ◆◆◆
Recorded live in 1976, Cooder cooks and struts his stuff on this grand tour of his abilities. The great Flaco Jimenez is on accordion. —*Jeff Tamarkin*

Jazz / 1978 / Reprise ◆◆◆
A tribute to Dixieland, with a stopover at the blues hotel. Joseph Byrd's arrangements on tunes by Bix Beiderbecke, Joseph Spence, et al., are inspired. —*Jeff Tamarkin*

Bop Till You Drop / 1979 / Reprise ◆◆
Cooder has disowned this early digital recording, and he's right; not only is the sound dry, but the music is rather lifeless. Although it has some bright moments, it's not his best. —*Jeff Tamarkin*

Long Riders / 1980 / Reprise ◆◆◆

Borderline / 1980 / Reprise ◆
Ry is offtrack here on covers of old rock & roll songs. The warmth of the earlier recordings is missing, and his already indistinguished vocals are hopeless here. —*Jeff Tamarkin*

The Slide Area / 1982 / Reprise ◆◆
Cooder is forgetting what he does best; his forays into soul and old rock & roll are interesting but not mouth-watering. Over-produced. —*Jeff Tamarkin*

Ry Cooder Live / 1982 / WEA ◆◆◆

Get Rhythm / 1987 / Reprise ◆◆◆
Self-producing this time, Cooder gets the old rock & roll right. Johnny Cash and Chuck Berry are pretty darn funky. Cooder can still play slide guitar like no one else. —*Jeff Tamarkin*

○ **Music by Ry Cooder** / 1995 / Reprise ◆◆◆◆
Since he's a limited vocalist with erratic songwriting skills, one could justifiably argue that the soundtrack medium is the best vehicle for Cooder's talents, allowing him to construct eclectic, chiefly instrumental pieces drawing upon all sorts of roots music and ethnic flavors (often, but not always, employing his excellent blues and slide guitar). This two-CD, 34-song compilation gathers excerpts from eleven of the soundtracks he worked on between 1980 and 1993 (three of the cuts, from the 1981 film *Southern Comfort*, are previously unreleased). As few listeners (even Cooder fans) are dedicated enough to go to the trouble of finding all of his individual soundtracks, this is a good distillation of many of his more notable contributions in this idiom, although it inevitably leaves out some fine moments. Still, it's well-programmed and evocative, often conjuring visions of ghostly landscapes and funky border towns. —*Richie Unterberger*

Sam Cooke (Sam Cook)

b. Jan. 22, 1931, Chicago, **d.** Dec. 11, 1964, Los Angeles, CA
Soul, R&B
Gospel, R&B, and pop singer/songwriter Sam Cooke enjoyed two careers of nearly equal duration and success, first in the religious, and later in the secular music fields. The son of a minister, Cooke began singing in gospel groups at an early age, and from 1950, when he was only 20, was the lead singer of the Soul Stirrers. His flexible tenor made him a stand-out star in gospel and an obvious candidate for secular stardom. He moved to performing non-religious material in 1956, which caused a split from the group and its record label, Specialty, as well as an ongoing controversy among music fans, just as his concentration on pop-oriented material over grittier R&B led some to question his intentions. Nevertheless, his pop successes were overwhelming. Keen Records released "You Send Me" (October 1957), Cooke's recording of a song written by his brother, and saw it top the charts. "I'll Come Running Back to You" (December 1957), released by Specialty in the wake of Cooke's success, topped the R&B charts. Cooke's hits of 1959 included "Everybody Likes to Cha Cha Cha" and "Only Sixteen," the former with a songwriting credit to "Barbara Campbell" (actually Cooke, Herb Alpert, and Lou Adler), the latter written by Cooke.

Cooke signed to RCA Victor Records on his 25th birthday in January 1960, though Keen scored one more hit with his "Wonderful World" (another "Barbara Campbell" composition). He then had his biggest hit since "You Send Me" with his own "Chain Gang" (July 1960). In 1962 and 1963, he released nine consecutive R&B Top Ten hits, including the chart-topping "Twistin' the Night Away" (January 1962) and "Another Saturday Night" (April 1963), both of which also made the pop Top Ten, and both of which were his compositions. (The notion that Cooke was some sort of puppet of White pop entrepreneurs was always belied by his songwriting as well as his acute business acumen, including the founding of his own record label, Sar.) Cooke's last giant single was the two-sided "Shake"/"A Change Is Gonna Come" (December 1964), released the same month as his untimely death.

Cooke proved a major influence on R&B singers like Otis Redding, rock singers like Rod Stewart, and pop singers like Art Garfunkel, all of whom covered his songs. His work has remained perennially popular, and in 1985 the release of the album *Sam*

Cooke Live at the Harlem Square Club, 1963, which showed him performing an uninhibited, soulful set before an African-American audience, further fueled the debate about him as a crossover artist. However that debate is resolved (if it ever is), Cooke's influence on popular music will remain profound, as many of his songs have long-since become standards. — *William Ruhlmann*

Encore / 1958 / Keen ◆◆◆
Superb vocals by the great Sam Cooke, with some sophisticated pop, wonderful ballads, and a few intense wailers that recall his great gospel material. This, and almost every other magnificent release by Sam Cooke from the '50s and early '60s, has been out of print for years. —*Ron Wynn*

Sam Cooke / Feb. 1958 / Diamond ◆◆◆
Sam Cooke was still honing his new style in the late '50s, and producers were constantly scraping off the rough, animated edges off his sound and steering him toward sweet, light songs. He did these superbly, but as this album shows, he remained at heart a gospel and soul man his entire career. —*Ron Wynn*

Hit Kit / 1959 / Keen ◆◆◆
Some smoking uptempo tunes, wailing ballads, and even interesting pop and novelty material. Sam Cooke was at his commercial peak in the early '60s, and if you ever find this anywhere, grab it quickly. It's well worth having. Someday, a major label will wise up and either put all Cooke's Keen, RCA, and Sar material back in print or put out a huge boxed set package. —*Ron Wynn*

Tribute to the Lady—Billie Holiday / 1959 / Keen ◆◆◆
An album that's seldom been seen and disappeared almost as quickly as it was released. Sam Cooke turned these songs inside out with twisting, awesome interpretations. It was one of the few times he was able to break out of the light pop/teen idol bag in a studio and pour his heart into great lyrics and numbers. —*Ron Wynn*

Cooke's Tour / 1960 / RCA ◆◆◆
Like so many other great Sam Cooke dates from the '50s and '60s, this has long been out of print. It's similar in style, performance quality, and sensibility to the *Live At The Copa* set, except that the sound isn't as good, since no major label has seen fit to remaster or fix it as the Copa tape was when it was discovered. —*Ron Wynn*

I Thank God / 1960 / Keen ◆◆◆
Cooke would periodically try to return to gospel, and there was plenty of vault material that Specialty would license or try to sneak past the watchful gospel audience. Those who feel that Cooke's gospel was his finest material will have that opinion validated, although it's doubtful that many people have ever heard or seen this, as it's been long out of print. —*Ron Wynn*

Swing Low / 1960 / RCA ◆◆◆
Compelling, beautifully sung material from the great Sam Cooke. Virtually every album he ever did, especially every great one, has long been out of print. Thankfully, people who grew up in the '50s and '60s got a chance to hear these before they got yanked. —*Ron Wynn*

○ **My Kind of Blues** / 1961 / RCA ◆◆◆◆
There's been talk that someone (RCA or ABKCO) is going to return the sessions from which this was garnered into print someday. I sure hope that's true, because anyone only familiar with either Cooke's gospel or pop has missed the boat if they haven't heard him doing the blues. It's a totally different experience, though also a transcendent one. —*Ron Wynn*

Twistin' the Night Away / Apr. 1962 / RCA Victor ◆◆◆
The title track was one of Cooke's most anthemic pop hits, while there are some other strong ballads scattered amidst the usual pop fluff and teen material. His voice sounded more soulful and dynamic, and he performed each number with equal intensity regardless of its quality. —*Ron Wynn*

Mr. Soul / Feb. 1963 / RCA ◆◆◆
A fantastic album and a collector's dream. Sam Cooke was arguably the greatest vocalist in the pop world during the early '60s, and he showed on this one both remarkable versatility and incredible pure talent. Vocalists from Marvin Gaye to Smokey Robinson have raved about Sam Cooke's '60s songs, while Otis Redding, Rod Stewart, and a legion of others used this and other '60s releases as a textbook. —*Ron Wynn*

○ **Night Beat** / Aug. 1963 / ABKCO ◆◆◆◆
Intense, spiraling uptempo numbers, gripping ballads, and simply marvelous performances by a legend who sadly wouldn't be around much longer. Originally released in August 1963, *Night*

Beat [RCA 2709] was reissued on CD on June 6, 1995 [ABKCO 1124]. —*Ron Wynn*

○ **Gospel Soul of Sam Cooke & The Soul Stirrers, Vol. 1** / 1964 / Specialty ◆◆◆◆
His pre-pop/soul days. The style is there, but turned toward God. —*Bruce Eder*

Sam Cooke at the Copa / Oct. 1964 / ABKCO ◆◆◆
Cooke's classic live album is a mixed bag—he was playing to a White supper-club audience and altered his sound accordingly, favoring ballads and folk songs over most of his celebrated classic soul numbers. The voice is there, and the style, but he never does cut loose completely, and the backing band is too clean. —*Bruce Eder*

○ **Gospel Soul of Sam Cooke & The Soul Stirrers, Vol. 2** / 1965 / Specialty ◆◆◆◆
More devotional music with the Soul Stirrers, at times overpowering. Includes "Wonderful," "I'm So Glad (Trouble Don't Last Always)" and "Farther Along." —*Bruce Eder*

Shake / Jan. 1965 / RCA ◆◆◆
The title track ranked among Cooke's finest uptempo pop tunes, a fine arrangement elevated into a great song through his vocal acrobatics. The album itself isn't among his greatest, although his voice has its usual hypnotic qualities. The uneven material and pop production brought it down a bit, but it's hard not to recommend any Sam Cooke album from the '60s, regardless of content. —*Ron Wynn*

☆ **Live at the Harlem Square Club** / Jun. 1985 / RCA ◆◆◆◆◆
Long believed lost, this live album—rejected for release in 1963 by Cooke's managers, who wanted to broaden his appeal to White listeners—captures Cooke playing to a largely Black crowd, and it couldn't be more different from his *At the Copa* live album. A hot, sweaty performance, with Cooke and a proper band luxuriating in his most soulful material in its most wrenching and impassioned form. —*Bruce Eder*

★ **The Man & His Music** / Feb. 1986 / RCA ◆◆◆◆◆
The ultimate Sam Cooke collection, and really the only one worth owning, covering his post-1957 career from his pop music breakthrough ("You Send Me") to his final impassioned soul statement, "A Change Is Gonna Come" (which is included in its seldom-heard uncut version). Few stones are left unturned, the sound is clean and sharp, and the tragedy of Cooke's early death is recalled with each play of this collection. —*Bruce Eder*

○ **His Earliest Recordings** / 1991 / Specialty ◆◆◆
A superb collection of 25 of the earliest recordings made by Sam Cooke, including "Touch the Hem of His Garment." —*Stephen Thomas Erlewine*

BOOK

◆◆◆◆◆ **You Send Me: The Life & Times of Sam Cooke**, by Daniel Wolff with S.R. Crain, Clifton White, & G. David (William Morrow & Co., 1995). A major work, following Cooke's music and life from his gospel days with the Soul Stirrers through his crossover to pop and soul success in the late '50s and early '60s. With lots of input from Crain (the founder of the Soul Stirrers) and White (Cooke's guitarist and arranger), Wolff unravels a lot of the ingredients to Cooke's success and influence: his gospel-soaked background, his determination to win over a broad audience, his aspirations as a producer and songwriter set on maintaining control of his art and product. Wolff interviewed dozens of friends and associates, such as Bumps Blackwell (the A&R man who was instrumental in convincing Cooke to record pop), Lou Rawls, and his latter-day manager, Allen Klein, for their inside takes on the immensely talented, and personally troubled, singer. Wolff deftly connects Cooke's success to the increasing influence of Black music and African-American pride on mainstream American culture, discusses all of his recordings in detail (including his little-heralded efforts as an enterpreneur and mentor for gospel/soul talent with his SAR label), and probes the mysterious, unexplained circumstances behind his violent, scandalous death in 1964. —*Richie Unterberger*

The Cookies

Group, Girl-Group
The forerunner of Ray Charles's Raeletts, the original Cookies were Margie Hendrix, Ethel "Earl-Jean" McCrea, and Pat Lyles. They recorded for Lamp (Aladdin) in 1954 and Jesse Stone

brought them to Atlantic in 1955. They recorded three sessions under the Cookies banner and scored a Top Ten R&B hit with "In Paradise" in 1956. The group also backed Joe Turner and Chuck Willis on their hit recordings in 1956 before being absorbed into the Charles empire and becoming The Raeletts. Almost six years later, a new trio emerged as The Cookies on Dimension, with only McRea from the first group in its lineup. They did backup vocals for Neil Sedaka, Little Eva, and Carole King, while scoring two Top Ten R&B, one Top Ten, and one Top 20 pop hit in 1962 and 1963. "Don't Say Nothin' Bad (About My Baby)" was their biggest, peaking at number three R&B (number seven pop) in 1963. "Girls Grow up Faster than Boys" was their final chart outing in November 1963. —*Ron Wynn*

● **Don't Say Nothin' Bad About the Cookies** / 1991 / Teenager ◆◆◆◆
This import compilation includes the hits "Chains" and "Don't Say Nothin' Bad About My Baby," and is jammed with obscure Goffin-King tunes. The problem is, most of them aren't anywhere nearly as good as the hits the team penned for the Cookies or other girl groups. It does include the obscure gem "Girls Grow Up Faster Than Boys," a sassy cut that's as good as the two hits. —*Richie Unterberger*

Coolio

Rap
Coolio (born Artis Ivey) is a native of Compton, CA, yet his variation of the P-Funk-inspired rap of Dr. Dre is calmer, less violent and funnier. Recorded with his DJ Bryan "Wino" Dobbs, Coolio's 1994 debut album, *It Takes a Thief* was a smash hit, selling over a million records and featuring the number three single, "Fantastic Voyage." —*Stephen Thomas Erlewine*

○ **It Takes a Thief** / 1994 / Tommy Boy ◆◆◆◆
Just when it looked like rap would completely succumb to the violent hyperbole and mean-spirited "realness" of gangsta rap, new blood entered the scene in 1994 to nudge the genre back toward friendlier turf. That new blood included Nas, Craig Mack, and Coolio, whose *It Takes a Thief* starts with the easy-rolling funk of Lakeside's "Fantastic Voyage" and goes from there, infusing rap with a much-needed sense of humor and the promise of good times. While Coolio is no simp—"County Line" playfully explores the hassles of welfare, while some tracks dip into gangsta territory—he manages to make rap a cool, inclusive journey. —*Eddie Huffman*

Alice Cooper

b. Feb. 4, 1948, Detroit, MI
Hard Rock, Heavy Metal
Originally, there was a band called Alice Cooper led by a singer named Vincent Damon Furnier. Under his direction, Alice Cooper pioneered a grandly theatrical and violent brand of heavy metal that was designed to shock. Drawing equally from horror movies, vaudeville, and Black Sabbath, Led Zeppelin, and the Stooges, the group created a stage show that featured electric chairs, guillotines, fake blood, and huge boa constrictors, all coordinated by the heavily made-up Furnier. By that time, Furnier had adopted the name for his adrogynous onstage personality. While the visuals were extremely important to the group's impact, the band's music was nearly as distinctive. Driven by raw, simple riffs and melodies that derived from '60s guitar-pop as well as showtunes, it was rock & roll at its most basic and catchy, even when the band ventured into psychedelia and art-rock. After the original group broke up and Furnier began a solo career as Alice Cooper, his actual music lost most of its theatrical flourishes, becoming straightforward heavy metal, yet his stage show retained all of the trademark props that made him the king of shock rock.

Furnier formed his first group, the Earwigs, as an Arizona teenager in the early '60s. Changing the band's name to the Spiders in 1965, the group was eventually called the Nazz (not to be confused with Todd Rundgrens' band of the same name). The Spiders and the Nazz both released local singles that were moderately popular. After discovering there was another band called the Nazz in 1968, the group changed its name to Alice Cooper. According to band legend, the name came to Furnier during a ouija board session, where he was told he was the reincarnation of a 17th century witch of the same name.

Comprised of vocalist Furnier—who would soon begin calling

himself Alice Cooper—guitarist Mike Bruce, guitarist Glen Buxton, bassist Dennis Dunaway, and drummer Neal Smith, the group moved to California in 1968. In California, the group met Frank Zappa and his manager Shep Gordon, who signed Alice Cooper to their new label Straight Records. Alice Cooper released their first album, *Pretties for You*, in 1969. *Pretties for You* captured the band in their formative stages, where they sounded more like a garage rock group than a heavy metal outfit, yet it was a small hit, peaking at number 193 on the U.S. charts. *Easy Action* followed early in 1970, yet it failed to chart. The group's reputation in Los Angeles was slowly shrinking, so the band moved to Detroit, the city where Vincent Furnier was born. For the next year, the group refined their bizarre stage show. Late in 1970, the group signed with Warner Brothers and began recording their third album with producer Bob Ezrin.

With Ezrin's assistance, Alice Cooper developed their classic heavy metal crunch on 1971's *Love It to Death*, which featured the number 21 hit single "Eighteen"; the album peaked at number 35 and went gold. The success enabled the group to develop a more impressive, elaborate live show, which made them highly popular concert attractions across the U.S. and eventually the U.K. *Killer*, released late in 1971, was another gold album, featuring the minor hit single "Under My Wheels."

Released in the summer of 1972, *School's Out* was Alice Cooper's commercial breakthrough, reaching number two in the charts and selling over a million copies. The title song became a hit single, cracking the Top Ten in the U.S. and hitting number one in the U.K. *Billion Dollar Babies*, released the following year, was the group's biggest hit, reaching number one in both America and Britain; the album's first single, "No More Mr. Nice Guy," became a Top Ten hit in Britain, peaking at number 25 in the U.S. *Muscle of Love* appeared late in 1973, yet it failed to capitalize on the success of *Billion Dollar Babies*. The album failed to go platinum and it peaked at number ten in America and a disappointing number 34 in Britain.

After *Muscle of Love* Furnier fired the rest of Alice Cooper, taking the name as his own official name; the rest of the band released one unsuccessful album under the name Billion Dollar Babies. Cooper hired guitarists Dick Wagner and Steve Hunter, bassist Prakash John, keyboardist Joseph Chrowski, and drummer Penti Glan as a backing band; all of the musicians had previously supported Lou Reed and both Wagner and Hunter made uncredited contributions to several Alice Cooper albums. In the fall of 1974, a compilation of Alice Cooper's five Warner albums, entitled *Alice Cooper's Greatest Hits*, became a Top Ten hit. Alice Cooper followed it with his first solo album, *Welcome to My Nightmare*, in the spring of 1975. *Welcome to My Nightmare* wasn't a great departure from his previous group and it became Top Ten hit in America, launching the hit acoustic ballad "Only Women Bleed." Released in 1976, *Alice Cooper Goes to Hell* was another hit, going gold in the U.S.

After *Alice Cooper Goes to Hell*, Cooper's career began to slip, partially due to changing trends and partially due to his alcoholism. Cooper entered rehabilitation in 1978, writing an album called *From the Inside* (1978) about his treatment with Bernie Taupin, Elton John's lyricist. During the early '80s, Cooper continued to release albums and tour, yet he was no longer as popular as he was during his early-'70s heyday.

Cooper made a successful comeback in the late '80s, sparked by his appearances in horror films and a series of pop-metal bands that paid musical homage to his classic early records. *Constrictor*, released in 1986, began his comeback but it was 1989's *Trash* that returned Cooper to the spotlight. Produced by the proven hitmaker Desmond Child, *Trash* featured guest appearances by Jon Bon Jovi, Richie Sambora, Kip Winger, and most of Aerosmith; the record became a Top Ten hit in Britain and peaked at number 20 in the U.S., going platinum. "Poison," a ballad featured on the album, became Cooper's first Top Ten since 1977. Since the release of *Trash*, he has continued to star in the occasional film, tour, and record. His latest album, *The Last Temptation of Alice Cooper*, featured contributions from members of Soundgarden. *—Stephen Thomas Erlewine*

Pretties for You / 1969 / Bizarre ✦✦✦

Alice Cooper's debut album had none of his legendary grotesque hard rock; instead, *Pretties for You* was an earnest, but flawed, stab at psychedelia which occasionally catches fire. *—Stephen Thomas Erlewine*

Easy Action / 1970 / Bizarre ✦✦✦

○ **Love It to Death** / Jan. 1971 / Warner Brothers ✦✦✦✦
The best studio album by Cooper features the classic "Eighteen." Other standouts: "Caught in a Dream," "Long Way to Go," and "Black Juju." *—Rick Clark*

○ **Killer** / Feb. 1971 / Warner Brothers ✦✦✦✦
Some of the more theatrical pieces undermine the album's strengths. It contains the hits "Under My Wheels" and "Be My Lover." *—Rick Clark*

○ **School's Out** / 1972 / Warner Brothers ✦✦✦✦
The title cut of one of Cooper's best albums was a Top Ten hit. *—Rick Clark*

○ **Billion Dollar Babies** / 1973 / Warner Brothers ✦✦✦✦
It's not as mindbendingly outrageous or hard-rocking as *School's Out*, *Killer*, or *Love It to Death*, but with its conscious attempt at pop crossover ("No More Mr. Nice Guy" and "Elected"), *Billion Dollar Babies* is just as perverse as the earlier records, as well as being more consistent than any of his other proper albums. Sometimes selling out just a little bit might not be such a bad thing. *—Stephen Thomas Erlewine*

Muscle of Love / 1973 / Metal Blade ✦✦

★ **Greatest Hits** / 1974 / Warner Brothers ✦✦✦✦✦
While he made many classic hard-rock singles, Alice Cooper never made a consistently enjoyable album, making *Greatest Hits* a necessity. It might not cover *all* of his best tracks, but everything you need to know is here. *—Stephen Thomas Erlewine*

○ **Welcome to My Nightmare** / 1975 / Atlantic ✦✦✦✦
Cooper's solo-artist debut contains "Only Women Bleed." It's the best of his solo efforts. *—Rick Clark*

Alice Cooper Goes to Hell / 1976 / Warner Brothers ✦✦

Lace & Whiskey / May 1977 / Metal Blade ✦

Alice Cooper Show / Dec. 1977 / Warner Brothers ✦✦

From the Inside / 1978 / Metal Blade ✦✦

Flush the Fashion / 1980 / Warner Brothers ✦

Special Forces / 1981 / Warner Brothers ✦

Zipper Catches Skin / 1982 / Warner Brothers ✦✦

Dada / 1982 / Warner Brothers ✦✦

Constrictor / 1986 / MCA ✦✦✦

Raise Your Fist and Yell / 1987 / MCA ✦✦✦

Prince of Darkness / 1989 / MCA ✦✦

○ **Trash** / 1989 / Epic ✦✦✦✦

Hey Stoopid / May 1991 / Epic ✦✦✦

Last Temptation / 1994 / Sony ✦✦✦

Les Cooper

b. Mar. 15, 1931, Norfolk, VA
R&B, Rock & Roll
A longtime denizen of New York's doo-wop scene, Cooper's only major hit was the 1962 instrumental "Wiggle Wobble." The Norfolk, VA, native was a member of the Empires and the Whirlers, and managed the Charts, before signing with Danny Robinson's Everlast imprint and cutting a vocal called "Dig Yourself" with his band, the Soul Rockers. Ironically, it was the flip side (a pounding instrumental called "Wiggle Wobble," featuring prominent King Curtis-styled tenor sax by ex-Charts lead singer Joe Grier) that gave Cooper his only chart ride. Follow-up efforts included the similar "Let's Do the Boston Monkey" for Enjoy. *—Bill Dahl*

● **Wiggle Wobble: Golden Classics** / 1963 / Collectables ✦✦✦✦
Cooper's soulful vocals and Joe Grier's yakety-sax combine for some scorching early-'60s R&B. *—Bill Dahl*

Michael Cooper

b. C. 1, England
Soul, R&B
Michael Cooper enjoyed quick success as a solo vocalist after the demise of Con Funk Shun. His LP *Love Is Such a Funny Game* yielded a huge hit in "To Prove My Love," which made it to number three on the R&B charts. His follow-up release, *Just What I Like*, in 1989, was also moderately successful. His most recent release, *Get Closer*, included appearances from jazz musicians Roy Ayers, Charles Tolliver, and Buddy Montgomery and was issued in 1992. *—Ron Wynn*

● **Love Is Such a Funny Game** / 1987 / Reprise ✦✦✦✦
Michael Cooper departed from Con Funk Shun in the late '80s and signed with Warner Bros. He landed a Top 10 hit single on his debut album, the song "To Prove My Love." Although he often sounded like a mirror image of Cameo's Larry Blackmon (who had built his delivery on an amalgam of Sly Stone, the Ohio Players, and Bar-Kays vocals), he did quite well with this release. —*Ron Wynn*

Just What I Like / 1989 / Reprise ✦✦✦
The second solo album for longtime Con Funk Shun lead vocalist Michael Cooper, and it didn't prove quite as successful as its predecessor. Cooper's vocal similarity to Cameo's Larry Blackmon again surfaced, but that didn't hurt things as much as a lack of standout tracks, lyrics, or arrangements. The production mixed urban contemporary and hip-hop-tinged tracks. —*Ron Wynn*

Get Closer / Sep. 15, 1992 / Reprise ✦✦

Cop Shoot Cop

Group, Alternative Pop/Rock

Starting with their intentionally confrontational (and controversial) name, New York City's Cop Shoot Cop are descended from the darker impulses of the early-'80s "no-wave" movement that produced noisy, disagreeable, anti-social, but often very intriguing bands such as Mars, DNA, and Teenage Jesus and the Jerks. As with those combos, the Cops eschew the impulse of pop altogether, preferring a rumbling, clattering, deafening, metallic sound that focuses on the band's two-bass, no-guitar attack. The song narratives tend toward simplistic doom-and-gloom observations that "life sucks, man"—a point they often belabor. But when this bummer-rock clicks, it's oddly compelling, if slightly intimidating stuff, crammed to the gills with the standard litany of contemporary urban angst: anomie, alienation, and boredom. Add to this the odd meters, the yelling (he never describes it as singing) by low-end bassist Natz, and forays into pure noise, and what you end up with is an anti-rock style that, despite its repetitive tendencies, is furious, frightening and powerful. Oddly, despite the inherent anti-commerciality of their music, as well as the band's disdain for corporate-controlled major labels, they did land a contract with Interscope Records (home of Helmet), part of the Atlantic family. Despite the more accessible sound of their recent records, Cop Shoot Cop remain an acquired taste, even for those who like their rock edgy and uncompromising. —*John Dougan*

Consumer Revolt / 1990 / Big Cat ✦✦

Suck City / 1992 / Interscope ✦✦✦

● **Ask Questions Later** / 1993 / Interscope ✦✦✦✦
Opening with the relentlessly stomping "Surprise, Surprise," this is Cop Shoot Cop at their harsh, semi-tuneful best (how is "Everybody Loves You When You're Dead" for a title?). Natz's monotone yelling could use a little variation, but all in all, this is a rampaging record that is undone only by its misanthropic singlemindedness. What makes *Ask Questions Later* the most successful Cop Shoot Cop record is that it takes more chances, and is as a result more rewarding. Not for the fainthearted, this record, despite its minor concessions to accessibility, is still a snarling, feral chunk of postmodern rock noise. —*John Dougan*

Release / 1994 / Interscope ✦✦✦
It's certainly not the case that each Cop Shoot Cop record gets more accessible; perhaps it's more the case that they grow on you with each release. *Release* doesn't have the highs of *Ask Questions Later,* but the rolling, tumbling sonic assault is still confrontational and better understood by those predisposed to their sound. Never ones to be accused of selling out, the Cops are in fine form here and have proven to the cynics that despite their antipathy toward the rock marketplace, they can peacefully coexist with the major-label powers that be and produce a consistently interesting body of work. —*John Dougan*

Julian Cope

b. Oct. 21, 1957, Deri, Mid Glamorgan, Wales
Alternative Pop/Rock

By the time Julian Cope called it quits with the Teardrop Explodes in 1982, he had already acquired something of a legendary status in English alternative pop, as a wildly creative oddball who fell somewhere between Syd Barrett and Jim Morrison. His solo albums blended '60s psychedelia, synth-pop, and garage rock into a wonderfully twisted stew, with his dry vocal delivery way up in the mix. Subject matter ranges from acid-tinged ruminations to unique manifestos on the state of the planet. Each of his efforts is worth seeking out, but *Peggy Suicide* is an ambitious project that consolidates Cope's many strengths to great effect. —*Rick Clark*

Fried / 1984 / Mercury ✦✦✦

World Shut Your Mouth / 1984 / Mercury ✦✦✦

Julian Cope / 1986 / Island ✦✦✦
This solo "mini-LP" contained five tracks and ran nearly 16 minutes. The first track was called "World Shut Your Mouth," but actually there had been no such song on the album of the same name, and this was an all-new recording. It revealed the solo Cope to be a straight-ahead rocker for the most part—"World" (which became Cope's first U.S. singles chart entry) was a guitar-driven anthem set to a martial beat, and Cope's cover of Pere Ubu's "Non Alignment Pact" fell just short of punk. Cope retained his punk anger in the lyrics, which included "Umpteenth Unnatural Blues," in which he expressed the desire for a violent death. Still, until that occurred, *Julian Cope* gave notice that its namesake had a claim to rock prominence. —*William Ruhlmann*

Saint Julian / Mar. 1987 / Island ✦✦✦
Former Teardrop Explodes leader Julian Cope adopted a harder, more direct rock style for his solo work, making it more accessible and bringing out the qualities of his commanding baritone. —*William Ruhlmann*

○ **My Nation Underground** / Oct. 1988 / Island ✦✦✦✦
Julian Cope's follow-up to *Saint Julian* is another hard-edged pop/rock collection, paced by its lead-off track, a medley of two 1965 hits, the Vogues' "Five O'Clock World" and Petula Clark's "I Know a Place," with Cope's apocalyptically altered lyrics—in his version, it's the missiles that blow, not the whistle. Cope follows this pessimistic vision throughout the album, but that doesn't keep him from making accessible music that drives home his message. —*William Ruhlmann*

Skellington / 1989 / CopeCo-Zippo ✦✦

Droolian / 1990 / MoFoCo-Zippo ✦✦✦

○ **Peggy Suicide** / Mar. 1991 / Island ✦✦✦✦
Peggy Suicide is Cope's idiosyncratic and complexly layered treatise on the state of the earth. Initially inspired by a vision that involved his own self-created mythological characters (Peggy Suicide as Mother Earth, Pollutio as destructive siren), Cope expands his cosmic tragedy beyond the larger political, social, and ecological issues with a healthy dose of mesmerizing psychedelic state-of-the-mind profiles. The unpolished production quality gives *Peggy Suicide* a more immediately believable delivery. Cope juxtaposes pure garage rock next to marimbas, loopy keyboard sounds, and loose-limbed percussion into a spellbinding tapestry. Among the many highlights are the ominous AIDS/death epic "Safesurfer" and "Drive, She Said," which is a trashy synthesis of Bowie's Velvet Underground sendups. —*Rick Clark*

● **Floored Genius: The Best of Julian Cope & the Teardrop Explodes 1979-1991** / Oct. 20, 1992 / Island ✦✦✦✦
A sprawling compilation that gives a good sense of the variety of Cope's career, even if it's a bit too scattered to be thoroughly listenable. —*Stephen Thomas Erlewine*

Jehovahkill / Dec. 8, 1992 / Island ✦✦
Idiot savant or fool on the hill? Eight albums on, *Jehovakill* does little to clarify the enigma. On first listen, you get the impression that Cope really has gone off the deep end this time. But patience with this 70-minute epic pays off. There is method to Cope's madness. Divided into three "phases", the disc makes an intriguing argument for looking to pre-Christian spirituality for a signpost out of our modern moral conundrums—even if music and lyrics deal with the theme rather more abstractly than the enclosed liner notes, photographs and poetry. While this disc is a fave of several music critics and Cope-ophiles, *Jehovakill* may be a bit of a sensory overload for many. The uninitiated might consider starting off with *Floored Genius*—a compilation of Cope's previous Teardrop and solo work. —*Roch Parisien*

Autogeddon / 1994 / American ✦✦
On *Autogeddon,* Julian Cope uses the automobile as a metaphor for his view of civilization in general, which he finds deplorable and inescapable. Listeners may be reminded of the solo albums of Syd Barrett, since Cope begins with his voice and acoustic guitar and adds electric instruments and percussion, often with the same uncertain tempos of Barrett's falling-apart arrangements. Jim Mor-

rison also comes to mind, especially on "Don't Call Me Mark Chapman," on which Cope eventually leaves music behind and just recites his lyrics as poetry. That poetry can be both obscure and threatening—it's not clear what he's talking about in the song, but maybe we don't really want to know. Few people work as hard at being self-indulgent as Julian Cope, and while he will part company with many fellow travelers on *Autogeddon*, it's hard to say whether that's because he's picked up speed or run out of gas. — *William Ruhlmann*

Cornells

Group, Surf

Whatever interest this L.A. surf combo generates stems from the fact that future Moby Grape guitarist Peter Lewis was a member. Composed mostly of the sons of Hollywood actors (guitarist Bob Linkletter's dad, Art, being the most famous of these), they cut an extremely obscure LP and several singles for the tiny Garex label. Their cover-dominated repertoire was of routine, if instrumentally competent, quality, and Lewis was the only member destined to make a mark on rock history. — *Richie Unterberger*

● **Surf Fever!** / 1995 / Sundazed ✦✦✦✦
CD reissue of their rare 1964 album (only 1,000 copies were pressed), with the addition of three bonus tracks from equally rare singles. Unexceptional, sax-driven instrumentals (save one vocal cut) that register fairly low on the surf voltage meter. — *Richie Unterberger*

Corrosion of Conformity

Group, Punk, Thrash, Heavy Metal

One of the first punk/metal fusion bands, Corrosion of Conformity (C.O.C. for short) were formed by guitarist Woody Weatherman in the early '80s. They built up a cult following with 1984's *Animosity*, but personnel shifts in 1986 led to their being dropped by their label. It took several years for a new lineup to come together, but 1991's *Blind* increased their audience by leaps and bounds. The band's current lineup features Weatherman, guitarist/vocalist Pepper Keenan, bassist Mike Dean, and drummer Reed Mullin. C.O.C. is known for its aggressive sound, intelligent political lyrics, and willingness to break away from both hardcore and metal conventions. — *Steve Huey*

● **Animosity** / 1985 / Combat ✦✦✦✦
Their most popular work to date, it has a lot of punk and hardcore overtones. Like Agnostic Front, they introduced a lot of metal listeners to punk and hardcore, and this was the album that did it. — *John Book*

Eye for an Eye / 1986 / Caroline ✦✦✦
One of their first recordings is very good. — *John Book*

Technocracy / 1987 / Combat ✦✦✦
There's a numb look at the realities of the world on this great set of music. — *John Book*

Blind / 1991 / Combat ✦✦✦
One of the best bands in hardcore turns around and moves into the thrash world with excellent results. Heavy like Metallica, it still captures that punk edge. — *John Book*

Deliverance / 1994 / Sony ✦✦

Elvis Costello

b. Aug. 25, 1955, Liverpool, England
Rock & Roll, Singer-Songwriter, New Wave, Pop/Rock

When Elvis Costello's first record was released in 1977, his bristling cynicism and anger linked him with the punk and new wave explosion. A cursory listen to *My Aim Is True* proves that the main connection that Costello had with the punks was his unbridled passion. He tore through rock's back pages taking whatever he wanted, as well as borrowing from country, Tin Pan Alley pop, reggae, and many other musical genres. Over his career, that musical eclecticism has distinguished Costello's records as much as his fiercely literate lyrics. Because he supports his lyrics with his richly diverse music, Costello is one of the most innovative, influential and best songwriters since Bob Dylan.

The son of British bandleader Ross McManus, Costello (b. Declan McManus) worked as a computer programmer during the early '70s, performing under the name D.P. Costello in various folk clubs. In 1976, he became the leader of country-rock group Flip City. During this time, he recorded several demo tapes of his original material with the intention of landing a record contract. A

copy of these tapes made its way to Jake Riviera, one of the heads of the fledgling independent record label Stiff. Riviera signed Costello to Stiff as a solo artist in 1977; the singer/songwriter adopted the name Elvis Costello at this time, taking his first name from Elvis Presley and his last name from his mother's maiden name.

With former Brinsley Schwarz bassist Nick Lowe producing, Costello began recording his debut album with the American band Clover providing support. "Less Than Zero," the first single released from these sessions, appeared in April of 1977. The single failed to chart, as did its follow-up, "Alison," which was released the following month. By the summer of 1977, Costello's permanent backing band had been assembled. Featuring bassist Bruce Thomas, keyboardist Steve Nieve, and drummer Pete Thomas (no relation to Bruce), the group was named the Attractions; they made their live debut in July of 1977.

My Aim Is True, his debut album, was released in the summer of 1977 to positive reviews; the album climbed to number 14 on the British charts but it wasn't released on his American label, Columbia Records, until later in the year. Along with Nick Lowe, Ian Dury, and Wreckless Eric, Costello participated in the *Stiffs Live* package tour in the fall. At the end of the year, Jake Riviera split from Stiff Records to form Radar Records, taking Costello and Lowe with him. Costello's last single for Stiff, the reggae-inflected "Watching the Detectives," became his first hit, climbing to number 15 at the end of the year.

This Year's Model, Costello's first album recorded with the Attractions, was released in the spring of 1978. A rawer, harder-rocking record than *My Aim Is True*, *This Year's Model* was also a bigger hit, reaching number four in Britain and number 30 In America. Released the following year, *Armed Forces* was a more ambitious and musically diverse album than either of his previous records. It was another hit, reaching number two in the U.K. and cracking the Top 10 in the U.S. "Oliver's Army," the first single from the album, also peaked at number two in Britain; none of the singles from *Armed Forces* charted in America. In the summer of 1979, he produced the self-titled debut album by the Specials, leaders of the ska-revival movement.

In February of 1980, the soul-influenced *Get Happy!!* was released; it was the first record on Riviera's new record label, F-Beat. *Get Happy!!* was another hit, peaking at number two in Britain and and number 11 in America. Later that year, two collections of B-sides, singles, and outtakes called *Taking Liberties* was released in America; in Britain, a similar album called *Ten Bloody Marys and Ten How's Your Fathers* appeared as a cassette-only release, complete with different tracks than the American version.

Costello and the Attractions released *Trust* in early 1981; it was his fifth album in a row produced by Nick Lowe. *Trust* debuted at number nine in the British charts and worked its way into the Top 30 in the U.S. During the spring of 1981, Costello and the Attractions began recording an album of country covers with famed Nashville producer Billy Sherrill, who recorded hit records for George Jones and Charlie Rich, among others. The resulting album, *Almost Blue*, was released at the end of the year to mixed reviews, although the single "A Good Year for the Roses" was a British Top 10 hit.

Costello's next album, *Imperial Bedroom* (1982), was an ambitious set of lushly arranged pop produced by Geoff Emerick, who engineered several of the Beatles' most acclaimed albums. *Imperial Bedroom* received some of his best reviews, yet it failed to yield a Top 40 hit in either England or America; the album did debut at number six in the U.K. For 1983's *Punch the Clock*, Costello worked with Clive Langer and Alan Winstanley, who were responsible for several of the biggest British hits in the early '80s. The collaboration proved commercially successful, as the album peaked at number three in the U.K. (number 24 in the U.S.) and the single "Everyday I Write the Book" cracked the Top 40 in both Britain and America. Costello tried to replicate the success of *Punch the Clock* with his next record, 1984's *Goodbye Cruel World*, but the album was a commercial and critical failure.

After the release of *Goodbye Cruel World*, Costello embarked on his first solo tour in the summer of 1984. Costello was relatively inactive during 1985, releasing only one new single ("The People's Limousine," a collaboration with singer/songwriter T-Bone Burnette released under the name the Coward Brothers) and producing *Rum, Sodomy and the Lash*, the second album by the punk-folk band the Pogues. Both projects were indications that he was moving toward a stripped-down, folky approach and 1986's

King of America confirmed that suspicion. Recorded without the Attractions and released under the name the Costello Show, *King of America* was essentially a country/folk album and it received the best reviews of any album he had recorded since *Imperial Bedroom*. It was followed at the end of the year by the edgy *Blood and Chocolate*, a reunion with the Attractions and producer Nick Lowe. Costello would not record another album with the Attractions until 1994.

During 1987, Costello negotiated a new worldwide record contract with Warner Brothers Records and began a songwriting collaboration with Paul McCartney. Two years later, he released *Spike*, the most musically diverse collection he had ever recorded. *Spike* featured the first appearance of songs written by Costello and McCartney, including the single "Veronica." "Veronica" became his biggest American hit, peaking at number 19. Two years later, he released *Mighty Like A Rose*, which echoed *Spike* in its diversity, yet it was a darker, more challenging record. In 1993, Costello collaborated with the Brodsky Quartet on *The Juliet Letters*, a song cycle that was the songwriter's first attempt at classical music; he also wrote an entire album for former Transvision Vamp singer Wendy James called *Now Ain't the Time for Your Tears*. That same year, Costello licensed the rights to his pre-1987 catalog (*My Aim Is True* to *Blood and Chocolate*) to Rykodisc in America.

Costello re-united with the Attractions to record the majority of 1994's *Brutal Youth*, the most straightforward and pop-oriented album he had recorded since *Goodbye Cruel World*. The Attractions backed Costello on a worldwide tour in 1994 and played concerts with him throughout 1995. In 1995, he released his long-shelved collection of covers, *Kojak Variety*. —*Stephen Thomas Erlewine*

☆ **My Aim Is True** / 1977 / Rykodisc ♦♦♦♦♦
Elvis Costello's debut album is a pop landmark that indicates the future that may exist for the spirit of punk in the wider genre of rock music. Backed by the American group Clover (featuring then-future Doobie Brother John McFee but not harmonica player Huey Lewis), Costello displays all the characteristics that would serve him throughout his career: a caustic wit he uses to savage himself and others, a broad imagination—"(The Angels Wanna Wear My) Red Shoes" is one of the best pieces of rock whimsy ever written, an unsentimental but compelling sense of romance ("Alison"), and an astonishing verbal facility, all enmeshed with a pop encyclopedist's musical knowledge. One of the greatest first albums in pop history. —*William Ruhlmann*

Live at the El Mocambo / 1978 / Columbia ♦♦♦

☆ **This Year's Model** / Jul. 1978 / Rykodisc ♦♦♦♦♦
Backed by his road band, the Attractions, his music becomes harder on the edges, suiting perfectly the bitterness of Costello's best song-for-song set. —*John Floyd*

★ **Armed Forces** / 1979 / Rykodisc ♦♦♦♦♦
Lavishly produced by Nick Lowe, and masterfully programmed, this is Costello's most political album and his most melodic. His bitterness is somewhat subdued, but his passion informs every song. —*John Floyd*

☆ **Get Happy** / 1980 / Rykodisc ♦♦♦♦♦
Featuring twenty tracks of energetic, amphetamine-driven soul, *Get Happy!!* captures Costello at his most vicious and clever. While his words and puns are pithy, it's the constant barrage of songs that make the album work. Not all of the songs are first-rate, but the great majority are. —*Stephen Thomas Erlewine*

Taking Liberties / 1980 / Columbia ♦♦♦
An interesting jumble of British B-sides and previously unreleased material, it is stylistically diverse and occasionally sublime. —*John Floyd*

○ **Trust** / Feb. 1981 / Rykodisc ♦♦♦♦
Some of the songs are too obtuse to really stick, but the Attractions turn the best of them into edgy and brittle mini-masterpieces. —*John Floyd*

Almost Blue / Nov. 1981 / Rykodisc ♦♦♦
Costello's "country record" is usually written off as a vanity project, but *Almost Blue* is quite a bit more than that. It's one of the most entertaining cover records in rock & roll, simply because of its enthusiasm. The album begins with a roaring version of Hank Williams's "Why Don't You Love Me" and doesn't stop. Costello sings with conviction on the tearjerking ballads, as well as barn-burners like "Tonight the Bottle Let Me Down." It's clear that Costello knows this music, and it's also clear who he learned it

from—Gram Parsons. Costello covers Parsons's "Hot Burrito No. 1" and "How Much I Lied," and all of the music on *Almost Blue* recalls Parsons's taste for hardcore honky-tonk and weepy ballads. It's to Costello's credit that he made a record relying on emotion to pay tribute. —*Stephen Thomas Erlewine*

☆ **Imperial Bedroom** / 1982 / Rykodisc ♦♦♦♦♦
This ornately orchestrated and lush set is Costello's version of *Blood on the Tracks*. It's a musically sophisticated and emotionally devastating tour through the crumbling heart of an incurable romantic. —*John Floyd*

Punch the Clock / 1983 / Rykodisc ♦♦♦
An upbeat set of fairly clear and concise pop songs, it is supplemented by some punchy horn charts. —*John Floyd*

Goodbye Cruel World / 1984 / Rykodisc ♦♦
During the making of *Goodbye Cruel World*, Costello was undergoing a multitude of personal problems, including a divorce, that resulted in a number of poor production decisions and ill-conceived, unformed songs. Like *Punch the Clock*, *Goodbye Cruel World* was produced by Clive Langer and Alan Winstanley, the top British hitmakers of the '80s. Consequently, most of the record suffers from a stiff, synthesized production that instantly dates the record. In some cases—like the duet with Daryl Hall "The Only Flame In Town," and the cover of the lost Hi R&B gem "I Wanna Be Loved"—the songs benefit from the shiny, streamlined production but it obscures the merits of the finest songs on the album. "Room With No Number," "The Comedians," "Sour Milk-Cow Blues," and "Peace In Our Time" all cry out for a simple, stripped-down presentation, but they're weighted down with stylized sounds and trendy synthesizers; however, once the sound of the album settles in, the strength of these songs is apparent. The remainder of *Goodbye Cruel World* isn't as memorable, primarily because Costello's uninspired vocals and the Attractions' muted performances fail to make the weaker songs musically compelling. —*Stephen Thomas Erlewine*

☆ **King of America** / Jan. 1986 / Rykodisc ♦♦♦♦♦
Although this is linked thematically to *Imperial Bedroom*, Costello's newfound clarity and the mostly acoustic accompaniment distinguish it from anything in his canon. Remarkable. —*John Floyd*

○ **Blood & Chocolate** / Feb. 1986 / Rykodisc ♦♦♦♦
A hard-rocking and inconsistent set is made worthwhile by "I Want You," "I Hope You're Happy Now," and "Next Time Round," all emotional stunners. —*John Floyd*

Out of Our Idiot / 1987 / Demon ♦♦♦
A wildly diverse collection of B-sides and rarities, *Out of Our Idiot* is a treasure for hardcore Costello fans, since many of his throwaways are as fine as his keepers. —*Stephen Thomas Erlewine*

Girls Girls Girls / 1989 / Columbia ♦♦♦
Elvis Costello assembled this compilation himself. It is highly idiosyncratic, not the least of its peculiarities being that the CD and cassette versions differ considerably. Costello describes a vague concept in his notes, but the collection of songs (47 on the CDs, 51 on the cassettes) seems a jumble. At least he demonstrates that songs from different periods work well together. A large part of Costello's oeuvre, including *some* of his best work, is represented. —*William Ruhlmann*

Spike / 1989 / Warner Brothers ♦♦
Throughout his career Elvis Costello has always been prolific; thus it was surprising, even given the change in record labels for the U.S., when he took a whole 20 months between *Blood & Chocolate* and this follow-up. But the musical growth he exhibits makes the wait worthwhile. The musical settings range from the stark folk of "Tramp the Dirt Down" to the pop sprightliness of "Veronica" (a collaboration with Paul McCartney that became Costello's first American Top 20 hit) and the New Orleans jazz sound of "Deep Dark Truthful Mirror," featuring the Dirty Dozen Brass Band. The lyrics are among his best. —*William Ruhlmann*

Mighty Like a Rose / 1991 / Warner Brothers ♦♦
The lyrical concerns here are cumbersome and pretentious, and the music is ponderous and indulgent. But a few decent songs—especially "The Other Side of Summer"—make this 1991 set worthwhile. —*John Floyd*

The Juliet Letters / 1993 / Warner Brothers ♦♦♦
Costello's collaboration with the Brodsky Quartet is an intriguing, if flawed, attempt at crossing pop with chamber music. Some songs rely too much on clever arrangements, but most of the

tracks are surprisingly successful and accessible. —*Stephen Thomas Erlewine*

○ **2 1/2 Years** / Oct. 12, 1993 / Rykodisc ✦✦✦✦
Rykodisc launched its Elvis Costello reissue series with *2 1/2 Years*, a box set featuring his first three albums together with the previously promotional-only *Live at the El Mocambo*, which is only available in the box. Costello fans know the studio albums by heart and will be pleased by the remastering and bonus tracks, while the highly sought-after *Live at the El Mocambo* proves that in addition to being an extremely talented songwriter, Costello was hell of a rocker. —*Stephen Thomas Erlewine*

Brutal Youth / 1994 / Warner Brothers ✦✦✦
Costello's first album with the Attractions since *Blood and Chocolate*, *Brutal Youth* suffers from soft, mushy production and the inclusion of too many songs. Apart from these two flaws, the record is highly enjoyable, recalling the stripped-down eclecticism of *Trust* and the force of *This Year's Model*. Costello's songs are strong and lean; it's his least affected and pretentious writing since *Blood and Chocolate*. —*Stephen Thomas Erlewine*

○ **The Very Best of Elvis Costello and the Attractions** / 1994 / Rykodisc ✦✦✦✦
A solid complement to Ryko's Costello reissue series if you don't want to pick up each individual album. Of course, the 22 tracks (drawn from his first 11 albums and, according to the liner notes, "hand-picked by Elvis himself") also sport the crisply remastered sound featured on the rest of the series. "The Very Best Of" halts abruptly at 1986's *Blood and Chocolate*, his last release for Columbia. —*Roch Parisien*

Kojak Variety / 1995 / Warner Brothers ✦✦
With *Almost Blue*, Elvis Costello wanted to be a honky-tonker. With *Kojak Variety*, he's a crooner, picking forgotten tunes by both minor and major artists (anyone from Screamin' Jay Hawkins to Bob Dylan). From his song selections to the pseudo-avant rock/R&B band, Costello doesn't make any obvious moves. Yet that doesn't mean that the record is difficult—it just shows the depths of Costello's affection for music and record collecting (which is also clear from his loving, detailed liner notes). Costello and his band (featuring guitarists James Burton and Marc Ribot, drummer Jim Keltner and Attraction Pete Thomas) play with gusto, tearing through the songs with the vigor of a bar band on a Friday night. Some of the rockers sound slightly forced, although there's no denying the power of Costello's passionate vocals, even if he stretches his range a little too much (Little Richard's "Bama Lama Bama Loo"). What matters here are the performances, and the majority of *Kojak Variety* is filled with fine interpretations. *Kojak Variety* does what any good covers album should do—it makes you want to seek out the originals. —*Stephen Thomas Erlewine*

Count Bishops

Group, Garage Rock
Although amounting to little more than a footnote in the early days of English punk rock, the Count Bishops were a fine, energetic, R&B-based band capable of kicking out a fierce racket of noise that sounded like a grimier version of seminal British R&B revivalists Dr. Feelgood. Originally fronted by journeyman American singer Mike Spencer, the Count Bishops' 1975 debut EP, *Speedball*, released on Ted Carroll's wonderful Chiswick Records, was a straight-ahead slice of R&B that featured the spooky, exhilarating "Train, Train." Surprisingly, the band unceremoniously dumped Spencer and recorded their self-titled debut with fellow Englishman Dave Tice, who had a voice so gruff it sounded as though he gargled with ground glass. A ripsnorting live record followed (by this time they had dropped "Count" from their name), but it was clear that the band was simply treading water. By 1979, the thoroughly mediocre *Cross Cuts* was released to public apathy, guitarist Zenon de Fleur was killed in a car wreck, and lead guitarist Johnny Guitar hooked up with Dr. Feelgood. The Bishops called it a career. —*John Dougan*

Speedball [EP] / 1975 / Chiswick ✦✦

● **Count Bishops** / 1977 / Dynamite ✦✦✦✦
Kicking off with a great cover of the Kinks' "I Need You," this solid, unpretentious debut album should belong in the home of every fan of English R&B from the Yardbirds to the Pretty Things to Dr. Feelgood. Guitarists Johnny Guitar and Zenon de Fleur keep it tight and simple, never wasting a note, and vocalist Dave Tice is so macho, it's enough to make you laugh. The originals are OK, if

somewhat predictable blues-based rave-ups, but the energy and good cheer more than make up for the album's derivative nature. Not a deep album by any stretch of the imagination, just good dirty fun. —*John Dougan*

Good Gear / 1977 / Lolita ✦✦

Live [12 Inch] / 1978 / Chiswick ✦✦✦
A hunk of greasy rock and R&B that's not the most original record you're likely to hear; it is fun, loud, sloppy and endearing. Vocalist Dave Tice's growl is a hoot, as are the Chuck Berry pyrotechnics of Johnny Guitar. Two great covers: Fleetwood Mac's barroom anthem "Somebody's Gonna Get Their Head Kicked in Tonight" and the Standells' "Good Guys Don't Wear White." As the old saying goes: made loud to be played loud! —*John Dougan*

Crosscut / 1979 / Chiswick ✦✦✦

Count Five

Group, Psychedelic, Garage Rock
This San Jose quintet scored one of the biggest garage-psychedelic hits of the '60s with "Psychotic Reaction," a derivative but riveting American adaptation of the Yardbirds' guitar rave-ups. The single reached number five in late 1966, but the group was unable to come anywhere close to duplicating its success. Their sole album and collectible follow-up flop singles, like "Psychotic Reaction," emulate the Yardbirds, Rolling Stones, and Who with less memorable results, although they have their moments. —*Richie Unterberger*

● **Psychotic Reaction: The Complete Psychotic Reaction** / 1994 / Performance ✦✦✦✦
Replaces previous Count Five collections as the most thorough retrospective of the group, with 18 of their tracks from the 1960s. —*Richie Unterberger*

Counting Crows

Group, Rock & Roll
With their angst-filled hybrid of Van Morrison, the Band, and R.E.M., Counting Crows became an overnight sensation in 1994. Only a year earlier, the band were a group of unknown musicians, filling in for the absent Van Morrison at the Rock & Roll Hall of Fame ceremony; they were introduced by an enthusiastic Robbie Robertson. Early in 1993, the band recorded their debut album, *August and Everything After*, with T-Bone Burnett; it was released in the fall. It was a dark, somber record, driven by the morose lyrics and expressive vocals of Adam Duritz; the only up-tempo song, "Mr. Jones," became their ticket to stardom. What made Counting Crows was how they were able to balance Duritz's tortured lyrics with the sound of the late '60s and early '70s; it made them one of the few alternative bands to appeal to listeners who thought that rock & roll died in 1972. —*Stephen Thomas Erlewine*

○ **August & Everything After** / 1993 / DGC ✦✦✦✦
Counting Crows became the surprise success story of 1994 with *August & Everything After*, which skillfully filters the classic rock of Van Morrison and the Band through the post-punk sensibilities of R.E.M. and the Cure. With his verbose lyrics and twisting melodies, lead singer and songwriter Adam Duritz resembles a cross between Morrison and Rick Danko, and his songs are more weathered than one might expect on a debut. Apart from the single "Mr. Jones," the album is rather gloomy, with melancholy, jangling guitars and a somber, solemn mood. Counting Crows crossed over because they were able to keep that gloom from resembling Joy Division or the Cure (or even *Automatic for the People*), instead sounding like something straight out of the classic years of 1968 to 1972. It's modern music for people who don't like modern music. —*Stephen Thomas Erlewine*

Country Joe & the Fish

Group, Psychedelic
One of the original and most popular San Francisco Bay Area psychedelic bands, Country Joe & the Fish, was formed by lead singer Country Joe McDonald (b. Jan. 1, 1942). The Berkeley group still had one foot in the jugband sound on their first EP, released in 1965 (featuring a folk version of their anthem "I Feel like I'm Fixin' to Die Rag"). By the time of their second EP in 1966, though, they had plunged full-tilt into the burgeoning psychedelic sound, with raga-ish, heavily distorted guitars and farfisa organ, displayed to its full glory on the instrumental "Section 43." Versions of songs from those limited edition EPs were combined with other material

for their first and best album, *Electric Music for the Mind and Body*. McDonald and his group combined protest politics, free love, and psychedelic drugs with a good-time humor on this 1967 release. After a similar, less impressive follow-up, the band began to disintegrate, and never recaptured the highs of their early days. McDonald went on to an intermittently successful, more folk-rock oriented solo career, achieving his greatest moment of notoriety with his version of "Fixin' to Die" (complete with the obscene "Fish Cheer") at the Woodstock festival. —*Richie Unterberger*

I Feel Like I'm Fixing to Die / 1967 / Vanguard ◆◆◆

● **Electric Music for the Mind and Body** / 1967 / Vanguard ◆◆◆◆
Their full-length debut is their most joyous and cohesive statement, and finds the band's psychedelic swirl of distorted guitar and organ at its most inventive. Ranging in mood from good-timey to downright apocalyptic, it includes most of their best tunes. —*Richie Unterberger*

Together / 1968 / Vanguard ◆◆

Here We Are Again / 1969 / Vanguard ◆◆

C J Fish / 1970 / Vanguard

○ **The Collected Country Joe & the Fish** / 1987 / Vanguard ◆◆◆◆
CJ & the F are well represented on *Collected Country Joe & the Fish (1965-1970)*, a 19-track compilation that traces their development from a politically oriented folk-jugband ensemble to a politically oriented rock and soul band. Most of the material comes from 1967, the band's high-water mark, and the centerpiece is the still-cutting "I-Feel-Like-I'm-Fixin'-to-Die Rag." —*William Ruhlmann*

The First Three EPs / 1987 / Decal ◆◆◆
The first recordings by Country Joe and the Fish (1965-1966) and his early solo material (1971). Includes "I-Feel-Like-I'm-Fixin'-to-Die Rag," "Superbird," and "Tricky Dicky." —*William Ruhlmann*

Dave Cousins

Folk, Art-Rock/Progressive-Rock
Leader/founder of Strawbs, Dave Cousins may be the most talented Dylan-influenced songwriter to come out of England. His work fairly resounds of both rebellion and antiquity, as though he were writing protest songs of the 18th or 19th centuries. Haunting melodies abound, carried by his raspy and sincere voice. Its beautiful sound is marred only by the same problem that plagued the Strawbs—his difficulty in finding proper musical backup and settings. —*Bruce Eder*

● **Two Weeks Last Summer** / 1972 / A&M ◆◆◆◆
Almost a lost Strawbs album, with moments of stately, haunting beauty and a wonderful title tune but harsh and unmelodic a little too often. (import) —*Bruce Eder*

Old School Songs / 1980 / PVC ◆◆◆
A mixed bag of songs that lacks the excitement of Cousins's electric recordings but is more pleasing with repeated listenings. —*Bruce Eder*

Bridge / 1994 / Road Goes on Forever ◆◆◆

Don Covay

b. Mar. 1938, Orangeburg, SC
Soul
An R&B and soul songwriting great, Don Covay compositions have been recorded by everyone from the Rolling Stones to Jimi Hendrix, Gladys Knight to Wilson Pickett, and many others. Covay was the son of a Baptist preacher. He sang in his family's gospel group, the Cherry-Keys, as a youngster. Covay was born in Orangeburg, SC, but grew up in Washington, D.C., and joined the Rainbows alongside Marvin Gaye, John Berry, and Billy Stewart in the '50s. Covay also performed as a solo singer with Little Richard, who recorded Covay as "Pretty Boy" on the Atlantic release "Bip Bop Bip." Covay had moderate success with the single "Pony Time," which he co-wrote with Berry, for the Arnold label in 1960. He began to hit his stride in 1964. Besides fronting Don Covay and the Goodtimers, he wrote "Mercy Mercy," "Sookie Sookie," and "See Saw," and had tunes recorded by Gene Chandler and Aretha Franklin. Covay did both blues and soul numbers for Janus and Mercury labels in the '70s. His biggest hit as a performer was "See Saw," which made it to number five on the R&B charts in 1965. But his most electrifying number was 1973's "I Was Checkin' Out She Was Checkin' In," which made it to number six. Covay

was also part of the short-lived Soul Clan, with Solomon Burke, Arthur Conley, Ben E. King, and Joe Tex in 1968. Their collaboration "Soul Meeting" made it to number 34, but wasn't quite the elaborate or explosive number everyone had envisioned. Covay made one LP for Gamble and Huff's Philadelphia International label in 1976, but *Travelin' in Heavy Traffic* proved a disappointment. Covay recorded for Newman in 1980, and got his last chart single with "Badd Boy." Some of his singles were reissued on a 1992 Mercury release, *Checkin' in with Don Covay*. An all-star gathering that included Ron Wood, Robert Cray, Bobby Womack, Iggy Pop, Peter Wolf, King, Todd Rundgren, Billy Squier, and Jimmy Witherspoon recorded a tribute album to Covay in 1993. —*Ron Wynn*

● **Mercy Mercy: The Definitive Don Covay** / 1995 / Razor & Tie ◆◆◆◆
Mercy Mercy: The Definitive Don Covay compiles 23 tracks from throughout the soul singer's career. Encompassing everything from the R&B stomp of "Bip Bop Bip" and "Pony Time" to the seductive soul of "I Was Checkin' Out While She Was Checkin' In" and "No Tell Motel," the disc makes a convincing argument that Covay was one of the great overlooked R&B/soul artists of the '60s. —*Stephen Thomas Erlewine*

Cowboy Junkies

Group, Alternative Pop/Rock
Although it was solely a way to gain attention, the Cowboy Junkies' name goes a long way in describing the Canadian band's sound. At its core, the group's music is based in country and folk traditions, except their tempos are slow and lethargic, their guitars are languid, and Margo Timmins's vocals are lovely, yet hauntingly detached.

The Cowboy Junkies have their roots in the Hunger Project, an unsuccessful Toronto-based group formed by guitarist/songwriter Michael Timmins and bassist Alan Anton in 1979. After the band failed, the duo moved to the United Kingdom and formed an experimental instrumental group called Germinal. It was also unsuccessful, so the two musicians moved back to Toronto, where they began playing with Timmins's sister Margo and his drummer brother, Peter. Under the name Cowboy Junkies, the group recorded their first album, *Whites off Earth Now!!*, in 1986, releasing it on a Canadian independent label. Two years later, they recorded *The Trinity Session* in an abandoned church, using only one microphone. The album may have only cost $250 to record, but it sparked a small sensation, with the band's reworkings of "Blue Moon," "I'm So Lonesome I Could Cry," "Walking After Midnight," and "Sweet Jane" earning them a diverse and dedicated cult following.

The success of *The Trinity Sessions* allowed the band to record on a bigger budget. The result was 1990's *The Caution Horses*, which featured more of Michael Timmins's original songs. *The Caution Horses* didn't earn as much press as their previous album, yet they maintained a sizable cult, which stuck by the band through their next two records, *Black-Eyed Man* (1992) and *Pale Sun, Crescent Moon* (1993). —*Stephen Thomas Erlewine*

Whites off Earth Now!! / 1986 / RCA ◆◆◆
Featuring only one original song, the Cowboy Junkies' debut *Whites Off Earth Now* captures the band forming their own sound through covers, including songs by Robert Johnson and Bruce Springsteen. It's not as captivating as their later releases, but it's fascinating to hear their signature country-on-valium sound develop. Margo Timmins sings beautifully. —*Stephen Thomas Erlewine*

● **The Trinity Sessions** / 1988 / RCA ◆◆◆◆
Recorded with one microphone in an abandoned church, their second album achieves a haunting ambience. —*John Floyd*

The Caution Horses / 1990 / RCA ◆◆
The country influences are clearer and more energetic here, but most of the original material (with the exception of "Sun Comes Up, It's Tuesday Morning") is boring. —*John Floyd*

Black Eyed Man / 1992 / RCA ◆◆◆
The Cowboy Junkies stick with their style of low-key songs steeped in country blues. Songwriter and guitarist Michael Timmins writes story-songs full of rain and street life and regret, and they are movingly sung by Margo Timmins. Two Townes Van Zandt songs, including his classic "To Live Is to Fly," fit right in. —*William Ruhlmann*

○ **Pale Sun, Crescent Moon** / 1993 / RCA ✦✦✦✦
Refreshed and revitalized, thanks to the incendiary guitar work of honorary Junkie Ken Myhr, without sacrificing trademark delicacy. —*Roch Parisien*

Cows

Group, Alternative Pop/Rock
Longtime denizens of the Minneapolis rock scene, the Cows are one of America's great degenerate punk-rock bands. Starting off as near-total incompetents, they have become more technically polished musicians over the past decade, but their white-hot noiserock has not been tamed one bit. In many ways, the Cows remain as gloriously messy, primitive and exciting as they were the day they started. Formed in the mid-'80s by idiosyncratic lead singer Shannon Selberg, the Cows appropriated the hardcore guitar blur that characterized fellow-Twin Citians Hüsker Dü, but stripped away any and all concessions to melodies, hooks, riffs—essentially anything that remotely resembled pop. What they offered was a blazing wall of distortion that was punk rock at its crudest; a feral racket that sounded as if the guitars were being played with metal files. Above the din was Selberg, free-associating surreal vignettes about, well, God knows what, but his squealing, shrieking and general lunacy provided the bizarre, often engaging focus. He plays trumpet, too—well, not so much play as blast a note or two when he's tired of ranting. After the release of their first album in 1987, the Cows were roundly derided as a talentless, tasteless joke (a charge that would be levelled a few years later against Babes in Toyland). However, they've stayed true to their anti-commercial stance and punk roots, releasing a handful of weird, loud, gleefully unhinged records that seem to get better (i.e., more focused and less obtuse) and retain the band's devotion to mania. —*John Dougan*

○ **Taint Pluribus Taint Unum** / 1987 / Treehouse ✦✦✦✦
Recommended to those who want to experience the Cows at their most impenetrable and noisy. This is not to say that this record is worthless, but it is relentless. And, if you tire of guitar feedback, screeched vocals and a rhythm section that only infrequently knows what it's doing, this may be more than you can handle. However, fans of Japanese noise acts like the Boredoms and some of John Zorn's more extreme jazzcore outfits might think this is pretty cool. —*John Dougan*

Daddy Has a Tail / 1989 / Amphetamine Reptile ✦✦

Effete & Impudent Snobs / 1990 / Amphetamine Reptile ✦✦

● **Cunning Stunts** / 1991 / Amphetamine Reptile ✦✦✦✦
The release of *Cunning Stunts* signaled a "maturity" to the Cows, but it really meant that riffs and hooks were starting to emerge from their usual tarpit of sound. Although Selberg's ranting and raving dominate the proceedings, it's guitarist Thor Eisenstrager who steals the show with his frenetic playing and bold experimentation. Not the pure noise of their earlier work, but certainly not an attempt at mainstream respectability either. The Cows are simply too frenzied and defiantly idiosyncratic for that to happen. —*John Dougan*

Peacetika / 1991 / Amphetamine Reptile ✦✦✦

○ **Sexy Pee Story** / 1993 / Amphetamine Reptile ✦✦✦✦
With an album title that sounds as though it was made up by a four-year-old, this follow-up to *Cunning Stunts* showed the Cows hitting their stride, producing another terrific, noisy, clamorous record stuffed to the gills with pure punk rock excitement. Never ones to miss an opportunity for humor, included on this disc is a great cover of "39 Lashes" from *Jesus Christ Superstar*, lyrics ("1,2,3,4 …") included. —*John Dougan*

Orphan's Tragedy / 1995 / Amphetamine Reptile ✦✦✦
It's been nearly a decade since their debut release, and the Cows show absolutely no sign of slowing down. *Orphan's Tragedy* squeals in a way that is reminiscent of early Cows, but Eisenstrager's guitar still dominates the mix with its overwhelming power. —*John Dougan*

The Cowsills

Group, Pop/Rock
The real-life antecedent to the Partridge Family, but an actual family and a better group, the Cowsills consisted of five teen and pre-teen siblings plus Mom. After some flop singles, producer Artie Kornfeld helped take the Newport, RI, group to number two in 1967 with "The Rain, the Park, the Other Things." The well-pro-

duced, well-harmonized single was actually a good slice of flower-power-pop, even if the group had nothing to do with psychedelia in real life, projecting an almost unbearably wholesome image. Mining the territory between the Mamas & the Papas and the Partridge Family, they had a few other hits in the late '60s, the biggest of which was their cringingly embarrassing version of the theme song to the Broadway hit *Hair*, which went to number two in 1969. Group member Susan Cowsill, surprisingly enough, resurfaced in the mid-'90s as a member of the alternative rock group Continental Drifters. —*Richie Unterberger*

The Cowsills / 1967 / MGM ✦✦
Featuring "The Rain, The Park, And Other Things," this really isn't half-bad mainstream late-'60s pop, with a heavy Mamas & the Papas fixation. It's not nearly as good as the Mamas & the Papas, of course, and doesn't stand up to in-depth listening. The CD reissue adds bonus tracks drawn from their themes for the movie *The Impossible Years* and the TV series *Love American Style*. —*Richie Unterberger*

● **Best of the Cowsills** / 1968 / Polydor ✦✦✦✦
Here's everything you wanted to hear from this family group ("The Rain, the Park & Other Things" (#2), "Indian Lake" (#10), "Hair" from the musical *Hair* (#2), among others) which was the real-life basis for the Partridge Family TV series. —*Larry Lapka*

Captain Sad and His Ship of Fools / 1968 / MGM ✦✦✦

We Can Fly / 1968 / MGM ✦✦✦

The Cowsills in Concert / 1969 / MGM ✦
Put most charitably, this 1969 set of covers of huge '60s hits like "Good Vibrations," "Please Mr. Postman," "Paperback Writer," and (we kid you not) "Sunshine Of Your Love" leaves itself open to all sorts of cruel jokes. Such as noting that all things considered, you're much better off with the original versions. Engineered by Val Valentin, who also worked on the Velvet Underground's *White Light/White Heat*—such are the ups and downs of the record business. The CD reissue includes a rare EP that (again, we kid you not) was originally recorded for the American Dairy Association. —*Richie Unterberger*

II by II / 1970 / MGM ✦✦

On My Side / 1971 / MGM ✦✦✦

Kevin Coyne

Group, Singer-Songwriter
There are plenty more heralded singer/songwriters, but few have produced more good work as have done so for longer than Kevin Coyne. Virtually unknown in America, Coyne has over 30 records, most of them very good, that deal primarily with outsiders: men, women and children arbitrarily shunted to the fringes of society, or worse, locked away and left alone. He can be extraordinarily compassionate and, in the blink of an eye, angry, anguished and accusatory. Perhaps the most durable and telling image of Kevin Coyne is the cover photo of his album *In Living Black and White*. On the front, Coyne is smiling and politely bowing to an unseen audience; the back of the album jacket is the same photo taken from the rear, with Coyne clutching an open straight razor.

Born in Derby, England in 1944, Coyne, like many rock & roll performers who came of age in early post-war Britain, was an art-school student who fell in love with American R&B.Living a bohemian life in late-'60s London, Coyne was employed for a while as a socio-therapist for alcoholics and the emotionally disturbed, jobs that would profoundly affect his approach to music. In 1969 his first band, Siren, signed to influential BBC DJ John Peel's specialty label Dandelion. Two years and two excellent records later, Peel dissolved his label and Coyne embarked on a solo career. Married with two children, Coyne supported both his family and musical career by returning to social work. In many ways, his solo debut, *Case History*, set the tone for his career. Based on his social work experiences, it was a riveting examination of the desperate search for love by those forcibly shunted to the fringes of society. With his bluesy voice wailing almost inconsolably, *Case History* is a naked examination of people (Coyne included) whose lives are in constant turmoil—betrayed, institutionalized, unwanted and mostly unloved. The characters in these songs cry out for attention, and Coyne, never one to buy into England's bureaucratic social work system, howls right along with them.

Case History was very nearly Coyne's swan song, but after a self-imposed exile from music, an opportunity to continue recording as a solo act with almost complete artistic freedom proved too powerful an incentive. In 1973, Coyne began a relationship with the then-fledgling Virgin Records, who seemed willing to embrace the decidedly non-commercial, difficult performer. For the next eight years, he recorded some of his best music and, somewhat surprisingly, attained a modicum of commercial success, albeit in Europe only. These were mostly edgy, folk-rock records tinged with an avant-garde feel for performance art (Coyne is a published poet too), clearly not easy listening by any stretch of the imagination; neither were these records overly pretentious or unapproachable.

By the early '80s, Coyne was recording for independent labels, making frustrating, semi-successful records that were erratically released and difficult to find. Exacerbating this bad situation were his worsening mental and physical states: chronic depression culminating in a nervous breakdown and alcoholism that, along with ending his marriage, nearly ended his life. By the end of the decade, he had relocated to Germany, formed a new band, fallen in love, and seemed to be sharpening his songwriting skills.

One can only guess at what the rest of the '90s will be like for Kevin Coyne, but chances are good that whatever he does, the music he records will always be interesting. Still, that assessment remains an educated guess, his recent recordings are nearly impossible to find, and most inquiries into his current activities, at least in this country, will doubtlessly yield the response, "Who's Kevin Coyne?" The good news is that in late 1994, there was a major CD reissue series (only in England, of course) of Coyne's work, including two late-'80s/early-'90s records (*Legless in Manila* and *Wild Tiger Love*) that went mostly unheard, even by fans. *—John Dougan*

○ **Case History** / 1971 / Dandelion ✦✦✦✦
Coyne's first solo recording is a triumphant, if occasionally bleak, look at life's outsiders. Using his time as social worker in a government-run mental hospital as a basis for his narratives, Coyne deals with issues of intense alienation, indifference, substance abuse (to which he was no stranger), and mental instability in a world that would rather forget these people existed, and a labyrinthine governmental bureaucracy that often denied their humanity. This is not a happy record, and is only infrequently hopeful, but it's never cynical, and neither does Coyne indulge in glib condescension. He acts as a subjective documentarian, and advocate for a group of people who desperately need one. Reissued on CD with extra tracks by the import label Dandelion/See For Miles in 1994. *—John Dougan*

● **Marjory Razorblade** / 1973 / Virgin ✦✦✦✦
Marjory Razor Blade was Coyne's return to rock & roll after a two-year "retirement" to go back to social work. A two-LP set in England, edited to a single disc in America, it contains some of his most stunning material and, arguably, his single greatest song, "House on the Hill." A harrowing tale of institutional life, as told by an overmedicated patient, it's as emotionally complex and well-written a song as one is likely to hear. Still, tracks like "Eastbourne Ladies," which pokes fun at stylish women at English seaside resorts, proves that Coyne the satirist is capable of making people laugh as well as cry. With so many albums available, it's difficult (close to impossible) to find one Coyne recording that's vastly superior to the others. However, if you bought this or *Case History*, you'd be listening to Coyne in his prime. *—John Dougan*

Blame It on the Night / 1974 / Virgin

Matching Head & Feet / 1975 / Virgin ✦✦✦

Heartburn / 1976 / Virgin

In Living Black & White / 1976 / Virgin ✦✦✦
As with *Marjory Razor Blade*, this live recording was edited down to one disc for American consumption. My advice is to find the 2-LP import and get the whole Kevin Coyne experience. Backed by a great band (perhaps his best), with dazzling guitar playing from soon-to-be Police guitarist Andy Summers, Coyne is in great form here, bellowing and braying the songs with inexhaustible energy. Excellent versions of "House on the Hill," the searing "Turpentine," and "Fat Girl" (about a depressed, overweight woman's suicide). A great record from start to finish. *—John Dougan*

Dynamite Daze / 1978 / Virgin

Millionaires & Teddy Bears / 1978 / Virgin ✦✦✦

Beautiful Extremes / 1978 / Virgin

Babble / 1979 / Virgin ✦✦✦
A match made in heaven: Coyne singing a series of songs about the successes and failures of communication between lovers with the female perspective provided by German chanteuse (ex-Henry

Cow/Slapp Happy/Art Bears) Dagmar Krause. Rather than sing duets, Coyne and Krause trade songs in a series of statements and responses. Occasionally the songwriting is thin, but the powerful singing and intense emotions more than make up for any lapses. This is a richly rewarding and frequently compelling record about love, communication and commitment that is never sanctimonious, obvious or cloying. Difficult to find (damn near impossible), but well worth the effort. *—John Dougan*

Bursting Bubbles / 1980 / Virgin

Sanity Stomp / 1980 / Virgin

○ **Boxed Set: Dandelion Years** / 1980 / Butt ✦✦✦✦
This three-disc box set includes both *Siren* and *Case History*, making it an essential release. The *Siren* material holds up extremely well, thankfully eschewing art-rock (which was becoming all the rage in late-'60s London) for a grubby, blues-based pub-rock sound. Coyne is in particularly good form (and good spirits), making this a wonderful glimpse into his early years. Unfortunately, in America, this box set seemed to disappear almost immediately after its release. Good luck finding a copy. *—John Dougan*

Pointing the Finger / 1981 / Cherry Red

Poloticz / 1982 / Cherry Red

Beautiful Extremes Et Cetera / 1983 / Cherry Red

Legless in Manila / 1984 / Collapse

Peel Sessions / 1990 / Dutch East India ✦✦
Until a multi-disc anthology comes out covering Coyne's 20-year-plus career, this single CD is a valuable entry for the benighted into Coyne's world. Although it doesn't pack the wallop of *Case History* or *Marjory Razor Blade*, it doesn't pull its punches or serve up filler and pass it off as inspiration (well, it does once on the silly "Eye Up Me Duck"). There is material recorded as late as 1990, for those wondering as to his recent whereabouts, and while this collection isn't dazzling, it's illuminating. *—John Dougan*

Cracker

Group, Alternative Pop/Rock
While he was the front-man for Camper Van Beethoven, it seemed that it would take nothing short of a miracle to make guitarist/singer David Lowery a favorite of mainstream rockers, but that's what his second band, Cracker, have become. Led by Lowery and guitarist Johnny Hickman, Cracker is much more straightforward than Camper; Cracker concentrates on rock and country, creating a twisted, rootsy rock & roll that sounds like a post-punk Rolling Stones or Little Feat. While their self-titled 1992 debut had moments of raw brilliance, Cracker's second album, 1993's *Kerosene Hat*, fulfilled their promise. Powered by the hit single "Low," the album was a hard-rocking meeting of traditional rock and post-punk sensibilities. Like Camper Van Beethoven's albums, it deserved to be heard by a wide audience; this time Lowery found a larger audience—*Kerosene Hat* eventually went gold. *—Stephen Thomas Erlewine*

○ **Cracker** / 1992 / Virgin ✦✦✦✦
Apart from David Lowery's tendency to slip in some smug, self-serving lyrics, Cracker's debut is a terrific rock & roll record, full of energetic three-chord bashers and surprisingly moving ballads. *—Stephen Thomas Erlewine*

● **Kerosene Hat** / 1993 / Virgin ✦✦✦✦
With their second album, Cracker has lost the smarmy self-righteousness that plagued their otherwise fine debut, replacing it with a surprisingly solid, rocking core. *Kerosene Hat* is David Lowery's least affected album yet—its humor is no stranger than the Stones' "Dead Flowers" or Little Feat's "Fat Man in a Bathtub," two groups that Cracker strongly recall throughout the album. *Kerosene Hat* is more blues- and country-based than their debut, but it sounds natural, since their songwriting has improved and the band has grown tighter. *—Stephen Thomas Erlewine*

The Cramps

Group, Rockabilly, Alternative Pop/Rock
They made their arrival during the first wave of punk-rock, but this New York (via Cleveland, OH) quartet (two guitars, drums, vocals, no bass) found their inspiration in the bizarre sounds of rockabilly and surf guitar and the seedy side of American junk-culture. At their best, the Cramps managed to pay homage to their musical heroes without aping them. *—John Floyd*

○ **Songs the Lord Taught Us** / 1980 / IRS ✦✦✦✦
Their first album is a brilliant tribute to their inspirers. Its well-chosen covers mingle with ferocious originals. —*John Floyd*

○ **Psychedelic Jungle** / 1981 / A&M ✦✦✦✦
Contained is their second album (not as wild as the first but still a ton of fun) and their debut EP material, featuring the epochal "Human Fly" and a pulverizing cover of Roy Orbison's "Domino." —*John Floyd*

Smell of Female / 1983 / Capitol/Enigma ✦✦✦
A live EP of new material, it is a tad lackluster. "Call of the Wighat" conjures the fire of the old days, and "I Ain't Nothin' but a Gorehound" is a career-defining anthem. —*John Floyd*

● **Bad Music for Bad People** / 1984 / IRS ✦✦✦✦
A solid collection of singles, B-sides, and album cuts, this decent introduction is made great by "Drug Train" and "New Kind of Kick." —*John Floyd*

Date with Elvis / 1986 / Big Beat ✦✦✦

Stay Sick! / 1990 / Capitol/Enigma ✦✦

Look Mom No Head! / 1991 / Restless ✦✦✦

Flamejob / 1994 / Warner Brothers ✦✦
The creases in the black leather show on the Cramps' *Flamejob*. Once, the band's demented rockabilly schtick was refreshing and entertaining, but at this point they're not only too old to pull off their gimmick, but they lack the songs to make the gimmick believable. —*Stephen Thomas Erlewine*

○ **Psychedelic Jungle/Gravest Hits** / IRS ✦✦✦✦

The Cranberries

Group, Alternative Pop/Rock
On the strength of the achingly lush ballad "Linger," the Cranberries' first album, 1993's *Everybody Else Is Doing It, So Why Can't We?*, was a surprise success. With its strummed acoustic guitars, soaring strings, and slight Celtic tint, "Linger" is a good example of the guitar-based, Sundays-style atmospheric pop of the Irish group. Although they were stars in Ireland, they hadn't had much success in the rest of Europe. Thanks to their American success, the band also became popular in Britain.

The Cranberries cemented their across-the-board success with their second album, *No Need to Argue*, which quickly sold over two million copies in America on the strength of the hit singles "Zombie" and "Ode to My Family." —*Stephen Thomas Erlewine*

● **Everybody Else Is Doing It, So . . .** / 1993 / PolyGram ✦✦✦✦
Dolores O'Riordan possesses one of those gorgeous, elastic voices that you can fall in love with on first listen and not tire of on the 20th. She yelps exotically to a vibrato guitar backing on "Dreams"; emotes seductively on "Pretty"; thickly breathes the lyrics to "Not Sorry"; and soars through the urgent pop roller-coaster of "How." The group paints a seamless, unobtrusive, almost orchestral backdrop that shatters into sonic shards at all the right moments of emphasis. —*Roch Parisien*

○ **No Need to Argue** / 1994 / PolyGram ✦✦✦✦
With their second album, *No Need to Argue*, the Cranberries have managed to avoid a sophomore slump by turning in a set of songs that builds on their debut's finest moments. With the exception of the distorted march of "Zombie," there aren't that many great departures from the band's atmospheric, melodic guitar-pop. Most of the credit goes to the gutsy, beautiful singing of Dolores O'Riordan, who manages to squeeze emotion out of even the most mundane lyrics ("Ode to My Family"). —*Stephen Thomas Erlewine*

Cranes

Group, Alternative Pop/Rock
Cranes were one of the major trance-pop/shoegazing groups of the early '90s, combining ethereal vocals and melodies with loud, droning guitars. Cranes were formed by brother and sister Jim (drums) and Alison Shaw (vocals) in 1988 in Portsmouth, England; guitarist Mark Francombe and bassist Matt Cope joined the band two years later. The group independently released their first album, *Fuse*, on cassette in 1990; a small local label released *Self Non Self* the same year to good reviews. Both sets of music led to a record contract with Dedicated, an English record label. Later that year, they released their first EP for the label, *Inescapable*, which earned them a lot of attention, including a *Melody Maker*

cover story; a second EP, *Espero*, also earned positive reviews, including a *Melody Maker* Single of the Week. The following year, the band released their first album, *Wings of Joy*, which received favorable reviews on both sides of the Atlantic, as well as earning the band a sizable cult following, including the Cure's Robert Smith; Smith picked Cranes to open for the Cure on their 1992 world tour, which earned them a larger audience. *Forever*, the group's second album, was released in 1993. It expanded their cult slightly, yet 1994's *Loved* found the band in a holding pattern, commercially. —*Stephen Thomas Erlewine*

Wings of Joy / Nov. 1991 / Dedicated ✦✦

● **Forever** / May 1993 / Dedicated ✦✦✦✦

Loved / 1994 / Arista ✦✦✦

Crash Test Dummies

Group, Alternative Pop/Rock
With their clever, smug lyrics and cloying folk-tinged melodies, the Crash Test Dummies are a perfect rock band for affluent '90s college students and yuppies. Their first album was a huge hit in their native Canada, but only gained a small cult following in other parts of the world. Thanks to former Talking Head Jerry Harrison's clean, radio-friendly production, the follow-up *God Shuffled His Feet* (1993), broke big in the States and, in turn, Europe. The first single from the album, "MMM MMM MMM MMM," became a worldwide Top Ten hit, making the group a minor sensation with their self-consciously bizarre lyrics and singer/songwriter Brad Roberts's deep baritone. —*Stephen Thomas Erlewine*

The Ghosts That Haunt Me / 1991 / Arista ✦✦✦
A fine debut album by these smug collegiate folk-pop humorists, featuring the alternative rock hit "Superman's Song." —*Stephen Thomas Erlewine*

● **God Shuffled His Feet** / 1993 / Arista ✦✦✦✦
Thanks to Jerry Harrison's remarkably clear and focused production, Crash Test Dummies' second album became a surprise hit. Apart from the relatively concise pop smarts of the singles "Mmm Mmm Mmm Mmm" and "Afternoons and Coffeespoons," *God Shuffled His Feet* isn't all that different from the band's first album. —*Stephen Thomas Erlewine*

Randy Crawford

b. Feb. 18, 1952, Macon, GA
Soul, Urban
Randy Crawford's initial notoriety came from her fiery vocal on "Street Life," a 1979 song that matched her with the Crusaders. It was included on the soundtrack for Burt Reynolds's film *Sharky's Machine*. Crawford was born in Macon and grew up in Cincinnati. She worked in clubs as a teen, accompanied by her father. Crawford was lead vocalist in a group that included bassist Bootsy Collins before touring as George Benson's opening act in 1972. Cannonball Adderley invited her to sing on his LP *Big Man*. Crawford recorded "Don't Get Caught in Love's Triangle," a song produced by Johnny Bristol, during a short stay on the label. She soon moved to Warner Brothers, and after "Street Life," recorded and toured Europe with the Crusaders. Crawford was tabbed Most Outstanding Performer at the 1980 Tokyo Music Festival. She remained with Warner Brothers through the '80s and early '90s, but has been unable to score either a big R&B hit or major crossover smash, despite having one of the most readily identifiable voices and distinctive approaches of any contemporary female vocalist. She's been more successful overseas, particularly in England, where such singles as "Knocking on Heaven's Door," "Rainy Night in Georgia," and "Last Night at Danceland" have gotten universal acclaim. —*Ron Wynn*

○ **Miss Randy Crawford** / 1977 / Warner Brothers ✦✦✦✦

Raw Silk / 1979 / Warner Brothers ✦✦✦
Actually, it's raw soul. —*Bil Carpenter*

● **Now We May Begin** / 1980 / Warner Brothers ✦✦✦✦
The Crusaders produced this 1980 album, one of the better Randy Crawford sets. The song "Last Night At Danceland" was a hit, while the album cut "One Day I'll Fly Away" got widespread radio airplay and did well in the international market. Crawford's quivering delivery and eclectic nature has made it difficult for record companies to target and market her material; this was one of the few times she penetrated the urban contemporary and R&B markets. —*Ron Wynn*

Everything Must Change / 1980 / Warner Brothers ✦✦✦

Secret Combination / 1981 / Warner Brothers ✦✦✦
Randy Crawford made even more noise on the urban contemporary and R&B front in 1981 with this album, one of her most successful ever from a chart and hit standpoint. The title track and the album cut "Rio De Janeiro Blue" were well-received. She continued smartly blending jazzy pop, slick ballads, and earnest, anguished numbers like her cover of "Rainy Night In Georgia." — *Ron Wynn*

Through the Eyes of Love / 1981-1991 / Warner Brothers ✦✦✦
Nice, highly stylized album by a versatile vocalist whose trembling sound and eclectic nature have made her tough for record labels to market. This album, like her others, was all over the idiomatic lot and expressively sung, if at times overproduced. — *Ron Wynn*

Windsong / 1982 / Warner Brothers ✦✦✦
Another strong album for Randy Crawford; the song "Imagine" remains one of the best R&B covers/versions around, while "One Hello" did well in Europe and made it to the charts, as did "Imagine," although it broke later in America. Crawford sang with consistency and character on every number. — *Ron Wynn*

Nightline / 1983 / Warner Brothers ✦✦✦
A nice combination of jazzy, sophisticated ballads, a few harder-hitting numbers, and some heartache material. The title track made it to the Top 30 on the R&B chart, and Crawford was a popular attraction on the urban contemporary and upscale R&B concert circuit. — *Ron Wynn*

Abstract Emotions / 1986 / Warner Brothers ✦✦✦
Randy Crawford continued her run of good '80s albums, generating more R&B chart hits with this '86 release, plus an international smash with "Almaz." The album even reached Britain's Top 20, while two of its singles were moderate American successes. — *Ron Wynn*

○ **Rich & Poor** / 1989 / Warner Brothers ✦✦✦✦
Modern soul with class. — *Bil Carpenter*

Crazy Horse

Group, Hard Rock
A hard-rock trio consisting of bassist Billy Talbot, drummer Ralph Molina, and guitarist Danny Whitten. They are known best as the on-again, off-again backup band for Neil Young, though they have recorded occasional albums themselves. Frank Sampedro replaced Whitten after his death in 1973. The current band is Talbot, Molina, singer Sonny Mone, and guitarist Matt Piucci. — *William Ruhlmann*

● **Crazy Horse** / 1971 / Reprise ✦✦✦✦
An exceptional hard-rock album by one of the finest garage-rock bands ever, *Crazy Horse* proves that the band doesn't need Neil Young to make tough, eclectic, and smart rock & roll. — *Stephen Thomas Erlewine*

Loose / 1971 / Reprise ✦✦

At Crooked Lake / 1973 / Epic ✦✦

Crazy Moon / 1978 / RCA ✦✦✦
The trio of Molina, Talbot, and Sampedro is frequently joined by compatriot Neil Young on an album of hard rock with a sound not unlike that produced by them on Young's records. — *William Ruhlmann*

Left for Dead / 1981 / Curb ✦✦

Papa John Creach

b. May 8, 1917d. Feb. 22, 1994
Folk-Rock
Violinist Papa John Creach first came to the notice of rock fans when he joined Jefferson Airplane and its spin-off group, Hot Tuna, in 1970. By that time, he was already in his early '50s, a veteran of jazz and blues associations, while his fellow band members were still approaching 30. Nevertheless, using an electrified violin, Creach added a new psychedelic edge to the Airplane in its final days. The band split in 1972, by which time Creach had begun to release solo albums on its custom label, Grunt. The Airplane was reorganized and relaunched as Jefferson Starship, and Creach was with it through its million-selling *Red Octopus* album in 1975. He continued to make solo albums through 1992, when he released *Papa Blues*. Papa John Creach died of heart failure in 1994 at the age of 76. — *William Ruhlmann*

● **Papa John Creach** / Dec. 1971 / Grunt ✦✦✦✦
At the time this album was recorded, Jefferson Airplane had expanded from a rock group into something of a San Francisco collective of musicians and launched its own record label, Grunt, necessitating a flow of product. As a result, there was a flurry of releases by the Airplane itself and several offshoots, with each of these records featuring several members of the loose aggregation informally dubbed PERRO (the Planet Earth Rock 'N' Roll Orchestra). Papa John Creach, violinist for the Airplane and its spin-off group, Hot Tuna, was the leader on this set, which featured members of the Airplane (Grace Slick, for example, duets with Creach on the lead-off track, "The Janitor Drives a Cadillac"), Quicksilver Messenger Service, and the Grateful Dead. The result sounds like the Airplane records of the period, with a bit more of Creach's electric violin soaring over the proceedings. — *William Ruhlmann*

Filthy! / 1972 / Grunt ✦✦✦
Papa John Creach's second album is a good collection mixing pop, jazz, R&B, and rock. Creach is only a modestly talented singer, but his violin playing soars, and there is more of that than vocals. Unlike his first album, on which he was joined by members of Jefferson Starship, here Creach is backed by Zulu, a competent band, on all but one track, Jorma Kaukonen's "Walking the Tou-Tou," on which Hot Tuna plays. — *William Ruhlmann*

Playing My Fiddle for You / 1974 / Grunt ✦✦✦
Fronting a six-piece band called Zulu, Papa John Creach produces a set of R&B, jump blues, ballads, and rock. A horn section augments the proceedings, as Creach and Zulu take on an instrumental version of "Milk Train" co-written by Grace Slick and featured on the 1972 Jefferson Airplane album *Long John Silver* and the similarly soaring "String Jet Continues." But "I Miss You So" is an old pop ballad, "Golden Dreams" is an airy instrumental, and "Playing My Music" is Creach's autobiography-in-song. A varied collection. — *William Ruhlmann*

I'm the Fiddle Man / 1975 / Buddah ✦✦

Rock Father / 1976 / Buddah ✦✦

The Cat & the Fiddle / 1977 / DJM ✦✦

Inphasion / 1978 / DJM ✦✦
Though he varies the approach a little, for example adding a Latin tinge on "Montuno Grande," this is for the most part a pop-rock vocal collection with more guitar than violin. Fellow violinists David LaFlamme from It's A Beautiful Day and Charlie Daniels lend a hand, as do Johnny "Guitar" Watson and Dr. John, but on the whole this isn't as funky as it wants to be. Creach has a distinctive instrumental style; there's no reason to turn him into a second-rate Boz Scaggs. — *William Ruhlmann*

○ **Papa Blues** / 1992 / Bee Bump ✦✦✦✦

○ **Best of Papa John Creach** / Buddah ✦✦✦✦

Cream

Group, Blues Rock, Hard Rock, Art-Rock/Progressive-Rock, Psychedelic
Cream's relatively short lifespan (it formed in July 1966 and broke up after a final concert on November 26, 1968) belies its overwhelming influence on the direction of subsequent rock music. The group helped define the blues-based hard rock/heavy metal genre that was a dominant force in popular music for decades afterward.

Cream was billed as a "supergroup" (the first group so billed), since it was made up of well-known talents from other groups: Eric Clapton (born Eric Patrick Clapp, Mar 30, 1945, Ripley, Surrey, England) (guitar, vocals) had been a member of the Yardbirds and John Mayall's Bluesbreakers; Jack Bruce (b. May 14, 1943, Glasgow, Scotland) (bass, vocals) had worked with the Graham Bond Organisation, Manfred Mann, and the Bluesbreakers; and Ginger Baker (born Peter Baker, Aug 19, 1939, Lewisham, London, England) (drums) also had been with Graham Bond.

Cream debuted with the U.K. hits "Wrapping Paper" and "I Feel Free," then released its debut album, *Fresh Cream* (December 1966), which hit the Top Ten in England. "Strange Brew" became their third British hit in June 1967. It was featured on *Disraeli Gears* (November 1967), another U.K. Top Ten hit that was their U.S. breakthrough and also included their first U.S. hit, "Sunshine of Your Love."

Cream's records, full of songs written by Bruce with lyricist Pete Brown, were more restrained and pop-oriented than their live shows, which featured extensive jamming. This was reflected in their third album, *Wheels of Fire*, a half-live half-studio double album that topped the American charts and featured the hits "White Room" and "Crossroads."

At their commercial peak, Cream announced in September 1968 that they would split up after a U.S./U.K. tour. They did, but also produced a final album, *Goodbye* (January 1969), featuring a last hit single, "Badge." —*William Ruhlmann*

Fresh Cream / Dec. 1966 / Polydor ✦✦✦
Cream's debut album was largely rooted in the blues, and included here highly charged versions of such standards as Willie Dixon's "Spoonful," Muddy Waters's "Rollin' and Tumblin'," and bassist Jack Bruce's "N.S.U."—which took on a whole new life on stage. On this record they sound somewhat flat and uninspired. —*Rob Bowman*

○ **Disraeli Gears** / Nov. 1967 / Polydor ✦✦✦✦
Cream's sophomore effort was a substantial step forward. Interestingly, part of the reason seems to be that they stopped covering American blues musicians and started writing their own psychedelic blues-based hybrids. "Sunshine of Your Love" was the big AM radio hit and "Tales of Brave Ulysses," "Strange Brew," and "S.W.L.A.B.R." received substantial FM play. —*Rob Bowman*

○ **Wheels of Fire** / Jun. 1968 / Polydor ✦✦✦✦
Wheels of Fire was a two-album set, one disc recorded in the studio, the second disc recorded live on stage in San Francisco. Side Three contains the definitive live version of what became Clapton's signature piece, Robert Johnson's "Crossroads," plus a version of "Spoonful" that clocks in just short of seventeen minutes. On such pieces, Cream approached blues-based rock with a jazz aesthetic, using the song as a framework to begin and end a performance. The strength of the performance is in the improvisation. When it worked, as it does on "Spoonful," they were brilliant. When it didn't, as on "Traintime" and "Toad," the band became excess incarnate. The studio disc contained their second Top Ten single, Jack Bruce's "White Room," as well as a stunning cover of Albert King's "Born Under a Bad Sign." Other tracks, particularly those written by Ginger Baker, do not hold up. —*Rob Bowman*

Goodbye / Jan. 1969 / Polydor ✦✦✦
As the title implies, this is Cream's farewell. By the time it was issued, the band had broken up. Three studio recordings that were left were coupled with extended live versions of "I'm So Glad," "Politician," and "I'm Sitting on Top of the World." The live tracks burn. Clapton, Bruce, and Baker each take credit for one of the studio tracks. Clapton's cut, "Badge," was co-written by George Harrison and remains what was surely the prettiest melody to ever grace a Cream recording. —*Rob Bowman*

Best of Cream / Jul. 1969 / Polydor ✦✦✦
The first of a long line of Cream anthologies, the 1969 *Best of Cream* (released originally on Atco, since reissued on Polydor) was a 10-track compilation featuring nearly all of Cream's U.K. and U.S. single hits. The exceptions were "Wrapping Paper" and "Anyone For Tennis," which were not much missed, especially when instead you got tracks like "Born Under a Bad Sign" and "Tales of Brave Ulysses." In fact, for a long time, *Best of Cream* served as the best one-record distillation of Cream. It has been superseded, however, by 1995's *The Very Best of Cream* (Polydor 314523752), which contains all of its selections and 10 more. —*William Ruhlmann*

Live Cream, Vol. 1 / Apr. 1970 / Polydor ✦✦✦
Cream was a band born to the stage. This is their most consistently brilliant album. Four of the five cuts appeared on *Fresh Cream*. The fifth, "Lawdy Mama," is a traditional blues piece that makes its first appearance here. All but "Lawdy Mama" are given extended jazz-based treatment. The dialog among the three musicians as the jams develop is fascinating. Foreground and background seem to dissolve as all three musicians take charge, using the full range of their instruments. Performances like this single-handedly raised the stakes of musicianship in rock. —*Rob Bowman*

Live Cream, Vol. 2 / Mar. 1972 / Polydor ✦✦✦
More live Cream concentrating on material from their *Disraeli Gears* and *Wheels of Fire* albums plus an extended workout on Freddie King's "Hideaway." —*Rob Bowman*

○ **Heavy Cream** / Oct. 9, 1972 / Polydor ✦✦✦✦
This 22-track double album presented consumers with a more extensive hits collection than *Best of Cream* (1969). The same hits were included, plus more of Cream's better album tracks, making

this the most comprehensive compilation of a band that only made four albums to begin with. —*William Ruhlmann*

Strange Brew: The Very Best of Cream / 1983 / Polydor ✦✦✦
What the title implies, all the finest tracks from the band's four studio albums. The best was brilliant. —*Rob Bowman*

★ **The Very Best of Cream** / 1995 / Chronicles ✦✦✦✦✦
There have been many compilations drawn from the four albums Cream originally released between 1966 and 1969. But the one most commonly available since the early 1980s was the 10-track *Strange Brew: The Very Best of Cream* (1983) (Polydor 811 639), a bare-bones collection focusing on the group's hit singles. Note, then, that this album, despite the similar title, is a newly compiled 1995 CD/cassette containing all of the recordings on *Strange Brew*, plus 10 more. It is thus the most comprehensive Cream anthology on the market, including all the group's essential tracks on a single disc with superior sound in a package containing good annotations. —*William Ruhlmann*

Steppin' Out [Bootleg] / Invasion Unlimited ✦✦✦
The best unreleased Cream to circulate widely, this collects 18 performances for the BBC between 1966 and 1968. Mostly very good sound, these fine straight-ahead renditions include most of the best tracks from their early albums, with the notable absence of their two biggest hits, "White Room" and "Sunshine Of Your Love." The two versions of the instrumental title track, one of Clapton's prime showcases in his Bluesbreakers days, are special highlights. These BBC sessions are available under a number of different guises; this particular package is the most thorough. —*Richie Unterberger*

Creation

Group, British Invasion, Psychedelic
No other band came closer to emulating the feedback-ridden autodestruction of the early Who than the Creation, who had a couple of minor British hit singles in 1966 with "Making Time" and "Painter Man." The sonic resemblance is hardly surprising; the Creation were produced by Shel Talmy, who also produced the Who's earliest records, and lead guitarist Eddie Phillips was even asked by Pete Townshend to join the Who as second guitarist. Phillips's feedback freakouts were grounded by solid mod power chords and British Invasion harmonies. The Creation produced several interesting singles between 1966 and 1968, and although they achieved brief stardom in Germany, they never made it big in the U.K. Ronnie Wood was briefly a member before the group disbanded in 1968. —*Richie Unterberger*

● **How Does It Feel to Feel** / 1982 / Edsel ✦✦✦✦
Unquestionably the best of the several Creation repackages floating around. Includes virtually all of their 1966-68 singles and a few other stray tracks of interest from the same period. —*Richie Unterberger*

Creation Rebel

Group, Reggae, Dub
The product of the fertile and prolific British producer, mixmaster and dub genius Adrian Sherwood, Creation Rebel was one of Sherwood's first endeavors as a producer. Originally the backing group for the late reggae great Prince Far-I, Creation Rebel worked with Sherwood from 1977-1980, recording some of the best reggae dub music this side of Lee Perry during the early English punk era. Languorous, funky, spacy and totally intoxicating, it's exciting to hear the awesome production/mixing talents of Sherwood in their early days. Similarly, the band (drummers Style Scott and Fish Clarke, bassist Clinton Jack, keyboardist Bigga Morrison, guitarist Crucial Tony, and percussionist Slicker) play with a grace, effortlessness and power that most studio bands would kill to achieve. With the band's talents so wonderfully used by Sherwood, this is without a doubt some of the best and most important non-rock music to be made in England in the late '70s. —*John Dougan*

Starship Africa / 1980 / 4D Rhythms ✦✦✦
Psychotic Junkanoo / 1981 / Statik ✦✦✦
Threat to Creation / 1981 / Cherry Red ✦✦
Lows & Highs / 1982 / Cherry Red ✦✦
● **Historic Moments, Vol. 1** / 1994 / On-U Sound ✦✦✦✦
Long out of print, CD technology has now made nearly all of the crucial recordings of Creation Rebel readily available. Both volumes (with another one in the offing) are absolutely essential dub

records, seductive and compelling play after play after play. Sherwood's avant-garde tendencies were in the early stages of development here, and he adds a daring bravado to the insistent, undeniable groove that Creation Rebel lays down. *Volume 1* is a little more song-oriented; *Volume 2* is a bit more adventurous (and slightly better). Both of these are essential for any reggae fan's library. However, those interested in experimentation will walk away from this experience with their lives changed for the better. —*John Dougan*

Creedence Clearwater Revival

Group, Rock & Roll
Even though Creedence Clearwater Revival hailed from the San Francisco area, the band's soul, which was steeped in R&B, rockabilly, blues, and stripped-down rock & roll, made it hard to believe they came from anywhere but the Mississippi Delta. At that time, Bay Area rock was dominated by bands like the Grateful Dead, Quicksilver Messenger Service, and Jefferson Airplane, whose idea of economical arrangements and a tight rhythmic pocket hardly existed.

John Fogerty, the band's lead vocalist/lead guitarist, brought a kind of passion to rock & roll that few recorded artists have ever delivered. In addition, his songwriting contributions to rock have unquestionably placed him in the ranks of American music legends like Chuck Berry, Willie Dixon, and Carl Perkins. Creedence's rhythm section, with Stu Cook (bass), Doug Clifford (drums), and Tom Fogerty (rhythm guitar), made every note count, doing for rock what Booker T. & the MGs did for Memphis soul.

Any lover of real, earthy rock should own most of Creedence's catalog, since this is the meat-and-potatoes of any decent rock collection. Then again, it is unimaginable that any lover of rock & roll could be unaware of this band. —*Rick Clark*

Creedence Clearwater Revival / 1968 / Fantasy ✦✦✦
The band's unique swampy crunch was already well-developed on this fine debut. It opens with a riveting version of Screamin' Jay Hawkins's hit "I Put a Spell on You." A gritty psychedelic version of Dale Hawkins's creation "Suzy Q" was Creedence's first hit. —*Rick Clark*

Bayou Country / 1969 / Fantasy ✦✦✦
John Fogerty's songwriting voice gains new focus, particularly in "Proud Mary," the band's most popular song, and "Penthouse Pauper." "Bootleg" features a powerfully spare groove, and "Born on the Bayou," with its rock-solid pulse and economical lead-guitar work, is one of the band's better attempts at stretching out. Nevertheless, the long jams found here cause the album to lose some steam. —*Rick Clark*

○ **Willy & The Poor Boys** / 1969 / Fantasy ✦✦✦✦
There's not a weak cut here, just more hits like "Down on the Corner" and the relentless wrong-side-of-the-tracks railing of "Fortunate Son." By the time of *Willy,* this California band had captured the spirit of the South more believably than most bands from that region. Versions of "The Midnight Special," "Cotton Fields," and instrumentals like the down-home "Poorboy Shuffle" and "Side O' the Road," with its Booker T. groove, helped underscore that perception. —*Rick Clark*

○ **Green River** / 1969 / Fantasy ✦✦✦✦
Fogerty tightens things up with this great collection of songs. It contains the truly great hits "Green River," "Lodi," and "Bad Moon Rising." "Wrote a Song for Everyone," "Cross-tie Walker," and "Tombstone Shadow" are classic Fogerty. There's a super version of "The Night Time Is the Right Time." —*Rick Clark*

○ **Cosmo's Factory** / 1970 / Fantasy ✦✦✦✦
"Ramble Tamble" and a masterful version of "I Heard It Through the Grapevine" may run a little too long, but the remainder of the album is letter-perfect. Pointing out highlights here is useless. Most of these tracks were hits as well. —*Rick Clark*

Pendulum / 1970 / Fantasy ✦✦✦
Creedence loses some steam here by wasting too much time on lengthy groove numbers like "Pagan Baby," "Born to Move," and "Rude Awakening" (number two), a horrible attempt at creating something serious-sounding, and an irritating waste of time. In spite of those miscalculations, most bands could only hope for as many good songs like "Have You Ever Seen the Rain?," "Hey Tonight," "It's Just a Thought," "Molina," and "(Wish I Could) Hideaway." —*Rick Clark*

○ **Creedence Gold** / 1972 / Fantasy ✦✦✦✦

Mardi Gras / 1972 / Fantasy ✦✦✦
Maybe Fogerty was running out of steam, but in the name of democratization, each of the other band members got to toss in their creative licks on this album. After so many great albums, this one sounds half-hearted. Only "Sweet Hitch-Hiker," "Someday Never Comes," and a cover of the Ricky Nelson tune "Hello Mary Lou" recall the band's earlier magic. —*Rick Clark*

○ **More Creedence Gold** / 1973 / Fantasy ✦✦✦✦

Live in Europe / 1973 / Fantasy ✦✦

★ **Chronicle, Vol. 1** / 1976 / Fantasy ✦✦✦✦✦
An essential disc for any serious lover of rock & roll, it contains almost all of the Creedence hits, plus a generous helping of key album tracks. —*Rick Clark*

The Royal Albert Hall Concert / 1980 / Fantasy ✦✦✦
This solid no-frills live document covers many of the band's hits, plus time for some meat-and-potatoes groove-jammin' with ten minutes of "Keep on Chooglin'." It beats the dismal *Live in Europe* by a long shot. —*Rick Clark*

☆ **Chronicle, Vol. 2** / 1986 / Fantasy ✦✦✦✦✦
A well-compiled set, it fills in most of the gaps left by *Vol. 1.* Sin of omission: Where's "Bootleg"?! —*Rick Clark*

Marshall Crenshaw

b. 1954, Detroit, MI
Rock & Roll, Pop/Rock
When Marshall Crenshaw's debut burst onto the 1982 music scene, his tight, well-crafted songs (part Buddy Holly/part Beatles) and exuberant performances were a fresh breeze at a time when robotic pop by Human League and Toni Basil, as well as soul-numbing ballads like Lionel Richie's "Truly," reigned on the airwaves. He even managed a Top 40 hit with the timeless-sounding "Someday, Someway." Crenshaw's albums have been mostly enjoyable. Only on 1989's *Good Evening* does Crenshaw seem creatively adrift. —*Rick Clark*

● **Marshall Crenshaw** / 1982 / Warner Brothers ✦✦✦✦
His incredible debut revealed Crenshaw to be a fully formed songwriter in the Beatles and Buddy Holly super-melodic pop tradition. Like the work of those influences, the best material here seems timeless. "Someday, Someway" (#36) was a moderate hit, even though it (and others like "Cynical Girl," "Girls," "The Usual Thing," and "Mary Anne") seemed written in stone. Crenshaw does include one fine cover of "Soldier of Love," recorded originally by Arthur Alexander and later by the Beatles. Criticism: Why has Warner chosen not to include Crenshaw's fine B-sides as bonus tracks from this period on this or his other CDs? —*Rick Clark*

○ **Field Day** / 1983 / Warner Brothers ✦✦✦✦
For those expecting a repeat of his fine debut effort, Crenshaw made an unexpected left turn and sought out in-demand producer Steve Lillywhite, whose credits (Psychedelic Furs, XTC, U2, Ultravox) read like an alternative rock Who's Who. The heavily treated drum sounds and walls of guitar may have initially put off some fans, but *Field Day* demonstrated that Crenshaw was making impressive strides as a songwriter and musician. "Whenever You're on My Mind" (a great single that should've been a hit), "Our Town," "All I Know Right Now," and "Monday Morning Rock" are highlights. —*Rick Clark*

○ **Downtown** / 1985 / Warner Brothers ✦✦✦✦
With the help of producer T-Bone Burnette and a handful of session sidemen, Crenshaw delivered a strong collection of originals and covers. Highlights include a version of Ben Vaughn's "I'm Sorry (But So Is Brenda Lee)" and Crenshaw's own "The Distance Between." This is one of Crenshaw's best efforts. —*Rick Clark*

○ **Mary Jean & 9 Others** / 1987 / Warner Brothers ✦✦✦✦
Not quite as strong as his first three full-length albums, *Mary Jean* does possess some standout tracks in "Calling Out for Love (At Crying Time)," a version of Peter Case's "Steel Strings," and the title cut. It was produced by Don Dixon, whose credits include the Smithereens. —*Rick Clark*

Good Evening / 1989 / Warner Brothers ✦✦
This effort drew heavily on outside material, with songs by Richard Thompson, Dianne Warren, John Hiatt, the Isley Brothers and Bobby Fuller. David Kershenbaum's production is typically

classy, but is unable to keep this from being Crenshaw's weakest release. —*Rick Clark*

Life's Too Short / 1991 / MCA ✦✦✦
Crenshaw changes labels and brings on producer Ed Stasium (Cavedogs, Living Colour, Smithereens). The result is a more vibrant, harder-rocking sound. Highlights include "Better Back Off," "Don't Disappear Now," "Face of Fashion," and "Fantastic Planet of Love." This is his strongest release since *Downtown*. —*Rick Clark*

Live: My Truck Is My Home / 1994 / Razor & Tie ✦✦✦
14 tracks taken from various sources (sound board tapes, etc.) from performances plucked from 1982, 1987, 1990, 1991, 1992 and 1994, respectively. Loads of great Crenshaw material ("You're My Favorite Waste of Time," "Cynical Girl"), explosive guitar that seldoms surfaces on his studio efforts the way it does here, and plenty of deadpan humor (the picture of Bo "Billy, Don't Be a Hero" Donaldson on the disc itself says it all) make this a great live album with quirks that keep it ahead of the pack. —*Cub Koda*

The Crests

Group, Doo-Wop
One of the most successful integrated doo-wop groups, the Crests waxed the classic ballad "16 Candles" in 1959. Formed in 1956, they began recording the next year for Joyce, where they inched onto the pop lists with "Sweetest One." Moving to the brand-new Coed logo, Johnny Maestro's (b. May 7, 1930) warm tenor made "16 Candles" a national smash, and pop/R&B hybrids like "The Angels Listened In" and "Step by Step" also did well. Maestro went solo in 1960, scoring the next year with "Model Girl" on Coed, while the Crests attempted to survive on their own. Maestro eventually reclaimed stardom as leader of Brooklyn Bridge, an 11-piece aggregation that hit with "Worst That Could Happen" in 1968. —*Bill Dahl*

● **The Best of the Crests** / 1990 / Rhino ✦✦✦✦
All of the Crests' hits, including the classic "16 Candles" and "Trouble in Paradise," are collected on this splendid 18-track disc. —*Stephen Thomas Erlewine*

The Crickets

Group, Rock & Roll
After the tragic death of Buddy Holly, his band, the Crickets, regrouped and continue to record and tour to this day. Drummer Jerry Allison and bassist Joe B.Mauldin had split from Holly shortly before his death, and with ex-Holly guitarist Sonny Curtis and vocalist Earl Sinks, they continued to record for Brunswick and Coral, notably the original versons of "I Fought the Law" and "More Than I Can Say." Moving to Liberty in 1961 with Jerry Naylor as their new singer, the Crickets recorded for Liberty into 1965 without having a hit of their own. Allison and Curtis were prolific session musicians, backing Bobby Vee, Eddie Cochran, Johnny Burnette, and the Everly Brothers in addition to Holly. With a lineup of Allison, Mauldin, and Gordon Payne, the Crickets garnered airplay in 1988 with "T-Shirt," a bouncy number produced by lifelong Holly fan Paul McCartney. —*Bill Dahl*

● **The Liberty Years** / 1991 / EMI America ✦✦✦✦
Thirty-one cuts of post-Buddy Holly material from his band the Crickets, who endured into 1965 on Liberty Records. Their energetic pop/rock sound often mirrored whatever trends were happening at the time. —*Bill Dahl*

The Critters

Group, Pop/Rock
In 1966, this New York group came off very much like a Lovin' Spoonful Jr., scoring a minor hit with a cover of John Sebastian's "Younger Girl," and then chalking up their only Top 20 single with the very Spoonful-esque original, "Mr. Dieingly Sad." The group's soft harmonies and pop-folk-rock were in a considerably lighter vein than their Kama Sutra labelmates', though. Much of their material was self-penned, though they also benefited from compositions by Jackie DeShannon and Brill Building tunesmiths Pete Anders, Vinnie Poncia, and Doc Pomus. Recording quite a few singles and an LP for Kama Sutra from 1965 to 1967, their gentle pop/rock was rather lightweight and forgettable, with the exception of their best singles. After a final Top 40 hit in 1967 ("Don't Let the Rain Fall Down on Me"), principal songwriter Don Ciccone was drafted, and the group struggled on with a couple albums for the Project 3 label before splitting. —*Richie Unterberger*

● **New York Bound: The Best of the Critters** / 1986 / Big Beat ✦✦✦✦
Both sides of all seven of their Kama Sutra singles, plus an album cut and previously unreleased track from the same era. Some pleasant harmonies and the occasional strong tune, but overall this is pretty insubstantial, and the group sounds nerdy when they try to rock out even just a bit. Includes exhaustive liner notes by British rock historian Brian Hogg. —*Richie Unterberger*

Jim Croce

b. Jan. 10, 1943, Philadelphia, PA, **d.** Sep. 20, 1973, Natchitoches, LA
Singer-Songwriter
A singer/songwriter whose enormous pop success of the early '70s was cut short by his death in a plane crash. A Philadelphia native who had worked the coffeehouse circuit for almost ten years when he was signed to ABC Records in 1971, Croce had a warm singing voice that served him well on his comic uptempo hits ("You Don't Mess Around with Jim," "Bad, Bad Leroy Brown") as well as his sincere ballads ("Operator"). The latter became predominant after his death, with "I Got a Name," "Time in a Bottle," and "I'll Have to Say I Love You in a Song," all of which were posthumous Top Ten hits. —*William Ruhlmann*

Croce / 1969 / Capitol ✦✦
You Don't Mess Around with Jim / 1972 / ABC ✦✦✦
Croce's debut ABC album was also his commercial breakthrough, topping the charts for five weeks, largely due to the comic, uptempo title tune, a story song about competing pool hustlers, although Croce also reached the Top 20 with the change-of-pace ballad "Operator (That's Not the Way It Feels)." Just after his death, ABC issued the LP track "Time in a Bottle," and a newly ironic message propelled it to #1. —*William Ruhlmann*

I Got a Name / 1973 / ABC ✦✦✦
● **Photographs & Memories: His Greatest Hits** / 1974 / Atlantic ✦✦✦✦
Photographs & Memories—His Greatest Hits is a compilation containing Croce's best songs and biggest hits, including the #1 hits "Bad, Bad Leroy Brown" and "Time in a Bottle." —*William Ruhlmann*

○ **Time in a Bottle/Greatest Love Songs** / 1977 / Atlantic ✦✦✦✦
Since it contains only his love ballads, fans who prefer his sweetly sentimental songs like "Operator" and "Time in a Bottle" to story-songs like "Bad, Bad Leroy Brown" and "You Don't Mess Around With Jim," will find *Time in a Bottle* the essential compilation; despite the amount of good material here, *Photographs and Memories* remains a better collection, since it presents both sides of the popular singer/songwriter. —*Stephen Thomas Erlewine*

○ **The 50th Anniversary Collection** / 1992 / Saja ✦✦✦✦
While it has too much material for the casual listener, the two-disc *50th Anniversary Collection* is the definitive package for the hardcore Jim Croce fan, covering all of his hits, as well as many forgotten album tracks. —*Stephen Thomas Erlewine*

Crosby & Nash

Group, Folk, Singer-Songwriter, Folk-Rock, Pop/Rock
This subset of Crosby, Stills, Nash & Young featured David Crosby (b. Aug 14, 1941) and Graham Nash (b. Feb 2, 1942) relying on their sweet harmonies and strong songwriting. The duo lasted from 1972 to the more-or-less permanent re-forming of Crosby, Stills & Nash in 1977. —*William Ruhlmann*

Graham Nash/David Crosby / Apr. 5, 1972 / Atlantic ✦✦✦
Nash and Crosby's first duo album after the demise of Crosby, Stills, Nash & Young produced a Top 40 hit, "Immigration Man." It also featured the excellent "Southbound Train," demonstrating the viability of C&N as a separate harmonic unit. —*William Ruhlmann*

Crosby-Nash: Live / 1975 / Atlantic ✦✦
○ **Wind on the Water** / Sep. 15, 1975 / MCA ✦✦✦✦
Among the finest of the splinter albums to come out of the CSNY camp, this album was paced by Crosby's leadoff track, the moving "Carry Me," and by its closer, the vocal showcase "To the Last Whale." —*William Ruhlmann*

Whistling Down the Wire / Jun. 1976 / ABC ✦✦
Maybe it took more than nine months to come up with another batch of first-rate material, or maybe David Crosby and Graham Nash were saving their first-rate material for the next Crosby,

Stills & Nash album, but *Whistling Down the Wire*, their third and final new studio album as a duo, was a distinctly second-rate effort. As usual, Crosby's loosely arranged jazz-blues tunes were offset by Nash's more pop-oriented songs, but this time around neither of them came up with anything memorable. Crosby seemed most comfortable on his "Dancer," an instrumental, while Nash expressed himself in poetic metaphors that were difficult to follow. — *William Ruhlmann*

The Best of Crosby & Nash / Oct. 1978 / Atlantic ✦✦✦

David Crosby

b. Aug. 14, 1941, Los Angeles, CA
Singer-Songwriter
Crosby was an original member of the groundbreaking '60s Los Angeles band, the Byrds. During his time with them, Crosby's smooth harmonic capabilities and airy lead-vocal style provided a major ingredient in their distinctive sound. He also wrote or co-wrote some wonderfully trippy songs during his stint with them, including "Lady Friend," "Everybody's Been Burned," "Draft Morning," "Dolphins Smile," "Why," "Eight Miles High," "What Happening?!?!," and "I See You," a song Yes recorded on their debut album. Crosby left the Byrds and helped found the richly harmonic, mellow acoustic-rock trio Crosby, Stills & Nash in 1968. They enjoyed enormous success in their first few years, but solo projects and Crosby's notorious drug problems (and subsequent late-'80s celebrity cleanup) resulted in the band's sporadic output. In 1989 Crosby released *Oh Yes I Can*, his first solo album since 1971, along with a best-selling autobiography called *Long Time Gone*. Four years later, he returned with *Thousand Roads*. — *Rick Clark*

● **If I Could Only Remember My Name** / Feb. 22, 1971 / Atlantic ✦✦✦✦
On his first solo album, the velvet-voiced hippie crooner invited half of Northern California to join him. It's vintage Crosby, ranking with the best of CSNY group efforts. — *Jeff Tamarkin*

Oh Yes I Can / Jan. 23, 1989 / A&M ✦✦✦
His post-rehab reintroduction to the world of creativity finds a reflective Crosby still in fine voice and trying a few new things with his music. — *Jeff Tamarkin*

Thousand Roads / May 4, 1993 / Atlantic ✦✦✦
For his third solo album, *Thousand Roads*, Crosby increased the participation of his guests and attempted to redefine himself as an artist. Where previously, whoever was playing or singing on the track, the song was a Crosby composition, on *Thousand Roads* Crosby acted primarily as an interpretive singer, penning only one of the ten songs and contributing to two others. The result certainly was a craftsmanlike set of songs written by pop professionals—Phil Collins, Jimmy Webb, Marc Cohn, John Hiatt, Paul Brady, Stephen Bishop—and produced by the cream of pop producers—Don Was, Glyn Johns, Phil Ramone. The failings were, first, that Crosby's individuality was lost and, second, that, as the list suggests, his choices were more calculated than inspired. The problem with David Crosby as a solo artist was not how to make him sound more conventional, it was how to make his unconventionality work. *Thousand Roads* solved the wrong problem; the album was Crosby's least successful in the record stores. — *William Ruhlmann*

It's All Coming Back Now / 1995 / Atlantic ✦✦
Recorded December 7, 1993, at the Whisky-A-Go-Go in Hollywood, California, this is a David Crosby live album and a good representation of his solo concert performance. In fact, it's a little better than usual, since Crosby is joined by singers Chris Robinson of the Black Crowes and his old partner Graham Nash. Crosby splits the 71-minute set just about evenly between more recent solo efforts—including two newly written songs—and faithful renditions of favorites from his Crosby, Stills, Nash & Young days. Inadvertently, the set list serves to confirm that the latter represent his best work, while at the same time we've heard songs like "Long Time Gone" and "Wooden Ships" so often in studio and live performances that there isn't much reason to have additional recordings of them. The album's chief virtue is in the expression of Crosby's personality, but there isn't enough of that. So, while these are often spirited performances, they don't add to our understanding of the artist the way a live album should. — *William Ruhlmann*

Crosby Stills & Nash (and Young)

Group, Singer-Songwriter, Folk-Rock, Pop/Rock
The musical partnership of David Crosby (b. Aug 14, 1941), Stephen Stills (b. Jan 3, 1945), and Graham Nash (b. Feb 2, 1942), with and without Neil Young (b. Nov 12, 1945), not only was one of the most successful touring and recording acts of the late '60s, '70s, and early '80s; with the colorful, contrasting nature of the members' characters and their connection to the political and cultural upheavals of the time, it was the only American-based band to approach the overall societal impact of the Beatles. The group was a second marriage for all the participants when it came together in 1968: Crosby had been a member of the Byrds, Nash was in the Hollies, and Stills had been part of Buffalo Springfield. The resulting trio, however, sounded like none of its predecessors and was characterized by a unique vocal blend and a musical approach that ranged from acoustic folk to melodic pop to hard rock. CSN's debut album, released in 1969, was perfectly in tune with the times, and the group was an instant hit. By the time of their first tour (which included the Woodstock festival), they had added Young, also a veteran of Buffalo Springfield, who maintained a solo career. The first CSN&Y album, *Déjà-vu*, was a chart-topping hit in 1970, but the group split acrimoniously after a summer tour. *4 Way Street*, a live double album issued after the breakup, was another #1 hit. (When it finally was released on CD in 1992, it was lengthened with more live material.) In 1974, CSN&Y reformed for a summer stadium tour without releasing a new record. Nevertheless, the compilation *So Far* became their third straight #1. Crosby, Stills and Nash reformed without Young in 1977 for the album *CSN*, another giant hit. They followed with *Daylight Again* in 1982, but by then Crosby was in the throes of drug addiction and increasing legal problems. He was in jail in 1985-1986, but cleaned up and returned to action, with the result that CSN&Y reunited for only their second studio album, *American Dream*, in 1988. CSN followed with *Live It Up* in 1990, and though that album was a commercial disappointment, the trio remains a popular live act; it embarked on a 25th anniversary tour in the summer of 1994 and released a new album, *After The Storm*. — *William Ruhlmann*

○ **Crosby, Stills & Nash** / May 29, 1969 / Atlantic ✦✦✦✦
A scintillating blend of personal poetry, topical politics, and splendid, spare production of some great music. — *Bruce Eder*

☆ **Déjà-vu** / Mar. 11, 1970 / Atlantic ✦✦✦✦✦
This was the group's triumph, displaying a broader musical scope than that found on the CSN debut record. Each of the four members contributed high-quality material, with Stills turning in the lead-off track, "Carry On," Nash contributing such standards as "Teach Your Children" and "Our House," Crosby presenting the title track, and Young adding the characteristic "Helpless." There was also the hit version of Joni Mitchell's "Woodstock." Flawless harmonies, thoughtful lyrics, accomplished playing: this is state-of-the-art 70s rock music and continues to be the best explanation of CSN&Y's enormous stature and enduring legacy. — *William Ruhlmann*

○ **Four Way Street** / Apr. 7, 1971 / Atlantic ✦✦✦✦
This 1992 expanded version of the original double live album (originally released on April 7, 1971) by CSN&Y is now an indispensible part of any collection, with additional Neil Young and Graham Nash material (and even a version of "King Midas in Reverse," the old Hollies tune) that any serious listener will want. Some of the extended guitar jams between Stills and Young ("Southern Man") go on longer than strict musical sense would dictate, but it seemed right at the time, and they capture a form that was far more abused in other hands after this group broke up. — *Bruce Eder*

● **So Far** / Aug. 1974 / Atlantic ✦✦✦✦
Released to coincide with CSN&Y's 1974 reunion tour, this compilation remains the best representation of the group's early work, featuring such hits as "Teach Your Children" and "Suite: Judy Blue Eyes." It also put the one-off single "Ohio/Find The Cost of Freedom" (CSN&Y's response to the shooting of four anti-war student protestors at Kent State University) on an album for the first time. — *William Ruhlmann*

CSN / Jun. 17, 1977 / Atlantic ✦✦✦
A fair and somewhat slick reprise, highlighted by "Dark Star." A valiant attempt to re-create the good spirits of the first album amid the malaise of the '70s. — *Bruce Eder*

Replay / Dec. 1980 / Atlantic ✦✦
Although this is a decent anthology of their hits and most well-known album tracks, with a few remixes, it's no substitute for the first album. —*Bruce Eder*

Daylight Again / Jun. 21, 1982 / Atlantic ✦✦✦
Originally a Stills and Nash project, but with the drug-addled Crosby added virtually in name only for commercial reasons (Timothy Schmit and Art Garfunkel provide many of the harmonies), this turned out better than expected, featuring Nash's reflective "Wasted on the Way" and Stills's "Southern Cross," both hits and respectable additions to the CSN repertoire. —*William Ruhlmann*

Allies / Jun. 6, 1983 / Atlantic ✦✦
A mediocre live album cobbled together from shows dating back six years, apparently released as a souvenir for people attending the group's '83 summer tour. —*William Ruhlmann*

American Dream / Nov. 3, 1988 / Atlantic ✦✦
There are some excellent songs here, notably Young's "This Old House" and Crosby's "Compass," but the quartet didn't really jell on its first new studio album in 14 years. Certainly, expectations were so high that the album seemed much worse than it really was, and in retrospect it seems a workmanlike effort simply lacking the spark that made this group so much more than the sum of its parts. —*William Ruhlmann*

Live It Up / Jun. 11, 1990 / Atlantic ✦✦
More than the harmonies or the scandals, what made CSN a major force was that they wrote great songs. That's what is missing on their first full-fledged trio album since *CSN* in 1977. They sing earnestly and well, and they are augmented, as ever, by the small, efficient army of players, such as Craig Doerge and Joe Vitale, who have made a career supporting them, but they just don't come up with the big songs they've led listeners to expect. (In fact, there are quite a few songs by others.) As a result, this is the least satisfying of CSN's studio albums. Not surprisingly, it flopped badly in record stores. —*William Ruhlmann*

○ **Crosby, Stills & Nash Box Set** / Oct. 1991 / Atlantic ✦✦✦✦
Seventy-seven tracks make up this four-CD boxed-set retrospective of the various permutations of Crosby, Stills & Nash (and Young) from 1968 to 1990. The set is dotted with fine unreleased tracks from abortive album sessions plus good choices of both solo work and well-known material. For a neophyte, it may be on the long side, but seasoned fans can welcome this lavish tribute. The sound quality alone justifies its purchase. —*William Ruhlmann & Bruce Eder*

After the Storm / Aug. 16, 1994 / Atlantic ✦✦

Christopher Cross (Christopher Geppert)

b. May 3, 1951, San Antonio, TX
Pop
Cross (born Christopher Geppert) came out of the blue in 1980 with his self-titled debut of slight soft pop. He managed to clean up at the following year's Grammys, beating out previous record-holder Frank Sinatra with a total of five awards. That album generated several substantial hits with "Ride like the Wind," "Never Be the Same," "Say You'll Be Mine" and the transcendent "Sailing," which went #1 and won Song of the Year. Cross briefly continued his success with several more hits like "Think of Laura," "All Right," and the #1 "Arthur's Theme (The Best That You Can Do)," from the movie *Arthur*, before sinking from sight. Cross's last album, the 1988 release *Back of My Mind,* failed to chart, indicating that what fan base he had enjoyed no longer existed. —*Rick Clark*

● **Christopher Cross** / Jan. 1980 / Warner Brothers ✦✦✦✦
This Michael Omartian-produced collection of light pop, which featured the atmospheric "Sailing," cleaned up at the 1980 Grammy presentations. Cross's rather thin tenor is given ample support from Michael McDonald, Don Henley, guitarist Eric Johnson, and other Los Angeles "A"-list session pros. —*Rick Clark*

Another Page / Jan. 1983 / Warner Brothers ✦✦✦
Christopher Cross had a lot to live up to in following his self-titled debut album, which had sold a million copies (now up to four million) and spawned four Top 40 hits, including the #1 "Sailing," and won him five Grammy Awards, including Album of the Year, Song of the Year, Record of the Year (the last two for "Sailing"), and Best New Artist. So, he took three years to make *Another Page,* which, unsurprisingly, sounded a lot like its predecessor. Cross concentrated on smooth pop arrangements, over which be sang greeting-card romantic sentiments in an innocent, Brian Wilson-like tenor.

No one would confuse the result with anything truly heartfelt or with real rock & roll, but Cross's soothing approach was still good enough to put two of his songs, "All Right" and "No Time For Talk," into the Top 40 and earn a gold record certification. Then, nearly a year after the album's release, TV soap opera *General Hospital* began featuring the maudlin ballad "Think of Laura," and *Another Page* suddenly had a third single, this one a Top Ten hit. —*William Ruhlmann*

Every Turn of the World / Nov. 1985 / Warner Brothers ✦✦
Having suffered a commercial decline with the ballad-filled *Another Page,* Christopher Cross took a harder rocking approach with his third album, *Every Turn of the World.* Gone were the L.A. session aces and the SoCal chorus of famous fellow pop singers, as Cross wielded his SynthAxe and producer/co-writer Michael Omartian his keyboards, along with a rhythm section, on a selection of uptempo songs, many of which had save-the-world themes. It didn't work. "Charm the Snake," the typically energetic lead-off single, sputtered on the charts, while Cross's core audience of "adult contemporary" ballad fans deserted him, and the album was a sales disaster. If anybody had tried turning over the LP and sampling tunes like the Beach Boys tribute "Love Found a Home," they would have discovered a couple of more characteristic Cross songs, but it was too little, too late. —*William Ruhlmann*

Back of My Mind / 1988 / Warner Brothers ✦✦
Since the spectacular success of his first album, Christopher Cross had suffered a steady commercial decline in its successors, and the slide continued with *Back of My Mind.* Having taken a more uptempo approach on *Every Turn of the World,* Cross returned to pop balladeering here, and though tracks like "I Will (Take You Forever)" certainly matched the work of such gutless peers as Peter Cetera and Richard Marx, who were eating up the charts in 1988, Cross was treated as a has-been, bleating out his songs of generalized romantic and filial devotion over synth-strings and drum programming. —*William Ruhlmann*

Crow

Group, Rock & Roll, Psychedelic, Garage Rock
During the late '60s and early '70s, Crow specialized in a raw R&B-influenced style of rock. This Twin Cities quintet (originally known as South 40 and formed from popular local bands Rave-Ons and Jokers Wild) enjoyed their greatest success in the late '60s with the horn-driven hit "Evil Woman." Crow continues to play to this day, fronted by original lead-singer Dave Wagner. —*Rick Clark*

● **Evil Woman–Best of Crow** / K-Tel ✦✦✦
A generous 18-track compilation of Crow, the keyboard-spiked garage pop-rock band who were one of the highlights of Minnesota's rock scene during the late '60s. With its extensive liner notes and excellent track selection, *Evil Woman—The Best of Crow* is the definitive Crow collection. —*Stephen Thomas Erlewine*

Sheryl Crow

b. Feb. 11, 1963
Rock & Roll, Singer-Songwriter
After many years of paying her dues as a backup singer for Don Henley, Eric Clapton, Rod Stewart, and Michael Jackson, Sheryl Crow finally got a chance to make her own album in 1993. Growing out of a series of informal jam sessions with L.A. studio veterans, the relaxed yet gritty blues-rock of *Tuesday Night Music Club* became a hit in the spring of 1994, thanks to the single "Leaving Las Vegas," a slightly surreal travelogue which only shows the beginning of her talent. Later that summer, the laidback "All I Want to Do" was released and it became an across-the-boards success, pushing *Tuesday Night Music Club* into the Top Ten and into multi-platinum status. —*Stephen Thomas Erlewine*

○ **Tuesday Night Music Club** / Aug. 3, 1993 / A&M ✦✦✦
Sheryl Crow's debut album *Tuesday Night Music Club* is a loose, melodic, gritty record with subtle country underpinnings. Throughout the album, she shows that not only does she have an impressive, bluesy voice, but is also a considerably talented songwriter, as "Leaving Las Vegas" and "Run Baby Run" prove. —*Stephen Thomas Erlewine*

Crowded House

Group, Pop/Rock
In 1985, New Zealand-born Neil Finn was left with the task of con-

tinuing with Split Enz after the departure of his brother (and founding member) Tim Finn. He opted instead to dissolve the Enz. Taking drummer Paul Hester with him, he formed a stripped-down trio with bassist Nick Seymour. After years of writing Split Enz's synth-pop hits like "I Got You" and "One Step Ahead," Neil concentrated on well-crafted, melodic songs and transparent production. This new Australian band was dubbed Crowded House for the state of congestion in the Los Angeles bungalow the band shared while recording with producer/keyboardist Mitchell Froom. Their self-titled 1986 debut album was a sleeper hit that waited until the third single, "Don't Dream It's Over," before jumping into the Top Ten. An excellent live act, Crowded House made quite a splash that year. Although their next two albums didn't match the chart success of the first, the consistently high level of quality has earned them many fans and critics' darling status. Tim Finn joined the band briefly for the *Woodface* album and tour.

Two years later, Crowded House added guitarist Mark Hart and recorded the acclaimed *Together Alone* with Youth, a former member of Killing Joke; the record was a hit everywhere except the U.S. During a U.S. tour in Spring of 1994, drummer Paul Hester left the band to spend more time with his family. —*Scott Bultman*

● **Crowded House** / 1986 / Capitol ✦✦✦✦
Their Top 40 debut is loaded with highly melodic, Anglo-pop gems. Strong, upbeat songwriting and vocal harmonies from this talented trio, featuring the hits "Don't Dream It's Over" and "Something So Strong." —*Scott Bultman*

Temple of Low Men / 1988 / Capitol ✦✦✦
Darker and more introspective, this still has fine songwriting and performances, including a guest appearance from Richard Thompson. Highlights include "Into Temptation," "Better Be Home Soon," and "When You Come." —*Scott Bultman*

○ **Woodface** / 1991 / Capitol ✦✦✦✦
This album has the great melodies of their first, the soul-searching depth of the second, and the great vocal harmonies of the reunited Finn brothers. It's a close contender for their most essential album. —*Scott Bultman*

○ **Together Alone** / 1993 / Capitol ✦✦✦✦
More experimental and musically varied than any of their previous releases, *Together Alone* finds Crowded House branching out into traditional Maori music and heavy guitars, as well as the shining pop songcraft that is Neil Finn's trademark. Picking up a new guitarist and adding the production skills of ex-Killing Joke member Youth, Crowded House energizes their sound without losing sight of Neil Finn's classic pop songwriting, as "Locked Out" and "Distant Sun" prove. —*Stephen Thomas Erlewine*

The Crows

Group, Doo-Wop
One of the first doo-wop groups, one of the first so-called "bird" groups, and one of the first acts of any kind to score a bonafide rock & roll hit record, the Crows were among the more important one-shot artists in rock & roll history. Discovered at New York's Apollo Theater in 1952, the Crows were one of the many groups pioneering doo-wop with their infectious, cheerful vocals and harmonies, use of nonsense syllables, and modified jump blues instrumental backing. Cut in 1953, "Gee," with its irresistible melody, naively enthusiastic street-corner singing, and Charlie Christian-like guitar solo, was far and away their best single. It was also their only successful one, although it needed almost a year to take off, reaching number 14 in the pop charts (and number two in the R&B charts) in early 1954. Recording about a half-dozen other 45s between 1952 and 1954, the group broke up with little fanfare only months after "Gee" fell off the hit parade. — *Richie Unterberger*

● **Gee, It's The Crows** / 1988 / Murray Hill ✦✦✦✦
16 sides covering their complete output for the Jubilee and Rama labels between 1952 and 1954, including all their singles, as well as 45s on which they backed Fatman Humphries (as the 4 Notes) and Lorraine Ellis. It's a respectable mix of uptempo numbers and ballads that will appeal to few listeners besides doo-wop aficionados. By far the best of the batch besides "Gee" is their final single, "Sweet Sue," a snazzy, uptempo cut with a thumping beat. "I Love You So," the flipside of "Gee," is also well-remembered by doo-wop fans, and was covered a few years later by the Chantels. Includes detailed liner notes and discography. —*Richie Unterberger*

Julee Cruise

Alternative Pop/Rock
Julee Cruise was the talent scout for composer Angelo Badalamenti when he was working on David Lynch's film *Blue Velvet* in 1985. Badalamenti discovered that her airy voice fitted a song for the film, so she wound up recording "Mysteries of Love" for the soundtrack. Three years later, she released her first album, *Floating into the Night*, which featured music by Badalamenti and lyrics by Lynch. Three tracks from the record made it onto the soundtrack to Lynch's television series, *Twin Peaks*, including the series' theme song, "Falling." Cruise had a bit part in the series. She released her second album, *Voice of Love*, in 1993. —*Stephen Thomas Erlewine*

● **Floating into the Night** / Sep. 12, 1989 / Warner Brothers ✦✦✦✦
Eerie and sensual vocals by a vocalist who can combine irony and humor with her lyrics, she sang the theme for the TV show *Twin Peaks*, which may give a small idea of what her music is all about. Somewhat different from what is considered "normal," Cruise's music often takes a few listens to get into, but may be addicting. —*John Book*

The Voice of Love / 1993 / Warner Brothers ✦✦✦

Cry of Love

Group, Pop/Rock
After a couple years of slogging it out down in the South, Cry of Love released its debut album, *Brother*, in 1993. Cry of Love was not cut from the same cloth as most of the '90s hard rock bands. Instead of sludgy Sabbath steals or punk rips or grunge, the band faithfully recreated the classic hard rock sounds of the '70s. From Bad Company to Lynyrd Skynyrd, all of the staples of classic rock could be heard in their music; guitarist Audley Freed wrote riffs that seemed like lost album tracks from 1975. And AOR fans paid tribute—they made "Peace Pipe" and "Bad Thing" major radio hits. —*Stephen Thomas Erlewine*

Brother / Dec. 1992 / Columbia ✦✦✦
While Cry of Love has the '70s hard-rock sound down pat, they only occasionally find songs that serve their skills well, as on "Peace Pipe" and the amazingly addictive Bad Company knockoff "Bad Thing." —*Stephen Thomas Erlewine*

The Cryan' Shames

Group, Pop/Rock
The Cryan' Shames were a big deal in Chicago in the mid- and late '60s, when a bunch of their singles hit the local Top Ten; some of them were small national hits as well. The biggest of these was "Sugar and Spice," a cover of a Searchers song (itself a cover of a Drifters hit) that made the Top 50 in 1966, and was later featured in the *Nuggets* anthology of '60s garage bands. In their original incarnation, the Shames leaned toward the pop end of the garage, but did quite a good job. Borrowing heavily from the Beatles, Byrds, and Yardbirds, guitarist Jim Fair wrote a clutch of energetic guitar pop-rockers with sparkling harmonies. After 1966, unfortunately, the group pursued an increasingly mainstream pop direction featuring saccharine arrangements and material. In this respect they uncannily mirrored the devolution of local rivals the New Colony Six, who also shifted from tough pop/rock to MOR in their bid for national success. —*Richie Unterberger*

● **Sugar & Spice (A Collection)** / 1992 / Columbia ✦✦✦✦
This 18-song compilation spans 1966 to 1969, and features their singles and key album cuts. Despite its good intentions, this well-packaged retrospective runs out of octane after the first half dozen songs. —*Richie Unterberger*

The Crystals

Group, Girl-Group
This Brooklyn female vocal group had R&B roots, but the Crystals were really a pop ensemble whose best songs perfectly expressed the romantic innocence of the early '60s. Barbara Alston, Lala Brooks, Dee Dee Kennibrew, Mary Thomas, and Patricia Wright were the original lineup formed by Benny Wells while still in high school. Wells served as their first manager. The remarkable producer Phil Spector heard them rehearsing and eventually signed them to his Philles label, where they had several classic songs. "There's No Other like My Baby" got things started in 1961, making it to number five on the R&B charts and to number 20 on the pop charts. "Uptown" cracked the R&B and pop Top 20, then came

"He's a Rebel," arguably their finest song and one of the era's landmarks. Darlene Love was lead vocalist, and both the song and the successful follow-up "He's Sure the Boy I Love" featured Love and the Blossoms, but were credited to the Crystals. The actual Crystals returned in 1963 minus Mary Thomas, who left to get married. They had two more huge hits, "Da Doo Ron Ron (When He Walked Me Home)" and "Then He Kissed Me" in 1963, each one making the Top Ten on both the R&B and pop lists. But the party ended in 1964, as their final two singles for Philles both flopped and relations between them and Spector degenerated. Wright left and was replaced by Frances Collins. They bought themselves out of their Philles contract in 1965 and signed with United Artists, only to get dropped a year later. They disbanded, then re-formed in 1971. Since then, various editions of Crystals have been plentiful on the oldies circuit, but at last account, only Kennibrew was still involved out of the originals. —*Ron Wynn*

● **The Best of the Crystals** / 1992 / ABKCO ✦✦✦✦
All of the Crystals' biggest hits are included on this comprehensive collection, which also features many forgotten singles and album tracks; while some of the lesser-known material might not match the standards of the classic singles, many songs do come close. — *Stephen Thomas Erlewine*

The Cucumbers

Group, Alternative Pop/Rock
This pop-rock quartet, based in Hoboken, NJ, was formed in 1982 by singer/guitarist Deena Shoskes and guitarist/singer Jon Fried. —*William Ruhlmann*

Who Betrays Me . . . and Other Happier Songs / 1985 / Fake Doom ✦✦✦
The Cucumbers write and perform catchy little rock songs about the uncertainties of love, especially the uncertainties about the self. "Who Betrays Me?" asks lead singer Deena Shoshkes, only to answer, "I do." And even when she and her love are happily "Walking And Talking," she seems to have trouble keeping his attention. —*William Ruhlmann*

● **The Cucumbers** / 1987 / Profile ✦✦✦✦
The doubtful lovers of "Who Betrays Me" are only a little better off here, as Shoshkes confesses that her boyfriend won't wash the dishes, but their relationship does have its good points: "Sometimes it's beautiful, sometimes it's too loud." There are a lot of things you could say that about. —*William Ruhlmann*

Where We Sleep Tonight / 1994 / Zero Hour ✦✦✦
On their first album in seven years, Cucumbers Deena Shoshkes and Jon Fried are still pondering the imponderables of love. In "Something Dangerous," Shoshkes tells her lover, "I'm afraid of you, and I love you"; seconds later, it's "I feel safe with you, and I love you." There are hints, however, that the duo's uncertain affection may be leading progeny. The album-opening "I'm Waiting" may be addressed to a lover or a coming baby, and "Your Little Ribcage," sung by Fried, presents the story from the inside. They're still quirky after all these years, in other words, and still employing a minimalist rock style reminiscent of the bands that were in the ascendant when they got together—early Talking Heads, B-52's, Devo. Some tracks boast more extensive instrumentation, notably horns, but the basic approach is still, well, basic, with a focus on the vocals and those odd observations. May they never change. —*William Ruhlmann*

The Cult

Group, Hard Rock
Singer Ian Astbury formed the Southern Death Cult in England in 1982 as a doom-rock band. Reorganized in 1983 with guitarist Billy Duffy as Death Cult, by 1984 the rock quartet, quickly moving toward heavy metal, had become simply the Cult. Their hard-rock set *Electric* (1987) was a commercial breakthrough. *Sonic Temple* (1989) was an even bigger success, hitting the Top Ten (#3 in the U.K.) and selling over a million copies. However, that proved to be the band's commercial peak, as subsequent records failed to chart as highly. After 1994's self-titled album failed to make an impression in either the U.S. or the U.K., the Cult disbanded in early 1995.—*William Ruhlmann*

Dreamtime / 1984 / Beggars Banquet ✦✦
Love / 1985 / Sire ✦✦✦
Apart from the monolithic rock & roll masterpiece "She Sells Sanctuary," *Love* is devoid of memorable riffs and melodies. — *Stephen Thomas Erlewine*

● **Electric** / 1987 / Sire ✦✦✦✦
After four years of evolving from a goth-rock band with two longer names (Southern Death Cult, Death Cult), the Cult emerged on this Rick Rubin production as a full-fledged heavy metal band. Billy Duffy pulls out monstrous guitar riffs and lead singer Ian Astbury declaims like a latter-day Jim Morrison. Contains "Love Removal Machine." —*William Ruhlmann*

Sonic Temple / 1989 / Sire ✦✦✦
A change of producer and drummers has no discernible impact on the Cult's driving metal assault. —*William Ruhlmann*

Ceremony / 1991 / Sire ✦✦✦
Ceremony continued the straightforward attack of *Sonic Temple*, and while the songs weren't quite as strong as those on the previous record, it delivered a bracing heavy metal roar. —*David Jehnzen*

Cult / 1994 / Sire ✦✦
As the years go by, the Cult become more traditional, which is a mixed blessing. At their best, the Cult can sound as powerful as any other hard-rock outfit, but they have trouble coming up with enough decent riffs and songs to fill an album. The band *sounds* good on *The Cult*—they've just neglected to write songs worthy of their skills. —*Stephen Thomas Erlewine*

Culture Club

Group, New Wave, Pop/Rock
Culture Club was a successful pop/rock group of the early '80s, led by singer Boy George O'Dowd (b. Jun 14, 1961). It was as well known for O'Dowd's flamboyant fashion sense as it was for its music, but when it was hot, it was hot: Culture Club racked up six straight Top Ten hits in 1983-1984.

The group was formed in London in 1981. In addition to O'Dowd, it consisted of bassist Mikey Craig (b. Feb. 15, 1960), guitarist Roy Hay (b. Aug. 12, 1961), and drummer Jon Moss (b. Sep. 11, 1957). They topped the charts with their debut single, "Do You Really Want to Hurt Me." The band's visual flair helped them in the U.S., where music video had recently become an important promotional tool, and the single hit Stateside by early 1983.

Culture Club's music was light, bouncy pop, topped by O'Dowd's appealing tenor. It was anything but outrageous, although O'Dowd's elaborate costumes made the group seem more daring than it was. *Kissing to Be Clever*, their debut album, was a million-seller and included "I'll Tumble 4 Ya," another Top Ten hit. The fall of 1983 brought a second album, *Colour by Numbers*, and more hits: "Church of the Poison Mind," "Karma Chameleon" (a #1), and "Miss Me Blind."

Unfortunately, the group's very novelty was its undoing. The third album, *Waking Up with the House on Fire* (1984) went platinum by momentum but its singles were not big hits, and the fourth album, *From Luxury to Heartache*, was a relative flop in 1986, the same year O'Dowd's heroin addiction became a matter of public knowledge. In 1987 O'Dowd cleaned up, split up Culture Club, and embarked on a solo career. —*William Ruhlmann*

○ **Kissing to Be Clever** / 1982 / Virgin ✦✦✦✦
Appealing lightly synthesized '80s pop music, featuring the infectious ballad hit "Do You Really Want to Hurt Me?" —*William Ruhlmann*

○ **Colour by Numbers** / 1983 / Virgin ✦✦✦✦
More melodic bouncy pop led by Boy George's engaging singing on "Karma Chameleon" and other songs. —*William Ruhlmann*

Waking up with the House on Fire / 1984 / Virgin ✦✦
The career of Boy George and Culture Club had been on a steady upward climb for two years by the fall of 1984, so the group had every reason to expect that their third album, *Waking Up With The House On Fire*, would enjoy similar success, but it was not to be. The lead-off single, "The War Song," put off many fans, and the problem may have been less the music on *Waking Up*, which was typically frothy and propulsive, than the passing of a fad. By late 1984, Boy George had been sideswiped in the image department by Michael Jackson, Prince, and Madonna. So, while it's true that *Waking Up* didn't contain any song as catchy as "Karma Chameleon," the album's real failure was one of timing. —*William Ruhlmann*

From Luxury to Heartache / 1986 / Virgin ✦✦
For their fourth album, *From Luxury To Heartache*, Culture Club jettisoned producer Steve Levine in favor of pop/R&B veteran Arif Mardin, seeking to reverse the commercial decline they had suf-

fered with their third album. When the danceable leadoff track, "Move Away," rose into the singles chart, that seemed like a good decision, and the rest of the album followed through with a pronounced drum sound and a relentless beat. The group's flamboyance was played down in an attempt to redefine Culture Club as dance floor favorites. But previously the group had enjoyed a broad-based pop appeal, and by focusing on one part of their constituency, they ultimately sacrificed the rest. What's more, to make this kind of music, you didn't need a group; all you needed was a lead singer and some synthesizers. No wonder Boy George went solo before the year was out. — *William Ruhlmann*

This Time: the First Four Years—Twelve Worldwide Hits / 1987 / Virgin ✦✦✦

● **At Worst . . . The Best of Boy George and Culture Club** / 1993 / Virgin ✦✦✦✦
The success of "The Crying Game" marked a comeback for Boy George, especially in the U.S., where his solo career had never taken hold beyond the dance clubs, and SBK (distributor of his label, Virgin) took advantage of his resurgence by compiling this 75-minute, 19-track album, which combines his former group Culture Club's biggest hits with selections from his solo work. The 10 Culture Club tracks are of a piece, from 1982's "Do You Really Want To Hurt Me" (which here leads off with an ominous voice intoning, "Popularity breeds contempt") to "Love Is Love," which wasn't a hit, but is a better choice than the missing "The War Song," which was. The solo tracks are a more mixed batch, and not only because Top 40 U.K. hits like "Keep Me In Mind," "Sold," and "To Be Reborn" are missing. They often rely on loud percussion tracks that strand Boy George's tender tenor somewhere in the distance. He remains most effective on rhythmic ballads, whether "Do You Really Want To Hurt Me," "Everything I Own" (his chart-topping first U.K. solo hit), or "The Crying Game." — *William Ruhlmann*

The Cure

Group, Alternative Pop/Rock
The Cure has become one of the most popular groups to emerge from Great Britain's post-punk gloom-rock trend of the late '70s, though it took a relatively long time to achieve its present prominence. Amid a variety of personnel changes, the constant in the group has been singer, songwriter, and guitarist Robert Smith (b. Apr. 4, 1957), whose teased hair and black eyeliner dominate the group's look. He formed the Cure as a trio in 1976 with Laurence Tolhurst (drums) and Michael Dempsey (bass). After some work for an independent label (including the single "Killing an Arab," based on Albert Camus's novel *The Stranger*), they released their first album, *Three Imaginary Boys*, in 1979.

In January 1980, Dempsey left and was replaced by Simon Gallup. More albums followed at yearly intervals, with the fourth, *Pornography*, finally breaking the U.K. Top Ten. The fifth album, *The Top*, became a U.K. Top Ten in 1984, a year that also produced the album *Concert—The Cure Live*. In 1985, *The Head on the Door* became the band's biggest U.K. hit yet, reaching # 7; it also broke the U.S. Top 100 list.

By 1986 the Cure had expanded to a quintet. In addition to Smith, Tolhurst (now on keyboards), and Gallup, the group had Porl Thompson on guitar and Boris Williams on drums. That year a compilation album, *Standing on a Beach—The Singles*, hit # 4 in the U.K.; in America it went gold in early 1987, finally establishing the Cure in the U.S.

In 1987 they released the double album *Kiss Me, Kiss Me, Kiss Me*, another success, and added Roger O'Donnell on keyboards. (Tolhurst subsequently departed.) In 1989 *Disintegration* produced the Cure's first big U.S. hit single, "Love Song" (#2). The album itself hit #12 and went platinum. *Wish*, released in the spring of 1992, entered the U.S. charts at #2. — *William Ruhlmann*

○ **Three Imaginary Boys** / Jun. 1979 / Fiction ✦✦✦✦
Bursting with high-energy playing and bare-bones production, the band's first album showcases Robert Smith's most concise songwriting. The now common themes of isolation and despair are present, this time presented in perfect three-minute form. *Three Imaginary Boys* ends up sounding like a more tuneful version of Wire's *Pink Flag*. — *Chris Woodstra*

○ **Boys Don't Cry** / Jan. 1980 / Elektra ✦✦✦✦
Combining the finer moments from *Three Imaginary Boys* with early singles, this is the best representation of the band's early pop-oriented days. A post-punk masterpiece. — *Chris Woodstra*

Seventeen Seconds / May 1980 / Elektra ✦✦✦
Still a pop album in many ways, the second proper album marks a move toward despair, depression and epic songwriting. The playing is slowed considerably with synthesizers barely rising above the minimalistic arrangements. The hooks are present but in smaller numbers. — *Chris Woodstra*

Faith / 1981 / Elektra ✦✦✦
Continuing the trend of the previous album, *Faith* is an even darker affair. Smith sings with suicidal resignation through eight somber epics, raising the tempo only for the single, "Primary." Typified by the title track and "Funeral Party," the album is chilling even though not particularly memorable. — *Chris Woodstra*

. . . Happily Ever After / 1981 / A&M ✦✦✦
A double album combination of *Seventeen Seconds* and *Faith*. An ideal package for two albums that flow together perfectly. — *Chris Woodstra*

○ **Pornography** / 1982 / Elektra ✦✦✦✦
This is possibly the quintessential Goth album. Layers of distorted guitars, heavily echoed vocals, and tribal drumming provide the "wall of doom" backdrop for lyrics like "It doesn't matter if we all die," taking the listener deep into Smith's disturbed psyche. *Pornography* marked the band's move from relative obscurity to cult status. — *Chris Woodstra*

The Walk / 1983 / Sire ✦✦

Japanese Whispers / 1984 / Sire ✦✦✦
This collection of the band's mid-'80s lightweight pop singles is a refreshing contrast to the somber albums which preceded it. — *Chris Woodstra*

The Top / 1984 / Sire ✦✦
Essentially a Robert Smith solo effort, this album lacks the direction of previous albums. Even experiments in different styles can't make up for a lack of real substance in the songs. Only the single, "The Caterpillar," leaves a lasting impression. — *Chris Woodstra*

Concert: Live / 1984 / Fiction ✦✦
A solid collection of the band's 1984 tour promoting *The Top*. Although the songs differ only slightly in their live form, this album works well as a "best of the early years" collection. — *Chris Woodstra*

○ **The Head on the Door** / 1985 / Elektra ✦✦✦✦
Head on the Door represents the band's creative high point and most accessible moment. The songs successfully walk a fine line between gloom and pop, including the danceable hits, "In Between Days" and "Close to Me." This move toward the mainstream made them stars in the U.K. and helped them make some inroads into the U.S. market. — *Chris Woodstra*

★ **Standing on a Beach: The Singles** / 1986 / Elektra ✦✦✦✦✦
The Cure's gloom-and-doom (but danceable) greatest hits, 1979-1985. Though not hits in the U.S., these helped set the stage for the group's later Stateside success. — *William Ruhlmann*

Kiss Me, Kiss Me, Kiss Me / 1987 / Elektra ✦✦✦
The Cure's breakthrough U.S. success, a double album containing "Why Can't I Be You?," "Just Like Heaven," and "Hot Hot Hot!!!" — *William Ruhlmann*

○ **Disintegration** / 1989 / Elektra ✦✦✦✦
The Cure became a top-selling group in the U.S. with this album, which sold a million copies and contains their #2 hit, "Love Song." — *William Ruhlmann*

Mixed Up / 1990 / Elektra ✦✦
An assortment of remixes, rerecordings, old singles, and one new song ("Never Enough"). Most of the remixes are quite radical, leaving only the bare bones of the original song. There are enough oddities and rare tracks on *Mixed Up* to make it necessary for Cure fans, but it's too specialized for casual listeners. — *Stephen Thomas Erlewine*

Wish / 1992 / Elektra ✦✦✦
Early notices for this album suggested that Robert Smith and company were getting more optimistic. To be sure, "Doing the Unstuck" contains the lyric "Kick out the gloom," but the chorus to that song is more ambiguous: "It's a perfect day to throw back your head and kiss it all goodbye." In fact, much of this album, from its dirge-like tempos to Smith's just-off-key vocals, bespeaks the depressed state typical of the Cure. There are oddly bouncy pop songs here and there too ("Friday I'm in Love") but the Cure remains the band its fans love to mope to. — *William Ruhlmann*

Show / 1993 / Elektra ✦✦
Concentrating on their recent, pop-oriented material, *Show* is a good, if unspectacular, representation of the Cure in concert. Only devoted fans need to own this album. —*Stephen Thomas Erlewine*

Paris / 1993 / Elektra ✦✦
Show featured mostly hit singles; *Paris* features the songs that built their cult, including "Close to Me" and "Letter to Elise." Consequently, most fans will find this the more interesting of the two live albums, and, out of the two records, it is the more consistent and satisfying. —*Stephen Thomas Erlewine*

Curtiss A

Group, Roots-Rock
Curtiss A (aka Curt Almsted) has been a fixture in Minneapolis rock since 1978, when he recorded with his punkish combo the Spooks. Never really a punk-rocker in the traditional sense, Almsted was more of a roots-rock wiseguy more influenced by John Lennon than John Lydon. In the late '70s and early '80s, he was a big part of the burgeoning pre-Replacements/Hüsker Dü Minneapolis rock scene which, at the time, included the Suburbs, Suicide Commandos, Flamin' Ohs, and Hypstryz. He recorded a great debut record, *Courtesy* (with future Replacement Slim Dunlap on lead guitar), which brought him and indie label Twin/Tone acclaim. Since his last album (1988's so-so *A Scarlett Letter,* with ex-NRBQ guitarist Al Anderson on board), he has kept an extremely low profile. —*John Dougan*

Courtesy / 1980 / Twin/Tone ✦✦✦
Courtesy erupts like a roots-rock fireball, with Curtiss A's throaty, thick voice wailing away like a man possessed. The band is a good one, and Slim Dunlap's guitar bobs and weaves, spitting out one great rockabilly lick after another. Most of the songs have a comic panache to them, and they're delivered with an infectious energy that never flags. Not a major record, but a pretty swell minor one by a once-hot regional talent. —*John Dougan*

Damage Is Done / 1984 / Twin/Tone ✦✦
● **Scarlet Letter** / 1988 / Twin/Tone ✦✦✦✦

Curve

Group, Alternative Pop/Rock
Considering Curve's towering monolith of guitar noise, dance tracks, dark goth, and airy melodies, it's strange that the two core members—guitarist Dean Garcia and vocalist Toni Halliday—met through David Stewart of the Eurythmics. Halliday met Stewart while she was a teenager and they remained friends for years; Garcia played on Eurythmics' *Touch* and *Be Yourself Tonight.* The two played together in State of Play, which released one album and two singles in the late '80s to little notice. After the failure of that band, Garcia and Halliday parted ways only to reunite in the beginning of the '90s. Renaming themselves Curve, Halliday and Garcia released three EPs that became independent hits in 1991. Although they were critically acclaimed as well, some members of the U.K. press attacked Halliday for not being a genuine member of the indie scene. Despite the negative press, their next EP and first album, 1992's *Doppelganger,* hit number one on the U.K.'s indie charts. By the time of the following year's *Cuckoo,* Curve had added two guitarists and a drummer, with Garcia moving to the bass. *Cuckoo* was noisier and more experimental than their previous releases, although it did have a couple of pop songs that were tighter than their usual singles. However, the album didn't make as big of splash in the U.K. as previous releases; Curve split several months after its release. —*Stephen Thomas Erlewine*

Pubic Fruit / 1992 / Charisma ✦✦✦
Pubic Fruit collects Curve's early EPs, which were as ambitious as *Doppelganger* yet not quite as well-constructed. Nevertheless, it's

an engaging listen for fans of the group. —*Stephen Thomas Erlewine*

○ **Doppelganger** / 1992 / Charisma ✦✦✦✦
Doppelganger established Curve's thick, neo-psychedelic sound, complete with swirling distorted guitars and trance-like melodies from Toni Halliday. While some of the songs were slightly weak, their vision is strong throughout. —*Stephen Thomas Erlewine*

● **Cuckoo** / 1993 / Capitol ✦✦✦✦
On its second album, Curve expands its adventurous soundscapes, which are often unfairly pigeonholed as dream-pop. Curve has larger ambitions than shoegazing, as *Cuckoo* proves. With more varied textures and better songs than *Doppelganger,* *Cuckoo* shows that Curve is only beginning to hit its stride. —*Stephen Thomas Erlewine*

Cypress Hill

Group, Rap
With their lazily menacing hip-hop, Cypress Hill became one of the biggest hip-hop groups of the early '90s. Powered by the slow, stoned production of DJ Muggs, the group's self-titled debut album became a sleeper sensation in 1991. B-Real's whiny vocals were balanced by the more straightforward rapping of Sen Dog, yet both of their lyrics were severely warped, whether they were telling surreal gangsta tales or celebrating marijuana. With its deliberate bass and beats, Cypress Hill's music sounded stoned—it was one of the most unique, creative sounds to hit hip-hop since the Bomb Squad. While preparing the group's second album, DJ Muggs produced a number of best-selling acts, including House of Pain and Funkdoobiest. All the while, the group earned notoriety for continuing to campaign for the legalization of marijuana.
    Cypress Hill's second album, 1993's *Black Sunday,* was an even bigger hit than their debut, selling over a million copies and earning a crossover hit with "Insane in the Brain." —*Stephen Thomas Erlewine*

★ **Cypress Hill** / 1991 / Ruffhouse ✦✦✦✦✦
With its slow, heavily stoned funk, surrealistic gangsta fantasies and whining delivery, *Cypress Hill* was a landmark hip-hop album of the early '90s, ushering in an era of marijuana and lazy funk. But it wasn't all good times—"How I Could Just Kill A Man" and "Hand on the Glock" were positively terrifying when delivered in their slow, blunted fashion. —*Stephen Thomas Erlewine*

○ **Black Sunday** / 1993 / Columbia ✦✦✦✦
It doesn't matter if *Black Sunday* follows the same formula as *Cypress Hill,* because it does so in such an intoxicating, convincing manner. Bolstered by the splendid singles "We Ain't Goin' Out Like That," "When the Sh— Goes Down," and "Insane in the Brain," *Black Sunday* is a surreal, stoned vision of contemporary hip-hop culture that is as funny as it is frightening. —*Stephen Thomas Erlewine*

Cyrkle

Group, Pop/Rock
Cyrkle's biggest hit in 1966, "Red Rubber Ball," was cowritten by Bruce Woodley, a member of the Seekers, and Paul Simon. With Tom Dawes and Don Dannemann as lead vocalists, the folk-tinged group managed by Beatles manager Brian Epstein came together at a Pennsylvania college and signed with Columbia. After "Red Rubber Ball" bounced up the charts, the group encored with another major seller, "Turn-Down Day." They made their last pop-chart appearance in late 1967. —*Bill Dahl*

● **Red Rubber Ball (A Collection)** / 1966 / Columbia ✦✦✦✦
Basically a two-hit wonder of the mid '60s ("Red Rubber Ball," "Turn-Down Day"), the Cyrkle had Beatles and Paul Simon connections and were themselves fine examples of lightweight folkie pop. Everything of note they ever did is on this album. —*Jeff Tamarkin*

D

D-Mob

Group, Dance-Pop
A British house-music crew, D-Mob enjoyed a flourish of popularity in 1989 and 1990, helping to introduce that style to the mainstream with the hit singles "We Call it Acieed" and "C'Mon and Get My Love." The latter featured vocalist Cathy Dennis, who went on to some solo success in 1991. —*Dan Heilman*

It Is Time to Get Funky / 1987 / FFRR ◆◆◆
● **Little Bit of This, Little Bit of That** / 1989 / London ◆◆◆◆
One of the better English dance/R&B/pop aggregations to emerge in the late '80s, D-Mob was really London mixer, producer, and disc jockey Danny D. His "albums" aren't really LPs in the classic sense, but more like inspired tapestries merging soul/R&B vocal snippets with waves of synthesized backbeats. It's not for serious listening, but is entertaining. —*Ron Wynn*

Trance Dance / FFRR ◆◆◆

Da Lench Mob

Group, Rap
Ice Cube produced this West Coast rap trio's 1992 project *Guerillas in Tha Mist*. It featured T-Bone, J-Dee and Shorty, and the title track proved an R&B and rap hit with a video loosely modelled on the film *Predator* that included an appearance by Cube. —*Ron Wynn*

● **Guerillas in Tha Mist** / 1992 / Atco ◆◆◆◆
Not surprisingly, Da Lench Mob has some similarities to their mentor and producer Ice Cube. Da Lench Mob elaborate Cube's hardcore fantasies with their group sound and contribute their own dose of scathing politics and controversy. Gangsta-rap fans should take note, if they haven't already. —*AMG*

Plant Of Da Apes / 1994 / Priority ◆◆◆
With the same aggressive style as partner Ice Cube, Da Lench Mob criticizes white society for the ills of the country. Preaching that blacks must help themselves, the group has some laid-back rhythms that contrast with their lyrics, but somehow it works. —*John Bush*

dada

Group, Alternative Pop/Rock
With their clean pop sound, catchy melodies, and clever lyrics, some journalists labeled dada the Police of the '90s, although the trio wasn't as musically adventurous as that group. Nevertheless, the band's debut record, 1992's *Puzzle*, was an updated version of the polished guitar-pop that the Police pioneered in the early '80s. On the strength of the single "Dizz Knee Land," the group earned a fair amount of press and sold a number of records. When they delivered their second album, *American Highway Flower*, in 1994, dada wasn't able to capitalize on the promise of their debut and the record slipped off the charts soon after its release. —*Stephen Thomas Erlewine*

● **Puzzle** / Aug. 1992 / IRS ◆◆◆◆
Guitar riffs permeate dada's pleasing debut *Puzzle*, wedded to thick slices of an equally important influence—'60s psychedelia. The L.A. trio offers plenty to keep the ears busy: the orchestral sadness of "Timothy," insidious melody of "Dog," strung-out ravings of "Here Today, Gone Tomorrow," and over-the-edge teen-angst of "Dizz Knee Land." Avoiding tedious jams, keeping the songs tight and memorable, and a taste in cover art worthy of L.A.'s best psychologists, help make this disc an intriguing puzzle. —*Roch Parisien*

American Highway Flower / 1994 / IRS ◆◆◆

Dag Nasty

Group, Punk
Dag Nasty kept roaring, D.C.-styled hardcore alive during the mid-'80s. Although the group were more accessible and melodic than Minor Threat, they never lost their bracing, blistering edge. Formed by former Minor Threat and Meatmen guitarist Brian Baker and ex-DYS vocalist Dave Smalley, Dag Nasty recorded their first album, *Can I Say* (1986), with D.C.-punk guru Ian MacKaye assisting on the production. The following year, Smalley left the group; he was replaced by Peter Cortner, who added more pop elements to the band's sound. Dag Nasty moved from MacKaye's Dischord label to Giant in 1988, releasing their last album, *Field Day*. Along with former Big Boy, Chris Gates, Baker formed the metal band Junkyard in 1989, which released two records on Geffen before fading away. —*Stephen Thomas Erlewine*

Can I Say / 1986 / Dischord ◆◆◆
Wig out at Denkos / 1987 / Dischord ◆◆◆
Loud and proud, a great band. —*John Dougan*
● **Field Day** / 1988 / Positive ◆◆◆◆
Energetic and smart. Undeniably great. —*John Dougan*
Four on the Floor / Epitaph
85 to 86 / Selfless

The Daily Flash

Group, Psychedelic, Folk-Rock
More than any other Seattle group of the '60s, the Daily Flash assimilated the folk-rock and psychedelic sounds of the day into a sound that was both forward-looking and commercial. Specializing in electric rearrangements of contemporary folk songs that emphasized their harmonies and 12-string guitar, the Flash were also capable of psychedelic rock, as on "Jack of Diamonds," which featured blistering feedback guitar. They cut a couple of regional singles and appeared with many of the leading psychedelic groups of the day in California, but never managed to launch their own career, or even record an album. They broke up in early 1968; guitarist Doug Hastings played briefly with Buffalo Springfield, and was a member of Rhinoceros. —*Richie Unterberger*

I Flash Daily / 1985 / Psycho ◆◆◆
An archival reissue that patches together an entire album by presenting both sides of their two singles with three previously unreleased studio recordings and a couple of lengthy live songs. As interpreters, the Flash showed a great deal of skill, adapting compositions by Eric Anderson, Dylan, Ian Tyson, and Fred Neil to full-blown folk-rock arrangements with a touch of baroque pop. As songwriters, their capabilities were undemonstrated; only one of the seven studio recordings on Side Two is a group original ("Jack of Diamonds" and Fred Neil's "Green Rocky Road" are erroneously credited to the band). Side Two is a bit of a waste, with a live 1967 cover of Herbie Hancock's "Canteloupe Island" and an okay live 1966 rendition of Dylan's "Queen Jane Approximately" (which they had covered on their first single). —*Richie Unterberger*

Dick Dale

Group, Surf

The father of surf music, guitarist Dick Dale to a large degree invented and defined the form in the early '60s with his pioneering use of Fender reverb, dazzling staccato playing, and thundering instrumentals that incorporated Middle Eastern and Latin melodic influences. Playing guitars strung for right-handers with his left hand (as Hendrix would years later), he had an agreement with Fender instruments to "road test" new amplification equipment before it was manufactured for the general public, and found that its hollow, sustained tones evoked the mood of surfing, then catching on in a big way in his Southern California stomping grounds. Dale's impact was largely limited to Southern California, but his influence was vast, helping inspire surf music and contributing several of the genre's most enduring classics, especially "Let's Go Trippin'" and "Miserlou" (both of which were covered by the Beach Boys on their early albums). In the 1990s, Dale made an unexpectedly successful comeback with newly recorded material that closely echoed his vintage sides. —*Richie Unterberger*

★ **King of Surf Guitar: Best of Dick Dale** / 1989 / Rhino ✦✦✦✦✦
From "Miserlou" on down, this is the best Dale document. —*Dan Heilman*

○ **Tribal Thunder** / May 1993 / Hightone ✦✦✦✦
The king of the surf guitar returns with a vengeance on his first new recording in almost a decade. Every track's a gem, but "Nitro" and the title track certainly do pack a particular wallop all their own. —*Cub Koda*

Unknown Territory / 1994 / Hightone ✦✦✦
Dick Dale's comeback continues to roll on with *Unknown Territory*, a record filled with blistering guitar and thundering rhythms. Listening to *Unknown Territory*, it's hard to believe that Dale is pushing 50—he plays with the vitality of a man half his age. —*Stephen Thomas Erlewine*

Roger Daltrey

b. Mar. 1, 1945, London, England

Rock & Roll

Lead singer of the British rock group the Who, 1962–1982 (plus a reunion tour in 1989). He launched a parallel solo career in 1973 with the album *Daltrey* and has also worked as a film and television actor. —*William Ruhlmann*

○ **Daltrey** / Apr. 1973 / MCA ✦✦✦✦
For his first solo album, Daltrey turned to Dave Courtney, who wrote the lyrics to all the songs and co-produced with Adam Faith, who wrote some of the music. The album turned out to be something of a showcase and springboard for the main composer, Leo Sayer; nevertheless, it demonstrates Daltrey's versatility as a singer outside a strictly hard-rock context. —*William Ruhlmann*

Ride a Rock Horse / Jun. 1975 / MCA ✦✦
By the time Roger Daltrey was ready to make his second solo album, Leo Sayer, upon whom he had relied to provide songs for his first, had launched his own successful singing career and was keeping his material for himself. Daltrey, therefore, called on his producer, Russ Ballard, who wrote three songs, including the chart single "Come and Get Your Love," and one P. Korda, who wrote another three. On this material, Daltrey took a pop/rock approach, somewhat less aggressive than his work with the Who. He also tossed in some R&B with a cover of Rufus Thomas's "Walking the Dog" and sang in something closer to his actual British accent in the Cockney raveup "Milk Train." *Ride a Rock Horse* lacked the overall quality and cohesion of *Daltrey*, but was still a respectable effort, especially since Daltrey's solo career remained a side issue at this time. —*William Ruhlmann*

One of the Boys / May 13, 1977 / MCA ✦✦✦
Roger Daltrey called on a wider circle of friends for his third album and came up with a more varied collection of songs, from Steve Gibbons's raucous title track to ex-Zombie Colin Blunstone's country-styled "Single Man's Dilemma." Daltrey also co-wrote three songs with producer David Courtney and Tony Meehan, and Beatle completists should note that Paul McCartney contributed a new song, "Giddy." But the best selections were Andy Pratt's "Avenging Annie," a stirring story song (and minor U.S. chart entry), and Murray Head's plaintive ballad "Say It Ain't So, Joe," both of which Daltrey sang as effectively as he had any Who song. The backup band included such notables as Who bassist John Entwistle, Wings guitarist Jimmy McCulloch, keyboardist Rod Argent,

and special guest guitarists Hank B.Marvin (of the Shadows), Alvin Lee (Ten Years After), Eric Clapton, Andy Fairweather-Low, and Mick Ronson. But Daltrey was never in danger of getting lost in the all-star session. Nevertheless, the album was not treated as a major release and found only modest commercial success. —*William Ruhlmann*

McVicar [O.S.T.] / Jun. 1980 / Polydor ✦✦✦
Though it is billed as an "Original Soundtrack Recording," *McVicar* is in effect a Roger Daltrey solo album. Daltrey, who starred in the film and co-produced it, sings on eight of the ten tracks. *McVicar* was Roger Daltrey's highest charting non-Who project, and for a simple reason: it sounds a lot like the Who. On his three previous solo albums, Daltrey had gone out of his way to avoid the hard rock sound of the Who. But here, using a set of backup musicians that included all the other members of the group—Pete Townshend, John Entwistle, and Kenney Jones—Daltrey employed his usual arena-shaking shout over Who-like music. Daltrey sounded more comfortable with such material than he had with the sometimes delicate pop of his other solo records, and you could hear his delight when he had a song like Russ Ballard's "My Time Is Gonna Come," more unadulterated hard rock, to work with. For Who fans, who had gone nearly two years without a new Who album, the soundtrack to *McVicar* was the next best thing. —*William Ruhlmann*

● **Best Bits** / Mar. 1982 / MCA ✦✦✦✦
A best-of from Daltrey's 1973-1980 work on MCA, including "Avenging Annie" and "Say It Ain't So, Joe." —*William Ruhlmann*

Parting Should Be Painless / 1984 / Atlantic ✦✦
Daltrey was much more successful, commercially as well as artistically, when his solo career was a side project. *Parting Should Be Painless*, the first album Daltrey made after the Who's breakup in 1982, contains some interesting tracks, including Bryan Ferry's "Going Strong," which gives you an idea what Roxy Music would sound like if Daltrey was its lead singer, and "Somebody Told Me," written by Dave Stewart and Annie Lennox of Eurythmics. But for the most part, it consists of mediocre material indifferently sung. —*William Ruhlmann*

○ **Under a Raging Moon** / Sep. 1985 / Atlantic ✦✦✦✦
Starting with Pete Townshend's "After the Fire," Daltrey moved to more of a hard-rock sound when his solo career no longer needed to stand in contrast to his work with the Who. As that song indicates, he isn't afraid to invoke the old group's spirit. —*William Ruhlmann*

Can't Wait to See the Movie / 1987 / Atlantic ✦
Rocks in the Head / Jul. 1992 / Atlantic ✦✦✦
Crucial to the creation of this album was Daltrey's meeting with guitarist/songwriter Gerard McMahon, since *Rocks in the Head*, which credits "Musical Direction and Production" to McMahon, also features him as primary backup musician and writer or co-writer of ten out of the 11 tracks. Daltrey himself is co-credited on seven, a new high for him, but it's hard not to feel that he is acting primarily as McMahon's mouthpiece. McMahon updates Daltrey for the '90s, constructing hard-edged tracks based on harsh electric or acoustic guitar textures, suggesting everyone from the Who to the Police. The result is an album that does nothing to diminish Daltrey's reputation. —*William Ruhlmann*

Celebration: Music Of The Who / 1994 / Continuum ✦✦✦
A Celebration: The Music Of Pete Townshend And The Who is the aural record of two concerts Roger Daltrey staged at Carnegie Hall in 1994 to pay tribute to his favorite composer. Backed by an orchestra and accompanied by various guest stars, including Linda Perry of 4 Non Blondes, Daltrey selected three songs each from *Who's Next* and *Quadrophenia*, one each from *Tommy*, *The Who By Numbers*, and *Who Are You*, and two non-Who Townshend songs, "After the Fire," which had appeared on his 1985 solo album *Under a Raging Moon*, and "The Sea Refuses No River," which had appeared on Townshend's 1982 solo album *All the Best Cowboys Have Chinese Eyes*. But while some of the arrangements present refreshing alterations, notably the Chieftains' take on "Baba O'Riley," this remains the kind of performance that works better as a one-time live event than as a record. —*William Ruhlmann*

Damn Yankees

Group, Hard Rock, Pop/Rock

For a brief time in the early '90s, the supergroup Damn Yankees enjoyed a considerable amount of success on the AOR circuit. Comprised of guitarist Ted Nugent, Styx guitarist/vocalist Tommy Shaw, Night Ranger bassist/vocalist Jack Blades, and drummer Michael Cartellone, the group came in on the tail-end of the heyday of polished pop-metal, and their music didn't stray from the radio-friendly format at all. With their first album they had some hits, including the Top Ten power ballad "High Enough" and the radio hit "Coming of Age." Although they were popular concert draws, their second album, released in 1992, wasn't as successful; in the following year, the group disbanded. — *Stephen Thomas Erlewine*

● **Damn Yankees** / 1990 / Warner Brothers ✦✦✦✦
This well-produced pop-metal debut included "Coming of Age" (#60) and "High Enough" (#3). — *Kenneth M. Cassidy*

Don't Tread / 1992 / Warner Brothers ✦✦✦
Damn Yankees' second album replicated the sound of their debut, but the songs on *Don't Tread* were missing the hooks that made the first record a hit. — *Stephen Thomas Erlewine*

The Damned

Group, Punk
While the Sex Pistols are often considered to be the first English punk band, a motley group of louts called the Damned managed to steal some of their thunder. Not only were the Damned the first punk band to release a proper album (1977's *Damned Damned Damned*), they released the first punk single in the U.K. ("New Rose"), and they were also the first to tour the U.S. Not only are the Damned historically important, but much of their music retained its power over the years; "New Rose" is a classic, breathless rocker and the album, produced by Nick Lowe and released on Stiff Records, followed through on its promise. However, they quickly fell out of favor with their second album, *Music for Pleasure*, which was produced by Nick Mason of Pink Floyd. With their credibility under attack from fans and the press, the band was dropped from Stiff; they briefly parted ways in 1978, with original members bassist Captain Sensible, drummer Rat Scabies, and singer Dave Vanian assembling a new version of the band at the end of the year. The new lineup's *Machine Gun Etiquette* was surprisingly good, yet it was the last good record the band ever released. During the '80s, the band's lineup changed several times with Vanian and Scabies remaining as the only original members; their '80s records are, not surprisingly, directionless, ranging from near power-pop to goth-rock and hard rock back to psychedelia. In 1989, the original Damned reunited for a successful U.S. tour; after the tour, the band called it quits for the last time. — *Stephen Thomas Erlewine*

★ **Damned Damned Damned** / Apr. 16, 1977 / Frontier ✦✦✦✦✦
With its raw, stripped-down production and primal three-chord bashing, the Damned's debut was a landmark punk album. It never deviated from the sound of "New Rose," but that didn't matter—with its simplistic approach and relentless energy, *Damned Damned Damned* defined an era. — *Stephen Thomas Erlewine*

Music for Pleasure / Nov. 1977 / Demon ✦✦
Quickly dismissed by critics at the time as a shocking mis-step, *Music for Pleasure* is not quite as bad as the Nick Mason (Pink Floyd) production would lead you to believe—though close. Its failure led to Stiff Records dropping them and the first of many temporary break-ups. — *Chris Woodstra*

○ **Machine Gun Etiquette** / 1979 / Roadrunner ✦✦✦✦
A newly reformed version of the Damned (with a new line-up) makes a surprising return to form with 1979's *Machine Gun Etiquette*, a psychedelic-tinged punk masterpiece. With the punk anthem "Smash it Up" and the U.K. hits "Love Song" and "I Just Can't Be Happy Today" the band proves that it hasn't given up the fight yet. — *Chris Woodstra*

The Black Album / 1980 / Chiswick ✦✦✦
The band's most accomplished and mainstream effort (at least attempt) to date, this sprawling double album obviously takes its inspiration from the Beatles' *White Album* for its title and attempts at stylistic diversity—ranging from power-pop to a bloated quasi-concept side to raw rock & roll. Unfortunately, despite several gems, the end result is a fairly inaccessible album. It was released as an edited single LP in America but was virtually overlooked. — *Chris Woodstra*

Live at Shepperton / 1982 / Ace ✦✦
While unnecessary, this live show from 1980 does an adequate job of capturing the band, flaws and all. Most of the favorites from the period are covered though (not suprisingly) no new light is shed on them. — *Chris Woodstra*

Strawberries / 1982 / Bronze ✦✦✦
A more cohesive album, *Strawberries*, finally achieves the pop sound and diversity they were looking for on *The Black Album*. Easily their finest moment since leaving punk behind, the band seems comfortable (and unexpectedly competent) stretching out with strings and horns embellishing the arrangements. — *Chris Woodstra*

Phantasmagoria / 1985 / Off Beat ✦✦✦
Now essentially Dave Vanian's vehicle, The Damned make an attempt to jump on the goth-rock bandwagon. Unfortunately for the band, they end up sounding more like a parody of the genre than anything else. Only on "Grimly Fiendish," which is pleasantly reminiscent of Madness crossed, and "Is It a Dream" does the band make a lasting impression with better-than-average Brit-pop. — *Chris Woodstra*

Anything / 1986 / MCA ✦
They didn't learn their lesson on *Phantasmagoria* and made another, even less-successful try at the goth-rock arena. A cover of Love's "Alone Again Or" is the albums sole saving grace. — *Chris Woodstra*

○ **The Light at the End of The Tunnel** / 1987 / MCA ✦✦✦✦
While it would have been much more effective if it was sequenced chronologically, *The Light At the End of the Tunnel* is a fine compilation of the Damned's long and surprisingly varied career. — *Stephen Thomas Erlewine*

Final Damnation / 1989 / Restless ✦✦
Chronicles the Damned's reunion concert, June 13, 1988, for a final run-through of the best material. — *William Ruhlmann*

Danzig

Group, Hard Rock, Heavy Metal
Most heavy metal bands that sing about Satan aren't threatening because their lyrics and music are never as menacing as their album covers. Danzig is the exception that proves the rule. Led by singer/songwriter Glenn Danzig, the band has created a dark, bluesy metal that walks the line between being horrifying and being a parody. As the band churns out a bluesy Sabbath/Zeppelin/AC/DC hybrid, he sings about death and evil, but with a knowing wink. All of the satanism is too exaggerated to be taken seriously, but beneath the cartoonish bluster there are some genuinely disturbing imagery and music. This duality, along with some undeniably powerful riffs, have made Danzig one of the best heavy metal bands since Metallica.

Before forming Danzig in the mid-'80s, Glenn Danzig performed with the seminal hardcore punk band the Misfits and a transitional metal/punk group, Samhain. With Danzig, his morbid visions flowered. Throughout the late '80s and early '90s, the band's cult grew steadily without the benefit of a hit. In 1994, a live version of the first album's "Mother" became a hit single, thanks to MTV's incessant airing of the video. *Danzig 4*, released in the fall of 1994, failed to capitalize on the success of "Mother," making it the band's first album not to significantly expand its audience. — *Stephen Thomas Erlewine*

● **Danzig** / 1988 / Def American ✦✦✦✦
Glenn Danzig's debut album with his new band has some incredibly dark and morbid lyrics, including such songs as "Twist of Cain" and "Mother." — *John Book*

Danzig II: Lucifuge / 1990 / Def American ✦✦✦
Danzig's second release is also their most diversified. They explore their blues roots here with a couple of boogies, a slow shuffle, and a slide number, throwing in a '60s-reminiscent ballad in waltz time for good measure. Glenn Danzig's theatrical vocals don't prevent these numbers from working surprisingly well, except when he attempts a Mississippi-delta accent on "Killer Wolf." The simple, somewhat standard blues-metal riffs of their debut are here, but not as plentiful, and the songs done in that style are generally more interesting. — *Steve Huey*

Danzig III: How the Gods Kill / 1992 / Def American ✦✦✦
Danzig's most accessible album to date has songs that could even cross over into mainstream audiences. Glenn Danzig's vocals aren't as raw as they used to be; they're rather more defined and

toned down like a real heavy metal vocalist. John Christ's guitar playing is great throughout, and it shows his progression from the band's debut. The cover artwork is by H.R. Giger. —*John Book*

Black Aria / 1993 / Plan 9/Caroline ✦✦
Hard-rocker Glenn Danzig's experimentation with opera and classical music is of interest to fans of his band, but most others will find it a bit precious and self-indulgent. —*Stephen Thomas Erlewine*

Thrall: Demonsweatlive / May 25, 1993 / Def American ✦✦✦
A combination of a few new studio tracks and some live recordings, *Thrall: Demonsweatlive* featured Danzig's first hit, a live version of "Mother," from the band's debut; throughout the EP, the band's energy matches the power of the single. —*Stephen Thomas Erlewine*

○ **4** / 1994 / American ✦✦✦✦
Danzig has experimented a bit with using texture and atmosphere instead of sinister metal riffs to evoke their trademark mood of evil, mostly on "How the Gods Kill". *4* pursues that direction to a greater extent than any previous album, with guitarist John Christ contributing more effects and fuller chord voicings. The band has also started to craft their songs, using different instruments and a few industrial sounds in the background of some tracks. Not all of the experiments are successful, but out of all their releases, the music here comes the closest to reflecting the darkness of Glenn Danzig's lyrics. —*Steve Huey*

Dirty Black Summer / Warner Brothers

Terence Trent D'Arby

b. Mar. 15, 1962, New York, NY
Soul, Urban, Pop/Rock
Terence Trent D'Arby emerged in 1987 amid a storm of publicity. Claiming his debut record was the best since *Sgt. Pepper*, his brash arrogance captured headlines throughout the U.K., eventually winding their way back to America—which, ironically, is the exact opposite of how D'Arby conducted his career.

During the early '80s, Terence Trent D'Arby was a soldier for the United States Army. While posted in Germany, he joined a funk band called Touch, which marked the beginning of his musical career. After leaving the Army, he moved to London, where he recorded the demo tape that led to his record contract with CBS. D'Arby's first single, "If You Let Me Stay," rocketed into the U.K. Top Ten upon its release. Its accompanying album, *Introducing the Hardline According to Terence Trent D'Arby*, was also a massive success, hitting number one and spending over a year in the top half of the chart.

D'Arby didn't have a major hit in the U.S. until 1988, when the sparse funk of "Wishing Well" hit number one. The ballad "Sign Your Name" followed it into the Top Five and *Introducing* ended up selling over two million copies.

All of the success—both commercial and critical—had D'Arby poised as a major act, artistically and popularly. D'Arby's mix of soul, rock, pop and R&B recalled Prince in its scope and sound, yet his sensibility was grittier and earthier. At least they were at first. By the time of his second album, 1989's *Neither Fish Nor Flesh*, his ambitions were more nakedly pretentious. The record carried the weighty subtitle "A Soundtrack of Love, Faith, Hope & Destruction" and attacked many self-consciously important themes, including homosexuality and environmental destruction. In addition to the self-import of the lyrics, the music added a variety of new textures, from Indian drones to straight-ahead-'50s R&B.

All of the added baggage was too much for his audience and *Neither Fish Nor Flesh* dropped off the charts quickly, without so much as one hit single. It took D'Arby a full four years to record a new album. When *Terence Trent D'Arby's Symphony or Damn*—an album containing many of the same ideas as *Neither Fish Nor Flesh*, only better executed—was released in 1993, it received favorable reviews, as well as some airplay on modern rock radio stations, and MTV. It was enough for D'Arby to regain some credibility, yet it wasn't enough to make the album a hit. Two years later, he released *TTD's Vibrator* which received the same fate as *Symphony or Damn*. —*Stephen Thomas Erlewine*

○ **Introducing the Hardline According to Terence Trent D'Arby** / 1987 / Columbia ✦✦✦
Introducing the Hardline According to Terence Trent D'Arby is a strong debut by this young, cocky Black British singer, who wrote virtually every note, played a multitude of instruments, and claimed that his was the most important album since the Beatles's

Sgt. Pepper. Hits included "If You Let Me Stay," "Dance Little Sister," "Sign Your Name," and the #1 "Wishing Well." His first album is a curious mixture of old and new styles. Although the production is quite modern, D'Arby shows his roots in the work of older artists, borrowing a page or two from Michael Jackson and Stevie Wonder, while James Brown appears to have had the strongest influence on D'Arby's stage presence. —*Rob Bowman*

Neither Fish nor Flesh / 1989 / Columbia ✦✦✦
D'Arby's sophomore effort was considered a disappointment by most. More experimental than the first, it was also less focused. If possible, his ego seemed to have grown even larger with D'Arby taking up to ten playing credits on any given track. —*Rob Bowman*

● **Terence Trent D'Arby's Symphony or Damn** / May 11, 1993 / Columbia ✦✦✦✦
Falling halfway between the modern R&B of *Introducing the Hardline* and the extravagent *Neither Fish Nor Flesh*, *Symphony or Damn* is Terence Trent D'Arby's most ambitious album yet. It's also his best, because it takes the fine songwriting of his debut and melds it to the sonic excesses of *Fish*. Sure, some of it is embarassing (it's hard not to cringe during the "Welcome to My Monasteryo" declaration at the beginning of the album), but more often than not, D'Arby's experimentations succeed, and succeed grandly, at that. —*Stephen Thomas Erlewine*

TTD's Vibrator / 1995 / Work ✦✦✦
Symphony or Damn was an impressive comeback for Terence Trent D'arby, putting together the melodic songcraft of his debut and the conceptual ambitions of *Neither Fish Nor Flesh*. *TTD's Vibrator* follows the same pattern of *Symphony or Damn*, only without the songs to support the ambitions. —*Stephen Thomas Erlewine*

Bobby Darin

b. May 14, 1936, Bronx, NY, d. Dec. 20, 1973
Pop, Pop/Rock
Who was the real Bobby Darin? Was it the finger-poppin' crooner, the slick '50s-rocker, or the introspective folkie of the late '60s? In the end, it really doesn't matter, for Bobby Darin was all of these things and played each of these roles exceedingly well.

The show-biz legend suffered from a number of hardships, health problems in particular, that in the end make his achievements even more impressive. He was one of the first of that breed of whitebread late-'50s pop singers, but Darin's sides do indeed rock. Best known for his ring-a-ding-ding style, Darin came across at the outset as a punk Sinatra; he was damn good, and he wasn't about to let you forget it. There was still the much underrated side of Darin that first turned to the music of Tim Hardin and then started his own record label to record the kind of music he felt deeply about, often at the revision of show-biz buddies who were confused by his moves.

Over the years, Bobby Darin has been bagged as kind of a jive, glossy cat and something of an also-ran. But in the end, quite the opposite was true; he gave everything to all his phases and acted honestly on his instincts and accomplished what most others would have never attempted. —*Steve Aldrich*

● **The Ultimate Bobby Darin** / Jun. 1988 / Warner Brothers ✦✦✦✦
It offers a thorough look at Darin's rock and pop hits, including "Mack the Knife," "Dream Lover," "Splish Splash," and the breathtaking "Beyond the Sea." —*John Floyd*

○ **Capitol Collectors Series** / 1989 / Capitol ✦✦✦✦
A compilation of Darin's mid-'60s singles, which showcase Darin's diversity even if the majority of the set leans heavily on his pop material. Comprehensive liner notes, intelligent track selection, and great fidelity make this worth picking up. —*Stephen Thomas Erlewine*

○ **Mack the Knife** / 1991 / Atco ✦✦✦✦
Darin's later hits, including "Mack the Knife," "Beyond the Sea," "Guys and Dolls," "Black Coffee," and "Artificial Flowers," are collected on this second volume of Atco's fine two-part retrospective. —*Stephen Thomas Erlewine*

○ **Splish Splash** / 1991 / Atco ✦✦✦✦
The first installment of a definitive two-volume Bobby Darin retrospective, *Splish Splash* concentrates on his earlier hits, including "Dream Lover," "Baby Face," "You Must Have Been a Beautiful Baby," "Multiplication," and the title track. —*Stephen Thomas Erlewine*

James Darren

b. 1936
Pop/Rock, Teen Idol
Even more than the typical teen idol, James Darren's roots in authentic rock & roll were tenuous. Darren began recording for Colpix in the late '50s at the beginning of a screen career which saw him star in numerous films, most notably *Gidget*. More at home with standard middle-of-the-road, show tune-like material than rock, and not much of a singer in any case, Darren was nonetheless marketed as a pop/rock performer to his predominantly young female constituency. He ran off quite a few novelty-tinged hit singles in the early '60s, of which "Goodbye Cruel World," which made number three, was the biggest and best. Top Brill Building songwriters—including the Goffin-King, Mann-Weil, and Pomus-Shuman teams, as well as Bob Crewe, Gloria Shayne, and Howard Greenfield—gave Darren material, albeit material that was well below their usual standards. He recorded quite a bit after his early '60s heyday, reaching the Top 40 in 1967 with "All" and charting as late as 1977 with "You Take My Heart Away." — *Richie Unterberger*

● **The Best Of James Darren** / 1994 / Rhino ✦✦✦✦
18 songs, mostly from the early '60s, that rank among the least impressive teen idol recordings, although they were far from the least popular. Includes all his Colpix hits, highlighted by "Goodbye Cruel World" and the uncharacteristically hard-driving late-'64 effort "Just Think of Tonight," as well as his later chart entries "All" and "You Take My Heart Away." —*Richie Unterberger*

DAS Efx

Group, Rap
With their first album, DAS Efx caused a minor revolution based on their speedy, quick-tongued stuttering; it helped that they backed their rhymes with thick, funky tracks. The album was a major success, scoring a Top Forty pop single and going gold. On their second LP, *Straight Up Sewaside*, the duo of Drayz and Skoob Effect slightly altered their approach. They downplayed the high speed stuttering, though they continued with the intense rhyming and confrontational themes that made their debut so memorable. —*AMG*

● **Dead Serious** / 1992 / East West ✦✦✦✦
Their raps are often lightweight, but this album has made an immediate and substantial impact in the hip-hop community. —*Ron Wynn*

Straight Up Sewaside / 1993 / East West ✦✦✦
It may not be as revolutionary or immediately memorable as the twisting rhymes of *Serious Business*, but the harder-edged styles of *Straight Up Sewaside* have enough slamming rhythms and rhymes to satisfy most fans. —*Stephen Thomas Erlewine*

Joe Dassin

Singer-Songwriter
The son of film director Jules Dassin, Joe Dassin began singing in folk clubs while enrolled at the University of Michigan during the late '50s and early '60s. After his education was completed, he acted in a handful of films for his father, playing minor roles. During this time, he signed a record deal to record several pop singles for Jacques Plait; they were released in France and its colonies to little sales. Dassin's career began to gain steam when his self-titled debut album started selling in North America; the foreign success was soon replicated back home. In 1967, he was the host of the first MIDEM festival at Cannes; the exposure made his vocal take on Plait's instrumental, "Les Dalton," a hit, establishing Joe Dassin as a French celebrity throughout the next two decades. —*Stephen Thomas Erlewine*

One Hour With Joe Dassin Vol.1 / CBS ✦✦
Joe Dassin, Vol.2: The Guitor Don't Lie / CBS ✦✦
Joe Dassin, Vol.3: Les Dalton / CBS ✦✦
Joe Dassin, Vol.4: Les Champs-Elysees / CBS ✦✦
Joe Dassin, Vol.5: Salut Les Amoureux / CBS ✦✦✦
Joe Dassin, Vol.6: Si Tu T'Appelles Melancolie / CBS ✦✦✦
○ **Joe Dassin, Vol.7: Le Jardin Du Luxembourg** / CBS ✦✦✦✦
○ **Joe Dassin, Vol.8: La Demoiselle De Deshonneur** / CBS ✦✦✦✦
● **23 Succes: Compact Longue Duree** / CBS ✦✦✦✦

David & David

Group, Pop/Rock
Although they only recorded one album, the Californian duo of David Baerwald and David Ricketts made some of the finest mainstream pop of the '80s. With its slick surfaces and memorable melodies, 1986's *Boomtown* was deceptively smooth; beneath the production, the songs were tales of despair and broken dreams in the Reagan era. David & David scored a surprise hit in 1986 with "Welcome to the Boomtown;" it was their only single that charted. Baerwald began a critically acclaimed solo career in 1990; Ricketts has not released anything since *Boomtown*. —*Stephen Thomas Erlewine*

● **Boomtown** / 1986 / A&M ✦✦✦✦
Los Angeles-musicians David Baerwald and David Ricketts joined forces to create subtle, moody, and darkly atmospheric rock, culminating in their Top 40 hit "Welcome to the Boomtown." —*Donna DiChario*

Dave Davies

Rock & Roll
Although he took a largely subordinate role to his brother Ray in the Kinks, Dave's fierce guitar work and hoarse but effective background (and occasional lead) vocals were key elements of the band's appeal. Dave also occasionally wrote songs for the Kinks that showed him to be a writer of considerable skill and wit, if not up to the same level as Ray. In the late '60s, Dave made some solo singles that met with critical success in Britain, although they were unknown in the U.S. "Death of a Clown" (also included on the Kinks' *Something Else* LP) made number three on the British charts in 1967, and the follow-up "Susannah's Still Alive" also did fairly well. Dave began to consider making a solo album, but after a couple other solo singles flopped, he seemed to lose heart and abandoned his plans (some unreleased solo tracks from this period turned up on the obscure Kinks bootleg *Good Luck Charm*). In the 1980s, Dave finally began a solo career in earnest, releasing a series of mainstream rock albums that found little critical or commercial acclaim. —*Richie Unterberger*

Afl 1: 3603 / 1980 / RCA ✦✦✦
Dave Davies / 1980 / RCA ✦✦
Glamour / 1981 / RCA ✦✦
Chosen People / 1983 / Warner Brothers ✦✦
● **The Album That Never Was** / 1987 / PRT ✦✦✦✦
When Dave Davies racked up a couple British hits in 1967, rumors were rife that the Kinks' lead guitarist would cut a solo album of his own. He never did—not in the '60s, anyway—and this album is a facsimile of what might have been, packaging some ultra-rare solo singles of the time with tracks that Dave wrote and sang on some of the Kinks' late-'60s records. They show him to be a fine, underappreciated singer and songwriter in a Dylanesque folk-rock mode. —*Richie Unterberger*

Spencer Davis Group

Group, British Invasion
His ferocious soul-drenched vocals belying his tender teenage years, Steve Winwood powered the Spencer Davis Group's three biggest U.S. hits during their brief life span as one of the British Invasion's most convincing R&B-based combos.
    Guitarist Davis formed the band with Winwood on organ, his brother Muff Winwood on bass, and drummer Peter York. Signing on with producer Chris Blackwell, the quartet got their first hit (the blistering "Keep On Running") from another of Blackwell's acts, West Indian performer Jackie Edwards. After topping the British charts in 1965, the song struggled on the lower reaches of the U.S. Hot 100.
    The group's two hottest sellers were self-penned projects. "Gimme Some Lovin'" and "I'm a Man" were searing showcases for the adolescent Winwood's gritty vocals and blazing keyboards and the band's pounding rhythms. Although they burned up the charts even on this side of the ocean in 1967, the quartet never capitalized on their fame with an American tour. At the height of their power, Winwood left to form Traffic, leaving Davis without his dynamic front man. The bandleader focused on producing other acts, including a Canadian ensemble called the Downchild Blues Band during the early '80s. —*Bill Dahl*

Their First LP / 1965 / Fontana ✦✦✦
The group's first album is basically a reflection of their early repertoire and very heavy on the R&B/soul standards. Dominated by
covers of Ike & Tina Turner, the Coasters, John Lee Hooker, Little
Walter, Brenda Holloway, and others, only three of the tunes are
original. Two of these are written by Stevie Winwood, the other by
Spencer Davis; Winwood's midtempo soul number "It Hurts Me
So" is easily the best of them. Winwood is in fine voice and the
group is energetic, but this is neither as good as their best work
nor nearly as good as the best British R&B albums of the era by
competitors like Them and the Rolling Stones. Includes their first
two British singles, "Dimples" and "I Can't Stand It." —*Richie Unterberger*

Autumn 66 / 1966 / Fontana ✦✦✦
At the peak of their popularity, the Spencer Davis Group's albums
were considerably less impressive than their hits and a bit thin on
imagination, although they were never less than competent. This,
their third LP, relies heavily on soul covers, as well as a few oft-
covered blues standards ("Midnight Special," "Mean Woman
Blues," "Dust My Blues"). Highlights are their second British #1
hit, "Somebody Help Me"; the decent group original "High Time
Baby," Winwood's organ-based instrumental "On the Green Light,"
and "When I Get Home," which (like "Somebody Help Me") was a
hit in Britain but not the U.S. —*Richie Unterberger*

Heavies / 1969 / United Artists ✦✦✦
A hodgepodge of some of the group's lesser-known tracks, this actually contains some of their better performances. The instrumental jam "Waltz For Lumumba" sounds like a prototype for some of
the ideas Winwood would employ in Traffic; the group original
"Hey Darling" is a smoldering, moody blues, "Mean Woman
Blues" and "Watch Your Step" are a couple of their best uptempo,
and most guitar-oriented, R&B covers, "Please Do Something" is a
good cover of a Don Covay tune, and "Back to My Life" was co-
written by Jackie Edwards, who was responsible for their first few
British hits. Put together by United Artists after the group had broken up to capitalize on Winwood's ascent to superstardom in Traffic, it's nonetheless a decent compilation of some of their more interesting odds and ends. —*Richie Unterberger*

● **The Golden Archive Series** / 1984 / Rhino ✦✦✦✦
The best compilation of their best moments. 14 songs, including
both of their U.S. hits, "I'm a Man" and "Gimme Some Lovin'"; the
U.K. chart-toppers "Keep On Running" and "Somebody Help Me,"
the smaller U.K. hit "When I Come Home," and several fine R&B
covers, all from 1964-66. —*Richie Unterberger*

● **Best of the Spencer Davis Group** / 1985 / EMI America ✦✦✦✦
This contains "Gimme Some Lovin'" and many good lesser-
known songs. —*Dan Heilman*

Tyrone Davis

b. May 4, 1938, Greenville, MS
Soul
Perennially a ladies' choice, Tyrone Davis just seems to naturally
appeal to women. That's not to say that gents haven't bought his
churning Chicago soul records too—his impressive hit-making career harks back to 1968, and there's no end in sight.
His mentor, noted singer Harold Burrage, coached his charge
well, and Davis debuted on wax in 1965 as "Tyrone the Wonder
Boy" on the local Four Brothers logo. Far more wondrous were
Davis's classy efforts for Chicago's Dakar label, commencing with
the remorseful R&B chart-topper "Can I Change My Mind" in
1968, continuing with "Is It Something You've Got" in 1969, and
the million-selling classic "Turn Back the Hands of Time" in 1970.
With Willie Henderson producing, the cats at Dakar were forging
a fresh, vital new Chicago soul sound, and Tyrone Davis was right
there at its forefront.
Davis remained with Dakar into 1976, his warm, assured vocals
powering the likes of "I Had It All the Time" and "Turning Point,"
before moving over to Columbia without missing a beat. These
days, Tyrone hops from one label to the next, seemingly with each
new release—but he's still no stranger to the urban contemporary
charts, and the women still love him. What more could he possibly
ask for? —*Bill Dahl*

○ **Can I Change My Mind** / 1969 / Dakar ✦✦✦✦
The title of Davis's greatest hit, and one of the genuine '60s soul
classics. This song broke Davis out of the pack and established
him as a star. It's by far the dominant song on this album of other-

wise nicely sung, expertly produced deep soul ballads and uptempo tunes. —*Ron Wynn*

○ **Turn Back the Hands of Time** / 1970 / Dakar ✦✦✦✦
The second Tyrone Davis album included another masterpiece, the
song that proved he wasn't going to be a one-hit wonder. It was
sung with bluesy conviction and soulful ardor, and helped make
the album a huge smash. It was his second number one R&B hit,
and his second single to make it into the pop Top 10. —*Ron Wynn*

I Had It All the Time / 1970 / Dakar ✦✦✦
Tyrone Davis scored another smash R&B hit with the title track,
although it wasn't a chart topper. Davis was about to exit the
Dakar label and did only one more album for them before signing
a big money deal with Columbia. This is prototype early '70s soul,
sparsely produced and wonderfully performed. —*Ron Wynn*

○ **Greatest Hits [Epic]** / 1972 / Epic ✦✦✦✦
A little short on running time, this is, nevertheless, the best CD
representation for now, showcasing the Chicago soulman's 1968-
1975 Dakar output. —*Bill Dahl*

It's All in the Game / 1974 / Dakar ✦✦✦
The final Dakar album before Tyrone Davis left to join Columbia.
It's right in line with his others: earthy ballads, heartfelt wailers,
and blues-oriented uptempo numbers. It was the end of an era, as
"deep" soul, already in decline, was about to be completely
swamped by the coming of disco. —*Ron Wynn*

○ **In the Mood with Tyrone Davis** / 1979 / Columbia ✦✦✦✦
His best overall Columbia album. Tyrone Davis surprised many
observers when the title cut smashed the embargo non-Southern
urban contemporary stations had on soul music and soared into
the Top 10, peaking at number six. The rest of the album was a bit
slick by past Davis' standards, but even the sappiest numbers were
performed with Davis' customary grit and soulfulness. —*Ron
Wynn*

I'll Always Love You / 1991 / Ichiban ✦✦
Tyrone Davis keeps making his familiar confessional soul, earthy
ballads, and bluesy uptempo wailers, now for the Atlanta-based
Ichiban label. There aren't any classics on this '91 set, but everything is produced in the classic Southern soul mode, with a minimum of electronic/synthesized backbeats and little trace of New
Jack influences. —*Ron Wynn*

● **Greatest Hits [Rhino]** / 1992 / Rhino ✦✦✦✦
Tyrone Davis combined influences from hard-edged, country-
tinged urban blues and more tightly arranged, horn-dominated
soul. He sang surging uptempo tunes, churning ballads, heartache
songs and tribute numbers, and moved from material dominated
by brassy arrangements to numbers reliant on his narratives and
persona. This 17-track CD begins with his earliest hits, such as
"Can I Change Me Mind" and "Is It Something You've Got," and
continues into smoother but no less urgent tunes such as "Turning
Point," "There Is Is," and "One Way Ticket." Because this collection
only covers his Dakar material, things end at 1976, after which he
left for Columbia. But for soul fans, Tyrone Davis' greatest music
came on Dakar. —*Ron Wynn*

Ronnie Dawson

b. 1939
Rockabilly
Late-'50s Dallas rockabilly guitarist and singer noted for his
shocking white brush cut and high-pitched, boyish vocals that
made him sound even younger than his teenage years. His clutch
of rare singles on regional labels are highly valued by rockabilly
collectors. Dawson sounded something like a raw, upper-register
Gene Vincent, and the connection is not entirely coincidental. He
shared Vincent's manager, and his greatest song, the manic "Action
Packed" (with its insistent "Hear me!" shouted refrain), was written by Jack Rhodes, who also wrote a couple of Vincent's best tunes
("Woman Love" and "B-I-Bickey-Bi-Bo-Bo-Go"). Dawson could also
sing convincingly on more grinding and bluesy numbers.
After a few singles, Dawson was briefly picked up by Swan
Records, which tried to mold him into a teen idol with unsuccessful results (commercially and artistically). After a fine single for
Columbia under the name Commonwealth Jones, Ronnie retreated to smaller labels once again for a time. He worked as a ses-
sion drummer for the semi-legendary Texas producer Major Bill
Smith, playing on Bruce Channel's "Hey Baby" and Paul & Paula's
"Hey Paula"; like most first-generation rockabilly singers, he tried
his hand at country music as well. His rediscovery was hastened

by the inclusion of "Action Packed" in Rhino's *Rock this Town* anthology of rockabilly classics, and he has resumed active performing and recording. —*Richie Unterberger*

● **Rockin' Bones** / 1990 / No Hit ◆◆◆◆
This 20-track CD has all his essential early recordings, with both sides of five singles (the Swan teen idol efforts aren't included). Besides "Action Packed," highlights are the subsequent A-sides "Do Do Do" and "Rockin' Bones," as well as a spooky rendering of "Riders in the Sky." The unreleased tracks include several raw demos he cut prior to his first single, as well as a few outtakes from his Columbia session that feature some harmonica work by Delbert McClinton. —*Richie Unterberger*

Bobby Day

b. Jul. 1, 1932, Fort Worth, TX, d. Jul. 15, 1990
Rock & Roll, Doo-Wop
An important cog in Los Angeles's doo-wop community during the '50s, Day wrote three often-covered early rock classics in 1957-1958. Day was part of the Hollywood Flames, one of the area's top R&B vocal groups, and briefly part of Bob and Earl, later to hit without Day on "Harlem Shuffle." Day formed his own group, the Satellites, in 1957, cutting the original "Little Bitty Pretty One" for Class Records. A nearly identical cover by Thurston Harris beat the original out, so Day countered with the driving "Rockin' Robin" in 1958, an R&B chart-topper. Its flip, "Over and Over," was a hit in its own right, although the Dave Clark Five's 1965 revival is better remembered today. Day waxed a few more hits for Class in 1959, including "That's All I Want" and a derivative "The Bluebird, the Buzzard & the Oriole," flitting from label to label during the 60s. —*Bill Dahl*

● **The Original Rockin' Robin** / 1991 / Ace ◆◆◆◆
Bobby Day's "Rockin' Robin" remains a classic. That and 25 other original recordings show up on this solid British import. —*Jeff Tamarkin*

Golden Classics / Collectables ◆◆◆

Best of Bobby Day / Rhino ◆◆◆
This 14-song vinyl release included out-of-print "Rockin' Robin" as well as Day's other major recordings. —*Jeff Tamarkin*

The Daybreakers

Group, Garage Rock, Pop/Rock
A garage-rock combo from Muscatine, IA, that cut only one single, "Psychedelic Siren" (1967), which was rediscovered by collectors upon its inclusion on the *Psychedelic Unknowns* anthology in the early '80s. They were a more or less average garage band of the time, led by songwriter, organist, and vocalist Al Collins, who became author of the Dick Tracy comic strip. In the early '70s, they evolved into the equally obscure Rox under the leadership of Bruce Peters, and pursued a more pop-oriented direction that recalled the late '60s Beach Boys and early Raspberries. —*Richie Unterberger*

History Of Eastern Iowa Rock Volume 1 / 1986 / Unlimited Productions ◆◆◆
18 songs, including both sides of their single and lots of previously unreleased demos, most dating from 1967-68. This is more progressive in slant than the usual archival garage release, with influences from the Doors, Rascals, and "White Room"-era Cream harmonies. The sound of the original garage band era is strongly felt via Al Collins' Farfisa organ, which is at the forefront of his often minor-key compositions. Also includes four demos in a much breezier pop vein by Rox, and some crummy oldies remakes by reunion versions of the band in the late '70s and 1980s. —*Richie Unterberger*

Taylor Dayne

Long Island, NY
Dance-Pop
Dance-pop diva Taylor Dayne (born Leslie Wonderman) had a remarkably quick ascent to stardom in the late '80s, sailing into the Top Ten with her first single, "Tell It to My Heart." Dayne began singing professionally after graduating from high school, performing with the rock group Felony and a new wave outfit called Next; neither band had any success. Once Dayne finished college, she began singing solo. Her first effort was a dance interpretation of the ballad "Tell It to My Heart;" her version led to a contract with Arista Records, who released the song in the fall of 1987. It soon became a hit, propelling her to stardom.

Taylor Dayne's first album, also titled *Tell It to My Heart* and released in early 1988, was a continuation of her dance-pop formula—no matter if the song was an uptempo number or a ballad, she belted out her vocals over the carefully-constructed synthesized backing tracks. The formula led to three more Top Ten singles from her debut: "Prove Your Love," "I'll Always Love You" and the number two "Don't Rush Me;" the album eventually sold over two million copies. *Can't Fight Fate*, Dayne's second album, was nearly as successful, spawning the hit singles "With Every Beat of My Heart," "I'll Be Your Shelter," and the number one "Love Will Lead You Back," as well as selling over a million copies. However, Dayne's fall out of the Top Ten was nearly as quick as her rise; "Heart of Stone," the fourth single from *Can't Fight Fate*, stalled at number 12 and only one of the singles ("Can't Get Enough of Your Love") from her third album, *Send Me a Lover*, cracked the Top 40 and even then, it only reached number 20. Despite her declining sales, Dayne remained a favorite of many dance-music fans. —*Stephen Thomas Erlewine*

● **Tell It to My Heart** / 1988 / Arista ◆◆◆◆
Taylor Dayne made a huge splash with the roaring dance/R&B title cut. Her big sound, flamboyant manner, and carefully calculated explosive delivery put her in the forefront at the time among female singers mixing soul and classic disco influences (Lisa Stansfield would soon emerge at the head of the class). The rest of the album is pleasant but inconsequential pop and dance filler. —*Ron Wynn*

Can't Fight Fate / 1989 / Arista ◆◆◆

Taylor Dayne / 1992 / Arista ◆◆◆

Send Me a Lover / Jun. 29, 1993 / Arista ◆◆

Dazz Band

Group, Funk
The Cleveland-based Dazz Band was one of the more popular funk groups of the early '80s. Bobby Harris formed the group in the late '70s, taking members from two Cleveland funk bands, Bell Telefunk and the Kinsman Grills house band. The end result was an eight-piece band featuring Harris, Skip Martin, III, Pierre DeMudd on horns and vocals, guitarist Eric Fearman, bassist Michael Wiley, drummer Isaac Wiley, keyboardist Kevin Frederick, and percussionist Kenny Pettus. Harris' concept for the group was "danceable jazz;" he shortened the description to "dazz" and called the group Kinsman Dazz. Under that name, the group had two small hits in the USA during 1978 and 1979. In 1980, they changed their name to the Dazz Band and signed to Motown.

Let the Music Play, the band's first release for the record label, was released in 1981. Once the group veered away from the more melodic, pop-oriented dance music that dominated their debut and started playing a tougher, more groove-oriented funk, the Dazz Band began racking up the hits. "Let It Whip," taken from their second album *Keep It Live* (1982), reached number five and won a Grammy Award for Best Performance by an R&B Vocal Duo or Group. While they never reached those heights again, the Dazz Band had a string of six consecutive Top 100 albums that ran until 1986; during that time, they scored two other Top 100 singles, "Joystick" and "Let It All Blow." In 1985, Fearman and Frederick left the band; they were replaced by Marlon McClain and Keith Harrison respectively. The Dazz Band switched labels to Geffen in 1986. That year they had their final charting album, *Wild and Free*. Soon after its release, the band switched to RCA. The group failed to have another hit and quietly faded away. —*Stephen Thomas Erlewine*

● **Greatest Hits** / 1987 / Motown ◆◆◆◆
A greatest-hits package from one of Motown's better '80s bands, it features "Let It Whip." —*Rick A. Bueche*

The dB's

Group, Alternative Pop/Rock, Power Pop/Anglo-Pop
Among the alternative bands who emerged during the '80s, the dB's clever songs, quirky vocals, and unique arrangements and production made them arguably the best practitioners of the smart power-pop movement that drew much inspiration from Big Star, the Move, the Byrds, and the Beatles, for example.

Regardless, principle singer/songwriters Chris Stamey (formerly of the North Carolina band Sneakers, and Alex Chilton sideman) and Peter Holsapple forged a sound together on their two

Scott Litt-produced albums (*Stands for Decibels, Repercussion*) that was truly distinctive. Stamey left to pursue a solo career, releasing several EPs and a couple of albums, of which *Fireworks* (released in 1991) is arguably his best.

After Stamey's departure, Holsapple forged ahead with the dB's, releasing *Like This* and *The Sound of Music*, two solid albums that delved deeper into a more Americanized roots-pop sound.

In early 1991, Holsapple and Stamey got together and released *Mavericks*, a charming collaboration that featured a cover of Gene Clark's "Here Without You," as well as some great originals like "Angels," "The Child in You," and "Geometry." *—Rick Clark*

● **Stands for Decibels** / 1981 / IRS ◆◆◆◆
Influences like the Beatles, Big Star, and the Move are detectable, but the dB's creatively synthesized those sounds into something unique and personal, with wonderfully twisted melodies, inside-out harmonies, herky-jerky grooves, and quirky arrangements. Every track is noteworthy. *—Rick Clark*

○ **Repercussion** / 1982 / IRS ◆◆◆◆
Their second effort is more polished, but none of their distinctive charm is missing. It has consistently fine material from top to bottom. *—Rick Clark*

Like This / 1984 / Rhino ◆◆◆
With Stamey gone, the trio (fronted by Peter Holsapple) dropped some of the band's previous eccentricities and got down to a more rootsy rock & roll approach, even touching on a little country. The melodies are still as catchy as ever. *—Rick Clark*

The Sound of Music / 1987 / IRS ◆◆◆
What Peter Holsapple calls "the band's most blatant attempt to make a commercial album" sounds like it—but it's also very enjoyable. There's some tremedous merges of melody and lyrics here, from the satiny pop of "I Lie," the funny kick of "Working for Somebody Else," and the folky Holsapple-Syd Straw duet, "Never Before and Never Again." *—Kit Kiefer*

Ride the Wild Tom Tom / 1993 / Rhino ◆◆
A wonderful collection of early demos—mostly pre-*Stands for deciBels*. Even though this isn't the place to start with the dB's, it is a must-own for fans of the band who already have the first two albums. *—Rick Clark*

Paris Avenue / 1994 / Monkey Hill ◆◆◆

De La Soul

Group, Rap
This trio of Long Island rappers consists of Posdnous (born Kelvin Mercer), Trugoy (born David Jolicoeur), and Mase. Their albums are lyrically keen and idiomatically diverse, sampling cuts from both the Coasters and the Turtles (the latter got them in some legal hot water), while espousing viewpoints that put them in the Afrocentric pocket yet don't wed them to any hard-and-fast religious or political position. Some have callled them hip-hop's first hippies; more to the point, they're among rap's sharpest and savviest performers.

De La Soul answered detractors who claimed they lacked edge with *Buhloone Mind State* in 1993. It was their answer to gangsta rappers who'd called them irrelevant, as they skewered that idiom for its obsessiveness with hardness and posturing. *—Ron Wynn*

★ **Three Feet High & Rising** / 1989 / Tommy Boy ◆◆◆◆◆
A remarkable debut that runs the gamut from absurdity ("Jenifa Taught Me" and "Plug Tunin' ") to hard-hitting social commentary ("Ghetto Thang" and "Say No Go"), and also contains the hit "Me Myself and I." De La Soul's inventiveness shines—not many rappers would be able to pull funky beats from Steely Dan and Turtles tracks. Throughout the album, a mock game show is interspersed between the songs, giving the entire recording a bizarre, humorous feel. *Three Feet High & Rising* would be incoherent if it wasn't for the sizable rhyming and musical talents of the trio. *—Stephen Thomas Erlewine*

○ **De La Soul Is Dead** / 1991 / Tommy Boy ◆◆◆◆
The title and cover (a picture of a broken pot of daisies) illustrate that De La Soul wishes to debunk their myth and shed the attention their debut album earned them. For the most part, the songs on the album are considerably less lighthearted than the ones on the debut, but are no less impressive—"Millie Pulled a Pistol on Santa" is one of the most chilling tales of child abuse ever recorded. *De La Soul Is Dead* is not easy to assimilate on the first listen, but the rewards are great. *—Stephen Thomas Erlewine*

○ **Buhloone Mindstate** / 1993 / Tommy Boy ◆◆◆◆
Continually trying to live up the revolution that was their debut, *Buhloone Mindstate* is a return to Daisy Age positive vibes. The beats are big, the samples are fresh, and the melodies are enticing. While the first two albums featured intros and side-lights along the way, *Buhloone Mindstate* has only fifteen tracks (eleven songs). With help from friends Guru, Maceo Parker, and Biz Markie, De La Soul approaches the perfection of *Three Feet High And Rising*, if not the initial effect. *—John Bush*

Deacon Blue

Group, Pop/Rock
Deacon Blue took their name from a particularly smooth song from Steely Dan, a group that set the precedent for sophisticated jazz-tinged pop. Not coincidentally, the Scottish group Deacon Blue followed a familiar path in their own career. Where Steely Dan relied on jazz, Deacon Blue's singer/songwriter Ricky Ross relied more on soul: This group wasn't afraid of being known for their pop singles. Even with their numerous British hit singles, the group was more serious than the average pop band, mixing in a fair dose of social criticism with their smooth melodies. Deacon Blue were U.K. favorites from their first album in 1988, yet they never gained a fair American audience. After struggling for a breakthrough hit for years, the group disbanded in the summer of 1994. *—Stephen Thomas Erlewine*

● **Raintown** / May 1987 / Columbia ◆◆◆◆
An inspiring debut of well-crafted adult pop, heavily under the influence of Prefab Sprout, it was originally released by CBS Records in the UK in May 1987. *Raintown* was released in the U.S. by Columbia Records in March 1988. *—Steve Aldrich*

○ **When the World Knows Your Name** / Apr. 1989 / Columbia ◆◆◆◆

Ooh Las Vegas / Sep. 1990 / CBS ◆◆◆
Collection of B-sides, previously unissued material. *—Steve Aldrich*

Fellow Hoodlums / Jun. 1991 / Columbia ◆◆◆
On their third album of new studio material, Ricky Ross and Deacon Blue continued to pursue their pop-folk-soul hybrid, a musical mixture seemingly unique to the lesser dominions of the British Isles. It's a sound in which the rhythm section usually is aping the Motown house band or the MG's, there are such acoustic instruments as guitars and fiddles (or keyboard on string settings) filling the middle section, and the tunes are topped by an expressive singer with lyrics full of yearning and local references. It doesn't always travel well, and, indeed, although *Fellow Hoodlums* entered the British charts near the top and produced three chart singles, the album was lost entirely in the U.S. *—William Ruhlmann*

Whatever You Say, Say Nothing / Mar. 1993 / Chaos/Columbia ◆◆◆
Abandoning the folkish feel of earlier records, Ricky Ross took Deacon Blue in a more rocking direction on the band's fourth new studio album, *Whatever You Say, Say Nothing*. It was as if, having failed at becoming the next Van Morrison, Ross decided to become the next Bono. Songs like "Bethlehem's Gate" were paced by relentless, martial drumming and rhythmic instruments that played pulse patterns rather than complete chords. Meanwhile, Ross adopted a high, breathy singing voice with lots of echo. The lyrics Ross sang had less to do with his old Glasgow neighborhood than with "Peace & Jobs & Freedom" "All Over the World." Many of Deacon Blue's British fans were willing to follow, but America still wasn't listening. *—William Ruhlmann*

Dead Boys

Group, Punk
Forming from the ashes of Cleveland's semi-legendary Rocket from the Tombs, the Dead Boys were one of the first punk bands to escalate the level of violence, nihilism, and pure ugliness of punk rock to extreme new levels. After they relocated to New York, ex-Rocket members guitarist Cheetah Chrome and drummer Johnny Blitz hooked up with guitarist Jimmy Zero, bassist Jeff Magnum, and vocalist Stiv Bators to form the Dead Boys. Their music wasn't very special; even by the relaxed standards of punk, it was loose and incompetent, bordering on the stupidity of heavy metal. "Sonic Reducer" and "Ain't It Fun," the band's two best songs, were hold-overs from former Rocket from the Tombs members David Thomas and Peter Laughner, who went on to form

Pere Ubu. What distinguished the Dead Boys, and what makes them notorious to this day, is their pure nastiness, much of it coming from Bators. Their two albums—*Young Loud and Snotty* and *We Have Come for Your Children*—are brutal, wallowing in their own self-serving nihilism; they embodied the punk stereotypes held by the mainstream. After two albums, the band split. Bators formed Lords of the New Church and the rest of the members slid into obscurity. In 1990, Bators died of injuries sustained from being hit by a bus in Paris. —*Stephen Thomas Erlewine*

● **Young Loud & Snotty** / 1977 / Sire ◆◆◆◆
A truly vulgar and tasteless slab of nihilistic punk rock, the Dead Boys' first album included the classic "Sonic Reducer," which was buried in a mess of relentless, sub-heavy metal pounding. —*Stephen Thomas Erlewine*

We Have Come for Your Children / 1978 / Sire ◆◆◆
Highlighted by the snarling "Ain't It Fun," the Dead Boys second album was as nasty and raw as their first. —*Stephen Thomas Erlewine*

Dead Can Dance

Group, Alternative Pop/Rock
Originally from Australia, this group has a purely European sound (Gregorian chants, Celtic, neo-gothic). Their songs are of lost beauty, regret, and sorrow, inspiration and nobility, and of the everlasting human goal of attaining a meaningful existence. —*Vladimir Bogdanov*

Dead Can Dance / 1984 / Warner Brothers ◆◆◆
Just experiments, without any definite style or direction. (Interesting only as a history of the group.) —*Vladimir Bogdanov*

Spleen & Ideal / 1985 / Warner Brothers ◆◆◆
Well-balanced in terms of both mood and style, this album brings you the whole new world of hopeless hope and aimless urge and search. —*Vladimir Bogdanov*

○ **Within the Realm of a Dying Sun** / 1987 / Warner Brothers ◆◆◆◆
Probably their most subtle and intelligent album. Touches the deepest levels of our identity. —*Vladimir Bogdanov*

Serpent's Egg / 1988 / Warner Brothers ◆◆◆
An interesting combination of Slavonic and European medieval music. —*Vladimir Bogdanov*

○ **Aion** / 1990 / Warner Brothers ◆◆◆◆
True medieval sound combined with all the variety of modern studio techniques. Not an imitation at all; just enriched with an old musical tradition. —*Vladimir Bogdanov*

● **A Passage in Time** / Oct. 1991 / Rykodisc ◆◆◆◆
Anthology; a best-of. —*Vladimir Bogdanov*

Into the Labyrinth / 1993 / Warner Brothers ◆◆◆

Toward the within / 1994 / Warner Brothers ◆◆◆
Dead Can Dance's albums are so meticulously constructed that the mere thought of a live album seems ridiculous. However, Dead Can Dance are more clever than the average band. When it came time for them to record a live album, they came upon an ingenious solution: instead of capturing their classics live, they decided to record an album of all-new material. Naturally, the result still appeals to the hardcore fan as much as the standard live formula, yet *Toward the Within* shows that Dead Can Dance's mesmerizing music continues to evolve, incorporating different strands of world music all the while. —*Stephen Thomas Erlewine*

Dead Kennedys

Group, Hardcore
Next to Black Flag and X, Jello Biafra's Dead Kennedys were the longest lasting of West Coast hardcore groups. Their music challenged everything and offended everybody, and Biafra's self-righteous morality made him a post-punk role model for thousands of pissed-off kids. In the late '80s, Biafra became a spokesperson for the indecency of music censorship. When the group disbanded in 1987, Biafra continued with Lard and solo projects. —*John Floyd*

★ **Fresh Fruit for Rotting Vegetables** / 1980 / Alternative Tentacles ◆◆◆◆◆
The DK's 1980 debut was as important to the West Coast hardcore scene as the Sex Pistols' *Bollocks* was to disenfranchised British punks. Despite a few clunkers, *Fresh Fruit* is an explosive and scalding blast of political and social fury, underpinned by Jello Biafra's wise-ass vocals and Klaus Flouride's pseudo-surf guitar wailing. Most of the band's best songs are here. —*John Floyd*

In God We Trust, Inc. / Feb. 1981 / Alternative Tentacles ◆◆◆
DK's anti-religion seven-song EP varies from all other material in thrashy-metallic nature. Each song is a speedy, essentially unintelligible gem of punk lore with super dominating guitars and heavier drums. It includes "Religious Vomit" and "Dog Bite" and culminates in a cover of the classic "California Uber Alles" entitled "We've Got a Bigger Problem Now," dealing with Ronald Reagan instead of Jerry Brown. —*Julian Katz*

○ **Plastic Surgery Disasters/In God We Trust, Inc.** / 1982 / Alternative Tentacles ◆◆◆◆
Their second effort captures their frenetic live set full of mayhem and confusion but with an underlying feeling of greatness. Nonconformist, anti-establishment sentiment is eloquently made sensible by talented frontman Jello Biafra. Punk at its best, musically and lyrically, it includes "Terminal Preppie," "Government Flu," and "Winnebago Warrior." —*Julian Katz*

Frankenchrist / 1985 / Alternative Tentacles ◆◆◆
More hyper-kinetic political punk rock. —*David Szatmary*

Bedtime for Democracy / 1986 / Alternative Tentacles ◆◆
This is the final political testimony from the DK. —*David Szatmary*

○ **Give Me Convenience or Give Me Death** / 1987 / Alternative Tentacles ◆◆◆◆
A useful compilation, it not only collects many essential non-album cuts but rounds up the best material from the otherwise desultory follow-ups to *Fresh Fruit*. —*John Floyd*

Dead Milkmen

Group, Alternative Pop/Rock
Philadelphia pop-punk quartet featuring vocalist Rodney Anonymous (who sometimes adds "Amadeus" or "Mellencamp" to his name), guitarist Joe Jack Talcum, bassist Dave Blood, and drummer Dean Clean. The Milkmen are renowned for their dumb, obnoxious sense of humor, which they frequently focus on pop culture. Some critics love them, some critics hate them, but all agree that the Milkmen are sophomoric and snotty. "Bitchin' Camaro," from their debut, *Big Lizard In My Backyard*, was a minor alternative-radio hit. The band got a small measure of publicity when Detroit Tiger infielder Jim Walewander praised them in interviews, and had a minor MTV hit with *Beelzebubba*'s "Punk Rock Girl." Unfortunately, they were never as consistently funny as they tried to be, and wound up dropped from Enigma after *Metaphysical Graffiti*. Their subsequent releases found them trying to learn how to be serious, and their popularity had almost disappeared by the time they broke up in 1994. —*Steve Huey*

● **Big Lizard in My Backyard** / 1985 / Enigma ◆◆◆◆
You can hardly refer to any Dead Milkmen album as a classic, but *Big Lizard* comes close. Stupid, sophomoric, and quite tuneful, this is when the jokes were still funny or, at the very least, still worth listening to. Features "Bitchin' Camaro" and the tastelessly funny "Takin' Retards to the Zoo." —*John Dougan*

Eat Your Paisley / 1986 / Enigma ◆◆◆
After *Big Lizard*, Milkmen albums are mostly inconsistent, hit-or-miss affairs. This one is more of a showcase for the dippy side of their sense of humor; only a couple tracks reproduce the snottiness of their debut. For real die-hards only. —*Steve Huey*

○ **Bucky Fellini** / 1987 / Enigma ◆◆◆◆
Another inconsistent outing, but this one is helped out by the dead-on "Instant Club Hit (You'll Dance to Anything)," a satire of pretentious alternative European dance artists, and a few cover tunes, including a parody of "Watching Scotty Grow" ("Watching Scotty Die"). —*Steve Huey*

○ **Beelzebubba** / 1988 / Fever ◆◆◆◆
Probably their best post-*Big Lizard* album, this contains some of the most memorable Milkmen tracks, including songs about wife-beating and drinking bleach, the anthemic "Life is Shit," and the MTV semi-hit "Punk Rock Girl." There are still a few clunkers, but those are outweighed (for the most part). Anonymous proves on "Stuart" that perhaps he would be funnier if he just forgot about trying to sing and instead delivered ranting monologues. —*Steve Huey*

Metaphysical Grafitti / 1990 / Enigma ◆◆
Too bad the songs on this one revert back to inconsistency, because Anonymous throws in a few more ranting monologues, which provide most of the album's best moments. Fans of the Milkmen's sense of humor may find this one worthwhile, however,

as there are a few good songs, and the album-closing monologue about Cousin Earl's maggot farm is easily the most disgusting thing the Milkmen have ever done, period. — *Steve Huey*

Smokin' Banana Peels / 1990 / Enigma ♦♦♦
This EP contains four new remixes of the title track, which originally appeared on *Beelzebubba*, but if you can wade through those, the second side is prime snotty, juvenile Milkmen. "The Puking Song" is probably the grossest *song* they ever recorded, so if you like their sense of humor, this one is worth it for that track alone. — *Steve Huey*

Soul Rotation / 1992 / Hollywood ♦
The Milkmen switch to Hollywood Records, a label owned by Disney, and it shows. The juvenile gross-out humor and snotty attitude that made the Milkmen great are gone. Extremely forgettable. — *Steve Huey*

Bill Deal & the Rhondels

R&B, Rock & Roll
Combining soul-inflected vocals with brassy, uptempo R&B-inspired grooves, Bill Deal & the Rhondels remain favorites on the Carolina "beach music" circuit to this day. The group was part of the Norfolk, VA, scene during the early '60s, and Deal played organ on Jimmy Soul's 1963 smash "If You Wanna Be Happy" on Legrand Records. The Rhondels apparently preferred reviving R&B obscurities to writing their own material, and it paid off—in 1969 their supercharged remake of the Maurice Williams hit "May I" gave the group their first hit, and they followed it up with a pair of blasting Tams covers, "I've Been Hurt" and "What Kind of Fool Do You Think I Am," all on the Heritage logo. The Rhondels charted for the final time in early 1970 with "Nothing Succeeds like Success." — *Bill Dahl*

● **Best of Bill Deal & The Rhondels** / May 1986 / Rhino ♦♦♦♦
It contains their biggest and best hit, a cover of "May I," first released by the Zodiacs. — *Dan Heilman*

The Dearly Beloved

Group, Garage Rock, Pop/Rock
Along with the Grodes, the Dearly Beloved were Tucson, AZ's top group in the mid-'60s, and made tentative passes at a national audience via contracts with White Whale and Columbia before the death of lead singer Larry Cox in 1967. Their seven singles are passable period pop/garage rock that don't measure up to the standards of literally hundreds of better obscure '60s garage groups throughout the country. Bassist Shep Gordon went on to join the Stone Poneys briefly, and play on albums by Tom Waits, Linda Ronstadt, and Jackson Browne. — *Richie Unterberger*

Rough Diamonds: The History Of Garage Band Music, Volume 6 / 1985 / Voxx ♦♦♦
16 tracks, including several of their singles, some previously unreleased 1966 Columbia demos, and a radio promo. "Keep It Movin'" and "Wait Till the Mornin'" are pretty catchy rockers, but otherwise this is rather generic stuff that doesn't warrant an archival release. Includes meticulous liner notes by Lee Joseph of the modern day garage revival band Yard Trauma. — *Richie Unterberger*

Death

Group, Thrash, Heavy Metal
Many listeners consider Death's vocalist/guitarist Chuck Schuldiner the father of death metal. Formed in 1983, the band didn't release their first album until 1987, but became known in the metal underground through their demos and savage live performances. More than any other metal band, Death obsessed over morbid violence and death, all at a pummelling, aggressive pace. With their bleak outlook and uncompromising metal, they gave birth to both the death metal and grindcore subgenres. Throughout the years, the band's lineup changed frequently with Schuldiner remaining the group's mastermind. — *Stephen Thomas Erlewine*

Spiritual Healing / 1980 / Combat ♦♦
● **Scream Bloody Gore** / 1987 / Combat ♦♦♦♦
Probably the first band to influence what is now known as "grindcore," this is classic is death-metal taken to the next level. — *John Book*

Leprosy / 1988 / Combat ♦♦♦
It's darker and a bit more morbid than "Scream Bloody Gore." — *John Book*

Human / 1991 / Combat ♦♦
Human started to break Death to a wider audience, after Chuck Schuldiner nearly disbanded the group. Schuldiner's playing has improved immensely since *Scream Bloody Gore*, as have his compositional skills. He writes strange, dissonant harmonized guitar lines and is one of the few death metal songwriters who changes moods and textures over the course of an album; *Human*'s second half is actually almost subdued by death metal standards. — *Steve Huey*

Individual Thought Patterns / Jun. 22, 1993 / Combat ♦♦♦
Schuldiner puts even more emphasis on the guitar harmonies, with the help of King Diamond guitarist Andy LaRocque. Bassist Steve DiGiorgio treats his instrument more like a third guitar, making for some unique ensemble interplay. This album cemented Death's reputation as not only one of death metal's founders, but also one of its most creative, musically proficient, and listenable bands. — *Steve Huey*

Symbolic / 1995 / Roadrunner ♦♦♦
The Best of Death / Combat ♦♦♦

DeBarge

Group, Urban, Pop
Motown hoped this family act would turn into another Jackson 5. Specializing in soft-pop tunes such as "All This Love" and "Time Will Reveal," family members include Eldra, Mark, Randy, Bunny, and Bobby. After hitting big with Richard Perry's "Rhythm of the Night" in 1985, El began receiving accolades for his fine tenor vocals and was singled out for a solo career in 1986. He went on to further success while the remainder of the family floundered at other record companies. — *Rick A. Bueche*

The Debarges / 1981 / Motown ♦♦♦
The introductory album for the DeBarge family. Their older brothers, Bobby and Tommy, had helped them land a deal with Motown through their connection playing with Switch. Although they sang tentatively on several songs and hadn't really meshed, they displayed enough potential to alert both the company and the urban contemporary/R&B audience that an interesting new group was on the scene. — *Ron Wynn*

All This Love / 1982 / Motown ♦♦♦
This album gave El DeBarge his first exposure as a artist/producer, with the Top Ten title track. — *Rick A. Bueche*

In a Special Way / 1983 / Motown ♦♦♦
A fine album for the DeBarge family. The title track was a deserved hit, and they were in the middle of their most productive period as a group. The star syndrome still hadn't hit, and the vocals, arrangements, and production weren't slick or cold. — *Ron Wynn*

● **Rhythm of the Night** / 1985 / Motown ♦♦♦♦
Their best Motown album includes the #1 title track. — *Rick A. Bueche*

● **Greatest Hits** / Dec. 1986 / Motown ♦♦♦♦
Included is all of their Motown work; most were Top 40 hits. — *Rick A. Bueche*

El DeBarge

b. Jun. 4, 1964, Grand Rapids, MI
Soul, Dance-Pop
El DeBarge was the lead singer of the '80s R&B group DeBarge throughout their career, including the hits "All This Love," "Love Me in a Special Way," "Who's Holding Donna Now," and "Rhythm of the Night." After leaving the group in 1985, he launched his solo career in 1986 with a self-titled debut album that featured the number three hit "Who's Johnny?," featured in the film *Short Circuit*. DeBarge has recorded several albums and singles since 1985; none of his subsequent efforts have been successful, apart from his appearance on Quincy Jones' 1990 hit "The Secret Garden (Sweet Seduction Suite)." — *Stephen Thomas Erlewine*

● **El DeBarge** / 1986 / Motown ♦♦♦♦
His first and, to date, best solo album includes "Who's Johnny" from the *Short Circuit* soundtrack. — *Rick A. Bueche*

Gemini / 1989 / Motown ♦♦♦
Despite some serious legal problems, El DeBarge emerged from the DeBarge family group as the best solo performer. This was his second album in the late '80s, and it got widespread chart and ra-

dio attention. Although it didn't generate as big a hit as anything from the prior release, there were three songs that were widely aired, and DeBarge eventually was recruited by Quincy Jones to be one of the singers on the hit "The Secret Garden," which De-Barge also co-wrote. —*Ron Wynn*

In the Storm / Mar. 17, 1992 / Warner Brothers ✦✦

Heart Mind & Soul / 1994 / Warner Brothers ✦✦

Chris DeBurgh

b. Oct. 15, 1948, Argentina

Pop

An art-rocker that occasionally writes pop-oriented material, Chris DeBurgh has never been as popular in his native Britain or the United States as was in other areas of the world. In America, he's only managed two Top 40 hits—1983's "Don't Pay the Ferryman" (number 34) and the number three ballad, "The Lady in Red" (1987). In Britain, he's had the same number of Top 40 singles—"The Lady in Red" was a number one hit and "Missing You" peaked at number three—yet he's had a number of minor hits. Nevertheless, he has gained an astounding popularity in other countries, particularly Norway and Brazil.

DeBurgh signed with A&M Records in 1974, releasing his debut album the following year. Before its release, he supported Super-tramp on their *Crime of the Century* tour, building himself a small fan base. His debut, *Far Beyond These Castle Walls*, was a folk-tinged stab at fantasy in the tradition of the Moody Blues that failed to chart upon its release in February of 1975. That July, he released a single from the album called "Flying." It didn't make an impression in the U.K., but it stayed on top of the Brazilian charts for 17 weeks. This became a familiar pattern for the singer/song-writer, as every one of his '70s albums failed to chart in the U.K. or U.S. while they racked up big sales in European and South American countries. In 1981, he had his first U.K. chart entry with *Best Moves*, a collection culled from his early albums. It set the stage for 1982's Rupert Hine-produced *The Getaway*, which reached number 30 on the U.K. charts and number 43 in the U.S., thanks to the eerie single "Don't Pay the Ferryman." DeBurgh's follow-up album, *Man on the Line*, also performed well, charting at 69 in the U.S. and 11 in the U.K.

DeBurgh had an across-the-board success with the languid ballad "The Lady in Red" in late 1986; the single became a number one hit in England (number three in America) and its accompanying album, *Into the Light*, reached number two in the U.K. (number 25 in the U.S.). That Christmas season, a re-release of De-Burgh's 1976 holiday song "A Spaceman Came Travelling" became a Top 40 hit in the U.K. *Flying Colours*, his follow-up to *Into the Light*, entered the British charts at number one upon its 1988 release, yet it failed to make the American charts. DeBurgh never hit the U.S. charts again and his commercial fortunes began to slide slightly in Britain in the early '90s, yet he retained a devoted following around the world. —*Stephen Thomas Erlewine*

Power of Ten / A&M

Far Beyond These Castle Walls / 1975 / A&M ✦✦

Chris DeBurgh's debut album clearly stated his musical roots in classic melodic rock and folk ballads; sometimes his songwriting developed into complete fantasy tales. —*Vladimir Bogdanov*

Spanish Train & Other Stories / 1976 / A&M ✦✦

Spanish Train and Other Stories is a sincere and daring attempt by the young songwriter, showing a great deal of intelligence and inherent musical culture. This album established DeBurgh's presence in Canada and Northern European countries. The irresistible "A Spacemen Came Travelling" became a British radio hit. —*Vladimir Bogdanov*

At the End of a Perfect Day / 1977 / A&M ✦✦

This album has a slightly transitional, transitory feel: there are fewer "stories" than on *Spanish Train* and there is a far-away, travelling flavor to many of the songs. While the majority are gentle, almost wistful ballads, "Brazil" stands out with its up-tempo latin rhythm. "Broken Wings" is the highlight, with its heartfelt tale of shattered dreams and fragile hope. —*Ali Sinclair*

Crusader / 1979 / A&M ✦✦✦

Although it features ambitious and sometimes overweighted compositions, *Crusader* still has DeBurgh's usual melodic beauty and straightforward rhythmic arrangments. —*Vladimir Bogdanov*

Eastern Wind / 1980 / A&M ✦✦

This transitional album was no doubt a step forward from *Spanish Train…*,but it never was a major success, except in Scandinavia, where it outsold the Beatles' *Let it Be*. —*Vladimir Bogdanov*

Best Moves / 1981 / A&M ✦✦✦

The Getaway / 1982 / A&M ✦✦✦

A powerful, strong collection of well-produced, well-balanced songs which show his vocal and writing skills at their best. "Don't Pay the Ferryman" is one of the best-known of all of his recordings, but there is something on *The Getaway* for every mood and temperament: "Borderline," a war-torn ballad, soars with pain and hope from its quiet piano backing with just-the-right touch of plaintive lead guitar; "I'm Counting on You" portrays a father's hopes and doubts: and "The Getaway" is fun, cheerful and strong. A good album and one of DeBurgh's best. —*Ali Sinclair*

The Very Best of Chris De Burgh / 1984 / Telstar ✦✦✦

Man on the Line / May 1984 / A&M ✦✦✦

Man on the Line was the Chris DeBurgh album that came between the modest breakthrough success of *The Getaway* and its Top 40 hit "Don't Pay the Ferryman" and the major career-making success of the gold-selling *Into the Light* and its Top Ten hit, "Lady in Red." To anyone who had liked "Don't Pay the Ferryman," it suggested that the song's virtues, especially DeBurgh's emotion-filled voice and the widescreen, melodramatic production style, were not unique to one performance. Whether treating the conflicting intimate emotions of "Much More than This" and "The Head and the Heart" or taking on political issues in "The Sound of a Gun" and the title track, DeBurgh gave all his vocals a theatrical urgency that was augmented by Rupert Hine's synthesized keyboard textures and a constant dance beat. The appropriately titled "High on Emotion" got halfway up the singles chart, but it wouldn't be until DeBurgh eased off with the elegant "Lady in Red" that he'd become a real household name in the U.S., as he had long been around the world. —*William Ruhlmann*

○ **Into the Light** / 1986 / A&M ✦✦✦✦

Chris DeBurgh's eighth album, *Into the Light*, released in his 11th year as a recording artist, finally broke him through to the two major record markets he had not conquered previously, the UK and the US. The reason was simple: The album contained a romantic ballad hit, "The Lady in Red," which topped the British charts and came close to doing the same thing in America. Heard within the context of *Into the Light*, however, DeBurgh's big anglo-American hit sounds like a slight tune, buried as the fourth track on the first side. On the rest of the album, it's easy to hear why DeBurgh was such a success in South America and Europe before his breakthrough. *Into the Light* is an album full of simple melodic songs set to two kinds of Eurodisco beats—medium tempo and slow tempo. DeBurgh delivers hooks as reliably as any pop performer; if a phrase, usually the song title, is worth singing once, it's worth singing 15 or 20 times more. In fact, these are songs for people for whom English is a second language. The imagery is all primary—sun, moon, fire, water—and the statements are all easily translatable into any European language (though they'd sound more complicated in German, of course). And the sentiments have a European tinge. In addition to the idealized love songs (including "The Lady in Red," which is part of that limited genre, of "Gee, honey, you really dolled yourself up" songs, along with Eric Clapton's "Wonderful Tonight"), DeBurgh has politics on his mind, though he expresses it in terms just as simple as those in the love songs. "Last Night" tells us war is bad, "Say Goodbye To It All" tell us war is bad, "The Spirit of Man" tells us to hang on anyway, and the album-closing trilogy, "The Leader/The Vision/What About Me?" introduces that perennial European favorite: fascist dictatorship. Which is bad, too, though DeBurgh gets close to the end before he gets around to saying so. —*William Ruhlmann*

Flying Colours / 1988 / A&M ✦✦✦✦

A number one album in Great Britain, *Flying Colours* is by far De-Burgh's most pop-oriented album. Crisp and clear arrangments, catchy melodies and simple lyrics make it a favorite of fans. —*Vladimir Bogdanov*

● **Lady in Red: Very Best of Chris DeBurgh** / 1991 / A&M ✦✦✦✦

This Way Up / 1994 / A&M ✦✦✦

Joey Dee & the Starliters

Group, Rock & Roll
Joey Dee led the house band at New York's Peppermint Lounge, immortalizing the joint in his 1961 chart-topper "Peppermint Twist." Born Joseph DiNicola in Passaic, NJ, Dee teamed with veteran producer Henry Glover to cut "Peppermint Twist" for Roulette, and the huge hit led to a starring role in the film *Hey, Let's Twist*. Most of Dee's hits, including a supercharged revival of the Isley Brothers' hit "Shout" in 1962, were firmly in the Twist mode, although he took a successful stab at a softer sound that year with a Johnny Nash tune, "What Kind of Love Is This." Dee gave several future stars early breaks with the Starliters, notably the Ronettes, three-quarters of the Young Rascals, and Jimi Hendrix. Dee is still active on the oldies circuit. —*Bill Dahl*

● **Best of Joey Dee & Starliters: Hey Let's Twist** / 1990 / Rhino ◆◆◆◆

Best of Joey Dee & Starliters—Hey Let's Twist is a representative early-'60s compilation by the man who made the "Peppermint Twist" a national craze. —*Bill Dahl*

Willie Dee

Rap
William "Willie Dee" Dennis was an original member of the Houston rap ensemble the Geto Boys. Willie Dee's 1990 debut *Controversy* certainly startled some with the track "F—-Rodney King," a no-holds-barred attack on King for purportedly selling out when he made his famous "Can't we all just get along?" comment. Dee followed that with *I'm Going Out like a Soldier*. —*Ron Wynn*

● **Controversy** / 1992 / Priority ◆◆◆
Former Geto Boy Willie Dee started his own controversy when he lit into Rodney King on this album. "F—- Rodney King" was a blistering indictment and denunciation, depicting King as a sellout, traitor and collaborator for asking his now-famous "Can't we all just get along?" question during the L.A. riots. Unfortunately, the rage Dee felt toward King or America in general wasn't effectively communicated, either on that cut or the rest of the album. The raps were unfocused, the beats predictable and the rhymes seldom catchy or inventive. —*Ron Wynn*

Deee-Lite

Group, Dance-Pop
Most dance bands based in the house movement of the early '90s concentrated more on the groove than the song; Deee-Lite did not. While they had a strong groove, they also had a strong sense of melody and song structure, as well as a campy, stylish retro-'70s look and a social conscience. Their music is a heady rush of beats, samples, and hooks, with pop songs—like the hit "Groove Is in the Heart"—that distinguish them from other dance combos. —*Stephen Thomas Erlewine*

● **World Clique** / 1990 / Elektra ◆◆◆◆
World Clique starts with a "Good Beat" and keeps them coming for the rest of the album. There are enough thick beats to satisfy house fans, plus enough hooks to cross over to the mainstream pop audience, as the success of "Groove is in the Heart" proved. At times, the retro-'70s shtick wears thin, but for the most part, *World Clique* is a sheer delight. —*Stephen Thomas Erlewine*

Infinity Within / 1992 / Elektra ◆◆◆
Although there are several good tracks and their political consciousness is commendable, *Infinity Within* falls short of the inventive beats and grooves of *World Clique*. —*Stephen Thomas Erlewine*

○ **Dewdrops in the Garden** / 1994 / Elektra ◆◆◆◆
Although it's more focused than *Infinity Within*, *Dewdrops in the Garden* only sporadically lives up to the promise of *World Clique*. —*Stephen Thomas Erlewine*

The Deep

Group, Psychedelic
Documentation is sketchy on this Philadelphia group, but apparently they were masterminded by one Rusty Evans, and included David Bromberg in an unspecified role. According to the skimpy liner notes, their album was the result of wee-hours freakout sessions at Cameo-Parkway studios. They took a middle ground between the Seeds, the 13th Floor Elevators, and Kim Fowley, with a thinly-produced, goofy psychedelia on which tomfoolery abounded. Though basically a silly exercise, the group had their

interesting moments, and certainly had a greater sense of melody than either Kim Fowley or the Seeds. —*Richie Unterberger*

Psychedelic Moods / 1987 / Cicadelic ◆◆◆
It's hard to tell whether these sessions—replete with fuzzy guitars, hallucinatory (and often silly) free-association lyrics. and ominous melodies—were intended seriously or not. Occasional folk-rockish tunes (some with male-female vocal duets) offer respite from the general chaos of some not untalented musicians doing their best to be psychedelically wild and crazy. Collectors should be aware that the version of the best song, "Trip #76," included here is for some reason much thinner and worse than the one issued on the psychedelic reissue compilation *Echoes Of Time*. —*Richie Unterberger*

Deep Purple

Group, Hard Rock, Heavy Metal
Formed in 1968, Deep Purple's initial success was on Bill Cosby's Tetragrammaton label with remakes of Joe South's "Hush" (#4) and Neil Diamond's "Kentucky Woman" (#38). When Tetragrammaton went under shortly afterward, Deep Purple switched to Warner, with a change in lineup, including the addition of dramatic lead singer Ian Gillan.

Their first effort on Warner, Jon Lord's *Concerto for Group and Orchestra*, was a ponderously overblown affair that died a quick death in the marketplace. From there on out, the band pursued a hard rock direction, generating their greatest successes on *Machine Head*, *Burn*, and the live double record set *Made in Japan*. In 1975 Deep Purple earned the dubious distinction of being named the "world's loudest band" in the *Guinness Book of World Records*.

Much of Deep Purple's appeal during their heyday (from 1970's *In Rock* to 1972's *Made in Japan*) came from the lightning-fast duels between keyboardist Jon Lord and lead guitarist Ritchie Blackmore.

Deep Purple successfully carried on after Blackmore, Gillan, and bassist Roger Glover departed (at different times), with a lineup featuring ex-Trapeze member Glen Hughes (bass, vocals), Tommy Bolin (lead guitar, vocals), and David Coverdale (lead vocals). Coverdale would later front the popular MTV/AOR band Whitesnake. —*Rick Clark*

Shades of Deep Purple / 1968 / Tetragrammaton ◆◆

The Book of Taliesyn / 1969 / Tetragrammaton ◆◆

○ **Deep Purple** / 1969 / Tetragrammaton ◆◆◆◆
This is worthwhile mainly for their psychezilla cover of Joe South's "Hush," which pits Ritchie Blackmore's flame-throwing guitar bursts against Jon Lord's chugging organ. —*Tom Graves*

Deep Purple & The Royal Philharmonic Orchestra: Concerto for Group and Orchestra / 1970 / Warner Brothers ◆

○ **Deep Purple in Rock** / 1970 / Warner Brothers ◆◆◆◆
The album on which Deep Purple decided they were rockers after all, they turned up the amps to prove it. Ian Gillan on vocals (added at this time) became the archetype for heavy metal screamers thereafter. Check out "Speed King," "Bloodsucker," and "Flight of the Rat" for your daily dose of high voltage. —*Tom Graves*

○ **Fireball** / 1971 / Warner Brothers ◆◆◆◆
Fireball solidified the band's reputation as purveyors of maximum-dosage heavy metal. Ritchie Blackmore steals the show with a wall of grinding chords and greased-lightning lead flourishes. At this juncture the band began to challenge Led Zeppelin's position as hard rock's most successful act. —*Tom Graves*

★ **Machine Head** / 1972 / Warner Brothers ◆◆◆◆◆
The definitive '70s heavy metal album, each locomotive song ("Highway Star," "Space Truckin'") blasts off like World War III. The highlight is the AOR staple "Smoke on the Water," which has a mandatory riff for anyone owning a guitar. It still fries ears twenty years after the fact. —*Tom Graves*

Purple Passages / 1972 / Warner Brothers ◆◆
A compilation of Deep Purple's early work released to cash-in on the group's *Machine Head*-inspired success, *Purple Passages* contains the highlights from their late-'60s records, including "Hush" and "Kentucky Woman." —*Stephen Thomas Erlewine*

Who Do We Think We Are / Jan. 1973 / Warner Brothers ◆◆◆
The last gasp for the classic Deep Purple lineup, *Who Do We Think We Are* isn't as rock-solid as their previous records, but its best moments, including the deliriously stupid "Woman from Tokyo," are bludgeoning hard-rock of the highest order. —*Stephen Thomas Erlewine*

○ **Made in Japan** / Apr. 1973 / Warner Brothers ◆◆◆◆
Not only could they kick ass in the studio, they could stir up a hor-
net's nest on stage too. This double-album (one CD) set recorded in
Japan includes most of their best material ("Highway Star,"
"Smoke on the Water") and pushes the metal envelope even fur-
ther. Ritchie Blackmore is in peak form throughout. — *Tom Graves*

Burn / 1974 / Warner Brothers ◆◆◆
Burn is Deep Purple's first album with lead singer David
Coverdale. While it's not quite up to the standards of *Machine
Head* and *Made in Japan*, it featured enough hot riffs and well-
constructed heavy rockers to make it a Top Ten success and an al-
bum rock favorite. — *Stephen Thomas Erlewine*

Stormbringer / 1974 / Metal Blade ◆◆

Come Taste the Band / 1975 / Metal Blade ◆◆◆
The addition of guitarist Tommy Bolin adds some fire to the performances on *Come Taste the Band*, yet the group didn't come up
with enough good songs to make the record memorable for anything besides Bolin's exceptional playing. — *Stephen Thomas Erlewine*

Made in Europe / 1976 / Metal Blade ◆◆

○ **When We Rock, We Rock and When We Roll, We Roll** / 1978 /
Warner Brothers ◆◆◆◆
When We Rock, We Rock & When We Roll, We Roll is a solid, if incomplete collection from their 1968-1974 peak years. — *Dan Heilman*

○ **Deepest Purple: The Very Best of Deep Purple** / 1980 / Warner
Brothers ◆◆◆◆

Perfect Strangers / 1984 / Mercury ◆◆

The House of Blue Light / 1987 / Mercury ◆

Nobody's Perfect / 1988 / Mercury ◆◆

Slaves & Masters / 1990 / RCA ◆◆

Knocking at Your Back Door / 1992 / Mercury ◆◆

The Battle Rages On / Jun. 1992 / Giant ◆◆

Best Of In The 80's / 1994 / Mercury ◆◆◆
The Best of Deep Purple in the 80's may be inconsistent and unsatisfying, but that's an accurate reflection of the group's career
during the decade. Even though its fitfully entertaining, *Best of*
features all of the highlights the group recorded during the '80s
and its preferable to the albums they released during that era. —
Stephen Thomas Erlewine

Def Leppard

Group, Hard Rock, Heavy Metal
Def Leppard's catchy, guitar-driven, power-pop/rock was one of
the most imitated styles of the '80s. Leppard's hit albums are polished syntheses of heavy, hummable guitar riffs, memorable pop
melodies, and simple teen-oriented lyrics. Originally the band (Joe
Elliot, vocals; Pete Willis, guitar; Steve Clark, guitar; Rick Savage,
drums; Rick Allen, drums) was associated with the new wave of
British heavy metal bands, releasing two albums (*On Through the
Night* and *High 'N' Dry*) that made a small impact on the U.S.
Robert "Mutt" Lange produced *High 'N' Dry*, which contained the
seeds of the signature Leppard sound. Before the recording of their
next album, Pete Willis left and was replaced by Phil Collen, who
used to play in the glam-rock band Girl. *Pyromania*, released in
1983, was a monster success selling over 6.5 million copies in the
U.S. and featuring three Top 40 hits ("Photograph," "Rock of Ages,"
and "Foolin' "). The album showcased the refinement of Def Leppard's twin-guitar attack, where both parts worked together to create a huge sound instead of merely repeating the riff. In 1984, the
group made two attempts to record a follow-up, one with the exhausted Lange and another with Jim Steinman, both ending with
the dismissal of the producer. On New Year's Eve, Allen lost his left
arm in an auto accident. Despite this, the band wanted Allen in
the group; he was equipped with a customized electronic drum kit
to ease his playing. In 1987, the long-awaited *Hysteria* (also produced by Lange) was released. Although *Hysteria* was a bigger
success than *Pyromania*, it took a considerable amount of time for
it to gain its sales—after 49 weeks, the album reached number
one. Recording for the follow-up to *Hysteria* was under way when
Clark was found dead in his apartment after a drinking binge in
January 1991. Def Leppard continued the album, with Collen playing all the guitars. *Adrenalize* shot to the top of the charts upon its
release in April 1992. Vivian Campbell, former guitarist for

Whitesnake, was announced as Clark's replacement in spring of
1992. — *Stephen Thomas Erlewine*

On through the Night / 1980 / Mercury ◆◆◆
Their US debut includes "Rock Brigade." — *AMG*

High 'n' Dry / 1981 / Mercury ◆◆◆
This includes "Bringing on the Heartache." — *AMG*

☆ **Pyromania** / 1983 / Mercury ◆◆◆◆◆
Although Def Leppard's first two workmanlike metal albums, *On
Through the Night* and *High 'n' Dry*, had already established the
band in both England and the U.S., it was *Pyromania* that broke
the sound (and sales) barrier for them. *Pyromania's* acute emphasis on pop sensibilities in songs like "Photograph" and "Rock Rock
('Til You Drop") over numbing thonk made the album a huge
crossover success with the more conservative AOR market. MTV
video saturation with key *Pyromania* songs didn't hurt either.
(Also available as a Mobile Fidelity Ultradisc) — *Tom Graves*

★ **Hysteria** / 1987 / Mercury ◆◆◆◆◆
If *Pyromania* was great pop-metal, *Hysteria* upped the ante a few
more notches. With dense, elaborate instrumental layering and
meticulous engineering, the album became known almost as
much for its production values as for its terrific music. Drummer
Rick Allen, who lost an arm in an automobile accident, adds an
even harder core of bottom end with his specially rigged drum kit.
As hardhitting as it is slicksounding, *Hysteria* became the standard-bearer for pop metal with anthemic tracks like "Rocket" and
"Pour Some Sugar on Me." One of the masterpieces of the '80s that
renewed the faith, for many, in sensible hard rock. — *Tom Graves*

Adrenalyze / 1992 / Mercury ◆◆◆
The jury may still be out on *Adrenalize*, but with the band's misfortunes (guitarist Steve Clark died of a drug overdose), they can
be forgiven for slipping a bit after the mega-success of *Hysteria*.
That's not to dismiss *Adrenalize*, however, which still has a heap-
ing helping of Leppard's patented Brit-pop crash-and-burn fusion.
— *Tom Graves*

Retro Active / Oct. 5, 1993 / Mercury ◆◆◆
It may be just a collection of B-sides and lost tracks, but *Retro-Ac-
tive* rocks harder and more convincingly than *Adrenalize*. It also
has twice the hooks, making it of interest to more than just hardcore Def Leppard fans. — *Stephen Thomas Erlewine*

Defunkt

Group, Funk
In its prime, Defunkt managed a successful merger of funk beats,
rock energy, jazz techniques and soloing, and an unpredictable,
free-wheeling avant-garde. The band was formed by trombonist
Joseph Bowie, brother of Lester Bowie. It was popular during the
early and mid-'80s, disbanded, then reunited in early '90s. — *Ron
Wynn*

Defunkt / 1980 / Hannibal ◆◆◆
Trombonist Joe Bowie's free-wheeling outfit Defunkt avoids categorization. They rip through soul, funk, free jazz, rock, and blues,
and stretch the limits of each one. The atmosphere on their records
is feverish; they don't do anything in an easy or simple manner.
Not everything they try works, but no Defunkt album is ever dull.
— *Ron Wynn*

A Defunkt Anthology / 1981-1983 / Rykodisc ◆◆◆
Defunkt were the '80s' most versatile pop band. They covered
avant-garde jazz, funk, rock, punk, and everything in between, and
could move from complex jams to tightly structured R&B at will.
This eclectic nature proved their undoing; they weren't straight
enough for the jazz market and they were too loose for the commercial audience. This eight-song anthology fully displays their
disparate influences and performance style, whether it be the
nearly 11-minute vocal/instrumental raver "Strangling Me with
Your Love," the short Charlie Parker cover "Au Private," or the furious remake of David Bowie's "Make Them Dance." — *Ron Wynn*

Thermonuclear Sweat / 1982 / Hannibal ◆◆◆
Another in their series of rampaging, outlandish Defunkt sessions
with trombonist Joseph Bowie and his comrades ripping through
funk, R&B, jazz, blues, rock, and many other things. Sometimes
they aim too high or try something that flops, but they keep right
on experimenting and eventually create something no other band
would even attempt. — *Ron Wynn*

● **In America** / 1988 / Antilles ◆◆◆◆
Ambitious attempt, erratic performance. — *Ron Wynn*

Avoid the Funk / 1988 / Hannibal ✦✦✦
As always, some hits and misses by jazz/funk ensemble. —*Ron Wynn*

Heroes / Dec. 1990 / DIW ✦✦✦

Crisis / 1992 / Enemy ✦✦

Live at the Knitting Factory / Knitting Factory Works ✦✦✦
Trombonist Joseph Bowie co-led and organized numerous editions of Defunkt, many with longtime section mate Charles "Bobo" Shaw. Shaw wasn't aboard for this '90 concert, but Bowie's crackling trombone solos remained a vital part of the group's sound. Guitarist Bill Bickford filled in the gap with an array of spicy, flashy riffs, colors and supporting phrases, while the other members smoothly handled the constantly changing atmosphere. Defunkt ripped through rock tunes, funk pieces, extended jazz vamps and blues, doing them all with humor and verve. —*Ron Wynn*

Del Amitri

Group, Folk-Rock, Pop/Rock
This Scottish quartet, who released its first album in 1985, delivers a Byrds-like country-flavored rock. During the latter half of the '80s, the band developed a cult following across Europe and began to make inroads in America. Their latest album, *Twisted*, was released in early 1995. —*David Szatmary*

Del Amitri / 1985 / Chrysalis ✦✦✦
The debut album features a bright countrified rock. —*David Szatmary*

● **Waking Hours** / 1989 / A&M ✦✦✦✦
The sound on this effort has more of a mainstream rock sheen to the production than the debut. —*David Szatmary*

○ **Change Everything** / Jun. 9, 1992 / A&M ✦✦✦✦
Del Amitri serves up a slice of Scottish folk-rock on 1992's *Change Everything*. Gritty vocals often hinting at sadness drape themselves over chiming guitars and tasty harmonies; vague memories of Van Morrison in his rockier days. —*Roch Parisien*

Twisted / 1995 / A&M ✦✦✦
Del Amitri hasn't changed their style for *Twisted*—they're still a bright, catchy folk-rock combo. However, the songs and performances don't match those on *Change Everything*. The songs don't have the same quality hooks, nor do the performances match anything on *Change Everything*, yet for fans of their sound, it's a fine effort. —*Sara Sytsma*

Del Fuegos

Group, Roots-Rock
Originally including Dan and Warren Zanes (who have the vocalist and guitarist duties, respectively), bassist Tom Lloyd, and drummer B.Woody Giessmann, this Boston-based band pounds out Rolling Stones-style rock. After critics panned the 1987 album *Stand Up*, Giessmann left the group. The band added horns for a more Stax-oriented sound on *Smoking in the Fields*. Guest appearances on their albums include James Burton and Tom Petty (*Stand Up*) and Rick Danko (*Smoking*). —*David Szatmary*

○ **The Longest Day** / 1984 / Slash ✦✦✦✦
An explosive garage-meets-roots-rock debut from the Boston rockers. —*David Szatmary*

● **Boston, Mass.** / 1985 / Slash ✦✦✦✦
It features more guitar-driven crunch. —*David Szatmary*

Spin Radio Concert / 1985 / BBE Sound ✦✦

Stand Up / 1987 / Slash ✦✦✦
A tone-downed, more bluesy effort, it includes guests James Burton and Tom Petty. —*David Szatmary*

Smoking in the Fields / 1989 / RCA ✦✦✦

The Del Lords

Group, Roots-Rock
No-nonsense New Yorkers who deliver their rock & roll with no frills or fancy stuff. Ex-Dictator Scott Kempner writes plainspoken, socially conscious songs, and the crunching riffs make the best of them ring like minor classics. —*John Floyd*

Frontier Days / 1984 / EMI America ✦✦✦
Their debut sports a low-budget sound but manages to capture their frenzied enthusiasm on some of their best work. —*John Floyd*

Johnny Comes Marching Home / 1986 / EMI America ✦✦✦

● **Based on a True Story** / 1988 / Enigma ✦✦✦✦
Kempner expands his songwriter range, but it's the celebratory party-man anthems like "The Cool and the Crazy" that make this the group's best work. —*John Floyd*

Howlin' at the Halloween Moon [Live] / 1989 / Enigma ✦✦

Live at Raji's / 1989 / Enigma ✦✦

Lovers Who Wander / 1990 / Enigma ✦✦✦
The band's most ambitious work, it has complex songs and a sound that expands on their previous attack. —*John Floyd*

Del Lords Live: Howlin' at the Halloween Moon / Enigma ✦✦

Del Tha Funkee Homosapien

Rap
The cousin of Ice Cube, Del Tha Funkee Homosapien issued his debut release in 1991, *I Wish My Brother George Was Here*, on Elektra. It was more comedic and less sophisticated and street-oriented than the follow-up, *No Need for Alarm*, in 1994. —*Ron Wynn*

● **I Wish My Brother George Was Here** / 1991 / Asylum ✦✦✦✦
This was a little more cutesy than expected, especially since Del Tha Funkee Homosapien was on the verge of making some credible political points. But it's hard to make good novelty and message songs at the same time, and the split focus made this release difficult to comprehend and tough to follow. Still, he displayed enough potential to suggest that better days lie ahead. —*Ron Wynn*

No Need for Alarm / 1994 / Elektra

Delaney & Bonnie

Group, Blues Rock, Pop/Rock
Husband and wife Delaney Bramlett (b. Jul 1, 1939) and Bonnie Bramlett (b. Nov. 8, 1944) recorded a series of blues- and country-influenced albums in the late '60s and early '70s. A variety of musicians played in Delaney and Bonnie's band, including Eric Clapton, Dave Mason, Duane Allman, Leon Russell, Rita Coolidge, Jim Gordon, Bobby Whitlock, and Carl Radle; Clapton, Gordon, Whitlock, and Radle formed Derek & the Dominoes after performing together on Delaney & Bonnie's 1969-70 tour. Delaney and Bonnie's records were a strong influence on Eric Clapton's style in the '70s. The group broke up after the Bramletts' marriage collapsed in 1972. —*Kenneth M. Cassidy*

● **Delaney & Bonnie & Friends on Tour with Eric Clapton** / Jun. 1970 / Atco ✦✦✦✦
Recorded with Eric Clapton, *On Tour* features Delaney & Bonnie's blend of country, rock, blues, and gospel. It includes "I'm Coming Home." —*Kenneth M. Cassidy*

The Best of Delaney & Bonnie / 1990 / Rhino ✦✦✦
This is a good overview of their brief career. —*Kenneth M. Cassidy*

The Delfonics

Group, Soul
A sweet ballad-oriented Philadelphia vocal trio, who proved highly popular in the late '60s and early '70s. Lead singer William Hart's high-pitched tenor effortlessly sailed into falsetto range on their first hit in 1968, "La-La—Means I Love You," a typically smooth ballad filled with swirling strings. Hart and co-producer Thom Bell wrote most of the group's early smashes, including the majestic "Didn't I (Blow Your Mind This Time)" in 1970. The group's hitmaking reign ended in 1974. —*Bill Dahl*

○ **La La Means I Love You** / 1968 / Bell ✦✦✦✦
The Delfonics didn't really make many albums; they issued singles collections, of which this was one of the best. The title track was among the most glorious "sweet" soul ballads in history, and the other tunes aren't far behind. Some beautiful harmonies, and the Harts are splendid. —*Ron Wynn*

○ **The Delfonics Super Hits** / 1969 / Philly Groove ✦✦✦✦
Another Delfonics anthology, and this was for a long time the best one available. It contained the chart-topping ballads and love songs that made them perhaps "sweet" soul's best unit, even though the Stylistics' Russell Tompkins, Jr. was probably the genre's most popular vocalist. There isn't a dud in this bunch. —*Ron Wynn*

The Sexy Sound of Soul / 1969 / Philly Groove ✦✦✦
The Delfonics, like many other soul bands and singers, liked to cover lots of different material. They didn't always exercise sound judgment in song selection, and that's the case on this album. While everything they do is sung with urgency and flair, there are times when they overdo the sappy love material. Still, there weren't many falsetto vocalists around who could hold their own with the Harts. —*Ron Wynn*

The Delfonics / 1970 / Bell ✦✦✦
The Delfonics were the most ethereal, heart-wrenching harmonizers among the "sweet" soul brigade, and their magic held even when they weren't utilizing it on quality material. That was the case at times on some of these songs, although even the weak tunes contained moments of glory. —*Ron Wynn*

Tell Me This Is a Dream / 1972 / Philly Groove ✦✦
Some signs of decline are starting to emerge on this release, mainly because they never replaced Major Harris. The Harts can still hit the shimmering, compelling high notes, but were beginning to run out of good songs and also were sabotaged by the lack of interest displayed from the label. —*Ron Wynn*

Alive & Kicking / 1974 / Philly Groove ✦✦
A medicore album by Delfonics standards, although there are a few good moments. But the magic was gone by the mid-'70s, and the Delfonics were being surpassed by their rivals, like Blue Magic and the Stylistics, who benefited from far superior songs. They kept trying, but didn't click nearly as often, nor as much as needed. —*Ron Wynn*

● **The Best of the Delfonics** / 1990 / Arista ✦✦✦✦
The Delfonics were arguably the premier sweet soul band of the late '60s and early '70s; their shimmering harmonies and William Hart's agonizing falsetto, coupled with Stan Watson's production and Thom Bell's arranging and writing touches, created many unforgettable love songs. While their hits have been frequently collected and reissued, this CD set, while short (37 minutes), includes among its 12 tracks every major hit except "Over and Over." Engineering guru Bill Inglot used original masters, fully capturing the trio's marvelous interaction, the songs' sweeping arrangements and the great mix of vulnerability, hurt, and poignance that characterized their finest hits. —*Ron Wynn*

○ **Golden Classics** / Collectables ✦✦✦✦
The Delfonics were arguably the greatest "sweet" soul trio of all time and certainly among the top two or three. Unfortunately, there are almost as many Delfonics anthologies as Sam Cooke collections, and most are just as bogus. This is actually a good one, and Collectables, a label notorious for poor-quality, badly transferred CDs, have done pretty well with their soul releases. —*Ron Wynn*

The Dell-Vikings

Group, R&B, Doo-Wop
One of the first integrated acts during rock & roll's infancy, the Dell-Vikings recorded a beloved classic in 1956, "Come Go with Me." The quintet was formed at Pittsburgh's Air Force Serviceman's Club in 1955 while the members were stationed there. They recorded their immortal "Come Go with Me," written by bass singer Clarence Quick, in the basement of a local deejay and sold the master to tiny FeeBee Records. When given national distribution on Dot, the upbeat tune proved a monster hit. Upon their discharge, four members split to form a new "Del Vikings" on Mercury, hitting in 1957 with "Cool Shake." Kripp Johnson, meanwhile, stayed with Dot, assembling a new lineup of "Dell-Vikings" that included a young Chuck Jackson, and hitting at precisely the same time with "Whispering Bells." All the confusion about the two groups may have ultimately sunk both, since those were the last hits for either lineup. —*Bill Dahl*

● **Del Vikings** / 1988 / Collectables ✦✦✦✦
Solid hits by one of doo-wop 's first integrated groups. —*Bill Dahl*

The Dells

Group, Soul, Doo-Wop
After nearly four decades of recording an incredible legacy of hits, the Dells have made only one personnel change in their entire professional career. Perhaps that's why the venerable R&B vocal group can boast such a remarkably consistent track record.
The quintet from Chicago's south suburbs has weathered stylistic shifts from doo-wop and soul to disco and urban contemporary,

and every permutation in between. Their harmony remains as striking as ever, with Marvin Junior's earthshaking lead enduring as the group's focal point.
Signing with Vee-Jay in 1955, their creamy vocal blend on "Oh, What a Night" gave the Dells their first major R&B hit the next year, but it would be nearly a decade before they returned to the winner's circle with another dreamy classic, "Stay in My Corner." By then Chicago's R&B sound had changed drastically—doo-wop was dead and soul was king—but the Dells adapted effortlessly, regularly scaling the charts for the Chess subsidiary Cadet with "There Is," "Always Together," "Give Your Baby a Standing Ovation," and a marathon remake of "Stay in My Corner" that afforded Junior's booming baritone room to roam.
Seemingly an indestructible force (turning up on the R&B charts as recently as 1984), the succinct harmonies of the Dells span entire generations of R&B history. —*Bill Dahl*

○ **There Is** / 1968 / Chess ✦✦✦✦
This rich 1966-1968 Chicago soul has little of the overproduction that marred the powerful R&B quintet's later Chess output. —*Bill Dahl*

○ **The Dells** / 1969 / Chess ✦✦✦✦
Tremendous vocals and production, coupled with superb ballads and good uptempo cuts. The Dells were never better than during the late '60s when they moved to Cadet and Charles Stepney's vision was fulfilled. Although he was never fully credited, lead singer Marvin Junior stands as one of soul's great vocalists, and he showed it repeatedly on this set. Johnny Carter's floating falsetto was another major weapon expertly utilized in the Dells' soul success. —*Ron Wynn*

○ **Love Is Blue** / 1969 / Cadet ✦✦✦✦
A fine album that included their excellent version of the title cut, some other stirring ballads, and some good uptempo tunes. The Dells were now in peak form, with Marvin Junior's booming voice and Charles Stepney's productions and good arrangements turning them into the hitmakers they never were in the doo-wop days. —*Ron Wynn*

○ **Oh, What a Night** / 1970 / Collectables ✦✦✦✦
Earlier doo-wop classics by the venerable Windy City R&B vocal group, this showcases their impeccable harmony on the gorgeous title track and similar fare. —*Bill Dahl*

Freedom Means / 1971 / Cadet ✦✦✦
A fine early '70s date, with the title track one of the more socio-political songs the Dells ever recorded. Both Marvin Jr. and Johnny Carter were in fine form, and while this was pretty basic material, they sang it with passion and exuberance. —*Ron Wynn*

Sweet As Funk Can Be / 1972 / Cadet ✦✦✦
Although not as striking as some other Dells albums, this was still good enough. There were some first-rate ballads, a few decent uptempo tracks, and plenty of fine lead vocals as always by Marvin Jr., with Johnny Carter's angelic answering falsetto coming in right on time. —*Ron Wynn*

Best of the Dells / 1973 / JCI ✦✦✦
The Dells were a good R&B/doo-wop ensemble, but they became a great soul group when they put Marvin Jr.'s glorious voice up front and when Charles Stepney began producing their songs. These are the finest cuts from the late '60s era, when they were challenging the Temptations as the dominant singing unit. —*Ron Wynn*

The Dells Greatest Hits, Vol. 2 / 1975 / Cadet ✦✦✦
This second volume of the group's greatest hits didn't get the widespread treatment of the first. It focused on their '70s material and had many fine cuts. It has since disappeared from listings and has probably been deleted. The Dells are another group crying out for boxed set treatment, especially with all the anthologies covering their doo-wop years. —*Ron Wynn*

○ **I Touched a Dream** / 1980 / 20th Century ✦✦✦✦
The last great Dells album, and one of the year's big surprises. The Dells were on another new label, and now were working with Carl Davis and Eugene Record (also of the Chi-Lites). The pair simply restored the Dells' strengths; each production made sure Marvin Junior's roaring leads and Johnny Carter's wavery falsetto were at the forefront. They also got them a superb ballad in the title track, a good message song in "It's All About the Paper," and other fine cuts. —*Ron Wynn*

★ **On Their Corner** / 1992 / Chess ✦✦✦✦✦
Excellent compilation of their late-'60s sides, like "Oh What a Night," "Stay In My Corner," "The Love We Had Stays on My Mind," and "Give Your Baby a Standing Ovation." —*Stephen Thomas Erlewine*

I Salute You / 1992 / Zoo ✦✦✦
The Dells formally celebrated their 40th anniversary with this nice 10-cut session, juggling overproduced urban contemporary and New Jack selections with classic, close harmony numbers that spotlighted Marvin Junior's still-impressive, swaggering baritone and Johnny Carter's always-mellow falsetto. The contemporary material wasn't horrible; even the rap insert on "Baby Don't Go Away Mad" wasn't overbearing, while the arrangements on the title track were acceptable. But it was the ballads that signaled that these were still the Dells; "Somebody's Gotta Move," "Oh My Love," and "Closer to You" had the familiar ingredients—steamy, inviting or even despairing lyrics. —*Ron Wynn*

○ **Dreams of Contentment** / 1993 / Vee-Jay ✦✦✦✦
The Dells never made it over the hump while at Vee-Jay, despite making many impressive singles. They were a top-flight doo-wop group, but they couldn't find a way to advance beyond the R&B margins. Only when they moved to Chess, changed their style, and made Marvin Junior the lead singer did they enjoy the success they deserved. Still, as this 24-track reissue shows, there wasn't anything wrong with their Vee-Jay output. They experimented on such numbers as "Lil Darlin'," "It's Not for Me to Say," and "It's Not Unusual" with jazz/pop harmonies and covers. In addition, songs like "Now I Pray" and "Pain in My Heart" are wonderfully sung and harmonized, even if they weren't huge sellers. —*Ron Wynn*

○ **Passionate Breezes: Best of 1975-1991** / 1995 / Mercury ✦✦✦✦

Cathy Dennis

Dance-Pop
Cathy Dennis' inspired singing stole D-Mob's "C'Mon and Get My Love," and her 1990 solo debut, *Move to This*, established her as a dance diva with a great, soulful voice that lacks substantial material. —*Stephen Thomas Erlewine*

● **Move to This** / 1990 / Polydor ✦✦✦✦
This house-influenced dance-pop debut features "Just Another Dream" (number nine), "Touch Me (All Night Long)" (number two), and "Too Many Walls" (number eight). —*Rick Clark & Dan Heilman*

Into the Skyline / May 1992 / Polydor ✦✦✦
You Lied to Me / Polydor ✦✦

Sandy Denny

b. Jan. 6, 1948, Wimbledon, England, d. Apr. 21, 1978
Folk-Rock
From her debut with Fairport Convention in 1968, Denny has been one of England's most important folk stylists and a major influence in rock as well, with a striking alto voice and daunting compositional style. Prior to her accidental death a decade later, Denny recorded a brace of superb solo albums with her former Fairport stablemate, guitarist Richard Thompson, and her husband Trevor Lucas (d. 1990). She left behind one classic song ("Who Knows Where the Time Goes"). Her major influence was Isla Cameron. —*Bruce Eder*

All Our Own Work / 1968 / Pickwick ✦✦✦
Sandy Denny / 1970 / Saga ✦✦✦
North Star Grassman and the Ravens / 1971 / Hannibal ✦✦✦
Some second thoughts and reapproaches to older work. —*Bruce Eder*

○ **Sandy** / 1972 / A&M ✦✦✦✦
Those seeking initiation into the ranks of Denny fans may consult listings for Fairport Convention and Fotheringay. Also, try this solo album, which features many of the same players (Richard Thompson, Dave Swarbrick, etc.) and contains a good collection of Denny originals along with her rendition of Dylan's "Tomorrow Is a Long Time." —*William Ruhlmann*

The Bunch / 1972 / A&M
Like an Old Fashioned Waltz / 1973 / Hannibal
Rendezvous / 1977 / Hannibal ✦✦✦
Stylistically varied, if not so fresh as her album *Sandy*. —*Bruce Eder*

Sandy Denny & The Strawbs / 1985 / Hannibal ✦✦✦
Pre-Fairport Denny with a British bluegrass band that later moved into progressive rock (without her). Her voice and a moody rendition of her classic "Who Knows Where the Time Goes" make it worthwhile. —*Bruce Eder*

○ **Who Knows Where the Time Goes 3-Set** / 1986 / Hannibal ✦✦✦✦
This magnificently produced multi-disc boxed set presents a complete portrait of Sandy Denny, the haunting singer, the melodic, mournful songwriter, and the mesmerizing bandleader of Fairport Convention and Fotheringay. Much of the material is previously unheard, but it's all of a piece with Denny's accomplished work on her solo albums and in her groups. The album makes the case for Denny as a major folk artist. —*William Ruhlmann*

● **The Best of Sandy Denny [Best of Box]** / 1989 / Hannibal ✦✦✦✦
Concise collection of key tracks. Excellent introduction. —*Bruce Eder*

Original Sandy Denny / 1991 / Trojan ✦✦✦
Denny's first recording, originally released in 1967, is her most traditional effort. Backed only by her own acoustic guitar, Denny's voice is assured, pure, and powerful on her debut. The album features traditional folk staples like "This Train," "Make Me AaPallet on Your Floor," and "Pretty Polly," as well as covers of Tom Paxton's "Ramblin' Boy" and "Milk and Honey." There are also a couple of songs by the obscure American songwriter Jackson Frank, one of which she would soon perform with Fairport Convention ("You Never Wanted Me"). Although this has little of the folk-rock cross-pollination that Denny would soon master with Fairport and others, it is still an impressive LP that shows her voice in as haunting and commanding form as her more renowned recordings. —*Richie Unterberger*

John Denver (John Henry Deutchendorf)

b. Dec. 31, 1943, Roswell, NM
Singer-Songwriter, Pop, Folk-Rock
In the '70s, John Denver's simple, melodic, light folk-pop made him one of the decade's biggest stars. In the '60s, he played with his idols the Chad Mitchell Trio, turning into a talented songwriter while he was with the group. Denver left for a solo career in 1969; later in the year, his "Leaving on a Jet Plane" became a big hit for Peter, Paul and Mary. In no time, Denver established himself as a star in his own right, with songs like "Take Me Home, Country Roads," "Rocky Mountain High," "Sunshine on My Shoulders," "Annie's Song," and "Thank God I'm a Country Boy" becoming pop standards of the decade. After the '70s were over, Denver's career began to lose its commercial momentum and he turned to social work, while recording the occasional album. Denver continues to record and perform in the '90s, consistently pleasing his fans. —*Stephen Thomas Erlewine*

● **Greatest Hits** / 1973 / RCA ✦✦✦✦
A good collection of his early (and best) era, 1969-1973. Note that John Denver re-recorded some of his hits for this collection. —*Dan Heilman*

○ **Greatest Hits, Vol. 2** / 1977 / RCA ✦✦✦✦
More pop, less folk, and more hits. —*Dan Heilman*

Depeche Mode

Group, Dance-Pop, Alternative Pop/Rock
In 1980, Depeche Mode (the name means "fast fashion") was formed in Basildon, Essex, England, by Andy Fletcher (b. Jul 8, 1961), Martin Gore (b. Jul 23, 1961), Vince Clarke, and Dave Gahan. All four played synthesizers, and Gahan sang. They were signed to tiny Mute Records in England in 1982 (distributed by Sire/Warner Bros. in the U.S.) and scored two Top 20 hits, "New Life" and "Just Can't Get Enough," and a Top Ten album, *Speak and Spell*, by the end of the year. At that point, Clarke quit and was replaced by Alan Wilder. The band's style—pop songs with ominous lyrics sung in Gahan's distinct baritone and backed by intricate synthesized dance music—did not change, and its commercial success continued as well.
The group only gradually built a following in the U.S., finally

breaking the Hot 100 with "People Are People," which reached #13 in 1985. The first album to reach the American Top 100 albums was *Black Celebration* in 1986; then *Music for the Masses* went gold in 1987. By 1989, Depeche Mode was big enough in the U.S. to play a concert at the Rose Bowl in California, and that show was recorded for the live album *101*. But it wasn't until the 1990 album *Violator* and the single "Enjoy the Silence" that Depeche Mode made the Top Ten in the U.S. By then, they'd also conquered the rest of the world and become one of the most popular "modern" or "alternative" rock groups of the '80s and early '90s. — *William Ruhlmann*

Speak & Spell / 1981 / Sire ✦✦✦
Vince Clarke's only album with Depeche Mode is dominated by him (he wrote nine of 11 tracks), and the band was never this imaginative or infectious again. Especially notable is the UK Top Ten hit, "Just Can't Get Enough," which remains the best single track they ever recorded. — *William Ruhlmann*

A Broken Frame / 1982 / Sire ✦✦✦

Construction Time Again / 1983 / Sire ✦✦✦
Intellectual songwriting from Martin Gore. — *Bil Carpenter*

○ **People Are People** / 1984 / Sire ✦✦✦✦

○ **Some Great Reward** / 1984 / Sire ✦✦✦✦
Depeche Mode's most consistent post-Clarke album contains some of its most provocative material, notably "Blasphemous Rumours" and "Master and Servant," which concern, respectively, religion and sexual domination. — *William Ruhlmann*

On the Crest of a Wave / 1984 / Castle

● **Catching up with Depeche Mode** / 1985 / Sire ✦✦✦✦
A U.S.-only compilation that's a well-put-together best-of, from the band's early singles to its current state. If you want to know what Depeche Mode is about, this is the record that will tell you. — *William Ruhlmann*

○ **Black Celebration** / 1986 / Sire ✦✦✦✦
Depeche Mode are frequently called gloom-mongers, and much of that criticism stems from this relentlessly bleak album, which is undoubtedly the most desolate record they have ever made. — *Stephen Thomas Erlewine*

○ **Music for the Masses** / 1987 / Sire ✦✦✦✦

101 / 1989 / Sire ✦✦✦

Violator / 1990 / Sire ✦✦✦
Depeche Mode's commercial breakthrough album is a mixed bag. Unlike their previous album, *Violator* truly *is* music for the masses. Throughout the album, occasional spells of catchy hooks emerge from beneath the thudding machines (most notably on the excellent "Personal Jesus" and the hit single "Enjoy the Silence"). On the strength of these flashes of melody, the album crossed over into the mainstream, but for the most part *Violator* is a dull, tedious drag. — *AMG*

Songs of Faith & Devotion / 1993 / Sire ✦✦✦
Depeche Mode attempted to reinvent themselves with *Songs of Faith & Devotion*, much as U2 did with *Achtung Baby*. In addition to their signature synthesizers, the group adds more guitar and strings to the music, frequently with rock and gospel flourishes that previously would have been unthinkable on a Depeche disc. Often these moments of departure are the most exciting on the album, like the terrific one-chord stomp of "I Feel You" or the nearly-soulful "Walking in My Shoes," which both feature animated vocals by Dave Gahan. Despite the new musical directions, there's nothing here that will alienate old fans; in fact, it might gain Depeche Mode a few new listeners. — *Stephen Thomas Erlewine*

Songs of Faith & Devotion Live / May 1993 / Sire ✦

Derek & the Dominos

Group, Rock & Roll, Blues Rock
Derek & the Dominos was a group formed by guitarist/singer Eric Clapton (born Eric Patrick Clapp, Mar. 30, 1945, Ripley, Surrey, England) with other former members of Delaney & Bonnie & Friends, in the spring of 1970. The rest of the lineup was Bobby Whitlock (b. 1948, Memphis, TN) (keyboards, vocals), Carl Radle (b. 1942, Oklahoma City, OK,–d. May 30, 1980) (bass), and Jim Gordon (b. 1945, Los Angeles) (drums). The group debuted at the Lyceum Ballroom in London on June 14 and undertook a summer tour of England. From late August to early October, they recorded the celebrated double album *Layla and Other Assorted Love*

Songs (November 1970) with guitarist Duane Allman sitting in. They then returned to touring in England and the U.S., playing their final date on December 6.

The *Layla* album was successful in the U.S., where "Bell Bottom Blues" and the title song charted as singles in abbreviated versions, but it did not chart in the U.K. The Dominos reconvened to record a second album in May 1971, but split up without completing it. Clapton then retired from the music business, nursing a heroin addiction.

In his absence, and in the wake of Allman's death in a motorcycle accident on October 29, 1971, the Dominos and *Layla* gained in stature. Rereleased as a single at its full, seven-minute length in connection with the compilation album *History of Eric Clapton* (Atco 803) (March 1972), "Layla" hit the Top Ten in the U.S. and the U.K. in the summer of 1972. (It would return to the U.K. Top Ten in 1982.) A live album, *Derek and the Dominos in Concert* (January 1973), taken from the 1970 U.S. tour, was also a strong seller.

Time has only added to the renown for the group, which is now rated among Eric Clapton's most outstanding achievements. The 1988 Eric Clapton box set retrospective *Crossroads* featured material from the abortive second album sessions. *The Layla Sessions* was a 1991 box set expanding that album across three CDs/cassettes. And *Live at the Fillmore* (1994) offered an expanded version of the *In Concert* album. — *William Ruhlmann*

★ **Layla & Other Assorted Love Songs** / Nov. 1970 / Polydor ✦✦✦✦✦
Quite simply, this is Eric Clapton's finest moment, full of gutsy, impassioned playing and tortured vocals. None of the love songs are simple, and the band rocks away their blues in a series of long jams that are never boring. — *Stephen Thomas Erlewine*

○ **Derek & The Dominos in Concert** / Jan. 1973 / Polydor ✦✦✦✦
While it isn't nearly as intense as *Layla*, *Derek & the Dominos In Concert* offers some fine playing by Clapton and his band and easily ranks among his best live albums. — *Stephen Thomas Erlewine*

The Layla Sessions / Sep. 1990 / Polydor ✦✦✦
Featuring two discs of outtakes and jams, the three-CD box *The Layla Sessions* manages to detract from the original by surrounding it with endless, dull instrumentals. Then again, all the unreleased material proves what a well-constructed album *Layla* is. — *Stephen Thomas Erlewine*

Live at the Fillmore / Feb. 22, 1994 / Polydor ✦✦✦
In his liner notes, Anthony DeCurtis calls *Live at the Fillmore* "a digitally remixed and remastered version of the 1973 Derek and the Dominos double album *In Concert*, with five previously unreleased performances and two tracks that have only appeared on the four-CD Clapton retrospective, *Crossroads*." But this does not adequately describe the album. *Live at the Fillmore* is not exactly an expanded version of *In Concert*; it is a different album culled from the same concerts that were used to compile the earlier album. *Live at the Fillmore* contains six of the nine recordings originally released on *In Concert*, and three of its five previously unreleased performances are different recordings of songs also featured on *In Concert*—"Why Does Love Got to Be So Sad?," "Tell the Truth," and "Let It Rain." The other two, "Nobody Knows You When You're Down and Out" and "Little Wing," have not been heard before in any concert version. Even when the same recordings are used on *Live at the Fillmore* as on *In Concert*, they have, as noted, been remixed and, as not noted, re-edited. In either form, Derek and the Dominos' October 1970 stand at the Fillmore East, a part of the group's only U.S. tour, finds them a looser aggregation than they seemed to be in the studio making their only album, *Layla and Other Assorted Love Songs*. A trio backing Eric Clapton, the Dominos leave the guitarist considerable room to solo on extended numbers, five of which run over ten minutes each. Clapton doesn't show consistent invention, but his playing is always directed, and he plays more blues than you can hear on any other Clapton live recording. — *William Ruhlmann*

Rick Derringer

b. Aug. 5, 1947, Celina, OH
Rock & Roll, Hard Rock
As a lead guitarist, Rick Derringer (born Rick Zehringer) was the frontman for the McCoys, a group of mid-'60s pop/rockers who recorded the #1 million-seller "Hang on Sloopy." The McCoys linked up with Texas guitarist Johnny Winter, and Derringer began producing and backing up Winter and his brother Edgar. Derringer's solo debut, *All American Boy*, generated his only hit with

the 1974 #23 "Rock and Roll Hootchie Koo." In 1976 he formed Derringer, a hard rock quartet that enjoyed moderate success. More recently, Derringer has produced Weird Al Yankovic's pop parodies. —*Rick Clark*

● **All American Boy** / 1974 / Blue Sky ✦✦✦✦
Derringer's first solo album, featuring great songwriting and performing, with his own version of his classic "Rock & Roll Hootchie Koo." —*Cub Koda*

Spring Fever / 1975 / Blue Sky ✦✦✦

Derringer / 1976 / Blue Sky ✦✦✦

○ **Live** / 1977 / Blue Sky ✦✦✦✦
A blistering live set from Derringer, featuring most of his best-known songs. —*Stephen Thomas Erlewine*

Des'ree

Group, Urban, Singer-Songwriter
With her second album, 1994's *I Ain't Movin',* soul singer Des'ree became a star. Des'ree's contemporary soul is smooth enough to fit into most urban contemporary playlists, yet it has enough grit and emotional style to attract fans of early-'70s R&B.Her first album—*Mind Adventures* (1992)—didn't attract an audience, yet her second record, 1994's *I Ain't Movin',* was a pop and R&B smash; thanks to the Top Ten hit "You Gotta Be," the record sold over a million copies. —*Stephen Thomas Erlewine*

Mind Adventures / 1992 / Epic ✦✦✦

● **I Ain't Movin'** / 1994 / Epic/550 Music ✦✦✦✦

Sugar Pie Desanto

b. Oct. 16, 1935, New York, NY
Soul, R&B
Desanto's earthy approach was suited equally to R&B and blues, and she cut both for Chess during the '60s. Discovered by bandleader Johnny Otis, who was responsible for her debut sides on Federal, Desanto scored her biggest R&B seller, "I Want to Know," for producer Bob Geddins of Veltone Records in 1960. After she signed with Checker, her 1964 "Slip-In Mules (No High Heel Sneakers)"—the answer to Tommy Tucker's "High Heel Sneakers"—sold well, and a 1966 duet with Etta James, "In the Basement," also garnered spins. Desanto wrote material for many of her labelmates before returning to the San Francisco Bay area in the '70s. —*Bill Dahl*

Sugar Pie Desanto / 1961 / Checker ✦✦✦
One of the least recognized, yet outstanding female soul singers of the early '60s, Sugar Pie Desanto could do coy, innocent songs, tough, hard-edged blues, romantic fluff, or heartache ballads. She was hurt by being on the same label as Etta James and not getting enough quality songs, as was the case with this set. —*Ron Wynn*

● **Down in the Basement** / 1989 / Chess ✦✦✦✦
Saucy, bluesy, mid-'60s R&B with a soulful edge, she had a Top Ten hit in 1960 with "I Want to Know." —*Bill Dahl*

Sugar is Salty / 1995 / Jasman ✦✦

Descendents

Group, Hardcore
One of Southern California's finest hardcore-era bands, the Descendents liberally sprinkled pop on their typically megavolume ceaseless-rush-of-guitar sound. Also, they featured a terrific lead singer in Milo Aukerman.
The Descendents released their first record, the 7-inch *Fat EP,* in 1981. After its release, Aukerman left the band, yet the group continued performing with guitarist Ray Cooper handling lead vocals. *Milo Goes to College,* their first full-length album, appeared in 1982. Following its release, drummer Bill Stevenson joined Black Flag and the band disappeared for a few years.
In 1985, the Descendents reunited, with Aukerman, Stevenson, Cooper, and bassist mTony Lombardo; this lineup's first album was *I Don't Want to Grow Up* (1985). The following year, the band recorded *Enjoy!* with a new bassist. For 1987's *All,* only Milo Aukerman and Bill Stevenson remained in the band's lineup. After its release, Milo left the group and the band evolved into All under the direction of Stevenson. The Descendents' records remain essential listening for fans of the late-'70s/early-'80s post-punk mosh scene. —*John Dougan & Stephen Thomas Erlewine*

Fat / 1981 / SST ✦✦✦

● **Milo Goes to College** / 1982 / SST ✦✦✦✦
Indisputably their best. Fast, furious, and funny, the Descendents never sounded this unabashedly joyous again. Essentially a farewell record (lead singer Milo was actually going to college), its songs are great slice-of-life tales of bored middle-class life in the perpetually sunny environs of L.A. —*John Dougan*

Bonus Fat / 1985 / SST ✦✦✦
A compilation of their superb first EP, plus assorted tracks. You'll never find a better culinary tune than "I Like Food." —*John Dougan*

I Don't Want to Grow Up / 1985 / SST ✦✦✦
O.K., so don't. Good but not great. —*John Dougan*

Enjoy / 1986 / SST ✦✦

All / 1987 / SST ✦✦✦
Although they were slowing down, this is primal stuff. —*John Dougan*

Liveage / 1987 / SST ✦✦✦
Great gig live in Minneapolis. —*John Dougan*

Hallraker: Live! / 1989 / SST ✦✦

● **Somery** / 1991 / SST ✦✦✦✦
A solid career overview. —*John Dougan*

Jackie DeShannon

b. Aug. 21, 1944, Hazel, KY
Singer-Songwriter, Folk-Rock, Pop/Rock
Few performers have enjoyed as versatile a career as Jackie DeShannon, and although she made a couple of well-remembered Top Ten pop hits in the '60s, she's never achieved the level of success or artistic recognition she deserves. Starting as a pop-rockabilly singer as a teenager in the late '50s, she quickly developed into one of the L.A. pop scene's hottest songwriters, penning hits for Brenda Lee, the Fleetwoods, and Irma Thomas, and often collaborating with fellow noted songwriter Shari Sheeley. One of the first established rock figures to see the potential for crossbreeding rock and folk, she was a crucial midwife to the birth of folk-rock, with the wonderful singles "Needles and Pins" and "When You Walk in the Room." Using the circular, jangling guitar lines that would become a prime feature of early folk-rock, both of those songs were covered by the Searchers for much bigger hits; she also wrote "Don't Doubt Yourself Babe," covered by the Byrds on their first album, and penned a couple of Marianne Faithull's early hits. In the mid-'60s, she also found time to write some songs with then-sessionman Jimmy Page, and perform as an opening act for the Beatles on the group's first big American tour.
DeShannon's famous affiliations and success as a songwriter have sometimes obscured her own enormous talents. She's a superb singer, capable of both sweet ballads and (more satisfyingly) a gutsy, soulfully husky delivery. She performed her own material with an honest, vulnerable, intelligent intensity that pre-figured the singer/songwriter movement by several years, and demonstrated command of pop, soul, hard rock, girl group, and country styles. Her greatest success, however, came not with her own material, but with Bacharach-David's "What the World Needs Now Is Love," which made the Top Ten in 1965. Perhaps as a result, she gravitated toward more middle-of-the-road pop sounds in the last half of the '60s, though she cut a good deal of strong material, by both herself and emerging writers like Randy Newman, Tim Hardin, and Warren Zevon. The soft-rock "Put a Little Love in Your Heart" gave her another Top Ten hit in 1969, and she made some well-received singer/songwriter albums in the 1970s. One of the songs from her '70s LPs, "Bette Davis Eyes," became a number one hit for Kim Carnes in 1981. —*Richie Unterberger*

○ **Jackie DeShannon** / 1965 / Sunset ✦✦✦✦
This album features DeShannon's hit version of Hal David and Burt Bacharach's "What the World Needs Now Is Love," but also included is DeShannon's rendition of her own standard, "When You Walk in the Room," and a co-composition with Randy Newman, "She Don't Understand Him Like I Do." —*William Ruhlmann*

This Is Jackie DeShannon / 1965 / Imperial ✦✦✦
Issued in the wake of her mammoth hit "What The World Needs Now Is Love" (included here), this album saw Jackie moving in an orchestrated ballad direction. If her work in that field doesn't hold up as well as her more rock-oriented material, she still did quite a good job of it, handling big production numbers like "Summertime," "Don't Let the Sun Catch You Crying," "I'm Gonna Be

Strong," and "Take Me Tonight" with soulful, full-throated gusto. Her best effort in this style, actually, was Bacharach-David's "A Lifetime of Loneliness," which was a small hit (and is featured on this LP). As was their wont with Jackie, Imperial/Liberty didn't help matters by pasting on a few old tracks from her early-'60s girl-group days; they're good, but out of place in the context of this album. A fairly strong but spotty recording by a great artist who was never afforded the opportunities to fulfill her potential. — *Richie Unterberger*

You Won't Forget Me / 1965 / Imperial ✦✦✦
This was also issued, with very minor track alterations, in 1964 on Liberty as *Breakin' It Up On The Beatles Tour!* This version, issued after her Top Ten 10 hit "What The World Needs Now Is Love," is much easier to find. It was probably the strongest album by this mercurial artist, who never seemed to corral enough top-rank material to produce a first-rate LP, despite recording dozens of fine songs throughout the '60s. Arranged by Jack Nitzsche, it's also her most girl-group and rock-oriented, featuring mostly original material, written alone or in collaboration with Nitzsche, Sharon Sheeley, and a young, unknown Randy Newman. Jackie also acquits herself well on a couple of Buddy Holly covers, "Oh, Boy" and "Maybe Baby." — *Richie Unterberger*

Put a Little Love in Your Heart / 1969 / Imperial ✦✦✦
DeShannon co-wrote her second Top Ten hit, the title track, with Jimmy Holiday and Randy Myers, and this album contains more of the fruit of their collaboration, including the followup, a Top 40 hit called "Love Will Find a Way." — *William Ruhlmann*

New Arrangement / 1975 / Columbia ✦✦✦
Excellent updating of DeShannon's sound. Includes her co-composition "Bette Davis Eyes," which Kim Carnes took to the top of the charts six years later. — *William Ruhlmann*

● **Pop Princess** / 1981 / EMI Australia ✦✦✦✦
Rhino and EMI have come out with fairly extensive CD compilations of DeShannon's work, but this 23-song Australian album—if it can be found—is probably the best. It concentrates almost solely on her '60s recordings (one 1959 track is included), which remains her most fertile era. It also has a few excellent singles that didn't make it onto either compilation. These include the early-'60s girl-group-type efforts "It's Love Baby," "Baby (When Ya Kiss Me)," "I Won't Turn You Down," and "Should I Cry?"— most written by De-Shannon, all flops, and all worth hearing. Later, more mainstream efforts like "A Proper Girl" and Jim Webb's "The Girls' Song" are also not included on other reissues, and also worth a listen. The gatefold package contains informative liner notes, photos, and an exhaustive discography which also lists dozens of songs she wrote for other performers. — *Richie Unterberger*

○ **The Best of Jackie Deshannon** / 1991 / Rhino ✦✦✦✦
This set contains all of De Shannon's best known singles, as well as other notable original songs like "Bette Davis Eyes." — *Rick Clark*

Trouble With Jackie Dee / 1991 / Teenager ✦✦
At first glance, this compilation of many rare DeShannon sides from the early and mid-'60s—most of which have not been reissued elsewhere—looks enticing. What it ends up proving, however, is that the prolific singer-songwriter wrote quite a few puffy tunes in addition to her classics. Most of the tracks on Side One came out as flop Liberty singles in the early '60s (the first of which was issued under the name Jackie Dee, hence the title of this compilation). Her 1959 debut "Buddy" is decent rockabilly, and her version of Leiber and Stoller's "Trouble" is okay, but the rest is surprisingly shallow teen idol fodder, including a duet with Bobby Vee. Side Two, from a slighty later vintage, is far gutsier and better, though several of these cuts have been reissued, like the dramatic "You Won't Forget Me" and the gospel-influenced "Glory Wave." The Buddy Holly covers are all right, and "Try to Forget Him" is good girl-group-type material, as is the obscure early Randy Newman composition "Did He Call Today Mama." "After Last Night" (not a DeShannon original), on the other hand, was done much better by the obscure girl group the Rev-Lons. You get the idea... these are the kind of artifacts that will appeal only to hard-bitten fans, though some of them aren't bad at all. — *Richie Unterberger*

● **What the World Needs Now ... : The Definitive Collection** / 1994 / EMI ✦✦✦✦
DeShannon's work is actually too diverse to be satisfactorily captured on an anthology, even one that includes 28 tracks, as this one does. Still, considering how hard the one DeShannon anthol-

ogy that might be better than this one is to find (the Australian import *Pop Princess*), this has to be cited as the recommended first purchase. Focusing on her output for Liberty between 1959 and 1970, it has all the essentials: her two Top Ten hits, the minor hits like "A Lifetime of Loneliness," the original versions of "Needles and Pins" and "When You Walk in the Room," and a host of fine girl-group, ballad, folk-rock, and singer-songwriter flop singles. From the collector's viewpoint, the most interesting songs are the rarities. The six previously unreleased tracks include the exuberant "Breakaway," a hit for Irma Thomas; the rocker "Dream Boy," cut in 1964 in Britain with Jimmy Page on guitar; and a cover of Tim Hardin's "Reason to Believe." A couple of interesting rarities are "For Granted" (from the little-seen movie *C'Mon, Let's Live a Little*) and the 45 version of "Splendor in the Grass," a somewhat sloppy folk-rock performance on which Jackie was backed by the Byrds. — *Richie Unterberger*

The Deviants

Group, Psychedelic
In the late '60s, the Deviants were something like the British equivalent to the Fugs, with touches of the Mothers of Invention and the British R&B-based rock of the Yardbirds and Pretty Things. Their roots were not so much in the British Invasion as the psychedelic underground that began to take shape in London in 1966-67. Not much more than amateurs when they began playing, they squeezed every last ounce of skill and imagination out of their limited instrumental and compositional resources on their debut, *Ptooff!*, which combined savage social commentary, over-heated sexual lust, psychedelic jamming, blues riffs, and pretty acoustic ballads—all in the space of seven songs. Their subsequent '60s albums had plenty of outrage, but not nearly as strong material as the debut. Lead singer Mick Farren recorded a solo album near the end of the decade, and went on to become a respected rock critic. He has intermittently performed and recorded as a solo artist and with reformed versions of the Deviants. — *Richie Unterberger*

● **Ptooff!** / 1967 / Edsel ✦✦✦✦
One of the more underappreciated psychedelic albums of the late '60s covers a lot of ground in its seven songs. Amphetamine, simplistic riffing that anticipates acts like the Stooges, an astonishingly pretty flower-child ballad, a musique concrete-like recitation, a scathing satirical hard rock ditty about garbage, a melodic instrumental for classical-style guitar, and a nine-minute psychedelic collage of stray licks and sounds from the social milieu of the British psychedelic underground. Packaged in a pop art-like poster, it was an inspired collision of punk attitude and psychedelic eclecticism. — *Richie Unterberger*

Disposable / 1968 / Sire ✦✦✦

No 3 / 1969 / Sire ✦✦
The Deviants' instrumental competence had improved by their third album, but the songwriting inspiration had dwindled. The fuzz guitar-drenched, repetitive, bluesy psychedelia has not dated well, and the satirical outrage of the lyrics—intended to be shocking at the time—sounds more silly and ham-fisted than clever. A couple of the best tracks are surprisingly similar to the best work of the Jimmy Page-era Yardbirds with their taut, vaguely Middle Eastern hard-rock guitar riffs. — *Richie Unterberger*

Willy Deville (William Boray)

b. Aug. 27, 1953, New York City
Rock & Roll
Singer/songwriter Willy DeVille led the band Mink DeVille from the mid-'70s to the mid-'80s, though it had a changing personnel and was basically a platform for him and his songs. In 1987, he launched a solo career, collaborating with Dire Straits guitarist Mark Knopfler on *Magic*. "Storybook Love," a track from the album, was used as the theme from the movie *The Princess Bride*, which Knopfler scored. DeVille moved to New Orleans, where he released *Victory Mixture* on the local Orleans label in 1990. In 1994, he signed to Rhino Records' Forward label and released *Backstreets of Desire*. — *William Ruhlmann*

Miracle / 1987 / A&M ✦✦✦
Willy DeVille moved from the group Mink DeVille to a solo recording career with very little stylistic change, which is no surprise given that the band was really a front for DeVille's songs and vocals. The big change on *Magic* is that DeVille collaborates with Dire Straits guitarist Mark Knopfler, whose distinctive fretwork is

prominently displayed, and who brings along bandmates like keyboard player Guy Fletcher and buddies like guitarist Chet Atkins. Nevertheless, the sound is still early- to mid-'60s pop/soul. The album contains DeVille's "Storybook Love," which was used by Knopfler in his score for the film *The Princess Bride* and is DeVille's best-known recording. — *William Ruhlmann*

○ **Victory Mixture** / 1990 / Orleans ✦✦✦✦
Backstreets Of Desire / May 17, 1994 / Forward/Rhino ✦✦✦

Devo

Group, Techno-Pop/Dance, New Wave
Made up of two sets of brothers (Mark and Bob Motherbaugh and Jerry and Bob Casale), Devo was one of the first new-wave groups to get mass-market attention. An Akron, OH, band, they had their own philosophy, "de-evolution"—a sci-fi/satirical view of postmodern cultural values complete with strange costumes and behavior. Their sound was appropriately nervous and jerky, with a heavy emphasis on synthesizers. Their debut album, *Q: Are We Not Men? A: We Are Devo!*, was produced by Brian Eno and featured a great cover of the Rolling Stones' "Satisfaction." After a less interesting second album, they rebounded with the self-produced album *Freedom of Choice*, containing the hit "Whip It." As one of new-wave's most cartoonish and successful bands, they helped define the genre with a minimalistic synth sound and a nihilistic attitude. Although each successive album provided a new look and theme, their sound became more glossy and less challenging, heading toward straight synth/dance-pop grooves. While both sets of brothers remain musically active on soundtrack work like *Pee Wee's Playhouse* and the theme for *Davis Rules*, most Devo discs of late have been repackage/remix efforts, live recordings, or instrumental works. — *Scott Bultman*

○ **Q: Are We Not Men? A: We Are Devo!** / 1978 / Warner Brothers ✦✦✦✦
Devo's debut shows why the band still has a small but rabidly dedicated following well after their artistic peak. Their sound here is mostly guitar-based, with odd melodies and crazily jerky rhythms. With songs about masturbation ("Uncontrollable Urge"), freaks ("Mongoloid"), and technology ("Space Junk"), plus their patented de-evolution philosophy (the anthem "Jocko Homo," about the regression of mankind) and a wickedly deranged deconstruction of "(I Can't Get No) Satisfaction," Devo took punk's anti-mainstream, D.I.Y. spirit and filtered it through the sensibilities of weirdoes, nerds, and outcasts, relentlessly (and bizarrely) satirizing American culture and briefly picking up, attitude-wise, where the Mothers of Invention left off. — *Steve Huey*

○ **Duty Now for the Future** / 1979 / Warner Brothers ✦✦✦✦
Most of the aural weirdness on Devo's second album comes from the band's experiments with homemade synthesizer technology. As a result, both the guitars and jerky rhythms play a lesser role in their sound. Although it isn't quite as interesting, it's still appropriately strange, and Devo still doesn't sound quite like anyone else. *Duty* is loosely structured around the theme of everyday corporate drudgery and its effects on individuals. — *Steve Huey*

Freedom of Choice / 1980 / Warner Brothers ✦✦✦
Freedom of Choice, arguably Devo's strongest musical effort, revolves around relationships, insecurity, and the lack of flexibility in the American psyche. Their arrangements achieve an effective balance between guitars and synths, and the band's highly stylized visual component, this time featuring "energy dome" hats, paid off in the video for "Whip It." The single went gold and helped the album sell over a million copies. — *Steve Huey*

New Traditionalists / 1981 / Warner Brothers ✦✦✦
With mainstream success on its hands, Devo decided that nobody was getting the point and chose direct statements of purpose ("Through Being Cool") over satirical absurdity. The minimalistic arrangements are mostly for synth, and a distinct note of bitterness has crept into the lyrics. The album can be viewed positively as the outcast's manifesto; others may find it heavy-handed (the band points out in "Beautiful World" that they're being sarcastic, something most fans would have recognized immediately) and see this as the point where Devo started to take itself a bit too seriously. — *Steve Huey*

Oh, No! It's Devo / 1982 / Warner Brothers ✦✦✦
By this point, too much of the band's endearing quirkiness had evaporated. Their sound here was not all that distinguishable from other new wave groups, and apart from a few songs, they simply

weren't as musically or lyrically as interesting as before. It was as if they had lost their focus after *New Traditionalists* and couldn't remember how to be naturally weird. — *Steve Huey*

Shout / 1984 / Warner Brothers ✦
E-Z Listening Disc / 1987 / Rykodisc ✦
Total Devo / 1988 / Enigma ✦✦
Now It Can Be Told (Devo at the Palace 12/9/88) / 1989 / Enigma ✦✦✦
Hardcore Devo / 1990 / Rykodisc ✦✦✦
The Rest: Greatest Misses / 1990 / Warner Brothers ✦✦✦
Smooth Noodle Maps / 1990 / Enigma ✦
● **The Greatest Hits** / 1990 / Warner Brothers ✦✦✦✦
This isn't the best Devo collection around; there's an import with better selections, but few distributors carry it and it's difficult to find. Devo's present-day cult is quite intense; if they would like your thing, chances are that you'll want as much as you can get, so start with *Q: Are We Not Men?* and buy the albums. If Devo simply sounds like an interesting novelty to you, or if you don't enjoy them enough to listen to their more uneven albums, this will suffice if you can't find the import. — *Steve Huey*

Hardcore, Vol. 2 / Aug. 23, 1991 / Rykodisc ✦✦✦
Devo Live: The Mongoloid Years / Oct. 1992 / Rykodisc ✦✦

Dexys Midnight Runners

Group, New Wave, Pop/Rock
When Dexys Midnight Runners were at their peak in the early '80s, U.K. critics hailed their lead singer/songwriter Kevin Rowland as a genius, capable of fusing soul, pop, Irish folk, new wave, and rock into one seamless, unique mix. Although the band wasn't able to fulfill their promise, the best of their music was remarkable. On their first album, *Searching for the Young Soul Rebels*, the group featured scores of horns along with accomplished songwriting from Rowland. It became a sensation in England, although it didn't dent the charts in America. After the album's release, three members of the band split and formed the Bureau, leaving Rowland to refashion Dexys Midnight Runners. What he came up with was a departure from the debut, although it shared the same spirit. Instead of soul, the band was rooted in folk and celtic music on their second album, *Too-Rye-Ay*, which produced the enormous international hit, "Come On Eileen." Rowland seemed lost in the wake of his success, lacking a new idea for his music; the last Dexys album was bland and directionless, as was his solo album, 1988's *The Wanderer*. Rowland hasn't been making music since the late '80s but his band's first records remain staring displays of passion and musical inventiveness. — *Stephen Thomas Erlewine*

○ **Searching for the Young Soul Rebels** / Jul. 1980 / EMI America ✦✦✦✦
While it's a fascinating fusion of punk and soul, Dexy's Midnight Runners' debut album isn't quite as wonderful as the band's cult claims it is, but it does offer a number of genuinely impressive and impassioned songs. — *Stephen Thomas Erlewine*

● **Too-Rye-Ay** / Aug. 1982 / Mercury ✦✦✦✦
For the second Dexy's Midnight Runners album, Kevin Rowland refashioned the band as country/folk/punk-rockers. Much like *Searching for the Young Soul Rebels*, *Too-Rye-Ay* is more interesting in theory than in practice, but it's the stronger of the two records, thanks to the irresistible hit single "Come On Eileen." — *Stephen Thomas Erlewine*

Geno / Mar. 1983 / EMI ✦✦✦
Geno is a compilation album containing the A- and B-sides of the first five singles released by Dexy's Midnight Runners in the U.K. between 1979 and 1981. Four of these singles made the British charts, three hit the Top 40, two the Top Ten, and one, "Geno," a tribute to American expatriate soul singer Geno Washington, went to number one. The first four singles, "Dance Stance," "Geno," "There There My Dear," and "Keep It," were made by the original Dexys lineup, which featured three horns and sported what in England was called a "northern soul" sound, i.e., the gutbucket R&B style of Booker T. & the MG's. But instead of a gritty soul singer up front, there was the adenoidal Kevin Rowland, who sang with a theatrical passion that was moving despite its pretentiousness. By the time of "Keep It," Rowland seemed to have nothing but posturing on his mind, after which the band split. Rowland re-

organized a new unit to make a final single, "Plan B," in the familiar style, but Dexys had only begun its series of drastic musical, fashion, and personnel shifts. — *William Ruhlmann*

Don't Stand Me Down / Sep. 1985 / Mercury ♦♦
In the three years between the release of *Too-Rye-Aye* and *Don't Stand Me Down*, bandleader Kevin Rowland once again revamped Dexy's Midnight Runners. Musically, Rowland had evolved a combination of the soul sound of the first album and the folkie approach of the second, retaining both the horns of the former and the strings of the latter. But long passages of *Don't Stand Me Down* were spoken, not sung, by Rowland in conversation with Adams. "Listen to This" proved that Rowland was still capable of turning out a catchy, Motown-derived pop song when he chose, but the bulk of *Don't Stand Me Down*, which sold disappointingly, must have sounded idiosyncratic to British listeners and nearly incomprehensible to Americans. — *William Ruhlmann*

Best of / 1994 / Mercury ♦♦♦

Diamond Head

Group, Hard Rock, Heavy Metal
Diamond Head was one of the best bands of the new wave of British Heavy Metal in the late '70s and early '80s, playing a tight and aggressive Zeppelin-derived style of hard rock. The band's power, unassuming sense of melody, and crunching guitars influenced a small generation of American metal bands, including Metallica. After several years of inactivity in the late '80s, the band re-formed in 1991 for a tour and an EP. — *Stephen Thomas Erlewine*

Lightning & The Nations / 1981 / Fan Club ♦♦♦

Four Cuts / 1982 / MCA ♦♦♦

Borrowed Time / 1982 / MCA ♦♦

● **Behold the Beginning** / 1986 / Metal Blade ♦♦♦♦
This NWOBHM band never got noticed in America until Metallica noted that Diamond Head was a major influence in their sound. The liner notes written by Metallica drummer Lars Ulrich. — *John Book*

Neil Diamond

b. Jan. 24, 1941, Brooklyn, NY
Pop, Pop/Rock
Neil Diamond built a career, first as a pop songwriter, and then as a pop singer, that has withstood the changing fashions of music, especially rock, over more than 25 years. Born in Brooklyn, Diamond was writing and recording in New York in his teens, though he graduated from Erasmus High School and attended New York University for a time. In 1965, he signed to Bang Records as an artist while also working as a songwriter. In 1966, he reached the Top Ten with his "Cherry, Cherry," while the Monkees took his "I'm a Believer" to #1. "Cherry, Cherry" was the first of five straight Top 20 hits, among them "Girl, You'll Be a Woman Soon."

Diamond began to develop into more of an individual writer in the mold of Bob Dylan and Paul Simon in the late '60s, and this led to his move to Uni Records in 1968, where he continued to score hits like "Sweet Caroline," "Holly Holy," and "Cracklin' Rosie," in a pop/rock style laced with gospel and country influences. His albums also began to go gold consistently as of 1969's *Touching You, Touching Me.*

Diamond signed a lucrative contract with Columbia Records in 1973 that began with his soundtrack to the film *Jonathan Livingston Seagull.* His 1976 album, *Beautiful Noise*, was produced by Robbie Robertson of the Band; it was his first album to go platinum. In 1980, Diamond starred in a remake of the film *The Jazz Singer.* Its soundtrack was another million-seller for him.

Diamond had developed into a dynamic live performer over the years, and his concert recordings were among his most successful. In the late '80s and early '90s, while updating his sound, he faded from the singles charts though his albums continued to sell consistently. And his shows continued to sell out: according to *Amusement Business*, he was the top concert draw in the U.S. for the first six months of 1992. — *William Ruhlmann*

Velvet Gloves & Spit / 1968 / MCA ♦♦♦

○ **Touching You, Touching Me** / 1969 / MCA ♦♦♦♦
Diamond's first regular album release to sell in substantial numbers, *Touching You, Touching Me* contains the gold Top Ten single "Holly Holy," a Diamond composition, but is mostly notable for its covers of standards by other songwriters: "Everybody's Talkin',"

"Mr. Bojangles," "Both Sides Now," and the chart entry "Until It's Time for You to Go." These helped signal that Diamond was thinking of himself less as a Brill Building hack than as a peer of Fred Neil, Jerry Jeff Walker, Joni Mitchell, and Buffy Sainte-Marie. — *William Ruhlmann*

○ **Tap Root Manuscript** / 1970 / MCA ♦♦♦♦
The follow-up to *Touching You, Touching Me* was an ambitious set of songs, all originals except for a Top 20 cover of "He Ain't Heavy ...He's My Brother," including the side-long suite "The African Trilogy" (which featured the hit "Soolaimon"), the #1 hit "Cracklin' Rosie" and "Done Too Soon." Going gold within two months, this album confirmed Diamond's breakthrough as a recording star. — *William Ruhlmann*

Stones / 1971 / MCA ♦♦

Moods / 1972 / MCA ♦♦♦

○ **Hot August Night** / 1972 / MCA ♦♦♦♦
This double-record set is the album that established Diamond's reputation as a live performer. Containing passionately performed versions of his biggest hits up to this time, it sold the best of any album he'd had so far, going gold the month of its release. — *William Ruhlmann*

Rainbow / 1973 / MCA ♦♦♦

Jonathan Livingston Seagull / Oct. 1973 / Columbia ♦♦♦
Columbia Records' multi-million-dollar signing of Diamond was questioned by industry-ites who felt president Clive Davis had paid too high a price. Davis had left the company by the time this, Diamond's first Columbia album, was released in October 1973, but it was posthumous vindication. The soundtrack to a forgettable film based on a trivial best-seller, *Jonathan Livingston Seagull*, sold two million copies, spinning off the singles "Be" and "Skybird," even if, in retrospect, it is not one of Diamond's more consistent efforts. — *William Ruhlmann*

★ **His Twelve Greatest Hits** / 1974 / MCA ♦♦♦♦♦
Actually, this is 12 songs that were hits for Diamond on Uni between 1969 and 1972. "Cracklin' Rosie" is here, along with Diamond's other chart-topper of the period, "Song Sung Blue," and the Top Ten hits "Sweet Caroline" and "Holly Holy." — *William Ruhlmann*

Serenade / Oct. 1974 / Columbia ♦♦
Neil Diamond's first regular album release for Columbia Records, following the success of the movie soundtrack *Jonathan Livingston Seagull*, *Serenade* is a slight effort characterized by Diamond's attempts to make pop sentiments seem more profound by grafting more auspicious art references onto them. But whether he's name-dropping Picasso or Longfellow, Diamond still has greeting card sentiments on his mind. Nevertheless, the catchiest of these autodidactic exercises, "Longfellow Serenade," which combines comments about "winged flight" with the exhortation, "Come on, baby, ride," was a Top Ten hit. — *William Ruhlmann*

Beautiful Noise / 1976 / Columbia ♦♦♦
A beautifully recorded concept album about Diamond's own emergence from the Brooklyn streets and from the Brill Building's Tin Pan Alley. Produced by Robbie Robertson. — *William Ruhlmann*

Love at the Greek / Jan. 1977 / Columbia ♦♦

I'm Glad You're Here with Me Tonight / Feb. 1977 / Columbia ♦♦

You Don't Bring Me Flowers / 1978 / Columbia ♦♦♦

September Morn / 1979 / Columbia ♦♦

○ **The Jazz Singer** / 1980 / Capitol ♦♦♦♦
Diamond's only notable screen appearance was his starring role in this remake of the 1927 movie that was Hollywood's first real talkie and originally featured Al Jolson. Diamond wrote a new score, featuring his biggest latter-day hits, "Love on the Rocks," "Hello Again," and "America," and as a result this soundtrack album became his biggest seller ever—five million copies and counting. — *William Ruhlmann*

Heartlight / 1982 / Columbia ♦♦
Although Diamond has continued to sell healthy quantities of his albums and to fill arenas for his concerts, *Heartlight* and its title song, which was a Top Ten hit, were his last record releases as what might be called a frontline artist, one who makes contemporary music for a contemporary audience and sells a million copies on release. It's a typical album for Diamond at this point, full of romantic sentiments rendered in highly-produced settings and em-

ploying the cream of L.A. studio musicians, but lacking the excitement of his early work and the ambition of his middle period. — *William Ruhlmann*

○ **12 Greatest Hits, Vol. 2** / May 1982 / Columbia ✦✦✦✦
Keying off the title of an earlier hits collection on another label, Columbia's *12 Greatest Hits Volume II* summed up Neil Diamond's first eight years with the label, 1973-1981, as well as his successful 1980 soundtrack for *The Jazz Singer* on Capitol Records. Five of the 12, "Longfellow Serenade," "You Don't Bring Me Flowers" (with Barbra Streisand), "Love on the Rocks," "Hello Again," and "America," were Top Ten hits. Another six, "Be," "If You Know What I Mean," "Desiree," "Forever in Blue Jeans," "September Morn," and "Yesterday's Songs," made the Top 40, and the last, "Beautiful Noise," was the title track of Diamond's best album of the period. The songs shared a catchiness that belied Diamond's shallow philosophizing and thinly veiled lust, and they made for a consistent collection out of what had been a series of uneven albums. And, since Diamond only made the Top Ten one more time, the album capped his hit-making days. This is the record to buy instead of investing in the Columbia catalog. — *William Ruhlmann*

★ **Classics: the Early Years** / 1983 / Columbia ✦✦✦✦✦
A terrific collection featuring his earliest and best songs, like "Kentucky Woman," "Girl, You'll be a Woman Soon," "Cherry, Cherry," "Thank the Lord for the Night Time," "Solitary Man," "I'm a Believer," and "Red Red Wine." — *Stephen Thomas Erlewine*

Primitive / 1984 / Columbia ✦✦
Headed for the Future / 1986 / Columbia ✦✦
Having stumbled with *Primitive*, Diamond attempted, with *Headed for the Future*, to re-establish himself as a contemporary artist, co-writing with Stevie Wonder, recording songs by Bryan Adams and Maurice White of Earth, Wind and Fire, employing nine producers and nine recording studios. The result was a slight upturn in sales and Diamond's last singles chart entry with the title track. But the album was also overblown and unfocused, record-making by committee, and Neil Diamond as an individual artist was getting lost in the process. — *William Ruhlmann*

Hot August Night 2 / 1987 / Columbia ✦✦
The Best Years of Our Lives / 1988 / Columbia ✦✦✦
Turning to David Foster as producer, Diamond made a more focused, if still somewhat overdone record that, with such songs as the title track and "This Time," was targeted at his adult audience, although he still made a play for the kids by covering Tracy Chapman's "Baby, Can I Hold You." — *William Ruhlmann*

Lovescape / Aug. 27, 1991 / Columbia ✦✦
Diamond's first album in 22 years to not even go gold, *Lovescape* was a major, if not very distinguished, effort in which Diamond covered "One Hand, One Heart" from *West Side Story* and duetted with Kim Carnes on his own "Hooked on the Memory of You." Six producers are credited on the 15 tracks, but all that money and effort once again results in an album in which the artist nearly gets lost. — *William Ruhlmann*

○ **The Greatest Hits (1966-1992)** / 1992 / Columbia ✦✦✦✦
Columbia has been Diamond's label since 1973, and it acquired the rights to his Bang material of 1966-1968. But MCA still controls the recordings from 1968-1973. That's why (although you won't find out by reading the album cover) this two-disc, 37-track retrospective consists of the original versions of such hits as "Cherry, Cherry" (1966) and "You Don't Bring Me Flowers" (1978) but covers the middle period with re-recordings and live renditions of 13 of Diamond's biggest hits. As such, this collection gets only a qualified recommendation. — *William Ruhlmann*

○ **Glory Road: 1968 to 1972** / 1992 / MCA ✦✦✦✦
A fine two-disc retrospective of Diamond's late-'60s and early-'70s tracks, it includes some of his biggest hits—"Cracklin' Rosie," "Sweet Caroline," and "Song Sung Blue," among others. If *His 12 Greatest Hits* doesn't offer enough material, *Glory Road* is the definitive retrospective of his years with Uni/MCA. — *AMG*

Up on the Roof (Songs from The Brill Building) / Sep. 28, 1993 / Columbia ✦✦✦
This is Diamond's equivalent of, say, one of Barbra Streisand's *Broadway* albums. It's Broadway that Diamond is returning to as well; specifically, the corner of 49th Street, where he and many others turned out songs for music publishers. Some of these songs were written there; most were only in the spirit of that modern

Tin Pan Alley. Handling the work of his then-rivals, such as "Spanish Harlem," "A Groovy Kind of Love," and "River Deep, Mountain High," Diamond adopts his usual hammy style. Peter Asher patented a neo-'60s production style in crafting oldies for Linda Ronstadt in the '70s, and he does the same thing here. Actually, this record sounds exactly like you would expect: just call to mind a familiar song like "Will You Love Me Tomorrow" and imagine what it would sound like if Neil Diamond sang it. Fans can decide for themselves whether it's valid and, perhaps more problematic, necessary. — *William Ruhlmann*

The Diamonds

Group, R&B, Doo-Wop
One of the leading cover groups of the mid 50s, the Diamonds adapted current R&B hits into pop gold of their own. Hailing from Toronto, the Canadian quartet signed with Mercury in 1955 and immediately zoomed up pop playlists with covers of the Teenagers' "Why Do Fools Fall in Love," the Willows' "Church Bells May Ring," and their biggest hit of all, a sanitized version of the Gladiolas hit "Little Darlin'." Fronted by David Somerville, the quartet hit with an original, the smooth dance outing "The Stroll." After weathering major personnel changes, the Diamonds notched their last hit in 1961. Somerville remains active as a solo, while various aggregations billed as the Diamonds populate the oldies scene. — *Bill Dahl*

● **The Best of the Diamonds** / Rhino ✦✦✦✦
"Little Darlin'," "The Stroll," and some of their lesser hits are all here. — *Dan Heilman*

Dick & Dee Dee

Group, Pop/Rock
A difficult-to-categorize male-female duo from L.A., Dick and Dee Dee had pretty fair success with material that drew from doo-wop, teen idol fare, pop, and even soul/R&B in the first half of the 1960s. The pair's biggest and best hit was their first, the moody, minor-key mid-tempo ballad "The Mountain's High," which reached number two in 1961. Much of their material (including "The Mountain's High") was written by Dick (full name Dick St. John), and the high, screechy (in a positive sense) vocals of Dee Dee in particular led some listeners to incorrectly assume they were African-American. They reached the Top 30 with a few more pop-oriented follow-ups—"Young and in Love," "Turn Around," and "Tell Me"—in the next couple of years, but got their second biggest smash with their toughest number, the blue-eyed soulish "Thou Shalt Not Steal," in 1964. A popular touring act in their day (appearing with the Beach Boys and Rolling Stones among others), they faded from view after the mid-'60s. — *Richie Unterberger*

● **The Best Of Dick & Dee Dee** / 1995 / Varese Vintage ✦✦✦✦
Well-chosen 12-song best-of includes all their chart hits. "The Mountain's High" and "Thou Shalt Not Steal" remain the clear highlights, though some of the rest is interesting early-'60s pop fare. Includes the rare 1965 single "Blue Turns to Grey," a Jagger/Richard cover produced by Andrew Loog Oldham that has the Stones themselves on backing instruments and vocals. — *Richie Unterberger*

The Dickies

Group, Punk
For the Dickies, punk rock wasn't a way to vent anger, it was a way to make fun of things. More than anything, the Los Angeles quartet was distinguished by their simplistic, nearly moronic, sense of humor. Basing their musical attack as well as their lyrical obsessions on early Ramones records, the Dickies played a speedy, hooky variation on standard three-chord rock, singing ludicrous, campy songs about things like the "Attack of the Mole Men." In addition to their wacky originals, the group recorded zany, jokey covers of rock & roll classics like "Paranoid," "Eve of Destruction," and "Communication Breakdown," as well as oddities like "Eep Opp Ork (Uh, Uh)," a pseudo-rockabilly number from a *Jetsons* episode.

The Dickies formed after the initial punk explosion of 1977. The band comprised vocalist Leonard Graves Phillips, guitarist Stan Lee, bassist Billy Club, keyboardist Chuck Wagon, and drummer Karlos Kaballero—all of the names were assumed, of course. Two years later, the group released their debut album, *The Incredible Shrinking Dickies* on A&M Records. Throughout their career, the Dickies only deviated slightly from the fast and catchy punk of their debut—their earlier records leaned toward the Californian hardcore punk that was popular at the time, while the later records slow down a little, approaching heavy metal territory. Over the course of six albums between 1979 and 1989, the group's audience never grew beyond a cult following. They stopped recording in the early '90s, but echoes of their music could be heard in Green Day's multi-platinum 1994 hit album, *Dookie*. — *Stephen Thomas Erlewine*

○ **The Incredible Shrinking Dickies** / 1979 / A&M ✦✦✦✦
The Dickies' first album was a blitzkrieg attack of silly humor and lightening-fast riffs, establishing the pattern the band would follow throughout their career. — *Stephen Thomas Erlewine*

○ **Dawn of the Dickies** / 1979 / A&M ✦✦✦✦
Featuring a more varied attack than their debut, *Dawn of the Dickies* manages to be a more listenable and effective record. — *Stephen Thomas Erlewine*

Stukas over Disneyland / 1983 / Restless ✦✦✦

We Aren't the World! / 1986 / Combat ✦✦✦
Originally released only on cassette, *We Aren't the World* is an exhaustive collection of 21 (mostly) live tracks from 1978-1985 that prove that the band hasn't changed that much over the years. The most interesting thing about the album is the presence of their four-song 1977 demo, which is the crudest and most scintillating rock & roll they ever captured on tape. — *Stephen Thomas Erlewine*

Second Coming / 1989 / Enigma ✦✦

● **Great Dictations (The Definitive Dickies Collection)** / 1989 / A&M ✦✦✦✦
Greatest Dictations compiles material from their first two albums and their early singles, providing an effective introduction to the band's goofy punk rock. — *Stephen Thomas Erlewine*

The Dictators

Group, Punk
Formed in 1974, NYC's Dictators were one of the finest and most influential proto-punk bands to walk the earth. Alternately reveling in and satirizing the wanton excesses of a rock & roll lifestyle and lowbrow culture (e.g., wrestling, TV, fast food), the Dictators, whose worldview was defined by bassist/keyboardist and former fanzine publisher (*Teenage Wasteland Gazette*) Andy (occasionally Adny) Shernoff and renegade rock critic/theorist Richard Meltzer, played loud, fast rock & roll fueled by a love of '60s American garage rock, British Invasion pop and the sonic onslaught of the Who. Driven by the guitar barrage of Scott "Top Ten" Kempner and Ross "The Boss" Funichello and fronted by indefatigable ex-roadie and wrestler Handsome Dick Manitoba (aka Richard Blum), it seemed that nothing stood in the way of the Dictators and mega-popularity. But that's not what happened. There were complications with record companies, personnel changes (one-time bassist Mark Mendoza left for Twisted Sister; original drummer Stu Boy King was replaced by Richie Teeter), radio hated them, critical response was lukewarm, and lots of audiences didn't get the jokes; supporters remained loyal and vociferous (especially Meltzer), but it didn't turn into anything tangible. Ironically, what didn't help at all was the rise of the New York punk scene, which only diverted attention away from them and onto bands they influenced (e.g., the Ramones). They did manage to release three fine albums, but by 1978, it was over, and the Dictators broke up in the face of the public apathy and overstated accusations of sellout that greeted what was to be their final album, *Bloodbrothers*. Since then, individual members have kept busy: Kempner put together the Del-Lords and now records as a solo act; Ross the Boss spent a few years in the goofy macho heavy metal band Manowar and later joined Shernoff and Manitoba in the punk/metal combo Manitoba's Wild Kingdom; Shernoff also works as a producer. In 1991, there was a brief reunion tour (with Top Ten) that proved they hadn't lost a step after all these years. — *John Dougan*

● **Go Girl Crazy** / 1975 / Epic ✦✦✦✦
A great debut release that went almost totally ignored in its day. Although Manitoba appears on the LP cover, it's Shernoff who does the bulk of the lead singing. Many of the songs—"The Next Big Thing," "Master Race Rock," "Teengenerate," and "(I Live For) Cars and Girls"—became live staples and are accurate example of the Dictators' style and abundant sense of humor. — *John Dougan*

Manifest Destiny / 1977 / Asylum ✦✦✦
By this time, Manitoba was considered the full-time lead singer (although Shernoff and Kempner sing plenty) and the band was hitting its stride. Despite a longish dud track that closes Side One

("Disease"), *Manifest Destiny* shows off the Dictators' strong (and often tender) pop smarts, especially on Shernoff's "Sleepin' with the Television On" and Kempner's "Hey Boys." Also, there's a fast and furious cover of the Stooges' "Search & Destroy." — *John Dougan*

Bloodbrothers / 1978 / Asylum ✦✦✦
Unjustly maligned at the time as an attempt to sell out to a more mainstream hard rock/heavy metal audience, *Bloodbrothers* (named after the novel by Richard Price) may, ironically, turn out to be the Dictators' best record (it's certainly the most consistent). It's non-stop, ragin' full-on from the moment Shernoff counts down the opening track "Faster and Louder" (which is) to the ferocious cover of the Flamin' Groovies classic "Slow Death" that closes the record. Sandwiched in between are a tribute to Richard Meltzer ("Borneo Jimmy"), a dark song about teenage prostitutes ("The Minnesota Strip") and a million-miles-per-hour love song, "Stay with Me." Critical history has dictated (pun intended) that the two earlier records are better, but when I need a 'Tators fix this is the one I play, over and over and over. — *John Dougan*

Live, Fuck 'em If They Can't Take a Joke / 1981 / ROIR ✦✦✦
Originally a cassette-only release of a reunion gig in New York in 1981 (since re-released on CD), this is a fine document of the Dictators' feral power and endless charm as a live act. The sound is only so-so, but it never interferes with the reckless abandon or fun the guys are having. Great guitar playing by Ross the Boss; Manitoba is in fine fettle too. — *John Dougan*

Bo Diddley (Ellas Otha Bates McDaniels)

b. Dec. 30, 1928, McComb, MS
R&B, Rock & Roll
Bo Diddley (born Ellas Otha Bates McDaniels) is one of the most influential R&B artists of all time. His music resists classification to this day. Though some critics dismiss him as a one-riff artist, nothing could be farther from the truth. His trademark rhythm (based on equal parts "hambone" beat and sanctified church shout) has many variations, textures, and subtleties, which reveal themselves to the listener with concentrated listening. Though his chart hits were few, the scope and breadth of his influence, both here and abroad, is wide indeed. A major innovator in guitar sounds and designs and a galvanizing live performer with a powerful singing voice and personality to match, his induction to the Rock & Roll Hall of Fame was no less than his due. The only musician in history to have a specific beat named after him, Bo Diddley stands as a true American music original. — *Cub Koda*

○ **Bo Diddley Is a Gunslinger** / 1963 / Chess ✦✦✦✦
One of Bo Diddley's better studio albums, *Bo Diddley Is a Gunslinger* features the classic "Ride On Josephine," as well as a raw version of "Sixteen Tons" and a rewrite of "Somewhere Over the Rainbow" called "Somewhere," among its many highlights. — *Stephen Thomas Erlewine*

○ **Bo Diddley's Beach Party** / 1963 / Checker ✦✦✦✦
A blistering live album. Currently out of print but well worth any search. — *Cub Koda*

○ **Bo Diddley/Go Bo Diddley** / 1986 / Chess ✦✦✦✦
Bo's first and second albums on one CD. — *Cub Koda*

★ **The Chess Box** / 1990 / MCA ✦✦✦✦✦
A two-CD boxed-set overview of Bo Diddley's music. The perfect place to start. — *Cub Koda*

○ **Rare & Well Done** / Sep. 10, 1991 / Chess ✦✦✦✦
Contains unissued and rare sides. The perfect companion piece to *The Chess Box*. — *Cub Koda*

Digable Planets

Group, Urban
One of the hottest hip-hop jazz groups to emerge in the '90s, Digable Planets combined a witty, loose rapping style similiar to the old "beat" poetry with improvisational backing to score a commercial and aesthetic success with their debut CD, *Reaching: A New Refutation of Time & Space. Reaching* proved to be both a critical and commercial success. Its follow-up, 1994's more street-oriented *Blowout Comb*, didn't achieve as many sales, yet it confirmed the group's status as one of hip-hop's most praised bands. — *Ron Wynn*

● **Reachin': A New Refutation . . .** / 1993 / Pendulum ✦✦✦✦
Digable Planets' debut album was one of the more successful fusions of jazz and rap, blending the two genres into a funky, seamless, stylish sound, without losing the integrity of jazz or hip-hop street credibility. —*Stephen Thomas Erlewine*

○ **Blowout Comb** / 1994 / Pendulum ✦✦✦✦
Digable Planets set the hip-hop world on its ear with their jazz-inflected debut, *Reachin'.* Their follow-up, *Blowout Comb,* not only offers a deeper exploration of their jazz roots, but also more politicized and harder-edged lyrics than their debut, even if it lacks a single song as impressive as "Rebirth of Slick (Cool Like Dat)." —*Stephen Thomas Erlewine*

Digital Underground

Group, Hip Hop
Nearly every rap posse from the '80s and '90s has borrowed from George Clinton's mountain of P-Funk, but this Bay Area conglomerate (led by rappers Shock-G and Humpty Hump) have mutated Clinton's boogie into the heaviest funk-fueled sound in rap. And their sense of humor is always dead on-target.

Digital Underground wasn't able to replicate the commercial success of their 1990 debut *Sex Packets,* yet their music has remained consistently strong, even if it all sounds a bit similar. —*John Floyd*

★ **Sex Packets** / Jan. 1990 / Tommy Boy ✦✦✦✦✦
This pulsating and wiggy debut is powered by the two instant classics "The Humpty Dance" and "Doowutchyalike." It's sometimes spotty, but worthwhile for aficionados. —*John Floyd*

This Is an Ep Release / Feb. 1990 / Tommy Boy ✦✦✦
Two decent remixes from their debut pad this half-hour mini opus. The new stuff ("Same Song," "Nuttin' Nis Funky") attests to the Underground's devotion to the funk and to their staying power. —*John Floyd*

○ **Sons of the P** / 1991 / Tommy Boy ✦✦✦✦
Their devotion to brother George Clinton mutates into a full-blown sort-of concept album. No truly great singles, but as a whole, this is their best album. —*John Floyd*

The Body Hat Syndrome / Tommy Boy ✦✦✦
With their third album, Digital Underground doesn't change their style much at all, but that isn't bad. Instead, *The Body-Hat Syndrome* is a goofily endearing mess of P-Funk inspired hip-hop, with enough good humor and beats to satisfy their fans. —*Stephen Thomas Erlewine*

Varetta Dillard

d. 1993
R&B
Varetta Dillard was a wailing, shouting mama who scored a trio of hits for Savoy in the early '50s. Dillard was born crippled, but that didn't stop her from being an excellent R&B vocalist. She had a great voice and sang flamboyant, suggestive lyrics with verve and fire. Dillard won two Amateur Night contests at the Apollo and was subsequently signed by Savoy in 1951. Her first hit was "Easy, Easy Baby" in 1952, followed by "Mercy, Mr. Percy," her trademark song, in 1953, and "Johnny Has Gone," an evocative tribute to Johnny Ace, in 1955. The latter two peaked at number six on the R&B charts. Dillard switched to gospel in the '60s, joining the Tri-Odds. She died in 1993. —*Ron Wynn*

● **Got You on My Mind, Vol. 1** / 1989 / Bear Family ✦✦✦✦
Bear Family issued a pair of CDs in 1989 presenting 51 of Varetta Dillard's songs. This disc, which contains 29 numbers, leads off with a curious novelty, "The Square Dance Rock." The other tunes are divided between earnest covers ("See See Rider Blues" and "Pennies From Heaven"), robust stompers ("Mama Don't Want [What Poppa Don't Want]") and teen laments ("Pray for Me Mother"). There's also an intriguing tribute piece, "I Miss You Jimmy (Tribute to James Dean)," prompting speculation as to whether the song was Dillard's idea or a company ploy to exploit Dean's tragic demise in 1956. Dillard makes most of these songs entertaining, and sometimes turns in a triumph. —*Ron Wynn*

● **The Lovin'bird, Vol. 2** / 1989 / Bear Family ✦✦✦✦
Bear Family's second CD featuring songs by R&B vocalist Varetta Dillard empties their vaults with a mix of comical novelty tunes, hard-hitting tracks and heartache numbers. Dillard moves from the hip silliness of the title track and "Mercy, Mr. Percy" to the anguished "What Can I Say" and "A Little Bitty Tear." She's also outstanding on "Scorched," "You Ain't Foolin' Nobody" and "Rules of Love." The disc's 22 tracks offer a portrait of a fine vocalist who

consistently sang with vigor and depth, regardless of a number's lyrical quality. —*Ron Wynn*

Dils

Group, Punk
The Dils were one of the biggest draws on the late '70s L.A. punk circuit. Led by harmonizing brothers Chip and Tony Kinman, the group played short, aggressive songs with political lyrics, often from a socialist viewpoint. During the group's four years of existence, it only released three 7-inch singles; all of their albums were posthumous, culled from the singles and various live performances. The group later evolved into Rank And File. —*Steve Huey*

● **Live!** / 1987 / Iloki ✦✦✦
A legendary early L.A. punk band, the Dils never got to record much during their lifetime (three seven-inches), so this posthumous release actually comprises a fair chunk of their recorded legacy. Ten of the fourteen tracks were taken from a cassette recording of a gig circa 1980. The fidelity, as you might expect, is not top-notch, but gets the job done as far as capturing their adrenaline rush. Dominated by singers Chip and Tony Kinman, this actually has a fair amount of harmonies and pop power chords considering the near-hardcore tempos. A chunky cover of Buddy Holly's "Modern Don Juan" is an unexpected nod to roots on this crude but effective set, which includes some considerably different versions of songs they recorded in the studio. The album closes with four songs from a show circa 1977 of distinctly raunchier fidelity and thrashier tempos. —*Richie Unterberger*

The Dils / 1990 / Lost ✦✦✦

The Dimensions

Group, Pop/Rock
There were many, many obscure garage bands in the mid-'60s that released limited editions of all-cover albums, to be given away at gigs and school. Most of these albums were virtually worthless except as time capsules, but there were a few scattered exceptions that proved the rule—LPs of this kind by T.C. Atlantic and the Litter became valued collector's items. The Dimensions were another example. Nothing is known about this Chicago college group, whose derivative but exciting album achieved a much greater audience when it was reissued for the '60s collector audience in the 1980s. —*Richie Unterberger*

From All Dimensions / 1966 / Eva ✦✦✦
Not an original bone in their body on this 1966 album of 12 covers, but the Dimensions did a good job as aspiring Rolling Stones. Killer versions of "Carol" and "Do You Love Me" highlight this timepiece, with the kind of crudely amplified raw guitars and frenetic drums that could not be reproduced by the most exacting current scientific methods. —*Richie Unterberger*

Dinosaur Jr.

Group, Alternative Pop/Rock
Led by J. Mascis' massive guitar roar and drawling vocals, Dinosaur Jr. were one of the most distinctive and influential alternative bands of the late '80s. Taking hardcore punk and Neil Young's splattered electric folk as their starting points, Dinosaur Jr. created a loud, sprawling rock & roll that frequently spun off into the white noise territory of Sonic Youth but just as frequently stayed in Mascis' lazily melodic, folk-based songs.

Initially, Dinosaur Jr. was a trio called Dinosaur. Mascis and bassist Lou Barlow played in a Massachusetts-area hardcore combo called Deep Wound, with Mascis on drums. After Deep Wound had run its course, former All White Jury drummer Murph was brought into the lineup and Mascis switched to guitar. The group released its self-titled debut for Homestead Records in 1985. Around the time of their second album, 1987's *You're Living All Over Me,* a '60s rock group called the Dinosaurs forced the band to change their name; at Mascis' suggestion, the band added "Jr."

The following year Lou Barlow recorded his last album with the band, *Bug;* he formed Sebadoh in the same year. Barlow wasn't immediately replaced. Instead, J. Mascis recorded the next album, *Green Mind* almost entirely by himself, which began a practice that Dinosaur Jr. would follow throughout their career. Frequently, Mascis recorded the majority of the album, with various musicians filling out the parts. Bassist Mike Johnston joined with 1993's *Where You Been* and Murph was kicked out before the sessions for 1994's *Without a Sound.*

Without Barlow, the band became more direct and accessible,

although Mascis' guitar would still frequently veer into wrenching noise. One of the few traditional lead guitarists in alternative rock, Mascis' fluid, feedback-drenched guitar expressed all of the emotions that his lyrics alluded to. Mascis also is one of the most respected songwriters in alternative rock; his songs have been covered by several artists, including the Cowboy Junkies. Since their first release in 1985, Dinosaur Jr. have influenced a generation of young guitar bands; along with the Pixies and Sonic Youth, they provide the link between the post-punk rock of Hüsker Dü and Replacements and the grunge rock of the '90s. —*Stephen Thomas Erlewine*

Dinosaur / 1985 / Positive ✦✦✦
With great angst-ridden songs, it's tense, with a Neil Young flavor. —*Robert Gordon*

☆ **You're Living All over Me** / 1987 / SST ✦✦✦✦✦
A colossal slab of snarling indie-rock guitar noise, Dinosaur Jr.'s second album was one of the landmark underground rock records of the late '80s; with its huge sheets of white noise and sighing melodies, it paved the way for the grunge movement of the early '90s. —*Stephen Thomas Erlewine*

○ **Bug** / 1988 / SST ✦✦✦✦
Bug is as noisy as *You're Living All Over Me*, but this time out, J. Mascis' songwriting has sharpened a bit, as evidenced by the brilliant single "Freak Scene." —*Stephen Thomas Erlewine*

Fossils / 1991 / SST ✦✦✦
A good collection of non-LP singles and rarities, *Fossils*' high points include strangely appropriate covers of Peter Frampton's "Show Me the Way" and the Cure's "Just Like Heaven." —*Stephen Thomas Erlewine*

● **Green Mind** / 1991 / Sire ✦✦✦✦
Many consider *Green Mind* to be a weak, uninspired effort, but Dinosaur Jr.'s major-label debut is a strong, varied album, featuring some of J. Mascis' best songwriting, as well as some of his best, most fluid guitar work. Essentially a solo effort by Mascis (Murph only appears on three tracks), *Green Mind* finds him stretching and expanding his traditional sonic assault with more acoustic guitars and tighter melodies. With its gentle Mellotron and lovely, sighing melody, "Thumb" stands as one of Mascis' finest songs; "Muck" is a surprisingly enjoyable stab at funk, "How'd You Pin That One on Me" is a great guitar workout, "Puke & Cry" and "I Live for That Look" are impressive folk-punk, and "The Wagon" rivals "Freak Scene" in its depiction of the underground scene. —*Stephen Thomas Erlewine*

Whatever's Cool with Me / Oct. 22, 1991 / Sire ✦✦✦
"Whatever's Cool With Me" is definitive Dinosaur Jr.—roaring rhythm guitars, legato solos, weary lyrics and a winding, penetrating melody. The other five B-sides on the EP are solid, but unremarkable, highlighted by a tongue-in-cheek rewrite of David Bowie's "Quicksand." —*Stephen Thomas Erlewine*

○ **Where You Been** / 1993 / Warner Brothers ✦✦✦✦
Dinosaur Jr.'s full-throttle punk roar keeps diminishing as time goes by, but that doesn't mean the music is any less powerful; if anything, it's getting stronger. *Where You Been* sounds similar to most other Dinosaur Jr. albums—there's no mistaking J. Mascis' trademark wrenching guitar and vocals—but the album is filled with terrific songs like "Get Me" and "Start Choppin'," even if the guitar meanders a bit too much. —*Stephen Thomas Erlewine*

Without A Sound / 1994 / Warner Brothers ✦✦
J. Mascis fired long-time drummer Murph before the recording of *Without a Sound*, which came as a surprise to Murph. Naturally, the change in personnel hasn't changed Dinosaur Jr.'s sound much; the only difference between *Without a Sound* and *Where You Been* is a more pronounced country leaning (particularly on the album's high point, the rollicking "I Don't Think So") and shorter, more concise performances. What hasn't changed are the overpowering fuzz tones of Mascis' guitar, which tend to hide his more expressive vocals; it also makes digging out the gems on this album a little more difficult than necessary. —*Stephen Thomas Erlewine*

Dio

Group, Hard Rock, Heavy Metal
Before he assembled Dio, Ronnie James Dio was a well-known figure in the heavy metal world. With Elf, Rainbow, and Black Sabbath, Dio was a top hard rock singer with a solid commercial appeal; he was responsible for reviving Sabbath's sagging fortunes in

the early '80s. After three years with Sabbath, he left to form his own band in 1983; it featured guitarist Vivian Campbell (who would later play with Whitesnake and Def Leppard), drummer Vinny Appice, ex-Rainbow bassist Jimmy Bain, and keyboardist Claude Schnell. For the rest of the '80s, Dio was one of the top metal bands, with a crunchier, more streamlined version of Sabbath's mystical vision. In 1990, Dio disbanded the group and returned to Black Sabbath for a brief time in 1991 and 1992; he soon left the band again, assembling a revamped version of Dio and began touring again. —*Stephen Thomas Erlewine*

○ **Holy Diver** / 1983 / Reprise ✦✦✦✦
Dio's first album was a platinum success, thanks to its crafty plundering of Black Sabbath's mystical imagery and heavy riffs. —*Stephen Thomas Erlewine*

The Last in Line / 1984 / Warner Brothers ✦✦✦
Even hardcore fans would be have a hard time pointing out the differences between Dio's debut, *Holy Diver,* and its follow-up, *Last in Line.* Like the band's first record, *Last in Line* was filled with a well-constructed, more pop-oriented version of Sabbath's thundering medieval fantasies and became a million-seller. —*Stephen Thomas Erlewine*

Sacred Heart / 1985 / Warner Brothers ✦✦✦
Intermission / 1986 / Reprise ✦✦
● **Dream Evil** / 1987 / Reprise ✦✦✦✦
On *Dream Evil,* Dio manages to record an album where the songwriting doesn't amount to an endless series of riffs. Instead, the record features real songs with actual melodies, making it their most accomplished album. —*Stephen Thomas Erlewine*

Lock up the Wolves / 1990 / Reprise ✦✦✦
Ronnie James Dio assembled a new version of Dio for *Lock up the Wolves,* to no apparant change in the band's sound. Nevertheless, the group's status in the metal community was beginning to slip, and the album was the lowest-charting Dio record apart from the live *Intermission.* —*Stephen Thomas Erlewine*

Strange Highways / 1994 / Reprise ✦✦

Dion & the Belmonts

Group, Rock & Roll, Doo-Wop
Like many teenagers from the '50s, Dion DiMucci (b. Jul. 18, 1939) developed his singing style from singing on street corners with neighborhood friends. Dion possessed a believable soulfulness in his delivery that enabled him to transcend the scads of doo-wop groups of the late '50s and early '60s. In 1957 Dion & the Timberlanes released their first single, "The Chosen Few" (Mohawk Records, then Jubilee Records). The band changed its name to Dion & the Belmonts (named after a Bronx avenue), signed to Laurie Records, and released their first big hit, the #22 "I Wonder Why." 1959 and 1960 were golden years for Dion & the Belmonts, with the million-selling hits "A Teenager in Love" (#5) and "Where or When" (#3).

In September 1960, Dion & the Belmonts parted ways. The Belmonts scored two more Top 40 hits with "Tell Me Why" (#18) and "Come on Little Angel" (#28). Meanwhile, Dion went solo and enjoyed a substantial string of thirteen Top 40 hits between 1960 and 1963. "Runaround Sue," "The Wanderer," and "Ruby Baby" were among the eight that went Top Ten. —*Rick Clark*

Runaround Sue / 1961 / The Right Stuff ✦✦✦
Includes the title track, "The Wanderer," the minor hit "The Majestic," covers of "Little Star," "In the Still of the Night," "Kansas City," "Dream Lover," and "Take Care of My Baby," and a few other songs that follow the blueprint of his early-'60s hits. The singing is good, but the best tracks are the hits, and they're on all the Dion compilations of note. —*Richie Unterberger*

Lovers Who Wander / 1962 / The Right Stuff ✦✦✦
A better-than-average early-'60s effort. Besides the oft-anthologized singles "Lovers Who Wander," "Little Diane," "Sandy," and "(I Was) Born to Cry," it has some hot covers ("The Twist," "Stagger Lee," and "Shout") that Dion makes his own. The haunting "Lost for Sure," which Dion co-wrote, is one of his best obscure Laurie-era tracks. —*Richie Unterberger*

○ **Dion** / 1968 / The Right Stuff ✦✦✦✦
Featuring his Top Five comeback single "Abraham, Martin And John," this folk-rock and blues-flavored effort remains his most fully realized album. In addition to the impressive anti-war original "He Looks a Lot Like Me," it contains mature interpretations,

arranged both acoustically and with strings, of songs by Fred Neil, Joni Mitchell, Leonard Cohen, Bob Dylan, and Lightnin' Hopkins (though the florid version of Jimi Hendrix's "Purple Haze" is embarrassing). The CD reissue adds the highly sought-after non-LP B-side "Daddy Rollin'," a Dion original that ranks as his most country blues-influenced performance. —*Richie Unterberger*

☆ **Everything You Always Wanted to Hear by Dion** / 1976 / Laurie ✦✦✦✦✦
The best overall collection of their classic sides. Includes "Teenager in Love," "Where or When," and "I Wonder Why." White New York doo-wop at its best. —*Cub Koda*

★ **24 Golden Greats** / 1983 / Arista ✦✦✦✦✦
This sampling of every phase of Dion's career spans from the late '50s to the early '70s. —*Dan Heilman*

○ **Greatest Hits** / 1987 / Columbia ✦✦✦✦
A solid compilation of Dion's solo sides, including "Donna the Prima Donna," "Ruby Baby," and others. —*Cub Koda*

○ **Bronx Blues: The Columbia Recordings** / 1991 / Columbia ✦✦✦✦
In the mid '60s, Dion turned away from teen-idol doo-wop material and cut several sides in a solid R&B/blues/folk vein. The best of those sides are collected here. —*Cub Koda*

Celine Dion

Group, Pop
In her native Canada as well as France, Celine Dion was a popular singer since she was a teenager. Dion's polished yet soulful adult contemporary pop didn't break in the U.S. until 1991 (when she released a record recorded in English), but when it did there was no stopping the hits; from "Where Does My Heart Beat Now" to the theme to *Beauty and the Beast,* Dion has been a fixture on the American pop charts since 1992. —*Stephen Thomas Erlewine*

○ **Unison** / 1990 / Epic ✦✦✦✦
A fine, polished American debut from this popular Canadian singer, featuring the hit singles "(If There Was) Any Other Way" and "Where Does My Heart Beat Now." —*Stephen Thomas Erlewine*

● **Celine Dion** / Mar. 31, 1992 / Epic ✦✦✦✦
Featuring the hit singles "Beauty and the Beast," "Love Can Move Mountains," and "If You Asked Me To," Celine Dion's follow-up to her successful American debut is an even stronger and more accomplished record than her previous album. —*Stephen Thomas Erlewine*

Dion Chante Plamondon / 1994 / Epic

The Colour of My Love / 550 Music/Epic ✦✦✦

Dire Straits

Group, Rock & Roll, Pop/Rock
In 1977 disco reigned and the new wave/punk movements were heralding the death of tired FM rock. It was then that Dire Straits came along with a unique blend of atmospheric blues-flavored rock and literate Dylanesque story-type lyrics. Singer, songwriter, and lead guitarist Mark Knopfler's dry, low-key vocal delivery and economical, clean guitar playing immediately hit a nerve with the public.

Aside from *Communiqué,* the band's sophomore effort, Dire Straits increasingly developed a cinematic approach to songwriting and production. *Love over Gold* is a particular highlight. It was only a natural sidestep for Knopfler to score the highly acclaimed soundtracks for *Local Hero* (1983) and *The Princess Bride* (1987). *Alchemy,* a double-record live set, was released in 1984.

In 1985 *Brothers in Arms* was released, becoming one of the biggest internationally selling albums of the '80s. The song "Money for Nothing" became free advertising for MTV, with the hook "I want my MTV."

Knopfler undertook various side projects, including the Notting Hillbillies and a fine duet album with Chet Atkins (*Neck and Neck*). Six years after the release of *Brothers in Arms, On Every Street* was released. —*Rick Clark*

☆ **Dire Straits** / Oct. 1978 / Warner Brothers ✦✦✦✦✦
Even after all the success, the debut is the best example of the intricate style of Dire Straits, dominated by the electric finger-picking of guitarist Mark Knopfler, his smoky voice and poetic lyrics. Features their first hit, "Sultans of Swing." —*William Ruhlmann*

Communiqué / Jun. 1979 / Warner Brothers ✦✦
Rushed out less than nine months after the surprise success of Dire Straits' self-titled debut album, the group's sophomore effort, *Communique* seemed little more than a carbon-copy of its predecessor with less compelling material. Mark Knopfler and co. had established a sound (derived largely from J.J. Cale) of laid-back shuffles and intricate, bluesy guitar-playing, and *Communique* provided more examples of it. But there was no track as focused as "Sultans of Swing," even if "Lady Writer" (a lesser singles chart entry on both sides of the Atlantic) nearly duplicated its sound. As a result, *Communique* sold immediately to Dire Straits' established audience, but no more, and it did not fare as well critically as its predecessor or its follow-up. —*William Ruhlmann*

○ **Making Movies** / Oct. 17, 1980 / Warner Brothers ✦✦✦✦
The third album displays Knopfler's expanding ambitions as a songwriter with, as the title suggests, a cinematic sweep on such songs as "Tunnel of Love" and "Romeo and Juliet." —*William Ruhlmann*

○ **Love over Gold** / Sep. 1982 / Warner Brothers ✦✦✦✦
The fourth Dire Straits album is their most atmospheric effort, featuring the spacious title track as well as the epic "Telegraph Road," with the extended guitar workout at its conclusion. —*Rick Clark*

Twisting by the Pool [EP] / Feb. 1983 / Warner Brothers ✦✦✦
Dire Straits followed the ponderous *Love Over Gold* five months later with a three-song EP paced by its title track, which lived up to its name by adopting a twist beat, making it the closest thing to exuberant rock 'n' roll this seemingly humorless band had ever attempted. "Two Young Lovers" had the same early rock feel, and even "If I Had You" was taken at a quicker tempo than had become common on Dire Straits albums. *Twisting by the Pool* didn't quite turn Dire Straits into a dance band, but it went a long way toward lightening up the group's image and repertoire. —*William Ruhlmann*

Alchemy: Dire Straits Live / Mar. 1984 / Warner Brothers ✦✦✦
There is an interesting contrast on this 94-minute double-disc live album (recorded at London's Hammersmith Odeon in July 1983) between the music, much of which is slow and moody, with Mark Knopfler's muttered vocals and large helpings of his fingerpicking on what sounds like an amplified Spanish guitar, and the audience response. The arena-size crowd cheers wildly and claps and sings along, when given half a chance, as though each song were an up-tempo rocker. When they do have a song of even medium speed, such as "Sultans of Swing" or "Solid Rock," they are in ecstasy. That Dire Straits' introspective music loses much of its detail in a live setting matters less than that it gains presence and a sense of anticipation. Alan Clark's keyboards help to fill out the sound and give Knopfler's spare melodies a certain majesty, but Dire Straits remains an overgrown pub band with a Bob Dylan fixation, and that's exactly how the crowd likes it. (The CD version of the album contains one extra track, "Expresso Love," which adds a needed change of pace to the otherwise slow-moving first disc.) —*William Ruhlmann*

○ **Brothers in Arms** / May 1985 / Warner Brothers ✦✦✦✦
Their biggest-selling album, containing the mega-hit "Money for Nothing" as well as "Walk of Life" and "So Far Away." —*William Ruhlmann*

● **Money for Nothing** / Oct. 1988 / Warner Brothers ✦✦✦✦
This best-of collection contains Dire Straits' biggest hits as well as some key album tracks. "Sultans of Swing," "Walk of Life," "Money for Nothing," plus a live version of "Telegraph Road" from *Love over Gold,* are among the highlights. Even though this may be a fairly representative sampler, listening to the better albums in their entirety is the best way to hear this band. —*Rick Clark*

On Every Street / Sep. 1991 / Warner Brothers ✦✦
It took Mark Knopfler more than six years to craft a followup to Dire Straits' international chart-topper, *Brothers In Arms,* but although *On Every Street* sold in the expected multi-millions worldwide on the back of the band's renown and a year-long tour, it was a disappointment. Knopfler remained a gifted guitar player with tastes in folk ("Iron Hand"), blues ("Fade to Black"), and rockabilly ("The Bug"), among other styles, but much of the album was low-key to the point of being background music. The group had long since dwindled to original members Knopfler and bassist John Illsley, plus a collection of semi-permanent sidemen who provided support but no real musical chemistry. This was not the comeback it should have been. —*William Ruhlmann*

On the Night / May 11, 1993 / Warner Brothers ◆◆
A live document of Dire Straits' 1991-92 world tour supporting the
On Every Street album, *On the Night* works sporadically, offering
enough good material to interest fans but not enough to win back
the commercial audience earned by *Brothers in Arms*. —*Stephen
Thomas Erlewine*

Dirty Looks

Group, Rock & Roll
Dirty Looks (not to be confused with the late-'80s metal band of
the same name) were formed in the late '70s in Staten Island, New
York. Composed of Patrick Barnes (guitar/vocals), Peter Parker
(drums/vocals) and Marco Sin (bass/vocals), the trio began playing
their hard-rocking power-pop at Max's Kansas City and CBGB's
where they were discovered by Stiff Records' Dave Robinson.
Robinson signed them, anticipating they were "the next big thing."
After releasing one brilliant single ("Let Go"), a good but unfortunately overlooked debut LP for Stiff, and a mediocre follow-up, the
band faded into obscurity. —*Chris Woodstra*

○ **Dirty Looks** / 1980 / Stiff ◆◆◆◆
The band's self-titled debut showed a lot of promise with its lean,
hard-driving power-pop and near-perfect single, "Let Go." Just
barely out of touch with the times, they drifted a little too close to
bar-band territory to fit in with the new wave of the time. —*Chris
Woodstra*

Turn It Up / 1981 / Stiff ◆◆◆
After failing with the edgy approach, the band enlisted Nick Garvey (ex-Ducks Deluxe/Motors) for production and moved toward
a slicker, more mainstream sound—a poor choice, considering that
Garvey was probably better suited to bring out the rock & roll side
of the band. None of the songs even approach the last batch. A sad
end to a band that could have been… —*Chris Woodstra*

The Disposable Heroes of the Hipoprisy

Group, Rap, Urban
Michael Franti's deep and defiant tones were the lure for this
short-lived group which didn't bill itself a rap band. Franti's resemblance in style, tone and timbre to Gil Scott-Heron, plus his
willingness to tackle targets ranging from television to fellow rappers won them immediate attention. There were charges that the
Disposable Heroes of the Hipoprisy were themselves engaging in
hypocrisy by not identifying with rappers, yet cashing in on the
genre's popularity. They issued only one album before disbanding.
—*Ron Wynn*

● **Hypocrisy Is the Greatest Luxury** / 1992 / 4th & Broadway
◆◆◆◆
Hard-hitting political rap that is excellent on the rhetoric and
lyrics but a bit weak on the grooves, it's closer to Gil Scott-Heron
than Public Enemy. —*AMG*

The Divinyls

Group, Pop/Rock
The Divinyls combined the raw, simple hard rock of AC/DC with
a new wave pop sensibility. Formed in 1981 in Sydney, Australia,
by vocalist Christina Amphlett and guitarist Mark McEntee, the
band's first release was a soundtrack for the 1982 Australian film
Monkey Grip, which featured an appearance by Amphlett. Taken
from the EP *Monkey Grip*, the single "Boys in Town" became an
Top Ten hit in Australia, leading to a contract with Chrysalis
Records. The band released their first full-length album, *Desperate*, in 1983. The record became a hit in Australia, but it didn't
make much of an impression in the U.S. or the U.K. *What a Life*,
their second album, appeared in 1985 and managed to chart in the
U.S. but its Australian sales did not equal *Desperate*. After the release of 1988's *Temperamental*, the Divinyls officially became a
duo, with original bassist Rick Grossman leaving the band to join
the Hoodoo Gurus. Three years later, the group released *Divinyls*.
The album became their first big hit album in America and
Britain, thanks to the single "I Touch Myself," a catchy, tongue-in-
cheek song about masturbation. In both countries, the song was
treated as a novelty and subsequent singles failed to chart. —
Stephen Thomas Erlewine

Desperate / 1983 / Chrysalis ◆◆◆
This Australian band, built around Christina Amphlett's hiccuping
vocals and Mark McEntee's rude grunge-guitar work, made an impressive debut with *Desperate*, a record that blends the thick cho-

rusy guitar sound of the Pretenders with a punkish hard rock reck-
lessness. Raw, ugly noises abound on this, their best studio album.
Highlights include "Take a Chance," "Only Lonely," and "Boys in
Town." —*Rick Clark*

What a Life! / 1985 / Chrysalis ◆◆
● **Essential** / 1987 / Chrysalis ◆◆◆◆
This good compilation contains key radio tracks, but some great
album sides are omitted. Still, it's a good place to start. —*Rick
Clark*

Temperamental / 1988 / Chrysalis ◆◆
Divinyls / 1991 / Virgin ◆◆◆
Only a couple of tracks of note: the highly song-crafted ode to
auto-eroticism, "I Touch Myself" (their biggest hit), and "Make Out
Alright." —*Rick Clark*

The Dixie Dregs

Group, Fusion
This Georgia-based instrumental fusion band developed quite a
following during the late '70s with their musical chops, band
chemistry, and complicated (but solidly melodic) compositions,
primarily written by guitarist Steve Morse. —*Rick Clark*

The Great Spectacular / 1975 / No Label ◆◆
Free Fall / 1977 / Polydor ◆◆◆
A potent debut, it presents the Dregs' melodic instrumental fusion
to fine effect. —*Jas Obrecht*

○ **What If** / 1978 / Polydor ◆◆◆◆
Of all the albums by the Dregs, this is the one to get. Steve Morse's
melodies have an otherwordly elegance on songs like "Night
Meets Light." The band plays with just the right amount of restraint. Ken Scott's production is, at turns, atmospheric and immediate. "Take It off the Top" is a fine rocker. —*Rick Clark*

Night of the Living Dregs / 1979 / Polydor ◆◆◆
This is a good half-live, half-studio set. —*Jas Obrecht*

Dregs of the Earth / 1980 / Arista ◆◆◆
Unsung Heroes / 1981 / Arista ◆◆◆
Industry Standard / 1982 / Arista ◆◆◆
● **Divided We Stand: Best of the Dixie Dregs** / 1989 / Arista ◆◆◆◆
A decent selection of their best work while signed to Capricorn, it
includes "Cruise Control," a live version of "Refried Funky
Chicken," and a healthy sampling from *What If*. —*Rick Clark*

Bring 'em Back Alive / Feb. 1992 / Capricorn ◆◆◆
Full Circle / 1994 / Capricorn ◆◆

Don Dixon

Rock & Roll, Singer-Songwriter, Pop/Rock
While his own records never reached a mass audience, Don Dixon
was one of the major figures in the post-punk Southern guitar pop
of the '80s. Dixon produced R.E.M., Let's Active, the Smithereens,
and Marti Jones during the decade, bringing his sharp pop sensibilities to their already highly melodic songs. But his true talents
shine in his solo albums. Dixon is successfully able to recall everything from Beatlesque pop and Southern soul to gritty country
and R&B with his lean, muscular pop; he adds an engagingly
twisted lyrical view to his effortlessly eclectic music, making him
one of the best subversive pop singer/songwriters since Nick
Lowe. —*Stephen Thomas Erlewine*

○ **Most of the Girls Like to Dance But Only Some of The Boys Do**
/ 1985 / Enigma ◆◆◆◆
Dixon put together *Most of the Girls Like to Dance but Only Some
of the Boys Like To* out of demos cut from 1981-1984. It's a kind of
best-of from a man with a pure pop sensibility and a wicked sense
of humor when it comes to matters romantic. (The 1986 CD version adds two songs to make a total of 16.) —*William Ruhlmann*

○ **Romeo at Juilliard** / Sep. 1987 / Enigma ◆◆◆◆
Dixon's domestic debut featured more of his skewed songs, and
here he was aided and abetted by such compatriots as Mitch
Easter and Marti Jones (who is his wife). —*William Ruhlmann*

Chi-Town Budget Show / 1989 / Enigma ◆◆◆
An intimate live album featuring many of the best songs from the
two previous albums. —*William Ruhlmann*

Eee / Sep. 20, 1989 / Enigma ✦✦✦

● **If I'm a Ham, Well You're A Sausage** / Mar. 3, 1992 / Restless ✦✦✦✦
While he is known mainly through his production work, this extensive best-of collection shows Dixon to be an equally sharp songwriter and performer. —*Chris Woodstra*

Romantic Depressive / Mar. 28, 1995 / Sugar Hill ✦✦✦
Don Dixon produces another set of well-crafted mid-'60s-style pop-rock songs on his Sugar Hill Records debut, playing most of the instruments and singing in his husky voice. The album title catches the tone of many of the lyrics, which turn on romantic reversals. Though Dixon continues to sound like a man who never got over the British Invasion of 1964, he does locate one song several years later, reminiscing in "Lottery of Lives" about a point in the Vietnam Era when his student deferment was in doubt. —*William Ruhlmann*

D.J. Jazzy Jeff & the Fresh Prince

Group, Rap
If you're looking for bubble-gum rap, these guys are your best bet. The Prince spins his teen-suburban tales in a pleasant, if facile fashion, and Jeff isn't bad on the turntable. Don't look for anything gritty or street-smart: when Jeff boasts that he can beat Mike Tyson, that's about as menacing as it gets. The Fresh Prince starred in the early-'90s TV sitcom, *The Prince of Bel Air.*

Will Smith, the "Fresh Prince" part of the team, has greatly expanded his horizons in the '90s. He appeared in the films *Six Degrees of Separation* and *Bad Boys,* and also tried to expand his hip-hop horizons enough to offset the talk that his raps had become hopelessy whitebread and irrelevant. *Homebase* in 1991 included "Dog Is a Dog" and the Top Ten pop hit "Summertime," with Smith's rap done in a leaner, harder fashion even if the lyrics were pretty much family hour. But by *Code Red* in 1993 it seemed Smith had made peace with his image and was back to laid back, pop-oriented material such as "Boom! Shake the Room," "I Wanna Rock," and "Can't Wait to Be with You" which had a guest stint from Christopher Williams. —*John Floyd*

Rock the House / 1987 / Jive ✦✦✦
A 10-song work originally issued on Pop Art Records and later picked up by Jive. Containing the hit "Girls Ain't Nothing But Trouble," which launched them as the kings of teen/clean rap, it had maximum crossover appeal yet retained a large following among the core hip-hop audience. —*Ron Wynn*

● **He's the D.J. I'm The Rapper** / 1988 / Jive ✦✦✦✦
Their commercial breakthrough contains their #12 hit, "Parents Just Don't Understand," and other good-time raps. —*Dan Heilman*

And in This Corner . . . / 1989 / Jive ✦✦✦
More wit and whim from Jeff and the Prince, this time with assistance from saxes, flutes, and trumpets. Though not as commercially successful as its predecessors, it's actually a more faithful rap work. —*Ron Wynn*

○ **Homebase** / 1991 / Jive ✦✦✦✦
After enduring a temporary sales slump, D.J. Jazzy Jeff and the Fresh Prince roared back with *Homebase.* They scored a huge pop and R&B hit with "Summertime," using Kool & the Gang's "Summer Madness" single for the music base while Will Smith rapped about romantic hopes and community barbeques. He landed another Top 20 single with "Ring My Bell," this time reworking Anita Ward's oldie while offering his own double-entendre take. Undoubtedly helped by the success of his television show, this album returned the duo to platinum status, even as Smith showed once more (protests to the contrary notwithstanding) that he was an accomplished pop rapper. —*Ron Wynn*

Code Red / Oct. 12, 1993 / Jive ✦✦✦
After years of proclaiming that he wouldn't do gangsta rap, the Fresh Prince finally succumbs to a harder-edged style on *Code Red.* And, surprisingly, he pulls it off well, thanks to sharp production and his endearing personality. —*Stephen Thomas Erlewine*

Ring My Bell / Jive ✦✦

DJ Quik

Rap
Compton rapper DJ Quik made a strong debut as a 20-year-old in 1991 with his debut *Quik Is the Name* on Profile. The single "Jus Lyke Compton" was an R&B hit, and both it and "Tonite" got some mild pop response. The second LP *Way 2 Fonky* peaked at 14 on

the pop albums chart in 1992, and was even more explicit and vulgar than its predecessor. —*Ron Wynn*

● **Quik Is the Name** / 1991 / Profile ✦✦✦✦
DJ Quik was 20 years old when he came roaring out of the chute in 1991 with the single "Tonite." It was a mild hit, while "Quik's Groove," "Born and Raised in Compton" and "Deep" were more appropriate for establishing Quik as another in the continuing line of hard West Coast rappers. While overdosing on the sexist references, Quik's furious pace and flippant style signaled that he could be a hip-hop force. —*Ron Wynn*

○ **Way 2 Fonky** / 1992 / Profile ✦✦✦✦
DJ Quik proved his mettle with "Jus Lyke Compton," a definitive bit of regional touting that proclaimed West Coast rap the style setter and all others followers. Whether or not you bought the line, you were hooked by the rap. Nothing else on the disc matched this single's intensity and wit, but it helped him earn a second straight gold LP. —*Ron Wynn*

Safe & Sound / 1995 / Profile ✦✦✦
Caught up with extolling his sexiness and success with women, DJ Quik raps about little else on his third album. The lyrics are funny though, and his G-funk grooves do help things. —*John Bush*

DMZ

Group, Garage Rock
Before Jeff "Monoman" Connolly formed Boston's seminal garage-rock terrorists the Lyres, he was in a late-'70s prototype known as DMZ. With the exception of a few musicians, DMZ and the Lyres were essentially same-sounding bands; DMZ just played with a little more speed and punk verve. Oddly enough, during the late-'70s signing frenzy of any band even remotely associated with the punk scenes in Boston and New York City, DMZ got a shot with Sire Records. The label, exhibiting near-total artistic myopia, teamed the band up with goofball has-beens Flo and Eddie as producers. While the resulting record was panned, it's far from a disaster, due mainly to DMZ's ferocity and trashy ebullience. Fans of mid-'60s rock such as the Seeds, ? & the Mysterians, and the Kinks, and who have an unending jones for speedy trash-rock and whiny Farfisa organs, will love DMZ. —*John Dougan*

DMZ / 1978 / Sire ✦✦✦
The infamous debut record. Flo and Eddie's production doesn't help, but DMZ's retrogressive sound did not, at the time, fit the punk model. As a result, they seemed curiously out of place when compared to the other Sire offerings, specifically the Ramones and Richard Hell and the Voidoids. Still, this record explodes from the turntable with the benzedrine grunge of "Mighty Idy" and doesn't let up. Sure, it could've been better, but it's not nearly as bad as has been alleged. —*John Dougan*

Relics / 1981 / Voxx ✦✦✦

● **Live 1978!!** / 1986 / Crypt ✦✦✦✦
Recorded in front of an audience of maybe 20 in a tacky little club called Barnaby's in beautiful Methuen, Massachusetts (you can hear the pinball machines being played in the background), this low-fi chunk of beer-soaked rock was recorded right after the release of their debut LP (Connolly plugs it repeatedly) and it's breathless, fast, furious and fun, fun, fun. Great originals, better covers and Monoman ragin' full-on. Sound quality is so-so, but who could ask for anything more? —*John Dougan*

DNA

Group, New Wave, Experimental
One of the great bands of the short-lived, New York City-based, late-'70s "no wave" avant-garde punk scene, DNA had what barely amounts to a recording career, yet still managed to record some crucial music. Originally comprised of guitarist Arto Lindsay, keyboardist Robin Crutchfield, and drummer Ikue Mori, DNA's music was sparse, loud and noisy—washes of keyboards punctuated by Lindsay's atonal, free-form guitar explosions. DNA made their recording debut in 1978 on a sampler of no-wave bands produced by Brian Eno (*No New York*), and, along with being one of the more interesting bands on the record, also exhibited the most promise. By the time they released their first record, Crutchfield had formed a new band, the far less interesting Dark Day, and DNA had replaced him with bassist Tim Wright, an original member of the seminal Cleveland band Pere Ubu. Now a power trio, and with Lindsay's guitar the manic focal point of this challenging music, DNA seemed poised to become one of the most exciting

bands in American avant-garde rock. Instead, they became increasingly enigmatic, rarely played outside of New York, and never recorded again. After breaking up in 1982, Lindsay formed the exciting Ambitious Lovers, who have released three tremendous albums fusing noise-rock with slick pop/soul and Brazilian music (Lindsay is a native of Brazil). He has produced records for Brazilian superstar Caetano Veloso. Ikue Mori is still performing avant-garde music in her native Japan. In 1993, thanks to John Zorn's great Japanese-import label (read: expensive), a DNA CD of previously unavailable live recordings was released. —*John Dougan*

● **A Taste of DNA** / 1981 / American Clave ✦✦✦✦
The title of this EP couldn't be more appropriate, clocking in at less than 10 minutes; this is a taste, but it will definitely make you hungry for more (it's a shame there isn't much more). Lindsay's guitar is out of control, and Wright's bass playing more than makes up for the loss of Crutchfield's keyboards. For fans of ebullient and exciting noise rock, this release will show you where the contemporary Japanese noise bands (e.g., the Bordeoms) got their inspiration. —*John Dougan*

Last Live at CBGB's / 1993 / Avant ✦✦✦
The sound quality isn't state of the art, but for those who were blown away by what this band could do then, hearing them shred through their live set is worth the effort (and money; Avant releases are expensive). Recorded at the world famous Bowery punk club in 1982, this is a churning, sonic fireball of bliss, despite the fidelity problems. —*John Dougan*

DOA

Group, Punk
A seminal Vancouver-based hardcore combo who shared common ground with the early Clash in both their lyrical commitment and their cogent musical structure. —*John Floyd*

Triumph of the Ignoroids [EP] / 1979 / Can. Friends ✦✦✦
The live first effort features the vocals and machine-gun-like guitar of frontman, Joey Shithead. —*David Szatmary*

Something Better Change / 1980 / Can. Friends ✦✦✦
This is the studio debut of Canada's premier hardcore outfit. —*David Szatmary*

● **Bloodied But Unbowed** / 1984 / Alternative Tentacles ✦✦✦✦
A compilation (1978-1983), it captures the wild, uninhibited exuberance of these Vancouver punksters. —*David Szatmary*

True (North), Strong & Free / 1987 / Profile ✦✦✦
Toned-down but still political hardcore. —*David Szatmary*

Talk—Action = Zero / 1988 / Restless ✦✦✦
More political mosh music from Canada's finest. —*David Szatmary*

The D.O.C.

Group, Rap
After the release of his debut album, the career of Texas-born rapper the D.O.C. was shattered by a car crash that almost took his life.
  Although he could no longer rap like he used to, his former producer Dr. Dre featured the rapper on his groundbreaking album *The Chronic*, which built on the foundation laid by the D.O.C.'s *No One Can Do It Better*; he was also featured on Snoop Doggy Dogg's *Doggystyle*. —*Stephen Thomas Erlewine*

★ **No One Can Do It Better** / 1989 / Ruthless ✦✦✦✦✦
This Texas-born rapper hooks up with Dr. Dre of N.W.A. fame to make an effective effort fusing funk, hip-hop, soul, and reggae, along with some tough, taut commentary and raps. Guest spots from Eazy-E, Miche'le, and MC Ren. —*Ron Wynn*

So How Ya Livin'? / 1991 / Star Song ✦✦
○ **Straight from the Basement of Kooley High** / Def Jam ✦✦✦✦
This rambling, wildly erratic session contained enough mildly amusing elements for a good record, but lacked coherence and focus. It seemed like a work in progress, and the raps fluctuated from being clever to silly to boring. The same held true for the production and rhymes. —*Ron Wynn*

Dr. Buzzard's Original Savannah Band

Group, Disco
Dr. Buzzard's Original Savannah Band was one of the most original musical ensembles of the disco era. They were formed in the Bronx in 1974 by Stony Browder, Jr. (b. 1949), his brother August

Darnell (born Thomas Browder, 1951), singer Cory Daye (b. 1952), Andy Hernandez (b. 1950), and Mickey Sevilla (b. 1953). The concept of the group was the re-creation of a '30s dance band...a la Cab Calloway, with witty lyrics and a disco beat. All of this was in evidence on their debut album, *Dr. Buzzard's Original Savannah Band*, released in 1976. It produced the dance-floor hit "Cherchez La Femme" and went gold. A follow-up album, *Dr. Buzzard's Original Savannah Band Meets King Pennett*, was less successful. After the release of a third album, *James Monroe HS Presents Dr. Buzzard's Original Savannah Band Goes to Washington*, the group fragmented, with Darnell and Hernandez going off to form Kid Creole & the Coconuts. Browder reorganized and issued a Dr. Buzzard's Savannah Band (dropping the "original") album titled *Calling All Beatniks!* in 1984. —*William Ruhlmann*

● **Dr. Buzzard's Original Savannah Band** / 1976 / RCA ✦✦✦✦
Dr. Buzzard introduced a big-band sheen to '70s dance music with the hit "Cherchez la Femme" and the rest of this charmingly neo-retro album. —*William Ruhlmann*

Doctor Dre

Urban
Hip-hop's reigning star and sales giant Andre "Dr. Dre" Young was originally a member of World Class Wreckin' Cru along with DJ Antoine "Yella" Carraby. They left that group to join Eric "Eazy-E" Wright, Lorenzo "M.C. Ren" Patterson and Oshea "Ice Cube" Jackson in creating N.W.A. Their 1989 album *Straight Outta Compton* shocked many observers with its explicit vulgarity and sexism, but it immediately shot them to the top, eventually becoming a double platinum record. N.W.A. stayed in the spotlight a couple of years, then splintered due to internal strife and the defection of Ice Cube and Eazy-E. Eazy-E, Ice Cube and Dr. Dre also had a falling out over fiscal matters involving their former label Ruthless Records and ex-agent Jerry Heller.
  Dre emerged as the head of his own organization and a solo star as a rapper/producer in 1993; his protégé Snoop Doggy Dogg became an equally huge star, rapping in a lower-key, off-rhythm fashion. Dre's commanding, brusque and menacing cadences, coupled with his skillful adoption of Parliament/Funkadelic and classic funk beats made *The Chronic* a rap juggernaut. —*Ron Wynn*

☆ **The Chronic** / 1993 / Death Row ✦✦✦✦✦
With its deeply funky George Clinton-inspired grooves, whining synthesizers, female backing vocals, and romantic gangsta tales, *The Chronic* redefined hip-hop for the 1990s. Dr. Dre's genius lies in keeping the funk loose but concise, creating perfect singles like "Down Wit Dre Day," "Let Me Ride," and "Nuthin' but a 'G' Thang." For all his musical genius, Dr. Dre remains an unspectacular rapper, which makes Snoop Doggy Dogg all the more remarkable. Snoop raps as much as Dre throughout *The Chronic*, and his surreally menacing drawl shows the reality behind the stylized portraits of sex and violence. —*Stephen Thomas Erlewine*

Dr. Feelgood

Group, Rock & Roll
Although they never strayed from their gritty R&B-based sound, Dr. Feelgood was a fixture on England's rock & roll scene since the early '70s. While their music wasn't particularly influential, their method of playing was. Dr. Feelgood constantly traveled England, playing to sold-out clubs across the country; with their devoted following, they helped create the pub-rock scene in the U.K.—venues where rough rock & roll bands could pound out anything from R&B to pop to simple, three-chord rock. By proving these clubs were profitable, the band helped pave the way for the success of punk rock in England; punk bands played the same bars and clubs that Dr. Feelgood, Brinsley Schwarz and other pub rockers played in the early '70s. Over the years, the band's lineup changed frequently with vocalist/harmonica player Lee Brilleaux being the only constant member. Brilleaux's energy never diminished as he got older; his consistently vibrant live performances were the reasons why Dr. Feelgood was such a concert draw.
  Even though he had been performing for over twenty years, Brilleaux remained a force to be reckoned with when he was on stage, right until his untimely death in April of 1994. —*Stephen Thomas Erlewine*

○ **Down by the Jetty** / Jan. 1975 / United Artists ✦✦✦✦
Dr. Feelgood's debut album is on a par with the early Rolling Stones albums as a demonstration of R&B fervor. Every track burns. —*Bruce Eder*

● **Malpractice** / Feb. 1975 / Columbia ✦✦✦✦
Guitarist Wilko Johnson's songs shine against such inspired covers as "Riot in Cell Block #9." And his Stonesy playing takes no prisoners. —*Bruce Eder*

Stupidity / 1976 / United Artists ✦✦
Despite a handful of fine moments, the live *Stupidity* doesn't quite capture Dr. Feelgood at its best. —*Stephen Thomas Erlewine*

○ **Sneakin' Suspicion** / 1977 / Columbia ✦✦✦✦
Wilko Johnson's last album with Dr. Feelgood continues to be dominated by his tough guitar playing, although fewer of his songs are heard. —*Bruce Eder*

○ **Be Seeing You** / 1977 / United Artists ✦✦✦✦
The Nick Lowe-produced *Be Seeing You*, Dr. Feelgood's first album with guitarist John Mayo, was only slightly weaker than the group's previous records. Although Mayo was still working his way into the band's sound, Dr. Feelgood retained their tough, hard-rocking appeal. —*Stephen Thomas Erlewine*

Private Practice / 1978 / United Artists ✦✦
Private Practice was Doctor Feelgood's first bland and uninspired record, due to the group's flat performances. —*Stephen Thomas Erlewine*

As It Happens / 1979 / United Artists ✦✦
The live *As It Happens* captures Dr. Feelgood at one of its weakest stages, as John Mayo was still finding his place in the group. Furthermore, the band relies on second-rate material throughout the record, making *As It Happens* a minor addition to the group's catalog. —*Stephen Thomas Erlewine*

Let It Roll / 1979 / United Artists ✦✦
Let It Roll was an improvement on the band's two previous records, yet it still wasn't up to the standards of *Sneakin' Suspicion* and *Malpractice*. —*Stephen Thomas Erlewine*

A Case of the Shakes / 1980 / United Artists ✦✦✦
A Case of the Shakes, the group's second album recorded with Nick Lowe, proved that Dr. Feelgood's last three records simply captured the band in a transitional phase. On *Shakes*, the band returns to form, ripping through a set of catchy three-chord rockers that are invigorated by Lowe's new wave-tinged production. —*Stephen Thomas Erlewine*

On the Job / 1981 / Liberty ✦✦
On the Job was another competent but unremarkable live record. —*Stephen Thomas Erlewine*

○ **Casebook** / 1981 / Liberty ✦✦✦✦
Casebook is an effective compilation, containing most of the highlights from Dr. Feelgood's first six years. —*Stephen Thomas Erlewine*

Fast Women & Slow Horses / 1982 / Chiswick ✦✦

Doctor's Orders / 1984 / Demon ✦✦✦

○ **Mad Man Blues** / 1986 / ID ✦✦✦✦
Lee Brilleaux and Dr. Feelgood sound positively revitalized on *Mad Man Blues*, a collection of raw versions of blues standards that is their best album since 1977's *Be Seeing You*. —*Stephen Thomas Erlewine*

Brilleaux / 1986 / Grand ✦✦✦

○ **Case History** / 1987 / EMI ✦✦✦✦

○ **Singles (The UA Years)** / 1989 / Liberty ✦✦✦✦

Live in London / 1990 / Grand ✦✦

Dr. Hook

Group, Country-Rock, Pop/Rock
This American country-rock band was originally named Dr. Hook and the Medicine Show. Formed in New Jersey in 1968, the original members included Ray Sawyer (b. 1937), Dennis Locorriere (b. 1948), Bill Francis, John David, and George Cummings. First coming to prominence with material written by Shel Silverstein, the looniness of their stage show transferred to records well, reaching its peak with the mega-hit "The Cover of the *Rolling Stone*" in 1972. They mellowed their style on record, hitting the charts with ballads as the decade wore on, but they were still crazy in live performances. Sawyer continues to front versions of the band to this day on various oldies package shows. —*Cub Koda*

● **Greatest Hits** / May 1987 / Capitol ✦✦✦✦
It includes "Sexy Eyes," "Sylvia's Mother," "Only Sixteen," "When You're in Love with a Beautiful Woman," and "Cover of the *Rolling Stone*." —*AMG*

Dr. John

Group, R&B, Rock & Roll, Pop/Rock
Dr. John (born Mac Rebennack) honed his skills playing '50s sessions during the heyday of New Orleans R&B. His solo work has alternately paid homage to his inspirations and incorporated those influences into his own distinct rhythmic roux. —*John Floyd*

○ **Gris Gris** / 1968 / Repertoire ✦✦✦✦
The most exploratory and psychedelic outing of Dr. John's career, a one-of-a-kind fusion of New Orleans Mardi Gras R&B and voodoo mysticism. Great rasping, bluesy vocals, soulful backup singers, and eerie melodies on flute, sax, and clarinet, as well as odd Middle Eastern-like chanting and mandolin runs. It's got the setting of a strange religious ritual, but the mood is far more joyous than solemn. —*Richie Unterberger*

Babylon / 1969 / Atco ✦✦✦
Dr. John's ambition remained undiminished on his second solo album, *Babylon*, released shortly after the groundbreaking voodoo-psychedelia-New Orleans R&B fusion of his debut, *Gris-Gris*. The results, however, were not nearly as consistent or impressive. Coolly received by critics, the album nonetheless is deserving of attention, though it pales a bit in comparison with *Gris-Gris*. The production is sparser and more reliant an female backup vocals than his debut. Dr. John remains intent on fusing voodoo and R&B, but the mood is oddly bleak and despairing, in comparison with the wild Mardi Gras-gone-amok tone of his first LP. The hushed, damned atmosphere and afterhours R&B sound a bit like Van Morrison on a bummer trip at times, as peculiar as that might seem. "The Patriotic Flag-Waiver" (sic), in keeping with the mood of the late '60s, damns social ills and hypocrisy of all sorts. An FM underground radio favorite at the time, its ambitious structure remains admirable, though its musical imperfections haven't worn well. To a degree, you could say the same about the album as a whole. But it has enough of an eerie fascination to merit investigation. —*Richie Unterberger*

Remedies / 1970 / Atco ✦✦

Sun Moon & Herbs / Sep. 1971 / Atco ✦✦✦

○ **Dr. John's Gumbo** / Apr. 1972 / Atco ✦✦✦✦
Dr. John's finest album offered a selection of classic New Orleans R&B, including "Tipitina" and "Junko Partner," updated with a dirty, funky beat. Two decades later, his interpretations sound as timeless as the original singles. —*Stephen Thomas Erlewine*

In the Right Place / Mar. 1973 / Atco ✦✦✦

Desitively Bonaroo / Apr. 1974 / Atco ✦✦✦

Hollywood Be Thy Name / 1975 / Beat Goes On ✦✦

City Lights / Feb. 1978 / Horizon ✦✦✦

Tango Palace / 1979 / Horizon ✦✦
Dr. John's second and final album for the Horizon jazz subsidiary of A&M Records finds him working with producers Tommy LiPuma and Hugh McCracken on a rollicking set that emphasizes his New Orleans roots while attempting to update his sound with '70s effects such as deep, plucked bass notes and occasional disco rhythms. The album leads off with "Keep That Music Simple," a somewhat caustic admonishment to musicians and the music business whose message is disregarded elsewhere on the record, as LiPuma and McCracken seek to cover all stylistic bases from funk to fusion to second line. Dr. John emerges from the production intact, but he is not quite as swampy as when heard at his best. —*William Ruhlmann*

○ **Dr. John Plays Mac Rebennack** / 1981 / Clean Cuts ✦✦✦✦

Brightest Smile in Town / 1983 / Clean Cuts ✦✦✦
Doctor John's second solo piano album finds him combining country, blues, and New Orleans standards with originals, half of them instrumentals and half of them containing vocals that sound like they were recorded off the piano microphone. This is not a high-tech recording, by any means, but in its unadorned way it does capture the flavor of Doctor John as directly as any record he's made. —*William Ruhlmann*

In a Sentimental Mood / Apr. 1989 / Warner Brothers ✦✦✦
On Dr. John's first major-label effort and first vocal studio album in ten years, he performs a set of pop standards including Cole Porter's "Love for Sale" and Johnny Mercer's "Accentuate the Positive." After starting out with a wild stage act and unusual costumes, Dr. John has evolved into a vocal stylist and piano virtuoso, which makes the idea of doing this sort of material appealing. And

he does it well, turning out a leisurely duet with Rickie Lee Jones on "Makin' Whoopee" that won a Grammy (Best Jazz Vocal Performance, Duo or Group) and giving sad feeling to "My Buddy." Maybe he has changed since the *Gris-Gris* days, but even a mellowed Dr. John is a tasty voice. — *William Ruhlmann*

Bluesiana II / 1991 / Windham Hill ✦✦✦
Previously, Windham Hill Records released *Bluesiana Triangle*, a jazz trio album by drummer Art Blakey, pianist Dr. John, and reed man David "Fathead" Newman. Blakey passed away in 1990, but in the spring of 1991, Dr. John and Newman organized this second Bluesiana session, featuring trombonist Ray Anderson, drummer Will Calhoun, bassists Essiet Okon Essiet and Jay Leonhart (on different tracks), and percussionist Joe Bonadio. The resulting music again justifies the name, blues played in a funky Louisiana style with plenty of room for extended jazzy soloing. Though much of the material was written by Dr. John and he does sing occasionally, this is not a conventional Dr. John vocal album. It does contain some excellent playing, however. — *William Ruhlmann*

Goin' Back to New Orleans / Jun. 23, 1992 / Warner Brothers ✦✦✦
Having cut an album of standards on his first Warner Brothers album, *In A Sentimental Mood* (1989), Dr. John turned for its followup to a collection of *New Orleans* standards. On an album he described in the liner notes as "a little history of New Orleans music," Dr. John returned to his hometown and set up shop at local Ultrasonic Studios, inviting in such local musicians as Pete Fountain, Al Hirt, and the Neville Brothers and addressing the music and styles of such local legends as Jelly Roll Morton, Huey "Piano" Smith, Fats Domino, James Booker, and Professor Longhair. The geography may have been circumscribed, but the stylistic range was extensive, from jazz and blues to folk and rock. And it was all played with festive conviction—Dr. John is the perfect archivist for the music, being one of its primary popularizers, yet he had never addressed it quite as directly as he did here. — *William Ruhlmann*

● **Anthology** / 1993 / Rhino ✦✦✦✦
Over his 35 years of recording, Mac "Dr. John" Rebennack has worn many hats, from '50s greasy rock & roller to psychedelic '70s weirdo to keeper of the New Orleans music flame. All of these modes, plus more, are excellently served up on this two-disc anthology. From the early New Orleans sides featuring Rebennack's blistering guitar work ("Storm Warning" and "Morgus The Magnificent") to the fabled '70s sides as The Night Tripper to his present day status as repository of the Crescent City's noble musical tradition, this is the one you want to have for the collection. —*Cub Koda*

Television / Mar. 29, 1994 / GRP ✦✦
Dr. John's debut for GRP doesn't deviate from any release he's made for several other labels. It's still his chunky, humorous take on New Orleans funk; these are his songs, visions and performances, and there's none of the elevator material or laid-back, detached fare that's a customary GRP byproduct. Such songs as "Witchy Red," "Spaceship Relationship" and the title selection are a delicate mix of seemingly outrageous but actually quite sharp commentary and excellent musical performances from Dr. John on keyboards, Hugh McCracken on guitar, and several other veterans, among them the great Red Tyler on tenor sax. While not quite as fiery as his classic sessions for Atlantic, if anyone can bring the funk to a company that's famous for avoiding it, it's Dr. John. — *Ron Wynn*

● **The Very Best Of Dr. John** / 1995 / Rhino ✦✦✦✦
The Very Best of Dr. John compiles the best moments from the comprehensive double-disc *Anthology*, making it a more effective, and cheaper, introduction for casual fans. —*Stephen Thomas Erlewine*

Afterglow / Jun. 20, 1995 / Blue Thumb ✦✦✦
Producer and GRP Records president Tommy LiPuma, a longtime associate of Dr. John's, revived his old Blue Thumb label as an imprint of GRP/MCA with this album, which served as something of a sequel to the last Dr. John/Tommy LiPuma collaboration, *In a Sentimental Mood*. On that earlier album, the two had covered pop standards. Here, they again turned to evergreens by the likes of Irving Berlin and Duke Ellington. But if *Sentimental Mood* was stylistically linked to the '20s and '30s, *Afterglow* was more a recreation of the late '40s and early '50s, with its big-band arrangements and the inclusion of jump blues numbers like Louis Jordan's "I Know What I've Got." Such songs allowed Dr. John plenty

of room to play his trademark New Orleans piano solos, and, in the second half of the record, some of the Doctor's own compositions were snuck in among the classics without disturbing the mood. Of course, the dominant sound remained Dr. John's gravel-and-honey voice, an even more appropriate instrument for these bluesier standards than it was for the *Sentimental* ones. — *William Ruhlmann*

John Doe

b. 1954
Roots-Rock
Bassist and co-lead singer of the Los Angeles punk rock group X during the '80s, John Doe launched a solo career when the group took a hiatus in 1987. He has also scored as an actor in such films as *Great Balls of Fire*. — *William Ruhlmann*

○ **Meet John Doe** / 1990 / David Geffen Co. ✦✦✦✦
From the rock-out sound, slashing guitars, and near-howl of the unison singing, not to mention the temper of the lyrics, the leadoff track, "Let's Be Mad," could be by X, Doe's former band. Elsewhere on his debut solo album he takes a less punky approach, but this is still a charged, rocking record. — *William Ruhlmann*

Bill Doggett

b. Feb. 16, 1916, Philadelphia, PA
R&B, Rock & Roll
Organist Bill Doggett cut one of the biggest-selling instrumentals of all time in 1956 with the two-part "Honky Tonk." He formed his first band in 1938 and sold the entire outfit to Lucky Milinder for a soda two years later. Doggett worked extensively with Millinder and Louis Jordan and recorded with Ella Fitzgerald before striking out on his own. He signed with King in Cincinnati around 1953, churning out a slew of sizzling instrumentals with Clifford Scott on tenor sax, Billy Butler on guitar, and Doggett on organ, notably "Ram-Bunk-Shush" in 1957 and in 1958, "Leaps and Bounds" and the often-covered "Hold It." Doggett continues to tour and record— he was recently featured on a disc by the King All-Stars, a distinguished group of alumni from the famous label. —*Bill Dahl*

● **Everybody Dance to the Honky Tonk** / 1956 / King ✦✦✦✦
This hugely influential jazz-laced R&B quartet plays their classic two-part instrumentals and several more groovers, with guitarist Billy Butler and saxist Clifford Scott incendiary throughout the album. —*Bill Dahl*

The Doggett Beat for Dancing Feet / 1958 / King ✦✦✦
Doggett's fatback organ cooks in tandem with Butler's licks and Scott's sax. —*Bill Dahl*

Dokken

Group, Hard Rock, Heavy Metal
Formed in Sacramento, CA, in the late '70s, Dokken's claim to fame was the harmonious vocals of Don Dokken and the engaging guitar work of George Lynch. Although their strength was heavy metal, they weren't afraid to record ballads, which brought them attention across the world. They soon toured around the world and became an important American metal band in the '80s, gathering a few hits along the way before splitting up in 1989 due to "personal indifferences." Don Dokken went solo and Lynch formed the Lynch Mob. Dokken reunited in 1994, releasing *Back in the Streets.—John Book*

Breakin' the Chains / 1982 / Elektra ✦✦
Dokken / 1983 / Elektra ✦✦✦
Tooth and Nail / 1984 / Elektra ✦✦
● **Under Lock & Key** / 1985 / Elektra ✦✦✦✦
This melodic heavy metal is played by a band that spawned a lot of copycats, both in sound and image. The album features strong vocals from Don Dokken and not-too-flashy guitar playing from George Lynch. —*John Book*

Back for the Attack / 1987 / Elektra ✦✦✦
○ **Beast from the East** / 1988 / Elektra ✦✦✦✦
The band's only live album was recorded in Japan. They do their best material, but, unfortunately, it was their last as a band. —*John Book*

Back in the Streets / 1994 / Elektra ✦✦✦
Dokken's reunion album was an impressive effort—the band sounded like they had never broken up and guitarist George Lynch, in particular, was in fine form. —*Stephen Thomas Erlewine*

Thomas Dolby

b. Oct. 14, 1958, Cairo, Egypt
Techno-Pop/Dance, New Wave
This British musician and producer was one of the first artists to explore the possibilities of synthesizers and digital samplers in a straight pop music context. Besides his dance hits "She Blinded Me with Science" and "Hyperactive!," Dolby has played on Foreigner's *4* album, produced albums for Joni Mitchell and Prefab Sprout, collaborated with George Clinton (on their respective solo albums and the Dolby's Cube project), and written music for the films *Howard the Duck* and *Gothic*.

He began his career working with Lene Lovich (he wrote "New Toy" for her) and with Bruce Wooley & the Camera Club, a group that also featured Trevor Horn (Yes, Buggles), Geoff Downes (Yes, Asia), and Matthew Seligman (Soft Boys). — *Scott Bultman*

○ **The Golden Age of Wireless** / Mar. 1983 / Capitol ✦✦✦✦
This contains Dolby's biggest hit, the humorously quirky "She Blinded Me with Science." Highlights include "Radio Silence," "Europa and the Pirate Twins," "Windpower," "One of Our Submarines," and "Airwaves"—a track that should've been a single. All in all, this is a very solid collection of early-'80s synth-pop. (*The Golden Age of Wireless* originally was released in May 1982 as Harvest/Capitol 12203. In the wake of the success of "She Blinded Me With Science," it was reissued in March 1983 with that track and another added (and two others dropped) as Harvest/Capitol 12271, later reissued on CD as Capitol 46009.) — *Rick Clark*

The Flat Earth / Feb. 1984 / Capitol ✦✦✦
A departure from the style of his debut, this moody and atmospheric album adds jazz and Joni Mitchell-esque elements to warm his synth-textures. Only "White City" and the single, "Hyperactive," feature the hard dance beats of his early hits. — *Scott Bultman*

Gothic Soundtrack / 1987 / Virgin ✦✦

Aliens Ate My Buick / Apr. 1988 / EMI-Manhattan ✦✦
Thomas Dolby didn't do his career much good by waiting four years between album releases. Pop music trends shifted away from the quirky synth-pop Dolby had pioneered in 1983-84, and though he employed a heavy funk beat aimed at the discos and even covered a George Clinton song, Dolby seemed less a true dancefloor king than a commentator on the same, especially in such songs as the (non-charting) single "Airhead," "Pop Culture," and "The Ability to Swing." Dolby's flirtation with film had also added an eclecticism to his style that embraced '40s jazz vocalese ("The Key to Her Ferrari") and European balladeering ("Budapest by Blimp"). As ever, Dolby was a man of many ideas, but on *Aliens Ate My Buick* they failed to add up to a coherent statement. — *William Ruhlmann*

Astronauts & Heretics / Jul. 1992 / Giant ✦✦✦

Gate to the Mind's Eye / Oct. 18, 1994 / Giant ✦✦✦
Soundtrack work suits Thomas Dolby, who here turns in a variety of musical settings for a computer animation video that include everything from moody electronic instrumentals and dance tracks to a '30s pop pastiche complete with horn section ("Nuvague"). Five of the nine tracks have vocals, two of which are contributed by Dr. Fiorella Terenzi. Dolby himself sings, raps, and even murmurs Napoleon's words of love to Josephine. As a non-visual listening, experience, it all seems scattered, but *The Gate to the Mind's Eye* demonstrates Dolby's continuing inventiveness. — *William Ruhlmann*

● **Best Of Thomas Dolby: Retrospectacle** / Apr. 4, 1995 / Capitol ✦✦✦✦
After what had seemed like a promising start with "She Blinded Me With Science" in 1983, Thomas Dolby only charted with two other singles in the U.S. (though he had nine chart singles in his native U.K., 1981-1992). This 16-track compilation, embracing both his Capitol/EMI and Warner Brothers recordings, demonstrates that Dolby deserved better. His synthesizer-based songs are consistently catchy and clever, and especially notable are early songs like "Urges" and "Leipzig" that have not previously appeared on a U.S. album. "One of Our Submarines," Dolby's cover of Dan Hicks's "I Scare Myself," and "Hyperactive" all hold up well. Some of the later (non-hit) material from the albums *Aliens Ate My Buick* and *Astronauts & Heretics* is less impressive; a better choice could have been made from those records. But for the most part, this is an efficient collection that justifies its name. — *William Ruhlmann*

Domino

Group, Rap
Domino's *Sweet Potatoe Pie* was a pop and R&B hit from his self-titled debut LP. The album was issued in December of 1993. — *Ron Wynn*

○ **Domino** / Mocity Music ✦✦✦✦
Rapper Domino's scattershot/stuttering rhyming (a near flawless imitation of early Das EFX) yielded a big hit with "Getto Jam," and is the hook for his self-titled CD. "Do You Qualify" offers a comic (if not comical) spin on a tale of mistaken identity and consensual sex, while "Money Is Everything" and "Sweet Potato Pie" provide Domino's insights into materialism and sexual conquest, and "Raincoat" is his safe sex lecture. He's not really a gangsta, satirist or protester; Domino's songs are delivered in a deadpan, half-sung, half-spoken fashion, and he's aided by tight production from DJ Battlecat and smart samples. — *Ron Wynn*

Fats Domino

b. May 10, 1929, New Orleans, LA
Rock & Roll, New Orleans R&B
New Orleans has produced many musical legends over the years but none have created a sound that was more recognizable, more influential, or more profitable than Fats Domino. Beginning with "The Fat Man" in 1949, Domino had an enviable run of chart success, selling more than 65 million records and chalking up 23 gold records. Although he's become a rock & roll deity—he was one of the first Rock & Roll Hall of Fame inductees—Domino made his name playing the same New Orleans R&B he'd always played. His best recordings were made for the Imperial label between 1949 and 1963. Of his scores of hits, "Ain't That a Shame," "Blueberry Hill," "I'm Walking," "Whole Lot of Lovin'," and "I'm Ready" were among the biggest. EMI's *They Call Me the Fat Man*, a 100-track box set, concisely chronicles Domino's sound and story. — *Jeff Hannusch*

Fats Is Back / 1968 / Reprise ✦✦✦
Producer Richard Perry's successful update of Domino's sound, complete with two most effective Beatles covers. — *Bruce Eder*

★ **My Blue Heaven: Best of Fats Domino** / Jul. 30, 1990 / EMI America ✦✦✦✦✦
A crisp, well-thought-out collection that says it all. — *Bruce Eder*

☆ **They Call Me the Fat Man . . . : The Legendary Imperial Recordings** / 1991 / EMI America ✦✦✦✦✦
Hardcore lovers of Fats Domino's rolling boogie-style piano playing and easy Cajun-inflected tenor voice (if they're ready to chunk down the change for a box set) should find this four-disc, 100-song compilation (which includes all of his Imperial hits) a thorough baptism. Sonically, this set is very impressive. Many times when old tracks are cleaned up during remastering, the life gets processed out, but that's not evident here. The 84-page booklet is a fan's delight, with first-rate annotation and plenty of photos. — *Rick Clark*

Fats Domino: Out Of New Orleans / 1993 / Bear Family

The Fats Man / 1995 / SMS

Don & Dewey

Group, R&B
Wailing in tandem like twin Little Richards, Don & Dewey cut numerous blistering rockers for Specialty from 1957 to 1959 without registering a single hit, only to see other acts revive their songs to much greater acclaim. Don Harris (b. 1938) and Dewey Terry (b. 1938) were born and raised in Pasadena, CA, joined a group called the Squires and recording for Vita before branching off on their own. Their Specialty output included the savage rockers "Jungle Hop," "Koko Joe" (written by Sonny Bono), and "Justine," the latter pair later covered by the Righteous Brothers. Don & Dewey's Specialty discography also includes the original "I'm Leavin' It Up to You," a hit for Dale & Grace; "Big Boy Pete," ditto for the Olympics; and "Farmer John," the Premiers' only smash. Don laid down his guitar for a violin during the '60s and, billed as "Sugarcane" Harris, sawed his rocked-out fiddle beside John Mayall and Frank Zappa. — *Bill Dahl*

● **Jungle Hop** / 1991 / Specialty ✦✦✦✦
Wild '50s rock & roll duets from Don "Sugarcane" Harris and Dewey Terry, backed by the same Specialty house band that recorded with Little Richard and others. A lot of these songs were

covered by other people, but *nobody* cut these guy's versions. — *George Bedard*

Don & Juan

Group, Doo-Wop

New York doo-woppers Roland Trone and Claude Johnson crafted one astonishing single ("What's Your Name") in 1962, then drifted into obscurity. —*John Floyd*

○ **What's Your Name: Golden Classics** / 1995 / Collectables ♦♦♦♦
The title cut, a hit during the early-'60s doo-wop revival, is the one to keep, but there's enough here to keep doo-wop pers happy. — *John Floyd*

Lonnie Donegan (Anthony James Donegan)

b. Apr. 29, 1931, Glasgow, Scotland
Pop/Rock

Born Anthony James Donegan (April 29, 1931) in Glasgow, Scotland, Lonnie Donegan was the son of a violinist with the Scottish National Orchestra who took up the guitar at an early age. It was while on military service that Donegan began playing professionally. He took his stage name, according to one version of the story, when he was on the same stage bill with jazz/blues guitarist Lonnie Johnson and the master of ceremonies accidentally introduced him as "Lonnie Donegan."

Donegan joined Ken Colyer's Jazzmen as a guitarist and banjo player, where he earned a special spot leading a small group combo in their shows. This group began presenting a small selection of American blues and work songs arranged for a trio of guitar, bass (Chris Barber), and washboard (Bill Colyer), which became known as skiffle music. Their sets proved popular, and when Barber left the Colyer band to form his own group, Donegan went along and got his own featured spots in the new group's sets.

Fate took a hand in 1955 when the Barber band recorded a ten-inch LP that included two songs, "Rock Island Line" and "John Henry," credited to the Lonnie Donegan Skiffle Group. "Rock Island Line," which Donegan learned from an American recording by legendary blues singer Leadbelly, was released as a single by English Decca, credited to Donegan, and became an instant hit, rising to number eight on the charts and spending 22 weeks among Britain's top-selling records. Although he never received any royalties for the sales of the record (he was paid a small session fee when the recording was made), Donegan became an overnight sensation and an instant star, especially among Britain's young people, who took to skiffle for its rhythmic vitality and the ease with which it could be played—a single guitar, a washtub bass, and a washboard and thimble gave you a basic skiffle band.

By the end of 1955, literally thousands of skiffle groups had sprung up throughout the country, and new artists—most notably Tommy Steele—were putting their own stamp on the skiffle sound. Donegan signed to Pye Records in mid-1955, and began a run of hits that continued unabated for seven years, highlighted by "Lost John" (#2), "Bring A Little Water Sylvie" (#7), "Don't You Rock Me, Daddy-O" (#4), "Cumberland Gap" (#6), "Does Your Chewing Gum Lose Its Flavor On the Bedpost Overnight" (#3), and a string of top-selling albums and extended play singles running all the way into 1961.

Donegan was a seminal influence on the Beatles, the Shadows, and virtually every other early rock band in England through his breakthrough as a skiffle star. While the skiffle boom had more or less faded as a major force by 1959, his own musicianship helped carry his career successfully until 1962, after which the hits stopped coming. He continued to record and perform occasionally, but also worked as a producer for Pye Records, whose biggest star he had been throughout the 1950s. A mid-1970s heart attack left Donegan sidelined for a time, and he moved to California to recuperate, but by 1978 he was back with his first chart entry in 15 years with *Putting On the Style*, an all-star skiffle-style album featuring Ringo Starr, Brian May, Peter Banks, Elton John, and other superstars who owed their entry into rock to Donegan's "Rock Island Line" and other early songs. Since then, he has periodically toured and recorded with new bands, and also appeared in small acting roles on British television. —*Bruce Eder*

● **The EP Collection** / 1992 / See For Miles ♦♦♦♦
In England, before the Beatles and the Rolling Stones came along, EPs (four-song extended play singles) outsold albums. This compilation of the best of Donegan's EPs is the definitive Lonnie Donegan collection, eclipsing any album or CD that existed previously

on his work. It is certainly the best hits compilation there ever has been on him, containing the 1956 hit "Rock Island Line" and its B-side, "Digging My Potatoes," plus 23 more fairly hard rocking tracks dating up through 1962, all very crisply remastered, with original artwork represented and a very detailed biography. — *Bruce Eder*

The EP Collection, Vol. 2 / 1994 / See For Miles ♦♦♦
Surprisingly strong (and nearly as important as Volume One) collection of the rest of Donegan's classic skiffle material, including the complete contents of his live EP *Donegan on Stage*. The novelty tunes share space with some surprisingly solid early rock & roll, and all of it is fast-paced and entertaining. —*Bruce Eder*

Putting on the Styles / Sequel ♦♦
This triple-CD collection is weaker than either of the See For Miles compilations listed above, with an over-reliance on the novelty tunes that skiffle acts tended to fall back on—it also doesn't contain the original hit "Rock Island Line." Little of what is here rocks as hard as the two EP collections listed above. —*Bruce Eder*

Ral Donner

d. Apr. 6, 1984
Rock & Roll

There was no more-accurate Elvis imitator than Ral Donner. In the early '60s, his hit singles were frequently mistaken for the King himself. The uncanny resemblance proved to be both the ticket to his success and the cause of his undoing. In 1961, his cover of an Elvis LP cut, "The Girl of My Best Friend," went into the Top 20; his follow-up, "You Don't Know What You've Got (Until You Lose It)" went to number four. After another Top 20 single in 1962 ("She's Everything"), Donner only managed a couple minor hit singles before falling into obscurity. Not a bad singer, he was so explicit in his Elvis adulation—particularly taking after the swooping, smoky style that Presley employed on slower numbers—that artistic growth into an identity of his own would have been difficult, if not impossible. Donner's resemblance to Elvis' voice was such that he was chosen to be the "voice" of Presley in the 1981 documentary film *This Is Elvis*. —*Richie Unterberger*

● **She's Everything** / 1988 / Murray Hill ♦♦♦♦
Includes all three big hits, three previously unreleased tracks, a few songs from his 1961 album, and some obscure cuts from singles. As early-'60s teen idol fare goes, it's not bad, but nothing else is as good as the three hits. The extreme resemblance to Elvis makes the album akin to experiencing a warm-up session by the King when neither he nor the material was particularly inspired. —*Richie Unterberger*

Donovan (Donovan Leitch)

b. Feb. 10, 1946, Glasgow, Scotland
Singer-Songwriter, British Invasion, Psychedelic, Folk-Rock

When Donovan first appeared on the British pop scene in the mid-'60s, he was touted as the British Invasion's answer to Bob Dylan. The unfortunate comparison led to a battle of the bands of sorts, immortalized in the Dylan documentary *Don't Look Back*, where Dylan shot down one of Donovan's pretty acoustic ditties with "It's All Over Now, Baby Blue." All of which has cast a harsher light on Donovan's early work than it merits. Certainly he wasn't as deep as Dylan, but the acoustic tracks he recorded in the mid-'60s, including the British hits "Catch the Wind" and "Colours," were affecting, thoughtful, and tuneful, especially considering he was still in his teens at the time.

In late 1965, Donovan hooked up with manager Allen Klein and a new producer, Mickie Most (who also worked with the Animals, Herman's Hermits, and Lulu), who steered the young singer away from acoustic folk and into psychedelic pop. His more excessively cosmic lyrics haven't worn well, but in general the combination was quite successful, with seductive and ornate arrangements backing Donovan's gentle musings, which could be more humorous and biting than he's been given credit for. Between 1965 and 1969, he scored a series of memorable hits, including "Sunshine Superman," "Mellow Yellow" (containing a Paul McCartney cameo), "Hurdy Gurdy Man" (with Jeff Beck), and "Atlantis." His initial pair of psychedelic albums, "Sunshine Superman" and "Mellow Yellow," were quite strong, but after a while his full-length efforts began to sound unduly repetitive and overly florid. By the early '70s, Donovan had begun to fade and struggle for relevancy, although he's been an active performer since, and has periodically mounted comebacks. —*Rick Clark & Richie Unterberger*

Catch the Wind / Jun. 1965 / Hickory ✦✦

Donovan's first album found the 19-year-old following in the footsteps of Bob Dylan, that is, the whimsical folkie Dylan of 1963. Even the hit "Catch the Wind" echoed Dylan's "Blowin' in the Wind," in form if not in content. Nevertheless, Donovan has his own charm and was already beginning to establish his own sound here. —*William Ruhlmann*

Fairytale / Nov. 1965 / Hickory ✦✦

Although it contains his hits "Colours" and "Universal Soldier," on which he moves to the more poetic and political styles of '64 Dylan, Donovan's second album still finds him aping his hero and falling dangerously behind the quickly moving musical trends of the '60s. By the time this album was released, folk had become folk-rock, and Donovan was in danger of being left behind the times. —*William Ruhlmann*

○ Sunshine Superman / Sep. 1966 / Epic ✦✦✦✦

Probably the singer/songwriter's best album, embracing folk, blues, and a druggy psychedelia, and driven by crisp rhythm guitars (especially on the title track). It starts to sound the same after a bit, but at its release, even this was a point of recommendation—it set a hazy, drugged-out mood. The use of the mono master helps, because it's punchier. —*Bruce Eder*

The Real Donovan / Sep. 1966 / Hickory ✦✦

Donovan left Hickory Records for Epic Records in a messy contractual battle in 1966, and Hickory, which retained his folk-based 1965 catalog, retaliated by releasing a series of compilations to compete with his new Epic work. This is the first one, containing hits like "Catch the Wind" and "Colours," as well as a few tracks previously available only in the U.K. —*William Ruhlmann*

Mellow Yellow / Jan. 1967 / Epic ✦✦✦

Despite the psychedelic pop nature of hit singles like the notorious title track, Donovan still retained some of his folkie charm on songs like "Writer in the Sun" (which he wrote when a contractual dispute led him to think his recording career was over). And "Sunny South Kensington" found him at his name-dropping, trendy best. —*William Ruhlmann*

For Little Ones / Dec. 1967 / Epic ✦✦

This children's album made up the second of the two-disc *A Gift from a Flower to a Garden*, and was released simultaneously as a separate album. With his whimsical style, Donovan is a natural children's artist, and this was the first of several recordings in this vein. —*William Ruhlmann*

Wear Your Love Like Heaven / Dec. 1967 / Epic ✦✦✦

Donovan's double album *A Gift from a Flower to a Garden* was simultaneously released as two single albums as well. This is the first, a psychedelic pop album containing the title track single and other like selections. —*William Ruhlmann*

A Gift from a Flower to A Garden / Dec. 1967 / Epic ✦✦✦

A blast from hippie past—a flower-decorated double album made up of precious trippy music spiced with a haunting melody or two ("Wear Your Love like Heaven"). —*Bruce Eder*

Like It Is, Was and Evermore Shall Be / Mar. 1968 / Hickory ✦✦✦

For its second repackaging of its 1965 material, Hickory used a fashionable psychedelic cover in an effort to make Donovan fans think this was a new album. Actually, containing his three hits, "Catch the Wind," "Colours," and "Universal Soldier," it was the strongest selection of his material yet assembled on one disc, even if most fans already had these recordings. —*William Ruhlmann*

Donovan in Concert / Jul. 1968 / Epic ✦✦

Donovan mostly eschewed his hits on this live album, which found him at the height of his Flower Power period, gently intoning folkish songs over a soft accompaniment of acoustic instruments. He's charming, but you can't help wondering whether his teenage fans (who scream when his father introduces him) weren't a little let down by the set list. It takes "Mellow Yellow" to bring them to life. —*William Ruhlmann*

Hurdy Gurdy Man / Oct. 1968 / Epic ✦✦✦

For this performer, this is a hard-rocking album, driven by some loud electric guitar subbing for sitar, which dresses up the plainer folk melodies and turns the title tune into a near-classic. —*Bruce Eder*

● Donovan's Greatest Hits / Jan. 1969 / Epic ✦✦✦✦

Entertaining but flawed collection of Donovan's psychedelic-era hits, fleshed out with too-languid re-recordings of his pre-CBS folk successes, including "Colours." It's unfortunate that the producers used the stereo versions, which don't sound nearly as good as the mono. —*Bruce Eder*

○ Barabajagal / Aug. 11, 1969 / Epic ✦✦✦✦

Donovan was moving beyond his hippie-dippie phase by this point, collaborating with the Jeff Beck Group on the title track, protesting the Vietnam War with "Susan on the West Coast Waiting," adapting the epic style of Beatles songs like "Hey Jude" on the hit "Atlantis" (which features Paul McCartney) and turning in two of his most charming, childlike songs in "Happiness Runs" and "I Love My Shirt." Overall, this may be Donovan's strongest collection of original songs, other than his compilations. —*William Ruhlmann*

The Best of Donovan / Oct. 1969 / Hickory ✦✦

Hickory's third repackaging of its 1965 acoustic Donovan material, with another misleading psychedelic cover, was intended to compete with Epic's *Greatest Hits* album of the same year. Anyone who still did not own a copy of "Universal Soldier," "Colours," or "Catch the Wind" could get them here. —*William Ruhlmann*

Open Road / 1970 / Epic ✦✦✦

Although it was a disappointing seller and signaled the start of Donovan's commercial decline, *Open Road* could have been a new beginning for the singer. Stripping down to a "Celtic rock" format that managed to be hard and direct, yet still folkish, Donovan turned out a series of excellent songs, notably the minor hit "Riki Tiki Tavi," that seemed to show him moving toward a roots-oriented sound of considerable appeal. Unfortunately, he was derailed by record company hassles and perhaps his own burnout, and *Open Road* turned out to be a sidestep rather than a step forward. —*William Ruhlmann*

Cosmic Wheels / Mar. 1973 / Epic ✦✦

Donovan came back after a three-year absence with this disappointing collection, which failed to recreate past triumphs and, in "The Intergalactic Laxative," proved embarrassing. —*William Ruhlmann*

Essence to Essence / Dec. 1973 / Epic ✦✦

Donovan had the best of L.A. session help here, but his writing remained cosmic ("Operating Manual for Spaceship Earth" was the title of the lead-off track), and he seemed to have lost the knack for appealing whimsy that had floated his career thus far. —*William Ruhlmann*

7-Tease / Nov. 1974 / Epic ✦✦

Donovan rocked a little harder, on this Norbert Putnam-produced, Nashville-recorded album, but to little greater effect than on his other comeback efforts. —*William Ruhlmann*

Slow Down World / May 1976 / Epic ✦✦

Donovan had become distinctly bitter about his status by this time, as indicated by the song "A Well Known Has-Been," but he gamely gave record-making another shot, although "Liberation Rag" found him trying a little too hard to keep up with the times and "Children of the World" found him much too preachy. —*William Ruhlmann*

Donovan / 1977 / Castle ✦✦

Donovan was reunited with his old producer, Mickie Most, and his old record company head, Clive Davis, for this label debut, which has a tight, sharp, punkish edge to it, notably on the lead-off track, "Local Boy Chops Wood." Unfortunately, no one paid attention. —*William Ruhlmann*

○ Spotlight / 1981 / PRT ✦✦✦✦

Donovan's acoustic, pre-psychedelic work was shoddily packaged in the United States, spread out over several albums in a haphazard fashion. This 24-track double LP reissue covers most of his work from this period (basically, 1965), including the hits "Catch the Wind" and "Colours," as well his cover of Buffy St. Marie's "Universal Soldier" and the memorable originals "Josie" and "Hey Gyp." This early phase is often unfairly dismissed as sub-Dylan musings by critics; Donovan was indeed the closest counterpart to Bob in the mid-'60s, but was distinctly more pop-oriented, and had a gentle, wistful songwriting voice all his own, even if it wasn't as complex as Dylan's. While this material lacks the punch of his best psychedelic work, it is of a consistently high standard, and lacks the occasional overly cosmic vision that has dated some of his later '60s recordings. While this reissue captures all the essential highlights of Donovan's pre-electric career, it's missing a few cuts and is packaged rather tackily; a comprehensive double CD compilation of the thirty or so tracks he recorded for the British Pye label during this time would be welcome. —*Richie Unterberger*

Lady of the Stars / 1983 / Allegiance ♦♦
Donovan rerecorded some old hits—"Season of the Witch" and "Sunshine Superman"—and cut some new songs for this independent label release. The result is a pleasant, but inconsequential effort. —*William Ruhlmann*

Classics Live / 1991 / Great Northern Arts ♦♦♦
Fresh stage recordings of Donovan's '60s hits, well-produced and arranged, and laced with a certain amount of humor from the passage of time and the druggy sensibilities behind them. "Sunshine Superman" is an intrinsically good song, although the infectious beat of the original Mickie Most-production is missed in spite of the good playing. —*Bruce Eder*

● **Troubadour: The Definitive Collection 1964-1976** / Aug. 4, 1992 / Epic ♦♦♦♦
This two-disc, 44-track retrospective album (initially released as a boxed set) chronicles Donovan's decade-long career at Epic Records, with the few folk hits he recorded before joining the label and a couple of early demos added. All the hippie hits of the '60s are included, plus a judicious selection of the less successful '70s recordings. Good liner notes by Brian Hogg and Derek Taylor. — *William Ruhlmann*

Early Years / 1994 / Griffin ♦♦♦

The Doobie Brothers

Group, Pop/Rock
The Doobie Brothers ("doobie" being slang for a marijuana joint) straddled FM rock and Top 40 pop better than most bands of the '70s, with their good-time grooves and melodies and solid musicianship. During the first part of their career (1970 to 1975), the Doobie Brothers scored with a batch of radio classics: "Listen to the Music" (#11), "Long Train Running" (#8), "China Grove" (#15), and the #1 hit "Black Water." With the arrival of soulful Steely Dan singer and keyboardist Michael McDonald, the Doobie Brothers took on a mellower, more sophisticated musical direction, giving passing nods to jazz and light funk along the way. "Takin' It to the Streets" (#13) showcased McDonald's contribution to fine effect. The 1977 album *Living on the Fault Line* is an artistic pinnacle of the band's new direction, but the #1 followup, *Minute by Minute*, was a much bigger success, containing the hits "What a Fool Believes" and the title cut.

By the time *One Step Closer* was released in 1980, the Doobies' brand of slick California pop reached the saturation point in fern bars across the land. The fact that Michael McDonald's aching vocals seemed to appear on every record from the West Coast ensured overkill. The band called it quits in 1981. The pre-McDonald lineup re-formed in 1987 and enjoyed a successful comeback. — *Rick Clark*

The Doobie Brothers / 1971 / Warner Brothers ♦♦♦
○ **Toulouse Street** / 1972 / Warner Brothers ♦♦♦♦
After a promising but ill-formed debut, the Doobie Brothers returned with *Toulouse Street*, a better-written and more energetically performed effort that became a platinum record on the strength of its catchy single, "Listen to the Music." —*Stephen Thomas Erlewine*

○ **The Captain & Me** / 1973 / Warner Brothers ♦♦♦♦
Their best early album features "China Grove." —*Dan Heilman*

What Were Once Vices Are Now Habits / 1974 / Warner Brothers ♦♦♦
Apart from the tight "Black Water," the Doobie Brothers' follow-up to their breakthrough *The Captain and Me* was a tepid affair, lacking the strong material of the previous album. —*Stephen Thomas Erlewine*

Stampede / 1975 / Warner Brothers ♦♦
With the addition of ex-Steely Dan guitarist Jeff "Skunk" Baxter, the Doobie Brothers became a more musically ambitious and accomplished band, without sacrificing their capability to rock & roll. However, *Stampede* suffers from the same flaw as *What Were Once Vices*—a lack of consistent material. —*Stephen Thomas Erlewine*

● **Best of the Doobies** / 1976 / Warner Brothers ♦♦♦♦
This formidable bunch of hard-rock hits appeared from 1972-1976. —*Dan Heilman*

○ **Takin' It to the Streets** / 1976 / Warner Brothers ♦♦♦♦
Jeff "Skunk" Baxter left after *Stampede* and keyboardist/vocalist Michael McDonald—who also recorded with Steely Dan—joined the band. Under McDonald's direction, the group departed from their trademark bluesy country-rock on *Takin' It to the Streets*, taking a laidback pop-soul that touched on jazz and White funk. The result was a commercial and artistic success, providing a blueprint for the band's next two records. —*Stephen Thomas Erlewine*

Livin' on the Fault Line / 1977 / Warner Brothers ♦♦♦
Livin' on the Fault Line follows the same pattern as *Takin' It to the Streets*, yet it lacks the fine songwriting of its predecessor. —*Stephen Thomas Erlewine*

○ **Minute by Minute** / 1978 / Warner Brothers ♦♦♦♦
Due to health problems, founding member Tom Johnson departed after *Livin' on the Fault Line*, leaving Michael McDonald as the leader of the Doobie Brothers. McDonald, in turn, wrote his finest set of songs for *Minute by Minute*," highlighted by the number one single "What a Fool Believes." —Stephen Thomas Erlewine

One Step Closer / 1981 / Warner Brothers ♦♦
One Step Closer was less impressive than *Minute by Minute* not only because it lacked the strong songwriting of the previous album, but because the band sounded tired and uninspired. Unsurprisingly, it was the final studio album the Doobie Brothers made before breaking up. —*Stephen Thomas Erlewine*

○ **The Best of the Doobies, Vol. 2** / 1981 / Warner Brothers ♦♦♦♦
This is the best of the Michael McDonald era. —*Dan Heilman*

Cycles / 1989 / Capitol ♦
The original lineup of the Doobie Brothers reunited in 1989, releasing *Cycles*. Thanks to a successful tour and single ("The Doctor"), the album went gold, but the music was just a rehashed version of the bluesy boogie of their early albums, only stiffer and less inspired. —*Stephen Thomas Erlewine*

Brotherhood / Apr. 15, 1991 / Capitol ♦♦

The Doors

Group, Rock & Roll, Psychedelic
The Doors, one of the most influential and controversial rock bands of the 1960s, were formed in Los Angeles in 1965 by UCLA film students Ray Manzarek (b. Feb 12, 1935), keyboards, and Jim Morrison (b. Dec 8, 1943—d.Jul 3, 1971), vocals, with drummer John Densmore (b. Dec 1, 1945) and guitarist Robby Krieger (b. Jan 8, 1946). The group never added a bass player, and their sound was dominated by Manzarek's electric organ work and Morrison's deep, sonorous voice, with which he sang and intoned his highly poetic lyrics. The group signed to Elektra Records in 1966 and released its first album, *The Doors*, featuring the hit "Light My Fire," in 1967.

From the start, the Doors' focus was the charismatic Morrison, who proved increasingly unstable during the group's brief career. In 1969, Morrison was arrested for indecent exposure during a concert in Miami, an incident that nearly derailed the band. Nevertheless, the Doors managed to turn out a series of successful albums and singles through 1971 when, upon the completion of *L.A. Woman*, Morrison decamped for Paris. He died there, apparently of a drug overdose. The three surviving Doors tried to carry on without him, but ultimately disbanded. Yet the Doors' music and Morrison's legend continued to fascinate succeeding generations of rock fans: In the mid-'80s, Morrison was as big a star as he'd been in the mid-'60s, and Elektra has sold numerous quantities of the Doors' original albums, plus reissues and releases of live material over the years, while publishers have flooded bookstores with Doors and Morrison biographies. In 1991, director Oliver Stone made *The Doors*, a feature film about the group starring Val Kilmer as Morrison. —*William Ruhlmann*

☆ **The Doors** / Jan. 1967 / Elektra ♦♦♦♦♦
One of the most remarkable debut albums in rock history introduced the powerful singing of Jim Morrison, his provocative lyrics, and the group's spare, direct guitar/organ sound. "Light My Fire" became an instant standard but the album also contained such Doors classics as "Break On Through (To the Other Side)," "Twentieth Century Fox," and, of course, that Oedipal odyssey "The End." — *William Ruhlmann*

Strange Days / Oct. 1967 / Elektra ✦✦✦
The band's second effort isn't as consistently stunning as their debut, but is overall a very successful continuation of the themes of their classic first album. Besides the hit "People Are Strange," it includes "You're Lost Little Girl," "Love Me Two Times," and "Moonlight Drive," which remain among the group's finest songs. — *Richie Unterberger*

Waiting for the Sun / Jul. 1968 / Elektra ✦✦✦
Singles like "Hello, I Love You" and "The Unknown Soldier" are on *The Best of the Doors*, but many of the standouts on this album are gentle songs like "Summer's Almost Gone," "Yes, the River Knows," and "Wintertime Love," which demonstrate that Morrison & company can be lyrical without losing their power. — *William Ruhlmann*

The Soft Parade / Jul. 1969 / Elektra ✦✦✦
Probably the most underrated Doors collection because the addition of horns and strings ("Wishful Sinful") turns it into a more exploratory album than their more basic music usually attempted. But "Tell All the People" is the group at its most revolutionary, and the long title track is among its most ambitious. This included the hit "Touch Me" as well as "Wild Child," one of their best rockers. — *William Ruhlmann*

○ **Morrison Hotel/Hard Rock Cafe** / 1970 / Elektra ✦✦✦✦
A bluesy, hard-rock album that nevertheless contains some of Morrison's most visionary poetry. — *William Ruhlmann*

○ **13** / Feb. 1970 / Elektra ✦✦✦✦
A one-disc hits compilation issued before the Doors' final album and thus lacking "Riders on the Storm," but nevertheless a good sampler of the singles that maintained the Doors' enormous popularity in the late '60s and remain rock standards today. — *William Ruhlmann*

Absolutely Live / Sep. 1970 / Elektra ✦✦
This sprawling collection demonstrated that, in concert, the Doors could be an enervating as well as an elevating experience. There are no hits, but there's a lot of Morrison-improvising, reciting poetry, sometimes singing. Not a record for the uninitiated. (Combined with *Alive, She Cried* and *Live at the Hollywood Bowl* for CD release under the title *In Concert*.) — *William Ruhlmann*

○ **L.A. Woman** / Apr. 1971 / Elektra ✦✦✦✦
Morrison's final testament shows him at the height of his ability to bring striking images to the lyrics of rock music, and the group produces some of its most trancelike music. — *William Ruhlmann*

Other Voices / Oct. 1971 / Elektra ✦✦
The Doors seem to have been planning to make this trio album even before Jim Morrison's death, since it was released shortly afterward. It has the Doors' characteristic instrumental sound and some effective songs, notably "Ships W/Sails," but there's no replacing Morrison's voice. — *William Ruhlmann*

Weird Scenes Inside the Gold Mine / Jan. 1972 / Elektra ✦✦✦
A two-LP compilation that fills in the Doors' hits not included on *13* and concentrates on some of their longer album tracks. — *William Ruhlmann*

Full Circle / Jul. 1972 / Elektra ✦✦
Ray Manzarek sometimes echoes Morrison's authoritative vocal style, and the band tries out a variety of different approaches on this second trio album, but the songs just aren't up to snuff, and Manzarek just isn't Morrison. When he tries "Good Rocking Tonight," you can't help thinking what Morrison could have done with the same material. — *William Ruhlmann*

American Prayer / Nov. 1978 / Elektra ✦✦
Poetry by Jim Morrison, with contemporary backing by the ex-Doors. For fanatics only. (*An American Prayer* was reissued on CD in revised and expanded form on May 23, 1995.) — *Jeff Tamarkin*

Alive, She Cried / Oct. 1983 / Elektra ✦✦
A more conventional concert album than *Absolutely Live*, containing an interesting reading of Them's "Gloria" and hits like "Light My Fire." (Combined with *Absolutely Live* and *Live at the Hollywood Bowl* for CD release under the title *In Concert*.) — *William Ruhlmann*

★ **The Best of the Doors** / 1985 / Elektra ✦✦✦✦✦
A well-chosen, 18-track compilation balancing the radio hits with the longer, more complex song poems. It's a good sampler, but this is one group for whom you need to hear the whole story. Reissued on CD in 1991 with one bonus track. — *William Ruhlmann*

Live at the Hollywood Bowl / Jun. 1987 / Elektra ✦✦✦
The Doors' most focused concert recording, from a show held on July 5, 1968, that also was filmed. There is also a home video of the show. (This album was combined with *Absolutely Live* and *Alive, She Cried* for release on CD under the title *In Concert*.) — *William Ruhlmann*

In Concert / 1991 / Elektra ✦✦✦
The Doors could be erratic live, as this double CD shows. Still, it's a fair example of their in-concert charms. — *Jeff Tamarkin*

○ **Live at the Matrix, San Francisco, March 10, 1967** / Bootleg ✦✦✦✦
Far and away the best unreleased Doors material out there, this is one of the highest fidelity live tapes of the era of any rock act, capturing the Doors just before "Light My Fire" made them superstars. More than any of their officially sanctioned live recordings, this showcases the Doors as a hard-working club unit, with a slightly raw feel not present on any other document. Morrison and the band are in top form on a selection of off-the-beaten tracks from their first albums, including "My Eyes Have Seen You," "Summer's Almost Gone," "Break On Through," and "People Are Strange." The blues/R&B covers are less compelling, but interesting in that several were never officially released by the group, including "Money," "I'm a King Bee," and "Summertime." — *Richie Unterberger*

Live In Seattle, June 5, 1970 / Bootleg ✦✦✦
An hour-plus, fairly good fidelity recording that ranks as the best live boot of their final days. Although much has been written about what a shambles Morrison was in at this time, the performances here are quite tight, and the extended renditions of warhorses like "Roadhouse Blues," "Five to One," "The End," and "When the Music's Over" are pretty interesting. Also has a version of "Mystery Train" and the unreleased original "Someday Soon." — *Richie Unterberger*

Rock Is Dead / Bootleg ✦✦✦
Around 1969, the group cut a semi-legendary 40 minutes or so of the rambling opus "Rock Is Dead," a tongue-in-cheek obituary that combines Morrison's poetry with offhand musical quotes from rock and blues oldies that simultaneously parody and pay homage to the band's inspirations. Not a vital piece of art by any means, but fascinating insight for Morrison/Doors aficionados, simultaneously reflecting the group's mystical vision and the burnout they were feeling as the pressure of commercial expectations, Morrison's dissolution, and legal hassles mounted. Available under a variety of different titles; *Love Me Tender*, if you can find it, adds some interesting late-'60s studio outtakes and farting around. — *Richie Unterberger*

BOOK

✦✦✦✦ **Break On Through: The Life And Death Of Jim Morrison**, by James Riordan & Jerry Prochnicky (William Morrow, 1991). Since the best-selling *No One Here Gets out Alive*, Morrison has been the subject of numerous books, most of them sloppy and sensationalistic. That, combined with the general repugnancy of much of the Doors' singer's behavior during his latter days, has inclined critics to ignore most of his biographies. This large (500+ pages), meticulously researched one is the best, drawing upon interviews with the surviving ex-Doors, with a lot of material in particular from their producer, Paul Rothschild. The focus of much of the book is upon the music, not the myth, and besides insider stories about how the band crafted their sound in the studio, the authors provide insightful descriptive critiques of all of the music on each of their albums. Morrison's extremely colorful life, on stage and off, is not neglected, and though it isn't glorified, the endless substance abuse, egotism, and overall grossness does get numbing, despite the brilliance of his art. His mysterious death, and the subsequent numerous (often far-fetched) theories surrounding it, are also examined in non-judgemental detail. — *Richie Unterberger*

Lee Dorsey

b. Dec. 24, 1924, New Orleans, LA, **d.** Dec. 1, 1986
Soul, R&B
The effervescent approach of Lee Dorsey perfectly summarizes the infectious charm of early-'60s New Orleans R&B. Dorsey specialized in good-humored music with a touch of second-line funk thrown in to make it all the more irresistible. Although he had al-

ready waxed a couple of singles, Dorsey caught the country by total surprise in 1961 with his deceptively simply nursery-rhyme-
style "Ya Ya" on Bobby Robinson's Fury label. Arranged by prolific
New Orleans pianist Allen Toussaint, the track proved an R&B
chart-topper and a major pop hit to boot.

Dorsey's laconic vocal charms served him well on "Ya Ya" and
the Earl King-penned followup "Do Re Mi," and the mid-'60s
found him working with Toussaint on the funky smashes "Ride
Your Pony" and "Working in the Coal Mine," this time for Amy
Records. It's little remembered that Dorsey was responsible for the
original 1970 version of Toussaint's "Yes We Can," revived to much
greater acclaim by the Pointer Sisters (who tacked on an extra
"Can"). From all accounts, Dorsey remained an exceedingly humble R&B star who preferred tinkering with cars to extensively
touring the country. He died of emphysema in 1986. —*Bill Dahl*

○ **Ya Ya** / 1962 / Relic ♦♦♦♦
This terrific overview of the good-humored New Orleans singer's
early-'60s classics (for Bobby Robinson's Fury label) features di-
rect-from-masters sound quality. —*Bill Dahl*

● **Holy Cow!: Best of Lee Dorsey** / 1985 / Arista ♦♦♦♦
A nice single-disc anthology featuring the best-known cuts and
biggest pop hits of New Orleans R&B and soul singer Lee Dorsey,
one of the Crescent City's best comic/novelty artists and a fine traditional R&B vocalist as well. The title track, "Working In A Coal
Mine," and "Ride Your Pony" are superb songs that use the second
line rhythm and boast outstanding arrangements, clever lyrics,
and great vocals. —*Ron Wynn*

Lee Dorsey / 1995 / Pickwick

Downliners Sect

Group, British Invasion
Of all the British R&B bands to follow the Rolling Stones' footsteps, the Downliners Sect were arguably the rawest. The Sect did-
n't as much interpret the sound of Chess Records as attack it, with
a finesse that made the Pretty Things seem positively suave in
comparison. Long on crude energy and hoarse vocals, but short on
originality and songwriting talent, the band never had a British
hit, although they had some sizable singles in other European
countries. Despite their lack of commercial success or appeal, the
band managed to record three albums and various EPs and singles between 1963 and 1966, with detours into country-rock and
an EP of death-rock tunes. Although they recorded afterwards, it is
the Sect's early work that continues to attract connoisseurs of '60s
garage and punk. —*Richie Unterberger*

● **The Sect** / 1964 / Columbia ♦♦♦♦
Their rawest and most R&B-oriented, firmly rooted in the same influences as the Stones and Pretty Things. Includes punk covers of
Chuck Berry, Bo Diddley, Muddy Waters, Jimmy Reed, et al., and a
few originals in the same vein. —*Richie Unterberger*

Nite at Gt Newport Street / 1964 / RBC ♦♦
Live demo disc, featuring the Sect at its rawest and most satisfying, complete with the zaniest, most satisfying cover of Bo Diddley's "Cadillac" ever recorded. Included complete on *The Definitive Downliners Sect. —Bruce Eder*

The Country Sect / 1965 / Columbia ♦♦
The funniest band on the British blues scene tries its hand at
American country-blues, with surprisingly good results—sort of
the Rolling Stones with a comically looser approach. —*Bruce Eder*

Sect Sing Sick Songs / 1965 / Columbia ♦♦
In 1965, the Downliners Sect managed to release not one, but two
records that counted as among the least commercial rock efforts of
the period. One was their album of country songs, and the other
was this, a four-song EP of death rock. On Side One, they cover
Jimmy Cross's gross "I Want My Baby Back" (now a Dr. Demento
standard) and "Leader of the Pack," changing the title to "Leader of
the Sect." Side Two has the lyrically indecipherable "Midnight
Hour" and a cornball teen lament entitled "Now She's Dead." Unusual concept, pedestrian execution, although they beat the
Cramps to it by a good dozen years or so. —*Richie Unterberger*

The Rock Sects In / 1966 / Columbia ♦♦♦
Their wildly erratic third album includes some tepid material, but
also has some of their best tracks, especially their vicious run-
through of the early British rock & roll standard "Brand New
Cadillac." It's most notable for the appearance—through God-
knows-what channels—of "Why Don't You Smile Now," which was
written by Lou Reed, John Cale, and two unknowns before the Velvet Underground formed. —*Richie Unterberger*

I Want My Baby Back / 1978 / Charly ♦♦♦
A collection of 1960s tracks that is now supplanted in value, content, and sound by the See For Miles Records *Definitive Downliners Sect. —Bruce Eder*

Showbiz / 1979 / Raw ♦

Be a Sect Maniac / 1983 / Out Line ♦♦
Dubious sound mars this collection, which is as close to a hits
compilation as existed—now irrelevant in the wake of the *Definitive Downliners Sect. —Bruce Eder*

Definitive Downliners Sect: Singles A's & B's / 1994 / See For
Miles ♦♦
Definitive, yes—both sides of all eight of their Columbia singles,
both sides of their one Pye single, their 1965 *The Sect Sing Sick
Songs* EP, their ultra-rare self-released *Gt. Newport Street* EP from
early 1964, and demos of "Cadillac" and "Roll Over Beethoven"
from '63 and '64 respectively. 29 songs in all, spanning 1963-67,
many of which didn't make it onto the three albums they released
during this period. Good? No, not really. As, performers the Sect
didn't only verge on inept, they were at times downright careless,
as if they couldn't be bothered to polish things a bit in the studio.
As (infrequent) songwriters, their talent was nearly nonexistent.
It's hard to believe anyone thought most of these sides had any
commercial potential, either in the band or at the record label; the
material is largely lackluster, and not even especially well-chosen
(a few of the songs on their first and third LPs would have been
much better bets). Highlights are the *Newport* EP, which at least
finds them playing things a bit straight and passionate, with a
ramshackle version of "Green Onions" and a good cut of Bo Diddley's "Nursery Rhymes"; the 1965 single "Bad Storm Coming" is
a fair moody number. That's a pretty low return on a band that enjoys a vociferous following among some collectors, although they
were really a pedestrian British R&B band with a propensity toward parched humor and odd novelty tunes that hasn't aged well.
—*Richie Unterberger*

Nick Drake

b. Jun. 19, 1948, Burma, **d.** Nov. 25, 1974
Singer-Songwriter, Folk-Rock
Mention the name Nick Drake and it's likely that Van Morrison or
Tim Buckley will be mentioned as well. If you asked fans to provide a one-word description of Drake's music, "haunting" would
surface most frequently. While his works were known to only a
cultish few in his lifetime, the legacy of Nick Drake looms ever
larger as the years have passed. In discovering the music, most
people gravitate to Drake's second album, *Bryter Layter,* a seemingly cheery and agreeable work that stands in sharp contrast to
the stark and desperate *Pink Moon.* Not even the lush, baroque orchestrations of *Five Leaves Left* can mask the real-life gloom, not a
studied pose, that Drake was unable to escape from. All three of
Drake's actual albums remain astonishingly valuable, with Joe
Boyd's production of *Bryter Layter* being a particularly standout
effort. That Drake's music has sold increasingly well in recent
years comes as little surprise, since Nick Drake has become a
most trendy namedrop among contemporary artists. It is safe to
say that the sad but beautiful music of Nick Drake will continue to
inspire for years to come. —*Steve Aldrich*

○ **Five Leaves Left** / 1969 / Hannibal ♦♦♦♦
Nick Drake's debut album skillfully augments his haunting folk-
based songs with tasteful string arrangements that accentuate the
gorgeous melancholy of his music. —*Stephen Thomas Erlewine*

○ **Bryter Layter** / 1970 / Hannibal ♦♦♦♦
While the strings on Nick Drake's second album are more prominent, they rarely take away from the impact of his music, which
significantly less sad on this record. However, *Bryter Layter* isn't
lighthearted—it's a reflective piece of music that gains power from
its own introspection. —*Stephen Thomas Erlewine*

○ **Pink Moon** / 1972 / Hannibal ♦♦♦♦
On his last album, Nick Drake strips away all of the excess instrumentation of his first two albums, keeping only the bare essentials. The result is a stark, brilliant album of despair, loneliness,
and alienation that is startling in its emotional power. —*Stephen
Thomas Erlewine*

★ **Fruit Tree** / 1986 / Hannibal ♦♦♦♦♦
Multi-disc album contains the complete works of this enigmatic
British singer/songwriter. —*William Ruhlmann*

Time of No Reply / 1986 / Hannibal ✦✦✦
A collection of ten previously unreleased tracks recorded between 1968 and 1974, the songs on *Time of No Reply* rank with Nick Drake's finest work. —*Stephen Thomas Erlewine*

Way to Blue: An Introduction to Nick Drack / 1994 / Hannibal ✦✦✦
A selection of 16 tracks from all three of his studio albums and the *Time Of No Reply* collection, compiled by Drake's producer, Joe Boyd. Of course the music is excellent, but Drake's albums stand so well on their own that this collection of piecemeal offerings hardly works as the best way to experience his distinctively haunting brand of folk-rock. —*Richie Unterberger*

Tanworth-In-Arden 1967/68 / Bootleg ✦✦✦
Long circulating as a tape among hardcore fans, these 18 solo acoustic songs were recorded by Drake at home; most or all of them were probably laid down before he had ever entered a studio. The sound quality is fuzzy, but given how little Drake recorded before his death, and how absolutely no unreleased material exists other than the four CDs included on his *Fruit Tree* box set, this is a Holy Grail (or at least a silver goblet) of sorts for Drake fanatics. Most of the material is in a far more traditional acoustic folk and blues vein than his official releases, which show a big leap in both songwriting maturity and instrumental sophistication. Here Nick sounds much like very early (acoustic) Donovan, covering traditional folk songs, "Summertime," "Get Together," and early Dylan; his originals are often quite derivative of these influences (and several compositions credited to Drake on the liner notes are in fact covers, or extremely derivative of existing standards). The best cuts—"Winter Is Gone," "The Reason Of The Seasons," "To the Garden"—show the emergence of a more idiosyncratic talent. Minor complaints: four songs from the original tape are missing (two do appear on *Fruit Tree*), some entertaining between-song banter has been eliminated, and there's a major typo in the CD title (this was in fact recorded in *Tanworth-In-Arden*). —*Richie Unterberger*

Dramarama

Group, Rock & Roll, Alternative Pop/Rock
Dramarama comes on like a hybrid of the Clash and the Replacements, playing a spiky, emotionally charged political rock & roll. After releasing a series of albums throughout the '80s and early '90s that were ignored by both the mainstream and the alternative audiences, they broke up in late 1994. —*Stephen Thomas Erlewine*

○ **Cinema Verite** / Nov. 1985 / Chameleon ✦✦✦✦
Cinema Verite begins a "trend" that will remain throughout Dramarama's recording career: some outstanding original tunes mixed with a couple well-chosen covers. In the case of the covers, they are generally tunes that are a little more obscure. For instance, on this album, in addition to the Velvet Underground's "Femme Fatale" the band has chosen a Bowie tune from *Diamond Dogs*. Start with this one and get them all. —*Jim Worbois*

○ **Stuck in Wonderamaland** / 1989 / Chameleon ✦✦✦✦
This is probably the second best album by Dramarama, one of the great overlooked bands of the '80s. John Easdale continues to grow as a writer and the band aptly handles all he gives them. One of the standouts on this record is "Last Cigarette" which, in both words and feel, captures the manic desperation of a smoker down to his last cigarette. The cover this time is Mott the Hoople's "I Wish I Was Your Mother." —*Jim Worbois*

○ **Box Office Bomb** / 1989 / Chameleon ✦✦✦✦
Dramarama expands their sound somewhat on *Box Office Bomb*. "It's Still Warm" is reminiscent of the Replacements while "Spare Change" has a psychedelic feel to it. The cover this time out is a tune from Patti Smith's *Radio Europa* album. —*Jim Worbois*

Live at China Club / 1990 / Chameleon ✦✦✦
● **Vinyl** / 1991 / Chameleon ✦✦✦✦
With *Vinyl*, Dramarama have captured everything that was good about '70s rock & roll. Hard driving, distorted, and muddy, this sounds more like a classic Rolling Stones album than the Stones themselves could have come up with in over a decade. The sound of a turntable needle on the run-out groove midway through (marking the end of side one) adds authenticity. A cover of the Stones' "Memo from Turner" is a nice touch too. —*Chris Woodstra*

Hi-Fi Sci-Fi / 1993 / Chameleon ✦✦✦
This album features some changes for Dramarama. Clem Burke (ex-Blondie) is now the drummer. There are *no* covers on this record. And, some interesting guests appear, such as Dwight Twilley (when's he going to make another record?), Neil Young's sister, Astrid, Benmont Tench, and Sylvain Sylvain (ex-New York Dolls and solo artist). Still, none of the changes or guests get in the way, making this another fine album. —*Jim Worbois*

Dramatics

Group, Soul
Popular Detroit R&B vocal aggregation that scored numerous hits for Volt and maintained their momentum through the disco era. The early Dramatics hits for Volt lived up to their billing with the emphatic vocals of Ron Banks (b. May 10, 1951) powering the funky "Whatcha See Is Whatcha Get," their first big-seller in 1971, and the R&B chart-topping ballad "In the Rain" the next year. The quintet was just as successful later in the decade, signing with ABC in 1975 and scoring repeatedly throughout disco-fever days. —*Bill Dahl*

Whatcha See Is Whatcha Get / 1971 / Stax ✦✦✦
This great debut album is a Tony Hestor creation. —*Richard Pack*

A Dramatic Experience / 1973 / Stax ✦✦✦
It's an anti-drug concept album. —*Richard Pack*

○ **Dramatically Yours** / 1973 / Stax ✦✦✦✦
One of their finest albums. The Dramatics had solidified their sound and personnel in the early '70s. L.J. Reynolds was now doing the leads, with Ron Banks' feathery falsetto and Willie Ford's booming baritone perfectly positioned at the top and bottom of the arrangements, and Reynolds and Lenny Mayes right in the center. Although they didn't generate much crossover success, they were on the R&B charts regularly with singles pulled from the album. —*Ron Wynn*

The Dells Vs. The Dramatics / 1974 / Cadet ✦✦✦
A fine set from both parties. The Dells and Dramatics were quite similar in their style, except that the Dells' signature soul sound came from the interaction of two, rather than three great singers. Each group took some songs on its own, and they also teamed on the single "Love Is Missing From Our Lives," the only song that proved a hit. The overall results were outstanding, although the album didn't do as well as anticipated. —*Ron Wynn*

○ **Drama V** / 1975 / ABC ✦✦✦✦
One of the best albums, featuring two great songs in "Who's Foolin'" and "Spaced Out Over You." They had found the perfect balance between solid uptempo funk tracks and sizzling love ballads, and there were temporarily no ego problems between the members. —*Ron Wynn*

The Dramatic Jackpot / 1975 / ABC ✦✦✦
The album that restored the group's soul credibility when it was issued in the early '70s. There had been some fallout from the splintering that resulted in Ron Banks going one way and other charter members the other. Banks' group had been dropped from Stax, and this was their first ABC album. It reached the Top 30 and gave them several chart hits as well. —*Ron Wynn*

● **The Best of the Dramatics** / 1976 / Stax ✦✦✦✦
A solid compilation, it includes the hits "Whatcha See Is Whatcha Get" (#9), "In the Rain" (#5), "Fell for You" (#45), and other equally good but lesser-known tracks. —*AMG*

Their Greatest Recordings / 1978 / At Ease ✦✦✦
Another good anthology, this one covering ABC and Cadet tracks. The Dramatics were encountering rough sledding at this point in their careers, but this collection reminded fans of their strengths: piercing harmonies, fine love tracks, and good leads by L.J. Reynolds and Ron Banks. —*Ron Wynn*

○ **10 1/2** / 1980 / MCA ✦✦✦✦
A celebratory album that marked their being together for over a decade, this was one of the group's best MCA/ABC albums, even though it didn't generate enormous success. "Welcome Back Home" and "Be with the One That You Love" were superbly performed and produced, while Reynolds' swaggering, soaring lead on "It Ain't Raining In Nobody's House But Mine" ranked among his best efforts. —*Ron Wynn*

Positive State of Mind / 1989 / Volt ✦✦✦
After a nearly six-year absence, the Dramatics regrouped in 1989. The new personnel included longtime veterans Ron Banks, L.J. Reynolds, William Howard, Willie Ford, and Lenny Mayes. This

was a well-produced, expertly sung soul work with a few urban contemporary production trappings, mostly drum tracks and synthesized backbeats. Sadly, the group found out that six years on the urban contemporary landscape was more like 60; they didn't get much response except from old fans happy they were back. – *Ron Wynn*

Stone Cold / 1990 / Volt ✦✦✦
The Dramatics had been through many breakups and reunions by the time of this '90 release. Their previous release didn't attract much attention for the revived Volt label, and unfortunately neither did this one. Ron Banks, L.J. Reynolds, Willie Ford, and company still sounded strong, and the harmonizing was marvelous, but there just wasn't much interest in '90 among the general urban contemporary/new jack/hip-hop audience in classic '70s soul. – *Ron Wynn*

○ **Best of Volt** / Stax ✦✦✦✦
The Dramatics were one of Stax's finest soul vocal groups, using Ron Banks' rising soprano, L.J. Reynolds' booming baritone, and Willie Ford's emphatic bass to create enticing love songs with excellent harmonizing at the top, in the middle, and at the bottom of the scale. Their albums tended to be erratic affairs, with outstanding love songs and sometimes dismal, formulaic dance tunes. This is one of many collections that spotlight their hits on the Stax/Volt label. – *Ron Wynn*

The Dream Academy

Group, Pop/Rock
A lush pop trio from Great Britain, featuring Nick Laird-Clowes, Gilbert Gabriel, and Kate St. John, that scored a #7 single in 1986 with "Life in a Northern Town." – *William Ruhlmann*

● **The Dream Academy** / 1985 / Reprise ✦✦✦✦
Classical influences (and not a little of *Sgt. Pepper*-era Beatles) can be heard on this lovely pop album, much of it co-produced by Pink Floyd's David Gilmour. Contains the hits "Life in a Northern Town" and "Love Parade." – *William Ruhlmann*

Remembrance Days / 1987 / Reprise ✦✦✦
A Different Kind of Weather / 1990 / Reprise ✦✦✦

Dream Syndicate

Group, Alternative Pop/Rock, Psychedelic
Of all of the so-called "paisley underground" Los Angeles bands of the '80s, the Steve Wynn-led Dream Syndicate was the one that gained the largest audience and was arguably the best of the lot. Instead of lifting their riffs from old Pink Floyd, Jefferson Airplane, or Byrds albums, Wynn relied on the darker sounds of the Velvet Underground and Neil Young, creating a dense, guitar-based pseudo-psychedelia that either soared on ballads or drilled on mid-tempo rockers; it was tailor-made for college radio success, where they received a fair amount of airplay. Dream Syndicate recorded several impressive records over their career, yet they never became big rock stars; the band called it quits in 1989, with Wynn pursuing a solo career. – *Stephen Thomas Erlewine*

The Days of Wine & Roses / 1982 / Slash ✦✦✦
Karl Precoda plays the kind of noisy guitar associated with the Velvet Underground, while lead singer Steve Wynn pursues his private demons on this perfectly realized low-budget '80s rock record. – *William Ruhlmann*

Medicine Show / 1984 / A&M ✦✦✦
This Is Not the New Dream Syndicate / 1984 / A&M ✦✦
Dream Syndicate / 1985 / Demon ✦✦✦
Out of the Grey / 1986 / Chrysalis ✦✦
50 in a 25 Zone / 1987 / Big Time ✦✦
Ghost Stories / 1988 / Enigma ✦✦✦
Paul B.Cutler plays the kind of noisy guitar associated with Neil Young and Crazy Horse, while lead singer Steve Wynn continues to pursue his private demons on what is nevertheless more of a mainstream rock record, maybe courtesy of Young's producer, Elliot Mazer. – *William Ruhlmann*

Dream Syndicate . . . Live at Raji's / 1989 / Enigma ✦✦✦
● **Tell When It's Over: The Best of Dream Syndicate** / 1992 / Rhino ✦✦✦✦
These fifteen tracks contain the cream of the crop of this Los Angeles band's independent and major label work. Among the highlights are "When You Smile," "Tell Me When It's Over," and "Hal-

loween" from their 1982 Ruby/Slash EP *Days of Wine and Roses*. The fine remastering captures their dense Velvet Underground-style rock in all its trashy glory. The booklet is loaded with a detailed history, many photos, lyrics, and track and personnel listings. – *Rick Clark*

Dream Theater

Group, Hard Rock
Originally known as Majesty, the nucleus of the band is comprised of John Petrucci (guitar), John Myung (bass), Mike Portnoy (drums), and Kevin Moore (keyboards; left the group in 1995), all of whom were trained at the Berklee School of Music. Dream Theater's music is an interesting thrash-influenced brand of progressive rock. After being dropped by MCA following the failure of their 1989 debut album, vocalist Charlie Dominici quit the band, and it appeared doubtful that they would be able to make it. However, the band somehow broke through on MTV with an edited version of *Images and Words'* "Pull Me Under." Petrucci has been hailed as a guitar hero of the future, being one of the few technically proficient guitarists to emerge in the '90s. – *Steve Huey*

Whey Dream and Day Unite / 1989 / Mechanic ✦✦✦
● **Images & Words** / 1992 / Atco ✦✦✦✦
Live At The Marquee / 1993 / Warner Music ✦✦
Awake / 1994 / Atlantic ✦✦

Dreamlovers

Group, R&B, Doo-Wop
Early 60s Philadelphia R&B vocal group. Their creamy ballad "When We Get Married" was a gorgeous throwback to doo-wop's heyday when it emerged in 1961, and the Dreamlovers cut several more fine group harmony items. Formed in 1956, the quintet supplied background vocals on Chubby Checker's mammoth rendering of "the Twist" and soloed on V-Tone before signing with Heritage Records and stepping forward with "When We Get Married," revived in 1970 by the Intruders. The Dreamlovers returned to the charts on a smaller scale the next year with another ballad on End, "If I Should Lose You." – *Bill Dahl*

The Best of the Dreamlovers, Vol. 2 / Collectables ✦✦✦
● **The Best of the Dreamlovers, Vol. 1** / Collectables ✦✦✦✦
Worthwhile early-'60s R&B vocal group. – *AMG*

DRI

Group, Hardcore, Thrash, Heavy Metal
D.R.I., which stands for Dirty Rotten Imbeciles, were one of the first bands to mix hardcore with thrash metal. Formed in Texas in the early '80s, they started out playing basic, straight-ahead hardcore. Their original lineup consisted of vocalist Kurt Brecht, drummer Eric Brecht, guitarist Spike Cassidy, and bassist Dennis Johnson. After moving to San Francisco for their second album, they started mixing heavy metal into their sound, and by their third record, it was impossible to tell which side of the dividing line they fell on (the two genres had become quite similar by then anyway). The band has experienced numerous personnel shifts over the years. On a Mexican tour supporting 1988's *Four of a Kind*, bass player John Menor was severely injured by a robber, but the band rebounded the next year with what many consider to be their best album, *Thrash Zone*. – *Steve Huey*

● **Dirty Rotten LP** / 1984 / Dirty Rotten ✦✦✦✦
Dealing with It / 1985 / Metal Blade ✦✦✦
Crossover / 1987 / Metal Blade ✦✦✦
Four of a Kind / 1988 / Metal Blade ✦✦
○ **Thrash Zone** / 1989 / Metal Blade ✦✦✦✦

The Drifters

Group, R&B, Doo-Wop
The Drifters were the longest-lasting of the '50s doo-wop groups simply because they were the best. What other vocal group from those days produced such 20th-century marvels as Clyde McPhatter and Ben E. King? What other group survived numerous personnel changes and changes in audience tastes, keeping their name in the charts for 12 straight years? Doo-wop is certainly full of mythological groups, celebrated as much for their obscurity as their music; the Drifters are the group that turned the myth into fact.

Clyde McPhatter was already an R&B star when Atlantic's Ahmet Ertegun signed him in 1953, thanks to his work with Billy Ward's Dominoes. After leaving them, McPhatter assembled a group to support his glorious, soaring vocals, and in 1953 the Drifters landed their first hit with Jesse Stone's "Money Honey." A slew of meticulously recorded classics followed: "Let the Boogie Woogie Roll," "Such a Night," "Honey Love," and "White Christmas" are among the best. McPhatter took off for a solo career in 1954 but was amply replaced by Johnny Moore, who was on hand when the group recorded three of their finest songs: "Ruby Baby," "Your Promise to Be Mine," and "Adorable."

Drifters manager George Threadwell disbanded the group in 1958 and found an ensemble called the Crowns, who had a lead singer named Ben E. King; a new Drifters was born. Under the wings of Jerry Leiber and Mike Stoller, this new outfit established their own identity in 1959 with the Latin-tinged "There Goes My Baby," a tour de force for King and the first R&B song to include strings, which ushered in a new era of Black music, known as soul. King departed in 1960, but thanks to a string of songs written by the likes of Doc Pomus and Mort Shuman, the Drifters, with Rudy Lewis and Johnny Moore taking leads, became a veritable hit factory. "Save the Last Dance for Me," "On Broadway," "Up on the Roof," and "This Magic Moment" all helped define the sound of soul music and define an era, with their tugging romanticism, dancing strings, and musical innovation and sophistication. — John Floyd

☆ **Let the Boogie Woogie Roll: Greatest Hits** / 1988 / Rhino ♦♦♦♦♦

Let the Boogie Woogie Roll—Greatest Hits is the definitive account of the early group (1953–1958) and Clyde McPhatter's greatest sides. —*Bruce Eder*

☆ **All-Time Greatest Hits & More: 1959–1965** / 1988 / Rhino ♦♦♦♦♦

All the Greatest Hits & More—1959–1965 is a towering and magnificent collection of some of the best popular R&B ever done this side of Sam Cooke. —*Bruce Eder*

★ **The Very Best of the Drifters** / 1993 / Rhino ♦♦♦♦♦
Combining all the greatest hits from both the Clyde McPhatter and Ben E. King eras, the single-disc *The Very Best of the Drifters* serves as the perfect introduction to the seminal R&B vocal group. —*Stephen Thomas Erlewine*

Drivin' N Cryin'

Group, Rock & Roll
This Georgia quartet boldly mixes country and bluegrass tunes alongside pedal-to-the-metal hard rock and, more often than not, manages to pull it off. It's an over-amped '90s version of the Buffalo Springfield style of earthy rock eclecticism. —*Rick Clark*

Scarred But Smarter / 1986 / Island ♦♦♦
Their debut boldly mixes everything from countryish sendups to death rock. It almost works. Certainly it's an engaging listen. Highlights include: "Stand Up and Fight for It," "Another Scarlet Butterfly," and "Saddle on the Side of the Road." —*Rick Clark*

Whisper Tames the Lion / 1987 / Island ♦♦♦
The juxtaposing of diverse genres continues, with greater success. It was produced by Anton Fier (Grapes of Wrath, Joe Henry). — *Rick Clark*

○ **Mystery Road** / 1989 / Island ♦♦♦♦
New guitarist Buren Fowler adds more punch to the band's sound. Kevin Kinney's mature songwriting grasp of various genres is shown to great effect, from reckless rockers from "Toy Never Played With" to more laidback tracks like "Peacemaker." —*Rick Clark*

● **Fly Me Courageous** / 1991 / Island ♦♦♦♦
This Atlanta quartet's most fully realized synthesis of aggressive hard rock, country-rock, and folk-rock includes visceral production by Geoff Workman. Standout tracks include the hyperdrive of "Rush Hour" and "Lost in the Shuffle," as well as "Around the Block Again," "Chain Reaction," "Build a Fire," and the title cut. —*Rick Clark*

Smoke / 1993 / Island ♦♦♦
As time goes by, Drivin' N Cryin' keep evolving into the heirs to the Southern rock throne. *Smoke*, while not as impressive or original as previous efforts, offers some crunching rock, but it really shines during the country-tinged acoustic numbers "What Difference Does it Make" and "When You Come Back." —*AMG*

Pete Droge

Singer-Songwriter, Alternative Pop/Rock
Singer-songwriter Pete Droge's career was helped immeasurably by his friendship with Pearl Jam guitarist Mike McCready. McCready helped Droge secure a deal with American Records to release his 1994 debut, *Necktie Second.* Droge is a rootsy rocker in the vein of Tom Petty and John Mellencamp, with the occasional introspective ballad. On the strength of the tongue-in-cheek single "If You Don't Love Me (I'll Kill Myself)" *Necktie Second* became an AAA hit. —*Stephen Thomas Erlewine*

Necktie Second / 1994 / Warner Brothers ♦♦♦

Ducks Deluxe

Group, Rock & Roll
If the old scientific adage is true—that for every action there is an equal and opposite reaction—than British pub-rockers Ducks Deluxe were purely and simply a reaction. With the mid-'70s English pop scene dominated by glitter/glam-rockers like Gary Glitter, the Sweet or blustery, chops-heavy art-rockers like Yes, Tull, Genesis, etc., then Ducks Deluxe represented none of the above. One of the first pub-rock bands, the Ducks played basic American-style blues and boogie with remarkable panache and thorough disregard for the whims of the zeitgeist. They never were hugely popular, but the unpretentious, do-it-yourself, working-class attitude they and their contemporaries (most notably seminal pub-rockers Dr. Feelgood) exuded influenced the English punk scene that was right around the corner. With friends like Dave Edmunds producing their records, the Ducks (guitarist/vocalist Sean Tyla, guitarist Martin Belmont, bassist Nick Garvey, and keyboardist Andy McMasters) came up with engaging, though not life-changing, records that celebrated the simple joys of rock & roll. Sure, much of it sounds like recycled Chuck Berry, but there's an infectious enthusiasm that the fan in you, who simply wants to hoist a pint of lager and hear some Little Richard, will love. Ironically, to get the biggest promotional boost in America, the Ducks Deluxe LP was released three years after they'd split up. This little bit of shift marketing came as a result of ex-Ducks going on to more prominent bands like the Motors, the Rumour and the Tyla Gang. —*John Dougan*

Jumpin' / 1975 / Skydog ♦♦♦

Don't Mind Rockin' Tonite / 1978 / RCA ♦♦♦
After RCA failed to do much for the band when the label released their self-titled debut record in 1974, the powers that be decided that this collection of material from their two previous LPs, along with some outtakes and B-sides, would engender more interest in the band now that they had some punk/new wave credibility. Well, it was a good thought, but it didn't work. Marketing avarice notwithstanding, this is a fine, loose-limbed, fast and funky record chock full of guitar bombs from Martin Belmont and some macho growling from Sean Tyla. The pure pop of "Love's Melody" (written by McMasters) is jarring in juxtaposition to all the blues-based grunting, but nothing detracts from the good vibe this record and the Ducks produced in their short existence. —*John Dougan*

Last Night of a Pub Rock Band / 1981 / Blue Moon ♦♦

● **Ducks Deluxe/Taxi to the Terminal Zone** / Edsel ♦♦♦♦
Both of the group's albums, *Ducks Deluxe* and *Taxi to the Terminal Zone*, compiled on one CD with one song from each removed to fit the format's time restriction—really a best-of, and worth any three Led Zeppelin albums. (import) —*Bruce Eder*

The Dukes of Stratosphear

Group, Alternative Pop/Rock, Psychedelic
The Dukes of Stratosphear (conceived in 1987) are the psychedelic alter-personalities of the English alternative pop/rock band XTC. —*Rick Clark*

● **Chips from the Chocolate Fireball** / 1987 / Geffen ♦♦♦♦
Fans of late-'60s psychedelia will love this affectionate Rutles-esque collaboration between XTC (posing as the Dukes) and producer John Leckie (Posies, Let's Active, House of Freaks). *Chips from the Chocolate Fireball* is loaded with playful tips of the hat to artists like the Move, the Electric Prunes, early Pink Floyd, the Yardbirds, Spirit, the Zombies, the Beach Boys, and (of course) the Beatles. By the way, this is a compilation of the Dukes's *25-O-Clock* EP and the full-length album *Psonic Psunspot*. —*Rick Clark*

Dumptruck

Group, Alternative Pop/Rock
Essentially a two-man project of Massachussetts natives Kirk Swan and Seth Tiven, with a rotating rhythm section, Dumptruck were, for a brief moment, among the favorites of U.S. college radio in the mid '80s, combining the jangly power-pop sound of the Southern alternative scene with intelligent lyrics and a melancholy twist. Swan left late in 1986, leaving Tiven to carry on for one more album, *For the Country,* before dissolving the band in 1988. The band reformed after settling legal disputes with their label in 1995 with a small-scale club tour of the US and a new record deal. —*Chris Woodstra*

D Is for Dumptruck / 1983 / Big Time ✦✦✦
Positively / 1986 / Big Time ✦✦✦
● **For the Country** / 1987 / Big Time ✦✦✦✦

Simon Dupree

Pop/Rock
There were countless British bands playing R&B and soul in the 1960s. A lot of them weren't that good, but then, they didn't have to be; playing workmanlike, competent soul covers guaranteed work in a country where interest in R&B was phenomenal, but tours by genuine African-American soul singers were rare. Simon Dupree & the Big Band, hailing from Portsmouth, were one of those relatively faceless, but relatively competent, bands. There was no "Simon Dupree"; the lead vocalist was actually Derek Shulman, and his band favored horn-driven '60s soul of the Stax/Volt variety. They recorded an album and a few singles, but nothing happened until they decided to jump on the psychedelic bandwagon in late 1967.

"Kites," with its haunting melody, interlude of spoken Chinese poetry, Mellotron, and gongs, was a Top Ten British hit. It wasn't at all characteristic of the band, who would have preferred to offer reheated soul, but was undoubtedly their most distinctive offering. They continued to adopt a quasi-psychedelic approach on a few subsequent singles, which were not terribly exciting, but retain a period British psychedelic charm. Indeed, Simon Dupree's psychedelic singles were far more distinctive than their soul ones, though they couldn't repeat the success of "Kites." But the psychedelic experience must have eventually gotten under their skin, because the group mutated into the progressive rock group Gentle Giant in 1970. —*Richie Unterberger*

● **Amen** / 1982 / Charly ✦✦✦✦
20 tracks, taken from various 1966-69 singles and their 1967 LP *Without Reservations.* "Kites" and obscure, psychedelic-influenced single tracks such as "For Whom the Bell Tolls," "Like the Sun Like the Fire," "Sleep," and "Thinking About My Life" generally shine over the derivative, organ-based soul material. Modestly enjoyable in spots, it's mostly of historical significance. —*Richie Unterberger*

The Duprees

Group, Doo-Wop
Specializing in updated renditions of '40s and '50s pop fare, the Duprees had a classy sound that harked back to an earlier era. Formed as the Parisians in Jersey City, they were discovered by George Paxton, who ran Coed Records in New York. Paxton convinced the quartet to change their name, and they hit big their first time out in 1962 with a polished revival of Jo Stafford's "You Belong to Me." Most sides cut for Coed were in the same big-band mold, including "My Own True Love" and "Have You Heard." Lead singer Joe Canzano (b. Apr. 3, 1943) left the group in 1964, and the Duprees moved to Columbia the next year with minimal success. —*Bill Dahl*

○ **You Belong to Me** / 1962 / Collectables ✦✦✦✦
Debut album, featuring the title track hit and 11 other doo-wop classics done in typical early-'60s NYC production style. —*Cub Koda*

○ **Have You Heard** / 1963 / Collectables ✦✦✦✦
Second album, companion piece to *You Belong to Me.* (Out of print) —*Cub Koda*

● **The Best of the Duprees [Rhino]** / 1990 / Rhino ✦✦✦✦

Duran Duran

Group, Dance-Pop, New Wave, Pop/Rock
The major teen-pop band of the '80s (Nick Rhodes, keyboards; John Taylor, bass; Simon Le Bon, vocals; Andy Taylor, guitar; Roger Taylor, drums) formed in 1978 in Birmingham, England, although the final lineup was not set until the addition of Simon Le Bon in 1980. Taking their name from a character in the Jane Fonda film *Barbarella,* their style of dance music was quickly drawn into the new romantic movement of the British punk/new-wave scene. These so-called haircut bands were inspired to their fashion-centered look and hip-synthesizer, neo-disco style by bands like Roxy Music. Duran Duran's lush arrangements and distinct vocal sound, combined with an aggressive new-wave, funk-rhythm section, caught the attention of the mass market. But it was their visual appeal and exotic/erotic videos for "Girls on Film," "Hungry Like the Wolf," and "Rio" on the newborn MTV that catapulted them into concert arenas and multi-platinum stardom. Although unabashed teen idols, the members tried to gain more critical respect with sideline efforts like Power Station (for John & Andy Taylor) and Arcadia (for LeBon, Roger Taylor, and Rhodes). After these experiments, the band went through a series of lineup changes and artistic wanderings as their teenage fans began to outgrow them. But none of their later works were as successful as *Rio* or *Seven and the Ragged Tiger.* With the end virtually in sight, Duran Duran released the hits/retrospective package *Decade* and one final studio album before the band temporarily disbanded.

In 1993, the band returned with a self-titled album that became a surprise success, thanks to two hit singles—"Ordinary World" and "Come Undone." Two years later, the band received some of the harshest reviews of their career for their covers album, *Thank You.* Even with the bad press, Duran Duran's version of Grand Masterflash's "White Lines (Don't Don't Do It)" received a significant amount of play in dance clubs. —*Scott Bultman*

○ **Duran Duran [First]** / 1981 / Capitol ✦✦✦✦
Duran Duran's self-titled debut effectively established their slick, catchy synth-pop sound. Featuring the decadent "Girls on Film" and "Planet Earth," the album set the pace for scores of new wave bands in the early '80s, which were subsequently dubbed the new romantics. —*Stephen Thomas Erlewine*

○ **Rio** / 1982 / Capitol ✦✦✦✦
Rio was Duran Duran's breakthrough album, selling over two million copies in the United States. The album's success was helped immeasurably by a series of slick, big-budget videos that featured the band cavorting in various exotic locations. However, the music on the album was as noteworthy as the accompanying videos. *Rio* featured more ambitious arrangements, with the group pursuing a more dance-oriented direction without losing its sense of pop songcraft. With the hit singles "Hungry like the Wolf," "Rio" and "Save a Prayer" forming the core of the record, *Rio* stands as their best, most accomplished record. —*Stephen Thomas Erlewine*

Seven and the Ragged Tiger / 1983 / Capitol ✦✦✦
Seven and the Ragged Tiger was released at the height of Duran Duran-mania and it shows. Throughout the album, the group replicates the sound of *Rio,* yet they have failed to write strong material. Although they are catchy, the singles "Union of the Snake" and "The Reflex" aren't on par with "Hungry like the Wolf" and "Rio." Only the brooding "New Moon on Monday" matches the inspired pop-craft of *Rio.* —*Stephen Thomas Erlewine*

Arena / 1984 / Capitol ✦✦
Seeing Duran Duran in concert in 1984 was like seeing a video come to life. The group put on a spectacular show, filled with impressive light shows and videos. Since the concerts featured so many visuals, the band could not vary the tempos greatly, resulting in music that nearly replicated the studio versions of the songs. *Arena* accurately reproduces the sound and feeling of these concerts. Duran Duran sounds tight and professional (probably due to studio overdubbing), yet Simon Le Bon sounds a little winded, possibly because of all the dancing he had to do during the course of the show. The new Nile Rodgers-produced single "The Wild Boys" was added to the album as bait and the strategy worked—peaking at number four, *Arena* was Duran Duran's highest-charting album and it sold over two million copies. Nevertheless, it's the most inconsequential album in their entire catalog, even if it's fun. —*Stephen Thomas Erlewine*

Notorious / 1986 / Capitol ✦✦✦
After a brief hiatus, Duran Duran returned as a trio in 1986 with *Notorious.* The spare groove of the title track made it clear that the band was trying to shed its teeny-bopper image and refashion themselves as a pop band for yuppies. Thanks to Nile Rodgers'

polished, radio-friendly production, *Notorious* was a success, as the band found a middle ground between synth-pop and White funk. —*Stephen Thomas Erlewine*

Big Thing / 1988 / Capitol ♦♦
Big Thing replicated the clean, mechanized funk of *Notorious*, yet the band failed to come up with a batch of strong songs. The naggingly catchy "I Don't Want Your Love" made it into the Top Ten, but the remainder of the album was bland and undistinguished. —*Stephen Thomas Erlewine*

● **Decade: Greatest Hits** / Nov. 15, 1989 / Capitol ♦♦♦♦
All their hits "Hungry like the Wolf" (#3), "Rio" (#14), "Is There Something I Should Know?" (#4), "Union of the Snake" (#3), "The Wild Boys" (#2), "Notorious" (#2), "I Don't Want Your Love" (#4), and the #1s "The Reflex" and "A View to a Kill" are included in a well-selected package. —*Dan Heilman*

Liberty / Aug. 13, 1990 / Capitol ♦
Apart from the greatest-hits collection *Decade*, *Big Thing* was the lowest-charting Duran Duran album to date, prompting the band to rework their sound for 1990's *Liberty*. Unfortunately, the group had no idea what direction they wanted to pursue. *Liberty* features everything from disco to guitar rock, adding elements of Motown, Philly soul, and new wave along the way. The stylistic diversity may have worked if the band had material to support it, but nothing on the record matched their best work—it didn't even match the finest moments of *Big Thing*. —*Stephen Thomas Erlewine*

○ **Duran Duran [1993]** / 1993 / Capitol ♦♦♦♦
Duran Duran came back out of nowhere in early 1993 with a new album and a huge hit, "Ordinary World." The group sounds more relaxed and mature than it did during their glory days, but not all that much has changed; instead of personifying the days of early-'80s synthesized dance-pop, the music is smooth dance-pop for the '90s. Taken on its own terms, *Duran Duran* works every bit as well as *Duran Duran*, *Rio* or *Seven and the Ragged Tiger*. "Ordinary World" and "Come Undone" are wonderful pop singles that sit between some passable album tracks and the occasional embarrassment, namely the wretched cover of the Velvet Underground's "Femme Fatale." In other words, Duran Duran are back and as good as they ever were. —*Stephen Thomas Erlewine*

Thank You / Apr. 1995 / Capitol ♦♦
An album of Duran Duran covering their "influences" was never something even the most dedicated fan wanted to hear, yet the band had the audacity to record *Thank You*, a collection of the group's favorite songs. Featuring songwriters as diverse as Bob Dylan and Sly Stone, *Thank You* works best when the band realizes the monumental silliness of their cover, as on "White Lines," which is performed with Grandmaster Flash himself, and the acoustic blues rendition of Public Enemy's "911 Is a Joke." Or, it works when they can reinvent material like Lou Reed's "Perfect Day" into a slick MOR ballad. When *Thank You* doesn't work, it's because the band doesn't quite get what made the original version special ("Lay Lady Lay" and "Watching the Detectives"). Too many plain, mediocre songs (the Doors' "Crystal Ship") prevent the album from being either unintentionally funny or genuinely successful. The record is solely a curiosity and not a very interesting one at that. —*Stephen Thomas Erlewine*

Ian Dury

b. May 12, 1942, Upminster, Essex, England
Rock & Roll, New Wave
When Ian Dury released his first record in 1977, he was 35 years old yet he fit in perfectly with the U.K. punk scene. Dury had energy to spare with his raucous rock & roll and surprisingly incisive lyrics. Although he could be angry and indignant, Dury's music wasn't full of bile—it was joyful noise-making. Dury never became a star in America—perhaps his thick Cockney accent was impenetrable—yet he became a beloved figure in the U.K., releasing records until 1984 and performing throughout the '80s and '90s. —*Stephen Thomas Erlewine*

○ **New Boots & Panties** / 1977 / Edsel ♦♦♦♦
Ian Dury's debut album positively seeths with energy, as he tears through a set of raw and funny punk rockers like the frenetic "Blockheads." However, the emotional core of the record lies in the slightly slower, but no less inspired, number like "Sweet Gene Vincent," "My Old Man," and "Wake up and Make Love with Me," which provide the context for his raging rockers. —*Stephen Thomas Erlewine*

Do It Yourself / 1979 / Edsel ♦♦♦
On his second album, Ian Dury began to move away from the exaggerated crude humor of his debut. *Do It Yourself* cleans up his act slightly without taming his willful eccentricity, but the most remarkable thing about the album is how Dury and the Blockheads explore dance and disco while retaining their punk spirit and vitality. —*Stephen Thomas Erlewine*

Laughter / 1980 / Stiff ♦♦♦
Dury's last album with Stiff was his first with former Dr. Feelgood guitarist Wilko Johnson as the chief Blockhead. Under Johnson's direction, the music was more eclectic than either of Dury's previous records, but the diversity sounded unfocused. *Laughter*'s best moments came when Dury and the Blockheads stuck to the three-chord rock that made them cult figures in the U.K. —*Stephen Thomas Erlewine*

Lord Upminster / 1981 / Polydor ♦♦
When Ian Dury left Stiff Records, he also left the Blockheads behind, recording *Lord Upminster* with reggae superstars Robbie Shakespeare and Sly Dunbar as producers. *Lord Upminster* turned out to be a set of uninspired funk that lack the joyful energy of his three previous records. —*Stephen Thomas Erlewine*

○ **Jukebox Dury** / 1981 / Stiff ♦♦♦♦

4000 Weeks Holiday / 1984 / Polydor

○ **Sex & Drugs & Rock & Roll** / 1986 / Edsel ♦♦♦♦

Apples / 1989 / WEA

The Bus Driver's Prayer and Other . . . / 1992 / Edsel ♦♦♦

● **Sex & Drugs & Rock 'n' Roll: Best of Ian Dury and the Blockheads** / 1992 / Rhino ♦♦♦♦
A fine eighteen-track collection, it features nearly every worthwhile track Ian Dury ever recorded. —*AMG*

Bob Dylan

b. May 24, 1941, Duluth, MN
Rock & Roll, Country-Rock, Singer-Songwriter, Folk-Rock
The greatest songwriter of his generation and a figure of incalculable influence on popular music from the '60s on, Bob Dylan is also, with the possible exception of Elvis Presley, the most important individual in rock music ever.

Dylan came from Minnesota to New York City in 1961, at the age of 19, as an acolyte of folksinger Woody Guthrie, although he had played rock music in the late '50s. He met Guthrie (who was slowly dying in a hospital) and was quickly taken up by the New York folk community. He signed to Columbia Records and, in March 1962, released his first album, *Bob Dylan*, consisting largely of folk-blues covers. By this time, however, he had begun to write original songs, many in the philosophical/political style of his Greenwich Village compatriots (though far superior in quality), the best early example being "Blowin' in the Wind." Many of these songs were on Dylan's second album, *The Freewheelin' Bob Dylan*, released in May 1963. That summer, the popular folk group Peter, Paul & Mary took "Blowin' in the Wind" to the Top Ten in the national charts. Thereafter, Bob Dylan songs became favorites among many pop and folk performers. As the result of such exposure, *Freewheelin'* became a chart hit in September 1963.

Dylan followed with two albums in 1964, the heavily protest-oriented *The Times They Are A-Changin'* and the more introspective *Another Side of Bob Dylan*. In 1965, he began recording and playing concerts with rock musicians, which vastly increased his following but also led to controversy within the folk community. His singles "Like a Rolling Stone" and "Positively 4th Street" were Top Ten hits, as were the albums *Bringing It All Back Home* and *Highway 61 Revisited*, and the "folk-rock" sound of his music could be heard on any number of other artists' records, many of them written by Dylan himself. Dylan undertook a world tour in 1966 to promote the double album *Blonde on Blonde*, which featured the Top Ten single "Rainy Day Women #12 & 35." That summer he was in a motorcycle accident and he withdrew from public view for a year and a half, meanwhile recording the informal material later released as *The Basement Tapes*.

When Dylan returned to action in late 1967, it was with the quieter *John Wesley Harding* album, followed in 1969 by the country-flavored *Nashville Skyline* and its Top Ten single "Lay Lady Lay." Critics expecting Dylan's more complex work were shocked and they savaged his two-disc *Self-Portrait* in 1970, though most saw *New Morning*, released only a few months later, as a return to form.

Dylan was not much heard from in the early '70s (he played at George Harrison's Bangladesh benefit concert in 1971, and in 1973 he appeared in the film *Pat Garrett and Billy the Kid* and wrote its score), but he returned in 1974 with a national concert tour and the #1 album *Planet Waves*. This was followed in 1975 by *Blood on the Tracks*, regarded by many as his best collection of the decade. The same year, Dylan organized a roving band of musicians as the Rolling Thunder Revue and toured the Northeast, later appearing in other parts of the country in 1976.

A film crew was part of the entourage, and Dylan put together a sprawling film, *Renaldo & Clara*, released in 1978. With that done, he went on an international tour and released a new album, *Street Legal*. In 1979, Dylan converted to Christianity and released the first of three overtly religious albums, *Slow Train Coming*.

The religious fervor became less apparent by the time of *Infidels* in 1983, and Dylan has released several excellent albums since, while touring more or less continually. The '80s and early '90s have also seen the welcome legitimate release of much previously unissued vintage Dylan material (some of it widely available on bootlegs). — *William Ruhlmann*

Bob Dylan / Mar. 19, 1962 / Columbia ✦✦✦
For the most part, Bob Dylan's debut album positions him as an interpretive singer of rural folk songs, and already influential at that. The Animals found "House of the Rising Sun" on this album, while Led Zeppelin borrowed "In My Time of Dyin'." But the most striking track is the Dylan original "Song to Woody," his tribute to Woody Guthrie, which leaves no doubt he intends to carry on in his mentor's footsteps. — *William Ruhlmann*

☆ **The Freewheelin' Bob Dylan** / May 27, 1963 / Columbia ✦✦✦✦
The most important collection of original songs issued in the '60s. "Don't Think Twice, It's All Right," "Girl from the North Country," "A Hard Rain's A-Gonna Fall," "Masters of War," and, especially, "Blowin' in the Wind" have long since become standards, and their sheer range, from bitter protest to wry romantic regret, is astonishing, not to mention the absurd apocalyptic humor of some of the album's other tracks. The songs were so strong that they put across Dylan's limited, rough vocal style at a time when such a voice normally would have seemed completely unacceptable in a professional singer. This album transformed the notion of what "good" singing was. — *William Ruhlmann*

○ **The Times They Are A-Changin'** / Jan. 13, 1964 / Columbia ✦✦✦✦
Dylan devoted most of his third album to hard, uncompromising topical or "protest" songs, starting with the anthemic title track and continuing through "The Lonesome Death of Hattie Carroll," "Ballad of Hollis Brown," "Only a Pawn in Their Game," and "With God on Our Side." — *William Ruhlmann*

☆ **Another Side of Bob Dylan** / Aug. 8, 1964 / Columbia ✦✦✦✦✦
The first of two transitional albums in which Dylan moved beyond protest, and then beyond folk music. Here, in songs like "Chimes of Freedom" and "My Back Pages," he suggested that social issues were much more complicated than the increasingly polarized times made them seem. His lyrics, meanwhile, also became more complicated and poetic. Other singers would mine this album for hits with "All I Really Want to Do" and "It Ain't Me, Babe." — *William Ruhlmann*

☆ **Bringing It All Back Home** / Mar. 22, 1965 / Columbia ✦✦✦✦✦
Dylan added a bluesy rock-band backing for the first half of this album, and the lyrics of the new songs are compendiums of allusions and witticisms—"Subterranean Homesick Blues," "Maggie's Farm," "Mr. Tambourine Man," "It's All Right, Ma (I'm Only Bleeding)." Even the love songs achieve a new poetic height—"She Belongs to Me," "Love Minus Zero/No Limit," "It's All Over Now, Baby Blue." — *William Ruhlmann*

☆ **Highway 61 Revisited** / Aug. 30, 1965 / Columbia ✦✦✦✦✦
Dylan only upped the ante, making more extensive use of a crack backup band including Al Kooper and Michael Bloomfield to play his signature song, "Like a Rolling Stone," and other articulate, poetic, and incredibly bitter songs, notably "Ballad of a Thin Man" and "Desolation Row." — *William Ruhlmann*

☆ **Blonde on Blonde** / May 16, 1966 / Columbia ✦✦✦✦✦
The bitterness was transmuted into humor and absurdity on this remarkable album, in which Dylan's gush of wordplay seems endlessly inventive, his wit razor sharp, and his world-weariness overwhelming. The music, meanwhile, has coalesced into a rock backing that influences every musician who hears it. — *William Ruhlmann*

★ **Bob Dylan's Greatest Hits** / Mar. 27, 1967 / Columbia ✦✦✦✦✦
A 10-song retrospective of the work of the most impressive—and most protean—singer/songwriter of the period 1963 to 1966. Please note that, while this album is listed as the "pick" of this period of Dylan's career due to its general accessibility, a full understanding of the popular music of the '60s is impossible unless the listener is familiar with its three predecessors. *Greatest Hits* combines folk-protest standards like "Blowin' in the Wind" and "The Times They Are A-Changin'" with his folk/rock hits "Like a Rolling Stone" and "Rainy Day Women #12 & 35." — *William Ruhlmann*

☆ **John Wesley Harding** / Dec. 27, 1967 / Columbia ✦✦✦✦✦
A quieter, simpler album than those Dylan had made in the mid-'60s, this "comeback" record nevertheless contained open-ended, parable-like songs, the most memorable of which has turned out to be "All Along the Watchtower." — *William Ruhlmann*

☆ **Nashville Skyline** / Apr. 9, 1969 / Columbia ✦✦✦✦✦
Dylan reached a sales peak with this album of simple, country-inflected songs (including "Lay Lady Lay"). — *William Ruhlmann*

Self Portrait / Jun. 8, 1970 / Columbia ✦✦
That Dylan was suffering writer's block should have been apparent from the skimpy *Nashville Skyline*, but he shocked his following by turning out this two-record set mostly devoted to covers of songs by the Everly Brothers and Simon and Garfunkel. A few tracks were drawn from Dylan's concert performance at the Isle of Wight on Aug. 31, 1969, and they proved ragged. For an audience accustomed to Dylan's classic '60s albums, this first album of the '70s was a crushing disappointment. — *William Ruhlmann*

○ **New Morning** / Oct. 21, 1970 / Columbia ✦✦✦✦
While retaining some of the bucolic, sunny outlook of his recent work, Dylan partially turned back to a grittier rock sound (Al Kooper again in the mix) and to the more ironic, poetic lyrics of his mid-60s songs. — *William Ruhlmann*

★ **Bob Dylan's Greatest Hits, Vol. 2** / Nov. 17, 1971 / Columbia ✦✦✦✦✦
A grab-bag of material dating back to 1963, this sprawling two-disc set is notable for its rarities, especially the 1971 single "Watching the River Flow" and the 1963 live performance of "Tomorrow Is a Long Time." — *William Ruhlmann*

Pat Garrett & Billy the Kid [soundtrack] / Jul. 13, 1973 / Columbia ✦✦
Dylan's soundtrack for this Sam Peckinpah-directed Western in which he co-starred consists of some folkish instrumentals, several takes of a ballad called "Billy," and "Knockin' on Heaven's Door," a simple song that has become one of his best-remembered compositions. — *William Ruhlmann*

Dylan / Nov. 16, 1973 / Columbia ✦
When Dylan signed to Geffen Records, Columbia Records retaliated by releasing this, which consists of outtakes from the sessions that produced his worst album, *Self Portrait*. There oughta be a law. — *William Ruhlmann*

Planet Waves / Jan. 17, 1974 / Columbia ✦✦✦
A companion work to its predecessor, *New Morning*, this first album to be recorded with Dylan's backup group, the Band, mixes pronouncements of marital and familial contentment with severe criticisms of the singer himself and others. Contains "Forever Young." — *William Ruhlmann*

Before the Flood / Jun. 20, 1974 / Columbia ✦✦✦
This double album chronicles Bob Dylan and the Band's U.S. tour of January and February 1974. It features souped-up performances of many of Dylan's hits and best songs as well as a good selection of work by the Band. — *William Ruhlmann*

★ **Blood on the Tracks** / Jan. 17, 1975 / Columbia ✦✦✦✦✦
A stunning, mature statement in which the songwriter faced the conflicting elements of his life, the uncertainties of life in general, and the virtues of kindness and generosity. Incidentally, he also invented new songwriting structures and composed some of the most appealing music of his career. Still perhaps Dylan's most listenable and compelling album, this best represents his post-'60s work. — *William Ruhlmann*

☆ **The Basement Tapes** / Jun. 26, 1975 / Columbia ✦✦✦✦✦
A two-disc set of ad hoc performances from 1967, albeit refurbished slightly for this release, *The Basement Tapes* provides the missing link between Dylan's long, poetic songs of the mid-'60s and the shorter, more direct songs of the late '60s. Some of the songs had already become well known: "Too Much of Nothing,"

"Tears of Rage," "This Wheel's on Fire," and "You Ain't Goin' Nowhere." — *William Ruhlmann*

○ **Desire** / Jan. 16, 1976 / Columbia ♦♦♦♦
A rough-and-tumble collection cut with a band Dylan was assembling for the *Rolling Thunder* tour. "Hurricane" recounts the tale of an unjustly imprisoned boxer, "Romance in Durango" and "Black Diamond Bay" are short stories in song, and "Sara" is a last plaintive plea from the singer to his wife. — *William Ruhlmann*

Hard Rain / Sep. 10, 1976 / Columbia ♦♦
A live album recorded on the second leg of the Rolling Thunder Revue tour in the spring of 1976 and similar to a TV special shown the month of its release. This was not the Revue at its best. Nevertheless, the album is notable for the radical reworkings of "Lay Lady Lay" and "I Threw It All Away." — *William Ruhlmann*

○ **Masterpieces** / Mar. 1978 / CBS ♦♦♦♦
The best-organized Dylan retrospective ever done up to this time, the Japanese *Masterpieces* (never released outside the Far East) spends three discs thoroughly presenting Dylan's best work from 1962 to 1976, including several rare singles never before released on an album. Remastered and reissued on CD in 1991. — *William Ruhlmann*

Street Legal / Jun. 15, 1978 / Columbia ♦♦♦
Using a big band assembled for a world tour, Dylan presents a group of songs, some of which are as imagistic—and as bitter—as his mid-'60s material. Particularly notable are the tone poem "Changing of the Guards" and the desperate but moving "Senor." — *William Ruhlmann*

At Budokan / 1979 / Columbia ♦
A two-disc accounting of Bob Dylan's 1978 world tour during one of its early stops. The songs have again been rearranged in a style many found too grandiose, but the band is frequently effective. — *William Ruhlmann*

Slow Train Coming / Aug. 18, 1979 / Columbia ♦♦♦
Among Dylan's best-played (members of Dire Straits participate) and best-produced recordings, this album reflects Dylan's religious conversion. At its best, on "Gotta Serve Somebody" and "When You Gonna Wake Up," the album presents cautionary messages similar to those Dylan had served up throughout his career. — *William Ruhlmann*

Saved / Jun. 20, 1980 / Columbia ♦♦
Just as fervent as he was on *Slow Train Coming*, Dylan is less inspired (sorry) as a songwriter here, and his preachiness is likely to be a bit much even for believers. — *William Ruhlmann*

Shot of Love / Aug. 12, 1981 / Columbia ♦♦
Dylan's need to sing only about his faith recedes, and his muse returns, notably on "Every Grain of Sand," one of his finest '80s songs. In 1985, this album was re-released with the non-LP B-side "The Groom's Still Waiting at the Altar," another of Dylan's better later songs, added. — *William Ruhlmann*

Infidels / Nov. 1, 1983 / Columbia ♦♦♦
Dylan emerged from his overt references to Christianity with his sense of moral outrage reawakened. He expressed it in songs defending Israel and attacking unions on this impassioned collection, which also includes "Jokerman," as impressive a piece of socially conscious poetry as he'd ever produced, and the love songs "Sweetheart Like You" and "Don't Fall Apart on Me Tonight." — *William Ruhlmann*

Real Live / Dec. 3, 1984 / Columbia ♦♦♦
A souvenir of Dylan's 1984 European tour that is notable for the revised lyrics to "Tangled Up In Blue." — *William Ruhlmann*

○ **Empire Burlesque** / Jun. 8, 1985 / Columbia ♦♦♦♦
Dylan's strongest song collection since *Blood on the Tracks*, this album also benefits from excellent backup work by members of Tom Petty's Heartbreakers, among others, and a remix by dance expert Arthur Baker. Dylan himself sounds unusually engaged as well, especially on such songs as "Emotionally Yours" (later an R&B hit for the O'Jays) and the moving autobiographical folk ballad "Dark Eyes." — *William Ruhlmann*

☆ **Biograph** / Oct. 28, 1985 / Columbia ♦♦♦♦♦
A five-LP, three-CD retrospective of Dylan's first 20 years of recording, with an emphasis on presenting some of the mountain of unreleased songs that began leaking out unofficially in the late '60s. The only reason this massive, brilliantly executed album is not listed as an essential pick is its expense—in fact, it's not a bad place to start in trying to appreciate the whole of Dylan's achievement. — *William Ruhlmann*

Knocked out Loaded / Aug. 8, 1986 / Columbia ♦♦
A hodgepodge of tracks recorded between 1984 and 1986, some written by others, some in collaboration. Mostly dispensable, it is saved from a "Poor" rating by the rambling "Brownsville Girl," co-written with playwright Sam Shepard. — *William Ruhlmann*

Dylan & The Dead / Feb. 6, 1989 / Columbia ♦
Oh Mercy / Sep. 22, 1989 / Columbia ♦♦♦
This stunning album demonstrated that, after more than 25 years, Dylan was perfectly capable of writing songs of topical concern, high poetry, and unflinching self-examination to match any of his best work of the '60s and '70s. — *William Ruhlmann*

Under the Red Sky / Sep. 11, 1990 / Columbia ♦♦
○ **Bootleg Series** / Mar. 26, 1991 / Columbia ♦♦♦♦
The floodgates opened with the release of this 58-song collection of outtakes and unreleased songs from throughout Dylan's career, an outpouring that demonstrated what all the bootleggers and their customers had known all along: that Dylan's throwaways were better than everyone else's keepers. It's amazing to think that, while turning out some of the most impressive albums of his time, Dylan was holding back material often equally good. — *William Ruhlmann*

Good As I Been to You / Oct. 27, 1992 / Columbia ♦♦♦
After a scattered decade's worth of albums ranging from terrific to terrible, Bob Dylan's second release of the '90s is a return to the acoustic folk that established his career. Naturally, it's not as breathtaking as *The Freewheelin' Bob Dylan* or his debut album, but it is an expert collection of standards by an expert folksinger. *Good As I Been to You* also proves he's a great guitarist, too. — *Stephen Thomas Erlewine*

World Gone Wrong / Oct. 28, 1993 / Columbia ♦♦♦
Although it follows the same formula as *Good As I Been To You*, *World Gone Wrong* cuts deeper. Dylan's collection of (mainly) obscure blues and folk songs is genuinely moving, one of his best albums of the past decade. On *World Gone Wrong*, Dylan says more with other people's songs than most do with their own, creating a vicious, worried commentary about modern society with a collection of traditional songs. — *Stephen Thomas Erlewine*

Greatest Hits, Vol. 3 / Nov. 15, 1994 / Columbia
Dylan's first greatest hits album was released in 1967, and his second in 1971. Twenty-three years later comes his third, and it's a reasonable compilation of the better-known songs he has produced over the period, notably standards like "Knockin' on Heaven's Door" and "Forever Young," Dylan chart hits like "Tangled Up In Blue" and "Hurricane," songs that have been covered extensively by other singers, such as "Ring Them Bells," and some of the better album tracks, such as "Changing of the Guard" and "Brownsville Girl." In an effort to span the period, a few lesser, later songs, such as "Silvio" and "Under the Red Sky" are included, while some stronger, earlier songs are not ("Simple Twist of Fate," "Senor," "Emotionally Yours," and "Everything Is Broken"). But on the whole, the selection is excellent, and this is the album to get for that Dylan fan who stopped listening to him at the end of his '60s. (Includes the previously unreleased 1989 track "Dignity.") — *William Ruhlmann*

MTV Unplugged / Apr. 25, 1995 / Columbia ♦♦
This show, taped for MTV, finds Dylan turning in an 11-song set, with eight of the songs dating from his 1963-67 heyday, including such standards as "The Times They Are a-Changin'" and "Like a Rolling Stone." ("John Brown," a powerful anti-war song from 1963, had not been released on a Dylan album previously.) The '70s are represented by "Knockin' on Heaven's Door," and the '80s by "Shooting Star" and "Dignity" (a trunk song, the studio version of which had emerged only the previous November on *Bob Dylan's Greatest Hits, Volume 3*). Dylan, accompanied by a competent five-piece band, approaches his material in a gentler fashion than on some of the originals—"The Times They Are a-Changin'" and "With God on Our Side," for example, seem sadder and less defiant than they did back in 1964. Otherwise, unlike some other *Unplugged* performances, this one doesn't offer a noticeably different view of the artist's work. But then, Dylan has been unplugged for much of his career, anyway. — *William Ruhlmann*

○ **Royal Albert Hall** / Bootleg ♦♦♦♦
Recorded in May 1966 during Dylan's British tour with the Hawks (soon to become the Band), this documents a landmark in the history of Dylan, folk-rock, and rock itself. Although Dylan had been recording electric rock & roll for a year at this point, his appear-

ances with a full band continued to arouse tremendous controversy and even hostility, as much of the folk audience that formed his original constituency viewed him as a sellout. He divided his sets between acoustic and rock formats; this bootleg comes from the electric half, in which he performed eight of his mid-'60s tunes, including "Like a Rolling Stone," "Just Like Tom Thumb's Blues," "Ballad of a Thin Man," the unreleased "Tell Me Mama," and radically reworked arrangements of "I Don't Believe You" and "One Too Many Mornings," which had appeared in plaintive acoustic versions on his albums. The songs are delivered with a fierceness and tight ensemble backing that exceeds the energy of his mid-'60s albums, and must have been quite a revelation for the more open-minded customers are heard heckling Dylan on this recording, to which he responds by heckling right back and charging into a stormy version of "Like a Rolling Stone" that holds nothing in reserve. It's been said that this isn't actually from Albert Hall, but wherever the tape dates from (it is certainly from the 1966 British tour), it's way, *way* overdue for official release, though most Dylan fans and many serious rock scholars have a copy already. — *Richie Unterberger*

○ **Carnegie Hall** / Bootleg ♦♦♦♦
Recorded by Columbia as a possible live release, but shelved, not for any reasons of artistic merit or sonic deficiencies. Bootlegged under a variety of titles, this is probably the best pre-electric-period unreleased Dylan concert to own, from the perspectives of fidelity, performance, and breadth of material. Besides featuring the core of his early repertoire, from "Times They Are A-Changin'" and "Mr. Tambourine Man" down to less celebrated numbers like "Spanish Harlem Incident" and "To Ramona," there are also a few unreleased or barely released tunes, the best of which is an acoustic version of "If You Gotta Go, Go Now." There are also a few duets with Joan Baez, which actually don't count among the highlights of this 95-minute program. —*Richie Unterberger*

BOOKS

♦♦♦ **Bob Dylan: Behind The Shades**, by Clinton Heylin (Summit Books, 1991). Not exactly a biography in the most conventional sense, this alternates between standard historical commentary and many quotes, from Dylan himself and many of his associates, progressing chronologically from his early life through 1990. Heylin's aim is to provide the most complete perspective yet on the man and focus more or less equally on all phases of his career, not just his most celebrated years in the 1960s. There's a lot of valuable information here, conscientiously arranged to allow for multiple perspectives and to deflate myths and rumors. Despite Heylin's noble attempt to treat Dylan's accomplishments in their totality, the fact is that for many fans, his work has declined precipitiously since the mid-1970s. This is not a matter of willful ignorance or inability to keep pace with Dylan's artistic growth, as some of his defenders charge, but a matter of heartfelt taste, shared by millions of listeners. As such, the first two-thirds or so of this 450-page book hold by far the greatest fascination for most Dylan fans; the remainder grows progressively less interesting, and some may find the final parts dispensable altogether. —*Richie Unterberger*

♦♦♦ **Bob Dylan: His Unreleased Recordings**, by Paul Cable (Schirmer, 1978). A most interesting concept for a book, one that should be pursued for other rock giants like the Beatles, Stones, Neil Young, the Dead, and others. This is a critical guide to the many unreleased recordings by Dylan from 1961-1976, quite a few of which stand up to the level of his officially released work. Bootleg guides do exist for some big groups (especially the Beatles), usually on extremely small presses; what makes them poor reading is that they are almost exclusively concerned with track listings, wads of dry discographical data, and different editions. Alone among such works, Cable, a good writer, concentrates on the music, discussing the song and performances with as much seriousness as conventional rock books give to officially released albums. And there's a lot of good insight and trivia to be found here, including detailed discussions of such major unreleased works as the publisher demos Dylan cut in the early '60s (including quite a few songs that he never got around to recording), professionally recorded live performances from 1964 and 1966 (the latter being the famous Royal Albert Hall bootleg) that were easily good enough to qualify for official release, and his unreleased sessions with the Band in 1967 and Johnny Cash in 1969. Besides pointing out the essential interest of the unreleased songs and alternative/live versions, Cable isn't afraid to call things as he sees them, enthusing over genuinely revelatory outtakes, coming down hard on half-baked jams and drunken performances. The book's value, though, decreases with age; since 1978 many of the most important unreleased performances have surfaced on official releases, and many other notable outtakes and live performances have been recorded and discovered that are not included in this book. The book's discography and cross-referencing of Dylan bootlegs is clumsy and also outdated, but there's still a lot of fascinating stuff to be found here. —*Richie Unterberger*

♦♦♦♦ **Bob Dylan**, by Anthony Scaduto (Grosset & Dunlap, 1971). Dylan's proven to be an elusive biographical subject; there are so many rumors and half-corroborated facts flying around his legacy, some perpetuated by the man himself. Scaduto's attempt is not perfect, but is about the best and most comprehensive, told clearly and intelligently, and drawing on first-hand recollections from many of his associates, especially from his early Greenwich Village days. The problem is not so much the content, but the erratic focus; the early '60s are documented in great detail, but the mid-'60s "electric" period, arguably the most fascinating era of his career, is treated somewhat cursorily in comparison. It's been suggested that this material is so rife with misleading and contradictory accounts that it's impossible to portray accurately, but it's nonetheless a gaping hole in the narrative; the late '60s and early '70s are also less detailed than the early chapters, although by this time, of course, Dylan was much less of a public figure. It only goes up through the early '70s, but one could argue that it covers the bulk of his most interesting years as it stands. —*Richie Unterberger*

E

(E)

Pop/Rock

Virginia singer/songwriter and multi-instrumentalist (E) projects a humorously idiosyncratic loser (Woody Allen-meets-Brian Wilson in the sandbox) mentality. In fact, (E)'s wistful melancholy and tainted hopefulness, as well as his delicately quirky melodicism and dense production smarts, recall the reclusive Beach Boy's better moments. —*Rick Clark*

● **A Man Called (e)** / 1992 / Polydor ◆◆◆◆
A Man Called (E) is a wonderful collection of pop gems, tapped from the soul of Beach Boys' *Pet Sounds, Tumbleweed Connection*-era Elton John, *White Album* Beatles, and early Todd Rundgren. (E) performed practically every instrument in this keyboard-rich production. Highlights from this impressive debut are "Hello Cruel World," "Fitting in with the Misfits," and "Are You and Me Gonna Happen?" —*Rick Clark*

○ **Broken Toy Shop** / Dec. 7, 1993 / Polydor ◆◆◆◆
On his second album, (E) offers more of the same highly crafted pop-rock that graced his debut; although the overall quality of songs is just a notch lower than his first album, *Broken Toy Shop* nevertheless features many delightful pop gems. —*Stephen Thomas Erlewine*

The Eagles

Group, Country-Rock, Pop/Rock

The Eagles were among the most successful rock groups of the '70s, and their blend of country, folk, and rock continues to sell well in catalogs. The group's four original members were Los Angeles session and group veterans assembled by producer John Boylan in 1970 as backup musicians for Linda Ronstadt on her *Silk Purse* album. They then served as her backup band for two years. The four were Glenn Frey (b. Nov 6, 1948), guitarist; Bernie Leadon (b. Jul 19, 1947), who played banjo and mandolin; Randy Meisner (b. Mar 8, 1948) on bass; and Don Henley (b. Jul 22, 1947) on drums. All four sang, though Henley and Frey took most leads. Signed to Ronstadt's label, Asylum, they issued their first album, *Eagles*, in June 1972. It was a moderate hit (going gold a year and a half later) and produced the Top 40 hits "Take It Easy" (written by Frey and Jackson Browne), "Witchy Woman," and "Peaceful Easy Feeling."

The second Eagles LP, a semi-concept album called *Desperado* (1973) that emphasized an "outlaw" image, was somewhat less successful. For their third album, *On the Border* (1974), the group added guitarist Don Felder. This was a breakthrough record, going gold in three months and producing the #1 hit "Best of My Love," which didn't top the charts until almost a year after the album's release, just in time to set up their fourth album. *One of These Nights* (1975), the first of four straight albums to top the charts, featured the title track, "Lyin' Eyes," and "Take It to the Limit," all Top Ten hits.

The Eagles released a greatest-hits album in 1976 (it now stands at 14 million sales, the best-selling hits record of all time) and suffered the loss of Leadon, who was replaced by former James Gang leader Joe Walsh (b. Nov 20, 1947). At the end of the year, they released *Hotel California*, which has now sold nine million copies. Its hits included the ominous title track, "New Kid in Town," and "Life in the Fast Lane."

In 1977, Meisner left the band and was replaced by former Poco member Timothy B.Schmit (b.Oct 30, 1947). It took the Eagles un-

til the fall of 1979 to complete *The Long Run*, another million-seller, featuring the chart-topper "Heartache Tonight" and Top Ten successes in the title track and "I Can't Tell You Why." The next year saw the release of a live album, but by 1981 the Eagles had split up. All five members have since released solo albums, the most successful of which have been by Henley and Frey.

In 1994, the Eagles reunited for a summer stadium tour and recorded an album as part of an appearance on the TV show *MTV Unplugged* that featured several new songs. The resulting album, *Hell Freezes Over* was released in November of 1994; it debuted at number one and sold over five million copies by June of 1995. —*William Ruhlmann*

The Eagles / Jun. 1972 / Asylum ◆◆◆
The Eagles' tentative debut album is notable for its single hits, "Take It Easy," "Witchy Woman," and "Peaceful Easy Feeling." (It also contains a rare Jackson Browne composition, "Nightingale.") The album has more of a bluegrass tone (courtesy of Bernie Leadon) than the band would later pursue. —*William Ruhlmann*

Desperado / Apr. 1973 / Asylum ◆◆◆
A concept album equating rock 'n' roll musicians with Old West outlaws, the Eagles' second album contains the hit "Tequila Sunrise," the song "Desperado," which has become a standard, and the recurring "Doolin-Dalton," co-written with J.D. Souther and Jackson Browne. —*William Ruhlmann*

On the Border / Mar. 1974 / Asylum ◆◆◆
A transitional Eagles album (and their commercial breakthrough), this contained songs like "Already Gone" and "James Dean" (co-written by Jackson Browne) that hark back to their earlier up-tempo rock style, but also "Best of My Love" and Tom Waits' "Ol' 55," ballads that showed off their harmonies and won them a whole new audience. —*William Ruhlmann*

One of These Nights / Jun. 1975 / Asylum ◆◆◆
The Eagles' breakthrough album, a convincing mix of heady rockers and lush ballads, featuring the Top Ten hits "One Of These Nights," "Lyin' Eyes," and "Take It to the Limit." —*William Ruhlmann*

★ **Their Greatest Hits (1971-1975)** / Feb. 1976 / Asylum ◆◆◆◆◆
The reason this is such a great greatest-hits album is that it includes almost all the best tracks from the Eagles' first four albums, eight Top 40 hits including the #1s "Best of My Love" and "One of These Nights," plus the favorites "Tequila Sunrise" and "Desperado." This is the essential Eagles for the period. (As of mid-1995, *Their Greatest Hits (1971-1975)* was the second-best-selling album of all time in the U.S., with certified sales of 22 million copies.) —*William Ruhlmann*

☆ **Hotel California** / Dec. 1976 / Asylum ◆◆◆◆
A concept album about the dissipated life of Southern California rock stars, from being the "New Kid in Town" to living "Life in the Fast Lane" to holing up in the "Hotel California" fearing it's all been "Wasted Time" and turning to "The Last Resort." This album and Pink Floyd's *The Wall* are aural versions of *A Star is Born* for the rock generation. —*William Ruhlmann*

The Long Run / Sep. 1979 / Asylum ◆◆◆
The long-awaited follow-up to *Hotel California* and the Eagles' last studio album proved a considerable disappointment, although it sold in the expected multimillions and included the hits "Heartache Tonight," "The Long Run," and "I Can't Tell You Why." —*William Ruhlmann*

Eagles Live / Nov. 1980 / Asylum ♦♦
The Eagles were always a yawn in concert, and this profit-taking recreation of their hits demonstrates the lifelessness they brought to live work. Today's fans should listen before forking over all those bucks to sit in the stadiums and experience it themselves. — *William Ruhlmann*

Eagles Greatest Hits, Vol. 2 / Oct. 1982 / Asylum ♦♦♦
This will save you from having to buy *The Long Run,* an inconsistent album best remembered for its hit songs, all of which are here, along with the ones from *Hotel California.* — *William Ruhlmann*

Hell Freezes Over / Nov. 8, 1994 / Geffen ♦♦
The Eagles were never a great live band, which makes the process of reinventing their hits slightly harder. But they are smart businessmen, so they realized that they didn't need to reinvent themselves; if they reunited, the public would only care about seeing the band again and just hearing the hits. When the Eagles finally reunited in 1994 for a mammoth tour, they began their tour with an *MTV Unplugged* set. The result is *Hell Freezes Over.* The band accentuates their country leanings, but everything winds up sounding much duller than their original recordings because they accentuate their relaxed vibe, not their rootsiness. Although the album sold well, it's not nearly as captivating as the original versions. — *Stephen Thomas Erlewine*

Jack Earls

Rock & Roll, Rockabilly
One of the more obscure names in the annals of Sun Records, Jack Earl's lone original single, "Slow Down" (covered by rock group the Paladins), is one of the shining crude examples of rockabilly. Never comfortable as a full-time musician, Earls moved from Memphis to Detroit to work full-time at the Chrysler plant, a job he maintains to this day. Occasionally playing and recording for small collector-oriented labels, Earls has a cracked-mountain tenor that is still intact and capable of scraping the paint off walls any time he feels like it. — *Cub Koda*

● **Let's Bop** / 1990 / Bear Family ♦♦♦♦
Complete collection of Earl's Sun recordings, raw rockabilly at its finest. — *Cub Koda*

Earth Wind & Fire

Group, Funk, Disco, Urban
Earth, Wind & Fire was the most successful R&B group of the second half of the '70s. EW&F was founded by Maurice White (b. Dec 19, 1942) and his brother Verdine (b. Jul 25, 1951) in Chicago in 1969, and they released their self-titled debut album on Warner Brothers in 1970. After the 1971 release of the second album, *The Need of Love,* White reorganized the group, bringing in Philip Bailey (b. May 8, 1951) as co-lead singer for the recording of the third album, *Last Days and Time* on Columbia.
EW&F encapsulated many strains of Black pop from before their time. Their high-pitched harmony vocals called to mind groups such as the Temptations, while their funkiness was reminiscent of Sly and the Family Stone, and their horn section sometimes evoked the work of James Brown and others. Over this, Maurice White laid his own brand of African-inspired kalimba music for a thorough synthesis that nonetheless bore a particular musical stamp unique to Earth, Wind & Fire.
The band began to break through with its fourth album, *Head to the Sky,* in 1973. EW&F's first R&B Top Ten hit was "Mighty Mighty," from their first gold album, *Open Our Eyes,* which went to #15 in the pop charts and also contained the R&B hit "Kalimba Story." EW&F's breakthrough to a mass audience, however, came in 1975 with the release of *That's the Way of the World,* the soundtrack to a film in which the group appeared. Led by its gold-selling #1 single, "Shining Star," the album topped the pop charts.
Equally successful were the partially live *Gratitude* (1975), *Spirit* (1976), *All 'n All* (1977), *The Best of Earth, Wind & Fire—Vol. 1* (1978), and *I Am* (1979). Several albums in the early '80s did almost as well, but after the relative failure of *Electric Universe* in 1983, EW&F disbanded. It re-formed for the 1987 release *Touch the World.*
Earth, Wind & Fire returned to the R&B/urban universe in 1990 with the LP *Heritage,* an attempt to update their sound with hip-hop and New Jack ingredients. Hammer and the Boys, as well as old school veteran Sly Stone, made guest appearances, but couldn't rekindle the old magic. They tried again in '93 with *Millennium,* switching labels to Reprise and ending a relationship with

Columbia dating back to 1972. Columbia issued a deluxe boxed set of their greatest hits in '92, *The Eternal Dance.* — *William Ruhlmann and Ron Wynn*

Earth, Wind & Fire / 1971 / Warner Brothers ♦♦♦
The debut album that launched the band in the early '70s. At the time, they were a collective band doing jazz-based funk in a manner similar to Kool and the Gang. Philip Bailey hadn't yet joined as a great falsetto lead singer, nor had Maurice White begun writing the great message songs or making the Egyptian connection. — *Ron Wynn*

The Need of Love / 1971 / Warner Brothers ♦♦♦
Earth, Wind & Fire began to attract some attention with their second release, especially Sherry Scott's inviting, if somewhat coy, lead vocal on the title track. They were still very close to first-generation jazzy funk on many tracks, but were starting to move in the direction that ultimately made them stars. — *Ron Wynn*

Last Days & Time / 1972 / Columbia ♦♦♦
Earth, Wind & Fire were nothing if not ambitious, and by the time of their third album, they had forged an individual sound by absorbing nearly everything that had gone before them in the previous ten years. It was as if they were trying to encapsulate every eclectic foray pursued by Motown, from catchy, rhythmic pop to churning funk, and even from Stevie Wonder singing borrowed folk songs like "Blowin' in the Wind" (here, Bailey did "Where Have All the Flowers Gone") to the schmaltzy, string-filled pop that spelled legitimacy to Motown. Not only that, they wanted to incorporate Sly and the Family Stone's horn-filled, gutbucket R&B and some of the fusion style of Weather Report. On *Last Days and Time,* they succeeded in pulling all that into their orbit, but they hadn't yet managed one crucial thing: they hadn't learned to write hits. That would come next. — *William Ruhlmann*

Head to the Sky / May 1973 / Columbia ♦♦♦
The album that made them the 1970s' top pop/funk and crossover R&B act. Their previous album had been better produced than anything on Warner Bros., and this one had excellent message songs, their finest playing, outstanding arrangements, and soaring vocals by Philip Bailey and Jessica Cleaves. The uptempo tracks were some of the best the group ever made. — *Ron Wynn*

Another Time / 1974 / Warner Brothers ♦♦♦
Once Earth, Wind & Fire became the top black music band in the world, Warner Bros. realized the mistake they had made in not giving Maurice White complete creative freedom. They rushed out this anthology featuring the group's early music, hoping to piggyback off their huge Columbia hits. These songs are certainly worth hearing again, but few people who hadn't originally purchased the Warner Bros. tracks were enticed to get them. — *Ron Wynn*

Open Your Eyes / Mar. 1974 / Columbia ♦♦♦
Earth, Wind & Fire were in peak form during the mid-'70s. Their fast songs had driving beats and excellent arrangements and were sung with the perfect mix of energy and conviction. The slow songs, particularly those featuring Philip Bailey, were moving and often anthemic. This album got them two Top 10 R&B hits and three songs on the charts, and kept their momentum going. — *Ron Wynn*

○ **That's the Way of The World** / Mar. 1975 / Columbia ♦♦♦♦
Sleekly produced '70s pop/R&B, highlighted by the stirring "Shining Star" and the atmospheric title track. — *William Ruhlmann*

○ **Gratitude** / Dec. 1975 / Columbia ♦♦♦♦
A two-record set that blended live and studio cuts and was a testimony to the band's immense popularity at the time. It was a huge success and even topped the charts for a time, something that live sets never did, especially live albums by black funk bands. Saxophonist Donald Myrick's blistering solos on the live cuts immediately put him in the spotlight, even though he'd been an active session musician for years, while Philip Bailey's spiraling, wondrous vocals were in the forefront throughout the record. — *Ron Wynn*

○ **Spirit** / Sep. 1976 / Columbia ♦♦♦♦
Another huge '70s album for Earth, Wind & Fire. The title track was among their biggest singles ever and represented another triumph for Philip Bailey. They had three other huge hits in 1976 and were without question the reigning kings of crossover black music. — *Ron Wynn*

All 'n All / Nov. 1977 / Columbia ♦♦♦
The Earth, Wind & Fire juggernaut kept rolling with this late '70s album. While they had turned more and more to the pop side, they had three more smash singles during this time, and their

stage shows became even more varied, entertaining, and ambitious. Although this album doesn't have the same passion or emphatic vocals as some of its predecessors, it was a worthy addition to their '70s legacy. —*Ron Wynn*

★ **The Best of Earth, Wind & Fire, Vol. 1** / Nov. 1978 / Columbia ✦✦✦✦✦

Hits compilation covering 1973-1978. —*William Ruhlmann*

I Am / Jun. 1979 / Columbia ✦✦✦

The gorgeous ballad "After the Love Has Gone" and the bouncy "Boogie Wonderland" (featuring the Emotions) lead this consistent collection. —*William Ruhlmann*

Faces / Oct. 1980 / Columbia ✦✦✦

Although they were catching more flak from critics for an alleged obsession with socio-political commentary and quasi-mystical references, R&B audiences hadn't yet tired of Earth, Wind & Fire. While this album admittedly had less memorable material and was more dependent on what had become production cliches and stock devices, it still landed plenty of hits on the charts. But it was becoming clear to even the most devoted fans that songs like "In the Stone" and "Let Me Talk" weren't their finest hour. —*Ron Wynn*

Raise! / Oct. 1981 / Columbia ✦✦

The end was near for Earth, Wind & Fire. This wasn't quite the disaster it was made out to be at the time, but it was their least distinguished overall album since the early days on Warner Bros., with the exception of their participation in the disastrous *Sgt. Pepper's Lonely Hearts Club Band* film soundtrack in 1978. "Let's Groove" was just a recycled mid-tempo tune from the mid '70s, and everything else sounded desultory and uninspired. It was no surprise that after two more albums White and company decided to take some time away from the scene. —*William Ruhlmann*

Powerlight / Feb. 1983 / Columbia ✦✦✦

Even though *Raise!* was an artistic disappointment, it was a commercial success. *Powerlight*, EW&F's first album in nine years to miss the Top Ten, showed that fans were catching on to the group's decline. There were still hits, at least on the R&B chart, in "Fall In Love with Me" and "Side by Side," but the formula was growing stale. —*William Ruhlmann*

Electric Universe / Nov. 1983 / Columbia ✦✦

Creatively exhausted, EW&F turned to L.A. studio hacks like David Foster (Chicago) and Martin Page (Starship) for their characteristically bland material. Typical was Page's lead-off track, "Magnetic," which, although a Top Ten R&B hit, could have been by anyone. There were no substantial pop hits, the album sold poorly, and EW&F split up. —*William Ruhlmann*

Touch the World / Oct. 1987 / Columbia ✦✦✦

Earth, Wind & Fire came close to recapturing their '70s glory on this late '80s vehicle, missing more because of stylistic changes on the black music scene than any failings on their part. Indeed, the song "System of Survival" did actually top the R&B charts for a week, and the overall album got favorable reviews and good support. It just wasn't the blockbuster effort that the group had routinely enjoyed in the past. —*Ron Wynn*

○ **The Best of Earth, Wind & Fire, Vol. 2** / 1988 / Columbia ✦✦✦✦

The second collection covering hit singles from the '70s' top funk and soul band, Earth, Wind & Fire. This anthology has recently been supplanted by a boxed set covering virtually all of their big Columbia singles and some early Warners material. If you enjoyed their disco and late '70s cuts more than the early tracks, this anthology is worth getting. —*Ron Wynn*

Heritage / 1990 / Columbia ✦✦

A disappointing comeback vehicle for Earth, Wind & Fire. They still had the seamless funk production and exuberant collective vocals, but there was no standout single, and the attempt at generating attention through Afrocentric commentary didn't raise any eyebrows or score any hits. —*Ron Wynn*

○ **The Eternal Dance** / Sep. 8, 1992 / Columbia ✦✦✦✦

Covering three discs and including all the hits, as well as a healthy selection of rarities, *The Eternal Dance* is not designed for the casual listener; only hardcore fans will remain enthralled through the numerous rarities. Most listeners will be content with the two greatest hits collections, but this comprehensive box set remains essential for hardcore Earth, Wind & Fire fans. —*Stephen Thomas Erlewine*

Millennium / Sep. 14, 1993 / Reprise ✦✦

Give them credit for sticking to their guns and delivering, as their return to Warner/Reprise, an EW&F album that sounds like something from the late '70s. The horns are in place, the songs are melodic, Philip Bailey is in good voice, and all of it seems irrelevant to the Black pop scene of 1993, which may be why (along with the band's failure to do a promotional tour) *Millennium* was only a modest seller with two minor hits, "Sunday Morning" and "Spend the Night." —*William Ruhlmann*

Sheena Easton

b. Apr. 27, 1959, Glasgow, Scotland
Pop/Rock

Easton came onto the pop scene in 1980 as an overnight sensation from England, due to her #8 UK hit "Modern Girl" (it later reached #18 stateside). Her first American hit, "Morning Train (Nine to Five)," went to #1 for two weeks. During the early '80s, Easton released a series of light dance-pop hits, but in 1984 she began to pursue hit material with more erotic implications, as in "Strut" (#7) and the Prince-penned "Sugar Walls" (#9). She sang with Prince on "U Got the Look" (#2), from his *Sign o' the Times* album in 1987. Easton has released several more singles and, in 1991, pursued an acting stint on Broadway with *Les Miserables*. —*Rick Clark*

○ **Greatest Hits** / 1989 / EMI America ✦✦✦✦

Easton's biggest and best tracks, including "Morning Train (Nine to Five)," "For Your Eyes Only," "Telefone (Long Distance Love Affair)," "Strut," and "Sugar Walls." —*Stephen Thomas Erlewine*

● **The World of Sheena Easton: The Singles Collection** / 1993 / EMI America ✦✦✦✦

All of Sheena Easton's biggest and best songs, including "Morning Train (Nine to Five)," "For Your Eyes Only," "Telefone (Long Distance Love Affair)," "Strut," and "Sugar Walls," are collected on this generous 19-track compilation. —*Stephen Thomas Erlewine*

The Easybeats

Group, Pop/Rock

The most successful Australian rock group of the 1960s, the Easybeats were nearly as popular as the Beatles in their homeland in the mid-'60s. In 1965 and 1966, they ran off a rapid string of seven Top Ten singles in Australia with peppy variations on the early Beatle and Merseybeat sound. With a nervous energy that featured staccato guitar lines, unexpected tempo changes, and strong original material, they also betrayed strong debts to the Kinks, The Who, and Small Faces, although their songs were generally cheerier and more lightweight. Like all of the aforementioned bands, the Easybeats stand as one of the earliest and foremost exponents of pure power-pop. In late 1966, the Easybeats moved to London and hooked up with legendary producer Shel Talmy (The Who, The Kinks) in an attempt to crack the international pop market. Against all the odds, they did so the first time out with the classic "Friday on My Mind," which hit the British Top Ten and the American Top 20. Some ill-chosen follow-ups, however, deflated their momentum, although the group—led by the increasingly adventurous combination songwriting/production team of guitarists George Young and Harry Vanda—were keeping up with the tenor of their times by expanding the scope of their lyrics and arrangements. Cuts like "Falling off the Edge of the World," "Come in You'll Get Pneumonia," and "Good Times" drew raves from peers like Lou Reed and Paul McCartney, although few listeners actually heard them at the time. After a few generally dispiriting years in London (during which they were nonetheless quite active in the studio), the group disbanded in late 1969 after a homecoming tour of Australia, where they had been superstars throughout the decade. Vanda and Young remained international cult figures with their extensive production work, and recaptured pop success for a time as masterminds of Flash & the Pan. —*Richie Unterberger*

Easy / 1965 / Repertoire ✦✦✦

Their first album, not available outside Australia until the 1990s. The Vanda-Young songwriting partnership had yet to dominate the band in their early days, and most of the (entirely original) material here comes from the pens of George Young and singer Stevie Wright. It's more Merseybeatish and less oriented toward power pop and staccato guitar attacks than their subsequent releases, which isn't really detrimental; it doesn't scale the peaks the band would shortly climb, but neither does it have the overdone good-time mania that made some of their efforts hard to take in more than limited doses. A fairly consistent, if not incredibly remarkable, relic from the Beat era, including their first big Australian hit, "She's So Fine." —*Richie Unterberger*

It's 2 Easy / 1966 / Repertoire ✦✦✦

Until this CD reissue, the Easybeats' second album, *It's 2 Easy*, had only been issued in Australia. Originally released in 1966, the LP features four Australian hit singles ("Women," "Come and See Her," "Wedding Ring," and "Sad and Lonely and Blue") and ten other original tunes in a peppy style reminiscent of the early Beatles. It doesn't come close to matching the actual quality of the early Beatles tunes, but it's also considerably higher in quality than the average British Invasion album in that it features entirely original material. Most of it was penned by guitarist George Young and singer Stevie Wright; guitarist Harry Vanda would not team up with Young to form the famous Vanda-Young partnership until "Friday In My Mind" later that year. This CD features a generous 11 bonus tracks that will be of considerable interest to specialist collectors, including various B-sides, EP tracks, mono versions, and outtakes from the mid-'60s, some of which have never been available outside Australia. The best of these are two tracks from a 1966 EP: the hard-hitting power-pop tune "I'll Make You Happy" and "Too Much," which recalls best of the Kinks' similar midtempo numbers from the same era. —*Richie Unterberger*

Volume 3 / 1966 / Albert ✦✦✦

The hardest Easybeats album to find (now available on CD) contains some of their rarest material, never issued outside of Australia. It's actually not worth making a special effort for unless you're a big fan of the group. Like their first two, Australia-only LPs, it's accomplished guitar pop/rock with a heavy British Invasion influence, but not outstanding. The best songs ("Sorry," "Funny Feelin' ") have been reissued on Easybeats anthologies. —*Richie Unterberger*

Friends / 1969 / Polydor ✦✦

Originally released in 1969, *Friends*, the Easybeats' last album, was a curiously half-baked and deflated affair, despite some interesting moments. The Australian group's trademark peppiness gave way to a world-weary tone, perhaps as a result of their rollercoaster ride through near-Beatle-like fame in their native land and limited success elsewhere. Apparently much of this collection was actually half-finished demos, which accounts for the fairly sparse feel on several tracks. The least successful songs are the forced rock & roll boogies, with overwrought vocals from lead singer Stevie Wright. The more pensive tracks, like the title tune, have an oddly compelling, hollow feel of resignation bordering on gloom that starkly contrasts with their more well-known mid-'60s material. The Harry Vanda/George Young songwriting team wrote all of the album's songs, including the group's final single, "St. Louis." This CD reissue adds 11 songs to the original LP from various late-'60s singles, obscure Australian compilations, and alternate mixes; all are reasonably enjoyable, none are particularly essential. —*Richie Unterberger*

The Shame Just Drained / 1977 / Albert ✦✦✦

For a group that really only scored one major international hit, the Easybeats' songwriting team—Harry Vanda and George Young—were very busy bees indeed in the studio in the late '60s. All but one of the songs on this 15-track compilation are taken from sessions between late 1966 and late 1968 that were unreleased at the time; five come from an album that was canned at the last minute. Apparently there were about 20 more outtakes where that came from. Don't pay any mind to the ridiculous claim in the sleeve note that "had all the material been released in the sequence (and quantity) it was created, then the Easybeats' impact might have been far more notable and we might today be comparing their albums alongside *Rubber Soul, Aftermath,* and other rock milestones." This is cheery late-'60s pop with mild psychedelic influences, echoing the Small Faces, the Turtles, and especially the Kinks. The cheeriness, in fact, verges on childish and sickly sweet in places. It's not bad, in fact it's occasionally pretty good; it's just not incredibly significant. By far the best track is "Mr. Riley of Higginbottom & Clive," a bit of dry class satire that compares well with Ray Davies' vignettes from the same era. —*Richie Unterberger*

○ **Absolute Anthology** / 1980 / EMI ✦✦✦✦

A 2-CD package from Australia, with ear-stunning sound and two hours of golden classics. The collection of choice. —*Bruce Eder*

Raven EP LP, Vol. 2 / 1982 / Raven ✦✦✦

A compilation of three EPs originally released on the Australian reissue label Raven, hence the strange title. The Easybeats recorded extremely prolifically during their five-year career, and this gathers about a dozen unreleased tracks, a few stray cuts that ended up on fairly rare LPs or EPs, and three (yes, three) Coke jingles. The best of these offerings are six demos from early 1965; all originals, they show the band at their most British Invasion-influenced and have a mawkish, innocent charm, though they're hardly classic. The rest of the material is typical mid- to late-period Easybeats: extremely clever insofar as quirky songwriting and guitar playing, cheerful almost to the point of being grating, and not nearly as lasting or important as their obvious reference points (the Beatles, The Kinks, The Who, and Small Faces). Also includes a couple unimpressive covers (of "Hound Dog" and the Nashville Teens' "Find My Way Back Home"). —*Richie Unterberger*

● **The Best of the Easybeats** / 1985 / Rhino ✦✦✦✦

A well-devised collection that pales in sound and content next to its Australian competitor. —*Bruce Eder*

Eazy-E

d. Mar. 26, 1995
Rap

After leaving N.W.A., rapper Eazy-E led a career that was filled with controversy and was considerably successful commercially, even if it never matched the creativity of his previous band. Eazy-E began his solo career in 1988 with *Eazy-Duz-It*; it was his only full-length album.

Eazy-E left N.W.A. after the 1991's *Niggaz4Life* hit the top of the charts. The break-up of N.W.A. was extremely bitter and Eazy in particular earned the wrath of Dr. Dre. Dre and Eazy carried out their feud on record throughout the early '90s.

Even though he released several hit EPs, Eazy's career was in decline when he announced he was suffering from AIDS in early March of 1995; he only learned that he had the disease in the previous month. Three weeks later, the rapper died on March 26, 1995—he was 31 years old. —*Stephen Thomas Erlewine*

● **Eazy-Duz-It** / 1988 / Ruthless ✦✦✦✦

Eazy-E's debut has something to offend just about everyone, regardless of leftist or rightist leanings or vehemence regarding issues of feminism. But at its best, *Eazy-Duz-It* is a fiery piece of hip-hop menace, marred only by E's incessant whine of a voice and his rampant sexism. Play at your own risk. —*John Floyd*

5150 Home 4 Tha Sick / 1992 / Priority ✦✦

Eazy-E issued this ill-conceived, stiffly rapped EP, which generated some quick response and then disappeared. —*Ron Wynn*

It's on (Dr. Dre 187um) Killa / 1993 / Ruthless ✦✦✦

Eazy-E fired back in the unending war of words with former N.W.A. comrade Dr. Dre on the EP *It's On (Dr. Dre 187um) Killa*. At the time of the EP's release, Eazy-E had already lost credibility in hip-hop circles for appearing at Republican fund-raisers and supporting one of the officers involved in the Rodney King incident. Thus, his charges that Dre is a fraud lack consistency and weight; in addition, his raps sound tired and lame throughout the disc. Where Eazy-E was once cocky, funny and often intriguing, he now sounds merely bitter. Besides the usual sexist and sexual posturing, he even reprises N.W.A.'s debut single "Boyz in tha Hood" again. The song was once an entertaining manifesto, but now it's just dated, "G" mix and all. —*Ron Wynn*

Temporary Insanity / Feb. 1993 / Priority ✦✦✦

Echo & the Bunnymen

Group, Alternative Pop/Rock

Echo & the Bunnymen's dark, swirling fusion of gloomy post-punk and Doors-inspired psychedelia brought the group a handful of British hits in the early '80s, while attracting a cult following in the United States. The Bunnymen grew out of the Crucial Three, a late '70s trio featuring vocalist Ian McCulloch, Pete Wylie, and Julian Cope. Cope and Wylie left the group by the end of 1977, forming Teardrop Explodes and Wah!, respectively. McCulloch met guitarist Will Sargent in the summer of 1978 and the pair began recording demos with a drum machine, which the duo called "Echo." Adding bassist Les Pattinson, the band made its live debut at the Liverpool club Eric's at the end of 1978, calling themselves Echo and the Bunnymen.

In March of 1979, the group released their first single, "Pictures on My Wall"/"Read It in Books," on the local Zoo record label. The single and their popular live performances led to a contract with Korova, a record label distributed by Warner Brother. After signing the contract, the group discarded the drum machine, adding drummer Pete de Freitas.

Released in the summer of 1980, their debut album *Crocodiles* reached number 17 on the U.K. charts. *Shine so Hard*, an EP released in the fall, became their first record to crack the U.K. Top 40. With the more ambitious and atmospheric *Heaven up Here* (1981), the group began to gain momentum, thanks to positive reviews and increased sales; it became their first U.K. Top Ten album. Two years later, *Porcupine* appeared, becoming the band's biggest hit (peaking at number two on the U.K. charts) and launching the Top Ten single, "The Cutter." Sergeant released a solo album, *Themes for Grind*, to little attention that summer as well.

"The Killing Moon" became the group's second Top Ten hit at the beginning of 1984, yet its follow-up, "Silver," didn't make it past 30 when it was released in May. *Ocean Rain* was released that same month to great critical acclaim; peaking at number four in Britain, the record became the Bunnymen's first album to chart in the U.S. Top 100. Later that year, McCulloch had a minor hit with his first solo single, an interpretation of Kurt Weill's "September Song." The following year was a quiet one for the band, as they released only one new song, "Bring on the Dancing Horses," which was included on the compilation, *Songs to Learn and Sing*. De Freitas left the band at the start of 1986 and was replaced by former Haircut 100 drummer Mark Fox; by September, de Freitas rejoined the group.

Echo and the Bunnymen returned with new material in the summer of 1987, releasing the single "The Game" and a self-titled album. *Echo & the Bunnymen* became their biggest American hit, peaking at number 51; it was a success in England as well, reaching number four. However, the album indicated that the group was in a musical holding pattern. At the end of 1988, McCulloch left the band to pursue a solo career; the rest of the band decided to continue without the singer. Tragedy hit the band in the summer of 1989, when de Freitas was killed in an auto accident. McCulloch released his first solo album, *Candleland*, in the fall of 1989; it proved a respectable commercial success, peaking a number 18 in the U.K. and number 159 in the U.S. Echo & the Bunnymen released *Reverberation*, their first album recorded without McCulloch, in 1990; although it replicated the group's classic sound, it failed to make the charts. McCulloch released his second solo album, *Mysterio*, in 1992. Two years later, Ian McCulloch and Will Sergeant formed Electrafixion, releasing their first album toward the end of the year. —*Stephen Thomas Erlewine*

○ **Crocodiles** / 1980 / Sire ✦✦✦✦
Arguments rage about these guys, but I prefer this—their debut—when their pop was spacier, moodier, and less coherent; in other words, before they started reading their press clippings. —*John Dougan*

A Promise / 1981 / Korova ✦✦
Shine So Hard / 1981 / Korova ✦✦
Heaven up Here / 1981 / Sire ✦✦✦
○ **Porcupine** / 1983 / Sire ✦✦✦✦
○ **Ocean Rain** / 1984 / Sire ✦✦✦✦
Lots of strings on this one, but the pop is still delivered with flair. Lacks direction, though. —*John Dougan*

● **Songs to Learn & Sing** / 1985 / Sire ✦✦✦✦
A fine anthology collecting all of the singles from their golden period of 1980 to 1985. In the end, Echo and the Bunnymen were a great singles band, so this is the ideal way to either get acquainted with the group or revisit them. —*Chris Woodstra*

Echo & The Bunnymen / 1987 / Sire ✦✦✦
Their "mature" record. Actually, the sound hadn't varied all that much since the early '80s; it just lost a little wallop. —*John Dougan*

Reverberation / 1990 / Sire ✦✦

Echobelly

Group, Alternative Pop/Rock
Led by vocalist Sonya Aurora Madan, Echobelly fuses the ironic, self-absorbed melancholy of the Smiths with stylish Blondie posturing, an interracial consciousness and a solid guitar crunch. Released in the winter of 1993, their first single won praise from the

British press, as well as from Morrissey. Following singles continued to build their fan base. *Everybody's Got One*, released in Britain in the late summer of 1994, earned positive reviews and became a moderate hit. The group wasn't able to break in America, yet they built up a rabidly devoted following in Japan. —*Stephen Thomas Erlewine*

● **Everybody's Got One** / 1994 / Epic ✦✦✦✦
Echobelly's debut album is a dynamite mix of brash ambition, undeniable energy, and smart pop songwriting. Lead singer Sonya Aurora Madan's swooping voice occasionally recalls the highly emotional phrasing of Morrissey, yet her lyrics never reach his grand self-pity. Instead, she is supremely confident ("I Can't Imagine the World Without Me"), which makes the melodic roar of the band all the more satisfying. Filled with soaring guitar hooks, propulsive energy, and wonderfully elliptical melodies, *Everyone's Got One* showcases a band who sounds as personal as the Smiths yet as confident as Blondie. —*Stephen Thomas Erlewine*

Eddie & the Hot Rods

Group, Rock & Roll, New Wave
Although their music might sound like conventional rock & roll today, Eddie & the Hot Rods played an important role in the birth of U.K. punk rock. The Hot Rods are the bridge between the pub rock of Dr. Feelgood and the punk rock of the Sex Pistols; tougher, louder, and wilder than Dr. Feelgood, the band gathered a large following in England's clubs, culminating with the release of their 1976 album *Teenage Depression*. At a time when pompous hard rock was dominating rock & roll, the simple pleasures of the joyous, R&B rockers on the album were a refreshing—and important—change of pace. Released during the beginning of England's punk revolution, 1977's *Life on the Line* featured an equally inspired set of songs that were more pop oriented than their predecessors. However, it was the last time Eddie & the Hot Rods had any impact in Britain. When *Thriller* was released in 1979, the band no longer was on the cutting edge; they couldn't compete with the bands they inspired. After one more lackluster album, the group called it quits; they reunited briefly in 1985. —*Stephen Thomas Erlewine*

○ **Live at the Marquee** / 1976 / Island ✦✦✦✦
Eddie & the Hot Rods were first and foremost a great live band so it makes perfect sense for their debut EP to show the band in their natural setting. *Live at the Marquee*, though only four songs (all covers), clearly shows how the band's wild and raw energy helped to inspire the punk explosion. —*Chris Woodstra*

Teenage Depression / 1976 / Island ✦✦✦
The band's first studio album is a fine effort in the spirit of Dr. Feelgood, bridging the gap between pub rock and punk rock. Wild, raw and rebellious—everything a rock & roll album should be. —*Chris Woodstra*

○ **Life on the Line** / 1977 / Island ✦✦✦✦
Life on the Line adds guitarist Graeme Douglas (ex-Kursaal Flyers) helping to bring out the band's pure pop sensibility. This is their finest moment and also their last really great album. Includes the brilliant "Do Anything You Want to Do," a British hit. —*Chris Woodstra*

Thriller / 1977 / Island ✦✦
Thriller reveals a band that has quickly slipped out of touch. They're unable to keep up with "the kids" anymore and they end up sounding like grumpy old rock & roll purists. As an added bonus, Linda McCartney makes a rare guest vocal appearance. —*Chris Woodstra*

Fish & Chips / 1980 / EMI ✦✦
Curse of the Hot Rods / 1990 / Hound Dog ✦✦
● **End Of the Beginning: Best of** / 1994 / Island [UK] ✦✦✦✦
A nearly flawless collection, *End of the Beginning* documents the band's golden period of 1976-1979 with the infectious singles, inspired live workouts, album tracks and a rarity or two for the collectors. An important part of punk rock's roots that shouldn't be missed. —*Chris Woodstra*

Duane Eddy

b. Apr. 26, 1938, Corning, NY
Instrumental Rock
One of the '50s most influential guitarists, and one of the more distinct. Unlike other guitarslingers of the era, Eddy forged a sound based on minimalism (and lots of twangy reverb). His best

hits ("Rebel Rouser," "Movin' and Groovin'," "Peter Gunn") feature simple reverb-drenched guitar riffs that usually provide a backdrop for a wailing sax. Eddy's chart run was brief (from 1958 to 1960), but his style is embedded in rock's fiber and continues to shape many young players. —*John Floyd*

○ **2 Classic Albums: Have 'twangy' Guitar Will Travel/$1,000,000 Worth of Twang** / 1959 / Motown ✦✦✦✦
Debut album, featuring "Rebel Rouser," "Ramrod," "Detour," "Three Thirty Blues," and "The Stalker." The album that inspired thousands of guitarists worldwide. —*Cub Koda*

○ **$1,000,000 Worth of Twang** / 1960 / Motown ✦✦✦✦
Solid best-of collection of Duane's earliest hits, including "Rebel Rouser," "Movin' & Groovin'," "Ramrod," and "Forty Miles of Bad Road." —*Cub Koda*

★ **Twang Thang: Anthology** / May 18, 1993 / Rhino ✦✦✦✦✦
Duane Eddy was America's first bona-fide rock & roll guitar hero, playing minimalistic riffs that any kid with a pawnshop guitar could aspire to with a little determination and elbow grease. This two-CD anthology offers the finest retrospective of his career available, with all facets of his career being well-documented, from the early hits to later collaborations with the famous rockers he initially inspired. Featuring just enough rarities to keep it from being merely a greatest-hits package, this truly showcases Duane at his best. —*Cub Koda*

Dave Edmunds

b. Apr. 15, 1944, Cardiff, Wales
Rock & Roll, Roots-Rock
Dave Edmunds may not be a musical innovator, but that doesn't mean he's not an original. Where other roots-rockers sound stiff and respectable, Edmunds sounds alive and passionate even on the tracks he recorded completely by himself. He's not much of a songwriter—all of his best compositions were co-written with Nick Lowe—but he has a great ear for material; he's able to not only pick the overlooked oldies, but new material that sounds like classic rock & roll (Elvis Costello's "Girls Talk," Graham Parker's "Back to Schooldays"). Edmunds' skills as a producer are formidable; he can replicate and update everything from the sound of Sun Studios and Phil Spector's wall of sound to the crisp guitars of the Everly Brothers and the driving rhythms of Chuck Berry. Although his records after 1982's *D.E. 7th* suffer from lackluster material and sound like he's trying to keep up with trends, all of the albums he recorded in the previous decade are brilliant recreations of the best of '50s and '60s rock & roll, played with energy and flair.

After spending some time as the lead guitarist of Love Sculpture, Edmunds built his own recording studio in the late '60s. In 1971, he had his only big hit single with a revamped version of Smiley Lewis' "I Hear You Knocking." As he recorded his own albums, he produced several other artists, including Brinsley Schwarz and the Flamin' Groovies. *Get It* featured former Brinsley bassist Nick Lowe, who also contributed several songs, including single "I Knew the Bride." Lowe and Edmunds formed Rockpile with guitarist Billy Bremner and drummer Terry Williams. Rockpile backed both Edmunds and Lowe on their solo records; during concerts everyone traded songs. With their support, Edmunds' solo records became more tougher and looser; the two albums he recorded entirely with the group—*Tracks on Wax 4* and *Repeat When Necessary*—are his finest.

Rockpile recorded one album as a group before they split in 1980. During the '80s, Edmunds produced several artists, including the Fabulous Thunderbirds, a Carl Perkins television special and the Everly Brothers. After releasing a couple of albums that lacked hit singless, he turned to Jeff Lynne for production help in 1983; the teaming resulted in two stiff, synth-dominated records. By 1990's *Closer to the Flame*, Edmunds had shed Lynne and returned to the straightforward rock & roll of his earlier records. 1994's *Plugged In* found Edmunds making a one-band record again, for the first time since *Subtle as a Flying Mallet*. —*Stephen Thomas Erlewine*

Rockpile / 1972 / Mamou ✦✦✦
Subtle As a Flying Mallet / 1975 / RCA ✦✦✦
○ **Get It** / 1977 / Swan Song ✦✦✦✦
Driven by the raucous rockers "Get Out of Denver," "I Knew the Bride," and "JuJu Man," *Get It* is one of Dave Edmunds' strongest albums. —*Stephen Thomas Erlewine*

○ **Tracks on Wax 4** / 1978 / Swan Song ✦✦✦✦
A piledriving set of new written-to-orders and covers is powered by Edmunds's dexterous vocals and the bar-band boogie of Rockpile. —*John Floyd*

○ **Repeat When Necessary** / 1979 / Swan Song ✦✦✦✦
His creative breakthrough mines the usual retro-terrain, only the nuevo-oldies are the best he's ever had. Both Edmunds's and Rockpile's finest moment. —*John Floyd*

Twangin' / 1981 / Swan Song ✦✦✦
Twangin..., Edmunds' first post-Rockpile album, is an inconsistent but enjoyable record, highlighted by the psuedo-New Wave of John Hiatt's "Something Happens," the insistent groove of "You'll Never Get Me Up (In One of Those)," and the gorgeous Everly Brothers-style ballad "(I'm Gonna Start) Living Again If It Kills Me." —*Stephen Thomas Erlewine*

○ **The Best of Dave Edmunds** / 1981 / Swan Song ✦✦✦✦
D.E. 7th / 1982 / Columbia ✦✦✦
While it follows the same formula as *Twangin', DE7* is a much stronger album, thanks to strong songs like "From Small Things (Big Things One Day Come)," "Bail You Out," and "Warmed Over Kisses (Left Over Love)." —*Stephen Thomas Erlewine*

Information / 1983 / Columbia ✦✦
Riff Raff / 1984 / Columbia ✦✦
Dave Edmunds Band Live: I Hear You Rockin' / 1987 / Columbia ✦✦✦
Closer to the Flame / 1990 / Capitol ✦✦
The Early Edmunds / 1991 / EMI ✦✦✦
● **The Anthology (1968-1990)** / 1993 / Rhino ✦✦✦✦
By trying to represent all aspects of his career accurately, this double-disc set overlooks a lot of Edmunds's finest material, but the 41 songs on *The Dave Edmunds Anthology (1968-1990)* do offer a good portrait of his career, from his beginnings with Love Sculpture, through Rockpile, and his solo hits. —*AMG*
Plugged In / 1994 / Forward/Rhino ✦✦

The Edsels

Group, Doo-Wop
A brief encounter with fame came for the Edsels (from the tiny mill town of Campbell, OH) when they did the doo-wop masterpiece "Rama Lama Ding Dong," its success coming only after diligent record collectors made the record a hit some three years after its release. —*Cub Koda*

● **Rama Lama Ding Dong** / 1992 / Relic ✦✦✦✦
A complete 16-track collection of the group's best sides, including the title track, one of the great nonsense doo-wop sides of all time. —*Cub Koda*

Jonathan Edwards

b. Jul. 28, 1946, Minnesota
Singer-Songwriter, Folk-Rock
This Minnesota singer/songwriter's claim to fame was the lightly upbeat ditty "Sunshine" (#4). Even though he was unable to match the success of that song, Edwards released a string of albums to a small but devoted following. His more recent efforts reflected a return to his bluegrass roots. —*Rick Clark*

● **Jonathan Edwards** / 1971 / Atco ✦✦✦✦
This album is best known for Edwards's hit, "Sunshine" and the song "Shanty," which radio stations around the country call "The Friday Song." If either of these songs is as far as you've gotten with this album, you are missing a great deal. Edwards has a great sense of melody, which means there is not a weak track on this record. Aside from the previously mentioned numbers, one or two of the songs on the record have taken on a life of their own. "Don't Cry Blue," for instance, has been knocking around bluegrass circles for some years. One listen and you'll know why this album has never gone out of print. —*Jim Worbois*

○ **Honky-Tonk Stardust Cowboy** / 1972 / Atco ✦✦✦✦
Edwards continues where the first record left off and continues to grow as an artist. In addition to his own fine songs, Edwards chose to include a few covers like Jesse Colin Young's "Sugar Babe," the

Mills Brothers' "Paper Doll" (complete with faux "trombone" solo), and the title track. The title track did receive some airplay on country radio in 1972 but was never the hit it should have been. If you find a copy of this one, grab it. —*Jim Worbois*

Have a Good Time for Me / 1973 / Atco ♦♦♦
While this album has no Edwards originals, the record is not short on good songs. Edwards has mainly covered tunes by three writers—Joe Dolce, Malcom McKinney, and Orphans' Eric Lillyequist (who has appeared on each of Edwards' records to this point)—each of whom has captured the style and essence of Jonathan Edwards. Highly enjoyable. —*Jim Worbois*

Lucky Day / 1974 / Atco ♦♦♦
Unlike many live albums where you get to hear the artist rehash their hits and rock the house, Edwards not only gives us a look at his musical roots (Merle Haggard, Jimmy Martin, and Gov. Jimmy Davis) but some surprises as well. One of the most surprising is a highly irreverent version of the Chi-Lites' hit, "Have You Seen Her?" with Edwards' seemingly improvised recitation. This is also the first of Edwards' records on which his band Orphan are credited by name. (Their records are also well worth checking out.) Recommended. —*Jim Worbois*

Rockin' Chair / 1976 / Reprise ♦♦
1976 found Edwards with a new label, new backing musicians, and a new producer, the then *very* hot Brian Ahern. Unfortunately, change is not always a good thing. The songs and the band are both very good, but the intimate feel of the early albums is missing here and that was one of the things that always made Edwards' records so appealing. That lack of intimacy seems to fall on the producer's shoulders and should not be held against the artist. Despite the flaws in production, this is still a fine collection of songs and performances from a regrettably overlooked artist. —*Jim Worbois*

Sailboat / 1977 / Reprise ♦♦
This just doesn't have the feel of a Jonathan Edwards album. It could be blamed on the relatively few Edwards originals, which leave the feeling that the creation of this record was more or less removed from the artist's hands. It's a pleasant enough collection, especially if you ever wondered what Jonathan Edwards would sound like singing other songwriters' songs. (His version of "Never Together" predates Carlene Carter's near hit by a year.) Still, if this is your first exposure to this artist, you may be tempted to skip the rest of his work and that would be a major mistake. —*Jim Worbois*

Live / 1980 / Chronic ♦♦♦
Blue Ridge / 1985 / Sugar Hill ♦♦

808 State

Group, House Music, Techno
With their sample-driven dance music, the pioneering Manchester-based 808 State is one of the first house groups to release trance/ambient dance records. Instead of being an incessant pounding, the beat in 808 State's music is hypnotic and mesmerizing; occasionally, their records feature a vocalist/rapper (including guest appearances by Bjork and New Order's Bernard Sumner) but the music is mainly instrumental. In the late '80s and early '90s, both their own records and their remixes were dance club staples. —*Stephen Thomas Erlewine*

○ **Newbuild** / 1988 / Creed State ♦♦♦♦
● **808 Utd. State 90** / 1990 / Tommy Boy ♦♦♦♦
One of the best house albums ever recorded, *Utd. State 90* is a hypnotic, trance-inducing collection of colorful samples and endlessly inventive rhythm tracks. —*Stephen Thomas Erlewine*

○ **Ex:el** / 1991 / Tommy Boy ♦♦♦♦
Gorgeous / 1993 / Tommy Boy ♦♦

Einstürzende Neubauten

Group, Industrial, Alternative Pop/Rock
The German-based industrial group (their name means "collapsing new buildings") brought new meaning to the genre by creating a roaring wall of noise, using many "found" instruments. Their music hinges on the drama wrenched from banging sheets of metal and oil drums, among other junkyard elements, with hammers, wrenches, and other tools. Guitars squeal in white-noise abandon, and their vocals sometimes conjure your worst nightmares. —*John Floyd*

Schwarz [EP] / 1981 / Zick Zack
Kollaps / 1981 / Zick Zack
Portrait of Patient O T / 1983 / Some Bizarre ♦♦♦
● **Strategies Against Architecture** / 1984 / Positive ♦♦♦♦
Radical noisy primitivism. Occasionally stunning. —*John Dougan*

2 X 4 / 1984 / ROIR ♦♦♦
Live noise with power tools. Fun! —*John Dougan*

1/2 Mensch / 1985 / Some Bizarre
Fuenf auf der Nach Oben Offenen Richterskala / 1987 / Some Bizarre
Haus Der Luege / 1989 / Rough Trade ♦♦
○ **Strategies Against Architecture, Vol. 2** / 1991 / Elektra ♦♦♦♦
Radical, noisy primitivism, part two. —*John Dougan*

○ **Tabula Rasa** / 1993 / Elektra ♦♦♦♦

The El Dorados

Group, R&B
One of the leading R&B vocal groups on Vee Jay Records, the Chicago-based El Dorados scored a large cross-over hit in 1955 with the infectious, jumping "At My Front Door." The group had only one other charting record—1956's "I'll Be Forever Loving You"—but they made several other fine records before their breakup in 1959. —*Stephen Thomas Erlewine*

● **Bim Bam Boom** / 1993 / Vee-Jay ♦♦♦♦
The El Dorados didn't enjoy sustained success or notoriety and really weren't a top-echelon doo-wop group. They did make one superb song in 1955: "At My Front Door" is a landmark of the genre; it had every ingredient, from a simple, catchy theme to first-rate harmonizing and Pirkle Moses' finest lead. The El Dorados made many other good tunes, and an occasionally inspired one like "I'll Be Forever Loving You" or "A Fallen Tear," before quitting Vee-Jay in a money dispute and subsequently disbanding. Almost their entire output is available on this 25-song reissue. It's a chance for fans to revisit triumphs and newcomers to hear why they did have a brief time in the spotlight. —*Ron Wynn*

Elastica

Group, Alternative Pop/Rock
Elastica's brief, angular and catchy punk rock became a hit on both sides of the Atlantic in 1995. While the group reworks both the sound and the image of new wave and punk rockers like Adam & the Ants, Wire, the Buzzcocks, and Blondie, the band's songs are more pop-oriented and hook-driven than most of their influences and Justine Frischmann's cool sexuality is earthier, yet more detached, than Debbie Harry.

Guitarist/vocalist Justine Frischmann began performing professionally in the early '90s, forming Suede with her boyfriend Brett Anderson. In addition to naming the band, Frischmann was the group's original guitarist and continued to perform with them once lead guitarist Bernard Butler joined. However, she left the group soon after her relationship with Anderson ended. Frischmann formed Elastica after leaving Suede in 1991. Recruiting guitarist Donna Matthews, drummer Justin, and bassist Annie Holland through advertisements, the final lineup of the band was set in 1993. Elastica released their first single, the roaring three-chord, two-minute punk rocker "Stutter," at the end of 1993. The single was a limited edition run and it quickly sold out, thanks to radio airplay and rave reviews. "Line Up" followed a few months later. It also sold very well, yet some critics claimed the band appropriated the melody from Wire's "I Am the Fly" for the song. For most of 1994, the group was relatively quiet, playing the occasional concert and recording; nevertheless, the band's name stayed in the British press, largely due to Frischmann's romance with Damon Albarn, the lead singer for Blur, England's most popular band of 1994. Released in the fall of the year, "Connection," their biggest hit yet, suffered the same criticism, this time for taking the keyboard riff from Wire's "Three Girl Rhumba." On the eve of the March 1995 release of their debut album, the group was taken to court by Wire's publishers, as well as the publishers of the Stranglers (who claimed Elastica's new single, "Waking Up," took the riff from the punk band's "No More Heroes"); both cases were settled out of court before the album was released.

Entering the charts at number one, Elastica's self-titled first album became the fastest-selling debut in the U.K., beating the record Oasis' *Definitely Maybe* set only seven months earlier. As well as being a popular success, the record received overwhelmingly positive reviews. Like Oasis, Elastica managed to have a hit single in America with "Connection"; the single was a major modern rock radio hit, as well as reaching the Top 60 on the singles chart. Elastica continued to make headway in America by replacing Sinead O'Connor on the 1995 Lollapalooza tour. —*Stephen Thomas Erlewine*

● **Elastica** / 1995 / David Geffen ✦✦✦✦
Elastica's debut album may cop a riff here and there from Wire or the Stranglers, yet no more than Led Zeppelin did with Willie Dixon or the Beach Boys with Chuck Berry. The key is context. Elastica can make the rigid artiness of Wire into a rocking, sexy single with more hooks than anything on *Pink Flag* ("Connection") or rework the Stranglers' "No More Heroes" into a more universal anthem that loses none of its punkiness ("Waking Up"). But what makes *Elastica* such an intoxicating record is not only how the 16 songs speed by in 40 minutes, but that the songs are nearly all classics. The riffs are angular like early Adam & the Ants, the melodies tease like Blondie, and the entire band is as tough as the Clash, yet they never seem anything less than contemporary. Justine Frischmann's detached sexuality adds an extra edge to her brief, spiky songs—"Stutter" roars about a boyfriend's impotence, "Car Song" makes sex in a car actually sound sexy, "Line Up" slags off groupies, and "Vaseline" speaks for itself. Even if the occasional riff sounds like an old wave group, the simple fact is that hardly any new wave band made records this consistently rocking and melodic. —*Stephen Thomas Erlewine*

Electric Flag

Group, Blues Rock
The Electric Flag were a horn-dominated rock band led by guitarist Michael Bloomfield (1944-1981) and featuring drummer and vocalist Buddy Miles, bassist Harvey Brooks (born Goldstein), and vocalist Nick Gravenites. Whereas later, more successful horn-based groups like Chicago and Blood, Sweat & Tears worked from jazz and pop influences, the Electric Flag used the Stax/Volt sound, James Brown, and B.B.King's large groups as role models. Bloomfield left after their first album, with Miles taking over the leadership role for the second album. They re-formed with Bloomfield in 1974 for one quick album released to scant acclaim, but its influence as a trendsetter far exceeds its record sales. —*Cub Koda*

Trip [O.S.T.] / 1967 / Edsel ✦✦✦
Before the Electric Flag had recorded their first album or even played live, they composed and performed the soundtrack to *The Trip*, the 1967 psychedelic exploitation film starring Peter Fonda, directed by Roger Corman, and written by Jack Nicholson. This odd but worthwhile relic is entirely instrumental, and as befits the subject matter, wildly eclectic, veering from ragtime and hurdy-gurdy music to basic soul-rock and sweeping, spacy psychedelia and harsh electronics. One of the funkiest snippets, "Flash, Bam, Pow," was later used by Fonda in *Easy Rider*. —*Richie Unterberger*

An American Music Band / 1968 / One Way ✦✦✦
○ **A Long Time Comin'** / 1968 / Columbia ✦✦✦✦
Ex-Butterfield Band guitarist/drummer Miles and others put this soul-rock band together in 1967. This debut is a testament to their ability to catch fire and keep on burnin'. —*Jeff Tamarkin*

You Are What You Eat [O.S.T.] / 1968 / CBS ✦✦
Electric Flag / 1969 / Columbia ✦✦
Best of Electric Flag / 1971 / Columbia ✦✦✦
Band Kept on Playing / 1974 / Atlantic ✦✦
Groovin' Is Easy / 1983 / Thunderbolt ✦✦✦
○ **Old Glory: The Best Of Electric Flag** / 1995 / Columbia/Legacy ✦✦✦✦
A near-definitive anthology, including almost all of the debut LP (but not every last item), key songs from the second album, and some previously unissued demos, alternate takes, and performances from the 1967 Monterey Pop Festival. —*Richie Unterberger*

Electric Light Orchestra

Group, Art-Rock/Progressive-Rock, Pop/Rock
Formed in 1971 from the ashes of one of Britain's greatest eccentric rock bands, Move, the Electric Light Orchestra drew heavily from the ornately lumbering "I Am the Walrus"-period Beatles. This is shown to extreme effect on their oddly engaging debut, *No Answer*. Of particular note is the track "10538 Overture."

Move expatriates Roy Wood, Jeff Lynne, and Bev Bevan formed the initial nucleus of ELO, but multi-instrumentalist Wood split after *No Answer* to form the bizarrely '50s-influenced Wizzard. Their sophomore release, *ELO II*, retained some of the off-key crunch of the debut, but it is clearly a transition to what became a very slick, highly orchestrated pop-hit factory. Between 1975 and 1981, ELO managed 17 Top 40 hits, among which were "Evil Woman" (#10), "Telephone Line" (#7), "Don't Bring Me Down" (#4), "Hold on Tight" (#10), "Shine a Little Love" (#8) and the wonderful "Can't Get It Out of My Head" (#9). ELO also scored a #24 hit with "Do Ya," which was the Move's only stateside chart hit. ELO increasingly became a side project to leader Jeff Lynne's successful outside artist productions, which included Brian Wilson, Dave Edmunds, Tom Petty, the Traveling Wilburys, Randy Newman, and George Harrison. —*Rick Clark*

○ **No Answer** / 1972 / Jet ✦✦✦✦
Their most lively album, this debut is driven by Roy Wood's manic musical sensibilities. An energetic offshoot of the Move's final album. —*Bruce Eder*

○ **On the Third Day** / 1973 / Jet ✦✦✦✦
ELO's sound came togther here, hooked around rocked-up classics and Jeff Lynne's guitar. —*Bruce Eder*

Electric Light Orchestra 2 / 1973 / Jet ✦✦
A middling second album with dull stretches that are almost balanced by the rip-roaring "Roll over Beethoven." —*Bruce Eder*

○ **Eldorado** / 1975 / Jet ✦✦✦✦
Pretentious pseudo-concept rock with some hot old-style rock & roll grace notes. —*Bruce Eder*

○ **Face the Music** / 1975 / Jet ✦✦✦✦
Superb production and a good song lineup featuring "Evil Woman" and "Strange Magic." —*Bruce Eder*

○ **Ole' Elo** / 1976 / Jet ✦✦✦✦
The early hits, marred only by the unnecessary cutting of "Roll over Beethoven." —*Bruce Eder*

A New World Record / 1976 / Jet ✦✦✦
A superbly crafted and dark-hued body of songs, all melodic and delectable. —*Bruce Eder*

Out of the Blue / 1977 / Jet ✦✦✦
An over-produced, overwrought piece of pop fluff masquerading as something important. —*Bruce Eder*

● **Elo's Greatest Hits** / 1979 / Jet ✦✦✦✦
Most of ELO's biggest and best hits—"Evil Woman," "Rockaria," "Telephone Line"—are included on this solid but slightly skimpy collection. —*Stephen Thomas Erlewine*

Discovery / 1979 / Jet ✦✦
Time / 1981 / Jet ✦✦
Secret Messages / 1983 / Jet ✦✦
Balance of Power / 1986 / Epic ✦✦
○ **Afterglow** / 1990 / Epic ✦✦✦✦
Although it contains all the hits and the remastering sounds superb, the three-disc box set *Afterglow* is likely to be more ELO than anyone but the most devoted fans would want from an anthology. —*Stephen Thomas Erlewine*

○ **Strange Music: The Best Of Electric Light Orchestra** / 1995 / Legacy/Epic ✦✦✦✦
Strange Music concentrates more on ELO's pop hits than *Afterglow*, which makes for a better, more listenable collection. All of the hits are accounted for, along with the group's '70s AOR staples, making it the one definitive collection. ELO may have been an album rock band but their best moments were individual songs; consequently, *Strange Music* doesn't ignore their best attributes, it accentuates them. —*Stephen Thomas Erlewine*

The Electric Prunes

Group, Psychedelic
The Electric Prunes were not so much a self-contained group as a front for some talented L.A. songwriters and producers; they by and large played the music on their records, but the vision and inspiration came from elsewhere. Nonetheless, they produced a few great psychedelic garage songs, especially the scintillating "I Had too Much to Dream Last Night," which mixed distorted guitars and pop hooks with inventive oscillating reverb. Songwriters Annette Tucker and Nancie Mantz wrote much of the Prunes' material, much of which in turn was crafted in the studio by Dave Has-

singer, who had engineered some classic Rolling Stones sessions in the mid-'60s. "Too Much to Dream" was a big hit in 1967, and the psychedelized Bo Diddley follow-up "Get Me to the World on Time" was just as good, and also a hit. Nothing else by the group made it big, and their initial pair of albums were quite erratic, although a few scattered tracks were nearly as good as those singles. Although they began to write more of their own material on their second album, their subsequent releases were apparently the products of personnel that had little to do with the original lineup. Their third LP, *Mass in F Minor*, was a quasi-religious concept album of psychedelic versions of prayers; a definitively excessive period piece, its best song ("Kyrie Eleison") was lifted for the *Easy Rider* soundtrack. None of the original Prunes were still in the lineup when the band dissolved, unnoticed, at the end of the '60s. *—Richie Unterberger*

● **Long Day's Flight** / 1986 / Edsel ◆◆◆◆
18-track compilation includes the best cuts from their first two albums, as well as a couple of non-LP singles. Pruned down to the best six or seven cuts, it would have made a ferocious EP; some of the material is simply unmemorable, as the band pounds away in a sub-Stones bluesy fuzz style in the mode of the Standells or Chocolate Watch Band. Besides the two hits, there are a few first-rate cuts that meld garage pop to inspired psychedelic production, like "Train for Tomorrow," "Hideaway," "Long Day's Flight," "You Never Had It Better," "Sold to the Highest Bidder" (featuring an organ made to sound like a balalaika), and their cover of Goffin/King's "I Happen to Love You." *—Richie Unterberger*

The Elegants

Group, R&B
This New York doo wop group earned notoriety for their masterpiece "Little Star" in 1958, which topped both R&B and pop charts. They were a White ensemble led by Vito Picone, with Arthur Venosa, Frank Tardogno, Carmen Romano, and James Mochella. All had been in other groups before uniting as the Elegants. They continued recording for Hull, United Artists, Limelight, Photo, IPG, and Laurie through the '50s, '60s and into the '70s, but never had another hit, despite cutting a number of solid ballads. There were two other editions in the mid-'60s, Vito Piccone with the Elegants and Vito & the Elegants. *—Ron Wynn*

● **Best of the Elegants** / Collectables ◆◆◆◆
One of the better white doo-wop groups from Long Island, although they didn't have many hits. All the members had worked in other bands before they came together in 1957. They did have one huge smash, the chart-topping "Little Star," which was both an R&B and pop hit and seemed to get their career as a group off to a bang. Unfortunately, it would be their only major record through the late '50s and early and mid-'60s. These are still nicely sung, with the emphasis on romantic wailers and tearjerkers. *—Ron Wynn*

Eleventh Dream Day

Group, Alternative Pop/Rock
One of the more underrated American bands currently occupying the ever-changing "alternative rock" scene, Chicago-based Eleventh Dream Day has managed to record three remarkable albums of driving rock & roll propelled by a swirling, intoxicating din of country-tinged, feedback-drenched guitars. As did the Los Angeles band X nearly a decade earlier, EDD deals intelligently with complex human and social relationships, the narratives spilling forth from the pens of Rick Rizzo and Janet Beveridge Bean. Unlike a number of alternative rock bands who simply cannot write songs EDD eschews a marketable pose and lets the music do the talking. Having been bounced from a major label to an indie, here's hoping the future is kind to them. *—John Dougan*

Prairie School Freakout / 1988 / Amoeba ◆◆◆

Beet / 1989 / Atlantic ◆◆◆
Beet only hints at what was to come, but in retrospect it holds up pretty well. The songs are strong, the playing is energetic, but this is not the place where the epiphanies are. *—John Dougan*

● **Lived to Tell** / 1991 / Atlantic ◆◆◆◆
The underrated album of 1991. *Lived to Tell* is a resounding triumph exhibiting all of Eleventh Dream Day's strengths without ever sounding like generic alternative rock. Sad, combative and raging, this is a record that reveals more with each play. *—John Dougan*

○ **El Moodio** / 1993 / Atlantic ◆◆◆◆
EDD got the big heave-ho from Atlantic when *El Moodio* stiffed. But I can't come up with a single reason as to why this album didn't make them the toast of MTV's Buzz Bin. Perhaps not as galvanizing as *Lived to Tell*, but there's no dross here, just lots and lots of guitars, passion and energy. *—John Dougan*

Ursa Major / 1994 / Atavistic ◆◆◆
Now recording for an indie label, guitarist Wink O'Bannon quit before the recording of *Ursa Major*, and Janet Bean was also consumed with her excellent side band Freakwater, but this record was winner number three. A tad more experimental (and some would argue less accessible, though not me) than earlier records, *Ursa Major* is still loaded with supple, pretty melodies and intense, rampaging guitars. *—John Dougan*

The Elgins

Group, Motown
The Elgins were actually a combination of soloist Saundra Edwards and a three-man male group called the Downbeats. Edwards, like Kim Weston and Brenda Holloway, was one of the finest vocalists in the Motown stable. As leader of the Elgins, the group scored some minor chart hits, including the original version of "Heaven Must Have Sent You" which became a major hit for Bonnie Pointer in 1979. Their only album featured some top rate material by Holland-Dozier-Holland. *—Rick A. Bueche*

○ **Darling Baby** / 1966 / VIP ◆◆◆◆
Savvy Saundra Edwards vocals and Holland-Dozier-Holland productions create some classy material here. *—Rick A. Bueche*

Yvonne Elliman

Disco
Yvonne Elliman had a brief moment in the spotlight during the middle of the '70s, yet she appeared on many of the decade's biggest hits as a backing singer. While she was in high school in Hawaii, she sang in a group called We Folk. She moved to London in 1949 and began singing at the Pheasantry folk club, located on Kings Road in Chelsea. It was here that songwriters Andrew Lloyd Webber and Tim Rice discovered her. The duo offered her the role of Mary Magdalene in their new rock opera, *Jesus Christ Superstar*, the role brought her instant fame. Elliman played the Magdalene in the film version of *Superstar*, for which she won a Golden Globe award; it also gave her a hit with "I Don't Know How to Love Him." The hit single became the title of her debut album, which was released in 1972. Pete Townshend helped Elliman prepare her second album, 1973's *Food of Love*. During this time, she appeared in the American production of *Jesus Christ Superstar* on Broadway, where she met Bill Oakes, the president of RSO Records; the two married soon afterwards. Oakes introduced her to Eric Clapton, inviting her to sing backup vocals on "I Shot the Sheriff." Elliman became part of the guitarist's band afterwards; she stayed with him for five years.

She joined RSO's roster in 1975, releasing the Steve Cropper-produced *Rising Sun*. Barry Gibb and Robin Gibb wrote the title song for Elliman's next album, 1976's *Love Me*; the song became a U.K. hit, paving the way for her greatest chart success, the *Saturday Night Fever* soundtrack. The Bee Gees wrote several songs on the soundtrack specifically for Elliman, including the number one single "If I Can't Have You." She never followed through on the song's success—she released two more albums before becoming solely a session musician. *—Stephen Thomas Erlewine*

● **The Very Best Of** / 1995 / Taragon ◆◆◆◆

Shirley Ellis

Soul
New York vocalist and composer Shirley Ellis was in the Metronomes before earning fame as co-composer and performer of some enjoyable soul novelty tunes in the mid-'60s. These included the Top Ten R&B hits "The Nitty Gritty" and "The Name Game." "The Name Game" was co-written with her manager and husband Lincoln Chase, and peaked at number four R&B and number three pop in 1965. She and Chase also collaborated on the follow-up, "The Clapping Song (Clap Pat Clap Slap)," which reached number 16 R&B, but also represented the end of the creative line for the trend. Ellis landed one final moderately successful, more conventional soul tune two years later, "Soul Time." All except "Soul Time" were recorded for Congress; she had moved to Columbia by 1967, when "Soul Time" was issued. *—Ron Wynn*

Shirley Ellis in Action / 1964 / Congress ✦✦✦
● **The Name Game** / 1965 / Congress ✦✦✦✦
Sugar, Let's Shing a Ling / 1967 / Columbia ✦✦✦

Lorraine Ellison

Group, Soul
A Philadelphia-born gospel singer (with the Ellison Sisters) turned soul diva, Ellison is best known for the poignant, apocalyptic "Stay with Me" (1966), a virtuoso display of vocal pyrotechnics written and produced by Jerry Ragovoy, which instantly garnered Ellison a cult following among her peers in the business. Ellison's stunning soprano, her phrasing by turns ethereal and triumphant, soars above Ragovoy's equally intense arrangements. Her technical perfection in the higher registers infuses each syllable with a purity that has rarely been equaled in the genre. —*Christine Ohlman*

● **Stay with Me** / 1969 / Line ✦✦✦✦
Produced by Jerry Ragovoy. Includes title track, covered by Terry Reid; "Try (Just a Little Bit Harder)," covered by Janis Joplin; "You Don't Know Nothing About Love," covered by Irma Thomas. Few soul albums have ever matched the intensity of this! —*Christine Ohlman*

Lorraine Ellison / 1974 / Warner Brothers ✦✦✦
Gospel-tinged effort includes a fine cover of Jimmy Cliff's "Many Rivers to Cross." —*Christine Ohlman*

Philadelphia's Queen of Soul / 1976 / Warner Brothers ✦✦✦

Joe Ely

b. Feb. 9, 1947, TX
Country-Rock
In the '70s, C&W was full of artists referred to as "outlaws," mavericks who bucked the stodgy Nashville music establishment by writing their own songs, recording with their road bands, and producing their own records. The genre produced a slew of acts, but Lubbock, TX. native Joe Ely epitomized the form. Unlike most of that era's big names, Ely remains a viable artist. He got his start back in the early '70s, working with Butch Hancock and Jimmie Dale Gilmore in a group called the Flatlanders. Their only album didn't go far, and the group broke up. (Rounder reissued the album in 1990.) Around the mid '70s, Ely formed an eclectic group that was able to swing from Cajun and Western to honky-tonk stomps and rockabilly; it was signed to MCA in 1977. Ely released an eponymous debut that year, using songs written by ex-Flatlanders Gilmore and Butch Hancock and throwing in some of his own road-worn, oddly poetic originals. The next year brought *Honky Tonk Masquerade*, the cornerstone of Ely's legacy and one of modern country's most ambitious albums. Further albums (especially *Live Shots*, recorded during his European tour with the Clash) brought Ely to the attention of rock fans and netted ecstatic reviews in country and pop magazines (but, mysteriously, produced no hits). MCA dropped Ely in 1983, and he woodshedded until 1987, when the independent Hightone label signed him and released *Lord of the Highway*. Another Hightone album followed before Ely (whose influence was being felt by the new breed of country neo-traditionalists) re-signed with MCA, releasing another live set and *Love and Danger*. He's yet to top his late-'70s achievements, but Ely remains an energetic and passionate live performer and an occasionally inspired songwriter. Writing him off could be perilous. —*John Floyd*

○ **Joe Ely** / 1977 / MCA ✦✦✦✦
Ely's first album came out while country's outlaw movement was in full swing, but *Joe Ely* took it one better. This is a roots-rocking country album with tunes by Jimmie Dale Gilmore ("Treat Me Like a Saturday Night") and Butch Hancock ("She Never Spoke Spanish to Me," "If You Were a Bluebird") that deserve the near-classic status their cult of fans has bestowed on them. —*Brian Mansfield*

● **Honky Tonk Masquerade** / 1978 / MCA ✦✦✦✦
Ely's best album, *Honky Tonk Masquerade* contains everything from Texas weepers ("Because of the Wind") to roadhouse rockers ("Fingernails"). Among the best tunes are Jimmie Dale Gilmore's "Tonight I Think I'm Gonna Go Downtown" and Butch Hancock's "West Texas Waltz." Nobody made country records like this in 1978. Come to think of it, they still don't. —*Brian Mansfield*

Down in the Drag / 1979 / MCA ✦✦✦
○ **Live Shots** / 1980 / MCA ✦✦✦✦
Ely partakes of the musical diversity of his hometown, Lubbock, TX, freely mixing country, rock, Tex-Mex, and hard honky-tonk music in excellent songs he writes himself or borrows from his friend Butch Hancock. This is a live best-of covering his first three albums, recorded on tour in England. —*William Ruhlmann*

Musta Notta Gotta Lotta / 1981 / MCA ✦✦✦

Hi-Res / 1984 / MCA ✦✦
The only one of Ely's MCA albums the label hasn't issued on CD, *Hi-Res* is a synthesizer-heavy record that came after Ely learned about Apple computers. Preferable versions of "Cool Rockin' Loretta" and "She Gotta Get the Gettin'" appear on *Live at Liberty Lunch*. —*Brian Mansfield*

Lord of the Highway / 1987 / Hightone ✦✦✦
After a long recording layoff, Ely picked up where he'd left off in 1984 with this typical collection, whose best songs—"Me and Billy the Kid" and "Are You Listenin' Lucky?"—were Ely originals. —*William Ruhlmann*

Dig All Night / 1988 / Hightone ✦✦✦
Milkshakes & Malts / 1988 / Sunstorm ✦✦✦

Live at Liberty Lunch / 1990 / MCA ✦✦✦
This live album was recorded over two days at Liberty Lunch in Austin, Texas. Ely's band has evolved from a country band with Tejano roots to a hard-rocking Texas ensemble highlighted by guitarist David Grissom, who later defected to John Cougar Mellencamp. —*Brian Mansfield*

○ **Love & Danger** / 1992 / MCA ✦✦✦✦
Ely is stark and restless. His muse still roams the highways in search of whatever, his romance doomed by a twist of fate. He's a more objective observer; a storyteller who captures the tragic side to the well-defined characters of "The Road Goes on Forever" and "Every Night About This Time."
Ely conveys much—if not most—of a song's emotion through his inspired electric guitar playing. The string-bending is at high-pressure intensity for "Love Is the Beating of Hearts," then drops deep, sonorous and echoed for "Slow You Down." —*Roch Parisien*

Embryo

Group, Art-Rock/Progressive-Rock
Since their inception in 1969, Embryo has been one Germany's most adventurous bands. —*Archie Patterson*

● **Reise** / 1979 / Schneeball ✦✦✦✦
Reise is an audio documentary of Embryo's end of the '70s "Journey" through the Middle East, a musical diary of their various experiences with master musicians and street players alike, from Bombay to the docks of Calcutta and beyond. No clinical exercise in musicology or studio session, it lives and breathes with the sounds and smells of music created from the creative flow of life in progress. Ethnic instruments, jazz, rock and chants combine to create a vibrant tapestry of sound on this magnificent double album. —*Archie Patterson*

Emerson, Lake & Palmer

Group, Art-Rock/Progressive-Rock
By the end of the '60s, many artists became swept up in the wake of the Beatles and their aggressive exploration of the possibilities of pop and rock. In the minds of many young, schooled musicians who found release in rock's energy, expanding the form by incorporating motifs and highly arranged extended compositions seemed an appealing notion. The results of this concept became known as art-rock.
Depending on your point of view, Emerson, Lake & Palmer was guilty of encouraging such tonal indulgence, or they delivered some of the genre's better moments. Pianist Keith Emerson had already met much success in Britain with his theatrical pyrotechnics in Nice. Greg Lake was the vocalist/bassist for the explosively dark King Crimson, and percussionist Carl Palmer backed up the heavy blues-based Atomic Rooster, a band that also contained eventual Fleetwood Mac member Christine McVie.
Months before the arrival of Emerson, Lake & Palmer's self-titled debut, expectations began running high about what the band would contribute to the expansion of rock. The debut was impressive, ranging from delicate acoustic piano and guitar interplay to explosive free-for-alls, but with the second album (*Tarkus*) it became obvious that the band often placed an enormous amount of

finesse on playing to the back of the bleachers, rather than focusing that energy into a consistently satisfying musicality.

Nevertheless, Emerson, Lake & Palmer became a staple of FM rock radio during the '70s, even scoring a couple of hits with "Lucky Man" (#48) and "In the Beginning" (#39). —*Rick Clark*

○ **Emerson, Lake & Palmer** / 1970 / Atlantic ✦✦✦

Lively, ambitious, largely successful debut album, made up of daring instrumentals ("Three Fates," "The Barbarian") and romantic ballads ("Lucky Man"), showcasing three very daunting talents. "Take a Pebble" is rewarding and pretentious enough to have been a Moody Blues track, except that the Moodies could never solo like Keith Emerson. The trio would never be as concise or precise in their work again. —*Bruce Eder*

Tarkus / 1971 / Atlantic ✦✦✦

A dark concept album, really as much an offshoot thematically of King Crimson's *Court of the Crimson King* (on which Lake played and sang) as anything derived by the trio, that reaches too far and takes itself too seriously much of the time. The title suite has some haunting moments, but the whole thing is too gloomy and pretentious for all but serious fans. —*Bruce Eder*

Pictures at an Exhibition / 1971 / Atlantic ✦✦✦

A live recording of the Mussorgsky piece which, despite its wildness, holds up well as a psychedelic art-rock showcase. —*Bruce Eder*

Trilogy / 1972 / Atlantic ✦✦✦

A major improvement over their second album (the convoluted concept effort *Tarkus*) and the group's first success with adapting the music of Aaron Copland ("Hoedown"), which became something of a signature of theirs. The title suite is a romantic, almost torch-song number, while "The Endless Enigma" is a curious mixture of pomp and mysticism. —*Bruce Eder*

○ **Brain Salad Surgery** / 1973 / Atlantic ✦✦✦✦

Science-fiction rock, virtually a soundtrack to a non-existent film. Well-produced and overpowering, but fully rewarding only on the tracks that fall outside the concept. —*Bruce Eder*

Ladies & Gentlemen (Welcome Back My Friends to the Show That Never Ends) / 1974 / Manticore ✦✦

For serious fans only. Not quite an adequate sounding document of their stage act. Others should stick with *Pictures at an Exhibition.* —*Bruce Eder*

Works, Vol. 1 / Oct. 1977 / Atlantic ✦✦✦

The trio's last great album, a double-disc set that essentially allowed each of the members a side of his own to produce and a fourth side on which they worked as a team. Emerson's Piano Concerto is over-extended but probably the best work of its kind (and there are quite a few from this period) by a rock figure. Lake's solo material is a little too soft and romantic, while Palmer comes off best, with a percussion/production tour-de-force. The group material (including "Fanfare for the Common Man") isn't a major advance (except in dimension) from the preceding record. —*Bruce Eder*

Love Beach / 1978 / Arista ✦✦

The Best of ELP / 1980 / Atlantic ✦✦✦

Black Moon / 1992 / Victory ✦

● **The Atlantic Years** / 1992 / Atlantic ✦✦✦✦

This double-disc set is a solid two-and-a-half hours' overview of ELP's career highlights, including "The Endless Enigma (Parts 1 & 2)," "Fugue," "Knife-Edge," "Take a Pebble," "Lucky Man," "From the Beginning," "Fanfare for the Common Man," "Still … You Turn Me On," Greg Lake's "Father Christmas," and excerpts from *Pictures at an Exhibition.* —*AMG*

The Return of the Manticore / Nov. 16, 1993 / Victory ✦✦

Coming from this notorious album-oriented art-rock band, the box set *Return of the Manticore* somewhat works against the very structured nature of their albums. For hardcore fans, the music might be disconcerting out of its proper context (although the first studio version of "Pictures at an Exhibition" will delight them), and there is way too much music for casual fans. All and all, the 2-CD *The Atlantic Years* compilation distills their career much more concisely and successfully, making it more worthwhile for most fans. —*Stephen Thomas Erlewine*

EMF

Group, Dance-Pop, Techno-Pop/Dance

One of the few British acts to experience success overseas, EMF

had a huge hit in 1991 with its throbbing, rock/dance/techno hybrid "Unbelievable." Other songs on the accompanying album, *Schubert Dip,* were good but none were as instantly memorable, although they had a follow-up hit with "Lies." By the time they released their second album, their brand of English dance pop was already passé in both the U.S. and the U.K. —*Stephen Thomas Erlewine*

● **Schubert Dip** / 1991 / EMI America ✦✦✦✦

Their debut album fuses dance music and rock, and includes the hit "Unbelievable." —*David Szatmary*

○ **Stigma** / 1992 / Capitol ✦✦✦✦

To everyone's surprise, EMF proved that they had the musical capability to be more than a one-hit wonder with their second album, *Stigma.* To no one's surprise, the record-buying public treated them as a one-hit wonder and the record bombed. Anyone who liked "Unbelievable" that cares to take a listen to *Stigma* will find much more than rewrites of their hit single; the band shows some skill and variety. —*Stephen Thomas Erlewine*

The Emotions

Group, Soul

A trio of sisters with a strong gospel base, the Emotions (based in Chicago) were one of the leading female R&B acts of the '70s. Lead singer Sheila Hutchinson and her sisters Wanda and Jeanette were only teenagers when they crashed the soul charts in 1969 with the engaging "So I Can Love You," but they sang gospel as children and enjoyed secular fame locally before signing with Memphis-based Volt and working with producers Isaac Hayes and David Porter. When Stax folded in 1975, the group hooked up with Maurice White of Earth, Wind & Fire, an association that led to the #1 pop/R&B hit "Best of My Love" in 1977.

Two years after *Best Of My Love,* Maurice White and the Emotions collaborated on "Boogie Wonderland," which was both a number two R&B and number six pop hit. They issued three more albums on White's ARC label from 1979 to 1981, but were unable to duplicate their earlier success. They moved to the Red label for the 1984 LP *Sincerely,* which included the single "All Things Come In Time." They issued three other singles from the album, but none made much impact, though each one charted. They then signed with Motown, but issued only one album, *If I Only Knew.* Sheila Hutchinson was a featured vocalist on Garry Glenn's "Feels Good to Feel Good" in 1987. Pam and Jeanette Hutchinson did background vocals on Helen Baylor's gospel song "There's No Greater Love" in 1990. Wanda Hutchinson and Jeanette sang on Earth, Wind and Fire's *Heritage* in 1990. —*Bill Dahl and Ron Wynn*

So I Can Love You / 1970 / Stax ✦✦✦

The Hutchinson sisters were an excellent gospel act billed as the Heavenly Sunbeams before they turned to secular material. This was their soul debut, and the title track was produced by Isaac Hayes and penned by Sheila Hutchinson. It was a nice bit of gospel-tinged soul, and was an indicator that the sisters weren't going to have any trouble turning to more earthly concerns. —*Ron Wynn*

Flowers / 1976 / Columbia ✦✦✦

Earth, Wind & Fire's Maurice White produced the excellent choral effect of this group. —*Rick A. Bueche*

● **Rejoice** / 1977 / Columbia ✦✦✦✦

This is the finest late-'70s soul collection available. —*Rick A. Bueche*

Sunbeam / 1978 / CBS ✦✦✦

The Emotions were beginning to encounter some problems in the late '70s, although their singing was still as emphatic and gospel-tinged as ever. But they didn't enjoy the same success on Maurice White's label as they did with Columbia. This was the first of three late-'70s and early-'80s albums they did for his ARC company, and although they did get two R&B chart singles, their biggest hit came on a collaboration with Earth, Wind & Fire from another project. —*Ron Wynn*

Come into Our World / 1979 / Columbia ✦✦✦

The Emotions were nearing the end of their association with Maurice White's ARC label and production company. This album had some competent uptempo tunes and good ballads, but neither the Hutchinsons' vocals nor the production and arrangements were as focused or distinctive as they had been in the past. The reaction from the R&B audience was equally mixed. —*Ron Wynn*

○ **Chronicle** / 1979 / Stax ✦✦✦✦
A fine collection of the Emotions' greatest hits, *Chronicle* also includes several songs that weren't as popular but were nearly as good. —*Stephen Thomas Erlewine*

○ **Best of Emotion** / 1979 / Stax ✦✦✦✦

New Affair / 1981 / Columbia ✦✦✦
This was the Emotions' final album for Maurice White's ARC label, and it wasn't among their more memorable outings. Their collective arrangements and harmonies were still solid, but the passion and energy that had marked their best singles was missing, while the production was routine and the arrangements lifeless and uninspired. They got a couple of moderate R&B chart hits out of it, but weren't the sparkling, vibrant ensemble they had been in the mid-'70s. —*Ron Wynn*

Sincerely / 1984 / Red Label ✦✦✦
The Emotions regrouped on a new label in the mid-'80s and seemed about to recapture their past glory. This album was their most exuberantly sung and tightly produced since the late '70s, but unfortunately times had changed, and their brand of Southern, gospel-inflected "deep" soul no longer packed much punch above the Mason-Dixon line. They were able to get three singles on the charts, but none were big hits. —*Ron Wynn*

Emperor

Group
Emperor is considered to be currently the best band on Norway's disturbingly violent death metal scene. Their dark, innovative sound is influenced by traditional Scandinavian folk and medieval music. Vocalist, keyboardist, and guitarist "Ihsahn" is the only major member who remains both in Norway and out of prison. Guitarist "Samoth" is serving a sentence for arson (he burned down a historical wooden church); bassist "Tchort" was convicted of burglary, knife assault, and desecration; and drummer "Faust" (b. Bard G. Eithun) is currently in prison for arson, burglary, and the murder of a homosexual acquaintance (Faust stabbed him several times outside the Olympic Park in Lillehammer). Their latest bassist, "Mortiis," who was a major part of Emperor's folk influence, left the band and moved to Sweden to pursue a solo career due to unspecified problems. It remains to be seen how the band will regroup. —*Steve Huey*

In the Nightside Eclipse / 1994 / Century Black
An excellent album combining black metal with synth arrangements and dark, haunting medieval chords and melodies. Emperor evokes moods of sorrow and loneliness in addition to death metal's typical noisy fury; the album, recorded in the Memorial Hall of Edvard Grieg, can almost be described as beautiful in places. This is an ambitious record, one highly recommended to anyone interested in bands not afraid to experiment or push the limits of the death metal genre. —*Steve Huey*

En Vogue

Group, Urban
Producers Denzil Foster and Thomas McElroy constructed the early '90s San Francisco Bay Area vocal quartet En Vogue. Members of the group include Dawn Robinson, Cindy Herron, Maxine Jones, and Terry Ellis.
En Vogue became an unexpected crossover smash when their debut *Born to Sing* produced several Top 40 hits in 1991. The 1992 followup, *Funky Divas*, also became a major hit and led some critics to call the dance-floor divas the "new Supremes."
In 1993, the group issued an EP, *Runaway Love*, and teamed with female rappers Salt-N-Pepa on the pop and Urban Top 10 hit "Whatta Man." —*John Floyd & Ron Wynn*

Born to Sing / 1991 / Atlantic ✦✦✦
A youthful unit with classic girl-group chops. —*Ron Wynn*

Remix to Sing / 1991 / East West ✦✦

● **Funky Divas** / 1992 / East West ✦✦✦✦
En Vogue are incredible singers, which is what makes *Funky Divas* a delight. Naturally, the singles are the high points on the album, but the rest of the album is hardly filler—it proves that En Vogue possess great talent. —*Stephen Thomas Erlewine*

Runaway Love / 1993 / East West ✦✦

Enchantment

Group, Soul
Enchantment's members all attended Detroit's Pershing High

School. Ed "Mickey" Clanton, Bobby Green, Davis Banks, Emanuel Johnson, and Joe Thomas began singing together in 1966. While "Gloria" was their first hit in 1976, the songs that followed it were actually their biggest records. "Sunshine" reached number three on the R&B charts, while "It's You that I Need" was their lone number one single, and a definitive performance featuring some energized exchanges and vocal group interaction, in 1978. They began on Desert Mn., switched to United Artists, then continued on Roadshow, RCA and Columbia into the mid-'80s. Their last release was "Feel like Dancing" on Prelude in 1984. —*Ron Wynn*

○ **Golden Classics** / Collectables ✦✦✦✦
A good collection of soul hits. —*Ron Wynn*

The Enfields

Group, Garage Rock
In 1966, this Wilmington, Delaware group released one of the best garage rock singles, "She Already Has Somebody," a moody, melodic original on par with the best efforts by the Zombies. Led by guitarist, singer, and songwriter Ted Mundy, they were popular in their region, and totally unknown elsewhere, releasing a few singles on a tiny local label. It may seem like a slim legacy, but the group's output stands considerably above the norm of the hundreds of other comparable American regional garage bands of the time, due primarily to Mundy's fine melodic songwriting, heavily influenced not only by the Zombies but by the Beatles and Beau Brummels. In 1967, Mundy formed Friends of the Family, which explored jazzier and more progressive directions, resulting in some interesting material. However, his work with the Enfields stands up best. —*Richie Unterberger*

○ **Enfields/Friends Of The Family** / 1993 / Get Hip ✦✦✦✦
All seven songs from the Enfields' four extremely rare singles, as well as eleven demos recorded by Friends Of The Family in 1967 and 1968. A well-above-average '60s obscurity. —*Richie Unterberger*

England Dan & John Ford Coley

Group, Pop
Successful mid- to late-'70s soft-pop duo. England Dan is Dan Seals, brother of Seals & Croft's Jim Seals. —*Rick Clark*

● **The Best of England Dan & John Ford Coley** / 1979 / Big Tree ✦✦✦✦
It contains "I'd Really Like to See You Tonight" (#2), "Nights Are Forever Without You" (#10), "We'll Never Have to Say Goodbye Again" (#9), and "Love Is the Answer" (#10). —*Dan Heilman*

England's Glory

Group, New Wave
Several years before Peter Perrett came to prominence in the new wave band the Only Ones, he was doing his best to imitate Lou Reed in an outfit called England's Glory. The group—dominated by Perrett's vocals and songs, and including future Squeeze bassist Harry Kakoulli—cut a bunch of demos in early 1973, but never got anywhere, on record or as a performing act. In the late '80s, long after the Only Ones had disbanded, many of these demos finally saw the light of day on an archival reissue. —*Richie Unterberger*

● **Legendary Lost Recordings** / 1989 / Skyclad ✦✦✦✦
Ten demos from January 1973 that mark Perrett as the most obsessed, and accurate, Lou Reed imitator ever captured on tape. No doubt the result of endless hours spent kneeling at Reed's 1972 *Transformer* album as it was spinning round the turntable, Perrett didn't miss a trick in emulating his hero of the moment. Tuneful power chords, sluggish keyboards, vulnerable-to-the-point-of-shaking love songs, and tossed-off, sing-speak vocals—it's all here, such an uncanny imitation that it could easily fool unwary listeners into believing they've stumbled on a stash of early-'70s Reed outtakes. No, it's not original, but it is pretty good—not as good as *Berlin*, but certainly better than some of *Transformer*, if not up to that album's best songs. Imagine Reed's 1972-73 work without the orchestration or anonymous session musicians, and you get the picture. Perrett isn't as good a singer or as direct a lyricist as Reed. But looking past the obvious imitation, Reed fans could do worse than check this out, and Only Ones fans will find this a fascinating glimpse into Perrett's beginnings. —*Richie Unterberger*

The English Beat

Group, Ska-Revival
One of the earliest and most important ska-revivalist groups,

Birmingham's the Beat formed in 1978 (the band had to change their name to the English Beat in the U.S. to avoid confusion with Paul Collins' band of the same name). The multi-racial band carved a distinct sound through the use of alternating lead vocals by guitarist Dave Wakeling and punk-toaster/rapper Ranking Roger, supported by a tight band consisting of Andy Cox (guitar), Dave Steel (bass) and Everett Moreton (drums). The addition of 50-year-old saxophonist Saxa, who originally played with Prince Buster and Desmond Dekker, gave the band credibility and fleshed out its sound. An opening spot for the Selecter led to the band's signing to 2-Tone, where they released the hit single "Tears of a Clown," a wonderful version of the Smokey Robinson classic. In 1980, the band decided to form their own 2-Tone inspired label, Go-Feet (distributed by Arista). A string of hit singles followed in the U.K., including "Mirror in the Bathroom." Their debut LP, *I Just Can't Stop It*, combined the early hits with other pop/ska-oriented material. "Stand Down Margaret," with its anti-Thatcher stance, found the band moving in a more political direction, leading to several benefit gigs for "radical" causes. Musically, the Beat slowed down the tempo for a more traditional reggae sound showcased on 1981's *Wha'ppen*. This direction failed to bring the chart success of its predecessor. Featuring a more pop-oriented approach, 1982's *Special Beat Service* helped the band increase its U.S. fan base through MTV exposure of "Save it for Later" and "I Confess," but the band members decided to call it quits later that same year. Wakeling and Ranking Roger went on to form General Public and Cox and Steel formed Fine Young Cannibals. *—Chris Woodstra*

☆ **I Just Can't Stop It** / 1980 / IRS ✦✦✦✦✦
The Beat's debut is a true masterpiece of the period, perfectly blending intense politics with a playful, yet driving dance beat. While the sound could be mimicked by other revivalists, the top-notch songwriting represented on this album is what set them apart. *I Just Can't Stop It* plays like a *Greatest Hits* album (most of their hits are found here) and still holds up today. *—Chris Woodstra*

Wha'ppen? / 1981 / IRS ✦✦✦
After the nearly perfect debut, the Beat seem somewhat directionless on *Wha'ppen*. No longer instantly danceable, the tunes have slowed to sub-Reggae tempo with more political content (though less focused this time around). The two unmemorable singles, "Drowning" and "Doors of Your Heart," failed to make an impact in the charts and only "Dreamhome in N.Z." leaves a lasting impression. *—Chris Woodstra*

○ **Special Beat Service** / 1982 / IRS ✦✦✦✦
The final Beat album focuses less on politics and more on the subject of personal relationships. Their most polished effort, the band leaves behind their early ska influences in favor of jangly pop that, at times, delves into African and Latin rhythms. Includes the flawless singles "Save It for Later" and "I Confess." *—Chris Woodstra*

● **What Is Beat?** / 1983 / IRS ✦✦✦✦
While the best introduction to Beat is still the first album, *What Is Beat* does a good job of collecting the hits from each of the three albums. The live tracks and remixes are a nice addition for completists but are generally unnecessary for anyone else. *—Chris Woodstra*

The Beat Goes on / 1991 / IRS ✦✦✦

Enigma

Group, Dance-Pop
With their 1991 hit, "Sadeness," Enigma brought the new age fascination with Gregorian chants and old world culture to the clubs; the resulting single was both unique and irresistible. The rest of the album followed that pattern successfully, although without quite matching the stunning success of the hit single. On their second album, 1994's *Cross of Changes*, some of the old world elements remained, but the new age angle came to the forefront in a set of slick, radio-friendly dance-pop. *—Stephen Thomas Erlewine*

● **MCMXC A.D.** / 1990 / Charisma ✦✦✦✦
Driven by the Gregorian chants of the hit single "Sadeness Part I," Enigma's debut album is an interesting fusion of New Age sensibilities and dancefloor rhythms. *—Stephen Thomas Erlewine*

The Cross of Changes / Feb. 8, 1994 / Charisma ✦✦✦
On Enigma's second album, their latent New Age tendencies come to the forefront and occasionally obscure their usually captivating dance tracks. *—Stephen Thomas Erlewine*

Brian Eno

b. May 15, 1948, Woodbridge, England
Electronic, Art-Rock/Progressive-Rock, Experimental
Brian Eno may not be a household name, but his influence has been felt on a number of rock's most unique records, some highly successful. Eno first made his appearance as a founding member of British art-pop rockers Roxy Music in 1971. Eno, who fancied himself a manipulator of "treated" sound rather than a formally titled musician, provided Roxy with sweeping tonal washes, peculiar noises, and bleeps and blips on electronic keyboards and tapes. After leaving Roxy Music, Eno pursued a fascinating career as a solo artist and producer.

Eno's solo career perhaps has been the most rewarding and respectable in the pantheon of rock art. His groundbreaking early work influences a slew of budding art-punk rockers, his experiments with synthesized atmospheria serve as intriguing Muzak for rock fans, and his innovative production skills have been enlisted by rockers as varied as David Bowie, U2, Ultravox, Devo, Talking Heads, and James. He's also collaborated with the likes of John Cale, Robert Fripp, Daniel Lanois, David Byrne, and his brother, Roger Eno.

Eno's interest in creating "sound landscapes" with sophisticated manipulations of echo and timbre led to the establishment of his "ambient music" ideal in the late '70s, through a series of influential solo albums and ethereal collaborations with Laraaji, Jon Hassell, and Harold Budd. By creating this new subgenre, he unwittingly became one of the fathers of new age music, a genre he was quick to criticize for not encompassing enough "evil and doubt." The intention and effect of Eno's style, however, is markedly different from the soothing sound-baths associated with many new age and contemporary electronic recordings, notoriously one-dimensional in their approach to sound construction. Eno makes soundscapes that challenge the listener; his music may be many things, but it is never easy listening.

In recent years, Eno has created increasingly sophisticated ambient soundtracks for his own multi-media installations, which have graced galleries in Venice, Milan, and Tokyo. Eno continues to release albums in both pop and contemporary instrumental genres. *—Rick Clark and John Floyd and Linda Kohanov*

○ **No Pussyfooting** / Nov. 1973 / EG ✦✦✦✦
Robert Fripp's collaboration with Brian Eno. A musical landscape made up of sedate guitar feedback echoed, repeated, and otherwise treated by tape recorder. Today this would be classified under "new age." The follow-up, *Evening Star,* is similar. *—William Ruhlmann*

○ **Here Come the Warm Jets** / Jan. 1974 / EG ✦✦✦✦
Eno's solo debut features complex but tight pop songs with bizarre and often hilarious lyrics, which puncture the treated guitar and keyboard textures. *—John Floyd*

○ **Taking Tiger Mountain (by Strategy)** / Nov. 1974 / EG ✦✦✦✦
They lack the vibrant and energetic rock-laced enthusiasm of *Here Come the Warm Jets,* but these experimentations within the pop format give art-rock a good name. *—John Floyd*

Evening Star / 1975 / Antilles ✦✦✦
Robert Fripp and Brian Eno's second collaboration is similar to their first, *No Pussyfooting,* in that it combines Fripp's interest in droning tape loops with Eno's taste in sound landscapes. Electronic instrumental music with a meditative air. *—William Ruhlmann*

★ **Another Green World** / Nov. 1975 / EG ✦✦✦✦✦
Eno's masterpiece contains a sumptuous aural melange of dense ambient instrumental snippets and rich, often beautiful pop melodies. This is one of those albums that should be enjoyed in one concentrated sitting. *—John Floyd*

○ **Discreet Music** / Dec. 1975 / EG ✦✦✦✦
Taking a cue from Satie's idea of "musique d'ameublement" (furniture music), music that just exists like furnishings in an apartment, played so as not to draw attention to itself (not really Muzak, a company which seeks to produce a more intentional work-product effect), Eno created several albums of what he termed "ambient music" which combined a softer style of pattern music (influenced by Bryars, Nyman, Harold Budd) with environmental noises. *Discreet Music* is probably the best of these, using an Oliveros-style tape delay arrangement to slowly change patterns of repeating sounds. *—Blue Gene Tyranny*

After the Heat / 1978 / Sky ✦✦✦
After the Heat is Eno's collaboration with Dieter Moebius and Hans-Joachim Roedelius of the German *avant-garde* group Cluster. It consists of slow-moving instrumentals full of repeated synthesizer sound patterns and sustained guitar notes in the "ambient" style familiar from Eno's collaborations with Robert Fripp and albums of his own, such as *Discreet Music*. (One song, "Broken Head," features recited vocals by Eno, and on another, "The Belldog," he sings. On "Tzima N'arki," he sings backwards.) — *William Ruhlmann*

☆ **Before & After Science** / May 1978 / EG ✦✦✦✦✦
This thrashing partial return to more basic song structures is punctuated by the exhilarating "King's Lead Hat." — *John Floyd*

Music for Films / Oct. 1978 / EG ✦✦✦

○ **Ambient 1: Music for Airports** / Mar. 1979 / EG ✦✦✦✦
Four subtle, slowly evolving pieces grace Eno's first conscious effort at creating ambient music. The composer was in part striving to create music that approximated the effect of visual art. Like a fine painting, these evolving soundscapes don't require constant involvement on the part of the listener. They can hang in the background and add to the atmosphere of the room, yet the music also rewards close attention with a sonic richness absent in standard types of background or easy-listening music. — *Linda Kohanov*

Ambient 2: The Plateaux of Mirror / 1980 / EG ✦✦✦

Possible Music / 1980 / EG

○ **My Life in the Bush of Ghosts** / Feb. 1981 / Sire ✦✦✦✦
Talking Heads singer David Byrne teams with art-rock guru Brian Eno to create this unique techno-tribal music by combining tapes of Third World vocalizations with African-like rhythm tracks. Dense and hypnotic, the recording of an exorcism is downright spooky. — *Scott Bultman*

○ **Ambient 4: On Land** / Apr. 1982 / EG ✦✦✦✦
Eno's most masterful ambient effort to date was created as a musical antidote to the confusion of life in New York City. An earthy sense of repose underlies intricate sonic essays. — *Linda Kohanov*

○ **Apollo: Atmospheres & Soundtracks** / 1983 / EG ✦✦✦✦

Music for Films, Vol. 2 / 1983 / EG ✦✦✦

Thursday Afternoon / 1985 / EG ✦✦✦

More Blank Than Frank / 1986 / EG ✦✦

○ **Desert Island Selection** / 1986 / EG ✦✦✦✦
A CD-only survey of Eno's first four albums, with songs hand-picked and annotations written by Eno himself. — *John Floyd*

Music for Films 3 / 1988 / Opal ✦✦✦

Ambient 3: Day of Radiance / 198z / EG ✦✦✦

Nerve Net / Sep. 1992 / Opal ✦✦
Nerve Net appears to be Eno's attempt to turn the page on his ambient work and strike out in a more cluttered, noisy, quasi-industrial direction for the '90s. While the liner notes would have us believe that his polyrhythmic dabbling is all very forward looking, this kind of stuff has all been done before. — *Roch Parisien*

The Shutov Assembly / Oct. 1992 / Opal ✦✦✦
If *The Shutov Assembly* is reminiscent of Brian Eno's earlier "ambient" music projects dating back to *Discreet Music* (1975), it shouldn't be surprising. Recorded between 1985 and 1990, the atmospheric, slow-moving sound patterns are more, the artist contends, like paintings than music. *The Shutov Assembly*, dedicated to Russian painter Sergei Shutov, is, like the similar works in his catalog (he cites *Music for Films, On Land, Music for Airports, Thursday Afternoon*, and *Nerve Net*, as well as *Discreet Music*), as much a concept as a record. — *William Ruhlmann*

○ **Eno Box 2** / 1993 / Virgin ✦✦✦✦
The first of two retrospective box sets devoted to the groundbreaking work of Brian Eno, *II* concentrates on his pop and vocal material, including some selections from the unreleased *My Squelchy Life*. Although his music still makes the most sense in the context of his albums, *II* is solid crash-course introduction to his work, which remains as revolutionary today as it was when it was released. — *Stephen Thomas Erlewine*

○ **Eno Box 1** / Mar. 22, 1994 / Virgin ✦✦✦✦
Box I features a cross-section of Eno's influential ambient music; while this music often works better in its original context, the box offers a good introduction to Eno's innovative instrumental work. — *Stephen Thomas Erlewine*

BOOK

✦✦✦ **Brian Eno: His Music And The Vertical Color Of Sound**, by Eric Tamm (Faber & Faber, 1989). Not a biography of Eno, but a book-length critical essay which originated as Tamm's doctoral dissertation. The first part discusses Eno's influences, and the influence Eno has exerted upon the world of popular music and contemporary composition; the second meticulously examines his recorded solo works, as well as some of his collaborations. This isn't light reading, though it's accessible, and some readers who aren't conversant with musical theory may find some of the more involved passages difficult. But it is exhaustively researched, taking from Eno's many writings and interviews from the '70s and '80s, and discusses topics such as Eno's use of the recording studio as instrument, his determination to cross-fertilize the worlds of pop music and art music, and his concentration upon sound colors and timbres rather than melody and lyrics. Familiarity with Eno's recordings is necessary to get a lot out of this, but his fans will be amply rewarded by this study. — *Richie Unterberger*

Eno/Cale

Group, Art-Rock/Progressive-Rock, Experimental
Composer and record producer Brian Eno (b. May 15, 1948) had been appearing on albums by former Velvet Underground member John Cale (b. Dec 3, 1940) since *Fear* in 1974 and had produced his 1989 album *Words for the Dying*, which appeared on Eno's Opal label through Warner Bros. So it was no surprise that the two would team up for a duo album, *Wrong Way Up*, as its follow-up. — *William Ruhlmann*

○ **Wrong Way Up** / 1990 / Opal ✦✦✦✦
Both Eno and Cale have always flirted with conventional pop music throughout their careers, while reserving the right to go off on less accessible experiments, which means they've always held out the promise that they would make something as attractive as this synthesizer-dominated collection, on which Eno comes as close to the mainstream as he has since *Another Green World* and Cale is as catchy as he's been since *Honi Soit*. The result is one of the best albums either one has ever made. — *William Ruhlmann*

Entombed

Group, Hard Rock, Thrash, Heavy Metal
Swedish death metal band comprised of guitarist Uffe Cederlund, vocalist Lars-Goran Petrov, guitarist Alex Hellid, bassist Lars Rosenberg, and drummer Nicke Andersson. In a genre where bands are ruled by conservatism and are loath to change their sound once it has been established, Entombed, like their contemporaries Sepultura and Death, are one of the few bands willing to experiment with their basic sound, incorporate other influences, or simply progress musically. They are considered by many to be the top band on Sweden's death metal scene. — *Steve Huey*

Crawl / 1990 / Earache ✦✦✦

● **Left Hand Path** / 1991 / Earache ✦✦✦✦
Competent if fairly standard death metal, with the familiar murky, detuned guitars and larynx-shredding vocals. Most of the album alternates between high-velocity pounding and slow grinding. — *Steve Huey*

○ **Clandestine** / 1992 / Earache ✦✦✦✦

Stranger Aeons / Jun. 23, 1992 / Earache ✦✦✦

○ **Wolverine Blues** / 1994 / Earache ✦✦✦✦
In spite of the tacky marketing gimmick (a tie-in with Marvel Comics), *Wolverine Blues* is one of the best death metal albums yet, helping to expand a rapidly stagnating genre. Entombed combine their heavily detuned guitars and brutal lyrics and vocals with classic rock and metal influences. The song structures owe more to traditional hard rock than to death metal, and, instead of alternating between extreme speed and slowness, the band spends much of the album in a crushing mid-tempo groove. But even though the music here is more accessible to fans of traditional metal, the band is still heavier than anything even approaching mainstream. — *Steve Huey*

John Entwistle

b. Oct. 9, 1944
Rock & Roll
John Alec Entwistle (b. October 9, 1944) is probably the most in-

fluential bassist in rock music. Before Entwistle came along as a member of the Who, bassists seldom stood out for their playing and few casual listeners knew or cared what purpose the four-stringed instrument served—after he came along, everyone knew. Born in Chiswick, Entwistle was a member of the Confederates with Pete Townshend while still in grammar school in 1959. Trained in both the piano and the French horn, he is one of the most musically accomplished teenagers ever to play in a skiffle band. Invited by Roger Daltrey to join his band, the Detours, Entwistle accepted, and was joined soon after by Townshend. With the addition of drummer Keith Moon, this band, later renamed the High Numbers and finally the Who, became part of the second wave of successful British invasion acts, getting their recording act together in 1964 and 1965.

The Who had started out with Daltrey and Townshend sharing guitar chores, until Daltrey gave the instrument up. The change to a single guitar was vital to Entwistle (nicknamed "The Ox"), who had to play extremely loud and complex parts to compensate for the absence of a rhythm guitar—the result was that, from the Who's first singles to their last, Entwistle's bass work was some of the most complex and audible in rock music. He played fills, counter-melodies, and all manner of material, and stood out doing it. Moreover, he tended to stand out precisely by not standing out—Townshend had his windmill strumming technique, Daltrey was the lead singer, and Moon was so animated on the drums that he was scary, but amid this pandemonium on stage, Entwistle simply stood there and played, providing an anchor that kept the band from flying off in all directions, both visually and musically.

As a songwriter, he wasn't nearly as prolific as Townshend, but Entwistle had a bizarre sense of humor that contrasted very nicely with Townshend. From "Boris The Spider" and "Whiskey Man" to "My Wife," Entwistle had a knack for capturing dark humor that lightened up every Who album, and even managed to contribute a couple of songs to Tommy. As a solo musician, however, his career has been somewhat more uneven than that of Townshend. Entwistle's first solo album, Smash Your Head Against the Wall (1971) was, in many ways, a lost Who album, recorded the way the bassist would've handled the group. His next album, Whistle Rhymes (1972), released the same week as Pete Townshend's Who Came First, was a rather more uneven album. Nine months later, Entwistle's third solo album, Rigor Mortis Sets In (1973), was released, to indifferent sales and critical response. It was nine years before another Entwistle solo album, Too Late the Hero, would appear. By that time, the Who had long passed their prime (Moon had died in 1978, and the group was in the midst of an awkward reassessment), and the record still managed to peak at number 71 in America. The band was to have retired following its farewell tour in 1982, but Entwistle's financial problems, coupled with the seeming demand for a reunion, led to another tour in 1989, which set the band members up well financially but was a critical disaster. —Bruce Eder

● Smash Your Head Against the Wall / 1971 / MCA ✦✦✦✦
Entwistle's first album is a killer, a loud, darkly humored, beautifully produced hard rock album that does sort of sound the way the Who might've with Entwistle as leader instead of Townshend and Daltrey. Every track is worthwhile, and even the cover art is some of the cleverest of its era. —Bruce Eder

Backtrack 14 (The Ox) / 1971 / Track ✦✦
Not really an Entwistle album, but a British-only collection of his tracks with the Who, up through "Heaven and Hell." This is still great fun, though, and quite a few of the songs never appeared in any other form (there is no CD version of this collection). —Bruce Eder

○ Whistle Rhymes / 1972 / MCA ✦✦✦✦
A disappointing second solo album, with an all-star lineup of sorts (Peter Frampton on guitar, etc.) but nothing to recommend the material, which is fairly tuneless and dull. —Bruce Eder

Rigor Mortis Sets In / 1973 / MCA ✦✦
More disappointment for fans of (possibly) rock's greatest bassist. The songs are better, and the dark humor is very pungent, but the record just lies there, with none of the energy of a Who album. —Bruce Eder

Mad Dog / 1975 / MCA ✦✦
Another forgettable record from Entwistle, who by now should have learned not to try and compete with his band when they had a current album in release. —Bruce Eder

Too Late the Hero / 1981 / Atco ✦✦

Enuff Z'nuff
Group, Hard Rock, Power Pop/Anglo-Pop
Because of their big hair and lipstick, Enuff Z'nuff is frequently tagged as another run-of-the-mill pop metal band. Although there is some truth to that—their guitars are as layered as Def Leppard's—their hearts lie with the trashy pop of Cheap Trick and the classic power-pop of Badfinger. Since very few bands have explored the connection between metal and power-pop, Enuff Z'nuff has received barely any airplay and sales, but loads of critical acclaim. And they have earned that praise—this is hard rock that is smarter than it seems, powered by an overwhelming sense of melody. —Stephen Thomas Erlewine

Enuff Z'nuff / 1989 / Atco ✦✦✦
○ Strength / 1991 / Atco ✦✦✦✦
While the guitars are loud, crunchy, and powerful, Strength succeeds because of Enuff Z'nuff's innate pop sensibility and their fondness for psychedelic flourishes. —Stephen Thomas Erlewine

● Animals with Human Intelligence / 1992 / Arista ✦✦✦✦
On Enuff Z'nuff's third album, the band finally makes their catchy, trashy fusion of Cheap Trick, Badfinger, Sweet, and Def Leppard sound completely original. —Stephen Thomas Erlewine

Enya
b. , Donegal, Ireland
Alternative Pop/Rock
Enya (Eithne Ni Bhraonain) is from Gweedore, County Donegal, Ireland, which she left in 1980 to join the Irish band Clannad, the group that already featured her older brothers and sisters. She stayed with Clannad for two years, then left, hooking up with producer Nicky Ryan and lyricist Roma Ryan, with whom she recorded film and television scores. The result was a successful album of TV music for the BBC. Enya then recorded Watermark (1988), which featured her distinctive, flowing music and multi-overdubbed trancelike singing; the album sold four million copies worldwide. It was followed by Shepherd Moons (1991), which confirmed Enya's status as a new age superstar. —William Ruhlmann

Enya / 1987 / Atlantic ✦✦✦
● Watermark / 1988 / Reprise ✦✦✦✦
The US was a little slower than the rest of the world to admire Enya's blend of ethereal multi-tracked vocals and subtly flowing music than the rest of the world, but this album's single, "Orinoco Flow (Sail Away)," which topped the charts elsewhere, was a Top 25 hit, and the album went gold. —William Ruhlmann

○ Shepherd Moons / Nov. 1991 / Reprise ✦✦✦✦
While it follows the same basic formula as the multi-million-seller Watermark, Shepherd Moons isn't quite as captivating, but that's only a relative term. Most of the album captures the same mystical, trance-inducing mood that made Watermark a success and Enya was rewarded accordingly—it sold as much as her previous album. —Stephen Thomas Erlewine

Epic Soundtracks
Alternative Pop/Rock
In the '70s, Epic formed the Swell Maps, with his brother, Nikki Sudden; the band influenced many groups, from Sonic Youth to the Lemonheads. Considering his past, it may seem strange that Epic returned in the early '90s after a long hiatus to write moving piano ballads. His first solo LP, Rise Above, featured J Mascis and Kim Gordon, among others. He returned two years later with a second album, Sleeping Star. —John Bush

● Rise Above / Bar/None ✦✦✦✦
Epic Soundtracks writes affecting piano ballads and midtempo pieces with an ease that belies how good these songs are. Though J Mascis (drums on two tracks) and Kim Gordon (voice on "Big Apple Graveyard") do contribute, this is Epic's show; he provides most of the music and all the magic. Many songs have a traditional feel and sound strangely familiar. —John Bush

Sleeping Star / 1994 / Bar/None ✦✦✦
Sleeping Star is not exactly identical to Epic's first album, but little has changed. The songs still have that traditional ballad feel; witness "Tonight's the Night (Rock 'N' Roll Lullabye)," a song that borrows heavily from the long history of ballad procedure. Not that any of this is bad. "Emily May" has a rolling piano line and up-

tempo rhythm that makes it the highlight of the disc. Most of the songs, however, are a bit too traditional to provoke any reaction by the listener. —*John Bush*

Episode Six

Group, British Invasion
Most famous for including bassist Roger Glover and singer Ian Gillan before they joined Deep Purple, Episode Six managed to release no less than nine British singles between 1966 and 1969 without coming close to a hit record or establishing a solid identity. Also prominently featuring organist/singer Sheila Carter-Dimmock, the group's 1966-67 singles were rather light pop/rock harmony numbers, with an occasional ballad and a bit of a soul influence. Light years removed from Deep Purple, Episode Six were nothing if not eclectic in their choice of material, trying their hands at numbers by the Hollies, the Beatles, the Tokens, and Charles Aznavour, as well as a British hot-rod tune (written by Glover). While their repertoire lacked focus, their singles were actually pleasant, and their fine cover of Tim Rose's "Morning Dew" would have been a deserving hit.

In 1967, they began to fuse pop and psychedelia with reasonably impressive results, especially the single "I Can See Through You" (written by Glover), one of the finest British psychedelic obscurities. Their final two singles showed the band going in a much more progressive direction, and anticipating some of the most indulgent art-rock of the '70s with "Mozart Versus the Rest," which assaulted one of the composer's most famous riffs with manic electric guitars. Episode Six folded in 1969, after Gillan and Glover had joined Deep Purple. —*Richie Unterberger*

Put Yourself in My Place / 1987 / PRT ✦✦✦
Although it's more a reflection of the pop trends of the day than an original vision, this compilation of their first seven singles (from 1966-67) is enjoyable listening, with some fine harmonies and reasonably strong material. Unfortunately, it's missing their final three singles from 1968 and 1969. —*Richie Unterberger*

● **Roots Of Deep Purple: The Complete Episode Six** / 1994 / Collectables ✦✦✦✦
This definitive 28-track anthology includes everything recorded by the group—all of their singles, solo efforts by a couple group members, and six previously unreleased songs. Although it's more a reflection of the pop trends of the day than an original vision, it's enjoyable listening, with some fine harmonies and reasonably strong material. —*Richie Unterberger*

EPMD

Group, Rap
Long Island rappers Erick Sermon and Parrish Smith (EPMD stands for Erick & Parrish Making Dollars) have confounded some observers by achieving monumental success despite utilizing minimal production and rapping skills. The deadpan, almost mushmouth, rapping style and simplistic insertion of samples and snippets throughout their three albums notwithstanding, such cuts as "You Gots to Chill" and "Rampage" have been hits. The duo are also accomplished producers and preside over the Hit Squad, a combine of rap acts including Redman, K-Solo, and Das Efx.

Sermon and Smith were unable to reconcile artistic differences and personality conflicts and dissolved their formerly successful partnership in 1993. Sermon issued his own CD, *No Pressure*, later that same year. —*Ron Wynn*

★ **Strictly Business** / 1988 / Priority ✦✦✦✦✦
In reality a collection of singles, EPMD's debut turns some clever samples (Steve Miller, Kool & the Gang, Bob Marley, Otis Redding) into an overpowering funk assault. "You Gots to Chill" is a classic. —*John Floyd*

○ **Unfinished Business** / 1989 / Priority ✦✦✦✦
Although this doesn't hit as hard as their debut, it does contain some good jabs at the quiet-storm, Black upwardly mobile crowd and also some slams at their doubters. —*Ron Wynn*

Business As Usual / 1991 / Def Jam ✦✦✦
A little to the processed side production-wise, but it boasts one good collaboration with LL Cool J on "Rampage." —*Ron Wynn*

○ **Business Never Personal** / Jul. 28, 1992 / Ral ✦✦✦✦
EPMD's terse, thick-tongued rapping style was back on point with their fourth album. Although behind the scenes turmoil finally split Erick Sermon and Parrish Smith up, they were together and cooking on this 1992 record. They scored their final signature sin-

gle with "Crossover," a dead-on commentary directed at rappers putting pop hopes ahead of hip-hop values. "Headbanger" and "Can't Hear Nothing but the Music" were other sterling tracks from their last great album. —*Ron Wynn*

Erasure

Group, Dance-Pop, Alternative Pop/Rock
After Vince Clarke left Depeche Mode in the early '80s, he formed the synth-based dance-pop band Yaz before forming Erasure in 1985 with singer Andy Bell. Clarke wrote and played the majority of the material; the extravagant Bell provided the duo with a voice and image. Like Depeche Mode or the Pet Shop Boys, Erasure sounds cold and detached while singing about love and alienation, yet they still have a knack for crafting successful pop singles like "Chains of Love." Over the years, the duo's following has expanded with each release and they have edged their way into the pop mainstream. —*Stephen Thomas Erlewine*

○ **Wonderland** / May 1986 / Sire ✦✦✦✦
Vince Clarke's inventive synthesizer music is immediately identifiable no matter who the singer is. Here the former Depeche Mode/Yaz leader does his electronic wonders behind another singer Andy Bell (who bears a certain vocal resemblance to Yaz's Alison Moyet). Clarke's irresistible music is the best argument there is for synthesizers, and Bell is an appealing front man. —*William Ruhlmann*

The Circus / Mar. 1987 / Sire ✦✦✦
Erasure broke through to mass acceptance in their native U.K. with their second album, *The Circus*, which contained four chart singles, three of which made the Top Ten. The album stayed in the charts more than two years. In America, the group's relentless synthesizer-based music, heavy beat, and emotive, romantically tinged vocals marked them as a dance music phenomenon. "Victim of Love" became a major club hit, and *The Circus* was Erasure's first album to reach the charts, however briefly. Vince Clarke and Andy Bell were simply continuing to turn out inventive pop tracks, the best (which is to say, the catchiest) being "Sometimes" and "Victim of Love." —*William Ruhlmann*

The Two Ring Circus / Dec. 1987 / Sire ✦✦✦
Originally released on two 45 rpm LPs, *The Two Ring Circus* was a remix version of songs from Erasure's second regular album release, *The Circus*. The first six tracks were extended, beat-heavy takes on such songs as "Sometimes" and "Victim of Love." The last three tracks were rerecordings with orchestra (and without synthesizer). *The Two Ring Circus* played to Erasure's core audience of dance musicians, though it would take their next regular album release to expand that following significantly. —*William Ruhlmann*

○ **The Innocents** / Apr. 1988 / Sire ✦✦✦✦
Erasure emerged from the dance clubs with this million-selling U.S. breakthrough album, which contains the Top 15 hits "A Little Respect" and "Chains of Love." —*William Ruhlmann*

Crackers International / Apr. 1989 / Sire ✦✦✦
This six-track EP helped bridge the gap between the April 1988 release of *The Innocents* and the October 1989 release of *Wild!* "Stop!" and "Knocking on Your Door" (both heard in original and 12" remix versions) were typical hi-NRG Erasure tracks, with driving dance beats and forceful tenor vocals by Andy Bell, but they did not embrace the broader pop audience the group had reached with the 1988 singles "Chains of Love" and "A Little Respect." "She Won't Be Home" was a Christmas song, reflecting the seasonal release of the EP in November 1988 in the U.K. —*William Ruhlmann*

Wild! / Oct. 1989 / Sire ✦✦
In the U.K., *Wild!,* Erasure's fourth album, topped the charts, just as its predecessor, *the Innocents*, had done, spinning off four hit singles in the process. But in America, where *the Innocents* had been Erasure's commercial breakthrough, it was a different story. Maybe it was the lead-off single, "Drama!," a hard-core dance track with ponderous lyrics about "the infinite complexities of love," but *Wild!* saw Erasure falling back on its disco audience rather than continuing to expand into the mainstream. The group tried different sounds, beginning with a piano instrumental and including the Spanish-flavored "La Gloria," but much of the material was just more of the synthesized dance tracks familiar from previous records. Despite their continuing appeal at home, Erasure seemed to be stagnating creatively. —*William Ruhlmann*

Chorus / Oct. 1991 / Sire ♦♦

Chorus, Erasure's fifth album, was a look back at its earliest synth-pop style, after the relatively eclectic approach taken on its predecessor, *Wild!* Vince Clarke's instrumental tracks employed familiar electronic keyboard sounds, rather like the synth-dance music of the early '80s that he pioneered with Depeche Mode and Yaz. That was good enough to give Erasure its third straight U.K. #1 and four more hit singles, but in the U.S., where the title track just stumbled into the lower reaches of the singles charts, the group had fallen back on a dance-oriented cult following, its music sounding dangerously old-fashioned. *— William Ruhlmann*

Abba-Esque / Jun. 30, 1992 / Mute ♦♦♦

A fun EP of ABBA covers, it's worthwhile for any Erasure fan. — *AMG*

● **Erasure Pop!: the First 20 Hits** / Nov. 24, 1992 / Sire ♦♦♦♦

Pop!—The First 20 Hits is exactly what it claims to be—a collection of Erasure's biggest singles, which makes it the best place to get acquainted with this synth-pop band. *— Stephen Thomas Erlewine*

I Say I Say I Say / May 17, 1994 / Mute/Elektra ♦♦♦

I Say I Say I Say, Erasure's sixth full-length album, was something of a new start for the group following its successful EP of ABBA covers and greatest hits compilation. And it earned them their long-awaited third U.S. Top 40 hit with "Always." But while the group maintained a mass following in Britain and a dance following in America, Erasure still seemed like proponents of a style that had long-since peaked and passed into decline, which may have accounted for the wistful, vaguely spiritual tone of Andy Bell's lyrics. Early on, Erasure had seemed to represent a radical change in the sound of pop music, but nine years, six albums, and several EPs later, they just seemed like another weightless British pop band who happened to use synthesizers a lot. *— William Ruhlmann*

Eric B & Rakim

Group, Rap, Funk

The Queens, NY, duo has the distinction of being the first of dozens of ensembles to construct a sound around James Brown samples. The rapid-fire boasts of Rakim and Eric B's inventive turntable techniques make their entire catalog worth investigating.

This once formidable duo, whose biting, sullen style was among the tightest and most influential during the '80s, called it quits in '93.—*John Floyd*

Microphone Fiend / 1982 / UNI ♦♦

★ **Paid in Full** / 1987 / 4th & Broadway ♦♦♦♦♦

Their debut contains new mixes of early singles ("I Ain't No Joke," "Eric B.Is President") and adds some prime stuff, including the monumental "Paid in Full," which became a heavily sampled item in the late '80s. *—John Floyd*

Just a Beat / 1988 / UNI ♦♦

☆ **Follow the Leader** / 1988 / UNI ♦♦♦♦♦

No immediate standouts, but Rakim's tongue-twisting boasts are sharper, and Eric B.is still a monster at the turntable. *—John Floyd*

Let the Rhythm Hit 'em / 1990 / MCA ♦♦♦

This subdued set works its magic more subtly, but the title is no joke. *—John Floyd*

Eric B. / 1995 / Nine ♦♦

○ **Don't Sweat the Technique** / MCA ♦♦♦♦

While it doesn't match their trailblazing work of the late '80s, *Don't Sweat the Technique* is a solid effort from this influential duo. *— Stephen Thomas Erlewine*

Eric's Trip

Group, Alternative Pop/Rock

A noise-pop quartet from Moncton, New Brunswick, Canada, that mixes pretty, folky ballads with garage-punk distortion fests (and occasionally marries the two). Formed in 1992, Eric's Trip could be considered part of the lo-fi movement that includes such bands as Sebadoh and Guided by Voices, but what sets them apart is the innocence and guilelessness in their songs, as well as their sweet boy-girl harmonies (courtesy of bassist Julie Doiron and guitarist Rick White). Although the amateurish production on the group's two albums (1993's *Love Tara* and 1994's *Forever Again*) is an acquired taste, Eric's Trip doesn't seem to need more than a four-track tape recorder in order to express themselves creatively. — *Heather Phares*

Love Tara / Jun. 1993 / Sub Pop ♦♦♦

● **Forever Again** / 1994 / Sub Pop ♦♦♦♦

Roky Erickson

Rock & Roll, Psychedelic

Aside from Syd Barrett, the Austin, TX, native Erickson is rock's most notorious looney-toon. After forming the 13th Floor Elevators, the quintessential acid-rattled '60s punk band, Erickson embarked on a solo career that has explored his emotional crumbling (due mostly to his nasty penchant for LSD). He's spent several years in institutions, and his voluminous and scattered solo catalog reflects the peculiarities of his vision. At its best, Erickson's music is truly scarifying. *—John Floyd*

Holiday Inn Tapes / 1987 / Fan Club ♦♦♦

Listeners primarily familiar with Erickson via his deranged vocals and compositions with the 13th Floor Elevators and as a solo act may be shocked by the low-key, acoustic intimacy of this album. Recorded on December 1, 1986 at the Holiday Inn Red River in Austin, Texas, Roky's acoustic guitar and vocals are the whole show on this ten-song performance. Going easy on the horror/monster/mystical imagery, Erickson reprises a couple of Buddy Holly classics, traditional folk tunes, and the Elevators' "May the Circle Remain Unbroken." Just to remind you that this is Roky Erickson, "The Singing Grandfather" (different versions of which open and close this album) begins with the line, "The singing grandfather will saw off your head." Sound (played into a portable recorder) is fair but quite listenable, and Roky's plaintive, yearning vocals are quite touching. His acoustic picking isn't bad either, although he stumbles or loses the beat once in a while (and for Roky, once in a while is quite an acceptable margin of error). This doesn't deliver the outrage that many have come to expect from Erickson, but shows a glimpse of the man behind the madness. *—Richie Unterberger*

● **You're Gonna Miss Me** / Sep. 27, 1991 / Restless ♦♦♦♦

Erickson's peculiar rock vision has been too schizophrenic to produce one essential album. *You're Gonna Miss Me—The Best of Roky Erickson* rounds up the finest cuts from Erickson's solo career, from a remake of "Bermuda" up to the slashing "Don't Slander Me" and "Don't Shake Me Lucifer." An alternately rocking and frightening compilation, it has fine liner notes by John Morthland. *—John Floyd*

The Escorts [U.K.]

Group, British Invasion

A distinctly lower-echelon Merseybeat band, the Escorts' commercial impact was slight indeed. Only one of their six singles made the British Top 50, and at number 49, at that. They covered "Dizzy Miss Lizzie" before the Beatles, and the single made some noise in Texas, but besides that they were unheard of beyond their Liverpool hometown. Their 45s were pleasant, moderately catchy, and featured close harmonies, but were basically unmemorable: The Escorts lacked a distinctive sound, and wrote virtually none of their own material (many of their A-sides were tame covers of U.S. rock and R&B hits; many of their B-sides were shallow Merseybeat numbers written by their manager). After a lineup change in 1966, the group recorded their sixth single with Paul McCartney on tambourine, showing a much more pronounced (though hardly impressive) soul feel. Guitarist Terry Sylvester left the Escorts near the end of their recording career to join the Swinging Blue Jeans, and eventually replaced Graham Nash in the Hollies in the late '60s. *—Richie Unterberger*

From the Blue Angel / 1982 / Edsel ♦♦♦

The only Escorts LP, this compiles both sides of their six 1964-66 singles. It's lovingly packaged, complete with a four-page history of the group, but one has to wonder whether the effort was really necessary for such a slight band. *—Richie Unterberger*

The Escorts

Group, Soul

Many live albums have been recorded behind prison walls, but few by actual inmates. Discovered by producer George Kerr, the Escorts were incarcerated at Rahway State Prison in New Jersey when they began recording for the Alithia imprint. The seven-member group scored four R&B hits during 1973 and 1974. Lead singer Reginald Hayes later recorded as a solo artist. *—Bill Dahl*

3 Down 4 to Go / 1973 / Collectables ◆◆◆
A good all-around session from these East Coast soul singers. Inferior recording, another Escorts collection. —*Ron Wynn*

● **All We Need Is Another: Golden Classics** / Collectables ◆◆◆◆
All We Need is Another—Golden Classics features fine uptempo soul tunes and good ballads. This is a collection of soul hits by an underrated local unit. —*Ron Wynn*

Esquerita (Eskew Reeder)

b. Greenville, South Carolina, **d.** 1986
Rock & Roll
With a six-inch pompadour, brocaded shirts, rhinestone shades, and a rhythmic, belligerent style of piano playing, Esquerita was the original Little Richard, years before Mr. Penniman tutti-frutti'd his way to stardom. Working around the Dallas-New Orleans circuit in the early '50s, Esquerita's shot at the big time came when Capitol Records decided they needed their own version of Little Richard, after signing their answer to Elvis, Gene Vincent. The resulting recordings, though smartly produced, stand as some of the most untamed and unabashed sides ever issued by a major label. Long revered by rock & roll fans the world over, they make Little Richard's Specialty sides look highly disciplined by comparison. Though Esquerita continued to record in a tamer style through the '60s, his Capitol sides stand as a monument to the potential of rock & roll's lunatic power and the off-kilter genius of Esquerita. —*Cub Koda*

Esquerita / 1984 / Capitol ◆◆◆
Exact reproduction of the rare 1959 debut album—once a valued collector's item and still a gas. (Import) —*Jeff Tarmarkin*

● **Capitol Collectors Series** / 1990 / Capitol ◆◆◆◆
One of the great lost rock & roll wildmen, Esquerita was as crazed as Little Richard (to whom he was an inspiration musically and visually). All of his key Capitol tracks can be found on this 28-song CD. —*Jeff Tarmarkin*

I Never Danced Nowhere! / Charly ◆◆◆
These 17 tracks were cut in New Orleans in 1962. Not as essential as the Capitol material, but fun. (Import) —*Jeff Tarmarkin*

Sock It to Me Baby / Bear Family ◆◆◆
Previously unreleased songs. For the fanatic only. —*Jeff Tarmarkin*

Vintage Voola! / Norton ◆◆◆
Nine-song vinyl rarities collection. Only serious Esquerita fans need apply. —*Jeff Tarmarkin*

Essential Logic

Group, New Wave
Susan Whitby was 15 years old and had been playing saxophone for a little more than six months when she joined her friend Marion Elliot (aka Poly Styrene) and formed the great English punk band X-Ray Spex. At this juncture, Whitby renamed herself Lora Logic and brought her honking and squawking to X-Ray Spex's guitar-propelled punk rock, staying long enough to record the seminal feminist-punk single "Oh Bondage, Up Yours!" Prior to the recording of their debut album, Logic abruptly left the band to follow her own quirky songwriting muse and formed the wonderfully named Essential Logic. Eschewing fast and loud guitars for off-kilter rhythms, "bluesy" sax playing and forays into dissonance and atonality, Essential Logic created some of the most liberating, exciting music of the early post-punk era. Along with her primitive, exhilarating sax playing, Logic displayed a wildly imaginative vocal style that conflated the subtle eroticism of Patti Smith with the epiglottal spasms of Yoko Ono. Singing, braying and screeching her implicitly (at times explicitly) feminist lyrics while her backing band crashed and bashed in the background, this was almost a punk version of that most despised of genres, art-rock. And while the subjects of most of her songs were serious (alienation, sexism, poverty, urban isolation) there was a bratty tongue-wagging raffishness to Logic (and band) that placed them a cut above the rest. After one album as Essential Logic, Lora Logic disbanded the group to go solo. After one great solo record, Logic left music to join a London-based Hare Krishna sect with old pal Poly Styrene. Recently, Styrene issued some music in England, and it was rumored that Logic played sax on the recording. But regardless of her current activities, Lora Logic's short recording career will always be marked by its intelligence, creativity and fun. —*John Dougan*

Beat Rhythm News / 1979 / Rough Trade
Never released in America, this is a stunning record that remains a benchmark of the punk era. From the bubbling, herky-jerky rhythms of "Quality Crayon Wax OK" to the gleeful honking of "Wake Up," this is the sound of five young English musicians disassembling rock & roll and remaking it in an entirely new way. It's more than just a different way of playing music; it, like the best punk rock, fills you with the feeling of being able to change the world. An underrated record of its time, it remains criminally overlooked by critics even today (with such notable exceptions as Greil Marcus and Jon Savage), as the history of punk is finally being written. —*John Dougan*

Pedigree Charm / 1982 / Rough Trade
After passing on *Beat Rhythm News*, it was no surprise that nearly three years later, no American release of *Pedigree Charm* was in the offing. And, like its predecessor, it remains a great forgotten album of the era. A little more controlled than her debut, *Pedigree Charm* never disappoints. If your ears have been opened wide by *Beat Rhythm News*, than denying yourself the many pleasures of this recording is senseless. —*John Dougan*

Gloria Estefan & Miami Sound Machine

Group, Dance-Pop, Pop
More than any other pop group, Miami Sound Machine and lead singer Gloria Estefan (b. Jan 9, 1957) have brought Latin-American (particularly Cuban) music into the mainstream. They originated out of the Miami Cuban community, and many of their early recordings were sung in Spanish. Their hits have included "Conga" (#10), "Bad Boy" (#8), "Words Get in the Way" (#5), "Anything for You" (#1), "1-2-3" (#9) and "Rhythm Is Gonna Get You" (#5).
In 1987, the group officially changed their name to Gloria Estefan and Miami Sound Machine. Not surprisingly, the following two years saw the direction of the group's music shift towards her vocals. In 1989, Estefan released her first solo album, *Cuts Both Ways*, which spawned the number one hit "Don't Wanna Lose You."
The following year the group's tour bus was in a serious accident when traveling in New York. Estefan's vertebra was broken and she underwent a successful surgery. Estefan and the group's career was postponed for nearly a year due to the accident. She released *Into the Light* in 1991, which showed her inching towards adult-contemporary territory. —*Rick Clark*

Eyes of Innocence / 1984 / Epic ◆◆
Gloria Estefan has a nice voice and does an interesting live show, but her albums are about as rigidly produced and routinely performed as anyone's this side of Julio Iglesias. This has some light Afro-Latin influences, but otherwise is generic pop. —*Ron Wynn*

Primitive Love / 1986 / Epic ◆◆◆
Gloria Estefan occasionally gets an above-average song, and her live show sometimes includes an Afro-Latin spot where she returns to her roots. Neither was the case on this mid-'80s set, which is certainly well produced, engineered, and arranged. If you're a fan, you enjoyed it. Otherwise, it was tough sledding. —*Ron Wynn*

○ **Let It Loose** / 1988 / Epic ◆◆◆◆
The group was still billed as "Gloria Estefan & Miami Sound Machine" on this album, which showed the singer and her bandleader husband, Emilio, retaining the jazzy, Latin flavor of their earlier music while moving determinedly into the pop mainstream and incidentally positioning Gloria as a superstar. Such goals were reached by a record that sold two million copies, went Top Ten, and produced the hits "Rhythm Is Gonna Get You," "Betcha Say That," "Can't Stay Away from You," "Anything for You," and "1-2-3." —*William Ruhlmann*

Cuts Both Ways / 1989 / Epic ◆◆◆
Dispensing with the "Miami Sound Machine" name, Estefan continued to successfully to mix Latin-tinged dance numbers with strong ballads on this million-selling Top Ten solo album, which included "Don't Wanna Lose You," "Get On Your Feet," and "Here We Are." —*William Ruhlmann*

Into the Light / 1991 / Epic ◆◆◆
With this successful album, Estefan demonstrated that she had recovered from her serious accident of 1990. The album contains the telling hit "Coming Out of the Dark" but showed her moving even farther toward the middle of the road and sacrificing her younger fans in the process—most of the singles from this album per-

formed better on the Adult Contemporary charts than on the Hot 100. —*William Ruhlmann*

● **Greatest Hits** / Oct. 6, 1992 / Epic ◆◆◆◆
All of Gloria Estefan's hits, with and without the Miami Sound Machine, are here, making *Greatest Hits* the best Estefan CD available. —*AMG*

○ **Mi Tierra** / Jun. 22, 1993 / Epic ◆◆◆◆
Estefan's all-Spanish album will cut down the amount of Top 40 radio play she receives, but her fans will be pleased with *Mi Tierra*, one of her more consistent albums. —*AMG*

Hold Me Thrill Me Kiss Me / 1994 / Epic ◆◆◆
A stretch for Estefan, and a genuinely worthy one, even if it sometimes strays too far from her Latin roots. This album of classic covers includes brilliant pop hits ("How Can I Be Sure," "Turn the Beat Around"), moments of genuine pathos ("Traces," "It's Too Late"), and some pure dreck ("You've Made Me So Very Happy"). While the record enhances Estefan's reputation as a savvy, sophisticated pop singer, it also lays bare her limitations, confirming that she's more stylist than soulstress. —*Eddie Huffman*

Melissa Etheridge

Rock & Roll, Blues Rock, Singer-Songwriter
Melissa Etheridge's gutsy electric blues-rock has earned her favorable comparisons to Rod Stewart and Janis Joplin, as well as a considerable fan base across America. Not only is she a solid live performer, but she has written several songs that have became AOR favorites since the late '80s, including "Bring Me Some Water" and "Similar Features." Although she earned some fans with her debut in 1988, her audience has increased with each new album. When she revealed that she is a lesbian in 1992, her commercial fortunes were not hurt at all; in fact, her audience continued to grow. Because it is rooted in the heart-break and turmoils of everyday life, Etheridge's music has a widespread appeal that makes her one of the top concert draws and AOR acts of the '90s. —*Stephen Thomas Erlewine*

● **Melissa Etheridge** / 1988 / Island ◆◆◆◆
A powerful debut with occasionally strident performances, it includes "Bring Me Some Water," a fine acoustic rocker. "Similar Features," a scathing indictment of a former lover, is a standout. —*Rick Clark*

Brave & Crazy / 1989 / Island ◆◆◆
A little more laidback offering than her self-titled debut, it includes reflective numbers like "Testify" and "You Used to Love to Dance." There are a few acoustic rockers like "My Back Door," "Skin Deep," and "Let Me Go." —*Rick Clark*

Never Enough / 1992 / Island ◆◆◆
Nothing here matches the raw power of "Bring Me Some Water," but this outing blends the thoughtful virtues of *Brave & Crazy* with the more rocking elements of her debut. Etheridge also synthesizes urban-dub rhythms and rap on tracks like "2001" (a single) and "Must Be Crazy for Me." It also includes the single "Ain't It Heavy." —*Rick Clark*

Yes I Am / 1993 / Island ◆◆◆
Etheridge's gutsy acoustic guitar-based rock is given a slightly more atmospheric treatment on this outing. Her voice is front and centre in the mix and the instrumentation conveys power, but there is an evenness to the dynamics here that keep her natural theatrical delivery from totally getting across. Nevertheless, "All American Girl" is a highlight, as is "I'm the Only One." A good album, it's not her best. —*Rick Clark*

Ethyl Meatplow

Group, Dance-Pop, Alternative Pop/Rock
Ethyl Meatplow was a short-lived, yet enormously accomplished, pseudo-industrial alternative/dance-rock outfit comprised of vocalist Carla Bozulich, guitarist Biff Barefoot Sanders, and drummer John Napier. Formed circa 1990, the group released three independent singles before their only album, 1993's *Happy Days Sweetheart*. The group earned a reputation for their live shows, which combined samples and electronics with live instrumentation. *Happy Days Sweetheart* earned good reviews in alternative/underground magazines yet the band split soon after its release. Bozulich became the vocalist for the pseudo-country-rock group the Geraldine Fibbers; she also sang on ex-Minutemen/fIREHOSE bassist Mike Watt's 1995 solo debut, *Ball-hog or Tugboat?*. —*Stephen Thomas Erlewine*

Happy Days Sweetheart / 1993 / Chameleon ◆◆◆

E.U.

Group
EU is one of the original DC go-go bands, but they never scored a pop hit until 1988, when "Da Butt" became a dance sensation, thanks to Spike Lee's *School Daze* movie. While they didn't record many great albums—1989's *Livin' Large*, which was riding on the success of "Da Butt," came the closest—each of their records has something that would appeal to hardcore funk fans. But, EU's strength was never captured on vinyl—it was their energetic, groove-oriented live shows that earned them a large following in the '80s, not their records. —*Stephen Thomas Erlewine*

Go Ju Ju Go / 1987 / E. Unlimited ◆◆◆

● **Livin' Large** / 1989 / Virgin ◆◆◆◆
Rare go-go tracks to get national exposure in 1989. —*Ron Wynn*

Cold Kickin' It / 1990 / Virgin ◆◆◆
Disappointing follow-up LP. —*Ron Wynn*

Eugenius

Group, Alternative Pop/Rock
Originally called Captain America, Eugenius is the second band from the talented Scottish guitarist/vocalist/songwriter Eugene Kelly. While Eugenius trades in the spare charm of the Vaselines for a more traditional, guitar-driven power-pop rush, the band is no less enjoyable; Kelly's talent for simple, unassuming pop songs hasn't disappeared and several of the band's best numbers rank with the best of his previous band. Like the Vaselines, Eugenius was helped by the support of Kurt Cobain who had the band open for Nirvana on their 1991 tour of Europe, as well as praising Eugene Kelly in many interviews. By the time Eugenius' second record was released in 1994, the band had earned their own audience. —*Stephen Thomas Erlewine*

● **Oomalama** / 1992 / Atlantic ◆◆◆◆
Eugenius' debut album is an infectious collection of fuzzy guitars and sweet pop melodies that slowly work their way into the subconcious. —*Stephen Thomas Erlewine*

Mary Queen of Scots / 1994 / Atlantic ◆◆◆
While it isn't as catchy or consistent as *Oomalama*, Eugenius' second album has enough strong songs to make it a worthwhile listen. —*Stephen Thomas Erlewine*

Europe

Group, Hard Rock
Originally a progressive rock group, Europe didn't achieve any success until they reworked their sound into a bombastic yet melodic pop-metal. In their first incarnation, the Swedish band was called Force. The band—featuring the core members Joey Tempest (vocals), John Norum (guitar), and John Leven (bass)—won a national talent contest in the early '80s, which led to a record contract. After releasing two albums in Sweden (*Europe* and *Wings of Tomorrow*), the band landed an international deal with Epic Records. By this time, Norum had left the group and was replaced by Kee Marcello; drummer Ian Haughland and keyboardist Michael Michaeli also joined the lineup.

Rechristening themselves Europe, the band released *The Final Countdown* in 1986. On the album, Michaeli's keyboards took a prominent role (they provide the main riff in the hit title track), which nicely complimented the band's smoother pop melodies. The change in style proved successful, as the record became a Top Ten hit in the U.S. and U.K.; both "The Final Countdown" and "Carrie" became Top Ten singles, as well. Delivered two years later, *Out of This World* continued the formula of the previous record. It also was a success, although its numbers didn't match those of *The Final Countdown*. Two years later, Europe released their final album, *Prisoners of Paradise*, to little attention. —*Stephen Thomas Erlewine*

Europe / 1983 / Epic ◆◆

Wings of Tomorrow / 1984 / Epic ◆◆◆
First album in the US. —*Robert DeFreitas*

● **The Final Countdown** / 1986 / Epic ◆◆◆◆
"Final Countdown" and "Carrie" were singles. —*Robert DeFreitas*

Out of This World / 1988 / Epic ◆◆

Prisoners in Paradise / 1991 / Epic ◆◆◆

Eurythmics

Group, Dance-Pop, Pop/Rock
Formed in December 1980 out of the ashes of the British band the Tourists, Eurythmics (comprising Dave Stewart and Annie Lennox) initially embraced the cool, clinical, synth-heavy sound of German ensembles like Kraftwerk or Can.

The musical element that immediately set Eurythmics apart from other techno artists was Lennox's powerful yet subtle voice, which could be extremely icy or soulful, depending on the requirements of the material. Stewart's production skills and multi-instrumental strengths usually provided all the right support.

Visually, Lennox toyed with androgyny as aggressively as David Bowie. As the '80s wore on, Eurythmics progressively infused soul and garage rock into their sound, producing an impressive string of hits. "Sweet Dreams (Are Made of This)", "Here Comes the Rain Again", "Would I Lie to You?", and a duet with Aretha Franklin, "Sisters are Doing It for Themselves", are among the numerous hits by Eurythmics. *— Rick Clark*

In the Garden / 1981 / RCA ✦✦
Eurythmics' debut album, *In the Garden*, is the missing link between the work of the Tourists, who included both Dave Stewart and Annie Lennox, and 1983's commercial breakthrough, *Sweet Dreams (Are Made of This)*. Co-produced by Kraftwerk producer Conny Plank at his studio in Cologne, Germany, it has some of the distant, mechanistic feel of the European electronic music movement, but less of the pop sensibility of later Eurythmics. The chief difference is in Lennox's singing; even when the musical bed is appealing, Lennox floats ethereally over it, and the listener doesn't focus on her. As a result, *In the Garden* wasn't much of a success, though when Eurythmics streamlined their sound and emphasized Lennox's dominating voice on subsequent releases, they found mass popularity. *— William Ruhlmann*

○ **Sweet Dreams (Are Made of This)** / Jan. 1983 / RCA ✦✦✦✦
Much commotion was caused by the MTV video clip for the hit title track from their breakthrough second album, which played up vocalist Annie Lennox's androgynous image. *— Donna DiChario*

○ **Touch** / Nov. 1983 / RCA ✦✦✦✦
The follow-up to the success of *Sweet Dreams* showed a more confident Lennox and Stewart, ready to expand their stylistic range. It contains the Top 40 hits "Here Comes the Rain Again", "Who's That Girl", and "Right by Your Side." *— Scott Bultman*

1984 (For the Love of Big Brother) / Nov. 1984 / RCA ✦✦
While it is not billed as an Original Motion Picture Soundtrack, this album does contain, as a jacket note indicates, "music derived from Eurythmics' original score of the motion picture *1984*, and it was treated as a side project for marketing purposes, not as Eurythmics' full-fledged fourth new studio album. Fair enough. Much of the album is instrumental, and the closest thing to a pop song, "Sexcrime (Nineteen Eighty-Four)" (which was a Top Ten hit in the U.K.), like the other vocal numbers, relates to the movie's future fiction theme. As such, the album is substandard if judged as an independent Eurythmics album, adequate if judged as a soundtrack. *— William Ruhlmann*

○ **Be Yourself Tonight** / May 1985 / RCA ✦✦✦✦
Showing sparks of Motown influence with the hit "Would I Lie to You?" and others, Stevie Wonder adds a harmonica solo to "There Must Be an Angel." *— Donna DiChario*

Revenge / Jul. 1986 / RCA ✦✦✦
On their fifth album, Eurythmics moved away from the austere synth-pop of their previous work and toward more of a neo-'60s pop/rock stance. "Missionary Man" (which went Top 40 as a single in the U.S. and charted in the U.K.) featured a prominent harmonica solo, while "Thorn in My Side" had a chiming guitar riff reminiscent of the Searchers and a fat sax solo. Of course, the primary element in the group's sound remained Annie Lennox's distinctive alto voice, which was still impressive even if the material was slightly less so. *Revenge* was a successful album, reaching the Top Ten in the U.K. and going gold in the U.S., but it was a disappointment compared to their last three albums. And creatively, it was a step down as well—there was nothing here that they hadn't done a little better before. *— William Ruhlmann*

Savage / Nov. 1987 / RCA ✦✦
If *Revenge*, Eurythmics' fifth album, marked a slight fall-off in the group's commercial and artistic accomplishments, *Savage*, their sixth collection, confirmed that decline. In the U.S., the album failed to generate a substantial hit single and sold poorly compared to previous efforts. In the more faithful U.K., the album hit the Top Ten and spun off four chart singles, but none that matched earlier hits. Musically, Eurythmics, for the most part, abandoned the more conventional pop/rock they recently had been pursuing, returning to the synthesized dance music and arch tone of their early hit "Sweet Dreams (Are Made of This)." But they still seemed less inspired than before. *— William Ruhlmann*

We Too Are One / Sep. 1989 / Arista ✦✦✦
Switching to Arista Records in the U.S., Eurythmics made their last album together with *We Too Are One*, and they went out in style. Calling upon a broad pop range, their seventh album was their best since *Be Yourself Tonight* in 1985. The sound was varied, the melodies were strong, and the lyrics were unusually well crafted. In retrospect, the album can be seen as a dry run for Annie Lennox's debut solo album, *Diva* (1992); songs like "Don't Ask Me Why" (which grazed the U.S. Top 40) serve as precursors to the dramatic ballads to come. There is, however, an air of romantic resignation throughout *We Too Are One*, appropriate to its valedictory nature. The disc spawned four chart singles in the U.K. and returned Eurythmics to number one in the album charts, but it did not substantially improve Eurythmics' reduced commercial standing in the U.S., confirming that it was time for Lennox and Dave Stewart to pursue other opportunities. *— William Ruhlmann*

● **Greatest Hits** / 1991 / Arista ✦✦✦✦
Whether cool and sophisticated or impassioned and soulful, this duo of singer Annie Lennox and guitarist Dave Stewart creates stylish and compelling rock. *— Donna DiChario*

Live 1983-1989 / 1993 / Arista ✦✦
The Eurythmics ruled the studio, not the stage, making this two-CD collection an interesting but not absorbing listen. *— Stephen Thomas Erlewine*

Betty Everett

Soul
Betty Everett sang gospel growing up in Greenwood, MS, before relocating to Chicago and moving into secular music. She began recording for Cobra in 1958, then joined Vee-Jay in the early '60s and started to land hit records. Her original version of "You're No Good," though sung with fire and verve, didn't make much impact until it was turned into a number one pop hit by Linda Ronstadt in 1975. Her next single, "The Shoop Shoop Song (It's in His Kiss)" was her first major release, peaking at number six pop in 1964. Her next success was the duet "Let it Be Me" with Jerry Butler, a soul version of the Everly Brothers tune that reached number five R&B that same year. Everett's finest song as a solo act was 1969's "There Comes a Time," which reached number two on the R&B charts and also cracked the pop Top 30 at number 26. Everett was now on Uni, where she remained until 1970. She continued recording for Fantasy until 1974 and made one other record for United Artists in 1978. *— Ron Wynn*

● **The Shoop Shoop Song** / 1993 / Vee-Jay ✦✦✦✦
Though sometimes classified as a "girl group" singer because of the Top Ten success of "The Shoop Shoop Song," Betty Everett's main thrust was much more in the R&B/soul vein. This excellent 25-track anthology of her 1963-65 material shows her facility with various soul, R&B, and pop styles. She had three other minor hits—the original hit version of "You're No Good," the energetic Goffin/King pop-rocker "I Can't Hear You," and Van McCoy's soulful "Gettin' Mighty Crowded"—all of which are featured here. But most of the other material is equally enjoyable, including other early efforts by McCoy, Valerie Simpson and Nick Ashford, and even P.F. Sloan (whose "Can I Get to Know You" is presented in a much earthier, slower version here than the Turtles' rendition several years later). This CD doesn't include her hit duets with fellow Chicago soulster Jerry Butler, but is a consistently enjoyable retrospective of an underrated singer who straddled the soul and pop worlds. *— Richie Unterberger*

The Everly Brothers

Group, Rock & Roll, Country-Rock, Pop/Rock
Don (b. 1937) and Phil (b. 1939) were sons of guitarist Ike Everly, said to be a teacher of finger-picking legend Merle Travis. As children, the brothers starred on an early radio program with their parents, going solo when their folks retired in the '50s. After recording in a country-duo style for Columbia with scant results, they switched to rock & roll on the Cadence label and had an immediate smash with "Bye Bye Love," going on to score over 25 Top

40 pop hits between 1957 and 1964. Their unerring harmonies melded well with crisp arrangements featuring top Nashville session players (among them Chet Atkins) and a bountiful supply of top-notch material, most of it coming from the prolific pens of Felice and Boudleaux Bryant. By the late '60s, the strain of touring, lack of record sales, and drug problems all led to their eventual and much-publicized split in 1973. Both recorded solo albums without success and reunited in 1983 to much critical acclaim, recording new material and touring with superb backup from a band led by guitarist Albert Lee. A major influence on any White rock & roll group singing two-part harmony (from the Beatles on down), they continue to impress and delight fans the world over. —*Cub Koda*

○ **The Everly Brothers [Cadence]** / 1958 / Rhino ✦✦✦✦
Although the Everlys hadn't quite fully matured as artists, their debut is a fine, consistent effort divided between original material and respectably energetic covers of early rockers by Little Richard, Gene Vincent, and Ray Charles. Besides their first few hits, it includes some superb, underappreciated tracks that are nearly as good, like "Should We Tell Him" and "I Wonder If I Care As Much." —*Richie Unterberger*

Songs Our Daddy Taught Us / 1958 / Rhino ✦✦✦
The Everlys had reached their commercial peak when they made this album of sparsely arranged traditional songs, a concept which was quite a surprise from a top rock & roll act, and considerably ahead of its time. It's actually not as enduring as their early rockers and pop ballads, but the singing is superb in their interpretations of standards like "Barbara Allen" and "Kentucky." —*Richie Unterberger*

○ **The Fabulous Style of the Everly Brothers** / 1960 / Rhino ✦✦✦✦
The best of their original Cadence albums, packed with hits ("Bird Dog," "All I Have to Do Is Dream," "When Will I Be Loved," "'Til I Kissed You") and other classic tracks ("Devoted to You," "Let It Be Me," "Since You Broke My Heart," "Like Strangers"). Almost all of the songs show up on their greatest hits collections, so it might be a superfluous purchase for all but serious fans, despite its top-drawer quality. —*Richie Unterberger*

○ **It's Everly Time** / 1960 / Warner Brothers ✦✦✦✦
While the Everlys' sound was diluted by more elaborate production in the '60s, that's not at all true on this LP, which is one of their very best. Not a stiff among the twelve tracks, most of which are barely known outside of serious Everly fans. Includes six stellar contributions by Boudleaux and Felice Bryant, one of Don Everly's best compositions ("So Sad"), and incredible harmony singing throughout. —*Richie Unterberger*

○ **A Date with the Everly Brothers** / 1961 / Warner Brothers ✦✦✦✦
Although the material is not on the killer level of *Everly Time*, there are some very fine songs on their second Warner LP. Includes "Cathy's Clown," their raucous cover of Little Richard's "Lucille," "Love Hurts" (which preceded Roy Orbison's hit version), and "So How Come" (covered by the Beatles in 1963 on the BBC). —*Richie Unterberger*

Gone, Gone, Gone / 1965 / Warner Brothers ✦✦
A jumble of tracks from varying sessions that, despite some excellent moments, was indicative of the general directionless of the Everlys' career at this point. The title song was their final Top 40 single of the '60s, and indeed one of their greatest performances. "The Ferris Wheel," also a 1964 single, was a decent, moody ballad that was a minor hit in both America and the U.K; for some reason, it was excluded from the double-CD compilation of their best '60s work, *Walk Right Back*. Otherwise, the album contains a few other songs cut in 1964, and some odds and ends from sessions in the early '60s. The Everlys, John D. Loudermilk, and the great Boudleaux/Felice Bryant songwriting team wrote almost all of the material on this album, but unfortunately it was not up to the standards of either the writers or the performers. —*Richie Unterberger*

Two Yanks in England / 1966 / Demon ✦✦✦
At first glance, this seems like a cash-in on the British Invasion. Recorded in London in 1966, no less than eight of the twelve songs were written by the Hollies (who released their own versions of many of the tunes). There are also covers of hits by the Spencer Davis Group and Manfred Mann. With a harder rock guitar sound (though not overdone or inappropriate) than previous Everlys discs, the duo's interpretations are actually worth hearing in their own right. The harmonies are fabulous, and indeed, the

Everlys improve a few of the Hollies' songs substantially. "So Lonely" and "Hard Hard Year," in particular, have a lot more force, transforming the tunes from decent Hollies album tracks to excellence. Because so much of the material is non-original, this couldn't be placed in the top rank of Everly Brothers recordings. But it is a good effort that shows them, almost ten years after "Bye Bye Love," still at the top of their game and still heavily committed to a rock & roll sound. This was a bold contrast to other '50s white rock & rollers with roots in country, most of whom had retreated to tamer country-oriented sounds by the mid-'60s. —*Richie Unterberger*

○ **Roots** / 1968 / Warner Brothers ✦✦✦✦
Considered one of the finest early country-rock albums, this showed the Everlys, unlike virtually every other top rock & roll act of the '50s, keeping abreast of contemporary rock and pop trends. In the manner of their 1958 LP *Songs Our Daddy Taught Us*, the concept was to cover songs by performers and composers that had been influential on the duo, including Jimmie Rodgers, Merle Haggard, traditional standards, and a couple of numbers by Ron Elliott of the Beau Brummels. Although this laidback, tasteful, acoustic-oriented recording isn't as outstanding as their classic early hits, the vocals are superb, conveying qualities of innocence tempered by experience. —*Richie Unterberger*

Nashville Tennessee Nov 1955 / 1981 / Bear Family ✦✦
Before beginning their rock & roll career with Cadence Records in 1957, the Everlys recorded one straight country single for Columbia in late 1955. Backed by the guitars, steel, bass, and fiddle of Carl Smith's Tunesmiths, this standard mid-'50s Nashville country offered little hints of the duo's further greatness, other than their shining harmonies. This four-song, 12-inch EP includes both sides of the single and two previously unreleased cuts from the same sessions. All four of the tunes were written by the Everlys themselves and are of mostly historical interest. —*Richie Unterberger*

The Reunion Concert / 1984 / Mercury ✦✦✦
Lively, if ultimately too slick, this concert recording ties up a few loose ends. —*Bruce Eder*

All They Had to Do Was Dream / 1985 / Rhino ✦✦✦
Alternate takes of much of their strongest material from the Cadence era, cut between 1957 and 1960. A bit more tentative than the familiar renditions, these aren't as good as the versions that ended up on official releases, but are enjoyable and fascinating glimpses at works in progress, and the singing is excellent throughout. Includes different versions of hits like "Wake Up Little Susie," "All I Have to Do Is Dream," "Till I Kissed You," and "When Will I Be Loved." —*Richie Unterberger*

★ **Cadence Classics: Their 20 Greatest Hits** / 1986 / Rhino ✦✦✦✦✦
Some of the best rock & roll ever recorded. Tough, melodic, innocent, and inventive. More than a road map for the Beatles' sound. —*Bruce Eder*

○ **Hidden Gems from the Warner Years** / 1989 / Ace ✦✦✦✦
This collects 14 songs that originally appeared on non-hit singles between 1962 and 1965; many of them had never been on LP. This material strongly counters the view that the Everlys faded artistically after "Cathy's Clown." The writing credits for these strong compositions read a bit like a who's who of early-'60s pop/rock, with contributions from Gerry Goffin, Mann/Weill, Doc Pomus & Mort Shuman, Sonny Curtis, Boudleaux and Felice Bryant, and the Everlys themselves. The singing is fabulous, and the arrangements still strong, rock-oriented, and tastefully produced. Tracks like "Nancy's Minuet" (1963), a great Don Everly original and one of their best paeans to lovelorn melancholia, and "You're the One I Love" (1964), a fine brooding midtempo rocker, stand with their very best work. Only three of these appear on the '60s Everlys anthology *Walk Right Back*, making this a necessary purchase for Everlys fans. —*Richie Unterberger*

○ **Classic Everly Brothers** / 1992 / Bear Family ✦✦✦✦
The three-disc box set *Classic Everly Brothers* collects all of their Cadence recordings, including alternate takes, as well as several early radio shows and the four tracks the duo recorded for Columbia in 1955. While this music is the most essential the brothers ever made, the disc of rarities is only of interest to devoted fans. Nevertheless, the sound on the box is stellar, the liner notes are excellent, and the whole package is wonderful; for hardcore fans, the set is worth the money. —*Stephen Thomas Erlewine*

○ **Walk Right Back: The Everly Brothers on Warner Bros.** / 1993 / Warner Archives ✦✦✦✦
This two-CD, 50-track compilation assembles the Everly Brothers' most memorable recordings of the 1960s. Although their work from this period has sometimes been criticized as inferior to their classic '50s recordings for Cadence, the best of these songs are a match for anything the duo recorded. As it happens, the strongest of these tunes are drawn from their first two albums for Warners in the 1960s, including the hits "Cathy's Clown" and "So Sad." In the following years, their material suffered from increasing inconsistency and ill-suited production. Yet the Brothers continued to intermittently hit the mark squarely—not only with early-'60s hits like "Crying In the Rain" and "Temptation," but neglected flop singles like "Nancy's Minuet" and "You're the One I Love," as well as the hard-rocking minor 1964 hit "Gone Gone Gone" (their last Top 40 single). They also showed a willingness to incorporate the hard-rocking beat of the British Invasion into their work that was not shared by any of the other major stars of the '50s. This compilation misses a number of fine B-sides and non-hit singles from the early and mid-'60s (check the Ace import collection *Hidden Gems* for those), and perhaps leans too heavily on their tepid late-'60s country-rock. But it's a good overview of a body of work which is often unfairly overlooked. —*Richie Unterberger*

○ **The Mercury Years** / Jul. 20, 1993 / Mercury ✦✦✦✦
Mercury Years collects all of the finest moments from their two 1980s albums; its best moments, like "On the Wings of a Nightingale," are surprisingly strong. —*Stephen Thomas Erlewine*

☆ **Heartaches & Harmonies Box Set** / 1994 / Rhino ✦✦✦✦✦
This four-CD, 102-song set includes all of their key performances, as well as many overlooked ones, dating from a previously unreleased 1951 radio performance of "Don't Let Our Love Die" to a 1990 live rendition of the very same tune. Opening with a disc's worth of classic Cadence performances, most of the next three CDs are given over to their largely overlooked Warner Bros. '60s output, including many interesting flop singles and album tracks, as well as top-notch rarities like an alternate version of the supremely moody "Nancy's Minuet" and the mid-'60s outtake "And I'll Go." Fine liner notes with detailed comments from the Everlys themselves, but it still manages to miss some great tunes (like the 1964 single "You're the One I Love" and various tracks from their late-'50s and early-'60s LPs), and shouldn't be considered a definitive collection of all their great performances. And the hard fact is, a lot of their post-1966 material (which comprises some of disc three and all of disc four) is kind of boring. —*Richie Unterberger*

BOOK

✦✦✦ **Walk Right Back: The Story Of The Everly Brothers**, by Roger White (Plexus, UK, 1984). There are a couple other Everlys bios from tiny publishers, but this is the best by a wide margin. It covers the duo's entire career, with considerable depth if not a great deal of pizzazz, from their days as child performers in Iowa, their phenomenally successful prime between 1957 and 1962, their commercially frustrating final decade (which included many fine recordings) before their bitter split in 1973, and their reunion a decade after that. White uses a lot of material, both first-hand and otherwise, from Don and Phil, Cadence label head Archie Bleyer, the Boudleaux & Felice Bryant songwriting team (which wrote many of their early hits), Chet Atkins, manager Wesley Rose, and several of their sidemen. The tone tends to be too uncritical—the Everlys released quite a few dogs, in addition to their wealth of great songs. But there are lots of interesting stories about their recording sessions and tours, the up-and-down relationship between the brothers, and a complete discography. —*Richie Unterberger*

Everything But the Girl

Group, Pop, Alternative Pop/Rock
A British pop duo with light jazz overtones, formed by Tracey Thorn (b. Sep 26, 1962) and Ben Watt (b. Dec 6, 1962) in 1983. —*William Ruhlmann*

Everything but the Girl / 1984 / Sire ✦✦✦
The music fad of the moment in 1984 in England was a revival of the early-'60s Brazilian pop sound of Antonio Carlos Jobim, Astrud Gilberto, and Stan Getz, updated to current sensibilities, and the two main practitioners were Sade and Everything but the Girl. On this revised version of their U.K. debut album, *Eden,* altered for

U.S. consumption, the duo of Tracey Thorn and Ben Watt performed their three U.K. chart singles, "Each and Every One," "Mine," and "Native Land," in a calm, unruffled style keyed to Thorn's warm, if slightly unfocused, vocal style. If the music had a flaw, it was that the sound, with its light sambas and steady ballads, spare instrumentation and careful sax solos, impressed more than individual songs did, perhaps because Thorn's way of phrasing meant you could listen to "Mine," for example, several times before catching on to its feminist theme. Still, Everything but the Girl was more direct and had less of the exotic affectation of Sade (which, however, may help explain why it was she, and not they, who succeeded in America). —*William Ruhlmann*

Eden / May 1984 / Blanco Y Negro ✦✦✦

Love Not Money / Apr. 1985 / Sire ✦✦✦
On their second album, Everything but the Girl took a more contemporary pop approach while retaining the spareness of their debut. They also upped the ante in their songwriting, tackling a range of issues from the Irish Troubles to the troubles of movie star Frances Farmer, with lots of criticism of the stratification and sexism of the current social and economic system thrown in. Tracey Thorn's careworn voice proved an excellent vehicle for such essentially pessimistic sentiments, and even if *Love Not Money* made for a dour listening experience, it was nevertheless compelling. (The "special U.S. edition" of the album, released by Sire Records, differed from the Blanco Y Negro version from the U.K. in that it featured the pop-sounding "Heaven Help Me" and a cover of the Pretenders' "Kid." Neither enhanced the album's commercial appeal; it made the Top Ten back home, but did not chart Stateside.) —*William Ruhlmann*

Baby, the Stars Shine Bright / Aug. 1986 / Sire ✦✦✦
On their third album, Everything but the Girl tries another departure on their craftsmanlike ballad style, hiring a full orchestra to give a lush backing to songs usually concerned more with sexual than national politics. Their last album, *Love Not Money,* may have boasted a considerable social agenda, but here Tracey Thorn sings of romantic disappointment and illicit liaisons, only occasionally bowing to such favorite themes as the lure of fame ("Country Mile"), fantasies about American movie stars ("Sugar Finney," which is "for Marilyn Monroe," and has the chorus, "America is free, cheap and easy"), and fears of fascism ('Little Hitler'). Thorn's throbbing voice is well-suited to the emotional concerns of the lyrics, and Ben Watt creates attractive, string- and horn-filled backings for them. So, Everything but the Girl has found yet another way effectively to vary what would have seemed to be a limited musical style. —*William Ruhlmann*

● **Idlewild** / Feb. 1988 / Sire ✦✦✦✦
Thorn and Watt made a couple of albums with a cocktail-jazz backup and one with strings before trying a small unit for the intimate songs of their most accessible recording. The setting is perfect for such moving compositions as "Love Is Here Where I Live" and "Apron Strings." Start here, then go on to the rest of this remarkable group's catalog. —*William Ruhlmann*

The Language of Life / Jan. 1990 / Atlantic ✦✦
It may have been the logical extension of Everything but the Girl's ersatz cool-jazz approach to finally go all the way by hiring veteran producer Tommy LiPuma and a studio full of fusion stars like Joe Sample (the Crusaders), Russell Ferrante (the Yellowjackets), Michael Brecker, and, finally, Stan Getz, whose early-'60s albums of Brazilian jazz are a main touchstone for the group. With such firepower, *The Language of Life,* at least musically, may be the album that Ben Watt and Tracey Thorn have been trying to make from the beginning. But it falls down in its songwriting, largely because of the near-disappearance of Thorn and her edgy lyrics; Watt takes over for a series of so-so love songs. And the bottom of the barrel is hit with a cover of Womack and Womack's "Take Me," intended as an erotic come-on and sounding more like a lullaby. —*William Ruhlmann*

Worldwide / Sep. 1991 / Atlantic ✦✦✦
Ben Watt and Tracey Thorn returned to the direct record-making style of their first two albums on *Worldwide.* Here, the music was carried largely by Watt's bank of keyboards. But the duo's lyrical concerns reflected their recent frenetic lifestyle. Sooner or later, every group that lasts makes a road album, and this was the one for Everything but the Girl, its songs nostalgically reminiscing about childhood back in England, along with reflections on the big-time touring life in America. Happily, there was still room for

a few of Everything but the Girl's complicated adult love songs, notably Thorn's "Understanding," though even that one talked about how love "depends on geography." The breezy subject matter contrasted with the more contemplative music. —*William Ruhlmann*

Acoustic / Jun. 1992 / Atlantic ♦♦
Acoustic presents two side projects in one. The first half of it consists of Everything but the Girl's covers of six songs by other contemporary performers. The second half contains two live recordings and four re-recordings of songs from Everything but the Girl's repertoire. All of the songs are performed with spare, acoustic instrumentation. The group's favorites are predictable—Bruce Springsteen, Elvis Costello, and Tom Waits at their quietest—and while the choices are indisputably good ones—"Alison," "Downtown Train," Cyndi Lauper's "Time After Time"—they are also familiar, and Ben Watt and Tracey Thorn don't bring anything new to them. Their own material is calm and contemplative anyway, so stripping away the synthesizers doesn't affect the arrangements much. *Acoustic* is a pleasant-sounding, inessential Everything but the Girl album. —*William Ruhlmann*

Amplified Heart / Jul. 19, 1994 / Atlantic ♦♦♦
Despite its title, *Amplified Heart* is one of Everything but the Girl's more acoustic works. A simple instrumentation of guitars and keyboards, augmented here and there by British folk-rock veterans like Richard Thompson, Danny Thompson, and Dave Mattacks, serves to set up a series of songs of romantic disillusionment. Declaring "My life is just an image of a rollercoaster, anyway" and "I don't understand anything," among other things, over and over the songs speak of confusion and disappointment deriving from failed love affairs. The approach is much more introspective than that taken on the group's last new original album, *Worldwide*, but Tracey Thorn and Ben Watt's musical restraint supports it well. This is an album to listen to when you've just broken up with your lover, or even when you're just in the mood to think about lost lovers from long ago—self-pity set to music. —*William Ruhlmann*

The Exciters

Group, Girl-Group
Despite the presence of lone male Herb Rooney, the Exciters made some of the best girl-group records of the early '60s. Led by vibrant-voiced Brenda Reid, the originally all-female quartet came from Jamaica, NY, as the Masterettes. After signing on with saxist Al Sears as their manager, they switched their name to The Exciters and cut "Tell Him" in 1962 for United Artists. Produced by Jerry Leiber and Mike Stoller, the brilliant uptown soul effort proved a major smash. Reid's roaring pipes were expertly spotlighted on the followups "He's Got the Power," "Get Him," and their original reading of "Do-Wah-Diddy," immortalized later that year by Manfred Mann. The group later appeared on Roulette, Band, Shout, and RCA. Reid and Rooney were married for a time, and Reid now performs with her children backing her. —*Bill Dahl*

● **Tell Him /EMI Legends of Rock 'n' Roll Series** / 1991 / EMI America ♦♦♦♦
This girl-group R&B has full-fledged, violin-laden productions backing Brenda Reid's soul-drenched lead vocals. —*Bill Dahl*

Extreme

Group, Hard Rock, Pop/Rock, Heavy Metal
Although guitarist and band mastermind Nuno Bettencourt's style was derived from Eddie Van Halen, his heart is with the progressive hard rock of Queen, as well as Beatlesque pop and touches of lounge jazz. Consequently, Extreme's music is never easy to classify; it's not just heavy metal, hard rock, or pop—their albums cover all of that territory, with a sweeping ambition and a social conscious to match. By the time of their second album, *Pornograffiti*, Bettencourt was already well-respected in the heavy metal world but it was the Everly Brothers-style acoustic ballad, "More than Words," that crossed them over into the mainstream—it hit number one and the follow-up single, the acoustic-based pop rocker "Hole Hearted," hit number four. Extreme's third album,

Extreme III: Three Sides to Every Story, was an over-ambitious follow-up that sold well at first, but didn't have the staying power of their previous album. Extreme's fourth album, 1995's *Waiting for the Punchline*, suffered from a similar lack of sales. —*Stephen Thomas Erlewine*

Extreme / 1989 / A&M ♦♦♦
Extreme's first album shows the band struggling to shed their influences, particularly Van Halen, and develop a style of their own; consequently, it's wildly uneven, but guitarist Nuno Bettencourt is always worth hearing. —*Stephen Thomas Erlewine*

● **Extreme II: Pornograffitti** / 1990 / A&M ♦♦♦♦
They're either MTV-ready mainstream pretty-boy hard rockers or sensitive acoustic balladeers singing lounge-lizard schmaltz—candy mint or breath mint. Exceptional lead-guitar chops are provided by Nuno Bettencourt, who also carries fine vocal work with lead singer Gary Cherone. It contains the left-field acoustic hit "More Than Words," and "Hole Hearted." "Song for Love" should have been an AOR hit. —*Rick Clark*

III Sides to Every Story / 1992 / A&M ♦♦♦
That sometimes-bombastic child of the '70s known as the "concept album" seems to be undergoing a revival of late. The latest perpetration of the genre is this third release from Boston's Extreme. Highlighted by the single "Rest in Peace," *III Sides to Every Story* stretches three separate musical movements—entitled Yours, Mine and The Truth, over 70 minutes of music. The disc packs a powerful anti-war message without being drearily pessimistic or nihilistic about its subject matter. Led by guitarist, songwriter and producer Nuno Bettencourt and singer Gary Cherone, Extreme have broken the mould of a standard hard rock band milking the occasional power ballad, to assemble a politically correct tour-de-force. —*Roch Parisien*

Waiting For the Punchline / 1995 / A&M ♦♦
Extreme's third album was lost in the thunder of grunge, selling far below expectations. The group fights back with *Waiting for the Punchline*, blasting out at the new wave of hard rockers by saying they'll be "Gone Tomorrow" and, presumably, gone tomorrow. Such proclamations would carry greater weight if they were supported by music that didn't replicate the soft melodic crunch of '80s pop-metal. Nuno Bettencourt remains a stunningly accomplished guitarist, but as a composer he's stuck in an increasingly restrictive formula. —*Stephen Thomas Erlewine*

Eyes

Group, British Invasion, Psychedelic
In 1965 and 1966, the Eyes released a clutch of singles which stand up to the Who's work from the same era in their blend of extremely innovative guitar feedback/distortion and anthemic mod songwriting. "When the Night Falls," "The Immediate Pleasure," "I'm Rowed Out," "You're Too Much," and the dry "My Generation" satire "My Degeneration" are revered highly by British Invasion collectors. The bursts of electronic mayhem were quite advanced for the time, though like the Who, they had hooks and harmonies to counterpoint the madness. They weren't as memorable as the Who, and didn't approach commercial success. After a much softer fourth single and an ill-conceived album of Rolling Stones covers (recorded under the name the Pupils), the group disbanded. —*Richie Unterberger*

● **Blink** / 1984 / Bam Caruso ♦♦♦♦
Includes both sides of their four singles, plus a couple of cuts from their LP of Rolling Stones covers. There's a big distance between the good and bad cuts on this compilation, although the best four or five tracks are good indeed. Comes with a four-page history of the band. —*Richie Unterberger*

Scene But Not Heard / 1987 / Bam Caruso ♦♦
A six-song EP of demos rescued from acetates, including early versions of "When The Night Falls," and "The Immediate Pleasure," along with a Radio London jingle and a cover of "Shakin' All Over." Raw in both sound quality and performance, it demonstrates (perhaps inadvertently) how much of the impact of their singles was attributable to excellent production. —*Richie Unterberger*

F

Shelley Fabares

b. 1944
Teen Idol

When Shelley Fabares was co-starring in *The Donna Reed Show* on television in the early '60s, she was reluctantly coerced into the recording studio to capitalize on her acting career. Her debut single, "Johnny Angel," went all the way to number one, and is an archetype of sorts for the entire teen idol era. One of the relatively few female idols, Fabares had a slight, innocuous voice, fleshed out with plenty of female backup singers and expert, if somewhat antiseptic, arrangements. The sequel to "Johnny Angel," "Johnny Loves Me," just missed the Top 20, and she had a few much smaller chart singles in 1962 and 1963. —*Richie Unterberger*

● **Best of** / 1994 / Sequel ✦✦✦✦
18 songs from 1962-65, most from her Colpix singles. Typically lightweight teen idol tunes, these do include some rare compositions by Barry Mann/Cynthia Weil and P.F. Sloan/Steve Barri, although, alas, they're throwaways that don't compare to their best work. Amidst the dross is an unexpectedly first-rate girl-group single from 1964, "He Don't Love Me," co-written by Jan Berry and featuring outstanding Spectoresque production from David Gates. —*Richie Unterberger*

Fabian

Pop, Teen Idol

Thanks to a series of performances on Dick Clark's "American Bandstand," Fabian rocketed to stardom in the late '50s. With his stylish good looks and mild rock & roll, he became one of the top teen idols of the era; luckily, he had the support of the legendary songwriting team of Doc Pomus and Mort Shuman, who provided him with "Turn Me Loose," "Hound Dog Man," and "I'm a Man," among other songs. Fabian's fame peaked in 1959 with the million-selling "Tiger" single; after that, he valiantly tried to become a movie star. When Congress fingered him as one of the performers who benefited from payola, his already ailing career was given a nearly fatal blow; under questioning, Fabian explained that his records featured a substantial amount of electronic doctoring in order to improve his voice. After the hearings, he starred in some more movies in the '60s, without regaining the audience of his peak years. —*Stephen Thomas Erlewine*

○ **The Best of Fabian** / 1995 / Varese Vintage ✦✦✦✦
Compared to some import collections that are available, this 10-song CD is on the skimpy side. But it does include all of his late-'50s and early-'60s chart hits, which should satisfy all but obsessively rabid collectors, and as a domestic release, it's considerably cheaper and more readily available than the other comps. —*Richie Unterberger*

The Fabulous Thunderbirds

Group, Blues Rock

The Fabulous Thunderbirds are one of the finest examples of Texas roadhouse R&B/electric blues. The original lineup featured the taut lead-guitar work of Jimmie Vaughan (Stevie Ray's brother). Kim Wilson, the band's frontman, is a master of rude harmonica playing. After years of fine album releases and endless gigging, this journeyman Austin band hit it big in 1986 with the #10 title cut from the Dave Edmunds-produced *Tuff Enuff*. Since then they've continued to enjoy a string of hits, including a remake of Sam & Dave's "Wrap It Up" (#50), "Stand Back" (#76),

and "Powerful Stuff" (#65), featured in the Tom Cruise film *Cocktail*. In 1990 Vaughan left the group and was replaced by Kid Bangham and Duke Robillard. The Fabulous Thunderbirds released *Walk That Walk, Talk That Talk*, the first album recorded with the new lineup, in 1991. The band released *Roll of the Dice* in the summer of 1995. —*Rick Clark*

○ **Fabulous Thunderbirds** / 1979 / Chrysalis ✦✦✦✦
Their debut album, with the original lineup of Wilson, Vaughn, Buck, and Ferguson stompin' through a roadhouse set of covers and genre-worthy originals. One of the few White blues albums that works. —*Cub Koda*

What's the Word / 1980 / Chrysalis ✦✦✦
Second album, equally powerful. Some of their best, including the off-kilter "Los Fabulosos Thunderbirds" and "Running Shoes." —*Cub Koda*

Butt Rockin' / 1981 / Chrysalis ✦✦✦

T Bird Rhythm / 1982 / Chrysalis ✦✦✦

Tuff Enuff / 1986 / Epic ✦✦✦
Their breakthrough success. The title track and soul covers point the band in a new, more mainstream direction. —*Cub Koda*

Portfolio / 1987 / Chrysalis ✦✦✦

Hot Number / 1987 / Epic ✦✦✦

Powerful Stuff / 1989 / Epic ✦✦

● **The Essential** / 1991 / Chrysalis ✦✦✦✦
Nice compilation of the early Chrysalis albums on one CD. —*Cub Koda*

Walk That Walk, Talk That Talk / Dec. 1991 / Epic ✦✦

○ **Hot Stuff: The Greatest Hits** / 1992 / Epic ✦✦✦✦
The best tracks from the Fabulous Thunderbirds' more rock-oriented years at CBS Associated Records are collected on this single-disc compilation. —*Stephen Thomas Erlewine*

Faces

Group, Rock & Roll

When Steve Marriott left the Small Faces in 1969, the three remaining members brought in guitarist Ron Wood and lead singer Rod Stewart to complete the lineup and changed their name to the Faces, which was only appropriate since the group now only slightly resembled the mod-pop group of the past. Instead, the Faces were a rough, sloppy rock & roll band, able to pound out a rocker like "Had Me a Real Good Time," a blues ballad like "Tell Everyone," or a folk number like "Richmond" all in one album. Stewart, already becoming a star in his own right, let himself go wild with the Faces, tearing through covers and originals with abandon. While his voice didn't have the power of Stewart, bassist Ronnie Lane's songs were equally as impressive and eclectic. Wood's rhythm guitar had a warm, fat tone that was as influential and enduring as Keith Richards' style.

Notorious for their hard-partying, boozy tours and ragged concerts, the Faces lived the rock & roll life-style to the extreme. When Stewart's solo career became more successful than the Faces', the band slowly became subservient to his personality; after their final studio album, *Ooh La La*, in 1973, Lane left the band. After a tour in 1974, they band called it quits. Wood joined the Rolling Stones, drummer Kenny Jones eventually became part of the Who, and keyboardist Ian McLagan came to become a sought-after supporting musician; Stewart became a superstar, although he never matched the simple charms of the Faces.

While they were together, the Faces never sold that many records and were never considered as important as the Stones, yet their music has proven extremely influential over the years. Many punk rockers in the late '70s learned how to play their instruments by listening to Faces records; in the '80s and '90s, guitar-rock bands from the Replacements to the Black Crowes took their cue from the Faces as much as the Stones. Their reckless, loose and joyous spirit has stayed alive in much of the best rock & roll of the past two decades. —*Stephen Thomas Erlewine*

○ **First Step** / 1970 / Warner Brothers ✦✦✦✦
On their first album, the Faces established the pattern they would follow throughout their four albums—a ragged mix of breakneck rockers ("Shake, Shudder"), sensitive yet gritty ballads ("Devotion"), folk songs ("Stone"), revelatory covers (Bob Dylan's "Wicked Messenger"), and relaxed, friendly rockers ("Three Button Hand Me Down"). Although two instrumentals on the second side is one too many (Ron Wood's "Pineapple and the Monkey" is pretty great), the Faces seldom got better than the first half of *First Step*. —*Stephen Thomas Erlewine*

☆ **Long Player** / 1971 / Warner Brothers ✦✦✦✦✦
With their second effort, the Faces grew more muscular and loose, rocking with loose abandon on "Bad N' Ruin" and "Had Me a Real Good Time," two of their best songs. At the same time, their ballads also improved, with Stewart's "Tell Everyone" and Lane's "Richmond" rivaling each other for the most touching number on the album. Out of the two live tracks, "Balling the Jack" goes on a little too long, but "Maybe I'm Amazed" is tremendous—the Faces tear into the song, transforming it from a McCartney ballad to a heartfelt cry of devotion. *Long Player* is a sloppy, terrific record; although it may have a couple of weak moments, it has the heart and soul of the band. —*Stephen Thomas Erlewine*

★ **A Nod Is As Good As a Wink … To A Blind Horse** / 1971 / Warner Brothers ✦✦✦✦✦
Boasting "Stay with Me," the only hit the Faces ever had, *A Nod is as Good ss a Wink* is their most consistent record, and arguably their best. "Stay With Me" and "Miss Judy's Farm" showcase the band at their best—they're all over the place, threatening to fall apart altogether before they snap it all back into place. Nobody rocked better than this, and the album is full of such terrific moments, including a rollicking cover of Chuck Berry's "Memphis." As with all of the Faces' albums, it's a little messy, but it is a classic rock & roll band at the top of their form. —*Stephen Thomas Erlewine*

Ooh La La / 1973 / Warner Brothers ✦✦✦
Although it's routinely lambasted as an uninspired effort or a sellout, *Ooh La La* is a tight rock & roll album, with its best moments—"Cindy Incidentally" and "Borstal Boy"—ranking among the Faces' best songs. —*Stephen Thomas Erlewine*

Snakes & Ladders / 1976 / Warner Brothers ✦✦✦
The best available overview of the Faces includes "Pool Hall Richard," "Cindy Incidentally," and "Stay with Me." (Import) —*Rick Clark*

The Factory

Group, Psychedelic
Before emerging as a cult star in the 1970s, Lowell George was a presence on the L.A. folk-rock/psychedelic scene in the 1960s. With his group, the Factory, he only managed to release one single during this time, although they cut a fair amount of unreleased material. At times they echo Kaleidoscope in their vaguely spacy, good-natured folkish rock; just as often, they take their cues from Captain Beefheart and Frank Zappa in their skewed blues-rock and obtuse songwriting. —*Richie Unterberger*

Lightning-Rod Man / 1993 / Rhino ✦✦✦
Lightning-Rod Man rescues 15 tunes cut by this unit, including the single and over a dozen outtakes and demos. Almost exclusively original material, most of these tracks were recorded in 1966 and 1967. They show the group pursuing a slightly eccentric folk-rock vision that neither bears much similarity to George's more famous work nor matches the best work done in this genre by their L.A. peers. A few songs cut towards the end of the decade feature a heavier, bluesier sound that show George edging in a different direction. Frank Zappa produced and played on a couple of the demos, and one-time Mothers of Invention members Elliot Ingber and Roy Estrada show up on a few others. An enjoyable vault find, but not a major revelation. —*Richie Unterberger*

Donald Fagen

b. Jan. 10, 1948, Passaic, NJ
Pop/Rock
Donald Fagen was one of the two masterminds behind Steely Dan, the seminal jazz-pop band of the '70s. Fagen's solo work has been a continuation of the band's work of the early '80s—carefully constructed and arranged, intricately detailed pop songs that are more substantial than their stylish surface may indicate. His 1982 solo debut, *The Nightfly*, was the best album he had made in years; it covered the same ground as the last two Steely Dan albums, yet surpassed it in terms of ambition and achievement.

After the success of *The Nightfly*, Fagen suffered a case of writer's block; for the rest of the decade he contributed music to the occasional film and briefly wrote a column for *Premiere* magazine in the mid-'80s. In the early '90s, he toured with the New York Rock & Soul Revue as he finished the material for his second album. With his former Steely Dan partner Walter Becker producing, 1993's *Kamakiriad* sounded like *Aja* recorded with '90s technology. It had some success on the adult contemporary charts, but it was overshadowed by the duo's decision to re-form Steely Dan and tour for the first time in nearly 20 years; the tour was a massive success. —*Stephen Thomas Erlewine*

★ **The Nightfly** / Oct. 1982 / Warner Brothers ✦✦✦✦✦
For his debut solo album after leaving Steely Dan, Fagen turned in a typically sophisticated jazz-pop collection tied to a lyrical theme concerning the late '50s and early '60s. One song takes the Kennedy administration's slogan, "The New Frontier," as a title, while another, "The Goodbye Look," is set in Cuba around the time of Castro's takeover. Steely Dan lovers will feel right at home. —*William Ruhlmann*

○ **Kamakiriad** / May 25, 1993 / Reprise ✦✦✦✦
After eleven years, Donald Fagen delivered his second album, *Kamakiriad*, in the summer of 1993. Where the sophisticated eclecticism of *The Nightfly* was warm and welcoming, *Kamakiriad* is insular; it takes several listens before all of the pieces fall into place. While all of the album *sounds* terrific, the melodies are subtler and tend to get buried under the meticulous arrangements. However, the hooks and melodies emerge after a couple of plays, as do Fagen's wry, witty lyrics. —*Stephen Thomas Erlewine*

Jad Fair

Alternative Pop/Rock
There are plenty of performers rock critics compliment by using the label "primitive," but few, if any, can hold a candle to the greatest American rock primitive, Jad Fair. With his fantastic and increasingly influential band Half Japanese or as a solo performer, Fair has constructed a prolific and extremely interesting career, writing and recording songs that display an uncomplicated emotional directness, unself-conscious (almost hokey) charm and warmth, and a genial simplicity that is simply beyond words. Although Fair's recent recordings are certainly more accessible—in some ways resembling those of another great American primitive, Jonathan Richman—his stock-in-trade is still the ability to compose and play music without any discernable (i.e., traditional) musical talent. Although he has "played" guitar since the mid-'70s, Fair, according to past and present members of Half Japanese, still can't name a chord, plays riffs almost by accident, and wouldn't have it any other way.

Fair's career as a solo artist began in 1980. It wasn't that he was particularly upset or unhappy with the direction he and brother David were leading Half Japanese, but rather that he needed another outlet with which to satiate his obsessive desire to make music. The first efforts were tentative, and in terms of the noise vs. music factor (more noise than music), akin to early Half Japanese records. But by the mid- to late '80s, Fair's solo records were becoming more accessible due to the contributions of celebrities and huge Half Japanese fans such as Dinosaur Jr.'s J Mascis, NRBQ's Terry Adams, Yo La Tengo's Ira Kaplan, and Gumball mastermind Don Fleming. And while the records got a little more polished, they certainly never lost a bit of Fair's childlike view of the world, nor his explosive, giddy belief in rock's liberating potential and endless possibilities. In Fair's world, love is the key to solving the world's problems, but his naivete-as-philosophy, while not deep, is never rank or manipulative (you always believe that he believes); and although he can sound cloying at times, the honesty and joy of this music will let you forgive his occasional excesses. By not being your typical singer-songwriter, Jad Fair has made the world a safe place for those who care passionately about rock & roll, but who don't feel the need to achieve any degree of virtuosity. —*John Dougan*

Everybody Knew . . . but Me / 1982 / Press ✦✦✦
Early, more extreme Jad. His singing is surrounded by metallic clattering and only the barest concessions to traditional pop song forms. The songs tend to be about love and, uh, love, but the rather limited narratives in no way detract from what is a mostly wonderful listening experience. Although this is an accurate portrait of what Jad was up to at the time, it's recommended for adventure seekers, noise-pop fans, and those who unequivocally loved the first two Half Japanese records. —*John Dougan*

● **Jad Fair and Daniel Johnston** / 1989 / Homestead ✦✦✦✦
Those not familiar with Daniel Johnston's work should know that his approach to pop songwriting is similar to Fair's, with the exception that he suffers from serious bouts with manic depression and severe delusional behavior. That said, this pairing of these two musical savants is a successful foray into pop music as therapy. Neither one is blessed with a great voice (or technically, a good voice), the songs tend to be about simple pleasure, and the instrumentation is sparse. Despite both of them having flashes of happiness, this is by and large not a happy record; it's more of a soul-baring exercise. —*John Dougan*

I Like It When You Smile / 1992 / Psycho ✦✦✦
This is the Fair release with the largest number of heavy hitters providing musical support (Terry Adams, J Mascis, Don Fleming) and some of it rocks in a radio-friendly (for Jad anyway) fashion that's downright jarring. But there is enough of the trademark Fair mania and out-of-tune playing (a downright messy, atonal cover of "On the Sunny Side of the Street") to keep diehards happy, while expanding the minds of newcomers to Jad Fair's warm and wonderful world. —*John Dougan*

Fairground Attraction

Group, Alternative Pop/Rock
British neo-skiffle pop quartet led by singer Eddi Reader (b. Aug 28, 1959, Glasgow, Scotland) and featuring guitarist Mark Nevin, guitaron player Simon Edwards, and drummer Roy Dodds. The group went to #1 in the U.K. with its single "Perfect" in May 1988 and released its debut album, *First of a Million Kisses*. Reader then quit, and the remaining members made *Ay Fond Kiss* before disbanding. —*William Ruhlmann*

○ **The First of a Million Kisses** / May 1988 / RCA ✦✦✦✦
The skiffle craze threatened to make a comeback in England with the success of the irresistible single "Perfect" and Eddi Reader's gorgeous singing. Alas, *First* turned out to be the last of Reader's association with Fairground Attraction, though they managed to release a second album without her. —*William Ruhlmann*

Fairport Convention

Group, Folk-Rock
Fairport Convention emerged at the end of the '60s, as something of a British response to the American West Coast sound. A wildly eclectic bunch at the outset, Fairport quickly jettisoned their original vocal front line, and abandoned the American singer/songwriter material they often relied on. With the band's third album, *Unhalfbricking*, guitarist Richard Thompson's songwriting skills took hold, and Sandy Denny emerged as England's premier female vocalist.

The album that was to follow, *Liege and Lief*, proved to be the crown jewel of Fairport's career. Inspired by earlier experiments with traditional British folk music, the band crafted a mixture of heavily reworked folk standards and sympathetic originals, topped by the brilliant singing of Denny. Sadly, it was to be her last (for a time), and after another album, Thompson was gone as well.

Fairport continued through the '70s with ever-changing lineups, and even a short-lived reunion with Denny, but despite making several fine, underrated albums, Fairport Convention eventually waved goodbye.

The mid-'80s saw a reborn Fairport, centering around three members from the band's classic era and continuing the legacy with several more fine albums. The complete Fairport story could occupy a massive volume in itself; just let it be known that the influence and importance of this band is substantial. —*Steve Aldrich*

○ **Fairport Convention [1st]** / Jun. 1968 / Polydor ✦✦✦✦
By far the most rock-oriented of Fairport's early albums, this was recorded before Denny joined the band (Judy Dyble handles the female vocals). Unjustly overlooked by listeners who consider the band's pre-Denny output insignificant, this is a fine folk-rock effort that takes far more inspiration from West Coast '60s sounds than traditional British folk. Good originals and excellent covers of a variety of obscure tunes by Joni Mitchell, Dylan, Emmitt Rhodes, and Jim & Jean. —*Richie Unterberger*

○ **What We Did on Our Holidays** / Jan. 1969 / Hannibal ✦✦✦✦
Sandy Denny's haunting, ethereal vocals give Fairport a big boost on her debut with the group. A more folk-based album than their initial effort, divided between original material and a few well-chosen covers. This contains several of their greatest moments: Sandy Denny's "Fotheringay," Richard Thompson's "Meet on the Ledge," the obscure Joni Mitchell composition "Eastern Rain," the traditional "She Moves Through the Fair," and their version of Dylan's "I'll Keep It with Mine." —*Richie Unterberger*

★ **Unhalfbricking** / Jul. 1969 / Hannibal ✦✦✦✦✦
Richard Thompson and Sandy Denny at their Fairport peak; three Dylan tunes, including the hit "Si Tu Dois Partir," and Denny's "Who Knows Where the Time Goes." This is worth owning just for the apocalyptic "A Sailor's Life." —*William Ruhlmann & Bruce Eder*

☆ **Liege and Lief** / Dec. 1969 / A&M ✦✦✦✦✦
This was Sandy Denny's exit album, highlighted by the scintillating "Tam Lin" and "Matty Groves." Voted the Best Folk Album of All Time by the readers of Britain's *Folk Roots* magazine, it features Thompson and Denny along with fiddler Dave Swarbrick. —*Stephen Winick & Bruce Eder & William Ruhlmann*

Full House / Jul. 1970 / Hannibal ✦✦✦
Denny and bass player Ashley Hutchings are gone. Thompson and Swarbrick take over as singers, while Dave Pegg (now also of Jethro Tull) plays bass. —*Stephen Winick*

Angel Delight / Jun. 1971 / A&M ✦✦✦
After Richard Thompson's departure, Fairport continued as a guitar-fiddle-bass-drums quartet, its dominant presence being violinist/singer Dave Swarbrick, who led the group in even more of a traditional British folk vein. But the loss of Fairport's big guns, Sandy Denny and Thompson, was felt, and this was a minor, if pleasant, effort. —*William Ruhlmann*

Babbacombe Lee / Nov. 1971 / A&M ✦✦✦
This concept album relates the story of John "Babbacombe" Lee, the man they could not hang. —*Stephen Winick*

Rosie / Mar. 1973 / A&M ✦✦✦
Simon Nicol, the last original member of Fairport, had departed by the time of this, the group's eighth album, replaced by two guitarists, Jerry Donahue and Trevor Lucas. The reconstituted band made a renewed effort at writing new material, the best of which was Dave Swarbrick's title tune (which featured ex-Fairporters Sandy Denny and Richard Thompson, and Thompson's future wife Linda Peters, as guests). —*William Ruhlmann*

Nine / Oct. 1973 / A&M ✦✦
The second album by the Mattacks/Pegg/Swarbrick/Donahue/Lucas lineup finds the last two asserting themselves more and moving Fairport Convention toward more of a conventional pop sound. But nothing here is particularly memorable. —*William Ruhlmann*

A Fairport Live Convention / Jul. 1974 / Island ✦✦✦
Fairport's first live album marked the return of Sandy Denny, and it's a fine collection that features some of the group's better known songs, including "Matty Groves" and "Sloth," and that displays their stylistic breadth. Scots-Irish roots are demonstrated in Dave Swarbrick's feature instrumental, "Fiddlestix," and he also gets to sing his recent song "Rosie." The band's earliest phase, as a group that covered American folk and rock & roll, is recalled with Bob Dylan's "Down in the Flood" and Chris Kenner's "Something You Got." And Denny's solo abilities are presented on "John the Gun." The big departure in the group's quality, of course, is Denny's reappearance. —*William Ruhlmann*

Rising for the Moon / Jun. 1975 / Island ✦✦✦
Fairport turned to rock producer Glyn Johns for a more contemporary sound on its tenth studio album. The band continued to suffer personnel changes, with Dave Mattacks leaving before the album was complete and being replaced by Bruce Rowland. On

her first studio album with Fairport since *Liege and Lief* six years before, Sandy Denny dominates the proceedings, writing or co-writing six of the 11 tracks, including the title track and the haunting "What Is True." With typical Fairport luck, however, this was Denny's last album with the group. — *William Ruhlmann*

● **Fairport Chronicles** / 1976 / A&M ✦✦✦✦
A well-chosen early best-of collection. — *William Ruhlmann*

Gottle O'Geer / May 1976 / Island ✦✦
Fairport Convention split in half in December 1975, with Sandy Denny, Trevor Lucas, and Jerry Donahue leaving; the remaining trio of Dave Swarbrick, Dave Pegg, and Bruce Rowland then made this contractual obligation album, which was credited to "Fairport Featuring Dave Swarbrick." As you might expect, it's fairly listless. — *William Ruhlmann*

Live at L. A. Troubadour / 1977 / Island ✦✦✦
With Fairport off the label, Island Records reached back and re-leased this live recording from 1970, featuring the last Richard Thompson lineup of the band. It was a forceful album, but it has since been superseded by *House Full*, a revised version of the same material. — *William Ruhlmann*

Bonny Bunch of Roses / Feb. 1977 / Vertigo ✦✦

Tipplers Tales / May 1978 / Vertigo ✦✦✦
Some of Fairport's finest traditional song performances are here, from yet another lineup. Singer/guitarist Simon Nicol, the only original Fairporter left, begins to take a more active role. — *Stephen Winick*

Farewell, Farewell / 1979 / Simon's ✦✦✦
This fine live album documents their farewell tour. — *Stephen Winick*

Moat on the Ledge / 1982 / Stony Plain ✦✦✦
Fairport Convention officially disbanded in 1979, only to become the hosts of a yearly folk festival/reunion concert every August in England. This album is taken from the 1981 show. It features original Fairport members Simon Nicol, Judy Dyble, and Richard Thompson, plus later members Dave Swarbrick, Dave Pegg, Dave Mattacks, and Bruce Rowland, and it's a good recapitulation of the band's style, with such numbers new to the repertoire as Bob Dylan's "Country Pie" and Thompson's "Woman or a Man." — *William Ruhlmann*

Glady's Leap / 1985 / Varrick ✦✦✦
After six years, Fairport re-formed and released this fine record featuring mostly newly composed material. — *Stephen Winick*

Expletive Delighted! / 1986 / Varrick ✦✦✦
The success of *Glady's Leap* led Simon Nicol, Dave Mattacks, and Dave Pegg to decide to re-establish Fairport Convention as a permanent recording and touring entity. So, they recruited multi-instrumentalist Martin Allcock and violinist Ric Saunders and recorded this album, the first Fairport record to consist entirely of instrumentals. It was a good way to introduce what might be called "Fairport Convention: The Next Generation" in the most traditional of the band's styles. — *William Ruhlmann*

House Full / 1986 / Hannibal ✦✦✦
A revised version of the 1977 album *Live at the L.A. Troubadour*, which, in turn, is taken from a concert performance by the Richard Thompson-led 1970 lineup of Fairport, one of its strongest units. Long versions of "Sloth" and "Matty Groves" dominate. — *William Ruhlmann*

○ **Heyday** / 1987 / Hannibal ✦✦✦✦
This collection of 14 BBC performances from 1968 and 1969 is just as outstanding as their late-'60s studio albums, and shows their mastery of an astonishing range of material. Most of these songs were not recorded on the group's official releases, and include covers of gems by Joni Mitchell, Eric Anderson, Johnny Cash, Leonard Cohen, Gene Clark, Richard Farina, the Everlys, and Bob Dylan. — *Richie Unterberger*

In Real Time: Live '87 / 1987 / Island ✦✦
All that's right and wrong with the surviving band. An electric and eclectic live album that's over-loud and over-done. — *Bruce Eder*

Red & Gold / 1989 / Rough Trade ✦✦

Five Seasons / Dec. 1990 / Rough Trade ✦✦✦
Fairport Convention's 17th studio album in 22 years finds them a competent, craftsmanlike unit led by Simon Nicol, who has developed into a strong singer. If they never aspire to the heights achieved with more impressive lineups, they nevertheless continue to find traditional and new material that suits them, sometimes by turning to newest members Ric Saunders and Martin Allcock, who are accomplished instrumentalists. — *William Ruhlmann*

Jewel in the Crown / 1995 / Green Linnet ✦✦✦
On their first album in five years, Fairport Convention, which now boasts a steady lineup (nearly a decade together!) for the first time in its history, carries on two traditions. The shorter-term one is the tradition of Fairport itself, a band intended to blend contemporary rock with folk, often in the form of work by current singer/songwriters, here including Clive Gregson and Leonard Cohen. The longer term one is the tradition of Scots-Irish music, with its jigs and reels and story songs that date back to the Middle Ages. Sometimes, the band combines the two traditions, recording songs like Steve Tilston's "The Naked Highwayman" and Ralph McTell and band member Maartin Allcock's "The Islands," which update traditional themes in interesting ways. (Allcock, by the way, has added an extra "A" to his first name since we last heard from him.) Simon Nicol, the only original member of Fairport Convention dating back to 1967, has developed into a sturdy baritone singer, and multi-instrumentalist Allcock carries the bulk of the musical burden. *Jewel in the Crown* is a well-balanced collection of songs that is true to the spirit of Fairport Convention and its antecedents. — *William Ruhlmann*

Andy Fairweather Low

b. Aug. 2, 1948
Pop/Rock
The seven million people who bought Eric Clapton's *Unplugged* album and the countless more who saw the MTV "Unplugged" TV show experienced the work of Andy Fairweather-Low, who served as Clapton's backup guitarist/vocalist. But probably few in that giant audience knew that Fairweather-Low had once been a teen idol and had an extensive recorded catalog in groups and as a solo star. Born in Cardiff, Wales, Fairweather-Low formed the Amen Corner in the mid-'60s, for which he served as lead singer. The group scored six U.K. hits from 1967 to 1969, the biggest of which was the #1 "(If Paradise Is) Half as Nice." Its success put Fairweather-Low's attractive face on the bedroom walls of teenage girls all over Britain. The Amen Corner broke up at the end of the '60s and evolved into the more progressive Fairweather, which scored a hit with "Natural Sinner" in 1970, but broke up in 1971. Fairweather-Low retired for several years, but returned as a solo artist in 1974 and made a series of albums through 1980, reaching the U.K. Top Ten with the singles "Reggae Tune" and "Wide Eyed and Legless." Gradually, however, he began to work as a sideman to more prominent British musicians, notably ex-Pink Floyd leader Roger Waters, and with the ARMS benefit group in 1987. He toured Japan with George Harrison and Eric Clapton in 1991 and has since been part of Clapton's backup band. — *William Ruhlmann*

Beginning from an End (Fairweather) / 1971 / Neon ✦✦

Spider Jiving / 1974 / A&M ✦✦✦
Fairweather Low has an appealing, gruff voice, and his songs show a talent for mixing unlikely elements—R&B and folk, for example, on the title tune, plus a real gospel fervor in "Drowning on Dry Land" and a schmaltzy ballad approach in "Dancing in the Dark." His true colors are revealed on "Keep on Rocking," but the album's U.K. hit is the aptly named "Reggae Tune." — *William Ruhlmann*

● **La Booga Rooga** / 1975 / A&M ✦✦✦✦
Fairweather Low's most successful record, this continues his eclectic approach, starting off with the steel-guitar-drenched cover "My Bucket's Got a Hole in It" and also featuring the cocktail lounge pop of "Champagne Melody" and the funky title track (a U.K. hit for the Surprise Sisters), plus his biggest solo single, the whimsical "Wide Eyed And Legless." — *William Ruhlmann*

Be Bop & Holla / 1976 / A&M ✦✦
Fairweather Low adds a tropical lilt to his repertoire with the lead-off track, "Shimmie-Doo-Wah-Sae," a song title that, along with the title tune, "Da Doo Rendezvous," and "Rhythm 'N' Jazz," demonstrates his affection for onomatopoeia and different musical genres. "Da Doo Rendezvous," with its strings and wistful tone, is the obvious followup to "Wide Eyed And Legless," but the problem is that it didn't follow up. Nor did this album fulfill the commercial promise of *La Booga Rooga*, which turned Fairweather Low, in record company eyes, from a breaking artist into dead meat. (Still,

you had to admire a sense of humor that allowed him to produce "Hot Poop," a song whose lyrics consisted entirely of its chord changes.) — *William Ruhlmann*

Andy Fairweather Low / 1976 / RCA ♦♦
Mega Shebang / 1980 / Warner Brothers ♦♦

Fairweather Low's last shot at solo stardom came with this outing for Warner Brothers, on which, producing himself, he took much the same approach he had in his '70s albums, mixing styles freely and putting them in his titles: "Night Time Djuke-ing," "Hard Hat Boogie," "3 Step Shuffle," etc. The beat was a bit more pronounced, and the tempos a bit more frantic, but this was a typical album on the whole for the artist, and the response was typical, too. No one bought it, and, after getting one last chance at success with the Local Boys in 1983, Fairweather Low paid the rent playing second-banana to more successful British rockers like Roger Waters and Eric Clapton. — *William Ruhlmann*

Faith No More

Group, Alternative Pop/Rock, Heavy Metal
With their fusion of heavy metal, funk, hip-hop, and progressive rock, Faith No More has earned a substantial cult following. By the time they recorded their first album in 1985, the band had already had a string of lead vocalists, including Courtney Love; their debut, *We Care a Lot*, featured Chuck Mosley's abrasive vocals but it was driven by Jim Martin's metallic guitar. Faith No More's next album, 1987's *Introduce Yourself*, was a more cohesive and impressive effort; for the first time, the rap and metal elements didn't sound like they were fighting each other.

In 1988, the rest of the band fired Mosley; he was replaced by Bay Area vocalist Mike Patton during the recording of their next album, *The Real Thing*. Patton was a more accomplished vocalist, able to change effortlessly between rapping and singing, as well as adding a considerably more bizarre slant to the lyrics. Besides adding a new vocalist, the band had tightened their attack and the result was the genre-bending hit single, "Epic," which established them as a major hard rock act.

Following up the hit wasn't as easy, however. Faith No More followed their breakthrough success with 1992's *Angel Dust*, one of the more complex and simply confounding records ever released by a major label. Although it sold respectably, it didn't have the crossover potential of the first album. When the band toured in support of the album, tensions between the band and Martin began to escalate; rumors that his guitar was stripped from some of the final mixes of *Angel Dust* began to circulate. As the band was recording its fifth album in early 1994, it was confirmed that Martin had been fired from the band.

Faith No More recorded *King for a Day, Fool for a Lifetime* with Mr. Bungle guitarist Trey Spruance. During tour preparations he was replaced by Dean Mentia. — *Stephen Thomas Erlewine*

We Care a Lot / 1985 / Mordam ♦♦
Introduce Yourself / 1987 / Slash ♦♦♦
● **The Real Thing** / 1989 / Slash ♦♦♦♦

An unusual combination of heavy metal, rap, and hard rock, appealing to head bangers and popsters alike. — *Donna DiChario*

○ **Angel Dust** / 1992 / Slash ♦♦♦♦

It's quite diverse and eclectic, with its range of styles going from lounge jazz to power-pop and all-out industrial grindcore. The songwriting shows a lot of talent, especially from Mike Patton, whose vocal range is used to its full potential on this album, the band's fourth. — *John Book*

King for a Day/Fool for a Lifetime / 1995 / Slash ♦♦

Faith No More's first album since the departure of guitarist Jim Martin is surprisingly direct and metallic, even lacking the keyboard flourishes that invigorated *Angel Dust* and *The Real Thing*. The sporadic ventures into '70s soul, skewed funk and vaguely experimental pop are present, yet they seem like they were dusted off for the occasion, repeating everything they said before. Without successful diversions, Faith No More is a standard metal band. They're competent, to be sure, yet they offer nothing out of the ordinary, except that odd song about enemas. — *Stephen Thomas Erlewine*

Marianne Faithfull

b. Dec. 29, 1946, London, England
Pop/Rock
Few stars of the 1960s have reinvented themselves as successfully as Marianne Faithfull. Coaxed into a singing career by Rolling Stones manager Andrew Loog Oldham in 1964, she had a big hit in both Britain and the U.S. with her debut single, the Jagger/Richards composition "As Tears Go By" (which prefaced the Stones' own version by a full year). Considerably more successful in her native land than the States, she had a series of hits in the mid-'60s that set her high, fragile voice against delicate orchestral pop arrangements—"Summer Night," "This Little Bird," Jackie De Shannon's "Come and Stay with Me." Not a songwriter at the outset of her career, she owes more of her fame as a '60s icon to her extraordinary beauty and her long-running romance with Mick Jagger, although she offered a taste of things to come with her compelling 1969 single "Sister Morphine," which she co-wrote (and which the Stones released themselves on *Sticky Fingers* later). In the 1970s, Faithfull split up with Jagger, developed a serious drug habit, and recorded rarely, with generally dismal results. Until late 1979, when she pulled off an astonishing comeback with *Broken English*. Displaying a croaking, cutting voice that had lowered a good octave since the mid-'60s, Faithfull had also begun to write much of her own material, and addressed sex and despair with wrenching realism. After allowing herself to be framed as a demure chanteuse by songwriters and arrangers throughout most of her career, Marianne had found her own voice, and suddenly sounded more relevant and contemporary than most of the stars she had rubbed shoulders with in the '60s. Faithfull's recordings in the 1980s and 1990s have been sporadic and erratic, but generally quite interesting; "Strange Weather," a Hal Willner-produced 1987 collection of standards and contemporary compositions that spanned several decades for its sources, was her greatest triumph of the decade. In 1994, she published her self-titled autobiography; the recent biography *As Tears Go By*, by Mark Hodkinson, is a more objective and thorough account of her life and times. One continues to look forward to unexpected twists on forthcoming recordings—a statement one can apply to few other performers who emerged during the 1960s. — *Richie Unterberger*

Marianne Faithfull / May 1965 / London ♦♦♦

Her erratic, self-titled debut features lovely baroque arrangements by Mike Leander and decent tunes like "As Tears Go By," Jackie DeShannon's "Come and Stay with Me" and "In My Time of Sorrow," and Bacharach-David's "If I Never Get to Love You," as well as fairly crummy covers of hits by the Beatles, Herman's Hermits, and Petula Clark. Look for the Japanese CD reissue: it adds six non-LP bonus tracks from mid-'60s singles, including a couple (the girl-groupish "The Sha La La Song," the melancholy "The Morning Sun") that rank among her best '60s recordings. — *Richie Unterberger*

Dreaming My Dreams / Jan. 1977 / Nems ♦♦♦

Marianne Faithfull's first new album in a decade revealed the weathered voice she later would put to good, if harrowing, use in a series of albums for Island Records starting with *Broken English* in 1979. Here, that voice was smoothed out and used for pop and country material including such songs as "I'll Be Your Baby Tonight," "I'm Not Lisa," and "It Wasn't God Who Made Honky Tonk Angels." Faithfull had loosened up considerably since the chaste schoolgirl days of "As Tears Go By," and *Dreaming My Dreams* suggested that her hard life could be analogous to that of a country music star. Faithfull didn't have the accent to match that assertion, but she did have the attitude. (Rereleased in slightly altered form as *Faithless* in March 1978.) — *William Ruhlmann*

Faithless / Mar. 1978 / Sony ♦♦♦

Marianne Faithfull's first new album in a decade revealed the weathered voice she later would put to good, if harrowing, use in a series of albums for Island Records starting with *Broken English* in 1979. Here, that voice was smoothed out and used for pop and country material including such songs as "I'll Be Your Baby Tonight," "I'm Not Lisa," and "It Wasn't God Who Made Honky Tonk Angels." Faithfull had loosened up considerably since the chaste schoolgirl days of "As Tears Go By," and *Faithless* suggested that her hard life could be analogous to that of a country music star. Faithfull didn't have the accent to match that assertion, but she did have the attitude. (Faithless was a slightly altered version of the January 1977 album *Dreaming My Dreams*. It was reissued on CD in 1991 with four bonus tracks.) —*William Ruhlmann*

● **Broken English** / Nov. 1979 / Island ◆◆◆

After a lengthy absence, Faithfull resurfaced on this 1979 album, which took the edgy and brittle sound of punk rock and gave it a shot of studio-smooth dance rock. Faithfull's whiskey-worn vocals perfectly match the bitter and biting "Why'd Ya Do It" and revitalize John Lennon's "Working Class Hero." —*John Floyd*

A Childs Adventure / Mar. 1983 / Island ◆◆

Faithfull pegged her comeback to a brutal survivalist persona, but by this fourth album of her second career, she had mellowed at least to the extent of constructing flowing song structures with her collaborators, Barry Reynolds and Wally Badarou, that eased the bitterness still found in many of her lyrics. *A Child's Adventure* is thus more listenable, but less compelling, than her other albums of the period. —*William Ruhlmann*

○ **Marianne Faithfull's Greatest Hits** / 1987 / ABKCO ◆◆◆

While missing a few fine album tracks, this is an excellent 16-song distillation of her '60s recordings. Includes all of her British and American hits—"As Tears Go By," "This Little Bird," "Summer Nights," and "Come and Stay with Me." Bonuses include "In My Time of Sorrow," an obscure mid-'60s folk-rocker co-written by Jackie DeShannon and Jimmy Page, and her 1969 single "Sister Morphine" (co-written with the Rolling Stones), predating the *Sticky Fingers* version; it's easily her most powerful performance of the decade. —*Richie Unterberger*

○ **Strange Weather** / Jul. 1987 / Island ◆◆◆◆

Faithfull's 1987 release recast her as a nicotine-stained chanteuse, approaching such standards as "Boulevard of Broken Dreams" and "Penthouse Serenade" with a ravaged, world-weary demeanor that recalls the latter-day recordings of Billie Holiday. She also tackles some blues and jazz material and turns "As Tears Go By" into the gut-wrenching torch ballad neither the Stones nor Faithfull could ever have done in the '60s. A dark, challenging masterpiece. —*John Floyd*

Blazing Away / Mar. 1990 / Island ◆◆◆

This live disc was recorded at the Brooklyn St. Anne's Cathedral. With a song list that stretches back to her '60s singles, this is something of a career overview. But the wisdom and maturity she applies to the material—both old and new—make this a document that attests to Faithfull's continued vitality and brave artistic commitment. —*John Floyd*

A Faithfull: A Collection of Her Best Recordings / Aug. 23, 1994 / Island ◆◆◆

This best-of basically covers the years 1979 to 1994, though it reaches back to 1964 for Marianne Faithfull's first recording and first hit, "As Tears Go By," and includes "She," slated for the upcoming 1995 album *A Secret Life*. Five of the 11 songs are drawn from Faithfull's strongest album, 1979's *Broken English*, including the bitter title track and "Why D'Ya Do It." Otherwise, compiler Chris Blackwell makes little attempt to present a balance among Faithfull's recordings—there is nothing at all from *Dangerous Acquaintances* or *A Child's Adventure*, and only one track each from *Strange Weather* and *Blazing Away*. But there is a good newly recorded cover of Patti Smith's "Ghost Dance" co-produced by Keith Richards and featuring other members of the Rolling Stones, and Blackwell rescues Faithfull's rendition of the title theme for the movie *Trouble in Mind* from the soundtrack album. It adds up to an excellent compilation that highlights Faithfull's strengths as a singer. —*William Ruhlmann*

Secret Life / Mar. 21, 1995 / Island ◆◆◆

For her first studio album comprised of mostly original material in over a decade, Faithfull enlisted noted composer Angelo Badalamenti (who collaborated with David Lynch for the *Twin Peaks* TV soundtrack) to write music for her lyrics and produce. Faithfull is still in rippingly fine voice, and her words still penetrate. But while Badalamenti's densely orchestral arrangements can be effectively noirish, they can also create an inappropriately cold and detached ambience, despite standout tracks like "Flaming September" and "She." —*Richie Unterberger*

BOOKS

◆◆◆ **Marianne Faithfull**, by Mark Hodkinson (Omnibus Press,

1991). Faithfull's recent autobiography was a saucily-related tale that dwelled mostly upon her experiences in the 1960s. This biography is a less saucy, more objective, and more thorough treatment, paying as much attention to her 1970s and 1980s recordings and experiences as her early life and career. It's well done, but perhaps a bit thin in source material. Although many still associate her primarily with her brief '60s pop success, Faithfull really didn't bloom as an artist until the late '70s, and the description of her early recordings and acting career can be of only marginal and slight interest, as seriously as Hodkinson approaches it. There's a lot about her days as a swinging '60s icon, and her junkie period in the '70s (and '80s, for that matter), all responsibly related and researched, but somehow not as compelling as one might expect from all the wild rumors and stories that have circulated around this charismatic figure. —*Richie Unterberger*

◆◆◆ **Faithfull**, by Marianne Faithfull & David Dalton (Little, Brown & Co., 1994). Faithfull's memoir devotes the greatest space to her days as a '60s icon, both as a pop singer in the middle of the decade and as Mick Jagger's girlfriend for several years afterwards. Faithfull speaks with a fair amount of candor about her colorful behavior, which found her intersecting with many of the day's leading musicians and artists, and descending into drug abuse by the 1970s. She's neither overly boastful nor apologetic about her checkered past, assigning herself a share fair of blame for her hard times, though the reader may start to get frustrated at her habitual cycles of drug dependency and bad relationships. Unlike most tales of this sort, though, the music side of things actually starts to get more interesting in the later part of the book, where she discusses her resurrection with the *Broken English* album of the late '70s and several other interesting projects in the '80s and '90s. For those who want the gossip, it contains many stories about Bob Dylan, Allen Ginsberg, Keith Richards, Andrew Loog Oldham, Chris Blackwell, and, of course, Mick Jagger. —*Richie Unterberger*

The Falcons

Group, Soul

Often credited as having cut the first true soul record in 1959 with "You're So Fine," a host of 60s soul stars called themselves Falcons at one time or another, including founder Eddie Floyd, Wilson Pickett, Sir Mack Rice, and 100 Proof Aged in Soul's Joe Stubbs. Originally an integrated R&B group headed by Floyd, the Falcons debuted on Mercury in 1955. Under the production aegis of Robert West, the Falcons' sound became more gospel-based as time passed, and with Stubbs as lead, the seminal "You're So Fine" was a major hit in 1959. Pickett screamed the gospel-fired ballad "I Found a Love" to national prominence on West's LuPine label in 1962, backed by guitarist Robert Ward's Ohio Untouchables. When Pickett went solo shortly thereafter, the members went their separate ways. West recruited another group, the Fabulous Playboys, who took over the Falcons name, but with little success. —*Bill Dahl*

● **I Found a Love** / 1986 / Relic ◆◆◆◆

A more incendiary collection, thanks to the addition of Wilson Pickett as the Falcons' front man. —*Bill Dahl*

○ **You're So Fine** / 1986 / Relic ◆◆◆◆

Prototypical early Detroit soul from this rough-edged vocal group that featured Eddie Floyd and Joe Stubbs. —*Bill Dahl*

Fall

Group, Punk, Alternative Pop/Rock

While the band's audience has never been expanded beyond a rabidly devoted cult following across the world, the Fall has had a significant impact on the post-punk music of the '70s, '80s, and '90s. Many fans of the group have gone on to form their own band, leaving the rock underground with a wealth of bands replicating and expanding the Fall's harsh, jagged guitar experimentalism.

Under the leadership of guitarist/vocalist Mark E. Smith, the band has released an enormous amount of albums since their debut in 1977. Every album is a complex, challenging piece of rock & roll yet none of them sounds the same; with each album, the Fall explores new territory, from guitar noise to club music. Through every incarnation, Smith has retained his reputation as one of rock's foremost experimental artists. —*Stephen Thomas Erlewine*

○ **Live at the Witch Trials** / 1979 / A&M ✦✦✦✦
○ **Dragon** / 1979 / Step Forward ✦✦✦✦
Totale's Turns (It's Now or Never) / 1980 / Rough Trade ✦✦✦
Grotesque / 1980 / Rough Trade ✦✦✦
○ **Slates** / 1981 / Rough Trade ✦✦✦✦
Early Years 77-79 / 1981 / Step Forward ✦✦✦
Hex Enduction Hour / 1982 / Kamera ✦✦✦
Room to Live / 1982 / Line ✦✦✦
Live in London, 1980 / 1982 / Chaos
A Part of America Therein, 1981 / 1982 / Cottage
○ **Perverted by Language** / 1983 / Rough Trade ✦✦✦✦
With the most prodigious catalog of all the late-'70s punk rock bands, the Fall's recorded output can be, for sanity's sake, broken down into three periods covering roughly 20 years. Early Fall (1977-1983) contains their harshest and most extreme music. Truthfully, only hardcore Fall fans will detect the differences among albums of any period, but with a catalog this large, collecting significant recordings of each era will help (and hopefully encourage) adventuresome neophytes to plunge headfirst into the dazzling, unpredictable world of the Fall. This is, to be sure, not every Fall album available; it is rather a subjective sampling. Perhaps of the early material, the best place to start is *Live at the Witch Trials*. Under the guidance of producer Bob Sargeant, this harnesses the essence of the Fall's early sound: jagged, colliding guitars, stiff, repetitive percussion, and Mark E. Smith's nasal, singsong ranting. It's dissonant, but not so harsh as to be totally unapproachable. In fact, Sargeant (who later went on to produce records by far poppier bands like the English Beat) accents the rhythmic bottom, so that even when the music lurches like a drunken Frankenstein's monster, it does swing enough to be captivating. Of course, this is assuming that Smith's vocals haven't prevented you from enjoying this (and really, they shouldn't). Tunes like "Rebellious Jukebox" and "Music Scene" will win you over with their caustic appeal. Both *Grotesque* and *Early Years 77-79* are more extreme. Extreme in the sense that traditional song form is almost totally dispensed with for a din of cacophony built around thuddingly simple guitar riffs. It's not totally alienating, but it's not where potential Fall fans (unless you have a jones for barely structured rock noise) should start. Oddly, despite both records being anti-rock to the point of almost being anti-music, there are some great songs that emerge through the trebly crashing and bashing ("Rowche Rumble," "Pay Your Rates," "Bingo Masters Breakout," and "New Face on Hell") Closing the early Fall period is *Perverted by Language*, which also starts the (what I call) "Brix Period." It was during this time that Smith married American guitarist Brix (birth surname unknown to this writer) who brought a stronger pop sense to the band. Suddenly, Fall albums, although still essentially abrasive, were more tuneful, and loaded with fuzztone garage-raunch guitar playing. Brix's first effort as a full-time Fall member is a winner, with tracks like "I Feel Voxish" and the parody of the excessively health-conscious "Eat Y'self Fitter" pushing the Fall into a new terrain that would bring them (surprise!) chart success in England. —*John Dougan*

Fall in a Hole / 1983 / Flying Nun
○ **The Wonderful and Frightening World Of.** / 1984 / Beggars Banquet ✦✦✦✦
Hip Priests & Kamerads / 1985 / Situation 2 ✦✦✦
○ **This Nation's Saving Grace** / 1985 / Beggars Banquet ✦✦✦✦
Driven by an unrelenting, tense performance by the band and filled with fractured melodies and elliptical guitar hooks, *This Nation's Saving Grace* is the Fall's masterpiece. —*Stephen Thomas Erlewine*

○ **Bend Sinister** / 1986 / Beggars Banquet ✦✦✦✦
○ **Palace of Sword's Reversed** / 1987 / Rough Trade ✦✦✦✦
○ **Domesday Pay-Off (Triad Plus)** / 1987 / Big Time ✦✦✦✦
Frenz Experiment / 1988 / Beggars Banquet ✦✦
I Am Curious Oranj / 1988 / Beggars Banquet ✦✦✦
The high point of the "Brix Period" may well have been the release of *Wonderful and Frightening World of the Fall*. Where before the music was tense, jumpy and anarchic, here it was focused, harder-hitting, and rocked more. To some, it signaled the end of the Fall, but that was an unfair assessment. Granted, the music changed slightly, but it didn't diminish the band's potency. And, for

all the time that Mark Smith had dominated the band, it was becoming clear that Brix's talents as a writer and musician were formidable and deservedly taking some of the spotlight. The records from *Wonderful* to roughly the end of the decade are solid, at times excellent forays into increasingly commercial rock. *This Nation's Saving Grace* could almost qualify as a dance record if it were a little smoother, but the songs are catchy, and for the Fall, almost upbeat. As far as solid groove goes, this is their toughest, funkiest record. Both *The Frenz Experiment* and *I Am Kurious Oranj* sound as if they were recorded on the same day, although the latter was a score commissioned for an experimental ballet. *Frenz* has a great cover of the Kinks' "Victoria," as well as production values never before heard on Fall records (high quality). *Oranj* isn't as completely satisfying, but was (so I am told) much better than the ballet. The anomalous release during this period was *A Palace of Swords Reversed*, which is a collection of non-LP tracks and assorted odds and sods from 1980-83. Despite its patchwork arrangement, it's a remarkably cohesive document and one of the Fall's best efforts. There was also a live recording made during this period (*Seminal Live*), but it's thoroughly mediocre and not worth the bother. —*John Dougan*

Seminal Live / 1989 / Beggars Banquet ✦✦
○ **458489 B Sides** / 1990 / Beggars Banquet ✦✦✦✦
★ **458489 A Sides** / 1990 / Beggars Banquet ✦✦✦✦✦
The Fall's singles collection covers their material between 1984 and 1989 and features some of their finest, most innovative work. —*Stephen Thomas Erlewine*

○ **Extricate** / 1990 / Fontana ✦✦✦✦
Peel Sessions / 1991 / Peerless ✦✦✦
Shiftwork / 1991 / Fontana
Code: Selfish / 1991 / Fontana ✦✦✦
○ **Kimble [Peel Sessions]** / 1993 / Dutch East India ✦✦✦✦
The Infotainment Scam / May 18, 1993 / Matador
15 Ways / 1994 / Matador
Middle Class Revolt / 1994 / Matador ✦✦✦
This is the late Fall period also known (by me anyway) as the "post-Brix" years. The Smiths had divorced around the time of *Extricate*, but Brix's presence could still be felt on Fall records. Some thought the mid-'80s signaled an end to the ragged, jagged Fall of old; the '90s must have made them apoplectic. Working with producers Rex Sergeant, Craig Leon, and Adrian Sherwood, the post-apocalyptic sound of the '70s had been smoothed to a sheen. There were still moments of anarchy and dissonance, but generally they were swaddled in synth-driven beats and high-tech production that smoothed out any remaining rough edges. Again, this was not a bad thing; after all Mark Smith was still upfront and still ranting, but even he was singing more, and shocking as that was, it made for even better music. Although *Shiftwork* and *Code: Selfish* are very good, they are almost indistinguishable from one another and the sameness works against them. That being said, let me contradict myself and suggest you buy *Code: Selfish*, which is notable for "Birmingham School of Business School" and a cover of Hank Williams' "Just Waiting." For this period, the place to start is *Extricate*, which proved beyond a doubt that the Fall were not too old to still be a part of this punk rock thang. Since this record follows on the heels of the Smiths' divorce, it's tempting to assume that Mark Smith's ranting has a more conspicuous target, but enigmatic as he tends to be, this is mere speculation. Still, "Sing! Harpy" and the title track will give you pause as to the source of Smith's considerable consternation. The band sounds great, especially longtime members Stephen Hanley and Craig Scanlon. Extra kudos to the solid backbeat provided by Simon Wolstencroft. During this time, Fall recordings were less likely to automatically be released in America. Still, hip American indie label Matador decided that these seminal punksters deserved better, and their last two records were made available in America (on vinyl no less!). *Infotainment Scam* is the better of the two, if only because *Middle Class Revolt* sounds carelessly conceived, but the sound that has defined the Fall in the '90s remains intact. In fact, *Infotainment Scam* was followed by the Fall's biggest American tour in some time, but it did little to stimulate interest and sales. A great collection of singles was also released during this time; *458489 A-Sides* is essential Fall—lean, mean and nasty. —*John Dougan*

Cerebral Caustic / 1995 / Permanent ✦✦

Georgie Fame

British Invasion, Pop/Rock
With his jazzy renditions of R&B and ska, English organist/vocalist Georgie Fame earned quite a following the early '60s before he and his band, the Blue Flames, had a number one single in the U.K. with the jazz-tinged pop of "Yeh Yeh." Fame had other similar hits in the U.K., but soon started to record straight jazz records as well as pop; he would continue this pattern throughout the '70s. During the '80s and '90s, he toured as Van Morrison's keyboardist, releasing the occasional album to favorable reviews. —*Stephen Thomas Erlewine*

R & B at the Flamingo / 1963 / RSO ♦♦♦
Recorded live at a London club in 1963, this is a bit stiffer than Fame's mid-'60s peak, but finds him gravitating towards his idiosyncratic blend of R&B and jazz. This R&B-oriented set includes covers of classics by Mose Allison, Smokey Robinson, Sonny Boy Williamson, and Rufus Thomas. —*Richie Unterberger*

● **20 Beat Classics** / 1982 / RSO ♦♦♦♦
The best compilation of Fame's work, finding his R&B-jazz fusion at its most potent (and most commercially successful) on these 20 cuts from the mid-'60s. Like a Mose Allison for the British Invasion, Fame sings and plays with a soulful verve on this set of blue-eyed soul. Includes the #1 British hits "Yeh Yeh" and "Get Away," although "Ballad of Bonnie and Clyde" is missing. —*Richie Unterberger*

Merrell Fankhauser

Group, Singer-Songwriter, Art-Rock/Progressive-Rock, Psychedelic
One of the most interesting cult figures in rock history, Fankauser's best work came as the leader of several interesting groups during the '60s and early '70s: the Impacts (instrumental surf), Merrell & the Exiles (solid British Invasion-style rock), Fapardokly (great Byrdsish folk-rock), the HMS Bounty (fine late '60s folk-rock), and MU (spaced-out progressive blues/psychedelia).

When MU broke up in the mid-'70s, Fankhauser began working as a solo artist, issuing a series of independent albums that continue to this day. These usually show him in a considerably mellower and more mainstream folk-rock mood than his best, earlier work, sometimes recalling Crosby, Stills & Nash, and often featuring violinist Mary Lee. —*Richie Unterberger*

● **The Maui Album** / 1988 / Reckless ♦♦♦♦
Fankhauser's first solo outing, originally titled *Merrell Fanhauser* and released in 1976, remains his best post-Mu work. Very light and serene folk-rock that owes little to trends of its era, predominantly acoustic in feel, often featuring Mary Lee on violin and harmony vocals. The 1988 reissue is enhanced by four previously unreleased Mu tracks, dating from 1974. —*Richie Unterberger*

Early Years 1964-1967 / 1994 / Legend Music ♦♦
Credited to Merrell & the Exiles, this is a selection of rarities and unreleased material by Fankhauser's mid-'60s band, essentially the one that cut the great rare psych-folk-rock album that was credited to Fapardokly. It's pretty much a collection of outtakes with a few rare non-LP singles thrown in, and as such doesn't measure up to the best of Fankhauser's '60s material. Often derivative of the British Invasion, folk-rock, and early '60s teen pop, it's not bad, just not terribly memorable, the fake British Invasion of cuts like "Send Me Your Love" ranking as the highlights. It also has his late '60s non-LP single cover of Fred Neil's "Everybody's Talkin'," although for some reason it's missing one of his mid-'60s non-LP 45s, "Can't We Get Along"/"That's All I Want from You"—it was reissued on a rarities tape that Merrell himself released, if you can find it. Future Mu and Captain Beefheart guitarist Jeff Cotton appears on most of the tracks; future Beefheart drummer John French.also appears on a few. —*Richie Unterberger*

Merrell Fankhauser & H.M.S. Bounty

Group, Singer-Songwriter, Art-Rock/Progressive-Rock, Psychedelic
After cutting some fine folk-rock and psychedelia on ultra-rare records with his group the Exiles, guitarist, singer, and songwriter Merrell Fankhauser moved to Los Angeles, retitled his backing group H.M.S. Bounty., and recorded a fine, if obscure, slice of pop-psychedelia in 1968, *Things*. The diverse offerings on the group's sole LP recalled such fellow Californian heavyweights as the Byrds, Buffalo Springfield, Moby Grape, and even Captain Beefheart. They weren't quite in the same league as those legends, but the album has a light and enigmatic air all its own, and is well

worth investigation by fans of late-'60s West Coast psychedelia. The group evolved into the interesting mystical avant-garde/blues/progressive rock group Mu in the early '70s. —*Richie Unterberger*

● **Things** / 1968 / Shamley ♦♦♦♦
Fine, tuneful '60s psychedelia with a pop edge, featuring Fankhauser's first-rate songwriting and warm vocals. About half of the tunes are excellent, especially the country-rocker "Your Painted Lives," the folk-rock ballad "Ice Cube Island," and "A Visit With Ashiya," one of the best raga-rock songs ever cut. The reissue adds a bluesy non-LP B-side, "Flying Home," that looks forward to the innovations of Mu; it also includes fine, lengthy liner notes detailing Fankhauser's fascinating and winding career. —*Richie Unterberger*

The Fantastic Deejays

Group, Garage Rock
Pittsburgh garage band whose high point was opening for a Rolling Stones concert in 1965. They might have been total unknowns in the grand scheme of things, but they actually managed to cut a few pretty nifty (mostly self-penned) singles on local labels in 1965 and 1966 that are well respected by '60s collectors. The trio featured two guitarists and a drummer—a bass-less lineup, a rarity in rock music to this day. Some of their singles were recorded at a local radio station, and indeed the crudeness of the production is fascinating, with mounds and mounds of reverb making the band sound like nothing so much as a garage punk version of Peter & Gordon. After five singles and an album, the group disbanded and evolved into the Swamp Rats, a harder-edged combo relying almost exclusively on nasty punk versions of big rock and R&B hits. —*Richie Unterberger*

● **Fight Fire** / 1984 / Eva ♦♦♦♦
A reissue of their 1966 LP, which included virtually all of their singles (a couple of the tunes were released in different 45 versions). Most of the songs are original compositions which emulate the lighter side of the Fab Four, and although they're pretty basic and a bit sloppy, they're catchy and executed with a raw sincerity that's hard to resist. At times they could rock out with a lot of grit as well, as on the title track, a cover of an obscure single by the Golliwogs (who would evolve into Creedence Clearwater Revival). Other highlights are a raw version of the Vogues' slick pop hit "You're the One" that is many times better than the original, and the absolute raunchiest version of the classic instrumental "Apache" ever laid down on wax. —*Richie Unterberger*

Fantastic Four

Group, Funk
Detroit R&B and soul group the Fantastic Four formed in 1955. "Sweet" James Epps, Robert and Joseph Pruitt, and Toby Childs were the original members. Childs and Robert Pruitt later departed, and were replaced by Cleveland Horne and Ernest Newsome. Their first single on Ric-Tic, "The Whole World Is a Stage," was their lone huge hit, peaking at number 6 on the R&B charts in 1967. The next release, "You Gave Me Something (And Everything's Alright)," reached number 12 that same year. Motown eventually purchased Ric-Tic, and they had another Top 20 R&B hit with "I Love You Madly," which came out in 1968 and was also issued on Soul. They enjoyed renewed appeal during the disco era with some singles on Westbound that were moderately successful, among them "Alvin Stone (The Birth & Death of a Gangster)" and "I Got to Have Your Love." Dennis Coffey produced "B.Y.O.F. (Bring Your Own Funk)" in 1979, but didn't have much luck with it. The Fantastic Four have remained active, and released "Working on a Building of Love" in 1990 for Britian's Motorcity label. —*Ron Wynn*

● **The Best of the Fantastic Four** / 1969 / Motown ♦♦♦♦
Includes all their Detroit recordings. —*Bill Dahl*

Fapardokly

Group, Psychedelic, Folk-Rock
An enigma in the world of '60s rock collectibles that would be barely worth explaining if the music wasn't so fine. There was never a group called Fapardokly; the twelve songs on their self-titled album were recorded by Merrell & the Exiles, a Southern California group headed by legendary cult folk-rocker Merrell Fankhauser. That group cut several singles for the tiny Glenn label, some of which are collected here, before heading off in a psy-

chedelic direction and mutating into HMS Bounty. The equally tiny UIP label decided to gather a few of the Glenn singles, add a few more psychedelically-oriented tracks that Merrill and his group had recorded, and release the package as the work of a group called Fapardokly. Although it was not recorded or intended as a unified work, it stands as one of the great lost folk-rock classics of the 1960s. Fankhauser went on to make more excellent obscure recordings with HMS Bounty in the late '60s and Mu in the early '70s. —*Richie Unterberger*

● **Fapardokly** / 1966 / Sundazed ✦✦✦✦
One of the most sought-after rock rarities of the '60s, this album was stylistically uneven, as can be expected from an LP cobbled together from recordings spanning a few years. About half, however, is sparkling psychedelic folk-rock, recalling *Fifth Dimension* Byrds with its shimmering twelve-string guitars, multipart harmonies, and occasional trippy lyrics. Although the early material is more pop-oriented and doesn't fit in as well, it's pretty solid as well, recalling the Zombies and (in the very earliest tracks) Ricky Nelson. "Lila," "Tomorrow's Girl," and "Super Market" are genuine lost '60s treasures, and much of the rest of the album isn't far behind. After a couple of European LP reissues, it was finally reissued on CD, with three bonus tracks, in 1995. —*Richie Unterberger*

Richard and Mimi Farina

Folk-Rock
Richard Farina was a noted counterculture author and folksinger in the early 1960s. Married for a time to folksinger Carolyn Hester, he was an early intimate of Bob Dylan, and in fact recorded a collectable album with Dylan (playing under the pseudonym "Blind Boy Grunt") and Ric Von Schmidt in 1963. After marrying Joan Baez's sister Mimi, he formed a folk-rock duo that released two acclaimed albums in the mid-sixties. Unlike folk-rock figureheads like the Byrds, the Farinas were far more firmly rooted in folk than rock.

Their recordings effectively flavored their material (mostly written by Richard) with jangling electric guitars and a rhythm section, ably assisted by such session players as guitarist Bruce Langhorne (who also played on Dylan's first electric recordings), bassist Felix Pappalardi, and harmonica player John Hammond. The Farinas themselves also played guitar, autoharp, and dulcimer. Least successful with blues, they recorded some effective Appalachian-flavored material, and several excellent bonafide midtempo folk-rockers and ballads. Their best songs effectively balanced worldwise, sardonic observations with good-natured, melodic optimism.

The Farinas' promising career ended prematurely with the death of Richard in a motorcycle accident on his birthday in 1966. His novel of the same year, Been Down So Long It Looks Like Up to Me, became a cult favorite. Since Richard's death, Mimi Farina has sporadically recorded and performed as a solo act. —*Richie Unterberger*

Celebrations for a Grey Day / 1965 / Vanguard ✦✦✦
The duo's debut effectively laid out their approach: Appalachian-like instrumentals that put the dulcimer to the fore alternate with strong contemporary folk compositions, which are by turns mournful and high-spirited. The world-weary "Reno Nevada" (a part of Fairport Convention's repertoire in their early days) is the duo's best song. —*Richie Unterberger*

Reflections in a Crystal Wind / 1965 / Fontana ✦✦✦
Basically a continuation of the first album with a slightly more electric feel, finding Richard developing deeper insight and a subtler touch. —*Richie Unterberger*

Memories / 1968 / Vanguard ✦✦✦
A posthumous collection of odds and ends, this actually holds considerable appeal for anyone who likes their pair of fully realized albums. The twelve songs include a few studio outtakes, a few solo turns by Mimi on compositions written by Richard but incompletely recorded at the time of his death, a couple performances from the 1965 Newport Folk Festival, and a couple of Joan Baez tracks from sessions for an aborted album Richard was producing with her. These leftovers are generally up to the standard of the two "real" albums, especially "The Quiet Joys Of Brotherhood" (covered by Fairport Convention) and "Morgan The Pirate" (a farewell to Bob Dylan, according to the sketchy liner notes). The two cuts by Baez (which Richard wrote or co-wrote), especially the compellingly melancholy "All The World Has Gone By," are excel-

lent, leading one to wonder if the projected album they came from would have been one of Baez's best if it had been completed. These may be leftovers, but it's a worthwhile collection nonetheless. —*Richie Unterberger*

● **Best of** / 1971 / Vanguard ✦✦✦✦
While a 26-song double album is not ordinarily recommended as the best introduction to such a short-lived act, the Farinas work was so consistent that it makes sense to pick up this compilation, which combines *Celebrations for a Grey Day* and *Reflections in a Crystal Wind* into one package. —*Richie Unterberger*

Chris Farlowe

b. Oct. 13, 1940, Essex, England
Soul, British Invasion
A British R&B singer of the mid '60s, Farlowe was discovered and heavily boosted by Mick Jagger, who produced his best and most successful sides. Alas, he lacked the commercial look needed for success. —*Bruce Eder*

● **The Chris Farlowe Collection** / 1991 / Sony ✦✦✦✦
Soulful Chris Farlow—The Immediate Collection is Farlowe's strongest work, featuring soulful and very powerful renditions of Mick Jagger/Keith Richards songs, spiced with other covers. —*Bill Dahl*

Mylene Farmer

Art-Rock/Progressive-Rock
Since 1985, Mylene Farmer (born in Quebec, but raised in France) and her musical collaborator Laurent Boutonnat have expanded the Birkin-Gainsbourg bedroom fantasy song into an entire cosmology of sighing songs pensive and melancholy and fitfully melodic dances in which *fin de siecle libertinism* is the motive principle and intoxicated hallucination the saving grace. It's popular throughout Euro-land and not unknown even in the US. —*Michael Freedberg*

Cendres De Lune / Polydor ✦✦

○ **Ainsi Soit Je . . .** / 1988 / ✦✦✦✦
Ambitiously stylish, this thick mix of powerful dance rhythms and sensual melodies is both accessible and subtle. Sometimes uneven in its overall composition, it offers superb sound quality of the mature artist. —*Vladimir Bogdanov*

● **L'antre . . .** / 1991 / ✦✦✦✦
Marked with the same stylistic integrity as her previous albums, this is without a doubt Mylene Farmer's masterpiece. Compositions are still elaborate and carefully designed but have now more refined transparent feel. Deep dark reflection of life, so typical for the artist, is enriched by the sparkling energy of her powerful, sometimes hysterical irony and calm confidence of her velvet soft voice. —*Vladimir Bogdanov*

Dionne Farris

Urban
After leaving Arrested Development in 1993, vocalist Dionne Farris recorded her own album, *Wild Seed Wild Flower* in 1994, which displayed a more pop-oriented contemporary R&B; the single "I Know" helped the album cross over into the mainstream. —*Stephen Thomas Erlewine*

● **Wild Seed—Wild Flower** / 1995 / Columbia ✦✦✦✦
On her debut solo album, Dionne Farris creates a hybrid of contemporary, pop and hip-hop. Like the hit single "I Know"—which features a greasy slide guitar over a percolating hip-hop beat—the album doesn't acknowledge boundaries, it combines them without thinking. —*Stephen Thomas Erlewine*

Fastbacks

Group, Alternative Pop/Rock
This Seattle quartet generates a sound alternating between punkish pop and poppish punk. Recording sporadically between 1982 and the present, the band benefits from sometime Young Fresh Fellows guitarist Kurt Bloch and the sneering vocals of Kim Warnick, who also doubles as bassist. They are an extremely underrated group. —*David Szatmary*

○ **. . . and His Orchestra** / 1987 / Pop Llama ✦✦✦✦
Recorded between 1981 and 1985, this album features 20 songs from a driving Seattle band that alternates between pop-ish punk and punk-ish pop. Fueled by Kurt Blocj's guitar. —*David Szatmary*

Very Very Powerful Motor / 1990 / Pop Llama ✦✦✦
Thanks to some tougher guitars and rawer vocals, *Very, Very Powerful Motor* is the most punkish album the Fastbacks have released, but the songs never lack strong melodies. —*Stephen Thomas Erlewine*

● **Zucker** / Jan. 29, 1993 / Sub Pop ✦✦✦✦
With its speedy, energetic riffs and bright melodies, *Zucker* is one of the Fastbacks' best albums. —*Stephen Thomas Erlewine*

Bike Toy Clock Gift / 1994 / Lucky ✦✦✦

Faster Pussycat

Group, Hard Rock, Heavy Metal
Sleazy Hollywood metal band (whose name was lifted from a Russ Meyer flick) Faster Pussycat released its first album in 1987 and peaked commercially two years later with the gold album, *Wake Me When It's Over*, and the Top Forty single, "House of Pain." Although their next album, 1992's *Whipped*, hit #90 on the charts, it fell off the charts quickly; with the alternative rock explosion, the hard rock audience had changed and had no patience for Faster Pussycat's trashy glam metal. —*John Book*

● **Faster Pussycat** / 1987 / Elektra ✦✦✦✦
This Los Angeles hard-rock glam band hit the big time in a big way. Fun and sleazy, it brings back the mood of bands from the '70s such as Aerosmith. —*John Book*

Wake Me When It's Over / 1989 / Elektra ✦✦✦
A bit more polished than the debut, it's not watered down. —*John Book*

Whipped / Aug. 1992 / Elektra ✦✦✦
Less of the neo-glam gloss and more serious themes than on past efforts, but Taime Downe and the gang haven't lost their wild edge and love of double entendre. —*AMG*

The Fat Boys

Group, Rap
More a comedy troupe than a rap posse, the Fat Boys marketed their obesity and goofiness with true savvy during the early '80s. Most of the songs dealt with their prodigious food intake, and Buff the Human Beat Box was always good for at least one laugh. The music ain't bad and, in 1984, they made a novelty for the ages: "Jailhouse Rap." —*John Floyd*

○ **Fat Boys** / 1984 / Sutra ✦✦✦✦
This rotund rap trio tipped the scales at 750 pounds. Their heft and Darren Robinson's verbal skills were the hooks that helped the Fat Boys land a gold record with their self-titled debut album. Even the lack of a standout single couldn't prevent the album from being a steady seller or limit the group's popularity. Such singles as "Human Beat Box" and "Jail House Rap" helped them quickly build a solid following that they retained until the end of the decade. —*Ron Wynn*

The Fat Boys Are Back / 1985 / WEA ✦✦✦

Big & Beautiful / 1986 / Sutra ✦✦
The train began derailing for the Fat Boys with their third album. It was their first that failed to go gold, and such songs as "Beat Box Is Rockin'," "Breakdown" and "Go for It" were indications that their novelty tunes and party rapping were becoming passe. They would make a brief comeback the next year fueled by the film *Disorderlies*, but the end was nearing for the trio. —*Ron Wynn*

● **The Best Part of the Fat Boys** / 1987 / Pair ✦✦✦✦
Everything you need by rap's fattest trio can be found on this concise sample of their first three albums. Included is "All You Can Eat," "Jailhouse Rap," and "Stick 'Em." —*John Floyd*

○ **Crushin'** / 1987 / PolyGram ✦✦✦✦
The Fat Boys enjoyed their biggest year in 1987. Their film *Disorderlies* proved much more commercially resilient than anticipated, and this LP earned their only platinum certification, while becoming the lone Fat Boys album to make the pop Top 10 (peaking at #8). They also landed a Top 20 single with an updated version of "Wipeout." —*Ron Wynn*

Krush on You / 1988 / Blatant ✦✦

Coming Back Hard Again / 1988 / Tin Pan Apple ✦✦✦
The last Fat Boys LP to make any noise, this sixth Sutra release proved their second most successful album, peaking at 33 and earning them their last gold record. It piggybacked on the success of "Louie Louie," their last chart single. They did try to adjust to

changing audience demands, cutting "Rock The House, Y'All" and "Powerlord," but the Fat Boys' strength remained novelty numbers and weight-based raps like "Big Daddy" and "Pig Feet," which had lost almost all their popularity. —*Ron Wynn*

On and on / 1989 / Tin Pan Apple ✦✦

The Fatback Band

Group, Funk
A seminal funk ensemble, the Fatback Band made many great singles through the '70s and early '80s, ranging from humorous novelty tunes to energetic dance vehicles and even occasional political/message tracks. The original lineup featured drummer Bill Curtis, trumpeter George Williams, guitarist Johnny King, bassist Johnny Flippin, saxophonist Earl Shelton, and flutist George Adam. Synthesizer player Gerry Thomas, saxophonist Fred Demerey, and guitarist George Victory were integral parts of the group during their peak years. They began recording for Perception in the early '70s, and had moderate luck with "Street Dance" in 1973. They moved to Event in 1974, and while funk audiences loved such songs as "Wicki-Wacky" and "(Are You Ready) Do the Bus Stop," they didn't generate much sales action. Their first sizable hit was "Spanish Hustle" in 1976, which reached number 12 on the R&B charts. They shortened their name to Fatback in 1977, and landed their first Top R&B hit with "I Like Girls" in 1978. Their 1979 single "King Time III (Personality Jock)" is widely considered the first rap single in many circles. But their biggest year was 1980. They scored two Top Ten R&B hits with "Gotta Get My Hands on Some (Money)" and "Backstrokin'," their finest tune. Fatback kept going through the mid-'80s, landing one more Top 20 hit with "Take It Any Way You Can Want It" in 1981. They were backed by the female vocal trio Wild Sugar in 1981-82, and Evelyn Thomas also provided the lead vocal for "Spread Love" in 1985, their last song for Spring. Fatback also recorded a pair of LPs for Cotillion in 1984 and 1985. —*Ron Wynn*

● **Best of the Fatback Band** / 1976 / Spring ✦✦✦✦
Although they earned their biggest hits under the guise of Fatback, their most enjoyable records were recorded as the Fatback Band. The often infectious funk arrangements and horn lines helped embellish what were without question forgettable group vocals. But there were few East Coast bands making more humorous and delightful singles than the Fatback Band, even if they never got significant airplay or sales, even within the R&B community. This anthology collects most of the tracks that either charted or were underground hits, including the wonderful "Wicky Wacky." —*Ron Wynn*

Father MC

Rap
Father MC straddles the line between hip-hop and new-jack-swing, which resulted in a #20 hit, "I'll Do 4 U," from his debut album *Father's Day*. Nearly two years after his debut, Father M.C. followed it with *Close to You*. Its success was almost guaranteed by Father MC's appearance on the CD *Uptown MTV Unplugged*. Father MC was formerly a dancehall reggae performer, and there was some reggae influence interspersed with the sentimental love lyrics and hip-hop production. —*Ron Wynn*

○ **Father's Day** / 1990 / Uptown ✦✦✦✦
One of the better applications of vintage soul and romantic R&B to hip-hop formula, along with one bit of verbal warfare between Father MC and female rapper Lady Kazan. —*Ron Wynn*

● **Close to You** / 1992 / Uptown ✦✦✦✦
Bronx rapper Father MC faked folks out on both sides of the style line when he released this 1990 debut. Those expecting 100 percent hardcore blanched at hearing sentimental love themes and straight R&B; others who thought he was strictly a New Jack Swinger were caught sleeping when the booming beats of the title track were cranked up on the box, or when Father MC matched one-liners with Lady Kazan on "I've Been Watching You." —*Ron Wynn*

I've Been Watching U / MCA ✦✦✦

Treat Them Like They Want To Be / MCA ✦✦✦

Everything's Gonna Be Alright / MCA ✦✦✦
Nearly two years after his debut and a few months after a successful number on the *Uptown Unplugged* CD, Father MC rolled in with his second disc. Things weren't nearly as varied or successful

as the debut, although he maintained his niche among New Jack types thanks to some creative production support. —*Ron Wynn*

Faust

Group, Art-Rock/Progressive-Rock, Experimental
While they never received much recognition while they were recording, the experimental, cut-and-paste approach of the German progressive rock group Faust influenced many of the noise and pre-industrial electronic bands of the late '70s and early '80s. Faust's music was never easy listening, with its tape experiments, electronics, and convoluted melodies, yet these were the very things that made the group influential. After releasing four albums between 1971 and 1973, the band split up. —*Stephen Thomas Erlewine*

○ **Faust** / 1971 / Recommended ✦✦✦✦
The impact of Faust cannot be overstated; their debut album was truly a revolutionary step forward in the progress of "rock music". It was pressed on clear vinyl, packaged in a clear sleeve, with a clear plastic lyric insert. The black X-ray of a fist on the cover graphically illustrates the hard core music contained in the grooves, an amalgamation of electronics, rock, tape edits, acoustic guitars, musique concrete and industrial angst. The level of imagination is staggering, the concept is totally unique and it's fun to listen to as well. —*Archie Patterson*

● **Faust So Far** / 1972 / Recommended ✦✦✦✦
Faust Tapes / 1973 / Cuneiform ✦✦✦
Faust 4 / 1973 / Blue Plate ✦✦✦
Munich & Elsewhere / 1986 / Recommended ✦✦✦

Fear

Group, Hardcore
With their blistering, nihilistic punk rock, Fear was one of the leading Los Angeles hardcore bands of the early '80s. More than most hardcore bands, Fear relied on shock techniques, dark humor, and vulgarity; frequently singer Lee Ving's lyrics were outright offensive, particularly concerning women and homosexuals. After two records, the band imploded and Ving pursued a successful acting career. —*Stephen Thomas Erlewine*

● **The Record** / 1982 / Slash ✦✦✦✦
Fierce punk-rock, Los Angeles '80s variety, distinguished by the raw vocals of lead singer Lee Ving. —*William Ruhlmann*

More Beer / 1985 / Restless ✦✦✦
Live . . . For the Record / Oct. 25, 1991 / Restless ✦✦

Charlie Feathers

b. Jun. 12, 1932, Hollow Springs, MS
Rockabilly
Charlie Feathers was one of the first country artists to record for Sam Phillips at the legendary Sun studios. He was there at the birth of rock & roll. Marketed during his tenure at the label strictly as a country artist, Feathers recorded a superb collection of singles for labels like Meteor, King, Kay, and Philwood, all in a highly charged rockabilly vein. Championed by the European rockabilly collector community in the early '70s, he has continued recording for a variety of labels—not varying, only improving, his original '50s style. Charlie Feathers is a superb stylist. His voice is a consummate instrument, full of nuances uniquely his own, whether he's rocking up a storm or singing the most mournful of country ballads. Though never commercially successful, Charlie Feathers nonetheless remains a shining example of raw American music at its finest. —*Cub Koda*

Live in Memphis / 1979 / Barrelhouse ✦✦✦
Loose early-'70s recordings. Great, but unfortunately out of print. —*Cub Koda*

● **Jungle Fever** / 1987 / Kay ✦✦✦✦
Boasting a generous twenty tracks, *Jungle Fever* is the best available compilation of Charlie Feathers' original rockabilly recordings; all of his best-known songs are collected here, including "Get with It" and "Tongue-Tied Jill." —*Stephen Thomas Erlewine*

Charlie Feathers / 1991 / Elektra/Nonesuch ✦✦✦
Recent recordings with Sun alumni. —*Cub Koda*

○ **Rock-A-Billy** / May 1991 / Zu-Zazz ✦✦✦✦
Superb collection of rare and unissued sides, 1954-1973, showcasing Feathers's mastery of rockabilly and country material. (Import) —*Cub Koda*

The Feelies

Group, Alternative Pop/Rock
The Feelies, consisting of Glenn Mercer (guitar/vocals), Bill Million (guitar/vocals), Keith DeNunzio (bass), Vinny DeNunzio (drums) and part-time member Anton Fier (drums), formed in New Jersey in 1977. In 1980, they released their debut avant-pop masterpiece, *Crazy Rhythms*, to critical acclaim but to no commercial response. Mercer and Million left the band dormant while working on outside projects such as the Trypes, Willies and Yung Wu; Fier left to work on his own Golden Palominos projects. Revived interest in the band, thanks in part to R.E.M.'s Peter Buck citing the band as an influence, led to a reactivated version of the Feelies in 1986, featuring Brenda Sauter on bass and Dave Weckerman on percussion. Produced by Peter Buck, *The Good Earth* was released in 1986 by Coyote to an enthusiastic college radio audience. They continued to be college radio mainstays for the rest of the decade, though mainstream success has eluded them. —*Chris Woodstra*

● **Crazy Rhythms** / 1980 / A&M ✦✦✦✦
The Feelies' debut picks up where the Velvet Underground and Television left off, using unconventional structures to create an album that is stark, nervous and detached. While it was virtually ignored at the time, *Crazy Rhythms* would prove to be a blueprint for much of the mid-'80s' guitar-based alternative rock. —*Chris Woodstra*

The Good Earth / 1986 / Coyote ✦✦✦
After a six year break, the Feelies return with R.E.M.'s Peter Buck producing. The result, not so suprisingly, is a fine alternative folk-pop album in the spirit of early R.E.M. Though not matching the debut's brilliance, *The Good Earth* creates a pleasant enough atmosphere and is a welcome return. —*Chris Woodstra*

○ **Only Life** / 1988 / A&M ✦✦✦✦
Only Life moves from the light acoustic strumming of 1986's *The Good Earth* into a slightly harder electric sound while still retaining much of the textured and atmospheric qualities that made its predecessor so charming. There is more of a return to the driving rhythms of the first album and the entire album has a feeling of the Velvet Underground revisited. —*Chris Woodstra*

Time for a Witness / 1991 / A&M ✦✦
By this time, the band is trapped by the formula. They *have* matured and found a slightly more relaxed sound, but the progress is minimal. The result is a close approximation of a Feelies album. —*Chris Woodstra*

Melissa Ferrick

Singer-Songwriter, Alternative Pop/Rock
Singer/songwriter Melissa Ferrick emerged in 1994 as part of a group of new female "alternative" singer/songwriters, much in the vein of Liz Phair. Ferrick began singing in coffeehouses after dropping out of college, eventually winding up in Boston. Her major breakthrough arrived one night when she replaced Morrissey's opening act less than an hour before showtime. Ferrick's performance impressed Morrissey and he invited her to open for him for the rest of the tour. The tour earned her a small cult following as well as a contract with Atlantic records. She released her debut album, *Massive Blur*, in 1994 to good reviews; the critical reception for her stripped-down second album, *Willing to Wait*, earned even stronger reviews. —*Stephen Thomas Erlewine*

Massive Blur / 1994 / Atlantic ✦✦✦
● **Willing To Wait** / 1995 / Atlantic ✦✦✦✦

Bryan Ferry

b. Sep. 26, 1945, Washington, Durham, UK
Pop/Rock
Bryan Ferry has been recording solo albums since Roxy Music's early- to mid-'70s heyday, in a bizarre and confounding hodge-podge of styles. His first few solos incorporated mostly eclectic covers that wander everywhere from early rock and soul hits up to Dylan and Beatles tunes; musically, they share a lot of common ground with his full-time group. —*John Floyd*

○ **These Foolish Things** / Oct. 1973 / Reprise ✦✦✦✦
As a side project during his Roxy Music tenure, Ferry recorded this album of drastic rearrangements of a variety of standards, most of them from the '60s. The Beatles, the Rolling Stones, and especially Bob Dylan never sounded like this before. —*William Ruhlmann*

Another Time, Another Place / Jul. 1974 / Reprise ✦✦✦
Same concept, different songs, as the suave Ferry recasts "Smoke Gets in Your Eyes," Sam Cooke, and several country standards. — *William Ruhlmann*

Let's Stick Together / Sep. 1976 / Reprise ✦✦✦
When Roxy Music broke up in 1976, Bryan Ferry's solo career moved from being a sideline to his main occupation. His initial post-Roxy single, "Let's Stick Together," was a U.K. hit, prompting the release of this cobbled-together album, which consists of outtakes from his two albums of pop covers and some alternate versions of Roxy songs, recorded from 1973 to 1976. It is thus more a marketing item than a real artistic statement, but it has some interesting moments. — *William Ruhlmann*

In Your Mind / Feb. 1977 / Reprise ✦✦
Although it is his fourth solo album overall, this is really Bryan Ferry's debut as a full-fledged solo artist, the follow-up to Roxy Music's 1975 album *Siren*. As such, however, it is a serious disappointment. Although its driving lead-off track, "This Is Tomorrow" (a U.K. Top Ten hit), is a good introduction, the album lacks the flair of Ferry's work with Roxy Music, and it signals that he will be less of a success without the group. — *William Ruhlmann*

The Bride Stripped Bare / Sep. 1978 / Reprise ✦✦
Ferry tried to recapture the feel of his first two solo albums with R&B covers like "Hold on (I'm Coming)" and "Take Me to the River" while carrying on the Roxy tradition with a few originals, but it didn't work. The commercial failure of this album sent Ferry back into the arms of his Roxy Music compatriots for a reunion of the more successful group. — *William Ruhlmann*

○ **Boys and Girls** / May 1985 / Reprise ✦✦✦✦
With the second (and presumably final) disbanding of Roxy Music, Ferry turned full time to his solo career, so this album is more of a follow-up to 1982's *Avalon*, the last Roxy album, than to 1978's *The Bride Stripped Bare*, the previous Ferry solo release. It brilliantly continues the ethereal dance-floor charm of *Avalon*. — *William Ruhlmann*

● **Street Life: 20 Greatest Hits** / Apr. 1986 / EG ✦✦✦✦
Covering both Ferry and Roxy Music's best-known songs, *Street Life* is the best introduction to the stylish art-rocker's career. — *Stephen Thomas Erlewine*

○ **Bête Noire** / Oct. 1987 / Reprise ✦✦✦✦
Enlisting Madonna producer Patrick Leonard to assist, Ferry matches his studiedly languorous vocals to densely percussive dance tracks. — *William Ruhlmann*

Taxi / Mar. 1993 / Reprise ✦✦
For Ferry, cover albums have become both artistic statements and a way to buy time. *Taxi*, delivered some six years after *Bete Noire*, is filled with the kind of contradictions inherent with such a dual purpose. Nothing on the album is particularly revelatory; it's his third album entirely composed of covers, so Ferry's slick, stylish approach is familiar. However, Ferry is such a singular singer that *Taxi* escapes being a worthless exercise. Although there are some songs that don't hit the mark, there are several moments (particularly "Will You Love Me Tomorrow" and "Amazing Grace") that make up for such missteps. — *Stephen Thomas Erlewine*

○ **Mamouna** / Sep. 20, 1994 / Capitol ✦✦✦✦
Ferry's first album of original material since *Bete Noire* finds the ex-Roxy Music singer in a familiar seductive mood. While working within his standard dance-oriented darkness, Ferry incorporates several new touches—namely, several pseudo-world music touches. None of it would have worked if Ferry hadn't blended them in so seamlessly with his stylish pop, which hasn't dated in the seven years that he's been away. — *Stephen Thomas Erlewine*

Fever Tree

Group, Psychedelic
A minor, if reasonably interesting, late '60s psychedelic group, Houston's Fever Tree are most famous for their single "San Francisco Girls," with its dramatic melody, utopian lyrics, and searing fuzz guitar. Most of their best material, ironically, was written by their over-30 husband-wife production team, Scott & Vivian Holtzman, who had previously written material for Tex Ritter and the *Mary Poppins* soundtrack. These odd bedfellows produced some fairly distinctive material with more classical/baroque influences and orchestral string arrangements than were usually found in psychedelic groups. Their pretty, wistful ballads (enhanced on their first album by arranger David Angel, who had also worked on

Love's classic *Forever Changes*) endure better than their dirge-like fuzz grinders, which epitomize some of the more generic aspects of heavy psychedelia. Releasing four albums (the third of which, *Creation*, included guest guitar by future ZZ Top axeman Billy Gibbons), their records grew weaker and more meandering with time, and the group disbanded in 1970. — *Richie Unterberger*

● **San Francisco Girls: The Best of Fever Tree** / 1986 / Era ✦✦✦✦
Well-chosen 16-song anthology featuring songs from their first three albums, leaning most heavily on their self-titled 1968 debut. Also has a couple of early singles and a thorough history of the band. — *Richie Unterberger*

Fiestas

Group, R&B
The lone moment of glory for the Fiestas, a Newark vocal group, came in 1959, with the perennial oldies radio favorite "So Fine." Lead vocalist Tommy Bullock, along with Eddie Morris, Sam Ingalis, and Preston Lane, took the song to number three on the R&B charts and number 11 on the pop charts. The follow-up, "Broken Heart," was a creditable heartache ballad in 1962 that also made it to number 18 on the R&B charts, but didn't enjoy any crossover appeal. Both songs were on the Old Town label. They continued recording for Old Town, as well as Strand and Vigor, through the '60s and into the mid-'70s, but never again enjoyed any hits. — *Ron Wynn*

● **Oh So Fine** / Ace (UK) ✦✦✦✦

5th Dimension

Group, Pop
They didn't sound anything like an R&B group, and their soaring, lighter-than-air harmonic blend frequently proved more palatable to pop audiences than to Black record buyers. But do not suggest, even for a second, that the 5th Dimension was in any way lacking in soul.

Formed as the Versatiles in 1965, the slick quintet changed its name at the request of Johnny Rivers, who had just signed them to his brand new label, Soul City. Up-and-coming songwriter Jimmy Webb supplied the group with their first pop smash "Up, Up and Away," in 1967, and the group's monumental rise mirrored the song's high-flying imagery. Another prolific composer, Laura Nyro, handed the 5th Dimension several megahits, notably "Stoned Soul Picnic" and "Wedding Bell Blues," but their biggest seller hailed from the groundbreaking musical *Hair*. The Grammy-winning "Aquarius/Let the Sunshine In" held down the #1 slot on the pop lists for six weeks in 1969.

After several more hits, Marilyn McCoo and Billy Davis, Jr., who had married while part of the group, successfully branched off as a duo, while Lamonte McLemore, Ron Townson, and Florence LaRue kept the 5th Dimension on the soul charts, losing a head-to-head battle with Diana Ross for hit status on "Love Hangover" in 1976. — *Bill Dahl*

● **Greatest Hits on Earth** / Sep. 1972 / Arista ✦✦✦✦
Until Rhino issued its anthology, this was the best hits package for the 5th Dimension, a group that in its peak was among the best at doing light-hearted pop with a soulful foundation. Certainly, they weren't a hardcore R&B or earthy singing group, but they did put some punch into songs that were really kind of silly otherwise, like "Wedding Bell Blues." — *Ron Wynn*

In The House / Jun. 20, 1995 / Click/Columbia ✦✦
The 5th Dimension attempts a comeback by redefining itself as a Quiet Storm R&B act, but gives the game away right off the bat by having themselves introduced by co-executive producer Dick Clark, who declares, "The 5th Dimension is in the house!" Suddenly, the enterprise seems as hip as a Publishers Clearinghouse commercial, and no amount of drum programming by producer Ollie E. Brown can rescue it. Nor does it help that the group insists on covering the Bee Gees' "How Deep Is Your Love" as well as the work of old friends Neil Sedaka and Laura Nyro. For better or worse, the 5th Dimension is what it is, even after 30 years. Back to Vegas, kids. — *William Ruhlmann*

54-40

Group, Alternative Pop/Rock, Roots-Rock
Vancouver's 54-40 take their name from James K. Polk's presidential campaign slogan "Fifty-Four Forty or Fight," which sought to expand the U.S. border northward. 54-50 formed in 1981 as a trio

consisting of Brad Merritt (bass), Darryl Neudorf (drums), and Neil Osbourne (vocals); they began touring the Western Canadian club circuit, without gaining much attention. In 1984, Phil Comarelli was added on guitar and vocals; Neudorf left shortly thereafter and was replaced by Matt Johnson (not The The's frontman). By the time of the band's self-titled album in 1986, their folk/roots approach had earned them favorable comparisons to R.E.M. Subsequent albums have found the band moving into harder-edged territory. A lack of U.S. interest led to 1992's exclusive Canadian release *Dear Dear*, but by 1994, continued success in their homeland helped to make a U.S. release possible for *Smilin' Buddah Cabaret*. —*Chris Woodstra*

Set the Fire / 1984 / Mo-Da-Mu ✦✦

● **54-40** / 1986 / Reprise ✦✦✦✦

Show Me / 1987 / Warner Brothers ✦✦✦

Fight for Love / Mar. 1989 / Reprise ✦✦✦

Dear Dear / 1992 / Columbia ✦✦
Vancouver's answer to R.E.M.'s thoughtful, hook-filled pop has consolidated all of its strongest elements for this, its fifth disc. As befits a Canadian perspective, Neil Osborne's lyrics are more rooted to earth than Michael Stipe's fanciful flights, but the songs have the same quality of stimulating both intellect and hips. Osborne makes the best of a limited vocal range by weaving a groove with his fellow musicians as if his voice was just another instrument. There's a lean, sinewy quality to the playing: focused energy with no excess fat. "Lovers and Losers," begins with Petty-like singspeak and smooth Southern shuffle before erupting to a ferocious conclusion. The most notable of several highpoints on *Dear Dear* are "You Don't Get Away (That Easy)," with its unsettling, echoed chorus, and the mystical, latin-tinged pop of "Book." —*Roch Parisien*

Figgs

Group, Alternative Pop/Rock
Comprised of Saratoga Springs, NY, natives Mike Gent (guitar, vocals), Pete Donnelly (bass), Guy Lyons (lead guitar) and Pete Hayes (drums), the Figgs specialize in bright punk-pop, with an accent on the pop; their roots lie in Elvis Costello, the Jam and Graham Parker, not the Buzzcocks. Released their debut album, *Lo Fi at Society High*, in 1994. —*Stephen Thomas Erlewine*

○ **Low-fi At Society High** / 1994 / Imago ✦✦✦✦

Fine Young Cannibals

Group, Dance-Pop, Pop/Rock
When the English Beat splintered in two, bassist David Steele and guitarist Andy Cox formed the Fine Young Cannibals with Roland Gift. Although the band's fusion of rock, Motown-style R&B, pop, and modern dance is tight and loaded with hooks, the real attraction is Gift's soaring falsetto—he sounds like a classic soul singer. Their 1985 debut album was critically acclaimed, but it was the 1989 follow-up, *The Raw & the Cooked*—with the number one singles "She Drives Me Crazy" and "Good Thing"—that made the band major hit makers. Apart from a remix album in 1990 and Gift's occasional film role, the group has been quiet since their breakthrough success. —*Stephen Thomas Erlewine*

Fine Young Cannibals / Dec. 1985 / IRS ✦✦✦
Roland Gift's vocals are the find here, backed by the R&B/pop music provided by ex-Beat members Andy Cox and David Steele. —*William Ruhlmann*

● **The Raw & The Cooked** / Feb. 20, 1989 / IRS ✦✦✦✦
FYC rode to massive success on the tender-and-terrified singing of Roland Gift and the neo-Motown sheen of the #1 hits "She Drives Me Crazy" and "Good Thing." —*William Ruhlmann*

The Raw & The Remix / Dec. 1990 / IRS ✦✦
Coming up on two years since the release of *The Raw & The Cooked*, and with no new album in sight, IRS Records put together various 12-inch remix versions of songs from the 1989 album and released this 59-minute collection. There are extended, alternate versions of such hits as "She Drives Me Crazy," "Good Thing," and "Don't Look Back." Off the dance floor, none of this improves on the originals. —*William Ruhlmann*

Fingerprintz

Group, New Wave
Now sadly relegated to footnote status, England's Fingerprintz

were one of the few bands that lent credibility to the marketing-inspired expression "new wave." Formed by Scottish-born singer/guitarist Jimmie O'Neill in 1978, the 'Printz slowed down punk's careening guitar rock, adding clever, rhythmic twists and turns and offering up deftly written stories about lust, angst and urban desolation. The problem was finding an audience; the music was certainly spot-on, but one can only guess as to what kept hordes of people away. Certainly it wasn't the quality of their recorded work, which, despite occasional concessions to slick production, is mostly smart, insightful songs. Perhaps it was simply a matter of being out of step with the zeitgeist or simply not getting a break. O'Neill decided to call it a day after the third and final 'Printz record, *Beat Noir*, in 1981. However, the story has a sort of happy ending: O'Neill and fellow 'Printz guitarist Cha Burns formed the Silencers in 1987, a band that reaped much greater commercial success than did the 'Printz. Ironically, the Silencers' records weren't nearly as good as that of the Fingerprintz. As of this writing, all three Fingerprintz records were long out of print, which is a thinly veiled recommendation for someone to compile a CD anthology. —*John Dougan*

● **The Very Dab** / 1979 / Virgin ✦✦✦✦
This is the most "punk"-like recording the 'Printz ever made, and its rough-hewn charm is immediately engaging. The songs, however, are not all light and happy pop songs, and that gives the record an extra edge. O'Neill and Burns's guitars are aggressive and intrusive (that's a compliment), and this record was one of the great left-field (and now long-forgotten) surprises of the late '70s. —*John Dougan*

Dancing with Myself / 1979 / Virgin ✦✦✦

Distinguishing Marks / 1980 / Virgin ✦✦✦
With producer Nick Garvey (ex-Ducks Deluxe and Motors) leading the way, *Distinguishing Marks* has all the rough edges smoothed away, but not so much as to have a negative impact on the music. O'Neill's songs are still loaded with dark emotional undercurrents and melodramatic narratives, but they aren't self-pitying, narcissistic exercises. In fact, this LP marked a maturational process that continued with their third and last record. Still, no record better sums up the excellence of Fingerprintz better than this one. —*John Dougan*

Beat Noir / 1981 / Virgin ✦✦✦
After being dropped by Virgin due to lack of interest in the American market, hipper-than-thou English indie label Stiff signed the 'Printz and released their oddest record. The songs didn't depart from O'Neill's usual concerns (angst, urban anomie); the rock/pop influences of the preceding records gave way to a funkier, more reggae, backbeat. More than any of their other recordings, *Beat Noir* is rhythmically dense, a little intimidating at first, but a joy once you get to know it. —*John Dougan*

Tim Finn

b. Jun. 25, 1952, Te Awamutu, New Zealand
Pop/Rock
This singer/songwriter keyboardist/guitarist was born in Te Awamutu, New Zealand. Influenced by his Catholic upbringing and the joyous communal singalongs of the native Maori people, Finn founded the '70s art-rock turned new wave band Split Enz. He led the band through several albums to borderline international success. The success of the between-albums solo project, *Escapade*, led to his leaving the band in 1983. The more ambitious second album, *Big Canoe* (1985) went virtually ignored (it was unreleased in the U.S. until the success of his brother's band Crowded House stirred up enough interest by 1988). Finn returned in 1989 with a self-titled album for Capitol Records. Despite good reviews, this too failed to make much impact. He joined his brother Neil's band, Crowded House, for their *Woodface* album but left mid-tour and released his fourth solo album, *Before and After* in 1993. In 1995, he joined with Hothouse Flowers' Liam O Maonlai and Andy White, releasing an album under the group name ALT. A collaboration between the Finn brothers is slated for late 1995. Finn's light melodic songs and soaring vocals, while influenced by classic British pop, reflect his unique homeland at the bottom of the world. —*Scott Bultman and Chris Woodstra*

Escapade / 1983 / A&M ✦✦✦
On his solo debut, Finn broke from Split Enz to exorcise these charming, light, melodic pop songs that didn't quite fit the band's style. Sweet and sappy, his soaring vocal style and introspective lyrics make this worthwhile. —*Scott Bultman*

○ **Big Canoe** / 1985 / Virgin ✦✦✦✦
Much production glitz here from producer Nick Launay, competing for attention with Finn's voice and songs. A very melodic and musical second solo effort, the highlights include "Don't Bury My Heart" and "Hyacinth." —*Scott Bultman*

● **Tim Finn** / 1989 / Capitol ✦✦✦✦
His third album is his most sparsely produced effort. Supported by Los Angeles session musicians and producer Mitchell Froom (Crowded House), Finn is as accessible here as he's ever been. Great melodies, well-turned phrases, and seamless backing vocals from brother Neil Finn of Crowded House make this one his best. —*Scott Bultman*

○ **Before & After** / 1993 / Capitol ✦✦✦✦
On his fourth solo album, Finn dabbles in dance-pop, pseudo-reggae, and folky ballads, with a different set of producers on nearly every track. While this leads to a certain lack of consistency, Finn's songwriting has never been stronger. He has the most success on the self-produced, stripped-down tracks where his strong sense of melody and knack for catchy pop hooks are allowed to be in the forefront. "Persuasion," co-written by Richard Thompson and "In Love with It All," written with his brother Neil Finn (Crowded House) are highlights. —*Chris Woodstra*

Firefall

Group, Country-Rock, Pop/Rock
When Firefall was formed in 1974, their pedigree included the Flying Burrito Brothers, the Byrds, and Spirit. Their first album (arguably their best) was a very commercial blend of tight harmonies and acoustic/electric, country-flavored pop/rock. Subsequent albums mined that approach, producing hits like "You Are the Woman" (#9), "Just Remember I Love You" (#11), and "Strange Way" (#11). —*Rick Clark*

○ **Firefall** / 1976 / Atlantic ✦✦✦✦
This debut effort, their best album, includes the hits "You Are the Woman" and "Cinderella." —*Rick Clark*

● **Greatest Hits** / Rhino ✦✦✦✦
A greatest-hits collection, it includes almost all the essential tracks. —*Rick Clark*

fIREHOSE

Group, Alternative Pop/Rock
In 1985, after D. Boon's tragic death at age 28 signalled the end of the Minutemen, bassist Mike Watt and drummer George Hurley threw in their lot with then-22-year-old former Ohio State University student, guitar player and Minuteman fanatic Ed Crawford to form fIREHOSE. Taking their group name from a line in Bob Dylan's "Subterranean Homesick Blues," fIREHOSE continued in the Minutemen tradition of breathtaking musicianship combined with caustic lyrical fusillades inspired by the writing of the Beat Generation and the erect-middle-finger indignation of the Blank Generation. However, with Crawford's decidedly folkie bent insinuating itself into the mix, fIREHOSE's songs began to expand into more traditional verse-chorus-verse songwriting symmetry. And although fIREHOSE never equalled the Minutemen's output in terms of sheer audacity and emotional depth, Crawford, Watt and Hurley recorded rock that was muscular, dense and daring, along with being tremendously heartfelt. They never patronized audiences or comported themselves as "rock stars"; they were instead the quintessential post-punk "peoples' band." Although they achieved wider notoriety than did the Minutemen (eventually recording for a major label), fIREHOSE called it quits in early 1994 after a desultory, dispirited final LP (*Mr. Machinery Operator*). Still, nearly all of their recorded work stands as some of the best late-'80s/early-'90s indie rock. —*John Dougan*

Ragin', Full-On / 1986 / SST ✦✦✦
The title is a bit of a misnomer, since this record seethes more than it rages, but all and all, it was a fine debut. Crawford (here he was referred to as Ed Fromohio) singing is tentative and a bit wan, but the songs are strong, and Watt and Hurley are one of rock's great rhythm sections. —*John Dougan*

● **If'n** / 1987 / SST ✦✦✦✦
On release number two, Crawford's guitar is assertive and drives the band more. Just as important, however, is that the songwriting has grown sharper and more compelling (especially on the romping "Sometimes") and Crawford sings with more reckless abandon here. No sophomore slump, not by a long shot. —*John Dougan*

Sometimes / 1988 / SST ✦✦
○ **Fromohio** / 1989 / SST ✦✦✦✦
A bit of a retrenchment and perhaps not a wholly successful record. Here, fIREHOSE sounds like a band reevaluating its place in the world and only occasionally coming up with compelling answers. An easy record to slough off as more of the same. But while it may not be an essential record, it isn't bad either. —*John Dougan*

Flyin' the Flannel / 1991 / Columbia ✦✦✦
If indie-rock purists were ready to scream "sellout" when fIREHOSE signed with Columbia, they were sorely disappointed when Crawford, Watt and Hurley released this louder-than-usual, revved-up hunk of clang and strum, that in no way repudiated fIREHOSE's reputation as a fiercely independent band. Less controlled and more traditionally "rock" than previous records, *Flyin' the Flannel* really is ragin' full-on and may well be their best. —*John Dougan*

Live Totem Pole / 1992 / Columbia ✦✦✦
A fun, mostly covers, 7-song EP that proves what a great live band fIREHOSE was. Ferocious and fast, the highlight is a rousing (and perhaps definitive) version of Superchunk's anti-slacker theme song "Slack Motherfucker." —*John Dougan*

Mr. Machinery Operator / Feb. 16, 1993 / Columbia ✦✦✦
fIREHOSE's final album was a pile-driving slab of post-punk rock, tamed by J. Mascis' production; occasionally, the guitars are too thick for the band's style of music, but overall, this was a fine way to close the book on their career. —*Stephen Thomas Erlewine*

Firehouse

Group, Hard Rock
Firehouse arrived at the tail end of the pop-metal explosion of the late '80s and early '90s, releasing their first album in 1991. Featuring vocalist C.J. Snare, Michael Foster, Bill Leverty, and Perry Richardson, the group's melodic, commercial hard rock had immediate chart success; their self-titled debut went platinum and featured two Top 20 singles, "Don't Treat Me Bad" and "Love of a Lifetime." The following year, Firehouse released their second album, *Hold Your Fire*, which managed to go gold, even as the mainstream was embracing a noisier, punkier hard rock. The band waited three years before releasing *Firehouse 3*, which showcased a softer, more MOR-oriented band; it was a moderate success. —*Stephen Thomas Erlewine*

● **Firehouse** / 1991 / Epic ✦✦✦✦
Hold Your Fire / Jun. 16, 1992 / Epic ✦✦✦
Firehouse 3 / 1995 / Epic ✦✦✦
Firehouse strip away most of their harder edges on their third album, the aptly titled *Firehouse 3*. Some of the songs still rock out, yet they are punctuated by the distorted guitars, not driven by them. Still, the group's strong point is their knack for power ballads. While none their ballads stray from the late-'80s formula, the group does them well—good enough to make the record a moderate hit, nearly five years after the style went out of fashion. —*Stephen Thomas Erlewine*

The Firm

Group, Hard Rock
The Firm (incorporated 1985) looked good on paper, with ex-Led Zeppelin guitarist Jimmy Page and former Free lead singer Paul Rogers. Unfortunately, precious little rose above the glut of mass-produced-sounding "rock" that gluted AOR radio in the '80s (or any other decade for that matter). Nevertheless, the Firm's self-titled debut album went #17, producing a hit with the #28 "Radioactive." The second album, *Mean Business*, reached #22. —*Rick Clark*

● **The Firm** / 1985 / Atlantic ✦✦✦✦
This atmospheric rock relies more on the vocals of former Bad Company singer Paul Rodgers than on the guitar of ex-Led Zeppelin Jimmy Page. —*Donna DiChario*

Mean Business / 1986 / Atlantic ✦✦✦
Instead of copying the finely crafted riffs of "Radioactive," the Firm's second and final album wallowed completely in the banal arena-rock that only occasionally appeared on the debut. —*Stephen Thomas Erlewine*

First Choice

Group, Soul

At their peak, First Choice did some sassy, strutting, triumphant disco-flavored soul material. This Philadelphia female trio began as the Debronettes in the late '60s while still high school students. Rochelle Flemming, Annette Guest, and Joyce Jones met writers/producers Norman Harris and Alan Felder in 1972. Their debut single on Wand, "This Is the House Where Love Died," didn't get much attention. But, in 1973, they moved to Philly Groove and made a big impression with "Armed and Extremely Dangerous." It peaked at number 11 on the R&B charts. They got their only Top Ten hit the next year with "The Player—Part 1," which peaked at number seven. "Guilty" reached number 19 that same year. First Choice moved from Philly Groove to Warner Bros. in 1976, but had only one successful record, "Doctor Love," in 1977. As disco and soul's fortunes declined, they failed to generate any more worthy material. *—Ron Wynn*

● Greatest Hits / 1995 / Salsoul ✦✦✦✦

Wild Man Fischer

b. 1945, Los Angeles, CA

Rock & Roll

A mentally disturbed street singer discovered by Frank Zappa, he recorded a double album for Zappa's Bizarre label, some of it with Zappa and the Mothers of Invention, the rest of it solo, giving full vent to nonmetrical original material. He recorded again for the Rhino label in 1977. An acquired taste to be sure, Fischer may surface again. *—Cub Koda*

● Evening with Wild Man Fischer / 1968 / Bizarre ✦✦✦✦

Fischer (aka Larry) proves to be the epitome of the bizarre. It includes the classics "Merry-Go-Round" and "The Taster." For those who lust for the unique. *—David Szatmary*

Wildmania / 1978 / Rhino ✦✦✦

Pronounced Normal / 1981 / Rhino ✦✦✦

Nothing Scary / 1984 / Rhino ✦✦

Fischer's most recent effort shows he hasn't changed. *—David Szatmary*

Fishbone

Group, Funk, Alternative Pop/Rock

Combining equal parts of deep funk, high energy punk, and frantic ska, the Los Angeles-based Fishbone were one of the most distinctive and eclectic alternative rock bands of the late '80s. With their hyper-active, self-conscious diversity, goofy sense of humor, and sharp social commentary, the group gained a sizable cult following during the late '80s, yet they were never able to earn a mainstream audience.

Led by vocalist/saxophonist Angelo Moore, the group formed in 1979 while the band was still in junior high; the original lineup comprised Moore, Chris Dowd, Kendall Jones, Walter Kibby, II, John Norwood Fisher, Fish, and Charlie Down. After performing in local clubs during the early '80s, the group signed with Columbia Records in the mid-'80s, releasing a self-titled EP in 1985. The following year, they released Fishbone released their first full-length album, *In Your Face*. While it was marred by a somewhat slick production, the sheer energy of their performances burned through the slightly polished surface. In 1987, the band released the Christmas EP *It's a Wonderful Life (Gonna Have a Good Time)*.

Truth and Soul (1988), Fishbone's second album, captured the band at their most ambitious, as they slammed back and forth between heavy metal and funk, throwing in an acoustic number and a cover of Curtis Mayfield's "Freddie's Dead" for balance. The album expanded their audience and charted at number 153. However, the band didn't record a new album for another three years. In the meantime, they made two EPs—*Ma and Pa* (1989) and *Bonin' in the Boneyard* (1990)—which basically comprised several B-sides. Before 1991's *The Reality of My Surroundings*, Charlie Down left the band and was replaced by John Bigham. *The Reality of My Surroundings* didn't depart from the band's wreckless eclectism, it refined it. The album was a hit, peaking at number 49 and receiving positive reviews. However, the record didn't establish the band as a mainstream success, nor did 1993's *Give a Monkey a Brain and He'll Swear He's the Center of the Universe*, despite their appearance at Lollapalooza Three. Nevertheless, the group has retained its dedicated following and they remain a pop-

ular concert attraction in the mid-'90s, a decade after their first record. *—Stephen Thomas Erlewine*

Fishbone / 1985 / Columbia ✦✦✦

What a debut! Fierce, funny, and ferocious. *—John Dougan*

In Your Face / 1986 / Columbia ✦✦✦

It's a Wonderful Life (Gonna Have a Good Time) / Oct. 1987 / Columbia ✦✦

○ Truth & Soul / 1988 / Columbia ✦✦✦✦

A perfect mix of their anarchic, chaotic debut with their more recent, thrashier sound still mixes uppity ska beats and licks with Sly and the Family Stone-style funk (good-feeling, choral, beautifully coordinated upbeat soul) and harder, Living Colour-style guitar-driven chops, but this time it comes together better than ever. It prances all over the musical spectrum but never loses its pace or identity. "Ma and Pa," "Freddie's Dead," and funk-punk anthem "Bonin' in the Boneyard." *—Julian Katz*

● The Reality of My Surroundings / 1991 / Columbia ✦✦✦✦

Give a Monkey a Brain and He'll Swear He's the Center of the Universe / May 25, 1993 / Columbia ✦✦

Fishbone's standard careening eclecticism is refined on *Give a Monkey a Brain*. Instead of freely flowing between different styles, as they did on *The Reality of My Surroundings*, the band's sound is reigned in (presumably in an attempt to make Fishbone palatable for the mainstream), making the album impressively diverse but frustrating; they never cut loose like they do in almost all of their concerts. Nevertheless, there's enough good material here to make it worthwhile for dedicated fans. *—Stephen Thomas Erlewine*

The Five Americans

Group, Garage Rock, Pop/Rock

In 1966-67, this Dallas group enjoyed some modest national success with the number five hit "Western Union," as well as a few other Top 40 entries, "I See the Light," "Zip Code," and "Sound of Love." Dominated by high, bubbling organ lines and clean harmony vocals, the group favored high-energy pop/rock far more than British Invasion or R&B-inspired sounds, although a bit of garage/frat rock raunch could be detected in their stomping rhythms. Recording prolifically throughout the last half of the '60s (often with ex-rockabilly star Dale Hawkins as producer), and writing much of their own material, they were ultimately too lightweight and bubblegumish to measure up to either the era's better pop/rock or garage bands. Their 1966 hit "I See the Light" is their toughest and best performance. *—Richie Unterberger*

● Western Union / 1968 / Sundazed ✦✦✦✦

20-song best-of includes all their big and small hits, as well as quite a few rarities and an extensive group history. *—Richie Unterberger*

The Five Keys

Group, R&B, Doo-Wop

A seminal pre-rock vocal group, the Keys are best remembered for the 1951 hit "The Glory of Love." Not quite as rollicking as most doo-woppers, they were steeped more in the traditions of the Ink Spots. *—John Floyd*

Golden Classics / Collectables

Capitol Collectors Series / 1989 / Capitol ✦✦✦

Worthwhile companion volume to *The Aladdin Years*, containing all of their Top 100 singles—"Ling Ting Tong," "Wisdom of a Fool," "Let There Be You," and "Out of Sight, Out of Mind"—as well as lesser-known tracks like "I Wish I'd Never Learned to Read" and "My Pigeon's Gone." *—Stephen Thomas Erlewine*

● The Aladdin Years / 1991 / EMI America ✦✦✦✦

This early '50s doo-wop has a highly polished, easy-on-the-ears sheen. Heavy on the ballads, it also has a few uptempo items. *—Bill Dahl*

The Five Royales

Group, R&B

The North Carolina-based Five Royales practically defined Black vocal group singing in the '50s, with their early sides cut for Apollo as well as their latter-day hits on King. Johnny Tanner's vocals anticipated the sound of Southern soul singing, and Lowman Pauling's stinging guitar licks influenced everyone from Steve Cropper to Eric Clapton. *—John Floyd*

The Five Royales Sing for You / 1959 / King ✦✦✦
An exact reproduction of their best original album, it doesn't have many hits, but the obscurities will keep you interested. —*John Floyd*

★ **Monkey Hips and Rice: the "5" Royales Anthology** / 1994 / Rhino ✦✦✦✦✦
The Five Royales certainly did their share of forgettable period-piece tunes, but they also had transcendent songs like "Think," "Just As I Am" and "Dedicated To The One I Love." They enjoyed a lengthy run, creating many hits plus a few gems, which are all available on this sparkling two-disc set. The opening disc sets the stage, showing their gospel origins and also the rather routine cuts the band did in its formative period. They began to evolve into a more substantial unit in the mid-'50s, and by the late '50s were a sterling unit cutting emphatic, appealing numbers. Most of these appear on the second disc. By the early '60s, they had run their course, but their legacy and impact was secure. This offers the most complete picture of the Five Royales and their superb music. —*Ron Wynn*

The Five Satins

Group, Doo-Wop
Fred Haven and the Five Satins were New Haven, Connecticut's favorite doo-wop sons. Their 1956 hit "In the Still of the Night" gave rock & roll one of its first cuddle anthems, and set the tone for several tasty followups. —*John Floyd*

● **In the Still of The Night** / 1990 / Relic ✦✦✦✦
Everything you need from this sumptuous and smoochy late-night doo-wop quintet is here. The title cut is a work of art worth listening to over and over. —*John Floyd*

The Five Stairsteps

Group, Soul
The Five Stairsteps were a Windy City family affair initially consisting of four brothers and a sister; later on, five-year-old Cubie Burke toddled aboard, and even mom and pop got into the act. Curtis Mayfield discovered the group at a talent contest, and they debuted in 1966 on his Windy C logo with the tender "You Waited Too Long," their first hit. Lead singer Clarence Burke Jr was only 15 years old in 1966, yet his attractive leads on "World of Fantasy" and "Come Back" displayed a wealth of emotion. The group enjoyed its biggest pop hit in 1970 with the classic "O-o-h Child" for Buddah. After a few years apart, the group re-formed and notched a final hit, "From Us to You," on George Harrison's Dark Horse label in 1976. Four of the Burkes recorded as the Invisible Man's Band, scoring a sizable seller in 1980 with "All Night Thing," and bassist Keni Burke has recorded as a solo artist. —*Bill Dahl*

● **Greatest Hits** / Collectables ✦✦✦✦
This hits package examines the adolescent Chicago soul group from their mid-'60s beginning through their 1970 bubblegum soul hit "O-o-h Child." —*Bill Dahl*

The Fixx

Group, New Wave, Pop/Rock
A London-based new wave group that managed to sustain a successful career in America for several years in the mid-'80s, the Fixx always flirted with mainstream pop with their catchy, keyboard-driven pop. Formed by college friends vocalist/keyboardist Cy Curnin and drummer Adam Woods in the early '80s, the pair advertised in the music press for additional members; the remaining members of the group—guitarist Jamie West-Oram, keyboardist Rupert Greenall, and bassist Charlie Barret—all responded to the ad. Taking the name the Portraits, the band recorded a single for Ariola Records, "Hazards in the Home," which failed to gather much attention. Within a year, the band had changed their name to the Fixx and recorded "Lost Planes," the single which led to a record contract with MCA.

The Fixx released their debut album, the Rupert Hine-produced *Shuttered Room*, in 1982. The record spawned to minor U.K. hits, "Stand or Fall" and "Red Skies," and spent a short time in the charts. In America, none of the singles were hits, yet the album stayed on the charts for nearly a year. After *Shuttered Room*, Barret left the group and was replaced by Dan K. Brown. *Reach the Beach*, released in 1983, established them as a hit-making force in the U.S. The terse, pulsating "One Thing Leads to Another" became a number four hit, sending the album into the Top Ten. *Reach the Beach* would go platinum by the end of the year,

launching two more Top 40 singles—"Saved by Zero" and "Sign of Fire." Despite all of their American success, the Fixx failed to break back into the British charts with *Reach the Beach*; in fact, they never had another British hit in their career.

The Fixx returned in 1984 with *Phantoms*. While it performed well—it peaked at number 19 and went gold—it didn't match the success of *Reach the Beach*; after it launched the number 15 single "Are We Ourselves?," the record fell off the charts. Although their audience was shrinking, the band kept their basic, synth-driven sound intact for 1986's *Walkabout*, which featured the hit "Secret Separation." After *Walkabout*, the Fixx stopped working with producer Rupert Hine, which resulted in a harder, more guitar-oriented sound for 1988's *Calm Animals*. The album charted at number 72, but it spawned no hit singles. *Ink* (1991) the group's last album, didn't reverse their declining fortunes, even though they tried to update their sound with an emphasis on guitars and slick, dance-ready beats. After the record failed to recapture their mainstream audience, the Fixx quietly faded away. —*Stephen Thomas Erlewine*

Shuttered Room / 1982 / MCA ✦✦✦
Their debut features "Stand or Fall" and "Red Skies." —*Larry Lapka*

○ **Reach the Beach** / 1983 / MCA ✦✦✦✦
This superb techno-pop includes "One Thing Leads to Another" and "Saved by Zero." —*Larry Lapka*

Phantoms / 1984 / MCA ✦✦✦

Walkabout / 1986 / MCA ✦✦✦

React / 1987 / MCA ✦✦

Calm Animals / 1988 / RCA ✦✦

● **One Thing Leads to Another: Greatest Hits** / 1989 / MCA ✦✦✦✦
All their hits are here, including "One Thing Leads to Another" (#4), "Are We Ourselves" (#15), "The Sign of Fire" (#32), "Secret Separation" (#19), "Stand or Fall" (#76), and "Saved by Zero" (#20). —*Larry Lapka*

Ink / 1991 / Impact ✦✦

Roberta Flack

b. Feb. 10, 1939, Ashville, NC
Soul, Urban
Flack has made a career out of giving composed readings of ultra-smooth ballads. The urbane restraint of her music has attracted fans of light commercial jazz and romantic urban R&B.Flack's biggest include "The First Time Ever I Saw Your Face" (#1), "Killing Me Softly with His Song" (#1), "Feel like Making Love" (#1), and "Making Love," as well as duets with Donny Hathaway, "Where Is the Love?" and "The Closer I Get to You." —*Rick Clark*

○ **First Take** / 1969 / Atlantic ✦✦✦✦
The album that launched Roberta Flack's career. She had been doing background vocals and also recording with Les McCann, who helped her land at Atlantic. The single "The First Time Ever I Saw Your Face" zoomed into the pop stratosphere after it was included in Clint Eastwood's film *Play Misty For Me*. —*Ron Wynn*

○ **Chapter Two** / Aug. 1970 / Atlantic ✦✦✦✦
A great album and the release that made Roberta Flack a major soul and R&B artist in the early '70s. She had a soft, compelling, alluring voice, and was able to convincingly switch gears and also convey anger, regret, hurt, or despair. Those who thought Flack was a one-hit wonder, or didn't think she could make the transition from doing jazz to other styles, were convinced otherwise. —*Ron Wynn*

Quiet Fire / Nov. 1971 / Atlantic ✦✦✦
Another super Roberta Flack album. She had now become one of the masters of what some described as "middle-class soul," restrained, elegant ballads sung in an exuberant but non-gospel fashion. It continued her string of Top 20 albums on both the R&B and pop side, and remains a staple on urban contemporary and adult contemporary outlets. —*Ron Wynn*

○ **Roberta Flack & Donny Hathaway** / Apr. 1972 / Atlantic ✦✦✦✦
A duet classic, and perhaps the most popular album Roberta Flack made. Their single "Where Is the Love" dominated urban contemporary radio for almost the entire year, while "You've Got a Friend" was just as influential and was later covered by numerous artists (of course they didn't write it, but a lot of folks thought they did). It did so well that Flack eventually did other duet material and also became very close to Hathaway. —*Ron Wynn*

○ **Killing Me Softly** / Aug. 1973 / Atlantic ✦✦✦✦
The title track was another smash for Roberta Flack, and the album continued in the same tradition as *Chapter Two* and *A Quiet Fire*. She made simmering ballads, declarative message songs, and better-than-average uptempo numbers, and at the time was among the top-selling female vocalists in any style. —*Ron Wynn*

Feel Like Makin' Love / Mar. 1975 / Atlantic ✦✦✦
Intimate set with title tune and "Mr. Magic." —*Bil Carpenter*

Blue Lights in the Basement / Dec. 1977 / Atlantic ✦✦✦
Soulful setting with the intoxicating "The Closer I Get to You" duet with Hathaway, "This Time I'll Be Sweeter." Background vocals by Deniece Williams, etc. Ahmet Ertegun produced. —*Bil Carpenter*

○ **The Best of Roberta Flack** / 1980 / Atlantic ✦✦✦✦
Showcases her biggest ballads, including "First Time Ever I Saw Your Face" (#1), "Feel Like Making Love" (#1), "Killing Me Softly with His Song" (#1), as well as her duets with Donny Hathaway, "Where Is the Love" (#5) and "The Closer I Get to You" (#2). —*Bil Carpenter*

Born to Love / Jul. 1983 / Capitol ✦✦✦
A duet set with Peabo Bryson on which they sing mood songs like "Tonight, I Celebrate My Love" and "You're Lookin' Like Love to Me." —*Bil Carpenter*

● **Softly with These Songs: the Best of Roberta Flack** / Jun. 22, 1993 / Atlantic ✦✦✦✦
While it includes almost everything on *Best of Roberta Flack*, *Softly with These Songs* covers material after 1980, including the hits "Tonight, I Celebrate My Love" and "Making Love," which makes it the preferable compilation. —*Stephen Thomas Erlewine*

The Flamin' Groovies

Group, Rock & Roll, Power Pop/Anglo-Pop
One of America's greatest, most influential, and legendary cult bands, the Flamin' Groovies came out of the San Francisco area in 1965 playing greasy, bluesy, rock & roll dashed with a liberal sprinkling of British Invasion panache in an era soon to be dominated by hippie culture and hyperextended raga-rock freakouts. Caught in a double bind of playing the wrong kind of music at the wrong time (as well as not looking the part), the Groovies were almost completely forgotten as the Fillmore/Avalon Ballroom scenes, dominated by the Dead, the Jefferson Airplane, et al., rendered them anachronistic. The plain truth, however, was that despite not being in tune with the zeitgeist, the Groovies made great music, and managed to sustain a career that lasted for over two decades.

What made the Groovies such a formidable band was the double dynamite supplied by guitarist Cyril Jordan and singer/wildman Roy A. Loney. Together they formed an uneasy partnership that guided the band through its most fertile period, from 1968-1971. In 1968, for next to nothing, the band recorded a seven-song EP entitled *Sneakers*. This little bit of DIY ingenuity resulted in a contract with Epic and the huge sum of $80,000 (1968 dollars, mind you) to be spent on their debut recording, *Supersnazz*. It was a great album that didn't sell but did get them dropped from Epic. Quickly signing with Kama Sutra, the Groovies closed the '60s and started the '70s with two terrific records (*Flamingo* and *Teenage Head*), but public apathy and the increasingly tempestuous relationship between Jordan and Loney led to the latter's departure for a solo career in 1971. Jordan, now free to run the band as a "benevolent" dictator and indulge his passion for a more folk-rock (read: Byrds) focus, hired guitarist/vocalist Chris Wilson, curiously added the apostrophe to their first name, and in 1972 moved the band to England.

Oddly enough, the Groovies had a larger, more enthusiastic following in Europe (especially in England and Germany) than they did in the States, and it seemed perfectly reasonable to assume that if great rewards were to be reaped, it would happen in Europe first. Hooking up with Dave Edmunds, who was keen to produce them, Jordan and company recorded a handful of songs as early as 1972. However, this seemingly natural collaboration yielded little until 1976, when the Groovies released their finest post-Loney effort, *Shake Some Action*. Loaded with ringing guitars, great covers, and Edmunds' spongy, bass-heavy production, *Shake Some Action* became a well-received album in punk-era Britain, as was the fine followup, *Flamin' Groovies Now*. This new notoriety brought renewed interest in the Groovies in America, but the string of good albums ended abruptly with the mostly covers and mostly forgettable *Jumpin' In The Night* in 1979. Clearly, the band

had run out of gas. That fact, however, did little to convince Cyril Jordan that the Flamin' Groovies in any form were no longer viable.

So, after five or six years of no new music—there were instead countless repackagings, anthologies, and lousy bootlegs—the band ended up in Australia, now reduced to Jordan and a bunch of unknowns (with the exception of longtime bassist George Alexander), shamelessly covering '60s material and living off the band's legend. Apparently Jordan, 20-plus years since the Groovies' first record, still flogs a version of the band to anyone willing to listen. Expectations for quality new music by the Groovies are at an all-time low. It should be noted that after his departure in 1971, Roy Loney, after a couple of music industry jobs, made (and still makes) some wonderful records with his band the Phantom Movers (with ex-Groovies drummer Danny Mihm). Loney still occasionally works behind the counter at Jack's Record Cellar in San Francisco (stop in and say hello), and has most recently been recording with the Young Fresh Fellows. —*John Dougan*

Sneakers [10 Inch] / 1968 / Snazz ✦✦✦

Supersnazz / 1968 / Epic ✦✦✦
For an unknown band, Epic sank a lot of money into this record, and wasn't happy when it didn't sell. But that's hardly the fault of the band, who sound great despite the intrusive overproduction of novice knob-twiddler Steve Goldman. Loney's yelping lead vocals are in fine form and the rest of the band rocks with a reckless abandon and stunning succinctness that was totally out-of-step with the times. —*John Dougan*

○ **Flamingo** / 1970 / Kama Sutra ✦✦✦✦
Licking their wounds after the Epic fiasco, the Groovies resurfaced on the much smaller Kama Sutra label and tore off this chunk of delirium that marked their best early '70s work. Jordan and second guitarist Tim Lynch fire off salvo after salvo of James Burton-tinged riffing, while Loney is, well, himself; his twitchy, rockabilly-styled vocalizing never wears thin. There's a great cover of Little Richard's "Keep a-Knockin'," and even better is Loney's hip and hilarious "Second Cousin." —*John Dougan*

○ **Teenage Head** / 1971 / Big Beat ✦✦✦✦
The last and best Flamin' Groovies record made with Roy Loney, *Teenage Head* is probably the most influential record they ever made. A favorite of the hip New York rock crowd (many of whom are thanked on the album jacket), this is a rip-snorter from the Loney/Jordan-penned "High Flyin' Baby" to the cover of Randy Newman's "Have You Seen My Baby?" The title track is a classic bit of teenage angst that sounds as fresh today as it did 24 years ago. —*John Dougan*

Slow Death / 1976 / United Artists ✦✦✦

○ **Shake Some Action** / 1976 / Sire ✦✦✦✦
The Groovies disappeared into the wilds of Europe after *Teenage Head*, which barely earned them a cult following over here. They went through a few personnel changes, honed their sound to an even finer point, and developed a few more musical smarts. Then came *Shake Some Action*, the debut of the Flamin' Groovies' Mark II, where they rocked out British-style for most of it (while still acknowledging their American roots), only louder and more passionately than any British Invasion band had played since 1964. The sound was a complete anachronism in the mid-'70s, but it got them noticed and earned them a cult following. The guitar sound is straight 1964 Beatles (a la "Not a Second Time") alternating with Kinks material of the same era, the vocals are the plaintive wailing of lovesick young rock gods, and the effect is stunning even 20 years on. Maybe the greatest British Invasion album since 1964. Reissued by Australia's AIM Records on CD, and well worth tracking down as an import. —*Bruce Eder*

○ **Still Shakin'** / 1976 / Buddah ✦✦✦✦
Buddah Records, the successor to Kama Sutra, seeing that the boys were finally getting their due in the rock press, put together this cool little cash-in effort, which combined the best tracks from *Flamingo* and *Teenage Head* with a bunch of outtakes into a sort of "best-of" the Mark I Groovies. The leftover tracks are even rawer and better than the released material, and this record only added to the passion that fans old and new felt for the band. —*Bruce Eder*

○ **The Flamin' Groovies Now!** / 1978 / Sire ✦✦✦✦
So the group is getting all kinds of great press, and even some radio play from their comeback album on Sire, and embark on a national tour, playing clubs like the Bottom Line in New York before

every rock V.I.P. who could wangle a ticket. And to accompany the tour, they put out an album of yet more British invasion-style (and pre-British invasion—they covered Cliff Richard & the Shadows' 1958 hit "Move It" alongside Beatles and Stones material) tracks. The sound on this record was a notable improvement over *Shake Some Action*, and the group had lost none of its flair for the period or the style, but there was also precious little new ground covered, which cost them some credibility with the press even if it didn't bother the fans at all. And their cover of the Gene Clark/Byrds classic rocker "Feel a Whole Lot Better" was one of the best remakes of a '60s classic ever recorded, outdoing the original at every turn (a few fans suggested that the Byrds might reunite to cover the Groovies' "Shake Some Action" in return). —*Bruce Eder*

Jumpin' in the Night / 1979 / Sire ♦♦♦
The Groovies' third British Invasion-revival style album was actually even better than the second, but Sire by this time was hedging its bets, replacing a cover of the Rolling Stones' "19th Nervous Breakdown" with Warren Zevon's "Werewolves of London" on the U.S. version. It didn't gain the band any added sales, and alienated hardcore fans, who had to buy the import to get the Stones cover. By this time, the record company was losing interest and the band was going through major personnel changes as well, and it would be a while before the Groovies turned up on another full-length album again. —*Bruce Eder*

Bucketful of Brains / 1983 / Voxx ♦♦♦

Flamin' Groovies Studio '68 / 1984 / Eva ♦♦♦
The very earliest Flamin' Groovies material ever to be issued, taken from live studio tapes cut on January 10, 1968. Lead singer Roy Loney's songs dominate this session, which also includes a couple of Lovin' Spoonful numbers and a version of the blues "Sportin' Life"; a couple tunes would later show up on their *Sneakers* EP. Most of this material is good-timey, blues/R&B-influenced rock, in the spirit of the earliest recordings of the Charlatans, Dead, and Big Brother. The jugband influence of the Lovin' Spoonful also pervades a few tracks, in an unimpressive fashion. This hardly stacks up with the best San Francisco rock of the time; its appeal will largely lie with Groovies fanatics (a not inconsiderable audience) looking for a glimpse of the group's roots. By far the most impressive track is "Good Morning, Mr. Stone," a seven-minute psychedelic workout with guitar work inspired by Jeff Beck, Pete Townshend, and Jorma Kaukonen, as well as a brief lift of a snatch of the Who's "A Quick One." —*Richie Unterberger*

The Gold Star Tapes / 1984 / Skydog
The Flamin' Groovies were off Sire Records, and without a major label contract, when this mysterious four-song EP turned up as an import in U.S. shops. The sound is ragged, as the material was taken from acetates rather than master tapes, and the work on this material was never really finished. But oh the covers of Byrds material like "She Don't Care About Time," and the Phil Spector '60s classic "River Deep, Mountain High," which makes every other rock band version of that song (even the one by the Easybeats) look anemic by comparison. —*Bruce Eder*

● **Groovies' Greatest Grooves** / 1989 / Sire ♦♦♦♦
More or less what it says, a 24-song best-of including much of their finest Sire Records material, including a few rarities and out-takes (including "River Deep, Mountain High," and most of their best Beatles and Dylan covers—but why no real Stones covers?), rounded out with a few of the better tracks from the pre-Sire Kama Sutra period. The notes are voluminous and enjoyable, and the music holds up even two decades later. An essential part of any serious rock record collection. —*Bruce Eder*

○ **The Rockfield Sessions** / 1989 / Aim ♦♦♦♦

Rock Juice / 1993 / National ♦♦♦

The Flaming Lips

Group, Alternative Pop/Rock
The Flaming Lips' latter-day psychedelia combines the swirling guitar of '60s psychedelia with the smart-ass humor of '80s post-punk, throwing in everything that comes in between. Even when the Lips come close to traditional rock & roll (like 1989's *Telepathic Surgery*), it still has an endearingly weird, catchy eclecticism, if not an infectious experimentalism. When the band jumped to a major label in 1992, their music didn't change—it was still the same druggy, alternative psychedelia that they flaunted on their 1985 debut. The group had a surprise hit single in late 1994 with "She Don't Use Jelly." —*Stephen Thomas Erlewine*

Flaming Lips / 1985 / Restless ♦♦♦
Good early stuff! —*John Dougan*

○ **Hear It Is** / 1986 / Restless ♦♦♦♦
Trippy, but rocks! —*John Dougan*

○ **Oh My Gawd!!! ... the Flaming Lips** / 1987 / Restless ♦♦♦♦
Convoluted, but with plenty of surprises. —*John Dougan*

Telepathic Surgery / 1989 / Restless ♦♦

In a Priest Driven Ambulance / 1990 / Restless ♦♦♦

Hit to Death in the Future Head / 1992 / Warner Brothers ♦♦♦
Filled with blazing guitars and elliptical melodies, the band's first album for a major label shows no signs of a sellout. —*Stephen Thomas Erlewine*

● **Transmissions from the Satellite Heart** / Jan. 1993 / Warner Brothers ♦♦♦♦
Not as bracingly weird as their previous records, the Flaming Lips' first album for a major label is still stranger than most music. With a good portion of the band now in Mercury Rev, the Flaming Lips veer closer to the inspired wackiness of They Might be Giants. *Transmissions From the Satellite Heart* is halfway between the pseudo-psychedlic guitar and flute explorations of Mercury Rev and the smartass, do-it-yourself jokiness of Ween, making it their most accessible, as well as consistent, album yet. —*Stephen Thomas Erlewine*

The Flamingos

Group, Doo-Wop
Both prolific and seminal in their influence and impact, The Flamingos may have been the greatest harmonizing vocal ensemble ever, and were certainly among the premier units of the doo-wop/R&B era. Cousins Jake and Zeke Carey moved to Chicago from Baltimore in 1950. They met Paul Wilson and Johnny Carter at the Church of God and Saints of Christ Congregation, a black Jewish church. They began singing in the choir, and the foursome met Earl Lewis (not the Channels' lead vocalist) through one of the members' sisters, who was his girlfriend at the time. They originally called themselves the Swallows, but had to change names when they found out that a Baltimore group already had the name. Carter suggested El Flamingos, which was changed to the Five Flamingos, and later the Flamingos. Ralph Leon of the King Booking Agency eventually became their manager. Sollie McElroy replaced Lewis as their lead singer in the early '50s, with Lewis joining the Five Echoes. They recorded with Chance in 1953, and "If I Can't Have You" attracted some attention and did well in the Midwest and on the East Coast. "That's My Desire" and "Golden Teardrops" were marvelously sung numbers, particularly "Golden Teardrops," with its sweeping harmonies on top and bottom framing McElroy's wondrous lead. But none of their great Chance recordings generated enough national attention to make the R&B charts, nor did the three numbers they recorded for Parrot. McElroy departed and was replaced by Nate Nelson. They enjoyed their first chart success with Checker in the late '50s, scoring a Top Ten R&B hit with "I'll Be Home" in 1956. They temporarily disbanded in 1956 and regrouped in 1957 with Nelson, Jake Carey, Paul Wilson, and Tommy Hunt as the lineup, and the group now a quartet. Zeke Carey returned in 1958, and they signed with End late that year. "I Only Have Eyes for You" in 1959 was their biggest hit, peaking at number three R&B and number 11 pop. It was a cover of a song that had been a huge hit for Eddy Duchin in 1934, and was the start of a productive period that saw the Flamingos issue four albums for End and get two more R&B Top 30 singles, one the Sam Cooke composition "Nobody Loves Me like You" in 1960. Hunt left in 1961, and the group returned briefly to Checker in 1964. They later recorded for Phillips, Julman, and Polydor, but couldn't regain their former standing. They remained among the genre's most beloved groups, and anthologies of their material on Chance and Checker have been reissued. In 1993, *The Flamingos Meet the Moonglows* was reissued by Vee-Jay. —*Ron Wynn*

★ **The Doo Bop She Bop: Best of the Flamingos** / 1990 / Rhino ♦♦♦♦♦
This splendid collection of smooth doo-wop includes "I Only Have Eyes for You" and the gorgeous "The Vow." Beautiful stuff. —*John Floyd*

Flash and the Pan

Group, New Wave
The best-known alter-ego of the Vanda/Young songwriting team

(the creative force behind the Easybeats), Flash & the Pan began simply as a between-production project in 1976. By 1979, the project had turned out a novelty hit with the single "Hey St. Peter." A second single, "Down Among the Dead," also became a hit throughout Australia and Europe, inspiring the release of the album *Flash & the Pan*. American radio began playing import copies which led to a deal with Epic Records. The album would soon reach the top 100 in the U.S. despite the lack of a supporting tour. They released two more albums with some minor success in the U.K. but failed to make much impact due to the part-time nature of the project. —*Chris Woodstra*

● **Collection** / 1994 / Epic ◆◆◆◆
This 15-track collection provides the best picture of the band. All of the singles, including the classic "Hey, St. Peter" and "Down Among the Dead Man," can be found here so this should satisfy most listeners. —*Chris Woodstra*

Fleetwood Mac

Group, Blues Rock, Pop/Rock
Fleetwood Mac, formed in 1967, initially began as one of Britain's great blues-influenced rock ensembles. Over the course of many lineup changes and a relocation to Los Angeles in 1974, "Big Mac" evolved into one of the most successful pop/rock units in commercial music history.

During the early years, Fleetwood Mac endured a succession of unstable (but brilliant) lead-guitarist/singer/songwriters in Peter Green, Danny Kirwan, and Jeremy Spencer. Green and Spencer eventually jumped ship for cultish religious pursuits, and Kirwan (who ended up in a psychiatric hospital) was fired in 1972 for refusing to go on stage at a Munich gig. Green, in particular, wrote some classics in "Oh Well," "Black Magic Woman" (later a hit for Santana), and "The Green Manalishi (With the Two-Pronged Crown)." Danny Kirwan contributed many of the standout tracks on albums like *Bare Trees*, including the haunting "Dust," the ethereal "Sunny Side of Heaven," and the propulsive title track.

Bob Welch, a Los Angeles resident, was brought on board in 1971. During his time with Fleetwood Mac, Welch penned some standouts as well, like "Hypnotized" and "Sentimental Lady." During all these changes, drummer Mick Fleetwood, bassist John McVie, and vocalist and keyboardist Christine McVie (also a fine songwriter) provided the glue for the proceedings.

In January of 1975 Welch left, and engineer and producer Keith Olsen turned the band on to a tape of Lindsey Buckingham and Stevie Nicks (who had previously released a much-sought-after debut on Polydor called *Buckingham Nicks*). They were hired onto Fleetwood Mac, and the rest is history.

Fleetwood Mac, the first album featuring the new lineup, became a goldmine, eventually hitting #1 in November 1976, fifteen months after its release. After much inner turmoil, Fleetwood Mac put out *Rumours*, which topped charts around the world and became one of the biggest albums in history. Mac never duplicated the impact of *Rumours*, but subsequent albums (*Tusk, Fleetwood Mac Live, Mirage, Tango in the Night*) have been substantial successes.

Buckingham (who left in 1987) and Nicks have enjoyed solid solo careers, and Christine McVie had a #10 hit in 1984 with "Got a Hold on Me" from her self-titled solo album.

Fleetwood Mac reunited with two new guitarists in 1989, releasing the lackluster *Behind the Mask*.

In November 1993, confirming the departure of Stevie Nicks and guitarist Billy Burnette, Fleetwood Mac announced the addition of vocalist Bekka Bramlett and veteran singer, songwriter, and guitarist Dave Mason to the band's lineup, joining Fleetwood and the McVies. —*Rick Clark*

○ **English Rose** / Jan. 1969 / Epic ◆◆◆◆
Under the direction of Peter Green, Fleetwood Mac is heard as a British blues group, although its most notable performances are on Green's original tunes "Black Magic Woman" and "Albatross," both British hits. —*William Ruhlmann*

○ **Pious Bird of Good Omen [Comp]** / Aug. 1969 / Blue Horizon ◆◆◆◆
This is a compilation of Fleetwood Mac's early period, 1967-1968, featuring both sides of its debut single, "I Believe My Time Ain't Long"/"Rambling Pony" and many blues covers, as well as the hits "Albatross" and "Black Magic Woman." —*William Ruhlmann*

Then Play On / Oct. 1969 / Reprise ◆◆◆
The most diverse and accomplished album by the Peter Green-led lineup. Features some wrenching, introspective originals that draw from both blues and progressive rock, highlighted by the doomy British hit single "Oh Well." —*Richie Unterberger*

Kiln House / Sep. 1970 / Reprise ◆◆◆
Fleetwood Mac's first album after the departure of their nominal leader, Peter Green, finds the remaining members, Mick Fleetwood, John McVie, Jeremy Spencer, and Danny Kirwan (plus McVie's wife Christine) trying to maintain the band's guitar-heavy, blues-rock approach, with the burden falling on Spencer and Kirwan. They don't embarrass themselves, but none of this is of the caliber of Green's work. —*William Ruhlmann*

Future Games / Nov. 1971 / Reprise ◆◆◆
By the time of this album's release, Jeremy Spencer had been replaced by Bob Welch and Christine McVie had begun to assert herself more as a singer and songwriter. The result is a distinct move toward folk-rock and pop; this album sounds almost nothing like "Peter Green's Fleetwood Mac." Welch's eight-minute title track has one of his characteristic haunting melodies, and with pruning and better editing could have been a hit. Christine McVie's "Show Me a Smile" is one of her loveliest ballads. Initial popular reaction was mixed: the album didn't sell as well as *Kiln House*, but it sold better than any of the band's first three albums in the U.S. In the U.K., where the original lineup had been more successful, *Future Games* didn't chart at all, the same fate that would befall the rest of its albums until the Lindsey Buckingham-Stevie Nicks era. —*William Ruhlmann*

● **Bare Trees** / Mar. 1972 / Reprise ◆◆◆◆
On *Bare Trees*, Fleetwood Mac married the gritty electric blues-rock of their earlier incarnations to the classic pop sensibilities that would later become fully realized in 1975's *Fleetwood Mac*. Bob Welch's "Sentimental Lady" and Christine McVie's soulful "Spare Me a Little of Your Love" are highlights. Danny Kirwin revealed an ability to compose highly melodic material that didn't constrain the band's legendary musical chemistry. —*Rick Clark*

Penguin / Mar. 1973 / Reprise ◆◆
Fleetwood Mac's first album made after the departure of Danny Kirwan features the additions of guitarist Bob Weston and singer Dave Walker. By now Bob Welch and Christine McVie were the dominant forces in the band, and all traces of blues-rock were gone, replaced by Welch's hypnotic melodies and McVie's romantic sentiments married to uptempo pop tunes. This album gave Fleetwood Mac its best U.S. chart showing yet, but the wonder is that this phase in the band's career wasn't even more popular. —*William Ruhlmann*

Mystery to Me / Oct. 1973 / Reprise ◆◆◆
At this point, Fleetwood Mac is a mainstream rock band whose songs alternate between guitarist/singer Robert Welch and keyboard player/singer Christine McVie. —*William Ruhlmann*

Heroes Are Hard to Find / Sep. 1974 / Reprise ◆◆◆
Welch's peak as a songwriter (with new highs by Christine McVie) is also his swan song with the group. —*William Ruhlmann*

Fleetwood Mac in Chicago / 1975 / Sire ◆◆
A two-record set culled from sessions the Peter Green/Danny Kirwan/Mick Fleetwood/John McVie edition of the band held at Chess Studios in Chicago in January 1969 with such blues legends as Otis Spann and Willie Dixon. Despite their care, the Brits hold their own on a set of standards. (Reissued on CD under the title *In Chicago 1969* on April 26, 1994.) —*William Ruhlmann*

☆ **Fleetwood Mac** / Jul. 1975 / Reprise ◆◆◆◆◆
The addition of Lindsey Buckingham and Stevie Nicks, plus the increasing quality of Christine McVie's songs, results in massive success. This #1 album, one of the finest collections of pop/rock in the decade, contains the hits "Rhiannon," "Over My Head," and "Say You Love Me." —*William Ruhlmann*

Original Fleetwood Mac / 1977 / Sire ◆◆
This collection of outtakes from the group's early days probably dates from 1967-68, and finds the band at their most reverently bluesy. Peter Green wrote most of the material on this set, which is quite similar to the band's first couple albums in its purist British take on traditional electric blues forms. The material, however, isn't nearly as strong as the best early Fleetwood Mac; not that the band should be faulted for that, as this is an outtake collection, after all. A couple of the tunes featuring Jeremy Spencer are actually taken from an audition that Spencer's pre-Fleetwood

Mac outfit, the Levi Set, recorded for the Blue Horizon label in England. The best track is the driving instrumental "Fleetwood Mac," and has been rumored to be an outtake from Green's days with John Mayall's Bluesbreakers. —*Richie Unterberger*

★ **Rumours** / Feb. 4, 1977 / Reprise ✦✦✦✦
Among the best-selling albums of all time, this brilliant song cycle about the travails of love features "Dreams," "Don't Stop," "Go Your Own Way," and "You Make Loving Fun." —*William Ruhlmann*

○ **Tusk** / Oct. 1979 / Reprise ✦✦✦✦
In some ways even more impressive than *Rumours*, this two-record set (compressed onto one CD by editing "Sara," one of its hits!) is an ambitious effort full of unusual arrangements and striking instrumental passages, plus a wealth of topflight song-writing. —*William Ruhlmann*

Fleetwood Mac Live / Dec. 1980 / Reprise ✦✦✦
Fleetwood Mac's first live album finds it at its popular height, pumping out hit after hit. To its credit, the group nevertheless puts out: Fleetwood drums like a demon and Buckingham plays fiercely. All the hits you'd expect are here, spread across two discs, and there's also a charming backstage rendition of the Beach Boys' "Farmer's Daughter." —*William Ruhlmann*

Mirage / Jun. 1982 / Reprise ✦✦✦
A tuneful, tastefully produced album that makes up in songcraft ("Hold Me," "Gypsy") what it lacks in the anguished passion that was once Fleetwood Mac's stock in trade. —*William Ruhlmann*

Jumping at Shadows / 1985 / Varrick ✦✦✦
Recorded live in Boston in 1969, this finds the Peter Green-era Mac at their best on seven lengthy but focused cuts. Includes versions of "Black Magic Woman" and "Oh Well," as well as a couple of straight blues covers and some Danny Kirwan material. —*Richie Unterberger*

Cerulean / 1985 / Shanghai ✦✦✦
From the same 1969 Boston gigs that produced *Jumping at Shadows*, this double album's appeal is more limited, with a heavier emphasis on straight blues boogie and eccentric fifties rock & roll parodies that featured Jeremy Spencer. Highlights are the 16-minute version of the British hit "Green Manalishi" and the 24-minute version of "Rattlesnake Shake." —*Richie Unterberger*

Tango in the Night / 1987 / Reprise ✦✦✦
Buckingham's final effort with the group strongly features his dramatic production techniques and striking guitar playing on his own "Big Love" and Christine McVie's terrific "Little Lies," among other tracks. —*William Ruhlmann*

● **Greatest Hits [Reprise]** / Nov. 1988 / Reprise ✦✦✦✦
A well-chosen best-of. The cassette version has three more tracks than the LP. —*William Ruhlmann*

Behind the Mask / Apr. 1990 / Reprise ✦✦
25 Years: the Chain / Nov. 24, 1992 / Reprise ✦✦✦
Overall, Fleetwood Mac's four-CD box set, *25 Years—The Chain*, contains a lot of great music, with plenty of the 1970s hits that made them one of the biggest bands in the world. It fails as a complete chronicle; not enough weight is given to the early, blues-based Mac with Peter Green, and there are too many songs (nearly a whole disc's worth) from the lightweight 1980s albums. Also, the haphazard song sequencing doesn't help matters—it doesn't make the case for Fleetwood Mac's music as a body of work, and it doesn't trace the evolution, which should be apparent from the diversity of the music. If nothing else, *25 Years—The Chain* offers evidence that Lindsey Buckingham was a brilliant pop composer and that the band's '70s success was well-deserved. —*Stephen Thomas Erlewine*

BOOK

✦✦✦ **Fleetwood Mac: Rumours 'N' Fax**, by Roy Carr & Steve Clarke (Harmony, 1978). The format of this book is essentially the same as Carr's fine *Illustrated Record* series: every recording the band did is analyzed in some depth, interspersed with lots of fine vintage photos and press clippings. The text also includes quite a bit of background information about what was happening in this volatile group's professional and personal lives, illustrating the reasons behind their odd metamorphosis from one of Britain's leading blues-rock acts through progressive rock and their eventual ascension (after major personnel changes) to mainstream pop superstardom. All very well done

and well-written, though there probably aren't many listeners who have a strong interest in all phases of Fleetwood Mac's career: those who followed them during the Peter Green era will probably skip the Buckingham-Nicks period altogether, and vice versa. —*Richie Unterberger*

The Fleetwoods

Group, Doo-Wop, Pop/Rock
An ultra-smooth White pop vocal trio who, in the late '50s, recorded some of the most delicate hits of the rock era. —*John Floyd*

● **The Best of the Fleetwoods** / 1990 / Rhino ✦✦✦✦
Rhino's *Best of the Fleetwoods* contains all of their hits ("Come Softly to Me," "Mr. Blue," and sixteen other songs) on a smartly assembled collection. —*Stephen Thomas Erlewine*

○ **Come Softly to Me: the Very Best of the Fleetwoods** / Aug. 10, 1993 / EMI ✦✦✦✦
While the single-disc collection *Come Softly to Me—The Very Best of the Fleetwoods* is a treasure for devoted fans, featuring alternate takes, radio commercials, a comprehensive discography, fine liner notes, and unreleased material. Casual listeners will find all of this material extraneous; they will find everything they need on Rhino's collection. —*Stephen Thomas Erlewine*

Flipper

Group, Alternative Pop/Rock, Hardcore
These San Francisco-based grunge boys were hardcore's most deliberately slovenly group, making feedback-drenched music that droned at a dreary pace. Their early singles ("Love Canal," "Ha Ha Ha," "Getaway") are essential West Coast punk nuggets. —*John Floyd*

● **Generic Album** / 1982 / Def American ✦✦✦✦
Slower-than-death riffing, screamed vocals, and the great "Sex Bomb." What a delight! —*John Dougan*

Gone Fishin' / 1984 / Subterranean ✦✦✦
Blow'n Chunks: Live / 1984 / Combat ✦✦
A good live album. —*John Dougan*
Public Flipper Limited / 1986 / Subterranean ✦✦✦
Sex Bomb Baby / 1988 / Subterranean ✦✦✦
American Grafishy / 1993 / Warner Brothers ✦✦

A Flock of Seagulls

Group, New Wave
A Liverpool new wave group with a name derived from the novel *Jonathan Livingston Seagull*, featuring lead singer/keyboard player Mike Score (b. Nov 5, 1957), his brother Ali (drums), Paul Reynolds (guitar), and Frank Maudsley (drums). They formed in 1979, hit with "I Ran (So Far Away)" in 1982, split up in 1986, and have since re-formed. —*William Ruhlmann*

Magic / 1981 / GNP ✦✦
○ **A Flock of Seagulls** / 1982 / Jive ✦✦✦✦
A Flock of Seagulls scored one big hit, "I Ran," in the driving, quick-tempo dance style that characterized most of their work. It's here, along with several similar tracks. —*William Ruhlmann*

Listen / 1983 / Jive ✦✦✦
The Story of a Young Heart / 1984 / Jive ✦✦
Dream Come True / 1986 / Jive ✦✦
● **The Best of a Flock of Seagulls** / 1987 / Jive ✦✦✦✦
Every good song A Flock of Seagulls ever recorded is available on this fine collection, including the new wave classic "I Ran (So Far Away)." —*Stephen Thomas Erlewine*

Flop

Group, Alternative Pop/Rock
Flop formed in 1989 when vocalist and guitarist Rusty Willoughby and drummer Nate Johnson left the group Pure Joy and joined up with guitarist Bill Campbell from Chemistry Set and bassist Paul Schurr from the Seers of Bavaria. After releasing a terrifically melodic, driving punk-pop album, *Flop and the Revenge of the Mopsqueezer*, on Frontier Records, the group was signed to Epic Records and produced an equally catchy major label debut in *Whenever You're Ready*. Apparently, Epic was not ready for Flop, and dropped the band shortly after their tour supporting the record. Now back with Frontier, Flop's sound has an extra edge to

it, making the band's brand of dry-witted, intelligent pop that much more intruiging. —*Heather Phares*

● **Flop & The Fall of The Mopsqueezer!** / Jan. 1992 / Frontier ✦✦✦✦

Whenever You're Ready / Sep. 21, 1993 / 550 Music/Epic ✦✦✦

World Of Today / 1995 / Frontier ✦✦✦

Flotsam & Jetsam
Group, Hard Rock, Thrash, Heavy Metal
Thrash band formed in 1985 in Phoenix by drummer Kelly Smith and bassist Jason Newsted. There were several personnel shifts, with Newsted joining Metallica in 1986 after Cliff Burton's death. The band's most productive lineup was led by vocalist Eric A.K., with Ed Carlson, Mike Gilbert, and Troy Gregory. —*Steve Huey*

● **Doomsday for the Deceiver** / 1986 / Metal Blade ✦✦✦✦
The classic debut album from this Arizona quintet features great songwriting and bass playing from Jason Newsted, who eventually left and joined Metallica. —*John Book*

○ **No Place for Disgrace** / 1988 / Elektra ✦✦✦✦
A different taste of American thrash, their major-label debut didn't hold back from anything: strong vocals, magnificent guitars, and excellent songs. It includes a cover of Elton John's "Saturday Night's Alright (For Fighting)." —*John Book*

When the Storm Comes Down / May 1, 1990 / MCA ✦✦

Eddie Floyd
b. Jun. 25, 1935, Montgomery, AL
Soul
Floyd came aboard the good ship Stax at the behest of his friend Al Bell and immediately made himself useful as a composer for labelmates Carla Thomas, William Bell, Otis Redding (originally intended to be the recipient of "Knock on Wood"), and Atlantic's Wilson Pickett.

Floyd's own mid-60s output included "Raise Your Hand," which utilized the same Booker T. & the MGs-powered thrust as "Knock on Wood," and "Big Bird," written partially in shocked response to the tragic death of Redding. Floyd remained loyal to Stax right up to its bitter demise, his engaging vocals resulting in major hits with the gentle "I've Never Found a Girl" and a lively remake of Sam Cooke's "Bring It on Home to Me."

Whenever Floyd re-teams with his old Stax pals—guitarist Steve Cropper, bassist Duck Dunn, and sometimes Booker T. Jones on organ—the long-ago Memphis magic instantly returns. With Floyd happily leading the throngs through "Raise Your Hand" and "Knock on Wood," it's 1966 all over again. —*Bill Dahl*

○ **Knock on Wood** / 1967 / Stax ✦✦✦✦
The finest album Eddie Floyd ever made for Stax, this late-'60s gem included both "I've Never Found a Girl" and "Knock on Wood," his two most magnificent hits and two Southern soul anthems. Floyd was never as transcendent or striking a vocalist as Otis Redding or even William Bell, but he was consistent and dependable. He was backed by both Booker T. and the MGs and the Memphis Horns (then called the Mar-Kay Horns). A recent CD reissue of this set adds several tracks, including some smoking duets with Mavis Staples. —*Ron Wynn*

○ **I've Never Found a Girl** / 1968 / Stax ✦✦✦
The title track was one of Floyd's biggest hits, while the other songs were fairly standard Southern soul, not particularly outstanding by Stax standards but well sung and performed. —*Ron Wynn*

You've Got to Have Eddie / 1969 / Stax ✦✦✦
Although he wasn't getting massive hits, Eddie Floyd continued to make solid Southern soul material in the late '60s. This album did have three moderately successful singles, but more importantly, every track features effective wailing leads and country/blues arrangements. An excellent example of the Stax sound. —*Ron Wynn*

California Girl / 1970 / Stax ✦✦✦
Eddie Floyd got the '70s underway in fine form with this release. The title track and two other singles, including a good version of "My Girl," made their way into the charts, and Floyd got good mileage out of the album, even though there were danger signs ahead for the Stax label. —*Ron Wynn*

Down to Earth / 1971 / Stax ✦✦
Another consistent release for Eddie Floyd, although it met with less success than most of his other releases. Only one single charted, and it didn't stay there long. But Floyd still sang with

hard-edged drive and conviction, and he had the reliable Stax studio pros and producers giving it the necessary support. —*Ron Wynn*

Baby Lay Your Head Down / 1973 / Stax ✦✦
Eddie Floyd got one of his last chart hits with the title track, a song that initially was being circulated as "Baby, Let Me Take You in My Arms." The rest of the album was formula soul, well produced, earnestly sung, and expertly played, but still formula material. —*Ron Wynn*

Soul Street / 1974 / Stax ✦✦✦
A worthwhile set. Funk's Memphis soul. —*Bill Dahl*

Experience / 1977 / Malaco ✦✦
Eddie Floyd resurfaced in the late '70s on the Jackson-based label that many felt would become the new Stax in the '70s and '80s. It didn't, but that's another story. This album did moderately well on a regional level, and a nice Floyd duet with Dorothy Moore even reached the middle of the R&B charts. But by the late '70s, soul was no longer palatable as a national sound. —*Ron Wynn*

● **Chronicle** / 1979 / Stax ✦✦✦✦
Singer/songwriter/producer Eddie Floyd, a former member of the Falcons, shines on originals such as "Soul Street" and "I've Got to Have Your Love" as well as covers such as Sam Cooke's "Bring It on Home to Me" and Smokey Robinson's "My Girl." This 1979 collection includes all of Floyd's singles between 1968-74.

○ **Rare Stamps** / 1993 / Stax ✦✦✦✦
A pair of remarkable soul hits, "Knock on Wood" and "I've Never Found a Girl," enabled Eddie Floyd to attain national success in 1968. But the longtime singer and composer, whose roots dated back to the Detroit group the Falcons in the late '50s, was a steady, if not spectacular, performer for many years before and after those two songs. Several of Floyd's finest pieces are compiled on the 25-track CD *Rare Stamps*, including a wonderful testimonial to Otis Redding, "Big Bird." There are also two super duets with Mavis Staples, "Never Let You Go" and "Ain't That Good," which rank with anything that the label issued. —*Ron Wynn*

The Flying Burrito Brothers
Group, Country-Rock
The Flying Burrito Brothers were formed in October 1968 from Byrds-expatriates Chris Hillman, Gram Parsons, along with Sneaky Pete Kleinow, all fresh from recording what was arguably the most important country-rock album—the Byrds' *Sweetheart of the Rodeo*. The Burritos took that concept and focused it into a brilliantly soulful country-rock sound.

Primary lead singer/songwriter Gram Parsons was capable of displaying heartbreaking vulnerability, as evidenced in tracks like "Hot Burrito #1." Parsons's influence and the band's overall concept laid the groundwork for many artists like the Eagles, Emmylou Harris, and much of today's cutting-edge country music. Parsons died of heart failure following a drug overdose on Sept 19, 1973, at the Joshua Tree Inn in Joshua Tree, CA. Burrito Brothers-cofounder Chris Hillman later formed the Desert Rose Band, which has scored numerous country hits. —*Rick Clark*

☆ **The Gilded Palace of Sin** / Feb. 1969 / A&M ✦✦✦✦✦
The birth of country-rock. Gram Parsons and Chris Hillman, aided by Sneaky Pete Kleinow and Chris Ethridge, create a hybrid by combining rock attitude with country sentiments and change the course of popular music. Really. —*William Ruhlmann*

○ **Burrito Deluxe** / Apr. 1970 / A&M ✦✦✦✦
The follow-up to the brilliant *Guilded Palace of Sin* finds the band somewhat directionless with Gram Parsons losing interest and playing a less active role. While the Parsons/Hillman-penned "Cody Cody" and a touching rendition of the Rolling Stones' "Wild Horses" capture some of the previous album's magic, *Burrito Deluxe* is somewhat of a letdown. Parsons left for a solo career shortly after. —*Chris Woodstra*

The Flying Burrito Brothers / May 1971 / A&M ✦✦✦
On their first post-Parsons album, the Burritos (now led by Hillman and Rick Roberts, and with future Eagle Bernie Leadon replacing Ethridge) make an honest step forward in country-rock. Includes the Roberts song "Colorado." —*William Ruhlmann*

The Last of the Red Hot Burritos / Apr. 1972 / A&M ✦✦
Last of the Red Hot Burritos, the fourth Flying Burrito Brothers album, was a live recording by the current lineup, led by sole original member Chris Hillman, billed as the group's swan song and

released after their breakup. By now, the Burritos had evolved into a competent country-rock band with a repertoire of country standards such as "Orange Blossom Special" (featuring Byron Berline on fiddle), but few of the originals by Gram Parsons and Hillman. *Last of the Red Hot Burritos* would have been a respectable, if unexceptional, way to go out, if in fact this had been the end of the group. But three years later, Kleinow and original bass player Chris Ethridge would resurrect the name, and there would be editions of the Burritos performing and recording, with legal, if not moral, legitimacy, long into the future. — *William Ruhlmann*

Bluegrass Special / 1974 / Ariola ♦♦

Honky Tonk Heaven / 1974 / Ariola ♦♦

○ **Close up the Honky-Tonks** / Jun. 1974 / A&M ♦♦♦♦
A&M Records seemed to close the book on the Flying Burrito Brothers with *Close Up the Honky-Tonks*, a 23-track, double-LP compilation. A combination best-of and odds-and-sods career wrap-up, the album contained one LP given over to tracks from the Burritos' first two records, *The Gilded Palace of Sin* and *Burrito Deluxe*, plus the non-LP single "The Train Song." The second disc presented 11 previously unreleased tracks, most of them cover songs, ranging from the Bee Gees' "To Love Somebody" to the Everly Brothers' "Wake Up, Little Susie." Co-founder Gram Parsons was featured on the five songs on Side Three, while Side Four came from the Rick Roberts era of the band. The Burritos would lack a one-disc best-of until A&M came up with the CD/cassette release *Farther Along* in 1988. So, for more than a decade, *Close Up the Honky-Tonks* was the definitive Burritos compilation, and even now, when it is out of print, it contains some excellent performances available nowhere else. — *William Ruhlmann*

Hot Burrito / 1975 / Ariola ♦♦

Flying Again / Sep. 1975 / Columbia ♦♦
The last that had been heard of the Flying Burrito Brothers was a 1973 European tour organized by Rick Roberts, replacement for founding member Gram Parsons, with a few hired guns. But with Parsons's growing posthumous legend, the band's name retained currency, and former bassist Chris Ethridge and former pedal steel guitarist "Sneaky" Pete Kleinow retained legal rights to that name. They brought in guitarist/fiddle player Floyd "Gib" Gilbeau, guitarist Joel Scott Hill, and former Byrds drummer Gene Parsons, and relaunched the Burritos with this album of competently played country-rock. Words like "travesty" and "insult" have been used to describe it, on the grounds that Ethridge and Kleinow were trading on Parsons's reputation, but on its own, the album is an adequate, if unremarkable set. Just don't pick it up looking for the old glory. (Out of print.) — *William Ruhlmann*

Sleepless Nights / Apr. 1976 / A&M ♦♦♦
A&M Records seemed to have exhausted its stock of Flying Burrito Brothers outtakes on *Close Up the Honky-Tonks* in 1974, but the continuing posthumous regard for Gram Parsons caused the company to unearth another seven tracks, six covers of country classics like "Tonight the Bottle Let Me Down" and "Green, Green Grass of Home," plus a version of the Rolling Stones' "Honky Tonk Women," all originally intended for what annotator Bud Scoppa called "a pure, honest country album" that the Burritos apparently never released. To this half-of-an-album, A&M added two tracks from *Close Up the Honky-Tonks* and three Parsons solo outtakes (with Emmylou Harris on backup vocals) licensed from Reprise Records. The result, credited to "Gram Parsons/The Flying Burrito Brothers," is a tribute to Parsons's heartbreaking tenor, especially because the tracks are little more than underproduced demos. It's not on par with *The Gilded Palace of Sin, Burrito Deluxe*, or *G.P.*, but should be of interest to fans. — *William Ruhlmann*

Airborne / May 1976 / Columbia ♦♦

Live from Tokyo / 1978 / Regency ♦♦
The second edition of the Flying Burrito Brothers, launched by "Sneaky" Pete Kleinow in 1975, turned out to have as many personnel shifts as the first edition put together by Gram Parsons in 1968. This lineup played familiar Burrito songs such as "Hot Burrito #2" and "Colorado," as well as a selection of honky-tonk country standards. Far from the greatest of Burrito Brothers bands, this one nevertheless was superior to later versions, and the music is efficiently played before an enthusiastic audience. As the group's live albums go, however, the one to get is still *Last of the Red Hot Burritos.* (*Live from Tokyo* was reissued by Relix Records in 1991 under the title *Close Encounters to the West Coast.*) — *William Ruhlmann*

Cabin Fever / 1985 / Relix ♦
This 1985 live album chronicles a Burritos lineup anchored by original member "Sneaky" Pete Kleinow and singer/guitarist Skip Battin, who first joined the band in 1976. It is in essence a Gram Parsons/Burritos/Byrds tribute album on which the band tries unsuccessfully to address Parsons classics like "Wheels" and "Hickory Wind" as well as the Byrds' "Mr. Spaceman." The sound quality is low and the performances substandard. Skimpy packaging fails to tell you where it was recorded or even who the other members of the band are. — *William Ruhlmann*

Live from Europe / 1986 / Relix ♦♦
Relix Records, which has curious ideas about marketing, released a second Flying Burrito Brothers live album in 1986, the year after it released the live *Cabin Fever*. The same lineup of original member "Sneaky" Pete Kleinow, guitarist Skip Battin and the previously uncredited rhythm section of bassist Greg Harris and Jim Goodall once again came off as a Burritos/Gram Parsons/Byrds tribute band, with a few of its own new originals thrown in. It was a reasonable enough concept for a live show, but back home on the record player versions of songs like "Christine's Tune (Devil in Disguise)" and "Citizen Kane" didn't hold a candle to the original recordings. Maybe to Relix and its Dead Head fans, who hew to the notion that all live shows should be taped and disseminated, this sort of release made sense, but not to average fans. — *William Ruhlmann*

Dim Lights, Thick Smoke & Loud, Loud Music / Mar. 1987 / Edsel ♦♦♦
The British Edsel label's *Dim Lights, Thick Smoke and Loud, Loud Music*, the first try at a Flying Burrito Brothers-compilation in a decade, is not a best-of. Because the label had recently reissued the Burritos' first two albums, *The Gilded Palace of Sin* and *Burrito Deluxe*, this 13-song collection is drawn from the rarities and outtakes first released on the A&M albums *Close Up the Honky-Tonks* and *Sleepless Nights* after the original group's (and Gram Parsons') demise. Specifically, as the album notes report, "… [It] brings together for the first time on one record all the Burritos' material that features Gram Parsons and that wasn't on those first two LPs." The songs are for the most part covers of country music standards presented as demos or working versions that probably never would have been released if it were not for Parsons' death. Parsons, of course, is the reason the Burritos continue to interest fans, and he sings well here, but this half-finished material does not compare to the first two albums. — *William Ruhlmann*

Back to Sweethearts of the Rodeo / 1988 / Disky ♦♦

★ **Farther Along: Best of** / 1988 / A&M ♦♦♦♦♦
Farther Along: The Best of the Flying Burrito Brothers is an excellent 21-track, 65-minute compilation of the Burritos. — *William Ruhlmann*

Close Encounters to the West Coast / 1991 / Relix ♦♦
The second edition of the Flying Burrito Brothers, launched by "Sneaky" Pete Kleinow in 1975, turned out to have as many personnel shifts as the first edition put together by Gram Parsons in 1968. This lineup played familiar Burrito songs such as "Hot Burrito #2" and "Colorado," as well as a selection of honky-tonk country standards. Far from the greatest of Burrito Brothers bands, this one nevertheless was superior to later versions, and the music is efficiently played before an enthusiastic audience. As the group's live albums go, however, the one to get is still *Last of the Red Hot Burritos.* (*Close Encounters to the West Coast* is a 1991 reissue of the 1978 Regency Records album *Live from Tokyo.*) — *William Ruhlmann*

Eye Of A Hurricane / 1994 / One Way ♦♦

Flying Saucer Attack

Group, Experimental
Forget all normal conventions of distorted static-rock; Flying Saucer Attack use distortion to create and enhance the effect of their songs, not as a masking tool to hide flaws. Closer to many ambient groups than U.S. indie-rock, the band has released two LPs, both distributed by Revolver USA. A third album compiled from early singles is also available. — *John Bush*

Flying Saucer Attack / 1994 / VHF

Distance / 1994 / VHF ♦♦♦
Distance is a compilation of early singles and unreleased tracks from the band's short career. Only half of the album's eight tracks could be considered songs; the rest are looped feedback workouts

that sound eerily ambient. Even the four "songs" are distorted beyond belief, producing a caterwaul reminiscent of My Bloody Valentine's prime work. —*John Bush*

Focus

Group, Art-Rock/Progressive-Rock
This Dutch progressive art-rock band (with a strange sense of humor) charted one hit in America, the novelty instrumental "Hocus Pocus" (#9), a song that featured wild yodeling and the frenetic lead-guitar work of Jan Akkerman. —*Rick Clark*

In and Out of Focus / 1970 / IRS ✦✦✦
This debut album is gentler and more low-key and vocal-oriented than their subsequent efforts; fans of Jan Akkerman's pyrotechnics may be disappointed by his relatively restrained presence, but others may be pleasantly surprised to find a more economic group than they remember. A fair collection of progressive rock tunes without a clear focus, the material is dominated by Thus Van Leer, often introducing classical sensibilities. But at least as often, it sticks with fairly conventional period folk-rock and blues influences, with occasional jazzy shadings. Akkerman's "House Of The King" is the most accurate Jethro Tull imitation ever recorded. —*Richie Unterberger*

○ **Moving Waves** / 1971 / IRS ✦✦✦✦
Included is the long version of the Top Ten hit "Hocus Pocus," plus the 23-minute suite "Eruption." —*Michael P. Dawson*

Focus III / 1972 / IRS ✦✦✦
A solid third effort, this double album (one disc) was marred only by some aimless jams. —*Michael P. Dawson*

Foetus

Group, Alternative Pop/Rock, Experimental
Under a variety of different names (You've Got Foetus on Your Breath, Scraping Foetus off the Wheel, etc.), Jim Thirlwell has explored his own violent, brutal obsessions on record since 1985. Everything that Foetus has released is filled with intense, abrasive violence and a total disregard for conventional pop structure—they have become the standard for industrial music terrorism. —*Stephen Thomas Erlewine*

Hole / 1984 / Thirsty Ear ✦✦✦

○ **Nail** / 1985 / Thirsty Ear ✦✦✦✦
Loud, stupid and relentlessly harsh. Sometimes funny, too! —*John Dougan*

Stinkfist / 1988 / Widowspeak ✦✦

○ **Thaw** / 1988 / Self Immolation ✦✦✦✦

Stink / 1988 / Some Bizarre ✦✦✦

● **Sink** / 1990 / Wax Trax! ✦✦✦✦
Painfully cool. Dance, I dare you! —*John Dougan*

Gash / 1995 / Colombia ✦✦✦

Dan Fogelberg

b. Aug. 13, 1951, Peoria, IL
Singer-Songwriter
When singer/songwriter and multi-instrumentalist Dan Fogelberg arrived in 1973 with his debut *Home Free*, reflective soft-folk/pop was making big inroads into a baby-boomer mass market coming of age.

Fogelberg had the good fortune to be previously acquainted (from his University of Illinois days in 1971) with ascending artist manager and industry power-broker Irving Azoff, who was managing R.E.O. Speedwagon at the time. Azoff took on Fogelberg and brought in Joe Walsh (another artist client of Azoff's) to produce the sophomore effort *Souvenirs*. It became Fogelberg's first chart success, generating a #31 hit with "Part of the Plan."

During the '70s and early '80s, Fogelberg became a mainstay on FM rock stations and soft adult-contemporary formats, easily managing to share air space with artists like the Eagles, Linda Ronstadt, Jimmy Buffett, and Jackson Browne. "Longer" (#2), "Same Old Lang Syne" (#9), and "Leader of the Band" (#9) were big hits indicative of Fogelberg's thoughtful mellow sound. His attempts at rock have generally failed to score as successfully, particularly the 1988 release *Exiles*. —*Rick Clark*

○ **Home Free** / 1973 / Columbia ✦✦✦✦
This debut, recorded in Nashville and produced by Norbert Putnam, is a nice blend of haunting acoustic-guitar-based numbers ("Stars," "Be on Your Way"), some supported by tasteful string-sec-

tion work ("To the Morning," "Wysteria," "Hickory Grove"). There are also a few country/light-rock items in "Anyway I Love You," "Long Way Home (Live in the Country)," and "More Than Ever." —*Rick Clark*

Captured Angel / 1975 / Epic ✦✦

Souvenirs / 1975 / Epic ✦✦✦
This Joe Walsh-produced effort includes Fogelberg's first hit, "Part of the Plan." Overall, this isn't as strong as the debut. —*Rick Clark*

○ **Netherlands** / 1977 / Epic ✦✦✦✦
Fogelberg returns to Norbert Putnam for this effort, which ranges from the heavily orchestrated, highly dramatic title cut to light CSN-style folk-rock like "Once Upon a Time." It's one of Fogelberg's better albums, in spite of his tendency for grandiose statement. —*Rick Clark*

Twin Sons of Different Mothers / 1978 / Epic ✦✦✦
This album contains duets with flutist Tim Weisberg. It's a nice diversion, featuring a good remake of the Hollies hit "Tell Me to My Face." There are some pleasant instrumental numbers here. Fogelberg scored a hit with "The Power of Gold" (number 24). —*Rick Clark*

○ **Phoenix** / 1980 / Full Moon ✦✦✦✦
Fogelberg's highest-charting album (#3) features his widest stylistic stretches, between the ultra-sentimental acoustic hit "Longer," to extended rockish numbers like "Face the Fire," "Wishing on the Moon," and the title cut. —*Rick Clark*

○ **The Innocent Age** / 1981 / Full Moon ✦✦✦✦
An ambitious song cycle, it details the experience of coming of age. Several of Fogelberg's biggest hits ("Leader of the Band," "Same Old Lang Syne," "Hard to Say," and "Run for the Roses") are on this set. —*Rick Clark*

Windows & Walls / 1984 / Full Moon ✦✦

● **Greatest Hits** / 1985 / Full Moon ✦✦✦✦
Even though this collection fails to address much of his best non-single material, most of his obvious hits are here (heavy on the sentimental), making this a fairly safe starting place for someone wanting to get into Fogelberg. —*Rick Clark*

High Country Snows / 1985 / Full Moon ✦✦✦
It's a well-recorded foray into more traditional acoustic country music. —*Rick Clark*

Exiles / 1987 / Full Moon ✦✦

The Wild Places / 1990 / Full Moon ✦✦

Dan Fogelberg Live: Greetings from the West / Jun. 1991 / Full Moon ✦✦

River of Souls / Sep. 28, 1993 / Full Moon ✦✦

John Fogerty

b. May 28, 1945, Berkeley, California
Rock & Roll
John Cameron Fogerty achieved fame as the lead singer/songwriter and guitarist in Creedence Clearwater Revival and has since gone on to a chart-topping solo career. Born in Berkeley, CA, Fogerty and his brother Tom organized the group that would become Creedence as the Golliwogs in the late '50s. As Creedence, they released nine Top Ten singles, all written by Fogerty, between 1969 and 1971, starting with the standard "Proud Mary." They also scored eight gold albums between 1968 and 1972, all fueled by Fogerty's simple, driving rock songs and his burly baritone, intoning deceptively poetic ("Bad Moon Rising") and even political ("Fortunate Son") lyrics.

Creedence split up in 1972. Fogerty at first confused his considerable following by releasing an album of covers, on which he played all the instruments, under the name the Blue Ridge Rangers in 1973. This was followed by a formal solo album, *John Fogerty*, in 1975, and then silence for more than nine years while the artist worked out business problems with Creedence's old label. But Fogerty returned at the end of 1984 with a Top Ten single, "The Old Man down the Road," and a #1 album, *Centerfield*. *Eye of the Zombie* was a less successful follow-up in 1986. —*William Ruhlmann*

Blue Ridge Rangers / 1973 / Fantasy ✦✦✦
Fogerty as a one-man country band paying tribute to his honky tonk roots. —*Jeff Tamarkin*

John Fogerty / 1975 / Asylum ✦✦
Forgettable post-Creedence exercise. —*Jeff Tamarkin*

● **Centerfield** / Apr. 1985 / Warner Brothers ✦✦✦✦
The comeback album that proved the ex-Creedence firebrand still
knew how to rock and make it count. Includes "The Old Man
down the Road" (#10), "Rock and Roll Girls" (#20), and "Centerfield" (#44). — *Jeff Tamarkin*

Eye of the Zombie / 1986 / Warner Brothers ✦✦
The disappointing follow-up to *Centerfield*, too high-tech and low-
profile. — *Jeff Tamarkin*

Foghat

Group, Hard Rock, Heavy Metal
Foghat specialized in a simple, hard-rocking blues-rock, releasing
a series of best-selling albums in the mid-'70s. While the group
never deviated from their basic boogie, they retained a large audience until 1978, selling out concerts across America and earning
five gold albums, as well as two platinum. Once punk and disco
came along, the band's audience dipped dramatically, yet the
group continued performing until 1980.

With its straightahead, three-chord romps, the band's sound was
American in origin, yet the members were all natives of England.
Guitarist/vocalist "Lonesome" Dave Peverett and drummer Roger
Earl were members of the British blues band Savoy Brown, who
left the group in the early '70s. Upon their departure, they formed
Foghat with guitarist Rod Price and bassist Tony Stevens. Foghat
moved to the United States, signing a record contract with
Bearsville Records, a new label run by Albert Grossman. Their
first album, *Foghat*, was released in the summer of 1972 and it became a hit on album rock; a cover of Willie Dixon's "I Just Want to
Make Love to You" even made it to the lower regions of the singles
charts. For their next album, the group didn't change their formula
at all—in fact, they didn't even change the *title* of the album. Like
the first record, the second was called *Foghat*; it was distinguished
by a picture of a rock and a roll on the front cover. Foghat's second
album was their first gold record, and it established them as a popular arena rock act. Their next five albums—*Energized* (1974),
Rock and Roll Outlaws (1974), *Fool for the City* (1975), *Night Shift*
(1976), *Foghat Live* (1977), *Stone Blue* (1978)—all were best-sellers
and all went at least gold. "Slow Ride," taken from *Fool for the
City*, was their biggest single, peaking at number 20. *Foghat Live*
was their biggest album, selling over two million copies. After
1975, the band went through a series of bass players; Price left the
band in 1981 and was replaced by Erik Cartwright.

In the early '80s, Foghat's commercial fortunes declined rapidly,
with their last album, 1983's *Zig-Zag Walk*, barely making the album charts. The group broke up shortly afterward, although they
have reunited for various tours in the late '80s and early '90s. —
Stephen Thomas Erlewine

Foghat (Rock and Roll) / 1973 / Rhino ✦✦✦
○ **Energized** / 1974 / Bearsville ✦✦✦✦
○ **Rock & Roll Outlaws** / 1974 / Bearsville ✦✦✦✦
Fool for the City / 1975 / Bearsville ✦✦✦
○ **Night Shift** / 1976 / Bearsville ✦✦✦✦
Foghat Live / 1977 / Bearsville ✦✦
Stone Blue / 1978 / Bearsville ✦✦✦
● **The Best of Foghat** / 1990 / Rhino ✦✦✦✦
Excellent blue-collar rock, it features "Slow Ride" and "Fool for the
City." — *Dan Heilman*

○ **The Best of Foghat, Vol. 2** / Jan. 24, 1992 / Rhino ✦✦✦✦
If *Best of Foghat* made you hungry for more, *Best of Foghat, Vol. 2*,
with no hit singles, only album tracks, and including two live cuts
and an outtake, should satiate your desire. — *Stephen Thomas Erlewine*

Wayne Fontana & The Mindbenders

Group, British Invasion
Lester Bangs said it best, in his essay on the British Invasion in
The Rolling Stone Illustrated History of Rock & Roll: "Wayne
Fontana and the Mindbenders may have been a one-shot group,
but what a shot. 'The Game of Love,' with its heavy bass, 'Louie
Louie' chording, Bo Diddley break and Fontana's rich, wailing vocals, was an instant classic, a perfect example of the rock and roll
band of no apparent distinction but with a masterpiece in them
anyway." Make that two masterpieces, although Fontana had split
for a solo career before the group topped the charts again with "A
Groovy Kind of Love." The Manchester, England group were com-

petent and energetic performers, but suffered the bane of many
early British Invasion acts in the ultra-competitive days of 1966—
they didn't write strong material for themselves. After some low-
charting follow-ups to "Game of Love," Fontana left for a solo career which saw him only gaining a couple British hits, "Come on
Home" and Graham Gouldman's "Pamela, Pamela." After "Groovy
Kind of Love," the Mindbenders had another British Top 20 hit
with "Ashes to Ashes," then cut a string of flop singles, and made a
memorable appearance in the *To Sir with Love* film. Graham
Gouldman was briefly a member before the group called it a day
in 1968, though he and Mindbenders singer/guitarist Eric Stewart
would work together again in 10CC. — *Richie Unterberger*

Hit Single Anthology / 1991 / Fontana ✦✦
In 1965, Wayne Fontana & the Mindbenders struck with one of the
British Invasion's greatest one-shots, the #1 hit "Game Of Love."
After Fontana split for a solo career shortly afterwards, the Mindbenders scored another mammoth hit that was nearly as memorable, "A Groovy Kind Of Love." This 23-song anthology—featuring
the most successful singles by Fontana and the Mindbenders, both
together and as separate entities—does not, unfortunately, offer
anything in the same league as those two smashes. They did manage a couple other U.K. hits, "Um Um Um Um Um Um" and "Just
A Little Bit Too Late" (both included here), in their original incarnation, but neither are especially memorable. Dependent upon
outside writers for virtually all of their material, Fontana & Co.
had little to distinguish them from literally hundreds of other middling British Invasion-era groups except their extraordinary luck
in latching on to a couple of pieces of great material. Upon splitting from the Mindbenders, Fontana pursued a Tom Jones-like
balladeering direction that has worn badly; the Mindbenders,
while remaining rock-oriented, offered nearly as little. Stick with
the two hit singles, on which they miraculously secured masterful
pieces of tuneful and dynamic British Invasion pop. — *Richie Unterberger*

● **Best Of Wayne Fontana & The Mindbenders** / 1994 / Fontana
✦✦✦✦
Well-chosen 20-track anthology, covering the hits and the best of
their rare 1964-68 singles, as well as a couple rare cuts from U.K.
LPs and EPs. It's actually a distinct improvement upon its U.K.
counterpart *Hit Single Anthology*, as it includes the fine "It's Getting Harder All of the Time/"Off and Running" single from the *To
Sir With Love* soundtrack, and eliminates some of the weak covers
and Wayne Fontana solo singles. — *Richie Unterberger*

Steve Forbert

b. 1955, Meridian, MS
Singer-Songwriter, Pop/Rock
Mississippi-born Forbert was one of the better received folk-based
singer/songwriters of the late '70s. In recent years, he has written
hits for country artists as well as continuing to record albums himself. — *William Ruhlmann*

○ **Alive on Arrival** / 1978 / Nemperor ✦✦✦✦
Forbert takes the folk-rock singer/songwriter format, already 13
years old at this point, and gives it a fresh, exuberant, almost
punkish appeal. — *William Ruhlmann*

○ **Jackrabbit Slim** / Oct. 1979 / Nemperor ✦✦✦✦
Forbert's more elaborately produced second album continues the
songwriting quality of his first and includes his #11 hit single
"Romeo's Tune." — *William Ruhlmann*

Little Stevie Orbit / Sep. 1980 / Nemperor ✦✦✦
Little Stevie Orbit was seen as a disappointment at the time of its
release because it did not generate a hit single on the order of
"Romeo's Tune," and thus failed to consolidate the commercial
success Steve Forbert had achieved with his second album,
Jackrabbit Slim. In retrospect, however, it is a spirited, rollicking
collection on which Forbert sounds increasingly comfortable
fronting a rock band on a series of light-hearted songs such as "I'm
an Automobile" and "If You've Gotta Ask You'll Never Know." It
may not have made him a superstar, but *Little Stevie Orbit* provided some strong additions to Steve Forbert's concert repertoire
for years to come. — *William Ruhlmann*

Steve Forbert / Jul. 1982 / Nemperor ✦✦
Steve Forbert hit quite a few stylistic bases on his fourth, self-titled
album, maybe too many. From the horn-filled, Motown-tinged "Ya
Ya (Next to Me)" to a faithful cover of Jackie DeShannon's mid-'60s

classic "When You Walk in the Room" to the lush, string-heavy "Oh So Close (And Yet So Far Away)" to the uptempo country two-step "You're Darn Right," Forbert couldn't be pinned down to a genre (certainly not folk-rock). But there was too little of the spunky tone of songs like "It Takes a Whole Lotta Help (To Make It on Your Own)" that had sparked Forbert's previous albums. (Unfortunately, Forbert's proposed fifth album was rejected by his record company in 1984, and it took him six years to follow this album.) — *William Ruhlmann*

Streets of This Town / Apr. 1988 / David Geffen Co. ◆◆◆
Coming back after a six-year layoff, Forbert displays a previously unheard edge of bitterness that only deepens his thoughtful lyrics. And he rocks harder than ever. — *William Ruhlmann*

The American in Me / Jan. 1992 / David Geffen Co. ◆◆◆
Steve Forbert never had a chance of living up to the "new Dylan" kiss of death that critics smeared on his collar with his first releases in the late 70s. Four albums of wit and optimism gave way to a six-year drought without a record contract. With *The American in Me*, Forbert has found a healthier, more balanced perspective. The pressures and uncertainties of growing up, taking on responsibilities, and looking back on missed opportunity makes up the central theme linking the disc's ten songs. This isn't a disc for the kids. It's for the parents out there who can still touch the rebel spirit within themselves and who have no desire to age gracefully. — *Roch Parisien*

● **Best of: What Kinda Guy?** / 1993 / Columbia/Legacy ◆◆◆◆
Excellent compilation featuring a generous 19 tracks, including his hit "Romeo's Tune." A great place to get acquainted with this underrated singer-songwriter. — *Stephen Thomas Erlewine*

Mission Of The Crossroad Palms / 1995 / Giant ◆◆◆
Steve Forbert turns in an album of craftsmanlike tunes on his seventh album, including story songs such as "It Sure Was Better Back Then" (a working man's reminiscence) and "The Trouble with Angels" (in which an ex-beauty queen robs the till to pay for her infertility treatments). There is also one of Forbert's philosophical treatises ("It Is What It Is [And That's All]") and the humorously multi-referential "Lay Down Your Weary Tune Again" (risky territory for a former New Dylan). But the best song may be Forbert's ode to infidelity, "Don't Talk to Me." The point, though, is that Forbert has flowered into a distinctive, broad-based songwriter and that, in E Street Band bassist Garry Tallent, he has found a sympathetic producer able to showcase his voice and lyrics properly. Now, if he could just re-connect with his audience. — *William Ruhlmann*

Force MD's

Group, Soul, R&B
Groundbreaking teen-soul crooners precipitated the New Jack balladry of the early '90s. — *John Floyd*

Touch & Go / 1981 / Tommy Boy ◆◆◆
The title track was a Top Ten R&B hit, and the Force MDs were at their best on this album. The leads, harmonies, songs, production, and arrangements never sounded better, and they certainly paved the way for the many New Jack vocal groups of the '90s. — *Ron Wynn*

○ **Chillin'** / 1986 / Tommy Boy ◆◆◆◆
A mid-'80s album featuring the Long Island hip-hop/doo-wop group the Force MDs. They predated the current hot trend featuring singing groups blending classic R&B and soul harmonies with hip-hop productions. While their sound now seems dated, it was quite revolutionary in its time. This album had three chart hits, and the group was then at its peak. — *Ron Wynn*

Step to Me / Sep. 4, 1990 / Tommy Boy ◆◆◆
The Force MDs were a dominant ensemble in the mid- and late '80s. They struck just the right chord between classicism and modernism with their hip-hop/doo-wop blend, and although this wasn't their biggest album, it still did quite well among both old and young black music fans. — *Ron Wynn*

● **For Lovers & Others: Greatest Hits** / 1992 / Tommy Boy ◆◆◆◆
Love Letters / Tommy Boy ◆◆◆
The Force MDs were rolling along when they issued this album in the mid-'80s. Their hip-hop/doo-wop fusion yielded two sizable hits, among them the Top Ten smash "Tears." The album did well among both R&B/soul fans and hip-hop/rap and urban contemporary audiences. — *Ron Wynn*

Forced Entry

Group, Hard Rock, Thrash, Heavy Metal
The small community of Mountlake Terrace, WA, is what the three-piece Forced Entry calls home. During their inception in the mid '80s, there was no active thrash-metal scene in the Seattle area. The band decided to change that situation with their musically diverse songs and intelligent lyrics. They are currently considered a major factor in the Seattle metal community. — *John Book*

Forced Entry / 1988 / Atom ◆◆
● **Uncertain Future** / 1989 / Combat ◆◆◆◆
They changed the world of thrash with their debut album in 1989, featuring eerie power chords, awesome vocals, and a tremendous bass guitar sound. For an album recorded on a low budget, the sound is impressive. This album has yet to be appreciated by the masses. — *John Book*

As Above So Below / 1991 / Combat ◆◆◆
More complex than *Uncertain Future*, it's just as good. The guitar playing of Brad Hull needs to be heard. — *John Book*

Foreigner

Group, Hard Rock, Pop/Rock
Foreigner was formed in 1976 by Mick Jones (ex-Spooky Tooth) and Ian McDonald (ex-King Crimson). The band was an instant success with the release of their debut album in 1977, which showcased the talents of guitarist Jones and lead singer Lou Gramm. Jones and Gramm also wrote most of the band's material. The songs, mainly hard rock, boasted strong melodies and memorable guitar riffs. The band never strayed far from this formula but, to keep things fresh, added some interesting touches. For example, Junior Walker's sax on "Urgent" and the gospel vocals of Jennifer Holliday and the New Jersey Mass Choir on "I Want to Know What Love Is" helped elevate these songs above the ordinary. Gramm left the band in the late '80s for a solo career. Foreigner recruited a new lead singer but Gramm's writing and distinctive vocals are sorely missed. — *Kenneth M. Cassidy*

Mr. Moonlight / Atlantic
Foreigner / 1977 / Atlantic ◆◆◆
No-nonsense rock & roll catapulted the band's debut all the way to the top of the charts with the hits "Cold as Ice" and "Feels like the First Time." — *Donna DiChario*

Double Vision / 1978 / Atlantic ◆◆◆
Building on the success of the first album, this followup yielded the Top 20 hits "Hot Blooded," "Double Vision," and "Blue Morning, Blue Day." — *Donna DiChario*

Head Games / 1979 / Atlantic ◆◆◆
○ **4** / 1981 / Atlantic ◆◆◆◆
The strength of Lou Gramm's powerhouse vocals and the band's synth-pop texturing carried this album to #1. It produced several major hits, including "Urgent," which featured a sax solo by Junior Walker, and "Waiting for a Girl like You." — *Donna DiChario*

○ **Records** / 1982 / Atlantic ◆◆◆◆
All the band's early (including those from *4*) radio-friendly hits are here in this collection of straightahead rock & rollers. It includes "Waiting for a Girl like You," "Hot Blooded," and more. — *Donna DiChario*

Best of Foreigner / 1982 / Atlantic
Agent Provocateur / 1984 / Atlantic ◆◆◆
Inside Information / 1987 / Atlantic ◆◆◆
Unusual Heat / 1991 / Atlantic ◆◆◆
● **The Very Best . . . and Beyond** / 1992 / Atlantic ◆◆◆◆
Very Best . . . and Beyond not only collects all the major hits from Foreigner's early years ("Feels Like the First Time," "Head Games," "Hot Blooded"), but also features their hits from the late '80s ("I Want to Know What Love Is," "Say You Will"), making the set preferable to *Records*. — *Stephen Thomas Erlewine*

Classic Hits Live / Atlantic ◆◆◆

Fotheringay

Group, Folk-Rock
A short-lived offshoot of Fairport Convention, featuring key member and leader Sandy Denny. A second album was planned but never completed; tracks from it turn up on the triple-CD Denny

anthology *Who Knows Where the Time Goes*. This is far more interesting and beguiling than their work with Fairport Convention, especially the Bob Dylan songs, but it lacks Fairport's precision and focus. —*Bruce Eder & William Ruhlmann*

○ **Fotheringay** / 1970 / Hannibal ✦✦✦✦
Also featured are Trevor Lucas and Jerry Donahue, both of whom eventually joined Fairport when Denny rejoined. The album is a close relative of Denny's other solo and group work and features several of her flowing ballads, showcasing her lovely voice. A footnote, but a pleasing one. —*Bruce Eder & William Ruhlmann*

The Foundations
Group, Soul
An integrated British R&B and pop group that were briefly international stars in the late '60s, the Foundations actually got more pop mileage out of "Baby, Now that I've Found You" than R&B success. Original lead vocalist Clem Curtis was from Trinidad and was replaced in 1968 by Colin Young, who was from Jamaica. The song was a pop Top 20 hit (it peaked at number 11). It didn't make it beyond number 33 on the R&B list. "Build Me up, Buttercup" was their other big hit, and also the title of their lone LP in 1969. The title track reached number three pop. A year later, they were history. —*Ron Wynn*

● **Best of the Foundations** / 1987 / PRT ✦✦✦✦

Four Seasons
Group, Pop/Rock
The Four Seasons were the most successful male vocal group of the rock era. Although the personnel has changed through the years (especially after the '60s), the group has nearly always been a platform for the singing of Frankie Valli (b. May 3, 1937). It was formed in Newark, NJ, in 1956, first as the Variatones and then as the Four Lovers, and featured Valli, brothers Tommy and Nick DeVito, and Hank Majewski. Under that name and with that lineup, they scored their first, minor hit, "You're the Apple of My Eye."
    Over the next five years, the Four Lovers became the Four Seasons, songwriter Bob Gaudio replaced Nick DeVito, Nick Massi replaced Hank Majewski, and the group began working with producer Bob Crewe. With this team—Valli singing lead, Gaudio and Crewe writing songs, and Crewe producing, plus Charlie Callelo arranging—the Four Seasons launched a series of teen-oriented hits in 1962 with the chart-topper "Sherry." The hits continued long into the Beatles era, totaling 13 Top Tens among 34 chart entries by the end of 1967. Valli also launched a solo career and had his own hits.
    After more personnel changes, the group's career seemed to take a backseat to Valli's in the early '70s, though they came back in a multiple-lead-singer format for another series of hits in the mid-'70s. —*William Ruhlmann*

The Genuine Imitation Life Gazette / Dec. 1968 / Rhino ✦✦✦
Frankie Valli & the Four Seasons go hippie in this concept album that stands out as one of the more bizarre entries in their catalog. —*Jeff Tamarkin*

★ **Anthology** / 1988 / Rhino ✦✦✦✦✦
Over the course of 20 tracks, *Anthology* covers all of the Four Seasons' essential hits, as well as Valli's solo "Can't Take My Eyes off You"; it's the definitive collection. —*Stephen Thomas Erlewine*

Rarities, Vol. 1 / 1990 / Rhino ✦✦✦
The Four Seasons did manage to hold their own for a while during the initial onslaught of the British Invasion, but it would be foolish to pretend that their albums and B-sides were as strong as those by the best British Invasion groups. Nevertheless, they did manage to issue some decent tracks aside from their hits during their prime that have been overlooked by all but die-hard fans. *Rarities, Vol. 1* collects 20 songs from the group's 1964-66 heyday, drawing heavily from their 1964 albums *Rag Doll* and *Dawn*. Several of the tunes were composed by the team of Bob Gaudio and Bob Crewe that wrote most of their biggest hits. They are indeed respectable, but simply not as memorable as their million-sellers, sometimes sounding like competent but lesser versions of smashes like "Dawn" and "Ronnie." One highlight is the odd death-on-the-surf ballad "No Surfin' Today," which shows a pronounced Southern Californian influence. As for rarities, you get a 1963 bowling commercial and a 1965 radio promo, and the second single by the notorious Wonder Who? This group, a thinly veiled pseudonym for the Seasons, scored the most unlikely Top

20 cover of a Dylan song ever with their castrato version of "Don't Think Twice, It's Alright." For their follow-up, the "group" tackled Shirley Temple's "On the Good Ship Lollipop"; both it and the flipside are included here, though they are less overlooked gems than historical novelties. —*Richie Unterberger*

Rarities, Vol. 2 / 1990 / Rhino ✦✦✦
More (or less) of the same. For fanatics only. —*Jeff Tamarkin*

Entertain You/Working My Way Back To You / 1995 / Ace ✦✦✦
This 69-minute, 24-track disc is part of a series released by British reissue label Ace collecting all of the Four Seasons' and Frankie Valli's recordings for the Vee Jay and Philips labels during the 1960s. Contained here is the material from the two pop-oriented albums the Seasons recorded for Philips in 1965 (a busy year, during which they also recorded an LP of Bacharach/David and Dylan standards and a "live" album actually cut in a studio). The first, *Entertain You*, released in March 1965, was a throwback to the group's earlier style of building an album of covers around a hit single, the one in question being "Bye, Bye, Baby (Baby Goodbye)," not one of their biggest. The Seasons could do songs like the Diamonds' "Little Darlin' " in their sleep and so the album wasn't one of their best. *Working My Way Back to You* (January 1966), on the other hand, not only featured a big hit in the title track, but also a collection of new songs, some of which could also have been hits. This set appends the group's September 1965 single, "Let's Hang On (To What We've Got)" as a bonus track. (Contains annotations and discography.) —*William Ruhlmann*

Four Tops
Group, Soul, R&B, Motown
The Four Tops are the most stable, consistent, and dependable of the successful R&B/pop vocal acts to emerge from Motown Records in the 1960s. Unlike the Temptations, they have had no personnel changes; unlike the Supremes and the Miracles, their lead singer never felt the need to step out on his own. At the same time, the Four Tops personified the musical hybrid Motown sought—they had the grittiness of gospel and R&B, but they were smooth enough to appeal to pop audiences.
    The group was formed in Detroit in 1953 by lead singer Levi Stubbs, Jr., Renaldo "Obie" Benson, Lawrence Payton, and Abdul "Duke" Fakir when they were still in high school. They recorded for several labels before signing to Motown in 1963. "Baby, I Need Your Loving" (July 1964), written and produced by the team of Brian Holland, Lamont Dozier, and Eddie Holland, was their first substantial hit, setting the pattern for a series of songs showcasing Stubbs's emotive wail set against the Benson-Payton-Fakir harmony line. Need and longing would be the hallmarks of Stubbs's singing on such songs as "Ask the Lonely" (January 1965), which launched a string of R&B Top Ten/pop Top 40 hits over the next two years. Its follow-up, "I Can't Help Myself" (April 1965), hit number one and was itself followed by "It's the Same Old Song" (July 1965), "Something About You" (October 1965), "Shake Me, Wake Me (When It's Over)" (February 1966), "Loving You Is Sweeter than Ever" (May 1966), a second #1, "Reach Out, I'll Be There" (August 1966), "Standing in the Shadows of Love" (November 1966), "Bernadette" (February 1967), "7 Rooms of Gloom" (May 1967), and "You Keep Running Away" (August 1967).
    At that point, the Holland-Dozier-Holland team left Motown, depriving the Four Tops of their writing and producing talent. The label at first had some trouble finding material for them, having them cover songs like "Walk Away Renee" and "If I Were a Carpenter." In 1970, however, they rebounded with "It's All in the Game," "Still Water (Love)," a duet with the Supremes on "River Deep—Mountain High," and "Just Seven Numbers (Can Straighten Out My Life)," all of which made the R&B Top Ten and the pop Top 40. They scored one more R&B Top Ten on Motown with "(It's the Way) Nature Planned It" before moving to Dunhill (later acquired by ABC, then by MCA) Records, where they enjoyed another string of hits, including "Keeper of the Castle" (October 1972), the goldselling "Ain't No Woman (Like the One I Got)" (January 1973), "Are You Man Enough" (June 1973), "Sweet Understanding Love" (September 1973), "One Chain Don't Make No Prison" (April 1974), and "Midnight Flower" (July 1974). They returned to the R&B Top Ten with "Catfish" (August 1976), and moved to Casablanca (since acquired by PolyGram) for the R&B number one "When She Was My Girl" (September 1981).
    The Four Tops returned to Motown in 1983, and by 1988 were signed to Arista. Their hit-making days presumably behind them,

they remain a solid concert act with a repertoire of favorites and a catalogue that continues to be repackaged successfully. — *William Ruhlmann*

○ **The Four Tops** / Oct. 1964 / Motown ✦✦✦✦
You'd be hard pressed to find two better singles on a debut album than "Ask the Lonely" and "Baby I Need Your Loving." These were the cornerstones of the Four Tops' first LP, and besides netting them one Top Ten and Top 20 pop single each, as well as a Top Ten and Top 20 R&B single, it established Levi Stubbs' resounding voice as another unforgettable one at Motown. Even the tunes that didn't do so well, like "Left with a Broken Heart" or "Without the One You Love (Life's Not Worth While)," were marvelously sung. It was a debut to remember. — *Ron Wynn*

○ **Second Album** / Nov. 1965 / Motown ✦✦✦✦
The Four Tops followed their fine debut album with an even more magnificent second effort. They landed their first number one pop and R&B hit with "I Can't Help Myself (Sugarpie, Honeybunch)." There was also "Shake Me, Wake Me," a great uptempo shouter that seemed a disappointment at number 18 (number nine R&B), but didn't lack vocal authority or production genius. The album also contained "It's The Same Old Song," a tidy little number that reached number five (number two R&B) and had one of the greatest lyric hooks and titles ever. — *Ron Wynn*

○ **On Top** / Jul. 1966 / Motown ✦✦✦✦
Their third album and a classic. The Four Tops never sounded better, more emphatic or compelling on Motown than in the mid-'60s, when they were getting great songs, production, arrangements, and musical support. — *Ron Wynn*

○ **Reach Out** / Jul. 1967 / Motown ✦✦✦✦
Although they were old hands by now, the Four Tops roared out of the gate in high style with this album, their most successful on the pop charts to that point. It didn't hurt that Levi Stubbs showed his flair for the oral narrative on "Bernadette," or that "Reach Out, I'll Be There" was their second single to top both the R&B and pop charts. The album peaked at number 11 on the charts, ending any worries that might have occurred when their prior release, *Four Tops on Broadway*, didn't excite anyone except their fans. — *Ron Wynn*

● **The Greatest Hits** / Aug. 1967 / Motown ✦✦✦✦
The first of what would be many greatest hits and anthology packages featuring the Four Tops. At this point, they had had enough chart hits for a good single album set, which is what this is. It has long since lost its value with the release of numerous superior packages. — *Ron Wynn*

Keeper of the Castle / 1972 / Motown ✦✦✦
The Four Tops finally left Motown in the early '70s, signing first with ABC/Dunhill. This was their debut for the label, and it was a moderate success. They did much more pop-oriented material than they ever did for Motown, and the title track was the first of several hits they would enjoy while on ABC. — *Ron Wynn*

★ **Anthology** / Jul. 1974 / Motown ✦✦✦✦✦
Until they get the deluxe box set CD treatment, this three-record/two-CD set qualifies as the ultimate Four Tops Motown statement. It includes all the landmark hits, plus good numbers from their final days at Motown in the 1970s (they did return in the mid-'80s), such as "Still Water" and "Just Seven Numbers." — *Ron Wynn*

Until You Love Someone: More of the Best (1965-1970) / 1993 / Rhino ✦✦✦
This compilation gathers 18 non-hit album tracks from eight LPs that the Four Tops cut for Motown between 1965 and 1970 (some of which appeared on B-sides). A major soul group they might have been, but the Tops' pinnacle was actually quite brief, and that's reflected in this collection. No less than two-thirds of the songs date from 1965 and 1966, six from 1965's *Second Album* alone. Not so coincidentally, all but one of those cuts were written by the legendary Holland/Dozier/Holland songwriting team. The production is faultless, the songs very characteristically HDH, and Levi Stubbs' lead vocals are unfailingly gritty and pleasurable. Yet none of these have the unforgettable hooks of their hit singles of the period like "Reach Out, I'll Be There" and "I Can't Help Myself." As enjoyable as the formula is, the uniformity of the sound limits this disc's appeal to serious Motown and soul collectors. Curiosities among the non-HDH cuts include little-known tunes by Smokey Robinson and Stevie Wonder, and a non-hit single from 1969, "What Is a Man." — *Richie Unterberger*

○ **The Best of the Four Tops (1972—1976)** / MCA ✦✦✦✦
This collection covers their best Dunhill tracks from the 1970s, which did include two big hits in "Ain't No Woman (Like the One I Got)" and "Are You Man Enough." "Keeper of the Castle" was also a Top Ten R&B single, and it seemed as if the Four Tops were in stride again. The Dunhill period yielded two more Top Ten R&B smashes with "One Chain Don't Make No Prison" and "Midnight Flower," and is a much better period than some fans consider. — *Ron Wynn*

Four Tunes

Group, R&B
This New York City group's origins dated back to the mid-'40s, when they were known as Deek Watson & the Brown Dots. Former Ink Spots member Watson, Pat Best, Jimmy Gordon, and Jimmie Nabbie were the founding lineup. The Four Tunes made their recording debut for Regis in 1945. They did a session for Manor in 1946 as the Sentimentalists, minus Watson, with Danny Owens taking his place. They then became the Four Tunes. Best and Watson's composition "I Love You for Sentimental Reasons" became a smash for Nat "King" Cole and several other performers, while Nabbie's "You Are My Love" was a hit for Jonie James. The Four Tunes did score a pair of triumphs themselves, with "Marie" peaking at number two on the R&B charts (number 13 pop) in 1953 and "I Understand Just How You Feel" becoming a number seven R&B hit in 1954. It was also their lone Top Ten pop single, peaking at number six. Both were for Jubilee Records. The Sid Bass Orchestra backed them on both songs. The Four Tunes continued until 1963. Nabbie maintained a solo career heading an Ink Spots ensemble. — *Ron Wynn*

○ **The Complete Jubilee Sessions** / 1992 / Sequel ✦✦✦✦

Samantha Fox

b. 1966
Dance-Pop
When she was 16 years-old, Samantha Fox rose to stardom in Britain as a topless model in the *Daily Sun* newspaper. Fox's popularity as a model soon led to a record contract. She released her first single, "Touch Me (I Want Your Body)," in 1986. "Touch Me" set the pattern for her career—frothy, sexually suggestive dance-pop, with good beats and sketchy melodies. Throughout her career, Fox always accentuated her sex appeal, making it take priority over her music. Nevertheless, she had a fairly long string of hits, beginning with the U.K. number three single "Touch Me." "Do Ya, Do Ya (Wanna Please Me)" followed her debut single into the British Top Ten.

Soon afterward, her records were released in America to nearly equal success. *Touch Me*, her debut album went gold with the title track hitting number four. Her next two singles didn't fare as well, yet "Naughty Girls (Need Love Too)"—taken from her second album, *Samantha Fox* (1987)—became a number three hit in the U.S. *Samantha Fox* also went gold, as did 1988's *I Wanna Have Some Fun*, but the hits dried up after that album. Fox has since tried her hand at acting. — *Stephen Thomas Erlewine*

○ **Touch Me** / 1986 / Jive ✦✦✦✦
This is her American debut. — *Larry Lapka*

Samantha Fox / 1987 / Jive ✦✦✦
Includes "Naughty Girls." — *Bil Carpenter*

I Wanna Have Some Fun / 1989 / Jive ✦✦
Sexy disco-pop. — *Larry Lapka*

Just One Night / 1991 / Jive ✦✦✦

● **Greatest Hits** / Sep. 29, 1992 / Jive ✦✦✦✦

Inez and Charles Foxx

Group, Soul, R&B
This brother/sister duo from Greensboro made a little noise on the soul scene in the '60s. They signed with Juggy Murray Jones' Symbol label in 1962. Their biggest hit was "Mockingbird," in 1963, which was a number five R&B and number seven pop smash. Their vocal tradeoffs and arrangement were primarily responsible for its appeal, though Foxx could do some sizzling numbers on her own. They continued with "Ask Me" and "Hurt by Love," then switched to Musicor. Their final moderate hit was "(1-2-3-4-5-6-7) Count the Days" in 1967 for Dynamo, which reached number 17 on the R&B charts. Inez Foxx had a solid LP on her own for Volt in

1969, *At Memphis*. But her solo songs for the label didn't generate much interest in the early and mid-'70s. James Taylor and Carly Simon later did a cover of "Mockingbird." —*Ron Wynn*

● **Mockingbird: The Best of Inez Foxx** / 1986 / EMI America ✦✦✦✦

Peter Frampton

b. Apr. 22, 1950, Beckenham, England
Pop/Rock
After years of toiling away as an exceptional journeyman guitarist and singer during the late '60s and early '70s, Peter Frampton struck mega-platinum with a double live album entitled *Frampton Comes Alive*. The huge success of that album, coupled with Frampton's pretty-boy looks, almost overshadowed his elegantly melodic musicianship.

The Herd was Frampton's first successful group, but he gained much visibility with the heavy English boogie band Humble Pie. Frampton left just when Humble Pie was becoming a major concert draw, and he released a great 1972 debut solo effort titled *Wind of Change*, following with the strong *Frampton's Camel*, *Somethin's Happening*, and *Frampton*.

Frampton Comes Alive was a neat summation of Frampton's first four solo albums; it also became the biggest-selling live rock album in history. Frampton's next studio album, *I'm in You*, was a hit, but a series of poor career moves (such as appearing in the ill-conceived movie *Sgt. Pepper's Lonely Hearts Club Band*) and a tragic auto accident undermined his momentum. Frampton continues to release periodic albums and tours regularly. —*Rick Clark*

○ **Wind of Change** / 1972 / A&M ✦✦✦✦
○ **Frampton's Camel** / 1973 / A&M ✦✦✦✦
   Somethings Happening / 1974 / A&M ✦✦✦
   Frampton / 1975 / A&M ✦✦✦
○ **Frampton Comes Alive** / 1976 / A&M ✦✦✦✦
Fueled by Frampton's voice-box guitar technique and accessible radio-friendly pop/rock songs like "Show Me the Way" and "Baby I Love Your Way," the double album *Frampton Comes Alive* became the biggest-selling live album in rock history, topping the ten million mark. It's a sensible place to start, since Frampton seems to be in his element here, and the song selection includes the cream of his first four albums. —*Donna DiChario*

   I'm in You / 1977 / A&M ✦✦✦
   Where I Should Be / 1979 / A&M ✦✦
   Breaking All the Rules / 1981 / A&M ✦✦
   The Art of Control / 1982 / A&M ✦✦
   Premonition / 1986 / Virgin ✦✦
● **Classics, Vol. 12** / 1989 / A&M ✦✦✦✦
This overview of Frampton's work may not be definitive but it is a nice sampler that includes all of his hits, plus some favorite album tracks. —*Rick Clark*

   When All the Pieces Fit / 1989 / Atlantic ✦✦
○ **Shine on: a Collection** / Oct. 20, 1992 / A&M ✦✦✦✦
This two-disc set is the essential collection for anyone looking for a great overview of Frampton. —*Rick Clark*

   Peter Frampton / Jan. 25, 1994 / Relativity ✦✦

Connie Francis

b. Dec. 12, 1938, Newark, NJ
Pop
Considered the leading pop female singer of her era, Connie Francis usually sang of her latest broken heart with a teardrop in her voice. The Newark, NJ, native started performing as a child, signing with MGM Records in 1955, but she suffered two years of bombs before the torch ballad "Who's Sorry Now" shot up the charts in 1958. Although she specialized in sobbing tales of woe, Francis proved she could rock with Neil Sedaka's "Stupid Cupid" in 1958 and "Lipstick on Your Collar" the next year. Francis scored two number one hits in 1960—the twangy "Everybody's Somebody's Fool" and "My Heart Has a Mind of Its Own," and she branched into acting with a starring role in *Where the Boys Are*, the archetypal spring-break movie. "Don't Break the Heart That Loves You" was Francis's last pop chart-topper in 1962, but she continued to rank high in the pop pantheon throughout the decade, with forays into ethnic and country idioms. —*Bill Dahl*

● **The Very Best of Connie Francis** / Oct. 1963 / Polydor ✦✦✦✦
Though many best-of's exist on the market, this one leans more heavily toward her earlier rock & roll hits. (Originally released in October 1963 as a 15-track LP by MGM Records [MGM 4167], *The Very Best of Connie Francis* was reissued in 1986 on CD with six bonus tracks by Polydor Records [Polydor 827 569].) —*Cub Koda*

Frankie Goes to Hollywood

Group, Dance-Pop
On the back of an enormous publicity campaign, Frankie Goes to Hollywood dominated British music in 1984. Frankie's dance-pop borrowed heavily from the then-current hi-NRG movement, adding a slick pop sensibility and production. What really distinguished the group was not their music, but their marketing campaign. With a series of slogans, T-shirts and homoerotic videos, the band caused enormous controversy in England and managed to create some sensations in the United States. However, the Frankie sensation was finished as soon as it was started; by the release of their second album *Liverpool* in 1986, the group's audience had virtually disappeared.

Based in Liverpool, Frankie Goes to Hollywood formed in 1980, comprising ex-Big in Japan vocalist Holly Johnson, vocalist Paul Rutherford, guitarist Nasher Nash, bassist Mark O'Toole, and drummer Peter Gill. Originally, the group was called Hollycaust, but they changed their name to Frankie Goes to Hollywood—taken from an old headline about Frank Sinatra's acting career—by the end of the year. The band didn't make anything of note until 1982, when they appeared on the British television program *The Tube* with a rough version of the video for "Relax." The appearance attracted attention from several record labels as well as record producer Trevor Horn. Horn contacted the band and signed them to his label, ZTT. Late in 1983, Frankie's first single, the Horn-produced "Relax" / "Ferry Cross the Mersey," was released. A driving dance number, "Relax" featured sexually suggestive lyrics ("Relax / Don't do it / When you wanna come") that would soon lead to great controversy.

Around the time of the release of "Relax," Frankie's promotional director Paul Morley, a former music journalist, orchestrated a massive, intricate marketing campaign that soon paid off in spades. Morley designed T-shirts that read "Relax" and "Frankie Says ...," which eventually appeared across the countries. The group began playing up their stylish, street-wise and campy homosexual imagery, especially in the first video for "Relax." The video was banned by British TV and a new version was shot. Similarly, Radio 1 banned the single, as DJ Mike Read labelled it "obscene;" the rest of the BBC radio and television networks quickly banned the record as well. Consequently, "Relax" shot to number one in January of 1984 and soon sold over a million copies. Frankie's second single, the political "Two Tribes," was released in June of 1984. The single, which was also produced by Trevor Horn, entered the charts at number one; it went gold in seven days. Sales of the single stayed strong thanks to the video, which featured impersonators of U.S. president Ronald Reagan and Soviet leader Chernenko in a wrestling match. "Two Tribes" stayed at number one for nine weeks and eventually sold over a million copies. While it was on the top of the charts, "Relax" went back up the charts, peaking at number two.

Frankie mania had taken England by storm, yet it took a while to catch on in America. "Relax" peaked at number 67 in the spring of 1984, while "Two Tribes" just missed the Top 40 in the fall. *Welcome to the Pleasuredome*, the band's Trevor Horn-produced debut double album, entered the U.K. charts at number one and their third single, the ballad "The Power of Love," also reached number one. *Welcome to the Pleasuredome* reached at number 33 in early 1985 in the U.S., prompting the re-release of "Relax;" this time around, it made it into the American Top Ten. The title track to the group's double album became their first single not to hit number one, peaking at number two. Both Frankie and Horn won BRIT Awards (Best British Newcomer, Best British Single for "Relax," and Best British Producer) in early 1985 and the group spent the rest of the year touring; the band also spent part of the year on tax exile in Eire, Ireland.

"Rage Hard," the first single from their second album, peaked at number four in the summer of 1986. It was followed by the release of *Liverpool*, which reached number five on the British charts. *Liverpool* was not produced by Trevor Horn and perhaps that was the reason why it failed to recreate the excitement of *Wel-*

come to the Pleasuredome. More likely is the fact that the group's moment in the sun had passed by late 1986.

Frankie Goes to Hollywood began their final tour in early 1987; by April, the band had broken up. Holly Johnson went on to pursue a solo career, which began in earnest in 1989, after a long legal battle with ZTT. Paul Rutherford also began a solo career, yet neither his nor Johnson's were particularly successful. — *Stephen Thomas Erlewine*

○ **Welcome to the Pleasuredome** / 1984 / ZTT/Island ✦✦✦✦
Upbeat British dance music with melodramatic vocals and lyrics that are sexually and politically provocative. The sound of Frankie Goes to Hollywood swept Britain in the years 1983-1985. Here is the wide-screen debut double album, containing the hits "Relax," "Two Tribes," "The Power of Love," and the title track. — *William Ruhlmann*

Liverpool / 1986 / ZTT/Island ✦✦

● **Bang! Greatest Hits** / 1994 / ZTT/Island ✦✦✦✦
This good collection includes all the worthwhile songs Frankie Goes to Hollywood ever recorded. — *AMG*

Alan Franklin Explosion

Blues Rock
Led by singer and rhythm guitarist Alan Franklin, this Florida group released a regional LP in 1970 that is highly valued by collectors. Non-specialists will probably wonder what the fuss is about, but although the record is not a classic, they were one of the better blues-rock acts of the era. Their reverent blues were in the mold of Fleetwood Mac and Canned Heat, with touches of garage and rockabilly. — *Richie Unterberger*

The Blues Climax / 1970 / Psycho ✦✦✦
A reissue of their 1970 LP, which is nearly impossible to find as an original pressing. White blues-rock of this sort has usually dated very badly. What Franklin has in his favor is engagingly raw, somewhat garage-like production and performance (the high-end snare drums are especially unusual for the genre), as well as relative economy; there are no long solos to be found on the six short cuts on Side One. Unfortunately, this doesn't hold true for "Climax," the unlistenable jam that takes up all of Side Two. — *Richie Unterberger*

Aretha Franklin

b. Mar. 25, 1942, Memphis, TN
Soul, R&B
Appropriately dubbed "Lady Soul," Aretha Franklin made several false starts before finding consistent artistic direction. It was only when she began integrating her gospel phrasing and passion (heard in its embryonic form on the Chess album) into secular material that she, like Ray Charles before her, elevated herself from the ranks of the also-rans. There were hints of what was to come in her Columbia recordings, but the flowering of Aretha Franklin coincided with her arrival at Atlantic. From the moment "I Never Loved a Man" broke through in early 1967, Aretha rarely took wrong step for five or six glorious years. When she went wrong, it was usually because of her poor choice of other people's songs to record, but even then, Aretha could sometimes turn dross into gold. By the late '70s, though, the partnership with Atlantic had become stale, and it took a deal with Arista to recharge her chart career. She still has the vocal chops, but many consider that market considerations alone will ensure she will never surpass the artistic high-water mark of her early Atlantic recordings. — *Colin Escott*

Aretha Arrives / 1967 / Atlantic ✦✦✦
Her second Atlantic album features hip "Aretha-fied" covers from Sinatra's "That's Life" to Question Mark & the Mysterians' "96 Tears." A great record utilizing King Curtis and the Muscle Shoals musicians heard on most of Aretha's classic Atlantic work, it includes "Baby I Love You." — *George Bedard*

○ **I Never Loved a Man (The Way I Love You)** / 1967 / Atlantic ✦✦✦✦
I Never Loved a Man The Way I Love You is Franklin's first Atlantic album—an electrifying breakthrough in her somewhat stymied (Columbia) career. The Muscle Shoals sound featured here became legendary. — *George Bedard*

○ **Lady Soul** / 1968 / Atlantic ✦✦✦✦
Great personnel again—King Curtis, Bobby Womack, Frank Wess, and others, including a guest spot by Eric Clapton. Several classic songs, including the lesser-known "Ain't No Way" by Carolyn

Franklin and the hits "Chain of Fools" and "Natural Woman." — *George Bedard*

○ **Aretha Now** / 1968 / Atlantic ✦✦✦✦
The 1968 release has more good covers and the hit "Think." — *George Bedard*

Aretha in Paris / 1968 / Atlantic ✦✦✦
Atlantic's Jerry Wexler once said that this concert album was an embarrassment to him, criticizing the inferior band (actually the musicians that usually accompanied her live in the late '60s). Composed of her first few big singles and cuts from her first three albums, it doesn't match the classic studio versions, and could be considered her least essential '60s Atlantic LP. That's not to say, though, that it doesn't sound pretty good, with fine if basic readings of a lot of her most popular late-'60s material, although the horns fall distressingly out of tune at a key point in the instrumental break of "Chain of Fools." — *Richie Unterberger*

○ **Soul '69** / 1969 / Atlantic ✦✦✦✦
One of her most overlooked '60s albums, on which she presented some of her jazziest material, despite the title. None of these cuts were significant hits, and none were Aretha originals; she displayed her characteristically eclectic taste in the choice of cover material, handling compositions by Percy Mayfield, Sam Cooke, Smokey Robinson, and, at the most pop-oriented end of her spectrum, John Hartford's "Gentle on My Mind" and Bob Lind's "Elusive Butterfly." Her vocals are consistently passionate and first-rate, though, as is the musicianship; besides contributions from the Muscle Shoals rhythm section, session players include respected jazzmen Kenny Burrell, Ron Carter, Grady Tate, David Newman, and Joe Zawinul. — *Richie Unterberger*

○ **Aretha's Gold** / 1969 / Atlantic ✦✦✦✦
The first compilation based on Franklin's successes of 1967-1968 on Atlantic. Included among the 14 selections here are all of the big hits (nine of which went Top Ten) that established Franklin's enduring reputation, from "I Never Loved a Man (The Way I Love You)" to "I Say a Little Prayer." It sometimes got as good as this afterwards, but it never got better. — *William Ruhlmann*

I Say a Little Prayer / 1969 / Atlantic

This Girl's in Love with You / 1970 / Atlantic ✦✦✦
The title song (a cover of Herb Alpert's "This Guy's in Love with You") might lead you to believe this is one of Aretha's more pop-oriented albums, but in fact, this is the only song of the sort on this solid and fairly earthy effort. Besides the hit singles "Call Me," and "Share Your Love With Me," it also includes her most well-known Beatle covers ("Eleanor Rigby" and "Let It Be"), and her interesting version of "The Weight," a Top 20 single featuring slide guitar by Duane Allman. — *Richie Unterberger*

○ **Spirit in the Dark** / 1970 / Atlantic ✦✦✦✦
Spirit in the Dark was one of Aretha Franklin's more overlooked albums from her Atlantic prime, despite the inclusion of a couple hit singles (the title track and "Don't Play That Song"). The disc includes five of her own compositions (the most she ever recorded for a single album) and her usual eclectic choice of cover material. On this record, the covers ranged from B.B.King and Dr. John to Jimmy Reed and Goffin/King's "Oh Not My Baby." The album also benefits from great backup players: both the Muscle Shoals rhythm section and the Dixie Flyers contributed to the sessions, and Duane Allman lends his guitar to a couple of tracks. Though it doesn't rank with her very best Atlantic LPs, it's an exuberant and remarkably consistent effort. The 1993 CD reissue has detailed liner notes on the songs and sessions by David Nathan. — *Richie Unterberger*

Live at Fillmore West / 1971 / Atlantic ✦✦✦
Aretha Franklin's 1971 LP *Live At Fillmore West* was as seminal a soul breakthrough as Albert King's visit had been for blues. It finally cemented her status beyond soul audiences as both a recording and live attraction, and it matched her with a phenomenal rhythm section in King Curtis and the Kingpens. Franklin adroitly mixed pop, rock and soul material throughout the three nights, including Stephen Stills' "Love the One You're With," Bread's "Make It With You," and The Beatles' "Eleanor Rigby," as well as tried and true favorites "Respect," "Don't Play That Song" and "Spirit in the Dark," which brought Ray Charles out of the audience for a spirited duet. There's more than enough here to make this absolutely essential, regardless of whether or not you have the original vinyl. — *Ron Wynn*

○ **Young Gifted & Black** / 1971 / Atlantic ✦✦✦✦

☆ **Amazing Grace** / 1972 / Atlantic ✦✦✦✦✦
Aretha Franklin disproved the notion that once you leave the church, you can't go back. She returned in triumph on this 1972 double album, making what might be her greatest release ever in any style. Her voice was chilling, making it seem as if God and the angels were conducting a service alongside Franklin, Rev. James Cleveland, the Southern California Community Choir and everyone else in attendance. Her versions of "How I Got Over" and "You've Got a Friend" are legendary. —*Ron Wynn*

Hey Now Hey / 1973 / Atlantic ✦✦✦
Hey Now Hey (The Other Side of the Sky) was just about Franklin's last gasp before succumbing to disco. This odd album, with its cheesy junky artwork contains some gems—notable are a poignant cover of Bernstein's "Somewhere," a sparkling "Moody's Mood," and the beautiful Carolyn Franklin composition "Angel." —*George Bedard*

With Everything I Feel in Me / 1974 / Atlantic ✦✦✦
This respectable but not-earth-shattering release was part of the gradual decline of Franklin's artistic and commercial achievements at Atlantic. The lead-off track, "Without Love," was a Top Ten R&B hit, and the title track, written by Franklin, was Top 20 R&B.There were a couple of familiar but completely rearranged Burt Bacharach tunes and a contribution from Stevie Wonder. Franklin was in good voice, and the studio band was accomplished, but this was all a far cry from the standard Franklin had set in the late '60s. It was also a far cry from the sales she enjoyed then: this was her first new album since her 1967 breakthrough to peak below the Top 30. —*William Ruhlmann*

Let Me in Your Life / 1974 / Atlantic ✦✦✦
A nice, if at times overbearing, mid-'70s Franklin set. She was still singing with the stunning delivery, amazing timing, and majestic soul that highlighted her late-'60s releases. Her version of "Until You Come Back to Me (That's What I'm Gonna Do)" is the only one that might be superior to Stevie Wonder's great original, while "I'm in Love" and the title cut are prime Franklin. —*Ron Wynn*

You / 1975 / Atlantic ✦✦
The first album that represented signs of stagnation. Aretha Franklin had issued two excellent albums in 1974, but in 1975 just didn't get enough quality songs to flesh out *You*. While she still put everything into them, often salvaging dismal lyrics and awkward production, Franklin only equaled past glories on the song "It Only Happens (When I Look at You)." Otherwise, it was a case of wonderful vocals but little else. —*Ron Wynn*

○ **Sparkle** / 1976 / Rhino ✦✦✦✦
Aretha Franklin's career was in a down period in the mid-'70s when she collaborated with Curtis Mayfield to sing his compositions for the film *Sparkle*. The film proved a non-event, but for Franklin it marked a return to glory. Once again she was the Queen of Soul, doing the chilling, spectacular leaps, cries, whoops and shouts that defined secularized gospel in the late '60s. The title cut was a sizable hit, while "Giving Him Something He Can Feel" became an anthem. Mayfield's lyrics and production shouldn't be overlooked; he added just the right amount of background trappings, and the Kitty Haywood Singers provided Franklin's best continuing backgrounds since the Sweet Inspirations. —*Ron Wynn*

Sweet Passion / 1977 / Atlantic ✦✦

Almighty Fire / 1978 / Atlantic ✦✦

La Diva / 1979 / Atlantic ✦✦

Love All the Hurt Away / 1981 / Arista ✦✦✦
Aretha Franklin's post-Atlantic material has the same problems as the Columbia cuts. There are too many songs in which the wondrous Franklin voice was simply inserted into otherwise routine situations, with singles issued to take advantage of her hard-earned credibility and reputation. The title cut was a nice duet between Franklin and George Benson, and there were some other decent songs, but this was overall a disappointment. —*Ron Wynn*

Jump to It / 1982 / Arista ✦✦✦
Aretha Franklin scored some hits with this early '80s album and managed to make concessions to urban contemporary tastes without totally distoring her classic soul sound. While it's certainly not in the class of past recordings, the title cut gave Franklin her first number one of the '80s, and "Love Me Right" was a decent followup. —*Ron Wynn*

Get It Right / 1983 / Arista ✦✦✦
Luther Vandross scored a popular success with *Jump to It*, but this followup is less impressive and proved less successful. Vandross wrote most of the material, including the #1 R&B title track and the R&B Top Ten hit "Every Girl (Wants My Guy)," although he also has Franklin tackle the Temptations hit "I Wish It Would Rain," in a painfully overwrought production. With this record, what had seemed to be an artist/producer marriage made in heaven hit the rocks. —*William Ruhlmann*

Never Grow Old / 1984 / Chess ✦✦✦
Actually credited to "Reverend C.L. Franklin and Aretha Franklin," this album was recorded live—very live-in church. The Reverend Franklin takes most of the leads on traditional gospel songs, with keyboard accompaniment, shouting and singing, although his daughter also has a couple of spotlights. The music is moving, and the audience is moved: one or two of them scream uncontrollably. —*William Ruhlmann*

Aretha's Jazz / 1984 / Atlantic ✦✦✦
A good anthology that covers various album cuts, B-sides, and assorted material in a jazz vein that Aretha cut for Columbia. It's great to hear her underrated piano playing given some more space, and Columbia should really reissue her Dinah Washington tribute album, from which they pulled a couple of these songs. Aretha wasn't a jazz vocalist from the standpoint of approach or inspiration, but she really can sing anything and showed it on these cuts, even if they weren't, for the most part, hits. —*Ron Wynn*

Who's Zoomin' Who? / 1985 / Arista ✦✦✦
Franklin continued finding ways to accomodate the urban contemporary production style and retain her soulfulness. The single "Freeway of Love" was a monster hit in both clubs and on radio, while the title track and "Another Night" also did well across the board. The cut with the Eurythmics even got a little attention at rock stations. —*Ron Wynn*

Aretha / 1986 / Arista ✦✦
Don't be confused by the generic title; this is a new Aretha Franklin album from 1986 and a moderately succesful one, notable for containing five R&B hits, four of which also made the pop charts: "Jumpin' Jack Flash" (produced by Keith Richards and featured in the Whoopi Goldberg movie of the same title), "Jimmy Lee" (#2 R&B), "I Knew You Were Waiting (For Me)" (a duet with George Michael that went #1 pop), "Rock-A-Lott," and "If You Need My Love Tonight" (a duet with Larry Graham). —*William Ruhlmann*

★ **30 Greatest Hits** / 1986 / Atlantic ✦✦✦✦✦
This contains all of her essential Atlantic hits, a matchless catalog of soul vocalizing that will never be topped. —*George Bedard*

One Lord, One Faith, One Baptism / 1987 / Arista ✦✦✦
Although nowhere as anthemic as *Amazing Grace* (what could be?), this was still much better than most contemporary gospel. There were socio-political speeches by Jesse Jackson and Carl Franklin for those who wanted earthly concerns addressed alongside spiritual ones, but the real impact came from Franklin's rousing voice and the contributions of such guest stars as Mavis Staples and Aretha's sisters Erma and Carolyn. If she hadn't issued *Amazing Grace* or *Aretha Gospel* as a teen, this set might have gotten better notices and more critical respect. Instead, it was virtually dismissed, and it deserves better than that. —*Ron Wynn*

Through the Storm / 1989 / Arista ✦✦✦
Having scored in the recent past with producer Narada Michael Walden and some star duets, Franklin and Arista turned out another album with the same approach but less successful results. The title duet with Elton John went Top 20, but its followup, "It Isn't, It Wasn't, It Ain't Never Gonna Be" was an embarrassing failure for both Franklin and the previously pop-perfect Whitney Houston. The rest was even less distinguished, including a song with the Four Tops and Kenny G and a remake of the old hit "Think." —*William Ruhlmann*

Jazz to Soul / 1992 / Columbia ✦✦✦
She's Billie Holiday. No, she's Ella Fitzgerald. No, wait, she's Dinah Washington. The conventional wisdom on Aretha Franklin's tenure at Columbia Records is that the label didn't know what to do with her, and that may be true, but you can't say they didn't try. On these 39 recordings, spread across two discs and cut between 1960 and 1965, Franklin and her producers look for ways to frame her obvious vocal talents, but always in terms of uptown jazz and

non-rock-pop formats. Much of the result is appealing, and it's only in light of the transcendent soul music Franklin made from her first day at Atlantic Records in 1967 that this work comes across as merely exploratory. "Show me the way to get to Soulville," she demands in 1964. She finally found the way, and that was that. — *William Ruhlmann*

☆ **Queen of Soul: The Atlantic Recordings** / 1992 / Rhino ✦✦✦✦✦
This four-disc, 86-track collection is a comprehensive look at Franklin's soul genius. All of her great Atlantic hits are here, as well as many key performances. —*AMG*

Greatest Hits 1980-1994 / 1994 / Arista ✦✦✦
○ **Very Best Of, Vol. 1** / 1994 / Rhino ✦✦✦✦
○ **Very Best Of, Vol. 2** / 1994 / Rhino ✦✦✦✦

Freakwater

Group, Country-Rock, Alternative Pop/Rock
An acoustic side project of the Eleventh Dream Day family tree, featuring Dream Day drummer/singer Janet Bean (who plays guitar in Freakwater) and her friend Catherine Ann Irwin with contributions from various other musicians. This is only "alternative rock" in the marketing sense; the Kentucky-bred singers largely stick to acoustic folk/country with close harmonies and strong Appalachian overtones, sometimes employing fiddle, pedal steel, mandolin, and dobro. Mixing strong original material (mostly written by Irwin) with traditional numbers and songs by the likes of Bill Monroe, Freakwater's albums stand as some of the finest maverick, progressive acoustic records of recent years. —*Richie Unterberger*

Freakwater / 1989 / ✦✦✦
Their debut, a short LP or a long EP, depending on how you look at it, presents plaintive, raw country-folk in a modern context without sounding forced. —*Richie Unterberger*

● **Dancing under Water** / 1991 / Amoeba ✦✦✦✦
A bit more polished than their debut, but hardly slick, with harmonies and the sobbing lead vocals of Irwin at the fore. This is recommended above the debut for a simple reason: the CD includes all of the songs from *Freakwater* as bonus tracks, eliminating the need to look for the first album. —*Richie Unterberger*

John Fred & The Playboys

Group, Rock & Roll, Pop/Rock
Remembered only for his fluke 1968 number one hit "Judy in Disguise," John Fred actually made quite a few records in the '60s. Though he was from Louisiana, Fred's vocals strongly recall Eric Burdon at times, and Georgie Fame's at others. A capable songwriter ("Judy in Disguise" was an original), he also cut several fine, deep Southern soul ballads that distinguish him as one of the best American White R&B singers. —*Richie Unterberger*

● **History of John Fred and the Playboys** / 1991 / Paula ✦✦✦✦
Eclectic 26-song assortment of pop/rock/soul/R&B.Highlights are his 1964 cover of John Lee Hooker's "Boogie Chillen," which stands up to the best early British R&B; the odd, moody "Agnes English" and "Sun City," which shows a strong Animals influence, and of course "Judy in Disguise." A 1958 track that he cut as a teenager recalls a frat-rock Frankie Ford with its low-wattage emulation of the New Orleans sound. Unfortunately there are little in the way of liner notes here, but the grooves prove Fred to be a versatile stylist with much greater depth than the usual one-shot. — *Richie Unterberger*

Freddie & the Dreamers

Group, British Invasion, Pop/Rock
Freddie & the Dreamers were the clowns of the British Invasion, playing their pop music for laughs while the other groups of the time were dead serious. Lead singer Freddie Garrity (b. Nov 14, 1940) began playing in skiffle groups in the late '50s, switching to rock & roll in the early '60s. After the Beatles broke the American market wide open, Freddie & the Dreamers followed in the flood of acts that tried to duplicate the overwhelming success of the Beatles. The group's hits were more numerous in the U.K. than in America, where they had only one Top Ten hit, the number one "I'm Telling You Now." As 1965 turned into 1966, the group stopped charting in the U.S. and the hits began to dwindle in the U.K.; by 1968 the original group disbanded. Garrity continues to tour with a new version of the Dreamers. —*Stephen Thomas Erlewine*

○ **The Best of Freddie & The Dreamers** / 1992 / EMI America ✦✦✦
Yes, "I'm Telling You Now" is here, and so is "Do the Freddie," an absurd attempt at fashioning a dance craze, but so are "How about Trying Your Luck with Me," "When I'm Home with You," and "Brown and Porters (Meat Exporters) Lorry." In other words, it's more than a definitive collection, with 25 tracks (many previously unreleased in the U.S.) and a comprehensive discography. —*Stephen Thomas Erlewine*

Free

Group, Blues Rock, Hard Rock
Free, an English quartet formed in 1968 with Paul Rodgers, Andy Fraser, Paul Kossoff, and Simon Kirke, took the then-popular heavy British blues-rock sound and stripped it down to a hard yet open minimalistic sound.

Rodgers quickly earned a reputation as one of the greatest singers of the genre, able to deliver lyrics with gritty dark sensuality as well as playful toss-offs. Drummer Simon Kirke was the hard rock equivalent to soul music's Al Jackson, speaking volumes with a no-nonsense groove. Paul Kossoff's wide sustain leads and rhythm work filled in the band's sounds, allowing Andy Fraser great freedom to pursue his inventive style of very spare, open but melodic, bass playing.

The band's sound coalesced into some great moments, particularly the #4 hit "All Right Now," "Fire and Water," and "The Stealer." After some lineup changes and an uneven final album (*Heartbreaker*) in 1973, Free disbanded. Rodgers and Kirke went on to form Bad Company. Fraser and Kossoff released spotty solo efforts, and Kossoff died of heart failure on March 19, 1976. —*Rick Clark*

Tons of Sobs / 1968 / A&M ✦✦
○ **Fire & Water** / 1970 / A&M ✦✦✦✦
This classic Free album features their biggest hit, "All Right Now," as well as key Free tracks, "Heavy Load," "Mr. Big," and the title track. —*Rick Clark*

Highway / Feb. 1971 / A&M ✦✦✦
Free Live / Sep. 1971 / A&M ✦✦
Free at Last / 1972 / A&M ✦✦✦
● **The Best of Free** / 1973 / A&M ✦✦✦✦
A solid compilation showcasing "All Right Now" and other semi-hits, this is a worthwhile sampler for the uninitiated. —*Dan Heilman*

Heartbreaker / 1973 / PolyGram ✦✦
● **Molten Gold: The Anthology** / Oct. 5, 1993 / A&M ✦✦✦✦
With their big riffs and bluesy melodies, Free virtually defined hard rock in the early '70s, and *Molten Gold: The Anthology* shows that this wasn't such a meager achievement. Throughout the two discs, it becomes clear that the key to Free's rock & roll was their rhythm section, which powered their riffs to perfection. This is the definitive Free, two discs of pure hard rock. —*Stephen Thomas Erlewine*

Free Spirits

Group, Fusion, Psychedelic
The beginning of jazz-rock is commonly dated in the late sixties, with the emergence of Blood, Sweat & Tears, the Electric Flag, and Miles Davis' *Bitches Brew*, but in fact a few sporadic efforts had made at reconciling the two forms before that. The Free Spirits, a New York group featuring the guitar, songwriting, and singing of Larry Coryell, may have been the first. Augmenting the usual guitar-bass-drums rock lineup with the tenor saxophone of Jim Pepper, the quintet's backgrounds were decidedly jazz. But their sound was considerably closer to rock, investing the early psychedelic sounds of the day with relatively adventurous, jazz-derived improvisation, horns (or one, anyway), and elastic song structures. They weren't avant-garde by any means; on their LP, their innovations were tailored to fit songs with vocals lasting between two and three-and-a-half minutes. The vocals were the weakest link in the band, and the free association of the lyrics has dated in some cases. But their moderate use of jazz idioms within pop and rock frameworks was innovative for its day, and remains unfairly overlooked. —*Richie Unterberger*

● **Out of Sight & Sound** / 1966 / ABC ✦✦✦✦
These tentative explorations into relatively uncharted jazz-rock territory retain an engaging, freewheeling verve and warm humor, although the lyrics are sometimes self-consciously hip and spacy. Coryell plays a sitar on "I'm Gonna Be Free," and "Blue Water Mother" employs the still-unusual device of two separate vocal tracks singing two entirely separate sets of lyrics. Obscure even in its day and long out-of-print, it's worth seeking out, though more for fans of '60s rock than jazz. —*Richie Unterberger*

Bobby Freeman

R&B
Bobby Freeman's energetic vocals punctuated two R&B dance hits in the late '50s and mid-'60s. The San Francisco performer started the Romancers as a 14-year-old and later formed the West Coast Vocaleers, whose sound was much more pop-oriented than the Harlem group of the same name. Freeman's single "Do You Want to Dance" just missed topping the R&B charts in 1958, staying at number two for two weeks (number five pop). It was one of three hits he enjoyed that year on Josie, although "Betty Lou Got a New Pair of Shoes" and "Need Your Love" only reached numbers 20 and 29, respectively. "C'Mon and Swim" parlayed the 1964 dance craze into his second Top Ten R&B hit, reaching number five. But the follow-up went to the water once too often, as "S-W-I-M" fizzled at number 56. Both were for Autumn. It was also Freeman's final visit to the R&B charts. —*Ron Wynn*

Do You Wanna Dance / 1958 / Collectables ✦✦✦
The title track is one of the great pieces of '50s R&B/rock and roll and was Freeman's moment of glory. The rest of the album is decent, occasionally above-average pop and light R&B, sung in an energetic fashion but not exactly spectacular stuff. It is fun, however, and if you can find the album, it's well worth getting. —*Ron Wynn*

● **Best of** / 1992 / Sequel ✦✦✦✦

Frente!

Group, Alternative Pop/Rock
Guitarist Simon Austin formed the Melbourne, Australian folk-pop band Frente! in 1991, bringing in Angie Hart, Simon Austin (guitar), Tim O'Connor and Mark Picton (replaced by Alastair Barden) to round out the lineup. Frente! entered the international spotlight in the summer of 1994 with their quirky acoustic version of New Order's "Bizarre Love Triangle." On the back of that single, *Marvin: The Album* entered the charts, with the single "Labor of Love" becoming a minor hit. —*Stephen Thomas Erlewine*

○ **Marvin the Album** / 1994 / Atlantic ✦✦✦✦

Doug E. Fresh & the Get Fresh Crew

Group, Rap
New Yorker Doug E. Fresh (born Doug E. Davis), got his initial notoriety for being the "human beatbox," able to approximate and imitate a rhythm machine. He had a string of hit singles with his then partner Ricky Dee in the early and mid-'80s, notably "The Show (Oh, My God)" in 1985, which included guest stints from jazz veteran trumpeter Jimmy Owens and synthesizer player Bernard Wright. Fresh had a long absence from the scene after 1988's *The World's Greatest Entertainer* and has just resurfaced with a new release on a small independent label. —*Ron Wynn*

○ **Oh, My God!** / 1986 / Reality ✦✦✦✦
Zany rhymes, slashing beats, with bits and pieces of everything from reggae to gospel to funk. —*Ron Wynn*

● **The World's Greatest Entertainer** / 1988 / Reality ✦✦✦✦
With the exception of the monster hit "Keep Rising to the Top," Fresh trimmed the religious zealotry and increased the lyrical and rhythmic potency. —*Ron Wynn*

Doin' What I Gotta Do / Apr. 27, 1992 / Bust It ✦✦

Glenn Frey

b. Nov. 6, 1948, Detroit, MI
Pop/Rock
Frey, previously a singer/songwriter and guitarist in the Eagles, launched a solo career upon the band's demise, starting in 1982. He also worked as a TV actor on "Miami Vice," "Wiseguy." Frey reunited with the Eagles in 1994 for a tour and the *Hell Freezes Over* album. —*William Ruhlmann*

No Fun Aloud / May 28, 1982 / Asylum ✦✦✦
Glenn Frey's debut solo album following the breakup of the Eagles was a modest pop/rock effort with none of the ambitiousness of his former group. Frey introduced a light tone in a series of songs, many of them co-written with Jack Tempchin and punctuated by Al Garth's tenor sax work. "I Found Somebody" and "The One You Love" became Top 40 single hits, and the album went gold, but anyone expecting Frey to shoulder the mantle of the Eagles was bound to be disappointed. —*William Ruhlmann*

○ **The Allnighter** / Jun. 1984 / MCA ✦✦✦✦
Frey breaks with the old Eagles sound on his second solo album, much of which has a bluesy, rocking feel. Includes the hits "Smuggler's Blues" and "Sexy Girl." —*William Ruhlmann*

Soul Searchin' / Aug. 1988 / MCA ✦✦
Eight years after the demise of the Eagles, Glenn Frey had settled into a career that involved writing the occasional movie theme song, taking the occasional acting role, and, every four years, turning out another album of light soul-pop tunes written with Jack Tempchin. *Soul Searchin'* showed him to be more interested in body building than record making (he was also appearing in health club before-and-after ads at this time, the two photos showing him as an Eagle—"Hard Rock"—and today—"Rock Hard"), and the songs here were so interchangeable with those on his first two albums he apologized for it in his note about "True Love," which became the album's sole Top 40 hit. The music was pleasant, but inconsequential, and suggested that Frey, living off his Eagles royalties, had come to think of his solo career as a hobby. —*William Ruhlmann*

Strange Weather / Jul. 1992 / MCA ✦✦✦
With his solo career fading, Glenn Frey got serious on his fourth album, but many of the album's sentiments sounded strange coming from him. "He Took Advantage" was subtitled "Blues for Ronald Reagan," but it came more than three years after Reagan's retirement, and Frey's 1984 song "Better in the U.S.A." could have served as Reagan's campaign song. On "I've Got Mine," Frey sang about how people in limousines don't care about "us," but when was the last time he was on the outside of a limousine looking in? Frey was out of his league going for the kind of philosophical/political territory better handled by his old partner Don Henley. So, although *Strange Weather* signaled a new commitment by Frey to his career, it missed the charts entirely. (The album concludes with "Part of Me, Part of You," an Eagles-like tune used in the 1991 film *Thelma and Louise*.) —*William Ruhlmann*

● **Glenn Frey Live** / Jul. 2, 1993 / MCA ✦✦✦✦
In the course of this 70-minute, 14-song live disc, recorded at the Stadium in Dublin on July 8, 1992, Glenn Frey divides the set list just about equally between solo material and old Eagles songs. As such, it provides a good sampler of Frey's career in total, from "Take It Easy" to "Smuggler's Blues." One might have hoped for a bit less of Frey's then-current solo album, *Strange Weather*, and a bit more of the Eagles (after this record, Frey returned for the group's reunion). At presstime, MCA planned a Frey hits compilation for the second half of 1995; until then, this will serve as the album best able to give listeners an idea of what his solo career has been like (and it is the only one to contain a version of "The Heat Is On," albeit not the hit recording. —*William Ruhlmann*

○ **Solo Collection** / 1995 / MCA ✦✦✦✦

Anni-Frid Lyngstad [Frida] (Anni-Frid Lyngstad)

Group, Pop/Rock
Frida, whose full name is Anni-Frid Lyngstad Fredriksson Andersson, was a Scandinavian solo singer in the 1960s and 1970s before she joined a group being put together by her boyfriend (and later husband) Benny Andersson, ABBA. ABBA was a massive international success especially during the second half of the '70s; the group disbanded at the start of the '80s, and Frida, who divorced Andersson, returned to solo work with the Phil Collins-produced *Something's Going On* in 1982. —*William Ruhlmann*

Frida / 196z / Columbia ✦✦

Frida Ensam / 1975 / Polar ✦✦

● **Something's Going on** / 1984 / Epic ✦✦✦✦

Shine / 1984 / Epic ✦✦✦

Friends of Distinction

Group, R&B
Los Angeles pop-influenced R&B group. Modeled after the 5th Di-

mension, the Friends of Distinction briefly carved out their own pop/R&B niche in 1969-70. Two members (Floyd Butler and Harry Elston) had been in the Hi-Fi's, (a group that spawned a pair of 5th Dimension members), and the Friends' breezy vocal blend was quite similar, although weighted toward the ladies (three women, two men). Their first RCA hit in 1969 was a vocal treatment of Hugh Masekela's hit instrumental, "Grazing in the Grass," and they encored with "Going in Circles," a mellow number that was a minor hit, and the dazzling "Love ME Or Let Me Be Lonely." —*Bill Dahl*

Friends of Distinction's Greatest Hits / 1973 / RCA ✦✦✦
● **Golden Classics** / Collectables ✦✦✦✦
The essential compilation from this wonderful soul ensemble. — *Ron Wynn*

Frightwig

Group, Hard Rock, Alternative Pop/Rock, Heavy Metal
Anyone interested in doing a genealogical study of the roots of riot grrrl rock must include this tremendously influential San Francisco band. Ferocious, funky feminists, Frightwig's debut LP was a brain-burning chunk of white-hot noise-rock, loaded with unsubtle sexual politics ("My Crotch Does Not Say Go") and fueled by punk-rock bravado that never let up. Flying in the face of every conventional (i.e., male-defined) attitude of a woman's place in contemporary rock, Frightwig simply got in your face and stayed there—if you didn't like it, tough shit. Sadly, they burned out after two records, reuniting in 1990 for a dispiriting EP that sounded more like a sophomoric dirty joke. A lot of feminist-inspired women rock bands of the '90s, like L7, Bikini Kill, and Bratmobile, owe a debt of gratitude to this pioneering band. Word is that they've reunited, and that their two seminal records are available on CD. Here's hoping for more good music. —*John Dougan*

● **Cat Farm Faboo** / 1984 / Subterranean ✦✦✦✦
Salacious and aggressive, this is an unholy racket the likes of which you've never heard before. It's a mess, but it's a glorious, fun-filled one. The only downside is a hectoring tone to some of the songs, but that's the revisionist in me speaking. From start to finish, this is 12 inches of blistering sonic carnage, which may not be your everyday choice for music, but would make a wonderful addition to your record collection (or CD library). —*John Dougan*

Faster, Frightwig, Kill! Kill! / 1986 / Caroline ✦✦✦
Its title a tribute to B-film sex and violence auteur Russ Meyer, this is Frightwig's greatest moment; more trad-rock (i.e., hard rock) oriented, but not losing any of its confrontational bite or over-the-top charm. Rabid fans of the first LP might feel that this was a step backwards, but they'd be missing the point. This is a tremendous record that will pole-axe from the get-go and leave you drooling at the finish. —*John Dougan*

Phone Sexy / 1990 / Boner ✦✦

Robert Fripp

b. May 16, 1946, Dorset, England
Art-Rock/Progressive-Rock, Experimental
Throughout his career, guitarist Robert Fripp has continually pushed the boundaries of pop music, as well as pursuing many avant-garde and experimental musical ideas. Fripp began playing professionally with the League of Gentlemen in the mid-'60s, providing instrumental support to many American singers that were touring England. During this time he began Giles Giles and Fripp with Pete and Mike Giles. The trio only released one album, 1968's *The Cheerful Insanity of Giles Giles and Fripp,* yet the group soon evolved into King Crimson.

Following the release of their 1969 debut album *In the Court of the Crimson King,* King Crimson became one of the most respected progressive rock acts of its era. From 1969 to 1974, Fripp was the one mainstay in the group, leading it through its various musical incarnations.

During this time, he pursued several side-projects away from King Crimson. Fripp recorded two albums with Brian Eno—*No Pussyfooting* (1972) and *Evening Star* (1974). Both of the albums featured the musicians experimenting with avant-garde techniques, including Fripp's "Frippertronics." "Frippertronics" featured layers of guitars and tape loops, producing a harmonically-rich, humming sound; it became a familiar sound on his records. Fripp also produced a handful of albums, mainly records by experimental jazz outfits.

In 1974, Fripp disbanded King Crimson and retired from music. Three years later, he returned to the business, playing on David Bowie's *"Heroes."* Soon afterward, he produced and played on Peter Gabriel's second self-titled album, as well Daryl Hall's *Sacred Songs.* Fripp released his first solo album, *Exposure,* in 1979. *God Save the Queen / Under Heavy Manner* appeared the following year and in 1981, he assembled a new lineup of King Crimson. While that band recorded and performed, he also led a new band which borrowed its name from his first group, the League of Gentlemen. After releasing three albums, the new version of King Crimson broke up in 1984; the League of Gentlemen split soon afterward.

Fripp released *God Save the King* in 1985 and began teaching guitar, dubbing his students and school the League of Crafty Guitarists; he released an album recorded with his Crafty Guitarists in 1986, the same year he released the first of two collaborations with his wife, Toyah Wilcox. Fripp re-formed the '80s lineup of King Crimson in late 1994, releasing *Thrak* in 1995. —*Stephen Thomas Erlewine*

No Pussyfooting / 1973 / EG ✦✦✦
His collaboration with Brian Eno. A musical landscape made up of sedate guitar feedback echoed, repeated, and otherwise treated by tape recorder. Today this would be classified under "new-age." The followup, *Evening Star,* is similar. —*William Ruhlmann*

Evening Star / 1976 / EG ✦✦✦
Fripp & Eno's second collaboration is similar to their first, *No Pussyfooting,* in that it combines Fripp's interest in droning tape loops with Eno's taste in sound landscapes. Electronic instrumental music with a meditative air. —*William Ruhlmann*

○ **Exposure** / 1979 / EG ✦✦✦✦
Although Fripp uses words like "commercial" and "MOR" to describe this music, and though parts of it contain more-or-less conventional pop-rock material, Fripp introduces a variety of tape loops and edits, vocal fragments and sound experiments, resulting in a unique musical sound collage. Guest artists include Phil Collins, Brian Eno, Daryl Hall, and Peter Gabriel. —*William Ruhlmann*

God Save the Queen/ Under Heavy Manners / Dec. 1980 / Polydor ✦✦✦
Despite the double title, this is a single album consisting of five examples of "Frippertronics," Fripp's word for his instrumental tape loop experiments, some also called "Discotronics" to indicate more of a rhythmic impulse. Talking Head David Byrne sings the words to "Under Heavy Manners," most of which consist of words ending in the suffix "ism." —*William Ruhlmann*

League of Gentlemen / 1981 / EG ✦✦✦
The League of Gentlemen was an instrumental group organized by Robert Fripp in 1980 featuring, in addition to his guitar, Barry Andrews on organ, Sara Lee on bass, and Jonny Toobad on drums, replaced by Kevin Wilkinson. This is their first album. It includes spoken word excerpts by Fripp's spiritual advisor, J.G. Bennett, and remarks about the music business by various unidentified people, sometimes heard over the music. That music is uptempo rock for the most part, dominated by Fripp's often jarring guitar parts, although some calmer pieces recall his ambient efforts. —*William Ruhlmann*

Let the Power Fall / 1981 / EG ✦✦✦
Let the Power Fall (An Album of Frippertronics). "Frippertronics" is the name Robert Fripp gives to his instrumental pieces constructed with an electric guitar and a tape recorder. It is characterized by long-lined instrumental passages with sustained notes that reverberate in interesting repetitions and variations. —*William Ruhlmann*

I Advance Masked / 1982 / A&M ✦✦✦
An instrumental collaboration between guitarists Andy Summers (formerly of the Police) and Robert Fripp (formerly of King Crimson). Much of it has the rock drive of Summers's work with the Police, along with Fripp's pattern work, making for a surprisingly diverse collection. —*William Ruhlmann*

○ **God Save the King** / 1985 / EG ✦✦✦✦

Network / 1985 / EG ✦✦✦
This is a 20-minute compilation EP consisting of three tracks from Fripp's *Exposure* album and featuring such sidemen as Phil Collins, Brian Eno, Daryl Hall, and Peter Gabriel, and two tracks from the League of Gentlemen album *God Save the King.* As such, it touches upon both Fripp's more pop-oriented work and his

more experimental work and makes a good introduction to him. — *William Ruhlmann*

The League of Crafty Guitarists Live / 1986 / EG ✦✦✦
A guitar teacher, Fripp assembled this group of seventeen acoustic guitar players from his students and played shows doing his instrumentals. It takes that many guitars, playing the same parts, to recreate the volume, sustain, and fullness Fripp usually gets by using a couple of electric guitars himself (and there's also some electric music to prove that point). But the tone achieved by the acoustics is unique and as tense as Fripp's music usually is, this record is also surprisingly vibrant. — *William Ruhlmann*

Kings / 1993 / EG

Bridge Between / 1994 / Discipline ✦✦✦

BOOK

✦✦✦ **Robert Fripp: From King Crimson To Guitar Craft**, by Eric Tamm (Faber & Faber, 1990). Tamm originally had the idea of writing a thesis on Fripp, but was persuaded by the guitarist himself that Eno would make a better topic. This combination biography/critique is a good deal more readable than Tamm's book on Eno, probably because the Eno volume drew on Tamm's thesis, whereas this bio was written more as a general interest book. Tamm intelligently analyzes Fripp's work from the late '60s through the late '80s, covering King Crimson, Frippertronics, the League of Gentlemen, his collaborations with Eno and others, and the League of Crafty Guitarists, referring to a good deal of previously published interviews. Fripp is a musician who guards his privacy and feels little obligation to play the media game; this, combined with Tamm's academic background, makes this more scholarly in tone than the average rock bio. Still, it's readable and accessible, not just in its musical criticism, but its portrait of a rock & roll enigma, who has also studied with Gurdjieff disciples, projects a persona of a super-rational theorist and technophile, and veers between fairly accessible work and almost willfully uncommercial projects. Of special interest is Tamm's eyewitness diary of one of Fripp's guitar seminars, in which Tamm participated as a student. — *Richie Unterberger*

Fred Frith

Art-Rock/Progressive-Rock, Experimental
Brilliant British avant-garde electric guitarist and multi-instrumentalist specializing in improvisation incorporating trace-elements of free jazz and progressive rock with lots of noise and "treated" guitars a la John Cage's "treated" pianos. Solo, duo, and group (see Henry Cow) recordings range from flat-out noise (*Guitar Solos, With Enemies Like These, Who Needs Friends*), to lovely, airy, almost lullaby-like compositions (parts of *Gravity*), to industrial dance music (side two of *Speechless*). Even the prettiest tunes have an edge, and the others (the majority) may make you re-evaluate what you consider music. Challenging and complex. It is hard to be halfway about Frith's music; you either love it or hate it. Definitely not for the weak-hearted, weak-minded, or weak-spirited. — *Niles J. Frantz*

With Enemies Like These Who Needs Friends? / Jul. 8, 1979–Jul. 17, 1979 / SST ✦✦✦

○ **Gravity** / 1980 / East Side Digital ✦✦✦✦

○ **Speechless** / 1981 / East Side Digital ✦✦✦✦

French Gigs / 1983 / AAA ✦✦✦

○ **Cheap at Half the Price** / 1983 / East Side Digital ✦✦✦✦
Cheap at Half the Price is the first solo album featuring Frith's vocals, but his rough-edged guitar experimentalism makes the album succeed. — *Stephen Thomas Erlewine*

Voice of America / Feb. 1984 / Rift ✦✦✦

Nous Autre / 1988 / Recommended ✦✦✦

● **Step Across the Border** / 1990 / East Side Digital ✦✦✦✦
Although it's theoretically a film soundtrack, *Step Across the Border* features tracks from all phases of Frith's varied career, making it a good introduction to his music. — *Stephen Thomas Erlewine*

Front 242

Group, Industrial, Alternative Pop/Rock, Techno
When the Belgian synth-dance group began recording in 1982, their style followed the cold, clinical work of Kraftwerk and Cabaret Voltaire yet their music had none of the dark mystery or threat of those early electronic bands. As the decade progressed, they captured that mystery; by the end of the decade, Front 242 were on the cutting edge of the experimental industrial dance groups, combining political sound bites with their dance samples and beats. Their 1988 club hit, "Headhunter," cemented their reputation and provided a good example of their aggressive style. After their 1988 album, *Front by Front*, the group left the seminal industrial record label Wax Trax for a major label, Epic. Front 242's first major label release, 1991's *Tyranny for You*, showed no concessions and was another strong statement. However, their subsequent albums in the '90s showed that the group was beginning to slip from the cutting edge, although each album had some highlights. — *Stephen Thomas Erlewine*

Geography / 1982 / Epic ✦✦✦

○ **Official Version (1986-1987)** / 1987 / Epic ✦✦✦✦
With its dense, claustrophobic mix of samples and relentless, hard beats, *Official Version* was the first consistently impressive Front 242 record. — *Stephen Thomas Erlewine*

No Comment / 1987 / Epic ✦✦

Back Catalogue / 1987 / Epic ✦✦✦
A collection of early 12-inch singles, *Back Catalogue* is the best way to get acquainted with Front 242's early days. — *Stephen Thomas Erlewine*

● **Front by Front** / 1988 / Epic ✦✦✦✦
While it reiterates the music of *Official Version*, *Front by Front* features a stronger political message, as well as their signature single, "Headhunter." — *Stephen Thomas Erlewine*

○ **Tyranny (for You)** / 1991 / Epic ✦✦✦✦
More aggressive and militant than its predecessors, *Tyranny (for You)* is an impressionistic, angry album that captured the underlying chaos of the early '90s with its dark, brutal rhythm tracks alone. — *Stephen Thomas Erlewine*

05:22:09:12 Off / 1993 / Epic ✦✦

06:21:03:11 up Evil / May 25, 1993 / Epic ✦✦✦
Although it isn't a bad album by any means, Front 242 seems at a loss for ideas on *06:21:03:11 Up Evil*, which lacks the sonic power and conceptual force of their three previous albums. — *Stephen Thomas Erlewine*

Fu-Schnickens

Group, Rap
This Brooklyn rap trio has been among the better humor-oriented hip-hop groups. They devised their name by combining the abbreviations FU (For Unity) with Schnicken, a term they invented designed to convey coalition. Their 1992 debut *F.U.—Don't Take It Personal* on Jive didn't yield any big hits. But the group hit paydirt when they collaborated with NBA star Shaquille O'Neal on the single "What's Up Doc." It got them widespread visibility and exposure, making their follow-up album eagerly anticipated. — *Ron Wynn*

○ **F.U.: Don't Take It Personal** / Feb. 25, 1992 / Jive ✦✦✦✦
What makes the Fu-Schnickens' debut album special isn't their beats, but their impressive verbal facility. Not only are they blindingly fast, but their lyrics are clever and inventive; the excitement of their rhyming makes the rote backing tracks invigorating. — *Stephen Thomas Erlewine*

What's up Doc / Jun. 8, 1993 / Jive

Fugazi

Group, Alternative Pop/Rock, Hardcore
Fugazi is as famous for its strident anti-corporate stance as they are for their music. Fugazi's leader, singer/guitarist Ian MacKaye, refuses to charge over five dollars for a concert and keeps the prices of their recordings low by releasing the band's recordings through his own record label, Dischord. As such, their vehement political stance can overshadow their musical accomplishments; they are one of the few bands that prove it's possible for hardcore punk to expand beyond its rigid structures. With the seminal D.C. hardcore band Minor Threat, MacKaye defined straight-edge hardcore; with Fugazi, he breaks and rewrites the very rules he established.

Since their 1988 debut EP, Fugazi has gained a substantial fan base without the help of mainstream press or MTV airplay; the band would rather talk to fanzines than to mainstream press, so they never talk to *Rolling Stone*. By the time of their 1993 album, they charted on *Billboard's* Top 200 without any commercial push. Through their anti-rock star stance, Fugazi have become rock stars. —*Stephen Thomas Erlewine*

Fugazi / 1988 / Dischord ✦✦✦

Margin Walker / 1989 / Dischord ✦✦✦

● **13 Songs** / 1990 / Dischord ✦✦✦✦
A CD combination of their first two EP's, *Fugazi* and *Margin Walker.* —*Meredith Erlewine*

Repeater + 3 Songs / 1990 / Dischord ✦✦✦
Not quite as polished as "13 Songs," but a great album. —*Meredith Erlewine*

Steady Diet of Nothing / 1991 / Dischord ✦✦

○ **In on the Kill Taker** / 1993 / Dischord ✦✦✦✦

Red Medicine / Jun. 1995 / Dischord ✦✦✦
On Fugazi's fifth LP, the band continue to move farther from their hardcore past. It's not that they've mellowed out; the aggression and fury at everything commercial and political is still there, but, as on 1993's *In on the Kill Taker*, Fugazi intersperse their uptempo rants with guitar-effects experimentation and slower tracks. The song-forms are more complex than on previous releases; while the album is not immediately captivating, repeated listenings reveal the music's depth and maturity—a more fulfilling form of appreciation, anyway. —*John Bush*

The Fugs
Group, Rock & Roll, Folk-Rock
Arguably the first "underground" rock group of all time, the Fugs formed at the Peace Eye bookstore in New York's East Village in late 1964. The nucleus of the band throughout its many personnel changes was Peace Eye owner Ed Sanders, and fellow poet Tuli Kupferberg. Sanders and Kupferberg had strong ties to the beat literary scene, but charged, in the manner of their friend Allen Ginsberg, full steam ahead into the maelstrom of '60s political involvement and psychedelia. Surrounded by an assortment of motley refugees from the New York folk and jugband scene (including Steve Weber and Peter Stampfel of the Holy Modal Rounders), some of whom could barely play their instruments, the group nonetheless were determined to play rock & roll their way—which meant rife with political and social satire, as well as explicit profanity and sexual references, that were downright unheard of in 1965. Starting on the legendary avant-garde ESP label, the Fugs' debut was full of equal amounts of chaos and charm, but their songwriting and instrumental chops improved surprisingly quickly, resulting in a great second album that was undoubtedly the most shocking and satirical recording ever to grace the Top 100 when it was released. After cutting an unreleased album for Atlantic, they moved on to Frank Sinatra's Reprise label, unleashing a few more albums of equally satirical material that was more instrumentally polished, but equally scathing lyrically. Breaking up around 1970, Sanders and Kupferberg have continued to write prose and poetry, and sometimes to write and perform music, both on their own and as part of Fugs reunions. By breaking lyrical taboos of popular music, they helped pave the way for the even more innovative outrage of the Mothers of Invention, the Velvet Underground, and others. —*Richie Unterberger*

The Fugs First Album / 1965 / Fantasy ✦✦✦
Engagingly sloppy, even raw performances on their debut, which draws on leftist politics, the poetry of William Blake, and the joys of sex. Some of this is wearily cacophonous, but "Slum Goddess," "Supergirl," "I Couldn't Get High," and "Nothing" are among their funniest songs. The CD reissue adds 11 bonus tracks: seven studio cuts from the same era (the sarcastic "CIA Man" is a highlight), three live songs from 1965, and an eight-minute spoken word piece. —*Richie Unterberger*

○ **Virgin Fugs** / 1966 / ESP ✦✦✦✦

● **The Fugs** / 1966 / ESP ✦✦✦✦
At the time of its release, the Fugs' second (self-titled) album contained the most outrageous lyrics ever heard on a Top 100 rock & roll LP. The group, with roots in New York's underground folk and poetry scenes, flung themselves wholeheartedly into all-out rock & roll on this 1966 record, which addresses concerns like free love, the madness of war, and government repression. The CD reissue of this classic includes two previously unreleased live performances and three tracks from the unreleased album they recorded for Atlantic in 1967. —*Richie Unterberger*

Tenderness Junction / 1967 / Reprise ✦✦✦
The band opted for a considerably more conventional rock sound more in keeping with the era's psychedelic tenor on their first major-label release. The material isn't as strong and the satirical humor not as biting as their earlier efforts, though it's characteristically witty stuff. Highlights include "Turn On/Tune In/Drop Out" and "War Song"; "Aphrodite Mass" is an ambitious if not terribly memorable five-part suite. —*Richie Unterberger*

It Crawled into My Hand, Honest / 1968 / Reprise ✦✦✦
It features the classic "Wide, Wide River." —*David Szatmary*

Belle of Avenue A / 1969 / Reprise ✦✦

No More Slavery / 1986 / New Rose ✦✦

Star Peace / 1987 / New Rose ✦✦

Full Force
Group, Rap
A Brooklyn production and songwriting sextet, Full Force became quite prominent in the mid and late '80s. Brian and Paul Anthony George teamed with their cousins Gerry Charles, Junior Clark, and Curt Bedeau. At one point they were producing sessions for Lisa Lisa, UTFO, and Roxanne Shante, and even worked with James Brown. They recorded a number of LPs for Columbia as performers, and scored five Top Ten R&B hits recording with Lisa Lisa and Cult Jam, the biggest being "All Cried Out" in 1986. It peaked at number three R&B and number eight pop. Their most recent effort was *Don't Sleep* in 1992, which paired them with longtime James Brown Revue contributor Bobby Byrd. —*Ron Wynn*

Full Force / 1985 / Columbia ✦✦✦
Although they were among the hottest production and performance combos on the scene in the mid- and late '80s, Full Force was never able to translate that magic to their own albums. This 1986 debut included the mildly entertaining "Alice, I Want You Just for Me!," but was mostly either uneventful love tunes, haphazard novelty pieces or unfocused and formulaic quasi-raps. —*Ron Wynn*

● **Get Busy 1 Time** / 1986 / Columbia ✦✦✦✦
The second Full Force release was a little better than the first, but still far from the levels they were scoring with Lisa Lisa & Cult Jam. Once more, they were unable to get any breakout or chart singles, and while songs like "Body Heavenly" and "Old Flames Never Die" may have contained potentially catchy lyrics, they lacked defined vocals, attractive arrangements or interesting production. —*Ron Wynn*

Full Force Get Ready 1 Time / 1986 / Columbia ✦✦✦

○ **Guess Who's Comin' to the Crib?** / 1987 / Columbia ✦✦✦✦
Full Force's third album did only marginally better than the first two; it peaked a little higher on the low end of the pop albums chart. They tried everything in their creative arsenal, from the bittersweet sentiments of "Love Is for Suckers (Like Me And You)" to the naughty double-entendre notions expressed on "Low Blow Brenda" and even a traditional soul number, "Take Care of Homework." Nothing clicked, and it probably didn't help matters that the album included the justifiable but shrill diatribe "Black Radio." —*Ron Wynn*

Smoove / 1989 / Columbia ✦✦✦

Don't Sleep! / Aug. 31, 1992 / Capitol ✦✦
Full Force tried a comeback in 1992, teaming with longtime James Brown confidant and vocal partner Bobby Byrd on *Don't Sleep*. All it did was show that a lot of folks evidently thought that Full Force was in retirement, as the album failed to get even a cursory glance from urban contemporary radio, and hip-hop/rap audiences weren't interested in 1980s legends. This was their first release for Capitol; there hasn't been another thus far. —*Ron Wynn*

Bobby Fuller Four
Group, Rock & Roll
With his blatant reverence for Buddy Holly, fellow Texan Bobby Fuller was a bit of an anomaly in the mid-'60s. With his Stratocaster guitar and brash, full sound, at his best Fuller sounded like Holly might have had he survived into the '60s. Cracking the Top 30 in 1966 with a cover of Holly's "Love's Made a Fool of You," and then the Top Ten with "I Fought the Law" (written by one-time Cricket Sonny Curtis), Fuller had just become a star when he died in mysterious circumstances in a parked car in Hollywood (the po-

lice thought it was a suicide, just about everyone who knew him disagreed). Fuller's relatively short period of national stardom actually crowned a good half-dozen years of recording, during which he released many outstanding tracks. After a few local singles in his hometown of El Paso in the early '60s, he moved to California with his combo in 1964, and briefly had aspirations of playing surf music before hooking up with producer Bob Keene. In the short time he recorded for Mustang in 1965 and 1966, he waxed quite a few fine tracks (most self-penned) besides his hits, including "Let Her Dance," "Another Sad and Lonely Night," "My True Love," "Never to be Forgotten," "Fool of Love," and "The Magic Touch." Rocking, tuneful and infectiously joyous, they showed Fuller to be a worthy inheritor of early rock & roll and rockabilly traditions without sounding self-consciously revivalist. While it's hard to imagine Fuller maintaining his success in the era of psychedelia, he no doubt would have gone on to produce interesting work. A talented and prolific songwriter and a studio wiz who drew from Eddie Cochran and (though only slightly) the full guitar sound of the British Invasion as well as Buddy Holly, he recorded a great deal of unreleased studio and live material that was issued in the 1980s, when the depth of his loss began to be appreciated. — *Richie Unterberger*

● **The Best of Bobby Fuller Four** / 1981 / Rhino ✦✦✦✦
A great 18-track compilation of his best work that is truly all killer, no filler. While there's some other good Fuller to be found, this is definitely the prime stuff from his mid-'60s recordings for Mustang: "I Fought the Law," "Let Her Dance," "The Magic Touch," "Love's Made a Fool Of You," "Fool of Love," "My True Love," and other equally fine if lesser-known sides. — *Richie Unterberger*

Bobby Fuller Tapes, Vol. 1 / 1983 / Rhino ✦✦✦
Not released until nearly 20 years after his death, this rare material—recorded in El Paso between 1960 and 1964—is less polished and even more overtly Buddy Holly-influenced than his mid-'60s tracks. But they're nearly as affecting and tuneful, and feature many strong Fuller originals. — *Richie Unterberger*

Live Again / 1984 / Eva ✦✦✦
According to legend, the Bobby Fuller Four were one hell of a live band. These previously unreleased live recordings from 1964 are indeed accomplished, but keep in mind that in those days, unestablished acts stuck mostly to well-known cover versions, and Fuller was no exception. Most of this set was composed of R&B/rock chestnuts along the lines of "Whole Lotta Shakin' Goin' On," "Night Train," "Peggy Sue," and "Little Bitty Pretty One"; there's a slight nod to the raging British Invasion with "From Me to You" and "House of the Rising Sun." Good though not imperfect fidelity on these cleanly executed but hardly revelatory interpretations. Fuller showed the true scope of his talents on his studio recordings of 1965 and 1966, and though this album demonstrates the band were first-class live players, it shows nothing of their originality. As such, it is only recommended to serious fans. — *Richie Unterberger*

Bobby Fuller Tapes, Vol. 2 / 1984 / Voxx ✦✦✦
The second major excursion into the vaults for previously unreleased Fuller material isn't nearly as interesting as Volume One, primarily because this collection of rare singles, alternate versions, live recordings, and outtakes from 1960-64 is composed mostly of cover versions. Still, Fuller's brash vocals and guitars are worth hearing, though they don't redefine Little Richard, Jerry Lee Lewis, and Buddy Holly's originals. The best of the lot are the versions of "Pretty Girls Everywhere," "Baby I Don't Care," and the sizzling five-minute instrumental version of "Miserlou." Also includes the original 1964 version of "I Fought The Law," the first-class Fuller rockabilly original "Bodine," and a haunting instrumental version of "My True Love." "Shakedown" is as raw and dirty as he ever got, but unfortunately, the version on this LP was mastered from a scratchy rare single (though the fidelity on the rest of the album is excellent). — *Richie Unterberger*

Bobby Fuller Instrumental Album / 1985 / Rockhouse ✦✦✦
In between his rockabilly roots in El Paso and hitting it big as a modern-day reincarnation of Buddy Holly in the mid-'60s, Bobby Fuller briefly entertained aspirations of playing surf music. Updated Holly and Cochranisms were really his true forte, so this album—mostly composed of surf and R&B instrumentals from 1964—doesn't measure up to his best work in the least. That's not to say it's bad. If nothing else, it's further evidence of how disciplined and versatile his band was. Much of the material was previously unreleased before this compilation, though collectors

should know that although the liner notes claim that the 1961 single by the Venturas on this LP features guitarist Jim Reese, Reese himself denies any knowledge of the group. — *Richie Unterberger*

I Fought the Law / The KRLA King of The Wheels / Nov. 1990 / Ace ✦✦✦
The first two albums by the legendary '60s rockers, with bonus tracks. For collectors only. (Import) — *Jeff Tamarkin*

Live at Pj's Plus! / Jul. 1991 / Ace ✦✦✦
Killer live show plus assorted rarities, by the ultimate '60s garage band. — *Jeff Tamarkin*

Fun Boy Three

Group, New Wave
U.K. trio of Terry Hall, Neville Staples, and Lynval Golding, a subset of the Specials, formed when that group split in 1981. Fun Boy Three had six U.K. Top 20 singles before they split in 1983. — *William Ruhlmann*

The Fun Boy Three / 1982 / Chrysalis ✦✦✦
Hall sings lead and Staples and Golding chant behind him on the group's beat-heavy ballads on such hits as "It Ain't What You Do ...," on which they are joined by Bananarama. — *William Ruhlmann*

Waiting / 1983 / Chrysalis ✦✦
David Byrne-produced second album contains the Boys' own version of their song "Our Lips Are Sealed," a hit for the Go-Go's. — *William Ruhlmann*

● **The Best of the Fun Boy Three** / 1984 / Chrysalis ✦✦✦✦
This collects all of the essential moments of the short-lived band. Two non-LP tracks are an added bonus: a cover of Gershwin's "Summertime" and their collaboration with Bananarama, "Really Saying Something." — *Chris Woodstra*

Annette Funicello

b. Oct. 22, 1942, Utica, NY
Teen Idol
The most popular of the Mouseketeers on the '50s TV program *The Mickey Mouse Club*, Annette Funicello was herded into the studio at the age of 16 to become the first female teen idol rock & roll star. Billed simply as "Annette" on most of her records, she hit the Top 20 five times in 1959 and 1960, and continued to record constantly in the early '60s as she moved into film stardom in a variety of California beach culture vehicles. While her records are lightweight trashy fun up to a certain point, they are surely no more than that. With her thin voice doubletracked and reverbed to achieve the necessary volume, the material was largely saccharine pop clap-trap flavored with the most banal elements of rock & roll. Kitschy overtones of Italian and Hawaiian popular music also figured strongly, and she even took stabs at surf and ska. She largely retired from recording in the mid-'60s to raise her family. — *Richie Unterberger*

● **Annette: A Musical Reunion With America's Girl Next Door** / 1993 / Disney ✦✦✦✦
This 2-CD, 47-song box set of material from her 1959-1965 heyday has everything you could possibly want to hear, including the hits "Tall Paul," "First Name Initial," "O Dio Mio," "Jo-Jo the Dog Faced Boy," and "Pineapple Princess." Curiosities include Paul Anka's "It's Really Love," which was eventually turned into the *Tonight Show* theme, and "The Monkey's Uncle," which features backup by the Beach Boys. — *Richie Unterberger*

Funkadelic

Group, Soul, Funk, Rock & Roll, Psychedelic
Funkadelic was the more politicized of George Clinton's psychofunk spinoffs. Where Parliament offered the butt-tugging ecstasy of "Tear the Roof off the Sucker" and "Flashlight," Funkadelic tackled racial conflict ("You and Your Folks, Me and My Folks"), government corruption ("America Eats Its Young"), and the power of the boogie ("One Nation Under a Groove"). They were never the singles act Parliament turned out to be, but Funkadelic tackled tougher issues and made them wiggle and wobble as surely as anything that ever bore Clinton's stamp. — *John Floyd*

Osmium / 1970 / Invictus ✦✦
An early Parliament release in which George Clinton and company are still perfecting their mix of straight soul and zany mythology. It's pretty tame compared to what would come in the future, but does reveal in bits and pieces the razor-sharp Clinton wit. —*Ron Wynn*

Funkadelic / 1970 / Westbound ✦✦✦
The music is serious but George Clinton is as tongue-in-cheek as ever. The album opens up with his voice, proposing "If you will suck my soul, I will lick your funky emotions," and proceeds in and out of that vein for forty minutes. This album is raw and pure funk, with often twangy guitars and deep, low yet prominent bass lines. It takes the quirky, basic groove of the Meters and renders it heavy and grungy, while maintaining the straightfaced humor that Clinton has made famous. —*Julian Katz*

Free Your Mind Your Ass Will Follow / 1970 / Westbound ✦✦✦
Not quite as promising as its title and classic cover would indicate, *Free Your Mind and Your Ass Will Follow* is full of faux religious rambling and spacey studio overdubs and effects, yet still manages to pull it off in the endearing Clinton style of blending soul, heavy metal, gospel, and bad sci-fi movies, coming up with gems such as "Friday Night, August the Fourteenth," and "Funky Dollar Bill." —*Julian Katz*

☆ **Maggot Brain** / 1971 / Westbound ✦✦✦✦✦
The best early Funkadelic record. There's some indulgent stuff here that may conjure some art-rock nightmares, but at its best—"You and Your Folks, Me and My Folks"—this is a brave and pioneering recording. —*John Floyd*

America Eats Its Young / 1972 / Westbound ✦✦✦
Some fantastic extended guitar jams and bitter, prophetic lyrics made this one of Funkadelic's most ambitious and remarkable albums. Few were ready in the early '70s for a black band that blended acid-rock riffs and angry rhetoric. It wasn't all political, however; there were also some silly, joyous tunes and the band's trademark biting satires on their rivals. —*Ron Wynn*

○ **Cosmic Slop** / 1973 / Westbound ✦✦✦✦
Another classic, with furious guitar riffs, inspired, bizarre lyrics, marvelous production, and loose, chaotic, brilliant arrangements. Funkadelic was the most musically ambitious, energized band in the Clinton empire, and every one of their Westbound albums was a triumph. —*Ron Wynn*

Standing on the Verge of Getting It on / 1974 / Westbound ✦✦✦

Greatest Hits / 1975 / Westbound ✦✦✦
This out-of-print (not on CD) collection of the early years rescues the best cuts from their spotty early records. An excellent work, it nevertheless excludes "You and Your Folks." —*John Floyd*

○ **Let's Take It to the Stage** / 1975 / Westbound ✦✦✦✦
The title track was one of their funniest funk jams, while the other songs run the gamut from blistering rock to zany R&B.George Clinton was in the midst of his greatest commercial/creative run, and this one ranks right alongside the other magical Funkadelic releases of the '70s. —*Ron Wynn*

○ **Hardcore Jollies** / 1976 / Warner Brothers ✦✦✦✦
Their major-label debut from 1976 lacks the manic drive of the early stuff, but tightens the grooves and adds some sharp melodies. —*John Floyd*

Tales of Kidd Funkadelic / 1976 / Westbound ✦✦✦
Some leftover jams, songs, and funk pieces from the Funkadelic era. George Clinton was in the midst of moving Funkadelic to another label, and the Westbound folk released a bunch of vault material to get another Funkadelic album on the market. There were still some fine cuts, but the random element prevented it from being a great album because it lacked the thematic organization and vision Clinton provided for the concept LPs. —*Ron Wynn*

○ **Best of the Early Years** / 1977 / Westbound ✦✦✦✦

★ **One Nation under a Groove** / 1978 / Warner Brothers ✦✦✦✦✦
The title cut is Clinton's supreme goodfoot manifesto, and for the first time in his career he pulls off a start-to-finish masterstroke. —*John Floyd*

○ **Uncle Jam Wants You** / 1979 / Warner Brothers ✦✦✦✦
It doesn't keep moving like its immediate predecessor, but this is where you'll find "Not Just Knee Deep," a wonderful piece of erotic esoterica. —*John Floyd*

○ **The Electric Spanking of War Babies** / 1981 / Warner Brothers ✦✦✦✦

Who's a Funkadelic / 1981 / Rhino ✦

Connections & Disconnections / 1981 / LAX ✦

★ **Music for Your Mother** / 1993 / Westbound ✦✦✦✦✦
This two-disc set collects all the great Funkadelic singles and B-sides and presents them in remastered glory. The list includes such gems as "Funky Dollar Bill," "Cosmic Slop," "Let's Take It to the Stage" and "I'll Bet You." Unfortunately, some of Funkadelic's finest efforts were album-length and/or suite pieces, so some brilliant material not issued on singles was omitted. But it's as comprehensive a collection as possible under the circumstances (lacking the later material owned by Priority), and Rob Bowman's notes are extensive and nicely done. —*Ron Wynn*

Billy Fury

b. Apr. 17, 1941, Liverpool, England, d. Jan. 28, 1983
Rock & Roll, British Invasion
England's best rock singer of the pre-Beatles era, Fury, born in Liverpool, was the most talented of England's Elvis clones and near-clones of the very early '60s; he also wrote some of his own songs. A strong singer with a very suggestive stage presence, Fury also had the benefit of a fine backing band, including rockabilly guitarist Joe Brown. His recordings from 1963 onward, backed by the Tornadoes (of "Telstar" fame), lack this power, but Fury still made the charts through the mid '60s, and, prior to his death in the mid '80s, retained the respect and admiration of the British establishment he helped to form. —*Bruce Eder*

● **Sound of Fury Plus 10** / 1988 / PolyGram ✦✦✦✦
The best rock album recorded in England before the rise of the Beatles (Andy White, the guest drummer on "Love Me Do," plays the skins on this too). A hard-rocking gem driven by Fury's powerful voice and Joe Brown's superb guitar. This reissue has ten bonus tracks. —*Bruce Eder*

The Future Sound of London

Group, Techno
Garry Cobain and Brian Dougans, i.e. Future Sound of London, first earned a U.S. release when their single, "Papua New Guinea," appeared on the *Cool World Sdtrk.* On *Lifeforms*, though, their first major release, the band has a more ambient feel. Eager to explore new possibilities, the duo released *ISDN*, a "live" album, actually recorded live in the studio and sent via computer to radio stations for broadcast. —*John Bush*

● **Accelerators** / 1991 / Jumpin' & Pumpin' ✦✦✦✦

Lifeforms / 1994 / Astralwerks ✦✦✦
Sprawled over two discs, the album explores a new direction in ambience which could be called eco-techno. Natural rhythms using water sounds and bird calls give the music an organic feel, light-years away from the "soulless" label with which techno has undeservedly been burdened. —*John Bush*

○ **ISDN** / 1995 / Astralwerks ✦✦✦✦
A "live" album, actually recorded live in the studio and sent via computer to radio stations for broadcast. Originally limited to only 10,000 copies, *ISDN* was later given a wide release due to demand for the album, which reportedly sold out in three days. The album documents another full-circle redirection for FSOL; the normal industrial-techno of their earlier days is back in place, but some tracks have what sounds like live drums, and "Far Out Son of Lung" has a jazzy feel with horns. *ISDN* makes for a diverse listening experience, even more so than *Lifeforms.* —*John Bush*

G

G. Love & Special Sauce

Group, Alternative Pop/Rock
Composed of guitarist/vocalist G. Love, percussionist Jeffrey Clemens, and string bassist Jimmy Jass Prescott, G. Love & Special Sauce are a Boston trio that melds blues and hip-hop together, creating a surreal, pseudo-intellectual sound that manages to adhere to its roots while being flip and irreverant. Released in 1994, their self-titled first album earned several positive reviews, as well as becoming a college radio favorite. — *Stephen Thomas Erlewine*

G. Love & Special Sauce / 1994 / Sony
Neither blues nor rap, but utilizing qualities of both, this debut from a trio of young Bostonians fits right in with much of indie-rock's take on rap. G. Love and co.'s drawled lyrics and relaxed instrumentation are even more laid-back than Beck's slacker nightmares. — *John Bush*

Warren G.

Rap
Warren G. is the younger brother of rapper Dr. Dre. Like his brother, Warren G. mines George Clinton's back catalogue for some funk, yet he reworks pop/rock groups like the Doobie Brothers into funky grooves. The rapper released his first album, *Regulate...G Funk Era*, in 1994; it was a multi-platinum success, thanks to the hit title track. — *Stephen Thomas Erlewine*

● **Regulate ... G Funk Era** / 1994 / Def Jam ✦✦✦✦
Dr. Dre's little brother Warren G proved that he was a talent in his own right with his debut record, *Regulate...G Funk Era*. With his music's slow, bass-heavy grooves and layers of synthesizers, Warren G does sound slightly similar to his older brother, but his album is more relaxed. But that doesn't mean he's soft. In fact, his casual mix of singing and speaking is often more evocative than Dre's standard thundering beats and whining keyboards. Plus, Warren G's sly, direct lyrics manage to convey the tragedy of the ghetto. — *Stephen Thomas Erlewine*

Peter Gabriel

b. May 13, 1950, England
Art-Rock/Progressive-Rock, Pop/Rock
Peter Gabriel was one of the founding members of Genesis when it was formed in 1965. Gabriel left Genesis in 1975 to pursue an idiosyncratic but highly successful solo career. He initially drew from the art-rock sounds of his time with Genesis but increasingly infused worldbeat and extremely dissonant rock, and eventually some R&B, into his sound.

Gabriel has always surrounded himself with first-class producers (Bob Ezrin, Robert Fripp, Daniel Lanois, Steve Lillywhite) who could sonically push the envelope into new frontiers. Thematically Gabriel's lyrics progressively abandoned the journey through the dark side of the psyche in favor of reaching out with awareness-elevating sentiment. That transition helped expand Gabriel's audience significantly in 1986 with the multi-platinum hit album *So*, which peaked at #2.

Gabriel followed *So* three years later with *Passion*, a collection of music used in the film *The Last Temptation of Christ*. It wasn't until 1992 that he delivered *Us*, the proper follow-up to *So*. Although it sold respectably and had a Top 40 hit, the "Sledgehammer" knock-off "Steam," it proved a relative commercial disappointment. — *Rick Clark*

○ **Peter Gabriel [1]** / 1977 / Atco ✦✦✦
His strong debut, produced by Bob Ezrin (Pink Floyd, Alice Cooper), features the hit "Solsbury Hill," which addressed Gabriel's breakup with Genesis. The sound reflects some of Genesis's art-rock sensibilities ("Moribund the Burgermeister"), while charting some more accessible styles (in Gabriel's eccentric fashion) like the fairly straightahead rock of "Modern Love." Other highlights include the portentous "Here Comes the Flood" and "Humdrum." — *Rick Clark*

Peter Gabriel [2] / 1978 / Atco ✦✦✦
King Crimson's Robert Fripp produced this followup. Overall, this effort is more uneven, but there are some real highlights in the form of "D.I.Y." and the aggressively dissonant rocker "On the Air." — *Rick Clark*

★ **Peter Gabriel [3]** / 1980 / Geffen ✦✦✦✦✦
On this, the third of three self-titled efforts, Gabriel teams up with producer Steve Lillywhite (XTC, Psychedelic Furs, U2) and produces a masterpiece. From the chilling opener, "Intruder," to "Biko," an impassioned tribute to murdered South African poet and activist Steven Biko, Lillywhite's experimental (and very left-of-center) approach to sound is a perfect match for Gabriel's convoluted tales from the dark side of human nature. Arguably, it is Gabriel's best work thus far. — *Rick Clark*

○ **Security** / 1982 / Geffen ✦✦✦✦
Produced by David Lord and Gabriel, this is really a transitional album, borrowing from the heavily treated approach to sound found on the Lillywhite work while embracing more worldbeat rhythms. The music is less dissonant. Thematically, Gabriel picks up the human-rights thread he started with "Biko" on "Wallflower." "Kiss of Life" suggests a hopefulness emerging in his work. It includes the hit "Shock the Monkey." — *Rick Clark*

Plays Live / 1983 / Geffen ✦✦✦
Gabriel has always been an excellent performer. This live set is excellent proof, in spite of some slight post-gig doctoring. Nevertheless, most of these songs work best in the arid confines of the studio atmosphere. — *Rick Clark*

Music from the Film "Birdy" / 1985 / Geffen ✦✦✦
This instrumental work was Gabriel's first major soundtrack undertaking. Fans of Gabriel's texturous arrangements and melodies (some here are drawn from earlier material) should check out this fine work. — *Rick Clark*

○ **So** / 1986 / Geffen ✦✦✦✦
After a four-year layoff from his last studio album (*Security*), Gabriel returned with his most upbeat record, infusing funk, worldbeat, and gospel. The more accessible production, by Daniel Lanois (U2) and Gabriel, helped make this album a worldwide commercial success. It includes the hits "In Your Eyes," "Sledgehammer," "Big Time." — *Rick Clark*

○ **Passion** / 1989 / Geffen ✦✦✦✦
For the soundtrack for Martin Scorsese's film *The Last Temptation of Christ*, Gabriel drew inspiration from field recordings of musicians in the Middle East, fusing those recordings with his own atmospheric sound tapestries for a powerful collection of music. — *Rick Clark*

Shaking the Tree: Sixteen Golden Greats / 1990 / Geffen ✦✦✦
This is an odd best-of collection. True, it includes his hits, but Gabriel isn't merely a singles artist. As a result, there are many important album tracks that are glaring omissions from a more

well-rounded picture of Gabriel's artistry. The title, no doubt, is an indicator of the tossed-off nature of this set. —*Rick Clark*

Us / 1992 / Geffen ♦♦♦
Us marks Peter Gabriel's first (non-soundtrack) studio effort since 1986's *So* and, more importantly, his most introspective and self-analytical work since leaving Genesis in 1975. Gabriel has done much to promote international music in recent years through his Real World record label, and he calls in a fistful of I.O.U.'s for *Us*. The most distinctive imports are exotic percussion sounds which percolate subtly throughout the recording. Intensely personal portrayals of love, longing, loss, and the dark emotions they can generate permeate atmospheric pieces such as "Blood of Eden," "Only Us," "Washing in the Water," and "Secret World." Gabriel makes group therapy a fascinating place to spend an hour and, thankfully, never loses sight of those rays of hope that pierce through from the other side. —*Roch Parisien*

Revisited / 1992 / Atlantic ♦♦♦
A good but useless compilation of Peter Gabriel's first two solo albums. *Revisited* contains some wonderful music, but fans would be better served by the individual albums, and casual fans will prefer *Shaking the Tree*, which has all of his big hits, including material featured here. —*Stephen Thomas Erlewine*

Secret World Live / 1994 / Geffen ♦♦
Peter Gabriel's second double-disc live album doesn't have the energy of *Plays Live*, which isn't surprising; his newer material is more subtle and doesn't easily lend itself to live performances. That's part of the reason why the *Secret World* tour was filled with cutting-edge visuals and stage effects. Unfortunately, it's very hard to record a light show, and the result is a thoroughly bland album. —*Stephen Thomas Erlewine*

Galactic Cowboys

Group, Hard Rock
Houston's Galactic Cowboys blend strong Beatlesque four-part harmonies with extended grunge-meets-art-rock song constructions. The band, along with producer Sam Taylor, imbues the sound and arrangements with a fine blend of playful humor and serious sentiment. —*Rick Clark*

● **Galactic Cowboys** / 1991 / Geffen ♦♦♦♦
This strong debut manages to incorporate four-part *Abbey Road*-style Beatles harmonies with extended multisectional Metallica-like heavy-metal ensemble work. There are many standout tracks on this collection, including "I'm Not Amused," "My School," "Why Can't You Believe in Me?," "Sea of Tranquillity," and the affecting crunch-rock ballad of "Someone for Everyone." —*Rick Clark*

Space in Your Face / Jun. 8, 1993 / Geffen ♦♦♦

Galaxie 500

Group, Alternative Pop/Rock
While many bands picked up on the Velvet Underground's more rocking traits, this Boston-based trio reveled in their slower doings. Sparse and not upbeat, they are not dour either. Galaxie 500 released three albums between 1987 and 1990 before lead singer/guitarist Dean Wareham left the band, effectively causing their breakup; Wareham formed Luna soon afterward. Bassist Naomi Yang and drummer Damon Krukowski have worked as Pierre Etoile and Damon & Naomi, and are currently in Magic Hour. —*Bruce Eder*

● **Today** / 1987 / Rough Trade ♦♦♦♦
Working the slow side of the Velvet Underground, it's melodic and intense. —*Robert Gordon*

Blue Thunder [EP] / 1989 / ♦♦♦

On Fire / 1989 / Rough Trade ♦♦♦

○ **This Is Our Music** / 1990 / Rough Trade ♦♦♦♦
With more of the same as on *Today*, they knew their trick and stuck to it. —*Robert Gordon*

Eric Gales Band

Group, Psychedelic
When guitar-slinger Eric Gales arrived on the scene in 1991 with his self-titled debut album, he was only 16, the product of a family of professional musicians. It's older brother (and bassist) Eugene Gales who provided much of the history and musical discipline behind Eric's Hendrix-influenced excursions. —*Rick Clark*

● **The Eric Gales Band** / 1991 / Elektra ♦♦♦♦
This is a heavily Hendrix-influenced mainstream AOR debut. In spite of some weak material, there are a few highlights with "Resurrection," the hit "Sign of the Storm," and the instrumental "High Anxiety." —*Rick Clark*

Picture of a Thousand Faces / 1993 / Elektra ♦♦♦
Like many a young hot-shot guitarist, Gales tends to overplay—it's all very fine wanting to be Hendrix, but maturity teaches that the notes you don't play can be equally important. Still, Gales' power trio has the talent and the chops to pull off the melodic Fender-on-hyperdrive approach, and it doesn't hurt that solid songs and vocal harmonies underpin the wailing.
Guitar solo fanatics will especially want to check out the powerhouse closing to "God only Knows," and the 8-minute, blues-injected cover of The Beatles' "I Want You (She's So Heavy)." —*Roch Parisien*

Rory Gallagher

b. Mar. 2, 1949, Ballyshannon, Ireland, **d.** Jun. 14, 1995
Blues Rock
Irish blues-rock guitarist and singer Rory Gallagher is surely one of the most exciting of the British blues acts to be seen live, and his recorded output over the years guarantees him a prominent place among the British blues stars.
Gallagher's band has undergone a number of personnel changes over the years, but his playing and singing haven't slipped one iota since his glory days, when he played to stadium-sized crowds in Europe in the late '60s and early '70s.
All of Gallagher's earlier releases have been reissued on American-based I.R.S., and his product is much more accessible than it was in the past. —*Richard Skelly*

Deuce / 1971 / Atlantic ♦♦♦

Rory Gallagher / 1971 / Atlantic ♦♦♦

Live in Europe/Stage Struck / 1972 / IRS ♦♦♦
Live recordings of many of his best tunes. —*Michael G. Nastos*

Tattoo / 1973 / Castle ♦♦♦
Studio recording done with a quartet. Every cut is solid. —*Michael G. Nastos*

○ **Irish Tour '74** / 1974 / IRS ♦♦♦♦
Double-album set recorded live at various venues in Ireland. Loaded with Gallagher's best material. A great album. —*Michael G. Nastos*

○ **Calling Card** / 1976 / IRS ♦♦♦♦
His best studio album. The Irish blues-rock guitarist plays like there's no tomorrow, even on mid-tempo tracks. He's an unsung hero on the guitar. —*Michael G. Nastos*

● **Edged in Blue** / 1992 / Edsel ♦♦♦♦

Gallon Drunk

Group, Alternative Pop/Rock
Gallon Drunk's dark, boozy rock & roll became a cult favorite in the U.K. in the early '90s. The band—James Johnston (vocals, guitar, organ), Mike Delanian (bass), Max Decharne (drums), and Joe Byfield (maracas), formed in 1990, releasing singles on their privately-owned Massive record label. Their early singles received favorable reviews and the band signed with Clawfist records in 1992. Gallon Drunk released their first major label record, *From the Heart of Town*, in 1993. —*Stephen Thomas Erlewine*

● **Tonite . . . The Singles Bar** / 1992 / Rykodisc ♦♦♦♦

You, the Night . . . & The Music / 1992 / Rykodisc ♦♦♦

From the Heart of Town / 1993 / Warner Brothers ♦♦♦

Game Theory

Group, Alternative Pop/Rock, Power Pop/Anglo-Pop
Led by Scott Miller, an Alex Chilton-influenced singer/songwriter, Game Theory produces smart alternative Anglo-power-pop, full of engaging quirky melodies and fairly obscure lyrics.
On the down side, Miller's voice can get a little whiney, and his earnest approximations to pitch (reminiscent of the Scruff's Steve Burns) may be an acquired taste for some. However, their Mitch Easter-produced albums, *Big Shot Chronicles, Real Nighttime*, and *Lolita Nation* are worth seeking out.
Big Star or dB's fans should love this band. Then again, they probably know about Game Theory already. —*Rick Clark*

Real Nighttime / 1985 / Alias ✦✦✦
This is the band's first effort with Mitch Easter (R.E.M., Let's Active) producing. Miller's Alex Chilton fixation comes to the fore here, and it generally works nicely. "24" was a breezy alternative college hit. Other highlights include "Curse of the Frontierland," with its Big Star-influenced guitar figure and the delicately reflective "If and When It All Falls Apart." —*Rick Clark*

○ **Big Shot Chronicles** / 1986 / Alias ✦✦✦✦
The band's sound and Miller's songwriting are more aggressive here, delivering an appealingly punchy power-pop sound. It's a fine album with many tracks to recommend; "I've Tried Subtlety" is a strong, over-amped T-Rex rocker, while "Like a Girl Jesus" shines with Easter's mildly psychedelic production touches. "Erica's World" is a wonderfully quirky rocker, and "Regenisraen" showcases the band's harmonic capabilities. —*Rick Clark*

○ **Lolita Nation** / 1987 / Enigma ✦✦✦✦
Many fans of the band claim that this is a creative peak for Game Theory. *Lolita Nation* is loaded with odd juxtapositions of experimental sounds and spoken passages. The material, while dazzling in places, is rather inconsistent. "The Real Sheila" and "We Love You, Carol and Alison" are highlights, and both of them are found on *Tinker.* —*Rick Clark*

Two Steps from the Middle Ages / 1988 / Enigma ✦✦
Miller's melodies and the band's overall execution sound largely devoid of any real sparks. —*Rick Clark*

● **Tinker to Evers To Chance (Selected Highlights 1982-1989)** / 1990 / Enigma ✦✦✦✦
For the uninitiated, this collection of highlights from 1982 to 1989 is the best place to start, containing a healthy selection from their later Mitch Easter-produced albums. —*Rick Clark*

Distortion of Glory / 1994 / Alias ✦✦
Distortion of Glory collects the band's early (and long out-of-print) EPs. An interesting look at their formative years but only fans need to bother. —*Chris Woodstra*

Gang of Four

Group, Alternative Pop/Rock, New Wave
Formed in 1977 by Leeds University students Jon King (vocals), Andy Gill (guitar), Dave Allen (bass) and Hugo Burnham (drums), Gang of Four (along with The Fall, Mekons and Liliput) produced some of the most exhilarating and lasting music of the early English post-punk era of 1978-1983. Fueled by the fury of punk rock and radical political theory, Gang of Four successfully welded the two in an inspired display of polemics and music that addressed the vagaries of life in the modern world (including love and romance) as matters of political inquiry. Despite the fact that this sounds rife with the potential for being long on rhetoric and short on groove, such was not the case. What made Gang of Four's polemical clang'n'roll so compelling was that it worked as harsh, bracing, and ultimately liberating rock & roll. With Allen and Burnham combining as a formidable and frequently very funky rhythm section, Gill didn't play guitar as much as emit thick wads of semi-tuneful distortion, while King "sang" in a dry, declamatory fashion similar to that of the Fall's Mark E. Smith. The rhythms were stripped down and jagged; at times Gill would dispense with guitar solos entirely and "play" non-solos, which were (surprise!) silence. Song titles sounded like the titles of radical political essays: "At Home He's a Tourist," "Damaged Goods," "It's Her Factory," "Love Like Anthrax," "To Hell with Poverty," all of it openly challenging the audience's preconceived notions about rock music, performance, the cult of celebrity and the nature of politics. And in doing so, GOF conveyed rage, confusion and loss of identity as well as any band of its time.

After three consecutive sensational albums, as well as a handful of EPs and singles, Allen left in 1982 to form the more danceable and less overtly political Shriekback, while Gill, King and Burnham recorded the misguided "radical soul/R&B" record *Hard* with veteran American producers Ron and Howard Albert (who'd previously worked with Stephen Stills' Manassas and Firefall). A near total disaster, *Hard* signalled that the end was nigh. Gill and King, who by this point had their slay-so on the band's musical and political direction, sacked Burnham, and the now Gang of Two released a so-so live album (*At the Palace*) and called it quits in 1984. But legends die hard, and Gang of Four experienced a mini-renaissance in the early '90s with the release of two excellent collections (*A Brief History of the Twentieth Century* and *The Peel Sessions Album*). King and Gill put together a new Gang of Four

and released the tepid but not disgraceful *Mall* in 1991. Despite the clumsy and haphazard finish, Gang of Four remains, to the ears of those opened wide by punk rock, an extremely important band. —*John Dougan*

Damaged Goods / 1978 / Fast Product ✦✦✦

★ **Entertainment!** / 1979 / Infinite Zero ✦✦✦✦✦
With songs like "Love Like Anthrax" and "Damaged Goods," you soon realize that the title of this release is heavy on sarcasm. Still, a decade and a half after its debut, *Entertainment!* still sounds direct, exciting and uncompromising. And, in spite of GOF's anti-pop tendencies, songs like "I Found That Essence Rare" explode into a singalong chorus that is delightfully shocking. True to their collectivist spirit, Gill, King, Burnham and Allen are a forceful musical unit, and the strength in this unity makes for a great fusion of punk, pop and politics. Easily one of the best records of the post-punk era. Issued on CD by Infinite Zero in 1995. —*John Dougan*

Gang of Four / 1980 / Warner Brothers ✦✦✦

○ **Solid Gold** / 1981 / Warner Brothers ✦✦✦✦
Another tongue-in-cheek title, another great record. A little more abstract and antipop than *Entertainment!, Solid Gold* is, arguably, the most abrasive record GOF ever made. Burnham and Allen play dance-defiant, choppy grooves, while King and Gill explore more contentious political terrain. Some of *Solid Gold's* best songs are the most challenging and confrontational ("Why Theory?" and "Paralysed"). Clearly hitting its stride as a band, by this time GOF was a force to reckoned with, and without a doubt post-punk's best band. —*John Dougan*

Another Day, Another Dollar / 1982 / Warner Brothers ✦✦✦

○ **Songs of the Free** / 1982 / Warner Brothers ✦✦✦✦
Recorded under the influence of Chic records and a burgeoning post-punk dance culture, *Songs of the Free* is the most accessible of GOF's first three records, but in no way indicates a compromise of principals or an egregious attempt to sell out. The more-polished arrangements, backup vocalists and slight studio sweetening does little to mask the sarcasm and ironic intent of songs like "I Love a Man In a Uniform" (a dance club "hit" in the early '80s) or the bitter "We Live as We Dream, Alone." A record that appeals to the aficionado as well as the benighted, *Songs of the Free* indicated that the GOF could simultaneously embrace and attack pop music without sounding disingenuous. Music for the mind and body. —*John Dougan*

Hard / 1983 / Warner Brothers ✦✦✦

At the Palace / 1984 / Mercury ✦✦

Peel Sessions / 1990 / Strange Fruit-Dutch East India ✦✦✦
One of the best *Peel Sessions* releases available, these 11 tracks were recorded for John Peel's BBC radio show in 1979 and 1981. Thrilling from start to finish, this features the Gang raw and live. —*John Dougan*

● **Brief History of the Twentieth Century** / 1990 / Warner Brothers ✦✦✦✦
A great starting point. This 20-track anthology covers all of GOF's best album material (even the one good song from the execrable *Hard*) and includes a wonderful liner essay by longtime GOF fan and fellow theorist Greil Marcus. Although *Entertainment!* is perhaps the most striking Gang release available, this compilation, due to its length, breadth and quality, is the best place to become acquainted with this formidable band. —*John Dougan*

Mall / 1991 / Polydor ✦✦

Gang Starr

Group, Rap
These Brooklyn rappers are near the top among hip-hop artists influenced by and interested in jazz. In 1989, longtime jazz and black-pop publicist Elliot Horne placed a poem he wrote with them, and the group used it as the foundation for the song "Jazz Music" on their debut *No More Mr. Nice Guy.* That track was later included on the soundtrack for Spike Lee's *Mo Better Blues.* The group has also used saxophonist and former *Tonight Show* bandleader Branford Marsalis and included acoustic as well as electric instruments on their follow-up release *Step in the Arena.* They've also discussed the jazz/rap connection in such magazines as *The Source* and *The Wire.* They did make a big gaffe on one cut though, crediting Dizzy Gillespie with playing the saxophone rather than the trumpet.

Both Gang Starr and their main man Guru have been in the

limelight in 1993 and 1994. Guru teamed with old and new jazz types Donald Byrd, Roy Ayers, and Ronnie Foster, as well as vocalist N'Dea Davenport and other guest stars for the session *Jazzmatazz*. He later did some New York club dates with some of the same musicians. Gang Starr issued *Hard to Earn* in March of 1994; it debuted on the Billboard R&B charts at number two.—*Ron Wynn*

No More Mr. Nice Guy / 1989 / EMI America ✦✦✦
Plenty of attitude although not so strong otherwise. —*Ron Wynn*

Step in the Arena / 1991 / Chrysalis ✦✦✦
It has its moments. —*Ron Wynn*

● **Daily Operation** / 1992 / Chrysalis ✦✦✦✦
Arguably the best example of the hip-hop/jazz coalition, Gang Starr's latest continues the trailblazing path. —*Ron Wynn*

○ **Hard to Earn** / Mar. 8, 1994 / Chrysalis ✦✦✦✦
Although they were pioneers in the hip-hop/jazz movement, Gang Starr is still primarily a rap group. They reaffirm that on their newest venture, a 17-track set that's much more on the hard-hitting hip-hop tip than a restating of their jazz connections. The disc also offers more evidence that Guru is among rap's finest wordsmiths and verbal improvisers; whether moving over a midtempo groove, doing autobiographical sketches, criticizing other rappers, or just describing his environment and feelings, Guru's tone and voice are an effective mix of striking and reflective. *Hard To Earn* ranks as one of 1994's outstanding rap albums. —*Ron Wynn*

The Gants

Group, Garage Rock, Folk-Rock, Pop/Rock
One of the relatively few garage bands from the deep south to make a national impression in the mid-'60s, the Gants hit the Top 50 in 1965 with their cover of "Roadrunner." Liberty Records then preceded to bleed the band dry by issuing three cover-heavy albums and five more singles in the next year and a half. They deserved better, because lead singer and guitarist Sid Herring was a performer and songwriter of some talent. Too Beatlesque to be considered a garage band in the usual mold, their original material approximated elements of the Fab Four's sound circa 1965 with a blend of mid-tempo acoustic and electric guitars, close harmonies, and a slight country feel. Herring himself sounded like Lennon, as he wasn't above reworking melodic phrases from "In My Life" and "From Me to You." The strong material tended to be dwarfed by their rushed, cover-heavy albums, and the group never had another hit after "Roadrunner." —*Richie Unterberger*

● **I Wonder** / 1988 / Bam Caruso ✦✦✦✦
This compilation distills the albums and singles down to 18 of their best tracks, concentrating on Sid Herring originals rather than the covers that dominated their LPs. Star tracks include the country-rock beat ballad "Spoonful of Sugar" (which recalls the material on *Beatles for Sale*), the Merseybeat imitation "I Don't Want to See Her Again," and the poignant folk-rocker "I Wonder." A few tracks with strings produced by future Bread leader David Gates in 1967 are okay, but don't fit the group's best qualities. Comes with a band history and discography, but a strike against this compilation for including a few inessential Top 40 covers and omitting "Roadrunner" and other original songs praised in the liner notes. —*Richie Unterberger*

Gap Band

Group, Soul, Funk
This Southern combo bopped around throughout the '70s, offering a rather pedestrian variety of boogie funk. After scaling down and retooling their sound, the Gap Band netted numerous hits with a big mod-funk sound that recalled everyone from Sly Stone to George Clinton and Rick James. —*John Floyd*

Gap Band / 1977 / Mercury ✦✦✦
Ronnie Wilson recruited his brothers Charles and Robert in the late '70s to cement a group vision and sound he'd begun in 1967, but hadn't honed due to constant personnel changes. The Wilsons' first album was titled *The Gap Band*, and it laid the groundwork for the George Clinton/Parliament-inspired sound that would become enormously popular with their second album. The debut lacked the production polish, spirited leads and exchanges, and breakout singles that distinguished their best releases. It did, however, contain teasers tipping listeners off that the Wilsons had a sound and style which would be commercially viable. —*Ron Wynn*

○ **Gap Band 2** / 1979 / Mercury ✦✦✦✦
The seeds planted with their debut flowered on *Gap Band II*. The Wilson Brothers now had their George Clinton/Parliament with a taste of Rick James schtick down perfectly, and the chunky riffs and enthusiastic group vocals began to attract attention. "Get Up and Dance (Oops)" was a party and club hit, and "Steppin' Out" had a good track, but lacked a lyrical hook. This album eventually went gold, and it helped make the Gap Band a national attraction. —*Ron Wynn*

○ **Gap Band 3** / 1980 / Mercury ✦✦✦✦
A masterpiece, one of the '80s great funk albums. It had the fabulous singles "Burn Rubber on Me" and "Humpin," and marked the fruition of their George Clinton-tinged vocals and humor/grinding Southwestern funk/blues approach. The Wilsons were just starting to hit their stride. —*Ron Wynn*

○ **Gap Band 4** / 1982 / Mercury ✦✦✦✦
Another smash album and their fourth funk masterpiece in a row, the Gap Band was still burning up the R&B charts in the early '80s. They had two singles from this album top the charts and a third make it to number two. Robert Palmer later covered "Early In the Morning," and the Wilson brothers were at the top of their game. —*Ron Wynn*

Gap Band 5 / 1983 / Mercury ✦✦✦
The beginning of the slump that eventually plagued their final releases. After making four magnificent albums, the Gap Band couldn't equal those heights on this one, although they did have some fine singles. "Outstanding" was excellent, and there were some good album cuts as well. It just wasn't the consistent gem its predecessors had been, although in retrospect, it was far superior to what came after it. —*Ron Wynn*

Gap Band 6 / 1985 / Total Experience ✦✦
Things were beginning to fade for the Gap Band by the time they issued this album in the mid-'80s. Their trademark funk sound seemed out of steam, and groups were starting to be shunted off the airwaves as hip-hop and urban contemporary were beginning to converge. It didn't help that this album contained the least inspired tracks since their late '70s debut. —*Ron Wynn*

● **Gap Gold** / 1985 / Mercury ✦✦✦✦
This brief but thorough best-of contains every major hit netted by the revamped, latter-day Gap Band, including such dance crushers as "You Dropped a Bomb on Me" and "Early in the Morning." —*John Floyd*

Gap Band 7 / 1986 / Total Experience ✦
The Gap Band had long since lost its commercial potency by the time they reached this album. There were still moments when the trademark brilliance would reassert itself, but these were few and far between. The arrangements sounded leaden, the songs limp, and the production tentative. —*Ron Wynn*

Gap Band 8 / 1987 / Total Experience ✦
Only a few fleeting cuts on the second side were a reminder of how great the Gap Band once sounded. They were truly going through the motions on this one, singing in listless fashion on the slow songs and never generating much energy or fire on the funk/dance tracks. The album still did decently, but it was a far cry from the brilliance they demonstrated on albums 1-4. —*Ron Wynn*

Straight from the Heart / 1988 / Total Experience ✦✦
The group's final album for the Total Experience label wasn't among their most memorable. The vocals were lifeless, the production and arrangements stagnant, and there was little energy or inspiration in the musical backdrops. It had the sound and feel of something churned out to satisfy contractual obligations, and the Band moved on to Arista and then to Capitol. —*Ron Wynn*

Round Trip / 1990 / Capitol ✦✦
The Gap Band made a mild comeback when they signed to Capitol. They tried to modify their Parliament/Funkadelic-influenced funk, toning down the bass and smoothing out the synthesized backbeat. they were partially successful on this release, getting one hit in "Addicted To Your Love." But the album lacked the fire or the flair of their past efforts, and was a signal that the Gap Band had seen its best days. —*Ron Wynn*

Jerry Garcia

b. Aug. 1, 1942, San Francisco, CA, d. Aug. 9, 1995
Rock & Roll

A singer/songwriter and guitarist in the Grateful Dead, Jerry Garcia has also worked extensively as a solo and in other configurations, starting in 1971. Garcia died of heart failure August 9, 1995. — *William Ruhlmann*

Hooteroll? / 1971 / Grateful Dead ✦✦✦
Howard Wales, who is co-credited on this album, is a keyboard player, and Jerry Garcia's first non-Grateful Dead album release finds the two, along with such Garcia band stalwarts as drummer Bill Vitt and bassist John Kahn, playing exploratory instrumental music that touches on jazz and rock. Originally released in 1971 on Douglas Records, the album was reissued on CD on Grateful Dead Records in 1987 with two added tracks. — *William Ruhlmann*

● **Garcia** / Jan. 1972 / Grateful Dead ✦✦✦✦
In essence, this is a Grateful Dead record, featuring as it does the band's leader/singer/guitarist, its drummer, and its lyricist. Except for the few instrumental/experimental cuts, the material has been incorporated into the Dead's concert repertoire. In fact, this is a perfect follow-up to the folk-rock song albums the Dead produced in 1970, *Workingman's Dead* and *American Beauty*—albums the band itself has never really followed up. — *William Ruhlmann*

Live at the Keystone / 1973 / Fantasy ✦✦
A live double album recorded in July 1973 by a band featuring Garcia with keyboardist Merl Saunders, bassist John Kahn, and drummer Bill Vitt. The set indicates Garcia's eclectic taste: the band covers Bob Dylan, Jimmy Cliff, Rodgers and Hart, and Arthur Crudup, among others. Somehow, though, it all has the same loosely structured, unhurried style familiar from Garcia's work with the Grateful Dead and dominated by his dense, considered, single-note guitar solos and calmly trembling tenor voice. — *William Ruhlmann*

Reflections / Jan. 1976 / Grateful Dead ✦✦✦
Again, a Dead album in everything but name, with several tracks featuring the entire band, perhaps most memorably on "It Must Have Been the Roses." — *William Ruhlmann*

Cats under the Stars / 1978 / Arista ✦✦✦
The first real "Garcia Band" album is paced by songs that would not sound out of place at a Dead concert. As a matter of fact, the album has garnered increased interest in the '90s as the Dead added the leadoff track "Rubin and Cherise" to its repertoire. — *William Ruhlmann*

Run for the Roses / 1982 / Arista ✦✦✦
One of the last Dead-related albums released before the band's hiatus from recording in the mid-'80s, this is a typical effort, with covers of the Beatles and Bob Dylan, plus a couple of minor Garcia-Hunter compositions. — *William Ruhlmann*

Almost Acoustic / Dec. 1988 / Grateful Dead ✦✦✦
Garcia got his start in bluegrass, and here he assembles the Jerry Garcia Acoustic Band (some of whom he started playing with) to handle a live set full of Jimmie Rodgers, Mississippi John Hurt, and traditional mountain music. — *William Ruhlmann*

Compliments of Garcia / 1989 / Grateful Dead ✦✦
On his second solo album, Garcia adopts an approach more typical of his solo live shows than the Grateful Dead, writing none of the material himself and tackling everything from Irving Berlin's "Russian Lullaby" to Smokey Robinson's "The Hunter Gets Captured by the Game." The songs are taken at slightly sluggish tempos compared to the originals, especially ones that used to be frantic rockers. Most of this material is beyond Garcia's limited vocal range, but he gets points for trying. (Since Garcia unimaginatively gave this album the same title as his first solo album, Deadheads differentiated between the two by referring to the *Compliments of Garcia* legend written on promotional copies of this album. In reissuing the album on CD in 1989, Grateful Dead Records adopted their title.) — *William Ruhlmann*

Jerry Garcia Band / 1991 / Arista ✦✦✦
A double live album recorded in 1990 and featuring extended versions of songs by Bruce Cockburn, Bob Dylan, Smokey Robinson, the Beatles, the Band, Los Lobos, and others. The Garcia Band serves a kind of songbook function for its listeners (as, indeed, does the Dead), which may mean that its chief virtue is as instruction: if you're familiar with the originals, you don't really need to hear Garcia's covers, but if, like many Deadheads, you don't hear much music outside the band's orbit, this may help lead you to other good music. — *William Ruhlmann*

○ **Jerry Garcia & David Grisman** / 1991 / Acoustic Disc ✦✦✦✦
A guitar-and-mandolin duet album, exquisitely produced, with this pair trying a variety of styles from Garcia's "Friend of the Devil" to the ambitious instrumental "Arabia." — *William Ruhlmann*

Not for Kids Only / Oct. 1993 / Acoustic Disc ✦✦✦
On their second duo album, Jerry Garcia and David Grisman play songs either written for or applicable to children, among them Elizabeth Cotten's "Freight Train" and "Teddy Bears' Picnic." It's a delightful record that lives up to its title, and also marks the development of Garcia/Grisman as a full partnership, with Grisman contributing as many vocals as Garcia and the two trading off on guitar and mandolin. — *William Ruhlmann*

Art Garfunkel

b. Oct. 13, 1941, Queens, NY
Pop
After Simon & Garfunkel, one of the most successful duos in pop history, split up in 1970, Art Garfunkel became a solo artist, as well as pursuing an acting career. Garfunkel's pure, high tenor had been one of the most distinctive elements of the duo's music, yet he wasn't responsible for the songwriting—Simon wrote all of the group's hits. Not surprisingly, Garfunkel relied on other songwriters, from Jimmy Webb and Randy Newman to rock & roll standards like "I Only Have Eyes for You," throughout his solo career. As a solo performer, he was never quite as successful as he was with Simon & Garfunkel, yet he did have a number of Top 40 hits in the mid-'70s.

Garfunkel didn't begin a solo career until 1973. Between 1970 and 1973, he acted, appearing in two Mike Nichols films, *Catch 22* and *Carnal Knowledge*. *Angel Clare*, his first solo record, was co-produced with Simon & Garfunkel producer Roy Halee and released in the fall of 1973. It established the style—a light, carefully arranged and constructed melodic soft-rock—he would follow throughout his solo career. The album became a Top Ten hit on the strength of the single "All I Know," which peaked at number nine. Two years later, he returned with the Richard Perry-produced *Breakaway*, the most successful album of his solo career. The record peaked at number seven, with a version of the Flamingos' "I Only Have Eyes for You" reaching number 18 on the U.S. charts; in Britain, the single topped the charts. That same fall, he reunited with Paul Simon for the first time, performing on *Saturday Night Live*. In December, Simon's "My Little Town," featuring Garfunkel on backing vocals, became a Top Ten hit.

In the fall of 1977, Garfunkel released his third album, *Watermark*, which primarily consisted of Jimmy Webb covers. However, when the first single from the album failed to chart, the album was reissued in early 1978 with a cover of Sam Cooke's "Wonderful World" that featured supporting vocals from Simon and James Taylor. Released as a single, "Wonderful World" peaked at number 17. The following year, *Fate for Breakfast* appeared. Although it performed well in Britain, reaching number two, the album signalled that his American audience was beginning to shrink: None of the singles made the Top 40 and the album only reached number 67. In the fall of 1979, he filmed two movies, *Bad Timing* and *Illusions*. *Scissors Cut*, a reunion with producer Roy Halee released in 1981, did nothing to reverse his sliding commercial potential—it didn't even break into the Top 100 albums.

After the release of *Scissors Cut*, Simon & Garfunkel reunited for a concert in New York's Central Park. The concert was so successful, the duo decided to embark on a year-long world tour. During the tour, tensions mounted between the pair and they split again after it was completed. After a lengthy quiet period, Garfunkel re-emerged in 1988 with *Lefty*, which spent a mere eight weeks in the American charts and failed to make the British charts. He did not release another album until 1993's *Up 'til Now*. — *Stephen Thomas Erlewine*

○ **Angel Clare** / Sep. 1973 / Columbia ✦✦✦✦
Garfunkel (he was billed without his first name here) had a lot riding on his debut solo album, and *Angel Clare*, named after a character in Thomas Hardy's novel *Tess of the D'Urbervilles*, lived up to the heightened expectations for the man who had sung "Bridge over Troubled Water" and other Simon and Garfunkel favorites. Garfunkel took no chances, issuing as the first single Jimmy Webb's "All I Know," which was arranged in a similar style to

"Bridge" and made the Top Ten. Elsewhere on the record, Garfunkel took a more spirited approach, notably on a version of Van Morrison's "I Shall Sing" that was reminiscent of Simon and Garfunkel's "Cecilia" and made the Top 40. Certainly, there was enough firepower on the record, which featured guitarists Jerry Garcia and J.J. Cale. But much of it was filled with stately, orchestra-laden ballads, sung by Garfunkel in his naive, breathy tenor. If Simon and Garfunkel had been the thinking man's Everly Brothers, Garfunkel alone turned out to be the thinking man's Johnny Mathis. — *William Ruhlmann*

Breakaway / Oct. 1975 / Columbia ✦✦✦
The second time around, Art Garfunkel turned to pop producer Richard Perry, who liked to record in studios rather than cathedrals and who replaced the angelic style of the first album with a lush pop approach. The result was Garfunkel's best-selling album. The title track and a cover of "I Only Have Eyes for You" reached the Top 40 (the latter topped the U.K. charts), though the most prominent song was the Simon and Garfunkel reunion single "My Little Town." But the album was full of wise pop choices, among them Bruce Johnston's "Disney Girls," Stevie Wonder's "I Believe (When I Fall in Love It Will Be Forever)," and Hal David and Albert Hammond's "1199 Miles from L.A." Perry proved that, given the right material and production, the problem of the relative sameness of Garfunkel's vocal approach could be overcome. — *William Ruhlmann*

Watermark / Oct. 1977 / Columbia ✦✦✦
The original idea was for Art Garfunkel to record an album of songs written by Jimmy Webb. But when the lead-off single, "Crying in My Sleep," failed to make the charts, Columbia Records withdrew the album and induced Garfunkel to put together a cover of Sam Cooke's "(What A) Wonderful World" with Paul Simon and James Taylor harmonizing. The single and a revised version of the LP then made the Top 40. But it's still a Garfunkel-Sings-Webb album, except for one song. And the initial idea was a good one: Garfunkel handles Webb's wistful pop songs well, and he has made good choices from Webb's songbook, dating back to the 1960s, though avoiding his big hits. The result is Garfunkel's most cohesive solo album. (The original version of *Watermark*, on test pressings and only a very few commercial copies, was available briefly in October 1977. The revised version, containing "[What A] Wonderful World," was released in January 1978.) — *William Ruhlmann*

Fate for Breakfast / Mar. 1979 / Columbia ✦✦
For his fourth solo album, Art Garfunkel opted to make a light contemporary pop record on the order of Breakaway, but for the most part the material was mediocre and the backup slick and unfeeling. "Since I Don't Have You" was an obvious choice for a singer who had scored with a similar '50s oldie, "I Only Have Eyes for You," but it was the album's only chart single, and *Fate for Breakfast* was as disappointing at the cash register as it was on the turntable. — *William Ruhlmann*

Scissors Cut / Aug. 1981 / Columbia ✦✦
After the disappointment of *Fate for Breakfast*, Art Garfunkel returned to old friends for his fifth solo album, co-producing with Roy Halee, who had worked with Simon and Garfunkel and on Garfunkel's debut album, *Angel Clare*, and singing several songs written by Jimmy Webb, who had written nearly all the songs on Garfunkel's third album, *Watermark*. But though *Scissors Cut* came closer to the sound of a good Garfunkel album, material remained a problem. "A Heart in New York," the LP's sole American chart single, was second-rate, as were many of the other compositions, Garfunkel scored a surprise number one hit in Great Britain with the Mike Batt-written and produced "Bright Eyes," the theme from the movie *Watership Down*, but that wasn't enough to make the album on the whole a success, Garfunkel then re-teamed with Paul Simon for a world concert tour, and it was five years before he was back in record stores with the seasonal release *The Animals' Christmas* and nearly seven years before his next regular solo album, *Lefty*. — *William Ruhlmann*

The Art Garfunkel Album / Oct. 1984 / CBS ✦✦
A U.K.-only compilation for the man who had topped the singles charts twice in Great Britain with "I Only Have Eyes for You" and "Bright Eyes." This is a reasonable reduction of Garfunkel's five solo albums to 14 tracks, highlighted by such songs as "All I Know," "I Shall Sing," and "(What A) Wonderful World." — *William Ruhlmann*

Lefty / Mar. 1988 / Columbia ✦✦
Art Garfunkel's first regular studio album in nearly seven years was a pleasant enough exercise that did nothing to arrest his commercial or artistic decline. The idea of covering "I Have a Love" from *West Side Story* was a good one, the obligatory '50s cover, "So Much in Love," was well performed, and "Love Is the Only Chain" was a good piece of material, even if better performed by authors Pam Rose and Mary Ann Kennedy (who joined Garfunkel on this recording). The version of "When a Man Loves a Woman," so far away from Percy Sledge's emotional original, served to illustrate Garfunkel's detached approach to his material. But much of the album consisted of second-rate songs, frequently written by Stephen Bishop. — *William Ruhlmann*

● **Garfunkel: Best of** / 1990 / Columbia ✦✦✦✦
This is a good overview of Garfunkel's solo work. Most of his airplay tracks are included here. — *Rick Clark*

Up 'til Now / Oct. 28, 1993 / Columbia ✦✦
Art Garfunkel gives his "deepest thanks to Mitchell Cohen at Columbia for the concept of this album." But what is the concept? It contains everything from the original Simon and Garfunkel recording of "The Sound of Silence" (from their *Wednesday Morning 3 A.M.* album) to tracks from previous Garfunkel solo albums, stray songs, apparently intended for albums never made, movie and TV themes, a live performance, and even a comedy routine with Paul Simon called "The Breakup"—you name it. So, perhaps the concept is what the Who called "odds and sods." In any case, it's also marginal. — *William Ruhlmann*

The Garrett-Sahm-Taylor Band
Group, R&B, Rock & Roll, Blues Rock
Not surprisingly, this group is also called the "Formerly Brothers," since all three members are alumni of other noted organizations (Paul Butterfield's Better Days, the Sir Douglas Quintet, Canned Heat, etc.). It was formed on an ad hoc basis after a chance gig at the Edmonton Folk Festival in 1986. — *William Ruhlmann*

○ **Return of the Formerly Brothers** / 1991 / Rykodisc ✦✦✦✦
Texan folk hero, Sir Doug Sahm meets underrated guitarist Amos Garrett and ex-Blasters keyboardist Gene Taylor and they cook like an Austin barbecue. — *Jeff Tamarkin*

Danny Gatton
d. Oct. 20, 1994
Rock & Roll, Rockabilly
In the early '50s, Gatton was a teen guitar prodigy, with a style that incorporated the flashy calisthenics of Jimmy Bryant, Joe Maphis, and Cliff Gallup (equal parts rockabilly fire and honkytonk dazzle). He retired for years to focus on his first love (restoring old cars) but returned in 1991 with a powerhouse solo album (*88 Elmira St.*) that was one of the best instrumental albums of the decade. He recorded several other equally accomplished albums before he committed suicide in 1994. — *John Floyd*

● **Unfinished Business** / 1987 / NRG ✦✦✦✦
Perhaps the most underrated guitarist there is. Gatton does it all, and dazzles at every turn. — *Jeff Tamarkin*

88 Elmira St. / 1991 / Elektra ✦✦✦
His first major-label recording after decades of flooring unsuspecting audiences. Gatton's guitar work is simply astounding. — *Jeff Tamarkin*

Redneck Jazz / 1991 / NRG ✦✦✦
Just like the title says. The music on this album is required listening for those who think they've heard it all. — *Jeff Tamarkin*

○ **Danny Gatton** / 1993 / Asylum ✦✦✦✦

Cruisin' Deuces / May 18, 1993 / Elektra ✦✦
Featured is more jaw-dropping guitar work from Gatton, the best guitarist you've never heard. — *AMG*

Relentless / 1994 / Big Mo ✦✦

Blazing Telecasters / Powerhouse ✦✦✦
Guitar freaks beware—when axe-killer Gatton and blues-whiz Principato get cookin' in this live set, sparks fly. — *Jeff Tamarkin*

Marvin Gaye (Marvin Pentz Gay, Jr.)
b. Apr. 2, 1939, Washington, DC, d. Apr. 1, 1984
Soul, R&B, Motown
Of the important R&B/pop artists to emerge on Motown Records in the 1960s, Marvin Gaye was one of two—the other being Stevie

Wonder—to adapt effectively to the musical changes of the 1970s. A singer of frothy dance hits and light romantic ballads early on, he turned to album-length treatments of social concerns and erotic pleasures, with complex music that took on elements of rock and funk.

The son of a minister, Gaye got his start singing in church and in the '50s was a member of the vocal group the Moonglows. He was an early recruit to Motown, for which he began recording on its Tamla label in 1961, the same year he married Anna Gordy, sister of Motown chief Berry Gordy, Jr. His first recording success came with "Stubborn Kind of Fellow" (September 1962), which reached the R&B Top Ten and entered the pop charts. "Hitch Hike" (December 1962) brought him into the pop Top 40 and "Pride and Joy" (May 1963) into the pop Top Ten.

Gaye continued to chart in 1964, sometimes in duets with Mary Wells and with Kim Weston, and his next major success came with "How Sweet It Is (To Be Loved By You)" (November 1964). Its follow-up, "I'll Be Doggone" (March 1965) topped the R&B chart, where nearly all of his singles would reach the Top Ten for the next eight years. His next major pop success was "Ain't that Peculiar" (September 1965), which also went to #1 R&B. Gaye enjoyed the biggest hit of his career with his sultry treatment of "I Heard It Through the Grapevine" (November 1968), which had been a #1 hit for Gladys Knight and the Pips only a year before. His next two singles, "Too Busy Thinking About My Baby" (April 1969) and "That's the Way Love Is" (August 1969) also hit the pop Top Ten.

Gaye was profoundly affected by the death of his singing partner Tammi Terrell of a brain tumor on March 16, 1970. (Their hits together had included "Your Precious Love" [August 1967], "If I Could Build My Whole World Around You" [November 1967], "Ain't Nothing like the Real Thing" [March 1968], and "You're All I Need to Get By" [July 1968]). He went into seclusion. At the same time, he was attempting to wrest greater creative control over his music from Motown. He re-emerged with a masterwork, "What's Going On" (February 1971), the centerpiece of his first pop Top Ten album *What's Going On* (May 1971), which also featured the hits "Mercy Mercy Me (The Ecology)" and "Inner City Blues (Make Me Wanna Holler)," songs that were a far cry from Gaye's '60s love songs.

Gaye next turned to movie scoring, producing the soundtrack to *Trouble Man* (December 1972), before topping the commercial success of *What's Going On* with the lusty *Let's Get it On* (August 1973). *Marvin Gaye Live!* (June 1974) and *I Want You* (March 1976) were also Top Ten hits, and *Marvin Gaye Live at the Palladium* (March 1977) returned him to the top of the pop charts with the irresistible funk song "Got to Give It Up."

Gaye suffered personal and business problems thereafter, however, divorcing Anna Gordy in an extraordinary settlement that awarded her the proceeds from his next album (he dubbed it *Here, My Dear* [December 1978]) and getting into a dispute over back taxes with the I.R.S. Gaye left Motown and the U.S., living in Europe for several years, then returned with the comeback album *Midnight Love* (November 1982) and its single "Sexual Healing." In 1984, Gaye was shot to death by his father during an argument. — *William Ruhlmann*

That Stubborn Kinda Fellow / Jan. 31, 1963 / Motown ✦✦✦
Vintage Gaye and Motown, following all the formulas that made the label the '60s' finest record company. The title track was an instant classic and is still among his finest '60s uptempo tunes. The other cuts are just as fantastic, and any doubts anyone might have had about Gaye were immediately and forever quashed with this album. — *Ron Wynn*

On Stage Recorded Live / Sep. 9, 1963 / Motown ✦✦✦
While the selections and overall production are spotty, there's nothing erratic or uneven about Gaye's vocals. This was his third Motown album and first live date, and he sounded refreshed, energetic, and triumphant. This came close to equaling his late '70s live set done in London and is among the best '60s live albums that Motown released. — *Ron Wynn*

When I'm Alone I Cry / Apr. 1, 1964 / Motown ✦✦
Hard as it may be to believe today, at the beginning of his career, Gaye was far more interested in crooning jazz standards than singing soul music, and took every opportunity to vent his jazz pipes in the studio. However much he may have wished otherwise, just about every listener agrees that he was a great soul singer, but a mediocre jazz vocalist. This album, cut at a time when he was already a rising soul star, consists of ten pop-jazz standards and is

really only of interest to collectors. Certainly it's competently done, but it's supper-club fare, in which Gaye comes off as a sub-Nat King Cole rather than his own man. The CD reissue, interestingly, presents the entire album in both mono and stereo versions. — *Richie Unterberger*

How Sweet It Is to Be Loved by You / Jan. 21, 1965 / Motown ✦✦✦
Another great album; Gaye was at this time Motown's finest solo vocalist (Smokey Robinson, Eddie Kendricks, David Ruffin, and Levi Stubbs were all heading groups). His vocal on the title track was both smooth and churning, celebratory and introspective. He could do no wrong during this period, regardless of content, tempo, or arrangement. — *Ron Wynn*

Tribute to the Great Nat King Cole / Nov. 1, 1965 / Motown ✦✦✦
A wonderful album that got buried when it was initially released. Nat "King" Cole was a primary influence on Marvin Gaye for Gaye's entire career, and he got a chance on this album to display his affection for sentimental, romantic fare and his skill in singing it. Motown finally had the good sense to get this out on CD in 1989. — *Ron Wynn*

Marvin Gaye and Kim Weston / 1966 / Motown ✦✦✦
Although they weren't as great a team as Gaye and Tammi Terrell, the Gaye/Weston duo turned out a few solid numbers. The finest was "It Takes Two," a steamy bit of uptempo soul that came close to equaling any fast duet number Gaye ever made at Motown. The rest was well done, but not quite on the same level. — *Ron Wynn*

Moods of Marvin Gaye / May 23, 1966 / Motown ✦✦✦
This is one of his better '60s albums. — *Rick A. Bueche*

☆ **Marvin Gaye's Greatest Hits, Vol. 2** / 1967 / Motown ✦✦✦✦✦
Other than the *Anthology* line, this was for quite a while the best single album set featuring Gaye's early and mid-'60s hits. There isn't a dud in the bunch, but both the *Super Hits* and Anthology line give you more cuts, while the boxed set has more variety. But this isn't by any stretch a bad release. — *Ron Wynn*

○ **I Heard It through the Grapevine** / 1968 / Motown ✦✦✦✦
Critic Dave Marsh picked the title cut as the finest American single of all time, and while that might be padding things, it would surely rank among them. Another Motown classic, superb ballads, striking uptempo tracks, great production and arrangements, and wonderful songs. — *Ron Wynn*

In the Groove / Aug. 26, 1968 / Motown ✦✦
An unusual concept album for Gaye, who showed he could handle dance, novelty, and uptempo tunes as surely and confidently as love ballads. Despite the lack of thematic variety and the sameness of the arrangements, Gaye's vocals were never subordinated to the beat. This has long since disappeared, although it's available on the collector's circuit. — *Ron Wynn*

Marvin Gaye & His Girls / Apr. 30, 1969 / Motown ✦✦✦
A wonderful anthology, one of the few instances where Motown recycling was justified. Gaye did masterpieces with Mary Wells, Diana Ross, and Kim Weston in addition to Tammi Terrell, and here's a chance to hear him with all of them. Since some of the original albums are either out of print or impossible to find, here's one concept album that's a must buy. — *Ron Wynn*

M.P.G. / Apr. 30, 1969 / Motown ✦✦✦
An underrated late '60s album, this one has sometimes been overlooked because it seemed like a generic throwaway. But it included some outstanding songs. Motown wisely has included it on their list of Gaye albums that got reissued on CD. — *Ron Wynn*

Easy / Sep. 16, 1969 / Motown ✦✦✦
Some splendid vocals by Gaye and Motown's customary excellent production, arrangements, and musical support. He and Motown were getting on increasingly edgy ground outside the studio, but they were still a potent team. — *Ron Wynn*

○ **Super Hits** / 1970 / Motown ✦✦✦✦
A fabulous anthology, one of the best ones Motown ever released. Both *Super Hits* packages were crammed full for albums of the era, and the sound and selections were first rate. Motown has issued the first volume on CD, but thus far not the second—a major mistake. — *Ron Wynn*

That's the Way Love Is / Jan. 8, 1970 / Motown ✦✦✦
The title cut was another Gaye classic, while much of the other material was equally impressive. Gaye was beginning to become disillusioned with Motown, but that hadn't affected his album out-

put or his singing. Anyone hearing this wouldn't have suspected that Gaye was about to unleash *What's Going On.* —*Ron Wynn*

☆ **What's Going on** / May 20, 1971 / Motown ✦✦✦✦✦
Shortly after Marvin Gaye turned 30, he became the first Motown artist with a measure of creative control. *What's Going On* was the result, surely Marvin's finest moment and, along with a number of Stevie Wonder's early-'70s releases, one of a handful of *great* Motown albums. A concept album, *What's Going On* chronicled a multitude of societal ills. Ironically, Motown owner Berry Gordy did not want to release it. He was convinced it held no commercial potential. Gordy couldn't have been more wrong: *What's Going On* catapulted Marvin Gaye into superstardom. Three #1 singles were pulled from the album: the title song, "Mercy Mercy Me (The Ecology)," and "Inner City Blues (Make Me Wanna Holler)." This was the first album where Marvin overdubbed his voice multiple times, creating a one-man vocal group. The result was a level of timbral integration in the harmonies that became a Gaye trademark. —*Rob Bowman*

Trouble Man / Dec. 8, 1972 / Motown ✦✦✦
Marvin Gaye turned to soundtracks in the early '70s, and came out with one that ranked right alongside the epic scores done by Curtis Mayfield and Isaac Hayes. The film itself was a typical '70s "blaxploitation" effort, but Gaye's vocals, seamless production, and a nice mix of uptempo funk, light ballads, and pseudo-macho camp were brilliant. —*Ron Wynn*

☆ **Let's Get It On** / Aug. 28, 1973 / Motown ✦✦✦✦✦
Let's Get It On is one of the most erotic recordings known to mankind. Inspired by Gaye's obsession with a teenage girl, Janis Hunter, who would later become his second wife, Side one is a self-contained suite. Side two, including "You Sure Love to Ball," is nearly pornographic. Over time, five songs would chart from the album, including one of his concert standards, "Distant Lover." —*Rob Bowman*

★ **Anthology** / 1974 / Motown ✦✦✦✦✦
With *Anthology* you can get an overview of Gaye's Motown work without having to plunk the money down for *The Marvin Gaye Collection* boxed set. The two-disc set contains most of his major hits (although not his number one hit "Let's Get It On"), including "Inner City Blues (Make Me Wanna Holler)," "Mercy Mercy Me (The Ecology)," "I Heard It Through the Grapevine," "Trouble Man," "I'll Be Doggone," "What's Going On," "Hitch Hike," "Can I Get a Witness," and "Pride and Joy," as well as his numerous duets with Kim Weston and Tammi Terrell, like "Ain't No Mountain High Enough," "Ain't Nothing like the Real Thing," "It Takes Two," and "Your Precious Love." —*AMG*

Live / Jun. 19, 1974 / Motown ✦✦✦
Some delightful ballads and not-so-great uptempo material make this a good, but not great, Marvin Gaye release. His silky tones were consistently fine, but the pacing on the album is jerky, as is the range of material. As a Gaye lover, it's well within the acceptable limits of Gaye concerts, but those who weren't huge fans probably should pass. —*Ron Wynn*

Greatest Hits / 1976 / Motown ✦✦✦
A good, if unessential, collection that recycles many songs available on many other packages. This is strictly for budget-conscious buyers and casual Gaye listeners; the CD version is pretty well mastered. —*Ron Wynn*

I Want You / Mar. 16, 1976 / Motown ✦✦✦
Featured are dynamic vocal and rhythmic arrangements. —*Rick A. Bueche*

Live at the London Paladium / Mar. 15, 1977 / Motown ✦✦✦
As fine a live album as Marvin Gaye ever made. The final track, the extended version of "Gotta Give It Up," still gets wide airplay at parties and in clubs. It was among his greatest uptempo hits ever, and the full treatment includes some wonderful instrumental work at the end accompanying Gaye's floating vocals and fleeing sighs. —*Ron Wynn*

○ **Here My Dear** / Dec. 15, 1978 / Motown ✦✦✦✦
On one of the stranger releases in popular music, *Here, My Dear,* Gaye stands emotionally naked. Over the course of this two-album set, Marvin chronicles the dissolution of his marriage (to company president Berry Gordy's sister Anna). The level of detail is nearly painful as Marvin accuses Anna of keeping him from seeing his son, having a restraining order issued against him, and holding their separation up for ransom. Marvin also tells us of his cocaine habit and his obsession with prostitutes. In a trace of irony not lost

on the singer, Anna received all royalties from the album as per their divorce agreement. Upon hearing it, she reportedly contemplated suing for invasion of privacy. —*Rob Bowman*

In Our Lifetime / Jan. 15, 1981 / Motown ✦✦✦
Another of Gaye's uneven, yet appealing releases. He was searching for the right songs and didn't always find them. He was also hurting again, suffering personal and professional problems that he ultimately failed to solve. This made his songs both poignant and painful, and that's what makes this album worth hearing, despite its problems. —*Ron Wynn*

○ **Midnight Love** / Oct. 1982 / Columbia ✦✦✦✦
Gaye's comeback album contains its share of fluff but "Sexual Healing" is one of the greatest R&B singles of all time. Black radio felt that way as well; the song stayed #1 for ten weeks, remaining on the charts for a total of 27 weeks. —*Rob Bowman*

Romantically Yours / 1985 / Columbia ✦✦✦
Longtime Motown impresario and former Gaye colleague Harvey Fuqua picked and mixed the tracks that comprised this mid-'80s Gaye retrospective. As you might expect, it was a far superior package to many other Gaye sets, both in content and sound quality. There are some wonderful ballads that sat in Motown's vault for reasons only they know, and a set that should have gotten much more publicity hype than a lot of the other recycled collections. —*Ron Wynn*

Dream of a Lifetime / May 1985 / Columbia ✦✦
An intriguing but deeply flawed set of vault items, unreleased performances, and alternate tracks. Some are sentimental and romantic, others are yearning or anguished. Almost anything Marvin Gaye released had some merit; this one has less than most, but still contains some gripping singing. —*Ron Wynn*

○ **Motown Remembers Marvin Gaye** / 1986 / Motown ✦✦✦✦
An odd collection of vault items, alternate takes, B-sides, and leftovers that the label issued in response to numerous bootleg sets that were running rampant in 1985, in the wake of Gaye's tragic death the year before at his father's hands. Many of these songs are quite flawed, yet Gaye's vocal treatments are seldom less than compelling, and sometimes unforgettable. —*Ron Wynn*

The Marvin Gaye Collection / 1990 / Motown ✦✦✦
Marvin Gaye has more than enough great music to make a superb box set, but the haphazard *Marvin Gaye Collection* isn't it. The four discs within the set are arranged thematically—one terrific disc of hits, one good disc of duets, one largely uninteresting disc of rarities, and one wildly uneven disc of ballads. By spreading out the material this way, Motown shortchanges Gaye's musical accomplishments; there is no sense of growth or innovation. Although many of the songs are wonderful, some of the selections are puzzling—they seem to be chosen because they're arcane, not because they're significant. This very quality makes *The Marvin Gaye Collection* essential for his most devoted fans; however, most fans will find this box set disappointing. —*Stephen Thomas Erlewine*

○ **Seek & You Shall Find: More of the Best (1963-1981)** / 1993 / Rhino ✦✦✦✦
Full of album tracks, B-sides, and live tracks, *Seek & You Shall Find: More of the Best* is a great compliment to Gaye's greatest-hits collections. —*AMG*

Norman Whitfield Sessions / 1994 / Motown ✦✦✦
All of Gaye's recordings with producer Norman Whitfield are collected on the appropriately titled *The Norman Whitfield Sessions.* The sessions proved beneficial to both Gaye and Whitfield, as they produced the classic "I Heard It Through the Grapevine." While nothing on the set matches that seminal cut, most of the music is captivating. Nevertheless, the disc will appeal mainly to the devoted Marvin Gaye collector, since most of the material is either alternate takes or outtakes. —*Stephen Thomas Erlewine*

○ **The Master 1961-1984** / Apr. 25, 1995 / Motown ✦✦✦✦
The average fan is better off with *Anthology,* which covers almost all of Gaye's true classics. But for those who want the hits and then some, and have the budget and interest to go further, this four-CD box set is an excellent retrospective of his career. The 89 tracks include all the chart hits (both on his own and with Mary Wells, Kim Weston, Tammi Terrell, and Diana Ross) and many interesting B-sides, album tracks, and misses. There are also over a dozen previously unreleased cuts, most dating from the early part of his career; they don't rank among his best work, but they're almost all good and interesting. With a long essay by his biographer, David

Ritz, this is the best overview of Gaye's evolution and versatility, and a much-recommended alternative to the previous Gaye box, *The Marvin Gaye Collection.* —*Richie Unterberger*

Gloria Gaynor

b. Sep. 7, 1949, Newark, NJ
Disco
Gaynor sang with the Soul Satisfiers band before being discovered at the Wagon Wheel in New York in the early '70s. Probably the first "disco queen," Gaynor helped popularize, through her music, the "segue" or "extended mix" that came to represent disco music. Her 1979 cut, "I Will Survive," became a woman's anthem in the vein of Helen Reddy's "I Am Woman." She continued to thrive in Europe during the '80s. —*Bil Carpenter*

● **Greatest Hits** / 1982 / Polydor ✦✦✦✦
Includes "Never Can Say Goodbye" and other disco hits. —*Bil Carpenter*

Paul Gayten

b. Jan. 29, 1920, New Orleans, LA, **d.** Mar. 26, 1991, Los Angeles, CA
New Orleans R&B
Paul Gayten, a seminal figure in New Orleans rhythm & blues, led a varied career in the music business as a bandleader, producer, label owner, and one-time overseer of the West Coast operation of Chess Records. A nephew of blues-piano legend Little Brother Montgomery, Gayten once led one of the top bands of New Orleans, but he gave up the performing life in 1956 to turn his attention to production and eventually to his own California-based Pzazz label (which featured Louis Jordan, among others). Gayten wrote Larry Darnell's 1949 classic "For You My Love" and recorded a few Top Ten hits of his own for Regal and DeLuxe (1947-1950), some of them with vocalist Annie Laurie. —*Jim O'Neal*

● **Chess King of New Orleans/The Chess Years** / 1989 / MCA ✦✦✦✦
Sizzling mid-'50s New Orleans R&B from this veteran. —*Bill Dahl*

○ **Regal Records in New Orleans** / 1991 / Specialty ✦✦✦✦
The early '50s New Orleans jump-blues and ballad material by pianist Paul Gayten and vocalist Annie Laurie are featured on this generous (27-track) disc. —*Bill Dahl*

○ **And Annie Laurie** / Specialty ✦✦✦✦
Stomping New Orleans R&B and barrelhouse blues by pianist/vocalist Paul Gayten and vocalist Annie Laurie. Although he moved to Los Angeles from New Orleans in the early '50s, Gayten never lost the second-line beat. The duo didn't enjoy as much success with this Specialty material as they did on Deluxe and Regal, but it's still wonderful, vibrant R&B in the great swing and bawdy tradition. —*Ron Wynn*

J. Geils Band

Group, Rock & Roll, Blues Rock, Pop/Rock
The J. Geils Band from Boston (formed 1967) embraced the idioms of doo wop, blues, and R&B at a time when many of their peers were diving headfirst into psychedelia. While everyone else grew their hair out, many of the Geils Band slicked their hair back like greasers. Jerome Geils was the band's lead guitarist, but it was Peter Wolf (Blankfield), a former WBCN-FM Boston DJ, who was the group's captivating frontman.

During the '70s, the J. Geils Band toured incessantly and enjoyed the occasional near-hit album or single, but the band struck multi-platinum with *Freeze Frame* (#1) in 1982, one of the biggest albums of that year. Excellent video exposure on the fledgling MTV helped considerably. With success came numerous problems, including substance abuse. A live album, *Showtime* (#23), followed before Wolf jumped ship for a solo career. The group's first post-Wolf studio effort (*You're Getting Even While I'm Getting Odd*) was a major stumble chartwise (#80), and the group disbanded shortly afterwards. —*Rick Clark*

○ **The J. Geils Band** / 1970 / Atlantic ✦✦✦✦
Their debut paid homage to the likes of Otis Rush, John Lee Hooker, and Motown through blistering covers, but originals such as "Wait" and "What's Your Hurry" more than hold their own. Magic Dick steals the show on this one. —*John Floyd*

The Morning After / 1971 / Atlantic ✦✦✦
Full House Live / 1972 / Atlantic ✦✦✦
Bloodshot / 1973 / Atlantic ✦✦
Ladies Invited / 1973 / Atlantic ✦✦✦
Nightmares . . . and Other Tales from the Vinyl Jungle / 1974 / Atlantic ✦✦✦
Hotline / 1975 / Atlantic ✦✦
Blow Your Face Out / 1976 / Atlantic ✦✦✦

○ **Monkey Island** / 1977 / Atlantic ✦✦✦✦
One of the great lost albums, *Monkey Island* is where the Geils Band make the blues their own. It's an elaborately produced, adventurous set that analyzes their commerical failure and looks for answers to hard-to-ask questions. Unlike their 1972 live album *Full House, Monkey Island* refuses to pander to blues conservatists or boogie-rock hammerheads; the album is steeped in the kind of pathos and bitterness that infuse the Stones' *Sticky Fingers.* The album flopped, but it remains the group's most personal statement. —*John Floyd*

Sanctuary / 1978 / EMI America ✦✦✦
The Geils sound is retooled into a streamlined shuffle that owes much to production and songwriting floriation of keyboardist Seth Justman. Their soul and blues chops are still apparent, but they've worked them into a sound that manages to elaborate on the experiments of *Monkey Island* while still paying homage to their early days. —*John Floyd*

○ **The Best of the J. Geils Band** / 1979 / Atlantic ✦✦✦✦
Pulling the decent material from this otherwise unspectacular mid-'70s albums makes this an adequate overview of the band's achievements. It's the best place to sample such minor hits as "Must of Got Lost" and "Give It to Me." —*John Floyd*

Love Stinks / 1980 / EMI America ✦✦✦
The title cut brought the band an across-the-board hit, and the near new wave production touches don't get in the way of the crack rhythm section or Geils's tasty leads. A new sound for a new decade. —*John Floyd*

○ **Freeze Frame** / 1981 / EMI America ✦✦✦✦
A stylistic retread, it nonetheless cemented the band's newfound popularity, thanks to the naggingly catchy "Centerfold" and the nuevo-funky "Flamethrower." "Piss on the Wall" and "Rage in the Cage" are blistering rockers. —*John Floyd*

Showtime! / 1984 / EMI America ✦✦
You're Gettin' Even While I'm Gettin' Odd / 1984 / EMI ✦✦
Flashback / 1988 / EMI America ✦✦✦
These are the products of their 1980-83 windfall. —*Dan Heilman*

● **Houseparty: Anthology** / 1992 / Rhino ✦✦✦✦
The superb two-disc anthology *Houseparty* concentrates on the rousing, full-throttle blues-boogie of their heyday, including a full album's worth of live material (ten songs from their three live albums). The pop success of *Love Stinks* and *Freeze-Frame* makes sense in the context of the set, but the songs that cut the deepest are the blues-rock numbers on the first disc and the live songs. Thankfully, the compilers (*Trouser Press* editor Ira Robbins and band members Peter Wolf and Seth Justman) end *Houseparty* with three songs from *Sanctuary,* helping secure the image of the J. Geils Band as one of America's top rock & roll groups. —*Stephen Thomas Erlewine*

Must Of Got Lost / 1995 / Rhino

Bob Geldof

b. Oct. 5, 1954, Dublin, Ireland
Pop/Rock
Geldof formed the punk group Boomtown Rats in 1975. During the band's existence, it moved from the pure energy and aggression of hits like "Looking After No. 1" to the more sophisticated, but still provocative, "I Don't Like Mondays" (its title derived from the answer given by a San Diego schoolgirl when asked why she'd killed her classmates). The band became a moderate success in the U.K., though it never really broke through in the U.S.

In the fall of 1984, Geldof watched a BBC documentary on Ethiopian poverty and was inspired to put together a charity single, "Do They Know It's Christmas." It featured a large number of British pop stars performing under the name Band Aid and became the best-selling single in U.K. history. Michael Jackson and Lionel Richie repeated the feat the following year in the U.S. with

"We Are the World." By then Geldof was involved in plans for a massive charity concert that eventually became Live Aid, two marathon shows held July 13, 1985, at Wembley Stadium in London and at JFK Stadium in Philadelphia, featuring a Who's Who of pop/rock talent. Millions were raised and distributed to the African poor. Geldof was nominated for a Nobel Prize and knighted, and his autobiography *Is That All?* became a U.K. bestseller.

In 1986, the Rats split and Geldof launched a solo career, again with greater success in England than in the U.S. — *William Ruhlmann*

● **Deep in the Heart of Nowhere** / 1986 / Atlantic ◆◆◆◆
On his first solo album, Geldof sheds the New Wave sound of the Boomtown Rats for a more straightforward classic Brit-rock approach, notably on the leadoff single, "This Is the World Calling" and on the "Waterloo Sunset" sequel "Love Like a Rocket," which features Eric Clapton. — *William Ruhlmann*

Vegetarians of Love / 1990 / Atlantic ◆◆◆
Geldof investigates his Irish folk roots, reveals himself to be a Dylan acolyte, and sends up his "Saint Bob" image on this varied and ambitious second album. — *William Ruhlmann*

The Happy Club / 1993 / Polydor

Gene

Group, Alternative Pop/Rock
To say that Gene sound like the Smiths is a bit like saying the Rolling Stones sound like Chuck Berry—although there are clear traces of their primary influence, the band has incorporated them into a familiar but re-energized sound. Gene don't treat the Smiths' catalogue as sacred texts; the music serves as a launching point for tales of debauchery and loneliness that Morrissey would never bother to chronicle. Gene's attack is more muscular and straight-forward as well, relying less on layers of guitars than a simple intertwining of two guitar parts. Before the release of their 1995 debut, the band had developed a dedicated following based on the strength of their singles "Be My Light, Be My Guide" and "Sleep Well Tonight" and extensive coverage in the British music weeklies. Upon its release, *Olympian* received mixed reviews, yet it sold well in the U.K.; however, the band failed to break big in the U.S. — *Stephen Thomas Erlewine*

○ **Olympian** / 1995 / Polydor ◆◆◆◆
Kicking off with the sprightly "Haunted by You," *Olympian* immediately conjures images of the Smiths, particularly "This Charming Man." Martin Rossiter's voice also sways like Morrissey, yet his band plays their songs as if they were hard rockers, bringing a desperate edge to their best material. Most of *Olympian's* finest moments were singles—aside from "Haunted by You," the epic sweep of "Sleep Well Tonight" and the gentle urgency of the title track, form the heart of the album; two other singles were added to the American version, including the stellar "Be My Light, Be My Guide." While Gene manages to carve out an identity indebted to the Smiths but not dominated by them, they also fail to produce an album of consistently compelling material—considering that it's a debut album, that's not a fatal flaw. And Gene's best material shows they are capable of transcending their influences. — *Stephen Thomas Erlewine*

General Public

Group, Ska-Revival, Pop/Rock
This U.K. duo of vocalist Dave Wakeling (b. Feb 19, 1956) and "toaster" Ranking Roger (b. Feb 21, 1961) was formed from the split of the English Beat in 1983. General Public released two albums before they split.

In 1994, General Public reunited and had a surprise hit single with their UB40-style interpretation of the Staple Singers' "I'll Take You There," taken from the *Threesome* soundtrack. — *William Ruhlmann*

● **All the Rage** / 1984 / IRS ◆◆◆◆
The vocal duo from the English Beat turn in an album of passionate pop-rock, little of which bears the ska style of the parent group. Most effective are the uptempo, Motown-style songs, especially the Top 30 hit "Tenderness." — *William Ruhlmann*

Hand to Mouth / 1986 / IRS ◆◆◆
Although it still has some of the pop smarts that informed *All the Rage*, General Public has toned down their ska and reggae roots, making *Hand to Mouth* a more professional, but less exciting, album. — *Stephen Thomas Erlewine*

Rub It Better / 1995 / Epic

Generation X

Group, Punk
An early London punk band (1978-1981), Generation X featured Billy Idol and Tony James (later to form Sigue Sigue Sputnik). Often criticized as being too commercially minded, Gen X was definitely the smoothest and most pop-oriented of their rebellious crowd. Their first album is considered the best, with the U.S. version offering a slightly improved song set. Their third and last, *Kiss Me Deadly*, was more an Idol/James project than a band effort and was produced by Keith Forsey, who shaped Idol's solo sound. This album contained an early version of "Dancing with Myself," which was eventually Idol's first big solo pop success. As to whether they were a band of crass opportunists or true champions of the punk spirit, Billy Idol's career and Sigue Sigue Sputnik's dubious distinction of having the first advertisement on a pop record speak volumes. — *Scott Bultman*

○ **Generation X** / 1979 / Chrysalis ◆◆◆◆
Generation X had punk attitude and subject matter on their debut album, which includes their answer song to the Who, "Your Generation," and the generic "One Hundred Punks." But the group's music already had more of a melodic mainstream rock sound than punk's raw assault, and frontman Billy Idol's snarl was straight out of Elvis Presley. — *William Ruhlmann*

Valley of the Dolls / 1979 / Chrysalis ◆◆◆

Kiss Me Deadly / 1981 / Chrysalis ◆◆◆
Idol and bassist Brian James rehearse for their post-Gen X careers, respectively as a solo artist and as the leader of Sigue Sigue Sputnik. This album contains the dance hit "Dancing with Myself." — *William Ruhlmann*

● **Best of Generation X** / 1985 / Chrysalis ◆◆◆◆
Collecting the highlights from their three uneven albums as well as their EP, *Best of Generation X* features nearly everything of value the band recorded. — *Stephen Thomas Erlewine*

Genesis

Group, Art-Rock/Progressive-Rock, Pop/Rock
Genesis has been both a successful progressive art-rock band of the 1970s and a successful pop/rock band of the 1980s and '90s, though fans of their earlier work and of their later work might not share the same taste in music. The group's evolution began at the elite British prep school Charterhouse, attended by all of its original members—Tony Banks (b.Mar 27, 1951, East Heatbly, Sussex, England) (keyboards), Peter Gabriel (b.May 13, 1950, London, England) (vocals), Anthony Phillips (guitar), Mike Rutherford (b.Oct 2, 1950) (guitar), and Chris Stewart (replaced by John Silver) (drums). This lineup signed to Decca Records in the U.K. and released *From Genesis to Revelation* (March 1969). Leaving school and turning professional, the group replaced Silver with John Mayhew, signed to Charisma Records, and released *Trespass* (October 1970). But by the time it appeared, Phillips and Silver had dropped out and been replaced by Steve Hackett (b. Feb 12, 1950, London, England) (guitar) and Phil Collins (b. Jan 31, 1951, London, England) (drums), and this unit made the third album, *Nursery Cryme* (November 1972).

Up to this point, Genesis hadn't sold enough records to make the charts, but they developed a highly visual stage show centered on Gabriel and toured extensively. Their fourth album, *Foxtrot* (October 1972), finally broke into the U.K. charts, and from then on they were a big success in their native country. Their live show was documented on *Genesis Live* (June 1973), which soared into the U.K. Top Ten. (From here on, every new Genesis album would reach the Top Ten in Britain.)

Selling England by the Pound (November 1973) spawned Genesis's first U.K. single hit, "I Know What I Like (In Your Wardrobe)," and was their first album to chart in the U.S., where it eventually went gold. An even greater success was the two-LP concept album *The Lamb Lies Down on Broadway* (November 1974). Then, just as Genesis seemed to be entering the top ranks of '70s rock groups, Peter Gabriel quit to start a solo career.

The remaining quartet auditioned singers but finally settled on drummer Phil Collins, whose voice bore some similarity to Gabriel's. They returned to action with *A Trick of the Tail* (March 1976), which turned out to be their most successful album yet. After *Wind and Wuthering* (January 1977) and a second live set, *Seconds Out* (November 1977), Hackett also decamped, and the remaining trio of Banks, Rutherford, and Collins continued on as Genesis, augmenting themselves with hired musicians on stage.

As their next album, *And Then There Were Three* (March 1978), demonstrated, fans liked Genesis even better as a trio than they had as a quartet or quintet. The album went platinum and produced Genesis's first U.S. Top 40 hit, "Follow You, Follow Me"; in the U.K., it was their first Top Ten hit.

By the time of *Duke* (April 1980), any resemblance to the art-rock style of the early Genesis was gone, and the result was another million-seller in the U.S. In the U.K., *Duke* was the first Genesis album to go to #1, and each of the band's next four studio albums would do the same.

Genesis's status was only enhanced by *Face Value* (February 1981), Collins's debut solo album, which was a far bigger hit than any Genesis album so far. Nevertheless, he stayed with the group, which now began to alternate periods of solo and band work. (Mike Rutherford achieved separate success as of the release of the self-titled debut album by his spin-off group, Mike & the Mechanics, in November 1985.)

Not surprisingly, *Genesis* (November 1981), the next Genesis album, was the group's biggest hit yet, soaring into the U.S. Top Ten. *Three Sides Live* (June 1982) was another concert collection, followed by *Genesis* (October 1983), which featured the group's first U.S. Top Ten hit, "That's All!"

Three years passed before the release of *Invisible Touch* (June 1986), long enough to build up tremendous demand among fans, who bought five million copies of it in the U.S. alone and put five of its songs into the Top Ten, including the #1 title song, "Throwing It All Away," "Land of Confusion," "Tonight, Tonight, Tonight," and "In Too Deep."

Genesis waited five years before releasing its next album, *We Can't Dance* (October 1991), which did not match the success of its predecessor, though with three million in U.S. sales and another five chart singles, including the Top Ten hit "I Can't Dance," it didn't do too badly. Following a world tour, Genesis released a two-part concert album under the title *Live/The Way We Walk, Volume One: The Shorts* (November 1992) which contained more concise pop songs, while *Volume Two: The Longs* (February 1993) contained more extended performances.

Genesis's popular momentum seemed to be slowing in the mid-'90s, as group albums and spin-off records ceased to trace new sales peaks with each release. But both its more challenging early work and its more radio-friendly later work had a major impact on the music of the 1970s and '80s. —*William Ruhlmann*

From Genesis to Revelation / Mar. 1969 / DCC ♦♦
The members of Genesis—Peter Gabriel, Tony Banks, Michael Rutherford, Anthony Phillips, and John Silver—were still teenagers and still attending the British boarding school Charterhouse when this, their debut album, was released in England in March 1969. It is thus juvenilia by definition and is further compromised by the record company addition of strings to make it sound like the Moody Blues. But there is already something there. Gabriel is an expressive singer, and the band turns in melodic pop songs that are surprisingly sophisticated. (The album was not released in the United States until August 1974. It has been re-released frequently, sometimes under the title *In the Beginning*.) —*William Ruhlmann*

Trespass / Oct. 1970 / MCA ♦♦
Genesis had changed considerably by the October 1970 release of their second album (which was their first to be issued in the U.S., by the Impulse! division of ABC-Dunhill Records, now part of MCA). For one thing, they'd finished school, turned professional and started playing out. For another, drummer John Silver had left and been replaced for the album by John Mayhew. (Before the release of *Trespass*, both Mayhew and Anthony Phillips left. The group then recruited guitarist Steve Hackett and former child actor Phil Collins as new drummer.) Genesis' individual sound began to appear on *Trespass*, with its complex structures and long songs. The driving rocker "Knife," at nine minutes the longest track, remains the highlight. —*William Ruhlmann*

Nursery Cryme / Nov. 1971 / Atlantic ♦♦♦
On their third album, released in the U.K. in November 1971 and in the U.S. in May 1972, Genesis is beginning to find a place in the British art-rock movement of the early '70s, as Peter Gabriel constructs elaborate musical set pieces, the most impressive of which is the 10 1/2-minute lead-off track, "The Musical Box." The dense structures, tempo changes, organ/guitar interplay, and fanciful

lyrics are not unlike what Yes was doing at the same time, and fans of that band will find music to their liking here. —*William Ruhlmann*

Foxtrot / Oct. 1972 / Atlantic ♦♦♦
On its fourth album, Genesis's ambitious music finally starts to show individual identity and accomplishment, mixing elaborate arrangements with stirring rhythms and highly poetic lyrics. Contains "Watcher of the Skies" and the 22-minute "Supper's Ready." —*William Ruhlmann*

☆ **Selling England by the Pound** / Jan. 1973 / Atlantic ♦♦♦♦♦
One of the best examples of '70s British art-rock, this album incorporates a variety of styles, showcasing the musical dexterity of the players as well as the lyrics to story-songs like "I Know What I Like (In Your Wardrobe)," the first Genesis British hit. —*William Ruhlmann*

Genesis: Live / Jun. 1973 / Atlantic ♦♦♦
Genesis' first live album was recorded in February 1973 and released in the summer in England, where it became the group's first Top Ten hit. In the U.S., it was held back from release until the spring of 1974, after *Selling England by the Pound* had begun to establish Genesis stateside. Although it lacks the visual element of Peter Gabriel's costumes and theatricality that made Genesis so effective, the album features some of its standout material of the time, including "Get 'Em out by Friday," "Musical Box," and "The Knife." —*William Ruhlmann*

★ **The Lamb Lies Down on Broadway** / Nov. 1974 / Atlantic ♦♦♦♦♦
This, the last Genesis album with Peter Gabriel, is a sprawling two-disc thematic album concerning a character named Rael. Keeping with that theme, it includes pastiches of Broadway show music, plus the group's typical mixture of folk, rock, and classical influences. If this is not the first Gabriel Genesis album to buy, it ultimately may prove the most satisfying. —*William Ruhlmann*

Trick of the Tail / Mar. 1976 / Atlantic ♦♦♦
At the time of its release in March 1976, Genesis' seventh studio album was a remarkable document if only because the group had managed to survive the departure of its frontman, Peter Gabriel, not only by locating a worthy (and similar-sounding) vocalist in drummer Phil Collins, but also by writing material that was respectable, even if it lacked Gabriel's vision and imagination. As a result, the album hit #3 in the U.K. and maintained the band's following in the U.S., assuring them a future. In retrospect, it isn't a very impressive effort (with the exception of "Robbery, Assault And Battery," which has some of the old spirit), although it gives hints of the pop assembly line Genesis would develop in the coming years. —*William Ruhlmann*

Wind and Wuthering / Jan. 1977 / Atlantic ♦♦
Less impressive than the first Genesis quartet album, *A Trick of the Tail*, *Wind and Wuthering* nevertheless marked another step in the band's gradual transformation into more of a pop act, containing its first U.S. (and only its second U.K.) chart single, "Your Own Special Way." —*William Ruhlmann*

Seconds Out / Nov. 1977 / Atlantic ♦♦
On its second live album (a double), recorded in 1976 and 1977, Genesis tried to make the case that its two manifestations, Genesis-with-Peter Gabriel and Genesis-without-Peter Gabriel, were actually one entity. They didn't really succeed, sounding instead like, on the one hand, the new post-Gabriel Genesis on side one and most of side four, and on the other hand, a Gabriel/Genesis soundalike band on sides two and three, on which Phil Collins handled Gabriel's vocals on such favorites as "Supper's Ready." —*William Ruhlmann*

And Then There Were Three / Mar. 1978 / Atlantic ♦♦♦
The birth of the modern Genesis, a pop-rock trio led by singer/drummer Phil Collins, playing tightly constructed, short, catchy songs. The best of the bunch here is "Follow You, Follow Me," a hit on both sides of the Atlantic. (The first Genesis gold album in the U.S.) —*William Ruhlmann*

Duke / Apr. 1980 / Atlantic ♦♦♦
Released in April 1980, *Duke* found Genesis completely geared up as a maker of concise, appealing pop singles, and it was an immediate, across-the-board hit, topping the U.K. chart and almost making the U.S. Top 10, while the singles "Misunderstanding" and "Turn It On Again" became radio favorites on both sides of the Atlantic. —*William Ruhlmann*

● **Abacab** / Sep. 1981 / Atlantic ✦✦✦✦

Genesis had perfected its rhythmic, densely chorded, passionate trio music with this, their first U.S. million-seller and Top Ten hit, which includes the Top 40 singles "Abacab," "No Reply at All," and "Man on the Corner." — *William Ruhlmann*

Three Sides Live / Jun. 1982 / Atlantic ✦✦✦

On its third live album (another double), Genesis brought listeners up to date on the trio version of the group and its recent hit singles from *Abacab* and *Duke*. The U.K. version of the album (Charisma GE 2002), despite the title, was an all-live album, while the American version (Atlantic SD 2-2000), had three live sides and a fourth side of studio material, including the Top 40 hit "Paperlate" (which appeared in the U.K. as part of an EP called *3 By 3*). — *William Ruhlmann*

○ **Genesis** / Oct. 1983 / Atlantic ✦✦✦✦

Genesis' third straight #1 studio album in the U.K. was also its biggest seller yet in the U.S., making the Top 10 and selling three million copies. Its big U.S. hit was "That's All," while Britain preferred "Mama." "Illegal Alien" and "Taking It All Too Hard" also charted. — *William Ruhlmann*

○ **Invisible Touch** / Jun. 1986 / Virgin ✦✦✦✦

The biggest Genesis hit to date, this multi-million-selling release features five Top Five hits, including the number one title track, "Throwing It All Away," "Land of Confusion," "Tonight, Tonight, Tonight," and "In Too Deep." — *William Ruhlmann*

We Can't Dance / Oct. 28, 1991 / Atlantic ✦✦✦

Genesis' first album in five years was another enormous hit, even if it failed to match the sales of 1986's *Invisible Touch*. In the U.K., it was the group's fifth straight studio album to hit number one; in the U.S., it was their fifth straight Top Ten and sold four million copies. "No Son of Mine" (something of an answer to "The Living Years," by Mike Rutherford's splinter group, Mike and the Mechanics) broke the group's string of Top Five singles by getting only to number 12, but it was followed by the number seven "I Can't Dance," as well as three more Top 25 hits: "Hold on My Heart," "Jesus He Knows Me" (a satire of evangelist preachers), and "Never a Time." — *William Ruhlmann*

Genesis Live: The Way We Walk, Vol. 1 (The Shorts) / Nov. 17, 1992 / Atlantic ✦✦

Live: The Way We Walk—Vol. 1: The Shorts is the first part of a two-disc live document of Genesis, supporting their 1991 album *We Can't Dance*. It concentrates on the shorter hit singles and will appeal to their mainstream fans. —*AMG*

Genesis Live: The Way We Walk, Vol. 2 (The Longs) / Feb. 9, 1993 / Atlantic ✦✦

Live: The Way We Walk—Vol. 2: The Longs features the extended compositions that made Genesis a trailblazer in the progressive rock field during the '70s. Fans of those albums will prefer this volume to the first installment. —*AMG*

Gentle Giant

Group, Art-Rock/Progressive-Rock
Gentle Giant (formed 1970) brought art-rock to new levels of mathematical complexity. Their pseudo-medieval arrangements and dissonant instrumental voicings dominated most of their albums, but later efforts found the band simplifying their sound into something less daunting. Radio-consultant Lee Abrams worked with the group's last album, *Civilian*, which failed commercially while alienating their cult following with its more mainstream sound. Lead-singer Derek Shulman has since gone on to a successful career as a major-record-label executive. —*Rick Clark*

Gentle Giant / 1970 / Polydor ✦✦
Acquiring the Taste / 1971 / Polydor ✦✦✦
Three Friends / 1972 / Columbia ✦✦✦
● **Octopus** / 1972 / Columbia ✦✦✦✦

The dull, small-sounding production of this album tends to mask the power of some of the material. However, mathematically inclined art-rockers may find pleasure in tracks like "The Advent of Panurge," "Raconteur Troubadour," and "Knots," with its complicated vocal-round interplay. —*Rick Clark*

In a Glass House / 1973 / Columbia ✦✦✦
The Power and the Glory / 1974 / Capitol ✦✦
A Giant Step / 1975 / Vertigo ✦✦
○ **Free Hand** / 1975 / One Way ✦✦✦✦

In spite of the band's continuing fascination with rhythmic complication, *Free Hand* contains a more rockish feel. "On Reflection" and "His Last Voyage" are nice showcases for the band's vocal arrangements and considerable dynamic performance skills. — *Rick Clark*

Interview / 1976 / Capitol ✦✦✦
○ **Pretentious** / 1977 / Vertigo ✦✦✦✦
Giant Edits / 1977 / Capitol ✦✦✦
Live: Playing the Fool / 1977 / Capitol ✦✦✦
The Missing Piece / 1977 / Capitol ✦✦
Giant for a Day! / 1978 / Capitol ✦✦✦
Civilian / 1980 / Columbia ✦✦
Greatest Hits / 1981 / Vertigo ✦✦✦

Barbara George

b. Aug. 16, 1942, New Orleans, LA
Soul, New Orleans R&B
George's "I Know (You Don't Love Me No More)" topped the R&B charts in 1961 and has proven a popular cover item ever since. The New Orleans native had never been in the studio before she brought her extremely catchy melody to Harold Battiste's fledgling A.F.O. label. Benefiting from her pleasing, unpolished vocal and a melodic cornet solo by Melvin Lastie, the tune caught fire, vaulting high on pop playlists. Amazingly, nothing else George did ever dented the charts, although she waxed some listenable followups for A.F.O. and Sue. —*Bill Dahl*

● **I Know (You Don't Love Me Anymore)** / 1962 / Collectables ✦✦✦✦

This catchy New Orleans R&B from the early '60s features coy and charming vocals by George. —*Bill Dahl*

Lowell George

d. Jun. 29, 1979
Rock & Roll
As Little Feat was disbanding in late 1978, their lead guitarist/songwriter Lowell George recorded a solo album, *Thanks, I'll Eat It Here*, that sounded as loose and funky as the band in their prime. After its release the following year, he set out on tour to support the album. Sadly, George died of a heart attack while on the road; he left behind a body of gritty, eclectic, and funky rock & roll. On the first five Little Feat albums, his songwriting and instrumental talents are more apparent than on his solo effort, yet that doesn't detract from the record's pleasures. — *Stephen Thomas Erlewine*

● **Thanks I'll Eat It Here** / 1979 / Warner Brothers ✦✦✦✦

While it's surprisingly short on original songs, Lowell George's solo album *Thanks I'll Eat Here* is as relaxed and funky as any Little Feat album from the last half of the 1970s. —*Stephen Thomas Erlewine*

Lightning-Rod Man / 1993 / Bizarre ✦✦✦

Before emerging as a cult star in the 1970s, Lowell George was a presence on the L.A. folk-rock/psychedelic scene in the 1960s. With his group the Factory, he only managed to release one single during this time. "Lightning-Rod Man" rescues 15 tunes cut by this unit, including the single and over a dozen outtakes and demos. Almost exclusively original material, most of these tracks were recorded in 1966 and 1967. They show the group pursuing a slightly eccentric folk-rock vision that neither bears much similarity to George's more famous work nor matches the best work done in this genre by their L.A. peers. At times they echo Kaleidoscope in their vaguely spacy, good-natured folkish rock; just as often, they take cues from Captain Beefheart and Frank Zappa in their skewed blues-rock and obtuse songwriting. In fact, Zappa himself produced and played on a couple of the demos, and onetime Mothers of Invention members Elliot Ingber and Roy Estrada show up on a few others. A few songs cut towards the end of the decade feature a heavier, bluesier sound that show George edging in a different direction. An enjoyable vault find, but not a major revelation. —*Richie Unterberger*

Georgia Satellites

Group, Rock & Roll

At a time when rock & roll didn't care about its roots, the Georgia Satellites came crashing into the charts with a surprise hit single to remind everybody where the music had come from. The hit single, 1986's "Keep Your Hands to Yourself," rocked as hard as an old Chuck Berry song, as well as being almost as clever. The Satellites weren't a back-to-basic roots band, either—their straightforward sound borrowed equally from Berry, the Rolling Stones, the Faces, Little Feat, and AC/DC, with a Southern backwoods bent. At their best, the Satellites were just a damn good rock & roll band, driven by the classic, yet fresh, songwriting of lead singer/guitarist Dan Baird. On the strength of "Keep Your Hands to Yourself," their first major-label album sold well, but the follow-up, *Open All Night*, did not; radio and MTV had treated the band as a kind of novelty—a bunch of hicks kicking out rock & roll offered a break between the slick pop-metal of Bon Jovi and Peter Gabriel's introspective pop. By the time they released *Open All Night* in 1988, no one was interested, even if the album was only slightly weaker than the debut. After one more album, 1989's *In the Land of Salvation and Sin*, the band called it quits. Guitarist Rick Richards joining Izzy Stradlin's Ju Ju Hounds three years later; Baird pursued a solo career and had a small hit in late 1992 with "I Love You Period." —*Stephen Thomas Erlewine*

○ **Georgia Satellites** / 1986 / Elektra ✦✦✦✦
Dirty Rolling Stones-like guitar grunge played by Rick Richards and topped by the adenoidal singing of Dan Baird. Especially enjoyable on the hits "Keep Your Hands to Yourself" and "Battleship Chains." —*William Ruhlmann*

Open All Night / 1988 / Elektra ✦✦✦
The Georgia Satellites' follow-up to their surprise hit is as loose and rocking as their previous album, but wasn't as successful. The few who did buy the album were treated to some of the rawest and funniest pure rock & roll of the 1980s, highlighted by the sleazy humor of "Mon Cheri" and the title track, as well as the stomping cover of the Beatles' "Don't Pass Me By." —*Stephen Thomas Erlewine*

In the Land of Salvation and Sin / 1989 / Elektra ✦✦✦
On the Georgia Satellites' final album, Dan Baird decides that he's a songwriter like Lowell George—a traditionalist who adds a healthy dose of ironic humor without losing respect for the music's roots. While his ambitions are ripe with pretensions, his band keeps him in check, and *In the Land of Salvation and Sin* is a terrific record, full of intelligent songs that are never pompous and never fail to rock like hell. —*Stephen Thomas Erlewine*

● **Let It Rock: The Best of The Georgia Satellites** / 1993 / Elektra ✦✦✦✦
Most of the band's best tracks are on this generous compilation, which not only features their hits ("Keep Your Hands to Yourself" and "Battleship Chains"), but also includes rarities like their sublime John Fogerty medley "Almost Saturday Night/Rockin' All Over the World" from the out-of-print *Rubaiyat* collection. —*Stephen Thomas Erlewine*

Gerardo

Rap

A rap performer whose Latino-flavored macho posturings (he frequently performs barechested with his pants unzipped) made him a minor sensation on both the dance and pop scene in 1991 with "Rico Suave" and "We Want the Funk." —*Cub Koda*

● **Mo' Ritmo** / 1991 / Interscope ✦✦✦✦
A hard mix of soul and Latin music, with guest George Clinton. —*Bil Carpenter*

Dos / Interscope ✦✦
Latino pop rapper Gerardo tried to follow the surprising success of *Mo Ritmo'* with *Dos*, and found that you can only ride a fluke so long. There was widespread audience indifference to this disc, which is understandable, since it's just the same feeble raps and limp rhymes foisted on an audience who enjoyed "Rico Suave" and "We Want the Funk," but were now weary of the formula. English, Spanish or Spanglish, teen-pop dreck still translates the same way. —*Ron Wynn*

Lisa Germano

Alternative Pop/Rock

Violinist Lisa Germano became known for her fluid, gutsy style

through her work with John Mellencamp, which is captured on the *Big Daddy* and *Lonesome Jubilee* albums. Germano's solo work is much darker and atmospheric than Mellencamp's albums; her 1991 solo debut, *On the Way Down from Moon Palace*, displayed some promising songwriting along with her acclaimed instrumental prowess. Germano's second album, 1993's *Happiness*, was even better, but the record didn't sell very well when it was first released on Capitol, prompting her to change record labels in 1994. She signed with 4AD, who released a resequenced and remixed *Happiness* in the spring of 1994; the new version of the album emphasized her music's underlying dark melancholy, which the original version only hinted at. —*Stephen Thomas Erlewine*

On the Way Down from Moon Palace / 1991 / Major Bill ✦✦✦
Words that come to mind on Germano's debut album—haunting, delicate, disturbing, abrasive, sparse, intimate, beautiful. The instrumentals, like the title track, "Dark Irie," and "Simply Tony," have a marvelous fragile beauty, while "Dig My Own Grave" is a herky jerky, rude acoustic rocker. Other highlights include "The Other One," "Guessing Game (Or the Music Business)," and "Hangin' with a Demon." —*Rick Clark*

● **Happiness** / 1993 / Capitol/EMI ✦✦✦✦
Germano's sophomore effort is a harrowing descent into black humor, anger, and general miserableness. With her deadpan little girl voice, Germano makes "You Make Me Want to Wear Dresses" sound like that is the last thing she wants to do, while she drives the point home on the transcendent dissonance of "Puppet." —*Rick Clark*

○ **Geek the Girl** / 1994 / 4AD ✦✦✦✦
Geek the Girl manages to eclipse both of Germano's previous albums by accentuating both the folkiness in her music and its awkward, dreamy qualities. The album is a song cycle about a young girl trying to come of age, both emotionally and sexually, but the story never overwhelms the tensely charming songs. It's musically richer than the average alternative angst-fest, incorporating traditional Italian melodies into Germano's folky songwriting, which touches on everything from unstructured stream-of-consciousness melodies to tight pop songs. But what makes *Geek the Girl* even more satisfying is that Germano doesn't take the easy way out and wallow in self-pity. Instead, she offers a glimmer of hope with the last two songs, making *Geek the Girl* a richly rewarding and moving record. —*Stephen Thomas Erlewine*

The Germs

Group, Punk

One of the first (but certainly not the best) Los Angeles punk groups. Lead singer Darby Crash was a live-fast-die-young nihilist who bemoaned of the stodginess of his sunny suburban surroundings. The group recorded from 1977 until 1979, when Crash died of a heroin overdose, just like his idol Sid Vicious. —*John Floyd*

○ **Gi** / 1979 / Slash ✦✦✦✦
It captures the black, foreboding explosiveness of West Coast punk during the late-'70s and highlights the sandpaper cries of Darby Crash (who died of a self-induced drug overdose shortly after the album was recorded). —*David Szatmary*

What We Do Is Secret / 1981 / Slash ✦✦✦

Germicide: Live at the Whisky 1977 / 1982 / ROIR ✦✦

● **M.I.A.** / Aug. 3, 1993 / Slash ✦✦✦✦
Everything the seminal L.A. punk band ever recorded is on *M.I.A.*, an exhaustive single-disc collection. At their best, the Germs were remarkably good—powerful, gut-wrenching guitars with surprisingly incisive lyrics; at their worst (as on the live tracks), they were messy and almost unlistenable. The Joan Jett-produced "G.I." holds up the best, but there are many quality tracks. It's too much for a single sitting, but *M.I.A.* has more than its share of great punk rock. —*Stephen Thomas Erlewine*

Gerry & the Pacemakers

Group, British Invasion

The second group out of the Liverpool starting gate in the early '60s, Gerry and the Pacemakers shared manager Brian Epstein and producer George Martin with the Beatles and even got their hand-me-down material—their first (U.K.) hit was "How Do You Do It," a song the Fab Four had declined to release. It was a #1 for Gerry.

The group was formed in 1959 by singer and guitarist Gerry

Marsden (b. Sep 24, 1942), with his brother Freddie (b. Oct 23, 1940) on drums, and Les Chadwick (b. May 11, 1943) on bass. Pianist Les Maguire (b. Dec 27, 1941) completed the lineup in 1961. They followed the same path to success as the Beatles, including making trips to Hamburg and hooking up with Epstein and Martin. And shortly after the Beatles topped the charts with "Please Please Me," Gerry and the Pacemakers did so with "How Do You Do It."

Like the Beatles, the group went over to America in 1964 and debuted on the "Ed Sullivan Show," resulting in a hit with their ballad "Don't Let the Sun Catch You Crying." Like the Beatles, they then made a movie (theirs was called *Ferry Cross the Mersey*). But unlike the Beatles, Gerry and the Pacemakers faltered commercially after 1964 and failed to develop musically the way their Liverpool neighbors did. As a result, they split up in 1966, with Gerry going solo. By 1975, he had put together a new Pacemakers group and toured on the oldies circuit, his voice still appealing and the Mersey Beat still bouncing. —*William Ruhlmann*

○ **The EP Collection** / 1987 / See For Miles ✦✦✦✦
A truly definitive collection, with all the hits and the most interesting non-hits. Includes the ultra-rare live *Gerry in California* concert recording from 1966. (Import) —*Bruce Eder*

● **Best of Gerry & The Pacemakers: The Definitive Collection** / 1991 / EMI America ✦✦✦✦
The title promises more than it really delivers in content, if not sound. It'll do for the casual listener. —*Bruce Eder*

Geto Boys

Group, Rap, Urban
Houston's Geto Boys have at times rivaled Public Enemy, 2 Live Crew, and Ice-T for their ability to generate controversial publicity. Among the most outrageous, outlandish, and frequently offensive gangsta-rap crews, they've released songs that include violent and perverse subject matter that some may find distasteful. They've also had problems with stores refusing to stock their albums, and in some cases even labels refusing to distribute them. The future of the group is now in doubt; Scarface's single album has been a big hit, Willie Dee has split to do a solo release and the remaining Geto Boys are working on their own projects. The inevitable greatest hits album appeared in 1993, which was an indication that there wouldn't be any fresh Geto Boys material for a long time, if ever. —*Ron Wynn*

○ **Grip It! on That Level** / 1990 / Def American ✦✦✦✦
The Geto Boys hit the national spotlight with this debut, which disgusted many, frightened a few others and won them a niche in hip-hop's growing "gangsta" constituency. From the sheer repulsiveness of "Let a Ho be a Ho" and "Do It Like a G.O." to the frightening nihilism of "Mind of a Lunatic" and "Life In the Fast Lane," this was one group definitely uninterested in pop/mainstream approval. The rapping ranged from surly to sleazy, the beats were sometimes popping, sometimes slashing, and even the most loyal fan would have a tough time finding something good to say about "Trigga Happy Nigga" or "Scarface." —*Ron Wynn*

○ **We Can't Be Stopped** / 1991 / Rap-A-Lot ✦✦✦✦
It contains their best song, the disturbing "Mind Playing Tricks on Me." —*Dan Heilman*

● **Geto Boys the Best Uncut Dope** / 1992 / Rap-A-Lot ✦✦✦✦
With various members opting for solo projects and the group disintegrating, Rap-A-Lot Records primed the pump one last time with what was essentially a greatest hits CD. It wasn't totally a retrospective because it included "Damn It Feels Good to Be a Gangsta," the ultimate genre definition piece and the last significant Geto Boys composition. "And My Word," "Actions Speak Louder Than Words" and "The Unseen" were other fresh jams that joined the Geto Boys anthems "Mind Playing Tricks on Me," "Assassins," "Scarface" and "Mind of a Lunatic," among others. The old/new menu made this the one to grab if one Geto Boys CD is all you need. —*Ron Wynn*

Till Death Do Us Part / Rap-A-Lot ✦✦✦
The Geto Boys' last album finds them expanding on the success of "Mind Playing Tricks on Me" with "Six Feet Deep," but more frequently, it keeps to their standard, grotesque gangsta rap with "Murder Ave." and "This Dick's for You." On these tracks, the whole shock formula seems like a worn-out trick and points the way to their eventual disbanding. —*Stephen Thomas Erlewine*

Ghost of an American Airman

Group, Pop/Rock
A powerful four-man group from Belfast that released its debut CD, *Life under Giants*, on the Hollywood label in 1992. Fronted by highly animated lead-singer Dodge, Ghost of an American Airman issued a 12-inch single, "I Hear Voices," in 1987 on Recoil Records. *Someday*, released the next year on the Plain Paper label, had a more infectious feel than their more mature, self-titled major-label disc. —*Bill Dahl*

● **Life under Giants** / 1992 / Hollywood ✦✦✦✦
Relentless alternative rock from northern Ireland. —*Steve Aldrich*

Ghost of an American Airman / 1993 / Hollywood ✦✦✦

Someday / Plain Paper ✦✦✦
This infectious out-of-print album is virtually impossible to grow tired of. —*Steve Aldrich*

Giant

Group, Hard Rock, Heavy Metal
Hard-rock quartet led by brothers Dann and David Huff (vocals and drums, respectively), both from Nashville. The group's other members are keyboardist Alan Pasqua and bassist Mike Brignardello; all are veteran session musicians. In 1990, the group had a top-20 single with the ballad "I'll See You In My Dreams." Dann Huff, Pasqua, and Brignardello all played on Amy Grant's *Heart In Motion*. —*Steve Huey*

Last of the Runaways / 1989 / A&M ✦✦✦
This debut effort contains the hit "I'll See You In My Dreams." Fans of mainstream AOR rock (a la Journey, Heart, Van Halen) should like this effort. "I'm a Believer" is a solid showcase for the band's journeyman chops, particularly lead vocalist/guitarist Dan Huff. —*Rick Clark*

Time to Burn / Dec. 1991 / Epic ✦✦

Steve Gibbons

Rock & Roll
I think it was a *Rolling Stone* critic who called Steve Gibbons "The English Bob Seger," which, as descriptions go, could have been much worse, but is really based on superficialities. Both guys are basically unpretentious, blue-collar rockers who achieved notoriety (Seger much more so than Gibbons) as veterans. But Gibbons' career wasn't long enough to witness the kind of decline and formulaic emptiness that marked Seger's career after 1980. Still, for a career that lasted for five albums, he didn't do too badly; three of them are good, and one (*Down in the Bunker*) is great. Backed by a crack band that included former Move bassist Trevor Burton, Gibbons fancied himself a modern day rock & roll outlaw: dark features, surly countenance, mean disposition. His songs were essentially Chuck Berry updates (in some cases, simply Chuck Berry covers) about thugs, dealers, and good lovin' gone bad. Tight with Who bassist John Entwistle, Gibbons was able to land a contract with the Who's American label MCA and share the same management company. The trouble was that being the English Bob Seger meant little, if anything, to most American rock fans (who preferred their own Seger by a wide margin), and Gibbons' career never amounted to much here; he was fairly popular in England, though. His last LP, 1980's *Street Parade*, was disappointing, and Gibbons seems to have vanished into thin air. —*John Dougan*

Short Stories / 1971 / Wizard ✦✦

Any Road Up / 1976 / MCA ✦✦✦

Rolling on / 1977 / Polydor ✦✦✦

Caught in the Act / 1977 / MCA ✦✦✦

● **Down in the Bunker** / 1978 / Polydor ✦✦✦✦
Although Gibbons' MCA recordings (*Any Road Up*, *Rollin'*, and *Caught in The Act*) are well worth searching for, if there was one Gibbons record that encapsulated what this journeyman rocker was all about, it was *Down in the Bunker*. Caustic, cool, with just a touch of goofball macho swagger, this was a critically lauded but publicly ignored record and one of the lost gems of the late '70s. For fans of unregenerate roots-rock or pub-rockers looking for a new buzz. —*John Dougan*

Street Parade / 1980 / RCA ✦✦✦

Saints & Sinners / 1981 / RCA ✦✦

On the Loose / 1986 / Magnum Force ✦✦

Debbie Gibson

b. Aug. 3, 1970, Long Island, NY
Dance-Pop, Pop/Rock

Debbie Gibson became a pop phenomenon in the late '80s, scoring a string of hit singles when she was only 17. Although she was still a teenager, Gibson showed signs of being a talented pop craftsman, capable of making catchy dance-pop in the style of Madonna, as well as lush, orchestrated ballads. Gibson's time at the top of the charts was brief, but it was quite successful, producing five Top Five singles, including two number ones, and two multi-platinum albums.

Gibson began writing songs in her early childhood, taking piano lessons from Morton Estrin (who also taught Billy Joel) from the age of five. At the age of six she wrote "Make Sure You Know Your Classroom," but it was "I Come from America," which she wrote at age 12, that earned wide recognition for her talents. "I Come from America" won $1,000 in a songwriting contest, prompting her parents to sign a management contract with Doug Breithart. Breithart helped Gibson learn several instruments, as well as teaching her how to arrange, engineer, and produce records; she would record over 100 of her own songs by 1985.

While she was still in high school, Debbie Gibson signed with Atlantic Records and began recording her debut album with producer Fred Zarr. "Only in My Dreams," her debut single, climbed to number four when it was released in the summer of 1987. It was followed in the fall by the dance-oriented "Shake Your Love," which also peaked at number four; the single also became a hit in Britain, reaching number seven. *Out of the Blue,* her debut album, was released in the fall of 1987, and by the spring of 1988, it had reached the American Top Ten. The title track became a number three hit that spring and it was followed by her first number one single, "Foolish Beat," making her the youngest artist ever to write, perform, and produce a number one single. Following the success of "Foolish Beat," Gibson graduated from Calhoun high school in Merrick, NY, with honors. "Staying Together," released in the fall of 1988, didn't perform as well as her previous four singles, stalling at number 22. By the end of 1988, *Out of the Blue* had gone triple platinum in the U.S.

"Lost in Your Eyes," the first single from her second album *Electric Youth,* became Gibson's biggest hit early in 1989, staying at number one for three weeks. *Electric Youth,* released in the spring of 1989, also hit number one, spending five weeks at th top of the charts. However, her popularity began to slip by the end of the year—"Electric Youth" just missed the Top Ten and her next two singles did progressively worse, with "We Could Be Together" unable to climb past number 71. At the end of 1990, she released her third album, *Anything Is Possible;* it peaked at number 41. Two years later, she released *Body Mind Soul,* which produced only one minor hit single, "Losin' Myself." After its release, she starred in a production of *Les Miserables.* Gibson returned to pop music in 1995, recording a duet of the Soft Boys' "I Wanna Destroy You" with the Los Angeles punk band the Circle Jerks and releasing a considerably softer album of her own, *Think with Your Heart,* which marked a departure from the dance-pop that made her famous. —*Stephen Thomas Erlewine*

● **Out of the Blue** / 1987 / Atlantic ✦✦✦✦

A smart, enthusiastic debut, Gibson has yet to top it. —*Dan Heilman*

○ **Electric Youth** / 1989 / Atlantic ✦✦✦✦

While it wasn't as carefree and effortless as her debut, *Electric Youth* contained several good hit singles, including "Lost In Your Eyes," "No More Rhyme," and the title track. —*Stephen Thomas Erlewine*

Anything Is Possible / 1990 / Atlantic ✦✦

Body Mind Soul / 1993 / Atlantic ✦

Giles-Giles-Fripp

Group, Art-Rock/Progressive-Rock

This trio formed late in 1967 by future King Crimson alumni Robert Fripp, Michael Giles, and Peter Giles. Their sound was a mix of elegant psychedelia and light jazz, rather akin to the Moody Blues. With the addition of Ian McDonald, Greg Lake, and Peter Sinsfield, the trio evolved into King Crimson. —*Bruce Eder*

The Cheerful Insanity / 1968 / Deram ✦✦✦

The Cheerful Insanity of Giles, Giles & Fripp is trippy light psychedelia, highlighted by Fripp's spacy, searing "Erudite Eyes" and the light pop of "Little Children." The CD reissue adds six bonus tracks: the previously unreleased "She Is Loaded" and "Under The Sky," and 45 mono and stereo versions of a few of the album cuts. —*Bruce Eder & Richie Unterberger*

Johnny Gill

b. 1967, Washington DC
Urban

Born in Washington, D.C., Johnny Gill was discovered by singer Stacy Lattisaw after singing in his family's group Wings of Faith from age five. His solo career began in 1983 with the Top 30 R&B single "Super Love." In duo with Lattisaw, he scored an R&B Top Ten hit in 1984 with "Perfect Combination." In 1988, Gill joined New Edition, replacing Bobby Brown. In 1989 he sang on two R&B hits: "Where Do We Go from Here," a #1 by Stacy Lattisaw, and "One Love," by George Howard. Gill finally scored as a solo singer in 1990 with the release of his album *Johnny Gill,* which sold a million copies, topped the R&B chart, and made the Top Ten in the pop chart. —*William Ruhlmann*

Perfect Combination / 1983 / Cotillion ✦✦✦

Adolescent pop-soul duet album with Lattisaw. —*Bil Carpenter*

Chemistry / 1985 / Atlantic ✦✦✦

It's worth having merely for the awesome pop ballad "Half Crazy." —*Bil Carpenter*

● **Johnny Gill** / 1990 / Motown ✦✦✦✦

Gill's long-in-coming solo breakthrough, featuring the hits "Rub You the Right Way," "My, My, My," and "Fairweather Friend." —*William Ruhlmann*

Provocative / Jun. 8, 1993 / Motown ✦✦✦

Basically, *Provocative* is a retread of *Johnny Gill,* but it's a retread done right, since Gill's voice is in prime form and the dueling production teams of Jimmy Jam & Terry Lewis and L.A. Reid & Babyface make the music smooth, stylish, and funky. —*Stephen Thomas Erlewine*

David Gilmour

b. Mar. 6, 1944, Cambridge, England
Art-Rock/Progressive-Rock

David Gilmour, lead guitarist of Pink Floyd, is one of rock's most distinctive players with his use of echoes, delays, and distorted sustain. His solo efforts have done well. —*Rick Clark*

David Gilmour / 1978 / Columbia ✦✦✦

This heavily atmospheric guitar rock is in the tradition of his Pink Floyd work. —*Donna DiChario*

● **About Face** / Feb. 1984 / Columbia ✦✦✦✦

More accessible than its predecessor, *About Face* is less about mood and more about well-crafted rock. Many highlights grace this underappreciated effort, including "Blue Light," "Love on the Air," and "All Lovers Are Deranged," which was co-written with Pete Townshend. —*Donna DiChario*

Gin Blossoms

Group, Rock & Roll

After an impressive debut EP, the Gin Blossoms rocketed out of the college pop charts and into the mainstream with their 1993 hit single, "Hey Jealousy." Combining the ringing guitar hooks of the Byrds and R.E.M. with a solid, rootsy drive, the band's breakthrough full-length album, *New Miserable Experience,* was filled with songs equally as strong as "Hey Jealousy," including the second hit single, "Found out About You." *New Miserable Experience* and its singles dominated radio and MTV for the following year—both "Hey Jealousy" and "Found out About You" were in heavy radio rotation nearly a year after their initial release—pushing the sales of their debut album over a million copies. —*Stephen Thomas Erlewine*

Up & Crumbling / 1992 / A&M ✦✦✦

● **New Miserable Experience** / 1992 / A&M ✦✦✦✦

Greg Ginn

Instrumental Rock, Punk, Alternative Pop/Rock

Greg Ginn was one of the most influential figures on independent/alternative rock in the 1980s. With Black Flag, the guitarist established many of the sounds and ethics of hardcore punk, from its faster-louder sound to its staunchly political and independent values. To distribute their band's records, Black Flag founded the SST record label; Ginn effectively controlled the company, determining its artistic direction, as well as reaping its meager financial gains. Throughout the '80s, the label would release some of the most important and influential post-punk bands of the decade, including Hüsker Dü, Sonic Youth, the Minutemen, Dinosaur Jr. and the Meat Puppets. While Black Flag was at the height of their career in the early '80s, Ginn led an instrumental trio called Gone. Both Black Flag and Gone broke up in 1986. The following year Ginn began Cruz Records; by the early '90s, he was the sole owner of SST, Cruz, and New Alliance Records. Ginn began his solo career in 1993 with *Getting Even*; it was followed a few months later by *Dick*. — *Stephen Thomas Erlewine*

Payday / 1993 / Cruz ✦✦✦

○ **Dick** / 1993 / Cruz ✦✦✦✦

● **Getting Even** / Jun. 29, 1993 / Cruz ✦✦✦✦

Girls Against Boys

Group, Alternative Pop/Rock
Girls Against Boys' dual-bass attack and Scott McCloud's wheezy sing-speak vocals (reminiscent of The Fall's Mark E. Smith) produce an energetic, if sometimes noisy, sound that would probably annoy listeners if it weren't for the Baltimore band's great Fugazi-influenced songs. The band has released three albums— *Tropic Of Scorpio*, *Venus Luxure No. 1 Baby*, and *Cruise Yourself*. — *John Bush*

Tropic of Scorpio / 198z / Adult Swim ✦✦✦

Venus Luxure No. 1 Baby / 1994 / Touch & Go ✦✦✦
"Go Be Delighted," "Learned It," "Bulletproof Cupid," and the crunching "Rockets Are Red," are powerful, bass-heavy tracks that work by themselves, but the album as a whole isn't consistent enough to merit repeated listenings. — *John Bush*

Cruise Yourself / 1994 / Touch & Go ✦✦✦
Much like *Venus Luxure*, GVSB's third full-length features some great singles, but the album fails to work on the whole. — *John Bush*

Gary Glitter (Paul Gadd)

b. May 8, 1940, Banbury, Oxfordshire
Rock & Roll
After many years of trying to become a star, Paul Gadd finally hit the winning formula in 1972—the glam rock king, Gary Glitter. Complete with extravagant makeup, silver outfits, and high boots, Glitter looked as trashy as his music sounded. Glitter and producer Michael Leander created pop records that weren't intended to be serious music—infectious singles that sounded perfect for the three minutes that they were playing; after they were finished, they seemed slightly embarrassing. With its mammoth drum beat, growling guitar, dumb instrumental hook, and incessant chorus of "hey!," his debut single, "Rock and Roll, Part Two," was a huge hit in both the U.K. and the U.S. Although he never had another hit in America, Glitter was a superstar in Britain throughout the mid-'70s, scoring three number one singles. Surprisingly, Glitter's cheerfully idiotic, catchy glam rock became somewhat influential over the next decade; Joan Jett covered several of his songs, as did the Human League, Generation X, Planet Control, and the Brownsville Station. — *Stephen Thomas Erlewine*

● **Rock 'n' Roll: The Best of Gary Glitter** / 1990 / Rhino ✦✦✦✦
Although he's best known for the knuckle-headed sports anthem "Rock & Roll Part Two," Glitter had plenty of other glam-rock delights that were equally as good, if not better. *Rock 'n' Roll—The Best of Gary Glitter* lovingly collects his best singles, from "Rock & Roll Part Two" to such unsung riff-rockers as "Do You Wanna Touch Me (Oh Yeah!)" and "I'm the Leader of the Gang (I Am!)." It's dumb, it's catchy, it's loud—everything good rock & roll should be. A nice guilty pleasure. — *Stephen Thomas Erlewine*

Global Communication

Group, Techno
Tom Middleton and Mark Pritchard formed the Evolution label in 1991 to release their own techno tracks. After three years of releases on Evolution and the Infonet label, the pair formed Global Communication to remix the Chapterhouse album, *Blood Music*. *76:14* was released to critical acclaim in 1994. A compilation of

the duo's early techno work, entitled *The Theory of Evolution*, is also available. — *John Bush*

Pentamerous Metamorphosis / 1994 / Dedicated ✦✦✦

● **76:14** / 1994 / Dedicated ✦✦✦✦
76:14 is the single most beautiful, haunting piece of work to emerge from the ambient-house genre. The tracks are referred to by their times so the listener won't be biased by song titles. The rhythms are slow and graceful; captivating synth dominates the melodies. — *John Bush*

The Go-Betweens

Group, Alternative Pop/Rock, New Wave
This Australian quintet was founded as a duo in 1977 by Robert Forster and Grant McLellan. The first of their six albums was released in 1982. When they broke up in 1990, Forster went solo and McLellan joined Steve Kilby in Jack Frost. — *William Ruhlmann*

Send Me a Lullabye / 1981 / Rough Trade ✦✦

Very Quick on the Eye-Brisbane, 1981 / 1982 / Man Made ✦✦✦

Before Hollywood / 1983 / Rough Trade ✦✦✦

Spring Hill Fair / 1984 / Sire ✦✦✦

Metal & Shells / 1985 / PVC ✦✦✦

○ **Liberty Belle & Black Diamond Express** / 1986 / Beggars Banquet ✦✦✦✦

○ **Tallulah** / 1987 / Big Time ✦✦✦✦
The addition of violinist and oboist Amanda Brown makes a crucial difference in the Go-Betweens' sound on this fifth album, giving it the elegance and pop sheen to back Forster and McLellan's intelligent, acerbic lyrics with the irony they deserve. — *William Ruhlmann*

○ **16 Lovers Lane** / 1988 / Beggars Banquet ✦✦✦✦
After several good albums (*Springhill Fair, Liberty Belle, Tallulah*) of polished pop, the Go-Betweens create the intimate compelling *16 Lovers Lane*, their best album. Among the album's many highlights are "You Can't Say No Forever," and the single "Was There Anything I Could Do?." — *Rick Clark*

● **1978-1990** / Aug. 27, 1990 / Capitol ✦✦✦✦
Fans of the Go-Betweens might have a few beefs concerning omitted key tracks from this compilation, but all in all, *1978-1990* is a solid introduction to the band's many virtues. Included are ample annotation and photos in the booklet. — *Rick Clark*

The Go-Go's

Group, New Wave, Pop/Rock
The Go-Go's were the most popular all-female band to emerge from the punk/new wave explosion of the late '70s and early '80s, becoming one of the first commercially successful female groups that wasn't controlled by male producers or managers. While their hit singles—"We Got the Beat," "Our Lips Are Sealed," "Vacation," "Head over Heels"—were bright, energetic new wave pop, the group was integral part of the Californian punk scene. And they did play punk rock, even if many of their rougher edges were ironed out by the time they recorded their first album, 1981's *Beauty and the Beat*. Even as they became America's darlings, the Go-Go's lived the wild life of rockers, swallowing as many pills and taking as much cocaine as possible, trashing hotel rooms and just generally being bad. More importantly, their earliest music—now collected on *Return to the Valley of the Go-Go's*—was raw and rocking; it may not have directly inspired the female alternative rockers and riot grrrls of the '90s, but it certainly foreshadowed it.

Originally formed in 1978 as the Misfits, the group featured Belinda Carlisle (vocals), Jane Wiedlin (guitar, vocals), Charlotte Caffey (lead guitar, keyboards), Margot Olaverra (bass), and Elissa Bello (drums); the group soon changed their name to the Go-Go's and began playing local parties and small clubs in California. In 1979, Gina Schock became the group's drummer. During that year, the band recorded a demo and supported the British ska revival group Madness in both Los Angeles and England. The Go-Go's spent half of 1980 touring England, earning a sizable following and releasing "We Got the Beat" on Stiff Records. An import copy of "We Got the Beat" became an underground club hit in the U.S., which meant the band was popular enough to sell out concerts yet they had a difficult time landing a record contract.

At the end of 1980, bassist Olaverra became ill and had to stop performing; she was replaced by Kathy Valentine, a guitarist who had never played bass before. Early in 1981, the Go-Go's signed with IRS Records. Released in the summer of 1981, their debut album, *Beauty and the Beat*, became one of the surprise hits of the year, staying at number one for six weeks and selling over two million copies; "Our Lips Are Sealed" hit number 20 and a re-recorded version of "We Got the Beat" spent three weeks at number two.

The following year, the group released *Vacation*. Although it sold well—the album made the Top Ten and it went gold, spawning the Top Ten hit single "Vacation"—it failed to keep the momentum of the first record. During the next year the band was unable to perform as Caffey recovered from a broken wrist. In 1984, the Go-Go's returned with *Talk Show*, their most musically ambitious album. While it had two Top 40 hits—the number 11 "Head over Heels" and "Turn to You"—it failed to even go gold. By the end of the year, Wielden had left the band; the Go-Go's broke up in May of 1985. Belinda Carlisle became the most successful solo artist, scoring a string of mainstream pop singles in the late '80s, including the number one single "Heaven Is a Place on Earth." For a while, Charlotte Caffey was in Carlisle's backing group; she eventually formed the Graces, who released *Perfect View* in 1990. Jane Wiedlin recorded two solo albums and acted in a few films. Wiedlin also organized the group's brief 1990 reunion, where they performed at a benefit for People for the Ethical Treatment of Animals; they also recorded a cover of "Cool Jerk" for their 1990 *Greatest Hits* album. The Go-Go's reunited once more in 1994, recording three new songs for the double-disc compilation *Return of the Valley of the Go-Go's;* after recording the songs, the group decided to continue as a full-time unit. — *Stephen Thomas Erlewine*

○ **Beauty & the Beat** / 1981 / IRS ✦✦✦✦

Vacation / 1982 / IRS ✦✦✦

Talk Show / 1984 / IRS ✦✦✦

● **Greatest** / 1990 / IRS ✦✦✦✦
An adequate collection of hits, it includes "Our Lips Are Sealed" (#20), "We Got the Beat" (#2), "Vacation" (#8), and "Head over Heels" (#11). — *Dan Heilman*

● **Return to the Valley of The Go-Go's** / 1994 / IRS ✦✦✦✦
Because it doesn't ignore the group's punk and new wave roots, the double-disc set *Return to the Valley of the Go-Go's* is far more entertaining than the single-disc collection *Greatest Hits*. All of the hits are included, as well as many rarities as good as anything they officially released. Not only is the music intoxicating, but the liner notes are filled with priceless photos and memorabilia, which makes the set the one definitive Go-Go's album. — *Stephen Thomas Erlewine*

Godflesh

Group, Hard Rock, Heavy Metal
Godflesh was formed in 1988 by ex-Napalm Death guitarist and Head of David drummer Justin Broadrick and bassist G.C. Green. The band's sound has been tagged as grindcore, with its heavy, ultra-detuned guitars and bass and plodding tempos. Industrial influences are also easy to spot in the drum machine and various noises, effects, and tape loops; depending on the album, the group's sound may run either way. Godflesh chiefly makes mood music, and the mood is one of intense, depressed rage. The group's discography is rather tangled, with various singles and EPs out in addition to their albums. Broadrick has drawn praise from the musical community for his unique guitar playing and musical style and has been hailed as a major innovator. — *Steve Huey*

Godflesh / 1988 / Combat ✦✦

○ **Streetcleaner** / 1990 / Combat ✦✦✦✦
Streetcleaner leans more towards the industrial end of Godflesh's sound, relying mostly on guitar textures and slow, pounding, ultra-detuned bass to carry the music, with some spat-out vocals as well. It gets very repetitive and rather dull in a few spots, but at its best, the music is pulverizing, jarring, and manages to hold attention by keeping the listener off balance with a variety of sounds, and even approaches being hypnotic. — *Steve Huey*

Slave State / 1991 / Earache ✦✦✦

● **Pure** / 1992 / Earache ✦✦✦✦

Selfless / 1994 / Earache ✦✦✦
Selfless is more subdued and moody, managing to be both dark and strangely soothing at the same time; Justin Broadrick even comes close to singing on occasion. The CD is over 78 minutes

long, so the band inevitably falls into repetition and meanders in spots. Fans of their heavier work may be disappointed, but most of *Selfless* works well as angry, depressed mood music. — *Steve Huey*

Merciless / 1994 / Earache ✦✦✦
A highly layered and textured EP with an abundance of sounds, effects, and tape manipulation, and even a simple melody on "Flowers." This ranks among their better work and holds attention more consistently than some of the group's long, full-length albums. — *Steve Huey*

Godz

Group, Psychedelic, Experimental
Few bands in the annals of rock & roll were stranger than the New York City-based Godz. Recording for the wonderfully idiosyncratic ESP-DISK label from the mid-'60s until the early '70s (although nothing they recorded after 1968 is worth hearing), the Godz coughed up some of the strangest, most dissonant, purposely incompetent rock noise ever produced. Part of the Lower East Side scene that produced post-Beat avant-hippie rockers/performance artists the Fugs and the Holy Modal Rounders, as well as honest-to-God beat performers like Allen Ginsberg, the Godz recorded the most extreme music while being secretive about themselves. As the late critic Lester Bangs noted in his essay (the only one I'm aware of concerning the Godz in a major rock publication—*Creem* 1971), the Godz "…are a pure test of one of the supreme traditions of rock & roll: the process by which a musical band can evolve from beginnings of almost insulting illiteracy to wind up several albums later romping and stomping deft as champs."

Despite Bangs' essay, there are few, if any, detailed histories about this enigmatic band. What is known is that the Godz consisted of guitarist Jim McCarthy, bassist Larry Kessler, autoharpist Jay Dillon, and drummer Paul Thornton. McCarthy, the ostensible leader of the group, went solo in 1973, but the Godz were pretty much over by that point. As to what happened after they split, McCarthy became a photographer, Kessler is a record dealer, Thornton is an actor and Dillon is living in the wilds of New Jersey, but none of that is as interesting as the three squalling bits of avant-garde noise/junk they recorded from 1966-68. Sounding like a prototype for Half Japanese or the Shaggs, the Godz play as if they discovered their instruments ten minutes before the tape started rolling. The singing is intentionally off-key, almost parodic, and the songs…well, they sound more like improvised snippets than actual compositions. And while that may not be your idea of pop music, this works, in large part due to the absolute glee and unself-consciousness with which the these clowns approached their peculiar brand of aural nonsense. You may not want to play this every day, but if your tastes run to the fringes of popular music, missing out on the Godz would be unforgivable.

Normally, there is a caveat with a listing such as this one indicating that the records are impossible to find—not true here! Although ESP-DISK recordings were never easy to find in the first place, Bernhard Mikulski, who runs the German label ZYX, is planning to reissue (assuming he hasn't already) the entire ESP-DISK catalog at very affordable prices. This means that the majesty of the Godz can be yours, and you won't need a second mortgage to buy expensive imports.

A final note: in the late '70s, there was a terrible Midwestern heavy metal band, also called the Godz, who made two execrable albums for Casablanca. There is absolutely no relation between the two bands, and music by the heavy-metal Godz should be avoided at all costs. — *John Dougan*

Contact High / 1966 / ESP
Clocking in at a hair over 25 minutes, *Contact High* is an unholy mess of a record. Opening with the track "White Cat Heat," which consists of clumsily strummed acoustic guitars, arhythmic percussion and Jim McCarthy and Larry Kessler screeching like a couple of, uh, cats in heat, it gets weirder. Best tracks are "1+1 Equals ?" and the hilarious "Lay in the Sun" (total lyrics: "All I want to do is lay in the sun"). For those who like their pop on the cutting edge, begin here and don't turn back. — *John Dougan*

Godz Two / 1967 / ESP
Only a label as adventurous as ESP would allow a band like the Godz to make second record, and *2* is as extreme as *Contact High*, and as good. A little more psychedelic sound here, but nothing that detracts from the Godz' relentless amateurish spirit and abilities. If you were sold on *Contact High*, having this is important. — *John Dougan*

Third Testament / 1968 / ESP
Although they went on to record into the 1970s, this is the last decent Godz record, primarily because it's the last one that incorporates their distinctive meandering and lack of technical merit with their growing interest in psychedelic rock. True Godz fanatics will tell you that *Third Testament* is a significant dropoff from *2*, but not to these ears. And while it doesn't pack the visceral wallop of *Contact High*, there's enough dementia here for a lifetime of fun. —*John Dougan*

Godzhunheit / 1970 / ESP

Alien / 1973 / ESP

Godz Bless California / 1973 / ESP

The Golden Palominos

Group, Alternative Pop/Rock
This progressive project band from New York, led by drummer Anton Fier, features an ever-changing lineup of current alternative players. At various times, the Golden Palominos have included Michael Stipe of R.E.M., John Lydon, Richard Thompson, Chris Stamey, Jack Bruce, Arto Lindsay, Carla Bley, Bob Mould, Syd Straw, and others. —*Iotis Erlewine*

The Golden Palominos / 1983 / Celluloid ✦✦✦
Leader Anton Fier (drums) and Bill Laswell (bass) serve as a rhythm section for a revolving group of rockers exploring avant-garde rock. Including Michael Stipe of R.E.M., John Lydon, Jack Bruce, Richard Thompson, Straw, Chris Stamey, and Arto Lindsay. —*William Ruhlmann*

○ **Visions of Excess** / 1985 / Celluloid ✦✦✦✦
There's a great eclectic mix of alternative rock songcraft and great musicianship from Jack Bruce, Richard Thompson, and others. Syd Straw shines on "(Kind Of) True" as does Michael Stipe on "Omaha." —*Scott Bultman*

Blast of Silence / 1986 / Celluloid ✦✦✦
Anton Fier, Syd Straw, and T-Bone Burnette serve up a fine selection of tracks with a country-rock slant, including a Lowell George cover and Peter Holsapple's "Diamonds." —*Scott Bultman*

A Dead Horse / 1989 / Celluloid ✦✦✦

○ **Thundering Herd: The Best of The Golden Palominos** / 1991 / Oceana ✦✦✦✦

○ **Drunk with Passion** / 1991 / Charisma ✦✦✦✦
Fier and Bill Laswell are joined by Stipe, Thompson, Carla Bley, and former Hüsker Dü singer/songwriter and guitarist Bob Mould on this album. —*William Ruhlmann*

● **A History (1982-1985)** / 1992 / Metrotone ✦✦✦✦
This is a fine sampler of the Golden Palominos' first two records. —*AMG*

● **A History (1986-1989)** / 1992 / Metrotone ✦✦✦✦
This is a fine sampler of the Golden Palominos' third and fourth records. —*AMG*

○ **This Is How It Feels** / 1993 / Restless ✦✦✦✦
Anton Fier and Bill Laswell use Lori Carson as their regular vocalist here, with three songs sung by Lydia Kavanagh. Guest musicians include Bootsy Collins, Nicky Skopelitis, and Bernie Worrell. The key figure, however, is Carson, who co-wrote all the songs on which she sings, making this, in effect, a Lori Carson solo album. Carson explores the argumentative, often brutal aspects of romance in songs that have a dreamy effect despite the involved rhythm tracks. Her double-tracked, interweaving vocals, with their repeated phrases and blunt sentiments, have a disorienting, yet compelling force. —*William Ruhlmann*

○ **Pure** / 1994 / Restless ✦✦✦✦
The Golden Palominos' manage to convey much of the same darkly seductive atmosphere as their other shimmering experimental pop records. —*Stephen Thomas Erlewine*

Bobby Goldsboro

b. Jan. 18, 1941, Marianna, FL
Pop
Singer/songwriter Bobby Goldsboro began his career in the early '60s as a guitarist in Roy Orbison's band. After departing for a solo career, Goldsboro's success has been marked by a long string of sentimental ballads, the most famous being "Honey," which held the number one spot for five weeks. Other hits included "See the Funny Little Clown," "Little Things," "Autumn of My Life," "Watching Scotty Grow," and "The Straight Life." —*Rick Clark*

● **Best of Bobby Goldsboro: Honey** / 1991 / EMI America ✦✦✦✦
A definitive 23-track collection of all the Bobby Goldsboro you'll ever need. —*Stephen Thomas Erlewine*

The Golliwogs

Group, Rock & Roll, Garage Rock, Pop/Rock
Of all the "vault" recordings by '60s rock groups that were unearthed and repackaged, few are less indicative of future fame and greatness than the Golliwogs'. With no changes in personnel, the group became superstars as Creedence Clearwater Revival. As the Golliwogs, they issued seven singles in the mid-'60s; all flops, they were eventually repackaged as a retrospective. These 45s liberally borrowed from the British Invasion and other rock and R&B trends of the day without displaying a shred of distinction, or even an especially high energy level. It doesn't take a genius to figure out what the problem is; over half the songs were sung not by John Fogerty, but his brother Tom. The half-dozen numbers sung by John are indeed more palatable, but even so, his songwriting had a ways to go before attaining maturity. The Golliwogs' recordings are interesting for their historical insight, but listeners shouldn't approach them expecting anything on the level of Creedence. —*Richie Unterberger*

Golliwogs (Pre Creedence) / 1975 / Fantasy ✦✦✦
Both sides of all seven of their singles, originally issued on Fantasy and Scorpio. It is odd to hear the group casting about for an identity; songs variously bring to mind the Zombies, Them, Merseybeat, even hints of the Beach Boys. "Fight Fire" was their best early number, and has a fairly high reputation among garage fans. The later cuts (all sung by John) show the group starting to develop a rootsier, funkier approach more in line with Creedence. Has early versions of "Walking on the Water" and "Porterville," which were included on the first Creedence album. —*Richie Unterberger*

Ian Gomm

Rock & Roll, New Wave
Former guitar player in England's greatest pub-rock band, Brinsley Schwarz, Gomm went on to an understated, yet fairly rewarding solo career in the late '70s and early '80s. Playing more power-pop than pub-rock as a solo artist, Gomm was a strong, if derivative, singer-songwriter whose clear, warm voice made up for the occasional banality of his lyrics. But even at his most obvious and cloying, Gomm was likable and winning, if only because of his sunny disposition and his way with a guitar riff. Curiously, after three good solo records, he pretty much disappeared. His best album is his first, *Summer Holiday*, which was released in England only. His American releases for Stiff/Epic (some of which included material from *Summer Holiday*) are solid, at times inspired, craftsmanship. —*John Dougan*

● **Gomm with the Wind** / 1978 / Stiff ✦✦✦✦
Part of the ill-fated marriage of the great English independent label Stiff and the massive distribution power of the CBS subsidiary label Epic, *Gomm With the Wind* was probably the most ignored of all the records released under this agreement but, like *Summer Holiday*, it's a sturdy piece of pop with Gomm acquitting himself quite nicely on Johnny Rivers' schmaltz-pop classic "Swaying to the Music (Slow Dancin')." —*John Dougan*

Summer Holiday / 1978 / Albion ✦✦✦
With his "hit" "Hold On" here, *Summer Holiday* is a wonderful record. Loaded with chiming guitars, snappy songs and Gomm's earnest vocals, only the world's meanest musical Scrooge could hate a record like this. By no means a record that will change your life; few people make records like this anymore, at least not without sounding smug and calculated. —*John Dougan*

What a Blow / 1980 / Stiff ✦✦✦

The Village Choice / 1982 / Albion ✦✦

Images / 1986 / Decal ✦✦

Gong

Group, Electronic, Art-Rock/Progressive-Rock
Gong slowly came together in the late '60s when Australian guitarist Daevid Allen (ex-Soft Machine) began making music with his wife, singer Gilli Smyth, along with a shifting line-up of supporting musicians. Albums from this period include *Magick Brother, Mystic Sister* (1969) and the impromptu jam session *Bananamoon* (1971) featuring Robert Wyatt from the Soft Machine, Gary Wright from Spooky Tooth, and Maggie Bell. A steady line-

up featuring Frenchman Didier Malherbe (sax & reeds), Christian Tritsch (bass), and Pip Pyle (drums) along with Allen (glissando guitar, vocals) and Gilli Smyth (space whisper vocals) was officially named Gong and released *Camembert Electrique* in late 1971, as well as providing the soundtrack to the film *Continental Circus* and music for the album *Obsolete* by French poet Dashiel Hedayat.

Camembert Electrique contained the first signs of the band's mythology of the peaceful Planet Gong populated by Radio Gnomes, Pothead Pixies, and Octave Doctors. These characters along with Zero the Hero are the focus of Gong's next three albums, the *Radio Gnome Invisible Trilogy*, consisting of *Flying Teapot* (1973), *Angel's Egg* (1974), and *You* (1975). On these albums, protagonist Zero the Hero is a space traveler from Earth who gets lost and finds the Planet Gong, is taught the ways of that world by the gnomes, pixies, and Octave Doctors and is sent back to Earth to spread the word about this mystical planet. The band themselves adopted nicknames—Allen was Bert Camembert or the Dingo Virgin, Smyth was Shakti Yoni, Malherbe was Bloomdido Bad de Grasse, Tritsch was the Submarine Captain and Pyle the Heap. Over the course of the trilogy, Tritsch and Pyle left and were replaced by Mike Howlett (bass) and Pierre Moerlen (drums). New members Steve Hillage (guitar) and Tim Blake (synthesizers) joined.

After *You*, Allen, Hillage, and Smyth left the group due to creative differences as well as fatigue. Guitarist Allen Holdsworth joined and the band drifted into virtuosic if unimaginative jazz fusion. Hillage and Allen each released several solo albums and Smyth formed Mothergong. Nevertheless the trilogy line-up has reunited for a few one-off concerts including a 1977 French concert documented on the excellent *Gong est Mort, Vive Gong* album. Allen also reunited with Malherbe and Pyle as well as other musicians he had collaborated with over the years for 1992's *Shapeshifter* album. —*Jim Powers*

Continental Circus / 1971 / Philips ✦✦✦

○ **Camembert Electrique** / 1971 / Charly ✦✦✦✦
An early Gong phase with Daevid Allen. A bit wacky, but a lot wonderful. —*Michael G. Nastos*

The Flying Teapot / 1973 / Charly ✦✦✦

Angel's Egg / 1973 / Charly ✦✦✦

You / 1974 / Virgin ✦✦

Shamal / 1976 / Virgin ✦✦✦

○ **Expresso** / 1976 / Virgin ✦✦✦✦
A studio album of excellent instrumental jazz/rock from percussionist Pierre Moerlen's band, featuring guitarist Allan Holdsworth's fluid guitar. —*Michael G. Nastos*

Gazeuse! / 1977 / Virgin ✦✦✦

Gong Est Morte, Vive Gong / 1977 / Tapioca ✦✦✦
Recorded live at the Hippodrome in Paris. Wildly eclectic, with Daevid Allen. —*Michael G. Nastos*

● **Live Etc** / 1977 / Virgin ✦✦✦✦
A live 2-fer of wild acid-tinged music from 1973-1975 concerts, with Daevid Allen, Steve Hillage, and Tom Blake. An essential album. —*Michael G. Nastos*

Expresso 2 / 1978 / Virgin ✦✦✦
French/German instrumentalists. Includes guitarist Allan Holdsworth and percussionist Pierre Moerlen. Very attractive music. —*Michael G. Nastos*

○ **Downwind** / 1979 / Arista ✦✦✦✦

Time Is the Key / 1979 / Arista ✦✦✦

P Moerlens Gong Live / 1980 / Arista ✦✦

Leave It Open / 1981 / Arista ✦✦✦

Breakthrough / 1987 / Eulenspiegel ✦✦

Shapeshifter / 1992 / Celluloid ✦✦✦

Goo Goo Dolls

Group, Hard Rock, Alternative Pop/Rock
Buffalo's Goo Goo Dolls are like the Replacements' goofier brothers—they have all the garage energy of the 'Mats, only without the depth of Paul Westerberg's songwriting. Still, that doesn't deny the pleasure of the band's sonic rush; they have enough hooks and melodies to please fans of both the Replacements and Cheap

Trick. As the Goo Goo Dolls make more albums, their songwriting keeps improving and the band gets tighter. 1993's *Superstar Car Wash* edged them into the mainstream, thanks to the single, "We Are the Normal," which was co-written with their idol Westerberg. —*Stephen Thomas Erlewine*

Goo Goo Dolls / 1987 / Mercenary ✦✦

Jed / 1989 / Death ✦✦

Hold Me Up / 1990 / Metal Blade ✦✦✦
A raucous rock record, full of sloppy riffs and energetic hooks; it sounds like the Replacements playing early Cheap Trick. —*Stephen Thomas Erlewine*

● **Superstar Car Wash** / 1993 / Warner Brothers ✦✦✦✦
A tighter, more polished album featuring the radio-ready collaboration with Paul Westerberg "We Are Normal," as well as several spirited hard-rockers. —*Stephen Thomas Erlewine*

○ **Boy Named Goo** / 1995 / Metal Blade ✦✦✦✦
Following the relative success of *Superstar Car Wash*, *A Boy Named Goo* sees the Goo Goo Dolls turning up the volume and grunge on their guitars, kicking out a batch of messy rockers. They still echo the Replacements in both attitude and sound, yet their affection for the band is genuine, making the record both an affectionate tribute and an enjoyable, rocking record. —*Stephen Thomas Erlewine*

Lesley Gore

b. May 2, 1946, New York, NY
Girl-Group
The most commercially successful solo singer to be identified with the girl group sound, Lesley Gore hit the number one spot with her very first release, "It's My Party," in 1963. Produced by Quincy Jones, who fattened the teenager's sound with double-tracked vocals and intricate backup vocals and horns, she reeled off a few more big hits in 1963 and 1964, including "Judy's Turn to Cry," "She's a Fool," "You Don't Own Me," "That's the Way Boys Are," and "Maybe I Know." She wasn't the most soulful girl group singer by a longshot, but she projected an archetype of female adolescent yearning. Her best songs survive as classics, particularly the irresistibly melodic "Maybe I Know" (written by Ellie Greenwich and Jeff Barry) and "You Don't Own Me," an anthem of independence with a feminist theme that was considerably advanced for early 1964. Gore's commercial fortunes dwindled as she entered college and the nation entered the mid-'60s, although she did make the Top 20 again with "Sunshine, Lollipops and Rainbows" (1965) and "California Nights" (1967). She played the cabarets after her days as an active recording artist, and eventually had some success as a songwriter for other performers. —*Richie Unterberger*

● **Anthology** / 1986 / Rhino ✦✦✦✦
Superlative compilation of Leslie's best sides, including "It's My Party," "Judy's Turn to Cry," and "You Don't Own Me." —*Cub Koda*

Graham Gouldman

British Invasion
Before forming 10cc with Eric Stewart, Graham Gouldman was a major presence in the British Invasion, writing hits for the Yardbirds, Hollies, Herman's Hermits, and others; "For Your Love," "Bus Stop," "Look Through Any Window," "Heart Full of Soul," and "No Milk Today" are among his most famous compositions. Gouldman wrote some of the finest tunes of the era, using haunting, shifting minor key melodies as well as similar efforts by the Zombies and Beatles. He also cut a lengthy string of flop singles, as a solo artist and with his group the Mockingbirds, and released a nifty solo album of his own in the late '60s. —*Richie Unterberger*

● **Graham Gouldman Thing** / 1968 / Edsel ✦✦✦✦
Gouldman issued this solo album in 1968, featuring his own versions of the hits "For Your Love," "Bus Stop," and "No Milk Today" with eight other original tunes. The album blends pensive, acoustic-guitar driven compositions with light orchestral arrangements. It's a pleasant record, but ultimately does not measure up to the monster hit covers of his tunes. He's only an adequate singer, and the slower, more elaborately produced versions of "Bus Stop" and "For Your Love" are not nearly as good as the hard-charging renditions by the Yardbirds and Hollies. A decent curio, though, highlighted by "Pawnbroker" and "Upstairs Downstairs," which would have fit in well on the Hollies' 1966-67 records. —*Richie Unterberger*

Animalolympics / 1980 / A&M ✦✦✦

Graham Central Station

Group, Funk
An exuberant mid-'70s funk group, Graham Central Station made some fine singles for Warner Bros. Former Sly & the Family Stone bassist Larry Graham renamed Hot Chocolate (not the British group) Graham Central Station after he moved from producing the group to playing with it. The group included Graham, guitarist David Vega, keyboardists Robert Sam and Hershall Kennedy, percussionist Patrice Banks, and drummer Willie Sparks. They utilized the identical funk cum rock and soul formula of Sly, though in not quite as imaginative a fashion. Their debut single, "Can You Handle It," reached number nine on the R&B charts, and they landed a number one record in 1975 with "Your Love." They recorded as Graham Central Station from 1974 to 1977, then as Larry Graham & Graham Central Station in 1978, and during their final year were called Larry Graham with Graham Central Station. —*Ron Wynn*

● Graham Central Station / 1973 / Warner Brothers ✦✦✦✦
  Release Yourself / 1974 / Warner Brothers ✦✦✦
  Mirror / 1976 / Warner Brothers ✦✦✦
  Now Do U Wanna Dance / 1977 / Warner Brothers ✦✦✦

Davey Graham

Folk
One of the most eclectic guitarists of the 1960s, Graham's mixture of folk, blues, jazz, Middle Eastern sounds, and Indian ragas was an important catalyst of the British folk scene. Like Sandy Bull and John Fahey—two folk-based guitarists with a similar taste for genre-bending experimentation—Graham could not be said to be a rock musician. But like Bull and Fahey, he shared the eagerness of the '60s psychedelic rockers to stretch out and incorporate unpredictable influences into his music. While he wasn't much of a singer, Graham's taste in material was broad and shrewd, encompassing blues, ragas, Joni Mitchell, Charles Mingus, and the famous instrumental "Anji," which Graham recorded in 1962, way before the more famous versions by Bert Jansch and Simon & Garfunkel. Besides cutting several albums of his own work in the 1960s with sympathetic, low-key rhythm sections, he also recorded with traditional folk singer Shirley Collins and British blues father Alexis Korner. Graham recorded only sporadically after the 1960s, although he performed with the renowned acoustic guitar wizards Stefan Grossman and Duck Baker. —*Richie Unterberger*

  Guitar Player . . . Plus / 1963 / See For Miles ✦✦✦
British guitarist Davy Graham established himself as one of the most innovative players in acoustic music with his 1963 debut, *The Guitar Player*. With this album, Graham became one of the first folk guitarists to fuse traditional virtuosity with crosscurrents from contemporary jazz and blues. Accompanied by drummer Bobby Graham (a top British session man who played on many British Invasion rock records, including several by the Kinks), Davy invigorates pop and traditional standards, as well as compositions by Sonny Rollins, the Adderleys, and Ray Charles. Neither jazz nor folk, Graham displays an eclectic bounce that was quite visionary for its time, and remains fresh today; in his subsequent 1960s recordings, he would branch out into Middle Eastern and psychedelic sounds as a natural extension of his experimental bent. As a significant bonus, the 1992 CD reissue of this album includes the three tracks from his rare 1962 EP *3/4 A.D.* One of these is the original version of "Anji," which was reworked by Simon & Garfunkel on one of their early albums; another features British blues-rock godfather Alexis Korner on second guitar. —*Richie Unterberger*

● Folk, Blues All Points In Between / 1985 / See For Miles ✦✦✦✦
Side One includes the entirety of his 1965 album *Folk, Blues And Beyond*; Side Two features seven tracks from three of his late-'60s LPs. The 1965 record was probably his most accomplished, as Graham handled blues, jazz, and Northern African music with aplomb. His other '60s recordings were more erratic, but the highlights gathered here matched his 1965 work, peaking with the original "No Preacher Blues," his folk-jazz cover of Joni Mitchell's "Both Sides Now," and the Indian-influenced "Blue Raga." —*Richie Unterberger*

Lou Gramm

b. May 2, 1950
Hard Rock, Pop/Rock
Lou Gramm was the powerful lead singer for the mainstream hard rock group Foreigner. During his solo career, Gramm has found continuing success with conservative power ballads like "Midnight Blue" (#10). —*Rick Clark*

● Ready or Not / 1987 / Atlantic ✦✦✦✦
Top-notch vocals propel these Foreigner-reminiscent rockers, including the hits "Midnight Blue" and "Ready or Not." —*Donna DiChario*

  Foreigner in a Strange Land / 1988 / Thunderbolt ✦✦✦
  Long Hard Look / 1989 / Atlantic ✦✦

Grand Funk Railroad

Group, Hard Rock
In spite of the fact that Grand Funk Railroad was almost universally reviled by the critical community, FM rock radio and millions of hard rock fans couldn't get enough. Conceived as a trio in 1968, Grand Funk got signed by Capitol after the label caught them live at the 1969 Atlanta Pop Festival. Unlike Cream or the Jimi Hendrix Experience, Grand Funk dispensed with wild interplay and focused on good-time boogie grooves and no-nonsense workmanlike arrangements. Their first album, *On Time* (#27), featuring Mark Farner's earnestly untrained tenor and buzz-saw guitar, Mel Schacher's buffalo-fart bass, and Don Brewer's bashola drumming, was an immediate hit.
The self-titled followup (#11) stripped down the band's sound to utter basics, but the third effort, *Closer to Home* (#6), showed the band utilizing strings and sound effects to widen their sound. By 1970, the band was one of the most popular band's in America; they broke the Beatles' record at Shea Stadium in 1971.
The band became a four-piece in 1973, and Todd Rundgren produced the hit albums *We're an American Band* (#2) and *Shinin' On* (#5). The Jimmy Ienner-produced *All the Girls in the World Beware!!!* (#10) continued their winning streak. Subsequent releases did progressively worse, and the band formally disbanded in 1983. —*Rick Clark*

  On Time / 1969 / Capitol ✦✦✦
○ Grand Funk / 1970 / Capitol ✦✦✦✦
  Live Album / 1970 / Capitol ✦✦✦
○ Closer to Home / 1970 / Capitol ✦✦✦✦
  E Pluribus Funk / 1971 / Capitol ✦✦
  Survival / 1971 / Capitol ✦✦✦
○ Mark, Don & Mel: 1969-71 / 1972 / Capitol ✦✦✦✦
  Phoenix / 1972 / Capitol ✦✦
○ We're an American Band / Nov. 1973 / Collector's Pipeline ✦✦✦✦
  All the Girls in The World Beware / 1974 / Capitol ✦✦✦
  Shinin' On / 1974 / Collector's Pipeline ✦✦
  Caught in the Act / 1975 / Capitol ✦✦
  Born to Die / 1976 / Capitol ✦✦
  Good Singin', Good Playin' / 1976 / EMI ✦✦✦
  Grand Funk Lives / 1981 / Full Moon ✦
  What's Funk? / 1983 / Full Moon ✦✦
○ More of the Best / 1991 / Rhino ✦✦✦✦
This set does a decent job of picking key tracks not found on the *Capitol Collectors Series* album. Included is the fuzz-bass-heavy "Paranoid" and boogie numbers like "Are You Ready?" and "Got This Thing on the Move." Fans may wish for a more incisive selection from their first three albums. —*Rick Clark*

● Capitol Collectors Series / 1991 / Capitol ✦✦✦✦
This is the place to start. All of Grand Funk's hits are here: the classic "We're an American Band," Todd Rundgren's perverse production of "Loco-Motion," their thudding remake of the Animals's "Inside Looking Out," the epic "Closer to Home/I'm Your Captain," "Heartbreaker," and other big favorites. —*Rick Clark*

Grand Puba

Rap
The lead rapper for Brand Nubian came out roaring on his own with *Reel to Reel* in 1992. It contained everything from unrelenting Nation of Islam propaganda to one number that seemed like

an updated "My Ding-a-Ling" with its shameless touting of Puba's sexual prowess. But overall, it showed he had the skills to flourish on his own. —*Ron Wynn*

● **Reel to Reel** / 1992 / Elektra ✦✦✦✦
Grand Puba's first solo album is an angry, righteous record, which is saved by his lyrical inventiveness, not his rhetoric. —*Stephen Thomas Erlewine*

2000 / 1995 / Elektra ✦✦✦
Grand Puba's second solo album continues his groundbreaking fusion of jazz and hip-hop, adding a harder, street-oriented edge for *2000*. The production saves the album, even when the songs are weak. —*Stephen Thomas Erlewine*

Grandmaster Flash (Joseph Saddler)

Group, Rap
Grandmaster Flash (born Joseph Saddler, Jan. 1, 1958) and the Furious Five (Cowboy, Keith Wiggins; Melle Mel, Melvin Glover; Kidd Creole, Danny Glover; Mr. Ness, Eddie Morris; and Rahiem, Guy Williams) were the most important group in the early days of rap music and, in fact, developed certain crucial aspects of the genre. Saddler was the DJ, providing the musical bed by manipulating records on turntables, scratching them, repeating particular instrumental sections, and thus creating new music out of collages of existing recordings. The most important such work was the single "The Adventures of Grandmaster Flash on the Wheels of Steel," released in 1981.

Most of the group's records, however, featured the interlocking raps of the five rappers, and the most significant of these was "The Message" (1982), led primarily by Melle Mel, which turned away from the party subjects of many current rap records to focus on urban social issues.

The group had split by 1984, with Melle Mel going off on his own. It later re-formed in 1987.

Grandmaster Flash resurfaced in the public consciousness in late 1993, thanks to interviews done in *Rolling Stone* and *The Source* and Rhino reissues featuring such legendary tracks as "White Lines" and "Grandmaster Flash on the Wheels of Steel." A comeback session was announced for sometime later in 1994, though no producers or record label were announced. —*William Ruhlmann*

☆ **The Message** / 1982 / Sugar Hill ✦✦✦✦✦
Grandmaster Flash & The Furious Five merged the Afrocentric consciousness expressed by such early rappers as Gil Scott-Heron and The Last Poets with b-boy production to create "The Message," an all-time rap anthem. It was the focal point of this LP, which also included "It's Nasty" and "Scorpio," two other strong cuts that might have been winners on their own. Unfortunately, rather than a starting point, this album proved to be their ultimate peak. —*Ron Wynn*

○ **Greatest Messages** / 1983 / Sugar Hill ✦✦✦✦

Work Party / 1984 / Sugar Hill ✦✦

They Said It Couldn't Be Done / 1985 / Elektra ✦✦

Stepping Off / 1985 / Sugar Hill ✦✦

The Source / 1986 / Elektra ✦✦✦
Grandmaster Flash's follow-up to *The Message* was his first minus the Furious Five. Things weren't the same from a compositional or performance standpoint, as his raps seemed weaker and his rhymes almost devoid of crispness, humor or insight. Only "Ms. Thang" and "Street Scene" offered any hint of the incisiveness or vision depicted in "The Message." —*Ron Wynn*

Da Bop Boom Bang / 1987 / Elektra ✦✦
The fire was gone and the imagination and flair diminished on this 1987 album. Grandmaster Flash sounded too tired on such cuts as "Big Black Caddy," "Get Yours" and "U Know What Time It Is" to recapture the spirit and bristling intensity that made "The Message" an anthem. He was sadly more effective doing nonsense like "Them Jeans." —*Ron Wynn*

On the Strength / 1988 / Elektra ✦
Grandmaster Flash & The Furious Five tried to regroup on this 1988 release, but old school hip-hop had been lapped by the charge of the new school. There was little interest or response to such cuts as "Tear The Roof Off" and "Boy Is Dope," while "Fly Girl" and "Magic Carpet Ride" sounded dated and weary. —*Ron Wynn*

○ **Greatest Hits** / 1989 / Sugar Hill ✦✦✦✦
Flash was the DJ and the Furious Five were the best multiple rappers around, moving from the music's low-rent dance origins (it was Flash who began cutting in repeated portions of other records) and party spirit to the "message" approach that took over in the mid 80s, prefigured in "The Message." Much of what came later, started here. —*William Ruhlmann*

★ **Message from Beat Street: The Best of** / 1994 / Rhino ✦✦✦✦✦
Grandmaster Flash was one of the most important, groundbreaking rap artists of the early '80s, and all of his most important records—with and without Melle Mel and the Furious Five—are collected on this essential 11-track disc, which includes the classic tracks "The Message" and "White Lines (Don't Don't Do It)." —*Stephen Thomas Erlewine*

Grant Lee Buffalo

Group, Alternative Pop/Rock
Under the leadership of guitarist/songwriter Grant Lee Phillips, Grant Lee Buffalo became a major buzz band in 1993 with their debut album, *Fuzzy*. The band's searching, often political, folk-rock has shades of everyone from David Bowie and John Lennon to R.E.M. and Bob Mould. Phillips' songwriting received a large amount of critical praise, as did their electrifying live performances. The band captured a larger following in Europe than their native America, earning near-universal critical praise upon the release of *Fuzzy*. During 1993, the band toured constantly, building a solid cult following all over the world. The following year they delivered their second record, *Mighty Joe Moon*. —*Stephen Thomas Erlewine*

● **Fuzzy** / 1993 / Warner Brothers ✦✦✦✦
While Grant Lee Phillips' songwriting is quite impressive, what makes Grant Lee Buffalo's debut album, *Fuzzy*, memorable is the band's muscular folk-rock. Equally adept at propulsive rock & roll and haunting ballads, the band turns Phillips' best songs into rough gems, as "Jupiter and Teardrop" and "Fuzzy" prove. —*Stephen Thomas Erlewine*

○ **Mighty Joe Moon** / 1994 / Warner Brothers ✦✦✦✦
With their second album, Grant Lee Buffalo strips back their sound to its bare essentials, which accentuates Grant Lee Phillips' rural myths. Not only does the approach make songs like "Lone Star Song" rock viciously, but it also makes the bittersweet beauty of ballads like the gorgeous "Mockingbirds" all the more poignant. —*Stephen Thomas Erlewine*

Eddy Grant (Edmond Montague Grant)

b. Mar. 5, 1948, Plaisance, Guyana
Ethnic Fusion, Pop/Rock
Grant was a member of the London group the Equals during the '60s; after they broke up, he established Coach House Studios in London in 1973 and founded the Ice Records label in 1974. He made records throughout the late '70s, gaining a following in the U.K. In 1982, he hit big with "Electric Avenue" in the U.S. While Grant has not been able to repeat the success of "Electric Avenue" in the U.S., he remains popular in other countries. —*Stephen Thomas Erlewine*

○ **Living in a Front Line** / 1979 / Ice ✦✦✦✦

Walking on Sunshine / 1979 / Ice ✦✦✦
The title cut was a monster hit, while "Living on the Frontline" and "The Frontline Symphony" were also gems. —*Ron Wynn*

○ **Killer on the Rampage** / 1982 / Portrait ✦✦✦✦
In his Barbados recording studio, Eddy Grant doesn't play reggae music so much as dance-oriented music with thoughtful lyrics. His big U.S. hit, "Electric Avenue," had a new-wave beat and a message about poverty. The rest of his album is also toe-tapping and timely. —*William Ruhlmann*

Born Tuff / 1984 / Portrait ✦✦✦

Going for Broke / 1984 / Portrait ✦✦✦

File under Rock / 1988 / Enigma ✦✦✦

Barefoot Soldier / 1990 / Enigma ✦✦✦
The popular term by the '90s is "world music," which is as good as any for Grant's bouyant sound, matched to the tough anti-apartheid message of the album's hit "Gimme Hope Jo'anna." —*William Ruhlmann*

Grapes of Wrath

Group, Alternative Pop/Rock
Grapes of Wrath was a jangly alternative folk-pop quartet formed in Kelowna, British Columbia, in 1983 by brothers Chris Hooper (drums) and Tom Hooper (bass) along with vocalist/guitarist Kevin Kane and keyboardist Vincent Jones. In 1984, they signed to Nettwerk Records and relocated to Vancouver where they recorded a four song self-titled EP that earned the band some initial local exposure. 1985's full-length *September Bowl of Green*, however, gave them national recognition and critical acclaim. Ready to make a stab at the U.S., they enlisted the help of Tom Cochrane (ex-Red Rider) for production of the follow-up *Tree House*. Though it failed to break big, it did yield a hit single in Canada with "Peace of Mind." Subsequent singles and two more albums, *Now and Again* (1989) and *These Days* (1991), did well in their homeland but earned little sales elsewhere. In 1992, Kane left the band and the remaining members went on to become Ginger. —*Chris Woodstra*

September Bowl of Green / 1986 / Capitol ✦✦✦
Their first LP shows a band unsure whether to follow R.E.M.'s folky-lead or post-punk's dreamy abstraction. Fortunately, the jangly guitars and harmonies win out for a pleasing, though unspectacular, debut. Highlights include the single "Misunderstanding," as well as "Love Comes Around" and "A Dream (About You)." The CD version adds two previously unreleased tracks. —*Chris Woodstra*

○ **Treehouse** / 1987 / Capitol ✦✦✦✦
Early comparisons to R.E.M. are clearly justified on *Treehouse*, a jangly folk-pop masterpiece. On this, their second album, the band seem considerably more confident and focused. Crisp and bright production, courtesy of Tom Cochrane (ex-Red Rider), compliment the glorious harmonies and melancholy songs perfectly. A sadly overlooked classic of '80s guitar rock. —*Chris Woodstra*

● **Now & Again** / 1989 / Capitol ✦✦✦✦
Producer Anton Fier, leader/drummer of the Golden Palominos, imbues this Vancouver quartet's third full-length album with a lush early-'70s sound, at times approaching an Elton John/*Tumbleweed Connection*-style blend of orchestration and occasional pedal-steel augmentation (by Sneaky Pete Kleinow). Chuck Leavell plays keys on this outing as well. Melodically, the band tends to sound samey, partly attributable to the band's rather light singing tonalities. Highlights include the reflective "All the Things I Wasn't." —*Rick Clark*

These Days / 1991 / Capitol ✦✦✦
John Leckie (the Posies, Let's Active) produces this followup to *Now & Again*, by giving the band a slightly heavier, more organic band-like sound. In spite of an improved performance edginess, the band still lacks the proper dynamics for their melodies to stand out in relief memorably. Leckie's production, while loaded with nice touches, fails to help the band in overcoming their limitations. —*Rick Clark*

● **Seems Like Fate 1984-1992** / 1994 / Nettwerk/EMI ✦✦✦✦
20 worthy folk-rock tracks and respectable liner notes. The blending of 7" single edits, live tracks, and previously unreleased versions adds a new twist to the group's harmonious, heartfelt material. —*Roch Parisien*

Grass Roots

Group, Pop/Rock
A Top 40 band with folk/rock and light soul influences, Grass Roots was looked down on as a largely faceless studio-spawned ensemble created by the songwriting/production team of Steve Barri and P. F. Sloane. But their sound was powerful as well as marketable, and their best song, "Let's Live for Today," contains the roots of Bruce Springsteen's sound and image. —*Bruce Eder*

Where Were You When I Needed You? / 1966 / Varese Sarabande ✦✦✦
Before the Grass Roots reached the peak of their pop-rock popularity, they were a much more folk-rock-oriented outfit. Indeed, this debut album is a matter of much confusion; apparently the original Grass Roots were pretty much a front for the songwriting team of P.F. Sloan and Steve Barri, who ended up performing on much of the album themselves. In any case, this is decent, though not top-of-the-line, early folk-rock, falling about halfway between the Byrds and more pop-oriented peers like the Turtles and the Mamas and the Papas. Highlights include the hit title track and other Sloan-Barri originals like "Lollipop Train," "Look Out Girl,"

"This Is What I Was Made For," and "You Baby," which was a hit for the Turtles. The CD reissue adds six bonus tracks from rare singles, the best of which is the uncharacteristically tough "Tip of My Tongue" (not the obscure Lennon-McCartney composition). —*Richie Unterberger*

● **Anthology: 1965-1975** / 1991 / Rhino ✦✦✦✦
A 2-CD set that contains "Midnight Confessions," "Let's Live for Today," and more. Extraordinary sound and brilliantly annotated. —*Bruce Eder*

The Grateful Dead

Group, Rock & Roll, Country-Rock, Psychedelic, Folk-Rock
The Grateful Dead are the longest-lived of the San Francisco "acid rock" groups of the '60s. In the '90s, after more than 25 years in action, the Dead were still playing to enough satisfied customers on the road (most of them "Deadheads") to make them one of the top-grossing concert acts in the music business.

The group was formed in 1965 by bluegrass enthusiast Jerry Garcia (b. Aug. 1, 1942—d. Aug. 9, 1995) on guitar and vocals, Ron "Pigpen" McKernan (b. Sep. 8, 1945—d. Mar. 8, 1973) on vocals and organ, Bob Weir (b. Oct. 16, 1947) on guitar and vocals, classical music student Phil Lesh (b. Mar. 15, 1945) on bass and vocals, and Bill Kreutzmann (b. Apr. 7, 1946) on drums. From the beginning, they brought together a variety of influences, from Garcia's country background to Pigpen's feeling for blues (his father was an R&B radio DJ) and Lesh's education in contemporary "serious" music. Add to that the experimentation encouraged at some of the group's first performances at novelist Ken Kesey's "acid test" parties—multimedia events intended to replicate (or accompany) the experience of taking the then-legal drug LSD—and you had a musical mixture of styles often played with extended improvisational sections that could go off in nearly any direction.

The band signed to Warner Brothers in 1967, experiencing some difficulties early on with the restrictions of standard recording practices and the company's interest in producing a conventionally commercial product. As a result, the group's first few albums were somewhat tentative but showed promise for the future, especially with the key additions of Mickey Hart as a second drummer in 1967 and Garcia's old friend Robert Hunter as the band's lyricist.

The Dead finally hit their stride with the release of *Live/Dead*, a double album, in 1969. (They were always more comfortable on stage than in the studio.) Two studio albums in 1970, *Workingman's Dead* and *American Beauty*, found them exploring folk-rock and more tightly constructed song forms and, along with extensive touring, won them a much larger audience.

In second half of the '70s, the Dead recorded a series of commercially-oriented albums for Arista, then concentrated on road work for the better part of the '80s. *In the Dark*, released in 1987, was their first studio album in seven years. It sold a million copies and produced the band's first Top Ten hit in "Touch of Grey." The Dead continued to tour, notably doing shows with Bob Dylan, and at the start of the '90s, they began to release vintage material on their own Grateful Dead Merchandising label.

Garcia died of heart failure on August 9, 1995; after his death, the future of the Grateful Dead was in question. —*William Ruhlmann*

The Grateful Dead / Mar. 17, 1967 / Warner Brothers ✦✦
The Grateful Dead's debut album finds them uncomfortable in the studio, rushing tempos and otherwise failing to reproduce the feel of their live shows. Nevertheless, the group covers much of its then-current repertoire, including such long-term favorites as "Beat It on Down the Line," "Cold Rain and Snow," and "New, New Minglewood Blues." —*William Ruhlmann*

Anthem of the Sun / Jul. 18, 1968 / Warner Brothers ✦✦✦
The Grateful Dead spent six months recording their second album in studios and at concerts. The result came closer to an accurate portrait of them, highlighted by the four-part, 12-minute "That's It for the Other One." Still, the extensive mixing and editing made the sound dense and uninviting, especially to those not yet converted to the group's approach. —*William Ruhlmann*

Aoxomoxoa / Jun. 20, 1969 / Warner Brothers ✦✦✦
The addition of poet Robert Hunter as lyricist marked the beginning of a consistent set of imagery in the Dead's words to match their musical interplay, especially on songs like "St. Stephen" and "China Cat Sunflower." But the aural experiments were still mak-

ing for trying listening as the Dead continued to search for a way to capture their concert feel on disc. — *William Ruhlmann*

○ **Live/Dead** / Nov. 10, 1969 / Warner Brothers ♦♦♦♦

Long, trancelike songs with allusive lyrics (such as the classic "Dark Star") and R&B workouts featuring Pigpen's bluesy voice characterize this album, which is the basic document in the early Dead catalog—it's what most fans would like them to sound like every night. — *William Ruhlmann*

☆ **Workingman's Dead** / May 1970 / Warner Brothers ♦♦♦♦♦

A folk-rock, tightly arranged Dead, singing (in harmony!) some of their best songs, from "Uncle John's Band" to "Casey Jones." — *William Ruhlmann*

★ **American Beauty** / Nov. 1970 / Warner Brothers ♦♦♦♦♦

Workingman's Dead, part two—more of the songs that have served as the band's basic repertoire ever since these albums were released. Includes "Box of Rain," "Friend of the Devil," "Sugar Magnolia," "Ripple," and, of course, "Truckin'.">— *William Ruhlmann*

Grateful Dead / Oct. 1971 / Warner Brothers ♦♦♦

The Dead's second double live album (now on a single CD) introduces a couple of excellent Garcia/Hunter compositions, "Bertha" and "Wharf Rat," and allows Bob Weir to indulge his taste for what Deadheads would come to call "cowboy songs": Merle Haggard's "Mama Tried" and Kris Kristofferson's "Me & Bobby McGee." The album became the Dead's first gold record, probably on the momentum of *Workingman's Dead* and *American Beauty*. It also failed to match *Live/Dead* as a concert album, so that, coming off the band's recent peaks, it seemed less effective than it was. Now, it seems like one of the Dead's better, more coherent records. (Not to be confused with *The Grateful Dead*, the band's debut album. They resorted to *Grateful Dead* as a title when Warner wouldn't let them call the album *Skull Fuck*). — *William Ruhlmann*

○ **Europe '72** / Nov. 1972 / Warner Brothers ♦♦♦♦

Released as a three-record set, *Europe '72* is now a double CD. But it's still a long album, notable for introducing more Garcia-Hunter songs, especially "Brown-Eyed Woman," and for incorporating onto one album the variety of musical styles to be heard at a Dead concert, as well as the sheer duration necessary to appreciate the experience. Which means that, while this may not be the place a new fan wants to start, it's a Deadhead favorite. — *William Ruhlmann*

History of the Grateful Dead, Vol. 1 (Bear's Choice) / Jul. 13, 1973 / Warner Brothers ♦♦♦

This is a contractual obligation album, a record given to Warner Brothers Records to complete the Dead's commitment to the label. It was recorded in February 1970 and is something of a tribute to the late keyboardist/vocalist Ron "Pigpen" McKernan, who is heard frequently. Pigpen highlights an 18-minute version of Howlin' Wolf's "Smokestack Lightnin'.">" But this is a nonessential Dead album. "Bear" is the band's friend/soundman/drug manufacturer Owsley Stanley. The album is misnamed: it does not provide a "history" and there was never any Volume 2. — *William Ruhlmann*

○ **Wake of the Flood** / Nov. 15, 1973 / Grateful Dead ♦♦♦♦

The Grateful Dead's first studio album in three years was also their first for their own record label. It's a strong collection, featuring such Garcia-Hunter songs as "Mississippi Half-Step Uptown Toodleoo," "Row Jimmy," and "Stella Blue," songs that would become concert staples, as well as Bob Weir's "Weather Report Suite." — *William Ruhlmann*

Skeletons from the Closet: The Best of The Grateful Dead / 1974 / Warner Brothers ♦♦♦

This is an 11-song compilation, five of whose songs come from *Workingman's Dead* or *American Beauty*. It presents a sampling of the Dead's 1967-1972 period, focusing on their more accessible material. In that sense, it is recommended to the uninitiated who want to get a feel for the group; not surprisingly, it is a perennial seller, turning up week after week on *Billboard* magazine's Top Pop Catalog chart. The initiated, however, despise it: In a survey of Deadheads conducted by *DeadBase*, it was rated above only *Dylan & the Dead* as the worst Grateful Dead album. — *William Ruhlmann*

Grateful Dead from the Mars Hotel / Jun. 27, 1974 / Grateful Dead ♦♦♦

The Grateful Dead's second independent album was an uneven one, containing favorites like "Scarlet Begonians," "U.S. Blues," and "China Doll," but also a fair amount of filler. — *William Ruhlmann*

For Dead Heads / 1975 / United Artists ♦♦

As part of its Grateful Dead and Round Records labels, the Dead released albums by group members and associates as well as full-fledged Dead albums. This is a label sampler, containing tracks from albums by the Dead, Jerry Garcia, Robert Hunter, Keith and Donna Godchaux, and Old and in the Way. — *William Ruhlmann*

○ **Blues for Allah** / Sep. 1, 1975 / Grateful Dead ♦♦♦♦

Opening with the suite that has become a concert favorite, "Help on the Way"/"Slip Knot!"/"Franklin's Tower," and also containing the anthemic "The Music Never Stopped," *Blues for Allah* is another Grateful Dead album containing a few band classics and a lot of filler. Note, however, that some fans seem to like the filler. In its survey of Deadheads, *DeadBase* found *Blues for Allah* to be the band's most popular studio album after *Workingman's Dead* and *American Beauty*. — *William Ruhlmann*

Steal Your Face / Jun. 26, 1976 / Grateful Dead ♦♦

A double live album recorded in October 1974 just before the start of a hiatus in performing by the Dead and not released until 20 months later, to coincide with the feature film *The Grateful Dead Movie*, shot at the same shows. It is universally hated by Deadheads, and why would anyone else want to listen to it? Primary evidence that the Dead needed to take a break from touring in 1974. — *William Ruhlmann*

● **What a Long Strange Trip It's Been** / 1977 / Warner Brothers ♦♦♦♦

This is a two-disc compilation of the Grateful Dead covering its tenure at Warner Brothers Records, 1967-1972, and as such the most extensive sampler of their work in existence. Well-chosen, it contains many of their best songs from the period and is notable for giving album release to the studio-recorded single version of "Dark Star," the Dead's most requested song. Relative newcomers to the band (those who bought *Skeletons from the Closet* and liked it) can get a stronger dose here, and then perhaps go on to the individual albums. Of course, Deadheads hate this record. — *William Ruhlmann*

Terrapin Station / Jul. 27, 1977 / Arista ♦♦♦

The best of the early Arista albums, containing the extended "Terrapin Station" suite. — *William Ruhlmann*

Shakedown Street / Nov. 15, 1978 / Arista ♦♦

Using Little Feat leader Lowell George as producer should have been a great idea, but somehow it didn't work out. The Dead have salvaged "Fire on the Mountain" and "I Need a Miracle" for live work from this collection, but it's one of their least satisfactory studio ventures. — *William Ruhlmann*

Go to Heaven / Apr. 28, 1980 / Arista ♦♦

Another misstep. Whatever the Dead were trying to accomplish in the studio, whether it was to expand their following into the mainstream or change their style, they failed here. Deadheads rank this as the group's worst-ever studio album, and it's hard to argue with them. The Dead stayed out of the studio for seven years after this. — *William Ruhlmann*

Reckoning / Apr. 1, 1981 / Arista ♦♦♦

Having given up on studio work after the disaster of *Go to Heaven*, the Dead recorded a series of concerts in New York and San Francisco in October 1980 for two live albums. This is the first, a set of acoustic material that will remind many listeners of the rustic feel of the classic *Workingman's Dead* and *American Beauty* albums, although much of it consists of traditional and bluegrass material favored by Jerry Garcia. (The original two-LP set was fit onto one CD in 1987 by eliminating the Dead's cover of Elizabeth Cotten's "Oh Babe It Ain't No Lie"). — *William Ruhlmann*

Dead Set / Aug. 1981 / Arista ♦♦♦

The second of the Dead's two live albums recorded at shows in October 1980, this presents an electric set featuring some material previously heard on Jerry Garcia solo albums and some of the group's less successful '70s material. As such, it is far from the Dead's best live album, but it is representative of their work at the time. — *William Ruhlmann*

○ **In the Dark** / Jul. 6, 1987 / Arista ✦✦✦✦
The comeback, with "Touch of Grey," "West L.A. Fadeaway," and
"Black Muddy River." For anyone who wondered how these old
hippies could have such a following 20 years after the hippies disappeared, here's the answer. — *William Ruhlmann*

Built to Last / Oct. 31, 1989 / Arista ✦✦
Supposedly, the Dead had broken their studio jinx with *In the
Dark* and finally learned how to make good albums without an
audience in front of them. So why was this followup such a letdown? Perhaps because they hadn't taken seven years to write
and perfect new material as they had with the previous album.
The dominant songwriter here was keyboard player Brent Mydland (who died the following year), while the crucial songwriting
team of Garcia and Hunter contributed only minor efforts. Chas-
tened, the Dead once again retreated from studio work. — *William
Ruhlmann*

Without a Net / Sep. 1990 / Arista ✦✦✦
A double-CD live album notable for featuring performances by
jazz saxophonist Branford Marsalis and the Dead's version of Traffic's "Dear Mr. Fantasy," a concert favorite. Unintentionally, the album serves as the epitaph to keyboard player Brent Mydland, who
died shortly after its completion, bringing about another change in
the band's direction. — *William Ruhlmann*

One from the Vault / Apr. 15, 1991 / Grateful Dead ✦✦✦
With this album, issued on the group's own merchandising label,
the Grateful Dead began to address the needs of an audience that
had long since taken to making their own tapes of every Dead
performance. Such an audience, of course, would be interested in
record releases containing vintage live shows, and the Dead began
by issuing this 16-year-old concert, which occurred shortly after
they completed their 1975 album *Blues for Allah* and while they
were nominally retired from live work. It contains all the material
featured on that album, plus such recent Dead songs as "U.S.
Blues" and such favorites as "The Other One." It made for a modest beginning to the Dead's archival investigations, and only whetted fans' appetites for what might follow. — *William Ruhlmann*

Infrared Roses / Nov. 1, 1991 / Grateful Dead ✦✦
Each Grateful Dead concert includes a long instrumental section,
part of which is devoted to a drum solo and part to group improvisation, the parts dubbed "Drums" and "Space" by Deadheads.
This two-disc set consists of excerpts from such performances, as
electronically treated by Dead soundman Bob Bralove. It is one of
the Dead's more esoteric releases and not to be confused with a
regular, song-filled album. For fans and aficionados of experimental music only. — *William Ruhlmann*

Two from the Vault / 1992 / Grateful Dead ✦✦✦
Two discs' worth of the Dead in all their psychedelic glory, this second volume of live material from the archives stems from two
shows in August 1968, when their improvisational headiness balanced out with Pigpen bringing the proceedings solidly back
down to Earth. For those who may have wondered what *Anthem
of the Sun* might have sounded like minus the studio collage
mix—here's the answer. — *Steve Aldrich*

Dick's Picks, Vol. 1 / Dec. 1993 / Grateful Dead ✦✦✦
This recording of a Grateful Dead concert performed in Tampa,
FL, on December 19, 1973, inaugurates a new series of archival releases that differs from the band's already established *From the
Vaults* series in that it is to feature somewhat lower fidelity, "what
you hear is what you get" tapes as the liner notes put it, subject to
editing problems, incompleteness, etc. Perhaps to make up for
that, this double-CD album was not offered to retail, but distributed only through mail order, and it was sold at a discount price.
For all that, this is a good, if laidback, Dead set, led off by a 14-
minute version of "Here Comes Sunshine." That song comes from
Wake of the Flood, which was the band's current album release at
the time, and much of that LP's other material turns up notably a
complete, 16-minute "Weather Report Suite," along with favorites
like "Truckin'" and "Playing in the Band" the latter at a running
time of 21 minutes. As promised, the recording quality is noticeably unenhanced, but Dead Heads won't mind, and casual fans
won't bother. — *William Ruhlmann*

Dick's Picks, Volume Two / 1995 / Grateful Dead ✦✦✦
The second of the Grateful Dead's low-fidelity archival series of
live concerts on CD finds the group in Columbus, OH, on Halloween 1971, This was a relatively low-key time for the band,
which had been reduced to a quintet by the temporary departure

of second drummer Mickey Hart and in which original keyboard
player/vocalist Ron "Pigpen" McKernan had been replaced by
Keith Godchaux. They open with a 23-minute version of "Dark
Star," segue into "Sugar Magnolia" and "St. Stephen," and conclude with a medley of "Not Fade Away" and "Going down the
Road Feeling Bad," filling one 58-minute disc. The performance is
representative of the group and the period, not perhaps as impressive as the Grateful Dead album, a live record released the month
this concert occurred. For non-Deadheads, all this will seem redundant; for Deadheads, it's another show to add to the collection.
— *William Ruhlmann*

Gravediggaz

Group, Rap
Gravediggaz's violent mixture of hardcore gangsta-rap and heavy
metal was labeled "horrorcore" by some in the press. The whole
incident is somewhat ironic, considering the heritage of the group.
The mastermind of the group, the Undertaker, is better known as
a Stetsasonic's Prince Paul (born Paul Huston), who has produced
De La Soul among other "alternative" hip-hop groups. The other
members include the Rzarector (Prince Rakeem of Wu-Tang Clan),
the Grym Reaper (Poetic), and the Gatekeeper (Fruitkwan; born
Arnold Hamilton). Gravediggaz's 1994 debut album *Six Feet Deep*
was a minor hit, breaking the Top 40 of the pop album charts and
containing the single "Diary of a Madman." —*Stephen Thomas Erlewine*

● **Six Feet Deep** / 1994 / Gee Street ✦✦✦✦
Horror-core, a rather suspect variation of gangsta rap, didn't make
the expected waves in the hip-hop world. Gravediggaz, however,
are more intelligent than their image conveys. *6 Feet Deep* is an
all-star effort including Prince Paul, MC Serch, Biz Markie, Masta
Ace, and Vernon Reid. Obviously the dominant theme, death is
tackled with good results on "Defective Trip" and "1-800 Suicide."
Big beats and jazzy samples carry the raps well. —*John Bush*

Dobie Gray (Leonard Victor Ainsworth)

b. Jul. 26, 1943, Brookshire, Texas
Soul, Pop/Rock
Journeyman soul singer, composer, and actor Gray has had a
checkered career, scoring hit records in two different decades, acting on Broadway, and appearing in the Los Angeles production of
Hair.
        After moving to Nashville in 1978, Dobie Gray resurfaced in the
late '80s as a country singer and performer. Previously he remade "The In Crowd" for an LP on Infinity, *Dobie Gray*, that was a
hit in England. David Ruffin also recorded his song "City Stars."
The LP *Back Where I Belong* in the early '80s was a competent bit
of country-soul, but failed to secure Gray a niche in Nashville's
tight-knit fraternity. He continues performing and making occasional appearances on The Nashville Network.—*Cub Koda and
Ron Wynn*

● **Best of Dobie Gray** / 1982 / MCA ✦✦✦✦

The Great Society

Group, Psychedelic
Before joining the Jefferson Airplane, Grace Slick sang lead and
played various instruments for the Great Society, who were nearly
as popular as the Airplane in the early days of the San Francisco
psychedelic scene. Instrumentally, the Great Society were not as
disciplined as the Airplane. But they were at least their equals in
imagination, infusing their probing songwriting with Indian influences, nifty minor key melodic shifts, and groundbreaking, reverb-
soaked psychedelic guitar by Grace's brother-in-law, Darby Slick.
Darby was also responsible for penning "Somebody to Love,"
which Grace brought with her to the Airplane, who took it into the
Top Five in 1967. The Great Society broke up in late 1966 after
recording only one locally released single; after the Airplane became stars, Columbia issued a couple of live albums of the Great
Society performing at San Francisco's Matrix Club in 1966. —
Richie Unterberger

● **Collector's Item** / 1966 / Columbia ✦✦✦✦
This CD reissue combines both of the Great Society's live albums
onto one disc, and features "Somebody To Love" in its original
slower, more menacing version. It also includes the Society's extended version of Grace Slick's "White Rabbit," along with several
other haunting originals which strike an exhilarating balance between tight songwriting and psychedelic jamming. This is far

more than a "Collector's Item"; it's a genuinely exciting glimpse into the birth of psychedelic music. —*Richie Unterberger*

BOOK

✦✦ Don't You Want Somebody To Love, by Darby Slick (SLG, 1991). As guitarist for the Great Society, the band Grace Slick sang in before she joined the Jefferson Airplane, Darby Slick was there at the beginning of the San Francisco acid rock sound. This is his first-hand account of those days, and it really doesn't measure up to the subject matter, although it will interest fans of the era. There are stories, ranging from interesting to dispensable, about the band and its most important Haight-Ashbury peers, such as Big Brother, the Airplane, and the Dead. There isn't nearly as much about the actual music of the Great Society as one would hope, given that they were an instrumental (if underappreciated) factor in launching the San Francisco sound with their unusual raga, jazz, and Middle Eastern influences. Far more space is devoted to capturing the milieu of the times—hanging out, getting stoned, chasing girls—and while it does succeed at doing that to some extent, Slick doesn't seem to realize that the music was far more interesting than his and his friends' personal lives and loves. Also problematic is the writing and editing, which can be jumpy and, at times, clumsy. —*Richie Unterberger*

Great White

Group, Hard Rock, Heavy Metal
For most intents and purposes, Great White wasn't that different from the glut of mid-'80s hard rock/heavy metal bands. Their songs were derivative of Led Zeppelin, AC/DC, and Mott the Hoople, and lead singer Jack Russell had Robert Plant's wail down cold. Despite their lack of originality, the band was a tight unit that knew the value of a good song—they covered Hunter twice, including their hit single "Once Bitten, Twice Shy." However, Great White could never write as clever and mean as Hunter, nor could they crank out the riffs like Jimmy Page or Angus Young, which made their time in the spotlight very brief. The band continues to record and tour in the '90s, but they have yet to regain the audience 1989's *Twice Shy* captured. —*Stephen Thomas Erlewine*

On Your Knees / 1982 / Enigma ✦

Great White / 1984 / EMI America ✦✦

With their self-titled second album, Great White improved on the faceless boogie of their debut, yet they still lacked material strong enough to earn them a large audience. —*Stephen Thomas Erlewine*

Shot in the Dark / 1986 / Capitol ✦✦✦

○ **Once Bitten ...** / 1987 / Capitol ✦✦✦✦

Once Bitten... was Great White's first consistent album, highlighted by the minor hit single "Rock Me." —*Stephen Thomas Erlewine*

Recovery: Live! / 1988 / Enigma ✦✦

A lackluster mixture of live tracks and covers of Led Zeppelin, Humble Pie, and Jimi Hendrix, *Recovery: Live!* is a slight addition to Great White's catalog. —*Stephen Thomas Erlewine*

○ **... Twice Shy** / 1989 / Capitol ✦✦✦✦

With *... Twice Shy* Great White followed through on the promise of *Once Bitten ...*, turning in a tight, hard-rocking album that featured well-chosen covers (Ian Hunter's "Once Bitten, Twice Shy") and impressive originals that replicated the classic arena rock sound of the '70s ("House of Broken Love," "Mistah Bone"). The result was the band's best album and its most popular—the album broke into the Top Ten and sold over two million copies. —*Stephen Thomas Erlewine*

○ **Hooked** / 1991 / Capitol ✦✦✦✦

Great White began to lose their audience with 1990's *Hooked*. Their previous album, *... Twice Shy*, had sold two million copies, yet *Hooked* only managed to go gold. Its disappointing performance wasn't an indication that the record was weak. While it replicates the hard rock formula of the group's two previous records, the album features several of Great White's best original songs. —*Stephen Thomas Erlewine*

Psycho City / Sep. 14, 1992 / Capitol ✦✦✦

● **The Best of Great White 1986—1992** / Oct. 25, 1993 / Capitol ✦✦✦✦

All of Great White's finest songs are collected on *The Best of Great White*. —*AMG*

Sail Away / May 10, 1994 / Zoo ✦✦

R.B.Greaves

Soul
R.B.Greaves has an interesting family background and history, one that's actually more significant than his R&B track record. Greaves was born on an Air Force base in what was then British Guyana and grew up on a Seminole reservation. The nephew of Sam Cooke, Greaves moved to England in 1963, and was lead singer of Sonny Childe & the TNT's. He had his moment of glory in 1969 with "Take a Letter Maria," a fine song blending soap opera narrative and soulful vocals that peaked at number two pop and number ten R&B.His remake of "Always Something There to Remind Me" stiffed, and he was soon off Atlantic's subsidiary label Atco. Greaves tried again in 1977, recording for the Bareback label. It didn't revive his career. —*Ron Wynn*

● **R.B.Greaves** / 1970 / Atco ✦✦✦✦

Green Day

Group, Alternative Pop/Rock
Although these brash, third-generation California punks had made a name for themselves in the independent scene in the early '90s, it wasn't until they signed to a major label that they became alternative stars. And when their major-label debut, 1994's *Dookie*, was released the infectious punk-pop of "Longview" became more than an alternative hit—it quickly crossed over into the mainstream. Green Day come off as bratty punks, not threatening revolutionaries, but it's actually for the music's benefit; without their healthy, snotty attitude, their speedy, loud guitars and highly melodic hooks wouldn't be nearly as appealing as they are. —*Stephen Thomas Erlewine*

1039/Smoothed out Slappy Hour / 1991 / Lookout ✦✦

Kerplunk / 1992 / Lookout ✦✦✦

Green Day's best independent record is fueled more by their attitude and sonic aggression than their riffs. —*Stephen Thomas Erlewine*

● **Dookie** / 1994 / Reprise ✦✦✦✦

After two albums of indie guitar punk, Green Day made the jump to the majors with *Dookie*. Based on MTV's constant playing of "Longview," the band became a major crossover success; *Time* even hailed the album as the best rock & roll record of 1994. While *Dookie* isn't that good, it is quite good. For once, Green Day has genuine songs and hooks to go along with their muscular, roaring guitars, making *Dookie* not only their most accessible album, but also their best. —*Stephen Thomas Erlewine*

Green Jelly

Group, Pop/Rock
Green Jelly began life as Green Jello in 1981 in Kenmore, New York. The name was chosen due to the band's poor opinion of that flavor, and they decided that it also appropriately reflected the quality of their music. The band never attempted to be good, deciding instead to "disguise their lack of ability with stupid props," as their liner notes put it. The group appeared on *The Gong Show* touting themselves as the world's worst band, but the real turning point came when they met Gwar in 1988 and learned how to sculpt props and costumes with latex, papier-mache, chicken wire, and couch cushions. They attracted a small, curious following with their bizarre, cartoonish look and wound up signing with Zoo Records as a video-only band. They released a video album called *Cereal Killer*, using simple, bubblegum metal songs as an excuse to dance around in silly costumes, and the clay-animation video for "Three Little Pigs" became an MTV hit, spawning the release of an EP and later the full soundtrack to the video album. With success came lawsuits for trademark infringement; the band was forced to change their name to Green Jelly and also had to put an edited version of "Cereal Killer" on their audio release, as the cereal companies whose mascots were murdered in the video did not take kindly to it. Band members, who have exceeded 74 in number over the years, perform under aliases such as Marshall Staxx and Jesus Quisp. It remains to be seen how much longer the

band will be able to sell records based on their visual weirdness, but they're still doing fine. —*Steve Huey*

● **Cereal Killer Soundtrack** / 1993 / Zoo ✦✦✦✦
More of a joke than a band, Green Jelly (formerly known as Green Jello) walks the fine line between being a fun novelty and being irritating. As expected, "Three Little Pigs" is the highlight of the album, but anyone who liked that surprise hit will find a couple other songs enjoyable, if not the whole album. —*AMG*

Three Three Three / 1994 / Pavement ✦✦

Green on Red

Group, Alternative Pop/Rock
A California band with a shifting lineup anchored by singer/songwriter and guitarist Dan Stuart, Green on Red evolved from the neo-psychedelic "paisley underground" band of the early '80s to a country-rock duo by the decade's end. —*William Ruhlmann*

EP / 1981 /

Green on Red / 1982 / Down There ✦✦✦

Gravity Talks / 1983 / Slash ✦✦✦

No Free Lunch / 1985 / One Way ✦✦

Gas Food Lodging / 1985 / Enigma ✦✦

The Killer Inside Me / 1987 / Mercury ✦✦

○ **Here Comes the Snakes** / 1989 / Restless ✦✦✦✦

Live at the Town & Country / 1989 / Polydor ✦✦

● **This Time Around** / 1989 / Mercury ✦✦✦✦
The tight production of Glyn Johns keeps things from getting too sloppy in these barroom ballads and raveups that mix country, folk, and rock, all keyed to Dan Stuart's appealing voice and desperate lyrics. —*William Ruhlmann*

Scapegoats / 1991 / China ✦✦✦

Too Much Fun / 1992 / Off Beat

Green River

Group, Alternative Pop/Rock
In the mid-'80s, Before the word "grunge" became a specific musical style, before Sub Pop was considered as a training league for major labels, many post-punk rock fans didn't believe Seattle had a worthwhile musical scene. Green River helped change that. With its ugly, loud, sub-Stooges guitar grind, Green River was the first band to make Sub Pop a hip underground label. At their best, the band made a powerful, brutal guitar rock that merged '70s heavy metal and '60s garage punk with '80s post-punk; at their worst, they were a sludgy, depressing mess.

Green River were together for three years before the band splintered apart. Singer Mark Arm and occasional guitarist Steve Turner formed Mudhoney, while guitarist Stone Gossard and bassist Jeff Ament formed Mother Love Bone after the band's demise, which would eventually turn into Pearl Jam. The roots of Mudhoney's garage grunge and Pearl Jam's revisionist '70s hard rock can be heard on Green River's two EPs and their one album. —*Stephen Thomas Erlewine*

Come on Down / 1985 / Positive ✦✦✦

○ **Dry As a Bone/Rehab Doll** / 1987 / Sub Pop ✦✦✦✦

● **Rehab Doll** / 1988 / Sub Pop ✦✦✦✦
Green River's only album is a brutal collection of primal Stooges-style guitar grind and punked-up metal riffing. The CD includes the equally powerful *Dry As a Bone* EP. —*Stephen Thomas Erlewine*

Al Green

b. Apr. 13, 1946, Forest City, AR
Soul, R&B
Born in 1946 in Forest City, AR, and raised in Grand Rapids, MI, Al Green became the premier soul singer in the '70s, in the process being the last great purveyor of a music whose time had come and gone. When he was thirteen, Green started singing with a family gospel group, the Greene Brothers. By 1967, he was singing secular and solo, scoring a hit with "Back Up Train" on the Hot Line Music Journal label. Touring the chitlin circuit on the strength of the record, Green found himself playing the same bill in Midland, TX, as Memphis trumpeter and producer Willie Mitchell. Mitchell signed Green to Memphis's Hi Records, and, as they say, the rest is history.

Between 1970 and 1977, Green placed 23 records on the R&B charts and 18 on the pop charts, including seven Top Tens. The Green/Mitchell/Hi rhythm-section sound was incredibly consistent, making most of the albums listed below somewhat interchangeable. The records are ultra cool; there is little overt sweat. Green's phrases are disjointed, generally behind the beat, always surprising. At regular intervals he dips into his unreal falsetto. Soft girl backup singing is employed, as is a string orchestra. Drummers Al Jackson and Howard Grimes eschew the cymbals, replacing them with a ride pattern on the tom-toms. All of this is executed in the context of compositions by Mitchell, Green, Jackson, and guitarist Teenie Hodges such as "Love and Happiness," "Take Me to the River," "Let's Stay Together," and "Tired of Being Alone." Green became "born again" in 1976, splitting from Mitchell a year later and electing to record gospel music only for most of the next decade and a half. In 1985, he reunited with Mitchell for the album *He Is the Light*. —*Rob Bowman*

Back Up Train / 1967 / Hot Line ✦✦
The album that launched the career of Al Green, the '70s' reigning soul king and '80s gospel giant. While there were some problems with material, Al Green's smooth, soulful, exuberant voice quickly established him as a dominant, compelling artist. He also still had the buoyant, innocent quality that, unfortunately, time and personal problems ultimately wore away. —*Ron Wynn*

Green Is Blues / 1970 / The Right Stuff ✦✦✦
The first album linking the soul-singing greatness of Al Green with the production brilliance and expertise of Willie Mitchell. The results were mutually beneficial; Green got the great production, arrangements, and backing from the Hi Rhythm section that often turned good songs into classics, and he sang with the conviction and talent that provided the final component in an artistically and commercially satisfying union. —*Ron Wynn*

○ **Gets Next to You** / 1971 / The Right Stuff ✦✦✦✦

○ **Let's Stay Together** / Feb. 1972 / The Right Stuff ✦✦✦✦
Green's third album for Hi and the first of a string of brilliant releases. The title song was the big hit but an extended version of the Bee Gees' "How Can You Mend a Broken Heart?" remained a staple for years. —*Rob Bowman*

☆ **I'm Still in Love with You** / Dec. 1972 / The Right Stuff ✦✦✦✦✦
Green's fourth album for Hi finds him exploring country-soul with an achingly beautiful take on Kris Kristofferson's "For the Good Times." The hits were the title song and "Look What You Done for Me." —*Rob Bowman*

☆ **Call Me** / Jul. 1973 / The Right Stuff ✦✦✦✦✦
Three R&B Top Ten hits, the title song, "Here I Am (Come and Take Me)," and "You Ought to Be with Me," dominate what is probably his finest album. Once again he tackles some country-soul, turning in moving versions of Hank Williams's "I'm So Lonesome I Could Cry" and Willie Nelson's "Funny How Time Slips Away." Green also returns to the gospel vein on "Jesus Is Waiting." —*Rob Bowman*

Livin' for You / Dec. 1973 / The Right Stuff ✦✦✦
A cut below the albums listed above, *Livin' for You* is still mighty fine. The title cut and "Let's Get Married" were both Top Ten R&B hits. —*Rob Bowman*

Al Green Explores Your Mind / 1974 / The Right Stuff ✦✦✦
Only one hit single this time out with "Sha-La-La (Make Me Happy)." *Explores Your Mind* also contains what may have become Green's best-known song, "Take Me to the River." —*Rob Bowman*

★ **Al Green's Greatest Hits** / Apr. 1975 / The Right Stuff ✦✦✦✦✦
The title says it all, ten songs that define Southern soul in the mid-'70s. —*Rob Bowman*

Al Green Is Love / Oct. 1975 / The Right Stuff ✦✦✦
Two more Top Ten hits with "L-O-V-E (Love)" and "Oh Me, Oh My (Dream's in My Arms)." —*Rob Bowman*

Full of Fire / Apr. 1976 / Hi ✦✦✦
Wonderfully sung, expertly produced and performed '70s soul by a vocal master and a superb support combo. Al Green and Willie Mitchell were so solidly attuned to each other that Green's albums were truly collaborative affairs, with the superb Hi Rhythm section filling in behind and underneath him effortlessly. —*Ron Wynn*

Have a Good Time / Dec. 1976 / Hi ◆◆◆

Al Green was riding right along, still singing with confidence, power, and authority. Although this was kind of a transition effort, with Green beginning to head toward gospel, his vocals retained their edge and relaxed fire. Mitchell and Hi Rhythm did their usual excellent supporting job. —*Ron Wynn*

☆ **Al Green's Greatest Hits, Vol. II** / Jul. 1977 / The Right Stuff ◆◆◆◆◆

As good as *Volume 1*, augmented by non-chart items that might have been hits anyway, like "Love and Happiness," "Take Me to the River," and "For the Good Times." —*Rob Bowman*

○ **The Belle Album** / Dec. 1977 / The Right Stuff ◆◆◆◆

Al Green severed his ties with longtime producer Willie Mitchell in 1977, establishing his own backup band and seizing the production reins. But he hadn't yet made the final break with soul; this was the last secular work he would make for many years, and it was brilliant, even though it didn't come close to equaling his previous commercial heights. In retrospect, many just didn't understand where he was going, while others were turned off by the blurred lyrical focus of songs like "Belle." But "I Feel Good" had as much danceable energy and soulful fire as any Green uptempo tune, and "Lovin' You" and "Dream" were sorely underrated compositions. —*Ron Wynn*

○ **Truth & Time** / 1978 / Hi ◆◆◆◆

○ **The Lord Will Make a Way** / 1980 / Myrrh ◆◆◆◆

One of my favorite gospel albums by Rev. Green. The R&B and pop hits had stopped coming but the sacred peaks were the equal of any of his secular material. In 1992 Green was still performing the title song and "In the Holy Name of Jesus." —*Rob Bowman*

○ **Tokyo Live** / 1981 / The Right Stuff ◆◆◆◆

A wonderful live set that serves as both a retrospective and a defining release showing that Green sang the same way regardless of musical and lyrical content. He did many of his greatest soul hits, performing them with the relaxed, powerful grace that made him the '70s' finest soul vocalist and the '80s' best male gospel artist. —*Ron Wynn*

○ **Higher Plane** / Feb. 1981 / Hi ◆◆◆◆

Another superior sacred recording, most notable for a stellar version of the Impressions' "People Get Ready." —*Rob Bowman*

○ **He Is the Light** / 1985 / A&M ◆◆◆◆

At the time of writing, this was Green's last truly great recording. Back with Willie Mitchell, the Hi rhythm section, and the Memphis Horns, Green has great material and delivers the goods. —*Rob Bowman*

○ **I Get Joy** / 1989 / A&M ◆◆◆◆

Some exuberant, rocking gospel and slower, less energetic, but equally reverent material from Rev. Al Green. Although he's not doing soul, Green still slips in some of the vocal maneuvers, sliding falsetto effects, and mannerisms that made his secular material electrifying. His '80s gospel albums were no less moving. —*Ron Wynn*

○ **Love Ritual** / 1989 / MCA ◆◆◆◆

Don't let the title lead you into thinking that these are second-rate leftovers, because this album (originally compiled for the British Demon label) is loaded with gems. Highlights are hard to pin down, but one surprise is a spirited version of the Beatles' "I Want to Hold Your Hand"; it should've been a single. Every track except "Ride Sally Ride" has been digitally remixed from the original multi-tracks. The sound is great, being faithful to the spirit of Willie Mitchell's production and mixing style, and the disc includes detailed liner notes. All in all, Green fans should pick up on this. —*Rick Clark*

○ **One in a Million** / 1990 / Word ◆◆◆◆

A compilation from Green's gospel recordings, it reveals the emotional depth of his religious work. —*Brian Mansfield*

Love Is Reality / 1992 / Word ◆◆◆

After years of refusing to sing anything but gospel, Green decided the time had finally come to fuse the godly and the secular elements of his soul. *Love Is Reality* made an overt play for the mainstream R&B market. Unfortunately, Christian dance-pop producer Tim Miner works from formulas, while Green runs on inspiration. Green sounded great, but the final result paled in comparison to the rest of his catalog. —*Brian Mansfield*

Vernon Green & the Medallions

Group, Doo-Wop

The Medallions, a Los Angeles doo-wop quartet with a predilection toward songs about speedy cars, formed in 1953. Their first single, "The Letter"/"Buick '59," on the Dootsie Williams Dootone label, was a regional hit, coupling a dreamy ballad with a joyriding rocker complete with automotive sound effects by the group. (Encores in the same vein included "Speedin',>" "Pushbutton Automobile," and "Coupe DeVille Baby;" there was even a "'59 Volvo"!). Williams's renamed Dooto label handed Green an opportunity to sing soul in 1973, and he recently reemerged with some doo-wop offerings on the Classic Artists imprint. —*Bill Dahl*

● **Golden Classics** / Collectables ◆◆◆◆

This Los Angeles doo-wop aggregation specialized in "rocking car songs" during the mid '50s. —*Bill Dahl*

Clive Gregson & Christine Collister

Group, Folk, Singer-Songwriter, Folk-Rock

Clive Gregson and Christine Collister were the most moving U.K. folk-rock duo to emerge since Richard and Linda Thompson. Gregson (b. Jan. 4, 1955) was the founder of Any Trouble, a rock quartet, in Manchester in 1975. The band's sound, and Gregson's songwriting and singing, reminded some of Elvis Costello, and Any Trouble was signed by Stiff, Costello's label. The band made several well-remembered but poor-selling albums, then split up. Gregson made a solo album, *Strange Persuasions*, in 1985, then hooked up with Collister. Gregson first introduced Collister into Richard Thompson's band (Gregson was backup guitarist at the time), then they began performing as a duo. The duo's first release was a homemade tape sold at gigs, later released as *Home and Away*. It was followed by their first formal album, *Mischief*, in 1988, and by a *Change in the Weather* in 1990. *Love in a Strange Hotel*, released later the same year, was an album of cover versions of Gregson and Collister's favorite songs. Their songs, all written by Gregson, are wry tales of the ins and outs of love, sung in Collister's heartbreaking voice. —*William Ruhlmann*

Strange Persuasions / 1985 / Demon ◆◆◆

○ **Home & Away** / 1986 / Flying Fish ◆◆◆◆

A collection of songs recorded during an early acoustic tour in 1986. The duo run through new originals, some songs from Gregson's Any Trouble days, and a few well-chosen covers in a warm, intimate setting. —*Chris Woodstra*

○ **Mischief** / 1987 / Rhino ◆◆◆◆

Clive Gregson's songs treat romance with ironic charm: "We're Not Over Yet" is a compendium of reasons why they ought to be over, and "Everybody Cheats on You" is about more than just romantic infidelity. Christine Collister gives the songs a depth that often keeps them from being a bit too glib and clever, as do the folk-pop arrangements. —*William Ruhlmann*

● **A Change in the Weather** / 1989 / Rhino ◆◆◆◆

The self-insight continues in Gregson's lyrics, but the concerns are expanded. Collister does a fine job covering "Tryin' to Get to You." —*William Ruhlmann*

Love Is a Strange Hotel / 1990 / Rhino ◆◆◆

A departure from the expansive arrangements of the previous two albums, *Love Is a Strange Hotel*, is a low key acoustic collection of covers. Even unlikely choices, like Aztec Camera's "How Men Are," and 10cc's "Things We Do for Love" are pulled off in their own charming way. —*Chris Woodstra*

○ **Welcome To The Workhouse** / 1990 / Special Delivery ◆◆◆◆

Welcome to the Workhouse is a collection of Gregson's home demos and outtakes and while most albums of this sort appeal only to the diehard fans, this one stands out as one of his finest moments. The recordings span 1980 to 1985 and provide a good bridge between his work with Any Trouble and his partnership with Christine Collister. —*Chris Woodstra*

The Last Word / 1992 / Rhino ◆◆◆

Gregson and Collister have perfected their now classic sound on their final effort. Their extraordinary harmonies have never sounded better on Gregson's moody songs mixing folk, jazz, country and blues. —*Chris Woodstra*

People & Places / 1995 / Compass ◆◆

Grenadine

Group, Alternative Pop/Rock
This independent-label rock supergroup consists of Jenny Toomey from Tsunami, Mark Robinson from Unrest and Air Miami, and Rob Christiansen from the Eggs. Formed in 1991, Grenadine has a slew of seven-inches to its credit, as well as two albums, *Goya* and *Nopalitos*, that show off the band's moody take on pop music. Toomey's compositions tend to be sullenly melodic, quiet epics that show off her rich, throaty voice, while Robinson's songs range from upbeat power-pop to odd, 1920s-style ditties reminiscent of Rudy Vallee and other crooners. An unusual band even by indie-rock standards, Grenadine allows its members to explore musical facets untouched by their other bands, making the group more than just a side project. —*Heather Phares*
○ Goya / 1992 / Shimmy Disc ✦✦✦✦

Grifters

Group, Alternative Pop/Rock
If Guided By Voices are the Beatles of the lo-fi scene, Grifters' big, bluesy racket is the Stones. Deliberately noisy, sloppy, and out-of-tune, Memphis' Grifters mask their melodies under a heavy static fuzz of distortion. After four singles, the band released their first album, *One Sock Missing*, in 1993. The indie-world began to take notice the next year when Grifters released their second LP, *Crappin' You Negative*. An EP followed in 1995. —*John Bush*
○ One Sock Missing / 1993 / Shangrila ✦✦✦✦
There's a point during second song, "She Blows Blasts of Static," where Grifters sound like a bad quality bootleg of Stones' demos. That's not an insult, but this especially caustic version of lo-fi indie-pop might be too much for some listeners. —*John Bush*

Grim Reaper

Group, Heavy Metal
Grim Reaper was a 1980s British metal band who played in the typical Euro-metal style of melodic vocals and simple riffs. They also had a very strong liking for demonic imagery and over-the-top theatrics. The group is best known to many '90s listeners through an episode of *Beavis and Butt-Head* in which their video for "See You in Hell" is commented on rather unfavorably. —*Steve Huey*
See You in Hell / 1984 / RCA ✦✦✦
Classy heavy metal, it has wonderful vocals. Fans of Anthrax's Joey Belladonna could appreciate this. —*John Book*
● Fear No Evil / 1985 / RCA ✦✦✦✦
Powerful American heavy metal in the style of Iron Maiden, this is Grim Reaper's best and most respected album. —*John Book*
Rock You to Hell / 1987 / RCA ✦✦

The Grodes

Group, Garage Rock, Pop/Rock
One of the more talented garage bands of the mid-'60s, with a more professional and pop/rock bent than the average garage outfit. The Grodes cut half a dozen singles between 1965 and 1967, several of which charted in their hometown of Tucson, AZ. They sported a pleasantly driving, melodic sound with obvious debts to the Beatles, Stones, Zombies, Kingsmen, Byrds, Mamas and Papas, and frat-rock, but ultimately didn't offer anything original enough to make them stand out from the pack. Their most lasting contribution arose when they briefly changed their names to the Tongues of Truth and cut the uncharacteristically tough punker "Let's Talk About Girls," which was covered in a much more famous version (later anthologized on *Nuggets*) by the Chocolate Watchband. The Grodes broke up in 1968, after briefly adding female singer Patti McCarron; lead singer and songwriter Manny Freiser married her and teamed up with her professionally in the soft rock duo Fire & Rain, who released an album for Mercury in 1973. —*Richie Unterberger*
Tongues Of Truth/The Grodes / 1983 / Voxx ✦✦✦
This rather cumbersomely titled compilation includes virtually everything the group released on their now-rare singles, both as the Grodes and the Tongues of Truth. Highlights are "Let's Talk About Girls," which is somewhat poppier than the more widely known Chocolate Watch Band version, and the driving garage-Mersey of "I Won't Be There" (included in both the official single release and a raw earlier unreleased version). Also features exten-

sive group history by Manny Freiser, who wrote and sang virtually all of the material. —*Richie Unterberger*

Group 1850

Group, Psychedelic
An interesting, if sometimes exasperating, late-'60s Dutch band that rank among the most accomplished and original Continental rock acts of the era, though they made little impression in English-speaking territories. Starting as a more or less conventional beat band in the mid-'60s, they had taken a turn for the more psychedelic and bizarre by 1967. Determined to drive into the heart of the psychedelic beast, their songs (performed in English) are quite eclectic for the era, shifting from doom-laden tempos with growling vocals to quite sunny, utopian passages with breezy harmonies. The group could be roughly labeled as a mixture of the early Mothers of Invention (whom they supported at a Dutch concert in 1967) and Pink Floyd without much of a sense of humor; their songs are intriguing and not without powerful hooks, and the lyrics ambitious (if often inscrutable), but one's attention tends to wander over the course of an album, or even during their lengthier songs. Their late-'60s LPs are highly esteemed by some serious psych/progressive collectors. —*Richie Unterberger*
Paradise Now / 1969 / Discophon ✦✦✦
The group play it spacier and lighter on their second album, with plenty of soaring guitars and keyboards and more diffuse compositions. The attractiveness of the ethereal sound almost obscures the fact that the songwriting lacks grist and cohesion. —*Richie Unterberger*
● 1967-1968 / 1993 / Mercury ✦✦✦✦
The entirety of their 1968 debut album *Agemo's Trip to Mother Earth*, as well as seven songs from somewhat more pop-oriented singles that preceded it. Dense and challenging stuff, owing more to the reckless groove of vintage psychedelia than progressive rock. —*Richie Unterberger*

Joe Grusheky & the Houserockers

Group, Rock & Roll
When Pittsburgh-based Joe Grushecky's band the Iron City Houserockers turned up on MCA Records in 1979, their driving bar-band rock & roll and working-class lyrics earned them critical kudos but also made them Johnny-come-latelies in a crowded field headed by Bruce Springsteen and including Bob Seger, John Cafferty, and John Mellencamp. Nevertheless, they managed to release four albums through 1983. Grushecky reorganized, keeping only the bass player for the new edition launched under his own name in 1989, but the approach and sound are the same. —*William Ruhlmann*
○ Love's So Tough / 1979 / MCA ✦✦✦✦
This is tough, R&B-based rock from the heartland. —*David Szatmary*
Have a Good Time (But Get out Alive) / 1980 / MCA ✦✦✦
More driving blues-rock fused with Springsteen-type politics from the Iron City Houserockers. —*David Szatmary*
Blood on the Bricks / 1981 / MCA ✦✦✦
Swimming with the Sharks / 1988 / Rounder ✦✦✦
○ Rock & Real / 1989 / Rounder ✦✦✦✦
Grushecky's songs of tough urban life are made all the more compelling by his rough voice and the aggressive playing of his band, though he can also turn tender on such songs as "Daddy's Little Angel." —*William Ruhlmann*
● Pumping Iron & Sweating Steel: The Best of The Iron City Houserockers / 1992 / Rhino ✦✦✦✦
A generous compilation of the best of an underrated rock and roll band from the late '70s and early '80s. Some of Joe Grushecky's songs on *Pumping Iron & Sweating Steel* equal the best of Bruce Springsteen, Tom Petty, and Bob Seger during this period. Fans of those artists will certainly find the Iron City Houserockers worth investigating. —*Stephen Thomas Erlewine*
End of the Century / Sep. 1992 / Razor & Tie ✦✦

Gryphon

Group, Art-Rock/Progressive-Rock
An English all-instrumental electric folk band, originally similar to Pentangle in their eclecticism (and, not coincidentally, signed to the same label, Transatlantic). They subsequently developed a

more intense playing style and went electric, eventually hooking up with Yes for one U.S. tour. Wind player Richard Harvey, who was classically trained and had a parallel career in movie music, was one of the more notable members, while Ernest Hart's rippling keyboards and guitarist Graeme Taylor's classically wrought elegance were key elements of the band's sound. —*Bruce Eder*

Gryphon / 1973 / Transatlantic ◆◆◆

Midnight Mushrumps / 1974 / Transatlantic ◆◆

● **Red Queen to Gryphon Three** / 1974 / Arista ◆◆◆◆
Apocalyptic electric folk-rock, utilizing traditional melodies pumped up and with heavily amplified organ and synthesizer and highly animated recorder and flute. The effect is rather Yes-like, sans vocals. This album achieves a *Close to the Edge*-style finale with the track "Checkmate." —*Bruce Eder*

Raindance / 1975 / Transatlantic ◆◆

Treason / 1977 / Harvest ◆◆

○ **The Collection** / 1991 / Progressive ◆◆◆◆

The GTO's

Group, Pop/Rock
The GTO's were a "groupie group" made up of young women familiar to musicians in the Los Angeles area. Most prominent among them was Miss Pamela who, as Pamela Des Barres, wrote the kiss-and-tell memoir *I'm with the Band.* —*William Ruhlmann*

○ **Permanent Damage** / 1969 / Bizarre ◆◆◆◆
Frank Zappa produced this combination of light pop songs and involved discussions of the ups and downs of groupie life. It's a sort of musical comedy documentary on record and, without doubt, unique. —*William Ruhlmann*

The Guess Who

Group, Pop/Rock
A Winnipeg, Canada, band called Chad Allen & the Reflections (formed 1962) enjoyed some success with a couple of regional 1963 hits ("Tribute to Buddy Holly," "Shy Guy") but quickly shifted over to the new British Merseybeat style and recorded a version of Johnny Kidd & the Pirates's "Shakin' All Over." The song became a #1 Canadian hit. As a publicity stunt, the record label (Quality) listed the artist as "Guess Who?," implying that it might be some big English act ghosting on the side. The ploy worked, and the American label Scepter picked them up, taking the record to #22. At the label's request, the Reflections changed their name to the Guess Who.
The band couldn't generate a followup hit, and it wasn't until 1968, when they met producer Jack Richardson, that things began looking up. Richardson mortgaged his house to help them record what became the album *Wheatfield Soul*. One of the tracks, "These Eyes," went to #6 Stateside, beginning a long string of excellent pop/rock hits.
1970 and 1971 were banner years for the Guess Who, with a pair of hit albums, *American Woman* (#9) and *Share the Land* (#14). During this time, they displayed a highly developed level of melodic skills. Burton Cummings had developed a compelling vocal style, and new lead guitarists Kurt Winter and Greg Leskiw forged out a distinctive sound. The band scored a few more hits before breaking up in 1975. Cummings experienced an uneven solo career after landing a million-selling #10 hit with his debut single, "Stand Tall." —*Rick Clark*

○ **Canned Wheat** / 1969 / RCA ◆◆◆◆
The group's second album, and probably their best long-player, with a couple of hits surrounded by some lyrical, well-crafted album tracks. —*Bruce Eder*

Share the Land / 1970 / RCA ◆◆◆
Hot on the heels of the hit *American Woman* album (whose title track was a number one stateside hit), the Guess Who delivered *Share the Land*, the band's most cohesive collection of pop-smart rock songs. Includes the hits "Do You Miss Me Darlin'?," "Hand Me Down World," "Hang on to Your Life" and "Share the Land." —*Rick Clark*

○ **The Best of Guess Who** / 1971 / RCA ◆◆◆◆
A fine single-disc collection of most of the band's greatest hits, it's perfect for listeners who don't want to invest in the double-disc *Track Record*. —*AMG*

So Long, Bannatyne / 1971 / RCA ◆◆
The Guess Who changed directions away from their hard pop/rock and came up with a more pianistic set of songs, like the orchestrated numbers "Sour Suite," "Goin' A Little Crazy" and jazzy "Grey Day." "Pain Train," not found on the excellent *Track Record*, is a highlight, as well as the hit single "Rain Dance." —*Rick Clark*

Live at the Paramount / 1972 / RCA ◆◆
An okay, but unexceptional, document of their stage performances from the post-Bachman era. —*Bruce Eder*

○ **The Best of the Guess Who, Vol. 2** / 1974 / RCA ◆◆◆◆

● **Track Record: The Guess Who Collection** / 1988 / RCA ◆◆◆◆
A perfect collection, covering the band's whole history on two CDs. Includes the hits "These Eyes" (#6), "Laughing" (#10), "Undun" (#22), "No Time" (#5), "American Woman/No Sugar Tonight" (#1), "Share the Land" (#10), and the noveltyish "Clap for the Wolfman" (#6). —*Bruce Eder*

Lonely One / 1995 / Intersound ◆◆

Guided By Voices

Group, Alternative Pop/Rock
Throughout the '80s, the Dayton, OH, guitar-pop group Guided By Voices released a series of independent albums; most of them never made it out of their own hometown. Led by vocalist Robert Pollard, the group featured a fluctuating lineup that recorded their albums in their spare time and rarely performed live. While their records are frequently muddy, full of tape hiss, and always lacking in clarity, their hooks are simple and catchy, and their songs are quite brief; their sound evokes Wire and mid-'60s British pop.
Guided By Voices became a hip name to drop in 1994, thanks to numerous accolades from Kim Deal, the leader of the Breeders. The group landed a slot on Lollapalooza's second stage and their album *Bee Thousand* received rave reviews. All the attention led to the reissue of all of their albums, as well as a record contract with the influential independent record label Matador. —*Stephen Thomas Erlewine*

Vampire on Titus / 1993 / SCAT ◆◆◆
After years of impressive but flawed records, *Vampire on Titus* was Guided By Voices' first consistent record, with more than half of the 18 songs being blessed with memorable melodies or hooks. The CD version includes *Propeller*, which showed Robert Pollard's songwriting beginning to become more refined and accessible. —*Stephen Thomas Erlewine*

● **Bee Thousand** / 1994 / Scat ◆◆◆◆
Sonically, *Bee Thousand* isn't that different from Guided By Voices' previous albums. The band still is creating brief, minimalistic homages to British Invasion pop and art-rock, except the songs are better-constructed, with hooks that are immediately memorable. —*Stephen Thomas Erlewine*

Box / 1995 / Scat ◆◆◆
Compiling all of Guided By Voices' '80s albums—*Devil Between My Toes, Sandbox, Self-Inflicted Aerial Nostalgia*, and *Same Place the Fly Got Smashed* (the vinyl version includes *Propeller*, which was on the *Vampire on Titus* CD)—and adding a collection of rarities called *King Shit and the Golden Boys, Box* is a bit of an intimidating listen for some devoted fans, let alone beginners. On each of their albums, Guided By Voices packs their records full of brief songs—if they reach the three-minute mark, it's an epic for the band. While that can make such a massive collection of music rather daunting; it all seems to speed by without much distinction, if you're listening casually, but on closer inspection, it withstands repeated listens. The first records, *Devils* and *Sandbox*, are unpolished versions of R.E.M.'s *Murmur*. On the next two albums, the group's distinctive, British Invasion-inspired abbreviated pop begins to coalesce; their music sounds more like messages than songs, albeit messages that are driven by undeniable hooks. Retailing for under $50, *Box* is a worthwhile investment for dedicated fans. —*Stephen Thomas Erlewine*

○ **Alien Lanes** / 1995 / Matador ◆◆◆◆
Featuring a slightly cleaner production and more straightforward melodies, *Alien Lanes*, the first record Guided By Voices released since their breakthrough *Bee Thousand*, is only slightly less impressive than their previous record. —*Stephen Thomas Erlewine*

Gumball

Group, Alternative Pop/Rock
When indie superstar and renowned record producer (Sonic Youth,

the Posies, Alice Cooper) Don Fleming decided to form his own group in the early '90s, he brought in his long-time collaborator drummer Jay Spiegel along with bassist Eric Vermillion to form Gumball. In Gumball, Fleming's obsession with pop culture and pop music from the Monkees to the Damned to Sonic Youth reached full fruition. Snatches of '60s guitar riffs sat next to '80s guitar noise and '70s punk rubbed shoulders with '70s schlock metal; all of it proved his knack for treating the worst pop music as serious rock, while dirtying respectable indie sonic tricks with sweet bubblegum pop. Unfortunately, much of their music sounds like the work of an expert record collector, not an expert musician, but at their best they can deliver some solid three-minute rock & roll thrills. —*Stephen Thomas Erlewine*

Gumball / 1990 / Primo Scree ✦✦✦

Special Kiss / 1991 / Primo Scree ✦✦✦

Wisconsin Hayride / 1992 / Columbia ✦✦✦
This fun, thrashing EP includes several covers that Gumball leader Don Fleming has found particularly inspirational over the years. —*AMG*

● **Super Tasty** / 1993 / Columbia ✦✦✦✦
Gumball's major-label debut will not only please their old fans, but may win some new ones with its trashy combination of indie guitar-rock and shameless pop melodies. —*Stephen Thomas Erlewine*

Revolution on Ice / 1994 / Epic ✦✦✦
Another inconsistent but enjoyable set of trashy, melodic punk-pop from Gumball, *Revolution on Ice* virtually duplicates all the pleasures of *Super Tasty*. —*Stephen Thomas Erlewine*

Guns N' Roses

Group, Hard Rock, Heavy Metal
At a time when pop was dominated by dance music and pop metal, Guns N' Roses brought raw, ugly rock & roll crashing back into the charts. They were not nice boys; nice boys don't play rock & roll. They were ugly, misogynist, violent; they were also funny, vulnerable, and occasionally sensitive, as their breakthrough hit "Sweet Child O' Mine" showed. While Slash and Izzy Stradlin ferociously spit out dueling guitar riffs worthy of Aerosmith or the Stones, Axl Rose screeched out his tales of sex, drugs, and apathy in the big city; bassist Duff McKagan and drummer Steven Adler were a limber rhythm section that kept the music loose and powerful. Guns N' Roses' music was basic and gritty, with a solid hard, bluesy base; they were dark, sleazy, dirty, and honest—everything that good hard rock and heavy metal should be.

Guns N' Roses released their first EP in 1986, which led to a contract with Geffen; the following year, the band released their debut album, *Appetite for Destruction*. They started to build a following with their numerous live shows, but the album didn't start selling until almost a year later, when MTV started playing "Sweet Child O' Mine." Soon, the album shot to number one and Guns N' Roses became one of the biggest bands in the world. By the end of 1988, they released *G N' R Lies*, which paired four new, acoustic-based songs with their first EP.

Guns N' Roses began to work on the follow-up to *Appetite* at the end of 1990. In October of that year, the band fired Adler, claiming that his drug dependency caused him to play poorly; he was replaced by Matt Sorum from the Cult. During recording, the band added Dizzy Reed on keyboards. By the time the sessions were finished, the new album had become two new albums. After being delayed for nearly a year, the albums, *Use Your Illusion I* and *II*, were released in the fall of 1991. The *Illusions* showcased a more ambitious band; while there were still a fair number of full-throttle guitar rockers, there were stabs at Elton John-style balladry, acoustic blues, horn sections, female backup singers, ten-minute songs with several different sections, and a good number of introspective, soul-searching lyrics. In short, they were now making art; amazingly, they were successful at it.

While the albums sold very well initially, the band soon fell out of favor. Stradlin left the band by the end of 1991 and with his departure the band lost their best songwriter. Once Nirvana's *Nevermind* hit the top of the charts in early 1992, there was a distinct division between what was cool in hard rock and what wasn't; Guns N' Roses—with all of their pretensions, impressionistic videos, models, and rock star excesses—were very uncool. The band didn't fully grasp the change until 1993, when they released their album of punk songs, *The Spaghetti Incident?*, it received some good reviews, but the band failed to capture the reckless spirit of not only the original versions, but their own *Appetite for Destruction*. By the middle of 1994, there were rumors flying that the band was about to break up, since Rose wanted to pursue a new, more industrial direction and Slash wanted to stick with their blues-inflected hard rock. —*Stephen Thomas Erlewine*

Live! Like a Suicide / 1986 / Uzi Suicide ✦✦✦

★ **Appetite for Destruction** / 1987 / Geffen ✦✦✦✦✦
Aggressive, brash, and well-executed hard rockers and ballads, they never stray from their chosen target. This major-label debut is one of the finest examples of late-'80s hard rock. "Welcome to the Jungle," "Sweet Child O' Mine," and "Paradise City" were key tracks from this classic. —*Donna DiChario & Rick Clark*

G N' R Lies / 1989 / Geffen ✦✦✦
The first side of *Lies* features their primitive independent debut EP, full of raw, vital rock & roll. Despite its disturbing lyrics, the second side is even more impressive musically, containing everything from the stark acoustic balladry of "Patience" to the country-rock boogie of "Used to Love Her." —*Stephen Thomas Erlewine*

○ **Use Your Illusion I** / Jan. 1991 / Geffen ✦✦✦✦
○ **Use Your Illusion II** / Feb. 1991 / Geffen ✦✦✦✦
Both CDs are full of what made classic rock classic; namely forceful band chemistry and an uncompromising spirit that approach staples like the Stones' *Exile on Main Street*, Led Zeppelin *IV*, or Aerosmith's *Rocks*. These two separately (but simultaneously) released volumes were a neat sidestep from the indulgent double-album concept. Musically, the band has never sounded better—or rawer. Lyrically, W. Axl Rose still spews out enough venom to offend half the planet, but you'd have to listen hard to catch it through the band-heavy sound mix. Nevertheless, Rose has seasoned his railings with some insights that the world around him isn't hopeless. In spite of his sloppy target shooting, his raw sentiments and delivery are bracing compared to the bulk of rock bands pounding the circuits. Highlights on volume one are "Right Next Door to Hell," "November Rain," "Perfect Crime," "You Ain't the First," and "Don't Cry." Volume two's standout tracks are "Civil War," "You Could Be Mine," "Locomotive," "Breakdown," and "Pretty Tied Up." Of the two albums, the first one is the better choice, but fans of hard rock should get both. —*Rick Clark*

Spaghetti Incident? / 1993 / Geffen ✦✦✦
As punk albums go, *The Spaghetti Incident?* lacks righteous anger and rage. As Guns N' Roses albums go, it's a complete delight, returning to the ferocious, hard-rocking days of *Appetite for Destruction*. The Gunners play Stooges and New York Dolls songs exactly as they do Nazareth—as straightahead, driving riff-rockers. After the epic *Use Your Illusions*, the band sounds like it's having fun, not caring about making "art" like "November Rain" or "Estranged." Unfortunately, the tacked-on Charles Manson song leaves a bad aftertaste, but not because of the song itself; the inclusion of the song seems like a publicity-seeking stunt, a way to increase their sales while trying to regain their street credibility. And as *The Spaghetti Incident?* proves, they didn't need to stoop so low. —*Stephen Thomas Erlewine*

Guru

Rap
The main cog behind Gang Starr, rapper/composer Guru stepped out on his own in 1994 with the album *Jazzmatazz*. He enlisted support from the hip-hop and jazz communities, getting everyone from Roy Ayers and Donald Byrd to N'Dea Davenport of the Brand New Heavies. Guru later did selected club dates with some of the *Jazzmatazz* personnel, before returning to straighter hip-hop on Gang Starr's *Hard to Earn*. —*Ron Wynn*

○ **Jazzmatazz, Vol. 1** / 1993 / Chrysalis ✦✦✦✦
Gang Starr's Guru has put together the best hip-hop/jazz outing issued yet, at least on these shores. Instead of merely wedding rap to recycled jazz samples, Guru and a cast of jazz, fusion, and R&B stars actually converge performance-wise, with the jazz musicians playing and the rappers and vocalists singing fresh material. The results are never less than enjoyable, and occasionally inspirational. Guru's deadpan rap style works, as do N'Dea Davenport's sultry vocals, and Roy Ayers, Donald Byrd, and Lonnie Liston Smith sound more convincing doing these songs than they have on any recent release of their own. —*Ron Wynn*

Arlo Guthrie

b. Jul. 10, 1947

Folk, Singer-Songwriter, Folk-Rock

Like his father Woody Guthrie, Arlo Guthrie has carved out a career as a folksinger and songwriter with a social conscience who leavens political messages with humor. Though Woody Guthrie was hospitalized for much of Arlo's youth, the youngster nevertheless grew up in a musical community that included Pete Seeger, Leadbelly, and Cisco Houston. He learned to play the guitar at age six and was performing in coffeehouses by his late teens.

Guthrie's early fame was based on his anti-Establishment shaggy-dog story in song, "Alice's Restaurant," actually a comic monolog about the singer's troubles with the police and the draft board that was extremely timely when it appeared on record in 1967. The *Alice's Restaurant* album became Guthrie's only gold record, but he made a series of folk-rock records through the '70s, filling them with his own songs and those of his contemporaries, notably Steve Goodman's "The City of New Orleans," which became Guthrie's sole hit single in 1972.

Guthrie's commercial fortunes, like those of most folkies, declined by the end of the '70s, and he made his last album for Warner Bros. in 1981. Since then, he has launched his own label, Rising Son, which has reissued his Warner albums and released his new recordings. He continues to tour extensively and to work for such causes as environmentalism. *— William Ruhlmann*

☆ **Alice's Restaurant** / 1967 / Reprise ♦♦♦♦♦
In 1967 when this LP came out it was totally radical, directly political and so deliciously funny that it deflated a great deal of the seriousness of the growing anti-war movement. In this one stroke Guthrie established himself as more than the son of the famous man and major star. Aside from the title cut, people often forget about the "Motorcycle Song" and "Chillin' of the Evening" which were on side two. *—Richard Meyer*

Arlo / 1968 / Rising Son ♦♦♦
On this LP Guthrie continued his monologue with an extended "Motorcycle Song" and other originals. *—Richard Meyer*

Running Down the Road / 1969 / Reprise
More of a rock & roll record with the hit "Coming into Los Angeles." *—Richard Meyer*

Washington County / 1970 / Reprise ♦♦♦
This album is more homey and roots flavored, with cuts like "Valley to Pray" with Doc Watson, and "Lay Down Little Doggies." It's a good relaxed effort. *—Richard Meyer*

○ **Hobo's Lullaby** / 1972 / Rising Son ♦♦♦♦
It contains his hit version of "City of New Orleans" and "1913 Massacre." *—Richard Meyer*

The Last of the Brooklyn Cowboys / 1973 / Rising Son ♦♦♦
A strong collection, it has good versions of "Ramblin' Round," "Gypsy Davey," "Love Sick Blues" and "Gates of Eden." *—Richard Meyer*

○ **Together in Concert** / 1975 / Reprise ♦♦♦♦
Separately and together, Arlo Guthrie and Pete Seeger delight in a live setting. *—William Ruhlmann*

○ **Amigo** / 1976 / Rising Son ♦♦♦♦
An excellent, rocking collection including Guthrie's adaptation of "Guabi, Guabi," a song about Victor Jara, and a knockabout cover of the Rolling Stones song "Connection." *—William Ruhlmann*

○ **The Best of Arlo Guthrie** / 1977 / Reprise ♦♦♦♦
This includes "Alice's Restaurant," the equally comic "Motorcycle Song," "Coming into Los Angeles," and "City of New Orleans." *—William Ruhlmann*

● **Precious Friend** / 1982 / Reprise ♦♦♦♦
A second excellent collection by Pete Seeger and Arlo Guthrie, veterans of two generations. *—William Ruhlmann*

Guy

Group, Urban

By bringing the minimalist swagger of hip-hop into the arena of '80s-style funk and soul, Guy (led by wünderkind Teddy Riley) forged a new R&B sound that continues to dominate the genre. Riley has been one of the most respected and sought-after hitmakers of the last decade, producing records for everyone from Heavy D. to Michael Jackson. The band went on hiatus during the early '90s, reuniting in 1995 to record their third album. *—John Floyd*

★ **Guy** / 1988 / MCA ♦♦♦♦♦
The hottest trend of the late '80s was New Jack Swing, in which hip-hop production met vintage R&B/soul singing. The man credited with perfecting this style, of course, was Guy's Teddy Riley. The New York City threesome roared out of the chute with this album, which eventually became a platinum success, and the hit "I Like" was extremely influential. "Spend the Night" and "Teddy's Jam" were other strong singles, but the key hit was "Groove Me," one of the year's hottest records and Guy's finest single. It had hypnotic beats, was superbly produced and featured riveting vocals. *—Ron Wynn*

○ **The Future** / Uptown/MCA ♦♦♦♦
The second and final album from New Jack trio Guy matched the platinum credentials of its predecessor, but didn't have the same dynamic grooves or inspired mix of soulful harmonies and futuristic beats. Once more, brothers Aaron and Damion Hall teamed with singer and producer Teddy Riley, but only the singles "I Wannna Get With U" and "Let's Chill" came close to generating the buzz and the heat of earlier hits. *—Ron Wynn*

Gwar

Group, Hard Rock, Heavy Metal

Gwar is thrash metal's answer to the more mainstream satire of Spinal Tap. Gory, sexually perverse, and scatological in the extreme, Gwar originally formed in Richmond, Virginia as an experiment in marketing strategy. The group claims to consist of all-powerful interplanetary warriors, created from the lowest filth in the universe, who have come to Earth to sexually enslave and/or slaughter the human race. All members perform under aliases and wear bizarre costumes made of latex and papier-mache. The main group consists of Oderus Urungus (vocals), Balzac the Jaws of Death (guitar), Flattus Maximus (guitar), Beefcake the Mighty (bass), and Jizmak the Gusher (drums), along with several other auxiliary characters. *—Steve Huey*

Hell-O / 1988 / Metal Blade ♦♦♦
Gwar's debut introduces their trademark cartoonish violence and silly gross-out humor (i.e. sex with a dead dog). However, with the absence of a lyric sheet, character bios, or liner notes to expand on the joke, there are better places to start. *—Steve Huey*

● **Scumdogs of the Universe** / 1990 / Metal Blade ♦♦♦♦
Their heaviest and probably most disgusting album, this brings in some monsters and villains to complement their standard sex & violence fare. Lines like "Maggots are falling like rain" pretty much tell the story. The quintessential Gwar album. *—Steve Huey*

○ **America Must Be Destroyed** / Sep. 1991 / Metal Blade ♦♦♦♦
More tales of perversity, mutilation, and horrible creatures. The subject matter broadens a bit, as they take aim at censorship advocates dumb enough to take them seriously ("The Morality Squad") and include a hilarious take on the power-ballad genre ("The Road Behind"), in which they reveal that they enjoy a good cry after senseless slaughters. *—Steve Huey*

The Road Behind / Oct. 6, 1992 / Metal Blade ♦♦

This Toilet Earth / 1994 / Metal Blade ♦♦♦
Not as consistently deranged as other Gwar releases, this one is at least the best-packaged, with fact sheets on all the characters and some truly hideous cartoons. *—Steve Huey*

H

Sammy Hagar

b. 1947, Monterey, CA
Hard Rock, Heavy Metal

After spending several years as the lead vocalist and rhythm guitarist for the mid-'70s hard rock band Montrose, Sammy Hagar began a solo career that produced several hits and made him an album rock favorite. Hagar became a true star once he joined Van Halen in 1985, but he was a popular hard rocker ever since his first album with Montrose.

After giving up a boxing career, Hagar began singing in the late '60s, performing with various California bands including Skinny, the Fabulous Catillas, Justice Brothers, and Dust Cloud. During this time, he built up a solid reputation in the Californian hard rock scene. Former Edgar Winter guitarist Ronnie Montrose asked Hagar to join his band, Montrose, in 1973. Hagar recorded two albums with Montrose before going solo in 1976, taking the group's bassist Bill Church. Montrose's drummer Denny Carmassi later joined Hagar's band, along with keyboardist Geoff Workman. Hagar's self-titled *Sammy Hagar* was his first chart entry; it eventually went gold. In 1979, he created a new supporting band featuring Workman, Church, guitarist Gary Pihl, and drummer Chuck Ruff. This lineup played on Hagar's most popular solo albums, including 1981's platinum *Standing Hampton* and 1982's gold *Three Lock Box*. After *Three Lock Box* and its number 13 hit single "Your Love Is Driving Me Crazy," Hagar toured with guitarist Neal Schon, bassist Kenny Aaronson, and drummer Mike Shrieve; the group recorded a live album under the name HGAS, as well as a studio version of Procol Harum's "A Whiter Shade of Pale." His 1984 album, *VOA* contained the hit single "I Can't Drive 55," which peaked at number 26.

In 1985, Hagar replaced David Lee Roth in Van Halen; his first album with the group was 1986's *5150*. Hagar released his last solo album, *Sammy Hagar,* in 1987; the title of the record was changed to *I Never Said Goodbye* in a MTV contest, but no copies of the record were ever issued with that name. — *Stephen Thomas Erlewine*

Nine on a Ten Scale / 1976 / Greenlight ✦✦

Sammy Hagar Two / 1977 / Capitol ✦✦✦

Musical Chairs / 1978 / Capitol ✦✦✦

All Night Long / 1978 / Capitol ✦✦✦

All Night Long is better than most hard rock live albums not only because Sammy Hagar is at his best when he's on stage, but because the set list includes only his best songs, eliminating the filler that tends to clutter his albums. — *Stephen Thomas Erlewine*

Danger Zone / 1979 / Capitol ✦✦

Street Machine / 1979 / Capitol ✦✦✦

Loud & Clear / 1980 / Capitol ✦✦✦

○ **Standing Hampton** / 1982 / Geffen ✦✦✦✦

After releasing several competent but more or less undistinguished albums on Capitol, Sammy Hagar switched to Geffen in 1981 and released *Standing Hampton,* a polished but tough record that showed a surprising amount of pop songcraft. The added production gloss and improved melodic sense proved commercially successful—the album was his first million-seller and it cracked the Top 30—and artistically successful as well; the record was the most consistent and memorable album he recorded to date, featuring the singles "I'll Fall in Love Again," "Baby's on Fire," and "There's Only One Way to Rock." — *Stephen Thomas Erlewine*

○ **Rematch** / 1982 / Capitol ✦✦✦✦

As Sammy Hagar's career was at its height in the early-'80s, Capitol, his '70s record label, released *Rematch,* a compilation of highlights from his six albums with the label. Like *All Night Long* before it, *Rematch* cuts away all the fat from Hagar's '70s catalog, leaving only his best rockers, including the scorching "I've Done Everything for You," "Plain Jane," "Turn up the Music," and "Trans Am (Highway Wonderland)." Even though the track listing is well-chosen, his Capitol records weren't as impressive as his albums for Geffen, meaning *Rematch* is only the best of a specific era of Hagar's career, not his entire career. — *Stephen Thomas Erlewine*

○ **Three Lock Box** / 1983 / Geffen ✦✦✦✦

Continuing the sleek, driving pop-oriented sound of Hagar's breakthrough *Standing Hampton, Three Lock Box* equals its predecessor, featuring such highlights as the double entendres of the title track and the hit single "Your Love Is Driving Me Crazy." — *Stephen Thomas Erlewine*

○ **Voa** / 1983 / Geffen ✦✦✦✦

VOA was the last album Hagar recorded before he became the lead singer of Van Halen and the record shows why he was invited to join the band. With songs like "I Can't Drive 55" he adds a simple melody to the song which never distracts from the all-important hard-driving riff. On "Two Sides of Love," he shows that he has the ability to pull off a power ballad, wrenching every bit of feeling out of the song. Like Hagar himself, *VOA* is never subtle, but in hard rock, that's a postive attribute. — *Stephen Thomas Erlewine*

Sammy Hagar / 1987 / Geffen ✦✦✦

Sammy Hagar, the singer's last solo album, was released a year after his first album with Van Halen, 1986's *5150*. Although it charted the highest of any of his records, peaking at number 14, it wasn't as successful as his three previous albums, suffering from a slick, synthesized production and a lack of consistent material. The power ballad "Give to Live" was a hit and a couple of the rockers raised above the pedestrian level, yet the overall product was rather faceless. Perhaps sensing the lackluster quality of the record, Hagar launched an MTV promotion to re-title the record; the winning entry was *I Never Said Goodbye.* No copies were released with the new title, although the 1994 *Unboxed* compilation called the album *I Never Said Goodbye,* not *Sammy Hagar.* — *Stephen Thomas Erlewine*

○ **The Best of Sammy Hagar** / Nov. 16, 1992 / Capitol ✦✦✦✦

A CD-era collection of Hagar's Capitol work that supplants *Rematch, The Best of Sammy Hagar* has a nearly identical track listing as the previous collection and suffers from the same flaws. — *Stephen Thomas Erlewine*

● **Unboxed** / 1994 / Geffen ✦✦✦✦

Collecting the best of Hagar's prime years at Geffen, *Unboxed* has most of his hits from the early '80s—including "I Can't Drive 55," "There's Only One Way to Rock," "Three Lock Box," and "Give to Live"—but there's a noticeable absence of "Your Love Is Driving Me Crazy," which was his biggest hit. Nevertheless, *Unboxed* is a good introduction to his best years. — *Stephen Thomas Erlewine*

Haircut 100

Group, New Wave

Combining light funk with frothy pop, Haircut 100 was one of the cleanest and most accessible new wave groups. Formed in 1980, the British band's core members were vocalist Nick Heyward, bassist Les Nemes, and guitarist Graham Jones; the following years drummer Memphis Blair Cunningham, saxophonist Phil Smith, and percussionist Mark Fox joined the group. Once the band was signed to Arista Records, they were put in the direction of producer Bob Sargeant, who helped them polish their stylish pop. Released in late 1981, Haircut 100's first single, "Favourite Shirts (Boy Meets Girl)," managed to reach number four in the U.K., establishing the group's widespread appeal. The band released their debut album, *Pelican West*, in early 1992. Their next single, "Love Plus One," was a bigger hit, making the band one of the hottest British pop groups of the year. However, their momentum crashed to a halt when Heyward decided to pursue a solo career. Fox became the lead vocalist in early 1983, yet Haircut 100 could not replicate their previous success; they broke up after the release of their second album, 1984's *Paint on Paint.* —*Stephen Thomas Erlewine*

● **Pelican West** / 1982 / Arista ✦✦✦✦
Led by Nick Heyward, this British band's debut effort featured the MTV hits "Love Plus One" and "Favorite Shirt (Boy Meets Girl)." —*Kenneth M. Cassidy*

Paint & Paint / 1983 / Polydor ✦

Bill Haley (William John Clifton Haley)

b. Jul. 6, 1925, Highland Park, MI, **d.** Feb. 9, 1981, Harlingen, TX
Rock & Roll, Rockabilly
The Bill Haley and the Comets recording of "Rock Around the Clock," which topped the charts for eight weeks in 1955, is remembered as the beginning of the rock era. Though it also represented Haley's peak as a performer, his career had begun some time before and would continue for a long time after. Born in Michigan, Haley began leading Western swing bands under various names in the late '40s, slowly starting to incorporate elements of R&B.Soon after he began recording for Essex in the early '50s, his backup band was named the Comets.

Because of his somewhat square image and his undeniably white sound, Haley, it could be argued, has been short-changed by latter-day rock historians. He was among the first performers—perhaps he was even the very first—of any color to combine R&B and C&W in a way that can readily be identified by listeners of any era as bonafide rock & roll. Although their initial impact was regional, his early '50s sides rank among his most exciting, steering country and Western and big band forms into uncharted regions that were more frenetic and reckless. Haley also wrote much of his own material, and one of his compositions, "Crazy, Man, Crazy," became one of the first Top 20 rock & roll hits in 1953. In 1954, he moved to the major Decca label, where his sides became increasingly formulaic, though for a time very successful, after "Rock Around the Clock."

It is his Decca sides, however, that are his most famous. In 1954, he went to number 12 with "Shake, Rattle and Roll," and in 1955 he hit with "Dim, Dim the Lights," "Mambo Rock," and "Birth of the Boogie." But it was "Rock Around the Clock," previously recorded and released as a B-side in 1954 and reissued as the theme song for the movie *Blackboard Jungle,* that became his biggest hit. At that time the band consisted of Haley on guitar and vocals, Danny Cedrone on lead guitar, Joey D'Ambrose on sax, Billy Williamson on steel guitar, Johnny Grande on piano, Marshall Lytle on bass, and Dick Richards on drums.

Following the success of "Rock Around the Clock," Haley and the Comets placed nine more records in the Top 40 over the next three years, among them the Top Tens "Burn that Candle" and "See You Later, Alligator." Haley was largely eclipsed as the king of rock & roll by Elvis Presley and other more flamboyant performers who followed him from 1956 on. Nevertheless, he continued to perform overseas and in oldies shows in the United States, and "Rock Around the Clock" even got back into the Top 40 in 1974. —*William Ruhlmann & Richie Unterberger*

Greatest Hits / 1985 / MCA ✦✦✦
All the casual fan really needs. —*Bruce Eder*

● **The From the Original Master Tapes** / 1985 / MCA ✦✦✦✦
The best-sounding Haley collection, but its 20 songs are probably ten more than anyone but the most hardcore fan needs. —*Bruce Eder*

○ **Rock The Joint!** / 1995 / Schoolkids ✦✦✦✦
A 22-track collection which collects sides from 1951-53. Those who haven't heard this material before will be astonished to discover bonafide rock & roll dating from three to four years earlier

than the era ('54-55) more commonly associated with the music's birth. Haley's sound is similar to the country-boogie of the late '40s, retaining the steel guitar prominent in much of the era's country music, but it's clearly more driving and forward-looking. The songs owe a lot of jump R&B, but are transformed into the basic model of rock & roll with slapping bass, ricky-tick drums, and extended electric guitar riffing. Listen to his version of Jackie Brenston's "Rocket 88" (which has itself been pegged as one of the first rock & roll records) and you'll be astounded to note the basics of rockabilly already in place—in 1951. The low buzzing, distorted guitar on "Green Tree Boogie" (also from 1951) is also a revelation, as is the guitar solo on 1952's "Rock The Joint," which is almost identical to the much more famous one on "Rock Around The Clock" a couple of years later. The later sides introduce a honking sax, which would become such a prominent feature in '50s rock & roll. Includes "Crazy Man Crazy," the first rock & roll song to make the Top 20. —*Richie Unterberger*

BOOK

✦✦✦ **Bill Haley: The Daddy Of Rock And Roll**, by John Swenson (Stein & Day, 1983). Haley usually isn't accorded as much respect as many other of rock & roll's founders, and this bio, which combines his life story with serious criticism of his music, does much to affirm his importance in getting the music off the ground. Haley was an also-ran country singer before he stumbled on rock & roll through a series of circumstances. The most interesting part of this compact volume deals with his early years, examining the little-known early '50s recordings in which Haley helped pioneer rockabilly, with the help of important sidemen, and industry figures who steered him toward R&B material. The sessions which yielded the seminal singles "Shake, Rattle & Roll" and "Rock Around the Clock" are also detailed, with particularly interesting comments from Decca producer Milt Gabler. Haley's long slide from superstardom, mirroring many other important early rock & rollers, is also documented, although this was alleviated by overseas popularity and occasional rock & roll revivals. —*Richie Unterberger*

Half Japanese

Group, Alternative Pop/Rock, Experimental
Depending on your point of view, Half Japanese is either a celebration of the pure, amateurish do-it-yourself rock & roll spirit or a pretentious, highly irritating example of self-conscious experimental rock at its most extreme. Formed by Jad and David Fair in 1977, the group started bashing out music in their parents' basement in Maryland, recording their debut EP by themselves. By the time the Fairs recorded their debut album, the three-record box set *1/2 Gentlemen/Not Beasts*, they had acquired a full-time drummer plus a saxophonist, yet their music was no less noisy and primitive; if anything, it was more atonal and difficult than before.

For the rest of their career, the band has proudly displayed nothing approaching instrumental virtuosity. David Fair left the band after their third record, rejoining briefly for 1988's *Charmed Life.* Throughout the years, the lineup has changed frequently—at times it has included Velvet Underground drummer Maureen Tucker and guitarist Don Fleming, as well as occasional contributions from Fred Frith and John Zorn—but Jad Fair has remained. That doesn't necessarily the mean the music hasn't changed; their later records are slightly more musically varied and accessible, yet no less challenging. Fair has released a few solo albums that are stranger (believe it or not) than the typical Half Japanese release. —*Stephen Thomas Erlewine*

○ **1/2 Gentlemen/Not Beasts** / 1980 / Armageddon ✦✦✦✦
As with any album that is three records long, *1/2 Gentlemen/Not Beasts* unwittingly shows Half Japanese's true roots. Over the three records, the band "covers" such minimalists as the Velvet Underground, the Stooges, and Jonathan Richman, as well as deconstructing such wordsmiths as Bruce Springsteen and Bob Dylan. Although they would have you believe that their untuned, almost unlistenable, instrumental clatter is the result of being so enthusiastic that they didn't bother to learn how to play their instruments, it's just the logical, inevitable intellectual extension of Richman's naivete and the Velvet Underground's stripped-down guitar. Half Japanese is consciously primitive and amateurish. —*Stephen Thomas Erlewine*

Loud / 1981 / Armageddon ✦✦✦

Horrible / 1983 / Press ✦✦

Our Solar System / 1984 / Iridescence ✦✦

Sing No Evil / 1984 / Iridescence ✦✦

Big Big Sun / 1986 / K ✦✦

Music to Strip By / 1987 / 50 Skidillion Watts ✦✦

● **Charmed Life** / 1988 / 50 Skidillion Watts ✦✦✦✦
While *Charmed Life* is the band's most accessible record, it doesn't even come close to the mainstream's concept of what constitutes pop music. Yet when Jad Fair sings about love and joy on *Charmed Life*, he is as straightforward and direct as he ever gets. *—Stephen Thomas Erlewine*

Velvet Monkeys / 1988 / K ✦✦✦

○ **Band That Would Be King** / 1989 / 50 Skidillion Watts ✦✦✦✦
Featuring contributions from John Zorn and Fred Frith, *The Band That Would Be King* is one of the most diverse and challenging records Half Japanese has recorded. It's also one of their most rewarding. *—Stephen Thomas Erlewine*

We Are They Who Ache with Amorous Love / 1990 / T.E.C. Tones/Elemental Music ✦✦✦

● **Greatest Hits** / 1995 / Safe House ✦✦✦✦
Half Japanese began their career with a three-LP box set, so it's little wonder that their *Greatest Hits* encompasses two CDs. Under the guidance of Jad Fair, the group has become more accessible over the years, but that's only a relative term. Fair has remained doggedly amateurish and noisy, letting the twisted pop structures peak out only once in awhile. There's a lot of subtle differences between albums which only fans can tell, so *Greatest Hits* serves as a good introduction to Half Japanese as well as a kind of roadmap of their career. *—Stephen Thomas Erlewine*

Hall & Oates

Group, Soul, Pop/Rock
During the mid-'80s, Daryl Hall and John Oates' record sales surpassed the Everly Brothers, making the two the most successful duo in rock history. From their first hit in 1974 through their heyday in the '80s, the duo's smooth, catchy take on Philly soul brought them enormous commercial success—including six number one singles and six platinum albums—yet little critical success. In retrospect, Hall & Oates' music was remarkably well-constructed and produced; at their best, their songs were filled with strong hooks and melodies that adhered to soul traditions without being a slave to them by incorporating elements of new wave and hard rock. By being pop craftsmen that kept up with the times, they were one of the few groups that kept blue-eyed soul alive during the '70s and '80s.

Daryl Hall began performing professionally while he was a student at Temple University. In 1966, he recorded a single with Kenny Gamble and the Romeos; the group featured Gamble, Leon Huff and Thom Bell, who would all become the architects of the highly-produced and orchestrated Philly soul sound. During this time, Hall frequently appeared on sessions for Gamble and Huff; he also formed his own group, the Temptones. In 1967, Hall met John Oates, a fellow Temple University student, while escaping a gang fight at a dance in Philadelphia's Adelphi Ballroom; Oates was leading his own soul band, the Masters, at the time. The two students realized they had similar tastes and began performing in an array of R&B and doo-wop groups. By 1968, the duo had parted ways, as Oates transferred schools and Hall formed the soft-rock band Gulliver with singer/songwriter Tim Moore and producer Tom Sellers; the group released one album on Elektra in the late '60s before disbanding.

After Gulliver's break-up, Hall concentrated on session work again, appearing as a backup vocalist for the Stylistics, the Delfonics, and the Intruders, as well as several others. Oates returned to Philadelphia in 1969, and he and Hall began writing songs and performing together. Their first material was more folk-oriented than their later songs, yet they eventually came to the attention of Chappell Music representative Tommy Mottola, who quickly became their manager, securing the duo a contract with Atlantic Records. On their first records—*Whole Oates* (1972), *Abandoned Luncheonette* (1973), *War Babies* (1974)—the duo were establishing their sound, working with producers like Arif Mardin and Todd Rundgren and removing much of their folk influences. At the beginning of 1974, the duo relocated from

Philadelphia to New York. During this period, they only managed one hit—the number 60 "She's Gone" in the spring of 1974.

After they moved to RCA in 1975, the duo landed on its successful mixture of soul, pop and rock, scoring a Top Ten single with "Sara Smile;" the song was written for Hall's girlfriend Sara Allen, who would later collaborate with him on many of Hall and Oates' biggest hits. The success of "Sara Smile" prompted the re-release of "She's Gone," which rocketed into the Top Ten as well. Released in the summer of 1976, *Bigger than the Both of Us* was only moderately successful upon its release, with the single "Do What You Want, Be What You Are" only barely making it into the Top 40. The record took off in early 1977, when "Rich Girl" became the duo's first number one single; the album would eventually go gold. *No Goodbyes*, a collection of their Atlantic work, was released in the spring of 1977 to capitalize on their current success. Hall and Oates' released *Beauty on a Back Street* that summer; although it would eventually go gold, it failed to repeat the success of *Bigger than the Both of Us*. During 1977, Hall recorded his first solo album, *Sacred Songs*, with guitarist Robert Fripp; it wasn't released until 1980.

Although they had several minor hits between 1977 and 1980—the largest being 1979's "Wait for Me," which reached number 18—the albums Hall and Oates released at the end of the decade were not as successful as their mid-'70s records. Nevertheless, they were more adventurous, incorporating more rock elements into their blue-eyed soul. The combination would finally pay off in late 1980, when the duo released self-produced *Voices*, the album that marked the beginning of Hall and Oates' greatest commercial and artistic success. The first single from *Voices*, a cover of the Righteous Brothers' "You've Lost That Lovin' Feeling," reached number 12, yet it was the second single, "Kiss on My List" that confirmed their commercial potential. "Kiss on My List" became the duo's second number one single, staying on the top of the charts for three weeks; its follow-up, "You Make My Dreams" hit number five. They quickly released *Private Eyes* in the summer of 1981; the record featured two number one hits, "Private Eyes" and "I Can't Go for That (No Can Do)," as well as the Top Ten, "Did It in a Minute." "I Can't Go for That (No Can Do)" also spent a week at the top of the R&B charts—a rare accomplishment for a White act. *H2O* followed in 1982 and it proved more successful than their two previous albums, selling over two million copies and launching their biggest hit single, "Maneater," which stayed at number one for four weeks; the record also included the Top Ten hits "One on One" and "Family Man." The following year, the duo released a greatest hits compilation, *Rock 'N Soul, Part 1*, that featured two new Top Ten hits—the number two "Say It Isn't So" and "Family Man."

In April of 1984, the Recording Industry Association of America announced that Hall and Oates had surpassed the Everly Brothers as the most successful duo in rock history, earning a total of 19 gold and platinum awards. Released in October of 1984, *Big Bam Boom* expanded their number of gold and platinum awards, selling over two million copies and launching four Top 40 singles, including the number one "Out of Touch." Following their contract-fulfilling gold album *Live at the Apollo with David Ruffin & Eddie Kendrick*, Hall and Oates went on hiatus. After the lukewarm reception for Daryl Hall's 1986 solo album, *Three Hearts in the Happy Ending Machine*, the duo regrouped to release 1988's *ooh yeah!*, their first record for Arista. The first single, "Everything Your Heart Desires," went to number three and helped propel the album to platinum status. However, none of the album's other singles broke the Top 20, indicating that the era of chart dominance had ended. *Change of Season*, released in 1990, confirmed that fact. Although the record went gold, it only featured one Top 40 hit—the number 11 single, "So Close." The duo hasn't released an album since 1990. *—Stephen Thomas Erlewine*

Whole Oates / 1972 / Atlantic ✦✦

Hall & Oates' debut album was a tentative effort, with the two singers' hesitantly working their way around slick, but relatively undistinguished material that displayed their folk roots more than any other record they would later make. *—Stephen Thomas Erlewine*

Abandoned Luncheonette / 1973 / Atlantic ✦✦✦

Abandoned Luncheonette, Hall & Oates' second album, was the first indication of the duo's talent for sleek, soul-inflected pop/rock, featuring the single "She's Gone," which would become a big hit in 1975, when it was re-released following the success of "Sara Smile." — *Stephen Thomas Erlewine*

War Babies / 1974 / Atlantic ♦♦
After crafting the fitfully accomplished blue-eyed Philly soul-pop of *Abandoned Luncheonette*, Hall & Oates retreated to a more rock-oriented sound on *War Babies*, recorded with producer Todd Rundgren. Some of the tracks work, but the duo's performance sounds forced through much of the record. — *Stephen Thomas Erlewine*

Daryl Hall & John Oates / 1976 / Intertape ♦♦♦
Switching to RCA, Daryl Hall & John Oates recorded a self-titled album that fulfilled their early promise as pop-savvy blue-eyed soul craftsmen. A few of the tracks fall flat—including the reggae-tinged "Soldering" and the pompous "Ennui on the Mountain"—but much of the album is lush and catchy, featuring ballads and mid-tempo numbers that are nearly as engaging as their break-through single "Sara Smile." — *Stephen Thomas Erlewine*

○ **Bigger Than the Both of Us** / 1977 / RCA ♦♦♦
Bigger Than the Both of Us continued the gold success of its predecessor by adding a cleaner, more pop-oriented gloss to the production, as well as fine songwriting that builds on the bright pulse of "Rich Girl." — *Stephen Thomas Erlewine*

No Goodbyes / 1977 / Atlantic ♦♦
Released after the success of their first RCA album, *No Goodbyes* is a compilation of their three Atlantic albums that includes three unreleased tracks. *No Goodbyes* concisely sums up the high points of the duo's early years (in particular, the soaring single "She's Gone"), and confirms the fact that the pair were still developing their signature style. — *Stephen Thomas Erlewine*

Beauty on a Back Street / 1977 / RCA ♦♦♦
Beauty on a Back Street isn't quite as accomplished as its two predecessors, yet it is more ambitious and diverse, as Hall & Oates begin to add some arena-rock conventions to their sound, particularly distorted guitars and anthemic choruses. On *War Babies*, they had tried a similar attack, but on *Beauty on a Back Street*, the duo's songwriting was stronger, which meant that the instrumental approach didn't overwhelm the actual songs. — *Stephen Thomas Erlewine*

Past Time Behind / 1977 / Mobile Fidelity ♦

Livetime / May 1978 / RCA ♦♦
A lackluster album recorded in the mid-'70s, *Livetime* proves that part of the success of Hall & Oates' singles lies in the studio, where they can carefully craft both the song and its presentation. In concert, many of the same songs fall flat, as the group tries to replicate their polished studio sound to little avail. — *Stephen Thomas Erlewine*

○ **Along the Red Ledge** / Sep. 1978 / RCA ♦♦♦♦
Continuing the more rock-oriented approach of *Beauty on a Back Street*, *Along the Red Ledge* is more successful than its predecessor, as the duo landed on a polished melodic pop/rock style that managed to retain their Philly soul influences without drowning their voices in distorted guitar flourishes. They would refine this sound two years later on *Voices*, the record that established them as pop/rock superstars. — *Stephen Thomas Erlewine*

X-Static / 1979 / RCA ♦♦
After coming up with a sleek and soulful template on *Along the Red Ledge*, Hall & Oates took a temporary detour on *X-Static*, concentrating on disco rhythms. A few tracks were successful—in particular, "Wait for Me"—but the record sounds unfocused and misguided. — *Stephen Thomas Erlewine*

○ **Voices** / 1980 / RCA ♦♦♦♦
This is the album that took Hall and Oates from being a successful '70s pop duo to being one of the four biggest singles acts of the '80s (the others: Michael Jackson, Prince, and Madonna). The sound is a wonderful pop pastiche, from the Beatlesque "How Does it Feel to Be Back" to the neo-Philadelphia soul of the hits "Kiss on My List" and "You Make My Dreams." — *William Ruhlmann*

○ **Private Eyes** / 1981 / RCA ♦♦♦♦
More bouncy, soulful rock & roll, led by the #1 hits "Private Eyes" and "I Can't Go for That (No Can Do)." — *William Ruhlmann*

○ **H2O** / 1982 / RCA ♦♦♦♦
From the Motown beat of "Maneater" to the lush ballad "One on One," Hall & Oates continue to make the top pop of the early '80s. Also contains "Family Man." — *William Ruhlmann*

★ **Rock 'n' Soul Pt. 1: Greatest Hits** / 1983 / RCA ♦♦♦♦♦
The best of Hall and Oates, 1974 to 1983, including their biggest 70s hits, "She's Gone," "Sara Smile," and "Rich Girl," plus the 80s chart-toppers and two new hits: "Say It Isn't So" and "Adult Education." — *William Ruhlmann*

Big Bam Boom / 1984 / RCA ♦♦♦
The last of the major Hall & Oates albums of the '80s features more of their patented soul-rock sound on the hits "Out of Touch" and "Method of Modern Love." — *William Ruhlmann*

Live at the Apollo / 1985 / RCA ♦♦
Hall & Oates' second live album was a better effort than 1978's *Livetime*, containing a collection of performances that are altogether more convincing, yet ironically, it fails to sound as exciting as their meticulously crafted studio albums. — *Stephen Thomas Erlewine*

Ooh Yeah! / 1988 / Arista ♦♦♦
Ooh Yeah!, Hall & Oate's first album for Arista Records, was their weakest studio effort since *X-Static*, both commercially and artistically. Although they still rely on their signature pop-soul sound, the duo's material is simply not up to par. Not that *Ooh Yeah!* is a total wash-out—the single "Everything Your Heart Desires" is as good as their early '80s hits—but the whole album is rather undistinguished. — *Stephen Thomas Erlewine*

Change of Season / 1990 / Arista ♦♦
Apart from the hit "So Close," *Change of Season* is largely undistinguished, relying more on sound than songcraft. Not surprisingly, it was Hall & Oates' lowest-charting album of original material since 1974's *War Babies*, even if it did go gold. — *Stephen Thomas Erlewine*

Kristen Hall
Folk, Singer-Songwriter
Atlanta based singer-songwriter, Kristen Hall has built a strong reputation in folk circles with her infectious Indigo Girls style of acoustic folk-rock. Her raspy voiced delivery of highly personal lyrics are the center of attention often times accompanied only by acoustic guitar. While her first album, released independently, consisted of minamalistic arrangements of nearly demo quality, subsequent releases have been bigger productions featuring high profile guests such as Emily Sailers of Indigo Girls, Cindy Wilson of the B-52's, and Jules Shear. — *Chris Woodstra*

Real Life Stuff / 1990 / Dog Gone ♦♦♦
An outstanding independent release from this Atlanta-based singer/songwriter. Her debut, a self-produced low-key folk album centered around Hall's raspy voice and guitar, gives the blueprint for her later releases. Well worth seeking out. — *Chris Woodstra*

● **Fact and Fiction** / 1991 / High Street ♦♦♦♦
This mainly acoustic album ranges from introspective ballads to catchy upbeat folk-rock anthems. Hall's world-weary voice, both rough and delicate, tells reflective tales of yearning and love lost while retaining an uplifting spirit. Guests include Emily Sailers (Indigo Girls) and Cindy Wilson (B-52's). — *Chris Woodstra*

○ **Be Careful What You Wish For** / 1994 / High Street ♦♦♦♦
Kristen Hall has a gutsy voice that never sounds forced. The rocking guitar-based arrangements have a sound not unlike some of John Hiatt's recent records. These are very personal songs, some with political centers such as "Proud Man," sung with commitment and deep emotion. The opening cut, "Cry Tomorrow," sets the tone of the album; she maintains the drive and quality through to the end. — *Richard Meyer*

Roy Hamilton
d. Jul. 20, 1969
Soul, R&B
An extremely influential vocalist despite having a rather short career, Roy Hamilton had both classical training and gospel experience. Hamilton studied commercial art in high school and was a heavyweight Golden Gloves boxer before starting his music career as a member of the Searchlight Singers. During the mid and late '50s, Hamilton's dramatic, searing voice and treatments of such songs as "You'll Never Walk Alone," "If I Loved You," "Ebb Tide," and "Unchained Melody" were enormously popular. "You'll Never Walk Alone" topped the R&B charts for two months in 1954, while "Unchained Melody" topped the R&B charts for three weeks, and was his only Top Ten pop hit. Jackie Wilson and Roy Brown were among the singers whose sound was affected by Hamilton,

while the Righteous Brothers did their own versions of "You'll Never Walk Alone," "Ebb Tide," and "Unchained Melody" (which later got new life via the film *Ghost*). Hamilton had to retire from 1956 to 1958 due to exhaustion. He suffered a stroke in 1969 and died at age 40. —*Ron Wynn*

● **Golden Classics** / 1991 / Collectables ♦♦♦♦

Hammer

Rap
Considered either the ultimate success story or consummate fraud, Oakland's MC Hammer, a one-time jack-of-all-trades for the Oakland Athletics baseball team, dominated the charts in 1990 with *Please Hammer Don't Hurt 'Em.* The single "U Can't Touch This," despite a rather feeble rap and recycle job on Rick James's single "Superfreak," was an enormous crossover smash. Hammer live puts on a fine show as far as dancing, sound, light effects, production, and such. But from a technical standpoint, everything, from his rhymes to his enunciation, qualifies as the ultimate in "wack" (weak) performance. He does have great taste in cover songs, picking choice items from Marvin Gaye, B.B.King, the Chi-Lites, and Prince, among others. He's since dropped the MC from his name.

After staying in the limelight as a race horse owner and Evander Holyfield's promoter, Hammer returned to the rap wars in 1994 with *The Funky Headhunter.* It featured a leaner, harder sound, with assistance and material provided by gangsta-rap producers, and featured Hammer sporting a more street look. He previewed the new style on Arsenio Hall's show early in the year, then issued the CD in March. It debuted at number two on Billboard's R&B charts, then dipped the next week to six. Skeptics voiced their doubts about the new Hammer, especially in the hip-hop press. —*Ron Wynn*

Let's Get It Started / 1988 / Capitol ♦♦♦
MC Hammer's debut effort established him as a hip-hop superstar, with energetic dance tracks under its pop-tinged choruses, highlighted by the single "Turn This Mutha Out." —*Stephen Thomas Erlewine*

★ **Please Hammer Don't Hurt 'em** / 1990 / Capitol ♦♦♦♦♦
MC Hammer's second album stands as the pinnacle of pop-rap crossover, with its hit singles "U Can't Touch This," "Have You Seen Her," and "Pray" forming its core. Hammer relied on pop choruses as much as hip-hop beats, which helped the album sell over ten million copies and stay on the top of the charts for 21 weeks. —*Stephen Thomas Erlewine*

Too Legit to Quit / 1991 / Capitol ♦♦♦
Hammer responded to hip-hop credibility charges by dropping the "MC" and releasing *Too Legit to Quit,* an album recorded with a live band. Although it sold over three million copies and had a hit in the title track and "This is the Way We Roll," the results were more well-intentioned than successful. —*Stephen Thomas Erlewine*

○ **The Funky Headhunter** / Mar. 1, 1994 / Giant ♦♦♦♦
The former M.C. Hammer resurfaced with a new musical identity and rap approach on this 1994 album. Getting help from new school producers and debuting a video on *The Arsenio Hall Show,* Hammer's sound was leaner, his rapping tougher and more fluid, and his subject matter harder and less humorous. The results seemed to have worked; *Funky Headhunter* peaked at number two on the R&B list, went gold and remained in the Top 30 midway through the year. —*Ron Wynn*

Peter Hammill

Electronic, Art-Rock/Progressive-Rock
Hammill's work as the leader of English prog-rockers Van Der Graaf Generator was always notable for its heavy moods and raw emotion. His solo work is even more intense, whether he's delivering a lump-in-the-throat ballad, railing with fury and scorn, or indulging his habit of using the studio as a combination confessional and psychiatric couch. Hammill's lyrics are always incomparably literate, passionate, and thought-provoking; his music is equally so. —*Michael P. Dawson*

Vision / 1978 / GIR ♦♦♦
Compilation of recordings from 1971-1975. Includes the campy "Imperial Zeppelin" and "Nadir's Big Chance," top early-period Hammill. —*Michael G. Nastos*

● **The Future Now** / 1978 / Blue Plate ♦♦♦♦
Premier rock with ethnic rhythms. Frustration turns into high art. The title cut, "Energy Vampires," and "Mediaeval" are particularly earthshaking. All originals. —*Michael G. Nastos*

Ph 7 / 1979 / Blue Plate ♦♦♦
Excellent followup. "Handicap and Equality" and "Factory X" easily rank with his best. Hamill is unique. —*Michael G. Nastos*

The Noise / 1993 / Rough Trade ♦♦
Loud, powerful and energetic music, balanced by poetical and clever lyrics. "The Entertainer" is an immediate success while "The Noise" is a prime example of Hammill's style of rhythmic and arrhythmic rock. A stab-in-the-back for the materialistic '90s society is cleverly disguised in the almost-pop "Great European Department Store," and the Finale—the slowly building, haunting "Primo on the Parapet"—reminds us to remember the past. Another unforgettable collection from Mr. Hammill. —*Ali Sinclair*

○ **Roaring Forties** / 1994 / ♦♦♦♦
From the cutting edge of "Sharply Unclear," through the insistent, throbbing "Talk Turkey," across the gentle instrumental bridges and into "A Headlong Stretch" (a twenty-minute, seven-part tempestuous journey through life) and all the way to the peaceful, gently-beautiful "Your Tall Ship," this album is an example of Hammill's musical, poetical and inspirational best. —*Ali Sinclair*

○ **Fireships** / Capitol ♦♦♦♦
Fireships is one of Hammill's most consistently quiet, intimate works; a collection of relationship odes similar in mood to 1984's *The Love Songs.* Hammill, even at his most reflective, is highly poetic and intense. Each of the nine numbers is given ample room to breathe, with most ranging between 5 and 7 minutes. A hint of tragedy, a smoldering fire, burns below the surface of even the most languorous numbers, like the highlight "His Best Girl." —*Roch Parisien*

Col. Bruce Hampton

Rock & Roll, Southern Rock
Equal parts psychedelicized Allman Brothers and boogiefied Grateful Dead (with a dash of Commander Cody thrown in), Col. Bruce Hampton and the Aquarium Rescue Unit have capitalized on the nuevo-hippie movement that's been sweeping the country. The Atlanta-born Hampton has been kicking around the Southern music circuit since the early '60s; as the Hampton Grease Band, he released *Music to Eat* in 1969. After '70s-era stints in the New Ice Age and the Late Bronze Age, Hampton formed the AQR, an eclectic congregation that's adept at everything from country-swing jazz to meltdown Southern boogie and over-amped gospel bluegrass. —*John Floyd*

● **Arkansas** / 1984 / Landslide ♦♦♦♦
This "Southern Captain Beefheart" misses, but this Colonel (Ret.) is original. —*Robert Gordon*

Col. Bruce Hampton & The Aquarium Rescue Unit / Sep. 1991 / Capricorn ♦♦♦

○ **Mirrors of Embarrassment** / Jan. 1993 / Capricorn ♦♦♦♦
Strange Voices / 1994 / LAN ♦♦♦

Happy Mondays

Group, Alternative Pop/Rock, Dance
Along with the Stone Roses, the Happy Mondays were the leaders of the late '80s/early '90s dance club-influenced Manchester scene, experiencing a brief moment in the spotlight before collapsing in 1992. While the Stone Roses were based in '60s pop, adding only a slight hint of dance music, the Happy Mondays immersed themselves in the club and rave culture, eventually becoming the most recognizable band of that drug-fueled scene. The Mondays' music relied heavily on the sound and rhythm of house music, spiked with '70s soul licks, and swirling '60s psychedelia. It was bright, colorful music that had fractured melodies that never quite gelled into cohesive songs.

With their second album, 1988's *Bummed,* the Happy Mondays became British superstars, particularly lead singer Shaun Ryder. *Pills'n'Thrills and Bellyaches,* released in 1990, marked the height of the band's popularity, creativity, and influence; although the record made the Top 100 albums chart in America, it didn't establish them as stars in the U.S.

After that, the fall was quick. By the time they released their last studio album, *Yes Please,* Manchester had disappeared from public consciousness; it sold respectably, but the group didn't have the commercial impact that they had just two years before. Besides the lack of public interest, Shaun Ryder had become addicted to heroin, tearing the band apart in the process. At a high-level record contract meeting, Ryder walked out for some "Kentucky Fried Chicken," which was the band's slang for heroin. Ryder never returned and the group quickly fell apart.

Shaun Ryder and the Mondays' full-time dancer Bez re-emerged in the mid-'90s with Black Grape. The band released their critically-acclaimed debut, *It's Great When You're Straight… Yeah!* late in the summer of 1995. Black Grape's sound pursued the same direction as the Mondays, only with a harder, grittier edge to their sound and lyrics.. —*Stephen Thomas Erlewine*

Squirrell & G Man Twenty Four Hour Part People Plastic Face Carnt Smile / 1987 / Factory ♦♦
Produced by John Cale, Happy Mondays' debut album is a haphazard affair that concentrates on bare-boned funk exercises, only occasionally landing on the colorful, swirlingly eclectic mixture of funk, hip-hop and pop that would become the band's signature sound. —*Stephen Thomas Erlewine*

○ **Bummed** / 1988 / Elektra ♦♦♦♦
The second album by the band, *Bummed*, established them as premier dance rockers and helped publicize the Manchester scene internationally. —*David Szatmary*

● **Pills 'n' Thrills & Bellyaches** / 1990 / Elektra ♦♦♦♦
The Mondays sound more kaleidoscopic and more soulful than ever, with '70s soul emerging as the primary stepping-off point. "Kinky Afro" lifts the groove from LaBelle's "Lady Marmalade" for a chilling effect. The group also covers John Kongos' "Step On." More varied and better produced than their previous efforts—the Manchester scene is likely to run out of ideas before the Mondays do. —*Brian Mansfield*

Live / 1991 / Elektra ♦♦
While the band frequently sounds stiff and Ryder frequently sounds stoned, *Live* is a better proposition than it sounds. Instead of relying strictly on the studio arrangements, the Happy Mondays open up their grooves some and play some new songs. It's an intriguing album, especially for dedicated fans, but it's not as convincing as *Pills N' Thrills* or *Bummed*. —*Stephen Thomas Erlewine*

Yes, Please / 1992 / Elektra ♦
By the time of 1992's *Yes, Please*, the Happy Mondays had succumbed to the excessive lifestyle they had so enthusiastically promoted. Lead singer Shaun Ryder, who had always acted as both the mouthpiece and musical visionary for the band, sounds as if he couldn't be bothered and the music reflects his disinterest. In the hands of Chris Frantz and Tina Weymouth (Talking Heads, Tom Tom Club), the group's music loses much of its distinctive, thuggish edginess, as well as its reliance on current dance trends, becoming faceless, undistinguished dance-pop sludge. *Yes, Please* was not a particularly good way to say goodbye. —*Stephen Thomas Erlewine*

Double Easy: The US Singles / 1993 / Elektra ♦♦♦
The Happy Mondays' drug-soaked vision worked best on individual songs, so the concept of a singles collection seems ideal. However, the band's two groundbreaking and popular albums—*Bummed* and *Pills N' Thrills and Bellyaches*—have distinct musical visions, and work better as records than *Double Easy*, which fails to be a captivating listen, even though it includes nearly every one of their finest songs. —*Stephen Thomas Erlewine*

Tim Hardin

b. Dec. 23, 1941, Eugene, OR, d. Dec. 29, 1980
Folk, Singer-Songwriter, Folk-Rock

A gentle, soulful singer who owed as much to blues and jazz as folk, Tim Hardin produced an impressive body of work in the late '60s without ever approaching either mass success or the artistic heights of the best singer/songwriters. When future Lovin' Spoonful producer Erik Jacobsen arranged for Hardin's first recordings in the mid-'60s, Tim was no more than an above-average White blues singer, in the mold of many fellow folkies working the East Coast circuit. By the time of his 1966 debut, however, he was writing confessional folk-rock songs of considerable grace and emotion. The first album's impact was slightly diluted by incompatible string overdubs (against Hardin's wishes), but by the time of his second and best LP, he'd achieved a satisfactory balance between acoustic guitar-based arrangements and subtle string accompani-

ment. It was the lot of Hardin's work to achieve greater recognition through covers from other singers, such as Rod Stewart (who did "Reason to Believe"), Nico (who covered "Eulogy to Lenny Bruce" on her first album), Scott Walker (who sang "Lady from Baltimore"), Fred Neil ("Green Rocky Road" has been credited to both him and Hardin), and most especially Bobby Darin, who took "If I Were a Carpenter" into the Top Ten in 1966. Beleaguered with a heroin habit since early in his career, Hardin's drug problems became grave in the late '60s; his commercial prospects grew dimmer, and his albums more erratic, although he did manage to appear at Woodstock. His end was not a pretty one: due to accumulated drug and health problems, as well as a scarcity of new material, he didn't complete any albums after 1973, dying of a drug overdose in 1980. —*Richie Unterberger*

Tim Hardin 1 / 1966 / Verve ♦♦♦
Hardin's official debut introduced a vocalist and composer of some talent, most effective on the gentle confessional tunes and least effective on the blues. Occasionally it suffered from inappropriate ornamental string arrangements, but it included some of his finest compositions, including "Reason To Believe," "How Can We Hang on to a Dream," and "Don't Make Promises." —*Richie Unterberger*

Tim Hardin 2 / 1967 / Verve ♦♦♦
Probably his best single album, on which he eschewed blues nearly entirely and forged a distinctive, folk-rock voice, occasionally embellished by tasteful full arrangements. "Lady Came from Baltimore," "Red Balloon," and especially "If I Were a Carpenter" rank among his best and most famous songs. —*Richie Unterberger*

This Is Tim Hardin / 1967 / Edsel ♦♦♦
Hardin's very earliest recordings from approximately 1964, not issued until the late '60s, when he had achieved some success with his albums for Verve. Accompanied by nothing besides his own guitar, Hardin's arrangements are far sparser and bluesier than his folk-rock work for Verve. Over half of the ten tracks are traditional blues numbers like "Hoochie Coochie Man" and "House of the Rising Sun," and even the four originals (one co-written by future Holy Modal Rounder Steve Weber) are in a very similar straight blues style. The material isn't nearly as distinctive as the best of Hardin's work, but the performances rank with Dave Van Ronk and Fred Neil as the best white blues/acoustic folk to emerge from the early-'60s Greenwich scene (indeed, Hardin covers Neil's "Blues on the Ceiling" here). The hollow, reverbed, one-man-sitting-alone-in-an-empty-room production gives this album a haunting, somber feel (though not to its detriment). While not as good as Fred Neil's similar material from this era, it's still well worth tracking down. —*Richie Unterberger*

Tim Hardin 3 Live in Concert / 1968 / Verve ♦♦
A great live recording, it captures Hardin at his peak as a performer. —*Kenneth M. Cassidy*

Tim Hardin 4 / 1969 / Verve ♦♦

The Best of Tim Hardin / 1969 / Verve ♦♦♦

Suite for Susan Moore & Damian / 1970 / Columbia ♦♦♦

Bird on a Wire / 1971 / Columbia ♦♦♦
His last new American release, it was a good one. —*Kenneth M. Cassidy*

Painted Head / 1973 / Columbia ♦♦♦

Archetypes / 1973 / MGM ♦♦

Nine / 1974 / Antilles ♦♦

○ **The Shock of Grace** / 1981 / Columbia ♦♦♦♦
His best from the '70s, including "Bird on a Wire" and "First Love Song." —*William Ruhlmann*

● **Hang on to a Dream: the Verve Recordings** / Feb. 22, 1994 / Polydor ♦♦♦♦
Double-CD set of 47 tracks that Hardin recorded for Verve between 1964 and 1966. His expressive, blues-inflected vocals and confessional songwriting are heard on covers and famous compositions like "If I Were a Carpenter," "Lady Came from Baltimore," and "Reason to Believe." The compilation includes every studio recording that Hardin released on the Verve label, as well as two alternate takes and 15 previously unreleased tracks. —*Richie Unterberger*

● **Reason to Believe** / PolyGram ♦♦♦♦
The great early work of this top-flight '60s singer/songwriter includes the title track, "If I Were a Carpenter," and "Misty Roses." —*Kenneth M. Cassidy & William Ruhlmann*

John Wesley Harding

Singer-Songwriter, Alternative Pop/Rock
John Wesley Harding takes his name from a Bob Dylan song and he's a modern-day folk singer, but with his biting, cynical, clever songwriting, his true forefather is Elvis Costello. On occasion, he also dips into the political commentary of Billy Bragg. Harding's records never slip into self-absorbed, singer/songwriter mush, thanks to his sharp melodies. At times, his approach is a little too much like Costello's for comfort, yet his lyrical and musical style is distinctly his own. —*Stephen Thomas Erlewine*

○ **It Happened One Night** / 1988 / Rhino ◆◆◆◆
This solo acoustic outing, recorded live in England in 1988, seems like an odd choice for a debut, but it comes off very well. Capturing both John Wesley Harding's folk roots and a wonderful sense of humor, *It Happened One Night* gives a very representative picture of the singer/songwriter. Included are early versions of songs appearing on the following two albums as well as unreleased gems such as his fun account of Live Aid ("July 13th 1985") and a cover of Prince's "Kiss." —*Chris Woodstra*

God Made Me Do It: the Christmas EP / 1989 / Sire ◆◆◆
On this four-song EP (plus "A Cosy Promotional Chat" with ex-Bonzo Dog Band Viv Stanshall), Harding, apparently at the behest of his label, wrote one seasonal song, the Bob Dylan-inspired "Talking Christmas Goodwill Blues," a free-association acoustic folk ditty. Amusing. —*Decibel Dennis MacDonald*

● **Here Comes the Groom** / 1989 / Sire ◆◆◆◆
His second album has him working in the studio with a band called the Good Liars, including Pete Thomas, and Bruce Thomas of the Attractions. Not surprisingly, *Here Comes the Groom* has a feel similar to classic Elvis Costello. Harding's articulate and biting vocal delivery, also reminiscent of Costello, retains a good dark sense of humor. —*Chris Woodstra*

The Name Above the Title / 1991 / Sire ◆◆◆
The follow-up to *Here Comes the Groom* continues in the same direction. This time the arrangements are filled out with horn sections and strings, but the overall folky feel remains. —*Chris Woodstra*

Why We Fight / Mar. 1992 / Sire ◆◆◆
This 1992 release is more low-key and moody than any of his previous work. The subject matter is darker, though the melodies are still catchy and instantly memorable as always, this time with smoother production. Even a discussion about Hitler ("Hitler's Tears") is musically irresistible, placing him in the ranks of Nick Lowe and Elvis Costello. —*Chris Woodstra*

Pett Levels: the Summer EP / 1993 / Sire ◆◆

Francoise Hardy

Pop, Girl-Group
Usually thought of as a middle-of-the-road popular singer, Francoise Hardy—at the beginning of her career, at least—covered more stylistic ground and owed more debts to pop/rock than she's given credit for. Immensely popular in her native France, the chanteuse first displayed her breathy, measured vocals in the early and mid-'60s. Her (mostly self-penned) recordings from that era draw from French pop traditions, lightweight '50s teen idol rock, girl groups, and sultry jazz and blues—sometimes in the same song. The material is perhaps too unreservedly sentimental for some (in the French tradition), but the songs are invariably catchy and the production, arrangements, and near-operatic backup harmonies excellent, at times almost Spector-esque. Fans of Marianne Faithfull's mid-'60s work can find something of a French equivalent here, though Hardy's material was stronger and her delivery more confident. Hardy quickly made attempts to capture the international market with English recordings. Although these weren't entirely unsuccessful ("All over the World" was actually a British Top 10 hit in 1965), by the late '60s she was concentrating on more mainstream, middle-of-the-road material and arrangements on both her French and English sessions. She has remained popular in France until the present. —*Richie Unterberger*

All over the World / 1988 / Vogue ◆◆
Several French stars attempted to cross over into broader international success by recording in English. Usually these failed due to clumsy pronunciation and disinterest in American and British markets. Francoise Hardy was more successful than most, both artistically and commercially. Her accent is slight and her phrasing accomplished on these English rerecordings of 18 of her most popular mid-'60s tunes. One of these, "All over the World," actually cracked the British Top 20 in 1965. And she actually managed to release several albums of English material in the States, though she never took off commercially. These performances are respectable, but you're still better off with the original French versions. Her native tongue lends itself better to her romantic and melodramatic melodies and arrangements, which remain distinctly French in spite of their liberal debts to American girl-group pop and production. The backing tracks are unchanged or only slightly altered on these rerecordings; the CD remastering is a bit awkward, placing her voice way up front. —*Richie Unterberger*

Story 1962-64 / 1989 / Vogue ◆◆◆
The *Story* series, with three separate volumes covering the period from 1962-1967, presents this immensely popular French chanteuse at her best. This first volume, which features 20 songs, is perhaps the most innocuous of the lot, which isn't to say it isn't good. Her 1962 single "Le Temps De L'Amour" is perhaps her best recording, featuring snaky spy guitars and a minor-key melody in an unlikely but wonderful marriage of early-'60s rock and a film-noirish atmosphere. —*Richie Unterberger*

● **Story 1964-65** / 1989 / Vogue ◆◆◆◆
Perhaps Hardy's finest compilation, although *Story 1962-64* is almost as good. This 20-song CD finds her at her most girl group-influenced; you don't need to understand French to catch the infectious melodies and sultry, almost hushed vocals. Highlights include the magnificently moody ballad "Tu Peux Bien"; "Non Ce N'est Pas Un Reve," with melodramatic Spectorish production that recalls the Righteous Brothers at their peak; and the tense, romantic yearning of "Il Se Fait Tard." All of these *Story* discs have apparently been remixed for CD release, although the differences are slight, giving more prominence to the percussion and Hardy's vocals. —*Richie Unterberger*

Story 1965-67 / 1989 / Vogue ◆◆◆
The third 20-song anthology of work from Hardy's early (and best) years is perhaps the least essential of the trio. Several of the ballads and acoustic numbers are unmemorable, suffering from weak material and/or soppy, orchestrated arrangements. These sometimes recall a modified Petula Clark, which can be good or (more often) bad. But the best cuts here stand up to her best material from the decade. "Surtout Ne Vous Retournez Pas" and "Qu'ils Sont Hereux" are among her best ballads, "Je Ne Suis La Pour Personne" is a snappy folk-rocker, and "Voila" is her best grandiose, heart-on-the-sleeve orchestral production. All of the aforementioned highlights were Hardy originals. In the late '60s, Hardy moved towards more middle-of-the-road material (often sung in English), perhaps in an attempt to crack the international market; the three volumes of *Story* remain her most impressive work. —*Richie Unterberger*

Roy Harper

b. Jun. 12, 1941, Manchester, England
Singer-Songwriter, Folk-Rock
Harper came out of the U.K. in the mid-'60s folk boom in the wake of Bob Dylan's success with songs filled with poetic insight and anger. Guest appearances on his albums over the years by the cream of British Rock (including Jimmy Page, Ian Anderson, Bill Bruford, and Paul McCartney) should have given Harper a larger following, but he has never translated the admiration of his contemporaries into anything beyond cult status. Led Zeppelin's "Hats off to Harper" was dedicated to Roy. —*Cub Koda*

Come out Fighting Ghengis Smith / 1967 / CBS ◆◆◆
From Harper's early period. Conservative compared to his later work, but no less vital. —*Michael G. Nastos*

Folkjokeopus / 1969 / World Pacific ◆◆
This Shel Talmy-produced album is as sprawling and unwieldy as its title. Always a determined eclectic, Harper tries to cover a lot of ground here, and while his effort is impressive, the result is unnervingly inconsistent. The influences of Bob Dylan, Bert Jansch, Donovan, and maybe even early Al Stewart hover over most of this folk-rock. Harper tries to cram too many musical and (especially) lyrical ideas together here, and several of his heart-on-the-sleeve narrative folktales ramble on for too long, with an obscurity that verges on maddening. Some pretty, melodic passages here and there, with adequate folk singing that cracks when he even approaches the upper register. The acoustic guitar work is uniformly excellent, making this confused late-'60s timepiece sound rather more impressive than it should. —*Richie Unterberger*

● **Stormcock** / 1971 / Chrysalis ◆◆◆◆
With only four tracks (three of which are quite long), this is Harper's most serious, focused work. Not as melancholy as Nick Drake, it has a similar moody appeal and features lots of fine acoustic guitar work. "The Same Old Rock" feature virtuosic acoustic lead from none other than Jimmy Page (playing under the pseudonym S. Flavius Mercurius), and one can detect Harper's influence in the acoustic-oriented Led Zep recordings of the early '70s. —*Richie Unterberger*

Lifemask / 1973 / Chrysalis ◆◆◆
Album with Jimmy Page. Side 1 has five tracks; side 2 includes "The Lord's Prayer" suite. —*Michael G. Nastos*

Flashes from the Archives of Oblivion / 1974 / Chrysalis ◆◆◆
Flashes from the Archives of Oblivion. 14 tracks recorded at various concerts in England. Some of his most influential work. An obscene cover photo. —*Michael G. Nastos*

Valentine / 1974 / Chrysalis ◆◆◆
Includes "Male Chauvinist Pig Blues" and "Magic Woman (Liberation Reshuffle)," which is dedicated to Harper's mates in Led Zeppelin. —*Michael G. Nastos*

○ **When an Old Cricketer Leaves the Crease** / 1977 / Chrysalis ◆◆◆◆
When an Old Cricketer Leaves the Crease is a premiere American release. Seven cuts written by Harper. Band mates include Bill Bruford and Chris Spedding. This is arresting folk/rock. —*Michael G. Nastos*

One of These Days in England / 1977 / Chrysalis ◆◆◆
Second American release. Includes 20-minute "One of Those Days in England." —*Michael G. Nastos*

Whatever Happened to Jugula / 1985 / Beggars Banquet ◆◆◆
Led Zeppelin guitarist Jimmy Page backs Harper up on this album and earns co-billing for his trouble. The guitar interplay turns out to be the highlight of the album. Harper displays a nihilistic attitude towards everything in general and quite a few things in particular. He sings of things dire and hopeless in his thin tenor, while standard-issue folk and rock play behind him. Not that he doesn't have a sense of humor about it—a sleeve note introduces the final song by saying, "The best thing to do with the next track is to take a hot soldering iron and pull it fairly swiftly across the track..." Given that the song features the sound of the artist urinating and that the chorus goes, "I'm really stoned," this may not be such a bad idea. —*William Ruhlmann*

Jet Harris

b. 1939
Instrumental Rock, Pop/Rock
One of the more intriguing footnotes of pre-Beatle rock in Britain, Jet Harris first made his mark as the bassist for the Shadows. As they were megastar Cliff Richard's backing group and the most popular instrumental rock band in Britain, it was a shock when Harris left the group to become a solo act. But with frequent assistance from Shadows drummer Tony Meehan, Harris scored a half-dozen hits in a year and a half. (Meehan himself rates as an interesting footnote in rock history, having turned down the chance to record the Beatles in early 1962 when he was a producer for Decca Records.) Harris' biggest hit, the brooding "Diamonds" (including, it's been said, session guitar work by a very young Jimmy Page), vied for the number one spot with the Beatles' own "Please Please Me" in the U.K. in early 1963. There could have been few better symbols for the changing of the guard in British rock & roll. Harris' recordings typified British rock, such as it was, in the early '60s: sullen, restrained, disciplined instrumentals (often based on popular themes). Harris' singles were relatively unusual in that they made prominent use of the bass as a lead instrument, and the best of them—"Diamonds," "The Man with the Golden Arm," and "Man from Nowhere"—had a menacing, shuddering bass reminiscent of the best James Bond soundtracks. More frequently, however, his instrumentals sounded like a tame Duane Eddy or worse, with cornball adaptations of western movie riffs. His occasional attempts at vocals were fairly mewling and embarrassing. Harris had a couple more big hits after the Beatles broke, but the revolution the group ignited—as well as a severe automobile accident, along with emotional problems in the wake of this early success—brought his career to a skidding halt in early 1964. Unbelievably, he turned up in the first lineup of the Jeff Beck Group in February 1967, but never recorded with Beck, who revamped his outfit after a few weeks of rehearsal. —*Richie Unterberger*

● **Diamonds & Other Gems** / 1989 / Deram ◆◆◆◆
Everything you could want is on this 20-track CD—all six of Harris' 1962-64 singles (several of which co-billed Meehan), a few rare LP and EP tracks, an unreleased song, a solo single by Meehan—every last available item, in fact, from Harris' heyday. An at times cool, but more often foolish, glimpse of British rock just before the Beatles changed the rules. It could have probably been boiled down to an EP of the few first-rate tracks without any harm done. —*Richie Unterberger*

Thurston Harris

d. Apr. 14, 1990
R&B, Rock & Roll
An Indianapolis native who recorded with the Lamplighters in 1953, Thurston Harris got his time in the spotlight with "Little Bitty Pretty One," a classic novelty number featuring the Sharps doing backgrounds. It was his one and only Top Ten R&B and pop hit, making it to number two R&B and number six pop in 1957 for Aladdin. Harris had another Top 20 R&B hit the next year, "Do What You Did." —*Ron Wynn*

● **Little Bitty Pretty One** / 1984 / EMI America ◆◆◆◆

Wee Willie Harris

Rock & Roll
In the first wave of rock & roll, England could only offer pale Elvis imitations or ancient pop singers masquerading as such. One exception to the rule was Wee Willie Harris. Dying his hair all manner of colors and wearing larger-than-life stage jackets that looked like the coat hanger was still inside, tight drainpipe trousers, and a huge polka-dot bow tie, Harris understandably stood out from the rest of the pack. Coming from the Three I's coffeehouse circuit in Soho, Harris had a love for hard American rock & roll and an ability to perform it with unrelenting energy that kept him actively performing and recording from the mid '50s onward, working everything from nostalgia packages to cruise ships across the Atlantic—anyplace where his humorous and dynamic stage show could have a forum. —*Cub Koda*

○ **Wee Willie Harris** / See For Miles ◆◆◆◆
The best account of this singularly British phenomenon. (Import) —*Bruce Eder*

Wynonie Harris

b. Aug. 24, 1915, Omaha, NE, **d.** Jun. 14, 1969, Los Angeles, CA
R&B, Jump Blues
One of the most popular and powerful singers to contribute to the birth of '40s rhythm & blues, Wynonie Harris achieved his greatest hits by rocking long and hard or by making his listeners laugh the same way. His two #1 hits were the Roy Brown-penned "Good Rockin' Tonight" and "All She Wants to Do Is Rock," while other chart records were often in a comic novelty vein. But his nickname was "Mr. Blues" and a blues powerhouse he was, as well as a humorist, showman, and "a profane and raucous individual," in the words of his lifelong friend Preston Love. Many of his 1946-1952 hits were recorded with top-flight jazz accompanists. Harris recorded sporadically afterwards but never again enjoyed the glory or success he'd known as one of the kings of jump blues. —*Jim O'Neal*

★ **Bloodshot Eyes: The Best of** / King/Rhino ◆◆◆◆◆
Wynonie Harris was a hard-living, rousing R&B shouter who made some of the most sexually explicit songs in modern popular music history. Harris didn't leave much to the imagination, but he also possessed a booming voice with wonderful tone and range, and the comedic skill to execute these tunes without becoming raunchy. There are many hilarious cuts on this 18-track anthology, among them "I Like My Baby's Pudding," "Grandma Plays The Numbers" and "Good Morning Judge." Harris roars, struts and wails over equally feverish arrangements, and earns a draw with Joe Turner on "Battle Of The Blues." These songs give a good portrait of a delightful, often spectacular vocalist who could be both provocative and compelling. —*Ron Wynn*

George Harrison

b. Feb. 25, 1943, Liverpool, England
Pop/Rock
As lead guitarist for the Beatles, George Harrison provided the band with a lyrical style of playing in which every note mattered.

This was not surprising, from a rock & roller whose idols included the legendary classical guitarist Andres Segovia. Harrison, then age 13, was one of millions of young Britons inspired to take up the guitar by British skiffle king Lonnie Donegan's recording of "Rock Island Line." But he had more dedication than most, and with the encouragement of a slightly older school friend—Paul McCartney—he advanced quickly in his technique and command of the instrument. Harrison developed his style and technique slowly and painstakingly over the several years, learning everything he could from the records of Carl Perkins, Duane Eddy, Chet Atkins, Buddy Holly, and Eddie Cochran. By age 15, he was allowed to sit in with the Quarry Men, the Liverpool group founded by John Lennon, of which McCartney was a member; by 16 he was a full-fledged member of the group.

The Beatles finally coalesced around Lennon, McCartney, Harrison, and drummer Ringo Starr in 1962, with Harrison established on lead guitar. The Beatlemania years, from 1963 through 1966, were a mixed blessing for Harrison. The Beatles' studio sound was generally characterized by very prominent rhythm guitar parts, and on many of the Beatles' early songs, Harrison's lead guitar was buried beneath the chiming chords of Lennon's instrument. Additionally, he was thwarted as a songwriter by the presence of Lennon and McCartney—the quality and prolificacy of their output left very little room on the group's albums for songs by anyone else. Despite these problems, Harrison grew markedly as a musician between 1963 and 1966, writing a handful of good songs and one classic ("If I Needed Someone"), and also making his first acquaintance with the sitar, an Indian instrument whose sound fascinated him.

In 1966, Harrison finally seemed to find his voice, with two of his songs on the *Revolver* album, "Taxman" and "Love You Too." In the wake of the group's decision to stop touring, Harrison's playing and songwriting grew exponentially. The period from 1966 onward was Harrison's richest with the Beatles. He displayed a smooth, elegant slide guitar technique that showed up on their last three albums, and contributed two classic songs, "While My Guitar Gently Weeps" and "Here Comes the Sun," along with "Something," which became the first Harrison song on the A-side of a Beatles single.

Although never known as a strong singer, Harrison's vocals were always distinctive, especially when placed in the right setting—for his first solo record following the group's 1970 break-up, *All Things Must Pass*, Harrison collaborated with producer Phil Spector, whose so-called "wall of sound" technique adapted well to Harrison's voice. *All Things Must Pass* and the accompanying single "My Sweet Lord" had the distinction of being the first solo recordings by any of the Beatles to top the charts following their break-up. Unfortunately, Harrison was later successfully sued by the publisher of the 1962 Chiffons hit "He's So Fine," which bore a striking resemblance to "My Sweet Lord."

Harrison followed *All Things Must Pass* with rock's first major charity event, *The Concert for Bangla-Desh*, which was staged as two shows at New York's Madison Square Garden in 1971 to help raise money for aid to that famine-ravaged nation. The second of the two all-star shows was released as a movie and a live triple album. Harrison's next studio album, *Living In the Material World*, initially sold well, but its leaner, less opulent production lacked the majestic force of *All Things Must Pass*, and it lacked the earlier album's mass appeal. Subsequent Harrison albums from the 1970s into the 1980s always had an audience, but except for *Somewhere in England* (1981), released in the wake of the murder of John Lennon with the memorial song "All Those Years Ago," none seemed terribly well-crafted or executed. During this same period, Harrison embarked on a successful career as a movie producer with the founding of Handmade Films, which was responsible for such hits as *Time Bandits* (1981), *Mona Lisa* (1986), and *Withnail and I* (1987).

In 1987, Harrison made a return to the top of the charts with his album *Cloud Nine*, which featured his most inspired work in years, most notably a cover of an old Rudy Clark gospel number called "Got My Mind Set on You," which reached number one on the charts. In 1988, Harrison, Bob Dylan, Tom Petty, Jeff Lynne, and Roy Orbison formed the Traveling Wilburys, who have since released two very successful albums. — *Bruce Eder*

Wonderwall Music / Dec. 2, 1968 / Capitol ✦✦
The first-ever solo album by a Beatle (although John Lennon's *Two Virgins* preceded it in the U.S.) is a film soundtrack combining Indian-influenced music (some of it played by Indian musicians)

with more conventional pop. It's no more essential than most film scores away from the films themselves, but demonstrates the range of Harrison's musical taste. — *William Ruhlmann*

Electronic Sound / May 26, 1969 / Apple ✦✦
On his second non-Beatles side project (one could hardly call them solo albums), Harrison produces two sidelong instrumental tracks using a variety of sound effects, edits, and other studio wizardry. A trifle. — *William Ruhlmann*

★ **All Things Must Pass** / Nov. 27, 1970 / Capitol ✦✦✦✦✦
Without a doubt, Harrison's first solo recording, originally issued as a triple album, is his best. Drawing on his backlog of unused compositions from the late Beatle era, George crafted material that managed the rare feat of conveying spiritual mysticism without sacrificing his gifts for melody and grand, sweeping arrangements. Enhanced by Phil Spector's lush orchestral production and Harrison's own superb slide guitar, nearly every song is excellent: "Awaiting On You All," "Beware Of Darkness," the Dylan collaboration "I'd Have You Anytime," "Isn't It A Pity," and the hit singles "My Sweet Lord" and "What Is Life" are just a few of the highlights. A very moving work, with a very significant flaw: the jams that comprise the final third of the album are entirely dispensable, and have probably only been played once or twice by most of the listeners that own this record. — *Richie Unterberger*

The Concert for Bangladesh / Dec. 20, 1971 / Capitol ✦✦✦
A unique live document showcasing Harrison near his best, with ex-Beatle Ringo Starr, Eric Clapton, and many other superstars. It has less-than-perfect sound but overall fine re-creations of his best work, with work by Bob Dylan as an added bonus. — *Bruce Eder*

Living in the Material World / May 30, 1973 / Capitol ✦✦✦
Harrison had a lot of songs stored up for his first major solo work, *All Things Must Pass*, and it launched his post-Beatles career with a bang. Two and a half years later, he released its follow-up, which, although it contained some good playing by his band of superstar friends and some good tunes, notably the number one hit "Give Me Love (Give Me Peace on Earth)," indicated that the first album had contained his best effort and the most he'd be able to do in the future would be to repeat it. — *William Ruhlmann*

Dark Horse / Dec. 9, 1974 / Capitol ✦✦
Rushed through in the preparations for Harrison's first (and last) North American tour, his third solo album found him with a strained throat and not enough first-rate material. Most embarrassing was a re-write of "Bye Bye Love" in which he commented on the romantic triangle between himself, his wife, and his best friend, Eric Clapton (who later married her). The title track and "Ding Dong, Ding Dong" were Top 40 hits. — *William Ruhlmann*

Extra Texture / Sep. 22, 1975 / Capitol ✦✦
"You," a Top 20 hit, was a terrific pop song, but much of this album is expendable, including an update of the old Beatles song "While My Guitar Gently Weeps" called "This Guitar (Can't Keep from Crying)." From the superstar status of *All Things Must Pass*, Harrison had declined rapidly. — *William Ruhlmann*

The Best of George Harrison / Nov. 8, 1976 / Capitol ✦✦✦
The Harrison material is matched with some Beatles numbers in a good but routine collection. — *Bruce Eder*

○ **33 & 1/3** / Nov. 24, 1976 / Dark Horse ✦✦✦✦
Having suffered the humiliation of being sued successfully over "My Sweet Lord," Harrison turned the ordeal into music, writing "This Song," a Top 25 hit. Even better was "Crackerbox Palace," which would have fit in nicely on any Beatles album. The rest was slight, although Harrison covering Cole Porter's "True Love" is an interesting idea. This was Harrison's first album on his Dark Horse custom label, formed after the completion of his contract with EMI/Capitol in June 1976 and initially distributed by A&M. — *William Ruhlmann*

George Harrison / Feb. 14, 1979 / Dark Horse ✦✦
Harrison's sixth solo studio album (released after a two-year hiatus) was another slight affair, boasting the Top 20 single "Blow Away," but otherwise unremarkable. "Not Guilty" was a Beatles-era song once short-listed for their *White Album*. "Here Comes the Moon" was a tepid sequel to "Here Comes the Sun." — *William Ruhlmann*

Somewhere in England / Jun. 1, 1981 / Dark Horse ✦✦
Harrison had trouble getting Warner Brothers Records, which now distributed his Dark Horse label, to accept this album (an early, rejected version even turned up in collecting circles). It finally ap-

peared, heavily revised, featuring a song originally intended for Ringo Starr with different lyrics, "All Those Years Ago." Now pitched as a tribute to the late John Lennon, the song (featuring Starr and Paul McCartney) became a substantial hit and carried the mediocre album, which also features two Hoagy Carmichael songs. — *William Ruhlmann*

Gone Troppo / Oct. 27, 1982 / Dark Horse ♦♦

Although George Harrison's solo career had faded from its early promise, through 1981 he could be counted on to turn in a gold-selling, Top 20 album containing a Top 20 single every year or so. Then came the disastrous *Gone Troppo*, a half-baked affair led by the minor single "Wake up My Love" that failed to make the Top 100 LPs. Clearly, Harrison could no longer treat his musical career as a part-time stepchild to his interests in car racing and movie producing if he wanted to maintain it. As it turned out, he didn't; this was his last album for five years. — *William Ruhlmann*

○ **Cloud Nine** / Nov. 2, 1987 / Dark Horse ♦♦♦♦

A great collection of bright, hard-rocking numbers, even embracing gospel. — *Bruce Eder*

○ **The Best of Dark Horse (1976-1989)** / 1989 / Dark Horse ♦♦♦♦

The best of a less-than-satisfying era. The only way to take it in. — *Bruce Eder*

Live in Japan / Jul. 1992 / Dark Horse ♦♦

George Harrison returned to the stage for the first time in years in 1991; that Japanese tour is documented on the fine double-disc set *Live in Japan*. Backed by a stellar supporting band led by Eric Clapton, Harrison turns in surprisingly strong versions of his best solo material; it easily surpasses Paul McCartney's double-disc *Tripping the Live Fantastic* or *Paul Is Live*. Not bad for a guy who doesn't like to give concerts. — *Stephen Thomas Erlewine*

○ **Beware Of Abkco!** / 1994 / Strawberry [Bootleg] ♦♦♦♦

Probably demos recorded shortly prior to the sessions for *All Things Must Pass*, this is Harrison playing solo, unaccompanied by anything but his voices and guitar, sometimes electric, but usually acoustic. The fidelity is absolutely marvelous, at the point of the top of the pyramid for an unreleased recording. The performances are very interesting, if often tentative; the 15 songs are divided equally between versions of some of the better *All Things Must Pass* tracks ("Art Of Dying," "Run Of The Mill," "Let It Down," "Beware Of Darkness," "If Not For You"), and songs that didn't end up making the final cut. Some of these were obviously too weak for inclusion on the final album, but others are good, or would have been strong contenders for the LP with more polishing of the songwriting and production ("Nowhere To Go," "Beautiful Girl," and "Tell Me What Has Happened To You") are standouts). One regrets that Harrison didn't take the time to work these into shape for the third disc of *All Things Must Pass*, instead of filling out the triple album with half-baked jams. — *Richie Unterberger*

All Things Must Pass: Acetate / 1994 / Black Dog [Bootlrg] ♦♦♦

Also packaged as *Songs For Patti*, this isn't as essential an item as *Beware Of Abkco!*, but is still a nifty addendum to the official *All Things Must Pass* release. Features alternate versions of songs from the LP, some of them substantially different early mixes (vocal and instrumental) without some layers of overdubs, some of them different takes entirely. Also includes a couple of songs that didn't make the final album; the haunting, though unfinished, "I Still Love You" is a noteworthy find. Sound ranges from good to outstanding. — *Richie Unterberger*

Jerry Harrison

b. Feb. 21, 1949
Pop/Rock
Former member of the Modern Lovers and Talking Heads, has recorded three solo albums and produced records for Violent Femmes, Fine Young Cannibals, BoDeans, others. — *William Ruhlmann*

The Red and Black / 1981 / Sire ♦♦♦

● **Casual Gods** / 1987 / Sire ♦♦♦♦

Harrison employs many of Talking Heads' auxiliary players and other guests (guitarists Chris Spedding, Robbie McIntosh) for an album that matches the mid-period Heads sound of dense funk rhythms and clever lyrics. — *William Ruhlmann*

Walk on Water / 1990 / Fly ♦♦

Wilbert Harrison

b. Jan. 5, 1929, Charlotte, NC, **d.** Oct. 26, 1994
Soul, R&B, Rock & Roll
Harrison cut the classic version of "Kansas City" in 1959. The Charlotte, NC, native's laconic vocal style first turned up on Henry Stone's Rockin' label in 1952, and he progressed to Deluxe, Chart, and Savoy before landing on Bobby Robinson's Fury imprint in 1959. With Jimmy Spruill wildly wringing out slashing bent notes on his guitar, Harrison's rocking revival of the Jerry Leiber/Mike Stoller classic "Kansas City" (first cut by Little Willie Littlefield in 1952) topped both the pop and R&B charts. Subsequent Fury 45s (including the sequel "Goodbye Kansas City") undeservedly bombed, and Harrison plied his trade for a time as a one-man band. But he wasn't through—"Let's Work Together," a slight rewrite of his Fury-era "Let's Stick Together," vaulted up the charts in 1970 after being recut for Sue. Like his other best-seller, "Let's Work Together" was prime cover material—for the likes of Canned Heat and Bob Dylan. And once again, he was unable to follow it up with anything of equal potency. — *Bill Dahl*

Listen to My Song / 1954-1957 / Savoy ♦♦♦

Interesting mix of R&B, blues, and light pop from journeyman vocalist Wilbert Harrison, who nonetheless scored two huge hits with "Kansas City" and "Let's Work Together." He was not a jazz vocalist, nor is the music, but R&B, blues, or early rock devotees will enjoy it. — *Ron Wynn*

● **Kansas City** / 196z / Relic ♦♦♦♦

Harrison's toughest late-'50s/early-'60s output for Fury Records features many songs in stereo for the first time. — *Bill Dahl*

○ **Greatest Classic R&B Hits** / 1989 / Grudge ♦♦♦♦

This is the only available CD for Harrison's late-'60s material, long after his 1959 classic "Kansas City." — *Bill Dahl*

Debbie Harry

b. Jul. 1, 1945, New York, NY
Pop/Rock
Singer/actress who was the lead vocalist in the new wave group Blondie, 1974-1982. Harry launched a solo singing career in 1981, as well as acting on stage and film, but she retired in 1983 to nurse seriously ill companion (and Blondie guitarist) Chris Stein. Stein recovered, and Harry returned to action in 1985. — *William Ruhlmann*

Kookoo / 1981 / Chrysalis ♦♦♦

Harry teams up with Chic for bass-heavy dance rock, notably on the hit "Backfired." — *William Ruhlmann*

○ **Rockbird** / 1986 / Geffen ♦♦♦♦

A return to the trashy, bubblegum-rock style of early Blondie, featuring the hit "French Kissin'." — *William Ruhlmann*

Once More into the Bleach / 1988 / Chrysalis ♦♦♦

A compilation disc containing Blondie and Debbie Harry solo hits in remixed, extended dance versions. — *William Ruhlmann*

● **Def, Dumb & Blonde** / 1989 / Sire ♦♦♦♦

Throughout *Def, Dumb & Blonde*, Harry switches between updated dance-pop (adding elements of hip-hop and house) and punky pop/rock, reminiscent of Blondie's first two records. It's a little inconsistent, yet it is thoroughly engaging, especially on "I Want that Man," which manages to bridge the gap between the two styles quite effectively. — *Stephen Thomas Erlewine*

Debravation / 1993 / Warner Brothers ♦♦♦

Recording with several star musicians, including members of R.E.M., Deborah Harry returns to a more rock-oriented approach on *Debravation*. Although the band is tight and Harry is in fine voice, the album suffers from weak material. — *Stephen Thomas Erlewine*

Mickey Hart

b. Sep. 11, 1943
Ethnic Fusion
Mickey Hart is a drummer, an ethnomusicologist, and an author. He joined the Grateful Dead as its second percussionist in 1967. In 1970, Hart left the Dead and cut the solo album *Rolling Thunder* in 1972, featuring various members of the Dead. Hart returned to the band in 1974.

Hart's musical activities outside the Dead have been extensive. In 1976, the Dead's Round Records label released *Diga* by the Diga Rhythm Band, an early experiment in worldbeat fusion put together by Hart. His interaction with drummers from around the world sparked an abiding interest in the role of the drum in other cultures—and a steadily expanding curiosity about non-Western musics. 1979 and 1980 saw the release of two albums of music from the film *Apocalypse Now*, much of it contributed by Hart. In 1983, Hart released albums under the heading *The World*. These began with a reissue of *Diga Rhythm Band* (an album by Babatunde Olatunji produced by Hart). Then came a series of albums of music Hart had recorded around the world. In 1989 Hart released *Music to Be Born By*, an album based on the heartbeat of his son in the womb, and 1990 saw the simultaneous release of Hart's first book, *Drumming at the Edge of Magic*, and an album, *At the Edge*. In 1991, another book and disc, both called *Planet Drum*, appeared. Both albums made the upper reaches of the new age and world-music charts. — *William Ruhlmann & Bob Tarte*

Rolling Thunder / 1972 / Grateful Dead ✦✦✦
This is the nearest thing to a conventional pop-rock album Mickey Hart ever made. It features Grateful Dead members Bob Weir, Jerry Garcia, and Phil Lesh, as well as other San Francisco rock musicians, and contains early versions of the Dead songs "Playing in the Band" and "Greatest Story Ever Told." — *William Ruhlmann*

Diga Rhythm Band / 1976 / Rykodisc ✦✦✦

The Apocalypse Now Sessions / 1980 / Rounder ✦✦✦
Hart's soundtrack work for *Apocalypse Now* expanded into these free-ranging, rather abstract tracks with fellow Grateful Dead drummer Billy Kreutzmann. — *Bob Tarte*

○ **Däfos** / 1983 / Rykodisc ✦✦✦✦
An established audiophile classic for its thrilling, nearly overpowering sonics, this percussion-based journey to a mythical country features Brazilian percussionist Airto Moreira and vocalist Flora Purim. — *Bob Tarte*

Music to Be Born By / 1989 / Rykodisc ✦✦✦
Hart plays off the sound of a pre-natal heartbeat to create a soothing ambient recording. — *William Ruhlmann*

At the Edge / 1990 / Rykodisc ✦✦✦
Sounds like we're at the edge of the rainforest on this atmospheric recording that uses a variety of unusual instruments and employs such musicians as Jerry Garcia, Babatunde Olatunji, Airto Moreira, and Zakir Hussain. — *William Ruhlmann & Bob Tarte*

Honor the Earth Powwow-Songs..Great Lakes Indians / 1991 / Rykodisc ✦✦✦

● **Planet Drum** / Dec. 1991 / Rykodisc ✦✦✦✦
A dazzling all-percussion workout with plenty of muscle and deep grooves featuring many of the world musicians from *At the Edge*. Loosely tied to Hart's book of the same name. — *Bob Tarte*

○ **Yamantaka** / Celestial Harmonies ✦✦✦✦

P.J. Harvey

Group, Alternative Pop/Rock
In terms of sound as well as subject, Polly Jean Harvey is the most challenging female singer/songwriter to emerge in the early '90s. With her band, PJ Harvey, she staked out a distinctly personal territory with her brutally honest, darkly humorous songs about sex, love, and hate. At their core, her songs are structured like the blues, but played with the raw aggression of punk. Harvey's voice is equally uncompromising, squeezing all of the emotion out of a song. The sheer overpowering sonic rush of her music can overshadow the fact that her songs are not bitterly angry and violent—they only sound that way; her music has a very human core.

PJ Harvey became an indie rock sensation, especially in their native Britain, with the 1992 release of their debut, *Dry*. All of the subsequent media attention helped her build a substantial cult following. Instead of expanding her cult, PJ Harvey's uncompromising second album, 1993's *Rid of Me*, only made her fans more devoted; in the fall of 1993, it was followed by *4 Track Demos*, a collection of Harvey's original recordings for the album, plus several unreleased songs.

During the *Rid of Me* tour, PJ Harvey's drummer and backing vocalist Rob Ellis left the band; for a short time, bassist Steven Vaughan also left, only to return by the end of the year. During 1994, Harvey broke up the original trio, recording her new album with a group of studio musicians, including Joe Gore, who played on Tom Waits' *Bone Machine*. Released in early 1995, the resulting *To Bring You My Love* was Harvey's most ambitious and accessi-

ble album to date. The album debuted in the American Top 40 and featured the alternative hit "Down By the Water." — *Stephen Thomas Erlewine*

○ **Dry** / 1992 / Indigo ✦✦✦✦
Dry is the stunning debut album from singer-songwriter Polly Jean Harvey's trio PJ Harvey. Although Harvey has her share of post-feminist anger, the album doesn't lack humor ("Dress" and "Sheela-Na-Gig"). However, Harvey really makes her mark through her music, a fierce combination of punk rage, sharp songwriting, and surprisingly melodic hooks. *Dry* is one of the most distinctive debut albums ever recorded. — *Stephen Thomas Erlewine*

○ **Rid of Me** / May 4, 1993 / Indigo ✦✦✦✦
Thanks to Steve Albini's production, PJ Harvey's second album is a harsher, more abrasive affair. Albini has taken the dynamics of Polly Harvey's songwriting to extremes; sometimes it's nearly impossible to hear the beginning of a song until an explosive rush of guitars obliterates the silence a minute later. Still, most of the uneasiness of *Rid of Me* can be mainly attributed to Harvey herself. Although the best songs here ("Rid of Me," "50 Ft. Queenie," "Yuri G," "Man-Sized") are better than the best on *Dry*, they're more difficult to listen to. Harvey's songs have become harder and angrier, but she hasn't completely stripped away the humor that enlivened *Dry*. *Rid of Me* is an impressive artistic achievement, but is difficult listening precisely because of its accomplishment. — *Stephen Thomas Erlewine*

4-Track Demos / Nov. 1993 / Indigo ✦✦✦
With Polly Harvey's voice acting as the focal point of these recordings, *4-Track Demos* isn't necessarily more accessible than the draining guitar attack of *Rid of Me*. Stripped-down, Harvey's songs function as raw nerve endings, accentuating the power of her songwriting. Her often-overlooked sense of humor is also more apparent, especially on the sublime "Reeling." All of these factors taken together make *4-Track Demos* an album that should be heard not just by Harvey's devoted fans, but by anyone with a passing interest in her or modern rock. — *Stephen Thomas Erlewine*

● **To Bring You My Love** / 1995 / Indigo ✦✦✦✦
PJ Harvey's third proper album is her first true solo album, recorded without the rhythm section that gave *Dry* and *Rid of Me* their savage roar. Instead, she has headed into the studio with Flood (U2/Depeche Mode/Nine Inch Nails), creating an album that is easily as dark as the blackest moments of *Rid of Me*, only with more sonic textures and colors, including the menacing rhythms of "Down By the Water," the bluesy stomp of "Meet Ze Monsta," and the layered guitars of "C'Mon Billy." Instead of diluting the impact of Harvey's music, the expanded pallette results in a more satisfying and uncompromising album that becomes more rewarding with each listen. — *Stephen Thomas Erlewine*

Juliana Hatfield

Alternative Pop/Rock
After leaving the Blake Babies, singer/guitarist Juliana Hatfield pursued a solo career that easily eclipsed her former band, both in commercial and artistic terms. Hatfield's thin, girlish voice accentuates her unassuming, catchy pop songs that can either be sweet and happy ("Spin the Bottle") or surprisingly honest and moving ("Ugly"). Her first solo album, 1992's *Hey Babe*, was a small gem, full of well-constructed songs that effortlessly evoked the pain and charm of adolescence; rarely had anyone captured teenagers from a female perspective so accurately. It was a college-radio hit that made a small dent in the mainstream, particularly with teenage girls. Afraid that she wasn't being taken seriously as an artist, Hatfield hooked up with a grungy male rhythm section for her next album, 1993's *Become What You Are*. She kept the effortless melody of her first album, while turning up the volume on the amplifiers, resulting in a more commercially successful album. After assembling a new band in late 1994, Hatfield returned in the spring of 1995 with *Only Everything*, which featured the minor hit single "Universal Heartbeat." — *Stephen Thomas Erlewine*

● **Hey Babe** / 1992 / Mammoth ✦✦✦✦
Hey Babe is Juliana Hatfield's terrific solo debut, filled with effortless melodies and catchy guitar riffs. Hatfield's thin, girlish voice can be slightly wearing over the course of an entire album, but her intelligent, hook-laden songs make up for that minor flaw. — *Stephen Thomas Erlewine*

Become What You Are / 1993 / Mammoth ✦✦✦
Although she desperately tries to hide behind a grungier guitar sound, Hatfield is still a talented practitioner of girlish power-pop. Because she tries so hard to put the innocent pleasures of her debut behind her, *Become What You Are* isn't as satisfying. Most of the loud rave-ups betray her true gifts with a melody, which most definitely has not disappeared; her hooks are so strong that she can bring over such cringe-inducing lyrics as those of "For the Birds" and "Mabel" rather effortlessly. Hatfield's strongest points are apparent on "Supermodel," "My Sister," and "Spin the Bottle"—catchy, honest, and incisive portraits of adolescence, rendered truthful by her girlish, sing-song vocals. Fortunately, her talents are strong enough to carry the album over the weak spots. — *Stephen Thomas Erlewine*

Only Everything / 1995 / Mammoth ✦✦✦
The Juliana Hatfield Three folded soon after the supporting tour for *Become What You Are*, yet Hatfield hasn't abandoned the basic approach of the band—she still rocks out, supporting her sing-song melodies with massive, grungy guitars. If anything, her new backing band rocks harder than the Hatfield Three, with a better, looser sense of rhythm as well. Even with the improved musicianship, Hatfield isn't able to deliver consistently impressive songs, occasionally relying on her cuteness to cover underdeveloped lyrics and pedestrian melodies. Most of the record doesn't drag, however—it's a fun, engaging pop album, yet it's best moments follow the strengths of her earlier songs, without doing much to expand her formula. — *Stephen Thomas Erlewine*

Donny Hathaway

b. Oct. 1, 1945, Chicago, IL, d. Jan. 13, 1979
Soul
Donny Hathaway was a marvelous composer and vocalist. His sound, delivery, and timbre have influenced singers from Stevie Wonder to George Benson, while his compositions have been recorded by an array of artists from Cold Blood to Jerry Butler, the Staple Singers, Carla Thomas, and Aretha Franklin. Hathaway was born in Chicago, but grew up in St. Louis and began singing gospel at age three. He attended Howard University on a fine arts scholarship and was a classmate of Roberta Flack. He began recording for Curtis Mayfield's Curtom label in 1969, then signed with Atco. His single "The Ghetto" was a mild hit, but the duet "You've Got a Friend" with Flack was his first Top Ten R&B hit. The duo would later score two number one hit duets, "Where Is the Love" and "The Closer I Get to You," each of which was also a Top Ten pop hit. The duo had two final hits, "You Are My Heaven" and "Back Together Again," in 1980, after Hathaway stunned everyone by committing suicide in 1979 at age 33. — *Ron Wynn*

Everything Is Everything / 1970 / Atlantic ✦✦✦
His debut, on this warm soul session. — *Bil Carpenter*

Donnie Hathaway / 1971 / Atlantic ✦✦✦
A wonderful album, with King Curtis playing sax. — *Bil Carpenter*

Live / 1972 / Atlantic ✦✦✦

Flack & Hathaway / 1972 / Atlantic ✦✦✦

○ **Extension of a Man** / 1973 / Atlantic ✦✦✦✦
This 1973 album (reissued on CD in 1993) was among Hathaway's most ambitious. It included a stunning two-part gospel tune, "I Love the Lord," a revamped version of "Valdez in the Country," a magnificent "We'll All Be Free" and a soulful remake of Blood, Sweat & Tears' "I Love You More Than You'll Ever Know." Hathaway's gorgeous voice and superb delivery, timing, pacing and style made him unsurpassed among soul artists of his generation, and his arranging skills were equally brilliant. This album ranks as a masterpiece, along with his self-titled debut. — *Ron Wynn*

In Performance / 1980 / Atlantic ✦✦✦
This live set is a must for serious fans. — *Bil Carpenter*

● **Collection** / 1990 / Atlantic ✦✦✦✦
A hits compilation including "The Ghetto" and "Givin' up Your Love Is Like (Givin' Up the World)," as well as the hit duets with Roberta Flack "Where Is the Love" and "You've Got a Friend." — *Bil Carpenter*

The Haunted

Group, Garage Rock
One of Canada's most popular homegrown rock groups in the 1960s, though they made no inroads to the rest of North America.

From the English-speaking community of Montreal, the group was very explicit in its desire to emulate the Rolling Stones, and most of their 1966-68 singles (as well as their sole LP, from 1967) were in a raunchy R&B/blues-rock style. As songwriters their range was pretty limited, and much of their material consisted of covers or thin rewrites of popular blues riffs. Their most successful single, "1-2-5," gained small fame when it was reissued on one of the first *Pebbles* compilations of garage singles in the 1970s. All of their material was reissued in the 1980s. — *Richie Unterberger*

● **Part One: Return From The Grave** / 1983 / Voxx ✦✦✦✦
Includes their most notable singles: the basic snotty Stones takeoff "1-2-5" (two versions), a cover of Them's "I Can Only Give You Everything," and their best original tune, "Eight O'Clock This Morning" (the B-side of "1-2-5"). Actually, some of the best tracks are eerily moody, slowed-down covers of Love's "A Message to Pretty," "Horror Show" (a ripoff of an early Small Faces track), and Joe South's "Untie Me" (although the Haunted's cover is based on Manfred Mann's version). Competent, at times exciting Stones-derived mid-'60s rock. — *Richie Unterberger*

Part Two: I'm Just Gonna Blow My Little Mind To Bits / 1983 / Voxx ✦✦
Combined with *Return From The Grave*, this comprises everything ever released by the Haunted. This volume isn't as good as the first, including a couple of poppy singles by the spinoff group Our Generation (formed by Haunted singer Bob Burgess after he split from the original lineup in 1967), bizarre French garage versions of "Purple Haze" and the Music Machine's "Talk Talk," and the group's extremely Hendrix-inspired final 1968 single. The title track, one of their B-sides, may sound like it would be an ultimate punk blowout, but it's actually a restrained and moody blues. A fairly thin LP, one for the completists. — *Richie Unterberger*

Richie Havens (Richard Pierce Havens)

b. Jan. 21, 1941, Brooklyn, NY
Folk, Singer-Songwriter, Folk-Rock
Born in the Bedford-Stuyvesant section of Brooklyn, Richie Havens moved to Greenwich Village in 1961 in time to get in on the folk boom then taking place. Havens had a distinctive style as a folksinger, appearing in such clubs as the Cafe Wha? His guitar set to an opening tuning, he would strum it while barring chords with his thumb, using it essentially as percussion while singing rhythmically in a gruff voice for a mesmerizing effect. Havens was signed to Douglas Records in 1965 and recorded two albums that gained him a local following. In 1967, the Verve division of MGM Records formed a folk section (Verve Forecast) and signed Havens and other folk-based performers. The result was Havens's third album, *Mixed Bag*. It wasn't until 1968 and the *Something Else Again* album, however, that Havens began to hit the charts—actually, Havens's fourth, third, and second albums charted that year, in that order. In 1969 came the double album *Richard P. Havens 1983*.

Havens's career benefited enormously from his appearance at the Woodstock festival in 1969 and his subsequent featured role in the movie and album made from the concert in 1970. His first album after that exposure, *Alarm Clock*, made the Top 30 and produced a Top 20 single in "Here Comes the Sun." These recordings were Havens's commercial high-water mark, but by this time he had become an international touring success. By the end of the '70s, he had abandoned recording and turned entirely to live work.

Havens came back to records with a flurry of releases in 1987: a new album, *Simple Things*; an album of Bob Dylan and Beatles covers; and a compilation. In 1991, Havens signed his first major-label deal in 15 years when he moved to Sony Music and released *Now*. — *William Ruhlmann*

○ **Mixed Bag** / 1967 / Verve ✦✦✦✦
Havens' first major-label album, and his best, featuring his distinctive interpretations of such songs as Dylan's "Just Like a Woman" and the scathing anti-war anthem "Handsome Johnny." (It should be noted that, while it is his best overall collection, *Mixed Bag* is a also characteristic album: If you like it, you'll probably like other Havens records, which adopt much the same style.) — *William Ruhlmann*

Somethin' Else Again / 1968 / Verve ✦✦✦

Alarm Clock / 1971 / Stormy Forest ✦✦✦

○ **The Great Blind Degree** / 1971 / Stormy Forest ✦✦✦✦

Richie Havens on Stage / 1972 / Stormy Forest ✦✦✦

Portfolio / 1973 / Stormy Forest ✦✦

Collection / 1987 / Rykodisc ✦✦✦

A compilation of Havens' 60s and early-'70s material. It leaves out some of his signature material, but it does include his version of "Here Comes the Sun." *—William Ruhlmann*

● **Resume: Best of** / 1993 / Rhino ✦✦✦✦

Havens' output has been so extensive that picking tunes for a single-disc anthology would be a difficult task for any label. Rhino has done a respectable job in compiling 17 selections, although there was no material from the LPs *Stonehenge* or *1984*, and while he certainly performed them his way, neither Ray Charles' "Drown in My Own Tears" nor Billie Holiday's "God Bless the Child" were among Havens' best songs. By comparison, "Handsome Johnny," "Freedom," "Here Comes the Sun," "The Klan" and "Just Like a Woman" had a strength and power that came partly from being ideally suited for Havens' style. This isn't the comprehensive or qualitative anthology Havens deserves; just a decent hits collection. *—Ron Wynn*

Cuts to the Chase / 1994 / Forward ✦✦✦

Guitarist/composer Richie Havens keeps making thought-provoking, poignant and intensely personal music, with few (if any) romantic songs and frank discussions of issues without violent or sexist rhetoric. This is Havens' first solo release in several years, and it contains only one original. But his covers of songs by Sting, Kris Kristofferson, Bob Lind and Marty Balin become his own memorable statements, while guitarist Billy Perry and guest guitarist Greg Chansky provide three new compositions. Although this doesn't have the same resonance as his great 1960s LPs, it's a worthy vehicle for the 1990s. *—Ron Wynn*

Dale Hawkins

Rockabilly

This Louisiana guitarist's 1957 hit "Suzy Q," with its crackling bluesy guitar and insistent cowbell, was one of the most exciting early rockabilly singles. Recording for Chess (as one of its few White artists) between 1956 and 1961, Hawkins never quite duplicated its success, either commercially or artistically, but came close enough on a number of occasions to warrant respect as one of the better rockabilly singers. His drawling delivery, sense of humor, affinity for blues, and sharp guitar work (which was actually provided by such ace players as Roy Buchanan, Scotty Moore, and James Burton) are heard to good effect on his 1958 album and a number of non-hit singles. Hawkins went on to become a producer of some note in the 1960s, working with the Five Americans and Bruce Channel. *—Richie Unterberger*

○ **Susie Q** / 1958 / Chess ✦✦✦✦

A way-above-average '50s rock & roll album, including both sides of Dale's first four singles. Highlights are "Suzie-Q," its killer B-side ("Don't Treat Me This Way"), and the goofy "See You Soon Baboon" and "Mrs. Mergitory's Daughter." *—Richie Unterberger*

● **Dale Hawkins** / 1972 / Chess ✦✦✦✦

My Babe / 1987 / Argo ✦✦✦

Rare singles and other interesting material that Hawkins cut, mostly for Chess, between 1958 and 1962. Includes his sole Top 40 hit besides "Suzie-Q" ("La-Do-Dada") and some fine rockabilly interpretations of blues hits. *—Richie Unterberger*

Ronnie Hawkins

Group, Rockabilly

Hawkins is a rockabilly singer who formed his original backing band, the Hawks, while attending the University of Arkansas. After auditioning unsuccessfully for Sun in 1957, he started working regularly in Canada the following year, eventually taking up permanent residence there. After one release on the Canadian Quality label, he signed with Roulette in New York in 1959, having hits with "Forty Days" and "Mary Lou." The live fervor of Hawkins (known as Mr. Dynamo) & the Hawks' show continued in Canada after all the original members except Levon Helm headed back to the US. Hawkins quickly hired Canadian players Robbie Robertson, Garth Hudson, Rick Danko, and Richard Manuel as the new Hawks. They stayed with him until 1963, but later became Bob

Dylan's backing group and went on to a career of their own as the Band. Hawkins has remained a legend in Canada, recording unrepentant rockabilly sides and gigging constantly. He's still the original Mr. Dynamo, capable of shaking the walls down any old time he feels like it. *—Cub Koda*

● **The Best of Ronnie Hawkins & His Band** / 1990 / Rhino ✦✦✦✦

In the late 1950s and early 1960s, Ronnie Hawkins was one of the few rock & rollers committed to performing and recording unapologetic rockabilly while others were returning to their country roots or going the teen idol route. This 18-song compilation focuses mostly on his initial burst of activity for Roulette in 1959 and 1960, with a few later odds and ends thrown in. While he deserves respect for keeping the torch of rock & roll's roots burning during some of its leaner years, he didn't match the greatness of rockabilly's kingpins. His voice and performance was energetic but not brilliant; his material was a bit pedestrian. The best of these tunes are "Mary Lou" (his sole Top 30 hit), "Forty Days" (an update of Chuck Berry's "Thirty Days"), and "One of These Days" (later covered by the Searchers). What he's really known for, of course, is giving a bunch of mostly Canadian kids their start as his backing band, the Hawks. A later edition of the Hawks eventually toured with Bob Dylan and evolved into the Band. Only two of these songs, though, feature that lineup (the 1963 single "Bo Diddley"/"Who Do You Love"). On "Who Do You Love" especially, Robbie Robertson lets rip with a roaring solo that's a good few years ahead of its time in its manic distorted intensity. It's by far the most exciting track on this compilation of a respectable but minor performer from rock's early days. *—Richie Unterberger*

Screamin' Jay Hawkins

b. Jul. 18, 1929, Cleveland, OH

R&B, Rock & Roll

Though capable of more conventional blues, sentimental ballads, and R&B, Screamin' Jay Hawkins will be forever remembered for the wild songs and onstage theatrics of his self-created brand of voodoo jive. His act has often featured him emerging from a casket to sing his best-known hit, "I Put a Spell on You." Other novelties, ranging from "Feast of the Mau Mau" to "Constipation Blues," may have stereotyped his talent, but on the other hand, his idiosyncracies have brought him TV and movie appearances that would have eluded him had he played his music straight. Regardless of style, Hawkins's recordings still display a remarkable voice, which would have been used for opera had Screamin' Jay had his way. *—Jim O'Neal*

● **Voodoo Jive: Best of Screamin' Jay Hawkins** / 1990 / Rhino ✦✦✦✦

Some maintain that Hawkins was a one-hit fluke and a one-dimensional performer with a limited singing voice and no other discernible skills. Others insist that Hawkins was a decent R&B and blues singer and an excellent entertainer and personality whose real talents were overshadowed by the success of "I Put a Spell on You." This anthology doesn't convincingly answer the argument, but it does collect 17 Hawkins singles from Okeh, Enrica and Phillips, including all of his major hits. The high (or low) point is perhaps 1969's "Constipation Blues." *—Ron Wynn*

Sophie B. Hawkins

Pop/Rock

A New York-based pop singer/songwriter, Sophie B.Hawkins' music ranges from dance-pop to chilly introspection. She began performing professionally as a percussionist with Bryan Ferry in the early '80s. Hawkins released her first solo album, *Tongues and Tails*, in 1992; it launched the number five hit "Damn I Wish I Was Your Lover." Released two years later, *Whaler* was a flop upon its release, yet a year later the single "As I Lay Me Down" broke into the singles charts. *—Stephen Thomas Erlewine*

● **Tongues and Tails** / 1992 / Columbia ✦✦✦✦

A New York eccentric type, Sophie B.Hawkins began her music career studying ethnic percussion. She moved to jazz, then was a drummer in a punk band while sidelining as an actor and performance artist. Hawkins' debut disc *Tongues and Tails* is as eclectic as her career choices. The songs ranges from the hook-filled mainstream pop of "Damn I Wish I Was Your Lover" to an off-centre rant about mothers in "Carry Me" that dissolves into feedback mayhem. Hawkins stitches together bits of jazz, folk, tribal, rock, and atmospheric new age noodling while efficiently camouflaging the seams. Somehow, it all works with repeated listens. The common thread is her distinctive, street-wise but unjaded voice. —*Roch Parisien*

Whaler / 1994 / Columbia ✦✦✦

Ted Hawkins

b. 1936, Biloxi, MS, **d.** Jan. 1, 1995
Soul, Singer-Songwriter

The enigmatic, elusive Ted Hawkins may be more familiar to passersby on the streets and beaches of Southern California than he is to blues concert audiences. A street musician with a street-wise yet sweet delivery of highly original songs, usually performed with only strummed acoustic guitar accompaniment, Hawkins first recorded for producer Bruce Bromberg in 1971. Peter Guralnick described Hawkins's "strikingly personal" music as "neither the blues nor gospel [but] a combination of the two, a rural adaptation of contemporary soul music." Hawkins died in 1995. —*Jim O'Neal*

● **Watch Your Step** / 1982 / Rounder ✦✦✦✦

Guitarist/vocalist Ted Hawkins was an instant sensation when this session was originally released in 1982. At a time when slick, heavily produced urban contemporary material was establishing its domination on the R&B scene, Hawkins' hard-edged, rough, cutting voice, plus his crisp acoustic guitar accompaniment and country blues roots, seemed both dated and extremely fresh. This 15-track CD includes four numbers with Hawkins backed by Phillip Walker and his band, and others ranging from the humorous "Who Got My Natural Comb?" to the poignant "If You Love Me" and two versions of the title track. He also teamed with his wife Elizabeth on "Don't Lose Your Cool" and "I Gave It All I Had" for moving duets. —*Ron Wynn*

○ **Happy Hour** / 1987 / Rounder ✦✦✦✦

Guitarist/vocalist Ted Hawkins' second Rounder date in 1986 enhanced his reputation. This CD version features Hawkins' memorable compositions, plus a wonderful version of Curtis Mayfield's "Gypsy Woman." Hawkins' vocals were even more gritty and striking, as was his acoustic guitar backing and chording. He teamed with his wife Elizabeth on "Don't Make Me Explain It," "My Last Goodbye" and "California Song," and with guitarist Night Train Clemons on "Gypsy Woman" and "You Pushed My Head Away." Hawkins blended soul and urban blues stylings with country and rural blues inflections and rhythms, making another first-rate release. —*Ron Wynn*

○ **The Next Hundred Years** / 1994 / DGC ✦✦✦✦

Hawkins' first album for DGC Records is a beautiful, understated record that easily ranks with his finest works. —*Stephen Thomas Erlewine*

Hawkwind

Group, Hard Rock, Art-Rock/Progressive-Rock

Hawkwind is a British acid-rock band led by Dave Brock, famous for long, spacey, improvisational jams. It gained notoriety playing at the 1970 Isle of Wight Festival headlined by Bob Dylan. Hawkwind wasn't on the bill—they set up outside the fence and played for free. Hawkwind's tendency to play gigs almost anywhere for free as well as press coverage resulting from drug busts gained them a cult following.

With a few moderately commercially successful albums under its belt, the group played at the 1972 London Roundhouse Greasy Truckers' Festival along with Gong and the Grateful Dead. They also appeared on one side of the live double album resulting from the festival. "Silver Machine," an out-take from the concert recording, was released as a single and became a huge surprise British hit and their only million seller.

Throughout its history, Hawkwind has had an incredible amount of personnel turnaround. Band members have included former Cream drummer Ginger Baker and sci-fi writer Michael Moorcock, who based his 1976 book *Time of the Hawklords* on the band members. Many former Hawkwinders have also released solo albums or formed offshoot groups. Lemmy was fired from the band in 1974; he went on to form the thrash metal pioneers Motorhead, who took their name from a Hawkwind B-side. —*Jim Powers*

Hawkwind / 1970 / One Way ✦✦✦

Includes their best-known hit, "Silver Machine." —*Michael G. Nastos*

● **In Search in Space** / 1971 / One Way ✦✦✦✦

Psychedelic rangers from England go one up on Pink Floyd and Tangerine Dream, and maybe Sun Ra too. Their best studio date. —*Michael G. Nastos*

Appeared on Greasy Truckers / 1972 / United Artists ✦✦

Doremi Farsolatido / 1972 / One Way ✦✦✦

○ **Space Ritual** / 1973 / One Way ✦✦✦✦

○ **Hall of the Mountain Grill** / 1974 / One Way ✦✦✦✦

○ **Warrior on the Edge of Time** / 1975 / Atco ✦✦✦✦

Road Hawks / 1976 / United Artists ✦✦✦

Astounding Sounds, Amazing Music / 1976 / Charisma ✦✦

○ **Masters of the Universe** / 1977 / United Artists ✦✦✦✦

○ **Quark Strangeness and Charm** / 1977 / Sire ✦✦✦✦

Still at it in an irreverent way. In many respects they are the standard for many of today's heavy metal bands. —*Michael G. Nastos*

Hawkwind 1967-1982 / 1986 / Samurai ✦✦✦

It Is The Business Of The Future To Be Dangerous / 1994 / Griffin ✦✦✦

Isaac Hayes

b. Aug. 29, 1942, Covington, TN
Soul, Funk, Disco, R&B

From the tough urgency of the Stax studio (for whom he was a prolific writer and arranger), Isaac Hayes went on to develop an overwrought style that utilized the potential of the album. To that point, most R&B and soul albums had been a mixture of two-and-a-half minute singles and filler. Hayes concocted mini-symphonies of extraordinary length, which, allied with his visual presence (shaved head, designer African clothes, shades, and bizarre jewelry), made him more than a musician: he became an instantly recognizable cultural icon in early-'70s Black music. One album title, *Black Moses*, was probably Hayes's own succinct self-appraisal. Some might argue that his legacy is better represented by his workaday compositions and his arrangements, which include Sam & Dave's immortal "Soul Man" and "Hold on, I'm Coming." —*Colin Escott*

Presenting Isaac Hayes / 1968 / Stax ✦✦✦

Isaac Hayes' earliest single efforts, and he hadn't yet perfected his lengthy raps and symphonic soul formula. These were rather the same type of songs he and David Porter turned into classics for many other Stax artists. They were mostly short, gospel and country-tinged soul ballads, vamps, and uptempo numbers. Hayes sang them well, his domineering baritone revealing itself as a potent weapon. While none of them did that well, the album revealed the enormous potential Hayes would begin to fulfill with his next album. —*Ron Wynn*

☆ **Hot Buttered Soul** / 1969 / Stax ✦✦✦✦✦

Isaac Hayes had already co-written many immortal soul singles in the late '60s when he began forging a solo career. Hayes helped focus attention on the album as a creative source in soul and R&B.This seminal album went against the grain in several ways. There were only four cuts, three of them at least nine minutes. There were two with extensive monologues, and he used symphonic backing and elaborate production. The album went gold, cracked the Top 100 and helped usher soul and R&B into the concept album era. It also featured some superb vocals and fine keyboard work by Hayes. —*Ron Wynn*

○ **Isaac Hayes Movement** / 1970 / Stax ✦✦✦✦

His second huge hit album and a great followup to the superb *Hot Buttered Soul*. Those critics who thought there was no way Hayes could repeat that triumph got fooled. He included a brillant remake of Jerry Butler's "I Stand Accused" and also did a 12-minute version of the Beatles' "Something," complete with a wailing violin solo from jazz-rocker John Blair. This album showed that Hayes was going to be around for a long time and perform just as consistently on his own as he did teaming with Porter. —*Ron Wynn*

To Be Continued / 1970 / Stax ✦✦✦

The third consecutive smash hit album for Isaac Hayes, with more anthemic raps and elaborate symphonic soul. This time he did his production/rap/movement routines remaking the songs "The Look of Love" and "You've Lost That Lovin' Feelin'." Once more, Hayes combined inspired vocals with equally creative production and arrangements, getting his third straight platinum album, something that was then unprecedented in R&B and soul circles for albums. —*Ron Wynn*

Enterprise / Aug. 1970 / Stax ◆◆◆

Black Moses / 1971 / Stax ◆◆◆

Isaac Hayes followed his Oscar-winning soundtrack LP *Shaft* with another two-record set blending remakes of soul and pop hits, extended monologues, symphonic orchestrations and backing, and other production devices that made him one of the 1970s' most successful producers and performers. Although *Black Moses* wasn't nearly as commercially dominant as earlier albums, it did make the Top Ten briefly and was on the charts for over 30 weeks. But it was also an indication that he was beginning to run a bit dry in the material department. —*Ron Wynn*

○ **Shaft** / 1971 / Stax ◆◆◆◆

Isaac Hayes surprised many in the film and R&B/soul world when he produced, arranged and composed the music for *Shaft*. Only three of the 15 tracks featured vocals, and Hayes displayed a finesse and capability with strings and mood pieces that his fans already knew he possessed from earlier albums, but which the general audience might have missed. This was a #1 pop LP and eventually earned Hayes an Oscar. It's also held up much better than the film. —*Ron Wynn*

In the Beginning / 1972 / Stax ◆◆◆

A repackaging of early Isaac Hayes material, which was done to take advantage of his then-huge presence in the industry. The only benefit to this was that the first album had done so poorly saleswise that it had been deleted, so those who missed it had another chance to get it. It has since been deleted again. —*Ron Wynn*

Live at the Sahara Tahoe / 1973 / Stax ◆◆

Schmaltzy, but cool. —*Bil Carpenter*

Joy / Dec. 1973 / Stax ◆◆

Isaac Hayes came close to recapturing his production and performance magic on this mid-'70s work. The title cut was a fine single, although it had to be split in two to fit radio formats. Otherwise, the songs alternated between classy ballads and fine uptempo cuts, neither of which did as well as expected. —*Ron Wynn*

Double Dynamite / 1974 / Stax ◆◆◆

Isaac Hayes not only was an innovative composer, songwriter, producer, and performer in the '60s and '70s, he was also an actor and appeared in several "blaxploitation" films during the early '70s. Hayes did double duty on these projects, writing and conducting the soundtracks for several, including the two featured on this twin-CD reissue. Neither *Truck Turner* nor *Tough Guys* was a particularly memorable film, but Hayes' effective use of symphony orchestras and strings against a vocal backdrop often made the music the best part of the movie. —*Ron Wynn*

Groove-A-Thon / 1975 / ABC ◆◆

Chocolate Chip / 1975 / ABC ◆◆◆

A fine mid-'70s album on which Isaac Hayes adapted to the disco era. His productions were already ideal for dancefloors, and he now updated his charts to include some stomping segments with horns and layered beats, while maintaining his soulful vocals on both uptempo tunes and ballads. This album got two Top 20 hits for Hayes, and was his last really big hit LP in the '70s. —*Ron Wynn*

○ **Best of Isaac Hayes** / 1975 / Enterprise ◆◆◆◆

A deep voice and an impeccable sense of the groove add up to some of the best R&B music of the early '70s. —*William Ruhlmann*

Disco Connection / 1976 / ABC ◆◆

Juicy Fruit / 1976 / ABC ◆◆

New Horizon / 1977 / Polydor ◆◆◆

A Man and a Woman / 1977 / ABC ◆◆

Soulful covers with Dione Warwick. —*Bil Carpenter*

For the Sake of Love / 1978 / Polydor ◆◆◆

Hotbed / 1978 / Stax ◆◆

Isaac Hayes didn't equal his past production, compositional, or performance greatness on this release, although much of the material was good. It just lacked the magic that had become almost routine with his '70s efforts. There were no magnificently narrated, drawn-out tales of romantic woe or any memorable arrangements. Instead, this was a routine, if well-done, session. —*Ron Wynn*

Don't Let Go / 1979 / Polydor ◆◆

A nice disco set. —*Bil Carpenter*

And Once Again / 1980 / Polydor ◆◆◆

Enterprise Greatest Hits / 1980 / Stax ◆◆◆

Royal Rappins / 1980 / Spring ◆◆

Sensual midtempo soul with Millie Jackson. —*Bil Carpenter*

Lifetime Thing / 1981 / Polydor ◆◆

U-Turn / 1986 / Columbia ◆

This was moderate to average quality material for most people, but well below par for Isaac Hayes. Nothing on this album came close to even resembling his great early '70s solo albums; nor were any of the tracks remotely near the caliber of what he and David Porter cranked out for Stax. This was possibly his least distinguished album, although he got a little airplay with the title cut. —*Ron Wynn*

● **Best of Isaac Hayes, Vol. 1** / 1986 / Stax ◆◆◆◆

A decent attempt to present some of Isaac Hayes' past hits on an anthology. But as one of R&B and soul's first concept and album artists, it's impossible to appreciate his contributions out of sequence. His early and mid-'70s albums helped change the course of contemporary black music production approaches, and that can't be understood by listening to condensed versions of hit singles, or even just by hearing the singles themselves removed from the album context. —*Ron Wynn*

● **Best of Isaac Hayse, Vol. 2** / 1986 / Stax ◆◆◆◆

These two compilations dutifully boil down Isaac Hayes's sometimes long-winded albums to their essential parts—in other words, they're both singles collections, highlighted by '70s landmarks such as "Theme from Shaft" and "By the Time I Get to Phoenix." Fanatics may want to investigate *Hot Buttered Soul* and *Black Moses*. —*John Floyd*

Love Attack / 1988 / Columbia ◆◆◆

Isaac Hayes seldom delivers less than a competent product, but he almost ended that streak with this late '80s effort for Columbia. It was one of his most inspired albums ever from a content standpoint, and while the production and arrangements got major label resources, they fell far short of past Hayes heights. Most fans were sorely disappointed, for there were high hopes when the news originally broke that Hayes had signed with the label. —*Ron Wynn*

○ **Greatest Hit Singles** / 1991 / Stax ◆◆◆◆

○ **Three Tough Guys/Truck Turner** / 1993 / Stax ◆◆◆◆

Branded / 1995 / Pointblank ◆◆◆

Raw and Refined / 1995 / Pointblank/Virgin ◆◆◆

Isaac Hayes launched a comeback in the spring of 1995 by releasing two records, *Branded* and *Raw and Refined*. *Branded* was a vocal album, while *Raw and Refined* was comprised of instrumental jams. Neither of them were a departure from the music Hayes made in the '70s—*Branded* was filled with laidback, lush soul and *Raw and Refined* was a deep, dirty funk workout—but they were effective reminders of Hayes' influence on '90s soul. —*Stephen Thomas Erlewine*

Justin Hayward

b. Oct. 14, 1946, Swindon, England
Rock & Roll

Justin Hayward (full name, David Justin Hayward) got his first guitar at age nine. In 1965, he joined pre-Beatles English rocker Marty Wilde as a member of his backing band the Wilde Cats. By the end of 1965, Hayward had four songs that he felt ready to record on his own, which led to former skiffle king-turned-producer Lonnie Donegan. It was Donegan's intention to record the songs himself, but Hayward insisted upon recording them, and Donegan duly agreed to serve as producer. Released by Pye Records on the last day of 1965, Hayward's solo recording debut "London Is Behind Me" vanished from sight without a trace. The follow-up, "I Can't Face the World Without You," was released by Parlophone on August 26, 1966, to similar results. It was at this same time that Hayward answered Eric Burdon's ad for a lead guitarist. But Burdon had already filled the spot and, offered the Moody Blues—who were in the market for a new guitarist/singer to replace Denny Laine, who had quit earlier that year—their pick of the responses filling mail sacks in his office. Hayward's letter was picked out by Ray Thomas, and he was called by Mike Pinder. A meeting between the two, and a subsequent meeting with the band brought Hayward into the Moody Blues line-up permanently.

For the first six months, the group continued doing the R&B-based repertory that they'd been known for prior to Hayward's arrival. Gradually, however, they began to work new songs into their stage act and their recording schedule, which took a big jump when the group was picked by Decca/London Records to participate in a stereo demonstration record mixing rock and orchestral sounds. The resulting album, *Days Of Future Passed* (1967), revived the band's fortunes, not least through the success of a Justin Hayward song called "Nights in White Satin." Although Hayward proved he could also rock out, he quickly became established as the romantic/mystic of the band, known not only for "Nights in White Satin" but songs such as "New Horizons" and "Your Wildest Dreams."

Hayward's career as a solo artist began in 1977 with the release of *Songwriter*, which displayed a somewhat leaner and more lively, acoustically textured sound than his work with the Moody Blues. He followed this up in 1980 with *Night Flight*, a major departure from his work with the group, with very much of a belated disco sound. During the next several years, Hayward devoted much of his attention to the revived Moody Blues, who had a full touring and recording schedule in front of them. His *Moving Mountains* (1985) was strongly reminiscent of his earlier work with the band, from the start of the 1970s. Since then, when he is not working with the band and writing new material (his "Your Wildest Dreams" is the biggest hit the group has had for the past decade, reaching number nine in America in 1986), Hayward seems to devote his time to reviving older Moody Blues songs in solo settings, as on the 1994 release *Classic Blue*, in which he sings Moody Blues songs with orchestral accompaniment. A guitarist of great skill and a unique sound, Hayward remains one of the few stars of the 1960s who retains a devoted international following in the 1990s, though most critics—as they have with the Moody Blues—have ceased to consider him a serious contemporary artist. —*Bruce Eder*

○ **Blue Jays** / 1975 / Polydor ◆◆◆◆
● **Songwriter** / 1977 / Polydor ◆◆◆◆
Hayward has always been at his best as a mystical/romantic, and *Songwriter* is the solo album that best displays these qualities around a relatively lean sound. From the gentle, lullaby-like "Raised on Love" to the ethereal mystical "Nostradamus," the album is a beguiling collection of material, more personal than his work with the Moody Blues. The material is richly scored, yet lean enough to seem like chamber music next to the Moody Blues' rock symphonies. —*Bruce Eder*

Blue Guitar / 197z / Threshold ◆◆◆
Nascence / 197z / Map City ◆◆◆
Night Flight / 1980 / Polydor ◆◆
An unfortunate and very late attempt to cash in on the disco boom, without much to recommend it to either disco fans or veteran Moody Blues fans. —*Bruce Eder*

Moving Mountains / 1985 / Atlantic ◆◆◆
A partial return to form for Hayward, with a lushly orchestrated sound that makes this record more representative of the Moody Blues than much of that band's actual output during the early '80s. Sort of Hayward's personal follow-up to *Days of Future Passed*, and nicely done but very dated for a '80s album. —*Bruce Eder*

Classic Blue / 1994 / Griffin ◆◆◆
Justin Hayward and an orchestra covering songs that he'd admired by other songwriters, this time on a grand scale that makes this record sound both sonically impressive and terribly pretentious. It's debatable whether the pop world needed Richard Harris's rendition of "MacArthur Park," but it definitely didn't need Hayward's even more cloying version 20-odd years later. —*Bruce Eder*

Roy Head

b. Jan. 9, 1943, Three Rivers, TX
R&B, Rock & Roll
Actually a country and rock vocalist rather than an R&B star, Roy Head nevertheless cut one of the great pieces of uptempo soul in the mid-'60s. "Treat Her Right" on Back Beat made it to number two on the R&B charts, and the fact that Head was White was soft-pedaled in R&B circles while the song made its way up the charts. Head was also an excellent entertainer, and his live shows of the period even included some fancy footwork clearly under the influ-

ence of James Brown. "Treat Her Right" also peaked at number two pop. Head later returned to country and rock. —*Ron Wynn*

● **Treat Me Right** / 1965 / Bear Family ◆◆◆◆
Read the title carefully; it's not "Treat Her Right," the title of Head's 1965 megasmash, but *Treat Me Right*, an entirely different song. Yes indeed, this is an exploitation release of material Head cut for a different label than the one that issued "Treat Her Right," repackaged after the hit to capitalize on its unexpected success. The final punchline is that, as exploitative as this LP is, it's quite good. The ten songs—mostly revved-up R&B, with a bit of country soul thrown in—are solid evidence of Head's stature as one of the finest white soul singers of the '60s. The small combo R&B arrangements are spare and tight, investing even overdone standards like "Money" with excitement. Long out of print, it still shows up in the used bins from time to time and is worth picking up. —*Richie Unterberger*

● **Treat Her Right: Best of Roy Head** / 1995 / Varese Vintage ◆◆◆◆
Treat Her Right: The Best of Roy Head collects the majority of the finest material the cult R&B-oriented rocker recorded during the '60s. —*AMG*

Jeff Healey Band

Group, Blues-Rock
What makes Jeff Healey different from other blues-rockers is also what keeps some listeners from accepting him as anything other than a novelty—the fact that the blind guitarist plays his Fender Stratocaster on his lap, not standing up. With the guitar in his lap, Healey can make unique bends and hammer-ons, making his licks different and more elastic than most of the competition. Unfortunately, his material leans toward standard AOR blues-rock which rarely lets him cut loose, but when he does, his instrumental prowess can be shocking.

Healey lost his sight at the age of one, after developing eye cancer. He began playing guitar when he was three years old and began performing with his band Blues Direction at the age of 15. Healey formed the Jeff Healey trio in 1985, adding bassist Joe Rockman and drummer Tom Stephen. The trio released a handful of self-released singles on their Forte record label, which led to a contract with Arista Records. The Jeff Healey Trio released their debut album, *See the Light*, in 1989 and the guitarist immediately developed a devoted following in blues-rock circles. Featuring the hit single "Angel Eyes," the record went platinum in the U.S. While the Jeff Healey Trio's subsequent records have been popular, none have been as successful as the debut. —*Stephen Thomas Erlewine*

● **See the Light** / Dec. 1989 / Arista ◆◆◆◆
An assured first effort, it contains the hits "Angel Eyes" and "Confidence Man." —*Dan Heilman*

Hell to Pay / 1990 / Arista ◆◆◆
A solid follow-up to Healey's impressive debut, *Hell To Pay* features some of the guitarist's hottest playing to date. —*Stephen Thomas Erlewine*

Feel This / Aug. 1992 / Arista ◆◆◆
By his third effort Healy and the band turn up the heat, while producer Joe Hardy gives it a live session feel. Healy's playing and singing have never been better. —*David Jehnzen*

Cover To Cover / 1995 / Arista ◆◆
Jeff Healey's collection of cover songs is fitfully entertaining, but his choice of material is predictable and when he does take a chance, such as on Stealer's Wheel's "Stuck in the Middle with You," he spends too much time trying to make it fit into his trademark stomping blues-rock style. —*Stephen Thomas Erlewine*

Heart

Group, Hard Rock, Pop/Rock
This Seattle band, led by sisters Ann and Nancy Wilson, has been a staple on FM-rock radio ever since their first hit in 1976, "Crazy on You." It was lead-singer Ann Wilson's powerful voice that gave the band an immediate appeal. Heart synthesized Led Zeppelin-style riff-heavy rock and shades of folk. Over the years, the band has continued to churn out hit after hit. In spite of a recent resurgence in the band's popularity, their hits are sounding increasingly formulaic.

A few of their hits are: "Magic Man," "Barracuda," "Straight On," "What About Love?," "Never," "These Dreams," "Alone," "There's the Girl," and a remake of Aaron Neville's "Tell It like It Is." —*Rick Clark*

○ **Dreamboat Annie** / Mar. 1976 / Capitol ◆◆◆◆
Their striking first album was one of the top-selling debuts ever. —*Dan Heilman*

○ **Little Queen** / May 1977 / Portrait ◆◆◆◆
Little Queen continued the arena-rock formula of Heart's debut album, streamlining the bombast of Led Zeppelin into a glossy, pop-friendly but tough variation of hard rock. And with material as catchy as "Barracuda" and "Little Queen," it didn't seem like the band was treading water—it seemed like they were using their strength to the best of their abilities. —*Stephen Thomas Erlewine*

Magazine / Apr. 1978 / Capitol ◆◆
A collection of early demos and outtakes released when the group changed record labels, *Magazine* accentuates Heart's folkie roots, but that's not what makes the album such an unengaging listen. Instead, the album is mediocre because most of the material is under-developed and directionless. —*Stephen Thomas Erlewine*

Dog & Butterfly / Sep. 1978 / Portrait ◆◆◆

Bebe Le Strange / Feb. 1980 / Epic ◆◆◆

● **Heart Greatest Hits/Live** / Nov. 1980 / Epic ◆◆◆◆
This set includes all of the significant rock radio hits that made Heart such a staple during the '70s and early '80s, such as "Barracuda," "Crazy on You," "Straight On," "Dreamboat Annie," "Even It Up," "Magic Man," "Heartless," and "Dog & Butterfly." Filling out the disc are six live tracks, including versions of Led Zeppelin's "Rock and Roll" and the Beatles' rave-up "I'm Down." —*Rick Clark*

Private Audition / May 1982 / Epic ◆◆

Passionworks / Aug. 1983 / Epic ◆◆

○ **Heart** / Jun. 1985 / Capitol ◆◆◆◆
Just when it seemed that Heart was yesterday's news on the radio, they changed labels and experienced a resurgence of huge success with this, their self-titled Capitol debut. Includes the hits "If Looks Could Kill," "What About Love?," "Never," "Nothin' at All," and "These Dreams." —*Rick Clark*

Bad Animals / May 1987 / Capitol ◆◆◆
The winning streak on the radio continues with hits like "Alone" and "Who Will You Run To." —*Stephen Thomas Erlewine*

Brigade / Mar. 26, 1990 / Capitol ◆◆

Rock the House Live! / Sep. 1991 / Capitol ◆◆
By 1991, Heart might have been expected to issue a live album or a hits compilation consolidating their second string of massively popular recordings made from the 1985 Heart album on. But the group felt they'd made a deal with the Devil, agreeing to record outside material in the name of achieving hit singles, but sacrificing their hard rock persona. As a result, in 1990, they made the harder rocking *Brigade*, and this live disc, recorded during the *Brigade* tour at the Centrum in Worcester, MA, on November 28, 1990, seemed intended not to demonstrate that Heart was the band of ballad hits like "These Dreams" and "Alone..." but instead an arena rock staple. Unfortunately, that meant filling the album neither with their early hard rock hits nor their later pop ones, but instead less familiar recent album tracks (six from *Brigade*), which made this a live album representative of one night, but not of Heart's career. —*William Ruhlmann*

Desire Walks on / Nov. 1993 / Capitol ◆◆
Without a strong single, *Desire Walks On* dissolves into a puddle of spineless contemporary AOR that Heart has performed much better on their recent albums. —*AMG*

The Heartbeats

Group, Doo-Wop
Lead singer James "Shep" Sheppard co-wrote a series of velvety doo-wop ballads for the Heartbeats during the mid-'50s; one entry, "A Thousand Miles Away," was a huge R&B seller in 1956. The Queens, NY, quintet began their string of street-corner classics with "Crazy for You" and "Darling How Long," culminating with "A Thousand Miles Away." The Heartbeats recorded for Hull, Rama, Roulette, Gee, and Guyden before packing it in. In 1961 the lead singer formed a new trio, Shep & the Limelites, and scored on the charts with a heartwarming sequel to his first hit, "Daddy's Home," for Hull. "Our Anniversary" also sold well for the trio the next year, but they broke up soon thereafter. Sheppard was found

dead in his auto on the Long Island Expressway in 1970. —*Bill Dahl*

● **The Best of the Heartbeats** / 1990 / Rhino ◆◆◆◆
This silky smooth New York quintet appeared from the mid '50s. The album includes five tracks by lead James Sheppard's early-'60s vocal trio, Shep & the Limelites. —*Bill Dahl*

For Collectors Only / Collectables ◆◆◆

Hearts & Flowers

Group, Folk-Rock
Of the many folk-rock groups in Southern California in the 1960s, Hearts & Flowers were one of the relatively few that were closer to "folk" than "rock." Founding guitarist Larry Murray was a member of the Scottsville Squirrel Barkers bluegrass group in the late '50s and early '60s; Chris Hillman and Bernie Leadon were also members of that group for a time. Murray teamed up with David Dawson and Rick Cunha to form Hearts & Flowers, a self-described "Georgia country-folk meets Hawaiian ukelele folk rock" group, in the mid-'60s. They released a couple albums of pleasant but inessential country-folk-rock in the late '60s. —*Richie Unterberger*

● **Now Is the Time for Hearts and Flowers** / 1967 / Capitol ◆◆◆◆
This debut album is an overlooked precursor to country-rock, echoing the late-'60s Byrds, Stone Poneys, Gene Clark, and most especially, as Brian Hogg points out in his lengthy liner notes, the Dillards. Earnest vocals and conscientious harmonies on this subdued, acoustic and countrified take on folk-rock, with mild Eastern/psychedelic dabs of autoharp. The songs mix original tunes with covers of Donovan, Tim Hardin, Hoyt Axton, Kaleidoscope, and Carole King. There's little to criticize, but it lacks the innovative spark that characterizes the best folk-rock of the time. —*Richie Unterberger*

Of Horses, Kids and Forgotten Women / 1968 / Capitol ◆◆◆

Reverend Horton Heat

Rockabilly, Alternative Pop/Rock
With his highly stylized, backwoods hick-preacher image, it would be easy to dismiss the Reverend Horton Heat as a poseur. But it would be wrong. Instead of treating rockabilly as a campy joke like the Cramps, the good Reverend rocks the hell out of his modern-day rockabilly, playing it as if it were the hardest of punk yet without any of the self-conscious trappings of either genre. Although his lyrics can be too silly, his music never is; it rocks harder than most of his punk and metal contemporaries. —*Stephen Thomas Erlewine*

○ **Smoke 'em If You Got 'em** / 1992 / Sub Pop ◆◆◆◆
Reverend Horton Heat's first album is filled with tongue-in-cheek songs and killer riffs, made all the more exciting by the good Reverend's raw, gutsy, punk-injected rockabilly licks. —*Stephen Thomas Erlewine*

● **The Full Custom Gospel Sounds** / 1993 / Sub Pop ◆◆◆◆
On Reverend Horton Heat's second album, the band sounds like it was having a race with the devil. All of their songs are played with a reckless abandon that makes their neo-rockabilly sound rawer and more vital than most punk or metal bands. —*Stephen Thomas Erlewine*

Liquor In The Front / 1994 / Interscope ◆◆◆
Al Jourgenson's production makes Reverend Horton Heat sound more like a heavy metal band than they actually are, but that usually doesn't distract from the primal pleasures of the group's jacked-up rockabilly roar. —*Stephen Thomas Erlewine*

Heaven 17

Group, Techno-Pop/Dance, New Wave
Heaven 17 explored the same territory as the Human League—which makes sense, since two of its members came from that seminal early '80s synth-pop band—but they weren't as instantly commercial and accessible as their chief rivals. Nevertheless, they were nearly as catchy and their seamless techno-synth-funk carried them through several albums; vocalist Glenn Gregory also made a difference, since he was a true singer in a field that was populated with emotionless frontmen and women. As the band's career progressed, their music became less innovative and more radio-friendly; after five albums, the group broke up in 1988. —*Stephen Thomas Erlewine*

○ **Penthouse & Pavement** / 1981 / Virgin ✦✦✦✦

Heaven 17 / 1982 / Arista ✦✦✦

○ **The Luxury Gap** / 1983 / Virgin ✦✦✦✦

How Men Are / 1984 / Virgin ✦✦

Pleasure One / 1986 / Virgin ✦✦✦

○ **Endless** / 1986 / Virgin ✦✦✦✦

○ **Teddy Bear, Duke & Psycho** / 1988 / Virgin ✦✦✦✦

● **The Best of Heaven 17: Higher & Higher** / Aug. 24, 1993 / Virgin ✦✦✦✦

Heavy D & the Boyz

Group, Rap

Jamaican-born Heavy D (born Dwight Myers) sports a 260-pound frame but can move and dance with agility and verve. He wisely chose sensitivity, rather than obesity or verbosity, as his framework, and many of his lyrics emphasize his search for a mate of similar qualities. He's also done good cover songs and penned cultural awareness tunes and tributes to black women.

Heavy D has managed perhaps the ultimate balancing act. He's remained a positive figure with close ties to his mother and is arguably the most admired male rap figure among African-American feminists. At the same time he's been willing to take chances musically, never embracing hardcore gangsta-rap, but yet able to include snatches of pop, R&B, reggae and funk into his music without being assaulted with cries of sellout. He's even survived the tragic death of longtime friend and original Boyz member Troy Dixon aka T-Roy in 1990. *Blue Funk* in 1993 is his most recent release. *—Ron Wynn*

Living Large / 1987 / Uptown ✦✦✦

This offers his first hit, a smartly done remake of "Mr. Big Stuff," plus charming romantic entries, though he sometimes overdoes the "overweight lover" routine. *—Ron Wynn*

○ **Big Tyme** / 1989 / Uptown ✦✦✦✦

Heavy D's commercial breakthrough is his best album. *—Dan Heilman*

● **Peaceful Journey** / 1991 / Uptown ✦✦✦✦

A continuation of the fine direction cemented in *Big Tyme*, this includes a first-rate rendition of the O'Jays/Third World hit "Now That We Found Love," plus strong message and romance cuts. *—Ron Wynn*

Blue Funk / 1992 / Uptown ✦✦✦

Although it didn't have a big hit, *Blue Funk* was another solid album of pop-oriented, R&B-tinged rap from Heavy D. *—AMG*

○ **Nuttin But Love** / 1994 / Uptown ✦✦✦✦

Heinz

b. 1942

British Invasion

A British teen idol in the early days of Beatlemania, Heinz (full name Heinz Burt) was the bassist for the Tornados, the instrumental group best remembered for topping the charts on both sides of the Atlantic with "Telstar." He was plucked from the group by producer Joe Meek to become a solo act, and hit the British Top Five with the Eddie Cochran tribute "Just Like Eddie" in 1963. Over the next couple years he had several other Top 30 hits, including "Country Boy," "You Were There," "Questions I Can't Answer," and "Diggin' My Potatoes." A lad with an awkward smile and shocking blond pompadour, Heinz couldn't sing well, and his songs were usually exceptionally dippy and trivial even for the time, albeit catchy. The material is elevated from the rubbish bin, however, by Meek's relentlessly imaginative production—ghostly choruses, stomping orchestras, and shudderingly compressed sound—and some remarkable lead guitar playing by sessionmen including Ritchie Blackmore, Jimmy Page, and much lesser known but quite talented players like Barry Tomlinson. On occasion, Heinz did get hold of tough rock tunes like "Big Bad Spider" and "I'm Not a Bad Guy," featuring blazing guitar leads that rank among the most unsung instrumental rock performances of the period. *—Richie Unterberger*

That's the Way It Was / 1986 / Rock Machine ✦✦✦

12-track compilation of the six singles Heinz cut for Columbia in 1964-66. Includes four minor songs not on *The Singles*, but is still missing "Just Like Eddie." Although this LP is easier to find, *The Singles* is a much stronger collection. *—Richie Unterberger*

● **The Singles** / 1987 / Triumph ✦✦✦✦

Hard-to-find 16-track reissue gathers most of the key A and B-sides from 1963-66, seriously marred only by the omission of "Just Like Eddie." Guilty pleasure of the first order, crammed with infectiously silly tunes, as well as virtuosic '60s British guitar work, especially on "Big Fat Spider," "Movin' In," "That Lucky Old Sun," and "I'm Not a Bad Guy." *—Richie Unterberger*

Helium

Group, Alternative Pop/Rock

Helium is essentially the project of Mary Timony, formerly of the girl-punk band Autoclave. Helium formed with Brian Dunton on bass and Shawn King Devlin in 1992, and started releasing seven-inches like "The American Jean" in 1993. 1994 saw the band release the *Pirate Prude* EP, an interesting but somewhat inaccessible exercise in mixing radical feminism with punk rock. *The Dirt of Luck*, released in 1995, was an improvement and embellishment of the sound laid forth in *Pirate Prude:* Heavy, sluggish guitars, spooky keyboards, and Timony's breathy alto laid over an understated rhythm section. That year, Polvo's Ash Bowie also joined the lineup, replacing Dunton on bass. Helium are a challenging listen, but also a rewarding one. *—Heather Phares*

Pirate Prude / 1994 / Matador ✦✦✦

The group's debut EP is an uncompromising introduction to Mary Timony's mix of radical feminism and warped pop sensibilities. Songs like "XXX," "OOO," and "Baby Vampire Made Me" are alluring and vicious, made all the more startling by their sonically droning and lyrically violent contrasts. Timony murmurs sentiments like your love is a fad/and you're a drag" and "you're gonna pay me with your life" in a schoolgirlish alto, adding to the intriguing contradictions in her work. Though it requires some concentrated listening, *Pirate Prude* ultimately rewards its listeners. *—Heather Phares*

● **The Dirt of Luck** / Apr. 1995 / Matador ✦✦✦✦

Helium's first full-length album expands on Timony's feminist lyrical bent and adds more colors to the band's musical palette. Full of what Timony calls "cartoon and monster movie music" *The Dirt of Luck* is a tight, focused album that is also diverse. The sludgy "Pat's Trick" mingles with the sweet-sounding and sweetly named "Honeycomb," which shares space with the nasty-sultry sounds of "Medusa" and the shimmery drone-pop of "Baby's Going Underground." It's tied together by the album's spacious sound and Timony's singing, which is fuller and richer than on the group's debut. *—Heather Phares*

Richard Hell & the Voidoids

Group, Punk

Some people will tell you Richard Hell was the main catalyst behind the birth of New York punk and its sensibilities. That's hardly true, but he's been around forever and did influence a number of budding punks (the Sex Pistols among them). In 1971 Hell and former high school buddy Tom Verlaine formed a group called the Neon Boys, who later became Television; he also cofounded the Heartbreakers with ex-New York Doll Johnny Thunders. In 1976 Hell formed the Voidoids, a caustic congregation that included guitarists Ivan Julian and Robert Quine and soon-to-be Ramones drummer Marc Bell. Hell's apocalyptic lyrics were steeped in alienated poetry, and his anguished howl of a voice set the pattern for scores of Bowery rockers. *—John Floyd*

● **Blank Generation** / 1977 / Sire ✦✦✦✦

Hell's debut isn't a masterpiece but it manages to re-create the intensity and exhilaration of the burgeoning days of American punk. "Love Comes in Spurts" defines Hell's romantic outlook, and the title cut is a classic piece of angst rock. *—John Floyd*

Destiny Street / 1982 / Combat ✦✦✦

It took five years for Hell to follow his debut, but *Destiny Street* is a moderately successful extension of *Blank Generation*. Some of the energy from the old days had disappeared, but Hell compensates with some fine ballads and another screwball classic, "The Kid with the Replaceable Head." *—John Floyd*

R.I.P. / 1984 / Combat ✦✦✦

Since Hell didn't record all that much, this cassette collection of live tracks and studio outtakes is an illuminating collection of antiques and curios. *—John Dougan*

Funhunt (Live at the CBGB & Max's 1978 & 1979) / 1990 / ROIR ✦✦

Hellecasters

Group, Roots-Rock
Comprised of three fine Telecaster-wielding guitarists (former Fairport Convention member Jerry Donahue, Desert Rose Band founder John Jorgenson, and session musician Will Ray), the Hellecasters won significant praise from guitar fanatics for the blistering roots and country-rock of their 1993 debut, *The Return of the Hellecasters. —Stephen Thomas Erlewine*

● **The Return of the Hellecasters** / 1993 / Pacific Arts ◆◆◆◆
The trio of lead guitarists that comprise The Hellecasters—John Jorgenson (a founding member of The Desert Rose Band), Jerry Donahue (a former guitarist with Fairport Convention) and long-time L.A. session-type Will Ray live up to that hype on *The Return Of.* The interplay between the three is seamless, as is the fusion of instrumental rock and country styles. The Telecaster can offer both a fluid, toney sound and a dry biting attack, and these Telemasters display ample examples of both ranges. The Hellecasters inject new life for the '90s into the instrumental guitar form. — *Roch Parisien*

Escape from Hollywood / 1994 / Rio ◆◆◆

Helmet

Group, Hard Rock, Alternative Pop/Rock, Heavy Metal
Led by ex-Band of Susans guitar monster and university-trained musician Page Hamilton, Helmet boils away nearly all of the excess of hard rock and heavy metal and serves up a thick wad of aural assault that values power, volume and simplicity. It's a concept that makes for compelling music, and Hamilton does a great job of creating songs that emphasize lacerating riffs, hypnotically repetitive distortion, and, at times, slower-than-a-lingering-death tempos. When the gears mesh on this monstrous machine, Helmet is one intimidating proposition. But by distilling hard rock to its feral core without the wit and panache that mark the careers of other, better, like-minded bands (e.g., Motorhead, the Melvins), one may not need a lot of Helmet to live a long and happy life. Hamilton does deserve credit for coming up with one killer record and scoring a sizable contract with a major label after the buzz surrounding their 1990 indie-label debut, *Strap It On. —John Dougan*

Strap It on / 1990 / Interscope ◆◆◆
Helmet's debut isn't as accomplished or powerful as *Meantime*, but it still provides enough gut-busting crunch to satisfy their fans. *—AMG*

● **Meantime** / 1992 / Interscope ◆◆◆◆
This is all the Helmet you will ever need. *Meantime* is a ferocious, sonic onslaught akin to hearing multiple explosions or living through a series of train accidents. Intense beyond description, *Meantime* will, with few exceptions, destroy nearly everything in its path, including Helmet's two other records. *—John Dougan*

○ **Betty** / 1994 / Interscope ◆◆◆◆
Although I cannot imagine wanting more Helmet than *Meantime*, if you've become a volume junkie and want a new fix, *Betty* might do the trick. Not as brutal or overpowering as *Meantime*, it has its moments, but indicates that Helmet's rage and fury may be changing into something slightly less aggressive. *—John Dougan*

Jimi Hendrix

b. Nov. 27, 1942, Seattle, WA, **d.** Sep. 18, 1970, London, UK
Rock & Roll, Blues Rock, Hard Rock, Psychedelic
Jimi Hendrix was one of rock's greatest pioneers on the electric guitar. Hendrix fused funky R&B with hard rock, developing and mastering fresh approaches to using feedback, distortion, and various sound effects. As a result of his early immersion in Muddy Waters, Elmore James, B.B.King, and Chuck Berry, as well as his work with the Isley Brothers and King Curtis, Hendrix's rhythm-guitar style utilized soul and blues licks and chord inversions as a starting place for many of his songs.

Much has been said about Hendrix's guitar playing, but he was also a formidable songwriter, using sensually trippy lyrics that sometimes drew inspiration from Dylan. "Purple Haze," "Fire," "Little Wing," "The Wind Cries Mary," and "Angel" are a few of Hendrix's classic titles. Along with Cream, Hendrix's group, the Jimi Hendrix Experience (with Mitch Mitchell on drums and Noel Redding on bass), is the most important trio of the rock era. After the demise of the Experience in July of 1969, Hendrix pursued a hard, funkier (slightly less imaginative) sound with Band of Gypsys, featuring Buddy Miles and Billy Cox. They released one self-ti-

tled live album in May of 1970. On September 18, 1970, Hendrix passed away due to complications brought on from a drug overdose. In spite of Hendrix's important place in the history of rock, and his great album sales, pop radio was resistant to much of his sound. As a result, Hendrix only had one Top 40 hit, a fiery version of Dylan's "All along the Watchtower," which peaked at #20. Other hits were "Crosstown Traffic" (#52), "Purple Haze" (#65), "Foxy Lady" (#67), "Up from the Skies" (#82), "Freedom" (#59), and "Dolly Dagger" (#74).

After a lengthy legal dispute, the rights to Hendrix's estate, including all recordings, returned to Al Hendrix, the guitarist's father, in July of 1995. *—Rick Clark*

☆ **Are You Experienced?** / 1967 / Reprise ◆◆◆◆◆
From the dissonant fanfare of "Purple Haze" to the hypnotic closing cadence of the title track, the Jimi Hendrix Experience's audacious debut built upon the experimental hard rock groundwork of groups like the Yardbirds, focusing it through a ferociously interactive trio format. Hendrix fused spacey Dylan-influenced imagery with R&B-derived song structures and chordal voicings to create an unique style. Tracks like "Fire," "Foxey Lady," "Manic Depression," the haunting "The Wind Cries Mary," and "May This Be Love" make this disc essential for any rock collection. *—Rick Clark*

☆ **Axis: Bold As Love** / 1967 / Reprise ◆◆◆◆◆
Continuing Hendrix's groundbreaking streak, this one matches his guitar pyrotechnics with a more refined collection of originals. The album features gorgeously unconventional ballads like "Little Wing," "Castles Made of Sand," "One Rainy Wish," and "Bold as Love," which shone alongside hyperspace rockers like "You Got Me Floatin'," "Up from the Skies," and the psychedelic hard jazz-rock free-for-all of "If 6 Was 9." *—Rick Clark*

● **Smash Hits** / Jan. 1968 / Reprise ◆◆◆◆
Smash Hits is a solid collection of his most popular radio tracks, as well as featuring the bluesy "Red House" and "Stone Free," which were not found on previous albums. *—Rick Clark*

☆ **Electric Ladyland** / Feb. 1968 / Reprise ◆◆◆◆◆
Hendrix's funky psychedelia reached a zenith on *Electric Ladyland*, one of the greatest albums of the rock era. His aggressively otherworldly production did as much for advancing the possibilities of recorded music as Phil Spector's "Wall of Sound" did in the early '60s. Hendrix's imaginatively fiery guitar work (and the Experience's brilliant interplay) here became the textbook source of inspiration for generations of musicians. Among *Electric Ladyland's* many highlights are "Voodoo Child (Slight Return)," with its kamikaze lead-guitar work, the transcendentally dense "Burning of the Midnight Lamp," the searing remake of Dylan's "All along the Watchtower," and the beautifully spacey "1983...(A Merman I Should Turn to Be)." *—Rick Clark*

○ **Band of Gypsys** / 1970 / Capitol ◆◆◆◆
Hendrix, sans the Experience, hooked up with bassist Billy Cox and drummer Buddy Miles to record this hard electric funk outing live at the Fillmore East in New York on December 31, 1969. While the rhythm section may have lacked the chops for wild free-form excursions, they provided Hendrix with a no-nonsense groove for his funkier R&B experiments. "Machine Gun," the album's highlight, features some of Hendrix's greatest playing. His dramatically violent soundscapes convey the horror of the war experience, with brilliantly controlled use of feedback and rapid-fire bursts of notes. *—Rick Clark*

○ **The Cry of Love** / 1971 / Reprise ◆◆◆◆
The posthumously released *The Cry of Love* revealed Hendrix turning toward a more subdued, less psychedelic style, with songs like "Night Bird Flying" and "Angel." Hendrix does deliver a few strong rockers with "Freedom," "Ezy Ryder," and "Astro Man." *— Rick Clark*

○ **Jimi Hendrix in the West** / 1972 / Reprise ◆◆◆◆
The live set features great versions of "Little Wing" and "Red House," but the highlight of the album goes to a ferocious version of "Johnny B.Goode" that borders on definitive. *—Rick Clark*

○ **Plays Monterey** / 1986 / Reprise ◆◆◆◆
Hendrix's show at the 1967 Monterey Pop Festival was the performance that broke him in the United States. While half of this was previously available as one side of an LP that also featured a side of live Otis Redding from the same event, this has his whole performances. Jimi and the Experience were in fine, lean, fiery form on this nine-song set, which showcased the most well-known tunes from the *Are You Experienced?* album and covers of "Killing

Floor," "Like a Rolling Stone," "Rock Me Baby," and "Wild Thing."
—*Richie Unterberger*

○ **Live at Winterland** / 1987 / Rykodisc ◆◆◆◆
Live at Winterland is one of the best representations of Hendrix's
live prowess. The great playing is further enhanced by a top-notch
mastering job. —*Rick Clark*

○ **Radio One** / 1989 / Rykodisc ◆◆◆◆
Just when it seemed that the only way to hear more unreleased
Hendrix was to put up with doctored Alan Douglas releases, Ryko
pulled this live 1967 BBC gem out of the hat. It includes versions
of "Day Tripper," "Killing Floor," "Love or Confusion," "Purple
Haze," and "Fire," among other tracks. It's definitely worth getting,
but only after you have purchased all of the other Hendrix albums
recommended in this section. —*Rick Clark*

● **The Ultimate Experience** / 1993 / MCA ◆◆◆◆
For an introduction to Hendrix, *The Ultimate Experience* is hard
to beat. All of the Jimi Hendrix Experience albums are sampled, in
addition to a couple of live tracks and "Red House." The Experience albums are mandatory listening, but *The Ultimate Experience* is a terrific compilation. —*AMG*

○ **Jimi Hendrix: Blues** / 1994 / MCA ◆◆◆◆
While Hendrix remains most famous for his hard rock and psychedelic innovations, more than a third of his recordings were
blues-oriented. This CD contains eleven blues originals and covers, eight of which were previously unreleased. Recorded between
1966 and 1970, they feature the master guitarist stretching the
boundaries of electric blues in both live and studio settings. Besides several Hendrix blues-based originals, it includes covers of
Albert King and Muddy Waters classics, as well as a 1967 acoustic
version of his composition "Hear My Train A-Comin'." —*Richie
Unterberger*

Jimi Hendrix: Woodstock / 1994 / MCA ◆◆◆
Hendrix's entire legendary set at Woodstock is featured on this set
for the first time. Hardcore Hendrix fans may enjoy this good-
sounding set, but it's a lot of endless jamming and general
noodling for even the average fan to ingest. Besides his incendiary
reading of "The Star Spangled Banner" and moments where the
playing really comes together, better live Hendrix sets can be
found elsewhere, like *Jimi Hendrix in the West.* —*Rick Clark*

Voodoo Soup / Apr. 1995 / MCA ◆◆◆
Voodoo Soup was supposed to be the outtake album that got it
right. Instead, it was another in a line of botched attempts to recreate Jimi Hendrix's unfinished final studio album. For most fans,
the re-recorded drum tracks by the drummer of the Knack was the
most unforgivable sin, yet the album is also poorly sequenced and
lacks the important "Room Full of Mirrors," among others. The
sound is polished to a disturbingly bright sheen, while the cover
art is garishly retro. —*Stephen Thomas Erlewine*

BOOKS

◆◆◆ **Jimi Hendrix: Inside The Experience**, by Mitch Mitchell
with John Platt (Harmony, 1990). More than almost any other
rock superstar, Hendrix has been subjected to different, at times
downright wildly varying historical accounts, making it difficult
to separate the likely from the unlikely. This book, not a biography but an oral history of sorts from the Experience drummer, is refreshingly straightforward. And, unlike some of the
authors and associates who have written about Hendrix,
Mitchell was very much there; in fact, he worked with Hendrix
more closely than any other musician, although some accounts
have painted the Experience (probably inaccurately) as a situation which constrained Hendrix creatively. Mitchell doesn't
have axes to grind, or a big ego to inflate, so what you get are
detailed, very interesting recollections of the tours, Hendrix's
methods of working in the studio, key gigs such as Monterey
and Woodstock, Jimi's influences, and the guitarist's innovative
use of equipment. With lots of good photos, a good book for
those more interested in the music than the mystique. —*Richie
Unterberger*

◆◆◆◆ **Jimi Hendrix: Electric Gypsy**, by Harry Shapiro & Caesar
Glebbeek (St. Martin's, 1991). Hendrix's life story is such a difficult, elusive subject to tackle that a definitive biography may be
an impossible goal. Although the memoirs by Mitch Mitchell,
Noel Redding, and producer Eddie Kramer all have their value,
for my money this is the best overall view of this extraordinarily complicated man's life and music. It's mammoth, weighing

in at over 700 pages, but purposefully detailed. The authors examine every stage of his development, and every facet of his
musicianship, from his R&B beginnings and his classic studio
recordings to his charismatic live performances and innovations in studio technique, amplification equipment, and, of
course, guitar playing. It draws upon a staggering mass of
archival materials—interviews, letters, press accounts of the period, memories of his many musical colleagues and professional associates. The many rumors and contradictory anecdotes could lead to a quagmire, but the book takes care not to
draw uninformed conclusions or pass judgement, presenting
many points of view and cautiously offering interpretations to
weigh. The large appendix is also quite valuable, offering a
lengthy discography (a project in itself given Hendrix's extraordinarily tangled recorded legacy), list of concerts performed, co-
pious documentation of his equipment and many guitars, and
family tree. —*Richie Unterberger*

Nona Hendryx

Soul, Disco
One-third of the pop/soul act Labelle (their big hit was "Lady Marmalade"), Nona Hendryx, by far and away, made the hippest solo
records of any member of that group (the others being Patti Labelle and Sarah Dash). After Labelle called it quits in 1976,
Hendryx released her self-titled debut record, which was an amazingly strong amalgam of soul and hard rock. It also went almost
completely ignored by critics, soul fans, and even Labelle fans, and
Hendryx took her strong, clear, booming voice and did lots of session work in the late '70s and early '80s. It was here that she fell in
with a hip crowd of musicians, specifically as a result of her time
singing backup for Talking Heads. This association with David
Byrne led to her working with Bill Laswell, who, along with his
band Material, helped her put together a second solo record entitled *Nona*. A strong album that's not as wild-eyed as her debut,
Nona did spark greater interest in Hendryx's considerable talents,
and since then, her solo career has been flourishing to the point
where she no longer needs studio work to supplement her income.
Although some of her late-'80s records sound a little formulaic,
Nona Hendryx is a dynamic, daring and extremely talented performer, who, as is often the case, doesn't receive the credit she's
due. But unlike Patti Labelle, who has chosen a career as the most
histrionic singer in MOR soul/pop, or the relative invisibility of
Sarah Dash, who sings backup for Keith Richards' X-Pensive
Winos, Hendryx has taken the road less traveled, and that has
meant a more aesthetically rewarding and interesting career. —
John Dougan

○ **Nona Hendryx** / 1977 / Epic ◆◆◆◆
Wearing skintight pants, black leather and brandishing a Bowie
knife on the LP cover, Nona Hendryx announces her intentions
loudly and clearly on her debut record. At the time, this record was
unpromotable (hell, it would be today), mainly because the record
company and radio stations didn't know what to do with a huge-
voiced African-American woman who was comfortable and capable of singing hard rock as well as soul music. So, as usual, they
turned their backs on the record and it disappeared almost as
quickly as it was released. Which is a shame, because it's a nasty,
relentless chunk of hard-edged rock'n'soul that was just a bit
ahead of its time. Long out of print, but worth searching for. —
John Dougan

Nona / 1983 / RCA ◆◆
After a few years doing session work, Hendryx, with help from the
band Material, came up with this winner that drops the hard rock
of her debut for a more Talking Heads-tinged pop/funk. Although
the songwriting could be a little sharper, Hendryx's powerful voice
gives the record focus and always commands your attention. Extra
musical emphasis provided by Sly Dunbar, Jamaladeen Tacuma
and Nile Rodgers. —*John Dougan*

The Art of Defence / 1984 / RCA ◆◆

The Heat / 1985 / RCA ◆◆◆

Female Trouble / 1987 / EMI America ◆◆◆

● **Skindiver** / 1989 / Private Music ◆◆◆◆
A transitional album from the word go, Hendryx plays synthesizer
and works with producer and former Tangerine Dream member
Peter Baumann, and the result is this lush (at times too lush) pop
record that sounds unlike anything else Hendryx recorded. Fans of
her previous work may be taken aback by this record, but the

dense, almost ambient, soundscapes she constructs and her always great singing make this a satisfying foray into uncharted territory. —*John Dougan*
You Have to Cry Sometime / 1992 / Shanachie ◆◆◆

Don Henley

b. Jul. 22, 1947, Gilmer, TX
Singer-Songwriter, Pop/Rock
Out of all of the Eagles, Don Henley had the most successful solo career. After the group broke up in 1982, Henley released his first solo album, *I Can't Stand Still*. Although it wasn't as successful as an Eagles record, the album peformed respectably, launching the number three single "Dirty Laundry" and going gold. *Building the Perfect Beast* followed two years later and established Henley as a solo star in his own right. Featuring the Top 10 hits "Boys of Summer" and "All She Wants to Do Is Dance," as well as the Top 40 singles "Not Enough Love in the World" and "Sunset Grill," the album sold over two million copies and stayed on the charts for over a year. Henley's third album, 1989's *The End of the Innocence*, was his most ambitious record yet, as well as his most commercially successful. The album sold over three million copies and stayed on the charts for nearly three years, launching the hit singles "The End of the Innocence," "Heart of the Matter," "New York Minute," "How Bad Do You Want It?," and "The Last Worthless Evening." Henley reunited with the Eagles in 1994, embarking on a worldwide tour. The group released a live album culled from an appearance on *MTV Unplugged* called *Hell Freezes Over;* the record also featured a handful of new studio tracks. *Hell Freezes Over* was a major success, selling over five million copies by the summer of 1995. However, the group decided not to pursue any more projects together and Henley continued working on his fourth solo album in 1995. —*Stephen Thomas Erlewine*

○ **I Can't Stand Still** / 1982 / Asylum ◆◆◆◆
This crisply produced and well-conceived debut is highlighted by "The Unclouded Day," "Johnny Can't Read," and "Dirty Laundry." —*John Floyd*

● **Building the Perfect Beast** / 1984 / David Geffen Co. ◆◆◆◆
His commercial breakthrough defined his solo formula with songs like "The Boys of Summer" and "All She Wants to Do Is Dance," which responded to political and romantic breakdowns. —*John Floyd*

The End of the Innocence / 1989 / David Geffen Co. ◆◆◆
A conceptual elaboration on his *Beast* album, this frames some wonderfully sarcastic rockers around "The Heart of the Matter," one of the finest ballads of the '80s. —*John Floyd*

Henry Cow

Group, Art-Rock/Progressive-Rock
The progressive-rock genre spawned many groups who became top-grossing arena acts—Pink Floyd and Genesis are two—as well as many who progressed right into obscurity. Henry Cow was one of the best-known and most widely traveled English bands of the progressive era (though only a cult-favorite in the U.S.), and their music has aged amazingly well over the last 20 years due to diverse influences (Oliver Messiaen, Kurt Weill, Frank Zappa, and Soft Machine were a few) and uncompromising creativity. The group functioned more or less as a collective, with a true group identity that changed from album to album as members came and went. This turnover was one factor in the consistent vitality of Henry Cow; another was the dedicated core of the band, a serious, politicized trio whose interest in improvisation served to leaven the complexity they supplied as primary writers.

Tim Hodginson played keyboards and reeds; Chris Cutler (later of Pere Ubu) played drums; Fred Frith provided a variety of instruments, specializing in strings (the guitar in particular); all of them sang. The three appear on all of the Henry Cow albums recorded between 1973 and 1978. Other longtime members included multi-reedist Lindsay Cooper, bassist John Greaves, and German singer Dagmar Krause, who worked with Frith and Cutler in the spinoff Art Bears band and later recorded bilingual renditions of songs by Brecht & Weill. Together, their sound was so mercurial and daring that they had few imitators, even though they inspired many on both sides of the Atlantic with a blend of spontaneity, intricate structures, philosophy, and humor that has endured and transcended the "progressive" tag.

Since the demise of Henry Cow, its members have continued in creative directions, mostly working in Europe with rock-based or improvising ensembles. Over the years they have reunited in various units, with resultant recordings being distributed worldwide through the Recommended Records network spearheaded by Chris Cutler. —*Myles Boisen*

Live at Dingwalls Dance Hall / 1973 / Greasy Truckers ◆◆

● **Legend** / 1973 / East Side Digital ◆◆◆◆
The first of their Virgin Records trilogy is a bold statement of humor and complexity, with a nod to Frank Zappa. —*Myles Boisen*

Unrest / 1974 / East Side Digital ◆◆◆
Cow furthers their commitment to improvisation and sonic experimentation. —*Myles Boisen*

Henry Cow / Oct. 1974 / Virgin ◆◆

In Praise of Learning / 1975 / East Side Digital ◆◆◆
A collaboration with Slapp Happy, this progressive and political operetta ended the group's influential Virgin period, pointing the way to future projects. —*Myles Boisen*

Concerts / 1976 / Caroline ◆◆◆
This two-fer of various compositions and improvisations document the group's busy life on the road in 1974-1975. Robert Wyatt guests on one side. —*Myles Boisen*

Western Culture / 1979 / East Side Digital ◆◆◆
With one side each by members Tim Hodgkinson and Lindsay Cooper, this isn't a truly collective effort but a good reunion in the Cow tradition. —*Myles Boisen*

Clarence "Frogman" Henry

New Orleans R&B
A bit more eccentric and unpredictable than Fats Domino, not as contemporary or inventive as, say, Lee Dorsey, New Orleans pianist Clarence "Frogman" Henry's vocals were consistently warm and humorous, his recordings always polished. Scoring an unexpected novelty hit with "Ain't Got No Home" in 1956, Henry disappeared from the charts for four years before roaring back with two smashes in the early '60s, "(I Don't Know Why) But I Do" and "You Always Hurt the One You Love." On his early '60s singles, Clarence added beefier horn sections that occasionally harked back to the spirit of Dixieland. Crescent City legends like saxophonist Lee Allen, and pianists Allen Toussaint and Paul Gayten, cropped up on his sessions; when Henry traveled to Memphis to record, he was backed by the all-star band of Bill Justis (guitar), Boots Randolph (sax), and Floyd Cramer (piano). He went on to record a fair number of singles for Chess' Argo subsidiary in the relaxed New Orleans R&B styles of his big hits until 1964. —*Richie Unterberger*

● **Ain't Got No Home: Best of Clarence "Frogman" Henry** / 1994 / MCA ◆◆◆◆
Ain't Got No Home includes 18 of these sides, most of which were previously unavailable on U.S. albums. —*Richie Unterberger*

The Herd

Group, Pop/Rock
Before '70s superstardom, even before Humble Pie, Peter Frampton got his first taste of celebrity as a singer and guitarist in the Herd, which chalked up several hits in Britain in 1967 and 1968. Frampton was only 17 when the single "From the Underworld" went into the British Top Ten in late 1967; "Paradise Lost" and "I Don't Want Our Loving to Die" were hits for the group in the first half of 1968. The Herd's brand of mod was extremely commercial, good-timey and pop-oriented, a bit like a muted and mainstream Small Faces. Much of their material (including all of the hits) was written by their management team of Ken Howard and Alan Blaikley, who had supplied songs for the Honeycombs (of "Have I the Right" fame). Frampton and keyboardist Andy Bown wrote most of the band's original tunes, and one presumes that the limitations of the Herd's overtly pop approach (which sometimes encompassed MOR ballads and orchestrated arrangements) were a factor in his decision to leave for Humble Pie after the Herd had issued just one album and a few singles. After a few Frampton-less singles, the Herd scattered; Andy Bown released a few solo albums, and has done session work with Frampton and Pink Floyd. —*Richie Unterberger*

● **Herd Featuring Peter Frampton** / 1994 / Fontana ◆◆◆◆
Their entire 1968 LP *Paradise Lost*, plus the eight non-LP tracks from 1967 and 1968 singles cut by the Frampton lineup. Rather precious and overtly British period pop-rock; "From the Under-

world," with its dense production and booming harmonies, is the highlight, and straightforward rock tracks with progressive and blues influences like "On Your Own" show the band's more serious aspirations. —*Richie Unterberger*

Herman's Hermits

Group, Pop, British Invasion

Herman's Hermits began life in 1963 in Manchester, England, as the Heartbeats, the group consisting of Keith Hopwood (b. Oct. 26, 1946, Manchester, England) (guitar), Karl Green (b. Jul. 31, 1947, Salford, England) (guitar, harmonica), Derek Leckenby (b. May 14, 1945, Leeds, England) (guitar), and Barry Whitwam (b. Jul. 21, 1946, Manchester, England) (drums). They got the name Herman's Hermits when they were joined by 16-year-old TV actor Peter Noone (b. Nov. 5, 1947, Manchester) (vocals, piano, guitar), who was thought to resemble the Sherman character on the *Rocky & Bullwinkle* TV cartoon. Pop producer Mickie Most, induced to see the group by their managers, thought Noone looked like a young John Kennedy and agreed to sign them. Most chose the group's material, from revamped oldies and pub songs to tunes submitted by professional songwriters like Gerry Goffin and Carole King, and produced the recordings, generally using Noone as singer and a group of studio musicians.

The result was two years of solid hits, starting with "I'm into Something Good," which topped the U.K. charts and broke the group in America. There were 11 Top Ten hits in the U.S. through 1967, among them the number one gold singles "Mrs. Brown You've Got a Lovely Daughter" and "I'm Henry VIII, I Am." Herman's Hermits had ten Top Ten hits in Britain through 1970. Inevitably, the group's teenage heartthrob appeal waned, and they never became the kind of self-sustaining musical unit that could outlive that initial infatuation. The group split in 1971, though it has re-formed, with and without Noone, for oldies performances. —*William Ruhlmann*

● **Their Greatest Hits** / 1973 / ABKCO ✦✦✦✦

Basic hits package, but too brief and under par sound-wise. (Originally released as a 15-track LP in 1973, *Their Greatest Hits* was reissued as a 16-track CD in 1987.) —*Jeff Tamarkin*

The EP Collection / Jan. 1990 / See For Miles ✦✦✦

This 22-track CD also features most of the major Herman hits, with a handful of obscurities thrown in. —*Jeff Tamarkin*

○ **The Collection** / Jun. 1990 / Castle ✦✦✦✦

All of the hits by Peter Noone and company, with room to spare for some nice surprises. —*Jeff Tamarkin*

Kristin Hersh

Singer-Songwriter, Alternative Pop/Rock

Kristin Hersh, the lead singer/songwriter of Throwing Muses, released her first solo album, the acoustic *Hips and Makers*, in early 1994; she followed it a couple of months later with the *Strings* EP, which featured versions of selected songs from the album recorded with a string quartet. After releasing the record, Hersh did a solo tour and finished the next Throwing Muses record, *University*, which was released in February 1995. —*Stephen Thomas Erlewine*

● **Hips and Makers** / 1994 / Sire/Reprise ✦✦✦✦

Hersh dug into her backlog of compositions for material of an intensely personal nature that she felt wouldn't be suitable for her band on her solo debut, *Hips And Makers*. In stark contrast to her work with Throwing Muses, *Hips And Makers* is almost entirely acoustic. Hersh embellishes her waifish voice and acoustic guitar with touches of cello and piano on this album, which offers a despairing and introspective tone that fails to submerge her considerable inner strength and fortitude. Recorded in a mere two weeks, this collection of haunting and confessional songs was produced by ex-Patti Smith Group guitarist Lenny Kaye, who has also produced Suzanne Vega. Hersh's voice and lyrical tone, however, are considerably brittler and coarser than Vega's. The opening track, "Your Ghost," features a duet with R.E.M. singer Michael Stipe. —*Richie Unterberger*

Strings / 1994 / Sire ✦✦✦

A beautiful EP featuring several tracks that didn't make *Hips and Makers*, as well as excellent rerecorded versions of several of the tracks that did. —*Stephen Thomas Erlewine*

The Hesitations

Group, Soul, R&B

Cleveland vocal group the Hesitations specialized in soulful treatments of blatantly pop melodies, epitomized by their biggest R&B smash, a stirring 1968 rendering of the theme from the movie *Born Free*. Although their initial bow on the R&B charts in 1967 was titled "Soul Superman," the Hesitations were best known for items like "The Impossible Dream" and "Who Will Answer," hardly typical soul fare. Lead singer George "King" Scott died from a gunshot wound in February of 1968. —*Bill Dahl*

Soul Superman / 1967 / Kapp ✦✦✦

A solid Cleveland singing group who never were able to make it past the second level in soul circles, even though they were an energetic harmonizing unit. Their debut album got them a mild hit with the title track, but didn't do much beyond that despite the glossy leads of George Scott and some emphatic group support underneath him. —*Ron Wynn*

The New Born Free / 1968 / Kapp ✦✦✦

The Hesitations came as close as they ever would during their existence as a group with their second album. The title cut made it to number four, and they made a run of concert and television appearances. But the album itself was simply too thin material-wise, and while they managed to get a second Top 20 hit in "The Impossible Dream," all that did was type them as a remake group. —*Ron Wynn*

● **Solid Gold** / 1968 / Kapp ✦✦✦✦

The pop-oriented R&B group sports soaring harmonies on this vinyl release. —*Bill Dahl*

Where We're at / 1968 / Kapp ✦✦✦

Tragedy would strike the Hesitations in 1968, when lead singer George "King" Scott was accidentally killed by a gun owned by group member Fred Deal. They went down as one of those bands that couldn't get over the hump, even though they were fine harmonizers and Scott had been an above average lead vocalist. This album exemplified their plight; it had the necessary components for success, but just didn't click. —*Ron Wynn*

Howard Hewett

Akron, OH

Soul, Urban

Among the great pure vocalists of the Urban Contemporary era, Howard Hewett has seldom found material worthy of his tremendous skills. He grew up in Akron, OH, and relocated to Los Angeles. Hewett danced on *Soul Train*, and became one-third of Shalamar with Jeffrey Daniel and Jody Watley in 1979. They had several big hits before Hewett departed for a solo career in 1985. He signed with Elektra, and his second single, "I'm for Real," was a number two R&B hit in 1986. The follow-up single, "Stay," also made the Top Ten, while "I Commit to Love" in 1987 reached number 12. Hewitt remained on Elektra through the '80s and into the '90s, earning another hit with "Strange Relationship" in 1988, and cutting duets with Dionne Warwick and Anita Baker. He's also been busy as a writer, producer, and session vocalist. Hewett co-wrote and produced "Frustration" for LaToya Jackson in 1984, and sang on her LP *Heart Don't Lie*. He did lead vocals on LPs by Stanley Clarke and George Duke in 1984 and 1986, a duet with Stacy Lattisaw on "Ain't No Mountain High Enough," and sang with Firefox in 1986, as well as doing backgrounds on a Donna Summer release. —*Ron Wynn*

● **I Commit to Love** / 1986 / Elektra ✦✦✦✦

It seemed that ex-Shalamar member Howard Hewett was off to a good start with his 1986 debut album. The single "I'm for Real" made it to number two and he had another song crack the Top Ten. That he never became a huge star was one of the '80s' more puzzling and frustrating stories in Black music. —*Ron Wynn*

Forever & Ever / 1988 / Elektra ✦✦✦

Howard Hewett's lack of solo success after leaving the group Shalamar was among the more frustrating stories of the late '80s. He had the vocal skills and the looks to be a major attraction, but couldn't get the consistently good material he needed. This 1988 album had three charts hits, including the superb "Once, Twice, Three Times," but just couldn't earn Hewett the star power he deserved. —*Ron Wynn*

Howard Hewett / 1990 / Elektra ◆◆◆
Allegiance / 1992 / Elektra ◆◆
It's Time / Calibre ◆◆

Richard X. Heyman

Power Pop/Anglo-Pop
Richard Heyman is a virtual one-man mid-'60s-style band. Fans of mid-period Beatles, Byrds, and Kinks should seek out Heyman's releases. —*Rick Clark*

Living Room / 1990 / Gold Castle ◆◆◆
Released on the unlikely Cypress Records label, this homemade debut effort shows Heyman's fully formed command of '60s Brit-pop and Byrds-style jangle. Material-wise, Heyman seems to lack focus. Heyman's voice, at times, lands somewhere between Petty, Hiatt, and Costello. Highlights include "Call out for the Military" and "Wouldn't That Be a Riot?" —*Rick Clark*

● **Hey Man!** / 1991 / Sire ◆◆◆◆
Heyman delivers a fine collection of largely self-performed tunes. His drumming is particularly fine, especially on "Sidetracked." "Falling Away" is a great power-pop song in the classic mid-'60s Anglo tradition. Other standouts include the Byrds/Petty-ish "In the Scheme of Things," the upbeat rocker "Private Army," the Beatley "Loud," and "Bad Business in Town." —*Rick Clark*

Nick Heyward

b. 1961, London, England
Alternative Pop/Rock, New Wave
This Haircut 100 frontman left his pop band at the peak of their success. Featuring the hit singles "Whistle down the Wind" and "Take That Situation," his solo debut, *North of a Miracle*, did well commercially, but *Postcards from Home* and *I Love You Avenue* failed to keep him in the spotlight. After five years of inactivity, *From Sunday to Monday* appeared in 1994. —*John Bush*

● **North of a Miracle** / 1983 / Arista ◆◆◆◆
Lushly orchestrated, this is sophisticated pop. —*Dan Heilman*

Postcards from Home / 1986 / Arista ◆◆

I Love You Avenue / 1988 / Reprise ◆◆

From Monday to Sunday / 1994 / Epic ◆◆◆
An album from former Haircut One Hundred frontman Nick Heyward is not likely to make many people's "most anticipated" list, but *From Monday To Sunday* is pure, exuberant power pop with melodies to kill for, chiming, British Invasion-style guitars, and nary a synthesizer in earshot. Depending on the track, the basic rock lineup is augmented by various combinations of real live cello, mandolin, clarinet, horns, piano, and organ. A couple of numbers lapse into the whitewashed sentimentality of old. But for the most part, Heyward delivers crisp, hummable pop songs, disposable but enjoyable. —*Roch Parisien*

John Hiatt

b. 1952, Indianapolis, IN
Rock & Roll, Country-Rock, Singer-Songwriter
One of the longest-gestating singer/songwriters of the last quarter-century, and one of the best, John Hiatt left his native Indianapolis in 1970 (after high school) to go to Nashville and write songs. He signed up with Epic Records and made two albums, *Hangin' Around the Observatory* (1974) and *Overcoats* (1975), which demonstrated his powerful songwriting ability but didn't draw customers. He signed to MCA in Los Angeles in the late '70s and released *Slug Line* (1979) and *Two Bit Monsters* (1980), still without gaining a commercial following. Then came a stint on Geffen that produced *All of a Sudden* (1982), *Riding with the King* (1983), and *Warming up to the Ice Age* (1985). All increased his visibility without really breaking through.

But in 1987, Hiatt went into the studio with old friends Ry Cooder and Nick Lowe, plus drummer Jim Keltner, and came out with his first chart album, *Bring the Family*. That album's follow-ups, *Slow Turning* (1988), *Stolen Moments* (1990), and *Perfectly Good Guitar* (1993) have demonstrated Hiatt's maturity as a writer and his flowering as a performer, resulting in some of the best singer/songwriter rock of the era. In 1992, Hiatt again teamed with Cooder, Lowe, and Keltner, this time in a group called Little Village that released a well-received debut album.

John Hiatt's songs have been covered by Rick Nelson, Dave Edmunds, the Searchers, Three Dog Night, Conway Twitty, Maria Muldaur, Rodney Crowell, Bob Dylan, the Neville Brothers, and many others. —*William Ruhlmann*

Hangin' Around the Observatory / 1974 / Epic ◆◆◆
John Hiatt mixed pop, folk, rock, R&B, country, and gospel on his debut album, immediately becoming an uncategorizable (and thus uncommercial) entity. Although this album was cut in Nashville, it owes more to Van Morrison than it does to Conway Twitty, and like the Belfast bluesman, Indianian Hiatt came to his influences somewhat secondhand, however sincerely he evoked them. What he really was, of course, was a singer/songwriter, albeit not in a style easily recognizable in 1974. The title indicates his position: Hiatt's songs show him an acute observer. But the performances require him to dig in, and although he does so with alacrity, the result is too diffuse. Nevertheless, Hiatt earned critical kudos for this album, and Three Dog Night (who knew good songwriting when they heard it) covered "Sure As I'm Sittin' Here," getting a Top 40 single out of it. —*William Ruhlmann*

Overcoats / 1975 / Epic ◆◆
John Hiatt is better at imitating Howlin' Wolf than he is James Taylor, and that he tries both here as well as Bob Dylan and Ben E. King is some indication of his ambition, if not his accomplishment. Conversely, be began to become more himself on his second album, at least on such songs as "I'm Tired of Your Stuff" and "I Killed an Ant with My Guitar," if not on the more lugubrious numbers, such as "Distance" or on the ones that sounded like publishing demos for a more popular singer, such as "Down Home." —*William Ruhlmann*

Slug Line / 1979 / MCA ◆◆◆
Conventional wisdom at the time was that MCA Records had signed John Hiatt (who had languished without a record contract for four years) with the idea that he would be their Elvis Costello—a singer/songwriter in the fashionable punk/new wave style. Certainly, Hiatt has stripped down and roughed up from his Epic records here, fronting a straight-ahead guitar rock band (that was capable, of course, of playing the obligatory reggae number), eschewing the stylistic diversity he reveled in before, and throwing out snappy, aphoristic lyrics in a highly processed voice. None of this quite turns him into Elvis Costello, although the mean streak he reveals would serve him well later. —*William Ruhlmann*

Two Bit Monsters / 1980 / MCA ◆◆◆
At the time of its release, *Two Bit Monsters* was perceived by critics who had caught up with John Hiatt on *Slug Line* as a less impressive followup to that record. In retrospect, it may be the better of the two albums, boasting an even more simplified musical approach and such notable songs (and future Rosanne Cash covers) as "Pink Bedroom" and "It Hasn't Happened Yet." Hiatt here was starting to emerge from the "new Elvis Costello" tag that had been affixed to him with *Slug Line*, but his reviewers, however well-meaning, seemed determined to keep him in that category. (In any case, record buyers were paying little attention—*Slug Line* was Hiatt's fourth straight album to miss the charts, and MCA dropped him as Epic had before.) —*William Ruhlmann*

All of a Sudden / 1982 / Geffen ◆◆◆
Hiatt's fifth album and his first for Geffen, his third record label, was given a somewhat inappropriate big-gloss production (all shimmering keyboards and filtered vocals) by Tony Visconti, known for his work with David Bowie. What counts with Hiatt, though, is the songs, and this album contains "I Look for Love," as knowing a dissection of the dating scene as anyone has yet attempted. —*William Ruhlmann*

○ **Riding with the King** / 1983 / Geffen ◆◆◆◆
One half of Hiatt's best Geffen album is played by him and Scott Matthews, while the other half features a band including Paul Carrack and Nick Lowe. But what matters is the songs: Hiatt's trenchant observations on life and love, especially the perceptive and painfully funny "She Loves the Jerk." —*William Ruhlmann*

Warming up to the Ice Age / Jan. 1985 / Geffen ◆◆◆
Hiatt turned to veteran country producer Norbert Putnam here, but the result still rocked hard, with the occasional soul touch (notably those obnoxious thumb-struck bass lines that are so prevalent in '80s music). Highlights here are "The Usual," later covered by Bob Dylan, and "She Said the Same Things to Me." There is also an odd duet with Elvis Costello on the old Spinners hit "Living a Little, Laughing a Little" (try and tell them apart). Critics' darling or not, when this album went into the tank, Geffen became the third label to drop Hiatt. —*William Ruhlmann*

★ **Bring the Family** / May 1987 / A&M ✦✦✦✦✦
Not only is the small-band playing impeccable, but this is Hiatt's best collection of songs, which is saying a lot for so talented a writer. "Memphis in the Meantime" is a knowledgeable look at the fame game, "Your Dad Did" perfectly skewers domestic life, and "Have a Little Faith in Me" is a touching evocation of persistent love. And that's just three of them. — *William Ruhlmann*

○ **Slow Turning** / 1988 / A&M ✦✦✦✦
Only a notch below *Bring the Family*, with such strong songs as "Drive South" and the wild criminals-on-the-loose song "Tennessee Plates." — *William Ruhlmann*

○ **Y' All Caught? the Ones That Got Away 1979-1985** / 1989 / Geffen ✦✦✦✦

Stolen Moments / Jun. 1990 / A&M ✦✦✦
John Hiatt's highest charting album yet is a step down from the dizzy heights of *Bring the Family* and *Slow Turning*, as he abandons his more acid commentaries and turns in a self-deprecating set full of promises of reformation and celebrations of marriage and family life. But the observations remain acute, and Hiatt's singing (so much camouflaged in his early days) is becoming his secret weapon. — *William Ruhlmann*

Perfectly Good Guitar / 1993 / A&M ✦✦✦
Perfectly Good Guitar is clearly a John Hiatt rock album, harking back to his mid-period *Riding with the King* days. It might disappoint some ardent admirers of the more subtle roots approach that defined Hiatt's peak "highway" twin-pack *Bring the Family* and *Slow Turning*, but most listeners should not be deterred by this perfectly good release. — *Roch Parisien*

Hiatt Comes Alive At Budokan? / Nov. 22, 1994 / A&M ✦✦✦
John Hiatt's first live album was recorded during a 1994 winter-spring tour of the U.S. (the title is a joke) and finds the singer/songwriter backed by the Guilty Dogs, a guitar-bass-drums trio. He doesn't need any more ammunition than that, not when he's got a set of 15 songs drawn from his last four critically acclaimed albums, including "Thing Called Love" and "Tennessee Plates." Hiatt gives his songs a rougher treatment than some of those who have covered them, his throaty voice giving even love songs like "Angel Eyes" an unsentimental force. In the absence of an A&M best-of, *Hiatt Comes Alive at Budokan?* makes a good sampler of his work, 1987-1993. — *William Ruhlmann*

Jessie Hill

b. Dec. 9, 1932, New Orleans, LA
New Orleans R&B
Loose and wild, Jessie Hill cut a New Orleans party classic with his crazed "Ooh Poo Pah Doo." The two-sided single, a 1960 Allen Toussaint production on Minit, has Hill shouting the nearly unintelligible lyrics over a strong Crescent City groove, while the flip is an instrumental featuring saxist David Lastie. Hill cut several more boisterous outings with Toussaint at the helm before heading to the West Coast, where he made a disappointing album for Blue Thumb in 1970. — *Bill Dahl*

Naturally / 1972 / Blue Thumb ✦✦
Hurts So Bad / 1982 / Capitol ✦✦✦
A good, occasionally great New Orleans vocalist, drummer, and pianist, better known for the time he spent playing with Huey "Piano" Smith than on his own. Hill did have one superb single in "Ooh Poo Pah Doo," but that wasn't on this batch of decent Southern soul and R&B tracks. There's nothing to get excited about, but they're all done with energy and conviction. — *Ron Wynn*

Y'all Ready Now ... Plus / 1987 / Charly ✦✦✦
● **Golden Classics** / Collectables ✦✦✦✦
Good-time New Orleans R&B from the early '60s, produced by prolific pianist Allen Toussaint. — *Bill Dahl*

Chris Hillman

b. Dec. 4, 1944, Los Angeles, CA
Country-Rock
This Californian has been perhaps the greatest influence on the country-rock/folk genre that's taken for granted today. He began as the mandolin player of the Scottsville Squirrel Barkers, a group which turned into the Hillmen, a bluegrass-oriented group based in California. Then came the Byrds, a legendary country-rock quintet that recorded Bob Dylan's "Mr. Tambourine Man" (in 1965) and the pioneer country-rock album *Sweetheart of the*

Rodeo, with Gram Parsons. Hillman and Parsons then formed the Flying Burrito Brothers in 1969. In the '70s Hillman performed as a solo act. In the '80s Hillman formed the Desert Rose Band and has been touring with them. — *David Vinopal*

○ **The Hillmen (Chris Hillman)** / 1971 / Together ✦✦✦✦
Recorded approximately two years before Hillman joined the Byrds, this album does as much to explain his background as the Byrds' *Sweetheart of the Rodeo* album. This fine bluegrass band also featured the Gosdin brothers, who not only had country hits during the '70s and '80s, but also made a fine record with Gene Clark. Worth looking for, not only for these reasons but also for some fine music. — *Jim Worbois*

Slippin' Away / 1976 / Asylum ✦✦✦
Having recently departed Souther, Hillman, & Furay, this album more heavily reflects his association with Manassa than anything he did with SH&F. A nice batch of songs overall but the high point for me is the killer version of the bluegrass standard "Take Me in Your Lifeboat" that closes the album. — *Jim Worbois*

Clear Sailin' / 1977 / Asylum ✦✦
This is not one of those records that transcends the period in which it was made. It could easily be confused with Fools Gold, Firefall, or any one of a number of bands from the late '70s. — *Jim Worbois*

Ever Call Ready / 1978 / A&M ✦✦✦
● **Morning Sky** / 1982 / Sugar Hill ✦✦✦✦
A back-to-the-roots album (of sorts), Hillman has given up the bass in favor of the mandolin and acoustic guitar for this mostly acoustic album of other people's tunes. The band is made up of people with whom Hillman has worked over the years and it's obvious they are comfortable together. Listening to this album is almost like eavesdropping on a group of friends making music in their living room. — *Jim Worbois*

○ **Desert Rose** / 1984 / Sugar Hill ✦✦✦✦
Bluegrass, country, and country-rock, Hillman played mandolin on this album, but his main instrument (with the Byrds and Desert Rose Band) is bass. — *Mark A. Humphrey*

Peter Himmelman

Singer-Songwriter, Pop/Rock
Minnesota-native Peter Himmelman was the leader of a pop/rock quintet called Sussman Lawrence that made two independent albums in the early '80s and earned him comparisons to such new wave singer/songwriters as Elvis Costello and Joe Jackson. The group became Himmelman's backup band for the release of his debut album, *This Father's Day* (1986), which earned him a contract with Island Records. He followed with *Gematria* (1987), *Synesthesia* (1989), and *Strength to Strength* (1991). By the last release, he had moved to Epic Records. — *William Ruhlmann*

This Father's Day / 1986 / Island ✦✦✦
Gematria / 1987 / Island ✦✦✦
● **Synesthesia** / 1989 / Island ✦✦✦✦
Inventive drum tracks highlight Himmelman's spare arrangements of songs that express a personal, poetic world view full of struggle and vulnerability. — *William Ruhlmann*

○ **From Strength to Strength** / 1991 / Epic ✦✦✦✦
"Woman with the Strength of 10,000 Men" is Himmelman's song of romantic devotion, but it's only one of the driven performances on an album whose song titles—"Crushed," "Midnight Walk in the Ruins"—express its sense of anguish and desperation. — *William Ruhlmann*

Flown This Acid World / Jun. 1992 / Epic ✦✦✦
Flown This Acid World's most powerful moment is album closer "Untitled"—a pointed, autobiographical story about a ride with a vociferously anti-Semetic taxi driver. It's a song that several parts of the world could use a strong dose of right now. Himmelman has a talent for zeroing in on some of the more unpleasant things about ourselves and society, coupled with an equal ability to rise above them while transporting the listener with him. — *Roch Parisien*

Skin / 1994 / 550 Music/Epic ✦✦✦

Hindu Love Gods

Group, Rock & Roll
Warren Zevon and a Michael Stipe-less R.E.M. engage in playful

electric blues-rock romps, plus some left-field song covers. Spirited playing and singing throughout make this effort fresher than many rock releases. —*Rick Clark*

○ **Hindu Love Gods** / 1990 / Giant ◆◆◆◆
Included is a great version of Prince's "Raspberry Beret." The production is immediate-sounding, generating the feel of a band knocking around in a rehearsal hall. There are plenty of charged versions of blues standards by Robert Johnson, Willie Dixon, and Muddy Waters, and the Love Gods also charge through a fun rendition of Terry Anderson's "Battleship Chains." —*Rick Clark*

His Name Is Alive
Group, Alternative Pop/Rock
His Name Is Alive create some of the most beautiful and complex independently-released music in recent memory, ranging from simple, folky ballads to electrifying guitar maelstroms. The brainchild of guitarist Warren Defever (also of shockabilly group Elvis Hitler), His Name Is Alive features the voices of Karin Oliver, Melissa Elliott, Denise James and Karen Neal, and the drumming of Damian Lang and Trey Many (also of Licorice). The band's sound is as ever-changing as its lineup; each of the group's releases, from the haunting, near-Gothic *Livonia* (named after the group's Michigan hometown) to the sunny-sounding *Mouth By Mouth*, shows innovation and continual change. —*Heather Phares*

Livonia / 1990 / Rykodisc ◆◆◆
The group's artiest release, *Livonia*, was recorded when Defever was a mere 19 years old. Karin Oliver's wide vocal range and elegant harmonies mix with Defever's guitar maelstroms and tape loops in a unique and usually successful way. "E-Nicolle," "How Ghosts Affect Relationships" and "Caroline's Supposed Demon" are good examples of *Livonia*'s mix of sonic beauty and experimentalism. —*Heather Phares*

○ **Home Is in Your Head** / 1992 / Rykodisc ◆◆◆◆
Home Is in Your Head completes His Name Is Alive's moody, neo-gothic period. A dark and disturbing, but also very beautiful record, *Home Is in Your Head* features song titles like "Put Your Finger in Your Eye," "Why People Disappear," "Chances Are We Are Mad" and "Are We Still Married?" The album is musically diverse, ranging from gentle folk ballads to ethereal instrumentals to harsh guitar blasts. The Rykodisc re-release also includes the group's *The Dirt Eaters* EP, which contains a creepy remix of "Are We Still Married?" as well as one of His Name Is Alive's best songs, "We Hold the Land in Great Esteem." —*Heather Phares*

● **Mouth by Mouth** / 1993 / 4AD ◆◆◆◆
His Name Is Alive's third release is actually half HNIA songs and half Dirt Eaters (HNIA's sister band) songs. The two groups' songs work together brilliantly, creating one of the best and most varied albums in alternative music. The Dirt Eaters' songs, like "Baby Fish Mouth," "In Every Ford," "Sick" and "The Dirt Eaters" are loud, catchy art-pop songs with lots of fuzzy, distorted guitars. His Name Is Alive's tunes, in contrast, feature the pristine harmonies and crisp cellos of "Cornfield," the pseudo-gamelan on "Sort Of," and the disturbing dead-calm of "Can't Go Wrong Without You" and "Ear." The light and shadow that the bands create with their harmonious yet distinct styles make *Mouth by Mouth* fascinating and rewarding on each listen. —*Heather Phares*

King of Sweet / 1993 / Perdition Plastics ◆◆
This release, on the miniscule Perdition Plastics label, is a limited edition of 2000. Nevertheless, it's an interesting collection of HNIA's odds and sods, including previously unreleased tracks and alternate takes and mixes of other songs. Sampling and tape loops are emphasized more on *King of Sweet* than on any of the band's previous releases, so its novelty and collector's value make it a must for fans of this unique and mesmerizing band. —*Heather Phares*

Robyn Hitchcock
b. 1952
Alternative Pop/Rock
British alternative singer/songwriter Robyn Hitchcock built up a large cult following and critical acclaim for his highly poetic, if somewhat obscure, songs, especially after his work began to be more generally available in the U.S. after 1985. Born in London, Hitchcock formed the Soft Boys with Andy Metcalfe and Morris Windsor in 1976; the band continued until 1981, when Hitchcock released his first solo album, *Black Snake Diamond Role*. This was followed by *Groovy Decay* (1982) and *I Often Dream of Trains*

(1984). In 1984, Hitchcock formed a backing band called the Egyptians, consisting of Metcalfe, Windsor, Otis Horns Fletcher, and Roger Jackson, and began playing concerts for the first time in two and a half years. The first recorded output of this band, and the first U.S. Hitchcock album, was *Fegmania!* (1985). It was followed by the live album *Gotta Let This Hen Out!* (1985), *Element of Light* (1986), and a compilation called *Invisible Hitchcock* (1986), all of which built up Hitchcock's following to the point that he was signed by A&M Records, resulting in his major-label debut *Globe of Frogs* (1988), which reached #111. *Queen Elvis*, Hitchcock's second A&M album, reached #139 in 1989. He then made *Eye* (1990), an acoustic solo album released on Twin/Tone Records. —*William Ruhlmann*

Black Snake Diamond Role / 1981 / Rhino ◆◆◆
Robyn Hitchcock's first album after leaving the Soft Boys isn't that far removed from the edgy, warped guitar-pop of his former band, which isn't surprising, considering the presence of former Soft Boys bassist Andy Metcalfe and drummer Morris Windsor. However, *Black Snake Diamond Role* removes much of the sharp, cutting guitars of *Underwater Moonlight* and replaces them with friendlier, ringing riffs. But that doesn't mean Hitchcock has gone soft—he's just refined his technique. And that doesn't mean his songwriting has improved. Cut by cut, *Black Snake Diamond Role* is weaker than *Underwater Moonlight*, but that's relative—the album contains pretty and twisted pseudo-psychedelic pop like "Brenda's Iron Sledge," "Acid Bird," "The Man Who Invented Himself," and "Do Policemen Sing?" which all rank among his finest songs. —*Stephen Thomas Erlewine*

Groovy Decay / 1982 / Combat ◆◆
For his second solo album, Robyn Hitchcock decided to work with producer Steve Hillage, a former member of Gong. Under his guidance, Hitchcock made an album that smoothed out his rough edges and obscured his quirks under layers of saxophones, trumpets, and processed guitars. Beneath the stilted production lay some of Hitchcock's weakest songs, most of which were under-developed melodically and lyrically. Some of the songs are worthwhile—"The Cars She Used to Drive" is the best stab at slick new wave pop, while "Fifty Two Stations" and "St. Petersburg" are powerful—but most of the album is simply lifeless. After its release, Hitchcock retired from music for nearly three years. In 1986, he released an alternate version of *Groovy Decay*, comprised mostly of songwriting demos, called *Groovy Decoy*. —*Stephen Thomas Erlewine*

○ **I Often Dream of Trains** / 1984 / Rhino ◆◆◆◆
Hitchcock was so shaken by the entire *Groovy Decay* disaster that he retired from recording for two years. When he returned in 1984 with *I Often Dream of Trains*, it was clear that the time off had affected his music. A collection of spare, acoustic-based pop-folk songs, *I Often Dream of Trains* is one of Hitchcock's most introspective and charming records. Instead of creating an impenetrably personal album, the stripped-down instrumentation actually opens up the songwriter's world, allowing the ballads ("Trams of Old London," "Cathedral," "Flavour of Night") to sit comfortably next to the jokes ("Uncorrected Personality Traits"). Alternating between acoustic guitars and solo piano, the music is never fragile, adding a strong support to Hitchcock's eccentric lyrics. —*Stephen Thomas Erlewine*

○ **Fegmania!** / Mar. 1985 / Rhino ◆◆◆◆
After the stripped-back collection *I Often Dream of Trains*, Hitchcock slowly formed a backing band called the Egyptians with ex-Soft Boys Andy Metcalfe and Morris Windsor and keyboardist Roger Jackson over the course of the next year. *Fegmania!*, the Egyptians' first album, was a distinct departure from both the Soft Boys and Hitchcock's previous solo work, featuring layered, intertwining guitars and keyboards that created lush and thick sonic textures. Even with the more detailed arrangements, the songs remained twitchy and off-kilter, with melodies that usually went in willfully unpredictable directions, yet remained catchy all the while. *Fegmania!* was Hitchcock's most consistent work to date, featuring such highlights as the Eastern-tinged "Egyptian Cream," the creepy "My Wife & My Dead Wife," and the relatively straightforward "The Man with the Lightbulb Head." —*Stephen Thomas Erlewine*

● **Gotta Let This Hen Out** / Oct. 1985 / Rhino ◆◆◆◆
Recorded at the Marquee in London shortly after the release of *Fegmania!*, the live *Gotta Let This Hen Out!* is a tense and exciting record, finding the raw energy that usually goes untapped in

Hitchcock's music. Although the album makes the Egyptians sound more like a rock & roll band than they actually were—they never played with such wreckless abandon before or since—the driving performances don't wreck the melodic and lyrical eccentricities of the songs; instead, the increased vigor gives the music a searing power, obliterating the notion that his songs are delicate and precious. The set list also accentuates Hitchcock's strengths, relying on his most accessible and melodic material, whether it's recent material like "Egyptian Cream," "Sometimes I Wish I Was a Pretty Girl," and "Acid Bird" or Soft Boys' tracks like "Kingdom of Love," "Only the Stones Remain," "The Face of Death," and "Leppo and the Jooves." —*Stephen Thomas Erlewine*

Groovy Decoy / Dec. 1985 / Relativity ✦✦
Four years after its release, Robyn Hitchcock pulled *Groovy Decay* from circulation, replacing it with *Groovy Decoy*, an alternate version of the record assembled mainly from demos he recorded with Soft Boys bassist Matthew Seligman; the album included some versions that are identical to the *Decay* material, as well as a handful of new songs. By and large, *Groovy Decoy* is a better record, with more immediate and gripping versions of the songs that comprised the original album, but the material remains some of the weakest Hitchcock has written. —*Stephen Thomas Erlewine*

○ **Element of Light** / 1986 / Rhino ✦✦✦✦
Element of Light, Hitchcock's second studio album with the Egyptians, remains one of his finest moments and offers a convincing argument for his talents as a pop craftsman. Using John Lennon's work for *Revolver* and *The Beatles* as a template, Hitchcock wrote an elegant set of songs for *Element of Light,* songs that contained all of his cryptic lyrical sensibilities, yet featured more refined melodies and song structures. The Egyptians play with a subtle grace, moving between the stately "Winchester" and light psychedelia of "If You Were a Priest" to the bracing attack of "Tell Me About Your Drugs" with ease. While it sacrifices some of the edgy tension of Hitchcock's earlier work, *Element of Light* is his most melodic and eerily beautiful record. —*Stephen Thomas Erlewine*

Invisible Hitchcock / 1986 / Rhino ✦✦✦
As the reference to the Soft Boys' rarities collection, *Invisible Hits,* suggests, *Invisible Hitchcock* gathers together a selection of obscurities and non-album tracks Robyn Hitchcock recorded between 1980 and 1986. Granted, the material is a bit uneven, but the album holds together well, as it emphasizes Hitchcock's gift for warped wordplay and appealingly convoluted melodies. Upon its original release, the running order for *Invisible Hitchcock* was considerably different in Britain and America; Rhino's 1995 reissue standardized the album, including all the material from both versions of the album (with the exception of "Grooving on an Inner Plane," which appeared as a bonus track on the company's reissue of *Black Snake Diamond Role*), as well as adding two songs that never appeared on either version of the record. —*Stephen Thomas Erlewine*

● **Globe of Frogs** / 1988 / A&M ✦✦✦✦
Hitchcock has a considerable catalog, but neophytes might wish to begin with this relatively recent collection, which finds him playing in a folk/rock style while singing highly imagistic lyrics, the tone of which can be suggested by noting some of the titles: "Balloon Man," "Tropical Fish Mandala," "Sleeping with Your Devil Mask," and "The Shapes Between Us Turn into Animals." Hitchcock is an original lyricist, well worth hearing, if not an acquired taste. —*William Ruhlmann*

Queen Elvis / 1989 / A&M ✦✦
Hitchcock earned some radio play for this album's lead-off track, "Madonna of the Wasps," which, like several tracks here, features the distinctive guitar of R.E.M.'s Peter Buck. —*William Ruhlmann*

○ **Eye** / 1990 / Rhino ✦✦✦✦
Robyn Hitchcock recorded *Eye,* his fourth proper solo album, after the disappointing *Queen Elvis. Eye* marked a return to the acoustic-oriented folk-pop of *I Often Dream of Trains,* featuring a collection of his most personal songs. Where *I Often Dream of Trains* was a kaleidoscopic journey through a colorfully twisted world, *Eye* sounds more confessional, although Hitchcock's exact lyrical sentiments can be difficult to sort out through his dense and willfully obscure imagery. Nevertheless, the immediacy of the music—which is delivered on acoustic guitars and piano—and the simple, delicate grace of Hitchcock's melodies make even the most cryptic lines sound direct and straightforward. —*Stephen Thomas Erlewine*

Perspex Island / 1991 / A&M ✦✦✦
While it's an uneven extension of the ringing guitar-pop of *Globe of Frogs, Perspex Island* contains Robyn Hitchcock's best pure pop single, the minor classic "So You Think You're in Love," which was written while he was in the Soft Boys. —*Stephen Thomas Erlewine*

Respect / Feb. 23, 1993 / A&M ✦✦
Through his years of leading influential psychedelic rockers the Soft Boys, his solo work, and seven releases with current combo The Egyptians, Robyn Hitchcock has earned recognition as a literate tunesmith in the tradition of great British eccentrics. Hitchcock uses conventional pop structures as a launching pad for whimsical, sometimes abstract, and often wildly imaginative flights. *Respect* is true to form, although his lyrics are at his most accessible here. Instrumentally, Hitchcock's layers of acoustic and electric guitars are accompanied not only by bass, keyboards and drums, but also—when called upon—by water jug, cheese grater, and frying pans. The intelligence and emotion of Robyn Hitchcock's work continues to reward. —*Roch Parisien*

Gravy Deco / Jan. 1995 / Rhino ✦✦
When Rhino reissued Robyn Hitchcock's catalog in 1995, the record company combined the material from *Groovy Decoy* and *Groovy Decay* onto one disc titled *Gravy Deco.* In any form, it's the weakest music he ever recorded, with a couple of songs—particularly the haunting "St. Petersburg," "Fifty Two Stations," and "America"—that make it worthwhile for dedicated fans. —*Stephen Thomas Erlewine*

You & Oblivion / Mar. 1995 / Rhino ✦✦
Released as part of Rhino's 1995 series of Robyn Hitchcock reissues *You & Oblivion* is the second collection of Hitchcock rarities, featuring demos, live tracks, and studio outtakes. Unfortunately, much of the material is second-rate, and some of the songs sound unfinished. Accentuating the frustratingly inconsisting musical quality of the record is the lack of liner notes and non-chronological sequencing, which makes the record confusing for casual listener and exasperating for hardcore fans. There are a handful of intriguing performances among the 22 tracks, yet most of *You & Oblivion* is a chore to listen to. —*Stephen Thomas Erlewine*

Allan Holdsworth

b. Aug. 6, 1948, Bradford, England
Progressive Rock, Fusion
A British electric guitar fusion virtuoso, Holdsworth began playing with progressive rock bands Gong and Soft Machine in the '70s, later becoming a sideman with the Tony Williams Lifetime, Bill Bruford, and Chuck Mangione. Holdsworth's melodic and precise style draws much inspiration from jazz horn phrasing. His most recent albums feature the Synth-axe, a guitarlike synthesizer controller. —*Scott Bultman*

Velvet Darkness / 1977 / Columbia ✦✦✦
The first solo album by this guitarist from such bands as Gong, Soft Machine, and the Tony Williams Lifetime includes several excellent acoustic guitar pieces. —*Paul Kohler*

Road Games / 1983 / Warner Brothers ✦✦✦
This excellent six-track EP features Chad Wackerman on drums and Jeff Berlin on bass. Great compositions. —*Paul Kohler*

● **Metal Fatigue** / 1985 / Enigma ✦✦✦✦
A terrific album by a most innovative guitarist and composer, it is truly first-class. —*Paul Kohler*

I.O.U. / 1985 / Enigma ✦✦✦
Brilliant compositions and musicianship appear on this independent release. Featuring vocal and instrumental material with outstanding guitar solos and P. Williams on vocals, it was recorded on a barge! —*Paul Kohler*

Atavachron / 1986 / Enigma ✦✦✦
Atavachron was a landmark album in the history of modern rock guitar instrumentals, because it marked the first time Holdsworth used a Synth-axe guitar synthesizer. The sounds and textures are incredible. —*Paul Kohler*

Sand / 1987 / Restless ✦✦✦
This instrumental album features more of the synth-guitar and regular guitar. Included are beautiful compositions and fiery guitar solos, with Chad Wackerman and Jimmy Johnson. —*Paul Kohler*

○ **Secrets** / 1989 / Intima ◆◆◆◆
A masterpiece from start to finish, it has nice chord changes and
wonderful solos. The album includes a mix of guitar and Synth-
axe. —*Paul Kohler*

Hole

Group, Alternative Pop/Rock
Throughout Hole's career, vocalist/guitarist Courtney Love's notorious public image has overshadowed her band's music. In its original incarnation, Hole was one of the noisiest, most abrasive alternative bands performing in the early '90s. By the time of their second album, 1994's *Live Through This*, the band had smoothed out
many of their rougher edges, as well as adding more melody and
hooks to their songwriting. Through both versions of Hole, Love's
combative, assaultive persona permeated both the group's music
and lyrics, giving the band a tense, unpredictible edge even at
their quietest moments.
Love formed Hole in Los Angeles in 1989, recruiting guitarist
Eric Erlandson through a newspaper add. Love had played with
numerous bands before Hole, including an early version of Babes
In Toyland and Faith No More. Erlandson and Love eventually
drafted bassist Jill Emery and drummer Caroline Rue into the
band, recording their first album with producer Kim Gordon, the
bassist of Sonic Youth. The violent and uncompromising *Pretty on
the Inside*, Hole's debut record, was released on Caroline Records
in 1991, to numerous positive reviews, especially in the British
weekly music press.
In early 1992, Courtney Love married Kurt Cobain, the lead
singer/songwriter of Nirvana. For a couple of months, the couple
were the king and queen of the new rock world; soon, that world
came crashing in. Cobain became addicted to heroin and the couple fought to keep custody of their baby after a piece in *Vanity
Fair* accused Love of shooting heroin while pregnant, charges
which she vehemently denied at the time; she would later admit
that she had taken small quantities of the drug. By 1993, their private world had settled down somewhat, with Cobain and Love
recording new albums with their respective bands.
Halfway through 1993, Love reassembled Hole with Erlandson,
adding bassist Kristen M. Pfaff and drummer Patty Schemel. Hole
was set to release their first major-label album, the more pop-oriented *Live Through This*, on DGC Records in April of 1994. Advance word on the album was overwhelmingly positive, with
many critics calling it one of the best records of the year. Four
days before the album was released, Kurt Cobain's body was discovered in the couple's Seattle home; he died of a self-inflicted
shotgun wound three days before.
Two months after Cobain's death, Kristen M. Pfaff was found
dead of a heroin overdose in a Seattle apartment. Two months
later, Hole began touring again, with bassist Melissa Auf Der Maur
taking Pfaff's place. "Doll Parts" was released as a single late in
1994, climbing into the Top 60 by the beginning of 1995. *Live
Through This* topped many critics' polls at the end of the year, including the *Rolling Stone* and *The Village Voice*. After *Live
Through This* went gold in the summer of 1995, Hole toured with
the fifth Lollapalooza tour. —*Stephen Thomas Erlewine*

Pretty on the Inside / 1991 / Caroline ◆◆◆
Hole's debut album is a brutal, scathing record, filled with primal
guitars and gut-wrenching vocals. All of the noise and angst is tied
together by the exceptional songwriting of Courtney Love, who always manages to provide a reason for anger, whether through her
lyrics or her music. —*Stephen Thomas Erlewine*

● **Live through This** / 1994 / DGC ◆◆◆◆
On their second album, Hole's sound matures without losing its vital edge. Love's songwriting is more melodic and succinct, which
makes the band's raging guitars and naked honesty all the more
effective. —*Stephen Thomas Erlewine*

The Hollies

Group, British Invasion, Pop/Rock
One of the best and most commercially successful pop/rock acts of
the British Invasion, when the Hollies began recording in 1963,
they relied heavily upon the R&B/early rock & roll covers that provided the staple diet for countless British bands of the time. They
quickly developed a more distinctive style of three-part harmonies
(heavily influenced by the Everly Brothers), ringing guitars, and
hook-happy material, penned by both outside writers (especially
Graham Gouldman) and themselves, eventually composing most

of their repertoire on their own. They ran off an awesome series of
hits in the U.K. in the '60s, making the Top 20 almost twenty
times. In the States, they were less successful, but still found a
wide audience with classic numbers like "Look Through Any Window," "On a Carousel," "Bus Stop," "Carrie Ann," and "Stop Stop
Stop," the last three of which reached the Top Ten. Lead singer Allan Clarke and guitarists Tony Hicks and Graham Nash dominated the band with their harmonies and songwriting, though
Bobby Elliott made a major contribution with his masterful drum-
work.
The best early Hollies records evoke an infectious, melodic
cheer similar to that of the early Beatles, although the Hollies
were neither in their class (not an insult: nobody else was) nor
demonstrated a similar capacity for artistic growth. They tried,
though, easing into somewhat more sophisticated folk-rock and
mildly psychedelic sounds as the decade wore on, especially on
their albums (which contain quite a few overlooked highlights).
Nash, supposedly frustrated by the group's reluctance to deviate
from their hit-making formula into more progressive pastures, left
the band in 1968 to join Crosby, Stills & Nash. That was really the
end of the group's peak era, although they had some typically
sparkling pop/rock hits in the late '60s and early '70s, especially
"He Ain't Heavy He's My Brother," "Long Cool Woman," and "The
Air That I Breathe." —*Richie Unterberger*

○ **In the Hollies Style** / 1964 / Beat Goes On ◆◆◆◆
Released only ten months after their debut album, *Stay with the
Hollies*, their second LP was a huge leap forward in every respect.
Their famous airtight harmonies were now in place, and the slop-
piness of the instrumental attack gone. Most important, the group
developed enormously as songwriters. Eight of the twelve tracks
were Hollies originals, and quite skillful in their mastery of the
British Invasion essentials of driving, catchy melodies and shining
harmonies. A couple of the covers are duds, but the "Nitty
Gritty/Something's Got a Hold of Me" medley is first-rate, and the
version of "It's in His Kiss" (retitled "It's in Her Kiss") respectable.
The Hollies weren't from Liverpool (though Manchester is fairly
close), but this nonetheless ranks of one of the very best Merseybeat albums not released by the Beatles themselves. It doesn't include any British or American hits, but "Come on Home," "To You
My Love," "Don't You Know," and "What Kind of Boy" (the last of
which was written for them by one Big Dee Irwin) will appeal to
any British Invasion fan. Surprisingly, none of the tracks were ever
released in the United States, making the reissue all the more desirable an item for British Invasion collectors from U.S. shores,
who most likely missed it entirely the first time around. —*Richie
Unterberger*

Stay with the Hollies / 1964 / Beat Goes On ◆◆
In *The Rolling Stone Illustrated History of Rock'n'Roll*, Lester
Bangs wrote of the Hollies, "During the British invasion, they
were mostly just bad, grinding out sloppy covers of 'Stay,' 'Do You
Love Me,' 'Lucille' and 'Memphis' in the most shamelessly churn-
'em-up, bash-'em-out Liverpudlian manner." While this is an unfair
overgeneralization, it's basically an accurate assessment of their
first album, which contains all of the above-mentioned cuts. The
group stuck to the tried-and-true rock/R&B cover staples of
dozens, if not hundreds, of British bands circa 1963 on this 14-cut
LP, which featured only one original composition. The Hollies'
harmonic blend had yet to fully coalesce; there's plenty of energy,
but the voices are adenoidal (and not always in perfect key) and
the performances almost embarrassingly callow. Nonetheless, the
album was a huge hit in Britain, reaching number two and staying
in the Top Ten for 18 weeks. "Stay" itself had been their first U.K.
Top Ten hit in late 1963, and the album's best track, the edgy
R&B/harmony rendition of "Watcha Gonna Do 'Bout It," was one
of their better early cuts. The group also covers Ray Charles, Roy
Orbison, Conway Twitty, "Rockin' Robin," and "Mr. Moonlight" (before the Beatles) on this set. —*Richie Unterberger*

Hollies / 1965 / Columbia/Legacy ◆◆◆
The Hollies' third album saw a band in the throes of transition between the Merseybeat and rock & roll with which they established
themselves, and the folk-rock and soul music that was blowing the
strongest winds of change in 1965. They clean up their backlog of
cover staples with versions of tunes by Lloyd Price, Buddy Holly,
and Roy Orbison, and delve into soul by taking on the Miracles'
"Mickey's Monkey" and Curtis Mayfield's "You Must Believe Me."
Their attempt at "Fortune Teller" won't make you forget the
Rolling Stones' version; nor, for that matter, are any of the other

covers impressive. That leaves five reasonably good originals, the best of which are the gorgeous "So Lonely" and the excellent Merseybeat knockoff "When I Come Home to You." They also sound Beatlesque on "I've Been Wrong," but "Too Many People" and their cover of Peter, Paul & Mary's "Very Last Day" hearken to a folk-rock direction. The album was issued in the U.S. as *Hear! Here!*, replacing "Mickey's Monkey" with their number one British hit "I'm Alive." —*Richie Unterberger*

Would You Believe / 1965 / Beat Goes On ✦✦✦
One of the less essential '60s albums by the Hollies, whose capabilities were arguably stretched by the two-album-a-year-pace-in-addition-to-three-hit-singles model established by the Beatles during this time. Their version of Paul Simon's "I Am a Rock" is nice, but the soul and early rock covers of Sam & Dave, Otis Redding, and Chuck Berry are pretty dispensable; the Hollies were not the Stones or the Animals, lacking their soul and interpretative imagination. Some of the originals are pretty ho-hum too (including the pathetic "Fifi the Flea," which was covered by the Everly Brothers). But every Hollies album of the '60s has some strong overlooked tracks. On this one, they're the surprisingly tough folk-rockers "Hard, Hard Year" and "I've Got a Way of My Own." The ultra-catchy "Don't You Even Care," written by Clint Ballard Jr. (also responsible for their number-one British hit "I'm Alive," as well as "The Game of Love" and "You're No Good"), is the real obscure gem here, and could have well been a hit under its own steam. The album's last song, "I Can't Let Go," was a big hit in Britain (and a small one in the U.S.) and one of the Hollies' best performances. The record was issued in America, in a slightly amended version, as *Beat Group!* —*Richie Unterberger*

For Certain Because / 1966 / Beat Goes On ✦✦✦
One gets the feeling that, as 1966 drew to a close amidst an incredible acceleration of innovations in the pop and rock world, the Hollies felt the need to prove themselves capable of artistic growth despite having established a very winning formula. *For Certain Because* was their first album entirely composed of original material, and echoed pop's increased sophistication with fuller, more adventurous arrangements and more personal, folk-rock-influenced compositions. Such was the intense competition of the time that this record couldn't hope to take on *Revolver*, *Aftermath*, or *Face to Face*, but it nevertheless remains an admirable effort that may stand as the group's most accomplished album (greatest hits packages excepted) of the '60s. The Hollies were very much a pop group, and didn't let their somewhat more sober and introspective compositions stand in the way of their glittering harmonies and jangling guitars. Occasional brass, banjo, bells, and vibrating piano embellish their basic rock instrumentation on this pleasant, if hardly earthshaking, work. The circus-like "Stop! Stop! Stop!," with its manic banjo, was a hit on both sides of the Atlantic; the good-natured "Pay You Back with Interest" a Top 30 hit in America; and the jazzy "Tell Me to My Face" was one of their best '60s album tracks. The LP was released as *Stop! Stop! Stop!* in the U.S. —*Richie Unterberger*

Evolution / 1967 / Epic ✦✦
The title of the album, along with the psychedelic shirts and artwork on the cover, sound a clarion call that the Hollies were aiming to keep up with the times on this mid-1967 release. Actually, they don't deviate too much from their formula of high harmonies and catchy tunes on this release, which stands as one of their less memorable '60s albums. If there are any expanded ambitions here, they're found in the eight cuts that feature modest orchestral arrangements directed by former Manfred Mann member Mike Vickers. When the band tries to stretch it a bit with clips of hard fuzz guitars or the embarrassingly dated "underwater" vocals of "Lullaby to Tim," it doesn't come off well. A couple of the better cuts are "Rain on the Window," a kind of downbeat sequel to "Bus Stop" with its Graham Gouldman-influenced melody line, and "Leave Me," which actually hearkens back to earlier British Invasion days with its strong Zombies influence. "Have You Ever Loved Somebody" is a good tune that was done better in cover versions by the Searchers and the Everly Brothers. No hits were featured on this LP, which was released in a slightly truncated form in the U.S. —*Richie Unterberger*

What Goes Around / 1983 / Atlantic ✦✦✦
Graham Nash rejoined the Hollies for one album for the first time in 15 years, which certainly beefed up their harmonies. He also co-produced, but he didn't bring any songs along, which makes this something less than one might have hoped. The group did get its

first U.S. hit in eight years and last so far with a remake of the Supremes' "Stop in the Name of Love." —*William Ruhlmann*

● **All Time Greatest Hits** / 1990 / Curb ✦✦✦✦
A 12 track all-singles compilation that includes the Hollies's biggest US hits on both Inperial ("Bus Stop," "Stop, Stop, Stop") and Epic Records from 1964 to 1975. —*William Ruhlmann*

● **Epic Anthology** / 1990 / Epic ✦✦✦✦
Epic Anthology: From the Original Master Tapes!. A 20-track compilation that picks up when the Hollies signed with Epic in 1967 and presents their biggest hits plus select album tracks and rarities through 1975. Includes "Carrie-Anne," "He Ain't Heavy, He's My Brother," "Long Cool Woman (In a Black Dress)," and "The Air That I Breathe." —*William Ruhlmann*

○ **Thirtieth Anniversary Collection 1963-1993** / 1993 / EMI America ✦✦✦✦
This three-CD, 57-track box set does a good if imperfect job of encapsulating the legacy of one of the British Invasion's better bands. This includes all of the Hollies' singles, A- and B-sides, from the '60s, as well as five previously unreleased tunes. The hits—"I'm Alive," "Bus Stop," "On a Carousel," and others—contain some of the finest beat harmonizing not done by the Beatles. The B-sides—many of them originals, some of them never before available in the United States—are often nearly equal in quality to the classic material. The compilation wisely touches upon only the essentials of their post-1970 singles ("Long Cool Woman" and "The Air That I Breathe"), and unwisely closes with three forgettable tracks from the early '90s. Don't be misled, however, that this box contains all of their best material—their early albums, though inconsistent, featured a fair number of strong original tunes which remain little-known beyond collector circles. It's a good set, with an excellent booklet and thoroughly annotated discography, but not definitive. —*Richie Unterberger*

Brenda Holloway

b. Jun. 21, 1946, Atascadero, CA
Soul, Motown
This sultry '60s addition to the Motown roster waxed several memorable ballads for the firm. One of Motown's first Los Angeles signings, Holloway's Tamla debut, "Every Little Bit Hurts," was a soaring ballad that sailed up the pop charts in 1964, while Smokey Robinson wrote and produced Holloway's 1965 smash "When I'm Gone." The voluptuous vocalist opened several concerts for the Beatles on their 1965 US tour, including their Shea Stadium show. In 1967 Holloway cowrote and recorded the original version of "You've Made Me So Very Happy," later a gigantic hit for Blood, Sweat & Tears. —*Bill Dahl*

Every Little Bit Hurts / 1964 / Motown ✦✦✦
The title track was one of Motown's grittiest singles ever, but it didn't put Brenda Holloway into the spotlight she deserved. Her sound and style were so gospel-tinged and powerful that she was out of place on a label that wanted more polished, sophisticated material. This album had some marvelous classics and stands as Holloway's finest. While Motown had many other superb soul artists, Holloway may have been one who'd have done better at Stax or any of the Southern outlets who specialized in rawer, "deep" country and gospel-tinged productions. —*Ron Wynn*

Artistry of / 1968 / Motown ✦✦✦

● **Greatest Hits & Rare Classics** / 1991 / Motown ✦✦✦✦
Brenda Holloway was Motown's second big solo female star, but she spent even less time at the label than Mary Wells. A hard-edged, gospel-tinged belter, Holloway scored two Top 20 hits in the mid-'60s with "Every Little Bit Hurts" and "When I'm Gone," and her single "You've Made Me So Very Happy" was later a huge smash for Blood, Sweat & Tears. Holloway lasted on Motown until 1967, then departed after becoming a born-again Christian. This album includes her biggest singles for Tamla, plus some other good, though not necessarily classic, 1960s soul numbers. —*Ron Wynn*

Brand New / Birthright ✦✦

Buddy Holly (Charles Hardin Holley)

b. Sep. 7, 1936, Lubbock, TX, d. Feb. 3, 1959, Mason City, IA
Rock & Roll, Rockabilly
An enormously important and influential performer, Buddy Holly started in his native Texas doing country music with boyhood friend Bob Montgomery, eventually adding R&B numbers to the

set list after meeting Elvis Presley. He recorded early rockabilly sides in Nashville, resulting in the Decca singles "Blue Days, Black Nights" (April 1956) and "Modern Don Juan" (December 1956). But success didn't come until he formed the Crickets and recorded in Norman Petty's New Mexico studio, producing the number one hit "That'll Be the Day" (May 1957). Holly and Petty experimented in the studio, utilizing double-tracking ("Words of Love" [June 1957]), different forms of echo ("Peggy Sue" [September 1957], a second gold-selling Top Ten hit), and close-miking techniques, now commonplace in the industry. Holly recorded under his own name and the name of the Crickets interchangeably ("That'll Be the Day" was credited to the group, "Peggy Sue" to him alone). With the Crickets, he had the further chart hits "Oh, Boy!" (October 1957) (another Top Ten), "Maybe Baby" (February 1958), and "Think It Over"/"Fool's Paradise" (May 1958), while "Rave On" (April 1958) was a Holly "solo" hit.

Holly went solo for real during 1958, however, marrying and re-locating to New York. He charted with "Early in the Morning" (July 1958) and "Heartbeat" (November 1958), and released "It Doesn't Matter Anymore"/"Raining in My Heart" (January 1959) before embarking on the Winter Dance Party package tour, during which, on February 3, he, the Big Bopper, and Ritchie Valens were killed in an airplane crash.

After Holly's death, much of his earlier pre-Crickets music was overdubbed by Petty, using the Fireballs, to keep up with fan demand for more product. In England, where "It Doesn't Matter Anymore" went to number one in the wake of his death, Holly continued to score hits through the mid-'60s, and he exerted tremendous influence on the developing beat groups both for his music and for his self-contained approach to his work—writing his own songs, playing them with his own group. As late as 1978, Holly could still top the U.K. charts with a hits collection, *20 Golden Greats*.

Buddy Holly's moment in the spotlight lasted barely 18 months, and the movie version of his life story only got it about half right, but his music still sounds fresh and continues to influence musicians to this day. —*Cub Koda & William Ruhlmann*

○ **The Chirping Crickets** / 1957 / MCA ✦✦✦✦
○ **Buddy Holly** / 1958 / MCA ✦✦✦✦
☆ **The Complete Buddy Holly** / 1979 / MCA ✦✦✦✦✦
Containing every note Buddy Holly ever recorded, this six-LP box is essential for hardcore fans. —*John Floyd*
○ **For the First Time Anywhere** / 1983 / MCA ✦✦✦✦
Powerful undubbed rockabilly sides. —*Cub Koda*
★ **The From the Original Master Tapes** / 1985 / MCA ✦✦✦✦✦
A 20-track best-of with superlative sound. —*Cub Koda*
Something Special from Buddy Holly / 1986 / Rollercoaster ✦✦✦
An import of more undubbed material from 1956. —*Cub Koda*
☆ **The Buddy Holly Collection** / 1993 / MCA ✦✦✦✦✦
The first comprehensive, remastered CD retrospective of Holly's work, including early tracks recorded in the Holly family garage, the Owen Bradley-produced singles, all the rockin' hits, orchestrated ballads, and tracks overdubbed with instrumentation after Holly's tragic death. Two discs, solid liner notes. —*Roch Parisien*

BOOK

✦✦✦✦ **Remembering Buddy**, by John Goldrosen & John Beecher (Penguin, 1987). One of the best rock biographies, tracing Buddy Holly's life from his roots in Lubbock, TX, through his success with the Crickets and his premature death in 1959. Both extremely well-written and extremely detailed, with lots of room for the Crickets and Buddy's family to tell stories and express their opinions. Producer Norman Petty also weighs in with views of the sessions, finances, and songwriting credits that, after several decades, often directly contradict those of the Crickets. Goldrosen brings an authoritative, enthusiastic, and balanced critical perspective to the work, paying special attention to Holly's innovations as a songwriter and a performer determined to establish creative control of the production of his recordings. This book is especially essential reading in light of the fact that many listeners got a substantially different, and often inaccurate, picture of Buddy's life through the film *The Buddy Holly Story*; this sets the record straight. Look for the 1987 edition, which includes lots of vintage photos and a complete discography added by Beecher. —*Richie Unterberger*

Hollywood Flames

Group, Doo-Wop
Long-lasting Los Angeles doo-wop aggregation with a very fluid personnel roster. Bobby Day was one of the group's founders in 1950, and they recorded prolifically for Hollywood, Specialty, Lucky, Swingtime, Money, and other firms before cutting their one major hit, the rocking "Buzz Buzz Buzz," in 1957 for Ebb Records. Earl Nelson, who was later half of Bob and Earl, sang lead on the tune, and some of their subsequent Ebb 45s were rocking novelties. Day went on to solo success with "Rockin' Robin," and the group managed one more chart item, "Gee," for Chess in 1961 with Donald Height as lead. —*Bill Dahl*

● **The Hollywood Flames** / 1992 / Specialty ✦✦✦✦
Rockers and doo-wop are included from this respected West Coast '50s R&B vocal group, including the Top Ten "Buzz Buzz Buzz." —*Bill Dahl*
○ **Buzz Buzz Buzz** / Specialty ✦✦✦✦

Eddie Holman

Soul
Holman's 1970 number two smash "Hey There Lonely Girl," with its creamy falsetto vocals and lush Philadelphia soul arrangement, is one of the most well-remembered one-shot soul hits. Actually, Holman had been recording since the early '60s, scoring some minor hits with "This Can't Be True" (1965) and "Am I a Loser (From the Start)" (1966). In 1969, he hooked up with Philadelphia producer Peter DeAngelis, best known for his work with teen idols Fabian and Frankie Avalon. His arrangements for Holman, however, rivaled Gamble & Huff's in quality, yielding some other minor R&B hits in 1969 and 1970 with "I Love You," "Don't Stop Now," and "Cathy Called," as well as a decent album in 1970. Most identified with his rich falsetto, Holman actually sang in a much more traditional vocal range on much of his material, some of which was written by himself or his wife Sheila. He largely vanished from sight after 1970, though he recorded for several labels in the 1970s. —*Richie Unterberger*

I Love You / 1970 / Varese Sarabande ✦✦✦
First-class romantic soul, featuring Holman's swooping vocals and lush Philly string and backup vocal arrangements. Includes "Hey There Lonely Girl" and his other minor R&B hits from the same period. The CD reissue adds three non-LP cuts from 1969 and 1970 singles. —*Richie Unterberger*

Holsapple-Stamey

Group, Power Pop/Anglo-Pop
Peter Holsapple and Chris Stamey were two of the principal singer/songwriters from the alternative power-pop band, the dB's. Much of the music from this collaboration is thoughtfully upbeat, guitar-driven folk-pop, with a few stylistic tips of the hat to the Byrds, Big Star, and mid-period Beatles. —*Rick Clark*

○ **Mavericks** / 1991 / Rhino ✦✦✦✦
A charming low-key power-pop effort, "Geometry" is a perfect Gary Lewis & the Playboys-style sendup. "Angels" is pure power-pop magic. The softer acoustic numbers, "Close Your Eyes" and "Anymore," recall the duo's work on Repercussions. —*Rick Clark*

Honey Cone

Group, Soul
This female trio formed in Los Angeles in 1969. They were all experienced background vocalists. Carolyn Willis had been in the Girlfriends and Bob B.Soxx & the Blue Jeans; Edna Wright was Darlene Love's sister and had sung in the Blossoms and Bob B.Soxx & the Blue Jeans; and Shellie Clark had been an Ikette and regular on *The Jim Nabors Hour* in 1969 and 1970. They were signed by legendary songwriters Holland—Dozier—Holland to their Hot Wax label. They had their first major hit in 1969 with "Girls It Ain't Easy," then garnered two consecutive R&B chart toppers in 1971 with "Want Ads" and "Stick-Up." "Want Ads" proved a '70s standard, also topping the pop charts. The Honey Cone scored two more R&B hits, "One Monkey Don't Stop No Show" and "The Day I Found Myself" in 1971 and 1972, before things began to slow down. They continued on Hot Wax through 1972. Wright later recorded as a solo act. —*Ron Wynn*

● **Greatest Hits** / HDH ✦✦✦✦

The Honeycombs

Group, British Invasion

Mostly renowned for their 1964 Top Five hit "Have I the Right," the Honeycombs were pretty much a front for producer Joe Meek and their songwriting-management team of Ken Howard and Alan Blaikley. With bee-sting guitar leads and lead singer Dennis D'Ell's wobbling vocals, which sounded like a Gene Pitney unable to hold notes, "Have I the Right" was a single that you either loved or hated, but couldn't forget. The relatively faceless group afforded Meek perhaps his fullest artistic expression in the studio; all the Honeycombs' singles and albums feature vari-speed vocals, ghostly organ, unpredictable clavoline runs, majestically thudding drums, and super-compressed sonics. The group managed a couple more minor American hits, "Is It Because" and the thrilling "I Can't Stop," as well as another British Top 20 hit, "That's the Way," and cut quite a few singles and two albums before Meek's death in early 1967 effectively finished the group as well. The Honeycombs' material can be annoyingly cloying and lightweight, but the eerie melodies and production continue to fascinate. *—Richie Unterberger*

● **The Honeycombs** / 1964 / Repertoire ✦✦✦✦

Most famed for their 1964 one-shot British Invasion hit "Have I the Right" and for being the first local band of any renown to feature a female drummer, the Honeycombs recorded a surprising amount of material in the mid-'60s. Even for collectors, this definitely falls into the "guilty pleasure" category. Lead singer Dennis O'Dell's wobbly voice sounds like a speeded-up Gene Pitney, and the material, though peppy and catchy, is exceedingly trite and innocuous. The group's chief asset, actually, was producer Joe Meek, who found the band to be a perfect vehicle for his eccentric production techniques. Meek used compression to the point of squashing, and used all manners of odd varispeed vocals, bee-stinging guitars, tinny keyboards, and echo to achieve a sound that was quite otherworldly by 1964 standards. Besides "Have I the Right," this 1964 debut LP includes the British Top 20 hit "That's the Way" (featuring drummer Honey Lantree on vocals) and the ghostly ballads "Without You It Is Night" and "This Too Shall Pass Away," though most of the rest of the material is slight. This 1990 reissue adds seven bonus tracks from non-LP singles, including a German recording of "Have I the Right" and the manic, irresistible "I Can't Stop," which was a minor hit for the band in the U.S. *—Richie Unterberger*

All Systems Go / 1965 / Repertoire ✦✦✦

Despite downwardly spiraling commercial fortunes, the Honeycombs recorded a second album in 1965 that featured as many intriguing production flourishes and oddball British pop songs as their first effort. No hits were included on this LP—and be warned that the version of their minor hit single "I Can't Stop" (probably their best song) featured here is an inferior, drastically slower remake. This album also includes a mighty obscure ballad by Ray Davies, "Emptiness," that was never recorded by the Kinks (or any other artist but the Honeycombs, for that matter). It's not much of a song, but it's a find for Kinks fanatics. The record's highlights are the sparkling guitars of "Love In Tokyo" and the soulful ballad "Something I Got to Tell You" (featuring drummer Honey Lantree on vocals), which sounds like an honest-to-god hit-that-never-was. The CD reissue of the album adds six non-LP cuts from 1965-66 singles. The best of these are the tense, overwrought ballad "Should a Man Cry?" and the uptempo "Can't Get Through to You," on which producer Joe Meek took his varispeed vocals and neurotic rhythms to their farthest extremes. *—Richie Unterberger*

Best Of The Honeycombs / 1988 / PRT ✦✦✦

The German Repertoire label has reissued both of the Honeycombs' studio LPs with bonus tracks; oddly, they don't include quite a few of the group's A-sides. All six of those missing singles can be found on this reissue, along with most of their other best-known songs. Two of these A-sides are standouts: "Is It Because," a small hit in the U.K., is a driving number, and "Eyes" one of the spookiest productions from a man (Joe Meek) who specialized in them. If you pick up this up thinking you'll forego the fanatically repackaged CDs for a 14-song greatest hits collection of this interesting but minor British Invasion band, be warned: the version of "I Can't Stop," the minor U.S. hit that was their best song, included here is not the original, but an inferior remake from their second album. *—Richie Unterberger*

The Honeydrippers

Group, Rock & Roll

The Honeydrippers were an ad hoc group put together by ex-Led Zeppelin lead singer Robert Plant and Atlantic Records executive Ahmet Ertegun to record a mini-album of '50s and '60s oldies in 1984. *—William Ruhlmann*

○ **The Honeydrippers, Vol. 1** / 1984 / Es Paranza ✦✦✦✦

Five-song EP features Robert Plant singing such oldies as the hit remake of "Sea of Love," with a backup that includes Nile Rodgers, Jeff Beck, and Jimmy Page. *—William Ruhlmann*

The Hoodoo Gurus

Group, Alternative Pop/Rock, Power Pop/Anglo-Pop

Australian kings of garage Anglo-pop/rock, the Hoodoo Gurus provided the '80s alternative music scene with a handful of fine trashy, tuneful classics in "Bittersweet," "Poison Pen," "Like Wow—Wipeout," "What's My Scene," "Come Anytime," and "Where Nowhere Is," among others. They incorporated the grunge of the Cramps with the '60s melodic pop-smarts of groups like the Kinks and the Turtles. *—Rick Clark*

○ **Stoneage Romeos** / 1983 / A&M ✦✦✦✦

Their debut effort is to garage-punk heaven. Highlights include the raveups "Let's All Turn On" and "Tojo"; "Dig It Up," a Cramps-style rocker; "My Girl," a slice of '60s girl/boy guitar-pop; and the grunge-ola "I Was a Kamikaze Pilot." Highly recommended. *—Rick Clark*

● **Mars Needs Guitars** / 1985 / Elektra ✦✦✦✦

This is the album that gave this Aussie band their break on the American college radio market, thanks to some classic tracks, "Bittersweet," "Poison Pen," "Death Defying," and "Like Wow-Wipe-out." The production is a little unfocused, lacking some of the punch the material demands and the trashy sparks of *Stoneage Romeos*. Nevertheless, the songs reflect considerable growth in the band's vision. *—Rick Clark*

○ **Blow Your Cool!** / 1987 / Elektra ✦✦✦✦

The Gurus alternate between appealing tuneful updates of Turtles-style guitar-pop ("Good Times," "What's My Scene") and wild workouts like "Where Nowhere Is" and "Hell for Leather." The anthemic "I Was the One" is a standout. The Bangles assist on backup harmonies on this effort. All in all, it's a solid effort. *—Rick Clark*

Magnum Cum Louder / 1989 / RCA ✦✦✦

The Gurus continue their once-every-two-year release schedule with this consistent effort that showcases vocalist Dave Faulkner's solid songwriting. "Come Anytime" is primo Gurus and the moody "Shadow Me" is also a highlight. Even though *Magnum Cum Louder* doesn't shine as brightly as previous efforts, it's still a stronger album than many efforts by groups mining this genre. *—Rick Clark*

Kinky / 1991 / RCA ✦✦✦

Kinky blasts out of the gate with pedal-to-the-metal speed, on the hard rocking put-down of substance abuse, "Head in the Sand." No doubt the inebriated fraternity crowd that worships this band will appreciate Faulkner's sentiments. All in all, this is one of the band's very best releases. *Kinky* portrays a band straddling their playful '60s garage rock esthetic with issues of adulthood, all the while playing as fiercely as ever. *—Rick Clark*

● **Electric Soup** / 1992 / RCA ✦✦✦✦

Gorilla Biscuit/B-Sides and Rarities / 1993 / RCA ✦✦✦

Crank / 1994 / Pavement ✦✦

Hootie & The Blowfish

Group, Pop/Rock

Hootie & the Blowfish's mainstream pop variation of blues-rock brought the band to the top of the charts in 1995. Formed at the University of South Carolina, the group features lead vocalist/guitarist Darius Rucker, Mark Bryan, Dean Felber, and Jim "Soni" Sonefeld; the name refers to two friends of the band, not Rucker and the group itself. *Cracked Rear View*, the group's first album was released in the fall of 1994 and a single, "Hold My Hand," worked its way into the Top Ten by the beginning of 1995. Its success propelled the album to number one, as well as launching a second hit, "Let Her Cry." *—Stephen Thomas Erlewine*

○ **Cracked Rear View** / 1994 / Atlantic ◆◆◆◆

Mary Hopkin
Pop, Folk-Rock
It was the British supermodel Twiggy who alerted Paul McCartney to the Welsh singer Mary Hopkin when Apple Records was looking for talent in 1968. The waifish soprano scored a huge, worldwide smash with her first Apple single, the melancholy but rabble-rousing ballad "Those Were the Days," in late 1968; it actually knocked the Beatles' own "Hey Jude" out of the number one position in the U.K. Paul McCartney lent Hopkin a further hand by producing her first album, and writing her second single, "Goodbye," which was also a hit. More comfortable with refined, precious ballads and folky pop than rock, Hopkin scored several more hit singles in the U.K., although she never entered the American Top 40 again. Her commercial success diminished as Apple's fortunes dwindled in the early '70s. —*Richie Unterberger*

● **Post Card** / 1969 / Capitol ◆◆◆◆
Paul McCartney produced this debut album of twee but pretty, romantic pop-folk. Besides "Those Were the Days," the highlights are Donovan's "Lord of the Reedy River" and "The Honeymoon Song," which Paul himself had sung with the Beatles way back in 1963 on the BBC. —*Richie Unterberger*

○ **Earth Song, Ocean Song** / 1971 / Capitol ◆◆◆◆

Those Were the Days / 1972 / Apple ◆◆◆

Nicky Hopkins
d. Sep. 6, 1994
Rock & Roll
Check the credits on any number of rock albums from the late '60s through the '80s, especially Rolling Stones albums, and you'll come across the name Nicky Hopkins. For almost two decades, he was the most in-demand session pianist in rock; the Beatles, Kinks, Who, Jeff Beck Group, Steve Miller Band, Jefferson Airplane—there was hardly a major rock band in the world that hadn't benefited from Hopkins' deft touch at the keyboards. Born in London in 1944, Hopkins honed his chops with Screaming Lord Sutch and British bluesmeister Cyril Davies before producer Shel Talmy absconded with him to provide keyboards on early Kinks and Who albums. Hopkins' biggest break was in 1967, when he worked with the Stones on *Their Satanic Majesties Request*; it was the start of a professional relationship with the band that would last until 1980. Hopkins only recorded three solo albums, the second of which, *The Tin Man Was a Dreamer*, was a surprisingly solid, engaging record that, frankly, no one thought he was capable of recording. Frail and often in ill health, Hopkins never toured much, preferring the studio to the road. Sadly, his chronic health problems culminated in his death in October 1994. —*John Dougan*

Revolutionary Piano / 1966 / CBS ◆◆

Jamming with Edward! / 1971 / Rolling Stones ◆

● **The Tin Man Was a Dreamer** / 1973 / Columbia ◆◆◆◆
Hopkins' best solo effort. With help from luminaries George Harrison and then-Rolling Stones guitarist Mick Taylor, *Tin Man* is a subtle, understated yet admirable record that will win you over with its low-key charm. Long out-of-print, but a fine, if nearly completely forgotten record. —*John Dougan*

No More Changes / 1976 / Mercury ◆◆

Bruce Hornsby & the Range
Group, Pop/Rock
Hornsby was born in Williamsburg, VA, and grew up in that combination college town and tourist center, later attending the University of Miami and the Berklee School of Music. He then spent years playing in bars and sending demo tapes to record companies. In 1980, he and his brother (and songwriting partner) John Hornsby moved to Los Angeles, where they spent three years writing for 20th Century Fox. There Bruce Hornsby met Huey Lewis, who would eventually produce him and record his material. Hornsby finally signed his band, the Range, to RCA in 1985.

Their debut album, *The Way It Is*, was released in August 1986. It eventually produced three Top 20 hits, the biggest of which was the socially conscious "The Way It Is," which featured Hornsby's characteristically melodic right-hand piano runs. The album stayed in the charts almost a year and a half, and sold two million

copies. Hornsby and the Range won the Best New Artist Grammy Award for 1986.

Hornsby's second album, *Scenes from the Southside*, was not as successful as his debut, though it sold a million copies, and produced the Top Ten single "The Valley Road." Hornsby also began to make his mark as a songwriter for others: Huey Lewis had a hit with his "Jacob's Ladder," as did Don Henley with "The End of the Innocence."

Hornsby's third album, *A Night on the Town* (1990), found him trying to break out of his signature sound into other areas. It was less successful than its predecessors but, along with the pianist's extensive session work, it signaled his determination to tackle new musical challenges. —*William Ruhlmann*

● **The Way It Is** / Aug. 1986 / RCA ◆◆◆◆
One of the best collections of new songs released in the 1980s, performed to perfection by a versatile band led by a seasoned (if new to the listener) artist. The songs provide an American panorama, in terms both of landscape and social mores. This is smart, compassionate music for thinking adults...and you can dance to it too. Includes "The Way It Is" and "Mandolin Rain." —*William Ruhlmann*

○ **Scenes from the Southside** / 1988 / RCA ◆◆◆◆
The Way It Is, part two, featuring some wonderful story songs, not only on the hits "Jacob's Ladder" and "The Valley Road" but also "Defenders of the Flag" and "The Road Not Taken." Hornsby continues to mine a rich American vein on this album. —*William Ruhlmann*

A Night on the Town / Jun. 1990 / RCA ◆◆◆
Hornsby's third album found him trying to break out of his signature sound into other areas. It was less successful than its predecessors but, along with the pianist's extensive session work, it signaled his determination to tackle new musical challenges. —*William Ruhlmann*

Harbor Lights / 1993 / RCA ◆◆◆
Bruce Hornsby dumped the Range with barely any public notice. Yet there is a difference in the music; more than any other Hornsby record, *Harbor Lights* is about playing. It's short on memorable songs and heavy on jazz improvisations. In short, Hornsby has taken the chops he has always had, honed them during his live shows with the Grateful Dead, and applied what he learned to adult contemporary radio. —*Stephen Thomas Erlewine*

Hot House / 1995 / RCA ◆◆◆
With 1993's *Harbor Lights*, Bruce Hornsby began abandoning the conventional pop/rock structures that had dominated his songwriting, turning toward an open-ended jazz-pop fusion. *Hot House* continues that direction, abandoning the three-to-four minute singles for longer pieces that showcases his musical skills. It's an impressive exercise that would be even more engaging if the actual songs had stronger melodies. —*Stephen Thomas Erlewine*

Hot Chocolate
Group, Soul, Funk
An interracial English funk and soul group, Hot Chocolate scored a pair of huge hits in the '70s, but were otherwise more enthusiastic than skilled. Lead singer Erroll Brown, guitarist Harvey Hinsley, keyboardist Larry Ferguson, bassist Tony Wilson, drummer Tony Connor, and conga player Patrick Olive were the original lineup. They recorded for Big Tree from 1975 to 1978, scoring a Top Ten R&B and pop hit with "You Sexy Thing" in 1975, which also was a gold single. They repeated the trick in 1978 with "Every 1's a Winner," once more earning a gold single in the process. No other Hot Chocolate song ever made it beyond number 40 on the R&B chart, and their albums never packed much commercial punch either. Wilson departed in 1975, and Olive switched to bass in his place. —*Ron Wynn*

● **The Very Best of Hot Chocolate** / 1993 / EMI ◆◆◆◆
British soul band Hot Chocolate were known mainly by Americans for their huge 1975 hit "You Sexy Thing." But this 19-song anthology reveals that the band deserves more attention than they received. Lead singer Erroll Brown was not only good with catchy dance tunes, but could deliver on romantic ballads, novelty tunes, inspirational material, or even message pieces such as "A Child's Prayer." The group was ahead of its time in other ways, having a racially mixed lineup in an era of increasing polarization, and also including reggae and rock elements in their production and sound. —*Ron Wynn*

Hot Tuna

Group, Rock & Roll, Blues Rock, Folk-Rock

Hot Tuna (formed October 1970) was an offshoot group led by Jefferson Airplane-guitarist Jorma Kaukonen and bassist Jack Casady. The group's self-titled debut was a live recording that covered versions of old blues tunes by Rev. Gary Davis and Jelly Roll Morton, as well as some originals that became required listening for those inclined toward the Airplane or Grateful Dead's more laidback material.

By the third album, *Burgers,* Hot Tuna increasingly drew upon their rock background, performing extended jams built around Casady's wide, lumbering bass sound and Kaukonen's tastefully texturous lead work. Even though the band seemed perpetually stuck in medium tempo, they were quite capable of generating sparks, which made them a popular concert draw for a number of years. — *Rick Clark*

○ **Hot Tuna** / 1970 / RCA ✦✦✦✦
This live set includes some solid originals, in particular the instrumental "Mann's Fate" and versions of tunes by Mississippi John Hurt and Rev. Gary Davis. Jorma Kaukonen contributes exceptionally tasteful acoustic-guitar work. Highlights include "Hesitation Blues" and "Death Don't Have No Mercy." — *Rick Clark*

First Pull Up, Then Pull Down / 1971 / RCA ✦✦✦
While the first Hot Tuna album had been an acoustic trio album featuring Jorma Kaukonen, Jack Casady, and Will Scarlet, this second album added violinist Papa John Creach and drummer Sammy Piazza, and most significant, it added electricity. Now, the sound was closer to Kaukonen's features in Jefferson Airplane. The highlight was the eight-minute "Keep Your Lamps Trimmed and Burning," although "Candy Man" also became a concert favorite. — *William Ruhlmann*

● **Burgers** / 1972 / RCA ✦✦✦✦
On this third effort, Hot Tuna turned in some blistering jams with "Sea Child" and "Sunny Day Strut." "Water Song" is a gorgeous instrumental, featuring some wonderful acoustic guitar and electric-bass interplay. David Crosby guests on background vocals. "Keep on Truckin'" was a moderate underground FM hit. — *Rick Clark*

The Phosphorescent Rat / 1973 / RCA ✦✦✦
Hot Tuna's first album made after the breakup of Jefferson Airplane found Jorma Kaukonen taking a firm hand: he's the author of nine out of ten songs. The walking tempos and familiar soaring, psychedelic guitar solos are in place, but much of the music is given over to Kaukonen's reflective lyrics, sung in his matter-of-fact voice, and there are strings on a couple of tracks. The group's fans, devoted as they were to its extended versions of blues standards, seem to have been unimpressed: the album was Hot Tuna's lowest-charting among those released during its 1970-1978 heyday. Probably a lack of enthusiasm at RCA, due to the demise of Jefferson Airplane, didn't help in the album's promotion, either. — *William Ruhlmann*

America's Choice / 1975 / RCA ✦✦✦
Hot Tuna returned to a heavier sound on their fifth album, which, although it again was dominated by Jorma Kaukonen's compositions, leaned more heavily on extended electric guitar solos and even included a Robert Johnson classic, "Walkin' Blues." Drummer Bob Steeler replaced Sammy Piazza as of this release. The result was a modest recovery from the disappointing sales of *The Phosphorescent Rat,* although not a complete return to form. — *William Ruhlmann*

Yellow Fever / 1975 / RCA ✦✦✦
Hot Tuna's second album of 1975 began with a cover of Jimmy Reed's "Baby, What You Want Me To Do" rendered in the group's characteristic noisy electric guitar style, an approach that was typical of this more-of-the-same album. By this point, Jorma Kaukonen seemed to have found a balance between his songwriting ambitions and the need to provide springboards for the group's boogie-all-night improvisations. Here, "Sunrise Dance with the Devil" and "Bar Room Crystal Ball" feature good lyrics and excellent hooks, yet still fit into Hot Tuna's heavy approach. — *William Ruhlmann*

Hoppkorv / 1976 / Grunt ✦✦✦
Unlike recent Hot Tuna albums, *Hoppkorv* found the group acting less as a mouthpiece for guitarist Jorma Kaukonen's compositions and more as a heavy rock cover band, handling such familiar material as Buddy Holly's "It's So Easy" and Chuck Berry's "Talkin' 'Bout You," although "Watch the North Wind Rise" was one of

Kaukonen's better tunes. Even on the originals, the tempo had picked up, the arrangements were shorter; nothing here ran as long as five minutes, and the sound had been filled out by the occasional addition of keyboards, second guitar, and background vocals. So, *Hoppkorv* was closer to a straightforward pop-rock album than many Hot Tuna releases, and for that, predictably, it got higher marks from critics, who appreciated the variety, and lower marks from Tuna fans, who found less music to boogie to. — *William Ruhlmann*

Double Dose / 1978 / Grunt ✦✦✦
Hot Tuna, now a quartet with the official addition of keyboardist Nick Buck, released this two-LP live album, its first concert material in seven years, and having thus summed things up, broke up as the album hit record stores. *Double Dose* gave a good sense of mature Hot Tuna as a vehicle for the musical interests of Jorma Kaukonen, who used the entire first side as an acoustic solo set, then included the excellent "Genesis" from his solo album *Quah* on Side B. Elsewhere, the electrified group alternated between Kaukonen's best Hot Tuna compositions and blues and rock standards. It was produced by Felix Pappalardi (Cream, Mountain), who gave Hot Tuna its best recorded sound; even though it's a "live" record, there seems to have been a lot of studio overdubbing. — *William Ruhlmann*

Final Vinyl / 1979 / Grunt ✦✦✦

Splashdown / 1984 / Relix ✦✦✦
This archival release is taken from a broadcast on New York radio station WQIV-FM on July 25, 1975, and features the duo of guitarist Jorma Kaukonen playing acoustic and bassist Jack Casady performing at the station. At the time, Hot Tuna recently had released its *America's Choice* album, but this set harks back to the group's 1970 debut album, *Hot Tuna,* both in its acoustic format and in the selection of mostly folk-blues standards. The performance also has an informality and intimacy that rivals the debut. Casual fans are likely to find the album redundant, but more fervent followers rejoiced when this album appeared nine years after the broadcast occurred and five years after the group's apparent demise. The album's title is derived from the re-entry of an Apollo spacecraft during the broadcast, which is mixed in with the performance of "Police Dog Blues." — *William Ruhlmann*

Historic Hot Tuna / 1985 / Relix ✦✦
Relix's second Hot Tuna release was another archival work, its two sides containing two KSAN-FM radio broadcasts from the spring and summer of 1971; one side was taped at the station, the other chronicles the band's appearance at the closing of the Fillmore West. In his liner notes, Jorma Kaukonen acknowledges that the band has encountered criticism for releasing such "so-called antique material," but counters that "If you like it, you like it...if you don't you don't." Hard-core Tuna fans will be pleased with the existence on record of these performances by a Hot Tuna that featured Kaukonen (acoustic guitar on Side One, electric on Side Two), Jack Casady, Papa John Creach, and Sammy Piazza. Others may find that the rudimentary sound quality and the generally restrained performing level render this inessential. — *William Ruhlmann*

Pair a Dice Found / 1990 / Epic ✦✦
Hot Tuna's first new album release in more than a decade, *Pair a Dice Found* was perhaps the band's most commercial, yet poorest selling, major-label effort. Unlike the Hot Tuna of the 1970s, this edition, again fronted by guitarist Jorma Kaukonen and bassist Jack Casady, was not a groove-oriented showcase for Kaukonen's songwriting and guitar prowess on old blues standards. Instead, Kaukonen had only three compositions on the record, while the closest thing to the old repertoire was the Jesse Fuller nugget "San Francisco Bay Blues." Second guitarist Michael Falzarano, in contrast, had five songs, and there was even a cover of the old Barry McGuire folk-rock protest hit "Eve of Destruction." Tuna fans ignored the release, and Epic failed to woo the new audience for whom the record seemed to be intended. — *William Ruhlmann*

Hothouse Flowers

Group, Pop/Rock

At the end of the '80s, Ireland's Hothouse Flowers was one of the most popular groups on the British Isles, with their larger-than-life blend of U2 and Van Morrison. Liam O'Maonlai fronts the band with a commanding passionate vocal presence, but sometimes their overwrought mega-production sound tends to reduce them to a variation of Commitments-style soul. Their first album, *Peo-*

ple, contains some fine moments: "Don't Go," "Forgiven," "Yes I Was," and the single "I'm Sorry." —*Rick Clark*

● **People** / 1988 / London ✦✦✦✦
This Irish sensation shoots for the big mystical picture, not unlike U2. Musically, it owes more to Van Morrison and various R&B rock influences. This debut is fairly solid from start to finish. Highlights are the prayerful "Forgiven," the affirmative "Yes I Was," and the exuberant hit single "I'm Sorry." —*Rick Clark*

Home / 1990 / London ✦✦✦

Songs from the Rain / 1993 / London ✦✦✦
Dublin's Hothouse Flowers deliver a colorful aural bouquet on third release *Songs from the Rain*, despite the greyish album title. The disc's highlight is "Isn't It Amazing," with loping rhythms, devotional lyrics and anthemic vocal chorus rendered with understated passion. Another personal favorite on the disc is the galloping "Spirit of the Land"—even if the wailing vocal finale evokes the heavy, pseudo-mystical rock of early-'70s Uriah Heep. —*Roch Parisien*

House of Love

Group, Alternative Pop/Rock
The post-Smiths guitar-pop of the House of Love was popular for a short time in the late '80s, as many college and alternative-rock fans became converts to their mixture of shiny ringing guitars, pseudo-psychedelic melodies and bursts of noise. The British group formed in 1986; it featured Guy Chadwick (vocals, guitar), Terry Bickers (guitar), Andrea Heukamp (vocals, guitar), Pete Evans (drums), and Chris Groothuizen (bass). Their demo tape attracted the attention of Alan McGee, the head of Creation Records. McGee signed the band for a single, "Shine On," which was released in May of 1987 to some critical acclaim; and its follow-up, "Real Animal," both sold poorly. Following a tour supporting the singles, Heukamp left the group. Instead of replacing her, the House of Love continued as a quartet, releasing their untitled debut album in the spring of 1988. Many U.K. critics called it one of the finest records of the year, and the band built up a cult audience.

The following year the band moved over to PhonoGram Records (PolyGram in the U.S.) and released two singles, "Never" and "I Don't Know Why I Love You," that failed to crack the British Top 40. By the end of 1989, Bickers left the group; he was replaced by Simon Walker. The House of Love's second untitled album (commonly called *Fontana*) was released in early 1990 to lukewarm sales and reviews; the band's revivalist guitar-pop didn't fit in with England's club-conscious pop scene, spearheaded by the Stone Roses and Happy Mondays. After the 1990 tour, Walker left the group and was replaced by Andrea Heukamp. The House of Love returned in early 1992 with *Babe Rainbow*, which received favorable reviews yet weak sales. The continuing lack of commercial success began to wear on the band, leading to their disbandment in 1994. —*Stephen Thomas Erlewine*

● **House of Love ['88]** / 1988 / Combat ✦✦✦✦
This brilliant debut established a pattern oft-imitated: a layered, swirling, guitar sound and outstanding songs as well. —*Steve Aldrich*

House of Love ['90] / 1990 / Fontana ✦✦✦
This is a German collection of early singles. —*Steve Aldrich*

Spy in the House of Love / 1990 / Fontana ✦✦✦
This is a collection of B-sides, outtakes, etc. —*Steve Aldrich*

Babe Rainbow / 1992 / Fontana ✦✦✦
Three albums back, House of Love was among the first to mine that distinctively British sound of fragile pop harmonies coupled to fuzzy, feedback-drenched guitars. Now that every other U.K. alternative music group is doing that very thing, House of Love has evolved. Superb, understated melodies still dominate *Babe Rainbow*, but the instrumentation is much more free-flowing and accessible. *Babe Rainbow* is the soundtrack to one of those grey-mood days that leaves you hanging in the balance somewhere between elation and despair. —*Roch Parisien*

Audience with the Mind / 1994 / PolyGram 3145 ✦✦

House of Pain

Group, Rap
This Irish rap ensemble headed by former Rhythm Syndicate member Everlast vaulted into national stardom in 1992 with "Jump Around" from their self-titled debut LP. After weathering

criticism about their hip-hop integrity, they returned in 1994 with harder, funkier *Same as It Ever Was*. —*Ron Wynn*

● **House of Pain** / 1992 / Tommy Boy ✦✦✦✦
It would be hard for nearly anyone to top the explosive, insanely catchy "Jump Around," so it's no great surprise to find that House of Pain isn't up to the task. At times, HOP comes close to duplicating the intoxicating power of their slamming single, but for the most part, their debut album is a repetitive circle of similar beats, misogyny, racism, and posturing lyrics. But the perfection of "Jump Around" almost makes up for the numerous faults. —*Stephen Thomas Erlewine*

○ **Same as It Ever Was** / 1994 / Tommy Boy ✦✦✦✦
House of Pain's second album finds the group getting harder, adding elements of jazz and dirty, street-oriented funk to their sound. *Same as It Ever Was* may not have a hit the size of "Jump Around"—and it may be plagued by misogynist lyrics—but it's a more focused, impressive effort. —*Stephen Thomas Erlewine*

Housemartins

Group, Alternative Pop/Rock
The Housemartins were formed in Hull, England, in 1984 and included singer/guitarist Paul Heaton, bassist Stan Cullimore, drummer Hugh Witaker, and Ted Key. They signed to the independent Go! Discs label in October 1985. Shortly after, vocalist Norman Cook (b.Jul 31, 1963) replaced Key. The group's first substantial success came with its third single, "Happy Hour," which reached #3 in the U.K. in June 1986. The Housemartins' debut album, *London 0 Hull 4*, reached the same position in the album chart. More success followed with the singles "Think for a Minute" and the chart-topping cover of Isley-Jasper-Isley's "Caravan of Love."

In 1987, the Housemartins continued to hit in the U.K., while suffering adverse press and personnel conflicts that eventually convinced them to split in 1988. They released two more albums, *The People Who Grinned Themselves to Death* (1987) and *Now That's What I Call Quite Good* (1988), the latter a double-disc compilation that has not been released in the U.S. Heaton went on to form the Beautiful South. —*William Ruhlmann*

● **London 0 Hull 4** / 1986 / Go! Discs ✦✦✦✦
The Housemartins had a bouncy pop-rock sound that was reminiscent of the British beat groups of the mid-'60s. This album is full of catchy tunes, although the lyrics are sometimes more serious than the music might suggest. —*William Ruhlmann*

○ **People Who Grinned Themselves to Death** / 1987 / Go! Discs ✦✦✦✦
Not quite on par with their debut, their second album nevertheless contains some bright moments of bouncy Brit-pop. The band takes a more abstract lyrical approach but the song craftsmanship can't be denied. The band broke up shortly after its completion. —*Chris Woodstra*

○ **Now That's What I Call Quite Good** / 1988 / Go! Discs ✦✦✦✦
A solid collection of singles, B-sides and rarities released only in the U.K. This, combined with the two proper albums, represents nearly all of the band's recorded output. Clocking in at over 70 minutes, this is not a bad place to start, though the actual albums should be heard as well. —*Chris Woodstra*

Cissy Houston

Soul
A terrific soul singer who is known primarily as Whitney Houston's mother rather than for her own considerable talents, Houston was born Emily Drinkard, and began her career as a member of her family's gospel group, the Drinkards. In the early '60s, she joined forces with a floating group of singers, known simply as "the Group" (including at various points Doris Troy and Dee Dee Warwick), to provide backup vocals on numerous soul, pop, and rock sessions. They contributed to many Atlantic sessions in particular, and Atlantic executive Jerry Wexler signed the act to the label in 1967. Named the Sweet Inspirations, they recorded some excellent gospel-flavored soul in the late '60s, managing a few hits (as well as continuing to back up other artists, most notably Aretha Franklin) before Cissy left to go solo at the end of 1969. Houston recorded an impressive album for Commonwealth United in 1970, *Presenting Cissy Houston*, which yielded a couple small R&B/pop hits, "I'll Be There" and "Be My Baby." Much in the

manner of the Sweet Inspirations, although the material consisted of fairly well-worn soul, rock, and pop tunes, the state of-the-art arrangements and gospelish vocals made them sound fresh. Her contract was sold to Janus Records later in the year, and while she issued a few fine singles there until the middle of the 1970s, she never received the support and promotion she deserved. A case in point was her little-known original version of "Midnight Train to Georgia," taken to the top of the charts about a year later by Gladys Knight & the Pips. Houston recorded several albums for Private Stock beginning in the late '70s, as well as continuing her regular work on sessions and commercial jingles. She recorded a duet with daughter Whitney ("I Know Him So Well") in 1987, and cut a duet album with veteran soul singer Chuck Jackson in 1992. —*Richie Unterberger*

● **Midnight Train to Georgia: The Janus Years** / 1995 / Ichiban/Soul Classics ✦✦✦✦
Fine 21-track compilation of almost everything she recorded between 1970 and 1975, including most of her 1970 album *Presenting Cissy Houston*, ten songs that were previously available only on singles, and a couple that were previously unreleased in the U.S. Highlights include excellent interpretations of two Bacharach-David classics ("I Just Don't Know What to Do with Myself," "This Empty Place") and Tim Hardin's "Hang on to a Dream," as well as the original version of "Midnight Train to Georgia." —*Richie Unterberger*

Penelope Houston

Singer-Songwriter, Alternative Pop/Rock
Houston is one of the most shocking reincarnations from the original punk era. She was the lead singer of the San Francisco band the Avengers, one of the very first full-out American punk acts, opening for the Sex Pistols on the last show of their legendary U.S. tour. After the group broke up in 1979, Houston worked for a time with Howard Devoto, and released a 1986 single fronting the short-lived -30-, finally releasing her debut album in 1988. To the shock of those who remembered her work with the Avengers, Houston had transformed into a folk-rock singer/songwriter with alternative rock sensibilities. As a solo act, her material emphasizes acoustic textures, haunting melodies, and her gentle soprano voice. Popular as a performing act in San Francisco, she has had trouble finding recording deals. Her similar, somewhat more fully produced second album did not appear until 1993 (a couple cassette-only releases mixing live and studio material appeared in the interim). Fans of singer/songwriters like Suzanne Vega, Shawn Colvin, and Christine Lavin looking for something similar but darker would do well to check Houston out. —*Richie Unterberger*

● **Birdboys** / 1988 / Subterranean ✦✦✦✦
A moody, melodic debut that evokes the spirit of Nick Drake and Sandy Denny with its brooding images of loss. Mandolins, accordion, acoustic bass, and sparse percussion (usually tambourines and bells) almost qualify this as a contemporary folk album, but Houston's biting and somber approach draws from her punk and alternative rock roots. The writing is inconsistent, and Houston's fragile voice is sometimes not as forceful as the material seems to demand, but overall this is one of the more underrated alternative music statements of the late 1980s. —*Richie Unterberger*

The Whole World / 1993 / Heyday ✦✦✦
Similar in tone to her debut, but bouncier and more engaging, prominently featuring her husband Mel Pappas on mandolin. Mature and introspective works that do their best to examine romance, innocence, aging, and compassion without sounding hackneyed, but it doesn't quite much the haunting power of her first album. —*Richie Unterberger*

Thelma Houston

b. Leland, MS
Soul, Disco, Motown
Houston was a protégé of composer Jimmy Webb in the late '60s. Despite a fairly consistent recording output, Houston's distinctively vigorous pipes have rarely appealed to the masses. Her biggest hit was the gold disco single "Don't Leave Me this Way" from her 1977 *Any Way You Want It* album on the Gordy label. —*Bil Carpenter*

○ **Sunshower** / 1969 / Dunhill ✦✦✦✦
Jimmy Webb produces this set, including a cover of "Jumpin' Jack Flash." —*Bil Carpenter*

Thelma Houston / 1973 / MoWest ✦✦✦
○ **Any Way You Like It** / 1977 / Motown ✦✦✦✦
With quality production from the mid-'70s, it includes great dance tracks. —*Rick A. Bueche*

Thelma & Jerry / 1977 / Motown ✦✦✦
The best of two albums Thelma Houston and Jerry Butler made during Houston's '70s stay at Motown. The pair were slick, smooth, and soulful, with Houston reigning in her gospel excesses and Butler finding a way to mesh his mellow style with her heated delivery. —*Ron Wynn*

I've Got the Music in Me / 1981 / Sheffield Lab ✦✦✦
An interesting, if uneven, release. Thelma Houston teamed with the band Pressure Cooker in the early '80s, doing a fusion/instrumental pop/R&B/soul work for Sheffield Labs. That affiliation ensured that it would be brilliantly engineered, and it sounded spectacular, especially for an early '80s release. Unfortunately, much of the musical output didn't match the mastering brilliance, despite an energetic effort from Houston. But her voice was too much for what was basically a warm-up caliber backing group. It would have been great to hear Houston doing these songs supported by the Tower of Power. —*Ron Wynn*

Throw You Down / 1990 / Reprise ✦✦
Thelma Houston raised a few eyebrows in 1990 when this album was released. She still had a soulful, galvanizing voice, and she was equally good at fitting into pop, dance, or R&B contexts. While the album itself wasn't a great effort and was strictly aimed at the crossover market, thanks to producer Richard Perry, the single "Out of My Hands" was one of Houston's best songs and among the better unpublicized gems of '90. —*Ron Wynn*

● **The Best of Thelma Houston** / 1991 / Motown ✦✦✦✦
This encompasses her Motown career. —*Rick A. Bueche*

Whitney Houston

b. Aug. 9, 1963, Newark, NJ
Soul, Dance-Pop, Urban, Pop
Coming from a solid musical background, this daughter of soul singer Cissy Houston and cousin of Dionne Warwick debuted in 1985. Her first album, *Whitney Houston*, was the first in *Billboard* chart history by a woman to enter at number one; it sold 14 million copies. She scored heavily on MTV with classy videos, helping to break the "color barrier" originally knocked down by Michael Jackson. Her second album, *Whitney*, was just as popular, scoring seven consecutive number ones in the U.S., shattering the previous record held by the Beatles.

After the disappointing performance of her third album, *I'll Be Your Baby Tonight*, Houston rocketed back to the top of the charts in late 1992 with the soundtrack from her first movie, *The Bodyguard*. The love theme from the movie, a version of Dolly Parton's "I Will Always Love You," broke all previous sales and airplay records, becoming the biggest single in pop music history; it also won her an almost innumerable amount of awards, including several Grammies.

With pure pop music melded to stunning beauty, Houston's star shines bright whether she is singing ballads, uptempo dance material, the national anthem, or cola commercials. Almost ten years after her first album, she is one of the biggest stars in pop music. —*Cub Koda & Stephen Thomas Erlewine*

● **Whitney Houston** / 1985 / Arista ✦✦✦✦
The legend of Whitney Houston began with this self-titled album. It marked her shift away from the experimental songs she did with the group Material and a move into heavily produced, very slick urban contemporary and adult pop. Although Houston had learned her craft working in New York nightclubs and singing in a Baptist church in Newark, she was steered into radio-friendly ballads that emphasized style over substance. The album did yield an unprecedented string of number one hits, but "Saving All My Love for You" and "How Will I Know" created an impression of an incredibly talented vocalist using only a minimum of her skills. It also contained one of her few legitimate soul workouts in "The Greatest Love of All." —*Ron Wynn*

○ **Whitney** / 1987 / Arista ✦✦✦✦
Whitney Houston became an international star with this album. It sold more than 13 million copies around the world, yielded a string of number hit singles across the board like "How Will I Know," "Saving All My Love for You," and "You Give Good Love," and established Houston as the era's top female star. She has since

gone to more than solidify that status, with other hit albums and now a budding film career. While this is a far cry from soul, it's the ultimate in polished, super-produced urban contemporary material. —*Ron Wynn*

I'm Your Baby Tonight / 1990 / Arista ✦✦
While Houston's voice always provides some interesting listening, this is somewhat of a disappointing release, with very few memorable songs. While she attempts to make a larger foray into dance music, she fails to make the crossover impact of artists such as Mariah Carey and Taylor Dayne. The two high points she does reach on this album come in the form of ballads—the uplifting tale or another's love being enough to provide happiness in "All the Man That I Need" and the powerful verses surrounding a love lost through one's own devices in "Miracle." —*Ashley S. Battel*

Steve Howe

Art-Rock/Progressive-Rock
Guitarist Steve Howe is mostly known for his work with the band Yes. Howe also was a member of Asia and GTR and has appeared on many albums as a sideman. Howe's playing embraces jazz, rock, folk, country, classical, and world music. —*Paul Kohler*

○ **Beginnings** / 1975 / Atlantic ✦✦✦✦
This excellent 1975 solo album from the ex-Yes guitarist contains vocal and instrumental material, with Howe playing everything but the kitchen sink. —*Paul Kohler*

The Steve Howe Album / 1979 / Atlantic ✦✦✦
Instrumental and vocal material with excellent acoustic guitar pieces. —*Bil Carpenter*

The Boddast Tapes / 1981 / Cherry Red ✦✦✦

The Early Years with Bodast / 1988 / Cfive ✦✦✦

● **Turbulence** / 1991 / Relativity ✦✦✦✦
An all-instrumental album, it features Howe on multiple guitars. —*Paul Kohler*

○ **The Grand Scheme of Things** / Aug. 24, 1993 / Relativity ✦✦✦✦
Those expecting longwinded guitar extravaganzas will be disappointed. Still, titles like "The Grand Scheme of Things," "At the Gates of the New World," "The Fall of Civilization," and "Road to One's Self" pretty well give away the truth that Howe has not parted with delusions of epic grandeur, despite the more understated approach. Cover by Roger Dean, just for old times sake. —*Roch Parisien*

Mothballs / 1994 / RPM ✦✦✦
Before joining Yes, Howe had nearly a decade's worth of experience with other groups under his belt. This is a first-rate 25-track compilation of his '60s work, with six previously unreleased cuts, starting in 1964 with the raw R&B/beat band the Syndicates, moving to soul-mod with the In Crowd, psychedelia with Tomorrow (six of the better tracks from their sole LP are included), and progressive rock with Bodast. Howe's playing is always interesting, and the material is pretty solid, serving almost as a road map of British rock trends of the '60s. It also includes the unreleased instrumental single he cut under his own name in 1967, a rare single by Tomorrow singer Keith West, and an unreleased track by the short-lived Canto, which was renamed Bodast. Although the six tracks by Tomorrow and the three by Bodast are easily available on separate CDs devoted to those groups, the remainder are quite hard to find. As a whole, it shows him as a player nearly the equal of Jimmy Page in versatility and imagination, although Howe's work from this time is much less widely recognized. —*Richie Unterberger*

H.P. Lovecraft

Group, Psychedelic
Featuring two strong singers (who often sang dual leads), hauntingly hazy arrangements, and imaginative songwriting that drew from pop and folk influences, H.P. Lovecraft were one of the better psychedelic groups of the late '60s. The band was formed by ex-folkie George Edwards in Chicago in 1967. Edwards and keyboardist Dave Michaels, a classically trained singer with a four-octave range, handled the vocals, which echoed the Jefferson Airplane's in their depth and blend of high and low parts. Their self-titled 1967 LP was an impressive debut, featuring strong originals and covers of early compositions by Randy Newman and Fred Neil, as well as one of the first underground FM radio favorites, "White Ship." The band moved to California the following year; their second and last album, *H.P. Lovecraft II,* was a much

more sprawling and unfocused work, despite some strong moments. A spin-off group, Lovecraft, released a couple LPs in the '70s that bore little relation to the first incarnation of the band. —*Richie Unterberger*

○ **H.P. Lovecraft** / 1967 / Philips ✦✦✦✦
With the exception of a couple of badly dated tracks, this is one of the best second-division psychedelic albums, with strong material that shows the immediately identifiable Edwards-Michaels vocal tandem at its best. According to the LP notes, the songs were largely inspired by novelist H.P. Lovecraft's "macabre tales and poems of Earth populated by another race." It's more haunting than gloomy, though, with deft touches of folk, jazz, and horns. —*Richie Unterberger*

H.P. Lovecraft II / 1968 / Philips ✦✦✦
Much more progressive than their first effort, the album also showed the band losing touch with some of their most obvious strengths, most notably their disciplined arrangements and incisive songwriting. The arrangements are more swirling and far denser on this follow-up. Unsurprisingly, the more concise, dual harmony numbers that bear the closest resemblance to the first album work best, especially "At the Mountains of Madness." —*Richie Unterberger*

● **At the Mountains of Madness** / 1988 / Edsel ✦✦✦✦
A superb double-album package of all of their studio material. Includes both LPs, historical liner notes, and a 1967 non-LP single (released prior to their debut) that is much poppier than their albums. —*Richie Unterberger*

Live May 11, 1968 / 1991 / Sundazed ✦✦✦
A most impressive document of the band in concert at the Fillmore West, with good, clear sound. Unlike many other groups of the era, H.P. Lovecraft could successfully replicate their fairly intricate vocal and instrumental arrangements on stage. The eight-song set (six from the first LP, two from the second) features all of their best songs; the extended versions of "Wayfaring Stranger" and "The Drifter" (clocking in at ten and eight minutes respectively) successfully embellish the original arrangements without succumbing to meandering jamming. Recorded between the first and second albums, the addition of bassist Jeff Boyan's backing harmonies creates subtle differences between the live and studio versions of tunes from the first LP. Lengthy liner notes top off a fine package. —*Richie Unterberger*

Hues Corporation

Group, Disco
A Los Angeles vocal trio that enjoyed two big hits in the mid '70s, notably "Rock the Boat" in 1974 for RCA. While it was lightweight, mainly pop work, it did take the Hues Corporation to number two on the R&B charts and get them their lone pop chart topper. The next single, "Rockin' Soul," peaked at number six on the R&B charts and number 18 on the pop charts. They had their final R&B hit the next year with "Love Corporation," which reached number 15, but it was evident that the audience was losing interest in their material. "I Caught Your Act" was the last release in 1977. H. Ann Kelley, Flemming Williams, and Bernard "St. Clair Lee" Henderson were the original lineup. Tom Brown replaced Williams after the success of "Rock the Boat". He was then replaced by Karl Russell in 1975. —*Ron Wynn*

● **Rock the Boat: Golden Classics** / May 1993 / RCA ✦✦✦✦

Jimmy Hughes

b . , Florence, AL
Soul, R&B
Jimmy Hughes established producer Rick Hall's fledgling Fame studio as an R&B mecca with his 1964 blues ballad "Steal Away." The ex-gospel singer hooked up with Hall in 1962 but it wasn't until the explosive "Steal Away" was issued on the Fame label that his career took off. With an intense, crying vocal style that was perfect for deep soul ballads, Hughes scored with the pleading "Why Not Tonight" in 1967, although the untypically uptempo "Neighbor, Neighbor" proved another giant hit. Hughes broke away from Hall and recorded an album for Volt before retiring from performing in the mid-'70s. —*Bill Dahl*

Steal Away / 1964 / Vee-Jay ✦✦✦
A classic pleading Rick Hall-produced ballad leads off this impressive debut album by the Alabama singer. It is available only on vinyl. —*Bill Dahl*

● **Why Not Tonight** / 1967 / Atco ✦✦✦✦
It's criminal that this Muscle Shoals soul classic isn't on CD—it includes aching, atmospheric lovelorn ballads and the ominous pounding hit, "Neighbor, Neighbor." —*Bill Dahl*

Something Special / 1969 / Volt ✦✦✦
Hughes in Memphis—fine, underrated Southern soul. —*Bill Dahl*

○ **A Shot of Rhythm & Blues** / 1980 / Charly ✦✦✦✦

○ **Soul Neighbours** / 1984 / Charly ✦✦✦✦

The Human Expression

Group, Psychedelic, Garage Rock
One of the many third-tier psychedelic groups crowding the Los Angeles scene in 1966 and 1967, the Human Expression's sound was typical of the time and place: minor-key, folk-rock-flavored material with spooky organ, fuzzy guitar, and some distorted special effects, sounding at times like a considerably more melodic Seeds. The band released only three singles on a tiny local label. "Love at Psychedelic Velocity" and "Optical Sound" became minor classics among garage band collectors, and were reissued on compilations many years later. —*Richie Unterberger*

● **Love At Psychedelic Velocity** / 1994 / Collectables ✦✦✦✦
Both sides of their three singles, a few demos of same, and four previously unreleased songs recorded by lead singer Jim Quarles shortly after he left the group. Spacy folk-rock psychedelia, with the ethereal "Optical Sound" and the punky "Love at Psychedelic Velocity" the highlights. Not bad, but for garage-psych specialists only. —*Richie Unterberger*

Human League

Group, New Wave, Dance-Pop
The Human League scored a number of hits in the '80s that crossed the line between post-new wave rock and dance-pop, though that was a very different style from the music the group played at first. The Human League was formed in Sheffield, England, in 1977 by synthesizer players Martin Ware (b. May 19, 1956) and Ian Marsh (b. Nov. 11, 1956), along with Addy Newton and singer Philip Oakey (b. Oct. 2, 1955). Newton was soon replaced by Adrian Wright and the lineup held for the first two Human League albums, *Reproduction* (1979) and *Travelogue* (1980).

Ware and Marsh left the Human League in October 1980 (they subsequently formed Heaven 17). Oakey and Wright recruited bassist Ian Burden (b. Dec. 24, 1957) and backup singers Joanne Catherall (b. Sep 18, 1962) and Susanne Sulley (b. Mar. 22, 1963), resulting in a much more pop-sounding version of the band. Synth player Jo Callis (b. May 2, 1955) was added to the group.

The Human League's third album, *Dare*, was its commercial and international breakthrough. Released in October 1981 in the U.K. and in February 1982 in the U.S., it went to number one in England and number three in the U.S., largely on the strength of the single "Don't You Want Me," which topped the charts in both countries. Subsequent hits in 1982 and 1983 included "(Keep Feeling) Fascination" and "Mirror Man."

Hysteria (1984), was far less successful, and the group agonized over a follow-up. *Crash* appeared in 1986, produced by Jimmy Jam and Terry Lewis (responsible for Janet Jackson's *Control*, among other hits). Largely a studio creation, it was nevertheless successful, producing the number one hit "Human." The Human League's sixth album, *Romantic?*, was released in 1990. —*William Ruhlmann*

Reproduction / 1979 / Virgin ✦✦

Travelogue / 1980 / Virgin ✦✦

○ **Dare** / 1981 / A&M ✦✦✦✦
Martin Rushent's fresh, clean production keeps the synthesized music from being too cluttered, while Philip Oakey's voice is used for its self-consciously melodramatic effect and contrasted with the untrained singing of Joanne Catherall and Susanne Sulley. The hits are "Don't You Want Me" and (in England) "The Sound of the Crowd," "Love Action (I Believe in Love)," and "Open Your Heart," but the album also works as a consistent piece. —*William Ruhlmann*

Love and Dancing / 1982 / A&M ✦✦✦

Fascination! / 1983 / A&M ✦✦✦

Hysteria / 1984 / Virgin ✦✦

Crash / 1986 / A&M ✦✦✦

● **Greatest Hits** / 1988 / A&M ✦✦✦✦
This well-chosen best-of contains the Human League's U.K. and U.S. hits from 1978 ("Being Boiled") to 1986, including the chart-toppers "Don't You Want Me" and "Human" and such non-album singles as "(Keep Feeling) Fascination" and "Mirror Man." It's a study in '80s dance-pop. —*William Ruhlmann*

Romantic? / 1990 / A&M ✦✦

Octopus / 1995 / East West ✦✦✦
After taking a five-year hiatus, Human League returned in 1995 with *Octopus*, a well-constructed record that shows little signs of musical change. *Octopus* alternates between adult contemporary ballads and seamlessly produced dance music. All of the music is competently performed, yet little of it makes a lasting impression. —*Stephen Thomas Erlewine*

Human Sexual Response

Group, New Wave
Although they were pegged to be the post-punk era's next big thing, Boston's Human Sexual Response did the opposite and crashed and burned after four years and two albums. But in their short existence, they created a substantial buzz in their hometown and on the East Coast for their arty and energetic live shows and their sophisticated postmodern pop. Fronted by four singers and backed by a power trio that featured the excellent guitar work of Rich Gilbert, HSR combined a punk rock ethos with a camp sensibility reminiscent of early Blondie. Prominent vocalist Larry Bangor offered songs like "What Does Sex Mean to Me" and the irreverent "Jackie Onassis" in a jittery tenor voice that conjured up sex, outrage and comedy in one neat package. Never eschewing controversy (Bangor was refreshingly outspoken about his homosexuality), HSR is the only American band in the annals of American rock & roll to perform a song entitled "Buttfuck" on television. After a promising debut record, HSR's second record was a comparatively dour affair, loaded down with art-rock pretensions and lifeless arrangements. After an almost unanimous critical drubbing, HSR played the New England circuit for another year and split in 1982. Rich Gilbert formed the cool (and loud) combo the Zulus, while drummer Malcolm Travis currently beats skins for Bob Mould in Sugar. —*John Dougan*

● **Figure 14** / 1980 / Eat ✦✦✦✦
The best record made by this promising band, *Figure 14* has the comic, campy qualities that made Human Sexual Response such a fun band, including "Jackie Onassis" and a screwy cover of "Cool Jerk." Bangor's singing might get a little irritating, but Rich Gilbert's big guitar always saves the day. In many ways, *Figure 14* is a classic piece of early-'80s new wave rock. —*John Dougan*

In a Roman Mood / 1981 / DFOTM ✦✦✦

○ **Fig. 15** / Feb. 13, 1992 / Eat ✦✦✦✦

Humble Pie

Group, Blues Rock, Hard Rock
When Humble Pie was formed in 1969, there was much excitement about the possibilities. After all, its founding members came from very popular English bands. Humble Pie comprised vocalist and guitarist Steve Marriott, previously with the Small Faces; Greg Ridley, former bassist for Spooky Tooth; Peter Frampton, the Herd's frontman and guitarist; and drummer Jerry Shirley of Little Women.

The band's initial albums (on Andrew Oldham's Immediate Records) were surprisingly laidback and melodic. 1971 turned out to be the band's breakthrough to major success, due to a hard and loud double live album, *Performance—Live at the Fillmore*, which went to #21. Frampton left shortly thereafter to pursue a successful solo career, and Humble Pie progressively turned toward an over-amped boogie style of rock. During the next two years, Humble Pie made three more forays onto the album charts with *Smoking* (#6), *Eat It* (#13), and *Lost and Found* (#37), an anthology of their earlier Immediate label work.

In spite of substantial album popularity, Humble Pie never had a major single, with their only chart titles being "I Don't Need No Doctor" (#73) and "Hot 'N' Nasty" (#52). The group disbanded in 1981 and Steve Marriott later passed away. —*Rick Clark*

○ **As Safe As Yesterday Is** / 1969 / Columbia ✦✦✦✦
Even though many think of Humble Pie as a boogie-rock band, their first two efforts, originally released on Immediate Records, possessed a healthy dose of tasty acoustical instrumentation. Steve Marriott and Peter Frampton applied themselves, through months of rehearsals, and came up with a solid collection of songs. Even though *Safe As Yesterday Is* is a little stronger than the pastoral *Town and Country*, both albums are worth seeking out. In 1972, they were sold as a double-record set titled *Lost and Found*, which is now out of print. —*Rick Clark*

Town & Country / 1969 / Sony ✦✦✦

Humble Pie / 1970 / A&M ✦✦✦

Rock on / 1971 / A&M ✦✦✦
By 1971, Humble Pie had taken on a much harder electric direction. Of their post-Immediate studio albums, this is probably their best. —*Rick Clark*

○ **Performance: Rockin' at the Fillmore** / 1971 / A&M ✦✦✦✦
This live, extended-play effort, recorded at the Fillmore, showcased the band in its element, with Steve Marriott's stratospheric wail and Peter Frampton's lyrical lead work in fine form. Frampton split to pursue a successful solo career after this album. —*Rick Clark*

Smokin' / 1972 / A&M ✦✦✦
With Marriott firmly in control, *Smokin'* featured grittier blues-based hard rock, with tracks like "Hot & Nasty," "C'mon Everybody," and the FM hit "Thirty Days in the Hole." —*Rick Clark*

○ **Lost and Found** / 1973 / A&M ✦✦✦✦
After the Top Ten success of *Smokin',* A&M prepared *Lost and Found,* which collected Humble Pie's first two albums in one package. The marketing ploy was a success and the record charted in the Top 40. —*Stephen Thomas Erlewine*

Eat It / 1973 / A&M ✦✦✦
Although the quality of the material is decidedly uneven, the double album *Eat It* is the last Humble Pie record to capture the rough and tumble spirit of their heyday. Nevertheless, all of side four—which was recorded live in Glasgow—is worthless. —*Stephen Thomas Erlewine*

Thunderbox / 1974 / A&M ✦✦
With *Thunderbox,* it's clear that most of the inspiration has left Humble Pie, as the band turns in a set of by-the-numbers boogie. —*Stephen Thomas Erlewine*

Street Rats / 1975 / A&M ✦✦
Even more undistinguished than *Thunderbox,* the limp blues-rock of *Street Rats* illustrates why Humble Pie threw in the towel after the release of this record. —*Stephen Thomas Erlewine*

Back Home Again / 1976 / Immediate

On to Victory / 1980 / Atco ✦
Five years after breaking up Humble Pie, Steve Marriott formed a new version of the band—featuring drummer Jerry Shirley, guitarist Bobby Tench, and bassist Anthony Jones—and recorded *On to Victory*. Unfortunately, *On to Victory* picks up exactly where *Street Rats* left off—it's a rote set of competent but faceless blues boogie. —*Stephen Thomas Erlewine*

Go for the Throat / 1981 / Atco ✦
Peaking at number 60, the resurrected Humble Pie's first album *On to Victory* was surprisingly successful, allowing the group to have another chance to record an album. The ensuing record, *Go for the Throat* was nearly identical to *On to Victory*, as the band ran through a set of bland, arena-ready blues-rock. The only difference was that the songs weren't as good as the last album, and those weren't very good to begin with. —*Stephen Thomas Erlewine*

○ **The Best of Humble Pie** / 1982 / A&M ✦✦✦✦
A brief but entertaining collection of Humble Pie's finest moments, *The Best of Humble Pie* is an effective introduction to the group's loud boogie. —*Stephen Thomas Erlewine*

● **Classics, Vol. 14** / 1987 / A&M ✦✦✦✦
If you are looking for the one place to go for Humble Pie, this best-of collection covers the essentials, such as "I Don't Need No Doctor," "Stone Cold Fever," "30 Days in the Hole," "Hot 'N' Nasty," "C'Mon Everybody," and "Take Me Back." —*Rick Clark*

Hot N' Nasty—The Anthology / 1994 / A&M ✦✦✦
Album rock artists that never made great albums, Humble Pie are well served by *Hot N' Nasty,* a double-disc set that collects the hits and highlights from throughout their career. —*Stephen Thomas Erlewine*

Ian Hunter

b. Jun. 3, 1946, Shrewsbury, England
Rock & Roll, Hard Rock
Hunter's post-Mott the Hoople work (most of it done in collaboration with guitarist Mick Ronson) has remained true to the boogie roots of his old group, while expanding his beautifully expressed romantic concerns. —*John Floyd*

○ **Ian Hunter** / 1975 / Columbia ✦✦✦✦
A spotty debut, but "Once Bitten Twice Shy," "Who Do You Love," and "I Get So Excited" rank with the best Mott the Hoople material. —*John Floyd*

All American Alien Boy / 1976 / Columbia ✦✦✦
Ian Hunter's second solo album lacked the consistently impressive songwriting of his first, and it suffered from overly-slick production, yet it had a handful of songs that made it worthwhile. —*Stephen Thomas Erlewine*

Overnight Angels / 1977 / Columbia ✦✦
For most of *Overnight Angels,* Ian Hunter sounds a bit uninspired—the music follows his patented literate hard rock formula, only without the stylistic embellishments and variations that made *Ian Hunter* and *All American Alien Boy* compelling listens. Nevertheless, there are a handful of tracks that make the record worthwhile for dedicated fans. —*Stephen Thomas Erlewine*

○ **Shades of Ian Hunter** / 1979 / Chrysalis ✦✦✦✦
A fine, if somewhat inconsistent, collection that features highlights from the early part of Ian Hunter's solo career as well as selections from Mott the Hoople's catalog, *Shades of Ian Hunter* is a good introduction to his work, even if it doesn't feature many of his best songs. —*Stephen Thomas Erlewine*

● **You're Never Alone with a Schizophrenic** / 1979 / Razor & Tie ✦✦✦✦
Hunter's post-punk return salutes the genre he helped spawn and brings that old Mott crunch to a fine set of energetic, if somewhat dated, rock & roll. —*John Floyd*

Ian Hunter Live / Welcome to the Club / 1980 / Chrysalis ✦✦✦
Recorded with guitarist Mick Ronson, *Ian Hunter Live / Welcome to the Club* is a tough, hard-rocking album that features material from both Ronson and Hunter. —*Stephen Thomas Erlewine*

○ **Short Back and Sides** / 1981 / Chrysalis ✦✦✦✦
Ian Hunter had been revitalized by punk rock, as *Short Back and Sides* shows. Featuring the Clash's Mick Jones on guitar, the music is a tougher and spikier take on Hunter's rock & roll, and his songwriting is at a near-peak. —*Stephen Thomas Erlewine*

All of the Good Ones Are Taken / 1983 / Columbia ✦✦✦
With its slightly dated and stiff sound, *All of the Good Ones Are Taken* is a step down from the vibrant *Short Back and Sides,* yet a handful of songs manage to break free of the restrictions placed on them by the production. —*Stephen Thomas Erlewine*

○ **Yui Orta** / 1990 / Mercury ✦✦✦✦
Overlooked upon its release, this is Hunter's most lyrically ambitious and mature disc, with tight rockers and melancholy ballads working gloriously off one another. —*John Floyd*

Ivory Joe Hunter

b. Oct. 10, 1914, Kirbyville, TX, d. Nov. 8, 1974, Memphis, TN
R&B
Best known for his classic ballads "I Almost Lost My Mind" and "Since I Met You Baby" (both #1 hits), Ivory Joe Hunter was one of the major '50s R&B stars to cross over into the pop market. Prior to that, he'd been a popular blues singer/pianist in the urbane West Coast style of the '40s. In the beginning he was a Texas barrelhouse blues pianist who recorded for the Library of Congress in 1933, and in later years, he did sessions as both a soul singer and a country & western artist. As a songwriter, Hunter claimed over 7000 compositions. His recorded output was so varied as to defy any overall categorization, but for the blues enthusiast the reissues of his '40s sides are of greatest interest. —*Jim O'Neal*

● **Since I Met You Baby: The Best of Ivory Joe Hunter** / 1994 / Razor & Tie ✦✦✦✦
Compiling all of Ivory Joe Hunter's pop hits as well as many of his finest singles, including "Since I Met You Baby," "Empty Arms," and "I Almost Lost My Mind," *Since I Met You Baby* provides the definitive portrait of the pianist. —*Stephen Thomas Erlewine*

Hunters & Collectors

Group, Alternative Pop/Rock

Hunters & Collectors developed a cult following in the American and Australian underground in the '80s. Originally, the band sketched out a noisy punk and funk fusion reminiscent of the Fall and Gang of Four, except with horns added into the mix. In the middle of the decade, the band turned into a driving, hard-hitting rock & roll band with a flair for pop melodies. The band formed in Melbourne, Australia, in 1981; over the years, numerous members went through the lineup, but the group's mainstays were Mark Seymour (vocals, guitar), Martin Lubran (guitar), John Archer (bass), Geoff Crosbie (keyboards), Doug Falconer (drums), Jeremy Smith (keyboards, saxophone), Greg Perano (percussion), Michael Waters (trombone), and Jack Howard (trombone). Hunters & Collectors released their debut single in 1982 and quickly followed it with two EPs and a self-titled full-length record; the band was briefly on A&M Records in America before switching to Slash. By the late '80s, the group had earned a cult following in America and their native Australia, as their sound became progressively more direct and melodic. However, they never were able to attain any commercial success and the band quietly disappeared in the early '90s. — *Stephen Thomas Erlewine*

Hunters & Collectors / 1983 / Virgin ✦✦✦

Fireman's Curse / 1983 / Virgin ✦✦

Jaws of Life / 1984 / Epic ✦✦✦

Way to Go Out / 1985 / White Label ✦✦

○ **Human Frailty** / 1986 / IRS ✦✦✦✦
As the title suggests, the band loses some of the edge of earlier releases on *Human Frailty,* revealing a softer, nearly vulnerable side. A more mainstream pop album, it includes the great love song "Throw Your Arms Around Me." — *Chris Woodstra*

○ **Fate** / 1988 / IRS ✦✦✦✦
The finest moment of their later period, *Fate* is a cohesive and tightly-produced album with an edge. "Back on the Breadline" received some attention through college and "Modern Rock" radio, making this the closest thing to an American breakthough the band has seen yet. — *Chris Woodstra*

Ghost Nation / 1990 / Atlantic ✦✦
Ghost Nation is a pleasant, though not distinctive album. Failing to build on the the previous effort, a lack of direction seems to hold the band back from being anything other than a second-string Midnight Oil. — *Chris Woodstra*

● **Collected Works** / 1990 / IRS ✦✦✦✦
A good collection of the band's recordings for IRS records in the mid-to-late '80s. This poppier side of the band is easily the most palatable of their work, though not definitive. Their varied career deserves better. — *Chris Woodstra*

Cut / 1993 / Mushroom ✦✦✦
Australia's Hunter's & Collectors have long been the source of some of Down-Under's most stately, dignified rock, while never forsaking an element of challenge. The group spices the standard instrumental lineup with trumpet, trombone and french horn which are used to create an almost-string-section-like moody canvas upon which the other instruments dance and paint. Mark Seymour's strong lyrics tackle several topical subjects, but are most successful when dealing with personal politics—especially the quest for self-purpose. While "Head Above Water" will be the party favorite, "Holy Grail" and "Closer Angel of Mercy" have an epic feel where all H&C's lyric and instrumental strengths converge. — *Roch Parisien*

Hüsker Dü

Group, Alternative Pop/Rock, Hardcore

Hüsker Dü and R.E.M. were the two American post-punk bands of the '80s that changed the direction of rock & roll. R.E.M. became superstars; Hüsker Dü never was more than a cult favorite. Nevertheless, their albums between 1981 and 1987 have proven remarkably influential; they provided the sonic blueprint for the roaring punk-pop hybrid that crossed over into the mainstream in the early '90s. Not only did they shape the sound of the music, they shaped the way independent bands made the transition to the major labels; they showed other bands that it was possible to record uncompromising music on a major label without losing any integrity or creative control. From the Replacements to Nirvana, the Pixies to Superchunk, nearly every major and minor

band that appeared in the alternative underground in the late '80s and '90s owed a major debt to Hüsker Dü, whether they were aware of it or not.

The band's two songwriters, guitarist Bob Mould and drummer Grant Hart, both had a knack for writing songs that essentially followed conventional pop structures, complete with memorable melodies, but were still punk songs. Hüsker Dü took the Buzzcocks' pioneering punk pop and made it harder, both musically and lyrically. Throughout their career, Hüsker Dü never lost their edge, never turned down their amplifiers, never compromised their music. While Hart and bassist Greg Norton were an unflailingly strong rhythm section, Mould would prove to be one of the most influential guitarists of the decade. With his slashing rhythms, distorted strumming, and blazing leads, he set the stage for the alternative guitar heroes of the late '80s and the '90s.

After releasing several good but unspectacular hardcore records, Hüsker Dü made *Zen Arcade* in 1984; the double album expanded hardcore in previously unimaginable ways. Instead of copying the strident political and social commentary of most hardcore, the band turned the focus inward, writing personal songs that were painfully honest. For the next three years, the band were consistently recording and touring, without a lapse in quality.

The band was at the top of its form in 1985, releasing two landmark albums (*New Day Rising* and *Flip Your Wig*) and one non-album single (a cover of the Byrds' "Eight Miles High"). In 1986, the band became one of the first post-punk groups to make the jump to the major label. Once they were there, they released two more albums before bitterly breaking up in 1988. After Hüsker Dü split, Grant Hart recorded a solo album before forming Nova Mob. Mould recorded two solo albums and then went on to form another punk-pop power trio, Sugar. Greg Norton became a chef in the band's hometown of Minneapolis. — *Stephen Thomas Erlewine*

Land Speed Record / 1981 / SST ✦✦
A brief live EP, *Land Speed Record* races through its songs without regard for melody or riffs. As a sonic blitzkrieg, it's quite impressive, yet little of the record makes a lasting impression. — *Stephen Thomas Erlewine*

Everything Falls Apart / 1982 / Reflex ✦✦✦

Metal Circus / 1983 / SST ✦✦✦
This five-songer, which followed a furiously paced debut, hinted that the confines of hardcore punk couldn't contain the group's collective vision. — *John Floyd*

☆ **Zen Arcade** / 1984 / SST ✦✦✦✦✦
Its four sides are linked by a muddled travelog concept, but this is a remarkable synthesis of hardcore sensibilities and rock & roll themes. "Turn on the News" may be their finest moment. — *John Floyd*

☆ **New Day Rising** / Jan. 1985 / SST ✦✦✦✦✦
From its thin and distorted production to the rich, tugging melodies, this one-ups *Zen Arcade* through its front-to-back consistency. — *John Floyd*

★ **Flip Your Wig** / Feb. 1985 / SST ✦✦✦✦✦
They finally got the professional production they've always deserved. While it's not the frontal assault of *New Day Rising,* the songs continue to get better, both lyrically and melodically. — *John Floyd*

○ **Candy Apple Grey** / 1986 / Warner Brothers ✦✦✦✦
The band's major-label debut coincidentally happens to be their most lyrically optimistic. Musically, it reiterates *Flip Your Wig.* — *John Floyd*

☆ **Warehouse: Songs & Stories** / 1987 / Warner Brothers ✦✦✦✦✦
Hüsker Dü's final record was also their second double-album. Much like *Zen Arcade, Warehouse* rarely loses momentum over its four sides. While the music here is the band's most accomplished and pop-oriented, it never loses its edge. — *Stephen Thomas Erlewine*

Everything Falls Apart and More / 1993 / Rhino ✦✦✦
Rhino's reissue of Hüsker Dü's shattering first studio album includes a couple of rare singles, making it a must-have for the band's fans, as well as anyone interested in hardcore punk rock. Anyone unfamiliar with Hüsker Dü's early work should brace themselves for a breakneck force like no other. Not for the faint of heart. — *Stephen Thomas Erlewine*

The Living End / Oct. 1994 / Warner Brothers ✦✦✦
Recorded on their final tour, *The Living End* is an invigorating document of Hüsker Dü's blistering live power, highlighted by a couple unreleased songs and a manic cover of "Sheena Is a Punk Rocker." —*Stephen Thomas Erlewine*

Willie Hutch (Willie Hutchison)

b. 1946, Los Angeles, CA
Soul, R&B
Hutch was a versatile figure at Motown, working with other artists as well as recording himself. Born Willie Hutchison in Los Angeles, he cut an album for RCA in 1969 before signing on with Berry Gordy's empire. Hutch first made his mark in 1973 by performing the soundtrack to a black exploitation flick called "The Mack." In the mid-'70s, his "Love Power" and "Party Down" were solid hits. —*Bill Dahl*

● **The Mack** / 1973 / Motown ✦✦✦✦
One of the great '70s soundtracks. An act called Sisters Love had a cameo in the blaxploitation film *The Mack*, and their manager suggested that Hutch do the soundtrack. The results included a pair of classic funk tunes, "Brothers Gonna Work It Out" and the title cut, and another score that far surpassed the quality of its film. —*Ron Wynn*

Making a Game out of Love / Motown ✦✦✦
Wille Hutch's second stint at Motown included a pair of decent albums as a solo artist. This was the second, and he landed a mild club hit with "Keep on Jammin.'" There were some nice ballads , but by the late '80s it was tough for slow songs to score that weren't produced in the slick urban contemporary format. —*Ron Wynn*

Brian Hyland

b. Nov. 12, 1943, Woodhaven, NY
Pop/Rock, Teen Idol
Initially aiming his output at teens, Brian Hyland grew up fast and cut a serious cover of "Gypsy Woman," a hit by the Impressions that went gold in 1970. The Queens, NY, native enjoyed his biggest hit at the age of 16—the tongue-twisting "Itsy Bitsy Teenie Weenie Yellow Polkadot Bikini," a ditty snapped up by Kapp Records after it was issued on the little Leader logo. Hyland moved to ABC-Paramount and sounded more adult by the time "Sealed with a Kiss" hit in 1962. A string of solid sellers, including "The Joker Went Wild" in 1966, preceded his remake of "Gypsy Woman," produced by Del Shannon and released on Uni. —*Bill Dahl*

● **Greatest Hits** / Rhino ✦✦✦✦
Included is everything from "Itsy Bitsy Teenie Weenie Yellow Polka Dot Bikini" to "Gypsy Woman." —*Larry Lapka*

I

Ian & Sylvia
Group, Folk, Folk-Rock
The '60s duo of Canadians Ian Tyson (b. 1933) and Sylvia Fricker (b. 1940) was notable for its combination of contemporary folk with the countryish music of rural Canada, once described as "country and Northwestern." Both singers wrote original songs that became standards (Tyson's "Four Strong Winds" and "Some Day Soon," Fricker's "You Were on My Mind"), and they championed the work of then-little-known writers such as fellow-Canadians Gordon Lightfoot and Joni Mitchell. *— William Ruhlmann*

Ian & Sylvia / 1962 / Vanguard ✦✦✦
Ian & Sylvia's debut album is their most standard affair, and indeed a fairly typical folk recording for the era, with such traditional warhorses as "Rocks And Gravel" (also recorded, but not released, by Dylan during this time), "C.C. Rider," and "Handsome Molly." What made the pair immediately distinctive was their superb vocal dueting, which was definitely a case of the sum being greater than its parts. Blended together, they canceled each other's weaknesses and gave the material great freshness and vigor. Ian's guitar and Sylvia's autoharp are backed by stellar playing from guitarist John Herald and string bassists Bill Lee (director Spike Lee's father) and Art Davis. *—Richie Unterberger*

○ **Four Strong Winds** / 1964 / Vanguard ✦✦✦✦
Ian & Sylvia hit their stride on their second LP, which features the first in a line of talented second guitarists (John Herald) they would use to augment their original guitar-autoharp-bass lineup. The album featured an assortment of largely traditional material that was unsurpassed in its time, encompassing bluegrass, spirituals, gospel, hillbilly, the French-Canadian standard "V'La L'bon Vent," a British prison song, and two tunes from the Cecil Sharp collection of Southern mountain folk songs of British origin. Two of the most impressive cuts, however, were contemporary compositions. One was their version of Bob Dylan's "Tomorrow Is a Long Time," one of the first obscure Dylan tunes to be committed to vinyl. The title cut, an Ian Tyson original, would prove to be the duo's first song to influence rock musicians, as the Searchers covered it shortly afterwards with a reverent version that was quite close to the original; Neil Young revived it in the late '70s. *—Richie Unterberger*

Northern Journey / 1964 / Vanguard ✦✦✦
The duo continue to fill out their sound on another collection of mostly traditional material, with John Herald (guitar), Monte Dunn (mandolin and guitar), and Eric Weissberg and Russ Savakus (bass) backing Ian & Sylvia's own guitar and autoharp. The few originals stand out much more than the traditional updates on this LP; Tyson's "Four Rode By" and "Some Day Soon" clearly point toward his future C&W/cowboy direction, and Fricker's "You Were on My Mind" remains their best (and best-known) song. *—Richie Unterberger*

Early Morning Rain / 1965 / Vanguard ✦✦✦
Side One of their fourth LP continues in the eclectic folkie style of their earlier albums, containing only one original (Tyson's "Marlborough Street Blues"). The other cuts include the fine Gordon Lightfoot title track, a Johnny Cash cover ("Come in Stranger") that heralded their increasing interest in country and western music, one of their finest interpretations of a bonafide traditional warhorse ("Nancy Whiskey"), and "Darcy Farrow," a fine obscure composition that could pass for a traditional standard (written for the duo by an unknown Californian singer/songwriter pair). Side

Two, however, with the exception of one traditional tune and another Lightfoot cover, is composed entirely of originals. The most notable of these is Tyson's "Song For Canada" (written with Pete Gzowski). A bittersweet plea for greater communication between French- and English-speaking Canadians, it could just as well be heard as a comment on any sort of deteriorating relationship. — *Richie Unterberger*

Play One More / 1966 / Vanguard ✦✦✦
Ian & Sylvia rely mostly on original material for the first time on this erratic record. For the first time, they employ full modern arrangements on four of the tracks, which sometimes works (their cover of Bacharach-David's "24 Hours From Tulsa") and sometimes doesn't (unfortunately for them, on one of their best compositions, "The French Girl"). They also cover songs by Phil Ochs and Scott McKenzie, and their own tunes range from solid numbers in their proven contemporary folk style ("Short Grass") to mediocre. Future Cream producer Felix Pappalardi plays bass. *—Richie Unterberger*

So Much for Dreaming / 1967 / Vanguard ✦✦✦
Ian & Sylvia's adjustment to folk-rock was sometimes fine, sometimes awkward, and this was another inconsistent, though generally worthwhile, effort. Highlights include "Circle Game," one of the very first recorded covers of a Joni Mitchell composition. Tyson's "Wild Geese" and "Child Apart" count as some of their better unheralded tunes, and the occasional muted orchestration worked well on "Circle Game" and the melancholy title track. On the other hand, the attempts at blues were abominable, the traditional ballads anachronistic, and some of the material (especially Fricker's) undistinguished. *—Richie Unterberger*

● **Greatest Hits** / 1987 / Vanguard ✦✦✦✦
This compilation (CVSD 5/6) captures much of their best work. Do not confuse it with the identically titled Vanguard album 73114, which includes only half the material found on this set. — *William Ruhlmann*

Long Long Time / 1994 / Vanguard ✦✦✦
After leaving Vanguard in 1967, Ian & Sylvia spent the next few years recording in a much more countrified style for MGM, Ampex (as figureheads of the band Great Speckled Bird), and Columbia. This compilation—ironically on Vanguard—draws from five albums they released between 1967 and 1971. While the duo's ambitions to expand their artistic horizons were admirable, the fact is that they were much more effective as eclectic folkies than country-pop-folk-rockers. The harmonies remained intact, but the material (mostly original) is often humdrum, the arrangements sometimes lackadaisical. A few cuts, like "Salmon in the Sea" and "Last Lonely Eagle," are reasonably strong; the higlights are the 1967 versions of "Hang on to a Dream" and "Reason to Believe," which were among the first Tim Hardin covers ever recorded. *—Richie Unterberger*

Ian & Sylvia / 1995 / Vanguard

Janis Ian (Janis Eddy Fink)
b. Apr. 7, 1951, New York, NY
Singer-Songwriter, Folk-Rock
A folk-pop singer/songwriter who gained fame at age 16 for her socially conscious ballad "Society's Child" and scored all over again at age 24 with "At Seventeen." Lately she is living and writing songs in Nashville. *—William Ruhlmann*

For All the Seasons / 1967 / Verve ✦✦✦
Sixteen-year-old Janis Ian's second album continues to probe a series of unusually mature issues, notably on the single "Insanity Comes Quietly To The Structured Mind," a meditation on suicide, and "Shady Acres," which is about old age. Producer Shadow Morton found interesting musical contexts for Ian's pronouncements, none of which was sufficiently provocative to score with the impact of "Society's Child." — *William Ruhlmann*

○ **Janis Ian** / 1967 / Verve ✦✦✦✦
An amazingly precocious set of songs, including the civil rights anthem "Society's Child" and songs touching on religion, prostitution, politics, and other urban concerns, all from the viewpoint of an intelligent teenager. — *William Ruhlmann*

Secret Life of J. Eddie Fink / 1968 / Verve ✦✦
Janis Fink is Ian's real name, and her concerns moved more toward the personal on her third album. "42nd St. Psycho Blues" was her unhappy commentary on what having a pop music career had been like, while "When I Was a Child" found her reminiscing regretfully about what had happened to her. Other songs waxed poetic, and producer Shadow Morton kept recreating the folk-rock sound of "Society's Child," but nothing here caught fire, and this album failed to chart, seeming to confirm that Ian would be a one-hit wonder, over the hill at 17. With a few years to think about it, of course, she'd have some trenchant things to say about that age. — *William Ruhlmann*

Present Company / 1971 / One Way ✦✦
Janis Ian's muse had subsided to a series of pretty-sounding but pedestrian piano tunes with sensitive-seeming but vague lyrics by the time of this, her fifth album, released the year she turned 20 by Capitol Records. Although the sound, when combined with far more substantial songs, would re-invigorate her career several years hence, *Present Company* went practically unnoticed when it came out, and it marked the end of Ian's juvenile efforts. — *William Ruhlmann*

Stars / 1974 / One Way ✦✦✦
From precocity to an accelerated maturity, Ian ruefully comments on the fame business in the title track, then turns deeply romantic on "Jesse," a hit for Roberta Flack. — *William Ruhlmann*

● **Between the Lines** / Mar. 1975 / Columbia ✦✦✦✦
"At Seventeen" is only one of a group of beautifully written, tastefully performed, and very moving songs. — *William Ruhlmann*

Aftertones / 1975 / Columbia ✦✦✦
Following only nine months after Ian's masterpiece, *Between the Lines*, *Aftertones* was something of a coda to that album, again tastefully produced by Brooks Arthur and featuring songs in the same mood. Although none came up to the standard of "At Seventeen," "I Would Like to Dance" presents much the same delicacy of expression. — *William Ruhlmann*

Miracle Row / 1977 / Columbia ✦✦✦
Janis Ian's career in the 1970s paralleled her career in the '60s—stimulated by a major hit early on, she made a series of albums that were successively less accomplished and less commercially successful. *Miracle Row*, her second followup to the top-selling *Between the Lines*, is a disturbing collection of tastefully written and performed songs about loneliness, desperation, drinking, and promiscuity. There was nothing as focused as "At Seventeen" or some of the songs on *Aftertones*, but the overall portrait of the singer was as painful, in a more mature way, as the one Ian presented in her later albums as a teenager. — *William Ruhlmann*

Janis Ian / 1978 / Columbia ✦✦
Janis Ian may have intended to signal a creative rebirth by using her own name as this album's title, the second time in her career she did so, but although the record was a more direct, low-key effort than its predecessor, *Miracle Row*, it didn't indicate any new directions. "Hotels & One-Night Stands" found the singer once again reflecting on life in the music business, while "Do You Wanna Dance?" used dancing as a metaphor for a desired romance for the umpteenth time. More extended metaphors, such as "The Bridge," were even less effective. With its piano textures and tasteful string arrangements, Janis Ian retained the artist's pretty sound, but much of the time the singer came off less confessional than merely self-involved. — *William Ruhlmann*

Night Rains / 1979 / Columbia ✦✦
When Janis Ian's self-titled 1978 album failed to crack the Top 100, it was clear that changes were in order. Here, she turns to producer Ron Frangipane and a surprising songwriting partner, Eu-

rodisco maven Giorgio Moroder, who brings in his dance tracks for "Fly Too High," which was intended for the motion picture *Foxes*. More appropriately, Ian also pairs with Albert Hammond for the lead-off track, "The Other Side Of The Sun." Even on her own, however, she is attempting a more timely pop style: "Memories" is as much of a disco cut as the Moroder one that makes the album more engaging on the surface than her recent releases, but less compelling. As a commercial move, all this was a failure: *Night Rains* failed to chart, a major comedown for an artist who had topped the chart only four years earlier. — *William Ruhlmann*

Restless Eyes / 1981 / Columbia ✦✦
Janis Ian turned to producer Gary Klein and a backup group of L.A. session aces after the commercial failure of *Night Rains*, and they gave her the kind of pop-rock album that people like Carly Simon turned out regularly. Despite the liner notes by former New York Times music critic Robert Shelton, little here was distinctive, and when the album failed to restore Ian's commercial fortunes, she retired for the second time at the age of 30. — *William Ruhlmann*

○ **Breaking Silence** / Jun. 8, 1993 / Morgan Creek ✦✦✦✦
Breaking Silence finds Ian ditching her past waifishness for a confident, mature, contemporary acoustic approach relying mostly on spare guitar and piano textures. Opening with "All Roads To The River" (also recorded by John Mellencamp), *Breaking Silence* includes among its highlights the Holocaust-survivor tale "Tattoo" and the dramatic half-a cappella, half-syncopated-rocker title track. — *Roch Parisien*

Ice Cube

Rap
Through his detailed, unflinching lyrical stance and his inventive phrasing, this former N.W.A. writer and rapper has become the finest mouthpiece gangsta-rap has produced. His posse, the Lynch Mob, construct sonic backdrops that kick with the force of the best Public Enemy. Ice Cube is a controversial but major figure in contemporary pop, and has recently begun an acting career with films, including 1991's *Boyz 'n the Hood.*

Ice Cube has arguably become rap's most controversial and widely known figure in the '90s. He's topped R&B, pop, and rap charts with his releases *AmeriKKKa's Most Wanted, The Predator,* and *Lethal Injection*. Cube has been the cover boy for every magazine from *Vibe* to *The Source*, and also joined the Nation of Islam. He currently ranks alongside Ice-T as perhaps the most feared personality in rap circles.

Whispers abounded that marriage and his decision to join the Nation of Islam were responsible for Ice Cube's weakest CD as a solo act. *Lethal Injection* went platinum, but the rage was more unfocused, the rhymes less fluid and thoughtful and the rapping less striking than on any other Ice Cube session. While his interviews sounded just as fierce, the speculation abounds that Ice Cube may have peaked as a creative force in hip-hop. — *John Floyd*

☆ **Amerikkka's Most Wanted [Clean]** / 1990 / Priority ✦✦✦✦✦
Cube gets some production help from Public Enemy's Bomb Squad and comes up with a stark and gripping portrait of life in America's inner cities. If you can get past the sexism, you'll find this debut to be one of rap's most unflinching bursts of rhythmic and political fury. — *John Floyd*

○ **Kill at Will** / 1990 / Priority ✦✦✦
A few remixes from the debut bog this one down, but the title track, which examines the emotional facets of gangland murder with brutal nakedness and accuracy, is Cube's best moment. — *John Floyd*

★ **Death Certificate** / 1991 / Priority ✦✦✦✦✦
His sexism is becoming even more repugnant, and his racism is sometimes misdirected, but this one perfectly articulates Cube's frustration and outrage at American injustice. — *John Floyd*

The Predator / 1992 / Priority ✦✦✦
Although Ice Cube makes a lot of noise throughout *The Predator,* he never actually says anything. For the most part, *The Predator* is Ice Cube by the numbers, spouting his standard line about women, police, drugs, and gangsters. The album doesn't sound weak at all; it's full of strong beats and muscular rhymes. Das EFX invigorate "Check Yo Self," "Wicked" is a classic single, and the light '70s groove of "It Was a Good Day" proves that Ice Cube doesn't need hardcore beats to succeed. If Ice Cube hadn't just blustered grandiosely, *The Predator* might have ranked among his previous efforts. — *Stephen Thomas Erlewine*

Lethal Injection / 1993 / Scarface ♦♦

It's difficult to explain the dip in quality of Ice Cube's recent CDs. Where Cube was once among hip-hop's most acerbic, gripping rappers, his voice sounds unconvincing and devoid of fury on such ostensibly political numbers as "Cave Bitch" and "Ghetto Bird." He takes repeated cheap shots at Christianity, but his pitch for Islam on "When I Get To Heaven" doesn't convey any sense of that religion's alternative views or allegedly superior stances. It's only on standard gangsta tracks that Cube comes close to resembling the incendiary figure who recorded *Kill at Will* and *Amerikkka's Most Wanted*. It's hard to believe, but could Ice Cube possibly be running out of things to say after only four solo albums? —*Ron Wynn*

Bootlegs & B-Sides / 1994 / Priority ♦♦♦

It's nothing but a collection of remixes and flip-sides, but Ice Cube's *Bootlegs & B-Sides* proves that he has always remained in step with the times and, more importantly, often set the standards for hip-hop. In fact, the record almost functions as an alternate best-of; none of the original single versions are included, but the material is so strong, it doesn't matter—these songs are essential listening, no matter what mix they are heard in. —*Stephen Thomas Erlewine*

Ice-T

Rap

Ice-T (born Tracy Morrow) has proven to be one of hip-hop's most articulate and intelligent stars, as well as one of its most frustrating. At his best, the rapper has written some of the best portraits of ghetto life and gangsters, as well as some of the best social commentary hip-hop has produced. Just as often, he can slip into sexism and gratuitous violence, and even then his rhymes are clever and biting. Ice-T's best recordings have always been made in conjunction with strong collaborators, whether it's the Bomb Squad or Jello Biafra. With his music, Ice-T has made a conscious effort to win the vast audience of white male adolescents, as his frequent excursions with his heavy metal band Body Count show. All the while, he has withstood a constant barrage of criticism and controversy to become a respected figure not only in the music press, but the mainstream media as well.

Although he was one of the leading figures of Californian hip-hop in the '80s, Ice-T was born in Newark, NJ. When he was a child, he moved from his native Newark to California after his parents died in an auto accident. While he was in high school, he became obsessed with rap while he went to Crenshaw High School in South Central Los Angeles. Ice-T took his name from Iceberg Slim, a pimp who wrote novels and poetry. Ice-T used to memorize lines of Iceberg Slim's poetry, reciting them for friends and classmates. After he left high school, he recorded several undistinguished 12-inch singles in the early '80s. He also appeared in the low-budget hip-hop films *Rappin',* *Breakin',* and *Breakin' II: Electric Boogaloo* as he was trying to establish a career.

Ice-T finally landed a major label record deal with Sire Records in 1987, releasing his debut album, *Rhyme Pays*. On the record, he is supported by DJ Aladdin and producer Afrika Islam, who helped create the rolling, spare beats and samples that provided a backdrop for the rapper's charismatic rhymes, which were mainly party-oriented; the record wound up going gold. That same year, he recorded the theme song for Dennis Hopper's *Colors*, a film about inner-city life in Los Angeles. The song—also called "Colors"—was stronger, both lyrically and musically, and more incisive than anything he had previously released. Ice-T formed his own record label, Rhyme Syndicate (which was distributed through Sire/Warner) in 1988, and released *Power*. *Power* was a more assured and impressive record, earning him strong reviews and his second gold record. Released in 1989, *The Iceberg / Freedom of Speech...Just Watch What You Say* established him as a true hip-hop superstar by matching excellent abrasive music with fierce, intelligent narratives and political commentaries, especially about hip-hop censorship.

Two years later, Ice-T began an acting career, starring in the updated blaxploitation film *New Jack City*; he also recorded "New Jack Hustler" for the film. "New Jack Hustler" became one of the centerpieces of 1991's *O.G. Original Gangster*, which became his most successful album to date. *O.G.* also featured a metal track called "Body Count" recorded with Ice-T's band of the same name. Ice-T took the band out on tour that summer, as he performed on the first Lollapalooza tour. The tour set up increased his appeal with both alternative music fans and middle class teenagers. The

following year, the rapper decided to released an entire album with the band, also called *Body Count*.

Body Count proved to be a major turning point in Ice-T's career. On the basis of the track "Cop Killer"—where he sang from the point-of-view of a police murderer—the record ignited a national controversy; it was protested by the NRA and police activist groups; the offices of Time-Warner. The record company initially supported Ice-T, yet they refused to release his new rap album, *Home Invasion*, on basis of the record cover. Ice-T and the label parted ways by the end of the year. *Home Invasion* was released on Priority Records in the spring of 1993 to lukewarm reviews and sales. Somewhere along the way, Ice-T had begun to lose most of his original hip-hop audience; now he appealed primarily to suburban White teens. In 1994, he wrote a book and released the second Body Count album, *Born Dead* which failed to stir up the same controversy as the first record—indeed, it failed to gain much attention of any sort. Nevertheless, Body Count was successful in clubs and Ice-T continued to tour with the band; they are scheduled to release a third album in 1996. —*Stephen Thomas Erlewine*

Rhyme Pays / 1987 / Sire ♦♦

Ice-T made his initial pop impact with this 1987 album. It earned him his first gold record, and while there were still lighter numbers like "I Love Ladies," it was also an early indication that the graphically violent images and sexist language of such songs as "Squeeze the Trigger," "Sex" and "Pain" would appeal across racial and economic lines. Ice-T was also trimming and tightening his rap approach, putting more menace in his tone and more edge in his rhymes. —*Ron Wynn*

○ **Power** / 1988 / Sire ♦♦♦♦

His second release is a quantum-leap improvement over his debut—better samples, a more pronounced and developed rapping style, and smarter material. Ice-T does marvelous homage to Curtis Mayfield with an excellent adaption of "I'm Your Pusherman" from the vintage *Superfly* soundtrack. —*Ron Wynn*

☆ **The Iceberg** / 1989 / Sire ♦♦♦♦♦

The Iceberg: Freedom of Speech...Just Watch What You Say is a brutal, occasionally brilliant condemnation of censorship, drug use, and societal injustice, marred only by a few conflicting ideals and his own sexism. —*John Floyd*

★ **O.G. Original Gangster** / 1991 / Sire ♦♦♦♦♦

T's masterpiece is an ambitious, sprawling examination of gangsta-rap culture that confronts all the relevant issues and even offers a few alternatives and solutions. It's also Ice-T's most musically visceral outburst. —*John Floyd*

Home Invasion / 1993 / Priority ♦♦♦

Given the fact that most of *Home Invasion* was recorded during and after the "Cop Killer" media firestorm, it comes as no surprise that the album is an uneven, muddled affair, not the clean, focused attack of *O.G. Original Gangster*. Instead of producing an album that illustrates his confusion through the music (like Public Enemy's claustrophobic "Welcome to the Terrordome"), Ice-T made a confused album, unsure in its musical and lyrical direction. *Home Invasion* does have some flashes of brilliance (about a third of the album, particularly the tribute to the gang truce, "Gotta Lotta Love"), but it takes a little digging to find the best material. —*Stephen Thomas Erlewine*

The Classic Collection / 1993 / Rhino ♦♦

Ice-T's early sound was far different from the material that later earned him fame and controversy. His voice was higher, his cadence less assured, his commentary and ideas rough and evolving, and his backdrops less sophisticated, with straight scratches rather than multiple edits and song samples. While he did rap about social problems, Ice-T was then just as concerned with proving his manhood on the mike as many East Coast types, and had to overcome initial skepticism about a West Coast rapper not being inherently soft. This collection reissues formative Ice-T, including such seminal raps as "6 in the Mornin'," "Killers," "Body Rock" and a 1992 autobiographical review of the old days, "Ice-A-Mix." It's also interesting to remember just how little furor there was in the mid-'80s over things that get people easy headlines in the 1990s. —*Ron Wynn*

Icehouse

Group, Alternative Pop/Rock

Though it has had varying personnel, Icehouse is essentially a vehicle for the work of Australian Iva Davies (b. May 22, 1955). Davies formed the first version of the band under the name Flowers in 1980 and began scoring hits in Australia with the group's first single, "Can't Help Myself." *Icehouse* was the name of Flowers' first album, but the group changed its name as it went international, to avoid conflicts with another band. They first reached the U.S. charts in 1981 with "We Can Get Together" but did not score a substantial hit until 1988, with "Crazy." This was followed by the Top Ten hit "Electric Blue," which was written by John Oates. — *William Ruhlmann*

○ **Icehouse** / 1981 / Chrysalis ✦✦✦✦
The debut album from Iva Davies and his band is stark, alienated synth-pop. Smooth and danceable, this offers tight musicianship but a definite angst-ridden quality. —*Scott Bultman*

Primitive Man / 1982 / Chrysalis ✦✦✦

Fresco / 1983 / Chrysalis ✦✦✦
A five-song EP, it includes material from *Primitive Man*, plus three others. The featured selection is "Hey Little Girl." —*AMG*

Sidewalk / 1984 / Chrysalis ✦✦✦

Measure for Measure / 1986 / Chrysalis ✦✦✦

Love in Motion / 1986 / Chrysalis ✦✦✦

○ **Man of Colours** / 1987 / Chrysalis ✦✦✦✦
The U.S. debut finds Davies, whose baritone suggests both David Bowie and Bryan Ferry, fronting a cohesive, synthesized pop sound on the hits "Crazy" and "Electric Blue." —*William Ruhlmann*

● **Great Southern Land** / 1989 / Chrysalis ✦✦✦✦
This ten-track compilation album of Icehouse's greatest hits of the '80s reveals the band's chameleonlike pop talent. British art-rock is the touchstone, although the group can also rock out. —*William Ruhlmann*

Icicle Works

Group, Pop/Rock
Icicle Works was an atmospheric guitar-pop band out of Liverpool, England, featuring guitarist/singer Robert Ian McNabb, bassist Chris Layhe, and drummer Chris Sharrock. They have worked with producer Ian Broudie, of Lightning Seeds fame. Icicle Works' output has been inconsistent throughout their career; their better songs are creative and melodic, while other work has been criticized as ponderous and pretentious. The group's sound has gradually become harder over the years, with several personnel shifts, leaving McNabb as the only remaining original member. —*Steve Huey*

Icicle Works / 1984 / Beggars Banquet ✦✦✦
The internationally successful debut includes their two biggest hits. —*Steve Aldrich*

○ **Small Price of a Bicycle** / 1985 / Beggars Banquet ✦✦✦✦
This is huge, wide-screen music; Icicle Works throw everything at the wall and most of it sticks. —*Steve Aldrich*

Seven Singles Deep / 1986 / Beggars Banquet ✦✦✦
Featured are remixed and extended versions of early singles. —*Steve Aldrich*

Understanding Jane / 1986 / Beggars Banquet ✦✦

Who Do You Want for Your Love? / 1986 / Beggars Banquet ✦✦

If You Want to Defeat Your Enemy Sing His Song / 1987 / Beggars Banquet ✦✦✦
This uneven album still has strong moments. —*Steve Aldrich*

Blind / 1988 / Beggars Banquet ✦✦
This is the final album with original line-up. —*Steve Aldrich*

Permanent Damage / 1990 / Epic ✦✦
Ian McNabb with short-lived second lineup. —*Steve Aldrich*

● **Best Of** / Beggars Banquet ✦✦✦✦

Billy Idol (William Broad)

b. Nov. 30, 1955, Middlesex, England
Hard Rock, Pop/Rock
Billy Idol represents the bridge between punk rock and hard rock/metal, a logical enough connection that somehow seemed unlikely until he made the transition. Idol left Sussex University in 1976 to join the punk movement, specifically the group of rabid Sex Pistols fans called the Bromley Contingent. Many of the members formed their own bands, and Idol began Generation X with

Tony James. Generation X became a moderate success during the punk heyday of the late '70s, especially in England, with Idol on snarling lead vocals.

When the band split in 1981, Idol went to New York and hooked up with manager Bill Aucoin (who had handled Kiss, among others). This resulted in Idol's grooming as more of a mainstream rock figure. His debut album, *Billy Idol*, came out in 1982 and spent two years on the charts as the result of such video hits as "White Wedding" and "Hot in the City." But it was Idol's second album, *Rebel Yell*, that was his big breakthrough, selling two million copies and spawning hits in the raucous title track and the ballad "Eyes without a Face." Idol followed it up with *Whiplash Smile* in 1986 and *Charmed Life* in 1990.

Idol's first commercial failure came in 1993, with *Cyberpunk*, his stab at techno-influenced rock. —*William Ruhlmann*

○ **Billy Idol** / 1982 / Chrysalis ✦✦✦✦
Billy Idol's self-titled debut album was a snarling take on hard rock, injected with the spite and attitude of punk and new wave. While the record is spotty, Idol pulls it all together on the classic single "White Wedding." —*Stephen Thomas Erlewine*

● **Rebel Yell** / 1983 / Chrysalis ✦✦✦✦
Tight rock arrangements featuring Steve Stevens's slashing guitar playing and Idol's vocal sneer. The dance-rock of "Rebel Yell" is alternated with power-ballads like "Eyes without a Face" for a well-rounded pop package. —*William Ruhlmann*

Whiplash Smile / 1986 / Chrysalis ✦✦✦
While *Whiplash Smile* is Idol's most ambitious album, it only comes to life on hard-rocking pseudo-rockabilly like "I Forgot to Be Your Lover." Unfortunately, there aren't many songs that are as good as that single on this album. —*Stephen Thomas Erlewine*

○ **Charmed Life** / 1990 / Chrysalis ✦✦✦✦
Like any Billy Idol album, *Charmed Life* is wildly inconsistent, but it has enough strong songs—like the gloriously tongue-in-cheek hard-rock of "Cradle of Love"—to make most of the filler on the record forgivable. —*Stephen Thomas Erlewine*

Cyberpunk / Jun. 29, 1993 / Chrysalis ✦✦
Cyberpunk, Idol's attempt to restyle himself as a futuristic cyber-rocker, only works when he falls back on his effortlessly catchy guitar hooks and melodies of his past hits (the first single, "Shock to the System," for instance). Unfortunately, most of the album is padded with pretentious speeches, sampled dialogue, and under-developed songs. Especially noteworthy is his techno-dance interpretation of the Velvet Underground's "Heroin" (featuring a repeated Patti Smith quote), which is one the worst covers ever recorded. —*Stephen Thomas Erlewine*

The Impacts

Group, Rock & Roll
Before beginning his career as a vocalist and songwriter, the multi-faceted Merrell Fankhauser was the lead guitarist of a surf group, the Impacts. He has repeatedly claimed in interviews that they recorded the original version of "Wipe Out," only to have the song and arrangement stolen by the Surfaris, who had a huge hit with it in 1963. The Impacts didn't get any hits themselves, but they did manage to release a respectable instrumental surf album on Del-Fi in 1962, as well as a few tracks on obscure compilation samplers issued in the early sixties. —*Richie Unterberger*

Wipe Out / 1962 / Del Fi ✦✦✦
Okay surf instrumentals, ranging from stompers to tropical-flavored slow tunes. Has some steel guitar, dirty sax, and the occasional hot lead (from Fankhauser), but nothing attains classic status. The version of "Wipe Out" is substantially different from (and not as good as) the Surfaris', featuring a saxophone and a raunchier feel. —*Richie Unterberger*

The Impressions

Group, Soul, R&B
The first Impressions hit, "For Your Precious Love," was an anachronism when released in 1958. Jerry Butler's robust, yearning vocal was a throwback to deep-South gospel, and Curtis Mayfield's arrangement was decidedly barebones. But this song also precipitated the changes coming in R&B; you can hear the groundwork for soul music being laid, from the melisma of Butler's phrasing to Mayfield's skeletal guitar. The song literally flew in the face of then-popular doo-wop formulas.

Butler left the group in 1960, but the pared-down trio, led by Mayfield, cut a path that altered the R&B map. Mayfield's high falsetto and the trade-off vocals of Fred Cash and Sam Gooden framed a new kind of R&B: smooth and graceful, at times lilting, soaked in the history of gospel, and, thanks to Mayfield's lyrical examinations of racism and urban decay, the catalyst for the wave of socially aware Black hits recorded in the '70s.

The group's hits varied from supple statements of affirmation ("It's All Right," "People Get Ready") and romantic declarations ("Talking About My Baby," "I'm So Proud") to songs that were sociopolitical ("Choice of Colors," "This Is My Country") or mystical ("Gypsy Woman"). Mayfield's outside production work yielded similar-sounding hits for the likes of Major Lance, Walter Jackson, and Billy Butler (and the sound of the Impressions was imitated by the likes of the Viscounts and the Knight Brothers). Their chart run ended by the late '60s, as did Mayfield's Midas touch; after recording the brilliant *Superfly* in 1972, his talents ran dry. Nonetheless, Mayfield's reputation as one of soul's supreme innovators cannot be exaggerated. —*John Floyd*

○ **The Impressions** / 1963 / Paramount ✦✦✦✦
A landmark soul date, one of the Impressions' finest albums. They showed once and for all that they would succeed as a trio, and also revealed to any who won't aware Curtis Mayfield's brilliance as a composer. The hits came pouring out of Mayfield in the mid-'60s, and "It's All Right" was just the first of many gems he would write, produce, sing the lead vocals on, and arrange. A fabulous album. —*Ron Wynn*

Keep on Pushing / 1964 / Paramount ✦✦✦
The Impressions moved over to Paramount in 1964, but had absolutely no problems continuing their soul dominance. Mayfield's title track and "I've Been Trying" were among the many monster tunes on this release. The Impressions had jelled and had the perfect combination of Mayfield's gripping leads and flickering guitar, plus perfect support by Sam Gooden and Fred Cash. —*Ron Wynn*

Never Ending Impressions / 1964 / Paramount ✦✦✦
The second Impressions album released on ABC Records more than equaled the high standards established by its predecessor. Mayfield's anthemic ballads and uptempo tunes were both superbly written and expertly produced and arranged. His vocals could be sparse, edgy, hard-hitting, or subdued, and the Gooden/Cash duo fit their voices into the material with precision. —*Ron Wynn*

● **Greatest Hits** / 1965 / MCA ✦✦✦✦
This skimpy but solid collection of Curtis Mayfield's early-'60s soul landmarks includes "It's All Right" and "Gypsy Woman," defining the formula of early-'60s soul. —*John Floyd*

The Impressions' Greatest Hits / 1965 / Paramount ✦✦✦
While it may have a been a bit early to issue a greatest hits album, you can't really argue with the quality of this mid-'60s anthology. It's no longer the package to obtain since MCA issued the excellent two-disc Mayfield anthology in 1992, and even ABC put out a good two-record vinyl set in the '70s. But as a single album venture, if you can find it, it's well worth getting. —*Ron Wynn*

○ **One by One** / 1965 / Paramount ✦✦✦✦
The Impressions continued a great run of hit singles and fine albums with this outstanding release, one of three that were issued on ABC in 1965. The structure by now was both fixed and marvelous; songs revolved around Mayfield's leads, superb production and arrangements, guitar licks and riffs anchoring the backdrop, and Fred Cash and Sam Gooden interacting with Mayfield on the choruses, bridges, and turnarounds. —*Ron Wynn*

○ **People Get Ready** / 1965 / Paramount ✦✦✦✦
Another majestic Impressions album, although the group was nearing the end of its stay on the ABC label. The title tune numbers among Mayfield's greatest compositions, and there are plenty of other solid songs throughout both sides. Their interplay, Mayfield's leads, and the production and arrangments are brilliant. —*Ron Wynn*

Ridin' High / 1966 / Paramount ✦✦✦
The Impressions were certainly dominating the charts and making wonderful albums in the '60s, and this one didn't break the string. They would depart from ABC in two years, but at this point there were no concerns, even though they didn't match the previous years' glittering array of hits. But their singing was no less emphatic or compelling, nor had Mayfield's writing, productions, or arrangements slipped. —*Ron Wynn*

The Fabulous Impressions / 1967 / Paramount ✦✦✦
The Impressions didn't make a bad album during their stint on ABC. They kept the string intact in 1967, with three more singles reaching the charts. Although Mayfield has now said in interviews that he felt the group was exhausting its repertoire of quality material during this period, it didn't sound like it from the performances on the LP. —*Ron Wynn*

○ **We're a Winner** / 1968 / Paramount ✦✦✦✦
The Impressions' final ABC album was a great one to exit the label. The title track was a chart topper and one of the year's great prophetic/inspirational compositions. Mayfield's voice had grown even more weary and poignant, and Cash and Gooden now were almost mystical in their ability to interact and come in at precisely the right moments with their accompaniment. The production and arrangements were excellent, as usual. —*Ron Wynn*

○ **The Young Mods' Forgotten Story** / 1969 / Curtom ✦✦✦✦
Curtis Mayfield was almost ready to leave the Impressions and began a remarkable solo career when they cut the brilliant *Young Mods' Forgotten Story*, which fully displays Mayfield's splendid skills as a lead vocalist, songwriter and arranger. He penned both moving love songs and provocative message tracks, with "Choice Of Colors" and "Mighty, Mighty (Spade & Whitey)" challenging audiences across the color line to address their prejudices. Mayfield managed to cram his ideas and sentiments into the restrictive pop frameworks of the time (no song longer than three minutes). —*Ron Wynn*

16 Greatest Hits / 1970 / Paramount ✦✦✦
As fine a single album anthology as existed for years of the Impressions, it's still among the best hits packages ever done of their material. Its value has lessened now only because of MCA's two-disc set and a two-album package that contained Impressions material with both Butler and Mayfield, plus Mayfield's own solo cuts. —*Ron Wynn*

○ **The Complete Vee-Jay Recordings** / 1993 / Vee-Jay ✦✦✦✦
The Impressions' early music has taken a back seat to what they did after Jerry Butler departed and Mayfield began doing the lead vocals, writing, producing and arranging. This excellent 18-track disc helps put the early years into focus, with Butler showcased on seven cuts and Mayfield on eight. The Impressions weren't a bad five-member harmony unit; they just were not a great one in an era when you had to be fantastic simply to break out of the pack. These are mostly nice love songs, and they aren't lyrically different from thousands of similar tracks, but they did deserve a better fate than to be dropped from the Vee-Jay label 1959. —*Ron Wynn*

Lasting Impressions / Curtom ✦✦✦
One of the final releases featuring Curtis Mayfield with the Impressions, the group had switched affiliations and were now recording for Curtis' label. It was a standard session for them—well-produced, with excellent compositions and Mayfield's usual stately vocals, plus their tight harmonies. —*Ron Wynn*

Incredible String Band

Group, Folk, Folk-Rock
Scotland-born Mike Heron (b. 1941) and Robin Williamson (b. 1943) led one of the most eclectic folk groups of the 1960s, starting as a duo and later expanding and electrifying into a folk-rock group. —*William Ruhlmann*

The Incredible String Band / 1966 / Rykodisc ✦✦✦
As much a showcase for individual performances as group ones, the ISB's debut was their most traditional effort, though Williamson and Heron modernized traditional British Isles music with their whimsical songwriting and vari-pitch vocals. It also has minor contributions from guitarist Clive Palmer, who would leave the group after this album. —*Richie Unterberger*

5,000 Spirits or the Layers of The Onion / 1967 / Elektra ✦✦✦
● **Hangman's Beautiful Daughter** / 1968 / Carthage ✦✦✦✦
Changing Horses / 1969 / Elektra ✦✦
Wee Tam / 1969 / Elektra ✦✦✦
Mixing English and American folk with what we now call "world music," the multi-instrumental Scottish duo of Robin Williamson and Mike Heron achieve a whimsical, delicate style that has never been duplicated. It reaches a peak here with such songs as "You Get Brighter." (*Wee Tam* is sometimes packaged with the simultaneously released *The Big Huge*, which is also recommended.) —*William Ruhlmann*

I Looked Up / 1970 / Elektra ✦✦✦

U / 1970 / Elektra ✦✦

○ **Relics of the Incredible String Band** / 1970 / Elektra ✦✦✦✦

The ISB's prolific output makes a compilation a virtual necessity, and this two-record set selects wisely from the seven albums the group released in the US between 1967 and 1970. From Robin Williamson's "First Girl I Loved" (covered by Judy Collins) and "Way Back in the 1960s" (recorded in 1967), to Mike Heron's "Air," and "This Moment," the ISB's eclectic, fanciful acoustic style is well portrayed. —*William Ruhlmann*

Liquid Acrobat As Regards the Air / 1971 / Elektra ✦✦✦

Earth Span / 1972 / Edsel ✦✦

No Ruinous Feud / 1973 / Edsel ✦✦✦

The ISB began to change its approach in 1971, cutting back on its sometimes open-ended song structures and adding a rock rhythm section to selected tracks. But it wasn't until this album that everything came together, resulting in a delightful collection of songs that range from reggae to light pop, along with the traditional folk styles that had always been the group's strong suit. —*William Ruhlmann*

Hard Rope & Silken Twine / 1974 / Edsel ✦✦

Seasons They Change / 1976 / Island ✦✦✦

On Air / 1994 / ✦✦✦

Indigo Girls

Group, Singer-Songwriter, Folk-Rock

The Indigo Girls (Amy Ray and Emily Saliers) have earned a devoted following with their thoughtful, introspective lyrics (rich in religious metaphor), sensitive folky delivery, and earthy harmonies. The dichotomy between Ray's edgier, rock-influenced delivery and Saliers's soft, reflective style creates enough tension to keep their concept interesting. —*Rick Clark*

Strange Fire / 1987 / Epic ✦✦

Their first proper album, *Strange Fire*, hints at future greatness with the duo's lush harmonies and shining acoustic guitars. Beautiful folk-pop but a diamond in the rough all the same. —*Chris Woodstra*

● **Indigo Girls** / 1989 / Epic ✦✦✦✦

This major-label debut is a strong showcase for this duo's harmonic skills and songwriting virtues. "Closer to Fine" (number 52) was a moderate hit. Emily Saliers's "History of Us" is particularly affecting. Other highlights include "Secure Yourself," "Tried to Be True," and "Kid Fears," which featured R.E.M.-vocalist Michael Stipe on backups. Hothouse Flowers also provides support. —*Rick Clark*

○ **Nomad Indians Saints** / 1990 / Epic ✦✦✦✦

Not as dynamic as *Indigo Girls*, this effort includes a few nice songs with "Welcome Me," "Watershed," and "Southland in the Springtime." The dichotomy between Ray's occasionally abrasive vocal strain and Saliers's delicately earthy alto is more apparent, making their delivery feel less focused. Their overreaching lyrics also undermined the success of this outing. —*Rick Clark*

Live: Back on the Bus Y'all / 1991 / Epic ✦✦

A spirited live set with Saliers and Ray backed by a full band, it features live and studio versions of their radio hit "1 2 3," and a version of Dylan's "All Along the Watchtower." —*Rick Clark*

Rites of Passage / Feb. 1992 / Epic ✦✦✦

Not straying too far from their nearly formulaic sound, *Rites of Passage* shows great strides in songwriting maturity. The tension between Amy Ray's harsher rock style and Emily Sailer's sweeter melodic sense makes for a beautiful combination. Only a ridiculous cover of Dire Straits' "Romeo and Juliet" misses the mark. —*Chris Woodstra*

Swamp Ophelia / 1994 / Epic ✦✦✦

The most sophisticated sounding Indigo Girls production to date, *Swamp Ophelia* features some fine material, like "Touch Me Fall," "Mystery," "Language or the Kiss," "Power of Two," and "Least Complicated." For the most part, Amy Ray's occasional over-the-top stridency is fortunately restrained, while Emily Saliers's warm, earthy voice continues to pull the listener into considering her lyrical sentiments. As usual, when the two sing together, it's a wonderful sound. —*Rick Clark*

James Ingram

b. Feb. 16, 1956, Akron, OH

Soul, Urban

Ingram began performing with the band Revelation Funk in the early '70s, moving from Akron, OH, to Los Angeles in 1973. During the '70s, Ingram supported Ray Charles on the road with backup vocals and piano, played keyboards behind the Coasters on Dick Clark's oldies revues, and was Leon Haywood's musical director. After hearing a demo of him singing "Just Once," Quincy Jones asked Ingram to perform on his new album. Released in 1980 on *The Dude*, the number 17 "Just Once" was Ingram's first success, resulting in three Grammy nominations—Best New Artist, Best Pop Male Vocal, and Best R&B Vocal—winning in the two latter categories. Throughout the '80s, Ingram had steady popular success singing duets, but all of his solo albums failed to make a dent in the charts; in 1990 he scored his first solo hit, "I Don't Have the Heart." —*Stephen Thomas Erlewine*

It's Your Night / 1983 / Qwest ✦✦✦

Middle-of-the-road ballads and light R&B.—*Ron Wynn*

Never Felt So Good / 1988 / Qwest ✦✦✦

James Ingram became a major artist in the '80s on the strength of his work with Quincy Jones and his duets with Patti Austin. He got plenty of urban contemporary airplay and exposure with this mid-'80s album, his last for Jones' Qwest label. It reinforced both the appeal of the urban production style (polished charts, great productions) and its problems (overly slick vocals and thematic sameness in the performances). —*Ron Wynn*

It's Real / May 23, 1989 / Qwest ✦✦

Contains his recent R&B hit. —*Ron Wynn*

● **The Power of Great Music: Best of James Ingram** / 1991 / Qwest ✦✦✦✦

Includes his Top 40 duets—"Yah Mo B There" (#19, recorded with Michael McDonald), "Somewhere Out There" (#2, recorded with Linda Ronstadt), "Baby, Come to Me" (#1, recorded with Patti Austin), and his first solo hit, "I Don't Have the Heart" (#1)— as well as songs that have scored the urban charts. —*Ron Wynn*

Always You / May 25, 1993 / Qwest ✦✦✦

America, the Dream Goes on / Philips ✦✦

Luther Ingram

b. Nov. 30, 1944, Jackson, TN

Soul

This Jackson, TN, Southern-soul singer was one of the top artists at Stax during the early '70s. Hooking up with producer Johnny Baylor's tiny KoKo label, Ingram appeared regularly on the R&B charts after Baylor brought his firm into the Stax fold in 1969. Ingram's intimate vocal approach was well suited to ballads, and his 1970 hit revival of "Ain't That Loving You (For More Reasons than One)" set the stage for his R&B chart-topping classic "(If Loving You Is Wrong) I Don't Want to Be Right" two years later. Long after Stax had folded, Ingram was still releasing hit singles—clear into 1987. —*Bill Dahl*

I've Been Here All the Time / 1972 / Koko ✦✦✦

Luther Ingram established himself as a comer on the Southern soul scene with his debut album for Koko. He moved from Jackson, Tennessee to New York, but then Stax contacted him, and he eventually began recording for Koko. Booming, energetic, and unsophisticated wailing was his stock-in-trade, plus a country/blues influence. —*Ron Wynn*

○ **If Loving You Is Wrong (I Don't Want to Be Right)** / 1972 / Koko ✦✦✦✦

Luther Ingram earned his biggest R&B and pop hit with the title track, one of the last hurrahs for gospel-tinged and country-flavored confessional soul. The song would later become a country hit for Barbara Mandrell. Ingram landed one other Top Ten R&B single with "I'll Be Your Shelter (In Time of Storm)," and the album contained some other earnest soul ballads that weren't hits in "I Can't Stop" and "Help Me Love." Ingram never again enjoyed similar crossover heights, and the tide was turning against deep soul in both pop and R&B camps. —*Ron Wynn*

○ **Luther Ingram** / 1986 / Profile ✦✦✦✦

Luther Ingram made a brief return to the R&B charts with this 1986 LP issued on a predominantly dance-oriented label, which mixed his classic soul voice with urban contemporary production. It wasn't an early new jack swing number, as there were no hip-hop or rap elements, but it did contain drum machine tracks and synthesizer-dominated arrangements. Otherwise, Ingram was still singing heartache ballads, doing confessional country-soul and sounding raw and urgent on "Baby Don't Go Too Far" and "Don't Turn Around." The album also contained an interesting, although flawed, remake of Bob Dylan's "Gotta Serve Somebody." —*Ron Wynn*

I Like the Feeling / Urgent! ✦✦✦
An overlooked late-'70s Southern soul gem from Luther Ingram. He didn't make any attempt to soften or dilute his raw, country and blues-tinged delivery and style. That resulted in the album not getting widespread attention, but it did get Ingram a pair of Top 40 R&B hits and did much better than a lot of other Southern soul issued at the same time. —*Ron Wynn*

● **Golden Classics / Collectables ✦✦✦✦**

The Ink Spots
Group, R&B, Pop
The Ink Spots played a large role in pioneering the Black vocal group-harmony genre, helping to pave the way for the doo-wop explosion of the '50s. The quavering high tenor of Bill Kenny presaged hundreds of street-corner leads to come, and the sweet harmonies of Carlie Fuqua, Deek Watson, and bass Hoppy Jones (who died in 1944) backed him flawlessly.

Kenny's impeccable diction and Jones's deep drawl were both prominent on the Ink Spots' first smash on Decca in 1939, the sentimental "If I Didn't Care." From there through 1951, the group was seldom absent from the pop charts, topping the lists with "We Three (My Echo, My Shadow, and Me)" (1940), "I'm Making Believe" and "Into Each Life Some Rain Must Fall" (both in 1944), and "The Gypsy" and "To Each His Own" (both in 1946).

Watson eventually split to form his own group, the Brown Dots, and appeared in numerous low-budget film musicals, while Kenny attempted a solo career, notching a top five hit in 1951 with the uplifting "It Is No Secret." Countless groups masquerading as the Ink Spots have thrived across the nation since the '50s. —*Bill Dahl*

★ **The Greatest Hits 1939-46 / MCA ✦✦✦✦✦**
The authentic Decca recordings showcase this seminal doo-wop vocal unit. —*Ron Wynn*

Inner City
Group, House Music
A Detroit group that mixes techno with funk, Inner City has recorded for Virgin since 1989. Vocalist Paris Grey and producer/composer/mixer Kevin Saunderson haven't had much pop or R&B success, but are more highly regarded on the dance circuit. Their debut for Virgin was called *Big Fun*. Their subsequent LP releases were *Fire* in 1990 and *Praise* in 1992. —*Ron Wynn*

● **Big Fun / 1989 / Virgin ✦✦✦✦**
Inner City was one of the few house music and non-pop dance acts to get a major label deal despite the great hype regarding house and dance at the end of the '80s. They were a prototype house unit, with a gospel-tinged vocal style atop the bubbling, multi-layered house beat. There weren't any standout singles, but it was about as authentic a dance production as you'll get on a major label. —*Ron Wynn*

Praise / 1992 / Virgin ✦✦✦

Fire / Virgin ✦✦✦
Inner City's second major label album wasn't any different than its first; more slithering synthesized backbeats and textured production underneath steamy vocals, with a decided gospel influence. It unfortunately didn't do any better than its predecessor commercially, but was a representative sampling of early '90s house. —*Ron Wynn*

Insect Trust
Group, Rock & Roll
One of the more interesting one-shot bands in rock & roll, the Insect Trust's most famous member was writer/critic/ethnomusicologist Robert Palmer, who played alto sax and clarinet. Less famous, but still a notable member, was guitarist/songwriter Luke Faust, who went on to add creative input for the Holy Modal Rounders' string of wonderful early/mid-'70s records. Although the Insect Trust released two albums, their 1968 debut on Capitol remains a mystery to me: never seen it, never heard it. In fact, I wasn't aware of their second and final LP, *Hoboken Saturday*

Night, until nearly a decade after its release and a few more years spent scrounging around used record stores before coming across a copy. Along with the loose-limbed music, *Hoboken Saturday Night* features musical contributions by heavy hitters (no pun intended) such as drummers Elvin Jones and Bernard "Pretty" Purdie, guitarist Hugh McCracken, and novelist Thomas Pynchon. The music ranges from surreal folk-rock (a la the Holy Modal Rounders and Fugs) to Booker T.-like pop-soul to flat-out free jazz. 25 years after its release, *Hoboken Saturday Night* sounds a bit dated, but its charm is irresistible, especially when Nancy Jefferies sings and the band cranks up its raucous onslaught of reeds and percussion. Never intended to be a traditional pop act, the Insect Trust should be best remembered for extending rock's boundaries and taking the genre to a much hipper level without resorting to a lot of banal technique. Good luck locating their records. —*John Dougan*

Insect Trust / 1968 / Capitol ✦✦✦

● **Hoboken Saturday Night / 1970 / Atco ✦✦✦✦**
Ebullient, warm and wonderful, *Hoboken Saturday Night* is a long-forgotten piece of rock trivia that deserves to be rescued from the archives of oblivion and reissued. When the band wasn't indulging in a bit of jarring, jazzy dissonance, they were coughing up some intelligent folk-rock ("Trip on Me") or kicking out some serious Booker T.-style jams ("Ducks"). Robert Palmer's horn blowing is mighty fine, as is Nancy Jefferies' wan, but oddly seductive, vocalizing. Long out-of-print, it would be sad if this were lost forever. —*John Dougan*

Inspiral Carpets
Group, Alternative Pop/Rock
Of all of the Manchester bands of the early '90s, Inspiral Carpets were arguably the least interesting. They didn't explore the deep psychedelia of the rave scene as thoroughly as the Happy Mondays, nor did they have the classic pop skills of the Stone Roses. What the band did have was some massive organ hooks, courtesy of Clint Boon; the organ recalled the classic garage punk of the '60s. When the Inspiral Carpets could write a song that matched the sheer pleasure of their sound—and they managed at least two on each album, as well as their U.K. hit singles—the group made some wonderful pop gems; unfortunately, their hit-miss ratio was too low to make their albums consistent. When the Manchester fad passed, the Inspiral Carpets were still around and managed to keep scoring hits in the U.K. by losing some of the dated club beats and experimenting with their music slightly, including a collaboration with Mark E. Smith of the Fall on their 1994 album. —*Stephen Thomas Erlewine*

Life / 1990 / Elektra ✦✦✦
An impressive but inconsistent debut that recalled '60s British pop more strongly than the current Manchester dance craze, *Life* nevertheless had some fine dance tracks that were made to be played in clubs. —*Stephen Thomas Erlewine*

● **Beast Inside / 1991 / Elektra ✦✦✦✦**
Inspiral Carpets' second album relies more on their organ-driven garage psychedelia than the previous *Life*, and the result is an engagingly diverse set of dance-oriented modern pop. —*Stephen Thomas Erlewine*

○ **Revenge of the Goldfish / 1992 / Elektra ✦✦✦✦**
Inspiral Carpets continue to get further away from their club-oriented dance roots on their third album; fortunately, their pop songwriting continues to improve, which is why *Revenge of the Goldfish* never sounds like the work of a bunch of has-beens. —*Stephen Thomas Erlewine*

Intelligent Hoodlum
Rap
New York rapper Intelligent Hoodlum (born Percy Chapman) served 20 months on Riker's Island for robbery in 1988, using the experience to immerse himself in works on African-American culture and the theology of the Nation of Islam. That combination underscores all of his work and makes his songs radiate with righteousness, anger, indignation, and frustration. It doesn't hurt that ace producer Marley Marl supplies the undergirding as well. —*Ron Wynn*

○ **Intelligent Hoodlum / 1990 / A&M ✦✦✦✦**
A great social commentary. "Arrest the President" is a great rap. —*Robert Gordon*

● **Tragedy: Saga of a Hoodlum** / Jun. 22, 1993 / A&M ✦✦✦
Onetime Riker's Island prisoner Intelligent Hoodlum speaks with genuine insight about inner city hell and chaos. His second album wasn't laden with posturing rhetoric or presented in an ambitiously produced package. Instead, it was a chilling, unapologetic chronicle of brutal, ugly, negative experiences relayed by someone neither celebrating nor regretting what he's seen and heard. There was no attempt to entertain, impress or amuse in his rapping or rhymes; this was just the straight dope. *—Ron Wynn*

The Intrigues
Group, Soul, R&B
A slick trio that served up funky Philly soul during the early 70s. Their biggest hit in 1969 on the Yew label, "In a Moment," was slickly arranged and produced by Bobby Martin and Thom Bell, although its flip, "Scotchman Rock," was a rocking throwback to simpler times. The Intrigues' lush 1971 hit on Yew, "The Language of Love," was coproduced by Van McCoy. After an extended absence from the R&B charts, the trio reemerged from the shadows in 1985 with "Fly Girl." *—Bill Dahl*

● **Golden Classics** / 1970 / Collectables ✦✦✦✦
Slickly produced Philly R&B from the late '60s and early '70s featuring smooth harmonies and crisp arrangements. *—Bill Dahl*

The Intruders
Group, Soul
One of the earliest hitmaking vehicles for producers Kenny Gamble and Leon Huff, the Intruders were a leading R&B act from the mid '60s to the mid '70s. Fronted by Samuel "Little Sonny" Brown, the Intruders hit in 1966 with "(We'll Be) United" and the next year with "Together" on Gamble Records. Their breezy "Cowboys to Girls" and "Love Is like a Baseball Game" garnered plenty of pop crossover action in 1968, and their slick cover of the Dreamlovers hit "When We Get Married" scored in 1970. The quartet enjoyed their last two important R&B hits in 1973—"I'll Always Love My Mama (Part 1)" and "I Wanna Know Your Name"—before switching to Gamble and Huff's TSOP logo. *—Bill Dahl*

The Intruders Are Together / 1967 / Gamble ✦✦✦
The greatest bad-singing group in soul history, Philadelphia's Intruders were famous for the flat, sometimes woefully out-of-tune, yet inspiring lead vocals of "Little Sonny" Brown and some wonderful harmonizing. This was among their finest albums, and the title cut is a soul anthem. *—Ron Wynn*

○ **Cowboys to Girls** / 1968 / Gamble ✦✦✦✦
The Intruders cracked the pop charts with the title cut, which is still their best-known song. It topped the R&B hit list and made it to number six on the pop side. The rest of the album wasn't quite that strong, but it did have two more wonderful ballads, and was their biggest LP overall. *—Ron Wynn*

○ **The Intruders' Greatest Hits** / 1969 / Gamble ✦✦✦✦
A great collection from a favorite group among soul fans, out-of-tune lead vocals and all. If you only wanted one Intruders album, this is the ideal set. There were some CD copies floating around of this that were horribly mastered, but hopefully that's been corrected. *—Ron Wynn*

When We Get Married / 1970 / Gamble ✦✦✦
The Intruders entered the '70s hot, getting three singles on the R&B charts in 1970. The title cut wasn't as definitive as some past efforts, but was sentimental enough to get both R&B and chart action. It was later covered by Larry Graham, although the Intruders didn't do the original. They were, for a time, the major act on Kenny Gamble's label before he and Leon Huff started Philadelphia International the next year. *—Ron Wynn*

Save the Children / 1973 / Philadelphia International ✦✦✦

○ **Super Hits** / 1973 / Philadelphia International ✦✦✦✦
This is a fine collection of hits by the '70s Gamble/Huff-produced soul team who brought you "Cowboys to Girls" and "Love Is like a Baseball Game." *—John Floyd*

● **Philly Golden Classics** / 1995 / Collectables ✦✦✦✦

INXS
Group, Rock & Roll, Pop/Rock
After several years as a moderately successful dance-oriented new wave band, INXS began to accentuate the underlying dance and funk elements of their music, as well as vocalist Michael Hutchence's Jaggeresque sexuality. With the strong, funky single

"The Original Sin," 1984's *The Swing* was the first album that featured their change in direction; for the first time, INXS had a hit outside of their native Australia. 1985's *Listen like Thieves* was even more successful, both commercially and artistically; its title track was a hit on the charts and on MTV, but it was "What You Need" and its stylish, funky rock & roll that gave them their first Top Ten hit outside of Australia. But that was nothing compared to the worldwide success of 1987's *Kick*, which sold over four million copies in the U.S. alone. From the slow, simmering sexuality of "Need You Tonight" to the lovely ballad "Never Tear Us Apart," the album had no less than four huge hit singles.
Although its 1990 follow-up, *X*, sold well, the record was a carbon copy of *Kick*, signalling the beginning of INXS' commercial decline. The band released their most consistent and musically adventurous album, *Welcome to Wherever You Are*, in 1992 but it had almost no impact on the chart; 1993's *Full Moon, Dirty Hearts* was even more disappointing, falling off the charts only a few weeks after its release. *—Stephen Thomas Erlewine*

Inxs / 1980 / Atlantic ✦✦
At the time of their debut album, INXS had not developed a signature style, playing a competent but unremarkable variation on droning new wave synth-pop. Although Michael Hutchence already exuded a powerful vocal charisma, the only time *INXS* springs to life is when the group hints at the R&B and dance roots that would form the basis of their biggest hits. *—Stephen Thomas Erlewine*

Underneath the Colours / 1981 / Atlantic ✦✦
Underneath the Colours, INXS' second album, was a nearly identical continuation of the new wave pop of their debut, yet the record featured better arrangements and songs, including the Australian hit "The Loved One." *—Stephen Thomas Erlewine*

Shabooh Shoobah / 1982 / Atlantic ✦✦✦
On *Shabooh Shoobah*, INXS finally hit upon a smooth, stylish fusion of new wave synth-pop and rock & roll that drew equally from the Stones' dirty R&B-inspired rhythms and AC/DC's loud crunch. However, the group hits their stride only on a handful of tracks. The droning synth riff of "Don't Change" masks a hard, funky groove and "The One Thing" is an infectious, catchy pop single, yet most of the album lacks memorable songwriting. *—Stephen Thomas Erlewine*

Dekadance / 1983 / Atlantic ✦✦
Over the course of four remixed tracks from *Shabooh Shoobah*, the *Dekadance* EP accentuates INXS' flair for catchy rhythms, yet the record only comes to life on the six-minute remix of "The One Thing," simply because it has a stronger melody than anything else on the EP. *—Stephen Thomas Erlewine*

The Swing / 1984 / Atlantic ✦✦✦
Consolidating the strengths of *Shabooh Shoobah*, *The Swing* is the first consistently impressive INXS album. With the Nile Rodgers-produced "Original Sin" acting as the centerpiece, *The Swing* retains the new wave pop sense and rock attack of their earlier albums, while adding a stronger emphasis on dance rhythms. At the same time, the group's songwriting had improved, with more than half of the album featuring memorable hooks. *—Stephen Thomas Erlewine*

○ **Listen Like Thieves** / 1985 / Atlantic ✦✦✦✦
INXS completes its transition into an excellent rock & roll singles band with this album. Unfortunately, the new configuration only works for three songs: "What You Need," "Listen like Thieves," and "Kiss the Dirt (Falling Down the Mountain)." But these three songs are so strong that the album cannot be dismissed completely. The album is worth its price just for "What You Need," a strong Stonesy groove with Michael Hutchence singing more warmly than he ever has. *—Stephen Thomas Erlewine*

○ **Kick** / 1987 / Atlantic ✦✦✦✦
Kick, INXS's commercial and artistic breakthrough, overflows with hit singles, including "Need You Tonight," "Devil Inside," "New Sensation," and "Never Tear Us Apart." The band's mix of Stonesy rock & roll, melodic pop, and dance-oriented beats has never sounded fresher—even the album tracks are fully developed songs that never seem like filler. It's easily their best album. *—Stephen Thomas Erlewine*

○ **X** / 1990 / Atlantic ✦✦✦
The follow-up to the smash *Kick* isn't quite as successful as its predecessor, but it packs quite a punch. Although "Suicide Blonde," "The Stairs," "Bitter Tears" and "Disappear" are as good as any-

thing on *Kick*, the album suffers from songs that sound too similar. *—Stephen Thomas Erlewine*

Live Baby Live / 1991 / Atlantic ✦
Recorded during their international 1990 tour, *Live Baby Live* is a lifeless live album. INXS sounds professional—they never miss a note—and that's part of the problem. All of the performances sound like the studio versions, stripped of their excitement and savvy productions, which were essential factors in making the songs hit singles. Consequently, the album is a thoroughly unenaging affair and the worst record INXS have recorded. *—Stephen Thomas Erlewine*

○ **Welcome to Wherever You Are** / Aug. 4, 1992 / Atlantic ✦✦✦
Although INXS needed to experiment badly, their attempt at self-reinvention, *Welcome to Wherever You Are*, didn't even come close to gaining commercial or critical acceptance. From the start of the album, it's clear that INXS is out to confuse the standard perceptions of the band; the first instrument on the album is an Eastern-flavored horn. Special recording effects and exotic rhythms and sounds are abundant on the album. Evidently, the pop audience didn't care about INXS anymore, since nobody bought the album. And that is a shame, since it is one of their strongest. *—Stephen Thomas Erlewine*

Full Moon, Dirty Hearts / 1993 / Atlantic ✦✦
Following the surprisingly adventurous and artistically successful *Welcome to Wherever You Are*, *Full Moon, Dirty Hearts* sounds tired and as calculated as *X*. While most of the exotic trappings of *Welcome* have been pared down, there is still the same sense of the band experimenting as a way to stay current. INXS sounds energetic throughout the album, but the experimentation is poorly executed and there is a serious lack of strong songs and singles, apart from two duets: "Please (You Got That …)" with Ray Charles and the title track, which features Chrissie Hynde. *—Stephen Thomas Erlewine*

● **The Greatest Hits** / 1994 / Atlantic ✦✦✦
While INXS have made a few consistent albums, singles are the best format for the group's stylish dance-rock. Throughout the '80s and early '90s, the group racked up nine Top 40 hits and seven of those singles hit the Top Ten. *Greatest Hits* collects all of those hits—including "Need You Tonight," "What You Need," "Devil Inside," "New Sensation," "Disappear," "Suicide Blonde," and "Never Tear Us Apart"—adding minor hits like "Original Sin" and "Listen like Thieves," but curiously bypassing the pivotal "Don't Change" and excellent "Bitter Tears," which was a bigger hit than several songs on the record. Nevertheless, *Greatest Hits* lives up to its title and provides a fine introduction to the band. *—Stephen Thomas Erlewine*

Iron Butterfly

Group, Hard Rock, Psychedelic, Heavy Metal
Formed in 1966, Iron Butterfly performed a heavy, minor-key style of psychedelic pop/rock. Their debut album, *Heavy*, was a promising start but the followup effort, *In a Gadda Da Vida* (#4) became the biggest-selling album in Atlantic Records history until the advent of Led Zeppelin. This was primarily due to the 17:05-minute title track, which became a staple on the emerging progressive-FM-rock format. An edited version became a #30 hit. The followup album, *Ball*, did one better at #3.
Besides "In a Gadda Da Vida," Iron Butterfly charted with "Soul Experience" (#75), "In the Time of Our Lives" (#96), and "Easy Rider (Let the Wind Pay the Way)" (#66), from the movie *Easy Rider*. The band attempted a reunion in 1975 with two albums, the #138 *Scorching Beauty* and *Sun and Steel*, before breaking up again. *—Rick Clark*

Heavy / 1968 / Atco ✦✦✦
Iron Butterfly's 1968 debut album *Heavy* established the band's trademark sound, relying on plodding, heavy guitar riffs and thundering drums. Most of the album was not particularly well-written—the riffs *were* the songs, not their foundation—but the band's overwhelmingly loud sonic attack occasionally made up for the weakness in the material. *—Stephen Thomas Erlewine*

○ **In a Gadda Da Vida** / 1968 / Atco ✦✦✦✦
The title song, in all its glory, is all you need. *—Dan Heilman*

Ball / 1969 / Atco ✦✦✦
Following the huge success of their second record, *In-a-Gadda-Da-Vida*, Iron Butterfly scored a second straight Top Five album with *Ball*. While it didn't have any acid-rock freak-out to compare with

the epic "In-A-Gadda-Da-Vida," *Ball* was a more ambitious album, as the group experimented with shorter, more melodic songs. Like any Iron Butterfly album, the quality of the material is wildly inconsistent, yet cut-for-cut, *Ball* is a more consistent album than their two previous records, as the group trimmed away some of the acid-rock excesses of their earlier records while retaining their brutally loud trademark heavy guitars. *—Stephen Thomas Erlewine*

Iron Butterfly Live / 1970 / Atco ✦✦
A dull document of Iron Butterfly's thundering live show, *Iron Butterfly Live* is noteworthy for its second side, which contains a 20-minute version of "In-A-Gadda-Vida." Even though it's only three minutes longer than the original version, it's three times as tedious. *—Stephen Thomas Erlewine*

Metamorphosis / 1970 / Atlantic ✦✦✦
On *Ball*, Iron Butterfly began to expand their sound, attempting to write more concisely. On *Metamorphosis*, the group continued their musical explorations, adding a layered production to their sound. However, only keyboardist/vocalist Doug Ingle was enthusiastic about the band's new musical direction and most of the group refused to participate in the recording of the album, claiming it strayed too far from Iron Butterfly's signature sound. The truth of the matter is the rest of the band was right—under Ingle's direction, the group tries stylistic diversions that they do not have the ability to accomplish, including funk and acoustic ballads. Nevertheless, this ambition makes for an interesting listen, since Iron Butterfly's albums can be weighed down by their relentless heaviness. Despite a handful of strong tracks—particularly the single "Easy Rider (Let the Wind Pay the Way)"—most of the album doesn't hold up on repeated plays. *—Stephen Thomas Erlewine*

Scorching Beauty / 1975 / MCA ✦✦
Five years after their breakup, Iron Butterfly reunited in 1975 and released *Scorching Beauty*, an undistinguished album that fell between the group's heavy acid-rock and mid-'70s arena rock conventions. *—Stephen Thomas Erlewine*

Sun and Steel / 1976 / MCA ✦
If the 1975 comeback *Scorching Beauty* was faceless, Iron Butterfly's 1976 follow-up, *Sun and Steel*, was an outright disastrous attempt at reshaping the band's signature sound to '70s hard rock conventions, lacking even the curiosity value of *Scorching Beauty*. *—Stephen Thomas Erlewine*

● **Light and Heavy: The Best of Iron Butterfly** / 1993 / Rhino ✦✦✦
Although the compilation is quite generous, featuring 21 tracks on CD, *Light and Heavy: The Best of Iron Butterfly* isn't all that entertaining, due to Iron Butterfly's difficulties with producing compelling material. All of the group's highlights from 1968-1970 are included, although the career-making, 17-minute "In-A-Gadda-Da-Vida" is presented in its three-minute single edit. Since that is the only Iron Butterfly song most listeners know, the lack of the full-length version could potentially sink the album, but the fact of the matter is, "In-A-Gadda-Da-Vida" gets quite repetitive over the course of nearly 20 minutes. While the quality of the rest of *Light and Heavy* is spotty—ranging from heavy psychedelic rock to light psychedelic pop—it is a more intriguing listen than *In-A-Gadda-Da-Vida*, even if it doesn't have the period-piece charm of the original hit record. *—Stephen Thomas Erlewine*

Iron Maiden

Group, Heavy Metal
From their origins as a bar band in the mid '70s to the present, England's Iron Maiden has become one of the most imitated bands in heavy metal. The man who has held the group together through the rough times is bassist Steve Harris. Some of their theatrics were somewhat tacky in the early days, but by the late '70s they were already gaining a respectable following. EMI released their self-titled debut album in 1980, featuring Paul Di'Anno on vocals and Dave Murray on guitar. In the US, the album was released on Harvest.
The band's second album helped them gain a huge following all over Europe and America, but within the band there were problems. Out went Di'Anno and in came Bruce Dickinson, former vocalist for the band Samson. Another change was the addition of guitarist Adrian Smith (who joined just before the *Killers* album, replacing Dennis Stratton), and it was this lineup (along with drummer Clive Burr) that took them over the top. The band's im-

pact has been immense, selling millions, and their sound has easily distinguished them from other bands. —*John Book*

○ **Iron Maiden** / 1980 / Capitol ◆◆◆◆
This is the debut album that started it all for this band; many of the songs remain all-time metal classics, including "Sanctuary" and "Running Free." —*John Book*

○ **Killers** / 1981 / Capitol ◆◆◆◆
Album #2 by Iron Maiden is not as aggressive or as addicting as their self-titled debut but still an essential part of their career. This was the last studio album to feature vocalist Di'anno; he later formed Paul Di'anno's Battlezone. —*John Book*

Maiden Japan / 1981 / Capitol ◆◆
A live EP recorded in Japan, this was the last Iron Maiden record to feature vocalist Paul Di'anno. —*John Book*

● **The Number of the Beast** / 1982 / Capitol ◆◆◆◆
The first Maiden album to feature ex-Samson vocalist Bruce Dickenson, this is powerful with some great guitar work from Dave Murray and Adrian Smith and fantastic bass playing from Steve Harris. This is the album that brought the band success in the US, and it features the classics "Run to the Hills" and the title track. —*John Book*

○ **Piece of Mind** / 1983 / Capitol ◆◆◆◆
The first Maiden album to feature drummer Nicko McBrain, *Peace of Mind* is easily one of their best efforts. Lead guitarists Adrian Smith and Dave Murray play their most creative work here, and the whole band is in top form. —*John Book*

Powerslave / 1984 / Capitol ◆◆◆
Iron Maiden gets more into lyrical themes this time around, featuring the 13-minute classic "Rime of the Ancient Mariner." —*John Book*

○ **Live After Death (The World Slavery Tour)** / 1985 / Capitol ◆◆◆◆
Documenting the band at their peak, this is a great live double album with a wide range of songs, going as far back as their first album. It's also available as a home video. —*John Book*

Somewhere in Time / 1986 / Capitol ◆◆
A somewhat controversial album, the band prominently used keyboards and synthesizers in their sound. It has lots of great songs, including "Heaven Can Wait." —*John Book*

○ **Seventh Son of a Seventh Son** / 1988 / Capitol ◆◆◆◆
The band's first attempt at a concept album includes keyboardist/synthesizer sounds, but is not as annoying as the *Somewhere in Time* album. A good set of songs includes "Can I Play with Madness?," "The Clairvoyant," and the haunting title track. —*John Book*

No Prayer for the Dying / 1990 / Epic ◆◆
The band's first label move since signing to EMI in 1979, it's probably their weakest album, songwise, but Bruce Dickinson shows that he is one of the best vocalists in heavy metal. —*John Book*

Fear of the Dark / May 12, 1992 / Epic ◆◆
On their tenth album, the band shows that they haven't lost their edge or power. No surprises—it's just what you'd expect from Iron Maiden. —*AMG*

Chris Isaak

b. Jun. 26, 1956, Stockton, CA
Rock & Roll, Pop/Rock
Chris Isaak clearly loves the reverb-laden rockabilly and country of Sun Studios. In particular, he transfers the sweeping melancholy of Roy Orbison's sweeping, classic melancholy MGM singles ("Crying," "Oh, Pretty Woman," "In Dreams") to the more stripped-down, rootsy sound of Sun. His stylized take on '50s and '60s rock & roll eventually made him into a star in the early '90s, thanks to the hit single "Wicked Game."

Isaak began performing after he graduated from college, forming the rockabilly band Silvertone. The group, which featured guitarist James Calvin Wilsey, bassist Rowland Salley, and drummer Kenney Dale Johnson, would become the singer/guitarist's permanent supporting band. Isaak released his first album, *Silvertone*, on Warner Brothers Records in 1985. It was crtically well-received, yet it didn't sell. Two years later, he released *Chris Isaak* which managed to scrape into the Top 200 album charts. After its release, the singer began an acting career with a bit part in Jonathan Demme's 1988 film, *Married to the Mob*; he would later have parts in *Wild at Heart* and *The Silence of the Lambs*.

Released in 1989, *Heart Shaped World* initially sold more than *Chris Isaak*, yet it didn't manage to break big until late 1990, when the single "Wicked Game" was featured in David Lynch's *Wild at Heart*. Soon, the single became a Top Ten hit; the album also made it into the Top Ten and sold over a million copies. Both 1993's *San Francisco Days* and 1995's *Forever Blue* mine essentially the same vein as *Heart Shaped World*, yet he has managed to keep the formula from growing stale; in the meantime, he has been able to score a handful of hits in both the pop and adult contemporary charts. —*Stephen Thomas Erlewine*

Silvertone / 1985 / Warner Brothers ◆◆◆

Chris Isaak / Dec. 1986 / Warner Brothers ◆◆◆

● **Heart Shaped World** / 1989 / Warner Brothers ◆◆◆◆
The album that really broke Isaak through to a mainstream audience, this features the title cut, "I'm Not Waiting," "Wrong to Love You," a driving rendition of "Diddley Daddy," and the surprise #6 hit "Wicked Game." Brooding and intense. —*Cub Koda*

○ **San Francisco Days** / 1993 / Warner Brothers ◆◆◆◆
Chris Isaak's records are eerily out of time; the production is too clean and sterile to sound as if it was recorded at Sun Studios (a sound he clearly admires), but his music doesn't fit neatly into the sounds of contemporary radio. Accordingly, his sound is original yet familiar, appealing both to fans of early-'60s rock & roll and a modern audience. At times, Isaak tries too hard to emulate his idols—for instance, his strained Orbison-esque falsetto on "Two Hearts"—but when he doesn't try too hard, the results are often startling. *San Francisco Days* is Isaak's most musically diverse album yet. —*Stephen Thomas Erlewine*

Forever Blue / 1995 / Warner Brothers ◆◆◆
Chris Isaak's albums all follow the same basic formula, yet he adds a grittier edge to *Forever Blue*. Kicking off with the bluesy stomp of "Baby Did a Bad Thing," where Isaak tries to sound like John Lee Hooker, the album is another of expertly crafted rock & roll, carefully crafted to sound like the early '60s. It's enjoyable, yet it never is as consistent as *Heart Shaped World* or *San Francisco Days*. —*Stephen Thomas Erlewine*

The Isley Brothers

Group, Soul, Funk, R&B
They're still at it: recording artists since 1957, and hitmakers for almost as long. Inevitably, their music has changed, but this group's chief claim to fame remains their secularization of gospel call-and-response. They found that particular groove on "Shout" (cut for RCA in 1959), later followed by "Twist & Shout" on Wand in 1962—definitely one of the ballsier twist records. Four years in the commercial wilderness followed before they signed with Tamla and came up with "This Old Heart of Mine."

They didn't work long on the Motown assembly line, though, and in 1969 revived their own T-Neck Records. Twenty years later they were still grinding out hits on the label, although their first T-Neck smash, "It's Your Thing," remains their biggest. Brothers have come and gone, as have sidemen—including Jimi Hendrix at one point. Still, the family that plays together stays together, although the group trading as the Isley Brothers today includes elements of Isley-Jasper-Isley (two younger brothers and a cousin), who had a hit with "Caravan of Love" in 1985.

The great second generation family unit 3 Plus 3 finally disbanded in 1984. At that time the original trio continued recording for Warner Bros., while the younger threesome worked as Isley/Jasper/Isley. When O'Kelly suffered a heart attack in 1986, Ronald and Rudolph continued without him. Ronald Isley's wife, Angela Winbush, contributed production and compositions, as well as sang backgrounds for the 1987 *Smooth Sailing* LP. Their most recent release was *Tracks of Life* in 1992. Ronald Isley became her manager and collaborator on her projects. After working together until 1990, Isley-Jasper-Isley split into various groups as well. Ernie Isley and Chris Jasper became solo artists. —*Colin Escott and Ron Wynn*

Twist & Shout! / 1962 / Sundazed ◆◆◆
On this album, the Isleys tried to mine the "Twist & Shout" groove for all it was worth. Produced by Bert Berns, over half the material was written or co-written by "Russell"; the same Russell who co-wrote "Twist & Shout," it was a pseudonym for Berns himself. Not that this was always necessarily a bad thing; "Twist & Shout" was a stone classic, and many of the other tunes do their best to emulate its groove with Latin rhythms and the Isleys' frayed,

gospelish vocals. Some of the tracks, though, do little more than rework the basic riff, and even the ones that aren't blatant rewrites don't measure up to the hit. The ballad "Time After Time" is a nice change of pace, and the brothers are never less than energetic and entertaining, but this is really not that strong as a whole. The CD reissue on Sundazed includes three bonus tracks: the previously unreleased (and unremarkable) "Crazy Love" and the cool singles "Twistin' With Linda" and "Nobody But Me," which are easily available on Rhino's *Story* compilation. —*Richie Unterberger*

The Famous Isley Brothers / 1963 / United Artists ✦✦✦
The Isley Brothers were floundering during the early '60s, unable to find the right company or formula for their gospel-based soul. This album had a few good songs, but simply wasn't the vehicle they needed to get over the top. —*Ron Wynn*

Take Some Time out for the Isley Brothers / 1964 / T Neck ✦✦✦
The Isley Brothers were slowly getting their act together in the mid-'60s. The vocal teamwork and harmonies had sharpened, and they began to move more in the direction of funk and rock as well as soul. This album didn't break them out, but was one of their better foundation efforts. —*Ron Wynn*

This Old Heart of Mine / 1966 / Motown ✦✦✦
A strong Holland-Dozier-Holland production. —*Rick A. Bueche*

Soul on the Rocks / 1967 / Motown ✦✦✦
The group's final Motown album yielded one good song and hit, but otherwise was a summation of everything that went wrong while they were there. They never got the in-house support or push they needed, and by now were disillusioned and going through the motions. That was probably suitable, for most of what they sang here was routine anyhow. —*Ron Wynn*

○ **Doin' Their Thing** / 1969 / Motown ✦✦✦✦
An underrated masterpiece. This album really began the 3 Plus 3 relationship between the older brothers and the younger generation. The single "It's Your Thing" became a national catch phrase and later turned up in a film the brothers financed. More importantly, they now saw that they could expand their stylistic frontiers and start doing funk and rock along with the soul. —*Ron Wynn*

○ **3 Plus 3** / 1973 / T Neck ✦✦✦✦
A masterpiece, one of the defining albums for '70s black music. The original Isley frontline of Ronald, Rudolph, and O'Kelly merged with the next generation featuring younger brothers Marvin and Ernie, plus cousin Chris Jasper. The lead single "That Lady" established their new sound and identity on Epic, and was just one of four monster songs that came from the album. —*Ron Wynn*

The Isley's Greatest Hits / 1973 / T Neck ✦✦✦
Yet another greatest hits album, this one covering '60s and early '70s material. It's of value only to those who feel they need every single Isley Brothers album ever issued. —*Ron Wynn*

○ **The Isley Brothers Live It Up** / 1974 / T Neck ✦✦✦✦
The album that cemented the revolution begun by the *3 Plus 3* LP. The title song was a blazing triumph, landing them on *Soul Train* and getting widespread pop and club attention, although it didn't prove to be their biggest hit in those areas. Ernie Isley made his first significant impact as a guitar soloist, and the group also began attracting fans who hadn't heard their earlier cuts, while alerting the faithful they were really back on the scene. —*Ron Wynn*

○ **The Heat Is on** / 1975 / T Neck ✦✦✦✦
Another spectacular album. The Isley Brothers had refined rock/disco and now had it down to a science. The uptempo tunes had extended vamps, slithering, driving backbeats, and funky rhythms, while the ballads were smooth and sentimental. Ernie Isley would get a track to blaze away on guitar, and the whole thing revolved around the group's non-stop excitement and intensity. —*Ron Wynn*

Harvest for the World / 1976 / T Neck ✦✦✦
The Isley Brothers kept their great string of hits going with this mid-'70s release. They enjoyed two more Top 10 R&B singles and several club smashes, and were making enjoyable, delightful music, both the uptempo songs and the ballads. —*Ron Wynn*

Everything You Always Wanted to Hear / 1976 / T Neck ✦✦✦
An intriguing title that ultimately didn't prove to be the case. Instead, it was another good but not comprehensive or definitive anthology, which still doesn't surpass or equal the Rhino three-disc package. —*Ron Wynn*

Go for Your Guns / 1977 / T Neck ✦✦✦
The Isley Brothers maintained their '70s roll, getting another chart topper with the single "The Pride" and turning out a first-rate rock/disco effort. They were among the dominant acts in the entire business and were ruling the R&B and urban contemporary airwaves at this time. —*Ron Wynn*

Showdown / 1978 / T Neck ✦✦✦
The Isley Brothers had perfected their rock/disco format by the late '70s, and each album had a set pattern. There were the hit singles, with their chunking beat, synthesized underpinning, and energetic collective vocals. Then came the album cuts, sentimental ballads wonderfully sung by Ronnie Isley. Then there was a cut designed to show off Ernie Isley's blistering guitar, which reflected the group's rock legacy and the influence of Jimi Hendrix. This contained another chart-topper in "Take Me To The Next Phase." —*Ron Wynn*

Winner Takes All / 1979 / T Neck ✦✦✦
This was the last great Isley Brothers album in the rock/disco style. Their vocals still retained the energy and exuberance of earlier works, Ernie Isley hadn't become so disgruntled that he simply recycled Hendrix cliches, and the group's production, songs, and arrangements weren't yet becoming stagnant. —*Ron Wynn*

Go All the Way / 1980 / T Neck ✦✦✦
Although regarded as the beginning of their decline, this 1980 album did get the Isley Brothers three more chart hits. But they were so locked into their uptempo dance/R&B, ballad, rock guitar solo format that each LP became more and more predictable. The internal difficulties that finally tore the group apart were also surfacing with this album. —*Ron Wynn*

Grand Slam / 1981 / T Neck ✦✦✦
Despite getting three more hits, including one Top 10 R&B song, the bloom was definitely off the Isley Brothers' rose. Stagnation and internal bickering were taking their toll, and the innocent, energetic air that sparked their '70s albums was gone. It had been replaced by a calculating, indifferent attitude that clearly affected their music. —*Ron Wynn*

Between the Sheets / 1983 / T Neck ✦✦✦
The title track was a huge ballad hit for the Isley Brothers and marked the end of an era. The great 3 Plus 3 collaboration between the brothers Ronnie, Rudolph, and O'Kelly and the second generation of younger brothers, Marvin and Ernie, plus cousin Chris Jasper, finally splintered over artistic differences. Neither ever attained the same levels apart as they did together. —*Ron Wynn*

○ **The Isley's Greatest Hits, Vol. 1** / 1984 / Epic ✦✦✦✦
Once the Isley Brothers' great 3 Plus 3 band split, it didn't take long for the anthology packages to be released. This set features many of their mid-'70s gems and is a good single set collection for the casual fan. But the hardcore lover would prefer getting all the Isley material in one package. —*Ron Wynn*

Smooth Sailin' / 1987 / Warner Brothers ✦✦✦
This was the first album the Isley Brothers made after O'Kelly suffered a heart attack and died in 1986. It's both poignant and painful, because Ronnie demonstrates the vocal presence and soulful character that always made his ballads so vital. Angela Winbush, who later became Ronnie Isley's wife, served as background vocalist, co-composer, and producer. —*Ron Wynn*

Spend the Night / 1989 / Warner Brothers ✦✦✦
They were down to a duo by the time this record was released. O'Kelly Isley had died of a heart attack a couple of years earlier. Ronnie Isley was the featured vocalist, and he still had a soaring, dynamic sound. Angela Winbush, whom he later married and who also served as manager, worked closely on the album, but the magic was clearly gone. At times, listening to this album was a chore for any longtime Isley Brothers follower. —*Ron Wynn*

The Best of the Isley Brothers / 1990 / Curb ✦✦✦
The songs that most people remember, the string of chart hits that the Isley Brothers did during their rock/disco period. They successfully blended driving, blistering uptempo tunes with collective vocals and silky smooth, sentimental romantic fare featuring Ronnie Isley. There's a better anthology available on Rhino, but this will certainly do for starters. —*Ron Wynn*

○ **Greatest Hits & Rare Classics** / 1991 / Motown ✦✦✦✦
Although the Isleys recorded some good stuff for Motown in the late '60s, it's generally true that the label's attempts to fit them into the standard Motown production line inhibited their creativity and

individuality. This 22-track retrospective of their Motown days is dominated by material from in-house songwriters like Eddie Holland, Smokey Robinson, and Ivory Joe Hunter, and doesn't rank among the Isleys' best work, though it's respectable enough. The best tracks—the Top Ten hit "This Old Heart Of Mine," "Behind A Painted Smile," and "Take Some Time Out For Love"—are available on the Rhino best-of, but Isleys fans will find this a worthwhile summary of their brief Motown stay. Includes the original versions of two of their biggest hits cut for other labels, "Twist & Shout" and "It's Your Thing." —*Richie Unterberger*

Shout!: the Complete Victor Sessions / 1991 / RCA ✦✦✦
A fine anthology featuring the late '50s and early '60s sessions of the Isley Brothers. The original three were then squarely in a classic rock and roll mode, with some shouting gospel-tinged vocals mixing with pile-driving arrangements. These songs for the most part weren't hits, but they were certainly spirited. —*Ron Wynn*

The Complete UA Sessions / 1991 / EMI America ✦✦✦
After the Isleys left Scepter, they recorded for United Artists for a year, a period that produced no hits but a wealth of muscular R&B.Although there's some overlap with the first volume of Rhino's anthology, this one is essential for fans of the Isleys. —*Stephen Thomas Erlewine*

★ **The Isley Brothers Story, Vol. 1** / 1991 / Rhino ✦✦✦✦✦
Rhino's two Isley Brothers compilations provide the definitive portrait of the group. *Vol. 1: Rockin' Soul (1959-1968)* focuses on the Isleys' R&B beginnings, including both parts of "Shout," "This Old Heart of Mine (Is Weak for You)," and "Twist & Shout." —*Stephen Thomas Erlewine*

★ **The Isley Brothers Story, Vol. 2** / 1991 / Rhino ✦✦✦✦✦
The Isley Brothers founded their own record label, T-Neck, in 1969, and along with the new label came a new direction and sound for the group. Funkier and harder, the Isleys charted more frequently than ever before in their career with such singles as "That Lady" (#6), "Fight the Power" (#4), and the #2 hit "It's Your Thing." This completes the picture that *Vol. 1* began and is essential for any collection of early-'70s soul. —*Stephen Thomas Erlewine*

Soul Kings, Vol. 1 / 1995 / SMS ✦✦✦

Isley/Jasper/Isley

Group, Soul, R&B
A spin-off from the Isley Brothers, bassist Marvin Isley, drummer/guitarist Ernie Isley, and their keyboardist cousin Chris Jasper worked in the Isley Brothers 3 Plus 3 band from 1969 until 1984. They signed with Columbia as a separate entity at that time, and had substantial success with their debut LP *Broadway's Closer to Sunset Boulevard*. Their 1985 release *Caravan of Love* included their only R&B chart-topping single in the title cut, which had a three-week reign at number one. They scored three other Top 20 singles in 1986 and 1987, "Insatiable Woman," "8th Wonder of the World," and "Givin' You Back the Love." —*Ron Wynn*

Broadway's Closer to Sunset Blvd / 1985 / CBS ✦✦

● **Caravan of Love** / 1985 / Epic ✦✦✦✦
The splinter group of Ernie and Marvin Isley, plus their cousin Chris Jasper, departed from the Isley Brothers 3 Plus 3 conglomerate in 1984, and for a while seemed ready to enjoy their own success. The album's title track topped the R&B charts and was an international smash; it was later covered by the Housemartins. But the trio began to suffer its own personality and direction conflicts and wouldn't survive them. —*Ron Wynn*

Different Drummer / 1987 / Epic ✦✦✦
The final album of three issued by the second generation of Isleys was a disappointment, and was marred by the personality problems and artistic differences that caused the original 3 Plus 3 group to disband. The singing was perfunctory, the production and arrangements routine, and they got little mileage from any of the material. —*Ron Wynn*

It's a Beautiful Day

Group, Folk-Rock, Pop/Rock
It's a Beautiful Day (formed 1967) featured the custom-made five-string violin work of former Utah Symphony member David LaFlamme, who also sang and wrote much of the material with his wife, Linda. —*Rick Clark*

● **It's a Beautiful Day** / 1969 / San Francisco Sound ✦✦✦✦
Even though *It's a Beautiful Day*'s lyrical content was basically hippie fluff, this debut was a production tour de force that sonically captured many of the distinctive elements of the San Francisco sound. The leadoff track, "White Bird" (number 118), became an FM rock-radio classic. Other highlights included "Hot Summer Day," "Girl with No Eyes," "Wasted Union Blues," and "Bulgaria." This domestic CD, which is hard to find, is sold at the top end of the import price scale, which might have been acceptable if the complete cover art (inside and out) and informative liner notes had been included. In spite of those drawbacks, the remastering is exceptional. —*Rick Clark*

Marrying Maiden / 1970 / San Francisco Sound ✦✦✦

Live at Carnegie Hall / 1972 / Columbia ✦✦

It's a Beautiful Day ... Today / 1973 / CBS ✦✦✦

1,001 Nights / 1974 / CBS ✦✦

Iveys

Group, Pop/Rock
Essentially the same as Badfinger, the Iveys landed on the Beatles' Apple label in late 1968 after Beatle personal assistant Mal Evans encouraged them to submit tapes to Paul McCartney. Their bright, melodic, and harmony-filled pop/rock sound immediately drew comparisons to the Beatles, and to the work of McCartney in particular. Their sole album (*Maybe Tomorrow,*) released in Europe in mid-1969, was an accomplished if somewhat lightweight collection of original material, reflecting the heavy influence of both McCartney and Ray Davies (indeed, the latter had expressed interest in producing the group before Apple picked them up). The LP gathered little attention, but after a name change to Badfinger, the replacement of bassist Ron Griffiths by Joey Molland, a commission to score the Peter Sellers/Ringo Starr film *The Magic Christian*, and a McCartney-penned hit single from the movie ("Come and Get It"), the group were on their way. Half a dozen of the tunes from *Maybe Tomorrow* ended up on Badfinger's first proper album, *Magic Christian Music*. —*Richie Unterberger*

Maybe Tomorrow / 1969 / Capitol ✦✦✦
Issued at long last in the U.S. in 1992, this is decent late-'60s British pop-rock, if somewhat less developed and more precious than Badfinger's prime efforts. Six of the better tracks were used on *Magic Christian*. The ones that got left behind are certainly not an embarrassment, with "Yesterday Ain't Coming Back," "Angelique," and "I've Been Waiting" (by far the album's hardest-rocking tune) ranking as the standouts. The CD reissue adds four rare cuts, two of them previously unreleased. —*Richie Unterberger*

J

Jackie & the Starlites

Group, Doo-Wop

Diminutive Jackie Rue's histrionic lead tenor distinguished the brief recording career of Jackie & the Starlites. They debuted in 1960 with their best-known ballad "Valerie" on Bobby Robinson's Fury label. After a few followups for Robinson, which included the solid-selling "I Found Out Too Late," the group recorded for another New York outfit, Hull/Mascot, before disbanding. Rue died of a drug overdose in the late '60s or early '70s. —*Bill Dahl*

○ **Valerie** / Relic ♦♦♦♦
Greasy Harlem doo wop in all its late-'50s glory from this unjustly obscure aggregation. —*Bill Dahl*

● **Meet the Bopchords: Golden Classics** / Collectables ♦♦♦♦

The Jackson 5

Group, Soul, Motown

The Jackson 5 was Motown's last great pop group and among the most successful singles acts of the '70s. The group consisted of five brothers—Jackie (b.May 4, 1951), Tito (b.Oct 15, 1953), Jermaine (b.Dec 11, 1954), Marlon (b.Mar 12, 1957), and Michael Jackson (b.Aug 29, 1958). They grew up in Gary, IN, and were first organized as a group by their father, Joe Jackson, in 1966. In essence, the group was a vocal ensemble centered on Michael, who, though the youngest, was clearly the most talented. The group came to the attention of Motown and was signed in 1969. Their first four singles, "I Want You Back," "ABC," "The Love You Save," and "I'll Be There," all hit number one in 1970; "Mama's Pearl" and "Never Can Say Goodbye" did almost as well in 1971.

In 1972, Motown launched both Michael Jackson and Jermaine Jackson as solo acts, and the group's efforts were gradually less successful in the following years, though "Dance Machine" was a big hit in 1974. In 1975, Jackie, Tito, Marlon, and Michael signed to Epic Records, adding brother Randy (b.Oct 29, 1961) and became the Jacksons (the name the Jackson 5 was owned by Motown). (Although Jermaine stayed at Motown, he rejoined the group in 1984.) —*William Ruhlmann*

Diana Ross Presents the Jackson 5 / 1970 / Motown ♦♦♦
This Gary, Indiana family ensemble exploded onto the national scene with immediate and long-lasting impact in 1970. This album's combination of youthful exuberance and innocence, coupled with Motown production magic, yielded quick results, as "I Want You Back" topped both R&B and pop charts. Michael Jackson, the nine-year-old lead singer, became a national darling. Once they hit the big time, there was controversy over whether Diana Ross actually discovered them, but there was no question that Motown had unveiled another superstar act. —*Ron Wynn*

○ **ABC** / 1970 / Motown ♦♦♦♦
A fabulous album, arguably their best on Motown. While the debut LP established the group's sound, this one cemented it and also made it clear that Michael was going to be a huge star for a long time. His blend of gentility, soul, and innocence sparkled on the title cut and throughout the album, while the songs, production, arrangement, and musical support were superb. —*Ron Wynn*

Third Album / 1970 / Motown ♦♦♦
The Jackson 5 solidified the audience they enjoyed with their first two albums by turning in a consistently produced and occasionally exciting third record. It included the fine ballad "I'll Be There" and another hit in "Mama's Pearl"; the group hadn't yet become hardened by Motown manipulation or troubled by internal dis-

sension. Michael Jackson was still widely beloved and seen as the 1970s' Frankie Lymon, and this LP became their third Top Ten album in a row. —*Ron Wynn*

Maybe Tomorrow / 1971 / Motown ♦♦♦
Another fine album, with Michael Jackson displaying surprising conviction and earnestness on the title track. The group was rolling along with a strong mix of novelty/dance hits, ballads, and soul covers, scoring massive pop success and turning up all over the airwaves. —*Ron Wynn*

○ **The Greatest Hits** / 1971 / Motown ♦♦♦♦
When this was issued, Motown was issuing a genuine greatest hits record. At the time it was essential. Now, it's just part of the overload of Jacksons hits packages floating around and has almost no value, since the newer sets have better sound. —*Ron Wynn*

Lookin' through the Windows / 1972 / Motown ♦♦♦
The Jackson 5 were still an engaging, delightful family unit when this album was released. They hadn't yet lost their innocent qualities and were also continuing to get first-rate material, production, and arrangements. They were three years away from the bitter fights that marred their exit from Motown, and Michael hadn't yet become a huge star. —*Ron Wynn*

Get It Together / 1973 / Motown ♦♦
Although they were still getting hits, there were some problems creeping into the Jackson 5's Motown albums. The main one was that the company was no longer in the forefront of black music production, and their '60s-style efforts were sounding dated. Only Michael Jackson's individual brilliance and the group's polished performances salvaged much of this material, and they soon openly expressed their disapproval. —*Ron Wynn*

Skywriter / 1973 / Motown ♦♦
The Jackson 5 slipped a bit with this album, although they still had two pop and R&B hits. But it wasn't anywhere near as dominant or popular an album as their earlier ones and wound up being one of their final three releases for Motown. They later did some recording with Stevie Wonder, Michael cut some solo material, and everyone except Jermaine headed for Columbia. —*Ron Wynn*

○ **Dancing Machine** / 1974 / Motown ♦♦♦♦
For a brief time, it seemed as if the magic was back between Motown and the Jackson 5. The title track was their best uptempo hit since "ABC," and put them back on top of the R&B charts for the first time in three years. It just missed topping the pop charts as well, peaking at number two. They even got a second chart hit from the album, and it restored their position within the pop and R&B communities. —*Ron Wynn*

★ **Anthology** / 1976 / Motown ♦♦♦♦♦
This three-LP set contains all 18 of the Jackson 5's pop-chart hits, plus solo hits by Jermaine and Michael, among its 33 cuts. It's the definitive collection and a good sampler of the sound of pop/R&B, ca. 1969–1975. —*William Ruhlmann*

The Jacksons / 1976 / Epic ♦♦♦
Epic turned the Jacksons over to Philly soul producers Kenny Gamble and Leon Huff for this smooth, danceable label debut featuring the discofied hit "Enjoy Yourself." —*William Ruhlmann*

Goin' Places / 1977 / Epic ♦♦♦
The Jacksons' move to Epic regenerated their enthusiasm and spirit for several years. The Gamble/Huff team brought them fresh material and new production ideas, as well as better tracks and arrangements than they'd gotten in quite a while on Motown.

This album got them R&B and pop hits and kept the family act in the spotlight for a little while longer. —*Ron Wynn*

○ **Destiny** / 1978 / Epic ✦✦✦✦
The Jacksons are finally turned loose to write and produce themselves, and the result is their best (non-hits collection) ever. The dance tracks still sound fresh ("Blame It on the Boogie," "Shake Your Body (Down to the Ground)"), and the ballads are heartfelt and smooth. This album is a dry run for Michael Jackson's adult solo career. —*William Ruhlmann*

○ **Triumph** / 1980 / Epic ✦✦✦✦
An excellent followup, featuring the hits "Can You Feel It" and "Heartbreak Hotel." —*William Ruhlmann*

Victory / 1984 / Epic ✦✦✦

2300 Jackson Street / 1989 / Epic ✦✦✦
This was the final gathering of the entire Jackson family, and it turned out to have both historical significance and some musical value. The team of L.A. and Babyface, then emerging as major producers, spearheaded the track "Nothin' Compares To U," and the title track was a nice autobiographical/family outing song. —*Ron Wynn*

The Jackson Five In The Beginning / 1994 / Motown

○ **Soulsation!** / 1995 / Motown ✦✦✦✦
A lavishly produced and lovingly assembled four-CD set, *Soulsation!* proves that the Jackson 5 were more than the puppets of record producers—they were dynamic performers that could enliven even weak material with their powerful charisma. However, the two-disc *Anthology* proves that point as well as this box set does. While they had some quality material that never was released as singles, the majority of their greatest songs were hit records; the album tracks add little to the story told by the hit singles. Nevertheless, both the Jackson 5 and their producers were talented craftsmen—they rarely cut anything that was embarrassing. *Soulsation!* collects the best of those moments, including all the hit singles. For dedicated listeners, there is no better way to listen to the group. —*Stephen Thomas Erlewine*

Chuck Jackson

b. Jun. 22, 1937, Latta, South Carolina
Soul, R&B
Chuck Jackson first hit as a member of the Dell-Vikings (1957-1959) before striking out on his own with a string of soulful pop classics ("I Don't Want to Cry," "Any Day Now") on Wand, a subsidiary of Scepter, during the early '60s. With a delivery by turns sophisticated and hoarsely sexy, he was part of a group of singers, Ben E. King among them, whose gospel-tinged style predated and influenced the singing of '60s soul men like Wilson Pickett. Jackson continues to be very active; in 1992 he received the prestigious Pioneer Award from the Rhythm and Blues Foundation. —*Christine Ohlman*

I Don't Want to Cry / 1961 / Charly ✦✦✦
Another solid anthology that covers the hits of Chuck Jackson. Unfortunately, Jackson did his best work at a time when soul greats at bigger labels dominated the charts. Hopefully, the many packages available now, both domestic and imported, will awaken the public to his greatness. —*Ron Wynn*

Any Day Now / 1962 / Trace ✦✦✦
A fine anthology covering many of Chuck Jackson's greatest soul singles. He was never an album artist, but made some of the most emphatic, soaring heartbreak/anguish records in soul annals. —*Ron Wynn*

Encore / 1963 / Wand ✦✦✦
Some wonderful soul ballads and good uptempo tunes, although nothing attracted much chart attention. Jackson simply couldn't get the same exposure for much of his material as Solomon Burke, Wilson Pickett, and others dominating the soul charts, although he was in their class vocally. —*Ron Wynn*

Chuck Jackson on Tour / 1964 / Wand ✦✦✦
Chuck Jackson's singles were outstanding, but he was even more electrifying live. This set features his exciting, robust vocals done before adoring, encouraging audiences whose cries and responses pushed him to even more spectacular performances. —*Ron Wynn*

Mr. Everything / 1965 / Wand ✦✦✦
Some shuddering, majestic soul vocals from Chuck Jackson, delivered with fierce conviction and energy. Although Jackson could be overly dramatic, there was no exaggerating the authority and

power he brought to ballads, and he deserves much more attention than he's received. —*Ron Wynn*

○ **A Tribute to Rhythm and Blues** / 1966 / Wand ✦✦✦✦
The first of two fantastic albums featuring Chuck Jackson's smashing, soaring vocals doing definitive treatments on R&B classics. Although never a "concept" or album artist, Jackson came closest on both volumes to doing a unified project, rather than just having singles slapped together on an album. —*Ron Wynn*

○ **A Tribute to Rhythm and Blues, Vol. 2** / 1966 / Wand ✦✦✦✦
The second volume in the series containing memorable expositions by Chuck Jackson of R&B gems. He never sang with more distinction, intensity, or energy than on these two volumes, and the second one is slightly superior to its predecessor. —*Ron Wynn*

Chuck Jackson Arrives / 1968 / Motown ✦✦✦
Inconsistent overall, it still has some great tracks. —*Richard Pack*

Goin' Back to Chuck Jackson / 1969 / Motown ✦✦✦
Yet another nice Chuck Jackson album that didn't generate anywhere near the reaction it merited. Jackson was prevented in the '60s from being in the spotlight by a glut of great performers, and also because he landed most of his hits in the early '60s and wasn't really in the mainstream at the peak of soul's commercial onslaught. —*Ron Wynn*

○ **Good Things** / 1991 / Kent ✦✦✦✦
Featured are twenty-four tracks, hits and unreleased material, from Wand Records. (Import) —*Richard Pack*

● **The Great Recordings** / 1995 / Tomato ✦✦✦✦
This 46-song, double-CD compilation of Wand-era recordings is the most extensive Jackson retrospective, though it doesn't include every last worthwhile track. It does contain his most important songs, as well as a few of his duets with Maxine Brown, but the programming leaves something to be desired, inserting some half-baked instrumentals, live cuts, and Elvis Presley covers among the prime stuff. —*Richie Unterberger*

Deon Jackson

b. Jan. 26, 1946, Ann Arbor, MI
Soul
Still in his teens when he began recording, Deon Jackson's 1966 smash "Love Makes the World Go Round" was an engaging piece of soft Detroit soul. The Ann Arbor, MI, product caught the ear of Detroit producer Ollie McLaughlin, who began recording him for his Carla label in 1962. Jackson's first couple of singles ended up on Atlantic with little commercial feedback, but when he cut "Love Makes the World Go Round" for Carla in 1965, he was an overnight sensation. Nothing else Jackson did equaled its success, although "Love Takes a Long Time Growing" and "Ooh Baby" were solid-selling encores. Jackson's lilting vocal style has served him well over the last 15 years as a lounge entertainer in suburban Chicago. —*Bill Dahl*

● **Golden Classics** / Collectables ✦✦✦✦
All the Carla hits are featured on these '60s recordings. —*Richard Pack*

Freddie Jackson

b. Oct. 2, 1956, New York, NY
Soul, Urban
Freddie Jackson ranks right behind Luther Vandross as the premier male vocalist of the '80s and early '90s in Urban Contemporary circles. He may in fact be a better pure soul singer, having had a solid gospel background. Jackson hasn't been able to duplicate Vandross' crossover appeal, however, although he's had a large number of R&B smashes. Since 1985, when his debut LP, *Rock Me Tonight*, was released on Capitol, Jackson has had many Top Ten R&B singles, and from 1985 until 1987, he had six number ones, another number two, and two others at number eight and number nine respectively. He finally departed Capitol in 1994 for RCA, looking for a fresh start. —*Ron Wynn*

● **Rock Me Tonight** / 1985 / Capitol ✦✦✦✦
An album that in the '80s launched this singer who rivaled to Luther Vandross for male R&B supremacy. Includes the hits "You Are My Lady" (#12), "He'll Never Love You (Like I Do)" (#25), and the #18 title track. —*Ron Wynn*

Just Like the First Time / 1986 / Capitol ✦✦✦
An excellent followup, featuring "Jam Tonight" (#32). —*Ron Wynn*

Don't Let Love Slip Away / 1988 / Capitol ✦✦✦
This is slick and smooth but retains a soul/gospel flavor. —*Ron Wynn*

Do Me Again / Oct. 29, 1990 / Capitol ✦✦✦
This album accents Jackson's strengths; no one sings with more conviction, earnestness and passion on love ballads, as he demonstrates repeatedly during such songs as "Love Me Down," "Do Me Again," "All Over You" (CD bonus cut) and "I'll Be Waiting For You." He has yet to record a captivating uptempo tune, but "I Can't Take It" came close. It's doubtful as to whether Jackson can overtake Vandross in the 1990s, but hopefully RCA will at least put him in the hunt. —*Ron Wynn*

Time for Love / Aug. 3, 1992 / Capitol ✦✦✦

Here It Is / Jan. 1994 / RCA ✦✦✦
After several years of R&B success but no crossover hits, vocalist Freddie Jackson left Capitol for RCA late in 1993. His RCA debut has several excellent performances, but unfortunately, there's no single standout cut. There are brilliantly sung numbers, ("Come Home II U," "I Love," "My Family") but there's no track that can stand alongside "Rock Me Tonight," "Nice And Slow" or any of a half-dozen other past Jackson hits. Jackson merits pop attention more than many others with a much larger profile. —*Ron Wynn*

○ **The Greatest Hits of Freddie Jackson** / Jan. 25, 1994 / Capitol ✦✦✦✦

Private Party / 1995 / Street Life ✦✦✦

J.J. Jackson
Soul
One of the most interesting obscure figures of '60s soul, Jackson scored a mammoth R&B hit in 1966 with one of the most infectious dance smashes of the decade, "But It's Alright." The New Yorker had worked as an arranger for Jack McDuff and Jimmy Witherspoon before his manager arranged for Jackson to come to England in 1966. Though "But It's Alright," with its classic stuttering guitar riff and sharp horn charts, sounded as authentic as any Stax/Volt single, it was actually recorded in the U.K. with British session musicians. Jackson—a mammoth, nearly 300-pound man who also played organ—was a grainy, good-natured belter in the mold of Otis Redding. A talented songwriter who penned much of his own material, he wrote the A-side of the Pretty Things' best mid-'60s R&B/raunch singles ("Come See Me"). Jackson never matched the success of "But It's Alright," but cut some singles which are highly valued by English "Northern Soul" connoisseurs. His hard-to-find 1969 and 1970 albums found him exploring, in the manner of most other soul stars of the time, increased social consciousness in his songwriting and increasingly sophisticated horn and string arrangements. He later surfaced as a Los Angeles disc jockey, leading to a cameo appearance in the film *Car Wash* that has been sampled by numerous rappers. —*Richie Unterberger*

○ **With the Greatest Little Soul Band** / 1967 / Strike ✦✦✦✦

The Greatest Little Soul Band / 1969 / MCA ✦✦

J.J. Jacksons Dilemma / 1970 / Perception ✦✦

● **The Great J.J. Jackson** / 1989 / See For Miles ✦✦✦✦
A reissue of his 1966 album, recorded in England with British producer Miki Dallon. Includes "But It's Alright," his version of "Come See Me" (actually recorded after the Pretty Things' rendition), and the effervescent, boastful "I Dig Girls." Much more solid than the average '60s soul album, it shows Jackson as a fine songwriter and infectiously throaty vocalist on a mixture of uptempo ravers and deep soul ballads. Somewhat similar to Otis Redding, but more pop-oriented, which is not necessarily a bad thing when you can make it work as well as J.J. does. —*Richie Unterberger*

Janet Jackson
b. May 16, 1966, Gary, IN
Dance-Pop, Urban, Pop/Rock
Janet Jackson is the ninth and last child in the musically talented Jackson family that includes the Jackson 5, Michael Jackson, and Jermaine Jackson. Janet Jackson performed on stage with her brothers at the age of seven. At ten, she acted in the TV series *Good Times* and was later seen in *Diff'rent Strokes* and *Fame*. She released her first album, *Janet Jackson*, in 1982 and her second, *Dream Street*, in 1984, but neither of these records was notably successful. Then, in 1985, Jackson turned to the production team of Jimmy Jam and Terry Lewis (formerly of the Time) for the al-

bum *Control*, which, ironically, emphasized the artist's new maturity and independence, even though most of the songs were co-compositions of the three. *Control* was a massive hit: it topped the charts, selling more than four million copies, and spawned five Top Ten hits, including the #1 "When I Think of You." The follow-up, *Rhythm Nation 1814*, did even better, spawning seven Top Ten hits, among them the #1s "Miss You Much," "Escapade," and "Black Cat." In 1991, Jackson signed a new recording contract with Virgin Records for a reported $32 million.

1993's *janet.* proved to be as successful as her previous two releases, featuring a series of Top Ten singles including "If" and "That's the Way Love Goes." —*William Ruhlmann*

Janet Jackson / 1982 / A&M ✦✦
Debut album of youth-oriented pop with "Young Love," a minor disco hit. —*Bil Carpenter*

Dream Street / 1984 / A&M ✦✦
After a style switch, this features more light rock and polished pop tunes. Includes the stellar cut, "You Don't Stand Another Chance." —*Bil Carpenter*

★ **Control** / 1986 / A&M ✦✦✦✦✦
Jam and Lewis tailor their contemporary dance-pop to the emerging personality of Jackson, who is attempting to take "Control" of her life on this record. In the course of that attempt, she comes across as an aggressive, independent woman, notably on "What Have You Done for Me Lately." But the album is primarily a production showcase; it may be tailored to Jackson's persona, but the real artists are Jam and Lewis. —*William Ruhlmann*

Control the Remixes / 1987 / A&M ✦✦

○ **Rhythm Nation 1814** / 1989 / A&M ✦✦✦✦
Jam and Lewis have more beats up their sleeves, and the singer's own personality is even more submerged than it was on *Control*, but this is the height of 80s dance-pop. —*William Ruhlmann*

Janet. / May 18, 1993 / Virgin ✦✦✦
Janet Jackson returns with *janet.*, a long (75 minutes), ambitious album declaring her sexual maturity. There are good moments here, but it's marred by the torturously long running time and the intros cluttering the entire album. With a CD player, it's possible to program these excesses out and enjoy *janet.* as a solid successor to *Control* and *Rhythm Nation 1814.* —*Stephen Thomas Erlewine*

Joe Jackson
b. Aug. 11, 1955, Burton-upon-Trent, England
Singer-Songwriter, New Wave, Pop/Rock
Although Joe Jackson initially appeared to fit in neatly with such new wave singer/songwriters as Elvis Costello and Graham Parker when he appeared in the late '70s, he has displayed a much broader range on his numerous record releases since. Born in Burton-on-Trent, England, Jackson studied music as a youth and earned a piano scholarship to the Royal College of Music, which he attended from 1971 to 1974.

Look Sharp!, his debut album released in March 1979, featured a fast-paced, guitar-driven rock style, with Jackson spitting out sometimes bitter, sometimes vulnerable lyrics, notably on the single "Is She Really Going Out with Him?," which hit number 21 in the U.S. The album got to number 20 and went gold. *I'm the Man*, an album in the same style released in October, got to number 22.

Jackson then began the first of his many changes of style. *Beat Crazy*, released in the fall of 1980, marked a sharp turn toward reggae and a drop in Jackson's commercial fortunes. *Joe Jackson's Jumpin' Jive* (1981) contained big-band and jump-blues standards from the '40s. In 1982, Jackson moved to New York City, adopting some of the sophisticated style of Cole Porter and some of the small-band jazz music found in the city's clubs for *Night and Day*, released in June. The album was Jackson's biggest hit, going to number four and producing the hit singles "Steppin' Out" and "Breaking Us in Two."

Jackson composed a film soundtrack, *Mike's Murder*, in 1983, then made *Body and Soul* in a style similar to *Night and Day*. It hit number 20 and included the Top 15 hit "You Can't Get What You Want (Till You Know What You Want)." In 1985 Jackson composed music for the Japanese film *House of the Poet*. Some of the music was later released on his album *Will Power*. Jackson's 1986 album was the three-sided *Big World*, which reached number 34. *Will Power*, issued in 1987, was an instrumental album combining classical and jazz styles. It was followed in 1988 by the double *Live 1980/1986* and the soundtrack to the film *Tucker*. After his next pop album, *Blaze of Glory* (1989), did not succeed commercially, Jackson jumped to Virgin Records, which issued *Laughter and Lust* (1991). — *William Ruhlmann*

★ **Look Sharp!** / Apr. 1979 / A&M ✦✦✦✦✦
Hyperactive new-wave rock overlaid with the intelligent, caustic world view of a man as angry as any punk, but far more perceptive. Includes the hit "Is She Really Going Out with Him?" — *William Ruhlmann*

○ **I'm the Man** / Oct. 1979 / A&M ✦✦✦✦
Nearly a re-write of *Look Sharp* and capturing all of its brilliance, *I'm the Man* is pure power-pop—hook filled, concise, and fun. Includes the wonderful "It's Different for Girls," a marginal hit in both the U.S. and U.K. — *Chris Woodstra*

○ **Beat Crazy** / 1980 / A&M ✦✦✦✦
Credited to the Joe Jackson Band, *Beat Crazy* completes Jackson's power-pop period. Jackson begins to stretch a bit stylistically, flirting with reggae and more experimental styles while in the confines of the three minute form he would later dismiss. Every bit as charming as the first two. — *Chris Woodstra*

○ **Jumpin' Jive** / 1981 / A&M ✦✦✦✦
A delightful trip back to '40s and '50s jump blues and big-band swing. With faithful covers of Louis Jordan and Cab Calloway, Jackson appears to be having fun, while helping a new generation discover these classics. — *Chris Woodstra*

○ **Night & Day** / 1982 / A&M ✦✦✦✦
Since Jackson has already demonstrated his broad musical tastes by turning from rock to "jumpin' jive" on his last album, that he was able to incorporate Latin, dance, and sophisticated ballad styles into his music wasn't so surprising. But that he could do it all so well was delightful. Includes "Steppin' Out" and "Breaking Us in Two." — *William Ruhlmann*

Body & Soul / 1984 / A&M ✦✦✦
Continuing in his move away from pop music that began with *Night and Day*, Jackson shows his love of '50s jazz with detail best represented by the cover photo (nearly identical to the Sonny Rollins album of the same name). Features his last U.S. hit, "You Can't Get What You Want" and the beautiful "Be My Number Two." — *Chris Woodstra*

Big World / 1986 / A&M ✦✦✦
A brilliant collection of songs, running over an hour, finds Jackson as biting as ever as he surveys the world, but also tenderly reflective on "Home Town." — *William Ruhlmann*

Will Power / 1987 / A&M ✦✦
Joe Jackson finally becomes the "serious composer" on *Will Power*. A good exercise in self-indulgence but little of anything else. — *Chris Woodstra*

Live . . . 1980–1986 / 1988 / A&M ✦✦✦
A double-disc live collection, *Live . . . 1980–1986* manages to effectively trace the development of Joe Jackson's diverse career. Drawing from four different periods in the songwriter's career—with each period featuring a new backing band—*Live* captures Jackson with his original new wave trio, a 1983 quintet that was dominated by keyboards, a horn-driven group from 1984, and a 1986 quartet that specialized in straightahead rock & roll. The resulting album highlights his musical diversity, not his songwriting, which means the record is more intriguing as a historical document than as casual listening — *Stephen Thomas Erlewine*

Blaze of Glory / 1989 / A&M ✦✦✦
A loose concept album about a second-generation rock & roller struggling to come to terms with maturity, *Blaze of Glory* holds together fairly well, as the story takes a backseat to individual songs. While that does mean that the concept is never fleshed out, the approach results in a handful of brisk, stylish pop songs—including "Nineteen Forever" and "Down to London"—that are more compelling than the story itself. — *Stephen Thomas Erlewine*

● **Stepping Out: The Very Best of Joe Jackson** / 1990 / A&M ✦✦✦✦
Jackson produced some of the finest singles of the new wave era; this import-only collection does a fine job of presenting the hits chronologically for a good career overview. While the early albums should be heard in their entirety, Jackson's later period is best previewed here. — *Chris Woodstra*

Laughter & Lust / 1991 / Virgin ✦✦✦
Jackson's work has sometimes been too didactic for its own good, but on *Laughter & Lust* he managed to balance the agenda with a nice blend of humor and heart. His perpetual disdain for the pop music industry found full flower in "Hit Single," in which Jackson

finds himself in "pure pop heaven," where angels only want to hear the hits, but not "the whole damn album." Other highlights are the classic acidic Jackson-style rocker "Obvious Song," the hyperkinetic "Jamie G," a faithful remake of Fleetwood Mac's "Oh Well," and Jackson's ode to the dynamics of love in "Stranger than Fiction." — *Rick Clark*

Night Music / 1994 / Virgin ✦
Joe Jackson's second attempt at "serious" composition, *Night Music* is an insufferable song cycle about writers' block. Jackson's lyrics are ponderous and elusive, his vocals are smug and self-important, and the unmemorable, low-key music is stiffly executed on a dry, lifeless synthesizer. What sinks *Night Music* is the total lack of involving music. *Will Power* may have been just as indulgent, yet the album had the occasional interesting twist in melodic lines and arrangements. On *Night Music*, everything from the production to the performance sounds processed, devoid of any defining characteristics. — *Stephen Thomas Erlewine*

Michael Jackson

b. Aug. 29, 1958, Gary, IN
Pop/Rock, Soul, Dance-Pop, Urban, Motown
As part of the Jackson 5, a group made up of his brothers, Michael Jackson was among the most popular singing stars of the '70s. On his own, he was the biggest pop star of the '80s. Jackson was always the visual and vocal focus of the Jackson 5, who broke through to national success on the Motown label in 1970, when he was 11, with the first of four straight #1 hits, "I Want You Back." Jackson was also promoted as a solo artist, and he scored his first hit, "Got to Be There," in 1971. Subsequent hits included his remake of "Rockin' Robin" and "Ben" in 1972.

Jackson's and the Jackson 5's fortunes declined somewhat after the early '70s, and the group moved to Epic at mid-decade, with Michael temporarily abandoning his solo career and subsuming his group leadership to other members of what was now called the Jacksons. The group gradually built back its popularity by writing its own material. Jackson returned to solo work in 1979 with *Off the Wall*, a mature combination of driving dance songs ("Don't Stop 'Til You Get Enough") and feelingly sung ballads ("She's Out of My Life") that outsold any previous group or solo effort, and spawned four Top Ten hits.

Jackson again recorded and toured with the Jacksons, but his next album, *Thriller* (1982), became a musical phenomenon. It was the biggest-selling album of all time, moving 20 million copies in the U.S. alone and including seven Top Ten hits. Clearly Jackson had grown beyond his brothers, but he stayed with them for one more album and tour in 1984.

His follow-up album, *Bad* (1987), accompanied by a solo world tour, sold six million copies domestically. Only six of its seven singles hit the Top Ten, but five in a row hit #1.

In late 1991, Jackson returned with *Dangerous*, which, by mid-1992, had sold four million copies and spawned the hits "Black and White," "Remember the Time," "In the Closet," and "Jam." Jackson's second world tour, launched in Europe in June 1992, continued into 1993.

Although numerous rumors had circled around Jackson throughout his career, his reputation remained clean. It wasn't until 1993 that he suffered serious damage to his image. Jackson was accused of child abuse by a teenage friend, sparking a major media frenzy. Through it all, Jackson vehemently denied the accusations. The civil case was settled out of court in early 1994. Jackson began working on *HIStory* soon after the settlement. *HIStory* contained one disc of Jackson's greatest hits and one disc of new material. It was released on June 20, 1995. — *William Ruhlmann*

Got to Be There / 1971 / Motown ✦✦✦
Fine production by various Motown producers. — *Rick A. Bueche*

Ben / 1972 / Motown ✦✦
Michael Jackson stunned everyone by scoring a huge hit with a song about a rat on this '73 release. He was just beginning to make his way outside the family unit, and the single actually did better on the pop side than on the R&B charts, topping the pop list but peaking at number five on the R&B survey. The remainder of the album was good to above-average pop, establishing for any doubters that Jackson was going to succeed, indeed thrive, on his own. — *Ron Wynn*

Music & Me / 1973 / Motown ✦✦✦
This was Michael Jackson's least successful album during his solo run at Motown. The songs were undistinguished, Jackson sounded tentative and uninterested vocally, and the production and

arrangements were routine at best, sometimes inferior. There's little wonder that Jackson at this point began to openly express his desires to expand his horizons and try a fresher, more contemporary approach. —*Ron Wynn*

☆ **Off the Wall** / 1979 / Epic ✦✦✦✦✦
If you were listening to the Jacksons's *Destiny* from the previous year, maybe you were less surprised than many that Michael Jackson was capable of making an album this accomplished and assured. From the first moments, he seems bursting with the wide range of music included, from the first side's clutch of irresistible dance tracks ("Don't Stop 'Til You Get Enough," "Rock with You," "Working Day and Night") to the light pop and ballads ("She's out of My Life," "Off the Wall") of Side 2. Throughout, Jackson's flexible tenor coos and growls by turns, always goosing the songs along. Deservedly a massive hit, this is less dated today than much of the dance music of that era. —*William Ruhlmann*

One Day in Your Life / 1981 / Motown ✦✦✦
Although Michael Jackson had long since moved on to Epic, Motown got a quick cash boost in the early '80s by issuing some tracks cut in 1975. The title song even came close to making the R&B Top 40 and reached the middle of the pop charts. Jackson was so hot at that point that anything with his name on it would sell something. But it's hardly first-class material, and it truly paled beside the material that Quincy Jones was producing at that point. —*Ron Wynn*

The Best of Michael Jackson / 1981 / Motown ✦✦✦
Michael Jackson's greatest hits, 1971–75, emphasize his waif-like charm and youth (he was 13 when the first of these songs appeared) in ballads such as "Got to Be There," "Ben" (even if it is a love song to a rat), and "I Wanna Be Where You Are." The upbeat cover of "Rockin" Robin" is equally appealing. —*William Ruhlmann*

★ **Thriller** / 1982 / Epic ✦✦✦✦✦
What impresses after a decade is Jackson's range of musical expression, one that touches the schmaltzy pop of Paul McCartney (his duet partner on "The Girl Is Mine") on one side and the hard rock of Van Halen (whose lead guitarist, Eddie Van Halen, is heard on "Beat It") on the other, with plenty of mainstream rock/pop and dance music in between. And it's no accident that the record found a home in so many record collections—there's good music here for everyone. And of course, by summing up the state of pop music, Jackson also redefined it—this was a high-water mark for pop music never equaled since, even in his subsequent music. —*William Ruhlmann*

○ **Anthology** / 1986 / Motown ✦✦✦✦
Michael Jackson's greatest hits (1971-1975) emphasize his waif-like charm and youth (he was 13 years old when the first of these songs appeared) in ballads such as "Got to Be There," "Ben" (even if it is a love song to a rat), and "I Wanna Be Where You Are." The upbeat cover of "Rockin' Robin" is equally appealing. The digitally remastered, double-CD version includes a few additional tracks. —*William Ruhlmann*

○ **Bad** / 1987 / Epic ✦✦✦✦
A partially successful attempt to remake *Thriller*. Interestingly, Jackson did not turn to a softer, more broadly commercial approach but instead upped the dance-rock ante. Songs such as "Dirty Diana" and "Smooth Criminal" found him striding forward in terms of rhythm and beat. And with seven hit singles out of ten tracks (five at #1), this, like *Thriller*, is in effect a Michael Jackson greatest-hits record, covering 1987-1989. —*William Ruhlmann*

Dangerous / 1992 / Epic ✦✦✦
Wisely, Jackson altered his creative process here, jettisoning producer Quincy Jones in favor of Teddy Riley and bringing in several songwriting collaborators. The result is an updated dance-floor success (the drums are way up in the mix), though the songwriting sometimes seem schematic. When Jackson is left more or less to himself, he is less R&B-oriented, notably on the pop ballad "Heal the World" and the guitar-driven pop/rock song "Black or White" (a Stones riff, though taken at a tempo the Stones never attempted). Rather than resting on his laurels, Jackson continues to work hard to maintain and further the quality of his work. —*William Ruhlmann*

HIStory: Past, Present And Future Book 1 / 1995 / Epic ✦✦✦
One of the most expensive albums ever made, both in production and marketing costs, Michael Jackson's double-disc *HIStory: Past, Present, and Future, Book I* is a monumental achievement of ego.

Titled *HIStory Begins*, the first disc is a collection of his post-Motown hits, featuring some of the greatest music in pop history (including "Billie Jean," "Don't Stop Til Ya Get Enough," "Beat It," "Rock With You," and "Wanna Be Startin' Somethin' "), as well as some of the most cloying ("Heal the World," "Black Or White"). It leaves some hits out—including "Off the Wall," "Human Nature," "Will You Be There," "In the Closet," and the number ones "Say Say Say" and "Dirty Diana"—yet it's filled with enough prime material to be thoroughly intoxicating. That can't be said for the second disc, called *HIStory Continues* and consisting entirely of new material—which also happen to be the first songs he released since being accused of child molestation. *HIStory Continues* is easily the most personal album Jackson has recorded. References to the scandal permeate almost every song, creating a thick atmosphere of paranoia. If Jackson's music had been the equal of *Thriller* or *Bad*, the nervous, vindicative lyrics wouldn't have been quite as overbearing, which would have saved the album from appearing as a mean-spirited attack. However, *HIStory Continues* reiterates musical ideas Jackson has been exploring since *Bad* and the songs aren't as fresh as the material on *Dangerous*. Jackson certainly tries to stay contemporary, working with R. Kelly and incorporating stronger elements of hip-hop rhythms, yet he has a tendency to smooth out all of his rougher musical edges with a fondness for show-biz schmaltz, as evidenced by his cover of Charlie Chaplin's "Smile." Occasionally, Jackson produces some well-crafted pop that ranks with his best material: Kelly's "You Are Not Alone" is seductive, "Scream" improves on the slamming beats of his earlier single "Jam," and "Stranger in Moscow" is one of his most haunting ballads. Nevertheless, *HIStory Continues* stands as his weakest album since the mid-'70s. —*Stephen Thomas Erlewine*

Tony Jackson

British Invasion
Tony Jackson was the original bassist and lead singer of the Searchers, handling the vocals on their first two British hits ("Sweets for My Sweet" and "Sugar and Spice") and much of their first two albums. For reasons which remain fairly obscure, he was eased out of the lead vocal spot in 1964, and split from the band in the middle of that year to go solo. With the Vibrations, he then recorded eight singles over the next couple years. Only the debut, a cover of Mary Wells' "Bye Bye Baby," made an impact on the British charts (reaching number 24), and the group disbanded around 1967. Jackson's solo records were similar in sound to the Searchers, perhaps harder rocking and more R&B-oriented, but were simply not in the same class as his former group; he was not a songwriter (though he did try a couple times), and his cover versions weren't as strong as the Searchers', in content or performance. —*Richie Unterberger*

● **Just Like Me** / 1991 / Strange Things (UK) ✦✦✦✦
All 20 tracks released by Jackson in the mid-'60s: all eight singles and four rock and soul covers from a rare Portuguese EP. Neither bad nor memorable, the best track is a folk-rockish cover of Mary Wells' "You Beat Me to the Punch," arranged in exactly the style the Searchers were using in their "Needles and Pins" days. Comes with lengthy history of the group on the inner sleeve. —*Richie Unterberger*

Wanda Jackson

b. Oct. 20, 1937, Maud, OK
Rockabilly
Fact: Wanda Jackson was the greatest female rockabilly singer of the late '50s and early '60s. Starting out as a Decca country singer in 1954, Oklahoma-born Wanda began her rock & roll career with Capitol in 1956 at age 18. Her trademark growl on the raveup "Fujiyama Mama" sounds like she gargled with nitroglycerine: explosive stuff. The Rhino compilation is evenly divided with Wanda's rocking sides, nine tracks cut between 1956–1960, with the remaining nine songs representing some of her best country output of 1958–1970. (For more of Wanda's rockabilly sides, seek out either the French Capitol *Only Rock & Roll* double-album set or the British Charly double album, *Let's Have a Party*.) —*Dennis MacDonald*

There's a Party Goin' on / 1959 / Capitol ✦✦✦
While this doesn't have most of Wanda's best rockabilly sides (check the compilation *Rockin' with Wanda* for those), it's a pretty solid and energetic set. About half of it is taken up with retreads of the "Let's Have A Party" theme and covers of early rock hits like

"Tweedlee Dee" and "Kansas City" which are, admittedly, well done. "Fallin'" and, especially, "Hard Headed Woman" are really fine cuts that rank among her best rock & roll performances. The real surprise of this album is the lightning-speed rockabilly riffing by Roy Clark; his playing on "Hard Headed Woman" is downright savage, almost enough to redeem all those horrible *Hee-Haw* programs. —*Richie Unterberger*

○ **Rockin' with Wanda** / 1960 / Capitol ✦✦✦✦
Absolutely the best collection of her rockabilly recordings, including her key 1956–60 singles—"Fujiyama Mama," "Mean Mean Man," "Hot Dog! That Made Him Mad," and others. A leading candidate for the best female rock & roll album of the 1950s. The British reissue adds four worthwhile bonus cuts, including the essential "Let's Have A Party." —*Richie Unterberger*

● **Rockin' in the Country: Best of Wanda Jackson** / 1990 / Rhino ✦✦✦✦
Perhaps the greatest of the rockabilly women, Wanda Jackson later turned to pure country. Rhino's *Best of Wanda Jackson—Rockin' in the Country* presents the best of both eras here on this 18-track collection. —*Jeff Tamarkin*

Faine Jade

Group, Psychedelic, Garage Rock
Long Island guitarist Faine Jade began performing and recording as a member of the Rustics in the mid-'60s, with basic, energetic, angst-ridden material that differed little from literally thousands of other like-minded garage bands across the country. After a single with the Rustics in 1966, Jade recorded a 45 under his own name in 1967, "It Ain't True," which was rescued from obscurity on the *Pebbles Vol. 8* compilation. His solo LP on the tiny R.S.V.P. label in 1968, *Introspection: A Faine Jade Recital*, showed a quantum leap in songwriting, with reflective, enigmatic lyrics and a swirling but disciplined melodicism. It has ranked among the most coveted collectibles of the psychedelic era, and resurfaced as an unauthorized reissue on a British label in the early '80s. After recording an album as a member of the country-rock Dustbowl Clementine in 1970, Jade has been mostly inactive. —*Richie Unterberger*

● **Introspection: A Faine Jade Recital** / 1968 / RSVP ✦✦✦✦
It's hard to imagine that a 20-year-old New York guitarist fresh out of garageland would have been infatuated with Syd Barrett in 1968. However, Faine Jade's 1968 album sounds as if he was besotted with Pink Floyd's first LP, which was barely known in the States at the time. Jade's vocals and songwriting uncannily evoke an American Syd Barrett with their evocative, cryptic lyrics, thick organs, and psychedelic guitar lines. "Cold Winter Sun," in particular, never fails to inspire comparisons to Barrett when played for those unfamiliar with Jade. Faine, it's fair to say, is somewhat blunted in comparison to Barrett's madcap edge. More laidback and grounded, he also deals more explicitly with hippie-era concerns like being hassled for being different and the necessity of being compassionate towards your brother, without being sappy or preachy. The 1994 CD *25th Anniversary Silver Series Edition* on Jade's Sandiland label was remastered from the first generation tapes by Faine himself. It also adds a few bonus cuts: backing instrumental demo tracks for a few of the songs, the previously unreleased brief instrumental "Piano Interlude," and a 1993 "reunion" performance. The extra tracks are of only minor interest, and it's disappointing that the *Introspection*-era demos released on *It Ain't True* were not included as well. —*Richie Unterberger*

It Ain't True / 1992 / Distortions ✦✦
Most of the material on this LP dates from Faine's 1966 days as a member of the Rustics, including their sole single ("Look at Me"/"Can't Get You out of My Heart") and seven rather crude demos from the same time. The band stalked the same reheated British Invasion territory that was being explored by most other garage groups of the era, sounding at times like a very raw and basic Zombies. With below-average (though not unlistenable) fidelity and clumsy execution, the Rustics actually rank below the norm of such groups; the songwriting is unimpressive, the material by and large unmemorable. Of more interest are the late-1967 demos of two cuts from *Introspection* ("I Lived Tomorrow Yesterday" and "Cold Winter Sun"), a demo of "It Ain't True," the best song of his "garage" era; and the previously unreleased "USA Now," a gentle early-1969 protest song that would have fit in on *Introspection*. Still, this can only be recommended to serious collectors. —*Richie Unterberger*

Mick Jagger

b. Jul. 26, 1943, Dartford, England
Rock & Roll, Pop/Rock
Lead singer/songwriter for the Rolling Stones. After occasional forays away from the group, especially into acting, Jagger finally launched a full-fledged solo career in 1985. —*William Ruhlmann*

She's the Boss / 1985 / Columbia ✦✦✦
Jagger employs a Who's Who including Herbie Hancock, Pete Townshend, and Jeff Beck for an album that replaces the familiar sound of the Stones with a more sophisticated but no less hard-rock sound. And the voice *is* familiar. Features the hit "Just Another Night." —*William Ruhlmann*

Primitive Cool / 1987 / Rolling Stones ✦✦✦
For his second solo album, Mick Jagger teamed up with producer Dave Stewart (Eurythmics), turning in a more adventurous and ambitious record. Of course, "adventurous" and "ambitious" are relative terms. In comparison to the carefully-constructed, state-of-the-art pop/rock of *She's the Boss*, *Primitive Cool* sounds lively, as Jagger puts some genuine conviction behind the funky "Peace for the Wicked" and the country stylings of "Party Doll." Nevertheless, the album, like *She's the Boss* before it, is designed to establish Mick Jagger as a solo star in his own right, and *Primitive Cool* is filled with attempts at contemporary rock and dance-pop. The nadir of his stabs at modern pop is the appalling single "Let's Work," where the rock star tells his fans to get off their asses and start working, all to a bouncy, aerobicized beat. However, most of the album is more appealing than the single, even if Jagger's writing seems forced on the numbers designed with the Top 40 in mind ("Shoot Off Your Mouth," in particular). Not surprisingly, the best moments on *Primitive Cool* occur when he stops seeing the album as a way to jumpstart his solo career and he concentrates on the music. While his emotionally unguarded songs ("War Baby" and "Party Doll") are the most affecting tracks on the record, songs like "Let's Work" are more indicative of Jagger's true feelings. —*Stephen Thomas Erlewine*

● **Wandering Spirit** / 1992 / Atlantic ✦✦✦✦
Jagger doesn't show any signs of wear on his third—and by far best—solo album. If anything, his voice seems to have developed a deeper bottom end without sacrificing any of the highs. This is not always an advantage—the forced falsetto and rhythmic pulse of "Sweet Thing" causes a nightmarish flashback to the Stones' disco flirtations in the mid-70s. But more times than not, this disc works. A lot of the credit goes to Jagger's backing band and producer Rick Rubin who keep things lean, mean, and simple. The economy of performance allows Jagger to remain credible on a wide variety of styles—he delivers a groovin', sultry version of Bill Withers' soul classic "Use Me," a passionate country ballad on "Evening Gown," and even pulls off an Irish traditional folk piece with "Handsome Molly." —*Roch Parisien*

Jags

Group, Power Pop/Anglo-Pop
Like so many of their peers, the Jags were a one-hit wonder of the UK power-pop explosion of the late '70s. The quartet was formed by the songwriting team of Nick Watkins (vocals) and John Adler (guitar), who enlisted the help of Steve Prudence (bass) and Alex Baird (drums). The band's debut for Island Records in 1979 was the memorable, though highly derivative, "Back of My Hand," which reached the U.K. Top 20. The followup, "Woman's World" barely scraped its way on to the charts. *Evening Standards* (1980) sold fairly well but as steam ran out of the power-pop craze, the band faded into obscurity releasing only one more album, *No Tie Like the Present*, in 1981. —*Chris Woodstra*

● **Evening Standard** / 1980 / Island ✦✦✦✦
The "Back of My Hand" single showed a lot of promise. Unfortunately, the debut album put an end to those hopes with its only slightly better-than-average watered down version of power-pop. The album is not completely without merit—just a disappointment. —*Chris Woodstra*

No Tie Like a Present / 1981 / Island ✦✦

The Jam

Group, Rock & Roll, Punk, Pop/Rock
The Jam were the most popular band to emerge from the initial wave of British punk rock in 1977; along with the Sex Pistols, the Clash, and the Buzzcocks, the Jam had the most impact on pop

music. While they could barely get noticed in America, the trio became genuine superstars in Britain, with an impressive string of Top Ten singles in the late '70s and early '80s. The Jam could never have a hit in America because they were thoroughly and defiantly British. Under the direction of guitarist/vocalist/songwriter Paul Weller, the trio spearheaded a revival of mid-'60s mod groups, in the style of the Who and the Small Faces. Like the mod bands, the group dressed stylishly, worshipped American R&B and played it loud and rough. By the time of the group's third album, Weller's songwriting had grown substantially, as he was beginning to write social commentaries and pop songs in the vein of the Kinks. Both his political songs and his romantic songs were steeped in British culture, filled with references and slang in the lyrics, as well as musical allusions. Furthermore, as the Jam grew more popular and musically accessible, Weller became more insistent and stubborn about his beliefs, supporting leftist causes and adhering to the pop aesthetics of '60s British rock without ever succumbing to hippie values. Paradoxically, that meant even when their music became more pop than punk, they never abandoned the punk values—if anything, Weller stuck to the strident independent ethics of 1977 more than any other punk band just by simply refusing to change.

Weller formed the Jam with drummer Rick Buckler, bassist Bruce Foxton, and guitarist Steve Brookes while they were still in school in 1975; Brookes quickly left the band and they remained a trio for the rest of their career. For the next year, the band played gigs around London, building a local following. In February 1977, the group signed a record contract with Polydor records; two months later, they released their debut single, "In the City," which reached the U.K. Top 40. The following month, the group released their debut album, also called *In the City*. Recorded in just 11 days, the album featured a combinations of R&B covers and Weller originals, all of which sounded a bit like faster, more ragged versions of the Who's early records. Their second single, "All Around the World," nearly broke into the British Top Ten and the group embarked on a successful British tour. During the summer of 1977, they recorded their second album, *This Is the Modern World*, which was released toward the end of the year. "The Modern World" made it into the Top 40 in November, just as the Jam were beginning their first American tour. Although it was brief, the tour was not successful, leaving bitter memories of the U.S. in the minds of the band.

This Is the Modern World peaked in the British charts at number 22, yet it received criticism for repeating the sound of the debut. The band began a headlining tour of the U.K., yet it was derailed shortly after it started when the group got into a nasty fight with a bunch of rugby players in a Leeds hotel. Weller broke several bones and was charged with assault, although the Leeds Crown Court would eventually acquit him. The Jam departed for another American tour in March of 1978 and it was yet another unsuccessful tour, as they opened for Blue Oyster Cult. It did nothing to win new American fans, yet their star continued to rise in Britain. Bands copying the group's mod look and sound popped up across Britain and the Jam itself performed at the Reading Festival in August. *All Mod Cons*, released late in 1979, marked a turning point in the Jam's career, illustrating that Weller's songwriting was becoming more melodic, complex, and lyrically incisive, resembling Ray Davies more than Pete Townshend. Even as their sound became more pop-oriented, the group lost none of their tightly controlled energy. *All Mod Cons* was a major success, peaking at number six on the U.K. charts, even if it didn't make a dent in the U.S. Every one of the band's singles were now charting in the Top 20, with the driving "Eton Rifles" becoming their first Top Ten in November 1979, charting at number three.

Setting Sons, released at the end of 1979, climbed to number four in the U.K. and marked their first charting album in the U.S., hitting number 137 in spring of 1980. At that time, the Jam had become full-fledged rock stars in Britain, with their new "Going Underground" single entering the charts at number one. During the summer, the band recorded their fifth album, with the "Taxman"-inspired "Start" released as a teaser single in August; "Start" became their second straight number one. Its accompanying album, the ambitious *Sound Affects*, hit number two in the U.K. at the end of the year; it was also the band's high-water mark in the U.S., peaking at number 72. "That's Entertainment," one of the standout tracks from *Sound Affects*, charted at number 21 in the U.K. charts as an import single, confirming the band's enormous popularity.

"Funeral Pyre," the band's summer 1981 single, showed signs that Weller was becoming fascinated with American soul and R&B, as did the punchy, horn-driven "Absolute Beginners," which hit number four in the fall of the year. As the Jam were recording their sixth album, Weller suffered a nervous breakdown, which prompted him to stop drinking. In February 1982, the first single from the new sessions—the double-A-sided "Town Called Malice"/"Precious"—became their third number one single and the band became the first group since the Beatles to play two songs on BBC's *Top of the Pops*. *The Gift*, released in March of 1982, showcased the band's soul infatuation and became the group's first number one album in the U.K. "Just Who Is the 5 O'Clock Hero" hit number eight in July, becoming the group's second import single to make the U.K. charts.

Although the Jam was at the height of its popularity, Paul Weller was becoming frustrated with the trio's sound and made the decision to disband the group. On the heels of the number two hit "The Bitterest Pill," the Jam announced their breakup in October of 1982. The band played a farewell tour in the fall and their final single, "Beat Surrender," entered the charts at number one. *Dig the New Breed*, a compilation of live tracks, charted at number two in December of 1982. All 16 of the group's singles were re-released by Polydor in the U.K. at the beginning of 1983; all of them re-charted simultaneously. Bruce Foxton released a solo album, *Touch Sensitive*, and Rick Buckler played with the Time U.K.; neither of the efforts were as noteworthy as the Jam biography the two wrote in the early '90s, which contained many vicious attacks on Paul Weller.

Immediately after the breakup of the Jam, Weller formed the Style Council with Mick Talbot, a member of the Jam-inspired mod-revival band the Merton Parkas. After a handful of initial hits, the Style Council proved to be a disappointment and Weller fell out of favor, both critically and commercially. At the end of the decade he disbanded the group and went solo in the early '90s; his solo albums have been both artistic and popular successes, returning him to the spotlight in the U.K. The legacy of the Jam is apparent in nearly every British guitar-pop band of the '80s of '90s, from the Smiths to Blur and Oasis. More than any other group, the Jam kept the tradition of three-minute, hook-driven British guitar-pop alive through the '70s and '80s, providing a blueprint for generations of bands to come. *— Stephen Thomas Erlewine*

In the City / 1977 / Polydor ✦✦✦

A spunky and abrasive debut, it mixes a mod's penchant for soul grooves with some fine piss-and-vinegar originals. *— John Floyd*

This Is the Modern World / 1977 / Polydor ✦✦✦

While it essentially repeats the formula of their debut, *This Is the Modern World* is an exciting, energetic record. *— Stephen Thomas Erlewine*

☆ All Mod Cons / 1978 / Polydor ✦✦✦✦✦

All Mod Cons marks a great leap for the band in songwriting maturity and sense of purpose. For the first time, they are able to build on rather than fall back on their influences, creating a sound all their own. Weller's story-song style, using invented characters, vivid British imagery, a youthful perspective and an impassioned delivery begs for the "voice of a generation" tag and clearly places him in the ranks of Ray Davies. Nothing short of a masterpiece. *— Chris Woodstra*

☆ Setting Sons / 1979 / Polydor ✦✦✦✦✦

Setting Sons was originally planned as a concept album about three childhood friends who, upon meeting up after some time apart, discover that they've grown apart. Though only about half of the songs follow the concept, Weller successfully depicts British life, male relationships and coming to terms with entry into adulthood. Oddly enough, while the lyrics are among Weller's darkest and most cynical, the production is their smoothest and the music is their most melodic to date. *— Chris Woodstra*

☆ Sound Affects / 1980 / Polydor ✦✦✦✦✦

A return to the expansive sound and love-and-politics of *All Mod Cons*, it's highlighted by the snarling "Pretty Green," "Set the House Ablaze," and "Start!," a fiery rewrite of the Beatles hit "Taxman." *— John Floyd*

The Gift / Jan. 1982 / Polydor ✦✦

A blatant stab at expanding their soul roots, it's pretty spotty, really, but "Town Called Malice," "Ghosts," and "Just Who Is the 5 O'Clock Hero?" are among the band's best work. *— John Floyd*

Dig the New Breed / Feb. 1982 / Polydor ✦✦✦
A live hodgepodge culled from material from 1977–1982, this rocking affair isn't bad, as far as live albums go. —*John Floyd*

★ **Snap!** / 1983 / Polydor ✦✦✦✦✦
A generous overview of the band's best, it includes many British-only singles that are musts for fans. Start with this one. —*John Floyd*

○ **Extras: a Collection of Rarities** / 1992 / Polydor ✦✦✦✦
Paul Weller has yet to receive his due in North America as one of Britain's major rock songwriters. His group The Jam began life in the late '70s as a Mod-revival combo influenced by The Who and The Small Faces. By 1982, backed by a palette of pop,soul, R&B and rock, Weller's lyrical insights into his country's psyche had positioned him as the Ray Davies of his generation. The exhaustive 26 tracks on *Extras* may not be the ideal introduction to newcomers, but make up an essential item for fans. As the title suggests, the disc collects single B-sides, demos of well-known songs, cover versions, and overlooked album tracks. Of special interest are two never-before- released numbers, a 1980 demo called "No One In The World," and "Hey Mister," recorded in 1979. U.K. music journalist Paolo Hewitt's 7-page essay is insightful, if a bit gushy. —*Roch Parisien*

○ **Greatest Hits** / 1992 / Polydor ✦✦✦✦
Greatest Hits covers nearly the same ground as *Snap*, with all the tracks but "Just Who Is the Five O'Clock Hero" included on the previous compilation. Granted, "That's Entertainment" is presented in the album version and "Funeral Pyre" in its original mix, but the album isn't quite as strong as *Snap*. Nevertheless, it has all of their hit singles, making it a thoroughly entertaining record, as well as an effective introduction to the group. —*Stephen Thomas Erlewine*

Live Jam / 1993 / Polydor ✦✦
Repeating none of the songs on *Dig the New Breed*, *Live Jam* is an energetic, exciting collection of concert material recorded during the band's early-'80s glory days. While it's an entertaining album, it's worthwhile listening only for dedicated fans. —*Stephen Thomas Erlewine*

James

Group, Alternative Pop/Rock
Since the release of their first EP in 1985, the English alternative folk-pop group James has always been on the verge of mainstream success, yet never quite becoming the superstars that they sometimes seem capable of becoming. For all their virtues, their albums have had their share of flaws, too; vocalist Tim Booth's tendency to go from a baritone to a falsetto within seconds was impressive at first, but soon grew tiresome and their songs were occasionally poorly arranged, making them sound directionless. However, James sounded off-kilter at times not because of a lack of talent, but because of the height of their ambitions—the band clearly aimed to be transcendent and important, not disposable. Since their first album, 1986's *Stutter*, each record has been drastically improved, with the band consistently reinventing and expanding their sound.

James' reached the Top Ten in the U.K. with a single from their live *One Man Clapping*, "Sit Down"; it showcased the band at their most direct and simple, which their next album did not. 1990's *Gold Mother* found the band incorporating elements of the current club scene of Manchester, their home town. James was never truly part of that musical trend, yet it helped them to re-sign with a major label in their country. Their next album, 1992's *Seven*, didn't have any of the dance inflections of their previous record, but it showed a significant step forward in their songwriting; 1993's *Laid* was even better, not only because of Brian Eno's atmospheric, melancholy production but because James reigned in their most excessive tendencies and recorded an album that fulfilled the promise they have always shown. *Laid* gave them their first hit in America, as well as some success in the U.K., although the band was publicly angry about what they believed to be a lack of support in their native country. *Laid* proved that James has just begun to hit their stride. —*Stephen Thomas Erlewine*

Stutter / 1986 / Sire ✦✦
On their debut album, James relied on a surging, powerful folk-rock that tended to obscure the fact that most of the songs were underdeveloped. Nevertheless, several of the tracks—including "Skullduggery" and "Why So Close," which was taken from the

early EP *Village Fire*—showed a great deal of potential. —*Stephen Thomas Erlewine*

Strip-Mine / 1988 / Sire ✦✦✦
With *Strip-Mine*, the band's second album, James' songwriting matures, as they incorporate anthemic pop melodies to their edgy, new wave-tinged folk-rock that recalled both the Smiths and U2. —*Stephen Thomas Erlewine*

One Man Clapping / 1989 / Rough Trade ✦✦✦
An excellent live album, it included exclusive material. —*Steve Aldrich*

Gold Mother / 1990 / Fontana ✦✦✦
Gold Mother was a significant departure from James' earlier records, as the group added a trumpeter and violinist to their lineup and began to experiment with the psychedelic dance-music craze that was currently sweeping Manchester. Instead of celebrating the hedonistic vibes of the Madchester scene, James used their new club-conscious and pop-oriented music to rail against injustice and social problems. Unfortunately, the music was so effective, it tended to drown out Tim Booth's heartfelt concerns, as well as his occasionally awkward melodies. —*Stephen Thomas Erlewine*

James (Sit Down) / 1990 / Fontana ✦✦✦
This is the U.S.-only revised edition of "Gold Mother." —*Steve Aldrich*

○ **Seven** / 1992 / Fontana ✦✦✦✦
James retreated from the dance inflections of *Gold Mother* on *Seven*. While they hadn't returned to the stripped-down folkiness of their first record, the group's songwriting had become more focused and direct, supporting fully-formed, memorable melodies, making *Seven* their most impressive record to date. —*Stephen Thomas Erlewine*

● **Laid** / 1993 / PolyGram 3145 ✦✦✦✦
James continued to refine and expand their songwriting on *Laid*, a dark, moody album of surprising emotional resonance. Brian Eno's atmospheric production makes *Laid* seem if it has only one tone initially, but with repeated listens, the peaks and valleys emerge as clearly as the details within the songs themself. Even the brightest songs, such as "Low Low Low" and "Laid," have a deep undercurrent of sadness, but it's a gorgeous melancholy, making *Laid* the band's most ambitious, accomplished and accessible album. —*Stephen Thomas Erlewine*

Wah Wah / 1994 / PolyGram ✦✦✦
While James was recording *Laid*, producer Brian Eno encouraged the band to wander into experimental jams to fuel their creative energies. The results are captured on *Wah Wah*, a free-form set of 22 loosely constructed songs. Although the record may be slightly indulgent, most of the music is quite impressive, proving that the depth James showed on *Laid* was far from a fluke. —*Stephen Thomas Erlewine*

James Gang

Group, Rock & Roll, Hard Rock
At the top of the '70s, Joe Walsh (James Gang lead guitarist and singer) blasted onto the music scene as the new kid on the block to watch. Walsh's distinctive staggered lead-guitar phrasing, bare-boned boogie riff-work, and tonal integrity immediately earned him high marks, and stories of Walsh upstaging Jimi Hendrix during their warmup slots with the Experience spread like wildfire.

Walsh backed up the buzz with the James Gang's second album, *Rides Again*, which was a tour de force of dynamic, hard trio rock. What James Gang drummer Jim Fox and bassist Dale Peters lacked in inventive fire (à la Cream or Jimi Hendrix Experience), they made up for in providing a rock-solid foundation for Walsh's soaring guitar flights and wide chordal sound washes.

After one more studio effort, *Thirds*, and a live album, Walsh split and went solo, leaving the James Gang to flounder around and produce a couple of minor FM rock hits before falling apart. —*Rick Clark*

Yer' Album / 1969 / One Way ✦✦✦
Yer' Album, the James Gang's first album, was a strong debut, thanks to the presence of guitarist Joe Walsh. Walsh helped bring the loud, bracing attack of British hard rock to American Southern rock boogie with his loud, crunching power chords and concise, biting leads. Most of the original songs on *Yer' Album* are underdeveloped and lack memorable melodies, yet the sound of the band is invigorating and forceful. —*Stephen Thomas Erlewine*

● **Rides Again** / 1970 / MCA ✦✦✦✦
With their second album *Rides Again*, the James Gang came into their own. Under the direction of guitarist Joe Walsh, the group—now featuring bassist Dale Peters—began incorporating keyboards into their hard rock, which helped open up their musical horizons. For much of the first side of *Rides Again*, the group tears through a bunch of boogie numbers, most notably the heavy groove of "Funk #49." On the second side, the James Gang departs from their trademark sound, adding keyboard flourishes and elements of country rock to their hard rock. Walsh's songwriting had improved, giving the band solid support for their stylistic experiments. What ties the two sides of the record together is the strength of the band's musicianship, which burns brightly and powerfully on the hardest rockers, as well as on the sensitive ballads. —*Stephen Thomas Erlewine*

○ **Thirds** / 1971 / One Way ✦✦✦✦
Thirds wasn't quite as satisfying as *Rides Again*, lacking the consistently strong songwriting of the previous album. Nevertheless, the interplay between the musicians is impressive throughout the record and whenever Walsh turns in a killer song, like "Walk Away" or "Midnight Man," the band drives it home for all it's worth. —*Stephen Thomas Erlewine*

Live in Concert / 1971 / Mobile Fidelity ✦✦✦
The James Gang earned a great number of fans through their live performances, so it made sense that they would release a live record within months of their successful third album. *Live in Concert* captures much of the energy of their live performances, with Joe Walsh's guitar solos catching fire on nearly every song. However, the record also makes it clear that he was beginning to outgrow the confines of the James Gang, as Fox and Peters struggled to keep up with his imaginative playing for most of the album. —*Stephen Thomas Erlewine*

Straight Shooter / 1972 / One Way ✦✦
Following the departure of Joe Walsh, drummer Jim Fox and bassist Dale Peters recruited guitarist Dominic Troiano and vocalist Roy Kenner and set about recording the James Gang's fourth studio album, *Straight Shooter*. Although Troiano was a competent player, he lacked Walsh's fiery passion and knack for crafting melodic solos. In addition to Troiano's workman-like performances, the band was saddled by a noticeable lack of strong material, since none of the members could write songs with memorable hooks. —*Stephen Thomas Erlewine*

Passin' Thru / 1972 / ABC ✦✦
Passin' Thru continued James Gang's dry period, as the band suffered from a dearth of memorable songs and Troiano exhausted his supply of guitar licks. Troiano left after the release of *Passin' Thru* and was replaced with ex-Zephyr guitarist Tommy Bolin, who helped revitalize the band. —*Stephen Thomas Erlewine*

○ **16 Greatest Hits** / 1973 / MCA ✦✦✦✦
This is a fine collection of the James Gang's best tracks. —*AMG*

Bang / 1973 / Atco ✦✦✦
Bang was the first record the James Gang recorded with Tommy Bolin, a former member of Zephyr. While the songs were still fairly undistinguished, Bolin's playing was imaginative and captivating, making the lack of interesting material forgivable. —*Stephen Thomas Erlewine*

○ **The Best of the James Gang** / 1973 / ABC ✦✦✦✦
A good collection of their innovative hard rock features "Walk Away" and "Funk 49." —*Dan Heilman*

Miami / 1974 / Atco ✦✦✦
Like *Bang* before it, *Miami* was a success solely because of the presence of guitarist Tommy Bolin. Bolin's energetic, muscular playing reinvigorated the James Gang, sparking the rest of the band into giving lively performances. Again, there was a noticeable lack of memorable songs, but *Miami* is worthwhile for guitar afficionados. —*Stephen Thomas Erlewine*

Newborn / 1975 / Atlantic ✦✦
Tommy Bolin left the James Gang after the release of *Miami*, leaving the band without a compelling lead guitarist once again. Fox and Peters broke up the group after his departure, but they reformed a year later, adding guitarist Richard Shack and vocalist Bubba Keith. The new version of the James Gang released their first album, *Newborn*, in 1975. The record was another collection of mediocre songs—a problem that plagued the band ever since the departure of Joe Walsh in 1971. On *Bang* and *Miami*, the group were able to disguise the absence of good songs with Bolin's

playing, but Shack could not compete with his predecessor's forceful, flowing style and *Newborn* suffered accordingly. —*Stephen Thomas Erlewine*

Jesse Come Home / 1976 / Atco ✦✦
Jesse Come Home was the James Gang's final album, and it's easy to see why. Ignoring the group's continuing failure to write strong songs, the main problem of the album lies in the bland, uninspired playing of the entire group. Shack may not have recaptured the power of Joe Walsh or Tommy Bolin, but that doesn't give Fox and Peters an excuse for phoning in their performances. After *Jesse Come Home* failed to make the charts, Fox and Peters wisely decided to call it a day, disbanding the James Gang for the last time. —*Stephen Thomas Erlewine*

Rick James (James Johnson)

b. Feb. 1, 1952, Buffalo, NY
Funk, Disco, Urban
In the late 1970s, when the fortunes of Motown Records seemed to be flagging, Rick James came along and rescued the company, providing funky hits that updated the label's style and saw it through into the mid-'80s. Actually, James had been with Motown earlier, though nothing had come of it. After growing up in Buffalo and running away to join the Naval Reserves, he ran away from the Navy to Toronto, where he was in a band with future Buffalo Springfield members Neil Young and Bruce Palmer, and with Goldy McJohn, later of Steppenwolf. As the Mynah Birds, they signed to Motown and recorded, though no record was ever released.

James had a journeyman's career playing bass in various groups before signing again to Motown as an artist, songwriter, and producer. His first single, "You and I," topped the R&B charts and reached the pop Top 40. "Mary Jane" (September 1978) was another hit. Both were on James's debut album, *Come and Get It!* (June 1978), which went gold. Subsequent efforts were not as successful, though *Bustin' Out of L Seven* (January 1979) featured the R&B bit "Bustin' Out" (April 1979). James returned to form with the #1 R&B hit "Give It to Me Baby" (March 1981), featured on the million-selling *Street Songs* (April 1981), which also featured the hit "Super Freak."

James turned his production attention to resuscitating the career of the Temptations, recently returned to Motown, and "Standing on the Top" (April 1982), credited to "The Temptations Featuring Rick James," was an R&B Top Ten. (He also produced recordings by Teena Marie and the Mary Jane Girls.) James' follow-up to *Street Songs* was the gold-selling *Throwin' Down* (May 1982), which featured the hit "Dance Wit' Me." The title song of *Cold Blooded* (August 1983) became James's third R&B #1, and the album also featured his hit duet with Smokey Robinson, "Ebony Eyes." James's greatest hits album *Reflections* (August 1984) featured the new track "17" (June 1984), which also became a hit. *Glow* (April 1985) contained Top Ten R&B singles in the title track and "Can't Stop," which was featured in the summer movie blockbuster *Beverly Hills Cop. The Flag* (June 1986) featured the hit "Sweet and Sexy Thing" (May 1986).

James left Motown for the Reprise division of Warner Bros. Records as of the album *Wonderful* (July 1988), which featured his #1 R&B hit "Loosey's Rap," on which he was accompanied by rapper Roxanne Shante. Nevertheless, his "punk funk" didn't seem to rest comfortably with the trend toward rap/hip-hop. In 1989, James charted briefly with medley of the Drifters hits "This Magic Moment" and "Dance with Me." In 1990, M.C. Hammer scored a massive hit with "U Can't Touch This," which consisted of his rap over the instrumental track of "Super Freak." That should have made for a career rebirth, but James has been plagued by drug and legal problems that have found him more frequently in court and in jail than in the recording studio. —*William Ruhlmann*

Come Get It! / 1978 / Motown ✦✦✦
An excellent debut set, "Mary Jane" was very risqué for its time. —*Rick A. Bueche*

Bustin' out of L Seven / 1979 / Gordy ✦✦✦

Fire It Up / 1979 / Gordy ✦✦✦

3 Times in Love / 1980 / Gordy ✦✦

Garden of Love / 1980 / Motown ✦✦
Rick James was riding high in the early '80s, although this album was the weakest of his hit string. Although he did get a couple of Top 20 R&B singles, this album was more of a formula job than ei-

ther its predecessor or successor, and had less exuberant vocals and more repetitive production and arrangements. But it didn't hurt James' then-soaring career much, and in retrospect was much better than some LPs he did later in the decade. —*Ron Wynn*

○ **Street Songs** / 1981 / Motown ✦✦✦✦
Rick James peaked on this album. His vocals were never more aggressive or better produced than on the singles "Super Freak" and "Give It To Me Baby." James became a crossover sensation, as the LP peaked at number three on the pop album chart and eventually went platinum. "Give It To Me Baby" topped the R&B charts for five weeks, while "Super Freak" was also a Top Ten single. —*Ron Wynn*

Throwin' Down / 1982 / Gordy ✦✦

Cold Blooded / 1983 / Motown ✦✦
The last gasp for Rick James, at one time the king of '80s punk/funk. He was close to the end by the time this came out, but got some fresh life from a surprising source. A ballad between James and Smokey Robinson, possibly the two least compatible male vocalists around, proved a big hit and regenerated James as a single artist for a few more years. But the remainder of the album marked his continual deterioration as a producer, arranger, songwriter, and performer. —*Ron Wynn*

● **Reflections: Greatest Hits** / 1984 / Motown ✦✦✦✦
A nice collection featuring the best uptempo and left-field ballad hits by Rick James. The anthology shows that James functioned best when riding the rhythm; he was a moderately talented (at best) vocalist better at yelling and exhorting than trying to interpret lyrics, pace a slow song, or vary a mood. The only significant ballad hit he had was a duet where the contrast between his voice and Smokey Robinson's generated enough response to sell the song. —*Ron Wynn*

You / 1985 / Gordy ✦✦✦

The Flag / 1986 / Motown ✦✦
Rick James had reached the end of the creative road by the time this was issued in the late '80s. Prince had taken the punk/funk hybrid and made it his own, while James' vocals and production lacked the spunk, rebellious air, and energy that had made him one of the early '80s more charismatic figures. These are leaden, woefully performed numbers, with no inspiration or conviction. The production and arrangements were just as uninspired. —*Ron Wynn*

● **Greatest Hits** / 1986 / Motown ✦✦✦✦
The best of his "punk-funk" includes "Super Freak," "Give It to Me Baby," and "You & I." —*Rick A. Bueche*

Wonderful / 1988 / Reprise ✦✦
Rick James had pretty much exhausted his bag of tricks by the late '80s. This album was little more than a shell of his former works, lacking the aggressiveness, energy, humor, or even the posturing that once gave his work a rebellious air. It was strictly a formula job, and wasn't even an up-to-date one. This plodding effort was quickly forgotten, even though James did land a number one R&B hit with "Loosey's Rap." —*Ron Wynn*

○ **Bustin' Out: The Very Best of** / 1994 / Motown ✦✦✦✦
A definitive double-disc anthology, it's essential for devoted fans. —*AMG*

Tommy James & the Shondells

Group, Pop/Rock
During the last half of the '60s, Tommy James & the Shondells were one of America's most successful pop acts, generating 14 Top 40 hits between 1966 and 1969. James formed the original Shondells at the age of twelve, in 1960. In 1963, they recorded a Jeff Barry-Ellie Greenwich song called "Hanky Panky" for the Snap label. Two years later, a Pittsburgh DJ picked up on the song and made it into a regional hit. James and the original Shondells parted ways because the band members didn't want to relocate from Indiana, and James formed a new Shondells by taking on a group called the Raconteurs. In 1966 they signed to Morris Levy's Roulette, which reissued "Hanky Panky" (it became a number one million-seller).

For the next two years, they embodied lightweight chewy pop with hits like "I Think We're Alone Now" and "Mirage." The group developed a heavier sound with the percussive 1968 hit "Mony Mony." In keeping with the times, they became more psychedelic, best captured in their number one "Crimson and Clover." The

Shondells continued to chart until James left for a moderately successful solo career in 1970. James's biggest hit was "Draggin' the Line." The Shondells changed their name to Hog Heaven to no appreciable success. During the '80s, the Shondells's material enjoyed a resurgence of popularity among various pop and rock artists. Joan Jett scored with "Crimson and Clover," while Billy Idol's version of "Mony Mony" and Tiffany's "I Think We're Alone Now" took turns at the number one position in November of 1987. —*Rick Clark*

● **Anthology** / 1990 / Rhino ✦✦✦✦
James and his band had a remarkable string of hits from the mid-'60s to the early '70s, largely because of an uncanny ability to keep current with fast-changing pop trends, from their first garage-band hit, "Hanky Panky," to their psychedelicized songs like "Crimson and Clover." Even more remarkable, the music holds up entertainingly today, and this well-annotated, 27-track compilation contains all the hits and more. —*William Ruhlmann*

Jan & Dean

Group, Surf, Pop/Rock
Besides the Beach Boys, no other vocal group captured the sound of California surf music with as much success—both commercial and artistic—as Jan & Dean. The duo actually began as a doo wop-soaked harmony act in the late '50s, reaching the Top Ten with the goofy "Baby Talk" and scoring minor hits with doo-wop updates of standards like "A Sunday Kind of Love" and "Heart and Soul." When the Beach Boys began their climb to superstardom, Jan & Dean changed gears and followed suit with a series of surf and hot rod hits that featured falsetto harmonies, chugging guitars, and Jan Berry's clean production. Brian Wilson himself sang backup vocals on their biggest hit (which he co-wrote with Jan), "Surf City," in 1963.

While they lacked the Beach Boys' depth and capacity for artistic growth, Jan & Dean's hits from 1963 and 1964—which also included "The Little Old Lady (From Pasadena)," "Drag City," "Honolulu Lulu," and the mini-soap opera "Dead Man's Curve"—are in the same class as the Beach Boys' early work in their infectious, energetic invocation of good times and California sunshine. They added an irresistibly reckless humor to the genre, and were wellcast as the fun-loving hosts of the classic 1964 rock & roll hootenanny film *The T.A.M.I. Show* (for which they performed the rip-roaring theme, "(Here They Come) From All over the World"). The duo's success, already on the wane a bit, was tragically cut short by Jan Berry's near-fatal auto accident in April 1966, which had been eerily foreshadowed by the lyrics of "Dead Man's Curve." —*Richie Unterberger*

● **Surf City: the Best of Jan & Dean** / 1990 / EMI America ✦✦✦✦
Remembered mostly for their surfing hits, Jan & Dean had a bit more range than they're generally given credit for. Their roots were in doo-wop, and after scoring surf and hot rod hits, they also cut some decent straight pop-rock songs and zany singles that verged on pop satire. *Surf City* includes just about all the material you'd want from the duo. The 22 songs include the big hits "Surf City," "Dead Man's Curve," and "The Little Old Lady (From Pasadena)," of course, but also feature nifty smaller successes like "Honolulu Lulu," "The New Girl In School," and "Ride The Wild Surf." The pair was second only to the Beach Boys in blending high, soaring harmonies with driving vocal surf'n'hot rod sounds. Of course, they weren't nearly as talented as Brian Wilson's group, but even their minor material has an irrepressible sense of fun and sparking L.A. pop-rock production and melodies. Other highlights include their rearrangement of the old standard "Linda" and the 1965 Top 40 hit "I Found a Girl," written by P.F. Sloan and Steve Barri. Sloan-Barri also penned their infectious theme for the classic rock film *The T.A.M.I. Show*, "(Here They Come) From All over the World," which deserved to be a bigger hit than it was. The only major omissions of this well-packaged set are their early, heavily doo wop-influenced hits "Jennie Lee," "Baby Talk," and "Heart and Soul," which weren't recorded for EMI. —*Richie Unterberger*

Jane's Addiction

Group, Alternative Pop/Rock, Hard Rock
Jane's Addiction were one of the most hotly pursued rock bands when they gained notice in Los Angeles in the mid '80s, with record companies at their feet. Flamboyant frontman Perry Farrell, formerly of the band Psi Com, has an undeniable charisma and an

interest in provocative art (he designed the band's album covers) and Jane's Addiction plays a hybrid of rock music—metal with strains of punk, folk, jazz, or you-name-it.

The quartet comprising Farrell, bassist Eric Avery, drummer Stephen Perkins, and guitarist Dave Navarro had already released their debut album as well, in the form of a live recording from the Roxy in Hollywood. Finally, Warner Brothers won the bidding war and released *Nothing Shocking* in 1988. The band's abrasive sound and aggressive atttitude (typified by the nude sculpture on the cover) led to some resistance, but Jane's Addiction began to break through to an audience: the album spent 35 weeks in the charts.

Ritual de lo Habitual followed in 1990 and was the band's commercial breakthrough, reaching the Top 20 and going gold. Farrell designed the travelling rock festival Lollapalooza as a farewell tour for Jane's Addiction. After the tour was completed at the end of the summer of 1991, the group split. Farrell would continue to be involved with the organization of the annual Lollapalooza festival for the next several years; he also formed Porno for Pyros with Perkins in 1992, releasing their debut record the following year. After a couple of quiet years—which included forming Deconstruction, a band that didn't release any records until 1994, with Avery—Navarro joined the Red Hot Chili Peppers at the end of 1993. —*William Ruhlmann*

Jane's Addiction / 1987 / Triple X ◆◆◆
Recorded live at the Roxy in Hollywood, Jane's Addiction's self-titled debut was an ill-formed attempt at melding post-punk brooding with thundering heavy metal and the self-conscious pretensions of '70s art-rock. Occasionally, the group manages a couple of fine songs—particularly the rolling, acoustic-based "Jane Says," which was re-recorded for their major-label debut, *Nothing's Shocking*—but the whole album begins to drag as the group hauls out a series of covers, including "Sympathy for the Devil" and the Velvet Underground's "Rock 'n' Roll," which makes Jane's Addiction sound like an undistinguished bar band. —*Stephen Thomas Erlewine*

○ **Nothing's Shocking** / 1988 / Warner Brothers ◆◆◆◆
The cover (a sculpture of two naked females joined at the hips with their hair ablaze) screams that this is an artsy album, and it is. Jane's Addiction, under the direction of lead vocalist Perry Farrell, brings the aesthetics of performance art to heavy metal. Some of the results are provoking, but the group's ambitions are usually irritating. Farrell's voice wears thin after a few songs, and it's not helped much by the post-Zeppelin stumble of the band—Dave Navarro may be a fluid guitarist, but he can't write riffs as powerful and catchy as Jimmy Page. Nevertheless, *Nothing's Shocking* works on occasion, particularly "Summertime Rolls" and the re-recorded version of "Jane Says." —*Stephen Thomas Erlewine*

● **Ritual De Lo Habitual** / 1990 / Warner Brothers ◆◆◆◆
Throughout the first half of *Ritual*, Jane's Addiction manages to groove, creating the best rock & roll of their short career. The two Bo Diddley knock-offs, "Stop!" and "Been Caught Stealing," in particular, sound tight and exciting, but on the second half, the indulgent ten-minute songs are hauled out, beginning with the insufferable *menage à trois* magnum opus "Three Days." Still, the band manages to salvage the album with the majestic "Classic Girl," one of their best songs. —*Stephen Thomas Erlewine*

Japan

Group, Art-Rock/Progressive-Rock
Japan was part of the short-lived "new romantic" movement in British pop. Members of Japan included brothers David Sylvian and Steve Jansen (original family name Batt, b. 1958 and 1959, respectively), Mick Karn (b. 1958), Richard Barbieri (b. 1957), and Rob Dean (b. 1959). Precursors to new-age music, Japan combined Eastern influences with synth-pop overlay, giving them a staunch UK following that has never translated into U.S. chart success. —*Cub Koda*

○ **Adolescent Sex** / 1978 / Ariola ◆◆◆◆
The debut album is vastly different from later work. —*Steve Aldrich*

Obscure Alternatives / 1978 / Ariola ◆◆◆
Continuing artsy glam rock formula of debut. —*Steve Aldrich*

Quiet Life / 1979 / Fame ◆◆◆
This transitional album turned the group from their original glam rock style to the later Roxy Music-influenced sound. —*Steve Aldrich*

● **Gentlemen Take Polaroids** / 1980 / Blue Plate ◆◆◆◆
This was the first fully realized album in the group's latter-day phase. —*Steve Aldrich*

○ **Tin Drum** / 1981 / Blue Plate ◆◆◆◆
A highly atmospheric effort, this early-'80s classic was strongly influenced by folk music of their namesake country. —*Steve Aldrich*

Assemblege / 1981 / Hansa ◆◆◆
First of the collections of Hansa-era tracks. —*Steve Aldrich*

Oil on Canvas / 1983 / Blue Plate ◆◆◆
An outstanding live album, it focused on *Tin Drum-* and *Polaroids*-era material. —*Steve Aldrich*

Exorcising Ghosts / 1984 / Virgin ◆◆◆
This is a compilation of Virgin-era material. —*Steve Aldrich*

Jason & the Scorchers

Group, Rock & Roll, Country-Rock
A country/hard rock band formed by Illinois native Jason Ringenberg in 1981, Jason and the Scorchers came careening onto the indie-rock scene seemingly out of nowhere (truth was, it was Nashville) with a debut EP whose most killer track (among a slew of killer tracks) was a fire-breathing cover of Bob Dylan's "Absolutely Sweet Marie." This amalgam of speedy hard rock fused with Ringenberg's decidedly country twang, along with the band's ability to deftly negotiate between Rolling Stones-style stomps and quieter, more melodic acoustic country music, led to Jason and the Scorchers becoming a critically lauded and fairly popular '80s band. Capitalizing quickly on the notoriety brought by their debut EP, the Scorchers kicked out two fine LPs (*Lost & Found* and *Still Standing*) that sounded perfect for radio, but not so slick as to sound manufactured. With Ringenberg's yowling voice pushed way up front, the band's sonic power came from the synchronous playing of Nashville rock veterans Warner Hodges (guitar), Jeff Johnson (bass), and Perry Baggs (drums). Sharing similar musical backgrounds that valued the music of Hank Williams and Johnny Cash as much as the Stones or Beatles, these guys could crank out mega-amped hard rock one minute and sound like the Flying Burrito Brothers the next, all of it done with great skill and excitement. Despite their obvious talent, by the release of 1986's *Still Standing*, it seemed as though the band wasn't going anywhere. They had achieved a modicum of success, but weren't able to break through to mass acclaim, partly because they came along just before the explosion of country radio in the late '80s/early '90s. Hence, rock radio was reluctant to play them because they sounded too country, and country radio thought they were too rock; it's an old story that usually spells doom for the band in question. After a three-year break that saw Johnson's departure, the Scorchers released a desultory third album (*Thunder and Fire*) that sounded like a desperate attempt at hard-rock credibility. They broke up soon after. Ringenberg went on to record country-oriented solo work, re-formed the original Scorchers in 1994, and released a modest reunion record (*A Blazing Grace*) that sounded like the Scorchers of old. —*John Dougan*

○ **Fervor** / 1983 / EMI America ◆◆◆◆
Their debut EP has "Absolutely Sweet Marie" (which you'll play over and over and over), as well as some wonderful country rock like "Hot Nights in Georgia." Ringenberg's twangy voice is a hoot to listen to, and Warner Hodges plays some great guitar. A wonderful, if too brief, record and a harbinger of some great rock and roll to come. R.E.M.'s Michael Stipe contributes a song ("Both Sides Of the Line") and some backup vocals. —*John Dougan*

○ **Lost & Found** / 1985 / EMI America ◆◆◆◆
Of the Scorchers' three full-length LPs, this is by far the best. There is so much pent-up energy and excitement on this record, it sounds as if it will fly off your turntable (assuming you still have a turntable) at any moment. With Hodges (as usual) driving this machine, Ringenberg's wild-eyed country-punk persona is here in full fury, and the good times never let up. This should have been the album that made them stars, but it did solidify their audience and place them in larger concert venues, where they tore it up. —*John Dougan*

Still Standing / 1986 / EMI Australia ◆◆◆
Produced by veteran hard rock producer Tom Werman, *Still Standing* is a fine record, but also shows subtle signs of the band in decline: the hard rock is stiffer, Hodges' guitar is smoother and more akin to the anonymous hard rock/heavy metal guitar sound that defined AOR radio in the '80s. That notwithstanding, there are

still songs like "Golden Ball and Chain," which sounds like an outtake from *Exile on Main Street* and, continuing with the Rolling Stones motif, a ripsnortin' cover of "19th Nervous Breakdown." A teensy bit disappointing in comparison to *Lost and Found*, but by no means a bad record or one to ignore. If you've liked the Scorchers up to this point, you'll want *Still Standing.* —*John Dougan*

Thunder & Fire / 1989 / A&M ◆◆◆

● **Essential, Vol. 1 (Are You Ready for the Country)** / 1992 / Capitol ◆◆◆◆

Jawbox

Group, Alternative Pop/Rock

Washington, D.C.'s Jawbox made indie news in 1994 not for their new album *For Your Own Special Sweetheart*, but for their major-label contract. Originally on independent stalwart Dischord Records (headed by Fugazi's Ian MacKaye), Jawbox was the first band from Dischord to jump ship and sign a contract with a major. Jawbox is headed by singer/guitarist Jay Robbins and bassist Kim Coletta. Drummer Adam Wade was replaced by Zachary Barocas for *For Your Own Special Sweetheart*, and a second guitarist, W.C. Barbot, joined in 1992 for the band's second album, *Novelty.* —*Matt Carlson*

Novelty / 1992 / Dischord ◆◆◆

On *Novelty*, Jawbox improved their music while burying the vocal tracks in the background. The new direction works well as the band blitzes through twelve songs that resemble early Joy Division filtered through early-'80s hardcore guitar aggression. Of special note is the 1991 single included on this disc, "Tongues" b/w "Ones And Zeros," which buzzsaw in an energetic yet playful rhythm guided by swirling harmonic guitar frenzy. —*Matt Carlson*

● **For Your Own Special Sweetheart** / 1994 / Atlantic ◆◆◆◆

For Your Own Special Sweetheart is Jawbox's best to date, as the band continued to mature musically. In fact, though many indie-stalwarts may have screamed "sellout," this album is more experimental, harsh, and emotionally draining than the band's previous records. While Jawbox stuns with a new, demented pop approach on tracks like "Savory" and "Chicago Piano," as Kim Coletta's bass playing roams more freely, the band still manages to aggressively pierce previous expectations with a gigantic wall of angular sound. —*Matt Carlson*

Jay & the Americans

Group, Doo-Wop, Pop/Rock

Jay and the Americans were a vocal group from Brooklyn formed by New York University students John ("Jay") Traynor, Kenny Vance (b. Dec 9, 1943), Sandy Deane (b. Jan 31, 1940), and Howie Kane (b. Jun 6, 1942). Marty Sanders (b. Feb 28, 1941) joined in 1961, the year before they scored their first hit, "She Cried." Traynor left the group after the hit and was replaced by David Blatt (b. Nov 2, 1938), who took the name "Jay Black." The group scored six more Top 40 hits through the end of 1965, all based around Black's dramatic (and near-operatic) tenor, among them "Come a Little Bit Closer" and "Cara Mia." They slowed down a little after that but came back in 1969 with a gold-selling version of "This Magic Moment" (the old Drifters hit). In total, they placed 18 records in the charts.

The group personnel altered in the late '60s and early '70s. Then-future Steely Dan members Donald Fagen and Walter Becker played in the backup group for a time. Vance recorded solo and eventually found success as a musical director of movies. Black kept the band going on the oldies circuit. When last heard at a benefit concert in New Jersey at the start of the '90s, he could still hit those high notes in "Cara Mia." —*William Ruhlmann*

● **Come a Little Bit Closer: The Best of Jay & the Americans** / 199z / United Artists ◆◆◆◆

Jay Black possesses one of the most remarkable voices in rock & roll. On *Come a Little Bit Closer—The Best of Jay & the Americans*, an exhaustive 28-song collection, you get all of the hits in superb fidelity, and plenty of bonuses. —*Jeff Tamarkin*

Jayhawks

Group, Country-Rock, Alternative Pop/Rock

On a series of independent albums in the late '80s, the Jayhawks staked out the same territory as Gram Parsons and Neil Young, recording some of the best, grittiest country-rock of the decade.

When the band signed to American Records in the early '90s, they started getting a substantial amount of press; many critics called their 1992 album, *Hollywood Town Hall*, one of the best of the year. While the Jayhawks do nothing particularly new, they do it well; not only do they sound like the classic country-rock of the '70s, they have the songs to support their sound, which keeps them from being an empty exercise in nostalgia. —*Stephen Thomas Erlewine*

The Jayhawks / 1986 / Bunkhouse ◆◆◆

Blue Earth / 1989 / Twin/Tone ◆◆◆

This fine debut is highlighted by good honky tonk songwriting. —*Dan Heilman*

● **Hollywood Town Hall** / 1992 / Def American ◆◆◆◆

Darn if that old Neil Young influence hasn't spun off another winner. Right from the distorted, rootsy, opening chords of lead track "Waiting for the Sun," you can tell that Minneapolis combo The Jayhawks is well versed in early Crazy Horse. Gary Louris' electric chording is off-set by Mark Olson's full-bodied acoustic guitar and harmonica textures. The disc was recorded partly in a home state, backwoods studio and partly in posher L.A. facilities. This contrast highlights the blend of—and tension between—rural and urban elements that give *Hollywood Town Hall* its edge. —*Roch Parisien*

○ **Tomorrow the Green Grass** / 1995 / American ◆◆◆◆

Even the title of the Jayhawks' follow-up, *Tomorrow the Green Grass*, shows that the band is headed for lusher pastures. The addition of a full-time keyboardist opens up their sound, as does the subtle string arrangements. The result is an album that is steeped in the early '70s, yet not in the dusty Gram Parsons tribute of *Hollywood Town Hall.* Instead, it sounds like what Parsons or Neil Young would have sounded like if they were produced in Nashville. —*Stephen Thomas Erlewine*

The JB's

Group, Soul, Funk, R&B

Maceo Parker joined James Brown's fabled band in 1964, Alfred "Pee Wee" Ellis joined the fold two years later, and Fred Wesley came on board in 1968. Ellis cowrote such classics as "Cold Sweat" and "Say It Loud—I'm Black and I'm Proud," and both he and Wesley at various points were musical director of the JB's. Parker was immortalized in Brown's famous incantation "Maceo, come blow your horn." Ellis also served as musical director for Van Morrison, while Wesley and Parker were part of the Parliament/Funkadelic gang at their peak in the mid and late '70s. The three of them have recorded in various permutations as Maceo and All the King's Men, Maceo and the Macks, the JB's, Fred Wesley and the New JB's, Fred Wesley and the Horny Horns, the John Book Horns and simply under any one of their individual names. In the '80s and early '90s, with the resurgence of interest in James Brown and Parliament/Funkadelic, the three horn men have been involved in a plethora of recordings. (Note: All of the albums made by Parker, Ellis, and Wesley in their various permutations have been included here; the artist credited with the album appears at the end of the review.) —*Rob Bowman*

Doing Their Own Thing / 1970 / House of the Fox ◆◆◆

Recorded and released after a mutiny by most of James Brown's late-'60s band, *Doing Their Own Thing* contains 12 slabs of superb early-'70s style funk. Mostly instrumental, radio play for the album and subsequent singles appears to have been blocked by Brown himself. (Credited to Maceo Parker.) —*Rob Bowman*

○ **Doing It to Death** / 1973 / People ◆◆◆◆

Extended live "funkafizing" including a ten-minute version of the #1 R&B hit "Doing It to Death." Written, produced, and arranged by James Brown. —*Rob Bowman*

Damn Right I Am Somebody / 1974 / People ◆◆◆

More of the same sparse, cutting-edge funk, including a Top 40 R&B hit in the title cut. (Credited to Fred Wesley & the JB's.) —*Rob Bowman*

Breakin' Bread / 1974 / People ◆◆◆

The last of the Fred Wesley and the JB's albums. "Breakin' Bread" and "Makin' Love" charted R&B. The funk is still much in evidence, although some new twists and turns manifest themselves on the "rapped" title cut. (Credited to Fred Wesley & the New JB's.) —*Rob Bowman*

○ **A Blow for Me: a Toot For You** / 1977 / Atlantic ◆◆◆◆

Produced by George Clinton and Bootsy Collins and recorded with the company of much of the P-Funk Mob, *A Blow for Me: a Toot for You* showcases a new, slinkier, more produced and less hard-edged edition of the J. B.Horns. The lead cut, a remake of Parliament's "Up for the Down Stroke," received a little R&B airplay. —*Rob Bowman*

New Friends / 1990 / Antilles ✦✦✦
Wesley and Parker in the company of jazz musicians Gerri Allen, Anthony Cox, and Robin Eubanks. This is by far the jazziest of Fred, Maceo, and Pee Wee's recordings, covering the likes of Thelonious Monk, Duke Ellington, and Dizzy Gillespie. Wesley also proves himself to be a fine jazz writer, "For the Elders" being particularly notable. —*Rob Bowman*

○ **For All the King's Men** / 1990 / 4th & Broadway ✦✦✦✦
Produced by Bill Laswell and Bootsy Collins, this five-cut CD EP includes Wesley, Parker, Bobby Byrd, Bootsy Collins, and Sly Stone on one cut. "Let 'Em Out" is a paean to free James Brown. That and "Sax Machine" appear in two different versions. Hilarious and serious-as-a-heart-attack funk all at once. (Credited to Maceo Parker.) —*Rob Bowman*

Roots Revisited / 1990 / Verve ✦✦✦
Ellis, Wesley, and Parker in the company of jazz keyboardist Don Pullen and Bootsy Collins. The first of a string of new recordings, *Roots Revisited* is half jazz, half soul, with a little funk thrown in for good measure. It's the first time these three have played jazz on record. The album includes wonderfully invigorating versions of Charles Mingus's "Better Get It in Yo' Soul" and the Impressions's "People Get Ready." —*Rob Bowman*

Mo' Roots / 1991 / Verve ✦✦✦
The second *Roots* installment, *Mo' Roots* was cut minus Pullen and Collins, leaning a little more toward the instrumental soul side. Three fine originals in conjunction with covers of Ray Charles, Marvin Gaye, Otis Redding, Horace Silver, and Lionel Hampton. —*Rob Bowman*

● **Funky Good Time: The Anthology** / 1995 / Polydor ✦✦✦✦
The J.B.'s recorded under various billings in the early '70s, including the JB's, Fred Wesley & the JB's, Maceo & the Macks, the First Family, the Last Word, and others. This double CD gathers 30 of the prime tracks by all of the above configurations from the first half of the '70s, including all nine of their chart hits and quite a few rare singles and long versions. Often, James Brown himself chirps in with incidental vocals (though this is mostly instrumental) and keyboards. The two-and-a-half hour program can start to sound monotonous if taken all at once, but it's prime, often riveting funk, jammed with lockstep grooves that vary between basic R&B vamps and imaginative, almost jazzy improvisation. —*Richie Unterberger*

The JB Horns / Gramavision ✦✦✦
On an album made up of eleven originals, the three horn men turn in a fine, if undistinguished mix of jazz and funk. Worth hearing just for Fred's rapping, the gently swinging "Mother's Kitchen," and the sly "Everywhere Is Out of Town." —*Rob Bowman*

Jefferson Airplane/ Starship

Group, Rock & Roll, Hard Rock, Psychedelic, Folk-Rock
Jefferson Airplane (formed July 1965), along with the Grateful Dead, Quicksilver Messenger Service, and Big Brother & the Holding Company, spearheaded the San Francisco rock sound of the '60s and the idealistic hippie message of free drugs and free sex.

Compared to many of the Bay Area statements of flower power and peace, Jefferson Airplane always possessed a darker, more revolutionary image. Frontperson Grace Slick (b. Oct 30, 1939) was a more-than-willing outspoken mouthpiece.

Musically, the band ranged from reflective acoustic gems (revealing their folk origins) to explosive excursions into psychedelia. Their performance of "Volunteers" at the legendary Woodstock festival was a highlight.

At the top of the '70s, Jefferson Airplane formed the RCA-distributed Grunt Records, on which they released their subsequent albums as well as albums by Papa John Creach and Hot Tuna. During this time, their counterculture tirades began to sound as tiring as the nagging, parental "Establishment."

In 1974, they become the Jefferson Starship. Their 1975 album, *Red Octopus*, became their biggest-selling album to date, generating lead singer Marty Balin's #3 hit "Miracles." Shortly thereafter, Grace Slick took a leave of absence until 1981. Singer Mickey Thomas (formerly with Elvin Bishop) joined in 1979 and helped usher the band into further mainstream rock-radio success.

After long-time band leader Paul Kantner left Jefferson Starship

in 1984, the band dropped the first word in its name. At that point it consisted of Mickey Thomas, Grace Slick, guitarist Craig Chaquico (b. 1955), bassist Pete Sears, and drummer Donny Baldwin. This unit immediately scored with the #1 hits "We Built This City" and "Sara" and the million-selling album *Knee Deep in the Hoopla*. Sears had left by the time of the 1987 follow-up, *No Protection*, which featured the #1 "Nothing's Gonna Stop Us Now" and the Top Ten "It's Not Over ('Til It's Over)." Slick then departed, and the remaining trio recruited keyboard player Mark Moragan and bassist Brett Bloomfield for the 1989 album *Love among the Cannibals*, which featured the Top 20 hit "It's Not Enough." In 1991, when RCA released a Starship greatest-hits album, the one new track on the album had been recorded by Thomas and studio musicians, leading to doubt that Starship remained a functioning band. —*William Ruhlmann*

Takes Off / Sep. 1966 / RCA ✦✦✦
The original group's pre-Grace Slick debut album, really closer in spirit to the Mamas & Papas in some respects, as a kind of folk-pop album. Signe Anderson and Marty Balin handle most of the vocals, and the instrumental textures are largely acoustic (Jorma Kaukonen contributes some excellent playing, however) and the political sensibilities are almost nonexistent. —*Bruce Eder*

★ **Surrealistic Pillow** / Feb. 1967 / RCA ✦✦✦✦✦
Their groundbreaking folk-based psychedelic album hit like a shot heard round the world. From "White Rabbit" and "Somebody to Love" to the sublime "3/5 of a Mile in 10 Seconds," the sensibilities are fierce, the material is melodic, and the performances, sparked by new member Grace Slick on most of the lead vocals, are magnificent and inspired. —*Bruce Eder*

After Bathing at Baxter's / Dec. 1967 / RCA ✦✦✦
The group's attempt to re-create the psychedelic drug experience as pure music fails in part—the material is too disjointed and the stretch for the listener (except in certain states of mind) is too great for the record to be enjoyable. But as an experiment, *Baxter's* is dazzling in its intensity and the playing is superb. —*Bruce Eder*

Crown of Creation / Sep. 1968 / RCA ✦✦✦
Majestic psychedelia that captures the mood of its era better than almost any other album. —*Bruce Eder*

Bless Its Pointed Little Head / Feb. 1969 / RCA ✦✦✦
A rough but very representative live album that succeeds where the *Baxter's* album failed in capturing the mood of psychedelic music in performance. The music is intense and driving, and the only unfortunate element of the album is that it dates from a period after Marty Balin's songs had largely been dropped from their set. —*Bruce Eder*

Volunteers / Nov. 1969 / RCA ✦✦✦
The band's most political album is a somewhat-dated statement but also a very joyous and rewarding one. "We Can Be Together" is still a compelling anthem. —*Bruce Eder*

Blows Against the Empire / 1970 / RCA ✦✦✦

The Worst of / Nov. 1970 / RCA ✦✦✦
Above-average '60s hits and major songs are featured on this well-chosen compilation. —*AMG*

Bark / Sep. 1971 / Grunt ✦✦

Long John Silver / Jul. 1972 / Grunt ✦✦

Thirty Seconds over Winterland / Apr. 1973 / RCA ✦✦
Well-produced document of the final days of the Airplane before it evolved into the Jefferson Starship. The singing and playing are all inspired, and the repertory is surprisingly melodic, considering the direction in which the group had been going. The highlight is a live version of the science-fiction anthem "Have You Seen the Saucers." —*Bruce Eder*

Dragon Fly / 1974 / RCA ✦✦✦

Early Flight / Apr. 1974 / RCA ✦✦
A beguiling collection of bluesy, druggy, and idealistic leftovers from the group's recorded output, partly supplanted by *2400 Fulton Street*, and sure to be further devalued by the upcoming boxed set, but still a handy little disc to have around. —*Bruce Eder*

● **Red Octopus** / 1975 / Grunt ✦✦✦✦
The masterpiece, and a massive seller, too. Grace Slick sings expressively, especially on "Fast Buck Freddie" and "Play on Love," but the real story is the integration of Marty Balin fully into the band, and again he brings a timeless ballad along in the hit "Miracles." —*William Ruhlmann*

Spitfire / 1976 / Grunt ✦✦✦

Earth / 1978 / Grunt ✦✦

From precocity to an accelerated maturity, Ian ruefully comments on the fame business in the title track, then turns deeply romantic on "Jesse," a hit for Roberta Flack. — *William Ruhlmann*

Freedom at Point Zero / 1979 / Grunt ✦✦✦

Amazingly enough, the band survives the departure of Grace Slick and Marty Balin, adding Mickey Thomas on vocals and scoring hits with "Jane" and Kantner's "Girl with the Hungry Eyes." — *William Ruhlmann*

○ **Gold** / 1979 / RCA ✦✦✦✦

Well-chosen best-of covering the years 1974-1979, after which the band personnel changed significantly. — *William Ruhlmann*

Modern Times / 1981 / RCA ✦✦✦

Slick comes back for one song, and "Find Your Way Back" becomes a hit. Also included is "Stairway to Cleveland," as gutsy a statement of purpose as any in rock. — *William Ruhlmann*

Winds of Change / 1982 / Grunt ✦✦

Nuclear Furniture / 1984 / Grunt ✦✦

● **2400 Fulton Street: an Anthology** / Mar. 1987 / RCA ✦✦✦✦

A more-than-adequate retrospective on the group (at least until the boxed set anticipated for late 1992 arrives), with every major song and a lot of oddball favorites as well, all remastered from sources far superior to those used on the original albums. Some of it will be redundant (virtually the whole *Surrealistic Pillow* album is here) but the quality and the order of the programming is rewarding. — *Bruce Eder*

Jefferson Airplane / Sep. 1989 / Epic ✦

Jefferson Airplane Loves You / Oct. 1992 / RCA ✦✦✦

A three-disc box set loaded with rarities, *Jefferson Airplane Loves You* is necessary for hardcore fans, but the double-disc *2400 Fulton Street* offers a better portrait of the band and is the essential purchase for casual fans. — *Stephen Thomas Erlewine*

Deep Space/Virgin Sky / 1995 / Intersound ✦✦✦

BOOK

✦✦ **The Jefferson Airplane**, by Ralph J. Gleason (Ballantine, 1969). Gleason was the pre-eminent San Francisco music journalist of the late 1960s, and helped launch *Rolling Stone*. The first part of this book, a basic overview of the San Francisco sound, is no great shakes. The second part, though, is necessary for the serious Jefferson Airplane fan, consisting of absolutely mammoth interviews with each member of the band (two with Marty Balin). Interviews with Jerry Garcia and Bill Graham round off the volume. — *Richie Unterberger*

Garland Jeffreys

Group, Soul, Rock & Roll, Singer-Songwriter
Multi-ethnic singer/songwriter who also performs in a variety of styles, especially rock and reggae, and has gained considerable critical acclaim during a career dating back to the '60s. — *William Ruhlmann*

Garland Jeffreys & Grinder's Switch / 1970 / Vanguard ✦✦✦

Garland Jeffreys / 1973 / Atlantic ✦✦✦

● **Ghost Writer** / 1977 / A&M ✦✦✦✦

Rock, reggae, and jazz mix on this album of striking urban songs that are both confessional and confrontational. Includes "Wild in the Streets." — *William Ruhlmann*

One Eyed Jack / 1978 / A&M ✦✦✦

American Boy & Girl / 1979 / A&M ✦✦✦

Rock'n'roll Adult / 1981 / Epic ✦✦

○ **Escape Artist** / 1981 / Epic ✦✦✦✦

Members of the Rumour and the E Street Band, among other top session people, give Jeffreys a sharp '80s rock sound on his typically well-written songs. Includes a cover of "96 Tears" that became a moderate hit. — *William Ruhlmann*

Guts for Love / 1983 / Epic ✦✦

○ **Don't Call Me Buckwheat** / 1992 / RCA ✦✦✦✦

After almost ten years away from recording, New York's Garland Jeffreys—best known for his 1977 album *Ghostwriter*—has made a remarkable return with *Don't Call Me Buckwheat*. Jeffreys spent most of the time off coming to terms with his mixed-race background, and this thematically consistent disc could easily serve as

a primer on the complexity of race relations in North America. Set mostly to pop-reggae rhythms—but with hints of Latin, doo-wop and hip-hop as well—songs like "Welcome to the World," "Color Line," "Racial Repertoire," and "Spanish Blood" bubble engagingly. Overall, Buckwheat offers much food for thought set in a musical recipe that makes the potent message easy to swallow. —*Roch Parisien*

Matador & More... / Jul. 14, 1992 / A&M ✦✦

Former label A&M Records takes advantage of Garland Jeffreys' excellent *Don't Call Me Buckwheat* album released earlier this year on BMG to issue *Matador and More ...*, a compilation of his material from the '70s. Not that the cash-in isn't warranted. Jeffreys' melting pot of singer/songwriter folk, urban R&B, and smooth reggae stylings backs lyrics that dissect a broad range of New York-inspired life-slices and emotions. The concluding eight-minute track "Spanish Town" still stands as Jeffreys' epic, steeped in atmosphere so thick you can almost feel the heat and smell the smells that wash over the song's setting. No liner notes are included save for a track-by-track listing of musicians. Shame Shame! —*Roch Parisien*

Jellybean

Group, Dance-Pop
While he had a taste of success when he worked with Madonna on her debut, Jellybean Benitez hasn't found the magic touch as a performer. The EP *Wotupski*, for EMI, started his solo career in 1984. Neither the single "Sidewalk Talk," a Madonna composition, nor "The Real Thing" did much, with "The Real Thing" being issued on Chrysalis. He did land a Top 20 pop single with "Who Found Who" in 1987, but the LP *Just Visiting This Planet* flopped. Benitez moved to East West in 1990, and his 1991 debut was *Spillin' the Beans*. —*Ron Wynn*

Wotupski / 1984 / EMI America ✦✦✦

This was actually an EP, not an album. Remix/production great Jellybean Benitez signed a separate artist deal with Liberty Records in the mid-'80s, and his first release was an EP that had some nice dance/pop cuts, including "Sidewalk Talk," a song written by Madonna. Outstanding sound and interesting arrangements. —*Ron Wynn*

Just Visiting This Planet / 1987 / Chrysalis ✦✦

Jellybean Benitez is one of the greatest producers and mixers in recent dance music history, but it's hard to call most of his releases as a leader "albums." They're impressively produced and arranged sequences, with faceless vocals running in and out of some superbly constructed arrangements. There's much on this album that's really ear-catching, but its lyric and performance content doesn't match its technical brilliance. —*Ron Wynn*

● **Jellybean Rocks the House** / 1988 / Chrysalis ✦✦✦✦

Jellybean Benitez made serious impact as a performer as well as a producer and remixer with this late '80s album, one of two he did with Chrysalis. He landed two chart hits and extensive urban contemporary radio airplay, plus serious club and dance attention. As always, the production, arrangements, and studio work were brilliant, more than enough to mask frequently routine vocals. —*Ron Wynn*

Spillin' the Beans / 1991 / Atlantic ✦✦

Super-producer/remixer Jellybean Benitez switched labels from Chrysalis to East West in 1990. This was his debut under the new pact, and it wasn't any different from his past albums, except that it didn't contain as many hits and also lacked the sparkling arrangements and glossy production of other Benitez albums. It still contained a few nice numbers, especially the song "What's It Gonna Be," but overall, it was Benitez's weakest album. —*Ron Wynn*

Jellyfish

Group, Power Pop/Anglo-Pop
In 1990 Jellyfish became a buzz band in certain circles of the music industry for their power-pop direction—essentially a Squeeze/Beatles/Beach Boys synthesis marketed with silly Alice in Wonderland-style psychedelic outfits.

For their second album, Jellyfish toned down their image, yet their music remained just as grandiose and colorful. —*Rick Clark*

● **Bellybutton** / 1990 / Charisma ✦✦✦✦

The beginning of the '90s brought a resurgence in Anglo-pop bands, and Jellyfish's debut, *Bellybutton*, was one of the best releases of that style. Highlights on this fine album are the Squeeze-influenced "Baby's Comin' Back," the hit single "The King Is Half-Undressed," and "I Wanna Stay Home," a beautiful pop ballad that draws its melodic and arrangement smarts from McCartney and Burt Bacharach. —*AMG*

Spilt Milk / 1993 / Charisma ♦♦♦
Jellyfish's second album is long on technique, stylistic flash, and hooks in the style of Queen, Badfinger, and the Beatles; unfortunately, very few of them stick. *Spilt Milk* sounds splendid while it's being played, when the hooks pile on top of each other, but the end result is slightly cold. Still, there are some pleasures here (particularly the single "The Ghost at Number One") that will make fans forgive the excesses. —*Stephen Thomas Erlewine*

The Jesters

Group, Doo-Wop
The archetypal New York street-corner group, with soaring falsetto and stirring harmonies. With Adam Jackson and Lenny McKay sharing lead duties, the Jesters recorded several classics of the doo-wop genre for Winley in 1957 and 1958, including "So Strange" and "The Plea." Jackson recast the group in 1960 for their last Winley releases, including an accurate remake of the Diablos tune "The Wind." —*Bill Dahl*

● **The Best of the Jesters** / 1969 / Collectables ♦♦♦♦
Falsetto-drenched late-'50s NYC-street-corner doo wop. —*Bill Dahl*

The Paragons Meet the Jesters / Relic ♦♦♦

The Jesus & Mary Chain

Group, Alternative Pop/Rock
This Scottish combo burst out of East Kilbraid in 1984 with a style that piled thick gobs of squalling guitars over tugging Beach Boy harmonies and the lyrical cynicism of Velvets-era Lou Reed. Brothers Jim and William Reid eventually toned down the feedback just a tad—replacing their rhythm section with a drum machine—and have managed to keep their sound fresh, primarily through clever melodies and the occasional inspired lyric hook. —*John Floyd*

● **Psychocandy** / 1985 / Def American ♦♦♦♦
This fuzzy, super-loud release introduced JMC to American audiences. —*John Floyd*

○ **Darklands** / 1987 / Warner Brothers ♦♦♦♦
This was the subdued, depressing followup to *Psychocandy*. —*John Floyd*

Barbed Wire Kisses / 1988 / Def American ♦♦
A singles and rarities collection, it fills in some gaps of this productive band's catalog. —*John Floyd*

Automatic / 1989 / Warner Brothers ♦♦♦
The drum-machine beats are too stiff, but this set contains their best songs, including the sorta-hit "Head On." —*John Floyd*

○ **Honey's Dead** / May 1992 / Def American ♦♦♦♦
If Mary Chain albums share that common thread with, say, the Ramones or Motorhead—in that as good as they are they're all pretty much interchangeable—then know that *Honey's Dead* still stands out. The Reid brothers deliver their concoction of melodic noise with craftsmen-like ability, and this latest collection stands above much of their previous output. —*Steve Aldrich*

Stoned & Dethroned / 1994 / Warner Brothers ♦♦♦
More subdued than any of their previous records, the Jesus & Mary Chain explore a calmer, almost acoustic-oriented direction for part of *Stoned & Dethroned*. Apart from the hit duet with Mazzy Star's Hope Sandoval, "Sometimes Always," the fuzz-drenched pseudo-psychedelic pop that has become the group's trademark is more effective than any of the band's musical experiments. —*Stephen Thomas Erlewine*

Hate Rock N' Roll / 1995 / American ♦♦
Hate Rock N' Roll was the group's second collection of rarities and B-sides. Like *Barbed Wire Kisses*, the album is fitfully entertaining, but only the scathing "I Hate Rock N' Roll" is an essential addition to their catalog. —*Stephen Thomas Erlewine*

Jesus Jones

Group, Dance-Pop, Alternative Pop/Rock
Jesus Jones' murky mix of samples, pop, dance tracks, and techno has resulted in one huge international hit single, "Right Here, Right Now" (taken from their second album, *Doubt*), that pretty much sums up all of the band's virtues—a strong melody and

hook, with a flair for making the dance club overtones mesh with the rock guitar. For their flaws, turn to their first album, which suffers from muddy beats, shapeless melodies, and intrusive samples, all of which plagued sections of *Doubt*. But when *Doubt* worked, as it did on "Right Here, Right Now," "International Bright Young Thing," and "Real, Real, Real," it showed that sample-driven dance club music could comfortably fit into pop music.

Based on the platinum success of *Doubt*, Jesus Jones' leader guitarist/vocalist Mike Edwards decided it was his mission to make techno palatable for the pop masses and recorded their follow-up album, 1993's *Perverse*, almost entirely on computer. The result was neither good pop music nor good techno; Jesus Jones' subsequent fall from the top of the U.S. and U.K. charts was as fast as their rise to the top. —*Stephen Thomas Erlewine*

Liquidizer / 1989 / SBK ♦♦♦
Sampling, synths, and political lyrics all find a home in this electrifying techno-pop debut album. Many of the cuts are from original demos; it includes "Info Freako" and "Broken Bones." —*Donna DiChario & Bil Carpenter*

● **Doubt** / 1991 / SBK ♦♦♦♦
More melodic singing by Edwards yielded the hit "Right Here, Right Now," a Beatlesque '90s diversion. The album is an optimistic response to Prince's pessimistic *Sign O' the Times*, a diatribe on the state of the world. —*Bil Carpenter*

Perverse / 1993 / SBK ♦♦
Perverse attempts to expand on the success Jesus Jones enjoyed with *Doubt*, not only commercially but artistically as well. The group made some history; this is the first album to be recorded entirely through a computer. Musically, *Perverse* is a synthesis of techno/rave dance music with traditional pop/rock songs and structures; it's an ambitious album that works sporadically. Bandleader Mike Edwards lost sight of most of the pop-song sensibility that made "Right Here, Right Now" an across-the-boards smash. Too often, the hooks are submerged beneath layers of computerized noise and aren't strong enough to pull themselves out. When *Perverse* clicks, Jesus Jones gives the listener an idea of how enjoyable a successful marriage of techno and rock could be. —*Stephen Thomas Erlewine*

Jesus Lizard

Group, Alternative Pop/Rock
Willfully abrasive and atonal, the Jesus Lizard has emerged as Chicago's leading guitar noise band. Formed by former Scratch Acid members bassist David Wm. Sims and vocalist David Yow with guitarist Duane Denison, their albums are almost indistinguishable from each other yet the band never sounds like they're repeating themselves. When it comes to scathing, disembowling guitar-driven pseudo-industrial noise, no one else can touch them. —*Stephen Thomas Erlewine*

Pure / 1989 / Touch & Go ♦♦
A five-song debut EP produced by Steve Albini, the Jesus Lizard's *Pure* expanded on the uncompromising hardcore of Scratch Acid while adding touches of Big Black's galvanizing pseudo-industrial rhythms. —*Stephen Thomas Erlewine*

Head / 1990 / Touch & Go ♦♦♦
Head, the Jesus Lizard's first full-length album, featured looser rhythms and a greater dynamic range than their debut EP, but that in no way diluted the impact of David Yow's manic vocals or the bracing force of Duane Denison's crushingly loud riffs. —*Stephen Thomas Erlewine*

● **Goat** / 1991 / Touch & Go ♦♦♦♦
Building upon the intense, spirited noise rock of their two previous records, *Goat* is the album where Jesus Lizard's twisted, post-hardcore punk comes into its own. Denison's acerbic guitar provides an appropriate setting for Yow's ranting tales of decadence and degradation. The Jesus Lizard never make a commentary about the urban filth they depict in their music—they're down in the grime because they like it there. —*Stephen Thomas Erlewine*

○ **Liar** / May 1992 / Touch & Go ♦♦♦♦
Jesus Lizard's third album, *Liar*, is their most focused set of bleak, grinding noise-rock, yet it lacks the wild abandon that made *Goat* so frightening. —*Stephen Thomas Erlewine*

The Jesus Lizard Show / Apr. 1994 / Collision Arts/Giant ♦♦
A scathing but inessential live EP, *Show* was the first recording the Jesus Lizard released in association with a major record label. Although the record's release was barely promoted and it made only

a small impact in the American underground, it prompted the band's long-time producer Steve Albini to sever ties with the band by the end of the year, simply because the Jesus Lizard released an album on a major-label. —*Stephen Thomas Erlewine*

Down / Oct. 1994 / Touch & Go ✦✦✦
Although the Jesus Lizard is in fine form throughout *Down*, the record is essentially a retread of *Goat* or *Liar*, featuring a slightly more accessible production. However, accessibility is a liability in the case of the Jesus Lizard, and the overall impact of *Down* suffers accordingly. —*Stephen Thomas Erlewine*

Jethro Tull

Group, Hard Rock, Art-Rock/Progressive-Rock
Centered around wildman flutist, singer, and songwriter Ian Anderson, Jethro Tull has been churning out an oddball synthesis of British Isles folk and progressive hard rock since the late '60s. During their heyday (the '70s), Tull became one of the biggest concert draws, due to Anderson and the band's clownish stage antics and their amazingly complex interplay.

Their earlier albums, *This Was* (#62), *Stand Up* (#20), and *Benefit* (#11), laid the groundwork for Tull's success, but it was 1971's *Aqualung* (#7) that put them over the top.

Not unlike many bands attempting to take rock to new levels through extended pieces, Tull released two back-to-back albums (*Thick As a Brick, Passion Play*) containing one musical piece on each. Unlike many of those bands, both of these albums went to number one.

Jethro Tull also managed a couple of hits with "Living in the Past" (#11) and "Bungle in the Jungle" (#12). The band continues to release albums and tour. —*Rick Clark*

This Was / 1968 / Chrysalis ✦✦✦
Tull incorporated jazz, folk, and blues-based rock into this impressive debut, which included "Dharma for One," "My Sunday Feeling," and "Song for Jeffrey." —*Rick Clark*

○ **Stand Up** / 1969 / Chrysalis ✦✦✦✦
Tull's second album was as impressive as *This Was*. Anderson's flute dominates this outing. The instrumental "Bouree" became a signature song for the band's early sound. Other highlights included "A New Day Yesterday," "Fat Man," and "Nothing Is Easy." (Also available as a Mobile Fidelity Ultradisc) —*Rick Clark*

Benefit / 1970 / Chrysalis ✦✦✦
Benefit was almost as strong as *Stand Up*. Anderson had yet to take the group into the realm of extended pieces. "Teacher," "Nothing to Say," and "A Time for Everything" are particularly nice. —*Rick Clark*

★ **Aqualung** / 1971 / Chrysalis ✦✦✦✦✦
It was with *Aqualung* that Tull became a staple on FM rock radio, thanks to dynamic riff-heavy tracks like "My God," "Hymn 43," "Locomotive Breath," "Cross-eyed Mary," "Wind-Up," and the title track. Thematically, many of these songs were vehicles for Anderson's railings about how organized religion had restricted man's relationship with God. —*Rick Clark*

Thick As a Brick / 1972 / Chrysalis ✦✦
○ **Living in the Past** / 1972 / Chrysalis ✦✦✦✦
Living in the Past was essentially an anthology of key tracks from Tull's first five albums. Included are extended live tracks as well as popular numbers like "Christmas Song," "Song for Jeffery," "Hymn 43," and their biggest hit, "Living in the Past" (number 11). The CD version has curiously omitted two of Tull's better early tracks—"Teacher" and "Bouree." Besides "Hymn 43," *Living in the Past* doesn't include any key tracks from *Aqualung*. —*Rick Clark*

A Passion Play / 1973 / Chrysalis ✦
War Child / 1974 / Chrysalis ✦✦
Minstrel in the Gallery / 1975 / Chrysalis ✦✦✦
Minstrel in the Gallery was Tull's most successful exercise in synthesizing Elizabethan folk with prog-rock. —*Rick Clark*

Too Old to Rock N' Roll, Too Young To Die / 1976 / Chrysalis ✦✦
M.U.: The Best of Jethro Tull / 1976 / Chrysalis ✦✦✦
M.U. is a decent sampling of hits and album picks, but not definitive. —*Rick Clark*

○ **Songs from the Wood** / 1977 / Chrysalis ✦✦✦✦
On *Songs from the Wood*, Tull's aggressive rock interplay and Ian Anderson's fascination with early folk melodies from the British Isles produced a particularly appealing collection of songs. "Cup of

Wonder" and "The Whistler" are particularly successful. —*Rick Clark*

Bursting Out / 1978 / Chrysalis ✦✦
Heavy Horses / 1978 / Chrysalis ✦✦
Stormwatch / 1979 / Chrysalis ✦✦
○ **A** / 1980 / Chrysalis ✦✦✦✦
With the addition of ex-Roxy Music violinist and keyboardist Eddie Jobson and ex-Fairport Convention bassist Dave Pegg, Tull produced their most overt (and fully realized) folk-rock album. "Batteries Not Included," "Black Sunday," and "Crossfire" are highlights. —*Rick Clark*

The Broadsword & The Beast / 1982 / Chrysalis ✦✦✦
Under Wraps / 1984 / Chrysalis ✦
Crest of a Knave / 1987 / Chrysalis ✦✦
○ **20 Years of Jethro Tull: Highlights** / 1988 / Chrysalis ✦✦✦✦
This is a distilled version of tracks taken from Tull's boxed set. Broken down into four parts, it includes a smattering of hits, live tracks, and some key album sides. It might not be definitive, but it does give the listener a good idea of the band's musical range. —*Rick Clark*

20 Years of Jethro Tull / 1988 / Chrysalis ✦✦✦
Fans of Tull should enjoy this collection that amply documents the band's entire career. There are loads of live performances, TV appearances, and good interviews. The sound quality is quite good. —*Rick Clark*

Rock Island / 1989 / Chrysalis ✦✦
Catfish Rising / 1991 / Chrysalis ✦✦
A Little Light Music / 1992 / Chrysalis ✦
25th Anniversary / Apr. 20, 1993 / Capitol ✦✦
Jethro Tull's 4-CD celebration of their quarter of a century in the music business is only worth the time of hardcore Tull fans. Two discs are full-length live performances (both discs contain two of the same songs), one disc is full of alternate versions of their most famous tracks, and a final disc of new remixes of "classic" tracks (which includes the third appearance of "A Song for Jeffrey" on the four CDs). Casual fans are much better served by one of the smaller collections. —*Stephen Thomas Erlewine*

Joan Jett

b. Sep. 22, 1960, Philadelphia, PA
Rock & Roll, Hard Rock
By playing pure and simple rock & roll without making an explicit issue of her gender, Joan Jett became a figure head for several generations of female rockers. Jett's brand of rock & roll is loud and stripped-down, yet with overpowering hooks—a combination of the Stones tough, sinewy image and beat, AC/DC chords and glam rock hooks. As the numerous covers she has recorded show, she adheres both to rock tradition and breaks with it—she plays classic three-chord rock & roll, yet she also loves the trashy elements (in particular, Gary Glitter) of it as well, and she plays with a defiant sneer. From her first band, the Runaways, through her hit-making days in the '80s with the Blackhearts right until her unexpected revival in the '90s, she hasn't changed her music, yet she's kept her quality control high, making one classic single ("I Love Rock-n-Roll") along the way.

Jett was born in Baltimore, MD; her family moved to Los Angeles when she was 12 years old. By the time she was 15, she had formed her first band and was performing around town. Kim Fowley, a Los Angeles record producer, discovered the band at one of their gigs and became their manager; soon, he renamed the all-female group the Runaways and secured them a contract with Mercury Records. At the time of their first record, the Runaways consisted of Jett on guitar and vocals, Lita Ford (guitar, vocals), Sandy West (drums), Jackie Fox (bass), and Cherie Currie (vocals). The band released three albums that never had much commercial success in America, yet were very popular in Japan; the group were popular in both the Los Angeles hard rock and punk scenes, which led to Jett's production of the Germs' first record, *G.I.* The Runaways group broke up in 1980 and Jett moved to New York to begin a solo career.

Teaming up with producer/manager Kenny Laguna, Jett independently released her self-titled debut album in 1980 in America, since no labels were interested in signing her. The record was a more traditional rock & roll record than the punky Runaways, yet it retained her previous band's defiant attitude. The record sold very well for an independent release, leading to a contract with Boardwalk Records, who reissued the album under the title *Bad Reputation*; it soon climbed to number 51 on the American charts.

Jett formed the Blackhearts between *Bad Reputation* and her second album, 1981's *I Love Rock-n-Roll*; the group included guitarist Ricky Byrd, bassist Gary Ryan, and drummer Lee Crystal. Released at the end of 1981, *I Love Rock-n-Roll* became her greatest success, sending her into the Top Ten. Originally the B-side of an Arrows single, the title track was an enormous success, spending seven weeks at number one in the spring of 1982. The follow-up single, a version of Tommy James and the Shondells' "Crimson and Clover," went Top Ten as well; a single of Gary Glitter's "Do You Wanna Touch Me (Oh Yeah)," taken from the *Bad Reputation* album reached number 20 in the summer of 1982. *Album*, released in 1983, went gold yet it had no hits that compared with either "I Love Rock-n-Roll" or "Crimson and Clover."

Jett starred in Paul Schrader's 1987 film *Light of Day*, which featured the Top 40 title song, yet she didn't have another Top Ten hit until 1988, when "I Hate Myself for Loving You," taken from the *Up Your Alley* album, hit number eight; the album became her second platinum record. After the album's success, her career had another slow period, with 1990's all-covers album *The Hit List* making it to number 36 and 1991's *Notorious* failing to chart. Between *Notorious* and 1994's *Pure and Simple*, a new generation of female rockers came of age and everyone from hard alternative rockers like L7 to the minimalist, riot grrrl punk rockers like Bikini Kill claimed Jett and the Runaways as an influence. *Pure and Simple* featured contributions from L7, Bikini Kill, Babes in Toyland's Kat Bjelland, and Circus Lupus; it received more press and positive reviews than any of her albums since the mid-'80s. In 1995, Jett recorded the live album *Evilstig* with the remaining members of the Gits, a Seattle punk rock band whose lead singer, Mia Zapata, was raped and murdered in 1993. On the record, Jett and the Gits performed the band's catalog with Jett singing Zapata's parts and playing guitar; the album offered further proof that Joan Jett is one of the unsung influences on punk and alternative rock. —*Stephen Thomas Erlewine*

Bad Reputation / 1981 / Blackheart ✦✦✦
Her debut suffers from a lack of one coherent sound, but it's an impassioned homage to her glitter-and-punk roots. —*John Floyd*

○ **I Love Rock & Roll** / 1981 / Blackheart ✦✦✦✦
The title track was an inescapable hit in 1981, and Jett's new band, the Blackhearts, gave her a big crunching hard rock sound. She could've used some better songs though. —*John Floyd*

○ **Album** / 1983 / Blackheart ✦✦✦✦
With her best set of songs and big-time production, this is an astonishing statement of purpose, full of gritty Rolling Stones-like boogie and a cover of Sly Stone's "Everyday People" that works better than you'd think. But it's all spectacular. —*John Floyd*

○ **Glorious Results of a Misspent Youth** / 1984 / Blackheart ✦✦✦✦
Another masterful blast of fury and celebration, it shifts from a blazing cover of the Runaway's "Cherry Bomb" to her best song, "I Got No Answers." Besides the Pretenders' early work, *Glorious Results*... ranks with the best rock of the '80s, focused through a female point of view. —*John Floyd*

Good Music / 1986 / Epic ✦✦✦
The production's a bit heavy but Jett's formula is still a winner. "Black Leather" and the title cut are fine rock anthems. —*John Floyd*

Up Your Alley / 1988 / Epic ✦✦
I Hate Myself for Loving You is a strikingly complex take on relationships and was a hit, but aside from a whopping cover of Chuck Berry's "Tulane," this album is pretty thin. —*John Floyd*

The Hit List / 1990 / Epic ✦✦
This one sidesteps the issue of poor songwriting by offering a full set of covers ranging from Roy Orbison to the Sex Pistols. It's all powerful, but it's also a step backward. —*John Floyd*

Notorious / 1991 / Epic ✦✦✦
Jett finally conceives an album where the ballads work as well as the barnburners. Included is a collaboration with Paul Westerberg of the Replacements. —*John Floyd*

● **Flashback** / 1994 / Blackheart ✦✦✦✦
While it includes a healthy share of rarities, nothing on Joan Jett's career overview, *Flashback*, is second rate. Even though she vascillated between punky hard rock and smoothed-out arena-rock

for much of the '80s, the disc accentuates her rebellious nature, making *Flashback* an effective introduction to her career. Besides, it rocks like hell. —*Stephen Thomas Erlewine*

Pure and Simple / 1994 / Warner Brothers ✦✦✦
A strong record showing that she has lost very little of her power, *Pure and Simple* contained contributions by several of Jett's fans, including members of L7 and Bikini Kill. —*Stephen Thomas Erlewine*

Jive Five

Group, Soul, R&B, Doo-Wop
One of the groups that was a major instigator in the move from '50s R&B to '60s soul, the Jive Five produced several outstanding hits for the New York Belton label during the early '60s. —*John Floyd*

● **The Jive Five** / 1989 / United Artists ✦✦✦✦
A superb twenty-track collection, it features the Jive Five's finest material, recorded in the early '60s for Lescay/Belton; songs include "Rain," "My True Story," "No Not Again," "What Time Is It?," and "Hurry Back." —*AMG*

○ **The Complete United Artists Recordings...** / 1992 / Capitol ✦✦✦✦
A superior 21-track collection, it highlights the Jive Five's material for United Artists, recorded in the mid-'60s. —*AMG*

Greatest Hits / Collectables ✦✦✦

My True Story / Relic ✦✦✦
These hard-hitting doo woppers testify on the title cut, "What Time Is It?," and on "Hully Gully Callin' Time." Eugene Pitts is one of the era's most evocative singers. —*John Floyd*

J.K. & Co.

Group, Folk-Rock
J.K. & Co. apparently consisted of one Jay Kaye, who recorded a little-known album, *Suddenly One Summer*, for White Whale in Vancouver around 1969. His florid, melodic songwriting betrayed obvious debts to Donovan and George Harrison; his low-key vocals also recall George's late Beatle efforts. The sappier excesses of his lyrics haven't dated well, but his soothing arrangements (with low-key organs and saxes), beguiling melodies, and good-hearted, meditative ambience make him one of the worthier obscurities of the late '60s. —*Richie Unterberger*

● **Suddenly One Summer** / 1969 / White Whale ✦✦✦✦
This sounds like the solo album that George Harrison might have made before he left the Beatles. Several songs have that solemn, spiritual, forlorn quality George perfected on cuts like "Long, Long, Long." With its languid guitars, organ, and somber mood, "Nobody" is so reminiscent of *All Things Must Pass* tracks like "Let It Roll" that one is inclined to believe that this album may have actually been recorded in the early '70s. Although the lyrics are blatantly hippieish, the music itself sets a dignified, almost stately mood with its intimacy and tasteful restraint. —*Richie Unterberger*

Jodeci

Group, Urban
A new jack swing ensemble whose debut LP was a huge hit, Jodeci pairs North Carolina brothers Joel and Cedric Halley and Dalvin and Donald Degrate, Jr., better known as "Devante Swing." *Forever My Lady* made them huge stars in 1991, selling over two million copies and securing a Top 20 pop hit with "Come and Talk to Me." "Forever My Lady" and "Stay" were also major R&B successes, as was their cover of Stevie Wonder's "Lately," which was issued on the *Uptown Unplugged* release. Jodeci followed that in 1994 with *Diary of A Mad Band*, which debuted at the top of the R&B charts. —*Ron Wynn*

Forever My Lady / 1991 / Uptown/MCA ✦✦✦
A pair of brother acts combined to form Jodeci, a singing group with one foot in the future and the other squarely in the past. Dalvin and Devante Swing teamed with Jo-Jo and K-Ci Halley for a debut album that mixed vintage soul singing with New Jack production and bravado. But it wasn't the hip-hop-flavored songs that earned them popularity; instead, urban contemporary audiences embraced the love tunes "Come and Talk To Me" and the title track, signaling the beginnings of a move away from New Jack Swing that's become a full-fledged retreat. —*Ron Wynn*

● **Diary of A Mad Band** / 1993 / Uptown/MCA ◆◆◆◆
Jodeci juggles New Jack Swing and vintage soul on their second album, and wind up with a jarring, mismatched release. The disc's love songs, particularly "Cry For You," "What About Us" and "My Heart Belongs To You," are tender, passionately sung, sincere expressions of romance and love. But they diminish these with a string of innuendo-laden come-on numbers, complete with explicit language, tired raps and samples, and the kind of sentiments and appeals better suited to a *Penthouse Forum* entry than an album. —*Ron Wynn*

The Show, The After Party, The Hotel / 1995 / Uptown ◆◆◆

Billy Joel

b. May 9, 1949, Long Island, NY
Singer-Songwriter, Pop/Rock
When pianist, singer, and songwriter Billy Joel came along in 1973 with his major-label debut *Piano Man*, he was perceived as an American alternative to *Tumbleweed Connection*-period Elton John. Both of them tended toward ornate and grand-sounding melodies and progressions, but Joel's musical attack was more assertive, and lyrically, he was a straight-shooter with somewhat of a chip on his shoulder. Joel's music embraces classic Brill Building and Broadway schools of song structure while drawing from the Paul McCartney side of the Beatles and genres like street-corner doo wop and early-'60s pop.

Joel's first hit, "Piano Man," portrayed him as a guy who endured the lounge-lizard circuit as an observer passing through. On his follow-up hit, "The Entertainer," the punkish pragmatism of his personality is further defined. It is an attitude, along with his decidedly non-rock melodies, that doesn't sit well with critics, but Joel's dynamic shows and his finely tuned compositional skills attracted a hardcore fan base.

Joel's initial success began to diminish until he hooked up with producer Phil Ramone (Paul Simon, Julian Lennon) and recorded the mega-platinum *The Stranger*. That album began a string of huge hit singles and albums that remains unabated.

Joel's numerous chart successes include "Just the Way You Are," "My Life," "You May Be Right," "It's Still Rock and Roll to Me," "Tell Her about It," "Uptown Girl," and "You're Only Human (Second Wind)." —*Rick Clark*

Cold Spring Harbor / 1971 / Columbia ◆◆◆
Joel's debut solo album finds him sounding like a romantic singer/songwriter with a strong sense of melody. The album's single, "She's Got a Way," later turned up in his concerts. The original 1971 album released by Family Productions was mastered wrong and speeds up the tape; in 1984, Columbia Records released a corrected version. —*William Ruhlmann*

Piano Man / Nov. 1973 / Columbia ◆◆◆
Joel presents a personal perspective of middle-class teen life in the suburbs ("Captain Jack," "The Ballad of Billy the Kid") followed by life in a cocktail lounge ("Piano Man"), and concludes, "Worse comes to worst, I'll get along." But his already apparent sense of melody and supple singing voice indicate much more promise than that. —*William Ruhlmann*

Streetlife Serenade / Oct. 1974 / Columbia ◆◆◆
Extending a mean streak he'd already revealed more than once, Joel looks upon the starmaking machinery that broke him the year before and scorns it. But he has such a gift for the putdown, notably in "Los Angelenos" and "The Entertainer," and the melodies are so good that you can't help singing along and agreeing with him. If you didn't already, that is. —*William Ruhlmann*

○ **Turnstiles** / May 1976 / Columbia ◆◆◆◆
Billy Joel's best, most consistent, most accessible record, even if not his best seller. From "Say Goodbye to Hollywood," which signals his return to the Big Apple with a drumbeat borrowed from the Ronettes, through the Sinatra ballad "New York State of Mind," the reflective "Summer, Highland Falls," and the hilarious "Miami 2017," Joel has never been more imaginative or more tuneful. Of course, "Angry Young Man" shows him to be as mean-spirited as ever, but the music carries even that one home. This record was the prototype to a virtual hit assembly line. —*William Ruhlmann*

○ **The Stranger** / Sep. 1977 / Columbia ◆◆◆◆
The breakthrough to superstardom, containing the hits "Just the Way You are," "Movin' Out (Anthony's Song)," "Only the Good Die Young," and "She's Always a Woman." All those are on *Greatest*

Hits—Vols. I & II, but "Scenes from an Italian Restaurant," one of Joel's most compelling story-songs, is not. —*William Ruhlmann*

○ **52nd Street** / Oct. 1978 / Columbia ◆◆◆◆
Joel consolidated his position with this somewhat harder rocking follow-up to *The Stranger*, which contained the hits "My Life," "Big Shot," and "Honesty." —*William Ruhlmann*

Glass Houses / Mar. 1980 / Columbia ◆◆◆
Billy Joel's response to punk, which, being a snotty kid himself, he felt a certain affinity with, and which allowed his usual belligerence unusually free rein (an aspect of his work that can be tolerated only because it is unflinchingly honest and as often directed at himself as at others). Again, most of the best songs are on the *Greatest Hits*, but this is the only place you can get "Sometimes a Fantasy." —*William Ruhlmann*

Songs in the Attic / Sep. 1981 / Columbia ◆◆◆
Joel used his first live album to refocus attention on his pre-*Stranger* catalog, turning in new versions of worthy songs like "She's Got a Way" and "Say Goodbye to Hollywood," both of which now became Top 25 hits. —*William Ruhlmann*

○ **The Nylon Curtain** / Sep. 1982 / Columbia ◆◆◆◆
Upon release, Joel's eighth studio album was hailed by critics who had previously scorned him because he had decided to take on social concerns—the stress of modern life in "Pressure," unemployment in "Allentown," and the Vietnam War in "Goodnight Saigon." In retrospect, those songs were the best of an uneven collection. —*William Ruhlmann*

○ **An Innocent Man** / Aug. 1983 / Columbia ◆◆◆◆
A brilliant evocation of popular styles of the early '60s, from doo-wop to R&B, that is much more than a period exercise because it obviously is so deeply felt and because it is so well executed. And no one has sounded quite so guilty as the singer of the title track, whether he realized it or not. —*William Ruhlmann*

● **Greatest Hits, Vols. 1 & 2 (1973-1985)** / 1985 / Columbia ◆◆◆◆
Long overdue, and exactly what it says it is. —*William Ruhlmann*

The Bridge / Jul. 1986 / Columbia ◆◆
The hits are "Modern Woman," "A Matter of Trust," and "This Is the Time," all melodic rockers in Joel's patented style. There is also "Baby Grand," a duet with Ray Charles. But, three years on, this wasn't a patch on *An Innocent Man* and suggested Joel's best work might be behind him. —*William Ruhlmann*

Kohuept (Live in Leningrad) / Oct. 1987 / Columbia ◆◆
Since Joel's concerts largely reproduce his studio recordings, and since he already has a greatest hits album out, a live record is inessential. The cachet of recording it in the old Soviet Union doesn't last over the years, and while the performances are fine, only completists need this record. Joel fans must have realized this, since the album was his first to miss the Top Ten in 11 years. —*William Ruhlmann*

Storm Front / 1989 / Columbia ◆◆◆
Joel caused a stampede for high school social science classes with the patter song "We Didn't Start the Fire," a cross between Gilbert and Sullivan and rock & roll that listed events in the news over the last 40 years, broken up by chants of the title. "I Go to Extremes" was a confession of emotional instability set to a strong melody and a rocking beat. There were also minor entries, such as "The Downeaster 'Alexa,'" which was about Long Island fishermen, and "Shameless," which Garth Brooks turned into a country smash. And, as usual, there was about a side's worth of worthless filler. —*William Ruhlmann*

River of Dreams / Aug. 10, 1993 / Columbia ◆◆◆
Joel has reached middle age and he is still restless and angry. Fortunately, this results in some fine, adventurous music, making *River of Dreams* his strongest effort since *The Nylon Curtain*. Joel explores all of his favorite musical territory on this album, reaching back to doo wop, moving through Beatlesque pop, towards his trademark balladry. —*Stephen Thomas Erlewine*

David Johansen

b. Jan. 9, 1950, Staten Island, NY
Rock & Roll, Hard Rock
The former lead singer with the New York Dolls, David Johansen went on to a solo career but failed to rise above cult status despite some fine albums. His live 1982 release, *Live It Up*, contains a great Animals medley that almost broke him into a wider market, but a persona change under the moniker "Buster Poindexter" put

Johansen over the top, with a big dance hit, "Hot Hot Hot." Subsequent efforts as Poindexter have lacked the freshness of the original concept, which drew from Caribbean dance grooves and '30s and '40s swing and cabaret styles. —*Rick Clark*

○ **David Johansen** / 1978 / Razor & Tie ✦✦✦✦
True, the best songs here ("Frenchette," "Funky but Chic," "Girls") are the ones Johansen brought with him from the Dolls. What's intriguing about his solo debut, though, is how well he pulls off ballads like "Donna" and "Pain in My Heart." And Johnny Rao's guitar work *almost* compensates for the absence of Johnny Thunders, the Dolls' guitarist. —*John Floyd*

In Style / 1979 / Razor & Tie ✦✦✦
Despite the presence of guitarist Mick Ronson, David Johansen's second solo album *In Style* wasn't a collection of blistering glamrock. Instead, Johansen began to expand the boundaries of his music, adding elements of disco, soul, and reggae. Occasionally, the soul inflections work, but the songs are by and large weaker than the ones on his first album, although any record with a song as beautiful as "Melody" is worthwhile. —*Stephen Thomas Erlewine*

Here Comes the Night / 1982 / Razor & Tie ✦✦
David Johansen returned to straightahead rock & roll with his third album, *Here Comes the Night*, but the combination of uninspired material and slick, professional music made the record his weakest effort to date. —*Stephen Thomas Erlewine*

○ **Live It Up** / 1982 / Razor & Tie ✦✦✦✦
A scorching live set from 1982, it also works as a career-defining best-of. Johansen drives his roadhouse band through a few old Dolls hits, the best cuts from his solo albums, and a medley of Animals hits that damn near outstrips the originals. And don't miss the two Motown covers. —*John Floyd*

Sweet Revenge / 1984 / Passport ✦✦✦
The live album *Live It Up* gave David Johansen a surprise MTV hit with an Animals medley and he attempted to continue his success with *Sweet Revenge*. Unlike his previous albums, *Sweet Revenge* is driven by synthesizers, but Johansen hasn't abandoned hard rock. The synths add a stylish sheen to his slyly powerful songs, which have some of his cleverest lyrics and melodies. Overall, the record is his strongest since his debut. —*Stephen Thomas Erlewine*

The Live at the Bottom Line / Feb. 2, 1993 / CBS ✦✦✦
Live at the Bottom Line is taken from a late-'70s show at the famous New York club and it captures David Johansen in all of his hard rock glory, even if the album isn't quite as impressive as *Live It Up*. —*Stephen Thomas Erlewine*

● **From Pumps to Pompadour: The David Johansen Story** / 1995 / Rhino ✦✦✦✦
Drawing from all three phases of David Johansen's career, *From Pumps to Pompadours: The David Johansen Story* is a comprehensive of the hard rocker's career. Only three songs date from his influential days with the New York Dolls ("Trash," "Personality Crisis," "Babylon"), but that has been the most well-documented period of his career. While his biggest hits—in fact, his only hits—are the five Buster Poindexter tracks at the end of the disc, the middle portion of the album, which selects the highlights from his overlooked solo albums of the late '70s and early '80s, is where most of the best material lies. From the sleazy rush of "Funky But Chic" to the savage Animals medley "We Gotta Get out of This Place / Don't Bring Me Down / It's My Life," the 11 solo tracks make a case for Johansen being one of the finest hard rockers of his era. —*Stephen Thomas Erlewine*

John's Children

Group, British Invasion, Psychedelic
Because Marc Bolan—soon to become T. Rex—was briefly a member, John's Children are perhaps accorded more reverence by '60s collectors and aficionados than they deserve. Still, they were an interesting, if minor, blip on the British mod and psychedelic scene during their relatively brief existence (1966-68), although they were perhaps more notable for their flamboyant image and antics than their music. Yardbirds manager Simon Napier-Bell recalled that they were "positively the worst group I'd ever seen" when he chanced upon them in France in 1966, yet he was conned into taking them on as clients. Not proficient enough to be trusted to play on their own records, their first single, "Smashed Blocked/Strange Affair," was recorded with sessionmen in late 1966. This disorienting piece of musical mayhem, opening with a crescendo of

swirling organs and an otherworldy over-reverbed vocal, was one of the first overtly psychedelic singles. Their improbable saga was launched when the single actually reached the bottom depths of the U.S. Top 100, cracking the Top Ten in some Florida and California markets. The group's U.S. company, White Whale, requested an album, which it shelved when it received an LP with the then-unthinkable title, *Orgasm*. The actual album consisted of mediocre studio material smothered in audience screams lifted from the *A Hard Day's Night* soundtrack, and was, bizarrely, actually released in 1971 (and reissued a decade later). Their second single, "Just What You Want—Just What You'll Get/But You're Mine," reached the British Top 40, and featured a guitar solo by recently departed Yardbird Jeff Beck on the B-side. A brief German tour followed, during with they managed to upstage the headliners, the Who (with their theatrics, not their music).

At this point, Marc Bolan joined the group for a time as their principal singer and songwriter; details are hazy, but he recorded at least one single with the group, "Desdemona" (which was banned by the BBC for the line "lift up your skirt and fly"), as well as several unreleased cuts that have surfaced on reissues. Bolan departed in a squabble with Napier-Bell, and the group released a couple more flop singles before disbanding in 1968. Their half-dozen singles rank among the most collectible British '60s rock artifacts, and the group—who actually managed some decent modish power-pop, once they'd learned their way around their instruments a bit—were acclaimed as pre-glam rockers of sorts by historians. Andy Ellison (the group's lead singer except during Bolan's brief tenure) recorded some decent pop singles at the end of the '60s, and members of John's Children were involved with the obscure British groups Jook, Jet, and Radio Stars in the 1970s. —*Richie Unterberger*

Legendary Orgasm Album / 1982 / Cherry Red ✦✦✦
The first readily available edition of *Orgasm*. The skimpy, vaguely Who-ish songs are nearly buried under the mountainous overdubs of hysterical teenage screams, making this a true artifact—and nothing more—of an era. The reissue includes excellent liner notes and four bonus tracks—the fine psychedelic single "Smashed Blocked" and its decent follow-up, "Just What You Want—Just What You'll Get," the B-side of which ("But You're Mine") is an unabashed ripoff of the Who's "I Can't Explain." Be warned that the version of "Strange Affair" (the B-side of "Smashed Blocked") included here has, for some inexplicable reason, been presented backwards! —*Richie Unterberger*

Instant Action / 1985 / Hawkeye ✦✦✦
A hard-to-find collection of 18 rare and unreleased tracks by the band. It doesn't include three of the four songs on their first two singles, but it includes their ultra-rare follow-ups, as well as some rawer, unreleased versions of those later singles and some Andy Ellison solo 45s. The material borrows from the poppiest aspects of the Who and sprinkles in some campy British psychedelia; Bolan's songs and vocals are quite T. Rex-like, even at this early stage. They manage to get a bit tougher with "Jagged Time Lapse," with crashing drums and power chords aplenty. Ellison's solo singles are quite interesting, especially the oddball folk-psychedelic "Cornflake Zoo" and the bizarre lounge/soul version of the Beatles' "Help!" (unlisted on the sleeve). Includes voluminous liner notes. —*Richie Unterberger*

● **Midsummer Night's Scene** / 1987 / Bam Caruso ✦✦✦✦
The A- and B-sides of all of their singles, plus the Andy Ellison solo number "It's Been a Long Time." It's missing some interesting material from *Instant Action*, but it's generally the best anthology available, as well as the only readily obtainable one. Comes with another set of fine, exhaustive liner notes—has a minor band ever been as well-documented by loving liner notes as John's Children has? —*Richie Unterberger*

Midsummer Night's Scene [E.P.] / 1988 / Bam Caruso ✦✦✦
A four-song 12" with the title cut (a single from the Marc Bolan era that never made it past the test pressing stage) and three previously unreleased tracks: Ellison's nifty solo cuts "Help" and "Casbah Candy," and "Hippy Gumbo" (a Bolan composition with the whole group). One for the collectors. —*Richie Unterberger*

It's Child's Play / 1989 / Zonophone ✦✦✦
Yet more unreleased tracks. This four-song seven-inch EP is actually fairly worthwhile, capturing a somewhat rawer and more rock-oriented sound than the official singles. Includes the Bolan compositions "Hot Rod Mama" and "Perfumed Garden," as well as a cover of the R&B tune "Daddy Rolling Stone," which the Who

had covered in a similar bashing power-chord style on the B-side of their second single. —*Richie Unterberger*

Elton John (Reginald Dwight)

b. Mar. 25, 1947, Pinner, England
Pop/Rock

Elton John was the single most successful pop artist of the '70s, and he continued to score hits for decades after his initial reign of popularity. Born Reginald Dwight in Pinner, England, he showed an early aptitude for the piano and received classical training, winning a scholarship to the Royal Academy of Music at the age of 11. But after six years he turned to pop music, and struggled as a songwriter, sideman, and member of unsuccessful groups for the rest of the '60s.

During this period, he hooked up with lyricist Bernie Taupin through a newspaper advertisement, and the two were signed as songwriters to publisher Dick James, who was to have a tremendous impact on John's early career.

A debut album sponsored by James, *Empty Sky,* flopped in 1969, but in 1970, with the album *Elton John* and the single "Your Song," Elton John took off, scoring especially well in America. For the next five years, his output—and the sales that material racked up—was enormous. John always had an ability to hit with ballads like the wistful "Daniel," then turn around and rock as hard as the Rolling Stones on a song like "Saturday Night's Alright for Fighting." There hardly seemed a day from 1972, when "Rocket Man" began a streak of 16 straight Top 20 hits (15 of which went Top Ten), to 1976, when John took a breather, that his songs were not dominating the airwaves and the record charts.

The late '70s seem to have been a period of recovery and indecision for the singer, but by 1980 he had settled into making one well-crafted album a year, and many of them tossed off hits, if not with such consistency as before. "Little Jeannie" (1980), "I Guess That's Why They Call It the Blues" and "Sad Songs (Say So Much)" (both 1984), and "Nikita" (1986) all showed John could still hit the upper reaches of the charts, especially with his trademark ballads. The late '80s again saw a slowing in John's record success, but by the start of the '90s he had gone public about drug and alcohol problems he said were behind him, and he looked poised for a new start.

After several more years of adult contemporary hits in the early '90s, John moved into films, writing the music for Walt Disney's 1994 film *The Lion King.* The soundtrack was an enormous success and John's version of "Can You Feel the Love Tonight" was his biggest hit in years. —*William Ruhlmann*

Empty Sky / 1969 / MCA ✦✦
Elton John's debut album released in his native U.K. in 1969 but not in the U.S. until 1975 is marred by the contrast of Bernie Taupin's airy lyrics and Steve Brown's down-to-earth production, between which John navigates uncertainly. The most memorable song later rerecorded is the pretty "Skyline Pigeon." —*William Ruhlmann*

Elton John / Aug. 1970 / MCA ✦✦✦
Ironically, Elton John's breakthrough album (and U.S. debut) is uncharacteristic of his other work, heavily featuring Paul Buckmaster's dramatic string arrangements. John is never overwhelmed by strings or choirs and turns in some powerful performances. Contains "Your Song." —*William Ruhlmann*

○ **Tumbleweed Connection** / Jan. 1971 / MCA ✦✦✦✦
Elton John's followup was a thematic album about the American Old West (a Taupin fascination) that allowed John to rock out on several numbers. There are no hits here (!) but the album stands up well two decades later on. —*William Ruhlmann*

Friends / Feb. 1971 / Paramount ✦✦✦
This is a soundtrack album including instrumentals not composed by or featuring Elton John, plus a few songs, notably the title track, which became a Top 40 hit. —*William Ruhlmann*

11-17-70 / Mar. 1971 / MCA ✦✦✦
Elton John's fourth album release in less than a year was a bootleg-beating live album culled from a concert broadcast on a New York radio station that also served the function of bridging the gap in the public perceptions of John as the soft balladeer of "Your Song" on the one hand and the piano-stool-throwing rock 'n' roller who was appearing in concert on the other. Here, John essayed songs like "Honky Tonk Women" and generally acted like a rock 'n' roll animal. —*William Ruhlmann*

○ **Madman Across the Water** / Nov. 1971 / MCA ✦✦✦✦
One of John's best-ever collections of songs, containing "Levon," "Tiny Dancer," and the title track, all of which survive in the memory better than they did in the charts. —*William Ruhlmann*

○ **Honky Chateau** / May 1972 / MCA ✦✦✦✦
Notable not only for the hits "Honky Cat" and "Rocket Man" but also for "I Think I'm Gonna Kill Myself" and "Mona Lisas and Mad Hatters." The first of John's seven U.S. #1 albums. —*William Ruhlmann*

Don't Shoot Me I'm Only the Piano Player / Jan. 1973 / MCA ✦✦✦
The hits were the ballad "Daniel" and the nuevo-retro rocker "Crocodile Rock," but there were also such excellent album tracks as "Elderberry Wine" and "I'm Going To Be A Teenage Idol" to keep things moving. —*William Ruhlmann*

○ **Goodbye Yellow Brick Road** / Oct. 1973 / MCA ✦✦✦✦
Almost certainly Elton John's biggest seller, save his first greatest hits collection. The hits on this sprawling double-disc set include "Saturday Night's Alright for Fighting," the title track, and "Bennie and the Jets," and the album tracks include "Love Lies Bleeding" and "Candle in the Wind" (which became a hit 15 years later in a live version). —*William Ruhlmann*

Caribou / Jun. 1974 / MCA ✦✦
Enjoying the hottest career in the music business at this point, Elton John was also amazingly prolific: *Caribou* was his eighth LP of new, original songs to be released within four years. Finally, the pace was beginning to tell. There were the expected hits in "The Bitch Is Back" and "Don't Let The Sun Go Down On Me," but the rest of this album was filler, with the nonsense song "Solar Prestige A Gammon" giving testimony to the facile and vapid approach to writing John and Taupin could take in their haste. —*William Ruhlmann*

★ **Greatest Hits** / Nov. 1974 / MCA ✦✦✦✦✦
A virtual time capsule of the pop music of the first half of the '70s. —*William Ruhlmann*

○ **Captain Fantastic & The Brown Dirt Cowboy** / May 1975 / MCA ✦✦✦✦
Bernie Taupin's most ambitious lyrical effort, *Captain Fantastic & the Brown Dirt Cowboy* is an autobiographical song cycle that also drew an unusually strong musical effort from John, resulting in perhaps his strongest overall record since *Tumbleweed Connection.* —*William Ruhlmann*

Rock of the Westies / Oct. 1975 / MCA ✦✦
The title signals that this album is short on ballads and long on bouncers; the hit was "Island Girl," but the real key to this album's thinness is that it came a mere five months after its ambitious predecessor, and even for Elton and Bernie, that's a bit too soon to expect much quality. —*William Ruhlmann*

Here & There / May 1976 / MCA ✦✦
One side from a May 1974 London concert, one side from a November 1974 New York concert, released a year and a half later for the 1976 summer buying season when the artist didn't have a new studio recording ready, this second Elton John live album looks suspiciously like product and sounds like it, too. —*William Ruhlmann*

Blue Moves / Oct. 1976 / MCA ✦✦
An unprecedented year in the making, the two-record *Blue Moves* was Elton John's opening farewell, a dreary song cycle full of self-pity and recycled melodies by an artist who had finally run out of gas. The inevitable hit was "Sorry Seems To Be The Hardest Word," although "Tonight," the album's other memorable song, was just as indicative of the low emotional ebb of the John-Taupin team. As the Mamas and the Papas once said in an LP title, "Farewell to the first golden era." —*William Ruhlmann*

☆ **Greatest Hits, Vol. 2** / Sep. 1977 / MCA ✦✦✦✦✦
More of the hottest hit streak of the decade, including such otherwise non-album singles as "Lucy in the Sky with Diamonds" and "Philadelphia Freedom." —*William Ruhlmann*

A Single Man / Oct. 1978 / MCA ✦✦✦
An unusually well-crafted album, and the beginning of John's comeback. "Part-Time Love" was the hit, but "Madness" and the instrumental "Song for Guy" were musical highlights. —*William Ruhlmann*

Victim of Love / 1979 / MCA ✦
As he had in 1977 with Thom Bell, Elton John turned to German disco producer Pete Bellotte in 1979, acting only as the singer over Bellotte's tracks. It was a disaster: there were no hits, and *Victim Of Love* was John's first new studio album not to go gold. This was the bottom of the decline John had been in artistically and commercially since 1976. — *William Ruhlmann*

The Thom Bell Sessions [EP] / 1979 / MCA ✦✦✦
In 1977, Elton John attempted to make a soul album using producer Thom Bell, known for his work with Philadelphia International Records, but it didn't work out. In 1979, John remixed three of the tracks and issued them on this 12-inch EP and on the single "Mama Can't Buy You Love," which went to #9. They didn't sound half-bad. — *William Ruhlmann*

Lady Samantha [Comp] / 1980 / DJM ✦✦✦
This is a 14-track, budget-priced rarities album covering non-LP B-sides, of which Elton John has released tons, and other oddities recorded between 1969 and 1974. For John fans, the album, released only in England, was a godsend, and even for more casual fans, much of it is rewarding. — *William Ruhlmann*

21 at 33 / May 1980 / MCA ✦✦✦
An ambitious songwriting effort featuring Tom Robinson's collaboration on "Sartorial Eloquence" and Gary Osborne's on "Little Jeannie," although the best songs are by the returning Bernie Taupin. "Chasing the Crown" and "Two Rooms at the End of the World." — *William Ruhlmann*

The Fox / 1981 / MCA ✦✦
Sounding like it contained outtakes from the superior *21 at 33*, *The Fox* found Elton John still hedging his bets, writing four songs with Bernie Taupin, but still collaborating with Gary Osborne, Tom Robinson, and James Newton Howard. And the album's number 21 single, "Nobody Wins," was a Eurodisco cover. Altogether, a bump on the comeback road and not an auspicious beginning to John's tenure at Geffen Records. The album has since been acquired by MCA. — *William Ruhlmann*

Jump Up! / Apr. 1982 / MCA ✦✦✦
John began finding his greatest successes with ballads in the 1980s, and this album still finds him mixing collaborators, including Tim Rice (with whom he would write the 1994 soundtrack to *The Lion King*), this time to good effect: Gary Osborne contributes "Blue Eyes," while Bernie Taupin effectively eulogizes John Lennon in "Empty Garden." Originally on Geffen, this album has since been acquired by MCA. — *William Ruhlmann*

○ **Too Low for Zero** / May 1983 / Geffen ✦✦✦✦
With Taupin (and his old band) on board full time, John turned out one of his best '80s albums—one full of remorse ("Cold As Christmas") and fierce reaffirmation ("I'm Still Standing"), not to mention such irresistible tunes as "Kiss the Bride" and "I Guess That's Why They Call It the Blues." — *William Ruhlmann*

Breaking Hearts / Jul. 1984 / Geffen ✦✦✦
This album was paced by its number five big ballad hit, "Sad Songs (Say So Much)," one of Elton John's most memorable latter day tunes. There were also two more Top 40 entries in "Who Wears These Shoes?" and "In Neon," but in retrospect, this is one of John's slighter albums of the '80s. — *William Ruhlmann*

Ice on Fire / Nov. 1985 / Geffen ✦✦
Elton John's relationship with Geffen Records seems to have been deteriorating by this point, and his regular output of one album a year was becoming rote. This one contains the #7 ballad "Nikita" and a pleasant uptempo song, "Wrap Her Up," but is otherwise undistinguished. The CD added the single "Act Of War," a raucous workout with Millie Jackson that immediately became the album's standout track. — *William Ruhlmann*

Leather Jackets / 1986 / Geffen ✦✦
This pedestrian throwaway of an album represents the end of Elton John's contractual commitment to Geffen Records and, as happens with these things, was buried, becoming perhaps the singer's worst-selling album ever. In retrospect, it deserved a better fate, but not much better. — *William Ruhlmann*

Greatest Hits, Vol. 2 / Apr. 28, 1986 / MCA

Elton John Live in Australia (With the Melbourne Symphony or / Jun. 1987 / MCA ✦✦
The first mystery is why Elton John would decide to mark his return to MCA Records with a live album of some of his wimpiest music swamped in strings. The second mystery is why he pressed on with this plan even though his voice was in such terrible shape

that, right after the concert, he underwent throat surgery. The final mystery is why the album did so well, and the answer to that may be that "Candle In The Wind," that wimpy tribute to Marilyn Monroe from *Goodbye Yellow Brick Road*, finally was released as a single in the U.S., where it soared to #6. So, go figure. — *William Ruhlmann*

○ **Greatest Hits, Vol. 3 (1979-1987)** / Sep. 1987 / Geffen ✦✦✦✦
The best of the Geffen years is very good indeed. — *William Ruhlmann*

Reg Strikes Back / Jun. 1988 / MCA ✦✦

The Complete Thom Bell Sessions / 1989 / MCA ✦✦✦
Elton John released a three-song EP from his abortive 1977 sessions with Philadelphia International producer Thom Bell in 1979. Ten years later, be issued a six-song EP containing the initial three tracks and three more that are unremarkable. The things an artist will do for record collectors... — *William Ruhlmann*

Sleeping with the Past / 1989 / MCA ✦✦
The past Elton John has in mind is the era of soul music of the mid-1960s to the mid-1970s, and although all the songs are new, he recreates it well here. The album's most notable selection is the ballad "Sacrifice," which amazingly became his first-ever #1 hit in the U.K. — *William Ruhlmann*

○ **To Be Continued . . .** / 1990 / MCA ✦✦✦✦
The inevitable Elton John boxed set is a four-disc, 68-track affair covering 25 years of the biggest pop star since the Beatles. Hit after hit is heard, plus good album tracks and rarities. There's a big booklet with commentary by John and his lyricist, Bernie Taupin. In a pinch, you can get by with the two MCA and one Geffen greatest hits collections, but for a complete overview of Elton John's career, this is the place to come. — *William Ruhlmann*

Greatest Hits, 1976-1986 / 1992 / MCA ✦✦✦
It covers much of the same ground as Geffen's *Greatest Hits—Vol. 3* but there's no denying that the hits on *Greatest Hits 1976-1986* are worth owning in any format by any Elton John fan. —*AMG*

The One / 1992 / MCA ✦✦
Elton John's latest album is a pleasant collection of adult-contemporary pop in the vein of the hit title track. —*AMG*

○ **Rare Masters** / 1992 / PolyGram ✦✦✦✦
A two-disc collection of rarities from the early '70s, it includes B-sides and the entire *Friends* soundtrack, which has previously been unavailable on CD. *Rare Masters* is essential for any hardcore Elton John fan. —*AMG*

Duets / Nov. 23, 1993 / MCA ✦✦
Unlike Frank Sinatra's album, John actually recorded in the studio with his duet partners, adding a spark to his album missing on Sinatra's *Duets*, even if his choices are nearly as bewildering. Some of the material doesn't work in the duet format, and his partners occasionally don't mesh with his current adult contemporary style. All of this makes *Duets* an ultimately disappointing record, even with the occasional successful track, like the kitschy number with drag queen RuPaul. —*Stephen Thomas Erlewine*

Made in England / 1995 / Rocket ✦✦✦
Made in England is more carefully constructed than many of Elton John's '90s albums. Unlike *One*, it's a cohesive album, with peaks and valleys, as well as featuring a grittier sound than his previous. Still, he doesn't rock out like he did in the early '70s, but he sounds more convincing on the record than he has in several years. —*Stephen Thomas Erlewine*

Mable John

Group, Soul
Born in 1930, she's the older sister of Little Willie John. After a nursing career, John was persuaded by family friend Berry Gordy to go into music. She was the first female artist on his Tamla label in 1959. Before they were even the Primettes, the Supremes backed some of John's blues sessions. Leaving the label in 1963 when it was moving towards the pop arena, John settled in at Stax in Memphis. There she recorded several soul classics such as her 1966 million seller "Your Good Thing (Is About to Come to an End)" which was backed by Booker T. & the MGs and written by the Isaac Hayes & David Porter songwriting team. After the death of her brother Willie in 1968, she fell into depression and temporarily left the business. Ray Charles persuaded her back into music as the lead singer of the Raelettes in the '70s. She continues to write songs for Charles, but has mostly devoted herself to charity work and running a soup kitchen from the church she pastors.

Fantasy, the owners of the Stax catalog, issued a 25-cut anthology, *Stay out of the Kitchen*, in 1993. It was the most comprehensive collection of Mable John material to date, and included some 18 unreleased singles recorded between 1966 and 1968. —*Bil Carpenter*

● **Stay out of the Kitchen** / 1993 / Stax ◆◆◆◆
If you're a fan and/or collector of deep Southern soul music from the '60s, you would have encountered in your listening some grade-A sides from one Mable John, most notably the politically incorrect "Don't Hit Me No More." A R&B veteran who did time as one of the Raelettes, her tenure at Stax Records was short, producing little in the way of substantial hits. But what Mable left behind in the vaults ends up shining like triple platinum here, 25 tracks of the best Southern soul you'll ever pop into the CD player. Even with Stax stars Steve Cropper, Al Jackson, Booker T., Isaac Hayes and David Porter all aboard, the real star of the proceedings is Ms. Mable, and better examples of the real thing are very hard to come by. —*Cub Koda*

Evan Johns & His H-Bombs

Group, Rock & Roll, Rockabilly
Johns (b. 1955) had fronted several bands in the Virginia/DC locale, coming to the attention of guitarist Danny Gatton and eventually doing vocals and writing the title track to Gatton's *Redneck Jazz* album. He formed the H-Bombs in the late '70s, recording an eponymous four-song EP on the tiny Deco label. After moving to Austin, TX, Johns joined the LeRoi Brothers in the early '80s. Johns was nominated for a Grammy for guesting on the *Big Guitars from Texas* album, a compilation of Austin's best. He re-formed the H-Bombs, carnival-barker voice and crazed guitar chops intact, and has continued into the '90s with a spate of frenzied, off-kilter albums ever since. —*Cub Koda*

○ **Evan Johns & The H-Bombs** / 1986 / Jungle ◆◆◆◆
Recorded between 1983 & 1985 and including Springsteen mates Garry Tallent and Danny Federici, this is the Texan band at its most brutal. —*Jeff Tamarkin*

● **Rollin' through the Night** / 1986 / Alternative Tentacles ◆◆◆◆
Bar-band bliss, originally recorded in 1982. —*Jeff Tamarkin*

Bombs Away! / 1989 / Rykodisc ◆◆◆
Still toasty, these Texan madmen drop the big one on this massive roots-rock riot. —*Jeff Tamarkin*

Rockit Fuel Only / 1991 / Rykodisc ◆◆◆
Few bands these days are as unpretentious and downright dangerous as Johns & friends. Not a cut here that doesn't cook. —*Jeff Tamarkin*

○ **Please, Mr. Santa Claus** / Aug. 23, 1991 / Rykodisc ◆◆◆◆
Put this nine-song mini-album CD in the Christmas stocking of any rock & roll fan. The "crash and burn" guitar style of Johns recalls Santo and Johnny ("Snowed In") and Jimmy Bryant ("Santa's Little Helper"), while his snarly vocals on the title track bring new meaning to "cool yule." Spiced with original instrumentals and a cover of "Telstar," this is a must for Evan Johns fans and those who want a little bite in their yuletide listening. —*Dennis MacDonald*

Eric Johnson

Rock & Roll
Very few post-Hendrix guitarists can match Eric Johnson's six-string magic. There's no hint of anger, angst, or sloppiness in any of his playing; instead, each note, each phrase, demonstrates his obsession with tone. Joyous celebrations, his solos seem to grow more magnificent with each listening. For years esteemed players proclaimed Eric Johnson one of rock's most imaginative and tasteful guitarists. Despite the praise, Johnson labored in relative obscurity in Austin, TX, until the 1986 release of *Tones*. His goal was to produce music that entertains and heals, and his playing married deep emotion to mind-boggling finesse. The album's collage of guitar tones ran from purest-of-pure Strat to Hendrix-approved psychedelia and majestic, violinlike textures. Johnson spent nearly two years producing his 1990 followup, *Ah Via Musicom*. Full of fire, light, and swirling thunder, it's an artistic triumph, as powerful a statement for Eric Johnson as *Electric Ladyland* was for Jimi Hendrix. —*Jas Obrecht*

Tones / 1986 / Reprise ◆◆◆
A landmark guitar recording. —*Jas Obrecht*

● **Ah Via Musicom** / 1990 / Capitol ◆◆◆◆
Strong songs and exquisite tones. —*Jas Obrecht*

Marv Johnson

b. Oct. 15, 1938, Detroit, MI, **d.** May 16, 1993
Soul, R&B, Motown
Johnson played an important role in the founding of the Motown empire, with his "Come to Me" the first release on Berry Gordy's Tamla label in 1959. The tuneful high-pitched tenor's impressive effort was snapped up by United Artists, who promptly issued his two biggest Gordy-produced hits, "You Got What It Takes" (first waxed by Bobby Parker on Vee-Jay) and "I Love the Way You Love." Johnson stayed with UA into the early '60s before returning home to Gordy in 1965 and staying to 1968. —*Bill Dahl*

○ **Marvelous Marv Johnson** / 1960 / Collectables ◆◆◆◆
Although he was one of the early artists who helped Motown become a pop and soul empire during the 1960s, Marv Johnson made better records while recording for United Artists in the late '50s and early '60s. This is one of several compilations chronicling his cuts prior to the Motown days. Although Berry Gordy produced a number of these, the ones that clicked weren't as clever, elaborate, or pop-oriented as Motown's finest cuts. Johnson had a soulful, flexible voice and is among the transitional artists who deserve more attention for their role in Motown's emergence. —*Ron Wynn*

More Marv Johnson / 1961 / United Artists ◆◆◆
Even many R&B and soul fans have overlooked the greatness of Marv Johnson, whose smooth, exuberant, and sometimes poignant style helped turn some weepy numbers into triumphant outings. He sounded uniformly great throughout this early '60s album, doing everything from light pop to anguished soul and singing with strength, conviction, and intensity. Unfortunately, with the exception of some greatest hits anthologies, there's very little Marv Johnson on today's market except on the collector's circuit. —*Ron Wynn*

I Believe / 1966 / United Artists ◆◆◆
A wonderful, sorely overlooked late-'50s and '60s soul singer, Marv Johnson had the misfortune to have early hits on Tamla, then a tiny label and not the giant wing of Motown it would become by the mid-'60s. He was a dynamic, aggressive vocalist who excelled at heartache ballads, and, as these songs repeatedly show, was among the finest of his era in building and pacing a song, delivering a lyric, and wrenching emotion out of whatever he was singing. —*Ron Wynn*

● **You Got What It Takes: The Best of Marv Johnson** / 1992 / EMI America ◆◆◆◆
EMI issued a single-disc anthology of Marv Johnson's material in 1992. It included all his R&B chart hits: "Come To Me," "You Got What It Takes," "I Love The Way You Love," and "Happy Days." —*Ron Wynn*

Ruby Johnson

Soul
A tremendous Southern soul vocalist whose ability to convincingly sing heartache ballads ranks with any active performer, Ruby Johnson never got a breakout single during the soul era. The Memphis vocalist began recording for V-Tone in 1960 and signed with Volt in the mid-'60s. But she did less than a dozen songs between 1962 and 1967, also recording for Nebs in Washington, D.C. Isaac Hayes and David Porter produced her songs, and they were backed by the Mar-Key Horns and Booker T. & the MGs. But none of the Volt tunes were hits, and later Johnson sessions at various studios were never issued. She left the business in 1974. Fantasy issued a definitive Ruby Johnson collection in 1993, *I'll Run Your Hurt Away*. It contained 20 outstanding singles, 14 of them previously unreleased. —*Ron Wynn*

○ **I'll Run Your Hurt Away** / 1993 / Stax ◆◆◆◆
There was such a surplus of talent in the Stax family, as with Motown, that inevitably some worthy artists were either overlooked or not promoted to the fullest. That's certainly the case with Ruby Johnson, a big-voiced, dynamic vocalist who could do wailing confessionals and tear-stained love songs with anyone. She did enjoy some regional success with a few singles, but now finally gets the deluxe treatment with a 20-song CD release. This is dramatic, often striking, and without question brilliantly sung soul music. It's sparsely produced, and the backing of Isaac Hayes, Steve Cropper, Duck Dunn, and others doesn't compete with the singer but buttresses the tracks and embellishes Johnson's powerful, assertive vocals. —*Ron Wynn*

Daniel Johnston

Alternative Pop/Rock

As with other talented but troubled artists such as Syd Barrett, Brian Wilson and Roky Erickson, Daniel Johnston fights a daily battle with the chronic mental illness that has plagued him nearly his entire life. However, despite recurrent bouts of delusional behavior wherein he has physically endangered himself and others, Johnston has carved out a respectable, influential career as a singer/songwriter of extraordinary talent that has grown since his first crudely recorded cassette was released in 1980. He has become the singer-songwriter of choice of the alternative/underground rock scene, and at various times has had his work championed by members of Sonic Youth, Yo La Tengo, Butthole Surfers, Half Japanese, Nirvana (Kurt Cobain was often photographed wearing a Daniel Johnston T-shirt), and numerous others.

Until recently, Johnston's recording were basically homemade affairs, his plain voice accompanied by crude piano and guitar playing. His narrative concerns focused mainly on lost love, the pain of miscommunication, his love for the Beatles and comic-book superhero Captain America. Johnston's music is unflinchingly direct, almost embarrassingly and painfully honest. Because of this and his increasingly erratic behavior, he was considered a local hero in his home of Austin, Texas (where he moved from rural West Virginia), but too extreme to engender the interest of a record label. That situation changed in 1985, when MTV filmed a program on the Austin music scene. Johnston's performance brought him almost overnight acclaim, and he went from local legend to national cult figure. Soon, many of his self-released cassette recordings (on his appropriately named Stress label) began showing up in hip record stores from Boston to L.A., and the buzz was that Daniel Johnston was the coolest. There was, however, a grim side to this "success," as if his mental illness was the primary component of his hipness; therefore, there was a feeling that those not close to him were marketing his illness as much as his talent. Sadly, Johnston's behavior wasn't helping, and he was institutionalized twice in the late '80s after his refusal to take medication led to two dangerous episodes.

In the late '80s, indie label Homestead issued some of Johnston's early recordings on vinyl and a full-blown appreciation of Johnston's work was well underway. Soon he was recording solo and with Half Japanese mastermind Jad Fair on the Shimmy Disc indie label, and most recently with Butthole Surfer Paul Leary, who may well be the best producer/musical accompanist Johnston has ever had. Johnston, to the amazement of virtually everyone, now records for Atlantic and, despite occasional behavioral lapses, seems more self-assured than ever. As a result, he has been recording some of the best music of his career: smart, ebullient pop with ringing guitars, primitive keyboards and a wonderfully naive way of looking at the world. Although he sometimes becomes sad and bitter, cynicism and self-pity aren't his style, and that makes the little tragedies and epiphanies he writes about all the more compelling. Daniel Johnston's world may seem small, but it's much bigger and friendlier than that of our wildest imaginations. —*John Dougan*

Songs of Pain / 1980 / Stress ♦♦

Don't Be Scared / 1982 / Stress ♦♦

The What of Whom / 1982 / Stress ♦♦

○ **Hi, How Are You** / 1983 / Homestead ♦♦♦♦

As with *Yip/Jump Music*, *Hi, How Are You* was a reissue of a cassette recording Johnston made in 1983, and as such it reflects the most fertile period of his early development. Like its predecessor, this is a friendly record marked by his increasing skill as a pop songwriter and his increasingly comfortable singing. His mood here is good, especially during the defiant "Keep Punching Joe," which eschews bitterness for personal resolve. Another important release. —*John Dougan*

Yip Jump Music / 1983 / Homestead ♦♦♦

As for his early music, this may be the best place to begin immersing yourself in the world of Daniel Johnston. Extremely primitively recorded with little instrumentation other than keyboards, Johnston's upbeat mood makes this a funny, sometimes moving exercise in obsessive behavior. Two things he thinks about a lot, the Beatles and Casper the Friendly Ghost, are the subject of songs, along with his usual examinations of unattainable love. Not the easiest record in the Johnston canon, but a rewarding one nonetheless. —*John Dougan*

Retired Boxer / 1984 / Stress ♦♦♦

○ **Continued Story** / 1985 / Homestead ♦♦♦♦

Respect / 1985 / Stress ♦♦♦

1990 / 1990 / Shimmy Disc ♦♦♦

Live at SXSW / 1990 / Stress ♦♦

● **Fun** / 1994 / Atlantic ♦♦♦♦

Johnston's major label debut is, arguably, his finest moment. With considerable help from Butthole Surfer Paul Leary, Johnston has never sounded so self-assured or confident before. Some of the songs are more polished, but they're never slicked up to such a degree that this sounds like a user-friendly approximation of Johnston's style; in fact, there are plenty of tracks that return Johnston to the keyboards ("Delusion & Confusion" and "My Little Girl") for his freewheeling, primitive workouts. Exhibiting some of his strongest songwriting to date, *Fun* is a rewarding record that never loses its initial, visceral appeal. —*John Dougan*

Freedy Johnston

Singer-Songwriter, Folk-Rock

A fine lyricist from Kansas who resettled in Hoboken, Johnston brought his heartland rock to the more brash Northeast, and after a shaky start has become a very exciting artist.

Johnston's 1992 album *Can You Fly?* received a generous amount of critical praise; his direct, Midwestern viewpoint graced some of the finest folk-rock of the decade. Two years later, the singer/songwriter had become a hot property and he followed through on his promise with the Butch Vig-produced *This Perfect World*, which easily matched *Can You Fly?* with its spare beauty. —*Bruce Eder*

● **Can You Fly** / Apr. 14, 1992 / Bar/None ♦♦♦♦

Freedy Johnston's second album is a supremely engaging set of folk-rock that showcases Johnston's considerable talent for writing melodic, literate songs. —*AMG*

Unlucky / 1993 / Restless ♦♦♦

This CD features Johnson's touring band and includes a great cover of "Witchita Lineman" as well as the acoustic demo of "The Lucky One." —*Richard Meyer*

○ **This Perfect World** / 1994 / Elektra ♦♦♦♦

The follow-up to the critically acclaimed *Can You Fly* is a collection of catchy, intelligent folk-rock that confirms Johnston's status as one of the 1990s finest singer-songwriters. —*Stephen Thomas Erlewine*

Grace Jones

b. May 19, 1952, Kingston, Jamaica

Dance-Pop, Disco

Entertainer and model Grace Jones has a European flair but a hard, stilted singing style. Jones is on the cutting edge of reggae-style dance music, although commercial success evades her.

Grace Jones renewed her career in the '90s, though she's done more acting than singing. She had a featured role in the Eddie Murphy film *Boomerang* in 1992. Her most recent release was *Bulletproof Heart* in 1989 for Capitol. —*Bil Carpenter*

Portfolio / 1977 / Island ♦♦♦

Broadway-styled disco. —*Bil Carpenter*

Fame / 1978 / Island ♦♦♦

Original, Euro-style disco. —*Bil Carpenter*

Muse / 1979 / Island ♦♦♦

A fine dance and club album, Grace Jones was still essentially a disco act when she recorded this album at the end of the '70s. The campy tendencies and flat vocals were subordinated to the array of cross-rhythms, textures, and production devices buttressing the tracks. Jones did some outstanding numbers during this era, but seldom utilized her voice beyond either a decorative or supporting role. She wasn't (and still isn't) a soulful or great singer, but future albums would demonstrate that she could do more things than mouth lines and insert herself in rhythm tracks. —*Ron Wynn*

○ **Warm Leatherette** / 1980 / Island ♦♦♦♦

Grace Jones teamed with the great reggae production duo of Sly Dunbar and Robbie Shakespeare on this '80 album, and made the transition from straight dance and club act into quasi-pop star with reggae and urban contemporary leaning. The single "Private Number" was one of her best, and the overall album had more energy and production gloss than previous LPs that had been aimed completely at the club market. It helped that Jones seemed enthused about the session and really put herself into the songs. — *Ron Wynn*

● **Nightclubbing** / 1981 / Island ✦✦✦✦
Actress, model and disco/reggae sensation Grace Jones enjoyed her greatest pop success with this album. Sly Dunbar and Robbie Shakespeare's production gave Jones a thin reggae veneer, while also providing her with a sensational hit in "Pull Up To The Bumper." The song's suggestive lyrics and quasi-reggae feel helped make it a club smash and Top 10 R&B hit. Jones alternated between being coy and aggressive on this record, which was one of the last hurrahs for Sly and Robbie's "taxi" beat pop-reggae sound. —*Ron Wynn*

Living My Life / 1982 / Island ✦✦✦
Grace Jones essentially retired from music after this album and became a film actress for three years. The album followed her definitive *Nightclubbing* and was a commercial disappointment, although it had some nice material and excellent production and arrangements. But she often sounded distant and detached, and not even the great support could totally overcome Jones' less than enthusiastic performances. —*Ron Wynn*

Island Life / 1985 / Island ✦✦✦

○ **Slave to the Rhythm** / 1985 / ZTT/Island ✦✦✦✦
An audio biography of Grace Jones, produced by Trevor Horn, it's a sonic treat along the lines of Yes's *90125* or Frankie Goes to Hollywood's first album (both produced by Horn). The music ranges from slick R&B runaway grooves to striking audio montages, interrupted occasionally by conversation about Jones's life. Serious ear candy! —*Scott Bultman*

Inside Story / 1986 / EMI ✦✦
Chic's Nile Rodgers produced this Grace Jones album as part of a new deal she signed in the late '80s with Manhattan. Unfortunately, she didn't remain on the label very long, even though this was among her better LPs and included a fine single in "(I'm Not Perfect) But I'm Perfect For You." There were rumors that Jones and Rodgers didn't get along, and perhaps they didn't, but the album wound up being one of her most commercially viable. —*Ron Wynn*

Bulletproof Heart / 1989 / Capitol ✦✦
'80s funk/dance done "Grace-fully." —*Bil Carpenter*

Howard Jones (John Howard Jones)

b. Feb. 23, 1955, Southampton, Hampshire
New Wave, Pop/Rock
Adept at overdubbing himself into a one-man band through his use of synthesizers and drum machines, Jones scored consistently on the charts in the early '80s with an inoffensive pop style on tunes like "New Song," "No One Is to Blame," and "Things Can Only Get Better." —*Cub Koda*

○ **Human's Lib** / 1984 / Elektra ✦✦✦✦
His debut album is almost entirely performed on synthesizers. The material on *Human's Lib*, like all of the following albums, is very inconsistent; Jones either writes hits or flops, with very little in between. Contains two of Jones's best songs, "New Song" and "What Is Love?" —*Iotis Erlewine*

○ **Dream into Action** / 1985 / Elektra ✦✦✦✦
This album shows the synthesizer pop idol at the height of his creativity—*Dream into Action* is definitely the most interesting of Jones's albums. It contains some of his best songs—"Things Can Only Get Better," "Life in One Day," and "No One Is to Blame." The CD includes two bonus tracks, "Bounce Right Back" and "Like to Get to Know You Well," both of which are worthwhile additions. —*Iotis Erlewine*

Action Replay / 1986 / Elektra ✦✦
This is a six-track mini-album that includes an updated version of "No One Is to Blame" featuring Phil Collins on percussion. This album really isn't worth buying, especially if you have the other Jones albums. —*Iotis Erlewine*

One to One / 1986 / Elektra ✦✦
This is Jones's most musically mature and toned-down album. The synthesizers are less overbearing than on the previous albums, yet the songs are mediocre. *One to One* reached number ten in the U.K., but did not fare as well in the U.S., peaking at number 56. This album features the revamped "No One Is to Blame," which is inferior to the original version. —*Iotis Erlewine*

Cross That Line / 1989 / Elektra ✦✦✦
After a three year wait, this album was a bit of a disappointment. Musically, it is his best yet, but it lacked a certain energy that the others had. The songs seemed to replace vivacity with length. The album didn't do very well on the charts; the number 13 single (U.S.), "Everlasting Love," was the biggest hit. Ironically, the best song on this album, "Out of Thin Air," does not use a single synthesizer but instead is a solo piano piece performed by Jones himself. After all those years of electronic music, a song featuring a real instrument is a welcome relief. —*Iotis Erlewine*

In the Running / 1992 / Elektra ✦✦
On his fifth album, *In the Running*, Howard Jones backs away from his trademark bouncy synth-pop in an attempt to secure a position in the adult-contemporary market. While his graceful keyboard playing is still impressive, he hasn't written a set of songs that supports his talent. Most of the record lacks strong hooks and melodies, making it nothing more than a pleasant, but bland and unmemorable, album. —*Stephen Thomas Erlewine*

● **The Best of Howard Jones** / Jun. 29, 1993 / Elektra ✦✦✦✦
The Best of Howard Jones successfully distills all the hits and highlights from his albums onto one disc. It could be all the Howard Jones you'll ever need. —*AMG*

Linda Jones

b. Jan. 14, 1944, Newark, NJ, **d.** Mar. 14, 1972
Soul
A word in support of an artist who will probably be passed over by 999 listeners out of 1000. Her biggest hit, the tastefully restrained "Hypnotized," came on the Loma subsidiary of Warner Brothers in 1967, but her later recordings for Turbo were probably the most gloriously histrionic soul records of all time. She started at a climax and worked up from there, transforming a ballad like "Let It Be Me" with her towering fury. It was pure gospel—and then some. Jones was already ill with diabetes when she cut those records, and she died in 1972 after collapsing backstage at the Apollo. —*Colin Escott*

● **Hypnotized** / 1967 / Collectables ✦✦✦✦
Linda Jones was a dynamic, sorely neglected late-'60s and early-'70s soul vocalist. There was no mild reaction to Jones' theatrical style; you were either amazed or appalled. She didn't deliver lyrics, she smashed and screamed them. This collection covers her bombastic hits, including the classic title track, "I'll Be Sweeter Tomorrow," "For Your Precious Love" and several others. Any vocalist picked by Gladys Knight and Patti Labelle as one of their favorites merits closer examination. Unfortunately, her premature death in the early-'70s prevented Jones from gaining much exposure, as did the fact that she recorded for a host of small independents. —*Ron Wynn*

Your Precious Love / 1988 / Turbo ✦✦✦
The best of the Turbo label tracks, it features superior sound quality. (Import) —*Richard Pack*

Marti Jones

Pop/Rock
This Ohio-based singer and former member of Color Me Gone went solo under the tutelage of producer Don Dixon (now her husband). With Dixon she made four albums (1984–1990) interpreting the best of current songwriters. —*William Ruhlmann*

○ **Unsophisticated Time** / 1985 / A&M ✦✦✦✦
Jones applies her smoky alto to a group of ironic love songs, the best of them written by producer Don Dixon. —*William Ruhlmann*

Match Game / 1986 / A&M ✦✦✦

● **Used Guitars** / 1988 / A&M ✦✦✦✦
This is another solid effort from Marti Jones. —*David Jehnzen*

Any Kind of Lie / 1990 / RCA ✦✦✦
After proving herself an ideal interpreter for the more literate songwriters of the day (Elvis Costello, Peter Holsapple, etc.), Jones writes most of her own material here (with Don Dixon). And it's just as good as, if not better than, the covers. —*William Ruhlmann*

Oran Juice Jones

Soul, Disco, R&B
Oran "Juice" Jones seemed on his way to stardom when the tough-talking single "The Rain" became a hit in 1986. Though born in

Houston, Jones grew up in Harlem and was one of the first signees to the Def Jam subsidiary label OBR, which was to be devoted to vintage soul and R&B acts. Jones was actually a good "sweet" soul singer, but that facet was obscured by his facade as a gangsta. His best single was a duet with Alyson Williams, "How to Love Again." After "The Rain" topped the R&B charts in 1986, Jones was unable to land any more hits with follow-up singles. —*Ron Wynn*

● **To Be Immortal** / 1986 / Original Black ✦✦✦✦
His debut featured the great single "The Rain," a song he hasn't touched since. —*Dan Heilman*

G.T.O.: Gangsters Takin' Over / Def Jam ✦✦✦

Juice / Columbia ✦✦✦

Rickie Lee Jones

b. Nov. 8, 1954, Chicago, IL
Singer-Songwriter
A singer/songwriter who emerged in 1979 with a million-selling album and the Top Ten hit "Chuck E's in Love." Born in Chicago, Jones grew up in Arizona and Washington state and was taught music by her father. Moving to Los Angeles in 1973, she started as a performer by doing rhythmic "beat" monologs. She began to gain notice after hooking up with singer/songwriter Tom Waits in 1977, and in 1979 Little Feat leader Lowell George recorded her "Easy Money" on his debut solo album. Signed to Warner Brothers, Jones recorded her own debut, *Rickie Lee Jones* (a combination of folk, jazz, and rock styles), its lyrical songs populated by bohemian characters and sung in Jones's slightly slurred voice. It hit, and Jones won the Best New Artist Grammy for 1979.

She returned in 1981 with the even more ambitious *Pirates*, which hit and went gold. *Girl at Her Volcano* was a 1983 EP made up mostly of cover songs. Jones's next full-length album was *The Magazine*, which hit the Top 50 in 1984. In the second half of the '80s, Jones married and gave birth to a daughter. She returned to recording with the Top 40 *Flying Cowboys* in 1989, and in 1991 she released another record of covers, *Pop Pop*. —*William Ruhlmann*

★ **Rickie Lee Jones** / Mar. 1979 / Warner Brothers ✦✦✦✦✦
One of the most impressive debuts for a singer/songwriter ever, this infectious mixture of styles not only features a strong collection of original songs (here are "Chuck E's in Love" and "Young Blood," but "Danny's All-Star Joint" and "Coolsville" are just as good) but also a singer with a savvy, distinctive voice that can be streetwise, childlike, and sophisticated, sometimes all in the same song. —*William Ruhlmann*

○ **Pirates** / Jul. 1981 / Warner Brothers ✦✦✦✦
If the songs are less immediately accessible than on Jones's first album, repeated listenings are likely to lead to even greater rewards. Open-ended song structures allow Jones to explore more fully her closely observed portraits of lowlife characters, and her singing remains entrancing. —*William Ruhlmann*

○ **Girl at Her Volcano** / 1983 / Warner Brothers ✦✦✦✦
This seven-song EP originally was released as a 10-inch record. It's a charming collection featuring Billy Strayhorn's standard "Lush Life," as well as the Left Banke hit "Walk Away Renee," which should give some sense of Jones's breadth. A minor, but enjoyable change of pace. —*William Ruhlmann*

The Magazine / Sep. 1984 / Warner Brothers ✦✦✦
The reason *The Magazine* was such a disappointment was that Jones had proven herself a major artist with her first two albums and turned into a self-conscious, pretentious, minor one on this, her third. Once, she made art by observing street people and describing them carefully; now she tried to make "Art" by navel-gazing. What a letdown. —*William Ruhlmann*

○ **Flying Cowboys** / Sep. 1989 / David Geffen Co. ✦✦✦✦

Pop Pop / Aug. 1991 / David Geffen Co. ✦✦✦

○ **Traffic from Paradise** / Sep. 14, 1993 / Geffen ✦✦✦✦
"Just give me many chances...time to learn to crawl," sings Rickie Lee Jones on this, her fifth album of new material in 14 years. Clearly, she's had a lot of chances already, and some have paid off big. Here, however, Jones has made a record of what sound like rough performances of musical ideas that might at some point become songs and then, with some work, acceptable recordings. As it is, the record is vague and unfocused, only aspiring to coherence when someone other than Jones is heard from, such as the two songs co-written by Leo Kottke. Too much of the time, Jones

sounds like she's singing half-forgotten songs, and the result is wispy and fragmentary. —*William Ruhlmann*

Tom Jones (Thomas Jones Woodward)

b. Jun. 7, 1940, Pontypridd, Mid-Glamorgan
Pop
Tom Jones became one of the most popular vocalists to emerge from the British Invasion. Since the mid-'60s, Jones has sang nearly every form of popular music—pop, rock, showtunes, country, dance, and techno, he's sung it all. His actual style—a full-throated, robust baritone that had little regard for nuance and subtlety—never changed, he just sang over different backing tracks. On stage, Jones played up his sexual appeal; it didn't matter whether he was in an unbuttoned shirt or a tuxedo, he was always radiated a raw sexuality, which earned him a large following of devoted female fans who frequently threw underwear on stage. Jones' following never diminished over the decades; he was able to exploit trends, earning new fans while retaining his core following.

Born Thomas Jones Woodward, Tom Jones began singing professionally in 1963, performing as Tommy Scott with the Senators, a Welsh beat group. In 1964 he recorded a handful of solo tracks with record producer Joe Meek and shopped them to various record companies to little success. Later in the year, Decca producer Peter Sullivan discovered Tommy Scott performing in a club and directed him to manager Phil Solomon. It was a short-lived partnership and the singer soon moved back to Wales, where he continued to sing in local clubs. At one of the shows, he gained the attention of former Viscounts singer Gordon Mills, who had become an artist manager. Mills signed Scott, renamed him Tom Jones and helped him record his first single for Decca, "Chills and Fever," which was released in late 1964. "Chills and Fever" didn't chart but "It's Not Unusual," released in early 1965, became a number one hit in the U.K. and a Top Ten hit in the U.S. The heavily orchestrated, over-the-top pop arrangements perfectly meshed with Jones' swinging, sexy image, guaranteeing him press coverage, which translated into a series of hits, including "Once Upon A Time," "Little Lonely One," and "With These Hands." During 1965, Mills also secured a number of film themes for Jones to record, including the Top Ten hit "What's New Pussycat?" (June 1965) and "Thunderball" (December 1965).

Jones' popularity began to slip somewhat by the middle of 1966, causing Mills to redesign the singer's image into a more respectable, mature tuxedoed crooner. Jones also began to sing material that appealed to a broad audience, like the country songs "Green, Green Grass of Home" and "Detroit City." The strategy worked, as he returned to the top of the charts in the U.K. and began hitting the Top 40 again in the U.S. For the remainder of the '60s, he scored a consistent string of hits in both Britain and America. At the end of the decade, Jones relocated to America, where he hosted the television variety program, *This Is Tom Jones*. Running between 1969 and 1971, the show was a success and laid the groundwork for the singer's move to Las Vegas in the early '70s. Once he moved to Vegas, Jones began recording less, choosing to concentrate on his lucrative club performances. After Gordon Mills died in the late '70s, Jones' son, Mark Woodward, became the singer's manager. The change in management prompted Jones to begin recording again. This time, he concentrated on the country market, releasing a series of slick Nashville-styled country-pop albums in the early '80s that earned him a handful of hits.

Jones' next image make-over came in 1988, when he sang Prince's "Kiss" with the electronic dance outfit, the Art of Noise. The single became a Top Ten hit in the U.K. and reached the American Top 40, which led to a successful concert tour and a part in a recording of Dylan Thomas's voice play, *Under the Milk Wood*. The singer then returned to the club circuit, where he stayed for several years. In 1993, Jones performed at the Glastonbury festival in England, where he won an enthusiastic response from the young crowd. Soon, he was on the comeback trail again, releasing the alternative-dance-pop album *The Lead and How to Swing It* in the fall of 1994; the record was a moderate hit, gaining some play in dance clubs.

No matter what style Tom Jones has appropriated, he has remained a genuine pop star, mainly because he has always delivered his hammy, melodramatic pop with a wink. By recognizing the camp in what he does, he has remained popular with hipsters; by never being condescending to his fans, he has remained popular with his devoted following. And that is why he is one pop/rock

star that always seemed more comfortable in Vegas than in swinging London. —*Stephen Thomas Erlewine*

It's Not Unusual / 1965 / Parrot ✦✦✦
Tom Jones' first American album was a well-produced set of
straightahead '60s pop, but the title track was not just the only hit
on the record, it was the only exceptional song. Nevertheless, the
rest of the album was comprised of pleasant filler that illustrated
Jones was blessed with a powerful voice. —*Stephen Thomas Erlewine*

What's New Pussycat? / 1965 / Parrot ✦✦✦
The soundtrack to *What's New Pussycat?* suffered from the same
lack of memorable material as *It's Not Unusual*, with only the title
track and "With These Hands" standing out among the album's 12
tracks, but the rest of the record was agreeable and well-produced.
—*Stephen Thomas Erlewine*

A-Tom-Ic Jones / 1966 / Parrot ✦✦
A-Tom-Ic Jones, Jones' cleverly titled third album, featured no major hit singles and failed to chart in the U.S. Given the quality of
the record, its lack of success isn't surprising. Jones sings well, but
he doesn't have the material to match his performance, making
the album noticeably weaker than his first two collections. —
Stephen Thomas Erlewine

Green, Green Grass of Home / 1967 / PolyGram ✦✦✦
With *Green, Green Grass of Home*, Tom Jones began to abandon
his teenage pop audience to concentrate on a more mature, middle of the road group of listeners. Although he did include uptempo R&B numbers like "Kansas City," the album's strongest moments occurred when he concentrated on standards and country
tunes like the title track, "My Mother's Eyes," and "That Old Black
Magic," or when he turned in laidback soul songs like "Any Day
Now." The album was still inconsistent, as Jones over-sang several
of the tracks, but it was easily the best album he had recorded to
date. —*Stephen Thomas Erlewine*

The Tom Jones Fever Zone / Jun. 1968 / Parrot ✦✦✦
As the title indicates, Tom Jones returned to uptempo, teen-oriented R&B and soul covers on his fifth album, *The Tom Jones
Fever Zone*. While the covers (including "Hold on, I'm Coming"
and "Keep on Running") were competent, it was material like the
rampaging "Delilah" that made the album worthwhile. —*Stephen
Thomas Erlewine*

Help Yourself / Dec. 1968 / Parrot ✦✦
The infectious title track was a Top 40 hit and it helped make *Help
Yourself* Tom Jones' first Top Ten album, but the record was
weighed down by lackluster material, making the album his
weakest set since *A-Tom-Ic Jones*. —*Stephen Thomas Erlewine*

This Is Tom Jones / Jun. 1969 / PolyGram ✦✦✦
On the back of his identically-titled hit television show, *This Is
Tom Jones* catapulted into the Top Ten. The album emphasized
Jones' broad-based appeal, as he worked his way through stan-
dards like "Fly Me to the Moon" and current pop hits like "Hey
Jude" and "Wichita Lineman," all delivered in a bombastic, heavily
orchestrated style perfectly suited to his forceful singing. —
Stephen Thomas Erlewine

○ **Tom Jones Live in Las Vegas** / Nov. 1969 / Parrot ✦✦✦✦
Tom Jones' greatest strength is as a showman, making *Tom Jones
Live in Las Vegas* one of his strongest records. As he tears through
his well-constructed show, the vocalist works the reserved crowd
into a near-frenzy, which makes him sing stronger and more dramatically. However, Tom Jones is at his best when he is at his most
melodramatic, so this isn't a flaw. Jones' impassioned performance
and the absence of weak material make *Live in Las Vegas* one of
his most consistent records. Not surprisingly, it was also his
biggest hit, peaking at number three on the American album
charts. —*Stephen Thomas Erlewine*

Tom / May 1970 / Parrot ✦✦
Tom continued Tom Jones' turn-of-the-decade winning streak,
climbing to number six on the album charts. However, the album
wasn't as strong as his previous studio collection, *This Is Tom
Jones*, featuring a set of R&B covers ("I Can't Turn You Loose," "I
Thank You," "Proud Mary") and pop confections ("Sugar Sugar")
that were too bombastic to be enjoyable. However, when Jones delivered ballads like "The Impossible Dream" or the hit "Without
Love (There Is Nothing)," the record kicked into high gear, as his
delivery matched the material as well as the arrangements. —
Stephen Thomas Erlewine

I (Who Have Nothing) / Nov. 1970 / Parrot ✦✦✦
Tom Jones fell out of the Top Ten with *I (Who Have Nothing)*, but
the title track was one of his biggest hits, as well as being one of
the best moments on this consistent, but average set, which also
featured fine versions of "To Love Somebody" and "Try a Little
Tenderness." —*Stephen Thomas Erlewine*

She's a Lady / May 1971 / Parrot ✦✦
Although the title track was Tom Jones' biggest hit and its double-
sided follow-up "Puppet Man" / "Resurrection Shuffle" was nearly
as good as its predecessor, *She's a Lady* featured one of Jones'
weakest collections of made-to-order songs, which were almost all
indistinguishable from each other. —*Stephen Thomas Erlewine*

Tom Jones Live at Caesars Palace / Nov. 1971 / Parrot ✦✦
Live at Las Vegas was Tom Jones' biggest album, so it made sense
that he followed it two years later with *Tom Jones Live at Caesars
Palace*, a record that was nearly identical to its predecessor. However, the performance was slightly weaker and his supper-club
schtick wasn't as entertaining the second time around. —*Stephen
Thomas Erlewine*

Close Up / 1972 / Parrot ✦✦
Close Up was Tom Jones' first album to not go gold since *Green,
Green Grass of Home*, and given the wildly inconsistent quality of
the material and performances, it's easy to see why the record was
only a minor hit. The hit single "Till" was a fine MOR ballad, but
its stilted follow-up "Young New Mexican Puppeteer" illustrates
the problem with the record: most of the songs were either cutesy
or vapid and occasionally—such as "Young New Mexican Puppeteer" and "Witch Queen of New Orleans"—they were both. —
Stephen Thomas Erlewine

The Body and Soul of Tom Jones / 1973 / Parrot ✦✦
Tom Jones continued to slide down the charts with *The Body and
Soul of Tom Jones*, even though it was a marginally better record
than the previous *Close Up*. Nevertheless, the majority of the material was limp, with only the minor hit "Letter to Lucille" and "If
Loving You Is Wrong (I Don't Wanna Be Right)" standing out
amidst the mediocrity. —*Stephen Thomas Erlewine*

○ **Darlin'** / 1981 / PolyGram ✦✦✦✦
In an attempt to resurrect his recording career, Tom Jones turned
to country music in the early '80s. *Darlin'*, his first attempt at
string-laden country-pop, was also his most successful. Jones
sounds revitalized for most of the record, breathing life into formulaic material like "Lady Lay Done" and "Dime Queen of
Nevada." His energetic performance makes the record surprisingly
effective and entertaining. —*Stephen Thomas Erlewine*

Love Is on the Radio / 1984 / London ✦✦
With *Love Is on the Radio*, Tom Jones began to return to mainstream pop/rock, which suited his vocal style better than the country-pop he had been singing for the past four years. However, the
songs on the album were decidedly lackluster, making the album
a tentative re-entry into the pop marketplace. —*Stephen Thomas Erlewine*

Tender Loving Care / 1985 / Mercury ✦✦
Tender Loving Care was a more confident album than the previous *Love Is on the Radio*, yet it still suffered from a stiff, synthesized production and a preponderance of tepid songs. —*Stephen
Thomas Erlewine*

○ **Things That Matter Most to Me** / 1987 / Mercury ✦✦✦✦
Things That Matter Most to Me compiles Jones' greatest country-
pop hits. Taken in one sitting, the singles sound stronger than they
do on the albums, and show that Jones can deliver country-flavored material convincingly. —*Stephen Thomas Erlewine*

Move Closer / 1988 / Jive ✦✦✦
Following the surprise success of "Kiss," his collaboration with the
art-dance outfit the Art of Noise, Tom Jones recorded *Move Closer*,
a collection of state-of-the-art late-'80s dance-pop. While the music
isn't as ambitious or provocative as "Kiss," most of the album was
well-produced and well-crafted, making it his best, most convincing record since *Darlin'*. —*Stephen Thomas Erlewine*

● **The Complete Tom Jones** / Aug. 17, 1993 / PolyGram ✦✦✦✦
Collecting almost all of his hit singles on one album, *Complete
Tom Jones* is the singer's most entertaining album, devoid of the
filler that clutters all of his studio records. —*Stephen Thomas Erlewine*

Lead & How to Swing It / 1994 / Interscope ✦✦✦
For some reason, some critics named Tom Jones as the most likely successor to Tony Bennett's throne as most unlikely hero to Generation X. So, Interscope signed the aging sex symbol and had him record with several of the hippest names in dance music—or at least the hippest names in dance music in 1991. And the result, the clumsily titled *Lead and How to Swing It*, is a record neither true to Tom Jones' core audience nor appealing to Gen Xers, simply because it doesn't feature Jones doing what he does best—famous songs written by other people. Instead, it's a set of written-to-order dance numbers that are immaculately produced and sung, yet hardly engaging. And they're devoid of the camp factor that made his version of Prince's "Kiss" so entertaining. —*Stephen Thomas Erlewine*

Janis Joplin

b. Jan. 19, 1943, Port Arthur, TX, d. Oct. 4, 1970
Rock & Roll, Blues Rock
Janis Joplin was one of the greatest White female singers to take on the blues. Hailing from Texas, Joplin journeyed to San Francisco in 1963 to sing, playing infrequent gigs with Jorma Kaukonen or Roger Perkins. She returned to Austin in 1966 to sort out her life, briefly giving up singing and making plans for marriage. Nevertheless, word that the Bay Area-band Big Brother & the Holding Company was looking for a singer lured Joplin back. With Big Brother, Joplin wowed audiences with her intensity and aching vulnerability. *Cheap Thrills*, a doctored-up live collection, topped a million sales. It contained incredible performances from Joplin and the band, particularly "Ball and Chain," "Summertime," "Combination of the Two," and the hit "Piece of My Heart."

On *Cheap Thrills*, the guitar interplay of Sam Andrew and James Gurley is among the finest examples of the psychedelic Bay Area style ever committed to disc. Joplin left for a solo career and released 1969's *I Got Dem Ol' Kozmic Blues Again Mama!*, which featured the track "Try (Just a Little Harder)." Joplin assembled the Full-Tilt Boogie Band and began recording the followup album. Unfortunately, Joplin's crippling drug and alcohol addiction got to her, and she was found dead Oct. 4, 1970, at the Landmark Hotel in Hollywood, of an accidental heroin overdose.

Pearl, which was Joplin's nickname, was assembled out of the sessions that had been recorded, and it went to #1. The album produced a #1 hit, as well, with a version of Kris Kristofferson's "Me and Bobby McGee." (See also Big Brother & the Holding Company.) —*Rick Clark*

I Got Dem Ol' Kozmic Blues Again Mama / 1969 / Columbia ✦✦✦
Joplin's only solo album to be released during her lifetime heavily employs horns and an R&B band feel, but the dominant sound remains Joplin's impassioned singing on such songs as "Try." —*William Ruhlmann*

○ **Pearl** / Feb. 1971 / Columbia ✦✦✦✦
Backed by a tight rock band, Full Tilt Boogie, Joplin puts her mark on everything but the bluesy "Cry Baby" to her hit version of Kris Kristofferson's "Me & Bobby McGee." —*William Ruhlmann*

In Concert / May 1972 / Columbia ✦✦✦
About half of this two-record set features Janis Joplin with Big Brother and the Holding Company in 1968, performing songs like "Down on Me" and "Piece of My Heart." The rest, recorded in 1970, finds her with her backup group, Full Tilt Boogie, mostly performing songs from *I Got Dem Ol' Kozmic Blues Again Mama!* Joplin puts herself out on stage, both in terms of singing until her voice is raw and describing her life to her audiences. Parts of this album are moving, parts are heartbreaking, and the rest is just great rock & roll. —*William Ruhlmann*

● **Janis Joplin's Greatest Hits** / Jul. 1973 / Columbia ✦✦✦✦
Well-chosen best-of gathers together tracks from Big Brother and the Holding Company and solo material. —*William Ruhlmann*

Janis / 1975 / Columbia ✦✦
This is a two-LP soundtrack to a documentary feature film about Joplin, and it contains some of the recordings she made prior to joining Big Brother and the Holding Company in 1966. —*William Ruhlmann*

Farewell Song / 1982 / Columbia ✦✦✦
A ragtag collection of odds and ends, live and studio, from both the Big Brother and solo era. The best cuts are on the *Janis* box in different versions, but serious fans will find some interesting items here, especially the *Cheap Thrills*-era outtakes and live perfor-

mances; "Misery 'N," "Farewell Song," and "Catch Me Daddy" were easily good enough to have qualified for inclusion on that album. —*Richie Unterberger*

○ **Janis** / Nov. 23, 1993 / Columbia/Legacy ✦✦✦✦
This 3-CD box set is the most thorough and valuable retrospective of Janis Joplin's career. Besides including all of her most essential recordings with and without Big Brother and the Holding Company, this 49-song package features quite a few enticing rarities; 18 of the tracks were previously unissued. These include a 1962 home recording of the Joplin original "What Good Can Drinkin' Do," which marked the first time her singing was captured on tape; a pair of acoustic blues tunes from 1965 with backup guitar by future Jefferson Airplane star Jorma Kaukonen, an acoustic demo of "Me and Bobby McGee," a 1970 birthday song for John Lennon, and live performances from her appearance on "The Ed Sullivan Show" in 1969. The real showstopper is the previously unissued, eight-minute version of "Ball and Chain" from Big Brother's first set at the 1967 Monterey Pop Festival (the cut on the *Monterey Pop* box set is from their second set). The more forgettable tracks from her solo albums are wisely excised, as are the Big Brother songs which did not feature her vocals. This is the rare multi-disc set of a major artist which manages to cover all the official milestones and present a bounty of worthwhile rarities at the same time. —*Richie Unterberger*

○ **18 Essential Songs** / 1995 / Legacy/Columbia ✦✦✦✦
While it contains more tracks than *Greatest Hits*, *18 Essential Songs* isn't as effective an introduction to Janis Joplin, as it tries to balance hit singles with alternate takes and rarities. There's plenty of fine music on the disc, to be sure, yet the sequencing and selection is a bit haphazard, making it a flawed but entertaining collection. —*Stephen Thomas Erlewine*

BOOKS

✦✦ **Pearl: The Obsessions And Passions Of Janis Joplin**, by Ellis Amburn (Warner Books, 1992). For all her talent and charisma, there was a great deal of sadness in Janis Joplin's life, which makes it difficult for any biography to avoid being kind of a bummer after a few hundred pages. Amburn documents the sex, drugs, alcohol, and emotional instability, and as with Jim Morrison, one is left with the feeling that her death was as inevitable as it was tragic. He doesn't ignore the rock & roll, and the author, besides drawing upon the memories of various friends and lovers, also talks quite a bit with most of the members of Big Brother and the Holding Company, as well as professional associates like San Francisco promoter Chet Helms. As with any performer of Joplin's mystique, there are a lot of sensational, and sometimes contradictory, tales flying around, making it difficult to ascertain how much of a true profile can be drawn. As for the music, there's quite a bit of information about her formative years, her ride to the top of the psychedelic wagon train with Big Brother, and her erratic solo career, in which she struggled with unsympathetic bands and material before appearing to have started to climb another peak shortly before her death. —*Richie Unterberger*

Margie Joseph

b. 1950, Pascogoula, MS
Soul, R&B
A talented journeywoman soul singer who had ten modest-to-tiny R&B hits in the 1970s, Joseph's style was often compared to Aretha Franklin's, though frankly the similarity is not overwhelming. Perhaps a midpoint between Franklin and Roberta Flack would be more appropriate; Joseph had a much softer delivery than Aretha, and lacked Franklin's gospelish firepower. After a few recordings for Volt in the late '60s and early '70s (including the small R&B hits "Your Sweet Loving" and "Stop! In the Name of Love"), Joseph moved to Atlantic in 1972, where she recorded for the next few years under the supervision of Arif Mardin. During this period, she had modest success with easygoing soul-pop singles, reaching the R&B Top Ten with a cover of Wings' "My Love." Moving around to different studios and producers (including Lamont Dozier) over the course of the rest of the '70s, she made the R&B Top 20 with "What's Come Over Me" (a duet with Blue Magic) and "Hear the Words, Feel the Feeling," but never really established a strong identity, though her material was pleasant enough. She recorded through the late '80s and remains an active performer, but hasn't really been heard from since the dance-flavored "Ready for the Night" was a small R&B hit in 1984. —*Richie Unterberger*

● **The Atlantic Sessions: The Best Of Margie Joseph** / 1994 / Ichiban/Soul Classics ◆◆◆◆
All eleven of her R&B chart singles from 1972 through 1984, as well as three album tracks from her early Atlantic days. Decent if unremarkable '70s soul with a sweet pop flavor. —*Richie Unterberger*

Journey

Group, Pop/Rock
During its 14-year existence (1973–1987), Journey altered its musical approach and its personnel extensively while becoming a top touring and recording band. The only constant factor was guitarist Neal Schon (b. Feb 27, 1954), a music prodigy who had been a member of Santana in 1971-1972. The original unit, which was named in a contest on KSAN-FM in San Francisco, featured Schon, bassist Ross Valory, drummer Prairie Prince (replaced by Aynsley Dunbar), and guitarist George Tickner (who left after the first album). Another former Santana member, keyboard player and singer Gregg Rolie, joined shortly afterwards. This lineup recorded *Journey* (1974), the first of three moderate-selling jazz-rock albums given over largely to instrumentals.

By 1977, however, the group decided it needed a strong vocalist/frontman and hired Steve Perry. The results were immediately felt on the fourth album, *Infinity* (1978), which had sold a million copies by the end of the year. (By this time, Dunbar had been replaced by Steve Smith.) *Evolution* (1979) was similarly successful, as was *Departure* (after which Rolie was replaced by Jonathan Cain). After a live album, *Captured* (1981), Journey released *Escape*, which broke them through to the top ranks of pop groups by scoring three Top Ten hit singles, all ballads featuring Perry's smooth tenor: "Who's Crying Now," "Don't Stop Believin'," and "Open Arms." The album topped the charts and had sold seven million copies by 1989.

Frontiers (1983), featuring the hit "Separate Ways," was another big success, after which Perry released a successful solo album, *Street Talk* (1984). When the group got back together to make a new album, Valory and Smith were no longer in the lineup, and *Raised on Radio* (1986) was made by Schon, Perry, and Cain, who added other musicians for a tour. This, however, was the end of Journey, as Perry and Cain went off to form Bad English. —*William Ruhlmann*

Journey / 1975 / Columbia ◆◆

Look into the Future / 1976 / Columbia ◆◆

Next / 1977 / Columbia ◆◆

Infinity / 1978 / Columbia ◆◆◆
This was the first album with vocalist Steve Perry. "Wheel in the Sky" was the band's first US-charting single, followed by "Anytime" and "Lights." It was the beginning of their climb up the charts with the trademark tenor of Steve Perry. —*Donna DiChario*

○ **Evolution** / 1979 / Columbia ◆◆◆◆
Journey got major US radio airplay with "Just the Same Way," "Lovin', Touchin', Squeezin'," and "City of Angels." —*Donna DiChario*

In the Beginning / 1979 / Columbia ◆◆
Selecting the highlights from Journey's first three albums, *In the Beginning* illustrates that the band was better at pop-oriented arena-rock than attempts at jazz and art-rock that comprised their early records. —*Stephen Thomas Erlewine*

Departure / 1980 / Columbia ◆◆◆
Featuring the driving "Any Way You Want It" and the Top 40 hit "Walks like a Lady," *Departure* didn't mark a departure from Journey's successful pop/rock formula, but overall the record was a little weaker than their previous two albums. —*Stephen Thomas Erlewine*

Captured / 1981 / Columbia ◆◆◆
A live double-album, it featured many of their late-'70s hits. —*Donna DiChario*

○ **Escape** / 1981 / Columbia ◆◆◆◆
Jonathan Cain (ex-Babys keyboardist) replaced Gregg Rolie on the band's most popular album to date. On the strength of the hits "Who's Crying Now" and "Don't Stop Believin'," this album spent more than a year in the Top 20. —*Donna DiChario*

○ **Frontiers** / 1983 / Columbia ◆◆◆◆
The ballads "Faithfully" and "Send Her My Love" reap the benefits of Steve Perry's crystal-clear vocals. —*Donna DiChario*

Raised on Radio / 1986 / Columbia ◆◆◆

● **Greatest Hits** / 1988 / Columbia ◆◆◆◆
A collection of Journey's '70s and '80s radio staples, the band's best-known rockers and ballads are here, including "Open Arms," "Who's Crying Now," "Any Way You Want It," and "Separate Ways (Worlds Apart)." —*Donna DiChario*

Time 3 / Dec. 1, 1992 / Columbia ◆◆◆
A three-disc box set of Journey is too much music for most listeners, although hardcore fans will be happy to know that all of their hits and best album tracks are included here. *Time 3* is more than comprehensive, but if you buy this you will never need to own another Journey album. —*AMG*

Joy Division

Group, New Wave
The unchallenged Kings of Angst, Joy Division would ultimately be recognized as England's most important band of the immediate post-punk era. Starting out as Warsaw, the band failed to distinguish itself beyond the psychotic-looking onstage behavior of singer Ian Curtis and the handful of sides the band issued were largely ignored. All of that changed with the release of Joy Division's debut album, *Unknown Pleasures*. The music was built around Peter Hook's dominant bass lines, winding their way around brooding minor-key melodies, while Curtis established himself as a Jim Morrison-like presence, with his rigid delivery and often disturbing lyrics. The album was hailed as an immediate classic.

As difficult and gloomy as Joy Division's music appeared to be, there was also an oddly warmer and sometimes beautiful side to this group, as evidenced by the non-LP single "Atmospheres." Their upcoming recorded work was highly anticipated, but just prior to its release came the shocking news that Curtis had taken his own life. The ensuing single, "Love Will Tear Us Apart" came packaged in tombstone style graphics, and housed Joy Division's masterpiece. The group continued as New Order; only their earliest work was directly connected with Joy Division's music, before finding a voice of their own, away from the spectre of Curtis. Despite the near-hysteria after Curtis's death and the numerous tortured souls who attempted to ape the formula, Joy Division's music stands as an impressive and still-riveting achievement. —*Steve Aldrich*

☆ **Unknown Pleasures** / 1979 / Qwest ◆◆◆◆◆
Their debut is a stark, almost Gothic, masterpiece of emotional destruction and inner pain, expressed both lyrically and musically. —*John Floyd*

☆ **Closer** / 1980 / Qwest ◆◆◆◆◆
An even gloomier set, their second album was released just after Curtis's death. Guitars take a back seat to swirling layers of synthesizer, while Curtis's lyrics expand to examine the decay of not only the heart but society. —*John Floyd*

Still / 1981 / Qwest ◆◆◆
A double album, it contains nine worthwhile studio outtakes, a live version of the Velvet Underground's "Sister Ray," and ten cuts from a 1980 gig. Of interest only to hardcore fans. —*John Floyd*

★ **Substance** / 1988 / Qwest ◆◆◆◆◆
Collecting some riveting and rare material previously available only on singles and compilations, this offers a more diverse portrait of the band and works as both an introduction and a supplement to the original release. —*John Floyd*

Permanent / 1995 / ◆◆◆
Featuring selected highlights from *Unknown Pleasures* and *Closer*, *Permanent* contains some of Joy Division's best songs, but the compilation isn't as useful as *Substance*, which featured early demos and B-sides, nor is it as mesmerizing as the band's two original studio albums. Consequently, *Permanent* is not only useless for dedicated fans, it's an incomplete and misleading introduction for casual fans, even though it contains a wealth of brilliant music. —*Stephen Thomas Erlewine*

Judas Priest

Group, Heavy Metal
Judas Priest was one of the most influential heavy metal bands of the '70s, spearheading the "new wave of British heavy metal" late in the decade. Decked out in leather and chains, the band fused the gothic doom of Black Sabbath with the riffs and speed of Led Zeppelin, as well as adding a vicious two-lead guitar attack; in do-

ing so, they set the pace for much popular heavy metal from 1975 until 1985, as well as laying the groundwork for the speed and death metal of the '80s.

Formed in Birmingham, England, in 1970, the group's core members were guitarist K.K. Downing and bassist Ian Hill. Joined by Alan Atkins and drummer John Ellis, the band played their first concert in 1971. Atkins' previous band was called Judas Priest, yet the members decided it was the best name for the group. The band played numerous shows throughout 1971; during the year, Ellis was replaced by Alan Moore; by the end of the year, Chris Campbell replaced Moore. After a solid year of touring the U.K., Atkins and Campbell left the band in 1973 and were replaced by vocalist Rob Halford and drummer John Hinch. They continued touring, including a visit to Germany and the Netherlands in 1974; by the time the tour was completed, they had secured a record contract with Gull, an independent U.K. label.

Before recording their debut album, *Rocka Rolla,* Judas Priest added guitarist Glenn Tipton. They released the record in September of 1974 to almost no attention. The following year they gave a well-received performance at the Reading Festival and Hinch departed the band; he was replaced by Alan Moore. Later that year, the group released *Sad Wings of Destiny,* which earned some positive reviews. However, the lack of sales were putting the band in a dire financial situation, which was remedied by an international contract with CBS Records.

Sin After Sin (1977) was the first album released under that contract; it was recorded with Simon Phillips, who replaced Moore. The record received positive reviews and the band departed for their first American tour, with Les Binks on drums. When they returned to England, Judas Priest recorded 1978's *Stained Class,* the record that established them as international force in metal. Along with 1979's *Hell Bent for Leather* (*Killing Machine* in the U.K.), *Stained Class* began the "new wave of British heavy metal" movement. A significant number of bands adapted Priest's leather-clad image and hard, driving sound, making their music harder, faster and louder; Iron Maiden, Motorhead, and King Diamond are some of the more significant bands that appeared in their wake. Until 1982, when speed metal began to capture the attention of adolescents, Judas Priest was one of the most popular heavy metal bands in the world.

After releasing *Hell Bent for Leather,* the band recorded the live album *Unleashed in the East* (1979) in Japan; it became their first platinum album in America. Les Binks left the band in 1979; he was replaced by former Trapeze drummer Dave Holland. Their next album, 1980's *British Steel,* entered the British charts at number three, launched the hit singles "Breaking the Law" and "Living After Midnight," and was their second American platinum record; *Point of Entry,* released the following year, was nearly as successful.

At the beginning of the '80s, Judas Priest was a top concert attraction around the world, in addition to being a best-selling recording artist. Featuring the hit single "You've Got Another Thing Comin'," *Screaming for Vengeance* (1982) marked the height of their popularity, peaking at number 17 in America and selling over a million copies. Two years later, *Defenders of the Faith* nearly matched its predecessor's performance, yet metal tastes were beginning to change, as Metallica and other speed/thrash-metal groups started to grow in popularity. That shift was evident on 1986's *Turbo,* where Judas Priest seemed out of touch with current trends; nevertheless, the record sold over a million copies in America on the basis of name recognition alone. However, 1987's *Priest...Live!* was their first album since *Stained Class* not to go gold. *Ram It Down* (1988) was a return to raw metal. It sold well—going gold in the U.S.—yet it failed to break outside their core group of fans. Dave Holland left after this record and was replaced by Scott Travis for 1990's *Painkiller.*

Like *Ram It Down, Painkiller* didn't make an impact outside the band's diehard fans, yet the group was still a popular concert act. During this time, Judas Priest was sued by the parents of a Nevada teenager who claimed *Stained Class* drove their child to suicide; the band testified in court and won the case. However, the group was not as unified as it appeared in court. Rob Halford began his own thrash band, Fight, and soon left Judas Priest. The rest of the band quietly faded away. Even if the band is no longer active, the records Judas Priest made during the '70s and '80s defined an entire era of hard rock and heavy metal, and helped popularize the genre throughout the world. —*Stephen Thomas Erlewine*

Rocka Rolla / 1974 / RCA ✦✦✦

While Judas Priest was still trying to find their footing on *Rocka Rolla,* the group managed to turn in an effective, lean debut album that suggested their potential. —*Stephen Thomas Erlewine*

Sad Wings of Destiny / 1976 / RCA ✦✦✦

Vintage Judas Priest from the mid-'70s, it's an excellent example of British heavy metal coming into its own and of a band beginning to gain acceptance on both sides of the Atlantic. The album includes "The Ripper" and "Victim of Changes," the latter of which demonstrates the full vocal range of Rob Halford. —*John Book*

Sin After Sin / 1977 / Columbia ✦✦✦

Sin After Sin was Judas Priest's first album for Columbia Records and it marked a noticeable improvement in their songwriting, as well as indicating the group was beginning to develop a signature sound. —*Stephen Thomas Erlewine*

○ Stained Class / Apr. 1978 / Columbia ✦✦✦✦

Judas Priest came into its own on *Stained Class,* a lean and lethal collection of brutal riffs. Halford's lyrics were deliberately morbid—"Beyond the Realms of Death" and "Saints in Hell" are about as bleak as heavy metal gets—but he sang them with a salacious glee, and the band hammered out a series of relentless power chords. *Stained Class* sounded like nothing else in heavy metal at the time and it sowed the seeds of the death metal movement of the '80s. —*Stephen Thomas Erlewine*

The Best of Judas Priest / 1978 / RCA ✦✦✦

Released after *Stained Class, The Best of Judas Priest* is an effective sampler of their first three albums, containing most of the highlights from *Rocka Rolla, Sad Wings of Destiny,* and *Sin After Sin.* —*Stephen Thomas Erlewine*

○ Hell Bent for Leather / Mar. 1979 / Columbia ✦✦✦✦

Hell Bent for Leather (titled *Killing Machine* in the U.K.) continued the style and sound of Judas Priest's breakthrough, *Stained Class,* yet its overall tone was lighter, as anthems like "Rock Forever" and the title track vied for space with "Evil Fantasies." While the lyrics weren't quite as dark as its predecessor's, the musical attack was just as heavy and the band's songwriting hadn't slipped at all. —*Stephen Thomas Erlewine*

○ Unleashed in the East (Live In Japan) / Oct. 1979 / Columbia ✦✦✦✦

Recorded live in Japan, this was the album that helped Judas Priest finally break through in America with support from critics and radio airplay. The album is an exceptional live performance. The songs chosen are a good example of their material from the '70s. —*John Book*

● British Steel / 1980 / Columbia ✦✦✦✦

British Steel added something that *Stained Class* and *Hell Bent for Leather* were missing—melody. Halford had managed to write some strong pop hooks for the album, particularly on the driving "Breaking the Law" and "Living After Midnight." Instead of diluting the group's power, the melodic hooks made them more forceful, arguably making *British Steel* their finest moment. —*Stephen Thomas Erlewine*

Point of Entry / 1981 / Columbia ✦✦✦

Point of Entry was another major-league success for Judas Priest. With well-written songs, solid musicianship from the entire band and powerful vocals from Rob Halford, Judas Priest helped define heavy metal in the '80s. Included is "Heading out to the Highway," "Hot Rockin'," and "Don't Go." —*John Book*

○ Screaming for Vengeance / 1982 / Columbia ✦✦✦✦

Screaming for Vengeance was Judas Priest's most successful album, featuring the hit single "You've Got Another Thing Comin'." While the group had backed away from the blitzkrieg attack of their late-'70s albums, they had increased the volume, turning in a set of thundering, heavy riffs that managed to stay melodic and catchy. The result was one of the band's finest albums; along with *British Steel,* it is their most accessible and memorable work. —*Stephen Thomas Erlewine*

Defenders of the Faith / 1984 / Columbia ✦✦✦

Defenders of the Faith was just as heavy as *Screaming for Vengeance,* but it lacked the well-constructed songs that made the previous record so impressive. Nevertheless, Judas Priest sounds tight and powerful throughout the record, which is one of the reasons why the album was another platinum success for the band. —*Stephen Thomas Erlewine*

Turbo / 1986 / Columbia ✦✦✦
Lacking the overwhelming power and heaviness of Judas Priest's two previous albums, *Turbo* was a streamlined collection that emphasized the group's pop leanings. However, the group's songs weren't quite as well written as their earlier material, making the record a muddled, unfocused affair. —*Stephen Thomas Erlewine*

Priest . . . Live! / 1987 / Columbia ✦✦
Judas Priest's first live album, *Unleashed in the East*, was a powerhouse but *Priest . . . Live!* was a sad, lackluster document of an aging heavy metal band desperately trying to hold on to their glory days. No matter how hard they tried, the group could not hide the fact that their power was declining rapidly. —*Stephen Thomas Erlewine*

Ram It Down / 1988 / Columbia ✦✦
Ram It Down recaptured some of the force of *British Steel* and *Screaming for Vengeance*, yet Judas Priest's songwriting was the weakest since *Sin After Sin*. Even though the guitars were as bracing as anything on *Defenders of the Faith* and the group performed with conviction, they could not save the album from mediocrity. —*Stephen Thomas Erlewine*

Painkiller / 1990 / Columbia ✦✦
Painkiller was a marginal improvement over the disheartening *Ram It Down*, featuring a tighter selection of songs and a menacing performance by the band. Nevertheless, the material wasn't up to Judas Priest's standards and the group seemed to have run out of things to say. A year after its release, Rob Halford left the band and the group quietly disappeared. —*Stephen Thomas Erlewine*

● **Metal Works '73–'93** / 1993 / Columbia ✦✦✦✦
Over two discs, *Metal Works '73–'93* winds its way through Judas Priest's 20-year career, hitting most of the high points as well as the low points and somehow managing to overlook seven of their eleven UK hits. Still, there isn't a better place to get acquainted with the band, which really was one of the most important metal acts of the late '70s and early '80s. —*AMG*

Phil Judd

New Wave
A founding member and early creative force behind New Zealand's Split Enz, Phil Judd quickly became disillusioned with the music industry and dropped out of the band in 1976. After rejoining Split Enz and leaving again, he formed his own three-piece band, the Swingers, who had some minor success in their homeland but fell apart by the early '80s. Judd released his first and only solo album in 1982, *Private Lives* (edited down to *The Swinger* EP in the U.S.). It was virtually ignored and Judd changed directions, focusing more on composing film music and pursuing art. In 1986, he joined with former Split Enz bandmates, Nigel Griggs and Noel Crombie along with guitarist Michael Den Elzen, to form Schnell Fenster. After two albums, the group broke up. Judd has since returned to film music and reportedly has some future solo projects in the works. Despite a lack of real commercial success, Judd's eccentric approach to pop music and skewed outlook have consistently provided (for those who stumble onto it) a welcome break from the mainstream. —*Chris Woodstra*

The Swinger / 1983 / MCA ✦✦✦
A six-song EP drawn from the Australian *Private Lives* LP. *The Swinger* picks up where Judd's previous band, The Swingers, left off. Quirky pop songs with slightly skewed subject matter are the focus but with a more radio-ready production. Unfortunately overlooked, this is his only solo work to date. —*Chris Woodstra*

● **Private Lives** / 1983 / Mushroom ✦✦✦✦
Sadly Judd's only full-length album, *Private Lives* never saw release outside of Australia/New Zealand but fans of his work with Swingers or Split Enz should seek this one out rather than the inferior, edited version—*The Swinger*. —*Chris Woodstra*

Jules & the Polar Bears

Group, Rock & Roll
After the demise of the Funky Kings, singer/songwriter Jules Shear formed his own band consisting of Stephen Hague (keyboards and, later, a noted producer), Richard Bredice (guitar), David White (bass), and David Beebe (drums). They were signed to Columbia Records in 1978 solely on the basis of Shear's demos—at the time, the band had never played live together. They recorded their first LP, *Got No Breeding*, in 1978 which quickly found critical acclaim, drawing favorable comparisons to Jackson Browne,

the Kinks, Bob Dylan, and Bruce Springsteen. Unfortunately, it failed to sell when Columbia tried to lump the band in with its new wave promotion. 1979's *Fenetiks*, another fine effort, went virtually unnoticed as well. A third LP, *Bad for Business*, was recorded, but Columbia decided to pass on it and the band folded. Shear moved on to a distinguished, though commercially unsuccessful, solo career, and Hague focused on production. The albums, especially *Got No Breeding*, remain cult favorites. —*Chris Woodstra*

● **Got No Breeding** / 1978 / Columbia ✦✦✦✦
Though it is packed with memorable hooks and Jules Shear's subtle twist-of-phrase, *Got No Breeding* was virtually ignored upon release, due in part to Columbia Records mis-marketing the band as part of the new wave. The Polar Bears were, in reality, just a good, hard-working rock band jamming with a sometimes over-enthusiastic Shear. The songs are among Shear's finest and the album is one of his most consistently enjoyable. —*Chris Woodstra*

Phonetics/Fenetiks / 1979 / Columbia ✦✦✦
The second Polar Bears album follows much of the same formula as *Got No Breeding*, with less memorable results. The band still rocks in places but the overall production is slicker and a little more synthesizer heavy. Shear's songwriting is top-notch ranging from the pure pop of "Good Reason" to the beautiful ballad "Real Enough to Love." His delivery seems more restrained this time around. —*Chris Woodstra*

Don Julian & the Meadowlarks

Group, R&B, Doo-Wop
An integrated group, formed at Los Angeles's Fremont High School, that cut some fine doo-wop during the mid '50s. With Julian's pleasingly cool lead vocals featured, the Meadowlarks recorded for RPM and Dootone, scoring a regional seller for the latter in 1955 with the smooth ballad "Heaven and Paradise." The Meadowlarks could rock too—"I Got Tore Up," also on Dootone, is a driving jump with rolling piano behind the quartet. As lead singer of the Larks, Julian hit the charts with "The Jerk" a decade later. —*Bill Dahl*

● **Golden Classics** / Collectables ✦✦✦✦
Mid-'50s Los Angeles doo-wop, with Julian supplying the floating leads. —*Bill Dahl*

Jungle Brothers

Group, Rap
An endlessly funky New York trio, Jungle Brothers have collaborated with like minds such as De La Soul and A Tribe Called Quest. Their love of James Brown goes deeper than mere sampling.
 Although the Jungle Brothers have received an enormous amount of critical acclaim, they have yet been able to score a commercial success as large as either De La or Tribe. —*John Floyd*

● **Straight out the Jungle** / 1988 / Warlock ✦✦✦✦
The trio's debut is powered by muscular funk riffs underpinned by an Afrocentric sensibility and a sharp sense of humor. —*John Floyd*

○ **Done by the Forces of Nature** / 1989 / Warner Brothers ✦✦✦✦
By injecting some vocal delicacy and some clever samples into their moderately militant message, they made a second album that elaborates on their own winning formula. —*John Floyd*

J. Beez Wit the Remedy / Jun. 22, 1993 / Warner Brothers ✦✦✦
Nearly four years after *Done by the Forces of Nature*, the Jungle Brothers return with a hazy, funky album, filled with their brand of literate hip-hop. Although they've made some stylistic progressions since the last record, it wasn't enough to be a completely groundbreaking release, nor was it commericial enough to break them out of their critically acclaimed/cult status. Instead, it was another solid, inventive album that didn't receive the attention it deserved. —*Stephen Thomas Erlewine*

Mickey Jupp

Rock & Roll
Like Dave Edmunds, guitarist/pianist/vocalist Mickey Jupp was a champion of traditional rock & roll during the late '70s, a time when it had been all but discarded. Unlike Edmunds, Jupp wrote the majority of his own material, which updated '50s rock & roll with a tongue-in-cheek irony.
 Jupp began his career with the Essex-based British R&B group

the Orioles in the early '60s. The band earned a devoted local following in the early '60s, yet they were never had the opportunity to record. The Orioles broke up late in 1965, after Jupp was arrested for not making alimony payments to his wife. Three years later, he returned to music, forming Legend, who laid the groundwork for the English pub rock of the early '70s. Following the release of their third album in 1971, Legend disbanded and Jupp took another lengthy break from music. When he was coaxed back into performing in 1975 by Lee Brileaux, the lead singer of Dr. Feelgood, pub rock was in its last days, yet Jupp was well-respected in the scene, since both Ducks Deluxe and Dr. Feelgood had recorded versions of his songs ("Cheque Book" and "Down at the Doctors," respectively).

Jupp released his first solo single, "Nature's Radio," on Arista Records in 1978. The single led to a contract with Stiff Records, who released the "Old Rock N Roller" single and the *Juppanese* album in 1978; the bulk of *Juppanese* was recorded with Rockpile and produced by Nick Lowe. Released the same year as his debut, *Mickey Jupp's Legend* featured material from his previous band. Following the release of *Juppanese*, Jupp joined Stiff's Rail Tour, although he left the lineup before it hit the U.S. because he was afraid of flying. Shortly afterward, he left Stiff Records and signed with Chrysalis in 1979. The same year he released *Long Distance Romancer*, which was produced by for 10cc members Kevin Godley and Lol Creme; like *Juppanese*, it failed to gain a large audience. Jupp moved over to A&M Records in 1982, releasing *Some People Can't Dance*. After releasing one more record on A&M, 1983's *Shampoo Haircut and Shave*, he was dropped from the label. Jupp spent the rest of the '80s and '90s touring the U.K., releasing the occassional album on independent labels. — *Stephen Thomas Erlewine*

● **Juppanese** / 1978 / Stiff ✦✦✦✦

Before he released his first solo album in 1978, Mickey Jupp's reputation as a songwriter had begun to grow, as pub rockers like Dr.

Feelgood and Ducks Deluxe were covering his compositions. As a performer, Jupp didn't fare as well. The main problem with *Juppanese*, his first solo album, is his lifeless vocals. The first half of *Juppanese* was recorded with Rockpile, the rock & roll group fronted by guitarist Dave Edmunds and bassist Nick Lowe. Because Jupp's strength is standard three-chord rock & roll, the first side of the album works the best; while it never captures the joyous energy of Rockpile's best moments, it is considerably tighter and rawer than the slick second side, where Jupp's non-descript voice struggles to be heard amid the studio professionalism. Even though it features several of Jupp's finest songs, including "You'll Never Get Me up in One of Those" and "Old Rock 'n' Roller," *Juppanese* doesn't include "Switchboard Susan," arguably his best song. Rockpile recorded the backing track for the album, yet Jupp refused to sing on it. Nick Lowe kept the tape, recording his own vocals for the song; his version is included on his 1979 album *Labour of Lust.* — *Stephen Thomas Erlewine*

Long Distance Romancer / 1979 / Chrysalis ✦✦✦

Long Distance Romancer, Jupp's first release for Chrysalis Records, continued the polished rock & roll of the second half of *Juppanese*, except it bettered it. Unlike Gary Brooker, producers Godley and Creme could exploit the slick, synth-based sound that Jupp was beginning to mine. However, the highly produced sound doesn't mesh with Jupp's main strength—direct, simple rock & roll. Instead of being powered by a driving beat, "Switchboard Susan" winds up sinking in the layers of keyboards and processed guitars. Yet the production does manage to save slight songs like "You Made a Fool out of Me," creating an album of pleasant pop/rock that never manges to really sink in. — *Stephen Thomas Erlewine*

Some People Can't Dance / 1982 / A&M ✦✦✦

Shampoo Haircut and Shave / 1983 / CBS ✦✦

X / 1988 / Waterfront ✦✦

K

Ernie K-Doe

New Orleans R&B
New Orleans vocalist Ernest Kador, Jr., had one unforgettable R&B hit in 1961, aided by Benny Spellman's authoritative bass vocal. "Mother-In-Law" topped the charts for five weeks, and was recorded for Minit. K-Doe originally sang with the Blue Diamonds, who recorded for Savoy in 1954. Their ranks included Huey "Piano" Smith, Billy Tate, Frank Fields and Earl Palmer. "Te-Ta-Te-Ta-Ta" did reasonably well as a follow-up single, peaking at number 21. It would be six years before K-Doe would get another chart hit; the singles "Later for Tomorrow" and a remake of "Until the Real Thing Comes Along" each gained only marginal success for Duke in 1967, his last releases to make any national noise. — *Ron Wynn*

● **Burn! K-Doe, Burn!** / 1989 / Charly ◆◆◆◆

Henry Kaiser

b. Sep. 11, 1952
Art-Rock/Progressive-Rock, Experimental
Guitarist Henry Kaiser is a prolific member of the San Francisco Bay Area music scene, as well as being a globally recognized leader of the "second generation" free improvisers who came of age in the '70s. His earliest musical inspiration came from the spiky sounds of English improvising guitarist Derek Bailey and the many guitarists in Captain Beefheart's Magic Band; later on Kaiser absorbed the subtle string textures of the American blues stylists and traditional music of Asia, particularly India, Korea, and Vietnam. His initial recordings documented solo projects and spontaneous groupings with other energetic improvisers like Fred Frith, the ROVA Saxophone Quartet, pianist Greg Goodman, and vocalist Diamanda Galas. Kaiser's restless creativity unearthed many new and unconventional electric guitar techniques during these years, and he combined these innovations with a strong sense of logic and concise development, often aided by sophisticated sound-processing devices. Recently Kaiser's projects have tended toward the rock sound of the '60s and '70s, with a special fascination for the music of the Grateful Dead. But he has simultaneously explored American folk along with the folk music of Vietnam and Madagascar. — *Myles Boisen*

○ **Aloha: Studio Solo** / 1981 / Metalanguage ◆◆◆◆
This two-fer was his first major statement of purpose as a multi-faceted soloist, leader, and producer. — *Myles Boisen*

● **With Enemies Like These, Who Needs Friends?** / 1987 / SST ◆◆◆◆
This is a CD compilation of Henry Kaiser and Fred Frith's guitar duo records. *With Enemies like These, Who Needs Friends?* is a masterpiece of studio improvisation and innovative guitar techniques. — *Myles Boisen*

○ **Devil in the Drain** / Oct. 1987 / SST ◆◆◆◆
His most fully realized instrumental solo work has fantastic structures from various creative directions on guitar and synclavier. — *Myles Boisen*

Re-Marrying for Money / 1988 / SST ◆◆◆
Improvised rock with San Francisco's Stench Brothers on bass and drums, it's an encyclopedia of twisted guitar playing. — *Myles Boisen*

○ **Those Who Know History Are Doomed to Repeat It** / May 1989 / SST ◆◆◆◆
Eclecticism reigns supreme here, on his first full exploration of pop music covers and Grateful Dead-style jamming. — *Myles Boisen*

Heart's Desire / 1990 / Reckless ◆◆◆
A live tribute to the psychedelic era, the versatile Henry Kaiser Band rocks nonstop. — *Myles Boisen*

○ **Hope You Like Our New Direction** / 1991 / Reckless ◆◆◆◆
From Buddy Holly to Beefheart, Virginia to Viet Nam, this musical tour takes you to every corner of Kaiser's wonderful world with lots of surprises. — *Myles Boisen*

○ **The A World out of Time: Henry Kaiser and David Lindley in Madagascar** / Jul. 20, 1992 / Shanachie ◆◆◆◆
A series of five CDs highlighting the best musicians of Madagascar collaborating here with avant-garde rock musicians Kaiser and Lindley. Features Madagascar's rising pop star Rossy and 72-year-old flute master Rakotofrah. — *Bob Tarte*

○ **Lemon Fish Tweezer: A History of Henry Kaiser's Solo Guitar Improvisations (1973-1991)** / Aug. 24, 1992 / Cuneiform ◆◆◆◆
This is a retrospective of Henry's boundary-smashing solo projects from the mid-'70s on. — *Myles Boisen*

Kajagoogoo

Group, New Wave
Kajagoogoo's light synth-pop and pretty, photogenic look made the group an instant sensation in the early days of MTV. Led by vocalist Limahl (born Chris Hamill), the group also featured Steve Askew (guitar), Nick Beggs (vocals, bass), and Stuart Crawford (vocals, synthesizer). Produced by Duran Duran's Nick Rhodes, Kajagoogoo's debut single "Too Shy" hit number one in the U.K. in early 1983; it peaked at number five in the U.S. As "Too Shy" and the following album *White Feathers* proved, the band may have shared some similarities with Duran Duran and Naked Eyes—they were pretty and they played immediately accessible, polished pop—yet Kajagoogoo was essentially a synth-pop variation of a bubblegum group. Like a bubblegum group, they were destined to have only one big hit; "Ooh to Be Ah" and "Hang on Now" both were Top 15 U.K. hits, yet neither made an impact in the U.S. At the end of the 1983, Limahl left for a solo career. Kajagoogoo continued with Nick Beggs as the lead vocalist, releasing *Islands* in 1984; it disappeared from the charts quickly. Meanwhile, Limahl scored a hit with the theme song from *The Neverending Story*. Perhaps in an attempt to gain some credibility, the group shortened their name to Kaja and released *Crazy People's Right to Speak*. It was a sales disaster and the band broke up the following year. Limahl continued to record, albeit without much chart success; eventually, his records were not released in either the U.S. or the U.K.—his last album, 1992's *Love Is Blind*, was only released in Germany. — *Stephen Thomas Erlewine*

○ **White Feathers** / 1983 / EMI ◆◆◆◆

Islands / 1984 / EMI ◆◆◆

● **Too Shy: the Singles . . . & More** / Sep. 7, 1993 / EMI ◆◆◆◆
As this collection proves, Kajagoogoo was a one-hit wonder. Only "Too Shy" stands out amidst the slick, bouncy new wave synth-pop that dominates the compilation, which covers material from all of the band's albums, as well as lead singer Limahl's solo career. Most of the music on the rest of the collection is pleasant, but

none of it is memorable. However, "Too Shy" is one of the best pop singles of the new wave era, driven by layers of bubbly synths, an inanely catchy chorus and Limahl's thin, airy vocals. —*Stephen Thomas Erlewine*

Kaleidoscope [U.K.]

Group, Psychedelic

No relation to the far better known American Kaleidoscope, though this British group was also psychedelic, and was active at almost exactly the same time in the late '60s. Highly esteemed by some collectors, Kaleidoscope epitomized certain of the more precious traits of British psychedelia with their fairytale lyrics and gentle, swirling folky sound. At times they sound like a far more melodic and accessible Incredible String Band. Their folky ballads have aged best, and although there's some period charm to be found throughout their two albums, it's all a bit too cloying to rank among the finest unknown psychedelia. Although they had a solid underground reputation in Britain, they never found wide success, and evolved into a similar group, Fairfield Parlour, by the end of the '60s. —*Richie Unterberger*

● **Tangerine Dream** / 1967 / Fontana ◆◆◆◆
Probably has the edge as the best of their two albums, but not by much. Includes several of their best songs: "Flight From Ashiya," "Dive Into Yesterday," "The Murder Of Lewis Tollani," and especially the fragile ballad "Please Excuse My Face." —*Richie Unterberger*

Faintly Blowing / 1969 / Fontana ◆◆◆
There's really not much difference between this and their debut album: if you like one, you'll like the other. It's perhaps more fully produced than their maiden effort, the standout being the ballad "Poem," which vies with "Please Excuse My Face" as their best composition. —*Richie Unterberger*

Kaleidoscope

Group, Psychedelic, Folk-Rock

Kaleidoscope were arguably the most eclectic band of the psychedelic era, weaving together folk, blues, Middle Eastern, and acid more often and more seamlessly than any other musicians. The California group was formed around the nucleus of multi-instrumentalists David Lindley and Chris Darrow in the mid-'60s. Adding fiddle, banjo, and various exotic string instruments to the traditional rock lineup, Kaleidoscope complemented their experimental sounds with taut and witty (if lyrically eccentric) songwriting. With the exception of their mawkish forays into old-timey music, their work holds up well. Their first three albums were their best, highlighted by the lengthy tracks "Taxim" and "Seven-Ate Sweet," which are groundbreaking fusions of Middle Eastern music and rock. —*Richie Unterberger*

○ **Side Trips** / 1967 / Epic ◆◆◆◆

Rampe Rampe / 1984 / Edsel ◆◆◆
Focusing on the more experimental and Middle Eastern-influenced side of the band, this five-track LP includes all three of their groundbreaking, ten-minute-plus jams—"Taxim," "Seven-Ate Sweet," and "Beacon from Mars"—as well as a couple of nifty shorter tunes that were left off the *Bacon from Mars* compilation. —*Richie Unterberger*

Bacon from Mars / 1986 / Epic ◆◆◆
The most intelligent compilation of their more accessible songs. Includes highlights of their first three albums, three tracks from non-LP singles, and a lengthy history of the band. —*Richie Unterberger*

● **Egyptian Candy (A Collection)** / 1991 / Epic ◆◆◆◆

Big Daddy Kane

Rap

Brooklyn-ite Big Daddy Kane (born Antonio Hardy, KANE is an acronym for King Asiatic Nobody's Equal) has nicely been able to balance his image as the ultimate hipster with the requisite solemnity and air of indignation and anger necessary to creditably deliver messages of Afrocentric awareness and Muslim reverence. He's done alternately inspirational, prophetical, ridiculous, and scandalous raps over his career, and has also managed to include duets with the maestro of love Barry White and legendary comedian Rudy Ray Moore, aka Dolemite, who laid waste to Kane in a dozens (insult-swapping) classic.

Big Daddy Kane has been a high profile figure the past couple

of years. Not only has he appeared in such films as *Posse* and *Gunmen*, but he also posed in Madonna's controversial photo book *Sex*, and issued a defiant disc *Looks like a Job for Big Daddy Kane* that offered no apologies for past actions and ridiculed unnamed individuals he claimed were fronting as gangsters.—*Ron Wynn*

● **Long Live the Kane** / 1988 / Cold Chillin' ◆◆◆◆
Kane's debut was his hottest. —*Dan Heilman*

○ **It's a Big Daddy Thing** / 1989 / Cold Chillin' ◆◆◆◆
A good application of funk sentiments and influence within a hip-hop context, particularly "I Get the Job Done." But Kane also veers into homophobic and sexist territory, notably on "Pimpin' Ain't Easy." —*Ron Wynn*

Taste of Chocolate / 1990 / Cold Chillin' ◆◆◆
Worth the purchase price for the exchange between Kane and Rudy Ray Moore (*Dolemite*), longtime champion of the underground Black comic circuit. Moore lays waste to Kane with relish. —*Ron Wynn*

Prince of Darkness / 1991 / Cold Chillin' ◆◆
More soul-based than his previous records, Kane not only has a slightly changed musical style on *Prince of Darkness*, but changes his rapping style to suit the sound, bringing a faster, twisting wordplay to his rhymes. When the change in style works—as in "I'm Not Ashamed"—the record is deadly, but when it doesn't, it's deadly boring; unfortunately, most of the record doesn't work. —*Stephen Thomas Erlewine*

Looks Like a Job for Big Daddy / May 25, 1993 / Cold Chillin' ◆◆◆
Looks Like a Job for Big Daddy Kane was a solid comeback record by Kane, bringing him back to the harder beats of his earlier albums. His rapping hasn't lost its spark, and the music is sparse and funky. However, it didn't have the same flair or innovation of *Long Live the Kane* and *It's a Big Daddy Thing*, and it fell off the charts quickly. —*Stephen Thomas Erlewine*

Kansas

Group, Art-Rock/Progressive-Rock, Pop/Rock

Popular prog-rock group from Topeka, whose ranks included Steve Walsh (vocals, keyboards), Kerry Livgren (guitar, keyboards), Rich Williams (guitar), Robby Steinhardt (violin), Dave Hope (bass), and Phil Ehart on percussion. Kansas' music leaned more towards progressive arena rock than the artsier, more symphonic music of other groups like Yes and King Crimson. Hits like "Carry On Wayward Son" and "Point of Know Return" cemented that reputation and resulted in multiplatinum success in the late '70s. Walsh, unhappy with the more commercial direction the band had taken, left the group in the early '80s and recorded a solo album. He was replaced by John Elefante. Without Walsh, their primary songwriter, the band lost direction and broke up in 1983. Livgren subsequently became a contemporary Christian artist. Walsh, Williams, and Ehart re-formed in 1986 with ex-Dixie Dregs guitarist Steve Morse and bassist Billy Greer joining the band. —*Steve Huey*

○ **Kansas** / 1974 / Kirshner ◆◆◆◆
This encouraging debut reflected an infatuation with English art-rock. —*Rick Clark*

○ **Song for America** / 1975 / Kirshner ◆◆◆◆
The title cut comprises some beautiful passages. While they never really attained the intensity of art-rock bands like Yes, this album is possibly Kansas's most fully realized artistic effort at testing the possibilities of the genre. —*Rick Clark*

○ **Leftoverture** / 1976 / Kirshner ◆◆◆◆
The rock hit "Carry on Wayward Son" catapulted Kansas (and this album) into the big arena rock circuit. —*Rick Clark*

Point of Know Return / 1977 / Kirshner ◆◆◆

Vinyl Confessions / 1982 / Kirshner ◆◆◆

● **The Best of Kansas** / 1984 / Epic ◆◆◆◆
It contains the essential rock radio hits "Dust in the Wind," "Carry on Wayward Son," and "Point of Know Return," as well as improved remastering from the original tapes. —*Rick Clark*

Power / 1986 / MCA ◆◆◆

In the Spirit of Things / 1988 / MCA ◆◆◆
Pink Floyd-producer Bob Ezrin gives Kansas a sonically impressive sound. Fans of orchestral mainstream rock will like this, particularly "One Man, One Heart," "One Big Sky," "House on Fire,"

and "The Preacher." Ex-Dixie Dregs guitarist Steve Morse and vocalist Steve Walsh shine. —*Rick Clark*

○ **Box Set** / 1994 / Epic ✦✦✦✦

Kashif
Soul, R&B
Onetime B.T. Express member Kashif had an impressive run as an Urban Contemporary performer and songwriter. He recorded for Arista from 1983 to 1986, and his singles "I Just Gotta Have You (Lover Turn Me On)," "Baby Don't Break Your Baby's Heart," and "Love the One I'm with (A Lot of Love)" all made the R&B Top Ten, the latter being a Capitol duet with Melba Moore. He moved to Capitol in 1986, then returned to Arista in 1987. His final hit was "Love Me All Over," another duet, this time with Meli'sa Morgan. This made it to number two R&B in 1987. Kashif took a hiatus from recording in 1990, devoting his time to holding seminars and conducting classes for aspiring performers about the music business. —*Ron Wynn*

Kashif / 1983 / Arista ✦✦✦
Kashif made his debut as an album artist on Arista with this release, which included some huge hits in "Stone Love," "Help Yourself to My Love," and "I Just Gotta Have You (Lover Turn Me On)." For a time, Kashif ruled the urban contemporary airwaves as completely as Luther Vandross does today, although he never made records that had the power or authority of Vandross', or for that matter, even a Freddie Jackson or Keith Washington. His songs were subdued, introspective, and slick. —*Ron Wynn*

Send Me Your Love / 1984 / Arista ✦✦✦
Kashif enjoyed another big hit album in the mid-'80s with this second Arista album that featured Al Jarreau on the cut "Edgartown Groove," and landed him one Top 10 and another Top 30 R&B hit. It was his best release from a performance standpoint; his vocals had more vigor and spirit than at any time before or since, and he toned down the production, varied the arrangements, and created a much more interesting and multi-faceted presentation than anticipated. —*Ron Wynn*

Condition of the Heart / 1985 / Arista ✦✦
Keyboardist and producer Kashif was a dominant figure in the mid- and late '80s. Besides this album of mild urban contemporary love songs, sentimental ballads, and occasional synthesized uptempo tracks, Kashif produced and wrote songs for Whitney Houston and sang on a Kenny G. album. This wasn't his most successful album, but it continued his run of chart hits and epitomized the slick, glossy brand of vocals that were in vogue for much of the '80s. —*Ron Wynn*

Love Changes / 1987 / Arista ✦✦
Kashif went the duet route on this late '80s release, working with both Dionne Warwick and Meli'sa Morgan and doing relatively well both times. Each duet cracked the R&B Top 20, and the collaboration with Morgan gave him a number two single. The album was otherwise as slick and overproduced as ever, and his singing went back to the subdued patterns of earlier works. But Kashif was still rolling along at the time, producing and writing other hits for Giorge Pettus and Johnny Kemp. Only a few months later, things changed radically in urban contemporary and R&B music, and Kashif's sound and style would quickly become passe. —*Ron Wynn*

● **Best** / 1994 / ✦✦✦✦

Katrina & the Waves
Group, New Wave, Pop/Rock
Led by ex-Soft Boys guitarist Kimberly Rew, Katrina and the Waves effortlessly evoked the irresistibly catchy guitar-pop of the mid-'60s with their first three albums in the early '80s. Not only could Rew write songs that were instantly memorable ("Goin' Down to Liverpool" and "Walking on Sunshine") but the band had a dynamic lead singer with the Kansas-born Katrina Leskanich, who could sound sweet or tough according to the material. After scoring a hit single with "Walking on Sunshine" in 1985, the band began to add a little bit of soul on their next album, *Waves*. While the experimentation was flawed, what really hurt the record was the fact that Rew only contributed two songs. *Waves* marked a downturn in their commercial fortunes, which was fixed with 1989's *Break of Hearts*, when the band turned into indistinguishable commercial hacks; they were rewarded with a Top 20 hit, "That's the Way." However, it marked the end of the road for the group, not only artistically, but literally, too—they disbanded a few

years later, without releasing another album. —*Stephen Thomas Erlewine*

Walking on Sunshine / 1983 / Attic ✦✦✦

Katrina and the Waves 2 / 1984 / Attic ✦✦✦

Waves / 1985 / Capitol ✦✦✦

Break of Hearts / 1989 / SBK ✦✦

● **Anthology** / 1995 / One Way ✦✦✦✦
Like most One Way collections, *Anthology* doesn't offer a comprehensive overview of the group. Instead, it resequences Katrina and the Waves' first American album and adds a couple of hits and album tracks from their second. While the compilation is haphazard, it does contain most of the group's best material, making it a worthwhile purchase. —*Stephen Thomas Erlewine*

Jorma Kaukonen
b. Dec. 23, 1940
Rock & Roll, Folk-Rock
Guitarist, singer, and songwriter Jorma Kaukonen was born and grew up in Washington, D.C., where he first turned to the guitar. He lived in the San Francisco Bay Area in the early '60s, playing backup to singer Janis Joplin in local clubs. In 1965, Kaukonen became a founding member of Jefferson Airplane, which soared to fame in 1967. Though Kaukonen's songs and vocals were not prominently featured in the band, his distinctive guitar-playing was crucial to its sound.

With bassist Jack Casady, Kaukonen formed a spinoff duo from the group in 1970 called Hot Tuna, and this became his primary musical vehicle after Jefferson Airplane split in 1973. Hot Tuna recorded a series of albums on which Kaukonen sang and played guitar through 1978. After that, Kaukonen worked as a soloist and with such groups as Vital Parts (1980), and he recorded occasional albums. Kaukonen reunited with Casady in Hot Tuna during the '80s, and both participated in the 1989 reunion of Jefferson Airplane. A Hot Tuna reunion album appeared the following year. —*William Ruhlmann*

● **Quah** / 1974 / Relix ✦✦✦✦
Brilliant acoustic album, with Tom Hobson, of Kaukonen originals and folk blues standards, the highlights being the beautiful "Genesis" and the Rev. Gary Davis's "I'll Be All Right" and "I Am the Light of This World." —*William Ruhlmann*

Jorma / 1979 / RCA ✦✦✦
Jorma Kaukonen's second solo album was released the year after Hot Tuna broke up and therefore represents his first major statement as a solo artist after nearly 15 years of group work. It was a real solo album, too, featuring Kaukonen alone on various overdubbed guitars, and the music contained his usual mix of folk and blues themes. But it was a big comedown from *Quah*, and the acoustic solo album held made during Hot Tuna's tenure, and not even as good as some of Kaukonen's work with Tuna, the band he'd left to make it. —*William Ruhlmann*

Barbecue King / 1980 / RCA ✦✦✦
One year after launching himself as a solo artist with *Jorma*, Kaukonen returned in a group context, co-billing this record to the rhythm section of drummer John Stench and bassist Denny De-Gorio under the name Vital Parts. The result was far more of a pop-rock album than anything Kaukonen had done before, with faster tempos and tighter arrangements. There was even a cover of "Love Is Strange." But no one seems to have told RCA that they had a potentially commercial album on their hands, and when this album failed to sell, Kaukonen and the label parted company. He would not return to the majors until the Jefferson Airplane reunion in 1989. —*William Ruhlmann*

○ **Too Hot to Handle** / 1985 / Relix ✦✦✦✦
On his first Relix album, *Magic*, Kaukonen was captured live reprising some of his best-known songs on acoustic guitar. On this followup acoustic release, he turns in a studio collection including some new songs and a few more remakes, among them "Death Don't Have No Mercy." The result doesn't match his solo acoustic debut, which Relix would license from RCA and reissue in 1987, but it reconfirms his guitar abilities, and new songs such as "Too Many Years" are welcome additions to his repertoire. —*William Ruhlmann*

Magic / 1985 / Relix ✦✦✦
Acoustic live album including such folk/blues favorites as "Walkin' Blues" and Kaukonen's Jefferson Airplane tunes "Embryonic Journey" and "Good Shepherd." —*William Ruhlmann*

K.C. & the Sunshine Band

Group, Disco

In the early '70s, two White men, Harry "KC" Casey (b Jan 31, 1951) and Richard Finch (b. Jan 25, 1954), created a racially integrated disco band that based its music on various soul styles. They became one of the most commercially successful groups of the early disco era. KC & the Sunshine Band's disco was funky enough to be a staple in the clubs, while remaining melodic and sweet enough to be huge pop hits. The group continued to have hits until the early '80s; their last hit single, "Give It Up," was credited to KC in the US. *—Bil Carpenter*

● **The Best of KC & The Sunshine Band** / 1990 / Rhino ✦✦✦✦
A percussive mix of steel drums, whistle flutes, and funky group harmonies, this most soulful disco set includes all of their hits—"Get Down Tonight," "Please Don't Go," "That's the Way (I Like It)," "I'm Your Boogie Man," "(Shake, Shake, Shake) Shake Your Booty," and KC's solo hit, "Give It Up." *—Bil Carpenter*

Paul Kelly & the Messengers

Group, Rock & Roll, Folk-Rock

Kelly is an Australian songwriter whose eye for detail and ability to transfer the listener into his world rivals Graham Parker's and (sometimes) Elvis Costello's. Kelly's best songs contain the episodic character of Bob Dylan's but with the rocking thwack of John Mellencamp and the occasional flash of the writer Raymond Carver. (Kelly's *So Much Water, So Close to Home* album takes its title and the inspiration for its title track from a Carver short story.) *—John Floyd & Kit Kiefer*

Stand on the Positive Side / 1977 / Warner Brothers ✦✦✦

Talk / 1981 / Mushroom ✦✦

Manila / 1982 / Mushroom ✦✦✦

Post / 1985 / White Label ✦✦

● **Gossip** / 1987 / A&M ✦✦✦✦
Their US debut offers 17 sublime examples of Kelly's compassionate and witty songwriting as well as the group's flexibility and charm. Highlights include "White Train," the gentle "Renwick Bells," "Darling It Hurts," and "Don't Ever Harm the Messenger." *—John Floyd & Kit Kiefer*

○ **Under the Sun** / 1988 / A&M ✦✦✦✦
This covers a lot of stylistic ground, including rockabilly, country, and punk throwbacks. A beautifully arranged set runs the gamut from Hoodoo Gurus-style raveups ("Dumb Things") to country-rock shuffles ("To Her Door") and pointed social criticism ("Bicentennial"), not to mention the golden title track. *—John Floyd & Kit Kiefer*

So Much Water, So Close to Home / 1989 / A&M ✦✦✦
A somewhat light release, but Kelly's writing continues to dazzle with a song written from the perspective of an abused wife and a touching interpretation of a Raymond Carver story. *—John Floyd*

○ **Comedy** / 1992 / Doctor Dream ✦✦✦✦
A diverse, startling record full of everything from folky social protest ("From Little Things Big Things Grow") to gorgeous pop ("Brighter"), it features a dazzling out-of-left-field homage to Jimmie Dale Gilmore's "Dallas from a DC-9" ("Sydney from a 727"). *—Kit Kiefer*

Wanted Man / 1994 / Vanguard ✦✦✦

R. Kelly

Group, Urban

Urban R&B producer/vocalist/multi-instrumentalist/songwriter R. Kelly and his supporting band Public Announcement began recording in 1992 at the tail-end of the new jack swing era, yet he was able to keep much of its sound alive while remaining commercially successful. While he's created a smooth, professional mixture of hip-hop beats, soul-man crooning, and funk, the most distinctive element of Kelly's music is its explicit carnality. Over the course of two albums, the singer has been able to make songs like "Sex Me," "Bump N' Grind," and "Your Body's Callin'" into hits because his production has been seductive enough to sell such blatant come-ons.

Kelly and Public Announcement released their debut album, *Born into the '90's*, at the beginning of 1992. It was an instant R&B smash, while earning a fair amount of pop airplay; "Honey Love" and "Slow Dance (Hey Mr. DJ)" were number one R&B hits, while

"Dedicated" was his biggest pop hit at number 31. *12 Play*, released in the fall of 1993, established R. Kelly as an R&B superstar. The first single pulled from the album, "Sex Me (Parts I & II)," became a gold single and the second, "Bump N' Grind" hit number one on both the pop and R&B charts in 1994; "Bump N' Grind" stayed on the top of the R&B charts for an astonishing 12 weeks, while it logged four weeks at the top of the pop charts. "Your Body's Callin'" was another gold single for Kelly, peaking at number 13 on the pop charts. In 1994, he also produced *Age Ain't Nothin' but a Number*, the debut album for Aaliyah, a 15 year-old R&B singer from Detroit; it featured two Top Ten pop singles, "Back & Forth" and "At Your Best (You Are Love)." Late in 1994, it was revealed that Kelly and Aaliyah had wed in August. The news sparked a small storm of controversy in the media, yet it didn't appear to hurt the careers of either singer. Kelly wrote and co-produced "You Are Not Alone," the second single from Michael Jackson's *HIStory* album, which was released in the summer of 1995. *—Stephen Thomas Erlewine*

Born into 90's / Jan. 14, 1992 / Jive ✦✦✦
One of the last popular new jack groups, this East Coast unit had some smash singles in '92 doing both conventional R&B/soul and hip-hop/new Jack tracks. They did both originals and covers, had an enthusiastic attitude, were well produced, and stayed on the urban contemporary outlets throughout the year. *—Ron Wynn*

● **12 Play** / Nov. 9, 1993 / Jive ✦✦✦✦
New jack swing may be on its way out as a primary R&B sound, but R. Kelly hasn't lost any points by employing it here. Kelly skillfully mixes '70s-style funk beats, '90s hip-hop production and his own raps, as well as those of Deandre Boykins and Carey Kelly. Sometimes things come perilously close to sounding corny and dated, but he manages to bring things off successfully. Kelly is a competent vocalist, but a master at striking and maintaining a heated mood, keeping a light touch no matter how explicit the language gets and giving this album distinction even as it mines territory that's essentially played out. *—Ron Wynn*

Johnny Kemp

Soul, R&B, Urban

Kemp began singing in nightclubs in his hometown of Nassau, Bahamas, when he was only 13. He moved to Harlem in 1979, developing his other talents as a dancer, songwriter, and actor. "Just Got Paid" was a Top Ten hit in 1988; he subsequently did a tune for the soundtrack of the motion picture *Sing*. *—Steve Huey*

Johnny Kemp / 1986 / Columbia ✦✦✦
Johnny Kemp got a lot of mileage out of a song written for him by Kashif, "Just Another Lover." The single was a huge hit in the mid-'80s and gave Kemp's debut album for Columbia a great start. Kemp, a session vocalist and composer who had worked with Millie Jackson, Glenn Jones, and Change while penning songs for the B.B.& Q. band, put plenty of effort and energy into these tracks, but too often expended his resources on routine material. But it was well produced, and he did well enough with the single to get a second album for the label. *—Ron Wynn*

● **Secrets of Flying** / Dec. 1987 / Columbia ✦✦✦✦
Johnny Kemp got an even bigger hit on his second album, "Just Got Paid," which has been absorbed into the general vernacular. He scored a number one R&B hit with it, but unfortunately peaked as an artist once it faded. The rest of the album wasn't anywhere near that level, and Kemp has never come close to duplicating either the song or getting compositions, production, and arrangements that could regenerate his career. The single was also noteworthy in that it was one of the first big hits co-produced by Teddy Riley, who went on to become an influential figure in new jack swing R&B. *—Ron Wynn*

Chris Kenner

b. Dec. 25, 1929, d. Jan. 25, 1976

New Orleans R&B

Kenner wrote a number of enduring New Orleans R&B classics, although subsequent cover versions eclipsed all but "I Like It Like That," his Grammy-nominated greatest hit in 1961. Kenner cowrote "Sick and Tired" with Fats Domino and charted with it in 1957 on Imperial, but Domino's version blew it out of the water. Signing with Joe Babashak's Instant label, Kenner's "I Like It like That," "Land of 1000 Dances," and "Something You Got" sported Allen Toussaint's rolling piano behind Kenner's raw vocals. *—Bill Dahl*

○ **Land of a Thousand Dances** / 1966 / Atlantic ✦✦✦✦
Slashing soul by the writer of the title cut, this is one of the great forgotten albums. —*David Szatmary*

● **I Like It Like That: Golden Classics** / 1987 / Collectables ✦✦✦✦
Vocalist Kenner's early-'60s sides for Instant, with Allen Toussaint laying down rolling piano behind him, represent New Orleans R&B at its most infectious. —*Bill Dahl*

Kenny & the Kasuals

Group, Garage Rock, Pop/Rock
This Dallas group—too accomplished to be called a garage band in the usual sense of the term—was pretty popular in their hometown in the mid-'60s, but never made any noise on the national level. It's ironic that much of their reputation rests on a live album of covers, *Impact*, that ranks among the most collectable LPs of the '60s, as the group actually wrote a lot of their own material. Starting in the mid-'60s as a sort of raucous Dave Clark Five-meets-the-Stones combo, the Kasuals progressed to acid-punk with their most popular local hit, "Journey to Tyme" (which would become one of the most valued singles by '60s garage collectors). They were a typical '60s group in that they also cut covers of popular R&B and British Invasion tunes, and sappy pop ballads that were mostly likely encouraged by the shortsighted local label owners for whom they recorded. The group tried their luck in New York City briefly, and split in late 1967. A spin-off group (without leader Kenny Daniels) released a promising single with progressive and folk influences under the name Truth, and the group reunited very briefly before splitting again after several members were drafted. Their material was reissued in Europe in the 1980s, along with a fair number of previously unreleased outtakes. —*Richie Unterberger*

● **Nothing Better To Do** / 1983 / Eva ✦✦✦✦
Both sides of all seven of their singles; all but two of the fourteen tracks are self-penned. Well-written '60s pop/rock with a raw touch. In the '90s, this was combined with the *Things Gettin' Better* reissue on one CD. —*Richie Unterberger*

Things Gettin' Better / 1984 / Eva ✦✦✦
15 previously unreleased tracks from all phases of their career (a couple are slightly different mixes, with the addition/subtraction of backup female vocals, of the songs from their lone sappy ballad single). An uneven mix of alternate takes, R&B covers, Tex-Mex, acid punk, and breezy pop, it's nonetheless about as strong as *Nothing Better To Do*. "Come on Kid" and "Revelation" are acid-punkers that should appeal to those who like "Journey to Tyme." In the '90s, this was combined with the *Nothing Better To Do* reissue on one CD. —*Richie Unterberger*

Nik Kershaw

b. Mar. 1, 1958, Bristol, England
New Wave, Pop/Rock
During the mid-'80s, Nik Kershaw managed to score a handful of pop hits and, in doing so, establish himself as a profitable commercial songwriter. Kershaw began his musical career by learning to play guitar when he was a teenager. In 1974, he joined his first band, Half Pint Hogg, which played nothing but Deep Purple covers. However, his musical ideas were not limited to heavy metal; after he left school, he joined a jazz-funk band called Fusion. Fusion released one album, *'Til I Hear from You*, in the late '70s. Once the group broke up, Kershaw signed to MCA Records with the help of Nine Below Zero's manager, Micky Modern.
    Kershaw released his first solo single, "I Won't Let the Sun Go Down on Me," in 1983; it peaked at number 47 on the U.K. charts. His next single, "Wouldn't It Be Good," hit number five in the U.K. and charted at number 46 in the U.S. Its success led to stardom in Britain for Kershaw; "I Won't Let the Sun Go Down on Me" was re-released in summer of 1984 and charted at number two, leading to a series of hit singles. Released in 1986, his third album *Radio Musicola* wasn't as successful as his previous albums. Kershaw subsequently retreated from performing and recording regularly. Although he released *The Works* in 1990, Kershaw's main musical contribution since the late '80s is as a songwriter; he's written several songs for other artists, including Chesney Hawke's hit single "The One and Only." —*Stephen Thomas Erlewine*

Human Racing / 1984 / MCA ✦✦✦
His debut, although rough around the edges, showed talent and promise, and includes "Wouldn't It Be Good." —*Scott Bultman*

○ **The Riddle** / 1984 / MCA ✦✦✦✦
Kershaw's second album, containing a remixed "Wouldn't It Be Good," finally garnered some deserved attention. The rest is his unique style of well-crafted synth-pop. —*Scott Bultman*

Radio Musicola / 1986 / MCA ✦✦
The Works / 1990 / MCA ✦✦✦
● **Anthology** / 1995 / One Way ✦✦✦✦

Chaka Khan

b. Mar. 23, 1953, Great Lakes, IL
Soul, Funk, Urban
The lead singer of the R&B band Rufus from 1972 to 1978, Khan went solo with *Chaka* and the single "I'm Every Woman." Since 1978 she has released several solo albums. The Grammy-winning Khan has also done vocal work for Prince, Steve Winwood, David Bowie, and Quincy Jones. —*William Ruhlmann*

Chaka / 1979 / Warner Brothers ✦✦✦
Naughty / 1980 / Warner Brothers ✦✦✦
What Cha' Gonna Do for Me / 1981 / Warner Brothers ✦✦✦
○ **Chaka Khan** / 1982 / Warner Brothers ✦✦✦✦
An excellent album from Chaka Khan, mixing tingling uptempo tunes with her characteristic soaring, glorious vocals. "Got to Be There" reached number five on the R&B charts, but it actually wasn't the album's high point. That was the marvelous "Be Bop Medley," which later led hardcore jazz purist Betty Carter to proclaim Khan the one female singer working outside the jazz arena with legitimate improvising credentials. —*Ron Wynn*

● **I Feel for You** / 1984 / Warner Brothers ✦✦✦✦
Smoothly produced funk outing features the Prince-composed title track, an R&B number one, and two more R&B Top 20 hits, "This Is My Night" and "Through the Fire." —*William Ruhlmann*

Destiny / 1986 / Warner Brothers ✦✦✦
Another fine, although more uneven than usual, album from Chaka Khan. "Love of a Lifetime" was the latest in her string of definitive singles, while she also elevated several otherwise mundane ballads and uptempo cuts. No matter what her personal situation, Khan seldom made a misstep on any of her albums during the early and mid-'80s, and this one might have been the least distinguished of the batch. —*Ron Wynn*

○ **C.K.** / 1988 / Warner Brothers ✦✦✦✦
A first-class release, despite the fact that it didn't pack the normal commercial punch. But it had excellent production, many outstanding selections, and uniformly dazzling, booming, triumphant vocals from Khan. She currently speaks with disdain about the record business, and it's probably due to the relative failure of great records like this to break out and really enjoy the success they merit that's disillusioned her. —*Ron Wynn*

Life Is a Dance (The Remix Project) / 1989 / Warner Brothers ✦✦
In lieu of a desperately needed greatest hits album, we'll have to settle for this reconfiguration of such Khan hits as "I'm Every Woman" and "Clouds." —*William Ruhlmann*

The Woman I Am / 1992 / Warner Brothers ✦✦✦
Love You All My Lifetime / Warner Brothers ✦✦✦

Kid Creole & the Coconuts

Group, New Wave, Disco
After leaving Dr. Buzzard's Original "Savannah" Band in 1980, August Darnell (born Thomas August Darnell Browder) conceived the Kid Creole persona: a kitschy lounge lizard that played disco, reggae, salsa, calypso—any kind of dance-derived music, really. With the help of Coati Mundi (born Andy Hernandez), Darnell developed a band that could fuse the disparate musical elements convincingly.
    Releasing their first album, *Off the Coast of Me*, in 1980, Kid Creole and the Coconuts built up a cult following during the first half of the decade. Their popularity had peaked by 1982, when their third album *Wise Guy* peaked at 145 on the U.S. charts. Nevertheless, the band remained new wave and dance club favorites until 1984, when their audience began to shrink. The group continued to release albums until 1990's *Private Waters in the Great Divide*, which barely made any impact. Since that album, Darnell and his band have been silent. —*Stephen Thomas Erlewine*

○ **Off the Coast of Me** / 1980 / Antilles ✦✦✦✦
Mixing disco, Caribbean music, and strains of big-band jazz, Kid Creole engages in a self-deprecating dialogue with his backup singers, the Coconuts, who dismiss him as "Mister Softee" and plead, "Can You Get Me Into Studio 54?" on this hilarious debut album. — *William Ruhlmann*

Fresh Fruit in Foreign Places / 1981 / ZE ✦✦✦
Musical gumbo of esoteric lilting, jazzy laidback disco, an acquired taste. — *Bil Carpenter*

○ **Wise Guy** / 1982 / Sire ✦✦✦✦
The ongoing adventures of Kid Creole continue on this bouncy collection that produced three British Top Ten hits, including "Annie, I'm Not Your Daddy" and "I'm a Wonderful Thing, Baby." — *William Ruhlmann*

Doppelganger / 1983 / ZE ✦✦✦

In Praise of Older Women & Other Crimes / 1985 / Sire ✦✦

I Too Have Seen the Woods / 1987 / Sire ✦✦

Private Waters in the Great Divide / 1990 / Columbia ✦✦✦

You Shoulda Told Me You Were / 1991 / Columbia ✦✦

● **Kid Creole Redux** / Mar. 17, 1992 / Sire ✦✦✦✦
Featuring the great majority of Kid Creole's singles, *Kid Creole Redux* is the perfect introduction to the eccentric dance-pop artist. — *Sara Sytsma*

Kid 'n Play

Group, Rap

They've recorded several decent albums with the aid of producer Hurby Luv Bug, but this duo is best known for their starring roles in the *House Party* film series.

The *House Party* movies helped Kid 'n Play's infectious pop-flavored hip-hop to crossover into the mainstream without losing much street credibility. — *John Floyd*

● **2 Hype** / 1988 / Select ✦✦✦✦
A solid debut with snatches of house, dance, and go-go. Despite minimal rapping abilities, the duo quickly captured a chunk of the hip-hop audience. — *Ron Wynn*

Funhouse / 1990 / Select ✦✦✦

Kid 'n Play's Fun House / 1990 / Select ✦✦✦
One of two releases from the twosome in 1990, this one has new cuts with funkier, looser foundations and more ambitious adult lyrics and rapping style. — *Ron Wynn*

House Party [O.S.T.] / 1990 / Motown ✦✦✦
Not strictly, or even mainly, their album, it does contain the singles "Funhouse" and "Kid vs. Play (The Battle)." Its prime importance was as the soundtrack from an extremely successful film of the same name, which launched the duo into cinematic stardom. — *Ron Wynn*

Face the Nation / Select ✦✦

Johnny Kidd & the Pirates

Group, Rock & Roll

One of England's top rock & roll outfits before the Beatles led the early '60s Beat Boom, Johnny Kidd & the Pirates are best remembered today for one international rock classic ("Shakin' All Over") and as a seminal influence on several more famous groups, most notably the Who.

Johnny Kidd (born Frederick Heath, November 23, 1935) had formed his first band, a skiffle group called the Five Nutters, in 1957. They quickly outgrew their skiffle roots and, after a short period fronting the Fred Heath Combo, he joined Alan Caddy (guitar), Tony Docherty (rhythm guitar), and Ken McKay (drums) in early 1958 in an outfit that was dubbed Johnny Kidd & the Pirates, who were spotted by an EMI Record representative and signed to the label.

The group cut their first record, the outstanding *Please Don't Touch*, in April 1959, highlighted by Heath's menacing vocals, which reached number 26 on the British charts. The group's subsequent records were an uneven mix of solid rhythm-and-blues based rock juxtaposed with awkwardly covered "standards."

In May of 1960, however, the band was in the studio to record one of those standards, "Yes Sir, That's My Baby," with an original B-side that they hadn't fully worked out. That B-side, a Heath original called "Shakin' All Over," became the A-side of a number one single that became the first original rock song in England to achieve the status of an international rock standard. Driven by Caddy's guitar and a mournful, ominous lead vocal by Heath, the song topped the charts and completely astonished everybody who heard it that such a track could have come from an English rock & roll band.

Unfortunately, like every other British label of the era, EMI was never sure how best to deal with rock & roll success, and the group was made to record any amount of dross in the wake of this success, amid some superb follow-up numbers ("A Shot of Rhythm and Blues," Bo Diddley's "I Can Tell," Willie Dixon's "I Just Want to Make Love to You").

Several membership changes followed, most notably the addition of Mick Green on lead guitar. The group was among the finest rock combos of the early '60s, with a wild stage act that had them playing in pirate regalia, but it never had enough consistent chart success to put it back in the top ranks of Britain's rock hierarchy, though they received a great deal of respect from the younger generation of rock & rollers.

Early in their career, the Who played on the same bill as Johnny Kidd & the Pirates, and it was through watching the Pirates at work that they arrived at their own sound of a solo singer backed by a guitar, bass, and drums; the band also added "Shakin' All Over" to their repertory, and immortalized their appreciation of Heath and company on their 1970 album *Live at Leeds*. Heath and his band struggled onward into the mid-'60s, even covering a remake of "Shakin' All Over." Green left in 1964 (replaced by future New Animals guitarist John Weider) to take over as a member of the Dakotas, Billy J. Kramer's backup band, and Heath put together a new combo during this period.

The mid-'60s seemed to be a more favorable period for Heath's brand of R&B-based rock & roll. He put together a group called the New Pirates, and was about to embark on a new phase of his career, when he was killed in a car crash on October 7, 1966. The New Pirates continued on for a time, with Johnny Carroll fronting the group until mid-1967, when they called it quits.

During the 1970's, however, the Pirates, with Mick Green back in the lineup, began playing together again, and they have continued to perform to this day in England, and recorded a handful of albums during the 1970's and 1980's, featuring Johnny Kidd-era material as well as new songs in their stage show. Among the New Pirates, bassist Nicky Simper went on to become a founding member of Deep Purple. — *Bruce Eder*

● **Hits & Rarities** / 1983 / See For Miles ✦✦✦✦
This collection is the best of three now available. It contains the strongest of Kidd's singles plus superb vault finds. Considered too rough for release in the '60s, they hold up splendidly. — *Bruce Eder*

○ **Complete Johnny Kidd** / 1994 / EMI ✦✦✦✦
A double CD of everything this underrated band ever recorded, assembled chronologically and beautifully remastered and annotated (with great pictures, too). This is the collection to own, especially since it has been issued at mid-price. And fans of the Who or the Small Faces can double the priority of owning this collection. — *Bruce Eder*

Greg Kihn

b. , Baltimore, MD
Rock & Roll, Pop/Rock

Greg Kihn began his career in his hometown of Baltimore, MD, working in the singer/songwriter mold but switched to straightforward rock & roll when he moved to San Francisco in 1974. In the following year, he became one of the first artists signed to Matthew Kaufman's now legendary Beserkley Records. Along with Jonathan Richman, Earthquake, and the Rubinoos, Kihn helped to carve the label's sound—melodic pop with a strong '60s-pop sensibility—a refreshing alternative to the bloated prog-rock of the time. In 1976, after his debut on the compilation *Beserkley Chartbusters*, he recorded his first album with his own band consisting of Ronnie Dunbar (guitar), Steve Wright (bass) and Larry Lynch (drums). Through the '70s, he released an album each year and built a strong cult following through constant touring, becoming Beserkley's biggest seller. In 1981, he earned his first bonafide hit with the Top 20 single, "The Breakup Song (They Don't Write 'Em)" from the *Rockihnroll* album. He continued in a more commercial vein through the '80s with a series of pun-titled albums; *Kihntinued* (1982), *Kihnspiracy* (1983), *Kihntageous* (1984), and *Citizen Kihn* (1985). He scored his biggest hit with 1983's "Jeopardy" (number two) from the *Kihnspiracy* album. One more single broke the Top 40, 1985's "Lucky," but by the time *Love and Rock and Roll* was released in 1986, the puns had run out and so had the hits. Kihn has kept a relatively low profile throughout the '90s, releasing only one album, 1994's *Mutiny*. —*Sara Sytsma*

Greg Kihn / 1976 / Beserkley ✦✦✦
This record has it all: good songs (mostly written by Kihn) with strong vocals and tight harmonies. If you only know Kihn from the hits, you owe it to yourself to go back and track this record down. If you're only just discovering him, start here and grow with the band. —*Jim Worbois*

○ **Greg Kihn Again** / 1977 / Beserkley ✦✦✦✦
A fine followup to *Greg Kihn* as Kihn continues to grow as an artist and songwriter. His version of "For You" received some favorable comments from Springsteen as well as first dibs on an original Springsteen tune for a later album. —*Jim Worbois*

Next of Kihn / 1978 / Beserkley ✦✦✦
For the first time, Kihn has written all the songs and, with the first track, has adopted a harder edge to his sound, at least on that particular track. Overall, not a bad record but more of a lateral move as an artist than a step forward. —*Jim Worbois*

With the Naked Eye / 1979 / Beserkley ✦✦✦
The awaited Springsteen cover finally pops up on this record, as does a cover of label-mate Jonathan Richman's "Roadrunner." The former allows some of the Kihn magic to shine through but the latter is just a straight read with none of the fun of the original. In between are some pleasant songs but nothing really memorable. —*Jim Worbois*

Glasshouse Rock / 1980 / Beserkley ✦✦
○ **Rockihnroll** / 1981 / Beserkley ✦✦✦✦
With this album Kihn finally has the hit he long ago deserved ("Breakup Song"). He also manages to recapture some of what made the early records so enjoyable. Once again, with both the material and the performance, Kihn sounds as if he is enjoying himself. —*Jim Worbois*

○ **Kihntinued** / 1982 / Beserkley ✦✦✦✦
A couple of the tracks, like "Everyday/Saturday" and "Testify," are more memorable than nearly anything on the previous record, but still not up to the potential Kihn hinted at on his first couple albums. —*Jim Worbois*

Kihnspiracy / 1983 / Beserkley ✦✦
With the help of the hit single ("Jeopardy") and saturation MTV airplay, *Kihnspiracy* became Kihn's highest charting album to date—eventually breaking the Top 20. Unfortunately, Kihn continued his decline into mediocrity with this overall uninspired effort. —*Sara Sytsma*

Kihntagious / 1984 / Beserkley ✦✦✦
Citizen Kihn / 1985 / EMI ✦✦
Kihn made his last appearance in the pop charts with this album. The single "Lucky" was a Top 40 hit but the remainder of the album is second rate. —*Sara Sytsma*

Love & Rock & Roll / 1986 / Beserkley ✦✦
Something of a return to form, Kihn delivers his finest album in years with a batch of solid originals and some well-chosen covers (including the Only Ones classic "Another Girl, Another Planet"). Unfortunately, by 1986, no one was all that interested anymore and the album went unnoticed. —*Sara Sytsma*

● **Kihnsolidation: The Best of Greg Kihn** / 1989 / Rhino ✦✦✦✦
A fine sampling of Kihn's pop sensibility. Drawing from each of his albums, it includes the hits "The Breakup Song" and "Jeopardy" as well as his better album cuts. —*Chris Woodstra*

Unkihntrollable (Greg Kihn Live) / 1991 / Rhino ✦✦
Mutiny / 1994 / Clean Cuts ✦✦

Killing Joke

Group, Alternative Pop/Rock
Heavy and slow, Killing Joke (at least early in their career) was a quasi-metal band dancing to a tune of doom and gloom. They eventually became less heavy and more arty (the latter seems almost impossible), more danceable even, but early on they made some urgent slabs of molten dynamite that oozed with the power of thick guitars, thudding drums and over-the-top singing. —*John Dougan*

● **Killing Joke** / 1980 / EG ✦✦✦✦
Killing Joke's self-titled debut album is a throttling merger of heavy metal, new wave, and noise. It's a dense, claustrophobic record that basically sketched out the path the band would follow over the next decade. —*Stephen Thomas Erlewine*

What's This for / 1981 / EG ✦✦✦
Revelations / 1982 / EG ✦✦
○ **Fire Dances** / 1983 / EG ✦✦✦✦
Night Time / 1985 / EG ✦✦✦
Brighter Than a 1000 Suns / 1986 / Virgin ✦✦✦
Outside the Gate / 1988 / EG ✦✦
○ **Extremities, Dirt & Various Repressed Emotions** / 1990 / Noise ✦✦✦✦
● **Incomplete Collection 1980-85** / 1990 / EG ✦✦✦✦
○ **Laugh? I Nearly Bought One!** / 1992 / Plan 9/Caroline ✦✦✦✦
Pandemonium / 1994 / Zoo ✦✦
Millennium / 1994 / Pavement
Wilful Days / 1995 / Caroline

King Crimson

Group, Art-Rock/Progressive-Rock
If the Moody Blues provided a heavenly Mellotron-soaked soundtrack for millions of late-'60s cosmic rockers, King Crimson (formed in 1969) balanced the scales with disturbingly dense and explosive sonic trips into the dark side. Even when the band was playing something relatively peaceful, there was a sense that something wasn't quite settled. Founded by guitarist Robert Fripp and saxophonist Ian McDonald, the group burst forth with an ornate, majestic, savage sound and an approach that owed a great deal to modern jazz. McDonald left after the first tour, followed by the rest of the band, except for Fripp, who re-formed the band in ever-changing configurations up through 1974, when the final breakup came. The latter-day King Crimson (with Adrian Belew on guitar with Fripp) is the most daring version but has virtually no connection with the original except its name. —*Bruce Eder & Rick Clark*

★ **In the Court of the Crimson King** / 1969 / EG ✦✦✦✦✦
Definitive debut album, which was almost too good (it took years for them to come up with a record as concise and distinctive), an orchestrated vision of apocalyptic doom dominated by Ian McDonald's Mellotron, Greg Lake's dignified voice, and the ferocious guitar playing of Robert Fripp. The latter would be the only survivor onto subsequent albums. —*Bruce Eder*

○ **In the Wake of Poseidon** / 1970 / EG ✦✦✦✦
A more carefully produced and better-crafted but more diffuse second album. Fripp took over the keyboards as well as all the compositional chores, with help from Gustav Holst (*The Planets*). —*Bruce Eder*

Lizard / 1970 / EG ✦✦✦
A more ornate and purely psychedelic venture, involving extended suites with more of a jazz feel to them. Guest performance by Yes's Jon Anderson on "Prince Rupert Awakes." —*Bruce Eder*

Islands / 1971 / EG ✦✦✦
A flawed album by what looked like the most stable Crimson lineup in some time (this band actually got to tour), with too much weak material expanded to mammoth proportions. The one compensation is the return of the sense of humor missing since the first two albums. —*Bruce Eder*

Earthbound / 1972 / Polydor ✦✦
○ **Larks' Tongues in Aspic** / 1973 / EG ✦✦✦✦
The new King Crimson makes their debut with a violin (courtesy of David Cross) now sharing center stage with Fripp's guitar, and the Mellotron pushed somewhat into the background. The material itself is the most experimental that Fripp had come up with up to that time, and John Wetton's vocals were the strongest since the departure of Greg Lake in 1970. —*Bruce Eder*

Red / 1974 / EG ✦✦✦
Some final thoughts before Fripp pulled the plug on Crimson—the material is longer, the playing more ferocious, and the whole album seems rushed toward the breaking point of dissolution for the band. The culmination of five years of doom-rock. —*Bruce Eder*

○ **Starless & Bible Black** / 1974 / EG ✦✦✦✦
An intriguing follow-up, and overall the band's most satisfying album. —*Bruce Eder*

USA / 1975 / Atlantic ✦✦✦
○ **Discipline** / 1981 / EG ✦✦✦✦
The new King Crimson, harder and heavier. —*Bruce Eder*
○ **Beat** / 1982 / EG ✦✦✦✦
A superior mid-'80s followup with better material. —*Bruce Eder*

3 of a Perfect Pair / 1984 / Warner Brothers ✦✦✦
The final chapter? Don't bet on it, but this would be a good way to end, if so. —*Bruce Eder*
○ **Essential King Crimson** / 1991 / Caroline ✦✦✦✦
○ **Frame by Frame** / 1991 / Caroline ✦✦✦✦
Frame by Frame is a four-disc box set, compiled by bandleader Robert Fripp, that does a good job providing primo samples of each of Crimson's musical periods. Sonically, the excellent remastering makes this the best this band has ever sounded on disc. Three of the discs cover their studio work, while the fourth is a collection of live work, spanning the band's entire career. Enclosed is a richly detailed diary (written by Fripp) of Crimson's entire history, plus interviews with band members, and glowing and hateful reviews from critics. Typical of Crimson, precious little of the music on this set would qualify for casual listening. However, those whose taste run towards the dark side of prog-rock will find this set rewarding. —*Rick Clark*
○ **The Great Deceiver (Live 1973-1974)** / 1992 / Caroline ✦✦✦✦
Four CDs full of live King Crimson from 1973 and 1974, an era that many consider their best. Although some songs are repeated, they're never played the same way twice. If you're a King Crimson fan, that's enough of an incentive for purchase; if you're not, the musical expertise of the band might convert you, providing you have the money for a box set. —*Stephen Thomas Erlewine*

Thrak / Apr. 1995 / Virgin ✦✦✦
King Crimson returned with a new record in 1995, featuring the same lineup that disbanded a decade earlier. With *Thrak*, the group picks up right where they left off; although they incorporate a couple of new technical tricks, the heart of the album echoes back to the early '80s with its dense, guitar-dominated sonic textures. —*Sara Sytsma*

King Curtis (Curtis Ousley)

b. Feb. 7, 1934, Ft. Worth, TX, **d.** Aug. 13, 1971, New York, NY
R&B, Soul
King Curtis was the last of the great R&B tenor sax giants. He came to prominence in the mid-'50s as a session musician in New York, recording, at one time or another, for most East Coast R&B labels. A long association with Atlantic/Atco began in 1958, especially on recordings by The Coasters. He recorded singles for many small labels in the '50s—his own Atco sessions (1958–1959), then Prestige/New Jazz and Prestige/TruSound for jazz and R&B albums (1960–1961). Curtis also cut a #1 R&B single with "Soul Twist" on Enjoy Records (1962). He was signed by Capitol (1963–1964), where he cut mostly singles, including "Soul Serenade." Returning to Atlantic in 1965, he remained there for the rest of his life. He had solid R&B single success with "Memphis Soul Stew" and "Ode to Billie Joe" (1967). Beginning in 1967, Curtis started to take a more active studio role at Atlantic—leading and contracting sessions for other artists, producing with Jerry Wexler and later on his own. He also became the leader of Aretha Franklin's backing unit, the Kingpins. He compiled several albums of singles during this period. All aspects of his career were in full swing at the time he was murdered in 1971. —*Bob Porter*

That's Alright / 1958–1967 / Red Lightnin' ✦✦✦
Collects mostly vocal cuts from various albums. Some duplication with Prestige albums. —*Ron Wynn*

The New Scene of King Curtis / 1960 / Original Jazz Classics ✦✦✦
Tenor and soprano saxophonist King Curtis made several R&B and pop recordings during his career, and also was a prolific session artist. What's not quite as well known was that he also made some jazz and blues recordings in the early '60s, among them this 1960 date that matched him with Wynton Kelly, Oliver Jackson, and Paul Chambers doing mostly hard bop, plus some blues backing Little Brother Montgomery. It was reissued on CD in 1985. —*Ron Wynn*

● **Instant Soul: The Legendary King Curtis** / 1994 / ✦✦✦✦
King Curtis has never been served with a comprehensive collection until *Instant Soul*, which features the best instrumental singles the distinctive, soulful, and influential tenor saxophonist ever recorded. —*Stephen Thomas Erlewine*
○ **Best of King Curtis** / Capitol ✦✦✦✦

King Diamond

Group, Heavy Metal
King Diamond started out with the influential Danish metal band Mercyful Fate, whose Gothic lyrics centering on themes of evil were much imitated by later groups. Diamond has an amazing vocal range, able to alternate between a low growl, mid-range melodicism, and an ear-piercingly high falsetto scream. In 1985, he left Mercyful Fate after two full-length albums to form a band named after himself with guitarist Andy LaRocque and a rotating lineup, releasing several concept albums with supernatural storylines and complex sub-themes and putting on highly theatrical stage shows, complete with actors portraying the characters in his songs. He rejoined Mercyful Fate when the band launched a successful comeback in 1993 and also reformed his own band with LaRocque, guitarist Herbie Simonsen, bassist Chris Estes, and drummer Darrin Anthony early in 1995. —*Steve Huey*

Fatal Portrait / 1986 / Roadrunner ✦✦✦
King Diamond's debut album is a bit uneven but still enjoyable. —*John Book*
● **Abigail** / May 1987 / Roadrunner ✦✦✦✦
Any King Diamond is good, but this is a top-notch performance. Excellent playing, powerful vocal effects, and a believable (and eerie) story line make this comparable to his days with Mercyful Fate. —*John Book*
○ **Them** / 1988 / Roadrunner ✦✦✦✦
This is a continuation of the storyline from *Abigail*. —*John Book*

The Dark Sides / 1988 / Roadrunner ✦✦✦
A compilation of essential non-LP tracks, it includes the classic "No Presents for Christmas." —*John Book*

Conspiracy / 1989 / Roadrunner ✦✦✦
Continuing where *Them* left off, it's a bit darker than that album. —*John Book*

The Eye / 1990 / Roadrunner ✦✦

Return of the Vampire / Roadrunner ✦✦✦

Dangerous Meeting / Roadrunner ✦✦

King's X

Group, Hard Rock
Known as the Edge since 1981, this Houston trio became King's X in 1986. Featuring Ty Tabor's lyrical guitar work, Jerry Gaskill's forceful drumming, and Doug Pinnick's emotive lead singing and distinctive bass work (sometimes on 12-string bass), King's X is a dense instrumental fusion between hard rock and prog-rock. Vocally, King's X exhibits a knack for rich three-part harmonies that, at times, recall *Abbey Road*-period Beatles. Thematically, they range from *Wizard of Oz*-style fantasy imagery to more complex spiritual (particularly Christian) metaphors. —*Rick Clark*

Out of the Silent Planet / 1982 / Megaforce ✦✦✦
Out of the Silent Planet (named after the first book of Christian writer C. S. Lewis's space trilogy) was a brilliant debut for King's X, featuring memorable melodies and sweeping harmonies. This debut's over-the-top performances and well-defined arrangements earned this band a substantial following from both metal and prog-rock audiences early on. —*Rick Clark*
● **Gretchen Goes to Nebraska** / 1989 / Megaforce ✦✦✦✦
King's X sophomore effort contained their smart blend of heavy and melodic rock to a fine effect. Many fans of the band consider this album their best; with fiery tracks like "Over My Head" and "Fall on Me" and ballads like "Summerland," it's easy to understand why. —*Rick Clark*
○ **Faith, Hope, & Love** / 1990 / Megaforce ✦✦✦✦
Faith, Hope, & Love was King's X's commercial breakthrough effort, containing the hit "It's Love." —*Rick Clark*

King's X / 1992 / Atlantic ✦✦✦
Their fourth album features harder sounds than previous efforts, but lack enough dynamic dimensionality to the arrangements to make it a consistently satisfying listen. It contains the hit "Black Flag," the album's highlight. —*Rick Clark*

Dogman / 1994 / Atlantic ✦✦✦
King's X sharpens their guitars a notch, adding a more modern touch to their Beatlesque progressive metal. That alone makes *Dogman* a tougher, more satisfying record that ranks among their best. —*Stephen Thomas Erlewine*

Ben E. King

b. Sep. 23, 1938, Henderson, NC
Soul, R&B
Swirling strings, subtly shaded orchestrations, and Ben E. King's assured baritone were a blueprint for uptown soul success during the early '60s. King and his vocal group, the Five Crowns, were in the right place at the right time when, in 1959, the manager of the Drifters decided to sack his entire group and solicit replacements. As new lead singer for the Drifters, King crooned the soulful smashes "There Goes My Baby," "Save the Last Dance for Me," and "I Count the Tears" before heading out on his own in 1960. The vocalist's own Atco singles mirrored the sumptuous production of his Drifter sides, and "Spanish Harlem," "Don't Play That Song (You Lied)," and the R&B chart-topping "Stand by Me" were all huge successes. King remained with Atco through 1969, then triumphantly returned to Atlantic in 1975 with another #1 soul hit, "Supernatural Thing (Part 1)."
With the re-release of "Stand by Me" as the theme to the 1986 film of the same name, King was in demand all over again, the stirring song improbably scaling the charts for a second time, despite being a quarter-century old. —*Bill Dahl*

○ **The Ultimate Collection** / 1987 / Atlantic ✦✦✦✦
The rich baritone of this ex-Drifter lead is matched by the majestic, violin-drenched, uptown soul arrangements on these early-'60s classics. —*Bill Dahl*

● **Anthology** / 1993 / Rhino ✦✦✦✦
This two-disc, 50-song box set thoroughly documents the recordings that Ben E. King cut for Atlantic. Starting as the lead voice of the Drifters on such hits as "There Goes My Baby" and "Save The Last Dance For Me," King went on to a successful solo career with a string of singles that matched his smooth, sexy baritone with tastefully arranged string sections and Latin rhythms. All of those early hits—"Stand By Me" and "Spanish Harlem"—were the biggest—are included here, along with non-hit 45s by the likes of Leiber/Stoller, Doc Pomus, Mort Shuman, Phil Spector, and Goffin/King that were nearly equal in worth. As the '60s progressed, Ben moved toward a more mainstream, heavier soul sound and less distinctive material, culminating in his parting from Atlantic in 1969. He returned to the label in the mid-'70s for a string of mainstream R&B successes. This compilation includes 16 non-LP singles from the '60s, which together with the hits constitute the definitive overview of this influential soul singer's work. —*Richie Unterberger*

Carole King

b. Feb. 9, 1942, Brooklyn, NY
Singer-Songwriter, Pop/Rock
During the early '70s, the singer/songwriter movement emerged as a reflective, folky alternative to rock and pop. Among the genre's more notable avatars were James Taylor, Joni Mitchell, Cat Stevens, and Carole King. Unlike many of the other artists, King was well-grounded in the pop songcrafting tradition, primarily from her tenure as a writer during the glory days at the Brill Building in New York. It was while she was at the Brill Building, beginning in 1958, that King met Neil Diamond and Paul Simon and began a very successful string of collaborations with Gerry Goffin, whom she would later marry. To list all of those hits would fill a page, but classics like "Up on the Roof," "(You Make Me Feel Like) A Natural Woman," "Will You Still Love Me Tomorrow," "The Locomotion," "Don't Bring Me Down," "Hey Girl," "One Fine Day," "Pleasant Valley Sunday," "Some Kind-A-Wonderful," and "You've Got a Friend" are just a few.
In 1962, King scored a number 22 hit as a solo artist with "It Might as Well Rain until September." With guitarist Danny Kortchmar and her second husband, bassist Charles Larkey, King formed the City, releasing an album titled *Now That Everything's Been Said* on Lou Adler's Ode label. The project fell apart and King focused on her solo career in 1970 with *Writer: Carole King*. That album went nowhere, but its followup, *Tapestry*, became one of the biggest-selling albums of the '70s, holding the number one position for fifteen weeks and remaining on the charts for 302 consec-

utive weeks. *Tapestry*, which featured a blend of old King standards and new compositions, fused the introspection of the singer/songwriter genre with a warm, homey soulfulness and believable passionate delivery.
Since then, King's intimate delivery and quality work have given her a long, rewarding career. In 1987, King was inducted into the Songwriters Hall of Fame.
A few of her may hits include "It's Too Late/I Feel the Earth Move" (#1), "So Far Away" (#14), "Sweet Seasons" (#9), "Jazzman" (#2), and "Nightingale" (#9). —*Rick Clark*

Writer / 1970 / Epic ✦✦✦
★ **Tapestry** / Mar. 1971 / Epic ✦✦✦✦✦
In the world of popular music, the word "classic" gets bandied about like the word "improved" on ad campaigns, ceasing to mean anything after a while. *Tapestry*, however, is a *classic*, no two ways about it. King (already a very successful songwriter) assembled a collection of her best-known songs, plus some new ones, and gave them intimate heartfelt readings. King's voice had a warm earthy quality, with just the right amount of urgency. Listing highlights is fairly pointless, as the whole album is stunning. —*Rick Clark*

○ **Music** / Dec. 1971 / Epic ✦✦✦✦
Without the reserve of self-penned standards to draw upon, *Music* lacked the powerful resonance of its predecessor, *Tapestry*. Nevertheless, songs like "Sweet Seasons," "Brother Brother," "Some Kind of Wonderful," and "Song of Long Ago" make this one of her better efforts. —*Rick Clark*

Rhymes & Reasons / Nov. 1972 / Epic ✦✦✦
On her second followup to *Tapestry* and third new album in less than two years, King turned entirely to new compositions, most of them co-written with Toni Stern, rather than relying partly on songs from her back catalog. The result was a thinner collection than *Tapestry* or *Music*, although the album still went to #2 and featured the Top 25 hit "Been To Canaan," as well as the warm love song "The First Day In August." —*William Ruhlmann*

Fantasy / Jun. 1973 / Epic ✦✦✦
By this time, King's work recalled the detached craftmanship of her days as a professional tunesmith. As a result, many of her post-*Tapestry* efforts lacked a certain sense of emotional investment in their performances. Regardless, *Fantasy* (an improvement over the previously released *Rhymes and Reasons*) produced three hits with "Believe in Humanity" (#28), "Corazon" (number 37), and "You Light Up My Life" (number 67). Other highlights include "A Quiet Place to Live" and "Directions." —*Rick Clark*

Wrap Around Joy / Sep. 1974 / Epic ✦✦✦
○ **Really Rosie** / 1975 / Caedmon ✦✦✦✦
This winning soundtrack collaboration for a children's TV special (with children's author Maurice Sendak) was a return to form for King. *Really Rosie* contains some of King's best solo material. This is an enjoyable listening experience for children and adults alike. —*Rick Clark*

Thoroughbred / Jan. 1976 / Epic ✦✦✦
After a series of solid but unexceptional albums, King re-collaborated with her first husband Gerry Goffin and produced her best album since *Tapestry*. Like *Tapestry*, much of *Thoroughbred* reflected a rich soulfulness. The only thing lacking was *Tapestry*'s amazing collection of standards. The emotive "Only Love Is Real" became a substantial hit. —*Rick Clark*

Simple Things / Jul. 1977 / Capitol ✦✦
Carole King moved to Capitol Records with this release and introduced as her lyric collaborator Rick Evers, who became her third husband. The new associations, however, did not signal an impressive new phase in her work. The rollicking "Hard Rock Cafe," which anticipated the chain of restaurants by a decade was the only moderate hit here, with most of the music well-meaning but lacking the distinctiveness of King's previous pop classics. Similarly, Navarro, her backup band, was adequate but no more. Despite the stimulus of a new label, *Simple Things* became King's first album since her breakthrough with *Tapestry* to peak below the Top 10. —*William Ruhlmann*

Welcome Home / 1978 / Capitol ✦✦
After seven straight gold-selling, Top 20 albums, *Welcome Home* demonstrated thoroughly that Carole King was on the wrong track. Her third husband, Rick Evers, who wrote lyrics for some of her songs and is pictured with her on the record cover, died of a drug overdose after this album was recorded in January 1978, but

before it was released in May, which seems emblematic of the problems here. They include "Venusian Diamond," a song that deliberately borrows gimmicks from Beatles records, and "Disco Tech." That's right, Carole King goes disco. There were no hits, although "Morning Sun" made a brief appearance in the Adult Contemporary chart, and there was certainly nothing that was up to King's usual standards. The album failed to make the Top 100 and effectively removed King from the top echelon of pop artists. — *William Ruhlmann*

○ **Her Greatest Hits** / Mar. 1978 / Epic ◆◆◆

All of King's major hits are here, plus a few key album tracks. It's a decent starting place for the uninitiated, but *Tapestry* is a richer listening experience. — *Rick Clark*

Touch the Sky / 1979 / Capitol ◆◆

Pearls: Songs of Goffin and King / 1980 / Scarface ◆◆◆

King reprises the early-'60s pop gems she wrote with Gerry Goffin, with fine results. — *Dan Heilman*

One to One / 1982 / Atlantic ◆◆

City Streets / Apr. 1989 / Capitol ◆◆

Carole King's first album in six years also marks her return to Capitol Records, for whom she recorded from 1977 to 1980. She tries updating her sound, with aggressive guitars played on a couple of cuts by Eric Clapton, synthesizers, and drum machines, while singing lyrics that declare her renewed passion and hope. King was never one of pop's deep thinkers, which got her into trouble when she started going cosmic in the late '70s, but here she restricts herself to a kind of willed optimism and determination, and she sings as though she means it. *City Streets* is thus King's most engaging record since her early '70s hits, and even if it's too late for her to reclaim her place in pop music, that's encouraging. — *William Ruhlmann*

Colour of Your Dreams / 1993 / Rhythm Safari ◆◆

The success of "Now And Forever," which was used as the opening-credits music for the summer 1992 film *A League Of Their Own*, seems to have earned Carole King another shot at record-making, albeit with an indie label. That song turns out to be one of the few highlights of a varied collection in which King sings some love songs and then turns to more serious fare, with dubious results. The best new songs here are two that reunite King with old partner Gerry Goffin, who still has a way with a romantic lyric. — *William Ruhlmann*

● **A Natural Woman: The Ode Collection (1968-1976)** / 1994 / Ode ◆◆◆◆

Carole King had already written an enormous amount of pop classics by the time she began her solo career in earnest in the late '60s. With her second album, *Tapestry*, King became one of the most popular and artistically successful singer-songwriters in the early '70s. King never matched the consistent brilliance of *Tapestry*, yet managed to record many fine songs during the rest of the decade. *A Natural Woman* collects all of her finest moments over the course of two discs. *Tapestry* is included in its entirety, along with the highlights from her other albums, making *A Natural Woman* the one essential King album—apart from *Tapestry* itself, of course. — *Stephen Thomas Erlewine*

Evelyn Champagne King

Soul, Disco

Once a sparkling, youthful star who seemed to be emerging as a perennial winner, Evelyn "Champagne" King didn't completely fulfill the potential she showed in her early records, but still became a very successful artist. She was reportedly discovered while subbing for her sister as a cleaning woman at Sigma Studios in her teens. Producer T. Life heard King singing Sam Cooke's "A Change Is Gonna Come." He took her to RCA, where her debut single vaulted King into prominence in 1978; both "Shame" and "I Don't Know if It's Right" were triumphant, explosive tunes that deserved their Top Ten R&B status. King kept making hits into the mid-'80s, topping the charts with "I'm in Love" and "Love Come Down," both spectacular vocals that elevated good arrangements into great ones. "Betcha She Don't Love You" and "Your Personal Touch" were her final RCA hits, and King moved to EMI-Manhattan in 1988. The song "Flirt" returned her to hit status, peaking at number three R&B.RCA issued a greatest hits/retrospective CD in 1993. — *Ron Wynn*

● **Love Come Down: The Best Of . . .** / Mar. 1993 / RCA ◆◆◆◆

Before the term "disco diva" was universally adopted, Evelyn "Champagne" King was hailed as dance music's reigning female vocalist. King was a sensation in disco's heyday, and she survived the backlash and prospered during the genre's evolution into dance music. She enjoyed a string of hits into the mid-'80s and was able to excel on rhythm-dominated material and sentimental ballads. This 15-track anthology includes her finest uptempo cuts ("Shame," "I'm In Love," and "Love Come Down," all done at the original hit length), plus underrated numbers such as "Don't Hide Our Love" and "Give Me One Reason." Those who remember King's hits will savor this collection, while others who missed her prime period will hear why she was so dominant. — *Ron Wynn*

The Kingsmen

Group, Rock & Roll

A rock & roll band from Portland, OR, the Kingsmen's one big hit "Louie, Louie" defined the garage-band style and became one of the all-time classics. The original lineup included Jack Ely (lead singer and guitar), Lynn Easton (drums), Mike Mitchell (lead guitar), Bob Nordby (bass), and Don Galucci (piano). After Ely had "incorrectly" taught the rest of the band the Wailers version of Richard Berry's "Louie Louie" (thus altering the basic rhythm into the now famous duh-duh-duh, duh-duh, duh-duh-duh, duh-duh riff that has become the only way anyone has played it since), they recorded it for fifty dollars at a primitive local recording studio with only three mikes, Ely hollering the lyrics into an overhead boom mike suspended ten feet in the air. Released on a local label, the record went nowhere after Paul Revere & the Raiders quickly covered it in the Northwest market, although it had quickly become a standard for all teen bands in that area. In 1964, the record started to break nationally, causing the breakup of the original lineup when Easton had copyrighted the group's name, informing the other members that he was now sole owner of the Kingsmen and its new lead singer. Ely formed his own Kingsmen, touring at the same time as Easton, who was lip-synching the record whenever possible. Only Easton and Mitchell were left from the original lineup, but they kept scoring big with frat-band versions of "Money" and "Little Latin Lupe Lu," reaching their peak with "The Jolly Green Giant," while Ely lavished in relative obscurity and Gallucci had formed Don & the Goodtimes. By the early '90s, history had redressed itself somewhat. While replacement members from the Easton version of the band toured as the "original" Kingsmen, Jack Ely finally received some of his due, headlining the 30th Anniversary Louie Louie tour. Though the song itself has been covered repeatedly, the version by Ely and the original lineup remains definitive. — *Cub Koda*

In Person / 1963 / Sundazed ◆◆◆

CD reissue of the group's first album, including the rock anthem "Louie Louie," issued here for the first time minus the annoying overdubbed crowd noises. Also nice is the inclusion of three bonus tracks. — *Cub Koda*

Vol. 2 / 1964 / Sundazed ◆◆◆

Supposedly another 'live' album, finally issued here without the audience overdubs. Highlights include "Little Latin Lupe Lu," "Long Green," and "David's Mood," plus two CD bonus tracks. — *Cub Koda*

The Kingsmen on Campus / 1965 / Wand ◆◆

Vol. 3 / 1965 / Sundazed ◆◆◆

The group's third album, again issued here without the overdubbed crowd noises. This features their hit "Jolly Green Giant" plus three CD bonus tracks. — *Cub Koda*

Up and Away / 1966 / Wand ◆◆

● **The Best of the Kingsmen** / 1989 / Rhino ◆◆◆◆

All the hits; great sound. — *Cub Koda*

The Kinks

Group, Rock & Roll, Hard Rock, British Invasion, Pop/Rock

Formed in 1963, the Kinks were one of the most influential groups to emerge from the first wave of the British Invasion.

The band's rather sloppy, but energetic ensemble work, coupled with singer/songwriter Ray Davies's (b. Jun 21, 1944) distinctly British point of view and excellent song sense, plus American producer Shel Talmy, generated a substantial body of classic albums.

They were a thoroughly British garage rock bridge (practically devoid of the overt American blues fascination practiced by the Animals or Rolling Stones) for those who desired an alternative to the bright clean tunefulness of the Beatles.

The Kinks's first stateside hit, "You Really Got Me" (#7), was built around what must be one of rock's most memorable (and influential) guitar riffs. Davies quickly followed suit with the similar (and equally fine) "All Day and All of the Night" (#7). Davies's intelligently barbed take on the British class system increasingly dominated their themes. Eventually, the Kinks gravitated toward conceptual albums. *Arthur, or the Decline and Fall of the British Empire* (released 1969, #105) was one of the first rock operas.

Lola vs. the Powerman & the Money-go-round (1970, #35) would produce their last hit for many years, "Lola" (#9), a song about a transvestite.

A label change to RCA found the band increasingly doing conceptual albums, with fairly spotty results and diminishing sales. Regardless of some good material, the band sounded stale on record compared to their earlier work.

In 1977 the Kinks signed with Arista and gradually enjoyed some substantial hits, including the 1983 hit "Come Dancing" (#6), which tied the highest charting record of their career, 1965's "Tired of Waiting for You." Other hits include "A Well-Respected Man" (#13), "Set Me Free" (#23), "Sunny Afternoon" (#14), and "Dedicated Follower of Fashion" (#36). The Kinks continue to do well as a live and recording unit. *—Rick Clark*

You Really Got Me / 1964 / Rhino ✦✦✦
The highlight of this rather spotty debut (consisting of a sampling of originals and covers the Kinks churned out at gigs) was, without a doubt, the title track, which single-handedly pioneered riff-oriented hard rock. "Stop Your Sobbing," a song later recorded by Pretenders, was also a standout track, but producer Shel Talmy's "Bald Headed Woman" was an absolute low point. *—Rick Clark*

Kinda Kinks / 1965 / Rhino ✦✦✦
Album number two featured a rewrite of "You Really Got Me," with the equally fine "All Day and All of the Night" (number seven). Ray Davies, however, delivered a strong set of tunes that went beyond riff-rockers with the exuberant "Come on Now," and "You Shouldn't Be Sad." His penchant for memorable melodies emerged with tracks like "Something Better Beginning" and "Tired of Waiting for You." *—Rick Clark*

☆ **Kink-Size/Kinkdom** / 1965 / Rhino ✦✦✦✦
This Rhino reissue contains the Kinks's third and fourth albums, *Kink-Size* (number 13) and *Kinkdom* (number 47), respectively, plus some non-album sides from the same period. *Kink-Size* featured the hit "Set Me Free" (number 23), another Kinks classic, as well as "Everybody's Gonna Be Happy." By the release of *Kinkdom*, the Kinks had developed an instantly identifiable sound, built around Davies's wavering lower tenor and the group's airy falsetto background vocals and ragged garage rock-like ensemble work. "Dedicated Follower of Fashion" (number 36), a noisy dance-hall rocker, was a wonderful poke at a Carnaby Street fop in his "frilly nylon panties." Other hits included "Who'll Be the Next in Line?" (number 34) and "A Well Respected Man" (number 13). This disc also includes the assertive "I'm Not Like Everybody Else," (originally written as a pitch for the Animals, and the B-side to "Sunny Afternoon". *—Rick Clark*

○ **Kink Kontroversy** / 1965 / PRT ✦✦✦✦
This great album is still only available as a British import. The Kinks sludge out some fine trashy rockers with "Where Have All the Good Times Gone?" (later re-recorded by Van Halen) and "Till the End of the Day" (number 50), a moderate hit. Other highlights included "It's Too Late," "You Can't Win," and "I'm on an Island." *—Rick Clark*

☆ **Face to Face** / 1966 / Reprise ✦✦✦✦✦
Face to Face was another extraordinary Kinks album, this time featuring the hit "Sunny Afternoon" (number 14) and other gems like "Holiday in Waikiki," "Fancy," "Too Much on My Mind," and "Rainy Day in June." *—Rick Clark*

Live at Kelvin Hall / 1967 / Reprise ✦✦✦
Outside of the Rolling Stones' *Got Live If You Want It* and the Beatles' *Live at the Hollywood Bowl*, this is the only readily available concert document of a British Invasion-era band, complete with all of the screaming fans. The Kinks slog through a version of "The Batman Theme," "I'm on an Island," "Milk Cow Blues," and a smattering of hits. *—Rick Clark*

☆ **Something Else by the Kinks** / 1967 / Reprise ✦✦✦✦✦
The followup to *Face to Face* was equally impressive, featuring the wistful "Waterloo Sunset," one of Davies's finest compositions. Other highlights included "Situation Vacant," "David Watts," "Love Me Till the Sun Shines," and Dave Davies's "Death of a Clown." Highly recommended! *—Rick Clark*

☆ **The Village Green Preservation Society** / 1968 / Reprise ✦✦✦✦✦
On *The Kinks Are the Village Green Preservation Society*, Ray Davies's eye for the little lyrical details that speak volumes about everyday people hit a zenith. Initially inspired by Dylan Thomas's portrayal of an indolent Welsh village (*Under the Milkweed*), this was the Kinks' finest conceptual album. Their first album produced without Shel Talmy, it projected an unassuming, low-key quality. It is amazing that this album failed to dent the charts. Fortunately, Warner has released it on CD. Highlights include "Picture Book," "Animal Farm," "Big Sky," "Johnny Thunder," "Wicked Annabella," and the title track. *—Rick Clark*

☆ **Arthur or Decline of the British Empire** / 1969 / Reprise ✦✦✦✦✦
After the commercial disaster of *Village Green Preservation Society*, Ray Davies turned his attentions to collaborating on a TV musical titled *Arthur (Or the Decline and Fall of the British Empire)* with writer Julian Mitchell. Even though the show got canned, the album received much acclaim, placing the Kinks back on the charts. "Victoria" (number 62) became a moderate hit. Other highlights included "Brainwashed," "Australia," "Shangri-la," and the title cut. *—Rick Clark*

○ **Lola vs. the Powerman & the Money-Go-Round, Part One** / 1970 / Reprise ✦✦✦✦
Thanks to the number nine hit single "Lola" (about an encounter with a transvestite), *Lola vs. the Powerman & the Money-Go-Round, Part One* became a comeback of sorts for the Kinks. Overall, this album is a Davies-eye view of life as an artist coping with the road ("This Time Tomorrow") and the music industry, which includes blackly humorous portrayals of the musician's union ("Get Back in Line"), music publishers ("Denmark Street"), making it big ("Top of the Pops"), and greed ("Money-go-round"). This might be a whinefest from a successful pop artist, but his observations aren't that far off base. Musically, the Kinks still had their ragged delivery, but they increasingly employed more acoustic instrumentation, giving the arrangements a slightly folky quality at times. *—Rick Clark*

Percy [O.S.T.] / 1971 / Pye ✦✦
Percy is a soundtrack to a BBC production, but that doesn't mean that Ray Davies didn't hide a few fine songs on the album. Recorded just as the Kinks were shifting from the wistfulness of *Village Green Preservation Society* and *Arthur* to the harder *Lola*, *Percy* tends to repeat some of the same ideas of *Arthur*. Nevertheless, "God's Children," "Animals in the Zoo," and the warped country of "Willesden Green" are fine songs—they just get somewhat lost in the incidental film music, which includes an instrumental version of "Lola." *—Stephen Thomas Erlewine*

○ **Muswell Hillbillies** / 1971 / Rhino ✦✦✦✦
For their first outing on the RCA label, the Kinks adopted a more laidback rootsy sound that even sported traces of country ("Holloway Jail") and dancehall/cabaret theater styles ("Skin and Bones," "Holiday," "Alcohol"). "Twentieth Century Man" is a nice medium-tempo rocker but lacks the reckless fire of their earlier efforts. *—Rick Clark*

Everybody's in Show-Biz / 1972 / Rhino ✦✦✦
One half of this release is a document of the Kinks' spirited live slopfest, including versions of "Top of the Pops," "Holiday," and the "Banana Boat Song." The other half contains a couple of gems like "Celluloid Heroes" and "Sitting in My Hotel," as well as "Motorway," and "Maximum Consumption." *—Rick Clark*

★ **The Kink Kronikles** / 1972 / Reprise ✦✦✦✦✦
Anyone wanting a well-chosen sampler of the best Kinks work, from half of their stay at Reprise, should start here. Many of the essential tracks are here. *—Rick Clark*

Great Lost Kinks Album / 1973 / Reprise ✦✦✦
An aptly titled collection; out of print for many years, there are even some Kinks cultists who have never been able to hear this ragtag but worthy collection of late-'60s and early-'70s outtakes and rarities. Most of these were recorded around the same time as the 1969 LP *Village Green Preservation Society*; these low-key, wry, bouncy tunes would have fit in well with that record. Lyrically, they're on the whole slighter than much of their late-'60s

work, perhaps accounting for why the group did not deign to release them at the time. Still, songs like "Rosemary Rose," "Misty Water," and "Mr. Songbird" would have hardly embarrassed the group, and rank as the highlights of this anthology. Besides 1969-era outtakes, it includes the single "Plastic Man," a couple of okay way-obscure B-sides featuring Dave Davies, and some songs penned for long-forgotten film and television productions. It also has the dynamite 1966 B-side "I'm Not Like Everybody Else," though that's easily available on reissue these days. That's not the case for most of the rest of this album; Kinks fans will find it quite worthwhile, and should be on the lookout for it in the used bins. —*Richie Unterberger*

Preservation: Acts 1 & 2 / 1973 / Rhino ♦♦♦
Initially intended as an extension of *The Village Green Preservation Society*, *Preservation* offered relatively little, in the way of great songwriting or spirited performances, something *Village Green...* had in spades. "Money Talks" is a nice mid-tempo rocker. The Rhino CD includes the single, "Preservation." —*Rick Clark*

The Kinks Present Schoolboys in Disgrace / 1975 / Rhino ♦♦
As the last of the Kinks' overt conceptual excercises, *Schoolboys...* was further proof that Ray Davies's best "plays" happened when he focused his observational skills into singular songs, rather than fleshing out an idea over the course of a whole album. Like *Soap Opera*, this is only recommended for hardcore completists. —*Rick Clark*

The Kinks Present a Soap Opera / 1975 / Rhino ♦♦
Davies's obsession with concept albums reached a nadir with *Soap Opera*. At this point, Davies and company were so busy pandering to their live audiences, they seemed to forget how to make truly memorable music. The lifeless production, indicative of this era of their music, didn't help matters either. Nevertheless, "You Make It All Worthwhile," "Face in the Crowd," and "Everybody's a Star" were highlights from this spotty set. —*Rick Clark*

○ **The Kinks' Greatest: Celluloid Heroes** / 1976 / RCA ♦♦♦♦
This is a good collection comprising the cream of the Kinks' RCA years. It includes "Sitting in My Hotel," "Twentieth Century Man," "Alcohol," and "Everybody's a Star." —*Rick Clark*

Sleepwalker / 1977 / Arista ♦♦♦
For their first release on Clive Davis's Arista label, the Kinks ditched the concept albums, and knuckled down to a workman-like, but unexceptional batch of songs. "Full Moon" and "Juke Box Music" are among the stronger tracks. —*Rick Clark*

Misfits / 1978 / Arista ♦♦♦
A slight improvement over *Sleepwalker*, *Misfits* boasted their first Top 40 hit in eight years, "A Rock'n'Roll Fantasy." —*Rick Clark*

Low Budget / 1979 / Arista ♦♦♦
Even though the Kinks enjoyed their most consistently satisfying album-chart success during their years at Arista, so much of this lacks the vision and execution of their work found on Reprise. Regardless of all that, the disco influenced pop-rocker "(Wish I Could Fly Like) Superman" was a number 41 hit. —*Rick Clark*

One for the Road / 1980 / Arista ♦♦
By this time, the Kinks enjoyed quite a bit of FM rock success, enough to make this servicable live album a hit. A singalong performance of "Lola" even resurrected itself to number 81 on the pop charts. —*Rick Clark*

Give the People What They Want / 1981 / Arista ♦♦♦
The Kinks delivered their interpretation of the mainstream FM rock sound on this effort, producing three moderate radio hits with "Destroyer" (number 85), "Better Things" (number 92) and the title cut. —*Rick Clark*

State of Confusion / 1983 / Arista ♦♦♦
State of Confusion had its share of glossy hard rock in the vein of "Low Budget" and "Destroyer," but the record came to life on the quieter numbers, whether it's the elegiac "Don't Forget to Dance," the wistful pop of "Long Distance," or the buoyant nostalgia of "Come Dancing," which became the group's biggest hit since "Tired of Waiting for You." —*Stephen Thomas Erlewine*

Word of Mouth / 1984 / Arista ♦♦♦
State of Confusion gave the Kinks their biggest single in nearly 20 years, but they didn't try to replicate the music hall-tinged pop of "Come Dancing" on its follow-up *Word of Mouth*, preferring to concentrate on straightahead hard rock. Most of the material was well-crafted, but only a few songs were distinctive, particularly the circular, synth-spiked minor hit "Do It Again." —*Stephen Thomas Erlewine*

○ **Come Dancing with the Kinks: The Best Of the Kinks 1977-1986** / Jul. 1986 / Arista ♦♦♦♦
A sampling of the their Arista years (1977-1986), most of the essential tracks are here, including all of their hits from that period. "Come Dancing," "A Rock 'n' Roll Fantasy," "Juke Box Music," "Destroyer," and "(Wish I Could Fly Like) Superman" are among the titles found here. —*Rick Clark*

Think Visual / Dec. 1986 / MCA ♦♦
Think Visual, the band's first album for MCA Records, represented an artistic dead-end for the Kinks, as Ray Davies continued to crank out a series of competent, but undistinguished hard rockers. Out of all the loud, riff-driven numbers, only Dave Davies' "Rock N' Roll Cities" made a lasting impression. Ray's gentler songs weren't among his most memorable, relying on slight melodies and underdeveloped lyrics. —*Stephen Thomas Erlewine*

The Kinks Live: the Road / 1988 / MCA ♦♦
The Kinks' second album for MCA was *The Kinks Live: The Road*, a tepid document of their workman-like arena-rock shows from 1987. At the time of recording, the group couldn't fill the arenas they were packing in the early '80s, so they began moving back to theaters. Perhaps the band resented being sent back to smaller venues, since they exhibited very little passion or excitement as they ran through their recent hits and old warhorses. The album also included a new, studio-recorded song called "The Road," which was a chronicle of the band's typical touring experiences. Like the rest of the record, the song wasn't anything special. —*Stephen Thomas Erlewine*

UK Jive / 1989 / MCA ♦♦♦
Even though the album was weighed down by its adherence to late-'80s state-of-the-art studio techinques, *UK Jive* was a noticeable improvement over the lackluster *Think Visual*. Featuring only a handful of hard rockers—including the excellent, snarling "Aggravation"—the album comprised pop songs that painted an unfocused portrait of modern British life. Although many of Ray Davies' finest songs were based on a similar concept, his songwriting on *UK Jive* was frustratingly inconsistent, ranging from the infectious bop of the title track to the ham-fisted anthem "Down All Days (To 1992)." With the loping "Looney Balloon," Davies wrote one of his finest songs of the '80s, but the only track that equalled its conviction was his brother Dave's spiteful protest "Dear Margaret." —*Stephen Thomas Erlewine*

★ **Greatest Hits, Vol. 1** / 1989 / Rhino ♦♦♦♦♦
If you are going to budget for only one Kinks disc, this is the one to get. It features all of their biggest '60s chart hits, plus some key B-sides. Nevertheless, their albums from this period feature many fine album cuts worth having, so consider this an excellent primer but not a definitive package. —*Rick Clark*

Lost & Found (1986-89) / 1991 / MCA ♦♦
The Kinks were on MCA Records for a remarkably brief time, recording three albums in three years, including one live record. During these three years, Ray Davies' songwriting was frequently uninspired and formulaic. Not surprisingly, the records didn't feature enough highlights to form an engaging compilation and *Lost & Found* is certainly the weakest of their "best-of" collections, featuring no hit singles at all. Although *Lost & Found* is a better album than either *Think Visual* or *The Kinks Live: The Road*, it isn't as consistent or engaging as *UK Jive*, which remains the only worthwhile record from their time at MCA. —*Stephen Thomas Erlewine*

Phobia / 1993 / Columbia ♦♦
Ray Davies continues to turn out three or four brilliant songs on albums that barely anyone will ever hear. For Kinks fans, that's enough to justify the purchase of any of their recent albums, and the harder-edged *Phobia* is no exception to that rule. —*AMG*

To the Bone / 1994 / Grapevine ♦♦
Since the mid-'70s, the Kinks have not been able to stop themselves from attempting their own variations on pop music trends, taking stabs at everything from bombastic heavy metal to sleek disco-flavored pop. On *To the Bone*, the group became another one of the scores of veteran rock acts to record an acoustic, "unplugged" album. However, the group's American popularity was at an all-time low in the mid-'90s and the band wasn't able to score a major-label record deal, let alone land a spot on MTV's prime-time ratings bonanza, *Unplugged*. So, the group financed their acoustic greatest hits record *To the Bone* themselves, releasing it on the U.K. independent label, Grapevine. Naturally, Ray Davies' songs

work well in such a stripped-back setting, but the album is nothing more than a pleasant diversion, featuring a lovely version of "Waterloo Sunset," possibly the most beautiful song of the rock & roll era. —*Stephen Thomas Erlewine*

BOOKS

♦♦♦ The Kinks: The Official Biography, by Jon Savage (Faber & Faber, 1984). While Johnny Rogan's thick Kinks study remains their most comprehensive biography, this is a worthwhile, if thinner, complement which doesn't overlap too much in coverage. Savage doesn't dig nearly as deep as Rogan does into the intense conflicts between the Davies brothers, or between the group and their managers. Perhaps that's because this is an authorized bio, but there's plenty of interesting stories about the music, which is the most important thing. Most crucially, Savage had access to the Davies brothers, and the book is packed with their recollections, as well as some from other band members, managers, and associates. Well-written and informative, with plenty of excellent photos. —*Richie Unterberger*

♦♦♦♦ The Kinks, by Johnny Rogan (Proteus, 1984). By far the best account of the Kinks' career, crammed with quotes from the members of the band (especially Ray Davies) and such important associates as producer Shel Talmy and early managerial figure Larry Page. Lots of stories about the conception and production of their classic singles and albums like *Something Else*, *Village Green*, and *Arthur*. Also interesting are the accounts of the explosive tensions within the group: the frequent feuds between Ray and Dave Davies, the belittling of drummer Mick Avory (who apparently didn't even play on some of the group's early records), the onstage fight in early 1965 that threatened to finish the group shortly after they became stars, the disorderly tours of America (from which they were banned by the musicians' union for three years in the '60s), and more. Contains mammoth, definitive discography, including bootlegs, foreign releases, and songs that Ray and Dave Davies wrote for other artists. —*Richie Unterberger*

Kiss

Group, Hard Rock, Heavy Metal

Rooted in the campy theatrics of Alice Cooper and the sleazy hard rock of glam rockers New York Dolls, Kiss became an favorite for American teenagers in the '70s. Most kids were infatuated with the look of Kiss, not their music. Decked out in outrageously flamboyant costumes and makeup, the band fashioned a captivating stage show featuring dry ice, smoke bombs, elaborate lighting, blood spitting and fire breathing that captured the imaginations of thousands of kids. But Kiss' music shouldn't be dismissed out of hand—it was a commercially potent mix of anthemic, fist-pounding hard rock driven by sleek hooks and ballads powered by loud guitars, cloying melodies and sweeping strings. It was a sound that laid the groundwork for both arena rock and the pop-metal that dominated rock in the late '80s.

Kiss was the brainchild of Gene Simmons (bass, vocals) and Paul Stanley (rhythm guitar, vocals), former members of the New York-based hard rock band Wicked Lester; the duo brought in drummer Peter Criss through his ad in *Rolling Stone* and guitarist Ace Frehley responded to an advertisement in *The Village Voice*. Even at their first Manhattan concert in 1973, the group's approach was quite theatrical; Flipside producer Bill Aucoin offered the band a management deal after the show. Two weeks later, the band was signed to the Neil Bogart's fledgling record label Casablanca. Kiss released their self-titled debut in February of 1974; it peaked at number 87 on the U.S. charts. By April of 1975, the group had released three albums and had toured America constantly, building up a sizable fan base. Culled from those numerous concerts, *Alive!* (released in the fall of 1975) made the band rock & roll superstars; it climbed into the Top Ten and its accompanying single, "Rock'N'Roll All Nite" made it to number 12. Their follow-up, *Destroyer*, was released in March of 1976 and became the group's first platinum album; it also featured their first Top Ten single, Peter Criss' power ballad "Beth."

A 1977 Gallup poll named Kiss the most popular band in America. Kiss mania was in full swing and thousands of pieces of merchandise hit the marketplace. The group had two comic books released by Marvel, they had pinball machines, makeup and masks, board games, and an animated television special, *Kiss Meet the Phantom of the Park*. The group was never seen in public without wearing their make-up and their popularity was growing by leaps

and bounds; the membership of the Kiss Army, the band's fan club, was now in the six figures. Even such enormous popularity had its limits and the band reached them in 1978, when all four members released solo albums on the same day in October. Simmons' record was the most successful, reaching number 22 on the charts, yet all of them made it into the Top 50. *Dynasty*, released in 1979 continued their streak of platinum albums, yet it was their last recorded with the original lineup—Criss left in 1980.

Kiss Unmasked, released in the summer of 1980, was recorded with session drummer Anton Fig; Criss' permanent replacement, Eric Carr, joined the band in time for their 1980 world tour. *Kiss Unmasked* was their first record since *Destroyer* to fail to go platinum and 1981's *Music from the Elder*, the first album recorded with Carr, didn't even go gold—it couldn't even climb past number 75 on the charts. Ace Frehley left the band after its release; he was replaced by Vinnie Vincent in 1982. Vincent's first album with the group, 1982's *Creatures of the Night*, fared better than *Music from the Elder*, yet it couldn't make it past number 45 on the charts.

Sensing it was time for a change, Kiss dispensed with their makeup for 1983's *Lick It Up*. The publicity worked, as the album became their first platinum record in four years. *Animalize*, released the following year, was just as successful and the group had recaptured its niche. Vincent left right after *Animalize* and was replaced by Mark St. John; St. John was soon taken ill with Reiter's Syndrome and left the band. Bruce Kulick became Kiss' new lead guitarist in 1984. For the rest of the decade, Kiss turned out a series of best-selling albums, culminating in the early 1990 hit ballad "Forever," which was their biggest single since "Beth."

Kiss were scheduled to record a new album with their old producer Bob Ezrin in 1990 when Eric Carr became severely ill with cancer; he died in November of 1991 at the age of 41. Kiss replaced him with Eric Singer and recorded *Revenge* (1992), their first album since 1989; it was a Top Ten hit and went gold. Kiss followed it with the release of *Alive III* the following year; it performed respectably, but not up to the standards of their two previous live records. In 1994, 20 years after the release of their first album, Kiss became a hip name, as both heavy metal and alternative rockers claimed the band as one of their childhood favorites, as did country superstar Garth Brooks. *Kiss My Ass*, a tribute album organized by the band, became a minor hit. All of the attention was a vindication for the group, who had never been hip nor critical favorites. —*Stephen Thomas Erlewine*

○ **Kiss** / Apr. 1974 / Casablanca ♦♦♦♦
Compared to their later albums, Kiss' self-titled debut is a raw, riveting dose of heavy metal. At the time of its recording, the group was still working out its sound, trying to develop their loud, lumbering guitar riffs into sleek, melodic heavy hooks. Kiss only succeeds in streamlining their bombast on a couple of tracks—"Deuce," "Black Diamond," "Firehouse," "Strutter"—but the rest of the record sounds vigorous and forceful, making up for the lapses in songwriting quality. —*Stephen Thomas Erlewine*

Hotter Than Hell / Nov. 1974 / Casablanca ♦♦♦
Hotter Than Hell is nearly an identical replica of Kiss' first album, which isn't surprising, considering how quickly it was recorded after their debut. *Hotter Than Hell* has a few highlights—"Parasite," "Let Me Go, Rock and Roll," "Got to Choose," and the title track—but overall the riffs weren't as catchy and the songs weren't as well-written as *Kiss*. —*Stephen Thomas Erlewine*

○ **Dressed to Kill** / Apr. 1975 / Casablanca ♦♦♦♦
With *Dressed to Kill*, Kiss began to write songs that delivered on the promise of their live shows. Driven by the pounding, but catchy, hooks of "Rock and Roll All Nite" and "She," the album increases the amount of melody Kiss works into their songs. Kiss also increases their sleaze content, delivering obvious, leering double entendres like "Room Service," "Love Her All I Can," and "Ladies in Waiting" throughout the record. But the hooks make the sleaze appealing, and when they can't come up with convincing melodies, the group has polished their sound enough to make the filler enjoyable. —*Stephen Thomas Erlewine*

★ **Alive!** / Oct. 1975 / Casablanca ♦♦♦♦♦
Given the wildly inconsistent quality of Kiss' first three albums, the high quality of *Alive!* comes as somewhat of a surprise. Then again, Kiss were showmen, not songwriters, which means they were always at their best when they were on stage. Part of that show—the makeup, the explosions, the lights, the dry ice—could not be replicated on record, but the group was invigorated by the live setting, adding passion and conviction to their thunderously

loud riffs. Of course, some of the material still falls flat, but most of *Alive!* seeths with energy, making their finest moments—"Rock and Roll All Nite," "Deuce," "Strutter," "Black Diamond," "She," "Hotter than Hell"—seem like hard rock classics. *—Stephen Thomas Erlewine*

○ **Destroyer** / 1976 / Casablanca ✦✦✦✦

Kiss followed the breakthrough Top Ten success of *Alive!* with *Destroyer*, the most pop-oriented record they had ever recorded. Under the direction of producer Bob Ezrin (Alice Cooper), the group's recorded sound became as theatrical as their live shows, featuring strings, sound effects, multi-layered guitars and vocals. That doesn't necessarily mean *Destroyer* is a better record than *Dressed to Kill*—it means the album is a set of slick pop/rock that hides its lack of improved songwriting with stylish production flourishes. Despite the presence of the throttling "Shout It Out Loud" and "Detroit Rock City," none of the rockers are quite as direct and memorable as "Rock and Roll All Night," but that's remedied by the heavily orchestrated proto-power-ballad "Beth." *—Stephen Thomas Erlewine*

○ **Rock and Roll Over** / 1976 / Casablanca ✦✦✦✦

Rock and Roll Over was Kiss' second straight number 11 album, and it was a marginally better album than the previous *Destroyer*, featuring a harder, more direct production and improved songwriting, as illustrated by the hit singles "Calling Dr. Love" and "Hard Luck Woman." *—Stephen Thomas Erlewine*

○ **Love Gun** / Jul. 1977 / Casablanca ✦✦✦✦

By the time of *Love Gun*, Kiss had perfected their gimmick, turning in a set of sleek, slick hard rock that celebrated its silly, tongue-in-cheek jokes and grotesque imagery. The group had polished all of the rough edges out of its sound, leaving a collection of hard-driving riffs that were more catchy than heavy. Songwriting was still a problem for the band, but *Love Gun* was one of their most consistent albums, featuring the concert staples "Christine Sixteen," "Plaster Caster," and "Love Gun." *—Stephen Thomas Erlewine*

Alive II / Nov. 1977 / Casablanca ✦✦✦

Kiss recorded *Alive!* after the release of their first three albums. *Alive II* appeared after *Love Gun*, their sixth studio album, giving the band three albums of new material for their new live record. Even with all the fresh material—including a side of new songs recorded in the studio—*Alive II* isn't nearly as energetic as Kiss' first live album. The problem with *Alive II* lies with the fact that the three albums that followed *Alive!* were better-produced than their first three records. Since the songs on *Destroyer, Rock and Roll Over*, and *Love Gun* were crafted in the studio, they weren't as raw or rocking as the songs that comprised Kiss' first albums, and consequently they didn't work quite as well on stage, where they were divorced from the detailed production of the original records. Nevertheless, songs like "Detroit Rock City," "Shout It Out Loud," and "Calling Dr. Love" benefitted from the live setting, with their riffs coming across more forcefully than the in-studio version. Overall, *Alive II* doesn't match the sheer power of Kiss' first live record. *—Stephen Thomas Erlewine*

● **Double Platinum (Greatest Hits)** / 1978 / Casablanca ✦✦✦✦

An imperfect collection, it still represents the best of their early peak years. *—Dan Heilman*

Dynasty / 1979 / Casablanca ✦✦✦

Although *Dynasty* was another Top Ten platinum success for Kiss, it marked the beginning of their turn-of-the-decade decline. Featuring a noticeable lack of memorable songs—only the hits "I Was Made for Lovin' You" and "Sure Know Something" stand out amidst the scores of undistinguished numbers—the record's main weakness is the workman-like performance of the band, which adds no style to their limp material. *—Stephen Thomas Erlewine*

Kiss Unmasked / 1980 / Casablanca ✦✦

Kiss Unmasked was the group's first album since *Destroyer* to not go platinum, and it's easy to see why. Driven by pedestrian riffs and melodies, none of the songs are memorable, and the group sounds uninspired throughout the record. Peter Criss left during the recording of the album; session drummer Anton Fig completed the record after Criss' departure. The change in drummers isn't evident in the music, but what the music does make clear is that it was time for Kiss to change their act. *—Stephen Thomas Erlewine*

Music from the Elder / 1981 / Casablanca ✦✦

On *Music from the Elder*, the first album the band recorded with Eric Carr, Kiss reworked their trashy metal aesthetic into a more ambitious and pretentious variation on hard rock. Recorded with an orchestra and a choir, the record sounded like nothing else in the band's catalog. While Kiss' desire to change musical direction was admirable, the stilted results aren't successful—in fact, they're frequently embarrassing. *—Stephen Thomas Erlewine*

Creatures of the Night / 1982 / Casablanca ✦

Ace Frehley left the band after *Music from the Elder* and the guitarist was replaced with Vinnie Vincent for *Creatures of the Night*, a return to the bombastic hard rock of Kiss' glory years. Although Vincent's playing is impressive, the group failed to write distinctive material, making the album sound like the work of a band well past their prime. *—Stephen Thomas Erlewine*

Lick It Up / 1983 / Mercury ✦✦✦

Kiss had been left scarred by the failures of *Music from the Elder* and *Creatures of the Night*, and they knew it was time for a makeover. So, for *Lick It Up*, the band removed their makeup and costumes for the first time in their careers, ensuring themselves a great deal of media coverage. The ploy worked, but what made *Lick It Up* a platinum success was the quality of the songwriting. While it wasn't up to the standards of *Dressed to Kill* and *Destroyer*, *Lick It Up* was state-of-the-art melodic heavy metal that returned the band to platinum status. *—Stephen Thomas Erlewine*

Animalize / 1984 / Mercury ✦✦

Animalize was more successful than the previous *Lick It Up*, but that's only because its predecessor had accomplished the job of restoring the band's reputation among adolescents. While it followed the same pattern as *Lick It Up*, most of the songs were second rate, with the noticeable exception of the smoldering "Heaven's on Fire." *—Stephen Thomas Erlewine*

Asylum / 1985 / Mercury ✦✦

Sonically, Kiss retained their revitalized roar throughout *Asylum*, turning in a tough, but supple performance that would have been more impressive if the songs were stronger. *—Stephen Thomas Erlewine*

Crazy Nights / 1987 / Mercury ✦✦✦

Like most of Kiss' '80s albums, *Crazy Nights* was an inconsistent set of power ballads and streamlined, polished hard rockers, but the hooks on the album were the strongest band had written since *Lick It Up*. *—Stephen Thomas Erlewine*

● **Smashes, Thrashes & Hits** / 1988 / Casablanca ✦✦✦✦

The companion volume to the above, from their later makeup-less period, includes "Lick It Up," "Let's Put the X in Sex," and "Love Gun." *—Dan Heilman*

Hot in the Shade / 1989 / Mercury ✦✦

Hot in the Shade continued Kiss' late-'80s winning streak, thanks to the hit power ballad "Forever." The rest of the album followed the familiar Kiss blueprint, with only a couple of the tracks meeting the standard of the hit single. *—Stephen Thomas Erlewine*

Revenge / 1992 / Mercury ✦✦✦

Revenge was supposed to be a triumphant return to Kiss' glory days of the mid-'70s, as the band reunited with producer Bob Ezrin, who was responsible for *Destroyer*. However, drummer Eric Carr died in 1991, making the whole affair more sombre and reflective than it was originally intended to be. Kiss replaced Carr with Eric Singer and proceeded to record the album that became *Revenge*. *Revenge* was the most brutal record they had recorded since the mid-'70s, driven by throttling riffs and relentless rhythms. Even though their sound had been considerably beefed up, their songwriting had only improved slightly, with "Heart of Chrome" being a particular standout. *—Stephen Thomas Erlewine*

Alive III / May 18, 1993 / Mercury ✦✦

Kiss' third live album was the weakest of the bunch, due to overly slick performances which tend to sound identical to the original studio versions and add no new dimensions to the songs. *—Stephen Thomas Erlewine*

Kitchens of Distinction

Group, Alternative Pop/Rock

Based in London, this trio plays atmospheric, dreamy music centered around Julian Swales' arpeggiated guitar, chords not commonly found in a rock context, and a great deal of effects, plus a melodic sensibility. Other band members include drummer Dan

Goodwin and vocalist/bassist Patrick Fitzgerald. Although having had some mild success, the band's approach has never quite won the following some might expect. Popular explanations range from the band's strange name to Fitzgerald's open homosexuality, but whatever the reason, the band still has not grown beyond cult status. —*Steve Huey*

● **Love Is Hell** / 1989 / A&M ✦✦✦✦
Well-crafted, spatial, melodic rock, and strong writing distances this group from similar swirly-guitar outfits. —*Steve Aldrich*

Strange Free World / 1991 / One Little Indian ✦✦✦
The strong followup to "Love Is Hell." —*Steve Aldrich*

The Death of Cool / Aug. 4, 1992 / A&M ✦✦✦

Cowboys and Aliens / 1995 / A&M ✦✦✦

Kix

Group, Hard Rock, Heavy Metal
Kix has been recording for over ten years, but they have had exactly one hit—the power ballad "Don't Close Your Eyes," from their 1988 album *Blow My Fuse*. But to call it a power ballad is to imply that the band was no different from the rest of the hard rock/heavy metal bands of the '80s and the truth is, they *were* different. Kix was different simply because they were much better—they had better hooks, they rocked harder, and they could write songs. They were also more clever than the average heavy metal band, yet that never meant they treated their adolescent anthems as jokes; it meant that they loved the music they were making so much that their albums sounded like a constant party. Naturally, they were critics' favorites and never became big stars, even in heavy metal circles; when Metallica was all the rage during the '80s, Kix's good-time metal was seen as wimpy by most metal fans. However, their albums hold up better than any of the pop metal bands that sold millions of records while Kix was struggling in the clubs. —*Stephen Thomas Erlewine*

○ **Kix** / 1981 / Atlantic ✦✦✦✦

Cool Kids / 1983 / Atlantic ✦✦✦

Midnight Dynamite / 1985 / Atlantic ✦✦✦

● **Blow My Fuse** / 1988 / Atlantic ✦✦✦✦
Their third album is an amazingly confident mixture of assured rock scorchers and self-respecting power ballads. —*John Floyd*

Hot Wire / 1991 / Atlantic ✦✦✦

Klaatu

Group, Pop/Rock
In August of 1976, the self-titled debut album by an unknown group called Klaatu was released on Capitol Records to little notice. The following February Steve Smith, a writer for the *Providence Journal* in Rhode Island, wrote an article titled "Could Klaatu Be the Beatles? Mystery Is a Magical Mystery Tour." The article began the rumor that Klaatu was "more than likely either in part or in whole the Beatles." These conjectures, fueled by a series of articles in trade magazines like *Billboard* created a huge amount of hype and Capitol did nothing to deny or confirm the rumors. Throughout 1977, record sales soared and radio stations ran "Is Klaatu the Beatles?" promotions. Reportedly, some of the "clues" as to whether or not Klaatu was the Beatles included backward messages, Morse code, references to the group's identities in the song lyrics, and the word "Beatles" hidden in various places on the record jacket. After several months of conjecture, the group's identity was revealed at the end of year—it wasn't the Beatles after all, it was Terry Draper (songwriter, vocalist, drummer), John Woloschuck, and Dee Long. Immediately, their record sales declined, and due to a backlash generated by the Beatles hoax their four subsequent albums failed to sell. The group broke up in 1981. —*Jim Powers*

○ **Klaatu** / 1976 / Capitol ✦✦✦✦

Hope / 1977 / Capitol ✦✦✦

Sir Army Suit / 1978 / Capitol ✦✦

Endangered Species / 1980 / Capitol ✦✦

● **Peaks** / 1993 / Attic ✦✦✦✦
Klaatu: three anonymous Toronto no-names who in 1976 were handed possibly the biggest simultaneous marketing boost and kiss-of-death in the history of pop: their debut album *3:47 E.S.T.* was widely rumoured to have been an anonymous recording by The Beatles. There's no denying the Fab Four influence in Klaatu's work, but this collection demonstrates that the trio had a larger

scope than they were usually given credit for. While *Peaks'* 17 tracks (72 minutes) offer a balanced and generous snapshot of Klaatu's five studio albums, one of the group's most popular songs—"California Jam"—and one of their best—"Everybody Took a Holiday"—were inexplicably omitted. —*Roch Parisien*

The KLF

Group, House Music, Alternative Pop/Rock, Techno
At the height of their career in the late '80s and early '90s, Bill Drummond and Jimmy Cauty were among the top figures in house music. All of their various permutations—Justified Ancients of Mu Mu, the Timelords, and, their most commercially successful group, the KLF—were very popular in the U.K.'s underground dance scene. The duo created with their liberal use of samples a dense, throbbing house mix filled that spat in the face of all pop and traditions. The best example of their flippant disregard for tradition is their surprise crossover single, "Justified and Ancient," which featured the standard-issue bass-heavy club beat with the vocals of country legend Tammy Wynette. After the success of the single, KLF announced they had broken up and that they were immediately pulling all of their recordings off the market. After a little time off, Drummond and Cauty resumed recording under a variety of different names. —*Stephen Thomas Erlewine*

Chill Out / 1990 / Wax Trax! ✦✦✦

○ **The What Time Is Love Story** / 1990 / KLF Communications ✦✦✦✦

● **The White Room** / 1991 / Arista ✦✦✦✦
Formerly known as Justified Ancients of Mu Mu, aka The Jams and the Timelords, the Kopyright Liberation Front (KLF) created dance music with as many samples as possible without getting busted. *White Room* is their debut and contains "Justified and Ancient," a surprise hit with Tammy Wynette on vocals. —*John Book*

Klymaxx

Group, Soul, Disco, R&B
All-female band formed in 1979 by producer Bernadette Cooper, who also played drums. The original lead vocalists were Lorena Porter Shelby and Joyce "Fenderella" Irby, who later left for a solo career. In 1990, the group became a trio, with Shelby, guitarist Cheryl Cooley, and keyboardist Robbin Grider. "I Miss You" was a major hit for the band in 1985. —*Steve Huey*

● **Never Underestimate the Power of a Woman** / 1981 / Solar ✦✦✦✦
This was Klymaxx's second and final Solar album, and they got even louder and more assertive and confrontational than on their debut. The title track was a clever outing, although it got a little too cute in spots. But "Meeting in the Ladies Room" was a huge hit, and the group seemed on its way as a viable alternative to standard women's vocal groups. None of them were exactly great instrumentalists, but they got mileage out of being guitarists, keyboardists, and drummers as well as singers. —*Ron Wynn*

Girls Will Be Girls / 1982 / Solar ✦✦✦
The R&B/funk/urban contemporary women's ensemble Klymaxx began their careers in the early '80s with this debut album on Solar. It was a historic occasion on many levels. This marked the beginning of the Jam/Lewis production combine, as Klymaxx was the first band they wrote songs for and produced. It also marked drummer Bernadette Cooper's entry into the arena as a bandleader, making them one of the rare African-American women's groups that was as much an instrumental as vocal unit. In fact, they got more attention for the fact that everyone except Loreana Porter played an instrument than for their harmonies, which were, to put it mildly, routine. Porter had a strong voice, but used it more to punctuate songs and shout than to interpret lyrics. —*Ron Wynn*

Girls in the Band / 1983 / Elektra ✦✦✦

Meeting in the Ladies Room / 1984 / Constellation ✦✦
Klymaxx enjoyed their biggest success on their debut album for MCA. It got them their biggest hit with "The Men All Pause," the kind of song that they only hinted at doing before and should have continued updating long afterward. This was the last go-round for the original band, and everyone seemed inspired and energetic. It had an air of brashness and uncertainty, one they unfortunately weren't able to maintain. —*Ron Wynn*

Maxx Is Back / May 15, 1990 / MCA ✦✦
Klymaxx made a bid to re-establish themselves in 1990 with a revised lineup and revamped sound. Now it was essentially a classic women's singing trio, with Loreana Porter's voice clearly the

strongest, and Robbin Gridder and Cheryl Cooper harmonizing around her and at times doing leads. They did more conventional urban contemporary material like "Good Love" and "Don't Run Away" and had almost eliminated the rock/funk and dance/pop trappings. It didn't work, at least from a commercial standpoint, but it was a good try. —*Ron Wynn*

Klymaxx / Constellation ✦✦✦
This was their least enjoyable and entertaining record. There had been some personnel shuffling and internal discord, and they had shifted labels; this self-titled late '80s album lacked clever novelty tracks, hard-hitting rock/funk tunes, and even sultry, innuendo-laden ballads. It just had faceless, routine filler, weak arrangements, and generic production. —*Ron Wynn*

KMFDM

Group, Industrial, Alternative Pop/Rock
KMFDM was one of Wax Trax's first industrial superstars, combining the corrosive scratching of their guitars with a hard, throbbing hip-hop derived beat. In the late '80s, the German trio (originally a quartet) became an underground sensation not only in America but in much of Europe; clubs became devoted to playing their style of abrasive, distorted guitar-driven dance music. KMFDM continues to be one of the major industrial bands of the '90s, with their recordings becoming even more aggressive, both musically and politically. —*Stephen Thomas Erlewine*

What Do You Know Deutschland / 1986 / Wax Trax! ✦✦
Don't Blow Your Top / 1988 / Wax Trax! ✦✦✦
○ **Uaioe** / 1989 / Wax Trax! ✦✦✦✦
● **Naive** / 1990 / Wax Trax! ✦✦✦✦
KMFDM's fourth full-length album is their strongest release to date. It's a claustrophobic wall of noise, driven by a relentless jackhammer beat. —*Stephen Thomas Erlewine*

Money / 1992 / Wax Trax! ✦✦✦
Sucks / 1993 / Wax Trax! ✦✦
Angst / 1994 / Wax Trax! ✦✦✦
Nihil / 1995 / Wax Trax! ✦✦

The Knack

Group, New Wave, Power Pop/Anglo-Pop
The Knack made a nod to the '60s power-pop sound, pushing the image of themselves as the American Beatles on their 1979 debut album cover. All of the members were experienced musicians and they didn't try to hide their attempt to market their way to the top. Cleverly crafted pop songs like their smash hit "My Sharona," which sold over five million copies, were aimed straight at the teen-pop market. "Good Girls Don't," the follow-up single to "My Sharona," was another strong hit. Their subsequent albums tried to repeat this initial success, even using blatant copies of previous songs, but failed. After the third album, the Knack folded; some members stayed together as the Game, while vocalist Doug Fieger started the band Taking Chances. In the '90s, the band re-formed with a new drummer, Billy Ward, but didn't make much of a splash. —*Scott Bultman*

● **Get the Knack** / 1979 / Capitol ✦✦✦✦
The band attempted to update the Beatles sound for the new wave era on their debut. A good idea that was well executed, but critics cried "foul" when millions sold after Capitol's pre-release hype (it went gold in 13 days and eventually sold five million copies, making it one of the most successful debuts in history). *Get the Knack* is at once sleazy, sexist, hook-filled and endlessly catchy—above all, it's a guilty pleasure and an exercise in simple fun. When is power-pop *legitimate* anyway? Includes the unforgettable hits "My Sharona" and "Good Girls Don't." —*Chris Woodstra*

. . . But the Little Girls Understand / 1980 / Capitol ✦✦✦
Mike Chapman summed it up best in the liner notes—"The songs are an assortment of feelings and emotions expressed redundantly as only the Knack can...This record is very dear to me and my bank manager." The self-deprecating title (which quotes Willie Dixon's "Back Door Man") isn't really an attempt to apologize but rather to let everyone know that they were in on the joke all along—and they're laughing all the way to the bank. This is essentially a rewrite of the debut especially evident on the lead-off single "Baby Talks Dirty." It's not as good as *Get the Knack* and didn't sell nearly as well, but it *is* a good time for those who don't take rock & roll too seriously. —*Chris Woodstra*

Round Trip / 1981 / Capitol ✦✦
By the time their third album was released in 1981, the *Knuke the Knack* backlash had been long forgotten but so had skinny ties. A slightly more low-key effort, *Round Trip* is a pleasant though unmemorable collection from a fast-fading era. The commercial failure of this album prompted the band to call it quits until reuniting in 1991. —*Chris Woodstra*

Serious Fun / 1991 / Charisma ✦✦
Nearly a decade since the failure of *Round Trip, Serious Fun* marks the reunited band's attempt at credibility through a harder-rocking sound. Though "Rocket O' Love" stirred up some regional radio interest, the album is their least fun to date. —*Chris Woodstra*

○ **Retrospective: The Best of the Knack** / Nov. 16, 1992 / Capitol ✦✦✦✦
A fine greatest hits set that collects the best from their debut and their two weaker follow-ups. —*Stephen Thomas Erlewine*

Knickerbockers

Group, Pop/Rock
In early 1966, the Knickerbockers hit the Top 20 with "Lies," the best and most accurate early Beatle imitation ever recorded; the lead vocals were a dead ringer for John Lennon, and the whole production could have fit in snugly on the second side of *A Hard Day's Night.* Actually a frat-rock band from New Jersey who didn't write much of their own material, they never made anything else as successful or good. A couple decent follow-ups, "One Track Mind" and the similarly mock British Invasion "High on Love," were small hits, but their albums were even blander than many of the era's other one-shot artists. Their three noteworthy singles were all featured in Rhino's *Nuggets* series, and everyone but '60s completists would be advised to stick with those tracks. Drummer and singer Jimmy Walker briefly replaced Bill Medley in the Righteous Brothers. —*Richie Unterberger*

Lloyd Thaxton Presents the Knickerbocker / 1965 / Challenge ✦✦
Jerk & Twine Time / 1965 / Challenge ✦✦
Even if you're a dedicated collector, you should think twice about chasing down this album, which consists almost entirely of British Invasion and R&B covers in the frat-rock style, and not done especially well. The CD reissue has three bonus tracks, and an interview with a couple members of the band. —*Richie Unterberger*

Lies / 1965 / Challenge ✦✦
Recorded in Hollywood, with songwriting contributions from such top session men of the day as Glen Campbell, Jim Seals, and Dash Crofts, this is, aside from the first-rate title track, an extremely generic mid-'60s set, with only one group original other than "Lies." The Knickerbockers never found an identity, alternating between frat-rock, flaccid pop-rock, and strange wall-of-sound productions in which the producers apparently had visions of turning them into the Walker Brothers. The CD reissue has three bonus tracks, and an interview with a couple members of the band. —*Richie Unterberger*

Stick with Us / 1985 / Line ✦✦
● **The Fabulous Knickerbockers** / 1988 / Sundazed ✦✦✦✦
This "best-of" collection includes the hits "Lies" (one of the greatest mid-'60s singles) and "One Track Mind." Tracks like "I Can Do It Better," "Rumors, Gossip, Words Untrue" and "High on Love" are more period highlights. This set contains ample annotation and great sound. —*Rick Clark*

Great Lost Album / Sundazed ✦✦✦
Those into the camp aspects of pop culture will enjoy the idealistic "The Coming Generation," or adolescent swinger fantasy poppers "Playgirl" and "The Pad and How to Use It"—complete with cheesy organ and garage rock guitar leads. —*Rick Clark*

Frederick Knight

b. Aug. 15, 1944
Soul, R&B
Frederick Knight's catchy "I've Been Lonely for So Long" was a sizable R&B hit on Stax in 1972, and he wrote and produced Anita Ward's across-the-board smash "Ring My Bell" in 1979. Knight cut his own "I've Been Lonely for So Long" in Birmingham, Alabama with a seasoned Southern soul crew behind him, and hit again in 1975 with "I Betcha Didn't Know That." —*Bill Dahl*

● **I've Been Lonely for So Long** / Stax ◆◆◆◆
Tuneful, early '70s Southern soul. —*Bill Dahl*

Gladys Knight & the Pips

Group, Soul, R&B, Motown

One of the great soul singers, Gladys Knight was a performer from her childhood years, forming the Pips with her brother Merald and a couple of cousins. They made the Top Ten in 1961 with the heavily doo-wop-influenced "Every Beat of My Heart," and recorded some fine, nowadays overlooked, pop-soul sides for the Fury and Maxx labels in the early and mid-'60s, sometimes under the direction of songwriter Van McCoy. A couple singles from this period, "Letter Full of Tears" and "Giving Up," made the Top 40, but Knight didn't hit her commercial stride until she moved to Motown in 1966. Steeped in the gospel tradition, like so many soul singers, Knight & the Pips developed into one of Motown's most dependable acts, although they never quite scaled the commercial or artistic heights of fellow stars on the label like the Supremes, Marvin Gaye, and the Temptations. With Norman Whitfield providing the production and much of the songwriting, the Pips fit into the mainstream of Motown's machine well, scoring big hits with some rabble-rousers (like "Friendship Train" and the original version of "I Heard It Through the Grapevine"), mainstream mid-tempo soul ("It Should Have Been Me" and "The End of Our Road,") and smooth ballads like "If I Were Your Woman."

In 1973, Knight had her biggest Motown hit with "Neither One of Us," which made number two; shortly afterwards, she and the Pips left Motown for Buddah. The group were briefly superstars in 1973–74, reeling off the smashes "Midnight Train to Georgia" (their only number one), "I've Got to Use My Imagination," and "Best Thing That Ever Happened to Me." This ranked as some of their best material, but Gladys soon moved toward an easy listening, adult contemporary direction, one that she's maintained to this day. Now performing separately from the Pips (who have retired), her days as a high-charting star ended after the mid-'70s, although she remains fairly popular. —*Richie Unterberger*

Letter Full of Tears / 1961 / Collectables ◆◆◆
A good anthology of early tracks by Gladys Knight and the Pips that were recorded for the Fury label in the early '60s. They were far from a polished act at the time, and didn't get the caliber of material or production they'd receive later at Motown. But the potential was shown on several tracks, notably the title cut, which the group did when Knight was only 12 years old. They later made another version of the song for Motown. This has better sound than some earlier Collectables titles. —*Ron Wynn*

Everybody Needs Love / 1967 / Motown ◆◆◆
Included are some fine Motown cuts. —*Rick A. Bueche*

○ **Greatest Hits** / 1970 / Soul ◆◆◆◆

Motown Legends / 1971 / Motown ◆◆◆
A nice outing, though not as comprehensive as the anthology and not as concise as the earlier greatest hits package. But it didn't contain much filler, and included every significant hit on Motown. If you want one collection, you couldn't go wrong with this one. —*Ron Wynn*

The Very Best of Gladys Knight & the Pips / 1971 / Pair ◆◆
Motown can't resist constantly scavenging its catalog, so out came this collection, which is supposed to be the VERY best, as opposed to the best or the greatest or the classic performances, etc. The songs are wonderful, but why they keep putting competing packages out that only muddy the waters and confuse people remains the most puzzling marketing question in popular music annals. —*Ron Wynn*

Neither One of Us / 1973 / Motown ◆◆◆
Although they left Motown (actually Soul) shortly after they cut this album, Gladys Knight and the Pips were at their performing peak during the early '70s. This magnificent title track featured stunning vocals by Knight and equally effective backing vocals from the Pips, and had several other outstanding songs on it. Why Motown never pushed them as much as they could have mystified many at the time, and while Knight and the Pips didn't surpass their Motown material at other labels, they created enough outstanding songs to justify their decision to leave. —*Ron Wynn*

All I Need Is Time / 1973 / Motown ◆◆◆
The final album that Gladys Knight and the Pips did for Motown (Soul) was a bittersweet one. It had a good mix of strong ballads and solid uptempo cuts, was superbly sung and produced, and the

Knight/Pips interplay and timing was perfect. Motown blundered badly in letting them go, and have been repackaging their singles for years ever since. —*Ron Wynn*

○ **Imagination** / Oct. 1973 / Pair ◆◆◆◆
Gladys Knight and the Pips left Motown for Buddah because they felt they would get more attention, a bigger push from the label, and better material. They made their point in a hurry with this album. Knight never sounded more triumphant or soulful than she did on every one of these songs, particularly the title track. This still stands as their finest overall album. —*Ron Wynn*

● **Anthology** / 1974 / Motown ◆◆◆◆
Atlanta family-group Gladys Knight & the Pips had performed together for 14 years before signing with Motown in 1966. Earlier recordings for Huntom (the master recordings were later sold to Vee-Jay), Fury, and Maxx had generated five chart hits, including the Top Ten R&B smashes "Every Beat of My Heart" and "Letter Full of Tears," but it was on the Motown subsidiary Soul that Glady Knight and company hit their stride. This compilation more than adequately covers this period of the Pips' career. Working primarily with producer Norman Whitfield from 1967 through 1969, the group created such Motor City classics as "Everybody Needs Love," "I Heard It Through the Grapevine," "The End of Our Road," and "Friendship Train." From 1970 through 1973 the Pips worked with a variety of Motown producers concentrating on ballads. Although they were perhaps a little less consistent, there was no shortage of hits, the most notable being 1970's "If I Were Your Woman" and 1973's "Neither One of Us (Wants to Be the First to Say Goodbye)." The updated double-CD version of *Anthology*, featuring digitally remastered sound, replaces about a dozen songs with different ones, though this 40-track collection still contains all of the essential hits and adds lengthy liner notes. Be aware that the three early-'60s hits that lead off the volume (on both versions of *Anthology*) are Motown re-recordings, not the originals. —*Rob Bowman*

Visions / 1983 / Columbia ◆◆◆
Leon Sylvers produced one of the finest uptempo hits Gladys Knight and the Pips ever made in "Save the Overtime for Me." It was the kind of jubilant, celebratory, rousing performance that had marked their best Motown singles, and it put some fresh life into what had become a stagnant group. The rest of this album wasn't that good, but it hardly mattered. They got a follow-up number five single, another chart hit with a third release, and were back in the game. —*Ron Wynn*

Every Beat of My Heart / 1989 / Chameleon ◆◆◆
The best collection of Knight's pre-Motown sides, including both of their big early-'60s hits (the title track and "Letter Full of Tears"), but concentrating more heavily on their mid-'60s sessions. These were overseen by Van McCoy, who supplied the group with several of his own compositions as well. McCoy was one of the most melodically ambitious pop/soul composers of the era, and his songs on this compilation—"Either Way I Lose," "Why Don't You Love Me," "Lovers Always Forgive"—are achingly beautiful and rife with unexpected key changes. His "Stop and Get a Hold of Myself," on the other hand, is a more conventional (but equally first-rate) uptempo soul stomper. If there's any criticism of these sides, it's that Knight and the group don't establish a strong identity, handling doo-wop-like ballads, girl-group-tinged pop, McCoy's idiosyncratic songs, and more modern pop-soul with chameleon-like skill. In the end, that doesn't detract from the strength of this CD, which is a collection of fine early to mid-'60s pop/soul. The major flaw is the inexplicable omission of the McCoy composition "Giving Up," a Top 40 hit for the group in 1964. —*Richie Unterberger*

● **Soul Survivors: The Best of Gladys Knight & the Pips** / 1990 / Rhino ◆◆◆◆
Soul Survivors—The Best of Gladys Knight & the Pips picks up where the Motown anthology left off, containing the most important singles that Gladys Knight and the Pips recorded for Buddah, Columbia, and MCA from the early '70s until the late '80s. The Buddah tracks, highlighted by the Jim Weatherly-written "Midnight Train to Georgia" and "Best Thing That Ever Happened to Me," contain some of Knight's most impassioned vocal performances. —*Rob Bowman*

Jean Knight

b. Jun. 26, 1943, New Orleans, LA
Soul, R&B
Knight filed her claim to fame in 1971 with her sassy #1 R&B hit,

"Mr. Big Stuff." Knight had previously recorded for Houston producer Huey Meaux, but it was her 1970 sojourn to Malaco Studios in Jackson, MS, that would make her a star. There she cut the teasing "Mr. Big Stuff," a #2 pop smash on Stax. Immediate followups included the similarly funky "You Think You're Hot Stuff." Knight returned to prominence in 1985 with her cover of Rockin' Sidney's wildly popular zydeco novelty "My Toot Toot." —*Bill Dahl*

● **Mr. Big Stuff** / 1971 / Stax ✦✦✦✦
Funky and hard-hitting, it was recorded at Malaco Studios. —*Richard Pack*

My Toot Toot / 1985 / Mirage ✦✦✦
New Orleans vocalist Jean Knight, who enjoyed a soul smash in the 1960s with "Mr. Big Stuff," scored a novelty winner in the 1980s with her version of what was the nation's most covered song in 1985, "My Toot Toot." There were Cajun, soul, country, blues, and pop versions, and labels were battling each other over the variations and licensing rights. Unfortunately, neither Knight's slightly soulful/humorous edition, nor the resulting album, which had a couple of good ballads, generated much attention beyond the curiosity stage. —*Ron Wynn*

Buddy Knox (Wayne Knox)

b. Jul. 20, 1933, Happy, TX
Rockabilly
The brand of Texas rockabilly that Buddy Knox cooked up around 1957 wasn't quite as raw as that of his Memphis cohorts at Sun, but it was just as commercially potent. Knox sported a light, almost gentle vocal style, and his band, the Rhythm Orchids, obliged with upbeat backing that suited him well. Formed at West Texas State University, the Rhythm Orchids also included Jimmy Bowen on upright bass, and it was Bowen's equally lighthearted vocal on "I'm Stickin' with You" that originally graced the flip side of Knox's first smash, "Party Doll." Roulette Records astutely picked up the master from the tiny Triple-D logo, separated the sides, and the fledgling firm enjoyed two giant hits for the price of one.

"Party Doll" soared to the very top of the pops, and Knox encored with the equally tuneful "Rock Your Little Baby to Sleep" and "Hula Love," which he performed in the 1957 rock flick *Jamboree*. Knox waxed the fine rockabilly-based "Swingin' Daddy," "Devil Woman," and a cover of Ruth Brown's "Somebody Touched Me" for Roulette before moving to Liberty and hitting with a pop-flavored rendition of the Clovers' song "Lovey Dovey" in 1960. Over three decades later, the Texas rocker remains a popular act on the oldies front. —*Bill Dahl*

● **The Best of Buddy Knox** / 1990 / Rhino ✦✦✦✦
This gentle, catchy Texas rockabilly has a pop slant. —*Bill Dahl*

Frankie Knuckles

Group, Urban
New York composer, producer, and former disc jockey Frankie Knuckles has emerged as a star on the house music scene. Knuckles began working as a DJ in 1971 and landed a residency at the club Better Days. While spinning records in a bath house he was offered a chance to own his own club in Chicago, the Warehouse. By the mid-'70s, Knuckles had made it a premier outlet and major player on the disco/dance circuit. He attracted international attention for his remix of First Choice's "Let No Man Put Asunder." Knuckles later remixed songs by Jamie Principle and teamed with Japanese keyboardist Satoshi Tomile. Their 1989 collaboration, "Tears," proved successful, as did Knuckles' debut, "You Can't Hide from Yourself," featuring vocalist Ricky Dillard. Knuckles became one of the first house music personalities signed to a major label deal when he joined Virgin in 1991. *Beyond the Mix* was his debut LP. —*Ron Wynn*

Beyond the Mix / 1990 / Virgin ✦✦✦

Cub Koda

b. Oct. 1, 1948, Detroit, MI
Rock & Roll, Blues Rock, Rockabilly
Founder and leader of the rowdy '70s rock group Brownsville Station ("Smokin' in the Boy's Room," "The Martian Boogie"), Koda has gone on to a solo career as a high-spirited archivist of obscure rock, blues, country, and R&B songs and artists. As a producer, Koda unearthed the "world's worst bar band," King Uszniewicz & the Uszniewicztones; as the frontman for Hound Dog Taylor's resurrected Houserockers, he recorded two raucous albums that are

encyclopedic in their array of blues songs and styles. But perhaps Koda's most lasting contribution to music is as a writer of liner notes and the long-running "Vinyl Junkie" column for the record-collecting magazine *Goldmine*. —*Kit Kiefer*

Cub Koda & the Points / 1980 / Fan Club ✦✦✦
Koda's first solo album after Brownsville Station. Highlights include "Jail Bait" and "Welcome to My Job." —*Stephen Thomas Erlewine*

It's the Blues / 1981 / Fan Club ✦✦✦
This is an intense, eclectic, wonderfully played set with the Houserockers. Lots of fun, it's 100% true to its title. —*Kit Kiefer*

Cub Digs Chuck / 1989 / Garageland ✦✦✦
Koda's tribute album to Chuck Berry, featuring blistering versions of "Johnny B.Goode," "Maybellene," and others. —*Stephen Thomas Erlewine*

○ **Live at B.L.U.E.S. 1982** / 1991 / Wolf ✦✦✦✦
Powerful blues with the Houserockers, raw and loud, with Koda shining on slide. There is a special appearance by Chicago legend Eddie Clearwater. —*Kit Kiefer*

Cub Digs Bo / 1991 / Garageland ✦✦✦
Koda's tribute album to Bo Diddley, including powerhouse renditions of "Mumblin' Guitar," "Roadrunner," and "Background to a Music." —*Stephen Thomas Erlewine*

● **Welcome to My Job: the Cub Koda Collection 1963-93** / 1993 / Blue Wave ✦✦✦✦
Covering everything from his pre-Brownsville Station days to two brand-new songs, *Welcome to My Job* is the definitive collection of Cub Koda's versatile solo career. —*Stephen Thomas Erlewine*

○ **Abba Dabba Dabba: A Bananza of Hits** / 1994 / Schoolkids ✦✦✦✦
Cub Koda's first album for Schoolkids Records is his wildest, funniest, and simply best album in years. —*Stephen Thomas Erlewine*

Kool & the Gang

Group, Funk, Urban, Pop/Rock
One of the leading funk outfits of the '70s and '80s, with gold and platinum platters galore. Formed by bassist Robert "Kool" Bell (b. 1950) as the Jazziacs in Jersey City, the Gang also featured his brothers Robert and Ronald Bell. The crew signed with De-Lite Records in 1969 and began churning out massively funky grooves, hitting full stride in 1973-1974 with "Jungle Boogie," "Hollywood Swinging," and "Higher Plane." The Gang topped the soul charts in 1979 with the high-stepping disco favorite "Ladies Night,"—the same year they hired J. T. Taylor as their new lead singer. "Celebrate!" a staple of every respectable wedding reception of the last dozen years, went platinum for the group in 1980, and their non-stop string of incendiary successes stretched into the mid 80s with "Fresh" and "Cherish." Taylor went solo in 1988. —*Bill Dahl*

Ladies' Night / 1979 / De Lite ✦✦✦
Kool and the Gang began their shift from funk to smooth pop and light R&B with this album. The title cut was a monster hit, and introduced lead singer J. T. Taylor and new producer Eumir Deodato. Deodato put the horns in the background, changed the arrangements, and replaced the prominent electric bass lines of Robert "Kool" Bell with lighter, synthesized rhythms and drum tracks. They were ready to move into new territory, but many fans of the wonderful '70s funk sound were dismayed. —*Ron Wynn*

Something Special / 1981 / De Lite ✦✦✦
The beginning of the change in the group's style could be heard on this album, although they wouldn't make the complete shift until the next release. But the horn lines were already being diminished, the backbeat toned down, and the vocals becoming less rowdy and more polished. They still had some funk influences, but you could hear the changes coming. They didn't have J. T. Taylor on board yet, so they couldn't do a complete musical makeover. —*Ron Wynn*

Celebrate / 1980 / De Lite ✦✦✦
The album that cemented Kool and the Gang's new status as pop icons in 1980. It ruled the pop and R&B charts for almost the entire year, and they got their first number one pop hit with "Celebration," the song that defined their new sound. J. T. Taylor emerged as a romantic idol, and they went on to sustain this success through the mid-'80s. —*Ron Wynn*

Kool & the Gang's Past Hits / 1981 / De Lite ✦✦✦
A decent anthology of funk material from Kool and the Gang, who were then riding high in a totally different vein. This wasn't as complete as some later greatest hits packages, but has a good set of tracks. You can find them elsewhere. —*Ron Wynn*

As One / 1982 / De Lite ✦✦✦
Kool and the Gang were in the midst of a hot streak in the early '80s, consistently scoring R&B and pop hits with their smooth, polished pop sound. While many of the tracks that scored from this album were in the silly/novelty vein, J. T. Taylor's silky voice could do no wrong, especially where female fans were concerned. The group had long since paid its dues on the funk and soul circuit, so it was good to see them raking in the big bucks. But while old fans didn't begrudge their success, they missed the classic, grinding funk. —*Ron Wynn*

In the Heart / 1983 / De Lite ✦✦✦
Kool and the Gang were in the midst of an impressive crossover hit string during the mid-'80s, and things didn't cool down with this album. The sappy "Joanna" was another R&B chart topper and reached the number two spot on the pop lists as well. By now, the memories of their hard-edged funk were long gone, and they ranked as the most successful black pop band of the '80s. J. T. Taylor was a matinee idol, hailed as the male singer of the moment. —*Ron Wynn*

Emergency / 1984 / De Lite ✦✦✦
Kool and the Gang stayed hot with this mid-'80s number, parlaying J. T. Taylor's creamy voice and their by now familiar light pop arrangements to repeated success on both the R&B and pop charts. They were now America's top black band, appearing all over the place and getting the attention they deserved but never received throughout the '70s. While nothing from this album was a chart buster, everything did well, and they maintained their position, which was all the album was intended to do anyhow. —*Ron Wynn*

Forever / 1986 / De Lite ✦✦✦
Kool and the Gang had their last fling with crossover success with this 1986 album—the last one with J. T. Taylor as their lead vocalist. They got three more chart hits, and while "Stone Love" or "Victory" didn't reach the number one spot on either survey, they both cracked the pop and R&B Top 10. They were like most of the hits the group enjoyed during their pop run—likable, lightweight, feel-good material without the punch of the past, but still viable. —*Ron Wynn*

● **Greatest Hits & More** / 1988 / Polydor ✦✦✦✦
The best of their later-era hits, featuring "Cherish" and the anthemic "Celebrate!" —*Cub Koda*

○ **Everything Is Kool & the Gang: Greatest Hits** / Jul. 25, 1988 / Mercury ✦✦✦✦
Kool and the Gang's long run as a recreated pop act in the '80s formally ended with this release of this late '80s anthology. It contained all the smooth pop winners sung by J. T. Taylor, who had already made his exit. It demonstrated how smooth, slick, yet also engaging a lead singer he'd been, and how the efforts of such producers as Deodato had successfully turned Kool and the Gang into superstars by erasing the funk beats, making the arrangements mellow and subdued, and also providing catchy, hook-filled songs like "Celebration" and "Ladies Night." —*Ron Wynn*

Sweat / Jan. 1989 / Mercury ✦
Things changed drastically for Kool and the Gang in 1989. J. T. Taylor departed, and they were caught without a standout lead singer for the first time since 1978. They had also transformed the sound so much that they couldn't go back to funk, which by now was passe anyhow. So they cranked out a completely faceless, aimless record, one so desultory that it was sad for both fans of the old and new sound to hear it. It's probably the worst album of their career. —*Ron Wynn*

● **The Best of Kool & the Gang** / May 18, 1993 / Mercury ✦✦✦✦
Although Kool and the Gang became pop superstars in the 1980s on the strength of J. T. Taylor's silky voice and several catchy arrangements, R&B fans regard their true glory days as the 1970s. The New Jersey-based ensemble patented a jazz-tinged funk approach keyed by Robert "Kool" Bell's bass lines, red-hot horn lines, chunky keyboards and guitar riffs, and functional vocals. Although they seldom ventured beyond the R&B charts during this era, their music had far more bite than their later pop hits. These 16 cuts pay homage to Kool and the Gang's funk roots, and should

be a revelation to those who only know them as the light ensemble behind J. T. Taylor. —*Ron Wynn*

Kool Moe Dee

Rap
One old-school rapper who's managed to thrive mixing it up with new-school types, Kool Moe Dee was a member of Harlem trio the Treacherous Three in the early '80s and was spotted by music veteran and producer Bobby Robinson. The trio eventually split from Robinson and joined rival Sugarhill Records, then disbanded when their contract expired. Dee hooked up with producer Teddy Riley, now the king of new-jack-swing efforts, and hit instant gold with the single "Go See the Doctor," an amazing safe-sex story that combines a cautionary message with a frenetic hypnotic beat. Since then, Dee has had a lengthy, disturbing sexist slant. He engaged fellow rapper LL Cool J in a continuing battle of words which was interesting for a while but degenerated into a stock formula.
Kool Moe Dee's past was celebrated in 1993 with the release of a greatest hits LP. —*Ron Wynn*

I'm Kool Moe Dee / 1986 / Jive ✦✦✦
A commanding debut, especially the smashing tune "Go See the Doctor," one of the best and most pointed cautionary sex songs ever. —*Ron Wynn*

○ **How Ya Like Me Now** / 1987 / Jive ✦✦✦✦
The title track was a big smash, and it marked the beginning of the lengthy Kool Moe Dee vs LL Cool J rap war. The second hit "Wild, Wild West" was also a masterpiece; the album's greatness overcomes its forays into sexism on "Stupid." —*Ron Wynn*

○ **The Best** / 1987 / Jive ✦✦✦✦
The value of this compilation has been diminished by the release of a superior 1993 hits package. This contains several of Kool Moe Dee's big records from the early '80s, and is a blueprint for both his rise and the emergence of the Kool Moe Dee/LL Cool J rivalry. —*Ron Wynn*

★ **Greatest Hits** / 1989 / Sequel ✦✦✦✦✦
As much as any single performer, Kool Moe Dee epitomized rap's rise from an East Coast underground genre to a national youth sound, and has been unceasing in his demands for respect and recognition. Dee was also among the first able to bring social significance to his material without being pedantic, and his songs (with the exception of "They Need Money") weren't littered with sexist and misogynistic rhetoric. This 15-song collection covers his biggest recordings, from novelty-type fare ("The Wild Wild West" and "Whosgotdaflava") to the safe sex number "Go See the Doctor," cultural battle cries like "Rise 'N' Shine" and "No Respect," and his "war" with LL Cool J that peaked with "Death Blow" and "How Ya Like Me Now." —*Ron Wynn*

Knowledge Is King / 1989 / Jive ✦✦✦
Another brilliant hit with "They Want Money," though he expands a disturbing anti-female line. But it's balanced by a stirring anti-drug, Afrocentric philosophy and a rap methodology that puts him near the top among hip-hop purists. —*Ron Wynn*

Funke Funke Wisdom / 1991 / Jive ✦✦✦
The single "Rise and Shine" was a summit meeting of rap theorists, with Dee joined by Chuck D from Public Enemy and KRS-One. Unfortunately, an overreliance on sexual posturing and macho imagery have begun to set in, weighing down an otherwise notable effort. —*Ron Wynn*

Al Kooper

b. Feb. 5, 1944, Brooklyn, NY
Rock & Roll, Blues Rock
Over the last thirty years, Al Kooper has managed to involve himself in many creative aspects of popular music. As a songwriter, Kooper co-wrote the #1 hit for Gary Lewis & the Playboys, "This Diamond Ring." Bob Dylan's "Like a Rolling Stone" and album *Highway 61 Revisited* benefited from Kooper's rolling Hammond B3 organ work. Kooper also played French horn and keys on the Rolling Stones' "You Can't Always Get What You Want." Kooper founded Blood, Sweat & Tears, producing and performing on their classic debut *The Child Is Father to the Man* (#47). He also did side projects with Stephen Stills and Michael Bloomfield, most notably *Super Session* (#12). As a producer, Kooper discovered Lynyrd Skynyrd, and produced their first three albums. Kooper's solo output has always been sporadic, due to the many other pro-

jects on his plate. More recently, Kooper has relocated to Nashville, where he produces and can be seen playing with the blues-rock band the Blue Bloods. —*Rick Clark*

I Stand Alone / 1969 / CBS ✦✦✦

You Never Know Who Your Friends Are / 1969 / CBS ✦✦

Live Adventures / 1969 / Edsel ✦✦✦
More jamming, this time at the Fillmore, with guest appearances by Elvin Bishop and Carlos Santana. —*Cub Koda*

● **Al's Big Deal (Unclaimed Freight)** / 1975 / Columbia ✦✦✦✦

Kraftwerk

Group, Techno-Pop/Dance, Electronic, Art-Rock/Progressive-Rock
In the mid-'70s, the German quartet Kraftwerk laid the ground work for most of the electronic and synth-rock bands that followed them in the next two decades. Each of the members played synthesizers, creating a cold, precise, almost mechanical music that was hypnotic in its repetitiveness. For the rest of the '70s, the band was on the cutting edge of rock and dance music, influencing numerous musicians in the process. As the '80s progressed, the group's records became less and less innovative, but they still made a number of albums that were very impressive; the band continues to record in the '90s.

Echoes of Kraftwerk's music can be heard in everyone from David Bowie and Tangerine Dream to Depeche Mode and the Human League. Hip-hop is also unwittingly in debt to many of the band's innovative use of electronics. But the underground techno scene of the '80s and '90s owes a great debt to Kraftwerk, as artists like the Aphex Twin, Orbital, Vapourspace, and the Orb bring the band's trance-like electronics to new heights, adding a warm, human dimension that the band never had when they recorded *Autobahn* in 1974. —*Stephen Thomas Erlewine*

Kraftwerk 1 / 1971 / Philips ✦✦

Kraftwerk 2 / 1972 / Philips ✦✦✦
The synthesis of man and machine was forged in the "power station," aka Kraftwerk. Ralf Hutter and Florian Schneider took the strum und drang of the industrial revolution and implanted it into a musical core that consisted of electronic soundscapes and metronomic rhythmic pulsations. The future sound of industrial music was fashioned on these two albums, in addition to the primal pulse that was later to become punk. —*Archie Patterson*

★ **Autobahn** / 1974 / Warner Brothers ✦✦✦✦✦
A cold, hypnotic album, the title song of which was an unlikely hit. —*Dan Heilman*

Radioactivity / 1975 / Capitol ✦✦✦

○ **Trans-Europe Express** / 1977 / Capitol ✦✦✦✦

○ **The Man Machine** / 1978 / Capitol ✦✦✦✦

○ **Computer World** / 1981 / Warner Brothers ✦✦✦✦

Electric Cafe / 1986 / Elektra ✦✦✦

Robotronik / 1991 / ✦✦

The Mix / 1991 / Elektra ✦✦✦

Robots / 1992 / Elektra ✦✦

○ **Model-Retrospective 1975-1978** / Cleopatra ✦✦✦✦

Billy J. Kramer & the Dakotas

Group, British Invasion
At the outset of the British Invasion in 1964, Billy J. Kramer with the Dakotas was one of the hottest bands of the movement's initial wave. Beatles manager Brian Epstein paired young Liverpool vocalist Kramer with the Dakotas and gave them a surefire hit—the Lennon/McCartney composition "Do You Want to Know a Secret?," which established the group in England. The group broke in America with the two-sided smash "Little Children"/"Bad to Me" in 1964 on Imperial, the latter another Lennon/McCartney effort. Their next two smashes, "I'll Keep You Satisfied" and "From a Window," were also penned by the prolific duo, although Kramer's last US hit, "Trains and Boats and Planes," was written by Burt Bacharach and Hal David. The group appeared in the popular 1964 movie *The T.A.M.I. Show*, but by 1967 the musicians and Kramer had gone their separate ways, the vocalist recording as a solo in Britain. —*Bill Dahl*

● **Best of Billy J. Kramer** / 1991 / EMI America ✦✦✦✦
A strong collection that presents all of his best—including a number of songs written by John Lennon and Paul McCartney—in excellent sound. —*Bruce Eder & Jeff Tamarkin*

Dagmar Krause

Art-Rock/Progressive-Rock
It seems odd to consider the work of Dagmar Krause in a book that deals specifically with rock, mainly due to her superb talent singing non-rock popular music. It is because of her association with German progressive rockers Slapp Happy, British avant-garde prog-rockers Henry Cow and the Art Bears that Krause becomes a suitable subject for inclusion in guides to rock & roll. And, ultimately, that's a good thing, because talent as formidable as hers should not go unheard, nor should it be relegated to some arcane status ostensibly beyond the interests of the "average" rock fan. Simply, Dagmar Krause is a great singer, and you'd be wise to own some of her recordings. A native of Hamburg, Germany, Krause began her professional career at 14 as a nightclub singer in the Reeperbahn sex district (made infamous by the wanton exploits of the pre-fame Beatles). At the time, Hamburg, along with numerous sex joints and prostitution, had a thriving avant-garde arts scene that attracted numerous European musicians interested in pursuing aesthetic freedom and musical experimentation. It was here she met Anthony Moore and Peter Blegvad and formed Slapp Happy.

Radical in both music and politics, the band relocated to London in the early '70s, eventually joining forces with progressives Henry Cow. After Cow's demise in 1980, Krause teamed up with former bandmates guitarist Fred Frith and drummer Chris Cutler in the wonderfully anarchic Art Bears, who disbanded after three excellent records. Now a solo act, Krause in 1978, starred in a London production of the Bertolt Brecht/Kurt Weill play *Mahagonny*. As much as anything she'd sung up to this point, Krause's elegant alto was perfectly suited to the emotionally and politically charged music of Brecht and Weill. Embracing this German song tradition with gusto, Krause went on to record the most stunning work of her career, culminating in two extraordinary releases, *Supply and Demand* and *Tank Battles* (the latter the music of Hans Eisler), that are eloquent arguments for Krause's eminence as a singer in the German song tradition (something for which she doesn't receive enough credit).

As a vocalist, Krause is arguably something of an acquired taste. Her husky, vibrato-laden alto can suddenly swoop into a breathtaking upper register with a power that belies her small, frail physique. Her English singing retains a heavy German accent, but whether she sings in German or English (which she often does on the same record), she retains her impeccable phrasing and ability to inject the most oft-heard lyric with almost palpable emotion. In fact, I'd go so far as to say that Dagmar Krause belongs in the pantheon of great contemporary European singers along with June Tabor and Anne Briggs. Unfortunately, Krause's last record, *Tank Battles*, was not released in the U.S., and if she's recorded anything since, it's been quietly released in Europe only. A sad state of affairs for such a talented vocalist. —*John Dougan*

● **Supply & Demand** / 1986 / Hannibal ✦✦✦✦
Although seeking out Krause's work with Slapp Happy, Henry Cow and the Art Bears is worthwhile, ultimately the democracy of a band means less Dagmar to listen to. Therefore, go straight to this amazing solo recording of Krause singing the music of Bertolt Brecht, Kurt Weill and Hans Eisler. It's approachable, accessible ("Mack the Knife" is here under its original title, "Moritat"), beautifully sung (her version of "Surabaya Johnny" is definitive) and very, very moving. The CD release adds a few tracks, but regardless of what configuration you may purchase, the stunning vocal ability of Dagmar Krause will transport you. —*John Dougan*

Tank Battles/Panzer Schlacht / 1988 / ✦✦✦
A worthy follow up-to *Supply and Demand*, this release focuses on Krause's interpretation of the music of Hans Eisler, a great German songwriter and contemporary of Brecht and Weill (though less well known). As usual, the singing is stunning, and the instrumental accompaniment, which features significant contributions by Lindsay Cooper and Danny Thompson, is impeccable. Krause recorded English and German versions of *Tank Battles* (hence the title *Panzer Schlacht*) and both are highly recommended. —*John Dougan*

Lenny Kravitz

New York
Soul, Rock & Roll, Psychedelic, Pop/Rock
As a musician and a producer, Lenny Kravitz is unquestionably gifted. He can successfully recreate the sound and feeling of count-

less groups from the past; his music recalls everyone from Lennon, Hendrix, and Bowie to the Velvet Underground, Curtis Mayfield and Prince. What Kravitz can't do is synthesize these influences into a distinctive style—every song on each of his albums sounds like it was recorded by a different artist. However, that's not entirely a bad thing, because Kravitz *can* reproduce the sound of his favorite artists exactly; "It Ain't Over 'Til It's Over" sounds like it was recorded in 1972, "Are You Gonna Go My Way" sounds like a forgotten track from 1968. His music might not be original, but it is quite enjoyable. Since his 1989 debut, *Let Love Rule*, Kravitz's songwriting and production skills have been consistently improving. His second album, *Mama Said*, gave him a number two hit with "It Ain't Over 'Til It's Over." *Are You Gonna Go My Way*, Kravitz's third album, was released in 1993; it was a stronger album than anything he had released in the past and it was his most commercially successful record yet. —*Stephen Thomas Erlewine*

○ **Let Love Rule** / 1989 / Virgin ✦✦✦✦
Kravitz played the majority of the instruments on this self-produced debut of catchy retro-pop. Most of the songs are exceptionally well-crafted, evoking everyone from the Velvet Underground and John Lennon to Prince and Sly Stone. Musically, *Let Love Rule* is an impressive debut, but lyrically Kravitz tends to rely on clichés and simple rhymes, including some embarssingly sophomoric lyrics from his current wife Lisa Bonet. Nevertheless, his musical talent obscures most of the lyrical shortcomings. —*Stephen Thomas Erlewine*

Mama Said / 1991 / Virgin ✦✦✦
Like his debut, Kravitz's second album, *Mama Said*, works best on the surface. *Mama Said* abandons the hippie folk leanings of *Let Love Rule* for a sleek update of Philly soul, acid rock, psychedelia, hard rock, and '60s pop. It's a more polished and musically accomplished record than his debut, resulting in the breakthrough number two hit single "It Ain't Over 'Til It's Over." Again, Kravitz plays the majority of the instruments, with Slash contributing some fine guitar to "Always On the Run" and "Fields of Joy." However, the music never sounds insular and self-involved, since Kravitz works in familiar pop idioms and has a knack for warm, organic production. Nevertheless, the lyrics—which mainly concentrate on the breakup of his marriage to actress Lisa Bonet—*are* insular and self-involved, but the music makes it easy to ignore what he's saying. —*Stephen Thomas Erlewine*

● **Are You Gonna Go My Way?** / 1993 / Virgin ✦✦✦✦
Opening with the pounding Hendrix-styled title track, Lenny Kravitz continues his rampage through the back pages of pop music history. On *Are You Gonna Go My Way*, Kravitz follows the same basic formula as *Mama Said*, concentrating on early-'70s soul and psychedelic hard rock, but his songwriting has improved, making the record his most consistent and coherent album. —*Stephen Thomas Erlewine*

Kreator

Group, Thrash, Heavy Metal
Formed in 1984 in Essen, Germany, when the death metal genre was still taking shape, Kreator (originally Tormentor) were one of the first European death metal bands. Led by vocalist/guitarist Mille Petroza, they were also one of the few death metal bands willing to experiment with the form or add any elements of individuality or subtlety. They became one of the more popular bands in the genre, particularly in Europe. —*Steve Huey*

Endless Pain / 1985 / Noise ✦✦✦
This essential speed-metal album from the mid '80s occurred when they were still a trio. —*John Book*

○ **Pleasure to Kill** / 1986 / Noise ✦✦✦✦
This influential dark speed-metal has a passion for death. —*John Book*

● **Terrible Certainty** / 1988 / Noise ✦✦✦✦
Angry speed-metal from Germany, this is the tightest and harshest album to date and is one of the best from the '80s. —*John Book*

Out of the Dark, into the Light / 1989 / Noise ✦✦✦
This EP (half studio songs, half live) was released before their major-label debut. —*John Book*

Extreme Aggression / 1989 / Epic ✦✦✦
Their major-label debut is just as good as their independent material. —*John Book*

Coma of Souls / 1990 / Epic ✦✦
Flag of Hate / Combat ✦✦✦
For those who can't consume Kreator in large doses, this six-song EP made the band a little more than an underground rage. —*John Book*

Renewal / Futurist ✦✦

Kriss Kross (Kris Kross)

Group, Rap
Rap successes come in the strangest packages. Kris Kross are two 13-year-olds from Atlanta who, with the help of 19-year-old producer Jermaine Dupri, released a gimmick-laden but fairly charming debut which promptly outsold nearly all of its competition in the summer of 1992. Whether they can turn their success story into a career remains to be seen.

While it wasn't a disaster, their 1993 follow-up *Da Bomb*, didn't match the levels of their debut, mainly because it didn't have a single as strong as "Jump" or "Warm It Up." —*John Floyd*

● **Totally Krossed Out** / 1992 / Ruffhouse ✦✦✦✦
The hottest rap duo of the summer of 1992, thanks to their penchant for wearing their clothes backward and the single "Jump," which crossed over to pop and R&B markets. —*Ron Wynn*

Da Bomb / 1993 / Ruffhouse ✦✦✦
Da Bomb sounds nearly identical to Kriss Kross' debut, but there are no singles that are as clever or catchy as either "Jump" or "Warm It Up." —*AMG*

KRS-One

Rap
KRS-One (born Kris Parker) was the leader of Boogie Down Productions, one of the most influential hardcore hip-hop outfits of the '80s. At the height of his career—roughly 1987–1990—KRS-One was known for his furiously political and socially-conscious raps, which is the source of his nickname, "The Teacher." Around the time of 1990's *Edutainment*, BDP's audience began to slip as many fans thought his raps were becoming preachy. As a reaction, KRS-One began to re-establish his street credibility with harder, sparer beats and raps. BDP's 1992's *Sex and Violence* was the first sign that he was taking a harder approach, one that wasn't nearly as concerned with teaching. KRS-One's first solo album, 1993's *Return of the Boom Bap*, was an extension of the more direct approach of *Sex and Violence*, yet it didn't halt his commercial decline. —*Stephen Thomas Erlewine*

○ **Return of the Boom Bap** / Sep. 28, 1993 / Jive ✦✦✦✦

Kursaal Flyers

Group, Rock & Roll, Power Pop/Anglo-Pop
The Kursaal Flyers bridged the gap between pub rock and power-pop, turning a handful of fine albums and great singles in their brief two year career. Comprised of Paul Shuttleworth (vocals), Graeme Douglas (guitar), Vic Collins (guitar, steel guitar, vocals), Riche Bull (bass, vocals), and Will Birch (drums), the band released their first album *Chocs Away* in 1975; it was followed soon afterward by *The Great Artiste*. Both records showed a grasp of country and roots-rock, as well as pure pop. They would begin to emphasize their pop elements with 1976's *Golden Mile*, released by CBS Records. The union with the major label helped the single "Little Does She Know" reach the British Top 20. Douglas left to join Eddie and the Hot Rods before the recording of their final album, *Five Live Kursaals* (1977); he was replaced by Barry Martin. The band broke up after the release of punk and power-pop injected *Five Live Kursaals*. Out of the members, Will Birch was the only one that stayed active—he formed the Records immediately after the Kursaal Flyers' disbandment. The Kursaal Flyers reunited in 1988, recording *A Former Tour de Force Is Forced to Tour*, which picks up right where they left off in 1977. —*Stephen Thomas Erlewine*

Chocs Away / 1975 / UK ✦✦
Great Artiste / 1975 / UK ✦✦✦
○ **Golden Mile** / 1976 / CBS ✦✦✦✦
Five Live Kursaals / 1977 / CBS ✦✦✦
● **In for a Spin: The Best of the Kursaal Flyers** / 1985 / Edsel ✦✦✦✦
A Former Tour de Force Is Forced to Tour / 1988 / Waterfront ✦✦✦

Kwamé & a New Beginning

Group, Rap

Kwamé's nice-guy personality—alternately humble and intelligent, outspoken and easy-stepping—offers a refreshing break from the usual bad-boy posturing of most of the rap pack. —*John Floyd*

The Boy Genius / 1989 / Atlantic ✦✦✦

● **Day in the Life: A Pokadelick Adventure** / 1990 / Atlantic ✦✦✦✦
Day in the Life—A Pokadelick Adventure is a strange but fun hip-hop journey. —*Dan Heilman*

○ **Featuring a New Beginning** / 1990 / Atlantic ✦✦✦✦
Queens rapper Kwamé stepped out with this 1989 debut, exhibiting a competent rap style and erratic, but sometimes catchy compositions. "Boy Genius" and "Mic Is Mine" were good boasting numbers and the best vehicles for his evolving rap style. "Pushthepanicbutton!!" and "U Gotz 2 Get Down" were less successful, sounding like Biz Markie or Marley Marl outtakes. —*Ron Wynn*

Nastee / 1992 / Atlantic ✦✦✦

Tasha Lambert joined Kwamé on his third album, but the union didn't generate much compositional fruit. The raps were unconvincing and the production a mish-mash of funk and soul snippets underpinning rhymes that were neither fluidly presented nor cleverly composed. —*Ron Wynn*

Kyuss

Group, Art-Rock/Progressive-Rock, Hard Rock

Kyuss got their start in the somewhat isolated environment of Palm Desert, California. Their current lineup includes vocalist John Garcia, guitarist Josh Homme, bass player Scott Reeder, and drummer Alfredo Hernandez. Their so-called "desert sound" combines punk with psychedelic blues influences, and their songs can be either structured or free-form jams. Glenn Danzig took the band on tour with him following their second album; their last two albums were produced by Masters of Reality's Chris Goss. —*Steve Huey*

● **Wretch** / 1991 / Dali ✦✦✦✦

Blues for the Red Sun / 1992 / Dali ✦✦✦

L

The La De Das

Group, Garage Rock, Pop/Rock
Aside from, perhaps, Ray Columbus & the Invaders, the La De Das were New Zealand's most popular rock group of the 1960s. As big fish in a very small pond, their work doesn't hold up to scrutiny in the company of the era's top American and English acts. But they did record some fine garage/pop numbers in the spirit of the Rolling Stones in the mid-'60s. A few of these ("How Is the Air up There?," "All Purpose Low") were big N.Z. hits, and they reached the Top Ten with covers of John Mayall's "On Top of the World" and a lame version of Bruce Channel's "Hey Baby." In 1968, they recorded a psychedelic-tinged children's concept LP, *The Happy Prince*; while ahead of its time, it sounds unbearably twee today. After a failed attempt to crack the British market, the group soldiered on for quite some time with pedestrian hard rock that—like even the best of their early work—was very derivative of overseas trends. —*Richie Unterberger*

● **La De Das/Find Us a Way** / CBS ◆◆◆◆
A double-LP reissue of their first two albums, covering their 1966-67 material, including nearly all of their best songs. Their debut (*La De Das*) is almost solely composed of R&B covers, with the exception of the hit "How Is the Air up There?" *Find Us a Way* is better, with more original compositions and a more mature soulful rock approach, including the snarling singles "Find Us a Way" and "All Purpose Low." —*Richie Unterberger*

Rock 'n' Roll Decade 1964-'74 / 1981 / EMI Australia ◆◆◆
A hefty double-album compilation, including most of their mid-'60s singles, the entire *The Happy Prince* LP, and a mixture of live and studio hard-rock material from the late '60s and early '70s. Includes exhaustive liner notes from Australian rock authority Glenn A. Baker, and their rare fine 1965 punk debut 45 "Little Girl," but the final three sides of this two-fer are pretty tedious going. —*Richie Unterberger*

La Dusseldorf

Group, Electronic
Klaus Dinger was an early member of Kraftwerk, co-founder of the cyber-punk duo Neu, and godfather of the ultimate German rock group, La Dusseldorf. —*Archie Patterson*

La Dusseldorf / 1976 / Radar ◆◆◆

● **Viva** / 1978 / Radar ◆◆◆◆
La Dusseldorf's *Viva* crystallized Klaus Dinger's progressive rock vision into a symphony of swirling guitars, rich keyboard melodies and driving percussive beats. The magnum opus "Cha, Cha 2000," will forever stand as one of the all-time anthems of futurist rock & roll. —*Archie Patterson*

Individuellos / 1981 / Teldec ◆◆◆

L.A. Guns

Group, Hard Rock, Heavy Metal
L.A. Guns was formed by former Guns N' Roses guitarist Tracii Guns in 1987. Teaming with ex-Girl vocalist Phil Lewis, former W.A.S.P. drummer Steve Riley, bassist Kelly Nickles, and guitarist Mick Cripps, Guns adhered to the Aerosmith-derived raunch of his former band. L.A. Guns released their self-titled first album in 1988, yet it wasn't until the following year's *Cocked & Loaded* that they truly broke big. On the strength of the hit single "The Ballad of Jayne," *Cocked & Loaded* went gold. Released two years later, *Hollywood Vampires* managed to hold their audience's attention,

peaking at number 42. Nevertheless, the band laid low for four years, waiting for grunge to fade away. When L.A. Guns released their fourth album, *Vicious Circle*, in early 1995, they retained a core group of followers, yet it failed to capture the mainstream's attention; it was their weakest-selling album to date. —*Stephen Thomas Erlewine*

○ **L.A. Guns** / Jan. 4, 1988 / Polydor ◆◆◆◆
Sleazy hard rock with enough hooks to pull the listener in, it's raw and tight and put together very well. —*John Book*

● **Cocked & Loaded** / 1989 / Polydor ◆◆◆◆
A more serious and polished effort, it has tighter and more accessible songs. —*John Book*

Hollywood Vampires / 1991 / Polydor ◆◆◆

Vicious Circle / 1995 / Polydor ◆◆

L.A. Star

Group, Rap
In 1990, L.A. Star provided a woman's perspective on the gangsta life at a time when there weren't many female rappers willing to operate in that arena. At the same time, she also included some material with a romantic side, though she couldn't afford to juxtapose vulnerability too close to combativeness. *Poetess* was a decent debut on Profile, but so far there hasn't been a follow-up. —*Ron Wynn*

○ **Poetess** / 1990 / Profile ◆◆◆◆
Good debut work from this South Bronx rapper; a frank, distressing portrait of inner-city life and times. —*Ron Wynn*

The La's

Group, Alternative Pop/Rock
When the La's released their debut album in 1990, it made immediate waves in the British pop scene, as well as American college radio. Drawing from the hook-laden, ringing guitars of mid-'60s British pop as well as the post-punk pop of the Smiths, the La's self-titled first album had a timeless, classic feel. It seemed like effortless music, yet that was not the case. From their inception in 1986 to the present day, lead singer/guitarist/songwriter Lee Myers has been a perfectionist with a nearly-obsessive eye for detail. Consequently, the La's have never been able to totally fulfill their promise.

Myers formed the group in Liverpool with bassist John Power, guitarist Paul Hemmings, and drummer John Timson. On the strength of their demo tapes, Go! Discs signed the band in 1987, releasing the single "Way Out"; it received good reviews, yet it wasn't a chart success. Similarly, the following year's "There She Goes" received good press yet stalled on the charts. With a new lineup featuring bassist James Joyce, guitarist Cammy (born Peter James Camell), and Lee's brother Neil on drums, the La's began recording their debut album that same year. The record didn't appear until 1990. Even though Myers claimed it was rush-released, the Steve Lillywhite-produced *The La's* received glowing reviews and strong sales; a re-released "There She Goes" entered the U.K. Top 20 and hit number 49 in America. For most of 1991, the band was on tour. At the end of the year, they went back to the studio to record their follow-up. This time, Lee Myers was in complete control and he took his time to perfect the album, re-recording tracks and rewriting songs. The La's disappeared without a trace from the pop music scene. Myers and a reconstituted band resurfaced in the spring of 1995, playing a handful of supporting concerts that featured a couple of new songs; the band began recording their second album the following summer. —*Stephen Thomas Erlewine*

○ **The La's** / 1990 / London ✦✦✦✦

This was one of the strongest debuts on the 1991 alternative music scene. "There She Goes" was a hit single with its appealing mid-'60s-influenced Brit Invasion sound and interweaving hooks. Most of the album should be a joy to hear for fans of alternative Anglo-pop. Highlights include "Son of a Gun," "Way Out," "Freedom Song," and "I.O.U." —*Rick Clark*

Labelle

Group, Soul, Funk, Disco, R&B

A girl-group from Philadelphia, they formed in 1962. Initially known as the Bluebelles, and then Patti LaBelle and the Bluebelles, the group's personnel consisted of Patti LaBelle, Cindy Birdsong, Sarah Dash, and Nona Hendryx. The quartet scored six R&B hits from 1962 through 1967 before Birdsong departed to join Diana Ross and the Supremes. Continuing as a trio, for the next seven years the group languished in obscurity. British manager Vicki Wickham remade their image in the early '70s and shortened the name to LaBelle. Decked out in ersatz futuristic garb, the threesome appeared as whirling dervishes delivering an explosive gospel/funk hybrid. Between late 1974 and late 1976, LaBelle enjoyed five R&B hits, the first, "Lady Marmalade," reaching the #1 spot on the R&B and pop charts. LaBelle split up in early 1977. —*Rob Bowman*

Pressure Cookin' / 1973 / RCA ✦✦✦

○ **Nightbirds** / 1974 / Epic ✦✦✦✦

The finest of the three LaBelle albums, *Nightbirds* was recorded in New Orleans with funkmeister Allen Toussaint handling the production chores and, one assumes, members of the Meters taking care of the session work. Worth the price of admission for the Bob Crewe-written "Lady Marmalade" alone, the album veers between the strutting New Orleans, horn-laden singles and more mainstream pop material. —*Rob Bowman*

● **Lady Marmalade: The Best of Patti and Labelle** / 1995 / Legacy/Epic ✦✦✦✦

Lady Marmalade: The Best of LaBelle features eight of the group's best tracks—including their two hits, "Lady Marmalade" and "What Can I Do for You?"—as well as eight of Patti LaBelle's R&B hits from the late '70s, which were among the funkiest tracks she ever recorded. —*Stephen Thomas Erlewine*

Patti Labelle (Patricia Holt)

b. May 24, 1944, Philadelphia, PA
Soul, Urban

Born Patricia Holt in Philadelphia, Patti LaBelle has enjoyed a 30-year-plus career, having sung early-'60s girl-group material, soul, funk, and '80s ballad and dance music. From 1962–1976 she was a founding member of both Patti LaBelle & the Blue Belles and LaBelle. She began her solo career in 1977. Over the ensuing six years, she scored a number of lower-range R&B hits with Epic, coming into her own on Gamble and Huff's Philadelphia International label in 1984 with the number one R&B hit, "If Only You Knew." She has been a consistent chartmaker ever since, renowned for a gospel-trained voice with stunning power and range, capable of exhilarating aural gymnastics. One of the most gifted, idiosyncratic voices in R&B.—*Rob Bowman*

Patti Labelle / 1977 / Epic ✦✦✦

Patti Labelle's solo debut for Epic closed the book on a 15-year collaboration with Nona Hendryx and Sarah Dash. She mixed light pop and soul covers on this outing, turning in earnestly sung renditions of "You Are My Friend" and the Skyliners' "Since I Don't Have You," but also doing curious material like "Dan Swift Me" and "You Can't Judge A Book By The Cover." Labelle was still finding her niche and hadn't yet become comfortable or established her now commonplace tendencies, such as the drawn-out lyric emphasis and the embellishments and lengthy holding of notes. —*Ron Wynn*

● **The Best of Patti Labelle** / 1986 / Epic ✦✦✦✦

This anthology includes the biggest pop hit that the trio Labelle scored, the classic "Lady Marmalade," plus other staples from Patti Labelle's solo phase, including "You Are My Friend," "Joy To Have

Your Love" and "I Don't Go Shopping." Labelle didn't make her best or most successful records while on Epic, so these aren't the tunes currently associated with her. They were decently produced and often well performed, but lack the depth of her best MCA cuts. —*Ron Wynn*

Winner in You / 1986 / MCA ✦✦✦

Patti Labelle enjoyed the biggest hit of her solo career when she switched labels from Philadelphia International to MCA. None of her albums had consistently clicked since she'd gone solo in 1977, but Labelle's 1986 MCA debut topped the pop album charts, anchored by the huge hit "On My Own." The duet with Michael McDonald dominated both the pop and R&B scenes, staying atop the R&B charts for four weeks and giving Labelle her first #1 pop single as a solo artist. She even earned a second Top 40 hit with "Oh, People," even though there was another fine single on the LP, "Kiss Away The Pain," that was ignored. Still, this album gave Labelle the elusive solo stardom she'd sought since 1977. —*Ron Wynn*

Be Yourself / 1989 / MCA ✦✦✦

This urban-R&B set includes some cuts produced by Prince. —*Bil Carpenter*

Burnin' / 1991 / MCA ✦✦✦

This was more a presentation and entertainment spectacle than a memorable production. Patti Labelle greeted special guests, had a reunion with former cohorts Sarah Dash and Nona Hendryx, and put her usual flourishes and energy into several cuts that lacked enough distinction to benefit from her fierce treatments. Although the album eventually went gold, it was an aesthetic disappointment. Not only were there few hits, but there weren't even any good singles. "Somebody Loves You Baby (You Know Who It Is)" at least had a demonstrative Labelle lead, while "Temptation" and "When You've Been Blessed (It Feels Like Heaven)" had decent production touches and frenetic vocals. —*Ron Wynn*

● **Over The Rainbow: The Atlantic Years** / 1994 / Ichiban ✦✦✦✦

The Bluebelles' stint with Atlantic in the '60s was not a great commercial success, yielding only a couple minor R&B hits ("I'm Still Waiting" and "Take Me for a Little While," both included here), but that wasn't due to any shortcomings on the records themselves, either in performance or material. Patti and the group recorded fine sides in pop-soul, Motown, Aretha Franklin, and early Philly soul styles, making full use of their powerful gospel-derived lead vocals and harmonies. This 22-track anthology features most of the singles (many previously non-LP) and some key album tracks that they recorded for Atlantic between 1965 and 1969, using top-notch writers like Carole Bayer, Pam Sawyer, Lori Burton, Bert Berns, Jeff Barry, Bacharach-David, Lorraine Ellison, Spooner Oldham, Dan Penn, and Curtis Mayfield (who produced some of the later sides), as well as the Bluebelles' own Nona Hendryx and Sarah Dash. Highlights include the original version of "Groovy Kind of Love" (a big hit for the Mindbenders), the Supremes-like "Tender Words," the dramatic "All or Nothing," and the moody Oldham-Penn ballad "Dreamer." —*Richie Unterberger*

○ **The Best of the Bluebelles** / Relic ✦✦✦✦

This anthology collects the early, often charming and sometimes overly cute singles from Patti Labelle and the Bluebelles. Besides the classic "I Sold My Heart to the Junkman" (which was really Labelle backed by the Starlets), there are lesser-known numbers like "Down The Aisle (The Wedding Song)" and "I'm Still Waiting." Overall, this is competent period-piece material, but it's clear that Labelle and company preferred more aggressive and assertive material and were never quite comfortable with most of these songs. —*Ron Wynn*

Laibach

Group, Industrial, Alternative Pop/Rock

Led by singer Milan Fras, Laibach was formed in what is now Slovenia in 1979 under the concept that Western rock was merely capitalism, its stars only businessmen, and its concerts political rallies for phony rebellion. The group has used fascist tinges to make points in much of its work and, early in their career, often appeared in concert in the uniforms of the Nazis who formerly occupied Slovenia. The group's music has encompassed industrial, rock, jazz, disco, ambience, tape loops, and the occasional Wagner-influenced horn part. Some of their efforts, such as *Let It Be* and *Sympathy for the Devil*, are parodies of Western pop stars; other work has been used for the New Slovenian Art theater troupe. —*Steve Huey*

Nova Akropola / 1985 / Wax Trax! ◆◆◆
Laibach / 1985 / SKUK ◆◆◆
The debut was initally released only in Yugoslavia. —*Steve Aldrich*
Rockapitulacija 1980-84 / 1985 / Walter Ulbright ◆◆◆
Two-LP box set compliation. —*Steve Aldrich*
● **Opus Dei** / 1987 / Wax Trax! ◆◆◆◆
Including teutonic versions of Queen's "One Vision," Opus' "Live Is Life," it's the best introduction to this group. —*Steve Aldrich*
○ **Let It Be** / 1988 / Mute ◆◆◆◆
Unique treatments of the entire Beatles LP of the same name. —*Steve Aldrich*
Sympathy for the Devil / 1988 / Mute ◆◆◆
Included are six variations of the Rolling Stones' classics. —*Steve Aldrich*
Kapital / 1992 / Elektra ◆◆◆
Nato / 1994 / Mute ◆◆
NATO is a collection of war-related covers (including Pink Floyd's "Dogs Of War" and Europe's "The Final Countdown"), each given the Laibach treatment with simple beats and rhythms, and a large choir on the choruses. —*John Bush*
Slovenska Akropola / SKUK ◆◆◆
This is a collection of rarities. —*Steve Aldrich*

The Lambrettas

Group, Power Pop/Anglo-Pop, Pop/Rock
This Brighton-based band featuring Jez Bird (guitar/vocals), Doug Saunders (guitar), Mark Ellis (bass) and Paul Wincer (drums), jumped on the mod-revival bandwagon of the late '70s, dressing in matching mohair suits and naming themselves after one of the mod-favored motor scooters. Led by Bird's catchy songwriting, the Lambrettas proved to be more (if only slightly more) than just Jam-sound-alikes, leaving behind mod-life arrogance/elitism in favor of a pure pop sensibility. The band signed to Elton John's Rocket Records in 1979 and after one failed single, "Go Steady," had a U.K. hit with their cover of Leiber and Stoller's "Poison Ivy." The follow-up singles "D-a-a-ance" and "Another Day (Another Girl)" also charted in the UK. The latter (originally titled "Page Three"), with its not-so-thinly veiled jabs at *The Sun* newspaper's practice of placing photos of topless women on page three, earned them some notoriety when the newspaper threatened legal action. *Beat Boys in the Jet Age*, their debut LP, released in 1979, collected the early singles and other similar-sounding originals. Though it did make it into the British charts, the mod-revival was fading fast. Subsequent singles and a second album, 1981's *Ambience*, were commercial flops despite efforts to break from the mod mold. The band called it quits in 1981 and faded quickly into obscurity. Bird regrouped the band in the '90s, playing small venues in England and recorded several demos for a new album to be released in 1996. —*Chris Woodstra*
○ **Beat Boys in the Jet Age** / 1980 / Rocket ◆◆◆◆
The band's debut picks up on all of the elements that made the early Jam albums brilliant—a certain reverence for '60s pop with a youthful, forward-looking attitude, punk's high-charged energy and strong songwriting. This sadly overlooked album features some of the era's best teen anthems. The CD version adds three bonus tracks. —*Chris Woodstra*
Ambience / 1981 / Rocket ◆◆◆
As the mod-revival was running out of steam, the band took a step away from the sound for a more mature and varied album. No longer is their main concern motor scooters, girls, and living for today as evident in the haunting "Good Times" and "Decent Town." Though it failed commercially, *Ambience* is a fine collection of Brit-pop worth seeking out. —*Chris Woodstra*
● **Best of the Lambrettas: The Singles Collection** / 1995 / ◆◆◆◆
Like so many bands of the era, the Lambrettas are best represented by their singles; *Best of the Lambrettas* collects all of the A and B-sides (as well as a newly recorded demo) in one place for the first time, providing the best introduction to the band. The songs are certainly of the time, but they've aged well, sounding as fresh as they did originally. —*Chris Woodstra*

Major Lance

b. Apr. 4, 1941, Chicago, IL, **d.** Sep. 3, 1994
Soul
Few vocalists better epitomize the breezy danceability of '60s

Chicago soul than whippet-thin Major Lance. Local deejay Jim Lounsbury discovered the loose-limbed singer and arranged his first contract with Mercury in 1959, but Lance needed expert guidance—and he received plenty from innovative producer Carl Davis after joining the Okeh label in 1962. Armed with exceptional dance material by Curtis Mayfield and the brass-heavy, often Latin-tinged charts of Jonny Pate, Lance blasted off with "The Monkey Time" and "Hey Little Girl" in 1963 and followed with the mysterious "Um Um Um Um Um Um" and "The Matador" the next year. When the influence of Mayfield and Davis dimmed, the hits became lesser in magnitude, and Lance left Okeh in 1968, bouncing from Dakar to Curtom to Volt with moderate success. Lance did a three-year prison stretch from 1978 to 1981 for drug dealing, but has been sighted on stage recently. —*Bill Dahl*
● **Best Of Major Lance: Everybody Loves A Good Time!** / 1995 / Legacy/Epic ◆◆◆◆
Delightful 40-song, double-CD compilation of Lance's best work for Okeh between 1962 and 1967, including all of the chart singles, quite a few misses and B-sides, five previously unreleased cuts, and some Curtis Mayfield songs from his debut LP. The later tracks, recorded after producer Carl Davis and songwriter Mayfield had moved on to other projects, suffer in comparison with Lance's 1963-65 output, as he tried to keep abreast of contemporary soul trends, especially Motown. For many listeners, a briefer best-of Lance compilation will suffice. But for soul fans, this is prime stuff, dominated by the classic Latin-influenced Chicago soul sound of the Davis-produced tracks. —*Richie Unterberger*

Mark Lanegan

Alternative Pop/Rock
The lead vocalist in the neo-psychedelic Screaming Trees favors a more brooding, quietly intense sound on his own. —*Bruce Eder*
○ **The Winding Sheet** / 1990 / Sub Pop ◆◆◆◆
A dark side of this Screaming Trees vocalist. —*Robert Gordon*
● **Whiskey for the Holy Ghost** / 1994 / Sub Pop ◆◆◆◆
As a member of the Washington state alternative rock group Screaming Trees, Lanegan sings a somewhat lightweight and goofy blend of punk, hard rock, and psychedelia. On his own, he pursues an altogether more somber, acoustic, and bluesier vision. Like his debut release *The Winding Sheet*, Lanegan's second effort features his deep, husky-voiced musings, evocative mystic imagery, and brooding meditations on mortality. His dark but passionate vision is underscored by forceful acoustic guitars, harmonica, and occasional female backup harmonies. Sonically, Lanegan strongly resembles post-punk god Nick Cave, but his vision is ultimately more optimistic and accessible. —*Richie Unterberger*

Daniel Lanois

Alternative Pop/Rock
Canadian Daniel Lanois has made a name for himself as a producer of very ambient albums. He has worked on successful projects with U2, Bob Dylan, the Neville Brothers, and Chris Whitley. Since his relocation to New Orleans, his thoughtful solo work reflects his fascination with the French Cajun rhythms. —*Rick Clark*
○ **Acadie** / 1989 / Opal ◆◆◆◆
Producer Lanois imbues this solo debut with his trademark otherworldly ambience on classics like "Still Water" and "Amazing Grace." Originals like the mystical "The Maker" and the soft French folk melodicism of "O Marie" are other highlights. —*Rick Clark*
● **For The Beauty of Wynona** / 1993 / Warner Brothers ◆◆◆◆
This remarkable followup to his great debut shows Lanois growing as a singer and songwriter. His production is a weirdly magical as ever. "Brother L.A." and "Lotta Love to Give" are highlights among the many delights this album offers. —*Rick Clark*

Larks

Group, Soul, R&B, Doo-Wop
After the demise of his previous doo-wop aggregation, the Meadowlarks, Don Julian assembled a new trio, called them the Larks, and cashed in on the Money label in 1965 with a floating soul dance number, "The Jerk." It was a huge R&B and pop hit, but numerous spinoffs, including "Soul Jerk," "Jerk Once More," and "Keep Jerkin'," went nowhere. —*Bill Dahl*
● **The Jerk: Golden Classics** / 1965 / Collectables ◆◆◆◆
Floating, three-piece, Impressions-style harmonies on a dance-heavy program. —*Bill Dahl*

Last Poets

Group, Soul, R&B, Fusion

A group of New York street poets, their raw, declarative, and nationalist material has been viewed in some quarters as a precursor to rap. The poets' messages were angry, witty, and striking in cadence, presentation, and impact. They also included in their rhymes praises for and tributes to jazz and jazz musicians, especially in the cut "Jazzoetry." Their early '70s debut work and their later albums have been reissued on disc by Celluloid. —*Ron Wynn*

This is Madness / 1971 / Celluloid ✦✦✦

A legendary set featuring a group of extremely controversial street poets. The Last Poets used offensive language brilliantly, talked in graphic detail about America's social and racial failures, and helped expose a wider audience to the sentiments of the '70s black nationalists. They were the forerunners of today's Afrocentric rappers, and also showed the way to a jazz/rap union now being explored on both sides of the Atlantic. This has been reissued on CD. —*Ron Wynn*

○ **Delights in the Garden** / 1977 / Casablanca ✦✦✦✦

Reactionist/revolutionist/humanist poets on fire. Highly recommended. With drummer Bernard Purdie. —*Michael G. Nastos*

Oh My People / 1984 / Celluloid ✦✦✦

Updated sound, same powerful message. —*Michael G. Nastos*

○ **Right On!** / Dec. 28, 1990 / Collectables ✦✦✦✦

The foundation work for latter-day rappers—Afro-centric themes, improvisational vocal styles, obscenity, and a political slant. —*Ron Wynn*

★ **Retro Fit** / 1992 / Ced ✦✦✦✦✦

○ **This Is Madness** / Nov. 13, 1992 / Metrotone ✦✦✦✦

Holy Terror / 1994 / P-Vine ✦✦✦

Latimore

Group, Soul, Funk, Disco, R&B

Deep-voiced Latimore's sultry mid-'70s output for Miami's Glades label was a steamy marriage of soul and blues. Initially billed as Benny Latimore, the Tennessean began recording for Miami mogul Henry Stone in 1965, and his late-'60s Dade singles are solid deep-soul. Dropping his first name on Glades, Latimore finally found stardom in 1973 with a jazzy reading of T-Bone Walker's "Stormy Monday." He topped the soul lists in 1974 with the anguished "Let's Straighten It Out," a simmering soul/blues hybrid, and encored with the incendiary "Keep the Home Fires Burnin'" the next year. Most of Latimore's Glades sides were produced in Miami by Steve "Everyday I Have to Cry" Alaimo, and when he wasn't cutting his own hits, Latimore acted as a house pianist for parent TK Records. Latimore moved to Malaco during the '80s, his appeal undiminished. —*Bill Dahl*

Latimore / 1973 / Glades ✦✦✦

More, More, More / 1974 / Glades ✦✦✦

Benny Latimore's tough-talking Southern soul began to make some inroads in the mid-'70s with this LP, which included his only #1 R&B hit, "Let's Straighten It Out." The singer, composer and keyboardist made no-nonsense, unsophisticated confessional soul and heartache ballads, plus an occasional uptempo number; at the time, he was making tunes with minimal production that put his coarse leads at the center. They were recorded for the Miami-based Glades label, and usually were regional rather than national hits. "Let's Straighten It Out" proved an exception. —*Ron Wynn*

It Ain't Where You Been / 1977 / Glades ✦✦✦

○ **Latimore 3** / 1977 / Glades ✦✦✦✦

○ **Dig a Little Deeper** / 1978 / Glades ✦✦✦✦

Singing in the Key of Love / 1982 / Malaco ✦✦

Benny Latimore has done the same thing as Denise LaSalle, joining Malaco in the late '70s and remaining faithful to its brand of Southern soul and country/blues staples while never attempting to make his productions and arrangements more contemporary. That was the case on this album, which had a few nice tracks but also sometimes got bogged down in pretension. Latimore hasn't yet duplicated the energy or the wit that made his early-'70s Glades albums some of the decade's best Southern soul efforts. —*Ron Wynn*

○ **Good Time Man** / 1985 / Malaco ✦✦✦✦

Benny Latimore's Malaco albums have been conservatively produced, geared toward Southern tastes and moderately successful on a regional basis. That's the case with this album, which didn't land national hits but was a generally good effort. Latimore's voice isn't as commanding as it was during his 1970s run, but he can still sing in a menacing fashion, deliver convincing heartache ballads, sound vulnerable or express tenderness and concern. Unfortunately, the lack of a great single and the decidedly non-urban contemporary sound doomed this to the fate of most Malaco LPs— little exposure above the Mason-Dixon line and little radio airplay. —*Ron Wynn*

Every Way But Wrong / 1988 / Malaco ✦✦✦

A good, if at times repetitive, album by Latimore, one of his better releases on Malaco. After he'd been on the label a while, the producers began to improve the kind of songs he was given, vary the production and arrangements more, and coax stronger, more impressive leads and vocal treatments from Latimore. They still couldn't match the quality of the Glades releases, but were coming closer. —*Ron Wynn*

I'll Do Anything for You / 1988 / Malaco ✦✦

Another satisfactory album on Malaco for Latimore, who hasn't yet hit his stride on the label. His singing was soulful, but not as effective or hard-hitting as on other numbers. The production and arrangements were good, but there wasn't the energy or swaggering air that marked Latimore's best releases. His tenure at Malaco has been a successful one, but the definitive, exciting records he cut in Florida during the early '70s remain the high point of Benny Latimore's career. —*Ron Wynn*

○ **Slow Down** / 1989 / Malaco ✦✦✦✦

This was Latimore's best Malaco release, and arguably his finest record in the '80s. It had both moving ballads and fine uptempo tunes, and his usually resourceful, deep soul vocals were stronger and more confident and animated. The song "One Man, One Woman, One Love" was the type of simple yet engaging number that the Malaco tunesmiths didn't deliver consistently enough for their acts in the late '80s. It was also the kind of song that had a vintage sound but a contemporary outlook. —*Ron Wynn*

The Only Way Is Up / 1991 / Malaco ✦✦✦

Southern soul, '90s-style. —*Richard Pack*

Catchin' Up / 1993 / Malaco ✦✦

Includes a fair reprisal of Clarence Carter's "I Smell a Rat." Latimore's smooth, low tenor delivers the goods best on the midtempo love songs, "Your Sweetness Is My Weakness," "Lay Another Log on the Fire!" or "Meet Me in the Middle of the Bed." But, on funk like "Skinny Little White Girl" or "Feed Your Hungry Man," the cuts would've fared better in the hands of Carter or perhaps Roy C. —*Bil Carpenter*

● **Straighten It Out: The Best of Latimore** / 1995 / Rhino ✦✦✦✦

All of Latimore's greatest hits are included on the 17-track collection *Straighten It Out: The Best of Latimore*, making the album the best overview of the seductive '70s soul balladeer's career. — *Stephen Thomas Erlewine*

Latin Playboys

Group, Rock & Roll

David Hidalgo and Louie Perez of Los Lobos hooked up with Tchad Blake and producer Mitchell Froom for this side project, a twisted and avant-garde take on roots music. Latin Playboys draw from blues, border music, experimental studio trickery, and cinematic sound textures on their ambitious self-titled 1994 album. All of the material was composed by Hidalgo and Perez, and shows a considerably more experimental direction than their work with Los Lobos. —*Richie Unterberger*

Latin Playboys / 1994 / Slash ✦✦✦

These are hardly "songs" in the conventional sense; more like eccentric sketches that create haunting moods. The players bounce back and forth between scratchy traditional Latin music, free-associating blues numbers, and spaced-out honky-tonk. Grounded in roots music, the lyrics and song structures are almost impressionistic in tone, creating an effect similar to listening to your car radio as stations drift in and out of reach while you drive along the Mexican border. —*Richie Unterberger*

Laughing Hyenas

Group, Alternative Pop/Rock, Hardcore

Formed by vocalist John Brannon and guitarist Larissa Strickland in 1985, the Ann Arbor, MI-based Laughing Hyenas specialize in a roaring, tortured bluesy post-punk that has its roots in the noisy sludge of the Stooges and the growling blues of Howlin' Wolf. The Laughing Hyenas released their first full-length album, *You Can't Pray a Lie*, in 1989. Throughout their career, Brannon and Strickland have remained the nucleus of the band; the current lineup features Ron Sakowski on bass and former Necros drummer Todd Swalla. —*Stephen Thomas Erlewine*

Merry-Go-Round / Nov. 1987 / Touch & Go ♦♦♦
You Can't Pray a Lie / Mar. 1989 / Touch & Go ♦♦
Though Brannon still shrieks and gnashes his throat on the Hyenas' second LP, *You Can't Pray a Lie*, the band takes a decisive step towards the musical setting of the moody dirges heard on future records. "Seven Come Eleven" is a rhythmic orgy of distortion and noise, while on "Lullaby and Goodnight," Brannon even manages to calm down a bit, a path he would follow more closely on all future Hyenas albums.—*Matt Carlson*

Life of Crime / Sep. 1990 / Touch & Go ♦♦♦
The Laughing Hyenas' problem up until *Life of Crime* was Brannon's dry-throat screams distracting attention from the music. The band's music, however, had reached a level of maturity on *Life of Crime* that couldn't be ignored. Melodies and rhythms are continually experimented with, as Strickland's guitar keys suddenly shift and as jazzy tempos provided by Kevin Strickland and Jim Kimball constantly lurch back and forth. The group blasts through the bass-heavy "Hitman," the harmonic force of "Here We Go Again," and the dynamic cover of the Weirdos' "Life of Crime." —*Matt Carlson*

○ **Crawl** / Oct. 19, 1992 / Touch & Go ♦♦♦♦
Due to musical differences, Kevin Strickland and Jim Kimball left the Laughing Hyenas to form Mule, and the Hyenas were vastly improved. On *Life of Crime*, guitarist Larissa Strickland usually just improvised above the musical direction of the rhythm section, but with the departure of primary musical force of the band, Strickland had to step up. And she did on *Crawl*, a four-song EP recorded with new drummer Todd Swalla and temporary bassist Kevin Reis. Each of the four songs blazes with guitar assertiveness, particularly the escalating title track and the sonic riffing of "Living In Darkness." —*Matt Carlson*

● **Hard Times** / 1995 / Touch and Go ♦♦♦♦
If *Crawl* was Larissa Strickland's chance to assert herself musically, "Hard Times" is John Brannon's. Early on, his excited shrieking merely detracted from the overall gloomy din of the music. But here, Brannon sings with an overwhelmingly emotive moan, punctuated with his guttural screams. Musically, Strickland's development on the guitar is extraordinary, as she tears through the supercharged Rolling Stones fervor of "Just Can't Win" or pulses with restrained energy on the climactic reverb-laden blues of "Each Dawn I Die." *Hard Times* feels like a blues album, but the feeling is sustained by emotion, not technical prowess. —*Matt Carlson*

Cyndi Lauper

b. Jun. 20, 1953, Queens, NY
Pop/Rock
As a guitarist, Lauper gigged with several bands in the '70s before co-founding Blue Angel in 1977, which released a highly acclaimed rock & roll album on Polydor three years later. She went solo in 1983 and became a musical and MTV sensation with her her pop-feminist song "Girls Just Want to Have Fun" and her tender ballad "Time after Time." She won the 1984 Grammy for Best New Artist.
    Although she has had several hits since her debut, most notably the hit ballad "True Colors," Lauper was never able to recapture the excitement that surrounded her debut, *She's So Unusual*. She was still recording in the '90s, scoring a hit every now and then. —*Bil Carpenter & Donna DiChario*

● **She's So Unusual** / 1984 / Portrait ♦♦♦♦
This quirky diva created a musical and MTV sensation with her pop-feminist "Girls Just Want to Have Fun" and her tender ballad "Time After Time." She won the 1984 Grammy for Best New Artist. —*Donna DiChario*

True Colors / 1986 / Portrait ♦♦♦
Included is the Top Five title track ballad and her Top 20 faithfully remade cover of Marvin Gaye's "What's Going On." Also included is the harder-edged "Change of Heart." —*Donna DiChario*

A Night to Remember / 1989 / Epic ♦♦
On *True Colors*, Cyndi Lauper began to edge her way into adult contemporary territory, but it was on her third album, *A Night to Remember*, that she concentrated all of her attention on becoming a self-consciously "mature" singer/songwriter. *A Night to Remember* doesn't work, but not because she's incapable of performing polished, well-crafted middle-of-the-road material—"Time after Time" and "True Colors" prove that she could convincingly deliver ballads. Instead, the album is a failure because it assumes that labored arrangements and precisely detailed production are tantamount to musical sophistication. Far from sounding sophisticated, *A Night to Remember* is bland and tedious, with only the seductive "I Drove All Night" making a lasting impression. —*Stephen Thomas Erlewine*

A Hat Full of Stars / 1992 / Epic ♦♦
A Night to Remember was a dull, unengaging affair, but Lauper's follow-up, *A Hat Full of Stars*, was even more repetitious and undistinguished, lacking a hit single like "I Drove All Night" to break the synthesized, sterile MOR tedium. —*Stephen Thomas Erlewine*

○ **12 Deadly Cyns** / 1994 / Epic ♦♦♦♦
Thankfully bypassing the Top Ten hit "The Goonies 'R' Good Enough," *12 Deadly Cyns* features almost all of Cyndi Lauper's Top 40 hits, tacking on a handful of new tracks at the end, including a "Hey Now (Girls Still Wanna Have Fun)," an updated version of her breakthrough hit single, "Girls Just Wanna Have Fun." As hits collections go, the album is fine, but with the exception of the ballad "True Colors" and the pop confection "Change of Heart," all of her finest songs and biggest hits were on *She's So Unusual*, which is a more consistent and entertaining album. —*Stephen Thomas Erlewine*

Lazy Cowgirls

Group, Punk
L.A. punk rock transplants originally from Indiana, the Lazy Cowgirls were a great, though mostly ignored high-speed rock band. Taking their stylistic cues from the Ramones and '60s R&B-influenced garage rock, the Cowgirls recorded some mighty fine records that can still scorch a hole in your cerebellum, providing you play them loud enough. Led by the short, balding lead singer Pat Todd, the Lazy Cowgirls hooked up with Flesheater/Divine Horseman mastermind Chris D(esjardins), who produced *Tapping the Source*. Stuffed to the gills with maximum-torque guitar spuzz, *Tapping the Source* set the standard for Cowgirls records to come: tuneful, loud, frenetic, full of a who-gives-a-shit attitude, and fun. In some ways they sounded liked a revved-up version of the Dictators without the comic teen-angst subtext. After a short stint on Greg Shaw's indie label Bomp, the Cowgirls became one of the first acts to sign with the very hip label Sympathy For The Record Industry, recording a messy but enjoyable live record and a great studio record, *How It Looks: How It Is*. Talented and capable of providing that punk rock buzz, the Cowgirls never seemed to get the break they deserved. Although they were well-received in the non-mainstream rock press, there was no snowball effect, many far less talented bands sold more records, and the Cowgirls called it a career in 1993. Better to burn out than to fade away, I guess. —*John Dougan*

Lazy Cowgirls / 1985 / Restless ♦♦♦
○ **Tapping the Source** / 1987 / Bomp! ♦♦♦♦
With former Flesheater Chris D at the controls, the Cowgirls' debut is a stoked and smokin' slab of clatter that wins you over with its smart attitude and very loud and fast guitars. Pat Todd is a wildman, and you get the sense that he was bouncing off the studio walls when this was recorded. Songs about boredom ("Bullshit Summer"), songs about assholes ("Can't You Do Anything Right"), and plenty of songs about just plain being fucked up makes this a great piece of punk rock, miles better than recent offerings by Green Day or Offspring. —*John Dougan*

Third Time's the Charm / 1988 / Grown Up Wrong ♦♦
Radio Cowgirl / 1989 / Sympathy For The Record Industry ♦♦♦
Not essential, but a fairly good representation of the kind of fury the Cowgirls could generate live. Mediocre recording quality doesn't help, but the pure energy the band exudes makes up for any technical shortcomings. The CD contains eight extra studio tracks. —*John Dougan*

● **How It Looks, How It Is** / 1990 / Sympathy For The Record Industry ✦✦✦✦
The final Lazy Cowgirls record is a scorching hunk of speed raunch that works in the classic way that Ramones records work: it's unrepentant punk rock. Nuance is thrown out the window, and this is full-bore, head-on, manic guitar panic. Pat Todd, with a voice that sounds like a high-speed drill when he sings in his limited upper register, gives that slightly psycho edge that made the Cowgirls a fairly intimidating proposition. Some of the tracks sound half-assed, but most of this raunch and rumble (especially "D.I.E. in Indiana" and "When It All Comes Down") is prime (and primal) scorch. Enjoy. —*John Dougan*

Amanda Lear

Disco
Amanda Lear first surfaced in the early '70s as a fetishistically-clothed album-cover model for Roxy Music. She was said to be a transsexual but, as she told *Interview* magazine, that was just a ruse dreamed up by her sponsor, David Bowie, to draw attention. Her importance to disco fans, however, begins in 1977, when, in Germany with production help from Tony Monn, she recorded *I Am a Photograph,* the first of six sleazy, hard-to-find albums in which she flaunts a voice so heavy with low notes you wonder if she really isn't a man after all. But no, Lear's slow notes are simply an exaggeration of the whisky-voiced sultryness created by Marlene Dietrich. Which isn't to say that Lear's lyrics—or the music's inverted proportions—don't exploit her mythology as a kinky concoction to the bursting point. —*Michael Freedberg*

○ **I Am a Photograph** / 1977 / Chrysalis ✦✦✦✦
Lear, previously known as a Roxy Music album cover model and a protégé of Salvador Dali, appears here as a cabaret countess. She enunciates sexually naughty suggestions in a smoke-and-velvet rasp. Her best subversions hit a dancer's most salacious fantasies dead on. Most of these songs support their studied lewdness with absurdly different music, creating tangible friction (i.e. "Alligator"—funk bottom, frothy violins on top) that makes Lear's tape-loop voice feel even naughtier. All of Lear's tempos assault disco norms, either as sleaze or ultra-fast high-energy. An album not to be missed. —*Michael Freedberg*

○ **Sweet Revenge** / 1978 / Chrysalis ✦✦✦✦
Producer Anthony Monn parades every effect known to Euro-dream imagery in support of Lear as disco vamp: whispers from inside a tunnel, rhythms that filter in subliminally, themes that scale up to soprano range, choirs of angels singing, guitar rhythm rock-ons, and, of course, Lear's voice. Lear's singing is perhaps Monn's greatest effect: androgynous, sultry, out of reach and horny at the same time, Lear works hard to pretend at playing the merciless siren. She can't properly sing even one note, but what's that got to do with anything? —*Michael Freedberg*

● **Super 20** / Ariola ✦✦✦✦
Collection / BMG ✦✦✦

The Leaves

Group, Folk-Rock
One of the first L.A. folk-rock groups to spring up in the wake of the Byrds in the mid-'60s, the Leaves are most remembered for recording the first—and one of the most successful—rock versions of "Hey Joe," which reached the Top 40 (and was a huge Californian hit) in 1966. None of their other releases approached this success (although "Too Many People" was a local hit), but the group recorded a fair number of strong covers and original songs during their brief existence. More explicitly Stones and Beatles-influenced than the Byrds, they didn't project as strong an identity as competitors like the Byrds or Love, despite displaying considerable talent for harmony rockers in both the folk-rock and British Invasion styles. After cutting some singles and a decent album for the tiny Mira label, they moved to Capitol, and disbanded after a disappointing follow-up (*All the Good That's Happening,* 1967) that offered less distinguished material and a more diluted sound. Leaves bassist Jim Pons went on to join the Turtles for a while in the late '60s. —*Richie Unterberger*

Hey Joe / 1966 / One Way ✦✦✦
Their spotty first album includes the hit title track, the strong beat ballad "Just A Memory," the Bo Diddley-esque folk-rocker "Dr. Stone," "Back On The Avenue" (a ripoff of the Stones' "2120 South Michigan Avenue"), and a pre-Monkees version of "Words." The

CD reissue on One Way adds five bonus tracks. —*Richie Unterberger*

All the Good That's Happening / 1967 / One Way ✦✦

● **1966** / 1982 / Fan Club ✦✦✦✦
Somewhat hard to find these days, this well-chosen best-of-compilation includes the best cuts from the *Hey Joe* album and a clutch of fine rare and unreleased tracks. Highlights among these are the raw, original 45 version of "Too Many People," the Beatlesque B-side "Funny Little World," a Byrds-like folk-rock cover of Dylan's "Love Minus Zero," and "Be With You," a superb ripoff of the Byrds' "All I Really Want To Do." Liner notes by Leaves member Jim Pons top off a fine package. —*Richie Unterberger*

Leaving Trains

Group, Alternative Pop/Rock
Self-styled politically incorrect hicks from California, the Trains' slophouse blues-inflected punkoid noise raunch can be alternately liberating and sophomoric. Led by "Falling" James Moreland, these guys are the quintessential mixed bag, but (at least early on) made some righteous, funny, self-deprecating rock. —*John Dougan*

Well Down Blue Highway / 1984 / Enigma ✦✦✦

● **Kill Tunes** / 1986 / SST ✦✦✦✦
A sizzling little platter that focuses on country/folk leanings with a fiery edge. Not quite uncontrolled. It's still as close to an undeniable record as they've ever made. —*John Dougan*

○ **Fuck** / 1987 / SST ✦✦✦✦
Their last really consistent record. Doomed to commercial failure, the title was much loved by anti-corporate rock snobs. It's still countrified, just sloppier, and is hampered by the 11-minute freakout "What the President Meant to Say." —*John Dougan*

Transportational D. Vices / 1989 / SST ✦✦✦
Sleeping Underwater Survivors / 1991 / SST ✦✦
The Lump in My Forehead / 1992 / SST ✦✦
The Big Jinx / Jun. 1994 / SST ✦✦✦

Keith Leblanc

Experimental
More than just a drummer for the apocalyptic dub/funk produced by Adrian Sherwood's On-U Sound productions, LeBlanc is also an accomplished solo artist who uses the same collage of sound and aural layering learned from years of playing in the Sherwood-produced band Tackhead. Admittedly, LeBlanc gets a lot of help from cohorts Doug Wimbish and Skip McDonald (the other two-thirds of Tackhead, originally part of Sylvia Robinson's Sugarhill studio band), as well as Sherwood himself, but that said, the recordings that bear his name have been exciting, experimental hunks of postmodern music that combine live playing with musique concrete, and spoken word segments with snippets from film and television. In other words: easy listening this ain't. LeBlanc's career started auspiciously with the release of the EP *No Sell Out,* which was a hip-hop deconstruction of a Malcolm X speech. an alternative scene "hit," it helped engender interest for LeBlanc's first full-blown solo effort, *Major Malfunction,* which gets its title from the description used by engineers of the Challenger space shuttle disaster; LeBlanc uses some of the tape-recorded reports from the disaster for effect. Not a big seller, *Malfunction* was followed by *Stranger than Fiction,* which was a bit of a letdown, but still had enough squalling noise and reggae-inflected creepiness to make it well worthwhile. Still working for Sherwood, LeBlanc hasn't released much of late, but his work up to this point has been extremely interesting. —*John Dougan*

○ **No Sell Out** / 1983 / Tommy Boy ✦✦✦✦
Actually, this wasn't an LP, but a 12" dance mix that featured snippets of speeches by Malcolm X (long before Spike Lee's film offered street cred to X merchandise) set to a churning mass of funk-dub supervised by Adrian Sherwood. A great record, *No Sell Out,* oddly enough, became a demi-hit because of its popularity in dance clubs. Early postmodern rock/funk/dub'n'roll at its best. —*John Dougan*

● **Major Malfunction** / 1986 / World ✦✦✦✦
It is more than a little disingenuous to refer to this as a Keith LeBlanc album. While his considerable drumming skills and compositional abilities are major parts of why this record is good, there are many other similarly important contributions made by

Adrian Sherwood's Tackhead gang (including Sherwood himself). That said, *Major Malfunction* is a wild, multifaceted piece of contemporary music that welds hard rock onto reggae onto musique concrete. With vocal sampling including everything from Apollo control to Margaret Thatcher, this is a complex, but extremely satisfying work. Avoid if your taste in music (or in Tackhead recordings) doesn't run to the extreme end of experimental. —*John Dougan*

○ **Stranger than Fiction** / 1989 / Enigma ✦✦✦✦
Another record with LeBlanc taking top billing, this is yet another exercise in Sherwood's wildly original Tackhead "empire." Unlike *Major Malfunction,* this is a little more restrained, but with people like Gary Clail and Sherwood involved, easy listening this ain't. LeBlanc gets all the writing credits, and he's done a great job of coming up with a challenging assortment of material. At times fiery and polemical, at others unhinged and dadaesque, *Stranger than Fiction* is another interesting, at times compelling work from this unique musical collective. —*John Dougan*

Led Zeppelin

Group, Hard Rock, Heavy Metal, Blues Rock
In 1968 the Yardbirds' commercial glory days were well behind them. The groundbreaking band had been the nurturing ground for some of the greatest guitarists of the rock era: Eric Clapton, Jeff Beck, and Jimmy Page. It was Page (the last of the three to come on board) who, along with manager Peter Grant, sensed a change in the times and sought to create a heavier, more aggressive sound for the developing album-oriented market.

Initially called the New Yardbirds, Led Zeppelin got its name from a Keith Moon (the Who's drummer) catchphrase ("going down like a lead zeppelin") concerning encountering bad gigs.

From the outset, Led Zeppelin (Jimmy Page, guitar; Robert Plant, vocal; John Paul Jones, bass and keys; John Bonham, drums) caused a stir with their incredibly heavy yet dynamic sound, their questionable plundering of old blues standards, and Plant's agitated banshee-wail of a voice. Their audacious self-titled debut, which went #10, displayed one of the greatest rock production jobs of all time, with its fine balance of room ambience and powerful immediacy. Throughout much of the '70s, Led Zeppelin reigned as the world's most successful rock band, breaking concert records and releasing ten Top Ten albums, eight of which went #1 or #2. In spite of their huge success, Led Zeppelin only had one Top Ten single, with the #4 "Whole Lotta Love." "Stairway to Heaven," the most requested song ever on rock radio, was never officially released as a single. Over the years, many bands have tried (and failed) to capture the raw power and sonic qualities of Led Zeppelin, but it was the band's shared vision that achieved their sound. They understood that enough to call it quits when Bonham died on Sept 25, 1980.

Fourteen years later Page and Plant reunited as a duo, recording the *No Quarter* album and touring Europe and America. —*Rick Clark*

☆ **Led Zeppelin** / 1969 / Swan Song ✦✦✦✦✦
Led Zeppelin's debut album provided a blueprint for its overall approach—hard rock with ornate guitar textures and powerful riffs, topped by singer Robert Plant's high-pitched singing on roaring rockers like "Good Times Bad Times" and "Communication Breakdown," plus drawn-out blues performances like "Dazed and Confused." —*William Ruhlmann*

☆ **Led Zeppelin II** / 1969 / Swan Song ✦✦✦✦✦
Perhaps the definitive heavy metal album, featuring "Whole Lotta Love." —*William Ruhlmann*

☆ **Led Zeppelin III** / 1970 / Swan Song ✦✦✦✦✦
After the bone-crunching hard rock of *Led Zeppelin II,* Page, Plant, Bonham, and Jones tracked a collection of more acoustic-flavored numbers. Songs like "Gallows Pole" and "Bron-Y-Aur Stomp" were essentially their trademark rockers played on folk instruments, but the reflective "That's the Way" and "Tangerine" indicated a new maturity. A handful of heavy riff-rockers like "Immigrant Song," "Out on the Tiles," "Celebration Day," and the hard blues raveup "Since I've Been Loving You" more than rounded out this solid (but transitional) effort. —*Rick Clark*

★ **Led Zeppelin IV** / 1971 / Swan Song ✦✦✦✦✦
The perfect mixture of Zeppelin's trademark heavy rock, plus some old-time rock & roll and the band's folkie influences, all of which culminated in its greatest song, "Stairway to Heaven." —*William Ruhlmann*

☆ **Houses of the Holy** / 1973 / Swan Song ✦✦✦✦✦
Houses of the Holy follows the same basic pattern as *Led Zeppelin IV,* but the approach is looser and more relaxed. Jimmy Page's riffs rely on ringing, folky hooks as much as thundering blues-rock, giving the album a lighter, more open atmosphere. While the psuedo-reggae of "D'Yer Mak'er" and the affectionate James Brown send-up "The Crunge" suggest that the band was searching for material, they actually contribute to the musical diversity of the album. "The Rain Song" is one of their finest moments, featuring a soaring string arrangement and a gentle, aching melody. "The Ocean" is just as good, starting with a typically heavy, but funky, guitar groove before slamming into an a cappella section and ending with a swinging, doo-wop-flavored raveup. With the exception of the rampaging opening number "The Song Remains the Same," the rest of *Houses of the Holy* is fairly straightforward, ranging from the foreboding "No Quarter" and the strutting hard rock of "Dancing Days" to the epic folk/metal fusion "Over the Hills and Far Away." Throughout the record, the band's playing is excellent, making the eclectism of Page and Plant's songwriting sound coherent and natural. —*Stephen Thomas Erlewine*

☆ **Physical Graffiti** / 1975 / Swan Song ✦✦✦✦✦
A lengthy two-disc set whose bluesy workouts (plus such new explorations as the Middle Eastern "Kashmir") mark it as the most "Zeppelinish" of Led Zeppelin albums. —*William Ruhlmann*

The Song Remains the Same / 1976 / Swan Song ✦✦
Led Zeppelin's initial popularity was based as much on its concerts as their albums, so it's strange that the group's only official live album is such an uninspired, boring affair. Released in conjunction with the pseudo-documentary film of the same name, *The Song Remains the Same* reproduces the very things that made Zeppelin concerts legendary—lengthy solos, intertwining interplay between Page and Plant, and ridiculously long songs ("Dazed and Confused" is nearly an entire half hour)—but the group's performance is not intoxicating, it's long-winded. As scores of bootlegs prove, Led Zeppelin could produce magic with the same formula, but *The Song Remains the Same* is excrutiatingly dull. —*Stephen Thomas Erlewine*

Presence / 1976 / Swan Song ✦✦✦
Presence scales back the size of *Physical Graffiti* to a single album, but it retains the grandiose scope of the double album. If anything, *Presence* has more majestic epics than its predecessor, opening with the surging ten-minute "Achilles Last Stand" and closing with the meandering, nearly ten-minute "Tea for One." In between, Zeppelin adds the lumbering blues workout "Nobody's Fault but Mine" and the terse, menacing "For Your Life," which is the best song on the album. These four tracks take up the bulk of the album, leaving three lighthearted throwaways to alleviate the foreboding atmosphere of the epics, as well as their pretensions. If all of the throwaways were as focused and funny as those on *Physical Graffiti* or *Houses of the Holy,* Zeppelin would have had another classic on their hands. However, the Crescent City love letter of "Royal Orleans" sags in the middle and the ersatz rockabilly of "Candy Store Rock" doesn't muster up the loose, funky swagger of "Hots on for Nowhere," which it *should* in order to work. The three throwaways are also scattered haphazardly throughout the album, making it seem more ponderous than it actually is, and the result is the weakest album they had yet recorded. —*Stephen Thomas Erlewine*

In through the out Door / 1979 / Swan Song ✦✦✦
Between *Presence* and *In through the out Door,* disco, punk, and new wave had overtaken rock & roll, and Led Zeppelin chose to tentatively embrace the pop revolutions, adding synthesizers to the mix and emphasizing Bonham's inherent way with a groove. The album's opening number "In the Evening," with its stomping rhythms and heavy, staggered riffs, suggests that the band hasn't strayed from their course, but by the time the rolling shuffle of "South Bound Suarez" kicks into gear, it's apparent that the group has regained their sense of humor. After "South Bound Suarez," the group tries a variety of styles, whether it's an overdriven homage to Bakersfield country called "Hot Dog," the layered, Latin-tinged percussion and pianos of "Fool in the Rain," or the slickly seductive ballad "All My Love." "Carouselambra," a lurching, self-consciously ambitious synth-driven number, and the slow blues "I'm Gonna Crawl" aren't quite as impressive as the rest of the album, but the record is a graceful way to close their career, even if it wasn't intended as the final chapter. —*Stephen Thomas Erlewine*

Coda / 1982 / Swan Song ✦✦✦
An odds-n-sods collection assembled after Bonham's death, *Coda* is predictably a hit-or-miss affair. The best material comes in later in the career, including the ringing folk stomp of "Poor Tom," the jacked-up '50s rock & roll of "Ozone Baby," and their response to punk rock, the savage "Wearing and Tearing." The rest of the album, sadly including the Bonham showcase "Bonzo's Montreux," is average, despite the presence of some stellar playing, especially on the early blues-rock blitzkrieg "I Can't Quit You Baby" and "We're Gonna Groove." —*Stephen Thomas Erlewine*

Led Zeppelin [Box Set] / 1990 / Swan Song ✦✦✦
Led Zeppelin's primary method of artistic expression was their albums. Although they had a handful of hit singles and selected album tracks were played endlessly on the radio, the true range of their music is only evident on the original albums, which were carefully sequenced and assembled. Consequently, the notion of a Led Zeppelin anthology is a bit strange—their records worked as individual pieces. Nevertheless, the four-disc box set *Led Zeppelin* includes most of their best and most famous material. Jimmy Page determined the set's running order, taking the songs out of their familiar contexts and placing them in a new, occasionally jarring, sequence, providing new insights to the band's music which dedicated fans will appreciated. *Led Zeppelin* is the only album in their catalog to include the classic B-side "Hey, Hey What Can I Do," as well as their unreleased version of Robert Johnson's "Travelling Riverside Blues" and a live medley of Page's "White Summer / Black Mountainside." Most fans will find these three tracks essential, but will balk at the price, especially since all of Zeppelin's albums have been re-mastered since the original release of the box set. Nevertheless, the box contains a wealth of brilliant music; however, all of it is better-heard in its original incarnation. —*Stephen Thomas Erlewine*

Led Zeppelin Remasters / 1992 / Swan Song ✦✦✦
A collection of most of Zeppelin's best-known tracks, this double-disc set only gives a slight idea of what the band accomplished in its career; stick with the original albums instead. —*Stephen Thomas Erlewine*

Boxed Set 2 / 1993 / ✦✦✦
Rounding up all of the studio tracks that didn't appear on the first box (as well as the pleasant, but unremarkable, "Baby Come On Home"), *Boxed Set 2* is the perfect way to complete a Led Zeppelin library begun with the first box set. —*Stephen Thomas Erlewine*

Complete Studio Recordings / 1993 / Atlantic ✦✦✦
Collecting all of Led Zeppelin's groundbreaking studio albums (as well as a reworked *Coda*) in one unattractive box, *The Complete Studio Recordings* is only necessary for hardcore fans wishing to replace their old records. Although the artwork inside the package is lavish, the box features no new material or remastering, making it completely irrelevant for those who already own the first two box sets. The music here is brilliant, but it's available in better, more attractive, and less expensive packages. —*Stephen Thomas Erlewine*

Albert Lee

b. Dec. 21, 1943, Leominster, England
Country-Rock, Rockabilly
Lee is an English guitarist, highly proficient in a multitude of styles but primarily gifted in country and rockabilly picking. The ultimate sideman on countless sessions over the last two decades, his Telecaster twangings have graced the recordings of Eric Clapton, Jerry Lee Lewis, and Emmylou Harris, to name just a few. Also notable as the music director when the Everly Brothers reunited a few years back, Lee has released a few solo albums of his own in the last few years, all of them informed by his clean, articulate picking. —*Cub Koda*

○ **Hiding** / 1979 / A&M ✦✦✦✦
Standard country-rock album. (Out of print) —*Jeff Tamarkin*

Albert Lee / 1982 / Polydor ✦✦✦
Disappointing rock effort still features brilliant guitar. —*Jeff Tamarkin*

○ **Country Guitar Man** / Nov. 1986 / Magnum ✦✦✦✦
This collection of Lee's early-'70s work with Head, Hands, & Feet is fairly remarkable, particularly Lee's guitar work. (Import) —*Jeff Tamarkin*

○ **Speechless** / Feb. 1987 / MCA ✦✦✦✦
One of the guitar world's best-kept secrets, the former Everly Brothers and Emmylou Harris sideman explores his roots in this instrumental jewel. Albert Lee co-produced this album. Very clean sound, very good cover of "Arkansas Traveler" featuring Lee on guitar, mandolin and piano; Jim Cox, Greg Humphrey, Sterling Biff Ball, and Chad Wackerman. —*Jeff Tamarkin & Chip Renner*

● **Gagged but Not Bound** / Mar. 1988 / MCA ✦✦✦✦
The master musician plays unworldly guitar on this acoustic/electric country-, rock-, and traditional-oriented masterpiece. Exquisitely recorded. —*Jeff Tamarkin*

○ **Black Claw & Country Fever** / Oct. 1991 / Line ✦✦✦✦
This collection of late-'60s material is raw yet engaging; the musicianship is stunning. (Import) —*Jeff Tamarkin*

Laura Lee

b. Mar. 9, 1945, Detroit, MI
Soul
A tough '60s soul singer with a salty sense of humor (aimed mostly at the men in her life), Laura Lee recorded at Rick Hall's FAME studio in Muscle Shoals for the Chess label, and later for Hot Wax. In songs like "Wanted: Lover, No Experience Necessary," "A Man with Some Backbone," and the anthemic "Women's Love Rights," the female experience was brazenly discussed, debated, kicked around, and, finally, celebrated. Her music laid the groundwork for artists like Millie Jackson and Denise LaSalle to expand this proud, sexy, brash-talking corner of "women's" soul music. Lee had a country/soul, romantic side as well, as shown on her splended version of the Penn-Oldham classsic "Uptight Good Man." Lee is a fine, versatile, saucy singer whose work deserves more attention. —*Christine Ohlman*

○ **That's How It Is: Chess Years** / 1990 / Chess ✦✦✦✦
Her '60s Chess recordings feature bone-chilling vocals. —*Richard Pack*

● **Greatest Hits** / 1991 / HDH ✦✦✦✦
Hot Wax-artist Laura Lee took the spirit of the feminist movement and gave it a hard-hitting R&B setting. Assertive titles like "Wedlock Is a Padlock" and "Rip Off" won her more acceptance on R&B stations. "Women's Love Rights," included here, dented the Top 40 charts at number 36. —*Rick Clark*

The Left Banke

Group, Pop/Rock
This New York group pioneered "Baroque'n'Roll" in the '60s with their mix of pop/rock and grand, quasi-classical arrangements and melodies. Featuring teenage prodigy Michael Brown as keyboardist and chief songwriter, the group scored two quick hits with "Walk Away Renee" (number five) and "Pretty Ballerina" (number 15). Chamber-like string arrangements, Steve Martin's soaring, near-falsetto lead vocals, and tight harmonies that borrowed from British Invasion bands like the Beatles and the Zombies were also key elements of the Left Banke sound. Though their two hits are their only well-remembered efforts, their debut album (*Walk Away Renee/Pretty Ballerina*) was a strong, near-classic work that matched the quality of their hit singles in songwriting and production.

Unfortunately the group, which showed such tremendous promise, was quickly torn asunder by dissension. Brown left in 1967, and most of the group's second and final album, *The Left Banke Too*, was recorded without him. While it still sported baroque arrangements and contained some fine moments, Brown's presence was sorely missed, and the record pales in comparison to their debut. Brown went on to form a Left Banke-styled group, Montage, which released a fine and underappreciated album in the late '60s. He later teamed up to form Stories with vocalist Ian Lloyd. —*Richie Unterberger*

● **There's Gonna Be a Storm: Complete Recordings 1966-69** / 1992 / Mercury ✦✦✦✦
Though it's missing a few rarities—namely the Steve Martin single for Buddha that reunited him with Michael Brown—this is the most definitive Left Banke compilation. It features the entirety of their two late-'60s albums, as well as a couple of singles that didn't make it onto LPs at the time (though they later appeared on Rhino's *History*) and a previously unissued cut, "Men Are Building Sand." Their debut 1967 LP, *Walk Away Renee/Pretty Ballerina*, is an underrated classic of the time, matching smart harmonies and

pop hooks to baroque orchestration. Its brilliance casts a bit of a shadow over the rest of this collection. The group's 1968 album *Too* suffered from bloated production and, more importantly, the absence of chief songwriter/arranger Michael Brown. In turn, the 1967 single Brown cut under the Left Banke moniker with singer Bert Sommer suffers from the absence of lead vocalist Steve Martin. By the time Brown and Martin tenuously reunited for a late-1969 single, some of the spark had gone. All of the aforementioned highs and lows of this prodigiously talented but strife-ridden group are on this disc. —*Richie Unterberger*

Leiber & Stoller

Group, Pop/Rock

A complete biography of the lives of Jerry Leiber and Mike Stoller and their contribution to rock & roll could easily take up the rest of this book. Very simply, Mike Leiber and Jerry Stoller are two of the most important songwriters of the early days of rock & roll. Although they had penned songs for R&B artists such as Jimmy Witherspoon, Floyd Dixon and Charles Brown in the early '50s, Leiber and Stoller more or less exploded onto the rock scene in 1953 by writing "Hound Dog" for Big Mama Thornton (later to be covered by Elvis). From that point on, the duo composed and produced a string of hits that include some of the most instantly recognizable songs in rock history. They were also pushing the art of rock songwriting (and record production) into, at the time, uncharted territory. As is noted by critic Greg Shaw in the *Rolling Stone Illustrated History of Rock and Roll*: "They were the true architects of pop/rock... Their signal achievement was the marriage of rhythm & blues in its most primal form to the pop tradition."

Few songwriters of this era had the Midas Touch as did Leiber and Stoller. A partial list of their credits include "Riot in Cell Block #9" (1953), "Love Me" (1956), "Charlie Brown" (1959), "Stand By Me" (1961), "On Broadway" (1963), and numerous songs for Elvis, including songs for the films *Jailhouse Rock* and *King Creole*. Along with wedding R&B with the pop tradition, Leiber and Stoller also introduced string arrangements to R&B records (The Drifters featuring Ben E. King, "There Goes My Baby") and by doing so created the foundation for a new era of soul music production that would come on the heels of the fading doo-wop style. Among the many artists and writers they influenced, few were more important than Phil Spector, who cut his teeth learning production techniques from them while they painstakingly assembled the great early Drifters tracks.

In 1964, Leiber and Stoller started their own record label, Red Bird, devoted to girl groups. Wisely, they also hired the talented songwriting duo of Ellie Greenwich and Jeff Barry, who were at their peak powers, composing some of the most lasting songs of the albeit brief heyday of girl-group music, including the Shangri-Las' "Leader of the Pack" and the Dixie Cups' "Chapel of Love." Leiber and Stoller, however, became disinterested in the business side of Red Bird and sold the label two years later, just as the girl group sound was on the wane. So, too, were the hitmaking days of Leiber and Stoller on the wane. They continued to write songs, mostly for the Coasters, but they no longer dominated the pop and R&B charts the way they once did. Still, they survived, taking on the august role of rock & roll elder statesmen, eventually landing a spot in the Rock and Roll Hall of Fame in 1987. Most recently, their songs were the basis of a successful Broadway musical entitled *Smokey Joe's Cafe*, which revived interest in their great body of work, and also brought the music of Jerry Leiber and Mike Stoller to a whole new audience. Not bad for a couple of guys who, in the words of Mike Stoller, never wanted to write rock & roll songs, just good R&B.—*John Dougan*

● **The Leiber-Stoller Big Band** / Jul. 15, 1960 / Atlantic ✦✦✦✦

The Lemon Drops

Group, Psychedelic, Garage Rock

Very obscure even by '60s garage band standards, the Lemon Drops released only one single, the ferocious raga-rocker "I Live in the Springtime," which found a home on *Pebbles Vol. 8*. In the mid-'80s, a couple albums' worth of unreleased material were issued that show the group to be one of the most talented garage-psych outfits. One of the relatively few garage groups to convincingly fuse raga-ish riffs with guitar raunch, the sometimes dippy lyrics of their all-original repertoire are offset by pretty harmonies, soaring melodies, and interesting flower-power production. Quite talented for their teenage years, they deserved a better fate than archival rediscovery by the garage rock cult. —*Richie Unterberger*

● **Crystal Pure** / 1985 / Collectables ✦✦✦✦

Combines the contents of both LPs issued on the Cicadelic label in the mid-'80s (*Crystal Pure* and *Second Album*) onto one CD, making this indeed the definitive collection. Almost all of their known tapes, covering both their searing electric garage/psych and softer, acoustic garage/folk sides. Dating from 1967 and 1968, this features a lot of original material that the band recorded in Chicago studios, as well as some drummerless home demos. These are endearing (and still moving) relics of an age of great exuberance, innocence, and hope. Good harmonies on the psychedelic ballads, which have been described as "garage-band Donovan." One of the best reissues of unknown '60s garage/psychedelic music. —*Richie Unterberger*

Lemon Pipers

Group, Pop/Rock

The Lemon Pipers included singer Ivan Browne, guitarist William Bartlett, keyboardist R.G. Nave, bassist Steve Walmsley, and drummer William Albaugh. The group is best known for their number-one bubblegum hit "Green Tambourine" and several followups, all written by the team of Paul Leka and Shelley Pinz. The group actually wanted to play more psychedelic music; they only recorded "Green Tambourine" because their label would have dropped them had they refused. They eventually got the artistic control they wanted and ended up dropping off the charts for good with their first self-produced album. They broke up in 1969, with Bartlett joining Ram Jam. —*Steve Huey*

○ **Green Tambourine** / 1967 / Buddah ✦✦✦✦

Jungle Marmalade / 1968 / Buddah ✦✦✦

● **Golden Classics** / 1994 / Collectables ✦✦✦✦

The Lemonheads

Group, Alternative Pop/Rock

Evan Dando was a hardcore punk when the Lemonheads released their first album, *Hate Your Friends*, in 1987; five years later, he was a teenage heart-throb, thanks to the memorable, punky power-pop of *It's a Shame About Ray*. Between those two albums, the rest of the band quit, leaving guitarist/vocalist Dando as the only Lemonhead. The membership wasn't the only thing that changed. Over the years, Dando began to accentuate his fondness for pure pop, which was apparent even on the band's harder earlier records. The Lemonheads moved to a major label in 1990 and released *Lovey*. Dando recorded most of the album by himself, which makes its mix of loud guitars, bright melodies, and charming, simple lyrics all the more impressive; this was the path he would follow to stardom. On the band's next album—1992's *It's a Shame About Ray*, which was recorded with a full band—Dando's songwriting blossomed. Not only could he write catchy, brash power-pop, he was able to seamlessly incorporate touches of folk and country-rock. Thanks to a loud, irreverent cover of Simon & Garfunkel's "Mrs. Robinson," the Lemonheads began getting mainstream attention; with their next album, 1993's *Come on Feel the Lemonheads*, the band gained an even bigger audience, even if the album was more inconsistent. Even with its lull spots, the album showed that Dando continued to grow as a songwriter, as his country influences became more pronounced and genuine. —*Stephen Thomas Erlewine*

Hate Your Friends / 1987 / Taang! ✦✦

Creator / 1988 / Taang! ✦✦

○ **Lick** / 1989 / Taang! ✦✦✦✦

On their last independent release, the Lemonheads turn in an engaging but incoherent album that bounces back and forth between inspired melodic punk-pop, hardcore, and the occasional ballad; the whole charming mess is highlighted by a muscular cover of Suzanne Vega's "Luka." —*Stephen Thomas Erlewine*

Create Your Friends / 1989 / Taang! ✦✦

The Lemonheads' first two albums show that beneath the band's relentless hardcore guitar grind, Evan Dando had written some very good songs with strong melodies. It just takes some effort to *hear* the melodies. —*Stephen Thomas Erlewine*

Lovey / 1990 / Atlantic ✦✦✦

Alternating between melodic hard rock and gentle country and folk-rock, *Lovey* is the band's most refined album to date, but only half the songs (including "Stove," "Half the Time," "(The) Door," and Gram Parsons' "Brass Buttons") make a lasting impression. —*Stephen Thomas Erlewine*

● **It's a Shame About Ray** / 1992 / Atlantic ◆◆◆◆

It's a Shame About Ray is a nearly perfect pop album—short, concise, and overflowing with memorable melodies. Although Evan Dando keeps every song between two and three minutes, he isn't cheating the audience by any measure; the 12-song, under-30-minute blitz of *It's a Shame About Ray* provides more quality music than most of today's bloated, 70-minute epics. Dando's songs prove that his true talents as a pop songwriter are just beginning to emerge. (Note: After the fall of 1992, the album was issued with the band's raucous power-pop take on Simon & Garfunkel's "Mrs. Robinson.") —*Stephen Thomas Erlewine*

Come on Feel the Lemonheads / 1993 / Atlantic ◆◆◆

More confused and muddled than *It's A Shame About Ray*, *Come on Feel the Lemonheads* has a number of power-pop pleasures, but they're buried among several lazy, half-hearted numbers and a ridiculous solo piano piece. When Evan Dando does hit home—as on "The Great Big No," "Down About It," and the cover, "Into Your Arms"—the results are irresistible; the moving, introspective "Favorite T" and the country-rock of "Being Around" and "Big Gay Heart" are also strong. Unfortunately, these songs are hard to find amidst the bloated directionlessness of the rest of the album. —*Stephen Thomas Erlewine*

John Lennon

b. Oct. 9, 1940, Liverpool, England, **d.** Dec. 8, 1980
Rock & Roll, Singer-Songwriter, Pop/Rock
John Lennon was a singer, songwriter, guitarist, record producer, author, actor, filmmaker, artist, and political spokesman, and one of the greatest figures in postwar popular music. Lennon was born in Liverpool, England, and became involved in music in the '50s. The group he founded as the Quarrymen eventually evolved into the Beatles, and from 1963 to 1970 they were the most successful rock group in history. Lennon, the group's leader, played an important part in that success, writing and singing many of its biggest hits and best songs.

Lennon began to record and perform outside the group in 1969, usually in the company of his wife, avant-garde artist Yoko Ono. The early Lennon-Ono records (and films and performance events) were experimental in nature, but as Lennon turned to recording as a solo performer, his work was more accessible to pop audiences, though his lyrical concerns were frequently political or scathingly personal. His first formal solo album was *John Lennon/Plastic Ono Band* in 1970, and he followed this with *Imagine* (1971), *Sometime in New York City* (1972), *Mind Games* (1973), *Walls & Bridges* (1974), and *Rock & Roll* (1975). Most of his recordings sold well, with *Walls & Bridges* topping the charts along with its single, "Whatever Gets You through the Night."

Lennon, who had separated from Ono in 1973, was reconciled with her in 1975 and thereafter retired from music to raise their son Sean. He and Ono re-emerged with the album *Double Fantasy* in 1980, and had plans for further recordings and performances at the time he was assassinated. —*William Ruhlmann*

Two Virgins: Unfinished Music No. 1 / Nov. 11, 1968 / Apple ◆◆

At the time of its release, this duo album by John Lennon and Yoko Ono gained its greatest notice for its cover, a photograph that depicted the two standing before the camera naked. The recording, too, can be described as naked, in that it contains no music that would interfere with one's ability to hear the normal sounds of life. The record is not unlike what you might get if you turned on a tape recorder for a random half hour in your home—snatches of inaudible conversation far away from the microphone, footsteps, wind, etc. Conceptual "music" in the Cageian sense, yes, but not popular music of the kind with which John Lennon had been previously associated in any sense at all. —*William Ruhlmann*

Life with the Lions: Unfinished Music #2 / May 26, 1969 / Apple ◆◆

John Lennon and Yoko Ono's second collaborative album consists of five tracks: all of Side One is taken up by "Cambridge 1969," a live recording at Lady Mitchell Hall in Cambridge of Lennon playing an electric guitar backup to Ono's singing and screaming. Side Two includes an a cappella rendering by Ono of "No Bed For Beatle John," which discusses the refusal of a hospital to give Lennon a bed so he could stay during his wife's troubled pregnancy; "Baby's Heartbeat," which is what it says it is; "Two Minutes Silence" in commemoration of Ono's miscarriage, which also is what it says it is; and "Radio Play," 12 minutes of a radio dial being turned back and forth to pick up random stations. If, as they sug-

gested, their lives were their art, then this is, too. Maybe. —*William Ruhlmann*

Live Peace in Toronto 1969 / Dec. 12, 1969 / Capitol ◆◆◆

Impromptu concert appearance, with Lennon singing a few rock & roll oldies plus his then-new single, "Cold Turkey," backed by guitarist Eric Clapton. Also 17+ minutes of Yoko Ono screaming and singing over guitar feedback. —*William Ruhlmann*

Wedding Album / 1969 / Apple ◆◆

The third and last of John Lennon and Yoko Ono's experimental albums to be released within a one-year period, *Wedding Album*, like *Unfinished Music No. 1—Two Virgins*, was in some ways more notable for its packaging than for its content. It came in a box containing a facsimile of the Lennons' wedding certificate and a photograph of a piece of wedding cake. The record itself contained two selections, one of which consisted of nearly 25 minutes of Yoko Ono's wailing, while the other, "John And Yoko," featured the two, one in each stereo speaker, calling out the other's name for more than 22 minutes. Employing such limited lyrics, Lennon is the more expressive, Ono the more penetrating. —*William Ruhlmann*

☆ **John Lennon/Plastic Ono Band** / Dec. 11, 1970 / Capitol ◆◆◆◆◆

A stark, harrowing set of songs in which Lennon recounts the horrors of his childhood ("Mother," "Working Class Hero"), the disillusionment of his adulthood ("I Found Out"), and his loss of faith in all idols ("God") including "Beatles." This album is one of rock's most personal—and most ambitious—statements. —*William Ruhlmann*

☆ **Imagine** / Sep. 9, 1971 / Capitol ◆◆◆◆◆

In addition to the justly revered title track (a #3 hit), this eclectic pop album also contains "Jealous Guy" (later a hit for Roxy Music) and "Gimme Some Truth" (later adopted by such punk rockers as Generation X). —*William Ruhlmann*

Sometime in New York City / Jun. 12, 1972 / Capitol ◆◆

The first album co-billed to John Lennon and Yoko Ono to actually contain recognizable pop music, *Sometime in New York City* found the Lennons in an explicitly political phase, expounding on such topical subjects as the Attica prison riot and the treatment of activists John Sinclair and Angela Davis. Especially in the case of Lennon's songs, there is an appealing rock style to the material, even if the lyrics limit the record's appeal. *Sometime in New York City* was originally released with a free bonus disc that contained a live medley of Lennon's "Cold Turkey" and Ono's "Don't Worry Kyoko," and an appearance by the Lennons at a Mothers of Invention concert. This slight material now makes the album a two-CD set, and it is priced accordingly. —*William Ruhlmann*

○ **Mind Games** / Nov. 2, 1973 / Capitol ◆◆◆◆

John Lennon retreated from the political tone of *Sometime in New York City* and returned to solo work here, managing a fitting followup to "Imagine" with the piano-based title track and also turning in one of his better ballads with "One Day (At a Time)." —*William Ruhlmann*

○ **Walls and Bridges** / Sep. 26, 1974 / Capitol ◆◆◆◆

Craftsmanlike pop-rock featuring the uptempo #1 hit "Whatever Gets You through the Night," its Top Ten followup, "#9 Dream," and some lovely album tracks. —*William Ruhlmann*

Rock 'n' Roll / Feb. 17, 1975 / Capitol ◆◆◆

It was a common practice in the early 1970s for artists to satisfy record companies' demands for frequent LP releases by recording albums of cover songs (see the Band's *Moondog Matinee* and David Bowie's *Pinups* for other examples). The story of John Lennon's covers album is a little more complicated, but the result is the same, with the artist tackling songs from the '50s by many of his favorites, from Gene Vincent to Lloyd Price. Of course, these are the kinds of songs that turned up on early Beatles albums, and while Lennon doesn't reinvent them as strikingly as his old group did, he gives them an affectionate, knowing treatment. —*William Ruhlmann*

○ **Shaved Fish** / Oct. 24, 1975 / Capitol ◆◆◆◆

Although superseded by *The John Lennon Collection* (see below), this greatest-hits album is the only place to find such singles as "Cold Turkey" and "Happy Xmas (War Is Over)." —*William Ruhlmann*

○ **Double Fantasy** / Nov. 17, 1980 / Capitol ◆◆◆◆

On an album made shortly before his death, Lennon explores his retirement, his artistic rebirth, and his relationship with his family on such songs as "(Just Like) Starting Over," "Woman," and

"Watching the Wheels," all of which were Top Ten hits. Lennon's songs are interspersed with surprisingly accessible contributions from Ono. — *William Ruhlmann*

★ **The John Lennon Collection** / Nov. 10, 1982 / Capitol ✦✦✦✦✦
Six of the seven Lennon tracks from *Double Fantasy*, plus nine of his best songs from 1969 to 1974, among them the singles "Give Peace a Chance," in its only LP appearance, and "Instant Karma!" — *William Ruhlmann*

Milk & Honey / Jan. 27, 1984 / Polydor ✦✦✦
Posthumous followup to *Double Fantasy*, featuring sometimes rough takes of perhaps unfinished songs that nevertheless sparkle with Lennon's wit and exuberance, among them the Top Five hit "Nobody Told Me." (Again, Ono's songs are interspersed with Lennon's contributions.) — *William Ruhlmann*

Live in New York City / Feb. 10, 1986 / Capitol ✦✦✦
This benefit concert, recorded August 30, 1972, marked John Lennon's last full-length concert appearance. The 55-minute video released 13 years later finds Lennon and wife Yoko Ono leading the band Elephant's Memory in a set of songs taken from Lennon's solo albums of the time, some of them with a heavily political theme. Nevertheless, hits like "Imagine" and "Instant Karma!" are also included, and Lennon is as witty and charismatic as ever. — *William Ruhlmann*

Menlove Ave. / Nov. 3, 1986 / Capitol ✦✦✦
John Lennon is heard in outtakes from the sessions for the albums *Walls and Bridges* and *Rock 'n' Roll*, including alternate versions of songs that turned up on those albums, as well as such original songs as "Rock and Roll People," previously heard only in a version by Johnny Winter. — *William Ruhlmann*

○ **Imagine: John Lennon [O.S.T.]** / Oct. 10, 1988 / Capitol ✦✦✦✦
A two-disc set containing a selection of Lennon's work with the Beatles and as a solo artist. This is the original soundtrack album. — *William Ruhlmann*

☆ **Lennon** / 1990 / Capitol ✦✦✦✦✦
Lennon is given a solid box-set treatment with this four-disc, 73-track collection. The set is so complete that there is essentially no need to go out and obtain any of his albums on disc. *Lennon* runs chronologically, from the Plastic Ono Band's "Give Peace a Chance," to "Grow Old with Me" from 1984's *Milk and Honey*. All the best stuff from *Live Peace in Toronto 1969* is here, as well as his live (with Elton John) versions of "I Saw Her Standing There" and "Lucy in the Sky with Diamonds." The book contains a generous collection of photos and lyrics to all of the songs. The A-to-Z color-coded index is overkill in lieu of any track information detailing where and when the songs were cut and who played on them. — *Rick Clark*

Julian Lennon

b. Apr. 8, 1963, Liverpool, England
Pop/Rock
Julian Lennon (son of Beatle John Lennon and Cynthia Twist) has had the mixed blessing of choosing a vocation that placed him firmly in his father's shadow. Lennon's similar vocal and melodic style on his successful #17 debut *Valotte* (in 1984) heightened the comparisons. Since then Lennon's albums haven't sold as well, but his releases have revealed increasing artistic growth. — *Rick Clark*

● **Valotte** / 1984 / Atlantic ✦✦✦✦
This strong debut showcases Julian's remarkable vocal resemblance to his father. — *Dan Heilman*

The Secret Value of Daydreaming / 1986 / Atlantic ✦✦✦
On *The Secret Value of Daydreaming*, the follow-up to his successful debut, Julian Lennon emphasizes his mainstream pop leanings by adding a tighter, more polished production which brings out the best in his songs. That is, it does when the songwriting is up to par. Lennon had some difficulty producing a consistent set of songs for his second album, with only a handful of tracks—including the hit "Stick Around"—standing out amidst the slick, immaculately-produced material. — *Stephen Thomas Erlewine*

Mr. Jordan / 1989 / Atlantic ✦✦
Julian Lennon did an about-face on *Mr. Jordan*, abandoning the polished mainstream pop of his first two albums for a darker, more rock-oriented sound. Lennon also changed his style of singing, choosing a deeper timbre that was eerily reminiscent of David Bowie—which was appropriate, because the thick gutiars that dominated the album were reminiscent of a kinder variation

on Bowie's early '70s hard rock. Although Lennon's new sound was promising, he only came up with one song, the minor hit "Now You're in Heaven," that could support his musical visions. — *Stephen Thomas Erlewine*

Help Yourself / 1991 / Atlantic ✦✦✦
Following the flawed *Mr. Jordan*, Julian Lennon returned to straightahead pop with *Help Yourself*, which recalled the work of his father more than any of his other records. On *Help Yourself*, Lennon never seemed to be cannibalizing his father's songs; instead, he appeared to be learning from the Beatles, writing songs that were more carefully constructed than his previous work. Most of the record featured strong hooks and melodies, indicative of his songwriting progression, with the gorgeous "Saltwater" as the best evidence of his improved songwriting abilities. — *Stephen Thomas Erlewine*

Annie Lennox

Pop/Rock
After the Eurythmics broke up in the early '90s, Annie Lennox released her first solo album, *Diva*. It was more commercially successful than any record her band has released since 1985. — *Stephen Thomas Erlewine*

● **Diva** / Apr. 28, 1992 / Arista ✦✦✦✦
Those expecting Annie Lennox to come out full guns blazing for her solo debut with the high energy Euro-electro-pop-meets-American-R&B of her Eurythmics work may have to wind their pacemakers down a notch. The enigmatic vocalist who made a career toying with different notions of gender now plays on the concept of fame—Lennox dressing up in the persona of a solitary *Diva* trapped by counterfeit glory. The framework offers an effective stage for Lennox's husky voice, showcasing her as much more of a chanteuse than in the past. But the music is strangely muted and understated. In fact, the album almost works best as one integrated mood-piece rather than a collection of individual songs. While Lennox succeeds in carving out a personality distinct from her Eurythmics days with *Diva*, one can't help but crave a shot of former partner Dave Stewart's musical muscle. — *Roch Parisien*

Medusa / 1995 / Arista ✦✦✦
Annie Lennox's second solo album reprises the slick R&B/pop approach of *Diva*, complete with sophisticated arrangements and impressive vocal workouts. Unfortunately, it was applied to a set of songs that are considered pop classics and Lennox's interpretations add nothing except the sheen of upper-class glamour. — *Stephen Thomas Erlewine*

Let's Active

Group, Alternative Pop/Rock, Power Pop/Anglo-Pop
Formed in 1981 by North Carolina musician/producer Mitch Easter, Let's Active was one of the premier bands of the Southern alternative-pop movement of the '80s. Easter is primarily known for his production of R.E.M.'s *Murmur* and *Reckoning*, yet that only scratches the surface of his work; at his Drive-In Studio, he produced numerous other bands during the decade. However, Easter's main project was Let's Active. Between 1983 and 1989, the band only released three albums and one EP, yet they showed a remarkable proficiency for ringing, melodic guitar pop as well as tangled neo-psychedelia. After their last album in 1988, the group split; Easter has concentrated on production work since then. — *Rick Clark*

○ **Afoot** / 1983 / IRS ✦✦✦✦
Afoot, their six-song debut EP, features Mitch Easter's own brand of Southern power-pop. With hook-filled and instantly lovable songs, Easter proves to be a master of the three-minute form. — *Chris Woodstra*

○ **Cypress** / 1984 / IRS ✦✦✦✦
The band stretch out a bit on their first proper LP. While it is still every bit a jangly guitar-pop effort, Easter seems to be enjoying the powers of his studio, experimenting in different electronic sounds and neo-psychedelic textures. "Waters Part," the failed single from the album is still one of his finest moments as a songwriter. — *Chris Woodstra*

Big Plans for Everybody / 1986 / IRS ✦✦✦
Essentially a Mitch Easter solo project, *Big Plans for Everybody* moves into darker territory than the previous album. Though Easter's trademark bright production and quirky songwriting still stand out, the mood is decidedly melancholy. — *Chris Woodstra*

Every Dog Has His Day / Aug. 22, 1988 / IRS ◆◆◆
Every Dog Has His Day features some of Easter's strongest songs in a harder-edged setting. Almost completely ignored, this is the band's last effort before disbanding indefinately. —*Chris Woodstra*

● **Cypress/Afoot** / 1989 / IRS ◆◆◆◆
This CD combines their first EP, *Afoot*, and their first album, *Cypress*. Featuring infectious hook-filled songs like "Every Word Means No" and "Waters Part," this perfect Southern power-pop is worth seeking out. —*Chris Woodstra*

Level 42

Group, Techno-Pop/Dance, New Wave, Pop/Rock
At the beginning of their career, Level 42 was a jazz-funk fusion band, following in the footsteps of such pioneers as Stanley Clarke. By the end of the '80s, they were a pop-R&B band with a number of hit singles to their credit. Featuring Mark King (bass, vocals), Phil Gould (drums), Boon Gould (guitar), and Mark Lindup (keyboards), the band formed in 1980. Before they released their first single, "Love Meeting Love," the band was pushed to add vocals to their music, in order to give their music a more commercial sound; they complied, with King becoming the lead singer. Released in 1981, their self-titled debut album was a slick soul-R&B collection that charted in the U.K. Top 20, resulting in the release of *The Early Tapes* by their former record label, Polydor. Level 42 had several minor hit singles before 1984's "The Sun Goes Down (Living It Up)" hit the British Top Ten. Released in late 1985, *World Machine* broke the band world-wide; "Lessons in Love" hit number one in Britain and "Something About You" hit number seven in America. Their next two records, *Running in the Family* (1987) and *Staring at the Sun* (1988), were a big success in the U.K., yet only made some headway in the U.S. Both of the Gould brothers left the band in late 1987; they were replaced by guitarist Alan Murphy and drummer Gary Husband. Murphy died of AIDS in 1991; he was replaced by the renowned fusion guitarist Alan Holdsworth for 1991's *Guaranteed*. —*Stephen Thomas Erlewine*

○ **Level 42** / 1981 / Polydor ◆◆◆◆
The album was produced by label owner Andy Sojka. Highlights include "Love Meeting Love," "Wings of Love," "Love Games," "Turn It On," and "Starchild." —*Bil Carpenter*

Strategy / 1981 / Elite ◆◆

Early Tapes / 1981 / Polydor ◆◆

Pursuit of Accidents / 1982 / Polydor ◆◆◆
Although they didn't really begin to have dance/pop hits until later in the '80s, the English group Level 42 provided some fine performances on this album. While vocals weren't their strong suit, they did a reasonable job of harmonizing and at least getting through the melodies, while the production and arrangements helped embellish and compensate for their singing inadequacies. Although such groups as the Pet Shop Boys and even Thompson Twins do this type of thing better, Level 42 at least isn't irritating or self-indulgent. —*Ron Wynn*

True Colours / 1983 / Polydor ◆◆◆
Level 42 was steadily perfecting and evolving their dance/pop, funk, and rock mix during the '80s, and when they hit the big time, the label began reissuing their earlier, less successful material. It's hard to understand why this didn't do as well as later albums like *World Machine*, *Running in the Family*, and *Staring at the Sun*, although the obvious reason would be that no singles ever broke that compared with the ones from those releases. But it was just as well produced, the songs were almost as cutely performed, and the arrangements are very similar. —*Ron Wynn*

○ **Standing in the Light** / 1983 / Polydor ◆◆◆◆

Physical Presence: Live / 1985 / Polydor ◆◆

○ **World Machine** / 1985 / Polydor ◆◆◆◆

Running in the Family / 1987 / Polydor ◆◆◆

Staring at the Sun / 1988 / Polydor ◆◆

● **Level Best** / 1989 / Polydor ◆◆◆◆
This hits CD draws heavily from *Running in the Family* (1987) and *World Machine* (1985) but offers a good introduction to this band. —*Scott Bultman*

Guaranteed / 1991 / RCA ◆◆◆

Physical Presence, Vol. 1 / Polydor ◆◆◆

LeVert

Group, Soul, Urban
As the offical offspring of the O'Jays, LeVert is a trio from Philadelphia who combine the sweet harmonies that their fathers provided with the "rope-a-dope" style that will keep them in the spotlight in the '90s. Great music all around, and powerful vocals from Gerald LeVert, who also has his own solo album. —*John Book*

Bloodline / 1986 / Atlantic ◆◆◆
When Eddie Levert's two sons, Gerald and Sean, teamed with Marc Gordon to form their own trio, everyone in the R&B community expected great things. They didn't get off to a good start when they recorded for the tiny Tempre label, but once they moved to Atlantic, Levert began building their image and reputation. They earned a number one R&B hit with "(Pop, Pop, Pop, Pop) Goes My Mind" and followed it with a Top 20 single in "Let's Go Out Tonight." Gerald's delivery, tone and approach mirrored his father's; their harmonies and production were contemporary, yet also reflected the O'Jays' influence. —*Ron Wynn*

● **The Big Throwdown** / 1987 / Atlantic ◆◆◆◆
Levert's second album started a run of hits that extended into the 1990s. They earned their first pop hit and second #1 R&B single with "Casanova," while "My Forever Love" was a solid follow-up and excellent ballad. Gerald Levert proved his mettle as a lead singer; although not as explosive as his father, he had a similar gift for communicating a lyric, and he teamed nicely with brother Sean and Marc Gordon on ballads. Levert's singles weren't as anthemic as the O'Jays', but they were established hitmakers on the urban contemporary scene. —*Ron Wynn*

○ **Just Coolin'** / Oct. 1988 / Atlantic ◆◆◆◆
Levert scored with both uptempo and ballad cuts on their third Atlantic album. The single "Pull Over" clicked with dance audiences and was aided by a video that neatly played off the lyrical hook. The title track was also an urban contemporary radio hit and successful single, although the overall record didn't match the level of its predecessor, despite eventually going gold. In fact, the first signs of creative stagnation that would really surface on their next release were evident on such songs as "Take Your Time" and "Join In The Fun." —*Ron Wynn*

Rope a Dope Style / 1990 / Atlantic ◆◆◆
Levert still sounded energetic and appealing on such cuts as "Nobody Does It Better" and "Hey Girl." Gerald Levert will never have the same command or dramatic presence as his dad, but he's developed into a sincere, effective vocalist. But when the raps begin on the title cut or "Nobody Does It Better," not only do they mar the song's pace, they split the listener's focus and change the mood. It doesn't help that neither rap was exciting, either lyrically or performance-wise. —*Ron Wynn*

For Real Tho' / 1993 / Atlantic ◆◆

Barbara Lewis

b. Feb. 9, 1943, South Lyon, Michigan
Soul
From a Detroit-area musical family (both parents had bands in the '30s and '40s), Barbara Lewis was writing songs at the age of nine. And could she sing! She wrote all the songs on her first album *Hello Stranger*, and the title cut was a major hit in 1963. Other classic Lewis hits include "Baby, I'm Yours" and "Make Me Your Baby." Even with only a few big hits, Lewis has achieved almost a cult status among her admirers. There is something unique about her songs and singing—an enchantment—that goes right to the heart. —*Michael Erlewine*

★ **Hello Stranger: The Best of Barbara Lewis** / 1994 / Rhino ◆◆◆◆◆
At last! Twenty great Barbara Lewis songs in glorious remastered digital sound. In fact, the sound is so good it's like hearing these classic sides for the first time. The only significant omission is the song "On Bended Knee," but then again, I would have liked a two-disc compilation. Thank you Rhino! —*Michael Erlewine*

○ **Golden Classics** / Collectables ◆◆◆◆
Smooth, snappy soul on these '60s recordings. —*Richard Pack*

○ **Hello Stranger** / Collectables ◆◆◆◆
"16 Smooth Sides By Detroit's Soulful Songstress" are featured on this compilation of singles and albums tracks, spanning 1962-68. Includes the number-one hit title track, as well as the girl-group-style Top Tenners "Make Me Your Baby" and "Baby I'm Yours," and

the original version of "Someday We're Gonna Love Again" (which was a hit for the Searchers). Some of the most velvety soul ever waxed. —*Richie Unterberger*

Gary Lewis (Gary Levital)

b. Jun. 31, 1946
Pop/Rock
The son of comedian Jerry Lewis formed this American rock group in 1964. After landing a gig at Disneyland, they were immediately signed to Liberty Records and handed over to pop production genius Snuff Garrett. Utilizing the best songwriters and studio players available, Garrett fashioned five Top Five hits in a matter of 18 months (15 in the Hot 100 by 1969) around Lewis's meager abilities, sometimes augmenting his voice in the studio with backup singers doubling his part. Lewis pretty well held his own against the British invasion, but the combination of his draft call in late 1966 and the rising tide of psychedelia put his days on the charts to an end. Still active on the oldies circuit, he fronts various backup bands under the name the Playboys. —*Cub Koda*

● **Legendary Masters Series** / 1990 / Capitol ✦✦✦✦
One of the most engaging pop acts of the mid-'60s, the Playboys benefited from strong songwriting (Al Kooper cowrote "This Diamond Ring") and studio personnel (courtesy of Leon Russell). It's still light, catchy pop with the enjoyable, unaffected vocals of Gary Lewis on top, and still fun. —*William Ruhlmann*

Huey Lewis & the News

Group, Pop/Rock
Before the formation of the News, Huey Lewis (born Hugh Cregg) had been part of the San Francisco band Clover from 1976 to 1980. During that time Clover (sans Lewis) backed up Elvis Costello on his debut *My Aim Is True*. Lewis also did session-sideman work on Nick Lowe's *Labour of Lust* and Dave Edmunds's *Repeat When Necessary*. Clover broke up in 1979 after bandleader John McFee split to join the Doobie Brothers.

Lewis returned to a day gig and started jamming at a local Marin County bar called Uncle Charlie's. It was there that the nucleus of the News was formed out of visiting musicians, many of whom had previously backed up Van Morrison.

The News's self-titled debut failed to sell, but "Do You Believe in Love?" went to #7. Their second album, *Picture This*, rose to #13 and produced a couple of moderate hits with "Hope You Love Me Like You Say You Do" (#36) and "Workin' for a Livin' " (#41). The next album, *Sports*, went multi-platinum and generated a number of hits.

Between albums the News scored a #1 hit, "The Power of Love," from the movie *Back to the Future*. Their followup album, *Fore* (#1), included five Top Ten hits: "Stuck with You," "Jacob's Ladder," "Hip to be Square," and "Doing It All (For My Baby)."

1988's *Small World* marked the beginning of Lewis's commercial decline which lasted until 1994, when the News became adult-contemporary favorites with their covers of classic soul songs. —*Rick Clark*

Huey Lewis & the News / 1980 / Chrysalis ✦✦
For most of their self-titled debut album, Huey Lewis & the News try to carve out their niche. While their basic idea is apparent—a cross between a driving bar band and catchy pop craftsmen—the group didn't write any songs to make their concept appealing. —*Stephen Thomas Erlewine*

○ **Picture This** / 1982 / Chrysalis ✦✦✦✦
Their second album broke through with the hits "Workin' for a Livin' " and "Do You Believe in Love?" —*Donna DiChario*

● **Sports** / 1983 / Chrysalis ✦✦✦✦
Their brand of spirited, no-frills rock & roll features the hits "I Want a New Drug," "The Heart of Rock & Roll," and "Walkin' on a Thin Line," and helped sell more than seven million copies of this album. —*Donna DiChario*

Fore! / 1986 / Chrysalis ✦✦✦
More pop/rock featuring the hits "Stuck with You," "Jacob's Ladder," and "Hip to be Square." —*Donna DiChario*

Small World / 1988 / Chrysalis ✦✦
Small World was another platinum hit for Huey Lewis & the News, but the album was noticeably weaker than their previous three records. Lewis tries to position himself as a socially-con-

scious rocker--no less than three tracks have the word "world" in their title—writing songs about the perilous state of the environment and urging everybody to live together peacefully, since "there ain't no livin' in a perfect world." Such sanctimonious and simple lyrical platitudes would be acceptable if the band had written a set of catchy pop to support them. Instead, the group decided to stretch out, exploring rootsy American music like the zydeco of "Bobo Tempo" and the bluesy "Old Antone's." None of the musical diversions work as well as the bouncy Top Ten hit "Perfect World." However, "Perfect World" is the only song that ranks with the group's best material—as "Give Me the Keys (And I'll Drive You Crazy)" proves, the News had failed to come up with hooks that rivaled their earlier hits. —*Stephen Thomas Erlewine*

Hard at Play / Jan. 1991 / EMI America ✦✦✦
As the title indicates, *Hard at Play* is a return to the straightahead blues-inflected pop/rock that made Huey Lewis & the News superstars in the early '80s. While the material wasn't as consistently strong as *Sports* or *Picture This*, the band rocked with a renewed vigor and a handful of songs, including the anthemic hit "Couple Days Off," were as catchy as their older hits. —*Stephen Thomas Erlewine*

Four Chords & Several Years Ago / 1994 / Elektra ✦✦
Four Chords & Several Years Ago was a set of well-performed R&B covers by Huey Lewis & the News. While it lacked the polished energy of their *Sports*-era hits ("The Heart of Rock N Roll," "I Want a New Drug," "The Power of Love"), the album was filled with pleasant, professional performances that proved the band still knew how to construct a hit single—both "(She's) Some Kind of Wonderful" and "It's Alright" were minor hits. Even though it was a well-crafted record that managed to avoid the group's tendency for bombast, *Four Chords & Several Years Ago* never managed to be a compelling listen; it sounded better on the radio than it did on the stereo. —*Stephen Thomas Erlewine*

Jerry Lee Lewis

b. Sep. 29, 1935, Ferriday, LA
Rock & Roll, Rockabilly
Jerry Lee Lewis, the self-proclaimed "Killer," is a man of prodigous appetites and talent. Egocentric and self-absorbed, Jerry Lee is the last of the original '50s wildmen. A child prodigy who quickly mastered his instrument, Lewis claims to have no influences, but his stylistic quirks point to boogie-woogie master Cecil Gant and country-piano man Moon Mullican. After being run out of Nashville (where he was told he could be signed if he strummed a guitar instead), he came to Memphis, where his audition tape got him hooked up to Sam Phillips's Sun label. In the space of four singles released in a year's time, the Killer was suddenly running neck and neck with Elvis for King of Rock & Roll honors. When Lewis married his 13-year-old cousin in 1958, his career promptly ground to a halt, leaving him to eke out a bleak existence in the honky-tonks of America. It took 12 years of his life to fight his way back, but Lewis is nothing less than American music's consummate survivor, and his reemergence (via the country charts, with a string of smashes) was no less than his due. There are few originals in '50s rock & roll, most taking their cue from Elvis or Little Richard, but Lewis is one of the major stylists in the history of American popular music—period. His distinctive piano style is tightly woven into the fabric of that instrument, while his vocal style is easily recognizable as well, whether tackling a mournful country weeper or storming through his prodigious catalog of rock & roll/R&B favorites, putting his individual stamp on each and every one. As he'll be the first to tell you, there is simply no one quite like the Killer. We shall not see the likes of him again in our lifetime. —*Cub Koda*

Jerry Lee Lewis / 1957 / Rhino ✦✦✦
Jerry Lee Lewis' debut album was a virtual greatest hits album, featuring "Whole Lotta Shakin' Goin' On." —*AMG*

Jerry Lee's Greatest / 1961 / Rhino ✦✦✦
Jerry Lee's second record followed the same formula as the first, mixing singles—including "Great Balls of Fire"—with album tracks that were nearly as good as the hits. —*AMG*

○ **The Greatest Live Show on Earth** / 1964 / Bear Family ✦✦✦✦
Combining two live albums originally issued in the '60s, Lewis proves that the onslaught of the British Invasion hadn't lowered his rocking quotient one single bit. Blazing performances. —*Cub Koda*

☆ **Live at the Star Club Hamburg** / 1965 / Rhino ✦✦✦✦✦
The Killer at his storming best, dragging his backup group, the Nashville Teens, by the scruff of the neck through a blazing set that earmarks this recording as one of the finest live albums ever made. —*Cub Koda*

★ **18 Original Sun Greatest Hits** / 1984 / Rhino ✦✦✦✦✦
Solid single-disc collection of the records that got Lewis into the Rock & Roll Hall of Fame on the first ballot; "Whole Lotta Shakin' Goin' On," "Great Balls of Fire," "High School Confidential," and "Breathless" being merely the tip of the iceberg. —*Cub Koda*

☆ **Classic** / 1989 / Bear Family ✦✦✦✦✦
Eight-disc boxed set of Lewis's complete output for Sun Records. Along with Muddy Waters's Chess recordings, Louis Armstrong's *Hot Fives & Sevens*, and Hank Williams's undubbed MGM sides, this box comprises one of the finest bodies of American music ever recorded. —*Cub Koda*

○ **Killer: the Mercury Years, Vol. 1 (1963-1968)** / 1989 / Mercury ✦✦✦✦
This three-volume set takes you through the best of the Mercury years, country, rock and gospel styles. —*Hank Davis*

○ **Killer: the Mercury Years, Vol. 2 (1969-1972)** / 1989 / Mercury ✦✦✦✦

○ **Killer: the Mercury Years, Vol. 3 (1973-1977)** / 1989 / Mercury ✦✦✦✦

★ **All Killer, No Filler: The Anthology** / 1993 / Rhino ✦✦✦✦✦
Excellent two-disc retrospective of Lewis's career, featuring all his rock and country hits. If the Bear Family box sets are too much for you to handle, this makes an indispensable alternative. —*Cub Koda*

○ **Locust Years . . . and the Return to the Promised Land** / 1994 / Bear Family ✦✦✦✦
Picking up where the eight-CD set *Classic* left off, eight-CD box *The Locust Years . . . and the Return to the Promised Land* rivals its predecessor in musical quality. Tracing Jerry Lee Lewis' '60s career at Smash Records, the first two discs find the pianist trying to replicate his rock & roll success; while the performances were good, it was clear he was out of touch with the times. During the third disc, he begins to concentrate on country music. The fourth, fifth, and sixth discs match his Sun recordings for consistently brilliant performances; several of the songs became big hits on the country charts, establishing him as a country star. The seventh disc chronicles an exciting unreleased show while the eighth disc is an unexceptional interview. For dedicated Jerry Lee Lewis fans, *The Locust Years* is every bit as essential as *Classic*. —*Stephen Thomas Erlewine*

● **Killer Country** / 1995 / Mercury ✦✦✦✦
Killer Country is a well-chosen selection of Jerry Lee Lewis' biggest and best country hits from the '60s and '70s, which feature some of his finest performances. —*Stephen Thomas Erlewine*

Young Blood / 1995 / Sire ✦✦
Jerry Lee Lewis made a comeback effort in 1995 with *Young Blood*. Although the Killer's performance is impressive—his voice continues to weather well with age and he hasn't lost much of his instrumental prowess—the selection of material is fairly uninspired and predictable. This wouldn't have been a problem if Jerry Lee was allowed to work with a top-notch backing band, elevating the pedestrian material to a new level. Instead, *Young Blood* was made like most albums in the mid-'90s—each song was constructed track-by-track, with the musicians laying down their parts at different times. Consequently, the record is stripped of most of its potential power, leaving behind a well-produced but thoroughly unengaging album. —*Stephen Thomas Erlewine*

BOOK

✦✦✦ **Hellfire: The Jerry Lee Lewis Story**, by Nick Tosches (Dell, 1982). Even by decadent rock & roll standards, Jerry Lee Lewis' story is not a pretty one: several broken marriages, scandal, tragic accidental deaths of brother and sons, ill health, run-ins with the law and tax authorities. He was, of course, a hell of a piano player and singer, who kept on rocking after his marriage to his 13-year-old cousin effectively ruined his career, finally turning to straight country in the late '60s to rejuvenate his commercial prospects. Tosches tells his story without undue romanticizing, often focusing on Lewis' turmoil between his impulses to preach the gospel (he grew up with his cousin Jimmy Lee Swaggart) and raise hell. A decent job, thoroughly covering

his poor beginnings in Ferriday, LA, his prime Sun years, his country comeback, and his general dissolution in the late '70s. Some readers may have appreciated a greater focus on the music, some of which is discussed cursorily; the decades' worth of trouble and bad-boy antics can be tiresome. —*Richie Unterberger*

Smiley Lewis

b. Jul. 5, 1920, **d.** Oct. 7, 1966
New Orleans R&B
Although he didn't have a lot of hits, Smiley Lewis was among New Orleans' most powerful, striking lead vocalists. A good guitarist as well as singer, Lewis began recording for Deluxe in 1947 under the name of Smiling Lewis. He attained his fame on Imperial as one of several artists whose songs were spiced by Dave Bartholomew's production, arranging, and bandleading acumen. With a brillant band featuring many superb musicians roaring behind him, Lewis enjoyed one Top 20 and three Top Ten R&B hits from 1952 to 1956, led by "I Hear You Knocking" in 1955. It was number two for two weeks, while "Bells Are Ringing" peaked at number ten in 1952 and "Please Listen to Me" reached number nine in 1956. "One Night" just missed the Top Ten at number 11 that same year. Though his version of "Shame Shame Shame" didn't make the charts, it was used in the soundtrack for the film *Baby Doll* in 1956. Lewis died of cancer in 1966. —*Ron Wynn*

● **The Best of** / 1992 / Capitol ✦✦✦✦
A strong sampling of some of the finest material the seminal New Orleans pianist ever recorded, *The Best of Smiley Lewis* isn't definitive, but it's a great introduction to his music. —*Stephen Thomas Erlewine*

Shame Shame Shame / Bear Family ✦✦✦
Exhaustive, multi-disc set comprising everything recorded on this New Orleans singer. With the songwriting talents of Dave Bartholomew aboard, utilizing the sound of the legendary J&M Studios, and the best Crescent City musicians available, this is truly New Orleans music at its very best. (Import) —*Cub Koda*

John Leyton

b. 1939
Pop/Rock
Like the better remembered Adam Faith, John Leyton had a lot of success in Britain in the early '60s with lugubrious teen idol pop that was only tenuously related to rock & roll. Not much of a singer, his hits are most notable for Joe Meek's inventive production, which utilized ghostly female backup vocals, varispeed pianos, and swirling wind effects. Most of Leyton's earliest (and most successful) material was written by Geoff Goddard, a songwriter who often penned compositions for Meek's acts; heavy on loner melodrama, it often used pseudo-Wild West galloping rhythms and lyrical themes. "Johnny Remember Me" and "Wild Wind" were huge hits for Leyton in 1961, and "Son this Is She" and "Lonely City" also made the Top 20 soon afterwards. But in 1963, Meek and Goddard's association with Leyton ended; that circumstance, combined with the British beat boom, cast Leyton adrift immediately, although he found a lot of acting work in television and film to keep him busy. —*Richie Unterberger*

● **Best Of John Leyton** / 1987 / See For Miles ✦✦✦✦
20 tracks from 1961–64, including all the hits and quite a few flops and B-sides. Most notable for the Meek-Goddard work on Side One, including his 1961-62 hits and intriguing obscurities like "Oh Lover." —*Richie Unterberger*

Gordon Lightfoot

b. Nov. 17, 1938, Orillia, Ontario
Folk, Folk-Rock
Canadian Gordon Lightfoot first began to gain recognition in the mid '60s as a songwriter when his compositions "For Lovin' Me" and "Early Morning Rain" became hits for Peter, Paul & Mary, and Marty Robbins topped the country charts with "Ribbon of Darkness." Lightfoot's own style was understated, his tasteful folk arrangements topped by a gentle burr of a voice. His albums began to appear in 1966, but it was not until the start of the '70s that he became a big success as a performer, scoring in 1970 with *Sit Down Young Stranger*, which contained his hit "If You Could Read My Mind," a song with a typically flowing melodic line and gently poetic lyrics.

Thereafter, the first half of the '70s were his. Lightfoot hit a peak in 1974 with *Sundown,* which went to number one, as did the title song when released on a single. Though he had developed a timeless style, Lightfoot was caught by the popular decline of folk-based music in the latter half of the 1970s, and has performed and recorded less frequently since, sometimes trying to conform to perceived commercial trends without success. But concert appearances in the early '90s confirmed that he remains an engaging performer and that his catalog of original songs is hard to match. — *William Ruhlmann*

○ **Sit Down Young Stranger** / 1970 / Reprise ◆◆◆◆
Lightfoot's Reprise albums are always tastefully constructed, with their careful finger-picking, restrained rhythm sections, and subtle string arrangements serving as a bed for the singer's sturdy baritone. What distinguishes the albums is the quality of Lightfoot's songwriting, and this one, featuring the title track as well as "Approaching Lavender" and "If You Could Read My Mind" has the best overall selection. — *William Ruhlmann*

Summer Side of Life / 1971 / Reprise ◆◆◆
This extraordinary release doesn't have big hits on it but contains some of his finest songwriting, from the political song "Miguel," to the wistful songs about divorce, "Same Old Loverman" and "Talking in Your Sleep," to the joyous "Cotton Jenny." This is highly recommended. — *Richard Meyer*

○ **Sundown** / 1974 / Reprise ◆◆◆◆
Lightfoot's commercial peak came with this album, which topped the US charts, containing both the #1 title song and the Top 10 hit "Carefree Highway." But songs like "Somewhere U.S.A." and "High and Dry" are textured, catchy folk/rock on a par with the better known tunes. — *William Ruhlmann*

○ **Gord's Gold** / 1975 / Reprise ◆◆◆◆

Summertime Dream / 1976 / Reprise ◆◆◆
Due to Lightfoot's tendency to re-record his hits when preparing compilations (the warning "caveat emptor" applies to the two volumes of *Gord's Gold*), this is the only place to find the original version of his number two "Wreck of the Edmond Fitzgerald." — *William Ruhlmann*

Waiting for You / 1993 / Reprise ◆◆◆
Anyone fearing that sobriety and serenity might dull Gordon Lightfoot's creative edge can rest at ease. Having apparently freed himself of several personal demons, *Waiting for You* delivers the most consistent Lightfoot to be heard since the late-'70s. While most tracks feature bass, drums, electric guitar, and/or keyboards (the synth washes sometimes overpower), for the most part the instrumentation is used sparingly, for color. The overwhelming feeling one derives from *Waiting for You* is of an intimate backporch session soaking up the sounds of a rejuvenated Gordon Lightfoot and his guitar. — *Roch Parisien*

★ **Gordon Lightfoot: the United Artists Collection** / Oct. 5, 1993 / EMI ◆◆◆◆◆
This double CD contains all four of the Toronto singer/songwriter's '60s studio albums (the live LP *Sunday Concert*, not included here, was also released in the '60s). On these records, his resonant vocals, lyrical ambition, and melodic strengths produced as close a rival to Bob Dylan as Canada ever fashioned during that decade, and foreshadowed work by other major Candian singer/songwriters of the late '60s, such as Joni Mitchell, Neil Young, and Leonard Cohen. "Early Mornin' Rain" (covered by fellow Canadian folkies Ian & Sylvia), the folk-rock protest number "Black Day in July," the epic "Canadian Railroad Trilogy," and his cover of Ewan McColl's "The First Time Ever I Saw Your Face" are all present, and are among the most popular tracks Lightfoot has issued during his long career. Featuring both acoustic and folk-rock recordings, this neatly bundles Lightfoot's early work into a listenable and fairly inexpensive package. — *Richie Unterberger*

Lightnin' Rod

Rap
A former member of the Last Poets, Lightnin' Rod helped pioneer the spoken-rhyme style that would one day become rap. His most renowned album, *Hustlers Convention,* told the story of an ill-fated ghetto "player" and featured backing instrumentation by an early incarnation of Kool & the Gang. — *Dan Heilman*

Hustlers Convention / 1972 / Oceana ◆◆◆
With music by Kool and the Gang, Rod recites a rhyming story of gamblers, pimps, and players. — *Dan Heilman*

Lightning Seeds

Group, Pop/Rock
Seeds founder Ian Broudie played guitar in Liverpool bands like Big In Japan and Original Mirrors, but he made his name in the music business producing artists like Echo and the Bunnymen, Icicle Works, and the Fall. He collaborated with Wild Swans singer Paul Simpson under the moniker Care, releasing several singles. The Lightning Seeds are essentially a one-man band, with Broudie bringing in help when he needs it. The band's melodic pop has been compared to the Pet Shop Boys, but without the electronics. — *Steve Huey*

● **Cloudcuckooland** / 1989 / MCA ◆◆◆◆
Bouncy pop by Ian Broudie, producer of such groups as the Fall and Echo & the Bunnymen. — *David Szatmary*

Sense / Feb. 18, 1992 / MCA ◆◆◆
There's a certain school of distinctly British pop music characterized by a reserved, dignified demeanor and pretty, fragile melodies. The Lightning Seeds is one exponent of the genre that also includes such groups as Beautiful South and Trashcan Sinatras. The Seeds, mainly the one-man project of Liverpool artist-producer Ian Brodie, has more of a groove than its peers. Many of the songs tend to fall in the New Order camp, except that the vocals are more upfront than the rhythm tracks. — *Roch Parisien*

Jollification / 1994 / Trauma/Interscope ◆◆

Liliput

Group, Alternative Pop/Rock
During the punk rock era of the late '70s, there were three bands composed of women who made some of the best, most adventurous, exhilarating and most critically derided music of the time. Two were the English bands the Slits and the Raincoats, and the third band, from Switzerland, was Liliput. Fans of all three bands will argue ad infinitum as to who was the better. As far as I'm concerned, they were equals, and depending on what day you asked me, I might give you a different answer as to who was better, but one thing is for certain: Liliput was an amazing band that recorded amazing music, and comparing what they accomplished to that of another band is a useless intellectual exercise. Besides, it detracts from valuable listening time.

Formed in Zurich in 1978 by guitarist Marlene Marder and bassist/vocalist Klaudia Schiff, they began with the name Kleenex until the threat of a lawsuit by corporate giant Kimberly-Clark (who had copyrighted the name Kleenex) forced them to become Liliput in 1980. Recording for the great English indie label Rough Trade, the then-Kleenex produced jumpy, aggressive, clamorous punk-noise that featured Marder's scratchy, semi-melodic guitar and Schiff's yelping vocals. Not punk rock in the fast, loud, economical sense, Liliput were forging a different kind of punk, one that was gleefully anarchic, avant-garde, unrestrained, and suffused with a giddy, almost palpable sense of joy. Listening to this music now, one gets the sense that there was a near-rapturous enjoyment that went into these recordings. Their tenure at Rough Trade was short, as was their interest in exploring career options beyond Europe. (I may be wrong, but I don't believe they ever toured America, nor did they release any music domestically.)

By 1982, when they released their only LP, they seemed perfectly happy remaining in Switzerland, running the band as part of numerous other artistic projects (painting, writing, etc.) they pursued. By the end of 1983, Liliput had disbanded, and the music they had recorded quickly achieved legendary, but mostly unheard, status. As for the band, they seemed destined to be relegated to the status of feminist-inspired punk rock footnote. All of this changed in 1993, when the Swiss label Off Course released a double-disc, 46-track compilation of the entire recorded output of Kleenex/Liliput. The result was one of the great reissues of the decade. The exuberance and excitement of Liliput's breathtaking music can be enjoyed once again, and a band that was almost forgotten returns with some of the most artful, contemporary, truly alternative music to be recorded under the genre identifier of punk rock. Also, fans of riot grrrl rock take note: this was a tremendously influential band. Although they eschewed extreme confrontation, there is a compelling sense of self that imbues this music and lit the way for a new generation of female musicians. — *John Dougan*

Some Songs / 1983 / Rough Trade ✦✦✦

● **Liliput** / 1984 / Rough Trade ✦✦✦✦
Little more needs to be said, other than that this is a tremendous, absolutely essential recording of feminist post-punk, loaded with scratchy, distorted guitars, elemental rhythms, and gleefully unhinged, screeching singing. The only way you can get it is to send $30 to Off Course Records, P.O. Box 241, CH-8025, Zurich, Switzerland. I suggest you do it immediately. —*John Dougan*

Bob Lind

Singer-Songwriter, Pop, Folk-Rock
Bob Lind's "Elusive Butterfly" was one of the most successful one-shots of the mid-'60s folk-rock boom, reaching the top five in early 1966. He never came close to matching that early triumph, although other acts brought his songs to a wider audience with their covers of Lind compositions like "Cheryl's Going Home" (Blues Project), "Counting" (Marianne Faithfull), and "Mr. Zero" (Yardbirds' lead singer Keith Relf). The beauty of Jack Nitzsche's intricate production on Lind's two 1966 LPs, favoring acoustic guitars and pretty string arrangements, is admirable, but Lind himself hasn't worn that well. His songs are wordy and on the didactic side; his voice is nervous and lacks emotional range; his melodies are pretty, but not enormously so. —*Richie Unterberger*

● **The Best of Bob Lind** / Jun. 29, 1993 / EMI ✦✦✦✦
This 25-song compilation includes the entire contents of his two 1966 LPs, as well as a 1967 single and two previously unreleased tracks. This period piece is highlighted by "Elusive Butterfly," the original versions of "Counting" and "Cheryl's Goin' Home," "Mr. Zero" (covered by Yardbird lead singer Keith Relf on a flop single), and the previously unreleased, gorgeous baroque rock song "English Afternoon." —*Richie Unterberger*

David Lindley

b. 1944, San Marino, CA
Rock & Roll, Blues Rock, Tex-Mex
You may remember listening to these great Jackson Browne albums from the '70s and thinking, "This guy not only writes and sings great songs, but he's an incredible guitar player and does great arrangements." Well, he did write and sing great songs, but the guitar playing and arrangements are by David Lindley, Los Angeles studio musician extraordinaire. Starting in 1981, Lindley has put out several albums under his own name with his always-changing band, El Rayo-X. He has wide-ranging musical influences: Tex-Mex, zydeco, reggae, blues, and rock & roll. His specialty seems to be taking a song and playing it in the style of a completely different genre of music, for example, a maniacal surf-music version of "Do Ya' Wanna Dance?" or a version of "I Fought the Law" with musicians from Madagascar. His own compositions are sometimes quite wonderful and always at least peculiar and droll. When he plays guitar (and often instruments of his own design), it's as good as it gets. If you grew up on '50s, '60s, and '70s rock & roll, this guy is the best thing going. —*Michael Katz*

○ **El Rayo-X** / 1981 / Asylum ✦✦✦✦
His debut album. Highly recommended! —*Michael Katz*

Win This Record / 1982 / Elektra ✦✦
His weakest album, but not without merit. For the afficianado. —*Michael Katz*

Mr. Dave / 1985 / WEA ✦✦✦
A great album, don't know why it wasn't released in the US. —*Michael Katz*

● **Very Greasy** / 1988 / Asylum ✦✦✦✦
His best. Unconditionally recommended. —*Michael Katz*

A World out of Time / 1992 / Shanachie ✦✦✦
Lindley and Henry Kaiser travel to Madagascar, where they record and play with some of that country's best musicians. Great world music. —*Michael Katz*

Arto Lindsay/Ambitious Lovers

Alternative Pop/Rock, Art-Rock/Progressive-Rock
After his tenure as guitarist in the great new wave band DNA, Arto Lindsay formed the equally exciting and (pun intended) ambitious Ambitious Lovers. Lindsay, a native of Brazil, began conflating the Brazilian pop music of his youth with the sonic density and avant-garde urgings he pursued as a member of the Lower East Side noise-rock scene. As a result, his recordings as leader of the Ambitious Lovers are not all atonal skronk, but rather a deft

blend of dance-pop and sonic adventurousness. With inestimable help from keyboardist and Ambitious Lover co-conspirator Peter Scherer, the first Ambitious Lovers release, *Envy*, retains more of a dissonant edge, and as such doesn't seem too far removed from Lindsay's days with DNA. The next record, *Greed* (noticing a pattern developing here?), was a slick, ebullient pop record that sounded like a direct descendent of the Brazilian pop recorded by giants such as Jorge Ben, Caetano Veloso and Gilberto Gil. With plenty of uptempo, danceable tracks, the noisy undercurrent was downplayed perhaps a bit more than noisemeisters would like, but the resulting album was nearly flawless—as was its follow-up, *Lust*, which, true to its title, was a touch more salacious, and undeniably great modern pop music. Assuming that the duo of Lindsay and Scherer will continue this thematic romp through the seven deadly sins, one can only wait with baited breath for *Sloth*. Although they don't sell records in the millions (or the hundreds of thousands for that matter), the Ambitious Lovers are one of the few bands to live up to their name record after record. —*John Dougan*

Envy / 1984 / EG ✦✦✦

Lisa Lisa & Cult Jam

Group, Soul, Dance-Pop, Disco
Based in Brooklyn, vocalist Lisa Lisa (born Lisa Velez) and her supporting band Cult Jam (Mike Hughes and Alex "Spanador" Mosley) were one of the most consistently pop-funk/R&B groups of the mid-'80s. Hughes and Mosley were also members of Full Force, the funk group that performed and produced the majority of Lisa Lisa and Cult Jam's albums.

Lisa Lisa and Cult Jam recorded their debut single, "I Wonder If I Take You Home," soon after forming in 1985, releasing it as an independent single. The group quickly signed to Columbia Records, which re-released the single; it climbed into the R&B Top Ten and the U.K. Top 20. The group amassed a number of hit songs throughout the '80s, yet by the end of the decade their success had begun to dry up; they disbanded after 1991's *Straight Outta Hell's Kitchen*. Lisa Lisa embarked on a solo career, releasing the commercially unsuccessful *LL 77* in 1993. —*Stephen Thomas Erlewine*

Lisa Lisa & Cult Jam w/ Full Force / 1985 / Columbia ✦✦✦
Lisa Velez's last name was forgotten after the single "I Wonder If I Take You Home" elevated Lisa Lisa and Cult Jam into the national spotlight. Her voice had the perfect mix of uncertainty, irony and edge, while Full Force's production was state-of-the-art for the time. There was also a fine ballad on the album, "All Cried Out," presenting Lisa Lisa's vulnerable side, and is arguably still her finest performance. Lisa Lisa and company eventually earned a platinum LP and were on their way. —*Ron Wynn*

● **Spanish Fly** / 1987 / Columbia ✦✦✦✦
Full Force was still hot as they produced a second consecutive platinum LP for Lisa Lisa & Cult Jam. This time, the group scored two number one pop hits with "Head To Toe" and "Lost In Emotion," and even "Someone To Love Me For Me" had its moments. Lisa Lisa was an ingenue one moment and a tough, hardened survivor the next. The album peaked at number seven on the pop charts, but was also the apex of their union. Lisa Lisa was already beginning to show signs of strain, and the bottom would fall out on the next release. —*Ron Wynn*

Straight to the Sky / 1989 / Columbia ✦✦✦
This includes the Top-40 hit "Little Jackie Wants to Be a Star." —*Bil Carpenter*

○ **Straight Outta Hell's Kitchen** / 1991 / Columbia ✦✦✦✦
There weren't many kudos handed out for this album, even though producers Robert Clivilles and David Cole (C&C Music Factory) did half the tracks. They were then the premier honchos in dance music and were enlisted to restore the luster to Lisa Lisa and Cult Jam. But the voice that was once effective in a variety of emotional situations now seemed lethargic and unconvincing, while Full Force's production efforts on the album's second half were even more disconcerting. —*Ron Wynn*

LL 77 / 1993 / Pendulum ✦✦
Once a major disco and hip-hop diva, Lisa Lisa has been missing in action for a number of years. She's returned without either Full Force or UTFO, and tried to tap into the hip-mama scene with this collection of tracks that blend cautionary numbers with laments, heartache tracks and dance-pop. Her voice is neither dynamic nor

memorable, but Lisa Lisa does a competent job of maintaining her energy level on such tracks as "Why Can't Lovers" and "Knockin' Down The Walls." Much of this is faceless, generic material; chances are that it will be a short comeback for Lisa Lisa. —*Ron Wynn*

Little Anthony & The Imperials

R&B, Doo-Wop

Formed in 1957, Little Anthony & the Imperials specialized in dramatic pop ballads. Fronted by tenor Anthony Gourdine (b. Jan 8, 1941), the Imperials charted with "Going Out of My Head" (#6), "Hurt So Bad" (#9), "Take Me Back" (#16), "Tears on My Pillow" (#4), and "I'm on the Outside Looking In" (#15). —*Rick Clark*

● **The Best of Little Anthony & the Imperials** / 1989 / Rhino ✦✦✦✦
"Little" Anthony Gourdine's angst-ridden leads were ideal for tear-jerkers and heartache ballads. Although this Brooklyn group began in the doo-wop era, they were much more effective on soul songs where group harmonies were low-key and Gourdine's voice was the major focus. This anthology includes "Hurt So Bad," "I'm On the Outside Looking In" and "Take Me Back," arguably their three finest hits, plus several others with equally theatrical vocals, but dissimilar chart performances. —*Ron Wynn*

Little Eva

Girl-Group

Little Eva Narcissus Boyd was a babysitter for Carole King and Gerry Goffin when the songwriting team was inspired to write "Locomotion," a song based on a dance that Eva would do around the house. Eva also got to sing on their demo, which impressed Don Kirschner enough to release it as it was. One of the greatest girl-group hits, "Locomotion," hit number one in 1962; the follow-up, "Keep Your Hands Off My Baby," was also written by Goffin-King. Almost as good as her debut, it reached the Top 20, and was even covered by the Beatles on stage in their early days (though they never recorded it in the studio). Unfortunately, Eva was then pigeonholed as a dance-craze singer and given inferior material. She never again reached the soulful heights of her first two singles; "Let's Turkey Trot" (1963) was her only other Top 20 hit. —*Richie Unterberger*

● **The Best of Little Eva** / 1988 / Murray Hill ✦✦✦✦
15 songs, most cut for the Dimension label between 1962 and 1964. Includes all the hits and some pleasant girl-group flops in a more lightweight style than "Locomotion." —*Richie Unterberger*

Little Feat

Group, Rock & Roll, Blues Rock

Little Feat was formed in 1970 when Frank Zappa encouraged his guitarist Lowell George to start his own band, after hearing George's original "Willin'." With Zappa-bass player Roy Estrada in tow, George enlisted drummer Richie Hayward (formerly of Fraternity of Man) and keyboardist Billy Payne. The band's name came from Jimmy Carl Black's (of the Mothers of Invention) kidding about George's shoe size. Their first albums blended blues, country, and rock with gritty finesse. *Sailin' Shoes* (their second album) is loaded with fine songs and the rudest rock they ever committed to tape.

With *Dixie Chicken* (considered by many to be Little Feat's best album), they added Kenny Gradney on bass and Sam Clayton on congas. The result was a New Orleans style of rhythmic gumbo and George's incredible slide guitar work. The title cut sums up many of the band's virtues, possessing a rubbery groove, off-kilter instrumental parts, and a classic, dryly humorous Lowell George tale. Subsequent albums increasingly sanded off the rough edges in favor of an eccentric fusion-like equivalent to the late-'70s Doobie Brothers.

Little Feat disbanded in April 1979 and Lowell George set out for a solo career, releasing the album *Thanks, I'll Eat It Here.* On June 29, 1979, George was found dead of a heart attack brought on from drug abuse.

In 1988 Little Feat reunited with former Pure Prairie League singer and guitarist Craig Fuller filling George's slot. Since then, the band has regained its status as a solid concert draw and has released several albums. —*Rick Clark*

Little Feat / 1971 / Warner Brothers ✦✦✦
Debut album finds Lowell George's songwriting, singing, and playing style in place on his signature song, "Willin'," as well as "Truck Stop Girl" and "Crazy Captain Gunboat Willie." —*William Ruhlmann*

○ **Sailin' Shoes** / 1972 / Warner Brothers ✦✦✦✦
A near-peak of songwriting ("Easy to Slip," "Cold, Cold, Cold," "Sailin' Shoes") distinguishes this second album, on which the band finds a perfect second-line groove and Lowell George sings and plays with blues authority. —*William Ruhlmann*

★ **Dixie Chicken** / 1973 / Warner Brothers ✦✦✦✦✦
A reconfigured group adds greater depth to the percussion, along with a rhythm guitarist who frees Lowell George to slide his way to heaven, and the songs—especially the title track, "Two Trains," and "Fat Man in the Bathtub"—are among George's best. —*William Ruhlmann*

○ **Feats Don't Fail Me Now** / 1974 / Warner Brothers ✦✦✦✦
Whereas earlier albums were carried by Lowell George, this one finds the band as a whole at a writing and performing peak, with Bill Payne and Paul Berrere especially standing out on such songs as "Rock and Roll Doctor," "Oh Atlanta," and "Skin It Back." —*William Ruhlmann*

○ **Waiting for Columbus** / 1978 / Warner Brothers ✦✦✦✦
Excellent double-disc live album. —*William Ruhlmann*

○ **Hoy-Hoy** / 1981 / Warner Brothers ✦✦✦✦
Compilation of best songs and odds and ends makes a good wrap-up to the Lowell George years. —*William Ruhlmann*

Let It Roll / Jul. 1988 / Warner Brothers ✦✦✦

Shake Me Up / Sep. 24, 1991 / Morgan Creek ✦✦
With this pedestrian third reunion album, Little Feat should have lost the right to use its noble name. Little of the band's original spark remained. —*William Ruhlmann*

Ain't Had Enough Fun / 1995 / Zoo ✦✦

Down on the Farm / Warner Brothers ✦✦
A scraped-together, post-breakup, contractual obligation album, for charitable fans only. —*William Ruhlmann*

The Last Record Album / Warner Brothers ✦✦✦
From this point on, Lowell George's role in Little Feat seems to have diminished, with the group's direction increasingly left in the capable, if less inspired hands of Bill Payne and Paul Barrere. The album does, however, contain two excellent George originals in "Down Below The Borderline" and "Long Distance Love." —*William Ruhlmann*

Representing the Mambo / Warner Brothers ✦✦
Having demonstrated on *Let It Roll* that they could produce an effective Little Feat soundalike record, the reconstituted band should have stopped while they were ahead. This follow-up shows a decline in songwriting, making the absence of Lowell George unmistakably apparent. —*William Ruhlmann*

Time Loves a Hero / Warner Brothers ✦✦✦
Lowell George's gradual disappearance from his own group continued here, with the album containing only one of his solo compositions, "Rocket in My Pocket," which wasn't one of his best. The title track and "Hi Holler," among other tracks, show Paul Barrere and Bill Payne to be talented substitutes, but this album, the original group's final studio effort, does not show them at their best. —*William Ruhlmann*

Little Richard (Richard Wayne Penniman)

b. 1935
R&B, Rock & Roll

With a six-inch-high pompadour topping a face dripping with eyeliner and pancake makeup, Little Richard (born Richard Wayne Penniman, 1935) came out of his native Macon, GA, to become one of the first Black artists not only to cross over to the national White pop charts, but to do it with an uncompromising set of recordings that virtually defined the inherent danger and wildness of rock & roll. Few records explode off a turntable the way the likes of "Tutti Frutti," "Long Tall Sally," "Rip It Up," "Lucille," or "Good Golly Miss Molly" do and Richard's banshee shrieks and propulsive beat (usually provided by crack New Orleans session players) were catnip to a young White audience who had never heard a Black gospel singer with the brakes off before. The hits kept coming, but by the late '50s Richard had quit show business to become a minister. The lure of success (his and the then-emerging Beatles) brought him back, recording dreadful remakes of his earlier hits for one label after another into the '70s and becoming a staple of the talk show circuit with his flamboyant costumes and chatter. The '90s now find him revitalized, making movie appearances and television commercials and recording new material.

Though his claim to be "the architect of rock & roll" may be disputed by some, any list of pioneering rock & rollers that doesn't include Little Richard near the top has just become too damn sophisticated for its own good. —*Cub Koda*

○ **Here's Little Richard** / 1957 / Specialty ✦✦✦✦

The Fabulous Little Richard / 1959 / Specialty ✦✦✦

★ **18 Greatest Hits** / 1985 / Rhino ✦✦✦✦✦
The one definitive package to own. —*Cub Koda*

○ **Shut Up!: a Collection of Rare Tracks, 1951-1964** / 1988 / Rhino ✦✦✦✦

○ **Specialty Box Set** / 1989 / Ace ✦✦✦✦
Check out this beautiful three-CD boxed set of all the important Specialty sides. —*Cub Koda*

○ **The Formative Years 1951-53** / Jul. 1989 / Bear Family ✦✦✦✦
Early Richard, pre-"Tutti Frutti." —*Cub Koda*

★ **Georgia Peach, The** / 1991 / Specialty ✦✦✦✦✦
Perhaps the greatest of Little Richard's greatest hits compilations, the 25-track *Georgia Peach* features all of his biggest hits in chronological order, as well as terrific singles that never were as big as "Tutti Frutti" and "Good Golly Miss Molly." On top of the sublime song selection and sound, the liner notes by compiler Billy Vera are splendid and insightful. —*Stephen Thomas Erlewine*

BOOK

✦✦ **The Life & Times Of Little Richard**, by Charles White (Harmony, 1984). Less a biography than an oral history, dominated naturally by recollections from Richard himself, with interjections from fellow musicians, relatives, and lovers; White provides the narrative links. It's no secret that Little Richard has one of the biggest egos of any entertainer of the 20th century, and thus one must be prepared for a lot of boasting and declarations of greatness. White's worshipful tone doesn't help matters, and nor do his occasional smugly unwarranted judgements (as when he asserts that John Lennon was "zero as a live musician" and "Lennon knew that artistically he was unfit to tune Richard's piano" because Lennon insisted on closing the 1969 Toronto Peace Festival after Richard). Beyond these considerable flaws, there are a lot of good stories (and occasional insights) about the music, touring, and records. It's especially strong in describing his mid-'50s peak, when he grafted his special outrage onto jump blues and New Orleans R&B to create some of the most exciting early rock & roll. Like most biographies of early rockers, it bogs down in recriminations against the fickle taste of the record industry, depictions of sleazy tours and substance abuse, and lurid sex as he soldiers on as a living legend in the '60s, '70s, and '80s. —*Richie Unterberger*

Little River Band

Group, Pop/Rock
Little River Band (formed 1975) enjoyed an impressive string of hits during the late '70s and early '80s with their rather mellow harmony-laden MOR pop. The original lineup included leadsinger Glenn Shurrock; guitarists Rick Furmoru, Beeb Birtles, and Graham Goble; Rugo McLachlan on bass; and Derek Pellicci on drums. Later members included David Briggs (guitar), George McArdle (bass), and lead singer John Faraham. —*Rick Clark & Larry Lapka*

● **Greatest Hits** / 1982 / Capitol ✦✦✦✦
All of their best are included—"Reminiscing" (#3), "Lady" (#10), "Lonesome Loser" (#6), "Cool Change" (#10), "The Night Owls" (#6), and "Take It Easy on Me" (#10). —*Larry Lapka*

Little Steven & the Disciples of Soul

Group, Rock & Roll
Steven Van Zandt (b.ca. 1951) grew up in the same south New Jersey shore scene as Bruce Springsteen and Southside Johnny Lyon and was closely associated with them. He was a member of Springsteen's band Steel Mill in 1969-1970 and the Bruce Springsteen band in 1971. He then worked with Southside Johnny, but rejoined Springsteen in the E Street Band in early 1975. This group went on to massive success, and Van Zandt worked closely with Springsteen, coproducing *The River* and *Born in the U.S.A.* while also producing and writing material for Southside Johnny and Gary US Bonds. In 1982, Van Zandt organized Little Steven and the Disciples of Soul, which released *Men without Women*.

He left the E Street Band under amicable circumstances in April 1984. In 1985 he organized the Top 40 hit single "Sun City," featuring a multitude of pop stars protesting apartheid in South Africa. —*William Ruhlmann & John Floyd*

Trail of Broken Treaties / 1979 / Manhattan ✦✦✦

● **Men without Women** / 1982 / Razor & Tie ✦✦✦✦
Little Steven's first album is a White-soul triumph, full of well-formed ballads, tough Stones-ish rockers, and the swagger and attitude of vintage Southside Johnny (for whom Van Zandt has produced and written). In effect, this is Van Zandt leading the E Street Band—Max Weinberg (d), Garry Tallent (b), Danny Federici (organ)—plus such other Northeast cronies as pianist Kevin Kavanaugh of the Asbury Jukes, ex-Rascals Felix Cavaliere and Dino Danelli, ex-Plasmatic Jean Beauvoir, and the La Bamba horn section. The result is a big sound that plays searing music. "Forever" was the album's closest thing to a hit, but its power and emotion still sound fresh a full decade after its release. —*John Floyd & William Ruhlmann*

○ **Voice of America** / 1984 / Razor & Tie ✦✦✦✦
The band has been pared down slightly, but the sound is just as big. This time Van Zandt has big issues on his mind, too, from the "disappeared" of South America to "Solidarity"; the best track is the plaintive anthem "I Am a Patriot." —*William Ruhlmann*

Freedom No Compromise / 1987 / EMI ✦✦✦

Revolution / 1989 / RCA ✦✦✦

Little Village

Group, Rock & Roll
An early-'90s supergroup, Little Village is composed of string wizard Ry Cooder, tunesmith John Hiatt, English bassist Nick Lowe, and session drummer extraordinaire Jim Keltner. All four musicians originally played as a unit in 1987 on Hiatt's breakthrough album *Bring the Family*. In that context, all but Hiatt were sidemen. Four years later they collectively wrote and recorded their self-titled debut CD. Although the record was a bit of a disappointment, the live shows were superb. —*Rob Bowman*

Little Village / 1992 / Reprise ✦✦✦
Given the personnel in the band, Little Village's first album was a somewhat uneven disappointment. That said, Nick Lowe has yet to make a truly poor recording and there is much here of merit. Particularly great is "Big Love" and the loose-limbed "The Action." —*Rob Bowman*

Little Willie John (William Edgar John)

b. Nov. 15, 1937, Cullendale, AK, d. May 26, 1968
Soul, R&B
He's never received the accolades given to the likes of Sam Cooke, Clyde McPhatter, and James Brown, but Little Willie John ranks as one of R&B's most influential performers. His muscular high timbre and enormous technical and emotional range belied his early age (his first hit came when he was 18), but his mid-'50s work for Syd Nathan's King label would play a great part in the way soul music would sound. Everyone from Cooke, McPhatter, and Brown to Jackie Wilson, B.B.King, and Al Green has acknowledged his debt to this most overlooked of rock and soul pioneers. His debut recording, a smoking version of Titus Turner's "All around the World" from 1955, set the pattern for a remarkable string of hits: "Need Your Love So Bad," "Suffering with the Blues," "Fever," "Let Them Talk," and his last, "Sleep," from 1961. His version of "Fever" was copied note for note by Peggy Lee and Elvis Presley, both of whom had bigger hits with it; John's version, however, remains definitive. His second hit, "Need Your Love So Bad," contains one of the most intimate, tear-jerking vocals ever caught on tape.

John had a volatile temper, fueled by a taste for liquor and an insecurity regarding his slight height (5 ft 4 in). He was known to pack a gun and knife; in 1966, he stabbed a man and was sent to the Washington State penitentiary, where he died of pneumonia in 1968. James Brown recorded a tribute album to John that year, and his material has been recorded by scores of artists from the Beatles to Fleetwood Mac to the Blasters. Nevertheless, Little Willie John remains a stranger to most listeners and has never received the respect his talent deserves.

Little Willie John was one of the first artists featured in Rhino's King reissues series. *Fever* was issued late in 1993, and the single-disc, 20-track anthology included such John releases as "Need Your Love So Bad," "Suffering with the Blues," and the title cut. —*John Floyd*

● **Fever: The Best of Little Willie John** / 1993 / Rhino ◆◆◆◆
Little Willie John had a commanding delivery, remarkable projection and a charismatic sound that was both instantly recognizable and unforgettable. His magical singles are all contained on this superb 20-track anthology, arguably the best single-disc set of John material available. It includes his best-known song, "Fever" (Peggy Lee's cover version became a huge smash), plus such marvelous numbers such as "Home At Last," "Heartbreak (It's Hurtin' Me)" and "You Hurt Me." While John was a dynamic heartache wailer, he could also do excellent dance/novelty and double-entendre tunes such as "Let's Rock While The Rockin's Good" and "Leave My Kitten Alone." This anthology demonstrates why he's still held in such high regard throughout the world of R&B and soul. —*Ron Wynn*

Live

Group, Rock & Roll, Alternative Pop/Rock
With their muscular R.E.M. and U2 hybrid, Live straddles the line between alternative rock credibility and mainstream radio accessibility. When their first album was released, it was a moderate commercial success, made all the more impressive considering the reluctance of radio to alternative-oriented music. *Throwing Copper*, their second album, shot to the top of college charts when it was released in the spring of 1994, as well as receiving a substantial amount of mainstream sales and play on pop radio. In early 1995, the number one album rock and modern rock single "Lightning Crashes" sent the album into the pop Top 10 and by the summer, *Throwing Copper* had sold over four million copies. —*Stephen Thomas Erlewine*

○ **Mental Jewelry** / 1991 / Radioactive ◆◆◆◆
Live's debut album was an impressive set of righteous, hard-driving alternative rock; *Mental Jewelry* was in the vein of such college-radio favorites as U2, but was more vulnerable and less sanctimonious. —*Stephen Thomas Erlewine*

● **Throwing Copper** / 1994 / Radioactive ◆◆◆◆
Not only did Live's songwriting improve on their second album, *Throwing Copper*, but their sound was much stronger; their hooks were powerful and memorable, their melodies were carefully crafted and catchy. The result was a major crossover hit, thanks to the singles "Selling the Drama," "I Alone," and "Lightning Crashes." —*Stephen Thomas Erlewine*

Living Colour

Group, Hard Rock, Heavy Metal
All-black metal band comprised of bandleader/guitarist Vernon Reid (a co-founder of New York City's Black Rock Coalition), singer Corey Glover, bassist Muzz Skillings, and drummer William Calhoun. Reid originally formed the band in 1984 as a trio. Mick Jagger was an early fan and helped them secure a deal with Epic. Living Colour's brand of metal also includes elements of jazz and funk, plus Reid's messy-but-lightning-fast guitar solos; the band drew praise from critics for its genre-straddling hybrid and political lyrics. Their debut album, *Vivid*, was a Top Ten smash. Skillings left the band in 1992 and was replaced by Doug Wimbish. Living Colour disbanded up early in 1995. —*Steve Huey*

● **Vivid** / 1988 / Epic ◆◆◆◆
Living Colour broke through on this debut album with their mixture of heavy metal, guitar heroics (courtesy of Vernon Reid), and thoughtful, sometimes scathing lyrics, suggesting a new direction for hard rock. This Top Ten million-selling album included the songs "Cult of Personality," "Open Letter (To a Landlord)," and the Top Forty hit "Glamour Boys." —*William Ruhlmann*

Time's Up / 1990 / Epic ◆◆◆
A powerful, uncompromising sophomore effort, featuring the radio hits "Type" and "Pride" as well as the provocative "Elvis Is Dead" and "Love Rears Its Ugly Head." —*William Ruhlmann*

Biscuits / 1991 / Epic ◆◆

Stain / 1993 / Epic ◆◆◆
With the addition of new bassist Doug Wimbish, Living Colour turns in a harder-edged effort with *Stain*, a record driven more by the shattering metal/jazz fusion riffs of Vernon Reid than any of their other albums. While the sheer sonic force of the album is impressive, the songs don't match the power of the music; nevertheless, the music is so strong that it usually overshadows the inadequate songwriting. —*Stephen Thomas Erlewine*

LL Cool J (James Smith)

Rap
The importance of LL Cool J (born James Smith, his moniker stands for Ladies Love Cool James) in rap cannot be exaggerated. By fusing the beatbox minimalism of Run-DMC with the b-boy snarl of his defiant lyrics, LL Cool J pushed the music into new terrain, opening the door for numerous hip-hop contenders and becoming a superstar in the process.
Since the across-the-boards success of *Mama Said Knock You Out*, LL Cool J's had trouble reclimbing the mountain from which he once stood tall. He predicted *14 Shots to the Dome* would be the ticket, and it did respectably, but lacked either the resonance or the power of *Mama Said*. —*John Floyd*

☆ **Radio** / 1985 / Def Jam ◆◆◆◆◆
LL Cool J's debut, produced by Rick Rubin, is a brilliant mix of hardcore street anthems ("I Can't Live Without My Radio," "Rock the Bells") and updated twists on the dozens ("That's a Lie"), with a couple of ballads thrown in. —*John Floyd*

Bigger and Deffer / 1987 / Def Jam ◆◆
On his second album, LL Cool J's ego goes to his head, resulting in a weak album of mild beats and inflated bragging, which is only partially saved by his first successful ballad, the syrupy "I Need Love." —*Stephen Thomas Erlewine*

○ **Walking with a Panther** / 1989 / Def Jam ◆◆◆◆
A sprawling followup to his stinko second album, it's his most ambitious. LL Cool J not only regroups the strengths that made his debut a winner, but shows a musical expansion of his art that bodes well for the future. Includes "I'm That Type of Guy," "Going Back to Cali," and "Big Ole Butt." —*John Floyd*

★ **Mama Said Knock You Out** / 1990 / Def Jam ◆◆◆◆◆
The future, Cool J 1990-style. He's mixing house and hip-hop into his minimalist backdrops, and he's finally come up with some decent love songs. With "The Boomin' System," he's created yet another essential rap anthem. Includes "Around the Way Girl," "6 Minutes of Pleasure," "Jingling Baby," and the title track. —*John Floyd*

14 Shots to the Dome / 1993 / CBS ◆◆◆
It's not the tour de force of *Mama Said Knock You Out*, but *14 Shots to the Dome* is a solid effort finding LL Cool J maturing gracefully and strongly, without selling out. *14 Shots* may not have sold as well as *Mama* either, but at least half of the album ranks with his best work. —*Stephen Thomas Erlewine*

Bill Lloyd

Power Pop/Anglo-Pop
As a solo artist, Bill Lloyd (half of the country duo Foster & Lloyd) displays his real passion: finely crafted Anglo-power-pop/rock—à la Byrds, Big Star, Badfinger—a must for any lover of this kind of music. —*Rick Clark*

Feeling the Elephant / 1987 / DB ◆◆◆
Originally released in 1986 on the Throbbing Lobster label, *Feeling the Elephant* was to be the debut for Lloyd's solo career until he got sidetracked with the successful country duo Foster & Lloyd. Lloyd might do country justice, but on *Feeling the Elephant*, his Anglo-pop/rock roots are everywhere to be found. From the urgent drive of "This Very Second," the album's opener, to the spacey melancholy of "Everything's Closing Down," the album exuberantly draws from the best elements of the Byrds, Big Star, Badfinger, mid-period Beatles, and early Who. Highlights include "It'll Never Get Better Than This" and "Lisa-Anne." —*Rick Clark*

● **Set to Pop** / 1994 / East Side Digital ◆◆◆◆
It's hard to find memorable melodies and smart lyrics as abundantly represented on one artist or band's album these days, as they are here. Picking a highlight is hard. For lovers of exceptionally melodic power-pop/rock, *Set to Pop* is a real find. —*Rick Clark*

Lobo (Kent Lavoie)

Group, Pop
Lobo (born Kent Lavoie) is one of those singer/songwriters who managed to be invisible to the public, while landing a 1972 #37 hit album, *Of a Simple Man*, and eight Top Forty hits, between 1971 and 1979. Among them were "Me and You and a Dog Named Boo" (#5), "I'd Love You to Want Me" (#2) and "Don't Expect Me to Be Your Friend" (#8). —*Rick Clark*

● **The Best of Lobo** / Jun. 15, 1993 / Rhino ✦✦✦✦
Anyone who has ever loved "Me and You and a Dog Named Boo"
will find plenty to explore on Lobo's *The Best Of*, which contains
18 tracks including "I'd Love You to Want Me," "Don't Expect Me to
Be Your Friend," "How Can I Tell Her," and, of course, "Me and You
and a Dog Named Boo." —*AMG*

Nils Lofgren

b. Jun. 21, 1951, Chicago, IL
Rock & Roll
Nils Lofgren formed Grin in 1969, a group with much promise
and little financial success. During the '70s and early '80s, Lofgren
pursued a spotty solo career while contributing some fine work
with Neil Young. Lofgren joined up with Bruce Springsteen's band
in 1986. A new deal with Massachusetts label Rykodisc produced
the moderate-hit album *Silver Lining* in 1991. —*Rick Clark*

● **Nils Lofgren** / 1975 / A&M ✦✦✦✦
After dismantling Grin in 1974, Lofgren signed a solo deal with
A&M, releasing a self-titled debut that neatly showcased his
strengths as a singer/songwriter and multi-instrumentalist. His
reading of Carole King's wistful chestnut "Goin' Back" is a highlight, as are fiery originals like "Keith Don't Go" (a tribute to the
Stones' Keith Richards) and "Rock & Roll Crook," with its wonderfully convoluted twin-guitar interplay. "Back It Up" is another gem.
—*Rick Clark*

Back It Up (Authorized Bootleg) / 1975 / A&M ✦✦✦

Cry Tough / 1976 / A&M ✦✦✦
Lofgren's only other worthwhile record. A little forced on the song-
writing side, but delivered with enough panache to make it work.
—*John Dougan*

I Came to Dance / 1977 / A&M ✦✦

Night After Night [Live] / 1977 / A&M ✦✦

○ **Nils** / 1979 / A&M ✦✦✦✦
Lofgren rebounded, after several spotty albums, with this effort,
which featured some of the strongest writing in his career, particularly "Shine Silently," "A Fool like You," "Steal Away," and the
powerful ballad "No Mercy." —*Rick Clark*

Night Fades Away / 1981 / MCA ✦✦

Wonderland / 1983 / MCA ✦✦
Unfortunately, this one got totally buried. "Across the Tracks," the
single, should have been given the push it deserved. A remake of
Bobby Womack's "It's All Over Now" is another highlight. —*Rick
Clark*

Flip / 1985 / Columbia ✦✦✦

○ **Classics, Vol. 13** / 1987 / A&M ✦✦✦✦
A solid 15-song compilation that gives a good sense of Lofgren's
career, but *Nils Lofgren* is a better introduction. —*Stephen Thomas
Erlewine*

Silver Lining / 1991 / Rykodisc ✦✦

Crooked Line / 1992 / Rykodisc ✦✦✦
Crooked Line evokes Lofgren's Youngian (not Jungian) roots, and
it's therefore appropriate that original mentor Neil guests on the
sessions. Mr. Young adds distinctive background vocals and harmonica to the country-folk ramble "You," and lets loose with some
grungy electric guitar for "Drunken Driver." Not that he steals any
of the limelight from Lofgren, who offsets his trademark tough
but melodic string-bending with tasteful acoustic pop forays like
"Shot At You." The guitarist leaves flashy pyrotechnics to others,
preferring to cut his material with direct, slashing simplicity. —
Roch Parisien

Loggins & Messina

Group, Pop/Rock
Kenny Loggins and Jim Messina were the most successful
pop/rock duo of the first half of the '70s. Loggins was a staff songwriter who had recently enjoyed success with a group of songs
recorded by the Nitty Gritty Dirt Band when he came to the attention of Messina, a record producer and former member of Buffalo
Springfield and Poco. Messina agreed to produce Loggins's first album, but somewhere along the way it became a duo effort that
was released in 1972 under the title *Kenny Loggins with Jim
Messina Sittin' in*. The album was a gold-seller that stayed in the
charts more than two years.
In the next four years, Loggins & Messina released a series of

gold or platinum albums, most of which hit the Top Ten. They
were all played in a buoyant country-rock style with an accomplished band. *Loggins and Messina* (1972) featured the retro-rock
hit "Your Mama Don't Dance." *Full Sail* (1973), *On Stage* (a double
live album, 1974), and *Mother Lode* (1974) all hit the Top Ten. *So
Fine* was an album of '50s cover songs. The pair's last new studio
album, *Native Sons*, came out at the start of 1976.
Loggins and Messina split for two solo careers by the end of
that year, their catalog completed by a greatest-hits album, *Best of
Friends*, and a live record, *Finale*. —*William Ruhlmann*

○ **Sittin' in** / Jan. 1972 / Columbia ✦✦✦✦
This debut album was credited to "Kenny Loggins with Jim
Messina" because the project had begun as a solo record by Loggins being produced by Messina. By the time it was finished, however, Messina had written or co-written six of the 11 songs, contributed "first guitar," and shared lead vocals on many tracks.
Messina's "Nobody but You" and "Vahevala," co-written by Loggins' brother Dave, were the singles chart entries, but today everybody remembers the album for Loggins' "House at Pooh Corner,"
which had earned Loggins his record contract, and "Danny's
Song," which Anne Murray took into the Top Ten the following
year. The only thing wrong with this record is that it was too perfect—with their infectious blend of country, folk, rock and
Caribbean music, L&M started out at the top of their game, and although they were able to match some of the material and performances on later records, the team never got any better than this.
—*William Ruhlmann*

○ **Loggins & Messina** / Oct. 1972 / Columbia ✦✦✦✦
The first full-fledged L&M album found the duo in good form as
songwriters, with Messina turning in the sparkling "Thinking Of
You" and the two collaborating on the hit single "Your Mama
Don't Dance" and "Angry Eyes." Their backup band was anchored
by multi-instrumentalist Al Garth and also featured keyboardist
Michael Omartian and Poco steel guitarist Rusty Young. —*William
Ruhlmann*

Full Sail / Oct. 1973 / Columbia ✦✦✦
This is every inch a followup to *Loggins And Messina*, including a
'50s rock & roll pastiche in the style of "Your Mama Don't Dance"
called "My Music" that hit #16 as a single. Other notable material
included Messina's island-rock anthem "Lahaina" and one of Loggins' sensitive-but-generic ballads, typically called "A Love Song."
But then, the charm of L&M was that they could get away with
something this sappy. Balance is the key to L&M albums, and it's
the chief talent (among many) that producer Messina brings to
them. Here, as on L&M's first two albums, he achieves a musical
flow that's exhilarating, and the record is only denied a "finest" rating because the quality of the songwriting doesn't quite match
those LPs. —*William Ruhlmann*

On Stage / Apr. 1974 / Columbia ✦✦✦
Having assembled a strong backup band, L&M were at their best
in concert, and this two-LP set catches all of their diverse talents,
from the tight, intricate rockers devised by Messina to the sensitive ballad skills of Loggins and the band's ability to stretch out on
the sidelong "Vahevala." —*William Ruhlmann*

Mother Lode / Oct. 1974 / Columbia ✦✦✦
From its brown-toned cover to its contents, Loggins & Messina's
fourth studio album is a sober, low-key, reflective affair. The band's
music, with its single flute, violin and horn lines, directed by
Messina's intricate guitar and mandolin playing, serves a series of
midtempo tunes expressing a lot of quiet dissatisfaction signalled
by titles like "Be Free," "Changes," and "Move On." As usual in a
Jim Messina production, all of this is elegantly, tastefully accomplished, but one could hardly come away from the record feeling
that all was well in the L&M camp. —*William Ruhlmann*

So Fine / 1975 / Columbia ✦✦

Native Sons / Jan. 1976 / Columbia ✦✦✦
Loggins and Messina's fifth and last album of new studio material
was also their least. No hit singles issued from a collection that
featured a new backup band and extensive use of strings on a set
of mediocre material. L&M's breakup at the end of the tour promoting this record seemed confirmation that they had exhausted
the possibilities of their partnership. —*William Ruhlmann*

● **The Best of Friends** / Nov. 1976 / Columbia ✦✦✦✦
It collects their biggest hits from "Your Mama Don't Dance" onward. —*Dan Heilman*

Finale / 1977 / Columbia ✦
Loggins and Messina's five-year partnership produced five albums of original material, one album of covers, a greatest hits album, and, with this post-breakup release, two double-LP live albums. The first of them, 1974's *On Stage*, displayed their concert abilities at the height of their career. This one, a profit-taking redundancy probably released because double live albums were fashionable in the wake of Peter Frampton's *Frampton Comes Alive*, chronicles their less-interesting last couple of years. Songs are contracted into medleys to get them over with, and even the ones at full length are better heard on the studio albums. —*William Ruhlmann*

Kenny Loggins

b. Jan. 7, 1948, Everette, WA
Pop/Rock
Singer, songwriter, and guitarist Kenny Loggins was born in Everett, WA, and moved to Los Angeles in his teens. He got a job as a staff writer and wrote four songs used on a Nitty Gritty Dirt Band album in 1970, among them the hit "House at Pooh Corner." This brought him to the attention of former Poco member Jim Messina, now a staff producer at CBS, who intended to produce Loggins's debut album. The two ended up in a duo, however, and Loggins & Messina made a series of successful albums during the '70s.

Loggins & Messina broke up in 1976, and Loggins went on to solo stardom with such million-selling albums as *Celebrate Me Home*, *Nightwatch* (which included the hit "Whenever I Call You Friend"), and *Keep the Fire*, all in the cheerful, sensitive style he had displayed in Loggins & Messina. Loggins also became known as the king of the movie soundtrack song, scoring Top Ten hits with "I'm Alright" (from *Caddyshack*), "Footloose" (from *Footloose*), "Danger Zone" (from *Top Gun*), and "Nobody's Fool" (from *Caddyshack II*). His own albums sold less well (and came less frequently) throughout the '80s. —*William Ruhlmann*

Celebrate Me Home / Apr. 1977 / Columbia ✦✦✦
This features the hit single "I Believe in Love" (number 66). "Lady Luck," "Why Do People Lie?," and the title cut are highlights on this relatively light MOR debut. —*Rick Clark*

Nightwatch / Jun. 1978 / Columbia ✦✦✦
This super-slick sophomore effort was Loggins's biggest chart success, aided in no small part by the singles "Whenever I Call You Friend" (number five), which featured a duet with Stevie Nicks, and "Easy Driver" (number 60). "Wait a Little While," and remakes of the Doobies' hit "What a Fool Believes" and Billy Joe Royal's "Down in the Boondocks" were further highlights. —*Rick Clark*

Keep the Fire / Oct. 1979 / Columbia ✦✦✦
Produced by Tom Dowd (Rod Stewart, Aretha Franklin, Allman Brothers), Loggins beefs up his sound a little with "Love Has Come of Age." He also enjoys more hits with "This Is It" (number 11) and the title cut (number 36). —*Rick Clark*

● **Kenny Loggins Alive** / Sep. 1980 / Columbia ✦✦✦✦
This extended live effort arrived on the wings of Loggins's number seven hit "I'm Alright," from the movie soundtrack of *Caddyshack*. The concert version included here is much better, stripped of some of the cute studio tricks found on the single. Most of the material comes from previously released studio tracks, which are given faithful (but livelier) readings. —*Rick Clark*

○ **High Adventure** / Sep. 1982 / Columbia ✦✦✦✦
Loggins continued his successful string of hit albums with this release. A light mainstream rock duet with Journey lead-singer Steve Perry, titled "Don't Fight It," reached number 17, while Loggins turned in a couple of MOR hits with "Heart to Heart" (number 15) and "Welcome to Heartlight" (number 24). As with all of his albums to this point, his sound is pleasant and well crafted. Loggins later enjoyed success with songs featured on soundtracks like *Caddyshack II*, *Top Gun*, and *Footloose*. —*Rick Clark*

Vox Humana / Mar. 1985 / Columbia ✦✦
Kenny Loggins turns to a more techno approach and stubs his toe commercially. He had established himself as a singles and soundtrack star (notably in 1984's *Footloose*) with this kind of uptempo, synthesized material, but in so doing lost his connection with his album audience, and, by taking such a stylistic sidetrack on his first regular LP in two-and-a-half years, failed to reconnect with fans who still remembered him from "House At Pooh Corner." In retrospect, they were wise; *Vox Humana* is ambitious but unaccomplished. —*William Ruhlmann*

Leap of Faith / 1991 / Columbia ✦✦
Kenny Loggins seems to have thought long and hard during the three years between *Back to Avalon* and this album, during which he underwent a divorce. The results can be heard on what is undoubtedly his most mature and heartfelt effort. He embraces environmental issues here, and tells his side of the unhappy marriage. He still isn't a cerebral sort, so the subject matter clashes somewhat with his typically simple expressions, but the effort helped him reconnect with his fans, who made this album something of a sleeper hit: although it was his lowest charting effort ever, it stayed in the charts longer than any album he'd made since the heyday of Loggins and Messina and went gold. —*William Ruhlmann*

○ **At His Best** / 1992 / Hollywood ✦✦✦✦

Outside: From the Redwoods / Aug. 10, 1993 / Columbia ✦✦✦
On his second live album, Kenny Loggins puts together a special show consisting of rearranged versions of old favorites like "What A Fool Believes" (complete with co-author Michael McDonald on vocals) and "Your Mama Don't Dance." It's Loggins' version of an "unplugged" performance (despite a substantial backup band), and as such a turning away from the technology-happy days of albums like *Back to Avalon* (which, by the way, is forgotten in a catalog promotion in the CD booklet), without quite returning to the more homegrown quality of early albums like *Celebrate Me Home*. The real question in Loggins' career is what will happen with his next set of new material, but as a placeholder, this release sbould be welcomed by his fans, who may find even "Footloose" tolerable in a barrelhouse piano arrangement. —*William Ruhlmann*

Back to Avalon / Columbia ✦✦✦
The title might have implied a return to form, but Kenny Loggins' commercial decline continued bere, despite the inclusion of "Nobody's Fool," the Top Ten theme from *Caddyshack II*, "Meet Me Half Way," the number 11 theme from *Over the Top*, and a cover of the Exciters' "Tell Him [Her]." Instead of addressing the concerns of his long-time fans, Loggins proceeded farther into contemporary sounds, employing multiple producers of the likes of Patrick Leonard (Madonna) and Peter Wolf (Starship), all to little effect. This was Loggins' first solo album to miss gold certification and made his career crisis official. —*William Ruhlmann*

The Lollipop Shoppe

Group, Psychedelic
Led by singer Fred Cole, who had formerly been in the Northwest punk band the Weeds, the Lollipop Shoppe's sole album (from 1967) ranks as one of the better psych-punk LPs, and indeed as one of the better one-shot rock records of the late '60s. Featuring Cole's choked, bitter phrasing, the group staked out the middle ground between the Seeds (who shared the same manager) and Love, with a bit of fellow L.A. psych-punkers the Music Machine thrown in. If comparisons must be made, they were definitely closer in tone to Love than the Seeds, with a mixture of raunch and reflection in the spirit of Arthur Lee. Cole was one of the few psychedelic performers to make a contribution during the punk era, surfacing in the Portland punk band the Rats in the late '70s. —*Richie Unterberger*

● **Just Colour** / 1967 / UNI ✦✦✦✦
Good brooding psych-punk with melancholy bite and melodic variety. The reissue adds a couple non-LP cuts from a 1968 single, complete with *Forever Changes*-like orchestration. —*Richie Unterberger*

Lone Justice

Group, Roots-Rock
Lone Justice in its original form, ca. 1983, was a quartet based in Los Angeles and featuring singer Maria McKee (b. 1964), guitarist Ryan Hedgecock (b. ca. 1960), bassist Marvin Etzioni, and drummer Don Heffington. The group played in a country-rock style on its debut album, *Lone Justice* (1985). By the time of the second album, *Shelter* (1986), it had turned more toward mainstream rock and become a sextet, with only McKee and Hedgecock remaining from the original unit. Then Lone Justice broke up, and McKee went on to a solo career. —*William Ruhlmann*

● **Lone Justice** / 1985 / David Geffen Co. ✦✦✦✦
Maria McKee has one of those aching, little-girl voices (not unlike Stevie Nicks'), and it's heard to great effect on these country-rock tunes, especially Tom Petty and Mike Campbell's "Ways to Be Wicked." —*William Ruhlmann*

Shelter / 1986 / David Geffen Co. ✦✦✦

Roy Loney & the Phantom Movers

Group, Roots-Rock

Bay Area native Roy Loney, a founding member of the great Flamin' Groovies, quit the band in the early '70s, ostensibly to pursue a solo career. Oddly, his first solo recording didn't appear until 1979, nearly seven years after leaving the Groovies. In the interim, Loney had taken a series of record industry jobs, at one point working as a sales rep for the now defunct ABC Records, and at the funky and fabulous Jack's Record Cellar in San Francisco. Despite the delay, Loney's return to rock & roll performance was auspicious; there was a tremendous EP, *A Hundred Miles an Hour*, dedicated to Sissy Spacek, which was followed by the wild and woolly full-length LP, *Out After Dark*. Eschewing the Byrdsian pop direction that former partner Cyril Jordan had now taken the Groovies, Loney's records were wild-eyed, rockabilly-fueled chunks of joyous noise, with much shaking, rattling and rolling provided by the great guitar playing of ex-Groovies James Ferrell and drummer Danny Mihm. Now fully integrated into the late-'70s/early-'80s rock scene, Loney, retaining his deservedly hip credentials, released a string of fine records from 1979–1983 on mostly small indie labels, eventually dropping out of sight in 1984. Actually, he just withdrew from the rock scene for a while and continued to play in the Bay Area and work at Jack's. In the late '80s, recording for roots-rock label Norton, Loney unleashed *The Scientific Bombs Away*, which was a terrific, if almost totally ignored record. Loaded with raving guitars, hiccuping vocals, and his thoroughly original sense of humor, Loney had made a triumphant return to rock. Too bad no one seemed to care. These days, Loney is recording new music with the Seattle band Young Fresh Fellows, and if the early results (a great cover of Sam the Sham's "I Couldn't Spell !!*@!") are indicative of what's to come, there will still be plenty of fine music coming from Roy A. Loney. —*John Dougan*

○ **Out After Dark** / 1979 / Solid Smoke ✦✦✦✦
After a protracted layoff from music, Loney came back in a big way with his first solo record. With help from ex-Flamin' Groovies Danny Mihm and James Ferrell, this is a feverish little slice of rock & roll, with Loney's overwrought, hiccuping vocals adding just the right bizarre touch. There's a great cover of "Return to Sender" and plenty of terrific and often funny Loney originals ("Born to Be Your Fool," "Used Hoodoo" and "Scum City"). Fans of roots-rock and the Loney-led Groovies years will love this. —*John Dougan*

Phantom Tracks / 1980 / Solid Smoke ✦✦
Perhaps not absolutely essential, this is a wonderful EP of live tracks an assorted studio hijinks. The real star of this record is guitarist Ferrell, who tears it up in a big way on "Down the Road Apiece" and "Hundred Miles an Hour." Big, big fun from start to finish. —*John Dougan*

Contents under Pressure / 1981 / War Bride ✦✦

○ **Rock & Roll Dance Party** / 1982 / Warner Brothers ✦✦✦✦
The title pretty much sums it up. Loney blows the dust off of the Groovies' great "Teenage Head" and gives it a revved-up treatment. The band is, as usual, hotter than hell, and Loney's punk, rave-up attitude is in full blossom. Not the deepest, most intellectually challenging record you'll ever hear, but who ever said that made for great rock and roll? —*John Dougan*

Fast & Loose / 1983 / Lolita ✦✦✦

Live / 1984 / Lolita ✦✦

● **The Scientific Bombs Away!!!** / 1988 / Norton ✦✦✦✦
Interestingly, this record was released in Australia a few months before it was released in America, which gives you an indication of the peculiarities surrounding Loney's career. Nevertheless, this is a fine and funky record, drenched in echo and with a crude, instantly likable rockabilly feel that puts the pedal to the metal and doesn't back down. After all these years, Loney can still crank it out and kick up a fuss. Just listen to "Bip Bop Boom" and "Boy, Man!" and you'll see what I mean. —*John Dougan*

Full Grown Head / 1994 / Shake/Cargo ✦✦✦
A frothy, irreverent blitz of '50s-style instrumental zingers, slamming garage rock, demented rockabilly, rumbling street-punk, cheesy Tex-Mex, and trashy R&B from the former Flamin' Groovies member. —*Roch Parisien*

Five or Six by Five Live / Norton ✦✦✦

Long Ryders

Group, Country-Rock, Roots-Rock

A '60s revisionist band from the early '80s, the West Coast-based Long Ryders were led by vocalist Sid Griffin. They blended Gram Parsons country and Bob Dylan rock & roll with their own everyman anthems. They netted a minor hit in 1984 with "Looking for Lewis and Clark" and broke up in 1988. —*John Floyd*

10 5 60 / 1983 / PVC ✦✦✦

○ **Native Sons** / 1984 / Frontier ✦✦✦✦
This updates the Byrds and Gram Parsons. —*Robert Gordon*

● **State of Our Union** / 1985 / Island ✦✦✦✦
American country-tinged rock & roll. —*Robert Gordon*

Two Fisted Tales / 1987 / Island ✦✦✦

Metallic B.O. / 1989 / Long Ryders Fan Club ✦✦✦

Longhouse

Group, Singer-Songwriter

A New York-based pop/rock group led by Lisa Herman, whose sound is characterized by extensive vocal harmonies provided by as many as six backup singers. Formed in 1985, they released their debut album in 1988. —*William Ruhlmann*

○ **Longhouse** / 1988 / Warner Brothers ✦✦✦✦
Lisa Herman represents the logical evolution of the doo-wop street-corner harmony style into an intricate vocal chorus, with her own alto up front, echoing the emotive style of Laura Nyro. And all in the service of a strong collection of catchy pop-rock songs with deeply emotional lyrics. One of the most auspicious debuts of the '80s. —*William Ruhlmann*

Loose Ends

Group, Soul, R&B

One of the top British dance and Urban Contemporary trios in the early '80s, Loose Ends formed in London. They were originally called Loose End, and included Carl McIntosh, Jane Eugene, and Steve Nichol. Virgin signed them in 1981, and their debut was written by Chris and Eddie Amoo of the Real Thing. The group changed its name to Loose Ends in 1983, and signed with MCA in America in 1984. Their single "Hanging on a String (Contemplating)" topped the R&B charts in 1985, and they repeated that achievement in 1986 with "Slow Down." Their last hit was "Watching You" in 1988, which reached number two. The group shuffled its lineup in 1990, with McIntosh now joined by Linda Carriere and Sunay Suleyman. They released *Look How Long*. McIntosh also produced several artists, notably Caron Wheeler. —*Ron Wynn*

● **Real Chuckeeboo** / 1984 / MCA ✦✦✦✦
This was the final album featuring British dance/R&B vocalists Jane Eugene, Steve Nichol, and Carl McIntosh. They had been quite successful on both sides of the Atlantic in the mid-'80s and were at the time of this release not only performing but writing and producing tracks for Juliet Roberts, Phyllis Hyman, Five Star, Peter Royer, Cheryl Lynn, and Lavine Hudson. Their focus may have been divided, because this was their least attractive and interesting album of the string with the core trio. It did have a fine single in "Watching You," and "Mr. Bachelor" was a nice concept cut. But it was no surprise that they split following the album. —*Ron Wynn*

A Little Spice / 1984 / MCA ✦✦✦

Zagora / 1985 / MCA ✦✦✦
Loose Ends was still in peak form on this late '80s release. "Slow Down" was an R&B chart topper and huge club smash, and they had two other songs become moderate hits. They had found the right mix of teasing vocals, clever lyric hooks, tight production, and good arrangements that weren't relentless in their backbeats, yet were also groove-oriented enough for dancers. —*Ron Wynn*

Look How Long / 1990 / MCA ✦✦✦
This is the British soul trio's best set of seamless, romantic groove ballads. —*John Floyd*

Tighten Up, Vol. 1 / 1994 / ✦✦

Lords of Acid

Group, House Music, Alternative Pop/Rock

Lords of Acid's exaggeratedly sexual acid house dance music gained a cult following with their 1991 album, *Lust*. Previously, the band had released three singles that laid the groundwork for the dense, throbbing *Lust* and its club hits, "Rough Sex" and "I Must Increase My Bust." Between their debut and their second album, 1994's *Voodoo-U*, the group added industrial elements to their sound and became a more straightforward, band-oriented group. At the time of their second album, Lords of Acid was led by Lady Galore (born Ruth Mcardle; vocals) and featured bassist Lord T. Byron (born Frank Vloeberghs), keyboard player Shai De La Luna, and drummer Mcguinnes (born Kurt Liekens). — *Stephen Thomas Erlewine*

● **Lust** / Oct. 25, 1991 / Antler Subway/Caroline ◆◆◆◆
Lords of Acid's debut album is the best representation of their dirty, sex-crazed acid-house dance music, featuring the club classics "I Sit on Acid" and "I Must Increase My Bust." — *David Jehnzen*

Voodoo-U / 1994 / Warner Brothers ◆◆
Previously an acid-house group, Lords Of Acid use more industrial sounds, along with some reggae and ska, on *Voodoo-U*. Songs such as "The Crab Louse" and "Drink My Honey" aren't recommended for queasy stomachs. — *John Bush*

Los Bravos

Group, Pop/Rock
In 1966, this Spanish quintet became one of the very few rock groups from a non-English-speaking country to have an international smash with "Black Is Black," which got to number four in the U.S. and number two in the U.K. Lead singer Mike Kogel's overwrought, pinched vocals sounded so much like Gene Pitney that many listeners assumed that "Black Is Black" was a Pitney single, and the strong resemblance remained intact throughout Los Bravos' career, both in the singing and arrangements. Indeed, with their brassy pop/rock songs and production, which sounded about halfway between New York mid-'60s pop/soul and Jay & the Americans, Los Bravos sounded far more like a mainstream American pop/rock group than a Spanish or British one. Most of their records were sung in English, and although they never made the American Top 20 again, they were far more popular in Europe, even placing another single in the British Top 20 in late 1966 with "I Don't Care." — *Richie Unterberger*

● **All The Best** / ◆◆◆◆
There's no label for this CD (though, oddly, it has the catalog #21670), but rest assured that it's easily available in specialty shops and mail-order collector catalogs, and in fact is much easier to locate than their original LPs. Good value, with 30 songs (about 90% of them in English), including "Black Is Black" and "I Don't Care," and a host of little-known tunes that usually follow the melodramatic, elaborately produced pop/rock mold of their hits. Fairly strong stuff, if not especially compelling. — *Richie Unterberger*

Los Cheyenes

Group, Garage Rock
Spain, unlike some other countries in continental Europe, was not a hotbed of garage rock in the 1960s, but there were a few Spanish bands. From the recorded evidence, the best of these were Los Cheyenes, a Barcelona group that wrote most of their riff-heavy material. They often sounded like an extremely raw variation of the early Kinks, with Merseybeat harmony and folk-rock influences as well. Unlike garage bands from most other non-English speaking countries, Los Cheyenes sang in their native tongue, and although it may make their stuff less approachable for some collectors, most of their EPs and singles were pretty strong. Not even all that successful in their own country, Los Cheyenes were pressured to commercialize their sound by their label, and broke up in 1967. — *Richie Unterberger*

● **Historia De La Musica Pop Espanola Vol. 0** / 1986 / ◆◆◆◆
All 16 of the tracks recorded by this interesting group, featuring every one of the EPs and singles they released between 1965 and 1967. Worth the search for garage/beat fans. — *Richie Unterberger*

Los Lobos

Group, Tex-Mex, Roots-Rock
Los Lobos were one of America's most distinctive and original bands of the '80s. They may have had a hit with "La Bamba" in 1987, yet that cover barely scratches the surface of their talents. Los Lobos are eclectic in the best sense of the word. While they draw equally from rock, Tex-Mex, country, folk, R&B, blues, and traditional Spanish and Mexican music, their music never sounds forced or self-conscious. Instead, all of their influences became one graceful, gritty sound. From their very first recordings their rich musicality was apparent; on nearly each subsequent record they have found ways to redefine and expand their sound, without ever straying from the musical traditions that form the heart and soul of the band.

After releasing an independent EP in the late '70s and an EP in 1983, Los Lobos delivered their first major-label album, *How Will the Wolf Survive*, in 1984; it received an enormous amount of critical acclaim, as well as a dedicated following of fans. In the next four years, they released a marginally successful attempt to make their wildly eclectic sound palatable for a pop audience (*By the Light of the Moon*), a soundtrack of old Ritchie Valens songs that was a hit (*La Bamba*), and an album of traditional Mexican music (*La Pistola Y El Corazon*). The band took two years off and returned with *The Neighborhood* in 1990; the album was a varied and powerful rock & roll record that was better than anything they had released in six years. *Kiko*, released in 1992, brought the band into more experimental territory, without ever abandoning their graceful songwriting. — *Stephen Thomas Erlewine*

...and a Time to Dance / 1983 / Slash ◆◆◆
Only seven songs but they're a perfect summation of what the band does and why it's important. This perfectly seamless fusion of Tex-Mex, R&B, and rock & roll has powerhouse covers of the Ritchie Valens hit "Come on, Let's Go" and the norteño classic "A Te Dejo en San Antonio" thrown in for good measure. — *Kit Kiefer*

● **How Will the Wolf Survive** / 1984 / Slash ◆◆◆◆
A broader spectrum of music without a measure of the all-out joy of *...and a Time to Dance, How Will the Wolf Survive?* features at least two raveup rockers ("Don't Worry Baby" and "I Got Loaded"), an irresistible shuffle ("Evangeline"), two traditional Mexican numbers ("Seranata Norteña" and "Corrida #1") and a stirring title tune. The album is well rounded and fully realized. — *Kit Kiefer*

By the Light of the Moon / 1987 / Slash ◆◆◆
A very gentle, very Catholic album, it's summed up by the trilogy of sad songs ("River of Fools," "The Mess We're In," "Tears of God") that closes out the album. — *Kit Kiefer*

La Bamba [O.S.T.] / Jun. 1987 / Slash ◆◆◆

La Pistola Y El Corazon / Sep. 1988 / Slash ◆◆◆
Los Lobos' album of traditional Mexican music isn't a history lesson, but a celebration of their heritage and its joyous music, which means that it's just as exciting and entertaining as their rock & roll records. — *Stephen Thomas Erlewine*

The Neighborhood / 1990 / Slash ◆◆◆
Recharged by their set of Mexican music, Los Lobos return with arguably their finest straight rock & roll record. *The Neighborhood* effortlessly combines rock, R&B, blues, and country into a singular, powerful sound that manages to be as darkly funky as "I Walk Alone" and "Georgia Slop" and as gently moving as "Emily." — *Stephen Thomas Erlewine*

○ **Kiko** / May 1992 / Slash ◆◆◆◆
With its highly textured layers of sound, *Kiko* sounds like nothing else Los Lobos has done. Although their sound is still based in roots music of all kinds (rock, folk, Mexican, country), the band has shaped it into a dense, impressionistic wall of sound that intensifies the emotions behind such carefully constructed and moving songs like "Two Janes," "Angels With Dirty Faces," and "Kiko and the Lavender Moon." It's certainly their most ambitious album, and it's arguably their best. — *Stephen Thomas Erlewine*

○ **Just Another Band from East LA: A Collection** / Aug. 31, 1993 / Slash ◆◆◆◆
Just Another Band From East L.A.: A Collection is a splendid double-disc collection that draws an accurate picture of Los Lobos, one of the most musically versatile bands of the 1980s. Featuring all of the band's hits and best-known songs, as well as several rare and previously unreleased tracks, there isn't a weak spot among the compilation's forty-one songs. — *Stephen Thomas Erlewine*

Los Mockers

Group, Garage Rock
The best group that South America produced during the 1960s, and not merely a novelty item. Formed in Montevideo, Uruguay, in the mid-'60s, the group relocated to Argentina in 1966 after winning a contract with EMI Argentina. Their sole LP and a few singles show the group to possess an uncanny ability to imitate early Rolling Stones songs without being that obvious about it.

Almost all of their material was original, sung in English by Polo Pereira, who (with a slight accent) emulates Mick Jagger's early snarl more accurately than anyone else from the time. You can detect apparent reference points to early Jagger/Richard tunes like "Off the Hook," and more sophisticated works like *Aftermath* ("Empty Harem" is complete with a "Paint It Black"-like guitar). The original lineup of Los Mockers disbanded in 1967, although other configurations using the same name recorded a few more discs in the late '60s. In the '80s and '90s, Los Mockers reached a much greater international audience than they did in their heyday via internationally distributed reissues of their mid-'60s work, and are widely respected by collectors as one of the best '60s garage groups. —*Richie Unterberger*

● **Los Mockers** / 1994 / Get Hip ◆◆◆◆
The best and most easily available of the several Los Mockers reissues that have appeared, built around their 1966 LP, with additional tracks from the '65–'67 era. No, of course, it's not nearly as good as the Rolling Stones. But it's fun, and much better than much of the (frequently inept) Stones-inspired U.S. garage music of the same era. —*Richie Unterberger*

Lothar & the Hand People

Group, Psychedelic
One of the weirder psychedelic groups of the late '60s, the New York-based Lothar & the Hand People took special pride in augmenting many of their tunes with the theremin, a then-futuristic instrument most famous for its use in horror movies (as well as the Beach Boys' "Good Vibrations"). Playing eccentric satirical rock, good-time folk-rock, and experimental psychedelia, their material wasn't nearly strong enough to elevate them to the rank of innovators. Although their first album is their best, they are most fondly remembered for the trance-inducing "Space Hymn," an FM radio favorite for many years. —*Richie Unterberger*

Presenting . . . Lothar & Hand People / 1994 / One Way ◆◆◆
This group may be one of the more fondly remembered psychedelic cult bands of the late '60s, but their debut album hasn't dated that well. Their determinedly freaky material has some period charm, but the songwriting and singing really aren't all that hot. There are other problems: the frequent use of "Lothar," the group's theremin, sounds gimmicky rather than futuristic. They vacillate between good-time New York psychedelia in the style of the Youngbloods (who did it much better) and satirical shock-rock of the Mothers (who also did it much better), and the styles don't mix especially well. What sounded adventurous and far-out at the time can be a bit flat and embarrassing out of the context of the era. The saving grace of the CD reissue is the addition of six bonus cuts from their first three singles. Of variable quality, they nonetheless show the Hand People playing it straighter and, for the most part, the psychedelic folk-rock on these rare tracks was more effective and tuneful than the material on their LPs. The undoubted highlight is the fabulous "L-O-V-E (Ask For It By Name)," an explosive slice of pop-psychedelia that ranks as one of the best hit-singles-that-never-were of the late '60s. —*Richie Unterberger*

Loud Family

Group, Alternative Pop/Rock, Power Pop/Anglo-Pop
After dissolving Game Theory, Scott Miller formed Loud Family, releasing their first album in early 1993. While the band continued the slightly experimental tendencies of the last Game Theory albums, it did so in a more concise power-pop setting. —*Stephen Thomas Erlewine*

● **Plants and Birds and Rocks and Things** / 1992 / Alias ◆◆◆◆
Former Game Theory frontman, Scott Miller, returns with a new band and his classic style of power-pop. With a sound similar to the experimental *Lolita Nation,* Miller builds on his former band's strong points while leaving behind much of its excesses. *Plants and Birds and Rocks and Things* will be pleasantly familiar to old fans and will no doubt inspire newcomers to seek out Game Theory albums. —*Chris Woodstra*

Tape of Only Linda / 1994 / Alias ◆◆◆

Love

Group, Psychedelic, Folk-Rock
Even revisionist rock criticism has overlooked the accomplishments of Arthur Lee and Love, one of the greatest groups to emerge from the psychedelia-shrouded scene of mid-'60s Los An-

geles. Their early work fused sharp pop hooks with the wiry crunch of early punk, producing instant classics such as "My Little Red Book" and "Seven and Seven Is;" you can hear Lee laying the groundwork for West Coast groups like the Doors and Moby Grape. By the late '60s, Lee moved the group into druggy psychedelic territory; 1967's *Forever Changes* is their best album, a symphonic explosion of lush, orchestrated textures and surreal lyrics. Surprisingly, the album still sounds fresh and innovative. —*John Floyd*

○ **Love** / 1966 / Elektra ◆◆◆◆
Their debut is both their hardest-rocking early album, and their most Byrds-influenced. Lee's songwriting muse hadn't fully developed at this stage, and in comparison with their second and third efforts, this is the least striking of the LPs featuring their classic lineup, with some similar-sounding folk-rock compositions and stock riffs. A few of the tracks are great, though: their punky rendition of Bacharach/David's "My Little Red Book" was a minor hit, "Signed D.C." and "Mushroom Clouds" were superbly moody ballads, and Bryan Maclean's "Softly To Me" served notice that Lee wasn't the only songwriter of note in the band. —*Richie Unterberger*

○ **Da Capo** / 1967 / Elektra ◆◆◆◆
Love broadened their scope into psychedelia on their sophomore effort, Lee's achingly melodic songwriting gifts reaching full flower. The six songs that comprised the first side of this album when it was first issued are a truly classic body of work, highlighted by the atomic blast of pre-punk "Seven and Seven Is" (their only hit single), the manic jazz tempos of "Stephanie Knows Who," and the enchanting "She Comes in Colors," perhaps Lee's best composition (and reportedly the inspiration for the Rolling Stones' "She's A Rainbow"). It's only half a great album, though; the seventh and final track, "Revelation," is a tedious 19-minute jam which keeps *Da Capo* from attaining truly classic status. —*Richie Unterberger*

★ **Forever Changes** / 1967 / Elektra ◆◆◆◆◆
It wasn't a hit, but *Forever Changes* continues to regularly appear on critics' lists of the top ten rock albums of all time, and it had an enormously far-reaching and durable influence that went way beyond chart listings. The best fusion of folk-rock and psychedelia, it featured Lee's trembling vocals, beautiful melodies, haunting orchestral arrangements, and inscrutable but poetic lyrics, all of which sound nearly as fresh and intriguing upon repeated plays. One of rock's most organic, flowing masterpieces, every song has a lingering, shimmering beauty, including the two penned by the band's other talented songwriter/guitarist/singer, Bryan Maclean. —*Richie Unterberger*

Four Sail / 1969 / Elektra ◆◆
Lee & Love started to lose focus by turning on the volume by this album. Hardly memorable. —*Jeff Tamarkin*

Out Here / 1969 / One Way ◆◆
Out *there* would have been more like it. This quasi-metal hour-plus recording had little in common with earlier Love. —*Jeff Tamarkin*

Love Revisited / 1970 / Elektra ◆◆◆

False Start / 1970 / One Way ◆◆◆
Clearly influenced by Hendrix at this stage, Arthur Lee began to lose sight of what Love once was. Some sparks but mostly misfires. Appropriately titled. —*Jeff Tamarkin*

Love Masters / 1973 / Elektra ◆◆◆

Reel to Real / 1974 / RSO ◆◆◆

Best of Love / 1980 / Rhino ◆◆◆

Love Live / Studio / 1982 / One Way ◆◆
Just like the title says—some live Fillmore East tracks and some studio stragglers. Nothing special. —*Jeff Tamarkin*

○ **Best of: Golden Archive Series** / 1986 / Rhino ◆◆◆◆
Well-chosen collection of Love's most celebrated tracks makes a case for Arthur Lee and company as one of the most creative, intense West Coast '60s rock bands. —*Jeff Tamarkin*

Out There / 1988 / Big Beat ◆◆◆

● **Love Story** / 1995 / Rhino ◆◆◆◆
Double-CD box contains most of their classic first three albums (including the entirety of *Forever Changes*), all three non-LP tracks from their 1966–68 prime, and highlights of the post-Bryan Maclean albums from the late '60s and early '70s. Great booklet of

liner notes and photos, but considering that all of those first three albums remain easy to find, and that the post-*Forever Changes* material is much inferior to the early recordings, it's not an essential purchase. The absence of "Revelation" from *Da Capo* is no big deal, but a few tracks from the debut are missing, including one of the better ones, "Mushroom Clouds." — *Richie Unterberger*

Love and Rockets

Group, Alternative Pop/Rock
Love and Rockets comprised guitarist/vocalist Daniel Ash, bassist/vocalist David J, and drummer Kevin Haskins, all former members of the pioneering goth band Bauhaus. However, the group didn't sound very similar to their first group. Instead, Love and Rockets emphasized the strains of psychedelia and glam rock that appeared underneath Bauhaus' gloomy drone, adding elements of pop songcraft, folk and R&B, as well as cryptic, self-important lyrics. For most of the late '80s, the group had a devoted cult following, resulting in a surprise Top Ten hit single, "So Alive," in 1989. During the early '90s, the group's audience steadily declined, although they still retained a number of loyal fans.

After Bauhaus broke up in 1983, David J recorded a solo album and collaborated with the Jazz Butcher, while Daniel Ash concentrated on a side-project, Tones on Tail. Haskins soon joined Tones on Tail, but the group folded in 1984. Haskins and Ash then attempted to reunite Bauhaus. David J agreed to the project but the band's lead vocalist Peter Murphy refused. Instead of pursuing an incomplete Bauhaus reunion, Ash, J, and Haskins formed Love and Rockets, taking their name from the underground comic book written by Jaime and Gilbert Hernandez.

Love and Rockets released their first album, *Seventh Dream of Teenage Heaven*, in 1985; it received mixed reviews but it began to build their following. *Express*, released the following year, was more successful, charting in both the U.S. and the U.K. On *Earth Sun Moon* (1987) the band retreated to more atmospheric musical territory, with the notable exception of the alternative/college radio hit "No New Tale to Tell," which helped the increase the group's fan base. *Love and Rockets*, released in 1989, broke the band into the mainstream, thanks to the T. Rex-inspired Top Ten single "So Alive." The album was nearly as successful, breaking into the Top 15 and going gold.

After the success of *Love and Rockets*, the members of the band concentrated on solo projects for nearly half a decade. Love and Rockets returned to recording in 1994 with *Hot Trip to Heaven*, which failed to make any inroads on the pop or alternative charts. — *Stephen Thomas Erlewine*

Seventh Dream of Teenage Heaven / 1985 / Beggars Banquet ✦✦✦
This album is filled with the dark, acoustic-driven work hinted at in their previous group, Bauhaus. — *Steve Aldrich*

○ **Express** / 1986 / Big Time ✦✦✦✦

● **Earth, Sun, Moon** / 1987 / Big Time ✦✦✦✦
Another solid LP. — *Steve Aldrich*

Love and Rockets / 1989 / Beggars Banquet ✦✦✦
Featured is their only US hit, "So Alive." — *Steve Aldrich*

Hot Trip To Heaven / 1994 / Warner Brothers ✦✦
Returning from a four-year absence, Love and Rockets attempts to update their sound with *Hot Trip To Heaven*. Adding several elements of the British house and ambient dance scenes to their sound doesn't make Love and Rockets sound hip. Instead, they sound like they're trying to figure out what the hell is going on. — *Stephen Thomas Erlewine*

Love Sculpture

Group, Blues Rock, Art-Rock/Progressive-Rock, Roots-Rock
A British blues-rock band of the late '60s that, despite being very good, would normally be relegated to footnote status if it were not for the fact that the lead guitarist of this trio was the soon-to-be-famous Dave Edmunds. Like many similar bands of the times, Love Sculpture was really a showpiece for Edmunds's guitar playing talents (which on the first LP are considerable), and little else. The covers are well chosen, slightly revved-up, but mostly reverent versions of blues classics. They had a fluke hit in 1968 with a cover of the classical piece "Sabre Dance" rearranged for guitar. After two LPs, Love Sculpture split up in 1970. Edmunds went on to solo success ("I Hear You Knockin' ") and a long, sometimes contentious re-

lationship with ex-Brinsley Schwarz bassist Nick Lowe, which culminated in the great band Rockpile. Still, Love Sculpture, though slightly dated, is a hoot to listen to today. And Edmunds, full of youthful bravado and dazzling technique, certainly knows his way up and down a fretboard. — *John Dougan*

○ **Blues Helping** / 1968 / Rare Earth ✦✦✦✦
As hyperkinetic blues albums by White English kids go, this is a good one. Dave Edmunds, armed only with a 1959 Gibson 335 and a 100-watt Marshall stack, cranks through these recognizable blues covers (with one original instrumental) with reckless abandon and gobs of technique. Backup support is handled by bassist John Williams and drummer Congo Jones, who do their best to keep up and provide a rhythmic foundation for Edmunds to wail over. Edmunds also handled nearly all the vocals, and as blues singers go, he's merely serviceable, but what makes this LP worthwhile is the revved-up guitar playing, especially when Edmunds shreds both Freddy King's "The Stumble" and Willie Dixon's "Wang Dang Doodle." — *John Dougan*

Forms & Feelings / 1969 / Parrot ✦✦✦

● **Singles A&B's** / 1990 / Harvest ✦✦✦✦

Darlene Love (Darlene Wright)

b. Jul. 26, 1938
R&B, Girl-Group
Amazingly, Darlene Love, a superb vocalist, hasn't had much of a track record as a solo singer, at least not in terms of hits. Love was a founding member of the Blossoms in 1957. They did several sessions and were resident singers on the television show *Shindig*. Love sang lead vocals on "He's a Rebel," which was credited to the Crystals, and "Zip-A-Dee-Doo-Dah," which was issued as Bob B.Soxx and the Bluejeans. She cut six singles for Spector's Phillies label, with "Wait Till My Bobby Gets Back Home" the most successful. Love became busy as an actress, but reunited with Spector for the 1977 single "Lord, if You're a Woman." Love appeared in all three *Lethal Weapon* films, and was also in the Royal Shakespeare Company's co-production of Stephen King's *Carrie*. Her 1990 LP, *Paint Another Picture*, failed to chart in America. Love later toured as a background vocalist with Cher. She appeared briefly on the soap opera *Another World* in 1993. — *Ron Wynn*

● **The Best of Darlene Love** / 1992 / ABKCO ✦✦✦✦
A terrific compilation of Love's Phil Spector-produced hits, it includes "(Today I Met) The Boy I'm Gonna Marry," "Wait Till My Bobby Gets Back Home" and the hits she sang for the Crystals, "He's a Rebel" and "He's Sure the Boy I Love." — *AMG*

The Loved Ones [Aus]

Group, Garage Rock
No relation to the '90s U.S. mod-revival band the Loved Ones, in 1966 and 1967, the Loved Ones recorded some of the best Australian rock singles of the '60s: "The Loved One," "Sad Dark Eyes," and "Everlovin' Man." A rock/R&B combo in the spirit of the early Animals and Them, with maybe some Pretty Things and garage drive mixed in, the Melbourne group were led by singer Gerry Humphreys' dark, anguished delivery. A moody angst hovers over their best songs, and may well have been an influence on another Melbourne lad, Nick Cave, especially the neurotic howl of "Sad Dark Eyes." The Loved Ones played more traditionally on the rest of their material, sticking closer to R&B conventions, although a sense of brooding mystery is found throughout their slim recorded repertoire. — *Richie Unterberger*

● **Magic Box** / 1985 / Raven ✦✦✦✦
13 studio tracks from 1966-67, including "The Loved One," "Sad Dark Eyes," and "Everlovin' Man," as well as three previously unreleased live cuts from the same era. The rest of the material is usually less fearsome and innovative, though much of it still carries an air of subdued menace. — *Richie Unterberger*

Loverboy

Group, Hard Rock, Pop/Rock
With a string of three multi-platinum albums, Loverboy was one of the most successful mainstream hard rock groups of the early '80s. Comprised of vocalist Mike Reno, guitarist Paul Dean, bassist Scott Smith, keyboardist Doug Johnston, and drummer Matthew Frenette, the band formed in Toronto, Canada, in 1980 and immediately signed with CBS Records. Later that year, their Bruce Fairbairn-produced debut album appeared. Featuring the slick, hard-

rocking singles "Turn Me Loose" and "The Kid Is Hot Tonite," the album went platinum in both Canada and America.

Loverboy recorded the follow-up, *Get Lucky*, in 1981. Driven by the anthemic "Working for the Weekend," the Fairbairn-produced record was a major success in the U.S. and Canada, yet it failed to gain an audience anywhere in Europe. Nevertheless, the band was a staple on AOR stations across North America, as well as a popular concert attraction. The band's good fortunes continued with the 1983 album *Keep It Up*. Again, Loverboy worked with Fairbairn, who kept their melodic yet tough sound intact; the album featured the hit single "Hot Girls In Love."

Loverboy's fortunes began to slip with 1985's *Lovin' Every Minute of It*, which was produced by Tom Allom (Judas Priest). Allom gave the band a harder edge, which didn't prove as commercially successful as their past records; nevertheless, the band's fans managed to make the album go platinum. Fairbairn returned from working with Bon Jovi to produce 1987's *Wildside*, yet the combination didn't prove as potent as before. After an extensive two year tour, the band returned to Canada. In 1989, the greatest-hits record, *Big Ones*, was released. The same year Reno and Dean announced plans to make solo records, which effectively put an end to the group. —*Stephen Thomas Erlewine*

○ **Loverboy** / 1980 / Columbia ✦✦✦✦
Their debut, with guitar-heavy pop-metal, included the Top 40 hit "Turn Me Loose" and the signature Loverboy tune, "The Kid Is Hot Tonite." —*Donna DiChario*

○ **Get Lucky** / 1981 / Columbia ✦✦✦✦
Although occasionally over-blown, songs like "Lucky Ones" and "Working for the Weekend" were made for blasting on the radio. —*Donna DiChario*

○ **Keep It Up** / 1983 / Columbia ✦✦✦✦
Loverboy kept up their string of multi-platinum albums with their third record, *Keep It Up*. Although it wasn't as consistent as *Get Lucky*, its finest moments were as good as anything on its predecessor, including the driving "Hot Girls in Love" and the Top 40 hit "Queen of the Broken Hearts." —*Stephen Thomas Erlewine*

Lovin' Every Minute of It / 1985 / Columbia ✦✦✦
While it was another platinum album, *Lovin' Every Minute of It*, was slightly weaker than Loverboy's first three records, due to a slip in songwriting quality. Although hits like "Lovin' Every Minute of It," "Dangerous," and "This Could Be the Night" were well-constructed arena-rock numbers, none of the album tracks were quite as catchy, resulting in the group's weakest record since their debut. —*Stephen Thomas Erlewine*

Wildside / 1987 / Columbia ✦✦
Although it went gold, *Wildside* made it clear that Loverboy's polished hard rock formula was running out of gas. The band wasn't able to come up with strong hooks for most of the record, with the Top 40 hit "Notorious" providing the only memorable moment on the album. —*Stephen Thomas Erlewine*

○ **Big Ones** / 1989 / Columbia ✦✦✦✦
Loverboy's biggest and best hits include "Turn Me Loose" (#35), "Lovin' Every Minute of It" (#9), "This Could Be the Night" (#10), "Hot Girls in Love," "Heaven in Your Eyes," and "Working for the Weekend" (#29). —*AMG*

● **Loverboy Classics** / 1994 / Columbia ✦✦✦✦
Like *Big Ones*, *Loverboy Classics* doesn't contain all of the band's singles, but it does feature a greater selection of hits and album rock favorites, including Mike Reno's duet with Ann Wilson "Almost Paradise," making it a better introduction to the group. —*Stephen Thomas Erlewine*

Lyle Lovett

b. Nov. 1, 1957, Houston, TX
Country-Rock, Singer-Songwriter
Lyle Lovett represents the increasing diversity of country music as it recovers from a commercial slump in the '80s. Highly literate (he has degrees in journalism and German from Texas A&M), the Houston-born singer comes from the eclectic tradition of Western swing, as filtered through the work of such wry '70s songwriters as Guy Clark and Townes Van Zandt. Lovett has a dry but absurdly hilarious sense of humor, as expressed on his first recorded song, "If I Had a Boat." ("And if I had a pony, I'd ride him on my boat.") But he also writes bitingly of love relations, as in "God Will," in which the singer tells his lover that God will forgive her, but he won't, "and that's the difference between God and me." Despite

some success in the country market and a Grammy award in the country category, it has been questionable since at least Lovett's second album, *Pontiac*, that his music could be categorized as country. But it's so multigeneric, with elements of folk, jazz, blues, and, lately, gospel, that it's hard to say exactly where it fits. At bottom, he's a singer/songwriter—and an amazingly imaginative one at that. —*William Ruhlmann*

○ **Lyle Lovett** / 1986 / Curb ✦✦✦✦
Lyle Lovett has an ironic overview of the world, expressed in songs he sings with the dead seriousness of the true comic. But he also has a finely defined sense of romantic troubles that sometimes isn't funny at all. Songs like "God Will" and "If I Were the Man You Wanted" mark him as one of the best new writers of the decade. —*William Ruhlmann*

★ **Pontiac** / 1987 / Curb ✦✦✦✦✦
Lovett's best overall collection of songs includes the gently absurd "If I Had a Boat," the subtly murderous "L.A. County," and the Henny Youngman-style "She's No Lady," among other gems. —*William Ruhlmann*

○ **Lyle Lovett & His Large Band** / 1989 / Curb ✦✦✦✦
On his third album, Lovett continues to explore a synthesis of country and big band. Included is his version of Tammy Wynette's country classic on "Stand By Your Man" and the bittersweet "I Married Her Just Because She Looks Like You." —*Rick Clark*

○ **Joshua Judges Ruth** / 1992 / Curb ✦✦✦✦
Lyle Lovett goes folk-gospel. To be fair, the country tag was never a comfortable fit for Lovett's eclectic musings. *Joshua Judges Ruth* distances him from the category without firmly boxing him into any new ones. There is a southern-fried gospel feel throughout much of the album, even if it's sometimes irreverent. "Church" best displays Lovett's surreal, dry wit, recounting a hunger-driven church rebellion complete with full gospel backing vocals. "She's Leaving Me," featuring guest vocals from Emmylou Harris, is the one sop offered to traditional country. Overall, though, the mood is sombre bordering on bleak. Like the album cover and insert photos, *Joshua* deals in shades of grey and themes of loneliness and death. What one misses the most on this release is the infrequent surfacing of Lovett's weird, playful sense of humor. —*Roch Parisien*

I Love Everybody / 1994 / Curb ✦✦✦
A collection of odds and ends that Lyle Lovett has written over the years (some of the tunes date back to the late '70s), *I Love Everybody* doesn't have the self-conscious artistic importance of *Joshua Judges Ruth*, and it's all the better for it. Instead, Lovett offers a set of relaxed, casual songs, accentuating his infamous, off-kilter sense of humor ("Skinny Legs," "Penguins"). At the same time, the songs offer hints of Lovett's sly, subtle sense of menace, particularly "Creeps Like Me." —*Stephen Thomas Erlewine*

Lene Lovich

New Wave
One of the more offbeat and memorable figures is new wave, Lene Lovich certainly drew much of her widely varied approach from her unconventional early experiences. Born of Yugoslavian father and British mother, she spent much of her childhood in Detroit, MI. At age 13, she moved to Hull, England, with her mother. She ran away to London shortly thereafter, where she worked several odd jobs ranging from bingo caller to go-go dancer to street busker. Around this time, she developed an interest in art and theater, enrolling at the Central School of Art. She took up the saxophone and, after a brief stint in a soul-funk band (with future collaborator Les Chappell), Lovich wrote a string of songs for French disco star Cerrone. In 1978, Stiff Records signed her after hearing her first recording, a remake of "I Think We're Alone Now." She quickly became one of Stiff's brightest stars, headlining package tours and earning several U.K. hits over the next three years with the unforgettable "Lucky Number," "Say When," "Bird Song," and "New Toy." Unfortunately, her theatrical quirkiness didn't translate well into LP length and as new wave dissolved, she disappeared from the music scene. After an eight-year absence, she returned in 1990 with *March*. It failed to ignite any further interest and she again went into retirement. —*Chris Woodstra*

● **Stateless . . . Plus** / 1979 / Rhino ✦✦✦✦
Stateless, her aptly-titled 1978 debut, is a new wave cult classic. Featuring her offbeat vocals and quirky synth-heavy production, this is her finest moment. Includes the great single, "Lucky Num-

ber." Now reissued on CD as *Stateless...Plus* with five extra tracks and extensive liner notes. —*Chris Woodstra*

Flex...plus / 1980 / Rhino ◆◆◆
Flex shows Lovich staying true to her unique sound, though it is somewhat watered down with super slick production. Now reissued on CD with six extra tracks as *Flex...Plus.* Includes the classic "New Toy" (written by Thomas Dolby). —*Chris Woodstra*

New Toy / 1981 / Stiff ◆◆◆

No-Man's-Land / 1982 / Stiff ◆◆

March / 1990 / Pathfinder ◆◆

The Lovin' Spoonful
Group, Folk-Rock, Pop/Rock
Right on the tails of the Beau Brummels and the Byrds, the Lovin' Spoonful were among the first American groups to challenge the domination of the British Invasion bands in the mid-'60s. Leader and principal songwriter John Sebastian was a young veteran of the Greenwich Village folk scene when he formed the band in 1965 with Zal Yanovsky, who'd already played primitive folk-rock of a sort with future members of the Mamas & the Papas in the Mugwumps. Between mid-1965 and the end of 1967, the group were astonishingly successful, issuing one classic hit single after another, including "Do You Believe in Magic?," "You Didn't Have to Be So Nice," "Daydream," "Summer in the City," "Rain on the Roof," "Nashville Cats," and "Six O'Clock." Like most of the folk-rockers, the Lovin' Spoonful were more pop and rock than folk, which didn't detract from their music at all. Much more than the Byrds, and even more than the Mamas and the Papas, the group exhibited a brand of unabashedly melodic, cheery, and good-time music, though their best single, "Summer in the City," was uncharacteristically riff-driven and hard-driving. More influenced by blues and jugbands than other folk-rock acts, their albums were spotty and their covers at times downright weak. As glorious as their singles were, the group lacked the depth and innovation of the Byrds, their chief competitors for the crown of best folk-rock band, and their legacy hasn't been canonized with nearly as much reverence as their West Coast counterparts. The Lovin' Spoonful were torn asunder by a drug bust in 1967; Yanovsky left the band, and the group was already on the wane when Sebastian effectively closed the chapter by leaving in 1968. Sebastian went on to moderate success as a singer/songwriter in the 1970s. —*Richie Unterberger*

Do You Believe in Magic / 1965 / Kama Sutra ◆◆◆
Their incredible debut, highlighted by the title tune, with the still-apt line "It's like tryin' to tell a stranger 'bout rock 'n' roll." This is a very eclectic LP, with Sebastian classics including the title tune, the follow-up hit "Did You Ever Have To Make Up Your Mind?," and "Younger Girl," later a hit for The Critters, plus adaptations of classic country blues and even covers of Fred Neil and the Ronettes. The liner notes are by Peter Stampfel of the Holy Modal Rounders. —*Gary Mollica*

Whats up Tiger Lily [O.S.T.] / 1966 / Kama Sutra ◆◆
This marks one of the first times a rock band wrote the whole score for a movie that they weren't starring in. There's lots of whimsy, mostly instrumental, and it includes the hit "Pow." "Introduction to Flick" is a brief monologue from the film's producer, Woody Allen. —*Gary Mollica*

Hums / 1966 / Pair ◆◆◆
Their third "real" album, and their fourth in 13 months, is quieter than previous efforts. There are eleven Sebastian originals, three of which became huge hits: "Summer In the City," "You and Me and Rain On the Roof" (as it's called on the label), and "Nashville Cats," along with "Lovin' You," later a hit for Bobby Darin. The album also features tributes to Fred Neil ("Coconut Grove") and Howlin' Wolf ("Voodoo In My Basement"). —*Gary Mollica*

Daydream / May 1966 / One Way ◆◆◆
The band's second LP was very strong; this time, most of the tunes are originals, with the exception of a cover of "Bald Headed Lema." Joe and Zally are featured on some lead vocals, and the album includes two more hits, "You Didn't Have to Be So Nice" and "Didn't Want to Have to Do It." Strangely enough, this has been the only Spoonful LP reissued on CD in the States. —*Gary Mollica*

○ **Best of Lovin' Spoonful, Vol. 1** / 1967 / Kama Sutra ◆◆◆◆
This is a nice collection of a dozen hits and LP tracks from their first two LPs, plus "Summer In the City." The original pressings came with individual pinups of the Spoonful. —*Gary Mollica*

You're a Big Boy Now / 1967 / Kama Sutra ◆◆◆
At the ripe old age of 22, John Sebastian wrote his second film score, this time for Francis Ford Coppola's New York-based comedy. There are thirteen tunes, mostly instrumentals, with two more hits, the title tune and the gorgeous "Darling, Be Home Soon." This was the final LP with Zal. —*Gary Mollica*

Everything Playing / 1968 / Kama Sutra ◆◆
The Spoonful's "hippie" LP has a gentle, almost unfinished feeling to it. Only "Priscilla Millionaira" rocks out with the old Spoonful zaniness; in fact, Zal covered it on his only solo LP. This was the first album with Jerry Yester, the final album with Sebastian, and the first to feature non-Sebastian originals. It contains the hits "Six O'Clock," "She Is Still A Mystery," and "Money." —*Gary Mollica*

○ **Best of Lovin' Spoonful, Vol. 2** / 1968 / Kama Sutra ◆◆◆◆
A stopgap LP put out after Sebastian's departure, featuring eleven tunes from *Hums* and *Everything Playing*, plus "Darlin' Be Home Soon." —*Gary Mollica*

Revelation Revolution '69 / 1968 / Kama Sutra ◆◆
The band is billed here as "The Lovin' Spoonful Featuring Joe Butler." Just when everybody had written them off after Sebastian's departure, this flawed gem came out of left field. Joe's smooth voice had graced a few tracks on all of the past LPs, in addition to having a few of his own tunes included. He comes into his own here, but unfortunately, his three originals are the weakest songs on the LP, especially the ultra-hip sound collage "War Games." However, the great pop team of Bonner and Gordon came up with three strong tunes, including the hit "Me About You" (previously done by the Turtles) and the fine "(Till I) Run With You" (the title of the LP as written on the label), with John Stewart supplying the best track, the gorgeous "Never Going Back." —*Gary Mollica*

★ **Anthology** / 1990 / Rhino ◆◆◆◆◆
Unquestionably the finest collection of a major band that did much to launch American folk-rock in the mid-'60s. *Anthology* jams 26 cuts onto a single CD, including all of their hits and some of their strongest album tracks, drawing mostly from their 1965–66 prime. As for the more interesting non-smashes, these include the original version of John Sebastian's "Younger Girl," which was a hit in a more commercial version by the Critters; the minor 1967 hit "She Is Still A Mystery," a dreamily psychedelic number that holds its own with their other standards, but has somehow been forgotten by oldies radio; and "Good Time Music," recorded early in 1965 for an obscure Elektra sampler (and a small hit in a cover version by the Beau Brummels). The most overlooked find here is the instrumental "Lonely (Amy's Theme)," from the early Francis Ford Coppola film *You're a Big Boy Now,* a lushly orchestrated, melancholy tune featuring Sebastian's wistful harmonica. There are also little-known Sebastian originals, with vocals, from *You're a Big Boy Now* and Woody Allen's early screen venture *What's Up, Tiger Lily?* The accompanying booklet features comments from Sebastian himself about some of the group's most famous songs. —*Richie Unterberger*

Nick Lowe
b. Mar. 25, 1949, Suffolk, England
Rock & Roll, Country-Rock, New Wave
After the seminal pub rockers Brinsley Schwarz broke up in 1974, Nick Lowe let his love for pop music in all of its trashy, sleazy glory blossom. At a time most artists were concerned about making art, he concentrated on returning to the days when rock & roll was about nothing except love, sex, good times, and rock & roll. The only thing was, Lowe paid tribute to classic rock and pop by twisting their conventions around; he took standard themes and melodies and turned them inside out with a wicked sense of humor. Lowe never sounded dated because at his heart he was a punk—his early records are ragged and raw, positively overflowing with energy. As his career moved into the '80s, he lost that wreckless energy, but he always remained an outsider laughing at the mainstream.

Lowe moved to Stiff Records in 1976, Britain's first independent record label, after releasing several flop singles on Liberty/UA. The label's first record was his "So It Goes"/"Heart of the City" single; it cost 45 pounds to make. Lowe became the label's in-house producer and he was behind the boards for nearly every one of the label's singles during their early days; by the end of the decade, he had produced an impressive array of artists, including Elvis Costello, the Damned, Graham Parker, the Pretenders, and Dr. Feelgood. During this time he recorded his first solo album, 1978's

Jesus of Cool, which was retitled *Pure Pop for Now People* in the U.S.

By the time his debut was released, he had formed Rockpile with guitarist Dave Edmunds, drummer Terry Williams, and guitarist Billy Bremner; the band functioned as a touring band for Lowe and Edmunds, as well as providing support on their records. Lowe's next album, 1979's *Labour of Lust* was recorded with Rockpile; it contained his only hit, "Cruel to Be Kind." After recording one album in 1980, Rockpile disbanded. Lowe began to experiment with country and Tex-Mex music on his '80s albums, without ever abandoning pop; the records were more polished, but they sold fewer copies than his earlier albums. However, he produced successful records by Carlene Carter, John Hiatt, the Fabulous Thunderbirds, and Paul Carrack during the decade.

While his days as a genuine musical force may be behind him, Lowe's albums have been consistently strong and when he's at the top of his form, he's an utterly original and inventive pop songwriter; his best songs make wading through his mediocre material worthwhile. *—Stephen Thomas Erlewine*

★ **Pure Pop for Now People** / 1978 / Columbia ✦✦✦✦✦
A masterpiece from a year that was full of them, this offers the best glimpse into his sometimes demented and ear-catching world. *—John Floyd*

☆ **Labour of Lust** / 1979 / Demon ✦✦✦✦✦
The grooves are tighter here than before, mixing the roots-rock sensibilities of Rockpile with his love of a good pop hook. It contains several minor hits, including "Cruel to Be Kind." *—John Floyd*

Nick the Knife / 1982 / Demon ✦✦✦
Lowe's first album since the breakup of Rockpile was a casually rocking record that recalled his former band, which isn't surprising, considering that both Billy Bremner and Terry Williams provide instrumental support. *—Stephen Thomas Erlewine*

The Abominable Showman / 1983 / Demon ✦✦
On *The Abominable Showman,* Lowe's fascination with country music begins to assert itself on a collection of songs that only seems lighthearted. While songs like "We Want Action" and "Tanque Ray" are nothing more than solid pop/rockers, "Time Wounds All Heels," "Raging Eyes," "Wish You Were Here," and "(For Every Woman Who Ever Made a Fool of a Man There's a Woman Who Made a) Man of Fool" are exceptionally well-written songs, full of subtle emotional power and catchy melodies. *—Stephen Thomas Erlewine*

Nick Lowe & His Cowboy Outfit / 1984 / Demon ✦✦✦
Thanks to a strong backing band, *Nick Lowe and His Cowboy Outfit* is his most musically satisfying album since *Labour of Lust.* Throughout the record, Lowe touches on all kinds of roots-rock, from Tex-Mex and three-chord garage rock to country and pop. And the great majority of the songs—from originals like the organ-driven rocker "Half A Boy and Half A Man" and the sly pop of "God's Gift to Women" to the excellent covers "You'll Never Get Me Up in One of Those" and "Breakaway"—are simply irresistible. *—Stephen Thomas Erlewine*

○ **The Rose of England** / 1985 / Demon ✦✦✦✦
Lowe's second album with his Cowboy Outfit is an even better record than their previous collection. *The Rose of England* retains the band's low-key charm, but they now have a better set of songs to work with. Lowe's originals rank with his best material, and the covers, including Elvis Costello's "Indoor Fireworks" and John Hiatt's "She Don't Love Nobody," are perfectly suited to his style. *—Stephen Thomas Erlewine*

Pinker and Prouder Than Previous / 1988 / Demon ✦✦✦
Pinker and Prouder Than Previous is Nick Lowe's most relaxed and casual album to date, but it never sounds tossed off or careless. Instead, Lowe's subtle mastery of pop, rock, R&B, and country results in an unassuming and thoroughly enjoyable set of clever, well-written originals and fine covers. *—Stephen Thomas Erlewine*

● **Basher: the Best of Nick Lowe** / 1989 / Columbia ✦✦✦✦
A superb collection spanning Lowe's solo career, it has a smattering of Rockpile's sides tossed in. A fine introduction, but start with *Pure Pop for Now People. —John Floyd*

Party of One / 1990 / Reprise ✦✦
While Dave Edmunds' production makes *Party of One* Nick Lowe's sharpest-sounding record in years, his songwriting isn't as strong as it has been in the past. Only "(I Want to Build a) Jumbo Ark," "What's Shakin' On the Hill," and "I Don't Know Why You

Keep Me On" rank with his best material. *—Stephen Thomas Erlewine*

○ **The Wilderness Years** / 1991 / Demon ✦✦✦✦
A wildly entertaining collection of outtakes, demos, and forgotten singles, *The Wilderness Years* captures Nick Lowe at the top of his form. Even seemingly slight songs like "Let's Go to the Disco" and "Bay City Rollers We Love You" are rough, melodic pop gems. The disc also contains some of Lowe's best performances, including the demo "Fool Too Long," the reckless single "Heart of the City," the "erstwhile Stiff advertising jingle" "I Love My Label," and a sublime version of Sandy Posey's "Born A Woman." The sheer quantity of brilliant material on *The Wilderness Years* makes it worthwhile even for Lowe's most casual fans. *—Stephen Thomas Erlewine*

○ **The Impossible Bird** / 1994 / Upstart ✦✦✦✦
Nick Lowe's best records have always been full of clever lyrics and undeniable pop craftsmanship; the exception is *The Impossible Bird.* For most of the 1980s, Lowe had been appropriating country and R&B influences, but *The Impossible Bird* is where he fully incorporates those styles into his songwriting. Lowe doesn't abandon his gift for melody; "Soulful Wind" and "12-Step Program (To Quit You Babe)" are as catchy as anything he's ever written. The difference is haunting songs like "The Beast In Me" and "Withered On the Vine," two rich, sad, introspective numbers that Lowe would never have put on previous albums. And that's what makes *The Impossible Bird* his best album since *Labour of Lust*—it's the most focused, mature, personal music of his career, without a single throwaway. *—Stephen Thomas Erlewine*

L7

Group, Hard Rock, Alternative Pop/Rock
L7's heavy, punk-inflected, riff-oriented guitar grind—a mix of the Ramones, Motorhead, and Joan Jett—was what earned them a dedicated following of fans in the early '90s, not the fact that they were female. While the band is strongly feminist, they never let their rhetoric stand in the way of their roaring guitars. L7 always relies on the sheer sonic aggression of rock, not its lyrical power.

When the group was on Sub Pop early in the '90s, the band sounded punkier and more abrasive; signing to a major label didn't cause them to lose that aggression—they just had a better production, courtesy of Butch Vig (Nirvana, Smashing Pumpkins, Sonic Youth). Featuring "Pretend We're Dead," 1992's *Bricks Are Heavy* was a major alternative hit; their second major-label album, the coarse *Hungry for Stink,* was released right before L7 toured with 1994's Lollapalooza. *—Stephen Thomas Erlewine*

L7 / 1990 / Epitaph ✦✦✦
Not as abrasive as either Hole or Babes In Toyland, L7 takes the middle ground between punk and heavy metal, with mixed results. L7 isn't as aggressive as Hole's Courtney Love or as incendiary as Babes' Kat Bjelland, nor do they have the same blend of melodicism and noisy guitars as Nirvana, as "Pretend We're Dead" proves. For the most part, *Bricks Are Heavy* is anticlimactic and rather tame, with the occasional track (most notably "Everglade") hinting that L7 might be a major contender in the future. *—Stephen Thomas Erlewine*

○ **Smell the Magic** / Jul. 12, 1991 / Sub Pop ✦✦✦✦
A wonderfully abrasive set of thrashing guitars and growling vocals. *—Stephen Thomas Erlewine*

● **Bricks Are Heavy** / 1992 / Slash ✦✦✦✦
While their major-label debut is hampered by Butch Vig's rather tame production, it does show that L7 has some strong pop sensibilities underneath their burning guitars, as "Pretend We're Dead" and "Everglade" prove. *—Stephen Thomas Erlewine*

Hungry for Stink / 1994 / Slash/Reprise ✦✦✦
While L7 sounds tremendous on *Hungry for Stink,* the band has neglected to write any songs. But when you're caught in the middle of a massive guitar grind this good, songs don't matter much. *—Stephen Thomas Erlewine*

L.T.D.

Group, Funk, Urban
L.T.D. is a horn-driven R&B/funk band that formed in 1968 in North Carolina; the name is an acronym for Love, Togetherness, and Devotion. The ten-piece band featured Jeffrey Osborne as the lead vocalist. During the '70s, the band accumulated several hit singles, including "(Every Time I Turn Around) Back in Love

Again." Osborne left the group in 1980; he was replaced by Andre Ray and Leslie Wilson. Though they had one more hit album, 1981's *Love Magic*, they weren't able to replicate the success they had with Osborne. —*Bil Carpenter*

● **Classics, Vol. 27** / 1987 / A&M ◆◆◆◆
Includes '70s hard-funk and orchestrated ballads like "Love Ballad" (#20) and "(Every Time I Turn Around) I'm in Love Again" (#4). —*Bil Carpenter*

Lulu (Marie MacDonald McLaughlin Lawrie)

Group, British Invasion, Pop/Rock
Most Americans first heard of Lulu when she soared to the top of the charts with the pop ballad "To Sir with Love," the theme to the film of the same name, in 1967. Actually, the Scottish singer—born Marie McDonald McLaughlin Lawrie—had been a star in Britain since 1964, when she hit the Top Ten with a raucous version of "Shout." Lulu's mid-'60s recordings (which included a version of "Here Comes the Night" that preceded Them's hit rendition) were often surprisingly rowdy and R&B-influenced. Although she didn't match Dusty Springfield, her Brenda Lee-like rasp could be quite gutsy and soulful. Her career was headed in a determinedly middle-of-the-road direction by the late '60s, which saw her hosting a British variety show and marrying Bee Gee Maurice Gibb (they have since divorced). Recording intermittently ever since, she raised a few eyebrows by traveling to Muscle Shoals studios to record her 1970 album *New Routes*, and releasing a single of David Bowie tunes (which Bowie also played on and co-produced) in 1973. —*Richie Unterberger*

Something to Shout About / 1965 / Decca ◆◆◆
Reissue of a 1965 LP, with many bonus tracks. In the U.K., Lulu first reached stardom as a gutsy belter of R&B tunes, delivered with a maturity and soulfulness that belied her teenage years. This 20-song compilation of material from 1964 to 1966 is the best CD reissue of her early work, although it's missing some of her better cuts. It includes her two mid-'60s British Top Ten hits, a cover of the Isley Brothers' "Shout" and the midtempo pop/soul tune "Leave a Little Love." Elsewhere, you get the spunky "I'll Come Running Over," which features Jimmy Page on guitar, and a raunchy cover of the obscure Rolling Stones song "Surprise Surprise" (also featuring Page). Most intriguing of all is the original version of "Here Comes The Night," later a hit for Them. Lulu performs it as an overwrought, pull-out-the-stops orchestral ballad; it's not nearly as successful as Van Morrison's rendition, but it's worth hearing. Unfortunately, this compilation doesn't include her surprisingly superb cover of "Heat Wave" from the same era. —*Richie Unterberger*

From Lulu . . . with Love / 1967 / Parrot ◆◆◆
Rush-released by Parrot to capitalize on the success of "To Sir With Love," this album may have been deceptively titled—it doesn't include "To Sir with Love," and the material dates from the mid-'60s, before she switched labels to Epic. But it's nonetheless a pretty good cross-section of her early sides, which saw her concentrating on rock and R&B rather than orchestrated pop ballads. Besides the British hits "Shout" and "Leave A Little Love," it has Bert Berns' "Here Comes The Night," which she recorded before Them's hit version; "I'll Come Running," one of her raunchiest tracks, which features Jimmy Page on guitar; "Surprise, Surprise," an unlikely cover of an obscure Rolling Stones tune; and good gutsy covers of the Knickerbockers' "Lies," Jerry Butler and Curtis Mayfield's "She Will Break Your Heart," and Van McCoy's "Take Me As I Am." —*Richie Unterberger*

● **From Crayons to Perfume: The Best of Lulu** / 1994 / Rhino ◆◆◆◆
By far the most wide-ranging retrospective of a singer who never found the consistently good material that her considerable talents deserved. Starting with her 1964 British hit cover of "Shout," it also includes the number one single "To Sir with Love" and a few of her other British Top Ten hits from the '60s, including the nice '65 soul ballad "Leave a Little Love" and the chirpy 1967 Neil Diamond tune "The Boat That I Row" (the flipside of "To Sir with Love," which wasn't a hit at all in the U.K.). Unfortunately, it gives short shift to the raunchy R&B she recorded in the mid-'60s, but it does include the sadly neglected, moody "Dreary Nights and Rows" (penned by "To Sir with Love" author Mark London) and the Top 40 orchestrated ballad "Best of Both Worlds," co-arranged by future Led Zepper John Paul Jones. You also get nifty covers of Tim Rose's "Morning Dew" and Nilsson's "Without Him," along

with a few songs she recorded with Atlantic (some with the Dixie Flyers) that gave her more sympathetic soul material than she was accustomed to, including the hit "Oh Me Oh My." There's also her semi-legendary 1974 single "Watch That Man"/"The Man Who Sold the World," a double-sided 45 of David Bowie covers produced by Bowie himself, and the theme song to the James Bond film *The Man with the Golden Gun*. This 20-song compilation doesn't gather together all her fine material by any means, but it's the only one to cover most of her career. —*Richie Unterberger*

Luna

Group, Alternative Pop/Rock
After Dean Wareham disbanded Galaxie 500 in the early '90s, he formed Luna, which followed in the same dreamy, slow style of his previous group, except the new band had a tendency to accentuate their melodies more frequently; in short, it was a lot like the Velvet Underground's third album, but not in a bad way at all. —*Stephen Thomas Erlewine*

○ **Lunapark** / 1992 / Elektra ◆◆◆◆
Luna's first album doesn't sound that different from Galaxie 500, except that Dean Wareham's pop sensibilites come to the forefront with his new band, which makes *Lunapark* more enjoyable than most of his old band's albums. —*Stephen Thomas Erlewine*

● **Bewitched** / 1994 / Elektra ◆◆◆◆
While it doesn't sound all that much different than their debut, Luna's second album is a stronger record, featuring improved playing and songwriting. —*Stephen Thomas Erlewine*

Lunachicks

Group, Alternative Pop/Rock
Part feminist-inspired riot grrrl band, part gross-out performance art, part hard rock band, New York City's Lunachicks are tastelessly in-your-face and proud of it (the back cover of their LP *Binge and Purge* showed them covered in fake vomit). Fronted by Theo Kogan, whose onstage gear consists of platform shoes, short dresses, surreal makeup, and huge wigs, the L-Chicks grind out a reasonable, messy amalgam of Ramones/Dictators high energy guitar rock. Song subjects include trashy '70s TV icons ("Jan Brady"), suffering after consuming too much junk food ("Binge and Purge"), and tabloid-style hysteria ("Babysitters on Acid"). Not particularly artful, the Lunachicks are wild and funny, and the music can be pretty hot, but the humor and the rock don't hold up after repeated spins. No matter what your tolerance for this kind of rock is, you'd be better off listening to L7, Bratmobile, Bikini Kill, Joan Jett or Huggy Bear first, and then finding time for the mixed blessings of the Lunachicks. —*John Dougan*

Lunachicks / 1989 / Plan 9/Caroline ◆◆◆
Babysitters on Acid / 1990 / Blast First ◆◆◆
● **Binge & Purge** / 1993 / Plan 9/Caroline ◆◆◆◆

Luscious Jackson

Group, Alternative Pop/Rock
With their dark hip-hop-influenced rock, Luscious Jackson recreates the dense, multi-cultural bohemian world of New York in a collage of sound, where Spanish guitars, jazzy keyboards, funky beats, and breathy vocals combine into one. Like the Beastie Boys, Luscious Jackson eclecticism doesn't acknowledge boundaries; instead, it takes freely from every kind of music, creating an amaglam that is distinctive and original. With their critically acclaimed 1993 debut EP, *In Search of Manny*, they earned a cult following; their first full-length album, 1994's *Natural Ingredients*, was even more eclectic and received terrific reviews. —*Stephen Thomas Erlewine*

● **In Search of Manny** / Oct. 11, 1993 / Grand Royal ◆◆◆◆
A darkly beautiful atmospheric EP where hip-hop is used as a basis for the folk-tinged songs, which paint detailed, textured portraits of the New York bohemian slacker scene. An impressive debut from this New York quartet. —*Stephen Thomas Erlewine*

○ **Natural Ingredients** / 1994 / Capitol ◆◆◆◆
Luscious Jackson's first full-length album, *Natural Ingredients*, features a brighter, more open sound than *In Search of Manny*, without losing the funky, organic feel of the EP. Musically, the band continued to refine their hip-hop influenced pop, adding stronger hooks and denser grooves. *Natural Ingredients* isn't as consistent or edgy as *In Search of Manny*, but the record fulfills their initial promise. —*Stephen Thomas Erlewine*

Lush

Group, Alternative Pop/Rock
Few bands live up to their names; Lush, however, does so in spades. Paced by Miki Berenyi's paper-thin voice (so thin you'll think she's on a respirator), Lush literally builds its music on a mountain of strummed guitars that approximates a rush of lava. Strong songwriting removes any tedium. —*John Dougan*

Sear / 1989 / Nesak ✦✦✦

○ **Gala** / 1990 / 4AD ✦✦✦✦
A little of it goes a long way, but this is where Lush shines. By this time, their pop craft was developed enough to warrant repeated listenings. Fans of folkie-style guitar, albeit with a touch more volume, will love this. —*John Dougan*

Mad Love / 1990 / Nesak ✦✦✦
This four-song EP captures Lush's sound well. —*Dan Heilman*

● **Spooky** / 1992 / 4AD ✦✦✦✦
While Lush features fragile, dual-female vocals layered over hypnotic melodies, the group has always taken a minimalist approach to its music. The vocal tracks are just as likely to be wedded to fuzzy guitar riffs and pounding rhythms. Everything kind of blurs and merges together in an urgent, often disturbing mix that belies the vocal sweetness. There are exceptions. Lush softens its stance on several fragile acoustic tracks, notably "Tiny Smiles," "For Love," and "Monochrome." Then like a shattered mirror, "Superblast!" and "Laura" offer a harsher extreme, shards of glass splintering through the songs without mercy. While Lush's bittersweet soundscapes will never grace mainstream dance floors or Top-40 radio, *Spooky* does make fascinating listening under headphones in the dark. —*Roch Parisien*

○ **Split** / 1994 / Warner Brothers ✦✦✦✦
Featuring improved songwriting and catchier, more muscular hooks, *Split* rivals *Spooky* as Lush's best album. —*Stephen Thomas Erlewine*

Frankie Lymon & the Teenagers

Group, Doo-Wop
Frankie Lymon (1942–1968) & the Teenagers were a New York doo-wop group consisting of Joe Negroni, Herman Santiago, Jimmy Merchant, and Sherman Garnes but centered around the extraordinary talents of their lead singer, thirteen-year-old Frankie Lymon. Lymon wrote their first big hit, "Why Do Fools Fall in Love." His wise-beyond-his-years vocal and performing abilities not only made the Teenagers a group several notches above the competition but made Lymon the first Black teenage pop star. Though only together for a brief 18-month period, Lymon & the Teenagers exerted an enormous influence, spawning several "kid" vocal groups and providing initial inspiration to Berry Gordy to model his entire Motown production approach around Lymon's original vocal style. Inexplicably, the group split into two factions at the height of their success, and neither had a hit again. Lymon died from a drug overdose at age 26. Diana Ross, Smokey Robinson, Len Barry, and his principal protégé, Michael Jackson (whose early recordings with the Jackson 5 are virtual re-creations of the early Lymon sound, merely updated) all show the influence of Frankie Lymon & the Teenagers's groundbreaking work. —*Cub Koda*

At the London Palladium / 1958 / Collectables ✦✦✦
An interesting live date featuring one of the truly tragic stories in American popular music annals. Frankie Lymon and the Teenagers capsulized what rock and roll was all about in the days before it became a corporate industry. Label head George Goldner was already producing Lymon as a single act when they toured London in 1957 and performed the concerts on this album. It's clear that there was far from a focused, cohesive operation by this time. This has been out of print for many years, although it was briefly back in circulation in England during the '70s. —*Ron Wynn*

○ **Frankie Lymon & Teenagers** / Aug. 1987 / Murray Hill ✦✦✦✦
This out-of-print five-record boxed set was obviously aimed at the hardcore fan and collector, and should be sought by those with more than a passing interest. —*Jeff Tamarkin*

★ **The Best of Frankie Lymon & the Teenagers** / 1990 / Rhino ✦✦✦✦✦
Frankie Lymon wrote "Why Do Fools Fall in Love?" at 13 and led his group, the Teenagers, to a brief stardom. They remain one of the finest examples of New York vocal group singing, and all of the essentials are on this album. —*Jeff Tamarkin*

Frankie Lymon & the Teenagers / 1994 / Bear Family ✦✦✦
Live, Rare & Unreleased / Live Gold ✦✦✦
A collection of 17 rare tracks. This isn't for everyone but will thrill the Lymon aficionado. —*Jeff Tamarkin*

The Complete / Bear Family ✦✦✦

Louie Lymon & the Teenchords

Group, R&B, Doo-Wop
Led by Lewis Lymon, the little brother of the far more successful Frankie Lymon, the Teenagers-soundalike, Teenchords, cut some solid singles beginning with 1956's "I'm So Happy" for the Fury logo. They also appeared in the 1957 movie *Jamboree*. —*Bill Dahl*

● **I'm So Happy** / 1992 / Relic ✦✦✦✦
Right off master tapes, this CD collects their complete output for Bobby Robinson's Fury label, 1956–1958. It features the title track, "Honey Honey," "Lydia," "I'm Not Too Young to Fall in Love," and "Your Last Chance." Classic examples of the mid-'50s "kiddie group" sound. —*Cub Koda*

○ **Meet the Kodaks** / Collectables ✦✦✦✦
A textbook example of concept albums pairing doo-wop vocal groups in shared settings. The Kodaks edge the Teen Chords on this one. —*Ron Wynn*

Lynch Mob

Group, Hard Rock, Heavy Metal
After Dokken broke up in 1989, George Lynch formed his own band, the Lynch Mob, with Dokken drummer Mick Brown. The band went through several personnel shifts and failed to meet commercial and sometimes musical expectations. Lynch called it quits and devoted his time to a 1993 solo album and a Dokken reunion record in 1995. —*Steve Huey*

Lynch Mob / 1992 / Elektra ✦✦✦

● **Wicked Sensation** / Elektra ✦✦✦✦
Ex-Dokken guitarist George Lynch and his new band sound a lot harder than Dokken. A great album as a band, it's not simply a showcase for Lynch. —*John Book*

Barbara Lynn

b. Jan. 16, 1942
Soul, R&B
A bluesy southpaw guitarist from Beaumont, TX, Barbara Lynn Ozen wrote her own ticket to hitdom with the 1962 smash "You'll Lose a Good Thing," an R&B chart-topper. Texas producer Huey Meaux brought Lynn to Cosimo's studio in New Orleans to cut the atmospheric downbeat tune, her debut single on the Jamie label. Followups included the bouncy "Oh! Baby (We Got a Good Thing Goin')"—better remembered through the Rolling Stones' faithful cover—and her minor 1966 hit on the often-covered "You Left the Water Running." Lynn remains active, currently recording for Antone's. Barbara Lynn resurfaced again in 1994, this time recording for Bullseye Blues. Her CD *So Good* included a new version of "This Is the Thanks I Get," but no reprise of "You'll Lose a Good Thing." —*Bill Dahl*

○ **You'll Lose a Good Thing** / 1962 / Jamie ✦✦✦✦
Barbara Lynn Ozen's smoky voice and fine guitar playing was one of the better blends of soul vocals and blues embellishment. Huey P. Meaux produced this early-'60s record, which featured the classic title track. Other Lynn numbers, like "I'll Suffer," were equally outstanding; Lynn was sometimes tough and confrontational, and tender, inviting or anguished at other times. Meaux didn't clutter the works with unnecessary firepower; his arrangements and charts were just enough to augment Lynn's sturdy vocals. Lynn also wrote ten of the 12 songs. —*Ron Wynn*

Good Thing / 1962 / Good Thing ✦✦✦
Sister of Soul / 1964 / Jamie ✦✦✦
Here Is / 1968 / Atlantic ✦✦✦
Guitarist and vocalist Barbara Lynn's Atlantic recordings have been recycled many times, including this recent import compilation. The mastering is good and the selection thorough, but a better choice might be the original Atlantic LP or any Japanese repo that's available. You can't go wrong with any collection that contains "You'll Lose A Good Thing," "I'll Suffer" and the other Atlantic classics. —*Ron Wynn*

○ **Barbara Lynn** / 1989 / Goodthing ✦✦✦✦
Yet another Barbara Lynn anthology, this one is more complete than its counterparts in that it includes her material on Jamie and other labels, as well as the Atlantic hits. Lynn actually recorded "You'll Lose A Good Thing" for Jamie, but it was later included on an Atlantic release. This has 17 songs from Jamie, Atlantic and Tribe sessions, including some that weren't big hits but should have been, like "This Is The Thanks I Get" and "It's Better To Have It." —*Ron Wynn*

So Good / 1993 / Bullseye Blues ✦✦
It's been a long time since Lynn has made a satisfying album, although she's given it a shot a few times. While this isn't flawless, it's a step in the right direction. The material isn't merely remakes or soul covers, but also includes a good version of Babyface's "I Love You Babe." Of course, Lynn couldn't desert classic soul, and she gives solid treatments to her own hit "This Is The Thanks I Get" and Tyrone Davis' "Can I Change My Mind." The familiar guitar riffs buttress her vocals, which still sound authoritative, even if the range and luster aren't quite as arresting. —*Ron Wynn*

● **Best of Barbara Lynn: The Atlantic Years** / 1994 / Ichiban/Soul Classics ✦✦✦✦
This 20-track collection gathers most of Lynn's output for Atlantic between 1968 and 1973, including most of her 1968 *Here Is Barbara Lynn* album and several non-LP singles. Commercially, Lynn's stay at Atlantic was not fruitful, yielding only a couple moderate R&B hits, the self-penned "This Is The Thanks I Get" and "Until Then, I'll Suffer" (both included). Artistically, this is fairly solid period soul, but a bit faceless. It seems as though Atlantic tried to fit Lynn into current soul trends; many of the 1968 tracks are quite derivative of Motown, and many of the later sides take a Memphis/Muscle Shoals approach. Those are fine influences, of course, but Lynn's strengths were her original songwriting and bluesy Southern phrasing. The most outstanding tracks are from her first Atlantic single, "This Is The Thanks I Get" and "Ring Telephone Ring," when much of her original relaxed Texas/New Orleans R&B style was still in evidence. The version of "You'll Lose A Good Thing" here, incidentally, is a remake, not the original 1962 hit. —*Richie Unterberger*

Lynyrd Skynyrd

Group, Southern Rock
From the time of their initial 1970 Sheffield, AL, demos to their tragic plane crash on Oct 20, 1977, the Jacksonville, FL, band Lynyrd Skynyrd fused the spirit of rock & roll with the truth and lyrical directness of great country music.

Lynyrd Skynyrd possessed a highly arranged approach to organizing their material. They also featured a powerful lead-guitar triumvirate in Allen Collins, Gary Rossington, and Ed King (later replaced by Steve Gaines), which augmented lead-singer/songwriter Ronnie Van Zant's no-nonsense tales of the common man's exploits.

Skynyrd was discovered playing in an Atlanta club by Blood, Sweat & Tears-founder Al Kooper in 1972. Kooper signed them to his new Sounds of the South record label and released *Pronounced Leh'Nerd Skin-Nerd* (#27), which included the classic "Freebird" (#19-1975/#38-1977), one of the most requested songs in rock history.

The band, which drew heavily from the hard English blues-rock sound (Free, Cream, Stones), had the good fortune to have a fan in the Who's Pete Townshend, who requested that Skynyrd open for the 1973 *Quadrophenia* tour. As a result, the band developed a strong fan base early in their career.

"Sweet Home Alabama" (#8) from *Second Helping* (#12) was the band's biggest single. Other singles included "Saturday Night Special" (#27), "What's Your Name?" (#13), "Double Trouble" (#80), and "You Got That Right" (#69).

Survivors of the 1977 plane crash played in various amalgamations (Rossington-Collins Band, Allen Collins Band, etc.). Lynyrd Skynyrd re-formed for a Tribute tour in 1987. After the tour, the reunited band began recording; they have since released a handful of albums. —*Rick Clark*

○ **Pronounced Leh'Nerd Skin-Nerd** / 1973 / MCA ✦✦✦✦
With the release of this debut album, Skynyrd was immediately recognized as one of the South's premier bands. The album's highlight is "Freebird," a song that, over time, has become one of the most requested rock songs in the history of radio. "Simple Man,"

"Gimmie Three Steps," and "Tuesday's Gone" are several other standards from this classic album. —*Rick Clark*

☆ **Second Helping** / 1974 / MCA ✦✦✦✦✦
The appropriately titled followup to their debut was equally impressive, containing their highest-charting hit, "Sweet Home Alabama" (#8). Unlike many albums, where the hit is the highlight, *Second Helping* is chock full of great tunes like "Working for MCA," "Call Me the Breeze," "Don't Ask Me No Questions," and "Ballad of Curtis Loew." —*Rick Clark*

Nuthin' Fancy / 1975 / MCA ✦✦✦
Frazzled by too much endless roadwork and too little songwriting preparation, *Nuthin' Fancy* is a step down from its impressive predecessor. Nevertheless, "Saturday Night Special," the album's opener, is a classic rocker. Other standouts include the Free-style "On the Hunt," "Whiskey Rock-A-Roller," and "Am I Losin'." —*Rick Clark*

Gimme Back My Bullets / 1976 / MCA ✦✦✦
On their first production with the legendary Tom Dowd (Rod Stewart, Eric Clapton, Allman Brothers), Skynyrd sounds relatively uninspired, even as they indignantly call for a return to platinum status with the Free-influenced title cut. Nevertheless, Van Zant's gift for plain-speaking lyrics and the band's undeniable chemistry help this record hold up better than many late-'70s AOR rock acts. —*Rick Clark*

One More from the Road / 1976 / MCA ✦✦✦
Recorded at Atlanta's Fox Theater and produced by Tom Dowd, Skynyrd returned to their original three-guitar lineup concept with the addition of Steve Gaines. Some might complain that *One More* failed to capture the energy of the band's shows, but overall it ranks as one of rock's finest live releases. Unfortunately, MCA abridged the CD, cutting out some key tracks and dialog. —*Rick Clark*

○ **Street Survivors** / 1977 / MCA ✦✦✦✦
The addition of lead guitarist and singer Steve Gaines goaded Ronnie Van Zant and the band into a dramatic rebirth. *Street Survivors* featured tighter songs, strong melodies, and an exciting element of vocal interplay between Van Zant and Gaines ("You Got That Right"). The contrast between Gaines's clean lead style, Collins's flash, and Rossington's thick-toned lyrical phrasing is something to behold. Without a doubt, it's Skynyrd's most cohesive body of work since *Second Helping*. —*Rick Clark*

Skynyrd's First and . . . Last / 1978 / MCA ✦✦✦
Pre-Al Kooper Skynyrd, recorded in Muscle Shoals, it may not be their best work, but shows without a doubt that this Jacksonville band was already heads and shoulders above many major-label bands, even before they were signed. —*Rick Clark*

★ **Gold & Platinum** / 1980 / MCA ✦✦✦✦✦
Compiled by Gary Rossington and Allen Collins after their tragic 1977 plane crash, *Gold & Platinum* contains most of the band's essential tracks. It would've been nice if annotations had been included, but this is a good primer. —*Rick Clark*

Legend / Oct. 5, 1987 / MCA ✦✦
Southern by the Grace of God: Lynyrd Skynyrd Tribute Tour—1 / 1988 / MCA ✦✦✦
Best: Skynyrd's Innyrds / 1989 / MCA ✦✦✦
Lynyrd Skynyrd 1991 / 1991 / Atlantic ✦✦
After the 1987 Tribute Tour, this reformed line-up of Skynyrd inked a deal with Atlantic and cut this album in Memphis with Tom Dowd producing. As a playing unit, the band still had a formidable delivery, but with the absence of Van Zant and Collins, it is obvious that there was a shortage of strong songs, with a distinctive point of view—a given throughout all of their pre-plane crash albums. However, "Smokestack Lightning," "Backstreet Crawler," and "Pure & Simple" (later remixed for the country market) are highlights. —*Rick Clark*

○ **Lynyrd Skynyrd [Box Set]** / 1991 / MCA ✦✦✦✦
This attractively packaged and well-chosen collection of the band's most popular tracks also includes early demos and other unreleased tracks. —*Rick Clark*

The Last Rebel / 1993 / Atlantic ✦✦
Endangered Species / 1994 / Capricorn ✦✦

The Lyres

Group, Punk, Garage Rock
Few bands in Boston rock & roll history have lasted as long, and

made as much good music, as the Lyres. Led by garage-rock obsessive, record collector, Farfisa organ king, and world-class megalomaniac Jeff "Monoman" Connolly, the Lyres rose from the ashes of Connolly's first band, DMZ. Sporting a similar high-energy trash-rock sound indebted to the Seeds, ? and the Mysterians, the Stooges, and the early British Invasion (especially early Kinks), the Lyres, for a brief, shining moment, were the kingpins of Boston's punk rock scene. Resembling venerable British blues-rockers Savoy Brown because of a constantly changing lineup (something like 40 musicians have passed through the ranks), the Lyres (or more specifically, Monoman) gleefully party on, oblivious of trends or the assorted vagaries of the alternative rock marketplace. A dinosaur in his own right? Perhaps, but as long as Jeff Connolly has his organ, a few guys behind him and a place to play, the simple joy that can only be had through rock & roll will exist in this world—hipness be damned! —*John Dougan*

○ **AHS: 1005** / 1981 / Ace of Hearts ♦♦♦♦
○ **On Fyre** / 1984 / Ace of Hearts ♦♦♦♦
Simply their best. *On Fyre* is a non-stop rave-up from the opening salvo of "Don't Give It up Now." Garage rock fans will want for nothing here: blistering tempos, manic intensity, hyperactive vocals, ultra-cheesy organ; it's a knock-down, drag-out rock & roll party, Lyres-style. —*John Dougan*

Lyres Lyres / 1986 / New Rose ♦♦♦
More emotionally complex and reflective than *On Fyre*, this could well be one of the most mature garage rock records ever recorded. That doesn't mean that energy and excitement are sacrificed for dour introspection—far from it. This is a total joy from start to finish, and a great place to hang out after a thousand or so spins of *On Fyre*. —*John Dougan*

Live at Continental / 1987 / Pryct ♦♦

A Promise Is a Promise / 1988 / Ace of Hearts ♦♦♦

Lyres Live 1983: Let's Have a Party!! / 1989 / Pryct ♦♦♦
Recorded live in the studio for Emerson College's great Boston music show Metrowave, these 13 slices of reckless abandon get about as close as one can to the "majesticity" (according to the guy introducing them) of a typical Lyres gig. Includes great versions of "Never Met a Girl Like You" and "Gonna Find a New Love." BYOB and crank it up! —*John Dougan*

● **Some Lyres** / 1994 / Taang! ♦♦♦♦
An excellent, if brief (12 tracks) part-career retrospective, part-collection of oddities that includes their 1979 debut single "How Do You Know" b/w "Don't Give it Up Now." Packaged as a parody of the Rolling Stones' controversial *Some Girls, Some Lyres* proves to be a valuable introduction. —*John Dougan*

M

Kirsty MacColl

Singer-Songwriter, Folk-Rock, Pop/Rock
Kirsty MacColl, daughter of folk singer-songwriter Ewan MacColl, began her own musical career while still in her teens, singing in a band called the Addix, and eventually signed to the legendary Stiff Records. Her first single, the modern girl-group gem, "They Don't Know," was released in 1979. Though it failed in the charts, it was later a major hit for Tracey Ullman. She switched to Polydor in the '80s and landed a U.K. Top 20 hit with the novelty song "There's a Guy Works Down the Chip Shop (Swears He's Elvis)." She followed the single with her first LP, *Desperate Character*, in 1981. In 1984, she married producer Steve Lillywhite and put her solo career on hold, raising their two children and working as a back-up singer. MacColl returned in 1989 with a more mature effort, *Kite*, which reached the U.K. Top 20. Since then, she has released two more albums, *Electric Landlady* (1991) and *Titanic Days* (1993), displaying great talent and diversity and above all, good pop sensibilities. —*Chris Woodstra*

Desperate Character / 1981 / Polydor ♦♦♦

Kite / 1989 / Charisma ♦♦♦
After nearly a decade's absence as solo performer, MacColl released the low-key *Kite*, a decidedly more mature effort. Her literate and sharp vocals are perfectly matched with lush, textured folk-pop arrangements. Johnny Marr contributes his distinctive guitar playing on several tracks. —*Chris Woodstra*

○ **Electric Landlady** / 1991 / Charisma ♦♦♦♦
MacColl is in peak form on the more experimental *Electric Landlady*. Playing with a different band on nearly every track, she effortlessly moves from the hip-hop of "Walking Down Madison," to the Latin-tinged "My Affair," to the Smiths' sound-alike "Children of the Revolution" (co-written by Smiths guitarist Johnny Marr). Overall, she builds on the folk-pop of her previous effort with much stronger material. Her lyrics have become more personal, mainly focusing on her relationship with and the recent death of her father. —*Chris Woodstra*

○ **Essential Collection** / 1993 / Stiff ♦♦♦♦
A fine collection of Kirsty MacColl's early singles for Stiff Records in the late '70s. She wrote effortlessly melodic three-minute pop singles that managed to recast the classic girl-group sound of the '60s into a style that was contemporary and timeless, much like how Rockpile energetically recast '50s and '60s rock & roll. Not only were these singles some of the best she's ever written, the singles were among the best pop songs of the era, including the original version of Tracey Ullman's hit "They Don't Know" and the infectious "There's a Guy Works Down the Chip Shop (Swears He's Elvis).". —*Chris Woodstra*

Titanic Days / Oct. 5, 1993 / IRS ♦♦♦
MacColl delivers another brilliant album with 1993's *Titanic Days*. The arrangements have become more ambitious, as evident in the jazzy "Bad" and the heavily orchestrated "Soho Square." The lyrics are still sharp with biting commentary, this time backed by a more dance-oriented pop. —*Chris Woodstra*

● **Galore** / 1995 / IRS ♦♦♦♦
18-track compilation. The strength of these collected forces may just be sufficient to overcome Kirsty MacColl's two fatal commercial "flaws": she spreads herself all over the musical map, and writes intelligent, often drily humorous lyrics about life and relationships that never pander to chart sentimentality. MacColl oozes a pure, fresh-scrubbed, girl-next-door quality that belies the so-

phistication of her songwriting without ever resorting to vacant innocence. —*Roch Parisien*

Craig Mack

Rap
Under the guidance of producer Sean "Puffy" Combs, the Long Island-native and former EPMD roadie Criag Mack became a sensation in 1994 with the pop-friendly hip-hop of his debut album *Project: Funk Da World* and the Top Ten single "Flava In Ya Ear.." —*Stephen Thomas Erlewine*

○ **Project: Funk Da World** / 1994 / Bad Boy ♦♦♦♦
Mack uses Dr. Dre's album-tested formula of syrupy P-Funk beats, but makes it his own with his rigorous delivery. Dancehall rhythms also surface, and he tackles issues (like black tradition) that Dre and Snoop wouldn't touch. In all, this LP isn't the stuff of a revolution, but Mack sure knows his way around a good groove. —*John Bush*

Mad Lads

Group, Soul, R&B
John Gary Williams, Julius Green, William Brown, and Robert Phillips were the original Mad Lads. They began recording for Volt in 1965, and landed a Top 20 R&B hit with the single "Don't Have to Shop Around." They followed that in 1966 with their lone Top Ten R&B single "I Want Someone," and had another Top 20 hit the same year with "I Want a Girl." The song regarded in most quarters as their finest, "Whatever Hurts You," made the R&B Top 30 in 1968. They never had a crossover single, but made several fine Southern soul cuts. Williams and Brown were replaced later by Sam Nelson and Quincy Clifton Billops, Jr., in 1966. —*Ron Wynn*

The Best of the Mad Lads / 1984 / Stax ♦♦♦
Including two late hits, this has no track duplication with their *Greatest Hits*. —*Richard Pack*

● **Greatest Hits** / Collectables ♦♦♦♦
The best from 1965 to 1968, from this connoisseur's vocal group, includes five hits. —*Richard Pack*

Mad River

Group, Psychedelic
One of the oddest San Francisco Bay Area bands of the late '60s, Berkeley-based Mad River cut two albums that are highly regarded by psychedelic collectors. After releasing a rare EP on a tiny local label in 1967, the band signed with Capitol and released their self-titled debut the following year. Perhaps the most ominous San Francisco band of the time, the group often sounded like an extremely dark version of Quicksilver Messenger Service, with a bit of Country Joe & the Fish's minor-key melodies thrown in. Their material veered between drawn-out angst jams and frenetic amphetamined numbers, spotlighting David Robinson's shimmering, blistering guitar leads and leader/songwriter Lawrence Hammond's mournful, quavering vocals. Unpredictably, their second and last LP (1969's *Paradise Bar & Grill*) found the band drifting into laidback country-rock with less memorable results. —*Richie Unterberger*

● **Mad River** / 1968 / Edsel ♦♦♦♦
The dark side of the psychedelic experience, sounding like a soundtrack to a bad trip with its bleak, enigmatic lyrics, swirling, somewhat dissonant arrangements, and relentlessly minor

melodies. The longer tracks meander at times, but the hell-bent jerking tempos of "Merciful Monks" and "Amphetamine Gazelle," as well as the chilling closing lullaby "Hush Julian," still pack a punch. The 1985 British reissue of this LP (on Edsel) adds extensive liner notes, and restores the album to its correct speed (the original master ran too fast). —*Richie Unterberger*

Paradise Bar & Grill / 1969 / Capitol ✦✦✦
The band chills out considerably here, largely eschewing the creeps for lazing-by-the-country-stream picking. Laurence Hammond's vocals are still uniquely pained, and cuts like "Equinox" and "Academy Cemetery" show traces of their facility for haunting guitar lines, but it doesn't come close to the impact of their debut. Countercultural hero Richard Brautigan makes an appearance on "Love's No Way To Treat A Friend." —*Richie Unterberger*

Madder Rose

Group, Alternative Pop/Rock
Madder Rose makes some of the sweetest pop music around today. Hailing from New York, guitarist Billy Cote, drummer Johnny Kick, bassist Matt Verta-Ray and guitarist/vocalist Mary Lorson created a brilliant debut in 1993's melodic and diverse *Bring It Down*. The combination of Lorson's dulcet voice and Cote's and Lorson's eloquent songs brought critical success but few commercial takers; 1994's equally graceful *Panic On* continued the band's trend of making great records to almost no notice. Hopefully, Madder Rose won't be destined to remain musical wallflowers, as the music contained in their two albums and numerous EPs surpasses many more successful bands in the college/power-pop vein. —*Heather Phares*

● **Bring It Down** / 1993 / Seed ✦✦✦✦
Madder Rose's first bursts with bright, jangly pop and punk songs. Songwriters Billy Coté and Mary Lorson deliver deleriously catchy tunes like "Beautiful John" and "Swim" as well as gentle, pensive ballads like "While Away" and "Lights Down Low," and harder-hitting songs like "Lay Down Low" and "20 Ft. Red." The creativity and versatility of *Bring It Down* makes it a strong and memorable debut. —*Heather Phares*

○ **Panic On** / 1994 / Seed/Atlantic ✦✦✦✦
Panic On is a more subdued affair than Madder Rose's effusive beginning. The title track, as well as most of the album, is a gentle but slightly dissonant mid-tempo pop song. Lorson's limpi, languid voice takes center-stage on this solid but somewhat underwhelming follow-up. —*Heather Phares*

Madness

Group, Ska-Revival
Madness was a British septet formed in 1976. They gained fame in the late-'70s ska-revival along with such bands as the Specials and the Beat. Unlike those contemporaries, however, the group had a comic, pop edge that turned it into a well-loved popular singles group. Members were Graham "Suggs" McPherson, vocals; Chas Smash, backup vocals; Chris Foreman, guitar; Mike Barson, keyboards; Lee Thompson, saxophone; Mark Bedord, bass; and Dan Woodgate, drums. The first of their 13 U.K. Top Ten hits was "One Step Beyond" in 1979.

Though the group's British subject matter and approach tended to preclude American success, Madness did manage one U.S. Top Ten hit, "Our House," in 1983. The group disbanded in 1986. —*William Ruhlmann*

○ **One Step Beyond** / 1979 / Sire ✦✦✦✦
The band's debut shows the band in peak form. More than just the silly novelty act portrayed on the cover, Madness offers a lighthearted approach to ska with an irresistible dance beat. Includes the favorites, "One Step Beyond" and "Night Boat to Cairo." A landmark ska-revival album. —*Chris Woodstra*

Absolutely / 1980 / Sire ✦✦✦
Their early ska-influenced material, featuring such UK hits as "Baggy Trousers," "Embarrassment," and "Return of the Los Palmas 7." —*William Ruhlmann*

Seven / 1981 / Stiff ✦✦✦
Their "nutty sound" seems to fall to the background somewhat on this move toward more mature songwriting. Expanding beyond the limited scope of ska, this is a fine pop effort at times dabbling in more experimental sounds such as sitars and Arabic rhythms. Includes the splendid single "It Must Be Love." —*Chris Woodstra*

○ **Rise & Fall** / 1982 / Stiff ✦✦✦✦
Madness Present the Rise and Fall marks the band's most mature effort and artistic statement. Completely devoid of their early ska influence, they paint a picture of British life in the spirit of the Kinks' *Village Green Preservation Society*. Though it was never released in the U.S., several tracks were later placed on the compilation *Madness*, including "Our House," their biggest Stateside hit. —*Chris Woodstra*

★ **Complete Madness** / 1982 / Stiff ✦✦✦✦✦
A smartly-assembled collection of their early singles. A good starting point for those interested in their self-described "nutty sound" ska/bluebeat. Pure fun. —*Chris Woodstra*

○ **Madness** / 1983 / Geffen ✦✦✦✦
A U.S. compilation album released to coincide with the success of "Our House." It includes that hit, its followup, "It Must Be Love," and such UK successes as "Tomorrow's Just Another Day," "Shut Up," "House of Fun," and "Grey Day." —*William Ruhlmann*

Keep Moving / 1984 / Geffen ✦✦
As the Clive Langer/Alan Winstanley production credit would indicate, *Keep Moving* is a slick sounding venture complete with appearances from Afrodiziak, TKO Horns, a full gospel choir, and even Michael Caine. Overbearing production aside, this is well-crafted Brit-pop that explores a brighter side than the previous album—though less memorable. —*Chris Woodstra*

Mad Not Mad / 1985 / Geffen ✦✦

Utter Madness / 1986 / Zarjazz ✦✦✦
Picking up where *Complete Madness* left off, this collection includes all of the key singles from 1982 to 1986. A good collection, though listeners would be better served by simply listening to *Rise and Fall* for a representation of this period. —*Chris Woodstra*

Madonna

b. Aug. 16, 1958, Rochester, MI
Dance-Pop, Pop/Rock
After a star reaches a certain point, it's easy to forget what they became famous for and concentrate solely on their persona. Madonna is such a star. Madonna rocketed to stardom so quickly in 1984 that it obscured most of her musical virtues. Appreciating her music became even more difficult as the decade wore on, as discussing her lifestyle became more common than discussing her music. However, one of Madonna's greatest achievements is how she manipulated the media and the public with her music, her videos, her publicity, and her sexuality. Arguably, Madonna was the first female pop star to have complete control of her music and image.

Madonna moved from her native Michigan to New York in 1977, with dreams of becoming a ballet dancer. She studied with choreographer Alvin Ailey and modelled. In 1979, she became part of the Patrick Hernandez Revue, a disco outfit who had the hit "Born to Be Alive." She travelled to Paris with Hernanadez; it was there that she met Dan Gilroy, who would soon become her boyfriend. Upon returning to New York, the pair formed the Breakfast Club, a pop/dance group. Madonna originally played drums for the band, but she soon became the lead singer. In 1980, she left the band and formed Emmy with her former boyfriend, drummer Stephen Bray. Soon, Bray and Madonna broke off from the group and began working on some dance/disco-oriented tracks. A demo tape of these tracks worked its way to Mark Kamins, a New York-based DJ/producer. Kamins directed the tape to Sire Records, who signed the singer during 1982.

Kamins produced Madonna's first single, "Everybody," which became a club and dance hit at the end of 1982; her second single, 1983's "Physical Attraction," was another club hit. In June of 1983, she had her third club hit with the bubbly "Holiday," which was written by Jellybean Benitez. Madonna's self-titled debut album was released in September of 1983; "Holiday" became her first Top 40 hit the following month. "Borderline" became her first Top Ten hit in March of 1984, beginning a remarkable string of 17 consecutive Top Ten hits. While "Lucky Star" was climbing to number four, Madonna began working on her first starring role in a feature film, Susan Seidelman's *Desperately Seeking Susan*.

Madonna's second album, the Niles Rodgers-produced *Like A Virgin*, was released at the end of 1984. The title track hit number one in December, staying at the top of the charts for six weeks; it was the start of a whirlwind year for the singer. During 1985, Madonna became an international celebrity, selling millions of records on the strength of her stylish, sexy videos and forceful personality. After "Material Girl" became a number two hit in March, Madonna began her first tour, supported by the Beastie Boys. "Crazy for You" became her second number one single in May. *Desperately Seeking Susan* was released in July, becoming a box office hit; it also prompted a planned video release of *A Certain Sacrifice*, a low-budget erotic drama she filmed in 1979. *A Certain Sacrifice* wasn't the only embarrassing skeleton in the closet dragged into the light during the summer of 1985—both *Playboy* and *Penthouse* published nude photos of Madonna that she posed for in 1977. Nevertheless, her popularity continued unabated, with thousands of teenage girls adopting her sexy appearence, being dubbed "Madonna Wannabes." In August, she married actor Sean Penn; the couple had a rocky marriage that ended in 1989.

Madonna began collaborating with Patrick Leonard at the beginning of 1986; Leonard would co-write most of her biggest hits in the '80s, including "Live to Tell," which hit number one in June of 1986. A more ambitious and accomplished record than her two previous albums *True Blue* was released the following month, to both massive commercial success (it was a number one in both the U.S. and the U.K., selling over five million copies in America alone) and critical acclaim. "Papa Don't Preach" became her fourth number one hit in the U.S. While her musical career was thriving, her film career took a savage hit with the November release of *Shanghai Surprise*. Starring Madonna and Sean Penn, the comedy received terrible reviews, which translated into disasterous box office returns.

At the beginning of 1987, she had her fifth number one single with "Open Your Heart," the third number one from *True Blue* alone. "La Isla Bonita," taken from the soundtrack of her third feature film *Who's That Girl?* was another Top Five hit, although the film itself was another box office bomb; the title track from the movie became her sixth number one single. 1988 was a relatively quiet year for Madonna, as she spent the first half of the year acting in David Mamet's *Speed the Plow* on Broadway. In the meantime, she released the remix album *You Can Dance*. After withdrawing the divorce papers she filed at the beginning of 1988, she divorced Penn at the beginning of 1989.

Like a Prayer, released in the spring of 1989, was her most ambitious and far-reaching album, incorporating elements of pop, rock and dance. It was another number one hit and launched the number one title track and "Express Yourself," "Cherish," and "Keep It Together," three more Top Ten hits. In April 1990, she began her massive *Blonde Ambition* tour, which ran throughout the entire year. "Vogue" became a number one hit in May, setting the stage for her co-starring role in Warren Beatty's *Dick Tracy*; it was her most successful film appearance since *Desperately Seeking Susan*. Madonna released a greatest hits album, *The Immaculate Collection*, at the end of the year. It featured two new songs, including the number one single "Justify My Love," which sparked another controversy with its sexy video; the second new song, "Rescue Me," became the highest-debuting single by a female artist in U.S. chart history, entering the charts at number 15. *Truth or Dare*, a documentary of the *Blonde Ambition* tour, was released to positive reviews and strong ticket sales at the end of 1991.

Madonna returned to the charts in the summer of 1992 with the number one "This Used to Be My Playground," a single featured in the film *A League of Their Own*, which featured the singer in a small part. Later that year, Madonna released *Sex*, an expensive, steel-bound soft-core pornography book that featured hundreds of erotic photographs of herself, several models, and other celebrities—including Isabella Rosselinni, Big Daddy Kane, Naomi Campbell, and Vanilla Ice—as well as selected prose. *Sex* received wretched reviews and enormous negative publicity, yet that didn't stop the accompanying album, *Erotica*, from selling over two million copies. *Bedtime Stories*, released two years later, was a more subdued affair than *Erotica*. Initially, it didn't chart as impressively, prompting some critics to label her a has-been, yet the album spawned her biggest hit, "Take a Bow," which spent seven weeks at number one. It also featured the Bjork-penned "Bedtime Stories," which became her first single not to make the Top 40; its followup, "Human Nature," also failed to crack the Top 40. Nevertheless, *Bedtime Stories*, marked her seventh album to go multiplatinum, ensuring her place as one of pop's most successful artists ever. — *Stephen Thomas Erlewine*

○ **Madonna** / 1983 / Sire ✦✦✦✦
Madonna's self-titled debut was one of the strongest dance records of the early '80s, featuring a state-of-the-art production and a handful of great songs. Although her voice was still quite thin at

this point, Madonna projected a powerful charisma, bringing slight material like "Everybody," "Physical Attraction," and "Burning Up" to life. However, it was on well-constructed pop songs like "Borderline," "Lucky Star," and "Holiday" that the record became truly impressive, as the material matched Madonna's performance. All three of the songs became hits and wrote the blueprint for dance-pop divas that dominated much of the remaining decade. — *Stephen Thomas Erlewine*

Like a Virgin / 1984 / Sire ✦✦✦
With monster hits like "Material Girl," "Dress You Up," and the title track, this album exploits the traits that defined her then-budding persona. — *John Floyd*

○ **True Blue** / 1986 / Sire ✦✦✦✦
A staggering album from an artist known for hot singles, the hits include "Papa Don't Preach," "Open Your Heart," and "True Blue." "Live to Tell," her best, is also to be found here. — *John Floyd*

Who's That Girl / 1987 / Sire ✦✦
In the strictest sense, *Who's That Girl* isn't a Madonna album—it's a soundtrack album to her 1987 comedy, featuring competent, but uninspiring dance-pop by Club Nouveau, Scritti Politti, Coati Mundi, Michael Davidson, and Duncan Favre. Madonna has four new tracks on the record, including the number one "Who's That Girl" and the number two "Causing A Commotion." Both of the hits aren't among her finest singles—neither song made her greatest-hits compilation, *The Immaculate Collection*—making it her weakest album. — *Stephen Thomas Erlewine*

You Can Dance / 1987 / Sire ✦✦✦
A decent assortment of extended dance remixes, it's deal for parties. — *John Floyd*

☆ **Like a Prayer** / 1989 / Sire ✦✦✦✦✦
Out of all of Madonna's albums, *Like a Prayer* is her most explicit attempt at a major artistic statement. Even though it is apparent that she is trying to make a "serious" album, the kaliedoscopic variety of pop styles on *Like a Prayer* is quite dazzling. Ranging from the deep funk of "Express Yourself" and "Keep it Together," to the haunting "Oh Father" and "Like a Prayer," Madonna displays a commanding sense of songcraft, making this her best and most consistent album. — *Stephen Thomas Erlewine*

★ **The Immaculate Collection** / 1990 / Sire ✦✦✦✦
A 70-minute singles package, it establishes once and for all Madonna's absolute mastery of the pop single. — *John Floyd*

Dick Tracy: "I'm Breathless" (Music from & Inspired by the Film) [st] / 1990 / Sire ✦✦
A collection of songs featured or inspired by the comic-book-turned-movie *Dick Tracy*, *I'm Breathless* is essentially Madonna's take on popular music from the '40s, particularly big band pop. Although her singing shows a surprising amount of range, the material tends to be nothing more than cutesy novelty numbers, like the double entendre-laden hit "Hanky Panky." *I'm Breathless* approaches greatness only on "Vogue," a hit single tacked on to the end of the record. Featuring an endlessly deep house groove and an instantly memorable melody, "Vogue" is a detached, affectionate celebration of transcendent pop and gay culture and stands as Madonna's finest single moment. — *Stephen Thomas Erlewine*

Erotica / Oct. 20, 1992 / Maverick ✦✦✦
While it didn't set the charts on fire like her previous albums, the ambitious *Erotica* contains some of Madonna's best and most accomplished music (including the hit singles "Deeper and Deeper" and "Rain"), even if it runs a bit long. — *Stephen Thomas Erlewine*

○ **Bedtime Stories** / 1994 / Maverick ✦✦✦✦
Perhaps Madonna correctly guessed that the public overdosed on the raw carnality of her book *Sex*. Perhaps she wanted to offer a more optimistic take on sex than the distant *Erotica*. Either way, *Bedtime Stories* is a warm album, with deep, gently pulsating grooves; the album's title isn't totally tongue-in-cheek. The best songs on the album ("Secret," "Inside of Me," "Sanctuary," "Bedtime Story," "Take a Bow") slowly work their melodies into the subconscious as the bass pulses. In that sense, it does offer an antidote to *Erotica*, which was filled with deep but cold grooves. The entire production of *Bedtime Stories* suggests that she wants listeners to acknowledge that her music isn't one-dimensional. She has succeeded with that goal, since *Bedtime Stories* offers her most humane and open music; it's even seductive. — *Stephen Thomas Erlewine*

Johnny Maestro & Brooklyn Bridge

Group, Doo-Wop

After making a name for himself as lead singer of the Crests, vocalist Johnny Maestro formed Brooklyn Bridge in 1967 and scored a gold record the next year on Buddah with a cover of the Fifth Dimension's heartbroken "Worst That Could Happen." Brooklyn Bridge was an amalgam of Maestro, the Del Satins (the vocal group that backed Dion on many of his early '60s solo hits), and a brassy outfit called the Rhythm Method. Brooklyn Bridge enjoyed several more hits in 1969 and 1970, and Maestro still performs on the oldies circuit. —*Bill Dahl*

● **The Best of the Crests Featuring Johnny Maestro** / Rhino ◆◆◆◆
○ **Greatest Hits** / Collectables ◆◆◆◆
Soft rock, including "Worst That Could Happen" and everthing else. —*Larry Lapka*

Best of Johnny Maesrtro & the Crests 1958-1961 / Ace ◆◆◆

Magazine

Group, New Wave

After leaving the Buzzcocks in 1977, vocalist Howard Devoto formed Magazine with guitarist John McGeogh, bassist Barry Adamson, keyboardist Bob Dickinson, and drummer Martin Jackson. One of the first post-punk bands, Magazine kept the edgy, nervous energy of punk, adding elements of art-rock, particularly with their theatrical live shows and shards of keyboards. Devoto's lyrics were combinations of social commentary and poetic fragments, while the band alternated between cold, jagged chords and gloomy, atmospheric sonic landscapes.

Magazine performed its first concert in the fall of 1977 and were signed to Virgin Records by the end of the year; by that point, Dickinson had left the group. The band recorded their first single, "Shot by Both Sides," as a quartet; Devoto had written the song with his former Buzzcocks partner, Pete Shelley. Appearing in early 1978, the single gathered good reviews on both sides of the Atlantic and charted in the U.K., peaking at number 41. Before they recorded their debut album, keyboardist Dave Formula joined the lineup. *Real Life*, released later in 1978, continued the confrontational, arty pop-punk of "Shot by Both Sides." Following their first tour, Jackson left the group and was replaced by John Doyle. The new lineup recorded the band's second album, *Secondhand Daylight* (1979). *Secondhand Daylight* was somewhat of a departure from the debut, featuring more keyboards, smoother rhythms, and streamlined lyrics from Devoto. Despite its ambitiousness, the record was poorly received by the press. During this time, McGeogh played with Siouxsie and the Banshees and Adamson, Formula, and McGeogh were part of Visage, along with Steve Strange. At the beginning of 1980, the band released their third album, *The Correct Use of Soap.*

In the summer of 1980, Magazine released "Sweetheart Contract," which became their second and last British chart hit, peaking at number 54. After it hit the charts, McGeogh left the band to become a full-time member of Siouxsie and the Banshees; he was replaced by Robin Simon. Magazine toured America and Australia, recording a live album called *Play.*, which was released at the end of 1980. Simon left at the end of the tour, with former Amazorblades guitarist Bob Mandelson taking his place. *Magic, Murder & the Weather* was released in the spring of 1981; it proved to be the Magazine's last album. Devoto left the group in May of 1981 to pursue a solo career and the band broke up shortly afterward. —*Stephen Thomas Erlewine*

○ **Real Life** / 1978 / Blue Plate ◆◆◆◆
A vital album and period classic, it fired the first shot in defining the UK post-punk scene. —*Steve Aldrich*

Secondhand Daylight / 1979 / Blue Plate ◆◆◆
○ **The Correct Use of Soap** / 1980 / Blue Plate ◆◆◆◆
Only a shade less brilliant than their debut, it featured outstanding work from guitarist John McCeoch. —*Steve Aldrich*

Play. / 1980 / IRS ◆◆
This is a live LP from 1980. —*Steve Aldrich*

Magic Murder & the Weather / 1981 / IRS ◆◆◆
Final studio album. —*Steve Aldrich*

About the Weather / 1981 / IRS ◆◆◆
After the Fact / 1982 / IRS ◆◆◆
A US compilation, it includes non-LP single sides. —*Steve Aldrich*

● **Rays & Hail** / 1987 / Virgin ◆◆◆◆
A comprehensive compilation that samples from all of the band's albums, as well as including the original single version of "Shot By Both Sides." —*Stephen Thomas Erlewine*

Scree (Rarities 1978-81) / Mar. 8, 1991 / Blue Plate ◆◆◆

Magma

Group, Fusion, Art-Rock/Progressive-Rock
French/German fusion rock band. Wild saxophone gymnastics of Yochko Seffer. —*Michael G. Nastos*

● **Mekanik Destruktiw Kommandoh** / 1974 / A&M ◆◆◆◆
Christian Vander is one of Europe's great modern composers. The music of his band Magma combines Wagnerian classicism and the spirit of John Coltrane into a completely unique fusion. *M.D.K.,* their third album, combines massed choral voices, classical jazz and ferocious rhythmic energy into a symphonic fusion that achieves amazing levels of creativity and intensity. —*Archie Patterson*

○ **Live** / 1984 / Utopia ◆◆◆◆
This bizarre and unique jazz-rock has sci-fi trappings. —*Michael P. Dawson*

Magnapop

Group, Alternative Pop/Rock
This Athens, Georgia band creates high-energy punk-pop with catchy hooks and literate lyrics. Formed in 1987 by singer Linda Hopper, guitarist Ruthie Morris, drummer David McNair and bassist Shannon Mulvaney, the group recorded a demo album with their friend Michael Stipe in 1992, which was released on Caroline Records. In 1994 the group released their "official" debut, *Hot Boxing,* on Priority. *Hot Boxing* was produced by another of the band's friends, Bob Mould, and features a more streamlined, intense approach than the quirky, off-kilter demos do. What makes Magnapop interesting (and different from many of the punk-pop bands out there) is the combination of Hopper's smooth, unhurried vocals and the furious lashings of Morrisson's guitar—it creates a tension that makes the group's songs all the more dramatic. An intelligent, underappreciated band. —*Heather Phares*

○ **Magnapop** / 1992 / Play It Again Sam ◆◆◆◆
This is a collection of demos and early singles produced by the band's friends, Michael Stipe and Bob Mould. *Magnapop* unveils the band as a punk-pop group with an arty bent, especially on songs like "Spill It" and "Favorite Writer." The cover of Big Star's "13" is a welcome addition to this good beginning. —*Heather Phares*

● **Hot Boxing** / 1994 / Priority ◆◆◆◆
On their official debut, Magnapop iron out the kinks of their sound, And come out a tighter but slightly less interesting band for it. The group are at their best on "Lay It Down," "Piece of Cake," and "The Crush, " where they mix punk-fueled energy and wistful lyrics. —*Heather Phares*

The Main Ingredient

Group, Soul, R&B
Originally formed in 1964 as the Poets, this New York soul group (Donald McPherson, Luther Simmons Jr, and Tony Sylvester) recorded for Red Bird before changing their name in 1966. After McPherson's death in 1971, Cuba Gooding became the lead singer, and the band scored three Top 40 hits, including "Everybody Plays the Fool," which went to #3.

The Main Ingredient tried it again in 1986, with Cuba Gooding returning to his lead spot. They recorded for Zakia, but didn't get much response to "Do Me Right." They kept trying, cutting a song on Polydor in 1989. Longtime group member Luther Simmons, who had left in 1975 to become a stock broker and then come back in 1980, returned to Wall Street and was replaced for this session by Jerome Jackson. —*Bil Carpenter & Stephen Thomas Erlewine*

● **The All-Time Greatest Hits** / RCA ◆◆◆◆
It wasn't until 1971 that the Main Ingredient's fortunes changed; when Cuba Gooding replaced Donald McPherson, his engaging voice helped make them part of the "sweet" soul trend. Gooding's leads made "Spinning Around (I Must Be Falling In Love)" and "Everybody Plays The Fool" huge hits, as well as "Just Don't Want To Be Lonely" and "Happiness Is Just Around The Bend." These and several other hits are featured on this anthology covering their prime years on RCA. —*Ron Wynn*

○ **Golden Classics** / Collectables ✦✦✦✦
The Main Ingredient were one of the few vocal groups able to be both classy and soulful. Cuba Gooding (father of talented film actor Cuba Gooding, Jr.) had the ability to sound earnest and anguished while singing sentimental, even sappy lyrics. Their polished harmonies made them mid-'70s romantic idols, and while they weren't as emphatic as trios like the Delfonics or Moments, they still cranked out many hit albums for RCA. This anthology collects their biggest chart hits and is a soul ballad bonanza. —*Ron Wynn*

Main Source

Group, Rap
New York rappers Main Source exploded into the hip-hop universe with *Breaking Atoms* for Wild Pitch in 1991. It featured the Large Professor's cutting, often cynical narratives about everything from police brutality to betrayal by friends. The one-time cohort of Producer Paul C., the Large Professor was joined by twin disc jockeys K-Cut and Sir Scratch. The single "Lookin' at the Front Door" proved a sizable hit, and Main Source seemed on its way. But nearly three years later, no second LP had been issued and the group was rumored to be disbanding. —*Ron Wynn*

● **Breaking Atoms** / 1991 / EMI America ✦✦✦
Sparkling raps, snazzy production, and an energetic set. —*Ron Wynn*

F—K What You Think / Mar. 22, 1994 / Wild Pitch ✦✦✦

Yngwie Malmsteen

b. Sweden
Hard Rock, Heavy Metal
By age twenty-one Yngwie Malmsteen had become one of the most admired guitarists on the planet. Raised in Sweden, the nineteen-year-old moved to California in 1983 and within two years had debuted on vinyl with Steeler, cut two albums with Alcatrazz, and self-produced a pair of much-lauded solo releases. Onstage, he was energy incarnate—tossing his Strat high in the air and catching it one-handed, playing with his teeth, and offering his instrument in symbolic sacrifice to the gods of feedback. The young Swede's technique was brilliant, with a sheer speed and picking control paralleled by few others. Solos were the heart of his art: roaring masterpieces, they cast high-drama melodies more closely related to Bach and Paganini than any rock forebears. With Yngwie's imprimatur, Paganini, Bach, and Beethovan suddenly became hot items among big-hairs and metal heads.

Meanwhile hordes of kids armed with copies of *Rising Force* and *Marching Out* scurried to guitar teachers to learn the mysteries of harmonic minor, phrygian, and diminished scales. There was no easy way around it; to approximate Malmsteen's style took hard work. The endless riffing, booze, and star trappings took quick tolls: Yngwie suffered from tendinitis throughout the *Marching Out* sessions. His prediction that he might someday be a racecar driver took a chilling turn in June 1987, when he wrapped his car around a tree. An injured picking hand and what he described as "severe brain damage" slowed his career until 1989, when he recorded *Trial by Fire*. Listening to 1990's *Eclipse*, one could argue that Yngwie's solos are stalled where they began, but that's a criticism he's quick to counter; "To be crazed about technique and to top whatever you've done before—I think that's very stupid and unnecessary. All I've tried to do is to maintain what I already had." —*Jas Obrecht*

○ **Rising Force** / 1984 / Polydor ✦✦✦✦
Sheer speed, dazzling execution. The result—the birth of the guitar hero. —*Jas Obrecht*

Marching Out / 1985 / Polydor ✦✦✦

○ **Trilogy** / 1986 / Polydor ✦✦✦✦
More commercial, it's still spectacular. —*Jas Obrecht*

Odyssey / Jan. 1988 / Polydor ✦✦
Important additions to his "solography," but no cigar. —*Jas Obrecht*

Live in Leningrad: Trial by Fire / 1989 / Polydor ✦✦

Eclipse / 1990 / Polydor ✦✦✦

● **The Collection** / 1992 / PolyGram ✦✦✦✦
This is a nice sampling of Malmsteen's finest songs and solos. —*AMG*

Fire and Ice / 1992 / Elektra ✦✦✦

The Mamas & the Papas

Group, Folk-Rock, Pop/Rock
The leading California-based vocal group of the '60s, the Mamas & the Papas epitomized the ethos of mid- to late-'60s pop culture: live free, play free, and love free. Their music, built around radiant harmonies and a solid electric-folk foundation, was gorgeous on its own terms, but a major part of its appeal lay in the easygoing Southern California lifestyle it endorsed.

Founder and leader John Phillips came out of early rock roots and a partly successful folk career, as did Cass Elliott and Denny Doherty, while Phillips's wife Michelle was an ex-model who also sang. They got together out of several failed folk groups just as the music was going electric, pulled up stakes in New York and headed west, where they signed with Lou Adler and wowed the world with a song called "California Dreamin'."

Phillips was a pop poet with a commercial edge, and a good arranger. The group had enviable chart success, lived well, and indulged themselves lavishly yet retained credibility with the counterculture. But it all came apart in a couple of years, as the quartet's intertwining romantic entanglements, coupled with their chemical excesses (detailed in separate books by John and Michelle Phillips), strangled their ability to work. By 1971 they were a fond memory, although a reconstituted version of the quartet has done well on the oldies circuit in the late '80s and early '90s. —*Bruce Eder*

The Mamas & the Papas / 1966 / MCA ✦✦✦
A last gasp, for fanatics only. —*Bruce Eder*

○ **If You Can Believe Your Eyes and Ears** / 1966 / MCA ✦✦✦✦
Radiant, full-length album. Superb songs. —*Bruce Eder*

The Deliver / 1967 / MCA ✦✦✦
That they do, with some brilliant covers. —*Bruce Eder*

● **16 Greatest Hits** / 1970 / MCA ✦✦✦✦
A good collection of their electric folk-pop hits, it includes "Monday, Monday" and "California Dreamin'." —*AMG*

Monterey International Pop Festival / 1971 / One Way ✦✦
A live concert curio, with uneven performances and recording quality, but it is unique. —*Bruce Eder*

○ **Creeque Alley** / 1991 / MCA ✦✦✦✦
They weren't the most important folk-rock group of the mid-'60s; the Byrds and others produced more enduring music. Yet the Mamas and the Papas were undoubtedly the most commercially successful folk-rock group of their time, racking up an astonishing nine Top 30 hits in little more than a year and a half. This 43-song double CD is by far the most comprehensive document of their legacy. It draws most heavily from their two 1966 albums (nine songs originate from their debut album *If You Can Believe Your Eyes and Ears* alone), when John Phillips's songwriting talent had yet to exhaust itself. Beyond the hits, the material is variable. Quite a few album tracks—especially "Got A Feelin'." "Straight Shooter," "Go Where You Wanna Go," "Once Was A Time I Thought," and their cover of Lennon/McCartney's "I Call Your Name"—were strong enough to have been hits under their own steam. Their slowed-down, California-ized versions of rock oldies are more problematic. And there's no doubt that their later material is less spirited and memorable than their initial burst of glory. The set includes various late-'60s and '70s solo recordings by each of the group's members (including small hit singles by John Phillips and Cass Elliott). Perhaps the most intriguing rarities are from the members' pre-Mamas days. These include commercial folk by the Big Three (featuring Cass Elliott) and primitive pop-folk-rock by the Mugwumps (including Elliott, Denny Doherty, and future Lovin' Spoonful member Zal Yanovsky). —*Richie Unterberger*

Melissa Manchester

b. Feb. 15, 1951, Bronx, NY
Pop/Rock
Melissa Manchester sang commercial jingles at 15 and later became a member of Bette Midler's Harlettes. With partners Peter Allen and Carole Bayer Sager, she wrote several modern-day adult standards. Manchester specialized in MOR hits, especially power ballads, thanks to her night-club background and her affiliation with Barry Manilow and Bette Midler. From 1975 to 1982, Manchester charted with "Midnight Blue", "Don't Cry out Loud", "Just You and I", "Just Too Many People", and the upbeat "You Should Hear How She Talks about You." —*Bil Carpenter & Rick Clark*

● **Greatest Hits** / 1983 / Arista ✦✦✦✦
Her own classic cuts like "Come in from the Rain" and "Fire in the Morning." —*Bil Carpenter*

Mandrake Memorial

Group, Psychedelic
If you lived in Philadelphia in the late '60s, you would remember the Mandrake Memorial well. They opened for many of the star rock bands that passed through the city, and in terms of local popularity, they were probably only second to the Nazz. Outside of Philadelphia, they were scarcely known whatsoever, though they did manage to produce some fine second-division psychedelia. As vocalists, they were only adequate, but they were accomplished players and interesting writers, dressing their solid melodies with liberal jazz and Middle Eastern influences. Guitarist Craig Anderton became a noted music technology writer, contributing to magazines such as *Electronic Musician*. —*Richie Unterberger*

● **Mandrake Memorial** / 1967 / Poppy ✦✦✦✦
By far their best album, this suite-like collection features some haunting, first-rate songs, such as "Bird Journey," "Here I Am," and "Dark Lady." With their harmonies and interplay between guitar, electric keyboards, and occasional sitar, they were very much a band of their age, but played with a drive and precision that anticipated progressive rock. —*Richie Unterberger*

Mandrill

Group, Soul, R&B
Mandrill may have been the most musically ambitious of all the funk bands, something that hurt them commercially. Mandrill albums blended lengthy jazz-oriented pieces with danceable ditties and merged soul, blues, rock, and Afro-Latin elements. The Wilson brothers Louis, Richard, and Carlos were the creative core of the Brooklyn group, aided by Omar Mesa, Claude "Coffee" Cave, Charlie Pardo, and Fudgie Kae. The seven members played over 20 instruments. They recorded for Polydor from 1972 to 1974, then resurfaced on Arista in 1977. They remained there until 1982, then cut a final session for Montage. Mandrill's best songs weren't easily condensed or edited into singles, and only one tune, "Fencewalk" in 1973, cracked the Top 20. But such songs as "Funky Monkey" and "Can You Dig It" scored in the clubs. —*Ron Wynn*

● **The Best of Mandrill** / 1975 / Polydor ✦✦✦✦
A fine, unpredictable band that was too eclectic for its own good. This Brooklyn group merged jazz, rock, funk, Latin, and R&B, were fine singers, and made some sensational extended jams and fine album cuts, as well as some hits, like "Hang Loose" and "Fencewalk." While you can't get the full range of their material from the anthology, it's a fine introduction to how creative and dynamic some '70s funk bands were. —*Ron Wynn*

Manfred Mann

Group, Art-Rock/Progressive-Rock, British Invasion, Pop/Rock
An R&B band that only played pop to get on the charts, Manfred Mann ranked among the most adept British Invasion acts in both styles. South African-born keyboardist Manfred Mann was originally an aspiring jazz player, moving toward R&B when more blues-oriented sounds became in vogue in England in the early '60s. Original Manfred Mann singer Paul Jones was one of the best British Invasion singers, and his resonant vocals were the best feature of their early R&B sides, which had a slightly jazzier and smoother touch than the early work of the Rolling Stones and Animals. It was a couple covers of obscure girl group songs, "Do Wah Diddy Diddy" (the Exciters) and "Sha La La" (the Shirelles), that broke the group internationally—"Do Wah Diddy Diddy" reached number one in the States, and "Sha La La" just missed the Top Ten. The Paul Jones lineup never duplicated this success, although "Come Tomorrow" and "Pretty Flamingo" were smaller hits. From 1964 to 1966, they took the approach of playing gutsy pop/rock on their singles (including the original version of "My Little Red Book") and soul and R&B on their albums, with occasional detours into jazz, Dylan (their cover of his then-unreleased "If You Gotta Go, Go Now" was a big British hit), and competent original material.

Jones left for a solo career and acting in 1966, and the group reformed around singer Mike D'Abo (Beatle friend Klaus Voormann was also in this aggregation on bass). Adopting an even more pop-oriented approach for the singles, with occasional psychedelic and progressive touches, the band ran off a string of Top Ten hits in

their homeland until 1969, although the only one to hit the jackpot in the U.S. was their cover of another unreleased Dylan song, "The Mighty Quinn."

Mann dissolved the D'Abo lineup in 1969 to form Manfred Mann Chapter Three with drummer Mike Hugg, who had been in the band since the beginning. The outfit's early jazz-rock efforts were interesting, but not very popular, and Manfred steered the ship back toward mainstream rock by forming yet another incarnation, Manfred Mann's Earth Band. The heavier, more synthesizer-oriented outfit made quite a few albums in the 1970s; 1976's *The Roaring Silence* made the Top Ten, and featured the number one hit "Blinded by the Light" (Mann also made the Top 40 with another Springsteen cover, "Spirit in the Night"). Ironically, despite Mann's oft-proclaimed preferences for serious explorations of jazz, blues, and progressive music, it's his pop/rock recordings that hold up best, and for which he'll be remembered most. —*Richie Unterberger*

● **The Manfred Mann Album** / 1964 / Ascot ✦✦✦
Manfred Mann's debut full-length U.S. platter was probably their strongest, and indeed one of the stronger British Invasion albums of the very competitive year of 1964. Besides the smash "Do Wah Diddy Diddy," it contained a number of fine soul and R&B covers. Standouts were the versions of "Untie Me" and Ike & Tina Turner's "It's Gonna Work Out Fine," as well as the strong pounding Paul Jones original, "Without You." —*Richie Unterberger*

○ **The Roaring Silence** / 1976 / Warner Brothers ✦✦✦✦
A later edition of Mann's band, which had a '70s hit with Bruce Springsteen's "Blinded by the Light" (on this album). —*William Ruhlmann*

○ **The R&B Years** / 1982 / See For Miles ✦✦✦✦
The Manfreds always took great pains to point out that their true love was R&B and jazz, not the pop/rock they sang on their hit singles, although they should have realized that their fans dug both approaches. Anyway, this 20-song compilation is a good taste of their purer sounds, taken from LPs, EPs, and singles cut by the band during the Paul Jones era (1963–66). Look to EMI's fine *Best of Manfred Mann* CD for the big hits; this has covers of R&B and soul cuts by the likes of Willie Dixon, Muddy Waters, and Screamin' Jay Hawkins, as well as some more-than-competent group originals in the same vein. "I'm Your Kingpin," "Without You," and "Hubble Bubble (Toil and Trouble)" rank among the better early self-penned British R&B, and their cover of Ben E. King's "Groovin'" is a stormer. Although Manfred Mann weren't quite as fine R&B interpreters as fellow British Invaders the Stones, Yardbirds, and Animals, they were quite respectable, and this is a good complement to the more wide-ranging EMI anthology. —*Richie Unterberger*

● **Best of: The Definitive Collection** / 1992 / Capitol ✦✦✦✦
For a guy who claimed to be a jazz buff and to despise pop, Manfred Mann (the keyboard player) sure knew a pop hit when he heard one. And here they are, including "Do Wah Diddy Diddy" and "Pretty Flamingo." —*William Ruhlmann*

Chapter Two: The Best Of The Fontana Years / 1994 / Fontana ✦✦✦

The departure of Paul Jones for a solo career in 1966 spelled major reorganization for Manfred and his troops, who recruited lead vocalist Mike D'Abo and bassist (and Beatle chum) Klaus Voormann. To the surprise of many, the new lineup rattled off seven Top Ten British hits in the next three years in a far less R&B-oriented style. Emphasizing harmonies and Manfred Mann's inventiveness as arranger and keyboardist (often employing the then-futuristic Mellotron), this represented the group's most commercial phase, with an upbeat approach that bordered on downright chipper. These 20 tracks include all the key singles from this time, as well as a few LP cuts. Frankly, this rather lightweight, prototypically cheery late-'60s British pop—sounding rather like a more commercial version of the *Odyssey & Oracle*-era Zombies—hasn't aged nearly as well as their far gutsier Paul Jones-era recordings. Only one of these songs was a hit in the U.S., but it was a big one—their great 1968 arrangement of the then-unreleased Bob Dylan song "The Mighty Quinn." —*Richie Unterberger*

Manhattans

Group, Soul, Urban, Doo-Wop
A venerable soul quintet from New Jersey, whose career has spanned the dawn of soul and the death of disco, although they have steadfastly preferred ballads over the years. Led initially by

George Smith, who died in 1970, the Manhattans first charted in 1965 with "I Wanna Be (Your Everything)." After a string of solid R&B sellers on Carnival and DeLuxe, Gerald Alston replaced the late Smith and the group moved to Columbia. In 1976 they struck pay dirt with the elegant platinum-selling ballad "Kiss and Say Goodbye," which topped both the pop and soul lists. Several more huge R&B hits preceded their uplifting 1980 gold record "Shining Star," and still more followed. —*Bill Dahl*

There's No Me without You / 1973 / Columbia ✦✦✦
Things changed considerably for the Manhattans in the early '70s. George "Smitty" Smith left the group and later died tragically. Gerald Alston replaced him and the group signed with Columbia. The title track of this album was their first huge hit with Columbia, and quickly showed them how much clout a smash on a major label meant. The single reached number three on the R&B charts, almost made the pop Top 40, and ensured that Alston's smoother, but equally powerful and declarative voice wouldn't have any problem fitting into their new sound. —*Ron Wynn*

○ **After Midnight** / 1980 / Columbia ✦✦✦✦
The finest Manhattan album in their second incarnation. The original group with George Smith had a slightly rougher, more traditional R&B/doo-wop sound, while the soul unit featuring Gerald Alston was smoother, but no less anthemic, especially on ballads. This album didn't make it as high on the pop charts as their self-titled '76 work, but had more consistently compelling tracks. "Shining Star" and "Girl Of My Dream" are masterful ballads. —*Ron Wynn*

● **Greatest Hits** / 1980 / Columbia ✦✦✦✦
This spotlights the biggest records from the Manhattans' second phase. After George "Smitty" Smith died, eventual replacement Gerald Alston brought them a fine heartache and love ballad stylist. The move to a major label in the early '70s also helped, as Columbia provided them much more publicity muscle and promotional assistance than they ever received at Carnival and Deluxe. During the mid-'70s and early '80s, they also earned their first crossover exposure with the #1 hit "Kiss And Say Goodbye," one of the songs featured on this anthology spotlighting their soul and pop hits for Columbia. —*Ron Wynn*

Black Tie / 1981 / Columbia ✦✦✦
A good, although not classic or spectacular, early '80s Manhattan album. The group dipped a bit from its peak of 1980, in part because the company chose to issue a greatest hits album in 1980 rather than just ride out an internal situation and wait for a fresh release. They got two more chart hits out of the album, but never regained the momentum or status they enjoyed in 1980. —*Ron Wynn*

Forever by Your Side / 1983 / Columbia ✦✦
Although this was a nice album, the Manhattans were beginning to encounter problems in the mid-'80s with Columbia. The hits were drying up, and although their harmonies and Alston's soothing leads were still first-rate, they had become strictly an R&B band in appeal and weren't generating any pop attention. They tried being even smoother and more romantic than ever, softening the production and toning down the group interaction. The results were some excellent singles in "Just The Lonely Talking" and "Locked Up in Your Love," but they couldn't move the album or the group ahead. —*Ron Wynn*

Back to Basics / 1986 / Columbia ✦✦✦
The Manhattans tried to return to the soul form of past years with this mid-'80s release. It contained songs written and produced by the great Bobby Womack and less pop/crossover arrangements and influences. Gerald Alston was preparing to leave the group, but still sang with his customary warmth and style. But the person who made the most impact on this album was new co-vocalist Regina Belle. She became an urban contemporary star in the Anita Baker/Dianne Reeves quasi-jazz vein, but on this album she was singing with more soul and less polish. Belle toured with the band that year and turned a lot of heads. It didn't do as well as some past Columbia efforts, but was a worthy final project for Alston. —*Ron Wynn*

● **Dedicated to You: Golden Carnival Classics, Pt. 1** / Collectables ✦✦✦✦
The first of two superb volumes covering the Manhattans' early years on the Carnaval label, the period many regard as their greatest. While they didn't come close to equaling the crossover/pop success they would enjoy with Columbia in their second incarna-

tion, these were the pure soul works. The group featured both a glorious George "Smitty" Smith and young Blue Lovett, and their songs were produced solely with soul/R&B audiences in mind. There was little of the slick, polished orchestrations or smooth arrangements that were the hallmark of the Columbia hits. Instead, Smith's aching, soaring leads and the group's alternately mellow and frenzied harmonies were the high points. No matter what the sound quality, both this album and its counterpart are essential purchases for soul fans. —*Ron Wynn*

○ **For You & Yours: Golden Carnival Classics, Pt. 2** / Collectables ✦✦✦✦
For many Manhattans fans, their earliest singles for Carnaval were their greatest. These featured the wondrous George "Smitty" Smith, a young Blue Lovett, and some classic heartbreak and anguished soul singles, such as the divine "I Wanna Be (Your Everything)." These haven't been available on anthologies very often, and haven't been available anywhere since the early days of the Solid Smoke series. While Collectables' reissues sometimes leave a lot to be desired in the sound category, these songs are so good and so rare that any anthology featuring them has to get the highest recommendation, regardless of technical merit. This is the second of two volumes covering this era. —*Ron Wynn*

Manic Street Preachers

Group, Hard Rock, Alternative Pop/Rock
Riding a conspicuous wave of hype out of their hometown of Cardiff, Wales, in the early '90s, the Manic Street Preachers were supposed to be (at least according to some wags in the British rock press) the saviors of British rock. So it was alleged that after they saved British rock, they were going to dominate the world pop market with their Stones/New York Dolls/Sex Pistols fusion. They were loud, made vaguely libertarian political declamations, and claimed that they were the products of a wanton consumer society, addicted to television and alienated by reality. They were the new generation and they had something to say—most of it bad. Well, the truth was, it was mostly hype, and the Manic Street Preachers managed to grind out mostly uninspired punk-derived hard rock. It did go over pretty well in England, but in America it was almost wholly ignored. Despite carrying their bizarre antics to occasionally ridiculous extremes (all of which garnered much media attention), the (second) strangest moment of this band's career came when guitarist Richey Edwards became incensed when the band's credibility was questioned by an English music journalist. Edwards produced a large knife and slashed the words "4 Real" into his own forearm, a stunt that got the band plenty of ink and required hundreds of stitches. After the release of their most recent record, portentously titled *The Holy Bible*, and just prior to a major U.K. tour, Edwards disappeared from a London hotel in January of 1995. His car was found several days later, but Edwards (who has a history of depression and substance abuse) has never been seen again, ostensibly bringing the band's career to a very bizarre conclusion. —*John Dougan*

● **Generation Terrorists** / 1992 / Columbia ✦✦✦✦
Gold Against the Soul / 1993 / Columbia ✦✦✦
○ **Holy Bible** / 1994 / CBS ✦✦✦✦
The Manic Street Preachers' final album was also their strongest, melding their aggressive, punky attack with a set of powerfully angry, well-written songs and hooks. *The Holy Bible* appeared in England in the fall of 1994 and was scheduled for U.S. release in early 1995 when Richey James disappeared, cancelling all plans for American release. —*Stephen Thomas Erlewine*

Barry Manilow

b. Jun. 17, 1946
Pop
Although he has never earned the respect of critics or the much of the public, Barry Manilow was one of the most successful recording artists of the '70s. Manilow began his pop music career by writing advertising jingles in the '60s; during this time, the Julliard-trained musician honed his pop instincts, as evidenced by the sheer number of successful advertisements he wrote. In 1972, he began accompanying Bette Midler on piano as she performed in New York City's gay bath-houses. Manilow arranged her first two albums, which helped him earn a record contract with Bell. His self-titled first album was a flop, yet his second featured the number one ballad "Mandy."

"Mandy" began a decade's worth of polished MOR hits for Manilow, which included the number one singles "I Write the Songs" and "Looks Like We Made It," as well as Top Tens "Could It Be Magic," "Copacabana (At the Copa)" and "I Made It Through the Rain." Manilow also became a popular live act during this time. By the mid-'80s, he decided to broaden his musical horizons by making records of jazz and pop standards. At the end of the decade, the widow of Johnny Mercer invited him to set music to a number of the great songwriter's unpublished lyrics; some of the results appeared on *Showstoppers*. — *Stephen Thomas Erlewine*

○ **Barry Manilow** / Sep. 1973 / Arista ✦✦✦✦

○ **Barry Manilow II** / Oct. 1974 / Arista ✦✦✦✦
Barry Manilow's second album was his breakthrough, since it contained his #1 gold single "Mandy," as well as the #12 "It's A Miracle." With its lush sound and appealing pop songs, this album set the pattern for Manilow's ongoing easy listening success through the rest of the 1970s and into the '80s. — *William Ruhlmann*

○ **Barry Manilow I** / 1975 / Arista ✦✦✦✦

○ **Tryin' to Get the Feeling** / Oct. 1975 / Arista ✦✦✦✦

This One's for You / Aug. 1976 / Arista ✦✦

○ **Live** / May 1977 / Arista ✦✦✦✦
Live was Manilow's only number one album. The performances are so seamless that it's practically a faithfully performed greatest-hits album. It includes the hit "Daybreak." — *Rick Clark*

Even Now / Feb. 1978 / Arista ✦✦✦

● **Greatest Hits, Vol. 1** / Nov. 1978 / Arista ✦✦✦✦
Manilow has had a load of albums, but essentially he is a singles artist. This first *Greatest Hits* collection is the place to start, for those desiring an introduction to one of the most successful MOR singers of all time. Among the songs included in this collection are "Mandy," "Looks Like We Made It," "Can't Smile Without You," "Tryin' to Get the Feeling Again," and "Daybreak." — *Rick Clark*

One Voice / Oct. 1979 / Arista ✦✦

Barry / Dec. 1980 / Arista ✦✦✦

If I Should Love Again / Sep. 1981 / Arista ✦✦

Here Comes the Night / Nov. 1982 / Arista ✦✦

● **Greatest Hits, Vol. 2** / Nov. 1983 / Arista ✦✦✦✦
Included is "Could It Be Magic," "This One's for You," "Weekend in New England," "Copacabana (At the Copa)," and "I Write the Songs." — *Rick Clark*

○ **2:00 AM Paradise Cafe** / Nov. 1984 / Arista ✦✦✦✦
With his contemporary pop career in decline and "classic pop" on the rise, Barry Manilow began to position himself as a long-term show business talent in the tradition of, say, Mel Torme, who turns up here to do a duet with him. So does Sarah Vaughan, and even when Manilow isn't hobnobbing with great singers of an earlier era, he's leading a band of jazz veterans like Shelly Manne and Gerry Mulligan in what are supposed to be new jazz-pop standards. So, can Barry Manilow become Harry Connick, Jr.? Well, not quite, but it's a nice try. — *William Ruhlmann*

○ **Swing Street** / 1987 / Arista ✦✦✦✦
Barry Manilow takes another stab at traditional jazz-pop, again enlisting support from those who have made a career at it, such as Diane Schuur. This time he includes some covers, such as "Summertime," the Schuur duet that also includes some sax from Stan Getz. But there are also his own originals, which don't compare, and he even adds lyrics to "Stompin' At The Savoy," firm evidence that he hasn't got the respect for tradition to make the transition from sweet to hot. — *William Ruhlmann*

○ **Greatest Hits, Vol. 3** / 1989 / Arista ✦✦✦✦
Vol. 3 isn't as consistently strong as the first two, since it consists mainly of his less successful tracks. This set contains "The Old Songs," "Memory," "Let's Hang On," "Somewhere Down the Road," "I Made It Through the Rain," and his Top Ten version of Ian Hunter's "Ships." — *Rick Clark*

Showstoppers / Sep. 10, 1991 / Arista ✦✦✦

Greatest Hits Box Set / 1992 / Arista ✦✦✦
For Barry Manilow fanatics, this lavish, expensive box set (which is filled with rarities) will be hard to live without, but more casual fans should stick with the *Greatest Hits* albums. — *Stephen Thomas Erlewine*

Singin' with the Big Bands / 1994 / Arista ✦✦

Aimee Mann

Singer-Songwriter, Pop/Rock
Because of its big video/radio 1985 hit "Voices Carry," Til Tuesday was pigeonholed as a one-hit wonder, but their three albums all featured some fine pop songwriting by singer/guitarist Aimee Mann. Several years after Til Tuesday's breakup and after some legal wrangling, Mann launched a solo career in 1993 with *Whatever*. Even if the album's sales were modest, she finally received some of the critical acclaim that she has always deserved. — *Stephen Thomas Erlewine*

● **Whatever** / May 11, 1993 / Imago ✦✦✦✦
Led by the instantly memorable power-pop of "I Should've Known," Aimee Mann's first solo album, *Whatever*, is a strong collection of pure pop singles and folk-tinged ballads proving that she is a very talented songwriter with a gift for melody, as well as a fine lyricist. — *Stephen Thomas Erlewine*

Mantronix

Group, Rap
Combining rap, funk, pop, reggae, and electronics, Mantronix was one of the most innovative hip-hop groups of the mid-'80s. Formed in 1984, the New York group comprised DJ/keyboardist Mantronik (born Curtis Khalee) and rapper MC Tee (born Tooure Embden). Mantronix's demo tape gained the attention of William Socolov, the head of the independent record label Sleeping Bag. The group released their first single, "Fresh Is the Word," in 1985; it was a big hit on the street and in the clubs, as was their debut album, *Mantronix*. The duo enhanced their reputation by producing Joyce Sims and 12.41. However, their second record, 1986's *Music Madness*, showed them in a holding pattern; soon afterward, their audience began to shrink and by the beginning of the '90s they had faded away. — *Stephen Thomas Erlewine*

● **The Album** / 1985 / Sleeping Bag ✦✦✦✦
Mantronix's finest album remains this intriguing mid-'80s debut, when Curtis "Mantronix" Kahleel and rapper M.C. Tee scored with what was then an imaginative and unusual mix of dance and hip-hop production styles and sensibility with soul and R&B vocals. They weren't house, or rap, or urban contemporary, but a wonderful hybrid of all these and more, including touches of dancehall reggae and even pop and funk. The album had two fine singles in "Bassline" and "Ladies," and made Mantronix a hot property. — *Ron Wynn*

This Should Move Ya / 1987 / Capitol ✦✦✦
Mantronix switched labels in the late '80s, moving from the independent Sleeping Bag to the major label Capitol. This was their second Capitol album, and it worked out fine. Although the lineup had now changed, with Bryce Luvah and D.J.D. on board rather than M.C. Tee, the group had another strong single in "Got To Have Your Love," and Capitol was providing Curtis "Mantronix" Kahleel with a bigger push and sharper production and sound. But the underground spirit that permeated Mantronix's Sleeping Bag albums was missing, as was the quirky air that marked their past singles. — *Ron Wynn*

In Full Effect / 1988 / Capitol ✦✦✦
The Capitol debut for Curtis "Mantronix" Kahleel, and the final album featuring rapper M.C. Tee. This album skirted the lower regions of the pop charts and had a less abrasive, smoother sound, although the patented dance/hip-hop/urban contemporary fusion hadn't been affected. But overall, it wasn't quite as risky or spirited as their Sleeping Bag records, which may have been the reason Tee departed. — *Ron Wynn*

The Incredible Sound Machine / Mar. 18, 1991 / Capitol ✦✦
Things had changed for the production/songwriting duo Mantronix by the early '90s. Curtis "Mantronix" Kahleel was still aboard doing remixes and production, but now the vocalists were Jade Trini and Bryce Luvah. They had one mildly interesting single with "Don't Go Messin' With My Heart," but otherwise, the formerly inspired mix of hip-hop/dance production and soul/R&B vocals wasn't as exuberant or as catchy. The studio work was equally as sharp, but they didn't generate as much attention in the dance, hip-hop, or urban contemporary markets. — *Ron Wynn*

The Mar-Keys

Group, Soul
Before Booker T. & the MG's, there were the Mar-Keys, who liter-

ally laid the groundwork for the Memphis Sound with their pow-erfully economic early-R&B instrumental sound. They enjoyed only one real hit with the #3 "Last Night," which was released in 1961 on Satellite Records, the predecessor to Stax.

Besides including Steve Cropper and "Duck" Dunn in the lineup, the Mar-Keys also had Wayne Jackson, who later formed the Memphis Horns, and Don Nix, who had a fairly successful ca-reer as a solo artist and producer. —Rick Clark

The Markeys / 1961 / Atlantic ✦✦✦
Do the Pop-Eye / 1962 / Atlantic ✦✦✦
The Great Memphis Sound / 1966 / Atlantic ✦✦✦
● **Back to Back** / 1967 / Atlantic ✦✦✦✦
Recorded live at Paris in 1967, when the Stax-Volt Revue was tour-ing Europe. This is just about exactly what you'd expect: solid, straight-ahead live versions of the instrumental group's best-known tunes, in good sound. Booker T. & the MG's take seven of album's ten tracks, including their hits "Green Onions" and "Hip Hug-Her"; the Mar-Keys do "Last Night" and a couple of other numbers. —Richie Unterberger

Mellow Jelly / 1968 / Atlantic ✦✦
Damifiknew / 1969 / Stax ✦✦✦
Memphis Horns / 1970 / Cotillion ✦✦✦
Memphis Experience / 1970 / Stax ✦✦
High on Music / 1976 / RCA ✦✦

The Marcels

Group, Doo-Wop
This Pittsburgh ensemble deserved a much better fate than being known primarily for a novelty-tinged cover of "Blue Moon." Bari-tone vocalist Richard F. Knauss teamed with Fred Johnson, Gene J. Bricker, Ron Mundy, and lead vocalist Cornelius Harp, an inte-grated ensemble. They named themselves after Harp's hairstyle, the marcel. The group did a string of covers as demo tapes that were sent to Colpix. The label's A&R director had them cut several oldies at RCA's New York studios in 1961, one of them being "Blue Moon." They used the bass intro arrangement from the Cadillacs' "Zoom" and the results were a huge hit. It eventually topped both the pop and R&B charts, and also was an international smash. The group eventually appeared in the film "Twist Around the Clock" with Dion and Chubby Checker. They eventually recorded an 18-cut LP for Colpix. Alan Johnson and Walt Maddox later replaced Knauss and Gene Bricker, making them an all-Black unit. The group did score another Top Ten pop single with "Heartaches," an-other cover of a pre-rock single. This peaked at number seven pop and number 19 R&B in 1961. They continued recording on Kyra, Queen Bee, St. Clair Rocky, and Monogram with varying lineups, but never again equaled their past success. —Ron Wynn

● **The Best of the Marcels** / 1990 / Rhino ✦✦✦✦
An outstanding vocal ensemble that is exceptional on nonsense/novelty tunes like "Blue Moon." —Ron Wynn

Little Peggy March

Girl-Group
At the age of 15, this small Philadelphian with a booming voice scored one of the biggest hits of the girl group era in 1963 with the chart-topping "I Will Follow Him" (which had already been a huge French hit for Petula Clark in 1962 under its original title, "Char-iot"). She had a couple more Top 40 hits in 1963 with "I Wish I Were a Princess" (featured in the John Waters film *Hairspray*) and "Hello Heartache, Goodbye Love." Her fortunes diminished in the U.S., though she kept recording for literally decades. Fairly popu-lar overseas, she also recorded a number of foreign language sides for European markets. She remains most known for her early girl group sides, which are quite tuneful and well-produced, if quite dated in their cutesy naivete. —Richie Unterberger

● **Boy Crazy!** / 1986 / Raven ✦✦✦✦
This won't win you any respect from your serious rock critic friends, but if you enjoy early-'60s pop and are willing to put up with a few smirks, this is lightweight pap of the first order. Most of this 20-song collection of early- and mid-'60s sides is quite infec-tious, in fact, with Peggy's sprightly vocals, songwriting that weaves together some of the better elements of Brill Building and teen-idol pop, and full production that goes heavy on the female backup vocals and light symphonic string arrangements. Includes

all her hits, as well as a couple surprisingly tough numbers and the California pop-influenced "He Couldn't Care Less." Also in-cludes rare, quality early compositions by Randy Newman ("Leave Me Alone") and Leon Huff ("Can't Stop Thinking About Him"). —Richie Unterberger

Bobby Marchan

b. Apr. 30, 1930, Youngstown, OH
Doo-Wop, New Orleans R&B
A premier female impersonator, Bobby Marchan was part of a troupe called the Powder Box Revue. Before going on his own, Marchan played with Huey "Piano" Smith and the Clowns, toured with Shirley & Lee, and led his own band, the Tick Tocks. He landed his lone number one hit in 1960, a powerhouse version of "There's Something on Your Mind" for Fire. He continued record-ing for various tiny labels, and in 1966 had a Top 20 R&B single with "Shake Your Tambourine" for Cameo. —Ron Wynn

There's Something on Your Mind / 1964 / Sphere Sound ✦✦✦
● **Golden Classics** / 1988 / Collectables ✦✦✦✦
A collection of falsetto doo-wop and Southern soul balladry from the '60s. —Bil Carpenter

Teena Marie

b. 1957, Santa Monica, CA
Dance-Pop, Disco
This protégé of Rick James was one of Motown's most successful White artists. In the early '80s, she was one of the label's most suc-cessful artists, as her combination of funk, rock, pop and R&B earned two gold albums; she was also an accomplished writer and producer as well. She left the label in 1983, moving to Epic; her chart success continued at first, yet her popularity shrunk by the end of the decade. She was inactive for most of the '90s. —Rick A. Bueche

Irons in the Fire / 1974 / Motown ✦✦✦
A fine album for white soul vocalist Teena Marie, although she was already becoming disenchanted with Motown. But she en-joyed a Top 10 R&B hit with "I Need Your Lovin'," and "You Make Love Feel Like Springtime" was another of the soaring album cuts that were never turned into the smash singles they could have been with some savvy marketing. Marie was laying the ground-work for the major career push she received when she jumped ship for Epic. —Ron Wynn

Emerald City / 1976 / Epic ✦✦
A puzzling album for Teena Marie, perhaps the most disappoint-ing of her career. She tried a concept work, doing thematically re-lated songs and longer, jazz-influenced ballads. Many of them were well sung; some were a bit self-indulgent, but overall, it was a nicely performed work. But it flopped, indicating that her fans preferred short, to-the-point soul tunes and hard-hitting dance or funk to more introspective, slow-to-develop pieces and socio-polit-ical commentary. —Ron Wynn

Wild & Peaceful / 1979 / Motown ✦✦✦
Her debut album, it was produced by Rick James. —Rick A. Bueche

Lady T / 1980 / Motown ✦✦✦
This is an underground treasure of funk and soul. —Rick A. Bueche

It Must Be Magic / 1981 / Motown ✦✦✦
Her greatest Motown album. —Rick A. Bueche

Robbery / 1983 / Epic ✦✦
Although there were several songs that hinted at her potential, Teena Marie didn't become a hit act as a white female soul vocal-ist until she joined Epic. This album served to introduce the con-cepts that would explode on the followup, and also begin to show-case the naturally exuberant and majestic Marie ballad sound. Motown was left looking stupid when Marie became one of the mid- and late '80s finest soul acts. —Ron Wynn

Starchild / 1984 / Epic ✦✦
This was the definitive album Teena Marie was never allowed to do while at Motown. She not only zoomed up the R&B charts, but even had a pop smash with "Lovergirl," and suddenly Motown ex-ecutives went scrambling for cover. "Mr. Dear Mr. Gaye" was one of the better tribute songs done to Gaye, although it didn't gener-ate the attention it deserved for Marie. The album wound up be-ing Marie's most successful. —Ron Wynn

● **Teena Marie's Greatest Hits** / 1985 / Motown ✦✦✦✦
The highlights of her career, it includes "I Need Your Lovin'"
(#37) and "Square Biz" (#50). —*Rick A. Bueche*

Naked to the World / Apr. 1987 / Epic ✦✦✦
This was the final big album for white soul vocalist Teena Marie.
While other females, many of them British, enjoyed success in the
late '80s and '90s by doing updated Barry White productions and
'70s-style disco tunes, Marie continued doing vintage soul and
R&B/funk. The single "Ooh La La La" was her last great song, topping the R&B charts and doing well internationally. Marie hasn't
duplicated its success since, and by '91 was without a label deal. —
Ron Wynn

○ **Greatest Hits** / 1991 / Epic ✦✦✦✦
More recent material, it features "Lovergirl" (#4), "Jammin'"
(#81), and "Ooo La La La" (#85). —*Rick A. Bueche*

Compact Command Performances / Motown ✦✦✦
Teena Marie had the distinction for many years of being not only
one of the rare white acts on Motown, but also one of its greatest
female soul singers. She hedged her bets by doing lots of uptempo
funk and dance-flavored tunes, but when she did ballads, even
overproduced ones, her strong, soaring voice had the kind of
earthy, direct quality attainable only by someone who really had
soul. While Motown's various special lines and concept packages
are often ripoffs, in this case it's certainly worth getting the Marie
package, especially because many of her albums didn't sell all that
well and are now hard to find. —*Ron Wynn*

Ivory / Epic ✦✦
Vocalist Teena Marie began the '90s recovering from an accident
in Texas that had broken six ribs. This album was an attempt to
recapture her earlier success, and included a song written and
produced by Soul II Soul's Jazzie B. Unfortunately, it didn't generate much action, and Marie was unable to halt the slide that had
begun in the mid-'80s. Despite some strong, often delightful and
energetic vocals, no single from the album exploded, and Marie
would soon find herself dropped from the label. —*Ron Wynn*

Marillion

Group, Hard Rock, Art-Rock/Progressive-Rock
Marillion was one of the leading art-rock bands of the '80s, paying
homage to the theatrical thrills of early Genesis before evolving
into a more straightforward hard rock. Over the years, the group
has been quite popular in the U.K., peaking in 1985 with the *Misplaced Childhood* album, but has never been more than a cult act
in the U.S.; they continue to tour and record in the '90s, with a
faithful cult of fans supporting their latest efforts. —*Stephen
Thomas Erlewine*

○ **Script for a Jester's Tear** / 1983 / Capitol ✦✦✦✦
Their strong debut shows the influence of Peter Hammill, Pink
Floyd, Rick Wakeman, Jethro Tull, and the much-ballyhooed re-
semblance to Genesis. —*Michael P. Dawson*

○ **Fugazi** / 1984 / Capitol ✦✦✦✦
Gut-wrenchingly powerful lyrics and dynamic prog-rock performance make this a classic! —*Michael P. Dawson*

Real to Reel / 1984 / EMI ✦✦
○ **Misplaced Childhood** / 1985 / Capitol ✦✦✦✦
A masterpiece of articulate and emotional lyrics, it has exciting
and colorful musical settings. The songs form a continuous album-length suite. —*Michael P. Dawson*

Clutching at Straws / Jun. 19, 1987 / Capitol ✦✦✦
The followup to *Misplaced Childhood* is even more personal and
often disturbing with its ruminations on alcohol abuse and self-be-
trayal. —*Michael P. Dawson*

The Thieving Magpie (la Gazza Ladra) / 1988 / Capitol ✦✦✦
A fine double-CD live set from their 1984 and 1987 tours, this was
Fish's last recording with Marillion and was named for the Rossini
piece they open their shows with. —*Michael P. Dawson*

Season's End / 1989 / Capitol ✦✦
An uneven but still tasty album, it features Steve Hogarth taking
over for the irreplaceable Fish. —*Michael P. Dawson*

Holidays in Eden / 1991 / IRS ✦✦✦
● **Six of One, Half-dozen of the Other** / 1992 / IRS ✦✦✦✦
A fine collection of Marillion's best and most popular tracks, *Six of
One, Half-dozen of the Other* offers a good introduction to the art-
rock group. —*Stephen Thomas Erlewine*

Brave / Feb. 8, 1994 / IRS ✦✦✦

Marilyn Manson

Group, Alternative Pop/Rock
A pet discovery of Trent Reznor's, this band was signed to his
Nothing label and was the opening act on Nine Inch Nails' tour
supporting *The Downward Spiral*. All band members play under
aliases combining a famous woman's name with the last name of
a serial killer: Mr. Manson (vocals), Daisy Berkowitz (guitars),
Madonna Wayne Gacy (synths), Twiggy Ramirez (bass), and Sara
Lee Lucas (drums). Their highly theatrical act is geared to shock
audiences and listeners and examines the seamy underbelly of
everyday American life and pop culture, which has begun to win
them a devoted cult. Critics of the band invariably say that their
shtick wears thin after a few songs and perhaps takes a few too
many cues from shock-rock master Alice Cooper. Still, the band is
making a name for itself, and it remains to be seen whether they
will sink or swim. —*Steve Huey*

○ **Portrait Of An American Family** / 1994 / Interscope ✦✦✦✦

The Mark Four

Group, British Invasion
Before changing their name, the Creation laid the foundation for
their Who-like distorted power chording as the Mark Four. The
group released four singles in 1964 and 1965 before renaming
themselves the Creation when they began to record for Shel
Talmy in 1966. The first two 45s are unremarkable covers of
R&B/rock standards, but the next couple featured fairly strong
mod/power-pop originals. "I'm Leaving" is particularly notable for
having one of the first extended guitar feedback passages in a rock
song. —*Richie Unterberger*

The Mark Four/The Creation / 1982 / Eva ✦✦✦
14-track compilation with all four of their singles, a couple songs
that were actually recorded by an unrelated Scottish group of the
time called the Mark Five (no kidding), and four Creation tunes,
two of which are fairly rare (a cover of "Like A Rolling Stone" and
the instrumental "Sylvette"). A real hodgepodge, but British Invasion aficionados will want to have the pair of 1965 Mark Four singles included here. —*Richie Unterberger*

Marky Mark & the Funky Bunch

Group, Rap
Few suspected Marky Mark, the younger brother of New Kids on
the Block vocalist Donnie Wahlberg, would still be around in the
mid-'90s while New Kids on the Block would be history. But
Marky Mark has survived through high profile underwear ads and
low grade, but popular enough, pop-rap. He's even overcome a homophobic controversy, and scored a number one hit with "Good
Vibrations" from his debut *Music for the People*; that single has
been his high point. Even though the second LP, *You Gotta Believe*, peaked at number 14, it didn't duplicate the platinum status
of the debut. —*Ron Wynn*

● **Music for the People** / 1991 / Interscope ✦✦✦✦
On the strength of the number one hit "Good Vibrations" and the
Top Ten follow-up "Wildside," Marky Mark & the Funky Bunch's
first album became a pop sensation. Unfortunately, the rest of the
album couldn't match the catchy, pop-oriented rap of the singles,
making the entire record a hit-or-miss affair. —*Stephen Thomas
Erlewine*

You Gotta Believe / 1992 / Interscope ✦✦✦
Marky Mark tried to keep riding the wave he had enjoyed with
Music for the People, but failed to score any pop or R&B hit, finding that it's much tougher to find another hit to scavenge or maintain a gimmick the second time around. He eventually enjoyed
moderate success with "You Gotta Believe," but a combination of
some ill-timed homophobic remarks in an interview and rather
limp material like "Bout Time I Funk You" and "I Run Rhymes"
extinguished whatever fires Marky Mark had previously lit. —*Ron
Wynn*

Biz Markie

Rap
A productive member of Marley Marl's posse, Markie is a contemporary master of comedic rap. He doesn't have much to say, but
songs such as "Picking Boogers" are worthy of the Fat Boys and
"Spring Again" is a classic summer single.

Biz Markie managed to dodge a potential career-ending bullet when a controversy involving a sample from Gilbert O'Sullivan's "Alone Again Naturally" was resolved. Markie had allegedly used the sample without permission, triggering a lawsuit. He gave his own spin to the controversy with the 1993 release *All Samples Cleared*. —*John Floyd*

○ **Goin' Off** / Feb. 23, 1988 / Cold Chillin' ◆◆◆◆
Biz Markie's debut album introduced his absurdly comical and extremely inventive musical style. While he talked about "Pickin' Boogers," hanging out at "Albee Square Mall," and made music with his mouth, the Biz never kept the music similar, with Marley Marl's production covering all of the bases, concentrating on a deeply funky R&B/dance beat. It was a funny, surrealistic minor masterpiece. —*Stephen Thomas Erlewine*

○ **The Diabolical Biz Markie: the Biz Never Sleeps** / Oct. 10, 1989 / Cold Chillin' ◆◆◆◆
Biz Markie's madcap humor was effectively utilized on this release. Markie relied on puns, quips, bad jokes and his disjointed rap style, creating material quite different from the hard-edged fare that now rules hip-hop. Some of it was funny, some of it stupid, but none of it vicious or offensive. The album contained the hits "Just a Friend" and "Spring Again." —*Ron Wynn*

I Need a Haircut / Aug. 27, 1991 / Cold Chillin' ◆◆◆
While others rap about gang strife, inner city turmoil, their proficiency on the mike or their sexual prowess, Biz Markie discussed bad haircuts and other such weighty matters on this release. This might be what the Coasters would sound like if they had grown up during the rap era. Sadly, there aren't many people on the '90s hip-hop scene interested in absurdist humor. —*Ron Wynn*

All Samples Cleared / 1993 / Cold Chillin' ◆◆
Biz Markie made sure he had permission for every sample featured on this album. Unfortunately, it seemed that the effort to get clearances took its toll on the creative process. The bizarre humor that made his earlier releases so entertaining was much less evident, as Markie now strained for results and mostly came up short. —*Ron Wynn*

● **Biz's Baddest Beats** / 1994 / Cold Chillin' ◆◆◆◆
Biz's Baddest Beats collects all of Biz Markie's hit singles, making the album a good introduction to his bizarrely humorous hip-hop. —*Stephen Thomas Erlewine*

Marley Marl

Rap
Ace producer Marl has worked with the likes of Roxanne Shanté, Biz Markie, Big Daddy Kane, MC Shan, and Master Ace. His style maintains its roots in old-school hip-hop while pushing the music to new, oftentimes blatantly accessible levels. —*John Floyd*

● **In Control, Vol. 1** / 1988 / Cold Chillin' ◆◆◆◆
Marl shows off his greatest stars, including Roxanne Shanté and Big Daddy Kane. —*Dan Heilman*

In Control, Vol. 2 / 1991 / Cold Chillin' ◆◆◆
Although the date carried his name, this was really a showcase for various rappers produced by Marley Marl. Everyone from Chuck D, LL Cool J and Heavy D to Chubb Rock, Def Jef and King Tee made an appearance on his second Cold Chillin' CD. Unfortunately this all-star lineup didn't hit any home runs, and the LP struck out. —*Ron Wynn*

The Marshall Tucker Band

Group, Southern Rock
One of the major Southern-rock bands of the '70s, the Marshall Tucker Band was formed in Spartanburg, SC, in 1971 by singer Doug Gray; guitarist Toy Caldwell (b. 1948); his brother, bassist Tommy Caldwell (b. 1950—d. Apr 4, 1980); guitarist George McCorkle; drummer Paul Riddle; and reed player Jerry Eubanks. The group's style combined rock, country, and jazz, and featured extended instrumental passages on which lead guitarist Toy Caldwell shone. The band was signed to Capricorn Records and released its debut album, *The Marshall Tucker Band*, in March 1973. They gained recognition through a tour with the Allman Brothers Band and found significant success during the course of the '70s, with most of their albums going gold. Their peak came with the million-selling album *Carolina Dreams* and its Top 15 single "Heard It in a Love Song" in 1977. The band was slowed down by the death of Tommy Caldwell in a car accident in 1980, and it faded from the album charts after 1982. Toy Caldwell left for a

solo career, and by the early '90s, Marshall Tucker consisted of Doug Gray, Jerry Eubanks, guitarist Rusty Milner, bassist Tim Lawter, drummer Ace Allen, and pianist Don Cameron. —*William Ruhlmann*

○ **The Marshall Tucker Band** / 1973 / AJK ◆◆◆◆
With flute and the occasional blast of horns, the Marshall Tucker Band were one of the most laidback Southern country-rock outfits of the late '70s. Their first album easily demonstrates this, and it still holds up well, with "Take the Highway," "Can't You See," and "Ramblin'" sounding particularly strong. —*Stephen Thomas Erlewine*

○ **Where We All Belong** / 1974 / AJK ◆◆◆◆
Although it runs a little long, *Where We All Belong* captures the sound of the Marshall Tucker Band coming into its own. Half the tracks are new studio recordings, which are more focused than their previous releases; the other half is a harder-edged, jam-oriented live set. Taken together, they show that the band was progressing musically. —*Stephen Thomas Erlewine*

○ **A New Life** / 1974 / AJK ◆◆◆◆
On their second release, the Marshall Tucker Band becomes slightly rootsier and bluesier without sacrificing any of the relaxed charm of their first record. Overall, it is a stronger, more consistent album, highlighted by "Southern Woman," "Blue Ridge Mountain Sky," and "Too Stubborn." —*Stephen Thomas Erlewine*

○ **Searchin' for a Rainbow** / 1975 / AJK ◆◆◆◆
With *Searchin' for a Rainbow*, the Marshall Tucker Band retreats somewhat from the grittier sounds of *Where We All Belong* without abandoning their country and blues roots. —*Stephen Thomas Erlewine*

Long Hard Ride / 1976 / AJK ◆◆◆
On *Long Hard Ride*, the Marshall Tucker Band's country influences come to the fore, resulting in a strong record that failed to gain many hits. Still, the final product is well worth listening to—it's one of their better releases. Be sure to listen for Charlie Daniels' guest appearance. —*Stephen Thomas Erlewine*

Carolina Dreams / 1977 / AJK ◆◆◆
Carolina Dreams marks a retreat from the more pronounced country leanings of *Long Hard Ride* to the more successful country-tinged pop-rock of "Heard It In a Love Song" and "Fly Like An Eagle." They gathered more hits with this approach, and although the hits hold up well, the rest of the album doesn't live up to their quality. —*Stephen Thomas Erlewine*

Best of Marshall Tucker / 1978 / Capricorn ◆◆◆

● **Greatest Hits** / 1978 / AJK ◆◆◆◆
If you are looking for a place to start with this band, *Greatest Hits* covers all the main bases. Included are "Can't You See" (number 75), "Heard It in a Love Song" (number 14), "Fire on the Mountain" (number 38), and "This Ol' Cowboy" (number 78). —*Rick Clark*

Together Forever / 1978 / AJK ◆◆◆
Together Forever boasts a more mainstream rock approach than any of its predecessors, halfway between the country-tinged *Long Hard Ride* and the pop-oriented *Carolina Dreams*. Although the band sounds good, the songs don't match the strength of their performances. —*Stephen Thomas Erlewine*

Running Like the Wind / 1979 / Warner Brothers ◆◆◆

Tenth / 1980 / Warner Brothers ◆◆◆

Dedicated / 1981 / Warner Brothers ◆◆◆

Tuckerized / 1981 / Warner Brothers ◆◆◆

Just Us / 1983 / Warner Brothers ◆◆◆

Greetings from South Carolina / 1983 / Warner Brothers ◆◆◆

Still Holdin' on / 1988 / PolyGram ◆◆

Southern Spirit / 1990 / Capitol ◆◆

Still Smokin' / 1992 / Cabin Fever ◆◆

Martha & the Vandellas

Group, Soul, Motown
One of Motown's finest female groups formed almost by accident. Martha Reeves had been in the Del-Phis and recorded solo for Checkmate, but in the early '60s was working as an A&R secretary at Motown, doing some background work on the side. She organized a group with Annette Beard and Rosalind Ashford in 1962. They roared into the spotlight with "Come and Get These Memories" in 1963, and Reeves' husky, alternately sensual and demure

leads made them a hit attraction through 1967. They scored number one R&B hits with "Heat Wave" and "Jimmy Mack" (both crossover Top Ten pop winners as well) and Top Ten R&B hits with "Quicksand," "Nowhere to Run," "My Baby Loves Me," "Honey Chile," and "I'm Ready for Love." Oddly, their finest song, "Dancing in the Streets," only reached number two. Beard departed in 1964, and was replaced by Betty Kelly, an ex-Velvelette. They disbanded from 1969 to 1971, then re-formed with Reeves and her sister Lois, plus Sandra Tilley. They split for good in 1972, as Martha Reeves went solo and Lois Reeves joined Quiet Elegance. Martha Reeves worked with various producers throughout the '70s, among them Richard Perry, and had only sporadic success recording for MCA, Arista, and Fantasy. She reunited with the Vandellas in 1989 and has continued performing with them ever since. She and original Vandellas Rosalind (Ashford) Holmes and Annette Beard recorded for Motorcity in England in 1989, and Lois Reeves also did a solo session with them, as did their brother Benny Reeves. —*Ron Wynn*

Heat Wave / 1963 / Motown ✦✦✦
Martha and the Vandellas began making their first noise on the pop and soul charts with this 1963 album. The title song was a classic, while there were also decent remakes of such vintage tunes as "Mocking Bird" and "My Boyfriend's Back." These proved that the group was a singles rather than an album act, and that a little more effort needed to be extended toward finding more material (they even put "Danke Schoen" on this album). But no one really cared, since "Heat Wave" was such a triumph. —*Ron Wynn*

Come and Get These Memories / 1963 / Motown ✦✦✦
Their debut album finds the Vandellas in a more lightweight and pop-oriented style than they would become known for, with some girl group and doo-wop roots still in evidence. As was often the case during this era, the best tracks were the singles: the title track (the group's first big hit), "There He Is (At My Door)," and the Shirelles-like "I'll Have To Let Him Go." Most of the material was written by Holland-Dozier-Holland, but beyond the singles, there aren't any exceptionally noteworthy cuts. —*Richie Unterberger*

○ **Dance Party** / 1965 / Motown ✦✦✦✦
Another collection of singles rather than a unified album, but who cared when the songs included "Dancing In The Street" and "Nowhere To Run," as well as "Wild One"? Martha Reeves was singing with as much energy, sensuality and joy as any Motown performer during the mid-'60s, and at least the filler for this record was "Hitch Hike" and "Jerk" instead of "Danke Schoen." —*Ron Wynn*

Watchout / 1966 / Motown ✦✦✦
The creative well was already starting to run a bit dry for Martha and the Vandellas, mainly because they were a singles band and seldom made a whole album worth a second listen. This proved no different, with the great singles "I'm Ready For Love" and "Jimmy Mack" anchoring an otherwise forgettable collection of filler, although "No More Tearstained Make Up" was a decent bit of period-piece heartache soul and "What Am I Going To Do Without Your Love" brushed the low end of the pop and soul charts. —*Ron Wynn*

Martha & the Vandellas Live! / 1967 / Motown ✦✦

Ridin' High / 1968 / Motown ✦✦✦

Sugar 'N Spice / 1969 / Motown ✦✦✦

Natural Resources / 1970 / Motown ✦✦✦

Black Magic / 1972 / Motown ✦✦✦
Martha and the Vandellas were nearing the end when this LP was issued. They reformed in 1971 with Martha's sister Lois Reeves and Sandra Tilley and made one last attempt at pop and soul glory. But while Reeves still had the old power, drive and fire, they weren't getting the inspiring songs or magnificent lyrics of their timeless 1960s hits. Instead, the best tunes, such as "Bless You," "No One There" or "Your Love Makes It Worthwhile," seemed like second-level material that would have simply filled out earlier releases. No hits resulted from this album, and Reeves would soon be a solo performer. —*Ron Wynn*

○ **Anthology** / 1974 / Motown ✦✦✦✦
Until the label issued the definitive two-disc set *Live Wire: The Singles 1962–1972* in 1993, this two-record set was the ultimate Martha Reeves & The Vandellas set. It's still worth hearing, as it contains all the essential hits from their early-'60s run. But the 2-CD set has better sound than the original vinyl, plus more extensive notes, discographical information and photos. —*Ron Wynn*

☆ **Martha & the Vandellas Greatest Hits** / 1987 / Motown ✦✦✦✦✦
The one definitive package to own, with all their biggest and best, including "Come and Get These Memories," "Heat Wave," and "Dancing in the Streets." —*Cub Koda*

● **Live Wire! the Singles (1962–1972)** / Sep. 7, 1993 / Motown ✦✦✦
This two-CD box set includes all of the top singles and many of their flipsides that Martha Reeves and the Vandellas cut for Motown. All the hits are here, of course; the collector will be especially interested in the B-sides and non-hit singles, many of which employed the songwriting talents of Motown regulars like Holland-Dozier-Holland and Mickey Stevenson. There's also the rare single (featuring Gloria Williamson on lead vocals) cut by the Vells in 1962, before Reeves took top billing and the group changed their name. Eight of these cuts have never been released on album before. Among the non-hits, there isn't anything to match "Heat Wave" or "Dancing In The Street," but Reeves' astonishingly powerful voice never falters. She was arguably Motown's most talented female singer, but the label's investment in her seemed to flag as the decade progressed. The later material lacks the distinction of her classic period, though the 1970 album track "I Should Be Proud" is a little-known (if somewhat heavy-handed) protest against the Vietnam War. —*Richie Unterberger*

● **Milestones** / 1995 / Motown ✦✦✦✦
Featuring 18 of Martha & the Vandellas' biggest hits and finest songs, *Milestones* is an inexpensive introduction to one of Motown's best girl groups. —*Stephen Thomas Erlewine*

The Marvelettes

Group, Soul, Motown
Probably the most pop-oriented of Motown's major female acts, the Marvelettes didn't project as strong an identity as the Supremes, Mary Wells, or Martha Reeves, but recorded quite a few hits, including Motown's first number one single, "Please Mr. Postman" (1961). "Postman," as well as other chirpy early '60s hits like "Playboy," "Twistin' Postman," and "Beechwood 4-5789," were the label's purest girl group efforts. Featuring two strong lead singers, Gladys Horton and Wanda Young, the Marvelettes went through five different lineups, but maintained a high standard on their recordings. After a few years, they moved from girl group sounds to uptempo and midtempo numbers that were more characteristic of Motown's production line. They received no small help from Smokey Robinson, who produced and wrote many of their singles; Holland-Dozier-Holland, Berry Gordy, Mickey Stevenson, Marvin Gaye, and Ashford-Simpson also got involved with the songwriting and production at various points. After the mid-'60s, Wanda Young assumed most of the lead vocal duties, Gladys Horton departing the group in the late '60s. While the Marvelettes didn't cut as many monster smashes as most of their Motown peers after the early '60s, they did periodically surface with classic hits like "Too Many Fish in the Sea," "Don't Mess with Bill," and "The Hunter Gets Captured By the Game." There were also plenty of fine minor hits and misses, like 1965's "I'll Keep Holding On," which is just as memorable as the well-known Motown chart-toppers of the era. The group quietly disbanded in the early '70s after several years without a major hit. —*Richie Unterberger*

○ **The Marvelettes' Greatest Hits** / 1966 / Motown ✦✦✦✦
A good collection spotlighting one of Motown's least appreciated great female groups. The Marvelettes not only gave the label its first number one pop hit, but strung together a good series of tunes, especially when Smokey Robinson was writing and producing them. They went from being a quintet to a quartet to a trio during their Motown years, but seldom failed to give an energetic performance. —*Ron Wynn*

Return of the Marvelettes / 1970 / Motown ✦✦✦
Things were pretty much gone for the Marvelettes when they tried an early-'70s comeback. By now Motown had pretty much lost interest in them, and they were down to one original in Katharine Anderson. This album didn't go down as one of their best, and the curtain closed on their careers shortly afterward, although Gladys Horton teamed in recent years with two newcomers on the nostalgia/oldies circuit. —*Ron Wynn*

● **Anthology** / 1975 / Motown ✦✦✦✦
This traces the group's Motown history, including the hits "Beechwood 4-5789," "Don't Mess with Bill," "The Hunter Gets Captured by the Game," "Please Mr. Postman," "That's How Heartaches Are

Made," "Too Many Fish in the Sea," and many others. —*Rick A. Bueche*

○ **Compact Command Performances** / 1982 / Motown ✦✦✦✦
A well-mastered, comprehensive collection, one of the best in this line. Groups like the Marvelettes are the ones that Motown should devote this type of anthology to, ensuring that they receive some measure of acclaim they didn't get during their heyday. The Marvelettes were great on teen/innocent material and also turned in some solid, more adult soul in their later years. —*Ron Wynn*

○ **Deliver: The Singles (1961-1971)** / Sep. 7, 1993 / Motown ✦✦✦✦
41 songs, featuring most of both the A-sides and B-sides, nine of which had never been issued on album before. The ace Motown songwriting and production stable was involved in virtually every one of these tracks, making for a surprisingly strong and consistent collection. Includes all the chart hits, as well as rarities like the Phil Spector-style single they released in 1963 as the Darnells. —*Richie Unterberger*

Marvin & Johnny

Group, R&B
Marvin Phillips was a constant presence in this swinging pair, but the role of his duet partner, Johnny, was variously held down by Emory Perry (who also handled the sax solos on many of their records), Carl Green, and even Marvin himself via overdubs. Phillips had recorded as a solo before teaming with Jesse Belvin in 1953 and hitting the R&B charts with "Dream Girl" for Specialty Records. Marvin recruited Perry for a series of rocking duets for Specialty, RPM, Aladdin, and other West Coast concerns. They cut the classic ballad "Cherry Pie" and its rocking hit flip, "Tick Tock," for RPM in 1954. —*Bill Dahl*

● **Flipped Out** / 1992 / Specialty ✦✦✦✦

Richard Marx

Pop/Rock
Before he released his first album, Richard Marx sang on commercials and was a backing vocalist for Lionel Richie. It was here that he learned his commercial pop skills. As soon as his first album was released in 1987, he shot to the top of the charts. Marx's first hit was the California rocker "Don't Mean Nothing," but his real strength lay with ballads; "Right Here Waiting" and "Hold on to the Nights" were adult contemporary and pop radio staples during the late '80s and early '90s. With his first two albums, he had a streak of three consecutive number one hits in America. With the release of his third album in 1991, his commercial fortunes started to slip somewhat, as the mainstream shifted away from the slick, well-constructed songs that are his forte; even if he isn't hitting the Top Ten with each single anymore, Marx remains a mainstay on adult contemporary and pop radio. —*Stephen Thomas Erlewine*

● **Richard Marx** / 1987 / Capitol ✦✦✦✦
Richard Marx's self-titled debut album was a finely crafted record of mainstream pop/rock. Marx understood how the melodies of uptempo rockers like "Don't Mean Nothin' " are driven by thick power chords and how arrangements are as important as melody in ballads like "Hold on to the Nights." Filled with carefully constructed radio-ready tracks, it was no surprise that the album became a huge hit. —*Stephen Thomas Erlewine*

○ **Repeat Offender** / 1989 / Capitol ✦✦✦✦
Marx's second album was almost as strong as his first, even if it showed that his songwriting has a tendency to slip into sappy, saccharine cliches. Nevertheless, it had contained some major hit singles—"Satisfied," "Right Here Waiting," "Angelia," "Children of the Night," and "Too Late to Say Goodbye." —*Stephen Thomas Erlewine*

Rush Street / Oct. 28, 1991 / Capitol ✦✦✦
While there are some strong songs on *Rush Street*, it isn't as consistently engaging as his first two albums. —*Stephen Thomas Erlewine*

Paid Vacation / Feb. 8, 1994 / Capitol ✦✦
Paid Vacation is Marx's calmest and most sophisticated album to date. —*Stephen Thomas Erlewine*

The Mary Jane Girls

Group, Soul, Dance-Pop
Members Joanne McDuffie, Candice Ghant, Kim Wuletick, and Yvette Marine were originally the backup singers for Rick James's concerts and records. He produced admirable dance hits for them

in the '80s, but as his fortunes declined, so did theirs, and they disbanded. —*Bil Carpenter*

Mary Jane Girls / 1983 / Motown ✦✦✦
Rick James was riding so high at Motown in the early '80s that they signed his backup band and let James produce a couple of albums for them. This self-titled debut actually proved to be better than anticipated. The foursome got four R&B hits from this album, with "All Night Long" just missing the Top 10. They were no great shakes as vocalists, but made up for it with a visual act that took male listeners' minds off the fact that were hearing, in some instances, minimal harmonies and leads. —*Ron Wynn*

○ **Only Four You** / 1985 / Motown ✦✦✦✦
Outstanding club music produced by Rick James, it includes the Top Ten hits "In My House" and "Wild & Crazy Love." —*Rick A. Bueche*

● **Best Of: In My House** / 1994 / Motown ✦✦✦✦

Dave Mason

b. May 10, 1946, Worchester, England
Pop/Rock
Mason was a founding member of the influential late-'60s group Traffic. He provided some of that group's best material on their first three albums, particularly "You Can All Join In" and "Feelin' Alright," a song that has been covered by numerous artists, including Joe Cocker and Three Dog Night. Mason left Traffic in 1970 and went solo, enjoying sporadic success during the '70s with his style of light melodic pop/rock. —*Rick Clark*

○ **Alone Together** / 1970 / MCA ✦✦✦✦
Mason's debut solo album remains his best effort, due to well-crafted tracks like the hit "Only You Know & I Know" and an appealing easy-going rock sound that presents a nice blend of acoustic and electric instrumentation. —*Rick Clark*

○ **Let It Flow** / 1977 / Columbia ✦✦✦✦
On *Let It Flow*, Mason delivered a super-slick bid for radio-friendly pop. He succeeded with three hits, "So High (Rock Me Baby and Roll Me Away)," "Let It Go, Let It Flow," and the richly harmonic "We Just Disagree." —*Rick Clark*

● **The Best Of Dave Mason** / 1995 / Columbia/Legacy ✦✦✦✦
The Best Of Dave Mason At Columbia would be a more accurate title, as this doesn't include work from his early-'70s LPs for Blue Thumb. The 19 tracks spotlight selections from seven albums that he recorded for Columbia. Including the hits "We Just Disagree," "Let It Go, Let It Flow," and "Will You Still Love Me Tomorrow," it charts his move from easygoing early-'70s FM rock to a more mainstream AOR pop sound. —*Richie Unterberger*

Massive Attack

Group, Alternative Pop/Rock, Dance
Massive Attack was one of the pioneers of the British dance genre labelled "trip-hop," a dark, seductive combination of hip-hop beats, atmospheric reverb-laden guitars and samples, soul hooks, deep bass grooves and ethereal melodies. Released in 1991, *Blue Lines* set the pace for much of the non-techno British dance of the decade, including that of Portishead and former Massive Attack member Tricky. Both of these acts managed to score more commercial success, including alternative hits in America, but much of their work builds on the concepts of Massive Attack. *Protection*, the group's second album, was a critical and underground hit in England during 1994, yet it made little impact in the United States when it was released early in 1995. —*Stephen Thomas Erlewine*

● **Blue Lines** / 1991 / Virgin ✦✦✦✦
At the time of its 1991 release, *Blue Lines* was a startlingly fresh album. Before Massive Attack, few dance collectives attempted to fuse hip-hop rhythms with hypnotic, trance-like pop melodies and soul instrumentation. All of the album has a dark, muted quality, making the tracks blend together seamlessly. While that might mean the songs are indistinguishable from each other, Massive Attack offer enough subtle variations in the rhythms and arrangements to keep the record a mesmerising listen. —*Stephen Thomas Erlewine*

Protection / 1994 / Virgin ✦✦✦
While it wasn't as fresh and innovative as *Blue Lines,* Massive Attack's second album, *Protection,* was a fine album that refined the group's atmospheric fusion of soul, pop and hip-hop, yet it offered no new musical ideas. —*Stephen Thomas Erlewine*

The Master's Apprentices

Group, Pop/Rock

One could easily make the case for designating the Master's Apprentices as the best Australian rock band of the '60s. Featuring singer Jim Keays and songwriter/rhythm guitarist Mick Bower, the band's earliest recordings combined the gritty R&B/rock of Brits like the Pretty Things with the minor-key melodies of the Yardbirds. The compelling "Wars or Hands of Time" and the dreamy psychedelia of "Living in a Child's Dream" remain undiscovered classics, although the latter was a Top Ten hit in Australia. Bower left the group after suffering a nervous breakdown in late 1967, and the Masters grew steadily less interesting, moving from flower-pop and hard rock to progressive and acoustic sounds. Plagued by instability (undergoing eight personnel changes between 1966 and 1968), the group moved to England in the early '70s, achieving some cult success with progressive rock albums before breaking up in 1972. —*Richie Unterberger*

The Master's Apprentices / 1967 / Regal Zonophone ✦✦✦
Debut mixes sloppy covers of popular '60s rock and soul tunes with some fine originals, most of which were reissued on the much more widely available best-of *Hands of Time.* Collectors will find this of most interest for the fairly strong original track "Theme for a Social Climber," which somehow didn't make it onto that compilation. The German CD reissue also includes their second album, *Masterpiece.* —*Richie Unterberger*

A Toast to Panama Red / 1972 / Regal Zonophone ✦✦

● **Hands of Time** / 1980 / Raven ✦✦✦✦
24-song compilation covering the group's most popular recordings from 1965–72. The eight Mick Bower-penned cuts from 1965–67 are the clear highlights; most of the rest, like much of the Australian rock of the time, is extremely derivative of British progressive rock trends. Includes excellent detailed history by renowned Australian rock archivist Glenn A. Baker. —*Richie Unterberger*

Masterpiece / 1991 / TRC ✦✦✦
The group had changed a lot in both personnel and style by the time they issued their second LP, two and a half years after their first. It's a respectable but oddly schizophrenic effort, finding them searching for an identity with competent forays into hard rock, early progressive rock, and poppy folk-rock, orchestral instrumental links between many of the tracks adding to the confusion (as there's no concept driving the LP). "A Dog, A Siren And Memories" ranks as the most accurate Simon & Garfunkel imitation ever. The German CD reissue also includes their first, self-titled album. —*Richie Unterberger*

Material Issue

Group, Power Pop/Anglo-Pop

A hard power-pop trio from Illinois, they draw much musical inspiration from early Who. Lyrically, they stay focused on adolescent love songs.

Material Issue's 1991 debut, *International Pop Overthrow,* had several radio hits ("Dianne" and "Valerie Loves Me") but their second album didn't receive much airplay—possibly because they suffered from a bit of a sophomore slump. With its glitzy, '70s-styled hard-rock production, 1994's *Freak City Soundtrack* put an end to their creative doldrums, even if it failed to gather much commercial attention. —*Rick Clark*

● **International Pop Overthrow** / 1991 / Mercury ✦✦✦✦
Produced by Jeff Murphy of Shoes, this major-label debut contained some power-pop gems like "Renee Remains the Same," "Dianne," "Valerie Loves Me," and the title cut. Fans of Cheap Trick and early Who should love much of this. Also check out their self-titled EP, which preceded this album. —*Rick Clark*

Destination Universe / Mar. 1992 / Mercury ✦✦✦

Freak City Soundtrack / Mar. 8, 1994 / Mercury ✦✦✦
Energetic pop-rock abounds on Material Issue's third album. "Goin' Through Your Purse" kicks things off sounding like a garage punk version of "Ballroom Blitz"-era Sweet. The single, "Kim the Waitress," fuses Byrds-style 12-string guitars and electric sitar with rich vocal harmonies. Other highlights include "Funny Feeling" and "The Fan." —*Rick Clark*

Johnny Mathis

b. 1935
Pop

Mathis (b. James Royce Mathis) made the smoothest makeout music ever recorded, and his rise to stardom in the mid '50s flew in the face of rock & roll's early domination. Staying almost exclusively with lushly orchestrated ballad material, Mathis racked up hit after hit and now has had albums in the charts for 30 years, an achievement few will better. —*Cub Koda*

○ **Open Fire, Two Guitars** / 1959 / Columbia ✦✦✦✦
A warm and intimate setting, with stellar guitar work from Al Caiola and Tony Mottola. —*Cub Koda*

★ **Johnny's Greatest Hits** / 1962 / Columbia ✦✦✦✦✦
The original greatest-hits package, which stayed on the charts for ten years; includes "Chances Are," "It's Not for Me to Say," "Wonderful! Wonderful!" and "The Twelfth of Never." It seldom gets more romantic than this. —*Cub Koda*

Dave Matthews Band

Rock & Roll

The South-African vocalist/guitarist Dave Matthews formed the Dave Matthews band in North Carolina in the early '90s. Featuring Matthews, Stefan Lessard, Leroi Moor, Boyd Tinsley, and Carter Beauford, the group's music presents a more pop-oriented version of the Grateful Dead, crossed with the worldbeat explorations of Paul Simon and Sting. The band built up a strong word-of-mouth following in the early '90s by touring the country constantly, concentrating on college campuses. In addition to amassing a sizable following, their self-released album *Remember Two Things* sold well for an independent release; soon, they were attracting the attention of majors. Signing with RCA, the Dave Matthews Band released their major-label debut, *Under the Table and Dreaming,* in the fall of 1994. By spring of 1995, the record had launched the hit single "What Would You Say" and sold over a million copies. —*Stephen Thomas Erlewine*

Remember Two Things / 1993 / Bama Rags ✦✦✦
Although the Dave Matthews Band's debut album *Remember Two Things* is hindered by a number of long-winded jams and an unfocused production, the record is an impressive showcase for their instrumental prowess. —*Stephen Thomas Erlewine*

● **Under the Table & Dreaming** / 1994 / RCA ✦✦✦✦
On their major-label debut, *Under the Table and Dreaming,* the Dave Matthews Band is helped by the lean production of Steve Lillywhite, who manages to reign in the group's tendency to meander. The result is a set of eclectic pop/rock which is accentuated by bursts of instrumental virtuosity instead of being ruled by it. That also means that the Dave Matthews Band is capable of turning out pop songs and as the hit single "What Would You Say" and "Ants Marching" illustrate, they have a flair for catchy hooks. —*Stephen Thomas Erlewine*

Ian Matthews

b. Jun. 1946, Lincolnshire, England
Folk, Singer-Songwriter, Folk-Rock

Ian Matthews (now spelled Iain to reflect his Celtic roots) has had a widely varied and complex recording career. He began as the lead singer for Fairport Convention after a short stint as the vocalist for a London-based surf band, Pyramid in 1966. During Fairport's 1969 *Unhalfbricking* sessions, he decided to leave due to growing musical differences with the band. After making his first solo album, *Matthews Southern Comfort,* he released two albums with a band of the same name. They had a hit with a version of "Woodstock."

Matthews left in 1971 for a second chance at a solo career, releasing two fine folk-rock albums for Vertigo. He then formed Plainsong while finishing the contractual obligation album, *Journey from Gospel Oak*—one of his finest recorded moments despite the conditions. Plainsong released one critically acclaimed album on Elektra and then disbanded while recording the second. His stay at Elektra ended after two more acclaimed yet overlooked country-folk albums. He began experimenting in different styles for the rest of the Seventies, often with uninspired and unsuccessful results. He did, however, have a US top ten hit in 1978 with "Shake It."

The Eighties were a relatively slow period for Matthews. Recording intermittently, he spent a few years as an A&R man for Island and later worked for Windham Hill. He relocated permanently to the US in the late Eighties. The Nineties have found him reviving his career with a return to his folk-rock roots, touring small clubs most of the year. —*Chris Woodstra*

Matthews Southern Comfort / 1969 / Decca ✦✦✦
This is a transitional album for Matthews. Having recently exited Fairport Convention, this record pays tribute to that period of his career in both material ("A Castle Far") and in the choice of musicians who back him (many of them from Fairport Convention). At the same time, songs like "A Commercial Proposition" indicate where Matthews is headed on 1971's *Later that Same Year*. —*Jim Worbois*

Second Spring / 1969 / Elektra ✦✦✦
With this album, Matthews' Southern Comfort is a real band and, in addition to Matthews, also includes Roger Swallow (ex-Marmalade) and Marc Griffiths (ex-Spooky Tooth). Though there is really nothing that makes this a memorable record, it's still quite a nice record overall. If you already know his work on Elektra, Mooncrest, or even *Later That Same Year*, it would be well worth your while to search this record out. —*Jim Worbois*

1 2 3 Too Good / 1970 / MCA ✦✦

Later That Same Year / Dec. 1970 / Line ✦✦✦
Best known for the hit "Woodstock," this is really the album on which Matthews first finds his direction. A nice mix of covers and originals, this record has held up nicely over the years. —*Jim Worbois*

○ **If You Saw Thro' My Eyes** / Jan. 1971 / Vertigo ✦✦✦✦
After leaving Southern Comfort, Matthews reunited with Fairport Convention members Richard Thompson and Sandy Denny and made one of his finest albums. Though the material and playing is superior to his previous work, it was unfortunately overlooked at the time. Now combined with his follow-up, *Tigers Will Survive* on CD (German import only), this is a must-have for fans. —*Chris Woodstra*

Tigers Will Survive / Nov. 1971 / Vertigo ✦✦✦
Recorded during two different periods of time broken up by a U.S. tour, his follow-up to *If You Saw Through My Eyes* lacks the focus of its predecessor. Still worthwhile if only for "Morning Star," one of Matthews' most beautiful originals. —*Chris Woodstra*

○ **Journeys from Gospel Oak** / 1972 / Mooncrest ✦✦✦✦
Billed as a contractual obligation record by the artist, *Journeys from Gospel Oak* is easily as good as Matthews' best work. It is most assuredly a companion piece to Plainsong's *In Search of Amelia Earhart* (an album loosely based on the disappearance of Amelia Earhart), this time loosely based around the night Hank Williams died. This album includes such solid tracks as Gene Clark's "Polly," "Bride 1945" by Paul Siebel, and the haunting Jimmy Webb tune, "Met Her on a Plane." A strong (but often overlooked record) and well worth the effort it takes to find a copy. —*Jim Worbois*

○ **Valley Hi** / 1973 / Elektra ✦✦✦✦
Often regarded as his best album, *Valley Hi* finds Matthews combining his folk-rock expertise with producer Mike Nesmith's country leanings. Highlights include the Nesmith penned "Propinquity" and Jackson Browne's "These Days." —*Chris Woodstra*

Some Days You Eat the Bear Some Days the Bear Eats You / 1974 / Elektra ✦✦✦
His final LP recorded for Elektra continues in the country spirit of *Valley Hi* with a stronger pop sensibility. Includes a brilliant rendition of Tom Waits' "Old 55" and the touching tribute to Hank Williams, "A Wailing Goodbye." —*Chris Woodstra*

Go for Broke / 1975 / Columbia ✦
More a hodge-podge than a proper album, Matthews gives us a mix of originals and mostly uninspired covers. One exception to the covers is one from the often overlooked Tim Moore (whose first two albums on Asylum are worth looking for). Still, this is mediocre at best. —*Jim Worbois*

Hit and Run / 1976 / Columbia ✦✦
This rather directionless record has Matthews covering himself ("Tiger Will Survive"), sounding like David Crosby (Terry Reid's "The Frame") and affecting a disco beat on a song that's very reminiscent of "Lady Marmalade" ("Times"). Still, long-time fans shouldn't write this one off. —*Jim Worbois*

Stealin' Home / 1978 / Rockburgh ✦✦
This album features Matthews's highest-charting single ("Shake It") which, on its own, isn't a bad song. It, along with one or two others, was written by John Boylan, an under-appreciated songwriter of the late '70s (he wrote some nice stuff, but his career

never really took off like some of his peers). While not one of Ian's stronger records, it is pleasant overall. —*Jim Worbois*

Siamese Friends / 1979 / Rockburgh ✦✦
Saddled with late-'70s production techniques, there is nothing, on the surface, to recommend this record. A close look at the songwriting credits, though, will reveal a beginning of Matthews's fascination with the work of great Jules Shear. (Matthews would later do an entire album of Shear's songs.) Still, even this track is burdened by a cheesy David Sanborn-style sax line. —*Jim Worbois*

Discreet Repeat / Rockburgh ✦✦
This is a nice cross-label compilation which features some of his best work (stuff recorded for Vertigo, Elektra, and Mooncrest) and some of his least interesting (nearly everything on CBS). If you are a fan of Matthews, you likely own all these records already. If not, this compilation will help you decide which areas of his career you will need to concentrate on in order to build your Ian Matthews collection. —*Jim Worbois*

Spot of Interference / 1980 / Rockburgh ✦✦✦
Matthews' makes an attempt at new wave and power-pop on this 1980 album. Surprisingly, he pulls it off quite well. Not his strongest work but certainly of interest to fans. Jules Shear's "Driftwood from Disaster" and the Wilde-Ainsworth (later the Rembrandts) "I Survived the 70's" stand out. —*Chris Woodstra*

Moods for Mallards / 1983 / Shanghai ✦✦
Once you get past the fact that the Ian Matthews of Matthews' Southern Comfort and Fairport Convention is now into power-pop, this isn't a bad record. The style isn't far removed from what the Romantics or the Kinks (or Peter Noone, for that matter) were doing about the same time. With that in mind, the cover of Prince's "When You Were Mine" doesn't seem as odd as it might. —*Jim Worbois*

Shook / 1983 / Teldec ✦✦

Walking a Changing Line / 1988 / Windham Hill ✦✦✦
On this, the first vocal album for Windham Hill, Matthews pays tribute to the songwriting of Jules Shear. While the song selection is first rate as always, the typical Windham Hill musical indulgences take away from the enjoyment of this disc. Worthwhile for curious fans of Matthews or Shear. —*Chris Woodstra*

Pure & Crooked / 1990 / Gold Castle ✦✦✦
Matthews' move from the freeways of L.A. to the active but relatively less jaded musical oasis of Austin also saw a return to his own songwriting after a five-year hiatus. The results married Matthews' honey tenor to a mostly up-tempo blend of pop, folk, and rock that evokes his best '70s work. His knack for a crisp, plaintive melody is keenly honed. If all this wasn't enough, the reissue adds five previously unreleased tracks, including an a capella pair and a live version of Danny Whitten's "I Don't Want To Talk About It" recorded in Hamburg, Germany. —*Roch Parisien*

● **Best of Matthews' Southern Comfort** / 1992 / MCA ✦✦✦✦
A fine 16-track collection drawing from Matthews' first solo effort and the two Matthews' Southern Comfort albums. Includes the band's hit version of "Woodstock." —*Chris Woodstra*

● **The Soul of Many Places** / 1993 / Elektra ✦✦✦✦
The Soul of Many Places compiles the best moments from Matthews' recording high point for Elektra (1972–1974). Featuring selections from *Valley Hi*, *Some Days You Eat the Bear...*, and Plainsong's *The Search for Amelia Earhart*, this is the best introduction to Matthews' finest work (all currently out-of-print in the U.S.). The inclusion of non-LP tracks makes this essential for fans as well. —*Chris Woodstra*

Orphans & Outcasts, Vol. 1 / 1993 / Dirty Linen ✦✦✦
An exceptional collection of demos, rarities and outtakes from Matthews' '70s period, *Orphans & Outcasts* is essential for fans. —*Chris Woodstra*

Skeleton Keys / May 18, 1993 / Rhino ✦✦✦
Matthews emerges from his experimental '80s period with a return to his classic acoustic country-folk sound. With his first album comprised solely of originals, he shows more focus than he has in nearly two decades. —*Chris Woodstra*

Dark Ride / 1994 / Watermelon ✦✦

Orphans & Outcasts, Vol. 2 / 1994 / Dirty Linen ✦✦✦
Volume 2 of the series, essentially a demos collection of the late '70s/early '80s material, is more interesting than the actual albums of the time. Fans of Matthews' folky early-'70s albums who could-

n't connect with this somewhat misdirected phase of his career should find this much more enjoyable. —*Chris Woodstra*

John Mayall

b. Nov. 29, 1933
Blues Rock

The elder statesman of British blues, it is Mayall's lot to be more renowned as a bandleader and mentor than as a performer in his own right. Throughout the '60s, his band, the Bluesbreakers, acted as a finishing school for the leading British blues-rock musicians of the era. Guitarists Eric Clapton, Peter Green, and Mick Taylor joined his band in a remarkable succession in the mid-'60s, honing their chops with Mayall before going on to join Cream, Fleetwood Mac, and the Rolling Stones, respectively. John McVie and Mick Fleetwood, Jack Bruce, Aynsley Dunbar, Dick Heckstall-Smith, Andy Fraser (of Free), John Almond, and Jon Mark also played and recorded with Mayall for varying lengths of times in the '60s.

Mayall's personnel has tended to overshadow his own considerable abilities. Only an adequate singer, the multi-instrumentalist was adept in bringing out the best in his younger charges (Mayall himself was in his thirties by the time the Bluesbreakers began to make a name for themselves). Doing his best to provide a context in which they could play Chicago-style electric blues, Mayall was never complacent, writing most of his own material (which ranged from good to humdrum), revamping his lineup with unnerving regularity, and constantly experimenting within his basic blues format. Some of these experiments (with jazz-rock and an album on which he played all the instruments except drums) were forgettable; others, like his foray into acoustic music in the late '60s, were quite successful. Mayall's output has caught some flak from critics for paling next to the real African-American deal, but much of his vintage work—if weeded out selectively—is quite strong, especially his legendary 1966 LP with Eric Clapton, which both launched Clapton into stardom and kick-started the blues boom into full gear in England. Mayall had relocated to the United States by the beginning of the 1970s, and although he's released numerous albums since and remained a prodigiously busy and reasonably popular live act, little of his post-1970 output is worthy of discussion. —*Richie Unterberger*

John Mayall Plays John Mayall / Mar. 26, 1965 / Decca ✦✦✦
Recorded live at the British club Klooks Kleek in late 1964 before Clapton joined (Roger Dean plays lead guitar), this is a fine set of early British R&B with a more pronounced rock feel (akin to the Rolling Stones) than Mayall's other '60s work. Mayall wrote all but one of the songs on this overlooked but driving, highly enjoyable LP that is recommended to connoisseurs of early British blues-rock. —*Richie Unterberger*

★ **Bluesbreakers with Eric Clapton** / Jul. 1966 / Deram ✦✦✦✦✦
One of the seminal blues albums of the '60s with the Bluesbreakers, capturing Clapton on a series of blues standards, after the pop leanings of the Yardbirds and before the heavy indulgence of Cream. —*William Ruhlmann*

Raw Blues / Jan. 1967 / Deram ✦✦
This is not, strictly speaking, a John Mayall album, but rather a various artists album containing among its 14 selections six recorded by Mayall, plus four tracks by Otis Spann, two by Champion Jack Dupree, and two by Curtis Jones. The three expatriate Americans had been recorded in sessions with British backup musicians, including Eric Clapton and Mayall himself. The Mayall tracks include two solo performances, one credited to the duo of Mayall and "Steve Anglo" (Steve Winwood), two pairing Mayall and Clapton, and one with Peter Green. Most of the playing is low-key blues, and Mayall holds his own with the homegrown competition. —*William Ruhlmann*

A Hard Road / Feb. 17, 1967 / Deram ✦✦✦
Eric Clapton is usually thought of as Mayall's most important right-hand man, but the case could also be made for his successor, Peter Green. The future Fleetwood Mac founder leaves a strong stamp on his only album with the Bluesbreakers, singing a few tracks and writing a couple, including the devastating instrumental "Supernatural." Green's use of thick sustain on this track clearly pointed the way to his use of this feature on Fleetwood Mac's hits "Albatross" and "Black Magic Woman," as well as providing a blueprint for Carlos Santana's style. Mayall acquaints himself fairly well on this mostly original set (with occasional guest horns), though some of the material is fairly mundane. Highlights include

the uncharacteristically rambunctious "Leaping Christine" and the cover of Freddie King's "Someday After A While (You'll Be Sorry)." —*Richie Unterberger*

○ **Crusade** / Sep. 1, 1967 / London ✦✦✦✦
The personnel changes in John Mayall's Bluesbreakers continued on his fourth album, and although Mayall had vowed not to, he had added two permanent horn players. Perhaps because he was putting out his second album within a year, Mayall wasn't able to fill up the record with his own compositions and turned to blues standards, which certainly didn't hurt the record overall. Mayall's heroes included Buddy Guy, Otis Rush, Freddie King, and Sonny Boy Williamson, and he did them proud. The album became his third straight U.K. Top Ten and, following the Bluesbreakers' first U.S. tour in the summer of 1967, his first charting album in America. —*William Ruhlmann*

The Blues Alone / Nov. 1967 / Deram ✦✦✦
The Blues Alone was the first Mayall "solo" album (without the Bluesbreakers). Mayall played and overdubbed all instruments except drums, which were handled by Bluesbreaker Keef Hartley. It also tried to serve notice that, despite his band being a spawning ground for several British stars by now, the real star of the group was its leader. But it didn't quite prove that, since Mayall, while certainly competent on harmonica, keyboards, and guitars, doesn't display the flair of an Eric Clapton or Peter Green, and the overdubbing, as is so often the case, robs the recording of any real sense of interplay. —*William Ruhlmann*

Diary of a Band, Vol. 1 / 1968 / Decca ✦✦
Diary of a Band, Vol. 2 / 1968 / Decca ✦✦
Blues Giant / 1968 / Decca ✦✦✦
Blues from Laurel Canyon / 1968 / Deram ✦✦✦
Bare Wires / Jun. 21, 1968 / Deram ✦✦✦
Bare Wires was the first Bluesbreakers album of new studio material since *A Hard Road*, released 16 months before. In that time, the band had turned over entirely, expanding to become a septet. Mayall's musical conception had also expanded—the album began with a 23-minute "Bare Wires Suite," which included more jazz influences than usual and featured introspective lyrics. In retrospect, all of this is a bit indulgent, but at the time it helped Mayall out of what had come to seem a blues straitjacket (although he would eventually return to a strict blues approach). It isn't surprising that he dropped the "Bluesbreakers" name after this release. (The album was Mayall's most successful ever in the U.K., hitting #3.) — *William Ruhlmann*

○ **The Turning Point** / 1969 / Deram ✦✦✦✦
Recorded just after Mick Taylor departed for the Stones, Mayall eliminated drums entirely on this live recording. With mostly acoustic guitars and John Almond on flutes and sax, Mayall and his band, as his typically overblown liner notes state, "explore seldom-used areas within the framework of low volume music." But it does work. The all-original material is flowing and melodic, with long jazzy grooves that don't lose sight of their bluesy underpinnings. Lyrically, Mayall stretches out a bit into social comment on "The Laws Must Change" on this fine, meditative mood album. —*Richie Unterberger*

Looking Back / Aug. 1969 / Deram ✦✦✦
Reasonably interesting collection of non-LP singles from 1964 to 1968, featuring almost all of the notable musicians that passed through the Bluesbreakers throughout the decade. "Sitting In The Rain" (with Peter Green) showcases fine fingerpicking, the haunting "Jenny" is one of Mayall's best originals, and "Stormy Monday" one of the few studio cuts from the 1966 lineup that briefly featured both Eric Clapton and Jack Bruce. The rest is largely passably pleasant and doesn't rank among Mayall's finest work. —*Richie Unterberger*

Back to the Roots / 1971 / Polydor ✦✦✦
For this double-LP, recorded in November 1970, John Mayall gathered together prominent musicians who had played in his bands during the past several years, including Sugarcane Harris, Eric Clapton, Johnny Almond, Harvey Mandel, Keef Hartley, and Mick Taylor. Mayall's compositions aren't all that impressive, but the sidemen frequently shine, especially Clapton. *Back to the Roots* hit #52 in the U.S. and #31 in the U.K., where it was Mayall's final album to reach the charts. It was reissued in altered form under the title *Archives To Eighties* in 1988. (See separate entry.) — *William Ruhlmann*

○ **Thru the Years** / 1971 / Deram ✦✦✦✦

A grab bag of rare tracks from the '60s, some of which stand among Mayall's finest. His debut 1964 single "Crawling up a Hill" is one of his best originals; this comp also includes a couple of 1964–65 flipsides that were never otherwise issued in the U.S. The eight songs featuring Peter Green include some top-notch material that outpaces much of the only album recorded by the Green lineup (*A Hard Road*), particularly the Green originals "Missing You" and "Out of Reach," a great B-side with devastating, icy guitar lines and downbeat lyrics that ranks as one of the great lost blues-rock cuts of the '60s. The set is filled out with a few songs from the Mick Taylor era, the highlight being the vicious instrumental "Knockers Step Forward." Look for the CD reissue and not the early-'70s double U.S. album of the same name, which includes a lot of superfluous material and omits the three 1964–65 songs from British 45s. — *Richie Unterberger*

Memories / Dec. 1971 / Polydor ✦✦✦

Having gone *Back To The Roots*, John Mayall returned to his forward-looking musical explorations with 1971's *Memories*, the true followup to *USA Union*, on which he retained bassist Larry Taylor, replaced Harvey Mandel with guitarist Jerry McGee of the Ventures, and dropped Sugarcane Harris, for an unusually small trio session. Actually, he was still looking back on a set of autobiographical lyrics about growing up, starting with the title track, and including "Grandad," and "Back From Korea." (Forced to compete with the simultaneous release of the London Records compilation *Thru the Years*, *Memories* managed to reach only #179 in the U.S. charts.) — *William Ruhlmann*

Latest Edition / 1974 / Polydor ✦✦✦

The title makes a virtue of necessity, as John Mayall introduces another all-new lineup (actually, bassist Larry Taylor is returning from an older edition). Two guitarists, Hightide Harris and Randy Resnick, lead the band in more of an uptempo R&B style than has been used in much of Mayall's music during the past several years, starting with the timely "Gasoline Blues" (1974 was the year of the gas lines, remember?) and going on to "Troubled Times" (which advises impeaching President Nixon). Still, this was a lackluster set, which is only appropriate since it was Mayall's swan song with Polydor, and the album became his first to miss the charts in the U.S. since 1967. — *William Ruhlmann*

Primal Solos / 1977 / Deram ✦✦

Fuzzy live tapes from 1966 and 1968 of dubious quality, in both sonics and performance. Side One has Clapton on lead and Bruce on bass on familiar Chicago blues standards by the likes of John Lee Hooker, Willie Dixon, and Sonny Boy Williamson. Side Two is from a couple of 1968 gigs with Mick Taylor, with three lengthy tracks that have little to recommend them. For fanatics only. — *Richie Unterberger*

Last of the British Blues / 1978 / One Way ✦✦✦

This was the last of the six albums John Mayall originally made for Blue Thumb/ABC Records between 1975 and 1978, about which he has said, "ABC released six of my albums as a tax write-off. A week after they were released you couldn't find them in any store." It's a live album on which Mayall fronts a quartet consisting of guitarist James Quill Smith (who sings lead on several songs), bassist Steve Thompson, and drummer Soko Richardson. The approach is rock-oriented, and the set list includes such Bluesbreakers favorites as Mose Allison's "Parchman Farm" and Freddie King's "Hideaway" (taken at a frantic tempo), along with the usual complement of generic Mayall originals, among them, a remake of "The Bear" from *Blues From Laurel Canyon*. — *William Ruhlmann*

Behind the Iron Curtain / 1985 / GNP ✦✦

On his first new album in four years (and first new U.S. release in seven years), John Mayall reclaims the "Bluesbreakers" name for the first time in 18 years to highlight a quintet featuring two lead guitarists, Coco Montoya and Walter Trout, along with a rhythm section of Bobby Haynes (bass) and Joe Yuele (drums). The album was recorded in concert in Hungary in June, 1985, and takes a fairly bluesy approach with lots of space for the guitarists to shine, a format similar to that of the Bluesbreakers lineups of 1965–1968. Sound quality is only fair, and this is not an inspired performance, but Mayall has latched onto a cohesive unit here, and the results are encouraging for the future. — *William Ruhlmann*

○ **The Collection** / 1986 / Castle ✦✦✦✦

This two-LP set is a compilation of John Mayall's Decca recordings, 19641968. It's a good, 22-track selection starting with songs from the Bluesbreakers album that featured Eric Clapton and pulling selections from other notable albums and from Mayall singles. This was a prolific period for the bandleader, and he is well-served by a coherent best-of that highlights his own compositions and some significant covers. — *William Ruhlmann*

Some of My Best Friends are Blues / 1986 / Decal/Charly ✦✦✦

The title is a giveaway that this compilation of John Mayall's Decca recordings of 19661967 is devoted to cover versions of blues standards rather than his own compositions. A thematically consistent set, it gathers together tracks from singles and EPs as well as relying heavily on Mayall's *Crusade* album, which was intended to showcase the blues masters. Four of the 11 tracks come from that album, and they include songs like "Oh, Pretty Woman" and "I Can't Quit You Baby." The guitar playing is by Peter Green, who provides some biting blues runs. — *William Ruhlmann*

Chicago Line / Aug. 1988 / Island ✦✦

John Mayall's first new studio album to be released in the U.S. in more than a decade shows that his current crop of Bluesbreakers—Coco Montoya, Walter Trout, Bobby Haynes, and Joe Yuele—who have been together longer than any previous outfit, play like a seasoned blues band, sparking each other (especially guitarists Montoya and Trout), and never falling into complacency. Mayall presides over the music without dominating it, which makes the Bluesbreakers more of a group than they've been since the '60s. — *William Ruhlmann*

A Sense of Place / Mar. 1990 / Island ✦✦✦

A Sense of Place represents Mayall's full-fledged return to major-label record-making, with all the good and bad things that implies, from a high-profile producer, R.S. Field, to the introduction of such cover material as Wilbert Harrison's "Let's Work Together" and J.J. Cale's "Sensitive Kind." Field uses a spare production style, light on atmosphere and heavy, as is the current fashion, on unusual percussion. This makes for an identifiable sound, to be sure, but you can't help thinking that it isn't what the Bluesbreakers sound like on a good night in a small club. The result, as intended, was Mayall's first chart appearance in 15 years, but as a commercial comeback, the record ultimately failed. — *William Ruhlmann*

○ **London Blues (1964-1969)** / 1992 / PolyGram ✦✦✦✦

Featuring forty tracks over two discs, *London Blues* is an excellent collection of most of the best moments from Mayall and the Bluesbreakers' early recordings, a time when Eric Clapton, Peter Green, and Mick Taylor all passed through the band. — *Stephen Thomas Erlewine*

○ **Room to Move (1969-1974)** / 1992 / Polydor ✦✦✦✦

The majority of Mayall and the Bluesbreakers' best material from the early '70s is collected on this 29-track, double-disc set. Although Clapton appears on a couple of songs, the playing on *Room to Move* isn't as universally breathtaking as it is on *London Blues*, but the collection is thoroughly listenable, and it does feature many fine musicians. — *Stephen Thomas Erlewine*

Wake Up Call / 1993 / Jive/Novus ✦✦✦

Fueled by Coco Montoya's searing but economical string-slashing, drummer Joe Yuele, and bassist Rick Cortes, John Mayall has managed to keep a stable core of Bluesbreakers together in recent years. Mayall rarely does the same album twice, and *Wake Up Call* finds him returning to a basic, physical sound after 1990's more progressive/highly produced *A Sense of Place*. The harp whiz has rarely flirted with the pop charts over the decades, a track record that will likely handicap the title track—a potential hit featuring guest vocalist Mavis Staples and some take-charge riffing from former mate Mick Taylor. For pure guitar joy though, Montoya turns the trick all on his own with barnburners "Loaded Dice" and "Nature's Disappearing". — *Roch Parisien*

Empty Rooms / Polydor ✦✦✦

This was John Mayall's studio-recorded followup to the live *The Turning Point*, featuring the same drumless quartet of himself, guitarist Jon Mark, reed player Johnny Almond, and bassist Steve Thompson. Mayall was at a commercial and critical peak with this folk-jazz approach; the album's lead-off track, "Don't Waste My Time," had become his sole singles chart entry prior to the LP's release, and although his former label, London, confused matters by releasing the two-year-old *Diary of a Band* [Volume 1] in the U.S.

just before this new album appeared in early 1970, the new crop of fans he'd found with *The Turning Point* stuck with him on this gentle, reflective release. *Empty Rooms* hit number 33 in the U.S.; in the U.K. it got to number nine. —*William Ruhlmann*

Ten Years Are Gone / Polydor ♦♦♦
Mayall returned to the studio in 1973 for this double album. The ten years Mayall had in mind, of course, were the previous ten, which had seen him start as a local musician in Manchester, England, and emerge a decade, almost two dozen albums, and nearly as many lineups later with an evolved jazz-blues style and an international following. The album allows the ensemble considerable room to solo on Mayall's typically simple, blues-based song structures, and the approach is perhaps excessively casual. The second LP is a live date recorded at the Academy of Music in New York, and here things stretch out even more: "Harmonica Free Form" clocks in at 12 minutes and "Dark of the Night" runs 17:41. —*William Ruhlmann*

U.S.A. Union / Polydor ♦♦
John Mayall's *Turning Point* band—Jon Mark, Johnny Almond, and Steve Thompson—broke up in June 1970 after a European tour. Mayall then assembled his first all-American band and recorded this album in July. It had more drive than the previous outfit, and Mayall turned to environmentalism on the leadoff track, "Nature's Disappearing." But much of his low-volume, reflective approach remained on an album that was still more of a jazz-pop outing than the blues sessions of his early career. *USA Union* had the highest U.S. chart peak of his career, hitting #22. But in the U.K., where its title confirmed Mayall's U.S. leanings, the album showed a big dropoff from his usual sales. —*William Ruhlmann*

Curtis Mayfield

b. Jun. 3, 1942
Soul, R&B
Few have had as much influence on Black music, in as many fields of endeavor, as Curtis Mayfield, starting from his early days with the Impressions back in 1958. His sinewy guitar work has become so woven into the basic fabric of R&B guitar that more people know the style than know the man who invented it. He was the first to exhibit racial pride, singing about it on hit singles with the Impressions in the early '60s through '70s. He scored big with the soundtrack to the blaxploitation film *Superfly* in 1972; by this time he had already been running his own record company for four years. Mayfield wrote hits for everyone from Major Lance to Jerry Butler. He continues to persevere today despite the tragic accident that almost took his life in 1990. Curtis Mayfield's stardom is assured by his massive talent.

A pair of tribute albums to Curtis Mayfield were recorded in 1993 and 1994. He also made appearances at the Grammy and Soul Train awards, getting standing ovations both times. He reactivated Curtom Records, and his classic early '70s solo LPs were reissued, as were some of his great film scores. —*Cub Koda & Colin Escott*

☆ **Curtis** / Sep. 1970 / Ichiban ♦♦♦♦♦
A masterpiece, and still one of the greatest urban soul albums of all time. Curtis Mayfield stepped into the spotlight and immediately showed that he would have no trouble away from the Impressions. While he had done many transcendent singles with them, he'd never made a song as searing in its indictments or immediately compelling as "(Don't Worry) If There's a Hell Below We're All Gonna Go." That was just one of many classic tunes, which retain their impact 25 years later. Those who don't think there were great message songs before the hip-hop era should check this one out and then come up with better songs done by Public Enemy, Ice-T, Boogie Down Productions, or anyone else. —*Ron Wynn*

○ **Roots** / 1971 / Curtom ♦♦♦♦
A fine followup to his hit debut album as a solo artist. Although he only scored one smash single, "Get Down," there were plenty of superb selections, expertly produced numbers, and fine arrangements. Mayfield, Marvin Gaye, Stevie Wonder, and Isaac Hayes were among the innovative composer/producer/performers that helped usher in the album age on the R&B/soul circuit. Mayfield was now doing concept works with a thematic unity and sophisticated style, rather than stringing together singles in the manner of '50s and '60s LPs. —*Ron Wynn*

☆ **Superfly** / Jul. 1972 / Curtom ♦♦♦♦♦
Curtis Mayfield's talents as an all-around artist became evident in the 1970s. This was one of many inspirational soundtracks Mayfield composed for films that seldom matched his musical tapestry. *Superfly* was a misunderstood film, but there were no questions about the music; such songs as "Freddie's Dead," "Pusherman" and the title track brought home the impact and scourge of drugs with clarity and power. Mayfield's singing was consistently magnificent, and the production and arrangements were equally superb. —*Ron Wynn*

○ **Curtis in Chicago** / 1973 / Curtom ♦♦♦♦
In the midst of a great run of superb albums, Curtis Mayfield cranked out a fine live set displaying how penetrating his music was in concert. He headed a fine combo, performed extended versions of several hits, sang with authority, earnestness, and conviction, and got an equally intense response from the audience. Sadly, this album is currently not available on CD. —*Ron Wynn*

○ **Early Years with the Impressions** / 1973 / ABC ♦♦♦♦
Until ABC/Paramount issued a good two-record anthology in the late '70s, and then MCA issued the definitive Mayfield/Impressions package in 1992, this was one of the better retrospective sets featuring some early Mayfield material with the Impressions. It still has value, but has been deleted. The Mayfield/Impressions two-disc set on MCA is weighted toward hits, while this one contained some quality album cuts that aren't on either of the later retrospectives. But since it's deleted and currently unscheduled for reissue, you're out of luck, other than on the collector's circuit. —*Ron Wynn*

○ **Back to the World** / May 1973 / Curtom ♦♦♦♦
Another stirring album by Curtis Mayfield, now in a groove on his own label. Mayfield's works issued challenges across the board, urging everyone to examine his or her prejudices and then seek a solution. While he always included one or two wonderful love songs for balance, these albums were largely examinations of American issues in the 1970s. He scored three R&B chart hits, with "Future Shock" just missing the Top 10, but that was icing on the cake. Mayfield's music had far more importance than simply getting hits. —*Ron Wynn*

Got to Find a Way / 1974 / Curtom ♦♦♦
Curtis Mayfield continued his run of excellent albums in the '70s with this followup to the huge hit *Superfly* soundtrack. This album had more love songs than some of his earlier material, although he didn't tone down his searing attacks on American injustice and hyprocisy. His vocals continued to be alternately poignant, urgent, and accusatory, while his lyrics, production, and arrangements were once again magnificent. —*Ron Wynn*

Sweet Exorcist / 1974 / Curtom ♦♦♦
Curtis Mayfield hit a stride during the '70s that was unparalleled among R&B/soul performers from an album standpoint. He was writing, producing, arranging, and performing on great album after great album, then distributing them on his own label as well. This one included the big hit "Kung Fu," plus the title song, and once more perfectly blended rigorous message tracks and steamy love songs. Sadly, it hasn't been reissued on CD and isn't on the list to be at this time. —*Ron Wynn*

○ **There's No Place Like America Today** / 1975 / Curtom ♦♦♦♦
Curtis Mayfield continued his string of powerful, assertive message albums with this mid-'70s release, but, as luck would have it, the only hit the album scored came with a love tune, "Only You, Babe." Still, the title tune, "Hard Times," "When Seasons Change" and "Blue Monday People" were unrelenting, unapologetic statements of frustration and anger. Mayfield also included "So In Love" and "Love to the People" to balance the menu, but the finest cuts addressed the inequities and injustices he saw being ignored. —*Ron Wynn*

Give Get Take Have / 1976 / Ichiban ♦♦♦

Short Eyes / 1977 / Curtom ♦♦

Never Say You Can't Survive / 1977 / Ichiban ♦♦
Curtis Mayfield was nearing the end of his run of marvelous albums on his Curtom label in the '70s. It was inevitable that the pace would catch up to him. He'd been doing spectacular albums—writing all the songs, singing leads, producing and arranging the material, but also producing other acts and crafting brilliant soundtrack projects on the side. This album wasn't awful; it still contained some nice songs. It just wasn't up to the level of past Mayfield albums. —*Ron Wynn*

Do It All Night / 1978 / Curtom ✦✦✦

Heartbeat / 1979 / RSO ✦✦

This was perhaps his weakest '70s album, although by many others' standards, it was a decent Curtis Mayfield album. But there was no anthemic message track or memorable love song. It was mostly well-produced and written, decently performed material a shade below usual Mayfield standards lyrically. But even poor Curtis Mayfield was worth hearing, and while this one wouldn't go down among his classics, it still contained some pleasurable selections. —*Ron Wynn*

Something to Believe in / 1980 / Ichiban ✦✦

This was one of the last albums Mayfield recorded on his Curtom label before financial problems forced him to temporarily suspend operation. It was a well-produced, often moving LP, although it didn't yield Mayfield any of the huge R&B hits he'd scored in the past. His voice has a somber, sometimes weary quality, and there's more stark, resigned material. He wasn't defeated, but at this point he didn't sound encouraged either. —*Ron Wynn*

The Right Combination / 1980 / RSO ✦✦✦

Honesty / 1983 / Epic ✦✦✦

Live in Europe / 1988 / Curtom ✦✦✦

An outstanding album spotlighting Curtis Mayfield's '70s band and compositions. Mayfield's hard-hitting socio-political tunes were fortified by his cutting tone and always poignant falsetto leads. The band included excellent rhythm players and a solid frontline, and the original two-album set was a winner on the R&B and urban contemporary circuit. —*Ron Wynn*

Take It to the Street / 1990 / Curtom ✦✦✦

One of his later albums, Curtis Mayfield revived his Curtom label in the mid-'80s after moving to Atlanta. He secured a distribution deal with Ichiban and was back in the ownership end. While this release didn't have the uniform excellence or consistent singles smashes of its predecessors, Mayfield remained an impressive vocalist, songwriter, and arranger. Even at less than top form, he could still provide many inspirational, memorable moments, and that was the case on this release. —*Ron Wynn*

○ **Of All Time: Classic Collection** / 1990 / Curtom ✦✦✦✦

This anthology spotlights Curtis Mayfield's hits biggest as a solo star since 1970. It includes his first hit as a lead artist, "(Don't Worry) If There's A Hell Below We're All Going To Go," plus "Superfly," "Freddie's Dead," "So In Love" and many other classics recorded for his Curtom label. Mayfield penned many masterful socio-political and protest tunes, but could also write poignant, expressive love songs. —*Ron Wynn*

★ **The Anthology 1961-1977** / 1992 / MCA ✦✦✦✦

An absolutely wonderful collection, it includes both the Impressions' '60s hits and Curtis Mayfield's early-'70s solo recordings on his Curtom label. All of the music on the two CDs (including "It's Alright," "People Get Ready," "Superfly," and "Freddie's Dead") is superb and the liner notes are excellent; it's the definitive Mayfield collection. —*AMG*

Percy Mayfield

b. Aug. 12, 1920, **d.** Aug. 11, 1984

Soul, R&B

After his #1 R&B lament "Please Send Me Someone to Love" established him as a subtly moving singer in 1950, a disfiguring auto accident forced Percy Mayfield to accentuate his songwriting skills instead. It was lucky for Ray Charles that he did, since the introspective composer penned some of Brother Ray's best material (notably "Hit the Road, Jack"). Based in Los Angeles, Mayfield proved to be one of his own best musical interpreters during the early '50s when he racked up seven Top Ten R&B sellers for Specialty Records. The despairing "Strange Things Happening," "The River's Invitation," and "Please Send Me Someone to Love" tabbed Mayfield as the poet laureate of R&B, a writer whose material has grown in stature with time (Johnny Adams recently cut a whole album of Mayfield tunes for Rounder). Although his own sound was based in sax and piano, Mayfield's recordings were apparently too gentle and troubling to weather the onslaught of early rock & roll. While under contract to Charles as a writer during the '60s, Mayfield cut a couple of nice albums for the Genius's own Tangerine logo, and he remained semi-active on the West Coast until his 1984 death. —*Bill Dahl*

○ **My Jug and I** / 1962 / Tangerine ✦✦✦✦

Known as the "poet laureate of the blues," Percy Mayfield remains arguably the genre's greatest singer / songwriter. This classic, long-out-of-print recording places him in front of the Gerald Wilson band featuring Ray Charles as producer / keyboardist. It first appeared on Charles' own label, Tangerine, and is perhaps Mayfield's finest outing. The songs, vocals, ensemble performances, arrangements, and instrumental solos are simply superb and combine to make this one of the greatest recordings of its kind. —*Larry Hoffman*

Bought Blues / 1969 / Tangerine ✦✦✦

Mayfield's Tangerine sides are eminently tasty. —*Bill Dahl*

★ **Poet of the Blues** / 1990 / Specialty ✦✦✦✦✦

This is the original 1950-1954 recordings by this influential songwriter and vocal stylist. The superb combo backing was led by Maxwell Davis. —*Hank Davis*

○ **Memory Pain** / Specialty ✦✦✦✦

More Specialty gems from the '50s, including many rarities. Gentle and plaintive. —*Bill Dahl*

For Collectors Only / Specialty ✦✦✦

As the title suggests, this gives a deeper look at Mayfield's early career. Alternate takes and unissued material are included. —*Hank Davis*

Mayhem

Heavy Metal

Formed around 1985, Mayhem was the first death metal band from Norway to make much of an impact in their homeland, which now has a burgeoning underground scene rife with violent, sometimes anti-Christian activity, as evidenced by Mayhem's non-musical history. Drummer "Hellhammer," who at one time worked in a mental hospital, is the only remaining member of the band's classic lineup. Lead vocalist "Dead" committed suicide in 1991 by shooting himself in the head; Hellhammer made a necklace using some of his skull fragments, and guitarist "Euronymous" (b. Oystein Aarseth) cooked and ate pieces of Dead's brain. Euronymous, in turn, was stabbed to death while in his underwear on August 10, 1993 by the band's bass player, "Count Grishnackh" (b. Christian Vikernes). Grishnackh's alleged motive was jealousy over the fact that Euronymous had a more evil reputation; he inflicted 23 separate wounds so as to outdo rival band Emperor's drummer "Faust," who was convicted in the stabbing death of a homosexual acquaintance. When police arrested him, they found over 150 kg of stolen dynamite in his house, complete with a plan to blow up a large church on a religious holiday. Grishnackh went on to form the techno-influenced Burzum while in prison, while Euronymous' parents successfully requested that his bass tracks be erased from Mayhem's latest album (which featured session vocalist "Attila"). The future of the band is somewhat unclear at this point. —*Steve Huey*

De Mysteriis Dom Sathanas / 1994 / Century Media/Grind Core

Released to acclaim after Euronymous' death, this is the most readily available Mayhem album in America. The music is fast and furious, and the stomach-turning vocals are unintelligible, but Mayhem avoid being simply standard by making subtle changes in their sound throughout the album and not falling into a rut or repeating themselves, as too many other death metal bands tend to do. This album may require a bit of patience, but it is worth it. —*Steve Huey*

Maze featuring Frankie Beverly

Group, Soul, Urban

Frankie Beverly & Maze may be the ultimate Urban Contemporary group, though they're much more soulful and funky than many of their counterparts. They began in Philadelphia as the Butlers, and later became Raw Soul. They moved to San Francisco in the mid-'70s and switched identities again to Maze. The lineup was lead singer Frankie Beverly, Wayne Thomas, Sam Porter, Robin Duke, Roame Lowry, McKinley Williams and Joe Provost. Ahaguna G. Sun later replaced Provost, and Sun was subsequently replaced by Billy "Shoes" Johnson. Ron Smith replaced Thomas, and Phillip Woo was added on keyboards in 1980. Though they've had only one number one R&B hit in their long tenure ("Back in Stride" in 1985), Maze's popularity is unquestioned, especially as a live act. They recorded for Capitol from 1977 until 1989, when they moved to Warner Brothers and issued another smash LP in

Silky Soul. Their most recent release was *Back to Basics* in 1993. —*Ron Wynn*

Golden Time of Day / 1978 / Capitol ✦✦✦

Inspiration / 1979 / Capitol ✦✦✦

○ **Joy and Pain** / 1980 / Capitol ✦✦✦✦

● **Live in New Orleans** / 1981 / Capitol ✦✦✦✦
A superb live album, one of the finest soul/funk concert dates ever released. Frankie Beverly and Maze managed to capture on this two-album set the energy, spontaneity, and nonstop excitement of their concerts, which have always been among the finest on the R&B/soul/funk circuit. The set functioned as both a greatest hits work and a wonderful introduction to people who'd never seen their live show. The album version of "Joy and Pain" became an international hit, and led to other singles being pulled and re-released in extended versions. —*Ron Wynn*

Maze / 1982 / Capitol ✦✦✦
Formerly known as Raw Soul, Frankie Beverly and his band took a new name when they relocated from Philadelphia to San Francisco, as well as broadening their style from mainly standard soul to a funk/soul hybrid. They signed with Capitol in the mid-'70s, and their first album under the new pact was their finest set, with Beverly's energetic lead vocals and an excellent band that included keyboardists Phillip Woo and Sam Porter, bassist Robin Duhe, and guitarist Ron Smith. They made an immediate impact with their hard-driving sound, not as strictly on the beat as the Dayton bands like the Ohio Players or Slave, but just as soulful. —*Ron Wynn*

○ **We Are One** / 1983 / Capitol ✦✦✦✦

Can't Stop the Love / 1985 / Capitol ✦✦✦

Live in Los Angeles / 1986 / Capitol ✦✦

Silky Soul / 1989 / Warner Brothers ✦✦✦
After being on Capitol through much of the 1970s and '80s, Maze moved to Warner Brothers in 1989 and scored immediate dividends with this album, containing some of the group's finest ballads ever. The title track was a poignant tribute to Marvin Gaye, a supporter and advocate of the group. Beverly also paid homage to Nelson Mandela, but didn't overdo the political message material. There were plenty of breezy and superbly crafted romantic numbers, while "Love's on the Run" was a decent uptempo number. The album helped re-establish the group as a major urban contemporary act and got them back on the charts for the first time in three years. —*Ron Wynn*

● **The Greatest Hits of Maze . . . Lifelines, Vol. 1** / Nov. 8, 1989 / Capitol ✦✦✦✦
When the Philadelphia band Raw Soul moved to San Francisco in the mid-'70s, they changed their name to Maze and made Frankie Beverly their lead singer. Beverly's personality and exuberance and their evolution into one of the tightest bands on the soul scene turned Maze into an institution. This collects formative hits from their years on Capitol, including "Golden Time of Day" and "Joy and Pain." It shows that they were both an enjoyable uptempo and funk band and a convincing ballad and love song ensemble. —*Ron Wynn*

Back to Basics / 1993 / Warner Brothers ✦✦

Mazzy Star

Group, Alternative Pop/Rock
David Roback, veteran of the California paisley-underground group Rain Parade, and singer Hope Sandoval, from Going Home, undertake a cold, reverberant alternative-folk sound, with occasional forays into electric psychedelia. —*Rick Clark*

She Hangs Brightly / 1990 / Capitol ✦✦✦
Roback and Sandoval slog through a collection of Velvet Underground-style pyschedelia and comatose folk. Sandoval's pleasantly detached vocal delivery complements the cold, highly reverberant production. It's good for encouraging numb disconnection from the planet. —*Rick Clark*

● **So Tonight That I Might See** / Sep. 27, 1993 / Capitol ✦✦✦✦
Treading a similar path as their debut, Mazzy Star generally succeed in their efforts to create an otherworldly, dream-state-like buzz with their lulling songs and layers of droning guitars. The duo offers a considerably warmer and more authentic persona on the pretty, acoustic-dominated songs than the droning trance-rock exercises. With its socially detached self-absorption, this CD is like a definitive soundtrack for the slacker elements of Generation X. —*Richie Unterberger*

M.C. Brains

Rap
Michael Bivins discovered Cleveland-born M.C. Brains (born James De Shannon) in 1992. With Bivins assistance and encouragement, M.C. Brains debuted on Motown with *Lovers Lane*. The single "Oochie Coochie" just missed the pop Top 20, while *Brainstorming* was a respectable follow-up. M.C. Brains style was pop/crossover rather than hard or gangsta, but he showed enough potential the first time out to indicate a second release would be justified. —*Ron Wynn*

○ **Lover's Lane** / 1992 / Motown ✦✦✦✦
MC Brains was discovered by former New Edition and current Bell Biv Devoe member Michael Bivins. He was 17 years old when this was released. Thus, it seemed appropriate that the teen angst/new jack number "Oochie Coochie" would be the lone hit, peaking at number 21 on the pop charts. There was nothing confrontational or angry about this one, the M.C. moniker notwithstanding. If there were any questions about MC Brains' (and Bivins') intentions, they were thoroughly answered by tracks like "Strawberry Lane" and "G-String." —*Ron Wynn*

M.C. Breed

Rap
Flint, MI, rapper M.C. Breed (born Eric Breed) came out hard, tough and fast on his 1991 debut *M.C. Breed & DFC.* "Ain't No Future in Yo' Frontin'" set the tone for a collection of confrontational, at times almost paranoid Afrocentric and/or gangsta tracks with occasional reggae flavoring. DFC were nowhere to be found on the 1992 follow-up *20 Below.* It opted to be even more explicit, angry and offensive than the debut, though such tracks as "Little Child Running Wild" and "Flash's Groove" provided some variety. Breed then issued *The New Breed* for Wrap in 1993. He came back strong with *Funkafied* in 1994, hitting the Top Ten on the R&B charts. It was also for Wrap, a label distributed by Atlanta-based Ichiban. —*Ron Wynn*

○ **MC Breed & Dfc** / 1991 / Ichiban ✦✦✦✦
MC Breed was 19 when he and DFC made their debut in 1991. Things got started on a positive front with the defiant cut "Ain't No Future In Yo' Fronting," a tough-talking, nicely rapped and rhymed assault on hypocrisy. "Black For Black" and "I Will Excel" were also worthy message cuts, while "Get Loose" and "Job Corp" added more good material. It was a solid but low-selling first album. —*Ron Wynn*

● **20 Below** / 1992 / Wrap/Ichiban ✦✦✦✦
MC Breed came out even harder and more combative on his second CD than he did on his debut. "Jealous Pimp" and "Ain't to Be F—. With" set the agenda squarely in gangsta territory, although he hedged his bets with "Life of A Flintstone" and "Whenever You Want Me." But apparently, audiences were also unsure as to whether MC Breed wanted to brandish a gun or hang out with Bugs Bunny. —*Ron Wynn*

The New Breed / 1993 / Wrap/Ichiban ✦✦✦
MC Breed was alone and rapping with fire and fury on this album. He continued changing his image to that of seasoned, prophetic gangsta commentator, rather than alternating between hard and light material. Breed's raps weren't always fluid, but his rhymes were frequently compelling. —*Ron Wynn*

Funkafied / Jun. 7, 1994 / Wrap/Ichiban ✦✦✦

MC5

Group, Rock & Roll, Hard Rock
This Detroit rock & roll band's musical and political stance helped sow the seeds of the British punk movement of the late '70s. Original members included Wayne Kramer (guitar), Rob Tyner (vocals), Bob Gaspar (drums), Pat Burrows (bass), and Fred "Sonic" Smith (guitar). They played around their native Detroit ca. 1966 as the Motor City Five. Both Gaspar and Burrows, who had shaped much of the band's early rhythmic drive, left before the band ever recorded and were replaced by Dennis Thompson (drums) and Michael Davis (bass). After two local singles went nowhere, manager John Sinclair (of the revolutionary White Panther Party) got them signed to Elektra, who recorded them live at Detroit's Grande Ballroom, where they enjoyed a fanatical local following. Troubles with the album's lyrical content (based in large part around the band's revolutionary sex, drugs, and rock & roll rhetoric) and Sinclair's conviction on drug charges saw the band

tone down its image for their second album, released on Atlantic. By the time their third album was released in 1971, the band was plagued by drugs and personal problems, and they broke up shortly thereafter. Though never commercially successful, the MC5 personified the Detroit high-energy sound and approach to rock & roll, and their style lives on in the work of punk and alternative bands around the world. —*Cub Koda*

★ **Kick out the Jams** / 1969 / Elektra ✦✦✦✦✦
The band in full cry at the Grande Ballroom, 1968; one of the most exciting live albums ever recorded. Highlights include the title track (uncensored on CD), "Ramblin' Rose," and "Borderline." —*Cub Koda*

○ **Back in the U.S.A.** / 1970 / Rhino ✦✦✦✦
Their second album is not so wild but still exciting. Great original material is included, like "Shakin' Street" (featuring vocal by Fred "Sonic" Smith), "The American Ruse," "The Human Being Lawnmower," and "Looking at You," which featured some fiery lead-guitar work by Wayne Kramer. —*Rick Clark*

○ **High Time** / 1971 / Rhino ✦✦✦✦
Their last studio album, with "Sister Anne" and "Baby, Won't Ya" as principal highlights. —*Cub Koda*

Babes in Arms / 1983 / ROIR ✦✦✦
Rare and unreleased sides. This includes their first singles, unavailable on album. —*Cub Koda*

M.C. Lyte

Rap
Though she's turned a bit in the pop direction on her latest release, Brooklyn rapper M.C. Lyte has done some inventive, distinctive material on her two prior releases. She's provided some of the better comebacks and put-downs aimed at out-of-control male egos and libidos, and she's also quite funny. It's to be hoped that the pop tinges on *Act like You Know* are merely an alternative, rather than a primary direction.

M.C. Lyte responded to fans questioning her direction on *Ain't No Other*, her 1993 album. This marked a return to the tough-talking, fat beats and no-nonsense personna that had characterized her most successful material. —*Ron Wynn*

Lyte As a Rock / 1988 / First Priority ✦✦✦
The debut from this femme rapper thrusts a middle finger toward the sexism of the male-dominated rap turf, through clever rhymes and a sharp sense of humor, ensuring that her feminism never exhausts and always enlightens. —*John Floyd*

● **Eyes on This** / 1989 / First Priority ✦✦✦✦
This expands on the promise of her debut, both musically (the samples are more dense) and lyrically (witness "Shut the Eff Up! (Hoe)" and the winningly arty "Cuppucino"). —*John Floyd*

Act Like You Know / 1991 / First Priority ✦✦

Ain't No Other / 1993 / First Priority ✦✦✦

M.C. 900 Ft Jesus

Group, Rap, Dance-Pop, Alternative Pop/Rock
Taking the name M.C. 900 Ft Jesus from an Oral Roberts' sermon, the Dallas native, Mark Griffin, began recording in the late '80s. M.C. 900 Ft Jesus' first records were bracing fusions of hip-hop, industrial, and spoken word, with hints of jazz. He became a favorite on college radio with his 1990 debut *Hell with the Lid Off* and 1991's *Welcome to My Dream*, yet he never established much more than a cult following. Laying low for a couple years, M.C. 900 Ft Jesus returned with his most popular record to date in 1994, *One Step Ahead of the Spider*. Featuring the hit single "If I Only Had a Brain," the record was calmer than his earlier work, incorporating more elements of jazz and funk; it was a hit on both alternative radio and MTV. —*Stephen Thomas Erlewine*

○ **Hell with the Lid Off** / 1990 / Nettwerk ✦✦✦✦
This is eccentric rap and hip-hop from White boy M.C. 900 Ft Jesus (Mark Griffin) and DJ Zero, a Texan who supplies some fierce cuts on the turntable. One of the few Caucasian rap artists that stays true to the traditions of rap, this album features "I'm Going Straight to Heaven," "Truth Is out of Style," and "Spaceman." —*John Book*

Welcome to My Dream / 1991 / Nettwerk ✦✦✦
Mark Griffin continues his weird ways and records an album that is more personal and political than the debut. Although not credited, DJ Zero is still part of the group. —*John Book*

● **One Step Ahead of the Spider** / 1994 / American ✦✦✦✦
M.C. 900 Ft Jesus reached his artistic maturity with *One Step Ahead of the Spider*, a dense set of jazzy hip-hop highlighted by the single "If I Only Had A Brain." —*Stephen Thomas Erlewine*

M.C. Ren

Rap
M.C. Ren (born Lorenzo Patterson) joined the list of NWA members gone solo in 1992 with *Kizz My Black Azz*. It peaked at number 12 and eventually went platinum despite being thoroughly unplayable on even the most underground radio station. The follow-up *Shock of the Hour* briefly topped the pop charts, but didn't have lasting power. On both releases, Ren has showed surprising facility and fluidity as a rapper. The rhymes haven't been anything special though, nor the beats. —*Ron Wynn*

Kizz My Black Azz / Jun. 30, 1992 / Priority ✦✦✦
It would be easier to dismiss M.C. Ren's obsessively violent and sexist lyrics if his music wasn't so tight and menacing. Taken on purely musical terms, *Kizz My Black Azz* is thrilling; when it's analyzed more deeply, the simplistic, disturbing lyrics unravel the achievements of the music. However, the production and beats are so deeply funky that they almost lift Ren's debut solo EP out of the swamp of violent, misogynist gangstas. Almost. —*Stephen Thomas Erlewine*

● **Shock of the Hour** / 1993 / Ruthless ✦✦✦✦
M.C. Ren's debut EP is uneven, but at least presents a lyrical vision when it's not spewing out familiar, tired, sexist cliches about women. Ren highlights American hypocrisy with a vengeance, and the title track foresees the nation's fiery end in an apocalyptic fury enabling black people to finally achieve justice. Both this tune and "Attack On Babylon" come closest to presenting a coherent, effective philosophy. Another provocative track is "Same Old S," a song that strips away any pretense of glamour around the gangsta lifestyle and outlines the brutality, paranoia and violence at its core. These tracks display M.C. Ren's potential as a hip-hop theorist; the others just fill out the CD. —*Ron Wynn*

Paul McCartney

b. Jun. 18, 1942
Pop/Rock
In the decade and a half after the demise of the Beatles in 1970, Paul McCartney became one of the most successful figures in popular music. Though he had more trouble scoring hits after the mid-'80s, McCartney embarked on a triumphant world tour in 1989 and premiered his first classical work, *Paul McCartney's Liverpool Oratorio*, in 1991. He launched his third "New World" tour, commemorating the release of his *Off the Ground* album, in 1993.

Born in Liverpool, McCartney teamed with John Lennon and George Harrison in the '50s to form the nucleus of the Beatles, who scored unprecedented worldwide success in the '60s, much of it fueled by McCartney's melodic songs. The bass player and singer was a musical chameleon, equally capable of performing the most tender love song, the most schmaltzy show tune, or the most raucous rocker, on command. McCartney scored a film (*The Family Way*) but otherwise restricted his musical activities to the group until the end of the '60s, when he launched his solo career with *McCartney*. In the early '70s, he formed a new group, Wings, and toured while recording frequently. Every new album hit the Top Ten, as did nearly every single. McCartney finally began to cool off in sales terms after the #1 album *Tug of War* in 1982, but artistically he continued to challenge himself, writing his own motion picture, *Give My Regards to Broad Street* (1984), and entering into a writing collaboration with Elvis Costello that resulted in hits for both of them. —*William Ruhlmann*

○ **McCartney** / Apr. 20, 1970 / Capitol ✦✦✦✦
McCartney's handmade solo debut has a rough-hewn, off-hand quality that invites the listener into his highly melodic, sometimes whimsical musical imagination. The best songs include "That Would Be Something" (lately revived by the Grateful Dead!), "Teddy Boy" (a Beatles outtake), and "Maybe I'm Amazed" (later a hit in a live 1977 version). —*William Ruhlmann*

Ram / May 17, 1971 / Capitol ✦✦✦
While lacking the polish of his later efforts, McCartney's second post-Beatles effort is brimming with melodies and intriguing ideas. Ultimately, it seems unfinished, but along the way one is treated to the delights of "Uncle Albert/Admiral Halsey" (a #1 hit),

"Heart of the Country," and "Back Seat of My Car." — *William Ruhlmann*

Wild Life / Dec. 7, 1971 / Capitol ✦✦
The first album credited to Paul McCartney's group Wings is a collection of slight material (most of it written by Paul and Linda McCartney). Worst is the lyrically challenged "Bip Bop," which even comes with a reprise! This was the album that gave evidence to anyone who'd ever dismissed McCartney as a lightweight. (The CD version of the album added three non-LP singles tracks: "Oh Woman, Oh Why," which had been the B-side of McCartney's first solo single, "Another Day," and both sides of the single "Mary Had A Little Lamb"/"Little Woman Love.") — *William Ruhlmann*

Red Rose Speedway / 1973 / Capitol ✦✦
After the debacle of *Wild Life*, Paul McCartney spent 1972 rebuilding his reputation with a series of one-off singles, then released this, his fourth post-Beatles album, which restored his commercial fortunes by hitting #1 and spawning the #1 single "My Love." Like *Ram*, the album is awash in interesting musical ideas, most of which aren't finished off, and what sound like dummy lyrics that were never replaced with good ones. The only substantive song other than the single is the lead-off track, "Big Barn Bed." (The CD version adds three non-LP B-sides: "I Lie Around," "Country Dreamer," and "The Mess." The last, a live cut that was the B-side of "My Love," is the best uptempo rocker of McCartney's solo career up to this point.) — *William Ruhlmann*

○ **Band on the Run** / Dec. 1973 / Capitol ✦✦✦✦
On his best post-Beatles album, McCartney uses his mastery of studio technique and gift for musical juxtaposition—from symphonic touches to hard rock to melodic acoustic music—in a wonderful collection of well-constructed songs, including the Top Ten hits "Helen Wheels," "Band on the Run," and "Jet." — *William Ruhlmann*

Venus & Mars / 1975 / Capitol ✦✦✦
A highly polished band album featuring the number one hit "Listen to What the Man Said," as well as "Letting Go" and "Venus and Mars/Rock Show," which served to introduce the McCartney & Wings world tour of 1975–1976. — *William Ruhlmann*

Wings at the Speed of Sound / 1976 / Capitol ✦✦
Released the same month as the start of Paul McCartney's first post-Beatles tour of the U.S., this album stayed at number one seven weeks and featured the number one single "Silly Love Songs" and the Top Ten "Let 'Em In." Without the hoopla, it's actually a mediocre effort not helped by having other members of Wings contribute songs, although it contains one of those lost McCartney gems, the rocker "Beware My Love." (The CD contains three bonus tracks culled from non-LP singles: "Walking in the Park with Eloise," "Bridge on the River Suite," and "Sally G.") — *William Ruhlmann*

Wings over America / Dec. 11, 1976 / Capitol ✦✦✦
McCartney made a favorable impression on his 1976 U.S. tour, convincing skeptics he could rock out when he chose and effectively mixing solo hits with Beatles oldies. This live album, originally issued on three LPs and now on two CDs, was more than a souvenir, containing an entire concert (edited from various shows), and finding McCartney performing effective versions of everything from "Lady Madonna" and "Yesterday" to "Hi Hi Hi" and "My Love." "Soily" is otherwise unavailable. "Maybe I'm Amazed" became a Top 10 hit, and the album was McCartney's fifth straight #1. — *William Ruhlmann*

London Town / Mar. 31, 1978 / Capitol ✦✦
London Town found Wings once again reduced to the trio of the McCartneys and Denny Laine. It was typically successful, hitting #2 and selling a million copies, with the bouncy single "With A Little Luck" topping the charts and the followups "I've Had Enough" and "London Town" making the Top 40. But the best tracks were "Deliver Your Children" and "Girlfriend," the latter discovered by Michael Jackson, who put it on his *Off The Wall* album the following year. (The CD contains the bonus track "Girls' School," which was a Top 40 single just prior to the album's release.) — *William Ruhlmann*

○ **Wings Greatest** / Nov. 22, 1978 / Capitol ✦✦✦✦
Most of McCartney & Wings's biggest hits, 1971–1978, among them the singles "Another Day," "Live and Let Die," "Junior's Farm," "Hi, Hi, Hi," and "Mull of Kintyre," which had not previously appeared on an album. — *William Ruhlmann*

Back to the Egg / 1979 / Capitol ✦✦
McCartney II / 1980 / Capitol ✦✦✦
Returning to an all-solo format, McCartney comes up with his best new studio album since *Band on the Run*, though ironically the album's hit is a live band version of "Coming Up," tossed in as a bonus. — *William Ruhlmann*

○ **Tug of War** / 1982 / Capitol ✦✦✦✦
McCartney turns to Beatles producer George Martin for a carefully constructed blockbuster album that features the #1 duet with Stevie Wonder, "Ebony and Ivory," and the Top Ten hit "Take It Away," plus McCartney's tribute to John Lennon, "Here Today." — *William Ruhlmann*

Pipes of Peace / 1983 / Capitol ✦✦
This was Paul McCartney's first new studio album, either as a member of the Beatles or as a solo artist, to miss the American Top 10—ever—and this was despite the inclusion of the long-running #1 duet with Michael Jackson, "Say Say Say." Explicitly pitched as a followup to *Tug of War*, *Pipes of Peace* was not as carefully crafted as its predecessor, despite the presence of producer George Martin. But that doesn't explain the commercial disappointment. Hereafter, McCartney would struggle to maintain the mass audience he had previously taken for granted. — *William Ruhlmann*

Give My Regards to Broadstreet / Jan. 1984 / Capitol ✦✦✦
McCartney's soundtrack to his poorly received feature film, this album contains rerecordings of Beatles songs and solo tunes, plus the hit single "No More Lonely Nights." — *William Ruhlmann*

Press to Play / Sep. 19, 1986 / Capitol ✦✦
This was Paul McCartney's first new studio album, either as a member of the Beatles or as a solo artist, not to go gold (i.e., sell half a million copies) upon initial release. It typically ranged from symphonic pop ("Only Love Remains") to rockers ("Pretty Little Head"), but was not one of McCartney's more impressive efforts. — *William Ruhlmann*

● **All the Best** / 1987 / Capitol ✦✦✦✦
Unfortunately, this second greatest-hits collection repeats many of the tracks from the first. But it does add the singles "C Moon" and "Goodnight Tonight" (previously unavailable on an album) and some of the bigger '80s hits, such as "Say Say Say" and "No More Lonely Nights." — *William Ruhlmann*

Flowers in the Dirt / 1989 / Capitol ✦✦✦
A well-constructed comeback album on which McCartney collaborates with Elvis Costello for the Top 30 hit "My Brave Face," recalls his father on "Put It There," rocks out on "Figure of Eight," and turns in one of those lovely McCartney ballads on "This One." — *William Ruhlmann*

Tripping the Live Fantastic / Oct. 1990 / Capitol ✦✦
Choba B CCCP / 1991 / Capitol ✦✦
This album of rock & roll oldies—"Lucille," "Twenty Flight Rock," etc.—was recorded in two days in July 1987, and released exclusively in the Soviet Union in 1988. It finally saw release in the U.S. in 1991 with one extra track, "I'm In Love Again," added. McCartney gives a spirited reading to the songs, which, it may be noted, are in some cases ("Ain't That A Shame," "Just Because") the same ones chosen by John Lennon for his similar *Rock 'N' Roll* album. But McCartney is characteristically more eclectic, including such ringers as "Summertime" and "Don't Get Around Much Anymore." — *William Ruhlmann*

Liverpool Oratorio / 1991 / Angel ✦✦
Paul McCartney was commissioned by the Royal Liverpool Philharmonic Orchestra to compose a work to mark its 150th anniversary and collaborated with composer/conductor Carl Davis on this 90-minute classical piece which features soloists Kiri Te Kanawa and Jerry Hadley in a vaguely autobiographical story of a Liverpudlian named Shanty. While ambitious for an untaught musician like McCartney, the assignment didn't inspire him to any heights of melodic or lyrical achievement. In both areas, the piece plods, suggesting that McCartney hasn't so much taken on the unfamiliar form as surrendered to it. Maybe he should have worked with George Martin (who scored "Yesterday" and "Eleanor Rigby") instead. — *William Ruhlmann*

○ **Unplugged (The Official Bootleg)** / May 1991 / Capitol ✦✦✦✦
A delightful acoustic performance in which McCartney resurrects some Beatles classics, some oldies, and some of his less well known solo songs in a live setting. — *William Ruhlmann*

Paul Is Live / Jan. 1, 1993 / Capitol ✦✦
McCartney's fourth live album in four years (including *Tripping the Live Fantastic—The Highlights*) is arguably his weakest yet, full of competent but utterly unnecessary versions of Beatles classics and recent McCartney numbers. Really, does anyone need to hear a live version of "Biker Like An Icon"? And after putting out two separate live albums from his previous tour, it smacks of overkill to release this record, which has the exact same band and tone as *Tripping the Live Fantastic*. —*Stephen Thomas Erlewine*

Off the Ground / Feb. 1993 / Capitol ✦✦
Paul McCartney gets an extra star for the song "Looking For Changes" from his latest *Off the Ground*. Its potent animal-rights message is married to a good tune, some sinewy playing, and a believable sense of commitment. Beyond this, the news is not as good. The advance hype pegged this release as a "return" to a harder, angry edge for cuddly Paul. The basic tracks were recorded live in the studio to impart an urgent feel. McCartney's social conscience may be active on songs like "Hope of Deliverance," "C'mon People," and "Peace In The Neighbourhood," but—more often than not—the album is awash in lame, gummy music and mawkish sentiment. —*Roch Parisien*

James McCarty
Pop/Rock
James McCarty was one of the founding members of one of the seminal British Invasion groups, the Yardbirds. After leaving the group, he formed the progressive rock outfit Renaissance with Yardbirds vocalist Keith Relf. McCarty left Renaissance in 1973; he wrote material for Dave Berry and Dave Clark, among others, before attempting to re-form Renaissance in 1976. Sadly, the band's plans were destroyed by Relf's death in 1976; the group continued as Illusion. In 1983, he joined former Yardbirds Chris Dreja and Paul Samwell-Smith in Box of Frogs. In the late '80s, McCarty launched his own solo album, which has produced four albums that meld his blues-rock heritage with new age philosophies and musical textures. —*Stephen Thomas Erlewine*

● **Out of the Dark** / 1994 / Higher Octave ✦✦✦✦
James McCarty's *Out of the Dark* is a richly layered album of meditative synthesized soundscapes that manage to incorporate hints of his roots in blues and rock & roll. —*Stephen Thomas Erlewine*

Van McCoy
b. Jan. 6, 1944, Washington, DC, d. Jul. 6, 1979
Soul, Disco
Producer/composer Van McCoy had a lengthy career in R&B, soul, and dance music, although he is best known by the general public for "The Hustle." But McCoy's experiences dated back to the '50s, when he sang with both the Marylanders and in the Starlighters with his brother. The Starlighters cut three singles for End in 1959. McCoy had his own label, Rock 'N, in 1960 and became an A&R man at Scepter/Wand from 1961 to 1964. He penned numbers for Chuck Jackson, the Shirelles, Jackie Wilson ("I Get the Sweetest Feeling"), and Ruby and the Romantics ("When You're Young and in Love"), and produced sessions by the Shirelles, Gladys Knight, and the Drifters. McCoy also ran Vando and Share and owned Maxx during the '60s, supervising such artists as Chris Bartley and the Ad-Libs. He later created Van McCoy Productions in 1968, and formed Faith, Hope & Charity in the early '70s before becoming a solo artist and signing with Avco. "The Hustle" was a number one R&B and pop hit in 1975, as well as a gold single. McCoy also had a Top Ten R&B hit with "Change with the Times" that same year, also on Avco. He continued on H&L and MCA through 1976. McCoy wrote and produced material for Gladys Knight & the Pips, Aretha Franklin, Linda Clifford, Stacy Lattisaw, Melba Moore, and Barbara Lewis before he died in 1979. —*Ron Wynn*

● **The Hustle and Best of Van McCoy** / 1976 / H&L ✦✦✦✦

McCoys
Group, Pop/Rock
This Indiana group were still in high school when they were tapped by the Strangeloves production team of Feldman-Goldstein-Gottehrer as a vehicle for their material in 1965. Their first effort, "Hang on Sloopy," was a monster number one smash, built around a riff and chorus that ranks with "Louie Louie" and "La Bamba" as a garage band perennial with its compelling, elemental simplicity. Featuring the lead vocals and lead guitar of a young Rick Derringer, they went on to cut a lot of similar chunky, innocuous pop/rock over the next couple years with fair success. The "Hang on Sloopy" soundalike "Fever" was their only other Top Ten entry, and the Ritchie Valens cover "C'Mon Let's Go" their only other Top 40 hit.

The McCoys recorded very little original material during their early years at Bang Records; most of it was supplied by the Feldman-Goldstein-Gottehrer production team, much of which consisted of unexceptional derivations of the "Hang on Sloopy" prototype. Notable exceptions were the folky "Sorrow," covered for a Top Ten hit by the Merseys in Great Britain (and covered by David Bowie on *Pin Ups* a decade later), and the adventurous Middle Eastern-tinged garage psychedelia of "Don't Worry Mother," their best cut besides "Hang on Sloopy." The McCoys proved unusually durable after their career as a teen pop band; in the late '60s, they broke from their Bang producers to record psychedelic and progressive rock for Mercury. Most of the group joined Johnny Winter's backup band in the early '70s, and in 1973 Rick Derringer joined the Edgar Winter group as lead guitarist and vocalist, after which he had a successful hard rock solo career. —*Richie Unterberger*

● **Hang on Sloopy: The Best of the McCoys** / 1995 / Legacy/Epic ✦✦✦✦
22-track compilation of their best mid-'60s material, including all the hits and tracks from their two Bang LPs, non-album singles, and a couple of previously unissued cuts. Much of this is rather forgettable if inoffensive, other than "Hang on Sloopy," "Fever," "Sorrow," and "Don't Worry Mother." —*Richie Unterberger*

Gene McDaniels (Eugene B McDaniels)
b. Feb. 12, 1935, Kansas City, MO
Soul, Pop
Gene McDaniels had some early '60s success with a pop-flavored R&B style. Born in Kansas City, he sang in Omaha choirs during the '40s and attended the Omaha Conservatory of Music. McDaniels led his own band in the '50s, then signed with Liberty. He had a Top Ten pop and Top 20 R&B hit in 1961 with "A Hundred Pounds of Clay," but the follow-up single, "A Tower of Strength," was his biggest. It was number five on both the R&B and pop charts, and "Point of No Return" just missed each list's Top 20. He appeared in the 1962 film *It's Trad, Dad*, which contained his song "Another Tear Falls." McDaniels continued to record for Liberty until 1965, then switched to Atlantic in the early '70s. He scored as a writer with the composition "Feel like Making Love," a number one pop and R&B hit for Roberta Flack in 1974. He also produced Merry Clayton and other performers. —*Ron Wynn*

● **A Hundred Pounds of Clay & Other Hits** / 1992 / CEMA ✦✦✦✦
Although he preferred singing jazz, blues and/or R&B, Gene McDaniels enjoyed some success in the late '50s and early '60s with highly arranged, elaborately produced and orchestrated pop. McDaniels was locked into short, sometimes humorous and/or vocally exaggerated romantic dilemma vehicles. He seldom got to explore serious themes or extend himself, instead hitting the hooks and then exiting backed by strings, female vocalists and/or a bombastic instrumental background. This anthology's 25 tracks include his biggest hits, "Tower of Strength," "Chip Chip," "Point of No Return," and the title track. There are also B-sides, unreleased cuts and singles that weren't hits, but more accurately reflected McDaniels' style. —*Ron Wynn*

McDonald & Giles
Group, Art-Rock/Progressive-Rock
After Ian McDonald and Michael Giles dropped out of King Crimson at the end of the band's first US tour in 1969, they formed a short-lived duo that featured eccentric, oddly relaxed art-rock with a lot of heart. If ever this genre was capable of producing charming music, this is it. McDonald subsequently went on to Foreigner, whence he made his fortune. —*Bruce Eder & Rick Clark*

○ **McDonald & Giles** / 1971 / EG ✦✦✦✦
This self-titled one-off (a Japanese import) by three expatriates of King Crimson is one of the great lost albums for fans of the art-rock genre. The whimsical themes and wonderfully creative musical interplay between the Giles brothers (Mike and Peter) and Ian McDonald keep this album from being bogged down in some of the ponderous elements of that style. Steve Winwood also guests on organ. "Suite in C," with its playful cut-and-paste motifs, and the extended concept piece "Birdman" are standouts. —*Rick Clark*

Michael McDonald

b. 1952, St. Louis, MO
Soul, Pop/Rock
There was a time during the early '80s when Michael McDonald's earnest soulful upper baritone seemed to appear on half the hits coming out of the West Coast, including ones by Christopher Cross, Nicolette Larson, Kenny Loggins, Toto, Donna Summer, Steely Dan, and hit duets with James Ingram and Patti LaBelle. McDonald's vocal presence was most felt as lead singer for the Doobie Brothers between 1975 and 1982 on hits like "What a Fool Believes" (#1), "Taking It to the Streets" (#8), and the #14 single "Minute by Minute." As a solo artist, McDonald scored with "I Keep Forgettin' (Every Time You're Near)" (#4) in 1982, off of his #6 debut *If That's What It Takes*. Other hits include "No Looking Back" (#34) and "Sweet Freedom" (#7). *—Rick Clark*

That Was Then / 1982 / Arista ◆◆◆

○ **If That's What It Takes** / 1982 / Warner Brothers ◆◆◆◆
Sweet, romantic blue-eyed soul, containing "I Gotta Try" (#44) and "I Keep Forgettin' (Every Time You're Near)" (#4). *—Bil Carpenter*

No Lookin' Back / 1985 / Warner Brothers ◆◆◆

● **Sweet Freedom: The Best of Michael McDonald** / 1986 / Warner Brothers ◆◆◆◆
A solid collection that features all of McDonald's greatest hits from the early '80s. *—Stephen Thomas Erlewine*

Take It to Heart / 1990 / Reprise ◆◆◆

Mike McGear

Pop/Rock
Mike McGear is actually Paul McCartney's brother; he changed his name in the mid-'60s shortly after the Beatles become famous, not wishing to be perceived as riding Paul's coattails. He was a member of the Scaffold, which recorded some fairly successful comedy-rock releases in the late '60s (their "Thank U Very Much" and "Lily Pink" singles were big British hits). In 1974, he recorded a solo album with plenty of help from Paul, who wrote or co-wrote almost all the songs, and sang backup; fellow Wings Linda McCartney, Denny Laine, and Jimmy McCullough also play and sing. The album, which unsurprisingly recalled the Wings, attracted some critical notice, but sold poorly. *—Richie Unterberger*

● **McGear** / 1974 / Rykodisc ◆◆◆◆
While McGear's album may be strongly reminiscent of Paul McCartney in important respects—the carefully crafted pop-rock arrangements and, of course, the vocals—no one's going to confuse it with Paul himself; the material, with a much more pronounced droll British satiric bent than McCartney's, simply isn't that strong. Mostly for Beatle aficionados, the CD reissue includes the previously unreleased bonus track "Dance The Do." *—Richie Unterberger*

Roger McGuinn

b. Jul. 13, 1942
Rock & Roll, Country-Rock, Folk-Rock
Before he helped found the influential mid-'60s group the Byrds, McGuinn (born Jim McGuinn) had been active as a sideman for Bobby Darin and folk artists like the Limeliters, the Chad Mitchell Trio, and Judy Collins. With the Byrds, McGuinn forged the distinctively bright 12-string Rickenbacker electric sound, which has inspired groups too numerous to name. His solo work hasn't risen to the level of his best work with the Byrds, but highlights include his self-titled debut, *Cardiff Rose*, and his 1991 comeback effort, *Back from Rio*. *—Rick Clark*

Roger McGuinn / 1973 / CBS ◆◆◆

Peace on You / 1974 / CBS ◆◆◆

Roger McGuinn & His Band / 1975 / CBS ◆◆◆

○ **Cardiff Rose** / 1976 / Columbia ◆◆◆◆

Thunderbyrd / 1977 / CBS ◆◆◆

○ **Back from Rio** / 1990 / Arista ◆◆◆◆
This comeback effort put McGuinn together with Tom Petty & the Heartbreakers, former-Byrds Chris Hillman and David Crosby, and other guest artists eager to pay tribute, like Michael Penn and Timothy B. Schmit. "King of the Hill" was a substantial FM rock hit. Other highlights include Elvis Costello's "You Bowed Down" and a fine version of Jules Shear's "If We Never Meet Again." The mainstream AOR production values make McGuinn sound like

he's guesting on a Tom Petty record—which is not a bad thing, just an observation. *—Rick Clark*

● **Born to Rock & Roll** / Mar. 1992 / Columbia ◆◆◆◆
A well-chosen overview of McGuinn's post-Byrds solo work, it includes "American Girl," "I'm So Restless," "Lover of the Bayou," "My New Woman," and "Peace on You." *—Rick Clark*

Barry McGuire

b. Oct. 15, 1935, Oklahoma City
Folk-Rock
Barry McGuire achieved one-hit wonder status for the 1965 folk-rock protest song "Eve of Destruction," which topped the charts. He began his career in folk music earlier in the decade and had been a member of the New Christy Minstrels, for whom he co-wrote the hit "Green, Green." McGuire was unable to follow up "Eve Of Destruction" despite several subsequent releases, but he found success in the Christian music field in the 1970s. He now devotes his time to a charity that sponsors poor children in Third World countries. *—William Ruhlmann*

● **Anthology** / 1994 / One Way ◆◆◆◆

Maria McKee

Rock & Roll, Country-Rock
While she was with Lone Justice, Maria McKee always showed promise; her gritty, soulful mix of R&B, rock, and country helped distinguish the band from the multitude of '80s roots rockers. When she released her first solo album in the late '80s, it suffered from the same problem as Lone Justice—lots of potential, but no delivery. However, 1993's *You Gotta Sin to Get Saved* showed McKee making good on her promise, with an album of impassioned rockers and ballads. *—Stephen Thomas Erlewine*

Maria McKee / 1989 / Geffen ◆◆◆
Three years after Lone Justice's last album, Maria McKee released her self-titled debut, which showed that her skills as a songwriter had grown considerably since her first band. Not only were her songs better, but McKee's singing had improved; while it was still a little thin, her voice had grown grittier and more soulful, which made her songs all the more convincing. Unfortunately, most of McKee's musical growth was obscured by Mitchell Froom's mushy overproduction. *—Stephen Thomas Erlewine*

● **You Gotta Sin to Get Saved** / Jun. 22, 1993 / Geffen ◆◆◆◆
A few years after an underappreciated solo album, former Lone Justice leader Maria McKee returns with *You Gotta Sin to Get Saved*, her best album yet. With Black Crowes and Jayhawks producer George Drakoulias at the helm, *You Gotta Sin to Get Saved* evokes the country-rock vibe of the early '70s (much like the aforementioned groups) without sounding like a studied replica. McKee sings a dynamic mix of originals and covers with genuine conviction, making *You Gotta Sin to Get Saved* an album that demands repeated plays. *—Stephen Thomas Erlewine*

Sarah McLachlan

Singer-Songwriter, Alternative Pop/Rock, Folk-Rock
Since her debut album in 1989, Sarah McLachlan's atmospheric folk-pop has gained a devoted following of fans, both in the U.S. and U.K. Each record has shown McLachlan growing both as a songwriter and a musician. In 1994, she began to work her way into the mainstream with her album *Fumbling Toward Ecstasy* and the single "Possession." *—Stephen Thomas Erlewine*

Touch / 1989 / Arista ◆◆◆
On her debut effort, McLachlan sets the stage for future greatness. While only in her early twenties, she shows insights beyond her years with highly personal and introspective lyrics. *—Chris Woodstra*

○ **Solace** / Sep. 10, 1991 / Arista ◆◆◆◆
With her second album, McLachlan shows a marked improvement in songwriting. Yearning lyrics flow perfectly with her 12-string guitar, a tight rhythm section, and strong Celtic influences. A fine folk-pop effort. *—Chris Woodstra*

Live EP / 1992 / Nettwerk ◆◆

● **Fumbling Towards Ecstasy** / Feb. 1, 1994 / Arista ◆◆◆◆
From the heavy dance beats of the opening single, "Possession," to the more delicate "Good Enough," McLachlan explores self-awareness and sensuality as well as a new world view in ways unrivaled

by her previous efforts. Lush arrangements back her powerful vocals to build a highly rewarding album. —*Chris Woodstra*

The Freedom Sessions / 1995 / Nettwerk ✦✦✦

A nice companion piece to *Fumbling Towards Ecstacy*, *The Freedom Sessions* offers seven early versions of songs from that album in a more stripped-down form. Also included is a cover of Tom Waits' "Ol'55." —*Chris Woodstra*

Malcolm McLaren

b. Jan. 22, 1946
Ethnic Fusion, Alternative Pop/Rock
He's been an artist, a clothing designer, a boutique owner, a personal manager (the New York Dolls, the Sex Pistols), a producer (Adam and the Ants, Bow Wow Wow), a songwriter, and finally a recording artist himself. —*William Ruhlmann*

● **Duck Rock** / 1983 / Island ✦✦✦✦

An amazingly eclectic collection of world music mixed with urban hip-hop, featuring the dance hit "Buffalo Gals." —*William Ruhlmann*

D'ya Like Scratchin' / Oct. 3, 1983 / Island ✦✦✦

Scratchin' / 1984 / Virgin ✦✦

○ **Fans** / 1984 / Island ✦✦✦✦

Selections from *Madame Butterfly* and *Carmen* recast as dance music—a wildly imaginative musical mixture, sometimes hauntingly beautiful. —*William Ruhlmann*

Swamp Thing / Nov. 11, 1985 / Island ✦

Waltz Darling / 1989 / Epic ✦✦✦

More stunning musical juxtapositions—*The Blue Danube* with bass playing by Bootsy Collins and a guitar solo by Jeff Beck, and more. —*William Ruhlmann*

Round the Outside! Round the Outside! / 1990 / Virgin ✦✦✦

Paris / 1994 / Island ✦✦

Malcolm McLaren has never been a musician, at least never in any accepted sense of the word. Rather, he's a self-promoter. Even when he was managing the Sex Pistols, most of his press conferences concentrated on what a great scam *he* had come up with, not the music itself. On his own records, he's been supported by first-rate musicians who manage to hide his half-baked concepts. On *Paris*, he has nothing to hide behind—the musicians fade into the background, since the record is essentially a love letter to Paris. And what a love letter! McLaren's overwrought prose is filled with bad rhymes and awkward imagery, making him sound like a lecherous old man, and the music doesn't help to remove that picture. Instead, the heavily orchestrated cabaret jazz backdrops tend to *accentuate* the sleaziness of McLaren's words. And that's what makes the record perversely fascinating: every element is so poorly conceived and executed that the entire thing appears to be an intentional joke. The only way he could make *Paris* any more pretentious and insufferable—and funnier—is if he released an instrumental version of it. Which he did, by the way. —*Stephen Thomas Erlewine*

Don McLean

b. Oct. 2, 1945, New Rochelle, NY
Folk, Singer-Songwriter
A singer/songwriter of a fiercely independent character, McLean dominated radio and record sales for weeks in 1971-1972 with his epic-length Buddy Hollyesque hit "American Pie." He could have gotten years more prominence by following it up and milking the sound; instead he wrote from a personal point of view, and achieved a level of respect more often associated with folksingers a good decade older than he is for valuing the past and himself more than chart action. —*Bruce Eder*

Tapestry / 1970 / MediaArts ✦✦✦

It took the success of Don McLean's second album, *American Pie*, to stimulate interest in his debut record, *Tapestry*. But once the new fans looked, they found that the album contained the same high level of pop-folk songwriting, if in a somewhat less epic form. "Castles in the Air" became a hit, and the album also contained McLean's version of his song "And I Love You So," which Perry Como successfully covered in 1973. —*William Ruhlmann*

○ **American Pie** / Jan. 1971 / EMI America ✦✦✦✦

The album that made McLean famous. The title track is the only real rocker, but the rest is intelligently produced and at times quite haunting, if a little angst ridden. —*Bruce Eder*

○ **Don McLean** / 1972 / United Artists ✦✦✦✦

Don McLean's followup to the overwhelmingly successful *American Pie* inevitably fell short of its predecessor, but it was a strong collection, containing the chart entry "If We Try" and "Dreidel," which should have been a hit, too. —*William Ruhlmann*

Playin' Favourites / 1974 / United Artists ✦✦✦

Homeless Brother / 1974 / United Artists ✦✦✦

McLean turned in more of a light pop effort here, with the charming "Wonderful Baby" topping the Adult Contemporary chart, an excellent cover of "Crying In The Chapel," and another strong original in "La La Love You." —*William Ruhlmann*

Solo / 1976 / United Artists ✦✦✦

A surprisingly rewarding and personal live double-album. —*Bruce Eder*

Prime Time / 1977 / Arista ✦✦

Chain Lightning / 1980 / Casablanca ✦✦

○ **Very Best of Don McLean, Favorites & Rarities** / 1980 / Capitol ✦✦✦✦

Fans of Don McLean should be thrilled with this comprehensive, digitally remastered, 42-track, double-disc set covering his hits, like "American Pie," "Castles in the Air," "Vincent," and "Everyday." There are also 18 previously unreleased tracks. Also included is an excellent set of liner notes, track annotations, and numerous photos from McLean's collection. —*Rick Clark*

Believers / 1982 / Millennium ✦✦

Love Tracks / 1987 / Capitol ✦✦✦

● **Greatest Hits Then & Now** / 1987 / Capitol ✦✦✦✦

An acceptable collection, with few surprises. —*Bruce Eder*

For the Memories, Vols. 1 & 2 / 1989 / Gold Castle ✦✦✦

McLean's brand of musical nostalgia, very much at the heart of his work, but not for all tastes or always interesting. —*Bruce Eder*

○ **Favorites & Rarities** / 1992 / EMI America ✦✦✦✦

Grant McLennan

Singer-Songwriter, Alternative Pop/Rock, Folk-Rock
A founding member of Australia's Go Betweens, McLennan added the more upbeat, pop elements. He's a craftsman of fine songs. —*Bruce Eder*

Watershed / 1991 / Beggars Banquet ✦✦✦

This cofounder of the Go Betweens succeeds with pop. It's marred by techno-dance attempts on a couple of tracks. —*Robert Gordon*

● **Horsebreaker Star** / 1995 / Beggars Banquet ✦✦✦✦

Intelligent, literate, pop-rock. Eighteen tracks (actually pared down for North America from its original 2-disc British release) recorded in the legendary pop hotbed of Athens, Georgia, the set offers an almost overwhelming embarrassment of unassuming, electro-acoustic, guitar-chiming, thinking-person's pop riches. Not all of *Horsebreaker*'s mood or McLennan's lyrics are "happy" by any means, but he exudes a warm, easygoing attitude at odds with the more fashionable, stark cynics of the day. —*Roch Parisien*

James McMurtry

Singer-Songwriter
With a voice as dry as a summer in his native Texas, singer/songwriter James McMurtry (son of famous author Larry McMurtry) is a first-rate storyteller, drawing from classic folk traditions and left-of-center poetic metaphors that rarely sound overreaching. —*Rick Clark*

● **Too Long in the Wasteland** / 1989 / Columbia ✦✦✦✦

On this impressive debut, McMurtry delivers a finely rendered series of musical snapshots that, at times, does for the drifters, dreamers, and losers of small-town America what Lou Reed did for the Big Apple—the Heartland as a wasteland. The characters that populate "Angeline" and "Terry" are portrayed with dignity, in a way that makes the listener care about what is being said. McMurtry's offhand vocal delivery is as dry as a Texas drought. This is one of the finest major-label singer/songwriter releases in years. —*Rick Clark*

Candyland / Jun. 2, 1992 / Columbia ✦✦✦

Like Dire Straits' Mark Knopfler (but with less mumble), James McMurtry offers a deep, personable (if plain) voice and delivery, equally suited to both country and rock. The instrumental backing veers between and blurs the two forms, the fluid dynamics rendering the distinction irrelevant. Whatever you call it, the music serves up a perfect backdrop to McMurtry's strong suit—his evocative, short-story lyrics. Eventually, rock appears to win out as guitars veer into overdrive on "Save Yourself" and "Storekeeper"; the disc finally closing with the wistful, acoustic "Dusty Pages." —*Roch Parisien*

Clyde McPhatter

b. Nov. 15, 1932, Durham, NC, **d.** Jun. 13, 1972
R&B
Along with Ray Charles and Sam Cooke, Clyde McPhatter was one of the most influential and important vocalists to emerge in the '50s. His unusually high, muscular vocals brought gospel fervor and sexual passion to the early-'50s hits of Billy Ward's Dominoes, with whom McPhatter cut the showstopping "Have Mercy Baby" and "The Bells." Ahmet Ertegun signed him to Atlantic in 1953, after McPhatter and Ward parted company, and assembled the Drifters around his gorgeous soprano. His solo career began in 1955, while he was serving in the Army; "Treasure of Love," "Without Love," and "A Lover's Question" were his best solo hits. He had some minor success with Mercury in the '60s but died in obscurity in 1972. —*John Floyd*

★ **Deep Sea Ball: The Best of Clyde McPhatter** / 1991 / Atlantic ✦✦✦✦✦
This 19-track compilation contains all of the top hits that McPhatter scored between 1956 and 1959. He also charted singles on MGM and Mercury, but the bulk of his best-remembered work is here, including "A Lover's Question" and "Treasure of Love." —*William Ruhlmann*

Meat Puppets

Group, Rock & Roll, Alternative Pop/Rock
One of the weirdest groups from the '80s and one of the more challenging, this Tempe, AZ, trio has confounded audiences and alternative standard-bearers by honing a singular style based on a genre (hardcore) that thrives on conformity. Their 1981 debut single was standard loud/fast punk, but by their second album the Pups became confident enough to flaunt their influences and their ambitions; traces of Captain Beefheart, Neil Young, ZZ Top, and Blue Öyster Cult seeped through the din of Curt Kirkwood's whining vocals and inventive guitar figures. Their sound has since become more streamlined, but they remain a unique and often-brilliant group, one of the best the '80s produced. —*John Floyd*

In a Car / 1981 / SST ✦✦
Meat Puppets / 1982 / SST ✦✦✦
Considering what they sound like these days, it's hard to imagine what an explosively noisy trio the Pups were around the time of their debut. There are bits and pieces of the country, folk and blues stylings that would show up on later recordings, but the first time out there was plenty of noise, feedback, arrhythmic bashing and screeched vocals. In other words, if you've become a Meat Pups fan on the strength of their last few records, this one will set your head spinning. It ain't nothing like anything else they've ever done. —*John Dougan*

○ **Meat Puppets II** / 1983 / SST ✦✦✦✦
More traditional songs, more noise, more great Curt Kirkwood guitar and vocals, this LP has been referred to as a seminal slice of country-punk and who am I to argue. This record was a startling mini-masterpiece, primarily because their debut record hadn't prepared anyone for this sudden stylistic shift. And, in typical Meat Puppets fashion, the pulled it off without batting an eye, as if they'd recording music like this for many years. One of the great rock records of the '80s. —*John Dougan*

● **Up on the Sun** / 1985 / SST ✦✦✦✦
Moving even farther away from the dissonance of their debut, the Pups, at this juncture were sounding more and more like a (gasp!) regular old rock band. But only a fool would consider their debut the best record of their career, clearly there was much more to this band than met the ear(s). Up on the Sun continues the postmodern country punk of *II* and offers up great greasy globs of guitar thanks to Curt Kirkwood's rapidly improving playing. There are some moments on this record that even leave rock behind in favor of folkie quietude, but for Meat Pups fans, they were turning into a formidable band unjustly ignored by the world. —*John Dougan*

○ **Out My Way** / 1986 / SST ✦✦✦✦
○ **Huevos** / 1987 / SST ✦✦✦✦
Punk ZZ Top wannabees. —*Robert Gordon*

Mirage / 1987 / SST ✦✦✦
Mirage signals the start of the period of the Meat Pups career when they began the transformation (subtle though it was) from a wonderfully messy punk band to a slightly less messy rock band. As usual, Curt's guitar is the star and at times he sounds like the psychedelic hippie-punk offspring of Doc Watson on tracks like "Confusion Fog." Still, the Pups were, in terms of playing, songwriting and production, light years beyond the first album, and that was a good thing. Unlike many maturing bands, the Meat Puppets are one of the few that remain consistently good without sounding as though they are pandering to an audience. —*John Dougan*

Monsters / 1989 / SST ✦✦✦
I lump these two records (*Huevos* and *Monsters*) together mainly because they are built around a similar "big rock" guitar sound. Curt had been listening to a lot of ZZ Top at this point (not a bad thing to do, I might add!) and the effect on the music of the Meat Puppets was obvious. Now playing Les Paul guitars and fancying a louder, more aggressive, fat, distorted wall of sound, the Pups sounded like world beaters on these two records. Old-time fans and purists were decidedly distraught when these records came out, for it sounded as though the Pups had simply decided to sound like just another country/blues tinged hard rock band, but that was only true on the more mediocre songs, the reality was that the Pups were now diamond hard and air-tight. The proof of this is in songs like "Bad Love," "Sexy Music," and "I Can't Be Counted On" (from *Huevos*) and "Attacked by Monsters," "Meltdown," and "Party Til the World Obeys" (from *Monsters*). At this point (later borne out by Kurt Cobain during Nirvana's *Unplugged* gig) the Pups had become a tremendously influential American rock band. —*John Dougan*

No Strings Attached / 1990 / SST ✦✦✦
An extremely well-thought-out two-LP sampler of the Pups from their SST days. Tracks go up to and include material from *Monsters*. SST released this after the band left the venerable indie label for London in 1990. An excellent anthology. —*John Dougan*

Forbidden Places / 1991 / London ✦✦✦
Few of the best bands that recorded for SST in the '80s (Husker Du, Minutemen, Black Flag) stayed with the label as long as did the Meat Puppets, and as a result, their leaving for a major label in 1990 seemed anti-climactic. *Forbidden Places*, while not as immediately gripping as some of the Meat Pups better records is a consistently enjoyable slice of psychedelic hard rock. The record's opening track, the annoying "Sam," got a lot of airplay on alternative rock stations, but it was not nearly as good (or indicative) of the rest of the music. It should be noted that Curt Kirkwood's singing, never a strength, sounds improved here. Had he been taking voice lessons? —*John Dougan*

Too High to Die / 1994 / London ✦✦✦
Still crazy after all these years, the Pups sound in fine fettle on this appropriately named recording, but a touch of sameness is starting to creep in making *Too High* probably the least essential of the band's later recordings. Being a laidback rock band can be cool, but it can also mean that falling into a rut is easier than taking on new challenges. But if the history of the Meat Puppets teaches us anything, it's that this band is capable of surprises—and plenty of them! —*John Dougan*

Meat Loaf

Group, Hard Rock, Pop/Rock
A rock singer (born Marvin Lee Aday) with a full, dramatic voice; also an actor who shot to fame with the multi-platinum album *Bat Out of Hell* in 1977.
After everybody had written him off as a has-been, Meat Loaf rocketed back to the top of the charts in 1993 with *Back into Hell: Bat Out of Hell II*, which became an enormous, multi-platinum hit. —*William Ruhlmann*

● **Bat out of Hell** / 1978 / Epic ✦✦✦✦
Meat Loaf's powerful, passionate voice serves as the messenger for Jim Steinman's over-the-top rock songs, which treat teenage angst in practically Wagnerian terms, while Todd Rundgren provides a clean, well-articulated Wall of Sound production in this kitsch masterpiece, which includes "Two Out of Three Ain't Bad" and "Paradise by the Dashboard Light." —*William Ruhlmann*

Meatloaf (Featuring Stoney) / 1979 / Prodigal
Dead Ringer / 1981 / Epic ✦✦✦
Meat Loaf collects a couple of Steinman songs, and he, Paul Jacobs, and Mack work at recreating the Rundgren production sound for an album of high-voltage rock. —*William Ruhlmann*

Midnight at the Lost & Found / 1983 / Epic ✦✦
Hits out of Hell / 1984 / Epic ✦✦✦
Bad Attitude / 1984 / Fame ✦✦
Blind Before I Stop / 1986 / Arista ✦✦
○ **Bat Out of Hell II: Back Into Hell** / 1993 / MCA ✦✦✦✦
The bottom line is pretty basic: if you still love (or live by) the original *Bat of Hell*, then this sequel will not disappoint … especially the 12-minute magnum opus "I'd Do Anything For Love (But I Won't Do That)." If you would rather chew off your own leg than be forced to sit through "Paradise By The Dashboard Light" ever again, then run fast. —*Roch Parisien*

Joe Meek
Group, Pop/Rock
Not an artist in the traditional sense of the term—he couldn't play or sing at all—producer Joe Meek has nonetheless been belatedly recognized as an important, even inimitable, figure of early British rock & roll. Like Phil Spector, Meek developed idiosyncratic production techniques that, much more than the artists he worked with, stamped a vision of mad genius on his recordings. In Meek's case, this usually amounted to super-compressed sound, wavering sped-up vocals, ghostly backing violins and choruses, spooky echo and reverb, ticky-tack varispeed piano, and all manners of Halloween and outer-space sound effects. The recordings were all the more remarkable for produced not in a state-of-the-art studio, but in Meek's own bedroom-sized facility, located over a shop within the flat he rented.

Meek couldn't rightly be compared to Phil Spector—he favored gawky, dippy teen-idol fare for gawky, dippy teen idols, not the gutsy soul and R&B-infused Wall of Sound. But he was a trailblazer in his own right—even before Spector, he set up shop as rock & roll's very first independent producer of note, making recordings on his own terms and leasing them to labels for distribution. In the United States, he only scored big with the Tornados' "Telstar" (the first British rock & roll record to top the American charts, a year before the Beatles) and the Honeycombs' "Have I the Right." In the U.K., he produced scores of records, many of them flops, and many others hits, for the Tornados, Honeycombs, Screaming Lord Sutch, John Leyton, Heinz, the Outlaws (featuring Ritchie Blackmore for a time), and many more. Highly prized by some collectors, these range from brilliant to insufferably insipid, though, as none other than Jello Biafra noted in the book *Incredibly Strange Music Volume 2,* "you can tell a Joe Meek record a mile away."

Meek's business and production methods may have been ahead of his time, but his actual musical tastes actually started to run behind the times with the advent of the self-contained groups of the British Invasion. He actually recorded a few respectable efforts in the R&B/mod vein, but his career was in a severe spiral by the time his life ended in tragic circumstances in early 1967, when he shot his landlady and himself. The existing CD compilations of his work don't actually do him justice; it's better to seek out the greatest hits collections of the artists mentioned above. John Repsch's book *The Legendary Joe Meek* (published in the U.K. only) is a good biography of this fascinating figure. —*Richie Unterberger*

Joe Meek Story, Vol. 1 / 1991 / Line ✦✦✦
Although one can hear the genesis of some of Meek's unique methods on this 20-track collection of 1960 releases, the material and performances are fairly insufferable, exhibit A in the lameness of much pre-Beatle British rock. Includes the super-rare (and silly) science fiction EP about intelligent life in outer space that he created with the non-futuristic sound effects and tape manipulation under the moniker "The Blue Men." —*Richie Unterberger*

Joe Meek Story: The Pye Years / 1991 / Sequel ✦✦✦
48-track double CD of Meek productions released on the British Pye label between 1960 and 1966 give a surprisingly scattershot and fragmented overview of his work, with an overabundance of weak early '60s-type teen idol and instrumental fare, despite some strong tracks by the Honeycombs, Riot Squad, and Glenda Collins. —*Richie Unterberger*

BOOK

✦✦✦✦ **The Legendary Joe Meek**, by John Repsch (Woodford House, U.K., 1989). Not many people listen to Meek's records anymore, but even if you're not one to dig out material by the Tornados or the Honeycombs, the story of his life is fairly fascinating. As a producer, Meek was one of a kind, and the book details his innovative uses of echo, compression, and all manner of wild arrangements, many recorded in his modest flat, with members of the band and orchestra sitting on the stairs or on the toilet at times to fit into the session. It's also the story of a man determined to do things his way at a time when the British recording industry was archaically stuffy, setting up his own production company to ensure control over his product. And it's the tale of a man pursued by demons and peculiar obsessions with the supernatural, whose unpredictable tantrums and behavior grew increasingly instable, culminating in his murder of his landlady in 1967, after which he turned the gun on himself. Repsch tells the story with sympathy and wit; supplemented by a complete discography, it's a valuable document of a little-discussed era in British pop. —*Richie Unterberger*

Megadeth
Group, Thrash, Heavy Metal
Megadeth formed in 1983 after Dave Mustaine left Metallica and moved to Los Angeles, where he met bassist Dave Ellefson. With guitarist Chris Poland and Gar Samuelson, they landed a contract with Combat Records, releasing their debut album in 1985. They became the first thrash band signed to Capitol Records. The next two albums on that label did extremely well, putting them among the top thrash bands with Metallica, Slayer, and Anthrax. Their music was very tight and the lyrics showed depth and intelligence. As far as Megadeth's impact on the world of heavy metal, they've lasted through many personnel changes and substance-abuse problems, while many other metal bands have since come and gone. —*John Book*

Killing Is My Business … and Business Is Good / 1985 / Combat ✦✦✦
Killing Is My Business…And Business Is Good is the album that started it all for ex-Metallica guitarist Dave Mustaine and his new band. This is a lot rawer than *Peace Sells…But Who's Buying?* —*John Book*

● **Peace Sells … But Who's Buying?** / 1986 / Capitol ✦✦✦✦
From the politics of war to the politics of the environment, Megadeth covered them all on an album that brought them from cult status to the eyes and ears of the mainstream. *Peace Sells… But Who's Buying?* is considered to be one of the best thrash albums of the '80s. —*John Book*

So Far, So Good … So What / 1988 / Capitol ✦✦✦
Although it featured a new drummer and guitarist, *So Far, So Good…So What* was a disappointment after the violent precision of *Peace Sells…But Who's Buying?* While there are some fine tracks, like "In My Darkest Hour," the album lacks focus and is marred by such ill-conceived songs as "Hook In Mouth" and a boneheaded cover of "Anarchy in the U.K." —*Stephen Thomas Erlewine*

○ **Rust in Peace** / Sep. 24, 1990 / Capitol ✦✦✦✦
After kicking drugs, Dave Mustaine returned with yet another new drummer and guitarist with *Rust in Peace*, a stronger collection than *So Far, So Good*, featuring some of Megadeth's most intricately constructed song riffs to date. —*Stephen Thomas Erlewine*

○ **Countdown to Extinction** / 1992 / Capitol ✦✦✦✦
Countdown to Extinction is proof that good ol' thrash can still survive in the '90s. Included are strongly written songs, wonderfully executed playing from the entire band, and believable lyrics ranging from suicide ("Skin O' My Teeth") to the destruction of civilization as we know it ("Ashes in Your Mouth"). It's arguably the band's best since their *Peace Sells…But Who's Buying?* —*John Book*

Youthanasia / 1994 / Capitol ✦✦✦
Megadeth's follow-up to the hit *Countdown to Extinction* lacks the focus of its predecessor, but *Youthanasia* makes up the difference with more accessible, radio-friendly production and tighter riffs. Unfortunately, they have abandoned some of the more experimental, progressive elements in their music, but those are hardly missed in the jackhammer riffs of tracks like "Train of Consequences." —*Stephen Thomas Erlewine*

The Mekons

Group, Punk, Alternative Pop/Rock

More than any band that came out of late-'70s England, the Mekons (the name taken from the popular low-tech British sci-fi show *Dr. Who*) have perhaps the most devoted fans of any band even remotely connected to punk rock. And why not? After 16 years together, this band, with an ever-shifting lineup (only Jon Langford and Tom Greenhaigh remain from the beginning), has produced some of the best rock & roll on the planet; be it amateurish rock-noise, cool synth-driven pop, guitar rave-ups, or postmodern country and western, the Mekons have done it all and done it with style, grace, and a ribald sense of humor.

Emerging from the same Leeds University "scene" that begat the Gang of Four, the Mekons weren't as overtly political as their Marxist-inspired brethren, but their punk-rock pedigree and unsubtle anti-Thatcher and Reaganisms did set them apart from the post-punk world's innumerable careerists and posers. Their early recordings were exceedingly low-fi affairs that valued emotion and energy over anything that remotely resembled musical proficiency. Songs like "Never Been in a Riot" and "32 Weeks" sound as if the band entered the studio, arbitrarily decided who was going to play what, and started the tapes rolling. It was fun, challenging and anarchic—principles to which the band has clung, musical genre notwithstanding, since their inception.

From the time of their debut album, *The Quality of Mercy Is Not Strnen*, the Mekons had turned into a slightly more accomplished post-punk band, who, like their pals in the Gang of Four, welded trebly guitars and shouted vocals over semi-funky rhythms tracks. The songs lacked focus, but this was a bizarre record that, for all of its oddly ingratiating music, offered little insight as to who was making it. This remained true for the couple of years or so as the band (basically Langford, Greenhaigh, Kevin Lycett and whoever else they could rope into a session) made one exciting, enigmatic and extremely difficult-to-find record after another.

In 1985, after it seemed the earth had swallowed them whole, the Mekons released the startling *Fear and Whiskey*, a ragged country album influenced by the ghosts of Hank Williams and Gram Parsons that was unlike anything they'd ever recorded. Thus began the second coming of the Mekons, who finally began to reach an underground/alternative rock audience that had missed them the first time around. Soon they began touring more frequently, putting on clamorous, exciting shows. Talented new members jumped on board, like violinist Susie Honeyman and singer Sally Timms, and even former Pretty Thing Dick Taylor was a Mekon for a while; records started coming out with more frequency and, despite considerable trouble from major labels that sent them back to the indies, could be found in nearly any record store. In the interim between *Fear and Whiskey* and their most recent record *Retreat from Memphis*, the Mekons have continually reinvented themselves: sodden country band, wiseass folk-rock band, cranked-up guitar band, troublemaking punk band; whatever the scenario, what has remained consistent throughout the Mekons' existence has been great, great music. *—John Dougan*

The Quality of Mercy Is Not Strnen / 1979 / Caroline ✦✦✦
Here's where it all began. Not the best Mekons album available, but *Quality*, along with their second album, *Devils Rats and Piggies*, and a *Special Message from Godzilla* (Red Rhino, 1980, now out-of-print) shows off the Mekons' noisy, avant-garde side. It's abrasive and not as user-friendly as their later records, but this was an exciting time for British punk-rock, and this music, as dense and difficult as it may be, reflects punk's seemingly limitless possibilities. Issued by Blue Plate on CD in 1990. *—John Dougan*

Mekons / 1980 / Red Rhino ✦✦

Devils Rats and Piggies a Special Message from Godzilla / 1980 / Red Rhino ✦✦

It Falleth like Gentle Rain from Heaven—The Mekons Story / 1982 / CNT ✦✦

○ **Fear & Whiskey** / 1985 / Sin ✦✦✦✦
A startling, unexpected record that sounds as wonderful now as it did when it was released. *Fear and Whiskey* uses American country music as its foundation, and the Mekons (ever the playful band) screw around with genre alternating between an honest-to-God reverence and flat-out parody. Don't expect sharply executed singing and playing; that's never been the Mekons' style. Instead, plan on a rambling, sodden opus of cowpunk with Hank Williams' ghost lurking in the shadows. In 1989, *Fear and Whiskey* was is-

sued on CD by the Minneapolis-based indie label Twin/Tone with extra material and retitled *Original Sin*. *—John Dougan*

Edge of the World / 1986 / Sin ✦✦✦
Hot on the heels of *Fear* came this terrific follow-up that mined the same cowpunk terrain as its predecessor. The new members (Timms, et al) sound fully integrated into the lineup, and the manic intensity doesn't let up for an instant. It's a party, but a very weird one indeed. *—John Dougan*

Honky Tonkin' / 1987 / Loud ✦✦✦
Finally, nearly a decade after the first Mekons release and after years of purchasing high-priced English imports, one of America's coolest indie labels manages to unleash the mighty Mekons domestically. The wonderful *Honky-Tonkin'* marks the Mekons' last overt country/cowpunk record as they slowly shifted into more guitar-oriented rock. Its title taken from the classic Hank Williams song, this is slightly less essential than *Fear* or *Edge*, but with songs as great as "If They Hang You" and the goofy "Sympathy for the Mekons," you most certainly need it as you build your Mekons collection. *—John Dougan*

○ **New York** / 1987 / Combat ✦✦✦✦
You know a band is great when they release odds and ends that are better than most other bands' painstakingly rendered studio efforts. *New York* is a shambling ode to life on the road that features live tracks, band commentary (including snoring), and a ratty version of the Band's "The Shape I'm In." Upon its release, I thought *New York* the province of Mekons fanatics, that the casual fan or curious would tire of its casual attitude, lack of focus, and its audio-verite documentary approach. Now I think that if you like the Mekons, there is no good reason not to possess this recording. Originally released on cassette, *New York* was reissued on CD by ROIR/Important in 1990. *—John Dougan*

So Good It Hurts / 1988 / Twin/Tone ✦✦✦
The second release for Twin/Tone showed the Mekons putting a bit of reggae and Latin rhythms into the more-folk-than-country mix. *So Good* sounds a tad subdued in comparison to earlier records, but that does not indicate a lackadaisical attitude or a softening of the band after nearly a decade of recorded work. In fact, its best moments ("Sometime I Feel Like Fletcher Christian") live up to the album's title. *—John Dougan*

○ **Original Sin** / 1989 / Twin/Tone ✦✦✦✦

● **The Mekons Rock 'n' Roll** / 1989 / A&M ✦✦✦✦
Asking a Mekons fan to select a favorite Mekons record is crazy—there isn't one, there are many. But, if the situation were such that a choice had to be made, this might be the record. Loud, unruly guitars, pissed-off vocals, the Mekons make an unregenerate, unapologetic punk rock record. This is a dark record, one that comfortably negotiates the dark recesses of rock and roll. They rip the messianic aspirations of U2's Bono ("Blow Your Tuneless Trumpet"), sing a tale of substance abuse that is both cautionary and parodic ("Cocaine Lil"), all the while cranking up a sonic tarpit of guitar noise. Bands this far on in a career, generally speaking, don't make records this good. But *The Mekons Rock 'n' Roll* is one of those cathartic records that only righteously indignant, justifiably pissed-off, grizzled veterans could make. Sadly, and perhaps unsurprisingly, it sold next to nothing and precipitated the band's departure from A&M, who didn't want to release another record like this one. *—John Dougan*

○ **Curse of the Mekons** / 1991 / Blast First ✦✦✦✦
It's amazing that as down and out as the Mekons were at this point, they could manage to summon up the emotional wherewithal to make a record as excellent as *Curse*, but they did. The title most definitely reflects the band's mindset at this time, but this is not the music of self-pity and despair ("We're right in all we distrust" yelps Greenhaigh on the title track); in fact, if it weren't for *Rock 'n' Roll*, this might be the Mekons' finest moment. Politically charged songs despairing about communism and capitalism, a return to C&W (Sally Timms' passionate reading of John Anderson's "Wild and Blue"), and a dig at America's status as the world's only post-Cold War superpower ("100% Song"). Heady stuff, and not all happy, but remarkably assured and very rewarding. *—John Dougan*

Mekons Story / 1993 / CNT ✦✦
Originally released in 1982, *The Mekons Story* (also known as *It Falleth like the Gentle Rain from Heaven*) is a collection of singles, odd tracks and assorted effluvia recorded between 1977 and 1982, that was thankfully reissued as a limited edition CD by

Chicago-based indie label Feel Good All Over. With a drunken-sounding David Spencer providing a between-cuts "history" of the band, this, more than any other Mekons recording, shows their crucial and comic post-punk development. After hearing this, you'll never believe it's the same band recording today. —*John Dougan*

○ **I Love Mekons** / 1993 / Quarterstick ✦✦✦✦
A series of rancorous disagreements with the high and mighty at Warner Bros. subsidiary Loud forced the Mekons into an unanticipated two years of silence that nearly scuttled the release this record and ended the band's career. Eventually, Warner relented (they had maintained the record was not good enough to release), and the increasingly restless Mekons fans were able to judge for themselves that this was another terrific Mekons record. More traditionally rock oriented and less prone to stylistic leaps than before, *I Love Mekons* is a strong, confident record that should have placed the Mekons at the forefront of the growing "alternative rock" market. It didn't, but often there's no accounting for taste. —*John Dougan*

Retreat from Memphis / 1994 / Quarterstick ✦✦✦
Retreat came hot on the heels of *I Heart* and was a similar sounding (almost too-similar) record, and while that might have dismayed the purists, it was obvious to those who'd paid attention that the Mekons couldn't make a bad record even if they tried, especially one this tuneful and stuffed to the gills with rampaging guitars. *Retreat* might not be the first Mekons record I'd buy, but as with virtually all of their recorded output, there is no earthly reason not to want this record. —*John Dougan*

Mel & Tim

Group, Soul, Disco
Mississippi cousins Mel Hardin and Tim McPherson had two tremendous hits in the late '60s and early '70s, one a classic novelty tune, the other a great slow wailer. They were signed to Gene Chandler's Bamboo label and their song "Backfield in Motion" remains a soul staple. It was both a Top Ten pop hit and number three R&B single. The follow-up was a decent effort, "Good Guys Only Win in the Movies," which made the R&B Top 20. But they were back in the hunt in a big way in 1972, as "Starting All over Again" peaked at number four R&B and number 19 pop. It was the duo's only Stax hit, although they continued recording for the company through the mid-'70s and were even in the film *Wattstax*, doing "I May Not Be What You Want." —*Ron Wynn*

○ **Good Guys Only Win in the Movies** / 1969 / Bamboo ✦✦✦✦
● **Starting All over Again** / 1972 / Stax ✦✦✦✦
Mel and Tim / 1973 / Stax ✦✦✦

Melanie

Group, Folk, Singer-Songwriter, Pop/Rock
Melanie is a folksinger who hit the charts after going electric with some sophisticated pop, rock, and gospel sounds. A product of the Woodstock-era counterculture, she was little more than a flower child with a raspy voice and uninteresting acoustic guitar sound, but she did some interesting covers of the Rolling Stones and Phil Ochs, as well as some intelligent originals. In 1972 her album *Gather Me* gave her a major hit with the suggestive "Brand New Key," and a good followup with the inspirational "Ring the Living Bell." Her later material matured rapidly into sophisticated and stylized pop music. —*Bruce Eder*

● **The Best of Melanie** / 1990 / Rhino ✦✦✦✦
18 songs from her 1968–1974 heyday, including all six of her Top 40 hit singles, and her unexpectedly passionate cover of the Rolling Stones' "Ruby Tuesday." —*Richie Unterberger*

John Cougar Mellencamp (John Mellencamp, a.k.a John Cougar)

b. Oct. 7, 1951
Rock & Roll
Indiana-native John Mellencamp is the American small-town boy who made good, selling millions of records while wresting artistic control from the record label and, all along, never disowning his Heartland roots. Unlike Springsteen, who has been lionized as a practically flawless all-American rocker for most of his career, Mellencamp seems utterly human, bull-headed, idealistic and preachy, indulgent, and very capable of sticking his foot in his mouth. In 1971 Mellencamp formed a glam rock band called

Trash. It basically went nowhere but his admiration for David Bowie's music led him to the artist's manager, Tony DeFries of MainMan Mgmt. DeFries landed Mellencamp a deal at MCA. When the album *Chestnut Street Incident* was released, Mellencamp discovered his last name had been changed to Cougar, courtesy of DeFries. That event is the beginning of a series of humiliating record-biz miscalculations that (not unlike Tom Petty) caused Mellencamp to cut an image as a regular guy out to beat the system. In 1982 Mellencamp (as John Cougar) scored the rock equivalent of winning a state lottery by selling five-million copies of *American Fool* (#1), which produced two huge hits, "Jack and Diane" (#4) and "Hurts So Good" (#1). Like anyone from the underbelly of the American middle class who wins big, Mellencamp underwent a running battle, trying to figure out how to stay sane while hanging onto the jackpot and trying to figure out why the gnawing vacuum deep inside him wouldn't go away. Ever since then, Mellencamp's albums have been public airings of the American Dream come true, undergoing an initiation through the Book of Lamentations. (In 1983 he added Mellencamp back to his name. In 1991 Mellencamp dispensed with the Cougar moniker all together.) Mellencamp's sound, while firmly rooted in rock, became increasingly earthy and acoustic until 1991's *Whenever We Wanted*, which was musically a return to a harder-edged sound.

Despite releasing a series of remarkably consistent records, Mellencamp had been in a bit of a commercial rut since 1989's *Big Daddy*. With its sinewy cover of Van Morrison's "Wild Night," 1994's *Dance Naked* put a halt to that decline; the duet with Me'Shell NdegeOcello was his biggest hit in years, appealing to a multitude of radio formats. —*Rick Clark*

Chestnut Street Incident / 1976 / Rhino ✦
Biography / 1978 / Riva ✦
John Cougar / 1979 / Riva ✦
Nothin' Matters & What If It Did / 1980 / Riva ✦✦
American Fool / 1982 / Mercury ✦✦✦
One of the biggest albums in 1982, *American Fool* established Mellencamp (then known as John Cougar) as a major star. His fatalistic ode, "Jack and Diane," and the radio rock sleeze-fest "Hurts So Good" were major hits. Even though Mellencamp was occasionally a clumsy lyricist, his small-town punk image, believable intentions, and rhythm-guitar-heavy rock were embraced by millions throughout the American Heartland. —*Rick Clark*

○ **Uh-Huh** / 1983 / Mercury ✦✦✦✦
After the mega-platinum *American Fool*, Mellencamp roughened up his sound and began adopting a more topical stance with hits like "The Authority Song," "Pink Houses," and the Stones-sounding "Crumblin' Down." —*Rick Clark*

○ **Scarecrow** / 1985 / Mercury ✦✦✦✦
Recorded at his home studio in Indiana, *Scarecrow* reflected Mellencamp's concern over the plight of the American farmer. The title track is one of the most fully realized statements of purpose in his artistic career. However, there are times when Mellencamp bludgeons the listener with heavy-handed polemics that lack focus. On the plus side, *Scarecrow* was loaded with great rock-radio singles like "Lonely Ol' Night," "R.O.C.K. in the U.S.A.," "Rumbleseat," and "Small Town." The raw noisy production did a good job of enhancing the sparks in Mellencamp's excellent band. —*Rick Clark*

★ **The Lonesome Jubilee** / 1987 / Mercury ✦✦✦✦✦
Here Mellencamp infused his Heartland rock with a strong dose of acoustic and country instrumentation in the form of fiddle, accordion, hammer dulcimer, dobro, banjo, and pedal steel. Thematically, he attempted to flesh out the big statements that predominated his previous album *Scarecrow*. In spite of the fact that Mellencamp's admonishments (with almost Biblical undertones) are delivered with the proselytizing earnestness of the recently converted, *Jubilee*'s spirited performances and memorable melodies make this one of his best efforts. Highlights include "Check It Out," "Paper in Fire," "Rooty Toot Toot," and "Cherry Bomb." —*Rick Clark*

Big Daddy / 1989 / Mercury ✦✦✦
Mellencamp went deeper into acoustic-dominated rock with *Big Daddy*, an album where his focus was fine-tuned through smaller, personalized settings and stories. As a result, *Big Daddy* contained some of Mellencamp's best material, with tracks like "Jackie Brown," "Mansions in Heaven," "Void in My Heart," and "Some-

times a Great Notion." *Big Daddy* is his most subdued album (except for such tracks as his remake of the Hombres's "Let It Out (Let It All Hang Out)," "Martha Say," and his number 15 hit whinefest "Pop Singer"). This was Mellencamp's first self-produced effort. The sounds are great but sometimes his vocals are buried way too deeply into the mix ("Mansions in Heaven") to be clearly intelligible. —*Rick Clark*

Whenever We Wanted / 1991 / Mercury ✦✦✦
Two years after Mellencamp released *Big Daddy*, he returned (sans the name Cougar) with electric guitars blaring away on material that represented the thematic extremes of his career. On "Get a Leg Up," (obviously concocted for radio airplay), Mellencamp resorted to his snotty *American Fool* personna, while on tracks like "Now More than Ever," "Love and Happiness," and the title track, he mined the concerns of his more recent work. "I Ain't Ever Satisfied" (not the Steve Earle song) pretty much summed up Mellencamp's mortality-aware desire to have it every way. All in all, this is a very strong album, and a must for fans of Mellencamp's brand of forthright Heartland rock. —*Rick Clark*

○ **Human Wheels** / 1993 / Mercury ✦✦✦✦
Arguably Mellencamp's best album to date, *Human Wheels* is a dark, somber portrait of America. Mellencamp's lyrics have been brooding with melancholy for years now, but on *Human Wheels* the music matches his words—the dark R&B and rock sounds as anguished as his voice. At one time, he would have sung "What If I Came Knocking" seductively, but here he sounds as if nothing would change if she answered the door. *Human Wheels* might not have the hit singles of *Scarecrow* and *The Lonesome Jubilee* or the punch of *Whenever We Wanted*, but it's more consistent and moving than any of those albums. —*Stephen Thomas Erlewine*

Dance Naked / 1994 / Mercury ✦✦✦
A short, stripped-down collection of basic rock & roll, *Dance Naked* isn't quite as powerful as *Human Wheels*, but it has more good songs in its 30 minutes than most 70-minute albums. —*Stephen Thomas Erlewine*

Mello-Kings

Group, R&B, Doo-Wop
Although White, the Mello-Kings from New York had no trouble sounding like an R&B group on their only national hit for Herald Records in 1957, "Tonite, Tonite." Bob Scholl took lead honors on the ballad, written by Billy Myles. Although they recorded for Herald into 1961, the Mello-Kings never repeated their initial success. —*Bill Dahl*

● **Tonight, Tonight** / 1960 / Relic ✦✦✦✦
Some Mello memories. —*Mark A. Humphrey*

Greatest Hits / Collectables ✦✦✦
This is sometimes spirited White doo-wop. —*Mark A. Humphrey*

Tonite Tonite / Relic ✦✦✦
A fine anthology from Relic containing the best singles from the Mello-Kings, a doo-wop group that recorded mostly for the Herald label. They did some nice slow tunes, as well as a few good jump and novelty/dance works. They weren't hitmakers, but this album offers as comprehensive an amount of their material as anyone would ever need or want. —*Ron Wynn*

Harold Melvin & the Blue Notes

Group, Soul, Doo-Wop
Starting out in 1954 in Philadelphia as a doo-wop group with Harold Melvin as lead singer, the Blue Notes first recorded for the New York-based Josie label two years later. They debuted on the R&B charts in 1960 on the Val-ue label with "My Hero." A 1965 release, "Get Out," with a lead vocal by John Atkins, also charted R&B Top 40 on Landa. But it was not until 1972, when drummer Teddy Pendergrass took over lead vocal chores and the group came under the wing of Kenny Gamble and Leon Huff and their Philadelphia International label, that Harold Melvin and the Blue Notes became consistent chart-makers.

Pendergrass's vocals smoldered with sensuality. Combined with the smooth group harmonies that had always been a Blue Note trademark, Gamble and Huff's superior writing, and lush productions, the superb TSOP house band records, such as "I Miss You," "If You Don't Know Me by Now," and "The Love I Lost" were staples on both Black and White radio from 1972 to 1975. Pendergrass went solo in 1975 and the Blue Notes' glory days came to an end. Recording subsequently for a number of labels (including

ABC, Source, MCA, and Philly World), Harold Melvin and the Blue Notes hit the R&B charts another ten times, often with lead vocals by Sharon Paige. Three of those 45s permeated the Top 20, one of which (1977's "Reaching for the World") reached as high as #6. The latter was the only one of the Blue Notes' post-Pendergrass recordings to break the Pop Hot 100. —*Rob Bowman*

○ **To Be True** / 1975 / Philadelphia International ✦✦✦✦
The best of their original albums, containing many hits and no filler, is out of print and not on CD. —*John Floyd*

★ **The Best of Harold Melvin & The Blue Notes** / 1995 / Legacy/Epic ✦✦✦✦✦
Although the ten-track disc is criminally brief, *The Best of Harold Melvin and the Bluenotes* contains most of their biggest hits and offers a good portrait of one of the finest soul groups of the '70s. —*Stephen Thomas Erlewine*

Melvins

Group, Alternative Pop/Rock, Heavy Metal
The Melvins were the first post-punk band to revel in the slow, sludgy sounds of Black Sabbath. Their music is oppressively slow and heavy, only without any of the silly mystical lyrics or the indulgent guitar solos—it's just one massive, oozing pile of dark slime. The Melvins' first record was released in 1987; they've released several albums since then, but it wasn't until 1993 that they went to a major label, thanks to their protégé, Kurt Cobain.

While the Melvins' can be dull and repetitious, their place in rock history is interesting, even if it is just a minor footnote. The band formed in Aberdeen, WA, the same town that produced Nirvana's Cobain and Chris Novaselic. For Nirvana and many other Seattle-area bands, the Melvins' sludge was inspirational; the younger bands took the Sabbath-styled heaviness of the Melvins, while adding an equally important pop song structure, which the group tended to lack. While all of their disciples became famous after Nirvana broke big in 1991 (including Mudhoney, which featured former Melvin bassist, Steve Turner), the Melvins only expanded their cult slightly. —*Stephen Thomas Erlewine*

Gluey Porch Treatments / 1987 / Boner ✦✦✦
When it comes to heavy music, Melvins are the reigning kings. This essential debut is mandatory for those into aggressive songs, the majority of which are played in a slow fashion, and those who want to hear power chords stretched beyond compare. It includes such songs as "Oh," "Steve Instant Newman," and "Over Fram Under the Excrement." —*John Book*

○ **Ozma** / 1989 / Boner ✦✦✦✦
The band's long awaited second album was definitely worth the wait. Now relocated in San Francisco, *Ozma* became an underground favorite, which was released exactly the same time the Seattle music scene exploded in Europe. Fierce guitar work from Osborne, intense drumming from Crover, and mind-numbing bass work from Lori Black makes *Ozma* one of the hardest (and harshest) albums of 1989. The CD version includes *Gluey Porch Treatments* in its entirety as a bonus. —*John Book*

Bullhead / 1991 / Boner ✦✦✦
Either a progression or a disappointment, *Bullhead* represented a slightly different sound for the group. The material on this album made an attempt at being actual "songs" rather than short examples of guitar execution, and the production is not as overpowering as their first two albums. But the progression of playing slightly faster songs did appeal to those who thought the band were running in molasses everyday. —*John Book*

○ **Eggnog** / 1991 / Boner ✦✦✦✦
Eggnog delivers on the goods, an EP that supplies what *Bullhead* failed to give. This record serves as a centerpiece for Melvins, showing what they've accomplished in the past and what they intent to execute in the future. The future lies in the 12-minute opus "Charmicarmicat." A holiday recording not recommended for the kids, or adults for that matter. —*John Book*

Lysol / 1992 / Boner ✦✦✦
Melvins take the Jethro Tull route by recording one lengthy song and releasing it as a full length album. *Lysol* is a progressive song in the vein of Jethro Tull's "Thick as a Brick" and "A Passion Play," as the band go through different tempo changes, musical moods and emotions during its 31-minute duration. This release also returns to the large sound they created on their first two albums; this takes heaviness to an all new plateau. The band's last album on an independent label. —*John Book*

○ **Houdini** / 1993 / Atlantic ◆◆◆◆
The Melvins changed nothing when they went to a major label. They still grind out the same slow, fuzzy, heavy sludge that remains the final word on "grunge." For those who have been wondering what all of the fuss is about, *Houdini* is a good way to catch up. —*Stephen Thomas Erlewine*

● **Stoner Witch** / 1994 / Atlantic ◆◆◆◆
Before the Melvins released *Stoner Witch*, they cleared out their systems by recording the defiantly unlistenable *Prick*. Everything *Prick* was, *Stoner Witch* isn't. For the first time, the Melvins' songwriting abilities match their ability for making noise, making *Stoner Witch* their finest moment to date. —*Stephen Thomas Erlewine*

Prick / 1994 / Reptile ◆◆
Even by Melvins standards, *Prick* is difficult to listen to. Filled with loud, distorted guitars but no discernable hooks or melodies, *Prick* is the band at their most experimental. The only problem is that the band isn't good at experimenting; they're good at making sludge rock. Even hardcore fans may find *Prick* rather tedious. —*Stephen Thomas Erlewine*

Members

Group, Punk, Ska-Revival
Formed in Surrey, England, in the summer of 1977, the Members were among the new wave of British bands jumping on the punk bandwagon. The band—composed of Nicky Tesco (vocals), Jean-Marie Caroll (guitar), Gary Baker (guitar), Adrian Lillywhite (drums) and Chris Payne (bass)—was among the first to successfully blend reggae rhythms with punk's attitude and aggression. Stiff Records saw some promise in the band and signed them early in 1978, releasing their first single, "Solitary Confinement." The success of the single (number 12 U.K.) led to their signing with Virgin Records. After replacing Payne with Nigel Bennett, they recorded *Live at the Chelsea Nightclub* which also made a brief appearance in the lower reaches of the U.K. charts. Around this time, the 2-Tone movement was stealing much of their limelight and their popularity began to fade. After one more album for Virgin in 1980, *1980 The Choice Is Yours*, they were dropped by the label. After a brief layoff, they returned in 1982 with *Uprhythm, Downbeat* (released in 1983 in the U.K. as *Go West*) broadening their sound with horns and a more serious attitude. "Working Girl" from the album became a cult classic in the U.S. through MTV exposure but mainsteam acceptance alluded them on both sides of the Atlantic. The band called it quits the following year. —*Chris Woodstra*

● **At the 1980 Chelsea Night Club** / 1979 / Caroline ◆◆◆◆
The only Members album worth owning, *Chelsea Nightclub* plays into the band's strengths and is loaded with their strongest songwriting (e.g. "Stand Up and Spit," "Off-Shore Banking Business"). —*John Dougan*

1980 the Choice Is Yours / 1980 / Virgin ◆◆
The band's sophomore effort finds them slipping drastically after a fine debut. It has its moments but the overall impression is a lack of inspiration and direction. —*Chris Woodstra*

Uprhythm, Downbeat / 1982 / Arista ◆◆◆
After the flop of *1980 the Choice is Yours*, the band took two years off to regroup and change strategies; the resulting *Uprhythm, Downbeat* (retitled *Going West* and released a year later in the U.K.) shows a more serious band (now a seven piece with a horn section) with a fuller sound. Their punk edges have been smoothed over leaving a slick reggae-funk-pop sound. While it fit nicely with the new wave era, it hasn't dated very well. Only the classic "Working Girl" leaves a lasting impression. —*Chris Woodstra*

● **Sound Of the Suburbs: A Collection Of the Members Finest Moments** / 1995 / Caroline ◆◆◆◆
True to its subtitle, this 18-track collection compiles the finest moments of the band's two-year stay at Virgin Records (1979-1980). While this period was the strongest for the band, it would have been nice to include a track or two from their final album, *Uprhythm, Downbeat* such as the near-hit "Working Girl." —*Chris Woodstra*

Men at Work

Group, New Wave, Pop/Rock
The Australian band Men at Work might still be a sensation relegated to the down under if it weren't for MTV's constant airing of their humorously oddball videos in America's heartland and FM radio's awareness that it was in dire need of some fresh faces. Men at Work's bar-band, Police-like pop/rock did have its share of hooks, particularly the sax line on their #1 international debut hit "Who Can It Be Now?" Their next single, "Down Under," went #1 as well. Both of those tracks came from *Business As Usual*, which held the #1 spot in 1982.

Their followup, *Cargo*, produced two more big hits with "Overkill" and the topical "It's a Mistake." A two-year layoff effectively killed the band's momentum. —*Rick Clark*

● **Business As Usual** / 1981 / Columbia ◆◆◆◆
Their smash debut contains "Who Can It Be Now" and "Down Under." —*Dan Heilman*

○ **Cargo** / 1983 / Columbia ◆◆◆◆
Men At Work's follow-up to their smash hit debut is a more varied collection, anchored by the fine ballad "Overkill" and the satiric "It's a Mistake." —*Stephen Thomas Erlewine*

Two Hearts / 1985 / Columbia ◆◆
By the time of their third album, Men At Work's music had become a bland, synthesized variation on mainstream pop, featuring none of the melodic sensibilities or subtle humor of their first two albums. Although the album went gold, it featured no Top 40 singles. The commercial performance of *Two Hearts* was a considerable disappointment after their first two multi-platinum records and the band broke up shortly after its release. —*Stephen Thomas Erlewine*

Men without Hats

Group, New Wave, Pop/Rock
The new wave synth-pop collective Men Without Hats was formed in 1980 by brothers Ivan and Stefan Doroschuk. Ivan was the leader of the group, writing the majority of the songs and providing the lead vocals; Stefan was the guitarist and the other members changed frequently throughout the course of their career. The group independently released their debut EP, *Folk of the '80s*, in 1980; it was reissued the following year by Stiff in Britain.

During 1982, the band consisted of Ivan, Stefan and keyboardist Colin Doroschuk, along with drummer Allan McCarthy; this is the lineup that recorded Men Without Hats' 1982 debut album *Rhythm of Youth*. Taken from their debut, the single "The Safety Dance" became a major hit, peaking on the American charts at number three in 1983. Driven by an insistent three-chord synthesizer riff, the song was one of the biggest synth-pop hits of the new wave era. The group wasn't able to exploit its success, however. *Folk of the '80s (Part III)* stalled at number 127 on the charts in America and made even less of an impact in other parts of the world. Thanks to the minor hit title track, 1987's *Pop Goes the World* was a bigger success, yet it didn't recapture the audience their first album had gained. Released two years later, *The Adventures of Women & Men Without Hats in the 21st Century* failed to chart, as did its followup, 1991's *Sideways*. The two albums' lack of success effectively put an end to Men Without Hats' career. —*Stephen Thomas Erlewine*

Folk of the 80's [EP] / 1980 / Trend ◆◆

● **Rhythm of Youth** / 1982 / Backstreet ◆◆◆◆
Men Without Hats' debut album *Rhythm of Youth* was a set of catchy, appealing synth-pop. Although the material on the album was wildly inconsistent, the group's energy was infectious, making up for the weaker songs. And when the band managed to write a solid melody—such as the hit single "The Safety Dance"—the results were quite memorable. —*Stephen Thomas Erlewine*

Folk of the '80s (Pt. III) / 1984 / MCA ◆◆◆
Men Without Hats' followup to their successful first album repeated the same formula as the debut with essentially the same results. Though *Folk of the '80s (Part III)* has its share of tedious material, the best songs on the album are as fun and charming as the finest moments from the debut. However, the band's audience had declined since the release of the first record, and *Folk of the '80s (Part III)* stiffed. —*Stephen Thomas Erlewine*

Pop Goes the World / 1987 / Mercury ◆◆◆
Men Without Hats made a minor comeback with 1987's *Pop Goes the World*, which featured the ingratiating electro-pop hit title track. Most of the songs on the record weren't as catchy as the hit, as the rest of the material emphasized beats and textures over hooks and melodies. —*Stephen Thomas Erlewine*

The Adventures of Women & Men Without Hats In the 21st Century / 1989 / PolyGram ✦✦

Sideways / 1991 / PolyGram ✦✦

Natalie Merchant

Pop/Rock

Natalie Merchant was the lead singer for 10,000 Mainiacs from their inception in the early '80s to her departure in early 1994. Merchant began a solo career the following year, releasing her solo debut, *Tigerlily,* in the summer of 1995. —*Stephen Thomas Erlewine*

○ Tigerlily / 1995 / Elektra ✦✦✦✦

Tigerlily, Natalie Merchant's first solo record, does sound different than 10,000 Maniacs. Instead of relying strictly on jangly folk-rock, Merchant continues the opening her music up as she did on *Our Time in Eden,* her last album with the Mainiacs. From the understated groove of "Carnival" to the rolling "San Andreas Fault," the added emphasis on rhythmic texture works, creating an intimate but not exclusive atmosphere that holds throughout the record, even when her occasionally sophomoric, sentimental poetry threatens to sink the album in the weight of its own preciousness (as in "River," her tribute to the late actor River Phoenix). —*Stephen Thomas Erlewine*

Mercury Rev

Group, Alternative Pop/Rock, Psychedelic

Considering the band's leader, guitarist Jonathan Donahue, spent a short time with the Flaming Lips, it's not surprising that Mercury Rev's music is a splendid, scattershot amaglam of psychedelia, pop, experimental noise, rock, free-form jazz, and movie soundtracks. What is surprising is that Donahue's songs are the band's most pop-oriented material, consolidating all of their colorful sonic rush into a three-minute blast. Vocalist David Baker's songs were more languid and less dependent on structure. It doesn't matter if it was a three-minute or a 12-minute song—it is always impossible to tell where Mercury Rev is coming from and where they are going.

After releasing two acclaimed albums in 1991 and 1993, Baker left the band acrimoniously and pursued a solo career. After releasing the "Everlasting Arm" single in 1994, Mercury Rev returned with *See You on the Other Side,* their first full-length album without Baker, in the summer of 1995. —*Stephen Thomas Erlewine*

○ Yerself Is Steam / 1991 / Columbia ✦✦✦✦

One of the most original debuts in years, Mercury Rev's *Yerself Is Steam* could be classified as '70s art-rock played with '90s postmodern sensibilities, but the band refuses to stay in one place. Instead of the self-absorbed excesses of Pink Floyd, there are elements of psychedelia, punk, free jazz, and warped pop. *Yerself Is Steam* only hints at the band's potential. Columbia's CD reissue includes the Velvet Underground pop of "Car Wash Hair" as a bonus track. —*Stephen Thomas Erlewine*

● Boces / Jun. 1, 1993 / Columbia ✦✦✦✦

Boces, Mercury Rev's second album, is an even stronger affair than their first, showcasing the possibilities of their truly mind-bending neo-psychedelic guitar rock. All of their flights into the netherworld are fascinating; even the eleven-minute songs seem too short. —*Stephen Thomas Erlewine*

See You on the Other Side / 1995 / Columbia ✦✦✦

Without David Baker, Mercury Rev's opens up, relying on the bright psychedelia of Jonathan Donahue's songwriting. While that means the band has a greater tendency to indulge themselves in noisy, free-form jams that don't lead anywhere, it also means that the music is more accessible, since Baker's dark hallucinations no longer dominate the group's experimental instrumental section. However, the music on *See You on the Other Side* isn't quite as compelling without the tension between Donahue's colorful pop and Baker's haunting voice and lyrics—which means that although they've progressed musically, they've lost an essential element of what made their first two records distinctive. —*Stephen Thomas Erlewine*

Freddie Mercury (Frederick Bulsara)

b. Sep. 5, 1946, Zanzibar, **d.** Nov. 24, 1991

Hard Rock, Pop/Rock

The lead singer for the popular '70s hard rock quartet Queen, Fred-

die Mercury also pursued a brief solo career. Before Queen released their first album, he had recorded a version of the Beach Boys' "I Can Hear Music" under the name Larry Lurex, yet he didn't record a true solo album until 1985's *Mr. Bad Guy.* In the year preceding the release of *Mr. Bad Guy,* Mercury had contributed the hit "Love Kills" to Giorgio Moroder's soundtrack to the revised silent film classic, *Metropolis,* as well as releasing the single "I Was Born to Love." None of the singles from *Mr. Bad Guy* fared as well as his previous solo singles. Mercury's first solo hit came in 1987's with a campy cover of the Platters' "Great Pretender," although it only charted in the U.K. That same year he recorded the "Barcelona" with opera singer Monserrat Caballe; the single would eventually hit the British Top Ten and it was followed by Mercury's second solo album, *Barcelona* (1988).

In 1991, Mercury recorded Queen's final album, *Innuendo,* before disappearing from the public view. It was revealed in November of 1991 that he was suffering from AIDS; he died on November 24, within 48 hours of announcing that he was ill. —*Stephen Thomas Erlewine*

● Mr. Bad Guy / 1985 / Columbia ✦✦✦✦

The Great Pretender / 1992 / Hollywood ✦✦✦

Mercyful Fate

Group, Heavy Metal

Danish band featuring vocalist King Diamond, guitarists Hank Shermann and Michael Denner, bassist Timi Hansen, and drummer Kim Ruzz. Mercyful Fate won a large cult following thanks to their dramatic lyrics, showing a Gothic obsession with evil and the occult, and Diamond's amazing vocal range, which shifted from a low growl to a banshee scream, plus the interplay of Shermann and Denner. The band broke up after two full-length albums owing to differences of opinion about what direction the group should take (Shermann wanted a more commercial approach). Diamond pursued a solo career in the mid-'80s. In 1993, the group reformed its original lineup, with the exception of Ruzz (King Diamond drummer Snowy Shaw joined instead). The results were quite successful, as the group seemed to pick up right where it left off, much to the delight of their fans. Hansen left after the first reunion record and was replaced by Sharlee D'Angelo. —*Steve Huey*

○ Melissa / Oct. 1983 / Megaforce ✦✦✦✦

A heavy Black Sabbath influence lingers on this album, some of the music even sounding like early Dokken. The vocal range King Diamond has (and the way he uses it) is still astonishing and has yet to be matched. —*John Book*

● Don't Break the Oath / 1984 / Roadrunner ✦✦✦✦

The feeling of being doomed still lingers with every listen of this very influential black-metal band from Denmark. This is vocalist King Diamond's tour de force. —*John Book*

The Beginning / 1987 / Roadrunner ✦✦✦

This is a compilation of the band's earlier material not found on their two albums. —*John Book*

Return of the Vampire / May 12, 1992 / Roadrunner ✦✦✦

Bell Witch / 1994 / Scarface ✦✦✦

In the Shadows / Scarface ✦✦✦

After an almost decade-long hiatus, Mercyful Fate's reunion did not disappoint; it was as if they picked up right where they had left off. There are more of King Diamond's Gothic tales of horror and the supernatural, and the music sounds better than ever. It doesn't have the historical significance of their early-'80s material, but that doesn't really matter; this is high-quality material from a tight veteran band. The CD features a rerecorded version of the underground classic "Return of the Vampire" with Lars Ulrich on drums. —*Steve Huey*

The Merry-Go-Round

Group, Pop/Rock

Like the Left Banke, the Merry-Go-Round were teen pop/rock prodigies who combined British Invasion pop melodies with baroque-pop studio polish. The L.A. group, dominated by singer and songwriter Emmitt Rhodes, had a couple huge local hits, "Live" and "You're a Very Lovely Woman," but achieved little national success before disbanding in 1969. A Paul McCartney soundalike and lookalike, Rhodes was blatantly influenced by McCartney's *Magical Mystery Tour*-era compositions, as one listen to "Pardon Me" (a ringer for "Fool on the Hill") will attest. Rhodes achieved modest commercial and critical recognition with his solo recordings in the early '70s. —*Richie Unterberger*

You're Very Lonely Woman / 1967 / A&M ✦✦✦

● **Best of the Merry-go-round** / 1985 / Rhino ✦✦✦✦
14-song compilation of songs from their sole album, plus a few rare singles. Highlights include "Live," "Come Ride," "Time Will Show The Wiser" (covered by Fairport Convention on their first album), and especially the gorgeous, haunting string ballad "You're A Very Lovely Woman." Solid, melodic late-'60s pop-rock with sophisticated arrangements, though it's sometimes lightweight. —*Richie Unterberger*

The Merseybeats

Group, British Invasion
The Merseybeats were one of the better Liverpool bands of the British Invasion, scoring several large and minor hits in the U.K., although they made no impact whatsoever in America. Friends of the Who (with whom they shared management for a time) and the Beatles, the band leaned toward mid-tempo harmony numbers, with the occasional ballads and ravers thrown in. Not nearly as distinguished as top-line British Invasion pop-rockers like the Hollies and the Searchers, the Merseybeats did have classy taste in cover material, recording the original version of Bacharach-David's "Wishin N' Hopin'" (a hit in the U.S. for Dusty Springfield), reaching the U.K. Top 40 with "I Stand Accused" (covered by Elvis Costello), and releasing covers of "Mr. Moonlight" and "Fortune Teller" before the Beatles and the Stones recorded their more famous versions. Like many of the original Liverpool bands, they were crippled by a lack of songwriting talent. After breaking up in 1966, members Tony Crane and Billy Kinsley formed the Merseys, who landed a huge British hit with "Sorrow" (covered by David Bowie on *Pin Ups*) the same year. —*Richie Unterberger*

The Merseybeats / 1964 / Fontana ✦✦✦
A very well-programmed 18-song collection representing the band's good and bad sides. The former includes crisp pop-rock ditties like "Don't Turn Around," "Last Night," and "It's Love That Really Counts," while the latter is mostly an over-reliance on show tunes. —*Bruce Eder*

● **Beat & Ballads** / 1982 / Edsel ✦✦✦✦
All of their British hits, and indeed most of the A- and B-sides they cut between 1963 and 1965—"I Think Of You," "Don't Turn Around," "Wishin 'N' Hopin'," "I Stand Accused." Also includes the 1964 single "Last Night," which flopped, but is one of the best obscure British invasion pop-rockers. —*Richie Unterberger*

The Merton Parkas

Group, Power Pop/Anglo-Pop
The Merton Parkas, taking their name from their home in South London (Merton) and the classic mod-wear (the parka) are another footnote in the British mod-revival of the late '70s (which itself was merely a footnote in music history). Formed by brothers Mick Talbot (keyboards) and Danny Talbot (vocals) along with Neil Wurrel (bass) and Simon Smith (drums) in 1978, they became one of the first third-wave mod-revivalists to release an album, *Face in the Crowd*, which featured the hit single "You Need Wheels." While many of the movement's followers took a more serious approach, the Merton Parkas tapped into the novelty side of the genre, becoming something of a mod version of Madness, though less innovative (and less interesting). Mick Talbot later teamed up with Paul Weller to form the Style Council in 1983. —*Chris Woodstra*

● **Face in the Crowd** / 1979 / Beggars Banquet ✦✦✦✦
The band's sole LP, while certainly flawed, offers a lightweight, novelty approach to the Jam-inspired mod-revival. A little too derivative to be taken seriously but there are some fun songs nonetheless such as the U.K. hit "You Need Wheels," "Plastic Smile," and the title track. —*Chris Woodstra*

The Singles EP / 1983 / Beggars Banquet ✦✦✦

Metal Church

Group, Heavy Metal
Formed in 1984, Metal Church consisted of vocalist David Wayne, guitarists Kurt Vanderhoof and Craig Wells, bassist Duke Erickson, and drummer Kirk Arrington. Their debut album, recorded when the thrash genre was still evolving, made a huge splash on the metal scene and hinted at great things to come for the band. However, in spite of some well-received work, the band never quite

topped their first album. Wayne left and was replaced by Mike Howe for *Blessing in Disguise*, Vanderhoof left after the album due to his dislike of touring and was replaced by Metallica guitar tech John Marshall. Vanderhoof remained the group's designated composer, but the band's sound became less and less distinctive. —*Steve Huey*

● **Metal Church** / 1985 / Elektra ✦✦✦✦
One of the first heavy metal bands out of Seattle to hit it big, this self-titled debut featured power ballads, fierce instrumentals and the customary "epic." It's arguably the band's best. —*John Book*

○ **The Dark** / 1987 / Elektra ✦✦✦✦

Blessing in Disguise / 1989 / Elektra ✦✦✦

Human Factor / 1991 / Epic ✦✦✦
A lighter sound than earlier albums, their first for Epic Records is still good. —*John Book*

Live in Dallas, Texas / Asylum ✦✦

Metallica

Group, Thrash, Heavy Metal
Metallica was easily the best, most influential heavy metal band of the '80s, responsible for bringing the music back to earth. Instead of playing the usual rock star games of metal stars of the early '80s, the band looked and talked like they were from the street. Metallica expanded the limits of thrash, using speed and volume not for their own sake, but to enhance their intricately structured compositions. The release of 1983's *Kill 'Em All* marked the beginning of the legitimization of heavy metal's underground, bringing new complexity and depth to thrash metal. With each album, the band's playing and writing improved; James Hetfield developed a signature rhythm playing that matched his growl, while lead guitarist Kirk Hammett became one of the most copied guitarists in metal. Lars Ulrich's thunderous, yet complex, drumming clicked in perfectly with Cliff Burton's innovative bass playing.

After releasing their masterpiece *Master of Puppets* in 1986, tragedy struck the band when their tour bus crashed while traveling in Sweden, killing Burton. When the band decided to continue, Jason Newsted was chosen to replace Burton; two years later, the band released the conceptually ambitious *And Justice for All*, which hit the Top Ten without any radio play and very little support from MTV. But Metallica completely crossed over into the mainstream with 1991's *Metallica*, which found the band trading in their long compositions for more concise song structures; it resulted in a Number One album that sold over seven million copies in the U.S. alone. The band launched a long, long tour which kept them on the road for nearly two years. By the '90s, Metallica had changed the rules for all heavy metal bands; they were the leaders of the genre, respected not only by headbangers, but by mainstream record buyers and critics. No other heavy metal band has ever been able to pull off such a trick. —*Stephen Thomas Erlewine*

☆ **Kill 'Em All** / 1983 / Elektra ✦✦✦✦✦
The origins of modern thrash-metal are here. One can hear traces of Judas Priest, the Scorpions, and Motorhead on some of the songs. In the 1987 reissue Elektra added "Am I Evil" and "Blitzkrieg" (from the European "Creeping Death" 12") but in a subsequent reissue have deleted both, making this a highly sought-after collectable. —*John Book*

○ **Ride the Lightning** / 1984 / Elektra ✦✦✦✦
Concise, direct, and to the point, it was originally released by the independent Megaforce label. This led to their being signed by Elektra. —*John Book*

★ **Master of the Puppets** / 1986 / Elektra ✦✦✦✦✦
The album that put thrash-metal into the spotlight and into the mainstream. This is one of the best albums of the '80s—period. It's also the last album to feature bassist Cliff Burton. —*John Book*

Garage Days Re-Revisited / 1987 / Elektra ✦✦✦
A blistering EP of covers of Metallica's favorite underground metal bands of the late '70s and early '80s, *Garage Days Re-Revisited* is one the band's purest blasts of raw, primal heavy metal. —*Stephen Thomas Erlewine*

○ **And Justice for All** / 1988 / Elektra ✦✦✦✦
The most sophisticated album in their career, this is also the first full-length release to feature ex-Flotsam & Jetsam bassist Jason Newsted. The thin sound quality stops this from being a masterpiece. —*John Book*

☆ **Metallica** / 1991 / Elektra ◆◆◆◆◆
Longtime fans may call this one a sellout but that's hardly the case. Instead, the group has increased the bottom end of their sound and keeps the riff-per-song limit down to about two. This may keep *Metallica* from alienating staunch metal-haters, but it's the quality of the songs—hits such as "Enter Sandman" and the ballad "Nothing Else Matters," but also "Holier Than Thou"—that has made this their most successful (and best) album to date. —*John Floyd*

Live Shit Binge and Purge / 1993 / Elektra ◆◆◆
Weighing in at three CDs and three videos, plus a bunch of tour memorabilia, the sheer bulk of *Live Shit Binge and Purge* scares off anyone but the most devoted fans, which is too bad. Although it is exhausting, this box provides ample proof of the brutal power of Metallica in concert—the entire program of a Mexico City concert is included, and it is awe-inspiring. For hardcore fans, *Live Shit* is a godsend. —*Stephen Thomas Erlewine*

Meters

Group, Soul, Funk, R&B
The top instrumental band in New Orleans during the late '60s and much of the '70s, both on their own and as a session crew (formed in 1966). Keyboardist Art Neville, guitarist Leo Nocentelli, bassist George Porter Jr, and drummer Zigaboo Modeliste played on numerous sessions for producer Allen Toussaint before they climbed the R&B charts themselves in 1969 with "Sophisticated Cissy" and "Cissy Strut" on the Josie label. They remained with Josie into the early '70s, issuing more funky hit instrumentals such as "Look-Ka Py Py" and "Chicken Strut" before spending the mid-'70s with the major labels Reprise and Warner. The quartet went their separate ways in 1977 but sometimes re-form for the New Orleans Jazz & Heritage Festival. —*Bill Dahl*

The Meters / 1969 / Josie ◆◆◆
While this isn't an album in the strictest sense, but a collection of singles, it was certainly welcomed when it was released. This featured some prime cuts from the Meters, the great New Orleans funk ensemble who began doing their own sessions in the late '60s. They only cut two albums for Josie, and both were monsters. Both were later deleted, although the hit singles have since been reissued. —*Ron Wynn*

○ **Look: Ka Py Py** / 1970 / Rounder ◆◆◆◆
The Meters' great 1960s singles anticipated the coming of funk. They made short, catchy tunes and scored occasional hits, particularly the single "Look: Ka-Py-Py," one of 12 outstanding tunes on this CD. These were the ultimate party/dance records, and they also showed the link between traditional African rhythms, New Orleans shuffle, second line sounds, soul and funk. Marvelous rhythm music at its hottest. —*Ron Wynn*

○ **Cissy Strut** / 1974 / Island ◆◆◆◆
The Meters made their anthemic funk cuts on Josie in the late '60s. The New Orleans crew backed Fats Domino, Lee Dorsey, and Aaron Neville before they started jamming on their own in the late '60s. Island issued this anthology of Josie material in the mid-'70s. It came out in the U.S. too. Rounder has since reissued some of this material. —*Ron Wynn*

Rejuvenation / 1974 / Reprise ◆◆◆
A nice, but not as definitive, mid-'70s Meters session. Their Reprise albums were never as transcendent, energetic, or freewheeling as the Josie tracks, but were better produced and engineered. This was one of the better sessions, and sometimes the Meters seemed to recapture that old New Orleans funk energy. But Reprise's attempts to bring them crossover success inevitably disrupted their chemistry, as they tried to blend a formulaic rock sensibility with the group's close-knit funk. —*Ron Wynn*

Best of the Meters / 1975 / Virgo ◆◆◆
A good collection of this quintessential New Orleans funk group's best '70s singles for the Reprise label. Of course they did their finest cuts for Josie, but turned in some reasonably good work on Reprise in a more rock/funk direction. "Hey, Pokey-A-Way" was probably the closest Reprise cut to matching the superb Josie singles. But these are the songs that got them gigs with the Rolling Stones and work with Paul McCartney and Robert Palmer, so they did have some value. —*Ron Wynn*

New Directions / 1977 / Warner Brothers ◆◆
This was perhaps the weakest Meters album, with rather mediocre vocals and songs, decent production and arrangements, but little of the fire or zeal that characterized their fine Josie dates and their

earlier rock/funk Reprise material. They were nearing the end of the line as a group anyhow, something that this material reflects. —*Ron Wynn*

Good Old Funky Music / 1990 / Rounder ◆◆◆
There are some good moments on this disc, culled from unissued material from the Meters's Josie heyday in the late '60s and early '70s, but there's too much filler. —*Bill Dahl*

The Meters Jam / 1992 / Rounder ◆◆
The 10 songs on this CD are a mixed bag, mainly because the Meters insisted on singing and simply weren't great vocalists. Their leads and harmonies on "Come Together" and "Bo Diddley," among others, were exuberant, but didn't add much to the proceedings. On the other hand, there haven't been many groups in any style that clicked any more smoothly and soulfully. Their inspired, funky playing almost overshadows the tepid vocals. —*Ron Wynn*

○ **Uptown Rulers: the Meters Live on The Queen Mary** / 1992 / Rhino ◆◆◆◆
A wonderful live concert from 1975, it showcases the powers of these New Orleans R&B legends. —*AMG*

● **Funkify Your Life** / 1995 / Rhino ◆◆◆◆
Two discs of the Meters is a lot to ask of most casual fans, yet for the devoted few, *Funkify Your Life* is essential. Featuring tracks from both their Josie and Warner years, the double-disc set captures some of the rawest New Orleans funk recorded in the Crescent City. —*Stephen Thomas Erlewine*

George Michael

b. Jun. 26, 1963, Watford, England
Dance-Pop, Pop/Rock
Yorgos Kyriatou Panayioutou (George Michael) achieved fame in the duo Wham! in his native U.K. in 1982. Through 1986, he and his partner, Andrew Ridgeley, scored hit after hit in a variety of styles from rap to uptempo pop to slow ballads. As songwriter and lead singer, Michael gradually overshadowed the group, and by the time they split, he was ready for a massively successful solo career. This began with the 1987 album *Faith*, which featured a series of chart-topping hit singles and sold more than seven million copies. That Michael had not achieved a similar critical success was evident from the title of his follow-up album, *Listen without Prejudice—Vol. 1*, which, though it sold a million copies, included two Top Ten hits, and hit #2, must be considered a major commercial disappointment. With *Vol. 2* apparently shelved, Michael contributed several songs to the charity album *Red Hot + Dance* in 1992, and one of them, "Too Funky," reached the Top 20.

After the failure of *Listen without Prejudice*, Michael engaged in a bitter legal battle with his record company, accusing them of not properly promoting the album and asking them to release him from his contract; he stated that he would refuse to release any records if he lost the lawsuit. He lost. After losing an appeal, Michael bought his way out his Columbia contract and signed with the music division of Dreamworks, a fledgling entertainment corporation founded by Steven Spielberg, Jeffrey Katzenberg, and David Geffen. —*William Ruhlmann*

★ **Faith** / 1987 / Columbia ◆◆◆◆◆
George Michael certainly looked like the biggest pop star to emerge in the second half of the '80s when he released this debut album after his years in Wham! It wasn't just that the record topped the charts for 12 weeks and sold seven million copies and that six of its nine tracks were Top Ten hits (four #1s, a #2, and a #5); it was that Michael, who wrote, arranged, and produced, seemed to have a broad understanding of all aspects of pop, from the rockabilly of the title track and the heartfelt ballad "Father Figure" to the R&B dance grooves of "I Want Your Sex" (indeed, the album also got to #2 on the Black charts.) —*William Ruhlmann*

○ **Listen without Prejudice, Vol. 1** / 1990 / Columbia ◆◆◆◆
Michael's follow-up to the massive success of *Faith* found him turning inward, trying to gain critical acclaim as well as sales. *Listen without Prejudice* is not an entirely successful effort; Michael has cut back on the effortless hooks and melodies that crammed not only *Faith* but also his singles with Wham!, and his socially conscious lyrics tend to be heavy-handed. But the highlights—the light, Beatlesque harmonies of "Heal the Pain," the plodding #1 "Praying For Time," "Waiting For That Day," and the Top Ten

"Freedom '90"—make a case for his talents as a pop craftsman. —*Stephen Thomas Erlewine*

Lee Michaels

Psychedelic, Pop/Rock
One of the most interesting second-division California psychedelic musicians, keyboardist Lee Michaels was one of the most soulful White vocalists of the late '60s and early '70s. Between 1968 and 1972, he released half a dozen accomplished albums on A&M that encompassed baroque psychedelic pop and gritty white, sometimes gospelish R&B with equal facility. A capable songwriter, Michaels was blessed with an astonishing upper range, occasionally letting loose some thrilling funky wails; for a time he played, live and in the studio, with the mammoth drummer "Frosty" as his only accompanist. In 1971, he landed a surprise Top Ten single with "Do You Know What I Mean," one of the best and funkiest AM hits of the early '70s, but Michaels was really much more of an album-oriented artist. His albums for Columbia in the mid-'70s were both commercial and critical disappointments, and he's rarely performed or recorded since. —*Richie Unterberger*

Carnival of Life / 1968 / A&M ✦✦✦
A strong, cheerful debut, awash in the Summer Of Love vibe, but featuring tight songs and arrangements. Although Lee played fewer instruments himself here than he would on his subsequent work, it introduces his organ/piano/harpsichord blend, heard to best effect on the uplifting opening track, "Hello." —*Richie Unterberger*

Recital / 1968 / A&M ✦✦✦
Michaels produced his second album himself and took over all the keyboard chores (he had played only sporadically on his first LP), accompanied by top-flight L.A. session players. Quite similar in sound and direction to his debut, it does show him expanding his songwriting horizons on tracks like "Grocery Soldier" and "The War." —*Richie Unterberger*

○ **Lee Michaels** / 1969 / A&M ✦✦✦✦
An abrupt but fairly successful change in direction, Lee's third album was recorded in a mere seven hours with drummer Frosty as his sole sideman, and is basically a reflection of his live set at the time. Far bluesier than his first two albums, Side one is a 20-minute medley; Side two features his superb interpretation of "Stormy Monday" and one of his best good-time numbers, "Heighty Hi." Some superb organ playing and thrilling high vocal trills, although Frosty's drum solo on the 20-minute track is tough to sit through. —*Richie Unterberger*

● **The Collection** / 1992 / Rhino ✦✦✦✦
Good 18-track overview of his A&M work, drawing from all six of the albums he released between 1968 and 1972. Includes "Do You Know What I Mean," "Stormy Monday," "Heighty Hi," "Hello," "The War," and "Carnival Of Life," as well as the 1969 non-LP B-side "Goodbye, Goodbye," and his only Top 40 single besides "Do You Know What I Mean," a cover of "Can I Get A Witness." —*Richie Unterberger*

Mickey & Sylvia

Group, R&B, Rock & Roll
Although this duo is primarily remembered as a one-hit act—for "Love Is Strange," which reached number one in 1957—they actually recorded quite a few exciting hybrids of R&B and rock & roll in the mid- and late '50s. Playing on countless '50s sessions for various labels (especially Atlantic and OKeh), Mickey Baker was one of the greatest guitar players of early rock & roll. With his partner (and former guitar student) Sylvia Robinson, he got to stretch out a bit from his usual role, with some trailblazing piercing, lean and bluesy leads. Vocally, Mickey & Sylvia had an engagingly playful, occasionally sly'n'sassy repartee that makes up in charm what it might lack in smoke and firepower. Their recordings were inconsistent, but at their best they offered a fetching blend of blues, Bo Diddley, calypso, and doo-wop.

After "Love Is Strange," whose devastating licks inspired countless guitarists, the duo notched a couple more substantial R&B hits. But although they recorded as late as 1965, they never approached the Top 20 again. Mickey Baker recorded as a solo artist and enjoyed a fairly successful career as an expatriate sessionman in France. Sylvia Robinson unexpectedly re-emerged with the number three pre-disco hit "Pillow Talk" in 1973, and cofounded the pioneering rap label Sugar Hill in the late '70s. —*Richie Unterberger*

Love Is Strange [Bear Family] / 1990 / Bear Family ✦✦✦
This two-CD, 60-song (!) set includes many alternate takes and a fair amount of previously unreleased material, spanning 1955 to 1964. A lot of the obscurities are in the close harmony, doo-wop vein, and are disappointingly short on verbal sparring and scorching Baker guitar. Lovingly packaged, but everyone except hardcore specialists should stick with the RCA compilation. —*Richie Unterberger*

● **"Love Is Strange" & Other Hits** / 1990 / RCA ✦✦✦✦
Unless you're a major R&B collector, it's likely you've never heard anything by this duo besides "Love Is Strange," their only major hit (and a great one). With 20 cuts from 1956-60, this disc reissues the bulk of their most interesting work. "Love Is Strange" will remain their most memorable tune after you've heard this, but on the whole, this is way-above-average '50s R&B/rock. If you're hungering for more great solos like the ones in "Love Is Strange," you'll find some here, especially in "There Oughta Be a Law" and the instrumental "Shake It Up," although his virtuosity doesn't dominate most of the songs. Some of these tunes are routine doo-wop, but a little over half the material is pretty strong, ranging from the calypso-rock they're best remembered for to ballads to straightahead R&B shouters, with King Curtis on sax. —*Richie Unterberger*

Bette Midler

b. Dec. 1, 1945, Patterson, NJ
Pop
Bette Midler counts singing as only one of her talents; at times, since 1972, when she first came to national recognition, it has seemed to be the least of her talents. Still, she has managed to score a number of major hits in a roller-coaster career as a recording artist. Born in Paterson, NJ, and raised in Hawaii, Midler early on showed an interest in singing and acting, and by the '60s she had moved to New York and gotten a role in the long-running Broadway hit *Fiddler on the Roof.* Midler developed a nightclub act that included comedy and singing of a variety of kinds of material, including show tunes, pop hits, and even a takeoff on the Andrews Sisters, and appeared with increasing frequency in New York with her accompanist, Barry Manilow. She was signed to Atlantic Records and released *The Divine Miss M* (1972), which went gold and included a Top Ten single cover of the Andrews Sisters' "Boogie Woogie Bugle Boy." *Bette Midler* (1973) was similarly successful.

Midler's album sales fell off during the rest of the '70s, though her records always reached the Top 100 in the album chart. But in 1979 she starred in the film *The Rose,* a fictional account of the life of Janis Joplin, and the title track became a Top Ten hit. 1980 saw the release of Midler's concert film, *Divine Madness,* and her best-selling book, *A View from a Broad.* Her next film, *Jinxed* (1982), however, was a major flop, and subsequent records didn't fare well. Midler made a cinematic comeback with *Down and Out in Beverly Hills* (1986), but it wasn't until 1989 that she had another pop hit, when her version of "Wind Beneath My Wings" from her film *Beaches* became a number one hit. This rejuvenated her singing career, and 1990's *Some People's Lives* became a Top Ten, million-selling album, with the song "From a Distance" hitting number two. Midler's soundtrack album to her 1991 film *For the Boys* was also a gold-selling hit. —*William Ruhlmann*

○ **The Divine Miss M** / 1972 / Atlantic ✦✦✦✦
Midler's early camp style is captured in this debut album, which features her torchy version of "Do You Want to Dance?," the bubbly remake of "Boogie Woogie Bugle Boy," and Buzzy Linhart's "Friends," all Top 40 hits. —*William Ruhlmann*

Bette Midler / 1973 / Atlantic ✦✦✦
This is an earthy mix of blues, R&B, and '40s boogie-woogie. —*Bil Carpenter*

○ **Songs for the New Depression** / 1976 / Atlantic ✦✦✦✦
Notable for a duet with Bob Dylan on "Buckets of Rain" and an excellent version of Tom Waits's "Shiver Me Timbers." —*William Ruhlmann*

Live at Last / 1977 / Atlantic ✦✦✦

Broken Blossom / 1977 / Atlantic ✦✦

Thighs & Whispers / 1979 / Atlantic ✦✦
A disco set. —*Bil Carpenter*

○ **The Rose** / 1979 / Atlantic ✦✦✦✦
The soundtrack to Midler's successful film, with the title track written by Amanda McBroom. —*William Ruhlmann*

○ **Divine Madness** / 1980 / Atlantic ✦✦✦✦
This record showcases Midler at her liveliest, during a concert at Pasadena Civic Auditorium. —*Larry Lapka*

No Frills / 1983 / Atlantic ✦✦✦
Top-40 pop and light rock. —*Bil Carpenter*

Mud Will Be Flung Tonight / 1985 / Atlantic ✦✦
An X-rated live comedy album. —*Bil Carpenter*

Beaches / 1989 / Atlantic ✦✦✦
The soundtrack to Midler's musical comeback film, featuring her version of "Wind beneath My Wings." —*William Ruhlmann*

Some People's Lives / 1990 / Atlantic ✦✦✦
Midler's most successful regular album release in some time, featuring "From a Distance." —*William Ruhlmann*

For the Boys / 1991 / Atlantic ✦✦✦
A film placing Midler in the Andrews Sisters' milieu of WWII was an inspired choice, and the soundtrack shows her abilities on period material as well as giving her a chance to sing a touching version of the Beatles' "In My Life." —*William Ruhlmann*

● **Divine Collection** / Jun. 22, 1993 / Atlantic ✦✦✦✦
Bette Midler's first compilation features most of her hits, including "Wind Beneath My Wings," "The Rose," "Boogie Woogie Bugle Boy," "From a Distance," and her version of "One More for My Baby (And One More for the Road)," recorded on one of the final episodes of *The Tonight Show* starring Johnny Carson. *Divine Collection* is the greatest-hits collection that Midler has needed for quite some time. —*AMG*

Midnight Oil

Group, Rock & Roll, Alternative Pop/Rock
An Australian quintet formed in 1978 and led by singer Peter Garrett. Other members: Peter Gifford, bass (replaced by Bones Hillman in 1987); Martin Rotsey, guitar; James Moginie, guitar and keyboards; and Rob Hirst, drums. The group came up playing for the surf crowd in Sydney bars but always had a serious, political side. Its first three albums, *Midnight Oil* (1978), *Head Injuries* (1979), and *Place without a Postcard* (1981), were released only in Australia. (They appeared in the U.S. in 1990.) Midnight Oil's first two U.S. releases, *10, 9, 8, 7, 6, 5, 4, 3, 2, 1* (1983) and *Red Sails in the Sunset* (1985) had only modest sales, but *Diesel and Dust* (1988) was a major hit, selling a million copies and featuring the Top 20 hit "Beds Are Burning." *Blue Sky Mining* went gold in 1990, and Midnight Oil released an album of concert recordings dating from 1982 to 1990, *Scream in Blue Live*, in 1992. —*William Ruhlmann*

Midnight Oil / 1978 / Columbia ✦✦
Generally speaking, Midnight Oil records pre-*10,9,8,7,6,5,4,3,2,1* are the sound of a band honing its skills, trying to find itself, and succeeding infrequently. Their debut is worth mentioning only because it's a virtually worthless record. In fact, the leap they made between their first release and their great mid-'80s output is all the more astounding. Sounding clumsy and unsure of themselves, the Oil's debut sounds like a record they were told to make rather than one they wanted to make. —*John Dougan*

Head Injuries / 1979 / Columbia ✦✦✦
Fortunately the same was not true on their second release, *Head Injuries* (great title). From start to finish this is a stoked and smokin' piece of punk-inspired hard rock with Garrett wailing away as though his life depended on it. Furious, relentless, chocked to the brim with solid songs, and fierce playing, *Head Injuries* is hands-down the best of the Oils' early output. —*John Dougan*

Bird Noises / 1980 / Columbia ✦✦

Place without a Postcard / 1981 / Columbia ✦✦✦
Place Without a Postcard, produced by the usually reliable Glyn Johns, is so-so, but a real letdown after the intensity of *Head Injuries*. The songs are very good and at its best, it hints at the consistency that was to mark the rest of their recorded work, but it never coalesces into a whole. Even after repeated plays, *Place Without a Postcard* is too much of a mess to recommend unequivocally. —*John Dougan*

○ **10, 9, 8, 7, 6, 5, 4, 3, 2, 1** / 1983 / Columbia ✦✦✦✦
Midnight Oil's first album to have a full-scale production, this album effectively brings out the band's driving rock sound, Peter Garrett's impassioned vocals, and the band's forthright political standpoint. —*William Ruhlmann*

○ **Red Sails in the Sunset** / 1985 / Columbia ✦✦✦✦

Species Deceases / 1985 / Columbia ✦✦✦

● **Diesel & Dust** / 1987 / Columbia ✦✦✦✦
On a thematic album dealing with the plight of Aborigines in Australia, this is Midnight Oil's most focused and compelling music. Its single most impressive song, "The Dead Heart," works powerfully, both as agit-pop and as moving rock music. Also included is the anthemic hit single "Beds Are Burning." —*William Ruhlmann*

Blue Sky Mining / 1990 / Columbia ✦✦✦
Diesel & Dust, only with less aggression. It's still a solid record. —*John Dougan*

Scream in Blue Live / May 5, 1992 / Columbia ✦✦
Scream in Blue Live is, thankfully, a very worthy addition to the group's catalogue. The Oils' music has always had more edge and power in a live setting, and this captures it perfectly. All that's missing is the visual dimension of frantic and imposing front-man Peter Garrett stalking the stage. Great songs that were delivered too tamely in their studio incarnations—"Dreamworld" from *Diesel and Dust* and "Stars of Warburton" from *Blue Sky Mining*, for example—erupt in full bloom live from the Brisbane Boondall Centre. Other highlights include "Progress," recorded in 1990 at a protest rally in front of Exxon head offices on 6th Avenue in New York, and a passionate plea for aboriginal rights that serves as an introduction to "Beds Are Burning." —*Roch Parisien*

○ **Earth & Sun & Moon** / Apr. 1993 / Columbia ✦✦✦✦
After the slightly uninspired *Blue Sky Mining*, Midnight Oil sound revitalized on *Earth & Sun & Moon*. Their most melodic, nearly Beatlesque effort is arguably their best yet. —*Chris Woodstra*

Mike + the Mechanics

Group, Pop/Rock
While Phil Collins was pursuing his solo career in 1985, Genesis bassist/guitarist Mike Rutherford formed the pop/rock band Mike + the Mechanics. Featuring Rutherford (bass), former Ace and Squeeze member Paul Carrack (vocals, keyboards), ex-Sad Cafe member Paul Young (vocals), keyboardist Adrian Lee, and drummer Peter Van Hooke, the group released their self-titled first album late in 1985. The record produced two Top Ten hit singles, "Silent Running (On Dangerous Ground)" and "All I Need Is a Miracle," which both peaked on the charts in early 1986. During 1986, Rutherford returned to Genesis and Carrack revived his solo career. Mike + the Mechanics didn't release another album until 1988's *The Living Years*. The record was a greater success than the first album, spawning the number one hit single "The Living Years." After its release, the group was inactive for another few years; they returned in 1991 with *Word of Mouth*, which failed to duplicate the success of their first two records. Four years later, Mike + the Mechanics released their fourth record, *Beggar on a Beach of Gold*. —*Stephen Thomas Erlewine*

● **Mike + the Mechanics** / 1985 / Atlantic ✦✦✦✦

○ **The Living Years** / 1988 / Atlantic ✦✦✦✦

Word of Mouth / 1991 / Atlantic ✦✦✦

Beggar on a Beach of Gold / 1995 / Virgin ✦✦

Milla

Folk-Rock
Milla Jovovich is an ex-teen supermodel/actress who recorded an unexpectedly interesting debut album, *The Divine Comedy*, in 1994. Far from the trite dance-pop released by most models angling for a music career, Jovovich's debut is largely acoustic and rooted equally in philosophy and her Slavic background—and it's surprisingly thoughtful and well-crafted. —*Heather Phares*

The Divine Comedy / Apr. 5, 1994 / SBK ✦✦✦
The singing supermodel's debut includes "Gentleman Who Fell," a good example of the lighthearted acoustic material included on this album. —*Heather Phares*

The Millennium

Group, Pop/Rock
Influenced by psychedelia and California rock, pop/rock producer Curt Boettcher (the Association) decided to assemble a studio supergroup that would explore progressive sounds in 1968. Millennium's resultant album would find no commercial success, and only half-baked artistic success, but nonetheless retains some period charm. Influenced in roughly equal measures by the Associa-

tion, the Mamas and the Papas, the *Smile*-era Beach Boys, Nilsson, the Left Banke, and the Fifth Dimension, Boettcher and his friends came up with a hybrid that was at once too unabashedly commercial for underground FM radio and too weird for the AM dial. It would have fit in better on the AM airwaves, though; the almost too-cheerful sunshine harmonies and catchy melodies dominate the suite-like, diverse set of elaborately produced '60s pop/rock tunes. —*Richie Unterberger*

● **Begin** / 1968 / Columbia ✦✦✦✦
A bit coy and sugary at times, this is nonetheless an interesting curio that has no shortage of hooks, even if it lacks the depth to back its aspirations toward hipness. The 1990 CD reissue adds two previously unreleased cuts. —*Richie Unterberger*

Steve Miller

b. Oct. 5, 1943, Milwaukee, WI
Blues Rock, Psychedelic, Pop/Rock
For my money, the best of the hippie-era San Francisco bands. Maybe that's because the Steve Miller Band actually hailed from Texas, and Miller and early Miller Band vocalist Boz Scaggs were blues fanatics who dabbled in psychedelic song structures and not vice versa. In the '70s Miller turned his tight blues machine into one of the decade's greatest and most consistent hit machines. His recent stuff, however has been sloppy and desultory, save one fine return to the blues. —*John Floyd*

○ **Children of the Future** / 1968 / Capitol ✦✦✦✦
Recorded in England with producer Glyn Johns (the Who, the Faces), this debut effort presented Miller as someone who was not only immersed in the blues but also fascinated with sound effects and sequencing, not unlike the Moody Blues or Pink Floyd. As a whole, this album flows nicely. Among the album's many highlights are "Baby's Callin' Me Home" (written by Boz Scaggs), "Stepping Stone," "Roll with It," "Junior Saw It Happen," and the spacey Mellotron-heavy ballad "In My First Mind." —*Rick Clark*

○ **Sailor** / 1968 / Capitol ✦✦✦✦
Less than six months after *Children of the Future*, Miller's solid followup proved that he wasn't a flash in the pan. Like its predecessor, *Sailor* dabbled in neat segues and effects, but to a lesser degree. Miller shines on the gently acoustic "Quicksilver Girl" and haunting "Dear Mary." *Sailor* has a couple of great rockers with "Living in the U.S.A." (Miller's first hit at number 94) and "Dime a Dance Romance," penned by soon-to-be-departing member Boz Scaggs. —*Rick Clark*

Your Saving Grace / 1969 / Capitol ✦✦✦
This effort is a little more subdued than *Brave New World*, with cuts like "Baby's House" and "Feel So Glad." However, Miller does lay down an authoritative groove on "Don't Let Nobody Turn You Around," while "Little Girl" features some excellent, tasty lead guitar work. Miller also included a spacey reworking of "Motherless Children." Lonnie Turner's daft "Last Wombat in Mecca" is the album's only low point. Considering this was the fourth album Miller released in two years, the weakness is hardly worth mentioning. —*Rick Clark*

○ **Brave New World** / 1969 / Capitol ✦✦✦✦
From the anthemic opening title cut, accelerating through to the crash-and-burn closer, "My Dark Hour" (a number 126 hit featuring Paul McCartney ghosting on drums, bass, and vocals under the pseudonym of Paul Ramon), *Brave New World* is a tour de force. Other standout tracks include Miller's atmospheric "Seasons," "Kow Kow," and "Space Cowboy," an FM rock classic. —*Rick Clark*

Revolution / 1969 / United Artists ✦✦
Number Five / 1970 / Capitol ✦✦✦
For this effort Miller went to Nashville, among other places, and recorded a wide range of material that covered everything from waxing poetic about eating hot chili to railing at the industrial military complex. In spite of this album's uneven material, it possesses many strong tunes, including "Going to Mexico," "Good Morning," and "Going to the Country" (a #69 hit). It also includes "Steve Miller's Midnight Tango," which charted at #117. —*Rick Clark*

Rock Love / 1971 / Capitol ✦
● **Anthology** / 1972 / Capitol ✦✦✦✦
This is a smartly assembled best-of collection that provides a good introduction to Miller's work up to this point. Those interested in digging deeper than this should check out *Brave New World*,

Sailor, Children of the Future, and *Your Saving Grace,* in that order. —*Rick Clark*

Recall the Beginning: A Journey From Eden / 1972 / Capitol ✦✦✦
After the miserable album *Rock Love*, Miller rebounded somewhat with *Recall the Beginning—A Journey from Eden*. One side is largely throwaway stuff, but the other half features a string of dreamy compositions that culminates with the haunting "Journey from Eden." "Love's Riddle," another track from that grouping, is also fine. —*Rick Clark*

The Joker / 1973 / Capitol ✦✦✦
While not so strong as some of his earlier work, *The Joker*'s title cut (built from a simple guitar riff) was Miller's first huge number one single. "Sugar Babe" and "Something to Believe In" were also highlights. Nevertheless, Miller's focus on basic catchy material laid the groundwork for his incredibly successful late-'70s albums. —*Rick Clark*

○ **Fly Like An Eagle** / 1976 / Capitol ✦✦✦✦
In his effort to create the ultimate playable album, Miller re-incorporated his interest in spacey sound effects and neat segues and synthesized them with a batch of tightly crafted light pop/rock tunes. The result generated a load of seamless hits like "Take the Money and Run," "Rock 'n Me," and the title track. —*Rick Clark*

○ **Book of Dreams** / 1977 / Capitol ✦✦✦✦
Recorded at the same time as *Fly Like An Eagle*, this album repeated the same formula, with the same big results. Hits included "Jet Airliner" (a slight reworking of an old R&B tune by Paul Pena), "Jungle Love," and "Swingtown." —*Rick Clark*

★ **Greatest Hits 1974-1978** / 1978 / Capitol ✦✦✦✦✦
This collection remains, to this day, Miller's most consistent-selling catalog item. It includes all of the hit singles and important album tracks from his biggest albums. —*Rick Clark*

Circle of Love / 1981 / Capitol ✦✦✦
After a four-year layoff, Miller returned with a truly weird album. One half of it is a wandering space-funk jam called "Macho City," the other half featured a couple of decent tunes, which were singles, "Heart Like a Wheel" (number 24), and "Circle of Love" (number 55). —*Rick Clark*

Abracadabra / 1982 / Capitol ✦✦✦
Even though the catchy title track became a number one hit, returning Miller to the limelight, this album lacked the focus and strong material to provide more staying power. —*Rick Clark*

Steve Miller Band: Live! / 1983 / Capitol ✦✦
This decent live album features a cross-section of hits, including "Living in the U.S.A." —*Rick Clark*

Italian X Rays / 1984 / Capitol ✦✦
Living in the 20th Century / Dec. 15, 1987 / Capitol ✦✦
Miller does a half-assed return to his blues roots with this outing, which was dedicated to Jimmy Reed. Among the more promising numbers was "Nobody but You Baby," but heavily processed rhythm tracks marred what might have been a strong album. —*Rick Clark*

Born 2B Blue / 1988 / Capitol ✦✦✦
After a string of incredibly spotty albums, Miller quits noodling around with synthesizers and gimmicky effects and knuckles down with a smooth collection of jazz standards. Utilizing the formidable talents of vibe player Milt Jackson, Phil Woods (alto sax), and Ben Sidran (keys and coproduction), Miller creates an album that is playful and sophisticated. While his guitar playing is downplayed, Miller shines on "Just a Little Bit," "God Bless the Child," and the swinging "Red Top." —*Rick Clark*

○ **The Best of Steve Miller (1968-1973)** / 1990 / Capitol ✦✦✦✦
Some duplication with *Anthology*, but this is a better initiation to the early days, including some cuts from *The Joker*. —*John Floyd*

Wide River / Jun. 8, 1993 / Polydor ✦✦
Steve Miller returns to the bluesy pop/rock sound that made his career so successful with *Wide River*, a pleasant collection of new songs that will appeal greatly to fans of "The Joker," "Take the Money and Run," and "Rock 'n Me." —*AMG*

○ **Steve Miller Band [Box Set]** / 1994 / Capitol ✦✦✦✦
This is one case where the project would have, more than likely, been better served if it was compiled without the help of the artist. This three-disc set is broken down into pre-"Joker" (vol. 1), post-"Joker" (vol. 2), and "Blues" (vol. 3). While Miller aced vol. 2's song

selection, and the third disc is enjoyably playable, it's obvious he holds much of his earlier work in disregard. It's hard to justify why he would perform horrible editing jobs and fade-outs on some of his best early work. Why didn't Miller just include *Anthology*, with a couple of extra cuts, as Disc One? The set does feature great sound and the liner notes and the pictures in the booklet are first-rate. —*Rick Clark*

Milli Vanilli

Group, Dance-Pop
The most notorious group of the '80s, bar none. Eurodisco producer Frank Farian (who created Boney M and Far Corporation) recruited two handsome, talentless dweebs to lip-sync to his prefab dance-pop ditties, such as "Girl You Know It's True" and "Blame It on the Rain." The group was an instant smash, selling millions of albums and winning a Best New Group Grammy. Farian later spilled the beans that the group didn't even sing on their records, creating an uproar that made them the enemies of scorned fans and critics; their Grammy was quickly revoked and the group ceased its existence. —*John Floyd*

● **Girl You Know It's True** / 1989 / Arista ✦✦✦✦
If you want to know what the defrocked duo *didn't* sing, pick up this infamous album, which includes the #1 singles "Blame It on the Rain," "Baby Don't Forget My Number," "Girl I'm Gonna Miss You," and the #2 title track. —*John Floyd*

Quick Moves: The Remix Album / Arista ✦✦
The value of Milli Vanilli product increased ten-fold when it turned out that they didn't even sing their songs. That posed an interesting problem for this project: how do you remix something that doesn't exist? —*Ron Wynn*

Stephanie Mills

b. Mar. 22, 1959
Soul, R&B, Urban
Mills is best known for her role as Dorothy in the stage show of *The Wiz*. She won a talent show at the Apollo Theater six weeks in a row at age nine. She appeared in the Broadway play *Maggie Flynn*, toured with the Isley Brothers, and released her debut album in 1973. She landed the part of Dorothy in 1975, recording an album for Motown during the show's four-year run. In 1980, she had a worldwide hit with "Never Knew Love Like This Before," which went Top Ten in the U.S. She was married for a short while to Shalamar's Jeffrey Daniels and worked with Teddy Pendergrass in 1981. In 1983, she landed a daytime television show on NBC. She also later played Dorothy in a revival of *The Wiz*. —*Steve Huey*

For the First Time / 1976 / Motown ✦✦
A collection of Stephanie Mills tracks from her days on Motown. Although you wouldn't know it from the packaging, this hearkens back to the early '70s, when Mills was splitting her time between being on Broadway in *The Wiz* and pursuing a recording career. She made an album for Motown produced by the team of Bacharach/David. It didn't generate much response, and she left them shortly after to sign with 20th Century Fox, where her singing career began in earnest. This has curiosity value, but little else. —*Ron Wynn*

What Cha Gonna Do with My Lovin ? / 1979 / 20th Century ✦✦✦
Down-tempo disco and fiery soul. —*Bil Carpenter*

Sweet Sensation / 1980 / 20th Century ✦✦✦
Soul and Top 40 mix. —*Bil Carpenter*

Stephanie / 1981 / 20th Century ✦✦✦

Tantalizingly Hot / 1982 / Casablanca ✦✦

Merciless / 1983 / Casablanca ✦✦✦

I've Got the Cure / 1984 / Casablanca ✦✦

● **In My Life: Greatest Hits** / 1985 / Casablanca ✦✦✦✦
Her hits on 20th Century. —*Bil Carpenter*

Stephanie Mills / 1985 / MCA ✦✦✦
Stephanie Mills made the move to MCA in the mid-'80s and kept right on rolling. Her self-titled debut included the solid number "Stand Back" and had a fine blend of uptempo/dance songs, soaring ballads, and light urban contemporary tunes. It was the first album matching Mills with producer Nick Martinelli, and their collaboration would be a fruitful one. —*Ron Wynn*

If I Were Your Woman / 1987 / MCA ✦✦✦
Sophisticated, zealous soul balladry. —*Bil Carpenter*

Home / 1989 / MCA ✦✦✦
Stephanie Mills enjoyed consistent success through the '80s, and this late '80s album was no exception. She had both an urban contemporary and then a club hit with original and remixed versions of "Something In The Way (You Make Me Feel)" and another major hit in "Comfort Of A Man." Her style matured during the decade, and she found a comfortable balance between bombastic, show business/show tunes interpretations and more soulful, earthy performances. —*Ron Wynn*

● **Best Of** / 1995 / Mercury ✦✦✦✦

Garnet Mimms

Soul, R&B
With his backing band the Enchanters in the early '60s, Garnet Mimms cut several fine, underrated R&B singles, including the hit "Cry Baby." After the Enchanters fell apart in 1964, Mimms pursued a solo career that merged a sophisticated R&B backing with his gospel-influenced singing. He made many terrific records that never hit the charts; it wasn't until 1977 that he had another hit, "What It Is." But in the '60s, Mimms made many records that should have been hits; they remain criminally unheard, but fans of '60s soul and R&B should seek them out. —*Stephen Thomas Erlewine*

● **The Best of Garnet Mimms/Crybaby** / 1993 / EMI ✦✦✦✦
Excellent compilation of this early soul singer, whose influence extended beyond his one big hit, the 1963 title track. Emerging from a gospel background and obscure doo-wop groups, Mimms invested the increasingly sophisticated R&B sound of the mid-'60s with both emotion and supple pipes. He never hit the top ten after "Cry Baby," but rang off a string of minor hits like "Baby Don't You Weep," "For Your Precious Love," "It Was Easier To Hurt Her," and "I'll Take Good Care Of You." Grittier than Motown, but not as down-home as Stax, Mimms married his vocals to the uptown production values and pop songwriting savvy of his producer Jerry Ragavoy to produce some of the more memorable early soul recordings. This 25-track anthology, covering his recordings for United Artists between 1963 and 1966, is unerringly consistent. It features all of his hit singles, highlights from the three albums he released during this period, and the original versions of "My Baby" (later one of Janis Joplin's signature tunes) and "Anytime You Want Me" (covered by the Who on a B-side in 1965). —*Richie Unterberger*

Ministry

Group, Industrial, Alternative Pop/Rock, Heavy Metal
When Ministry released their first EP in 1981, it seemed impossible that the band would become one of the biggest industrial terrorists of the late '80s and '90s. On their first album and EP, the band was a synth-funk duo, more similar to the Human League than Einsturzende Neubauten. Yet lead singer/guitarist Al Jourgensen was smart enough to abandon that sound and begin constructing a terrifying new form of dance music. Using heavy guitar, synthesizers, samples, distorted vocals, massive drums, noise, and tape effects, Ministry created some of the first industrial dance records that cross over to a mass audience. And it wasn't because Jourgensen diluted the power of the music. Although the band sometimes approached conventional song structures that were simply fueled by jack-hammer guitars, the real reason Ministry appealed to heavy metal fans as much as the alternative crowd is because of how the band looked. Instead of the faceless, abrasive drone of KMFDM or Skinny Puppy, Ministry acted like rock stars, dressing in leather and sunglasses, playing a relentlessly heavy guitar rock that happened to have a dance beat and synthesizers. After years of slowly building a large fan base, the band completed their cross over into the mainstream with 1992's *Psalm 69*; the album's success confirmed that Ministry was one of the most popular hard rock and industrial bands of the early '90s. —*Stephen Thomas Erlewine*

With Sympathy / 1983 / Arista ✦✦

Twitch / 1986 / Sire ✦✦

Twelve Inch Singles (1981-1984) / 1987 / Wax Trax! ✦✦✦
Included are all of their best-known hits and great songs before they got signed by a major label (Sire). Early techno-industrial music from the early '80s. —*John Book*

○ **The Land of Rape and Honey** / 1988 / Sire ◆◆◆◆
Considered to be one of Ministry's best albums, this is the one that crossed them over from the industrial-alternative scene into the heavy metal crowds. It's very heavy and enjoyable from start to finish. —*John Book*

○ **The Mind Is a Terrible Thing to Taste** / 1989 / Sire ◆◆◆◆

In Case You Didn't Feel Showing Up (Live) / 1990 / Sire ◆◆
A live album recorded during their most recent tour, *In Case You Didn't Feel Like Showing Up (Live)* demonstrates that a band that used a lot of technological wizardry in the studio is fully capable of playing its music on stage. It's also available as a home video on Warner/Reprise. —*John Book*

● **Psalm 69: The Way to Succeed & The Way To Suck Eggs** / 1992 / Sire ◆◆◆◆
Although this is Ministry's most accessible album, it is not a sell-out. Al Jourgensen and company never let the intensity up, with the machine-like grind of the rhythm section constantly driving the same sixteenth-note rhythms again and again. "Just One Fix" is the best track on a remarkable, intense album, which also includes the single "Jesus Built My Hotrod." —*Stephen Thomas Erlewine*

Mink DeVille (Willy DeVille)

Group, Rock & Roll, Pop/Rock
From 1977 to 1985, NYC singer and guitar slinger Willy DeVille recorded six albums with his band, Mink DeVille. He wrote street-tough songs but was a romantic at heart, showing his inspiration to be closer to Ben E. King and the Drifters than to Lou Reed. Mink DeVille got lumped in with other bands in the burgeoning NYC punk underground, which perhaps helped the band get gigs but also made them misunderstood. —*Dennis MacDonald*

○ **Mink DeVille** / 1977 / ERA ◆◆◆
Energetic, no-holds-barred, smoking rock with R&B roots. —*David Szatmary*

Return to Magenta / 1978 / ERA ◆◆
This is the followup to DeVille's self-titled debut. (Out of print) —*David Szatmary*

Le Chat Bleu / 1980 / ERA ◆◆◆

● **Savoir Faire (A Compilation)** / 1981 / Capitol ◆◆◆
Collecting tracks from Mink Deville's first three albums, *Savoir Faire* is a good introduction to the band's raw, stripped-down R&B-influenced rock. —*Stephen Thomas Erlewine*

Coup de Grace / 1981 / Atlantic ◆◆◆

Where Angels Fear to Tread / 1983 / WEA ◆◆◆

Sportin' Life / 1985 / Atlantic ◆◆◆

Cabretta / 1987 / Capitol ◆◆

Minor Threat

Group, Hardcore
Minor Threat was the definitive Washington, D.C. hardcore band, writing the rules for straight-edged, hardcore punk rockers. Led by Ian MacKaye, the band was one of the first to reject drugs and alcohol, leading a call for self-awareness, as well as having a fiercely intelligent political bent to their music. Each of their songs were short, sharp, and lethal, made all the more frightening by MacKaye's raging vocals. Minor Threat wouldn't have been half as invigorating and powerful as they were if they didn't have his literate, intelligent lyrics; they were simple, direct, and vicious, much like the band's music. After two years of recording, the band broke up in 1983; MacKaye went on to form the more successful—but no less uncompromising—Fugazi, yet Minor Threat remains his most influential band. —*Stephen Thomas Erlewine*

○ **Out of Step** / 1983 / Dischord ◆◆◆

Minor Threat / 1984 / Dischord ◆◆◆

★ **Complete Discography** / 1988 / Dischord ◆◆◆◆◆
Everything the seminal hardcore band Minor Threat ever recorded is collected on this single disc; it's the ultimate statement of straight-edged, razor-sharp early-'80s hardcore. —*Stephen Thomas Erlewine*

Minutemen

Group, Alternative Pop/Rock, Hardcore
At their best, the Minutemen made eclecticism seem as effortless as breathing: in songs that seldom lasted more than a minute (hence their name), this San Pedro, CA, trio touched on everything

from jazz and funk to anarchist punk, bohemian beat poetry, and '70s dinosaur rock. Their songs (mostly written by either vocalist and guitarist D. Boon or bassist and vocalist Mike Watt) seethed with political outrage; their wry sense of humor (often pointed at themselves) separated them from the dead-serious punk brats on the West Coast, as did the diversity of their music. Their career was cut short in 1985 when Boon died in a car crash. Watt and MM drummer George Hurley formed fIREHOSE in 1986. —*John Floyd*

Paranoid Time / 1980 / SST ◆◆◆

Punch Line / 1981 / SST ◆◆◆
With lyrics that sound lifted from William Carlos Williams' poetry, this is a hit of punk rock unlike anything else available at the time. With dense, compact songs (18, and the record isn't even 30 minutes long) that spin off into the stratosphere in their jagged, funky way, it's an exhilarating, totally original record—one that alleged alternative rockers of today probably would never think of making. A bold indication of the great music that was to come. —*John Dougan*

○ **Buzz or Howl under the Influence of Heat** / 1983 / SST ◆◆◆◆
Not wasting an instant, the Minutemen recorded *Buzz or Howl* in a near-improvisatory frenzy. The arrangements seem looser and the lyrics more Beat-inspired in their harsh, epigrammatic imagism ("Dreams Are Free, Motherfucker"). With only eight tracks, this record began a larger critical examination of the Minutemen due to its dazzling music. The racket and wailing kicked up by Boon, Watt and Hurley was indisputably great—and original. It was clear from this recording that it was only a matter of time (the next record to be exact) before the Minutemen exploded with a major work(s). —*John Dougan*

○ **What Makes a Man Start Fires?** / 1983 / SST ◆◆◆◆
At the time this record was released, nothing in punk rock (or in any kind of rock, for that matter) sounded like the Minutemen. And although their earlier EPs and singles had provided glimpses at what kind of band they were, *What Makes a Man...* was an amazingly confident display of talent proving that this was one of the best young bands in America, and that punk rock (or in this instance, hardcore) could no longer be defined simply as yowling guitar rant. On this record, Boon's guitar is all over the place, as Hurley and Mike Watt begin to assert themselves as punk rock's greatest rhythm section. As usual, brevity is the soul of the Minutemen's wit, but unlike earlier recordings, the songs here are more expansive and complex. —*John Dougan*

Politics of Time / 1984 / SST ◆◆◆
Not a follow-up to *Double Nickels* as much as it was an interesting assortment of odds and ends recorded during the band's infancy and pre-Minutemen days when they were called the Reactionaries. Unsurprisingly, the quality of some of these recordings is less than high quality, but the energy and excitement come through. Side Two is arguably the most interesting, with Martin Tamburovich on lead vocals; this is perhaps the most exhaustive collection of Reactionaries material on record. Perhaps not an essential record, but a good one nonetheless. —*John Dougan*

★ **Double Nickels on the Dime** / 1984 / SST ◆◆◆◆◆
Today it seems hard to believe that a record as amazing as this was released the same month as Husker Du's *Zen Arcade*, and it seemed that many critics at the time were knee-deep in either record. An astonishing record, *Double Nickels* remains the Minutemen's finest moment. It was on this record that the music, political activism, and band chemistry coalesced into a forceful document of rage during the height of the Reagan Administration's marketable "me-first" jingoism. Boon's guitar sputters, clanks and cajoles, while Watt and Hurley explode in rhythmic splendor. The songs, now more explicitly political, question U.S. covert military operations in Central America and challenge accepted approaches to American political history; as well as the crassness and narcissism of popular culture and the business machinations of corporate rock & roll. Daring, justifiably pissed-off and accusatory, this is a benchmark work of the era that hasn't lost an ounce of power since the day it was released. In fact, it gets better with age. —*John Dougan*

1980-1983 / 1985 / SST ◆◆◆

○ **My First Bells** / 1985 / SST ◆◆◆◆
A superb collection of all Minutemen recordings from their first EP (*Paranoid Time*) up to and including *What Makes A Man Start Fires*. Rather than going crazy looking for those hard-to-find bits of

vinyl, here's the whole shootin' match from 1980–83 in one spot. Cheap at twice the price. —*John Dougan*

○ **Project: Mersh** / 1985 / SST ✦✦✦
"Mersh" is San Pedro slang for commercial, and as the hilarious cover art by D. Boon indicates, the Minutemen were a long way from establishing any kind of toehold in the commercial rock marketplace. But that didn't slow them down from recording, nor did it force them to reevaluate what they had done up to this point. The Minutemen were true punk rockers, and commercial success (and I'm talking huge mega-unit-selling success here, not simply making a solid middle-class life for oneself) was treated more as an accident, not as an aspiration. *Mersh* is only a six-song EP, but it sated the appetites of hungry Minutemen fans awaiting the first full-length record in the wake of *Double Nickels*. This proved that there was plenty more good stuff on the way, especially in Mike Watt's "Take out Test" and Boon's incredible "The Cheerleaders" and "King of the Hill." Added bonus is a hilarious run-through of Steppenwolf's "Hey, Lawdy Mama." —*John Dougan*

○ **3-Way Tie (For Last)** / Oct. 1985 / SST ✦✦✦
D. Boon's death in December 1985 was one of rock's most tragic occurrences. And, a decade later, I find that it still affects the way I listen to this, the "final" Minutemen record. Boon was hitting his stride here; the songs were emphatic, smart and marked by his increasing sociopolitical awareness. Boon did not suffer fools gladly, and this record (as does the best of the Minutemen) retains a strong sense of moral indignation (listen to "The Price of Paradise" and "The Big Stick"). One fact that shouldn't be lost in eulogizing over Boon was the significant role Mike Watt was playing in the band. This hadn't happened overnight, but with each successive record Watt's confidence as a bass player and songwriter was growing, and by the time of *3-Way Tie*, his skills were in full flower—so much so that one side of the record is called Side D., the other Side Mike. Dense and driving, this is a bittersweet moment closing an excellent band's career. —*John Dougan*

○ **Post-Mersh, Vol. 1 (Punch Line/What Makes a Man Start Fires)** / 1987 / SST ✦✦✦✦

○ **Post-Mersh, Vol. 2 (Buzz or Howl under the Influence)** / 1987 / SST ✦✦✦✦

Ballot Result / 1987 / SST ✦✦✦
Originally, this was to be a major work entitled *3 Dudes/6 Sides/3 Studio/3 Live*. For the live recording, ballots were enclosed in copies of *3-Way Tie* and Minutemen fans were given the chance to vote on the 30 songs they'd like to hear on the three live sides. Unfortunately, Boon's death scuttled the project, but Hurley and Watt managed to piece together this two-LP set based on the ballots that were sent in. A fine collection of live tracks that go back to 1980, this is a classy way to say goodbye, and proves what muscle the Minutemen had onstage. —*John Dougan*

○ **Post-Mersh, Vol. 3** / 1989 / SST ✦✦✦✦

Miranda Sex Garden

Group, Alternative Pop/Rock
This creatively named band was formed when the members were studying vocal music together and started busking in the streets of London. *Madra*, their first album, is largely a capella, and composed entirely of traditional British songs. Their later releases— like 1993's *Suspiria* and 1994's *Fairytales of Slavery*—saw the group moving in a more rock/industrial direction, pitting their smooth voices upon layers of distortion, feedback, and heavy drums. —*Heather Phares*

○ **Madra** / 1990 / Mute ✦✦✦✦
The group's first album consists of madrigals and traditional songs, most of them from the 18th century or earlier. A dance remix of one of the songs, "Gush Forth My Tears," became a surprise club hit. Musically, *Madra* is nothing more than the voices of Miranda Sex Garden in all their pristine clarity—the album is completely *a capella*. the vocals and material are exceptionally beautiful; *Madra* is a unique and refreshing listen. —*Heather Phares*

● **Suspiria** / 1993 / Mute ✦✦✦✦
The group's second full-length album finds Miranda Sex Garden going in a rock direction. Loud guitars and pounding drums mix with droning cellos and sawing violins on songs such as "Open Eyes." Even the group's vocal style is more pungent and aggressive, with the heretofore dulcet tones of the group now transforming into wild, banshee-like shrieks and snarls. Despite the radical

changes in direction, the group still manages to create a powerful and individual album in *Suspiria*. Along with *Madra*, it's one of the group's best efforts. —*Heather Phares*

Fairytales Of Slavery / 1994 / Mute ✦✦
Fairytales Of Slavery continues the heavy direction of *Suspiria* and goes a step further by including industrial rhythms and sounds as well as powerful guitars and drums. Members of the seminal industrial group Einstürzende Neubauten appear on the album, giving it industrial credentials. The vocal role of hte group is downplayed, unfortunately; Miranda Sex Garden seems more concerned with sounding hard and menacing on this album than singing well. —*Heather Phares*

Iris / Elektra ✦✦✦
The *Iris* EP introduces instrumentation to the group's entrancing vocal harmonies. For the most part it's a success, giving an edgy and gothic sound to their classical style. —*Heather Phares*

The Misfits

Group, Hardcore
Long before Danzig (the band) sold tons of records and showed up with regularity on MTV, Glenn Danzig (the guy) sang for the Misfits. Crawling out of the swamps of New Jersey in the late '70s, the Misfits were part of the early hardcore scene populating New York's trend-setting underground rock Bowery hangout, CBGB's. But while other bands favored skinheads and Doc Martens boots, Danzig and pals drew their look from early goth-punks like the Damned's Dave Vanian. Playing tuneful, ferocious speed-punk, Danzig's big baritone bellowed lyrics that sounded torn from '50s and '60s grade-Z gore flicks (e.g. "Mommy, Can I Go Out and Kill Tonight?," "Vampira," "Last Caress"). As scary as they tried to be, there was always something cartoonish about the Misfits, and that made their horror-punk less shocking and more tastelessly funny (and sometimes just tasteless). Still, they were a potent rock band, capable of some thunderously good music. Some would argue that the Misfits are an underappreciated band, but with Glenn Danzig now so successful, he's probably having the last laugh. Danzig split up the Misfits in 1983 and then formed the gloomier, more ghoulish (and not nearly as good) Samhain. Danzig (the band) debuted in 1988. —*John Dougan*

○ **Walk among Us** / 1982 / Ruby ✦✦✦✦
With imagery lifted from sci-fi flicks and gory horror films, Glenn Danzig and Co. sound all revved up and ready to go on their debut record. With Ramones-influenced punk that occasionally veers into speedy, unintelligible hardcore, this is a ferocious, relentless record that makes no apologies for its capacity to alienate listeners. Ugly, unrepentantly nasty, and essential. Issued on CD in 1988. —*John Dougan*

Earth A.D. / 1983 / Plan 9/Caroline ✦✦✦

Legacy of Brutality / 1985 / Plan 9/Caroline ✦✦✦
A collection of outtakes released two years after the band called it a day, *Legacy* is a pretty intimidating proposition that provides an excellent historical overview. Going back to 1978 for some tracks, this collection has its inconsistent moments, but its strengths overwhelm its weaknesses. —*John Dougan*

● **The Misfits** / 1986 / Plan 9/Caroline ✦✦✦
Purists may disagree, but for the benighted, this is the best place to start. A 20-track anthology that gives you the most Misfits for your money, everything that made the Misfits great is here, including the odd remix, alternate take and re-edited version. The band is loud and defiant, as is Danzig, whose considerable vocal chops are well displayed here. The perfect music for an evening of headbanging or watching gore films. —*John Dougan*

○ **Die Die My Darling** / 1987 / Plan 9/Caroline ✦✦✦✦

The Missing Links

Group, Garage Rock
One of the best Australian bands of the '60s, though they weren't even stars in their home country, the Missing Links started as a very raw, Kinks-like combo, gaining a number two hit in New Zealand with "We 2 Should Live"/"Untrue." The first lineup folded in 1965, and a second, with entirely different personnel, took the name. This aggregation cut the rawest Australian garage/punk of the era, and indeed some of the best from anywhere, sounding at their best like a fusion of the Troggs and the early Who, letting loose at times with wild feedback that was quite ahead of its time. They didn't find commercial success, and split after several singles,

an EP, and an album. Various members turned up in other Australian groups like Running Jumping Standing Still and Python Lee Jackson; the most notable of these was guitarist Doug Ford, who joined Running Jumping Standing Still and then graduated to the Masters Apprentices, the best Australian band of the '60s other than the Easybeats. —*Richie Unterberger*

● **The Missing Links** / 1984 / Raven ✦✦✦✦
Their lone album is an uneven affair. The best cuts, "Wild About You," "Some Kinda Fun," "You're Drivin' Me Insane," "Mama Keep Your Big Mouth Shut," and "Speak No Evil," are tremendous '60s punk, with blistering, feedback-ridden guitar and cord-shredding vocals. The rest is rather ordinary group originals and covers, save "H'Tuom Tuhs," a nearly-six-minute backwards version of "Mama Keep Your Big Mouth Shut" that was quite experimental for 1966, if not terribly listenable. —*Richie Unterberger*

The Links ... Unchained! / 1984 / Raven ✦✦
This four-song EP is worth tracking down if you're into the group, and if you can find it, but inessential otherwise. Contains rough-hewn covers of "Wooly Bully," James Brown's "I'll Go Crazy," and Them's "One More Time"; the best track, "Don't Give Me No Friction," is available on the compilation *Raven EP-LP, Vol. 1*. —*Richie Unterberger*

Missing Persons

Group, New Wave, Pop/Rock
Los Angeles-based quintet, 1980–1986, featuring former members of Frank Zappa's band, including drummer Terry Bozzio, Warren Cuccurillo, Patrick O'Hearn, Chuck Wild, and lead singer Dale Bozzio. —*William Ruhlmann*

Missing Persons / 1982 / Capitol ✦✦✦
○ **Spring Session M** / 1982 / Arista ✦✦✦✦
Rhyme & Reason / 1984 / Capitol ✦✦✦
Color in Your Life / 1986 / Capitol ✦✦
● **The Best of Missing Persons** / 1987 / Capitol ✦✦✦✦
The two main qualities of this band, heard on this compilation taken from their three albums and one EP, are the untutored singing of Dale Bozzio and the technical facility of the musicians, expressed in the inventive guitar and keyboard arrangements. High-quality '80s rock. —*William Ruhlmann*

Mission of Burma

Group, Punk
Of all the punk-inspired bands that came out of Boston in the early '80s, none were better than Mission of Burma. Arty without being too pretentious, capable of writing gripping songs and playing with ferocious intensity, guitarist Roger Miller, bassist Clint Conley, drummer Peter Prescott and tapehead Martin Swope, galvanized the city's alternative rock scene, and despite a too-short existence, set a standard for excellence that has rarely been equalled.

Burma's music is vintage early-'80s post-punk: jittery rhythms, odd-shifts in time, declamatory vocals; an aural assault similarly employed by bands such as the Gang of Four, Mekons and Pere Ubu—Burma's peers as well as their influences. Also, conspicuously present in the mix was the proto-punk of the Stooges and Velvet Underground (with just a dash of Led Zeppelin and Roxy Music), bands that inspired Burma's darker songwriting impulses and tendencies towards longish, repetitive jams capable of boring holes into your skull. What Burma added was a sonic texture through the use of extreme volume. Roger Miller's guitar enveloped the band in thick, distorted cascading chords, erupting into squealing solos and (intentional) squalls of feedback. With Prescott and Conley furiously bashing in support, the band's sound was extremely physical (ask anyone who saw them live) to the point of leaving you feeling slightly bruised, battered, but extremely happy.

After releasing an explosive single ("Academy Fight Song," still one of punk rock's greatest songs) on Boston's then-hippest indie label Ace of Hearts, Burma released two excellent records in just over a year: *Signals, Calls, and Marches* EP and their only full-length studio album *Vs.* The former was poppier, but in a breath-takingly intense way; the latter dark and ominous, lacking in riff-heavy punch, but still delivering a wicked blast of aural chaos. Unbeknownst to fans, this was the beginning of the end. The massive volume, a key element in Burma's sound, had taken its toll on the band members, especially Miller, who developed a severe case of

tinnitus that hastened the band's demise. (Always the trooper, Miller played the band's final tour wearing a protective headset used on shooting ranges to prevent his ears from absorbing more punishment.) After a bittersweet farewell tour in 1983, the shows were released as a live LP entitled *The Horrible Truth About Burma*, an occasionally thrilling example of their considerable stage prowess.

Miller has since gone on to a career as a solo artist and with his non-touring band Birdsongs of the Mesozoic. Prescott formed the wonderful Volcano Suns who released a half-dozen records all worth checking out before starting a new band Kustomized with ex-Bullet Lavolta singer Yukki Gipe. Clint Conley produced the first Yo La Tengo record and then left the music business and reportedly works as a television producer in New Jersey. —*John Dougan*

○ **Signals, Calls, and Marches** / 1981 / Ace of Hearts ✦✦✦✦
"That's When I Reach for My Revolver" is a must-hear punk anthem. —*Robert Gordon*

Vs. / 1982 / Ace of Hearts ✦✦✦
Assaulting and musically sound, this is a great American punk album. —*Robert Gordon*

The Horrible Truth About Burma [EP] / 1985 / Ace of Hearts ✦✦
Now re-released on CD, it's a wonderful sample of the power of Mission of Burma live. An assaultive "Peking Spring" and great covers of the Stooges "1970" and Pere Ubu's "Heart of Darkness" make this essential listening. —*John Dougan*

Mission of Burma [EP] / 1987 / Taang! ✦✦
Forget / 1987 / Taang! ✦✦✦
● **Mission of Burma** / 1988 / Rykodisc ✦✦✦✦
A stunning, long (80 minutes) career overview of this magnificent band that includes all of *Signal, Calls, and Marches, Vs.* and the single "Academy Fight Song." Only two tracks from *Horrible Truth* are here, and recent converts will want to find the original album to hear Burma's sonic madness in its entirety. Very simply a great release from a great band, whose best moments have served as inspiration for hundreds of younger bands. —*John Dougan*

Let There Be Burma / 1990 / Taang! ✦✦✦
With so little material available it's common for outtakes and assorted ephemera to be released to a ravenous horde of uncritical fans. These are interesting, but non-essential releases. The Rykodisc release serves as the most exhaustive and authoritative document. Caveat Emptor: *Let There Be Burma* is a re-release of *Mission of Burma* (not to be confused with the Rykodisc release) and *Forget* on one disc. —*John Dougan*

Mr. Big

Group, Hard Rock, Pop/Rock, Heavy Metal
Mr. Big was no more than a side project for bassist Billy Sheehan, who had just left David Lee Roth's band and was once an original member of Talas. Mr. Big was immediately considered a super-group when they released their debut, simply because of Sheehan, but with Eric Martin (vocals), Paul Gilbert (guitar), and Pat Torpey (drums) they were simply a hard working metal band who loved to play loudly and were very good at it. Even as heavy as they are, they gained a huge audience when an acoustic ballad off their second album, "To Be with You," reached #1 on the Billboard singles charts in 1992. —*John Book*

Mr. Big / 1989 / Atlantic ✦✦
Bassist Billy Sheehan (formerly of David Lee Roth's band) formed this band with guitarist Paul Gilbert of Racer X; both musicians contribute impressive instrumental work even if the songs aren't worthy of the effort. —*AMG*

● **Lean into It** / 1991 / Atlantic ✦✦✦✦
Mr. Big abandons the virtuoso guitar and bass of Paul Gilbert and Billy Sheehan for the majority of *Lean into It*, and the result is a big, shiny mainstream rock album. It also translated into chart success with the hit campfire-singalong ballad "To Be With You." Elsewhere, Mr. Big provides some tracks to satisfy the new fans, along with plenty of head-spinning solos from Gilbert and Sheehan to satisfy their old audience. —*Stephen Thomas Erlewine*

Mr. Mister

Group, Pop/Rock
This Los Angeles-based pop/rock quartet came out of nowhere in 1985 with a #1 sophomore release, *Welcome to the Real World*,

which produced three huge hits in "Broken Wings" (#1), the anthemic "Kyrie" (#1), and "Is It Love?" (#8). —*Rick Clark*

I Wear the Face / 1984 / RCA ✦✦✦

An uneven, but impressive debut comes from these L.A. songwriters/session musicians with already significant credentials. —*AMG*

● **Welcome to the Real World** / 1985 / RCA ✦✦✦✦

Here are the major pop hits "Broken Wings," "Kyrie," and "Is It Love" from this band of session musicians and songwriters. —*Kenneth M. Cassidy*

Go On / RCA ✦✦

The Misunderstood

Group, Psychedelic, Garage Rock

Of the thousands of U.S. garage bands that struggled in the 1960s without achieving international success, the Misunderstood were not only among the very best, but among the very few to progress beyond basic garage sounds to music that has been (belatedly) recognized as nearly as accomplished and innovative as that of the British Invasion bands that touched off the garage explosion in the first place. Formed in Riverside, CA, in 1963, the group began as a basic R&B/rock combo in the tradition of the Stones and Animals. After the addition of steel guitarist Glenn Campbell, they rapidly moved toward a proto-psychedelic sound with guitar feedback, sustain, Middle Eastern influences, and exploratory song structures that strongly echoed the Yardbirds. With the encouragement of local expatriate British radio announcer John Ravenscroft (who would shortly become one of Britain's most influential DJs as John Peel, a designation he holds to this day), the band moved to England in 1966 in an attempt to find a sympathetic audience. The group cut six songs (a few of which were issued as extremely rare singles) that found them anticipating the early innovations of groups like Pink Floyd and Jimi Hendrix. The group were praised by the British press and up-and-coming acts like Pink Floyd and the Move, but were hounded by U.S. draft authorities and internal problems, and disbanded in confusion around early 1967. Campbell kept the Misunderstood name alive briefly with a couple unimpressive singles before forming Juicy Lucy, who had a small British hit with a cover of "Who Do You Love?" The group's other guitarist, Tony Hill (actually a Britishman who joined the band after they arrived in England), joined High Tide, who recorded some progressive rock albums. The Misunderstood finally gained some measure of the respect due them with a well-packaged reissue of their best material in the early '80s. —*Richie Unterberger*

● **Before the Dream Faded** / 1982 / Cherry Red ✦✦✦✦

One of the great lost '60s albums. Side One includes all six of the tracks they recorded in England in 1966, with magnificent guitar work and nervy, ambitious (if a bit overtly cosmic) songwriting that combines some of the best aspects of the Jeff Beck-era Yardbirds and Syd Barrett's Pink Floyd. Remember that Pink Floyd and Hendrix had yet to record when these sides were waxed; they aren't derivations, but genuinely innovative and groundbreaking performances. Side Two contains seven pre-psychedelic demos from their U.S. garage days in the mid-'60s that, while not nearly as important as their 1966 work, are solid, crunching R&B-soaked rock in the tradition of their chief British influences. —*Richie Unterberger*

Golden Glass / 1984 / Cherry Red ✦✦✦

Only Glenn Campbell remains from the original lineup on this album of 1969 material. Competent blues-rock, with some commendable steel guitar work by Campbell, it's nonetheless a pale shadow of the group's psychedelic recordings. Instead of picking this up, be on the lookout for a three-song EP (also called *Golden Glass*) that includes wild psychedelic covers of "Shake Your Money Maker" and "I'm Not Talkin'" by the original lineup in early 1966, and the eight-minute 1969 track "Golden Glass," which is probably the best cut from the last version of the band. —*Richie Unterberger*

Joni Mitchell

b. Nov. 7, 1943

Singer-Songwriter, Folk-Rock

One of the most important artists to emerge from the singer/songwriter era of the early '70s. Mitchell first gained notice as a songwriter when her "Both Sides Now" was a hit by Judy Collins in 1968. That same year, Mitchell released her debut album, *Joni Mitchell*. It was followed by *Clouds* in 1969 and *Ladies of the*

Canyon in 1970, the latter containing the much-covered songs "Big Yellow Taxi" and "Woodstock." *Blue*, her 1971 album, was her first to hit the Top 20 and has now sold over a million copies. *For the Roses* in 1972 was Mitchell's first gold album and included her first Top 40 hit, "You Turn Me on, I'm a Radio."

Mitchell's 1974 album, *Court & Spark*, was a commercial breakthrough, producing two hit singles, selling a million copies, and being nominated for several Grammys. She followed it with a live album, *Miles of Aisles*, that duplicated its success. From the mid-'70s on, Mitchell's work became more complicated and less folk/pop-oriented. *Hejira*, for example, paired her acoustic guitar with the bass improvisations of Jaco Pastorius, and *Don Juan's Reckless Daughter* contained an impressionistic sidelong song. Her most experimental album was *Mingus* (1979), which found her setting lyrics to the last tunes written by jazz composer Charles Mingus, at his request. The live *Shadows and Light* (1980), recorded with jazz guitarist Pat Metheny, also leaned in this direction.

Since 1982, Mitchell has adopted a slightly more accessible approach in a series of albums that take into consideration contemporary pop sounds. They have gained critical respect and sold moderately well. —*William Ruhlmann*

Joni Mitchell / Mar. 1968 / Reprise ✦✦✦

David Crosby produced this debut album, on which Mitchell sings in a formal, restrained style and writes in a wordy, poetic style, which is nevertheless touching on such songs as "I Had a King" and "Michael from Mountains." —*William Ruhlmann*

Clouds / May 1969 / Reprise ✦✦✦

Contains Mitchell's version of "Both Sides Now," as well as the exuberant "Chelsea Morning" and such vulnerable love songs as "I Don't Know Where I Stand." Grammy Award-winner for best folk performance. —*William Ruhlmann*

○ **Ladies of the Canyon** / Apr. 1970 / Reprise ✦✦✦✦

Contains several Mitchell standards, including "For Free," "Big Yellow Taxi," "Woodstock," and "The Circle Game." —*William Ruhlmann*

☆ **Blue** / Jun. 1971 / Reprise ✦✦✦✦✦

An extraordinarily revealing study in romance and dependency that begins with the girlish infatuation of "All I Want" and ends with the downcast but determined "The Last Time I Saw Richard." The spare music is dominated by Mitchell's newly expressive singing and her guitar and dulcimer work. —*William Ruhlmann*

○ **For the Roses** / Nov. 1972 / Asylum ✦✦✦✦

Mitchell rails against the music industry and defends the position of the artist in isolation, at the same time moving toward more of a pop sound, notably on the Top 25 hit "You Turn Me On, I'm a Radio." —*William Ruhlmann*

★ **Court & Spark** / Jan. 1974 / Asylum ✦✦✦✦✦

Mitchell's commercial peak came with this polished collection, which features the backup of a clutch of jazz-oriented session aces. "Help Me" was a Top Ten hit, and "Free Man in Paris" reached #22. —*William Ruhlmann*

Miles of Aisles / Nov. 1974 / Asylum ✦✦✦

Like most live albums, this two-record set was a profit-taking release on which the artist re-presented many of her old songs for a new acceptance now that she had a larger pop audience. Backed by the pop-jazz ensemble the L.A. Express, Mitchell reprised the best from her first five albums, pointedly ignoring *Court & Spark* and including two new cuts, "Love Or Money" and "Jericho." —*William Ruhlmann*

○ **The Hissing of Summer Lawns** / Nov. 1975 / Asylum ✦✦✦✦

Mitchell turned her back on stardom with this admirable, idiosyncratic effort. —*Dan Heilman*

Hejira / Nov. 1976 / Asylum ✦✦✦

Spare recordings prominently featuring the bass of Jaco Pastorius. Mitchell sings of life on the road, literally and figuratively. —*William Ruhlmann*

Don Juan's Reckless Daughter / Dec. 1977 / Asylum ✦✦

A big chunk of the pop audience Mitchell had earned with *Court & Spark* in 1974 deserted her in 1975 and 1976 when the follow-ups, *The Hissing of Summer Lawns* and *Hejira*, proved more difficult works. With this pretentious double album, Mitchell lost many of the loyal fans who'd stuck with her from the beginning but who now, as she spread her obscure poetic observations and thin melodies across whole sides of the album, found her disengaged from the close, personal observations that filled her best songs. This was Mitchell's last album to go gold. — *William Ruhlmann*

Mingus / Jun. 1979 / Asylum ✦✦✦
Mitchell sets lyrics to Charles Mingus's last melodies in collaboration with the composer and a Who's Who of prominent jazz musicians. — *William Ruhlmann*

Shadows & Light / Sep. 1980 / Asylum ✦✦
On her second double live album, Mitchell fronted a band that included fusion-jazz stars Pat Metheny, Lyle Mays, Michael Brecker, and Jaco Pastorius, who gave considerable validity to the jazzy compositions she had been writing over the last five years. — *William Ruhlmann*

Wild Things Run Fast / Oct. 1982 / Geffen ✦✦✦
On her first new studio album of original material in five years and her debut for Geffen Records, Joni Mitchell achieved more of a balance between her pop abilities and her jazz aspirations, meanwhile rediscovering a more direct, emotional lyric approach. The result was her best album since the mid-'70s. — *William Ruhlmann*

Dog Eat Dog / Oct. 1985 / Geffen ✦✦
Joni Mitchell here turned to guests like Michael McDonald, Thomas Dolby, Don Henley, James Taylor, and Wayne Shorter, continuing to straddle the worlds of California folk/pop and fusion jazz. Musically, it worked, although as a lyricist, Mitchell again took off after abstractions (one song railed against "the three great stimulants of the exhausted ones/Artifice, brutality and innocence"), such that, even when you could figure out what she was talking about, you didn't care. — *William Ruhlmann*

Chalk Mark in a Rain Storm / Mar. 1988 / Geffen ✦✦

Night Ride Home / Feb. 19, 1991 / Geffen ✦✦✦

Turbulent Indigo / 1994 / Warner Brothers ✦✦✦

Moby

Techno
During the late '80s and early '90s, Moby established himself as one of the leading DJs and artists in the American and English techno and rave scenes. Moby was a devout Christian and vegetarian, making him an anomaly in the hedonistic world of raves; his throbbing music, not his message, is what earned him a devoted cult following. By the time he signed to a major label in 1993, his bright, danceable techno was going out of style, being replaced by a new wave of ambient artists, yet he continued to make records that were among the best dance music of the decade. — *Stephen Thomas Erlewine*

○ **Moby** / 1992 / Instinct ✦✦✦✦
After a string of singles on the Instinct label, Moby released a self-titled album of his brand of high-energy techno. Though the beats aren't terribly original, the instrumentation is, and added vocal samples freshen the songs. This is challenging, decidedly un-repetitive music, and Moby's take on the *Twin Peaks* theme in "Go" is magnificent. — *John Bush*

Early Underground / 1993 / Instinct ✦✦✦
A fifteen-track compilation of Moby's early career, collected from seven releases, this album fails to show the diversity which makes his self-titled LP such a joy. The tracks here are acceptable techno, but they won't appeal to those who think repetition a sign of artistic deficiency. Most of the vocal samples are typical house/techno fare, but "Go (Original)" is a worthy song. — *John Bush*

Ambient / 1993 / Instinct ✦✦✦
Hoping to cash in on the ambient-house craze, Instinct Records released a collection of Moby's softer tracks. (To his credit, he had recorded these songs long before.) The album is quite good; it showcases his talent for majestic orchestral sounds and melodic synth layered over slower beats and percussion. — *John Bush*

● **Everything Is Wrong** / 1995 / Elektra ✦✦✦✦
For his first major label album, Moby pulled out all the stops, trying to fit as many different styles into 50 minutes. From fast break-beats to pseudo-industrial trash, ambient trance to dance-pop, Moby tries it all. It's not quite a statement of genius—for all the bluster, there really isn't that much difference between his songs, which are nearly all standard three-chord progressions, it's all in the production. What ties everything together is Moby's understanding of the beat. The pulse holds steady throughout the

record, making it sound like a very good night at a club. — *Stephen Thomas Erlewine*

Moby Grape

Group, Rock & Roll, Country-Rock, Psychedelic, Folk-Rock
There was no shortage of rock & roll in San Francisco in the late '60s. The Grateful Dead, the Jefferson Airplane, Big Brother and the Holding Company—the names go on and on. Moby Grape was, for a short while, one of the great ones. With a triple-guitar attack, the Grape presented taut, deftly arranged rock tunes, eschewing the jam-all-night approach of their contemporaries. They handled a ballad as well as a blistering rocker, and they weren't afraid to throw a country lick or a sweet harmony into the mix.

A combination of overhype and internal disarray killed the Grape after several years, and they never recaptured the brilliance of that debut. But 25 years later most of the original members were still working together, their brief discography regarded highly by a battery of loyal fans. — *Jeff Tamarkin*

○ **Moby Grape** / Jun. 1967 / San Francisco Sound ✦✦✦✦
Some consider this 1967 debut to be the most impressive of the San Francisco rock revolution. Not a wasted moment, and the Grape do jam. — *Jeff Tamarkin*

Wow/Grape Jam / 1968 / San Francisco Sound ✦✦✦
Disappointing followup includes indulgent jam session with guest musicians. — *Jeff Tamarkin*

Truly Fine Citizen / 1969 / Columbia ✦✦

Moby Grape '69 / 1969 / Columbia ✦✦✦

○ **20 Granite Creek** / 1971 / Reprise ✦✦✦✦

Moby Grape '84 / 1984 / San Francisco Sound ✦✦✦
The Grape go country-rock and pull it off. — *Jeff Tamarkin*

● **Vintage: Very Best** / May 11, 1993 / Columbia/Legacy ✦✦✦✦
It's hard to imagine a better-produced package of Moby Grape's work than this two-disc, 48-track condensation of their best late-'60s recordings. The first disc of this set centers around their entire 1967 self-titled debut LP (included in its entirety), which mixed blues, country, and folk influences with hard-charging psychedelic rock & roll. The result was one of the Summer of Love's more enduring works. The second disc boils their wildly inconsistent 1968–69 material down to a fairly strong and coherent selection. While it doesn't match the peak of the group's initial burst, it features some strong folk and country-rock originals that wear much better in the absence of the bloated jams and half-baked hard rock that could make their albums a chore to sit through. Each disc includes interesting demos, outtakes, and live performances that round out the legacy of this prodigiously talented but ill-fated band, which was overcome by internal strife and label/management difficulties after their promising debut. — *Richie Unterberger*

Modern English

Group, New Wave
British punk quintet from Colchester formed in 1979 and featuring singer and guitarist Robbie Grey, guitarist Gary McDowell, bassist Mick Conroy, keyboard player Stephen Walker, and drummer Richard Brown. By 1990, personnel changes had left the group a trio of Grey and Conroy, with keyboardist, guitarist, and singer Aaron Davidson. — *William Ruhlmann*

Mesh & Lace / 1981 / 4AD ✦✦✦

● **After the Snow** / 1982 / 4AD ✦✦✦✦
Modern English had evolved into a synthesizer-driven power-pop band by the release of this second album, which features their signature hit, "I Melt with You." Ignore the 1990 remake on Tee Vee Toons. — *William Ruhlmann*

○ **Ricochet Days** / 1984 / Sire ✦✦✦✦

Stop Start / 1986 / Sire ✦✦✦

Pillow Lips / 1990 / TVT ✦✦✦

The Mojo Men

Group, Psychedelic, Garage Rock, Pop/Rock
One of the earliest San Francisco rock bands, the Mojo Men had local hits on the Autumn label with "Dance with Me," "She's My Baby," and a cover of the Rolling Stones' "Off the Hook" in the mid-'60s. Their early sides displayed a raunchy but thin approach taken from the mold of British Invasion groups like the Stones

and Them. In 1966, after female drummer Jan Errico joined from the San Francisco folk-rock group the Vejtables, they moved to Reprise and pursued folkier psychedelic pop directions, and had a Top 40 hit with a baroque arrangement of Buffalo Springfield's "Sit Down I Think I Love You" in 1967. In their later days, they developed more intricate arrangements and harmonies that reflected the influence of the Mamas and the Papas and the Jefferson Airplane, although they weren't in the same leagues as those groups. Their many singles never fully displayed the band's considerable songwriting and vocal talents, and after changing their name to The Mojo and finally just Mojo, they disbanded in the late '60s. —*Richie Unterberger*

Dance With Me / 1984 / Eva ♦♦♦
A ragtag collection, drawn from their first seven singles and a few unreleased tracks. The later tracks, featuring Errico, are much more ornate productions that sound like a somewhat less refined Mamas & the Papas. A wealth of unreleased material (much of it original) that has circulated among collectors shows them to be a much more interesting group than this album would indicate; unfortunately, this anthology (the only one available) focuses on their more simplistic and derivative numbers. —*Richie Unterberger*

The Mojos

Group, British Invasion
Known mostly (if at all) in the States for doing the original version of "Everything's Alright" (covered by David Bowie on his *Pin Ups* album), the Mojos were one of the best Liverpool groups of the British Invasion. Besides "Everything's Alright"—a Top Five raver in the U.K.—they never scored any other British hits of note, though a couple squeezed into their top thirty. At times, they could be pretty wimpy, with jerky vocals and material that would have been at home with Gerry & the Pacemakers. But at other times, with their electric keyboard-driven sound, they echo the much tougher Manfred Mann. Way below the Beatles and even the Searchers in terms of quality, they were, except for the Swinging Blue Jeans and maybe the Merseybeats, the best of the rest in their home city. —*Richie Unterberger*

● **Working** / 1982 / Edsel ♦♦♦♦
This compilation includes 16 tracks recorded by the group between 1963 and 1965, taken from rare singles and their sole EP. This stuff isn't exactly timeless, but it has a giddy Merseybeat enthusiasm that remains infectious. Comes with a detailed history of the band. —*Richie Unterberger*

Moments

Group, Soul, R&B
One of the most consistent R&B aggregations of the '70s, the Moments enjoyed a string of major hits throughout the decade. The Hackensack, NJ, trio introduced themselves and the Stang label with "Not on the Outside" in 1968, and topped the R&B charts in 1970 with the gold-plated "Love on a Two-Way Street," produced by Sylvia Robinson (one half of Mickey and Sylvia). Other major soul smashes by the Moments included "If I Didn't Care" and "All I Have" in 1970, "Sexy Mama" in 1973, and another #1 R&B item, "Look at Me (I'm in Love)," in 1975. Members Harry Ray, Al Goodman, and William Brown changed their billing to Ray, Goodman & Brown in 1978 and topped the soul lists the next year with the slickly harmonized "Special Lady" on Polydor. The renamed trio remained potent soul hitmakers through the '80s. —*Bill Dahl*

● **Greatest Hits [Sequel]** / 1994 / Sequel ♦♦♦♦
○ **The Greatest Hits** / Chess ♦♦♦♦
This album collects "Love on a Two-Way Street," "Sexy Mama," and other worthy tracks. —*Dan Heilman*

Eddie Money

b. Mar. 2, 1949
Pop/Rock
Since his 1977 self-titled debut, Eddie Money (born Edward Mahoney) has enjoyed a long career as a purveyor of mainstream guitar pop/rock. Money scored quite a few hits in the early to mid-'80s, peaking with the number four 1986 hit "Take Me Home Tonight." After that, his albums didn't command the marketplace they once did. His other hits include "Baby, Hold On" (#11), "Two Tickets to Paradise" (#22), "Shakin'" (#63), "I Wanna Go Back" (#14), "Think I'm in Love" (#16), and "Walk on Water" (#9). —*Rick Clark*

○ **Eddie Money** / 1977 / Columbia ♦♦♦♦
The debut album of his raspy-voiced, pop/rock tunes charted in the Top 40 and went platinum. —*Donna DiChario*

Life for the Taking / 1978 / Columbia ♦♦♦
Eddie Money's second album wasn't as consistent as his debut, featuring on a slicker production that relied heavily on current pop trends, including disco and arena rock. Nevertheless, the record had a couple of good tracks, including the single "Can't Keep A Good Man Down." —*Stephen Thomas Erlewine*

Playing for Keeps / 1980 / Columbia ♦♦
If *Life for the Taking* made concessions to pop trends, *Playing for Keeps* was sunk by Eddie Money's attempt to fit into the mainstream. While his production had never been raw, the sound of the album was entirely too glossy for album rock radio, while Money couldn't write songs with enough memorable hooks to earn him radio play. The result was one of his weakest albums. —*Stephen Thomas Erlewine*

No Control / 1983 / Columbia ♦♦♦
On *No Control*, Eddie Money found the perfect middle ground between AOR production and pop hooks, with the singles "Think I'm In Love" and "Shakin'" sending the rocker back into platinum territory. —*Stephen Thomas Erlewine*

Where's the Party / 1985 / Columbia ♦♦
After the comeback of *No Control*, Money produced the lackluster *Where's the Party* Although the album replicated the formula of its predecessor, it lacked a collection of hook-filled songs, which made *Where's the Party* Money's lowest-charting record to date. —*Stephen Thomas Erlewine*

○ **Can't Hold Back** / 1986 / Columbia ♦♦♦♦
It featured his biggest-selling single—"Take Me Home Tonight," an upbeat duet with Ronnie Spector of the Ronettes. —*Donna DiChario*

Nothing to Lose / 1988 / Columbia ♦♦♦
Throughout his career, Eddie Money has followed a successful album with another record that sounded remarkably similar to its predecessor and *Nothing to Lose* was no exception to the rule. However, *Nothing to Lose* was marginally better than *Playing for Keeps* and *Where's the Party*, featuring a handful of well-crafted mainstream pop songs, including the Top 10 hit "Walk on Water." —*Stephen Thomas Erlewine*

● **Greatest Hits: Sound of Money** / 1989 / Columbia ♦♦♦♦
Money's albums are often uneven combinations of solid tracks and filler. This collection has all the hits with none of the misses, including "Baby Hold On," "Two Tickets to Paradise," and "No Control." —*Donna DiChario*

Unplug It In / Nov. 3, 1992 / Columbia ♦♦
Eddie Money was one of the first rockers to make an attempt to capitalize on MTV's successful *Unplugged* series, releasing this record in 1992. Like any "unplugged" recording, the album features a collection of the rocker's biggest hits performed acoustically. However, Money's songs have always been big, anthemic pop-rockers, which benefitted from their slick studio production, which doesn't make them good candidates for acoustic treatments. *Unplug It In* confirms this fact, as even his best songs sound limp in these stripped-back arrangements. —*Stephen Thomas Erlewine*

Zoot Money's Big Roll Band

Group, British Invasion
London-based pianist and R&B enthusiast Zoot Money (real name George Bruno) put together this combo in 1964, and for a time achieved notable success on the club circuit, before he and lead guitarist Andy Summers gave up the Big Roll Band to join one of the later line-ups of the Animals, during their psychedelic era. Money also played on the Animals' 1983 reunion tour and the accompanying album. —*Bruce Eder*

● **Live at Klook's Kleek** / PolyGram ♦♦♦♦
One of the most accomplished pieces of British R&B to actually get captured on record, with influences ranging from Memphis to Motown, and some excellent playing by a youthful Andy Summers. —*Bruce Eder*

Monie Love

Rap, Urban
London-born Simone Wilson aka Monie Love was featured on Queen Latifah's single "Ladies First" while still a teen. Her CDs as

a leader have been erratic, often suggesting much more than they delivered, though they've usually contained at least one strong single. After *Down to Earth*, Love issued *In a Word or Two* in 1993. —*Ron Wynn*

Down to Earth / 1990 / Warner Brothers ✦✦✦
The mood moves through vibrant, concerned, bemused, and resigned. Nice samples and good production. —*Ron Wynn*

● **In a Word or 2** / 1993 / Warner Brothers ✦✦✦✦
Monie Love's second CD was more ambitious, taking a harder, less pop tone and approach. She spoke frankly and with clarity about such topics as promiscuity and self-esteem, while her rapping was more focused, her beats starker and more forceful, and the rhymes less gimmicky. —*Ron Wynn*

The Monkees

Group, Pop/Rock
To nonmusical TV executives aware that the pop market was exploding in 1965, the idea of auditioning cute actors to star in a show featuring a fabricated group called the Monkees (Davy Jones, Michael Nesmith, Peter Tork, and Mickey Dolenz) seemed like marketing genius. The public agreed, and the show was a huge success for several years.

The Monkees could sing, and Mike Nesmith actually was a singer/songwriter, and guitarist. They also had access to the best material the professional songwriting world had to offer, covering songs by Neil Diamond, Goffin & King, Harry Nilsson, David Gates, Boyce & Hart, Mann & Weil, Leiber & Stoller, Paul Williams, and many more. As a result, the Monkees were a veritable pop-hit machine, charting with "Last Train to Clarksville" (#1), "I'm a Believer" (#1), "A Little Bit Me, a Little Bit You" (#2), "Daydream Believer" (#1), "Valerie" (#3), "Pleasant Valley Sunday" (#3), "I'm Not Your Stepping Stone" (#20), and many others. After the initial success, the Monkees lobbied for more artistic control and got it. The result, *Headquarters*, was number one on the charts and the album went gold. Nevertheless, the high quality of material soon diminished and, with the demise of the show, the Monkees called it quits in 1971.

Michael Nesmith went solo and recorded some fine country-rock albums, scoring a hit with "Joanne" (#21). He also became very involved with video production, forming the Pacific Arts Corporation in 1977.

A well-orchestrated Monkees campaign returned the band and their show to new popularity in 1986, thanks in part to much MTV coverage. In August 1986, seven of their albums returned on the charts. Rhino Records released an extensive four-CD boxed set in 1991. —*Rick Clark*

The Monkees / Oct. 1966 / Rhino ✦✦✦
The Monkees did virtually nothing besides sing lead vocals on their full-length debut; poor Peter Tork didn't even get to do that, his contribution being limited to one of the six guitar parts on "Papa Gene's Blues." Given that it wasn't a project of high integrity, it wasn't bad—in fact, much of this is reasonably gutsy pop/rock, including their TV theme song, the hits "Last Train To Clarksville" and "Take A Giant Step," and various decent songs by top Brill Building tunesmiths like Goffin/King, Boyce/Hart, and David Gates. Nesmith was allowed one composition ("Papa Gene's Blues") that indicated his country-rock direction. The CD reissue includes unremarkable bonus tracks of alternate versions of the Monkees theme and a couple of songs that would turn up on subsequent LPs. —*Richie Unterberger*

More of the Monkees / Jan. 10, 1967 / Rhino ✦✦✦
Second album, same as the first, virtually: a huge single ("I'm A Believer"/"Steppin' Stone"), a couple of token Mike Nesmith songs (including "Mary, Mary," previously recorded by the Paul Butterfield Blues Band and a rap hit for Run-D.M.C. in 1988), tunes by Boyce/Hart, Goffin/King, Neil Diamond, Jeff Barry, Neil Sedaka, and Carole Bayer, no participation from the group other than lead vocals. The band was quite upset at their lack of input at the time, but it's relatively decent (if quite harmless) pop/rock, featuring one of their best album tracks, "She." Like all of the Rhino CD reissues, it adds marginally interesting bonus tracks of unreleased alternate versions, including an early take of "I'm a Believer." —*Richie Unterberger*

Headquarters / May 22, 1967 / Rhino ✦✦✦
For their third album, the Monkees were determined to wrest control of the creative process, and with producer Chip Douglas functioning as frequent bassist and auxiliary member, they were in-

deed able to play most of the instruments and write much of the material. It would be nice to report that the result far exceeded previous efforts and established the group as visionary artists, but in fact this was, again, pleasantly inoffensive pop/rock. There was more of a country flavor and a sense of personal involvement, though the group still tapped songwriting pros like Boyce/Hart and Mann/Weil for about half the songs. Standouts included Nesmith's "You Just May Be The One," one of his best Monkee tunes, and Tork's "For Pete's Sake," which became the show's closing theme. The CD reissue includes six unreleased tracks and alternate takes, a couple of which (Nilsson's "All Of Your Toys" and Nesmith's "The Girl I Knew Somewhere") rank among their finest. —*Richie Unterberger*

○ **Pisces, Aquarius, Capricorn & Jones Ltd.** / Nov. 14, 1967 / Rhino ✦✦✦✦
One of their better efforts, featuring the double-sided hit "Pleasant Valley Sunday"/"Words," and some of their best album tracks, like "She Hangs Out," "Star Collector," and "Cuddly Toy," the last of which was one of the first Nilsson songs to be covered by a major artist. As usual, some of the country-rockers and half-baked psychedelic tunes are tedious, though a couple tracks are notable for featuring some of the first uses of a Moog synthesizer on a rock record. The CD reissue adds some previously unissued alternate mixes, as well as the killer soulful B-side "Goin' Down," which ranks as one of their very best tracks despite its obscurity. —*Richie Unterberger*

The Birds, The Bees & The Monkees / Apr. 22, 1968 / Rhino ✦✦
Not one of their better efforts, dominated almost wholly by session musicians (with the occasional songwriting and instrumental contribution by Mike Nesmith) and containing too many sickly sweet Davy Jones-sung numbers. It does have the hits "Daydream Believer" and "Valerie," as well as Nesmith's "Tapioca Tundra," which just inched into the Top 40, but overall the material is pretty weak. The CD adds some previously unissued songs and alternate takes, the only one of interest being Peter Tork's "Lady's Baby," which sounds like a Buffalo Springfield outtake with its laidback country/folk/rock flavor. —*Richie Unterberger*

○ **Head** / Dec. 1, 1968 / Rhino ✦✦✦✦
Like the film from which it came, the soundtrack to *Head* was far from a masterpiece, but had some inspired moments. The spacy "Porpoise Song," written by Gerry Goffin and Carole King, was their final Top 20 hit, the tough-rocking "Circle Sky" was probably the best song Mike Nesmith wrote for the group, "Can You Dig It" was one of Peter Tork's best contributions, and "As We Go Along" and "Daddy's Song" are little known songs by Carole King and Nilsson, respectively. As a listening experience, it's made more difficult by the juxtaposition of music and dialogue from the film. The CD reissue adds bonus unissued jingles and alternate takes, highlighted by a live version of "Circle Sky." —*Richie Unterberger*

Instant Replay / Feb. 15, 1969 / Rhino ✦✦
By 1969's *Instant Replay*, it was all over but the funeral. Peter Tork had already left the fold and the songs were little more than disjointed solo vehicles for the remaining three, combined with older unreleased tracks from the vaults. This afforded far too much rope for schmaltzy Jones ballads, although Nesmith salvages the day once again with tasty country inflections on the wistful "Don't Wait For Me" and "While I Cry." This otherwise slight collection—for intensive Monkees fans only—is at least beefed up by some interesting previously unreleased songs, rather than just alternate mixes. —*Roch Parisien*

The Monkees Present / Oct. 1969 / Rhino ✦✦
Like *Instant Replay*, *The Monkees Present* was incoherent collection of pop and country-rock. Although most of the album was well-produced but bland, Mike Nesmith's contributions, particularly "Listen to the Band," indicated that he was continuing to grow as a songwriter. However, his handful of songs couldn't save the album from being a rather desultory affair. After the record's release, Nesmith left the band to pursue a solo career. —*Stephen Thomas Erlewine*

Changes / Jun. 1970 / Rhino ✦
For most intents and purposes, the Monkees had broken up before the recording of *Changes*, their final record. Peter Tork and Mike Nesmith had left the band, leaving only Mickey Dolenz and Davy Jones. Although Dolenz was a relatively accomplished songwriter, he only contributed one song to *Changes*, which meant both he and Jones were vehicles for a variety of professional songwriters,

particularly Jeff Barry, who also produced the majority of the album. Most of the material was bland pop, featuring a couple of R&B and soul inflections to liven up the sound. Neither Dolenz or Jones sounds inspired by the material, which isn't surprising—out of the 12 songs, only Boyce and Hart's "I Never Though It Peculiar" makes any sort of impression. The lack of worthwhile material and the slick, passionless production easily make *Changes* the weakest record the Monkees released. Until they reunited for *Pool It*, that is. —*Stephen Thomas Erlewine*

Pool It / 1986 / Rhino ✦
Failed '80s reunion album is more "fake" sounding than anything from their prime. Stick to the originals. —*Jeff Tamarkin*

● **Then & Now . . . the Best of the Monkees** / 1986 / Arista ✦✦✦✦
The best of the single-CD collections, with 25 tracks, most of them true Monkees classics. —*Jeff Tamarkin*

Live 1967 / 1987 / Rhino ✦✦
Still believe the Monkees didn't play their own music? This concert recording proves otherwise, and you know what? They played well! —*Jeff Tamarkin*

Missing Links / 1987 / Rhino ✦✦✦
A fine selection of rarities and oddities that every Monkee maniac with more than a passing interest should own. —*Jeff Tamarkin*

Missing Links 2 / 1990 / Rhino ✦✦✦
19 rare and unreleased tracks that, like the rest of the Monkees' output, ranges from excellent to insufferable, with plenty of mediocre material between. The highlights are the sprightly pop-rocker "All The King's Horses" (a 1966 Mike Nesmith original) and alternate versions of two of the group's best singles, "Words" and "Valerie." These alternate takes aren't exactly better, but they are definitely different and less elaborately produced. Most of the rest is either lightweight 1966 pop-rock or weedy 1968 Mike Nesmith country-rock tunes that foreshadow his solo work; several cuts are alternate versions of songs that were hardly notable efforts in the first place. An exception is the live 1968 recording of the unusually forceful Nesmith original "Circle Sky," which was featured in their movie *Head* (although a studio version was substituted on the actual soundtrack album). Odds and ends like an instrumental banjo piece by Peter Tork and a Spanish Christmas carol are pleasant but inessential. A thoughtfully compiled CD, it nonetheless really gives this group more respect than they're due by treating these artifacts with such importance. —*Richie Unterberger*

○ **Listen to the Band** / 1991 / Rhino ✦✦✦✦
A four-CD boxed set that includes every Monkees track a fan could want, and probably much more. Excessive, but a collector's dream. —*Jeff Tamarkin*

BOOK

✦✦✦✦ **The Monkees Tale**, by Eric Lefcowitz (Last Gasp, 1985). The Monkees were not remotely on the level of the Beatles, as some revisionists would have you believe; nor were they the no-talents they've sometimes been accused of being. This fine, if a bit slim, bio takes the appropriate middle road, evaluating their music and acting seriously, but not hesitating to point out their shortcomings. An excellent, straightforward account, this reveals the truth behind some oft-heard myths, with the help of behind-the-scenes reports from key handlers like record producer Chip Douglas and Bob Rafelson and Bert Schneider (producers of the group's TV show). Has a lot of interesting studio and tour stories, documenting their struggle with Don Kirshner for a modicum of artistic freedom, an in-depth examination of their cult movie *Head*, profiles of each Monkee, lots of photos, and complete discography/videography. —*Richie Unterberger*

The Monks

Group, Rock & Roll, Garage Rock
One of the strangest stories in rock history, the Monks were formed in the early '60s by American G.I.s stationed in Germany. After their discharge, the group stayed on in Germany as the Torquays, a fairly standard "beat" band. After changing their name to the Monks in the mid-'60s, they also changed their music, attitude, and appearance radically. Gone were standard oldie covers, replaced by furious, minimalistic original material that anticipated the blunt, harsh commentary of the punk era. Their insistent rhythms recalled martial beats and polkas as much as garage rock, and the weirdness quotient was heightened by electric banjo, berserk organ runs, and occasional bursts of feedback guitar. To

prove that they meant business, the Monks shaved the top of their heads and performed their songs—crude diatribes about the Vietnam war, dehumanized society, and love/hate affairs with girls—in actual monks' clothing.

This was pretty strong stuff for 1966 Germany, and their shocking repertoire and attire was received with more confusion than hostility or warm praise. Well-known in Germany as a live act, their sole album and several singles didn't take off in a big way, and were never released in the U.S., it was rumored, because the lyrical content was deemed too shocking. They disbanded in confusion around 1967, but their album—one of the most oddball constructions in all of rock—gained a hardcore cult among collectors, and has ironically made them much more popular and influential on an international level than they were during their lifetime. Bassist Eddie Shaw's 1994 autobiography, *Black Monk Time,* is a fascinating narrative of the Monks' stranger-than-fiction story. —*Richie Unterberger*

● **Black Monk Time** / 1966 / Repertoire ✦✦✦✦
The Monks' only album is packed with angst anthems on the order of "Shut Up," "I Hate You," "Complication," and "Drunken Maria." The CD reissue adds their two later non-LP singles, making it a complete document of the Monks' entire recorded legacy. —*Richie Unterberger*

BOOK

✦✦✦✦ **Black Monk Time**, by Thomas Edward Shaw & Anita Klemke (Carson Street, 1994). It's rare that a lengthy book is devoted to an obscure cult rock group, and rare that the story of such a group merits so much space. *Black Monk Time* is an exception. Written by former Monks bassist Eddie Shaw and his wife, this is the firsthand account of one of the strangest rock groups of all time. With humor and insight, Shaw writes of the band's transformation from a cover band formed by American soldiers stationed in Germany in the early '60s to the bizarre, blank-generation-punks-before-their-time outfit they became in the mid-'60s. Even if you've never heard the Monks (and most people haven't), this is fascinating reading, covering the joys and heartbreak of a struggling band from the inside: the intense personality conflicts, the tragicomic foulups on stage, at the recording studio, and on the road, the groupies, the substance abuse, the difficulty in playing up to an image (and few images were stranger than the Monks'), the trials of keeping a band together in the face of limited success, and above all, the sense of displacement as an American band based in Germany, and as a group playing bleak minimalist garage rock at the height of the British Invasion. It's a strange trail indeed, with occasional intersections with superstars like the Kinks and, in their final days, Jimi Hendrix (for whom the Monks opened when Hendrix was just starting his solo career). Hard to find, but fully worth the search. —*Richie Unterberger*

Chris Montez

b. Jan. 17, 1943
Rock & Roll
One of the leading rockers in the Los Angeles Hispanic community after the tragic death of Ritchie Valens, Chris Montez later mellowed out under the tutelage of Herb Alpert and tallied several MOR-style hits. His first smash was on Monogram in 1962, "Let's Dance." It was a grinding rocker with roller-rink organ. Montez changed his attitude after signing with A&M. With Alpert producing, Montez adopted an easygoing approach on "Call Me," "The More I See You," and "Time after Time," all solid sellers in 1966. The formula quickly faded, however, and his final chart entry came the following year with "Because of You." —*Bill Dahl*

● **All-Time Greatest Hits** / 1991 / DCC ✦✦✦✦
Montez began as a Ritchie Valens-style rocker and reemerged as a crooner of pop ballads in the mid-'60s. He excelled at both styles, each of which is amply documented here. —*Jeff Tamarkin*

Ronnie Montrose

Hard Rock, Heavy Metal
Guitarist Ronnie Montrose began his career as a backing musician, playing with Van Morrison, Boz Scaggs and Edgar Winter. He finally formed his own band in 1973. Named after the guitarist, Montrose also featured vocalist Sammy Hagar, bassist Bill Church, and drummer Denny Carmassi; they released their debut album in 1974 and Church was replaced by Alan Fitzgerald shortly after

its release. Released the following year, *Paper Money* confirmed the band's status as one of the more popular hard rock acts of their era. However, Hagar was fired after completing the *Paper Money* tour. Bob James replaced him and keyboardist Jim Alcivar joined the band, yet Montrose's next two albums—1975's *Warner Brothers Presents Montrose* and 1976's *Jump on It*—were commercial failures.

Ronnie Montrose broke up the band after the release of *Jump on It* and began his own solo career with the all-instrumental *Open Fire* (1978). Montrose then formed another hard rock group, Gamma. Gamma recorded three albums between 1979 and 1982. After they broke up in 1982, Montrose began his solo career again. Alternating between hard rock and jazz-rock, he has released six albums since. —*Stephen Thomas Erlewine*

WB Presents Ronnie Montrose / 1975 / Warner Brothers ♦♦

Jump on It / 1976 / Warner Brothers ♦♦♦
This hard-rockin' album, produced by Edgar Winter, includes vocalist Bob James. —*David Szatmary*

Territory / Oct. 1986 / Passport ♦♦

Mean / 1987 / Enigma ♦♦

● **Speed of Sound** / 1988 / Enigma ♦♦♦♦
The perfect showcase for guitar-whiz Montrose, who wails against an unlikely backdrop of ex-Mitch Ryder drummer Johnny Bee Badanjek and the sound of synthesizers. —*David Szatmary*

Diva Station / 1990 / Enigma ♦♦

Mutatis Mutandis / 1991 / IRS ♦♦♦
Out of his many solo albums, *Mutatis Mutandis* remains one of his best efforts. —*John Book*

Music from Here / 1994 / Fearless Urge ♦♦♦

Moody Blues

Group, Art-Rock/Progressive-Rock, British Invasion, Pop/Rock
Although they're best known today for their lush, lyrically and musically profound (some would say bombastic) psychedelic-era albums and singles, the Moody Blues started out as one of the better rhythm-and-blues based combos of the British invasion. The Moody Blues' history began in Birmingham, England, where one of the more successful bands during that time was El Riot and the Rebels, co-founded by Ray Thomas (harmonica, vocals; b. Stourport-on-Severn, December 29, 1941) and Mike Pinder (keyboards, vocals; b. Birmingham, December 27, 1941). Pinder left the band, first for a gig with Jackie Lynton and then a stint in the army. In May of 1963, he and Thomas reunited under the auspices of the Krew Cats. They were good enough to get overseas bookings in Germany, where English rock bands were the rage in the country's more notorious red light districts. Upon their return to Birmingham in November of 1963, the entire English musical landscape was occupied by 250 groups, all of them vying for gigs in perhaps a dozen clubs. Thomas and Pinder decided to try and go professional, recruiting members from some of the best groups working in Birmingham. This included Denny Laine (vocals, guitar; b. Jersey, October 29, 1944), Graeme Edge (drums; b. Rochester, Staffordshire, March 30, 1941), and Clint Warwick (bass, vocals; b. Birmingham, June 25, 1939). The Moody Blues made their debut in Birmingham in May of 1964, and quickly earned the notice and later the services of manager Tony Secunda. A major tour, including some London dates, was quickly booked, and the band landed an engagement at the Marquee Club, which resulted in a contract with England's Decca Records less than six months after their formation. The group's first single, "Steal Your Heart Away," released in England during September of 1964, didn't touch the British charts.

Their second single "Go Now," recorded in the fall of 1964 and released in November of that year, fulfilled every expectation and more, reaching number one in England during a 14 week chart run; in America, it peaked at number 10. Following it up was easier said than done. Despite their fledgling songwriting efforts and the access they had to American demos, this version of the Moody Blues never came up with another single success. By the end of the spring of 1965, the frustration was palpable within the band, but nothing seemed to help their chart status.

The group decided to make their fourth single, "From The Bottom of My Heart," an experiment with a different sound. "I think 'From the Bottom of My Heart' was the real turning point for the band," Pinder commented in 1994. "That was where we began try-

ing to experiment with sound, writing with ideas that were more sophisticated—we developed a style, using reverb on the vocal, and getting various kinds of sounds and effects out of the piano that we hadn't done before." Unfortunately, the single only reached number 22 on the British charts following its release in May of 1965. Ultimately, the grind of touring coupled with the strains facing the group, became too much for Warwick, who exited in the spring of 1966, and by August of 1966 Laine had left as well. Warwick was replaced by John Lodge (b. Birmingham July 20, 1945). His introduction to the band was followed in late 1966 by the addition of Justin Hayward (b. Swindon October 14, 1946).

The reconstituted Moody Blues set about keeping afloat financially, mostly playing in Europe, recording the occasional single. Their big break came from Deram Records, an imprint of their Decca label, which in 1967 decided that it needed a long-playing record to promote its new "Deramic Stereo." The Moody Blues were picked for the proposed project, a rock version of Dvorak's *New World Symphony*, and immediately convinced the staff producer and the engineer to abandon the source material and permit the group to use a series of its own compositions that depicted an archetypal "day," from morning to night. Using the tracks laid down by the band, and orchestrated by conductor Peter Knight, the resulting album *Days of Future Passed*, became a landmark in the band's history.

The mix of rock and classical sounds was new, and at first puzzled the record company, but eventually the record was issued. This album, and its singles "Nights In White Satin" and "Tuesday Afternoon," hooked directly into the musical sides of the Summer of Love and its aftermath. *In Search of the Lost Chord* (1968) abandoned the orchestra in favor of the Mellotron, which quickly became a part of their signature sound.

By the time of 1969's *To Our Children's Children's Children*, the group found themselves painted into something of a corner. Working in the studio with the process of overdubbing, they'd created albums that were essentially the work of 20 or 30 Moody Blues. Beginning with *A Question of Balance* (1970), the group made the decision to record albums that they could play in concert, reducing their reliance on overdubbing and toughening up their sound. By the release of *Seventh Sojourn* (1972)—a chart-topping album—the strain of touring and recording steadily for five years was beginning to take its toll, and following an extended international tour, the band decided to take a break from working together, which ultimately lasted five years. During this era, Hayward and Lodge recorded a very successful duet album, *Blue Jays* (1975), and all five members did solo albums. By 1977, however, the group members had made the decision to reunite, a process complicated by the fact that Pinder had moved to California during that period. Although all five participated in the resulting album, *Octave* (1978), there were stresses during its recording, and Pinder was ultimately unhappy enough with the LP to decline to tour with the band. The reunion tour was a success, with Patrick Moraz brought in to replace Pinder on the keyboards, and the album topped the charts.

The group's follow-up record, *Long Distance Voyager* (1981), was even more popular, though by this time a schism was beginning to develop between the band and the critical community. The Moody Blues continued to play songs that ran toward the mystical and romantic, and were beginning to seem out-of-step with the rest of the music world, at least to the rock press, whose members made no secret of their contempt for the group's sound. Although they continued to reach the middle levels of the charts, and even ascended reasonably close to the top with the Hayward single "In Your Wildest Dreams" (1986), the Moody Blues were no longer anywhere near the cutting edge of music. By the end of the 1980s, they were perceived as a nostalgia act, albeit one with a huge audience. Then, in 1992, the group began making appearances on stage supported by full orchestra, something they had never done before, and the response was phenomenal—arena-sized crowds, sold-out shows, and a new enthusiasm by the fans for the old songs. In 1994, a four CD set called *Time Traveller* was released. In early 1995, the group—having completed a U.S. tour—began work on another studio album. —*Bruce Eder*

The Magnificent Moodies / 1965 / Polydor ♦♦♦
The definitive collection of the band's rhythm-and-blues period, containing every track known to exist. All—except for "Go Now," which sounds very tinny here—are beautifully remastered, and annotated with great (if occasionally inaccurate) detail. About a dozen of the 20-odd songs here are among the finest R&B tracks

recorded during the British Invasion. Out-of-print in America, but worth finding. —*Bruce Eder*

○ **Days of Future Passed** / 1967 / Polydor ♦♦♦♦
The reconstituted Moody Blues, with Justin Hayward and John Lodge established on guitar, bass, and vocals, venture into progressive rock territory with the London Festival Orchestra and have their first major success, both with the album and the singles "Nights in White Satin" and "Tuesday Afternoon." The material seems pretentious but really rocks pretty hard, and the orchestral interludes, courtesy of the late Peter Knight, have an epic sweep that still dazzles the ear. In 1967, a lot of people hungry for something to put on the turntable after *Sgt. Pepper* turned to this, and turned it into an international hit with good reason. —*Bruce Eder*

In Search of the Lost Chord / 1968 / Polydor ♦♦♦
The Moody Blues discover drugs and mysticism as a basis for songwriting, and come up with a compelling psychedelic album, filled with songs about Dr. Timothy Leary and the astral plane and other psychedelic-era concerns, all resplendent in sweeping choruses and an elegant mix of conventional rock instruments augmented by flutes, sitars, tablas, cellos, and electronic orchestrations. Beautiful and elegant. —*Bruce Eder*

○ **On the Threshold of a Dream** / 1969 / Polydor ♦♦♦♦
Mysticism gives way to science-fiction on this album, which abandons Indian sitars and tablas in favor of more traditional sounding orchestrations (created on the Mellotron), and also rocks a little harder in spots than their previous records. —*Bruce Eder*

To Our Children's Children's Children / 1969 / Polydor ♦♦♦
The Moody Blues' most personal album was also, oddly enough, the poorest seller among their psychedelic period releases, taking longer to go gold. The material here dwells on time, space, and distance, with a curious mood of loneliness to several of the songs. The last of the band's "studio"-based albums (that is, built up with multiple overdubs, regardless of the difficulty in recreating the material on stage), it has a very lush, rich sound, although the group avoids extended suites of the kind on their previous two albums. And Hayward's "Gypsy" and "Watching and Waiting" are among the best songs in their history. —*Bruce Eder*

Question of Balance / 1970 / Polydor ♦♦♦
A return to a harder rocking sound in the studio, beginning with the rippling "Question" and including the oft-overlooked "Tortoise and the Hare" (a great rock number in concert), as well as the gorgeous "And the Tide Rushes In." —*Bruce Eder*

● **Every Good Boy Deserves Favour** / 1971 / Polydor ♦♦♦♦
The most well realized of the band's psychedelic era albums, filled with gorgeous melodies, superbly crafted songs, and a dazzling array of keyboard and guitar pyrotechnics—"Emily's Song," "Nice to Be Here," and "My Song" are among the best work the group has ever done, and "The Story in Your Eyes" is the best rock number they've ever cut, with a riveting beat and the kind of insights one expected more out of George Harrison at his best. —*Bruce Eder*

Seventh Sojourn / 1972 / Polydor ♦♦♦
The group's hardest rocking album, and one that closed their psychedelic period. The songs generally lack the rich Mellotron orchestrations of the earlier records, and most of the songs are built around John Lodge's and Graeme Edge's driving rhythm section— "New Horizons" was the most romantic number the band had debuted since "Nights in White Satin," while "I'm Just a Singer in a Rock 'n Roll Band" showed the sudden emergence of John Lodge as a major songwriter in the group. —*Bruce Eder*

○ **This Is the Moody Blues** / 1974 / Polydor ♦♦♦♦
A double-D best-of covering the group's 1967–1972 period, its tapes recompiled and remastered for the compact disc reissue. The selection is reasonably complete, although it leaves out one excellent number for every two that are included, and the individual CDs are probably a better investment. The new liner notes by John Tracy are also thoughtful and informative. —*Bruce Eder*

In the Beginning / 1975 / Deram ♦♦♦
A deliberately misleading attempt to resell the "Go Now"-era R&B material in a psychedelic style package. Protests from the band, coupled with a nasty reaction from fans, resulted in its being deleted very quickly, making it a genuine rarity. —*Bruce Eder*

Caught Live + 5 / 1977 / PolyGram ♦♦♦
An unusual mixture of three live sides cut at Royal Albert Hall in 1969 and a group of old, previously unreleased studio sides (the latter now included on the *Prelude* CD) from 1967–69, intended to

herald the band's return to recording and touring in 1978. The live material is a little sloppy but has a fair amount of energy (several of the band members now believe they were too stoned to have played well at the show)—after a long delay, the concert reportedly has been okayed for CD reissue. The studio material isn't anywhere near their best, but several of them stand up on their own, and fill in some holes in the band's history. —*Bruce Eder*

Octave / 1978 / Polydor ♦♦♦
The group's first post-reunion album is uneven in spots, but Justin Hayward's songwriting and singing maintains its haunting romantic edge, and John Lodge shows a newly prominent and energetic voice as a composer. Keyboard-player Mike Pinder exited after finishing this album, leaving behind one song on the record. —*Bruce Eder*

Long Distance Voyager / 1981 / Polydor ♦♦♦
The group's biggest-selling album of the '80s also marked a turning point in their fortunes, where they began losing even the mainstream critics. The music has drive, and is extremely well played and produced (this was the only album the band ever got to do at their own, custom-designed Threshold Studios), but also seemed very dated in its time, with a '60s sensibility that was out of place. —*Bruce Eder*

The Present / 1983 / Polydor ♦♦
The group's best years were clearly behind them, as evidenced by this record, which lacked much of the energy of their previous efforts and seemed predictable throughout. Reasonably well-played but very much limited in interest to the band's hardcore fans. —*Bruce Eder*

● **Voices in the Sky: Best of the Moody Blues** / 1985 / Polydor ♦♦♦♦
A good sampling of the Moody Blues' greatest hits from the 1960s and '70s; it's fine for those who only want the hits. —*Stephen Thomas Erlewine*

The Other Side of Life / 1986 / Polydor ♦♦♦
The group's best album in several years benefitted mostly from the presence of the Top Ten single "Your Wildest Dreams," which managed to turn their status as dinosaurs from the '60s psychedelic era into a plus, with a great beat to boot and a very entertaining video featuring young British psychedelic rockers the Mood Six playing the young Moody Blues. The rest was fairly routine, alas, but the single was strong enough on its own terms to revive interest in the group one more time out. —*Bruce Eder*

Prelude / 1987 / Polydor ♦♦♦
A collection of little known "transitional" period tracks in the group's history, dating from the period after guitarist/vocalist Denny Laine exited, and after Justin Hayward and John Lodge replaced them, but before the band had fully hit upon a new sound. Some of the stuff is suprisingly Beatle-esque, and "Love and Beauty" marks the group's first use of the Mellotron and the layered vocals that would define their later psychedelic-era sound. And all of this is rounded out by the presence of the late-'60s studio tracks that filled out their 1978 compilation *Caught Live + 5.* This disc, out-of-print in America, for fans it is worth tracking down as an import. —*Bruce Eder*

○ **Greatest Hits** / 1989 / Polydor ♦♦♦♦
All of the Moody Blues' best songs and biggest hits from the 1980s are collected on *Greatest Hits*; it's the most mainstream pop-oriented material the band has ever recorded. —*Stephen Thomas Erlewine*

A Night at Red Rocks With The Colorado . . . / 1993 / Polydor ♦♦♦
Having succeeded in the '80s by drawing on '60s nostalgia with a song ("Your Wildest Dreams") and video, the Moody Blues in the '90s began tailoring entire shows to recapture their '60s glory days—and they succeeded. Performing on tour with a series of regional orchestras, they brought the majesty of their old studio sound onto the stage for the first time on songs like "Nights in White Satin" and "Tuesday Afternoon," and audiences reponded by turning them into one of the top concert draws of the decade. This album and the accompanying video is beautifully recorded (and the video looks gorgeous, too) and performed, and the group—caught amid the splendor of one of the prettiest outdoor concert venues in the West (Stevie Nicks has also done a video there) and with the orchestra backing them up on half the numbers, rise to the occasion with a drive and eloquence that they

haven't shown on stage in many years. An essential recording and video for any fan of the group. —*Bruce Eder*

Time Traveller / 1994 / PolyGram ✦✦✦

When the Moody Blues were due for the box set treatment, it would have been uncharacteristic for the production to be lacking in overstated grandiosity. On that count, this 4-CD retrospective does not disappoint, including the bulk of their most famous work (from their 1967–72 albums), lots from their later records and side projects, and a few rarities. There's not a great deal of reason for anyone but fanatics to fork out for this package; the albums (which were specifically programmed to work as separate entities) remain readily available, there's too much late stuff and Hayward/Blue Jays tracks, and there's nothing from the Denny Laine era. The three non-LP 1967 cuts that open the set are available on the double import LP *A Dream* (still possible to find), an album that also has the additional 1967 B-side "Really Haven't Got The Time," which somehow doesn't make it onto *Time Traveller*. As consolation, the liner notes are pretty good and extensive, and the first printings of the box include a bonus disc of a 1992 concert with the Colorado Symphony Orchestra. —*Richie Unterberger*

Moonglows

Group, R&B, Doo-Wop

Among the most seminal R&B and doo-wop groups of all time, the Moonglows' lineup featured some of the genre's greatest pure singers. The original lineup from Louisville included Bobby Lester, Harvey Fuqua, Alexander Graves, and Prentiss Barnes, with guitarist Billy Johnson. They were originally called the Crazy Sounds, but were renamed by disc jockey Alan Freed as the Moonglows. The group also cut some recordings as The Moonlighters. Their first major hit was the number one R&B gem "Sincerely" for Chess in 1954, which reached number 20 on the pop charts. They enjoyed five more Top Ten R&B hits on Chess from 1955 to 1958, among them "Most of All," "We Go Together," "See Saw," and "Please Send Me Someone to Love," as well as "Ten Commandments of Love." Fuqua, the nephew of Charlie Fuqua of the Ink Spots, left in 1958. He recorded "Ten Commandments of Love" as Harvey & the Moonglows with Marvin Gaye, Reese Palmner, James Knowland, and Chester Simmons before founding his own label, Tri-Phi. Fuqua created and produced the Spinners in 1961 and wrote and produced for Motown until the early '70s. The Moonglows disbanded in the '60s, then reunited in 1972 with Fuqua, Lester, Graves, Doc Williams, and Chuck Lewis. They recorded for RCA and a reworked version of "Sincerely" eventually charted, but wasn't a major hit. —*Ron Wynn*

○ **Their Greatest Hits** / 1984 / Chess ✦✦✦✦

Before MCA issued the definitive two-CD anthology containing every significant Moonglows single, this mid-'80s anthology was a good sampler covering seminal material from the vocal group that championed "blow" harmony. The Moonglows' finest tracks—among them "Sincerely," "The Ten Commandments Of Love," and "Twelve Months Of The Year"—featured brilliant vocals from Bobby Lester or Harvey Fuqua. The sound was acceptable, and the annotation was brief but thorough. This is no longer in print, but the MCA collection eclipses it anyway. —*Ron Wynn*

● **Blue Velvet/The Ultimate Collection** / 1993 / Chess ✦✦✦✦

Few rivaled the Moonglows in musical sophistication, inventiveness or flair. They could sing gorgeous heartache ballads, rollicking uptempo rhythm tunes, creditable period-piece novelty numbers, wonderful pop covers or shattering originals. This two-disc set contains 44 outstanding numbers, with every major Moonglows anthem and several others that weren't big hits but deserved to be, such as "Penny Arcade" and "Love Is A River." This collection updates and expands the *Greatest Sides* single LP release briefly available when Sugar Hill had the Chess catalog in the 1970s. It wisely restricts material to the era when they were at their best, the 1950s, and includes an excellent booklet. —*Ron Wynn*

Gary Moore

Blues Rock, Hard Rock

England's Gary Moore played guitar with Colosseum before joining a side band created by Thin Lizzy vocalist Phil Lynott called Greedy Bastards. Moore was then asked to join Thin Lizzy in 1977, which is where he gained a lot of attention with his musicianship. After two years with them, Moore was asked to leave, so Moore

then became a solo artist. Although more popular in Europe and Japan, Moore remains an idol among many American guitarists, and his albums continue to sell well around the world. He also does a lot of session work with artists of all types. —*John Book*

○ **Back on the Streets** / 1979 / Grand Slamm ✦✦✦✦

Corridors of Power / 1982 / Mirage ✦✦✦

After the War / 1989 / Virgin ✦✦✦

● **Still Got the Blues** / 1990 / Charisma ✦✦✦✦

Relieved from the pressures of having to record a hit single, he cuts loose on some blues standards as well as some newer material. Moore plays better than ever, spitting out an endless stream of fiery licks that are both technically impressive and soulful. It's no wonder *Still Got the Blues* was his biggest hit. —*David Jehnzen*

Blues Alive / 1992 / Virgin ✦✦✦

● **After Hours** / 1992 / Charisma ✦✦✦✦

Not wanting to leave a good thing behind, Moore reprises *Still Got the Blues* on its follow-up, *After Hours*. While his playing is just as impressive, the album feels a little calculated. Nevertheless, Moore's gutsy, impassioned playing makes the similarity easy to ignore. —*David Jehnzen*

○ **The Early Years** / Jan. 1992 / WTG ✦✦✦✦

Jackie Moore

Soul

One of the relatively few artists who emerged in the early '70s to enjoy a run of success with a southern soul-based sound, this Florida singer recorded her best material for Atlantic in Miami with noted session players like the Memphis Horns and the Dixie Flyers. Putting her earthy pop-soul to ballads and mid-tempo material, much of it written and crafted by producer Dave Crawford, Moore had a half-dozen R&B hits for the label; the biggest, "Precious, Precious" (1970) and "Sweet Charlie Babe" (1973), were also small pop hits. In 1972 and 1973, she cut some tunes in Philadelphia's Sigma Sound Studios with a slicker feel, with generally successful results. There was nothing especially earthshaking about Moore's style or material, but it was solid stuff with a grittier feel than much of the soul music in vogue at the time. After leaving Atlantic, she had one more sizable R&B hit, "Make Me Feel like a Woman" (1975). —*Richie Unterberger*

● **Precious, Precious: The Best Of Jackie Moore** / 1994 / Soul Classics ✦✦✦✦

Retrospective of her 1970–73 Atlantic material includes all of her hits and a few of her misses. Four of the tracks have never been released on album before. —*Richie Unterberger*

Melba Moore

b. Oct. 27, 1945
Soul

Melba Moore has been an extremely successful actress and performer since her early days in such plays as *Hair* and *Purlie*. She began recording for Buddah in 1975, and has continued with Epic, EMI, and Capitol. She has done duets with Lilo Thomas, Kashif, and Freddie Jackson, and was instrumental in helping to discover and get Jackson started by signing her to Hush Productions, a firm run by her husband Beau Higgins. Moore's flamboyant, octave-leaping style has been featured on ballads and dance/disco material, but her biggest hits were "A Little Bit More" (with Freddie Jackson) and "Falling". Both were R&B chart-toppers in 1986, recorded for Capitol. Other R&B Top Ten hits include "Love's Comin' at Ya" for EMI in 1982, "Livin' for Your Love" in 1984, "Love the One I'm With (A Lot of Love)" with Kashif in 1986, and "It's Been So Long" in 1987, all three for Capitol. —*Ron Wynn*

● **The Best Of** / 1995 / Razor & Tie ✦✦✦✦

Thurston Moore

Alternative Pop/Rock

A member of the critically-acclaimed art/punk rock band Sonic Youth, Moore has been involved in numerous side projects including the Dim Stars and Even Worse. But his first solo album was recorded during and immediately after his wife (and SY bassist) Kim Gordon's pregnancy in 1994 with ex-Half Japanese guitarist Tim Foljahn and Sonic Youth drummer Steve Shelley. *Psychic Hearts* has an appropriately offhand feel, but is far from sloppy. The album is saved from rock-star indulgence by well-written songs and an unpretentious attitude. —*Heather Phares*

● **Psychic Hearts** / 1995 / DGC ✦✦✦✦
Moore's solo album is full of surprisingly straightforward and catchy (though definitely off-kilter) pop songs. The title track, "Queen Bee and Her Pals," "Patti Smith Math Scratch" and "Ono Soul" are hip, knowing tunes that capture the essence of Moore's songwriting. "Elegy for All the Dead Rock Stars" is a mesmerizing, epic guitar piece that closes the album on a beautiful and poignant note. —*Heather Phares*

Morbid Angel

Group, Thrash, Heavy Metal
Morbid Angel was formed in 1984 by guitarist Trey Azagthoth in his home of Tampa, Florida because he wanted to elevate "the standards of the rapidly proliferating death-metal genre." Azagthoth brought his band over to England for a few shows with Napalm Death, and soon they were signed to Earache Records, a label designed to expose the true underground scene of heavy metal. Often called, sick, brutal, disgusting, and energetic, Morbid Angel eventually got a deal in America when Earache was distributed by Relativity Records. The band, although still underground, has become a major influence for bands in Florida (where there are many death-metal bands) and other parts of the U.S., as well as Europe. —*John Book*

Altars of Madness / 1989 / Earache ✦✦✦
Speed-metal, death-metal, black-metal: call it what you want but only the strong can survive with this one. This is the forefront of metal from Florida. —*John Book*

Abominations of Desolation / 1991 / Earache ✦✦
The band's actual, self-financed debut, which was recorded in 1986 but not released due to the band's dissatisfaction with the results. This was only available as a bootleg until Earache decided to release the original recordings. —*Steve Huey*

● **Covenant** / 1994 / Giant ✦✦✦✦
Covenant started to bring Morbid Angel up out of the underground, as MTV gave them wider exposure on its late *Headbanger's Ball*. Guitarist Trey Azagthoth plays complicated, heavily detuned riffs, some with a lightning-fast picking style and others in a slower groove. Drummer Pete Sandoval is one of the genre's fastest, and his jackhammer style helps complete Morbid Angel's core sound. Their incredible chops and non-stop intensity may be exactly what you've been looking for, or you may find the lack of variation wearisome. —*Steve Huey*

God of Empt. . . . .s / 1994 / Giant ✦✦

Domination / 1995 / Giant ✦✦✦
Guitarist Erik Rutan joins the fold and contributes several of his own compositions. The group's sound is better than ever and perhaps a bit more groove-oriented, but this is mostly standard Morbid Angel, with the typical problems: the bass drums are played too fast to be recorded properly and end up sounding like a fast clicking underneath the songs. There is also very little variation on the band's signature sound, and since they rarely give themselves or the audience a rest, their intensity often borders on self-caricature. This will either be just what you want or will strike you as irritating and comically overdone. —*Steve Huey*

Blessed are the Sick / Combat ✦✦✦
Florida's best in death-metal is more technical than "Alters..." and even more gloomy. —*John Book*

Morphine

Group, Rock & Roll, Alternative Pop/Rock
Morphine has managed to create a bluesy, bare bones rock & roll without any guitars. Leaving the amps behind, the band relies on sliding bass lines, a squawking baritone saxophone, and understated, powerful drums. With their second album, 1993's *Cure for Pain*, Morphine began receiving favorable reviews in mainstream publications, as well as earning a sizable cult following. —*Stephen Thomas Erlewine*

Good / Sep. 8, 1992 / Rykodisc ✦✦✦
While somewhat uneven, the stark simplicity of the band's stripped-down approach and the barking exchanges between the sliding bass and baritone sax make Morphine's debut album a worthwhile listen. —*Stephen Thomas Erlewine*

○ **Cure for Pain** / Sep. 1993 / Rykodisc ✦✦✦✦
With stronger songwriting and a darker, more menacing atmosphere, Morphine's second album improves on their debut. —*Stephen Thomas Erlewine*

● **Yes** / 1995 / Rykodisc ✦✦✦✦
From the start of *Yes*, it's clear that Morphine has stripped away a lot of their pretenses and have just set out to rock. Well, that's not entirely true. *Yes* still is highly-stylized, with Mark Sandman sounding like an English major that took his Charles Bukowski to heart and the band adhering to its no-guitar / no-keyboard policy (with the exception of a couple of acoustic guitar ballads, that is). But Morphine rocks out more fearlessly than before, making the music sound alive, not the product of a conscious conceit. From the growling "Honey White" to the dirty "Super Sex," it provides an immediate gratification that previous Morphine records never quite delivered. —*Stephen Thomas Erlewine*

Van Morrison

b. Aug. 31, 1945
Singer-Songwriter, Pop/Rock
For years, the works of Leadbelly, Robert Johnson, Hank Williams, Howlin' Wolf, Jimmie Rodgers, and other legends of American folk-music forms have inspired subsequent generations of artists to capture the blues within themselves. Many artists may have had the style or inflections down textbook perfect, but with an end result as insubstantial and hollow as the false-fronted buildings of a Hollywood movie set; no matter how much the outside had been dirtied up, investigation usually reveals that the place had truly never been lived in. Irishman Van Morrison is one of those truly gifted artists who goes way beyond the props. There seems to be an almost mystical connection between the soul of the blues and his voice and vision. As a result, Morrison's blues aren't limited to any one form of music; he takes in all that moves him.

While fronting the group Them in the mid-'60s, Morrison's intense passion set him apart from the generally poppy British Invasion sound, with songs like "Mystic Eyes," "Here Comes the Night," and the classic "Gloria."

Morrison went solo in 1967 and scored a Top Ten hit with "Brown Eyed Girl." In 1968 he signed with Warner Brothers and released the brilliant label debut *Astral Weeks*, a synthesis of jazz and folk. Cut in 48 hours, it defied pop-radio airplay with its lengthy open-ended compositions. Morrison followed with a series of R&B-influenced albums, many of which are some of the greatest albums ever released in the rock era.

Much of Morrison's music has aged very gracefully, largely due to his commitment to artistic vision rather than fads or trends. Over the years, his work has mellowed with dignity, getting deeper into Christian mystical spirituality. —*Rick Clark*

Blowin' Your Mind! / 1967 / Bang ✦✦✦
Although his first solo album is remembered for containing the immortal pop hit "Brown Eyed Girl," *Blowin' Your Mind!* is actually a dry run for Van Morrison's masterpiece, *Astral Weeks*. Songs like "Who Drove The Red Sports Car" look to that song cycle, even as "Midnight Special" nods to Morrison's R&B past. But it is the agonizing "T.B. Sheets"—all nine-and-three-quarters minutes of it—that dominates this record and belies its trendy title and pop association. "T.B. Sheets" takes the blues and reinvents it as noble tragedy and humiliating mortality. It is where Van Morrison emerges as an artist. (*Blowin' Your Mind!* was superseded by *Bang Masters*, which contains all of its tracks except "He Ain't Give You None," presented in an alternate take, plus Morrison's other recordings for Bang, in 1991.) —*William Ruhlmann*

☆ **Astral Weeks** / Nov. 1968 / Warner Brothers ✦✦✦✦✦
Recorded in a concentrated burst over a couple of days, *Astral Weeks* is one of the most uncompromising albums ever recorded by a major artist. Containing eight cuts that were more like impressionistic sound renderings than conventional melodic song structures, *Astral Weeks* treated the social outsiders that populated its grooves (the transvestite in "Madame George" or the dealer in "Slim Slow Rider") with dignity and compassion. Morrison's free-associative wail, over a sympathetic rhythm section that predominately drew from folk and jazz, made *Astral Weeks* an album that defied passive listening. His intonation might vary too much for some ears, but if you really *listen*, his soulful vocal flights will (as Dylan said concerning the function of art) practically stop time. Bassist Richard Davis's lyrical counterpoint and Modern Jazz Quartet drummer Connie Kay's sensitive rhythmic shadings are among this album's most stunning musical elements. Listing highlights is practically pointless, as *Astral Weeks* should be taken as a whole. —*Rick Clark*

Best of Van Morrison [Bang] / 1969 / Bang ◆◆◆
In the wake of the success of *Astral Weeks*, Bang Records, Van Morrison's previous label, issued this compilation without his permission. It contains five songs taken from *Blowin' Your Mind!*, including "Brown Eyed Girl," plus five previously unreleased recordings from 1967, all written by Morrison. (*The Best of Van Morrison* was superseded by *Bang Masters*, which contains all of its tracks except "He Ain't Give You None," presented in an alternate take, plus Morrison's other recordings for Bang, in 1991.) — *William Ruhlmann*

☆ **Moondance** / Feb. 1970 / Warner Brothers ◆◆◆◆◆
After *Astral Weeks*, Morrison switched gears for *Moondance*, a flawless collection of more accessible R&B-rooted material, which drew from easygoing swing ("These Dreams"), upbeat shuffles ("Come Running"), gospel-influenced song structures like "Crazy Love," and "Caravan," the latter a celebration of radio that didn't pander to that medium's more self-congratulatory nature. The jazzy title cut is a classic, as is "Into the Mystic," a song that essentially encapsulated Morrison's artistic bent. *Moondance*'s tasteful production imbued the music with a timeless quality. — *Rick Clark*

○ **His Band & Street Choir** / Oct. 1970 / Warner Brothers ◆◆◆
It is a noticeable step down from the amazing *Moondance*, primarily in the sense that some of the material and performances lack Morrison's characteristic edge. Nevertheless, Morrison's immersion into R&B helped produce his highest-charting track, "Domino" (number nine), as well as two lesser hits, "Blue Money" (number 23) and "Call Me up in Dreamland" (number 95). — *Rick Clark*

○ **Tupelo Honey** / Oct. 1971 / Warner Brothers ◆◆◆◆
The pastoral *Tupelo Honey* was another fine Morrison album, which ranged from the R&B rock of "Wild Night" (#28) to the folky gospel of the title cut, a heavenly love letter. — *Rick Clark*

○ **Saint Dominic's Preview** / 1972 / Warner Brothers ◆◆◆◆
Rarely has there ever been so joyous a rocker as "Jackie Wilson Said (I'm in Heaven When You Smile)" (number 61), with its brilliantly arranged cascading horn lines. That's just one of many delights found here. From the inspirational title cut's tale of resolve to the primally prayerful "Listen to the Lion," *Saint Dominic's Preview* stands as one of Morrison's finest albums. This is one of the few Warner reissues that actually was given a fine remastering for CD. — *Rick Clark*

Hard Nose the Highway / Aug. 1973 / Warner Brothers ◆◆◆
Although it marks a decline from the astonishing run of five great albums Van Morrison had made from 1968 through 1972, *Hard Nose the Highway* is still a respectable, if uneven, effort, notably containing "Snow In San Anselmo" (which features the Oakland Symphony Chamber Chorus) and "Warm Love." Nevertheless, it marked the end of Morrison's greatest period of creativity and accomplishment. — *William Ruhlmann*

○ **It's Too Late to Stop Now** / Jan. 1974 / Warner Brothers ◆◆◆◆
This dynamic double-disc set finds Morrison covering everything from his early work with Them, through *Astral Weeks*, to his early-'70s Warner hits and album tracks. Morrison is in great vocal form, and the band, the Caledonia Soul Orchestra, is exceptionally hot. Any fan of Morrison's should own this one. — *Rick Clark*

○ **Veedon Fleece** / Feb. 1974 / Warner Brothers ◆◆◆◆
His most willfully introspective album since *Astral Weeks*, *Veedon Fleece* (written in Ireland) is almost a classic, full of delicately rendered reflections and more open-ended vocal excursions. Morrison runs out of steam slightly during the second half of the proceedings, but not enough to keep this from being a pretty magical album. Highlights are "You Don't Pull No Punches but You Don't Push the River," "Fair Play," "Linden Arden Stole the Highlights," "Streets of Arklow," and "Comfort You." — *Rick Clark*

A Period of Transition / 1977 / Warner Brothers ◆◆◆
On paper, the collaboration of Morrison with Dr. John looked awfully good. While *A Period of Transition* failed to live up to the potential, it did have some wonderful songs, like "Heavy Connection" and "It Fills You Up" (a particular favorite). The flat-sounding mixes tend to rob the sparks out of the music, making some of this album's more expressive moments sound forced. — *Rick Clark*

Wavelength / 1978 / Warner Brothers ◆◆◆
The self-produced *Wavelength* marked an improvement over *A Period of Transition*, producing a near-hit (number 42) with the title cut. Other highlights included "Santa Fe," co-written with Jackie DeShannon. — *Rick Clark*

○ **Into the Music** / 1979 / Warner Brothers ◆◆◆◆
Five years after Van's last great album (*Veedon Fleece*), he returned with one of his finest albums, *Into the Music*, which fused the earthly with the spiritual. Highlights included "Bright Side of the Road," "Full Force Gale," "Angelou," and a version of "It's All in the Game." Not the first place to go to discover Morrison, it's a masterful album nonetheless. — *Rick Clark*

Common One / 1980 / Warner Brothers ◆◆◆
Van Morrison's most meditative album since *Veedon Fleece*, *Common One* painted a pastoral portrait dominated by such extended pieces as "Summertime In England" and "When The Heart Is Open," each of which was more than 15 minutes long. The result could be soothing, but also enervating. — *William Ruhlmann*

○ **This Is Where I Came In** / 1982 / Bang ◆◆◆◆
This umpteenth repackaging of Van Morrison's Bang Records material is notable for containing the most complete set of the recordings yet issued on a single disc. Fifteen tracks are crammed onto this LP, which constitutes the entire set of Bang masters with the exception of the B-side single "Chick-A-Boom." (*This Is Where I Came In* was superseded by *Bang Masters*, which contains all of its tracks except "He Ain't Give You None," presented in an alternate take, plus "Chick-A-Boom" and a couple of previously unreleased recordings, in 1991.) — *William Ruhlmann*

Beautiful Vision / 1982 / Warner Brothers ◆◆◆
Beautiful Vision improved upon its meandering predecessor, *Common One*, first by having some stronger melodies, and second by having a song as mystically upbeat as "Cleaning Windows." — *Rick Clark*

The Inarticulate Speech of the Heart / Mar. 1983 / Warner Brothers ◆◆◆
Van Morrison's final album for Warner Brothers Records was one of his more uncompromising efforts, including the two-part instrumental title track and "Rave On, John Donne," a spoken tribute to one of Morrison's influences. — *William Ruhlmann*

A Sense of Wonder / 1985 / Mercury ◆◆◆
Van Morrison's U.S. label debut with PolyGram (which had issued his *Live At The Opera House Belfast* album in England earlier) is a strong effort, mixing some of his familiar influences—R&B, poetry, mysticism—on such characteristic tracks as "Tore Down A La Rimbaud." It might be fair to say that, by now, Morrison's fans had heard what he had to say and the rest was just repetition, but he continued to write and perform at a high level at this mature stage in his career. — *William Ruhlmann*

○ **Live at the Grand Opera House Belfast** / 1985 / Polydor ◆◆◆◆
Not so fiery as *It's Too Late to Stop Now*, it's still an enjoyable set, featuring "It's All in the Game," "Cleaning Windows," and other tracks from this period. — *Rick Clark*

No Guru, No Method, No Teacher / Jul. 1986 / Mercury ◆◆◆
With "Ivory Tower," Van Morrison produced another excellent rocker in his familiar style, while "In The Garden" took him to one of his more spiritual, religious spaces. — *William Ruhlmann*

○ **Poetic Champions Compose** / 1987 / Mercury ◆◆◆◆
The hypnotic string arpeggios and rolling rhythms of "The Mystery," the gentle exhortation of "Did Ye Get Healed," and even reverberant cocktail-jazz instrumentals like "Spanish Steps" help make the meditative *Poetic Champions Compose* one of Morrison's better albums during the '80s. — *Rick Clark*

○ **Irish Heartbeat** / 1988 / Mercury ◆◆◆◆
Although still purposeful, Van Morrison's '80s albums were becoming repetitive when he took a break for this collaboration with the Chieftains on traditional Irish songs. The result takes him back to his earliest days and finds him singing with renewed conviction. This album should appeal to all fans of Irish music as well as Morrison lovers. — *William Ruhlmann*

○ **Avalon Sunset** / 1989 / Polydor ◆◆◆◆
Avalon Sunset's evocative melodies and almost prayful sentiments make this one of Morrison's finest albums during the '80s. Some might find this album's rich orchestration a little too close to easy listening, but repeated listenings reveal it adds a quiet dignified elegance and atmospheric unity to the proceedings not unlike the strings on Marvin Gaye's trancendent *What's Going On*. "I'm Tired Joey Boy," "Orangefield," "Have I Told You Lately?," "I'd Love to Write Another Love Song," and the supplicatory "When Will I Learn to Live in God?" are among the many highlights. *Avalon Sunset* is the mature, timeless work of an artist beyond fashion. — *Rick Clark*

★ **The Best of Van Morrison [Mercury]** / Jan. 1990 / Mercury
✦✦✦✦✦

This is a strong collection of many of Van Morrison's best songs. Of particular note is the inclusion of "Wonderful Remark," previously only available on *The King of Comedy* soundtrack. That alone makes this worth having. Many of the key Them tracks are here ("Gloria," "Here Comes the Night"), as is Morrison's classic "Brown Eyed Girl." Even though it's a strong sampler, it fails to draw a complete-enough picture of the depth of his work. Sonically, this CD is quite impressive. —*Rick Clark*

Enlightenment / Feb. 1990 / Mercury ✦✦✦
Morrison dispensed with the super-reflective spirit that dominated many of his albums from the '80s and returned to a more relaxed, almost playful effort with *Enlightenment*. "In the Days before Rock 'n' Roll" is a particular highlight. Not one of his best albums, it's still a nice change of pace. —*Rick Clark*

Hymns to the Silence / 1991 / Polydor ✦✦✦

○ **The Bang Masters** / 1991 / Epic ✦✦✦✦
An excellent sound and packaging of Morrison's work at Bert Bern's Bang label, the tracks range from the morose "T. B. Sheets," to his pop standard "Brown Eyed Girl." This is a must for fans who want to go deeper than just obtaining his obviously classic albums. —*Rick Clark*

○ **The Best of Van Morrison, Vol. 2** / 1993 / PolyGram ✦✦✦✦
Unlike *Volume One*'s dependence on his early Warner Brothers catalog, this collection exclusively features his later Polygram work and pre-Warners sides with his old band Them. While not as strong, there are some wonderful tracks, such as "When Will I Ever Learn to Live in God?," "Coney Island," "Enlightenment," "Hymns to the Silence," and "The Mystery." —*Rick Clark*

Too Long in Exile / Jun. 8, 1993 / Polydor ✦✦
Too Long in Exile marks a welcome return to the earthy secular world, an embrace of rootsy R&B and smoky jazz, a street album that ranks with Morrison's best. He weaves a kind of magic with a funky "Good Morning Little Schoolgirl" and the confessional blues of "Bigtime Operator," a story-song recounting some harrowing early experiences within the music industry. Instrumentally, the album is driven by a smooth horn section, Van's harmonica, and British vet Georgie Fame's virtuoso Hammond B-3. The proceedings stall briefly towards the end with a pair of vapid jazz pieces and noodling instrumental backing that does little justice to a W.B. Yeats text, but searing closer "Tell Me What You Want" moves things right back into club territory. —*Roch Parisien*

A Night in San Francisco / 1994 / Polydor ✦✦✦
Van Morrison's third commercially released live album takes a show format that frequently spotlights the backup band, led by organist/singer Georgie Fame and featuring singers Brian Kennedy and James Hunter, as well as saxophonist Candy Dulfer and blues singers John Lee Hooker, Junior Wells, and Jimmy Witherspoon. Even Morrison's daughter Shana comes on to sing his "Beautiful Vision." The material is not limited to Morrison compositions, either. In fact, it isn't so much that Morrison & Co. cover a variety of rock, pop, blues, R&B, and jazz standards as that many pieces are medleys that contain complete songs and quotes from others, rather in the way that a jazz soloist wil suddenly throw in a few bars of a familiar tune. Those who want to see Morrison as an esoteric singer/songwriter rather than a showman may find this album a mongrel creation, but it's undeniably lively, and that's the first requirement of a live album. —*William Ruhlmann*

○ **Payin' Dues** / 1994 / Charly ✦✦✦✦
A most fascinating double disc. The first contains the tracks found on *Bang Masters*; the bonus CD contains 31 previously unreleased acoustic ditties. The word ditties is a description, not a value judgment. According to one account, Morrison cut these purely out of necessity to fulfill his Bang contract, delivering the most unusable material possible. All of the cuts are between 45 and 90 seconds, divided between the inane (numerous nonsensical variations on "La Bamba," "Twist And Shout," and "Hang On Sloopy") and the viciously uncommercial ("The Big Royalty Check," "Ring Worm," "Blow In Your Nose"), along with a few silly variations on "Madame George." Along with Lou Reed's *Metal Machine Music*, this ranks as the least commercial music ever recorded by a major rock artist, and the nastiest spit in the eye of commercial expectations and contractual obligations. It's much more listenable than *Metal Machine Music*, though, and funnier. If you haven't picked up the *Bang Masters* collection, the addition of this off-the-wall

material (which may never find release in the U.S.) makes *Payin' Dues* a recommended alternative. —*Richie Unterberger*

Days Like This / 1995 / Polydor ✦✦
Van Morrison is a songwriter. He's paid to write about romance. We know this because he tells us on "Songwriter." A list of cliches, presumably intended to be ironic, the song unintentionally reveals the real problem with *Days Like This*—Van Morrison is going through the motions. *Days Like This* smooths over the rougher edges of the R&B-dominated *Too Long in Exile* without returning the meditative, jazzy explorations of his '80s works. Instead, the ensuing album is a completely competent yet completely uninspired pop-R&B workout, with Van sounding as if he couldn't care less about the words leaving his mouth. And that, in a way, explains the empty rhymes of "Songwriter"—it's just a job and Van will get paid no matter what he turns out. —*Stephen Thomas Erlewine*

Morrissey

b. May 22, 1959
Alternative Pop/Rock
With the Smiths, singer/songwriter Morrissey established himself as a post-punk hero, becoming the spokesman for millions of disaffected teenagers and young adults with his literate, biting, and sensitive lyrics and dramatic vocals. After the band broke up in 1987, he pursued a solo career, releasing his first album the following year. While he released several excellent singles in the late '80s, he ultimately began to sink into his persona without producing enough quality songs. After 1991's self-absorbed *Kill Uncle*, many critics considered him as a has-been, with his best work in the past. Thanks to the explosive, Mick Ronson-produced *Your Arsenal*, Morrissey regained his credibility; it was almost universally acclaimed as one of the best albums of the year and many said it was his best work since the Smiths' masterpiece *The Queen Is Dead*. His fan base continued to grow, both in size and devotion. With 1994's *Vauxhall and I*, he even had a hit single ("The More You Ignore Me, the Closer I Get") scrape the Top 50 singles chart in America, which would have been unthinkable when "Hand in Glove" was released a decade earlier. —*Stephen Thomas Erlewine*

○ **Viva Hate** / 1988 / Sire ✦✦✦✦
Morrissey pairs with Stephen Street for an album very much in the mold of his Smiths work, i.e., melodic rock dominated by jangly guitar serving as a musical bed for the singer's idiosyncratic lyrical interests and unconcerned delivery on such songs as "Everyday Is like Sunday" and "Hairdresser on Fire." —*William Ruhlmann*

○ **Bona Drag** / 1990 / Sire ✦✦✦✦
This collection of less than successful singles somehow plays nicely in the context of an album. As in the case of the Smiths, many found the *Hatful of Hollow* collection to be a favorite; the same formula works again here. It's far preferable to *Kill Uncle*, the proper album that followed. —*Steve Aldrich*

Kill Uncle / 1991 / Sire ✦✦
Clive Langer and Alan Winstanley provide a pop production dominated by keyboards for this typically catchy collection, with typically off-kilter songs like "(I'm) The End of the Family Line." —*William Ruhlmann*

● **Your Arsenal** / 1992 / Sire ✦✦✦✦
Nothing could prepare you for the shock of this album. From the opening shot, this is the most overt rock & roll of Morrissey's career. The inspired choosing of Mick Ronson as producer solidifies the link to the '70s glam influences here. And Morrissey serves up his best material since *The Queen Is Dead*. *Your Arsenal* cannot be viewed as anything less than a major comeback. —*Steve Aldrich*

○ **Vauxhall & I** / 1994 / Sire ✦✦✦✦
While it isn't a gutsy rock & roll record like *Your Arsenal*, *Vauxhall and I* is equally impressive. Filled with carefully constructed guitar-pop gems, the album contains some of Morrissey's best material since the Smiths. Out of all of his solo albums, *Vauxhall and I* sounds the most like his former band, yet the textured, ringing guitar on this record is an extension of his past, not a replication of it. In fact, with songs like "Now My Heart is Full" and "Hold On To Your Friends," Morrissey sounds more comfortable and peaceful than he ever has. And "The More You Ignore Me, the Closer I Get," "Speedway," and "Spring-heeled Jim" prove that he hasn't lost his vicious wit. —*Stephen Thomas Erlewine*

World of Morrissey / 1995 / Sire ✦✦

Released to coincide with Morrissey's brief winter tour of England in 1995, *World of Morrissey* follows none of the accepted rules for compilations. It's not a hits collection, nor is it a "best of"—the disc is filled with album cuts, live tracks, a couple of B-sides and a new single, all of which dedicated Morrissey fans already own. However, the choice of songs does mean something—the choice of the vaguely threatening "Spring-heeled Jim" over "Now My Heart Is Full" and the sad "Billy Budd" over "The More You Ignore Me, the Closer I Get" makes the calm *Vauxhall & I* seem darker than it is. But that melancholy is cut by the sly taunt of "Have-A-Go Merchant" and the perennial "Last of the Famous International Playboys," as well as a long, bizarre crawl through "Moon River." Only hardcore fans will notice such subtle matters as running orders; for them, *World of Morrissey* is a mix tape. —*Stephen Thomas Erlewine*

The Motels

Group, New Wave, Pop/Rock

By the time the Motels scored with their 1982 hit album *All 4 One* (#16), they had spent ten years in Los Angeles's alternative scene, going through enough lineup changes (particularly drummers) to make Spinal Tap proud. At the time of their self-titled 1979 debut album, the Motels featured dramatic vocalist Martha Davis, guitarist Jeff Jourard, keyboardist/saxophonist Martin Jourard, bassist Michael Goodroe, and drummer Brian Glascock. *The Motels* earned positive reviews upon its release, but the group wasn't able to translate the critical success into commercial success. During the recording sessions for their second album, 1980's *Careful,* Jeff Jourard was replaced by Davis' boyfriend Tim McGovern, formerly of Captain Kopter and the Fabulous Twirlybirds. Although the album sold more copies than their debut, it didn't break the band into the mainstream.

All 4 One, released in 1982, was their commercial breakthrough, spawning the Top 10 single "Only the Lonely" and going gold. Featuring the Top 10 hit "Suddenly Last Summer," the Motels' 1983 followup, *Little Robbers,* was equally successful. On *Shock* (1985), the group had succumbed to a West Coast mainstream rock sound. Although the album produced the minor hit "Shame," it was clear that the band was running out of steam. The Motels broke up two years later. —*Rick Clark*

The Motels / 1979 / Capitol ✦✦✦

Careful / 1980 / Capitol ✦✦✦

○ **All 4 One** / 1982 / Capitol ✦✦✦✦

○ **Little Robbers** / 1983 / Capitol ✦✦✦✦

Shock / 1985 / Capitol ✦✦

● **The Best of the Motels: No Vacancy** / 1990 / Capitol ✦✦✦✦

Mother Love Bone

Group, Hard Rock, Heavy Metal

When other Seattle bands were releasing singles and EPs of hard garage grunge, Mother Love Bone had their sights set on the arenas, making a grandiose heavy metal that recalled Zeppelin and Aerosmith with a slight punk fervor; in a sense, the band was a response to Guns 'N Roses' sleazy guitar boogie. Considering that guitarist Stone Gossard and bassist Jeff Ament formed the rhythmic core of the Stooges-soaked Green River, it was a little strange that the band played it so safe, but that was mainly due to the lead vocalist, Andrew Wood. Wood was a modern day hippie, preaching love and understanding, as well as a healthy dose of sex. Most of the hooks came from Gossard and Ament, but Wood was the focal point. The band was set to make their stab at the big time with 1990's *Apple,* but Wood died of a heroin overdose before it was released; the *Temple of the Dog* album, featuring Gossard, Ament, Soundgarden's Matt Cameron and Chris Cornell, and vocalist Eddie Vedder, was released as a tribute to him.

Gossard and Ament went on to form Pearl Jam, which took many of the hard rock elements of Mother Love Bone, except it was rawer and more honest. Also, Pearl Jam had a distinctive lead vocalist and lyricist in Eddie Vedder, who easily eclipsed the macho posturings of Wood. —*Stephen Thomas Erlewine*

Shine / 1989 / Stardog ✦✦✦

An EP by one of the most promising bands from Seattle, this record contributed to the buzz about the Seattle music scene. —*John Book*

○ **Apple** / 1990 / Polydor ✦✦✦✦

This is the first and last album by a band that almost made it. Comparisons to Led Zeppelin, Deep Purple, and Marc Bolan can be made from the abundance of strong material and great vocals from Andrew Wood. This group could've reached the level that Nirvana gained in 1991. —*John Book*

● **Stardog Champion** / 1990 / Stardog ✦✦✦✦

Released after the phenomenal success of Pearl Jam, *Mother Love Bone* collects everything Mother Love Bone ever released. Their resurrection of the epic hard rock of the 1970s was quite good, but also derivative. While Wood was a fine singer, he wasn't a very original vocalist and often sounded very similar to Robert Plant. *Mother Love Bone* is the definitive collection of the band, and worth the time of fans of Pearl Jam and the Seattle scene. —*Stephen Thomas Erlewine*

Mother's Finest

Group, Soul, R&B

This sextet's late-'70s albums for Epic mixed rock, funk, and soul, but never clicked commercially, although the single "Love Changes" did make the R&B Top 30. The group began in Chicago in the late '60s, with vocalists Glenn Murdock and Joyce Kennedy, guitarist Garry Moore, bassist Jerry Seay, drummer Barry Borden, and keyboardist Michael Keck. They moved temporarily to Miami, before settling in Atlanta. They had one RCA LP, then recorded for Epic until the mid-'80s. Kennedy had a solo LP for A&M in 1984; Mother's Finest then resurfaced and tried again on Capitol with *Looks Could Kill* in 1989. —*Ron Wynn*

Mother's Finest / 1974 / RCA ✦✦✦

● **Another Mother Further** / 1977 / Epic ✦✦✦✦

Pioneering funk, with "Baby Love." —*Bil Carpenter*

Mother Factor / 1978 / Epic ✦✦✦

Mother's Finest came closest with this album to getting some deserved attention. The album stayed on the pop charts for over 20 weeks, generating a mild R&B hit, and the group did some support tours. Unfortunately, it didn't have the one breakout single they needed, or even an album cut that could become a cult winner. Instead, it ended up being a close-but-no-cigar proposition, although it did keep them viable enough to secure another contract with a new label. —*Ron Wynn*

○ **Live** / 1979 / Epic ✦✦✦✦

Mother's Finest tried to smash the embargo blocking black rock acts with this live record. It was the closest any album came to actually conveying the kind of nonstop excitement, spontaneity, and unpredictability of their live shows, although it also showed how vocally erratic they could be in performance. The failure of a band that had as exciting a vocalist as Joyce Kennedy and did both solid rock and fine grinding funk proved one of the '80s' more puzzling questions. It couldn't just be attributed to racism either, because Mother's Finest actually did better among white audiences than black ones. —*Ron Wynn*

Iron Age / 1982 / Epic ✦✦✦

One Mother to Another / 1983 / Epic ✦✦

Looks Could Kill / 1989 / Capitol ✦✦

Mother's Finest predated Living Colour by several years. They were a Chicago band that first relocated to Dayton, then settled in Atlanta. They achieved a genuine synthesis of rock licks, funk beats, and wailing soul lyrics, thanks to dynamic vocalist Jean "Joyce" Kennedy and Glenn Murdoch. They had in James "Moses" Moore the kind of sparkling, inventive guitarist able to provide either crackling funk or exploding rock. But by the time they made this late-'80s album, Mother's Finest were on their third record label, still unable to attain success. There was a little media buzz when the album was initially released, but it quickly died on the vine. —*Ron Wynn*

Black Radio Won't Play This Record / 1992 / RCA ✦✦✦

Mötley Crüe

Group, Hard Rock, Heavy Metal

As far as commercial appeal goes, Mötley Crüe was one of the top heavy metal bands in the '80s, exploiting every trend in metal and hard rock without seeming crass or opportunistic. *Shout at the Devil* had them embracing a theatrical, Kiss-styled Satanism; *Theater of Pain* saw them ride the line between glam and pop-metal; *Girls, Girls, Girls* had them toughening up their image with leather and harder guitars, reaching for a street credibility; *Dr. Feelgood* had them sharpening the guitars of the previous album while adding a pop sensibility that took them straight to the top of the charts. Throughout their changes, the Crüe remained joyously sleazy and stupid, with their Zeppelin/Aerosmith-based hard rock making them high school favorites across the country. After the success of *Dr. Feelgood*, singer Vince Neil was fired from the band. When the band re-emerged in 1994 with their new vocalist John Corabi, they had changed their image again, falling somewhere between Ministry, Stone Temple Pilots, and Soundgarden in an attempt to recapture the new alternative metal audience. *Mötley Crüe*, the new lineup's first album, was a commercial disppointment, spending 10 weeks on the charts and only going gold. — *Stephen Thomas Erlewine*

Too Fast for Love / 1981 / Elektra ✦✦
Sleazy heavy metal before all the hype took over their home of Los Angeles, their debut album was remixed from the original on their own Leathur label. — *John Book*

Shout at the Devil / 1983 / Elektra ✦✦✦
Possibly the best mainstream heavy metal band of the '80s, and their best album to date. — *John Book*

Theater of Pain / 1985 / Elektra ✦✦✦
Powered by a sneering remake of Brownsville Station's "Smokin' in the Boy's Room" and the classic power ballad "Home Sweet Home," *Theater of Pain* was Mötley Crüe's biggest hit up to that point, even if the rest of the album wasn't as strong as its hit singles. — *Stephen Thomas Erlewine*

○ **Girls, Girls, Girls** / 1987 / Elektra ✦✦✦✦
With *Girls, Girls, Girls*, Mötley Crüe toughens up their music as well as their image, turning in an album of greasy, sleazy hardrock boogie that, at its best, rivals Aerosmith. — *Stephen Thomas Erlewine*

○ **Dr. Feelgood** / 1989 / Elektra ✦✦✦✦
Producer Bob Rock gives the Crüe a high-gloss, corporate rock sheen, eliminating most of the band's self-indulgent tendencies. Thanks to a detox program, the Crüe itself sounds tighter, giving *Dr. Feelgood* a mindless but strong catchiness. *Dr. Feelgood*'s four Top 40 hits—the title track, the ballad "Without You," the driving "Kickstart My Heart," and caustic "Don't Go Away Mad (Just Go Away)"—form the heart of the album, but solid album tracks like "S.O.S. (Same Old Situation)" help make *Dr. Feelgood* arguably the band's best album. — *Stephen Thomas Erlewine*

● **Decade of Decadence** / 1991 / Elektra ✦✦✦✦
It is a collection of some of their hits and the best of their album material. — *John Book*

Mötley Crüe / 1994 / Elektra ✦✦
On *Mötley Crüe*, their first album recorded without vocalist Vince Neil, the band revamped their trademark dirty but melodic heavy metal, adding elements of '90s grunge and alternative metal. The group's new vocalist John Corabi is a hoarse shouter without the charisma of Vince Neil, so he wasn't able to put a distinctive spin on the pedestrian grind the rest of the band churned out. The Crüe seem to have equated grunge with seriousness, since very few of the songs on the record recall the hedonistic atmosphere of their '80s albums. Unfortunately, this also means the group have neglected to write memorable hooks and riffs, which makes *Mötley Crüe* the weakest effort in their catalog. — *Stephen Thomas Erlewine*

Motörhead

Group, Hard Rock, Thrash, Heavy Metal
English metal band Motörhead formed in 1975. Led by bassist Ian "Lemmy" Kilminster, the band was originally named Bastard but soon changed to Motörhead (American slang for speed freak), a name that suited their style of playing very well. Along with guitarist Larry Wallis and drummer Lucas Fox, Lemmy and the boys brought the concept of the power trio to new heights, using the bass almost as a lead instrument behind a wall of noise emanating from the other two instruments. They attracted a huge following in England during the late-'70s punk-rock era with their combination of breakneck speed and deafening volume. Though Lemmy remains as the only original member (having revamped the lineup several times over), and their style hasn't progressed much in almost 20 years, their hardcore fans wouldn't have it any other way. — *Cub Koda*

Motörhead / 1977 / Roadrunner ✦✦✦

○ **Overkill** / 1979 / Roadrunner ✦✦✦✦
Motörhead's second album followed the same pattern as the first—it was a relentless collection of fast, loud and simple heavy metal—but the songwriting was more melodic and consistent than the debut. — *Stephen Thomas Erlewine*

○ **Bomber** / 1979 / Roadrunner ✦✦✦✦
By the time of Motörhead's third album *Bomber*, it was clear that the band had one basic sound and nothing else. However, that didn't mean the group was boring—the lethal attack of their buzzing guitars and Lemmy's hoarse vocals never became tedious because of the immediacy of the group's sound, as well as their talent for coming up with memorable riffs and tightly written songs. *Bomber* sounded no different than Motörhead's two previous albums, but the group had lost none of its impact and the album featured "Dead Men Tell No Tales," one of their finest songs. — *Stephen Thomas Erlewine*

○ **Ace of Spades** / 1980 / Roadrunner ✦✦✦✦
The forefathers of thrash on one of their better-known albums, *Ace of Spades* features guitarist "Fast" Eddie Clark, who later left and formed Fastway. Highlights include "(We Are) The Road Crew" and the title track. — *John Book*

○ **No Sleep Til Hammersmith** / 1981 / Roadrunner ✦✦✦✦

Iron Fist / 1982 / Roadrunner ✦✦✦
This is also a pretty good early album from the band. — *John Book*

★ **No Remorse** / 1984 / Roadrunner ✦✦✦✦✦
No Remose is a solid collection (in spite of the omission of the band's Chiswick recordings), consisting of key album, EP, and single tracks. Included are Motörhead standards like "Killed by Death" and "Please Don't Touch." Unfortunately, this Roadracer reissue of the 1984 release omits "Leaving Here" and "Louie Louie." Overall, *No Remose* is a great intro to the band's earlier thrash sound. — *Rick Clark*

○ **Orgasmatron** / 1986 / Sinclair ✦✦✦✦
For *Orgasmatron*, Motörhead enlisted producer Bill Laswell, who assisted the band in achieving a dense wall of sound, which sounded a little too compressed. Highlights include "Built for Speed," "Deaf Forever," and the title track, an incredible aural sludgefest that borders on psychedelic. — *Rick Clark*

Rock 'N' Roll / 1987 / Sinclair ✦✦✦

○ **1916** / 1991 / WTG ✦✦✦✦
Produced by Pete Solley and Ed Stasium, *1916* is Motörhead's most diversified effort, including humorous sendups like "Ramones" (a tribute to the New York speed punkers) and "Angel City" (a love letter to Los Angeles), as well as grim topics, like the dying World War I soldier's perspective in the title track. Motörhead manages to cover all this territory without ever losing their basic sonic integrity. All in all, *1916* is arguably this band's finest release thus far. — *Rick Clark*

March or Die / Jul. 14, 1992 / WTG ✦✦
1992 seems to be the year of accessibility for veteran heavy metallurgists. Lemmy Kilmister and his hoary band of rockers Motörhead remain as dependable as ever on their 15th outing *March or Die*. The original punk-metal fusion band (going back to 1977) continues to play it raw as sushi. But, like many oldtime noisemongers, Motörhead have come out this summer with their most user-friendly and well-produced work. The toned down fury even allows for an emotive ballad-duet with Ozzie Osbourne on "I Ain't No Nice Guy," with guest guitar courtesy of Slash from Guns 'N Roses. The piledriving Name In Vain, a bulldozer cover of Ted Nugent's "Cat Scratch Fever," and the title track's ominous, deathmetal rap will please the hardcore following. — *Roch Parisien*

Motors

Group, Rock & Roll, New Wave, Power Pop/Anglo-Pop
After several years in England's pub-rock scene, ex-Duck Deluxe members Nick Garvey and Andy McMaster formed the Motors in 1977 with vocalist Bram Tchaikovsky and drummer Ricky Slaughter. Their first album was a splendid piece of guitar-driven pop/rock highlighted by the single "Dancing the Night Away." *Approved By* was the album that earned them the U.K. hits "Airport" and "Forget About You;" the record saw the band's songwriting improving with forceful melodies and invigorating performances. After that record, the Motors split up; Garvey and McMaster used the band's name for the 1980 album *Tenement Steps*, which didn't

equal the spark of their first two records. —*Stephen Thomas Erlewine*

Motors 1 / 1977 / Virgin ✦✦✦
Their debut features a reworked version of pub rock with an edgier punk feel. Includes the catchy single "Dancing the Night Away," the high point of the album. —*Chris Woodstra*

○ **Approved by the Motors** / 1978 / Virgin ✦✦✦✦
Their second album shows a marked improvement over the debut, with a stronger melodic base and catchier songs including the British hits "Airport" and "Forget About You." The CD version adds three bonus tracks. —*Chris Woodstra*

Tenement Steps / 1980 / Virgin ✦✦
The band, now reduced to Nick Garvey and Andy McMaster, is a little too ambitious and overproduced. While not their best album, it does include one of their finest songs, "Love and Loneliness," making it worthwhile for those who liked the first two albums. Essential for collectors if only for the uniquely shaped sleeve. —*Chris Woodstra*

● **Airport: The Motors' Greatest Hits** / 1995 / Caroline ✦✦✦✦
A solid collection of the band's best moments, *Airport* provides a good introduction for the uninitiated, drawing from the brilliant first two albums and the lesser *Tenement Steps*. —*Chris Woodstra*

Mott the Hoople

Group, Rock & Roll, Hard Rock
Originally a Herefordshire, England, band named Silence, Mott the Hoople was signed to Island in 1969 by A&R man Guy Stevens, who suggested that they change their name (inspired by a Willard Manus novel) and dump their lead singer, Stan Tippens, in their search for a stronger identity. Tippens was made road manager (he later worked for the Pretenders), and Ian Hunter (an engineering apprentice) was brought in to sing and play piano. Stevens, in turn, became the band's manager and producer. Between 1969 and 1972, Mott cut four albums, two of which contained some great rock & roll. Nevertheless, the band's future looked bleak, due to diminishing sales with each release. A happenstance pairing with ascending glam rock star David Bowie caused a fortuitous turn of events, which culminated in a new record deal (Columbia) and sound. The result of their collaboration was the Bowie-produced *All the Young Dudes*, a blatant glam sendup. The title cut became Mott's first hit, and in the time one could say the words "image makeover," Mott was camping it up, teetering around the stage in makeup and cartoonish platform shoes. Their followup effort, *Mott*, was the band's finest artistic statement, loosely addressing the travails of rock "stardom." After that, Mott began to lose its focus, and the departure of lead singer/songwriter Ian Hunter hastened the band's demise. They eventually broke up in 1976. Hunter later enjoyed a moderately successful cult following with his solo career. As a songwriter, he scored some substantial hits with artists like Great White ("Once Bitten Twice Shy") and Barry Manilow ("Ships"). —*Rick Clark*

○ **Mott the Hoople** / 1969 / Atlantic ✦✦✦✦
Mott the Hoople, with its hard-rock variation of Dylan's *Blonde on Blonde* sound, stands as one of the band's better efforts. This debut sported some fine originals, particularly "Backsliding Fearlessly" and "Rock and Roll Queen," as well as some unusual (but hip) song covers, like Sonny Bono's "Laugh at Me" and Doug Sahm's "At the Crossroads." The Kinks' garage-riff standard "You Really Got Me" got a high-octane instrumental treatment. Only on the middle section of the lengthy "Half Moon Bay" does *Mott the Hoople* lose momentum. The fidelity on this disc (and *Brain Capers*) rivals the sound of a good vinyl import version. —*Rick Clark*

Mad Shadows / 1970 / Atlantic ✦✦

Wildlife / 1971 / Atlantic ✦✦

☆ **Brain Capers** / 1971 / Atlantic ✦✦✦✦✦
After a couple of fairly dismal efforts, Mott rebounded with one of the great lost hard rock albums of the '70s. Released with practically no fanfare whatsoever, *Brain Capers* sank without a trace. Certainly, in the decade that produced Styx and Journey, *Brain Capers* (from the audaciously titled "Death May Be Your Santa Claus," to the closing "The Wheel of the Quivering Meat Conception") convincingly drew a line in the sand, revealing most everything called "rock" to be a fraud. Some of this was due, in part, to the return of Guy Stevens at the production helm. Among the album's highlights are versions of Dion's "Your Own Backyard," the Youngbloods' "Darkness Darkness," and Ian Hunter's powerful

"The Journey," "Sweet Angeline," and the previously mentioned "Death …". —*Rick Clark*

○ **All the Young Dudes** / 1972 / Columbia ✦✦✦✦
Just as Mott was about to pack it in due to their amazing lack of public acceptance, David Bowie entered the picture, and with the recording of a few cannily conceived songs, containing strong gay allusions (Bowie's "All the Young Dudes" and Mott's "Sucker" and "One of the Boys"), Mott went from potential has-beens to avatars of the glam rock movement. The Bowie-produced album contained a version of Lou Reed's "Sweet Jane" and Mick Ralphs's "Ready for Love," one of his finest bits of writing to date. As on many albums of that genre, the production sounds tight-assed, stiff, and dry. Nevertheless, Mott makes the proceedings rock fairly convincingly. —*Rick Clark*

Rock & Roll Queen / 1972 / Atlantic ✦✦✦

☆ **Mott** / 1973 / Columbia ✦✦✦✦✦
Regarded by many to be their finest album, this self-produced effort was a loosely conceived concept album about the ups and downs of rock & roll success. *Mott* contained two U.K. hits with "All the Way from Memphis" and "Honaloochie Boogie." Other highlights were "The Ballad of Mott the Hoople," "Whizz Kid," "Violence," and "Drivin' Sister." The sound of this reissue is a little on the muddy side. Nevertheless, of their Columbia-period albums, this is the one to get. —*Rick Clark*

○ **The Hoople** / 1974 / Columbia ✦✦✦✦

Mott the Hoople Live / 1974 / Columbia ✦✦✦

Drive on / 1975 / Columbia ✦

Greatest Hits / 1975 / Columbia ✦✦✦

Shouting and Pointing / 1976 / CBS ✦

★ **The Ballad of Mott: A Retrospective** / 1993 / Columbia ✦✦✦✦✦
Mott the Hoople were punks without realizing it. Combining a heavy-metal roar with the sneering hipster stance of 1965 Bob Dylan, Mott the Hoople made some of the best, most original rock & roll of the early '70s. This two-disc set chronicles their Columbia recordings, with four tracks from their early Atlantic albums thrown in for good measure. Because of David Bowie's production of *All the Young Dudes* and their stage costumes, Mott was tossed into the glam-rock scene, but their music was often wittier and meaner than other glam-rock bands. This made the group an enormous element in the punk/new wave movement. Although it isn't definitive because it doesn't contain enough material from *Mott the Hoople* or *Brain Capers*, *The Ballad of Mott* is all the Mott most people will need. Nearly all of the songs from their two classic Columbia albums, *All the Young Dudes* and *Mott*, are included, as is a generous selection of tracks from *The Hoople* and a number of B-sides and unreleased tracks. While the band didn't receive much attention at the time, their music still sounds vital over 20 years later. —*Stephen Thomas Erlewine*

○ **Backsliding Fearlessly: The Early Years** / 1994 / Rhino ✦✦✦✦

Bob Mould

b. 1961
Alternative Pop/Rock
After Hüsker Dü fell apart in late 1987, guitarist/singer Bob Mould took a year off before re-emerging with his solo debut, *Workbook*, in 1989. Compared with the sonic fireworks of his previous band, the largely acoustic *Workbook* was a shock, but a pleasant one. The following year, Mould released *Black Sheets of Rain*, a devastatingly brutal record overflowing with raging guitars; the only thing that tied the two records together was their merciless introspection and consistently strong songwriting. After *Black Sheets*, Mould formed a new trio, Sugar, which released its first album in 1992. —*Stephen Thomas Erlewine*

● **Workbook** / 1989 / Virgin ✦✦✦✦
Mould takes a less raucous, more coherent approach than on his Hüsker Dü work for this solo debut, which combines somewhat pessimistic lyrics with majestic guitar parts matched to a prominent cello. —*William Ruhlmann*

Black Sheets of Rain / May 1990 / Virgin ✦✦✦
A scalding, monolithic collection of soul-baring lyrics and primal guitars, *Black Sheets of Rain* is extremely powerful musically, but is also slightly monotonous. Nevertheless, the record features several inspired songs from Mould, including the catchy single "It's Too Late." —*Stephen Thomas Erlewine*

Poison Years / 1994 / Virgin ✦✦✦

Drawing heavily from *Black Sheets of Rain*, this anthology of Mould's time at Virgin doesn't give enough space to the brilliant *Workbook*, but it does have several fiery live tracks, including a harrowing version of Richard Thompson's "Shoot Out the Lights." — *Stephen Thomas Erlewine*

Mountain

Group, Hard Rock

Founded in 1969 by Cream producer, bassist, and vocalist Felix Pappalardi and 250-pound vocalist and lead guitarist Leslie West (from the Long Island group the Vagrants), Mountain specialized in bottom-heavy mid-tempo hard rock. The band was rounded out by organist Steve Knight and drummer Corky Laing's George-of-the-jungle-style pounding. West's distinctive sustain-drenched lead sound and economical phrasing made him one of the most emulated guitarists at the turn of the '70s.

During their existence, Mountain hit the charts with *Mountain Climbing!* (#17) (which included the #21 hit "Mississippi Queen"), *Nantucket Sleighride* (#16), and *Flowers of Evil* (#35). — *Rick Clark*

● **Mountain Climbing!** / 1970 / Columbia/Legacy ✦✦✦✦
This includes the hit "Mississippi Queen." All in all, this is Mountain's strongest studio effort. — *Rick Clark*

Nantucket Sleighride / 1971 / Columbia ✦✦✦

Mountain Live / 1972 / Windfall ✦✦

Flowers of Evil / 1972 / Windfall ✦✦✦

○ **The Best of Mountain** / 1973 / Columbia ✦✦✦✦
This collection contains most of the band's recorded highlights, except for the curious omissions of "Dreams of Milk and Honey" (from the debut *Leslie West—Mountain*) and "Silver Paper" (from *Mountain Climbing!*). Included are "Mississippi Queen" (number 21), "The Animal Trainer and the Toad" (number 76), "For Yasgur's Farm" (number 107), and their version of Jack Bruce's "Theme for an Imaginary Western." — *Rick Clark*

Avalanche / 1974 / Columbia ✦✦

Twin Peaks / 1974 / Columbia ✦✦

○ **Over The Top** / 1995 / Columbia/Legacy ✦✦✦✦
Over The Top is right. Two discs of Mountain, complete with all the AOR hits, unreleased tracks, two newly recorded songs, a nearly six-minute guitar solo and a twenty-minute jam is a bit much for anyone but the most devoted Leslie West fans, yet the number of rarities and classy packaging make the set a necessary item for the dedicated. — *Stephen Thomas Erlewine*

Mouse & The Traps

Group, Garage Rock, Pop/Rock

This Tyler, TX group from the mid-'60s is most known for their uncanny imitation of *Highway 61*-era Dylan, "A Public Execution." Featured on the *Nuggets* compilation, it is to Dylan what the Knickerbockers' "Lies" is to the Beatles: one of the few rip-offs so utterly accurate that it could easily fool listeners into mistaking it for the original article. Spearheaded by singer and songwriter Ronnie Weiss, the group actually recorded quite a few decent singles between 1965 and 1969, without approaching any sort of national recognition. "Mouse" never got as explicitly Dylanesque again, but there's no doubt that Weiss often recalled a non-atonal Dylan with his nasal delivery, and several of their singles were a much more melodic, pop-oriented extension of Dylan's mid-'60s sound. Recording almost exclusively original material, they were one of the better regional groups of the time, and also waxed some capable Texas punk-psychedelia and good-time pop-rockers. — *Richie Unterberger*

● **Public Execution** / 1982 / Eva ✦✦✦✦
19-song compilation includes most of their '60s singles, as well as the 1966 single they recorded under the name Positively Thirteen O'Clock with singer Jimmy Rabbit. Most of the songs are original material of a pretty high standard; a good buy for '60s specialists. — *Richie Unterberger*

The Move

Group, Art-Rock/Progressive-Rock, Pop/Rock

A quintet (later reduced to four) of mod-poseurs from Birmingham led by guitarist/oboist/songwriter/singer Roy Wood, the Move wasted a lot of time and energy on image and squandered

some great music. Influenced by the Beatles, Eddie Cochran, Duane Eddy, and any number of R&B sources (they even covered "Zing Went the Strings of My Heart," a Coasters number that goes back to Judy Garland in the 1930's, in creditable doo-wop style), they were equally comfortable doing merry psychedelic pop ("Flowers in the Rain") or pumping their amperage up to planet-cracking levels ("Hello Susie"). They seemed impervious to personnel shifts, which were many, and even got stronger with the addition of Jeff Lynne, a guitarist/songwriter with an even bigger Beatles fixation, in 1970. At around the same time, Wood devised the notion of an offshoot group called the Electric Light Orchestra, which was supposed to co-exist with the Move but instead replaced it, ironically enough without Wood. — *Bruce Eder*

○ **The Move** / 1968 / Repertoire ✦✦✦✦
The Move's debut album was a solid effort of mod-pop-psychedelia, boasting a number of fine Roy Wood compositions: the British hits "Flowers in the Rain" and "Flower Brigade," the original version of "Cherry Blossom Clinic," and the lesser-known but equally worthy "Yellow Rainbow" and "Walk Upon The Water." The three routine covers (of Eddie Cochran, the Coasters, and Moby Grape) that pad the album dilute it only slightly. The German CD reissue adds seven bonus tracks from late-'60s singles, but if you can live with vinyl, you should still seek out the A&M double LP compilation *the Best of the Move*, which has the entire debut album and even more of their late-'60s and early-'70s 45s. — *Richie Unterberger*

Something Else From The Move / 1968 / Regal Zonophone ✦✦✦
When the Move were reaching the peak of their popularity after a burst of fine psychedelic-tinged power pop singles, they issued this rather odd live five-song, 12" EP consisting entirely of covers. If nothing else, it proves the Move were a dynamic live act with an eclectic range, to say the least, as they cover tunes by the Byrds, Love, Eddie Cochran, Jerry Lee Lewis, and Spooky Tooth on this set. They really burn it up, in fact, on the Byrds' "So You Want To Be A Rock And Roll Star" and Love's "Stephanie Knows Who," with spinning and frenetic guitar work. The rest of the set is more routine, coming off more as a tribute to some of their idiosyncratic favorites. — *Richie Unterberger*

☆ **Shazam** / 1970 / A&M ✦✦✦✦✦
The single most accomplished album to be recorded by any of the Birmingham rock bands (which include the Moody Blues), *Shazam* is sort of *Sgt. Pepper* with an attitude, a mixture of expansive progressive-rock worthy of the Beatles and high energy music honed by years of playing loud on stage. The rendition of Tom Paxton's "The Last Thing on My Mind" pushes these guys simultaneously into Byrds and Jimi Hendrix territory, while "Beautiful Daughter" is one of the most unabashedly pretty records of this era, and "Cherry Blossom Clinic Revisited" is defiantly strange. The album only exists as an import from Japan, paired up on one CD with the earlier *Flowers in the Rain* album (all songs in print domesticallly or a better German version filled out with five live tracks from London's Marquee Club, off of the super-rare *Something Else* EP). — *Bruce Eder*

Looking On / 1971 / Capitol ✦✦
Probably their weakest album, finding the group trying to blend progressive elements with lumpy hard rock boogie on obscure, extended tracks. The songs do look forward to the Electric Light Orchestra, for good or ill, in the helium-like high harmonies and the wide palette of instruments. Most of the multi-instrumentation is provided by Roy Wood, who picks up oboe, sitar, slide guitar, cello, and saxophone in addition to his usual guitar chores. Includes the British Top Ten single "Brontosaurus." — *Richie Unterberger*

Message from the Country / 1971 / One Way ✦✦✦
The group's last good album, weaker than *Shazam* but pleasant enough in its *White Album* way. — *Bruce Eder*

Split Ends / 1972 / United Artists ✦✦✦
Basically an improved version of *Message from the Country*, replacing that album's weakest tracks with some fine British singles, especially "Tonight," "Chinatown," and "Do Ya." With the release of all of these tracks and the entire *Message from the Country* album on the 1994 reissue *Great Move!*, fans no longer have to seek out this package. — *Richie Unterberger*

○ **Best of the Move [A&M]** / 1974 / A&M ✦✦✦✦
Really the best of the group's early period, ranging from delightfully trippy ("Here We Go Round the Lemon Tree," "Flowers in the Rain") to the downright weird ("Zing Went the Strings of My

Heart," "Night of Fear") singles and album sides that helped establish the group's reputation for eccentricity. —*Bruce Eder*

Black Country Rock / 1993 / Gold Standard ✦✦✦
This quasi-legal compilation of 26 BBC performances from the late 1960s, in reasonable to excellent fidelity, shows the Move's astonishing versatility and range of influences. Ten of these are live-in-the-studio run-throughs of original material, including most of their early British hits—"Night Of Fear," "Fire Brigade," "Flowers in the Rain," "I Can Hear The Grass Grow," and "Blackberry Way." More interesting from a historical perspective are the 16 covers, showing an eclectic range that must have been the equal of any major group of the time—the Byrds, Simon & Garfunkel, Tim Rose, Love, Jerry Lee Lewis, Eddie Cochran, Neil Diamond, Jackie Wilson, Janis Joplin, Johnny Cash, Moby Grape, and the Beach Boys all come in for the Move's accomplished chunky rock, harmony-laden treatment. The covers of the Byrds' "Goin' Back" and Paul Simon's "Sounds Of Silence" are particularly nifty. It's not recommended to anyone except serious fans, but that small audience could hardly wish for a better collection of rarities from the group's salad days. —*Richie Unterberger*

★ **Great Move! The Best Of The Move** / Jun. 15, 1994 / EMI ✦✦✦✦✦
The title is really a misnomer; it includes much of the best of the Move, but can hardly stake a claim as a definitive collection, as it only covers their final years in the early '70s. Which isn't to say it isn't good. This is basically a spruced-up version of their final album, *Message From The Country* (1971), with the addition of five bonus tracks from early-'70s singles. *Message From The Country* itself was an erratic affair, alternating between lumbering forays into hard rock, revivalist roots rock and country, and some of Roy Wood and Jeff Lynne's most inspired Beatlesque progressive compositions. The singles, most of which were previously issued on the *Split Ends* compilation, include some of their most memorable moments. "Tonight" (a British hit) is Roy Wood at his most tuneful, wistful, and folk-rockish; "Chinatown," though not quite as good (and not quite as big a British hit), is in much the same vein; and "Do Ya," redone with much more success by ELO, one of their catchiest all-out rockers. Wood also gets into heavy sounds on the Top Ten British hit "California Man." Includes informative liner notes by respected rock critic Ira Robbins. —*Richie Unterberger*

BBC Sessions / 1995 / Band Of Joy ✦✦✦

The Moving Sidewalks

Group, Psychedelic, Garage Rock
Before forming ZZ Top, Billy Gibbons was the lead guitarist of this Houston group, which released one album and a few singles in the late '60s. Their single "99th Floor" became one of the most famous vintage garage 45's after its inclusion on *Pebbles Vol. 2,* but the Sidewalks actually leaned much more heavily towards psychedelic and blues-rock. In fact, the group supported Jimi Hendrix at one of his early U.S. gigs, and Gibbons became one of Hendrix's first boosters on these shores; strange as it may seem, Hendrix was quite impressed with Gibbons himself, even at this early juncture. The Moving Sidewalks never developed into anything more than a regional act, and are known primarily as a starting point for Gibbons. —*Richie Unterberger*

● **99th Floor** / 1982 / Eva ✦✦✦✦
All 15 songs recorded by the group, including their entire album (*Flash*) and three singles. "Every Night A New Surprise" is the only psych-punk number besides "99th Floor" on this LP of extremely Hendrix-influenced originals, with a bit of Stevie Winwood-like soul here and there, as well as an unusual heavy psychedelic treatment of "I Want To Hold Your Hand." —*Richie Unterberger*

Alison Moyet

b. Jun. 18, 1961
Pop/Rock
Alison Moyet, a British pop singer with a remarkably bluesy voice, began her professional career with synth-pop duo Yazoo (Yaz in the U.S.) in the early '80s. In 1983, Moyet began a solo career, releasing her debut album, *Alf* the following year. *Alf* was a major success in Britain, hitting number one on the charts and launching the hit singles "Invisible," "All Cried Out," and "Love Resurrection;" it was a minor hit in the U.S., with "Invisible" cracking the Top 40. During 1985, Moyet toured with a jazz band led by John Altman; the group recorded a version of Billie Holiday's "That Ole Devil Called Love," which became her biggest British hit, even though the group received poor reviews.

In 1986, Moyet had another major U.K. hit with "Is This Love?," which was released while she was recording her second solo album. *Raindancing* appeared in 1987 and it was another big British hit, peaking at number two and featuring the Top 10 hits "Weak in the Presence of Beauty" and "Love Letters." The record wasn't quite as successful in the U.S., peaking at number 94. In 1991, she released her third album, *Hoodoo,* which was her most musically ambitious collection to date. However, it didn't match the commercial success of her previous albums, failing to chart in America. *Essex,* her fourth album, appeared in 1994 and she released a greatest hits collection, *Singles,* the following year. —*Stephen Thomas Erlewine*

● **Alf** / 1984 / Columbia ✦✦✦✦
Moyet's debut attempted a gradual transition from the electronic-pop backgrounds of her Yaz work. She succeeded to the tune of three U.K. hits—"Love Resurrection," "All Cried Out," and "Invisible." — *William Ruhlmann*

Raindancing / 1987 / Columbia ✦✦✦

○ **Hoodoo** / 1991 / Columbia ✦✦✦✦
Moyet's voice has never sounded bigger or more expressive than it does on this disc. The arrangements span popular African-American music from the Delta to the dance floor, and every tune is delivered with an amazing emotional intensity. —*J. Poet*

Essex / 1994 / Columbia ✦✦✦

Mtume

Group, Soul, Disco, R&B
A former jazz percussionist, Mtume moved into Urban Contemporary and funk in the late '70s, and became one of the more successful producers and performers in both styles during the '80s. The son of the great jazz saxophonist Jimmy Heath, Mtume was a conga player and percussionist who recorded and toured with Miles Davis and was featured on albums by the Heath Brothers, Sonny Rollins, Herbie Hancock, Joe Henderson, and Freddie Hubbard. He even recorded as a bandleader for Strata-East before turning to funk in the late '70s. Mtume's band included the sassy, sultry vocalist Tawatha Agee, keyboardist Phil Fields, and bassist Ray Johnson. They had a number one R&B hit with "Juicy Fruit" for Epic in 1983 and a number two single in 1984 with "You, Me and He." They recorded for Epic until the late '80s. Agee went solo in 1987. Their final Top Ten hit was "Breathless" in 1986. Mtume also teamed with another ex-jazz musician, Reggie Lucas, who had also been in Davis' '70s band. They produced and/or wrote for such artists as Stephanie Mills, Roberta Flack/Donny Hathaway, Phyllis Hyman, Gary Bartz, Sadane, Lou Rawls, Rena Scott, and Eddie Henderson in the late '70s. The duo worked on the LP *In Search of the Rainbow Seekers* for Epic in 1980. Mtume worked on his own as a producer with several artists, among them Levert, Tyrone Brunson, Roy Ayers, Henderson, Tease, and Sue Ann. — *Ron Wynn*

Kiss This World Goodbye / Nov. 1978 / Epic ✦✦

In Search of the Rainbow Seekers / 1980 / Epic ✦✦✦

You & Me / 1984 / Epic ✦✦✦

You, Me & He / 1984 / Epic ✦✦✦
This was one of Mtume's late-'80s "sophisti-funk" projects, with a mix of socially conscious lyrics, love songs, and uptempo cuts, plus collective vocals and sparing production and arrangements. The title cut was a huge R&B hit, peaking at number two and even generating some crossover pop action. Mtume got two other R&B smashes, one in the Top 20, and the album proved one of his best. —*Ron Wynn*

● **Juicy Fruit** / 1985 / Epic ✦✦✦✦

Native Son / 1985 / MCA ✦✦✦
Mtume participated in the soundtrack for this poorly distributed, uneven remake of the film conceived out of the landmark novel by Richard Wright, who appeared in an earlier version. Oprah Winfrey was in the cast for this edition, but her presence didn't ensure them the widespread distribution or publicity necessary to salvage it. The soundtrack was quite similar to the film—strong at times, but disjointed and ultimately disappointing. —*Ron Wynn*

Theater of the Mind / Epic ✦✦✦
Former jazz percussionist James Mtume moved into soul and funk in the 1980s, and then changed gears again in the mid- and late '80s. This was one of an album series Mtume called "sophisti-

funk" LPs, with a denser, sparser sound than his previous works and devoid of string or horn support. Mtume managed to both get R&B chart hits like "P.O.P." and also make some biting, satirical comments about materialism and commercialism. —*Ron Wynn*

Mu

Group, Art-Rock/Progressive-Rock, Psychedelic
This intriguing early '70s Southern Californian group featured the talents of singer/songwriter Merrell Fankhauser (who was also at the helm of cult classics in the '60s by Fapardokly and HMS Bounty) and Jeff Cotton, previously slide guitarist with Captain Beefheart. Their sole album (from 1971) is a gem of the late hippie era, combining the fractured blues-based tangents of Beefheart with the loose flow and stoned lyricism of bands like the late '60s Grateful Dead. After a couple more singles, Mu moved to Maui and cut a fair amount of unreleased material before breaking up around 1974. Their eponymous album, as well as a lot of their unreleased material, was reissued in the 1980s. —*Richie Unterberger*

● **Mu** / 1971 / Reckless ✦✦✦✦
One of the best overlooked albums of the early '70s. Daring rhythms and song structures that build off the blues without following the standard three-chord/12-bar progressions, occasional modal jazzy sax by Cotton, and great slide guitar combine to form one of the most unclassifiable recordings of the time, with a high-spirited lightness that avoids the heavy excesses that sometimes burdened late-period psychedelia. —*Richie Unterberger*

End of an Era / 1988 / Reckless ✦✦✦
17 songs recorded after their relocation to Maui in 1974. More subdued and acoustic than the *Mu* LP, but still worthwhile, with Crosby, Stills, & Nash-like harmonies, melancholy melodies, and almost prototypically hippie-ish lyrics about visitations from other planets, searches for lost lands, mystical love, and the like. —*Richie Unterberger*

Mudhoney

Group, Alternative Pop/Rock, Garage Rock
With their fuzzed-out guitars and Mark Arm's straining vocals, Mudhoney defined '80s and '90s grunge rock. In fact, their 1988 debut single "Touch Me, I'm Sick" is the definitive grunge song— an obnoxious, dirty song driven by massively distorted guitars and a screaming vocal. It was a terrific, invigorating song that the band rewrote on each album that followed, but that's alright because Mudhoney only has one other song—a slow, sludgy Stooges grind. But their limitations are ultimately endearing; the band is a punk band, not like a '70s or '80s group, but like a '60s garage band, kicking out the same three chords with an unbridled enthusiasm. Leave the serious themes to Nirvana, Pearl Jam, Soundgarden, and Alice in Chains—Mudhoney takes the same themes but makes them sleazy and trashy, like the Russ Myers' film they named themselves after. Their records are inconsistent but when they are good, they are great. —*Stephen Thomas Erlewine*

● **Superfuzz Bigmuff (& Early Singles)** / 1988 / Sub Pop ✦✦✦✦
Combining the band's first EP with a handful of early singles, highlighted by the classic "Touch Me, I'm Sick," this disc showcases Mudhoney at their most furious and fine. *Superfuzz Bigmuff* keeps the overextended riffing and hyper-vocalizing down to a minimum, focusing on maximum-torque, metallic garage raunch. A release that provides as much bite as bark. —*John Dougan & Meredith Erlewine*

Mudhoney / Jul. 1989 / Sub Pop ✦✦✦
Mudhoney's first full-length album cut away the acid-rock excesses of their debut EP, concentrating on a tighter, punkier sound, highlighted by the raging "You Got It (Keep It Out of My Face)." —*Stephen Thomas Erlewine*

○ **Every Good Boy Deserves Fudge** / 1991 / Sub Pop ✦✦✦✦
It's no great stylistic breakthrough, but what Mudhoney record is? Instead, it's another solid album of fuzzed-out three-chord garage rockers. There's nothing as great as "Touch Me, I'm Sick" or "In 'N' Out of Grace," but song for song, it's their most consistent album. —*Stephen Thomas Erlewine*

Piece of Cake / Oct. 1992 / Reprise ✦✦✦
While their first major-label album isn't as raw as their earlier singles, Mudhoney hasn't lost their apathetic, slacker attitude. Full of short jokes between tracks (ranging from a rip on techno music to 28 seconds of flatulence), *Piece of Cake* is a muddled album show-

ing flashes of brilliance. The thundering opener, "No End In Sight," and the pulverizing single "Suck You Dry" fill the hammering grunge quotient, while the band veers off into slower territory on other tracks and is almost equally successful. The fuzz guitars never let up. —*Stephen Thomas Erlewine*

Five Dollar Bob's Mock Cooter Stew / 1993 / Reprise ✦✦✦
A stopgap EP that sounds like it was recorded in a garage, *Five Dollar Bob's Mock Cooter Stew* has some of Mudhoney's rawest and best rock & roll. —*Stephen Thomas Erlewine*

○ **My Brother The Cow** / 1995 / Reprise ✦✦✦✦
Mudhoney doesn't have an expansive musical vocabulary, they're all about grunge. Naturally, they don't abandon it now that it's no longer hip—they just keep going and going. In fact, they make it harsher and nastier, stripping melody off of the songs. The guitar hooks growl, occasionally sinking their teeth in and Mark Arm has never sounded quite so pissed off. *My Brother The Cow* isn't much for songs—it's nearly all sneering attitude—yet the sound is positively galvanizing. —*Stephen Thomas Erlewine*

The Muffs

Group, Alternative Pop/Rock
Led by guitarist/vocalist Kim Shattuck, the Muffs follow the punk-pop tradition of the Ramones and Buzzcocks, churning out of fuzzy, hook-driven three-minute pop singles. The group released their self-titled debut in 1993 without gaining much attention. Recorded after a lineup change which brought former Redd Kross bassist into the group, 1995's *Blonder and Blonder* received more attention, thanks to their association with neo-punk sensations Green Day, though it failed to break through to a wider audience. —*Stephen Thomas Erlewine*

● **The Muffs** / May 11, 1993 / Reprise ✦✦✦✦
The Muffs leave the garage behind and retrogress to caves for this self-titled release. Shattuck tries almost too hard to sound grungy and amateurish, then blows her cover with some cool melodies on "Everywhere I Go". There's a certain charm to the group's 3-chord riffing and primitive rhythms (provided by the male half of the quartet) that seems to have most appeal when driving a vehicle beyond the posted speed limit on a hot, sunny day. But stretched over 16 tracks, the forced minimalism begins to wane in appeal. —*Roch Parisien*

○ **Blonder And Blonder** / 1995 / Reprise ✦✦✦✦
While the band has changed significantly since their debut, the Muffs' second album, *Blonder and Blonder*, sounds nearly identical to their first. It's all a brightly colored collection of fuzzed-out guitars, Kim Shattuck's screaming pop melodies and punk rhythms, delivered with just the right touch of abandon and just the right amount of polish. Even though the band is long-time friends with Green Day, the repetition of the formula hits a little too close for comfort. Shattuck's songs aren't quite as strong as Billie Joe's, yet her hooks catch hold often enough to make *Blonder and Blonder* enjoyable for most fans of punk-pop. —*Stephen Thomas Erlewine*

Maria Muldaur

b. Sep. 12, 1943
Pop/Rock
Singer Maria Muldaur was born Maria D'Amato in New York City. In the 1960s, she was a member of the New York-based Even Dozen Jug Band and later of the Boston-based Jim Kweskin Jug Band, which also included her husband, Geoff Muldaur, from whom she was divorced in 1972. She found solo success with the sultry single "Midnight at the Oasis," which was featured on her debut solo album, *Maria Muldaur*, in 1973, and she followed with several similar albums, though her commercial success declined. In the 1980s, Muldaur began performing as a Christian artist. She continues to work the club circuit successfully. —*William Ruhlmann*

● **Maria Muldaur** / 1974 / Reprise ✦✦✦✦
Waitress in a Donut Shop / 1974 / Reprise ✦✦✦
Maria Muldaur's followup to her gold-selling debut album includes her second (and final) hit single "I'm A Woman" and presents a pleasant folk-blues mixture of material including everything from contemporary songs by Wendy Waldman and Anna McGarrigle to Skip James blues tunes and Fats Waller's "Squeeze Me," all given Muldaur's earthy, enthusiastic treatment. —*William Ruhlmann*

○ **Sweet Harmony** / 1976 / Reprise ✦✦✦✦
Southern Winds / 1978 / Reprise ✦✦
Open Your Eyes / 1979 / Reprise ✦✦
○ **Sweet & Low** / 1983 / Tudor ✦✦✦✦
○ **Gospel Night** / 1988 / Takoma ✦✦✦✦
Meet Me At Midnite / 1994 / Black Top
○ **Louisiana Love Call** / Black Top ✦✦✦✦

Mumps

Group, New Wave
The Mumps were one of the most obscure, but distinctive, New York bands of the late '70s, performing an absurdly theatrical fusion of pop, punk and glam rock. Led by vocalist Lance Loud, the group's music was an affectionate satire of '70s kitsch culture, predating the similar obsessions of the B-52's by a number of years. The Mumps rocked as hard as the New York Dolls, while writing clever pop hooks that updated trashy garage and bubblegum singles of the '70s.

Although they never even earned a large underground following, the group was a favorite of many punk rockers of the era (including the Ramones, Blondie, the New York Dolls, X, Television, the Cramps, Devo, and the Go-Go's), as well as '80s alternative rockers like R.E.M., Game Theory, and Sparks.

In addition to Lance Loud, the core linup of the Mumps also featured keyboardist Kristiann Hoffman, guitarist Rob Duprey, bassist Kevin Kiely, and drummer Paul Rutner. Over the years, the lineup changed slightly, with Loud, Hoffman, and Duprey remaining the constant members in each incarnation of the band. The Mumps only released two singles while they were active in the late '70s, but in 1994 Eggbert Records released a CD called *Fatal Charms* that compiled everything the band ever recorded, including outtakes, alternate takes, and live rehearsals. *Fatal Charms* proves that the Mumps' music remains vibrant, creative, and intoxicatingly bizzare nearly 20 years after it was recorded. — *Stephen Thomas Erlewine*

○ **Fatal Charm** / 1994 / Eggbert ✦✦✦✦

Elliott Murphy

b. Mar. 16, 1949
Singer-Songwriter, Folk-Rock
A New York-based folk-rock singer/songwriter who emerged with the acclaimed *Aquashow* in 1973 and has since built a cult following in the U.S. and Europe. — *William Ruhlmann*

● **Aquashow** / 1973 / PolyGram ✦✦✦✦
Highly literate songs played with an instrumentation (rock band, harmonica, piano, and organ) and in a manner strongly reminiscent of mid-'60s Bob Dylan. The lyrics provide a telling portrait of suburban life. — *William Ruhlmann*

Lost Generation / 1975 / RCA ✦✦✦
Night Lights / 1976 / RCA ✦✦
○ **Just a Story from America** / 1977 / Columbia ✦✦✦✦
Murphy travels to England for a streamlined rock sound featuring session aces such as guitarist Mick Taylor and drummer Phil Collins. But it's the songs, such as "Drive All Night," "Rock Ballad," and the title tune, that make the album a standout. — *William Ruhlmann*

Party Girls/Broken Poets / 1984 / Dejadisc ✦✦✦
Backed by a seasoned three-piece band, Murphy again turns in a high-quality rocking collection, spearheaded by "Three Complete American Novels" and "Blues Responsibility." (Import) — *William Ruhlmann*

Milwaukee / 1986 / EMIS ✦✦✦
Murphy adopts a more contemporary rock sound (with production on two tracks by Talking Head Jerry Harrison) for songs often touching on hard and desperate themes. — *William Ruhlmann*

○ **Diamonds by the Yard** / Jun. 19, 1992 / Razor & Tie ✦✦✦✦
Diamonds by the Yard compiles 17 tracks Murphy recorded in the '70s, offering an effective overview of his career. It's also necessary, since nearly all of his albums are out of print in America. — *David Jehnzen*

Peter Murphy

Alternative Pop/Rock
After leaving Bauhaus and a short-lived group with ex-Japan member Mick Karn, Peter Murphy launched a solo career in 1986. Murphy's solo albums are a combination of Bauhaus' goth and the synth-based art-rock of Bowie, Roxy Music, and Japan. As his career progressed, he began writing in the stylistic restrictions of a pop song, as well as adding some dance-rock elements. — *Stephen Thomas Erlewine*

Should the World Fail to Fall / 1986 / Beggars Banquet ✦✦
Love Hysteria / 1988 / Beggars Banquet ✦✦✦
● **Deep** / 1990 / Beggars Banquet ✦✦✦✦
This contains Murphy's dramatic alternative rock hit "Cuts You Up." Forceful grooves and thick (somewhat dissonant) arrangements and production propel material reminiscent of David Bowie's work with Brian Eno. — *Rick Clark*

Holy Smoke / Apr. 14, 1992 / Beggars Banquet ✦✦✦
Cascade / 1995 / Beggars Banquet ✦✦

Music Explosion

Group, Pop/Rock
One-hit-wonder Ohio garage band that reached number two in 1967 with "Little Bit O'soul," a great gutsy pop/rock number with a classic bass-organ riff. Whatever personality they may have had was coated in the studio by producers Jeffrey Katz and Jerry Kasenetz, who would soon help create bubblegum with acts like the 1910 Fruitgum Co. and the Ohio Express. The Music Explosion didn't have nearly as juvenile a sound as those groups, but they never latched onto another piece of material nearly as attention-grabbing as "Little Bit O'soul," entering the Top 100 only once more with the tiny hit "Sunshine Games." — *Richie Unterberger*

Little Bit O'soul / 1967 / Performance ✦✦✦
14 tracks taken from their sole album and several non-hit singles. Nothing comes close to matching the ultra-catchy "Little Bit O'soul," and in fact, on the whole it's quite mediocre and unmemorable. — *Richie Unterberger*

● **Anthology** / 1995 / One Way ✦✦✦✦

Music Machine

Group, Psychedelic, Garage Rock
Most famous for "Talk Talk," a Top 20 single from 1966 that was one of the most manic '60s garage-punk hits, the Music Machine had much more depth and songwriting talent than the typical one-hit wonders of the day. Lead singer and songwriter Sean Bonniwell's strangled lyrics and dark, verbose vision paced the group's wiry psychedelic guitar lines and ominous, minor-key Farfisa organ. Only one album was released with the original lineup, and the group's ferocious energy was diluted on subsequent recordings. Despite chalking up only one more minor hit single ("The People In Me"), the Music Machine recorded quite a few excellent, imaginatively produced singles and album tracks that find them exploring the darker side of psychedelia with compelling intensity and imagination. — *Richie Unterberger*

○ **(Turn On) the Music Machine** / 1966 / Original Sound ✦✦✦✦
Bonniwell Music Machine / 1968 / Warner Brothers ✦✦✦
● **Best of the Music Machine** / 1984 / Rhino ✦✦✦✦
Besides "Talk Talk" and "The People In Me," this features the best cuts from their first LP, some fine non-LP singles that rank among the best obscure gems of the psychedelic era, and some decent previously unissued cuts. The package is enhanced by detailed liner notes by Sean Bonniwell. — *Richie Unterberger*

My Bloody Valentine

Group, Alternative Pop/Rock
My Bloody Valentine is ear-splittingly loud, constructing their records with layers of sound and noise. It may sound unlistenable at first, but the sheer sonics of the band are beautiful and shimmering, with the vocals only adding another texture to the overall sound; underneath the white noise, the band plays simple, melodic pop. Comparisons to the Jesus and Mary Chain or Sonic Youth may be inevitable, but My Bloody Valentine is much more atmospheric than either band; their distorted noise is not confrontational or aggressive, it is rolling sheets of gorgeous dissonance. After several years of independent label releases, the band released the monolithic *Loveless* in 1991 which increased their cult dramatically. Although they haven't released a record since

Loveless, their fan base has not diminished. —*Stephen Thomas Erlewine*

This Is Your Bloody Valentine / 1985 / Tycoon ✦✦✦
With the original line-up, it's different from other releases. —*Steve Aldrich*

Ecstacy / 1987 / Lazy ✦✦✦
This mini-LP was later fleshed out to full length in Lazy 12 reissue. —*Steve Aldrich*

○ **Isn't Anything** / 1988 / Creation/Sire ✦✦✦✦
The first of My Bloody Valentine's two landmark albums, *Isn't Anything* combines delicate, brittle melodies and big guitars. "Lose My Breath" and "No More Sorry" highlight Belinda Butcher's understated but charismatic voice, while guitars take the spotlight on "Cupid Come." Songs like "Sue Is Fine" and the seminal "Feed Me with Your Kiss" point towards the band's future sound of fuzzed-out, multi-tracked guitars and blissful male-female vocal harmonies. An underrated and surprisingly accessible album. —*Heather Phares*

Ecstacy & Wine / 1989 / Lazy ✦✦✦
This is a combination of *Ecstasy* mini-LP and *Strawberry Wine* EP. —*Steve Aldrich*

○ **Glider** / 1989 / Sire ✦✦✦✦

● **Loveless** / 1991 / Sire ✦✦✦✦
One of the best and most influential albums in '90s alternative rock, *Loveless* puts the band's innovative sonic style over lyrical substance. And the sonic styles of *Loveless* change constantly: Drums bludgeon the listener's ears and fade into nothingness; guitars whine like chainsaws and hum like cellos. The intricate mix of feedback, guitar washes and dreamy harmonies on songs like "Til Here Knows When" and "Blown a Wish" is awe-inspiring; though it takes My Bloody Valentine many years of work to complete their albums, it's easy to understand why when the results are this breathtaking. —*Heather Phares*

My Life with the Thrill Kill Kult

Group, House Music, Alternative Pop/Rock
Most house-based dance music is either completely devoid of content or has a fairly serious political consciousness. Not so with My Life with the Thrill Kill Kult. With its schlocky mix of samples, synths, beats, Satan, and sex, the group is a hyped-up, stylized psychdelic dance troupe that revels in bad taste of all kinds. And the sheer tastelessness of their records gained a large cult following in the early '90s, culminating in their *Sexplosion!* album and its single, "Sex on Wheels." —*Stephen Thomas Erlewine*

I See Good Spirits & I See Bad Spirits / 1988 / Wax Trax! ✦✦✦

Kooler Than Jesus / 1990 / Wax Trax! ✦✦

○ **Confessions of a Knife** / 1990 / Wax Trax! ✦✦✦✦

● **Sexplosion!** / 1991 / Interscope ✦✦✦✦
A trashy kaleidoscope of an album, it's full of campy samples and pulsating rhythm tracks, highlighted by the single "Sex on Wheels." —*David Jehnzen*

13 Above the Night / 1994 / Interscope ✦✦

The Mystic Tide

Group, Psychedelic, Garage Rock
Of the many garage bands who released unrecognized and obscure singles in the mid-'60s, the Mystic Tide were one of the very best. The Long Island group released four singles on their own labels in the 1966 and 1967, mostly for distribution at their own gigs (and apparently they didn't sell too well there either). While the production on these is fairly raw, the group had genuine original talent, pursuing a dark, psychedelic vision with overloaded distorted guitar breaks. Their tunes (all written by guitarist Joe Docko) combined the minor-key melodies of British Invasion groups like the Zombies with the raunch of acts like Them. Unlike most other American groups following this path, however, they added a mysterioso (at times vaguely Middle Eastern) element that echoed the innovations of groups like the Doors, the Velvet Underground, and the very early Pink Floyd and Soft Machine, though the Mystic Tide most likely didn't hear any of these groups. Their sound and outlook were perhaps too foreboding for even local success, and the group disbanded in 1967, ironically finding a much greater audience when their singles were reissued for psych/garage collectors in the 1980s. —*Richie Unterberger*

● **Solid Ground** / 1994 / Distortions ✦✦✦✦
Both sides of their four singles, plus three earlier demos in a lighter, more Zombies-like style. The grinding "Frustration" and the ominous "Running Through The Night," featuring Docko's prickly psychedelic guitar, are garage classics; the lengthy instrumental "Psychedelic Journey" anticipates Pink Floyd's "Interstellar Overdrive"; and "I Search For A New Love" has delightful interweaving harmonies. The final seven tracks on this 18-cut single were recorded by Docko in the late '60s, with a lumbering, sub-Hendrix approach (including two Mystic Tide remakes). Fortunately, their placement at the end of the CD means that they can be ignored with ease by discriminating listeners. —*Richie Unterberger*

Mystics

Group, Doo-Wop
Doc Pomus and Mort Shuman wrote "Hushabye," this Brooklyn quintet's only big hit, for the Laurie label in 1959. With Phil Cracolici as lead, "Don't Take the Stars" barely charted later that year. The Mystics made an impressive comeback in 1981 with an album on Ambient Sound and a starring role on a doo-wop-drenched episode of PBS-TV's award-winning musical program "Soundstage." —*Bill Dahl*

● **16 Golden Classics** / Collectables ✦✦✦✦
Late-'50s/early-'60s Italian-American doo-wop from the street corners of Brooklyn, NY. —*Bill Dahl*

N

Naked Eyes

Group, Techno-Pop/Dance, New Wave
This quintessential early-'80s MTV synth-pop duo, made up of
Pete Byrne (vocals) and Rob Fisher (keyboards), hit it big with
"Promises, Promises" and a remake of Dionne Warwick's "Always
Something There to Remind Me" (#8). —*Rick Clark*

○ **Naked Eyes** / 1983 / EMI America ♦♦♦♦
A sterling synthesizer debut features their hit remake of "Always
Something There to Remind Me." —*Larry Lapka*

Burning Bridges / 1983 / EMI ♦♦♦

Fuel for the Fire / 1984 / EMI America ♦♦

● **Promises, Promises: the Very Best of Naked Eyes** / Apr. 19, 1994
/ EMI America ♦♦♦♦
Promises, Promises features every worthwhile song Naked Eyes
ever recorded, making it the definitve collection. —*AMG*

Napalm Death

Group, Hard Rock, Heavy Metal
Napalm Death are the kings of grindcore, a subgenre of metal that
takes the extremes of hardcore punk, thrash metal, and industrial,
making a music that is extreme, brutal, metallic, and brief; many
of their songs are under two minutes in length, some are as short
as five seconds. With their harsh, uncompromising albums, the
band has gained a cult following in America and Europe since
their first album in 1987. —*Stephen Thomas Erlewine*

Scum / 1987 / Earache ♦♦♦
Perhaps the first real grindcore album, Napalm Death's debut
packs in 28 tracks, some of which clock in at less than ten seconds.
They can't really be called "songs"; they're mostly furious blasts of
punk- and thrash-influenced noise with unintelligible, disgusting
vocals about injustice. An influential album and a classic of its
kind. —*Steve Huey*

○ **From Enslavement to Obliteration** / 1988 / Earache ♦♦♦♦
Their second album only ups the ante, incorporating influences
from the so-called NYC "avant-noise" scene (typified by bands like
Sonic Youth, Swans, Live Skull, etc.) and lengthening the tracks.
This was the last full-length album with their original sound; Lee
Dorrian left to form Cathedral, and the revamped lineup took a
more conventional (although only slightly more listenable),
thrash-influenced approach. —*Steve Huey*

● **Harmony Corruption** / 1990 / Earache ♦♦♦♦
The kings of grindcore have disturbing lyrics and fast-paced music with no remorse. —*John Book*

○ **Death by Manipulation** / 1991 / Earache ♦♦♦♦
This is a compilation of three EPs from their home of England. —
John Book

Utopia Banished / Jun. 23, 1992 / Earache ♦♦
Blinding guitar speed (for it's own sake?), a brutal, no-mercy psy-
chobabble of indecipherable vocals, and pummelling percussion
characterize Napalm Death on *Utopia Banished.* —*Roch Parisien*

Fear Emptiness Despair / 1994 / Sony ♦♦♦
Incredible as it may seem, this is Napalm Death's major-label debut. They haven't toned things down a bit, keeping their noisy,
thick, atonal guitar sound and Barney Greenway's painful-sound-
ing vocals. For those keeping track, original bassist Shane Embury
is still with the group. —*Steve Huey*

Steve Nardella

Rock & Roll, Blues Rock
Nardella is a strong, American-roots-music performer, equally
adept at rockabilly and lowdown blues. His first known recording,
behind Detroit bluesman Bobo Jenkins on "Shake 'Em on Down,"
also featured the debut work of Austin, TX, mainstay Sarah Brown
and Fran Christina of the Fabulous Thunderbirds. Nardella
formed the local Boogie Brothers band with Brown, Christina, and
John Nicholas (Asleep at the Wheel, Guitar Johnny & the Guitar
Rockers), backing any blues legend who came into their native
Ann Arbor, appearing on Atlantic's *1972 Ann Arbor Blues & Jazz
Festival* behind Johnny Shines, and doing their own solo turn. After the nucleus of the band moved to Boston with Nicholas,
Nardella formed the Silvertones with local guitar hot-shot George
Bedard, recording one fine album for the Blind Pig label. Nardella
has continued on his own since then, expanding his musical gen-
res beyond just straight blues forms and turning out some interesting music along the way. —*Cub Koda*

It's All Rock & Roll / 1979 / Blind Pig ♦♦♦
Extraordinary rock, R&B, and rockabilly influences all come out of
Nardella's love for blues. As well as posessing a strong voice,
Nardella is also an electrifying guitarist in the Chuck Berry mold,
Nardella's a rare bird, with more talent than he can harvest. —
Michael G. Nastos

● **Daddy Rollin' Stone** / 1993 / Schoolkids ♦♦♦♦
Hard rocking music from a mix of rock, rockabilly, and R&B on
Silvertones-member Nardella's solo outing. —*AMG*

Nas

Rap
Queensbridge, New York native Nas (born Nasir Jones) appeared
on Main Source's "Live At The BBQ," and his first album *Illmatic,*
appeared in 1994. The LP also showcased the skills of DJ Premier,
Large Professor, Pete Rock, and Q-Tip. It's billed as a "reality storybook;" Nas' raps detail the harsh realities of inner-city life with an
honest quality. —*John Bush*

○ **Illmatic** / 1994 / Columbia ♦♦♦♦

Johnny Nash

b. Aug. 19, 1940
Soul, Pop/Rock
Native-Texan Johnny Nash experienced his first chart success in
1958 with the #23 hit "A Very Special Love." By the end of the
'60s, Nash had begun recording in Jamaica and formed his own
record labels, Joda and Jad. He became one of the first artists to
bring reggae into the pop mainstream, with the 1968 #5 hit "Hold
Me Tight," 1972's #1 "I Can See Clearly Now," and a 1973 #12 version of Bob Marley's "Stir It Up." —*Rick Clark*

● **I Can See Clearly Now** / 1972 / Epic ♦♦♦♦
This is West Indian music for a pop audience, rhythmic and
melodic. Nash helped open the mass-market doors to reggae. The
title song and "Stir It Up" are winners. —*Hank Davis*

The Reggae Collection / 1993 / Epic ♦♦♦
Nash was the first American singer to incorporate reggae
rhythms, and as such deserves a lot of credit for paving the way
for the acceptance of bonafide Jamaican performers. His own pop-
soul-reggae concoctions, though, were often rather watery in comparison to the real thing. This brings together 20 of the reggae-
style tracks he cut between 1968 and the mid-'70s, including his

hits "Hold Me Tight," "Cupid," and "Stir It Up"; the version of "I Can See Clearly Now" is an alternate take. This leans too heavily on his 1972-75 Epic material without enough of his late-'60s work; the small hit "You Got Soul" is missing, and the delightfully light and soaring "Hold Me Tight" towers over most everything else here. Almost half the tracks were previously unreleased or previously unavailable in the U.S. —*Richie Unterberger*

The Nashville Teens

Group, British Invasion
The Nashville Teens' "Tobacco Road" was one of the British Invasion's better one-shot hits. Their 1964 rearrangement of John Loudermilk's folkish tune, built around insistently hammering riffs and soulful dual lead vocals, was their only Top 20 entry in the U.S. Although they never had another hit in America and only had one other sizable hit in the U.K. (Loudermilk's "Google Eye"), the group continued to record singles throughout the rest of the '60s. The Teens never came close to matching their one taste of glory, commercially or aesthetically. Their ragged R&B covers didn't remotely match the Stones, Yardbirds or Pretty Things, and without any songwriting talent to speak of, they drifted rather aimlessly in search of an identity or style, stabbing at straight pop, folk-rock, and hard rock. Keyboardist John Hawken joined Renaissance in the late '60s. —*Richie Unterberger*

Tobacco Road / 1964 / London ✦✦✦
A representative album by the group, with lots of loud R&B, but not rough or tough enough to compete with the Rolling Stones, Kinks, et al. —*Bruce Eder*

Nashville Teens / 1974 / New World ✦✦✦
A mid-'70s reissue with some hard-to-find tracks that are actually superior to much of the released tracks from the 1960s. Probably the best single album by this band. —*Bruce Eder*

Remembering / 197z / Decca ✦✦✦

Live at the Red House / 1984 / Shanghai ✦✦

● **Best of the Nashville Teens** / 1993 / EMI ✦✦✦✦
The group recorded a fair amount of material in the '60s, almost all of which is included on this 24-track anthology, which contains their sole album (from 1964) and several singles. They had no songwriting talent (only two of these tunes are originals); and they drifted rather aimlessly in search of an identity or style, stabbing at straight pop, folk-rock, and hard rock. Some Shel Talmy-produced numbers from 1966 are of mild interest, as are some nicely arranged folk-pop tunes from 1965 (which suffer from mediocre vocals), but even British Invasion completists will be unimpressed by this collection. As a final insult, the mix of "Tobacco Road" which leads off this set is notably inferior to the familiar hit vinyl version. —*Richie Unterberger*

Naughty by Nature

Group, Rap
One of the finest new rap posses received some help from Queen Latifah on their 1991 debut and landed a huge hit with the naggingly incessant "O.P.P."
Naughty By Nature scored another huge hit with their next release. *19 Naughty III* featured "Hip Hip Hooray," which rivaled "O.P.P." as a crossover smash and national catchphrase in '93. —*John Floyd*

● **Naughty by Nature** / 1991 / Tommy Boy ✦✦✦✦
This leering trio's first single, "O.P.P.," dominated the airwaves in the fall of 1991 on the strength of its home-truth bedroom message and its butt-hugging beat. Fans of the single will find plenty more in NBN's rollicking debut album. —*John Floyd*

○ **19 Naughty III** / 1993 / Tommy Boy ✦✦✦✦
With its slamming beats and infectious hooks (exemplified by the hit single "Hip Hop Hooray"), *19 Naughty III*, Naughty by Nature's second album, proves that they're not a one-hit-wonder group. Although the music is terrific, the lyrical posturing and misogyny can grow tiresome. —*Stephen Thomas Erlewine*

Poverty's Paradise / 1995 / Tommy Boy ✦✦✦
For their third album, Naughty By Nature do little to truly change their style. Some of the beats are little slower and funkier, some of the rhymes are more dexterous, some of the rhythms are a little more complex—yet nothing distinguishes *Poverty's Paradise* from the group's two previous, and superior, records. —*Stephen Thomas Erlewine*

Nazareth

Group, Hard Rock
The Scottish hard rock quartet Nazareth had a handful of hard rock hits in the late '70s, including the proto-power ballad, "Love Hurts." Formed in 1968, the band featured vocalist Dan McCafferty, guitarist Manny Charlton, bassist Pete Agnew, and drummer Darrell Sweet. The band had relocated to London by 1970, and they released their self-titled debut album in 1971. Both *Nazareth* and 1972's *Exercises* received favorable attention by British hard rockers, but it was 1973's *Razamanaz* that moved them into the U.K. Top Ten (both "Broken Down Angel" and "Bad Bad Boy" were hit singles). *Loud N' Proud* and *Rampant* (both 1974) followed the same formula, yet it was slightly less successful.
Released the following year, *Hair of the Dog* established Nazareth as an internationally popular hard rock band. Featuring their revamped version of the Everly Brothers' "Love Hurts," the album sold over a million copies in the U.S. Until the end of the '70s, the band continued successfully as a quartet, releasing a series of Top 100 albums. In 1979, they added former Sensational Alex Harvey band guitarist Zal Cleminson to their lineup; he left after recording two albums—1979's *No Mean City* and 1980's *Malice in Wonderland*—and was replaced by former Spirit keyboardist John Locke. Following the live 1981 album *'Snaz*, guitarist Bill Rankin also joined the group; Locke left soon after his addition and Rankin switched to keyboards.
By this time, their commercial appeal had dwindled across both the U.K. and the U.S. After 1985's *Play the Game*, Nazareth was left without a record contract, so the band was put on hiatus for a few years. They returned in 1992 with *No Jive*, which failed to gain an audience in America and Europe. —*Stephen Thomas Erlewine*

Nazareth / 1971 / A&M ✦✦✦

Exercises / 1972 / Warner Brothers ✦✦✦

Razamanaz / 1973 / A&M ✦✦

Rampant / 1974 / A&M ✦✦

Loud & Proud / 1974 / A&M ✦✦✦

● **Hair of the Dog** / 1975 / A&M ✦✦✦✦
Hair of the Dog is Nazareth's biggest hit, as well as their best album, containing both the thundering title track and their cover of "Love Hurts," which turned out to be the blueprint for the heavy-metal power ballads that dominated the pop charts of the late '80s. —*Stephen Thomas Erlewine*

○ **Classics, Vol. 16** / 1987 / A&M ✦✦✦✦
Classics, Vol. 16 collects all of Nazareth's hard rock radio hits, making it a preferable alternative to their frequently spotty albums. —*Stephen Thomas Erlewine*

The Nazz

Group, Psychedelic, Power Pop/Anglo-Pop
The Nazz (named after a Yardbirds song, "The Nazz Are Blue") was a Philadelphia-based quartet formed in 1967 by guitarist and songwriter Todd Rundgren, bassist Carson Van Osten, drummer Thom Mooney, and vocalist and keyboard player Robert "Stewkey" Antoni. Rejecting the free-form psychedelic rock and hippie fashions of the day, the group harked back a couple of years to the British Invasion, performing short, catchy pop songs, mostly written by Rundgren (sometimes with a hard rock edge), and sporting suits and Beatle haircuts. They released their debut album, *Nazz*, in 1968 and scored a minor hit single with Rundgren's plaintive ballad "Hello, It's Me" in 1969 (it recharted in 1970, and Rundgren had a Top Five hit with a new version in 1973). Critics and a growing audience were charmed but the Nazz fell apart in 1969, largely because of Rundgren's ascendancy. Predictably, he went on to his greatest success after the split. —*William Ruhlmann*

○ **Nazz** / 1968 / Rhino ✦✦✦✦

Nazz Nazz / 1969 / Rhino ✦✦

○ **Nazz III** / 1970 / Rhino ✦✦✦✦

● **The Best of Nazz** / 1983 / Rhino ✦✦✦✦
Contains good examples of the band's powerful uptempo material ("Open My Eyes"), the kind of Rundgren pop material that defined the group to its pop audience ("Hello, It's Me"), and some interesting covers ("Kicks," a previously unreleased "Train Kept A-Rollin'"). —*William Ruhlmann*

Me'Shell Ndegecello

R&B, Singer-Songwriter

Me'Shell Ndegecello blurs sexual conventions as much as any artist since Prince; more importantly, she blurs musical boundaries, too, creating a funky rock & roll that can veer off into sweet pop or dance-club bliss. Her 1993 debut, *Plantation Lullabies*, was critically acclaimed and scored a minor hit with "If That's Your Boyfriend (He Wasn't Last Night)," but she really began to receive mainstream attention with her hit 1994 duet with John Mellencamp, "Wild Night." —*Stephen Thomas Erlewine*

○ **Plantation Lullabies** / 1993 / Maverick ✦✦✦✦

Fred Neil

b. 1937, St. Petersburg, FL
Folk, Singer-Songwriter, Folk-Rock

Moody, bluesy, and melodic, Fred Neil was one of the most compelling folk-rockers to emerge from Greenwich Village in the mid-'60s. His albums showcased his extraordinarily low, rich voice on intensely personal and reflective compositions, sounding like a cross between Tim Buckley and Tim Hardin. His influence was subtle but significant; before forming the Lovin' Spoonful, John Sebastian played harmonica on Neil's first album, which also featured guitarist Felix Pappalardi, who went on to produce Cream. The Jefferson Airplane featured Neil's "Other Side of This Life" prominently in their concerts, and dedicated a couple songs ("Ballad of You and Me and Pooneil" and "House at Pooneil Corner") to him. As the B-side of "Crying," Neil's "Candy Man" was one of Roy Orbison's bluesiest efforts. Most famously, Harry Nilsson took Fred's "Everybody's Talkin'" into the Top Ten as the theme to the movie *Midnight Cowboy*. Always an enigmatic recluse, Neil retreated to his home in Coconut Grove, FL, after achieving cult success, and hasn't released anything since a live album in 1971. —*Richie Unterberger*

○ **Bleecker & MacDonald** / 1964 / Elektra ✦✦✦✦
Neil's Greenwich village coffeehouse roots are in strongest evidence on this album (later retitled *Little Bit of Rain*). The drummerless (but not entirely acoustic) LP is also his bluesiest recording. The uniformly strong tracks include "Other Side of This Life" and "Candy Man." —*Richie Unterberger*

● **Very Best of Fred Neil** / 1986 / See For Miles ✦✦✦✦
It doesn't include any of his Elektra tracks, but this is a good compilation of his Capitol work, including all of the 1967 album *Fred Neil* (which featured Stephen Stills) and four tracks from his follow-up LP *Sessions*. Contains "Everybody's Talkin'," "Green Rocky Road," and the beautiful "The Dolphins." —*Richie Unterberger*

Vince Neil

Group, Hard Rock, Heavy Metal

Vince Neil was the lead singer of the heavy metal band Mötley Crüe during the '80s. Following the group's multi-platinum mainstream breakthrough *Dr. Feelgood*, the rest of the band fired Neil in 1992. He embarked on a solo career in 1993, teaming with former Billy Idol guitarist Steve Stevens for *Exposed*; the record performed respectably, yet it failed to match Mötley Crüe standards. —*Stephen Thomas Erlewine*

Exposed / Apr. 27, 1993 / Warner Brothers
Anyone who loved Neil's sneering vocals throughout his years with Mötley Crüe will be delighted to find that he hasn't changed a thing for his first solo album. Anyone who wasn't enamored with the Crüe's sleazy raunch might be surprised by the strength of ex-Billy Idol sideman Steve Stevens' lively guitar, which stands heads and shoulders above the Crue's Mick Mars in both technique and personality. —*Stephen Thomas Erlewine*

Bill Nelson

Art-Rock/Progressive-Rock

As the guiding light of Bebop Deluxe, the Yorkshire-born Nelson was a guitar hero who combined the passionate excess of Jimi Hendrix with a cold, calculated intellectualism. As a solo artist, he often forsakes the guitar entirely in favor of keyboards and splicing tape, crafting a body of work that ranges from thumping funk (of a cerebral sort) to synth-pop and ambient murmurs. —*Michael P. Dawson*

Quit Dreaming & Get on the Beam / 1981 / Enigma ✦✦✦
One of Nelson's rockier efforts, it's similar to his work with Red Noise. —*Michael P. Dawson*

Sounding the Ritual Echo / 1981 / Enigma ✦✦✦
Instrumental theatre music, it was originally a bonus LP with *Quit Dreaming*. —*Michael P. Dawson*

● **Love That Whirls (Diary of a Thinking Man** / 1982 / Capitol ✦✦✦✦
Love That Whirls (Diary of a Thinking Heart) is infectious synthesizer-driven pop. —*Michael P. Dawson*

Summer of God's Piano / 1984 / Enigma ✦✦✦
This is the first volume of *Trial by Intimacy*, a four-disc collection of short instrumental pieces. —*Michael P. Dawson*

Catalogue of Obsessions / 1984 / Enigma ✦✦✦
The fourth volume of *Trial by Intimacy*. —*Michael P. Dawson*

Two-Fold Aspect of Everything / 1984 / Enigma ✦✦✦
This double CD collects rare tracks and demos. —*Michael P. Dawson*

Vistamix / 1984 / Epic ✦✦✦
A ten-song compilation. —*Michael P. Dawson*

Das Kabinet/La Belle et Bete / 1985 / Enigma ✦✦✦
Featured are two excellent soundtrack projects on one CD. —*Michael P. Dawson*

Chamber of Dreams (music from the Invisibility Exhibition) / 1986 / Enigma ✦✦✦
The second volume of *Trial by Intimacy*. —*Michael P. Dawson*

Chance Encounters in the Garden / 1987 / Enigma ✦✦✦
It's a double CD of instrumental miniatures. —*Michael P. Dawson*

Pavilions of the Heart & Soul / 1989 / Enigma ✦✦✦
The third volume of *Trial by Intimacy*. —*Michael P. Dawson*

Rick Nelson (Eric Hilliard Nelson)

b. May 8, 1940, Teaneck, NJ, d. Dec. 31, 1985
Rock & Roll, Country-Rock

Ricky Nelson made it a little safer for "respectable" American teenagers to rock. When 16-year-old Ricky cut his debut single in 1957—a timid cover of Fats Domino's "I'm Walkin'," allegedly on a dare from his girlfriend—the sneering image of Elvis Presley was still taboo in many households. Nelson, the nonthreatening, cleancut youth, commanded the perfect vehicle for spreading his rocking message—his family's beloved TV sitcom, *The Adventures of Ozzie and Harriet*.

With a genuine passion for Sun-style rockabilly and the searing lead-guitar work of Joe Maphis initially and later the brilliantly inventive James Burton (from "Believe What You Say" on), Ricky signed with Imperial later in 1957. He waxed one incendiary rocker after another, including "Stood Up," "Waitin' in School," and "It's Late." He introduced them via those TV airwaves, thus ensuring gold record status well into the '60s.

As the demand for unrelenting rock & roll slowly faded, Ricky's sound softened as well, with smoother material such as "Never Be Anyone Else But You" in 1959 and his 1961 chart-topper "Travelin' Man." A much-publicized name switch to Rick on his twenty-first birthday reflected that maturity.

But Nelson never forgot his roots, not even during the lean mid-'60s on Decca, when he ran dry of fresh material and revived too many old Tin Pan Alley standards that should have stayed buried. Returning triumphantly to the top in 1972 with the introspective *Garden Party*, Rick Nelson proved emphatically that he was more than just another teen-idol hunk, right up to his fatal plane crash on New Year's Eve of 1985.

Like his idols at Sun, this kid was born to rock—and showed America that it was no sin. —*Bill Dahl*

Ricky / 1957 / United Artists ✦✦✦
This debut is filled with bopping covers and Joe Maphis on lead guitar. —*Bill Dahl*

○ **Ricky Nelson** / 1958 / Imperial ✦✦✦✦
His second Imperial album is a classic, introducing the brilliant guitar of James Burton. —*Bill Dahl*

○ **Songs by Ricky** / 1959 / Imperial ✦✦✦✦
More first-class rockers by Ricky, and James Burton is amazing. —*Bill Dahl*

○ **Rick Is 21** / 1961 / Imperial ✦✦✦✦
...and he celebrates with some fine rock & roll, including "Hello Mary Lou." —*Bill Dahl*

Album Seven / 1962 / Imperial ✦✦✦
This underrated set contains several exceptional rockers. —*Bill Dahl*

Rick Nelson Sings for You / 1963 / MCA ✦✦✦
Still rocking at this point, it includes James Burton's ringing lead guitar. —*Bill Dahl*

For Your Sweet Love / 1963 / Decca ✦✦✦
His first Decca album is also his best, with a searing cover of "I've Got a Woman." —*Bill Dahl*

○ **Garden Party** / 1972 / MCA ✦✦✦✦
This comeback introduced Nelson to a new generation. —*Bill Dahl*

★ **Legendary Masters** / 1990 / EMI America ✦✦✦✦✦
Nelson at his early (1957-1960) best. His youthful vocals are backed by fiery rockabilly pioneers Joe Maphis and James Burton. —*Bill Dahl*

Best of 1963-1975 / 1990 / MCA ✦✦✦
No longer Rockin' Ricky, but Responsible Rick, his Decca output was wildly inconsistent. The early efforts like "Fools Rush In" and "String Along" still feature guitarist James Burton prominently. —*Bill Dahl*

○ **Best of Rick Nelson, Vol. 2** / 1991 / Capitol ✦✦✦✦
Focusing primarily on Rick's early-'60s material for Imperial, this 27-cut disc is not quite as rocking as Volume One, but still offers plenty of worthy moments. It includes all of his massive, midtempo teen idol ballad hits of the era: "Young World," "A Wonder Like You," "Teenage Idol," "It's Up To You," and the #1 hit "Travelin' Man." Teen ballads they might have been, but James Burton's masterful guitar licks and Nelson's assured, committed delivery placed them leagues above other teen-idol hits of the period. Of more interest to serious fans are the inclusion of several minor hit singles and covers of R&B tunes. And of course, there's the first-class rockabilly hit "Hello Mary Lou" (penned by Gene Pitney), perhaps his best recording of the decade. His surprisingly raucous cover of "Summertime" features, amazingly, the same bass line used as a hook on the Blues Magoos' psych-pop-garage hit "We Ain't Got Anything Yet" years later. The pleasures of this CD are modest but consistent. —*Richie Unterberger*

Stay Young: The Epic Recordings / Epic ✦✦✦
Stay Young is an entertaining overview of Rick Nelson's country-tinged years at Epic, proving that he recorded plenty of worthwhile material in the '70s. —*Stephen Thomas Erlewine*

BOOK

✦✦ **Ricky Nelson: Idol For A Generation**, by Joel Selvin (Contemporary Books, 1990). Sometimes dismissed as a teen idol during the early days of rock criticism, Nelson achieved belated respect as a rock & roller of real significance and talent. That doesn't mean, however, that his life was all that fascinating, and there really isn't enough material to construct a lengthy first-rate biography, although Selvin does a decent, workmanlike job with what he has. Nelson's records were good, but his creative input and vision rather slight, relying a good deal on his backup musicians, a good supply of outside material, and the enormous promotional value of weekly television exposure. So there's some interesting stuff about his early Imperial sessions, though not a great deal, and the details of his television and film career won't be of much interest to those who appreciate Ricky primarily from a musical perspective. The stylistic and commercial founderings of his final two decades, which saw him exploring early country-rock, hitting the charts a final time with "Garden Party," and generally becoming adrift in personal and economic problems, are covered thoroughly, but the music he made during this time was simply not nearly as significant as his early classics, and it doesn't make for scintillating reading. —*Richie Unterberger*

Nerves

Group, New Wave
They could've been contenders had they stayed together long enough, but the Nerves, despite their brief existence, were one of the most exciting bands in power pop. Formed by Jack Lee, Peter Case and Paul Collins in 1975, their career was over by 1978, but they produced a great EP that featured the power-pop classic "Hanging On the Telephone," which was later recorded (and wonderfully so) by Blondie. Ultimately, having three talented song-

writers in one band hurried the demise of the Nerves, and all three principles found greater happiness and success with their new bands, although Jack Lee (arguably the most talented songwriter of the three) had the shortest career and eventually dropped out of sight after a fine solo record (*Jack Lee's Greatest Hits Vol. 1*) in 1981. Case went on to form the Plimsouls, who recorded two good records and a transcendent pop song, "A Million Miles Away." After breaking up in 1984, Case recorded as a roots-rock solo act for the rest of the decade and into the '90s, although there is a rumor he's put the Plimsouls back together. Collins formed the Beat (later Paul Collins's Beat), who were merely OK, and has done little since the mid-'80s. —*John Dougan*

● **Nerves [EP]** / 1976 / Nerves ✦✦✦✦
There was only one EP; it had four songs, and each one is great. Although I'm sure this record has vanished from the face of the earth, if you run across it, snatch it up; it's wonderful. Best song: Paul Collins' "Working Too Hard." There is a French import release from 1986 that includes outtakes and some related ephemera. But, sadly, this EP stands as the sum total of a great band. —*John Dougan*

Notre Demo / 1981 / Good Vibration ✦✦✦

Michael Nesmith

b. Dec. 30, 1943, Houston, TX
Country-Rock, Singer-Songwriter, Folk-Rock
You'll get very little argument that Michael Nesmith's songs are the highlights of the Monkees' catalog. If given a chance on his own, Nesmith might have beat Gram Parsons in a race to invent country-rock. When he ceased to be "Monkee Mike," Nesmith created rootsy country music, unaffected by the often cynical approach of numerous contemporaries. Nesmith's stature as an outside producer grew, and he eventually shed much of the country influence of his writing before ultimately shelving his musical career entirely. What remains is a sizable body of solo work that too few have investigated. Now that it is readily available again, it would be well worth the effort to check out. —*Steve Aldrich*

Mike Nesmith Presents the Wichita Train Whistle Sings / 1968 / Dot ✦✦
Nesmith stepped away from the Monkees for this instrumental rendering of many of the songs he'd written for the Monkees. Looking back on the record, with its experimentation with musical styles, it seems to point to some of the music Nesmith would make on Pacific Arts. For that reason, the album is somewhat interesting, though it's certainly not a necessity for your Nesmith collection. —*Jim Worbois*

Loose Salute / 1970 / Pacific Arts ✦✦✦
With this record, Nesmith's momentum builds as this album is even better than the first. While the single from this album didn't do as well as his previous hit, it was a better song and kicks off the album nicely. Also, steel player extraordinaire, "Red" Rhodes, is beginning to take a more dominant role in the sound of the band. Of special interest are Nesmith's third go at recording "Listen to the Band," a fine cover of Patsy Cline's "I Fall to Pieces," and his renewed interest in Latin rhythms. —*Jim Worbois*

○ **Magnetic South** / 1970 / Pacific Arts ✦✦✦✦
This fine collection not only features Nesmith originals (and his first solo hit) but one of the most interesting versions "Beyond the Blue Horizon" ever committed to vinyl. For nearly six minutes we follow a day-in-the-life of the singer, from the minute he wakes in the morning and goes off to work on his tractor, till the time he returns at day's end. Also, at least two of the Nesmith originals were songs from his Monkee days but the Monkee versions of these songs would not be heard until the issue of the *Missing Links* series nearly 20 years later. —*Jim Worbois*

Nevada Fighter / 1971 / Pacific Arts ✦✦✦
This album stands in contrast with the previous two, in part because of the use of several members of Elvis's band which gives the album a slightly different sound. Also notable is the fact that Nesmith only wrote half the tracks. Still the songs he wrote were as strong as anything he'd written to this point and the covers he chose fit well with the feel and spirit of his own material. —*Jim Worbois*

Tantamount to Treason / 1972 / Pacific Arts ✦✦✦
Tantamount to Treason has a lazy feel to it, perhaps inspired by the beer recipe Papa Nes includes in the album's liner notes. That laziness is the reason the album is not as listenable as the previous

three records, since you almost need to be "in the mood" to put this one on. That said, it's still quite a nice album and is worth tracking down. — *Jim Worbois*

○ **And the Hits Just Keep on Comin'** / 1972 / RCA ✦✦✦✦

If you don't own this record, there is a huge hole in your collection. Nesmith's own version of "Different Drum" (a song which introduced Linda Ronstadt to many of us back in 1968 and which most of us had only heard Nesmith do as a speeded up, mumbled "audition" on an old Monkees episode) may be the key to lure you in but every song is a gem. This is easily some of Nesmith's finest work as both a songwriter and an artist. Also, between Nesmith and Red Rhodes, the sound is so full that it's easy to forget that a full band wasn't used in creating this record. — *Jim Worbois*

○ **Pretty Much Your Standard Ranch Stash** / 1973 / Pacific Arts ✦✦✦✦

Despite the comment inside the cover that "After two or three months this album may lose potency although some of the aroma may linger" this record holds up some 20 years later as one of Nesmith's finest. He continues to mix originals and a nice selection of covers as before but somehow this record feels more "comfortable" than his previous efforts. This seems to be, in part, due to the strong musical bond between Nesmith and steel player, Red Rhodes. If the "Buy This Record" inducement on the front cover doesn't make this a must for your collection, one listen to the music inside will! — *Jim Worbois*

The Prison / 1974 / Rio ✦✦

If Nesmith's albums are listened to in chronological order, this record is startling in how different it is to his previous work, especially the previous two records. It may even be a little off-putting. Accepted on its own, it's actually a nice album. That said, it's not one of those records one feels compelled to listen to more than a few times. — *Jim Worbois*

Michael Nesmith & the First National Band / 1976 / Island ✦✦✦

From a Radio Engine to the Photon Wing / 1977 / Pacific Arts ✦✦

"Rio" is probably the best-known song on this album as well as the most memorable song on the album. Most of the tracks seem to be meant to evoke a mood more than to be actual songs and, for that reason, tend to be a bit more interesting on their own rather than as a collection. — *Jim Worbois*

Live at Palais / 1978 / Pacific Arts ✦✦

On this album, which was recorded while on tour in Australia in 1977, Nesmith reintroduces some of the music from his years on RCA. These are not mere copies though as each song is performed differently, and, in each case, is presented as a longer version than the original. These songs obviously still mean something to their writer. — *Jim Worbois*

Infinite Rider on the Big Dogma / 1979 / Pacific Arts ✦✦✦

This is easily Nesmith's most interesting record from the '70s Pacific Arts material, and the one that most often calls for repeated listenings. By this time, he was getting heavily into video so a number of these tracks were also turned into music videos (check out the Grammy-winning *Elephant Parts*). While not a must, it's still a record worth searching out. — *Jim Worbois*

Newer Stuff / 1989 / Rhino ✦✦✦

This compilation of later solo material is often glossy and overreaching but still quite impressive. — *Jeff Tamarkin*

● **The Older Stuff: Best of Michael Nesmith (1970-1973)** / 1991 / Rhino ✦✦✦✦

Post-Monkees country-oriented material is proof that at least one member of the "pre-fab four" possessed genuine musical talent. — *Jeff Tamarkin*

Tropical Campfires / 1992 / Rio ✦✦✦

Nesmith plays desert music—quiet, contemplative, dignified—embellished, as the album title suggests, with splashes of lush tropical rhythms. His yearning vocals are ably supported by a cast of crack sessioneers, including the legendary Red Rhodes on pedal steel. Nesmith pens nine of the disc's 12 tracks, the others being covers of the samba chestnut "Brazil" and two Cole Porter tunes. Somehow, *Tropical Campfires* makes for exceedingly pleasant (if mellow) listening overall. The disc's highlight is Nesmith's weepy "Moon over the Rio Grande;" close your eyes and hear the campfire crackle and the coyotes wail. — *Roch Parisien*

● **Complete** / 1993 / Pacific Arts ✦✦✦✦

All of Michael Nesmith & the First National Band's three albums are collected on this superb two-disc set proving what a surprisingly inventive musician the former Monkee is. — *Stephen Thomas Erlewine*

Garden / 1994 / Rio Royal ✦✦

The Neville Brothers

Group, Soul, Funk, R&B

After more than two decades of performing together and alone, the Nevilles returned to their home turf, New Orleans, in 1977. The music they began making was grounded in that city's rhythms and folklore. Individually, the first Neville to get on record was Art, who joined the Hawketts and scored with "Mardi Gras Mambo" (1955) and on his own with "Cha Dooky Do" (1958). Then Aaron made his mark with "Over You" (1960) and the anthemic "Tell It Like It Is" (1966). The details of how Art, Aaron, Charles, and Cyril passed through the Meters, the Wild Tchoupitoulas, and other outfits to form their family band would defy a genealogist, and their less-than-successful debut on Capitol suggested that it was hardly worth the trouble. But then came *Fiyo on the Bayou* on A&M in 1981. Since then, the brothers have gone from strength to strength, plundering their New Orleans heritage and combining it with an eclectic mix of material to produce music that is virtually without category. Exposure in the band has finally enabled Aaron Neville to gain recognition as one of the truly great, eccentric voices in Black music. *Rolling Stone* and then Linda Ronstadt offered their seals of approval, with the result that the brothers are now both funky and chic. — *Colin Escott*

○ **Fiyo On The Bayou** / Apr. 1981 / A&M ✦✦✦✦

A brilliant updating of New Orleans R&B sound to include strains of Cajun, rock, and reggae on standards ranging from "Hey Pocky Way" to "The Ten Commandments of Love" and "Sitting in Limbo." — *William Ruhlmann*

○ **Neville-Ization** / Jun. 1984 / Black Top ✦✦✦✦

It took Black Top Records two years to put this record out after the Neville Brothers recorded it live at Tipitina's in New Orleans in September 1982, and one reason may be that it presents a mediocre, going-through-the-motions set. At their best, the Nevilles achieve a transcendent musical mixture, and even at the level of mere professionalism they're an impressive unit, but this just isn't the live album of which they are capable. — *William Ruhlmann*

★ **Treacherous: A History of the Neville Brothers 19** / 1986 / Rhino ✦✦✦✦✦

The music of the Neville Brothers was more a matter of rumor than documentation to most record buyers outside the New Orleans area until 1986, when Rhino Records finally gathered together their various solo and group records dating back 30 years and presented their story coherently on this two-disc set. Suddenly, it all makes sense, and the Nevilles' mixture of styles emerges as a singular American genre unto itself. This record is a revelation. — *William Ruhlmann*

Uptown / Mar. 1987 / EMI America ✦✦

The Neville Brothers displayed their eclecticism on this lone EMI album. They played with some high class guest stars, including Branford Marsalis, Jerry Garcia, Ronnie Montrose, Carlos Santana, and Keith Richards. But despite these excellent musicians and the Nevilles' usual tight playing and exuberant collective vocals, once more, the album failed to either get them a huge hit or faithfully recreate the quality of their live shows. — *Ron Wynn*

○ **Yellow Moon** / 1989 / A&M ✦✦✦✦

The Neville Brothers made a bid for pop/rock stardom with this well-produced album for A&M, their first under a new pact with the label mid in the late '80s. It was certainly as solid as any they cut for A&M; the vocals were both nicely arranged and expertly performed, the arrangements were basically solid, and the selections were intelligently picked and sequenced. The album charted and remained there for many weeks, while the Nevilles toured and generated lots of interest. It didn't become a hit, but it did respectably and represents perhaps their finest overall pop LP. — *Ron Wynn*

Brother's Keeper / 1990 / A&M ✦✦✦

All of the Neville Brothers' recent albums for A&M have been frustrating, uneven propositions, with great performances followed by disjointed numbers, and the studio productions seldom conveying the excitement and fire this group routinely generates in concert. The same holds true for this release, even though it got more pop exposure and chart penetration than any previous Neville Brothers album. But despite their energetic vocals and often superb instrumental interaction, this release still didn't come close to presenting the Neville Brothers on a good night, much less a great one. —*Ron Wynn*

○ **Treacherous Too!: History of** / 1991 / Rhino ✦✦✦✦
Okay, there's no such thing as secondhand revelation, but the Neville Brothers had more than enough stray tracks from their decades of local music-making around New Orleans to justify this second, single-disc followup to Rhino's first Nevilles history. There's more of an emphasis on novelty material here, but once again you can hear the roots of the Nevilles' cross-genre appeal in pop, R&B, and soul music dating back to the 1950s. Since most of these songs were recorded as singles, they have an immediate surface appeal, but repeated listenings also bring out the sounds of the tight session bands (including members of the Meters) who backed the Nevilles up. Actually, it's only the five 1980s tracks from just-okay albums like *Neville-ization* and *Uptown* that keep this collection from classic status, not the older stuff. —*William Ruhlmann*

Live on Planet Earth / Apr. 19, 1994 / A&M ✦✦✦
Clearly, this is intended to be the definitive live document of a band that has always been defined by its live work. Clocking in at 71 minutes, the album was culled from a world tour. The rhythm section of drummer Willie Green and bassist Tony Hall keeps up a steady groove from song to song, and the Nevilles trade off lead and harmony vocals on original songs that range across their career and add everything from Bob Marley compositions to "Love The One You're With" and "Amazing Grace." They Neville-ize all comers, throwing them into the pot and coming out with a tasty gumbo. If there's anything missing, it's the small club atmosphere from which the Nevilles emerged: this is a wide-screen treatment of a music that gained impact from its intimacy but now seeks to form a global conga line. —*William Ruhlmann*

Aaron Neville

b. Jan. 24, 1941, New Orleans, LA
Soul, R&B, Pop/Rock
Although Neville is often compared to singer Sam Cooke in terms of sheer vocal refinement, he has a voice and style uniquely his own. Today he is well known as part of the New Orleans sound of the Neville Brothers. Yet, aside from the 1967 number one R&B hit "Tell It Like It Is," few have heard his incredible early solo recordings. Many of the first recordings of Aaron Neville, in the early and mid-'60s, were arranged, produced, and often written by the brilliant Allen Toussaint—another talent only now being really appreciated. Most of these sides were cut for the Minit (and later) Parlo labels. Songs like "She Took You for a Ride" and "You Think You're So Smart" on Parlo are masterpieces. While his more recent work, including that with Linda Ronstadt, makes for pleasant listening, it lacks the sheer persuasion of his early songs. Aaron has recorded his early work often, and it is important to hear the originals. The early sides of Aaron Neville are just waiting to be heard.
    Aaron Neville has been venturing more into other waters besides R&B. 1993's *The Grand Tour* included a remake of a George Jones song that got Neville a little country attention, and he announced plans in 1994 to do a complete country album. He was also one of several R&B artists who teamed with country stars for the *Rhythm, Country and Blues* session. Neville was paired with Trisha Yearwood, and the duo also performed together in a benefit concert for the LP held in Los Angeles in April 1994. The LP made history by debuting in the Top Ten on the pop, R&B, and country charts. —*Michael Erlewine and Ron Wynn*

Greatest Hits / 1957 / Curb ✦✦✦
● **Tell It Like It Is** / 1967 / Curb ✦✦✦✦
Eleven of Neville's best Parlo cuts, including those mentioned above, are included on one CD. His biggest solo smash from 1966, plus more songs in the same style. Sublime stuff. —*Bill Dahl*

Like It 'tis / Oct. 14, 1967 / EMI America ✦✦✦
An excellent vinyl compilation of Neville's early-'60s Allen Toussaint-produced Minit singles, this includes the amusingly macabre 1960 rocker "Over You." —*Bill Dahl*

○ **Orchid in the Storm** / Dec. 1986 / Rhino ✦✦✦✦
Aaron Neville's wondrous singing on this poorly distributed EP was overlooked by many still unaware of his stunning falsetto. But Neville covered doo-wop, soul, and even country on this project, singing with a soaring conviction and poignancy that made it a delightful, though short, set. Rhino has thankfully reissued it on CD. It's actually closer to representing Neville's real style than his recent much-hyped, overproduced pop records. —*Ron Wynn*

Show Me the Way / Aug. 1989 / Charly ✦✦✦
Here are 22 of his early Minit recordings, many of them incredible. —*Michael Erlewine*

Warm Your Heart / 1991 / A&M ✦✦✦
This new set finds Neville's wavering vocals as elegant as ever on a ballad-oriented program. —*Bill Dahl*

The My Greatest Gift / 1991 / Rounder ✦✦✦
The songs that made Neville famous among soul and R&B fans were done years before he became a recognized star, for tiny Southern labels. The 12 tracks on this anthology were recorded in the late '60s, when Neville's soaring falsetto, emphatic delivery and gut-wrenching treatments were locked out of the pop mainstream. Although this isn't the definitive version of "Tell It Like It Is," it's far from a throwaway. On "Love Letters," "Hercules," "Mojo Hannah" and "Where Is My Baby," Aaron Neville tackled the soul mountain and conquered it. —*Ron Wynn*

The Grand Tour / 1993 / A&M ✦✦
The Tattooed Heart / 1995 / A&M ✦✦✦
● **Tell It Like It Is: Golden Classics** / Collectables ✦✦✦✦
One of many collections covering Aaron Neville's superb early R&B and soul classics. The burly Neville, whose delicate, feathery voice stands in vivid contrast to his muscular body, made great heartache ballads, uptempo wailers, and brilliantly sung originals for tiny New Orleans labels, often not even getting widespread soul airplay. Now that's he's hot property, the domestic anthologies are coming out left and right. This one is as good as any other, although for my money the import labels have still done a better job on early Neville than the American companies. —*Ron Wynn*

Art Neville

b. 1937
Soul, R&B, Rock & Roll
New Orleans vocalist and keyboardist. As a founding member of the Meters and Neville Brothers, Neville helped immeasurably to shape the contemporary New Orleans funk sound. Neville's first band, the Hawketts, tasted local success in 1954 with the carnival perennial "Mardi Gras Mambo" on Chess. He cut some nice solo singles for Specialty during the late '50s, notably "Cha Dooky-Doo," as well as contributing two choruses of storming piano to Jerry Byrne's 1958 classic "Lights Out." "All These Things," a gentle ballad, also did well locally in 1962 on the Instant logo. He assembled the Meters in the mid-'60s and the instrumental quartet proved the Crescent City's answer to the MG's until their 1977 breakup. That's when Art and his siblings formed the Neville Brothers, and today they reign as the leading musical export from New Orleans. —*Bill Dahl*

○ **His Specialty Recordings 1956-1958** / 1992 / Specialty ✦✦✦✦
● **That Old Time Rock 'n' Roll** / Specialty ✦✦✦✦
A good collection that gives the lesser-known Neville some attention. —*Ron Wynn*

Mardi Gras Rock & Roll / Ace ✦✦✦

New Age Steppers

Group, Experimental
Rallying around the considerable talents of British producer/modern dub mastermind Adrian Sherwood, the New Age Steppers were not so much a band as they were a loosely knit aggregation of musicians from some of Britain's best avant-garde post-punk/funk bands. There was Ari Upp from the Slits, Mark Stewart from the Pop Group, and John Waddington and Bruce Smith from Rip, Rig & Panic. Along with the usual gang of suspects employed by Sherwood's dynamically creative On-U Sounds (George Oban, Style Scott, Eskimo Fox) studio, the sound of the New Age Steppers was that of cut-and-paste dub mixing, psychedelic swirls of found sounds, dissonant aural collages, sinewy reggae riddims and odd, semi-tuneful vocals. Not for the faint of heart, the music created by Sherwood and his Steppers was among the most exhil-

arating and consistently challenging to come out of Britain during the early post-punk era. It wasn't always accessible, but it has few peers in terms of ingenuity and daring. Highly recommended to those whose musical tastes occasionally reside on pop's radical, experimental fringes. —*John Dougan*

● **Massive Hits, Vol. 1** / 1994 / On-U Sound ✦✦✦✦
While there are numerous recordings by the New Age Steppers, many of them are out of print or extremely difficult to find. This release is the first in a series cataloguing the "band's" amazing existence. *Volume 1* takes most of its tracks from 1983's *Foundation Steppers*, adding a few tracks from their 1980 debut. It's wildly inventive music and thankfully made easily available on CD. And while the title is tongue-in-cheek (there were no hits to speak of), this music is most definitely massive. —*John Dougan*

New Colony Six

Group, Garage Rock, Pop/Rock
Chicago's New Colony Six originally emerged as a tough, British Invasion-styled outfit prominently featuring Farfisa organ and a novel (at the time) Lesley guitar. Scoring a huge local hit with "I Confess," their early recordings—exemplified by their 1966 debut album, *Breakthrough*—featured first-class original material that gave the sound of Them and the Yardbirds a more commercial, American garage-based, vocal harmony approach. The rest of the '60s saw the band gradually abandoning their roots for middle-of-the-road pop with horns and strings. Continuing to rack up major local hits and minor national ones, they finally cracked the U.S. Top 30 with "Love You So Much" (1968) and "Things I'd Like to Say" (1969). —*Richie Unterberger*

○ **Colonized! The Best of New Colony Six** / 1993 / Rhino ✦✦
In the mid- and late '60s, the New Colony Six were one of Chicago's most successful pop/rock groups, scoring many regional hits and hitting the national Top 30 with "I Will Always Think About You" and "Things I'd Like to Say." Both of those tracks are included on this 20-track retrospective, which documents the group's evolution from masterful garage rockers to pop/rock softies. In this case, this was certainly not a change for the better. The Six's 1966 LP *Breakthrough* was one of the finest obscure rock albums of the 1960s, marrying American pop hooks and harmonies to tough organ-dominated British R&B in the spirit of Them. Four songs from that album are included on this compilation, as well as a non-LP single (a cover of Bo Diddley's "Cadillac") from the same period. With personnel changes, the group devolved into a pedestrian mainstream pop/rock outfit that owed more to Gary Puckett than their gritty British Invasion roots. Discriminating listeners are advised to stick with their early material. —*Richie Unterberger*

● **At the River's Edge** / 1993 / Sundazed ✦✦✦✦
22 tracks, including all of the worthwhile songs from their classic *Breakthrough* album, a non-LP single, and most of their second album, *Colonization*. The only New Colony Six package worth owning. —*Richie Unterberger*

New Edition

Group, Urban, Pop/Rock
When Maurice Starr assembled New Edition in the early '80s, he never could have guessed that the group would produce some of the biggest, most influential urban R&B stars of the following decade. At the time of their first record, Bobby Brown, Ralph Tresvant, Ricky Bell, Mike Bivins, and Ronald Davoe were barely in their teens, yet they had impressive voices and a natural charisma which sent them to the charts with their first single, "Candy Girl." Their second album was even bigger, featuring the number two single "Cool It Now." New Edition's songs were either light funk or sweet ballads, yet they followed their formula well even if much of it seems quaint now, especially compared to their groundbreaking solo work.

Brown left the band after their third album, being replaced by Johnny Gill. The band released two more albums before splitting. After the group was finished, they each became successful as solo artists in the early '80s. —*Stephen Thomas Erlewine*

○ **Candy Girl** / 1983 / Warlock ✦✦✦✦
When Maurice Starr uncovered the talents of a Roxbury vocal group in the early '80s, he envisioned a second Jackson 5. That was the direction he took New Edition in in its early days, and this album includes such overt Jackson 5 ripoffs as "Candy Girl" and the

title track. None of the toughness or street touches that emerged on their later material were evident on this slick, pop-oriented session. Ralph Tresvant, Ronald DeVoe, Michael Bivins, Ricky Bell and Bobby Brown were all aged 13 to 15 when this was released. —*Ron Wynn*

○ **New Edition** / 1984 / MCA ✦✦✦✦
Maurice Starr's vision peaked with this second album by New Edition. They were now thoroughly Jackson 5 clones and were reaping similar commercial dividends thanks to the teen angst cuts "Cool It Now" and "Mr. Telephone Man." They earned their first platinum album, one Top Ten hit and another Top 20 pop single (both songs topped the R&B charts) and were among the hottest acts in either pop or R&B during this stretch. —*Ron Wynn*

All for Love / 1985 / MCA ✦✦✦
New Edition's voices and focus were changing in the late '80s. They'd moved away from the kiddie-pop/soul of the early '80s and were singing harder, adult love material and cutting uptempo funk tracks, although there weren't many of those on this session. While sometimes things got a bit sappy lyrically and seemed repetitive at other times, the group compensated with their strongest harmonies and vocal performances to date. —*Ron Wynn*

Under the Blue Moon / 1986 / MCA ✦✦✦
Changes were on the horizon for New Edition. They had become enormously successful by aping the Jackson 5, but were undergoing internal trauma as original member Bobby Brown bolted amid rumors of dissatisfaction with the group's direction. This album featured their covers of 1950s and '60s standards and were among early examples of the retro trend now so prominent in urban contemporary camps. While they didn't do this type of material nearly as well as the Force MD's, they at least brought fresh attention to such songs as "Earth Angel" and "Tears On My Pillow." —*Ron Wynn*

Heart Break / 1989 / MCA ✦✦✦
The arrival of Johnny Gill's lusty baritone and production tactics of Jimmy Jam and Terry Lewis temporarily revived the sagging careers of New Edition. Jam and Lewis gave them current beats, let Gill take the lead on romantic numbers, and put punch and edge into their arrangements. This proved New Edition's biggest album since 1985's *All For Love*, and such songs as "Can You Stand The Rain," "If It Isn't Love" and the autobiographical "Where It All Started" signaled the end of the Jackson 5 ties. But it was also the precursor to more internal dissension. —*Ron Wynn*

● **Greatest Hits, Vol. 1** / 1991 / MCA ✦✦✦✦
For anyone who missed New Edition in either its Jackson 5 imitation phase or final days as a funkier, more aggressive urban contemporary vocal group with a slight dance influence, this collection contains examples of both incarnations. Kiddie-pop hits such as "Candy Girl," "Cool It Now" and "Mr. Telephone Man" are included, along with their final hits "If It Isn't Love," "Can You Stand The Rain" and the appropriately titled "Is This the End." This anthology shows how dominant New Edition was during the 1980s and early '90s. —*Ron Wynn*

New Kids on the Block

Group, Urban, Pop/Rock
After his success with New Edition, producer Maurice Starr decided to replicate the group, substituting the young black teenagers for suburban White kids. The result was New Kids on the Block, which quickly eclipsed the popularity of Starr's previous group. Comprising Boston area singers Donnie Wahlberg, Jordan Knight, Jon Knight, Danny Wood, and Joe McIntyre, the New Kids were awkward and enthusiastic on their 1986 debut, which wasn't surprising considering that the oldest members were barely 16 years old. With their next album, 1988's *Hangin' Tough*, the group's image had toughened up and they had the material to support it. From the saccharine ballad "I'll Be Loving You Forever" to the title track's stab at funk, the band had a seemingly endless streak of hits in 1988 and 1989; their Christmas album even went double platinum. New Kids mania continued with 1990's *Step by Step*, even if it sold five million copies less than *Hangin' Tough*, it still sold three milion copies. But that was the end of the road for their short time in the sun—they were the subject of an endless amount of jokes and were getting no respect. Besides, their audience was growing up. In 1994, they returned with the Starr-less *Face the Music*, which actually showed a remarkable musical maturity—

they were a credible urban R&B outfit—but hardly sold anything, even if they were packing theaters on tour. In June of 1994, the band announced that they had acrimoniously parted ways and all of the members were now pursuing solo careers. —*Stephen Thomas Erlewine*

New Kids on the Block / 1986 / Columbia ◆◆◆
Debut with "Be My Girl." —*Bil Carpenter*

● **Hangin' Tough** / 1988 / Columbia ◆◆◆◆
Good songs collected by New Kids mastermind Maurice Starr highlight this smash, including "I'll Be Loving You Forever," "You Got It (The Right Stuff)," "Please Don't Go Girl," and the title track. Tight, warm, even soulful harmony on the ballads. —*Dan Heilman & Bil Carpenter*

Step by Step / 1990 / Columbia ◆◆◆
In an attempt for some respect, the group wrote some cuts on *Step by Step*, a more serious, harder-sounding album. Although the title track was #1 for three weeks and the followup, "Tonight," went Top Ten, they couldn't replicate the success of *Hangin' Tough*. —*Bil Carpenter*

Face the Music / 1994 / Columbia ◆◆◆
The New Kids return after much ridicule and doubt with the defensive *Face the Music*, and, surprise!—it isn't bad at all. Sure, they've changed their style a bit—their new jack R&B is a bit rougher, the lyrics are a touch nastier, and their hip-hop sounds a little more *real*—but none of it sounds fake, and the best tracks on the album might impress even the most jaded listener. —*Stephen Thomas Erlewine*

New Order

Group, Dance-Pop, Techno-Pop/Dance, Alternative Pop/Rock, New Wave
Of all of the synth-based post-punk bands that emerged in the '80s, New Order is the most important. After Ian Curtis hung himself, the remaining members of Joy Division—Bernard Sumner, Peter Hook, and Stephen Morris—picked up the pieces and formed New Order, adding keyboardist Gillian Gilbert. While the group alleviated some of Curtis' most morbid tendencies, their music still was serious; the band also adhered to pop melodies and structure more frequently than Joy Division. New Order exploited synthesizers and electronics to their fullest, creating a detached, yet strangely human soundscape that managed to convey the emotional alienation of the Thatcher and Reagan era. The band was also not afraid to use disco as the basic rhythm in their music, laying the groundwork for the house scene in the U.K. at the end of the decade, as well as the cold, detached synth-dance pop that dominated the charts in America and the U.K. for most of the beginning of the decade. In the U.K., New Order were stars, yet they never developed anything larger than a cult following in America.

After 1991's *Technique*, the band members concentrated on solo projects (Sumner in Electronic, Hook in Revenge, Gilbert and Morris in the Other Two), fueling rumors that they had broken up. In 1993, they returned with *Republic*, which earned them their first genuine hit single in America, "Regret." After a tension-filled tour, the members resumed their solo projects, again sparking rumors of the band's split. —*Stephen Thomas Erlewine*

Movement / 1981 / Factory ◆◆◆
New Order's debut album *Movement* bridges the gap between the dance-rock the group would later develop and Joy Division's languid, morbid drone. *Movement* pointed the way towards New Order's future by featuring more synthesizers than any of Joy Division's records, as well as more accessible hooks and melodies. —*Stephen Thomas Erlewine*

○ **Power Corruption and Lies** / 1983 / Qwest ◆◆◆◆
Synthesized dance music at moderate tempos, plus calmly sung, distanced lyrics, makes for an entrancing effect. —*William Ruhlmann*

○ **Low Life** / 1985 / Qwest ◆◆◆◆
New Order's messages are no less dire here, but the tempos are faster, the singing more engaged, and the melodies more distinct. In fact, "Love Vigilantes" is positively catchy. —*William Ruhlmann*

○ **Brotherhood** / 1986 / Qwest ◆◆◆◆
Brotherhood repeated the formula of *Low Life*, but instead of being a mere retread of its predecessor, the new album was a refinement of the innovations of the previous album, as the group's

songwriting became tighter and more accessible, as the single "Bizarre Love Triangle" proved. —*Stephen Thomas Erlewine*

★ **Substance** / 1987 / Qwest ◆◆◆◆◆
A collection of New Order singles—some of their best work—little of which had previously turned up on albums or in the U.S. —*William Ruhlmann*

○ **Technique** / 1989 / Qwest ◆◆◆◆
Technique expands New Order's trademark sound by adding elements of dense acid house rhythms, the occasional acoustic guitar, and a greater reliance on pop melody. All of the subtle experimentation made *Technique* one of their most intriguing and successful records. —*Stephen Thomas Erlewine*

Republic / May 11, 1993 / Qwest ◆◆◆
New Order's most pop-oriented record actually resulted in a hit single in the U.S., the pleasantly catchy "Regret." However, most of the album finds New Order repeating ideas that are now almost a decade old. —*Stephen Thomas Erlewine*

★ **Best of New Order** / 1995 / Qwest ◆◆◆◆◆
Instead of presenting New Order as a progressive dance band as *Substance* did, the *Best Of New Order* showcases New Order the pop band, condensing their hit singles onto one disc. A couple of remixes are thrown in (Shep Pettibone takes over "Blue Monday"), but it is still a concise explanation of why the group was one of the most important of the '80s. —*Stephen Thomas Erlewine*

New Race

Group, Hard Rock
An interesting one-time-only band, New Race was proof that good music can occur when "teachers" and "students" get together. In this instance, the "teachers" were ex-Stooges guitarist Ron Asheton and ex-MC5 drummer Dennis Thompson, who joined forces with "students" Deniz Tek, Rob Younger and Warwick Gilbert, the latter three members of the seminal Australian punk band Radio Birdman. Tek was a Michigan native who'd emigrated to Australia in the early '70s, bringing his love of high-energy Detroit proto-punk with him. After Birdman's demise, he contacted Asheton and Thompson to come to Australia and form this ad-hoc touring outfit. New Race toured Australia once in 1981, playing mostly small halls and releasing one legit live LP and a few low-fi bootlegs. While the resulting record, *The First and the Last*, benefits from a significant amount of in-studio sweetening (backing vocals are added, guitar solos overdubbed), it's still an exciting, guitar-fueled rave-up. Fans of the early-'70s Motor City sound or early Aussie punk wouldn't want to be without it. —*John Dougan*

○ **The First and the Last** / 1982 / Statik ◆◆◆◆
If you can ignore the obvious post-production trickery, this is a grimy little hunk of fun that never disappoints. Playing mostly Birdman and MC5 covers (with a couple of songs from Asheton's band Destroy All Monsters), this is the sound of good mates having a good time, and there is plenty of white-hot guitar mania supplied by Tek and Asheton. If you can find it, don't pass it by. —*John Dougan*

New York Dolls

Group, Rock & Roll
The New York Dolls were the bridge between the Rolling Stones, the MC5, and the Sex Pistols and the punk rock movement of the late '70s. Their highly charged, reckless, guitar-heavy sound and lead singer David Johansen's fey stage antics, coupled with the group's inclination toward androgyny, made for a nice diversion in 1973, when their self-titled Todd Rundgren-produced debut came out. Unfortunately, the Dolls were too raw for most of the public, including those who claimed to love rock & roll. As a result, the band became more of a media event and critics' darlings.

The Shadow Morton-produced followup, *Too Much, Too Soon*, proved that the Dolls were more than a one-shot wonder. It included a wonderful version of Archie Bell & the Drells's "There's Gonna Be a Showdown." The Dolls lost their deal with Mercury Records and were briefly managed by the outrageous Malcolm McLaren (who later handled the Sex Pistols). They eventually broke up in 1977. Of the five, Johansen has enjoyed the most success as a solo artist, later under the pseudonym Buster Poindexter. Guitarist Johnny Thunders became a punk legend, releasing a series of wildly inconsistent records—both with his post-Dolls band, the Heartbreakers, and on his own—before his death in 1990. —*Rick Clark*

☆ **New York Dolls** / 1973 / Mercury ✦✦✦✦✦
Their debut suffers from Todd Rundgren's murky production, but "Personality Crisis," "Pills," and "Frankenstein" manage to break through the clutter. —*John Floyd*

★ **Too Much, Too Soon** / 1974 / Mercury ✦✦✦✦✦
Their second (and last) album mixes well-chosen soul/R&B covers with a slew of striking Johnny Thunders-David Johansen originals. It's good enough to make their early demise even more regrettable. —*John Floyd*

○ **Rock & Roll** / 1994 / Mercury ✦✦✦✦
Rock & Roll contains all of the original material from the Dolls' two classic albums and adds a couple of outtakes and rarities. So why isn't it as much fun as *New York Dolls* or *Too Much Too Soon?* For starters, the Dolls' versions of "Pills," "Stranded In the Jungle," "Don't Start Me Talkin'," and "(There's Gonna Be A) Showdown" weren't filler, they were essential to the overall feeling of the albums. And that brings us to the main problem of *Rock & Roll*—it isn't sequenced in an inviting manner. Instead of showcasing the New York Dolls in all of their trashy glory, the disc manages to make them sound rather tedious, which is something their proper albums certainly aren't. Nevertheless, there's plenty of fine music here, and hardcore fans will want the rarities. But the original albums remain the best way to hear the Dolls. —*Stephen Thomas Erlewine*

Randy Newman

b. Nov. 28, 1943
Singer-Songwriter
Randy Newman, nephew of Lionel and Alfred Newman (Hollywood composers and arrangers), was already steeped in a rich creative environment when he chose to pursue music as a career. Newman's first attempt as a solo artist was the 1961 Dot single "Golden Gridiron Boy," which was produced by Pat Boone. Even though the record went nowhere, Newman embarked on a successful songwriting career, with songs cut by the Fleetwoods, Jerry Butler, Cilla Black, Judy Collins, Manfred Mann, Nilsson, and Three Dog Night, among others. Since 1968, when he released his self-titled Warner Bros. debut, Newman has employed a seductive blend of ragtime, rolling Fats Domino-style rock & roll, blues, and classic Hollywood cinema-style melodies (with a touch of Stephen Foster), which has been effective in luring the listener into the twisted mindsets of the characters that populate many of his songs. Since Newman often sang from the protagonist's point of view, he rarely wasted time moralizing his position. In 1978, Newman's tongue-in-cheek acerbity produced a hit with "Short People" (#2), off of *Little Criminals* (#9), but it also rankled many, who thought the single was mean-spirited. Even Newman's fans began to wonder about the literalness of his sentiment with the 1979 album *Born Again* (#41), which mercilessly skewered each of the protagonists represented.

In 1981 Newman did the soundtrack for the movie *Ragtime*, beginning a successful career in film scoring. Newman has continued to sporadically release solo albums that are many cuts above the average release. —*Rick Clark*

○ **Randy Newman** / 1968 / Reprise ✦✦✦✦
Randy Newman creates something new under the sun," read the banner on the back of Newman's debut album, but it wasn't so much that as that, in keeping with the intended irony of the statement, Newman was intent upon taking cliches and using them to satirize social conventions, a popular parlor game in the late '60s. Thus, we have "Love Story" (predating the sappy book/movie of the same title), in which the lovers retire to Florida and pass away, "So Long Dad," in which a son squares things with his old man, and "Davy The Fat Boy," in which an affectionate friend exploits the title character. But there were also songs like "Living Without You" and "I Think It's Gonna Rain Today," which were so painfully lonely you wished they weren't so sincere. Taken together, this was an audacious first album by a major, if extremely quirky, talent. —*William Ruhlmann*

★ **12 Songs** / 1970 / Reprise ✦✦✦✦✦
Randy Newman's droll humor and ability to render ludicrous settings (through the eyes of protagonists who were obviously not playing with full decks) made *12 Songs* an instant classic to the handful of people lucky enough to hear it. The bare-bones production, along with assistance from guitarist Ry Cooder, gave the record a homey immediacy. Highlights are hard to single out but "Mama Told Me Not to Come" (later a hit for Three Dog Night),

"Yellow Man," "Lucinda," and "Uncle Bob's Midnight Blues" are great. —*Rick Clark*

Randy Newman Live / 1971 / Reprise ✦✦✦
This live set basically reprises much of his first two albums, without adding much to their interpretation. There are a few new tunes, the only standout being a song that Frank Sinatra passed on, called "Lonely at the Top." —*Rick Clark*

☆ **Sail Away** / 1972 / Reprise ✦✦✦✦✦
Sail Away was Newman's first synthesis of his satirical writing and his impressive orchestral arrangement skills. The result was one of his very best albums. The title cut was a brilliantly twisted take on slaves coming on a ship from Africa, set to a score that owed much to Stephen Foster. "Burn On," Newman's sentimental-sounding ode to the polluted Cuyahoga River (in Cleveland, OH), and his perverse "You Can Leave Your Hat On" (later popularized by Joe Cocker in the movie *9 1/2 Weeks*) are among the many great songs to be found on *Sail Away*. —*Rick Clark*

☆ **Good Old Boys** / 1974 / Reprise ✦✦✦✦✦
On *Good Old Boys*, Newman increasingly focused his obsessions on the South, but his slant seemed to be rooted more in Steppin' Fetchit and Shirley Temple *Little Rebel* Hollywood films than in reality. As distorted as viewing things through that particular lens may be, the South in *Good Old Boys* is undeniably poignant. "Louisiana 1927" is an affecting account of a spring flood, while "Marie" (a love song from a drunk) is one of the most touching songs written in popular music. The grand, sweeping melodies and arrangements are quite simply beautiful. Newman's sloppy, soulful mumble and understated piano keep this great record from tumbling into drippy sentimentality. —*Rick Clark*

Little Criminals / 1977 / Reprise ✦✦✦
On *Little Criminals*, Newman's penchant for satirically illuminating the quirks in human nature earned him a million-selling #2 hit with "Short People," a song that dealt with the issue of bigotry. It also earned him the loathing of thousands of short people who failed to get the message. Aside from that controversy, *Little Criminals* was relatively tame by Newman standards. "Baltimore," "Sigmund Freud's Impersonation of Albert Einstein in America," and "Rider in the Rain" were among the standout tracks. —*Rick Clark*

Born Again / 1979 / Reprise ✦✦✦
It was on his sixth studio album that Newman's caustic humor seemed to become mean-spirited. His characters had always been small-minded creeps, but on *Born Again*, they weren't presented with any sympathy, and the hand of the author was apparent. Newman was as clever as ever, but crueler than usual, except for "The Story Of A Rock And Roll Band," which trashes Electric Light Orchestra, a band
deserving of such ridicule. —*William Ruhlmann*

○ **Trouble in Paradise** / 1983 / Reprise ✦✦✦✦
After the mean-spirited 1979 release *Born Again*, Newman regrouped and released *Trouble in Paradise*, an album that employed more lyrical subtlety and was more successful at skewering its terminally character-disordered targets ("Christmas in Capetown," "Song for the Dead," "My Life Is Good"). "The Blues," a dryly humorous duet with Paul Simon, was a moderate hit at #51. "I Love L.A." failed to chart, in spite of extensive exposure. Musically, Newman downplayed the timeless feel of his best work in favor of a trendier, clean West Coast-pop sound. As a result, this effort doesn't age so well. *Trouble in Paradise* may not be Newman's best work, but fans will enjoy it. —*Rick Clark*

● **Retrospect** / 1983 / WEA ✦✦✦✦
To date, Warner Brothers in the U.S. has not released a compilation of Randy Newman's best work, but the U.K. division has, and here it is. From "Political Science" to "God's Song," these 16 songs should show any listener the depth of Randy Newman's talent as a songwriter and provide some big horse laughs along the way. —*William Ruhlmann*

○ **Land of Dreams** / 1988 / Reprise ✦✦✦✦
After a five-year layoff, Newman returned with the solid *Land of Dreams*, an album that was by turns gentle and reflective ("Something Special," "Falling in Love") or subtly scathing. Among the topics explored in *Land of Dreams* are Newman's childhood memories in New Orleans ("Dixie Flyer," "New Orleans Wins the War"), a beautifully twisted ode to patriotism ("Follow the Flag"), and an explanation from a father to his son ("I Want You to Hurt Like I Do"), concerning the passing down of abusive ways. The cynical

"It's Money That Matters" barely dented the charts at #80. Interestingly, Jeff Lynne helped produce this album; only two albums earlier, Newman was skewering Lynne's band ELO for representing some of the worst elements of the music biz. —*Rick Clark*

Thunderclap Newman

Group, Rock & Roll
John "Speedy" Keene was an old crony of the Who, and had written "Armenia City in the Sky," which appeared on *The Who Sell Out* LP. The unlikely Andy Newman played terrific pub-style piano and looked much like a postal clerk, which in fact, he was. Jimmy McCullough, the guitarist, looked to be a mere teenager, and so he was. It was this combination, plus the production efforts of Pete Townshend, that offered the album, *Hollywood Dream*. As the now-classic single, "Something in the Air" had long preceded it, the album delivered the goods in a similar fashion, fueled by Keene's reedy vocals and Newman's charming honky-tonk piano. *Hollywood Dream* has remained an anglophile fave; sadly, it was to be Thunderclap Newman's only album. Even if you own the original LP, make sure to check out the recently expanded edition of the compact disc. —*Steve Aldrich*

● **Hollywood Dream** / 1969 / PolyGram ◆◆◆◆
Thunderclap Newman seized the sound of an era with their 1969 hit, "Something in the Air," as beautiful a call for pacifism as you'll ever hear. That song is included on this expanded version of their Pete Townshend-produced debut, which features a strange but enticing mix of off-kilter originals and clever covers (such as the Dylan nugget "Open the Door Homer"). —*John Floyd*

Olivia Newton-John

b. Sep. 26, 1948, Cambridge, England
Pop/Rock
Olivia Newton-John ranks at #12 in chart researcher Joel Whitburn's ranking of the most successful singles artists of the '70s. The biggest of her 15 Top Ten hits, "Physical," came in the '80s, when it spent ten weeks at number one. Born in Cambridge, England, but raised in Australia, she returned to her native country after winning a talent contest at 16 and spent several years struggling before she scored a Top Ten U.K. hit in 1971 with a cover of Bob Dylan's "If Not for You." But it was not until 1973 that Newton-John made her real American breakthrough with the first of five straight gold-selling Top Ten hits, "Let Me Be There." She scored two number one albums in 1974 and 1975 with *If You Love Me, Let Me Know* and *Have You Never Been Mellow*. (Newton-John's simultaneous success on the country charts and her winning of Grammy and Country Music Association awards in country categories were controversial in Nashville.)

Newton-John's career cooled in 1976 and 1977, but in 1978 she appeared in the film version of the retro-'50s musical *Grease*, which not only added to her hit total but also moved her image from sweetness and innocence to a more aggressive posture. She capitalized on the change and on the disco wave for songs like the sexually provocative "Physical," and enjoyed a new vogue as a dance-pop singer in the early '80s. Her last Top Ten hit, "Twist of Fate" was in 1984, also the year Newton-John married actor Matt Lattanzi. She has since released the gold-selling *Soul Kiss* in 1985, *The Rumour* in 1988, and released *Warm and Tender* (1989), an album of children's lullabies. —*William Ruhlmann*

● **Back to Basics** / 1992 / Geffen ◆◆◆◆
An artist well-defined by her hit singles, Olivia Newton-John has had a stylistically varied career, as is illustrated on *Back to Basics: The Essential Collection 1971-1992*, a set that ranges from her teary ballad "I Honestly Love You" to that bouncy paean to getting horizontal, "Physical." Fans may quibble that such hits as "Let Me Be There" and "Make a Move on Me" are not included, but Newton-John's two greatest-hits albums are out of print, and this is the only collection to combine both her good-girl and bad-girl personae. —*William Ruhlmann*

Nice

Group, Art-Rock/Progressive-Rock
Formed in 1967, Nice was keyboardist Keith Emerson's theatrical testing ground before he formed Emerson, Lake & Palmer in 1970. The group never really sold stateside, but their audacious stage antics and extended trashings of classical pieces made them popular in Europe. —*Rick Clark*

The Thoughts of Emerlist Davjack / 1967 / Columbia ◆◆◆
An okay, but unambitious first album, heavily influenced by Jimi Hendrix. Lacking discipline, but full of surprises. —*Bruce Eder*

Ars Longa Vita Brevis / 1968 / Columbia ◆◆◆
Leonard Bernstein, Bach, and Sibelius interpreted through a musical lens forged by Brubeck, Monk, and a mad keyboard player named Keith Emerson. —*Bruce Eder*

● **Nice** / 1969 / Columbia ◆◆◆◆
Their final statement, with rippling organ passages and a great lineup of songs, plus 20 minutes of a legendary Fillmore live gig. —*Bruce Eder*

Autumn 67, Spring 68 / 1972 / Charisma ◆◆
Elegy & Five Bridges / 1975 / Mercury ◆◆◆
A farewell record of live cuts and outtakes, not showing the band to its best advantage. A good appendix to their superior Immediate recordings on Columbia. —*Bruce Eder*

Stevie Nicks

b. May 6, 1948
Pop/Rock
A singer/songwriter who gained fame as a member of Fleetwood Mac starting in 1975 and launched a concurrent solo career in 1981, resulting in five gold or platinum albums through 1991. —*William Ruhlmann*

○ **Bella Donna** / 1981 / Modern ◆◆◆◆
Nicks' major attributes—her passionately ragged voice and emotionally vulnerable songwriting—are much in evidence on her debut solo album, given a clean rock production by Jimmy Iovine. Includes "Stop Draggin' My Heart Around" (with Tom Petty & the Heartbreakers), "Edge of Seventeen," and "Leather and Lace" (a duet with Don Henley). —*William Ruhlmann*

The Wild Heart / 1983 / Modern ◆◆◆
Rock a Little / 1985 / Modern ◆◆◆
The Other Side of the Mirror / 1989 / Modern ◆◆
● **Timespace: Best of Stevie Nicks** / 1991 / Modern ◆◆◆◆
All the hits, some well-selected album tracks, and two new ones on a generous best-of. —*William Ruhlmann*

Street Angel / 1994 / Modern ◆◆◆
Released in 1994, *Street Angel* could've easily been the follow-up to Nicks's debut thirteen years earlier, thanks to production that sounds frozen in her early-'80s heyday. Overall, the material isn't that strong; the opening track, "Blue Denim," is the highlight here. —*Rick Clark*

Maybe Love Will Change Your Mind / 1994 / Atlantic ◆◆◆

Nico (Christa Paffgen)

b. Oct. 16, 1938, d. Jul. 18, 1988
Art-Rock/Progressive-Rock, Experimental
One of the most fascinating figures of rock's fringes, Nico hobnobbed, worked, and was romantically linked with an incredible assortment of the most legendary entertainers of the 1960s. The paradox of her career was that she herself never attained the fame of her peers, pursuing a distinctly individualistic and uncompromising musical career that was uncommercial, but wholly admirable and influential. Nico first rose to fame as a European supermodel, also landing a bit part in Fellini's *La Dolce Vita* film and giving birth to a son by Alain Delon. In 1965, she attracted the attention of Rolling Stones manager Andrew Loog Oldham, who gave her a chance to record for his Immediate label, though the resulting single, which also featured Brian Jones and Jimmy Page on guitars, flopped. Shortly afterwards, she moved to New York, where Andy Warhol installed her as a vestigial presence and occasional lead singer for the Velvet Underground. The band never really accepted her as a bonafide member, and she departed in 1967, but not before contributing unforgettable deadpan vocals to three of the songs on their classic 1967 debut album.

Nico embarked on a solo career, recording folk-rock flavored songs for her debut *Chelsea Girl* album with assistance from Jackson Browne, Lou Reed, and John Cale. Her 1969 follow-up, *The Marble Index*, was a dramatic departure that unveiled her doom-laden, gothic persona, produced by Cale and prominently featuring her deep vocals, impenetrable lyrics, and ghostly harmonium. Her subsequent 1970s albums explored much the same territory, with assistance from Cale and influential art-rockers like Eno and Phil Manzanera. Her career fell into disarray during the rest of the '70s and the '80s, as she struggled with a massive drug habit and tangled personal life. She released several live albums on various labels, but the ill-planned *Drama of Exile* and the more successful *Camera Obscura* were her only coherent studio efforts until she died of a cerebral hemorrhage in Ibiza in 1988.

The original goth-rocker, Nico's albums are demanding and bleak, but map a unique and starkly powerful vision that has become more influential with age. An intimate of Bob Dylan, Jackson Browne, the Velvets, the Stones, Jim Morrison, Iggy Pop, and others, her fascinating story is recounted in the biography *Nico: The Life & Lies of an Icon*, by Richard Witts, published in Great Britain by Virgin books; *The End*, by James Young, is a seedy look at her drug-addled final years by a member of her touring band. — *Richie Unterberger*

● **Chelsea Girl** / 1967 / Polydor ✦✦✦✦
Nico's distanced, German-accented voice is presented over austere strings and, in one case, electric guitar on a series of songs reminiscent of her work with the Velvet Underground and written by Velvets John Cale and Lou Reed. Other songs (some unrecorded elsewhere) were written by a young Jackson Browne. — *William Ruhlmann*

The Marble Index / 1969 / Elektra ✦✦✦
The quirky, orchestrated folk-rock of Nico's 1968 debut album *Chelsea Girl* in no way prepared listeners for the stark, almost avant-garde flavor of her 1969 follow-up, *The Marble Index*. Produced by former Velvet Underground partner John Cale, the chanteuse presented an uncompromisingly bleak, Gothic soundscape on her second album. Dominated by spare harmonium and Nico's deep, brooding vocals, this album unveiled her singularly morose songwriting (her first record featured none of her compositions). Owing more to European classical and folk music than rock, it found little favor with 1969 audiences. But like the work of the Velvet Underground, it proved to be quite influential in the long run on a future generation of black-clad goth-rockers. The 1991 reissue of this recording adds two previously unreleased songs, "Roses in the Snow" and "Nibelungen." — *Richie Unterberger*

○ **Desert Shore** / 1971 / Reprise ✦✦✦✦
John Cale produces, arranges, and plays almost all the instruments on this atmospheric collection of songs well suited to Nico's droning delivery. — *William Ruhlmann*

The End / 1974 / Island ✦✦✦
The most remote and Teutonic of Nico's studio albums features Roxy Music guitarist Phil Manzanera, Brian Eno on synthesizer, and John Cale (who also produced) on a dozen instruments. After five Nico originals, it concludes with chilling readings of the Doors' "The End" and "Das Lied Der Deutschen." — *Richie Unterberger*

Drama of Exile / 1981 / Aura ✦

Do or Die! / 1982 / ROIR ✦✦

Camera Obscura / 1985 / Beggars Banquet ✦✦

(Live) Heroes / 1986 / Performance ✦✦✦
A six-track mini-album, four songs recorded live, including David Bowie's title track, which is perfectly suited to the Nico treatment. — *William Ruhlmann*

Peel Sessions / 1988 / Dutch East India ✦✦✦
In February 1971, Nico recorded a four-song session for the BBC that included songs from three of her solo albums. "No One Is There" and "Frozen Warnings" had appeared on 1969's *The Marble Index*, and "Janitor of Lunacy" on 1970's *Desert Shore*, "Secret Side" would appear on 1974's *The End*. Frequently bootlegged over the years, this official release presents the performance at the right speed in pristine sound. These renditions are about as bare-boned as they come, with no accompaniment save Nico's own harmonium. In both material and performance, she leans toward the more wistful and Gothic of her numbers. They don't differ drastically from the LP versions, but it's an interesting addition to fans' collections. — *Richie Unterberger*

Hanging Gardens / 1990 / Restless ✦✦✦

BOOK

✦✦✦✦ **Nico: The Life & Lies Of An Icon**, by Richard Witts (Virgin, UK, 1993). Biographies of cult musicians are sometimes stretched thin to approach book length. That is not at all the case with Nico, not only a fascinating individual in her own

right, but one who had a gift for intersecting with the life of numerous rock and film celebrities, from Fellini to the Rolling Stones and Velvet Underground. This is a lengthy, absorbing biography of her life and times, poking through the many myths she liked to build around herself to arrive at some sort of responsible guess at the truth. Much of the mystique built around Nico is generated by her experiences in the 1960s, and these are covered in depth, from her appearance in the film *La Dolce Vita* to her failed attempt at pop stardom in mod London to the Velvet Underground. It also spares no detail in her long and sad decline, which found her making influential avant-rock records, unmarketable avant-garde films, and playing and performing in the 1980s mostly to support her consuming drug habit. Includes fascinating recollections from John Cale, Jackson Browne, Iggy Pop, Fellini, and others. — *Richie Unterberger*

Night Ranger

Group, Hard Rock, Heavy Metal
Featuring ex-Ozzy Osbourne guitarist Brad Gillis and former Montrose keyboardist Alan Fitzgerald, Night Ranger was one of the most popular mainstream hard rock bands of the mid-'80s. The group formed in the early '80s in San Francisco; in addition to Gillis and Fitzgerald, the members included Jack Blades (vocals, bass), Jeff Watson (guitar), and Kelly Keagy (drums). After a few local gigs, promoter Bill Graham managed to get them supporting slots on Judas Priest, Santana, and Doobie Brothers concerts. Night Ranger's first album, *Dawn Patrol* (1982), reached number 38 on the U.S. charts, yet it was 1983's *Midnight Madness* that established the band as a commercial force. Featuring the AOR hit "(You Can Still) Rock in America" and the number five single "Sister Christian," the record peaked at number 15 and sold over a million copies. 1985's *7 Wishes* was just as successful, reaching number ten on the charts. Night Ranger's audience began to diminish after 1987's *Big Life*. Fitzgerald left the following year and the band released their last album, *Man in Motion*, which failed to go gold or spawn any Top 40 singles. Night Ranger broke up the next year. Jack Blades joined the supergroup Damn Yankees, which also featured Ted Nugent and Tommy Shaw. — *Stephen Thomas Erlewine*

○ **Dawn Patrol** / 1982 / Camel ✦✦✦✦
Featured is the hit "Don't Tell You Love Me." — *Larry Lapka*

○ **Midnight Madness** / 1983 / Camel ✦✦✦✦
Featured is the hit "Sister Christian." — *Larry Lapka*

7 Wishes / 1985 / Camel ✦✦✦
Featured is "Sentimental Street." — *Larry Lapka*

Big Life / 1987 / MCA ✦✦

Man in Motion / 1988 / Camel ✦✦

● **Night Ranger's Greatest Hits** / 1989 / Camel ✦✦✦✦
Night Ranger's albums were usually hit-or-miss affairs. Without exception, the strongest songs on the records were the singles, which combined their hard rock crunch with pop hooks. *Greatest Hits* collects all of their Top 40 singles, including "Sister Christian," "When You Close Your Eyes," and "Sentimental Street," as well as lesser hits "(You Can Still) Rock in America" and "Sing Me Away" and album rock radio hits like "Restless Kind" and "Eddie's Comin' Out Tonight," making it a definitive compilation. — *Stephen Thomas Erlewine*

Live in Japan / 1990 / MCA ✦✦
This is an okay live concert. — *Larry Lapka*

The Nightcrawlers

Group, Garage Rock, Folk-Rock
Florida group that scored a modest hit in 1967 with the cutesy folk-rocker "The Little Black Egg." Group member Chuck Conlon wrote most of the material on their sole album and several singles, with a sparse folk-rock sound that comes off as a poor person's Beau Brummels. — *Richie Unterberger*

● **The Little Black Egg** / 1967 / Eva ✦✦✦✦
18 songs, including their album and three non-LP singles. It's pretty thin and forgettable, with the exception of "The Little Black Egg" and the single "My Butterfly," an incredibly accurate early Who imitation complete with high harmonies, ringing guitar, and airplane take-off instrumental breaks. — *Richie Unterberger*

Willie Nile

b. 1949
Rock & Roll

A New York-based singer/songwriter whose 1980 debut album sparked much critical attention and the usual Bob Dylan comparisons, but which really anticipated the jangly guitar-rock revival later led by such acts as R.E.M. Willie Nile re-emerged in 1991 with *Places I Have Never Been* on Columbia. —*William Ruhlmann*

● **Willie Nile** / 1980 / Razor & Tie ✦✦✦
Strong songs full of urban observations, sung with urgency in Nile's high, thin voice and backed by guitar-driven music and the propulsive drumming of ex-Patti Smith Group member Jay Dee Dougherty. It all adds up to one of the best debut albums of the early '80s. —*William Ruhlmann*

Golden Dawn / 1981 / Razor & Tie ✦✦✦

Places I Have Never Been / 1982 / Columbia ✦✦

Harry Nilsson

b. Jun. 13, 1941, d. Jan. 15, 1994
Singer-Songwriter, Pop/Rock
Though he was best known as a singer, Harry Nilsson first gained recognition as a songwriter in the mid-'60s, when his songs were recorded by the Ronettes, the Modern Folk Quartet, and the Monkees. By the time Three Dog Night took his "One" into the Top Five, Nilsson had released two albums of his own on RCA. Neither of them was a hit, but Nilsson did score with his cover of Fred Neil's "Everybody's Talkin'" when it was used as the theme song of the film *Midnight Cowboy*. Nilsson wrote his own film and television scores and in 1970 made an album of songs written by Randy Newman. His career was not helped by his disinclination to undertake live appearances.

Nevertheless, Nilsson broke commercially with his late-1971 album, *Nilsson Schmilsson*, which contained his version of Badfinger's "Without You," a number one hit, and his own novelty number, "Coconut," which also hit the Top Ten. *Son of Schmilsson*, another appealing collection, was successful the following year. Nilsson's next album was a collection of standards sung against an orchestra conducted by noted '50s arranger Gordon Jenkins, *A Little Touch of Schmilsson in the Night*.

Nilsson had always been a favorite of the Beatles (he was sometimes rumored to be joining the group), and he engaged in projects with Ringo Starr (a film called *Son of Dracula*) and John Lennon (who produced Nilsson's *Pussy Cats*) in the mid-'70s. After Lennon's murder, Nilsson became an outspoken advocate of gun control and devoted much of his time to the cause. In the early '90s, he was holding showings of his art in galleries and starting a comeback in music. His comeback never materialized—Nilsson died of a heart attack on January 15, 1994, while he was preparing a new album and RCA Victor was compiling a two-CD retrospective, *Personal Best*. —*William Ruhlmann*

○ **Pandemonium Shadow Show** / 1967 / RCA ✦✦✦✦
It's no wonder that Nilsson was taken up by members of the Beatles after they heard this album, which demonstrated that the singer understood better than most the eclectic whimsy that had given birth to *Sgt. Pepper's Lonely Hearts Club Band*. Contains the bittersweet "1941" and "Cuddly Toy," which was covered by the Monkees. —*William Ruhlmann*

○ **Aerial Ballet** / 1968 / RCA ✦✦✦✦

Harry / 1969 / RCA ✦✦✦

○ **Nilsson Sings Newman** / Feb. 1970 / RCA ✦✦✦✦
Nilsson turns out to be a wonderful interpreter of the work of Randy Newman, his light voice making Newman's satiric humor even drier than when the composer himself sang the songs. —*William Ruhlmann*

The Point / 1971 / RCA ✦✦✦

Aerial Pandemonium Ballet / 1971 / RCA ✦✦✦
Nilsson selected tracks from his 1967 album *Pandemonium Shadow Show* and his 1968 album *Aerial Ballet*, and did some re-recording and remixing to produce this 1971 reconfiguration. Whatever you make of it, it does contain a version of "Everybody's Talkin'," plus Nilsson's recording of his composition "One," which was a hit for Three Dog Night. —*William Ruhlmann*

○ **Nilsson Schmilsson** / Nov. 1971 / RCA ✦✦✦✦
Nilsson's most successful album was a bouncy Richard Perry production, whose catchy songs were deepened by the singer's puckish humor. Contains the hits "Without You," "Jump into the Fire," and "Coconut." —*William Ruhlmann*

○ **Son of Schmilsson** / Jul. 1972 / RCA ✦✦✦✦
The humor is starting to take over on this followup but the songs are still entertaining, and the session players, including "George Harrysong" and "Richie Snare," make for a great backup band. Contains the hits "Spaceman" and "Remember (Christmas)," as well as the ultimate putdown song, "You're Breaking My Heart." —*William Ruhlmann*

A Little Touch of Schmilsson in the Night / 1973 / RCA ✦✦
Nilsson was nearly a decade ahead of Linda Ronstadt and other nouveau crooners in hiring a conductor/arranger of the pre-rock era (in this case Gordon Jenkins) and recording an album of standards before a full orchestra. And he did it better than most, proving to be a marvelous interpreter of songs like "What'll I Do?" and "Makin' Whoopee!" His version of "As Time Goes By" became a minor hit. —*William Ruhlmann*

Son of Dracula / Apr. 1, 1974 / RCA ✦✦

○ **Pussy Cats** / Aug. 19, 1974 / Edsel ✦✦✦✦
A dark, disjointed album of covers (including "Subterranean Homesick Blues," "Rock Around the Clock," and "Many Rivers to Cross"), the John Lennon-produced *Pussy Cats* is the strangest album Nilsson ever recorded; it's an aural document of Lennon and Nilsson's notorious, alcohol-soaked "lost weekend"—the sheer chaos of the album effectively evokes their aimless hedonism. —*Stephen Thomas Erlewine*

Duit on Mon Dei / 1975 / RCA ✦✦✦

Sandman / 1975 / RCA ✦✦

That's the Way It Is / 1976 / RCA ✦✦

Knnillssonn / 1977 / RCA ✦✦

● **All-Time Greatest Hits** / 1978 / RCA ✦✦✦✦
Nilsson's albums tended to hang together well, but that didn't keep him from throwing off singles, at least in the late 60s and early 70s. This collection contains all ten of his chart singles (including "Everybody's Talkin'"), plus his version of his song "One," which was a hit for Three Dog Night. —*William Ruhlmann*

● **Personal Best: The Harry Nilsson Anthology** / 1995 / RCA ✦✦✦✦
Spanning two discs, *Personal Best: The Harry Nilsson Anthology* is a comprehensive overview of Nilsson's varied career, including all of the hits and many significant album tracks, yet it offers too much material for the casual fan, who would be better served by *All-Time Greatest Hits*. —*Stephen Thomas Erlewine*

Nine Inch Nails

Group, Industrial, Alternative Pop/Rock
Nine Inch Nails, the one-man band of Trent Reznor, brought industrial music to the masses with 1989's *Pretty Hate Machine*. With its electronic rush, incessant beats, and distorted guitars, the album appeared to be like much industrial music on the surface, yet Reznor wrote pop songs, not the soundtrack to a personal horror movie. NIN's scarred, harsh soundscapes were bleak enough, yet Reznor's lyrics rise the despair and self-loathing to new heights; at times, his relentless darkness can veer dangerously close to self-parody.

Pretty Hate Machine wasn't a hit when it was released; it charted in 1990 and stayed on the charts for years afterward. By the time Reznor assembled a band for the first Lollapalooza tour in 1991, the group had a sizable following that only grew with NIN's ferocious performances on the tour. Legal troubles with his record company delayed the release of a second album; in 1992, he released a stop-gap EP, *Broken*, that was harder and more abrasive than the debut, yet still conformed to conventional song structures; it debuted in the *Billboard* Top Ten. With their second full-length album, Reznor showed his true roots—'70s progressive rock. *The Downward Spiral* was promoted as a concept album, a cohesive piece of work; it also featured ex-King Crimson guitarist Adrian Belew. Still, NIN is able to straddle two seemingly opposing genres easily, gaining alternative and mainstream hard rock fans alike; whether he likes it or not, Trent Reznor is the man that made industrial palatable for pop fans. —*Stephen Thomas Erlewine*

● **Pretty Hate Machine** / 1989 / TVT ✦✦✦✦
The reason *Pretty Hate Machine* gained a huge cult following is that Trent Reznor didn't make an industrial album in the strict sense of the term; his songs are pop songs played in an industrial style. Meanwhile, he constructs a towering monument of angst

and hatred in his lyrics, perfect for legions of alienated adolescents. As Reznor says, "I'd rather die than give you control," and he proves it throughout *Pretty Hate Machine*. Full of hooks, beats, and abrasive noise, *Pretty Hate Machine* gave a generation of adolescents a martyr as well as a great way to vent anger. —*Stephen Thomas Erlewine*

○ **Broken** / 1992 / Interscope ✦✦✦✦
After the unexpected success of *Pretty Hate Machine*, Trent Reznor found himself unable to enjoy it. Instead, he became embroiled in an ugly lawsuit with his record company, which prevented him from releasing any new material for three years. Although *Broken* is only an EP, the wait was more than worth it. Those who fell in love with the pseudo-industrial *Pretty Hate Machine* will likely be alienated by the raging, angry assault of *Broken*. Instead of blaming everyone else for his troubles, Reznor turns his anger inward. "Wish" and "Happiness in Slavery" are busier, angrier, and noisier than anything on *Pretty*; the songs still have hooks, but the hooks are the noise. The anger on *Broken* is real, not feigned; for those who can stomach undiluted rage, *Broken* is a masterpiece. (Note: There are two bonus tracks at 98 and 99 that equal the other six songs.) —*Stephen Thomas Erlewine*

Fixed / Nov. 1992 / Interscope ✦✦✦
Even more than *Broken*, the limited-edition *Fixed* EP sounds like an attempt by Reznor to whittle down the size of his audience. The remixes on *Fixed* totally distort all of the original meanings and intents of the original versions on *Broken*; it's the closest Reznor has come to pure industrial music. While the remixes completely rearrange the songs, *Fixed* is additional proof that NIN is not a flash in the pan. A bold artistic move, and not for the faint of heart. —*Stephen Thomas Erlewine*

The Downward Spiral / 1994 / Interscope ✦✦✦
Although Trent Reznor designed *The Downward Spiral* as a concept album about despair and anger, these are familiar themes for Nine Inch Nails; it's up to the music to carry the album. And it does carry the album, featuring harder guitars and more brutal beats. However, the songwriting has slipped and the aggression sounds forced. —*Stephen Thomas Erlewine*

Further Down The Spiral / 1995 / Nothing/Interscope ✦✦
While it's marketed as an EP, *Further Down The Spiral* is essentially the single for "Hurt," which is included here in its live version, the same version that's used in the video. However, what makes the disc worth investigating is the remixes. Like *Fixed* before it, *Further Down The Spiral* deconstructs and reassembles the tracks from the platinum *The Downward Spiral*, reconfiguring the music ways that are frequently more interesting and challenging than the original versions. —*Stephen Thomas Erlewine*

Nirvana

Group, Alternative Pop/Rock
With one album, Nirvana changed rock & roll. Before "Smells like Teen Spirit" and *Nevermind* were released in 1991, alternative and post-punk rock had never been considered profitable or commercial. Nirvana changed the record industry's conception of what was mainstream, as well as the public's. *Nevermind* marked a shift in the mainstream, when punk rock finally reclaimed the rock & roll mainstream for themselves. Other post-punk bands that crossed over into the mainstream had done so slowly; by the time U2 and R.E.M. became superstars in 1987, their audiences were large enough to guarantee them a hit album. Besides, neither band had as much raw guitars and naked angst as Nirvana; they were as close to a punk band as possible in the '90s.

Nirvana combined strands of rock from all eras into one explosive burst of rage. Combining the melodic pop of the Beatles, the '70s sludge of Black Sabbath, and the spiky song structure of the Pixies with the fierce indie ethics of the American indie underground of the '80s, the band came up with a signature pop-punk that was distinctly their own.

Bleach, their 1989 debut, made the band underground darlings and led to a major-label contract. In 1990, Dave Grohl became Nirvana's permanent drummer, teaming with bassist Chris Novoselic to form the fiercest rhythm section in rock. Guitarist/vocalist Kurt Cobain's new songs surpassed anything on their debut; his songs were stunning, concise bursts of melody and rage, that occasionally spilled over into haunting, folk-styled acoustic ballads.

Nevermind wasn't expected to sell over 100,000 copies; by early 1992, the album was the top-selling record in the country. However, the band's personal fortunes weren't as smooth. During 1992,

Cobain developed a debilitating heroin habit which strained relations with the rest of the band. By the beginning of 1993, Cobain had admitted that he had just detoxed from heroin, which he claimed he used to fight a chronic stomach problem. Nirvana released their third album, *In Utero*, in September of 1993; the album debuted at number one and soon went double platinum. The band launched a U.S. tour in October; all of the articles about the band portrayed a happier, calmer Cobain.

Those images began to unravel in March of 1994, when he overdosed on champagne and tranquilizers while on vacation in Rome. For all of March, rumors were flying about Nirvana's future. All of the rumors stopped on April 8, when Cobain's body was discovered at his home in Seattle; he had died three days earlier of a self-inflicted gunshot wound.

Since his death, Cobain has been equally revered and reviled; he wasn't universally mourned because he wasn't universally loved. Even after *Nevermind*, Nirvana's music was too raw for many listeners. But that doesn't mean that Cobain was not gifted or that his music was not important. Nirvana proved to both the record companies and the public that post-punk-music and culture had a prominent place in mainstream culture. More importantly, the band made some undeniably great music. —*Stephen Thomas Erlewine*

☆ **Bleach** / 1989 / Sub Pop ✦✦✦✦
At the time, *Bleach* was a stellar piece of Seattle sludge, state-of-the-art indie-rock. Although it still stands as one of the best albums in the Sub Pop catalog, it pales next to their other work. *Bleach* is clearly a debut album; there is a fair amount of filler, and the band sometimes collapses into a sub-Sabbath murk, but "School," "Love Buzz," "Blew," and "Negative Creep" are outstanding, furious rockers, and the gorgeous, Beatlesque ballad "About A Girl" signals the heights the band would reach on their next album. —*Stephen Thomas Erlewine*

★ **Nevermind** / 1991 / DGC ✦✦✦✦
If "Smells Like Teen Spirit" was the only good song on *Nevermind*, the album wouldn't have inspired the popular revolution that it did. Although the "Louie Louie"-meets-the-Pixies teen angst of "Teen Spirit" is what crossed Nirvana over, what made the album so remarkable was the quantum leap in Kurt Cobain's songwriting. The throttling punk rockers "Breed" and "Territorial Pissings" demolish anything on *Bleach*, and the haunting "Something in the Way" and "Polly" show Cobain's full range. Even better are "In Bloom," "Drain You," "On A Plain," and "Lithium," which fully combine both the melodicism and the sonic roar that Nirvana does so well. And the record wouldn't sound half as good as it does without Dave Grohl, who pushes every song to the limit. —*Stephen Thomas Erlewine*

○ **Incesticide** / Dec. 1992 / DGC ✦✦✦✦
More than anyone else, Nirvana itself was caught completely off guard by the overwhelming success of *Nevermind*. While Cobain wondered what to do next, the band put out *Incesticide*, a collection of B-sides, live performances, outtakes, demos, and "rare" singles. The first half of the album is terrific, but after "Beeswax" the entire enterprise collapses into half-baked ideas and outtakes that deserved to stay that way. The first half is filled with BBC sessions previously only available on the Japanese import *Hormoaning*, the B-sides "Been A Son" and "Son of A Gun," and a Sub Pop single. The price of the CD is justified by the first two tracks, the "Dive"/"Sliver" single, which was released just before *Nevermind* was recorded. —*Stephen Thomas Erlewine*

☆ **In Utero** / 1993 / DGC ✦✦✦✦
Despite all of the pre-release rumors predicting a noisy all-out sonic assault, *In Utero* is not an alienating alternative rock monster. Instead, *In Utero* retains all of the melodic splendor of *Nevermind*, injecting it with a raw roar louder and harder than anything on *Bleach*. However, Kurt Cobain remains a pop songwriter, and the melodies don't get buried under the Steve Albini's sonic assault, as "Heart-Shaped Box" and "Pennyroyal Tea" prove. The songs are among Cobain's best, making *In Utero* a successful follow-up to a landmark, groundbreaking album. —*Stephen Thomas Erlewine*

☆ **MTV Unplugged In New York** / 1994 / DGC ✦✦✦✦
Sadly, *MTV Unplugged* stands as Nirvana's last album. While it's an album of covers and old songs, it ranks as one of the band's most cohesive records. Instead of relying on the trio's overpowering sonic force, *Unplugged* concentrates on Kurt Cobain's subtly shaded songwriting and Nirvana's deceptively simple musical

power. Every version of their previously recorded songs, with the possible exception of "On A Plain," dramatically improves the original, and the covers reveal more about Cobain than he intended. By the time Nirvana close with a wrenching, spine-chilling version of Leadbelly's "Where Did You Sleep Last Night" the emotional complexity of Nirvana's music is clear. It's also clear that they could have made even greater music. —*Stephen Thomas Erlewine*

Mojo Nixon

Rock & Roll, Alternative Pop/Rock
Mojo Nixon parlayed an irrepressible personality, a wicked sense of humor, and a taste for high-energy rockabilly into success on a series of novelty albums, and even a place as an MTV VJ. The latter was surprising, since Nixon had first gained notice for a song on his and Skid Roper's second album, *Frenzy* (1986), called "Stuffin' Martha's Muffin," an ode to the joys of intimate contact with MTV VJ Martha Quinn. The song was typical of Nixon's lyrical approach, which he followed with relentless mirth through the course of four albums on which Roper (a mostly silent partner) contributed incidental instrumental backup. *Bo-Day-Shus!!!* (1987), for example, contained "Elvis Is Everywhere," one of the more outrageous tributes to the King. Debunking famous names came more naturally to Nixon, however, and *Root Hog or Die* was introduced by the *National Enquirer*-headline leadoff song "Debbie Gibson Is Pregnant with My Two Headed Love Child." Gibson didn't comment, but when Nixon (now separated from Roper) issued his first solo album, *Otis*, containing the song "Don Henley Must Die," the ex-Eagle was heard to say that the singer needed a laxative. —*William Ruhlmann*

Mojo & Skid / 1985 / IRS ✦✦
Get Out of My Way / 1986 / Restless ✦✦✦
Frenzy / 1986 / IRS ✦✦✦
Arguably the duo's best album, highlights include "I'm Living with the Three-Foot Anti-Christ," "The Amazing Bigfoot Diet," and two songs any working musician should understand, "Where the Hell's My Money?" and "I Hate Banks." By the way, the *Get Out of My Way* mini-LP, which included some of Nixon's Christmas tunes, is also part of the *Frenzy* CD. —*Rick Clark*

○ **Bo-Day-Shus!!!** / 1987 / Enigma ✦✦✦✦
On *Bo-Day-Shus!!!*, Nixon and Roper want you to know that "Elvis Is Everywhere" (but you knew that anyway—right??). They explore the junk-food underbelly of American culture with thoughtful odes like "B.B.Q.U.S.A.," "I'm Gonna Dig Up Howlin' Wolf," and "We Gotta Have More Soul." Declarative odes like "I Ain't Gonna Piss in No Jar" and "Don't Want No Foo-Foo Haircut on My Head" are indications of the duo's sensitivity to politically correct issues. —*Rick Clark*

○ **Root Hog or Die** / 1989 / IRS ✦✦✦✦
With the help of Jim Dickinson and a few sidemen, Skid Roper and Mojo Nixon plow through thoughtful numbers like "Debbie Gibson Is Pregnant with My Two-Headed Love Child," "She's Vibrator Dependent," and "Louisiana Liplock." Nixon indulges his Elvis fixation with "(619) 239-KING," and a version of "This Land Is Your Land" mutates into a pitch for Mojo World. —*Rick Clark*

● **Unlimited Everything** / 1990 / Enigma ✦✦✦✦
This fairly complete overview of Nixon and Roper's most popular work is a good place to start for the uninitiated. —*Rick Clark*

Otis / 1990 / IRS ✦✦✦
After *Root Hog or Die*, Mojo went solo and enlisted a primo group of rude rock sidemen from the Del-Lords, X, Beat Farmers, and Dash Rip Rock. Nixon did a good job making the transition from the bare-bones duo approach to a full band. His putdown of "serious" pop rockers like Don Henley ("Don Henley Must Die") gained quite a bit of publicity. —*Rick Clark*

The Notorious B.I.G.

Rap
The Brooklyn-born rapper the Notorious B.I.G. (born Chris Wallace) first gained attention for his work on Mary J. Blige's "What's the 411?" When he delivered his debut album, *Ready To Die*, in 1994, it became one of the most popular hip-hop releases of the year. In June of 1995, his single "One More Chance" debuted at number five in the pop singles chart, tying Michael Jackson's "Scream / Childhood" as the highest-debuting single of all time. —*Stephen Thomas Erlewine*

● **Ready To Die** / 1994 / Bad Boy ✦✦✦✦
With the galvanizing deep funk of *Ready To Die*, the Notorious B.I.G. scores one of the most impressive rap debuts since Dr. Dre's seminal *The Chronic*. While *Ready To Die* takes its throbbing bass grooves from that P-Funk-saturated album, the Notorious B.I.G. writes more acute and evocative lyrics, as well as being a more skillful rapper. —*Stephen Thomas Erlewine*

NRBQ (New Rhythm & Blues Quintet)

Group, Rock & Roll
Formed in 1967 in Florida as New Rhythm & Blues Quintet, the original lineup included pianist Terry Adams, guitarist Steve Ferguson, bassist Joey Spampinato, vocalist Frank Gadler, and drummer Tom Staley. After recording two albums for Columbia (including one with Carl Perkins), which went nowhere, guitarist Al Anderson joined in 1971, replacing Ferguson. Gadler left in 1972; Staley was replaced by drummer Tom Ardolino in 1974.

This versatile and witty quartet is at home with everything from atonal jazz to rockabilly to country swing to pop jangle to roadhouse R&B. But they don't always give eclecticism a good name; although there's something worth hearing on each of their albums, the Q's humor is often corny, and their penchant for indulging their every artistic whim means that even their best albums are padded with silly hokum. They've been doing the same stuff for nearly 30 years and have amassed a fanatical cult following. At times, NRBQ can sound like the greatest rock band in the world.

After two decades without any line-up shakeups, Anderson left the band after the release of their 1994 album, *Message for our Mess-Age*, to pursue a career writing country songs; he toured as Carlene Carter's guitarist immediately after his departure. NRBQ replaced Anderson with Spampinato's brother, Johnny. —*Cub Koda & John Floyd*

NRBQ / 1969 / Columbia ✦✦✦
The Q's debut is as succinct a summation of what this band was about than perhaps anything they've released since. After opening the record with a storming version of Eddie Cochran's "C'mon Everybody," they take a breath and leap headlong into a raucous version of Sun Ra's "Number 9." Add to that a songwriting collaboration between Terry Adams and jazz composer Carla Bley, and the great guitar playing of Steve Ferguson (really great on "Stomp"), and you've got the makings of a tremendously important record by a furiously eclectic and always wonderful band. —*John Dougan*

Boppin' the Blues / 1970 / ✦✦
Scraps / 1972 / Polydor ✦✦✦
A spotty album, it contains a few necessary gems, like "Magnet" and "It's Not So Hard." —*John Floyd*

Workshop / 1973 / Kama Sutra ✦✦✦
○ **Scraps/Workshop** / 1976 / Annuit ✦✦✦✦
When vinyl was still the prevailing form of sound reproduction, these two long-lost records were rereleased in this fantastic double set, which is probably out of print, but (assuming it hasn't been issued on CD) is worth ferreting out. Both records feature the debut of Al Anderson's superb guitar, and, (trivia buffs take note) *Scraps* is the only time in the band's history they were a quintet with lead vocalist Frank Gadler (who's very good). Both records are chock full of classic Q: "Howard Johnson's Got His Hojo Working on Me," "C'Mon If You're Comin'," "Get That Gasoline," and "Magnet." Also making these records indispensable is Joey Spampinato's best-ever Beatles impression "It's Not So Hard," maybe the best pop song the Q ever recorded. Buyers note: parts of *Workshop*, along with an assortment of outtakes, was issued by Rounder in 1986 as an album entitled *RC Cola & a Moon Pie*. —*John Dougan*

All Hopped Up / 1977 / Rounder ✦✦✦
A fairly consistent and ballsy offering, it contains early classics such as "Ridin' in My Car" and "That's Alright." —*John Floyd*

● **NRBQ at Yankee Stadium** / 1978 / Mercury ✦✦✦✦
More than just NRBQ's best record, but one of the great records of the '70s (maybe ever!). This album contains the strongest batch of new Q songs on one record, many of them the best and most memorable songs in the band's long and storied career. Starting with Terry Adams' herky-jerky "Green Lights" to the rollicking "I Want You Bad," the band has rarely sounded better. The record's gem, however, is an Al Anderson song left over from their previous record (*All Hopped Up on Red Rooster*), "Ridin' In My Car." A song about lost love and blown chances, it has Al's characteristic wry sensibility and (non-fatal) heartache, all wrapped up in a ebullient pop

package driven by Terry Adams' melodic keyboard riffing and Tom Ardolino's amazingly assertive drumming. *Yankee Stadium* should have been a huge album, but Mercury booted it and never capitalized on the band's fanatical support base. Caveat emptor: when this record was issued by Mercury on CD just a couple of years back, they inexplicably left off "Ridin' In My Car." As to whether that idiotic oversight has been rectified, I haven't a clue. —*John Dougan*

○ **Kick Me Hard** / 1979 / Rounder ✦✦✦✦
This is a decent mix of tough rockers and cheesy pop. —*John Floyd*

○ **Tiddlywinks** / 1980 / Rounder ✦✦✦✦
After being unceremoniously dumped by Mercury after *Yankee Stadium*, NRBQ returned to that warm embrace of Rounder and recorded a string of fine records that started with *Kick Me Hard*. This lineup was to remain intact for nearly 20 years, but here, fairly early on, the synchronicity among the quartet was apparent; it was as if they'd been playing together forever, and the music excelled as a result. The songwriting was getting better too: Al, Terry and Joey were dividing the chores but never losing the group's cohesiveness. At times, Terry's songs would be a little too goofy, and Joey's heartfelt pop might dip into saccharine sweetness now and again, but never so much so that it becomes a huge problem. Of these two excellent records, *Kick Me Hard* lives up to its title, especially during the bluesy organ workout "Don't You Know" and the riff-happy "All Night Long" (great solo by Al). *Tiddlywinks* is carried by "Me And the Boys" (later to be recorded by Bonnie Raitt) and Al's beautiful "Never Take the Place of You." —*John Dougan*

Grooves in Orbit / 1983 / Bearsville ✦✦✦
Back to a major label, NRBQ came up with a solid record that, again, didn't significantly increase their audience, even though many musicians (Elvis Costello, Bonnie Raitt) were singing their praises. Although very good, *Grooves* is not significantly better (actually it's not any better) than *Kick Me Hard* or *Tiddlywinks*. Both sides end with a whimper rather than a bang, and it seems that the band was developing an overreliance on recycling material (their cover of Johnny Cash's "Get Rhythm" shows up on *Yankee Stadium*). Still, the crucial stuff ("Rain at The Drive-In" and "Smackeroo") fit the bill. —*John Dougan*

Tap Dancin' Bats / 1983 / Rounder ✦✦✦
While the Q was recording *Grooves* for Bearsville, Rounder released this bizarre chunk of odds and sods that featured the band's experimental side. Ask anyone who's ever gone to an NRBQ gig and they'll tell you that the Q are as likely to play Sun Ra as they are Carl Perkins, or sometimes fuse the two. *Tapdancin' Bats* has such supremely strange moments: their paean to wrestler/actor Lou Albano, "Captain Lou," a crazy novelty song from the '50s, "Rats In My Room," some straightahead (but slightly skewed) rock and roll, and the title track, a dissonant jazz blurt that sounds like Ornette Coleman. Truly inspiring stuff. —*John Dougan*

She Sings, They Play / 1985 / Rounder ✦✦✦
During the mid-'80s, bassist Joey Spampinato married country music legend Skeeter Davis, and what better way to celebrate than with a record that featured Skeeter's great voice with the Q backing her up. To those who have little patience for classic country performers, and who simply want to hear NRBQ rock, this is probably a minor work. But, for the rest of us, it's an unfettered joy. —*John Dougan*

RC Cola & a Moon Pie / 1986 / Rounder ✦✦
This abridged version of *Workshop* (one of their finest early albums) includes some previously unreleased and rare material. —*John Floyd*

Lou and the Q / 1986 / Rounder ✦✦
Silliness abounds on this wacky meeting of the "Q" with pro-wrestling manager Lou Albano. —*Jeff Tamarkin*

God Bless Us All / 1987 / Rounder ✦✦✦
Go figure this: Rounder decides to release two live recordings in succession. Granted, NRBQ had long been known for great live shows, but these records, while certainly enjoyable, seem a little perfunctory, and only hint at the kind of excitement the band was capable of generating live. Still, on *God Bless Us All*, Al tears through an inspired "Crazy Like a Fox" and the whole band cranks on "Shake, Rattle and Roll." *Diggin'* has a pounding "It Comes to Me Naturally" and the country standard "Scarlet Ribbons." Both records are fun, but neither is essential unless you're a completist. —*John Dougan*

Diggin' Uncle Q (Live) / 1988 / Rounder ✦✦
Wild Weekend / 1989 / Virgin ✦✦
Another year, another shot with a major label. Actually, of all the recent Q releases, *Wild Weekend* got the most ink and promotional support out of the box. Helping it along was a video for the title track, as well as mostly favorable critical notices. It's a good record, but not a great one. The good stuff rocks with the power, swing and sway of classic Q, whereas the bad stuff (not really bad, just mediocre) serves as filler. Another great Al Anderson song ("Boys Life") and a wonderful, whimsical one from Terry ("Little Floater"). —*John Dougan*

● **Peek-A-Boo: Best of NRBQ (1969-1989)** / 1990 / Rhino ✦✦✦✦
A two-CD set that does a great job of hitting the band's high spots, without sacrificing any of the freewheeling stylistic leaps or engaging lunacy that has made NRBQ one of America's longest-lived bands. If you're interested in a career overview and little more, this is the ideal release. However, it is my considered opinion that anyone who loves this stuff (and to emphatically use a double negative, there's nothing not to love) will have their appetite whetted for more. Not a slow spot, ill-chosen track or bad decision among the 35 songs, this is as great a statement for NRBQ as one of the best rock bands America has ever produced. Few bands, genre notwithstanding, have been able to effortlessly recombine styles, be so defiantly off-the-wall, and rock like all get-out for so long and still sound so good. God bless them all. —*John Dougan*

Honest Dollar / 1992 / Rykodisc ✦✦
If legendary American rockers NRBQ would issue an album of songs as wistful and infectious as *Honest Dollar*'s opener "Ridin' in My Car," they would be huge stars. But then they wouldn't be NRBQ, the band for which repetition and predictability equals death. *Honest Dollar* features 17 wildly diverse live tracks spanning the last decade's-worth of NRBQ life on the road, 11 of which have never previously been set to disc by the group. The collection serves as a perfect introduction to NRBQ's rootsy, off-center pop fused with blues, jazz, country, and rockabilly. NRBQ are obviously too spontaneous and diverse for their own commercial good, but offer a heady experience for anyone willing to ride this musical roller-coaster with an open mind. —*Roch Parisien*

Stay with We: The Best of NRBQ / 1993 / Columbia ✦✦✦
Featuring 24 songs including eight unreleased tracks, *Stay with We* is the definitive compilation of NRBQ's early years at Columbia. —*Stephen Thomas Erlewine*

Message for the Mess Age / 1994 / Forward/Rhino ✦✦✦
Sadly, the last record with Al on guitar (he's since been replaced by Joey's brother Johnny, ex-guitar slinger for the Incredible Casuals and Four Star Combo) isn't a knockout, but the material is strong and makes one optimistic for the Q's next 25 years. Al does contribute another achingly beautiful song, "A Better Word For Love," and even the goofy moments ("Girl Scout Cookies" and the spell-my-name-right-anthem "Spampinato") don't sound nearly as forced as they occasionally have in the past. We're lucky to still have 'em around. —*John Dougan*

Ted Nugent

b. 1948
Hard Rock, Heavy Metal
Nugent started in a local Detroit teen band, the Lourds, and formed the Amboy Dukes in late 1965 or early 1966. He scored his first hit with "Journey to the Center of Your Mind" in 1968. Several albums using the Amboy Dukes tag followed, with the personnel changing with almost every album. Nugent went solo in 1975, marking his greatest success to date with one album after another in the charts; he put his solo career on hold to become a member of the group Damn Yankees in 1990. He resumed his solo career in 1995 with *Spirit Of The Wild*. A powerful, high-decibel guitarist, Nugent's energy more than makes up for whatever subtleties he lacks. —*Cub Koda*

Call of the Wild / Jul. 1973 / Bizarre ✦✦✦
Journeys & Migrations / 1974 / Mainstream ✦✦
Ted Nugent / 1975 / Epic ✦✦✦
○ **Free for All** / 1976 / Epic ✦✦✦✦
Ted Nugent's career kicked into gear with his second solo album, *Free-for-All* which was a collection of storming hard rockers sung by Meat Loaf, who had yet to establish himself as a star in his own right. —*Stephen Thomas Erlewine*

○ **Cat Scratch Fever** / 1977 / Epic ✦✦✦✦
Driven by a set of hard-driving, catchy riffs and numerous gut-wrenching solos, *Cat Scratch Fever* remains Ted Nugent's best studio album. —*Stephen Thomas Erlewine*

Weekend Warrior / 1978 / Epic ✦✦✦
Weekend Warriors, Nugent's followup to the career peaks of *Cat Scratch Fever* and *Double Live Gonzos!*, isn't quite as strong as his two previous albums, but it remains one of his better albums, featuring a handful of prime hard rockers. —*Stephen Thomas Erlewine*

○ **Double Live Gonzo** / 1978 / Epic ✦✦✦✦
This is the ultimate document of Nugent's mountain-man persona. —*Dan Heilman*

State of Shock / 1979 / Epic ✦✦

Scream Dream / 1980 / Epic ✦✦✦

● **Great Gonzo: The Best of Ted Nugent** / 1981 / Epic ✦✦✦✦
Featuring all of his hard-rock standards from the 1970s, *Great Gonzos: The Best of Ted Nugent* is a better collection than the double-disc *Out of Control*, since there isn't a bit of filler. —*Stephen Thomas Erlewine*

Intensities in 10 Cities / 1981 / Epic ✦✦

Nugent / 1982 / Atlantic ✦✦

Penetrator / 1984 / Atlantic ✦✦

Little Miss Dangerous / 1986 / Atlantic ✦✦

● **Ted Nugent and the Amboy Dukes** / 1987 / DCC ✦✦✦✦
Featuring the psychedelic classic "Journey to the Center of the Mind," as well as several other similar-sounding acid-rockers, *Ted Nugent and the Amboy Dukes* is the best record Nugent with his first band. —*Stephen Thomas Erlewine*

If You Can't Lick 'Em . . . Lick 'Em / 1988 / Atlantic ✦✦

○ **Out of Control** / Jun. 22, 1993 / Epic ✦✦✦✦
Out of Control is two CDs of prime Nugent, covering his days with the Amboy Dukes as well as his lengthy solo career. It's the definitive collection of the Motor City Madman. —*AMG*

○ **Spirit Of The Wild** / 1995 / Atlantic ✦✦✦✦
Spirit Of The Wild ranks as one of Ted Nugent's finest moments because it cuts away the filler and keeps the wildman's tendency for indulgence in check. A fair amount of the material does concern itself with the wilderness, which fits right in with his '90s reinvention as a conservative family-values spokesman. That doesn't mean that it's a tame record—it means that Nugent sounds committed again, since that passion for hunting and family flows throughout his performance. —*Stephen Thomas Erlewine*

Gary Numan (Gary Webb)

b. 1958
Techno-Pop/Dance, Electronic, New Wave
Gary Numan managed to incorporate the electronic innovations of Kraftwerk, Brian Eno, and David Bowie into pop music, creating some of the first synth-pop hits of the new wave era. Numan originally performed under the name Tubeway Army, which had a chart-topping British single with "Are 'Friends' Electric?" The first record he released under his own name, 1979's *Pleasure Principle*, featured the international hit "Cars"; the single hit number one in the U.K. and reached the U.S. Top Ten. Throughout the early '80s, Numan was one of the most popular artists in the U.K., amassing several Top Ten hits and two number one albums. Around 1983, his career began to slip, as each record became indistinguishable from each other. Even as he fell out of the Top Ten, Numan held on to his die-hard fans. He continued to record into the '90s. —*Stephen Thomas Erlewine*

First Album / 1978 / Atco ✦✦

Tubeway Army / 1978 / Beggars Banquet ✦✦✦
Gary Numan's first album, recorded with his backup band Tubeway Army and released under their name, is a tentative but intriguing effort, as the keyboardist works synthesizers and electronic textures into basic, guitar-driven post-punk song structures. —*Stephen Thomas Erlewine*

● **The Pleasure Principle** / 1979 / Arista ✦✦✦✦
Gary Numan perfected his combination of Kraftwerk-influenced synth-drone and pop melodies on *The Pleasure Principle*, the first album he released under his own name. —*Stephen Thomas Erlewine*

○ **Replicas** / 1979 / Atco ✦✦✦✦
On *Replicas*, Gary Numan tooke top-billing over Tubeway Army, which was appropriate, considering that Numan's synthesizers were now the dominant instruments in the band's music. The new direction was successful, both artistically and commercially, with the the cold, catchy single "Are 'Friends' Electric?" reaching the top of the U.K. charts. —*Stephen Thomas Erlewine*

That's Too Bad / 1979 / Beggars Banquet ✦✦✦

○ **Telekon** / 1980 / Atco ✦✦✦✦
After the synthesized triumph of *The Pleasure Principle*, Gary Numan brought some guitars back into his sound on *Telekon*. Unlike *Tubeway Army*, which was dominated by guitars, the instrument is used to flesh out the keyboard-created textures on *Telekon*, which makes the album one of his most intriguing and creative records. —*Stephen Thomas Erlewine*

Dance / 1981 / Atco ✦✦✦

Living Ornaments '79 / 1981 / Arista ✦✦

Living Ornaments '80 / 1981 / Beggars Banquet ✦✦

○ **I Assassin** / 1982 / Atco ✦✦✦✦
Although it showcases his trademark sound to a fine effect, the repetitive, formulaic songwriting of *I, Assassin* suggests that Gary Numan had hit a brick wall with his robotic, synthesized pop. —*Stephen Thomas Erlewine*

New Man Numan / 1982 / Virgin ✦✦✦

Warriors / 1983 / Beggars Banquet ✦✦

The Plan / 1984 / Beggars Banquet ✦✦

Berserker / 1984 / Numa ✦✦✦

1978-1979, Vols. 2 & 3 / 1985 / Beggars Banquet ✦✦

● **Exhibition** / 1987 / Beggars Banquet ✦✦✦✦
Exhibition compiles Gary Numan's classic synth-pop singles as well as several album cuts and live tracks, making it a good introduction to his music. —*Stephen Thomas Erlewine*

Absolution / 1995 / Numa ✦✦

Nutmegs

Group, R&B, Doo-Wop
The floating lead tenor of Leroy Griffin distinguished the Nutmegs's 1955 R&B smash "Story Untold," an East Coast doo-wop classic. Hailing from New Haven, CT, the quintet signed with Herald Records and debuted with "Story Untold." Another smooth ballad issued later that year, "Ship of Love," also scaled the R&B charts. The Nutmegs made several more solid singles for Herald but without recapturing their initial success. —*Bill Dahl*

● **Greatest Hits** / Relic ✦✦✦✦
Fine East Coast doo-wop, including the classic "Story Untold" and "The Ship of Love," only available on vinyl for now. —*Bill Dahl*

N.W.A.

Group, Rap
This Compton, CA, ensemble once held the title of "most controversial rap act," but in recent months others have surfaced to share some of the heat. The original posse, including Ice Cube, Eazy-E, Arabian Prince, MC Ren and the D.O.C., made their first release in 1987. *N.W.A. and the Posse* was mainly a party/fun record but cuts like "Boyz N' the Hood" and "Dope Man" should have been a warning to alert ears of what was coming. Anyone who missed the debut was certainly caught by surprise when the 1988 follow-up, *Straight Outta Compton*, came along. The stark, brutal depictions of gang strife and urban warfare, the coarse, obscene language and the complete amoral tone, plus the anti-authority number "F**k Tha Police" earned N.W.A. scorn from middle-class types of all colors and also attempts from the FBI to get retailers not to stock it. Since that high point, N.W.A. has really become less an entity and more an amalgam of solo acts. Ice Cube, Eazy-E, Arabian Prince, D.O.C., and MC Ren have all done separate projects; Cube has not only left the group but has engaged in bitter, heated public feuds with them; and D.O.C. suffered a near-fatal car crash that took him out of circulation for quite some time. The EP *100 Miles and Runnin'* (1990) was half-hearted, and the group's 1991 release *Efil4zaggin* (Niggaz4Life backwards) elicited some controversy but nothing close to past albums. Amidst gargantuan clashes of egos, N.W.A. dissolved the following year, leaving behind an enormously influential body of work. —*Ron Wynn*

○ **N.W.A. and the Posse** / 1987 / Priority ✦✦✦
This is a hodgepodge of early singles from N.W.A. and some of their Compton contemporaries (including D.O.C.). The highlights are N.W.A.'s "Boyz-N-the-Hood" and "Dope Man." —*John Floyd*

★ **Straight Outta Compton** / 1989 / Priority ✦✦✦✦✦
This is a scalding, relentless, and always jolting look at life in the ghettos of South Central Los Angeles. You may not agree with their relish of violence or the rampant sexism, but this series of inflammatory and bruising vignettes is a visceral landmark on a par with the MC5 or the Sex Pistols. —*John Floyd*

100 Miles and Runnin' / 1990 / Priority ✦✦
After the revolutionary (in more than one sense of the word) *Straight Outta Compton*, N.W.A. could hardly go any further, especially with the departure of Ice Cube, by far the most gifted of the crew. *100 Miles and Runnin'* was released as a stop-gap while N.W.A. prepared their next full-length release, and also to try and stop Ice Cube's success. It reprises all of the gangsta/bitch fantasies of *Compton*, but with no insight or humor and very little reality. Nothing much of interest. —*Stephen Thomas Erlewine*

Niggaz4life / 1991 / Priority ✦✦✦
This is where N.W.A. went off the deep end and became a self-parody. Their tales of urban horror have no reality anymore and simply aren't dangerous or menacing. But that was all that was expected of them; the majority of N.W.A.'s audience was always white, and suburban kids glommed onto the silly fantasies of *Efil4zaggin* by the thousands, rocketing the album to the upper reaches of the charts. While the tracks sound great (Dr. Dre is unquestionably the only talent left), there is nothing here. —*Stephen Thomas Erlewine*

Judy Nylon

Experimental
A New York singer who sprang from the early-'80s avant-garde Lower East Side noise-rock scene (aka "no wave"), Judy Nylon led a brief but interesting career. Abandoning New York for London in 1981, she joined forces with singer Pat Palladin, forming the indelicately named duo Snatch. Snatch was a truly hit-and-miss artsy-fartsy duo, attracting the attention of Brian Eno who, despite working with them, didn't improve their wan, bloodless sound. More successful, however, was brilliant British reggae/dub/psycho-funk producer Adrian Sherwood, who produced Nylon's only solo recording, *Pal Judy*, in 1982. Superficially reminiscent of Patti Smith, Nylon's Beat-inspired lyrical extrapolations are well suited to Sherwood's expansive sonic collage. It's a tremendously seductive record that certainly gave rise to the opinion that Nylon was embarking on an interesting solo career. Instead, *Pal Judy* is all we have to show for Nylon the solo artist. Ex-cohort Palladin recorded a great record of covers (*Copy Cats*) with Johnny Thunders, but has also been absent from music for over a decade. —*John Dougan*

Pal Judy / 1982 / ROIR ✦✦✦
With Adrian Sherwood's amazing production technique providing the foundation, Nylon takes off on this dark, moody exercise in postmodern pop that includes an incredible downtempo version of "Jailhouse Rock." Oddly, *Pal Judy* disappeared almost immediately after its release, and it wasn't until the American label ROIR rediscovered it and reissued it on cassette and CD nearly a decade later that it was put into wide release. And it's a good thing, because it represents Nylon's finest moment, as well as more great work by Sherwood. —*John Dougan*

Laura Nyro

b. Oct. 18, 1947, Bronx, NY

Singer-Songwriter
While Laura Nyro remains best known for providing hit material for a number of late-'60s acts, it's a mystery why she never had a smash of her own. Essential college-dorm-room listening for the era, and often bagged as a sort of East Coast answer to Joni Mitchell, in reality Nyro was in a class by herself. Nyro's songs were steeped in classic R&B and framed in stark settings, her vocal gymnastics often accompanied only by her own piano work. Any doubts as to where her music came from were erased by the album *Gonna Take a Miracle*, a brilliant collection of soul covers recorded with the resurrected Patti LaBelle. It was also one of the first albums of all-outside material by a major rock-era songwriter. In the '70s Nyro became more reclusive, releasing only the occasional album letting us in on

a bit of her home life. Even now, the promise of new Laura Nyro material is still cause for much hope. —*Steve Aldrich*

More Than a New Discovery / 1967 / Verve/Forecast ✦✦✦
A collection given over to the more conventional, if high-quality early Nyro songs that later became hits (and standards) in the hands of other performers. The album includes "Wedding Bell Blues," "Stoney End," and "And When I Die." (Also released under the title *More Than A New Discovery* and reissued on Columbia Records in 1973.) —*William Ruhlmann*

● **Eli and the 13th Confession** / 1968 / Columbia ✦✦✦✦
The hits (for others) keep coming—"Sweet Blindness," "Eli's Comin'," and "Stoned Soul Picnic" are all here, sung by their author—but Nyro not only proves herself a powerful singer in her own right, comfortable in styles from jazz to gospel/R&B to stark balladry, she also begins to turn to a more introspective, personal writing and singing which no one will be able to replicate. —*William Ruhlmann*

○ **New York Tendaberry** / 1969 / Columbia ✦✦✦✦
A stunning musical journey through love, loss, religion, and eroticism, by turns passionate, inspired, and suicidal, this is Nyro's most accomplished, most idiosyncratic record, and one of the greatest singer/songwriter works ever made. Using a wide vocal range and her often delicate piano work with deftly added instrumental touches, Nyro creates an aural landscape that spans the extremes of human emotion. It's not listed as her "pick" album only because it's not the place to start; rather, it's the logical conclusion of her musical development. —*William Ruhlmann*

Christmas and the Beads of Sweat / 1970 / Columbia ✦✦✦

○ **Gonna Take a Miracle** / 1971 / Columbia ✦✦✦✦
A joyous change of pace, this album presents inspired readings of pop/R&B hits of the 60s, songs like "Jimmy Mack" and "Nowhere to Run," produced by creamy-smooth soul producers Gamble & Huff and sung rapturously by Nyro, with gorgeous backing by Patti Labelle, Sarah Dash, and Nona Hendryx. —*William Ruhlmann*

The First Songs / 1973 / Columbia ✦✦✦
Columbia Records acquired Laura Nyro's 1967 debut album from Verve Forecast and reissued it in 1973, by which time such songs as "Wedding Bell Blues," "Stoney End," and "And When I Die" had become enormously successful copyrights for Nyro. —*William Ruhlmann*

Smile / 1976 / Columbia ✦✦✦
This warm comeback album is Laura Nyro's *Double Fantasy*, a return to action by a mature artist, who retains her emotional power but has worked through her problems and beaten back her demons to emerge as a "Sexy Mama." —*William Ruhlmann*

Season of Lights . . . Laura Nyro in Concert / 1977 / Columbia ✦✦
Trying to make the most of Laura Nyro's comeback, Columbia Records released this live album, most of whose songs come from her trio of stunning records of 1968-1970, *Eli and the Thirteenth Confession*, *New York Tendaberry*, and *Christmas and the Beads Of Sweat*. There's not really much hope of besting those performances, but this is a decent effort, even if not essential. —*William Ruhlmann*

Nested / 1978 / Columbia ✦✦✦

Mother's Spiritual / 1984 / Columbia ✦✦
Laura Nyro's romantic passion has been replaced by motherly nurturing, a respectable if less compelling development in the work of an artist whose concerns are always private and personal. Political concerns for women's rights and environmentalism, while clearly deeply felt, are not well integrated into her overall perspective or particularly insightful. —*William Ruhlmann*

Live at the Bottom Line / 1990 / Cypress ✦✦✦
Laura Nyro's first album in five years, reflecting another return to action in the music business, is a pleasant mixture of her own hits ("Stoned Soul Picnic"), other people's, and promising new material such as "The Japanese Restaurant Song." —*William Ruhlmann*

Walk the Dog & Lite The Lite (Run The Dog Darling Lite Delite) / Aug. 17, 1993 / Columbia ✦✦✦
Laura Nyro effectively recreates her emotional, piano-based sound on her first new studio album in nine years. By now, the political stands are a part of her persona, expressed as directly as her emotional ones, and this is a well-rounded portrait of a mature artist. —*William Ruhlmann*

O

Oasis

Group, Alternative Pop/Rock

Oasis shot from obscurity to stardom in 1994, become one of Britain's most popular and critically-acclaimed bands of the decade; along with Blur and Suede, they are responsible for returning British guitar-pop to the top of the charts. Led by guitarist/songwriter Noel Gallagher, the Manchester quintet adopts the rough, thuggish image of the Stones and the Who, crosses it with Beatlesque melodies and hooks, distinctly British lyrical themes and song structures like the Jam and the Kinks, and ties it all together with a massive, loud guitar roar, as well as a defiant sneer that draws equally from the Sex Pistols' rebelliousness and the Stone Roses' cocksure arrogance. Gallagher's songs frequently rework previous hits from T. Rex ("Cigarettes and Alcohol" borrows the riff from "Bang a Gong") to Wham! ("Fade Away" takes the melody from "Freedom"), yet the group always puts the hooks in different settings, updating past hits for a new era.

Originally, the group was formed by school mates Liam Gallagher (vocals), Paul "Bonehead" Arthurs (guitar), Paul McGuigan (bass), and Tony McCaroll (drums). After spending several years as the guitar technician for the Stone Roses-inspired group the Inspiral Carpets, Noel Gallagher returned to Manchester to find that his brother had formed a band. Noel agreed to join the band if he could have complete control of the group, including contributing all the songs; the rest of the band agreed and under the new name Oasis, they began a year of intensive rehearsing.

After playing a handful of small club gigs, the band cornered Alan McGee, the head of Creation Records, and forced him to listen to their demo. Impressed, he signed the band. The group released their first single, "Supersonic," in the spring of 1994; it edged its way into the charts on the back of positive reviews. With a melody adapted from "I'd Like to Teach the World to Sing," "Shakermaker" became a bigger hit in the early summer. Released a month before their debut album, the soaring ballad "Live Forever" was a major hit in England. The group's first record, *Definitely Maybe*, became the fastest-selling debut in British history, entering the charts at number one. Oasis mania continued throughout 1994, as the group began playing larger theaters and each new single outperformed the last. However, tensions in the group began to build—Liam and Noel refused to do joint interviews because they always fought—and Noel Gallagher briefly left the band at the end of a difficult fall American tour; he soon rejoined and the band headed back to England. As "Supersonic" began to climb the U.S. album rock and modern rock charts, the non-LP, string-laden "Whatever" hit number two over the British Christmas season.

At the beginning of 1995, the group concentrated on America, promoting the single "Live Forever." The song became a major hit on MTV, album rock, and modern rock radio stations, peaking at number two and *Definitely Maybe* went gold in the U.S. Returning to England after a sold-out American tour, the group recorded a new single, "Some Might Say." On the eve of its release, drummer Tony McCaroll parted ways with the band, with Alan White taking his place. "Some Might Say" entered the charts at number one upon its May release; its success led to all of their previous singles re-entering the indie charts. Oasis spent the rest of the summer completing their second album, *Morning Glory*, which was released in October of 1995. —*Stephen Thomas Erlewine*

● **Definitely Maybe** / 1994 / Epic ♦♦♦♦

Definitely Maybe manages to encapsulate much of the best of British rock & roll, from the Beatles to the Stone Roses, in the space of eleven songs. Their sound is louder and more guitar-oriented than any British band since the Sex Pistols, and the band is blessed with the excellent songwriting of Noel Gallagher. Gallagher writes perfect pop songs, offering a platform for his brother Liam's brash, snarling vocals. Not only does the band have melodies, but they have the capability to work a groove with more dexterity than most post-punk groups. But what makes *Definitely Maybe* so intoxicating is that it already resembles a greatest hits album. From the swirling rush of "Rock 'n' Roll Star," through the sinewy "Shakermaker," to the heartbreaking "Live Forever," each song sounds like an instant classic. —*Stephen Thomas Erlewine*

Billy Ocean

b. 1950, Trinidad
Soul, Pop/Rock

Born in Trinidad, Billy Ocean emigrated to the U.K. as a child. He worked as a tailor while pursuing music on the side in the '60s, then broke through with the Motown-flavored "Love Really Hurts without You," which hit number three in the U.K. in 1976. Ocean continued to have U.K. hits through the end of the '70s but didn't achieve mass success in the U.S. until 1984, when "Caribbean Queen (No More Love on the Run)" became a number one hit, the first of seven Top Ten hits over the next four years. —*William Ruhlmann*

Billy Ocean / 1975 / GTO ♦♦

City Limit / 1980 / GTO ♦♦

Nights (Feel Like Getting Down) / 1981 / Epic ♦♦♦

Billy Ocean was on his way to superstardom with this album, his first big hit release on Epic. The title song was his first R&B Top 10 record, and he got another couple of chart singles before beginning his run of R&B and pop hits. It also demonstrated his equal ability doing exuberant uptempo dance tunes and convincing, if at times oversung and vapid, ballads. Epic was later left red-faced when an act they developed moved over to Jive/RCA and went platinum. —*Ron Wynn*

Inner Feelings / 1982 / Epic ♦♦

Billy Ocean went from international superstar to falling completely off the charts in one of the most amazing rise and fall stories of the 1980s and early '90s. This was an early, introductory self-produced session for Epic, with Ocean still feeling his way around America after having enjoyed huge success on Britain's club circuit. There were some decent ballads and uptempo dance tunes, but little to suggest that Ocean was on his way to becoming Britian's pop/dance king and an urban contemporary and pop superstar in America as well. —*Ron Wynn*

○ **Suddenly** / 1984 / Jive ♦♦♦♦

Billy Ocean vaulted into international stardom with this album in 1984. The album peaked at number nine, was on the charts for over a year and a half, and yielded him three R&B hits that were all also pop smashes. Ocean would sing on the soundtrack for the film *The Jewel Of The Nile*, make sellout appearances around the world, and appear regularly on television and videos. At this point he was a bigger pop star than R&B artist, as two of his three hits did better across crossover vehicles than R&B tunes. —*Ron Wynn*

○ **Love Zone** / 1986 / Jive ♦♦♦♦

Billy Ocean was riding atop the charts when he issued this album in '86. The title track contained both a fine arrangement and Ocean's emphatic lead vocal, and was a huge hit. He topped the

R&B charts twice that year with both "Love Zone" and "There'll Be Sad Songs (To Make You Cry)," each of which was also a huge pop smash, the latter topping the pop chart. This was arguably his finest album, and was certainly his most successful. —*Ron Wynn*

Tear Down These Walls / 1988 / Jive ✦✦✦
Things were beginning to slip a bit for Billy Ocean in the late '80s. While he was still a successful attraction, this album wouldn't reach the multiplatinum levels of its predecessors. Ocean's voice also lacked the resonance and authority it had on earlier dance tunes and wasn't as convincing or confident on ballads. He still landed a couple more hits, and one additional chart topper (R&B and pop) with "Get Outta My Dreams, Get Into My Car," but the decline was starting. —*Ron Wynn*

● **Greatest Hits** / 1989 / Jive ✦✦✦✦
Contains his cool '80s disco hits "Caribbean Queen" and "Get outta My Dreams, Get into My Car" and piano-based ballads like "There'll Be Sad Songs to Make You Cry." —*Bil Carpenter*

Time to Move on / Jun. 8, 1993 / Jive ✦✦

Phil Ochs

b. Dec. 19, 1940, El Paso, TX, **d.** Apr. 9, 1976
Folk, Singer-Songwriter, Folk-Rock
Depending on your point of view, you might find Phil Ochs to be an idealistic American hero or the ultimate '60s casualty. Relocating to New York City from Ohio with a college journalism background and already well-versed in the emerging political left, Ochs found his niche as a topical singer/songwriter and quickly became a favorite in the Village's blossoming folk scene of the early '60s. When Bob Dylan eventually moved into the rock arena, Ochs became the folk protest movement's de facto king. By 1967 Ochs had realigned his management and record company and his music as well. He responded to the musical changes of the day with a trilogy of three heavily arranged albums that were far from the simplicity of the earlier three. These albums also graphically documented a deeply troubled singer, in terms of both his personal life and the now full-blown radical politics of the period. When the left-wing movement died, evidently so did much of Ochs's muse. Ochs could never grasp why his status in the rock world never matched what he achieved in folk music. His final studio album, with the self-deprecating title, *Phil Ochs's Greatest Hits*, proved to be a harrowing look back at his life and a clairvoyant pointer to his short-lived future. While some elements of his music carry a dated air about them, many of the same causes ring true today, and Ochs remains one of the '60s most fascinating characters. —*Steve Aldrich*

All the News That's Fit to Sing / 1964 / Hannibal ✦✦✦
All the News That's Fit to Sing is his bittersweet debut and is a vital and topical album of its time. —*Bruce Eder & William Ruhlmann*

○ **I Ain't Marching Anymore** / 1965 / Carthage ✦✦✦✦
A strident, searching, and haunting echo of the '60s. —*Bruce Eder*

○ **Phil Ochs in Concert** / 1966 / Elektra ✦✦✦✦
It's since been revealed that some or all of these tracks were not "in concert" at all, but recorded in the studio, with audience noise dubbed on afterwards. Nevertheless, this is Ochs' finest acoustic album. As a lyricist, he was moving from the singing journalist mode to more abstract symbolism, but still attacked U.S. imperialism, knock-kneed bleeding hearts, and even organized religion with an uncompromising sensitivity. Some haunting, wistful ballads transcended topical concerns entirely, including the beautiful love song "Changes" and "There But For Fortune" (a British hit for Joan Baez). —*Richie Unterberger*

★ **Pleasures of the Harbor** / 1967 / A&M ✦✦✦✦✦
Moving from his acoustic base to elaborate musical arrangements, Ochs also turns largely away from his topical material to more lyrical and poetic songs, though the caustic "Outside a Small Circle of Friends" and the apocalyptic "The Crucifixion" clearly retain his social and political focus. —*William Ruhlmann*

Tape from California / 1968 / A&M ✦✦✦
A somewhat manic production, highlighted by reasonably successful straightforward rock (the title track) and one of the great '60s anti-war songs, "The War Is Over," a perfect combination of droll commentary with jaunty backing. Most of the rest of the tracks fall into the over-orchestrated malaise that, to a lesser degree, afflicted *Pleasures of the Harbor*. —*Richie Unterberger*

Phil Ochs's Greatest Hits / 1970 / Edsel ✦✦✦
Not really his greatest hits (the title was intended as irony). This is his final, troubled studio album, and a good companion to *Gunfight at Carnegie Hall* —Bruce Eder

○ **Gunfight at Carnegie Hall** / 1975 / Mobile Fidelity ✦✦✦✦
Most unusual. Ochs does Elvis and Buddy Holly songs exceptionally to an angry audience and plays out his own internal conflicts at the same time. —*Bruce Eder*

○ **Chords of Fame** / 1976 / A&M ✦✦✦✦
A fine collection on vinyl only, but worth having for the liner notes. Note that this out-of-print double LP is the only album to combine Ochs's Elektra work (1964-1966) with his A&M work (1967-1970). The two CD samplers cover the same ground separately. —*Bruce Eder & William Ruhlmann*

A Toast to Those Who Are Gone / 1987 / Rhino ✦✦✦
14 previously unreleased demos, all of excellent fidelity; while no dates or sources are given for these sessions, an educated guess would put them in his earliest, most topical period, circa 1964-65. Most of these feature just Phil and acoustic guitar, and sound as strong as the material officially released on his first Elektra LPs. The other, equally fine cuts seem to date from a later period, and show him delving into intensely personal, non-political concerns. —*Richie Unterberger*

The War Is Over: The Best of Phil Ochs / 1988 / A&M ✦✦✦
Not his best by a longshot, but a cross-section of his better A&M recordings. —*Bruce Eder*

Broadside Tapes 1 / 1989 / ✦✦✦
This album of previously unreleased songs was recorded casually in the 104th St. Offices of *Broadside* Magazine. They were intended as demos for transcription but are in fact quite good performances. —*Richard Meyer*

○ **There and Now: Live in Vancouver** / 1990 / Rhino ✦✦✦✦
Definitive Ochs (along with *Gunfight at Carnegie Hall*). A "lost" 1968 concert featuring his most beloved songs. The real "best-of." —*Bruce Eder*

BOOK

✦✦✦✦ **Death Of A Rebel: A Biography Of Phil Ochs**, by Marc Eliot (Franklin Watts, 1989). Phil Ochs was a troubadour in the best tradition of American commentary and dissent. No one could hope to be as noble as the songs he wrote, but in Ochs' case, the gap between life and art was fairly wide. Alcoholism, failed aspirations toward stardom, and failed relationships contributed to the mental disorders which led to his suicide in 1976. This bio is a decent portrait of America's leading protest singer, with a cast of supporting characters and cameos from many of the era's leading folk and folk-rock performers, from Dylan on down to Judy Henske, David Blue, and Jim & Jean. It follows his life from his struggling beginnings in Greenwich Village through his attempts (some quite artistically successful) at pop stardom with rock arrangements after his move to L.A. in the late '60s, his harassment by the FBI, his struggles with record companies and producers, and his artistic famine and loss of idealism in the '70s. Well balanced between coverage of his art and private life, marred only by some minor chronological and factual inconsistencies when his work is placed in the context of the rock and folk of the '60s. Look for the improved, revised edition, not the original 1979 printing. —*Richie Unterberger*

Sinéad O'Connor

b. 1967, Dublin, Ireland
Alternative Pop/Rock
From Dublin, Ireland, Sinéad O'Connor came onto the music scene in 1987 with a powerful image of a woman who could express great sensitivity while not losing any qualities of inner strength. In public, O'Connor's seemingly audacious pronouncements about the state of the world around her may have put off those unaccustomed to a woman so forthright with her feelings; nevertheless, it's that courageousness that has endeared her to millions of fans. O'Connor's second album, *I Do Not Want What I Haven't Got*, was a worldwide hit. Musically, O'Connor draws from hard synth-rock, Celtic folk, and funk. Her dramatic alto explores sound in much the same way as Peter Gabriel applies varied tonal dynamics.

After the success of *I Do Not Want What I Haven't Got*, O'Connor seemed a bit directionless. Two years later, she released an album of big-band covers, *Am I Not Your Girl?*, a strange record that was a commercial disappointment. Even worse, the singer suffered a tidal wave of bad publicity when she tore a photo of the Pope on *Saturday Night Live*, saying "Fight the Real Enemy." For the next year, O'Connor laid low, recording a new album which was released in the fall of 1994. —*Rick Clark*

○ **The Lion and the Cobra** / 1987 / Ensign ♦♦♦♦

The Lion and the Cobra was an impressive showcase for this Dubliner's vocal and writing skills. On this self-produced effort, O'Connor incorporates bits of hard rock, folk, synth-pop, and light funk onto standout tracks like "I Want Your (Hands on Me)," "Jerusalem," and "Mandinka," a wonderful synth-rocker. —*Rick Clark*

● **I Do Not Want What I Haven't Got** / 1990 / Ensign ♦♦♦♦

O'Connor's debut might have been a strong showing, but her followup, *I Do Not Want What I Haven't Got*, was a stunner. Her songwriting skills were much more incisive and, vocally, O'Connor exhibited a greater range of interpretive skills. Highlights include "The Emperor's New Clothes," "I Am Stretched on Your Grave," "Jump in the River," "Black Boys on Mopeds," and the international hit "Nothing Compares 2 U," which was penned by Prince. —*Rick Clark*

Am I Not Your Girl? / 1992 / Ensign ♦♦

Based on O'Connor's version of "You Do Something to Me" (a highlight on the *Red Hot & Blue* album), an album of pop standards performed with a big band might have actually worked. At times, such as on "Success Has Made a Failure of Our Home" and "Don't Cry for Me Argentina," *Am I Not Your Girl?* does work. However, O'Connor runs into trouble with acknowledged standards and songs heavily identified with other vocalists. She doesn't offer a new perspective on these songs, and her airy voice is buried by overwrought string arrangements. Plus, there's O'Connor's bizarre two-minute rant on love, hatred, herself, and the Catholic Church. —*Stephen Thomas Erlewine*

Universal Mother / 1994 / Ensign ♦♦♦

O'Connor's first album of original material since her breakthrough *I Do Not Want What I Haven't Got* is nearly as confused as her big-band album, *Am I Not Your Girl?* O'Connor has lost her sense of conceptual unity, which makes her most extreme moments quite embarrassing ("Red Football" and the white hip-hop of "Famine"). Every so often, she manages to pull off a number that shows why her first two albums were so startling and captivating, but through most of *Universal Mother*, O'Connor sounds lost and confused. —*Stephen Thomas Erlewine*

Offspring

Group, Alternative Pop/Rock

Offspring's metal-inflected punk became a popular sensation in the 1994, selling over a four million copies on an independent record label. While the group's credentials and approach follows the indie-rock tradition of the '80s, sonically they sound more like an edgy, hard-driving heavy metal band, with their precise, pulsing power chords and Brian "Dexter" Holland's flat vocals.

Featuring Holland, guitarist Kevin "Noodles" Wasserman," bassist Greg Kriesel, and drummer Ron Welty, the Offspring released their first album, *Ignition*, in 1993. It was an underground hit, setting the stage for the across-the-board success of 1994's *Smash*. The Nirvana-soundalike "Come out and Play," the first single from the album, became an MTV hit in the summer of 1994, which paved the way to radio success. The band was played on both alternative and album rock stations, confirming their broad-based appeal. "Self Esteem," the second single, followed the same soft verse/loud chorus fomula and stayed on the charts nearly twice as long as "Come out and Play." The group got offers from major labels, yet they chose to stay with Epitaph. While they were able to play arenas in the U.S., their success didn't translate in foreign countries. Nevertheless, the band's popularity continued to grow in America, as "Gotta Get Away" became another radio/MTV hit in the beginning of 1995. The Offspring recorded a version of the Damned's "Smash It Up" for the *Batman Forever* soundtrack in the summer of that year; it kept the band on the charts as they worked on their third album. —*Stephen Thomas Erlewine*

Ignition / 1993 / Epitaph ♦♦♦

● **Smash** / 1994 / Epitaph ♦♦♦♦

The Offspring's second album for Epitaph did the impossible: it landed in the Top Five, unheard of for independent records. The Offspring crossed over due to the raucous, Eastern-tinged single "Come out and Play (Keep 'Em Separated)," which stopped and started just like Nirvana, only without the Seattle trio's recklessness. The record stayed in the charts because the Offspring sounded relentlessly heavy, no matter how much the band claimed to be punk. Their tempos are slower than traditional hardcore, and their attack is as heavy as Metallica. But they acted like they were punk, with odes to no "Self Esteem" and singing about fighting in school. Nothing on the album matches the incessant catchiness of the singles, but *Smash* is a solid record, filled with enough heavy riffs to keep most teenagers happy. —*Stephen Thomas Erlewine*

Ohio Express

Group, Bubblegum

Ohio Express and the 1910 Fruitgum Co. were two of the leading late-'60s bubblegum rock groups. Under the aegis of producers Jerry Kasenetz and Jeff Katz, both of these rather anonymous bands surfaced repeatedly on the late-'60s pop charts for Buddah Records, spearheading the bubblegum rock craze. With Joey Levine taking the vocals on their early hits, the Ohio Express roared up in 1968 with "Yummy Yummy Yummy" and "Chewy Chewy," a pair of million-sellers. Future 10CC leader Graham Gouldman fronted the Express on their final chart bow in 1969, "Sausalito (Is the Place to Go)."

At the same time, another Kasenetz-Katz discovery, New Jersey's 1910 Fruitgum Co., was bubbling over with the obnoxiously catchy "Simon Says," "1,2,3, Red Light," and "Indian Giver," another gold record triumvirate. Like their labelmates, their mercurial chart run was history before 1969 was over. —*Bill Dahl*

● **Very Best of the Ohio Express** / 1970 / Buddah ♦♦♦♦

The Ohio Players

Group, Soul, Funk

Originally formed in 1959 as an instrumental R&B group, the Ohio Untouchables (as they were then known) provided backup on the Falcons' records. After the Untouchables broke up, two of the members (Clarence "Satch" Satchell and Marshall "Rock" Jones) formed a new outfit called the Ohio Players and began working as the house band at Compass Records. In the early '70s, the Ohio Players had a steady stream of funky, sexual hit singles, including the number ones "Fire" and "Love Rollercoaster." As the decade progressed, their sound gradually transformed into a throbbing disco pulse and their sales slowly tapered off. —*Stephen Thomas Erlewine*

Pain / 1972 / Westbound ♦♦♦

The Ohio Players perked up ears around the soul world with their early '70s debut. This was prototype jazz-rock/funk, particularly the title cut, with its layered bass lines, Marvin Pierce's crackling trumpet solo, and Sugarfoot's prickly guitar accompaniment. While the arrangements had a skeletal sound due to Westbound's rather meager engineering, the energy, flip/flamboyant attitude, and vocal assertiveness provided an early read on what would prove to be one of the 1970s' finest funk bands. —*Ron Wynn*

Ecstacy / 1973 / Westbound ♦♦♦

Pleasure / 1973 / Westbound ♦♦♦

This was the first Ohio Players album to get sizable mileage and attract some attention. "Funky Worm" was their initial number one R&B hit, got them into the pop Top 20, and alerted the funk and R&B community to the group's mix of sizzling beats, a jazz-rock sensibility, and exuberant collective vocals. They were almost ready to break, and this was an early indication of the band's potential. —*Ron Wynn*

Climax / 1974 / Westbound ♦♦♦

This was the lull before the storm. The Ohio Players had left Westbound, where they perfected their shuddering funk sound, and moved to Mercury. In just a few short weeks, they would explode with their greatest album and begin a string of classic funk records. Meanwhile Westbound issued this vintage session, in which their older material seemed a little thin and light, but was still enjoyable. It would quickly be eclipsed by what came next. —*Ron Wynn*

○ **Fire** / 1974 / Mercury ✦✦✦✦

The Ohio Players peaked as a funk band with this record, which became their lone #1 pop hit. The title track was a #1 pop and R&B single, while "I Want To Be Free" was perhaps their best non-dance or novelty hit. The horn charts were catchy and energetic, guitarist Leroy "Sugarfoot" Bonner was in his prime, and the vocals were silly but hypnotic. —*Ron Wynn*

○ **Skin Tight** / 1974 / Mercury ✦✦✦✦

This earned the Ohio Players their first gold album, as well as a number-two R&B single with the title cut. The group was honing its punchy funk arrangements and exuberant vocal style, and "Skin Tight" was the first song since "Funky Worm" to earn both R&B and pop attention. It was also their debut album on Mercury, and it did so well that their old label Westbound rushed out a compilation of old cuts called *Climax*. —*Ron Wynn*

Rattlesnake / 1975 / Westbound ✦✦✦

Greatest Hits / 1975 / Westbound ✦✦✦

With the Ohio Players established funk superstars on Mercury in the mid-'70s, Westbound rushed out a collection of their best early songs, many of which were outstanding. This is actually a worthwhile anthology, particularly since many people missed "Pain," "Funky Worm," and other pre-Mercury hits. Unfortunately, this is not currently on CD reissue lists. —*Ron Wynn*

○ **Honey** / 1975 / Mercury ✦✦✦✦

A huge hit album, their second most successful LP ever, peaking at the number two spot on the R&B charts, although it didn't generate any pop action (none of their albums ever crossed over). The album cover, with its photo of a gorgeous woman having hot honey poured on her, wouldn't even make it to the drawing board in the current environment; it generated a firestorm in the mid-'70s when it turned out that one of the women used got burned. Many think the title track was a hit, but it was actually the single "Sweet, Sticky Thing" that cemented the LP's hit status. That and "Love Rollercoaster" were R&B chart toppers; "Honey" didn't even chart. —*Ron Wynn*

★ **Ohio Players Gold** / 1976 / Mercury ✦✦✦✦✦

A strong overview of their biggest hits and best moments, including "Fire" (#1), "Fopp" (#30), "Skin Tight" (#13), and the shattering "Love Rollercoaster" (#1). —*Stephen Thomas Erlewine*

Contradiction / 1976 / Mercury ✦✦✦

Angel / 1977 / Mercury ✦✦

Arguably the greatest of the Dayton funk bands, the Ohio Players had peaked by the time this album was issued in the late '70s. Internal dissent would soon split them apart, and it seemed that they had run out of catchy funk hits and inspiration. There were remnants of the old spirit, fire, and energy, but often the collective vocals sounded detached, and the classic horn lines and guitar/bass/keyboards interaction stiff. They still made great album covers. —*Ron Wynn*

Mr. Mean / 1977 / Mercury ✦

This album hit the charts after the group was defunct, and had sentimental value if little musical distinction. They had long since lost the magic and cohesion that made them the definitive Dayton funk ensemble. The vocals, even Sugar's Sly Stone/Bar-Kays inflections, were bland, while everything else, from production to arrangements and vocals, were a shell of past works. —*Ron Wynn*

Ohio Players / 1977 / Trip ✦✦✦

Jass-Ay-La-Dee / 1978 / Mercury ✦

The group was already in massive decline by the time this album was released. They had officially disbanded, and this album was rushed out by Mercury to fill the void. It sounded like a wrap job as well; their vocals were never great, but they were at least exuberant. Now, they were lifeless, as were the arrangements, horn charts, musical backing, and compositions. Only Ohio Players completists ever purchased it, and they're the only ones who would ever own it. —*Ron Wynn*

Tenderness / 1981 / Boardwalk ✦✦

The Ohio Players were near the end of the line when they issued this album for the Boardwalk label. It featured the same roster that had made so many strong hits for Mercury, but they sounded tentative and unfocused, which was probably justified, since most of the songs were undistinguished and the production and arrangements were muddled. This proved a completely forgettable proposition all around.—*Ron Wynn*

● **Funk on Fire: The Mercury Anthology** / 1995 / Mercury Funk Essentials ✦✦✦✦

The O'Jays

Group, Soul, R&B, Urban

Perhaps the reigning vocal group of the '70s and '80s, the O'Jays began in Canton as the Triumphs in 1958. The original lineup was Eddie Levert, Walter Williams, William Powell, Bobby Massey, and Bill Isles. They recorded as the Mascots for King in 1961 and were renamed by Cleveland disc jockey Eddie O'Jay. Isles departed in 1965 and Massey left in 1971 to become a producer, making the group a trio. They got their first chart single in 1963 for Imperial, for whom they recorded until 1967. The O'Jays' first major hit was "I'll Be Sweeter Tomorrow (Than I Was Today)" for Bell in 1967, which reached number eight on the R&B charts. They continued on Bell and Neptune until they attained stardom in 1972 on Philadelphia International. "Back Stabbers" was the first of eight number one R&B hits they would get on the label from 1972-1987. Others included "Love Train, " "Give the People What They Want," "I Love Music," "Livin' for the Weekend," "Message to Our Music," "Use Ta Be My Girl," "Darlin' Darlin' Baby (Sweet, Tender, Love)" and "Lovin' You." They also had eight other Top Ten R&B hits and four other Top Ten pop smashes, while "Love Train" also topped the pop charts in 1973. They moved to EMI in 1987 and continued recording. Their most recent release was *Heartbreaker* in 1993. —*Ron Wynn*

Comin' Through / 1965 / Imperial ✦✦✦

The O'Jays were a fledgling five-member outfit when they issued their debut album in 1965. They generated a little attention with the dance/novelty tune "Do the Wiggle," and also issued a pair of good ballads in "Lonely Drifter" and "Lipstick Traces." None of these songs were as masterfully produced or arranged as the epic Gamble/Huff material, but it did reveal the potential they had for R&B stardom. This album has been out of print for years, although some of the songs have surfaced on anthologies. —*Ron Wynn*

Back on Top / 1968 / Bell ✦✦✦

A fine album, their last for the Bell label. George Kerr was still working with them, and they were now down to three members. The harmonies weren't quite polished, and Eddie Levert, Walter Williams, and William Powell hadn't rounded into form, although at times they flashed signs that things were coming together. But this album has more nostalgic than musical value, although those who only heard the O'Jays on Philadelphia International should check it out to discover their roots in '50s doo-wop and '60s soul. —*Ron Wynn*

○ **O'Jays in Philadelphia** / 1969 / Philadelphia International ✦✦✦✦

The O'Jays' first album with the Gamble/Huff production team was a landmark for all parties involved. A respected but journeyman soul outfit since the early '60s, the singers benefited immensely from distinctive, innovative production; in the O'Jays, Gamble and Huff found what may have been the best vehicle for framing their lush arrangements. Gamble and Huff write most of the material; Thom Bell handles about half the arrangements. There weren't any monster hits, but the result was considerably above the average late-'60s soul album, with strong songs and propulsive strings and brass that clearly blueprinted the Philadelphia soul sound. —*Richie Unterberger*

☆ **Back Stabbers** / 1972 / Philadelphia International ✦✦✦✦✦

Although you could lean toward *Ship Ahoy*, it would be hard to argue with the general assessment that this is their greatest album. Certainly no other single in 1973 was as transcendent and definitive as "Love Train," without question their greatest track. "Back Stabbers" isn't far behind it; the message, harmonies, Eddie Levert's lead, and the group's refrains are all testimonies to soul's glory, and Gamble and Huff were in peak form. There were other good songs on the record, like "Listen to the Clock on the Wall" and "Shiftless, Shady, Jealous Kind of People," but they were completely blown away by "Love Train" and "Back Stabbers." —*Ron Wynn*

○ **Ship Ahoy** / 1973 / Philadelphia International ✦✦✦✦

The "other" O'Jays album masterpiece, *Ship Ahoy* combined shattering message tracks and stunning love songs in a fashion matched only by Curtis Mayfield's finest material. From the album cover showing a slave ship to the memorable title song and incredible "For the Love of Money," Gamble and Huff addressed every social ill from envy to racism and greed. Eddie Levert's leads were consistently magnificent, as were the harmonies, production and arrangements. "Put Your Hands Together" and "You Got Your Hooks In Me" would be good album cuts, but on *Ship Ahoy* they were merely icing on the cake. —*Ron Wynn*

○ **Survival** / 1975 / Philadelphia International ✦✦✦✦
The O'Jays followed the spectacular *Backstabbers* and *Ship Ahoy* with the good, but not on the same level, *Survival*. It was unrealistic to expect masterpieces every time out, and the LP included many strong ballads and good message tracks. But while it may not have been as epic in its performances and compositions, it was certainly the other albums' equal in sales strength. The group had two number one R&B hits in 1975, "Give The People What They Want" and "I Love Music (Part 1)." In addition, the title track made the charts as the B-side to "Let Me Make Love To You," another rousing ballad. —*Ron Wynn*

Family Reunion / 1975 / Philadelphia International ✦✦✦
The O'Jays were in one of their most productive periods during the '70s. The Gamble/Huff team was giving them consistently strong material, often classic songs, and their three-member harmonies and shared leads were galvanizing, particularly those by Eddie Levert. The title track did well, but the album tended to be overlooked because it was sandwiched between *Survival* and *Message In Our Music*. Yet it attained more pop attention than the more heralded (and probably superior) *Ship Ahoy*. —*Ron Wynn*

★ **Collector's Item** / 1977 / Philadelphia International ✦✦✦✦✦
After enjoying an impressive string of gold and platinum albums, the O'Jays had this collection of their biggest hits on Philadelphia International released in 1977. There was no way to lose with such songs as "Back Stabbers," "Love Train," "For the Love of Money" and "I Love Music." Unfortunately, Philadelphia International haphazardly sequenced the collection, ignoring chronological and stylistic considerations and just sticking tracks on the two sides without any attention to pacing. That gaffe aside, it's a worthy anthology for the casual listener, although the hardcore fan should look elsewhere. —*Ron Wynn*

So Full of Love / 1978 / Philadelphia International ✦✦✦
This was the biggest hit album the O'Jays ever enjoyed, even though it wasn't as aesthetically transcendent as *Ship Ahoy*. But it came at the right time; there weren't many great group albums being produced in R&B at the time, and that's what this really was, even if Eddie Levert took most of the leads. "Use Ta Be My Girl" was a triumphant success, while "Brandy" was the prototype album cut that became a hit through popular demand. —*Ron Wynn*

When Will I See You Again / 1983 / Philadelphia International ✦✦✦
The O'Jays didn't have any big crossover hits or R&B chart-toppers with this album, but it was still a fine effort. The production and arrangements were outstanding, the harmonies and leads nicely done, and there were several fine songs. It produced some R&B chart singles, although nothing proved a smash. If anything, it was proof that sometimes no matter what the artists and producers do, it just doesn't succeed to the extent that it should or they hoped. —*Ron Wynn*

From the Beginning / 1984 / Chess ✦✦✦
The O'Jays weren't always a trio, nor did they begin on Philadelphia International or sing hard-edged three-member soul. This collection of earlier, sometimes awkward, but energetic singles by the four-member edition was issued as part of the Chess collection during the era when Sugar Hill had the masters. It has since been deleted, although it's certainly worth getting if you can find it. —*Ron Wynn*

● **Greatest Hits** / 1984 / Philadelphia International ✦✦✦✦
When the O'Jays left Columbia for EMI, the company promptly issued this greatest hits package, although they opted to put fewer tracks on it than on the 1977 *Collector's Item*. So, the logical question would be, why would anyone want it? Probably because they've made *Collector's Items* extremely difficult to locate, and also because this mid-'80s release had better mastering of such seminal O'Jays items as "Love Train" and "For the Love of Money." While it has gaping holes as a single-disc anthology, this release provides an acceptable overview of the group's Epic/Philadelphia International/TSOP material. —*Ron Wynn*

Love & More / 1984 / Philadelphia International ✦✦✦
A nice mid-'80s album, although the O'Jays weren't scoring the huge hits that often anymore. But they had matured, were still singing wonderful adult ballads, doing an occasionally exuberant uptempo tune, and regularly selling out mid-sized arenas and black community engagements. Eddie Levert's throaty vocals and their close harmonies remained engaging and impressive; their material was just a bit below its peak levels of the '70s. —*Ron Wynn*

Let Me Touch You / 1987 / EMI America ✦✦✦
The O'Jays made tight three-member harmonies and alternating leads from Eddie Levert, Walter Williams, and Sammy Strain a successful formula throughout the '80s, and this album included a superb ballad, "Lovin' You." It was an R&B chart topper, one of two Top Ten singles from the album, and continued a good run for the group on Philadelphia International. —*Ron Wynn*

Serious / Mar. 1989 / EMI America ✦✦
The O'Jays wrapped up the '80s with another fine album, generating some mild pop attention. They experimented with New Jack production a bit, but otherwise retained their customary tight harmonies and the piercing leads of Eddie Levert, with Walt Williams and Sammy Strain sometimes taking the spotlight. The O'Jays wisely understood that changes on the black music scene would prevent them from being an all-things-to-all-ages group, so they continued making the poignant, exuberant ballads that retained their appeal among the adult segment of the urban contemporary population. —*Ron Wynn*

Emotionally Yours / Jan. 21, 1991 / EMI America ✦✦✦
A fine early-'90s release demonstrating that the trio of Eddie Levert, Walter Williams, and Sammy Strain still packed a solid punch on ballads and uptempo songs, and were making the adjustment to New Jack production and hip-hop influences. But while they occasionally used rapper Jaz, the O'Jays' strengths remained their energized harmonies and the soulful leads of Levert, as well as Williams and Strain at times. Their sound remains timeless and appealing, dependent on material, but superb when they get quality songs. —*Ron Wynn*

Heartbreaker / 1993 / EMI America ✦✦✦
The O'Jays have made concessions to changing tastes, adopting drum samples and synthesized backing, and including some new jack swing material. But they wisely haven't tampered with their strength, lush three-part harmonies anchored by the earnest lead vocals of Eddie Levert. This release contains several intense, urgent ballads, many of them written by group members. Outside of Carlton Hunt's raps on "Trouble" and "Can't Let You Go," many numbers aren't much different from the classic material that made them superstars in the '70s; that's both part of the music's charm and something that might trouble fans hoping the group would experiment with the vocal arrangements as well as the production. —*Ron Wynn*

○ **Love Train: The Best Of The O'Jays** / 1994 / Epic/Legacy ✦✦✦✦
All of the band's monster 1972-76 Philadelphia International hits are here, as well as a couple of small ones. The essay by Robert Palmer is good, but at a mere 10 tracks, the selection is unaccountably skimpy. —*Richie Unterberger*

Give The People What They Want / 1995 / Epic/Legacy ✦✦✦
Give The People What They Want collects 11 of the O'Jays' politically-oriented songs, including the hit title song and "Ship Ahoy." Since most of these tracks were not singles, it's a good supplement to an O'Jays' greatest-hits collection. —*Stephen Thomas Erlewine*

Let Me Make Love To You / 1995 / Epic/Legacy ✦✦✦
Like *Give The People What They Want*, *Let Me Make Love To You* is a concept compilation, collecting 10 of the O'Jays' most underappreciated love ballads, including the title track, which was a minor hit, "Stairway to Heaven," and "Listen to the Clock on the Wall." Again, the disc is not a hits collection, but a sampling of some of the group's finest album tracks and forgotten singles, and in that context, it's very enjoyable. —*Stephen Thomas Erlewine*

Ol' Dirty Bastard

Rap
A member of the Brooklyn hip-hop congregation the Wu-Tang Clan, Ol' Dirty Bastard released his first solo album in the spring

of 1995, after the Clan imploded. Produced by fellow Wu-Tang member Prince Rakeem, Ol' Dirty Bastard's *Return to the 36 Chambers* sounds identical to the Clan's 1993 debut album, *Enter the Wu-Tang (36 Chambers)*. —*Stephen Thomas Erlewine*

● **Return of the 36 Chambers** / 1995 / Elektra ✦✦✦✦
On a break from the Wu-Tang Clan, Ol' Dirty Bastard hands in a defiantly vulgar record, *Return to the 36 Chambers*. Choosing not to stray from the hardcore style of the Clan, Ol' Dirty Bastard keeps the sound and makes it looser lyrically. Nothing on the record stands out as an equal to *Enter the 36 Chambers*, but the good times keep flowing and "Brooklyn Zoo" could be one of the classics of 1995. —*Stephen Thomas Erlewine*

Olympics
Group, R&B
A sub-Coasters R&B group scored in 1958 with the great novelty hit "Western Movies." In 1965 they recorded the original version of "Good Lovin'," later covered by the Rascals. Despite the rumors, they were not the same group as the Marathons ("Peanut Butter"). —*John Floyd*

● **All-Time Greatest Hits!** / 1991 / Sandstone Music ✦✦✦✦
Somewhat more comprehensive than their Rhino package, this 26-track gem is the definitive homage to this good-time R&B crew. —*Jeff Tamarkin*

○ **Best of the Olympics** / Rhino ✦✦✦✦
Most, but not all, so it should be titled *Most of the Best Of.* —*Jeff Tamarkin*

○ **Doin' the Hully Gully/Dance By the Light of the Moon** / Party Time / Ace ✦✦✦✦
Featuring 26 tracks, this single-disc contains three complete Olympics albums—*Doin' the Hully Gully, Dancy By the Light of the Moon*, and *Party Time*. For any serious fan, it's indispensible, and even casual fans will be well-served by the collection. —*Stephen Thomas Erlewine*

One Dove
Group, Techno
One Dove's 1993 debut album, *Morning Dove White*, featured production by techno mastermind Andrew Weatherall. Under his direction, the band became one of the hippest names in techno and alternative circles in late 1993. —*Stephen Thomas Erlewine*

● **Morning Dove White** / Oct. 19, 1993 / FFRR ✦✦✦✦
A nearly perfect mixture of techno and pop, *Morning Dove White* succeeds because the hooks and melodies are given priority along with the rhythm tracks. Vocal parts float in and out of the mix, wrapping themselves around melodic, muscular guitar and keyboards; the hypnotic single, "White Love," sets the direction for the album. —*Stephen Thomas Erlewine*

100 Proof (Aged in Soul)
Group, Soul, Funk
As part of legendary songwriting trio Holland-Dozier-Holland's early-'70s Hot Wax/Invictus Records artist roster, 100 Proof's gritty soul reflected more of a Stax sensibility than a Motown one. "Somebody's Been Sleeping in My Bed" was their biggest hit, going number eight pop. —*Rick Clark*

100 Proof Aged in Soul / 1972 / Hotwax ✦✦✦
Somebody's Been Sleeping in My Bed / 197z / Hot Wax ✦✦✦
● **Greatest Hits** / 1990 / HDH ✦✦✦✦
Great tracks and great sound quality abound on this Eddie Holland production. —*Richard Pack*

Alexander O'Neal
b. Nov. 14, 1953, Minneapolis, MN
Soul, Urban
This Minneapolis soul man cut his teeth in the Time but was bounced (for looking "too Black") before they signed with Warner Brothers. His tough, ballsy voice has the same grain and range as Otis Redding's. Like that master, O'Neal is comfortable with pumping dance-floor burners and slinky couch-cuddlers. He's certainly the best singer Jimmy Jam and Terry Lewis have ever produced, and the strength of his material and his robust voice make him a candidate for Greatest Soul Singer of the last ten years. —*John Floyd*

Alexander O'Neal / 1985 / Tabu ✦✦✦
Former Time member Alexander O'Neal made a smashing debut as a lead artist in the mid-'80s. The Jam/Lewis duo found the ideal balance for O'Neal between dance/funk uptempo tunes and urgent urban contemporary ballads. They scored with "If You Were Here Tonight" and "A Broken Heart Can Mend," as well as "Innocent." Suddenly, O'Neal was among the top male urban artists, and continued having hits into the '90s. —*Ron Wynn*

○ **Hearsay** / 1986 / Tabu ✦✦✦✦
Alexander O'Neal almost achieved the breakout he needed for crossover success with his second album. It cracked the Top 30 on the pop album chart, earned a gold record, and included O'Neal's two strongest uptempo tunes, "Fake" and "Criticize." Jam and Lewis linked the material with "party" dialogue and patter, providing their finest and tightest production for any O'Neal record. The beats were catchy, the songs hook-laden, and O'Neal's voice alternately explosive, sensitive and bemused. —*Ron Wynn*

○ **My Gift to You** / 1988 / Tabu ✦✦✦✦
Old and new standards as sung by O'Neal. Funky. —*Michael Erlewine*

All Mixed Up / 1988 / Tabu ✦✦
This lengthy and intelligently programmed set of remixed hits is culled mostly from *Hearsay*. —*John Floyd*

○ **All True Man** / 1991 / Tabu ✦✦✦✦
Alexander O'Neal's biggest weakness was timing; he came along during an era when individual soul singers and romantic balladeers had lost their prominence in the urban contemporary equation. While O'Neal had more ruggedness and natural ebullience than any vocalist except Luther Vandross and Freddie Jackson, his songs could never generate the attention they deserved. Although this album went gold, it couldn't get enough of a breakout single to keep it on the charts long enough. Likewise, O'Neal's voice was never more versatile, convincing or urgent than on such cuts as "Hang On," "Midnight Run" and "Sentimental." —*Ron Wynn*

All True Love / 1991 / Tabu ✦✦✦
Most soul and R&B male vocalists excel at slow, simmering love tunes and merely execute uptempo ones; Alexander O'Neal reverses the process. So it was no surprise that *All True Love* contained several excellent dance-based tunes and no memorable love ballads. Despite some production clutter with multi-tracked female vocalists and overblown strings, O'Neal scored on such numbers as "What Is This Thing Called Love" and "All True Man," prime Jimmy Jam/Terry Lewis numbers. For some reason, Jam and Lewis sought to thematically link several songs on the CD into a portrait of '90s urban angst, without success. —*Ron Wynn*

Love Makes No Sense / 1993 / Tabu ✦✦✦
● **This Thing Called Love: Greatest Hits of** / 1993 / CBS ✦✦✦✦
While it can be argued that Alexander O'Neal's track record doesn't merit any greatest hits or best-of compilations, that didn't deter Tabu from issuing this compilation. It presented O'Neal's finest uptempo and ballad singles, displaying his ferocity on such cuts as "Fake" and "Criticize," plus his range and passion on "Never Knew Love Like This." —*Ron Wynn*

The Only Ones
Group, Rock & Roll, Punk, Power Pop/Anglo-Pop
Led by the raffish and slightly scuzzy romance-obsessed Peter Perrett, the Only Ones were one of the punk era's most underrated bands. Not as confrontational as the Sex Pistols, as politically indulgent as the Clash, or as stripped-down as the Ramones, the Only Ones played not-so-fast guitar rock that sounded deeply indebted to the New York Dolls and other mid-'70s proto-punks. Singing his intelligently crafted pop songs in a semi-tuneful whine of a voice and backed by a band that effectively combined youthful exuberance with gracefully aging veterans (non-punk drummer Mike Kellie had done time with early-'70s clod-rockers Spooky Tooth, bassist Alan Mair was nearly 40!), Perrett was an astute chronicler of the vagaries of modern, dysfunctional love. Despite a career that lasted from 1978-1981 and one certifiable "hit" song to their credit (the brilliant "Another Girl, Another Planet") the Only Ones became the archetypal contenders that never broke big, despite assurances from fans and critics that they couldn't miss.

Although they split up in 1981 after only three records, the Only Ones, due in large part to "Another Girl, Another Planet," became more influential than one would have guessed. Listen to Paul Westerberg and you'll hear more than a little Peter Perrett (in fact, the Replacements covered "Another Girl"); look at the number of Only Ones releases over the past decade (a half-dozen at least) and you soon realize that a significant cult surrounding the band grew after their breakup. Ironically, it was the posthumous release of the sessions for John Peel's BBC show that, more than any of the proper studio releases, accurately displayed the muscle and smarts of this fine band. There have been many rumors surrounding Perrett's life after the Only Ones, many of them involving an alleged heroin addiction. As of this writing, he doesn't seem to be planning a return to rock & roll any time in the near future. —*John Dougan*

○ **The Only Ones** / 1978 / CBS ♦♦♦♦
"Another Girl, Another Planet" is here, but then again, it surfaces on a number of Only Ones records. The best of their studio releases, this record is a tuneful anomaly of mid-'70s rock that stands in stark contrast to the prevailing punk zeitgeist. Still, the band (even the old guys) play with an infectious enthusiasm, and Perrett, despite his tendency towards adenoidal Dylanesque vocals, is particularly winning. —*John Dougan*

● **Special View** / 1979 / Epic ♦♦♦♦
In America, Epic couldn't decide whether or not to release any Only Ones recordings, so they came up with this half-way measure: a sampler. *Special View* took the strongest tracks from their debut, added tracks from their so-so second album, *Even Serpents Shine*, and the result was (surprise) a great record. All these years later, *Special View* is as good a sampler of early Only Ones as anyone could have hoped for and should be considered an important purchase, although I think it's no longer in print. —*John Dougan*

○ **Even Serpents Shine** / 1979 / CBS ♦♦♦♦
Only a shade removed from the standard of debut LP. —*Steve Aldrich*

Baby's Got a Gun / 1980 / Epic ♦♦♦
Less consistent than their first two efforts, it's still rewarding. —*Steve Aldrich*

Remains / 1984 / Closer ♦♦
Included are demos and unfinished studio tracks. —*Steve Aldrich*

○ **Alone in the Night** / 1986 / Dojo ♦♦♦♦
Possibly the best of the available compilations. —*Steve Aldrich*

○ **Peel Sessions** / 1989 / Dutch East India ♦♦♦♦
Frankly, one could argue an eloquent case either way as to why *Special View* or the *Peel Sessions* are the most important Only Ones recordings. I tend to recommend the *Peel Sessions*, because it's rougher, a little meaner, and the Only Ones were in the midst of their 15 minutes of fame as a rock band; plus, there's a swagger here that's missing on other recordings. —*John Dougan*

Live / 1989 / Edsel ♦♦
Not essential, but if you've fallen under Peter Perrett's spell, you owe it to yourself to hear what a fine live band they were. Recorded in London in 1977 in the Ones' pre-CBS days, this is a "punkier" sounding band, a little ragged, but wonderful. To no one's surprise, "Another Girl" is here and it's great. —*John Dougan*

Live in London / 1990 / Skyclad ♦♦♦
Essentially a greatest-hits live package, this contains many of the aforementioned tracks, but adds bits and some hots-on guitar spuzz. —*John Dougan*

The Immortal Story / 1992 / CBS ♦♦♦
The "Official" compilation consists of best-ofs, including alternate takes and rare tracks. —*Steve Aldrich*

Yoko Ono

Pop/Rock, Experimental
Over the years, Yoko Ono has received an unfair treatment in the press. From being pegged as the reason the Beatles broke up to being called talentless, Ono has been dragged through the press more times than any one person deserves. And she did have talent, although it was primarily as a conceptual and visual artist. As a musician, she is allegedly influential on many post-punk bands, though it is highly unlikely anyone outside of the B-52s actually listened to her records. With her abrasive, frequently atonal pop and rock experimentations, Ono did predict, if not influence, the sound of some experimental post-punk bands, including Public Image Limited. Ono could be even more effective when she conformed to pop songwriting, turning in some surprisingly moving

straightforward pop/rock. If you can wade through the pretensions—as well as grow accustomed to her shrill voice—you may find some rewarding music among her many records. —*Stephen Thomas Erlewine*

● **Walking on Thin Ice Compilation** / 1992 / Rykodisc ♦♦♦♦
A single-disc distillation of the *Ono Box* which covers everything the curious listener needs to know. If you still need more after listening to *Walking on Thin Ice*, the *Ono Box* is a must-buy. —*Stephen Thomas Erlewine*

○ **Ono Box** / 1992 / Rykodisc ♦♦♦♦
Although it inspires countless jokes, the music on the six-disc *Ono Box* is, by and large, quite impressive. In terms of experimental rock & roll, Ono was certainly one of the leaders in the 1970s, creating intense, almost atonal rock that demanded to be accepted on its own terms. Nearly twenty years later, some of the music sounds dated, but much of it sounds remarkably contemporary. Nevertheless, the box is rarely dull and makes a strong case for her musical talents. —*Stephen Thomas Erlewine*

Onyx

Group, Rap
The hip-hop trio Onyx ushered in a new development in 1993; rap in the mosh pit. Their shouting, in-your-face brand of high volume rapping didn't sit well with everyone, but their debut CD *Bacdafucup* included a huge crossover smash with "Slam." —*Ron Wynn*

○ **Bacdafucup** / 1993 / Ral ♦♦♦♦
With their simple, brutal production and shouted rhymes, Onyx's debut album was a menacing, threatening record, relying more on sheer aggression than musical competence. Still, that aggression could produce undeniably classic tracks, like their breakthrough single, "Slam." —*Stephen Thomas Erlewine*

Opal

Group, Alternative Pop/Rock, Psychedelic
The neo-psychedelic group Opal formed in the mid-'80s, featuring former Rain Parade guitarist David Roback and former Dream Syndicate bassist Kendra Smith. Initially, the group was called Clay Allison, yet the group dropped the name after one single; Roback, Smith, and drummer Keith Mitchell released the remaining Clay Allison tracks underneath their own name in 1984, on the *Fell from the Sun* EP. After its release, the group adopted the name Opal and released an EP, *Northern Line*, in 1985. *Happy Nightmare Baby*, their first full-length album, followed in 1987. Smith left the group during the *Happy Nightmare* tour, effectively putting an end to the band. Roback continued with vocalist Hope Sandoval; the group then metamorphosed into Mazzy Star. —*Stephen Thomas Erlewine*

● **Happy Nightmare Baby** / 1987 / SST ♦♦♦♦
Early Recordings / 1989 / Rough Trade ♦♦♦

The Orb

Group, Techno
Originating from Dr. Alex Paterson's ambient-house sets at a popular London chill-out club with Jimmy Cauty of the KLF, the Orb resurrected slower, more soulful, electronic rhythms (reminiscent of Pink Floyd and Tangerine Dream) on their debut LP, *The Orb's Adventures Beyond the Ultraworld*. With partner Kris Weston (aka Thrash), Paterson gained an audience with "Little Fluffy Clouds." A welcome turn for frenzied club-kids worn out by years of harsh techno, the Orb's live dates featured amazing light shows, visuals, and a relaxed, positive vibe rarely found in previous electronic circles. *U.F.Orb*, released in 1992, continued the Orb's popularity. As the ambient-house genre began to take off, though, the duo were grounded by legal trouble with their label, Big Life, and spent almost two years trying to sever ties with the company.
 The Orb finally reemerged in 1994 with the EP *Pomme Fritz* and an album the following year, *Orbus Terrarum*. While ambient-house has spawned legions of imitators, including many new-age bandwagon-jumpers, the Orb move on, restless to explore new vistas of sound and rhythm. —*John Bush*

Huge Ever Growing Pulsating Brain That Rules From the Center of the Ultraworld / 1989 / Island ♦♦♦
Pink Floyd-like space music with a variety of water noises. *A Huge Ever Growing Pulsating Brain That Rules From the Center of the Ultraworld* is suited to those interested in psychedelia and the bizarre. —*David Szatmary*

○ **The Adventures Beyond Ultraworld** / 1991 / Big Life ✦✦✦✦
The Orb's first full-length album expands on the strengths of their debut EP, resulting in one of the most compulsively listenable techno albums ever recorded. —*Stephen Thomas Erlewine*

● **U.F.Orb** / Mar. 1992 / Big Life ✦✦✦✦
So far, the Orb haven't made an album better than *U.F.Orb*, a hypnotic series of trance-inducing rhythms and interweaving synths that never grows boring, even at its 74-minute length. —*Stephen Thomas Erlewine*

○ **Live 93** / 1993 / Island ✦✦✦✦
Although the thought of an Orb live album may raise some eyebrows, the resulting 2-CD set is amazing, a complete representation of the group in concert and living proof that techno is indeed alive, as well as recorded, art form. Besides, the consistent Pink Floyd jokes on the record (as well as the brilliant cover art) are hilarious. —*Stephen Thomas Erlewine*

Pomme Fritz / 1994 / Island Red ✦✦
After a long absence, Orb returned with this EP, a very experimental work which won't appeal to most listeners. Still, "Alles Ist Schoen" features a great ambient groove. —*John Bush*

Orbvs Terrarvm / 1995 / Island ✦✦✦
The perfect response to a music-scene swamped by what Paterson himself called "lame ambient noodling for seventy minutes." The melodies and dub lines of the first two albums are still in the mix, though they are overpowered by harsh percussion and noisy synth. This creates an unsettling affect on first listen though, after repeated plays, the brilliance of *Orbus Terrarum* becomes clear. The hilarious vocal samples on "Slug Dub," taken from a children's story, make it the highlight of the disc. —*John Bush*

Roy Orbison

b. Apr. 23, 1936, Wink, TX, **d.** Dec. 6, 1988
Rock & Roll, Rockabilly, Pop/Rock
Roy Orbison was the most unlikely of early rock & rollers, the physical and charismatic antithesis of Elvis Presley, Jerry Lee Lewis, and Little Richard. But he forged a style that was as singular as any in rock, assuming the role of pop's master paranoic. He cut some rockabilly for Sun in the late '50s, but it's his string of brilliant '60s hits, produced with Frank Foster for Monument, that established Orbison's formula. His best singles delve into the darkest areas of a soul torn by romantic confusion and terror; "Only the Lonely" and "Running Scared" epitomize Orbison's near-operatic ballad formula. Although he also recorded some convincing and tough pop ("Oh, Pretty Woman," "Candy Man"), his reputation rests on his bleak, uncompromising broken-heart laments, which have influenced rockers from Del Shannon to Bruce Springsteen and Elvis Costello. After spending most of the '70s and '80s on the oldies circuit, Orbison revived his career through an association with a group called the Traveling Wilburys. He died in 1989, just weeks after releasing *Mystery Girl*, the album that put him back on the charts. —*John Floyd*

Crying / 1962 / Sony ✦✦
Roy Orbison's second album was above-average considering the slight standards of the time, but was a fairly slight effort nonetheless. In its favor, the album features nearly all original material by Orbison and some of the writers who frequently tailored songs for him, such as Boudleaux and Felice Bryant and Joe Melson. The trademark early Orbison production flourishes, with swooping strings and full vocal choruses, are also present. What's missing is truly first-rate songwriting. With the exception of "Love Hurts," the title track, and the epic hit "Running Scared," most of the cuts lean toward the Big O's more sentimental side, and are pleasantly forgettable. Of the obscure cuts here, the best are the uptempo "Nite Life" and "Let's Make A Memory," with its bouncing string arrangement, but neither could be classified among his best early work. —*Richie Unterberger*

There Is Only One / 1965 / PolyGram ✦✦
Orbison explains in the liner notes that MGM will allow him "a new climate of freedom" as an artist, but the results of his first album for the label were unimpressive. He forsakes much of the rock & roll foundation of his classic early-'60s hits for Nashville country and western on most of the LP, complete with barroom piano. The material (mostly written by Orbison with various collaborators) doesn't approach the magnificence of his best work, and his version of his composition "Claudette" isn't nearly as good as the Everly Brothers' hit rendition from 1958. The highlight is the strange, almost rambling minor hit single, "Ride Away." —*Richie Unterberger*

Fastest Guitar Alive / 1968 / Columbia Special Products ✦✦
Orbison's one bid for film stardom, *The Fastest Guitar Alive*, was an unqualified flop. The soundtrack fares slightly better, but only slightly. With ten songs clocking in at a mere 27 minutes, most of the tunes—which Roy composed with longtime collaborator Bill Dees—borrow from the cheesiest elements of cowboy music, with quasi-Mexican guitar riffs, silly Indian chants, and uneasy spaghetti-Western pathos. For all its ill-conceived failure, it includes what may be his best obscure tune, the little-anthologized "Whirlwind." With its galloping rhythm, emotive operatic vocals, swirling strings, and ghostly backing vocals, it recalls the best uptempo ballads that he recorded during his early-'60s heyday at the Monument label. In 1968, of course, few listeners were interested. —*Richie Unterberger*

○ **All-Time Greatest Hits of Roy Orbison** / 1976 / Monument ✦✦✦✦
The All-Time Greatest Hits of Roy Orbison is an essential collection. It rounds up 20 of the Big O's best '60s recordings, with some fine album tracks thrown in. —*John Floyd*

★ **For the Lonely: 18 Greatest Hits** / 1988 / Rhino ✦✦✦✦✦
For the Lonely: Roy Orbison Anthology (1956-1965) offers the usual Monument hits along with a few Sun tunes—18 in all. Buyers beware: the vinyl version contains more cuts than the CD. —*John Floyd*

○ **The Legendary Roy Orbison** / 1988 / Sony ✦✦✦✦
While the Rhino set, *For the Lonely: Roy Orbison Anthology (1956-1965)*, is the most essential single-disc release of Orbison's work, *The Legendary Roy Orbison* tries to flesh out the picture considerably with a four-disc, 75-track boxed set. It may be overkill for some, and certain tracks feel like pointless inclusions, but fans who want more than just a hits collection should like this set. The enclosed booklet contains a wealth of photos and the annotation is passionate and informative. —*Rick Clark*

The Classic Roy Orbison (1965-1968) / 1989 / Rhino ✦✦✦
The hits dried up when Orbison left the Monument label for MGM in 1965. The 14 recordings here, taken from singles and LP tracks, feature arrangements and production not far removed from his classic Monument era. The singing is wonderful, but stacked up against his classic hits, a lot is missing. Lacking the ace songwriting of his best work, there's lots of midtempo, melodramatic rock balladry here, but somehow nothing nearly as gripping as his best compositions. —*Richie Unterberger*

○ **Mystery Girl** / 1989 / Virgin ✦✦✦✦
Roy's comeback is remarkable in that every song, from "You Got It" and "She's a Mystery to Me" to "The Only One," proves that the formula of his '60s stuff is still vital 30 years later. This album really deserved a followup. —*John Floyd*

○ **The Sun Years 1956-58** / Apr. 1989 / Bear Family ✦✦✦✦
It contains Orbison's complete Sun output, featuring many undubbed recordings and the pile-driving "Domino." —*John Floyd*

Rock Legends / 1990 / RCA ✦✦✦
A compilation of rare and early works by Roy Orbison and Little Richard that makes odd bedfellows of two extremely dissimilar performers, borne out of the necessity of cleaning out old vault material to capitalize on the CD reissue explosion. The first eight tracks belong to Little Richard, who won a recording contract with RCA after winning a talent contest in Atlanta. These sides, cut in 1951 and 1952, show barely a hint of his later wildness, owing far more to the jump blues R&B of Roy Brown and others. Orbison's seven songs were cut in the late '50s, between his rockabilly days at Sun and his ascent to stardom on Monument. You can hear tentative explorations of the soaring romanticism that he'd find his niche with in 1960, but the material is basic, weak, typical late-'50s teen fodder, courtesy of Roy himself and noted songwriters John Loudermilk, Boudleaux Bryant, and Felice Bryant. The yearning "Seems To Me" (written by Boudleaux, who would write many fine hits for Orbison and the Everly Brothers) is the only track which begins to even approximate his future glory. This cheese'n'chalk compilation is only recommended to those wishing to glean historical insight into these giants' beginnings, though it may well be that the Little Richard fanatic isn't necessarily a Roy Orbison devotee (and vice versa). —*Richie Unterberger*

BOOK

✦✦ **Only The Lonely**, by Alan Clayson (St. Martin's, 1989). One of the great early rock & roll musicians, Orbison's public image wasn't nearly as colorful as those of peers such as Elvis, Jerry Lee Lewis, or Johnny Cash. That makes maintaining interest over the course of a full-length biography a challenge, but Orbison's death in the late '80s created a need for a book, and Clayson made a reasonable attempt to fulfill it. Drawing heavily on archival quotes from an extremely wide range of sources, some quite obscure, Clayton focuses primarily upon the music, and Orbison's creative collaborations with such key colleagues as Monument producer Fred Foster and songwriting partners Bill Dees and Joe Melson. Orbison's story was not empty of real-life drama—he lost a wife and two sons in separate, devastating tragedies—but it's the drama of his music that exerts lasting fascination, and Clayson properly concentrates on that. The post-1964 years, which saw him fall from the charts and drift artistically, are pretty thin going unless you're a very devoted fan. — *Richie Unterberger*

Orbital

Group, Techno-Pop/Dance, Techno
As with most ambient-house practitioners, the brothers Phil and Paul Hartnoll have techno backgrounds. Unlike many artists, however, Orbital have not deserted their roots. Instead, they weave their Kraftwerk-influenced rhythms and melodies in with slower ambient tracks. Their first two full-length albums, both self-titled (but known as the green and the brown albums) are closer to collections of singles than true LPs. *Snivilization*, a more unified LP, appeared in 1994. —*John Bush*

○ **Orbital** / Oct. 1991 / FFRR ✦✦✦✦
○ **Orbital +** / 1992 / FFRR ✦✦✦✦
 Halcyon / 1993 / FFRR ✦✦✦
● **Snivilization** / 1994 / FFRR ✦✦✦✦
The Hartnoll brothers' most consistent album, *Snivilization* has a unified feel that works from uptempo opener, "Forever," to the finale, "Attached," a glorious ten-minute ambient climax. Sandwiched between is Kraftwerk-influenced techno that works well on the dancefloor as well as the living room. Also check out aggro-industrial thrasher "Quality Seconds," and "Kein Trink Wasser," with its complex and infectious piano medley. —*John Bush*

 Diversions / FFRR ✦✦✦

Orchestral Manoeuvres in the Dark

Group, Techno-Pop/Dance, New Wave
Featuring the core members Paul Humphreys and Andy Mc-Cluskey, the Liverpudlian synth-pop group Orchestral Manoeuvers in the Dark formed in the late '70s. Humphreys and Mc-Cluskey began performing together in school, playing in the bands VCL XI, Hitlerz Underpantz, and the Id. After the Id split in 1978, McCluskey was with Dalek I Love You for a brief time. Once he left Dalek, he joined with Humphreys and Paul Collister to form Orchestral Manoeuvers in the Dark. The group released their first single "Electricity" on Factory Records; the record led to a contract with the Virgin's subsidiary DinDisc. Using their record advance, McCluskey and Humphreys built a studio, which allowed them to replace their 4-track recorded with drummer Malcolm Holmes (formerly of the Id) and Dave Hughes (formerly of Dalek I Love You).

In 1980, the group released their self-titled debut album, which featured the U.K. Top Ten single "Enola Gay." *Organisation* appeared the same year; Hughes was replaced by Martin Cooper after its release. The band's next few albums—*Architecture & Morality* (1981), *Dazzle Ships* (1983), *Junk Culture* (1984)—found the band experimenting with their sound, resulting in several U.K. hit singles. Recorded with two new members, Graham and Neil Weir, *Crush*, their most pop-oriented album, found more success in America than in Britain, as the single "So in Love" hit number 26 on the charts. "If You Leave," taken from the *Pretty in Pink* soundtrack was their biggest American hit, climbing to number four in 1986. *The Pacific Age* was released the same year, yet America was the only country where it was popular. Shortly after its release, the Weir brothers left the band, followed by Holmes, Cooper, and Humphreys. McCluskey continued with the band, releasing *Sugar Task* in 1991; in the meantime, Humphreys formed the Listening Pool. —*Stephen Thomas Erlewine*

○ **Orchestral Manoeuvres in the Dark** / 1980 / Virgin ✦✦✦✦
 Organisation / 1980 / Virgin ✦✦✦

○ **Architecture & Morality** / 1981 / Virgin ✦✦✦✦
 Dazzle Ships / 1983 / Virgin ✦✦✦
○ **Junk Culture** / 1984 / A&M ✦✦✦✦
○ **Crush** / 1985 / A&M ✦✦✦✦
 The Pacific Age / 1986 / A&M ✦✦
● **The Best of O.M.D.** / 1988 / A&M ✦✦✦✦
 Sugar Tax / 1991 / Virgin ✦✦✦
 Pandora's Box / 1993 / Atlantic ✦✦✦
 Liberator / Jun. 29, 1993 / ✦✦

Original Surfaris

Group, Surf
Not to be confused with the famous Surfaris, the ones who did "Wipe Out," this entirely separate surf group from Orange County, CA, was forced to change their name when the other Surfaris got a big hit. A respectable band in their own right, they managed to record a few very obscure singles and compilation LP tracks, as well as an unreleased album. Their best tracks, "Bombora," "Surfari," and "Latin'ia," boast the spooky reverb guitar lines and Latin-influenced minor melodies that were hallmarks of much of the best instrumental surf music, although the bulk of their recordings were run-of-the-mill. —*Richie Unterberger*

○ **Bombora!** / 1995 / Sundazed ✦✦✦✦
Originally slated to be released in 1963, this album was withdrawn due to litigation over the use of the Surfaris name, and retrieved from the vaults in the mid-'90s. A fair but unexceptional instrumental surf collection; the best cuts (most notably the title track) have appeared on compilations. —*Richie Unterberger*

The Originals

Group, Soul, Motown
Detroit soul vocal group. Led by Freddie Gorman, the Originals took the R&B world by storm in 1969, although they had worked at Motown for years as invaluable background vocalists. Gorman recorded as a solo for Berry Gordy in 1961 and co-wrote "Please Mr. Postman" for the Marvelettes, and the Originals cut a version of Leadbelly's "Goodnight Irene" for Gordy's Soul subsidiary in 66 with ex-Falcon Joe Stubbs as lead. But Stubbs had split to form 100 Proof Aged in Soul by the time the quartet waxed the beautiful doowop throwback "Baby I'm for Real," a R&B chart-topper in 69 that was co-written and lushly produced by Marvin Gaye. The same combination also produced "The Bells," another major hit in 1970. Former solo act Ty Hunter joined the group in 1971, and the Originals continued to chart into the next decade. —*Bill Dahl*

○ **Naturally Together** / 1970 / Soul ✦✦✦✦
The group's third Motown album didn't fare nearly as well as the previous two, which both made the lower regions of the pop charts. Despite some wonderful production by Clay Murray and fine ballad and uptempo leads from Crathman Spencer and Henry Dixon, they couldn't generate much national action, even though it had one wonderful song in "God Bless Whoever Sent You," which peaked at #14 R&B. —*Ron Wynn*

● **Motown Superstar Series, Vol. 10** / Motown ✦✦✦✦
The Detroit-based Originals began singing in 1966, with tenor vocalists Crathman Spencer and Henry Dixon, bassist Freddie Gorman and baritone Walter Gaines. Marvin Gaye helped bring them to Motown and later wrote or co-wrote three of their singles, including the anthemic "Baby, I'm For Real." That single, their other major hit, "The Bells," and the third Gaye single, "We Can Make It Baby," are among the tunes on this anthology. They weren't a great group, but their two hits are as gripping and wonderfully produced and arranged as any Motown material. —*Ron Wynn*

The Orioles

Group, R&B, Doo-Wop
A smooth, early-'50s group best known for the 1953 hit "Crying in the Chapel," the Orioles were arguably the most important R&B vocal group of the late '40s and early '50s; as much as anyone, they were responsible for the shift from the straight pop harmonies to doo-wop.—*John Floyd*

○ **Jubilee Sides** / 1993 / Bear Family ✦✦✦✦
This exhaustive six-CD box set shows you all the reasons why The Orioles, led by smooth-as-silk vocalist Sonny Til, were one of the most pivotal, if not the most important, of all the early Black vocal

groups. The group's honey-smooth harmonies perfectly frame Til's soaring, sexy vocals against the simplest of backgrounds on their earliest sides, while later sessions with full orchestras surprisingly do little to intrude, with interesting results. With typical Bear Family completeness, this rounds up everything the group cut for Natural-Jubilee from two different tenures with the label. —*Cub Koda*

★ **Sing Their Greatest Hits** / Collectables ◆◆◆◆◆
This Orioles hit package is about equal to any other that's available, but pales next to the Bear Family boxed set. The now defunct Murray Hill also had a great Orioles box several years ago. Save your money and grab the Bear Family if you really want the real story on the Orioles. —*Ron Wynn*

For Collectors Only / Collectables ◆◆◆

Orlons

Group, Girl-Group
A predominantly female group from Philadelphia, the Orlons had some dance and novelty gems in the early '60s for Cameo-Parkway. Lead vocalist Rosetta Hightower, Marlena Davis, Steve Caldwell and Shirley Brickley scored with "The Wah Watusi" in 1962; it was a number five R&B and number two pop hit, while the follow-ups, "Don't Hang Up" and "South Street," were also Top Ten R&B and pop successes. "Not Me" was their fourth consecutive R&B Top Ten winner in 1963, and it peaked at number 12 pop. It was also their last, although "Cross Fire!" reached number 19 on the pop charts. But their other singles fizzled, and Davis and Caldwell left in 1964, replaced by Audrey Brickley. When Hightower moved to England in 1968, the Orlons disbanded. —*Ron Wynn*

● **Best of Orlons** / 1977 / London ◆◆◆◆

Ozzy Osbourne (John Osbourne)

b. Dec. 3, 1948, Birmingham, England
Heavy Metal
Ozzy Osbourne has been ridiculed over the years, yet he has had an immeasurable effect on heavy metal, while he was in Black Sabbath and as a solo artist. Osbourne doesn't have a great voice—it's thin and it doesn't have much range—yet he has a good ear and a great dramatic flair. Over the course of his career, his band has featured some of the most innovative and distinctive guitarists in hard rock, including the late Randy Rhoads. As a showman, his instincts are nearly as impeccable; his live shows have been overwrought spectacles with gore and glitz that have endeared him to adolescents around the world. Indeed, Osbourne has managed to establish himself as an international superstar, capable of selling millions of records with each album and packing arenas across the world, capturing new fans with each record.

Ozzy Osbourne began his professional career with Black Sabbath, who released their first album in 1970. Throughout the '70s, the group carved out a distinctive brand of slow, gloomy heavy metal that became the essence of metal for many listeners. Osbourne left the band in 1979, embarking on a solo career. Supported by a band featuring ex-Uriah Heep drummer Lee Kerslake, former Rainbow bassist Bob Daisley, and ex-Quiet Riot guitarist Randy Rhoads, the singer recorded *Blizzard of Ozz*; the group would adopt the album's title as their name. Released in 1981, *Blizzard of Ozz* had some of the same ingredients as Black Sabbath—the lyrics focused on the occult and the guitars were loud and heavy—yet he was supported by a group that was more technically proficient and capable of pulling off varying the standard metal formulas. The record hit number seven on the U.K. charts; it peaked at number 21 in the U.S., staying on the charts for over two years and going platinum. Before the band began their first U.S. tour in 1981, Kerslake and Daisley left the band; they were replaced by former Pat Travers Band drummer Tommy Aldridge and ex-Quiet Riot bassist Rudy Sarzo. This is the group that recorded Osbourne's second album, *Diary of a Madman*; the album charted at number 16 in the U.S. and also became a platinum seller. Following its release, Daisley returned to the group and Aldridge left; former Rainbow keyboardist Don Airey was added to the lineup at this time, as well.

During Osbourne's 1982 tour, guitarist Randy Rhoads died in a bizarre plane accident, leaving a gaping hole in Osbourne's band, since Rhoads essentially determined the musical direction of the group. He was replaced by Brad Gillis, a former member of Night Ranger. Gillis' first record with Osbourne was *Speak of the Devil*, a live album of Black Sabbath material released to combat Sabbath's

live album, *Live At Last*. After the release of *Speak of the Devil*, Osbourne reshaped the lineup of his band, adding guitarist Jake E. Lee. The new group recorded *Bark at the Moon*, which repeated the success of the first two records. For the rest of the decade, Osbourne's band continued to change, yet the only lineup changes that mattered were the guitarists. Lee left the band in 1987 and was replaced by Zakk Wylde, who led Osbourne's group into the '90s. Even as Osbourne approached his 50th birthday he remained one of the biggest stars in heavy metal, capable of selling well over a million records with each album. —*Stephen Thomas Erlewine*

○ **Diary of a Madman** / 1981 / Jet ◆◆◆◆
The follow-up was rushed, and it shows: Rhoads didn't even have time to lay down a real solo on "Little Dolls" (the solo used was intended only as a guide). Even so, Rhoads' classical training manifests itself even more, and the compositions generally increase in sophistication (especially the epic title track). One wonders how much the Osbourne/Rhoads combination would have accomplished had Rhoads not been killed in a plane crash five months after this recording. —*Steve Huey*

○ **Blizzard of Ozz** / 1981 / Jet ◆◆◆◆
Ozzy's solo debut not only re-established him as a viable attraction, it also introduced the ample talents of guitarist Randy Rhoads, whose classically-influenced style had a huge impact on rock guitar in the '80s. Say what you will about Ozzy, but the music here is simply great; Osbourne/Rhoads collaborations like "Crazy Train," "Mr. Crowley," and "Revelation (Mother Earth)" still stand today as all-time heavy metal classics. —*Steve Huey*

Speak of the Devil / 1982 / Jet ◆◆◆
A live album recorded from Osbourne's 1982 tour, it features powerful new versions of Black Sabbath classics. It caused a minor controversy, since Sabbath (with Ronnie James Dio as vocalist) released their first live album (*Live Evil*) at the same time, also with early Black Sabbath material. Ozzy's band at the time featured drummer Tommy Aldridge (now with House of Lords), Night Ranger guitarist Brad Gillis, and bassist Rudy Sarzo, later a member of Whitesnake. (Sarzo was also a founding member of Quiet Riot, an early incarnation of which featured a young guitarist named Randy Rhoads.) —*John Book*

Bark at the Moon / 1983 / Epic ◆◆◆

● **Tribute** / 1987 / Epic ◆◆◆◆
This live double album, released five years after Randy Rhoads' death, showcases a hard-rock guitarist whose all-around ability was arguably second only to Eddie Van Halen. Osbourne leads his best band lineup through the entire *Blizzard* repertoire, plus a few *Diary* and Sabbath numbers. Of special note are Rhoads' unaccompanied solos, leaving no doubts about his virtuosity, and the studio outtakes of his short solo piece "Dee." Rhoads' entire output is absolutely essential for guitar freaks, but he sounds even better live than in the studio. —*Steve Huey*

No Rest for the Wicked / 1989 / Epic ◆◆

Just Say Ozzy / 1990 / Epic ◆◆

○ **No More Tears** / 1991 / Epic ◆◆◆◆
While looking for fresh inspiration, Osbourne started writing songs with Motörhead's Lemmy Kilmister, the kind of collaboration metal fans dream about. As a result, the songs on *No More Tears* are more compact, the sound denser, the musical payoffs more immediate. And not that Ozzy's mellowing in old age or anything, but *No More Tears* contains two of his best ballads—"Mama, I'm Coming Home" and "Time After Time." —*Brian Mansfield*

Live & Loud / 1992 / Epic ◆◆◆
Fans will be pleased with this live set from Osbourne, which isn't as consistent as *Tribute* but does feature a hot new band and songs that aren't available on any other live Osbourne album. —*AMG*

The Other Half

Group, Psychedelic
This obscure San Francisco '60s band gained a degree of notoriety in the '80s when their punk-garage single "Mr. Pharmacist" was included on one of Rhino's *Nuggets* compilations and covered by the Fall. Actually, most of the Other Half's material was far less garage than psychedelic, featuring the sustain-laden guitar of Randy Holden, one of the best Jeff Beck-inspired axemen of the '60s. Boasting decent songwriting and a just-out-of-the-garage approach to Haight-Ashbury psychedelia, the group cut a little-heard, fairly strong album, as well as a few rare singles, in 1967 and

1968. Holden, who had previously played in the L.A. psychedelic garage band Sons of Adam, went on to join Blue Cheer and record on his own. —*Richie Unterberger*

● **Mr. Pharmacist** / 1982 / Eva ✦✦✦✦
15-song reissue includes their entire 1968 LP and several non-LP singles. Besides a bad ten-minute jam and a couple other weak tracks, this is good stuff that often recalls early Love at their rawest. Includes a fine version of the obscure composition "Feathered Fish," which has been variously credited to Arthur Lee and Country Joe McDonald. —*Richie Unterberger*

The Other Two

Group, Dance-Pop, Techno-Pop/Dance, Alternative Pop/Rock
Gillian Gilbert and Stephen Morris—respectively, the keyboardist/guitarist and percussionist/programmer for New Order—released their first full-length album, *The Other Two and You*, in 1994. Before its release, they had recorded the hit single "Tasty Fish" in 1991 and worked on various film and television scores, including *America's Most Wanted*. —*Stephen Thomas Erlewine*

The Other Two and You / 1993 / Qwest ✦✦✦
A side project from Stephen Morris and Gillian Gilbert of New Order, *The Other Two & You* provides some melancholy, synth-pop kicks for devoted fans of the seminal Manchester group, but it won't appeal to those that were never fond of that sound in the first place. —*Stephen Thomas Erlewine*

The Outlaws

Group, Rock & Roll
No relation to the country-rock band, these British Outlaws cut nine singles and an album between 1961 and 1964; most of their material was instrumental. With an ever-changing lineup, this group (which never achieved any major hits) was pretty much a front for legendary British producer Joe Meek's eccentric production techniques. Around simple guitar instrumentals that borrowed heavily from the Shadows and a skewed sense of American cowboy themes, Meek soaked their basic sound with plenty of reverb and oddball sound effects. At times, the group approaches a compressed, goofy space-age sound that recalls another, much more famous Meek-produced band, the Tornados (of "Telstar" fame). Their recordings are especially interesting to collectors for the presence of future Deep Purple guitarist Ritchie Blackmore on the eight cuts from 1963-64. When given a loose reign, Blackmore unleashes some dazzling solos that were as advanced as any of the more renowned early British guitar heroes. Their final single, "Keep a Knockin'"/"Shake with Me," has some especially mind-bending lightning riffs that rank among the most exciting guitar work of the British Invasion, even if they were virtually unheard at the time. —*Richie Unterberger*

● **Ride Again: The Singles As & Bs** / 1990 / See For Miles ✦✦✦✦
All 18 of the songs from their singles are included on this collection. It's all quite dated decades later, but not without its period charm, and the production was actually quite innovative for its period. —*Richie Unterberger*

Outrageous Cherry

Group, Alternative Pop/Rock
This Detroit group explores the sunnier side of droning alternative pop. With songs like "Pale Frail Lovely One" and "Till I Run Out," their sweetly wistful sound makes their sound as delectable as their name. Matthew Smith (vocals, guitars) writes hook-filled, deceptively simple songs that are filled out by Chad Gilchrist (bass), Larry Ray (lead guitar) and Deb Agnollli (the band's drummer, who has the style and sound of the Velvet Underground's Mo Tucker). Outrageous Cherry's engaging and refreshing take on 1960s pop promises big things for this up and coming band. —*Heather Phares*

○ **Outrageous Cherry** / 1994 / BarNone ✦✦✦✦
The group's debut contains 12 fun, fuzzy drone-pop tracks like "Pale Frail Lovely One," "Til I Run Out" and "The Stare." A promising, entertaining beginning. —*Heather Phares*

The Outsiders

Group, Pop/Rock
The Outsiders started in Cleveland, OH, as a garden-variety bar band led by guitarist and songwriter Tom King. The addition of vocalist Sonny Geraci infused the band with new life. Signed to Capitol Records in 1967, the group scored big with the single "Time Won't Let Me," their finest moment.

Personnel changes and management conflicts stalled the band's career but not before they had racked up several hits. —*Cub Koda*

● **Capitol Collectors Series** / 1991 / Capitol ✦✦✦✦
All their best in one neat little package. Includes "Time Won't Let Me," "Respectable," and "Girl in Love." —*Cub Koda*

The Outsiders [Dutch]

Group, Psychedelic, Garage Rock
Not to be confused with the Cleveland pop/rock group that had a Top Ten hit in 1966 with "Time Won't Let Me," these Outsiders (from Amsterdam, Holland) could issue a serious claim for consideration as the finest rock band of the '60s to hail from a non-English speaking nation. Led by singer and songwriter Wally Tax, the group were quite comparable to England's Pretty Things in their fine raw, punky R&B/pop with basic but riveting hooks. Like the Pretty Things, the Outsiders (who sang entirely in English) made similar psychedelic/progressive ventures in the late '60s that cut loose from their R&B roots without losing sight of them entirely. Recording several albums worth of material (consisting wholly of original compositions) between 1965 and 1969, the group tempered their punky, almost proto-hardcore ravers with melancholy, pensive folk-rockers and unpredictable production touches ranging from baroque mandolins and harpsichords to found radio static. The Outsiders' music was fraught with tension, the punkish rhythms playing against the melodic tunes, the R&B sensibilities against the pop hooks, often within the same song. Unknown on an international level to all but the most fervent '60s collectors, a lot of fine music awaits those who have yet to discover the Outsiders. Wally Tax moved to the U.S. in the early '70s, where he recorded one album as the leader of the band Tax Free. —*Richie Unterberger*

○ **The Outsiders** / 1967 / Pseudonym ✦✦✦✦
Their super-raw debut album, a few songs of which were recorded live. Some of this is too melodically primitive and clumsy to survive the ages, but tracks like "Filthy Rich," "Won't You Listen," and "If You Don't Treat Me Right" are comparable to little else of the era with their savage, Pretty Things-on-speed mood and hyper-fast tempos. The CD reissue adds several bonus tracks. —*Richie Unterberger*

○ **CQ** / 1968 / Polydor ✦✦✦✦
Their final LP (now available on CD) is one of the finer unsung psychedelic records of the late '60s. Heavy echoes of Syd Barrett-era Pink Floyd, Hendrix, and psychedelic-era Pretty Things, with adroit shifts from crunching rock and soft, almost folky passages to spacy phase-shift bits and just plain dementia. The album has an ominous and creepy, but rocking, ambience that still cuts deep. —*Richie Unterberger*

● **Best Of The Outsiders** / 1979 / MFP ✦✦✦✦
16-song compilation collects most of their singles, ranging from raunchy cuts like "Touch" and "I'm Only Trying To Prove Myself" to tuneful, forceful folk-rockish cuts like "I've Been Loving You So Long" and "Summer Is Here." Very consistent and strong, only a couple clunkers. —*Richie Unterberger*

C.Q. Sessions / 1994 / Pseudonym ✦✦✦
A double CD comprising 29 alternate takes, some instrumental and some vocal, of songs from the classic *C.Q.* album, one of the finest obscure psychedelic records. Besides one or two different alternate versions of each of the 13 songs from that record, it also has alternate versions of sides from non-LP singles they released around the same time ("Do You Feel Allright" & "You Remind Me"), as well as four songs (some instrumental) that never made it onto any official release. Some of the tracks are quite close to the finished versions, and some are quite different, but it's a pretty fascinating look at works in progress, and the sound quality is uniformly excellent. The audience for this reissue is, to say the least, extremely specialized and limited, but if you're a fan of this group, it's worth picking up. It also includes five bonus tracks from excruciatingly rare (and quite good) earlier non-LP singles from 1965 and 1966, when they were a much more R&B/beat-oriented outfit. —*Richie Unterberger*

P

The Pagans

Group, Punk

Of all the bands that burst out of Cleveland in the mid- to late-'70s punk explosion, one of the most unjustly ignored was the Pagans. Despite breaking up in 1979 (they have, however, reunited several times since), these grimy bohunks played fast'n'loud piss-and-vinegar garage rock that valued alienation and, at times, extreme bad taste. Led by the honking rasp of Mike Hudson and the rapid-fire guitar of Mike "Tommy Gunn" Metoff, the Pagans never played it safe, nor did they enter the rock & roll wars wanting to win any friends. And this, ultimately, was a good thing, for like their pals the Dead Boys, their anti-star pose and *carpe diem* attitude meant that their best songs (and there are quite a few) sound as if they were set to auto-destruct at the tune's end. Although their don't-give-a-shit attitude lends itself more than once to some sexist japes and homophobic ranting, the Pagans were ultimately nonplussed by who they offended. In fact, listening to any of their vintage material (1977-79), you'd think that offending everyone was their artistic *raison d'etre*. As Treehouse Records president Mark Trehus opines in the liner notes to the great collection *Buried Alive*, "The Pagans were as unwrought, impudent and gnarly a buncha rock'n'roll bedlamites as America's ever spewed outta its queasy underbelly." Little more need be said. — *John Dougan*

The Pagans / 1983 / Terminal ✦✦✦

● **Buried Alive** / 1986 / Treehouse ✦✦✦✦
Nasty, loud and vulgar, this is the best collection of the Pagans' music and one of the great, although almost completely forgotten, American punk rock records. After hearing such endearing "classics" as "What Is This Shit Called Love," you can see why Tesco Vee and his Meatmen covered it years later. Even better are the living-in-nowhere anthem "The Street Where Nobody Lives" and "Dead End America." Seventeen tracks, and each one's a killer, even the ones that make you wince. — *John Dougan*

Live-The Godlike Power of the Pagans / 1987 / Treehouse ✦✦✦

Street Where Nobody Lives / 1989 / Resonance ✦✦✦

Jimmy Page (James Patrick Page)

b. Jan. 9, 1944, Heston
Rock & Roll, Hard Rock

James Patrick Page is one of the most successful rock guitarists to come out of England in the '60s. Born in Heston, Page was playing recording sessions in London studios while still in his teens, and his guitar can be heard on many of the records made there in the mid-'60s. Page turned down an initial offer to join the Yardbirds, then changed his mind and worked with the group until its demise in 1968. He then formed Led Zeppelin, which was the predominant hard rock/heavy metal band in popular music until 1980. After the group split, Page was less active, though he formed another hard rock quartet, the Firm, in the mid-'80s. He released his own solo album in 1988.

In 1993, Page released his collaboration with former Whitesnake vocalist David Coverdale, *Coverdale/Page*. While it featured some fine playing by Page, it was hampered by lackluster songs. Following a tour, the duo broke up.

Page reunited with Robert Plant in 1994 for an *MTV Unplugged* television show and an album, *No Quarter*, both of which featured revamped versions of Led Zeppelin songs. They also launched a tour that ran into 1995. — *William Ruhlmann*

Death Wish II / 1982 / Swan Song ✦✦

Outrider / 1988 / David Geffen Co. ✦✦
Page's debut solo album is a heavy guitar treat employing a varying cast of sidemen, including drummer Jason Bonham and Page's old Led Zeppelin partner Robert Plant, who co-writes and sings one song. — *William Ruhlmann*

Session Man, Vol. 1 / 1989 / Bomp! ✦✦✦
Prior to his tenure in the Yardbirds and Led Zeppelin, Jimmy Page played numerous recording sessions in England. This is a compilation of his work from 1963 to 1968, including a solo single, some previously unreleased Yardbirds material, and various obscure British artists. — *William Ruhlmann*

Session Man, Vol. 2 / 1991 / Bomp! ✦✦✦
With more obscure acts than the previous volume, it also includes such name artists as Brenda Lee and Billy Fury, plus a live Yardbirds cut. — *William Ruhlmann*

Jimmy's Back Pages: The Early Years / 1992 / Sony ✦✦✦
Before joining the Yardbirds, Jimmy Page was Britain's premier session guitarist, guesting on innumerable dates from the Who and the Kinks on down to total unknowns. This 22-track compilation includes some of his more notable uncredited solos, when Jimmy was the man to give a song or a session an extra lift with his licks. As you might expect, the quality is variable, encompassing charming but wimpy Merseybeat, energetic but generic covers of '50s rock classics, and sub-Stones R&B. There are some great moments here, though. The Primitives' sides are respectable raw British R&B, and Les Fleur De Lys are like a poppier Who. Jimmy really lets rip on his solo for the First Gear's "Leave My Kitten Alone"; it's probably the best one he recorded prior to joining the Yardbirds. This also includes the rare single cut by Nico in Britain in 1965 before joining the Velvet Underground, which has a folk-ish sound in the vein of Marianne Faithfull; the A-side is a cover of Gordon Lightfoot's "I'm Not Saying," and the B-side is a somber acoustic ballad co-written by Page himself. The set ends with its one smash hit, Donovan's "Sunshine Superman." — *Richie Unterberger*

● **Coverdale/Page** / 1993 / A&M ✦✦✦✦
A fitfully entertaining collaboration with former Whitesnake singer David Coverdale, *Coverdale/Page* shows that Jimmy Page can still write the occasional killer riff, but has trouble pulling together cohesive songs. — *Stephen Thomas Erlewine*

Page/Plant

Group, Rock & Roll, Hard Rock

After years of rumors, Led Zeppelin guitarist Jimmy Page and vocalist Robert Plant reunited in 1994, recording the *No Quarter: Jimmy Page and Robert Plant Unledded* album for *MTV Unplugged*. Plant and Page didn't invite bassist John Paul Jones to join the reunion, choosing to assemble a band comprised of studio musicians. *No Quarter* performed respectably and the duo's subsequent 1995 tour was a sold-out success. — *Stephen Thomas Erlewine*

○ **No Quarter: Jimmy Page & Robert Plant Unledded** / 1994 / Atlantic ✦✦✦✦
Page and Plant's long-awaited reunion wasn't the blockbuster success it was predicted to be, but then again, they didn't play by the rules. Instead of rerecording their most famous material, the duo chose some of the most challenging and diverse Led Zeppelin material and wrote three originals to match. *No Quarter* doesn't cele-

brate Page and Plant's title of the Kings of Bombast; it focuses on their role in popularizing ethnic musics, from Arabia to the Celtic islands. So, it might not thrill fans of "Whole Lotta Love," but there's more invention on *No Quarter* than the standard reunion album. And, from the sounds of "City Don't Cry," "Yallah," and "Wonderful One," the partnership between the two remains fruitful. — *Stephen Thomas Erlewine*

The Painted Faces

Group, Psychedelic, Garage Rock
A psychedelic-garage band that prominently used ominous minor keys and organ, the Painted Faces recorded a few singles in 1967 and 1968 whose popularity was largely limited to their home state of Florida, where "Anxious Color" was a sizable hit. A garage band of average or a bit above-average worth, they featured mostly original material, and sounded somewhat like a garage Doors at times, with some pop, soul, and folk- rock influences as well. They were moving in a more progressive rock direction when their drummer was drafted in 1968, after which they disbanded. They achieved some notoriety in the 1980s when their singles "Anxious Color," "I Lost You in My Mind," and "I Think I'm Going Mad" showed up on '60s garage compilations. — *Richie Unterberger*

Anxious Color / 1994 / Distortions ✦✦✦
19-song compilation includes all seven of the tracks they released during their lifetime, as well as a dozen previously unreleased cuts from 1967 and 1968. A fair, though not remarkable, collection of a band that leaned toward the moodiest end of the garage-psych spectrum. Taken from copies of the singles and the like, the sound quality on some of the material (especially on Side Two) is even funkier than it usually is on compilations of this nature. — *Richie Unterberger*

The Palace Brothers

Group, Alternative Pop/Rock
Known alternately as Palace, Palace Songs and Palace Brothers, this outfit is the project of guitarist/vocalist Will Oldham. Palace Brothers takes the harsher side of country and folk and reworks it into devastatingly spare, intense indie-rock. Oldham's voice whimpers and whines like a centegenarian, and the simplicity and effortlessness of the songs suggest that they are timeless. While Palace Brothers are definitely a high concept group, the music speaks for itself. — *Heather Phares*

There Is No-One What Will Take Care of You / Jun. 14, 1993 / Drag City ✦✦✦
The name says it all. Dramatic, desperate country-indie rock that focuses on the dark side of life. — *Heather Phares*

● **Palace Brothers [EP]** / 1994 / Drag City ✦✦✦✦
Oldham's second EP is even more spartan and gaunt-sounding than Palace's debut. Strumming away on an acoustic guitar, his feeble voice barely topping a whisper, Oldham croaks out tunes of quiet despair like "Pushkin" and "I Am a Cinematographer." — *Heather Phares*

Viva Last Blues / 1995 / Drag City ✦✦✦
Viva Last Blues continues Oldham and company's trend of spare acoustic tunes with sad, world-weary themes. Palace seems to be refining and honing both their playing and songwriting skills with each album. — *Heather Phares*

Pale Saints

Group, Alternative Pop/Rock
This British band formed in 1987, and starting with their first full album in 1990, *Comforts of Madness*, displayed a knack for writing tunes both effervescent and ethereal. The original linneup included Chris Cooper, Ian Masters and Graeme Naysmith, to which current vocalist/guitarist Meriel Barham was added in late 1990. Masters left after 1992's *In Ribbons*, and despite the loss of its founding member and chief songwriter, Pale Saints has endured with Barham at the helm. Bassist Colleen Browne joined for 1994's strong third album, *Slow Buildings*. Pale Saints' songs range from whimsical, airy Brit-pop to elongated, droning soundscapes, but on the majority prove enjoyable. — *Heather Phares*

Comforts of Madness / 1990 / 4AD ✦✦✦
The group's debut contains some of their finest jangly songs as well as some of their most evocative soundscapes. — *Heather Phares*

● **In Ribbons** / 1992 / 4AD ✦✦✦✦
In Ribbons introduces Meriel Barham's sweet vocals and guitars to the Pale Saints. The group's second album continues the group's winning ways with light, delicate pop and ethereal melodies. A good introduction to Barham and Master's singing and songwriting. — *Heather Phares*

Slow Buildings / 1994 / 4AD/Warner Brothers ✦✦✦
Pale Saint's third album finds them carrying on without Masters, who had previously written the bulk of the group's material. While his absence is noticeable, it's not disastrous. *Slow Buildings* is an album of competent pop like "Will You Be My Angel' and "Fine Friend" and some experimental instrumentals like "King Fade" and "Henry." — *Heather Phares*

Robert Palmer

b. Jan. 19, 1949
Pop/Rock
British singer (and occasional songwriter), with a strong taste for R&B, Caribbean, New Orleans, and other rhythmic styles. He made a series of well-received albums in the '70s but finally broke through commercially in the '80s, singing in the Duran Duran side-project band Power Station and later on his own with his *Addicted to Love* in 1986. — *William Ruhlmann*

○ **Sneakin' Sally through the Alley** / 1974 / Island ✦✦✦✦
On his debut solo album, Palmer employs members of the Meters and Little Feat for a musical gumbo enriched by his husky, percussive voice. — *William Ruhlmann*

○ **Pressure Drop** / 1976 / Island ✦✦✦✦
Palmer's own songs (especially the silky "Give Me an Inch" and "Work to Make It Work") and the backing of Little Feat help make this a worthy followup to *Sally*. — *William Ruhlmann*

○ **Some People Can Do What They Like** / 1976 / Island ✦✦✦✦
Palmer's "Keep in Touch," "Man Smart, Woman Smarter," and "Spanish Moon" (the latter by Little Feat's Lowell George) pace *Some People Can Do What They Like*, another terrific collection. — *William Ruhlmann*

Double Fun / 1978 / Island ✦✦✦
Palmer produces and writes more songs than usual, resulting in the hit "Every Kinda People" and a somewhat lighter, more pop approach. — *William Ruhlmann*

○ **Secrets** / 1979 / Island ✦✦✦✦
Palmer scores his biggest hit single of the '70s with the uptempo rocker "Bad Case of Loving You (Doctor, Doctor)" on an album that also includes a wonderful version of Todd Rundgren's ballad "Can We Still Be Friends." — *William Ruhlmann*

Clues / 1980 / Island ✦✦✦
A move toward fast-paced electronic dance-rock. It's successful about half the time, especially on Palmer's UK hits "Looking for Clues" and "Johnny and Mary." (Rod Stewart Xeroxed "Johnny and Mary" for his hit "Young Turks" the following year.) — *William Ruhlmann*

Maybe It's Live / 1982 / Island ✦✦
Five oldies recorded in concert and five new songs, among them Palmer's first big UK hit, "Some Guys Have All the Luck." (Rod Stewart had a U.S. hit version two years later.) — *William Ruhlmann*

Pride / 1983 / Island ✦✦
Robert Palmer continued to move toward techno-rock here, cutting a cover of the System's "You Are In My System" that, for once, did little to illuminate the original. — *William Ruhlmann*

○ **Riptide** / Nov. 1985 / Island ✦✦✦✦
Palmer's commercial breakthrough, much of it in the hard rock style of his one-shot band Power Station, and featuring the hits "Discipline of Love," "Addicted to Love" (a number one hit), "Hyperactive," and "I Didn't Mean to Turn You On." — *William Ruhlmann*

Heavy Nova / Jun. 1988 / EMI America ✦✦
Robert Palmer cloned his hard rock *Riptide* style for its follow-up, his debut album on EMI, and was rewarded with the number two hit "Simply Irresistible," even if the formula was beginning to sound thin. — *William Ruhlmann*

● **Addictions, Vol. 1** / 1989 / Island ✦✦✦✦
Thirteen-track compilation containing Palmer's biggest hits, not only the ones on Island but also the Power Station singles and "Simply Irresistible," from Palmer's first EMI album. —*William Ruhlmann*

Don't Explain / 1990 / EMI America ✦✦
Robert Palmer's second EMI album, which turned out to be a sales disappointment, seems to combine two different musical concepts in its 18 tracks. The first is a straightforward, rhythm-heavy Robert Palmer rock album that takes up about the first half of the record. The second is a soundtrack for a planned musical that a Palmer bio describes as "a futuristic comedy using telling songs from the '40s to the present day," some produced by jazzman Teo Macero. These include songs like Bob Dylan's "I'll Be Your Baby Tonight" (done reggae style), Marvin Gaye's "Mercy Mercy Me" and "I Want You," and Rodgers and Hammerstein's "People Will Say We're In Love." The idea looks forward to Palmer's next album, *Ridin' High*, which is comprised entirely of standards, but the mixture of rhythm tracks and string-filled arrangements here makes for a confusing mixture. —*William Ruhlmann*

Ridin' High / 1992 / EMI America ✦✦
Addictions, Vol. 2 / May 5, 1992 / Island ✦✦✦
Apart from "I Didn't Mean to Turn You On," there are no big hits, only album tracks and failed singles, all of which are quite good. Unfortunately, the majority of the material has been remixed, remade, or has new vocal tracks; the album may sound great, but it isn't an accurate retrospective. —*Stephen Thomas Erlewine*

Honey / 1994 / EMI America ✦✦

Pansy Division

Group, Punk
A San Francisco band that celebrates deep subculture fringes of gay life, Pansy Division gained mainstream attention when they supported Green Day on their 1994 tour. Consequently, the band became the de-facto leaders of the punk rock "queer-core" movement and developed a small mainstream following. —*Will Grega*

● **Undressed** / 1993 / Lookout ✦✦✦✦
Sex punks tunefully and loudly wagging their penises and preferences about. The most successful track here is a departure for the band, the Byrds-influenced "Boyfriend Wanted." —*Will Grega*

○ **Deflowered** / 1994 / Lookout ✦✦✦✦

Pantera

Group, Heavy Metal
Pantera's massively brutal, aggressive, jagged heavy metal earned them a large cult following in the early '90s. During the early '80s, the band explored several different styles of hard rock; sometimes they sounded like Kiss and Aerosmith, others Def Leppard. After several years of struggling the band changed their tune in 1988, becoming rougher and harder, much like Metallica. Guitarist Diamond (aka "Dimebag") Darrell rejected an offer to join Megadeth, concentrating on Pantera's new direction. The change in style proved successful; 1992's *Vulgar Display of Power* became an underground metal hit, eventually scaling *Billboard's* Top 50. When their new album, *Far Beyond Driven*, was released in 1994, the band debuted at number one. Some chart-watchers were surprised, but anyone that followed their rise from obscurity to *Vulgar Display of Power* knew that Pantera was one of the most popular metal bands of the early '90s. —*Stephen Thomas Erlewine*

Power Metal / 1988 / Metal Magic ✦✦
○ **Cowboys from Hell** / 1990 / East West ✦✦✦✦
Technical thrash from Texas, this is the album that put them in the spotlight and opened the door for thrash bands who were a little different. —*John Book*

● **Vulgar Display of Power** / 1992 / East West ✦✦✦✦
A burning, disemboweling collection of brutal riffs, pulverizing speed, and hoarse, shouted vocals, *Vulgar Display of Power* is the record that established Pantera as the most vicious and popular heavy metal band of the early '90s. —*Stephen Thomas Erlewine*

Far Beyond Driven / 1994 / East West ✦✦✦
Far Beyond Driven finds Pantera in a bit of a holding pattern. Although the riffs are still lethally fast, the band shows no signs of musical development, and the songs aren't any better than those

on *Vulgar Display of Power*. Nevertheless, there's enough primal metal here to satisfy most of their fans. —*Stephen Thomas Erlewine*

Paramounts

Group, British Invasion
Were it not for the fact that three of the four Paramounts went on to form the nucleus of Procol Harum, this British R&B band would be totally forgotten today. Singer keyboardist Gary Brooker, guitarist Robin Trower, and drummer B.J. Wilson were all members of this group, which released six singles between 1963 and 1965. Drawing heavily upon R&B and soul classics like "Poison Ivy," "A Certain Girl," and "Bad Blood," the Paramounts were among the less original first-wave British bands. The group wrote little of their own material, and didn't leave a distinctive imprint on their covers. Brooker's vocals were soulful, but Trower was afforded little opportunity to stretch out on guitar, and their recordings offer no hints of the psychedelic and progressive rock of Procol Harum. —*Richie Unterberger*

● **Whiter Shades of R&B** / 1983 / Edsel ✦✦✦✦
16-song compilation hunts down every last scrap recorded by the band: both sides of their six singles, a cut released only on a French EP, and three previously unreleased tracks. The group professed dislike of the pop numbers thrust upon them by their record company in 1965, but Jackie DeShannon's "Blue Ribbons" and P.F. Sloan's "You Never Had It So Good" are actually among the more memorable tunes. It also includes a surprisingly interesting 1966 version of Charles Mingus' "Freedom" (unreleased until this reissue). A modestly enjoyable collection of mostly historical significance. —*Richie Unterberger*

Paris

Rap
This San Francisco rapper debuted in 1990 with *The Devil Made Me Do It* for Tommy Boy, then moved to the independent Scarface label with *Sleeping with the Enemy* in 1992. His fiercely Afrocentric themes were reminiscent of the Last Poets or Gil Scott-Heron, but didn't generate as much response as anticipated. They did cause lots of controversy in other circles however, leading to allegations of "reverse" racism. —*Ron Wynn*

Devil Made Me Do It / 1990 / Tommy Boy ✦✦✦
San Francisco rapper Paris's debut album featured several angry, Afrocentric numbers (the CD included four selections that didn't make it onto the vinyl LP, and two that weren't on the cassette). There was little here designed to make anyone feel good, and it was Paris, not Sister Souljah, who effectively described racism's impact on the psyche of oppressed people with his composition "Hate That Hate Made." —*Ron Wynn*

● **Sleeping with the Enemy** / 1993 / Scarface ✦✦✦✦
It took several months and a change of record labels before it was released, but Paris' *Sleeping With the Enemy* was the most incendiary political hip-hop album released since Ice Cube's *Death Certificate* in 1991. Paris' production may rely on beats that have been done before, but in no way does that detract from the strength of his militant rhymes or the controlled, vicious anger of the music. —*Stephen Thomas Erlewine*

○ **Guerrilla Funk** / 1994 / Scarface ✦✦✦✦
Guerrilla Funk wasn't quite as scathing as the previous *Sleeping with the Enemy*, but that's only a relative term. Paris hasn't tempered his rage at all, he's just expanded his range, adding more societal issues to his hit list. In addition, the music hasn't lost any of its potency, making *Guerrila Funk* a worthy match for one of the most incindieary hip-hop albums of the '90s. —*Stephen Thomas Erlewine*

Mica Paris

Urban
Though she has yet to attain stardom, English vocalist Mica Paris has a wonderful voice and individualistic delivery and approach. She sang in the Spirit of Watts gospel group before touring and recording in the late '80s with Hollywood Beyond. She signed with 4th and Broadway/Island in the '80s and then issued her debut *So Good*. Her second LP, *Contribution*, was released in 1990. Paris moved to Polydor for her third LP, *Whisper a Prayer*, in 1993. She also recorded with Will Downing in 1989, doing an updated version of "Where Is the Love." —*Ron Wynn*

So Good / 1988 / Island ✦✦✦
British songstress Mica Paris generated some excitement on both sides of the Atlantic with her debut album in 1988. Part of the buzz came from the fact that her tone, huge sound and approach were much more soul and R&B-oriented than the ultra-smooth and polished urban contemporary commonplace at the time. It also had some dance touches and was looser and more attractive than many of the releases coming from pop and disco divas. — *Ron Wynn*

● **Contribution** / 1990 / 4th & Broadway ✦✦✦✦
Despite improved production, even stronger vocals and some excellent material, Mica Paris didn't enjoy the same response with her second release that her debut enjoyed. She even ventured into New Jack territory, utilizing rappers Rakim and Danny D, and recorded some Prince material. But the set's best song, the sizzling "South Of The River," was a radio bust, and Paris simply couldn't get enough momentum generated to make the album a success. — *Ron Wynn*

Whisper a Prayer / Jun. 8, 1993 / Island ✦✦

Graham Parker

b. Nov. 15, 1950
Rock & Roll, Pop/Rock
Graham Parker is the quintessential angry young man; his early albums are full of righteous passion, vicious sarcasm, and great, powerful rock & roll. Graham Parker is also the quintessential bitter old man; while the occasional good song pops up here and there, his later albums are weighed down by petty anger, disgust, and frustration. But when he was at the top of his form in the late '70s, Parker was a singer/songwriter like no other. Backed by his superb band the Rumour, he turned out a series of clever, concise songs that bristled with energy; his songs drew heavily from R&B, rock & roll, and rockabilly without ever sounding dated. Parker's music sounded vital because of his unrestrained passion, as well as the way his lyrics and song structures redefined and subverted the traditions of the '50s and '60s.

Howlin Wind, his 1976 debut album, earned him scores of lavish critical praise, as did its follow-up, *Heat Treatment,* released the same year. In 1977, he formed the Rumour and released the inconsistent, but occasionally exceptional *Stick to Me.* Parker left Mercury in 1978, leading to his classic attack on the record label, "Mercury Poisoning"; the company rushed out a live album to fulfill his contract. With 1979's *Squeezing out Sparks* in 1979, Parker had made his finest record; again, he received an overwhelming amount of critical acclaim but no sales.

After *Squeezing out Sparks,* Parker began to sink into his own cynicism as he tried to refashion his sound for the mainstream marketplace; he had only one hit from the four albums he released between 1980 and 1985–"Wake Up (Next to You)" in 1985. Following that minor chart success, his songs became more direct, as shown by 1988's *The Mona Lisa's Sister,* the best thing he had released in years. It began a string of strong albums that were sometimes undone by his own relentless pessimism. By this time, the anger that fueled his early records had turned into mere bitterness. However, when Parker can keep his sniping to a minimum, he is as good as he has ever been. — *Stephen Thomas Erlewine*

☆ **Howlin Wind** / Jul. 1976 / Mercury ✦✦✦✦✦
Parker comes across as both tough-minded and optimistic (maybe the word is "determined") on his debut album, on which he sings with conviction against the cohesive backing of the Rumour. — *William Ruhlmann*

○ **Heat Treatment** / Oct. 1976 / Mercury ✦✦✦✦
Essentially *Howlin Wind—Vol. 2,* as Parker and the Rumour demonstrate that their initial burst of high-quality songs can extend to a second album, in the same year as their debut. — *William Ruhlmann*

Pink Parker / Mar. 1977 / Mercury ✦✦✦
This is a seven-inch EP, pressed on pink vinyl, containing Graham Parker and the Rumour's killer version of "Hold Back The Night." — *William Ruhlmann*

○ **Stick to Me** / Oct. 1977 / Mercury ✦✦✦✦
Graham Parker and the Rumour's third new studio album to be released in 18 months finds the bandleader running short of top-flight material; "Thunder And Rain" and "Watch The Moon Come Down" are up to his usual standards, but songs like "The Heat In Harlem" find him dangerously out of his depth. As a result, al-

though fiercely played, this star-crossed release (it had to be re-recorded when the first version suffered technical problems) is a cut below Parker's first two albums. — *William Ruhlmann*

The Parkerilla/Live / 1978 / Mercury ✦✦
This is an ill-conceived live album (probably put out as a contract breaker with Mercury) on which Graham Parker and the Rumour sing songs from the substandard *Stick to Me* album and even use up a whole side of the original two-LP version on a studio re-recording of "Don't Ask Me Questions." With this release, what had seemed like one of the most promising careers of the second half of the 1970s suddenly seemed to be on the rocks. — *William Ruhlmann*

○ **Mercury Poisoning** / Feb. 1979 / Arista ✦✦✦✦
This is a 12-inch promotional single containing Graham Parker and the Rumour's notorious explanation-in-song for the debacle of their career on Mercury Records. Complaining that he's "the best kept secret in the West," Parker condemns his former label in one of his catchiest songs ever. — *William Ruhlmann*

★ **Squeezing out Sparks** / Mar. 1979 / Arista ✦✦✦✦✦
Older and more bitter, Parker delves deeper into his demons, and the Rumour just plays harder. Parker's best album, and one of the best albums of the decade. — *William Ruhlmann*

○ **The Up Escalator** / May 1980 / Arista ✦✦✦✦
On his last album with the Rumour, Parker goes for mainstream rock success, employing the widescreen production style of Jimmy Iovine and such guests as Bruce Springsteen. It didn't sell, but it was a great try. — *William Ruhlmann*

○ **Another Grey Area** / Mar. 1982 / Razor & Tie ✦✦✦✦
Parker begins to make his peace with human imperfection (though he can still be sharp-tongued) and starts to look for love ("It's All Worth Nothing Alone"), backed by a smooth session band and a clean Jack Douglas production, which cool his usual fire without putting it out. — *William Ruhlmann*

The Real Macaw / Jul. 1983 / Razor & Tie ✦✦✦
Parker finds love, and manages to write about it without losing his usual wit ("Last Couple on the Dance Floor"). He also re-employs Rumour guitarist Brinsley Schwartz and goes back to the uptempo pub rock of his 70s albums. — *William Ruhlmann*

Steady Nerves / Mar. 1985 / Elektra ✦✦✦
Graham Parker moves to his third record label (following stints at Mercury and Arista), forms a backup band called the Shot (again led by guitarist Brinsley Schwarz) and continues alternately arguing with existence ("Break Them Down") and praising his romantic life ("Wake Up [Next To You]"). — *William Ruhlmann*

Mona Lisa's Sister / Apr. 1988 / RCA ✦✦
Graham Parker moves to his fourth record label (actually, his fifth, if you count Atlantic, which dumped him before releasing an album) for one of his less inspired efforts. When he sings "Get Started, Start A Fire," he seems to be talking to himself, and when he resorts to covering the old Sam Cooke hit "Cupid," he seems to be grasping for material. — *William Ruhlmann*

Live! Alone in America / Jul. 1989 / RCA ✦✦✦
Graham Parker's second commercially released live album is a solo affair that finds him connecting with his audience and singing a lot of his 1970s favorites. — *William Ruhlmann*

Human Soul / Jan. 1990 / RCA ✦✦
On *Human Soul,* Graham Parker begins to retreat further into his domestic life, writing an album that includes a side of romantic ruminations and a side of social commentary. With a band that comprises guitarist Brinsley Schwarz, bassist Andrew Bodnar, and Attractions Steve Nieve (keyboards) and Pete Thomas (drums), Parker's music is subtlely diverse, adding elements of worldbeat, reggae, pop, and folk to his R&B-fueled rock & roll; however, most of the impact of the music is lost by the slick, radio-ready production. When Parker stays at home on the first half of *Human Soul,* he makes his most impressive music, from the sultry come-ons of "Call Me Your Doctor" to the reassuring "My Love's Strong." He tends to lose his focus on the latter half of the record, when he writes about subjects that don't directly affect his homelife. Taken in conjunction with the self-conscious musical eclecticism, the lyrical stretches make *Human Soul* an intriguing, but flawed, record. — *Stephen Thomas Erlewine*

Struck by Lightning / Feb. 1991 / RCA ✦✦✦
Struck by Lightning was the culmination of Graham Parker's previous two records, where he increasingly began to chronicle domestic tasks and affairs of the married heart. For such an intimate

subject, Parker wisely decided to scale back the musical ambition of *Human Soul* on *Struck by Lightning*, recording a lean, stripped-down album that relies heavily on acoustic guitars. Appropriately, his lyrics were some of the most concise he has written in years, breathing life into tales like "The Kid With the Butterfly Net" and "Wrapping Paper." Parker's music is similarly simple and tuneful, making *Struck By Lightning* his best effort since the early '80s. —*Stephen Thomas Erlewine*

Burning Questions / Jul. 20, 1992 / Capitol ♦♦
After *Struck by Lightning*, Graham Parker was dropped by RCA Records. He moved to Capitol in 1992, releasing another installment in his musical diaries called *Burning Questions*. A more open and polished affair than the previous record, *Burning Questions* concentrates on broader issues than *Struck By Lightning*, yet the scope is similarly scaled-back. And it's clear from "Long Stem Rose," "Oasis," and "Mr. Tender" that his heart is with his home, not with the sputtering rage of "Here It Comes Again" and "Short Memories." —*Stephen Thomas Erlewine*

The Best of Graham Parker 1988-1991 / Sep. 1992 / RCA ♦♦♦
All of the highlights from Graham Parker's brief stint at RCA are here on this single-disc compilation. —*AMG*

Live Alone! Discovering Japan / 1993 / Demon ♦♦
Live Alone! Discovering Japan isn't all that different than *Live! Alone in America*. Parker runs through a set largely comprised of his classics, adding some newer material in for good measure. It's an engaging disc—he remains not only a convincing performer, but also somewhat of a showman, cracking jokes throughout the album—but it's only of interest to hardcore fans, who will find it a pleasant, but decidedly minor, addition to their collection. —*Stephen Thomas Erlewine*

○ **Passion Is No Ordinary Word: the Graham Parker Anthology 1976-1991** / Sep. 21, 1993 / Rhino ♦♦♦♦
With its smart song selection and entertaining liner notes, *Passion Is No Ordinary Word* is an excellent 2-CD anthology covering Parker's entire career, complete with such rarities as "Mercury Poisoning" and "I Want You Back (Alive)" among such signature songs as "White Honey" and "You Can't Be Too Strong." A terrific introduction to Parker's career. —*Stephen Thomas Erlewine*

12 Haunted Episodes / 1995 / Razor & Tie ♦♦♦
12 Haunted Episodes, Graham Parker's first album recorded for an independent label, is appropriately intimate and warm, recalling the simplicity of *Struck by Lightning*, but with a gentler approach. Parker makes no concessions to commerical radio on the record, dispensing with the slick productions that tended to plague his albums for the past decade or so. That doesn't mean the record is raw—it means that it's more personal and intimate. At its core, *12 Haunted Episodes* is not that different than Parker's records since *The Mona Lisa's Sister:* Most of the songs are love songs to his wife and daughter, or they're tales of an aging rebel, trying to keep his youthful fire alive as he grows older. However, the songs are measured and reflective, signalling that he's settling gracefully into his middle age. When Parker does get bitter—such as his attack on capitalism, "Disney's America"—it doesn't seem vengeful, it seems regretful, which helps make *12 Haunted Episodes* his most mature album to date. —*Stephen Thomas Erlewine*

Ray Parker, Jr.

b. May 1, 1954, Detroit, MI
Soul, Dance-Pop, Urban
Highly successful R&B vocalist through the 80s. His career peaked in 1984 with his monstrously popular movie theme "Ghostbusters." Born in Detroit, Parker built an enviable reputation as an ace Los Angeles session guitarist. He formed Raydio in 1977 and immediately hit with "Jack and Jill" on Artista, and his assured mid-tempo approach resulted in heavy pop airplay on "You Can't Change That" in 1979 and the 1981 R&B chart-topping "A Woman Needs Love (Just Like You Do)." Going solo the next year, Parker continued to rack up the sales for Arista, culminating with a gold record for "Ghostbusters," a #1 pop and R&B item. Parker continues to record in an urban contemporary vein. —*Bill Dahl*

The Other Woman / 1982 / Arista ♦♦♦
● **Greatest Hits** / 1982 / Arista ♦♦♦♦
It contains "The Other Woman," among his other hits, recorded both as a solo act and with Raydio. —*Dan Heilman*

Woman out of Contol / 1983 / Arista ♦♦
Chartbusters / 1984 / Arista ♦♦♦
A good anthology covering the pop/soul hits of Ray Parker, Jr. as a solo artist. Although a talented musician, songwriter, and producer, Parker will invariably be considered more of a novelty and trendy comic figure than anything else, since such songs as "Ghostbusters" are little more than happy fodder. His songs also had a kiddie-pop sensibility, even when he addressed romantic or serious issues. The fact that his voice always had a light, nasal sound didn't help matters. —*Ron Wynn*

After Dark / 1987 / David Geffen Co. ♦♦♦
This was the closest Ray Parker Jr. ever came to doing adult soul. His debut for Geffen included the song "I Don't Think That Man Should Sleep Alone." This was his last big hit, and despite the title, said some serious things about male/female intimacy and relationships. Parker's voice sounded more somber, introspective, and varied than on anything before or since. —*Ron Wynn*

I Love You Like You Are / 1991 / MCA ♦♦
Ray Parker, Jr.'s big hit days had faded by the time he switched labels to MCA in the early '90s. He made a comeback bid with this album, which had a heavy pop flavor. It did yield him a mild hit with "She Needs To Get Some," although it also generated a little controversy regarding the song's sexual/sexist direction. Parker's vocals were never great, but they seemed more weary than anything else. His past hits had succeeded with him striking either a bemused or a comical/teasing stance; now he sounded tired, detached, and even a little angry. —*Ron Wynn*

Robert Parker

b. Oct. 14, 1930, Crescent City, Louisiana
Soul, R&B
Parker's dance raver "Barefootin' " was one of the biggest hits to come out of New Orleans during the mid 60s. Parker played sessions as a saxophonist back in 1949 with the legendary pianist Professor Longhair, and his 1959 solo debut for Ron, "All Night Long," was a scorching two-part instrumental. But Parker's underutilized vocal talents suddenly emerged in 1966, when his highly infectious "Barefootin' " became a giant hit on tiny Nola. Only one other Parker single, "Tip Toe," charted the next year, but Parker remains a popular attraction in his hometown. —*Bill Dahl*

● **Barefootin'** / 1966 / Collectables ♦♦♦♦
Originally issued in 1987 on vinyl by England's Charly, this collection includes Parker's main claim to fame, the 1966 R&B and pop dance smash "Barefootin' "; its flip side, "Let's Go Baby (Where the Action Is)"; both sides of a 1969 single Parker cut for Silver Fox; and a number of '70s recordings the erstwhile sax player waxed for Sansu Enterprises. Much of the CD, including the title cut, is infectious New Orleans R&B of a high caliber, but other tracks find Parker attempting to cut mainstream funk and disco, usually with less-than-inspiring results. If possible, find the Charly release, because Collectables, in their typically shoddy manner, do not bother to provide songwriting credits, let alone track credits or liner notes. A good policy is to buy Collectables only if there is no other anthology of the same material issued anywhere else in the world, no matter what the price difference. —*Rob Bowman*

Van Dyke Parks

b. 1941
Singer-Songwriter, Experimental
Composer, arranger, producer, and musician Van Dyke Parks has had a varied career in popular music without ever getting near the popular mainstream. Parks worked as a songwriter in the early '60s and became a producer, handling such mid-'60s acts as Harper's Bizarre. He was enlisted by Brian Wilson to write lyrics for what turned out to be an abortive album project called *Smile* (now one of the legendary lost albums of the '60s), resulting in such songs as the hit "Heroes and Villains." Parks released his own album, the eclectic *Song Cycle*, to critical acclaim and minimal sales in 1968. He then did session work with a variety of artists, not releasing his second album, *Discover America*, which revealed his immersion in Trinidadian music, until 1972. *Clang of the Yankee Reaper*, another eclectic collection, followed in 1975. But Parks maintained his "day job"—film work on scores by Ry Cooder and others, writing and arranging for Shelley Duvall's children's TV series, and other pursuits. Finally, in 1984, came the brilliant *Jump!*, a concept album based on the Uncle Remus tales of Joel Chandler

Harris. It was followed in 1989 by *Tokyo Rose,* which concerned the state of American-Japanese relations. — *William Ruhlmann*

● **Song Cycle** / 1968 / Warner Brothers ✦✦✦✦
Parks demonstrated an audacious musical imagination on this debut album, which effectively deployed a full orchestra, along with electric instruments, balalaikas, accordions, and an "authentic folk choir," plus nature sounds and God knows what else to produce a unique soundscape. A unusual piece of music and a stunning accomplishment. — *William Ruhlmann*

○ **Discover America** / 1972 / Warner Brothers ✦✦✦✦
Parks turns to the music of Trinidad here, especially as it was heard in the '40s, which means tributes to "Bing Crosby" and "The Four Mills Bros.," not to mention "G-Man Hoover" and "FDR in Trinidad," played on steel drums and other indigenous instruments. A charming, idiosyncratic genre exercise. — *William Ruhlmann*

The Clang of Yankee Reaper / 1975 / Warner Brothers ✦✦✦
Expanding from the Caribbean approach he took with *Discover America,* Van Dyke Parks explores more arcane Americana on an album that ranges from New Orleans to the islands to the classics. Only the title track bears a co-composing credit for the artist, but Parks' exuberant, eclectic musical personality is the unifying force in an collection of music that varies from the Sandpipers' "Another Dream" to Pachelbel's "Canon In D." — *William Ruhlmann*

○ **Jump!** / Feb. 1984 / Warner Brothers ✦✦✦✦
An exhilarating song cycle based on the Uncle Remus tales. It incorporates the styles of Stephen Foster, ragtime, 30s movie-soundtrack music, you name it, all in the service of playful, touching lyrics that correspond to the source material, without actually aping it. A delight from start to finish. — *William Ruhlmann*

Tokyo Rose / Jul. 1989 / Warner Brothers ✦✦✦
One can hear "America" as played on a Japanese koto on this history of relations between East and West, which covers everything from the "Trade War" to baseball with Parks's typically eclectic and broad musical imagination. A charming album. — *William Ruhlmann*

Parliament

Group, Soul, Funk, R&B

Parliament started as a doo-wop group centered around a barber shop owned and operated by George Clinton in New Jersey in the late '50s. One 45 was released on the APT label before Clinton and company headed off to Detroit. Updating their sound to reflect the innovations of Motown, Parliament had a (#3 R&B/#20 pop) hit with "(I Wanna) Testify" for Revilot in 1967. Leaving Revilot before the group's contract had legally expired, Clinton lost the right to the name for a few years.

Putting his backup band up front, Clinton signed with Detroit's Westbound label and called the group Funkadelic. By 1971 Clinton regained title to the original name and shortened it to Parliament, while still recording as Funkadelic as well. Parliament's records tended to be more R&B dance-oriented, while Funkadelic leaned toward the psychedelic side of rock & roll.

Parliament was signed first to Invictus and then to Casablanca. In the mid and late '70s, they were at the forefront of funk music, playing crazed shows that included spaceships landing on stage and articulated Clinton's acid-tinged funk cosmology, where the pro-funk and anti-funk forces battled it out. Characters such as Sir Nose D'Void of Funk were routinely forced to give up the funk and dance at the end of Parliament's concerts. Hits included "Up for the Down Stroke," "Chocolate City," "Tear the Roof Off the Sucker (Give Up the Funk)," and "Flash Light." Group members included Fuzzy Haskins, Bernie Worrell, Bootsy Collins, Fred Wesley, Maceo Parker, Eddie Hazel, Gary Shider, and Michael Hampton. Offshoots included the P-Funk All-Stars, Bootsy's Rubber Band, the Brides of Funkenstein, Fred Wesley & the Horny Horns, and Parlet. — *Rob Bowman*

○ **Osmium** / 1970 / Invictus ✦✦
The first album issued by the group that was then known as the Parliaments. It was tame compared to what came later and was basically routine group soul and funk, although the Clinton wit still came to the fore at times. But its value has increased tremendously, and now no serious Parliament or Clinton fan can afford not to have it. — *Ron Wynn*

○ **Up for the Down Stroke** / 1974 / Casablanca ✦✦✦✦
The first album by Clinton's revamped Parliament remains a perfect introduction, although its best songs are on their *Greatest Hits.* — *John Floyd*

Chocolate City / 1975 / Casablanca ✦✦✦
The title track was a masterpiece, one of George Clinton's satirical triumphs. Whether you think it was a political work or not, everything clicked—the production, comic lead vocals, lyrics, and arrangements. The remainder of the album wasn't quite that strong, but was still excellent. It mixed every Clinton element: chaotic jamming, quirky outlook, hilarious vocals, and that sense of the casually absurd that Clinton championed. — *Ron Wynn*

○ **Clones of Dr. Funkenstein** / 1976 / Casablanca ✦✦✦✦
George Clinton had his otherworldly, controlled, chaotic vision well in gear for this album. He milked the Frankenstein notion, creating a mad scientist and sonically documenting his warped funk notions. Clinton got instrumental assistance from a crack corps that included keyboardist Bernie Worrell, saxophonist Maceo Parker and trombonist Fred Wesley, plus numerous vocalists, guitarists, and instrumentalists. The album went gold, although it wasn't as inspired or successful as *Mothership Connection.* But such songs as "Dr. Funkenstein," "I've Been Watching You (Move Your Sexy Body)," and "Everything Is On The One" were quintessential Parliament jams. — *Ron Wynn*

☆ **Mothership Connection** / 1976 / Casablanca ✦✦✦✦✦
This was *the* Parliament masterpiece. It mixed creative and clever satirical takeoffs on James Brown, Sly Stone and classic black radio with the kind of loose, inventive improvising seldom heard in R&B or soul circles. The narratives were swift and humorous and the music crackling, fast-moving and progressive. The title cut, "Tear The Roof Off The Sucker (Give Up The Funk)," and others marked the beginning of Clinton and Parliament/Funkadelic's evolution into national celebrities. — *Ron Wynn*

☆ **Funkentelechy Vs the Placebo Syndrome** / 1977 / Casablanca ✦✦✦✦
Funkentelechy Vs. the Placebo Syndrome offers an even better introduction to the group than the singles collection, by presenting the most intelligible and rhythmically unstoppable glimpse into Clinton's P-Funk world. — *John Floyd*

Live: P-Funk Earth Tour / 1977 / Casablanca ✦✦✦
One of the few live sets that accurately depict the flavor of an epic event. George Clinton's massive P-Funk tour, with all the spinoff groups and support personnel, gave some incredible shows in the late '70s. Concerts would last three to four hours and run together in an amazing display of controlled chaos. Songs were openended, the pace was nonstop, and it was much more like a ritual than a concert. This album perfectly conveyed the concert's feel and quality. — *Ron Wynn*

Motor Booty Affair / 1978 / Casablanca ✦✦✦
Another concept album, only this time the concept is about water and not being able to swim and not wanting to swim. This album is worth hearing, in spite of its occasional Frank Zappa-isms. — *John Floyd*

Gloryhallastoopid / 1979 / Casablanca ✦✦✦
Although at the time this album was viewed as a disaster, there has been some critical reassessment in the past years. It was certainly not as inspired, brilliantly executed or memorable as any one of many 1970s Parliament or Funkadelic gems, but it did have its own humorous/bizarre outlook. Clinton was being torn in many directions and plagued by money problems, so he didn't give it the attention it probably needed. Still, it deserves a revisit by Clinton fans who tossed it aside in disgust the first time around. — *Ron Wynn*

Trombipulation / 1980 / Casablanca ✦✦
The final album issued before Parliament temporarily disbanded. Clinton's empire was being besieged, and while he didn't completely lose his gifts, the impact could be heard on the album. The spontaneity, bizarre comic wit and wisdom, as well as the production and arranging greatness, weren't as evident. There were no epic jams, classic satirical numbers, or magnificent message tracks. Instead, it was more a worthy goodbye, one that fortunately hasn't been final. — *Ron Wynn*

○ **Greatest Hits (The Bomb)** / 1984 / Casablanca ✦✦✦✦
This is a solid if scanty assortment of their best singles. — *John Floyd*

★ **Tear the Roof Off** / May 18, 1993 / Casablanca ✦✦✦✦✦
Two discs of the hardest funk ever recorded, *Tear the Roof Off* is essential for both the casual fan and the hardcore collector. In addition to the presence of the full-length versions of all their hits, several 12" mixes make their first appearances on CD here. Without the music on *Tear the Roof Off*, contemporary music would not sound as it does today. —*AMG*

Live 1972-1993 / 1994 / Aem ✦✦
A scatter-shot multi-disc collection, *Live 1972-1993* provides a good overview of the number of incarnations of Parliament/Funkadelic, even if it is a bit too inconsistent to be essential listening. —*Stephen Thomas Erlewine*

★ **The Best of Parliament: Give Up the Funk** / 1995 / Mercury Funk Essentials ✦✦✦✦✦
Best of Parilament supplements *Greatest Hits (The Bomb)* by offering a better selection of tracks, as well as more songs. —*Stephen Thomas Erlewine*

Alan Parsons Project

Group, Art-Rock/Progressive-Rock
Engineer/producer Alan Parsons and his colleague, songwriter and lyricist Eric Woolfson, formed the Alan Parsons Project in 1975. Throughout their career, the Alan Parsons Project has recorded concept albums (including adaptations of Poe and Asimov books), with a revolving cast of session musicians. 1982's *Eye in the Sky* was their greatest success; the title track charted in the Top Ten on the pop charts and the album went platinum. Although they haven't been able to repeat that success, the group has maintained a devoted cult audience. —*AMG*

○ **Tales of Mystery & Imagination** / 1975 / Mercury ✦✦✦✦
This "project," led by former Beatles engineer Alan Parsons, was recorded at Abbey Road and featured a session group including Terry Sylvester and Arthur Brown (he of the "Crazy World"). It made its first and best album (if not its most popular one) by interpreting the ominous poems and stories of Edgar Allan Poe. Heavy on synthesized keyboards and dramatic choral parts, it's rock soundtrack music minus the film. The group went on to make a series of similar followups, notably including *I Robot* and *Eye in the Sky*, but this is the place to start. —*William Ruhlmann*

○ **I Robot** / Jun. 1977 / Arista ✦✦✦✦
The Alan Parsons Project was established as a top record-seller with *I, Robot*, their second album. Musically, the record continued the ideas of their debut. Thematically, the record was an exploration of the science fiction concept of a world run by machines and mechanized human beings, particularly robots. —*Daevid Jehnzen*

Pyramid / Jun. 1978 / Arista ✦✦✦
Even though it didn't break into the Top 10 like its predecessor *I, Robot*, *Pyramid* was another hit for the Alan Parsons Project, going gold and peaking at number 26. Thematically, it was an exploration of mystic mideastern myths and traditions, particularly pyramids and the like. —*Daevid Jehnzen*

Eve / Sep. 1979 / Arista ✦✦
Eve continued the Alan Parsons Project's string of best-selling albums, peaking at number 13 and going gold. Musically, it reiterated the group's first three records, while thematically it explored the perplexing nature of women. Although the concept is certainly intriguing, Parsons' lyrical outlook is rather cold, opening him to charges of misogyny. —*Daevid Jehnzen*

○ **The Turn of a Friendly Card** / Nov. 1980 / Arista ✦✦✦✦
The Turn of a Friendly Card was the Alan Parson Project's second straight number 13 album, but it proved more successful than either *Pyramid* or *Eve*, going platinum and spending over a year on the charts. Musically, the group had matured, offering intricate, carefully-crafted pop songs that were exacting in detail. Thematically, the record seemed to be their slightest effort to date, as it superficially explored the midieval ramifications of a card game. Dig a little deeper, however, and the record reveals itself to be a rumination about destiny versus the choice of self-determination. Features the hit, "Games People Play." —*Daevid Jehnzen*

○ **Eye in the Sky** / Jun. 1982 / Arista ✦✦✦✦
Eye in the Sky was the Alan Parsons Project's most successful record, peaking at number seven and going platinum, as the title track hit number three. Musically, it expanded the ideas of *Turn of a Friendly Card*, adding some softer edges and lusher textures; despite its hit single, *Eye in the Sky* worked better as a whole, not as

a series of songs. Thematically, the album was a snapshot of an Orwellian future, ruled by the all-seeing "Eye in the Sky," who watches over its populace with a calm, menacing glee. —*Daevid Jehnzen*

● **The Best of the Alan Parsons Project** / 1983 / Arista ✦✦✦✦
Although the Alan Parsons Project is a quintessential album-rock act, their most effective statements were made on singles, and this collection features their best songs, including "Eye in the Sky" and "Games People Play." —*Stephen Thomas Erlewine*

Ammonia Avenue / Feb. 1984 / Arista ✦✦✦
While it wasn't as successful as *Eye in the Sky*, *Ammonia Avenue* was yet another gold album for the Alan Parsons Project—even if it would turn out to be their last. Like the lilting single "Don't Answer Me," the album is filled with meticulously-crafted, synthesized textures that straddle the line between conceptually sweeping art rock and smooth, accessible pop. Thematically, *Ammonia Avenue* is the most simple and streamlined album the group recorded, as it explored the decaying relations between the genders, as well as the rapidly deteriorating situations between people in general, as the modern world spins out of control, snapping off ties and relations between humans. However, Parsons and Woolfson offer a glimmer of hope with "Ammonia Avenue," which is where all the unvarnished answers lie. —*Daevid Jehnzen*

Vulture Culture / Mar. 1985 / Arista ✦✦
As the title suggests, *Vulture Culture* explores the tendencies the modern world has to feed off of each other, circling around for the losers, since you either "use it or you lose it." Musically, it's a bit tougher and more ambitious than *Ammonia Avenue*, though it basically reiterates the same themes as its predecessor, only in a more abstract way. —*Daevid Jehnzen*

Stereotomy / Nov. 1985 / Arista ✦✦
According to the Random House Dictionary, "stereotomy" is the technique of cutting solids, as stones, to specified forms and dimensions. On their album *Stereotomy*, the Alan Parsons Project paints a portrait of a man that has been cut into a specific shape according to the demands of society, as he thirsts after the "Limelight" but is consigned to "Urbania" and relies on "Beaujolais" to ease the pain. Most of the album is devoted to long, sweeping instrumental passages which makes the album one of the group's most ambitious records, but not one of their most accessible. —*Daevid Jehnzen*

Gaudi / 1987 / Arista ✦✦
One of Alan Parsons' most personal albums, *Gaudi* is a meditative tribute/biography of the life of Antonio Gaudi, a Catalan architect. Gaudi's most ambitious and elaborate work was the Sagrada Familia Cathedral is Barcelona, which included in its architecture a timetable which was designed to run for hundreds of years; he is buried in this cathedral, which was never finished. Fortunately, Alan Parsons was able to finish *Gaudi*, and it is breathtaking in its scope, if not in its accomplishment. Although the group does some amazing things musically, it doesn't quite work as a coherent album, which may be the reason it was one of the group's least commercially successful efforts. —*Daevid Jehnzen*

○ **The Best of the Alan Parsons Project, Vol. 2** / 1988 / Arista ✦✦✦✦
The Alan Parsons Project didn't have as many hits between 1983 and 1988 as they did between 1976 and 1983, so the task of compiling a second volume of greatest hits was somewhat difficult. Instead of conquering this problem head on, the compilers ignore it, choosing a selection of album tracks from the group's first six albums as well as adding the hit "Don't Answer Me" and several tracks from *Stereotomy*, *Vulture Culture*, and *Ammonia Avenue*. It's an effective sampler of some of their more ponderous work. —*Daevid Jehnzen*

The Instrumental Works / 1988 / Arista ✦✦
Part of the charm of the Alan Parsons Project was always their gumption, how they dared to make albums that were linked together both by their synth-driven art-rock but also by their lyrics, which almost always told a story. *Instrumental Works* selects all the instrumentals from their concept albums. Since these songs had a place on the original albums in their original sequence, they don't quite make as much sense on a different disc. Even so, the group shows its musical dexterity on these pieces. —*Daevid Jehnzen*

Try Anything Once / Oct. 26, 1993 / Arista ✦✦✦

Gram Parsons (Cecil Ingram Connor)

b. Nov. 5, 1946, Winterhaven, FL, **d.** Sep. 19, 1973, Joshua Tree, CA
Country-Rock

Parsons is considered the founder of country-rock. Like Hank Williams, Parsons lived hard and died young, but not before leaving behind a fine recorded legacy. This included stints with the International Submarine Band, the Byrds, the Flying Burrito Brothers, and finally as a solo artist. Parsons strove to break down the barriers between country and rock. He stripped country music down to its basics, while making its concerns more contemporary. For his two solo albums on Reprise, he is backed up by, among others, Elvis Presley's band and Emmylou Harris. The duets with Harris are superb. Harris has since gone on to re-record most of Parsons's material on her solo albums. His influence has also been acknowledged by the Rolling Stones, Elvis Costello, Dwight Yoakam, and Rodney Crowell. In his field, Parsons is the artist all others must be measured against. His music fits comfortably into any rock or country fan's collection. —*Kenneth M. Cassidy*

Gram Parsons Int Sub Band (Safe at Home) / 1967 / Shiloh ✦✦✦
Safe at Home represents some of Gram Parsons' earliest recordings as a part of the International Submarine Band. Arguably the first country-rock album, this more than hints at Parsons' greatness to come. This charming document is essential listening. —*Chris Woodstra*

★ **G.P./Grievous Angel** / 1973 / Reprise ✦✦✦✦✦
Parson's two best albums appear on one compact disc. Seeking to synthesize his own ideas with those of classic country and rock, Parsons hired Merle Haggard's recording engineer (he had approached Haggard himself about producing) and members of Elvis Presley's band, including pianist Glen D. Hardin and guitarist James Burton. The result had its roots in everything but sounded like nothing else. Parson's songs were the musings of a wounded soul, and his taste in others' material ran from Harlan Howard to the J. Geils Band. On *Grievous Angel*, Emmylou Harris emerges from the background to provide an angelic foil for Parsons's lost folkie voice. —*Brian Mansfield*

Sleepless Nights / 1976 / A&M ✦✦✦
Sleepless Nights is a collection of unreleased Gram Parsons material recorded while he was in the Flying Burrito Brothers. Most of the material are covers, yet the selection demonstrates how Parsons closed the gap between rock and country. —*Stephen Thomas Erlewine*

○ **Gram Parsons & the Fallen Angels** / 1981 / Sierra ✦✦✦✦
A good live document of Parsons's last tour, it was recorded at radio station WLIR in New York. —*Kenneth M. Cassidy*

○ **Warm Evenings, Pale Mornings, Bottled Blues** / 1992 / Raven ✦✦✦✦
Although all of Parson's albums are essential, this import-only collection provides an excellent sampling of his entire career including his stints with the Shilos, the International Submarine Band, the Byrds (complete with Parsons' vocals restored), the Flying Burrito Brothers, and the solo years. —*Chris Woodstra*

BOOK

✦✦✦✦ **Gram Parsons: A Musical Biography**, by Sid Griffin (Sierra, 1985). As the title implies, this focuses on the music, not the sometimes volatile personal life, of the country-rock innovator. Griffin, a member of the '80s alternative folk-country-rock group the Long Ryders, provides the narrative links between the essence of the volume, which consists of several interviews, both brief and indepth. These cover quite a few bases: Jim Stafford (of "Spiders and Snakes" fame, who played with Parsons in high school), Paul Surratt (from the Shilos, Gram's first professional band), Jon Nuese (guitarist for the International Submarine Band), Peter Fonda (for whom Parsons wrote a 1967 single), Kim Fowley, and Emmylou Harris, as well as reprints of interviews with Gram himself. Especially valuable is the mammoth interview with ex-Byrd and Flying Burrito Brother Chris Hillman, Parsons's closest musical collaborator. Lots of fine vintage photos, though the worshipful tone of Griffin's text could have used some editing. —*Richie Unterberger*

Billy Paul

b. Dec. 1, 1934, Philadelphia, PA
Soul

Billy Paul had a good run in the '70s as an R&B vocalist, though he'd been recording since the '50s, when he debuted on Jubilee. Paul was featured on radio broadcasts in Philadelphia at age 11, and had an extensive jazz background. He worked with Dinah Washington, Miles Davis, and Roberta Flack, as well as Charlie Parker, before forming a trio and recording for Jubilee. His original 1959 recording of "Ebony Woman" for New Dawn was later re-recorded for Neptune as the title of his 1970 LP. He signed the next year with Philadelphia International, and scored his biggest hit with "Me & Mrs. Jones" in 1972, topping both the R&B and pop charts. Paul had one other Top Ten R&B single, "Thanks for Saving My Life," in 1974. He remained on Philadelphia International until the mid-'80s. Paul recorded one LP for Total Experience in 1985, *Lately,* and another for Ichiban before announcing his retirement in 1989 in London. But he's since done several club dates, both in America and overseas. —*Ron Wynn*

Ebony Woman / 1970 / Epic ✦✦✦
Billy Paul originally recorded "Ebony Woman" in 1959, but it didn't make much noise. It served as the title track for a good, though uneven, mid-'70s release. Paul never equaled the success of "Me & Mrs. Jones," but was a consistent attraction for Philadelphia International in the early '70s. His albums used the same formula as this one—some adult ballads, one or two dance-oriented tunes, and some in-between numbers that tapped his background as a jazz singer but weren't done in such a sophisticated manner that they angered the R&B faithful. —*Ron Wynn*

○ **Going East** / 1971 / Philadelphia International ✦✦✦✦

● **360 Degrees of Billy Paul** / 1972 / Philadelphia International ✦✦✦✦
This jazzy soul set includes his hit "Me & Mrs. Jones." —*Bil Carpenter*

War of the Gods / 1973 / Philadelphia International ✦✦✦
Billy Paul got reasonably good mileage out of this album, which never had any huge hits but remained on both the pop and R&B charts for several weeks and got good album cut radio airplay. It was well sung, done in stylish and soulful fashion, and had one good message song in "Am I Black Enough For You." It was Paul's second R&B hit and a good followup to "Me & Mrs. Jones." —*Ron Wynn*

Feelin' Good at the Cadillac Club / 1973 / Gamble ✦✦
Although Billy Paul actually recorded this in the early '70s, the company didn't issue it until he already had a couple of successful releases under his belt because of its jazz direction and flavor. It was one of three Paul albums released in 1973, his biggest year as an artist. Paul might have been successful in jazz; if he emerged in the '80s or '90s doing this kind of supper-club/cabaret fare, he would immediately be routed into the adult contemporary and Quiet Storm market and probably be a huge hit. —*Ron Wynn*

Billy Paul Live in Europe / 1974 / Philadelphia International ✦✦
Former jazz vocalist Billy Paul found R&B success in the '70s on Philadelphia International doing a mix of anguished ballads, sophisticated originals, and reworked standards. But Paul was not a great live vocalist either as a jazz or soul singer, something that was evident on this mid-'70s set. No matter how polished or well-rehearsed the backing band, Paul's flaws couldn't be covered as smoothly in a concert setting, and they're revealed along with his strengths—timing, a good delivery, and decent range and interpretative skills. —*Ron Wynn*

Got My Head on Straight / 1975 / Philadelphia International ✦✦✦

When Love Is New / 1975 / Philadelphia International ✦✦✦

● **Greatest Hits** / 1983 / Philadelphia International ✦✦✦✦

Pavement

Group, Alternative Pop/Rock

With their fractured songs, unexpected blasts of feedback, laconic vocals, cryptic lyrics, and defiant low-fidelity, Pavement is one of the most influential and distinctive bands to emerge from the American underground in the '90s. For several years before their first full-length album, the group had been releasing a series of singles and EPs on small, obscure labels. During this period, Pavement was essentially a studio project featuring guitarists/vocalists Stephen Malkmus and Scott Kannberg.

By the time of Pavement's first album, 1992's *Slanted & Enchanted*, Malkmus and Kannberg had added drummer Gary Young to the lineup. *Slanted & Enchanted* took the world of rock criticism by storm; before the album was even available promotionally, critics were lavishly praising it. Initially, the band's following was based more on the press instead of word of mouth, but soon word began to spread on the street as well as in the magazines. During 1992, a permanent lineup of Pavement was established, as the group added bassist Mark Ibold and percussionist Bob Nastanovich.

Before Pavement recorded their second album, the band kicked Gary Young out of the group, due to his erratic behavior and performances; he was replaced by Steve West. Pavement's second album, 1994's *Crooked Rain, Crooked Rain*, saw the band toning down its extreme sonics for a laidback record that emphasized songs over sound. The album helped the band consolidate its position as alternative stars and critic's darlings, as well as expanding their cult; they charted in the lower reaches of *Billboard*'s Top 200 Album chart and had an alternative rock hit with "Cut Your Hair."

The following year, Pavement released their third album, sprawling *Wowee Zowee*. It was the first album that featwhich debuted higher than *Crooked Rain* in the charts without the benefit of an alternative radio or MTV hit single on the level of "Cut Your Hair." In the summer of 1995, the group toured with Lollapalooza. — *Stephen Thomas Erlewine*

★ **Slanted & Enchanted** / May 1992 / Matador ✦✦✦✦✦
Slanted & Enchanted is like listening to a college radio station that you can barely tune in—melodies are interrupted by shards of white noise, only to have several "sha-la-la's" bring it back into focus. — *Stephen Thomas Erlewine*

Watery, Domestic / Nov. 1992 / Matador ✦✦✦
Released between *Slanted & Enchanted* and *Crooked Rain, Crooked Rain*, the *Watery, Domestic* EP captures Pavement in a transitional phase, as the band began to abandon the static-laden guitar-rock of their early recordings and started to move toward a cleaner sound. Most of the innovations of *Watery, Domestic* have to do with recording techniques, yet the songs are certainly fine. The cleaner production brings Pavement's inherent fractured melodicism into sharper focus, which benefits "Texas Never Whispers," the wistful "Frontwards," and the bright, nearly jangly "Shoot the Singer," but the slow grind of "Lions (Linden)" would have been mesmerising irregardless of the production, or the lack of it. — *Stephen Thomas Erlewine*

Westing (by Musket & Sextant) / 1993 / Drag City ✦✦✦
A collection of all of Pavement's low-fidelity early singles and EPs, which feature considerably less melody than *Slanted & Enchanted*. It's nice to have this rare material on one CD, although the music is defiantly anti-CD. Those who boarded the train with the acclaimed *Slanted & Enchanted* should catch up on what they've missed. — *Stephen Thomas Erlewine*

○ **Crooked Rain, Crooked Rain** / 1994 / Matador ✦✦✦✦
Although it's much calmer than the critically acclaimed *Slanted & Enchanted*, *Crooked Rain, Crooked Rain* shares the same spirit of the band's debut—it's a messy, impossibly catchy catalog of pop music and culture. On their second full-length album, Pavement have abandoned much of the low-fi squalor of their earlier work, opting for a laidback, subdued sound that borders on country-rock and jazz-rock at times, and pure pop and rock & roll at others. In other words, it's more accessible than *Slanted & Enchanted* but just as distinctive and original. Ultimately, *Crooked Rain, Crooked Rain* revamps rock history and reinvents it for the slacker generation. — *Stephen Thomas Erlewine*

○ **Wowee Zowee** / 1995 / Matador ✦✦✦✦
With its vast array of musical styles, *Wowee Zowee* isn't as accessible as *Crooked Rain, Crooked Rain* or as immediate as the bracing, noisy pop of *Slanted & Enchanted*. Pavement never abandon their warped pop aesthetic, they simply expand it, incorporating elements of folk-rock, English music-hall, soul, jazz, country, as well as adding asides to such contemporaries as Suede ("We Dance"), Ween ("Brinx Job") and Stereolab ("Half a Canyon"). Alternating between majestic epics like "Grounded" and ragged narratives like "Rattled by the Rush" and "Father to a Sister of Thought," to song fragments like "Brinx Job" and the punkish "Serpentine Pad," the record might seem disjointed at first. After repeated listens, the songs play off each other, creating a dense collage of '90s rock & roll that recasts the past and present into one rich, kalidescopic and blissfully cryptic world view. — *Stephen Thomas Erlewine*

Freda Payne

b. Sep. 19, 1945, Detroit, MI
Soul
A Detroit soul/jazz/pop vocalist. Multitalented and beautiful, Payne crashed the soul and pop playlists in 1970 with a series of powerful sides for Holland-Dozier-Holland's Invictus imprint. Payne's early musical experience was quite varied, and she debuted on the jazz-oriented Impulse! label in 1965. Her 1970 blockbuster, "Band of Gold," made Payne a pop star with its strident message and insistent bassline, and she encored with "Deeper & Deeper." The controversial antiwar anthem "Bring the Boys Home" proved her biggest R&B seller the next year. Payne hosted a TV gabfest during the '80s. — *Bill Dahl*

○ **Band of Gold** / 1970 / HDH ✦✦✦✦
The title track was Payne's first number one hit, and it still has a jubilant, celebratory feel 23 years later. She had a smooth, polished, trained voice, shaped by her years as a jazz singer. The Holland/Dozier/Holland team recreated her as a pop/soul vocalist, carefully producing, arranging, and writing her material to allow the soft and sophisticated qualities emerge and yet also strike some chords among fans who wanted fire and soul. This was their greatest success. — *Ron Wynn*

Contact / 1971 / Invictus ✦✦✦
Freda Payne's second Invictus album was a significant success, making it onto the pop charts. She found her niche in the early '70s, doing silky, sophisticated pop/soul with excellent production, arrangements, and material supplied by the Holland/Dozier/Holland team. They wisely didn't try to make her a sassy or hard-edged vocalist, putting her voice in string and horn-dominated charts and emphasizing her soothing, lightly sensual side. — *Ron Wynn*

Freda Payne / 1974 / MGM ✦✦✦
Payne's brand of glossy pop/soul clicked when she got the right material; even when she didn't, Payne's experience and training as a jazz vocalist made her performances interesting, and that was the case on this collection. The songs are even smoother and more cabaret- and supper-club-oriented than her hits, and show Payne carefully pacing songs, interpreting lyrics, and displaying a soft, yet emphatic vocal style. — *Ron Wynn*

● **Greatest Hits** / 1991 / HDH ✦✦✦✦
Payne, an old childhood friend of Holland and Dozier, had already worked with Pearl Bailey, Duke Ellington, and Quincy Jones when she signed to Hot Wax/Invictus. Her biggest claim to fame was the number three hit "Band of Gold," which eventually sold more than five million copies. Interestingly, Payne was reluctant to do the song. She garnered some moderate successes with the followup singles, "Deeper and Deeper" and "Cherish What Is Dear to You," but her heartfelt plea to end the Vietnam War, "Bring the Boys Home," hit a nerve with the public and became a number 12 hit. — *Rick Clark*

Peaches & Herb

Group, Soul, Pop/Rock
The sweet harmonies of two different women billed as Peaches allowed Herb Fame to bridge the 60s soul era and 70s disco days resulting in major hits for Peaches & Herb in both decades. The original pairing—Fame and Francine Barker—burst onto the soul scene in 1966 with the charming "Let's Fall in Love" on Columbia's Date subsidiary. Covers of the Five Keys's "Close Your Eyes" and Ed Townsend's "For Your Love" gave the duo two sizable R&Bers the next year. By the turn of the decade, the original Peaches & Herb were hit-making history, but after an extended hiatus, Fame considered Linda Green to be ripe for the picking as his new Peaches, and they actually bettered the earlier incarnation in sales. "Shake Your Groove Thing" went gold on Polydor in 1978, and the cooing, slow-dance classic "Reunited" went platinum the following year, topping both the R&B and pop lists. — *Bill Dahl*

Let's Fall in Love / 1967 / Date ✦✦✦
The first of two albums by the duo Peaches and Herb issued in 1967. This debut LP started slowly as the title track got good response, then exploded when the songs "For Your Love" and "Close Your Eyes" became huge soul hits and even attracted some pop attention. They continued rolling along until 1970, when Barker left to get married. Fame was left without a partner until 1975, when McCoy arranged for Fame to meet and work with Linda Green, reviving Peaches and Herb. — *Ron Wynn*

○ **For Your Love** / 1967 / Date ✦✦✦✦
The original Peaches and Herb, former sales assistant Herb Fame and vocalist Francine Barker, were teamed by Van McCoy. Their debut album sounded a bit trite at times, but was redeemed by a couple of wonderful duets. This was their second album of 1967, rushed out to keep the momentum going from the response to the two chart hits from their debut. They remained hot with an entertaining version of "Love Is Strange," which had sparkling production and nice harmonies. —*Ron Wynn*

● **Sweethearts Of Soul** / 1994 / Original Sound ✦✦✦✦

● **Peaches & Herbs' Greatest Hits** / Epic ✦✦✦✦
A vinyl collection of the lovey-dovey DC duo's late-'60s finest, this includes "Reunited" and "Let's Fall in Love." —*Bill Dahl*

Pearl Jam

Group, Alternative Pop/Rock, Hard Rock
Pearl Jam rose from the ashes of Mother Love Bone to become the most popular American rock & roll band of the '90s. After vocalist Andrew Wood overdosed on heroin, guitarist Stone Gossard and bassist Jeff Ament assembled a new band, bringing in Mike McCready on lead guitar, Dave Krusen on drums, and vocalist Eddie Vedder. Naming themselves Pearl Jam, the band recorded their debut album, *Ten*, in the beginning of 1991. *Ten* didn't begin selling in significant numbers until early 1992, after Nirvana made mainstream rock radio receptive to alternative rock acts. Soon, Pearl Jam outsold Nirvana, which wasn't surprising. Pearl Jam fused the riff-heavy stadium rock of the '70s with the grit and anger of '80s post-punk, without ever neglecting hooks and choruses; "Jeremy," "Evenflow," and "Alive" fit perfectly into album rock radio stations that were looking for new blood.

Krusen left the band shortly after the release of *Ten;* he was replaced by Dave Abbruzzese. Pearl Jam's audience continued to grow during 1992, thanks to a series of radio and MTV hits, as well as a successful appearance on the second Lollapalooza tour. Despite their status as rock & roll superstars, the band refused to succumb to the accepted conventions of the msuci industry. The group refused to release any videos or singles from their second album, 1993's *Vs.* Nevertheless, it was another multi-platinum success, debuting at number one and selling nearly a million copies in its first week of release. On their spring 1994 American tour, the band decided not to play the conventional stadiums, choosing to play smaller arenas, including several shows on college campuses.

Pearl Jam cancellled their 1994 summer tour, claiming they could not keep ticket prices below twenty dollars because Ticketmaster was pressuring promoters to charge a higher price. The band took Ticketmaster to the judicial department for unfair business practices. As the band fought Ticketmaster, they recorded a new album in the spring and summer of 1994. After the record was completed, the group fired Dave Abbruzzese, replacing him with former Red Hot Chili Peppers and Eleven drummer Jack Irons

Vitalogy, the band's third album, was appeared at the end of 1994. For the first two weeks, the album was only available on as a limited vinyl-only release, but the record charted in the Top 60. Once *Vitalogy* was available on CD and cassette, the album shot to the top of the charts and quickly became multi-platinum. Pearl Jam continued to battle Ticketmaster in 1995, but the Justice Department eventually ruled in favor of the ticket agency. In early 1995, the band recorded an album with Neil Young. Vedder toured with his experimental side project Hovercraft in the spring of 1994 as Stone Gossard founded an independent record company. Mad Season, Mike McCready's side-project with Layne Staley of Alice in Chains, released their first album, *Above*, in the spring of 1995.Comprised entirely of Neil Young songs, *Mirror Ball* appeared in the summer under Young's name; although the individual members of the band were credited, the name Pearl Jam did not appear on the cover due to legal complications. —*Stephen Thomas Erlewine*

★ **Ten** / 1992 / Epic Associated ✦✦✦✦✦
The first Seattle band to hit the big time after Nirvana, Pearl Jam was not anyone's pick to be successful. Yet, Pearl Jam's brand of hard rock made them more accessible than any other Seattle band, including Nirvana. Pearl Jam's music is not as confused as Mudhoney, as melodic as Nirvana, as menacing as Alice In Chains, or as bloated as Soundgarden. *Ten* is remarkably clear-headed and

clean, and very politically correct—a perfect soundtrack for the 1990s. The muscular, melodic rock of "Jeremy," "Alive," and "Evenflow" brought Pearl Jam crossover success, helping *Ten* climb into the Top Ten and sell over nine million copies. —*Stephen Thomas Erlewine*

○ **Vs.** / 1993 / Epic Associated ✦✦✦
On the first listen, it appears that Pearl Jam's second album has no songs as instantly stunning as the best songs on *Ten*, but after a couple of plays, *Vs.* reveals its strengths. Instead of copying *Ten*'s signature clear, dark hard rock, *Vs.* is rawer and more open, with a number of different textures. From the pulverizing assault of "Go," "Animal," and "Leash" to the folkier, more reflective "Daughter," "Elderly Woman Behind the Counter in a Small Town," and "Indifference," Pearl Jam proves that their initial success was no fluke. Occasionally, the band falls into treacherous politically correct waters (the silly "Glorified G" and the meandering "W.M.A."), but for most of the album, Pearl Jam locks hold, and the best results are riveting. —*Stephen Thomas Erlewine*

○ **Vitalogy** / 1994 / Epic Associated ✦✦✦✦
Thanks to its stripped-down, lean production, *Vitalogy* stands as Pearl Jam's most original and uncompromising album. While it isn't a concept album, *Vitalogy* sounds like one. Death and despair shroud the album, rendering even the explosive celebration of vinyl "Spin the Black Circle" somewhat muted. But that black cloud works to Pearl Jam's advantage, injecting a nervous tension to brittle rockers like "Last Exit" and "Not For You," and especially introspective ballads like "Corduroy" and "Better Man." In between the straight rock numbers and the searching slow songs, Pearl Jam contributes their strangest music—the mantra-funk of "Aye Davanita," the sub-Tom Waits accordion romp of "Bugs" and the chilling sonic collage "Hey Foxymophandlemama, That's Me." Pearl Jam are at their best when they're fighting, whether it's TicketMaster, fame, or their own personal demons. —*Stephen Thomas Erlewine*

Ann Peebles

b. Apr. 27, 1947, St. Louis, MO
Soul
Ann Peebles was the queen of Willie Mitchell's Memphis-based Hi Records roster during the '70s, when Al Green was its undisputed king. Sung in a voice as bittersweet as it is riveting, her always-dramatic recordings include one undisputed masterpiece, "I Can't Stand the Rain," cited as a favorite by John Lennon and most recently covered by Tina Turner. Other covers abound—Robert Palmer took "I'm Gonna Tear Your Playhouse Down," and Bette Midler claimed "Breakin' Up Somebody's Home." Backed by the brilliant Hi rhythm section and flawlessly produced by Mitchell, Peebles sang and wrote (often in partnership with husband Don Bryant) of the feminine perspective on the darker side of love—sometimes untrusting love, but love, for better or worse. Her work represents, with elegance and grit, some of the best of Memphis soul.

After a long absence from recording, Ann Peebles returned to the wars with the CD *Full Time Love* in 1992 for Bullseye/Rounder. While it didn't get much exposure or recognition in urban circles, it was a wonderfully sung and well-produced attempt at giving Peebles some contemporary tweaking without losing her gritty qualities. —*Christine Ohlman and Ron Wynn*

This Is / 1969 / Hi ✦✦

Straight / 1970 / Hi ✦✦✦

○ **Part Time Love** / 1971 / Hi ✦✦✦✦
The title track was a masterpiece, and everything else on this dynamic early '70s soul session is a jewel. Ann Peebles may have been the most overlooked great soul singer, male or female, who emerged in the '70s. Hi couldn't strike crossover gold twice, and Al Green was becoming a superstar. But Peebles deserved a better fate than obscurity, as this collection of soul wailers and weepers proves. —*Ron Wynn*

○ **Straight from the Heart** / 1972 / Hi ✦✦✦✦

○ **I Can't Stand the Rain** / 1974 / Hi ✦✦✦✦
The title song was an instant classic, and its lyrics are among the most moving and gripping in soul annals. This was Ann Peebles' finest album for Hi Records, and it should have been a massive success. Instead, while it's celebrated in Europe and now considered an anthem, it floundered and barely scraped the pop charts, although the single was her biggest R&B hit. It's sad and ridicu-

lous that the only Ann Peebles session presently available on CD is the one she did for Bullseye Blues in '92. —*Ron Wynn*

○ **If This Is Heaven** / 1978 / Hi ✦✦✦✦
Another exceptional album by Ann Peebles, who was cutting remarkable records for Hi in Memphis that no one noticed except for deep soul junkies. Her voice was alternately anguished, angry, defiant, and resigned, while Willie Mitchell and the Hi Rhythm Section provided minimal, yet spectacular backing. Peebles seldom toured, preferring to stay in Memphis around her family. But she had a voice only surpassed among female soul vocalists by Aretha Franklin and equalled by Carla Thomas. —*Ron Wynn*

Handwriting Is on the Wall / 1979 / Hi ✦✦✦
Some fabulous down-home, earthy soul from Ann Peebles, a Southern treasure. Peebles was the finest female singer to pass through the Hi Records operation, and Willie Mitchell achieved with her the same kind of wonderful records he made with Al Green, although they didn't get identical commercial success. Any and all of the albums Ann Peebles did with Hi are classics; sadly, most of them haven't been reissued. —*Ron Wynn*

● **Ann Peebles' Greatest Hits** / MCA ✦✦✦✦
Backed by the vaunted Hi rhythm section and produced by Willie Mitchell, this includes her original "Come to Mama" and "I Can't Stand the Rain." These are classics of the '70s Memphis soul idiom. —*Bill Dahl*

Teddy Pendergrass

b. Mar. 26, 1950
Soul, Urban
In 1970, Pendergrass joined Harold Melvin and the Blue Notes as their drummer and lead vocalist; he sang on all of the group's Top 40 hits. Pendergrass left the group in 1976 and scored eight Hot 100 hits before he suffered an auto accident that left him partially paralyzed. He made a comeback two years later with *Heaven Only Knows*, which did not fare all that well commercially despite "Hold Me," a Top 50 duet with a young Whitney Houston. Subsequent albums also did not sell particularly well. —*Stephen Thomas Erlewine*

○ **Teddy Pendergrass** / 1977 / Philadelphia International ✦✦✦✦
The skeptics had their suspicions allayed quickly when Teddy Pendergrass' debut album as a solo singer cracked the Top 40. Its lead single, "I Don't Love You Anymore," was among his best uptempo tunes, and the followup ballad "The Whole Town's Laughing At Me" ended any speculation that he was returning to Harold Melvin & The Blue Notes. While many thought the album would launch him to consistent R&B success, almost no one thought he would be R&B's biggest male star in a couple of years. —*Ron Wynn*

○ **Life Is a Song Worth Singing** / 1978 / Philadelphia International ✦✦✦✦
This was the album that convinced anyone who had doubts about the wisdom of Pendergrass leaving Harold Melvin and The Blue Notes that he had made a good decision. Although he only got one R&B hit from the album, there were enough strong ballads and uptempo cuts to show that Pendergrass had the sound, personality, and style to cut it on his own. He would shortly become R&B's greatest male attraction, but in the interim, Philadelphia International was laying the ground work. —*Ron Wynn*

Teddy Live / 1979 / Philadelphia International ✦✦
Until his tragic auto accident, Teddy Pendergrass was the number one male attraction on the R&B and urban contemporary circuit. His "For Women Only" concerts make Luther Vandross shows seem tame in comparison. He was a certified sex symbol and matinee idol. This album, recorded when he was at his peak in both popularity and appeal, shows why he was so beloved. His voice had a swagger and come-on quality, but he also had good range, knew how to project, and never rushed or hurried through a ballad. —*Ron Wynn*

Teddy / 1979 / Philadelphia International ✦✦✦
Teddy Pendergrass scored his greatest hit album with his third solo release, cementing his position at the end of the '70s as the reigning matinee idol and romantic balladeer among male R&B vocalists. This album cracked the pop Top 10, dominated the R&B charts, and ruled the airwaves through much of 1979. While the overt sexual orientation of a song like "Turn Off The Lights" blinded some to the fact that Pendergrass' animated vocal was as soulful as you'd ever hear outside the gospel/blues/country axis of

the South, this album confirmed that Pendergrass had found his niche and would be a dominant singer into the '80s. —*Ron Wynn*

It's Time for Love / 1981 / Philadelphia International ✦✦✦
Teddy Pendergrass showed no signs of slowing down in the early '80s. This was another R&B smash and crossover hit, again putting him the Top 20. He got two good R&B singles, remained a popular concert attraction, and demonstrated good rapport with Stephanie Mills on several duets. They teamed so well together that Pendergrass eventually appeared on stage with her during a tour of England. —*Ron Wynn*

This One's for You / 1982 / Philadelphia International ✦✦
In the immediate period after Teddy Pendergrass' tragic, near-fatal car accident, many wondered what would happen to his career. Philadelphia International rushed out a pair of albums containing unissued tracks that hadn't made the cut from past albums. This was the first one, released in the summer of 1982. It actually managed to have two singles crack the R&B Top 40, although neither moved very far beyond that. It was evident on several tracks why they hadn't been issued; the ballads weren't as powerful or sensual, and the uptempo numbers lacked style and hooks. —*Ron Wynn*

Heaven Only Knows / 1983 / Philadelphia International ✦✦
With Teddy Pendergrass undergoing tortuous rehabilitation from his near-fatal car crash, Philadelphia International was faced with the loss of its single greatest star. The company didn't sit back and mourn; they rushed out a pair of albums containing unissued tracks in both 1982 and 1983. This was the second release, and it had a few nice cuts, although it was evident why much of it hadn't been released in the first place. —*Ron Wynn*

Love Language / 1984 / Asylum ✦✦✦
Teddy Pendergrass delighted both R&B and music fans in general when he debuted on a new label with this album in 1984. It was his first album of fresh songs in two years, and Elektra put some muscle behind it. It also helped that he had a good duet with Whitney Houston, a song included in the film *D.A.R.Y.L.*, and generally better material than Philadelphia International had trotted out on the two albums of unissued vault tracks released in the interim. The album made it into the pop Top 40 and was a triumph of the spirit. —*Ron Wynn*

Workin' It Back / 1985 / Asylum ✦✦✦
A most appropriate title, as Pendergrass was making his comeback following the tragic car accident. The album took a long time to make an impact, but finally wound up a modest success. He wasn't able to generate much response to any single, but the fact that he continued his comeback was welcome news, owing to speculation that he was going to retire due to mixed response to his earlier release. —*Ron Wynn*

● **Greatest Hits** / 1987 / Philadelphia International ✦✦✦✦
This collection covers Pendergrass' run of big hits from the Philadelphia International era, including "I Don't Love You Anymore," "Close The Door" and "Turn Off The Lights." —*Ron Wynn*

Joy / 1988 / Elektra ✦✦✦
Teddy Pendergrass finally made it back to the top in 1988, when the title track from this album spent two weeks at the head of the R&B list. The song even got mild pop attention, and the album was the first since his accident to really reflect the new Pendergrass sound. He sang in a slower, somber, yet appealing way quite different from the swaggering, openly sexual/macho posturing of the late '70s and early '80s. This was a weary but not beaten Pendergrass, whose manner and delivery underscored the resilient theme in *Joy's* lyrics. —*Ron Wynn*

Truly Blessed / 1991 / Elektra ✦✦✦
Teddy Pendergrass' return to recording and performing after the tragic accident that resulted in permanent paralysis was among the greatest stories of the 1980s. Pendergrass had to learn to sing all over again, with restraint, sensitivity and control now his keys rather than volume and presence. This 1991 album wasn't quite as moving as 1988's *Joy*, but it still included several poignant numbers, especially the title track, which addressed his survival, neither downplaying the problems nor overstating his genuine happiness about still being alive. —*Ron Wynn*

Penetration

Group, Punk
The only summation one can make of the career of English punks Penetration is, what a disappointment. In 1977, Penetration re-

leased a classic chunk of punk rock defiance titled "Don't Dictate." With Pauline Murray's impassioned vocals (sounding a bit like X-Ray Spex's Poly Styrene) leading the way, this was a blazing piece of anti-authoritarian rant, loud, snotty and proud. Sadly, it was to be the one song they remained best noted (assuming there are people who still remember Penetration) for. The problem was that they traded in barely competent but energetic bashing and thrashing for a more "mature" new wave/"punkish" rock sound. As a result, their debut LP, *Moving Targets*, although it has its moments, never lived up to the promise of "Don't Dictate." Still, Pauline Murray was a force to be reckoned with. Easily one of the best singers to come out of English punk rock, she made the band interesting even when the songs weren't there, the production was overwrought and the whole enterprise was terribly uneven. It was to the surprise of no one that by 1980 she was fronting a new band, The Invisible Girls, who based on Murray's strengths became known as Pauline Murray and.... Still, major success eluded Murray, and she has since moved into singing more elegant, mainstream pop/rock, remaining one of England's best unknown singers. —*John Dougan*

● **Moving Targets** / 1978 / Blue Plate ◆◆◆◆

Danger Signs / 1979 / Virgin ◆◆◆

Coming up for Air / 1979 / Virgin ◆◆◆

○ **Race Against Time [Official Bootleg]** / 1979 / Cliffdayn ◆◆◆◆
Although Penetration's debut, *Moving Targets*, is smoother and better produced, it doesn't pack the raw wallop and bristling energy of this collection of demos and live recordings cut from 1977-79. The live side, recorded in the band's hometown of Newcastle, provides the greatest thrills per song, but ultimately the Penetration saga is one of missed opportunity and overinflated expectations. Most importantly, "Don't Dictate" is here in demo form, and it still sounds pretty great, although the version that shows up on the CD reissue of *Moving Targets* sounds better. —*John Dougan*

Aquarian Symphony / Kigher Key ◆◆

Penguins

Group, Doo-Wop
These West Coast doo-woppers were led by vocalists Curtis Williams and Cleve Duncan. "Earth Angel," from 1954, was their biggest hit. —*John Floyd*

● **Authentic Golden Hits** / 1993 / Juke Box Treasures ◆◆◆◆
At long last, a well-thought-out compilation that gathers up all of the group's best sides for Dooto Records, including the original versions of the classics "Earth Angel" and Hey, Senorita" in their original, unedited form. —*Cub Koda*

Earth Angel / Ace ◆◆◆
A 21-track anthology from the Du Tone label, it's a deeper look at the group's '50s sides and style, built around the title track that sold five-million copies worldwide. (Import) —*Hank Davis*

○ **Golden Classics** / Collectables ◆◆◆◆
Unadorned West Coast doo-wop from the originators of "Earth Angel." Back-seat music. —*Hank Davis*

Michael Penn

Singer-Songwriter, Pop/Rock
Michael Penn was one of the best singer/songwriters to emerge in the late '80s, capable of melding Beatlesque pop melodies with wordplay that rivals Elvis Costello. *March*, in 1989, was critically acclaimed and had a surprise hit single with "No Myth." Although his second album, 1992's *Free-for-All*, didn't have a hit on the size of "No Myth," it displayed his folk roots alongside his pop sensibilities. —*Stephen Thomas Erlewine*

● **March** / 1989 / RCA ◆◆◆◆
A solid debut album, it includes the hit "No Myth." —*Kenneth M. Cassidy*

Free-for-All / 1992 / RCA ◆◆◆
Free For All, Michael Penn's second album, isn't as immediately accessible as *March*, but his cryptic lyrics and twisting melodies will work their way into your memory if given some time. —*Stephen Thomas Erlewine*

Pentangle

Group, Folk
A major British folk group of the late '60s and early '70s led by master guitarists John Renbourn and Bert Jansch and featuring singer Jacqui McShee, Pentangle combined traditional folk styles with contemporary songs and arrangements. —*William Ruhlmann*

Sweet Child / 1968 / Reprise ◆◆◆
A double album, one comprised of studio recordings, the other of a 1968 concert. No other Pentangle LP covered as much ground as this one, which included original material, Scottish folk songs, jazz, and blues, as well as instrumentals and numbers which spotlighted McShee, Jansch, and Thompson as soloists. "In Time" is a sparkling guitar duel between Jansch and Renbourn that ranks as one of the highlights in both of their careers. —*Richie Unterberger*

The Pentangle / 1968 / Reprise ◆◆◆
A thrilling debut, which saw five virtuosos creating a progressive folk album that added up to more than the sum of its parts. Divided between traditional and original material, highlights included their arrangement of "Bruton Town" and the seven-minute instrumental "Pentangling." —*Richie Unterberger*

○ **Basket of Light** / 1969 / Edsel ◆◆◆◆
Although *Sweet Child* is usually cited as the group's high-water mark, *Basket of Light* finds them at their most progressive and exciting. Highlights of this album—which actually reached the Top Five in the U.K.—include the buzzing jazz dynamics of "Light Flight," their moving rendition of the traditional folk song "Once I Had A Sweetheart," their reinvention of the girl-group smash "Sally Go Round The Roses," and "Springtime Promises," one of their finest original tunes. —*Richie Unterberger*

● **Essential, Vol. 1** / 1986 / Transatlantic ◆◆◆◆

● **Essential, Vol. 2** / 1986 / Transatlantic ◆◆◆◆

○ **A Maid That's Deep in Love** / 1987 / Shanachie ◆◆◆◆
Currently, only this 9-track compilation is available to remind listeners of this British traditional folk/rock quintet, which provided Fairport Convention's main competition in the late '60s and early '70s. Much of it is lovely, notably McShee's haunting singing and Jansch's finger-picking. But a more complete picture is provided by the two volumes of *Essential* Pentagle on Transatlantic in the U.K., which may be found in US record racks. —*William Ruhlmann*

Pere Ubu

Group, Alternative Pop/Rock, New Wave, Experimental
Named for the French absurdist play by Alfred Jarry, Pere Ubu was one of the most important and long-lived bands of the punk/new wave era (formed in September 1975 in Cleveland). The current edition of the band features original members David Thomas (vocals) and Scott Krauss (drums). Another current member, Tony Maimone (bass), joined the group in 1976. Pere Ubu was organized by Thomas and fellow rock journalist Peter Laughner (guitar, bass) for the purpose of recording the apocalyptic single "30 Seconds over Tokyo." By spring of 1976, Pere Ubu had recorded a second single, "Final Solution," and traveled to New York, where they gained exposure. The band was then reorganized, minus Laughner, who died the following year. Mercury Records signed Pere Ubu and issued their debut album, *The Modern Dance*, in February 1978. Its combination of uncompromising rock, featuring odd noises and Thomas's high-pitched singing, earned the group critical hosannas and commercial indifference beyond a loyal cult, a situation that would continue for most of their existence. That existence was fitful. Pere Ubu was dropped by Mercury and signed by Chrysalis, which released *Dub Housing* and *New Picnic Time* (both 1979), after which the group split again. But they were back to release *The Art of Walking* in 1980 (on Rough Trade). *360 Degrees of Simulated Stereo* (1981) was an archival live album, and *Song of the Bailing Man* (1981) was the last album before another split. 1985 saw the release of a compilation, *Terminal Tower*, and in 1987, Pere Ubu was reorganized, releasing the slighly more commercially accessible albums *The Tenement Year* (1987), *Cloudland* (1989), and *Worlds in Collision* (1991). —*William Ruhlmann*

○ **Datapanik in the Year Zero** / 1978 / Atlantic ◆◆◆◆

○ **Dub Housing** / 1978 / Rough Trade ◆◆◆◆

○ **The Modern Dance** / 1978 / Blank ◆◆◆◆
Aggressive punk rock, punctuated by found sounds and noises and topped by Thomas's remarkably affecting near-falsetto shriek. It's not easy listening, but it's powerful and daring, and has lost none of its impact since release. —*William Ruhlmann*

○ **New Picnic Time** / 1979 / Rough Trade ✦✦✦✦
The last album from the late '70s version of Ubu is extreme dada, with a beat (sometimes). —*Myles Boisen*

Art of Walking / 1981 / Rough Trade ✦✦✦
An early-'80s recording with guitarist Mayo Thompson, this is a buoyant and groovy accompaniment to Thomas's surrealism. —*Myles Boisen*

390 Degrees of Simulated Stereo (Live) / 1981 / Rough Trade ✦✦
This odds and ends sampler of early band activities (concerts, singles, and other crazy tidbits) is for collectors only. —*Myles Boisen*

Song of the Bailing Man / 1982 / Rough Trade ✦✦✦
David Thomas becomes more obtuse as the band heads toward breakup again. —*Myles Boisen*

★ **Terminal Tower** / 1985 / Twin/Tone ✦✦✦✦✦
The songs on *Terminal Tower—An Archival Collection*, many of them taken from Pere Ubu's first singles, demonstrate what helped make them one of the most original and challenging bands of the American New Wave of the '70s. Be warned that songs like "30 Seconds over Tokyo" and "Final Solution" will have a polarizing effect on the listener: either this on-the-edge rock is just what you've been looking for, or it isn't. —*William Ruhlmann*

○ **The Tenement Year** / 1988 / Enigma ✦✦✦✦
Since the re-formed version of Pere Ubu reins in (slightly) the group's more extreme tendencies, this album, which nevertheless presents David Thomas's unique vision and the band's somewhat off-kilter approach to rock more or less intact, may be the place for neophytes to get their feet wet with a highly unusual group. This one should give you the idea—then you're on your own. —*William Ruhlmann*

○ **Cloudland** / 1989 / Fontana ✦✦✦✦
David Thomas returns to his favorite boyhood themes, with his new pop band in tow. —*Myles Boisen*

One Man Drives / 1989 / Rough Trade ✦✦
A second live compilation, *One Man Drives While the Other Man Screams*, is more unified than *360 Degrees…*, with lots of their best material. —*Myles Boisen*

Worlds in Collision / 1991 / Fontana ✦✦✦
Their latest shows a definite commercial aspiration. It's still good, but lacks personality. —*Myles Boisen*

Story of My Life / 1993 / Imago ✦✦✦
Although it is the most pop-oriented record Pere Ubu ever cut, *Story of My Life* didn't make much of a dent even in alternative radio. Nevertheless, there are many fine pop tunes here, occasionally spiked with some of their trademark experimentalism, although the music isn't as challenging as it was years before. —*Stephen Thomas Erlewine*

Carl Perkins (Carl Lee Perkins)

b. Apr. 9, 1932, Lake City, TN
Rock & Roll, Rockabilly
The history of rock & roll guitar would have a gigantic gaping hole without the pioneering efforts of Carl Perkins. He taught Eric Clapton and George Harrison how to play, years before he met either one, and the early Beatles albums were peppered with their versions of Perkins rockabilly classics. Born dirt-poor and ambitious, Perkins started playing the honky-tonks in his native Tennessee with his brothers, fusing elements of hillbilly music with Black blues. He started recording for the Sun label a few months after Elvis, but he was cast as a straight country singer, albeit a fine one, in the Hank Williams mold. Every great singer needs a great lead guitarist, and Carl found one in himself, his combination of fingerpicking chording and rapid spitfire licks becoming instantly recognizable. Turned loose to rock out at his third session, Perkins did just that, producing the ultimate rockabilly anthem, "Blue Suede Shoes." Hitting the #1 slot on the pop, R&B, and country charts, Carl's future seemed assured when he almost perished in a car accident, just as Elvis became a worldwide phenomenon. Minor hits followed (now all acknowledged as classics of the genre), but Carl's star was on the wane. After becoming a member of the Johnny Cash TV show in the '60s (writing hits for Cash and others in the country field), he experienced a comeback when England went rockabilly crazy in the early '70s. Elected to the Rock & Roll Hall of Fame on the second ballot, Carl Perkins keeps on pickin', the ultimate rockabilly survivor. —*Cub Koda*

★ **Original Sun Greatest Hits** / 1986 / Rhino ✦✦✦✦✦
Essential, primal rockabilly, including "Everybody's Trying to Be My Baby," "Matchbox," "Honey Don't," "Boppin' the Blues," "Glad All Over," and the original "Blue Suede Shoes." —*Hank Davis*

Honky Tonk Gal / Apr. 1989 / Rounder ✦✦✦
Quirky, obscure, and offbeat, this is a much deeper look into Perkins's Sun period, with emphasis on hillbilly roots. —*Hank Davis*

○ **The Jive after Five: Best of Carl Perkins (1958-1978)** / 1990 / Rhino ✦✦✦✦
His later CBS work, much of it is excellent. —*Hank Davis*

○ **The Classic** / Feb. 1990 / Bear Family ✦✦✦✦
Simply the most comprehensive collection imaginable, included are all of his essential Sun tracks and alternate takes on five discs. All the 1958-1962 CBS sides are here, plus his 1963-1964 Decca sessions. It is indispensable for the serious fan and completist. —*Hank Davis*

Restless: The Columbia Recordings / May 12, 1992 / Columbia ✦✦✦
A strong collection of Perkins' singles for Columbia, concentrating on the late '50s and early '60s; some of his finest songs, including "Pink Pedal Pushers" and "Jive After Five," are included here. —*Stephen Thomas Erlewine*

The Persuaders

Group, Soul
This group made a pair of marvelous heartache ballads in 1971, but have the unfortunate legacy of having their finest cuts turned into pop hits via covers. Lead singer Douglas Scott, whose nickname appropriately was "Smokey," Willie Holland, James Barnes, and Charles Stodghill formed in New York in 1969. They signed with Atlantic in the early '70s, and had their lone R&B chart topper in 1971, the shattering classic "Thin Line Between Love & Hate." It was also their only gold single. The follow-up was nearly as strong; "Love's Gonna Pack Up (And Walk Out)" reached number eight on the R&B charts, but had no crossover appeal. They continued on Win & Lose until 1973, then moved to Atco, where "Some Guys Have All the Luck" was a number seven R&B single in 1973. It was their final hit, though they kept recording into the late '70s, doing their last session for Calla. Besides the Pretenders re-doing "Thin Line Between Love & Hate," Rod Stewart had a Top Ten pop hit with his version of "Some Guys Have All the Luck" in 1984. —*Ron Wynn*

● **Thin Line between Love & Hate** / 1974 / Collectables ✦✦✦✦
A gritty soul unit, adept at tragic encounter tunes. The title song is a soul anthem. —*Ron Wynn*

Best Thing That Ever Happened to Me / 1974 / Atco ✦✦✦

It's All About Love / 1976 / Calla ✦✦✦

The Persuaders / 1989 / Atco ✦✦✦

The Persuasions

Group, Soul, R&B
A cappella singing has been part of the African-American musical tradition since the days of slavery. Despite the recent success of the hi-tech a cappella group Take 6, the tradition has suffered a steady decline to the point where it is rare even in gospel circles. The Persuasions, though, are resolutely a cappella. Their chart successes have been minimal (two fleeting R&B entries in 1974-1975), but they carry forward the tradition without appearing ossified. Airplay will probably always elude them—and with it the really big breakthrough—but their music has been a consistently enjoyable sidebar, and never one that has simply reeked of revivalism. —*Colin Escott*

○ **Acappella** / 1970 / Bizarre ✦✦✦✦
The first Persuasions release, recorded live in Los Angeles. The sound is a little two-dimensional, but this recording captures the spirit of joy in live harmonizing, which is the very essence of the Persuasions. Includes great takes on the Temptations's "Don't Look Back" and the Drifters's "Up on the Roof," making manifest the intrinsic connection between '50s doo-wop and '60s group singing. —*Rob Bowman*

○ **We Came to Play** / 1971 / Collectables ✦✦✦✦
Better produced than their debut, *We Came to Play* continues what became a formula for the Persuasions—covering '50s and '60s classics (the latter most usually taken from the Motown and

Curtis Mayfield portfolios), the occasional Tin Pan Alley standard, and judiciously chosen pop/rock covers. In the '70s, a cappella singing was a lost art the Persuasions were determined to keep alive. —*Rob Bowman*

○ **Street Corner Symphony** / 1972 / Capitol ✦✦✦✦
On this, their highest-charting recording, the Persuasions give more of the same, including gorgeous reworkings of Bob Dylan's "The Man in Me" and the Impressions' "People Get Ready." —*Rob Bowman*

○ **Spread the Word** / 1972 / Capitol ✦✦✦✦
Why the Persuasions were never able to generate much action while on commercial labels is a mystery. They made fine albums for A&M and Capitol, but just couldn't get any hits. While it was true that '70s tastes were geared more towards funk, "sweet" soul, and vocal groups with elaborate arrangements and production, there still should have been room for the Persuasions' classic harmonizing. At any rate, this was one of a couple of fine albums they made in the early '70s for Capitol. It's long out of print, and probably won't be reissued any time soon, if ever. —*Ron Wynn*

We Still Ain't Got No Band / 1973 / MCA ✦✦✦
Maintaining their high level of consistency, the Persuasions shy away from Motown here and delve into the blues, tackling Jimmy Hughes's "Steal Away" and a medley of Jimmy Reed's "Baby What You Want Me to Do?" and "Bright Lights, Big City." Superb. —*Rob Bowman*

More Than Before / 1974 / A&M ✦✦✦
An often spectacular mid-'70s date by the Persuasions, singing at the peak of their harmonizing powers and on a major label that gave them great production and engineering. Even on songs that weren't first-rate, their interaction, Jerry Lawson's soaring leads, and the bass/baritone support of Jimmy Hayes and Herbert Rhoad were magnificent. —*Ron Wynn*

Live in the Whispering Gallery / 1976 / Hammer N Nails ✦✦
Tremendous vocals, wonderful harmonies, and genuine audience reaction are the selling points for this concert recording. While the response sometimes seems a bit contrived, there's nothing artificial about the blistering uptempo or moving ballads that the Persuasions provided, whether doing love tunes, novelty items, protest works, folk, or pop. —*Ron Wynn*

● **Chirpin'** / 1977 / Elektra ✦✦✦✦
After two ill-advised albums for A&M with instruments, the Persuasions returned to their a cappella roots. No longer popular enough to chart, the music was in no way diminished. Highlights include a swinging version of the gospel standard "It's Gonna Rain" and a dramatic reading of Tony Joe White's "Willie and Laura Mae Jones." —*Rob Bowman*

Comin' at Ya / 1979 / Flying Fish ✦✦✦
Smooth a cappella music comes from this top quartet. —*AMG*

No Frills / 1984 / Rounder ✦✦✦
The Persuasions celebrated their 20th anniversary with this 1986 set blending classics and more contemporary material. They covered vintage songs from the Drifters and Clyde McPhatter, included a lengthy, more modern/dance tune in Candi Station's "Victim" and added a holiday number with "What Are You Doing New Year's Eve." They brought back former second tenor Joe Russell for four tracks, among them the concluding "Slip Sliding Away." There was also a creditable gospel selection "I Wonder Do You Love The Lord Like I Do." Bev Rohlehr provided an interesting additional element with a woman's voice in the harmonies on six cuts. —*Ron Wynn*

Good News / 1988 / Rounder ✦✦✦
The Persuasions were among the finest a cappella quartets of the 1970s and '80s. This 1982 album, which was reissued on CD in 1991, included a nice rendition of the title track, outstanding treatments of "All I Have To Do Is Dream" and "I Won't Be The Fool Anymore," plus a credible cover of Sam Cooke's "Cupid." The only shaky moments are on the "Swanee River Medley," which came closer to camp than probably intended. But that one oversight notwithstanding, the Persuasions continued their tradition of excellent a cappella albums while on Rounder. —*Ron Wynn*

Pet Shop Boys

Group, Dance-Pop, Disco, Techno-Pop/Dance
With their detached, intellectual, and often very funny lyrics and relentlessly hip, melodic, synth-driven disco, Neil Tennant and

Chris Lowe were one of the most commercially successful groups in America and England in the late '80s, scoring a consistent string of hit singles through 1991. Through four albums and several singles, the Pet Shop Boys explored every dance trend from disco to house, creating beautifully lush, haunting soundscapes with their synthesizers and drum machines. By the time the *Very* was released in 1993, the popular audience had shifted away from dance-pop and they had difficulty receiving mainstream airplay and MTV wouldn't air their videos. However, the duo continued to sell respectably while they continued to expand and redefine their music. —*Stephen Thomas Erlewine*

Please / 1986 / EMI America ✦✦✦
A collection of immaculately-crafted and seamlessly-produced synthesized dance-pop, the Pet Shop Boys' debut album *Please* sketches out the basic elements of the duo's sound. At first listen, most of the songs come off as mere excuses for the dance floor, driven by cold, melodic keyboard riffs and pulsing drum machines. However, the songcraft that the beats support is surprisingly strong, featuring catchy melodies that appear slight because of Neil Tennant's thin voice. Tennant's lyrics were still in their formative stages, with half of the record failing to transcend the formulaic constraints of dance-pop. The songs that do break free—the crass "Opportunities (Let's Make Lots of Money)," the lulling "Suburbia," and the hypnotic "West End Girls"—are not only classic dance singles, they're classic pop singles. —*Stephen Thomas Erlewine*

Disco / Oct. 1986 / EMI America ✦✦
Released at the height of dance-pop in 1986, the Pet Shop Boys' remix album *Disco* defiantly asserted the roots of the current trend with the title. And with its long remixes, *Disco* is designed to be pumped at a dance floor. As casual listening, it gets a bit tedious, but even at these extended lengths, the melodic craft of the Pet Shop Boys' material shines through. —*Stephen Thomas Erlewine*

○ **Actually** / Jun. 1987 / EMI America ✦✦✦✦
With their second album *Actually,* the Pet Shop Boys perfected their melodic, detatched dance-pop. Where most of *Please* was dominated by the beats, the rhythms on *Actually* are part of a series of intricate arrangements that create a glamorous but disposable backdrop for Neil Tennant's tales of isolation, boredom, money, and loneliness. Not only are the arrangements more accomplished, but the songs themselves are more striking, incorporating a strong sense of melody, as evidenced by "What Have I Done To Deserve This?," a duet with Dusty Springfield. Tennant's lyrics are clever and direct, chronicling the lifes and times of urban, lonely, and bored yuppies of the late '80s. And the fact that dance-pop is considered a disposable medium by most mainstream critics and listeners only increases the reserved emotional undercurrent of *Actually,* as well as its irony. —*Stephen Thomas Erlewine*

Introspective / Apr. 1988 / EMI America ✦✦✦
Featuring a mere six tracks, most of them well over six minutes in length, *Introspective* was a move back to the clubs for the Pet Shop Boys. Over the course of the album, the incorporated various dance techniques that were currently in vogue, including Latin rhythms and house textures. The title isn't entirely an arch joke, however. Like *Actually, Introspective* was an exploration of distant, disaffected yuppies, which naturally resulted in a good deal of self-analyzation. Melodically, the essential song structures were as strong and multi-layered as the previous album, yet that was hard to hear beneath the varying rhythmic textures that composed the bulk of each track. Nevetheless, the mixes are more compelling than the remixes on *Disco* and the songs include several of their best numbers, including "Left to My Own Devices" and "Domino Dancing," as well as the reconstruction of "Always On My Mind" and a cover of Blaze's club classic, "It's Alright." —*Stephen Thomas Erlewine*

○ **Behavior** / 1990 / EMI America ✦✦✦✦
Behavior was a retreat from the deep dance textures of *Introspective,* as it picked up on the carefully-constructed pop of *Actually.* In fact, *Behavior* functions as the Pet Shop Boys' bid for mainstream credebility, as much of the album relies more on pop-craft than rhythmic variations. Although its a subtle manouever, it would have been rather disasterous if the results weren't so captivating. Tennant takes this approach seriously, singing the lyrics instead of speaking them. That doesn't necessarily give the album added emotional baggage—all of the distance and detachment in

the duo's music is not a hinderance, it's part of the concept—but it does result in an ambitious and breathtaking pop album, which manages to include everything from the spiteful "How Can You Expect To Be Taken Seriously?" to the wistful "Being Boring." — *Stephen Thomas Erlewine*

★ **Discography: The Complete Singles Collection** / 1991 / EMI America ✦✦✦✦✦
Most of the Pet Shop Boys' albums are well-crafted and thoroughly intriguing in their own right, but dance-pop is a medium that is driven by hit singles. *Discography* collects all the duo's numerous hit singles, including a handful of non-albums tracks, in their original 7-inch single mix, which occasionally varies from the album version, particularly in the case of the *Introspective* material. Presented chronologically, the singles not only demonstrate the band's increasing musical sophistication, they illustrate what fine songwriters Tennant and Lowe are. These 19 songs form one of the most consistent and innovative bodies of work of its era. Some of the production techniques have dated slightly, but the music has remained impressive. — *Stephen Thomas Erlewine*

○ **Very** / 1993 / ERG ✦✦✦✦
Because they work in a field that isn't usually taken seriously, the Pet Shop Boys are often ignored in the rock world. But make no mistake—they are one of the most talented pop outfits working today, witty and melodic with a fine sense of flair. *Very* is one of their very best records, expertly weaving between the tongue-in-cheek humor of "I Wouldn't Normally Do This Kind of Thing," the quietly shocking "Can You Forgive Her?" and the bizarrely moving cover of the Village People's "Go West." Alternately happy and melancholy, *Very* is the Pet Shop Boys at their finest. — *Stephen Thomas Erlewine*

Disco 2 / 1994 / Capitol ✦✦
The Pet Shop Boys' second remix record is more long-winded than their first, suffering not only from too many pointless remixes, but a surprising lack of cohesiveness, making it for devoted fans only. — *Stephen Thomas Erlewine*

Alternative / 1995 / EMI ✦✦✦
Alternative is a double-disc set of the Pet Shop Boys' B-sides. Far from being a superfluous collection, the album contains a wealth of prime material, including several tracks that surpass those the duo put on their albums. Consequently, the set is worthwhile not only for hardcore fans, but for listeners with a passing interest in the group. — *Stephen Thomas Erlewine*

Peter & Gordon

Group, British Invasion
As part of the first wave of the British Invasion, Peter Asher (b. Jun 22, 1944) and Gordon Waller (b. Jun 4, 1945) recorded a number of highly successful, lushly orchestrated pop singles that blended Phil Spectorish production sensibilities with Everly Brothers-style harmonies. Their hits included "I Go to Pieces" (#9), "World Without Love" (#1), "Lady Godiva" (#6), "Woman" (#14), "To Know You Is to Love You" (#24), and a version of Buddy Holly's "True Love Ways" (#14). — *Rick Clark*

● **Best of Peter & Gordon** / 1991 / Rhino ✦✦✦✦
This duo synthesized Beatles and Everly Brothers harmonies into a wonderfully seamless string of mid-'60s British Invasion lite-pop hits. The popular songs are all contained here, with great sound and well-rendered liner notes. — *Rick Clark*

Tom Petty & the Heartbreakers

Group, Rock & Roll
Since 1976, Tom Petty & the Heartbreakers have been one of America's finest rock & roll bands, combining the ringing guitars of the Byrds with the gritty rhythmic drive of the Rolling Stones. Petty's tales of American losers and dreamers were simple and direct, but emotionally charged. The Heartbreakers were a lean, tight band that could handle hard rock & roll and melodic pop equally well. The group gained critical attention and solid sales with their first album, but 1979's *Damn the Torpedos* was their commercial breakthrough, selling over two million copies; it couldn't have come at a better time, since Petty filed for bankruptcy before its release.

During the '80s, Petty sold consistently well, as he expanded his sound with the release of each album. In 1989, he released his first solo album, *Full Moon Fever*, which became his biggest hit yet. That momentum carried over into the next Heartbreakers release,

1991's *The Great Wide Open*, which went platinum. As they were preparing their next album, the group released a greatest hits album in 1993 which contained the hit single, "Mary Jane's Last Dance"; it proved that nearly two decades after he began recording, Tom Petty remains a vital artist. — *Stephen Thomas Erlewine*

Tom Petty & the Heartbreakers / 1976 / Gone Gator ✦✦✦
Originally released on Denny Cordell's Shelter label, the 1976 self-titled debut was a real sleeper until the single "Breakdown" became Petty's first hit almost a year and a half later. This album's release coincided with the advent of the punk and new wave movements. The lean, edgy production and arrangements only enhanced that perception, in spite of the fact the the songs clearly drew inspiration from the Byrds and '60s Anglo-rock. Among the highlights are the gritty riff-rocker "Strangered in the Night" (which features Dwight Twilley), "American Girl" (a song so shamelessly influenced by the Byrds that even Roger McGuinn covered it), "Hometown Blues" (later covered by Rosanne Cash), and "The Wild One, Forever." — *Rick Clark*

You're Gonna Get It! / 1978 / Gone Gator ✦✦✦
Not quite so strong as the debut, *You're Gonna Get It* exhibited a denser, Rickenbacker-heavy guitar sound. Petty's voice was practically buried in the mix, particularly on the rockers. Nevertheless, this album does have some great songs, particularly "I Need to Know" and "Listen to Her Heart." Each of the first two CDs clocks in at around thirty minutes' playing time. It would've been nice if Petty were true enough to his well-advertised principles (concerning giving consumers value for their money) to fit these two albums on one disc when he re-released them on his own Gone Gator label. — *Rick Clark*

☆ **Damn the Torpedoes** / 1979 / MCA ✦✦✦✦✦
Petty switched producers to Jimmy Iovine, and together they created the masterful *Damn the Torpedoes*. For once, Petty's voice was up front in the mix, giving him much more character. The band never sounded so full or punchy before this. *Torpedoes* opens with a seamless string of great rockers, "Refugee," "Here Comes My Girl," and "Even the Losers." Other highlights include "Century City" and "Don't Do Me Like That." — *Rick Clark*

○ **Hard Promises** / 1981 / MCA ✦✦✦✦
Pre-album publicity made much of the fact that Petty was taking issue with his record label (MCA) over gouging his fans with a list-price increase on this album. Petty won, reinforcing the notion that he was a principled people's artist. The aptly titled *Hard Promises* became another platinum hit. Even though *Hard Promises* is a slight step down from its predecessor, there is plenty of strong material. "The Waiting," one of Petty's finest songs, is the stylistic epitome of his Byrds fixation. Other standouts include the rockers "Kings Road," "A Thing About You," and the darkly humorous "Something Big." — *Rick Clark*

Long after Dark / 1982 / MCA ✦✦
The highlights of this album, "Straight into Darkness," "Change of Heart," "Deliver Me," and "You Got Lucky," may be some of Petty's best, but much of *Long after Dark* suffers from weak melodies and flat-sounding production. — *Rick Clark*

Pack up the Plantation: Live! / 1985 / MCA ✦✦
A solid-as-a-brick live set, featuring incredible symbiotic playing from all the Heartbreakers. — *Cub Koda*

Southern Accents / 1985 / MCA ✦✦✦
Produced by Dave Stewart, *Southern Accents* is an ambitious album, attempting to incorporate touches of psychedelia, soul, and country into a loose concept about the modern South. Occasionally, the songs work; "Rebels" and "Spike" are fine tunes, and "Don't Come Around Here No More" and "Make It Better (Forget About Me)" expand the Heartbreakers' sound nicely. But too often, the record is weighed down by its own ambitions. — *Stephen Thomas Erlewine*

Let Me up (I've Had Enough) / 1987 / MCA ✦✦✦
After the failed *Southern Accents*, Petty and company return to a fairly straightahead collection of rock & roll. Except for a handful of strong tunes like the free-associative rocker (co-written with Dylan) "Jammin' Me," "Runaway Trains," and "My Life/Your World," much of this album feels like the product of an uninspired band. — *Rick Clark*

○ **Full Moon Fever** / 1989 / MCA ✦✦✦✦
Recorded as a casual side project, Petty's first solo album possessed more flashes of brilliance than most of his albums put together. It also produced four hits, with "Free Fallin'," "A Face in

the Crowd," "Runnin' Down a Dream," and "I Won't Back Down." Another highlight was a great remake of the Byrds's "I'll Feel a Whole Lot Better." Petty ought to moonlight more often. —*Rick Clark*

Into the Great Wide Open / 1991 / MCA ✦✦✦
This is Petty's first Heartbreakers album after his multi-platinum solo effort, *Full Moon Fever*. The band sounds a little more lively than on the previous two efforts, and the material is generally better than much of their previous two studio albums. However, *Full Moon Fever* is a stronger album, overall. —*Rick Clark*

★ **Greatest Hits** / 1993 / MCA ✦✦✦✦✦
All of Petty's biggest hits collected, along with two new tracks—the excellent "Mary Jane's Last Dance" and a cover of Thunderclap Newman's "Something In the Air"—on one essential disc. Everything from "American Girl" to "Free Fallin' " is included, with sixteen tracks proving that Petty is one of the best rockers of the past fifteen years. —*Stephen Thomas Erlewine*

○ **Wildflowers** / 1994 / Warner Brothers ✦✦✦✦
Under the guidance of producer Rick Rubin, Tom Petty turns in a stripped-down, subtle record with *Wildflowers*. Coming after two albums of Jeff Lynne-directed bombast, the very sound of the record is refreshing; Petty sounds relaxed and confident. Most of the songs are small gems, but a few are a little too laidback, almost reaching the point of carelessness. Nevertheless, the finest songs here ("Wildflowers," "You Don't Know How It Feels," "It's Good to Be King," and several others) match the quality of his best material, making *Wildflowers* one of Petty's most distinctive and best albums. —*Stephen Thomas Erlewine*

Pezband

Group, Rock & Roll, Power Pop/Anglo-Pop
Hailing from the same state as Cheap Trick (Illinois), the Pezband were a mostly fine, occasionally wonderful, power-pop band that specialized in hook-filled hard rock with sweet multi-part harmonies. Led by the strong, blues-inflected singing of Mimi (a guy) Betinis and the rampaging Jeff Beck-influenced guitar playing of Tommy Gawenda, the Pezzers' first LP (released in 1977) was not as hard and heavy as Cheap Trick, nor did it exhibit the berserk panache of their fellow Illini. But that all changed with their second LP, *Laughing in the Dark*, which contained a high quotient of good-to-great songs, excellent production by Jesse Hood Jackson, and a wonderful lack of smugness and calculation that was slowly infiltrating every power-pop band in America. A huge public reaction, however, was not forthcoming. The band had its supporters (like most of the editorial staff of *Trouser Press*), but power-pop/hard rock from Illinois was dominated by Cheap Trick, and everybody else had to find a place in the pecking order. For bands like the Pezband, that meant far less coverage than they deserved. There was also another issue: the band didn't deliver another record as good as *Laughing*, nor could they recapture the excitement and messy mania of their live show (forever preserved on an excellent pair of EPs, *Too Old, Too Soon* and *Thirty Seconds Over Schaumburg*) in the studio. Hence, the rest of their recorded output is serviceable, but only hints at what the band was truly capable of doing. It's too bad, because they were such unpretentious, likable guys. By the early '80s, the Pezband had virtually vanished from the music scene, but a Chicago-based independent label (in 1994!) released some outtakes and other previously unreleased material, and the word is that Mimi Betinis is putting the band back together. Cautious optimism is suggested. —*John Dougan*

Pezband / 1977 / Passport ✦✦

● **Laughing in the Dark** / 1978 / Radar ✦✦✦✦
Without a doubt, the best Pezband record available. Side One offers an especially strong trio of rock-pop songs ("Love Goes Underground," "I'm Leavin'," and "Stop! Wait a Minute"). Sadly, many other bands got more press, and this record was lost in the shuffle. The good news is that if you found it in a used record store (assuming there still are a few in your neighborhood), you could probably get it for $2. Some may dismiss it as formulaic, and that might be true, but no one ever said that formula couldn't be fun. —*John Dougan*

Too Old, Too Soon Live at Dingwalls / 1978 / Passport ✦✦✦
A great four-track live EP recorded at the much-missed club Dingwalls in London. Side One features rough and ready versions of "Stop! Wait A Minute" and "Lovesmith"; Side Two features a manic "Not Fade Away" and a thoroughly great romp through the

Swinging Blue Jeans' "Hippy Hippy Shake." Power pop with the accent on power. —*John Dougan*

○ **Thirty Seconds Over Schaumburg** / 1978 / PVC ✦✦✦✦
The title is a tongue-in-cheek reference to the Chicago suburb from whence they came. The music is loud, ferocious and wonderful. Tommy Gawenda is a little out of control here (too many multi-chorus solos), but after all is said and done, this record proves what a great live band the Pezband were. Extra point for a rippin' version of Jeff Beck's "Blue Wind" and its neat segue into the Yardbirds' "Stroll On." —*John Dougan*

Cover to Cover / 1981 / Passport ✦✦✦

PFM

Group, Art-Rock/Progressive-Rock
Italy's leading progressive-rock outfit of the early '70s, PFM would've remained a purely Italian phenomenon had it not been for their being signed by Emerson, Lake & Palmer to the latter's Manticore label. Their sound was more distinctly rooted in the pre-classical era than that of their Germanic counterparts. In addition to electric keyboards (synthesizers, etc.), they also relied on violin and flute (recorder, actually) as major components of their music. Their name, by the way, was short for Premiata Forneria Marconi, the name of the bakery that originally sponsored them. —*Bruce Eder*

● **Photos of Ghosts** / 1972 / Manticore ✦✦✦✦
Their phantasmagorical debut English-language album (sung phonetically, natch), filled with beautifully melodic, classically based songs; strong inclinations toward psychedelia; and a refreshingly open and airy sound, distinct from the thick Germanic textures of competing classical rock bands. (Out of print) —*Bruce Eder*

World Became the World / 1974 / Manticore ✦✦✦
A less interesting follow-up album with fewer memorable melodies and less distinctive songs. —*Bruce Eder*

Liz Phair

b. Apr. 17, 1967
Singer-Songwriter, Alternative Pop/Rock
For several years, singer/songwriter Liz Phair recorded homemade tapes under the name *Girlsound*; one of the cassettes reached Matador Records which offered her a contract. Phair's first album, the double-length *Exile in Guyville*, was released in the early spring of 1993; by the end of the year, it was topping nearly every critic's poll in America. During the course of the year, Phair became the figure-head for the new movement of female artists, particularly those in alternative rock. Combining elements of both traditional singer/songwriters and alternative rockers, Phair stands as an original; although her roots are identifiable, nothing in her music sounds derivative.

Whip-Smart, Phair's 1994 followup to *Exile in Guyville*, was a commercial success, debuting at number 27, but it received mixed reviews. "Supernova," the first single pulled from the album, was a Top 10 alternative radio hit. In the summer of 1995, Phair released *Juvenilia*, an EP that featured the first commercial release of selected *Girlsound* material. —*Stephen Thomas Erlewine*

★ **Exile in Guyville** / 1993 / Matador ✦✦✦✦✦
Liz Phair's stunningly accomplished and ambitious debut album *Exile in Guyville* is loosely based on the Rolling Stones' classic *Exile on Main Street*, retelling that album's weary tales of love and sex from a female perspective. While there is some anger here ("Fuck and Run" and "6' 1' "), there are also love songs ("Never Said"), lust songs ("Flower"), haunting character sketches ("Canary" and "Explain It to Me"), and exceptional narratives ("Divorce Song," "Stratford-On-Guy," and "Help Me Mary"). While her lyrics are literate without being pretentious, what makes the album so impressive is her musical diversity; from rock & roll to folk, from experimental rock to just a piano and a voice, *Exile in Guyville* is an endlessly inventive album that only gets better with repeated plays. —*Stephen Thomas Erlewine*

Whip-Smart / 1994 / Matador ✦✦✦
Few debut albums are as startlingly accomplished as Liz Phair's *Exile in Guyville*. Fewer still receive as much praise, which left Phair in a catch-22 with her second album. *Whip-Smart* is a continuation of both the sound and attitude of her acclaimed debut. At first, it may seem that Phair is merely reiterating herself, but repeated listenings reveal that *Whip-Smart* is a more concise and direct record. In fact, her debut never had a single as powerful as the

fuzz-drenched "Supernova," nor did it have anything as infectious as the sing-song chorus of "Whip-Smart." Phair hasn't abandoned her talent for haunting ballads, either. But the best moments of *Whip-Smart*—the one-two punch of "Go West" and "Cinco De Mayo," as well as "Supernova" and the title track—show that Phair is continuing to improve not only as a songwriter, but as a musician. —*Stephen Thomas Erlewine*

○ **Girlysound** / Bootleg ✦✦✦✦
Before signing to Matador Records, Phair recorded a wealth of home demos that were only circulated, primarily to acquaintances, on cassette. In fact, it was a tape of this material that brought Phair to the attention of Matador in the first place. Featuring just Liz and her low-volume electric guitar, with layers of overdubs enabling Liz to harmonize with herself, this collection of over 20 low-fi, intensely personal songs has circulated among literally thousands of Phair fans, making this one of the most popular and sought-after alternative rock bootlegs of all time. A few of the tracks found their way onto her first couple of albums in drastically reworked versions, including "Stratford-On-Guy," "Flower," "Johnny Sunshine," "Whip-Smart," "Never Said," "Shane," and "Chopsticks." These stripped-down versions aren't necessarily better (although "Whip-Smart" sounds much less tongue-in-cheek and more effective in its original incarnation), but they are fascinating to hear in such bare-bones arrangements. The substantial majority of these have not been released by Phair, and while some are clearly tentative drafts or awkward, half-baked efforts, others are as tuneful and provoking as anything on her official albums. Phair is arguably a more powerful performer when stripped to her essentials of voice and guitar, and this tape is as vital to her legacy as her Matador discs. —*Richie Unterberger*

Sam Phillips

Pop/Rock
Sam Phillips the singer, not the former head of Sun Records, is a California-based singer/songwriter, whose 1987 debut album, *The Turning* (released under her given name of Leslie Phillips) was a contemporary Christian recording issued by Myrrh and produced by fellow Christian and then-future husband T-Bone Burnette. He also handled the boards for Phillips's two secular albums, which have garnered considerable critical praise. —*William Ruhlmann*

○ **The Indescribable Wow** / 1988 / Virgin ✦✦✦✦
T-Bone Burnette surrounds Phillips's voice, which has both a little-girl bounce and a teenage ache in it, with neo-'60s pop arrangements on songs whose lyrics are often more serious than the inevitably cute-sounding production. But that only means that, once the music has seduced you, the words surprise you. —*William Ruhlmann*

Cruel Inventions / 1991 / Virgin ✦✦✦
A somewhat less accessible but nevertheless impressive followup. —*William Ruhlmann*

● **Martinis & Bikinis** / 1994 / Virgin ✦✦✦✦
Sam Phillips' third album is a remarkably rich and varied set of Beatlesque pop, distinguished by her exceptional songwriting. —*Stephen Thomas Erlewine*

Phish

Group, Rock & Roll
Phish has gained a devoted cult since the release of their 1988 debut album, *Junta*. Most of their support derives from their concerts; their wildly eclectic music—incorporating rock, folk, country, bluegrass, jazz, and pop—catches fire in an improvised setting. On record, their experimentations can sometimes fall flat, but often the band's rich musical diversity and goofy charm usually carries them over the dull spots. —*Stephen Thomas Erlewine*

○ **Junta** / 1988 / Elektra ✦✦✦✦
Phish's debut album is a bit long-winded and unfocused, yet it establishes their dedication to musical exploration effectively. —*David Jehnzen*

Lawn Boy / 1991 / Elektra ✦✦✦
The Phish boys play real good in a variety of styles, writing amusing, surrealist lyrics full of non-sequiturs and don't seem to take themselves too seriously. —*J. Poet*

○ **A Picture of Nectar** / Aug. 1991 / Elektra ✦✦✦✦
A wildly eclectic album in the vein of the Grateful Dead, *A Picture of Nectar* is the best studio example of Phish's genre-jumping good-time rock & roll. —*David Jehnzen*

Rift / 1993 / Elektra ✦✦
Rift, Phish's follow-up to their major-label breakthrough *A Picture of Nectar*, follows the same pattern as its predecessor, but doesn't live up to the surprising, adventurous music on *Nectar*. Instead, most of the album sounds like an uninspired retread, as the band tries to fashion their songs into a loose concept album. The concentration on thematic unity tends to rob Phish of the loose spontaneity that makes them unique and makes *Rift* a bland, tedious listen. —*Stephen Thomas Erlewine*

Hoist / 1994 / Elektra ✦✦✦
Hoist is the most concise album Phish has recorded, but that's not necessarily a complement. Phish's strength is not songcraft or hooks; it's their love of free-form song structures and extended jams. When the group's sound is reduced to its core, as it is on *Hoist*, it isn't quite as compelling. Nevertheless, the album is an improvement on the dismal *Rift*, and features several fine cuts. —*Stephen Thomas Erlewine*

● **A Live One** / 1995 / Elektra ✦✦✦✦
Phish's strength has always been its live shows, and *A Live One* shows why. Given the opportunity, they take their songs in every direction, winding through several different sounds within the course of a song. *A Live One* also features seven previously unreleased songs, making it worthwhile listening for even casual fans. Then again, most fans of Phish will want to hear everything the group has ever played. —*Stephen Thomas Erlewine*

Phranc

Folk-Pop
Born in 1959, in Southern California, a young Jewish woman attends 13 years of Hebrew School and loves to swim. Who knew that little pigtailed Suzy Gottlieb who fooled around with the guitar at age nine was to come out as a lesbian separatist, then a punk rocker, then a radical folksinger named Phranc, effective at dissolving prejudice and barriers, and the only lesbian solo artist to perform out to mainstream audiences?

Tracing her lyrical roots to Allan Sherman (she has listened to *My Son the Folksinger* since age five), Phranc has toured with The Smiths and The Pogues, appeared in the film *The Fall of Western Civilization* with her band, Nervous Gender, has been interviewed for *People Magazine*, and has released three albums, *Folksinger* (1985, Rhino Records), the campy *I Enjoy Being a Girl* (1989, Island Records), and, most recently, *Positively Phranc* (1991, Island Records).

Phranc credits the strong foundation in her lesbian youth with allowing her to make the transition between radical separatist and affirmative lesbian missionary. Experiencing consistent, positive, role models; living and working within a disciplined, politically thoughtful collective; and being shown personal tolerance all cultivated the inner reserve and confidence necessary for confronting and thriving within the straight world. Though Phranc's early path often was unproductive, sometimes wild, and occasionally self-destructive, she, nonetheless, retained a firm commitment to coming out and staying out with her own opinions as well as with her lesbian identity. —*Laura Post*

Folksinger / 1985 / Island ✦✦✦
Her debut of modern acoustic folk with a rock edge includes voice, guitar, and harmonica. —*AMG*

● **I Enjoy Being a Girl** / 1989 / Island ✦✦✦✦
Her pop breakthrough features songs like "Take Off Your Swastiska." She doesn't mince words, and as with the great folksingers of the past, her music is just as good as the message. Politics infused with humor and irony, it's got a great cover! —*AMG*

Positively Phranc / 1991 / Island ✦✦✦
This is harder and more electric, with a song about Billy Tipton and a wonderful a cappella cover of the Beach Boys classic "Surfer Girl." —*AMG*

Charlie Pickett

Alternative Pop/Rock
To this guitar playing native of Dania, FL, punk rock meant old Rolling Stones and mid-'60s garage rock more than the Ramones and Sex Pistols, and that devotion to a hyped-up roots-rock sound was what made Charlie Pickett such a fine performer. With his backing band the Eggs (later called the MC3), Pickett was an anomaly in the era of punk aggression and new wave marketabil-

ity, playing covers by British old-wavers Johnny Kidd and the Pirates and Manfred Mann when the prevailing cry of underground rockers was "no future." Still, Pickett's unobtrusive, straightahead style endeared him to both punks and new-wave thrillseekers, and after a so-so debut live LP (*Live at the Button*), he quickly fired off a couple of good-to-great records steeped in a blues-influenced, roots-rock sound with plenty of guitar fireworks supplied by John Salton. Pickett's best moments came in the mid-'80s recording for Twin/Tone under the watchful eyes of producer (and ex-Suicide Commando) Chris Osgood, who finally gave Pickett the kind of muscular, grimy sound he needed. (This sound was very reminiscent of the sound Jimmy Miller gave the Stones on *Exile On Main Street*.) But moderate success and the support of enthusiastic rock critics was all Pickett could muster. His last LP, *The Wilderness*, was good, but received little acclaim, and by the '90s Pickett seemed destined to remain a regional phenomenon. —*John Dougan*

Live at the Button / 1982 / Open ♦♦

● **Cowboy Junkie Au-Go-Go [EP]** / 1984 / Open ♦♦♦♦
The title says it all. A blues-inflected, rootsy joyride through the gutters of rock and roll. Pickett's big, brawling voice is a joy to hear, and John Salton's guitar makes a joyful noise. Although at the time post-punk roots rock revisionists (e.g., Jefferey Lee Pierce) were getting lots more ink, Pickett's records, while not as self-consciously arty, were certainly as good. And this may well be his best. Lone caveat: this is an EP. It was, however, rereleased on compact disc in 1989 with *The Wilderness*. —*John Dougan*

Route 33 / 1986 / Twin/Tone ♦♦♦
Chris Osgood turned out to be Charlie Pickett's most sympathetic producer, and it shows on this fine record. With help from demi-big shots like Jim Duckworth and Maureen Tucker, Pickett sounds relaxed and confident here, and friendliness practically oozes from the grooves. This should've been a much bigger record than it was, and in spite of a couple of mediocre tracks that ramble on a bit too long, it still sounds mighty good 10 years after. —*John Dougan*

The Wilderness / 1988 / Safety Net ♦♦♦

Wilson Pickett

b. Mar. 18, 1941, Prattville, AL
Soul, R&B
The Wicked Pickett, as he dubbed himself, first achieved a measure of success as the apoplectic lead tenor on the Falcons's "I Found a Love" in 1962. Fleeting success followed (his original of "If You Need Me" was scooped up by Solomon Burke), before he signed with Atlantic Records in 1964. After a couple of false starts, he was shipped down to Memphis and came back with "In the Midnight Hour." It was followed by similarly compelling entries such as "Don't Fight It," "634-5789," "Mustang Sally," and a hysterical revival of Chris Kenner's mid-tempo shuffle, "Land of 1000 Dances." Scouring old albums, one will also notice that Pickett never lost his feel for a slow ballad, despite his reputation as the prince of the dance floor. Some have charged that Pickett went on to reduce spontaneous emotion to a cliché, and most of his later records certainly reinforce that notion, but at his considerable best, Pickett was an immensely compelling performer at any tempo. The hit movie *The Commitments* hinted broadly at the esteem in which vintage Pickett is held. Sampled at his best, he was a titan. —*Colin Escott*

In the Midnight Hour / 1965 / Atlantic ♦♦♦
Wilson Pickett's first album, from 1965, was a bit of a hodgepodge, including singles from as far back as 1962. Three of these tracks were actually issued as singles by the Falcons (for whom Pickett sang lead) before he started his solo career; others were issued as singles before Pickett broke through as a national star with the title track. This 12-track album doesn't really suffer as a result, however. Besides the all-time classic "In The Midnight Hour," it includes the Mann/Weil-penned single "Come Home Baby," covered by several rock and soul artists; "Don't Fight It," which reached the R&B Top Ten in late 1965; "I'm Gonna Cry," a 1964 single Pickett wrote with fellow soul legend Don Covay; and "I Found A Love," the Falcons single that made the R&B Top Ten in 1962. Working with several collaborators (including Steve Cropper), Pickett himself wrote most of the tunes on this album. The record also featured the first recordings he made with the Stax rhythm section in Memphis—a combination that would yield much fine soul music

throughout the rest of the '60s. The 1993 CD reissue of this album features extensive liner notes and session details. —*Richie Unterberger*

○ **The Exciting Wilson Pickett** / 1966 / Atlantic ♦♦♦♦
Less of a hodgepodge than his debut *In The Midnight Hour* album, Pickett's second LP established—if there had been any doubt—his stature as a major '60s soul man. The 12 tracks include his monster hits "634-5789," "Ninety-Nine And A Half (Won't Do)," "In The Midnight Hour," and "Land of 1000 Dances" (the last of which was his first Top Ten pop hit). Collectors will be more interested in the non-hit cuts, which are of nearly an equal level. These include covers of the R&B standards "Something You Got," "Mercy Mercy," and "Barefootin' "; several original tunes written in collaboration with Memphis soul greats Steve Cropper, Eddie Floyd, and David Porter; and Bobby Womack's "She's So Good To Me." It all adds up to one of the most consistent 1960s soul albums. The CD reissue of this 1966 record features detailed liner notes and session documentation. —*Richie Unterberger*

○ **The Wicked Pickett** / 1966 / Atlantic ♦♦♦♦
A fabulous album, done when Pickett was in the midst of his best period at Atlantic. It had everything—great songs, wonderful production and arrangements, and a hungry, galvanizing Wilson Pickett hollering, screaming, shouting, and soaring on anything he covered, from ballads to uptempo dance and midtempo wailers. It also has been deleted at present. —*Ron Wynn*

○ **The Sound of Wilson Pickett** / 1967 / Atlantic ♦♦♦♦
A masterpiece, perhaps his finest '60s album. This wasn't a hits collection, but a batch of great singles. His version of "Funky Broadway" may still be the best; it was certainly the most swaggering and posturing, punctuated by his screams and jubilant cries. Pickett was all over the R&B charts in 1967, and this was one of three albums Atlantic issued on him that year. Each one was a classic. —*Ron Wynn*

I'm in Love / 1968 / Atlantic ♦♦♦
Bobby Womack's title track, which was a masterpiece of hurt and heartache, became in Wilson Pickett's hands a smashing, surging tale that managed to register the hurt Womack had in mind, but also contained plenty of fire and energy as well. No one except James Brown could put as much crunching power behind a scream as Pickett, but he was also a first-rate soul vocalist who showed often that he could do more than just yell and bellow. —*Ron Wynn*

Midnight Mover / 1968 / Atlantic ♦♦♦
The title track was another of Pickett's smoking '60s soul singles; he rode the beat perfectly, and then concluded the song with a series of bloodcurdling screams and triumphant exhortations. He turned in several other equally assertive, defiant, and excellent uptempo and ballad performances, continuing a run of great Atlantic albums. —*Ron Wynn*

Hey Jude / 1969 / Atlantic ♦♦♦
There were some in the soul world who scratched their heads when Wilson Pickett covered "Hey Jude" in 1969. They couldn't be found when the song became a Top 20 hit, one of five R&B smashes Pickett enjoyed that year. His cover was both outlandish and right on the button; the remainder of the album is just old-fashioned, urgent, gritty Southern soul. It's unfortunately out of print at present; hopefully, Rhino will put it back into circulation at some point. —*Ron Wynn*

Right on / 1970 / Atlantic ♦♦♦
Wilson Pickett encountered a momentary slump in 1970, as this album was his first for Atlantic in many years that stayed locked in the bottom rungs of the pop Top 200 albums. Pickett did get a fluke novelty hit with "Sugar, Sugar," maybe his worst soul smash ever. The album wasn't a total disaster, but everyone forgot about it quickly when Atlantic rushed out *Wilson Pickett in Philadelphia* later that year. —*Ron Wynn*

○ **Wilson Pickett in Philadelphia** / 1970 / Atlantic ♦♦♦♦
A landmark album, one of Pickett's all-time best and without question his finest '70s date. "Engine, Engine, Number 9" was a return to the great funky days of the '60s. The edited single was a big radio and crossover hit, while the extended version was a club smash. It revived his career, although he was now feuding with Atlantic and would take almost a year and a half to follow this with any new material. Hopefully, Rhino will have the good sense to put this back out on CD for a new generation to savor. —*Ron Wynn*

Don't Knock My Love / 1971 / Atlantic ✦✦✦
His final definitive Atlantic session. The title track was vintage Pickett—a driving, syncopated bass and surging horn arrangement punctuated by his aggressive, spiraling lead and concluding with a robust shout and defiant exhortation. That set the stage for some sharp ballads and a couple of other nice uptempo cuts. "Don't Knock My Love, Part 1" was Pickett's last number one R&B hit and a Top 20 pop smash. He left Atlantic shortly after the album peaked on the charts, returning to RCA and never enjoying similar success again. —*Ron Wynn*

Join Me and Let's Be Free / 1972 / RCA Victor ✦✦
Wilson Pickett kept trying with RCA, going back to them in the mid-'70s after scoring one more hit album with Atlantic. He tried doing material with less soul and more pop production touches, toned down the familiar screams and cries, and stuck more to the melody. The results were unsatisfying all around. —*Ron Wynn*

Miz Lena's Boy / 1973 / RCA Victor ✦✦
A funny title, and a little bit better material and production for yet another Pickett attempt on RCA. He got a couple of chart hits, although the album itself didn't fare well. But it just wasn't the same; no longer was he roaring and belting out lyrics over a driving beat. Instead, he seemed like a mellow, almost restrained pop/soul type. —*Ron Wynn*

Tonight I'm My Biggest Audience / 1974 / RCA Victor ✦✦
A curious mid-'70s session for Pickett, one that left many people wondering if either he or RCA knew what was happening. The songs were mostly weak ballads or overproduced uptempo pop; Pickett's voice sounded disjointed, and his screams and cries woeful. This was his second RCA album, and it was no surprise when he left the label. —*Ron Wynn*

American Soul Man / 1987 / Motown ✦✦
If Wilson Pickett had arrived at Motown 20 years earlier, the reaction would have been frenzied. But by the time he joined them in 1987, the once-great company was in the throes of a horrible slump. Pickett's late-'80s album for them was painful. It wasn't half bad as far as production and arrangements, and Pickett's vocals were better than anticipated. But the songs sounded third-rate, and while he did get one single onto the lower rungs of the charts, "Don't Turn Away," this wasn't the Pickett everyone loved or wanted to hear. —*Ron Wynn*

○ **A Man and a Half: Best of Wilson Pickett** / 1992 / Rhino ✦✦✦✦
This tribute to the soulful career of the Wicked One is simply one of the most fabulous compilation reissues of 1992. From the fire-breathing kick-off of "I Found a Love," Pickett's debut recording with the Falcons, through all the great Atlantic hits, this 2-disc set spotlights some of the greatest singing ever recorded. Songs like "In the Midnight Hour," "Mustang Sally," and "Land of 1000 Dances," helped define '60s soul music. Great liner notes by Leo Sacks and equally great photos. A must for your collection. —*Christine Ohlman*

★ **Very Best of** / 1993 / Rhino ✦✦✦✦✦
A terrific single-disc collection of all of Pickett's biggest hits; it's the place to go for casual fans. —*Stephen Thomas Erlewine*

Pink Floyd

Group, Art-Rock/Progressive-Rock, Psychedelic
Practically from its inception in 1965, Pink Floyd was on the cutting edge of psychedelic rock experimentalism, utilizing feedback, sound effects, light shows, unorthodox lyrical themes, and spacey productions. It was band member Syd Barrett (b. Jan 6, 1946) who gave the band its moniker, inspired by Georgia bluesmen Pink Anderson and Floyd Council. Barrett's trippy songwriting on their debut album, *The Piper at the Gates of Dawn* (UK #6), set the band even further apart from most bands of the time. Barrett, however, left the band due to psychological deterioration encouraged by drug abuse, leaving bassist Roger Waters (b. Sep 9, 1944) to take over the primary songwriting duties.

The band's sonic explorations achieved focus with 1973's seamless *The Dark Side of the Moon* (#1), an album that firmly placed them in the big time. Followup albums *Wish You Were Here* (#1), *Animals* (#3), *The Wall* (#1), and *The Final Cut* (#6) enjoyed phenomenal success.

Waters revealed an increasingly vitriolic spirit in his conceptual themes as he addressed the breakdown of individual dignity in the face of a perceived Orwellian post-World War II social order.

It should be said that guitarist Dave Gilmour's (b. Mar 6, 1946) soaring guitar work and songwriting contributions on *The Wall's* "Comfortably Numb" gave him a high profile in the band. After *The Final Cut*, Waters and the band acrimoniously split up in 1983, leaving them to pursue various solo efforts, with moderate success.

Gilmour re-formed Pink Floyd in 1987 with drummer Nick Mason (b. Jan 27, 1945) and keyboardist Rick Wright (b. Jul 28, 1945), releasing *A Momentary Lapse of Reason* (#3), which sparked a flurry of lawsuits between Waters and the band over the ownership of the name. While the album lacks the thematic bite of Waters's input, the band's sound is intact, helping the album become a worldwide hit. The new Pink Floyd's success continued in 1994, when *The Division Bell* topped the charts upon its release. —*Rick Clark*

☆ **The Piper at the Gates of Dawn** / Aug. 5, 1967 / Capitol ✦✦✦✦✦
The debut album combines long, group-written, largely instrumental compositions with shorter, whimsical, eclectic pop songs written by lead singer and guitarist Syd Barrett (his only full-length album appearance with the group). A wonderful evocation of the distinctly British take on '60s psychedelic music. (Note: Avoid the out-of-print LP version *Pink Floyd*, Tower 5093, which abridges the original UK album.) —*William Ruhlmann*

Tonite Let's All Make Love in London / 1968 / CBS ✦✦✦
Peter Whitehead's 1967 film *Tonight Let's All Make Love in London* was an attempt to document the mid-'60s Swinging London pop scene at its peak. The soundtrack was an instant collector's item, divided between interview snippets with such scenemakers as Michael Caine, David Hockney, Julie Christie, and Mick Jagger, and marginal incidental music by unmemorable pop acts produced by Rolling Stones manager Andrew Loog Oldham (Vashti and Twice As Much). The Small Faces' contribution, "Here Comes The Nice," is easily available elsewhere. Allen Ginsberg (misspelled "Alan" on the original sleeve) reads the poem that gave the film its name. The chief attraction of this CD reissue is the addition of two lengthy, otherwise unavailable cuts by the original Pink Floyd lineup in 1967 (mere snippets had appeared on the original LP). Their 16-minute version of "Interstellar Overdrive" (rerecorded for their first LP) starts off scintillatingly, then degenerates into a rather aimless jam. The 12-minute "Nick's Boogie," not available in any other version, is a considerably more aimless, free-form instrumental piece dominated by scraping guitars. Even in its expanded CD reissue, this album will only appeal to hardcore collectors. —*Richie Unterberger*

The Saucerful of Secrets / Jun. 29, 1968 / Capitol ✦✦✦
A transitional album on which the band moved from Barrett's relatively concise and vivid songs to spacy, ethereal material with lengthy instrumental passages. Barrett's influence is still felt (he actually did manage to contribute one track, the jovial "Jugband Blues"), and much of the material retains a gentle, fairy-tale ambience. "Remember A Day" and "See Saw" are highlights; on "Set The Controls For The Heart Of The Sun," "Let There Be More Light," and the lengthy instrumental title track, the band begin to map out the dark and repetitive pulses that would characterize their next few records. —*Richie Unterberger*

More / Jul. 1969 / Capitol ✦✦
Commissioned as a soundtrack to the seldom-seen French hippie movie of the same name, *More* was a Floyd album in its own right, reaching the Top 10 in Britain. The group's atmospheric music was a natural for movies, but when assembled for record, these pieces were unavoidably a bit patchwork, ranging from folky ballads to fierce electronic instrumentals to incidental mood music. Several of the tracks are pleasantly inconsequential, but this record does include some strong compositions, especially "Cymbaline," "Green Is The Colour," and "The Nile Song." All of these developed into stronger pieces in live performances, and better, high-quality versions are available on numerous bootlegs. —*Richie Unterberger*

Ummagumma / Nov. 1969 / Capitol ✦✦✦
A two-disc set, the first disc containing a definitive live set, the second experimental contributions from each of the band members. —*William Ruhlmann*

Atom Heart Mother / Oct. 1970 / Capitol ✦✦✦
Pink Floyd started to stretch out its long numbers here, with the orchestrated title track taking up an entire side of the album. Still not as focused as they would be, the group nevertheless was beginning to show the musical ambition that would lead to their later successes. —*William Ruhlmann*

○ **Relics** / May 1971 / Barclay ◆◆◆◆
A singles collection from the Syd Barrett era, containing the British hits "Arnold Layne" and "See Emily Play," among other psychedelic nuggets. — *William Ruhlmann*

○ **Meddle** / Oct. 30, 1971 / Capitol ◆◆◆◆
With *Meddle*, Pink Floyd instrumentally arrived at an airy ensemble sound, which would eventually find full flower on their 1973 classic *The Dark Side of the Moon*. This approach is particularly evident on "Echoes," a periodically languorous jam that takes up one half of the album. Nevertheless, there are enough sonic concepts and pleasant melodies at work on this album to make it worthwhile to the Floyd fan looking to dig deeper than *The Dark Side of the Moon* or *The Wall*. —*Rick Clark*

Obscured by Clouds / Jun. 1972 / Capitol ◆◆
Like *More*, *Obscured by Clouds* was a soundtrack album Pink Floyd threw together quickly for a film by Barbet Schroeder. Songs like "Free Four" show Roger Waters developing the songwriting skill that would catapult Pink Floyd to mass stardom with its next new release, *The Dark Side of the Moon*. — *William Ruhlmann*

Nice Pair / 1973 / Capitol ◆◆◆
A reissue of Pink Floyd's first two albums, *The Piper at the Gates Of Dawn* and *A Saucerful Of Secrets*, as a two-record set. — *William Ruhlmann*

★ **Dark Side of the Moon** / Mar. 24, 1973 / Capitol ◆◆◆◆◆
Pink Floyd's instrumental prowess and mastery of sound effects, married for the first time to bassist Roger Waters' lyrics about madness, "Time," "Money," and other concerns make for the most impressive mood music of the decade (and sales of 25 million copies so far). —*William Ruhlmann*

☆ **Wish You Were Here** / Sep. 12, 1975 / Columbia ◆◆◆◆◆
A concept album paying tribute to Syd Barrett ("Shine on You Crazy Diamond") and lambasting the music industry ("Have a Cigar"). —*William Ruhlmann*

Animals / Oct. 2, 1977 / Columbia ◆◆◆
Consisting of heavily reworked songs that had long been a part of Pink Floyd's live repertoire and were now given an Orwellian overview, *Animals* found Pink Floyd acting as the mouthpiece for Roger Waters' increasingly vitriolic takes on modern life. The result was one of its less successful later efforts. —*William Ruhlmann*

☆ **The Wall** / Nov. 1979 / Columbia ◆◆◆◆◆
This is Roger Waters's two-disc meditation on the travails of a rock star, whose unhappy life causes him to build a psychological barrier between himself and the rest of the world. Contains the #1 hit "Another Brick in the Wall (Part 2)" and the concert favorite "Comfortably Numb" (cowritten by David Gilmour). —*William Ruhlmann*

Collection of Great Dance Songs / Nov. 1981 / Columbia ◆◆
Anyone who knew anything about Pink Floyd knew that a dance band they were not, so this profit-taking, holiday-season compilation, courtesy of Columbia Records, was intended ironically. Arguably the quintessential album band, Pink Floyd is not well-served by compilations, especially one on which the two parts of "Shine On You Crazy Diamond" are edited together and there's a re-recording of "Money." Stick to the full-length versions. — *William Ruhlmann*

Works / 1983 / Capitol ◆◆
Capitol Records gets into the Pink Floyd compilation game, but why bother when all you have in mind is the same old tired tracks, plus one previously unreleased song appropriately called "Embryo?" — *William Ruhlmann*

The Final Cut / Apr. 1983 / Columbia ◆◆◆
A Roger Waters solo album in all but name, containing the composer's response to Britain's Falklands War in the form of a massive condemnation of war and government. — *William Ruhlmann*

A Momentary Lapse of Reason / 1987 / Columbia ◆◆
A David Gilmour solo album in all but name, heavily featuring the kind of atmospheric instrumental music and Gilmour guitar sound typical of the Floyd before the now-departed Roger Waters took over but lacking Waters' unifying vision and lyrical ability. — *William Ruhlmann*

Delicate Sound of Thunder / Jan. 2, 1988 / Columbia ◆◆ —*Rick Clark*
This live album documents their 1987-1988 world tour.

○ **Shine on [Box Set]** / Nov. 17, 1992 / Columbia ◆◆◆◆
A lavish and expensive nine-CD box set of Pink Floyd's greatest hits—which are all albums, naturally. Seven albums (*A Saucerful of Secrets*, *Meddle*, *The Dark Side of the Moon*, *Wish You Were Here*, *Animals*, *The Wall*, and *A Momentary Lapse of Reason*) have been digitally remastered; when the 8 discs are set together on the shelf, their spines form the prism and rainbow from the cover of *The Dark Side of the Moon*. *Shine on* also includes an extra disc of early singles, housed in a digi-pak, and a hardcover book with plenty of pictures and text. Since there is no previously unreleased material included on the set, the only incentive for hardcore fans who already own the albums is the packaging and remastering, both of which are impressive. *Shine on* is certainly worth the investment for those who don't already own the music. —*Stephen Thomas Erlewine*

The Division Bell / 1994 / Columbia ◆◆
The second post-Roger Waters Pink Floyd album is less forced and more of a group effort than *A Momentary Lapse Of Reason*—keyboard player Rick Wright is back to full band member status and has co-writing credits on five of the 11 songs, even getting lead vocals on "Wearing The Inside Out. Some of David Gilmour's lyrics (co-written by Polly Samson and Nick Laird-Clowes of the Dream Academy) might be directed at Waters, notably "Lost For Words" and "A Great Day For Freedom," with its references to "the wall" coming down, although the more specific subject is the Berlin Wall and the fall of Communism. In any case, there is a vindictive, accusatory tone to songs such as "What Do You Want From Me" and "Poles Apart," and the overarching theme, from the album title to the graphics to the "I-you" pronouns in most of the lyrics, has to do with dichotomies and distinctions, with "I" always having the upper hand. Musically, Gilmour, Nick Mason, and Wright have largely turned the clock back to the pre-*Dark Side Of The Moon* Floyd, with slow tempos, sustained keyboard chords, and guitar solos with a lot of echo. — *William Ruhlmann*

Pulse / 1995 / Columbia ◆◆
Pink Floyd claim they had no intention of recording another live album when they began the *Division Bell* tour, but performing *The Dark Side of the Moon* in its entirety convinced the group to release another double live set, called *Pulse*. There's no question that the group is comprised of talented musicians, including the number of studio professionals that augmented the trio on tour. Whether they're inspired musicians is up to debate. A large part of Pink Floyd's live show is based on the always impressive visuals; on the *Division Bell* tour, they closed each show with an unprecedented laser extravaganza. In order for the visuals and the music to coincide, the group needed to play the sets as tightly as possible, with little improvisation. Consequently, an audio version of this concert, separated from the visuals, is quite dull. Pink Floyd play the greatest hits and the new songs professionally, yet the versions differ only slightly from the original recordings, making *Pulse* a tepid experience. (The first edition of the album featured a blinking red light—a symbolic representation of the "pulse"—in the spine of the disc and cassette.) —*Stephen Thomas Erlewine*

○ **Dark Side of The Moo** / Bootleg ◆◆◆◆
Look at the title carefully; it's not the Floyd *meisterwerk*, but a wittily titled (and packaged, with *Atom Heart Mother*-like cows on the cover) bootleg of their rarest studio tracks. Presented in 99-100% of their original fidelity, these include some choice and necessary items that would cost you quite a bit to assemble piece by piece. From the Syd Barrett era, we have "Candy And A Currant Bun," the brilliant B-side to their debut "Arnold Layne" single, and "Apples And Oranges," the legendary flop single from late 1967. Other late-'60s (post-Syd) flop singles include the pleasant psychedelic ballads "It Would Be So Nice" and "Point Me At The Sky." A number of the other tracks, including their contributions to the *Zabriskie Point* soundtrack, the original studio version of "Astronomy Domine" (cut off the U.S. version of the first LP), and the different "Interstellar Overdrive" that showed up on the *Tonite Let's All Make Love in London* soundtrack, have appeared on CD since the mid-'80s issue of this bootleg. If you're not inclined to spend an additional $50 or so tracking these down, it certainly makes sense to spring for this, if you can find it. —*Richie Unterberger*

○ **Rhapsody in Pink (The Psychedelic Years: The Incredible BBC** / Bootleg ◆◆◆◆
Packaged under various titles, this is *the* collection of material to hunt for if you're looking for unreleased Floyd from the post-Barrett, pre-*Dark Side* era. Bootleg fidelity doesn't come any better

than this; it's one of the very few occasions where you could argue that the sound may actually be *better* than most official releases. These BBC airshots from the late '60s and early '70s focus on rather obscure material: "Julia Dream," "If," "Green Is the Colour," "Embryo," and the never-released "Murderistic Women" (a blueprint for "Careful With That Axe, Eugene"). There are also full-bore workouts of "Echoes" and "Atom Heart Mother Suite" that, depending on one's taste, could be argued to exceed the officially issued versions. The double LP, still findable, contains about 85 minutes of music and is a great value. —*Richie Unterberger*

Saucerful of Outtakes / Bootleg ♦♦♦

There is a huge demand for Syd Barrett material, and, alas, a very limited supply. This is probably the best compilation of unreleased Barrett-era Floyd, though the material and sound quality are erratic. "Lucy Leave" and "I'm a Kingbee" are the band's very first demos, showing a much more R&B-oriented outfit, and the live version of "Astronomy Domine" is pretty good. The BBC sessions contain a bunch of songs from the classic *Piper at the Gates of Dawn* album, in muffled, hissy fidelity that is nonetheless an improvement on many previous bootlegs. These include two of the most coveted Barrett-Floyd treasures, the unreleased songs "Vegetable Man" and "Scream Thy Last Scream," chaotic but fascinating pieces which illustrate Syd's descent into madness more vividly than anything else he recorded with the group. Be on the lookout, though, for much clearer studio outtakes of these two songs (perhaps recorded with Floyd, perhaps solo) that have appeared on bootlegs throughout the years. —*Richie Unterberger*

BOOK

♦♦♦♦ **Saucerful Of Secrets: The Pink Floyd Odyssey**, by Nicholas Schaffner (Harmony, 1991). It's kind of surprising that it took so long for a reasonably thorough Pink Floyd bio to appear, but it was written by the right man for the job. Schaffner, who previously penned first-rate volumes on the Beatles and the British Invasion, does his usually meticulous but entertaining job of weaving a storehouse of facts with vivid critical description of the band's music and astral horizons. Appropriately, he devotes a good third of the book to the band's most fascinating and productive period—their 1966-68 flower-power beginnings, when they were very much dominated by Syd Barrett, a name unknown even now to many Pink Floyd fans. Barrett's truly tragic descent from genius into madness (documented more fully in the Barrett bio *Crazy Diamond*) inspired and hounded the band throughout their existence, but didn't prevent them from becoming international megastars. Schaffner documents their ascent from underground psychedelic favorites to stadium giants with aplomb, drawing from a good deal of first-hand material from band members and key associates such as their first manager, Peter Jenner. The book's chief flaw is one which afflicts the biographies of most rock stars of the period: after a point (in Floyd's case, about the mid-'70s), the story simply gets much less interesting. —*Richie Unterberger*

The Pirates

Group, Rock & Roll

Originally organized as the trio backing Johnny Kidd, this band continued working long after the latter's death in a mid-'60s automobile accident. Behind lead guitarist Mick Green, who has played with just about everybody over the years (most recently on Paul McCartney's Russian album, *Choba B CCCP*), they embraced their punk roots in the late '70s and early '80s and still do a great show, even without a "real" lead singer. —*Bruce Eder*

● **Out of Their Skulls** / 1977 / Warner Brothers ♦♦♦♦

Well representative of the latter-day group. Includes both live and studio material, with a savage "Shakin' All Over" as the highlight, and some loud and wonderfully grungy rockabilly. —*Bruce Eder*

Gene Pitney

b. Feb. 17, 1941

Pop/Rock

Between 1961 and 1968, Gene Pitney's seamless pop sound scored sixteen Top 40 hits, with songs like "Town Without Pity" (#13), "Only Love Can Break a Heart" (#2), "(The Man Who Shot) Liberty Valance" (#4), "It Hurts to Be in Love" (#7), and "I'm Gonna Be Strong" (#9). Pitney, with his expressive tenor voice, was one of the few artists who successfully bridged the gap from early-'60s light pop to the British Invasion sound. Much of this came from

his extensive music-industry background as a producer, engineer, and songwriter, penning hits for Ricky Nelson, the Crystals, Roy Orbison, and others. He also worked with producer Phil Spector and had a knack for identifying upcomers like Al Kooper and Randy Newman. Pitney's shrewd business sense, coupled with the compliance of manager/publisher Aaron Schroeder, positioned him to record with much more favorable artistic control and greater participation in publishing and royalties. —*Rick Clark*

● **Anthology 1961-1968** / 1986 / Rhino ♦♦♦♦

The voice still sounds surreal, like no one else in pop music, and this collection of hits exudes class. Emotional, pained, stunning. Pitney is a master—rock's Caruso. —*Jeff Tamarkin*

○ **Gene Pitney & George Jones** / 1994 / Bear Family ♦♦♦♦

○ **More Greatest Hits** / 1995 / Varese Sarabande ♦♦♦♦

A very worthy supplement to *Anthology*; in fact, it's almost as good. Has a lot of minor hits, some of which ("I Must Be Seeing Things," "Backstage") rank among his best; "Nobody Needs Your Love," an early Randy Newman composition that was a #2 hit in England in 1966; Pitney's own versions of his compositions "Hello Mary Lou" and "Today's Teardrops," much better known via their interpretations by Rick Nelson and Roy Orbison, respectively; and interesting album tracks and flop singles. All cuts are from the '60s, except the 1989 version of "Something's Gotten Hold Of My Heart," performed as a duet with Marc Almond. —*Richie Unterberger*

Pixies

Group, Alternative Pop/Rock

With their jagged, roaring guitars and undeniable pop melodies, the Pixies were arguably the best American alternative rock band of the late '80s. Many critics accused the band of being pretentious, amateurish college students just wanting to make noise, and some of that criticism is rather accurate; their records are filled with squealing guitar noise that could only be made by enthusiastic, inexperienced musicians and rabid rock fans. But the band was able to meld punk and post-punk indie guitar rock, classic pop, surf rock, and stadium-sized riffs with singer/guitarist Black Francis' (born Charles Thompson) bizarre, fragmented lyrics about space, religion, sex, mutilation, and pop culture; while the meaning of his lyrics may have been impenetrable, the music was direct and forceful. The Pixies' busy, brief songs, extreme dynamics and subversion of conventional song structures was very influential on many bands of the '90s; Nirvana, in particular, cited them as one of their favorite bands, admitting that "Smells like Teen Spirit" was a Pixies rip-off.

By the time of their last album, 1991's *Trompe Le Monde*, the band was increasingly becoming a solo project for Black Francis; bassist/vocalist Kim Deal barely sang on the record and was reportedly angry that she wasn't allowed any space for her songs on the last two albums. After a tension-filled final tour opening U2's 1992 Zoo TV stadium extravaganza, Black Francis informed the band in early 1993 that they were officially broken up. He inverted his stage name to Frank Black and released his first solo album three months later. Lead guitarist Joey Santiago played with Black; drummer David Lovering joined Cracker. At the time, Deal was already at work on the Breeders' second album, which became a much bigger commercial success than any Pixies record. —*Stephen Thomas Erlewine*

○ **Come on Pilgrim** / 1987 / 4AD/Elektra ♦♦♦♦

The band's first mini-album is actually some of the demos that the group gave to 4AD. The label was so impressed by the group's potential that it releasd eight of the demos (paid for by Black Francis' dad). It's easy to see why they were impressed; *Come on Pilgrim* contains some of the group's best material, from the eerie opener "Caribou" to the propulsive pop of the final track, "Levitate Me." Not one of the eight tracks on *Come on Pilgrim* is a ringer; "I've Been Tired," "Nimrod's Son," and "Ed Is Dead" also prove that the Pixies' debut is one of their finest efforts. —*Heather Phares*

☆ **Surfer Rosa** / 1988 / 4AD/Elektra ♦♦♦♦♦

Surfer Rosa is one of the seminal art-punk albums of the '80s. It mixes thrashy guitars, boy-girl harmonies and strange lyrics in a way that still sounds fresh and innovative. Joey Santiago's prickly guitar work, Black Francis' psychotic shriek of a voice, Kim Deal's steady bass and luminous vocals and David Lovering's formidable drumming unite in some blazing punk and unique pop. "Bone Machine," "Broken Face," "Oh My Golly!" and "Vamos" zip along at a fearsome rate, taking no prisoners. But the Pixies' beauty is just as apparent on *Surfer Rosa*. Tracks like Deal's "Gigantic" and Francis' "Where Is My Mind" provide refreshing contrasts to the rest of the album's incandescent energy. —*Heather Phares*

★ **Doolittle** / 1989 / 4AD/Elektra ✦✦✦✦✦
The group's third album (and their first for Elektra) continues the Pixies' winning streak. With Gil Norton producing, the band's raw edge is smoothed and streamlined into something too clever to be just punk but too edgy and neurotic to be simply pop. Driving spurt tunes like "Debaser" and "Wave of Mutilation" coexist with raw, disturbing tracks like "Dead," "Tame" and "Gouge Away." But a always, the Pixies exhibit their schizophrenic pop sensibilities and also produce melodic and catchy tunes like "Here Comes Your Man" and "La La Love You." —*Heather Phares*

○ **Bossanova** / 1990 / 4AD/Elektra ✦✦✦✦
The Pixies' fourth album dives deeper into the group's twin fascinations of surf pop and science fiction. Much of the hyperkinetic punk energy of the first three albums is missing, resulting in a kinder, gentler, but no less iconoclastic band. "Is She Weird," "Rock Music," "Allison" and "All over the World" are some of the album's highlights, as well as "Havalina," which shows off Deal's glorious voice. —*Heather Phares*

Trompe le Monde / 1991 / 4AD/Elektra ✦✦✦
The band's final album is not so much a return to their early, aggressive soun as it is a fusion of their raw energy and eccentricity. It's both arty and rousing, especially on fun tracks like "Subbacultcha," "Palace of the Brine," "D Equals RxT," and "U-Mass." Beautiful and offbeat songs like "Bird Dream of the Olympus Mons," "The Navajo Know," and "Letter to Memphis" confirm that the Pixies were and are one of the most individual talents in alternative music. —*Heather Phares*

Plainsong

Group, Folk-Rock
A quartet formed by Ian Matthews in 1972 with Andy Roberts, Bob Ronga and Dave Richards. They released the brilliant *In Search of Amelia Earhart* the same year to critical praise but little commercial success. While working on their followup, the more country oriented *Plainsong III*, Ronga quit and Matthews and Richards were unable to agree on the direction the band would take musically. They disbanded before the album's completion. In 1993, a revived interest in the band inspired a new studio album, *Dark Side of The Room* as well as a BBC recording of a promotional tour from 1972. —*Chris Woodstra*

● **In Search of Amelia Earhart** / 1972 / Elektra ✦✦✦✦
The theme of this album is loosely based on the disappearance of Amelia Earhart and features four tunes penned by Matthews including the spooky "For the Second Time" and "Call the Tune." Matthews also shows his ability to pick top-notch material by covering Paul Siebel's "Louise," the Jim & Jesse classic "Diesel on My Tail" and Rick Cunha's "Yo Yo Man" (a song Cunha attempted to chart with a year later). —*Jim Worbois*

Dark Side of The Room / 1993 / Line ✦✦✦
Matthews and company regrouped for this 1993 album. Though losing much of the charm of their first album, it is certainly in league with Matthew's latest work. —*Chris Woodstra*

○ **On Air-original BBC Recordings** / 1993 / Band Of Joy ✦✦✦✦
Voices Electric / 1994 / Line ✦✦

Robert Plant

b. Aug. 20, 1948
Hard Rock, Pop/Rock
British hard rock/heavy metal singer Robert Plant had released a couple of singles and worked with a number of bands before he hooked up with Jimmy Page's New Yardbirds, subsequently renamed Led Zeppelin, around the time of his 20th birthday in 1968. For the next 12 years, Plant was one of the biggest rock stars on the planet. He gradually developed as a singer, branching out into other styles within Zeppelin's hard rock framework, and he blossomed as a songwriter as well.

Plant launched a solo career in 1982 with the album *Pictures at Eleven*, a gold-selling hit. He did even better the following year with *Principle of Moments*. It sold a million copies, included the Top 20 hit "Big Log," and led to his first post-Zeppelin concert tour. Surprisingly, Plant then organized a one-off mini-album, *The Honeydrippers—Vol. One*, recording some rock oldies with a superstar pickup band. He faced greater consumer resistance with his third

solo album, *Shaken 'n' Stirred*, perhaps because joint appearances with Page led an audience to desire for a Zeppelin reunion. To an extent, Plant fed that desire with *Now & Zen*, which sampled Zeppelin tracks and featured Page. It was another million-seller. Plant's 1990 follow-up, *Manic Nirvana*, went gold. —*William Ruhlmann*

○ **Pictures at Eleven** / 1982 / Swan Song ✦✦✦✦
The directions in which Plant seemed to be heading in the later Zeppelin records—toward lighter, more melodic music, tempered with sometimes odd rhythms—are continued on his first solo album, which finds him singing more and screaming less. It wasn't Led Zeppelin, but then, that was the whole point. —*William Ruhlmann*

● **Principle of Moments** / 1983 / Es Paranza ✦✦✦✦
Plant reinvents rock and pop oldies in much the way Led Zeppelin did old blues songs. "Other Arms" recasts "Lay Down Your Arms," as Plant declares, "I'm not a prisoner of the big parade," while "In the Mood" retools an old pop theme. The playing is propulsive (thanks to guest drummer Phil Collins) and Plant's singing unusually supple. —*William Ruhlmann*

Shaken 'N' Stirred / 1985 / Es Paranza ✦✦✦
Robert Plant continued to expand the horizons of his music with his third album, *Shaken 'N' Stirred*, adding elements of worldbeat to his increasingly atmospheric and synth-driven pop-rock. Although the experimentation is admirable, and occasionally successful, the most successful tracks on the album are straightforward numbers like "Little By Little." —*Stephen Thomas Erlewine*

Now & Zen / 1989 / Es Paranza ✦✦✦
Robert Plant hires a new band, prominently featuring keyboardist Phil Johnstone, and also adds a backup singer for a fuller sound. At the same time, the appearance of Jimmy Page on "Tall Cool One," a Top 25 hit, casts a glance back at Plant's Led Zeppelin days. —*William Ruhlmann*

Manic Nirvana / 1990 / Es Paranza ✦✦
Manic Nirvana essentially continued the revitalized hard-rock crunch of *Now & Zen*. Unlike the previous record, *Manic Nirvana* played it a little closer to the vest, concentrating on a set of lean, driving riff-rockers instead of ponderous Led Zeppelin pomp. While the overall result is successful—especially on the frenzied "Hurting Kind," the technicolor stomp of "Tie Die on the Highway," and the affectionate rockabilly cover "Your Ma Said You Cried in Your Sleep Last Night"—the album sounds like a holding pattern instead of a step forward. —*Stephen Thomas Erlewine*

Fate of Nations / May 27, 1993 / Atlantic ✦✦✦
At first, *Fate of Nations* seems so light and airy that it slips away through the layers of acoustic guitars, violins, and keyboards. Upon further listenings, more textures appear, and the album gains a calm sense of tension and reflectiveness. It's also Plant's most personal record ever; he addresses the death of his son in the beautiful "I Believe." Simultaneously, *Fate of Nations* is a political album—"Great Spirit" and "Network News" are two of the most socially conscious songs Plant has ever written. Yet, the album is never heavy-handed and doesn't fall into sermonizing or sentimentality. Plant has always had a folkie heart; on *Fate of Nations*, he wears it on his sleeve. —*Stephen Thomas Erlewine*

Plasmatics

Group, Punk, New Wave
Although their "fame" lasted for a full 15 minutes, few bands entered rock & roll with such a controversial reputation as did the Plasmatics. Founded by Rod Swenson (a porn film producer who fancied himself the next Malcolm McLaren), the Plasmatics were fronted by sex film "star" Wendy O. Williams, a muscular, raspy-voiced "singer" who generally wore little onstage. (Her most radical bit of fashion accessorizing consisted of covering her nipples with black electrical tape.) Almost as captivating was guitarist Richie Stotts, a tall, gangly geek who fancied garters and stockings and a blue mohawk; he also liked to smash his guitar against his head until he drew blood. Playing the New York punk circuit (i.e., CBGBs), the Plasmatics became notorious for their extreme stage shows, which, early on, culminated in Williams firing blanks from a sawed-off shotgun and taking a chainsaw to a human dummy filled with stage blood, sending a spray of fake gore throughout the club and anticipating the fake carnage of GWAR by nearly a decade. The music, however, was another story: mostly sub-literate punk rock loaded with lots of quasi-sci-fi totalitarianism and con-

sumer nightmares of Orwellian proportions that on record didn't work without the stage pyrotechnics, something I'm sure Swenson and the 'Matics understood completely as the stage shows quickly became more elaborate: cars were blown up, guitars were sawed in half (oddly, the dummy disappeared), equipment was set on fire—it was a Beavis and Butt-Head wet dream come to life.

None of this translated into significant record sales. While Williams became something of a demi-celebrity in punk circles, especially after she was busted (and brutalized by police) in Milwaukee for "public indecency," the Plasmatics were (gee, what a surprise) all show and no substance. Stotts, apparently on a quest for legitimacy, quit the band, and the focus became Wendy O. rather than the bunch of unknowns backing her up, even though one of her backup musicians was future Ramones producer and one-shot hard rock solo artist Jean Beauvoir. Williams eventually went solo, worked with Lemmy from Motörhead, and roped in Kiss's Gene Simmons to produce her totally useless album W.O.W. By the end of the '80s she was recording rap tracks and acting in B-films. Her career since then is pretty much a mystery, one that's perhaps best left unsolved. —*John Dougan*

New Hope for the Wretched / 1980 / Stiff ♦♦

● **Beyond the Valley of 1984/Metal Priestess** / 1981 / PVC ♦♦♦♦
If you're interested in actually listening to the Plasmatics (though I'd guess watching a video of them performing would be infinitely more satisfying) this is the only recording worth getting. More of a heavy metal than a punk record, it was reissued with their EP *Metal Priestess*, so you can get more bang (pun intended) for your buck. There are songs here worth playing more than once, and the outrage and vituperation seems real, even if it is a pose. Notable trivia: the drummer is ex-Alice Cooper tubman Neil Smith, a veteran of the *Killer* and *Billion Dollar Babies* Cooper era. —*John Dougan*

○ **Metal Priestess** / 1981 / PVC ♦♦♦♦

Coup D'Etat / 1982 / Capitol ♦♦♦

Plastic People of the Universe

Group, Experimental
This band's debut may well have been one of the most amazing and radical records to be released during the punk era (or any era for that matter), recorded under the most extreme conditions in the years before punk rock was a reality (1973-74). Prague's Plastic People of the Universe, and the band they later became, Pulnoc, remain one of rock & roll's great stories of triumph and how great music can be produced and survive even in the most hostile of environments. The band was founded in 1968 soon after 500,000 Soviet troops invaded Czechoslovakia. With the Kremlin not being particularly fond of Western-style rock that wasn't sanctioned by the state, the Plastic People, to paraphrase the Jefferson Airplane, quickly became outlaws in the eyes of Moscow (and the ruling Soviet government in Prague). From 1970 until the "Velvet Revolution" of 1989 that ended Soviet domination, the Plastic People lived a mostly illegal existence, with two of their members, Ivan Jirous and Jaroslav Vozniak, doing lengthy stretches in prison. Influenced by Zappa, English progressive rock/radical politicos Henry Cow, Captain Beefheart, and the Velvet Underground, the Plastic People appropriated the avant-garde leanings and anti-authoritarian outrage of these bands while working in their own sense of dread and desperation. Remember, according to Soviet law, they could not record, press and distribute albums or play gigs; still, they did all three surreptitiously, with the help of their numerous artist friends who made up an indefatigable support network known as the Invisible Organization.

Although all of their music remained unheard outside of Eastern Europe (or Czechoslovakia for that matter), their first record was released in the West in 1978. *Egon Bondy's Happy Hearts Club Banned* was not a proper record in the sense that the Plastic People entered a studio with the intent to record a "rock" record that would be placed into mass circulation. The reality was that these were grubby, low-fi demo recordings made by friends on primitive equipment and released without the band's knowledge. It also marked the first time the poetry of Czech dissident Egon Bondy was heard outside of Czechoslovakia. Bondy wrote lyrics that meshed perfectly with the Plastic People's cacophonous sound: harsh, dissonant soloing over repetitive odd-metered rhythms. It remains dense, challenging music, totally oblivious to the state-approved pop music.

A ferocious government crackdown on the Plastic People and

their supporters occurred in 1976. Many of them were jailed, their meager instruments and recording equipment confiscated or destroyed, all in the hope that this troublesome group of avant-garde artistic political radicals would finally be stopped. The problem was that Czech government officials didn't realize that the music of the Plastic People was being listened to in the West (thanks to favorable reviews of *Egon Bondy's* in the British music press and in America in the *Village Voice*) and that groups such as Amnesty International were now wondering why these musicians were being persecuted and jailed without trial. Although never reaching the fever pitch of, say, Nelson Mandela's incarceration, it wasn't long before the plight of the Plastic People became better known to an outraged Western pop community. After being released from prison, the band managed two more releases in the '80s that were (and still are) extremely difficult to find, unless you lived in New York.

After 15 years of struggle, incarceration, harassment and violence, the Plastic People quietly disbanded in 1984, but in no way stopped their anti-government activities. Finally, in 1988, a year before the "Velvet Revolution" and the ascendancy of the poet Vaclav Havel (a longtime supporter and occasional lyricist for the Plastic People) to the presidency, the band was given government permission to perform under the name Pulnoc ("Midnight"). With three original Plastic People in the group (Milan Hlavsa, Josef Janicek, and Jiri Kabes), Pulnoc recorded an extraordinary debut for Arista in 1991 (*City of Hysteria*), and a difficult-to-find live cassette recorded at New York's vaunted experimental performance space P.S. 122. Unlike the radical, dissonant sounds of the Plastic People, Pulnoc had a more traditional guitar-based rock sound and production polish, but its accessibility in no way detracts from its greatness as a record. For reasons unknown to me, there has been little music from Pulnoc since *City of Hysteria*. But, whatever the case, this story had a much happier ending that anyone could have anticipated. Although much work is required in finding what little recorded work they made, the payoff is well worth the effort. — *John Dougan*

● **Egon Bondy's Happy Heart Club Banned** / 1978 / Invisible ♦♦♦♦
Sounding like a meeting between Zappa, Henry Cow and Allen Ginsberg, this is a wild, politically charged chunk of avant-garde agit-prop. Bondy's poetry may not be the most lyrical you've ever heard, but his imagery is striking in its desperation and anger. Lots of honking saxes courtesy of Vratislav Brabenec, who is a big-time blower in the style of German free-jazz player Peter Brotzmann. For those whose love for late-'60s/early-'70s progressive rock is boundless, this is absolutely essential. But, even if you're squeamish about anything labeled art-rock, don't pass this by; the raw emotions and intense idealism in the face of oppression, despite their being sung in a language you don't speak (there are English lyrics on the LP jacket), are very moving. —*John Dougan*

Passion Play / 1980 / Bozi Mlyn ♦♦♦

Plastikman

Techno
Richie Hawtin, aka Plastikman, is a Windsor, Ontario native, and is just as renowned for his DJ skills as for original works. His +8 label is the home of some of the most influential techno of the past few years. Using Roland 808s and 303s, dinosaurs of the techno field, he creates intriguing, minimalist tracks with a lean beat and spare acid-sounding synth. In the one-year period beginning November, 1993, Hawtin released three albums—*Sheet One, Musik* and *Recycled Musik. —John Bush*

Sheet One / 1994 / Nova Mute ♦♦♦

● **Musik** / 1994 / Nova Mute ♦♦♦♦

The Platters

Group, R&B, Doo-Wop
During the '50s and early '60s, this Los Angeles vocal quartet, featuring the soaring tenor of lead singer Tony Williams (b. Apr 15, 1928), successfully straddled the line between teen and adult audiences with their romantically charged material. The Platters charted 35 Top 100 hits while on Mercury Records. Their hits, many of which were penned by manager Buck Ram, included "Only You (And You Alone)" (#5), "The Great Pretender" (#1), "My Prayer" (#1), "Twilight Time" (#1), "Smoke Gets in Your Eyes" (#1), "Harbor Lights" (#8), "(You've Got) The Magic Touch" (#4), and "Enchanted" (#12). —*Rick Clark*

The Very Best of the Platters / 1991 / Mercury ✦✦✦
The Platters' twelve biggest hits are featured on this brief, but solid, collection; it's fine for those who don't want to spend the money on the double-disc set. — *Stephen Thomas Erlewine*

★ **The Magic Touch: An Anthology** / 1991 / Mercury ✦✦✦✦✦
Double-disc set of all their best sides, including "The Great Pretender," "Smoke Gets in Your Eyes," "Only You," "Harbor Lights," and the title track. Great annotation and impeccable sound. All compilations should be done this well. — *Cub Koda*

Four Platers And One Lovely Dish / 1994 / Bear Family ✦✦✦
○ **All the Hits and More** / 1995 / Double Gold ✦✦✦✦

The Pleazers
Group, Garage Rock
In the mid-'60s, the Pleazers were one of the only New Zealand groups competently playing tough, British Invasion/R&B-styled rock & roll; they were probably only second to the La-De-Das in their homeland in this regard. They managed to record about half a dozen singles, an LP, and an EP, gaining a few hits in New Zealand and playing some stints in Australia during their brief life. Mixing typical covers of the time with fairly strong original material, the Pleazers were not an extraordinary band; in the United States or Britain, they would have been just another decent regional act. Tough rock bands were still a rarity in New Zealand, though, and so the Pleazers are still remembered there as trailblazers of sorts. — *Richie Unterberger*

A Midnight Rave With The Pleazers / 1987 / Raven ✦✦✦
18-song compilation drawn from their various releases, focusing mostly on their original material. Competent British Invasion-style rock, usually in a Stonesy style, though sometimes in a poppier vein. — *Richie Unterberger*

Plimsouls
Group, New Wave, Power Pop/Anglo-Pop
With their sharp guitar hooks, memorably sweet melodies, and raggedly beautiful harmonys, the Plimsouls made music that invigorated power-pop in the early '80s. Led by Peter Case's strong songwriting, the group only released two albums and an EP before breaking up in 1983, yet their records sound fresh and exciting more than a decade after their split. — *Stephen Thomas Erlewine*

● **The Plimsouls ... Plus** / 1981 / Rhino ✦✦✦✦
Now reissued as *Plimsouls...Plus* with bonus tracks from the *Zero Hour* EP, the band's first album showcases their blend of power-pop and gritty Southern soul. Hook-laden and filled with raw energy, this is a lost masterpiece that shouldn't be missed this time around. — *Chris Woodstra*

○ **Everywhere at Once** / 1983 / Geffen ✦✦✦✦
The second album retains all of the fiery spirit of the debut with a smoother production. This album holds up much better than many others of the period. Includes the infectious "A Million Miles Away." — *Chris Woodstra*

One Night in America / 1988 / Fan Club ✦✦

PM Dawn
Group, Rap, Urban
Comprised of brothers Prince B (Attrell Cordes) and DJ Minute Mix (Jarrett Cordes), the early '90s group PM Dawn straddled the gap between hip-hop and smooth '70s-style soul, creating an innovative urban R&B that owed as much to pop as it did to rhythm and blues. The brothers recorded their debut single, "Ode to a Forgetful Mind," in 1988. PM Dawn didn't release a full-length album until 1991. The record, *Of the Heart, of the Soul, of the Cross: The Utopian Experience*, was an immediate hit, thanks to the single "Set Adrift on Memory's Bliss," which sampled Spandau Ballet's new wave hit "True." Both the album and the single received glowing reviews, as did the 1993 follow-up *The Bliss Album?*, which featured the hit singles "I'd Die Without You" and "Looking Through Patient Eyes." — *Stephen Thomas Erlewine*

● **Of the Heart, of the Soul and of the Cross ...** / 1991 / Gee Street ✦✦✦✦
Of the Heart, of the Soul and of the Cross: The Utopian Experience is a standout release, sandwiching psychedelic tinges, political/social discourse, and invigorating raps and production. Includes the hit "Set Adrift on Memory Bliss." — *Ron Wynn*

○ **The Bliss Album?** / 1993 / Gee Street ✦✦✦✦
It's inaccurate to label PM Dawn a hip-hop band, since their sensibility lies with smooth ballads and mellow soul; they only use hip-hop to underscore their songs. In many ways, *The Bliss Album?* is a more focused album than their debut, containing such brilliant ballads as "I'd Die Without You" and "Looking Through Patient Eyes." When Prince Be tries to go harder, as on "Plastic," the results are well-intentioned, but seriously flawed—they don't have the strength or power to pull off hardcore material. But when they stick to their pop-friendly R&B, PM Dawn is often quite remarkable; *The Bliss Album?* was the rare second album to expand on, rather than duplicate, the achievements of the debut. — *Stephen Thomas Erlewine*

Poco
Group, Rock & Roll, Country-Rock
Founded by Jim Messina and Richie Furay during the dying days of Buffalo Springfield, with Randy Meisner (who dropped out shortly before the recording of their first album), Rusty Young, and George Grantham, the band built a solid reputation in Los Angeles as an innovative country-rock ensemble. Their first album, *Pickin' up the Pieces*, was one of the strongest debut records of its era, a blend of country and western influences, Beatlesque harmonies, and mainstream rock, all within one cover. They began developing a major national reputation with the release of their second album, *Poco*, at the same time that the group's membership entered what proved to be a virtually constant state of flux. By the mid-'70s, the band had become an established fixture in the middle reaches of the national charts but Messina and Furay were long gone. The band continued recording well into the late-'70s on MCA after leaving Epic, and their following was strong enough to justify a posthumous live album from Epic at the same time. The original quintet, which never did get to record, finally went into the studio under the auspices of RCA in the late-'80s. — *Bruce Eder*

○ **Pickin' up the Pieces** / 1969 / Epic ✦✦✦✦
Their debut album, which is as accomplished as anything by Buffalo Springfield, also recalls the Beatles and the Byrds in its musical orientation. — *Bruce Eder*

Poco / May 6, 1970 / Epic ✦✦✦
Their still fresh, and very Beatlesque, debut album is a fine continuation from the early Buffalo Springfield. — *Bruce Eder*

From the Inside / 1971 / Epic ✦✦
A most unusual record, produced by Memphis guitarist Steve Cropper. Much harder-edged than the rest of the group's output, this album is much more a solid rock album and relies less on the harmony sound than their other records. — *Bruce Eder*

Deliverin' / Jan. 13, 1971 / Epic ✦✦✦
The first of two live albums, and consisting of mostly new material—a major country-rock success, capturing not only the lyricism and upbeat approach of the band, but also the infectiously positive attitude of its fans. — *Bruce Eder*

A Good Feelin' to Know / Oct. 25, 1972 / Epic ✦✦✦
The title track is a failed attempt at a hit single, but the record as a whole is a much more pure rock album than they were known for. — *Bruce Eder*

Crazy Eyes / 1973 / Epic ✦✦✦
Richie Furay's final album with Poco is a mixed effort, containing Gram Parsons's "Brass Buttons" and Furay's title track, a song about Parsons, who died shortly after the album's release. — *William Ruhlmann*

Seven / 1974 / Epic ✦✦
Poco's first album as the quartet of Rusty Young, George Grantham, Timothy Schmit, and Paul Cotton finds them expanding as songwriters, with even Young contributing "Rocky Mountain Breakdown." — *William Ruhlmann*

Cantamos / Dec. 1974 / Epic ✦✦
This album marks the emergence of Rusty Young as a composer of merit. Side one rocks out hard and fresh while the second side deals with lost love and broken-hearted romance. Much of the magic of their earlier albums has been recaptured. — *Jim Chrispell*

○ **Head over Heels** / Jul. 1975 / MCA ✦✦✦✦
Keeping the songs short and to the point, Poco lets loose with a fine batch of material. This time out, they even cover the Becker-Fagen song "Dallas" with great verve. Less country, but a lot more pop. — *Jim Chrispell*

○ **The Very Best of Poco** / Sep. 1975 / Epic ✦✦✦✦
A well-chosen double LP compilation (now on one CD) chronicling Poco's Epic Records period, 1969-1974. —*William Ruhlmann*

Rose of Cimarron / 1976 / One Way ✦✦✦
Lushly-produced pop/rock, *Rose of Cimmaron* hosts an array of sidemen, most notably Al Garth, formerly of Loggins & Messina and keyboardist Steve Ferguson. The country influence is nearly abandoned except for the Rusty Young tune "Company's Comin'/Slow Poke." Great tunes with great arrangements throughout. —*Jim Chrispell*

Live / Apr. 1976 / Epic ✦✦
Epic Records released this live album, recorded in November 1974, in 1976, long after the band had left the label. It's not bad, but it isn't a patch on Poco's previous live effort, *Deliverin'*. —*William Ruhlmann*

Indian Summer / 1977 / MCA ✦✦✦
Although highly listenable, this album marks the slow descent of a band once at the forefront of the country-rock movement. High points include the title track and the mini-suite entitled "The Dance" Donald Fagen of Steely Dan adds synths here and there. —*Jim Chrispell*

Legend / Nov. 1978 / MCA ✦✦✦
The departure of Timothy B. Schmit to the Eagles should have signalled the end for Poco. However, they turned in a surprisingly tight set here and got their first Top 40 hit with "Crazy Love." —*Jim Chrispell*

Songs of Richie Furay / 1979 / Epic ✦✦✦
Richie Furay was one of Poco's co-founders, and he wrote many of its strongest songs between 1969 and 1973. If you want to take Poco in those terms, here's your chance. —*William Ruhlmann*

Songs of Paul Cotton / 1979 / Epic ✦✦
An Epic Records compilation gathering together Paul Cotton compositions from Poco's years on the label, 1971-1974. —*William Ruhlmann*

Under the Gun / 1980 / MCA ✦✦
A deliberate followup to *Legend*, *Under The Gun* was a workmanlike but unremarkable effort. —*William Ruhlmann*

Blue and Gray / 1981 / MCA ✦✦
A concept album about the Civil War, not well executed. —*William Ruhlmann*

Cowboys & Englishmen / 1982 / One Way ✦
Poco's contractual obligation album to get off MCA Records (which had taken over ABC Records). A throwaway effort at a time when their career needed rejuvenation, not another wound. (Originally released on LP by MCA Records, *Cowboys & Englishmen* was licensed to One Way Records for CD reissue.) —*William Ruhlmann*

Backtracks / 1982 / MCA ✦✦✦
A nine-song compilation of Poco's tenure at ABC (later MCA) Records, 1975-1982, judiciously chosen. Later expanded for CD release and retitled *Crazy Loving: Best Of Poco 1975-1982*. —*William Ruhlmann*

Cowboys & Englishmen / 1982 / One Way ✦✦
Merely a shadow of their former selves, Poco seems to have lost their way. This album includes covers of Gordon Lightfoot's "Ribbon of Darkness," J.J. Cale's "Cajun Moon," and the Everly Brothers' "The Price of Love." —*Jim Chrispell*

Ghost Town / 1982 / Atlantic ✦✦
Surprise! Just when they had been written off by even the most loyal fans, Poco rebounds nicely here. Songs "Shoot for the Moon," "When Hearts Collide," and the title track are pleasant reminders of a band that once was. —*Jim Chrispell*

Inamorata / 1984 / Atlantic ✦✦
Poco was down to the duo of Rusty Young and Paul Cotton by this point, which may be why, having been visited in the studio by former members Richie Furay, Timothy Schmit, and George Grantham, they structured the credits in such a way that you might think the old group had reformed. Not so. Rather, this was a mediocre (and final) effort by an act long past its prime. —*William Ruhlmann*

Crazy Loving: Best of Poco 1975-1982 / 1989 / MCA ✦✦✦
In the wake of Poco's success with *Legacy*, MCA Records resurrected their 1982 best of, *Backtracks*, added tracks to fill it out to respectable CD length, threw in some liner notes and reissued it

under a new title. It's not Poco's best period, but this is a good selection that will satisfy most casual listeners. —*William Ruhlmann*

Legacy / Aug. 1989 / RCA ✦✦
A reunion of the "Original Poco" could not stand up to the hype that surrounded its release. Jim Messina does his best on the hit "Call It Love" and Randy Meisner covers Richard Marx's tune "Nothin' to Hide." Other selections fall short of the mark. —*Jim Chrispell*

● **The Forgotten Trail (1969-1974)** / 1990 / Epic ✦✦✦✦
This definitive 2-CD collection is full of wonderful moments and great songs, so it is the obvious starting point. —*Bruce Eder*

The Pogues (Pogue Mahone)

Group, Alternative Pop/Rock
The Pogues combined traditional folk of all stripes (with an emphasis on Irish folk) with rock muscle, producing some of the most original and remarkable music of the '80s. Originally known as Pogue Mahone (Gaelic for "kiss my ass"), the group (Shane MacGowan, vocalist and songwriter; Philip Chevron, guitar; Spider Stacy, tin whistle; Andrew Ranken, drums; James Fearnley, accordion; Darryl Hunt, bass; Jem Finer, banjo; Terry Woods, mandolin) formed in 1982. The Elvis Costello-produced *Rum Sodomy & the Lash* proved MacGowan was a gifted songwriter and earned the band several U.K. hits. Original bassist Caitlin O'Riordan left the band in 1985 and married Costello; O'Riordan was replaced by Hunt. The Pogues signed to Island, releasing *If I Should Fall from Grace with God*, arguably their best album, in 1988. MacGowan's health began to deteriorate due to drug use, culminating in a breakdown in the fall of 1990; Joe Strummer toured with the band after his departure.

MacGowan resurfaced on a one-off Christmas single with Nick Cave; he formed a new band late in 1993. The Pogues continued with Spider Stacy on lead vocals, releasing a new album in 1993; it received a lukewarm critical and commercial reception. By the beginning of 1994, there were rumors that the band had decided to call it quits. —*Stephen Thomas Erlewine*

Red Roses for Me / 1984 / Enigma ✦✦✦
The Pogues' debut was hampered by an unfocused production, which lets the band run loose over the traditional numbers but gives Shane MacGowan's originals a careening power that belies the fact that he was still finding a distinctive voice. —*Stephen Thomas Erlewine*

○ **Rum Sodomy & the Lash** / 1985 / MCA ✦✦✦✦
A triumph, produced by Elvis Costello. Shane MacGowan has never sounded so intense, nor has the band played with such authority. A classic melding of punk-era-defined sensibilities and the magic of Celtic traditionalism. Features a stirring version of Eric Bogle's classic "And the Band Played Waltzing Matilda." —*John Dougan*

● **If I Should Fall from Grace With God** / 1987 / Island ✦✦✦✦
The Pogues' third album is another fiery, eclectic meld of traditional Celtic music and rock played with punk venom. The band can easily keep up with the breakneck pace of songs like "Bottle of Smoke," which is what makes the album so appealing. Overall, this album has more of a rock spirit than *Rum Sodomy & the Lash*, and MacGowan's songs show significant strides in quality. —*Stephen Thomas Erlewine*

Peace and Love / 1989 / Island ✦✦✦
Shane MacGowan was still in fine form on *Peace and Love*, even as he began to sink deeper into drug and alcohol abuse. Although his lyrics remained sharp and incisive, his toxic excesses make his already poor enunciation virtually incomprehensible. Fortunately, the rest of the Pogues were in fine form on *Peace and Love*, turning an eclectic set of folk-rockers that touched on everything from jazz to R&B. It didn't have the kinetic flair of *Rum Sodomy & the Lash* or *If I Should Fall from Grace With God*, but its rich, diverse musicality almost made up for that shortcoming. —*Stephen Thomas Erlewine*

Hell's Ditch / 1990 / Island ✦✦✦
Under the direction of Joe Strummer, the Pogues turned in a harder record with *Hell's Ditch*. Although the band's sound is sharper and tougher than it was on *Peace and Love*, the music on *Hell's Ditch* is wildly eclectic, as the record follows a loose sonic travelogue, touching on Spanish, Italiian, and African music. Shane MacGowan's epic stories match the ambitiousness of the al-

bum—in fact, the lyrics are more convincing and detailed than the supporting music. Even if MacGowan's involving tales can't erase the incoherent musical ideas of the record, *Hell's Ditch* remains a fascinating and intriguing listen. —*Stephen Thomas Erlewine*

Yeah Yeah Yeah Yeah / 1990 / Island ♦♦

A relentless, Motown-styled raveup, "Yeah Yeah Yeah Yeah," was one of the Pogues finest moments and one of their hardest rockers. It was a British hit in 1988, yet it took two years for an EP of the same name to appear. The EP is one the group's most rock-oriented efforts—it even features a version of the Rolling Stones' "Honky Tonk Women"—but it's not entirely successful, with the noticeable exception of the title track. —*Stephen Thomas Erlewine*

○ **Essential Pogues** / 1991 / Island ♦♦♦♦

Essential Pogues doesn't cover *Red Roses for Me* or *Rum Sodomy & the Lash*, so it isn't a definitive collection. However, it does capture the majority of the highlights from their Island albums and functions as a good introduction to the band. One complaint: the tedious extended remix of "Yeah, Yeah, Yeah, Yeah," was included instead of the punchy, energetic original single. —*Stephen Thomas Erlewine*

Waiting for Herb / 1993 / Chameleon ♦♦

Without Shane McGowan, the Pogues are a competent Irish folk-rock band with several strong songs, yet they lack the fire of their earlier albums. For the diehard, *Waiting for Herb* will be necessary, even if it is a little disheartening. —*AMG*

The Pointer Sisters

Group, Soul, Urban, Pop/Rock

Versatile Ruth, Anita, June, and Bonnie Pointer regularly scored pop and soul hits throughout the '70s and '80s in a chameleonic variety of styles. Formed in Oakland, with their first successes for Blue Thumb Records blending funky rhythms with a novel nostalgic attitude (beginning with their 1973 revival of Allen Toussaint's "Yes We Can Can"), leading up to their first #1 R&B item in 1975, "How Long (Betcha' Got a Chick on the Side)."

Bonnie signed with Motown in 1978 and kicked off her own string of R&B hits with "Free Me from My Freedom/Tie Me to a Tree (Handcuff Me)." (June and Anita also tried the solo route during the '80s, without leaving the fold.)

By 1979, when the remaining trio covered Bruce Springsteen's "Fire," the Pointers were headed in a more contemporary direction on the Planet label, and "He's So Shy" (1980), "Slow Hand" (1981), "Automatic," and the anthemic "Jump (For My Love)" (the last two both 1984) were savvy ditties that blazed trails across the R&B and pop charts.

The Pointer Sisters enjoyed renewed exposure and recognition in 1994. They teamed with Clint Black on "Chain of Fools," one of several projects teaming R&B and country acts for the release *Rhythm, Country and Blues* and also issued a new release on RCA. —*Bill Dahl*

The Pointer Sisters / 1973 / MCA ♦♦♦

The Pointer Sisters stepped out of session anonymity and into stardom with their '73 debut. After working with Elvin Bishop, Esther Phillips, and many others, the foursome got into the spotlight in a hurry with "Yes We Can Can." They did a mix of jazzy pop, scat, light R&B, and even some country, and their harmonies and shared leads were reminiscent of both cabaret acts and early-'60s female ensembles. The album cracked the pop Top 20 and established them as a viable frontline singing act. —*Ron Wynn*

○ **Steppin'** / 1975 / Blue Thumb ♦♦♦♦

The second Pointer Sisters album didn't do as consistently well as its predecessor, although it earned them their second gold album and also won them a country Grammy for the song "Fairy Tale." They may have been the most unlikely country success story of all time, with their sassy attitudes and irreverent stage show, but they appeared all over the country landscape that year, even at the Grand Ole Opry. Regrettably, it was an indication of how wide the splits are musically and demographically that "Fairy Tale" didn't even chart on the R&B side. —*Ron Wynn*

Having a Party / 1977 / Blue Thumb ♦♦

This would have to be deemed their first flop album, but there were extenuating circumstances. Bonnie Pointer would soon bolt from the band, and they were also preparing to jump labels. It didn't help that they had a weak crop of songs as well; even Stevie Wonder's writing help couldn't save "Bring Your Sweet Stuff Home To Me." The Sam Cooke cover did make the lower rungs of the

R&B charts, but this qualifies as their least memorable album during the 1970s. —*Ron Wynn*

Energy / 1978 / Planet ♦♦♦

The Pointer Sisters regrouped and switched labels in the late '70s. Bonnie went solo and moved to Motown, while the others signed with superstar manager/producer Richard Perry's Planet label (affiliated with RCA). Their Planet debut was a huge success, equaling their Blue Thumb career-launching release and exceeding any other 1970s release, while eventually becoming their third gold album. It also quickly ended any speculation that they might not be as potent with three voices rather than four. —*Ron Wynn*

Priority / 1979 / Planet ♦♦♦

A moderately successful, but nicely sung release by the Pointer Sisters. They were then in a quasi-rock phase, and a good version of Bruce Springsteen's "Fire" gave them an R&B hit. They didn't have any huge smashes, and the production and arrangements leaned toward the tentative side. But they were getting their three-part harmonies down and weren't far from entering another run as crossover attractions. —*Ron Wynn*

Special Things / 1980 / Planet ♦♦♦

The Pointer Sisters continued riding high into the 1980s with their third Planet album. They enjoyed a huge pop and R&B hit in 1980 with "He's So Shy," and another strong single in "Could I Be Dreaming." The album gave them a solid rebound sales-wise from the mixed results of *Priority* and signaled that they hadn't lost their appeal. At this time, the group was doing better among pop audiences than with soul and R&B crowds. —*Ron Wynn*

○ **Black & White** / 1981 / Planet ♦♦♦♦

The Pointer Sisters were beginning to hit their stride on Planet with this album. They earned their second number-two pop hit with "Slow Hand." "Should I Do It" was a throwback to the camp and novelty tunes that launched their careers, while they also did a cover of "Someday We'll Be Together" and handled other straight pop pieces such as "Take My Heart, Take My Soul" and "Sweet Lover Man." —*Ron Wynn*

○ **So Excited** / 1982 / Planet ♦♦♦♦

The Pointer Sisters put the title track on the charts twice; this was the original version, which peaked at #30 and was the cornerstone for this 1982 album. There was also the mild hit "American Music," which spoke to their eclecticism, and the less successful "If You Wanna Get Back Your Lady" and "Heart Beat." They were still carefully building their fan base, mixing soul-oriented cuts with lighter pop ones and not letting any single sister dominate the spotlight. —*Ron Wynn*

○ **Greatest Hits** / 1982 / Planet ♦♦♦♦

A good anthology covering their '70s and '80s hits. There are now at least six Pointer Sisters anthologies, covering all of the Blue Thumb, Planet, and RCA material. This one was issued on vinyl and can't match the digital sound quality of some later Pointer Sisters releases, but has more than enough hit material to satisfy even their hardcore fans. —*Ron Wynn*

○ **Break Out** / 1983 / Planet ♦♦♦♦

The Pointer Sisters landed the biggest album of their careers with this Richard Perry-produced glossy pop package. The album eventually became a double-platinum success, while "Automatic," "Jump" and "Neutron Dance" were all pop and R&B hits. There was little surprise on these cuts, but the Pointer Sisters sang them with class and zest. —*Ron Wynn*

Contact / 1985 / RCA ♦♦♦

This was the first album that the Pointer Sisters did directly for RCA. Richard Perry produced once again, and they scored their biggest hit in quite a while with the single "Dare Me," while several other songs from the album charted in subsequent months. They were about to move to Motown, and Anita was making noises about a solo career. She finally did issue her own session, but didn't stay out of the fold very long. —*Ron Wynn*

Pointer Sisters / 1985 / MCA ♦♦♦

This group's early hits are included. —*Rick A. Bueche*

Hot Together / 1986 / RCA ♦♦

The Pointer Sisters didn't fare so well on RCA at the end of the '80s. Their harmonies and sound seemed tame in the wake of the hip-hop, dancehall, and New Jack revolution. The songs were superbly performed and well produced and arranged, but just too sedate for the period. They had a couple of singles make the low end of the R&B charts, but while the album did decently, it was far from the heights they had enjoyed only three years earlier. —*Ron Wynn*

Sweet & Soulful / 1987 / RCA ✦✦

Serious Slammin' / 1988 / RCA ✦✦✦

● **Jump: Best of the Pointer Sisters** / 1989 / RCA ✦✦✦✦
Jump covers their hits for the Planet record label. They had moved beyond their camp/novelty origins and away from their country flirtation, and were comfortable making exuberantly sung, conservatively produced, soul-tinged pop. During this period, they scored a number of crossover smashes, including "Jump," "He's So Shy," "Automatic" and "Slow Hand"; all of their 1980s hits are included on this album. —*Ron Wynn*

Right Rhythm / 1990 / Motown ✦✦
A switch to Motown didn't do wonders for the Pointer Sisters, as they hit the label during its nadir. They got substandard songs, only routine production and arrangements, and didn't sound very inspired on any number. They only stayed at the label a short time, and while the album hasn't been deleted, it's no wonder they returned to RCA. —*Ron Wynn*

Only Sisters Can Do That / 1993 / EIG ✦✦

● **The Best of the Pointer Sisters** / 1993 / RCA ✦✦✦✦

Poison

Group, Hard Rock, Pop/Rock, Heavy Metal
A hard rock quartet consisting of singer Bret Michaels, guitarist C. C. Deville, bassist Bobby Dall, and drummer Rikki Rockett, Poison was formed in Harrisburg, PA, in 1983, though the band members relocated to Los Angeles early on, where their highly visual approach (drummer Rockett was also a hairdresser who advised them on clothes, hair, and makeup) made them favorites in the city's glam-rock underground. C. C. Deville left the band in early 1992.

Deville's replacement, Richie Kotsen, appeared on 1993's *Native Tongue*, an attempt to become a grittier, serious rock band; he was fired during the subsequent tour. —*William Ruhlmann*

Look What the Cat Dragged in / 1986 / Capitol ✦✦✦
Glam-metal gets revived with the Los Angeles group, Poison, who turned many heads with their hook-filled songs as well as their looks. Although subsequent albums were more diverse, this one was loose and fun without a care for safety. Includes their first hit, "Talk Dirty to Me." —*John Book*

● **Open up & Say ... Ahh!** / 1988 / Capitol ✦✦✦
This, the group's most popular album, presents its taste for straightforward hard rock ("Nothin' but a Good Time"), for acoustic ballads ("Every Rose Has Its Thorn"), and for its roots in simple pop-rock ("Your Mama Don't Dance"). —*William Ruhlmann*

○ **Flesh & Blood** / 1990 / Capitol ✦✦✦✦
On their third album, vocalist Bret Michaels puts in his best performance. "Unskinny Bop" and the anthemic "Something to Believe In" were both Top Ten hits. —*John Book*

Swallow This Live / 1991 / Capitol ✦✦✦
A two-disc concert release that captures Poison in all its excess (six-and-a-half-minute drum solo, nine-and-a-half-minute guitar solo) and hard-rock glory, with live versions of the hits that are better produced and more impassioned than the original studio cuts. —*William Ruhlmann*

Native Tongue / Feb. 8, 1993 / Capitol ✦✦
Ditching most of their party anthems, as well as guitarist C.C. Deville because he allegedly wasn't up to par, Poison adds guitar whiz Richie Kotzen and makes a bid for respect. Leader Bret Michaels has decided to accentuate the populist strains of ballads like "Something to Believe In" throughout *Native Tongue*. It often falls short—Kotzen's playing is too proficient for the lite-metal hooks that the rest of the band have mastered—but Poison gets points for trying, and they do come up with some tracks, like the single "Stand," that could stand with some of their previous anthems. —*Stephen Thomas Erlewine*

The Police

Group, New Wave, Pop/Rock
In 1977, Sting (a British ex-schoolteacher born Gordon Sumner) and Stewart Copeland (a young drummer from the U.S.) met up with guitarist Andy Summers (of Soft Machine), and the three formed the final lineup of the Police—the rock group that would

later take the early '80s by storm. The band's debut album, *Outlandos d'Amor*, which sported jazz and reggae rhythms in a pop/rock format, was released in 1978. The album, with such classic songs as "Roxanne," was popular with college radio, marking the beginning of the band's ascent to fame. The follow-up, *Regatta de Blanc*, was released the next year; with its bouncy, lively songs, it hit number one in the U.K. for four weeks. *Zenyatta Mondatta*, released in 1980, achieved the same success on the U.K. charts and became the band's first album to place into the U.S. Top Ten. *Ghost in the Machine* was a success as well, and in 1983 *Synchronicity* was released and went multi-platinum. It was number one on the U.S. charts for 12 weeks, winning three Grammy Awards, including Song of the Year for the single "Every Breath You Take." In 1985 the three band memebers split to pursue solo careers. Apart from reuniting in 1986 to record a new version of "Don't Stand So Close to Me" for their stellar compilation *Every Breath You Take—The Singles*, the band has remained inactive. —*Iotis Erlewine*

○ **Outlandos d'Amour** / 1978 / A&M ✦✦✦✦
The Police's first album, although fairly rough, is still an impressive first effort. Although "Can't Stand Losing You" was their first hit (it made the Top 50), the best-known track on this album is definitely "Roxanne," still a favorite among college-radio stations. The influence of the punk era on this album is evident, as is bass player Sting's jazz background. A great deal of fun. —*Iotis Erlewine*

Regatta de Blanc / 1979 / A&M ✦✦✦
The very title, *Regatta de Blanc* (rough French for "White reggae"), describes the style of the Police's second album. This speedy mix of reggae and mainstream rock spawned two number one U.K. hits with "Message in a Bottle" and "Walking on the Moon." The reggae influence is most noticeable in the rhythms, especially on the tracks "Bring on the Night," "Walking on the Moon," and "The Bed's Too Big Without You." —*Iotis Erlewine*

○ **Zenyatta Mondatta** / 1980 / A&M ✦✦✦✦
This album, although a bit rough around the edges, marks a transitional point in the band's career. "Don't Stand So Close to Me" became a number one hit on the U.K. charts, and the band edged further into the mainstream. The sound became more pop oriented on this album, with songs like "De Do Do Do, De Da Da Da" and "Canary in a Coalmine," although they retained their unique sense of rhythm. For a good introduction to early Police, this album is a wise choice. —*Iotis Erlewine*

Ghost in the Machine / 1981 / A&M ✦✦✦
One of the Police's best songs, "Every Little Thing She Does Is Magic" (#3), is featured on this album, but as a whole, *Ghost in the Machine* is bland. Besides being poorly mixed (the music overpowers the vocals), the songs lack the musical simplicity and direction that is so appealing in the earlier albums. —*Iotis Erlewine*

Synchronicity / 1983 / A&M ✦✦✦
A departure from early Police, this album completed the band's transition into mainstream pop while, at the same time, becoming more musically refined. *Synchronicity* had the complexity of *Ghost in the Machine* without the boredom. The Police get louder and angrier, making this a stronger, more driving album. *Synchronicity* contains some of the band's most well-known work: "Every Breath You Take," which went number one on both the U.S. and the U.K. charts; "Wrapped around Your Finger"; and "King of Pain." The pinnacle of the band's career, it went multi-platinum and secured the Police's claim to the title of "Rock-gods" in the early '80s. With the exception of Andy Summers's "Mother," there is not a bad song on the album. The CD contains the bonus track "Murder by Numbers." (Also available as a Mobile Fidelity Ultra-Disc.) —*Iotis Erlewine*

★ **Every Breath You Take: the Singles** / 1986 / A&M ✦✦✦✦✦
A collection of singles from the five Police albums, this provides a consistent sampling of some of the Police's best work, from "Roxanne" to "Every Breath You Take." It's a good overview of the band's work and an excellent place to get an introduction to their music. This also includes a 1986 remake of "Don't Stand So Close to Me," featuring all three members of the band. —*Iotis Erlewine*

○ **Message in a Box** / 1993 / A&M ✦✦✦✦
All of the studio recordings the trio made during their short career (except for a couple of foreign-language recordings, remixes, and live tracks) are collected together on the four-disc *Message in a Box*. There are enough rarities in this attractive, sonically impres-

sive package to justify its purchase for hardcore fans; for anyone who doesn't own any Police, it is an easy way to have the entire collection at once, but casual fans will be more satisfied by *Every Breath You Take: The Singles.* — *Stephen Thomas Erlewine*

Live / 1995 / A&M ◆◆

Featuring two complete concerts from two different stages in the band's career, the double-disc *Live* is a comprehensive portrait of the Police's onstage prowess. Of the two shows, the first is rawer. Recorded on the *Zenyatta Mondetta* tour, the band still had enough spiky power to seem like a punk/new wave band and they tear through their best songs, including a killer version of "So Lonely." At the time of the second disc, the group were one of the most popular acts in the world, playing arenas around the world. Somewhat predictably, the sound is slicker, yet it doesn't affect the impact of the music. When they were slick, the Police didn't seem manufactured, they seemed elegant. Neither of the concerts offers anything remarkably different than the studio versions, they just accentuate the underlying musical themes of the records. However, dedicated fans will not be disappointed by the overall quality of *Live.* — *Stephen Thomas Erlewine*

Pop Group

Group, New Wave

Warning: this band's name is loaded with irony; there is little if anything "pop" about them. So, if you happen across any of their albums and think you're getting something that sounds like a cross between the Raspberries and the Beatles, don't say you weren't warned. Emerging in the late-'70s post-punk era, this militant gang of leftist radical politicos from Bristol, England specialized in a funk-driven cacophony of sound that was abrasive, strident, and ultimately very exciting. Railing against Margaret Thatcher's Tory government, the state of pop music, racism, sexism, etc., the Pop Group were not the easiest band of the early post-punk era to listen to, but those who made the effort were in for an interesting melange of primitive rhythms and avant-garde guitar racket. Led by the squalling "vocals" of Mark Stewart (which were little more than chanted political slogans), the Pop Group were unabashedly and stridently radical to the point of being hectoring. But, unlike others of their ilk, the music was so challenging, joyfully noisy, and downright weird that it was easy to cut them a little slack, even when their finger-pointing and ranting became a bit much. Never intending to make a serious run at the pop charts, the Pop Group imploded after three albums, the third being a collection of outtakes and assorted ephemera. They did, however, contribute some talented people to other bands, most notably Gareth Sanger, who formed the wild and woolly Rip, Rig and Panic (named after a Rahsaan Roland Kirk LP), which also featured the lead vocals of a then-teenage Neneh Cherry; and the aforementioned Stewart, who went on to flourish in Adrian Sherwood's On-U stable of artists, recording with the Maffia and Tackhead. Despite its raw, inherent anti-commerciality, the Pop Group's dissonant agit-prop rock did influence a contemporary generation of political bands like Fugazi, Fun-da-Mental, and Rage Against the Machine. — *John Dougan*

● The Pop Group / 1979 / Radar ◆◆◆◆

Abrasive, but interesting, the Pop Group's debut is perhaps the most succinct summation of their angry and defiant approach to rock and roll. Although at times resembling the discordant funk of fellow post-punk radicals the Gang of Four, the Pop Group leave rhythm behind almost as quickly as they find it, and the result is a clattering din of sound resembling an aural collage. I like it, but even I'll admit it's a bit meandering and overly experimental to take in one sitting. The longish, guitar-driven track "We Are Time" is the strongest cut, establishing a solid groove that won't let go. — *John Dougan*

Y / 1979 / Radar ◆◆◆

For How Much Longer Do We Tolerate Mass Murder? / 1980 / Rough Trade ◆◆◆

If the title doesn't tip you off as to what this record will probably sound like, then you're hopeless. More accusatory than their debut (only because the lyrics are more clearly recorded), and more funk-powered. Oddly, what hurts this is a lack of experimentation, but with the Pop Group, it's always too much of one thing and not enough of another. An interesting experiment that is as maddening as it is satisfying. — *John Dougan*

We Are Time / 1980 / Rough Trade ◆◆◆

Iggy Pop (James Newell Osterberg)

b. 1947

Hard Rock

After the disbandment of the proto-punk group the Stooges, vocalist Iggy Pop (born James Osterberg) embarked on a solo career that flirted with the mainstream while keeping his fiery punk spirit alive. Pop laid low for a couple of years following the breakup of the Stooges, resurfacing in 1977 with two David Bowie-produced albums, *The Idiot* and *Lust for Life.* These records expanded his trademark full-throttle rock & roll, incorporating a more pop-oriented approach that increased his audience; *The Idiot* remains his highest-charting album, peaking at number 72 in America.

However, Pop soon returned to straightforward, raging hard rock with the double-punch of *TV Eye Live* (1978) and 1979's *New Values,* which was recorded with former Stooges guitarist James Williamson. Although he kept changing his backing band, both 1980's *Soldier* and 1981's *Party* followed the same blueprint as *New Values.* Released in 1982, the Chris Stein-produced *Zombie Birdhouse* (which appeared on Stein's private label, Animal) was the most varied collection Pop had created since *Lust for Life.*

After the release of *Zombie Birdhouse,* Pop took some time off, reappearing four years later with the Bowie-produced *Blah-Blah-Blah;* the record became his highest-charting album since *The Idiot.* He followed it in 1989 with *Instinct,* another return to basic hard rock. Released the following year on Virgin Records, the Don Was-produced *Brick by Brick* was his most accessible and commercially successful album, producing his first Top 40 hit, "Candy." Pop began an acting career during the next few years, appearing in John Waters' *Cry Baby.* Pop's first album since *Brick By Brick* was *American Caesar* (1993), which was yet another return to punky hard rock. — *Stephen Thomas Erlewine*

○ The Idiot / 1977 / Virgin ◆◆◆◆

Although it appears that producer David Bowie directed the proceedings a bit too carefully, remaking Iggy Pop entirely in his own image, *The Idiot* proves that Iggy was equally responsible for the menacing electronic music. *The Idiot* was an effective reinvention on the part of Iggy Pop partially because it removed him completely from the primal heavy guitar grind of the Stooges. A different musical direction in itself would be meaningless if Iggy and Bowie hadn't produced a set of songs that supported the new, synth-driven style. "Funtime" is essentially a sleazy, mid-tempo rocker that is re-energized by its context, but most of the album explores the various subtexts within the bleak, keyboard-dominated soundscapes. Iggy's lyrics are some of his best, as he faithfully recreates the hedonistic underworld of jet-setting "Nightclubbing," with both humor and rage. Several of the songs—including "Funtime," "China Girl," and "Nightclubbing"—have become post-punk standards, but that doesn't remove the jarring, disturbing sound of the record. In its own quiet way, *The Idiot* is as discomforting as *Fun House.* — *Stephen Thomas Erlewine*

● Lust for Life / 1977 / Virgin ◆◆◆◆

The pounding drums that open *Lust for Life* instantly signal that the album is a brighter, harder-rocking affair than *The Idiot.* While black humor was an undercurrent throughout *The Idiot,* it is brought to the front on *Lust for Life,* both musically and lyrically. Using the title track as a template, the record not only rocks, it swings and it swings hard. Bowie wrote most of the music for the record and it reflects his musical ambition, careening from the hard rock of the title track to the strutting piano of "The Passenger," the jaunty ironic sing-along of "Success," to the stylized R&B of "Tonight." While Iggy Pop spent most of the decade trying to escape the pop leanings of *Lust for Life,* he never made a better record. — *Stephen Thomas Erlewine*

TV Eye / 1978 / RCA ◆

A desultory live album recorded on a 1977 tour of America, *TV Eye* captures Iggy Pop at his most self-indulgent and his most uninspired. — *Stephen Thomas Erlewine*

New Values / 1979 / Arista ◆◆◆

On *New Values,* Iggy Pop teamed back up with Stooges guitarist James Williamson, creating a set of tough hard rock that was highlighted by the sly humor of "I'm Bored" and the driving title track. — *Stephen Thomas Erlewine*

Soldier / 1980 / Arista ✦✦✦

Recorded with an ad-hoc punk supergroup (Glen Matlock, Barry Andrews, Ivan Kral, Steve New, and Klaus Kruger), *Soldier* rages on with a lean precision, giving Iggy's occasionally weak and bitter lyrics the extra kick they need. —*Stephen Thomas Erlewine*

Party / 1981 / Arista ✦✦

Party attempts to recapture the loose hard-rock professionalism of *Soldier*, even adding the Uptown Horns to the mix. However, the music winds up sounding stiff and anything but a party, even when Iggy tries to make the group unwind with the standards "Time Won't Let Me" and "Sea of Love." —*Stephen Thomas Erlewine*

Zombie Birdhouse / 1982 / IRS ✦✦

With the help of Chris Stein (Blondie), Iggy Pop attempts a self-consciously eclectic musical exploration with *Zombie Birdhouse*. By and large, the attempts are admirable, as Iggy turns in a set of songs that range from social commentary and urban folk to bizarre poetry and philosophical ruminations. Instead of singing, Iggy alternately raps and sings over sonic backdrops that have touches of hard rock, folk, and electronic music. It's an ambitious effort that never quite works and keeps listeners at a distance. —*Stephen Thomas Erlewine*

○ **Choice Cuts** / 1984 / RCA ✦✦✦

Following the success of David Bowie's version of "China Girl," RCA assembled *Choice Cuts*, a compilation of Iggy Pop's two albums for the label. Actually, "compilation" is a misleading word: Side one of *Choice Cuts* features side one of *The Idiot*, while side two features side one of *Lust for Life*. It effectively illustrates the differences between the records, and includes most of the prime material from each collection, yet the two albums are necessary listens in their entirety, making *Choice Cuts* an engaging but useless compilation. —*Stephen Thomas Erlewine*

Blah Blah Blah / 1986 / A&M ✦✦✦

Iggy Pop reunited with producer David Bowie for *Blah Blah Blah*. While it adopts a number of different musical styles, the record isn't as cohesive or as ambitious *The Idiot* or *Lust for Life*. Instead, it acts as an Iggy sampler, offering a variety of material that is all competently performed, but with the notable exception of a cover of Johnny O'Keefe's "Real Wild Child (Wild One)," rarely compelling. —*Stephen Thomas Erlewine*

Instinct / 1988 / A&M ✦✦

After the pop-oriented smorgasbord of *Blah Blah Blah*, Iggy Pop teamed with producer Bill Laswell for the lackluster *Instinct*, a return to the pounding grind his early '80s albums, not the classic grime of the Stooges. In fact, Laswell allows Iggy's backing band, led by ex-Sex Pistols guitarist Steve Jones indulge their tendency to wallow in a heavy metallic mud, making *Instinct* his most tedious record. —*Stephen Thomas Erlewine*

○ **Brick by Brick** / 1990 / Virgin ✦✦✦

Instinct suggested that Iggy Pop had run out of ideas. *Brick By Brick* put an end to that speculation. While it's easily the most mainstream record, Iggy has ever recorded, it rivals his two Bowie-produced 1977 albums in terms of sheer accomplishment. Under the direction of producer Don Was, Iggy twists through a number of styles, recorded with an ever-shifting assembly of studio musicians like David Lindley and Waddy Wachtel, members of Guns N' Roses, John Hiatt, John Mellencamp's drummer Kenny Aronoff, and the B-52's singer Kate Pierson. Iggy's duet with Pierson on the pure pop of "Candy" is the highlight, yet the record also features Iggy at his toughest ("Home," "Butt Town," "I Won't Crap Out," "Pussy Power") and his most sensitive "Moonlight Lady." Although there was potential for a slick, mainstream sell-out with *Brick By Brick*, Was has helped Iggy turn in a well-crafted and thoroughly enjoyable album. And with Iggy, a consistent album is a rare occurence. —*Stephen Thomas Erlewine*

American Caesar / 1993 / Virgin ✦✦✦

Turning on themes of jealousy, hate, abuse, and corporate profits (it's not pretty, but then neither is Iggy), Caesar marks his first album in decades backed by a permanent group. This likely explains why several songs echo the energy and sound of his legendary proto-punk band the Stooges. Unquestioned highlight is a dishevelled and humorously political rendition of "Louie Louie." *American Caesar* is a raw, sometimes ugly, but ultimately very real album. —*Roch Parisien*

Popol Vuh

Group, Neo-Classical, Progressive Electronic, Ethnic Fusion

One of Germany's premiere progressive electronic bands, Popol Vuh was founded in 1969 by keyboardist Florian Fricke. The band took its name from the Mayan Indian bible, and, in fact, the group's first album *Affenstunde (The Time of the Monkey King)* was a strong reflection of Fricke's interest in Mayan lore. Over the course of nearly 20 albums, Popol Vuh combined sacred musical traditions and instruments from around the world with classical, jazz, and rock elements. It also created quite a stir as one of the first bands to use the Moog synthesizer in the early '70s. As such, the band influenced several generations of electronic and contemplative artists. Popol Vuh also gained considerable attention for its scores to films by the celebrated German director Werner Herzog, including *Nosferatu* and *Aguirre, the Wrath of God*. —*Linda Kohanov*

○ **In Den Garten Pharads** / 1972 / Pilz ✦✦✦✦

"In Pharaoh's Garden" was the first true work of "Sacred Music" by Florian Fricke, guiding light of the mythical group Popol Vuh. Consisting of two extended works, his mixture of electronics and church organ with assorted winds and percussives, conjures up visions of the celestial light. Deeply emotional and filled with mysticism, this album marked the dawning of new age music, and still today is a wonder to behold. —*Archie Patterson*

● **Tantric Songs** / 1991 / Celestial Harmonies ✦✦✦✦

Tantric Songs/Hosianna Mantra is new age devotional-rock chamber music that is spacey and spacious on this pairing of two early albums (from 1973 and 1978) on one CD. —*Michael P. Dawson*

Porno for Pyros

Group, Alternative Pop/Rock

Perry Farrell's post-Jane's Addiction band, Porno for Pyros, followed the same path as his previous band, combining art-rock, punk, heavy metal, and funk into one shrieking whole. On their self-titled 1993 debut, Farrell's pretensions got out of hand at times, resulting in some ridiculously self-absorbed conceptual pieces sitting next to some straightforward rockers and pop songs; it sold well at first, but soon slipped down the charts. While he prepared new Porno material in 1994, Farrell returned to the organization of Lollapalooza—the traveling rock festival he conceived—for the first time since 1992. —*Stephen Thomas Erlewine*

Porno for Pyros P / 1993 / Warner Brothers ✦✦✦

Although Porno for Pyros was supposed to sound radically different than Jane's Addiction, Porno sounds like Jane's without the Zeppelinesque grandeur of David Navarro. Their self-titled debut should please Perry Farrell's fans, although it does shows signs of the limits of his vision. —*Stephen Thomas Erlewine*

Portishead

Group, Dance-Pop, Alternative Pop/Rock

Led by keyboardist Geoff Barrow, the British group Portishead combined hip-hop rhythms and samples, jazzy melodic textures, and pop/rock instrumentation into a alluringly dark, atmospheric sound, distinguished by the seductive vocals of Beth Gibbons. The group's 1994 debut album, *Dummy*, earned glowing reviews, landing on many critics' year-end Top Ten lists. *Dummy* crossed over into the mainstream in both America in Britain in late 1994, thanks to the hit single "Sour Times." —*Stephen Thomas Erlewine*

○ **Dummy** / 1994 / PolyGram ✦✦✦✦

Dummy plays a romantic film noir, filled with reverb, sighing strings, dark erotic arrangements, and the doomed, sighing vocals of Beth Gibbons. —*Stephen Thomas Erlewine*

The Posies

Group, Alternative Pop/Rock, Power Pop/Anglo-Pop

This Seattle-based power-pop quartet is influenced by the Move, Big Star, Badfinger, and the Beatles. The songwriting and harmonic skills of Jonathon Auer and Kenneth Stringfellow are particularly striking, at times sounding like Graham Nash-period Hollies. —*Rick Clark*

Failure / 1988 / Pop Llama ✦✦✦

Failure is worth looking up, not so much because it represents a mature work but because it's a nice diamond-in-the-rough portrait of a band with a deep creative resource and a strong sense of pop history. —*Rick Clark*

● **Dear 23** / 1990 / DGC ◆◆◆◆
From the Move-influenced "My Big Mouth" to the delicate, wistful "Everyone Moves Away," through tracks that would do Badfinger or Big Star proud, like "Apology," "Golden Blunders," and "Suddenly Mary," *Dear 23* is Anglo-pop/rock heaven. John Leckie's larger-than-life production might be a little overwhelming at times, but overall it highlights this band's gorgeous harmonies and arrangements to great effect. *—Rick Clark*

Frosting on The Beater / 1993 / DGC ◆◆◆
The Posies turn up the rockets for their third album with an appealingly huge wall of guitars and bashola drumming. For the most part, the melodies and harmonies are still intact, but song for song, *Frosting On the Beater* doesn't hold up to *Dear 23*. Nevertheless, songs like "Different Door," "Solar Sister," and "Flavor of the Month" are wonderful. *—Rick Clark*

Poster Children

Group, Alternative Pop/Rock
Poster Children are a high-energy punk-pop band that formed in 1987 in Champaign, Illinois. Playing what they call "post wave" music, their three full-length releases illustrate why they have a die-hard cult following: Their ability to write hard-yet-melodic songs, and their do-it-yourself philosophy, which includes driving their own tour bus, creating all of their own artwork and T-shirt designs, and having their own record label. A long-time college favorite, Poster Children continue to gain fans with each hyperkinetic release. *—Heather Phares*

Toreador Squat / 1988 / Poster Children ◆◆
● **Daisychain Reaction** / Jul. 1990 / Reprise ◆◆◆◆
Poster Children's second album continues in a hard-yet-accessible pop-punk vein. "If You See Kay" and "Cancer" are two stand-out tracks on this intense record. *—Heather Phares*

Tool of the Man / 1993 / Sire ◆◆◆
The group's third album is slightly less interesting than the first two albums, but songs like "Tommyhaus" still showcase their melodic and dynamic power. *—Heather Phares*

Junior Citizen / 1995 / Sire ◆◆◆

Powder

Group, Psychedelic
One of the many fine '60s groups that barely got to record, let alone reach a wide audience, Powder were one of the most Anglophile American bands of the decade. Hailing from San Mateo, CA (near San Francisco), the group stood apart from their peers in that they were neither psychedelic nor garage, specializing in power-pop with ringing, crashing guitars and harmonies. Most of their material was extremely reminiscent of the Who circa *A Quick One* and *The Who Sell Out*, and while it was undoubtedly derivative, it was also well done. Sonny and Cher tried to help Powder get an album out after the group backed them on a 1968 tour, but it was shelved, although a lot of material was recorded. Powder leaders Tom and Rich Frost released some records on their own, including the minor hit "She's Got Love," and an album of unreleased Powder material was finally released in 1993. *—Richie Unterberger*

Biff! Bang! Powder / 1993 / Distortions ◆◆◆
Composed of fourteen 1968 demos, you could be forgiven for thinking you'd stumbled into a room of Who outtakes (with an occasional detour into folk-rock), with strong (at times blatant) echoes of tracks like "Happy Jack" and "So Sad About Us." Nonetheless, it's fun stuff, and the strongest original tracks, like "Turn Another Page" and "Gladly," stand up well on their own. *—Richie Unterberger*

Power Station

Group, Pop/Rock
Pop/rock supergroup consisting of drummer Tony Thompson (Chic), guitarist Andy Taylor, bassist John Taylor (both from Duran Duran), and singer Robert Palmer. They hit the Top Ten with the singles "Some Like It Hot" and T. Rex's "Bang a Gong (Get It On)." Palmer did not want to tour, so he was replaced by Michael Des Barres, but the band split soon after. John Taylor returned to Duran Duran, while Andy Taylor pursued a solo career, working with ex-Sex Pistols guitarist Steve Jones. *—Steve Huey*

The Power Station / 1985 / Capitol ◆◆◆
Under the direction of guitarist Andy Taylor, the Power Station is an attempt to break free from the constraints of Duran Duran's polished synth-pop, adding elements of funk, courtesy of Chic drummer Tony Thompson, as well as straightahead hard rock, courtesy of vocalist Robert Palmer. Everything is polished with a glossy sheen, which makes the record sound quite similar to Duran Duran, although with out their sense of popcraft. Only the cover of T. Rex's "Bang A Gong (Get It On)" and the single "Some Like It Hot" work up enough energy to make them memorable, but most of the album falls flat. *—Stephen Thomas Erlewine*

Duffy Power

b. Sep. 9, 1941
Blues Rock, British Invasion
Power is a lost figure of the '60s who drifted into the inner circle of British blues after a middling career as a teen idol in the early '60s. He recorded one of the first Beatle covers (on an early 1963 single of "I Saw Her Standing There"), and never experienced acclaim as a commercial pop singer or blues vocalist. But he recorded some fine, little-known blues-cum-R&B/rock sides in the '60s, some of which featured present and future members of the Graham Bond Organisation, Cream, and Pentangle. The pleasures of Power are subtle and not easily captured in print. He doesn't have the best voice, and will never be mistaken for a Steve Winwood or Eric Burdon. But his original material is strong, his arrangements imaginative, and his performance sincere; he's grounded in the blues, but doesn't fall into shopworn clichés, bringing a lot of himself and the innovations of British '60s rock into the picture. *—Richie Unterberger*

○ **Blues Power** / 1992 / See For Miles ◆◆◆◆
Most of the recordings on *Blues Power* were originally released on Power's self-titled album on the tiny U.K. Spark label in 1969. Duffy says in the liner notes of this reissue that the album was never intended for release, and that these sessions were acoustic demos for an LP that never got produced with the arrangements he had envisioned. That may be so, but it's still a worthy document of this underrated British bluesman at his most bare-boned and haunting. With just his guitar and harmonica, Power runs through both moody originals and covers of R&B/blues standards (with the Beatles' "Fixing a Hole" thrown in) that are rearranged and drastically stripped down. This reissue includes the 15 tracks from the 1969 release, a couple more from the same sessions that were issued on the extremely obscure *Firepoint* compilation album, and three from the mid-'60s (also included on the *Little Boy Blue* reissue) that also explore acoustic moods, forming a picture of Power's most intimate work. *—Richie Unterberger*

● **Little Boy Blue** / 1992 / Edsel ◆◆◆◆
His best recordings, as noteworthy for the players on the album as Power himself. Laid down sometime in the mid-'60s, Power (who sings and plays occasional guitar and harp) is backed by a rotating ensemble including, at various points, John McLaughlin and Jack Bruce (before they gained fame), as well as future Pentangle members Danny Thompson and Terry Cox. Neither as rock-oriented as the Stones nor as strictly revivalist as Alexis Korner (with whom Power played for a time), this is one of the best British blues recordings, cutting straight down the middle between gutbucket blues and soulful R&B. Divided equally between Power originals and R&B blues covers, the material and performances are spare, powerful, and as consistent as any '60s British blues album. Unfortunately, these sessions were unissued for several years, surfacing briefly under the title *Innovations* in 1970 on the British Transatlantic label. This reissue on another tiny British label is equally obscure, but should not be missed by fans of '60s British R&B. *—Richie Unterberger*

○ **Just Say Blue** / 1995 / Retro ◆◆◆◆
While not up to the level of the other vintage Power compilations available (*Little Boy Blue* and *Blues Power*), this is a worthwhile supplement to those CDs, featuring 21 tracks of rare and unreleased material cut by the singer from 1965 to 1971. The first half, focusing on his 1965-67 output, is the more interesting portion by a considerable margin, as much for the jazz-blues-R&B fusion of the arrangements (featuring contributions from Jack Bruce, John McLaughlin, Ginger Baker, and Pentangle's Danny Thompson and Terry Cox) as Power's singing. The early-'70s songs that make up the remainder of the disc have a more pedestrian blues-rock feel, but there are some good, inspired moments, with cameos by Rod Argent, Thompson, Cox, and Alexis Korner. *—Richie Unterberger*

Johnny Powers

Rock & Roll, Rockabilly

Rockabilly Johnny Powers' story is one of the more intriguing the genre has to offer. Detroit-born, the young John Pavlick made the standard '50s beeline from teenage country singer to teenage rockabilly singer after being bit by the Elvis bug. After several now legendary local recordings for Fortune and Fox, he landed a deal with Sun Records in Memphis, from which two singles were issued. Power's style was then and still is today raw, full throated, fully engaged rockabilly, a wholesale committment to the moment. After his stint on Sun, Powers became the first white artist to be signed to the fledgling Motown label. As the '60s moved into the '70s, Johnny's career found him on the other side of the studio glass, producing hits with Tim Tam & The Turn-Ons' "Wait A Minute" and Jack Kittel's oddball country sickie "Psycho." Still active today, Johnny Powers is proof positive of rock's ability to produce a true survivor who also is a true believer in the strength that lies within the music itself. — *Cub Koda*

New Spark (For an Old Flame) / 1994 / Schoolkids ✦✦✦

● **Long Blond Hair** / Norton ✦✦✦✦

An excellent 23-track retrospective of Powers' early career. All the landmark Fox (the title cut), Fortune ("Honey Let's Go to a Rock'n' Roll Show") and Sun ("With Your Love, with Your Kiss") singles from the '50s are here, along with a batch of unissued material from the same time frame. Great, true, high powered rockin' that makes up in raw enthusiasm what it may sacrifice in commercial pleasantries. — *Cub Koda*

Prefab Sprout

Group, Pop/Rock

Prefab Sprout, featuring singer/songwriter Paddy McAloon, are an adult-alternative/smart-pop quartet from England, who integrate their music with a Steely Dan-like sophistication in an airy bed of texturous synth-work and acoustic instrumentation. — *Rick Clark*

Swoon / 1984 / Epic ✦✦✦

Their full-length album debut is rough around the edges, but shows the band reaching beyond the tried and clichéd. — *Scott Bultman*

○ **Two Wheels Good** / 1985 / Epic ✦✦✦✦

A strong album debut of atmospheric, breathy, and clever pop music, it features Thomas Dolby's tight production. Earthy and ethereal at the same time, the album was released overseas as *Steve McQueen*, but with a different name for the US version due to protests from the actor's estate. — *Scott Bultman*

Steve McQueen / 1985 / Kitchenware ✦✦✦

○ **From Langley Park to Memphis** / 1988 / Epic ✦✦✦✦

A good but inconsistent record, it includes shining tracks like "The Golden Calf," "Cars and Girls," and "I Remember That." Paddy McAloon begins to explore his fixation with pop icons like Elvis and Springsteen. A must for fans. — *Scott Bultman*

Protest Songs / 1989 / Kitchenware ✦✦

○ **Jordan: The Comeback** / 1990 / Epic ✦✦✦✦

A stunning masterwork with 19 tracks (over 70 minutes) tied together by recurrent themes of God and Elvis, this one is stylistically all over the map—gospel, soul, rock, and pop. The pop songwriting has acknowledged influences from Jimmy Webb and Paul McCartney. — *Scott Bultman*

● **A Life of Surprises: The Best of Prefab Sprout** / 1992 / Epic ✦✦✦✦

This hits package offers a well-chosen set and two previously unreleased tracks, "The Sound of Crying" and "If You Don't Love Me." The 16 tracks draw more selections from the *From Langley Park to Memphis* LP than the other albums, but this is a good single-disc introduction to Prefab Sprout's music. — *Scott Bultman*

Elvis Presley (Elvis Aron Presley)

b. Jan. 8, 1935, Tupelo, MS, **d.** Aug. 16, 1977, Memphis, TN
Rock & Roll, Pop/Rock

Elvis Presley was the defining figure of rock & roll music. He is the biggest record seller in history. During his lifetime, especially in the 1950s, he was the focal point for the emergence of rock & roll culture, and he made some of the genre's seminal recordings. Since his death, he has become a pervasive American icon.

Elvis Presley did not invent rock & roll. In fact, as an artist who did not write songs and whose abilities as an instrumentalist were

only rudimentary, he was essentially a transitional performer, bridging the gap between pre-rock singers such as Dean Martin, whom he openly admired, and later rock stars such as the Beatles. But by fusing the existing entertainment industry to the emerging genres of country and blues, he helped turn a hybrid into a national phenomenon. He was the foremost popularizer of rock & roll, and the name "Elvis" became synonymous with the music itself.

Presley grew up in Memphis, TN. He first recorded for the local Sun Records label, owned by Sam Phillips, which issued his initial singles, "That's All Right (Mama)"/"Blue Moon of Kentucky"(July 1954), "Good Rockin' Tonight"/"I Don't Care If the Sun Don't Shine" (September 1954), and "Milkcow Blues Boogie"/"You're a Heartbreaker" (January 1955), before reaching the Top Ten of the country charts wih "Baby, Let's Play House"/"I'm Left, You're Right, She's Gone" (April 1955).

Both sides of Presley's fifth Sun single, "Mystery Train"/"I Forgot to Remember to Forget" (August 1955) also reached the country charts, with the latter hitting #1. In November 1955, Phillips sold Presley's contract to RCA Victor Records, along with his master tapes. Presley would record for RCA Victor from then on. (The Sun material is available on the *The Sun Sessions* CD [1987] [RCA Victor 6414].)

Starting with "Heartbreak Hotel" (January 1956), Elvis Presley dominated the popular music of the second half of the 1950s. That single topped the pop charts as did "I Want You, I Need You, I Love You" (May), "Hound Dog"/"Don't Be Cruel" (July), and "Love Me Tender" (September), and the albums *Elvis Presley* (March) and *Elvis* (October), all in 1956 alone. "Love Me Tender" was the title song of Presley's first motion picture, which opened in November.

The following year was more of the same, as Presley went to #1 with "Too Much" (January 1957), "All Shook Up" (March), "(Let Me Be Your) Teddy Bear" (June), and "Jailhouse Rock" (September), and the albums *Loving You* (the soundtrack to his second movie) (July) and *Elvis' Christmas Album* (November).

Drafted by the Army, Presley entered the service in March 1958, which slowed down his hit-making slightly, but he still managed to reach the top of the charts with "Don't" (January), "Hard Headed Woman" (June), and "A Big Hunk O' Love" (June 1959), and stay in the movie theatres with *King Creole* (June 1958), all work done before his induction.

Presley's return to civilian status in March 1960 was marked by a renewed flurry of success with the number one singles "Stuck on You" (March), "It's Now or Never" (July), and "Are You Lonesome Tonight" (November 1960), and the soundtrack album *G.I. Blues* (October). Such recordings found him moving more to the ballad material, as his rebellious '50s image gave way to a more conventional star persona in the '60s. But his "comeback" continued into 1961, as he topped the charts with "Surrender" (February) and the albums *Something for Everybody* (June) and *Blue Hawaii* (October).

After 1961, Presley gave up performing live and concentrated almost exclusively on making movies and recording soundtracks. His records continued to sell, if at a slightly less frantic pace. "Good Luck Charm" (February 1962) and the soundtrack to *Roustabout* (November 1964) went to number one, and Presley was a frequent visitor in the Top Ten, but, especially after the U.S. arrival of the Beatles in February 1964, the King of Rock & Roll began to seem a figure from an earlier time. His records disappeared from the Top Ten after "Crying in the Chapel" (April 1965), which had been recorded back in October 1960, and the *Harum Scarum* soundtrack (October 1965).

Presley turned his career around with a second comeback launched by a television special broadcast in December 1968. The centerpiece of the show was a performance in the round in which Presley performed many of his '50s hits with the original backing musicians, wearing a black leather suit and evoking the rebellious image of old. A soundtrack album drawn from the "comeback special," *Elvis* (December 1968), returned him to the Top Ten.

Presley began to take greater care with his recordings, returning to Memphis to make records not intended for movie soundtracks. The result was his first Top Ten single in four years, "In the Ghetto" (April 1969) and the gold album *From Elvis in Memphis* (May 1969).

Presley gave up acting in favor of a return to live work, starting in Las Vegas in July 1969. His next single, "Suspicious Minds" (August 1969), was his first chart topper since 1962.

Presley's '70s career as a live performer followed a similar pattern to his '60s career as a singing movie star—early success followed by a gradual decline. He reached the Top Ten with "Don't Cry Daddy" (November 1969), "The Wonder of You" (May 1970), and "Burning Love" (August 1972), and topped the charts with the TV soundtrack album *Aloha from Hawaii Via Satellite* (February 1973), but gradually the releases became less-considered and there were more live recordings. Presley's health declined and his weight increased, and his death in August 1977 has been blamed on a number of factors, including the excessive ingestion of prescription drugs, though the official cause of death was heart failure.

Since his death, Presley has gone beyond legend to become a cultural stereotype, with dozens, if not hundreds, of professional imitators curling their lips and slurring their words in tribute to him, and the lunatic fringe continually reporting sightings of him in convenience stores. His home, Graceland, has become something of national shrine. Meanwhile, RCA Victor has reissued his work in a dizzying variety of configurations, gradually coming to give it the respect and consideration it deserves. *—William Ruhlmann*

☆ **Elvis Presley** / Mar. 1956 / RCA ✦✦✦✦✦
While RCA had the material, they opted to play it safe and combine five Sun outtakes with seven new recordings and release the Hillbilly Cat's first album. This is a great way to begin a career! The best material here is on a par with the Sun singles. While "Blue Suede Shoes" is a cultural cornerstone of sorts, hearing Elvis's version of Clyde McPhatter's "Money Honey" is still, after four decades, revelatory. *—Neal Umphred*

Loving You / Jul. 1957 / RCA ✦✦✦
Purporting to be the soundtrack to Elvis's second film, this album collects songs used in the film on one side with new material on the other. The weakness of a couple of the movie tunes and the fact that the new songs were leftovers from the sessions used to produce Elvis's first gospel EP and latest single add up to his weakest album offering, although any album with "Got a Lot O' Living to Do" is alright. *—Neal Umphred*

○ **Elvis' Golden Records, Vol. 1** / Mar. 1958 / RCA ✦✦✦✦
This is the greatest-hits album by which all greatest-hits album need be measured. Fourteen sides sold umpteen bejillion records in the previous two years. The only discrepancy is the inclusion of "That's When Your Heartaches Begin," which failed to reached the Top 40 as the flip of "All Shook Up," at the expense of "I Was the One," "My Baby Left Me," and "Playing for Keeps," each much bigger hits. *—Neal Umphred*

King Creole / Aug. 1958 / RCA ✦✦✦
In which, backed by blaring horns, Elvis takes on New Orleans for the soundtrack to his fourth film. The arrangements work great on the uptempo numbers: "Hard Headed Woman" and "Trouble" are classics, "Dixieland Rock" and "New Orleans" should be, "Crawfish" is unlike anything Elvis would ever record again, and "King Creole" is probably the best title tune for a movie Elvis ever got. Had a couple more rockers been included, this could be more highly recommended. *—Neal Umphred*

○ **For LP Fans Only** / Feb. 1959 / RCA ✦✦✦✦
RCA was desperate while Elvis was in the army, so they scraped together odds and ends and some Sun material. This quaint early album appeared circa 1959. *—Hank Davis*

○ **A Date with Elvis** / Sep. 1959 / RCA ✦✦✦✦
The companion volume to *For LP Fans Only*, this one collects five "enhanced" Sun sides (leaving the tenth side unavailable on album for almost twenty years), three from the *Jailhouse Rock* EP, and a *Love Me Tender* EP leftover. *—Neal Umphred*

☆ **Elvis** / Oct. 1956 / RCA ✦✦✦✦✦
Almost any rocker of the '50s could have claimed this as their best album. While there are some excellent rhythm numbers ("Rip It Up," "Paralyzed," and the too-country "When My Blue Moon Turns to Gold Again"), the album's standout is the panting "Love Me." *—Neal Umphred*

○ **50,000,000 Elvis Fans Can't Be Wrong: Elvis' Golden Records, Vol. 2** / 1960 / RCA ✦✦✦✦
The beginner is pointed toward the first two gold record sets, which contain the obvious hits that make up oldies fare, and the not so well known, such as—in the case of this second volume—the smoldering "One Night" and the rousing "I Need Your Love Tonight." *—Neal Umphred*

Elvis Is Back! / Apr. 1960 / RCA ✦✦✦
The first album after the Army, *Elvis Is Back!* captures him at his secular best, which is nonetheless moved by gospel undertones. The sheer intensity of the performances from both Elvis on vocals and rhythm guitar, and the all-star band (which, aside from the regulars, includes Floyd Cramer, Hank Garland and Boots Randolph) overcomes any shortcomings the material might offer. "Make Me Know It," "Fever," "The Girl of My Best Friend" (a hit for sound-alike Ral Donner here and for Elvis abroad) could have been chart-toppers. "Dirty, Dirty Feeling," "Reconsider Baby," and "Such a Night" are among the very best—and "dirtiest"—numbers Elvis had ever cut. *—Neal Umphred*

G.I. Blues / Oct. 1960 / RCA ✦✦✦
Elvis was out of uniform in March and laying down vocals for his first big musical production in April. The confections that make up the soundtrack for *G.I. Blues* were the most trite collection of songs in his career, with the slight but affecting "Wooden Heart" the standout. Still, Elvis's enthusiasm makes even the puff listenable; one can't imagine even considering listening to this music had any other singer on the planet recorded them (except Bob Dylan). *—Neal Umphred*

☆ **His Hand in Mine** / Dec. 1960 / RCA ✦✦✦✦✦
Presley cut several gospel albums over the course of his career, most of them overblown affairs. This one's easily his best; stripped down arrangements with Elvis passionately involved every note of the way. *—Cub Koda*

Something for Everybody / Jun. 1961 / RCA ✦✦✦
Within a year, the emotional involvement and the sense of joie de vivre of both *Elvis Is Back!* and *His Hand in Mine* was replaced by the more stunted professionalism of *Something for Everybody*. While certainly not a compliment, the title was not meant as a total put-down. There are some excellent moments on this LP ("I Want You with Me" would have made a credible single) but, for the first time, it is the "rhythm numbers" that pull down the overall excellence, not the ballads. In the midst of restraint, he cut "Feel So Bad," a scorcher that reached the upper reaches of the charts in 1961 and heated up the first side of *Golden Records, Volume 3*. *—Neal Umphred*

Blue Hawaii / Oct. 1961 / RCA ✦✦✦
The soundtrack of what was to be Elvis's biggest movie called for an Hawaiianesque flavor, and, while Presley's vocals are excellent throughout, much of the material is of a throwaway caliber. Of course, any session that produces "Can't Help Falling in Love" is memorable, but said sessions also gave us "Rock-A-Hula Baby," which was a worldwide hit despite being as dumb as the title implies! Within a matter of months, critical fans would look back at *this* album as a high point. *—Neal Umphred*

Pot Luck with Elvis / Jun. 1962 / RCA ✦✦✦
This album continued the decline begun with *Something for Everybody*. While there are several excellent, continually underrated tracks ("Gonna Get Back Home Somehow," "Night Rider," "(Such An) Easy Question" and, of course, "Suspicion"), this album sounds like a collection of filler, the ballads especially tending towards the lugubrious. A good if unexceptional album. *—Neal Umphred*

Girls! Girls! Girls! / Nov. 1963 / RCA ✦✦
An even lamer attempt at a Hawaiian backdrop produced a nice cover of the old Drifters number as the title tune and "Return to Sender," an excellent mid-tempo R&B-ish hit. The ballads are pleasant, though hardly memorable. Elvis is still singing well, especially considering the material and the arrangements. That would change shortly. While the movies Elvis made during the '60s and their accompanying soundtracks did produce a reliable source of income, they were against Elvis in the long run. The initial enthusiasm that accompanied even the silliest of plots in 1960-62 was replaced by inevitable boredom. The Colonel's response to his boy's growing disillusionment was to find sillier scripts, reduce the budgets allotted for other actors and props, and accept songs the nonsense of which boggles the imagination. Still, during this time, especially those first few years when a movie meant having some fun, Elvis also cut a number of tracks for lesser, nonmusical films, including several affecting ballads for *Wild in the Country*. In 1963 Elvis teamed up with the luscious Ann-Margret, recording some of his most spirited singing in years for *Viva Las Vegas*. Had RCA Victor collected the best of these sessions, along with the standouts "Summer Kisses, Winter Tears,"

"King of the Whole Wide World" and "Follow That Dream," a surprisingly solid album could have been issued. Alas, these tracks were scattered to the winds, showing up on EPs, B-sides and budget albums over a period of ten years. If one needs to delve into this period, an easy rule of thumb is that the further into the decade the soundtracks go, the less likely they are to please. — *Neal Umphred*

○ **Elvis' Golden Records, Vol. 3** / Sep. 1964 / RCA ✦✦✦✦
This third package of gold captures most of the hits from 1960-1962 and is a marvelous album, a model in selection and programming. The songs are all excellent, Elvis was in a period that is always overlooked by fans, critics and biographers, the band often cooked and the production and engineering were flawless. Much of what Elvis achieved here on songs like "(Marie's the Name) His Latest Flame" and "Little Sister" has not been duplicated elsewhere in the field of rock & roll, although the influences are sprouting up in contemporary country. — *Neal Umphred*

Elvis for Everyone / Jul. 1965 / RCA ✦✦✦
To fill in the blank space between soundtracks (yes, it had come to that), RCA gathered a dozen leftovers stretching back to 1954 (!) and assembled this album with a cover that lives up to the title. There is no attempt at programming a logical compilation, a set that might tell us something about Elvis. As usual, everything is treated as so much fodder for the unwashed masses. *And* this was his best album in two years! — *Neal Umphred*

○ **How Great Thou Art** / Mar. 1967 / RCA ✦✦✦✦
Between 1966 and 1968, Elvis recorded just enough studio material to fill one complete secular album and *How Great Thou Art*, a far more polite (and slightly surreal) reading of traditional religious material than the previous outing, a half-dozen years earlier. The performances throughout are superb, the sound impeccable; this actually beat *Sgt. Pepper* as the Best Engineered Album of 1967 in the Grammys! This album is also much closer to mainstream gospel and may not be so immediately accessible to the unconverted; don't let that steer you away from an otherwise great record. — *Neal Umphred*

○ **Elvis** / 1968 / RCA ✦✦✦✦
Presley's return from the cold began in earnest with those "live" sessions in front of a hand-picked audience in the summer of 1968. With both his future *and* his past on the line, Elvis sang with enough passion to scare the meek and enough humor to cause the jaded to pause. — *Neal Umphred*

Elvis Gold Records, Vol. 4 / Feb. 1968 / RCA ✦✦✦
This is one of Elvis's most misunderstood albums. At the time of release the reviews almost without exception discussed how Elvis's gold was drained up and he was reduced to filling up the fourth volume with B-sides. Actually there was more than enough gold for the set: "Wooden Heart," "Can't Help Falling in Love," and "Return to Sender" are the most obvious. "A Mess of Blues," "Witchcraft," and "Please Don't Drag That String Around" are fine uptempo numbers while "Love Letters" and "It Hurts Me" are among the best ballads Elvis—or anyone else—recorded during the decade. — *Neal Umphred*

☆ **NBC TV Special** / Dec. 1968 / RCA ✦✦✦✦✦
After years of making abysmal movies, Presley appeared before a live audience, scared to death. That he more than rose to the challenge is evidenced here, a masterly performance highlighted by the jam-session segment with DJ Fontana and Scotty Moore, where Presley plays electric guitar and knocks out drop-dead versions of "Baby, What You Want Me to Do" and "Tiger Man." — *Cub Koda*

☆ **From Elvis in Memphis** / May 1969 / RCA ✦✦✦✦✦
Presley returned to Memphis, recording thirty-odd songs in Chips Moman's America Sound Studios in 1969, leading to his artistic and commercial resurgence ("In the Ghetto" and "Suspicious Minds") and what may be his single greatest album, *From Elvis in Memphis*. The first track opens with Elvis's hoarsely shouting "I had to leave town for a little while..." and then announces—in no uncertain terms—that he's back. A brilliant selection of material, Elvis sings like his life depended on it. (It didn't; his career did.) The musicians (all regulars from Chips Moman's American Sound Studios) cook and the overdubbed horns and background vocals are among the most appropriate ever used on a White singer's record. — *Neal Umphred*

○ **From Memphis to Vegas / From Vegas to Memphis** / Nov. 1969 / RCA ✦✦✦✦
One half of the imponderably titled *From Memphis to Vegas / From Vegas to Memphis*, (later issued as a separate album, *Elvis in Person at the International Hotel*) captures Elvis from the summer of 1969 while the exhilaration of conquest was still evident. It's a nice compromise between mere entertainment and the revelatory: the first few songs are old hits to pull you in; the second side opens with a roaring medley of "Mystery Train" and Rufus Thomas's "Tiger Man" and leads to a staggering seven-minute "Suspicious Minds." The studio album, ten tracks from the previous Memphis sessions, are a letdown and, even at the time of release, the two-fer concept seemed ill conceived. Had the best of the rest of the Memphis material been collected on a single album and titled *Suspicious Minds*, it's possible this album could have leapt to number one and outsold the first. — *Neal Umphred*

On Stage: February 1970 / Jun. 1970 / RCA ✦✦
On Stage: February 1970, is a bit more tame than *Elvis in Person* but provides Elvis with a chance to cover a number of then-contemporary hits, which he carries with aplomb. Actually, two numbers, "Yesterday" and "Runaway" were recorded for the previous album in August past, so the title is only 80% accurate. As for the live albums that were to follow, you had to have been there. — *Neal Umphred*

○ **Worldwide 50 Gold Award Hits, Vol. 1** / Aug. 1970 / RCA ✦✦✦✦
A combination of the two four-LP *Worldwide* boxes, this 2-CD set contains each of the fifty sides that RCA credits with accumulated worldwide sales in excess of 1,000,000 copies! And in chronological order of release in mono! One can either trace the obvious decline of the artist into entertainer, or marvel at how good the bad stuff sounds in context. Million-selling B-sides and EPs that most assuredly had topped the seven-digit figure but were routinely ignored by most compilations are also included. If all you want in your collection from Elvis is the most obvious hits, this is the one to go with. — *Neal Umphred*

○ **In Person at the International Hotel Las Vegas** / Nov. 1970 / RCA ✦✦✦✦
When Elvis and the Colonel decided it was time to start appearing live again, they assembled a crackerjack band (featuring guitarist James Burton) and took on Vegas full bore. Easily the King's best live album, the highlights on *In Person (at the International Hotel, Las Vegas)* include "Johnny B. Goode," the "My Babe/Mystery Train/Tiger Man" medley, and "Suspicious Minds." — *Cub Koda*

Almost in Love / Nov. 1970 / RCA ✦✦✦
The Camden series is, except for diehards, of negligible interest. The first couple of Elvis titles drew the consumer in with a couple of tasty recent outtakes (1968's "Tiger Man" and a pair from the 1969 Memphis sessions) and then padded the albums out with soundtrack items that were, for the most part, better forgotten. Even at the budget price they were an iffy buy. Not so this one, which collects ten single sides from both the movies and the studio in an interesting package that illuminates the dichotomy that was Elvis Presley in the two years prior to the NBC special. "Clean up Your Own Backyard" and "U.S. Male" are very interesting country explorations while "Long Legged Girl (With the Short Dress On)" and "A Little Less Conversation" are so awful they need to be heard by everyone! — *Neal Umphred*

○ **That's the Way It Is** / Dec. 1970 / RCA ✦✦✦✦
Returning to the more familiar haunts of Nashville in 1970, Elvis & Co. recorded three-dozen tracks, the best of which are on a par with the Memphis recordings from the preceding year. From these, two albums emerged, both flawed, both excellent. *That's the Way It Is*, purporting to be the soundtrack from the documentary of the same name, contains eight of those sides, with Elvis at his most delicious ease. The live recordings are negligible and sink the album's basic level *except* for Elvis's magnificent "I Just Can't Help Believin'." — *Neal Umphred*

○ **Elvis Country** / Jan. 1971 / RCA ✦✦✦✦
Elvis Country was the second album from the June 1970 sessions. It is Elvis's best single album from the '70s and one of his very best ever. Every performance has something to offer; one can argue about the outstanding selection, although one tends away from the pleading of "I Really Don't Want to Know" to the raving "(I Washed My Hands In) Muddy Water." Even "Snowbird" is sung with passion! — *Neal Umphred*

You'll Never Walk Alone / Mar. 1971 / Special Music ✦✦✦
Another budget album, this one collects various gospel items from
sundry sources ("Let Us Pray" was the closer to what may be
Elvis's most outrageous piece of celluloid, 1969's *Change of Habit*)
and orbiting them around the four tracks from 1957's *Peace in the
Valley* EP (no longer a part of *Elvis's Christmas Album*, which had
been deleted and then resurrected as a budget Camden album
with a slightly revamped lineup). Not in the league of Elvis's regular catalog gospel albums, it's stirring nonetheless. —*Neal
Umphred*

○ **He Touched Me** / Apr. 1972 / RCA ✦✦✦✦
As if to make up for not recording in the studio for all those Hollywood years, Elvis took the first few years of his comeback dead
serious. As it stands, *He Touched Me* blends the earthiness of the
1960 gospel album with a bit of the preternatural churchiness of
the 1966 recordings. This is a fine record and you don't need to be
a Christian to dig this music. —*Neal Umphred*

Aloha from Hawaii Via Satellite / Feb. 1973 / RCA ✦✦✦

Elvis / Jul. 1973 / RCA ✦✦✦
Ten tracks, all leftovers from previous projects, appeared in an
ugly cover with nothing on the back except ads for other Presley
Product. Still, what was left off of Elvis's albums is more revealing
than what went on: "It's Still Here" and "I Will Be True" are Elvis
at the piano sans backing and they are glorious. Worth the price of
the whole damn album. Period.—*Neal Umphred*

Raised on Rock / Oct. 1973 / RCA ✦✦✦
In July 1973, Elvis returned to Memphis, this time to the source of
Southern soul, Stax Studios. Apparently, the very idea of working
with Elvis was intimidating and the Stax musicians couldn't overcome their awe, so Elvis had to leave the building. In his absence,
the rhythm tracks were laid down. He then returned to add his vocals, a practice only used during the last few years of the soundtracks, when he was too bored to show up and work. From all of
this, five songs were attempted, one completed, and they're instantly forgettable. Elvis returned in December to Stax with a mix
of his band and some Nashville cats, recording eighteen tracks in
a week. In between, he had tried a session at his Palm Springs
home that didn't work, although three almost ponderously sincere
ballads were completed. All in all, RCA had thirty new Elvis songs,
enough quality material for two strong albums of 12 tracks each.
Unfortunately, the material was issued as three cheesily packaged
albums of a mere ten tracks each. *Raised on Rock, Good Times*
and *Promised Land* all have something to offer, but the lesser material dilutes the impact of the strong and the sound ranges from
O.K. to atrocious, thus producing more evidence of Presley's growing mediocrity. —*Neal Umphred*

○ **Elvis: A Legendary Performer, Vol. 1** / Jan. 1974 / RCA ✦✦✦✦
The *Legendary Performer* series—there were four on Elvis—collected hits, non-hits, and previously unreleased studio and live
recordings with snippets of interviews. While their importance has
been diminished by the various collections that have been released since, many of which robbed the "rare" tracks from here,
the albums are essential *as* albums nonetheless. Each one was issued with a booklet that included rare photos, old posters, session
notes and Elvis memorabilia with captions that were generally a
bit fannish. Should the reader take the four volumes and painstakingly transfer the material to tape in its correct chronology, he or
she would have a more rational overview of Presley's career than
the label has yet compiled. —*Neal Umphred*

Good Times / Mar. 1974 / RCA ✦✦✦
Refer to *Raised on Rock*. —*Neal Umphred*

Recorded Live on Stage in Memphis / Jun. 1974 / RCA ✦✦✦
This oft-ignored album, recorded in March 1974 at Memphis's Mid-
south Coliseum (formerly the center of controversy when the proposed title, the Elvis Presley Coliseum, was poo-pooed), is easily
the strongest live package of the '70s, the one worth having. Elvis
is in exceptional vocal form and, between all the stuff that showed
up on every other live album of the period, there is a great "Trying
to Get to You" and strong versions of "My Baby Left Me" and
"Lawdy, Miss Clawdy," material he otherwise left unnoticed. —
Neal Umphred

Elvis Today / May 1975 / RCA ✦✦✦
Elvis Today is often cited by writers as Elvis's uncertain return to
his Sun origins. There really isn't that much difference from the
trio that resulted from 1973's Stax sessions, with the lesser tracks
being a bit more substantial. The sound is better but the packag-

ing had become, at this point, practically offensive: One color
close-up after another, almost all from the *Aloha from Hawaii* special (or that pre-bloated period), back covers with no noted or technical data, just ads for other Presley Product. Still, an album with
"Susan When She Tried," "T-T-R-O-U-B-L-E," and a hilariously appropriate reading of "I Can Help" is worth listening to any time. —
Neal Umphred

○ **The Sun Sessions** / Mar. 1976 / RCA ✦✦✦✦
It only took Elvis and the Colonel (no, sorry, the order is wrong:
the Colonel and Elvis) twenty years to compile the greatest music
the King ever made onto one coherent package, and they did that
only because RCA of Great Britain had done it the year before and
imported copies were selling out all over the US. So, what does
one say about sixteen sides the equal of which one might have to
search adjectives for? That Elvis's Sun recordings stand as the
Rosetta Stones of rock & roll and modern country & western. Or,
that along with perhaps *King of the Delta Blues Singers*, it is one
of the handful of absolutely essential—and continually
influential—collections ever released? Or, does one complain that
no one took the time to find the original tapes, using the tampered
album (refer to *For LP Fans Only* and *A Date with Elvis*) masters
instead? Oh, well, at the very least, it was worth the wait. —*Neal
Umphred*

From Elvis Presley Boulevard, Memphis, Tennessee / May 1976
/ RCA ✦✦✦
By 1976 Elvis was recording at home in Graceland, cutting what
would be the final recordings of his career. Filled with bathos and
showing little rock & roll vitality, these remain interesting
nonetheless, as it implied his accepting his age somewhat and attempting to combine old-fashioned, melodramatic soul with contemporary country-pop. While the pain and decay are evident—especially in hindsight—Elvis could still sing: "Hurt" is excellent, one
of his best and, on "Danny Boy," Elvis reaches with an aching
falsetto that closes the song, appropriately. Still, this is hardly the
album to begin your collection with. —*Neal Umphred*

Moody Blue / Jul. 1977 / RCA ✦✦
For some reason, this album sold briskly on release, heading for
the most respectable sales an Elvis album had had in years. Then,
nothing. This is not one of his best, combining a few recently
recorded tracks (October, back in his home studios), with leftovers
from the February sessions, and a couple of live tracks, one of
which had previously been released on the already deleted
Recorded Live on Stage in Memphis. The first 250,000 copies were
pressed on blue vinyl. All subsequent pressings were due to be on
black. When the news of Elvis's passing reached RCA, they
switched back to blue. The few copies of AFL1-2428 on black vinyl
are worth $200. —*Neal Umphred*

○ **Elvis: A Legendary Performer, Vol. 3** / Nov. 1979 / RCA ✦✦✦✦
Refer to the comments on *A Legendary Performer—Vol. 1*. —*Neal
Umphred*

Elvis Aron Presley / Aug. 1980 / RCA ✦✦✦
An eight-record boxed extravaganza, it promised so much and delivered so little. Averaging 12 minutes per side, this could have
easily been a six album set with a considerably pared down retail
price. The packaging is as ugly as to defy description, including inner sleeves that fell apart after sliding the albums in a couple of
times. The programming of the discs by theme or concept was interesting but the box stands as a condemnation of the way that
Presley was perceived by RCA. There is some good, previously unavailable material here; the side titled *Elvis at the Piano* contains
four tracks of just that, including the complete take of "It's Still
Here" from 1971 and the lovely but inexplicably never-heard-be-
fore "Beyond the Reef" from the *How Great Thou Art* sessions. —
Neal Umphred

This Is Elvis / Mar. 1981 / RCA ✦✦✦
This two-LP set comes from the movie of the same name. The material is not programmed randomly, which certainly doesn't help
tell the story of Elvis, but the selections are good and there was
some new material. Mainly this functions as a primer of sorts and,
if it assists in getting novices to view the film, then it did its job. —
Neal Umphred

Elvis: The Beginning Years, 1954 To '56 / 1983 / Louisiana
Hayride ✦✦✦
At the start of his career, Elvis played many engagements for the
Louisiana Hayride, the most popular country radio show except
for the *Grand Ole Opry*. Nine surviving airshots from those days

are compiled on this album, including a few of his classic Sun singles, the otherwise unavailable covers "Tweedle Dee" and "Maybellene," and a very raw "Hound Dog." The sound isn't bad considering the source; Elvis' vocals are always clear, the guitar sometimes bright and sometimes not, the bass all but inaudible. No one's buying this for high fidelity, though; what you want is a glimpse of the man at his peak before his live audience, and on that account, this comes through, with energetic performances that form a valuable historic document. —*Richie Unterberger*

○ **A Golden Celebration** / 1984 / RCA ✦✦✦✦
This box is what the first one should have been, with six albums of unreleased material: Sun outtakes, Elvis's complete television appearances from 1956, more exhilarating stuff from *The 1968 NBC Special*. The packaging is a great leap forward, the sound impeccable, and the selections are of value both aesthetically and historically. Recommended to everyone, it is desperately needed on CD. —*Neal Umphred*

☆ **Reconsider Baby** / 1985 / RCA ✦✦✦✦✦
Since Elvis's death in 1977, the market has been inundated with an array of repackages, most of them artless, pointless and, a fan might wish, profitless. Part of the 50th Anniversary celebration, *Reconsider Baby* offered little that was new, but the concept—Elvis as an R&B singer—was overdue. The selection is impossible to argue with, the programming perfect, and the album makes its argument aptly. —*Neal Umphred*

○ **The Number One Hits** / 1987 / RCA ✦✦✦✦
Number One Hits contains 18 #1 records from the charts of *Billboard*, who somehow didn't rank "Crying in the Chapel," "In the Ghetto," "Burning Love," and "Way Down" as chart-toppers, although other national surveys did. In fact, according to RCA, every copy of "Way Down" was sold out within days after Presley's death, not just here but all over the planet, and somehow, amazingly, it didn't even make the magazine's Top Ten! —*Neal Umphred*

★ **The Top Ten Hits** / 1987 / RCA ✦✦✦✦✦
The one definitive collection to own, 38 essential tracks are spread over two CDs. Think of any of Elvis's biggest chartbusters, they're all here. —*Hank Davis & Cub Koda*

☆ **The Memphis Record** / 1987 / RCA ✦✦✦✦✦
Coming hot off the heels of his breakthrough NBC special in 1968, Presley returned to Memphis to record for the first time in 12 years and laid down 20 tracks in the space of four days. He was hot, he was inspired, and it's all here. —*Cub Koda*

★ **The Complete Sun Sessions** / 1987 / RCA ✦✦✦✦✦
The place where rock & roll begins. "That's All Right," "Baby, Let's Play House," "Mystery Train," "Milkcow Blues Boogie," and "Good Rockin' Tonight," plus fascinating outtakes like "When It Rains, It Really Pours." The cornerstone of any rock & roll collection, and great notes by Peter Guralnick too. —*Cub Koda*

○ **Essential Elvis: The First Movies** / 1988 / RCA ✦✦✦✦
A great collection of movie-soundtrack alternates, including great, eye-opening versions of "Jailhouse Rock" and "Got a Lot of Livin' to Do." —*Hank Davis &Cub Koda*

Stereo '57: Essential Elvis, Vol. 2 / 1988 / RCA ✦✦✦
The second volume of *Essential Elvis* offers Elvis in binaural stereo from the January 1957 sessions that produced several hits. (RCA Victor generously filled the disc out with mono masters of the remaining songs to give the consumer a complete version of the sessions.) This is a lot of fun; the gaffes are numerous, obvious, and hilarious, and for ears raised on multi-track recording, it must be amazing to hear an entire record recorded live in the studio! —*Neal Umphred*

Hits Like Never Before: Essential Elvis, Vol. 3 / 1990 / RCA ✦✦✦
A whopping 24 alternates of takes from his 1958 sessions. This has some substantially different versions of most of his big late-'50s hits—"I Got Stung," "A Fool Such As I," "I Need Your Love Tonight," "Wear My Ring Around Your Neck," and "A Big Hunk O' Love"—as well as alternates of songs from the *King Creole* film. Not exactly essential, but decent stuff. —*Richie Unterberger*

☆ **Million Dollar Quartet** / 1990 / RCA ✦✦✦✦✦
For years available only as a poor-fidelity bootleg, this is Elvis jamming in the Sun studios with Carl Perkins, Jerry Lee Lewis, and others on a set of primarily gospel and hillbilly material. Loose as a goose, with a true jam-session spirit to it, it offers a fascinating glimpse of one of the few times Presley let his true musical soul

come up for air with somebody (Sam Phillips) there to record it. —*Cub Koda*

☆ **The King of Rock 'n' Roll: Complete 50s' Masters** / 1992 / RCA ✦✦✦✦✦
This boxed five-CD set contains every studio recording Elvis made from 1954-58 in chronological order on the first four discs; the fifth is a collection of outtakes and alternates. The sound is the best heard on CD by Elvis with virtually every track taken from an original tape of a first-generation safety copy. The great booklet has more notes from Peter Guralnick. *Absolutely* the single finest package RCA of America has ever released on Elvis Aaron Presley and indispensable to any collection that pretends to deal with American music. —*Neal Umphred*

☆ **From Nashville to Memphis: the Essential 60's Masters** / 1993 / RCA ✦✦✦✦✦
Continues the tradition of first-quality sound remastering and packaging. Much of Elvis' '60s work is arguably not as essential as the '50s stuff, but this meticulous five-disc/130-track set makes an impressive case for the defense. A thick booklet contains riveting liner notes, full-color photos, complete discography and session listings; a sheet of RCA album cover stamps tops off the set. —*Roch Parisien*

If Every Day Was Like Christmas / 1994 / RCA ✦✦✦
All of Elvis Presley's catalogue Christmas material has been remastered and compiled on this single-disc. RCA has taken the same masterful care with this 24-track collection as with the Elvis box sets. Sound quality is exceptional. Includes 3 unreleased alternate performances, solid liner notes and a closing "Christmas message from Elvis." —*Roch Parisien*

○ **Amazing Grace: His Greatest Sacred Songs** / 1994 / RCA ✦✦✦✦

Heart and Soul / 1995 / RCA ✦✦
The concept that seems to be guiding this, one of the latest in a long line of rehash repackages, is a focus on romantic ballads. You get well-worn hits like "Love Me Tender," "Can't Help Falling In Love," and "Suspicious Minds," not-so-well-worn hits like "She's Not You," the original version of "The Girl Of My Best Friend" (covered by Ral Donner for a big hit), and other odds and ends on this 22-track compilation. Not appealing for either the novice or serious fan, the rarities, if you could call them that, are a stereo version of "I've Lost You" and a version of "Bridge Over Troubled Water" with the dubbed applause removed. Only regular pilgrims to Graceland need to get in line. —*Richie Unterberger*

Legend Begins / Magnum ✦✦✦
An absolutely astounding collection of early Elvis live performances, starting with his initial appearance on the Louisiana Hayride in 1954. Of particular note is the five-song performance from the Eagle's Hall in Houston, Texas (March of 1955), as well as the inclusion of Hayride performances of LaVern Baker's "Tweedlee Dee" and Chuck Berry's "Maybellene," two songs Presley never recorded commercially. Although this material has been around the block numerous times, its improved fidelity and legal issuance here makes this a true cornerstone for any '50s Presley collection. (British import) —*Cub Koda*

BOOKS

✦✦✦✦ **Elvis: The Illustrated Record**, by Roy Carr & Mick Farren (Harmony, 1982). At the time this book appeared, there were no serious critical studies of Elvis' work. This remains the volume that, as the authors intended, "set the record straight." Features in-depth criticism, with enthusiastic but considered analysis, of every record Elvis made. Naturally—thankfully, actually—the early Sun and RCA sessions, as well as some isolated later critical triumphs like the late '60s albums, are covered in the most depth, with a scholarship that is both meticulous and compelling. Elvis' relatively brief eras of brilliance were punctuating by long ones of excruciating mediocrity, and the authors do not fail to point out the shortcomings of his many soundtracks and uninspired singles. Indeed, the stretch between 1961 and 1968 can make for pretty thin gruel, and these parts are inevitably much less interesting than the highlights, though the authors do a good job of dismissing, or lightly skipping over, his bad records with curt humor that doesn't waste words. Includes some good essays summarizing specific eras of his career, tons of sleeves and photos, and an exhaustive discography including bootlegs. —*Richie Unterberger*

✦✦✦✦ **Last Train To Memphis: The Rise Of Elvis Presley**, by Peter Guralnick (Little, Brown & Co., 1994). There are many biographies of Elvis, most of them cheap and shoddy productions that focus on the most sensational and morbid aspects of the King's life (though he did give them a lot to focus on). Guralnick is one of the top authorities on early rock & roll, and the natural candidate to write a biography that is both accurate and focused upon his art and music as much as his personal life. The first volume of a projected multi-part work, this covers what, for the majority of his fans, are his most interesting years, ending just after he leaves the United States in late 1958 to serve as a member of the army in Germany. The early years are thoroughly documented (there are almost 500 footnotes alone): the grinding poverty, the gospel influences, the months of pestering Sun Records to record him, the sculpting of his early rockabilly sound in the Sun Studios, the wild early tours, the early managers, the meteoric rise to fame after his contract was sold to RCA, the hangers-on he felt compelled to surround himself with from Memphis, the induction into the army. Lots of detail and balanced perspective between his personality and his music, only marred by some surprisingly perfunctory appraisals of some of his early sessions, particularly the ones at RCA. —*Richie Unterberger*

Billy Preston

b. Sep. 9, 1946
Soul, R&B
It's advantageous to get an early start on your chosen career, but Billy Preston took the concept to extremes. By age ten, he was playing keyboards with gospel diva Mahalia Jackson, and two years later, in 1958, he was featured in Hollywood's film bio of W. C. Handy, *St. Louis Blues,* as young Handy himself. Preston was a prodigy on organ and piano, recording during the early '60s for Vee-Jay and touring with Little Richard. He was a loose-limbed regular on the mid-'60s ABC-TV *Shindig* series, proving his talent as both vocalist and pianist, and he built an enviable reputation as a session musician, even backing the Beatles on their *Let It Be* album. That impressive Beatles connection led to Preston's big break as a solo artist with his own Apple album, but it was his early-'70s soul smashes "Outa-Space" and the high-flying vocal "Will It Go Round in Circles" for A&M that put Preston on the permanent musical map. Sporting a humongous Afro and an omnipresent gap-toothed grin, Preston showed that his enduring gospel roots were never far removed from his joyous approach, less so now than ever. —*Bill Dahl*

Sixteen Year Old Soul / 19-z / Derby ✦✦✦

Early Hits / 1965 / Exodus ✦✦✦

○ **Most Exciting Organ Ever** / 1965 / Vee-Jay ✦✦✦✦
The hyperbole of the title aside, Preston did produce some flamboyant organ solos and keyboard work throughout this album. His use of bass pedals, dazzling intervals, octave jumps, phrases, and chordal maneuvers were impressive. This hasn't been reissued by Vee Jay, and certainly should be if the label hasn't lost the masters. It's another side of Preston, one that became lost as he gained more and more popularity in the '70s as a singer. —*Ron Wynn*

Wildest Organ in Town! / 1966 / Capitol ✦✦✦
A late '60s Capitol set with Preston displaying his jazz/blues side as an organist. Unfortunately, nothing on this album caught fire, even in the R&B community, and Preston would soon go on to work for Ray Charles and the Beatles. His early prowess as a flashy organ equivalent of Jimi Hendrix has been largely forgotten or overlooked, and the fact that this album hasn't been in print for many years hasn't helped. —*Ron Wynn*

Club Meeting / 1967 / Capitol ✦✦✦

Greazee Soul / 1969 / Soul City ✦✦✦

○ **Billy Preston** / 1969 / Buddah ✦✦✦✦

○ **That's the Way God Planned It** / 1969 / Apple ✦✦✦✦
A great bit of gospel/soul in the title cut, and otherwise a fine record that didn't make Billy Preston a huge star but alerted everyone that he was more than just a talented keyboard player backing the Beatles. This was one of two albums Preston did on the Beatles' Apple label, and while nothing made the charts, it was a good introduction for those unaware of Preston's multiple skills. —*Ron Wynn*

Encouraging Words / 1970 / Capitol ✦✦✦

I Wrote a Simple Song / 1971 / A&M ✦✦

Music Is My Life / 1972 / A&M ✦✦
Although this was an erratic album, keyboardist and vocalist Billy Preston landed his lone number-one pop hit with "Will It Go Round In Circles." Preston tried everything from gospel and message tracks to rock and pop, but outside of "Circles," nothing else generated even a listen. Among Preston album cuts, "God Loves You" and "Ain't That Nothin' " are quite interesting. —*Ron Wynn*

Everybody Likes Some Kind of Music / 1973 / A&M ✦✦✦

Original Billy Preston: Soul'd Out / 1973 / GNP ✦✦
A moderately interesting set of tracks that GNP issued in the mid-'70s trying to take advantage of the fact that Billy Preston was a huge star at the time. There's nothing here remotely as interesting as any of his hits, but there are bits and pieces that show his skill as a keyboardist and vocalist. It has long since disappeared, and it's no loss to the Preston legacy. —*Ron Wynn*

Genius of Billy Preston / 1973 / Springboard ✦✦✦
A low-budget anthology that collects some good Preston recordings, but issued them in such a flimsy-sounding package that it diminishes the value. This label may or may not still be in existence, so if they are, perhaps you'll find this around one day. If not, there are better hits and anthologies packages around. —*Ron Wynn*

● **The Best of Billy Preston** / 1988 / A&M ✦✦✦✦
It contains several fun pop hits, including "Will It Go Round in Circles" and "Outa-Space." —*Dan Heilman*

The Pretenders

Group, Rock & Roll, New Wave, Pop/Rock
Over the years, the Pretenders have become a vehicle for guitarist/vocalist Chrissie Hynde's songwriting, yet it was a full-fledged band when it was formed in the late '70s. With their initial records, the group crossed the bridge between punk/new wave and Top 40 pop more than any other band, recording a series of hard, spiky singles that were also melodic and immediately accessible. Hynde was an invigorating, sexy singer that bended the traditional male roles of rock & roll to her own liking, while guitarist James Honeyman-Scott created a sonic palate filled with suspended chords, effects pedals, and syncopated rhythms that proved remarkably influential over the next two decades. After Honeyman-Scott's death, the Pretenders became a more straightforward rock band, yet Hynde's semi-autobiographical songwriting and bracing determination meant that the group never became just another rock band, even when their music became smoother and more pop-oriented.

Originally from Akron, OH, Hynde moved to England in the early '70s, when she was in her 20s. British rock journalist Nick Kent helped her begin writing for the *New Musical Express;* she wrote for the newspaper during the mid-'70s. She also worked in Malcolm McLaren's Sex boutique before she began performing. After playing with Chris Spedding, she joined Jack Rabbit; she quickly left the band and formed the Berk Brothers, as well as recording a single under the name the Moors Murders.

In 1978, Hynde formed the Pretenders, which eventually consisted of Honeyman-Scott, bassist Pete Farndon, and drummer Martin Chambers. Later in the year, they recorded a version of Ray Davies' "Stop Your Sobbing" with Nick Lowe as their producer. Released on Stiff Records, the single made it into the British Top 40 in early 1979, supported by positive reviews. "Kid" and "Brass in Pocket," the group's next two singles, also were successful. Their self-titled debut album was released in early 1980 and eventually climbed to number one in the U.K. The Pretenders were nearly as successful in America, with the album reaching the Top Ten and "Brass in Pocket" reaching number 14.

During an American tour in 1980, Hynde met Ray Davies and the two fell in love. Following a spring 1981 EP, *Extended Play,* the group released their second album, *Pretenders II.* Although it fared well on the charts, it repeated the musical ideas of their debut. In June of 1982, Pete Farndon was kicked out of the band, due to his drug abuse. A mere two days later on June 16, James Honeyman-Scott was found dead of an overdose of heroin and cocaine. Pregnant with Davies' child, Hynde went into seclusion following Honeyman-Scott's death. In 1983, two months after Hynde gave birth, Farndon also died of a drug overdose.

Hynde regrouped the Pretenders at the end of 1983, adding former Average White Band guitarist Robbie McIntosh and bassist

Malcolm Foster; the reconstituted band released "2000 Miles" in time for Christmas. The new Pretenders released *Learning to Crawl* early in 1984 to positive reviews and commercial success; it became the highest-charting Pretenders album in the U.S., reaching number five. Hynde married Jim Kerr, the lead vocalist of Simple Minds, in May of 1984, effectively ending her romance with Ray Davies.

Apart from a performance at Live Aid, the only musical activity from the Pretenders during 1985 was Hynde's appearance on UB40's version of "I Got You Babe." Hynde assembled another version of the Pretenders for 1986's *Get Close*. Only McIntosh and herself remained from *Learning to Crawl*—the rest of the album was recorded with session musicians. *Get Close* showed the Pretenders moving closer to MOR territory, with the bouncy single "Don't Get Me Wrong" making its way into the American Top Ten in 1987. Hynde recorded another duet with UB40 in 1988, the old Dusty Springfield song, "Breakfast in Bed." For most of 1988 and 1989, she devoted her time to animal rights causes.

Hynde's marriage to Kerr fell apart in 1990 and the Pretenders recorded *Packed!*, which failed to ignite the charts in either America or Britain. She was relatively quiet for the next few years, re-emerging in 1994 with *Last of the Independents*, which was hailed as a comeback by some quarters of the press. The album did return the Pretenders to the Top 40 with the ballad "I'll Stand by You." The tougher "Night in My Veins" received airplay on alternative rock stations, where Hynde was being hailed as a mother to the new wave of female rockers. —*Stephen Thomas Erlewine*

☆ **Pretenders** / 1980 / Sire ✦✦✦✦✦
Chrissie Hynde's tough-girl persona, allied with the aggressive onslaught of Pete Farndon, James Honeyman Scott, and Martin Chambers, makes this the top debut album of its year and prime evidence of the enlivening influence punk had on mainstream rock. —*William Ruhlmann*

○ **Pretenders II** / 1981 / Sire ✦✦✦✦
A well-named followup, since this album successfully repeats the formula of the debut, from its punky leadoff track, "The Adultress," to its catchy pop-rock single, "Talk of the Town," and even to its Kinks cover, "I Go to Sleep." But if you liked the first one ... —*William Ruhlmann*

☆ **Learning to Crawl** / 1984 / Sire ✦✦✦✦✦
Half the band is dead, Chrissie Hynde has taken time off to have a baby, and the world has changed. The Pretenders are now a front for Hynde, solo artist, an adult rock singer/songwriter and, on such songs as "Middle of the Road," "Back on the Chain Gang," and "My City Was Gone," a damn good one too. —*William Ruhlmann*

Get Close / 1986 / Sire ✦✦✦
By now, Hynde is writing songs to her child and taking on social issues. But the chiming guitars are gorgeous, and Hynde's caught-in-the-throat voice has never been more expressive. —*William Ruhlmann*

★ **The Singles** / 1987 / Sire ✦✦✦✦✦
Although the singles-only format makes the Pretenders sound more pop-oriented than they were, especially in the beginning, this album essentially addresses the legacy of punk in the 10 years after its peak, tracing a heritage back to mid-'60s Merseybeat and forward to a more rock-based pop music. It also makes the case for Chrissie Hynde as a major artist. —*William Ruhlmann*

Packed! / May 1990 / Sire ✦✦
It may be true that Chrissie Hynde's songs on *Packed!* are the weakest in her career, but they are not the sole reason why the album is such a bland, uninspiring affair. In the hands of producer Mitchell Froom, Hynde's stylistic retreads become even more unfocused and lackluster. Froom's production lacks any edge, making the pleasant but pedestrian songs bland and featureless. Only a cover of Hendrix's "May This Be Love" and "When Will I See You," a collaboration with guitarist Johnny Marr, stand out admit the number of undistinguished tracks on *Packed!*. —*Stephen Thomas Erlewine*

Last of the Independents / 1994 / Sire ✦✦✦
Chrissie Hynde rebounded from the directionless *Packed!* with *Last of the Independents*, a tough album that proves she can mature without losing her edge. Most of the record crackles with the lean power of *Learning to Crawl*, occasionally stopping for a lushly-produced numbers recalling *Get Close*. Although the record goes on a little too long and there's a couple of weak songs, particularly the anthemic "I'm A Mother," but *Last of the Independents*

re-established Hynde as a powerful and insightful rocker. —*Stephen Thomas Erlewine*

Pretty Things

Group, Art-Rock/Progressive-Rock, British Invasion
Of all the original British Invasion groups, perhaps none is as underappreciated in the United States as the Pretty Things. Featuring the hoarse vocals of Mick Jagger-lookalike Phil May and the stinging leads of guitarist Dick Taylor (who actually played in early versions of the Rolling Stones with Jagger and Keith Richards), the Pretties recorded a clutch of raunchy R&B rockers in the mid-'60s that offer a punkier, rawer version of the early Stones' sound. Their first two albums, as well as a brace of fine major and minor British hits (of which "Don't Bring Me Down" and "Honey I Need" were the biggest), feature first-rate original material and covers, and remain the group's most exciting and influential recordings. Unfortunately, the band remained virtually unknown to American audiences, most of whom would first hear "Don't Bring Me Down" on David Bowie's *Pin Ups* album (which also included a version of the Pretties' "Rosalyn").

After their initial run of success, the group took a sharp left turn into psychedelia with the orchestrated album *Emotions* (1967), impressive singles that owed more to Pink Floyd than Bo Diddley, and, most significantly, *S.F. Sorrow* (1968). The first rock opera, *S.F. Sorrow* was a major influence upon Pete Townshend, who released his much more successful opera, *Tommy*, with the Who the following year. Founding member Taylor left shortly after *S.F. Sorrow*, and the group continued to record progressive rock and hard rock with less impressive results through the mid-'70s, although *Parachute* (1970) was named by *Rolling Stone* as album of the year. The group reunites sporadically for occasional gigs and recordings in their early R&B vein. —*Richie Unterberger*

Emotions / 1967 / Fontana ✦✦✦
In accordance with their label's (and not the band's) wishes, the Pretties were teamed with a middle-aged orchestra directed by Reg Tilsley on this album, which saw the Phil May-Dick Taylor songwriting team making an effort to move beyond R&B knock-offs into more sophisticated territory. Sometimes the arrangements (dubbed onto tracks without much involvement from the group) worked; more often, they were an unnecessary hindrance. An interesting failure, it contained some genuinely top-rank originals that saw the group expanding their vision into social observation and tentative psychedelia, including "My Time," "The Sun," and especially the moody, folk-rock-ish "Death of a Socialite." —*Richie Unterberger*

S.F. Sorrow / 1968 / Edsel ✦✦✦
No amount of scrutiny can disguise the fact that this rock opera—built around a short story by Phil May—is ultimately a bit of a confusing effort. Although it may have helped inspire *Tommy*, it is, simply, not nearly as good. That said, it was first, and has quite a few nifty ideas and production touches. —*Richie Unterberger*

Parachute / 1970 / Rare Earth ✦✦✦
The last Pretty Things album to explore interesting territory, this progressive rock is grounded by some solid harmonies and riffs, but is ultimately not nearly as compelling as its *Rolling Stone* Album of the Year award would suggest. —*Richie Unterberger*

The Singles A's & B's / 1977 / Harvest ✦✦✦
Thirteen tracks from their progressive/psychedelic era, 1967-71. Of special interest is the non-LP 1967 single "Defecting Grey," a brilliant cop of Syd Barrett-era Pink Floyd. Its B-side ("Mr. Evasion") and the follow-up single "Talkin' About the Good Times"/"Walking Through My Dreams" were also non-LP, and also rank among the more coveted rarities of the early British psychedelic era. —*Richie Unterberger*

Electric Banana / 1991 / Repertoire ✦✦
As chart activity became slim for the Pretty Things around 1967, they started a sideline of recording songs specifically for film soundtracks. This compilation features their vocal contributions to these projects, and consists mostly of fairly pedestrian psychedelic-tinged rock of a lower standard than either their 1967-68 singles or the *S.F. Sorrow* album. Highlights are the driving fuzzy rocker "Alexander" and an early version of the *S.F. Sorrow* track "I See You." —*Richie Unterberger*

● **Get a Buzz: The Best of the Fontana Years** / 1992 / Fontana ✦✦✦✦

It's missing a few good tracks, but this is a good retrospective of their British Invasion-era work, running through the 1967 *Emotions* LP. Includes all their major singles—"Rosalyn," "Don't Bring Me Down," "Honey I Need," "Midnight to Six Man," "Come See Me." —*Richie Unterberger*

On Air / 1992 / Band Of Joy ✦✦

15 BBC airshots of the Pretty Things, cut between 1964 and the early to mid-'70s (no dates are included in the liner notes). To this day, the Pretty Things are one of the most underappreciated British Invasion bands in the United States. Failing to score a hit in this country, they emulated the best aspects of the early Rolling Stones in the U.K., moving from raunchy rock/R&B to psychedelia and progressive rock by the end of the '60s. The most exciting cuts on this disc are the six songs from the mid-'60s, which found them mining the line between rock and R&B. "Deflecting Grey," their Syd Barrett-esque single from 1967, is also heard in its live-in-the-studio version. That said, this compilation really is for fanatics only. These alternate versions have good fidelity, but don't differ notably from their official releases; if anything, they are a bit tamer. The last half of the disc, drawn from their progressive/hard rock days, is a bit of a waste, and downright turgid in comparison with their early work. —*Richie Unterberger*

Alan Price

b. Apr. 19, 1941, Fatfield, Co Durham
Rock & Roll, British Invasion
As the organist in the first Animals lineup, Alan Price was perhaps the most important instrumental contributor to their early run of hits. He left the group in 1965 after only a year or so of international success (he can be seen talking about his departure with Bob Dylan in the rockumentary *Don't Look Back*) to work on a solo career. Leading the Alan Price Set, he had a top ten British hit in 1966 with a terrific reworking of "I Put a Spell on You," complete with Animal-ish organ breaks and bluesy vocals. His subsequent run of British hits between 1966 and 1968—"Hi-Lili-Hi-Lo," "Simon Smith and His Dancing Bear," "The House that Jack Built," "Don't Stop the Carnival"—were in a much lighter vein, drawing from British music hall influences. "Simon Smith and His Dancing Bear," from 1967, was one of the first Randy Newman songs to gain international exposure, though Price's version—like all his British hits—went virtually unnoticed in the U.S. A versatile entertainer, Price collaborated with Georgie Fame, hosted TV shows, and scored plays in the years following the breakup of the Alan Price Set in 1968. His greatest achievement since the '60s is his score to Lindsay Anderson's *O Lucky Man*, where his spare and droll songs served almost as a Greek chorus to the surreal, whimsical film (Price himself has a small role in the movie). His 1974 concept album *Between Today and Yesterday* was his most critically-acclaimed work. —*Richie Unterberger*

The World of Alan Price / 1970 / Decca ✦✦✦

Best-of compilation of his '60s solo work, including all his hits. "I Put a Spell on You" is fabulous, one of the best British '60s hits that never made it big in the States. The rest is surprisingly disappointing good-timey pop, sometimes in a jazzy Georgie Fame mold, at times verging on vaudevillian. —*Richie Unterberger*

● **O Lucky Man** / 1973 / Warner Brothers ✦✦✦✦

Price's keyboard-dominated score to the Lindsay Anderson film works well on its own, with incisive tunes that dole out equal measures of cynicism and sympathy. The infectiously poignant "Poor People" is a highlight. —*Richie Unterberger*

Lloyd Price

b. Mar. 9, 1933, Kenner, LA
Rock & Roll, New Orleans R&B
Having taken New Orleans by storm in 1952 with his often-covered #1 R&B hit "Lawdy Miss Clawdy" and a raft of sizzling encores, Lloyd Price yearned for new horizons in 1958, when he signed with ABC-Paramount Records. Price wanted to be a pop star, and it didn't take him long to achieve his goal. Price's pleading style worked brilliantly on his initial New Orleans sides for Specialty Records, resulting in a string of 1952-1953 R&B hits, but his later ABC output left the second-line rhythms behind in favor of prominent female choruses and giant supper-club-style horn sections. His socko reading of the old Crescent City chant "Stagger Lee" deservedly topped the R&B and pop lists in 1958, and he fol-

lowed it with the utterly pop-styled "Personality" and "I'm Gonna Get Married," another pair of R&B #1s that sported no hint of Price's New Orleans roots. As the '60s dawned, Price insisted on interpreting a variety of Tin Pan Alley standards on his albums, although "Come into My Heart" and "Lady Luck," both hits, swung with a brassy, R&B-based drive. Price formed his own Double-L logo in 1963, issuing hits by Wilson Pickett and one for himself—a Vegas-oriented treatment of "Misty." Price seemed to prefer the business end of show biz after that, rather than focusing on his singing career. —*Bill Dahl*

● **Greatest Hits** / 1990 / Curb ✦✦✦✦

Price's biggest hits are included (vintage 1957-1959), like "Personality" and "Stagger Lee." Catchy, brassy, and over-arranged. —*Hank Davis*

○ **Lawdy!** / 1991 / Specialty ✦✦✦✦

Only five years earlier than the pop hits, but what a difference! Wonderful New Orleans R&B, it includes the memorable "Lawdy Miss Clawdy." —*Hank Davis*

Primal Scream

Group, Alternative Pop/Rock, Dance, Rock & Roll
Primal Scream might be the greatest charlatans of the '90s. With their third album, *Screamadelica*, the band was hailed as great musical innovators, dragging rock & roll kicking and screaming into the drug-soaked dance club scene of the early '90s. As it turns out, the record was merely a means to an end—Primal Scream just wants to be rock stars and they don't care what they actually sound like, as long as they get there.

On their first two albums, the band recycled '60s and early '70s guitar pop and hard rock to some acclaim in the U.K., but it was 1991's *Screamadelica* that established Primal Scream as major stars in England and earned them a cult following in America. *Screamadelica* took the classic early '70s rock of the Stones and the Faces and submerged it in techno and house dance music, creating a blissed-out, colorful pseudo-psychedelic extravaganza. It was a distinctive, innovative album, but Primal Scream's actual contribution to the sound of the record is questionable. What carried the album was its admittedly amazing production, mainly provided by Andrew Weatherall; there were few songs that could actually be attributed to the group and those that could were blatantly derivative.

Primal Scream's true roots appeared on their follow-up album, 1994's *Give out but Don't Give Up*, which saw the band accentuating the classic rock currents that ran beneath their music and refashioning themselves as retro-rockers like the Black Crowes. Of course, that may again be the work of their producers—R&B veteran Tom Dowd, George Clinton, and Black Crowes mastermind George Drakoulias—but either way, the band lost many of its fans in the dance world while gaining a new audience of rockers. —*Stephen Thomas Erlewine*

Sonic Flower Groove / 1987 / Elevation ✦✦

Primal Scream's debut album draws from a variety of influences, pulling together strands of '60s pop with psychedelia, noisy protopunk, and the detached cool of the Velvet Underground. However, most of the album is only impressive conceptually, as the group didn't write enough solid hooks to make their fusions memorable. —*Stephen Thomas Erlewine*

Primal Scream / 1989 / Mercenary ✦✦

On their self-titled second album, Primal Scream improves on their debut by turning in a handful of pop songs that manage to fulfill portions of their grand ambitions, yet the record remains a bit too unfocused to be memorable. —*Stephen Thomas Erlewine*

● **Screamadelica** / Oct. 8, 1991 / Sire ✦✦✦✦

Screamadelica is an impressive, innovative album that seamlessly combines classic rock with the throbbing beat of the dance club. While it doesn't contain any concise pop songs besides "Movin' On Up," the album is remarkably consistent and proved that it was possible to inject some true grit into the highly stylized world of techno, house, and rave. —*Stephen Thomas Erlewine*

Give out but Don't Give Up / Sep. 1993 / Sire ✦✦✦

The rock undercurrents that ran throughout *Screamadelica* come to the forefront on the tired *Give out but Don't Give Up*. While Primal Scream turn out a couple of good songs, "Jailbird" and "(I'm Gonna) Cry Myself Blind," the band sounds too mannered to be a truly successful ripoff of the Stones and Faces. And the colorful, reckless experimentation of their previous album is sorely missed. —*Stephen Thomas Erlewine*

Primus

Group, Alternative Pop/Rock

Primus is all about Les Claypool; there isn't a moment on any of their other records where his bass isn't the main focal point of the music, with his vocals acting as a bizarre side show. Which isn't to deny guitarist Larry LaLonde or drummer Tim "Herb" Alexander any credit—no drummer could weave in and around Claypool's convoluted patterns as effortlessly as Alexander and few guitarists would as willingly push the spotlight away like LaLonde, so he can produce a never-ending spiral of avant-noise. All of this means that they are miles away from being another punk-funk combo like the Red Hot Chili Peppers; Claypool may slap and pop his bass, but there is little funk in the rhythm he and Alexander lay down. Instead, they're a post-punk Rush spiked with the sensibility and humor of Frank Zappa. Primus doesn't want to make you dance, they want to play music; songs are secondary to showcasing their instrumental prowess.

Primus' music is willfully weird and experimental, yet it's not alienating; the band was able to turn their goofy weirdness into pop stardom. At first, the band was strictly an underground phenomenon but in the years between their third and fourth albums, their cult grew rapidly. 1991's *Sailing the Seas of Cheese* went gold shortly before the release of *Pork Soda.* By the time of the album's 1993 release, Primus had enough devoted fans to make *Pork Soda* debut in the Top Ten. After touring for a year—including a headlining spot on 1993's Lollapalooza—Claypool revived his Prawn Song record label in 1994 and released a reunion record by Primus' original lineup under the name Sausage. In the summer of 1995, Primus released their fifth album, *Tales From The Punch Bowl.* —Stephen Thomas Erlewine

Suck on This / Jan. 1990 / Caroline ✦✦✦

Originally released on their own Prawn Song label (a parody of Led Zeppelin's Swan Song Records), this is their debut, recorded live in a small club and featuring all of the greatness this trio has. It's hard, thrashy funk and punk with a sense of humor. The reissue on Caroline sounds a little muddy. Find the original vinyl pressing on Prawn, which sounds more like a CD than the CD. —*John Book*

Frizzle Fry / Feb. 1990 / Caroline ✦✦✦

Some of the songs seem rushed on their first studio album. —*John Book*

○ **Sailing the Seas of Cheese** / 1991 / Interscope ✦✦✦✦

The band's major-label debut features an appearance by Tom Waits on "Tommy the Cat" (originally found on *Suck on This*). Guitarist Larry Lalonde, formerly with Possessed and Blind Illusion, shows his death-metal roots on some of the songs on this album. —*John Book*

○ **Miscellaneous Debris** / 1992 / Interscope ✦✦✦✦

What makes this 5-song EP of covers Primus's best release is the material. For once, Les Claypool's crew plays actual songs instead of sketching out a few ideas as an excuse for jamming. As a result, *Miscellaneous Debris* isn't as weird and alienating as previous albums, and often their reinterpretations—from the clever ribbing of XTC's "Making Plans for Nigel" and Pink Floyd's "Have A Cigar" to the relatively respectful readings of the Meters, the Residents and Peter Gabriel's "Intruder"—show flashes of brilliance, largely due to the loose yet focused musicianship. —*Stephen Thomas Erlewine*

● **Pork Soda** / 1993 / Interscope ✦✦✦✦

Apart from the bizarre murder tale "My Name is Mud," few tracks on *Pork Soda* rival "Tommy the Cat" or "Jerry Was A Race Car Driver"; another troubling sign of a lack of songwriting ideas is that one track, "The Pressman," was originally released on *Suck on This.* However, the overall quality of the playing is so good that it almost doesn't matter that the songs are frequently simplistic and occasionally awful. Primus continue to improve as musicians, so *Pork Soda* is hardly a terrible album—in fact, it's their best, most consistent effort to date, even though it would benefit from some editing. —*Stephen Thomas Erlewine*

Tales From The Punch Bowl / 1995 / Interscope ✦✦

For most listeners, the differences between Primus albums is so small, they're not even noticeable. With each record, the group improves instrumentally, which isn't surprising since they're a musician's band. On *Tales From The Punchbowl*, the group consolidates the qualities that made them arena rock favorites, featuring the same novelty tunes ("Wynona's Big Brown Beaver") and instrumental workouts that have always appeared on Primus' albums. Nevertheless, there's not much to distinguish the record from previous performances—there's only so much the group has to say, after all. —*Stephen Thomas Erlewine*

Prince (Prince Rogers Nelson)

Group, Soul, Funk, Urban, Pop/Rock

Few artists have created a body of work as rich and varied as Prince. During the '80s, he emerged as one of the most singular talents of the rock & roll era, capable of seamlessly tying together pop, funk, folk, and rock. Not only did he release a series of groundbreaking albums, he toured frequently, produced albums and wrote songs for many other artists, and recorded hundreds of songs that still lie unreleased in his vaults. With each album he has released, Prince has shown remarkable stylistic growth and musical diversity, constantly experimenting with different sounds, textures, and genres. Occasionally, his music can be maddeningly inconsistent because of this eclecticism, but his experiments frequently succeed; no other contemporary artist can blend so many diverse styles into a cohesive whole.

Prince's first two albums were solid, if unremarkable, late '70s funk-pop. With 1980's *Dirty Mind*, he recorded his first masterpiece, a one-man *tour de force* of sex and music; it was hard funk, catchy Beatlesque melodies, sweet soul ballads, and rocking guitar-pop, all at once. The follow-up, *Controversy*, was more of the same, but *1999* was brilliant. The album was a monster hit, selling over three million copies, but it was nothing compared to 1984's *Purple Rain.*

Purple Rain made Prince a superstar; it eventually sold over ten million copies in the U.S. and spent twenty-four weeks at number one. Partially recorded with his touring band the Revolution, the record featured the most pop-oriented music he has ever made. Instead of continuing in this accessible direction, he veered off into the bizarre psycho-psychedelia of *Around the World in a Day* (1985), which nevertheless sold over two million copies. In 1986, he released the even-stranger *Parade*, which was in its own way as ambitious and intricate as any art-rock of the '60s; however, no art-rock was ever grounded with a hit as brilliant as the spare funk of "Kiss."

By 1987, Prince's ambitions were growing by leaps and bounds, resulting in the sprawling masterpiece *Sign O' the Times*. Prince was set to release the hard funk of *The Black Album* by the end of the year, yet he withdrew it just before its release, deciding it was too dark and immoral. Instead, he released the confused *Lovesexy* in 1988, which was a commercial disaster. With the soundtrack to 1989's *Batman* he returned to the top of the charts, even if the album was essentially a recap of everything he had done before. The following year he released *Graffiti Bridge*, the sequel to *Purple Rain*, which turned out to be a considerable commercial disappointment.

In 1991, Prince formed the New Power Generation, the most versatile and talented best band he has ever assembled. With their first album, *Diamonds and Pearls*, Prince reasserted his mastery of contemporary R&B; it was his biggest hit since 1985. The following year, he released his twelfth album, which was titled with a cryptic symbol; in 1993, Prince legally changed his name to the symbol. In 1994, he independently released "The Most Beautiful Girl in the World" single, which became his biggest hit in years. Late in the summer of 1994, he released *Come* under the name of Prince; the record was a moderate success, going gold.

After *Come*, Prince agreed to release *The Black Album* officially in November of 1994. In early 1995, he immersed himself in another legal battle with Warner, as the record company refused to release his new record, *The Gold Experience*. By the end of the summer, the disputes had been resolved and the album was released in the fall. —*Stephen Thomas Erlewine*

For You / 1978 / Warner Brothers ✦✦✦

Prince's debut is a fairly conventional blend of erotic funk, highlighted by the horny "Soft and Wet" and subverted by too much mediocre material. —*John Floyd*

Prince / 1979 / Warner Brothers ✦✦✦

The followup makes his rock leanings more apparent, culminating in the Hendrix guitar-driven single "I Wanna Be Your Lover." —*John Floyd*

☆ **Dirty Mind** / 1980 / Warner Brothers ♦♦♦♦♦
This delirious, hard-on masterpiece is dedicated to the joy of sex. The guitars are revved up a few notches, the funk has more muscle, and the songs make explicit just how unique (and sometimes twisted) Prince's vision can be. —*John Floyd*

Controversy / 1981 / Warner Brothers ♦♦♦
Synthesizers move to the forefront and, though the sound is riveting, and while "Do Me, Baby" and the title cut are among his best, this is a tad short on decent songs. —*John Floyd*

☆ **1999** / 1982 / Warner Brothers ♦♦♦♦♦
This double-album mingling of politics and sex features Prince's sturdiest dance grooves and his first crossover hits ("Little Red Corvette," "Delirious," and the title track). This album is a near-masterpiece. —*John Floyd*

☆ **Purple Rain** / 1984 / Warner Brothers ♦♦♦♦♦
Upon its release, the soundtrack from Prince's big-screen debut sounded as if his artistry had blossomed fully. Today it remains essential for the singles, like "When Doves Cry" and "Let's Go Crazy." Elsewhere, it retreads familiar ground. —*John Floyd*

Around the World in a Day / 1985 / Paisley Park ♦♦♦
Prince got his first negative reviews when this album was originally issued. Cries of ripoff and imitator were leveled his way, while defenders rushed into the fray. The album was hardly the flop it's been perceived as. While it did reflect Prince's love of the Beatles' psychedelic period, it also topped the charts for three weeks and ultimately yielded the hits "Pop Life" and "Raspberry Beret." But Prince would return to a harder, funkier sound the next time out, and the album seems a logical end to a direction he began with *Purple Rain*. —*Ron Wynn*

○ **Parade (Music from the Motion Picture "Under the Cherry Moon")** / 1986 / Paisley Park ♦♦♦♦
Another soundtrack (from Prince's second film, *Under the Cherry Moon*) that boasts some strong singles ("Kiss," "Mountains," and "Anotherloverholenyohead") and some dreary, neo-psychedelic filler. —*John Floyd*

☆ **Sign O' the Times** / 1987 / Paisley Park ♦♦♦♦♦
This two-disc, one-man-band romp through everything he does best goes from galvanizing grooves (one of which was recorded with the Revolution) to some slinky smoochers, which show for the first time sympathy and genuine affection for his romantic objects. This is Prince's greatest album. —*John Floyd*

Black Album / 1987 / Warner Brothers ♦♦♦
Recorded in 1987 but shelved until 1994 in favor of *Lovesexy, The Black Album* is a sinister funk-fest, long on the boogie but short on anything really remarkable. —*John Floyd*

Lovesexy / Feb. 1988 / Paisley Park ♦♦♦
Lovesexy was a better album, anyway. It's not perfect, but it does find Prince attempting to make clear his philosophy, which likens sex to godliness and vice versa. It doesn't fully convince, but "Anna Stasia" and "I Wish U Heaven" should keep you interested. —*John Floyd*

Batman / 1989 / Paisley Park ♦♦♦
The soundtrack for the hugely successful film is a mildly amusing set of competent funk, but nothing he hasn't done better elsewhere. —*John Floyd*

Graffiti Bridge / Aug. 21, 1990 / Paisley Park ♦♦♦
Prince was shooting for the top of the charts with *Graffiti Bridge*, and he missed. The movie was a disaster, causing the soundtrack to sell very poorly. Despite its poor showing, *Graffiti Bridge* is not a bad album; in fact, it's often very good. Prince wrote all of the songs, but only performed a little over half the tracks, leaving the rest for the Time, Mavis Staples, and Tevin Campbell. With the exception of the Time's slamming "Release It" and Campbell's "Round and Round," the best songs are the ones Prince performed himself. The George Clinton collaboration "We Can Funk," the psycho-blues of "The Question of U," the sinewy single "Thieves in the Temple," and the pop/rock of "Can't Stop This Feeling I Got," "Tick, Tick, Bang," and "Elephants & Flowers" make *Graffiti Bridge* a thoroughly enjoyable listen. — *Stephen Thomas Erlewine*

○ **Love Symbol Album** / Oct. 13, 1992 / Paisley Park ♦♦♦♦
The New Power Generation is the most talented and versatile band Prince has ever fronted, and they fulfill their potential on *Symbol*. Although the NPG factored heavily on *Diamonds and Pearls*, it still sounded like a solo Prince album. *Symbol* sounds like a band performing together, working off of each other's strengths and weaknesses. Opening with the dance smash "My Name Is Prince" and the deep funk of "Sexy M.F.," *Symbol* has Prince's best dance tracks since the *Black Album*. But Prince wasn't content; he decided to run the gamut of modern pop/R&B/dance, and the music is uniformly accomplished and excellent. Unfortunately, he also decided to make a "rock soap opera," so the music is saddled with ridiculous lyrics and annoying sound bridges by Kirstie Alley. However, *Symbol* has some of the finest, most inventive music of Prince's career. —*Stephen Thomas Erlewine*

★ **The Hits 1** / 1993 / Paisley Park ♦♦♦♦♦
★ **The Hits 2** / 1993 / Paisley Park ♦♦♦♦♦
○ **The Hits/B-Sides** / 1993 / Paisley Park ♦♦♦♦
While it isn't a truly comprhensive set, Prince's singles collection does contain most of his biggest hits. The two volumes are available separately or packaged together with a third disc of B-sides; apart from the glorious "Erotic City," the flip sides are only of interest to devoted fans. —*Stephen Thomas Erlewine*

Come / 1994 / Warner Brothers ♦♦
Released after Prince announced his retirement and his intention of never using the name "Prince" again, *Come* is something of a surprise: an album of reportedly all new material, released by "Prince," not "The Artist Formerly Known As Prince." After listening to *Come*, its purpose becomes clear—it's a record fulfilling a contract, nothing more and nothing less. Some of the songs are good, but there's nothing on *Come* that Prince hasn't done before; he even sounds bored on certain tracks. On top of that, the album has no obvious singles, making it a nightmare to sell. Not surprisingly, the album flopped. —*Stephen Thomas Erlewine*

John Prine

b. Oct. 10, 1946, Maywood, IL
Singer-Songwriter
He's from the Bob Dylan school of talented folkies who like to play with words. But unlike most Dylanites, Prine also evokes the sly, dry humor of Woody Guthrie, and his broken-hearted laments are never chauvinistic and only seldom wallow in self-pity. If he's never made one album as great as prime Dylan, that's because he isn't Dylan; he makes great albums that flaunt his own personality, not the personality of his inspirations. —*John Floyd*

☆ **John Prine** / 1971 / Atlantic ♦♦♦♦♦
A revelation upon its release, this album is now a collection of standards: "Illegal Smile," "Hello in There," "Sam Stone," "Donald and Lydia," and, of course, "Angel from Montgomery." Prine's music, a mixture of folk, rock, and country, is deceptively simple, like his pointed lyrics, and his easy vocal style adds a humorous edge that makes otherwise funny jokes downright hilarious. —*William Ruhlmann*

Diamonds in the Rough / 1972 / Atlantic ♦♦♦
John Prine's second album was a cut below his first, only because the debut was a classic and the followup was merely terrific. "Sour Grapes" showed Prine's cracked sense of humor and "Souvenirs" his sentiment. Even if it was the second rank of his writing, *Diamonds in the Rough* demonstrated that Prine had an enduring talent that wasn't exhausted by one great album. —*William Ruhlmann*

○ **Sweet Revenge** / 1973 / Atlantic ♦♦♦♦
A bold and brilliant stab at (almost) straight country, it tempers Prine's cynical streak with the tone of a jaded humorist and social commentator. —*John Floyd*

Common Sense / 1975 / Atlantic ♦♦♦
A brash album, it's full of aggressive rock rhythms and morose tunes. Even the Chuck Berry cover, "You Never Can Tell," is shot full of melancholy. —*John Floyd*

○ **Prime Prine** / 1976 / Atlantic ♦♦♦♦
Atlantic Records' compilation of John Prine's first four albums was good for its time (and became his only gold record) but has been superseded by Rhino's *Great Days* anthology. —*William Ruhlmann*

○ **Bruised Orange** / 1978 / Asylum ♦♦♦♦
Despite some brilliant songs, Prine's followup albums to his stunning debut were uneven until this, his fifth, produced by his friend Steve Goodman. Here, Prine's always finely-tuned sense of absurdity once again collides with his ability to depict pain sympathetically for a whole album, typified by "That's the Way That the

World Goes 'Round," a neat statement of his philosophy, and "Sabu Visits the Twin Cities Alone," perhaps the best depiction ever written of life on the road in the entertainment business. — *William Ruhlmann*

○ **Pink Cadillac** / 1979 / Oh Boy ♦♦♦♦

Storm Windows / 1980 / Oh Boy ♦♦♦
A relaxed effort, it's defined by straightforward love songs and subdued vocals. Modest but quite nice. — *John Floyd*

Aimless Love / 1984 / Oh Boy ♦♦♦
John Prine moved to his own independent label, Oh Boy, after stints at Atlantic and Asylum (later, he acquired his Asylum albums and reissued them on Oh Boy). On this label debut, he is under no commercial pressures, but that seems to make him more low-key, less striking. "The Oldest Baby in the World," "Somewhere Someone's Falling in Love," and "Unwed Fathers" are good examples of his new sweetness, which is as winning as, if less impressive than, his witty older songs. — *William Ruhlmann*

German Afternoons / 1986 / Oh Boy ♦♦♦
Another straight country set, but unlike *Sweet Revenge*, this is a sleepy-town stroll, highlighted by some beautiful ballads and snappy accompaniment by the New Grass Revival. — *John Floyd*

○ **Live** / 1988 / Oh Boy ♦♦♦♦
With years of experience playing club dates, John Prine has evolved into a very entertaining live performer, and this album, originally a double-LP and now a single CD, presents him at his intimate best, telling funny stories and performing his most impressive material in unadorned arrangements. — *William Ruhlmann*

● **The Missing Years** / Sep. 1991 / Oh Boy ♦♦♦♦
Prine took five years between his ninth studio album and this, his tenth—enough time to gather his strongest body of material in more than a decade. From the caustic "All the Best" to the cliche compilation "It's a Big Old Goofy World," Prine's gifts for emotional revelation and off-the-wall humor are on display in abundance, and he's aided by excellent production (courtesy of Heartbreaker Howie Epstein) and strong backup musicians. *The Missing Years* won the 1991 Grammy Award for Best Contemporary Folk Album. — *William Ruhlmann*

★ **The John Prine Anthology: Great Days** / Aug. 17, 1993 / Rhino ♦♦♦♦♦
Prine's career has been rich but scattered, and *Great Days* gathers together almost all of his finest moments, providing a comprehensive introduction to one of the best songwriters of the past twenty years. — *Stephen Thomas Erlewine*

John Prine Christmas / 1994 / Oh Boy ♦♦♦
An eight-song EP of new and old works with a holiday theme. Knowing John Prine's sense of humor, you can expect that much of this is not to be taken straight, so when he sings of "Christmas In Prison" or, in the live version of the romantic kiss-off "All The Best" starts talking about nailing the trains to the dining room table, you find you're in for a Christmas celebration unlike any other. — *William Ruhlmann*

Lost Dogs And Mixed Blessings / 1995 / Oh Boy ♦♦♦

P.J. Proby (James Marcus Smith)

b. Nov. 6, 1938, Houston, TX
British Invasion
Like the Walker Brothers, he wasn't British, he sang more ballads than rock & roll, and he was far more successful in the U.K. than the States. Texan P.J. Proby was pretty hot stuff in England for a time, as much—indeed, probably more—for his then-risqué stage act, which saw him incorporate split pants into his act after they (he claimed) accidentally ripped during a performance. Artistically, this is a case when the taste of the British listening public could be called into question. Proby sang in a pinched facsimile of Elvis and Gene Pitney that grew increasingly pained as it approached the upper register. A few of his hits were MOR ballads like "Somewhere" and "Maria," but he did manage an infectious Merseyish rocker on his first (and biggest) British smash, "Hold Me." In the United States, he is most remembered for recording the Lennon-McCartney composition "That Means a Lot" in 1965 (which the Beatles themselves never released), and his sole Top 40 U.S. hit (from 1967), the Cajun-flavored "Nicki Hoeky." — *Richie Unterberger*

I Am P.J. Proby / 1964 / Liberty ♦♦♦

● **Legendary P.J. Proby at His Very Best: Vol. 2** / 1987 / See For Miles ♦♦♦♦
Oddly, this is a better compilation than Volume One, which focused more on his ballads; this is oriented towards his rock and soul recordings. Includes "Hold Me," "Nicki Hoeky," the 1964 British Top 20 single "Together," and "Just Call and I'll Be There" (also recorded by Francoise Hardy in French), where Proby sounds like the loser in a Gene Pitney soundalike contest. Spanning from 1964 to 1968, most of the rest consists of rock and soul covers that range from passable to horrid. — *Richie Unterberger*

Proclaimers

Group, Pop/Rock
When the Scottish duo of Craig and Charlie Reid emerged in 1987, they were immediately compared to the Everly Brothers. Considering their energetic, melodic folk-rock, the comparison made some sense, even though the Proclaimers didn't really sound like the Everlys. Instead, the band were a post-punk pop band, aggressively displaying their thick accents on sweet, infectiously melodic songs about love. After two albums in the late '80s, the band disappeared for several years, suffering from personal problems and severe writer's block. When their 1988 song "I'm Gonna Be (500 Miles)" was used in the 1993 film *Benny & Joon*, the duo began to receive massive radio airplay in America, sending them into the Top Ten in the U.S., as well as the rest of the world; it was their first taste of real success. Luckily, the band was close to completing their third album at the time, leaving them in a position to capitalize on their success. However, when the album was released the following year, it received little attention. — *Stephen Thomas Erlewine*

This Is the Story / 1987 / Chrysalis ♦♦♦

● **Sunshine on Leith** / 1988 / Chrysalis ♦♦♦♦
The Proclaimers' second album is a delightful set of folk-pop, highlighted by the belated hit single, "I'm Gonna Be (500 Miles)." — *David Jehnzen*

Hit the Highway / Mar. 22, 1994 / Chrysalis ♦♦
After six years, the Proclaimers delivered their third album. While it was a strong record with many fine songs, it lacked a knockout single. Consequently, the duo wasn't able to follow through on the success of "I'm Gonna Be (500 Miles)." — *David Jehnzen*

Procol Harum

Group, Art-Rock/Progressive-Rock, Psychedelic
Formed in 1967, Procol Harum incorporated a weighty classicism into their sound, with occasional traces of R&B and rock & roll. This British group was originally formed around the core of lyricist Keith Reid and singer/songwriter Gary Brooker, who hailed from the R&B club band the Paramounts. Their first collaboration, the stately "A Whiter Shade of Pale," was loosely built off of Bach's "Air on a G String." A band was formed (named after Reid's cat), and in short order, Procol Harum had a record deal and an international hit on their hands. Part of the success of the band's sound was due to Matthew Fisher's stately organ work and Robin Trower's lyrical blues-based lead-guitar playing, which appeared on Procol's second and third albums—*Shine on Brightly* and *A Salty Dog*.

In spite of further lineup changes (eventually incorporating most of the Paramounts), Procol Harum enjoyed even greater chart success during the early '70s, particularly *Live in Concert with the Edmonton Symphony Orchestra* (#5). By this time, the band seemed to be trading on its past glories, with flashes of their earlier brilliance briefly resurfacing on their 1974 release *Exotic Birds and Fruit* (#86). Procol Harum eventually broke up in 1977, after the spotty *Something Magic*. — *Rick Clark*

○ **Procul Harum** / 1967 / Deram ♦♦♦♦
Their spectacular debut showed remarkable songwriting and became a late-'60s classic, due to the immense popularity of "A Whiter Shade of Pale," which made their reputation. — *Cub Koda & Dan Heilman*

○ **Shine on Brightly** / 1968 / A&M ♦♦♦♦
Procol's ambitious sophomore effort expanded upon their symphonic-style rock, particularly the 18-plus-minute conceptual opus "In Held 'Twas in I." The title track was another highlight. — *Rick Clark*

○ **A Salty Dog** / 1969 / A&M ✦✦✦✦
Procol's synthesis of blues and grand classically inspired melodies reached an apex on their third album. The tasteful production featured sweeping orchestrations, subtle sound effects, and dynamic arrangements. *A Salty Dog* became one of Procol's signature numbers. —*Rick Clark*

Home / 1970 / A&M ✦✦✦
With Matthew Fisher gone, Procol embraced a harder, more rock-oriented approach best displayed on the herky-jerky riff-rocker "Whiskey Train," a Robin Trower showcase. —*Rick Clark*

Broken Barricades / 1971 / A&M ✦✦✦

Procol Harum Live: in Concert with the Edmonton Symphony Orchestra & The Da Camera Sin / 1972 / A&M ✦✦✦
With the help of the Edmonton Symphony Orchestra (Canada), Procol Harum does an impressive job re-creating their more stately numbers, complete with sound effects and a full choir. "Conquistador" became a number 16 hit. —*Rick Clark*

○ **The Best of Procol Harum** / 1973 / A&M ✦✦✦✦
A fine wrap-up of the band's 1967-73 output, it documents their most creative era. —*Dan Heilman*

Grand Hotel / 1973 / Chrysalis ✦✦

Exotic Birds & Fruit / 1974 / Chrysalis ✦✦✦
Procol's eighth studio effort recalled their best early work. —*Rick Clark*

Procol's Ninth / 1975 / Chrysalis ✦✦

Something Magic / 1977 / Chrysalis ✦✦

● **Classics, Vol. 17** / 1987 / A&M ✦✦✦✦
This best-of collection covers the hits, plus a decent collection of album tracks. —*Rick Clark*

Prodigal Stranger / 1991 / Zoo ✦✦

Professor Longhair (Henry Roeland Byrd)

b. Dec. 19, 1918, Bogalusa, LA, **d.** Jun. 30, 1980, New Orleans, LA
Rock & Roll, New Orleans R&B
Born Henry Roeland Byrd and known affectionately as "Fess" to most New Orleans residents, Professor Longhair began his musical career as a street entertainer in the early '30s. In the late'40s he was playing piano, leading small combos with arcane names such as the Four Hairs Combo and Professor Longhair & his Shuffling Hungarians. He worked as part of Dave Bartholomew's big band in 1949, then began a series of recordings for various labels, including Star Talent, Mercury, and Atlantic. For the next 20 years Professor Longhair continued to record for obscure labels but remained on the fringes of the New Orleans scene, forced to supplement his meager earnings from music with odd day jobs.

In 1971 he re-created the Four Hairs Combo for an appearance at the New Orleans Jazz & Heritage Festival. This inaugurated the comeback phase of his musical career and attracted the interest of a small but dedicated cadre of college students who undertook his rehabilitation as part of a burgeoning roots revival.

As he stated, "I'm a little rowdy with my playing," and the synthesis he developed of calypso and rhumba rhythms, boogie-woogie, and street-parade music became the basis for young groups like the Neville Brothers and the Radiators as they sought to translate their own respective musical visions of the New Orleans "good time" heritage. Despite his often unorthodox approach, Fess remained true to the essence of New Orleans music in never straying too far from the basic maxims of "freedom, freedom, and fun."

At the time of his death in 1980, he was the most popular and revered musician in New Orleans. His passing left a vacuum in the city's longstanding piano traditions, seemingly closing the book on an illustrious musical heritage. —*Bruce Boyd Raeburn*

★ **Fess: Professor Longhair Anthology** / 1993 / Rhino ✦✦✦✦✦
An essential two-CD set covering the highlights of Professor Longhair's career, including all of his best-known songs and performances. —*Stephen Thomas Erlewine*

Prong

Group, Hard Rock, Heavy Metal
Could be the perfectly named heavy metal band. From the ashes of New York speed-thrash, Prong plays slower, stripped-down metal without the egregious marketing flourishes (i.e., sexism, Satanism). Perhaps a tad derivative, Prong makes up for its lapse in stylistic originality with speed and power. —*John Dougan*

Primative Origins / 1987 / Sound League ✦✦✦
Prong's debut recording got accepted in England way before the U.S. —*John Book*

Force Fed / 1988 / In-Effect ✦✦✦
Brutal and bloody, Prong achieves maximum riff thrust here as Tommy Victor's guitar penetrates the wall-of-steel sonic boom. A dense and forceful album, worth many headbangs. —*John Dougan*

○ **Beg to Differ** / 1990 / Epic ✦✦✦✦
Technical thrash with a band who continues to stretch the boundaries of their genre. —*John Book*

○ **Prove Your Wrong** / 1991 / Epic ✦✦✦✦
Tighter riffs and stronger songwriting on *Prove Your Wrong* helped Prong expand their cult substantially. —*AMG*

Whose Fist Is This Anyway / 1992 / Epic ✦✦

● **Cleansing** / 1994 / Epic ✦✦✦✦
The aptly titled *Cleansing* offers a cleansing of Prong's sound, tightening up their trademark drilling guitars while adding some slight techno and industrial touches, which only heightens the tension. Thankfully, none of this compromises the band, but only strengthens their already muscular metallic roar. In fact, it helps makes *Cleansing* their most varied and best record yet. —*Stephen Thomas Erlewine*

The Psychedelic Furs

Group, Alternative Pop/Rock
The Psychedelic Furs, whose name belies their punk-influenced music, were formed in England in 1977 by brothers Richard Butler (vocals) and Tim Butler (bass), along with saxophone player Duncan Kilburn and guitarist Roger Morris. By the time they released their self-titled debut album in 1980, the group had become a sextet, adding guitarist John Ashton and drummer Vince Ely. That album, featuring Butler's hoarse voice (the tone of which suggested John Lydon without the sneer) was a bigger hit in England, where it reached the Top 20, than in the U.S.

Talk Talk Talk (1981) did better, reaching the U.S. Top 100 and producing two British singles-chart entries, one of which was "Pretty in Pink," later also a hit in the U.S. when a new version was used as the title song of a film. *Forever Now* (1982) saw the band reduced to a quartet with the departure of Kilburn and Morris. The rest moved to the US, turned to producer Todd Rundgren, and scored a U.S. Top 50 hit with "Love My Way." Ely then left, and the remaining trio of the two Butlers and Ashton made *Mirror Moves* (1984), the biggest Psychedelic Furs hit yet.

The film *Pretty in Pink* helped spread their name further before the release of their next album, *Midnight to Midnight* (1986), which consequently got to #12 in the U.K. and the Top 30 in the US and included the Top 30 U.S. hit "Heartbreak Beat." *Book of Days* (1989) marked the return of Vince Ely but was a considerable commercial disappointment. *World Outside* (1991) also failed to find an audience. The Psychedelic Furs then folded up shop, and Richard Butler launched a new group, Love Spit Love. —*William Ruhlmann*

○ **The Psychedelic Furs [1st LP]** / 1980 / Columbia ✦✦✦✦
This auspicious debut finds the sextet turning out thick, noisy rock (especially in the saxophone-guitar combination) through which Richard Butler's voice cuts like a buzzsaw. Best track: "Imitation of Christ." —*William Ruhlmann*

○ **Talk Talk Talk** / 1981 / Columbia ✦✦✦✦
An even better followup makes explicit the Furs' connection to the Velvet Underground (their name comes from the Velvets' song "Venus in Furs"). Their strongest overall collection, this includes the original (superior) version of "Pretty in Pink," "Dumb Waiters," and the definitive Psychedelic Furs song, "Into You Like a Train." —*William Ruhlmann*

Forever Now / 1982 / Columbia ✦✦✦
Actually, Todd Rundgren's much-vaunted clean, sharp production style has very little effect on the Furs' sound, which is still pretty noisy and still dominated by Butler's hoarse, slightly scornful voice on such songs as "Love My Way," "President Gas," and the title track. —*William Ruhlmann*

Mirror Moves / 1984 / Columbia ✦✦✦
On *Mirror Moves*, the Psychedelic Furs began to move toward a slicker, accessible pop-rock sound. By and large, the extra gloss works, as the group turns in a set of catchy rockers that manages

incorporate some mainstream concessions into their signature sound without losing their personality. It may not be as exciting as their first four records, but they pull off the streamlined pop on *Mirror Moves* with considerable panache. —*Stephen Thomas Erlewine*

Midnight to Midnight / 1987 / Columbia ✦✦✦
Midnight to Midnight continues the streamlining of the Psychedelic Furs. Unlike the previous *Mirror Moves*, *Midnight to Midnight* loses the essential character of the Furs' sound, as the production relies on a sleek, stylish pop production. Although the results don't have much to do with the group's early records, it's an entertaining record, filled with its share of pop thrills, including the single "Heartbreak Beat." —*Stephen Thomas Erlewine*

● **All of This and Nothing** / 1988 / Columbia ✦✦✦✦
Not a perfect Furs compilation, but this 12-track look back does contain the notable tracks from the albums *Mirror Moves* and *Midnight to Midnight*, plus some of the necessary ones from the albums listed above and a good new song, "All That Money Wants." —*William Ruhlmann*

Book of Days / 1989 / Columbia ✦✦

World Outside / 1991 / Columbia ✦✦✦

B-Sides & Lost Grooves / 1994 / Columbia/Legacy ✦✦✦
As the title suggests, *B-Sides & Lost Grooves* is a collection of Psychedelic Furs obscurities culled from throughout their career. Predectiably, some of the tracks fall flat, but the great majority of the album is engaging, make the record a worthwhile complement to the group's first four albums. —*Stephen Thomas Erlewine*

Public Enemy

Group, Rap
Without question, the most talked about rap group ever and among the most controversial and publicized bands of its day in any genre. Carlton Ridenhour, a Long Island college student and former radio disc jockey, has parlayed a booming voice, congenial, yet forceful, personality, and the articulation skills necessary to cogently present often inflammatory viewpoints into a hugely successful performance, marketing, and proselytizing empire. As Chuck D, Ridenour is Public Enemy's theorist, lyricist, and head rapper. He's quoted constantly, seen on television around the world, and idolized by legions of black and white youth. Through five albums, Public Enemy has served as the hip-hop vanguard, rapping about issues of race, rage, and inequality without lapsing (too often) into vicious sexism or homophobia, though they've been tagged with charges of anti-Semitism. They did eventually cut loose former minister of information Professor Griff, following a flap about comments he made in an interview, but the group has been able to ride out storms over lyric content and maintain popularity without any stylistic compromise. Hank Shocklee, Terminator X, Flavor Flav, and the rest of the Bomb Squad and crew also deserve praise, especially Shocklee and Terminator X, whose dynamite production keeps things anchored through hard-hitting, rapid-fire snippets and impressive studio techniques. Flav's absurdist raps and onstage antics provide some welcome levity and comic relief.

After laying low for nearly three years, the reaction was swift and mostly unfavorable when Public Enemy's first new full-length album since *Apocalypse 91* was unveiled in 1994. Not only did *Rolling Stone* and *The Source* give *Muse Sick-N-Hour Mess Age* bad reviews, but the album sold poorly, disappearing from the charts quickly. In the summer of 1995, Chuck D. announced that Public Enemy was retiring from live performances, giving the members time to pursue other studio projects. —*Ron Wynn*

○ **Yo! Bum Rush the Show** / 1987 / Def Jam ✦✦✦✦
When their debut was released in 1987, very few rap groups even approached Public Enemy's musical or political stance. Listening to the first album now, it's surprising how few of the songs are actually political—the sheer force of the sound fools the listener into thinking Chuck D is saying more than he actually is. Still, "Megablast," "Public Enemy No. 1," and "Miuzi Weighs a Ton" carry a small amount of political rhetoric. Much sparer than later releases, the album is carried over the top by Chuck D's bulldozer roar. —*Stephen Thomas Erlewine*

★ **It Takes a Nation of Millions** / 1988 / Def Jam ✦✦✦✦✦
Arguably the best hip-hop album ever made, *It Takes a Nation of Millions* was a huge leap forward not only for Public Enemy, but for all of hip-hop. PE's signature sound—a barrage of found

sounds, densely woven samples, and noisy tape loops—was evident for the first time, courtesy of the Bomb Squad. Chuck D's lyrics, full of revolutionary rhetoric yet managing to avoid being hysterical, matched the aural onslaught. The group's political stance would be meaningless if the music didn't put it over the top throughout, and that does happen on "Black Steel in the Hour of Chaos," "Night of the Living Baseheads," "Rebel Without a Pause," "Don't Believe the Hype," and "Bring the Noise," in particular. There isn't a weak moment on the album. A landmark recording. —*Stephen Thomas Erlewine*

☆ **Fear of a Black Planet** / 1990 / Def Jam ✦✦✦✦✦
Nothing could quite match the pure, concentrated fury of *It Takes a Nation of Millions* and Public Enemy tried to replicate it on their third album. *Fear of a Black Planet* is much more experimental than its predecessor, boasting an impressive array of textures from pseudo-reggae to crushing hip-hop. Chuck D's phrasing and vocalization have matured; he even sounds seductive on "Pollywanacraka." The basic theme of *Fear of a Black Planet* is an exploration of American racism, concentrating on interracial relationships and White injustice. The relative lack of heavy beats and the wall of rage caused some to cry sellout, but *Fear* is hardly that. —*Stephen Thomas Erlewine*

☆ **Apocalypse 91 . . . The Enemy Strikes Black** / 1991 / Def Jam ✦✦✦✦
In response to the accusations that *Fear of a Black Planet* was a sellout, Public Enemy lashed out with *Apocalypse '91 . . . The Enemy Strikes Black*, an album of hard, noisy funk, much closer to *Millions* than to *Fear*. Having dealt with White racism on their previous album, Public Enemy sets their sights on correcting problems in the Black community. On "1 Million Bottlebags," "Nighttrain," "Shut 'Em Down," and "By the Time I Get to Arizona," Chuck D offers some of his hardest-hitting rhymes, matched to equally hard rhythm tracks. Public Enemy even offers solutions on a few tracks, a rarity in the rap world. Although the Imperial Grand Ministers of Funk have replaced the Bomb Squad (who are listed as executive producers) as the main production team, Public Enemy's sound didn't change drastically. —*Stephen Thomas Erlewine*

Greatest Misses / Sep. 15, 1992 / Def Jam ✦✦
For the first time in their career, Public Enemy sounds unsure of the direction of their music. *Greatest Misses* is half original tracks and half remixes, and consequently sounds muddled. Public Enemy sounds like it's treading water throughout the new songs; none of them are particularly bad, but unlike all of their previous material, none of it is groundbreaking. None of the remixes are awful, but they are neither revelatory nor insightful and often miss the original intent of the song. —*Stephen Thomas Erlewine*

Muse Sick-N-Hour Mess Age / 1994 / Def Jam ✦✦
Public Enemy took a full three years between *Apocalypse 91* and *Muse Sick-N-Hour Mess-Age*. During that time, numerous hip-hop styles had come and gone, making Public Enemy seem hopelessly outdated by the time they actually released their fifth record. With the exception of the *Greatest Misses* compilation, *Muse Sick* didn't fare as well on the charts as the group's three previous albums, nor was it well-received critically, receiving the poorest reviews of any of the group's efforts. And, again discounting *Greatest Misses*, *Muse Sick* is PE's weakest album. Conceptually, it's all over the place, as Chuck D strikes out at a number of his usual targets but without the focused, intelligent rage of *Nation of Millions* or *Fear of A Black Planet*. Similarly, the music careens out control, as they try to incorporate recent hip-hop innovations to their signature sound. Nothing on the record sounds forced, but the album does sound directionless, which tends to cancel out the number of solid tracks on the album. Public Enemy doesn't necessarily seem outdated or musically bankrupt on *Muse Sick-N-Hour Mess-Age*— they just appear unsure of themselves. —*Stephen Thomas Erlewine*

Public Image Limited

Group, Alternative Pop/Rock, New Wave, Experimental
Public Image Ltd. (PiL) originally was a quartet led by singer John Lydon (formerly Johnny Rotten b. Jan 31, 1956) and guitarist Keith Levene, who had been a member of the Clash in one of its early lineups. The band was filled out by bassist Jah Wobble (John Wordle) and drummer Jim Walker. It was formed in the wake of the 1978 breakup of Lydon's former group, the Sex Pistols. For the

most part, it devoted itself to droning, slow-tempo, bass-heavy noise rock, overlaid by Lydon's distinctive, vituperative rant.

The group's debut single, "Public Image," was more of an up-tempo pop/rock song, however, and it hit the U.K. Top Ten upon its release in October 1978. The group itself debuted on Christmas Day, shortly after the release of its first album, *Public Image.* Neither the single nor the album was released in the U.S.

Metal Box, the band's second U.K. album, came in the form of three 12-inch, 45 RPM discs in a film cannister. It was released in the U.S. in 1980 as the double album *Second Edition.* (By this time, PiL was a trio consisting of Lydon, Levene, and Wobble.) The third album, not released in the U.S., was the live *Paris in the Spring* (1980). Lydon and Levene, plus hired musicians, made up the group by the time of *The Flowers of Romance* (1981), the much-acclaimed fourth album, which reached #11 in the U.K.

In 1983, PiL scored its biggest U.K. hit, when "This Is Not a Love Song" reached #5. By this time, however, Levene had left, and the name from here on would simply be a vehicle for John Lydon. A second live album, *Live in Tokyo,* appeared in England in 1983.

1984 saw the release of *This Is What You Want ... This Is What You Get,* only PiL's third album to be released in the U.S., though it now had six albums out. It marked the start of Lydon's move toward a more accessible dance-rock style, a direction that would be pursued further in *Album* (1986) (also called *Cassette* or *Compact Disc,* depending on the format), notably on the hit "Rise," as well as on *Happy?* (1987) and *9* (1989). In 1990, PiL released the compilation album *The Greatest Hits, So Far,* and in 1991 came the new album, *That What Is Not.*

After completing his memoirs in late 1993, Lydon decided to put an end to PiL and pursue a solo career. — *William Ruhlmann*

Public Image Ltd / 1978 / Warner Brothers ◆◆◆
Public Image Ltd. finds the group trying to develop a musical identity, creating an album that falls half-way between defiant rock & roll and self-consciously experimental musical explorations. Although the driving "Public Image" is the best moment on the record, the rest of the album is intriguing, if flawed. — *Stephen Thomas Erlewine*

Paris Au Printemps / 1980 / Virgin ◆◆
Pairs au Printemps (Paris in the Spring) is an engaging live album that draws from PiL's first two records, but it's only of interest to dedicated fans. — *Stephen Thomas Erlewine*

○ **Second Edition** / Jul. 1980 / Warner Brothers ◆◆◆◆
A two-disc deconstruction of traditional rock music, its tempos steady but slow, its bass track mixed high as in a reggae dub album, and Lydon's droning voice, with its scornful lyrics, wafting in the back. It is what PiL called it at the time, "anti-rock & roll," and it's fascinating. — *William Ruhlmann*

Flowers of Romance / 1981 / Warner Brothers ◆◆◆
The drums are loud and sharp, and Lydon wails like some sort of Middle Eastern street singer on this forbidding but rewarding album. — *William Ruhlmann*

Live in Tokyo / 1983 / Virgin ◆◆
Live in Tokyo doesn't capture PiL at its best moment. Lydon is supported by a set of anonymous backing musicians, as he tries to squeeze some added milage out of the hit single "This Is Not a Love Song." The group's performance is bland and the entire record seems rather opportunistic, making it the weakest entry in PiL's catalog. — *Stephen Thomas Erlewine*

○ **This Is What You Want ... This Is What You Get** / 1984 / Virgin ◆◆◆◆
Lydon adds keyboards, horns, and even a violin, double-tracks his vocals, and writes shorter songs with faster tempos. *This Is What You Want ... This Is What You Get* doesn't quite add up to a pop album, but you can dance to it. Contains the UK hit "This Is Not a Love Song." — *William Ruhlmann*

○ **Album/Compact Disc/Cassette** / 1986 / Elektra ◆◆◆◆
Hot guitars and 4/4 time signatures make this sound more like a hard-rock album than anything Lydon's done since the Sex Pistols. And the hit single "Rise" is actually a catchy number, believe it or not. — *William Ruhlmann*

○ **Happy?** / 1987 / Virgin ◆◆◆◆
Continuing with the deceptively pop-oriented studio sheen of *Album, Happy?* is a set of outwardly friendly material, which reveals its fractured melodies and concepts upon closer inspection. Song for song, *Happy?* isn't quite as strong as *Album,* but it continues its predecessor's sound to a fine effect. — *Stephen Thomas Erlewine*

9 / 1989 / Virgin ◆◆◆
Not only does *9* expand on the pop leanings of the two previous PiL albums, it adds elements of dance music and funk. At first, the record might seem a bit too slick, but it reveals more subtexts with each listen, although the music isn't quite as involving as the songs on *Album* and *Happy?.* — *Stephen Thomas Erlewine*

● **The Greatest Hits So Far** / 1990 / Virgin ◆◆◆◆
Fourteen tracks, recorded between 1978 and 1990, that trace PiL from the punk energy of the first single, "Public Image" (not previously released in the US), through the anti-rock of "Death Disco" and "Flowers of Romance" to the almost-pop of "This Is Not a Love Song" and "Rise" and the best of the late '80s material. — *William Ruhlmann*

That What Is Not / 1992 / Virgin ◆◆
Former Sex Pistol vocalist John Lydon has once again unleashed his Public Image Ltd. project, this time with a more basic, unrelenting rock & roll attack than ever before. The audio assault of guitarist John McGeoch and bassist Allan Dias perfectly complements Lydon's frenzied, strangled bleating throughout. As usual, Lydon succeeds in being all of satirical and fatalistic, confrontational and self-deprecating. The album's opening words set the tone: "What does it mean, What does anything mean." It's spat out as a statement rather than a question. "Covered" unpredictably tosses sampled vocals, bluesy harmonica, and the Tower of Power horns into the mix. *That What Is Not* can be a difficult PiL to swallow, but the heady side-effects make the effort worthwhile. — *Roch Parisien*

Gary Puckett & Union Gap

Group, Pop/Rock
Late '60s pop/rock group. Very popular during the late '60s, this San Diego-based band rode Gary Puckett's soaring vocal cords to pop gold. Formed in 1967 and signed to Columbia, the band's smooth accessibility and full-bodied pop arrangements quickly led to four 1967-68 million sellers: "Woman, Woman," "Young Girl," "Lady Willpower" and "Over You." Puckett notched his last couple of chart entries as a solo, including a Paul Simon tune, "Keep the Customer Satisfied." — *Bill Dahl*

● **Greatest Hits** / 1970 / Columbia ◆◆◆◆
All you would ever need from the "Lady Willpower" man, and more. — *Dan Heilman*

Pulnoc

Group, Alternative Pop/Rock
This Czechoslovakian ensemble, a descendant of the outlawed underground group Plastic People of the Universe, is a synthesis between early-'70s art-rock and early Velvet Underground. — *Rick Clark*

● **City of Hysteria** / Oct. 8, 1991 / Arista ◆◆◆◆
The only recording by any former Plastic People members to be released on a major American record label is a stunning bit of guitar rock helped by the beautiful singing of Michaela Nemcova. Egon Bondy is back, penning the lyrics to "Destroying Angel (White Mushrooms)," and Nemcova takes a beautiful lead vocal on the definitive version of the Velvet Underground's great "All Tomorrow's Parties." Although this disc was hyped upon its release (especially by Jello Biafra), I think that hardcore Plastic People fans were offput by the smooth sound, beefy guitar and high-tech production. Boy, were they ever shortsighted. — *John Dougan*

Pulp

Group, Alternative Pop/Rock
Formed in the early '80s by vocalist Jarvis Cocker, the English pop group Pulp went through numerous incarnations in the '80s, although none of the lineups ever made an album. In 1994, the band released their first album *His n' Hers.* Pulp's music was in the tradition of Roxy Music / Bowie-esque synth-pop and it captured the attention of Britain, as the band earned positive reviews and a Top 10 single with "Do You Remember the First Time?" The following year, the band confirmed its status as pop stars with the single "Common People," which debuted in the Top Ten upon its release and led to a headlining slot at the Glastonbury festival. — *Stephen Thomas Erlewine*

● **His n' Hers** / 1994 / PolyGram 3145 ◆◆◆◆
Jarvis Cocker's update on Bryan Ferry's lounge lizard persona works because recognizes the sleaziness beneath the style. Instead of chronicling the lives and times of jet-setting club-hoppers,

Cocker sneaks into the closet of his girlfriend to watch her sister have sex, reveals a fetish for pink gloves among other things, and remembers the first time. Pulp's fake, synthetic backdrop sound like they were constructed on bargain Casio keyboards, adding an extra layer of seaminess to Cocker's songs. That sense of cheap, faux-glamor is essential to the success of *His n' Hers*, Pulp's debut album. It's the sound of a poor man giving up everything he has so he can act out his expensive, elegant fantasies. He may never get there, but the approximation of glamor is more appealing and compelling than the reality, which is what gives *His n' Hers* a grand tragic romanticism. — *Stephen Thomas Erlewine*

Pure Prairie League

Group, Country-Rock
Pure Prairie League fused singer/songwriter pop with mellow country-rock. They scored several hits from the mid '70s to early '80s, with "Let Me Love You Tonight," "I'm Almost Ready," "Still Right Here in My Heart," and their most popular track, "Amie." — *Rick Clark*

Let Me Love You Tonight & Other Hits / 1971 / PolyGram ◆◆◆
● **Bustin' Out** / 1972 / RCA ◆◆◆◆
Bustin' Out was this band's most distinctive album, featuring very bright, thin-sounding acoustic guitars and dramatic string arrangements, courtesy of David Bowie's lead player Mick Ronson. "Amie" became a standard of sorts for the college coffeehouse crowd. Other highlights include "Jazzman," "Early Morning Riser," "Boulder Skies," "Call Me Tell Me," and "Angel," a song originally recorded on J. D. Blackfoot's *The Ultimate Prophecy*. — *Rick Clark*
○ **Pure Prairie League** / 1972 / RCA ◆◆◆◆
For all those who think the Eagles are the be all and end all of country-rock, you owe it to yourself to search out this album. Any track here (or on the followup, *Bustin' Out*) holds up as well, if not better than, anything by the Eagles. This album also proves that Craig Fuller is a grossly underrated songwriter. A country-rock must! — *Jim Worbois*

Two Lane Highway / 1975 / RCA ◆◆◆
With the departure of Fuller, the face (and sound) of Prairie League changed considerably. Larry Goshorn (ex-Sacred Mushroom) has replaced Fuller as the main songwriter in the band. And, while the overall album isn't up to it's predecessors, there are still some nice moments including the title track, "Runner" and a humorous tribute to country music legend, Merle Haggard. — *Jim Worbois*

If the Shoe Fits / 1976 / RCA ◆◆
PPL continues in the same vein as the last LP with only a couple of George Powell tunes bearing any resemblance to the sound of the first two records. Not a bad record, but it's becoming harder to find any traces of what made this band so special. — *Jim Worbois*

Dance / 1976 / RCA ◆◆
It's getting more difficult to find positive things to say about the band's records by this time. Aside from some fine playing by Andy Stein (ex-Lost Planet Airman), JD Call's superb pedal steel work, and the track "All the Way," there isn't much to recommend this album. — *Jim Worbois*

Live Takin' the Stage / 1977 / RCA ◆◆
Live, PPL fairly accurately re-created their studio sound. Which makes one wonder, why buy this record if you have all the previous albums? The band doesn't seem to feel they have anything to prove so they walk through these tracks adding nothing. If you already like these songs, stick with the studio versions since nothing is added on this one. — *Jim Worbois*

Just Fly / 1978 / RCA ◆◆

Can't Hold Back / 1979 / RCA ◆
Another shake-up finds Goshorn and longtime steel player, JD Call, gone. Goshorn has been replaced by future modern-country star, Vince Gill, as both main writer and leader of the group. By this time, they are PPL in name only as there is no resemblance between this and the original band. In fact, if you play "Rude Rude Awakening" next to the Eagles "One of These Nights," it would be difficult to distinguish between the two bands. — *Jim Worbois*

Firin' Up / 1980 / Casablanca ◆
This last gasp effort provided the band with their highest charting single, "Let Me Love You Tonight." By now, the band's sound was nearly indistinguishable from Firefall and many other bands of

the period. A sad end to a band that had begun with such promise. Single aside, there is no reason to look for this album. — *Jim Worbois*

Something in the Night / 1981 / Casablanca ◆◆
○ **Amie & Other Hits** / 1981 / RCA ◆◆◆◆
This best-of collection contains all the hits and most of the essential album cuts, including a healthy sampling from *Bustin' Out*. — *Rick Clark*

Home on the Range / 1983 / Pair ◆◆

Mementos 1971-1987 / 1987 / Rushmore ◆◆◆
● **Best of Pure Prairie League** / 1995 / Mercury Nashville ◆◆◆◆
Containing most of their hits and key album tracks, *Best of Pure Prairie League* provides an effective introduction to the country-rock group. — *Sara Sytsma*

James and Bobby Purify

Group, Soul
James (b May 12, 1944) and Bobby (b Sep 2, 1939) of this Southern soul duo were not actually brothers but cousins. James Purify and Robert Lee Dickey joined forces for some classic Southern soul duets during the mid '60s. Producer Papa Don Schroeder brought the soulful Floridians to Muscle Shoals in 1966 to record at Rick Hall's Fame studios, and the result was the gorgeous midtempo "I'm Your Puppet." The Dan Penn/Spooner Oldham ballad proved their biggest hit for the Bell label, although "Let Love Come between Us" and their revival of the Five Dutones's "Shake a Tail Feather" also made some major noise in 1967. When Bobby mutinied, James went it alone for a while before recruiting a new Bobby (Ben Moore), and they picked up right where the old duo left off. — *Bill Dahl*

● **Best of James Purify** / 1985 / Arista ◆◆◆◆
The Purify cousins made decent, occasionally excellent confessional soul tunes for Bell from 1966 to 1968, the best of them being "I'm Your Puppet," "Shake a Tail Feather" and "Let Love Come Between Us." While some compared them to Sam & Dave, they were actually more like Mel & Tim, since they didn't have songs anywhere as transcendent as those Isaac Hayes and David Porter were giving Sam & Dave. — *Ron Wynn*

Pussy Galore

Group, Alternative Pop/Rock
You either loved them or loathed them (some did both) but it was difficult to ignore the bawling, intentionally crude, anti-musicianship coughed up by Pussy Galore. A bunch of scuzzy-looking juveniles from Washington D.C.—their name coming from Honor Blackman's character in the James Bond film *Goldfinger*—and led by a young punk rockin' bohemian hipster wannabe named Jon Spencer, Pussy Galore created an unholy metallic ruckus that has part serious avant-garde noise wail, part bullshit pose. Considering their limited skills, narcissistic tendencies, and drug-cult mythologizing, their is a sizeable body of work from this band. The problem is that it's mostly hit-and-miss, which is a polite way of saying a little Pussy Galore goes a long way.

A serious discussion of Pussy Galore music attributes must thoroughly ignore technical ability; they have none. Spencer and guitarists (no bass) Julia Cafritz and Neil Hagerty locked horns in a badly played riff-fest with drummer ex-Sonic Youth drummer Bob Bert sounding as if he's dropping pots and pans of the floor. Surprisingly, with all of their hip attitude and condescending, arty indifference, Pussy Galore was capable of creating some great trash rock. However, I would argue that these moments were accidental, the byproduct of doing something long enough you eventually get it right.

Really the only difference between good Pussy Galore music and bad is that the latter is boring and the former is not—that is unless you have an extremely high tolerance for low-rent nihilism. As their noisiest and most frantic (e.g., the two fine EPs, *Groovy Hate Fuck* and *Sugarshit Sharp*) there is a messy ebullience to this muck that undercuts their normal snotty, calculatedly offensive shtick. And they did have a sense of humor as they proved on their 1986 cassette-only release a track-by-track cover of the Rolling Stones' classic *Exile on Main Street*. This release is not recommended to Stones fans. Still, for a band that no one predicted would have a long life, Pussy Galore has turned out many interesting side projects and bands since their demise in 1990. Spencer went on to form Boss Hog, and the more recent and much better Jon Spencer Blues Explosion, while also adding his distinctively smartass touch to recent recordings by the Gibson Bros; while Neil Hagerty joined forces with Jennifer Herrema and formed Royal Trux. —*John Dougan*

○ **Groovy Hate Fuck** / 1986 / Vinyl Drip ✦✦✦✦

Exiles on Main Street / 1986 / ✦✦✦

1 Yr. Live / 1986 / (no label) ✦✦

Right Now / 1987 / Caroline ✦✦✦

○ **Pussy Galore, Right Now!** / 1987 / Caroline ✦✦✦✦

○ **Sugarshit Sharp** / 1988 / Caroline ✦✦✦✦

Both of these records (*Groovy Hate Fuck* and *Sugarshit Sharp*) come highly recommended if only because as EPs, filler is kept to a minimum. *Groovy Hate Fuck* lives up to its title: it's a mess of a record thrown together by a bunch of bored kids who want to be as offensive as possible. On that level it's a near total success. Don't be shocked by the song titles (e.g., "Cunt Tease," You Look Like A Jew," "Dead Meat"), simply enjoy the violent, sonic chaos they whip up. It's very energetic. *Sugarshit Sharp* is even better. Side one is a cover of Einsturzende Neubauten's "Yu Gung," side two is more death-grunge rendered with a maximum of noise and minimum of panache. But at under 30 minutes it's free of a lot of arty-farty jerking around. —*John Dougan*

Dial 'M' for Motherfucker / 1989 / Caroline ✦✦

Historia De La Musica Rock / 1990 / Caroline ✦✦✦

● **Corpse Love: The Firstyear** / Feb. 14, 1992 / Caroline ✦✦✦✦

With the exception of *Corpse Love*, a pretty good career anthology, I recommend all of Pussy Galore's full-length records with this caveat: Not a one of them is strong all the way through. All have their moments (especially *Right Now*) but after a while (a short while) you'll be able to anticipate every one of their moves, and the cacophonous anti-rock thrash and bash becomes samey sounding. Freaks for this stuff will want all three records, but as trashy noise rock goes there are better bands, and certainly plenty who are less patronizing to their audiences. —*John Dougan*

Pylon

Group, New Wave

Let it be known that R.E.M. wasn't the only great band to come from the college town of Athens, GA; Pylon emerged in the early '80s as one of the best bands from this arty, exciting scene. True, their success never came close to that of R.E.M. (or the B-52s for that matter), but they approached post-punk dance music in a unique manner and recorded some exciting music. Slightly more avant-garde that the B-52s, and more willing to take risks, Pylon featured the ecstatic whoopin' and hollerin' of lead singer Vanessa Briscoe-Hay (formerly Vanessa Ellison). Helped by the sturdy rhythm section of drummer Curtis Crowe and bassist Michael Lachowski, and the scratchy, forceful guitar of Randy Bewley, Pylon created bizarre song shards that were giddy, surreal and propulsive.

Despite good word-of-mouth, numerous critical huzzahs and the hip production pals Chris Stamey and Gene Holder (of the dB's), Pylon called it quits after LP number two (*Chomp*) in 1983. Ironically, there seemed to be plenty of bands appropriating Pylon's jittery, art-dance rock, but none were doing it with their panache and spirit. After a layoff of about six years, the band reunited to promote a great anthology entitled *Hits* in 1989. Enjoying playing together after such a long time, Pylon released a new LP, *Chain* in 1990, that enhanced their reputation as an influential cult band, but did little to expand their cult audience. Still, Pylon may not sell huge amounts of records, but they are still stars, regardless of how much they were overshadowed by their peers. —*John Dougan*

Gyrate / 1980 / DB ✦✦✦

○ **Chomp** / 1983 / DB ✦✦✦✦

● **Hits** / 1989 / DB ✦✦✦✦

While searching out the two Pylon LPs (*Gyrate* and *Chomp*) is recommended, a better place to start would be this anthology which includes practically everything they recorded. It's dance music with an arty tinge, but it's never cold, off-putting or less than groove-filled. In fact, Pylon proved to be a better band than the more lauded B-52s. But that's an argument you'll want to start after you've heard this record. —*John Dougan*

Chain / 1990 / Dog Gone ✦✦✦

The reformed Pylon acquit themselves nicely on Chain, but never deliver a knockout blow. Stylistically speaking, there are no big changes here, but the exuberance and emotion carry even the most rote workouts. —*John Dougan*

Q

Queen

Group, Hard Rock, Art-Rock/Progressive-Rock, Pop/Rock
Queen was a quartet that combined elements of hard rock, heavy metal, and art-rock, adding other styles along the way for an often-majestic sound that also contained a distinct element of campy humor. The group was formed in England in 1971 by singer Freddie Mercury (b. Frederick Bulsara, Sep 5, 1946–d. Nov 24, 1991), guitarist Brian May (b. Jul 19, 1947), bassist John Deacon (b. Aug 19, 1951), and drummer Roger Taylor (b. Jul 26, 1949). They released their first album, *Queen*, in 1973, and it first reached the charts in the U.S. (going gold in 1977). It wasn't until the following year that Queen broke through in its native country, getting a Top Ten hit with "The Seven Seas of Rhye" and reaching the album chart with *Queen II*. *Sheer Heart Attack*, later the same year, was a substantial hit on both sides of the Atlantic (a number two U.K. hit with "Killer Queen," number 12 in the U.S.).

The biggest of Queen's early albums, however, was *A Night at the Opera* (1975), which topped the U.K. chart, made the Top Five in the U.S., and included the gold-selling single "Bohemian Rhapsody," the longest-running U.K. number one in 18 years (in 1992, bolstered by an appearance in the film *Wayne's World*, it would be a hit all over again in the U.S.). *A Day at the Races* (1976) was also a substantial hit, though it couldn't match its predecessor.

Queen turned to a harder rock approach for 1977's *News of the World*, which included the Top Five hit "We Are the Champions," still a sporting-event favorite. *Jazz* (1978) and *Live Killers* (1979) were successful, if less substantial albums, but Queen took a sharp stylistic turn for *The Game* in 1980 and was rewarded with two uncharacteristic number one hits, the rockabilly-tinged "Crazy Little Thing Called Love" and the disco-rock "Another One Bites the Dust."

Though Queen scored gold in the U.S. with the subsequent releases *Hot Space* (1982) and *The Works* (1984), the group was in a gradual commercial decline throughout the '80s. It returned to gold-selling status with *Innuendo* in 1991, but singer Freddie Mercury died of AIDS in November of that year. That set off a sales bonanza in Europe and, belatedly, in the U.S., with a giant benefit concert held in Mercury's honor at Wembley Stadium in England in April 1992. Posthumous releases began to appear, with a boxed set promised. *— William Ruhlmann*

Queen / Sep. 1973 / Hollywood ✦✦
Queen had already staked out a distinct identity by the time of their debut album, led by Freddie Mercury's big-voiced flamboyance and Brian May's slabs of hard rock guitar, all in the service of surprisingly poppy tunes. The most memorable track is the lead-off song, "Keep Yourself Alive." *— William Ruhlmann*

Queen II / Apr. 1974 / Hollywood ✦✦✦
Following Queen's debut album by only seven months, *Queen II* was the record that broke the group in its native country, where it hit #5 and spun off the #10 single "The Seven Seas of Rhye." It is a less impressive album than its predecessor, however, and today seems one of the weakest entries in Queen's catalog. *— William Ruhlmann*

○ **Sheer Heart Attack** / Nov. 1974 / Hollywood ✦✦✦✦
An effective demonstration of the range of Queen's musical tastes, from the guitar pyrotechnics of "Brighton Rock" to the vocal histrionics of "Killer Queen" and the on-the-road diary "Now I'm Here." *— William Ruhlmann*

☆ **A Night at the Opera** / Dec. 1975 / Hollywood ✦✦✦✦✦
In case there was any doubt that Queen was devoted to over-the-top effects, this massively overdubbed combination of hard rock and opera, paced by May's monster guitar riffs and Mercury's million-voiced choir and emotive solo singing, should have erased it. Contains "Death on Two Legs," "You're My Best Friend," and, of course, "Bohemian Rhapsody." *— William Ruhlmann*

A Day at the Races / Dec. 1976 / Hollywood ✦✦✦
A Day at the Races was the inevitable second-best followup to *A Night at the Opera*, the album that made Queen a superstar act. The group's patented brand of hard rock and melodic overstatement was in place on such songs as "Tie Your Mother Down" and "Somebody To Love" (the two hit singles), so that anyone who loved the previous album would at least like this one. *— William Ruhlmann*

News of the World / Nov. 1977 / Hollywood ✦✦✦
In the balance between Queen's operatic tendencies and its desire to rock out, the rock side once again gained an upper hand on this release. Not that the bombast lessened, but songs like "We Will Rock You" were actually dry runs for the stripped-down approach of *The Game*, and even "We Are the Champions" was a ballad. Well, almost. *— William Ruhlmann*

○ **Jazz** / Nov. 1978 / Hollywood ✦✦✦✦
Despite its commercial success, Queen's albums were hit-and-miss affairs, with every step forward (*News of the World*) seemingly followed by a misstep (*Jazz*). What they meant by the title has never been clear, and the single "Bicycle Race"/"Fat-Bottomed Girls," although it became a minor hit on career momentum, is not among the group's more memorable efforts. After this, it was time for a new direction, and happily, Queen found it with *The Game*. *— William Ruhlmann*

Live Killers / Jun. 1979 / Hollywood ✦✦
At an artistic and commercial crossroads, Queen paused to release a two-LP live album chronicling their first five years of music-making. Like most such efforts, it was basically redundant, although pleasant for fans. *— William Ruhlmann*

○ **The Game** / Jul. 1980 / Hollywood ✦✦✦✦
The basic elements of Queen's approach, from May's heavy guitar to Mercury's vocal army, were in attendance here, but the album owes its success to its novelties, especially "Another One Bites the Dust" and "Crazy Little Thing Called Love." *— William Ruhlmann*

Flash Gordon / Dec. 1980 / Hollywood ✦✦
This was a movie soundtrack, and it represented a relatively minor effort for Queen. *— William Ruhlmann*

★ **Greatest Hits** / Oct. 1981 / Elektra ✦✦✦✦✦
They may not have started out that way, but by 1981 Queen definitely was perceived as a singles act. This record gathers their biggest US/UK hits, 1973–1981, including the collaboration with David Bowie, "Under Pressure." Not to be confused with the 1992 Hollywood Records (61625) release also called *Greatest Hits*, which isn't as good but has the advantage of being in print. *— William Ruhlmann*

Hot Space / May 1982 / Hollywood ✦✦✦
After turning out a movie soundtrack and a greatest hits LP, Queen finally got around to following up its chart-topping 1980 album *The Game* with *Hot Space*. Taking a cue from the spare, rhythmic style of the previous album's hits, "Another One Bites The Dust" and "Crazy Little Thing Called Love," the band took an austere, beat-heavy dance floor approach again, but without as

much distinctiveness. The biggest American hit, "Body Language" (#11 U.S., #25 U.K.) was typical, with Freddie Mercury intoning "Give me your body" over and over. The album also contained the year-old single "Under Pressure," by Queen & David Bowie. — *William Ruhlmann*

The Works / Feb. 1984 / Hollywood ♦♦
Despite the presence of the hit singles "Radio Ga Ga" and "I Want to Break Free," *The Works* was Queen's weakest album to date, featuring a set of under-developed songs that lacked memorable hooks and melodies. — *Stephen Thomas Erlewine*

A Kind of Magic / Jun. 1986 / Hollywood ♦♦
A Kind of Magic was a more diverse and ambitious collection than *The Works*, but it also suffered from a lack of memorable, fully-developed songs. Again, it was a massive succes in Britain, entering the charts at number one, but it failed to return Queen to superstar status in the U.S. — *Stephen Thomas Erlewine*

The Miracle / May 1989 / Hollywood ♦♦
Queen had subsided to also-ran status in the U.S. by the time of this, its next-to-last studio album, but, with its return from disco to elaborate pop-rock, it continued to reign in its native U.K., where this album hit #1 and produced five Top 25 singles in "I Want It All," "Breakthru," "The Invisible Man," "Scandal," and "The Miracle." The approach is similar to that on Queen albums like *Sheer Heart Attack*, with overdubbed vocal choirs, elaborate arrangements, and Brian May's extended guitar runs. But as a recreation of that style, it lacked freshness. — *William Ruhlmann*

Innuendo / Feb. 1991 / Hollywood ♦♦
Queen's final new studio album before the death of lead singer Freddie Mercury was its third straight U.K. chart topper, but a more modest success in the U.S., although "Headlong," "Innuendo," and "I Can't Live Without You" earned AOR radio play, and the album was Queen's first in seven years to go gold. *Innuendo* was very much in the tradition of Queen's slightly comic, operatic hard rock style of the mid-1970s, with "Headlong" delivering heavy-handed guitar playing and hooks and "I'm Going Slightly Mad" displaying Mercury's campier side. (As of this record, Queen's entire catalog dating back to 1973, previously on Elektra and Capitol, was acquired for U.S. distribution by Hollywood Records, a subsidiary of Disney, which reissued its albums on CD.) — *William Ruhlmann*

● **Greatest Hits** / 1992 / Hollywood ♦♦♦♦
This is going to take a little explaining. In 1981, when it was contracted to Elektra Records in the U.S., Queen released an album called *Greatest Hits* (Elektra 564), which contained 14 songs that chronicled singles from 1973 to 1981. In 1990, Hollywood Records acquired CD rights to Queen's catalog, by which time the Elektra *Greatest Hits* had gone out of print on vinyl. Hollywood released *Classic Queen*, a compilation that covered Queen's hits from 1982 to its demise in 1991, with a few older songs thrown in. Then it released this album, its version of *Greatest Hits*, which is a 15-track album that deletes the songs from the first *Greatest Hits* which appeared on *Classic Queen* (among them Queen's biggest hit, "Bohemian Rhapsody") and adds a few tracks from the 1973–1982 era that did not appear on the original release. The Elektra *Greatest Hits* LP had a superior selection, but it's gone now, so you're stuck with this. (New fans don't seem to have minded, as this new *Greatest Hits* sold better than the first one.) — *William Ruhlmann*

○ **Classic Queen** / Mar. 10, 1992 / Hollywood ♦♦♦♦
Essentially, this 17-track album is a second-volume Queen's *Greatest Hits*, picking up the story from that album's 1981 release and taking it to the end of Queen's career. But the album also contains a few tracks—"Bohemian Rhapsody," "Keep Yourself Alive," and "Under Pressure"—that appeared on that first set, as well as a couple—"Stone Cold Crazy" and "Tie Your Mother Down"—from the same era. The remaining 12 tracks, culled from *The Works, A Kind Of Magic, The Miracle*, and *Innuendo*, represent songs that were not big hits in the U.S. Nevertheless, with a resurgence of interest in Queen and the second coming of "Bohemian Rhapsody," courtesy of *Wayne's World*, this album returned Queen to platinum status and the U.S. Top Five for the first time since the early '80s. — *William Ruhlmann*

Live at Wembley / Jun. 2, 1992 / Hollywood ♦♦
This solid live two-disc set from Queen offers a glimpse of their live power; fans will be pleased by the band's performance. — *AMG*

At The BBC / 1995 / Hollywood ♦♦
A collection of early Queen material recorded for the British Broadcasting Corporation, *At The BBC* captures the band in their formative stages, as they were sketching out a cross between heavy metal and bombastically melodic pop. Several classic Queen songs, including "Killer Queen," are included and the performances are fascinating for hardcore fans, but there are only seven tracks on the album and it lists at full-price, which doesn't make it a bargain by any stretch of the imagination. — *Stephen Thomas Erlewine*

Queen Latifah

b. New Jersey
Rap
The New Jersey-born Queen Latifah (born Dana Owens, Latifah is an Arabic word meaning sensitive and delicate) has almost single-handedly opened the doors for female rappers in the '90s, belying the sexism that permeates the male side of the genre. Her versatility suggests she'll be around for a long while.

Queen Latifah's moved into television as part of the cast for the hit Fox situation comedy *Living Single*. While there was far from universal praise for the series, even its detractors had positive things to say about her portrayal of a magazine editor. She also moved to Motown from Tommy Boy, and her CD *Black Reign* was her finest since *All Hail the Queen*. — *John Floyd*

● **All Hail the Queen** / 1989 / Tommy Boy ♦♦♦♦
Her genius is two-fold. She preaches Afrocentrism through clever, versatile, and educated raps, and they're coming from a clever, versatile, and educated feminist. The whole shebang is funky beyond belief. — *John Floyd*

Nature of a Sista' / 1991 / Tommy Boy ♦♦♦
Her feminism becomes even more focused on this followup. With an equally diverse and creative set list, Latifah is becoming the female voice in a male-dominated genre. — *John Floyd*

○ **Black Reign** / Nov. 16, 1993 / Motown ♦♦♦♦
Black Reign marked Latifah's move to Motown, and was also a return to the tough-talking, lyrically frank, frequently controversial material that established her as arguably the finest female rapper. "Coochie Bang" and "Weekend Love" were harsh and explicit attacks on would-be hit-and-run lovers, while "Just Another Day" and "I Can't Understand" examined the continuing inequities plaguing inner-city youth, and "Superstar" took a pointedly unglamorous view of her situation and the perils of hip-hop supremacy. — *Ron Wynn*

Queensryche

Group, Hard Rock, Art-Rock/Progressive-Rock, Heavy Metal
During the early '80s, Queensryche was a standard heavy metal band, sounding like a cross between Iron Maiden and Judas Priest. In the middle of the decade, the band shifted to a more progressive sound, adding elements of '70s art-rock, particularly Pink Floyd, to their music. Queensryche came into their own on 1988's *Operation Mindcrime*, a concept album about a media-dominated future. With *Empire* two years later, the band crossed over into the mainstream with the hit "Silent Lucidity." Four years later, the band returned with *Promised Land*; the album went gold with little radio support and minimal airplay on MTV, proving that the group had not lost their devoted fans. — *Stephen Thomas Erlewine*

Queensryche / 1983 / EMI America ♦♦
Their first EP (released in 1983) would have been forgotten if it wasn't for the band's dedication. — *John Book*

The Warning / 1984 / EMI America ♦♦♦
This is good heavy metal with dominant synthesizer work. — *John Book*

Rage for Order / 1986 / EMI America ♦♦♦

○ **Operation Mindcrime** / 1988 / EMI America ♦♦♦♦
Seattle's best kept secret is let out of the box with a concept album that brought comparisons of Pink Floyd and the Who. Fantastic lyrics with a great story line, powerful playing by the band, and powerful vocals by Geoff Tate made them finally noticed by fans a year after its release. — *John Book*

● **Empire** / 1990 / EMI America ♦♦♦♦
This band knows what they want and how to get it. Masterfully produced (recorded digitally), this is the album that made the band international superstars. — *John Book*

Promised Land / 1994 / EMI America ✦✦✦
Queensryche returned from a four-year absence with *Promised Land* only to find the hard rock land very different than the one they left in 1990. But Queensryche did something smart. Instead of trying to adjust themselves to fit into the world that their Seattle brethren had created, they simply stayed the same. Not only was the record a commercial success—it went gold in four months—but it was also an engaging album. *Promised Land* lacks the conceptual unity and consistent songwriting of *Operation Mindcrime*, but it makes it clear that the band hasn't run out of ideas yet. —*Stephen Thomas Erlewine*

? & the Mysterians

Group, Garage Rock
Originally formed in Flint, MI, in 1962, this group took its name from the obscure science-fiction movie, *The Mysterians*. They recorded the anthemic "96 Tears" for the local Spanish music label Pa-Go-Go in 1966. It was immediately picked up for national consumption by Cameo-Parkway, going on to be one of the most covered garage band classics of the '60s. Lead singer Question Mark (real name listed as both Rudy Martinez and Reeto Rodriguez) continues to front a version of the band on oldies package shows across the U.S. —*Cub Koda*

● **96 Tears** / 1966 / Cameo ✦✦✦✦
A true garage band classic, featuring the title track and 11 others straight from the band's set list. (Out of print.) —*Cub Koda*

Action / 1966 / Cameo ✦✦✦

○ **96 Tears Forever** / 1985 / ROIR ✦✦✦✦
This is a band that definitely got by on attitude, as this collection of lesser tracks shows. —*Dan Heilman*

Quicksilver Messenger Service

Group, Psychedelic
The band that became Quicksilver Messenger Service originally was conceived as a rock vehicle for folk singer/songwriter Dino Valenti (b. Nov 7, 1943), author of "Get Together." Living in San Francisco, Valenti had found guitarist John Cipollina (b. Aug 24, 1943–d. May 29, 1989) and singer Jim Murray. Valenti's friend David Freiberg (b. Aug 24, 1938) joined on bass, and the group was completed by the addition of drummer Greg Elmore (b. Sep 4, 1946) and guitarist Gary Duncan (b. Sep 4, 1946). As the band was being put together, Valenti was imprisoned on a drug charge and he didn't rejoin Quicksilver until later.
They debuted at the end of 1965 and played around the Bay Area and then the West Coast for the next two years, building up a large following but resisting offers to record that had been taken up by such San Francisco acid-rock colleagues as Jefferson Airplane and the Grateful Dead. Quicksilver finally signed to Capitol toward the end of 1967 and recorded their self-titled debut album in 1968 (by this time, Murray had left). *Happy Trails*, the 1969 follow-up, was recorded live. After its release, Duncan left the band and was replaced for *Shady Grove* (1970) by British session pianist Nicky Hopkins. By the time of its release, however, Duncan had returned, along with Valenti, making the group a sextet.
This version of Quicksilver, prominently featuring Valenti's songs and lead vocals, lasted only a year, during which two albums, *Just for Love* and *What About Me*, were recorded. Cipollina, Freiberg, and Hopkins then left, and the remaining trio of Valenti, Duncan, and Elmore hired replacements and cut another couple of albums before disbanding. There was a reunion in 1975, resulting in a new album and a tour, and in 1986, Duncan revived the Quicksilver name for an album that also featured Freiberg on background vocals. —*William Ruhlmann*

○ **Quicksilver Messenger Service** / May 1968 / Capitol ✦✦✦✦
The band's debut effort was a little more restrained and folky than some listeners had expected, given their reputation for stretching out in concert. While some prefer the mostly live *Happy Trails*, this is inarguably their strongest set of studio material, with the accent on melodic folk-rockers. Highlights include their cover of folksinger Hamilton Camp's "Pride of Man," probably their best studio track; "Light Your Windows," probably the group's best original composition; and founding member Dino Valenti's "Dino's Song" (Valenti himself was in jail when the album was recorded). "Gold and Silver" is their best instrumental jam, and the 12-minute "The Fool" reflects some of the best and worst traits of the psychedelic era. —*Richie Unterberger*

○ **Happy Trails** / Mar. 1969 / Capitol ✦✦✦✦
Quicksilver was heard at its best on this partially live album, which contained a 25-minute version of Bo Diddley's "Who Do You Love." —*William Ruhlmann*

○ **Shady Grove** / Dec. 1969 / One Way ✦✦✦✦
Even though the opening title track featured all the elements that made Quicksilver one of the great Bay Area bands (particularly John Cipollina's vibrato-laden lead guitar), *Shady Grove* was a transitional album. The addition of pianist Nicky Hopkins (Rolling Stones, Steve Miller) gave the band more colors to work with. One of Quicksilver's better albums, *Shady Grove* shines brightest on tracks like "Joseph's Coat," the dazzling Hopkins keyboard instrumental showcase "Edward (The Mad Shirt Grinder)" and the title cut. The sound on this disc isn't particularly good. —*Rick Clark*

Just for Love / Aug. 1970 / One Way ✦✦✦
With the return of Gary Duncan and the recording debut of founder Dino Valenti, *Just for Love*, Quicksilver's fourth album, marked their debut as the band they were intended to be. The ironic thing about that is that, led by singer/songwriter Valenti, they were a much more pop-oriented band than their fans had come to expect. On *Just for Love*, Quicksilver finally was Valenti's backup group (he wrote all but one of the songs), and while this gave them greater coherence and accessibility, as well as their only Top 50 single in "Fresh Air," it also made them less the boogie band they had been. And it meant the band's days were numbered. —*William Ruhlmann*

What About Me / Dec. 1970 / One Way ✦✦✦
Recorded in part at the same 1970 sessions that produced *Just for Love*, *What About Me* was a similar effort, again dominated by Dino Valenti's songwriting and singing. It was also the swan song of the band, with guitarist John Cipollina, pianist Nicky Hopkins, and bassist David Freiberg dropping out after its completion. —*William Ruhlmann*

Quicksilver / Nov. 1971 / Capitol ✦✦✦

Comin' Thru / Apr. 1972 / Capitol ✦✦

○ **Anthology** / Mar. 1973 / Capitol ✦✦✦✦
A two-record set chronicling Quicksilver's recorded history from 1967 to 1971 and including most of their best tracks. Now out of print, this collection has been superseded by the Rhino album *Sons Of Mercury*. —*William Ruhlmann*

Solid Silver / Oct. 1975 / Capitol ✦✦
A one-off reunion album featuring the lineup of Dino Valenti, John Cipollina, David Freiberg, Greg Elmore, and Gary Duncan. Valenti again dominates, and the band is cohesive, but its creative spark is gone. —*William Ruhlmann*

Maiden of the Cancer Moon / 1983 / Psycho ✦✦✦
A double album of live material from 1968, this duplicates a lot of the material on *Happy Trails* and adds considerably more. This erratic collection reflects Quicksilver's best and worst qualities: the hard-driving blend of raga/folk/psychedelic rock is fine, the blues jams are fairly awful. Besides "Who Do You Love?" and "Mona" (two versions), this LP has covers of "Back Door Man," "Smokestack Lightning," Buffy St. Marie's "Codine," and versions of most of the songs from the first Quicksilver LP. The rendition of "The Fool" here eclipses the studio take, and the performance of "Gold And Silver" is fine except for the "Toad"-like drum solo. John Cipollina's slithery leads are consistently fine, and Quicksilver fans will find this worth the search. —*Richie Unterberger*

Peace by Piece / Jul. 1986 / Capitol ✦
A travesty. Guitarist Gary Duncan, apparently the owner of the Quicksilver name, rounds up David Freiberg for a few background vocals, along with some Bay Area regulars and records an album that has nothing to do with Quicksilver Messenger Service and isn't any good. —*William Ruhlmann*

● **Sons of Mercury (1968-75)** / 1991 / Rhino ✦✦✦✦
This thorough two-disc best-of contains Quicksilver's most familiar material from its various lineups, plus some rarities. The only thing keeping this from being essential is the exclusion of the complete live version of "Who Do You Love," over a single edited version. —*William Ruhlmann*

○ **Best of Quicksilver Messenger Service** / 1992 / CEMA ✦✦✦✦

Quiet Riot

Group, Hard Rock, Heavy Metal
In the early '80s, Quiet Riot became one of the first metal bands to

hit the top of the pop charts with their remake of Slade's "Cum on Feel the Noize." By that time, Quiet Riot had been recording for a number of years, experiencing several changes. During the late '70s, the band was a straightahead metal group, distinguished only by the talented young guitarist Randy Rhoads; he left in 1979 to join Ozzy Osbourne's band, causing Quiet Riot to change their sound slightly, adding more pop elements to their hard rock. It paid off with 1983's *Metal Health*, which hit number one. However, their following albums didn't have the same crossover appeal and started to slip down the charts. Throughout the '80s, the band was a solid concert attraction even if their albums didn't sell particularly well. In 1988, the band broke up; vocalist Kevin DuBrow assembled a new version of Quiet Riot in 1993 for a tour and an album. — *Stephen Thomas Erlewine*

● **Metal Health** / 1983 / Pasha ◆◆◆◆
On the strength of their gloriously stupid cover of Slade's "Cum On Feel the Noize," Quiet Riot shot to the top of the charts with *Metal Health*. While it was easily the best thing the band ever recorded, it is very inconsistent, but the album does contain some of the best dumb heavy metal of the early '80s. — *Stephen Thomas Erlewine*

Condition Critical / 1984 / Pasha ◆◆◆
Condition Critical, Quiet Riot's followup to their number one, multi-million commercial breakthrough *Metal Health,* is nearly identical to its predecessor. Not only do they repeat the hard-driving pop-metal hybrid to the last detail, they even throw in another Slade cover. Like *Metal Health,* the Slade cover on *Condition Critical* ("Mama Weer All Crazee Now") is the finest moment on the record—it's the only time the riffs have a solid hook and the melody is memorable. However, the rest of the record is well-produced and sounds good, even if the quality of the songs is somewhat poor. — *Stephen Thomas Erlewine*

QR III / 1986 / Pasha ◆◆

Quiet Riot / 1988 / Pasha ◆

○ **Randy Rhoads Years** / 1993 / Rhino ◆◆◆◆
A fine collection of Quiet Riot's earliest records, *The Randy Rhoads Years* captures the influential guitarist in his formative years. That alone would have made the disc essential for his fans, but it also includes some prime unreleased material, making it all the more desirable. — *Stephen Thomas Erlewine*

Terrified / 1993 / Moonstone ◆◆

R

Radial Spangle

Group, Alternative Pop/Rock

Radial Spangle are an eclectic trio from Oklahoma City. The group's first album, 1993's *Ice Cream Headache*, has a cavernous, echoing sound filled with plinking guitars and feedback, over which the vocals of Alan Laird and April Tippens hover. 1994's *Syrup Macrame* shows a vast improvement, mixing loud, abrasive "city songs" with loopy, gentle "country songs." Similar to Sonic Youth and Mercury Rev, Radial Spangle lacks the pretensions of those groups, instead writing songs about sunflowers and birthdays. It's a welcome change. —*Heather Phares*

Ice Cream Headache / 1993 / Beggars Banquet ✦✦✦
Ice Cream Headache features Radial Spangle's soft, dreamy, pop side and their more inaccessible sonic experiments. "Canopy and Shoe" and "Birthday" are two good examples of the former, and "White Paper Basket" is a good example of the latter. An uneven debut, it still contains enough listenable material to make it worthwhile. —*Heather Phares*

● **Syrup Macramé** / 1994 / Beggars Banquet ✦✦✦✦
The band's second album sees them follow their pop instincts, and the result is unexpectedly tight and catchy. While some noodling stil exists on *Syrup Macramé*, it's more amusing than tedious. The humor and lightheartedness of the recording make up for some of the band's pretensions. —*Heather Phares*

Radiators from Space

Group, Punk

Truth be told, this is one of my all-time favorite band names. Punk rockers from Dublin, the Radiators played, like a lot of bands did at the time, fast, loud, and gnarly rock & roll. They never made it big (not even in punk circles), only recorded two records (the second one, *Ghostown*, is only OK), and were a dead issue by 1979. What caused their demise? No one knows for sure; bands like the Radiators came and went so quickly in the early days of punk (raise your hands, all those who remember the Cortinas) that this year's model quickly became yesterday's news. That's the way it is in rock & roll, but too often that means that good bands like the Radiators were given far less notice than they deserve. While I couldn't tell you what happened to many of the Radiators, their most "famous" member is Philip Chevron, who went on to play guitar and write some fine songs for the Pogues. —*John Dougan*

○ **TV Tube Heart** / 1977 / Chiswick ✦✦✦✦
Predating many English punk records by nearly a year, *TV Tube Heart* is a tuneful mess of crash-and-bash full-throttle punk rock. Better than a lot of the more hyped bands of the time (like the Cortinas!), the Radiators pull out all the stops and came up with a winner first time out. Sadly, they couldn't repeat the excitement of this record. Still and all, this is a great artifact of the era. —*John Dougan*

Ghostown / 1979 / Chiswick ✦✦✦

Radio Birdman

Group, Punk

Although the best-known band of the early Australian punk scene of the late '70s was the Saints, the first band to wave the punk rock flag in the land down under was Radio Birdman. Formed by Australian emigre Deniz Tek (originally from Ann Arbor, Michigan) and Aussie surfer-turned-vocalist Rob Younger in 1975, Radio Birdman's approach to rock & roll was rooted in the high-energy, apocalyptic guitar rant of the Stooges and MC5, sprinkled liberally with a little East Coast underground hard rock courtesy of Blue Oyster Cult. Their first EP, *Burn My Eye*, released in 1976, was a great record and, nearly 20 years later, still remains a seminal chunk of Aussie punk. Loud and snotty, with Younger bellowing his guts out and Tek on a search and destroy mission with his guitar, this was a great debut that set the stage for the impending deluge of Aussie punk bands waiting in the wings. After the release of their debut LP, *Radios Appear* (the title comes from a lyric in the Blue Oyster Cult song "Dominance and Submission"), a year later, Radio Birdman seemed poised to break Aussie punk worldwide. And although the American label Sire (then the home of the Ramones) was quick to sign them and distribute *Radios Appear* internationally, there was a gap of three years before they released a second album (*Living Eyes*). During that time, two things happened: dozens of other Aussie punk bands stole their thunder, and Radio Birdman split up almost immediately after *Living Eyes* was released. Sire never released the record outside of Australia, and Radio Birdman, who should have been the biggest band in Aussie punk, were now highly-regarded punk forefathers. After the band split in 1981, various members were busy forming other bands; space limitations prevent an exhaustive look at their post-Birdman careers. Tek formed the New Race with Younger, ex-Stooges guitarist Ron Asheton and ex-MC5 drummer Dennis Thompson, released a handful of solo singles and EPs, and became a surgeon (!); Younger started his own band, the New Christs, and produced records by the second generation of Aussie punk bands influenced by Radio Birdman, most notably the Celibate Rifles; other Radio Birdman alumni ended up in assorted Aussie bands such as the Lime Spiders, Hoodoo Gurus and Screaming Tribesmen. Now the grand old man of Aussie punk, Tek has formed an unnamed, part-time project with Celibate Rifles guitarist Kent Steedman that rocks with the same reckless abandon Radio Birdman did when they were changing the course of Australian rock forever. —*John Dougan*

Burn My Eye [EP] / 1976 / Trafalgar ✦✦✦
This is where Aussie punk got the kick in the pants it needed to become a worldwide phenomenon. Tough to locate the original, but it has been reissued more than once as an affordable import. The title track alone (later recorded by the Celibate Rifles) is worth the price of the record. —*John Dougan*

● **Radios Appear** / 1977 / Sire ✦✦✦✦
Starting off with a rip-snortin' cover of the Stooges' "T.V. Eye," this is primal (and prime) Birdman, with Tek and Younger firmly ensconced in the eye of this guitar-fueled hurricane. Tek's originals are pretty strong, especially the grimy tale of urban desolation "Murder City Nights" and the noisy freakout "Descent Into the Maelstrom." One of Australia's great rock and roll bands in all of their glory. —*John Dougan*

Living Eyes / 1981 / WEA ✦✦✦

Under the Ashes / 1988 / WEA ✦✦✦
I've seen this box set exactly once (in Minneapolis to be exact), didn't pick it up and have regretted it almost daily ever since. If you've caught the fever of this band and are inclined to have their complete recorded works—buy it! Also available as a multi-CD box. Well worth the investment. —*John Dougan*

Radiohead

Group, Alternative Pop/Rock

Radiohead's combination of British pop sensibilities and noisy,

Pixies-derived post-punk managed to cross into the mainstream while keeping a fair amount of alternative credibility. Consisting of vocalist Thom E. Yorke, Johnny and Colin Greenwood, Ed O'Brien, and Phil Selway, the Oxford-based group were relative unknowns in their homeland when the brooding single "Creep" became an American hit in 1993. "Creep" carried their debut album, *Pablo Honey*, into the charts, as well as into gold record status; soon, the single also became a hit in Britain. However, the group wasn't able to produce any successful follow-up singles, and the record disappeared from the charts by the end of the year. Radiohead delivered their second album, *The Bends*, in spring of 1995. Although it received positive reviews and sold well upon its British release, the record was still-born in America. After a couple of months, radio and MTV began playing "Fake Plastic Trees," making the single an alternative hit and pushing *The Bends* into the charts. *—Stephen Thomas Erlewine*

Pablo Honey / 1993 / Capitol ✦✦✦
Oxford, England's Radiohead often wear their cleverness on their collective sleeve for debut release *Pablo Honey*. There is great potential here. Thom Yorke has a great singing voice that ranges from moody angst to soaring falsetto. It's hard to define the music which displays both good pop sense and a sometimes skillful use of controlled noise. British singles such as "Creep" (an ode to self-loathing) and band anthem "Anyone Can Play Guitar" are marvy and essential. "Blow Out" closes *Pablo Honey* in full accordance with all truth in advertising legislation. *—Roch Parisien*

○ **Bends** / 1995 / Capitol ✦✦✦✦
With one stroke, Radiohead casts off the albatross of their obsession-inducing hit "Creep" and, at the same time, fight off the dreaded sophomore jinx. *The Bends* is a work of remarkable, fragile, but sinewy beauty. Producer John Leckie perfectly balances Thom Yorke's pivotal choirboy vocals, Jon Greenwood and Ed O'Brian's distorted, Nirvana-ish guitar thrusts, and the flexible Colin Greenwood/Phil Selway rhythm axis. *—Roch Parisien*

Rage Against the Machine

Group, Alternative Pop/Rock
On the strength of their fiercely political debut album, Rage Against the Machine became an alternative rock sensation in 1993. Combining a technically advanced post-punk guitar roar with an amateurish stab at hip-hop, the band's sound is polarizing: you believe either they're the most uncompromising rockers on earth or they're whining, simplistic hypocrites (after all, how many revolutionaries sign to Sony). Either way, with their fiery, militant rock, the band managed to gain more fans than most stridently political bands, as well as earning a considerable amount of critical acclaim for their abrasive sound. *—Stephen Thomas Erlewine*

● **Rage Against the Machine** / Nov. 3, 1992 / Epic ✦✦✦✦
Rage Against the Machine's debut album is overflowing with barely contained anger that comes across better in the scalding music than the half-baked, cliched lyrics. *—Stephen Thomas Erlewine*

Rage to Live

Group, Country-Rock
In 1978, I had the misfortune to see Rage to Live founder Ed Tomney's original band the Necessaries open for Johnny Thunders's Gang War (featuring Wayne Kramer) and the Clash at Clark University in Worcester, MA. After their set of mostly forgettable, ponderous pop-punk, a waggish friend of mine who had accompanied me to the gig dismissed them as the "Un"-Necessaries and assumed they were out of our lives forever. Now here I am writing about Tomney's post-Necessaries project, Rage to Live, an excellent pop band. Man, life can be weird. Joining forces with singer Glenn Morrow (himself an ex-member of the terrific Individuals), Rage to Live played elegantly rockin' (if that's possible) pop that was part of the "Hoboken Sound" of post-punk New York, which gave the world great bands like the Feelies, the dBs, and the criminally underrated Wygals. Rage to Live fit into this scene like hand in glove, and despite recording only two albums (both of which have been issued on one CD), made some wonderful music. Their self-titled debut is a little tentative, but the songwriting and presentation are very strong, making *Rage to Live* one of the great left-field surprises of the mid-'80s. After the second album (*Blame the Victim*), RTL were no more. Tomney, indulging in his artier instincts, began working with Jonathan Borofsky, and Morrow has been keeping a low profile. *—John Dougan*

Rage to Live / 1986 / Bar/None ✦✦✦

● **Blame the Victim** / 1990 / Bar/None ✦✦✦✦
Caveat emptor: Only the CD release of *Blame the Victim* carries tracks from Rage to Live's debut, and the CD is what you want. There's no reason to scrimp and save and miss out on any of the many wonderful songs this band has recorded, like "Countdown to My Imagination" and the pre-grunge grungefest of "Joker's Punch." Some excellent lead guitar is contributed by Television's Richard Lloyd, adding considerably to the fun. *—John Dougan*

Railway Children

Group, Alternative Pop/Rock
Consisting of vocalist Gary Newby, Brian Bateman, Guy Keegan, and Stephen Hull, the Railway Children gained a small cult following in their native England in the late '80s. When the members were still teenagers, the group began releasing singles on Factory Records. Recalling the intricate guitar-pop of the Smiths, their singles evoked the ringing hooks of '60s British pop and the post-punk pop attitude of the '80s. The band released their debut album, *Reunion Wilderness*, in 1987; the album led to a contract with Virgin Records. Railway Children's second album, *Recurrence* (1988), smoothed out the rougher edges of their early independent records, leading to several minor hit singles. Released in 1990, *Native Place* captured the band in a transitional phase, as they were incorporating dance elements into their sound. *—Stephen Thomas Erlewine*

Reunion Wilderness / 1987 / Virgin ✦✦✦

● **Recurrence** / 1988 / Virgin ✦✦✦✦

Native Place / 1990 / Virgin ✦✦✦

Rain Parade

Group, Alternative Pop/Rock, Psychedelic, Power Pop/Anglo-Pop
Formed in Los Angeles in the early '80s, Rain Parade were one of the major bands of the psychedelic revival of the mid-'80s, a movement that was called the "paisley underground" by some critics. Initially led by David Roback (vocals, guitar, percussion), the group also featured his brother Steve (vocals, bass), Matthew Piucci (vocals, guitar, sitar), Eddie Kalwa (drums), and Will Glenn (keyboards, violin). Rain Parade's self-released debut single, "What She's Done to Your Mind," led to a contract with Enigma Records. Released in 1983, their first album *Emergency 3rd Rail Power Trip* received positive reviews and became a hit on college radio; the record gained enough attention to earn them a contract with Island Records. Before they could make the transition to Island, Dave Roback left the band to form Opal; he was replaced by John Thoman. Around the same time, drummer Mark Marcum replaced Eddie Kalwa; this new lineup recorded the 1985 live album, *Beyond the Sunset*. The following year, Rain Parade released their major label debut, *Crashing Dream*, yet it failed to recapture the audience *Emergency 3rd Rail Power Trip* had gained them. Two years later, the band released their last album, *Explosions in the Glass Palace*. *—Stephen Thomas Erlewine*

○ **Emergency 3rd Rail Power Trip** / 1983 / Restless ✦✦✦✦
A popular band among the West Coast Paisley Underground movement during the early '80s, they drew inspiration from '60s California 12-string pop, as well as from the Velvet Underground. Pleasantly trippy, in a sleepwalking kind of way, the highlights are: "1 Hr 1/2 Ago," "What She's Done to Your Mind?," and "This Can't Be Today." *—Rick Clark*

Explosions in the Glass Palace / 1984 / Enigma ✦✦✦

Beyond the Sunset / 1985 / Restless ✦✦✦

● **Crashing Dream** / 1986 / Island ✦✦✦✦

Raincoats

Group, Punk, New Wave
The Raincoats were one of the most experimental bands that immediately followed the initial burst of punk rock in the late '70s. With their minimalistic approach to guitar-driven folk-rock, the band developed a distinctive, jagged sound, punctuated by a shrill violin. The Raincoats were also one of the first all-female post-punk bands, which wasn't common in the late '70s and early '80s. When they were recording, the band gained a small cult following in their native England and an even smaller audience in America;

they broke up in 1984. Nearly ten years later, the band became a hip name in alternative rock, thanks to Kurt Cobain's mention of the group in the liner notes to a Nirvana album. Geffen picked up the rights to the Raincoats' catalog and reissued their albums in late 1993 and 1994. The band reunited and toured with Nirvana in the U.K. before heading out on their own tour of the U.S. in 1994. —*Stephen Thomas Erlewine*

● **The Raincoats** / 1979 / Geffen ✦✦✦✦
Picking the "best" Raincoats is more an intellectual exercise than it is a work of thoughtful criticism. So, to make it easy for the benighted, all three studio releases are absolutely essential. Their live cassette is wonderful, but I wouldn't start there. Better yet, start with their debut, a soaring, daring, avant-garde-influenced folk-punk record. Don't let the words "avant-garde" scare you off; the Raincoats are not harsh or unapproachable. In fact, this music, even at its most dissonant, is stunning and captivating. There's a great cover of the Kinks' "Lola" that's so skewed and obtuse, I'm sure Ray Davies never dreamed it could sound this way. Reissued by Geffen on CD with extra tracks in 1995. —*John Dougan*

○ **Odyshape** / 1981 / Geffen ✦✦✦✦
It was the late Kurt Cobain (with some help from labelmates Sonic Youth) that initiated Geffen's reissue of the Raincoats' catalog. And listening to *Odyshape*, it's easy to see why Cobain loved them so. There's an emotional directness about these songs that hooks you from the start. Mostly you hear about emotions and situations, sometimes indirectly, almost as if you are eavesdropping on a conversation. Then it hits you: it's almost like you're talking to old friends. That's the way the Raincoats' music worked: it's deceptively simple, but extremely complicated. Also, as on this record, it makes demands of the listener. But songs like "Red Shoes" and "Dancing in My Head" say this far more eloquently. Reissued by Geffen with extra tracks in 1995. —*John Dougan*

○ **Kitchen Tapes** / 1983 / ROIR ✦✦✦✦
Rough, loose-limbed, warm, exciting and everything you'd expect from the Raincoats onstage. Bolstered by the heavy percussion of Richard Dudanski and Derek Godard, this recording pulsates, while the band dances around the beat tossing in shards of guitar, vocals and violin. Excellent liner essay by Greil Marcus. —*John Dougan*

○ **Moving** / 1984 / Geffen ✦✦✦✦
What a wonderful cacophony of sounds! The Raincoats' last record (until their reunion EP of 1995) is a triumph of excitement and intensity equaling that of their previous studio work. Some of these songs are from the live tape and are in sharper (and I'd say better) form here. Yet another important record by one of the most important bands of the post-punk era. Reissued by Geffen with extra tracks in 1995. —*John Dougan*

Bonnie Raitt

b. Nov. 8, 1949, Cleveland, OH
Blues Rock, Singer-Songwriter, Pop/Rock
In 1989, Bonnie Raitt, singer/songwriter and guitarist, finally hit major success after almost twenty years of performing with the aptly titled *Nick of Time* (#1). The album came at a time when the market was ready for something earthy, and fortunately Capitol Records, who had just signed Raitt, had the foresight to encourage her love of sexy folk-blues, R&B, and intelligently thoughtful sentiment. Raitt, who has always championed quality songwriters like John Prine, John Hiatt, Terry Adams, Jackson Browne, and Jerry Williams, is quite an accomplished songwriter herself, penning songs for *Nick of Time* that equal anything she has covered.

Before Raitt's late-'80s success, she had enjoyed a few moderate successes and a respectable cult following. By 1986, with the release of *Nine Lives*, Raitt's career seemed to be stagnating, and Warner Bros. (her label of fifteen years) cut her loose.

Raitt's soulful guitar playing, particularly slide, has sadly been overlooked. Lesser male players have graced the covers of major music magazines. Hopefully, her time of recognition in that area will arrive as well. —*Rick Clark*

Bonnie Raitt / 1971 / Warner Brothers ✦✦✦
By the time Raitt recorded this impressive self-titled debut, she had developed quite a set of blues chops playing with artists like Mississippi Fred McDowell, Howlin' Wolf, and other blues greats. In fact, she enlisted Chicago-bluesmen Junior Wells and A.C. Reed to aid in the proceedings, which are relaxed and earthy. —*Rick Clark*

● **Give It Up** / Sep. 1972 / Warner Brothers ✦✦✦✦
Raitt's sophomore release is a classic. Of all the albums from her days with Warner, this is the one that put together her folky singer/songwriter sensitivities with her love for country-blues. *Give It Up*, which took thirteen years to go gold, showcased an intelligent song selection, with tracks by Jackson Browne ("Under the Falling Sky"), Eric Kaz ("Love Has No Pride"), and Joel Zoss ("Been Too Long at the Fair"). Her self-penned "Love Me like a Man" highlighted her impressive guitar technique. —*Rick Clark*

○ **Takin' My Time** / 1973 / Warner Brothers ✦✦✦✦
Raitt continued her streak of quality albums with *Takin' My Time*. Like her previous efforts, Raitt drew from the cream of the songwriting crop. Randy Newman's "Guilty" and Jackson Browne's "I Thought I Was a Child" are highlights. —*Rick Clark*

Streetlights / 1974 / Warner Brothers ✦✦✦
This album was undermined by slick production and unnecessary orchestration. At the time, Raitt seemed to be fighting the production by Jerry Ragovoy. Versions of Joni Mitchell's "That Song About the Midway" and Allen Toussaint's "What Is Success?" are the main highlights of the album. —*Rick Clark*

Homeplate / 1975 / Warner Brothers ✦✦✦
On this return to form, Raitt shines with some great songs, particularly "Good Enough," "Your Sweet and Shiny Eyes," and "Run like a Thief." —*Rick Clark*

Sweet Forgiveness / Apr. 1977 / Warner Brothers ✦✦
One of Raitt's lesser efforts, it includes her version of Del Shannon's "Runaway" (number 57), a minor hit despite being pretty lifeless-sounding. Even though the production isn't quite as slick as *Streetlights*, the relatively weak selection of material is this album's failing. —*Rick Clark*

The Glow / 1979 / Warner Brothers ✦✦✦
With the success of "Runaway," Warner felt it was time to take Raitt all the way by pairing her up with hit-producer Peter Asher (Linda Ronstadt, James Taylor). Gone is the natural earthiness Raitt possessed on her first albums. In its place was an airbrushed slickness—from the cover photo all the way down to the grooves. A rendition of Isaac Hayes and David Porter's "Your Good Thing" and an original, "Standing by the Same Old Love" are among *The Glow's* few highlights. The single from this album was a Robert Palmer song, "You're Gonna Get What's Coming" (number 73). —*Rick Clark*

○ **Green Light** / 1982 / Warner Brothers ✦✦✦✦
Raitt dumps the slick stuff and goes for the grit with this energetic set, featuring her band, which included keyboardist Ian MacLagan, whose credits included the Stones and Faces. Raitt's sensitive electric slide-guitar work was finally out front in the mix. It's one of her very best albums. Raitt does spirited versions of NRBQ's "Green Light" and "Me and the Boys." Other standouts include the wreckless rockers "Willya Wontcha" and "I Can't Help Myself." "River of Tears" is a powerful track that Raitt has dedicated to the memory of Little Feat's Lowell George in shows over the years. —*Rick Clark*

Nine Lives / 1986 / Warner Brothers ✦✦✦
Bonnie Raitt's ninth and final album for Warner Bros. Records was a star-crossed affair that began in 1983 in a session with producer Rob Fraboni, which was a typical Raitt mixture of different genres and songwriters, from Jerry Williams ("Excited") and Eric Kaz ("Angel") to reggae star Toots Hibbert ("True Love Is Hard To Find") in a style similar to her 1982 LP *Green Light*. This record seems to have been rejected by Warner, but three years later Raitt returned to the studio with Bill Payne (Little Feat) and George Massenburgh and cut a group of commercial-sounding songs by the likes of Bryan Adams and Tom Snow. *Nine Lives* splits the difference between the two sessions, with four tracks rescued from '83, and five added from '86, plus the theme from a forgotten Farrah Fawcett movie ("Stand Up To The Night" from *Extremities*). The result is predictably scattered and strained, and it was Raitt's lowest-charting album since her debut. Not surprisingly, it was also the last straw in her relationship with Warner. —*William Ruhlmann*

● **Nick of Time** / Mar. 1989 / Capitol ✦✦✦✦
Few comebacks have been as celebrated as Raitt's multi-platinum hit *Nick of Time*, an album that included some of her strongest performances as a musician and singer. The determined "I Will Not Be Denied" seemed to say it all. Her poignant self-penned title

cut revealed Raitt as a mature songwriter, on the level of the best writers whose work she had covered. She dug deep with some solid roadhouse R&B in "Love Letter," "Road's My Middle Name," and "Real Man." Her playful version of John Hiatt's "Thing Called Love" was another highlight. All in all, this is a very seamless album. Highly recommended. —*Rick Clark*

○ **The Bonnie Raitt Collection** / 1990 / Warner Brothers ✦✦✦✦
A good (not great) sampler of Raitt's years at Warner, it's also a good starting place. —*Rick Clark*

○ **Luck of the Draw** / Jun. 1991 / Capitol ✦✦✦✦
This proves that middle-aged rockers don't have to shrivel up and die. It also hints that middle-aged problems make for better rock & roll than the preoccupations of angst-ridden collegiates. —*John Floyd*

○ **Longing in Their Hearts** / Mar. 14, 1994 / Capitol ✦✦✦✦
On the followup to the followup (and another million-selling #1 hit), Bonnie Raitt contributes more than her usual share of original songs, writing four songs herself and setting a lyric of her husband's to music for a fifth. Elsewhere, she draws on such strong writers as Richard Thompson and Paul Brady, all for a collection devoted to devotion. Song after song expresses passion, usually with happy results—this is not the album of a woman with the blues. Even when she's dressing down a parent in her own "Circle Dance," Raitt offers forgiveness and understanding. There, and in other songs, the object of her emotion rarely seems to be perfect, but she takes that in and loves him, anyway. Co-producer Don Was provides a detailed production in which single elements—an accordion, a harmony vocal by Levon Helm or David Crosby—effectively color arrangements and complement Raitt's always soulful singing. —*William Ruhlmann*

The Ramones
Group, Punk
With a crisp, militaristic shout of "1-2-3-4" introducing a sonic barrage the likes of which had never been heard, the Ramones declared that rock & roll had become fatuous and ostentatious, embarrassingly prissy, and way too serious. They cranked up the volume, took out the stuffing, and let it be known that henceforth endless solos, pseudo-poetry, and concept albums were being relegated to the dustbin, to be mocked and scorned as digressions.

Perhaps all this quartet from Queens, NY, was really doing was reminding those who had strayed that simple is often best, that the first rockers had the right idea (just get a guitar and make some noise with it), that one should not have to study in a conservatory to play rock. The Ramones stripped it back to the basics, a few chords and some d-u-m-b words, and before they knew it they'd been congratulated—and blamed—for inventing something called punk-rock.

They kept it up for nearly two decades, staying true to their original vision. Upon the release of their 1995 album *Adios Amigos,* they announced that they were breaking up. Maybe they weren't able to rid the world of the scholarly approach to rock after all, but they sure "shook it up good." —*Jeff Tamarkin*

○ **Ramones** / 1976 / Sire ✦✦✦✦
Punk rock begins here. The cartoon kings of Queens at their most primitive and threatening. Rock's mainstream didn't know what hit it. —*Jeff Tamarkin*

○ **The Ramones Leave Home** / 1977 / Sire ✦✦✦✦
The disappointing second album was still hipper than, well, Peter Frampton or something. —*Jeff Tamarkin*

○ **Rocket to Russia** / 1977 / Sire ✦✦✦✦
The epitome of "stoopidity"—the Ramones at their peak. Includes "Rockaway Beach," "Teenage Lobotomy," and other fine examples of Ramonedom. —*Jeff Tamarkin*

○ **Road to Ruin** / 1978 / Sire ✦✦✦✦
Power ballads, even a (gasp!) "country" tune, but also "I Wanna Be Sedated." In other words, the Ramones get versatile but remain on target. —*Jeff Tamarkin*

It's Alive / 1979 / Sire ✦✦✦
A double-album live set that relies heavily on the Ramones first three albums, *It's Alive* captures the whiplash frenzy of the group at their peak. —*Stephen Thomas Erlewine*

End of the Century / 1980 / Sire ✦✦✦
The Ramones as produced by Phil Spector. Not a disaster but not all it should've been. —*Jeff Tamarkin*

Pleasant Dreams / 1981 / Sire ✦✦✦
The group reportedly wasn't happy with this Graham Gouldman-produced album, but it holds up well—one of their more solid '80s releases. —*Jeff Tamarkin*

Subterranean Jungle / 1983 / Sire ✦✦✦
On *Subterranean Jungle* the Ramones returned to their basic formula after the heavyhanded pop experiments of *End of the Century* and the heavy *Pleasant Dreams.* While they've slowed the tempo down slightly, the record remains an infectious slice of powerful rock & roll. —*Stephen Thomas Erlewine*

○ **Too Tough to Die** / 1984 / Sire ✦✦✦✦
With the Ramones' original drummer Tommy Erdelyi producing, the group returns to simple, scathing punk rock on *Too Tough to Die.* The group takes the big guitar riffs of *Subterranean Jungle,* and makes them shorter and heavier. The Ramones rhythms are back up to jackhammer speed and the songs are down to short, terse statements. The results read like a reaction to hardcore punk, but the Ramones are more melodic than any hardcore band, as well as smarter than most. Apart from the occasional foray into pop, such as the surprisingly effective Dave Stewart-produced "Howling at the Moon," the album is a sterling set of lethal punk, the best the Ramones had made since the end of the '70s. It was also the last great record they would ever make. —*Stephen Thomas Erlewine*

Animal Boy / 1986 / Sire ✦✦✦
The Ramones get d-u-m-b again and score with a back-to-basics roaring set. —*Jeff Tamarkin*

Halfway to Sanity / 1987 / Sire ✦✦
Halfway to heavy metal anonymity. —*Jeff Tamarkin*

○ **Ramones Mania** / 1989 / Sire ✦✦✦✦
The best of the Ramones, or, how to pack 30 songs onto one CD—not all of their "hits" but a crash course in stripped-down genius. —*Jeff Tamarkin*

Brain Drain / 1989 / Sire ✦✦
It's the end, the end of the '80s, and the Ramones have seemingly run out of new ideas. —*Jeff Tamarkin*

★ **All the Stuff & More, Vol. 1** / 1990 / Sire ✦✦✦✦✦
The first two albums, *Ramones* and *Leave Home,* condensed onto one CD, plus bonus tracks. —*Jeff Tamarkin*

☆ **All the Stuff & More, Vol. 2** / 1990 / Sire ✦✦✦✦✦
The third and fourth albums, *Rocket to Russia* and *Road to Ruin,* combined the present Ramones at their peak on one CD plus bonus tracks. —*Jeff Tamarkin*

Loco Live / 1991 / Sire ✦✦
Ramones in the '90s, still kickin' ass. Still no guitar solos. Hope they never change. —*Jeff Tamarkin*

Mondo Bizarro / 1992 / Radioactive ✦✦
Although *Mondo Bizarro* is a serious attempt to revamp the Ramones, it doesn't work. Fond memories of the hard, fast punk band of the 1970s taint dull power ballads like "Poison Heart" and the by-the-book rock & roll of the rest of the album. —*Stephen Thomas Erlewine*

Acid Eaters / 1994 / Radioactive ✦✦
Tearing through a bunch of psychedelic and garage-rock classics from the 1960s, the Ramones regain much of the fun and abandon of earlier records, making *Acid Eaters* easily their best record in a decade; the guest appearances of Pete Townshend ("Substitute") and ex-porn star Traci Lords ("Somebody to Love") help make the record a blast. —*Stephen Thomas Erlewine*

Adios Amigos / 1995 / Radioactive ✦✦✦
The Ramones announced before the release of *Adios Amigos* that the record would likely be their last—unless it sold in massive quantities, that is. While it's hardly their best effort, *Adios Amigos* is an admirable way to bow out. The Ramones haven't progressed much since the mid-'80s, yet they have recaptured a bit of the inspiration that fueled their last great album, *Too Tough to Die.* Even with the extra kick of energy, there are moments on the album that veer too close to self-parody—even the grungy stomp through Tom Waits' "I Don't Wanna Grow Up," one of the record's best moments, seems forced. Still, the weakest moments of the record outshine the best songs on the stiff and over-produced *Brain Drian* and *Mondo Bizarro.* They might not have been on the top of their game, yet the Ramones knew that a record like *Adios Amigos* was the right way to call it a day—it rocks and it rolls, and it's not an embarrassment. —*Stephen Thomas Erlewine*

Willis Alan Ramsey

Singer-Songwriter
Few artists have sustained a devout cult following from only one album as Willis Alan Ramsey has. In a way, it's understandable. Ramsey's 1972 self-titled debut, on Denny Cordell's Shelter label, contained some real gems: "Satin Sheets," "Ballad of Spider John," "Painted Lady," and "Muskrat Love," a song that became a huge hit for Captain & Tennille. — *Rick Clark*

○ **Willis Alan Ramsey** / 1972 / DCC ✦✦✦✦
One of the great (and sadly overlooked) albums of the '70s, Willis Alan Ramsey's self-titled debut had great impact among Austin's progressive country-folk songwriters. Although best known as the writer of "Muskrat Love," which Captain & Tennille took to the Top Ten, Ramsey's muse was rooted much deeper in American lore and folk music. Influences from Robert Johnson to Jimmie Rodgers to Woody Guthrie can be felt if not actually heard on these eleven highly original tracks. Unfortunately, Ramsey, a unique talent with a clear and idiosyncratic artistic vision, hasn't been heard from since. — *Tom Graves*

Rancid

Group, Punk
Rancid is a punk revivalist band that came to national attention in late 1994 with their second album, *Let's Go*. Comprised of Tim Armstrong, Lars Frederiksen, Matt Freeman, and Brett Reed, Rancid reworks the sound of 1977, sounding like an updated version of the Clash's roar. — *Stephen Thomas Erlewine*

● **Let's Go** / 1994 / Epitaph ✦✦✦✦
Whatever Rancid lacks in innovation, it makes up with sheer energy. The group rushes through *Let's Go* with an invigorating wrecklessness, sounding like a less-serious, party-ready version of Clash. It's almost impossible to understand what vocalist Tim Armstrong sings at any given moment, yet their is no great meaning in what Rancid says—the message is in the buzzing guitars and speeding rhythms. It doesn't hurt that the band can throw out the occasional memorable hook or melody, like the single "Salvation," as well. — *Stephen Thomas Erlewine*

Rank & File

Group, Rock & Roll, Alternative Pop/Rock
Formed by brothers Chip and Tony Kinman after they split up their hardcore punk band the Dils (who recorded the great L.A. punk single "Class War"), Rank and File were at times a dazzling roots-rock post-punk band that stumbled early in its career, only to flame out much too quickly and finally collapsing with an embarrassing thud. Their debut record, *Sundown*, was a gem of tuneful, Byrdsian pop, with a healthy dollop of Gram Parsons and Merle Haggard to boot. The Kinmans' singing was distinctive; they weren't traditional harmony singers a la the Everly Brothers, but rather sang synchronized upper and lower octaves. The songwriting was wry, heartfelt and cliche-free; the band (which at the time featured the guitar of the immensely talented Alejandro Escovedo) rocked with gusto, but never bombastically, preferring nuance and subtlety over volume and simplicity. In fact, the Kinmans were so into cowpunk and so far from their hardcore punk beginnings that they even landed a spot on PBS's revered country music showcase *Austin City Limits*. The sophomore record *Long Gone Dead* was an excellent follow-up, but the self-titled third album (it's never a good sign when a band releases a self-titled record three records into a career), recorded three years after *Long Gone Dead*, was absolutely awful; the songs went nowhere, and the singing and playing, which had previously been so precise and artful, was now buried under a thicket of cliched hard-rock-isms. After listening to Side One, you knew these guys were done for. Sad, really. In a stunning repudiation of Rank and File's roots-rock style, the Kinmans' next project was the execrable Blackbird, an ill-conceived try at synth-pop, that went a long way toward making them laughingstocks. Former guitarist Alejandro Escovedo formed the excellent (but also short-lived) True Believers with his brother Javier, and since their breakup has recorded a number of interesting solo records. — *John Dougan*

● **Sundown** / 1982 / Rough Trade ✦✦✦✦
This was the era of post-punk Los Angeles, and bands like X, the Blasters and Rank and File made great records. *Sundown* is Rank and File's great contribution to this scene, and despite the bizarre and egregious career moves of the Kinman brothers over the past decade-plus, *Sundown* is as strong, tuneful and compelling as the day it was released. With their voices locking together imperfectly and Alejandro Escovedo's guitar providing sharp counterpoint, this is a great chunk of cowpunk that would please even the most doctrinaire country traditionalist, as well as beat the hell out of nearly all of the new generation of country hacks. Not bad for a couple of punks from L.A. — *John Dougan*

○ **Long Gone Dead** / 1984 / London ✦✦✦✦

Rank & File / 1987 / Rhino ✦✦✦

Rare Earth

Group, Soul, Pop/Rock
Rare Earth started life as the Sunliners, a premier bar band of the Detroit circuit. Rumored to know over 5000 songs, their penchant for jamming "psychedelic" versions of Motown tunes caught the ear of session-man Dennis Coffey, who got them signed to the label's Rare Earth subsidiary in 1969. The group's name changed at the same time. Their formula worked like a charm throughout the '70s, with their best sides produced by Motown staffer Norman Whitfield. Massive personnel changes led to an eventual breakup. Drummer and lead vocalist Pete Rivera is still active on oldies shows, while an ersatz version of the group with two original members mines a similar circuit. — *Cub Koda*

● **Greatest Hits & Rare Classics** / 1991 / Motown ✦✦✦✦
This CD includes all singles releases by Motown's premier rock group. — *Rick A. Bueche*

The Rascals

Group, Soul, Pop/Rock
The Young Rascals from New York (formed 1965) successfully integrated soul and rock into a sound that earned the band considerable success on pop and R&B radio formats with songs like "Good Lovin'" (#1—a remake of the Olympics' 1965 R&B hit), "Groovin'" (#1), "People Got to Be Free" (#1), "A Beautiful Morning" (#3), and "How Can I Be Sure" (#4), as well as other hits, many of which were penned by keyboardist Felix Cavaliere (b. Nov 29, 1944) and vocalist and percussionist Eddie Brigati (b. Dec). The Young Rascals possessed an explosive rhythm section with jazz drummer Dino Danelli (b. Jul 23, 1945) and guitarist Gene Cornish (b. May 14, 1945). "Young" was dropped from the band name, as they wanted to portray a more serious image. As the Rascals progressively immersed themselves in indulgent album projects like *Freedom Suite* (#17), their audience shrank. The band called it quits in 1972, after dismal commercial success with their last three albums, *Search and Nearness* (#198), *Peaceful World* (#120), and *The Island of Real* (#180), which were actually pretty good. — *Rick Clark*

Young Rascals / 1966 / Warner Brothers ✦✦✦
A vital, driving debut album, with a nice, grungy garage-band feel to it. The old mono LPs of this album are a real treat. — *Bruce Eder*

○ **Groovin'** / 1967 / Warner Brothers ✦✦✦✦
A smooth, soulful collection. Carefully and subtly crafted production wrapped around superb songs. — *Bruce Eder*

Once upon a Dream / 1968 / Rhino ✦✦✦
In 1967 they shortened their name to just the Rascals and began to put more social consciousness into their songs. Includes "It's Wonderful." — *Ron Wynn*

○ **Time Peace: The Rascals' Greatest Hits** / 1968 / Atlantic ✦✦✦✦
Arguably the greatest greatest-hits album of the '60s. A White-soul classic. — *Bruce Eder*

○ **The Ultimate Rascals** / 1986 / Warner Brothers ✦✦✦✦
A somewhat-impressive collection marred only by substandard sound. — *Bruce Eder*

○ **Anthology (1965-1972)** / 1992 / Rhino ✦✦✦✦
Anthology is the most comprehensive overview of one of the greatest bands of the '60s. All 18 of their hits as well as important album cuts (including tracks from their Columbia releases) are here on this double-disc, 44-track set. — *Rick Clark*

● **Very Best of the Rascals** / 1994 / Rhino/Atlantic ✦✦✦✦
Although Rhino issued a deluxe two-CD set covering the Rascals a few years ago, this single disc set contains enough essential songs for you to get the point. The Rascals, along with the Righteous Brothers, defined blue-eyed soul singing, making records that were as churchy, earthy, and convincing as anything that came out of the South or Motown in the '60s, backed by tight, anthemic

arrangements and excellent combo playing. The 16 cuts include their first hit, "I Ain't Gonna Eat Out My Heart Anymore," and continues on into their flirtation with psychedelia in 1970. The only quibble is their failure to include "Look Around," a socio-political cut from the *Freedom Suite* album that's just a cut below "People Got To Be Free" or "A Ray of Hope." —*Ron Wynn*

The Raspberries

Group, Power Pop/Anglo-Pop
Led by Eric Carmen (b. Aug 11, 1949), the Raspberries (from Cleveland, OH) brought out their exuberant Beatles-style Anglo-pop and matching outfits at a time in the early '70s when art-rock, concept albums, and serious "statements" were being heralded. It was a time when pop for pop's sake was decidedly uncool. Capitol Records accentuated the band's teenybopper appeal by marketing their self-titled debut with a raspberry-scented scratch-and-sniff sticker on the cover. The band's dynamic first single, "Go All the Way" (#5), was a huge hit.

Carmen's tenor had the range of Paul McCartney, and he had the goods to write a handful of truly great guitar pop hits. Lead guitarist Wally Bryson, who filled out their sound with a Beatles-meets-Free crunch, also contributed some solid material. Unfortunately, the public increasingly cooled off on the band, unwilling to buy into harder-rocking single releases like "I'm a Rocker," "Ecstasy," and the truly amazing "Tonight."

Drummer Jim Bonfanti (b. Dec 17, 1948) and bassist Dave Smalley (b. Jul 10, 1949) left in 1973, frustrated over the group's image problems. They were replaced by drummer Michael McBride and bassist Scott McCarl.

The 1973 follow-up effort, *Starting Over*, documented the dreams and frustrations of wanting to be pop stars. The track "Overnight Sensation (Hit Record)" went to #18, but the album ended up being one of the great lost pop albums of the '70s. The group disbanded shortly afterward, and Eric Carmen went on to pursue a sporadically successful solo career that resembled Barry Manilow more than rock & roll. —*Rick Clark*

Raspberries / 1972 / Capitol ♦♦♦
An excellent first effort, highlighted by "Go All the Way," "Don't Want to Say Goodbye," "I Saw the Light," and "Come Around and See Me." At the time, audiences thought they heard echoes of Paul McCartney's work with the Beatles, and they weren't far wrong, in terms of what the group was capable of. —*Bruce Eder*

○ **Fresh** / Dec. 1972 / Capitol ♦♦♦♦
The second best of the four albums issued by the band, with "I Wanna Be with You," "If You Change Your Mind," and "Drivin' Around" as highlights amid some overall incredibly superb rock craftsmanship. The band's sound is overall more confident, and more powerful. —*Bruce Eder*

Side Three / 1973 / Capitol ♦♦♦
The group's most accomplished album, almost Beatles-like in its richness, romanticism, cleverness, and even its packaging, which is one of the few "novelty" jacket designs (it's shaped like a basket of . . . you guessed it) that works. The band was at its peak and it showed in "Ecstasy" and "Last Dance," among numerous others. —*Bruce Eder*

Starting Over / 1974 / Capitol ♦♦♦
The band's last album is something of a disappointment, much louder and punchier than their previous work but lacking the elegance that characterized their overall sound. None of the songs is bad, and some are quite good, but they sound like they're going through the motions at this point, and they did break up soon after. —*Bruce Eder*

○ **Raspberries' Best** / 1975 / Capitol ♦♦♦♦
A fair best-of, and the original packaging had some of the most complete sleeve notes of any album of its era, telling everything one needed to know about the band and its history. —*Bruce Eder*

★ **Capitol Collectors Series** / 1991 / Capitol ♦♦♦♦♦
Twenty songs covering an entire cross-section of the group's history, with more superb notes, and this time superb sound as well. Short of having the second and third albums (only out on CD in Japan), the best the group has to offer. —*Bruce Eder*

Ratt

Group, Hard Rock, Heavy Metal
Ratt's brash, melodic heavy metal made the Los Angeles quintet one of the most popular rock acts of the mid-'80s. The group had

its origins in the '70s group Mickey Ratt, which had evolved into Ratt by 1983; at that time the band featured vocalist Stephen Pearcy, guitarist Robbin Crosby, guitarist Warren D. Martini, bassist Juan Groucier, and drummer Bobby Blotzer. The band released their self-titled first album independently in 1983, which led to a major label contract with Atlantic Records. Their first album under this deal, 1984's *Out of the Cellar*, was a major success, reaching the American Top Ten and selling over three million copies. "Round and Round," the first single drawn from the album, hit number 12, proving the band had pop crossover potential. While their second album, 1985's *Invasion of Your Privacy*, didn't match the multi-platinum figures of *Out of the Cellar*, it also reached the Top Ten and sold over a million copies. By that time, the band could still sell concerts across the country and were a staple on MTV and AOR radio. Both *Dancin' Undercover* (1986) and *Reach for the Sky* (1988) continued the band's platinum streak and their audience had only slipped slightly by the time of their final album, 1990's *Detonator*. In 1992, Pearcy left Ratt to form his own band; his departure effectively put an end to the group. —*Stephen Thomas Erlewine*

Ratt / 1983 / Time Coast Communications ♦♦♦

○ **Out of the Cellar** / 1984 / Atlantic ♦♦♦♦
The first album by Los Angeles's Ratt brought them instant success and a number of memorable hits. The cover featured actress Tawny Kitaen. —*John Book*

○ **Invasion of Your Privacy** / 1985 / Atlantic ♦♦♦♦
They may have been influenced by Aerosmith but at this stage Ratt were recording songs that were powerful as well as masterful hits. This album also showed they were a lot more than a hit-making machine. —*John Book*

Dancin' Undercover / 1986 / Atlantic ♦♦♦
This is the band's last album before falling into a slump when their imitators got more attention. —*John Book*

Reach for the Sky / 1988 / Atlantic ♦♦

Detonator / 1990 / Atlantic ♦♦

● **Ratt & Roll 8191** / 1991 / Atlantic ♦♦♦♦
A greatest-hits package, it has the best of Ratt's impressive ten-year career. —*John Book*

Lou Rawls

b. Dec. 11, 1935
Soul, R&B, Pop/Rock
When Chicago-born Lou Rawls croons a soulful love song, his deep-hued pipes rumble with simmering passion. Rawls did the usual gospel apprenticeship before breaking out on a landmark jazz album with pianist Les McCann's trio for Capitol that launched his secular career. But it took Rawls a while to establish himself as a soul artist—perhaps he was perceived as a little too sophisticated and jazzy (although his uncredited responses on Sam Cooke's "Bring It on Home to Me" certainly proved he could wail). "Love Is a Hurtin' Thing" instantly changed that notion when it topped the R&B charts in 1966, and the unyielding "Dead End Street" and "Your Good Thing (Is About to End)" perpetuated his success.

After memorably delivering Bobby Hebb's powerful "A Natural Man" in 1971, Rawls joined forces with Philadelphia producers Kenny Gamble and Leon Huff in 1976, emerging with the silky "You'll Never Find Another Love like Mine," another gigantic R&B and pop smash tailor-made for nattily sweeping across the classiest disco dance floors. The disco era's long gone now, but Rawls maintains elegantly. He's still as cool as cool can be. —*Bill Dahl*

○ **Lou Rawls Sings/Les McCann Plays Stormy Monday** / 1962 / Capitol ♦♦♦♦
A highly popular soul-jazz duo in the '60s, this reissue spotlights the Lou Rawls/Les McCann team in peak form. Rawls sang gritty blues and R&B, while McCann added funky keyboard solos and accompaniment. The album was an early indicator that McCann would be a steady, consistent seller working the same territory as Ramsey Lewis. This 1990 reissue included three bonus cuts. —*Ron Wynn*

Black and Blue / 1963 / Capitol ♦♦♦
Super blues and jazzy soul by Lou Rawls from an early period on Capitol. He hadn't yet found the hit formula, but was cutting some superb singles. His voice had a resonance and strength developed for years on the gospel trail, and also during his work backing

Sam Cooke. Even though he didn't get any hits, it's well worth the cost if you can find this album. —*Ron Wynn*

Live! / 1965 / Capitol ◆◆◆
Riding high on the success of his mid-'70s soul and R&B dates, Philadelphia International issued this live recording featuring Rawls doing the straight blues, jazzy ballads and pre-rock standards he normally reserved for clubs and concerts. There were none of the big radio hits here; instead, Rawls covered such songs as "Six Cold Feet of Ground," "Blues for A Four String Guitar" and "Everyday I Have the Blues." It also didn't stay on the charts very long, and Gamble and Huff got back to commercial basics the next time out. Still, it's one of his finest and most representative albums. —*Ron Wynn*

○ **Soulin'** / 1966 / Capitol ◆◆◆◆
Lou Rawls began his roll onto the R&B and pop charts with this '67 work. He was now doing soul material, songs where his gospel background and instincts took over, and he simply wailed, soared, and shouted, rather than interpreting or working with blues progressions. He scored a huge hit with "Love Is A Hurtin' Thing" and had finally found a successful formula. —*Ron Wynn*

Too Much / May 1967 / Capitol ◆◆◆
Lou Rawls was in the midst of a hot streak at Capitol, scoring smash singles and winning Grammy awards. This was one of three albums he released in 1967, all of which made the pop Top 40 albums chart. It was superbly produced and arranged by David Axelrod, with Rawls being bluesy, soulful, anguished, triumphant, and resigned. He displayed both a variety of moods and a vocal mastery at its peak. Unfortunately, this has also been deleted. —*Ron Wynn*

That's Lou / Aug. 1967 / Capitol ◆◆◆
Rawls topped his success of the previous year with an even bigger hit album. He won a Grammy for "Dead End Street" and got good notices for a followup cut about the joys and pains of being a celebrity. David Axelrod gave Rawls the production and arranging support he needed, keeping everything squarely in the background and letting Rawls' voice stay at the center and be the focus of the song. —*Ron Wynn*

You're Good for Me / 1968 / Capitol ◆◆◆
Things were beginning to cool a bit for Lou Rawls following the period when he topped the R&B charts, got great crossover exposure, and won a Grammy. This album didn't have the impact or sustained appeal of past works, although it was just as well produced and arranged, and Rawls sang with his usual vigor and impact. The songs were a bit below the normal standard, but it was otherwise a fine album—just not quite as potent. —*Ron Wynn*

Feelin' Good / 1968 / Capitol ◆◆◆
Lou Rawls had enjoyed three smash albums in a row, so it wasn't too surprising when this release failed to equal their success. David Axelrod couldn't work his production magic this time, and there weren't any big hits or tracks Rawls could turn into successes, even though he sang with his normal drive and style. It was inevitable for an artist who was never a trendy vocalist and always depended on first-rate songs. —*Ron Wynn*

○ **All Things in Time** / Oct. 1976 / Philadelphia International ◆◆◆◆
Fine Philly-sound disco and warm romantic ballads. —*Bil Carpenter*

○ **Unmistakably Lou** / 1977 / Philadelphia International ◆◆◆◆
Lou Rawls was riding another hot streak in the late '70s, his career rejuvenated by a string of fine albums and singles on the Philly International label. This was the followup to his huge hit LP *All Things In Time*. He only had one R&B chart song from the album, but in ways, his vocals are superior to those on the prior album. Where the Gamble/Huff production team's efforts on the preceding project rivaled Rawls' vocals, he took the spotlight this time, while their arrangements and productions were more on the subdued side. —*Ron Wynn*

○ **When You Hear Lou, You've Heard It All** / 1977 / Philadelphia International ◆◆◆◆
A smooth, often delightful album that kept Lou Rawls squarely in the love/romantic/mellow circle that he'd been scoring in throughout the late '70s. Gamble and Huff were really trimming the productions and keeping things laid-back and casual, while Rawls' emphatic, smoky vocals carried the day. They weren't getting huge pop hits, but were on the R&B charts steadily, and the album just missed the pop Top 40. —*Ron Wynn*

Let Me Be Good to You / 1979 / Philadelphia International ◆◆◆
An above-average album that did much better than anyone thought it would at the time. The title track just missed the R&B Top 10, and the album almost made the pop Top 40, although it wasn't on the charts for a long time. Rawls was still singing in a confident, relaxed, earnest, convincing fashion, and the Gamble/Huff production team continued to keep his voice at the forefront and give him minimal arranging support. —*Ron Wynn*

Sit Down & Talk to Me / 1980 / Philadelphia International ◆◆◆
A fine late-'70s Rawls album on Philadelphia International. He had temporarily enjoyed some disco success, but had returned to the blend of jazzy pop, soul, and blues that best showcased his skills. While his voice was now deeper and rougher, his timing, delivery, and overall technique had matured to the point where anything he sang was impressive. Rawls enjoyed a pair of moderate hits from the album and showed that he was still able to turn out quality sessions. —*Ron Wynn*

○ **Stormy Monday** / 1985 / Blue Note ◆◆◆◆
Lou Rawls has enjoyed success in almost every musical arena, from traditional gospel to R&B, soul, pop, and blues. This was his strictest jazz material, as he received excellent backing from the Les McCann trio. McCann, himself a pretty fair singer, played funky keyboards and fronted the trio, while Rawls did shouting stompers and blues, mellow ballads, standards and pre-rock pop, with the bulk of this material being blues and ballads. —*Ron Wynn*

○ **At Last** / 1989 / Blue Note ◆◆◆◆
He's never deserted either blues or jazz, but Lou Rawls hasn't always found a receptive audience for these styles at notoriously conservative major labels. That wasn't the case on this 1989 album, on which Rawls performed straightahead jazz and pre-rock pop or blues, and was backed by an all-star lineup including Ray Charles, Cornell Dupree, Steve Khan, Richard Tee and Dianne Reeves. His voice had an exuberance and fervor that spoke volumes about how happy he was in the setting. —*Ron Wynn*

It's Supposed to Be Fun / 1990 / Blue Note ◆◆◆
When Lou Rawls returned to Blue Note, he was given creative carte blanche to cut the kind of albums he'd made in the 1960s and '70s. This meant a return to recording jazzy standards, blues covers and sophisticated, yet soulful R&B. There were examples of all these styles on this 1990 album, but it lacked either the big name guest stars who participated on *At Last* or the same relaxed and informal air. Rawls still sounded confident and assured, but the production and material weren't as demanding or accomplished. —*Ron Wynn*

● **The Best of Lou Rawls** / Capitol ◆◆◆◆
A nice collection of Rawls' Capitol singles, which include his number one hit "Love Is A Hurtin' Thing" and many other fine chart singles, all produced by David Axelrod. Rawls got in a groove during his Capitol years, singing songs that had a soul feel but a jazz and blues base. In some ways, he's never made better songs than his late-'60s and early-'70s stint at Capitol. —*Ron Wynn*

○ **Lou Rawls and Strings** / Capitol ◆◆◆◆
While the strings are overdone at times, Rawls fits his voice into the situation with verve and flair. He never tried to overpower or work against the support, moderated his voice, and paced each song to ensure that he would hit a vocal peak at the right point. The album still didn't generate much sales response, but it remains one of Rawls' most stunning works on any label. —*Ron Wynn*

James Ray

b. 1941
Soul, R&B
The Washington, DC, native's 1962 hit, "If You Gotta Make a Fool of Somebody," inspired a raft of covers, while one of his lesser-known efforts, "I've Got My Mind Set on You," provided George Harrison with a recent big-seller. Ray's pop-slanted R&B output for Caprice Records, including his less successful followup "Itty Bitty Pieces," was arranged by pianist Hutch Davie. All three of the songs cited above were written by prolific New York tunesmith Rudy Clark. —*Bill Dahl*

● **Golden Classics** / 1976 / Caprice ◆◆◆◆
An overlooked R&B stylist whose best songs were triumphs of form over thin lyrics. —*Ron Wynn*

The Records

Group, Power Pop/Anglo-Pop
A U.K. quartet, active from 1979 to 1982, employing a jangly-guitar, '60s-pop approach. The band was led by songwriter and guitarist Will Birch and also featured John Wicks, Phil Brown, and guitarist Huw Gower. Their first album, *Shades in Bed*, was released in the U.S. as *The Records* and featured the minor hit single "Starry Eyes." Gower left, replaced by American Jude Cole for *Crashes* (1980). Their last album, *Music on Both Sides* (1982), featured a quintet of Birch, Wicks, Brown, Dave Whelan, and Chris Gent. *— William Ruhlmann*

○ **The Records** / 1979 / Virgin ✦✦✦✦
Virtually every song here is a catchy guitar-driven pop song with sweet harmonies, from the single "Starry Eyes" through "Teenarama" and "Another Star." The album includes a bonus record containing the Records' versions of such oldies as the Kinks' "See My Friends" and Spirit's "1984." *— William Ruhlmann*

Crashes / 1980 / Virgin ✦✦✦
The Records' second album is just as tuneful and nearly as catchy as its predessor though none of the songs have the punch of "Starry Eyes." "Girl in the Golden Disc" and "Hearts Will be Broken" are the highlights. Unfortunately, the band's take on the brilliant "Hearts in Her Eyes" (a song written by Will Birch and covered more successfully by the reunited Searchers the previous year) is lackluster and somewhat of a letdown. *— Chris Woodstra*

Music on Both Sides / 1982 / Virgin ✦✦✦
With a tighter, harder-rocking five-man lineup, the Records returned with *Music on Both Sides*. Despite the usual strong material courtesy of the John Wicks/Will Birch partnership, the album failed to make an impact. This would be their last album. *— Chris Woodstra*

● **Smashes Crashes and Near Misses** / 1988 / Virgin ✦✦✦✦
The Records may not have been great innovators but they undeniably made some of the best singles of the era. *Smashes Crashes and Near Misses*, a 20 track collection, is the definitive proof of the band's generally overlooked brilliance. Anyone interested in power-pop should start here. *— Chris Woodstra*

A Sunny Afternoon in Waterloo / 1988 / Waterfront ✦✦
Paying for the Summer of Love / 1990 / Skyclad ✦✦
A collection of demos recorded prior to their first album, *Paying for the Summer of Love* provides an interesting look at the songs in their formative stages but only true fans need to seek this one out. *— Chris Woodstra*

The Red Hot Chili Peppers

Group, Alternative Pop/Rock, Funk
A quartet with varying personnel, anchored by lead singer Anthony Kiedis and bassist Flea (born Michael Balzary), the Red Hot Chili Peppers play a hybrid rock incorporating punk, funk, rap, and metal. Though the mixture was ahead of its time when the group was first organized in the early '80s in Los Angeles, the music industry has since caught up to it, which earns the group the right to call itself the forerunner of an approach now adopted by such acts as Living Colour and Faith No More, and also means the Peppers themselves have finally hit the big time. In 1988, guitarist Hillel Slovak died of an overdose and the band reorganized, with John Frusciante on guitar and Chad Smith on drums. This lineup scored a commercial breakthrough with *Mother's Milk*, which went gold after its release in 1989. They ascended to real star status with the release of *Blood Sugar Sex Magik*, which sold two million copies and included the Top Ten hit "Under the Bridge." In mid-1992, Frusciante left the group and was replaced by Arik Marshall.

Marshall was replaced by Jesse Tobias in 1993. Tobias's tenure with the group was extremely brief; after a couple of months, he was replaced by ex-Jane's Addiction guitarist Dave Navarro. *— William Ruhlmann*

○ **Red Hot Chili Peppers** / 1984 / EMI America ✦✦✦✦
Red Hot Chili Peppers' debut album sketched out their funk-metal hybrid quite effectively, especially on the warped deep groove of "True Men Don't Kill Coyotes." Even though their fusion of heavy guitars and slapping bass was audacious, their first effort didn't quite gel into a cohesive album. *— Stephen Thomas Erlewine*

○ **Freaky Styley** / 1985 / EMI America ✦✦✦✦
Under the guiding hand of George Clinton, the Red Hot Chili Peppers turned in a nastier, funkier album their second time around with *Freaky Styley*. It also didn't hurt that it was the first album the group recorded with Hillel Slovak; he was performing with What Is This at the time the debut was recorded. Even though Slovak and Clinton help make the music more exciting, their contributions didn't necessarily mean that *Freaky Styley* was more coherent than the debut—it just meant that it was more compelling *— Stephen Thomas Erlewine*

The Uplift Mofo Party Plan / 1987 / EMI America ✦✦✦
If the Red Hot Chili Peppers' first two albums were incoherent, *The Uplit Mofo Party Plan* is a downright mess, with the band being torn between their metallic-punk instincts and their funk ambitions. Part of the album works, particularly the fierce "Fight Like A Brave," but most of the record reveals the group's tendency to wallow in shallow sexist chants, culminating in the sophomoric "Party on Your Pussy." *— Stephen Thomas Erlewine*

Abbey Road [EP] / 1988 / EMI America ✦✦
Mother's Milk / 1989 / EMI America ✦✦✦
While *Mother's Milk* is not their most adventurous or best release, it's a good album, which expanded the Red Hot's cult. Mainstream listeners were attracted to the band in large part because of their cover of Stevie Wonder's "Higher Ground," the best song on *Mother's Milk*. Other highlights include "Knock Me Down," "Taste the Pain," "Nobody Weird like Me," and "Sexy Mexican Maid." *— Meredith Erlewine & Stephen Thomas Erlewine*

○ **Blood Sugar Sex Magik** / 1991 / Warner Brothers ✦✦✦✦
It isn't just that the world has finally come around to the Peppers's funk-rock mixture, it's that, with the help of producer Rick Rubin, they've found a focus and that, as musicians, they've reached a sufficient level of competence to execute their ideas. The result is their best album, containing the hit "Under the Bridge." *— William Ruhlmann*

● **What Hits!?** / 1992 / EMI America ✦✦✦✦
A sampling of tracks from the band's ten-year career, it includes the hit "Under the Bridge," plus "Higher Ground" and "Fight like a Brave." *— AMG*

Out in L.A. / 1994 / EMI America ✦✦
A tepid collection of remixes and obscurities, *Out in L.A.* is only of interest to devoted Chili Peppers fans, and even they might have their patience tested by this overly-long compilation. *— Stephen Thomas Erlewine*

Red House Painters

Group, Alternative Pop/Rock
With their slow, atmospheric, weaving alternative folk-rock, Red House Painters have earned considerable critical acclaim and a cult following. Prolific to a fault, the band released their first EP late in 1992, following it with two full-length albums the next year. On each record, leader Mark Kostelich's introspective melancholia is detailed over a spare, moody soundscape that is occasionally interrupted with bursts of distorted guitar. At their best, Red House Painters are absorbing and hypnotic; at their worst, they are long-winded and boring. Since they are still developing their style, it's understandable that they occasionally fall into their own mire; fortunately, they are often more mesmerizing than dull. *— Stephen Thomas Erlewine*

○ **Down Colorful Hill** / 1992 / 4AD ✦✦✦✦
○ **Red House Painters** / May 25, 1993 / 4AD ✦✦✦✦
A slow, stark mood piece, with its folk-pop roots in the somber meditations of Nick Drake, Love's *Forever Changes*, and fellow San Franciscans American Music Club, *Red House Painters* will either mesmerize or act as a cure for insomnia, depending on your mood. *— Stephen Thomas Erlewine*

● **Ocean Beach** / 1995 / 4AD ✦✦✦✦
Red House Painters has always been Mark Kozlik's project, but *Ocean Beach* represents the first record that is almost entirely a solo project. Not that that distinction has made a great change in the music—*Ocean Beach* is a spare, gentle, nearly painfully introspective folk-rock album that draws more from Simon & Garfunkel than Bob Dylan. Kozlik's reigns the droning experimental tendencies of the group's first full-length album yet he is more generous with his melodies and arrangements than the band's second untitled record. While Red House Painters remains very arty

and self-conscious, *Ocean Beach* shows the singer-songwriter breaking out of his shell ever so slightly, bringing more fully developed songs and melodies with him. —*Stephen Thomas Erlewine*

Red House Painters [untitled] / ✦✦✦

Leon Redbone

Folk, Pop

Leon Redbone got his start in Toronto at the start of the '70s, then (as now) performing songs primarily of the teens, twenties, and thirties and accompanying his affectionate crooning baritone (which some found funny, either intentionally or unintentionally) with simple, syncopated guitar-playing. Folk stars such as Maria Muldaur and Bob Dylan spread the word, and Redbone eventually signed to Warner Bros., for whom he recorded three albums (*On the Track* (1976), *Double Time* (1977), and *Champagne Charlie* (1978)) whose sales were increased by his appearances on the TV show "Saturday Night Live." His recordings from 1981 on were infrequent and on small labels, but he made a good living as the voice (on and off screen) in many TV commercials. —*William Ruhlmann*

● **On the Track** / 1976 / Warner Brothers ✦✦✦✦
Debut album contains a typical collection of campy oldies ("Ain't Misbehavin'," "Lulu's Back in Town"), accompanied by a varied cast including folkie Don McLean and jazz stars Milt Hinton and Ralph McDonald. —*William Ruhlmann*

○ **Double Time** / 1977 / Warner Brothers ✦✦✦✦

Takin' My Time / 1977 / Warner Brothers ✦✦✦

From Branch to Branch / 1981 / Atlantic ✦✦✦

○ **Leon Redbone Live** / 1985 / Pair ✦✦✦✦
A live setting is just about ideal for a performer like Redbone, and he does not disappoint on this two-record set, which features "Diddy Wah Diddy," "Champagne Charlie," and other favorites. —*William Ruhlmann*

○ **Red to Blue** / 1985 / August ✦✦✦✦
Redbone's best overall album veers from country to jazz to folk to blues. Backup includes members of Vince Giordano's old-time jazz band, Dr. John, David Bromberg, and the Roches on songs ranging from "Lovesick Blues" to Bob Dylan's "Living the Blues," and with two Redbone originals, as well. —*William Ruhlmann*

Champagne Charlie / Oct. 11, 1988 / Warner Brothers ✦✦

Christmas Island / 1989 / Private Music ✦✦✦
The enigmatic Leon Redbone gives his time-warp treatment to a predictable bunch of Christmas standards. Fans of Redbone's low-key camp style will enjoy this, particularly the duet with Dr. John on "Frosty the Snowman." —*Rick Clark*

Sugar / 1991 / Private Music ✦✦✦

Up a Lazy River / 1992 / Private Music ✦✦✦

Whistling in the Wind / 1994 / Private Music ✦✦✦

Otis Redding

d. Dec. 10, 1967
Soul

We are left to guess the direction Otis Redding's music would have taken had he lived. His last hit, the gently affecting "Dock of the Bay," pointed away from the impassioned soul ballads with which he'd made his name and strayed further yet from the Little Richard imitations with which he'd begun his career. Like many others during the mid-'60s, Redding discovered what was special about his music in Memphis. He had been recording sporadically and unsuccessfully for three or four years when he arrived at Stax and cut "These Arms of Mine." It gave us everything we could expect from him for the next few years: the almost exaggeratedly impassioned vocals couched in the sparse elegance of the Stax/Volt rhythm and horn sections. Wrenching ballads such as "I've Been Loving You" and "That's How Strong My Love Is" were judiciously mixed with uptempo stomps like "Mr. Pitiful" and "Respect." The individual albums inevitably contain some duds, but Otis rarely fired blanks on his singles. Redding's appearance at the Monterey Pop Festival and on the West Coast club circuit was beginning to spread word of his music beyond the traditional confines of the R&B market when he was tragically killed in a plane crash in December 1967. —*Colin Escott*

○ **Pain in My Heart** / 1964 / Atco ✦✦✦✦
Redding's first release. Includes the title track, a deep-soul gem, plus "These Arms of Mine" and "Security." —*Christine Ohlman*

○ **The Great Otis Redding Sings Soul Ballads** / 1965 / Atco ✦✦✦✦
Redding's second album includes "Mr. Pitiful," "That's How Strong My Love Is," "Chained and Bound." He moves out of the country-soul genre into his own stompin' thing. —*Christine Ohlman*

☆ **Otis Blue** / 1966 / Atco ✦✦✦✦✦
Pretty essential if you can only afford individual albums. Three Sam Cooke covers, including "Shake" and "A Change Is Gonna Come" are included, as well as "I've Been Loving You Too Long," "Satisfaction," and the original version of "Respect." —*Christine Ohlman*

☆ **The Dictionary of Soul** / 1966 / Atco ✦✦✦✦✦
If you can only afford one Redding album, start here. Includes "Try a Little Tenderness," "My Lover's Prayer," "Fa-Fa-Fa-Fa-Fa (Sad Song)." One of the best album covers ever! —*Christine Ohlman*

The Soul Album / 1966 / Atco ✦✦✦
Includes "Chain Gang," "Good to Me," and "Cigarettes and Coffee." —*Christine Ohlman*

○ **King and Queen** / 1967 / Atco ✦✦✦✦
Eleven duets by the undisputed ruler and his consort Carla Thomas. Includes "Tramp" and "Lovey Dovey." Sweet and soulful! —*Christine Ohlman*

Live in Europe / 1967 / Atco ✦✦✦
Ten of Redding's biggest hits, live before an ecstatic audience. Includes "Respect," "I Can't Turn You Loose," "Try a Little Tenderness," etc. Soul rave-up! —*Christine Ohlman*

○ **In Person at the Whisky a Go Go** / 1968 / Rhino ✦✦✦✦
Redding captured live in 1966, at the peak of his form! —*Christine Ohlman*

○ **The Dock of the Bay** / 1968 / Atco ✦✦✦✦
Includes the posthumously released classic title track plus the great "Ole Man Trouble." —*Christine Ohlman*

The Immortal Otis Redding / 1968 / Atco ✦✦✦
His later sides, including the wonderful "I've Got Dreams to Remember" and the super-funky "Hard to Handle." Produced by Steve Cropper. Redding on the border of a new soul frontier as a writer and performer, before his untimely death. —*Christine Ohlman*

Love Man / 1969 / Rhino ✦✦✦
Includes the heart-fixin' title track, plus "Free Me," "Look at That Girl," "Direct Me." —*Christine Ohlman*

Tell the Truth / 1970 / Rhino ✦✦✦
Another posthumously released collection, including "The Match Game" and "Tell the Truth." —*Christine Ohlman*

The Best of Otis Redding / 1972 / Atco ✦✦✦
This was another anthology that was definitive for many years, but lost a lot of value once Rhino began with its CD reissues. Atlantic hasn't bothered to reissue it as a CD, so it's only available on cassette. The original sound was decent and the range of selections good, and it still can be a nice introduction to Redding's greatness. There wasn't much information available beyond the minimum details. —*Ron Wynn*

Recorded Live / 1982 / Atlantic ✦✦
Various Redding classics recorded live. This was an interesting idea, but has since lost value as more and more Redding concert sets have been reissued. It's currently unavailable on CD, but for a sampler of how fantastic Redding was live, it's a good buy as a cassette. The sound isn't great, and there's some inconsistency in the performances, but the good stuff more than compensates for the rough spots. —*Ron Wynn*

○ **The Otis Redding Story** / 1989 / Atlantic ✦✦✦✦
A few previously unissued tracks, plus *all* the hits, from "These Arms of Mine" (1962) through "Dock of the Bay" (1967). A magnificent tribute to a magnificent career. It's a little expensive but it'll completely rock your soul! —*Christine Ohlman*

Remember Me / 1992 / Stax ✦✦✦
Twenty-two previously unreleased tracks, finished and unfinished, from the Stax vaults. Includes outtakes, remakes, cover tunes, and some very tasty never-before-heard originals. A historically important release covering all of Otis's remaining studio material. —*Christine Ohlman*

Good to Me: Live at the Whiskey A Go Go, Vol. 2 / 1993 / Stax
✦✦✦

Despite the deluge of reissues and anthologies, there still remains some unreleased Otis Redding material. There are two pluses about this new release of vintage Redding cuts, four of them newly issued. The first is that it's live, and Redding was always worth hearing in that context. The second is that the bonus cuts are invigorating, frenetic workouts with Redding blazing through the verses and then reworking and reshaping them in fiery vocal improvisations. The only negative, if there is one, is that there are better versions of "Ole Man Trouble" and "Pain In My Heart" available on other Redding releases. —*Ron Wynn*

★ **The Very Best of Otis Redding** / 1993 / Rhino ✦✦✦✦✦
For a single-disc collection, *The Very Best of Otis Redding* is unbeatable. All of his biggest hits are here—it's a dynamite album, essential for any lover of soul. —*Stephen Thomas Erlewine*

☆ **Otis! the Definitive Otis Redding** / 1993 / Rhino ✦✦✦✦✦
Although it includes the same studio tracks, *Otis!* supplants the previous, excellent *Otis Redding Story* by adding improved liner notes and sound, as well as a fourth disc of prime live material gathered from various performances. —*Stephen Thomas Erlewine*

☆ **The Very Best Of Otis Redding, Vol. 2** / 1995 / Rhino ✦✦✦✦✦

Redman

Rap

New Jersey rapper Redman made his initial impact with *Whut? Thee Album* in 1992. He blended reggae and funk influences with topical commentary and displayed a terse, though fluid rap style that was sometimes satirical, sometimes tough and sometimes silly. Redman returned in 1994 with his second album, *Dare Iz a Darkside*, which was a harder album than his debut. —*Ron Wynn*

● **Whut? Thee Album** / Sep. 22, 1992 / Chaos ✦✦✦✦
Redman's debut album is a minor masterpiece, fueled by the thick, P-Funk-influenced production of Erick Sermon. Redman's rhyming is forceful and intelligent, and he's never afraid to lighten his rhetoric with humor. Plus, the deeply funky grooves forming the core of the album never grow tiresome or repetitive. —*Stephen Thomas Erlewine*

Dare Iz a Darkside / 1994 / Ral ✦✦✦

Reducers

Group, Rock & Roll

Roaring their way out of the boring landscape that is New London, Connecticut, the Reducers were one of the great underrated bands of the '80s. The band recorded, in just under two years, three albums of punk- and pub-rock-inspired rowdy rock & roll, chock full of wiseass ruminations on life and love. The Reducers were post-punks with a formalist approach to rock & roll: two guitars, bass, and drums that echoed mid-'60s British Invasion and American garage rock. What made them different from the average retro-rock bar band was being hip, funny and smart more than most, plus having two ace song writers in Hugh Birdsall and Peter Detmold, who wrote wry and comically desperate songs like "Let's Go" ("Let's go to London/where all the music's good/Let's go to Paris/they've got a lot of nice food), "Rocks" (as in "New London hardly ever"), and the brilliant "Maximum Depression." Ultimately, what may have sunk the Reducers, or at the very least, limited the breadth of their audience, was their almost willful lack of pretension. There were absolutely no gimmicks, false pretenses towards stardom, or slick attitude; they were the real deal, working-class guys who played rock and roll because it meant the hope of a better life and (maybe) a ticket out of New London. This fire and determination, while not making them stars, made even their weakest songs still sound like they meant it. The title of their third album, *Cruise To Nowhere*, was unintentionally prophetic, as the band slipped into a crack in the earth by the end of 1986. A CD compilation of their "greatest hits" was released in the early '90s, but all three Reducers albums belong in the home of any self-respecting rock fan who shares an affinity for Dr. Feelgood, the Sex Pistols, and ? and the Mysterians, and lives in a place like New London. —*John Dougan*

● **Let's Go** / 1984 / Rave On ✦✦✦✦
A nearly forgotten record, *Let's Go* may well be a roots-rock (demi) masterpiece. Sounding like the Count Bishops meeting the Sex Pistols, the Reducers grind through some great material, including the insistent, life-affirming title track, and never remove their feet

from the accelerator. There's a liberating quality to this music, and the feeling of exuberant release the band puts across is almost palpable. Don't pass this by. —*John Dougan*

Reducers / 1984 / Rave On ✦✦✦

Cruise To Nowhere / 1985 / Rave On ✦✦✦

Shinola / 1995 / Rave On ✦✦✦

Lou Reed

b. Mar. 2, 1942, Freeport, Long Island, NY
Rock & Roll

Lou Reed would be important even if his career had ended with the passing of the Velvet Underground. It didn't though, and Reed has forged a rich and varied solo career spanning some twenty albums. Not everything he has released has been great but the best is formidable, and most is worth investigating. Equally interested in poetry and guitar/bass/drums rock & roll, Reed has always felt that rock & roll can be made interesting and valid for those over 40. Just as authors and film directors are supposed to get better at their craft as they get older, why not rock & roll musicians? Similarly, books and films routinely deal with subject matter other than the "I love you, you love me" school, so why not rock & roll? Reed's solo career is proof that such goals are attainable. Born in Brooklyn, Reed guided the Velvet Underground from 1965 to 1970. His first, eponymously titled solo album came out in 1972. From his second album, *Transformer*, came his only chart hit in "Walk on the Wild Side." Peaking in popularity in the mid-'70s with the *Rock & Roll Animal* and *Sally Can't Dance* albums, Reed became increasingly hostile, frustrated, and erratic. Cleaning himself up in the '80s, from 1982's *The Blue Mask* through 1992's *Magic and Loss*, he has made some of the finest, most engaging non-formulaic rock music ever conceived. —*Rob Bowman*

Lou Reed / 1972 / RCA ✦✦✦
Reed's first solo album, with "Walk It & Talk It," "Wild Child," and "Lisa Says" being particular standouts. —*Cub Koda*

○ **Transformer** / 1972 / RCA ✦✦✦✦
Produced by David Bowie and Mick Ronson, *Transformer* has a lushness and beauty to its production and arrangements that Reed's material had never before received. The hit single "Walk on the Wild Side" was a fluke brought about by the actions of one fill-in disc jockey at the BBC. The song chronicles several personages from Andy Warhol's Factory retinue, including speed-freaks and transvestites giving head; it is boggling to this day that it got by AM radio programmers. Other Reed classics such as "Vicious" and "Satellite of Love" get similar treatment. —*Rob Bowman*

Berlin / 1973 / RCA ✦✦✦
Relations between Bowie and Reed had been strained during the recording of *Transformer*, so for his third solo album, Reed hired Canadian studio whiz Bob Ezrin. Ezrin and Reed concocted a brilliant album-length concept loosely constructed around the song "Berlin," from Reed's first solo album. Reed, of course, wrote the basic songs (several stemming back to demos recorded but not released by the Velvet Underground), and Ezrin and Allan MacMillan wrote orchestral arrangements for each track. Recording in London, Ezrin assembled a dream band including Jack Bruce, Steve Winwood, Aynsley Dunbar, and two relatively unknown guitar heroes, Steve Hunter and Dick Wagner, while Reed's writing and singing has never been better. A number of reactionary writers thought that orchestration automatically meant somehow compromising one's authenticity, while others found the level of depression and vitriol in the story more than they wanted to bear. —*Rob Bowman*

Rock & Roll Animal / 1974 / RCA ✦✦✦
Retaining guitarists Hunter and Wagner from the *Berlin* sessions, Reed hired a rhythm section consisting of Prakash John on bass, Pentti Glan on drums, and Ray Colcord on keyboards. Two shows were recorded at New York's Academy of Music in 1973. Behind Reed the band produced fierce near-heavy-metal twin-guitar apotheosis for ninety minutes. Just under half of the concert made it onto this album. An FM radio staple at the time, *Rock & Roll Animal* includes searing versions of the Velvet Underground classics "Sweet Jane," "Heroin," "White Light/White Heat," and "Rock 'n' Roll," plus "Lady Day" from *Berlin*. —*Rob Bowman*

Sally Can't Dance / 1974 / RCA ✦✦✦
Following the self-conscious artiness of *Berlin*, *Sally Can't Dance* was Lou Reed's blatant stab at commercial success, featuring beefed-up guitar riffs, horn charts, and the occasional slick

melody. The move paid off—it was his only album to reach the Top 10—but it's an inconsistent record, complete with lackluster material, terrific rockers ("Sally Can't Dance" and "Kill Your Sons"), and one of Reed's best ballads, "Billy." —*Stephen Thomas Erlewine*

Lou Reed Live / 1975 / RCA ◆◆◆
Most of the rest of the above-mentioned concert. Three songs from *Transformer*, two songs from *Berlin*, and the Velvet Underground's "I'm Waiting for the Man." Just a shade less visceral than *Rock 'n' Roll Animal. —Rob Bowman*

Metal Machine Music / 1975 / RCA Victor ◆
A double-record of galvenizing white-noise, *Metal Machine Music* gained instant notoriety when it was released, inspiring reams of rock criticism speculating whether the album was a serious attempt at avant-garde music or not. Considering that the record was a relentless series of layered, overlapping loops of guitar feedback, it probably was intended as a mammoth fuck you not only to the fans he acquired with *Sally Can't Dance*, but to his dedicated followers, critics, and record company. Regardless of Reed's intentions, *Metal Machine Music* is the most uncompromising work he ever released, featuring no lyrics, no hooks, no songs, no melodic themes—there's nothing but endless layers of noise. It's not necessarily unlistenable—in the two decades since its release, the atonal guitar experiments of Sonic Youth and their offspring have made *Metal Machine Music* sound downright conventional. It is boring, however. There is no variation in the processed noise, making the record's four sides unbearably tedious. —*Stephen Thomas Erlewine*

○ **Coney Island Baby** / Feb. 1976 / RCA ◆◆◆◆
Coney Island Baby was an album of renewal for Reed. The year 1974 had witnessed one of his worst albums ever in *Sally Can't Dance*, and, early in 1975, in reaction to a career spinning out of control, he had released the lyric-less sonic feedback assault of *Metal Machine Music*. *Coney Island Baby* was a return to peak songwriting form. The title track reflected Reed's early love of doo-wop. It is probably the grandest love song of his career. "Kicks" is a rather frightening internal study of a diseased mind that eventually turns to murder. As with most of Reed's writing in the '60s and '70s, he draws no conclusion; he simply paints a picture. —*Rob Bowman*

Rock & Roll Heart / Nov. 1976 / Arista ◆◆
Lou Reed continued the relaxed, R&B-inflected rock & roll of *Coney Island Baby* with *Rock & Roll Heart*, released the same year as its predecessor. Reed's quick turnaround with *Rock & Roll Heart* is an indication of the inherent flaws of the album. Musically, it's appealing, but the record contains a set of lackluster songs which fail to match the gentle, humane songs that formed the core of *Coney Island Baby. —Stephen Thomas Erlewine*

● **Walk on the Wild Side: The Best of Lou Reed** / 1977 / RCA ◆◆◆◆

Live: Take No Prisoners / 1978 / Arista ◆
Live: Take No Prisoners isn't so much a live album as it is a constant barrage of vicious, mean-spirited jokes by a third-rate, failed comedian. Throughout the double-album set, the songs take a back seat to Lou's rambling monologues, which include a number of personal attacks, including one on rock critic Robert Christgau. Instead of reinforcing Reed's clever wit, the record makes him seem rather pathetic and—considering this was recorded during the height of punk—even pathetic. And the music, performed by an anonymous pick-up band, is shockingly bland, providing no support for Reed's streetwise show-biz shitick. —*Stephen Thomas Erlewine*

Street Hassle / 1978 / Arista ◆◆◆
Reed's second album for Arista has a few weak spots, but most of it, including the 11-minute title song, is unmitigated brilliance. The sound is rather odd as Reed began experimenting with Manfred Schunke's binaural recording process. Some tracks on the album are part live and part studio while others are near totally live or totally studio. *Street Hassle* includes Reed's tongue-in-cheek take on racial stereotypes, "I Wanna Be Black," and a quite strange reinterpretation of the Velvet Underground's "Real Good Time Together." —*Rob Bowman*

The Bells / 1979 / Direct Disk ◆◆◆
Like *Street Hassle*, *The Bells* is a conceptual *tour-de-force*, as Lou Reed delivers some of his most open and poetic material over a sonic backdrop that recalls rock & roll, but owes more to streamlined jazz. It's one of his most intriguing records, as well as being

of one his most giving and humane albums. —*Stephen Thomas Erlewine*

Growing up in Public / 1980 / Arista ◆◆
As the title suggests, *Growing up in Public* is a musical diary of Lou Reed entering middle age. Conceptualy, the record is intriguing and the lyrics are well-crafted on occasion, but the album is filled with too much mediocre, formulaic music to make it a compelling listen. —*Stephen Thomas Erlewine*

Rock & Roll Diary / 1980 / Arista ◆◆◆
An excellent wrap-up of his best work (1967-80), both with and without the Velvet Underground, this is the perfect place to start. —*Dan Heilman*

○ **The Blue Mask** / 1982 / RCA ◆◆◆◆
Reed took nearly two years off at the end of the '70s to dry out and clean up. When he did return to recording, it was with a vengeance. In an odd quirk of fate Reed had re-signed with RCA and he had also gone back to a lineup of two guitars, a bass, and drums. *The Blue Mask* sounds immaculate. The guts of Reed's sound are still present in no uncertain terms but there is also a richness to the finished mix that is striking. The bass player, Fernando Saunders, became Reed's right-hand man for the next several years, and guitarist Robert Quine was Reed's ideal foil for this and the subsequent *Legendary Hearts*. The result was Reed's best album since *Berlin*. His songwriting had taken a quantum leap since cleaning up. The maturity was inspiring, as was the breadth of the material. —*Rob Bowman*

○ **Legendary Hearts** / 1983 / RCA ◆◆◆◆
Continuing with Quine and Saunders, coupled with a different drummer in Fred Maher, Reed delivered his second superb album in a row. This was a more subdued affair than *The Blue Mask* but the writing was no less impressive. —*Rob Bowman*

● **New Sensations** / 1984 / RCA ◆◆◆◆
After a few challenging (and critically acclaimed) albums, Reed dispensed with densely literate (and dissonant) excursions into the dark side of the human psyche and delivered a solid, upbeat (and at times humorous) collection of accessible rock & roll. Reed celebrated love ("I Love You Suzanne"), poked fun at power-plays between the genders ("My Red Joystick"), and, as the title track suggested, generally looked forward with optimism. Reed's dirty-electric rhythm, Fernando Saunders's elastic bass work and Fred Maher's forceful drumming provide a solid bed of ragged but tight ensemble work behind Reed's dry narratives. —*Rick Clark*

Mistrial / 1986 / RCA ◆◆◆
After three successive accomplished and mature albums, Lou Reed made an attempt to stay current with the stilted *Mistrial*. Six of the songs are driven by drum machines, which certainly gives the music a robotic feel. However, Reed doesn't help the situation any by turning in a set of songs that are stripped back to their bare rhythms, lacking memorable hooks and melodies. All of these spartan arrangements are designed to attract attention to the lyrics, which aren't among his finest efforts. Reed is in a social protest mode, particularly attacking violence, in both its domestic and global incarnations. Instead of personalizing the material, he relies on platitudes, which tend to make the processed chords and beats of the music even more grating. Nevertheless, he ends the album with two ballads that showcase many of his finer musical and lyrical skills. —*Stephen Thomas Erlewine*

○ **New York** / 1989 / Sire ◆◆◆◆
Reed's first album in three years hailed another peak in his recording career. In the past he had always painted pictures of any given social situation. Positive or negative, he had never stated a point of view. On *New York* he rails. Sporting a new band, including bass virtuoso Rob Wasserman and Reed's brother-in-law, guitarist Mike Rathke, Reed indicts everyone from slum lords to polluters. *New York* contains, perhaps, his finest writing. —*Rob Bowman*

○ **Songs for Drella** / Jul. 1990 / Sire ◆◆◆◆
Reed and former Velvet Underground partner John Cale reunite to create a song cycle based around the life of Velvet's mentor Andy Warhol. Recorded with just the two of them, the range of sound and mood is masterful. Reed's ballads give way to angst-ridden feedback-charged guitar freakouts. This is an astonishingly moving album. —*Rob Bowman*

○ **Magic and Loss** / 1992 / Sire ◆◆◆◆
Magic and Loss marks the third installment of a trilogy featuring mature, thematic works from Lou Reed, following 1989's *New York* (universal metaphor for urban decay) and 1990's collabora-

tion with John Cale, *Songs for Drella* (a tribute to Andy Warhol). The disc is inspired by the loss of two of Reed's close friends to cancer in 1991, an experience that proved cathartic for the artist. The songs—a generous 14 tracks over 58 minutes—tend not to stand out as distinctive pieces, but work very much as an organic whole. An exception is "Power and Glory," featuring vocal backing from Little Jimmy Scott, startling in its contrast to Reed's understated monotone. The artist succeeds in making the project inspirational, a chronicle of how the magic of life transforms loss into something greater. —*Roch Parisien*

Between Thought and Expression: The Lou Reed Anthology / 1992 / RCA ✦✦✦
Over the course of 45 songs on three CDs or cassettes, *Between Thought and Expression* chronicles the first 16 years of Lou Reed's solo work, from his debut, self-titled album that followed his 1970 departure from the Velvet Underground, through the RCA and Arista years that culminated in 1986's *Mistrial*. On the way, the anthology delivers stellar moments from Reed's David Bowie-produced *Transformer* period, several pieces from the hauntingly doom-laden *Berlin*, and the '70s guitar anthem "Sweet Jane" from *Rock & Roll Animal*. The set includes five previously unreleased tracks, one non-LP B-side, and two soundtrack-only numbers. The tracks were selected and remastered with Reed's participation, and the refurbished sound is a revelation, particularly on the early material. —*Roch Parisien*

○ **Sweet Jane** / Oil Well [Bootleg] ✦✦✦✦
This recording of a 1972 radio show has been available in numerous guises for many years; the label listed is merely about the easiest to find as of the mid-'90s. This is inarguably among the finest of Reed's solo work, released or unreleased, split evenly between Velvet Undergroud classics and highlights from Reed's early solo albums, with a band featuring Dick Wagner and Steve Hunter on guitars. The sound is very good, Reed's singing is great, and the band plays in a raw and urgent manner that Lou should have employed on his solo albums, but didn't. The Velvets songs are well done and considerably different from the originals, and the versions of solo classics like "Vicious," "Walk On The Wild Side," "I'm So Free," "Berlin," and "Satellite Of Love" slay the studio takes to shreds. Essential for Reed fanatics. —*Richie Unterberger*

BOOK

✦✦✦✦ **Lou Reed: The Biography**, by Victor Bockris (Hutchinson, UK, 1994). He may have claimed in one of his songs to be just an "average guy," but that's one thing Lou Reed decidedly is not. Average guys don't get several weeks of electroshock treatments as a teenager, hang out with renowned poet Delmore Schwartz as an undergraduate, set the blueprint for punk and alternative rock as the leader of the Velvet Underground, ingest impressive quantities of amphetamines for years on end, and live with a transvestite for several years. Drug use, bisexuality, and egotistic behavior are often tawdry, private matters that don't necessarily make for compelling rock bios. But in Reed's case, perhaps more than any other rock star's, these topics are not just useful for understanding his work, but worn quite nakedly on his sleeve in his actual music and lyrics. Bockris, the author of the only full-length study of the Velvet Underground (*Uptight*), details Reed's odyssey from teenage misfit through the Velvets, glam rock, and venerated elder statesman of New York underground rock with lots of detail in this 450+-page work. The author didn't accumulate information from a great many first-hand sources (and many of these are fellow journalists), but does present a great deal of information gleaned from interviews and reviews from the '60s to the early '90s. What emerges is a portrait of a fascinating, enigmatic artist and person who often helps bring down his most productive musical and professional relationships because of a need to always be in control. Unlike most bios covering several decades worth of output, this maintains more or less equal interest all the way through, with plenty of interesting stories about the Velvets, all of his solo albums, and his partnerships with such noted cohorts as John Cale, Andy Warhol, and Robert Quine. The chief flaw is that Bockris sometimes offers surprisingly scant description and analysis of Reed's recorded work, often relying heavily on previously published reviews. —*Richie Unterberger*

R.E.M.
Group, Alternative Pop/Rock
R.E.M., along with their English counterparts the Smiths, mark the

point when post-punk turned into alternative rock. When their first single, "Radio Free Europe," was released in 1981 it created a massive buzz in the American underground that continued to grow through the release of their first full-length album, 1983's *Murmur*. What made R.E.M. so different from other guitar-driven pop bands of their time was the subtlety of their influences; although they were clearly influenced by punk, they didn't sound like any punk group. Instead, Peter Buck's arpeggiated rhythm guitar recalled the Byrds and the Velvet Underground, while Mike Mills was reminiscent of the melodic bass lines of the Beach Boys and the Beatles. But the band was never a retro-group or pop revivalists—Bill Berry's strong drumming and Michael Stipe's mumbled vocals and abstract lyrics place them squarely into the post-punk era. While their influences are discernable, the clean, atmospheric folk-rock of their early records are clearly their own.

Murmur was adored by critics, as well as earning legions of listeners in the college rock underground. Even with Stipe's inaudible, cryptic lyrics, the band's guitar pop was highly melodic and accessible, yet it didn't fit into the strict confines of AOR or Top 40 radio; consequently, it stayed in the American underground, gaining an enormous following over the years, as well as countless imitators. Yet, R.E.M. continued to improve with each record, continually expanding their fan base through constant touring and uniformly excellent albums. By the time they had their first hit single in 1987—the Top Ten "The One I Love"—their underground fans were devoted enough not to be scared off by the success; besides, R.E.M. had not compromised their music in order to sell records.

During the late '80s, the band became genuine rock stars, selling out arenas across the world. Stipe was becoming the focal point for many of the new fans, as well as the press, but R.E.M. had always functioned as a band, not as a backing group and a singer. Their albums were always the result of a collaborative effort between their members, which is the reason they continued to be musically inventive in the '90s.

Although the band didn't tour at all in the first half of the '90s, they were at the height of their popularity, releasing a three multi-platinum albums and scoring several Top 40 hits; in addition to their commerical success, countless bands cited R.E.M. not only as a musical influence, but as an ideological model. After releasing the lush pop of *Out of Time* in 1991 and the haunting acoustic melancholia of *Automatic for the People* in 1992, R.E.M. returned to loud rock & roll in 1994 with the *Monster* album. Following its release, the group embarked on their first worldwide tour since 1989. —*Stephen Thomas Erlewine*

Chronic Town / 1982 / IRS ✦✦✦
R.E.M.'s debut EP *Chronic Town* expanded the catchy, jangling pop of their first single, "Radio Free Europe," by making it murkier and more cryptic, but no less melodic or memorable. Stipe may mumble the lyrics throughout the record, but that doesn't detract from the quiet grace of "Gardening at Night" and "Carnival of Sorts (Box Cars)," or the ringing guitars of "Stumble." —*Stephen Thomas Erlewine*

☆ **Murmur** / 1983 / IRS ✦✦✦✦✦
All of R.E.M.'s imitators base their homages on this strange, eerie album. Out of all of their albums, none have the mood this one has—it's the aural equivalent of the creeping kudzu on the cover. The music belongs to no time—the guitars and rhythms may have their roots in 1960s pop and folk, but the vocals couldn't have been produced before 1977 and the punk-rock movement. —*Stephen Thomas Erlewine*

☆ **Reckoning** / 1984 / IRS ✦✦✦✦
The guitar still rings and chimes, the vocals still mumble, but the rhythm section is brought toward the front of the mix and the sound is brighter. While the mood has changed (it isn't out of time like *Murmur*), the songs are better—nothing on *Murmur* had the power of "(Don't Go Back To) Rockville" and "So. Central Rain." —*Stephen Thomas Erlewine*

○ **Fables of the Reconstruction** / 1985 / IRS ✦✦✦✦
Fables of the Reconstruction is R.E.M.'s most folk-oriented record, but it never strays from the band's highly developed pop sensibilities, as "Can't Get There From Here," "Green Grow the Rushes," and "Driver 8" prove. —*Stephen Thomas Erlewine*

☆ **Lifes Rich Pageant** / 1986 / IRS ✦✦✦✦
This is not R.E.M.'s most successful album, but it captures the band at an important crossroads. The ringing guitars of *Murmur* and *Reckoning* remain ("Fall on Me," "Flowers of Guatemala," "What If We Give It Away?"), but the bombastic directness of their next two

albums is anticipated with tracks like "Just a Touch," "Begin the Begin," and their cover of "Superman." An important transitional album. —*Stephen Thomas Erlewine*

Dead Letter Office / 1987 / IRS ♦♦♦

For the fans: a collection of B-sides and outtakes, including a drunken cover of Roger Miller's "King of the Road" and three Lou Reed songs. An entertaining album that will leave the unconverted scratching their heads and the fans delighted. The CD version includes their fine 1982 debut EP *Chronic Town*. —*Stephen Thomas Erlewine*

☆ **Document** / 1987 / IRS ♦♦♦♦♦

The breakthrough. R.E.M.'s first Top Ten (and Top 40) single, "The One I Love," is included, as is the anthem "It's the End of the World As We Know It (And I Feel Fine)." Those two songs illustrate the difference in the band—loud guitars, driving rhythms, and clear (or at least clearer) vocals. "It's the End of the World..." may be unintelligible, but Stipe's vocals are audible throughout the album, even though the lyrics are murky. —*Stephen Thomas Erlewine*

● **Eponymous** / 1988 / IRS ♦♦♦♦

Basically a singles collection from R.E.M.'s first five albums, *Eponymous* gives the listener a sense of R.E.M.'s change from a folk-rock band to a rock band. The songs are intelligently selected, distilling most of the best moments from their first five albums for I.R.S. Included is the original single of "Radio Free Europe," different mixes of "Gardening at Night" (where it's actually possible to hear the vocal) and "Finest Worksong," and the previously unreleased (and unspectacular) "Romance." (Note: An import collection, *The Best of R.E.M.*, doesn't have the rarities, but has 16 songs, including the remainder of *Eponymous*, plus many other important songs from their I.R.S. years. Worth the couple of extra dollars for the beginner.) —*Stephen Thomas Erlewine*

Green / 1988 / Warner Brothers ♦♦♦

Green is R.E.M.'s most disjointed and strange recording. Alternating between eerie acoustic numbers and all-out guitar rave-ups, there is no cohesion here. Nevertheless, there is some good material: the goofy "Stand," the veiled confessions of "Hairshirt" and "World Leader Pretend," the guitar workout of "Turn You Inside Out," the mocking "Pop Song 89," and the charming untitled eleventh track. —*Stephen Thomas Erlewine*

○ **Out of Time** / 1991 / Warner Brothers ♦♦♦♦

In contrast to the directness of *Green* and *Document*, this may seem like a return to the abstractness of the early years, but that isn't the case. *Out of Time* is among R.E.M.'s best work—a mature, balanced, graceful collection of pop songs quite different from *Murmur* and *Reckoning*. Buck, Berry, and Mills switch instruments frequently, keeping the music fresh and exciting. —*Stephen Thomas Erlewine*

☆ **Automatic for the People** / Jul. 1992 / Warner Brothers ♦♦♦♦♦

After electing not to support the success of *Out of Time* with a tour, R.E.M. promised a hard, driving guitar-rock album by the end of the next year. Fortunately, R.E.M. delivered *Automatic for the People*, a beautifully sad album that is the anything but hard rock & roll. A dark, brooding meditation on loss of all sorts, *Automatic for the People* is arguably R.E.M.'s finest moment. Largely acoustic, with lush string arrangements by John Paul Jones, *Automatic for the People* is sorrowful and nostalgic without being crass, shallow, or pandering. Whether it's the adolescent memories of "Nightswimming" and "Find the River," the celebrity deaths of "Monty Got A Raw Deal" and "Man on the Moon," or the consolations of "Everybody Hurts" and "Sweetness Follows," R.E.M. never falls into false sentiment. —*Stephen Thomas Erlewine*

Monster / 1994 / Warner Brothers ♦♦♦

Monster is indeed R.E.M.'s long-promised "rock" album; it just doesn't rock in the way one might expect. Instead of R.E.M.'s trademark anthemic bashers, *Monster* offers a set of murky sludge, powered by the heavily distorted and delayed guitar of Peter Buck. Stipe's vocals have been pushed to the back of the mix, along with Bill Berry's drums, which accentuates the muscular pulse of Buck's chords. From the androgynous sleaze of "Crush With Eyeliner" to the subtle, Eastern-tinged menace of "You," most of the album sounds dense, dirty and grimy, which makes the punchy guitars of "What's the Frequency, Kenneth?" and the warped soul of "Tongue" all the more distinctive. *Monster* doesn't have the conceptual unity or consistently brilliant songwriting of *Automatic*,

but it does offer a wide range of sonic textures that have never been heard on an R.E.M. album before. —*Stephen Thomas Erlewine*

The Rembrandts

Group, Pop/Rock
The Rembrandts are focused around Phil Solem and singer/songwriter Danny Wilde (both originally in the Los Angeles band Great Buildings) and feature a pleasantly melodic folk-pop/rock with harmonies that, at times, draw inspiration from the Everly Brothers. —*Rick Clark*

○ **The Rembrandts** / 1990 / Atco ♦♦♦♦

This promising debut contains "Just the Way It Is," which was a minor hit. —*Dan Heilman*

Untitled / 1992 / Atco ♦♦♦

● **LP** / 1995 / East West ♦♦♦♦

Most of the merits of the Rembrandts' third album, *LP*, were overshadowed by the massive success of "I'll Be There for You," the infectious theme from the hit Generation X sitcom *Friends*. Included on *LP* at the last minute—the first pressings didn't list the song on the album cover—"I'll Be There for You" received saturation radio airplay, topping the adult contemporary charts, yet it was never released as a single, forcing fans of the song to by the entire album to own the song. While the Monkees guitar riffs and layered harmonies are not entirely representative of the Rembrandts—it makes them out to be a bubblegum band—the record is filled with smart, hook-laden guitar pop that won't disappoint old Rembrandts fans or listeners attracted by the hit. —*Stephen Thomas Erlewine*

Renaissance

Group, Art-Rock/Progressive-Rock
The history of Renaissance is essentially the history of two separate groups, rather similar to the two phases of the Moody Blues or the Drifters. The original group was founded in 1969 by ex-Yardbirds members Keith Relf and Jim McCarty as a sort of progressive folk-rock band, who recorded two albums (of which only the first, self-titled LP came out in America, on Elektra Records) but never quite made it, despite some success on England's campus circuit.

The band went through several membership changes, with Relf and his sister Jane (who later fronted the very Renaissance-like Illusion) exiting and McCarty all but gone after 1971. The new line-up formed around the core of bassist Jon Camp, keyboard player John Tout, and Terry Sullivan on drums, with Annie Haslam, an aspiring singer with operatic training and a three-octave range.

Their first album in this incarnation, *Prologue*, released in 1972, was considerably more ambitious than the original band's work, with extended instrumental passages and soaring vocals by Haslam. Their breakthrough came with their next record, *Ashes Are Burning*, issued in 1973, which introduced guitarist Mick Dunford to the line-up and featured some searing electric licks by guest axman Andy Powell. Their next record, *Turn of the Cards*, released by Sire Records, had a much more ornate songwriting style and was awash in lyrics that alternated between the topical and the mystical.

The group's ambitions, by now, were growing faster than its audience, which was concentrated on America's East Coast, especially in New York and Philadelphia—*Scheherazade* (1975) was built around a 20-minute extended suite for rock group and orchestra that dazzled the fans but made no new converts. A live album recorded at a New York concert date reprised their earlier material, including the "Scheherazade" suite, but covered little new ground and showed the group in a somewhat lethargic manner. The band's next two albums, *Novella* and *A Song for All Seasons*, failed to find new listeners, and as the 1970's closed out, the group was running headlong into the punk and new wave booms that made them seem increasingly anachronistic and doomed to cult status.

Their 1980's albums were released with less than global or even national fanfare, and the group split up in the early '80s amid reported personality conflicts between the members. During 1995, however, both Haslam and Dunford made attempts to revive the Renaissance name in different incarnations, and Jane Relf and the other surviving members of the original band were reportedly planning to launch their own "Renaissance" revival which, if nothing else, may keep the courts and some trademark attorneys busy for a little while. —*Bruce Eder*

Renaissance / 1969 / Elektra ✦✦✦
The original group's debut album was a then-groundbreaking meld of progressive rock with classical and jazz influences. The album is a little clunky by today's standards, and far druggier than the later group in its ambience (cofounders Keith Relf and Jim McCarty were the heavily psychedelic half of the final lineup of the Yardbirds, which made them anathema to Jimmy Page), but vocalist Jane Relf had a striking individual style, and the classical influence was unique for its time. —*Bruce Eder*

○ **Prologue** / 1972 / One Way ✦✦✦✦
The debut of Renaissance Mark II, featuring Annie Haslam on lead vocals and John Tout on keyboards, is a solid meld of classical and rock, most of the material built around long, highly developed instrumental lines and Haslam's soaring three-octave range. Nineteenth-century European classical influences (especially Chopin) abound, in a mix of electric and acoustic rock. Reissued on CD by One Way Records in the '90s. —*Bruce Eder*

Ashes Are Burning / 1973 / One Way ✦✦✦
With electric guitarist Andy Powell sitting in on the title track, Renaissance delivered its best, and first fully-formed album, mixing Russian, French, and Indian influences in musical settings that are both lively and elegant. The title track is one of the few lengthy progressive rock pieces of the era that holds up, and the rest of the material runs the gamut from folk ("Carpet of the Sun") to Impressionist ("At the Harbor"), all of it hauntingly beautiful and enlivening. Reissued in 1993 by One Way Records, with excellent sound. —*Bruce Eder*

Turn of the Cards / 1974 / Sire ✦✦✦
An extension of *Ashes Are Burning*, even better produced and more unified thematically, but slightly lacking in the freshness and vibrancy of its predecessor, and the classicism is the strongest element. Some of the material has an almost topical basis, which made it most unusual for progressive rock at the time. —*Bruce Eder*

○ **Scheherazade & Other Stories** / 1975 / Repertoire ✦✦✦✦
The group's most ambitious album is slightly disappointing because the material in the title track seems somewhat repetitive, and the orchestra is mixed a little too far down. The rest of the material is livelier and, in some ways, more impressive and memorable. —*Bruce Eder*

Illusion / 1976 / Island ✦✦✦
The group's second album is more polished in its sound, but the record never found an audience because it has never remained in print for very long or been very easy to find. The classical influence is more pronounced and Jane Relf stretches out further in her vocalizing, as the original group evolved somewhat in the direction of Renaissance Mark II. —*Bruce Eder*

Live at Carnegie Hall / 1976 / Sire ✦✦
Originally a double LP, this record showcased the group's live sound in full, including a performance of "Scheherazade" in concert with a 30-piece orchestra. All of the material (drawn from *Ashes Are Burning* onward) is stretched out from the studio originals, and not all of it really works on record. —*Bruce Eder*

Novella / 1977 / Sire ✦✦
By this time, the formula behind the group's sound was becoming predictable, as were many of the songs, although this record and its successor retained some interest for more than hard-core fans. —*Bruce Eder*

A Song for All Seasons / 1978 / Sire ✦✦
The last gasp for the group as anything resembling a band with an international following, this was their last record to get any serious exposure. The material lacks any of the life that resonated from the early-'70s releases, and even the classical pretentions now seem dullish if pretty. —*Bruce Eder*

In the Beginning / 1978 / Capitol ✦✦✦
This compilation of the *Prologue* and *Ashes Are Burning* albums should be great, but it isn't. The sound is flat and two major songs from *Ashes* were cut mercilessly. Good for a glimpse at the band. —*Bruce Eder*

Azure d'Or / 1979 / Sire ✦✦
Rock Galaxy / 1980 / RCA ✦✦
Camera Camera / 1981 / IRS ✦✦
Time-Line / 1983 / IRS ✦✦
● **Tales of 1001 Nights, Vol. 1** / 1990 / Sire ✦✦✦✦
○ **Tales of 1001 Nights, Vol. 2** / Mar. 27, 1990 / Sire ✦✦✦✦
Less satisfying than the first volume with fewer memorable melodies, although it's worth a listen. —*Bruce Eder*
Other Woman / HTD ✦✦

Diane Renay

Girl-Group
A one-shot artist from the waning days of the girl group sound, Philadelphian Diane Renay made number six in early 1964 with "Navy Blue." From the same white-bread mold as Lesley Gore and Little Peggy March, but not as talented as either, most of her material was written by her producer, Bob Crewe (most famous for his work with the Four Seasons). After her follow-up "Kiss Me Sailor" made the Top 30, she vanished from sight, although the surprisingly tough and soulful single "Watch Out Sally" was one of the best obscure girl group songs. —*Richie Unterberger*

○ **Navy Blue** / 1964 / 20th Century ✦✦✦✦
Passable lightweight teen girl-group pop, most written by producer Bob Crewe. European reissues add some bonus tracks, the most noteworthy being the single "Watch Out Sally," one of the bitchiest girl-group revenge tales ever cut. —*Richie Unterberger*

REO Speedwagon

Group, Pop/Rock
REO Speedwagon may not have been the most talented arena rock band of the '70s, but they were almost certainly worked harder than any other group on the same circuit. In 1971, they released their first album of competent hard rock, but they didn't chart until 1974 with *Ridin' the Storm Out*. That album was recorded with temporary vocalist Michael Murphey, who would later have some solo success of his own; regular vocalist/rhythm guitarist Kevin Cronin rejoined the band in 1975. The first album released after Cronin rejoined REO was only moderately successful but 1977's *REO Speedwagon Live/You Get What You Play For* began a string of gold and platinum albums, culminating with the 1980 album *Hi Infidelity*, which sold over seven million copies in America. Although their style had shifted to a slick, mainstream AOR rock and they were known for the power ballads, their hits didn't stop coming until 1990, when the band's support dropped off sharply; their 1991 album didn't even chart. However, the band remains a solid touring attraction and they continue to release albums into the '90s. —*Stephen Thomas Erlewine*

R E O Speedwagon / 1971 / Epic ✦✦✦
○ **R.E.O. 2** / 1972 / Epic ✦✦✦✦
REO Speedwagon began to come into its own with its third album, *Ridin' the Storm Out*. Over the years, the record became a platinum-seller, but it originally charted at number 171, due to the strength of their series of opening shows for more successful rock acts. While the group still had elements of their bar-bad boogie, they began to streamline their approach on this album. Although it only resulted in one minor hit, with the title track scraping the bottom of the singles charts, the record was one of their most consistent efforts. —*Stephen Thomas Erlewine*

○ **Ridin' the Storm Out** / 1973 / Epic ✦✦✦✦
Lost in a Dream / 1974 / Epic ✦✦
This Time We Mean It / 1975 / Epic ✦✦
R.E.O. / 1976 / Epic ✦✦
Live: You Get What You Play For / 1977 / Epic ✦✦✦
REO Speedwagon built their audience through constant touring. Often, their live shows were more exciting than their records, which is what makes *You Get What You Play For*, a live run-through of their greatest hits, one of their better records of the era. —*Stephen Thomas Erlewine*

○ **You Can Tune a Piano But You Can't Tuna Fish** / 1978 / Epic ✦✦✦✦
You Can Tune A Piano, But You Can't Tuna Fish was REO Speedwagon's biggest hit of the '70s, featuring the singles "Roll with the Changes" and "Time for Me To Fly." —*AMG*

Nine Lives / 1979 / Epic ♦♦♦

○ **Decade of Rock & Roll '70-80** / 1980 / Epic ♦♦♦♦
This is a well-chosen recap of REO's dues-paying years. —*Dan Heilman*

○ **Hi-Infidelity** / 1982 / Epic ♦♦♦♦
The band's breakthrough album with the masses. Heavy on the syrupy ballad formula that brought them success. —*Cub Koda*

Wheels Are Turnin' / 1984 / Epic ♦♦♦
Wheels Are Turnin' was REO Speedwagon's most popular post-*High Infidelity* album, selling over two million copies and featuring the number one single "Can't Fight This Feeling," as well as "I Do'wanna Know" and "One Lonely Night." —*AMG*

Life As We Know It / 1987 / Epic ♦♦

● **The Hits** / 1988 / Epic ♦♦♦♦
This collects their chart hits and some old favorites. —*Dan Heilman*

Good Trouble / 1988 / Epic ♦♦♦

The Earth, a Small Man, His Dog and a Chicken / 1990 / Epic ♦

Second Decade of Rock & Roll / 1991 / Epic ♦♦♦
The Second Decade of Rock & Roll isn't as strong a compilation as *The Hits*, lacking the focused concentration of the previous compilation, but it does contain fair amount of highlights from REO Speedwagon's '80s albums. —*AMG*

The Replacements

Group, Rock & Roll, Alternative Pop/Rock
Minneapolis band the Replacements blasted onto the scene with a perfectly inspired blend of irreverence, sloppiness, and heart, the stuff from which great rock & roll is created.

Paul Westerberg, the band's primary singer/songwriter, has produced an impressive body of work that ranges from moronically inspired rock to reflective numbers possessing heartbreaking vulnerability. No other band from the post-punk age has worn such an interesting and complex heart on their torn-up sleeve or used an imperfect voice to such great advantage. On their initial releases (*Sorry Ma, Forgot to Take out the Trash*, *Stink*, and *Hootenanny*), the band puked out frantic song-bites (many less than two minutes long) with clown punk titles like "I Hate Music," "Shiftless When Idle," "White and Lazy," "F*** School," and "God Damn Job."

Let It Be, their fourth release, reflected a new maturity without sacrificing their spirit of reckless fun. The next two efforts, *Tim* and *Pleased to Meet Me*, maintained the magic.

Since then, the Replacements have had some lineup changes and softened their ragged-but-right sound with *Don't Tell a Soul* and the more acoustic-oriented followup, *All Shook Down*, their final album.

They were called "the last great band of the '80s" by *Musician*. You'd better believe it. —*Rick Clark & John Floyd*

Sorry Ma, Forgot to Take out the Trash / 1981 / Twin/Tone ♦♦♦
Sorry Ma, Forgot to Take out the Trash is a thrashy, Ramones-like debut. "Johnny's Gonna Die," "I'm in Trouble," and "Takin' a Ride" hint at things to come. —*John Floyd*

The Replacements Stink / 1982 / Twin/Tone ♦♦♦
Stink works better than *Sorry Ma, Forgot to Take out the Trash* not only because it's shorter and thereby eliminating the filler that cluttered the debut, but also because the band is faster *and* messier, making songs like "Kids Don't Follow," "Fuck School," and "God Damn Job" invigorating rock & roll. —*Stephen Thomas Erlewine*

○ **Hootenanny** / 1983 / Twin/Tone ♦♦♦♦
A hodgepodge of hard rock, country, punk—everything. It's patchy, but "Color Me Impressed," "Willpower," and "Within Your Reach" are among their best. —*John Floyd*

☆ **Let It Be** / 1984 / Twin/Tone ♦♦♦♦♦
This is where they realized their potential and consolidated their diversity into a masterpiece that screams, cries, comforts, and antagonizes. Highlights include "Unsatisfied," one of Westerberg's finest songs and vocal performances, as well as the reckless swinging "I Will Dare," and the playful "Androgynous." —*John Floyd*

☆ **Tim** / 1985 / Sire ♦♦♦♦♦
Their major-label debut isn't a great leap forward but their raggedness is retained, and Westerberg contributes anthems of rebellion and insecurity, like "Bastards of Young" and "Hold My

Life." Also included is a hard-rockin' nod to alternative radio (with Alex Chilton), "Left of the Dial." —*John Floyd*

The Shit Hits the Fans / 1985 / Twin/Tone ♦
An effective document of the Replacements' chaotic mid-'80s concerts, the cassette-only *The Shit Hits the Fans* was recorded at a 1984 show in Oklahoma City without the band's consent. After the show was completed, one of the band's roadies confiscated the tape from a patron that was bootlegging the show. Appropriately, the sound quality is quite poor, but the band's sloppy, drunken energy can be infectious, particularly when they try to cover bands like the Rolling Stones and Thin Lizzy. or even R.E.M., for that matter. —*Stephen Thomas Erlewine*

★ **Pleased to Meet Me** / 1987 / Sire ♦♦♦♦♦
Pared down to a trio, the band offers a complex set of ballads and guitar blazers and continues its examination of the effects of rock stardom. Producer Jim Dickinson (Ry Cooder, Big Star) gives the group a piledriver sound, like a boombox with the loudness up to ten. "Alex Chilton," a hard-rocking ode to Big Star's founder; "Can't Hardly Wait," with its great Memphis groove and Box Tops-style horn and string parts; and the haunting "Skyway" are among this album's highlights. —*John Floyd*

Don't Tell a Soul / 1989 / Sire ♦♦♦
The full-blown production made some cry sell out, but *Don't Tell a Soul* contained a heightened level of melodicism that produced some wonderful moments, particularly the expansive "Darlin' One," "Talent Show," "Achin' to Be," and their first #1 AOR hit, "I'll Be You." With that song, Westerberg practically achieved the magic he so much admired on Big Star's records. If *Don't Tell a Soul* hadn't been a Replacements album, its appealingly sloppy melodic power-pop would have, more than likely, earned rave reviews. This contains their most desolate work, highlighted by "I'll Be You" (their first #1 AOR hit), "Talent Show," the expansive psychedelia of "Darlin' One," and the creepy "Rock & Roll Ghost." —*John Floyd*

○ **All Shook Down** / 1990 / Sire ♦♦♦♦
More a Westerberg solo album than a band effort, this is a delicate, acoustic-based set, which finds him finally facing the perils of adulthood. But don't worry, he hasn't become a Jackson Browne-ian simp. —*John Floyd*

The Residents

Group, Experimental
The Residents are one of rock's oddest and most mysterious groups. Their identity has been a closely guarded secret for two decades. In rare public appearances, they are typically disguised as giant eyeballs decked out in tuxes and top hats. But behind all the weirdness is...more weirdness—primitive mutations of popular songs by the likes of Elvis, James Brown, and Hank Williams, frightening nursery rhymes, elaborate mythological epics that span several albums, and pure sonic explorations. Like the most adventurous modern composers, the Residents understand the emotive power of sound; early works like *Eskimo* are unforgettably evocative. Their later projects contain subtle social commentary. Even when the parody verges on self-parody, the music retains shock value and sophistication. —*Myles Boisen*

○ **Meet the Residents** / 1974 / East Side Digital ♦♦♦♦

○ **Third Reich & Roll** / 1975 / East Side Digital ♦♦♦♦

○ **Eskimo** / 1979 / East Side Digital ♦♦♦♦
A CD re-issue of the 1979 record. A wild vision of what original polar Eskimo life was like before government housing came along in the late '60s. Contains "The Walrus Hunt," "Birth," "Artic Hysteria," "The Angry Angakok," "A Spirit Steals A Child," "The Festival of Death." A totally engaging tone-poem, filled with humor, pathos, shamanism, and all the other great things, with skillful electronic sound-painting, and always the right touch. —Blue *Gene Tyranny*

○ **The Commercial Album** / 1980 / East Side Digital ♦♦♦♦
40 brief stories, homilies, instrumentals, slices of life, each exactly 60 seconds long —"The Coming of the Crow," "Nice Old Man," "My Work Is So Behind," "Die in Terror," "Floyd," "Act of Being Polite," etc. . . . each unique in vocals and instrumentation, and each weirdly humorous, momentarily stunning. —Blue *Gene Tyranny*

★ **God in Three Persons** / 1988 / Rykodisc ♦♦♦♦♦
Employing the same stress scheme as Poe's "The Raven" throughout its 62 minutes, "God in Three Persons" is an extended work in talking-blues style for narrator, electronic instruments, and a cho-

rus providing humorous comments not found in the libretto. As in all Residents pieces, the voices are modified electronically and the musical elements are deceptively minimal—most of its 14 episodes have only two chords, which still manage to instantly produce the correct atmosphere (Wagnerian thirds for mythic import, tonic-dominant in triplets for '50s teenage love story, etc.). There are only passing riffs, more like comments, and the only melody in the whole piece is a wheezy organ quote of the standard doxology hymn "Holy, Holy, Holy (God in Three Persons)." The subject matter is, in part, the derivation of religious and other symbolic images from the naturally erotic, but that's only part of it. Give this one a listen. —Blue *Gene Tyranny*

Paul Revere & the Raiders

Group, Rock & Roll, Pop/Rock

In 1959, two natives of Caldwell, ID, met and decided to form a band. Paul Revere (b. Jan 7, 1942) and Mark Lindsay (b. Mar 9, 1942) called their group the Downbeats, after the jazz magazine. At first the group was largely instrumental, featuring Revere's pounding roadhouse piano (in the style of Jerry Lee Lewis) and Lindsay's sax playing. The band was renamed Paul Revere & the Raiders in 1960, after a pressing plant owner suggested Revere ought to capitalize on his memorable name.

Their first single was an instrumental called "Beatnick Sticks," a takeoff on "Chopsticks." Their third single, an instrumental called "Like Long Hair" was their first national hit, getting them played on Dick Clark's *American Bandstand.* Eventually Clark became one of the most important people in furthering the band's career.

Columbia signed the band, and Terry Melcher was given the job of producing them and toughening up their sound. Beginning with "Steppin' Out," the band had a long stretch of substantial hits, aided by their residency on Dick Clark's *Where the Action Is* TV show.

Melcher managed to get songwriters Barry Mann and Cynthia Weil to give the Raiders an antidrug song, "Kicks," (originally written for the Animals) and it became one of their biggest hits. Mann and Weil supplied the followup, "Hungry."

Other hits included "Good Thing," "Him or Me—What's It Gonna Be?," "Indian Reservation," "Just like Me," and "The Great Airplane Strike." Mark Lindsay concurrently pursued a solo career, scoring a hit with "Arizona" during the latter part of the Raiders's existence. Paul Revere continued to perform with a modified lineup of Paul Revere & the Raiders. —*Rick Clark*

○ **Legend of Paul Revere** / 1990 / Columbia/Legacy ✦✦✦✦
This two-CD anthology, with 55 songs, may be a lot more Raiders than the average fan would want. But go for it and be amazed at how consistently strong this rocking band from the Great Northwest was. Includes all the hits. —*Jeff Tamarkin*

● **The Essential Ride '63-'67** / 1995 / Columbia/Legacy ✦✦✦✦
A much more sensible buy than the double-CD *Legend Of Paul Revere,* this 20-track compilation focuses on their toughest (and therefore best) material. Has all the big early hits, and about half the songs weren't on *Legend,* most notably their fine pre-Monkees version of "Steppin' Stone." Note that the version of "Hungry" here is an alternate take, good or bad news depending on whether you have the original hit rendition already. —*Richie Unterberger*

Revolting Cocks

Group, Industrial, Alternative Pop/Rock

Revolting Cocks have been the sleaziest and ugliest industrial band in the land since their debut album in 1986. Over the years, their records have featured many musicians, but the core members of the band are Ministry's Al Jourgensen, ex-Fini Tribe member Chris Connelly, and Belgian producer Luc Van Acker. Combining samples, guitars, synths, and pounding dance rhythms, their records are a trashy synthesis of the most extreme industrial noise, the silliest pop culture, and classic art-rock. Because of their irreverence, they are the industrial band that is the most fun to listen to, if not the best or most influential. —*Stephen Thomas Erlewine*

○ **Big Sexy Land** / 1986 / Wax Trax! ✦✦✦✦
You Goddamned Son of a Bitch / 1988 / Wax Trax! ✦✦
● **Beers, Steers & Queers** / 1990 / Wax Trax! ✦✦✦✦
A sleazy set of campy, vulgar samples and rhythms, *Beers, Steers & Queers* is the Revolting Cocks' most entertaining record. —*David Jehnzen*

Linger Ficken' Good . . . / 1993 / Warner Brothers ✦✦✦
Revolting Cocks' major-label debut treads no new ground but contains a giddy, demented reworking of Rod Stewart's "Do Ya Think I'm Sexy," that has to be heard to be believed. —*AMG*

The Rezillos

Group, Punk, New Wave

One of Scotland's great punk bands, the Rezillos came on like gangbusters with a hip attitude, a revved-up band (featuring soon-to-be Human Leaguer Jo Callis) and the remarkable pipes of Ms. Fay Fife. With a flair for garish '60s pop-art artifacts (something I'm positive influenced the B-52s), the Rezillos were decidedly less serious than their punk contemporaries, but their debut album *Can't Stand the Rezillos* is a cheesy classic. —*John Dougan*

Mission Accomplished . . . but the Beat Goes On / 1979 / Sire ✦✦✦
● **Can't Stand the Rezillos** / 1993 / Sire ✦✦✦✦
Nearly everything this energetic new wave band ever recorded is on this splendid one-disc compilation. —*Stephen Thomas Erlewine*

Emitt Rhodes

Singer-Songwriter, Pop/Rock

Hawthorne, California native, Emitt Rhodes made his first mark in the music world in 1967 as the leader of the baroque-pop band the Merry-Go-Round. The band achieved some marginal success with the Rhodes-penned "Live," and "You're a Very Lovely Woman," recording one album of *Magical Mystery Tour*-inspired pop. When the band broke up in 1969, Rhodes set up a home studio in his parent's garage and began his solo career, engineering and playing all instruments himself. The strength of his initial demos, now showing a strong Paul McCartney influence, helped him get signed to ABC/Dunhill. His critically-acclaimed, self-titled debut managed to break into the Top 40 in 1971 but pressure from his record company forced him to rush-release a follow-up, *Mirror,* the same year. *Mirror* was predictably a lesser effort, barely charting. By the time of the third album, 1973's *Farewell to Paradise,* Rhodes was running into legal problems with ABC, since he was unable to fulfill his contract, which demanded he deliver a new album every six months. Dissillusioned, he retired from the performing side of the business, working instead as an engineer and studio operator for Elektra/Asylum. Though he hasn't released an album since *Farewell to Paradise,* he continues to write and demo new songs. —*Sara Sytsma*

○ **Emitt Rhodes** / 1970 / One Way ✦✦✦✦
Rhodes turns in a fine performance, much in the style of Paul McCartney's first solo album. Like McCartney, Rhodes wrote all the songs, played all the instruments and recorded the album at home. There the comparison ends. Songs like "With My Face on the Floor" and "She's Such a Beauty" are the kinds of songs that pop into your head 20 years later and get you as excited as the first time you heard them. —*Jim Worbois*

The American Dream / 1971 / A&M ✦✦✦
If you wish to get an overview of the early career of Emitt Rhodes, this may be the place. Consisting of tracks recorded by his former band, Merry-Go-Round, as well as some "later" material on which he is backed by some of L.A.'s finest, this record will only serve to whet your appetite. "You're a Very Lovely Woman" is strong inducement to look for further Merry-Go-Round material, while a song like "Pardon Me" points the way to Rhodes's first Dunhill album. —*Jim Worbois*

Mirror / 1972 / Dunhill ✦✦✦
Rhodes continues strolling down the same road as McCartney and has discovered some of the same potholes. Like McCartney, Rhodes is insulated from outside influences (especially peers) and the work isn't nearly as exciting or adventurous as the first time out. This is still a pleasant record but this is not the Emitt Rhodes album one would be inclined to grab first. —*Jim Worbois*

Farewell to Paradise / 1973 / Dunhill ✦✦
● **Listen, Listen: The Best of Emitt Rhodes** / 1995 / Varese Sarabande ✦✦✦✦
Listen, Listen is an extensive, 21-track overview of Rhodes' commercially underappreciated career. A chronological collection, the disc begins with his work with the Merry-Go-Round (six tracks—nearly all of the band's finest moments), covers his solo years with highlights from the three albums as well as a rare single from

1972 ("Tame the Lion") and ends with a track from a 1980 aborted solo album. —*Chris Woodstra*

Cliff Richard (Harry Webb)

Group, Rock & Roll

Britain's answer to Elvis Presley, Richard (born Harry Webb) dominated the pre-Beatles British pop scene in the late '50s and early '60s. An accomplished singer with a genuine feel for the music, Richard's artistic legacy is nonetheless meager, as he was quickly steered toward a middle-of-the-road pop direction. Several of his late '50s recordings, however, were genuinely exciting Presley-esque rockers—especially his first hit, "Move It" (1958)—and gave British teenagers their first taste of genuine homegrown rock & roll talent. Backed by the Shadows—clean-cut instrumental virtuosos who became legends of their own—Richard embarked on a truly awesome string of hit singles in Britain, scoring no less than 43 Top 20 hits between 1958 and 1969. One of these, although it was by no means one of the more successful, was an actual Mick Jagger/Keith Richards composition (the ballad "Blue Turns to Grey").

In his homeland, Richard's popularity was diminished only slightly by the rise of the Beatles, but in his prime, he had a much rougher time in the U.S., hitting the Top 40 only twice (with "Living Doll" in 1959 and "It's All in the Game" in 1963). Richard belatedly cracked the U.S. Top Ten in 1976 with "Devil Woman," and racked up a few other hits ("We Don't Talk Anymore," "Dreaming," "A Little in Love") in a mainstream pop/rock style. He remains an institution in Britain, where he is one of the nation's most popular all-around entertainers of all time. —*Richie Unterberger*

● **20 Rock 'N' Roll Hits** / 1979 / EMI ✦✦✦✦
Concentrating mostly on his 1958-59 material, this has Cliff's most untamed recordings (bearing in mind that they're still pretty polished compared to most U.S. rockabilly). Includes his first brace of hits—"Move It," "High Class Baby," "Mean Streak," and "Never Mind"—along with the megasmash "Livin' Doll," which pointed the way toward the pop ballad path he would follow in the '60s. —*Richie Unterberger*

○ **Cliff Richard & the Shadows** / 1984 / EMI ✦✦✦✦
Cliff Richard & the Shadows rock out like nobody's business on this classic live album (arguably rock's first authorized and professionally recorded concert album). Recorded in February 1959 at EMI in front of 500 screaming fans, the sound is raw and raunchy by British standards of the time. (Import) —*Bruce Eder*

Keith Richards

b. Dec. 18, 1943, Dartford, Kent, England
Rock & Roll

One of the few White guitarists with strong blues roots who has been able to take the form to new places, Richards's contribution to the vocabulary of rock guitar cannot be overestimated. His heavy reliance on Delta blues open tunings (mostly played on guitars with only five strings) has provided licks that are part and parcel for any player who wants to get the joint rocking and the dance floor packed. Though much has been made of his lifestyle, and time has reduced his voice to a sore-throated husk, it is as a guitarist and songwriter that Richards has ultimately established his reputation. —*Cub Koda*

● **Talk Is Cheap** / 1988 / Virgin ✦✦✦✦
Richards's lone solo album includes "Take It So Hard," "Struggle," "I Could Have Stood You Up," and "Make No Mistake," with a classic Hi Rhythm Section groove and featuring great guest vocals by Sarah Dash. —*Cub Koda*

Live at the Hollywood Palladium (Dec 15, 1988) / 1991 / Virgin ✦✦✦
A nicely ragged live album that captures Richards and the Winos at the top of their form. —*Stephen Thomas Erlewine*

Main Offender / 1992 / Virgin ✦✦✦
Richards's second solo album is even more delightfully focused than his first. Highlights include "Wicked as It Seems," "Eileen," and the searing "999." New Rolling Stones albums should rock this hard. —*Cub Koda*

Lionel Richie

b. Jun. 20, 1949, Tuskegee, AL
Soul, Urban, Pop

After he left the Commodores in 1981, Lionel Richie became one of the most successful solo artists of the early '80s, earning a string of thirteen Top Ten hits between 1981 and 1987, including five number one singles ("Endless Love," "Truly," "All Night Long (All Night)," "Hello," "Say You, Say Me"). Between 1986 and 1992 he didn't release any new material, but in 1993 he re-emerged with a new album that sold well, but not up to the standards he set a decade earlier. —*Stephen Thomas Erlewine*

○ **Lionel Richie** / 1982 / Motown ✦✦✦✦
Lionel Richie was perhaps the dominant songwriter and performer of the early '80s. His overwhelmingly sentimental love tunes were massive crossover hits, and he turned awkwardness into an art form. This was his first big album, and it peaked at #3 on the pop album chart, eventually selling over four million copies and staying on the charts for 140 weeks. —*Ron Wynn*

● **Can't Slow Down** / 1983 / Motown ✦✦✦✦
The Lionel Richie gravy train was in full throttle on this second big hit album, which eventually sold over eight million copies. Richie earned the 1984 Grammy for Album of the Year, and such tunes as "Hello," "Running With the Night," "Stuck On You" and "Love Will Find A Way" were all over the R&B, pop, and even country airwaves. —*Ron Wynn*

Dancing on the Ceiling / 1986 / Motown ✦✦✦
Lionel Richie had a slump of sorts after the incredible success of *Can't Slow Down*. This record, which came some three years later, only sold four million instead of eight million copies, stayed atop the pop album charts for only one month instead of two, and only had a few pop hits in "Love Will Conquer All," "Say You, Say Me," "Se La" and "Deep River Woman." —*Ron Wynn*

Back to Front / 1992 / Motown ✦✦✦
After six silent years, *Back to Front* is a respectable comeback from Lionel Richie, although it rarely catches fire or is as memorably melodic as his records from the early '80s. —*Stephen Thomas Erlewine*

Jonathan Richman

b. 1951, Boston, Massachusetts
Rock & Roll, Pop/Rock

Jonathan Richman (b. 1951) is a certifiable rock weirdo. In 1971 he and the Modern Lovers cut some demos for Warner Bros (produced by John Cale) that funneled the influence of the Velvet Underground into the twisted vision of a high-school geek. Those demos were finally released in 1976, but everything he's done since then has pushed the parameters of cuteness into theme albums (*Jonathan Goes Country*, etc.), amplifying Richman's lighthearted approach. —*John Floyd & Cub Koda*

☆ **Modern Lovers** / 1976 / Rhino ✦✦✦✦✦
This is a reissue of the 1971 John Cale-produced demos that unknowingly precipitated what would eventually become punk rock. As he states on "Roadrunner," he's in love with the modern world but also with girls. His odes to a lack of love make for a cogent debut. —*John Floyd*

Live / 1977 / Rhino ✦✦✦
○ **Jonathan Richman & the Modern Lovers** / Jan. 1977 / Beserkley ✦✦✦✦
Richman's second collection of Modern Lovers, over which he was billed (eventually, the group name would be dropped) had a lighter rock & roll sound than the first. In fact, as often as not, Richman played acoustic guitar. And his lyrical concerns had similarly lightened up, to the point of childlike whimsy on such songs as "Hey There Little Insect" and "Here Come the Martian Martians." But the focus was still Richman's unabashed vocalizing (the word "sings" is put in quotes on the back cover), giving the whole album an amateurish charm. —*William Ruhlmann*

○ **Rock 'N' Roll with the Modern Lovers** / Feb. 1977 / Rhino ✦✦✦✦
Rock 'N' Roll with the Modern Lovers. Richman branches out to Japanese music, a "South American Folk Song," and even "Egyptian Reggae" (the last earning him a UK Top 5 hit), but the real highlight on *Rock 'N' Roll with the Modern Lovers* is that ode to a totaled car, "Dodge Veg-O-Matic." —*William Ruhlmann*

Back in Your Life / 1979 / Beserkley ✦✦✦
○ **The Original Modern Lovers** / 1981 / Bomp! ✦✦✦✦
There's a good deal of confusion about when the demos on this album were recorded; the liner notes claim that they were made in 1972, before John Cale produced the tracks that eventually composed their official debut release (although it has been reported

that the Cale sessions date from 1971). Anyway, the fidelity on these cuts (produced by Kim Fowley) is less than optimal, but the performances are probably the best that the original lineup managed to lay down during their haphazard existence, and the truest to the band's vision. Includes fiery takes of many of their best songs ("Roadrunner," "Astral Plane," "I'm Straight," "I Wanna Sleep"), and some Richman originals are not to be found anywhere else. —*Richie Unterberger*

Jonathan Sings / 1983 / Rough Trade ✦✦✦

Having a Party with Jonathan Richman / 1983 / Rounder ✦✦✦

○ **Rockin' & Romance** / 1985 / Twin/Tone ✦✦✦✦
While it is generally true that many of Richman's post-1980 albums are all but interchangeable, with their earnest naive cheerfulness, this stands as one of the best, if you like his schtick and need to make a choice. The production is sparse, accentuating the acoustic guitar and the doo-wop harmonies (both male and female), with light but purposeful drums. Jonathan covers his usual terrain here: juvenilia ("My Jeans," "The U.F.O. Man," "Chewing Gum Wrapper"), cultural heroes ("Vincent Van Gogh," "Walter Johnson"), and optimistic paeans to the simple pleasures of life ("The Beach"). Heart-warming and melodic stuff that might well sound insipid in the hands of others. —*Richie Unterberger*

It's Time for Jonathan Richman / 1986 / Upside ✦✦✦

● **Beserkley Years** / 1987 / Rhino ✦✦✦✦
After the first Modern Lovers album, Richman's records were enjoyable but fairly spotty. Thankfully, *The Beserkley Years* collects the best moments from his '70s records, when his cuteness was endearing, not irritating. With "Roadrunner," "Pablo Picasso," "Here Come the Martian Martians," "Important In Your Life," "Ice Cream Man," and "Dodge Veg-O-Matic" forming its core, this collection is a definitive portrait of his goofy, catchy minimalist pop and rock. —*Stephen Thomas Erlewine*

Modern Lovers 88 / 1988 / Rounder ✦✦✦
One of his better '80s efforts, and certainly one of the most basic, performed in an acoustic trio format. It's nonetheless quite rocking, with heavy debts to doo-wop and Bo Diddley rhythms, and a jolly (though not sappy) summertime campfire feel. Some of his best uptempo tunes are here, including "I Love Hot Nights," "California Desert Party," and "Gail Loves Me." —*Richie Unterberger*

Jonathan Richman / 1989 / Rounder ✦✦✦

Jonathan Goes Country / 1990 / Rounder ✦✦✦

○ **I, Jonathan** / 1992 / Rounder ✦✦✦✦

Jonathan, Te Vas a Emocionar! / 1994 / Rounder ✦✦

Precise Modern Lovers Order / 1994 / Rounder ✦✦✦
Live material recorded in various locations, circa 1971-1973 (the exact dates have become muddied with time). The fidelity and performances are fairly funky—this is essentially a high-quality bootleg—but the band (augmented by original guitarist John Felice on the earliest cuts) attacks the material with a fair amount of elan. Includes most of their best songs—"Roadrunner," "Girlfriend," "She Cracked," "I'm Straight," "Pablo Picasso"—as well as rarities like "The Mixer," "Womanhood," "Dance With Me," and a cover of the Velvet Underground obscurity "Foggy Notion." —*Richie Unterberger*

You Must Ask The Heart / 1995 / Rounder ✦✦

Ride

Group, Alternative Pop/Rock
Trancelike vocals and dance grooves, coupled with walls of ambient distorto-guitar, are this Oxford, England, quartet's stock in trade. In the style of Echo & the Bunnymen, psychedelic dance-pop is filtered through early Pink Floyd psycho-drone. —*Rick Clark*

● **Nowhere** / 1990 / Sire ✦✦✦✦
Rackety, reverberant, psychedelic drone-rock from Oxford, England. Fans of hypnotic detached singing against numbing waves of dissonance should find this somewhat interesting, particularly the throbbing "Polar Bear," the lumbering yet airy "Vapour Trail," the fairly accessible "Taste," and the reckless "Here and Now." The title cut is an effective fusing of early Pink Floyd sonic freakout and industrial noise sludge. —*Rick Clark*

○ **Smile** / Jan. 1990 / Sire ✦✦✦✦
Their first two EPs from Britain's Creation label appear on one American collection. Sonically, it is muddier than *Nowhere* (if that can be possible), but the tuneful crash-and-burn of "Like a Daydream" is one of their best. —*Rick Clark*

Going Blank Again / Oct. 1991 / Sire ✦✦
Ride's second full-length album finds the band in a holding pattern. While the loud, atmospheric guitars and gorgeous melodies *sound* good, it isn't a big departure from *Nowhere*, and it doesn't point the band in a new direction. Fortunately, they experienced a creative rebirth on their next album. —*Stephen Thomas Erlewine*

Carnival of Light / 1994 / Sire ✦✦✦
A thoroughly impressive, assured set of swirling guitar psychedelia that recalls classic British pop without ever sounding dated. —*Stephen Thomas Erlewine*

The Righteous Brothers

Group, Soul, Pop/Rock
The Righteous Brothers vocal duo consists of Bill Medley and Bobby Hatfield (both b. 1941). Generally regarded as the popular originators of "blue-eyed soul," they originally formed as the Paramours in a stronger doo-wop style, eventually tackling harder R&B material in a more gospel-oriented fashion, prompting the name change. The duo's early recordings featured the hit "Little Latin Lupe Lu," written by Medley. The song quickly became a garage-band staple of the '60s, successfully covered by both the Kingsmen and Mitch Ryder. With producer Phil Spector, they scored Top Ten hits consistently with classic ballad material like "You've Lost That Lovin' Feelin' " and "Unchained Melody," the latter featured prominently in the movie *Ghost*. Even with label and production changes, the hits kept coming through the end of the '60s, when they went their separate ways. They reunited in 1974-1975, had another Top Ten smash with "Rock and Roll Heaven," and are still performing today to appreciative audiences. Their 21 entries on the *Billboard* Hot 100 chart and contribution to the music makes their eventual induction into the Rock & Roll Hall of Fame a given. —*Cub Koda*

★ **Anthology 1962-1974** / 1989 / Rhino ✦✦✦✦✦
Excellent two-CD retrospective covering the hits from the early Moonglow R&B sides up to "Rock and Roll Heaven." The definitive overview. —*Cub Koda*

Live 1967 / Live Gold ✦✦✦
Great live performance from Anaheim Stadium, running the gamut from familiar hits to doo-wop and gospel favorites. With dynamic singing and energetic backing, this one catches them pretty much at the top of their form. —*Cub Koda*

Billy Lee Riley

b. 1933
Rockabilly
Billy Lee Riley is a rockabilly singer and multi-instrumentalist. An alumni of Sun Records, he was one of the most crazed, unabashed rockers that label had to offer—in the company of Jerry Lee Lewis, Carl Perkins, and Sonny Burgess, that's saying a lot. Proficient at harmonica, guitar, bass, and drums, Riley contributed as a sideman to many a classic Sun session, and his combo the Little Green Men (most notably guitarist Roland Janes and drummer J.M. Van Eaton) in time became the Sun house band. Riley recorded for a number of labels in a variety of styles, especially effective with blues. Though never commercially successful, Riley's Sun recordings of "Flying Saucer Rock 'n' Roll" and "Red Hot" (both covered in wooden renditions by Robert Gordon) remain landmarks of the genre. —*Cub Koda*

● **Classic Recordings, 1956-1960** / Jul. 1990 / Bear Family ✦✦✦✦
All the classic Sun sides, plus later Memphis recordings in a brilliant 2-CD set. Raw rockin' at its finest. —*Cub Koda*

Rip, Rig & Panic

Group, Fusion
Named after a terrific '60s jazz album by Rahsaan Roland Kirk, Rip, Rig & Panic answered the question: what happens when avant-garde post-punks collide headlong with a pop/soul singer and play a mutated form of jazz? A loosely knit collection of ex-Pop Group members (Gareth Sanger and Bruce Smith) and young stars-to-be (Neneh Cherry), Rip, Rig & Panic formed in 1980 as quintessential avant-garde bohemians, eschewing pop for a more primal, percussive foundation (slightly reggae, slightly Afro-pop), upon which was layered free-jazz blowing and honking, soulful singing, and Cecil Taylor-inspired piano mania. But, as intense as this music was, it wasn't done with a dry academic seriousness; quite the contrary, Rip, Rig & Panic were all about fun and play-

fulness. Even the song titles ("Constant Drudgery is Harmful to Soul, Spirit & Health" and "Those Eskimo Women Speak Frankly") sounded more like surreal announcements than they did traditional, catchy song titles. Arguably the most likable bunch of avant-garde types ever to record music, Rip, Rig & Panic called it a day after three mostly wonderful, if somewhat inconsistent records. If your taste in music, even fringe music, is such that a strong melodic focus is necessary, than perhaps this probably won't be your cup of tea. However, if you don't mind a little chaos with your funk, then give this heady mix a chance; it will work its way into your heart, head and feet. As for the members, Bruce Smith joined Public Image Ltd. for a spell, and Neneh Cherry became a huge pop star (deservedly so) with her first solo record. — *John Dougan*

● **God** / 1981 / Virgin ✦✦✦✦
With Gareth Sanger leading the charge, Rip, Rig & Panic's debut is much more user-friendly than anything recorded by Sanger's previous band, the always abrasive Pop Group. This record gallops along from start to finish, honking and buzzing along the way, with loads of odd vocalizing and feral, primal, repetitive rhythms. Not the most significant album to come out of the early days of English post-punk, but one that still delivers plenty of smiles 15 years later. — *John Dougan*

I Am Cold / 1982 / Virgin ✦✦✦
With additional help from ex-Slits singer Ari Upp and Cherry's stepfather, noted jazz trumpeter Don Cherry, *I Am Cold* is a slightly more mature work, but the exuberance and all-out craziness that marked their debut is here in full force. A little rambling, but an approach to music unlike one you've heard before. — *John Dougan*

Attitude / 1983 / Virgin ✦✦✦
○ **Kneep Deep in Hits** / ✦✦✦✦

Rising Sons

Group, Blues Rock, Folk-Rock
No one knew quite what to make of this L.A. band in the mid-'60s, which unbelievably included Ry Cooder, Taj Mahal, Kevin Kelly (later in the Byrds), and even Ed Cassidy (briefly) in the same lineup. They only managed one single on Columbia before breaking up in 1966, but they also got to lay down an album's worth of unreleased material, which was finally issued over 25 years later. Their languid, bluesy, folksy sort of sound anticipated future recordings by outfits like Moby Grape, Buffalo Springfield, the Dead, and even the country-rock Byrds. — *Richie Unterberger*

● **Rising Sons featuring Taj Mahal & Ry Cooder** / 1992 / Columbia/Legacy ✦✦✦✦
Their lone single and unreleased album form the core of this 22-track reissue, which features imaginative rearrangements of standards like "Corrine, Corrina," an obscure Dylan cover ("Walkin' down the Line"), rocking originals, a confident performance of Goffin/King's "Take A Giant Step" (later Mahal's signature tune), and nifty guitar interplay between Mahal and Cooder throughout. Overall, it sounds a lot more like it belongs in 1967-68 than 1965-66. This archival release has value above and beyond historical interest. — *Richie Unterberger*

The Rising Storm

Group, Garage Rock
While still at prep school in the mid-'60s, this New England group recorded one of the rarest and most respected garage band albums, divided equally between outside and self-penned material. This effort was distinguished from many other recordings of the sort not by the respectable covers (of material by Them, Wilson Pickett, Love, and fellow Boston garage bands the Remains and the Rockin' Ramrods), but by the beautiful, haunting original folk-rock ballads. Disbanding upon graduation, they were rediscovered by hardcore '60s collectors over 15 years later, and actually reunited for a live recording at their alma mater in the early '80s. — *Richie Unterberger*

○ **Calm Before the Rising Storm** / 1968 / Remnant ✦✦✦✦
Back in Anover Again / 1983 / Arf! Arf! ✦✦✦
● **Calm Before . . . /Alive Again at Andover** / 1992 / Arf! Arf! ✦✦✦✦
This CD reissue combines their original LP with the live reunion recording. It's the original album, unsurprisingly, that you want this for, featuring some melodic folk-rock compositions that were among the best garage music ever recorded. — *Richie Unterberger*

Johnny Rivers (John Ramistella)

b. Nov. 7, 1942
Pop/Rock
Johnny Rivers, intent on getting a break in the music business, left his Baton Rouge home for New York and Nashville. DJ Alan Freed suggested the name change to Rivers, since he originated from the Delta South. After a series of movies and song cuts and a stint with Louie Prima, Rivers gained attention on the Los Angeles club scene, particularly at the Whiskey a Go-Go, where he recorded his debut, *Johnny Rivers at the Whiskey a Go-Go*, for Imperial Records. Versions of Chuck Berry's "Memphis" and "Maybellene" hit, launching a series of live hit singles that reflect his tendency to draw from the blues and old rock & roll. Rivers scored with "Secret Agent Man," capitalizing on the then-current fascination with foreign espionage. After that he increasingly turned his attentions to a lusher MOR formula with the number one "Poor Side of Town," "Baby I Need Your Lovin,' " "The Tracks of My Tears," and the haunting "Summer Rain." During the '70s, Rivers had a comeback with several remakes of old rock hits, as well as a hit with the romantic "Swayin' to the Music (Slow Dancin')." Besides his artistry, Rivers displayed good commercial instincts by discovering and signing the 5th Dimension and assisting the career of writer Jimmy Webb. Rivers continues to perform, sounding like he hasn't aged a day since his biggest hits. — *Rick Clark*

Last Boogie in Paris / 1974 / Atlantic ✦✦
Rivers delivered a set of well-known oldies for this 1973 concert, as well as his hit "Summer Rain" and a 10-minute tribute to "John Lee Hooker." Competent and uninspiring, the backing is provided by the session men comprising his L.A. Boogie Band, who epitomize early-'70s slick professionalism. — *Richie Unterberger*

● **The Best of Johnny Rivers** / 1987 / EMI America ✦✦✦✦
A fine single-disc collection, *Best of Johnny Rivers* features most of his biggest hits, making it a good purchase for those who don't want the definitive double-disc set. — *Stephen Thomas Erlewine*

○ **Anthology** / 1991 / Rhino ✦✦✦✦
One of the great interpretive singers in rock & roll, Rivers made every song his own, and this 2-CD package is proof that he rarely faltered. — *Jeff Tamarkin*

○ **Changes/Rewind** / 1993 / Capitol ✦✦✦✦
Johnny Rivers took a dramatic step during the late '60s, embracing adult standards and recording several Jimmy Webb compositions. These were solemn, literate tales of woe, anguish and turmoil requiring lyric interpretation and careful vocal pacing. They were also heavily produced numbers with string sections and background vocalists. The change didn't hurt Rivers' career; indeed, it won him new critical attention as a serious ballad stylist and landed him some hits. This single-disc collection covers 23 songs from two LPs, *Changes* and *Rewind*. Besides the big hit covers "Tracks of My Tears" and "Baby, I Need Your Loving," there is arguably his greatest ballad, "Poor Side of Town." While not everything worked, this material showed another side of Johnny Rivers and expanded his popularity. — *Ron Wynn*

The Rivieras

Group, Rock & Roll
A South Bend, IN, rock & roll band, the Rivieras' one big hit was one of the last great gasps of pure American rock & roll before the British invasion took over the charts. Original members Otto Nuss (organ), Doug Gean (bass), Marty "Bo" Fortson (vocals and guitar), Joe Pennell (guitar), and Paul Dennert (drums) were local teen ballroom heroes. They recorded a supercharged version of the Joe Jones R&B semi-hit "California Sun" featuring a powerful drum intro and the now-famous signature guitar and organ riff. The song became a hit in the midst of the first flush of Beatlemania, only nudged out of the #1 spot on the national charts by "I Want to Hold Your Hand." Although several equally fine 45s and two albums followed, the band's relatively young ages, coupled with numerous personnel changes caused by the draft and the changing musical climate, caused the band to break up by 1966. Nuss, Gean, and Fortson reunited the Rivieras in the mid '80s, recording and doing local shows, sounding as great as ever. Though their time in the spotlight was brief, their one big hit continues to define for future generations everything that's pulsatingly great about American teen-band rock & roll. — *Cub Koda*

● **California Sun** / 1964 / Sonet ✦✦✦✦
Import reissue of their first album. —*Cub Koda*

○ **Campus Party** / 1965 / Riviera ✦✦✦✦
Second album; classic frat-band sound. Out of print and impossibly rare but worth the search at any cost. —*Cub Koda*

The Rivingtons

Group, R&B, Doo-Wop
The Rivingtons were a West Coast vocal group featuring Al Frazier, Carl White, John "Sonny" Harris, and Turner "Rocky" Wilson Jr. Though they are best known for their string of early-'60s novelties, the Rivingtons in reality had a rich tradition of doo-wop in their background, going back to their original recordings for Federal as the Lamplighters in 1953. They did extensive backup group work throughout the '50s between their own stray releases under a number of different names; the Sharps (singing on the original "Little Bitty Pretty One" and "Over and Over" by Thurston Harris), the Tenderfoots, the Rebels (they do all the backups on the Duane Eddy hits), the Four After Fives, the Crenshaws. They even sang backup on Paul Anka's first record, credited as the Jacks! In 1962 they became the Rivingtons and hit pay dirt with their first record, the self-penned "Pa Pa Ooh Mow Mow," one of the truly great rock & roll songs to make a virtue of sheer gibberish. They hit the charts again a year later with "The Bird's the Word," capitalizing on a current West Coast dance fad that teenagers were doing to "Pa Pa Ooh Mow Mow." A landlocked surf-teen combo from Minnesota called the Trashmen combined the two songs, revved up the beat to warp factor nine, and scored a massive hit with "Surfin' Bird." Despite no further chart success, their place in rock & roll history (both for the classic performances they recorded and for being the inspiration behind one of the great noise-rock anthems of all time) is assured. —*Cub Koda*

Doin' the Bird / 1963 / Liberty ✦✦✦
● **The Liberty Years** / 1991 / EMI America ✦✦✦✦
An excellent 23-track CD with detailed notes and great sound, featuring both sides of all their original-issue 45s (including the insane followup "Mama Ooh Mow Mow") plus all the tracks from their lone Liberty album, *Doin' the Bird.* —*Cub Koda*

Robbie Robertson

b. Jul. 1943
Singer-Songwriter, Pop/Rock
The chief songwriter and lead guitarist of the Band, Robertson dissolved the group in late 1976. He then acted in and produced *Carny,* wrote and/or chose the music for the soundtracks of Martin Scorsese's *Raging Bull, King of Comedy,* and *The Color of Money,* and in 1987 released his first solo album. Relatively inactive in the late '80s, Robertson's second solo album, *Storyville,* was not released until 1991. —*Rob Bowman*

● **Robbie Robertson** / 1987 / Geffen ✦✦✦✦
Robbie Robertson's first solo album, released eleven years after the Band called it quits at *The Last Waltz,* found the singer/guitarist mining radically new territory. Hiring Daniel Lanois as co-producer, Robertson crafted an album that owed very little to the Band's roots-Americana sound. Instead, Robertson opted for a quirky, enigmatic modern approach, using drum programs, the stick, and guest musicians such as U2, Peter Gabriel, and Bill Dillon. If the album had a weakness, it was in the vocal department. Robertson had only sung lead on a couple of songs with the Band. His reedy ghost of a voice can be quite effective but wears a bit thin over the course of a whole album. Ultimately that is a minor complaint, as the songwriting, arrangements, playing, and sound-painting are superb. Highlights: "Broken Arrow" and "Somewhere Down the Crazy River." —*Rob Bowman*

Storyville / 1991 / Geffen ✦✦✦
Robertson's second album was four years in the making. Once again he set out to explore an approach and sound markedly different from any of his previous work. The album is conceptual, roughing out a story over ten songs set in New Orleans's legendary turn-of-the-century Storyville red-light district. Co-produced by Robertson, Stephen Hague, and Gary Gersh, the record was recorded in New Orleans with members of the Neville Brothers, Mardi Gras Indians, the Meters, and the Zion Harmonizers. Legendary New Orleans arranger Wardell Quezergue contributed stunning horn charts. More aggressive than Robertson's first solo release, *Storyville* is perhaps a little less mysterious and enigmatic. —*Rob Bowman*

Music for the Native Americans / 1994 / Capitol ✦✦✦
With *Storyville,* Robbie Robertson's music began to directly incorporate more world music influences; *Music for the Native Americans* makes that connection more explicit. Most of the album is quite evocative, recalling an American version of Peter Gabriel's Mediterranean exploration *Passion.* Robertson writes some fully formed songs, but most of the record is devoted to instrumental, incidental film music, and that's where he fully explores new musical territory. *Music for the Native Americans* is a soundtrack, yet contains some of Robertson's most challenging and complex music. —*Stephen Thomas Erlewine*

Smokey Robinson & the Miracles (William Robinson)

Group, Soul, R&B, Urban, Motown
Bob Dylan called him "America's greatest living poet." Certainly, he was—and is—one of America's greatest living voices; he has brought his thrilling high tenor to a wide variety of material, most of it marked by his innate good taste. Smokey Robinson's association with Motown-founder Berry Gordy goes back to the late '50s, when Gordy produced and co-wrote the singles that the Miracles recorded for Chess and Roulette. Subsequently, the Miracles were one of the first acts to record for Tamla—and one of the first to break; "Shop Around" was a hit in 1960 and was followed by 38 more before Robinson quit the group in 1972. He also wrote for other acts (including "The Way You Do the Things You Do" and "My Girl" for the Temptations and "My Guy" and "Two Lovers" for Mary Wells).

Perhaps Robinson's masterpiece was "Tracks of My Tears," which he recorded with the Miracles. Its success was all the more surprising because the group had largely confined themselves to dance-oriented novelties before then. Robinson's contributions to Motown as an artist, writer, and producer were rewarded with a vice presidency, although the group's momentum was sagging. Their career was temporarily bolstered in 1970 when "Tears of a Clown" (cut three years earlier) became their first #1 pop hit. Robinson went solo two years later, and his solo albums trace the journey of a man who peaked early in life but has never lost the creative spark. —*Colin Escott*

Shop Around / 1962 / Motown ✦✦✦

Cookin' with the Miracles / Nov. 1962 / Motown ✦✦✦
Their second album shows Smokey and Motown starting to "uptownize" with energetic strings, although it's still one of the Miracles' most uptempo and R&B-oriented efforts. A solid set, with virtually all the material coming from the pens of Robinson and Berry Gordy, although half of the tracks—comprising the best tunes, such as "That's The Way I Feel," "Ain't It Baby," and "Determination"—are available on the Smokey/Miracles box set. The CD reissue adds "Mighty Good Lovin'" as a bonus track. —*Richie Unterberger*

Fabulous Miracles / Feb. 1963 / Motown ✦✦✦

○ **Going to a Go-Go** / Nov. 1965 / Motown ✦✦✦✦
This was the first truly great Miracles album, and their first to crack the Top Ten on the LP chart. The title song was arguably Robinson's finest uptempo composition (along with "Get Ready"), and the album also contained the majestic ballads "Ooh Baby Baby" and "My Girl Has Gone," plus Robinson's signature tune, "Tracks of My Tears." After those heavyweights, it didn't matter what else was there, but "In Case You Need Love" and "My Baby Changes Like The Weather" were the kind of afterthought gems Motown churned out with regularity during their prime. —*Ron Wynn*

Make It Happen / Aug. 1967 / Motown ✦✦✦
This album was re-released under the title *The Tears of a Clown* after that song, which appears on the album, became a hit single in 1970. —*William Ruhlmann*

The Tears of a Clown / Aug. 1967 / Motown ✦✦✦
The title track revisited the arena of heartache and confessional soul that few have ever exploited more skillfully and memorably than Smokey Robinson. This album was actually an example of corporate greed at work; it was only grafting a new title onto an old album. Motown merely reissued *Greatest Hits, Vol. 2* with a fresh title to fill the gap as internal problems were preventing the completion of a new Miracles record. Of course, most of the songs were great, since "More Love" and "Love I Saw In You Was Just A Mirage" were among the many fine tunes on the album. But it was

just an early example of the label's constant recycling of their hits, which is now standard operating procedure. —*Ron Wynn*

Hi, We're the Miracles / 1969 / Motown ✦✦✦
A wonderful late-'60s album from the period when Smokey Robinson was still producing, writing for, and singing with the Miracles. They scored five R&B chart hits in 1969, among them the transcendent ballad "Baby, Baby, Don't Cry" and the equally fine "Doggone Right," as well as his version of "Abraham, Martin and John." It's one of the few Miracles releases closer to being a genuine album than a collection of singles. —*Ron Wynn*

Time out For . . . / Jul. 1969 / Motown ✦✦✦
Smokey Robinson was in peak form on this 1969 album, even though he would end his involvement with the group three years later. His voice was still splendid, his delivery and soaring falsetto magical, and his writing and production skills keen. The album boasted "Doggone Right" and "Here I Go Again" as its prime hit material, and was done with the soulful charm and elegance that marked every Miracles record from the mid-'60s until Robinson went solo in 1972. —*Ron Wynn*

★ **Anthology** / 1973 / Motown ✦✦✦✦✦
Detroit vocal group the Miracles were a fixture at Motown from day one. Driven by Robinson's superior writing and smooth, silky falsetto, the Miracles placed a stunning 48 singles on the Billboard charts, 39 of those with Smokey in tow. Virtually all of them are included on this collection. Songs such as "Ooh Baby Baby," "The Tracks of My Tears," and "The Tears of a Clown" define much that was good about the '60s. The 1995 double-CD reissue is digitally remastered, and includes virtually the same tracks, adding a couple previously unreleased songs and extensive liner notes. —*Rob Bowman*

Smokey / Jun. 1973 / Motown ✦✦✦
○ **Pure Smokey** / Mar. 1974 / Motown ✦✦✦✦
☆ **A Quiet Storm** / Mar. 1975 / Motown ✦✦✦✦✦
The landmark artistic release of Smokey Robinson's solo career. This album didn't equal the sales of his '80s LPs, but was extremely influential. Robinson linked the songs conceptually and produced the album with almost no breaks between selections. *A Quiet Storm* was as influential as Marvin Gaye's *What's Going On* or Isaac Hayes' *Hot Buttered Soul*. It also spawned the rise of a new sound—soul aimed at an adult audience. Many radio stations aired various unedited cuts from this LP late at night or after dark. Soon an entire format was developed that emphasized adult ballads and played album cuts as much as, if not more than, edited singles. This format was called "Quiet Storm." —*Ron Wynn*

Smokey's Family Robinson / Feb. 1976 / Motown ✦✦
Smokey Robinson sets up groove-based arrangements that take their tone from Sonny Burke's electric piano rhythms, but his own personal songwriting stamp often gives way to the percolating funk, notably on the single "Open" (#10 R&B, #81 Pop), which attempts to do what Marvin Gaye did the following year with "Got To Give It Up," but, with its prominent "backup" vocals, only succeeds in confusing the listener. The second side is more ballad-oriented, but there are no great songs even when the focus is on the singer. —*William Ruhlmann*

Where There's Smoke . . . / May 1979 / Motown ✦✦✦
This album was a considerable return to form, Smokey Robinson's most commercially successful solo LP up to this point (and highest-charting record in 11 years), entirely due to the single "Cruisin'" (number four Pop and R&B), his biggest pop hit since "The Tears of a Clown." Motown doesn't seem to have recognized that track's potency, leading off with the flop "Get Ready" (a disco treatment of the old Temptations hit) before turning to "Cruisin'" as a second single several months after the LP's release. *Where There's Smoke* . . . then took off and peaked at number 17 more than six months after first appearing. Although the LP is divided into "Smoke" and "Fire" sides, both sides start out with rhythmic songs and gradually slow down to near-ballad speed, with the sensuous "Cruisin'" the final "Fire" track. In retrospect, the album may be uneven and a touch too disco-ish in places, but in 1979-1980, *Where's There's Smoke* . . . brought Smokey Robinson back into the limelight. —*William Ruhlmann*

Warm Thoughts / Feb. 1980 / Motown ✦✦✦
On his followup to "Cruisin'," Smokey Robinson goes right back to that lazy, romantic style with "Let Me Be The Clock" (#4 R&B, #31 Pop), which leads off the aptly named *Warm Thoughts*. Robinson seems to have taken the success of "Cruisin'" as his op-

portunity to distance himself from disco and return to his more familiar ballad style, even injecting a touch of his old wordplay in "Into Each Rain Some Life Must Fall." Side Two begins with the more uptempo "Melody Man," which was arranged, co-written, and co-produced by Stevie Wonder, but for the most part this is the bedroom Smokey Robinson, and that got him to #14 on the LP chart, his highest solo peak yet. —*William Ruhlmann*

Being with You / Feb. 1981 / Motown ✦✦✦
Smokey Robinson landed his first big album of the 1980s with this release. The title track soared to the top of the R&B charts and stayed there, while it just missed topping the pop charts. Robinson's wonderful lead vocals, timing, dramatic delivery, and overall technique were as impressive as ever, and he got two more chart hits from the album. It eventually became his most successful LP ever from a commercial standpoint, although his artistic landmark as a solo artist remains *A Quiet Storm*. —*Ron Wynn*

Yes It's You Lady / 1982 / Motown ✦✦
Surprisingly, having scored his biggest solo success with the self-penned, self-produced *Being with You*, Smokey Robinson turned to an outside producer and outside writers for the followup. Both of the singles from *Yes It's You Lady*, which was produced by George Tobin, "Tell Me Tomorrow" (number three R&B, number 33 Pop) and "Old Fashioned Love" (number 17 R&B, number 60 Pop) were mid-tempo rhythm numbers written by Gary Goetzman and Mike Piccirillo. Robinson's own compositions, notably the title track, which would have made a perfect follow-up to "Being with You," were de-emphasized. The result was a retreat from the careful career-building Robinson had been engaged in since 1979; the album peaked at only number 33 after three straight Top 20 LPs. It was as though, having established himself as a solo voice, Robinson was now content to be "Cruisin'." —*William Ruhlmann*

Touch the Sky / 1983 / Motown ✦✦
Smokey Robinson took back the production reins from George Tobin and reinstated his producing/arranging partnership with Sonny Burke for *Touch the Sky*. The two took a more rhythmic approach, with Burke contributing drums and synthesizers. R&B listeners responded, notably on the title track (#68 R&B) and "I've Made Love To You A Thousand Times" (#8 R&B), but Robinson was shut out of the Hot 100, and as a result *Touch The Sky* continued his slide in LP sales, peaking at only #50 on the Pop chart, although it hit #8 R&B. —*William Ruhlmann*

○ **Blame It on Love and Other** / 1983 / Motown ✦✦✦✦
A fine compilation covering recent Smokey Robinson love songs and hits. While some of these lack the staying power and integrity of the Miracles' hits, they were certainly superior to much of what was being marketed as romantic fare. Robinson's ageless falsetto, masterful lyrics, and professionalism have enabled him to survive numerous trends and changes in both the business and his audience. The success of these tracks reaffirmed his special qualities as one of the greatest performers in the history of American music. —*Ron Wynn*

Essar / 1984 / Motown ✦✦
Essar marks the low point of Smokey Robinson's solo career. Co-producer and arranger Sonny Burke, a long-time Robinson recording partner, provides nearly all the tracks, dominating the sound with his synthesized keyboards. On songs like "And I Don't Love You" (#33 R&B), it's hard to identify the result as a Smokey Robinson record. This may help explain why *Essar*, Robinson's second straight album not to generate a Hot 100 Pop chart entry, was his lowest charting studio album on the Pop LPs list (#141). But it also flopped with R&B fans, peaking at #35 and becoming his first album not to generate at least one Top 10 R&B hit. —*William Ruhlmann*

Smoke Signals / 1985 / Motown ✦✦✦
One Heartbeat / Feb. 1987 / Motown ✦✦✦
Another superb Robinson album. He continued scoring hit singles throughout the 1980s, and this time out, the song "Just To See Her" was another huge pop and R&B smash, and the title track did almost as well. Robinson was thriving, despite the fact that hip-hop was steadily gaining strength, and New Jack Swing would soon force its way into the urban contemporary spotlight. —*Ron Wynn*

○ **Compact Command Performance** / 1989 / Motown ✦✦✦✦

Love, Smokey / 1990 / Motown ✦✦✦

Smokey Robinson entered another decade, his fifth as a performer, writer, and producer, with another fine album. He didn't have anything quite as evocative or successful as "Just To See Her" from his previous release, but did make it onto the pop charts for a few weeks. Robinson long ago established his greatness, so at this point any other hits he garners are just icing on the cake. The same year this was issued, Robinson also became a vice-president at Motown. —*Ron Wynn*

Double Good Everything / 1991 / SBK ✦✦✦

○ **Whatever Makes You Happy: More of the Best . . .** / 1993 / Rhino ✦✦✦✦

Solid compilation of 18 of the most interesting non-hits from Smokey's (and Motown's) golden era. Culled from 11 albums, this is an intelligent and consistent overview of Robinson's relatively unknown tunes. These cuts show the stylistic evolution of Motown as surely as any greatest hits collection, moving from bluesy, raucous R&B to assembly-line soul to songs reflecting the lyrical and instrumental innovations of the psychedelic era. Robinson's peerless soul songwriting and the Miracles' smooth harmonies remained constant no matter what the era, making this a much more fluid set than you might expect. Ultimately, the songs don't boast hooks quite as memorable as their classic hit singles, despite their similarities in structure and production. The early-'60s tracks are perhaps the record's most interesting, displaying a gritty, almost salacious approach that had yet to be toned down by slicker production values. Dominated by Robinson originals, this collection also includes scattered covers of "Money" and hits by the Temptations and Supremes, as well as the original version of "From Head To Toe," later covered by Elvis Costello. —*Richie Unterberger*

☆ **Thirty-Fifth Anniversary Box** / 1994 / Motown ✦✦✦✦✦

This splendid four-disc box set covers all the essential tracks Smokey Robinson and the Miracles ever recorded. —*AMG*

Tom Robinson Band

Group, Rock & Roll, New Wave

Although his career had pretty much flamed out by the start of the '80s, there were few punk-era major label performers as intensely controversial as Tom Robinson. Cutting his teeth with folk-rockers Cafe Society (who released a Ray Davies-produced record on the head Kinks' Konk label in 1975), Robinson roared into the spotlight in 1978 with a great single ("2-4-6-8 Motorway") and a much-ballyhooed contract with EMI. What was remarkable about this was that Robinson was the kind of politically conscious, confrontational performer that major labels generally ignored: he was openly gay and sang about it ("Glad to be Gay"), vociferous in his hatred for then British Prime Minister Margaret Thatcher, helped form Rock Against Racism, and generally spoke in favor of any leftist political tract that would embarrass the ruling ultra-conservative Tory government. His debut album, 1978's *Power in the Darkness*, was an occasionally stunning piece of punk/hard rock agit-prop that, along with being ferociously direct, was politicized rock that focused more on songs than slogans.

However, by the release of the second album, the Todd Rundgren-produced *TRB Two*, the songs were getting weaker and Robinson began sounding like a boring idealogue. Similarly the band, even terrific guitarist Danny Kustow, sounds as if on automatic pilot. By the end of the '70s, Robinson had been dropped by EMI and signed to maverick major IRS as a solo act. In a wise move, he ditched the hard rock polemics of the TRB for a more sophisticated pop/rock sound, but found his audience dwindling. A brief period of silence ended with him, somewhat surprisingly, signing with Geffen and releasing *Hope and Glory*, a politically-tinged, but mostly mainstream rock record that featured a cover of that decidedly non-punk song, Steely Dan's "Rikki Don't Lose That Number," with Robinson deftly exploring the song's homoerotic subtext. Still, it wasn't enough to resuscitate his career and for the remainder of the decade Robinson released English-only albums that tried the patience of even long time fans.

As to his current whereabouts, Robinson is rumored to be married to a woman (!) and raising a family in England. He's still writing songs and occasionally performing, but it can be safely assumed that whatever he's doing, it's light years away from the radical energy and excitement of *Power in the Darkness*. —*John Dougan*

● **Power in the Darkness** / 1978 / Capitol ✦✦✦✦

This is angry British political punk at its best. —*David Szatmary*

TRB Two / 1979 / Harvest ✦✦✦

A heartfelt record of political rock, Robinson made interesting albums after this one, but never again sounded as passionate, defiant and full of himself. The band's secret weapon was guitarist Danny Kustow whose playing makes even the most obvious and unsubtle moments enjoyable. Earnest and likeable, this is hands-down the best Tom Robinson record available (yes, even better than any of the TRB anthologies). The original American LP release included a bonus EP, with "Glad to be Gay" (which doesn't hold up well) and the embarrassingly simplistic feminist ode "Right on Sister." *TRB Two* is only recommended to those who will appreciate a warmed-over version of *Power in the Darkness*; more slogans, less substance. —*John Dougan*

Sector 27 / 1980 / Fontana ✦✦

Tom Robinson Band / 1981 / Fame ✦✦✦

○ **North by Northwest** / 1982 / IRS ✦✦✦✦

Cabaret '79 / 1982 / Panic ✦✦

Hope and Glory / 1984 / Geffen ✦✦✦

Robinson's only two interesting post-Power records. *North by Northwest* features contributions by Peter Gabriel and a far less noisy pop/rock sound. It's an insinuating record, one that was dismissed cavalierly upon its release, but Robinson's songwriting is mostly good even when his singing (never much to write home about in the first place) is inadequate or just plain bad. *Hope and Glory* is good too, if only because it rocks a little harder and the simple, but emotional track "War Baby" is here. Neither of these records is the place to begin with Robinson, but the work is better than you'd expect. —*John Dougan*

Still Loving You / 1986 / Castaway ✦✦

Midnight at the Fringe / 1987 / Dojo ✦✦

○ **The Collection of 1977-1987** / 1987 / EMI ✦✦✦✦

Back in the Old Country / 1989 / Connoisseur ✦✦

Last Tango / 1989 / Line ✦✦

We Never Had It So Good / 1990 / Musidisc ✦✦

Love Over Rage / 1994 / Scarface ✦✦✦

Pete Rock & C.L. Smooth

Group, Rap

Mt. Vernon New Yorkers Pete Rock, a producer and disc jockey, and rapper C.L. Smooth emerged in 1992 as both a powerhouse performance duo and as prolific producers. Their album *Mecca and the Soul Brother* was a solid hit, notably the cuts "They Reminisce Over You (T.R.O.Y.)" and "Straighten It Out." They later collaborated with Mary J. Blige for a remix of her song "Reminisce" that effectively merged the two tracks in a re-edited hit. Their next album, *The Main Ingredient*, appeared in 1994. They've also done many productions for both hip-hop acts and Urban Contemporary artists like Johnny Gill. —*Ron Wynn*

○ **All Souled Out** / 1991 / Elektra ✦✦✦✦

This strong debut release combines jazz and hip-hop to an impressive effect. —*AMG*

● **Mecca and the Soul Brother** / 1992 / Asylum ✦✦✦✦

C.L. Smooth's clever raps and Pete Rock's snazzy production put this duo into the hip-hop big time with their second album. There were tremendous message cuts and attractive general material, and it was simply an excellent album on every level. It includes the hit single "They Reminisce Over You (T.R.O.Y.)." —*Ron Wynn*

The Main Ingredient / 1994 / Elektra ✦✦✦

Pete Rock & C.L. Smooth's sequel to the groundbreaking *Mecca and the Soul Brother* wasn't quite as focused or innovative as its predecessor, but *The Main Ingredient* included several first-rate tracks, making the album a succcessful followup. —*Stephen Thomas Erlewine*

Rocket from the Crypt

Group, Alternative Pop/Rock

Pledging to never play a venue with a stage, singer/guitarist John Reis formed San Diego's Rocket From The Crypt in the summer of 1990 after becoming disillusioned with the hardcore punk band he was in called Pitchfork. Joining with current Rocketeers bassist Petey X and guitarist ND, in addition to now departed drummer

Sean and backing vocalist Elaina, Reis and company released *Paint as a Fragrance* in 1991.

Though the album caused a lot of people to take notice, a lineup change ensued; Atom became the drummer, and Apollo 9, a drinking buddy of Reis' who played sax in high school, joined as saxophonist. After the successful independent *Circa: Now!* was released on Cargo Records in 1992, a major-label bidding war resulted in Rocket From The Crypt signing with Interscope Records (in addition to Reis' other band, Drive Like Jehu, which features another former Pitchfork member, Rick Fork). Interscope then re-released *Circa: Now!* in 1993, and the single "Ditch Digger" spent some time in MTV's Buzz Bin. Eventually, a sixth member—JC 2000 on horn—was added in 1994, which preceded the release of a new 10-inch record, "The State of Art is on Fire," in 1995. —*Matt Carlson*

Paint As a Fragrance / 1991 / Headhunter ✦✦✦
This record lurches through ten solid songs, which, though as aggressive as punk's roots, offer much more than your typical power-chord mosh pit anthems. John "Speedo" Reis stuns with his soulful, Sammy Davis, Jr.-meets-Eddie Cochran lead vocals, while backing vocalist Elaina adds rich harmony. In addition to more immediate punk scorchers, Rocket From The Crypt also explores other musical terrain; the band gears up with rockabilly-laden guitar riffs, which are then unleashed with some dissonant guitar harmonies and breakneck piano. —*Matt Carlson*

● **Circa: Now!** / 1993 / Headhunter ✦✦✦✦
Originally released on Cargo/Headhunter before the group was picked up by Interscope, *Circa: Now!* finds Speedo's army redirecting its sound slightly by adding saxophone and slowing the tempo down on some tracks. Of course, Rocket From The Crypt still imbues every second of these with unflinching power. The saxophone of Apollo 9, though sparsely decorated and subtly buried throughout the album, adds 1950s R&B flair on "Hairball Alley" and "March of Dimes." And though a majority of the songs pack a more direct wallop than *Paint As a Fragrance,* the record still finds room to settle down on the lush '60s pop of "Little Arm." —*Matt Carlson*

All Systems Go / 1994 / Headhunter ✦✦✦
This collection of Rocket From The Crypt's singles, issued for the first time on CD, captures the band in both of its incarnations—direct, no-nonsense punk maestros ("Live the Funk" and "Jumper K. Balls") and playful mood-swingers ("Lefty" and "Chantilly Face"). But *All Systems Go* makes its best excuse with "Pigeon Eater" and "The Paste That You Love," by far Rocket's best songs, released together as a Merge 45 in early 1994. —*Matt Carlson*

○ **State of Art is on Fire** / 1995 / Sympathy For The Record Industry ✦✦✦✦
Certainly Rocket from the Crypt's most furious punk exploit to date, the 10-inch EP *The State of Art is on Fire* burns straight to the point. Rocket relinquishes its usual musical homage to rockabilly and R&B, and instead blazes through six explosive songs that don't slow down until the final track, "Human Spine." Reis' lyrics add more fuel to the fire, while Apollo 9 and JC 2000 blast their horns against the wall of sound. —*Matt Carlson*

The Rockin' Ramrods

Group, Pop/Rock
Along with the Remains, the Rockin' Ramrods were Boston's premier rock band in the mid-'60s. Unlike the Remains, they didn't gain even a modicum of exposure beyond their city, and are far more obscure even to '60s collectors. They were a decent if not significant group, sounding kind of like a Beatlized frat band, and relying largely upon original material, much of it penned by bassist Ronn Campisi. Over the course of more than half a dozen singles between 1963 and 1966, they competently tackled garage grunge, wild instrumentals, and some very pleasant hard pop/rock originals with prominent keyboards, somewhat in the manner of an Americanized early Manfred Mann. "Bright Lit Blues Skies," their best song, was a hit in the Boston area, but they achieved no other success of note before disbanding. —*Richie Unterberger*

● **I Wanna Be Your Man** / 1984 / Eva ✦✦✦✦
Both sides of all eight of their singles. Not one of the rawest or most distinguished mid-'60s garage bands, but one of the more tuneful and consistent, highlighted by the first-class originals "Bright Lit Blue Skies," "Mr. Wind," and "Cry In My Room," as well as two of the better garage treatments of Lennon/McCartney

songs, "I Wanna Be Your Man" and "I'll Be On My Way." —*Richie Unterberger*

○ **The Best Of The Rockin' Ramrods** / 1995 / ✦✦✦✦
A strange compilation that spans several stages of the group's evolution. There are eleven songs (one previously unreleased) from their mid-'60s prime, presented in much better sound than on the Eva reissue, but six of the songs from the eight singles they recorded during this time are missing. Then there are eleven tracks (one previously unreleased) from the obscure 1968 MGM LP by Puff, a spinoff group that did not feature Ramrods leader/singer/songwriter Ronn Campisi, although, oddly, he wrote all of the material. The Puff cuts are light, sophisticated pop/rock with lots of harmonies and slight psychedelic touches; mildly interesting, it's much less hard-rocking than the other "Bosstown" groups MGM was giving a big push to in 1968. The CD finishes with three unreleased songs recorded by a 1971 incarnation of the Ramrods. A wealth of genuine Rockin' Ramrods unreleased material from their 1966-67 prime that has circulated among a few '60s/garage collectors was not tapped at all. Though less comprehensive, much harder to find, and of lower fidelity, the French import on Eva—which includes both sides of every one of their eight early singles—still gets the nod over this less cohesive batch. —*Richie Unterberger*

Rockpile

Group, Rock & Roll, Pop/Rock
During the late '70s, Rockpile was the touring band for both Dave Edmunds and Nick Lowe. Like Edmunds, the band was passionate about traditional rock & roll. Like Lowe, the band played with a reckless, trashy abandon. Driven by the powerful rhythm section of drummer Terry Williams and Lowe's bass, guitarists Billy Bremner and Edmunds were free to spit out crushing rock, blues, rockabilly, and country licks. With their fierce live energy and unpretentious rock & roll, the band fit easily into the post-punk new wave at the end of the decade.

Although they only released one album as a group—1980's *Seconds of Pleasure*—the band provided support for most of the albums Lowe and Edmunds recorded in the late '70s. After the rushed release of *Seconds of Pleasure,* the band toured one last time before splitting apart, largely due to mismanagement. All of the members continued to occasionally collaborate with each other throughout the '80s. —*Stephen Thomas Erlewine*

○ **Seconds of Pleasure** / 1980 / Columbia ✦✦✦✦
Rockpile's only proper album is an inspired collection of old-fashioned rock & roll, which sounds vital because of the band's unrelenting energy and Nick Lowe's consistently inventive songwriting. The CD includes the bonus EP of Everly Brothers covers that was included in the album's original pressing. —*Stephen Thomas Erlewine*

Jimmie F. Rodgers

Folk, Pop/Rock
It's hard to call Jimmie Rodgers (no relation to country great Jimmie Rogers) a rock & roller, exactly, but a lot of the rock audience listened to him and bought his records during his late-'50s prime. With his high, sweet voice, acoustic guitar, updates of traditional folk songs, brisk tempos, and muted rock-influenced arrangements, he was a distant forefather of folk-rock. And he was briefly a superstar, landing "Honeycomb," "Kisses Sweeter than Wine," "Oh-Oh, I'm Falling in Love Again," "Secretly," and "Are You Really Mine" in the Top Ten within about a year's span in 1957-1958. An original and ingratiating performer, Rodgers' records began to sound like lesser repeats of themselves fairly quickly, and his minor hits are sometimes cloying in a sing-song way. Rodgers had a long dry spell after 1960, but re-emerged with a couple of Top 40 hits in 1966 and 1967, "It's Over" and "Child of Clay." At the end of 1967, his career went into a final tailspin after he suffered severe head injuries in a controversial incident involving a Los Angeles police officer. —*Richie Unterberger*

● **The Best of Jimmie Rodgers** / 1990 / Rhino ✦✦✦✦
18-track collection includes every one of his hits, as well as interesting obscurities like "Woman from Liberia." —*Richie Unterberger*

Tommy Roe

b. May 9, 1942
Rock & Roll, Bubblegum

Widely perceived as one of the archetypal bubblegum artists of the late 60s, Tommy Roe cut some pretty decent rockers along the way, especially early in his career—many displaying some pretty prominent Buddy Holly roots. In fact, Roe's initial pop smash, 1962's chart-topping "Sheila," was quite reminiscent of Holly's "Peggy Sue," utilizing a very similar throbbing drum beat and Roe's hiccuping vocal. The singer had previously cut the song for the smaller Judd label before remaking it in superior form for ABC-Paramount. The infectious "Everybody"—another hot item the next year—was waxed in Muscle Shoals at Rick Hall's Fame studios, normally an R&B-oriented facility (it's not widely known that Roe wrote songs for the Tams, a raw-edged soul group from his Atlanta hometown).

Once Roe veered off on his squeaky-clean bubblegum tangent, he stuck with it for the rest of the decade. His lighthearted "Sweet Pea" and "Hooray for Hazel" burned up the charts in 1966, and he was still at it three years later when he waxed his biggest hit, "Dizzy," and "Jam Up Jelly Tight." —*Bill Dahl*

● **Greatest Hits** / 1993 / ◆◆◆◆
Supplants previous anthologies as the best Roe collection available. 18 songs spanning 1962 to 1971, including all the big singles, with thorough liner notes. —*Richie Unterberger*

The Rolling Stones

Group, Rock & Roll, British Invasion
The Rolling Stones are the definitive rock & roll band and, by now, the longest-lived rock & roll band to remain consistently popular throughout their (30-year) career. The group came together in London, where singer Mick Jagger (b. Jul 26, 1943) and guitarist Keith Richards (b. Dec 18, 1943), who had been grade school classmates, joined with guitarist Brian Jones (b. Feb 28, 1942–d. Jul 3, 1969) and a rhythm section then consisting of pianist Ian Stewart, bassist Dick Taylor, and drummer Mick Avory (later of the Kinks) at a debut show at the Marquee on July 12, 1962. Taylor was replaced soon after by Bill Wyman (b. Oct 24, 1936), and Avory eventually by jazz drummer Charlie Watts (b. Jun 2, 1941).

The Rolling Stones played an eight-month residency at the Crawdaddy Club in 1963, during which they signed a management contract with Andrew "Loog" Oldham (who demoted Ian Stewart to road manager) and a recording contract with Decca. The group was devoted to playing Chicago blues and its offshoots, notably the rock & roll of Chuck Berry, and its early records were either covers of such music or extremely derivative originals. The Stones' first single, for example, was a cover of Berry's "Come On." It was followed by "I Wanna Be Your Man," a song written for the Stones by John Lennon and Paul McCartney.

The Stones' first really successful single, however, was a version of Buddy Holly's "Not Fade Away," which reached #3 in England and became their first American chart entry. Their next five U.K. singles all hit #1, and by 1965 they had established themselves as second only to the Beatles as the most popular British rock group, a position they held until the Beatles broke up.

The important factor setting the Stones apart from their lesser competition was that they successfully moved from being a blues-rock cover band to being a band that performed primarily original pop/rock material with a blues base. Jagger and Richards turned into a songwriting team as early as 1964, and by 1965 such Stones hits as "The Last Time" and "(I Can't Get No) Satisfaction" were scoring on both sides of the Atlantic.

The Stones toured extensively in the mid-'60s, with their success partially attributable to frontman Mick Jagger, who became the most prominent lead singer in rock. They followed many of the trends of the '60s as the decade wore on, and their involvement with drugs curtailed their ability to play in the U.S. after 1966. By that time, like the Beatles and others, their musical horizons had expanded to include a variety of eclectic styles. Unlike the Beatles, however, the Stones were never really comfortable with psychedelia, and after their 1967 *Sgt. Pepper* knock-off, *Their Satanic Majesties Request*, they returned to a more basic hard rock style on the single "Jumpin' Jack Flash" and the album *Beggars Banquet*.

In 1969, the Stones re-emerged as a concert attraction after firing Brian Jones (who died shortly after) and hiring guitarist Mick Taylor (b. Jan 17, 1948), who in turn was replaced by Ron Wood (b. Jun 1, 1947) in 1976. They released the single "Honky Tonk Women" and the album *Let it Bleed* and embarked on an American concert tour that culminated in the disastrous Altamont Festival. Despite that debacle, after the Beatles' split the following year,

the Stones were undisputed in their claim to being "the greatest rock & roll band in the world."

In the '70s, the Stones toured every three years and released a series of million-selling, chart-topping albums, despite guitarist Keith Richards's descent into heroin addiction. The drug problem came to a head when Richards was arrested in Toronto in 1977. He subsequently cleaned up, however, and took a more active role in the Stones' creative efforts, resulting in improved albums in the late '70s and early '80s.

The band played a world tour 1981-1982 and continued actively into the mid-'80s, but when Jagger made a solo album in 1985 and then refused to tour behind the Stones's 1986 *Dirty Work* album, their long career together seemed to be over. Richards reluctantly began work on a solo album and publicly voiced his anger. Jagger released a second solo album in 1987 and toured Japan in 1988, but by the time of the release of Richards's solo album, *Talk Is Cheap*, the Stones were in discussions about a reunion. A new album, *Steel Wheels*, was recorded and released in 1989, accompanied by another world tour lasting into 1990.

Bill Wyman left the group for good after the *Steel Wheels* tour. For a couple of years, the Stones had no bassist; they signed a multi-million dollar deal with Virgin Records in 1992 as a four-piece. After all four members released solo records in 1992 and 1993, the band began auditioning bassists during rehearsals for their new album. Released in the summer of 1994, *Voodoo Lounge* was recorded with former Miles Davis and Sting bassist Darryl Jones; after the album's release, he was named as Wyman's permanent replacement. —*William Ruhlmann*

○ **Rolling Stones [British import]** / Apr. 16, 1964 / London ◆◆◆◆
The imported edition of the group's first album is superior in sound to the American version, with some curious differences in the songs as well ("Tell Me" runs longer). —*Bruce Eder*

○ **The Rolling Stones (England's Newest Hitmakers)** / May 30, 1964 / ABKCO ◆◆◆◆
The group's debut album, a bit bluesier and more acoustically textured than the sound they later became famous for, with the influence of Slim Harpo and Muddy Waters getting equal time with Chuck Berry and Bo Diddley. "Carol," "King Bee," and "Route 66" are just a few of the indispensable highlights. —*Bruce Eder*

☆ **12 X 5** / Oct. 17, 1964 / ABKCO ◆◆◆◆◆
A much more rock-oriented album than their debut, *12 X 5* is the album that solidified the group's Chuck Berry and Bo Diddley-based sound, and on which guitarists Keith Richards and Brian Jones first flexed their muscles. —*Bruce Eder*

○ **The Rolling Stones Now!** / Apr. 1965 / ABKCO ◆◆◆◆
The group's second album is a louder blues record, moving toward rock, with Mick Jagger beginning to stretch out as a vocalist and the band hardening its sound. "Everybody Needs Somebody to Love" and "Mona" are among the best parts of a near-perfect record. —*Bruce Eder*

○ **Out of Our Heads** / Aug. 1965 / ABKCO ◆◆◆◆
The first of the American patchwork albums, assembled from sessions on two continents and some London concerts, and it all works—"Satisfaction" was the hit, but "I'm Alright" was a concert favorite for years. —*Bruce Eder*

○ **December's Children** / Dec. 1965 / ABKCO ◆◆◆
A much more artful collection, compiled from various singles and album sessions. The blues material is subservient to rock numbers like "Get off of My Cloud" and elegant R&B such as "You Better Move On." —*Bruce Eder*

○ **Big Hits High Tide and Green Grass** / Mar. 1966 / ABKCO ◆◆◆◆
Big Hits—Vol. 1 (High Tide & Green Grass) is a concise collection of the group's early hits, without any surprises. —*Bruce Eder*

☆ **Aftermath** / Jun. 1966 / ABKCO ◆◆◆◆◆
The group's most accomplished studio record of the '60s, and the first to feature all Jagger-Richards originals. The sound also expands here to embrace the mild psychedelic/Eastern sound of "Paint It Black," and the barrier-bursting 10-minute-plus "Goin' Home," highlighted by Brian's workout on blues harp. —*Bruce Eder*

Got Live If You Want It / Nov. 4, 1966 / ABKCO ◆◆
Glorious, majestic, raunchy, completely out-of-tune concert album, marred by the inclusion of two phony live tracks. The sound here is crisper than what you would have heard at the show itself, and the roughness of the sound and the mix preserves the power and fury of the band and its audience (which rioted at the opening of

the Royal Albert Hall show where part of this record was made). — *Bruce Eder*

☆ **Between the Buttons** / Jan. 1967 / ABKCO ✦✦✦✦✦
A spaced-out, trippy mix of psychedelia, vaudeville, and Dylan homages that has worn well despite the inclusion of two hits ("Let's Spend the Night Together" and "Ruby Tuesday") that had nothing to do with the rest of it. A self-conscious album, and very theatrical. — *Bruce Eder*

Flowers / Jun. 1967 / ABKCO ✦✦
Somewhat repetitive collection of odd B-sides and unanthologized singles that is worth owning just for the Bo Diddley-styled "Please Go Home." — *Bruce Eder*

Their Satanic Majesties Request / Nov. 1967 / ABKCO ✦✦✦
Underrated psychedelic venture by the Stones, who seem to lack confidence in their abilities and material (and lacked a producer at the time as well). The dross is balanced out by a couple of minor hits ("2000 Light Years from Home," "She's a Rainbow") and a couple of brilliant album tracks ("2000 Man" and "Citadel"). — *Bruce Eder*

☆ **Beggars Banquet** / Nov. 1968 / ABKCO ✦✦✦✦✦
The group's newly matured sound came together on this album, a mixture of blues and politics that proved almost too controversial to release at the time. "Salt of the Earth," "Parachute Woman," "Street Fighting Man," and "Jigsaw Puzzle" make it worthwhile. — *Bruce Eder*

○ **Through the Past Darkly (Big Hits, Vol. 2)** / Sep. 1969 / ABKCO ✦✦✦✦

☆ **Let It Bleed** / Nov. 28, 1969 / ABKCO ✦✦✦✦✦
A coda to the Brian Jones era, and the start of the Mick Taylor era, with a dazzling collection of numbers ("Gimme Shelter," "Midnight Rambler," "Love in Vain," "You Can't Always Get What You Want," "Let It Bleed," etc.), most of which figured prominently in the group's subsequent tour. — *Bruce Eder*

☆ **Get Yer Ya-Ya's Out** / Sep. 4, 1970 / ABKCO ✦✦✦✦✦
This live album, released largely to counteract the effect of the bootleg *Liver Than You'll Ever Be*, captured the new-era Stones in their top form, doing all of the key material from their preceding pair of albums. — *Bruce Eder*

☆ **Sticky Fingers** / Apr. 23, 1971 / Virgin ✦✦✦✦✦
A ballsy, bluesy masterpiece made up of leftovers and works in progress from the preceding two years, including "Wild Horses," "Brown Sugar," and "Sister Morphine." — *Bruce Eder*

● **Hot Rocks 1964-1971** / Jan. 1972 / ABKCO ✦✦✦✦
This import double-disc anthology contains their biggest hits on London, as well as many of their most popular album tracks. A stereo version of "Satisfaction" is the highlight, and worth the price, even though the US mono version is also pretty cool. — *Bruce Eder*

☆ **Exile on Main Street** / May 12, 1972 / Virgin ✦✦✦✦✦
Originally rock's most musically successful double album, this epic collection has aged magnificently. Includes the hit "Tumbling Dice," as well as "Rocks Off," "Happy," "Rip This Joint," and "Sweet Virginia." — *Bruce Eder*

● **More Hot Rocks (Big Hits and Fazed Cookies)** / Nov. 1972 / ABKCO ✦✦✦✦
Highlighted by a unique stereo edition of "It's All Over Now." Often thought of as secondary, this anthology is really a lot more interesting than *Hot Rocks*. — *Bruce Eder*

Goats Head Soup / Aug. 31, 1973 / Virgin ✦✦✦
Compared to the monumental *Exile on Main Street, Goats Head Soup* is bound to sound inferior, and it does. Nevertheless, the album doesn't deserve its bad reputation. It might be careless and decadent, but that excess is quite intoxicating, as the nasty rocker "Star Star" and the finely crafted ballad "Angie" prove. — *Stephen Thomas Erlewine*

It's Only Rock and Roll / Oct. 18, 1974 / Virgin ✦✦✦
It's uneven, but at times *It's Only Rock and Roll* catches fire. The songs and performances are stronger than those on *Goats Head Soup*; the tossed-off numbers sound effortless, not careless. Throughout, the Stones wear their title as the "World's Greatest Rock & Roll Band" with a defiant smirk, which makes the bitter cynicism of "If You Can't Rock Me" and the title track all the more striking, and the reggae experimentation of "Luxury," the aching beauty of "Time Waits for No One," and the agreeable filler of

"Dance Little Sister" and "Short and Curlies" all the more enjoyable. — *Stephen Thomas Erlewine*

Metamorphosis / Jun. 1975 / ABKCO ✦✦
A motley assortment of 1960s outtakes, apparently compiled by the Stones' former managers to squeeze every last drop from the group's songwriting backlog. Most of the cuts are demos of weak Jagger/Richard songs that became flop singles for other artists; it's likely that some of the Stones don't even play on much of the album. The versions of "Out Of Time" and "Heart Of Stone" are abominable when compared to the more widely known original renditions. The late-'60s outtakes that make up most of Side Two (including a rare Bill Wyman original, "Downtown Suzie") probably do feature the actual group, but quite simply don't cut it. And did we mention the atrocious cover design? A couple exceptions make the LP worth picking up for Stones fanatics: a decent mid-'60s cover of Chuck Berry's "Don't Lie To Me," and "If You Let Me," a nice folk-rock outtake from *Between The Buttons*. Note: the British version contains two additional tracks. — *Richie Unterberger*

Made in the Shade / Jun. 6, 1975 / Rolling Stones ✦✦
Made in the Shade was a haphazard collection that collected hit singles from the Stones' first four albums on Rolling Stones Records (*Sticky Fingers* through *It's Only Rock & Roll*), adding a handful of album tracks for good measure. The material here is first-rate, but the sequencing and selection make little sense and the album doesn't offer a comprehensive portrait of the group's early-'70s successes. — *Stephen Thomas Erlewine*

Black & Blue / Apr. 20, 1976 / Virgin ✦✦✦
Ron Wood's first album with the Stones finds the band working through a number of reggae and funk-tinged numbers, trying to expand their sound. Consequently, songs are sacrificed for grooves; only the ballads "Memory Motel" and "Fool to Cry" are fully developed, but the grooves that dominate the album are strong enough to make the record successful. — *Stephen Thomas Erlewine*

Love You Live / Sep. 23, 1977 / Rolling Stones ✦✦
Recorded on the supporting tour for 1976's *Black & Blue*, the double-album set *Love You Live* is an adequate live album, capturing the Stones' transition from a lean, lethal rock & roll band to accomplished show men. As show men, they aren't as compelling as they are when they're rockers, but the show-biz glitz of Mick Jagger's arena-rock schitck remains thoroughly entertaining, even when it robs the music of its power. — *Stephen Thomas Erlewine*

☆ **Some Girls** / Jun. 9, 1978 / Virgin ✦✦✦✦✦
A nasty, hard-rocking album, *Some Girls* finds the Stones turning out an effortlessly brilliant and eclectic set of material, encompassing the disco pulse of "Miss You," the sleazy snarl of "When the Whip Comes Down," the campy country of "Far Away Eyes," the moving ballad "Beast of Burden," and Keith's best outlaw song, "Before They Make Me Run." — *Stephen Thomas Erlewine*

Emotional Rescue / Jun. 23, 1980 / Virgin ✦✦✦
While it isn't a great album, *Emotional Rescue* is good. The Stones made a set of skillfully crafted pop/rock, which embraces disco and new wave to a greater extent than *Some Girls*. When *Emotional Rescue* is on, as on "She's So Cold," "Where the Boys Go," "Send it To Me," and the hypnotic, pulsing title track, it is damn good. — *Stephen Thomas Erlewine*

Sucking in the 70's / Mar. 12, 1981 / Rolling Stones ✦✦
This is a superior collection of tracks and an end-of-decade flashback. — *Bruce Eder*

○ **Tattoo You** / Aug. 30, 1981 / Virgin ✦✦✦✦
Tattoo You remains the Stones' last great album. While the rockers on Side One provide some sparks, the heart of the album lies in the second side, with the gorgeous ballads "Worried About You" and "Waiting On a Friend." — *Stephen Thomas Erlewine*

Still Life / Jun. 1, 1982 / Rolling Stones ✦
Like *Love You Live* before it, *Still Life* showcases the Stones as pure entertainers, although the band adds enough rhythmic grit to keep the record from sinking into pure show-biz formula. Nevertheless, it isn't nearly enough grit to make it rock as hard as *Get Yer Ya-Ya's Out*. Or even *Love You Live*, depressingly enough. — *Stephen Thomas Erlewine*

Undercover / Nov. 7, 1983 / Virgin ✦✦✦
A glorious return to form, with topical politcs, sex, and decadence all colliding to create some memorable sparks. In addition to the title track, "She Was Hot" was also a hit, and managed to create a

fair amount of controversy with its subject matter and the accompanying video clip. —*Bruce Eder*

Rewind (1971-1984) / 1984 / Rolling Stones ♦♦♦
A collection of material from 1971-1984. —*Bruce Eder*

Dirty Work / 1986 / Virgin ♦♦♦
At its best, *Dirty Work* captures the friction between Mick and Keith during the album's recording; at its worst, it's simply a competent collection of hard rock, spiked with some unnecessary synthesizers. —*Stephen Thomas Erlewine*

☆ **Singles Collection: the London Years** / 1989 / ABKCO ♦♦♦♦♦
The best individual collection of their classic hits ever assembled, for sound and content. —*Bruce Eder*

Steel Wheels / 1989 / Virgin ♦♦♦
The band's best album of the '80s, embracing blues, classic rock, and even psychedelia ("Continental Drift"). —*Bruce Eder*

Flashpoint / 1991 / Rolling Stones ♦♦
The live follow-ups and a fond look back on 25 years of decadence. —*Bruce Eder*

Voodoo Lounge / 1994 / Capitol ♦♦♦
While *Voodoo Lounge* sounds amazingly like the Stones' classic records from the early '70s, it's rather inconsistent and too long to make it one of their major works. Instead, it's simply another solid Stones record, with some fine tracks and typically strong playing. —*Stephen Thomas Erlewine*

○ **Bright Lights, Big City** / Bootleg ♦♦♦♦
As you'd expect, there are a ton of Rolling Stones bootlegs, but there isn't a great deal of essential material from the '60s to be found on them. The exceptions are these outtakes from 1963 and 1964, which have popped up under quite a few guises, but most frequently under the *Bright Lights, Big City* title. The five early-1963 demos were cut shortly before they signed with Decca, and capture the band at their bluesiest and blackest; when Brian Jones was being frozen out of the Stones in the late '60s, it's said that he would play these for listeners as examples of the purity of the group's original vision. With clear fidelity, the standards of these performances are well up to official release; "Baby What's Wrong," "Road Runner," and "I Want to Be Loved" are downright electrifying. The four 1964 cuts were recorded at Chess Studios, and again (with the possible exception of the jam "Stewed And Keefed") are well up to release quality, with fine, spare readings of "Hi-Heel Sneakers," Howlin' Wolf's "Down In The Bottom," and Big Bill Broonzy's "Tell Me Baby." Essential for serious fans. —*Richie Unterberger*

BBC Sessions / Bootleg ♦♦♦
The Rolling Stones' BBC sessions haven't been accorded the same deluxe bootleg treatment as those of the Beatles, for two big reasons: they didn't record nearly as much for the Beeb as the Fab Four, and (unlike the Beatles) didn't record many tracks that they didn't release on record. Good fidelity tapes exist of a few dozen of their mid-'60s BBC airshots, and fans will find them worth picking up. Heavy on R&B covers (the Stones, like the Beatles, didn't record for the BBC after 1965), the tracks, as is par for the course on radio sessions, don't better or usually even equal the studio renditions, but have an interesting rougher live feel. They did manage to let rip on a half-dozen or so unreleased covers, and these items are naturally the most interesting, especially their takes on "Memphis, Tennessee" and their incendiary "Roll Over Beethoven," which is perhaps even better than the well-known Beatle version. —*Richie Unterberger*

BOOKS

♦♦♦ **The Rolling Stones: An Illustrated Record**, by Roy Carr (Harmony, 1976). Though flawed, this is the best critical survey of the Stones' work, reviewing every releases through *Black and Blue*. That leaves nearly 20 years uncovered, but it could be argued that it nonetheless encompasses just about everything worthwhile. The inconsistency of depth is frustrating; some albums are discussed rather cursorily, and *Between the Buttons* is, unbelievably, dismissed as a trivial affair in the course of several sentences. On the other hand, there are a lot of critical insights and details about the recording and production of masterpieces from "I Wanna Be Your Man" on through "Paint It Black," Beggar's Banquet, and the rest of their classic material. A running diary of notable incidents and quotes from the band is interspersed throughout, along with photos, a lengthy interview with Mick Jagger, and the most comprehensive discography and tour itineraries (complete with bootlegs and session appearances) of their prime years ever assembled. —*Richie Unterberger*

♦♦♦♦ **The True Adventures Of The Rolling Stones**, by Stanley Booth (Vintage, 1984). The Rolling Stones' story is a diffuse and murky one that doesn't lend itself nearly as well to retelling as the Beatles'. This book, originally titled *Dance with the Devil*, is not the most linear of these efforts, but it is the best. Memphis journalist Booth, a friend of the band (particularly Keith Richards), traveled with them through much of their famous late 1969 tour of America. In the account that he finally published 15 years later, he alternates between first-hand reportage of the tour and a history of the band, from their scuffling blues beginnings in the early '60s through their rise to fame and the death of Brian Jones. Not much is spared in either part of the tale; the fierce infighting that resulted in the ouster (which, to a large degree, was self-imposed) of Jones, the backstage groupies and drugs, the violence at Altamont, the pushy businessmen and promoters, the decadent ennui of a megastar touring band are all here, documented entertainingly without undue moralizing. Especially interesting are the sections on Altamont, of course, and the recording of several tracks at Muscle Shoals for *Sticky Fingers*, to which Booth was an eyewitness. —*Richie Unterberger*

Henry Rollins

Alternative Pop/Rock
In the '90s, Henry Rollins emerged as a post-punk renaissance man, without the self-conscious trappings that plagued such '80s self-conscious artists as David Byrne. Since Black Flag's break-up in 1986, Rollins has been relentlessly busy, recording albums with the Rollins Band, writing books and poetry, performing spoken word tours, writing a magazine column in *Details*, acting in several movies, and, most surprisingly, appearing on MTV as an occasional VJ. All the while, he has kept his artistic integrity, becoming a kind of father figure for many alternative bands of the '90s.

The Rollins Band's records are uncompromising, intense, cathartic fusions of hard rock, funk, post-punk noise, and jazz experimentalism, with Rollins shouting angry, biting self-examinations and accusations about the grind. On his spoken word albums, he is remarkably more relaxed, showcasing a hilariously self-depricating sense of humor that is often absent in his music. —*Stephen Thomas Erlewine*

○ **Hot Animal Machine** / 1987 / Texas Hotel ♦♦♦♦
A good solo effort, raw and powerful. This CD includes the EP *Drive By Shootings*. —*John Dougan*

Live / 1987 / Eksakt ♦♦

Do It / 1988 / Texas Hotel ♦♦♦

Life Time / 1988 / Texas Hotel ♦♦♦

○ **Hard Volume** / 1989 / Texas Hotel ♦♦♦♦

Turned on / 1990 / Quarterstick ♦♦♦
A perfect example of the Rollins Band at work was recorded live in Vienna, Austria, in 1989 with some of his best songs from that era. Recorded digitally, but the CD treats the entire recording as one track. —*John Book*

● **The End of Silence** / 1992 / Imago ♦♦♦♦
Intense is the only word that can describe Henry Rollins, and his band is the most intense unit recording today. *The End of Silence* is arguably the Rollins Band's best effort to date, full of angry, abrasive hardcore/jazz fusion, highlighted by the crushing "Low Self Opinion." —*Stephen Thomas Erlewine*

○ **Deep Throat** / Feb. 1992 / Quarterstick ♦♦♦♦
All of Rollins' early spoken-word releases are gathered in the reasonably priced six-disc box set *Deep Throat*. As with each of his spoken albums, Rollins is incisive, moving, self-effacing, and very funny; it's worth the price of the discs. —*Stephen Thomas Erlewine*

● **Rollins: The Boxed Life** / 1993 / Imago ♦♦♦♦
Rollins' spoken-word records are comedy records, more like Lenny Bruce or Richard Pryor than Andrew Dice Clay or Eddie Murphy. Underneath all the laughter there are some serious themes; the humor is drawn from pain. But the main reason to hear *The Boxed Life* (or any of Rollins' spoken-word records) is that he's a superb storyteller with a wicked sense of humor. Some of the topics are squeamish (animal testing, safe sex, depression) and there

is a generous helping of profanity, but it is genuinely funny and moving. — *Stephen Thomas Erlewine*

○ **Weight** / Apr. 12, 1994 / Imago ✦✦✦✦
The latest effort from the Rollins Band is able to mix the musicians' love for jazz with a blindingly direct hard-rock assault, making a twisted form of metal-jazz. Rollins' lyrics have also begun to move away from his relentless self-examination, adding a touch of the self-effacing humor that distinguishes his spoken records. The new lyrical dimension adds depth to the band's music, making *Weight* the most impressive album they have released to date. — *Stephen Thomas Erlewine*

The Romantics

Group, Power Pop/Anglo-Pop, Pop/Rock
In the early '80s, the Romantics were a terrific rock band, joyously tearing through loose, infectious power pop gems like the classic "What I Like About You." After two albums of energetic pop/rock, the band shifted its direction to a slicker, more radio-friendly pop; the change of style worked, resulting in the hit singles "Talking in Your Sleep" and "One in a Million" in 1983. Surprisingly, their drummer Jimmy Marinos left after their success; the band recorded one more album in 1985 before breaking up.
　　In the early '90s, "What I Like About You" began appearing in television commercials, leading the band to reunite. They have recorded one EP and have toured several times since re-forming. — *Stephen Thomas Erlewine*

○ **The Romantics** / 1979 / Epic ✦✦✦✦
The cover, featuring the four members decked out in identical red leather outfits with the *de rigeur* skinny ties, leaves no doubt as to the album's content. This is your basic artifact of the era—lusty, girl-crazed, teen anthems sung to hard-driving, puchy power-pop. "What I Like About You" was the hit but any of these songs could have been hits. It's easy to dismiss this band but few albums provide this much guilty pleaure. — *Chris Woodstra*

National Breakout / 1980 / Epic ✦✦✦
Their sophomore effort follows much of the same formula of the debut. Unfortunately, none of the songs had the instantly endearing catchiness of "What I Like About You" and the album failed to live up to the optimistic title's promise. — *Chris Woodstra*

Strictly Personal / 1981 / Epic ✦✦✦
Strictly Personal, the Romantics' commercial breaktrough, loses much of the innocence (and fun) of the first two albums, with its slicker production. "Talking in Your Sleep" and "One in a Million" both broke the Top Ten but the album offers little else. — *Chris Woodstra*

In Heat / 1983 / Nemperor ✦✦✦

Rhythm Romance / 1985 / Nemperor ✦✦
Power-pop was very much of the moment; bands who held on as late as 1985 had to lose the silly ties and modify their sound or face ridicule. The Romantics certainly followed the rules with *Rhythm Romance*. This time the band is pictured on the cover dressed in *black* leather and bigger hair. They've become full-fledged arena rockers complete with a big arena-slick production …and an utterly forgettable batch of songs. — *Chris Woodstra*

● **What I Like About You (& Other Romantic Hits)** / 1990 / Nemperor ✦✦✦✦
The title track was their finest hour but there are a couple of other hits here too. — *Dan Heilman*

Made in Detroit / 1993 / Westbound ✦✦

Romeo Void

Group, New Wave
A post-punk quintet formed in San Francisco in 1979, consisting of singer Debora Iyall (b. 1956), bassist Frank Zincavage, guitarist Peter Woods, drummer Jay Derrah (replaced by John Stench and then Larry Carter), and saxophone player Ben Bossi. They released several albums on 415 Records (distributed by CBS) from 1981 to 1984. Iyall then left for a solo career. — *William Ruhlmann*

It's a Condition / 1981 / 415 ✦✦✦
Iyall's distanced vocal style, plus the group's steady beat, make sentiments such as "Love Is an Illness" believable. Iyall is the Mae West of punk rock: When she says, "Talk dirty to me," it doesn't sound as though she cares whether you do or not. — *William Ruhlmann*

○ **Never Say Never** / 1982 / Columbia ✦✦✦✦
Benefactor / 1982 / Columbia ✦✦
"I might like you better if we slept together," Iyall sings in "Never Say Never," and so coins her ultimate putdown line, which is, typically, in the form of a come-on. — *William Ruhlmann*

Instincts / 1984 / Columbia ✦✦✦

● **Warm, in Your Coat** / May 5, 1992 / Columbia ✦✦✦✦

Ronettes

Group, Girl-Group
Before Phil Spector took them under his wing in the early '60s, the Ronettes had already recorded several singles and were regionally successful. But the Spector-produced records are what everyone remembers and for a good reason—they featured some of his biggest, best productions along with equally impressive sounds. Beneath his monumental wall of sound, lead vocalist Ronnie Bennett, who would later marry Spector, sang songs of teenage love in a plain, girlish voice; "Be My Baby," the group's first and biggest hit, was the pinnacle of the group's talent, as well as being one of the producer's finest moments. None of their following singles (including "Baby, I Love You," "(The Best Part Of) Breakin' Up," and "Walking in the Rain") were quite as successful commercially, although they were nearly as strong artistically. While Spector was inactive in the mid-'60s, the Ronettes were also inactive; together they re-emerged in 1969, to a small commercial reception. After Ronnie divorced Spector in 1973, she formed a new version of the Ronettes that lasted for three years; after the group disbanded, she launched a solo career. — *Stephen Thomas Erlewine*

Today's Hits / 1963 / Phillies ✦✦✦

○ **Fabulous Ronettes** / 1964 / Phillies ✦✦✦✦

The Ronettes / 1965 / Colpix ✦✦✦

○ **The Ronettes: The Early Years** / 1965 / Rhino ✦✦✦✦
The early Ronettes songs weren't as immaculately produced or as evocative as Phil Spector's productions. Their sound was more generic and resembled other girl groups like the Shirelles or Chiffons. They recorded for Colpix and Dimension during 1961 and 1962, with Ronnie Bennett doing most of the leads, while her sister Estelle and cousin Nedra added soothing harmonies and backgrounds. At times, as on "My Guiding Angel" or "You Bet I Would," they came close to the appealing mix of innocence and earnestness that characterized their later (and greatest) tracks. But despite getting material from such songwriters as Jackie DeShannon and Carole King, many of these cuts were more serviceable than classic. Still, this is the foundation for the sound that exploded in the mid-'60s. — *Ron Wynn*

★ **The Best of the Ronettes** / 1992 / ABKCO ✦✦✦✦✦
For a couple of years, the Ronettes made music that was as moving and unforgettable as any made during the rock era. Their voices merged sensuality, longing, anguish, and sentimentality, with Ronnie Spector's angelic leads framed by Phil Spector's sweeping production, the lyrics of Ellie Greenwich, Jeff Barry, Barry Mann, Cynthia Weil, Spector, and others. While such songs as "Walking In The Rain," "Be My Baby," "Baby, I Love You," and "(The Best Part) Of Breakin' Up" may seem hopelessly naive and possibly sexist in today's cynical world, they're still classic love poems. Ronnie Spector's voice retains its allure and appeal, and the 18 tracks on this CD will never become dated. — *Ron Wynn*

○ **Complete Colpix & Buddah Sessions** / Sequel ✦✦✦✦

BOOK

✦✦ **Be My Baby**, by Ronnie Spector with Vince Waldron (Harmony, 1990). As the lead singer of the Ronettes, Ronnie Spector (nee Bennett), was one of rock's great female vocalists, although her peak was extremely brief. That's because her career ended, more or less forcibly, when she became Mrs. Phil Spector. One could argue, based on the life story presented here, that her early ascent to stardom, and her suffocating marriage to the domineering Spector, didn't allow her to fully mature as an individual. She comes off as a quite naive and dependent, if likable, individual, fazed by Spector's musical prowess and wealth, and subsequently virtually imprisoned as his dream goddess— an unrealistic vision that no one could have satisfied. There are some good times from the two years or so of stardom, including stories of hanging out with the Beatles and the Rolling Stones, and working with Spector on the great Ronettes singles. These are outweighed by, well, a ton of dirt on Spector himself, who proved to be a sadistic tyrant during much of the couple's stormy marriage. Not a bad read for Ronettes/girl group fans, but heavier on the soap opera than the music. *—Richie Unterberger*

Mick Ronson

d. Apr. 12, 1993
Rock & Roll
Mick Ronson first made a name for himself as guitarist for David Bowie on such great '70s albums as *The Man Who Sold the World, Hunky Dory, Ziggy Stardust* and so forth. He was also the guitarist and creative foil for Ian Hunter's (Mott the Hoople) solo work. As a producer, Ronson worked with Morrisey (*Your Arsenal*) and Rich Kids. Ronson's string arranging skills were considerable and can be heard on Pure Prairie League's *Bustin' Out* album. Ronson passed away in 1993 of liver cancer. *—Rick Clark*

● **Slaughter on Tenth Avenue** / 1974 / RCA ◆◆◆◆
Surprisingly, Ronson's solo debut still isn't out on CD. It might not be a great album (Ronson's singing is sometimes overly affected), but his take on Richard Rodgers' "Slaughter on 10th Avenue" is worth the price of admission. *—Rick Clark*

Play Don't Worry / 1975 / RCA ◆◆◆

Heaven & Hull / 1994 / Epic ◆◆◆
A fitting final testament for one of rock's ultimate guitarists who passed away in the midst of completing this disc. Includes strong, collaborations with Def Leppard's Joe Elliott, David Bowie, Ian Hunter, and John Mellencamp, and all the guitar you could wish for. *—Roch Parisien*

Linda Ronstadt

b. Jul. 15, 1946, Tuscon, AZ
Country-Rock, Pop, Pop/Rock
With roots in the Los Angeles country and folk-rock scenes, Linda Ronstadt became one of the most popular interpretive singers of the '70s, earning a string of platinum-selling albums and Top 40 singles. Throughout the '70s, her laidback pop never lost sight of her folky roots, yet as she moved into the '80s, she began to change her sound with the times, adding new wave influences. After a brief flirtation with pre-rock pop, Ronstadt settled into a pattern of adult contemporary pop and Latin albums, sustaining her popularity in both fields. No matter what she is singing, her full, sweet voice has not lost much of its power over the years.

While Ronstadt was a student at Arizona State University, she met guitarist Bob Kimmel. The duo moved to Los Angeles, where guitarist/songwriter Kenny Edwards joined the pair. Calling themselves the Stone Poneys, the group became a leading attraction on California's folk circuit, recording their first album in 1967. The band's second album, *Evergreen, Vol. 2*, featured the Top 20 hit "Different Drum," which was written by Michael Nesmith. After recording one more album with the group, Ronstadt left for a solo career at the end of 1968.

Ronstadt's first two solo albums—*Hand Sown, Home Grown* (1969) and *Silk Purse* (1970)—accentuated her country roots, featuring several honky tonk numbers. Released in 1971, her self-titled third album was a pivotal record in her career. Featuring a group of session musicians that would later form the Eagles, the album was a softer, more laidback variation of the country-rock she had been recording. With the inclusion of songs from singer/songwriters like Jackson Browne, Neil Young, and Eric Anderson, *Linda Ronstadt* had folk-rock connections as well; it was one of the records that established the slick Californian country-pop sound that became very popular during the '70s.

Don't Cry Now, released in 1973, followed the same formula to greater success, yet it was 1974's *Heart Like a Wheel* that perfected the sound, making Ronstadt a star. Featuring hit versions "You're No Good," "When Will I Be Loved," and "It Doesn't Matter Anymore," *Heart Like a Wheel* reached number one and sold over two million copies; Ronstadt also won a Grammy award for her performance of Hank Williams' "I Can't Help It (If I'm Still in Love with You)" on the record.

Released in the fall of 1975, *Prisoner in Disguise* followed the same pattern as *Heart Like a Wheel* and was nearly as successful. *Hasten Down the Wind*, released in 1976, suggested a holding pattern, even if it charted higher than *Prisoner in Disguise*. *Simple Dreams* (1977) expanded the familiar pattern of rock oldies and new contributions by adding a more rock-oriented supporting

band, which breathed life into the Rolling Stones' "Tumbling Dice" and Warren Zevon's "Poor Poor Pitiful Me." The record became the singer's biggest hit, staying on the top of the charts for five weeks and selling over three million copies.

With *Living in the U.S.A.*, released the following year, Ronstadt began experimenting with new wave, recording Elvis Costello's "Alison;" the album was another number one hit. On 1980's *Mad Love*, she made a full-fledged new wave record, recording three Costello covers and adopting the synth-laden, quirky sound of many early '80s bands. While the album was a commercial success, it signalled that her patented formula was beginning to run out of steam. That suspicion was confirmed with 1982's *Get Closer*, which was her first new album since *Heart Like a Wheel* that failed to go platinum.

Sensing it was time to change direction, Ronstadt starred in the Broadway production of Gilbert & Sullivan's *Pirates of Penzance*, as well as the accompanying movie. *Pirates of Penzance* led the singer to a collaboration with Nelson Riddle, who arranged and conducted her 1983 collection of pop standards, *What's New*. While it received lukewarm reviews, it was a considerable hit, reaching number three on the charts and selling over two million copies. Ronstadt's next two albums—*Lush Life* (1984) and *For Sentimental Reasons* (1986)—were also albums of pre-rock standards recorded with Riddle; each subsequent record sold less than the previous album, yet all three were chart successes.

At the end of 1986, Ronstadt returned to contemporary pop, recording "Somewhere out There," the theme to the animated *An American Tail*, with James Ingram; the record became a number two hit. She also returned to her country roots in 1987, recording the *Trio* album with Dolly Parton and Emmylou Harris, which peaked at number six on the album charts. That same year, Ronstadt recorded *Canciones De Mi Padre*, a set of 13 traditional Mexican songs which became a surprise hit, selling over a million records. Two years later, she recorded *Cry Like a Rainstorm—Howl Like the Wind*—her first contemporary pop album since 1982's *Get Closer*. Featuring four duets with Aaron Neville, including the number two hit "Don't Know Much," the album sold over two million copies. Ronstadt returned to traditional Mexican and Spanish material with 1991's *Mas Canciones* and 1992's *Frenesi*; neither album performed as well as *Canciones De Mi Padre* and *Frenesi* fell off the charts after one week. She returned to pop with 1994's *Winter Light*, which failed to generate a hit single, as did 1995's *Feels like Home*. *—Stephen Thomas Erlewine*

Hand Sown Home Grown / 1969 / Capitol ◆◆

Linda Ronstadt's debut album is a transitional effort, as the vocalist began to abandon the folk leanings of the Stone Poneys for a relaxed country-rock approach. Several of the songs are well-performed, but the majority of the music is unfocused and Ronstadt occasionally sounds unsure of herself. *—Stephen Thomas Erlewine*

Silk Purse / 1970 / Capitol ◆◆◆

While it followed the same musical approach of the debut, *Silk Purse* was an improvement on *Hand Sown Home Grown*, featuring more confident vocals from Linda Ronstadt and a stronger selection of songs, including "Lovesick Blues" and "Long Long Time." *—Stephen Thomas Erlewine*

Linda Ronstadt / 1971 / Capitol ◆◆◆

Linda Ronstadt's self-titled third album captured the singer moving away from the rootsier charms of her first two albums, towards a more polished take on country rock. Supported by the Eagles throughout the record, Ronstadt turns in a strong performance, aided by a fine selection of material, including "Rock Me On the Water," "Crazy Arms," "I Still Miss Someone," and "I Fall to Pieces." *—Stephen Thomas Erlewine*

Don't Cry Now / 1973 / Asylum ◆◆◆

Don't Cry Now expanded the pop/rock concessions of *Linda Ronstadt*, and the result was the singer's first genuine hit record, peaking at number 45 on the charts. *—Stephen Thomas Erlewine*

○ **Different Drum** / 1974 / Capitol ◆◆◆◆

Different Drum collects the highlights of Linda Ronstadt's first three solo albums, adding five Stone Poneys tracks, including the hit "Different Drum," for good measure. It misses some fine tracks from her solo records, but the album remains a fine introduction to her early years. *—Stephen Thomas Erlewine*

☆ **Heart Like a Wheel** / 1974 / Capitol ✦✦✦✦✦
Ronstadt's breakthrough album, and her most perfectly realized.
Solid from top to bottom, featuring the title track, "When Will I Be
Loved?," "Desperado," and "You're No Good." Essential. —*Cub
Koda*

○ **Prisoner in Disguise** / 1975 / Asylum ✦✦✦✦
Linda Ronstadt followed the commercial and critical breakthrough success of *Heart Like a Wheel* with *Prisoner in Disguise,*
a record that essentially repeated the formula of its predecessor.
While it lacked the consistency of *Heart Like a Wheel,* it was a
thoroughly enjoyable, highlighted by sturdy remakes of the Motown classics "Tracks of My Tears" and "Heat Wave." —*Stephen
Thomas Erlewine*

● **Greatest Hits, Vol. 1** / 1976 / Asylum ✦✦✦✦
A concise collection of her chart successes. —*Dan Heilman*

Hasten Down the Wind / 1976 / Asylum ✦✦✦
Again, Linda Ronstadt repeats her slick, Californian pop/country-
rock formula on *Hasten Down the Wind.* When the material is
first-rate—such as "That'll Be the Day" or "Crazy"—Ronstadt's performances are terrific, but on the sub-par songs—such as the three
Karla Bonoff numbers—she's dragged down with her material. —
Stephen Thomas Erlewine

○ **Retrospective** / 1977 / Capitol ✦✦✦✦
A nice compilation of primarily country-influenced, pre-hit material. —*Cub Koda*

○ **Simple Dreams** / 1977 / Asylum ✦✦✦✦
Featuring a broader array of styles than any previous Linda Ronstadt record, *Simple Dreams* reconfirms her substantial talents as
an interpretive singer. Ronstadt sings Dolly Parton ("I Never Will
Marry") with the same conviction as the Rolling Stones ("Tumbling Dice"), and she manages to update Roy Orbison ("Blue
Bayou") and direct attention to the caustic, fledgling singer/song-
writer Warren Zevon ("Poor Poor Pitiful Me" and "Carmelita"). The
consistently adventerous material and Ronstadt's powerful performance makes the record rival *Heart Like a Wheel* in sheer overall
quality. —*Stephen Thomas Erlewine*

Living in the U.S.A. / 1978 / Asylum ✦✦✦
On *Living in the U.S.A.,* Linda Ronstadt made the ill-advised move
to incorporate some current musical trends, such as new wave,
into her successful formula. While some of the record sounds
good, the majority of the album is poorly executed, particularly
her take on Elvis Costello's "Alison." —*Stephen Thomas Erlewine*

○ **Greatest Hits, Vol. 2** / 1980 / Asylum ✦✦✦✦
Her next dozen hits, more formulaic in content, but bigger on the
charts. —*Cub Koda*

Mad Love / 1980 / Asylum ✦✦
Linda Ronstadt made a full-fledged, new wave-influenced pop album with *Mad Love.* It's an unfocused, stilted effort that suggested
her career at the top of the charts was coming to a close. —*Stephen
Thomas Erlewine*

Round Midnight with Nelson Riddle and his Orchestra / 1981 /
Asylum ✦✦✦

Get Closer / 1982 / Asylum ✦✦
Get Closer was another successful album for Ronstadt, even
though it didn't perform up to her plaitnum standards. Part of the
reason for the relative lack of success was the lackluster material,
which again signals that Ronstadt had lost touch with the mainstream pop scene. —*Stephen Thomas Erlewine*

What's New / 1983 / Asylum ✦✦✦
Instead of trying to compete with a newer, fashion-conscious pop
marketplace, Linda Ronstadt removed herself from the rat race,
recording an album of tradtional-pop standards with Nelson Riddle. Ronstadt's voice isn't always showcased to a fine effect on
these songs, but the record is an interesting change of pace. And it
would have been more interesting if she hadn't repeated its formula on her next two records. —*Stephen Thomas Erlewine*

Lush Life / 1984 / Asylum ✦✦✦

For Sentimental Reasons / Feb. 1986 / Asylum ✦✦✦

Canciones De Mi Padre / 1987 / Asylum ✦✦✦
Rondstadt's first all-Spanish album is a heartfelt tribute to her her-
itage. It also contains some of her finest performances of the '80s.
—*AMG*

○ **The Trio** / 1987 / Warner Brothers ✦✦✦

Cry Like a Rainstorm—Howl Like the Wind / 1989 / Asylum
✦✦✦
On the strength of the hit duet with Aaron Neville, "Don't Know
Much," *Cry Like a Rainstorm—Howl Like the Wind* returned
Linda Ronstadt to the top of the charts. The album was a collection
of well-constructed adult contemporary pop, which suits her voice
better than than the traditional-pop she recorded during the mid-
'80s. Musically, *Cry Like A Rainstorm* isn't as adventerous as *Canciones De Mi Padre,* nor is it as consistent as *Trio,* the album she
recorded with Emmylou Harris and Dolly Parton, but it is her
most satisfying mainstream pop album she has made since the
late '70s. —*Stephen Thomas Erlewine*

Mas Canciones / 1990 / Asylum ✦✦✦

Frenesi / 1992 / Asylum ✦✦
Frenesi is Linda Ronstadt's third in as series of Spanish language
releases. This one—inspired by her work on the soundtrack to the
film *Mambo Kings*—tackles Afro-Cuban pop and jazz. While some
tracks, especially "Entre Abismos," swing mightily, there's little
that sounds street level or rootsy about these sessions. I can't help
picturing a wind-up lounge band holding court at some tourist-
trap Holiday Inn in Acapulco. —*Roch Parisien*

Winter Light / 1994 / Asylum ✦✦✦

Feels Like Home / 1995 / Asylum ✦✦

Tim Rose

Singer-Songwriter, Folk-Rock
A nearly forgotten singer/songwriter of the '60s, Tim Rose's early
work bore a strong resemblance to another Tim working in
Greenwich Village around 1966-67, Tim Hardin. Rose also favored
a throaty blues-folk-rock style with pop production flourishes,
though he looked to outside material more, wasn't quite in
Hardin's league as a singer or songwriter, and had a much harsher,
even gravelly vocal tone. Before beginning a solo career, Rose had
sung with Cass Elliott in the folk trio the Big Three, a few years
before she joined the Mamas and Papas. Signed by Columbia in
1966, his 1967 debut album (which actually included a few previously released singles) is considered by far his most significant
work. Two of the tracks were particularly noteworthy: his slow
arrangement of "Hey Joe" inspired Jimi Hendrix's version, and
"Morning Dew," Rose's best original composition, became something of a standard, covered by the Jeff Beck Group, the Grateful
Dead, Clannad, and others. Some non-LP singles he recorded
around this time have unfortunately never been reissued, and although he made several other albums up through the mid-'70s,
none matched the acclaim of the first one. —*Richie Unterberger*

○ **Retrospective** / 1977 / Capitol ✦✦✦✦

● **Morning Dew** / 1988 / Edsel ✦✦✦✦
A retitled reissue of Rose's self-titled debut. A fairly strong singer-
songwriter set, divided about equally between originals and imaginative covers, showing strong blues and folk leanings as well as
forays into orchestrated pop-rock. Includes "Morning Dew" and
"Hey Joe." —*Richie Unterberger*

Diana Ross (Diane Earle)

b. Mar. 26, 1944, Detroit, MI
Soul, Disco, Pop/Rock
As a solo artist, Diana Ross is one of the most successful female
singers of the rock era. If you factor in her work as the lead singer
of the Supremes in the 1960s, she may be *the* most successful.

With her friends Mary Wilson, Florence Ballard, and Barbara
Martin, Ross formed the Primettes vocal quartet in 1959. In 1960,
they were signed to local Motown Records, changing their name to
the Supremes in 1961. Martin then left, and the group continued
as a trio. Over the next eight years, the Supremes (renamed "Diana Ross and the Supremes" in 1967, when Cindy Birdsong replaced Ballard) scored 12 number one pop hits. After the last one,
"Someday We'll Be Together" (October 1969), Ross launched a solo
career.

Motown initially paired her with writer/producers Nicklaus
Ashford and Valerie Simpson, who gave her four Top 40 pop hits,
including the number one "Ain't No Mountain High Enough" (July
1970).

Ross branched out into acting, starring in a film biography of
Billie Holiday, *Lady Sings the Blues* (November 1972). The sound-

track went to number one, and Ross was nominated for an Academy Award.

She returned to record-making with the Top Ten album *Touch Me in the Morning* (June 1973) and its chart-topping title song. This was followed by a duet album with Marvin Gaye, *Diana & Marvin* (October 1973), that produced three chart hits. Ross acted in her second movie, *Mahogany* (October 1975), and it brought her another chart-topping single in the theme song, "Do You Know Where You're Going To." That and her next number one, the disco-oriented "Love Hangover" (March 1976), were featured on her second album to be titled simply *Diana Ross* (February 1976), which rose into the Top Ten.

Ross's third film role came in *The Wiz* (October 1978). *The Boss* (May 1979) was a gold-selling album, followed by the platinum-selling *Diana* (May 1980) (the second of her solo albums with that name, though the other, a 1971 TV soundtrack, had an exclamation mark). It featured the number one single "Upside Down" and the Top Ten hit "I'm Coming Out."

Ross scored a third Top Ten hit in 1980 singing the title theme from the movie *It's My Turn.* She then scored the biggest hit of her career with another movie theme, duetting with Lionel Richie on "Endless Love" (June 1981). It was her last big hit on Motown; after more than 20 years, she decamped for RCA. She was rewarded immediately with a million-selling album, titled after her remake of the old Frankie Lymon and the Teenagers hit, "Why Do Fools Fall in Love," which became her next Top Ten hit. The album also included the Top Ten hit "Mirror, Mirror."

Silk Electric (October 1982) was a gold-seller, featuring the Top Ten hit "Muscles," written and produced by Michael Jackson, and *Swept Away* (September 1984) was another successful album, containing the hit "Missing You," but Ross had trouble selling records in the second half of the 1980s. By 1989, she had returned to Motown, and by 1993 was turning more to pop standards, notably on the concert album *Diana Ross Live: The Lady Sings...Jazz & Blues, Stolen Moments* (April 1993). Motown released a four-CD/cassette boxed set retrospecive, *Forever Diana*, in October 1993, and the singer published her autobiography in 1994. — *William Ruhlmann*

○ **Diana Ross** / May 1970 / Motown ✦✦✦✦
This remains arguably her finest solo work at Motown and perhaps her best ever; it was certainly among her most stunning. Everyone who doubted whether Diana Ross could sustain a career outside the Supremes found out immediately that she would be a star. The single "Reach Out And Touch (Somebody's Hand)" remains a staple in her shows, and is still her finest message track. — *Ron Wynn*

Lady Sings the Blues / Dec. 1971 / Motown ✦✦✦
Her biggest album as a solo act, Diana Ross forever ended any association with the Supremes after this film. She not only got an Oscar nomination and more roles, she really did capture the spirit and flavor, if not the sound and timbre, of Billie Holiday's music; her performance was the film's only saving grace. — *Ron Wynn*

Last Time I Saw Him / Dec. 1973 / Motown ✦✦✦
An odd entry into the early-'70s Diana Ross sweepstakes, this album became a hit many months after it was initially issued. It was one of three Ross LPs Motown released in 1973, and it succeeded only after an album of duets between Ross and Marvin Gaye had peaked. The single eventually cracked both the R&B and pop Top 20, and the album became moderately successful nearly a year after its initial debut date. — *Ron Wynn*

Live at Caesar's Palace / May 1974 / Motown ✦✦✦
An entertaining, lavish, and sometimes a bit pretentious concert album from Diana Ross. It was the first album that really presented how a typical Ross live performance sounded, and that proved both complimentary and negative. The staged conversations, often awkward monologues, and rough pacing were balanced by some excellent performances, and the album was produced well enough to keep her voice at the core of the sound. It's not an essential purchase, but it's worth getting if it turns up in an oldies collection. — *Ron Wynn*

Diana Ross / Feb. 1976 / Motown ✦✦✦
Diana Ross landed one of the decade's definitive singles with "Love Hangover," instantly making this a major hit album. While it surprisingly didn't sell as well as some 1980s LPs, the single was a double chart-topper and a huge club hit for much of the next two years. It vaulted the album into the pop Top 10 and even managed to break the followup single onto the charts. — *Ron Wynn*

Baby, It's Me / Sep. 1977 / Motown ✦✦✦
A moderately successful late-'70s album for Diana Ross. She was evolving into celebrity/stardom status, and her albums were increasingly filled with less soulful, more sophisticated, heavily produced and arranged ballads and light pop. She still sounded glorious on most of them, but now the edge, sensuality, and energy that had made her Motown songs classics was steadily eroding in favor of a more stylized, almost show-business kind of singing. — *Ron Wynn*

The Boss / May 1979 / Motown ✦✦✦
Great dance material is featured, again by Ashford & Simpson. — *Rick A. Bueche*

Diana / May 1980 / Motown ✦✦✦
This is a funky Chic production. — *Rick A. Bueche*

Why Do Fools Fall in Love / Oct. 1981 / Capitol ✦✦✦
The irony of a 37-year-old woman having a huge hit covering an anthem for a bunch of teenagers aside, Diana Ross enjoyed tremendous success with this early '80s album. It was her second platinum album of the 1980s and eventually did better than any other LP she issued in the decade, except for *Diana*. It also started Ross on a run of youthful hits that would include "Work That Body," "Mirror, Mirror," and the ultimate vanity song, "Muscles." — *Ron Wynn*

● **All the Great Hits A** / Oct. 1981 / Motown ✦✦✦✦
Yet another Motown anthology/greatest hits package. The songs are fine and the mastering is good. It's really a question of choice and need. If you want everything, get either the new Ross boxed set or the original anthology. If you only want a few hits, then either this or any other package will suffice. — *Ron Wynn*

Silk Electric / Oct. 1982 / RCA ✦✦✦
Diana Ross continued her steady pace in the early '80s, scoring a hit single with the curious song "Muscles." She was now established as a stylist and show-business celebrity, and seldom evoked the soulful or sensual air that characterized her past material. The songs were also more elaborately produced, the arrangements designed to accent the carefully calculated pauses, sighs, and coos, and the compositions more suggestive in their lyrics than convincing or compelling. — *Ron Wynn*

Ross / Jun. 1983 / RCA ✦✦
A noble, if failed, experiment. Diana Ross teamed up with Steely Dan producer Gary Katz for this, her third outing on RCA. Katz brought in the usual suspects, not only buddies like Michael McDonald and Donald Fagen (each of whom contributed a song and keyboards), but also session aces like Jeff Porcaro and Greg Phillinganes. The result, on the five tracks Katz handled, has that precise, icy sound those guys always get, not a sound that meshes well with Ross. No better are the two tracks contributed by Ray Parker, Jr., or Ross's own effort, "Girls," which closes things out. As a result, *Ross* was Diana Ross's first album since 1978 not to even go gold. (Not to be confused with Diana Ross's 1978 album [Motown 907] of the same name.) — *William Ruhlmann*

Eaten Alive / Aug. 1985 / RCA ✦✦✦
Diana Ross got a lot of mileage from this album, although it didn't duplicate the success she'd enjoyed with *Swept Away*. The title track was a Top 10 R&B hit, thanks in part to Michael Jackson's presence on background vocals, and another single also made the charts. Ross wasn't the powerhouse she was in the 1970s, but she was still doing well enough to keep making records. — *Ron Wynn*

Red Hot Rhythm & Blues / May 1987 / RCA ✦✦✦
Diana Ross made one of her better albums in quite a while, although this late-'80s number didn't fare as well as anticipated. But "It's Hard For Me to Say," co-produced and co-written with Luther Vandross, was the first heartache tune Ross had done in many years with a real, poignant edge to it, while "Cross My Heart" was a decent commercial number. Of course, the tune that ended up making the most noise was "Dirty Looks," another of Ross' patented cute, quasi-sophisticated numbers. — *Ron Wynn*

Workin' Overtime / Jun. 1989 / Motown ✦✦
Diana Ross made a bid for new stardom by returning to Motown with a deal giving her profit participation in the company and creative control in 1989. This album was the first product of that new contract, and the results weren't very encouraging. There were no moderate or even small hits, and the album quickly dropped off both the R&B and pop charts within a couple of weeks of its release. Ross sounded completely lost, and the production, arrange-

ments, and compositions sounded weak and thin next to the dominant New Jack and hip-hop works. —*Ron Wynn*

Forever Diana: Musical Memoirs / Oct. 5, 1993 / Motown ✦✦
Plagued by inferior sound and a weak track selection, *Forever Diana* is a major disappointment for fans. Only one disc is devoted to the Supremes, with Ross's spotty solo career occupying the other three discs, featuring decidedly poorer sound than previous Motown releases. Besides poor audio, the liner notes are skimpy and incomplete. Ultimately, *Forever Diana* is a wasted opportunity. —*Stephen Thomas Erlewine*

David Lee Roth

b. Oct. 10, 1955, Bloomington, IN
Hard Rock, Pop/Rock, Heavy Metal
With Van Halen, vocalist David Lee Roth raised the role of a heavy metal frontman to a performance art. After the band's commercial breakthrough with the *1984* album, Roth released *Crazy from the Heat*, a 1985 EP that displayed his blatant pop roots, covering everything from the Beach Boys to Louis Prima. With two hit singles, *Crazy from the Heat* confirmed Roth's solo commercial potential, prompting his decision to leave Van Halen in June of 1985.

For his first full-length album, 1986's *Eat 'Em and Smile*, Roth hired guitarist Steve Vai and bassist Billy Sheehan for a grossly exaggerated take on heavy arena rock. It was a mammoth hit, as was the more pop-oriented follow-up, *Skyscaper*. After *Skyscraper*, Vai and Sheehan left to form their own bands (the Steve Vai Band and Mr. Big, respectively). Roth put together a new band for 1991's *A Little Ain't Enough*, which was his first album to not go platinum. Sensing that it was time for a change, he tried to refashion himself as a slick hard rock singer/songwriter with 1994's *Your Filthy Little Mouth*, but it resulted in his least successful album yet. —*Stephen Thomas Erlewine*

○ **Crazy from the Heat** / 1985 / Warner Brothers ✦✦✦✦
For his first solo effort, Roth stripped away the gonzo guitars that are Van Halen's trademark and accentuated his lounge-lizard-as-rock-star persona, resulting in an EP that succeeds because of that persona, not because the music is anything special. Certainly, he doesn't add anything to "California Girls" and "Just a Gigolo/I Ain't Got Nobody" other than his joking, over-the-top vocals. Then again, that's all he needs to do. —*Stephen Thomas Erlewine*

● **Eat 'Em & Smile** / 1986 / Warner Brothers ✦✦✦✦
This flamboyant frontman is flanked by bassist Billy Sheehan and guitar-shredder Steve Vai, blazing the solo trail with these big and bawdy rockers, like "Goin' Crazy!" —*Donna DiChario*

Skyscraper / 1988 / Warner Brothers ✦✦✦
On his second full-length solo album, Roth turns down the guitars, adds more melody, and makes a more polished, but less interesting record, highlighted by the soaring pop of "Just Like Paradise." —*Stephen Thomas Erlewine*

A Little Ain't Enough / Apr. 1991 / Warner Brothers ✦✦
Recorded with a new backing band, *A Little Ain't Enough* doesn't feature the gonzo instrumental kick of *Eat 'Em and Smile*, nor is it a stab at pop-craft like *Skyscraper*. Instead, it's an attempt to regain the energy that fueled Van Halen's early albums, but Roth can't work up enough steam to make the driving riffs convincing or memorable. —*Stephen Thomas Erlewine*

Your Filthy Little Mouth / Mar. 8, 1994 / Warner Brothers ✦✦
Although the title wouldn't indicate it, *Your Filthy Little Mouth* was a retreat from the thundering hard rock of *A Little Ain't Enough*. David Lee Roth kept some of the piledriving guitar riffs that always gave his records a foundation, but he added a smoother pop sensibility, along with self-consciously clever lyrics in an attempt to become a mature hard-rocker for all aging yuppies. It didn't work, either commercially or artistically, since most of the songs didn't have enough hooks to make them memorable. —*Stephen Thomas Erlewine*

Roulettes

Group, British Invasion
An underrated British band, the Roulettes featured future Argent alumnus Russ Ballard on lead guitar. They were originally formed as a backing group for vocalist Adam Faith, whose records, although few in number, were of a very high caliber and had some of the musical virtues evident in the better-known work of the Beatles and the Searchers: soaring harmonies behind strong lead

vocals, crisp guitar playing, and a knack for memorable hooks. —*Bruce Eder*

Stake & Chips / 1965 / Parlophone ✦✦✦
An unusual album, marred only by some ill-chosen cover versions. (import) —*Bruce Eder*

● **Russ, Bob, Pete and Mod** / 1983 / Edsel ✦✦✦✦
A superb collection of singles, B-Sides, and album tracks. All are enjoyable and memorable, especially the track "I'll Remember Tonight." (Import) —*Bruce Eder*

Roxette

Group, Pop/Rock
It's tempting to write Roxette off as nothing more than a shallow pop/rock band, but their shameless hooks are precisely what makes them so enjoyable. Roxette has a knack for writing extremely catchy and simple hooks and melodies that are sweet but not saccharine; it's radio-friendly pop, but the hooks don't wear thin with repeated plays. The duo of guitarist Per Gessle and vocalist Marie Fredriksson released an album in 1986 that didn't display much of their talents, but the infectious follow-up, 1988's *Look Sharp*, brought them to the top of the charts in America and England; 1991's *Joyride* was almost equally successful. After a couple of years off, Roxette returned with a new album in 1994. —*Stephen Thomas Erlewine*

Pearls of Passion / 1986 / EMI Sweden ✦✦

● **Look Sharp!** / 1988 / EMI America ✦✦✦✦
A fun, dynamic debut, it features the hit singles "The Look" (#1), "Dressed for Success" (#14), "Listen to Your Heart" (#1), and "Dangerous" (#2). —*Dan Heilman*

○ **Joyride** / 1991 / EMI America ✦✦✦✦
Their second album, featuring infectious, solid song construction from Gessle and dynamite singing from Fredriksson. "Knock on Every Door," "Watercolours in the Rain," and the title track are among the highlights. —*Cub Koda*

Tourism (Songs from Studios, Stages, Hotelrooms & Other Strange Places) / 1992 / EMI America ✦✦✦
A completely live hits package from Roxette's first world tour (1991-1992), this features both concert and in-studio performances of some of their biggest hits, including "Joyride," "The Look," and "It Must Have Been Love." It was recorded in their native Stockholm, as well as in Zurich, Buenos Aires, and Sydney, Australia. —*AMG*

Crash! Boom! Bang! / 1994 / EMI America ✦✦

Roxy Music

Group, Art-Rock/Progressive-Rock
Roxy Music scored enormous success in its native England in the '70s, first as a leader of the glam-rock movement and later for its sophisticated sound. The group was formed in London in 1971 around lead singer Bryan Ferry (b. Sep 26, 1945). Personnel came and went until the group solidified by the time of its 1972 debut album with a lineup of Ferry, reed player Andy Mackay (b. Jul 23, 1946), guitarist Phil Manzanera (b. Jan 31, 1951), keyboardist Brian Eno (b. May 15, 1948), and drummer Paul Thompson (b. May 13, 1951). The band's original bassist, Graham Simpson, left during the album sessions and was replaced initially by Rik Kenton, though the group employed a series of bassists throughout its career.

Roxy Music was a Top Ten U.K. hit in the summer of 1972, spinning off the Top Ten single, "Virginia Plain." *For Your Pleasure* (1973) did even better, getting to number four. Eno had left the band by the time it made its third album, *Stranded* (going on to an extensive career as a solo artist and record producer), and was replaced by Eddie Jobson (b. Apr 28, 1955), who played violin and keyboards. *Stranded* was another U.K. hit, going to number one, and it was followed by *Country Life*, Roxy Music's first album to sell in even modest numbers in the U.S. *Siren* (1975) contained the American Top 30 hit "Love is the Drug" (number two in the U.K.).

At the point of American commercial breakthrough, however, Roxy Music disbanded, with Ferry, Mackay, Manzanera, and Jobson going off to solo careers. The group re-formed in 1978, minus Jobson, and recorded *Manifesto* (1979), after which Thompson left. The remaining trio released *Flesh and Blood* and *Avalon* (the latter was Roxy's only U.S. gold album), albums made in a smooth, melodic art-rock style before the group folded again in 1983. —*William Ruhlmann*

Roxy Music / 1972 / Reprise ✦✦✦

For Your Pleasure / 1973 / Reprise ✦✦✦
For Your Pleasure, Roxy's schizophrenic second album, vacillates between campy rockers like "Do the Strand" and "Editions of You" (both UK hits) and creepy mood pieces like "In Every Dream Home a Heartache" (an ode to an inflatable sex doll) and the title cut, which showcases lead singer Bryan Ferry's ghoulish croon over an instrumental track that would work well on *Twin Peaks.* —*Rick Clark*

○ **Stranded** / 1973 / Reprise ✦✦✦✦
On *Stranded,* their first album without sound-manipulator Brian Eno, Roxy affected a more sophisticated, self-absorbed stance with elegant numbers like "A Song for Europe" and "Psalm." Roxy's penchant for fine oddball pop/rockers continued with "Street Life" (a number nine U.K. hit), "Amazona," and the soaring "Serenade." —*Rick Clark*

★ **Country Life** / 1974 / Reprise ✦✦✦✦✦
Arguably their best album, *Country Life*'s everything-and-the-kitchen-sink art-rock production and steely dissonance reached a pinnacle with tracks like the "The Thrill of It All," "All I Want Is You," and "Casanova." "Out of the Blue," one of their finest songs, showcased Eddie Jobson on a powerfully phase-shifted violin solo. The beautifully unsettling "Bitter-Sweet" reflected Bryan Ferry's flirtation with Germanic melodicism and fascist imagery. —*Rick Clark*

☆ **Siren** / 1975 / Reprise ✦✦✦✦✦
Siren provided Roxy Music with their first international hit, the coolly funky "Love Is the Drug" (number 30). Except for "Sentimental Fool," "Both Ends Burning," and "Whirlwind," most of this album fails to deliver the power or memorable melodies of either *Country Life* or *Stranded.* —*Rick Clark*

Viva! / 1976 / Reprise ✦✦
While their studio work is the place to start with this group, this is a good live set. —*Rick Clark*

Manifesto / 1979 / Reprise ✦✦✦
After a four-year layoff, Roxy shed their aggressively dense rock sound and returned with a more streamlined (but still weird) danceable pop. Detractors claimed that the band had lost their edge, but *Manifesto* introduced Roxy Music to a new audience looking for a sophisticated alternative to generic late-'70s disco. Highlights include "Angel Eyes," "Dance Away," and the title cut. —*Rick Clark*

Flesh + Blood / 1980 / Reprise ✦✦
Flesh + Blood finds Roxy making a further transition away from dissonant arrangements. The sleepwalking delivery of "In the Midnight Hour" is oddly fascinating, as is the discoish streamlining of the Byrds' classic "Eight Miles High." Nevertheless, many of the originals lack any memorable qualities. —*Rick Clark*

☆ **Avalon** / 1982 / Reprise ✦✦✦✦✦
From the beautifully longing romanticism of Bryan Ferry's melodies to the dreamy soundscapes rendered by Rhett Davies, Roxy Music, and Bob Clearmountain, *Avalon* is fashion-plate cool, yet somehow exudes a weird, intoxicating kind of detached soulfulness that makes this one of the most elegant-sounding releases ever committed to disc. —*Rick Clark*

High Road / 1983 / Reprise ✦✦✦

○ **Atlantic Years (1973-1980)** / 1983 / Atco ✦✦✦✦
Atlantic Years 1973-1980 provides the cream of *Flesh + Blood* and *Manifesto* (as well as a couple of key tracks from Roxy's earlier work on Reprise). Overall it lacks the substance of the original 1977 Atco *Greatest Hits* package, which was an essential showcase for their earlier work. —*Rick Clark*

○ **Street Life: 20 Greatest Hits** / 1986 / Reprise ✦✦✦✦
This compilation is a more general (not entirely satisfactory) overview of Roxy tracks and Bryan Ferry's urbane dance-pop hits. —*Rick Clark*

Heart Still Beating / Oct. 30, 1990 / Reprise ✦✦

Royal Trux

Group, Alternative Pop/Rock
From the noisy demise of underground kingpins Pussy Galore came two interesting bands. The first was Jon Spencer's blues deconstruction unit the Jon Spencer Blues Explosion; the second was Neil Hagerty and Jennifer Herrema's dissonant junkie nightmare

known as Royal Trux. Interestingly, both bands started out as avant-noise combos playing little that resembled traditional rock & roll. That doesn't mean the music they made was bad; it was rather a little difficult to figure out when they were really into it or simply pulling your chain. What was amazing is that after a protracted period of making harsh, nearly inaccessible records, both bands, by the mid-'90s, were making records that sounded like '70s rock, only with gobs more attitude and noise.

Early Royal Trux records (two self-titled records and *Twin Infinitives*) are, to say the least, extreme. Herrema and Hagerty play mostly beat-to-shit, thrift-store guitars, howl over the noise, and let a crappy little drum machine keep a beat. Both were raging junkies, and running the risk of turning this into a tabloid piece, the music sounds it. It's messy, self-indulgent, and on-the-nod, but's it's also jarring, exciting and full of potential. Both Herrema and Hagerty "play" like they couldn't care less about what they were doing (and they probably couldn't), but there's a spark here— maybe an accidental one, but a spark that makes these messy chunks of distortion more interesting than your average underground rant, although I can certainly understand why people hate this stuff. It's not what you'd call friendly, inviting music. Most wouldn't even consider it music.

Although their drug problems escalated (in a fit of Miles Davis-inspired bravado, Herrema and Hagerty allegedly spent a recording advance by their label Drag City on smack, only to ask the impoverished indie label for more money to make the record), they eventually got sober around the time of *Cats & Dogs,* their most lucid and last recording for Drag City. Now employing three other musicians and sounding like and honest-to-God rock band, Royal Trux was making music that sounded grimy and raunchy, the way the Stones did in the mid-'70s. It was an amazing and unexpected turnaround, but well worth the wait.

After exhibiting a little stability, Royal Trux was gobbled up by Virgin as part of the post-Nirvana/Pearl Jam alternative-rock signing frenzy. While purists were hissing sellout (as they always do), Royal Trux hooked up with Neil Young producer David Briggs and cut *Thank You,* a great, greasy glob of low-fi rock fueled by cigarettes and junk food. Hagerty's guitar playing still gleefully wanders into noiseland, but he's just as likely to cough up a '70s hard rock riff or two. Herrema actually sings now, but her voice still hasn't improved much beyond a one-octave catgrowl. Still, Royal Trux seems to have made it; and at the start of the decade, few people would have made that prediction. —*John Dougan*

Twin Infinitives / 1991 / Drag City ✦✦✦

○ **Royal Trux** / Oct. 5, 1992 / Drag City ✦✦✦

○ **Cats & Dogs** / Jun. 14, 1993 / Drag City ✦✦✦✦
Recorded for America's number one low-fi underground label, *Cats & Dogs* was the first indication that Royal Trux could do more than whip up a tornado of distortion. A little more less focused than *Thank You,* it still has its moments of splendor, especially when it sounds as though it's going to fall apart and, suddenly, comes back together. —*John Dougan*

● **Thank You** / 1995 / Virgin ✦✦✦✦
I realize that this runs contrary to the beliefs of longtime Royal Trux fans, but the more Royal Trux resembles a standard rock band, the better they sound. If you want a little guitar skronk with your sci-fi surrealism (as in Herrema's lyrics), but like a little funky backbeat now and again, this is Royal Trux at their scuzzy best. It's still not for the weak, nor for those who like pretty melodies or great musicianship. But for the rest of us who like the occasional run through the jungle, songs like "The Sewers of Mars" and "You're Gonna Lose" are prime chunks of non-commercial alternative rock. It's a safe bet to assume that more '90s bands will continue to appropriate '70s rock stylings, but few will do it with the panache of Royal Trux. —*John Dougan*

Rubinoos

Group, New Wave, Power Pop/Anglo-Pop
For a brief moment, San Francisco's the Rubinoos seemed to be the last hope for pure pop music, carrying on the tradition of the Raspberries. The band was formed in 1973 by teenage friends Jon Rubin (vocals, guitar) and Tommy Dunbar (guitar, keyboards, vocals) along with Royse Adler (bass) and Donn Spindt (drums) but it wasn't until 1977 that they made their recording debut for Beserkley Records. The single, a cover of Tommy James' "I Think We're Alone Now," made an appearance in the lower reaches of

the U.S. charts, giving the indie label their first hit. The same year, their self-titled debut LP received rave reviews all around but failed commercially. 1979's *Back to the Drawing Board*, another solid collection of bouncy pop songs again went ignored despite its classic single "I Wanna Be Your Boyfriend." The band effectively broke up the following year. Rubin and Dunbar returned in 1983, using the band name one more time for the Todd Rundgren produced *Party of Two* EP. "If I Had You Back" from the EP saw some airplay on MTV but it failed to ignite enough interest for the band to go on. They reunited in the late '80s and have since issued collections of lost recordings from the early '80s though new recordings have yet to be released. —*Chris Woodstra*

● **The Rubinoos** / 1977 / Beserkley ✦✦✦✦
This little gem is a celebration of pop music. There's no other way to describe this record. Catchy tunes with a touch of tongue-in-cheek, mixed with exuberance and joy make this record as much fun as when it was first released. —*Jim Worbois*

Back to the Drawing Board / 1979 / Beserkley ✦✦✦
Overall, this is not quite as strong a record as the first one but still, not to be missed. There are some fine original tunes on this record and one quite interesting cover, "Hold Me," taken from *Three Faces of Eve*. —*Jim Worbois*

Party of Two / 1983 / Warner Brothers ✦✦
New label, new look, new sound. Presumably, the label thought that teaming the band with Todd Rundgren would give them the exposure (and possibly, recognition) they deserved. Unfortunately, you get a record that sounds like another Todd Rundgren project. For instance, "Faded Dream" sounds more like a McCartney throw-away than a Rubinoos track. —*Jim Worbois*

Basement Tapes: Studio Demos Circa 1980-1981 / 1994 / One Way ✦✦✦

Garage Sale / 1994 / Big Deal ✦✦✦

Rufus & Chaka Khan

Group, Soul, Funk
Rufus was one of the most commercially successful funk bands of the mid-'70s, primarily because lead vocalist Chaka Khan was a dynamic singer, capable of making even the band's pedestrian material seem interesting. Their self-titled debut album suffered from a lack of strong single material, but the follow-up featured Stevie Wonder's "Tell Me Something Good," which he wrote specifically for the band after hearing Khan sing; it became a number three hit single. After that song, the hits kept coming until the end of the '70s. Chaka Khan began a solo career that eventually eclipsed Rufus' success in 1978, continuing to record with the band until 1983; the group fell apart shortly after her departure. —*Stephen Thomas Erlewine*

Rufus / 1973 / MCA ✦✦

○ **Rufusized** / 1974 / MCA ✦✦✦✦
With the addition of guitarist/songwriter Tony Maiden, Rufus delivers one of their best albums. It features the hits "Once You Get Started" and "Please Pardon Me (You Remind Me of a Friend)." —*Rick Clark*

● **Rags to Rufus** / 1974 / MCA ✦✦✦✦
From the hard-funk opener of "You Got the Love" to the Stevie Wonder-penned "Tell Me Something Good," *Rags to Rufus* is a fine showcase for Chaka Khan's amazing vocals. —*Rick Clark*

Rufus Featuring Chaka Khan / 1975 / MCA ✦✦✦
Rufus continued their string of successful albums with this 1975 release, featuring the mellow soul of "Sweet Thing," a number five million-seller, as well as jolting funk tunes like "Dance with Me." —*Bil Carpenter*

Ask Rufus / 1977 / MCA ✦✦✦
This solid album includes "Hollywood" (number 32) and "At Midnight (My Love Will Lift You Up)" (number 30). —*Rick Clark*

Street Player / 1978 / ABC ✦✦✦

Numbers / 1979 / ABC ✦✦

○ **Masterjam** / 1979 / MCA ✦✦✦✦

Party 'Til You're Broke / 1981 / MCA ✦✦

Camouflage / 1981 / MCA ✦✦✦

Stompin' at the Savoy (live) / 1983 / Warner Brothers ✦✦
This double record includes three sides of live hits and one side of new studio cuts, including "Ain't Nobody." —*Bil Carpenter*

Seal I Red / 1983 / Warner Brothers ✦✦✦

Ain't Nobody / 1984 / Warner Brothers ✦✦✦

Run-D.M.C.

Group, Rap
The most famous exports from Hollis, Queens, NY, expanded the boundaries of rap in ways Grandmaster Flash could only imagine. Through their early singles they built up a devoted street following and, without ever diluting their music, managed to bust their grooves into the White pop mainstream. They've lost their edge in the '90s but their influence is still felt.

Run-D.M.C. bounced back from the aesthic graveyard in 1993 with *Down with the King*. The album linked them with the hip-hop generation that had grown up admiring them, and the trio also sported a new look (shaved heads) and philosophy (Born-Again Christians). The title track was a huge hit and the disc ended speculation that they were finished on the hip-hop scene. —*John Floyd*

☆ **Run-D.M.C.** / 1984 / Profile ✦✦✦✦✦
Their album debut features all the early singles, including "It's Like That" and "Rock Box," which stripped rap down to the bare essentials and introduced slews of innovations, lyrically and musically. —*John Floyd*

☆ **King of Rock** / 1985 / Profile ✦✦✦✦✦
Run-D.M.C. scored their first platinum LP and roared into pop consciousness with this 1985 LP. Such cuts as "King Of Rock," "Rock the House" and "Can You Rock It Like This" were definitive, and their tough tone, clipped style and posturing attitudes set the hip-hop agenda for several years. —*Ron Wynn*

☆ **Raising Hell** / 1986 / Profile ✦✦✦✦✦
The collaboration with Steven Tyler and Joe Perry on "Walk This Way" made this the most successful rap album of its time, but the blistering title track, the pulsating "You Be Illin'," kept it in the Top Ten. It is a masterful and important release, not just for rap but for modern music. —*John Floyd*

Tougher Than Leather / 1988 / Profile ✦✦✦
After the epic *Raising Hell*, it was almost a drop in the bucket for Run-D.M.C. to get only a platinum LP for *Tougher Than Leather*. It included the mild hit "Mary Mary," but was also an indication that all was not well with the trio creatively. There was an ominous quality to "I'm Not Going Out Like That," and such cuts as "Miss Elaine" and "Beats to the Rhyme" signaled that their run to the top was in its final stages. —*Ron Wynn*

Back from Hell / 1990 / Profile ✦✦✦
Run-D.M.C.'s popularity was decreasing dramatically in the late '80s and early '90s, which helps explain the hard-edged *Back from Hell*. In an attempt to allign themselves with the new generation of gangsta rappers, Run-D.M.C. stripped their beats back to a minimum and concentrated on tough rhymes like "Pause." Even if the group's new musical direction was necessary in order from them to stay alive in the hip-hop community, it resulted in a surprisingly successful record that demonstrates Run-D.M.C.'s superior musical and lyrical skills. —*Stephen Thomas Erlewine*

★ **Greatest Hits** / 1991 / Profile ✦✦✦✦✦
A few necessary items are missing, but this provides a great introduction to the most influential posse in rap. —*John Floyd*

Down with the King / May 4, 1993 / Profile ✦✦✦
After 1990's lackluster *Back from Hell*, most hip-hop fans thought that Run-D.M.C. was no longer capable of delivering a solid record. *Down with the King* proved those doubters wrong. Although it didn't burn up the charts like *Raising Hell* and wasn't as innovative as their first album, *Down With the King* showed that they remained strong and talented; it also didn't hurt that the production was provided by several of the 1990s' most talented artists, including Public Enemy, Pete Rock, Naughty by Nature, and Q-Tip. —*Stephen Thomas Erlewine*

The Runaways

Group, Hard Rock, Heavy Metal
This rock & roll band featured vocalist Cherie Currie and guitarists Joan Jett and Lita Ford. Organized by producer Kim Fowley in 1976, their raw, punkish style became a cult item in Japan and Europe, but unfortunately never connected with any kind of mainstream success stateside until Jett and Ford each went solo. —*Cub Koda*

○ **Queens of Noise** / 1977 / Mercury ✦✦✦✦
Their definitive statement, with Joan Jett taking over lead-singing chores on six of the ten tracks. The title cut says it all. (Japanese import) —*Cub Koda*

● **The Best of the Runaways** / 1987 / Mercury ✦✦✦✦
A good collection of the Runaways' finest moments, *Best of the Runaways* is the only consistently enjoyable disc from these trashy hard-rockers. —*Stephen Thomas Erlewine*

Todd Rundgren

b. Jun. 22, 1948, Upper Darby, PA
Pop/Rock
Over the course of his lengthy career, Todd Rundgren (b. Jun 22, 1948) has created some of popular music's finer moments, as well as some of its most frustrating. He has proved to be a master of great pop melodies (with influences from Beatles to Philly Soul) and heartfelt lyrical sentiment, while also releasing albums of tedious prog-rock that only a diehard fan could care about. At times Rundgren's productions seemed to have existed independently of the music, rather than enhancing it; nevertheless, Rundgren is an influential Renaissance man in the history of rock. Rundgren's first taste of success came with the psychedelic pop/rock group Nazz, in 1967. "Hello, It's Me" (number 71/number 66) charted twice, while the heavily phased riff-rocker "Open My Eyes" became a signature tune of sorts. Rundgren left Nazz (future Cheap Trick guitarist Rick Nielson was his replacement) and pursued a solo career with the 1970 debut *Runt*. *Something/Anything?*, Rundgren's third album, was his finest showcase as a songwriter. It was during this time that Rundgren began making a name for himself as an innovative producer. Over the years he has worked on projects for Badfinger, New York Dolls, Foghat, Patti Smith, Cheap Trick, XTC, Meat Loaf, and others. In 1974 Rundgren formed Utopia, a quartet that helped fulfill his prog-rock tendencies. By the late '70s, Rundgren was actively exploring the medium of rock video, opening his own computer video studio in Woodstock, NY. He continues to produce various artists and to release solo albums that enjoy a solid cult success. —*Rick Clark*

○ **Runt** / Sep. 1970 / Bearsville ✦✦✦✦
Runt, Todd Rundgren's debut, might have been a little uneven, but its homemade production, spirited arrangements, and great tunes, like "We Gotta Get You a Woman" and "I'm in the Clique," made this one of the most appealing albums of his career. —*Rick Clark*

Runt: Ballad of Todd Rundgren / Jun. 1971 / Rhino ✦✦✦
Rundgren's sophomore release didn't contain the flashes of brilliance found on *Runt*, but "Be Nice to Me," "Parole," and "Remember Me" are standouts on this relatively low-key effort. —*Rick Clark*

★ **Something/Anything?** / Feb. 1972 / Bearsville ✦✦✦✦✦
From beginning to end, *Something/Anything?* is Rundgren's best album, featuring the hit singles "I Saw the Light," and "Hello, It's Me." There are also a load of gems like "It Wouldn't Have Made Any Difference," "Wolfman Jack," and "Couldn't I Just Tell You?," one of the finest power-pop tracks ever cut. Rundgren plays every instrument and sings all the parts on three-fourths of this self-produced release. Even though Rundgren had flashes of brilliance after *Something/Anything?*, he never came up with an album with performances and material as consistently satisfying. —*Rick Clark*

○ **A Wizard a True Star** / Mar. 1973 / Bearsville ✦✦✦✦
Rundgren's keen sense for writing tight pop songs is almost nowhere to be found on this over-the-top production job. That's not to say that *A Wizard a True Star* doesn't have its virtues. Rundgren's take on *Peter Pan*'s "Never Never Land" is otherworldly, and his Philly-soul medley is quite fine. "International Feel" and "Just One Victory" are other standout tracks. —*Rick Clark*

Todd / Feb. 1974 / Bearsville ✦✦

Todd Rundgren's Utopia / Oct. 1974 / Bearsville ✦✦
After five solo albums released between 1970 and 1974, Todd Rundgren organized the band Utopia, although he also maintained a solo career. At this point, the group, a sextet featuring Kevin Ellman on percussion, Moogy Klingman and Ralph Schukett on keyboards, M. Frog Labat on synthesizers, and John Siegler on bass and cello, had little independent existence, as indicated by its billing, but later it would be a more equal unit. On this debut album, TR's U plays extended compositions—three of the

four tracks run over 10 minutes each, with "The Ikon" clocking in over half an hour—in a hard rock/heavy metal/progressive rock mode with little of Rundgren's usual melodic appeal. —*William Ruhlmann*

Initiation / May 1975 / Bearsville ✦✦✦
Todd Rundgren returned to solo billing here, although his studio musicians included current and future members of Utopia, and he remained interested in dense, extended compositions like "A Treatise On Cosmic Fire," which takes up all of Side 2. The most memorable track on the album, however, was "Real Man," which hit #83 on the singles chart. —*William Ruhlmann*

Another Live / Oct. 1975 / Bearsville ✦✦
By the time of its second album, Todd Rundgren's Utopia had altered its personnel, with M. Frog Labat replaced by Roger Powell on synthesizers and John ("Willie") Wilcox taking over the drum chair in the sextet. It remained a vehicle for Rundgren's harder rocking tendencies, although this album, recorded live, was more kinetic, featuring group versions of such Rundgren favorites as "Heavy Metal Kids" and his signature song, "Just One Victory," plus a cover of the Move/ELO oldie "Do Ya." —*William Ruhlmann*

Faithful / Apr. 1976 / Bearsville ✦✦✦
One half of this outing features Rundgren delivering almost letter-perfect versions of '60s classics like "Good Vibrations" and "Rain," which are impressive in their attention to detail but sound strangely lifeless. On the other half of the album, he delivers some of his best work since *Something/Anything?*, particularly on "Black & White" and "When I Pray." —*Rick Clark*

RA / Feb. 1977 / Bearsville ✦✦✦
By the time of its third album, Utopia had become an independent band, without the possessive "Todd Rundgren's" attached to it, and it was stripped down to a quartet of Rundgren, Roger Powell (keyboards), Kasim Sulton (bass), and John ("Willie") Wilcox (drums). Rundgren shared writing and lead vocal chores with his bandmates. Ironically, the result sounded more like Rundgren's solo work than Utopia's first two albums, mixing Bernard Herrmann movie music with the show music approach of "Magic Dragon Theatre" and a typically Rundgrenesque ballad style on "Eternal Love," which was written by Powell and Sulton and sung by Sulton. All of that was on Side One, however, with Side Two largely given over to "Singing and the Glass Guitar," the kind of extended, progressive rock compositions that must have helped inspire *This Is Spinal Tap*. —*William Ruhlmann*

Oops Wrong Planet / Sep. 1977 / Bearsville ✦✦✦

Back to the Bars / 1978 / Bearsville ✦✦✦
A double live album, *Back to the Bars* presented Todd Rundgren at his most accessible, accompanied both by Utopia and by some of his other long-time sidemen, performing his most melodic pop-rock songs, from "Hello, It's Me" to "Love In Action," and even suggesting his roots in soul pop with covers of "Ooh Baby Baby" and "La La Means I Love You." —*William Ruhlmann*

○ **Hermit of Mink Hollow** / Apr. 1978 / Bearsville ✦✦✦✦
By the release of this album, Rundgren had ditched the homemade charm of *Something/Anything?* for a warbly hard rock/pop sound. Tracks like "Determination," "Out of Control," "You Cried Wolf," and "Fade Away" best exemplify that approach. "Can We Still Be Friends?" became a number 29 hit. —*Rick Clark*

Adventures In Utopia / Jan. 1980 / Bearsville ✦✦✦
At this point in Todd Rundgren's career, he seems to have juggled a schedule of alternating one year's solo work, during which he'd record two albums, with a year's worth with Utopia, during which he'd also record two albums. Thus, in January, 1980, Utopia returned for the first of two albums, *Adventures In Utopia*. Having moved Utopia in more of a pop direction with *Oops! Wrong Planet*, Rundgren & Co. went even farther this time and were rewarded with two hit singles, "Set Me Free" (#27) and "The Very Last Time" (#76), while the album, reaching #32, was Utopia's highest-charting ever and bettered any Rundgren solo release except *Something/Anything?*. Anyone who enjoyed the pop sound of Rundgren's early work would feel comfortable here. —*William Ruhlmann*

Deface the Music / Oct. 1980 / Bearsville ✦✦✦
On his solo album *Faithful*, Todd Rundgren had devoted a side of the LP to remaking elaborate studio recordings like the Beach Boys' "Good Vibrations" exactly. On Utopia's sixth album, it took a slightly different tack on the same notion, recording original songs

in the style of the Beatles, as the Beatles evolved from "I Want To Hold Your Hand" to their more psychedelic efforts. The result is not unlike Eric Idle's parody album *The Rutles*. — *William Ruhlmann*

Healing / Feb. 1981 / Rhino ♦♦
Todd Rundgren's first solo studio album in nearly three years was one of his entirely self-contained efforts: he wrote, played, sang, produced, and engineered everything. It found him retreating from the hard rock sound of recent efforts toward a more soulful, almost ambient approach. But though songs such as "Compassion" were in Rundgren's patented "Hello, It's Me" ballad style, there were no real classics this time around. (The original Bearsville Records LP package contained both a 12-inch record and a seven-inch, 33 1/3 r.p.m. record with the tracks "Time Heals" and "Tiny Demons." The Rhino version, which contains those tracks, is a September, 1987, CD reissue.) — *William Ruhlmann*

Swing to the Right / Mar. 1982 / Bearsville ♦♦
After Todd Rundgren's 1981 solo year with *Healing*, Utopia returned to action with two 1982 albums, the first of which was this R&B-flavored effort, a far cry from the band's progressive rock beginnings, which even featured a cover of "For The Love Of Money." Maybe because things at Bearsville were winding down (this was the last Rundgren or Utopia album on the label), *Swing to the Right* missed cracking the Top 100 on the LP chart, but songs like "Lysistrata," a Rundgren pop tune based on the Greek anti-war play, showed the group was still in good form on occasion. — *William Ruhlmann*

Utopia / Sep. 1982 / Network ♦♦

○ **The Ever Popular Tortured Artist Effect** / Jan. 1983 / Rhino ♦♦♦♦
This album, one of Rundgren's best do-it-yourself efforts of the '80s, contains his number 63 hit "Bang the Drum All Day" and a swell remake of the Small Faces's "Tin Soldier." — *Rick Clark*

Oblivion / Jan. 1984 / Passport ♦♦
Utopia moved from major label to indie status with *Oblivion*, which retained the band's pop/rock sound on such songs as "Itch In My Brain," "Love With A Thinker," and "Crybaby." Although sung by Kasim Sulton, "Maybe I Could Change" was in Todd Rundgren's "I Saw The Light" pop ballad style. — *William Ruhlmann*

A Cappella / Sep. 1985 / Rhino ♦♦
Todd Rundgren was used to playing all the instruments on his albums himself. Here, he went one step further: all the sounds on this record come from Rundgren's voice, albeit sampled and filtered and edited to sound like instruments. Strip away the trickery, however, and you have a typical Rundgren pop collection, none of whose songs are among his best. — *William Ruhlmann*

● **Anthology (1968-1985)** / 1989 / Rhino ♦♦♦♦
Anthology is a fairly comprehensive overview of Rundgren's entire career, starting with "Open My Eyes," by Nazz, and including "Something to Fall Back On," from Rundgren's 1985 solo album *A Cappella*. All of his radio hits are included, as well as many important album tracks. Nevertheless, there are several key tracks missing, like "Wolfman Jack," "International Feel/Never Never Land," and Nazz's "Forget All About It" and "Hang on Paul." Like all of Rundgren's reissues on Rhino, *Anthology* has been given a first-class remastering job. — *Rick Clark*

Nearly Human / May 1989 / Warner Brothers ♦♦♦
Included are strong songs and extraordinary recording. — *Jas Obrecht*

Second Wind / Jan. 1991 / Warner Brothers ♦♦
Todd Rundgren's last major label album was recorded in July, 1990, at the Palace of Fine Arts Theatre in San Francisco before a live audience, although under recording studio conditions, with a backup band that included some local talent: Roger Powell of Utopia, Vince Welnick (who would join the Grateful Dead later in the year) and Prairie Prince of the Tubes, Ross Valory of Journey, and Jenni Muldaur. It's a mixed set, containing three songs Rundgren wrote for the off-Broadway musical *Up Against It*, which was based on an unproduced screenplay British playwright Joe Orton wrote in the 1960s for the Beatles. Those songs have a Kurt Weillish tone, while songs like "Love Science" are uptempo R&B and lead-off track "Change Myself" is in Rundgren's familiar pop-rock style. On the whole, though, there's nothing to get excited about here. — *William Ruhlmann*

No World Order / Jul. 6, 1993 / Forward ♦
Every Todd Rundgren album seems to have a gimmick, and on this one, the trick is that he recorded almost four hours of musical fragments of four to eight seconds each and put them on an interactive CD so that they could be combined in a nearly infinite number of ways. If you have a CD-I, that is. If you only have a regular old CD player, this non-interactive version presents 10 songs and six variations on them. Rundgren has added rap to his arsenal, his lyrics are more political, and many of the tracks seem aimed at the dance floor. Rundgren fans will be put off, while the new jack swingers won't bother to listen. But the real problem is that it's just not very good. — *William Ruhlmann*

○ **The Best of Todd Rundgren** / 1994 / Rhino ♦♦♦♦
No World Order Lite / 1994 / Alchemedia ♦
The Individualist / 1995 / Pony Canyon International ♦♦

Rush
Group, Hard Rock, Art-Rock/Progressive-Rock
Inspired by Cream, Led Zeppelin, and Jimi Hendrix, the Toronto, Canada, power-trio Rush formed in 1969, comprising guitarist Alex Lifeson (b. Aug 27, 1953), bassist Geddy Lee (b. Jul 29, 1953), and original drummer John Rutsey—later replaced by Neil Peart (b. Sep 12, 1952). Their first few albums were rather pedestrian hard rock, but the addition of Peart in 1974 prodded the group into a more complicated, heavy art-rock mode: King Crimson and Yes meet Led Zeppelin.

"The Trees," metaphorically addressing the Quebec secessionist movement (off of 1978's #47 *Hemispheres*) became a controversial rock-radio hit. The 1980 album *Permanent Waves* (#4), containing two substantial AOR hits with "Freewill" and "Spirit of the Radio" (#51), marked the beginning of a golden period for the band, which peaked with the #3 followup *Moving Pictures*.

Rush briefly flirted with a more synthesized sound, sublimating the band's natural interplay. Fortunately, recent albums indicate Rush is back in top form with *Presto* and *Roll the Bones*. — *Rick Clark*

Rush / 1974 / Mercury ♦♦
Caress of Steel / 1975 / Mercury ♦♦
Fly by Night / 1975 / Mercury ♦♦
All the World's a Stage / 1976 / Mercury ♦♦♦
○ **2112** / 1976 / Mercury ♦♦♦♦
This is Rush's first successful stab at a concept album. Like many of Rush's albums during the '70s, this one deals with a futuristic scenario where an individual triumphs over an impersonalized high-tech society. — *Rick Clark*

A Farewell to Kings / 1977 / Mercury ♦♦♦
Rush continues to explore their sci-fi fantasy themes and lofty concepts with this effort, which featured "Closer to the Heart," a substantial FM rock hit that also went number 76 pop. — *Rick Clark*

Hemispheres / 1978 / Mercury ♦♦♦
Included is the FM hit "The Trees," which can be found on *Chronicles*. Their extended pieces here aren't among their best, but the playing and dynamics of the arrangements keep things fairly interesting. — *Rick Clark*

○ **Permanent Waves** / 1980 / Mercury ♦♦♦♦
The cumulative effect of endless tours and obvious growth with each studio effort, Rush hit it big with this effort, delivering with their best material to date. "Spirit of the Radio" (#51), "Freewill," and "Entre Nous" (#110) were big FM rock hits. "Jacob's Ladder" was another highlight. — *Rick Clark*

★ **Moving Pictures** / 1981 / Mercury ♦♦♦♦♦
On *Moving Pictures*, Rush's aggressive prog-rock hit a zenith, with challenging playing that never became formless or devoid of good melodic integrity. The trio's active ensemble work reached new levels of interplay. "Tom Sawyer," "Limelight," "Red Barchetta," and the instrumental "YYZ" are standouts. — *Rick Clark*

○ **Exit Stage Left** / 1981 / Mercury ♦♦♦♦
A good live collection, it's possibly the best of their three such releases. — *Rick Clark*

○ **Signals** / 1982 / Mercury ♦♦♦♦
This is the third in a trio of great albums. "Digital Man" and "Analog Kid" are powerful riff-rockers. "New World Man" was a number 21 hit, and "Subdivisions" was an FM rock favorite. The soundstage lacks some of the ambience found on *Moving Pictures*, but the performances still pack quite a punch. — *Rick Clark*

Grace under Pressure / 1984 / Mercury ♦♦

Power Windows / 1985 / Mercury ♦♦♦
It's an improvement over the sterile techno-crap of the 1984 release *Grace under Pressure*. "Big Money" recalls the highlights of *Moving Pictures*, while "Manhattan Project" and "Territories" also shine. —*Rick Clark*

Hold Your Fire / 1987 / Mercury ♦♦♦
Even though the playing is typically exceptional, the clinical production keeps this album from really catching fire. "Time Stand Still," "Force Ten" and "Turn the Page" are among the highlights. —*Rick Clark*

A Show of Hands / Jan. 2, 1988 / Mercury ♦♦♦
A solid document of their live work, it concentrates on later albums. —*Rick Clark*

○ **Presto** / 1989 / Atlantic ♦♦♦♦
Presto, Rush's 13th album of new studio material, and their first for Atlantic, showed this Canadian trio coming out from under a succession of bloodless-sounding techno-excursions (*Grace under Pressure, Hold Your Fire*) and going for a much more open, accessible sound. From beginning to end, the arrangements reflect more straightahead rock playing than on any of their other albums. *Presto* contains some of Neil Peart's best lyrics, and along with *Moving Pictures*, smartly presents many of Rush's virtues in their best light. —*Rick Clark*

● **Chronicles** / 1991 / Mercury ♦♦♦♦
Anyone wanting an essential overview of this Canadian band's prog-rock work should start here. All of their FM rock hits and most of the important album tracks are here. —*Rick Clark*

Roll the Bones / 1991 / Atlantic ♦♦♦
Roll the Bones continues with the organic-sounding hard prog-rock spirit of *Presto*, and it's equally fine. After many years of albums and touring, it's obvious that Rush has maintained its edge as a musical unit. The playing and material are primo throughout. Highlights include "Neurotica," "Big Wheel," "Ghost of a Chance," and the title cut. —*Rick Clark*

Counterparts / 1993 / Atlantic ♦♦
A solid collection of songs, it includes the AOR rock radio tracks "Stick it Out," "Animate," and "Nobody's Hero," the band's statement on the AIDS situation. The playing is typically top-notch, but the type of reverbs and equalization setting on this Peter Collins production make the band sound colder and more distant than usual. —*Rick Clark*

Leon Russell

b. Apr. 2, 1941
Singer-Songwriter, Pop/Rock
Leon Russell has had a widely varied career as an artist, a songwriter, a record-label owner, a producer, and an in-demand session sideman. As part of Phil Spector's "Wall of Sound" wrecking crew, Russell played on hits by the Crystals. He also played on Herb Alpert's *Taste of Honey* and the Byrds's *Mr. Tambourine Man* and played and arranged tracks for Gary Lewis & the Playboys. Russell also toured with Delaney & Bonnie and briefly with Paul Revere & the Raiders when Revere was drafted. Russell organized Joe Cocker's Mad Dogs & Englishmen tour, which led him to tours with Bob Dylan, Eric Clapton, and the Rolling Stones, and a performance at George Harrison's Concert for Bangladesh.

In 1970 Russell formed Shelter Records with English producer Denny Cordell. The label eventually released albums by Willis Alan Ramsey, Dwight Twilley, and Phoebe Snow, among others. In October 1971, the Carpenters had a huge hit with Russell's "Superstar." (Years later, another composition, "This Masquerade," became a career-making hit for George Benson.)

All of this visibility set the stage for Russell's lucrative solo career, which fused gospel, blues, country, rock, and light jazz behind his quirky warble of a voice. Russell had seven Top 40 albums, with 1972's *Carney* peaking at #2 for four weeks. "Tightrope" (#11), "Lady Blue" (#14), and a double-sided single remake of Hank Williams's "Roll in My Sweet Baby's Arms"/"I'm So Lonesome I Could Cry" (#78) are a few of Russell's hits. In 1992, he released a comeback effort, *Anything Can Happen*. —*Rick Clark*

○ **Leon Russell** / 1970 / DCC ♦♦♦♦
Russell's self-titled debut features his strongest set of songs and performances, with tracks like "A Song for You," "Dixie Lullaby," "Shoot out at the Plantation," and "Delta Lady," which became one of Joe Cocker's early signature songs. The CD includes a brief version of Dylan's "Masters of War." —*Rick Clark*

○ **And the Shelter People** / 1971 / DCC ♦♦♦♦
Released hot on the heels of his Mad Dogs & Englishmen tour with Joe Cocker, Russell released this spirited outing, which included covers of tunes by George Harrison ("Beware of Darkness") and Dylan ("It's a Hard Rain Gonna Fall," "It Takes a Lot to Laugh, It Takes a Train to Cry") and some fine originals: "Alcatraz," "Home Sweet Oklahoma," "Stranger in a Strange Land" (an FM hit), and the title cut. The CD includes three bonus versions of Dylan tunes. —*Rick Clark*

Asylum Choir II / 1971 / Dunhill ♦♦
Of all Russell's early work as an artist, this record is the weakest; in particular, songs like "Tryin' to Stay Alive" and "When You Wish Upon a Fag" feel dated. Nevertheless, *Asylum Choir II* is still a pretty nice record. Especially noteworthy is Russell's own version of "Hello, Little Friend"; Joe Cocker would later record the definitive version of the song. (The 1995 CD reissue features five bonus tracks.) —*Jim Worbois*

● **Carney** / 1972 / DCC ♦♦♦♦
Carney became Russell's highest charting album with the aid of the oddball #11 hit "Tightrope." Also included is "This Masquerade," a song that later became an international hit for George Benson. "If the Shoe Fits" is a great putdown of pop-star sycophants. Other highlights include "Manhattan Island Serenade" and "Cajun Love Song." —*Rick Clark*

Hank Wilson's Back / 1973 / DCC ♦♦♦
A skewed but interesting Hank Williams tribute album, with capable country backing. —*Cub Koda*

Leon Live / 1973 / DCC ♦♦♦
A solid concert offering which showcases Russell's strengths (and weaknesses) as a live performer, with A-1 support throughout. —*Cub Koda*

Looking Back / 1974 / Olympic ♦♦

Stop All That Jazz / 1974 / DCC ♦♦

Will O' the Wisp / 1975 / DCC ♦♦♦

Anything Can Happen / Sep. 1992 / Virgin ♦♦♦
Bruce Hornsby's active participation in Leon Russell's first recording in ten years is both a blessing and a curse. A blessing, because without Hornsby's encouragement, co-songwriting, production, and musical backing, the project would probably never have happened. A curse, because Hornsby imprints too much of his own personal style and mushy, middle-of-the-road keyboard washes on the sessions. Despite Russell's long layoff, the unique, drawling rasp that gave us "Tightrope" and "Delta Lady" in the early-'70s is still intact. However, the cloying instrumental backings to such tracks as "Angel Ways" and "Faces of the Children" have Hornsby engraved all over them. —*Roch Parisien*

The Rutles

Group, Pop/Rock
Originally broadcast on network TV in 1978, ex-Monty Python member Eric Idle's satire of the Beatles legend was one of the very few successful rock parodies; only Spinal Tap, perhaps, has outdone it. One of the key elements of this mock "rockumentary" was the brilliantly executed "soundtrack" by Python associates and ex-Bonzo Dog Band member Neil Innes (he also played the character loosely based upon John Lennon in the film itself). As an actual peer of the group in the '60s (the Bonzos even appeared in the *Magical Mystery Tour* film), Innes was well qualified to satirize the Fab Four phenomenon in song. With the exception of Idle, each of the four "Rutles" played their own instruments on the recording in addition to acting in the film. —*Richie Unterberger*

● **The Rutles** / 1978 / Rhino ♦♦♦♦
Neil Innes delivered catchy, harmony-laden tunes that deftly and lovingly parody every phase of the moptops' career, from their Hamburg/Cavern Club days through "Get Back" (here retitled "Get up and Go"). In between are fully realized send-ups of "If I Fell," "I Want to Hold Your Hand," "Penny Lane," "Lucy In The Sky," "I Am the Walrus," "All You Need Is Love," and more. "Ouch!," their hilarious mockery of "Help!," is perhaps the album's highlight. The 1990 CD reissue adds six very worthwhile "bonus tracks" that were used in the special, but were unavailable on the original 1978 Warner album, making for 20 cuts in all. —*Richie Unterberger*

Ruts

Group, Punk, Ska-Revival
The Ruts were part of a second wave of English punk bands following the Sex Pistols and the Clash. They incorporated sounds from both bands as well as a major dose of reggae, with straightforward political lyrics. The group featured singer Malcolm Owen, guitarist Paul Fox, bassist John "Segs" Jennings, and drummer Dave Ruffy. Owen died of a drug overdose in 1980, after which the group changed its name to the Ruts D.C. (Da Capo) and added saxophone and keyboard player Gary Barnacle. They later worked with famed reggae producer the Mad Professor. However, without Owen, the group's original spirit was never quite the same. — *Steve Huey*

○ **The Crack** / 1979 / Virgin ✦✦✦✦
Find it and buy it. This is an overlooked gem of speedy guitars and reggae skank! — *John Dougan*

Grin & Bear It / 1980 / Virgin ✦✦✦

Animal Now / 1981 / Virgin ✦✦

Rhythm Collision / 1982 / Bohemian ✦✦✦

Rhythm Collision Dub, Vol. 1 / 1987 / ROIR ✦✦

Live and Loud!! / 1987 / Link ✦✦

You Gotta Get Out of It / 1987 / Virgin ✦✦

● **Something That I Said-The Best Of the Ruts** / 1995 / Choice Cuts ✦✦✦✦

Mitch Ryder (William Levise)

Group, Soul, Rock & Roll
Mitch Ryder & the Detroit Wheels blended the Motown-soul sound with over-revved Midwestern rock & roll. Mitch Ryder's (born William Levise) gutsy soul shouting and superhuman screams were some of the most electrifying sounds to charge AM radio in the mid-'60s, landing somewhere between the Rascals' Felix Cavaliere and Wilson Pickett. The Wheels sported two strong lead guitarists in Joe Cubert and Jim McCarty (later in Cactus and Detroit), and they were pushed along by one of the great unsung rock drummers of all time, John ("Johnny Bee") Badanjek.

It was producer Bob Crewe who signed the band to his New Voice label, releasing a string of high-octane raveups in "Jenny Take a Ride" (#10), "Little Latin Lupe Lu" (#17), "Devil with a Blue Dress On/ Good Golly Miss Molly" (#4), "Sock It to Me-Baby!" (#6), and "Too Many Fish in the Sea" (#24). In spite of all the hits and visibility, Mitch Ryder & the Detroit Wheels were victims of the era, making loads of money for Crewe and New Voice, but ending up broke. — *Rick Clark*

● **Rev-Up; the Best of Mitch Ryder & the Detroit Wheels** / 1990 / Rhino ✦✦✦✦
Perhaps the most raucous White soul band of the '60s, Ryder and the Detroit Wheels scored a series of hits, 1966-1968, by souping up rock and R&B ravers to fever pitch. This is hard party music. — *William Ruhlmann*

S

Sade (Helen Folsade Adu)

Group, Urban, Pop
Sade's smooth, silky jazz-tinged pop-oriented R&B earned several hits and a large following in the mid-'80s. Borrowing the spirit, if not the sophisticated sound, of her idols Billie Holiday and Nina Simone, her music was lush and stylish, helped considerably by her talented supporting band. After her 1988 album, *Stronger than Pride*, Sade disappeared for several years, reappearing in 1992 with *Love Deluxe*, which returned her to the spotlight, selling over a million copies in the first few months after it was released. —*Stephen Thomas Erlewine*

Diamond Life / 1984 / Portrait ♦♦♦♦
Former model Sade made an immediate and huge impact with her 1985 debut album. Her sound and approach were deliberately icy, her delivery and voice aloof, deadpan and cold, and yet she became an instant sensation through such songs as "Smooth Operator" and "Your Love Is King," where the slick production and quasi-jazz backing seemed to register with audiences thinking they were hearing a jazz vocalist. Sade won the Best New Grammy Award for 1985, and *Diamond Life* sold more than two million copies. —*Ron Wynn*

Promise / 1985 / Portrait ♦♦♦
Sade's second LP improved on the performance of her debut, as "Sweetest Taboo" was a huge hit and "Never As Good As The First Time" landed in both the R&B and pop Top 20. She was once again the personification of cool, laid-back singing, seldom extending or embellishing lyrics, registering emotion or projecting her voice. This demeanor made her more desirable in the minds of many fans and was perhaps the ultimate misapplication of the notion of sophistication. But this album topped the pop album charts and eventually went triple platinum. —*Ron Wynn*

Stronger Than Pride / 1988 / Epic ♦♦♦
After two LPs with little or no energy, Sade demonstrated some intensity and fire on her third release. Whether that was just an attempt to change the pace a bit or a genuine new direction, she had more animation in her delivery on such songs as "Haunt Me," "Give It Up" and the hit "Paradise." Not that she was suddenly singing in a soulful or bluesy manner; rather, Sade's dry and introspective tone now had a little more edge, and the lyrics were ironic as well as reflective. This was her third consecutive multiplatinum album, and it matched the two-million-plus sales level of her debut. —*Ron Wynn*

◗ **Love Deluxe** / Oct. 20, 1992 / Epic ♦♦♦♦
Sade's fourth album included the hit "No Ordinary Love" and marked a return to the detached, cool jazz backing and even icier vocals that made her debut album a sensation. Although Sade's style is more suggestive than hypnotic, and her production and arrangements are in an urbane mode rather than a jazz one, she's maintained her popularity among the fusion and urban contemporary audiences. This release also included "Mermaid," "Pearls" and "Feel No Pain." —*Ron Wynn*

Best of Sade / 1994 / Epic ♦♦♦♦
It's easy to dismiss Sade as makeout music for Calvin Klein Obsession models, but the group created an impressive body of work over the course of a decade, a series of moody singles with cool jazz passion and the kick of good R&B. All the hits are here, of course, from "Smooth Operator" to "No Ordinary Love." —*Eddie Huffman*

Doug Sahm

b. Nov. 6, 1942, San Antonia, TX
R&B, Rock & Roll, Tex-Mex
Since his days with the Sir Douglas Quintet in the '60s, Doug Sahm has been preaching the gospel of Texas music traditions. He's mastered everything from barrio Latin rock to Western swing to shuffle blues to doo-wop to Cajun, yet his work always bears his distinctive stamp. He's recorded a ton of albums with a wide array of sidemen and, regardless of the style, his laconic, reefer-headed vision comes through. Everything he's recorded is worth hearing but most of it has been out of print for decades. But the stuff that's in print offers an adequate estimation of the beautiful music he's made for the last 30 or so years. —*John Floyd*

● **Juke Box Music** / 1989 / Antone's ♦♦♦♦
Sahm shimmies and strolls through this set of doo-wop and R&B covers, a gorgeous slow-dancing gem. —*John Floyd*

○ **Best of Doug Sahm (1968-1975)** / 1992 / Rhino ♦♦♦♦
In 1972, Atlantic bought out Sahm's contract with Mercury, giving him the freedom to create an all-star ensemble of musicians. Throughout the year, Sahm recorded with the likes of Bob Dylan, Dr. John, and David Bromberg, producing a typically rich body of work released on two albums in late 1973. Rhino has collected various cuts from the albums, adding five previously unreleased tracks on CD only, and giving an excellent portrait of Sahm's music. —*Stephen Thomas Erlewine*

St. Etienne

Group, Alternative Pop/Rock, Dance
Formed by U.K. rock journalist Bob Stanley and Pete Wiggs in late 1988, St. Etienne became one of the leading British dance-pop bands of the early '90s, combining elements of house, techno, pop, disco, and hip-hop in a melodic, hypnotically rhythmic music that not only was popular in dance clubs, but had crossover appeal. Considering their detached, intellectual approach to pop, it's not surprising that the group has experienced its greatest success in Europe—particularly in England—and has only been a cult band in America. After a series of female singers, Sarah Cracknell became their permanent lead vocalist during the recording of their debut album, 1991's *Foxbase Alpha. —Stephen Thomas Erlewine*

○ **Foxbase Alpha** / Jan. 14, 1992 / Warner Brothers ♦♦♦♦
● **So Tough** / 1993 / Warner Brothers ♦♦♦♦
British duo Bob Stanley and Pete Wiggs deserve recognition as genius pop svengalis of their generation. Eerie, dreamy, moody, hypnotic, all those cliche terms don't disguise the fact that under the name Saint Etienne, they craft superb, digital aural candy on their latest release *So Tough*. While delicately-applied Prophet, Roland, Moog, and Emax sampler synths comprise the duo's main stock in trade, their key weapon is Sarah Cracknell's waifish vocals. —*Roch Parisien*

Tiger Bay / 1994 / Warner Brothers ♦♦♦
While its not as consistently engaging as *So Tough, Tiger Bay* has a number of excellent, innovative dance-pop tracks. —*Stephen Thomas Erlewine*

Hug My Soul / 1994 / Warner Brothers ♦♦♦

Saints

Group, Punk
Roaring out of Brisbane, Australia, in 1977 with the punk-era clas-

sic "(I'm) Stranded," the Saints, despite going through numerous incarnations, have been a part of rock & roll for nearly 20 years, thanks mainly to their indefatigable leader (and founder) Chris Bailey. Although they haven't played anything that passes for punk rock since about 1978, and despite extended dormant periods, the Saints have never officially broken up (at least I'm unaware of it), and Bailey always seems to have another version of the band and record ready to release. Saints fans fall into two distinct camps: the punk-era fans (up to about 1980) and the mature pop fans, which for American audiences begins with the release of *All Fool's Day* in 1987. I will here admit my biases and tell you that I am more of a fan of the punk era than of the mature pop era. This has nothing to do with the overall quality of the music; Bailey recorded two fine records with the late-'80s incarnation of the band. It's simply that the feral assault of their first three records (when co-founder Ed Kuepper was in the band) is more interesting and exciting. After Kuepper left in 1979 and the band became Bailey's show, the twists and turns he took them through (horns, folk/blues arrangements, as well his numerous solo excursions) produced some good music, but it was mostly too scattershot and lacked focus. It was simply too difficult to wade through the mediocre material.

Punk-era Saints was exactly what you'd expect: buzzsaw guitars, Bailey's pissed-off, nasal vocals, and locomotive rhythms supplied by bassist Kym Bradshaw and drummer Ivor Hay. After the LP *(I'm) Stranded* became a modest hit in England, the follow-up record, *Eternally Yours,* showed some changes (more varied tempos, acoustic guitars) that would set the stage for their third record, *Prehistoric Sounds,* which combined horn arrangements into a punkish sort of R&B. It was at this point that the Saints were beginning to change enough to not resemble the band they were just a scant two years earlier. Kuepper left to form the arty Laughing Clowns and eventually made a number of records as a solo act. Bailey, however, got to keep the name the Saints and soldiered on, taking time here and there to record his own solo records.

To most Americans, the Saints were a dead issue, if they were still an issue at all. *(I'm) Stranded* caught on with punk aficionados, but hardly anyone else; *Eternally Yours* came and went without a trace, and *Prehistoric Sounds* was never domestically released (neither were any of the post-Kuepper Saints records of the early '80s). So, by the time *All Fool's Day* was released in 1987, there were many who thought the Saints were a brand new band—and they were right. Gone were the rapid-fire guitar sound and bellowing vocals, replaced by sophisticated pop arrangements and more technically accomplished singing. The music was strong, intelligent pop that was better than much of the late-'80s "new wave." The next LP, *Prodigal Son,* wasn't as good, but did nothing to hurt the reputation of the "new" Saints. Oddly enough, Kuepper has recently gotten together with Celibate Rifles guitarists Kent Steedman and Dave Morris and performed under the name the Aints. Gigging in Sydney, they generally play a set of *(I'm) Stranded*-era material, and have even recorded a couple of low-fi live discs. It's all done for laughs, and I bet they're a hoot. As for Bailey, he's a credible performer who will continue to release interesting records, with or without the Saints. *—John Dougan*

● **I'm Stranded** / 1977 / Sire ✦✦✦✦

Around the time Sire was scooping up every band under the sun that played like the Ramones, they had the smarts to sign the Saints, who were creating great punk rock. Along with the title track, there are rough and ready bits of speedburn, like "Erotic Neurotic," and very unpunk-like tracks in terms of song length, six minutes of "Messin' With the Kid" (not the Junior Wells song). Toss in a pisstake of Elvis' "Kissin' Cousins," and you've got the makings of a fine slice of history. I still think this is their best record, for a lot of reasons, but primarily for its energy, high spirits and smarts. *—John Dougan*

○ **Eternally Yours** / 1978 / Sire ✦✦✦✦

Retaining much of the raw punk raunch that fueled *(I'm) Stranded, Eternally Yours* adds horns to a couple of tracks as the Saints attempt to play a little high-speed R&B. This record doesn't have the recklessness of the first one, but there are plenty of strong songs, especially the music industry critique "Know Your Product." Recommended to those who want to repeat the buzz of the first LP, but need different songs. Incidentally, after the success of the first record, this was a major flop and doubtlessly precipitated Sire's decision to drop them. *—John Dougan*

○ **All Fool's Day** / 1987 / TVT ✦✦✦✦

Call this the second coming of the Saints, but the only thing this record has in common with previous Saints recordings is Chris Bailey. Still, it's a sharp, tuneful and (ahem) mature work that shows Bailey's increasing confidence as a singer and songwriter. One listen to songs as grabbing as "Celtic Ballad" or the great "Just like Fire Would" (which is kind of a neat pun) will convince you that despite the differences, the new Saints were a good band for completely different reasons than the old Saints. *—John Dougan*

Sallyangie

Group, Folk

The Sallyangie, the British folk duo of Sally Oldfield and her brother Michael, were signed upon the recommendation of guitarist John Renbourn of the Pentangle. Sally was 21 years old, and Michael a mere 16, at the time of their late-'60s album *Children of the Sun,* which was produced by the legendary Shel Talmy (who also produced Pentangle). Not surprisingly, the result was crystalline, gentle contemporary British folk with similarities to Pentangle, but considerably more low-key. The Oldfields collaborated on the writing of all of the material on their sole outing. Mike Oldfield went on to join Kevin Ayers' band and achieve stardom as a progressive rock guitarist and composer with *Tubular Bells,* while Sally recorded less successful but equally ambitious art-rock albums as a solo act. *—Richie Unterberger*

Children of the Sun / 1969 / Warner Brothers ✦✦✦

A gentle, fairy-tale ambience pervades on this album of harmony folk tunes, on which Sally's high trills generally overshadow Mike's vocal contributions. *—Richie Unterberger*

Salt-N-Pepa

Group, Rap

Queens, NY, rappers Sandy Denton, Cheryl James, and DJ Dee Dee Roper have been prime female stars since 1986, when *Hot, Cool & Vicious,* with its single smash "Push It," made them stars. The duo has been able to shift gears at will, sometimes being naughty, other times nice, letting the beat propel their rhymes on one song, and then slicing their exchanges off it on the next. They've done numbers with feminist viewpoints, then turned around and echoed the conventional wisdom regarding male/female relationships in another number. But contradictions aside, they're among the tightest, most accomplished rap outfits active, and their records have held up well. Salt -N-Pepa made the pop big time with *Very Necessary* in 1993. The huge hit "Whatta Man" teamed them with En Vogue. They also did commercials for the NBA and various products, while finding themselves the rap act of choice for the upper class. At the same time, they recaptured the Black audience that they'd previously lost with more lightweight material like *A Salt with a Deadly Pepa.* The group also took more control over their image and production, wresting the reins from long-time producer Hurby Astor. *—Ron Wynn*

○ **Hot, Cool & Vicious** / 1987 / London ✦✦✦✦

One of the earliest female rap groups, they hit the big leagues with this debut that includes the pulsating "Push It" and the salacious "Tramp." *—John Floyd*

A Salt with a Deadly Pepa / 1988 / London ✦✦✦

A concept album musically, if not lyrically, this one fleshes out one terrific single, "Shake Your Thing," with a sharpening of the trio's sensibilities and talents. *—John Floyd*

A Blitz of Hits: The Hits Remixed / 1990 / London ✦✦

As remix albums go, Salt-N-Pepa's is fine, but their hit singles lose a bit of their magic in these extended forms. *—Stephen Thomas Erlewine*

● **Blacks' Magic** / 1990 / London ✦✦✦✦

Another concept album, this time the themes celebrate Black education and awareness, with some concise feminism included. *—John Floyd*

○ **Very Necessary** / 1993 / PolyGram ✦✦✦✦

Driven by the ferociously sexy "Shoop," Salt-N-Pepa's latest album matches the drive of that hit as well as the best of their earlier classics, making it one of the best albums of their successful career. *—AMG*

Sam & Dave

Group, Soul

Perhaps no act epitomized soul music as the secularization of gospel more than Sam & Dave. The original pairing of Sam Moore and Dave Prater met in Florida in 1961, and they recorded unsuccessfully for several years before being signed to Atlantic Records in 1965. Atlantic persuaded their Memphis affiliate Stax Records to produce them, and in December that year the writing and production team of Isaac Hayes and David Porter delivered the crisply soulful "You Don't Know Like I Know." Hayes and Porter became the "eminences grises" behind Sam & Dave, while Holland-Dozier-Holland pulled the strings behind the Supremes. They wrote, they produced—and the result was a string of hits, including "Soul Man," "Hold on I'm Comin'" and "I Thank You," songs that survive as the very epitome of Southern soul. Certainly, Sam & Dave's hits are among the most soulful ever to crack the Hot 100. Their albums often bore the hallmarks of hasty execution, though. The dissolution of the partnership between Stax and Atlantic virtually sealed the fate of Sam & Dave; there were a few more hits (and, later, a revival of interest thanks to the Blues Brothers), but the glory days were over.

Sam Moore's solo career was reinvigorated by his participation in the *Rhythm, Country & Blues* project in 1994. The CD, which paired country and R&B artists in various duets, teamed Moore with Conway Twitty in what turned out to be one of Twitty's last sessions. They did "Rainy Night in Georgia." Rhino issued *Sam & Dave: Sweat'N'Soul*, a two-disc anthology of their greatest recordings, in 1991. —*Colin Escott*

Sam & Dave / 1962 / Roulette ✦✦✦
Sam Moore and Dave Prater cut one album for Roulette before coming to Stax, where they acheived soul superstardom. They displayed their potential on this set, although they didn't have the musical support, production greatness, or magnificent songs that they received at Stax. But Moore's earthy leads and Prater's gritty contrasts were already emerging, if in rough fashion. Since this was practically deleted the day after it was issued, forget about finding it unless you're willing to pay ripoff prices in a collector's auction or at a specialty store, or find someone who doesn't know what they're doing throwing it out one day in a garage sale. —*Ron Wynn*

○ **Hold On, I'm Comin'** / 1966 / Atlantic ✦✦✦✦
The finest single Sam and Dave album, featuring the superb title track and several other brilliant works. They were the greatest soul duo ever, with Sam Moore's crackling leads, Dave Prater's less intense but equally effective contrast, and their perfect harmonizing, supported by wonderful compositions, production, and arrangements by David Porter and Isaac Hayes. Atlantic wisely has kept this in print on CD. —*Ron Wynn*

○ **Double Dynamite** / 1967 / Atlantic ✦✦✦✦
This was the second Sam and Dave album to enjoy significant crossover appeal. The 1967 record included such hits as "Said I Wasn't Gonna Tell Nobody," "Soothe Me," and "When Something Is Wrong With My Baby." Isaac Hayes and David Porter were now rolling as songwriters, and even though the record didn't attain big pop numbers, the singles clicked with both soul and pop audiences. More importantly, Sam and Dave's teamwork and vocal interaction were establishing them as major stars. —*Ron Wynn*

○ **Soul Men** / 1967 / Rhino ✦✦✦✦

I Thank You / 1968 / Rhino ✦✦✦
Straight reissue of an original Atlantic album, one of Sam & Dave's better efforts. Highlights include "Wrap It Up," "These Arms of Mine," "Don't Turn Your Heater On," "If I Didn't Have A Girl Like You," and the #9 title track. —*Stephen Thomas Erlewine*

○ **The Best of Sam & Dave** / 1969 / Atlantic ✦✦✦✦
For many years this late-'60s Atlantic collection was the finest value available to soul fans who hadn't purchased the original albums. But Rhino's extensive 1993 two-volume set supplanted this collection, although it's still a nice set and is ideal for anyone who didn't want the B-sides and extra tracks from Rhino. Atlantic had the good sense to reissue it on CD in the mid-'80s, and it's still available. —*Ron Wynn*

Back at 'Cha! / 1976 / United Artists ✦✦✦
The great soul duo of Sam Moore and Dave Prater made a gallant attempt at a comeback with this mid-'70s release, but the times had changed dramatically, and there wasn't much demand on the urban contemporary horizon for an aging Southern soul duo. Their harmonies were still solid, although the leads and shared vocals were a little on the faded side. It was great to hear the two singing together again, but the combination of changed audience

tastes and uneven material proved too much of an obstacle for Sam and Dave to get back in the spotlight. —*Ron Wynn*

★ **Sweat 'N' Soul** / 1993 / Rhino/Atlantic ✦✦✦✦✦
Sam Moore and Dave Prather were the ultimate soul duo; one a high-voiced wailer, the other a low-toned blaster. They came together in the mid-'60s to form a superb duo, singing tunes penned by soul's finest writing tandem, Isaac Hayes and David Porter. They made a host of great singles before ego battles broke them apart. This 50-cut, two-disc anthology not only has every song of significance, but plenty of obscure worthwhile items, like a "Stay In School" promo, some overlooked material done with the Dixie Flyers, and a couple of numbers cut by Moore as a single act in the early '70s. The sound quality, annotation, and song sequencing are as outstanding as the songs themselves. —*Ron Wynn*

★ **The Very Best Of Sam & Dave** / 1995 / Rhino ✦✦✦✦✦
Sam & Dave's absolutely essential songs are collected on this distillation of the double-disc set *Sweat'N'Soul*. —*AMG*

Samples

Group, Rock & Roll, Pop/Rock
With their relaxed, slightly jazzy pop, the Samples have become one of the most popular touring bands of the early '90s. After a bad experience with a major label, the band began releasing their own records independently, building support through a grass-roots network of fans. Through constant touring, the Samples were able to keep building their network of fans. They were also busy in the studio, recording three albums between 1992 and 1993. With none of their albums deviating from their folky, Sting-meets-the-Grateful Dead pop, their albums are virtually indistinguishable from each other. However, none of them are bad—each record has a couple of first-rate songs, showing why they are concert favorites across the country. —*Stephen Thomas Erlewine*

○ **The Samples** / May 1989 / What Are? ✦✦✦✦
The Samples' self-titled debut was a bit polished compared to their later efforts, but the roots of their rootsy, laidback, eclectic style are apparent throughout the album. —*Sara Sytsma*

● **Underwater People** / 1992 / What Are? ✦✦✦✦
All of the Samples' records feature a pleasant mix of pop, jazz, and blues, but *Underwater People* is the only album to feature consistently strong songwriting throughout the entire record. —*Stephen Thomas Erlewine*

No Room / 1992 / What Are? ✦✦✦

The Last Drag / Sep. 1993 / What Are? ✦✦✦
The Last Drag follows the same formula as the other Samples records, but it's a bit disjointed and overlong, preventing it from becoming a consistently enjoyable album. Nevertheless, there are several fine moments on the album—it just takes a little longer to find them. —*Sara Sytsma*

Autopilot / 1994 / What Are? ✦✦✦

Carlos Santana (Devadip Carlos Santana)

Group, Rock & Roll, Blues Rock, Fusion
Santana is the name of a band that has successfully married elements of blues, rock, and Latin music and enjoyed international acclaim for more than two decades. It is also the name of the guitarist, Carlos Santana, who has led that band and made other recordings over the same period of time. In its original manifestation, the Santana Blues Band was a group of equals, with Carlos named as leader only because of a musicians union requirement that such a designation be made. The group was formed in San Francisco in the mid-'60s and first gained recognition in the same dance halls that hosted the psychedelic rock groups of the era, although, with its Latin and African roots, Santana never quite fit in with the psychedelic sound. The group came under the direction of promoter Bill Graham and had already scored a contract with Columbia when it appeared at the Woodstock Festival in August 1969. Personnel at that time, in addition to Carlos, included Gregg Rolie (vocals and keyboards), Dave Brown (bass), Mike Shrieve (drums), Armando Peraza (percussion and vocals), and Mike Carabello and Jose Areas (percussion).

Santana, the debut album, was a massive success, including the #4 hit "Evil Ways." *Abraxas* (1970) did even better, topping the charts for six weeks and featuring the hits "Black Magic Woman" and "Oye Como Va." For *Santana III* (1971), the group expanded to a septet with the addition of guitarist Neal Schon, though an additional six sidemen were listed in the album credits. This album was #1 for five weeks.

Guitarist Santana released a live duet album with drummer and vocalist Buddy Miles (later a member of Santana) in 1972; then came the fourth Santana Band album, *Caravanserai*, on which different musician credits were listed for each track, none of them including bassist Dave Brown or percussionist Mike Carabello. The album was a Top Ten hit. Carlos released another duet album in 1973 with guitarist John McLaughlin (the two shared a guru), followed by *Welcome*, credited to "The New Santana Band," its only remaining original members being Santana, Mike Shrieve, Armando Peraza, and Jose Areas (Rolie and Schon had decamped to found Journey).

In subsequent years, "Santana" for the most part referred to Carlos and a band of hired musicians playing in the established Santana style, while the leader also made occasional solo albums that varied the style somewhat. In 1992, Santana ended his long association with Columbia and signed to Polydor, which set up a custom label for him, calling for him to sign his own new acts. — *William Ruhlmann*

○ **Santana** / Aug. 1969 / Columbia ✦✦✦✦
A brilliant combination of rock with Latin and African influences, prominently featuring the organ playing and husky vocals of Gregg Rolie; the energetic, precise drumming of Mike Shrieve; and, especially, the soaring, immediately identifiable guitar sound of Carlos Santana. Justifiably a massive hit and the prototype for an assembly line of similar records. Contains "Evil Ways" and "Soul Sacrifice." — *William Ruhlmann*

☆ **Abraxas** / Sep. 1970 / Columbia ✦✦✦✦✦
Excellent continuation of the first album, with songwriting credits to four of the six band members, plus a terrific version of Tito Puentes's "Oye Como Va." The hit was a cover of the Fleetwood Mac song "Black Magic Woman." — *William Ruhlmann*

○ **Santana III** / Sep. 1971 / Columbia ✦✦✦✦
Completes a trilogy of tightly constructed, exciting band albums filled with percolating, multirhythmic percussion and fiery guitar work. The last album that is the work of the Woodstock-era Santana band. — *William Ruhlmann*

Carlos Santana & Buddy Miles! Live! / Jun. 1972 / Columbia ✦✦
From December 1971 to April 1972, Carlos Santana and several other members of Santana toured with drummer/vocalist Buddy Miles, a former member of the Electric Flag and Jimi Hendrix's Band of Gypsys. The resulting live album contained both Santana hits ("Evil Ways") and Buddy Miles hits ("Changes"), plus a 25-minute, side-long jam. It was not, perhaps, the live album Santana fans had been waiting for, but at this point in its career, the band could do no wrong, and the album went into the Top 10 and sold a million copies. (Reissued on CD on September 6, 1994.) — *William Ruhlmann*

○ **Caravanserai** / Oct. 1972 / Columbia ✦✦✦✦
On *Caravanserai*, individual personnel credits were included for each song, suggesting changes in the band's lineup. But perhaps more significant than the personnel shifts was the changed musical direction of the band. The album cover depicted a desert scene complete with camels, and the opening track was called "Eternal Caravan Of Reincarnation," which should give some indication of the global and spiritual concerns addressed in the music. Tempos were slower, there were more instrumentals, and the overall sound had little of the fiery Latin-rock feel of previous Santana efforts. The result was an album with no hit singles and a fall-off in sales, although *Caravanserai* still made the Top 10 and sold a million copies. — *William Ruhlmann*

Love Devotion Surrender / 1973 / Columbia ✦✦✦
A duo album by John McLaughlin and Carlos Santana, this recording presents the two guitarists attempting jazz-fusion versions of the work of John Coltrane and McLaughlin compositions. Santana's fire is dampened somewhat by the solemn proceedings, but his commercial power held: this was the sixth straight Santana-related album to go gold, but the first to miss the Top 10. — *William Ruhlmann*

Welcome / Nov. 1973 / Columbia ✦✦✦
On the group's fifth album, "The New Santana Band," as it was called, was an octet. Musically, the album was something of a companion piece to Carlos Santana's duet album with John McLaughlin, *Love Devotion Surrender*, even including a song by that title and, like the earlier record, containing compositions by

McLaughlin and John Coltrane. In addition to the jazz influences, there was also a new blues sound courtesy of Leon Thomas, a smooth-voiced singer in the Joe Williams tradition. The record was musically adventurous, but as Santana continued to diverge from its Latin rock roots, its popularity eroded. — *William Ruhlmann*

○ **Lotus** / May 1974 / Columbia ✦✦✦✦
Recorded in Japan in July 1973, this massive live album, originally on three LPs and now on two compact discs, was available outside the United States in 1974, but held back from domestic release until long into the CD age. It features the same "New Santana Band" that recorded *Welcome* and combines that group's jazz and spiritual influences with performances of earlier Latin rock favorites like "Oye Como Va." — *William Ruhlmann*

● **Greatest Hits** / Jul. 1974 / Columbia ✦✦✦✦
This 10-song sampler presents the best of Santana, 1969-71, the period of its greatest popularity. The hits include "Black Magic Woman," "Evil Ways," "Everybody's Everything," and "Oye Como Va." But note that this is a bare minimum of prime Santana. Not only does the sampler choose from only Santana's first three albums, but it leaves out such seminal numbers as "Nobody To Depend On" and "Soul Sacrifice." Those looking for a more extensive overview should consider *Viva Santana!* — *William Ruhlmann*

Illuminations / Sep. 1974 / Columbia ✦✦
For his third duet album, Carlos Santana, who had been performing the works of John Coltrane, paired with Coltrane's widow, harpist/keyboardist Alice Coltrane, on this instrumental album. Side One includes several contemplative, string-filled numbers, while Side Two presents Santana's recreation of John Coltrane's late free jazz style in "Angel Of Sunlight." Columbia Records can't have been pleased at Santana's determined drift into esoteric jazz: *Illuminations* was the first of the nine Santana-related albums so far released in the U.S. not to go gold. — *William Ruhlmann*

Borboletta / Oct. 1974 / Columbia ✦✦✦
Borboletta was the first new Santana Band studio album in 11 months and the group's sixth overall. Once again, individual credits were listed for each song. The main problem was that the band seemed to be coasting; Carlos turned in the usual complement of high-pitched lead guitar work, and the percussionists pounded away, but the Santana Sound had long since taken over from any individual composition, and the records were starting to sound alike. That, in turn, started to make them inessential; *Borboletta* spent less time in the charts than any previous Santana album. — *William Ruhlmann*

○ **Amigos** / Mar. 1976 / Columbia ✦✦✦✦
By the release of *Amigos*, the Santana Band's seventh album, only Carlos Santana and David Brown remained from the band that conquered Woodstock, and only Carlos had been in the band continuously since. Meanwhile, the group had made some effort to arrest its commercial slide, hiring an outside producer, David Rubinson, and taking a tighter, more uptempo, and more vocal approach to its music. The overt jazz influences were replaced by strains of R&B/funk and Mexican folk music. The result was an album more dynamic than any since *Santana III* in 1971. "Let It Shine" (#77), an R&B-tinged tune, became the group's first chart single in four years, and the album returned Santana to Top Ten status. — *William Ruhlmann*

Festival / Jan. 1977 / Columbia ✦✦✦
Santana's follow-up to its comeback album, *Amigos*, was another David Rubinson-produced effort that moved back toward more of a Latin-rock feel, although it retained an essentially pop focus— "The River" was the first real vocal ballad on a Santana album. If any doubt still existed that the group was no longer a band of equals but a platform for its lead guitarist, the current lineup dispelled that; Carlos Santana was now the only original member of the band left. Although the album went gold, the lack of a hit single hurt the album's commercial standing; its number 27 peak was the lowest yet for a Santana Band album. — *William Ruhlmann*

Moonflower / Oct. 1977 / Columbia ✦✦✦
Santana, which was renowned for its concert work dating back to Woodstock, did not release a live album in the U.S. until this one, and it's only partially live, with studio tracks added, notably a cover of the Zombies' "She's Not There" (#27) that became Santana's first Top 40 hit in five years. The usual comings and goings in band membership had taken place since last time; the track listing was a good mixture of the old—"Black Magic Woman," "Soul

Sacrifice"—and the recent, and with the added radio play of a hit single, *Moonflower* went Top Ten and sold a million copies, the first new Santana album to do that since 1972 and the last. — *William Ruhlmann*

Inner Secrets / Oct. 1978 / Columbia ✦✦
Since he had joined Santana in 1972, keyboard player Tom Coster had been Carlos Santana's right-hand man, playing, co-writing, co-producing, and generally taking the place of founding member Greg Rolie. But Coster left the band in the spring of 1978, to be replaced by keyboardist/guitarist Chris Solberg and keyboardist Chris Ryne. Despite the change, the band soldiered on, and with *Inner Secrets* they scored three chart singles: the disco-ish "One Chain (Don't Make No Prison)" (#59), "Stormy" (#32), and a cover of Buddy Holly's "Well All Right" (#69), done in the Blind Faith arrangement. (There seems to be a Steve Winwood fixation here.) The album also featured a cover of Traffic's "Dealer." The singles kept the album on the charts longer than any Santana LP since 1971, but it was still a minor disappointment after *Moonflower*, and in retrospect seems like one of the band's more compromised efforts. — *William Ruhlmann*

Oneness: Silver Dreams Golden Realities / Mar. 1979 / Columbia ✦✦✦
This is the first Carlos Santana solo album. It features members of the Santana band as backup, however, so the difference between a group effort and a solo work seems to be primarily in the musical approach, which is more esoteric and more varied than on a regular band album. The record is mostly instrumental and given over largely to contemplative ballads, although there is also, for example, in the song "Silver Dreams Golden Smiles," a traditional pop ballad sung by Saunders King. — *William Ruhlmann*

Marathon / Sep. 1979 / Columbia ✦✦
Marathon marked the addition of keyboard player Alan Pasqua and singer Greg Walker's replacement by singer/guitarist Alex Ligertwood in the Santana lineup. Otherwise, the album was notable for consisting entirely of band-written material, although those songs were in the established rock/R&B style evolved on albums like *Amigos*, *Festival*, and *Inner Secrets*. The formula seemed to be wearing thin by now, however, as, even with a Top 40 hit in "You Know That I Love You" (#35), *Marathon* became the first Santana album to fall below the 500,000-sales mark necessary for gold record certification. (It has since made the mark.) — *William Ruhlmann*

The Swing of Delight / Aug. 1980 / Columbia ✦✦
For his second "solo" album, Carlos Santana used Miles Davis's famed '60s group—Herbie Hancock, Wayne Shorter, Ron Carter, and Tony Williams—plus members of the current Santana band, for a varied, jazz-oriented session that was one of his more pleasant excursions from the standard Santana sound. (Originally released as a double-LP, *The Swing Of Delight* was reissued on a single CD.) — *William Ruhlmann*

Zebop! / Apr. 1981 / Columbia ✦✦
On *Zebop!*, a Santana band featuring newcomer Richard Baker on keyboards tried to preserve the better elements of the first and third trilogies of Santana albums—there was a heavy component of Latin-flavored percussion topped by Carlos's biting lead guitar work, and there were also three pop cover songs in Cat Stevens' "Changes," J.J. Cale's "The Sensitive Kind," and Russ Ballard's "Winning." The double strategy worked. "Winning" (#17) became Santana's first Top 20 single in a decade, "The Sensitive Kind" (#56) also charted, and the album was Santana's first Top Ten, gold-selling hit in four years. — *William Ruhlmann*

Shango / Aug. 1982 / Columbia ✦✦
Shango is notable for featuring the return, in the role of co-producer and co-songwriter, of original Santana keyboardist Greg Rolie. The main producer, however, was Bill Szymczyk (James Gang, Eagles), who gave Santana an unusually sharp rock sound resulting in two more hit singles, "Hold On" (number 15) and "Nowhere to Run" (number 66), although the band once again slipped below Top Ten, gold-selling status, with the album peaking at only number 22, and even this was the highest Santana would get from here on out. — *William Ruhlmann*

Havana Moon / Apr. 1983 / Columbia ✦✦✦
The third Carlos Santana solo album marks a surprising turn toward 1950s rock 'n' roll and Tex-Mex, with covers such as Bo Diddley's "Who Do You Love" and Chuck Berry's title song. Produced by veteran R&B producers Jerry Wexler and Barry Beckett, the album features an eclectic mix of sidemen, including Booker T. Jones of Booker T & the MG's, Willie Nelson, and the Fabulous Thunderbirds. *Havana Moon* is a light effort, but it's one of Santana's most enjoyable albums, which may explain why it was also the best- selling Santana album outside the group releases in 10 years. — *William Ruhlmann*

Beyond Appearances / Feb. 1985 / Columbia ✦✦
Seven months in the making, and appearing two and a half years after Santana's last album, *Beyond Appearances* was produced by Val ("Bette Davis Eyes") Garay in a hot 1980s style replete with prominent synthesizers and drum machines. In the interim, the band had undergone changes, with Alphonso Johnson replacing David Margen on bass, Chester D. Thompson and David Sancious replacing Richard Baker on keyboards, Chester Cortez Thompson replacing Graham Lear on drums, and singer Greg Walker rejoining. Garay co-wrote "Say It Again" (#46), Santana's final Hot 100 entry (a remake of Curtis Mayfield's "I'm The One Who Loves You" hit #102), but this latest pop interpretation of the Santana sound did not endear it to fans, and, at a peak of #50, *Beyond Appearances* was the lowest charting Santana album yet. — *William Ruhlmann*

Freedom / Feb. 1987 / Columbia ✦✦✦
Freedom marked several reunions in the Santana band, which was now a nonet. In addition to Carlos, the band consisted of percussionists Armando Pereza, Orestes Vilato, and Raul Rekow, returning drummer Graham Lear, bassist Alphonso Johnson, returning keyboardist Tom Coster, keyboardist Chester Thompson, and, on lead vocals, Buddy Miles, who had made a duet album with Santana 15 years before. Credited as an "additional musician" was keyboard player Greg Rolie, an original member. The music also marked a return from the hyper-pop sound of Val Garay on *Beyond Appearances* to a more traditional Santana Latin rock style. Thus, *Freedom* was a literal return to form, but, unfortunately, not to the quality of early Santana albums. And the group's commercial decline continued, with the LP getting to only #95. — *William Ruhlmann*

○ **Blues for Salvador** / Oct. 1987 / Columbia ✦✦✦✦
On previous "solo" albums, Carlos Santana had made noticeable stylistic changes and worked with jazz, pop, and even country musicians. On this, his fourth Carlos Santana release, the line between a "solo" and a "group" project is blurred; this record is really a catchall of Santana band outtakes and stray tracks. For example, included are an instrumental version of "Deeper, Dig Deeper" from *Freedom* and an alternate take of "Hannibal" from *Zebop!*, as well as "Now That You Know" from the group's 1985 tour. Given the variety of material, the album is somewhat less focused than most Santana band albums, but there are individual tracks that are impressive, notably "Trane," which features Tony Williams on drums. (*Blues For Salvador* won the Grammy Award for Best Rock Instrumental Performance.) — *William Ruhlmann*

○ **Viva Santana!** / Aug. 1988 / Columbia ✦✦✦✦
A lovingly assembled two-disc retrospective set that collects the best of the Santana band, along with many interesting rarities. — *William Ruhlmann*

Spirits Dancing in the Flesh / Jun. 1990 / Columbia ✦✦✦
Following a 1989 20th anniversary reunion tour to promote *Viva Santana!*, Carlos Santana reorganized the band as a sextet and recorded *Spirits Dancing In The Flesh*, Santana's 15th and final studio album for Columbia Records. It was an unusually eclectic collection, featuring songs by Curtis Mayfield ("Gypsy Woman"), the Isley Brothers ("Who's That Lady"), and Babatunde Olatunji ("Jin-Go-Lo-Ba"). For all those influences, it was more of a straightforward, guitar-heavy rock album than usual. Coming more than three years after Santana's last new album, *Freedom*, it sold to the band's core audience only, reaching #85. — *William Ruhlmann*

Milagro / 1992 / Polydor ✦✦✦
Santana signed to Polydor in 1991 after 22 years with Columbia Records. Their label debut has a somewhat elegiac tone, beginning with a stage introduction by the late promoter Bill Graham, and featuring an excerpt from a speech by Dr. Martin Luther King, Jr., solos taken from Miles Davis and John Coltrane, and music written by Bob Marley, Coltrane, and Gil Evans. Despite the presence of all these heroic ghosts, however, *Milagro* is only an average Santana release, familiar-sounding but undistinguished, and it failed to arrest the band's commercial slide, becoming the first new Santana studio album not to crack the Top 100. — *William Ruhlmann*

Sacred Fire: Santana Live in South America / Oct. 19, 1993 / Polydor ✦✦

For its third live album, Santana introduced a new bass player, Myron Dove, and added guitarist Jorge Santana (Carlos Santana's brother) and singer Vorriece Cooper to bring the band up to nine members. Adopting the mantle of Bob Marley, the band played "Esperando," which borrowed Marley's characteristic audience chant. Much of the album, however, is given over to repeating Santana's earliest hits—"No One To Depend On," "Black Magic Woman," "Soul Sacrifice," etc.—which should please the band's new record label (it's always good to have versions of the hits in your catalog), but which make the album inessential for fans. *Sacred Fire* spent one week at #181 in the charts, the worst performance ever for a Santana album. —*William Ruhlmann*

Santana Brothers / Sep. 27, 1994 / Island ✦✦
This is a trio album featuring Carlos Santana, his brother Jorge, and his nephew, Carlos Hernandez. —*William Ruhlmann*

Joe Satriani

b. 1956
Hard Rock, Fusion, Pop/Rock
Joe Satriani was one of the best, most influential rock guitarists of the late '80s, equally capable of fast flights of blinding technique as well as sweet, lyrical passages. What also separates Satriani from most technically gifted guitar virtuosos is that he treats a song as a song, not as an excuse to shred. For these reasons, he appeals not only to guitarists, but also to many rock fans who have never touched the instrument—his breakthrough 1987 album, *Surfing with the Alien*, was the first rock instrumental album in years to chart in the Top 30 on *Billboard's* Top 200 Albums. Since then, he has added vocals to his records; while his voice can't compare to his guitar, it added another dimension to an artist that was already more versatile than the majority of contemporary musicians.

Before Satriani became a recording star, he taught guitar is San Francisco; several of his students became famous, influential guitarists in their own right, before he even recorded his first album in 1988. Metallica's Kirk Hammett was the first of his students to hit the big time, followed by Steve Vai and Larry LaLonde of Primus. —*Stephen Thomas Erlewine*

Joe Satriani / 1985 / Rubina ✦✦✦
This ultra-rare (fewer than 500 copies were pressed) five-song EP produced by Satriani, features songs in which all of the sounds were created with a guitar. A cult classic. —*Paul Kohler*

Not of This Earth / 1986 / Combat ✦✦✦
The major debut from this San Francisco guitarist is an eclectic mixture of sounds and styles. —*Paul Kohler*

● **Surfing with the Alien** / 1987 / Combat ✦✦✦✦
Hard-hitting, intense, and foot-to-the-floor guitar playing, it's all instrumental. —*Paul Kohler*

Dreaming #11 / 1988 / Combat ✦✦
This live mini-CD features 20 minutes of fiery guitar playing. —*Paul Kohler*

Flying in a Blue Dream / Feb. 1990 / Combat ✦✦✦
His first album to feature Satriani's vocals has a total playing time of over 66 minutes. —*Paul Kohler*

The Extremist / Jul. 1992 / Combat ✦✦✦
Satriani returned to the all-instrumental format for *The Extremist*. It's a smart move, and not just because he's a better guitar player than he is a singer. Whether it's guitar-god rock like "Friends" and the neo-folk "Rubina's Blue Sky Happiness," Satriani always shows that he's got a real knack for melody—his voice may hide that, but his guitar only emphasizes it. —*Brian Mansfield*

○ **Time Machine** / 1993 / Combat ✦✦✦✦
Satriani has proven to be one of the most technically gifted and influential guitarists of the '80s, and the two-disc *Time Machine* compiles his long out-of-print first EP with several live tracks, making it a good showcase for his considerable talents. —*Stephen Thomas Erlewine*

Savage Rose

Group, Art-Rock/Progressive-Rock
One of the most well-known rock groups from Continental Europe, Denmark's Savage Rose recorded a wealth of intriguing and eclectic progressive rock in the late '60s and '70s. In their early work, one hears faint echoes of the Airplane, Doors, Pink Floyd, and other psychedelic heavyweights, combined with classical, jazz,

and Danish-Euro folk elements. Their arrangements rely heavily on an incandescent, watery organ that sounds like nothing so much as psychedelic aquarium music. The most striking aspect of the band's sound, however, was the vocals of lead singer Annisette. Her childish wispy and sensual phrasing can suddenly break into jarring, almost histrionic wailing, like a Janis Joplin with Yoko Ono-isms, and eerily foreshadows Kate Bush's style.

Stars in their native land, Savage Rose also achieved a bit of underground success abroad, and several of their albums were released in North America. Between 1968 and 1978, the group released nine albums, moving from vaguely psychedelic rock and the heavily gospel-influenced *Refugee* to the nearly classical ballet score *Dodens Triumf* and the folky, nearly all-Danish *Solen Var Ogsa Din* (their first eight albums were sung entirely in English). Always a radical band, the Black Panthers even invited the group to play at a benefit for Bobby Seale after hearing one of Savage Rose's records—they took the extremely radical step of ending their professional and recording career around 1980 in order to use their music to support revolutionary causes. Although they actually continued to make music and perform, they were only heard at benefits and free concerts (actually playing in Lebanese hospitals, schools, and refugee camps at the P.L.O.'s invitation). They continue to perform to this day, and have actually been back in the studio to record in recent years. —*Richie Unterberger*

● **Savage Rose** / 1968 / Polydor ✦✦✦✦
Their debut is their lightest and most charming effort. Waltzing melodies give way to thunder-of-doom bass runs, and the storybookish lyrics have a forlorn, yearning quality. With its oddly hollow sound, one is never really sure whether the tone is supposed to be playful or ominous. —*Richie Unterberger*

In the Plain / 1969 / Polydor ✦✦✦
The band takes a more aggressive and soul-oriented approach on their second album, but the material isn't as strong, and much of the ethereal ambience that made their first LP special is lost. It does include the terrific, rollicking "Evening's Child," as well as the pre-doom & gloom workout "A Trial In Our Native Town." —*Richie Unterberger*

Travelin' / 1969 / Polydor ✦✦✦
More excursions into soul-rock territory dominate one of their less distinguished albums. Highlights include the more serene and melodic cuts ("Travelin'," "Sailing Away") and the shockingly titled (for 1969) "My Family Was Gay," with its rather straightforward hints of incest. —*Richie Unterberger*

Your Daily Gift / 1970 / Gregar ✦✦✦
Their most well-known album, singled out for praise by critic Greil Marcus in his anthology *Stranded*. About half of this is fairly undistinguished heavy progressive-psychedelic rock, but the other half ranks among their most fragile and best material—the group were always better when they waxed reflective than when they tried to rock out. The lengthy, bittersweet, melancholy title track (complete with weepy European sidewalk cafe accordion) is one of their finest moments. —*Richie Unterberger*

Refugee / 1971 / Gregar ✦✦✦
Their most gospel and soul-influenced recording. Recalls Janis Joplin's more generic solo recordings, albeit with a more subdued feel. —*Richie Unterberger*

○ **Dodens Triumf** / 1972 / Polydor ✦✦✦✦
An unheralded landmark in art-rock, this features Savage Rose keyboardist Thomas Koppel's score for a ballet by Flemming Flindt (the title translates to "Triumph of Death"). Nearly entirely instrumental (one song features Annisette on vocals), this is one of the finest classically-influenced rock records. Moody and melancholy, at times almost doomy, yet always melodic, this 40-minute selection of haunting pieces prominently features the group's unique underwater organ sound, and makes for compelling listening. —*Richie Unterberger*

Babylon / 1972 / Polydor ✦✦✦
With contributions by noted jazz saxophonist Ben Webster and the American gospel quintet the Stars of Faith, this is (along with *Refugee*) their most R&B-influenced recording, at times achieving a churchy, old-time New Orleans-like feel. —*Richie Unterberger*

Wild Child / 1973 / Polydor ✦✦✦
One of their better efforts. The R&B influence retreats in favor of a tender, melodic approach emphasizing the organ, piano, and accordions on a strong set that favors their European folk influences. —*Richie Unterberger*

Sole Var Ogsa Din / 1978 / Sonet ✦✦✦
A welcome return to their lightest and wispiest styles, with clear, shimmering instrumental textures that are almost like sonic waterfalls. Their enigmatic, moody song structures and melodies remain, with the most histrionic edges of Annisette's vocals toned down. As all but two of the songs are in their native Danish, this can perhaps be considered their most personal effort as well. — *Richie Unterberger*

The Savages

Group, Garage Rock
Little is known about this mid-'60s group, which have variously been reported to be from Bermuda, or a group of Americans who were based in Bermuda when their sole LP, *Live 'N Wild*, was recorded. That album, recorded live at the Princess Hotel in Bermuda (according to the liner notes), stands as one of the best '60s full-length garage platters. Composed almost wholly of original material, the group played top-notch tunes with heavy echoes of the Beatles, Searchers, and Byrds, with a much greater melodic sense than the typical American garage combo, though a pleasing rawness is evident throughout. — *Richie Unterberger*

● **Live 'N Wild** / 1984 / Resurrection ✦✦✦✦
One of the few ultra-rare garage albums that lives up to the raves you'll come across in specialist fanzines, by one of the few groups of the genre that were equally capable of garage raunch and moody, melodic ballads (the Rising Storm were about the only other one in their league in this regard). Don't bother looking for the original LP, which fetches hundreds of dollars on auction lists; the reissue is much easier to find. — *Richie Unterberger*

Savoy Brown

Group, Blues Rock
Along with John Mayall's Bluesbreakers and the Byrds, English blues-influenced rock band Savoy Brown should win some kind of distinction for having the most line-up changes—almost a different one for each of their fourteen albums on Deram between 1967 and 1978. Lead guitarist Kim Simmonds was the constant element throughout. Among the band's expatriates were members of Foghat. — *Rick Clark*

○ **Blue Matter** / 1969 / Deram ✦✦✦✦
A great album, a classic which includes "Louisiana Blues" and "Train to Nowhere." — *Michael G. Nastos*

○ **Raw Sienna** / 1970 / Deram ✦✦✦✦
A blues-rock standard. — *Michael G. Nastos*

● **The Savoy Brown Collection (Chronicles Series)** / Jul. 20, 1993 / PolyGram ✦✦✦✦
This double -D set is all you may ever need of Savoy Brown. It includes their biggest hit, "Tell Mama." Like all Polygram *Chronicles* sets, this features great sound, smart track selections, thoughtful liner notes, and good photos. What more could you ask for? — *Rick Clark*

Leo Sayer

b. May 21, 1948, Shoreham-on-Sea
Pop/Rock
Leo Sayer (born Gerard Sayer) had a string of highly-polished mainstream pop hits in the late '70s. Sayer began his musical career as the leader of the London-based Terraplane Blues Band in the late '60s. He formed Patches with drummer Dave Courtney in 1971; Courtney used to play with British pop star Adam Faith. Faith was beginning a management career in the early '70s, so Courtney brought Patches to his former employer in hopes of securing a contract. Patches failed to impress Faith, yet he liked Sayer and chose to promote him as a solo artist. Sayer began recording some solo material written with David Courtney at Roger Daltrey's studio; the Who's lead singer liked the Sayer/Courtney originals enough to record a handful himself, including the hit "Giving It All Away." Sayer's debut single, "Why Is Everybody Going Home," failed to make any impact, yet 1973's "The Show Must Go On" hit number one in the U.K.; a cover by Three Dog Night stopped Sayer's version from charting in the U.S. The following year he released his first album, *Silver Bird*.

Silver Bird was followed quickly by *Just a Boy*, which included two more British hit singles, "One Man Band" and "Long Tall Glasses (I Can Dance);" "Long Tall Glasses" managed to break Sayer into the American Top Ten in early 1975. Sayer's working re-

lationship with Courtney was severed during the recording of his third album, *Another Year* (1975). The following year, he released *Endless Flight*, which was co-written with former Supertramp member Frank Furrell; featuring the number one singles "You Make Me Feel like Dancing" and "When I Need You," the record became his biggest hit in both the U.S. and the U.K., selling over a million copies in America. Following *Endless Flight*, Sayer became a fixture in the American Top 40, yet his hits began to dry up in England.

Sayer began the '80s with the American number two hit, "More than I Can Say," yet it was his last big single in the U.S. His last chart entry in America was the early 1981 hit "Living in a Fantasy;" the U.K. hits didn't stop until 1983, after "Till You Come Back to Me" scraped the charts. After laying low for the rest of the decade, he attempted a comeback in 1990 with *Cool Touch*, yet it fell on deaf ears. — *Stephen Thomas Erlewine*

● **All the Best A** / 1993 / Chrysalis ✦✦✦✦

Boz Scaggs (William Royce Scaggs)

b. Jun. 8, 1944, Ohio
Soft Rock, Pop/Rock
Boz Scaggs got his start in 1959, playing with Steve Miller in the Dallas band, the Marksmen. It was Miller who taught Scaggs guitar. Scaggs and Miller eventually formed the Steve Miller Band, with Scaggs leaving after their classic second album, *Sailor*. *Rolling Stone* editor Jann Wenner helped Scaggs secure a solo artist deal with Atlantic. Scaggs's self-titled debut (produced by Wenner) failed to sell in spite of critical praise and the presence of sidemen like Duane Allman on the album. A deal with Columbia in 1970 was more fruitful, with each of Scaggs's albums selling in increasing numbers. In 1976 Scaggs achieved major stardom, thanks to the elegant urban pop of *Silk Degrees*. Over the next five years, he released a string of sophisticated R&B-influenced pop hits. In recent years, Scaggs' output has been very sporadic, as he became a restaurant owner in San Francisco. — *Rick Clark*

○ **Boz Scaggs** / 1969 / Atlantic ✦✦✦✦
Produced by Jann Wenner and featuring crack accompaniment by the Muscle Shoals house band, Scaggs's solo debut is a near-masterwork, mingling the pathos and heartbreak of vintage honky tonk with the celebration and release of Southern soul. The highlights of the album also flaunt its diversity: "Loan Me a Dime," an extended blues dirge, which features some of Duane Allman's finest work, and "Waiting on a Train," Scaggs's marvelous revamping of Jimmie Rodgers's classic hobo song. — *John Floyd*

Moments / 1971 / Columbia ✦✦✦
Scaggs's first album for Columbia is so low-key you barely notice the magic conjured on this set of introspective ballads. That is, until you really *listen*. — *John Floyd*

○ **Boz Scaggs & His Band** / Dec. 1971 / Columbia ✦✦✦✦

○ **My Time** / 1972 / Columbia ✦✦✦✦
Scaggs's last rock & roll gasp, the ballads that would become his trademark are already surfacing, but you need this one for "Full-Lock Power Slide" and "Dinah Flo," two scorching rockers that give this album the muscle it needs. — *John Floyd*

Slow Dancer / 1974 / Columbia ✦✦✦
Uneven production by Motown's Johnny Bristol. — *Bil Carpenter*

○ **Silk Degrees** / Feb. 1976 / Columbia ✦✦✦✦
Scaggs reached his commercial peak with this elegant collection of soulful urban pop, thanks to hits like the ultra-smooth disco of "Lowdown" (number three), the revved-up "Lido Shuffle" (number 11), and "We're All Alone," Scaggs's finest ballad. — *Rick Clark*

Down Two Then Left / Nov. 1977 / Columbia ✦✦

Middle Man / Apr. 1980 / Columbia ✦✦✦

● **Hits!** / Nov. 1980 / Columbia ✦✦✦✦
In spite of the inclusion of "Dinah Flo," *Hits!* primarily focuses on Scaggs's '80s pop hits like "Lowdown," "Jojo," "Break Down Dead Ahead" and "Look What You've Done to Me." — *Bil Carpenter*

Other Roads / 1988 / Columbia ✦✦
Boz Scaggs ended his retirement in 1988 and returned from running a restaurant to cut this session. It had his patented folk/soul mix and a few decent songs, but wasn't anywhere as ambitious or polished as any of his previous four platinum albums. Perhaps there really is truth to the old saying about going home again. His voice still had its introspective, bemused tone, but the production, arrangements, and compositions lacked conviction, power, or com-

mercial appeal. He did get one hit with the single "Heart Of Mine," but Toto's backing was more hindrance than help. —*Ron Wynn*

○ **Some Change** / Apr. 5, 1994 / Virgin ✦✦✦✦
This album has a nice organic feel to it that many of Scaggs's more commercially successful albums lacked. Scaggs plays a lot more guitar here and his singing has a relaxed soulfulness. This is one of his very best albums. —*Rick Clark*

Scandal

Group, Pop/Rock
Guitarist Zack Smith formed the mainstream pop/rock band Scandal after playing in various groups, including ones that featured Dee Murray and Davey Johnson of the Elton John band. Scandal's lineup was secured in 1982, with the addition of vocalist Patty Smyth; the rest of the band included bassist Ivan Elias, keyboardist Benji King, and drummer Frankie La Rocka. After opening for acts like the Kinks and Hall and Oates, the band released their debut single, "Goodbye to You," in 1982; their self-titled debut album followed soon afterward. *The Warrior* was released two years later. The title track was a Top Ten hit and the album went platinum. However, Smyth left for a solo career the following year, causing the band to break up. —*Stephen Thomas Erlewine*

● **Scandal** / 1982 / Columbia ✦✦✦✦
The Warrior / 1984 / Columbia ✦✦✦

Scarface

Rap
Brad "Scarface Akshen" Jordan was an original member of the Houston rap group the Geto Boys. He became the latest Geto Boy to go solo with *Mr. Scarface Is Back* in 1991. *The World Is Yours* and *The Diary* followed in 1993 and 1994, the latter featuring Ice Cube on one track. His albums have had some impact, but other than Bushwick Bill, most of the Geto Boys did better together than apart. —*Ron Wynn*

● **Mr. Scarface Is Back** / 1991 / Rap-A-Lot ✦✦✦✦
Scarface became the latest Geto Boy to try it solo with this 1991 album. He created a memorable message track in "A Minute to Pray and a Second to Die," a song that should have been a crossover sensation. Few gangsta numbers have more vividly and effectively chronicled the litany of hopelessness and violence plaguing the nation's inner cities. Other cuts, like "Body Snatcher," "Born Killer" and "Diary of a Madman," were less compelling and more chilling. —*Ron Wynn*

○ **The Diary** / 1993 / Rap-A-Lot/Noo Trybe ✦✦✦✦
Scarface's debut album after the break-up of his controversial band, the Geto Boys, *The Diary* is just that—a journal of the trials of inner-city life. Related with his rhythmic, deep-voiced delivery, this gangsta album has some of the deepest, darkest beats around, and one track with guest Ice Cube. —*John Bush*

The World Is Yours / Rap-A-Lot ✦✦✦
The second album from former Geto Boy Scarface didn't contain any single cut as moving or hypnotic as "A Minute To Pray And A Second To Die," but it proved even more popular. It also was an indication that the Geto Boys were kaput, as everyone continued cutting solo albums, and talk of a proposed new Geto Boys album went from probable to possible to the backburner. —*Ron Wynn*

Scarlets

Group, Doo-Wop
A '50s R&B vocal group. Before vocalist Fred Parris formed his Five Satins, he was lead singer of the Scarlets, a New Haven, CT, group that cut four highly prized singles for Bobby Robinson's Red Robin label in 1954-1955, notably "Dear One." —*Bill Dahl*

○ **Golden Classics** / Collectables ✦✦✦✦
Dreamy '50s East Coast doo-wop by the group who developed into the Five Satins. —*Bill Dahl*

Schnell Fenster

Group, Alternative Pop/Rock
An eclectic New Zealand-based band comprised of former Split Enz members Phil Judd (guitar/vocals/keyboards), Noel Crombie (drums), Nigel Griggs (bass) and Michael Den Elzen (guitar). The band formed in 1986 and released their first album, *Sound of Trees,* in 1988 in Australia. A warm reception in their homeland

prompted an American contract with Atlantic Records the following year and a worldwide release for the album in 1990. Without a supporting tour outside of their homeland and poor promotion, the album quickly faded. The followup, 1990's *OK Alright A Huh Oh Yeah,* suffered the same fate, this time with a release limited to Australasia. While promoting the album, Crombie developed tinnitus, forcing them to postpone the tour. They eventually broke up, with the members eventually playing a more active role behind the scenes in the music business. —*Chris Woodstra*

● **Sound of Trees** / 1990 / Atlantic ✦✦✦✦
The band's debut picks up where Split Enz left off in the mid-'80s, exploring some of the funkiness first heard on *Time and Tide* and the jazzy stylings of *Conflicting Emotions.* The always interesting Phil Judd turns in another quirky batch of lyrics as only he can sing, proving that his return was long overdue. —*Chris Woodstra*

OK Alright a Huh Oh Yeah / 1992 / WEA ✦✦
Though the songs aren't quite as strong as those on the debut, *OK Alright a Huh Oh Yeah* is still a solid effort, worthwhile for longtime Split Enz fans. Released only in Australia. —*Chris Woodstra*

Schoolly D

Rap
Opinion has been widely mixed about the merits of Philadelphia rapper Jesse B. Weaver Jr. aka Schoolly D. Long before the debate about gangsta-rap lyrics became an easy way to get national newsprint, there was outrage over Schoolly D's explicit and undiluted narratives on inner city strife. *Saturday Night* in 1987 and *Smoke Some Kill* in 1988 had city officials openly endorsing removal of the albums from record stores. He has continued in the same vein, with *Am I Black Enough for You,* his most recent release in 1993. Schoolly D's rather lackluster rapping style and repetitive material doesn't place him in the forefront of hip-hop creators, but he does merit mention (or blame, depending on your perspective) for being an early gangsta proponent. —*Ron Wynn*

Schoolly D / 1986 / Jive ✦✦
It was unclear on this self-titled LP whether Schoolly D wanted to be a comic or a poet, a philosopher or a storyteller, and whether he wanted to concentrate on topical issues or lighter material. Perhaps it was a reflection of the uncertainty in his raps and the muddiness of his rhymes, because no clear vision or direction emerged on this record. —*Ron Wynn*

○ **Saturday Night** / 1987 / Jive ✦✦✦✦
Philadelphia rapper Schoolly D functions better as an absurdist commentator exploring the netherworld of inner city chaos than as a political philosopher or Afrocentric advocate. This 1987 album was among his best, precisely because he chose to be bizarre rather than prophetic and kept things freewheeling instead of didactic. —*Ron Wynn*

● **The Adventures of Schoolly D** / 1987 / Rykodisc ✦✦✦✦
This collects his early singles, cut before his bad-ass rep subverted whatever creativity he had left. —*John Floyd*

Smoke Some Kill / 1988 / Jive ✦✦
Philadelphia rapper Schoolly D was among the earliest gangstas to generate censorship threats. This 1988 LP included lewd descriptions of genitalia, vivid commentary on drug use and its impact, plus "Gangster Boogie II" and "Black Man." Schoolly D's rapping was erratic and often seemed disjointed, while his rhymes hardly flowed. It was more chaotic than creative, but did manage to generate considerable East Coast controversy among more sedate types. —*Ron Wynn*

Am I Black Enough for You? / 1991 / Jive ✦✦✦
While Schoolly D's attempts to present Afrocentric philosophy and call for self-determination were commendable, he failed to present them in either a musically satisfying or lyrically convincing manner. This 1989 album did little beyond rip white society for its ills and injustices in a fashion merging the worst excesses of rambling propaganda and irrational nationalism. —*Ron Wynn*

How a Blackman Feels / Oct. 14, 1991 / Capitol ✦✦
○ **Welcome to America** / 1994 / Ruffhouse ✦✦✦✦
Schoolly D returns with a spare, dark attempt to recapture the gangsta audience he helped create back in the 1980s; it helps that the record contains the best music he has ever recorded, although the best moments can't hide the fact that Schoolly D doesn't have the lyrical grace of the rappers that followed his footsteps. —*Stephen Thomas Erlewine*

Klaus Schulze

Electronic

One of the cornerstone figures in the German electronic scene, this pioneering synthesist has recorded nearly two dozen solo albums over the past 20 years. His music has grown and changed with the evolution of technology, but his concept of long-form, highly rhythmic sequencer music pulsing under soaring melodies has remained constant. Though he established his own identity years ago, Schulze was briefly a member of Tangerine Dream, appearing on one album, *Electronic Meditation*, in 1970. He did not, however, cave in to convention or engage in cheap pop-electronic exploits, as did his former TD colleagues in the mid '80s and beyond. Still, Schulze's collaborations with former Santana drummer Michael Shrieve brought a new level of percussive intensity to his music, as well as a wider audience from the progressive rock world. The availability of Schulze's music has always been inconsistent in the U.S., and many Americans have no idea how strong his influence has been on electronic music worldwide. (He was, for instance, the inspiration behind Kitaro's initial investigations of synthesizer music.) Schulze continues to perform throughout Europe and is tireless in releasing new recordings, some of which are better than others. When Schulze does hit the nail on the head, his music is immensely powerful. —*Linda Kohanov*

○ **Cyborg** / 1973 / A&M ✦✦✦✦

One of the original members of Tangerine Dream, *Cyborg* was Klaus's second solo album. From the early days of electronic experimentation in the pop field, still today it stands as one of the most powerful examples of ambient pulse music ever conceived. The dense layers of rhythm and synthetic tone colors melt into a seamless, flowing soundscape of melody, motion and spatial effects. It's a monumental double album of "cosmic music." —*Archie Patterson*

○ **Timewind** / 1975 / Blue Plate ✦✦✦✦

Two masterful sequencer essays make effective use of minimalistic patterns to suspend and ultimately erase all sense of objective "clock-time" experience. —*Linda Kohanov*

Mirage / 1977 / Island ✦✦✦

Mirage gives the listener impressionistic sequencer work depicting winter landscapes. —*Linda Kohanov*

X / 1978 / Gramavision ✦✦✦

Schulze's tenth solo release marks the peak of his most influential period of work. Presented with a classic sense of German drama, this double CD artfully combines the composer's synthesizers and sequencer patterns with live drums and full orchestra. Intense, driving, long-form pieces frame surreal, abstract sounds. Each of six pieces is named for a historical figure Schulze admires, beginning with a 24-minute selection titled "Friedrich Nietzsche." —*Linda Kohanov*

● **Beyond Recall** / 1991 / Venture ✦✦✦✦

Schulze is in a more sedate and reflective mood here, with acoustic guitar samples creating lyrical melodies. —*Linda Kohanov*

Scorpions

Group, Heavy Metal

A German metal band formed in 1970 by Rudolf and Michael Schenker, the Scorpions also included vocalist Klaus Meine, bassist Lothar Heimberg, and drummer Wolfgang Dziony. The original lineup stayed intact for three years, until Michael quit in 1973 to join UFO. The band broke up briefly and was re-formed at the end of the same year by Rudy Schenker with Meine; guitarist Uli Roth, bassist Francis Buchholz, and drummer Jorgen Rosenthal (replaced in 1975 by Rudy Lenners). Lenners was replaced in 1977 by Herman Rarebell. Roth left to form Electric Sun in 1978, replaced by Matthias Jabs, the two of them in and out of band during the '80s. Undoubtedly the biggest group to come out of Germany, the Scorpions have survived in a genre not noted for longevity, cutting several classic sides along the way. —*Cub Koda*

Fly to the Rainbow / 1974 / RCA ✦✦✦

First U.S. release features the title track, "Speedy's Coming," "Drifting Sun," and "They Need a Million." Early meisterwerk from these German hard rockers. —*Cub Koda*

○ **In Trance** / 1975 / RCA ✦✦✦✦

Still rockin' hard in the '70s, this one features "Robot Man," "Dark Lady in Trance" and "Top of the Bill." —*Cub Koda*

○ **Virgin Killers** / 1976 / RCA ✦✦✦✦

Features the title track, "Hell Cat," "Backstage Queen," "Polar Nights" and "Yellow Raven." —*Cub Koda*

Taken by Force / 1978 / RCA ✦✦

Tokyo Tapes / 1978 / RCA ✦✦✦

Tokyo Tapes pulled this German band out of obscurity and into the spotlight. A quality sampling of their early material, it's a performance that is considered one of the band's best. Includes "All Night Long," "Back Stage Queen," and "Flight to the Rainbow." —*John Book*

○ **Lovedrive** / 1979 / Mercury ✦✦✦✦

Well-written songs and powerful singing from Klaus Meine are some of the reasons given for calling *Lovedrive* one of the best Scorpions ever. Rudolf Schenker and Matthais Jabs provide many of this album's highlights, with lots of great guitar. —*John Book*

● **The Best of the Scorpions** / 1979 / RCA ✦✦✦✦

Rock Galaxy / 1980 / RCA ✦✦

Animal Magnetism / 1980 / Mercury ✦✦✦

○ **Blackout** / 1982 / Mercury ✦✦✦✦

The band experiments with pop smarts in a few of the songs, while retaining the solid hard rock sound they have molded over the years. *Blackout* provided this German band with their first major hit, "No One like You" (#65). —*John Book*

○ **The Best of the Scorpions, Vol. 2** / 1984 / RCA ✦✦✦✦

○ **Love at First Sting** / 1984 / Mercury ✦✦✦✦

Love at First Sting was the Scorpions' U.S. commercial breakthrough, thanks to the single "Rock You like a Hurricane." —*Sara Sytsma*

World Wide Live / 1985 / Mercury ✦✦✦

Savage Amusement / 1988 / Mercury ✦✦✦

● **The Best of Rockers 'n' Ballads** / 1989 / Mercury ✦✦✦✦

This good collection spotlights the band's best tracks from the '80s, including "Rock You Like a Hurricane," "Rhythm of Love," "No One Like You," and "Still Loving You." —*AMG*

○ **Crazy World** / 1990 / Mercury ✦✦✦✦

Crazy World featured the Scorpions' biggest (and best) hit single, the reflective ballad "Wind of Change," which was the highlight on one of the band's most consistent, accomplished albums. —*Stephen Thomas Erlewine*

Jack Scott (Jack Scafone Jr.)

b. Jan. 24, 1936, Windsor, Ontario

Rock & Roll, Rockabilly

Jack Scott sounded tough, like someone you wouldn't want to meet in a dark alley unless he had a guitar in his hands. When he growled "The Way I Walk," wise men (and women) stepped aside. Despite his snarling rockabilly attitude, Scott hailed from Ontario, Canada, and grew up near Detroit, developing a love for hillbilly music along the way. His first sides for ABC-Paramount in 1957 exhibited a profound country-rock synthesis, and after moving to the Carlton label, Scott hit the charts the next year with the tremulous ballad "My True Love," backed by his vocal group, the Chantones. Flip it over, however, and you have the hauling rocker "Leroy," all about some wacked-out tough guy who's content to remain behind the bars of his local jail.

Scott's pronounced emphasis on acoustic guitar distinguishes atmospheric rockers like "Goodbye Baby," "Go Wild Little Sadie," "Midgie," and "Geraldine." But his principal pop success came with tears-in-your-beer country-based ballads—"What in the World's Come Over You" and "Burning Bridges" were massive smashes on Top Rank in 1960, and he recorded an entire album's worth of Hank Williams covers for the firm the same year.

Scott continued to vacillate between cowboy crooner and rough-edged rocker throughout the '60s, recording for Capitol and Groove. He still occasionally turns up on the oldies circuit, and he still looks and sounds like a man you seriously don't want to mess with. —*Bill Dahl*

Classic Scott / Bear Family ✦✦✦

○ **Greatest Hits** / Curb ✦✦✦✦

This collects the cream of Scott's late-'50s hits. —*Dan Heilman*

Scratch Acid

Group, Alternative Pop/Rock, Hardcore

The Austin, TX, post-hardcore noise group Scratch Acid laid the groundwork for much of the distorted, grinding alternative punk rockers of the '90s. Formed in 1982, the band originally featured Steve Anderson (vocals), David Wm. Sims (guitar), Brett Bradford (guitar), David Yow (bass), and Rey Washam (drums). Anderson was soon kicked out of the group and the band performed as an instrumental outfit for a short while. Yow moved to vocals and the band released a self-titled EP in 1984. Two years later, they released the full-length *Just Keep Eating* and the scathing *Berserker* EP. Following a long tour that took them through America and Europe, Scratch Acid split in May of 1987. Sims and Washam joined with Steve Albini to form the consciously caustic Rapeman. After Rapeman split, Sims reunited with David Yow to form the Jesus Lizard in 1989, which picked up where Scratch Acid left off. —*Stephen Thomas Erlewine*

Scratch Acid / 1984 / Rabid Cat ✦✦

Just Keep Eating / 1986 / Rabid Cat ✦✦✦

○ **Berserker** / 1987 / Touch & Go ✦✦✦✦
Loud, crazed, and fast. Cool and corrosive! —*John Dougan*

● **Greatest Gift** / 1991 / Touch & Go ✦✦✦✦

The Screaming Blue Messiahs

Group, Alternative Pop/Rock, Hard Rock
This band is very high on my "whatever happened to…" list. At times they played with such ferocity and complete over-the-top abandon that it was easy to proclaim them one of the best English bands in ages. But after three records (all very good) and about five years together (1984-89), they vanished without a trace—a mystery that's never been solved to my satisfaction. Led by bald, bullet-headed guitarist/singer Bill Carter (who looked a little like British actor Bob Hoskins), the Messiahs specialized in loud, rampaging, rockabilly-tinged sonic bomblets of songs. Carter wielded his instrument like a cross between Wilko Johnson and Pete Townshend; he was a deft soloist, but it was his tricky, complex rhythm playing that gave the band sheet after sheet of supercharged sound for a foundation. As impressive was his voice: at times comically bawling, other times mumbling and imperceptible; in the course of a verse, Carter could sound righteously indignant, or suddenly frightened and confused. Add to this terse, highly imagistic songs, mostly about American iconography and popular culture (cars, guns, the Flintstones), and it made for extreme, confrontational, and very, very exciting rock & roll.
There was a significant enough buzz generated from their first EP (*Good & Gone*) that Elektra signed them for their debut, and *Gun Shy* was a compelling debut. With Carter's ferocity barely contained (and even when it is, you can hear him seethe), *Gun-Shy* practically exploded from the get-go and was a much-needed tonic to the faux-soul and nth-generation synth-pop England was delivering at the time. Supporting the record with a series of great live shows didn't hurt either, and the Messiahs were staring next-big-thing-dom square in the face. The sophomore disc, *Bikini Red*, was even better. Packing a ferocious wallop accentuated by the production of famed English producer Vic Maile (Dr. Feelgood, Motorhead), and the goofy "I Wanna Be a Flintstone" (along with an equally goofy video) made them flavor of the second on MTV. But things seemed to be stalling, and by the time LP number three, *Totally Religious*, was released, it seemed as though the zeitgeist had passed the Messiahs by. Too bad, because they were as raucous and unpredictable as anything that had come since the early days of punk. —*John Dougan*

Good & Gone / 1984 / Big Beat ✦✦✦

Gun Shy / 1986 / Elektra ✦✦
Starting off with the hyperactive pub-rock sound of "Wild Blue Yonder," this is a great debut record. Taking its cues from punk rock, the Messiahs crank up the intensity with songs like "Smash the Marketplace" and the ominous "Let's Go Out to the Woods Tonight." If *Gun-Shy* stumbles, it's probably because it's a tad restrained (given the energy, volume and power these guys generated live), as if it were assumed that audiences simply might not be able to handle it all at once. Still, that's a minor complaint. This record will knock you out. —*John Dougan*

● **Bikini Red** / 1987 / Elektra ✦✦✦✦
The Messiahs' follow up to *Gun-Shy* was this devastating hunk of noise, which didn't pull any punches when it came to raw emotion and intensity. Side One, especially, is a rave-up from the gut-bustin' raunch of "Sweet Water Pools" to the closer "Big Brother Muscle." As always, Carter's obsessions are a little hard to understand, but the images and lyric fragments fly at you like shards of

broken glass; you'll remember when they hit you. "I Wanna Be a Flintstone" kicks off Side Two, and it remains as funky and funny as it was the first time I heard it. Great production work by Vic Maile (RIP). —*John Dougan*

Totally Religious / 1989 / Elektra ✦✦✦
The final chunk of squalling guitar rant from the Messiahs doesn't reach the relentless highs of *Bikini Red*, but it's pure mania nonetheless, and a sure shot for those who lapped up the first two waxings. The titles alone ("All Gassed Up" and "Four Engines Burning [Over the USA]") clue you in that this is no mellow fest. My suggestion is, get 'em all and triple your fun. —*John Dougan*

Live in Concert / ROIR ✦✦✦

Screaming Trees

Group, Alternative Pop/Rock, Hard Rock, Psychedelic
Putting their post-punk guitar noise within traditional hard-rock song structure, the Screaming Trees crafted a new form of psychedelia. Instead of the long, spacy trips of the late '60s, the band took the sonic explorations of indie guitar bands and used it for a mind-altering journey instead of expressions of aggression. Their late '80s releases on SST are raw, on the level of the label's other groups but trading angst for a drug-inspired mysticism that is too realistic and gritty for the Screaming Trees to be called hippies. When the band signed to a major label in the early '90s, some of the rough edges in their sound were smoothed out, yet they continued to produce some fine hard rock, incorporating more traditional rock styles (like the country-tinged "Dollar Bill") that kept the band's sound from growing stale. —*Stephen Thomas Erlewine*

Clairvoyance / 1986 / Velvetone ✦✦✦

○ **Even If and Especially When** / 1987 / SST ✦✦✦✦
The Screaming Trees were still trying to define their style on their second album, *Even If and Especially When*, but that makes it one of their most intriguing and exciting efforts. —*Stephen Thomas Erlewine*

Invisible Lantern / 1988 / SST ✦✦✦
Solid neo-psychedelic pop. —*Robert Gordon*

Buzz Factory / 1989 / SST ✦✦✦

○ **Uncle Anesthesia** / 1991 / Epic ✦✦✦✦
Major-label bucks don't detract from their punch. —*Robert Gordon*

● **Anthology: SST Years** / 1991 / SST ✦✦✦✦
A scalding collection of their finest moments from the late '80s. —*Stephen Thomas Erlewine*

Sweet Oblivion / Mar. 1992 / Epic ✦✦✦
The Screaming Trees' first album on Columbia is a step down from *Uncle Anesthesia*, but when the band kicks their '90s psychedelic hard-rock into gear on "Dollar Bill" and the spectacular "Nearly Lost You," the shortcomings of the rest of the album are easy to ignore. —*Stephen Thomas Erlewine*

Scritti Politti

Group, New Wave, Dance-Pop, Pop/Rock
An early synth-pop band, Scritti Politti was formed in 1977 by Welshman Green Gartside (b. Jun 22, 1956). Over the years, Scritti Politti has also included Nial Jinks (bass), Tom Morley (drums), David Gamson (keyboards), and Fred Maher (drums), and produced polished pop/funk efforts like *Cupid & Psyche 85* and *Provision*. —*Scott Bultman*

Songs to Remember / 1982 / Rough Trade ✦✦✦
Scritti Politti's debut album was an infectious set of catchy, well-crafted pop songs that demonstrate Green Gartside's talent for deceptively simple hooks and melodies. —*Stephen Thomas Erlewine*

● **Cupid & Psyche 85** / 1985 / Warner Brothers ✦✦✦✦
On their second album, Scritti Politti essentially was Green Gartside, who directed drummer Fred Maher, keyboardist David Gamson, and a multitude of studio musicians through a state-of-the-art, immaculately constructed set of catchy, synth-pop on *Cupid & Psyche 85*. The results are as impressive as *Songs to Remember*, and produced the hit singles "Perfect Way" and "Wood Beez (Pray like Aretha Franklin)." —*Stephen Thomas Erlewine*

Provision / 1988 / Warner Brothers ✦✦

Seal

Soul, Dance-Pop, Pop/Rock
Seal's mix of classic soul melodies and contemporary dance

rhythms and instrumentation made him a pop star after the release of his debut album in 1991. "Crazy," his Top Ten hit single, and the dance hit "Killer" are the best examples of his fusion of soulful pop and '90s club culture and sound. —*Stephen Thomas Erlewine*

○ **Seal [91]** / 1991 / Sire ✦✦✦✦
This debut album features great dance music, some acoustic tunes, and moody ballads, highlighted by the hit singles "Crazy" and "Killer." —*John Book*

● **Seal [94]** / 1994 / Sire ✦✦✦✦
This self-titled second album continues Seal's richly produced style of dance-influenced pop with a soul. Themes of unconditional love, compassion, and spirituality prevail throughout. A fine album, it includes the hit "Prayer for the Dying." —*Rick Clark*

Seals & Crofts

Group, Singer-Songwriter, Pop
The '70s were big years for this soft acoustic-pop duo, who had previously enjoyed success with the late-'50s/early-'60s group, the Champs (remember "Tequila"?). From 1971 to 1978, Jim Seals (b. Oct 17, 1941) and Dash Crofts (b. Aug 14, 1940) charted 14 times with hits like "Summer Breeze" (#6), "Diamond Girl" (#6), "Hummingbird" (#20), "We May Never Pass This Way Again" (#21), "I'll Play for You" (#18), "You're the Love" (#18), and "Get Closer" (#6).
Besides their pleasant tenor harmonies, both of them were multi-instrumentalists, showcasing instruments like mandolin and fiddle on some of their material. —*Rick Clark*

Year of Sunday / 1972 / Warner Brothers ✦✦✦
○ **Summer Breeze** / 1972 / Warner Brothers ✦✦✦✦
○ **Diamond Girl** / 1973 / Warner Brothers ✦✦✦✦
● **Greatest Hits** / 1975 / Warner Brothers ✦✦✦✦
This album has all their hits, including "Summer Breeze," "Hummingbird," "We May Never Pass This Way (Again)," "Diamond Girl," and "When I Meet Them." —*Dan Heilman*

Seam

Group, Alternative Pop/Rock
Seam began as a trio out of Chapel Hill, North Carolina, with Sooyoung Park (guitars, vocals) and Lexi Mitchell (bass) of Bitch Magnet and Mac McCaughan of Superchunk (drums). Their first album *Headsparks*, released in 1992, was filled with the slow, affecting melodies and vocals that would become their trademark. After the release of that record, McCaughan left the group to pursue Superchunk full-time, and the rest of Seam moved headquarters to Chicago. Bob Rising replaced McCaughan and Craig White joined on as an additional guitarist, turning Seam into a quartet. 1993's *The Problem With Me* featured this new lineup and slightly more upbeat sounds. *Are You Driving Me Crazy*, released in 1995, features an entirely lineup except Park (the band currently consists of drummer Chris Manfrin, bassist William Shin, and guitarist Reg Shrader) but continues in the line of moody and challenging Seam releases, making their musical quality a constant in a constantly changing band. —*Heather Phares*

Headsparks / 1992 / Homestead ✦✦✦
● **The Problem with Me** / 1993 / Touch & Go ✦✦✦✦

The Searchers

Group, British Invasion, Power Pop/Anglo-Pop, Pop/Rock
Founded in 1957 by John McNally (guitar/vocals), the Searchers were originally one of thousands of skiffle groups formed in the wake of Lonnie Donegan's success with "Rock Island Line." The Searchers' immediate competitors included bands such as the Wreckers and the Confederates, both led by Michael Pender (guitar, vocals), and the Martinis, led by Tony Jackson (guitar/vocals). By 1959, McNally and Pender were working together as a duet; later in the year, Jackson joined as the lead vocalist. After drummer Norman McGarry left the Searchers he was replaced by Chris Crummy, who quickly renamed himself Chris Curtis. Other changes were in the works as Jackson built and learned to play a customized bass guitar. Learning his new job on the four-stringed instrument proved too difficult to permit him to continue singing lead, and McNally and Pender brought in a fifth member, Johnny Sandon (b. Billy Beck). Johnny Sandon & the Searchers lasted from 1960 through February of 1962, and were extremely popular on the dance hall and club circuit in Liverpool. Sandon cut out for a career on his own, with another band called the Remo Four in early 1962.

Meanwhile, the Searchers, now a quartet with Jackson once again lead singer, became one of the top acts on the Liverpool band scene, playing textured renditions of American R&B, rock & roll, country-and-western, soul, and rockabilly. The group was signed to Pye Records in mid-1963 and their first single, a cover of the Drifters' "Sweets for My Sweet," was released in August of 1963, hitting number one on the British charts. While the Beatles quickly outdistanced all comers, the Searchers did, indeed, go to the top of the charts with two of their next three singles, "Needles And Pins" and "Don't Throw Your Love Away." Another record, "Sugar And Spice," written by their producer Tony Hatch under the pseudonym Fred Nightingale, stalled at the number two spot. Over the next nine months, the band staked out a sound that was one of the most distinctive in a rock scene crawling with hundreds of bands. Their music was built around the sound of a crisply played 12-string guitar, coupled with strong lead vocals and carefully, sometimes exquisitely arranged harmonies, so that they could credibly cover American R&B standards like "Love Potion No. 9" or Phil Spector-based girl group pop like "Be My Baby." Their 1964 singles included a venture into folk-rock before the genre had been "invented" in the press, in the form of a cover of Malvina Reynolds' "What Have They Done To the Rain." Interestingly, their 12-string guitar sound would become a key ingredient in the success of the Byrds, who even took the riff from "Needles And Pins" and transformed it into the main riff of "Feel A Whole Lot Better."

In July of 1964, with the group riding the upper reaches of the British charts, and with their third album in nine months in release, it was announced that Tony Jackson was leaving the Searchers to form his own band, and would be replaced by Frank Allen, who had been playing bass with Cliff Bennett & the Rebel Rousers. The turning point for the band came in 1965, as the British and international fascination with the Liverpool sound faded away. The Searchers began casting their net wider for material to cover, in addition to coming up with one original hit, the Curtis/Pender-authored "He's Got No Love." By the beginning of 1966, the group's string of chart hits seemed to have run out, and Chris Curtis exited in early 1966, claiming to have become exhausted from the group's constant touring.

The Searchers, with Johnny Blunt on drums, continued working and had their last hit, "Have You Ever Loved Somebody," which barely cracked the Top 50 in October of 1966. The group continued working, however, playing clubs and cabarets in England and Europe. Blunt exited at the end of the 1960s, but was replaced by Billy Adamson, and this line-up of the Searchers continued intact until the mid-1980s, working for 35 weeks a year throughout Europe with an occasional U.S. visit. Although they played as part of Richard Nader's "Rock 'n Roll Revival" shows, they never became an "oldies" act, always adding new material, including originals and covers of work by songwriters such as Neil Young to their sets, and in 1972, the band cut a new single ("Desdemona") and an album for British RCA.

At the end of the 1970s, their recording fortunes were revived once again as Seymour Stein, the head of Sire Records, signed the Searchers for two albums. Those records, *The Searchers* and *Love's Melodies*, were the best work the group ever did, highlighted by achingly beautiful yet vibrant and forceful playing and singing, and an unerring array of memorable hooks and melodies. Those two albums were followed by a series of tracks recorded for their original label, Pye Records, in the early 1980s. The group held their audience well into the 1980s, playing before crowds of as large as 15,000 along one U.S. tour. In 1985, after playing together for 26 years, Pender and McNally split up, with McNally continuing to lead the Searchers (with Adamson and Allen, with Spencer James added on second guitar and vocals), while Pender formed Mike Pender's Searchers, consisting of Chris Black (guitar, vocals), Barry Cowell (bass, vocals), and Steve Carlyle (drums, vocals). Both groups have toured extensively and the Searchers under McNally have recorded on occasion. —*Bruce Eder*

Sugar & Spice / 1963 / Castle ✦✦✦
The Searchers' 1963 debut LP was typical of most early British Invasion albums, built around one hit ("Sugar And Spice," a number-one hit in the U.K.) and eleven covers of American rock & roll standards. This wasn't destined to be remembered as an artistic statement along the lines of *With the Beatles*, but it's better than

the average period artifact, due to the group's always enjoyable harmonies and arrangements. Actually, nearly half of the tracks are first-rate. Their energetic rave-up of the Coasters' "Ain't That Just like Me" was actually a minor U.S. hit; "All My Sorrows" was an excellent arrangement of a Glenn Yarborough song that foreshadowed folk-rock; and "Hungry for Love" has the irresistibly saccharine appeal of Gerry & the Pacemakers' early hits. —*Richie Unterberger*

Meet the Searchers / 1963 / Castle ✦✦
The Searchers' second LP is arguably the most dispensable of their early albums now available on CD. "Sweets For My Sweet," the cover of the Drifters song, gave the band their second number-one single in Britain. That worthy cover version leads off the album, followed by their fine rendition of the obscure R&B song "Alright" (actually covered in turn by a number of garage bands) and "Love Potion #9," which would turn out to be their biggest U.S. hit a year later, though it was never issued as a single in Britain. It's all downhill from then on, with routine covers of hits like "Money," "Stand By Me," "Da Doo Ron Ron," and "Twist And Shout" which aren't going to make anyone forget the originals, or for that matter the Beatles' own versions of "Money" and "Twist And Shout." Their neatly arranged covers of "Where Have All The Flowers Gone" and the Everly Brothers' "Since You Broke My Heart" are decent, if not earthshaking. —*Richie Unterberger*

○ **It's the Searchers** / 1964 / Castle ✦✦✦✦
Perhaps the best studio album by a band that is really best represented by greatest hit collections. This 1964 LP includes the classic hits "Needles And Pins" and "Don't Throw Your Love Away." It also features some of their best LP cuts, on which they applied their famed harmonies to American material that was both strong and obscure. The best of these covers are Bacharach/David's "This Empty Space" (originally by Dionne Warwick), the Jackie DeShannon-penned "Can't Help Forgiving You," the Drifters' "I Count The Tears," the folkish "Sea Of Heartbreak," and "Where Have You Been" (which was also part of the Beatles' repertoire during their Hamburg days). The harder-rocking songs don't lend themselves as well to the group's talents, which always (with some notable exceptions) lay more in the folk-rock and Merseybeat direction than R&B/rockabilly. —*Richie Unterberger*

Take Me for What I'm Worth / 1965 / PRT ✦✦
The Searchers were not only slipping in popularity by the time of this release, but were also slipping considerably behind the prevailing musical trends of the times. Maybe that's why they offered more original tunes (four) than usual. Still, the group sounded pretty much like they always did in the mid-'60s, though this is perhaps one of their weaker albums. Their interpretation of P.F. Sloan's anthemic protest folk-rock title track is good, and gave the group their final British Top 20 hit. But, as usual, their R&B covers (of Fats Domino and Marvin Gaye) are inoffensively second-rate and dated, and the originals equally inoffensive and unmemorable. Their cover of the Ronettes' "Be My Baby" is competent but ill-advised; nothing's going to compete with the original. The harmonies and arrangements are never less than pleasant and professional, but even big fans of the group will count this among their lesser relics. It does, however, include a couple of their better album tracks: a cover of the obscure Jackie DeShannon composition "Each Time" and, especially, a fine acoustic reading of Ian Tyson's "Four Strong Winds." —*Richie Unterberger*

Second Take / 1972 / RCA ✦✦
If you actually find this record, consider yourself lucky. Cut by the band with their longest-standing lineup (drummer Billy Adamson replacing Chris Curtis), the material still sings, though the remakes of the early hits lacks the crispness and punch of the originals. And it features their early-'70s bid for chart success, "Desdemona." —*Bruce Eder*

○ **The Searchers** / 1979 / Castle ✦✦✦✦
○ **Love Melodies** / 1981 / Sire ✦✦✦✦
These two albums (*The Searchers* and *Love Melodies*) represent the Searchers at their peak as a recording outfit, having maintained their original mid-'60s emphasis on excellent harmonies and crisply played guitars but also absorbed lessons from such '70s pub-rockers as Brinsley Schwarz and roots-rock expert Dave Edmunds. The material is some of the most beautiful recorded anywhere in this era, and anyone lucky enough to spot a copy of either of these records—neither of which has yet shown up on compact disc—should grab them. —*Bruce Eder*

Silver Searchers / 1984 / PRT ✦✦
The best "best-of" on the band done up to the mid-'80s, with decent if not too extensive notes and fair sound. This collection was supplanted by Rhino's *Greatest Hits* and *The Searchers' 30th Anniversary Collection* in the early '90s. —*Bruce Eder*

● **Greatest Hits** / 1985 / Rhino ✦✦✦✦
The best American best-of on the band, and the most desirable for those on a budget, with superior sound to the *Silver Searchers* collection. —*Bruce Eder*

Play the System: Rarities, Oddities & Flipsides / 1987 / PRT ✦✦✦
Exactly what the title says: 18 tracks from 1963-67, including 14 non-LP B-sides, three non-LP A-sides, and the odd 1964 EP-only cut "The System," which was used in a 1964 film. The ten songs on Side One are a pleasure for fans of the early Searchers sound, and also serve as a showcase for the group's songwriting talents, as all but one are originals. Rarely surfacing on album, let alone on A-sides, it was only on B-sides that the band deigned to (or was allowed to) pen their own material. It's not like these are brilliant works on the level of Lennon-McCartney or Ray Davies, but they're very pleasant numbers highlighting the Searchers' strengths: melodies, harmonies, and clean arrangements. "It's All Been a Dream" and "Saturday Night Out" are good, energetic Merseybeat tunes, "This Feeling Inside" recalls the early Hollies, "Don't Hide It Away" is a good moody, downbeat tune, and "Till I Met You" an exquisite ballad. Side Two is a different story, showing the group trying to keep apace of '60s trends toward more sophisticated lyrics and arrangements with far less success than, say, the Hollies. It's not so much that the group weren't up to the task as performers; it's simply that the material (all dating from 1966-67, except the closing track "The System") is weak. The collection, with fine liner notes from Brian Hogg, can nonetheless be unreservedly recommended to Searchers fans on the strength of the first side alone. —*Richie Unterberger*

EP Collection / 1989 / See For Miles ✦✦✦

German, French + Rare Recordings / 1990 / ✦✦
While this anthology does collectors a service by gathering many of the group's rarest recordings in one place, you've really got to be a hard-bitten fanatic to find this import worthwhile. This 24-song compilation includes the group's German versions of hits like "Sugar And Spice" and "Goodbye My Love," as well as their (poorly accented) French renditions of "Don't Throw Your Love Away" and "Sugar And Spice" (again). A half-dozen other German and French re-recordings of 1963-64 B-sides and album tracks, some quite obscure even in their original English versions, are included as well. As you might expect, the group simply rerecorded their vocals over the original backing tracks for the Continental market, which most likely preferred the English versions anyway. The CD also includes drummer Chris Curtis' rare and forgettable 1966 single, as well as a clumsy medley of their greatest hits and ten dreadful, undocumented tunes that date from well after their mid-'60s heyday. Fans looking for decent rare Searchers should seek out the *Play The System* LP, which compiles '60s B-sides and rarities of considerably higher quality. —*Richie Unterberger*

○ **30th Anniversary Collection** / 1992 / Sequel ✦✦✦✦
Although it's missing one or two fairly strong tracks, this three-CD, 84-song set is a pretty definitive collection of the group's best '60s material, for those who want to go beyond the greatest hits. Besides including all of their key A- and B-sides, it has an entire disc of their best '60s album tracks. The rarities disc includes foreign-language versions, outtakes, mid-'60s BBC performances, and solo discs by Tony Jackson and Chris Curtis. Highlights here include an alternate take of "Someday We're Gonna Love Again," a BBC version of "Blowin' in the Wind," and the previously unreleased "Once Upon a Time" (recorded by Dusty Springfield). The package includes liner notes, discography, and a family tree. —*Richie Unterberger*

Live at the Star Club / 1994 / PolyGram ✦✦✦
Of all the British bands that recorded at the Star Club in 1962/63, the Searchers gave the best performance—polished, exciting, and utterly professional, lacking the finely honed 12-string guitar sound that their subsequent hits would display but still a fine testament to their early work and history. —*Bruce Eder*

Sebadoh

Group, Alternative Pop/Rock
After leaving Dinosaur Jr., Lou Barlow formed Sebadoh. Instead of

working like a traditional rock band and collaborating on each song, Sebadoh acts as a backing band for the material of each individual band member. Consequently, their albums can be a little schizophrenic, covering all kinds of indie guitar-rock from R.E.M.-style pop to Dinosaur-style melancholy and Sonic Youth sonic explosions, all recorded in ragged lo-fidelity. Fortunately, each member is a talented songwriter, managing to wear their influences without sounding exactly like any of them; they are one of the most unique bands of the early '90s. Sebadoh's artistic breadth makes them critical and cult favorites; their jagged playing and oblique songwriting guarantees that they will never cross over into the mainstream, but that has never seemed a concern of the band. —*Stephen Thomas Erlewine*

III / 1991 / Homestead ✦✦✦

Smash Your Head on the Punk Rock / 1992 / Sub Pop ✦✦✦
Smash Your Head on the Punk Rock is a low-fi masterpiece, full of noise and subversive pop songs. —*Stephen Thomas Erlewine*

○ **Bubble & Scrape** / 1993 / Sub Pop ✦✦✦✦
Nearly as impressive as *Smash Your Head, Bubble & Scrape* shows that Sebadoh continues to grow as songwriters, turning out a number of rough, fractured pop gems. —*Stephen Thomas Erlewine*

● **Bakesale** / 1994 / Sub Pop ✦✦✦✦
With *Bakesale*, Sebadoh has trimmed down to Lou Barlow, Jason Loewenstein, and Bob Fay, with Barlow and Loewenstein taking on the lion's share of the songwriting. Maybe the change in personnel was needed, because *Bakesale* is their most accessible, concise work to date. Without the noise that usually envelops their records, the solid, unconventional pop songwriting of Barlow and Loewenstein shines through brightly. —*Stephen Thomas Erlewine*

Freed Weed / Positive ✦✦
The epitome of lo-fi, these 47 skeletal bits-of-songs were recorded by Lou Barlow and Eric Gaffney long before their Sebadoh days. Collects their first two self-released cassettes. Only for the curious or the collector. —*John Bush*

John Sebastian

b. Mar. 17, 1944, New York City
Singer-Songwriter, Folk-Rock, Pop/Rock
Born in New York City, the son of a classical harmonica player, John Sebastian grew up in the Greenwich Village coffeehouses and was a popular sideman to various folk artists prior to forming the folk-rock band, the Lovin' Spoonful, for which he served as lead singer and songwriter in the mid-'60s. When the Spoonful broke up, Sebastian went solo, appearing at the Woodstock Festival in 1969 and releasing the Top 20 *John B. Sebastian* album in 1970. Subsequent efforts were less successful, but in 1976 Sebastian scored a number one hit with "Welcome Back," the theme song from the TV series *Welcome Back, Kotter*. Sebastian continues to tour and play on occasional sessions; he released his first album since the '70s in 1993. —*William Ruhlmann*

○ **John B. Sebastian** / 1970 / MGM ✦✦✦✦
A strong debut solo album spotlighting Sebastian's warm voice and optimistic, melodic folk-pop songwriting. —*William Ruhlmann*

The Four of Us / 1971 / Reprise ✦✦✦

○ **Cheapo-Cheapo Productions Presents** / 1971 / Reprise ✦✦✦✦
Cheapo-Cheapo Productions Presents is an exuberant solo appearance at which Sebastian's humor and wit are at their apex. A wide variety of songs, from old folk-blues standards to Spoonful favorites. Makes you wish you'd been there. —*William Ruhlmann*

Tarzana Kid / 1974 / Reprise ✦✦✦

Welcome Back / 1976 / Reprise ✦✦✦

● **The Best of John Sebastian** / 1989 / Rhino ✦✦✦✦
A 16-track selection from Sebastian's solo albums from 1970 to 1976, including the hit "Welcome Back." —*William Ruhlmann*

Tar Beach / 1993 / Shanachie ✦✦✦
A low-key comeback album from Sebastian, showing that his melodic folk-pop hasn't lost its charm in the seventeen years since he recorded his last record. —*Stephen Thomas Erlewine*

Jon Secada

Urban, Pop
With only one album, Jon Secada became one of the biggest adult

contemporary artist of the '90s, selling over six million albums worldwide. Secada's smooth mix of R&B, pop, and Latin music appealed to a number of different audiences. What separates him from the overly slick sound of most adult contemporary artists are his considerable songwriting skills; he's able to write sweet, affecting ballads that rarely seem contrived. As well as becoming a huge pop star, Secada is one of the hottest Latin artists recording in the '90s; his Spanish language album *Otro Dia Mas Sin Verte* was *Billboard*'s number one Latin album in 1992 and won a Grammy for Best Latin Pop album. —*Stephen Thomas Erlewine*

● **Jon Secada** / 1992 / SBK ✦✦✦✦
Secada, formerly a backup singer for Gloria Estefan, provides an impressive mix of appealing Top Ten dance singles and powerful ballads in his English album debut. Notable cuts from this self-titled album include "Just Another Day" and "Angel," both of which have accompanying Spanish versions on the release, with Estefan and Secada collaborating on their lyrical content. Estefan also provides background vocals on "Otro Dia Mas Sin Verte," the Spanish version of "Just Another Day." If these titles are any indication of his future work, Secada will definitely be an impact artist to look for in the coming years. —*Ashley S. Battel*

Heart, Soul & a Voice / May 24, 1994 / SBK ✦✦✦
While there aren't as many obvious singles on Jon Secada's second album, his voice sounds better than ever, making it a worthwhile sophomore effort. —*Stephen Thomas Erlewine*

Secret Affair

Group, Power Pop/Anglo-Pop
Secret Affair, consisting of Ian Page (vocals, trumpet, piano, organ), David Cairns (guitar, backing vocals), Dennis Smith (bass, backing vocals), and Seb Shelton (drums), formed in 1978. Taking their inspiration from the Jam, the group was quickly seen as one of the shining stars of the mod-revival movement of the late '70s. They received their most important early exposure by supporting the Jam on small-scale tours in England and followed with several mod package tours with bands such as the Purple Hearts. Their first single, "Time for Action," was the perfect youth anthem for the time and certainly one the most memorable and successful of the movement. The band released its first album, *Glory Boys*, late in 1979 on their own label, I-Spy (distributed by Arista in the U.K. and Sire in the U.S.). Both the album and their subsequent singles charted but by the time 1980's *Behind Closed Doors* was released, the revival was dissolving and they were too firmly rooted in the movement to change their arrogant stance. The band began to break up when drummer Seb Shelton left in 1980. They held on until 1982, releasing one more album, *Business as Usual*, to an uninterested public; the members went their separate ways shortly after its release. —*Chris Woodstra*

● **Glory Boys** / 1979 / Sire ✦✦✦✦
Glory Boys clearly placed Secret Affair at the top of the mod-revival's third wave. The songs are top notch, building on rather than ripping off the Jam's sound—a refreshing change from the second and third rate sound-alikes the revival usually produced. Ian Page's arrogant, self-important lyrics are a little too much in places, but overall, this was a promising debut. —*Chris Woodstra*

Behind Closed Doors / 1980 / I Spy ✦✦✦
Unfortunately, Secret Affair couldn't match the bite of *Glory Boys* with the follow-up. They've gotten better with the formula sound but the songs really don't measure up this time out. —*Chris Woodstra*

Business As Usual / 1982 / Arista ✦✦
The aptly-titled third album shows a band that held on for too long without progressing. —*Chris Woodstra*

Neil Sedaka

b. 1939
Pop, Pop/Rock
An excellent songwriter, Sedaka came from a doo-wop background (working with an early version of the Tokens). He sharpened his skills with Juilliard training, and enjoyed much success with a number of pre-Beatles-era hits. Though the British Invasion stopped the flow of hits, he re-entered the charts in the mid-'70s with a string of chart-toppers that extended into the following decade. A major influence on Elton John, Sedaka continues performing today. —*Cub Koda*

● **All-Time Greatest Hits** / 1975 / RCA ✦✦✦✦
Includes "Calendar Girl," "Happy Birthday, Sweet Sixteen,"
"Breaking Up Is Hard to Do," and other sprightly pop numbers. —
Dan Heilman

○ **Oh! Carol & Other Hits** / 1990 / RCA ✦✦✦✦
This early-'60s album with the title track and other pop material is
one step removed from White doo wop. —*Dan Heilman*

○ **All-Time Greatest Hits, Vol. 2** / Aug. 1991 / RCA ✦✦✦✦
This companion volume to the above is equally fine. —*Dan Heilman*

The Seeds

Group, Psychedelic, Garage Rock
The Seeds (formed in 1965 in Southern California) produced five
albums of magically limited garage-psychedelia extolling the
virtues of sex and drugs and drugs and sex. Sky Saxon, the band's
self-absorbed singer/songwriter, evidently understood arrested development quite well, making the Seeds records a pretty enjoyable
'60s punk sleazefest.

The urgent trashola snarl (and corny "Rawhide"-style backup
vocals) of "Pushin' Too Hard," it helped give them their only
hit. "Can't Seem to Make You Mine," probably their best song, was
later affectionately covered by Alex Chilton as the B-side of his
"Bangkok" single. Both of those songs can be found on their self-
titled debut. Even though subsequent albums recycled the basic
formula of the Seeds, their second album, *A Web of Sound*, is
worth checking out. —*Rick Clark*

Web of Sound / 1966 / GNP ✦✦✦
A more ambitious, but less successful venture into teenage rages
and lusts. —*Bruce Eder*

● **The Seeds** / 1966 / GNP ✦✦✦✦
Punk sneers, cheesy organ, and an attitude. A garage-band classic.
—*Bruce Eder*

● **Evil Hoodoo** / 1988 / Bam Caruso ✦✦✦✦
The only serious attempt at a best-of Seeds retrospective features
16 songs culled from their half-dozen or so '60s albums. Besides
"Pushin' Too Hard," it features their sole other hit single of any
magnitude ("Can't Seem To Make You Mine"), as well as other
fairly well-remembered cuts like "The Wind Blows Your Hair,"
"Tripmaker," "Falling Off The Edge Of My Mind," "Mr. Farmer,"
and "Up In Her Room." Non-converts to the Sky Saxon legend may
be excused for wondering what all the fuss is about: even distilled
to 16 cuts, the melodies and arrangements are almost inter-
minably monotonous. Comes with an extensive group history by
rock archivist Brian Hogg. —*Richie Unterberger*

Seefeel

Group, Techno
Seefeel began life on England's Too Pure label (PJ Harvey, Moon-
shake, Stereolab). After two EPs (collected on *Polyfusia*), *Quique*
appeared in the U.S. in early 1994 on Astralwerks. Mark Clifford
and company do use guitars, bass, and female vocals, but they are
looped over and over to create a repetitive but beautiful drone-
rock, not unlike Spacemen 3. Previously thought of as an indie-
band with electronic pretensions, Seefeel signed to Warp Records
in early 1995. —*John Bush*

Quique / 1993 / Astralwerks ✦✦✦
With titles like "Climactic Phase 3" and "Filter Dub," the songs on
Quique are precise works which begin with a tape loop of guitar
or bass, and slowly change with added instruments, some synth-
work, and vocal repetitions. —*John Bush*

● **Polyfusia** / 1994 / Astralwerks ✦✦✦✦
This album collects Seefeel's first two EPs, *More Like Space* and
Pure, Impure. Better than their album, *Polyfusia* also includes two
good remixes by Aphex Twin. —*John Bush*

The Seekers

Group, Pop, Folk-Rock
During the '60s, this quartet from Australia deftly bridged folk vo-
cal-ensemble work with shades of British Invasion pop. Their stirring harmonies and memorable melodies earned them a series of
big hits, as first the Seekers (on Capitol) and, with a totally different lineup, as the New Seekers on Elektra. Their biggest hits were
"Georgy Girl" (#2), "I'll Never Find Another You" (#4), and the #7
"I'd Like to Teach the World to Sing (In Perfect Harmony)," a song

that also became a theme song for a Coca-Cola ad campaign.
Their work on Capitol is their best. —*Rick Clark*

○ **Come the Day** / 1966 / Columbia ✦✦✦✦
Their best album, with their biggest hit and the Simon-Woodley
songs. Also includes a killer rendition of Tom Paxton's "The Last
Thing on My Mind." U.S. title is *Georgy Girl*. —*Bruce Eder*

● **Capitol Collectors Series** / 1992 / Capitol ✦✦✦✦
The Seekers' rich folky harmonies, fronted by the clear alto of Judith Durham, are given an excellent presentation on this 23-song
anthology. All of their Capitol hits are here, including "Georgy
Girl," "A World of Our Own," "Come the Day," and "I'll Never Find
Another You." Typical of *Capitol Collectors Series* reissues, this set
contains ample annotation, track info, and photos. —*Rick Clark*

○ **The Seekers** / EMI ✦✦✦✦
A compilation featuring over one hour of hits and key album
tracks on this British import. Completely comprehensive, with the
best sound ever. —*Bruce Eder*

Bob Seger

b. May 6, 1945
Rock & Roll, Pop/Rock
At his best, Detroit rocker Bob Seger has produced some incredibly clearheaded music speaking to and about the working class's
fleeting joys, shortchanged dreams, and grinding existence. Many
of the people who populate Seger's material possess some kind of
resolve and dignity. Seger grew up as one of these people, and he's
never really forgotten it. Musically, Seger's influences range from
Chuck Berry to Creedence Clearwater Revival, the Rolling Stones,
and Bob Dylan to Bruce Springsteen and the Eagles, all merged
together in a Heartland rock stew. Seger's first hit was the 1969
heavy soulful stomper "Ramblin' Gamblin' Man" (#17). For years
after that, he consistently landed regional Top Ten hits that never
saw the light of day anywhere else in the country. That was until
the release of 1976's *Live Bullet*, a great concert album that encapsulated Seger's career to that point with an impassioned delivery.
It became his first million-seller, charting at #34. His next two studio efforts, *Night Moves* (#8) and *Stranger in Town* (#4), were
artistic highlights. By this time, Seger had become a major arena
attraction. He stumbled on the mediocre *Against the Wind*, reducing once-effective sentiment to hack wordplay, but he regained his
focus on *The Distance*. His latest effort, *The Fire Inside*, is solid but
fails to mine any new territory. Blessed with a voice that could
sing the phone book and sound great, Seger has even scored hits
with his most pedestrian work. Nevertheless, he has created a
body of work that, at its best, celebrates the spirit of rock in the
face of mortality with a hard-won wisdom. —*Rick Clark*

○ **Ramblin' Gamblin' Man** / 1968 / Capitol ✦✦✦✦
The title track on Seger's Capitol debut is one of the all-time-great
rock & roll stompers with its bone-crunching 2- and 4-drum
groove and gospel-choir backup. Other highlights include the incredibly hard-rocking anti-war track "2 + 2 Equals ?," and "Down
Home," a rude harmonica-driven rocker that sports an absolutely
addled rhythm section. In spite of some cornball psychedelic-pe-
riod mixes, *Ramblin' Gamblin' Man*, with its reckless over-the-top
delivery, is Seger's hardest-rocking album. Throughout many of
these tracks, Seger wails like a banshee. Seger's later rock hits
sound absolutely tame next to this stuff. —*Rick Clark*

Noah / 1969 / Capitol ✦✦

Mongrel / 1970 / Capitol ✦✦✦

Back in '72 / 1973 / Reprise ✦✦

Smokin' O.P.'s / 1973 / Capitol ✦✦✦
Smokin' O.P.'s was a fine showcase for Seger's workmanlike rock
& roll approach. "Heavy Music," an original, became a huge Detroit hit. Other highlights included Seger's versions of such standards as "Bo Diddley," "Let It Rock," and "Turn on Your Lovelight."
—*Rick Clark*

○ **Seven** / 1974 / Capitol ✦✦✦✦

○ **Beautiful Loser** / 1975 / Capitol ✦✦✦✦
After several years of relative obscurity, Seger emerged with this
rather reflective effort. The hard-rocking "Katmandu," however,
was a substantial hit in the Midwest. —*Rick Clark*

○ **Live Bullet** / 1976 / Capitol ✦✦✦✦
A blistering live show from Cobo Hall, containing raucous ver-
sions of early material like "Nutbush City Limits" and "Get Out of
Denver" as highlights. —*Cub Koda*

★ **Night Moves** / 1976 / Capitol ◆◆◆◆◆
Seger's breakthrough album, a classic of blue-collar rock, features such standouts as the wistful "Mainstreet," the no-frills rock of "Rock and Roll Never Forgets," and the title track, a reflective coming-of-age masterpiece. Throughout, Seger believably details the characters in his songs with compassion. —*Rick Clark*

○ **Stranger in Town** / 1978 / Capitol ◆◆◆◆
It's not quite as strong as *Night Moves,* but *Stranger in Town* continues Seger's streak of great songwriting and performance. Highlights include the relentless rockers "Hollywood Nights" (number 12) and "Feel like a Number." Seger's facility with the ballads "Still the Same" (number four) and "We've Got Tonight" (number 13) produced substantial hits. —*Rick Clark*

Against the Wind / 1980 / Capitol ◆◆◆
Against the Wind became Seger's first number one album, producing the hits and key album-rock-radio tracks, "Fire Lake" (number six), "You'll Accomp'ny Me" (number 14), "The Horizontal Bop" (number 42) and the number five title cut. However, after two fine albums, Seger's lyrical abilities and melodic skills began to reveal a cookie-cutter sameness. His singing still had plenty of passion. —*Rick Clark*

Nine Tonight / 1981 / Capitol ◆◆◆
Features the title-track contribution to the *Urban Cowboy* movie soundtrack and an effective cover of "Trying to Live My Life Without You." —*Cub Koda*

○ **The Distance** / 1982 / Capitol ◆◆◆◆
The Distance was a strong rebound after the spotty *Against The Wind,* featuring his rocking Chuck Berry-like auto-worker's tribute, "Makin' Thunderbirds," the resolute rock anthem "Even Now," and a fine version of Rodney Crowell's "Shame on the Moon." —*Rick Clark*

Like a Rock / 1986 / Capitol ◆◆◆

The Fire Inside / Aug. 19, 1991 / Capitol ◆◆

● **Greatest Hits** / 1994 / Capitol ◆◆◆◆
For over twenty years, Bob Seger has been one of the best mainstream rock & rollers in America, developing a distinctive body of honest, hard-rocking songs. More songs that can be put on this single-disc set, unfortunately. While many of Seger's trademarks are here—"Turn the Page," "Old Time Rock N' Roll," "Night Moves"—there is no "Rock and Roll Never Forgets," "Katmandu," "Shame on the Moon," or any of his pulverizing early records, when he was as tough as fellow Michigan rockers the MC5 and the Stooges; this is one time when a double-disc set would have held enough quality material. Nevertheless, what is here is fine and contains enough first-rate material to satisfy most fans. —*Stephen Thomas Erlewine*

Selecter

Group, Ska-Revival
Despite being the band that got the least press during the ska revival of the early '80s, the Selecter, despite only recording one undeniably fine record, deserved better than they got. Hailing from Coventry, England, the same hometown as ska pals the Specials, the Selecter's secret weapon was lead singer Pauline Black, arguably the best lead singer of the ska revival, who gave the jumpy and jittery songs an edge that veered into haunting drama. Although they got off to a roaring start with their debut record, 1980's *Too Much Pressure,* the second record, *Celebrate the Bullet,* was a strained follow-up that led to the band's rapid demise.

Black spent some time singing solo, and eventually rejoined guitarist Neol Davis in a Selecter reunion in the early '90s that has seen them become dance club favorites. According to those attending recent Selecter shows, the vibe is strong and the music great. However, don't expect a recording renaissance any time soon. —*John Dougan*

● **Too Much Pressure** / 1980 / 2 Tone/Chrysalis ◆◆◆◆
At the time of its release, *Too Much Pressure* was relegated to second-class status behind the debut records by Madness and the Specials. Now it's easy to see that this record was the equal to the Specials record, and (I realize I'm getting into trouble here) better than the first (and second) Madness records. Pauline Black is the key and she makes songs like "On My Radio" and the title track classic chunks of Caribbean-influenced pop rather than mere stylistic mimicry. Much better that the weak second record, *Celebrate the Bullet,* or the 1989 anthology, *Selected Selecter Selections.* —*John Dougan*

Celebrate the Bullet / 1981 / 2 Tone/Chrysalis ◆◆
Celebrate the Bullet failed to live up to the promise of the band's debut. It has its moments but those can all be found on the collection, *Selected Selecter Selections.*—*Chris Woodstra*

○ **Selected Selecter Selections** / 1989 / 2 Tone/Chrysalis ◆◆◆◆
It features the greatest hits from their two studio albums. —*David Szatmary*

Out on the Streets / 1992 / Trojan ◆◆

Out in the Streets Again / 1994 / Triple X ◆◆

Sepultura

Group, Heavy Metal
Formed in Belo Horizonte, Brazil, in 1984, Sepultura includes Max Cavalera (guitar, vocals), Igor Cavalera (drums), Paulo Jr. (bass), and Andreas Kisser (guitar), who took over for Jairo T in 1987. Their name is the Portuguese word for grave. Their early work combined the compositional style of Metallica with the extreme sounds of the nascent death metal scene. Lyrically, they have been passionately preoccupied with the poor social and political conditions in Brazil, which makes them one of the few death metal bands with something to say. Their first recording, *Bestial Devastation,* was done with a Brazilian band called Overdose; it was badly recorded and badly circulated. A couple of albums, *Morbid Visions* and *Schizophrenia,* followed before the band signed with Roadrunner Records and came to international attention with *Beneath the Remains.* Their followup, *Arise,* proved to be their big breakthrough, becoming at that time the biggest-selling album in Roadrunner's history. 1993's *Chaos A.D.* became their highest-charting album, entering *Billboard'*s top 40, and was hailed as arguably the best death metal album thus far. In the summer of 1995, the band was preparing to go into the studio to record a followup album. —*Steve Huey*

Morbid Visions / 1986 / Roadrunner ◆◆
This was America's first listen to what Brazil had to offer in the world of thrash. Before this, most bands were only known through trading tapes or demos in the underground. The sound quality isn't too good, though. —*John Book*

Schizophrenia / 1987 / Roadrunner ◆◆◆
There's a little experimentation on this album. —*John Book*

○ **Beneath the Remains** / 1989 / Roadrunner ◆◆◆◆
Excellent thrash that immediately goes into the conciousness of the listener, this was the first metal band from Brazil to gain international acclaim. —*John Book*

○ **Arise** / Apr. 2, 1991 / Roadrunner ◆◆◆◆
Sepultura's breakthrough release still wears the band's Metallica influences proudly, featuring harmonized guitar lines and soft, non-distorted passages to go with some Kirk Hammett-style solos and extremely powerful grooves. And, of course, there are some sections taken at death metal's typical high-velocity tempos. Nothing really innovative appears here, but the band is intense, passionate, and energetic, and the music is quite well done. —*Steve Huey*

● **Chaos A.D.** / 1993 / Roadrunner/Epic ◆◆◆◆
Everything comes together for Sepultura on *Chaos A.D.* The band's strident political dissidence is more focused than ever. Death metal's standard thick, heavy guitars and hoarsely shouted vocals are here, but Sepultura draw on the influences of their native Brazil, audible in many of the rhythms and the acoustic instrumental "Kaiowas," to offer a much wider musical range than usual for the genre. The band's songwriting has become almost airtight, giving up the Metallica-esque passages and breakneck speed and concentrating instead on creating texture and dissonance. But it's the unbelievably powerful rhythmic base provided by Igor Cavalera that gives *Chaos A.D.* its knockout punch and helps make it one of the best metal albums ever, a remarkable achievement. —*Steve Huey*

The Sex Pistols

Group, Punk
The Sex Pistols may have only been together for two years in the late '70s, but they changed the face of popular music. Through their raw, nihilistic singles and violent performances, the band revolutionized the idea of what rock & roll could be. In England, the group was considered dangerous to the very fabric of society and were banned across the country; in America, they didn't have the same impact, but countless bands in both countries were in-

spired by the sheer sonic force of their music, while countless others were inspired by their independent, do-it-yourself ethics. Even if they didn't release any singles by themselves, there was an implicit independence in the way they played their music and handled their career. The band gave birth to the massive independent music underground in England and America that would soon include bands that didn't have a direct musical connection to the Sex Pistols' initial three-minute blasts of rage, but couldn't have existed without those singles.

Guitarist Steve Jones and drummer Paul Cook were regulars at a boutique owned by their manager, Malcolm McLaren; bassist Glen Matlock worked at the store. Vocalist John Lydon, who would later perform under Johnny Rotten, met the rest of the group at the shop and was asked to join the band. While the band played simple rock & roll loudly and abrasively, Rotten arrogantly sang of anarchy, abortion, violence, fascism, and apathy; without Rotten, the band wouldn't have been threatening to England's government—he provided the band's conceptual direction, calculated to be as confrontational and threatening as possible. The publicity caused by their caustic first single "Anarchy in the U.K." caused the band to be dropped by their record label, EMI. Matlock was fired before their next single "God Save the Queen," which was released on Virgin; it was banned by the BBC. Matlock's replacement was Sid Vicious, a street tough who, unlike the rest of the band, couldn't play his instrument.

After releasing one album in 1977, the band headed over to the U.S. for a tour in January of 1978; it lasted fourteen days. Rotten left the band after their show at San Francisco's Winterland Ballroom on January 14, heading back to New York; he would soon form Public Image Limited later that year. McLaren tried to continue the band but Cook and Jones soon turned against him. In the following years, an endless stream of outtakes, repackages, and live shows have appeared but their one proper album, *Never Mind the Bollocks—Here's the Sex Pistols* remains their most concise and effective record; without it, popular music would have been much different. —*Stephen Thomas Erlewine*

★ **Never Mind the Bollocks** / 1977 / Warner Brothers ✦✦✦✦✦
Never Mind the Bollocks (Here's the Sex Pistols) is a delightfully vulgar and viscerally pulverizing debut. Everything you need is here, including "God Save the Queen," "Pretty Vacant," "Holidays in the Sun," and "Anarchy in the U.K." —*John Floyd*

○ **The Great Rock & Roll Swindle** / 1979 / Warner Brothers ✦✦✦✦
The soundtrack to a muddled film from 1979, it's loaded with rubbish, but there are some live and studio cuts that should be heard. (Import) —*John Floyd*

○ **Flogging a Dead Horse** / 1980 / Virgin ✦✦✦✦
This collects the band's seven British singles. There are some duplicates with *Never Mind the Bullocks*, but the B-sides can't be found elsewhere. (British import) —*John Floyd*

Charlie Sexton

b. 1969, Austin, TX
Pop/Rock
Sexton was a Texas boy guitar wizard, playing behind Joe Ely by age 13 and going on to work with Bob Dylan, Keith Richards, Ron Wood, and former Eagle Don Henley. Sexton's good looks and technical wizardry had him pegged to be the next big thing coming out of Texas behind Stevie Ray Vaughan and the Fabulous Thunderbirds, but he was done in by over-produced albums and scathing reviews from the rock critics. He recently formed the band Archangels with members of Stevie Ray's Double Trouble. —*Cub Koda*

● **Pictures for Pleasure** / 1985 / MCA ✦✦✦✦
His debut album, with solid songs and playing. —*Cub Koda*

Charlie Sexton / 1989 / MCA ✦✦✦
An about-face, with more emphasis on Sexton's guitar playing and Texas roots. —*Cub Koda*

○ **Under The Wishing Tree** / 1995 / MCA ✦✦✦✦

The Shadows

Group, British Invasion, Pop/Rock
Originally Cliff Richard's backing band, this British quartet began recording on their own in 1960 and had a major hit with the instrumental "Apache." They were built around guitarists Hark Marvin and Bruce Welch, with an ever-changing rhythm section (Jet Harris and Tony Meehan, the original bassist and drummer, were

the most famous, and went on to success on their own in the early '60s). Often erroneously thought of as England's answer to the Ventures, the Shadows's sound was polished, crisp, clean, and metallic, making up for its inherent sterility and lack of soul with a knack for drawing out melodies in their most haunting form. They continue to record in the '90s. —*Bruce Eder*

● **20 Golden Greats** / 1977 / EMI ✦✦✦✦
As fine a cross-section of their best work that has been (or ever will be) assembled. Highlighted by "Apache," but with lots of other fun. (Import) —*Bruce Eder*

Shadows of Knight

Group, Garage Rock
"The Stones, Animals and Yardbirds took the Chicago Blues and gave it an English interpretation. We've taken the English version of the Blues and re-added a Chicago touch." The Shadows of Knight's self-description was fairly accurate. Although this mid-'60s garage band from the Windy City did not match the excellence of either their British or African-American idols, the teen energy of their recordings remains enjoyable, if not overwhelmingly original. The group took a tamer version of Them's classic "Gloria" into the American Top Ten in 1966, and also took a Yardbirdized version of Bo Diddley's "Oh Yeah" into the Top 40 the same year. Their patchy albums contained a few exciting R&B covers in the Yardbirds/Stones style and a few decent originals in the same vein. The group's original lineup splintered quickly, and the Shadows faded in the late '60s after briefly pursuing a more commercial pop sound. —*Richie Unterberger*

○ **Gloria** / 1966 / Dunwich ✦✦✦✦

Back Door Men / 1967 / Dunwich ✦✦✦

Shadows of Knight / 1969 / Super K ✦✦✦

○ **Gee-El-O-Are-I-Ay** / 1985 / Edsel ✦✦✦✦
Boils the Shadows' legacy down to 16 essential tracks. Contains "Gloria," "Oh Yeah," and the flop singles "Bad Little Woman" and "I'm Gonna Make You Mine," as well as the better tracks from their first two LPs, including the impressive originals "Light Bulb Blues" and "Gospel Zone." —*Richie Unterberger*

Raw 'N Alive at the Cellar, Chicago 1966! / 1992 / Sundazed ✦✦✦
This is one of the very few live garage band tapes from the mid-'60s of relatively decent sound quality (considering the standards of the era). The song selection of this set should also please fans of one of the most famed '60s garage bands, captured here at a club in their home turf of Chicago in December 1966. The 13 songs include live versions of many of the tunes from their first (and best) album, as well as a six-minute workout of their lone national hit "Gloria" and a couple of Solomon Burke covers. However, it's not essential if you already have the original albums, or the fine best-of compilation released in the U.K. on Edsel, *Gee-El-O-Are-I-Ay*. These versions are very close in arrangement to the officially released ones, but the performance is less accomplished, as it were, and the sound quality worse. An interesting artifact that nevertheless has little appeal beyond '60s garage collector circles, although the very brief quotes from the Mothers of Invention's "Help I'm A Rock" are most curious and unexpected. —*Richie Unterberger*

● **Dark Sides: The Best of Shadows of the Knight** / 1994 / Rhino ✦✦✦✦
More easily available to North Americans than the British Edsel best-of, but not necessarily an improvement. Adds some tracks from both the original lineup and their unimpressive, more pop-oriented singles from the late '60s, and has more comprehensive liner notes, but also omits a few decent covers that are on the U.K. compilation, particularly their smoking, over-the-top version of "I Just Want To Make Love To You." —*Richie Unterberger*

The Shaggs

Group, Alternative Pop/Rock
In 1969 the Shaggs, comprising three sisters, Dorothy, Betty, and Helen Wiggin, entered a Revere, MA, recording studio under the encouragement and financial support of their father, Austin Wiggin. The recording engineer, upon hearing the band, tactfully suggested that they weren't ready to be a recording unit, but their father insisted on catching the band on tape "while they were hot." The result of this session, their first album, was called *Philosophy of the World*. Their followup effort, the appropriately titled *Shaggs'*

Own Thing, actually reflects some growth in the area of technical facility.

Depending on your point of view, this is the most hilarious-sounding mish-mash of ineptitude ever committed to CD, or it's an unconscious musical realization of everything great naive American art desires to be, believably innocent. Either way, you'll either love them or hate them. *—Rick Clark*

● **Philosophy of the World** / 1969 / Rounder ◆◆◆◆
This release compiles the Wiggins sisters' (otherwise known as the Shaggs) two releases *Philosophy of the World* and *Shaggs' Own Thing.* Anyone with unconventional tastes interested in taking a harrowing trip into the twilight zone of naive Americana pop should check this out. *—Rick Clark*

Shai

Group, Urban
At the end of 1992, the four-man urban contemporary vocal group Shai shot to the top of the R&B and pop charts with their debut album, *...If I Ever Fall in Love,* and its number one title track. Although they sometimes lack quality material, the smooth silkiness of their voices usually makes such weaknesses easy to ignore; the group has remained hot on the R&B charts, even if they haven't duplicated the pop success of their first single. *—Stephen Thomas Erlewine*

○ **...If I Ever Fall in Love** / 1992 / Gasoline Alley Music ◆◆◆◆
Apart from the gorgeous title track, most of the material on *If I Ever Fall in Love* is underdeveloped; although Shai sounds terrific, their material doesn't match their vocal talents. There are occasional signs of promise, but the single is the only flat-out impressive track here. *—Stephen Thomas Erlewine*

The Shakers

Group, Pop/Rock
The concept of a Uruguayan band in the mold of the *Hard Day's Night*-era Beatles may seem absurd, but it did happen in the mid-'60s. What's more, the Shakers were fairly successful in mimicking the jangle of the early Beatles sound, writing most of their material, with a decent grasp of the British Invasion essentials of catchy tunes and enthusiastic harmonies. While the grammar is fairly broken and pidgin, soundwise the Shakers were actually superior to many of the bonafide Mersey groups; if you like the Beatle sound as heard on tracks like "I Should Have Known Better" or "I'll Be Back," you'll like this stuff. Popular in their native land, the Shakers were understandably unable to compete on an international scale, although their 1965 album, *Break It All,* was actually issued in the States. Today they enjoy respect from hardcore '60s collectors, and much of their material is available on reissues. *—Richie Unterberger*

Break It All / 1965 / Audio Fidelity ◆◆◆
Solid mid-tempo Beatles derivations characterize their debut LP. Still easy to find decades after its original release, but look for the recent Australian reissue on Raven if you have trouble finding it. *—Richie Unterberger*

● **All The Best** / 1992 / EMI Brazil ◆◆◆◆
22 songs from 1965-68, including some substantially different takes and mixes from the *Break It All* LP, a few songs from their second 1966 album *Shakers From You,* some singles, a delightfully raucous British Invasion-ized version of "It's My Party," and some tracks which show them going into a harder mod direction. A pricy but worthwhile import. *—Richie Unterberger*

Shakespear's Sister

Group, Pop/Rock
Comprised of Siobhan Fahey and Marcella Detroit (born Marcy Levy), Shakespear's Sister formed in late 1988. Fahey had several hits as a member of Bananarama and Levy was the backup vocalist for Eric Clapton in the late '70s. After their first single flopped, Shakespear's Sister's second single, "You're History," made it into the U.K. Top Ten. *Sacred Heart,* their 1989 debut, also made it into the Top Ten. Most of the material on *Sacred Heart* and the 1991 follow-up *Hormonally Yours* was written with producer Richard Feldman, who gave the band a polished, synth-laden R&B feel, along the lines of the Eurythmics. "Stay," the first single from *Hormonally Yours,* was a Top Five hit on both sides of the Atlantic; the follow-up single, "I Don't Care," cracked the U.K. Top 20, yet failed to make the U.S. Top 40. Despite their success, the duo broke up the following year. *—Stephen Thomas Erlewine*

Sacred Heart / 1989 / FFRR ◆◆◆
● **Hormonally Yours** / 1991 / London ◆◆◆◆
This engaging collection includes adult-contemporary synth-pop in the vein of their hit "Stay." *—AMG*

Shalamar

Group, Soul, Disco, Urban
Shalamar was the creation of Dick Griffey, the booking agent for the television R&B program *Soul Train,* and British R&B producer Simon Soussan. The group's first single, the 1977 Motown medley "Uptown Festival," featured a bevy of faceless studio musicians; once it became a hit, Griffey decided to form a performing group under the name Shalamar. Through *Soul Train* Griffey found Jody Watley, Jeffrey Daniels, and Gerald Brown, the three vocalists that became Shalamar; Brown was quickly replaced by Howard Hewitt in 1978.

Shalamar's string of poppy dance-soul hits began in 1979 with "Take That to the Bank;" later that year, "The Second Time Around" hit the Top Ten. Throughout the early '80s the group were favorites on the U.S. R&B scene, as well as scoring a number of British hit singles. Watley and Daniels left the group in 1982 and were replaced by Delisa Davis and Micki Free in 1984; Watley went on to stardom as a solo act. The following year Shalamar won a Grammy award for "Don't Get Stopped in Beverly Hills," which was featured in *Beverly Hills Cop.* Hewitt left for a solo career in 1986, signaling the end of the band's career as hit-makers. Sidney Justin replaced Hewitt and the group recorded 1987's *Circumstantial Evidence,* which was a commercial disappointment. The group faded away soon after the release of 1990's *Wake Up.* *—Stephen Thomas Erlewine*

○ **Big Fun** / 1979 / Solar ◆◆◆◆
This Top-40 disco set includes "Second Time Around." *—Bil Carpenter*

Friends / 1982 / Solar ◆◆◆
Features sophisticated dance and romantic music. *—Bil Carpenter*

● **Greatest Hits** / 1982 / Solar ◆◆◆◆
Heartbreak / 1984 / Solar ◆◆
Charter Shalamar member Howard Hewitt tried to revive their early-'80s dance/soul magic with a new lineup in the mid-'80s. He brought in Micki Free to replace Jeffrey Daniels and Delissa Davis for Jody Watley. This was the reworked trio's debut, and they seemed as if they might make it. They managed to score several hits in 1984, combining film soundtrack numbers with album cuts. But it wasn't as energetic or appealing as the original Shalamar material; Hewitt was basically carrying the load, and when he left a year later, the ball game was over for Shalamar. *—Ron Wynn*

Sham 69

Group, Punk
I doubt there would be much disagreement with the assertion that of all the British punk bands of the late-'70s, Sham 69 was the worst band to have a career lasting more than two records. Negligibly talented like their punk brethren the Cortinas and Eater, and specializing in simplistic political vituperation, shouted vocals and roaring guitars, Sham 69 was remotely interesting in the heady days of 1976-78, only to quickly descend to joke status (in America anyway) by the turn of the decade.

Led by vocalist and lyricist Jimmy Pursey, Sham's basic attack was "leftist" slogans chanted repeatedly over a wall of fast distorted guitars that exploded into shout-a-long choruses (all the better for their yob fans to participate). Unsurprisingly, this begat chart success (in England only) where the band released five, albeit indistinguishable, hit singles in their first year. Flushed with success, Pursey adopted the role of principal spokesman, erstwhile politico, and punk careerist, roles for which (except for the latter) he showed little talent. In 1980, shortly after the release of the album *The Game,* Pursey, in a move that indicated a tremendously inflated self-worth, broke up Sham 69 for a solo career; his four subsequent solo records exhibit a dearth of creativity and talent.

His solo career stalled, Pursey saw an opportunity to milk punk rock nostalgia for a few pounds and reformed Sham 69. Exhibiting careerist proclivities and excessive crassness, the new Sham simply played like the old Sham, and Pursey fobbed the whole thing off as a retrenchment by an aging punk rocker to his "roots." Mostly it was pathetic, but based on Sham 69's history, totally unsurprising. *—John Dougan*

○ **Tell Us the Truth** / 1978 / Sire ✦✦✦✦
The first and only Sham 69 record released in America is the only one worth listening to, primarily because their fakery had not gotten in the way of their loud and proud shouting and bashing. And, given the rush of excitement that greeted most English punk rock records at the time, it was easy to get sucked in to this record's raffish, working-class charm. One side studio, one live side, it's intensely derivative, but dumb fun in a sophomorically liberating way. —*John Dougan*

○ **That's Life** / 1978 / Polydor ✦✦✦✦
A good follow-up to their debut *Tell Us the Truth*, this one includes "Hurry Up Harry." —*David Szatmary*

Hersham Boys / 1979 / Polydor ✦✦✦
First, the Best & The Last / 1980 / Polydor ✦✦✦
The Game / 1980 / Polydor ✦✦✦
This is a more experimental effort by these punkers. —*David Szatmary*

● **Live and Loud** / 1987 / Link ✦✦✦✦
A blazing 1979 live set, it captures these Hersham punks at their best and includes many of their hit U.K. singles. —*David Szatmary*

Shamen

Group, Alternative Pop/Rock, Techno-Pop/Dance
Combining swirling psychedelic rock with hardcore hip-hop rhythms, the Shamen were one of the first alternative bands to appeal to dance clubs as much as indie rockers. Comprised of Colin Angus, Peter Stephenson, Keith McKenzie, and Derek McKenzie, the Scottish quartet had its roots in the early '80s neo-psychedelic group Alone Again Or. The Shamen officially formed in 1986 and released their first album, *Drop*, the following year. *Drop* was filled with varying guitar textures, recalling many late-'60s rock groups. After the record's release, Angus immersed himself in the emerging acid house/hip-hop club scene, which prompted the departure of Derek McKenzie; he was replaced with William Sinnott, who helped reshape the band's sound into a dense, rhythmic pulse that relied heavily on samples, drum machines, and loud guitars. The band debuted their revamped sound in 1988 with a stage show that featured sexually explicit visuals along with impassioned political rhetoric. During 1988, Peter Stephenson and Keith McKenzie departed, leaving Angus and Sinnott to perform as a duo.

With their 1989 album *In Gorbachev We Trust*, the Shamen expanded their following in Britain and began attracting American listeners. The duo continued to concentrate on dance music throughout 1989, adding rappers to their live shows. Just as the band was heading toward mainstream acceptance, Will Sinnott drowned off the coast of the Canary Islands on May 23, 1990. With the Sinnott family's encouragement, Angus continued the Shamen and the group did indeed begin to score hits, particularly in the U.K. where they amassed five Top 20 singles between 1991 and 1992; "Move Any Mountain (Progen 91)" managed to make it into the American Top 40 at the end of 1991, as well. However, the Shamen fell out of favor during 1993 and their 1994 album *Different Drum* failed to gain much of an audience. —*Stephen Thomas Erlewine*

Drop / 1987 / Communion ✦✦✦
In Gorbachev We Trust / 1989 / Edsel ✦✦
● **En-Tact** / 1990 / Epic ✦✦✦✦
○ **Boss Drum** / 1992 / Epic ✦✦✦✦
Different Drum / 1994 / ✦✦✦

Shampoo

Group, Pop/Rock
Shampoo are a duo of punk-rock Barbie dolls barely out of their teens, hailing from Plumstead, England. Jacqui Blake and Carrie Askew both handle vocals in a highly energetic and barely intelligible fashion, and both have enough attitude and downright sass to make critics on both sides of the Atlantic go ga-ga over their primitive punk and sly innuendoes. Even though their talent is barely discernible, Shampoo are a knowing and clever joke and loads of fun. *We Are Shampoo*, their full-length debut, features all of the jaw-dropping singles released in Britain, including their anthem, "Trouble," which was featured in the *Mighty Morphin Power Rangers* soundtrack. —*Heather Phares*

We Are Shampoo / 1995 / IRS ✦✦✦
The attitude that Jacqui and Carrie have in spades is what holds together their debut, *We Are Shampoo*. "Trouble" is the highlight of the collection, but songs like "Shiny Black Taxi Cab" and "Skinny White Thing" are good for plenty of fun as well. —*Heather Phares*

The Shangri-Las

Group, Rock & Roll, Girl-Group
Street-tough and smart, the Shangri-Las were like nothing that had come before in the history of rock & roll female groups. Hailing from Queens, NY, the group comprised two sets of sisters (one set identical twins, at that). They cranked out 11 hits in the space of two years, all of them enduring classics of the girl-group genre. Masterminded by oddball writer and producer George "Shadow" Morton, these narratives have a disturbing edge—tales of girls who run away from home, doomed girls who go all the way with bad boys; the spectre of death hangs over most of their songs. Eerie and creative production makes fatalistic melodramas such as "I Can Never Go Home Anymore" (1965) truly haunting—and the girls' voices, ranging from New York-snotty to wistful and breathy, are ideally utilized.

The epitome of "biker girls in heat," their live presentation devastated audiences on package shows, while their offstage antics left a string of trashed hotel rooms, tour buses, and male groupies in their wake. The formula of teen-biker melodramas with a tough-as-nails image worked like a charm until they were eclipsed by the progressive rock movement of the late '60s. —*Cub Koda & George Bedard*

● **Golden Hits of the Shangri-Las** / 1984 / PolyGram ✦✦✦✦
It includes all the eerie three-minute melodramas from one of the all-time great girl groups: "Leader of the Pack," "Remember," "I Can Never Go Home Anymore," "Past, Present, and Future." —*George Bedard*

○ **At Their Best** / Collectables ✦✦✦✦

Del Shannon (Charles Westover)

b. Dec. 30, 1934, Coopersville, MI, **d.** Feb. 8, 1990
Rock & Roll
Del Shannon (born Charles Westover) came out of Grand Rapids, MI, in 1961 with a sound that no one had ever heard before. A rocker by inclination in a time when rock was supposedly dead, his first single, "Runaway," became a monster hit and a half with its catchy guitar hooks, great beat, and Shannon's strong yet vulnerable vocal (which leaped to falsetto range without compromising his manliness).

Shannon had several follow-up hits, none quite as memorable or driving, and in 1963 also became the first American artist to cover a Beatles song ("From Me to You"). By 1964, however, he began concentrating equally on songwriting and production, and wrote "I Go to Pieces," a romantic rocker that became a hit for Peter and Gordon. He made numerous attempts at finding a new and successful sound, signing with Liberty, which was able to sell his records in England and other parts of Europe but not stateside. An attempt at updating his sound, first with Andrew "Loog" Oldham, and later with Dave Edmunds and Tom Petty as producers, met with very limited success. In the mid-'80s, however, Shannon seemed poised for a comeback when "Runaway" emerged as a hit in an updated version by Todd Rundgren from the TV show *Crime Story*. Unfortunately, just as he was completing a comeback album on MCA, Shannon took his own life. —*Bruce Eder*

○ **I Go to Pieces** / 1990 / Edsel ✦✦✦✦
A British import and an indispensable complement to the Rhino hits package. Sixteen important tracks, capturing Shannon's sound at its most achingly beautiful. —*Bruce Eder*

★ **Greatest Hits** / 1990 / Rhino ✦✦✦✦✦
An almost-perfect collection of his best tracks from the U.S. catalog. The gaps can (and should) be filled by his album *I Go to Pieces*. —*Bruce Eder*

The Liberty Years / 1991 / EMI America ✦✦
Not the record to start with. An artist in search of a style, with some interesting attempts at finding one. —*Bruce Eder*

Rock On! / Oct. 1, 1991 / Gone Gator ✦✦✦

Roxanne Shanté

Rap

Roxanne Shanté (born Lolita Gooden) was walking outside a New York housing project called the Queensbridge when she heard three men talking about how the trio U.T.F.O. had cancelled their appearance at a show they were promoting. Gooden offered to make a rap record that would get back at U.T.F.O, who'd previously recorded "Roxanne, Roxanne," a song about a woman too stuck up to notice them. The three, Tyrone Williams, disc jockey Mister Magic, and producer Marley Marl, took her up on the idea, with Marl producing "Roxanne's Revenge." The song was confrontational, sneering, boastful, and even borderline obscene, and it spawned 102 additional answer records. Since then, she's had two albums. The original "Roxanne's Revenge" was issued by Pop Art. Eventually U.T.F.O. threatened to sue Shanté for using their B-side as the musical foundation. She settled with them and recut the song with a different, though related, track.

Roxanne Shanté's fortunes have been thin since the heyday of the "Roxanne, Roxanne" rush. She did share a number one R&B and a Top Ten pop hit with Rick James in 1986, "Loosey's Rap," but has otherwise found the going tough. Her last release was *Go Down but Don't Bite It*, a 1992 album that proved much less interesting, alluring, sensual or even offensive than its title would suggest. —*Ron Wynn*

● **Bad Sister** / 1989 / Cold Chillin' ◆◆◆◆
Her debut album doesn't quite live up to the promise of her early singles, which can be found on various rap compilations. —*Dan Heilman*

Def Mix #1 / 1989 / Pop Art ◆◆

Roxanne / Columbia ◆◆◆

Sandie Shaw (Sandra Goodrich)

b. Feb. 26, 1947, Dagenham, Essex
British Invasion

British singer Sandie Shaw had a string of girl group-styled singles in the mid-'60s before she retired in the early '70s. Shaw was discovered by pop singer Adam Faith in 1963, who led her to his manager, Eve Taylor; she released her debut single, "As Long As You're Happy," the following year. It didn't hit the charts, yet her next record, "(There's) Always Something There to Remind Me," hit number one in the U.K.; the single hit number 52 in the U.S., yet Shaw was never as big a star in the States as she was in the U.K. For the next three years, she had a string of hits—most of them written by her producer Chris Andrews—that kept her at the top of the charts. In 1967, Taylor began to move Shaw into cabaret territory; the approach proved a success when the Bill Martin/Phil Coulter song "Puppet on a String" hit number one. She recorded one more Coulter song, "Tonight in Tokyo," before returning to Chris Andrews. However, none of her further work with Andrews resulted in hit singles. Released in early 1969 her English version of the French "Monsieur Dupont" managed to crack the Top 20; it would turn out to be her last hit.

In 1970, Shaw tried to become a family entertainer, yet those plans were scuttled by a failed marriage and scandalous rumors that circulated in the British newspapers. She subsequently retired for the rest of the '70s. Shaw returned to recording in the early '80s when BEF, a Heaven 17 side-project, prompted her to record "Anyone Who Had a Heart," an old Cilla Black hit. The Smiths' lead singer Morrissey began championing her in interviews, as well, which led her to record a version of the band's "Hand in Glove" supported by the Smiths themselves; the single briefly appeared on the U.K. charts. Shaw recorded a version of Lloyd Cole's "Are You Ready to Be Heartbroken?" in 1986; like "Hand in Glove," it scraped the bottom of the pop charts. In 1988, she recorded an entire album, *Hello Angel*; although it featured songs by the Smiths and the Jesus and Mary Chain, it failed to make a large impression on the pop charts. —*Stephen Thomas Erlewine*

● **64/67 Complete Sandie Shaw Set** / 1994 / Sequel ◆◆◆◆
A double-disc set that features all of her big hits as well as all of her minor ones, this provides the definitive portrait of the British girl group vocalist. —*Stephen Thomas Erlewine*

○ **Collection** / Castle ◆◆◆◆
Collection is an effective overview of Sandie Shaw's entire career, from her early hits to her '80s collaborations with the Smiths. It covers more ground than the double-disc *Complete* but it doesn't have quite as much prime material. —*Stephen Thomas Erlewine*

Jules Shear

b. Mar. 7, 1952, Pittsburgh, PA
Singer-Songwriter, Pop/Rock

Singer/songwriter Shear (born in Pittsburgh) is best known for hits he's written for others, notably "All Through the Night" for Cyndi Lauper and "If She Knew What She Wants" for the Bangles. He has been a member of the groups the Funky Kings, Jules and the Polar Bears, and the Reckless Sleepers in addition to making solo albums. He was also an early host of the successful MTV series *Unplugged*. —*William Ruhlmann*

○ **Watch Dog** / 1983 / EMI ◆◆◆◆
His first solo album following the breakup of the Polar Bears, *Watch Dog*, features a new-found maturity in songwriting with an eclectic mix of styles from ultra-smooth pop to R&B-inflected rockers. Shear sounds much more comfortable on his own, even under Todd Rundgren's heavy-handed production. Highlights includes "All Through the Night" (a hit for Cyndi Lauper), "Whispering Your Name," and the more experimental, Brian Wilson-inspired "Longest Drink." Another unjustified commercial sleeper. —*Chris Woodstra*

Eternal Return / 1985 / EMI America ◆◆◆
Seemingly unfazed by *Watch Dog's* failure, Shear again produces a slick, pop delight in *Eternal Return*. Shear explores a more soulful side in songs like "Steady" and the yearning "You're Not Around" while perfecting his hook-laden melodies. Despite being perfectly in line with the mid-'80s sound, this one also slipped through the cracks. The Bangles would later find a hit in the lead-off track, "If She Knew What She Wants." —*Chris Woodstra*

Demo-Itis / 1987 / Enigma ◆◆
Of interest mainly to fans, this collection of demos shows Shear's true talent, free of the often smothering production that plagued his previous albums. In addition to early versions of old favorites, several songs that never made it on the LPs appear for the first time. —*Chris Woodstra*

The Third Party / 1989 / IRS ◆◆◆
Shear sings his songs with no more accompaniment than the acoustic guitar of Marty Willson-Piper of the Church. The results are stark but impressive. —*William Ruhlmann*

○ **The Great Puzzle** / 1992 / Polydor ◆◆◆◆
Full-band production gives a pop sheen to Shear's excellent songs, notably the ballad "We Were Only Making Love." —*William Ruhlmann*

● **Horse of a Different Color (1976-1989)** / 1994 / Razor & Tie ◆◆◆◆
This retrospective covers everything from Shear's work with Funky Kings, Jules & the Polar Bears, and Reckless Sleepers, to his solo work. Of particular note is the beautiful Byrds-like "If We Never Meet Again" and "If She Knew What She Wants," later recorded by the Bangles. —*Rick Clark*

Healing Bones / 1994 / PolyGram ◆◆◆
While Shear's albums are always packed with craftsmanlike songwriting, the production and arrangements often end up dating them. What sets *The Healing Bones* apart from most of his back catalog is a certain timelessness of the sound. The songs are definitely among his finest. Includes a cover of the Walker Brothers' classic "The Sun Ain't Gonna Shine Anymore." —*Chris Woodstra*

Sheila E.

b. Dec. 12, 1959, Oakland, CA
Dance-Pop, Pop/Rock

Before she became a solo artist in 1984, drummer Sheila E. played with Azteca, the Latin jazz-fusion band led by her father, percussionist Pete "Coke" Escovedo; she also played on two of his solo albums recorded for Fantasy Records. Prince discovered Sheila E. around 1983 and had her sing on "Erotic City," the B-side to his number one 1984 single, "Let's Go Crazy." Prince also helped her secure a record contract with Warner Brothers; she released her debut album, *Sheila E. in the Glamorous Life*, in 1984. Written by Prince, the title track hit the U.S. Top Ten and her second single, "The Belle of St. Mark," charted in both the American and British Top 40. The following year she released *Sheila E. in Romance 1600*, which featured the number 11 hit "A Love Bizarre." Her self-titled album was released in 1987, yet it didn't have the commercial impact of her two previous records. Shelia E. joined Prince's band for the 1987 *Sign O' the Times* tour and is featured prominently in the resulting film documentary of the same name. Four years later, she returned with her fourth album, *Sex Cymbal.* —*Stephen Thomas Erlewine*

● **The Glamorous Life** / 1984 / Warner Brothers ✦✦✦✦
Prince-influenced debut. —*Bil Carpenter*

○ **Romance 1600** / 1985 / Paisley Park ✦✦✦✦
This set includes "A Love Bizzarre." —*Bil Carpenter*

Sheila E. / 1987 / Paisley Park ✦✦✦
This set includes dance cut "Koo Koo" and adult contemporary cut, "Hold Me." —*Bil Carpenter*

Sex Cymbal / 1991 / Warner Brothers ✦✦
A striking set of percussive, rhythm-section-based funk. —*Bil Carpenter*

Shellac

Group, Alternative Pop/Rock
After Big Black, Steve Albini's first band, broke up at the height of their popularity, he moved on to produce stellar albums by the Pixies, the Breeders, Nirvana, PJ Harvey, and the Poster Children, among others. After his second band, Rapeman, broke up due to controversy surrounding the name, Albini formed Shellac two years later with veteran producer and bassist Tom Weston and drummer Todd Trainer. After three 7"s on Touch & Go, the band released an album, *At Action Park,* in 1994. —*John Bush*

● **At Action Park** / Sep. 1994 / Touch & Go ✦✦✦✦
Although Steve Albini's grating guitar has not changed significantly since the birth of Big Black, the rumbling bass of Bob Weston and Todd Trainer's commanding drum work provide a much richer framework for his melodies than in the past. As usual, Albini shows the darker side of life; "Le Porno Star" and "The Admiral" could be taken straight from Big Black songs. Shellac's rhythmic start-stop brand of hard rock works so well, listeners will think the band has been playing together for years. —*John Bush*

Pete Shelley

New Wave
Pete Shelley, the leader of the seminal punk band the Buzzcocks, actually had recorded a solo album in 1974, two years before the Buzzcocks had formed. Released in 1979, *Sky Yen* was a collection of electronic music that didn't sound much like his full-time band's blistering guitar-pop, yet it did contain the roots of his solo career. After the Buzzcocks disbanded in 1981, Shelley began a solo career which incorporated the electronic experimentations of *Sky Yen* with the pop sensibilities of his punk singles. Released in 1982, *Homosapien* showcased this musical merger and resulted in the U.K. hit single, "Homosapien." The following year Shelley released *XL 1,* which added more guitar to his dance-oriented synth-pop. Three years later he released his final solo album, *Heaven & the Sea,* which failed to capture an audience. Shelley then joined the short-lived band Zip; after its breakup, he rejoined the reunited Buzzcocks in 1988. —*Stephen Thomas Erlewine*

Sky Yen / 1979 / Groovy ✦✦

● **Homosapien** / 1982 / Genetics ✦✦✦✦

XL 1 / 1983 / Genetics ✦✦✦

Heaven & the Sea / 1986 / Mercury ✦✦✦

The Shells

Group, Doo-Wop
Recording for the tiny Johnson label, the Shells cut some fine doo-wop during the late '50s. With Nate Bouknight as lead singer, the Shells debuted with "Baby Oh Baby" in 1957 and continued to wax impressive 45s without much commercial interest. Three years later, record collectors Donn Fileti and Wayne Stierle promoted the track anew, and it actually hit the pop charts on its second time around. By 1962, when the quintet cut "Happy Holiday," Ray Jones had taken over as lead. —*Bill Dahl*

● **Golden Classics** / 1989 / Collectables ✦✦✦✦
Tasty late-'50s R&B group harmonies. —*Bill Dahl*

○ **Badder Than Badd** / 1993 / Juke Box Treasures ✦✦✦✦
Another entry in JBT's acapella series, this collects 20 studio tracks of the group doing a mixture of original material penned by producer Wayne Stierle as well as several genre classics. —*Cub Koda*

The Sheppards

Group, Doo-Wop
This seminal six-piece outfit from Chicago, centered around the twin lead vocals of Millard Edwards and Murrie Eskridge, had few hits, but their Apex and Constellation recordings from the late '50s and early '60s are pre-soul gems. —*John Floyd*

★ **Golden Classics** / 1989 / Collectables ✦✦✦✦✦
These obscure but absolutely brilliant '60s vintage recordings walk the line between R&B and soul. Contained are some of the most gorgeous ballads ever sung. —*John Floyd*

Mike Sheridan

British Invasion
A British Invasion group from Birmingham that had no hits on either side of the Atlantic, Mike Sheridan & the Night Riders gained what little notoriety they possess from the fact that Roy Wood played guitar with them before joining the Move. The band managed to release six singles between 1963 and 1966, most including Wood, the final two under the name Mike Sheridan's Lot. Their recordings have a basic, middle-of-the-pack British Invasion sound, divided between competent covers and modestly enjoyable three-chord originals. Wood doesn't take a prominent role on either guitar or vocals (Sheridan sang lead almost all of the time), although the group managed to lay down one undistinguished Wood original, "Make Them Understand," which marked the first appearance of a Wood composition on record. The group did have one great moment in them, the 1965 single "Take My Hand," which is great British Invasion pop in the mold of the best early Hollies. —*Richie Unterberger*

● **Birmingham Beat** / 1984 / Edsel ✦✦✦✦
Everything ever recorded by the group: both sides of their six singles, plus a couple previously unissued tracks. —*Richie Unterberger*

The Shirelles

Group, Girl-Group
The Shirelles were instrumental in defining the girl group sound, and were one of the style's most successful acts between 1960 and 1963, when they placed six singles in the Top Ten. Bridging doo-wop and uptown New York pop-soul, the group projected a beguiling mixture of tenderness and innocence that was grounded in R&B as much as pop/rock. Forming as high school classmates in New Jersey, the Shirelles came under the wing of manager Florence Goldberg, who also ran the Scepter label. Many of their classic early sides featured innovative, occasionally string-laden production by Luther Dixon, who also penned several of their greatest songs. Top Brill Building songwriters like Goffin-King, Bacharach-David, and Van McCoy also supplied the group with material. "Will You Love Me Tomorrow," "Baby It's You," "Foolish Little Girl," "Soldier Boy," "Dedicated to the One I Love," and "Mama Said" were their biggest hits, but they also cut a number of delightful less famous sides, including "Boys," which (like "Baby It's You") was covered by the Beatles on their first LP. After mid-1963, the Shirelles were unable to dent the Top 40, although they recorded some excellent songs, including the original version of "Sha La La" (covered for a hit by Manfred Mann). The group recorded well into the '70s, updating their sound into a more soul-oriented mode that was lacking in comparison. —*Richie Unterberger*

Baby It's You / 1962 / Scepter ✦✦✦
The best songs on here—the title track, "Big John," "A Thing Of The Past," "Make The Night A Little Longer," "Soldier Boy," and "Putty In Your Hands"—are available on the Rhino best-of double album. Still, it's a pretty solid effort for its day, featuring state-of-the-art orchestral early-'60s New York girl group production and decent songwriting. —*Richie Unterberger*

The Shirelles & King Curtis Give A Twist Party / 1962 / Scepter ✦✦✦
A rather strange concept for an early-'60s album, pairing the Shirelles, then at the peak of their success, with R&B/soul sax great King Curtis. It's not so much a collaboration as an alternation; Curtis gets three instrumentals to himself, and sings "I Got A Woman" and another cut. King does duet with the girls on "I Still Want You," and the Shirelles handle the rest of the material, mostly written by their chief producer/songwriter Luther Dixon, in a much more uptempo vein than their famous singles. No hits

on this record, which is respectable but not terribly exciting, and a bit schizo in concept. —*Richie Unterberger*

★ **Anthology (1959-1967)** / 1988 / Rhino ✦✦✦✦✦
One of the most consistently creative and danceful of the '60s girl groups, the Shirelles were a hit-making machine. "Soldier Boy," "Dedicated to the One I Love," "Will You Still Love Me Tomorrow?," and 13 others can be found here. —*Jeff Tamarkin*

Golden Classics / Collectables ✦✦✦
The Shirelles were for many the ultimate 1960s women's vocal group; their hits have been collected and recollected on numerous packages. My own choice is the Rhino anthology, either in the complete or condensed versions. All the others, including this one, are inferior from a packaging, selection, and mastering standpoint. It's no better or worse than any of the others, except for Pair's cheap ripoff job. —*Ron Wynn*

Lost & Found / Ace ✦✦✦

Shirley & Lee

Group, New Orleans R&B
Shirley Goodman's (b. Jun 19, 1936) screechy vocals and Leonard Lee's (b. Jun 29, 1936—d Oct 23, 1976) bluesy retorts added up to R&B gold during the '50s for the young Crescent City duo. The teenagers' debut on Aladdin, the Dave Bartholomew-produced "I'm Gone," was a major R&B hit in 1952. Shirley and Lee caught fire in 1955-1956 with three rocking smashes: "Feel So Good," the R&B chart-topping "Let the Good Times Roll," and "I Feel Good," all written by Lee. The pair stayed on Aladdin into 1959 before moving to Warwick and re-doing "Let the Good Times Roll." The "Sweethearts of the Blues" broke up after a few 1962-1963 singles for Imperial. In 1974 Goodman returned under the sobriquet of Shirley and Company with a #1 R&B smash, the disco-fied "Shame, Shame, Shame," for producer Sylvia Robinson on the Vibration logo. —*Bill Dahl*

● **Legendary Masters** / EMI America ✦✦✦✦
The "Sweethearts of the Blues" in all their glory, it includes "Let the Good Times Roll" and more. —*Dan Heilman*

Michelle Shocked

b. 1962, Texas
Singer-Songwriter, Alternative Pop/Rock, Folk-Rock
According to her own, undoubtedly semi-fictional account, Michelle Shocked was born in Dallas, TX, in 1962, where she spent her early childhood travelling around army bases. In 1977, she ran away from her Mormon fundamentalist mother to live with her father who introduced her to country bluesmen Big Bill Broonzy and Leadbelly as well as contemporary songwriters Guy Clark and Randy Newman. She spent the next several years exploring the folk underground, spending the early '80s in Austin, where she began honing her own songwriting skills. Shocked left Texas in 1983, travelled throughout the U.S. and became an activist in the squatter's movement. According to the legend, in 1986, while volunteering at the Kerrville Folk Festival, English producer Pete Lawrence was impressed by her campfire-side playing and recorded her on his Sony Walkman. The recordings surfaced in the fall of that year as *The Texas Campfire Tapes* on Cooking Vinyl Records and became a surprise hit in England, eventually topping the independent charts. The success led to her signing with Mercury Records in 1988. *Short Sharp Shocked,* produced by Pete Anderson in 1988, displayed even more talent, combining the informal, tradition-rooted folkiness of *The Texas Campfire Tapes* with a strong post-modern feminist perspective and punk attitude. The album quickly earned her respect among the alternative community and critics. In an unexpected move, Shocked returned in 1989 with *Captain Swing,* a '40s-style big-band swing outing that shocked her fans initially but had no shortage of strong material. In 1992, she took something of a step back with *Arkansas Traveller,* a rootsy collection of songs based on the blackface minstrelsy that covered all forms of early American, homegrown music. In 1993, Mercury finally became fed up with her confusing style jumping and refused to release her proposed gospel album. She then left on a solo tour, selling her newly recorded, independently produced (with Tony Berg), *Kind Hearted Woman.* Late in 1995, Shocked began legal action against Mercury Records. —*Chris Woodstra*

The Texas Campfire Tapes / 1986 / Mercury ✦✦✦
Her debut, recorded live around a campfire on a Walkman, is a wildly overrated but interesting introduction to her talents. —*John Dougan*

● **Short Sharp Shocked** / 1988 / Mercury ✦✦✦✦
With the great miss-you song "Anchorage," this is Shocked's strongest record from start to finish. Rich and evocative, there's hardly a clinker in the bunch. Special credit to Pete Anderson for a sympathetic production job. —*John Dougan*

Captain Swing / 1989 / Mercury ✦✦✦
Whoa, stop right there. Read the title. This is swing music like your parents listened to. That's right, Goodman, Herman, the lot. Includes "On the Greener Side." —*John Dougan*

○ **Arkansas Traveler** / Oct. 1991 / Mercury ✦✦✦✦
Part three of the trilogy that began with *Short Sharp Shocked, Arkansas Traveler* focuses this time on American roots music of the South, mainly rural-blues and country; according to her theory in the album's liner notes, all of these songs are based on the legacy of blackface minstrels. Recorded with a mobile studio at various non-conventional locations around the country, it features an amazing array of guest musicians including Pops Staples, Doc Watson, and Gatemouth Brown. Those who were put off by the unexpected direction of *Captain Swing* will certainly welcome this return to form—her best since *Short Sharp Shocked.* —*Chris Woodstra*

Kind Hearted Woman / 1994 / no label ✦✦✦
Shocked released *Kind Hearted Woman* on her own, selling it exclusively at live shows, when she ran into troubles with Mercury Records. Accompanied by only her own Stratocaster playing, she has produced her most touching, personal document to date. A very difficult album to track down but worth seeking out. —*Chris Woodstra*

Shoes

Group, Power Pop/Anglo-Pop
If there was a band that typified all that was good about that post-punk permutation known as power-pop, it was the Shoes. This Zion, IL, quartet burst from their studio home with a string of terrific records that took Beatles-inspired pop and sprinkled it liberally with their own airy melodies and steady, sturdy playing. —*John Dougan*

○ **Black Vinyl Shoes** / 1977 / Black Vinyl ✦✦✦✦
A homemade demo that became their first national release, this is a dazzling collection of pop songs driven by thick sheets of guitar and warm, emotive singing. —*John Dougan*

○ **Present Tense** / 1979 / Elektra ✦✦✦✦
Their major-label debut suffers from a bit of overwhelming post-production, but there isn't enough interference to ruin this great collection of tunes. The CD version is a two-fer which combines *Present Tense* with *Tongue Twister.* —*John Dougan*

Tongue Twister / 1981 / Elektra ✦✦✦
After a short stint at Bomp!, the Shoes were snapped up by Elektra for their major label debut. The songs are good, the sound is right but something is missing. Maybe it's because they were saddled with a co-producer. Still, not to be missed. On the CD issue, *Tongue Twister* has been combined with *Present Tense.* —*Jim Worbois*

○ **Boomerang/Shoes on Ice** / May 1982 / Black Vinyl ✦✦✦✦
In an early interview, the Beatles were asked why they chose their name, to which Paul McCartney replied, "for all you know, we might have been called the Shoes." Fortunately, there *is* a band called the Shoes and this is one of the finest pop albums ever made. Back on their own territory and producing their own records, this is the album that *Tongue Twister* should have been. It stands as one of their best. A live EP, *Shoes on Ice,* which came with the initial pressing of the album, has now been added to the CD version.—*LAG*

Silhouette / 1984 / Black Vinyl ✦✦✦
Now reduced to a three-piece (John Murphey, Jeff Murphey and Gary Klebe), the band recorded their fifth album independently in their home studio in Illinois. A pleasant, though unexceptional album, *Silhouette* is a softer, more keyboard-dominated effort. Without an American outlet (they left Elektra prior to recording), this album was only available in Europe until the band's own label, Black Vinyl Records, reissued it in the late '80s. —*Chris Woodstra*

● **Shoes Best** / 1987 / Black Vinyl ✦✦✦✦
A 22-song compilation, this is a wonderfully comprehensive overview of this wonderful band. Good liner notes by former *Trouser Press* head honcho Ira Robbins. —*John Dougan*

Stolen Wishes / 1989 / Black Vinyl ✦✦
The Shoes still sound good and they obviously still enjoy what they are doing, but the tunes on *Stolen Wishes* don't stand up to some of their earlier work. Still, the Shoes never released a bad album, so you won't be out anything if you take a chance on this one. —*Jim Worbois*

Propeller / 1994 / Black Vinyl ✦✦
Shoes returned in 1994 with *Propeller,* proving they're still vital with a harder-edged sound while managing to retain their classic melodies. —*Chris Woodstra*

Fret Buzz / 1995 / Black Vinyl ✦✦✦

Shonen Knife

Group, Alternative Pop/Rock
At their best, the Japanese punk-pop band Shonen Knife is an irresistible delight, combining sweet Beatlesque pop with buzzing Ramones power chords, singing about the schlockiest things pop culture has churned out. At their worst, the band's cuteness seems contrived, as if they were using their fractured English and obsession about Barbie Dolls, ice cream, and Hello Kitty as a deliberately cloying, cutesy marketing ploy. Even worse, at times it seems that their fans are not laughing with the band, they're laughing *at* their fascination with American kitsch culture and their bad English. Nevertheless, when taken on a strictly musical level, Shonen Knife's best records are truly intoxicating, rocking hard with a melody you can hum for days. —*Stephen Thomas Erlewine*

○ **Pretty Little Baka Guy** / **Live In** / 1986 / Rockville ✦✦✦✦
The CD reissue of this album adds eight live tracks (some that go as far back as 1982, when they were barely teens!) and makes this hands-down the best Shonen Knife record available. On *Baka Guy,* their pop culture obsessions are clearly and humorously articulated ("I Wanna Eat Choco Bars" and "Ice Cream City"), and the record includes the best song ever about public bath houses, "Public Bath." Too often, cute, condescending terminology is used to describe Shonen Knife as though they were candy-floss teddy bears instead of a rock band. So, let's get one thing straight: this is a great rock & roll record by one of Japan's great rock & roll bands. —*John Dougan*

○ **Shonen Knife** / 1990 / Positive ✦✦✦✦
A superb collection of material previously available only in Japan on the albums *Burning Farm* and *Yama No Attchan,* covering Shonen Knife's early career from 1983-85. The purist in me has become increasingly disappointed with Shonen Knife's records, as they sound more and more like generic alternative rock. On these recordings there is a nearly palpable sense of joy that comes with the discovery that you've mastered four chords, can keep a steady beat and are now considered a band. Also, this material is unforced, almost carefree and has little of the calculation that's creeping into their more recent work. Very simply, fabulous pop music. —*John Dougan*

○ **712** / 1991 / Rockville ✦✦✦✦
"Good morning Shonen Knife freaks!" is the cry that opens *712,* Shonen Knife's last indisputably great record. The playing and songwriting have matured here, but not to the point where it begins to sound sterile or overly sophisticated. Of course, what would a Shonen Knife record be without a few goofy tributes to junk culture, as in "Fruit Loop Dreams" and "Expo '90"? There's a surprising cover of John Lennon's "Luck of the Irish" with vocal help from Redd Kross's Jeff MacDonald. Note: the song "Blue Oyster Cult" is not a tribute to the band; it's about food poisoning from eating raw oysters. —*John Dougan*

● **Let's Knife** / 1993 / Capitol ✦✦✦
Song titles "Twist Barbie," "Flying Jelly Attack," and "I Am A Cat" offer an accurate snapshot of this Japanese band... then there's the environmental anthem (?) "Bear Up Bison": "He has a right to live though he's ill ill ill-shaped/He's on the way to extinction/We only want what's best for him/Bear up bison never say die!" There's something fascinating about having Western culture thrown back at us in this quirky, unpretentious manner, and Shonen Knife are well on their way to becoming a cult favorite—for those who "get" it. —*Roch Parisien*

Rock Animals / 1994 / Virgin ✦✦
The least essential of all Shonen Knife's releases, *Rock Animals* is a fair-to-middling record made by a band that seems to be trying too hard. There are some good songs here ("Catnip Dream" and the very sexy "Quavers"), but the sound is too big and overpro-

duced, which removes the intimacy that made their earlier records so great. Hopefully, they haven't reached the end of the line when it comes to good records. But *Rock Animals* doesn't leave one optimistic. —*John Dougan*

Showmen

Group, New Orleans R&B
Norman "General" Johnson's first group was based in New Orleans, but their best hit—"It Will Stand," from 1961—became a rock & roll anthem with global appeal. In the '70s, Johnson led the Chairmen of the Board ("Give Me Just a Little More Time"). —*John Floyd*

○ **It Will Stand** / Collectables ✦✦✦✦
A nice collection featuring the stuttering, sputtering vocals of General Norman Johnson and company, otherwise known as the Showmen. The title track was one of the great pieces of rock and R&B testimony. They never quite equaled it, although they produced some fine ballads and good uptempo tunes. "It Will Stand" wasn't a hit the first time out of the box; it didn't make it onto the R&B charts until 1964, three years after it had peaked at number 61 on the pop charts, and then it only reached number 80. —*Ron Wynn*

Shriekback

Group, Alternative Pop/Rock
A U.K. dance-rock band, 1982-1989, with varying personnel. The only constant member was keyboard player Barry Andrews, a former member of XTC. The original lineup was a trio also featuring former Gang of Four bassist Dave Allen and guitarist and vocalist Carl Marsh. They reached the U.S. charts with their first album, *Care,* in 1983, and the U.K. charts with their second, *Jam Science,* in 1984. *Oil & Gold* (1985), *Big Night Music* (1987) and *Go Bang!* (1988) also made the lower reaches of the U.S. charts, but the group's real home was in discos devoted to the kind of electronic, industrial-noise dance music of such peers as Ministry. Hits include "Nemesis" and "My Spine (Is the Bassline)." —*William Ruhlmann*

○ **Care** / 1983 / WEA ✦✦✦✦
Jam Science / 1984 / Arista ✦✦✦
○ **Oil & Gold** / 1985 / Island ✦✦✦✦
Big Night Music / 1986 / Island ✦✦✦
Go Bang / Mar. 1988 / Island ✦✦✦
● **The Dancing Years** / 1990 / Island ✦✦✦✦
An idiosyncratic compilation devoted to remixes and extended dance versions and lacking some of the group's best-known songs, though it *is* very danceable and gives a good sense of what Shriekback sounded like. If possible, find the U.K. import *The Infinite,* a good best-of, covering the early years. —*William Ruhlmann*

Sacred City / Sep. 14, 1992 / World Domination ✦✦

Jane Siberry

b. 1956, Canada
Singer-Songwriter, Alternative Pop/Rock
This Canadian singer/songwriter has been compared to both Joni Mitchell and Laurie Anderson, perhaps because she mixes traditional folk styles with various electronic effects and because of quirky lyrics that border on humor. —*William Ruhlmann*

Jane Siberry / 1981 / East Side Digital ✦✦
Siberry's first (low-budget) recording is her most conventional and folk-oriented, but already she is warning us that "Writers Are a Funny Breed" and is showing the offbeat perspective that will charm listeners later on. —*William Ruhlmann*

○ **No Borders Here** / 1983 / Open Air ✦✦✦✦
The sound has a new-wave rock energy. The songs poke fun at "Extra Executives" as well as the artist, who muses that she'd probably be famous by now if she weren't such a good waitress. — *William Ruhlmann*

The Speckless Sky / 1985 / Open Air ✦✦✦
The Walking / Jul. 1988 / Reprise ✦✦✦
Bound by the Beauty / 1989 / Reprise ✦✦✦
Siberry has by now mastered an ability to make her unorthodox song forms (changing time signatures, surprising alterations of melody) work for her, and she's struck a balance between revealing too much and too little in her lyrics, so that such songs as "The

Life Is the Red Wagon" really do reveal all the levels she's given it. And "Everything Reminds Me of My Dog" is one of the funniest and best songs of the year. — *William Ruhlmann*

○ **When I Was a Boy** / Aug. 3, 1993 / Reprise ♦♦♦♦
Considering the three year delay since her last release (which reportedly saw one completed album scrapped altogether), Siberry has obviously gone through some intense soul searching to determine where her muse was to take her next. Judging by *When I Was A Boy*, she ended up retreating to some neutral ground that drew on several elements of her previous work without really taking things anywhere new. This is a very personal, introspective album, its ambient textures consistent with the ambient work that production collaborators Brian Eno and Michael Brook are well known for. Even average Siberry is still better than most of what gets foisted on the public as female vocalist pop these days. It's just that one has come to expect more from her—like surprises and wonder—rather than the sound of treading water. — *Roch Parisien*

● **A Collection 1984-1989** / 1994 / Duke/MCA ♦♦♦♦
This collection doesn't shy away from Jane Siberry's more extended, difficult, but ultimately rewarding work found on *The Walking*. Otherwise, this 14-track compilation gathers all the most accessible Duke Street-period material produced by a very unique vocalist—from "Mimi On The Beach" and "The Waitress" to "Bound By The Beauty." Missing in action: anything from her debut indie release or *When I Was A Boy*. — *Roch Parisien*

The Silver Jews
Group, Alternative Pop/Rock
Not quite a side project, but not quite a full band, the Silver Jews are a "sister band" of the wonderfully sprawling, beyond-diverse group Pavement. And what a sister: The Jews' leader, D.C. Berman, is joined by Pavement's guitarist/vocalist Steven Malkmus and percussionist Bob Nastanovich, creating a sound that's definitely homespun, sometimes lighthearted and other times emotional. Countrified ballads rest comfortably alongside experimental noise-fests on the group's two releases, 1993's *The Arizona Record* EP and 1994's *Starlite Walker*. Not surprisingly, *The Arizona Record* is a more rackety, unkempt affair than the full-length *Starlite Walker*, which was recorded in an actual studio in Tennessee. — *Heather Phares*

The Arizona Record [EP] / 1993 / Drag City ♦♦♦
D.C. Berman, Stephen Malkmus and Bob Nastanovich recorded this EP on a Walkman, and it sure shows. About as lo-fi, avantgarde and willfully experimental as you can get on a shoestring budget, it sounds like it was lots of fun to record. While it's not essential listening, it gives a sense of history to the group's other recordings. — *Heather Phares*

● **Starlite Walker** / 1994 / Drag City ♦♦♦♦
Starlite Walker was recorded in an actual studio in Tennessee and contains lots of gorgeous pop songs penned by Berman and Malkmus. The album has an appealingly off-handed, laidback feel that gives simple but eloquent songs like "New Orleans," "Trains Across the Sea" and "Advice to the Graduate" an added intimacy and resonance. Aside from a couple of instrumentals, *Starlite Walker* is filled with enjoyable, folky-countrified pop that improves with each listen. — *Heather Phares*

Gene Simmons
Rock & Roll
Gene Simmons (not the Kiss guy) had a number 11 hit in 1964 with the novelty "Haunted House," but his heart was actually in the rich and rootsy rock, soul, and country traditions of his home base of Memphis. Born in Tupelo, MS, Simmons relocated to Memphis after recording some rockabilly for Sun Records, which actually only got around to issuing one single from his sessions. Moving to the Hi label in the early '60s, he recorded several singles and an album, but "Haunted House" was the only one that met with success before his last single for the company in 1966. With his white Southern R&B, Simmons echoed such fellow travelers as Roy Head, Bruce Channel, and post-rockabilly Dale Hawkins, although he was not as gritty or talented as any of them. He was a likable performer, though, and gave the Hi label some of its first taste of success. — *Richie Unterberger*

● **Goin' Back to Memphis** / 1987 / Hi ♦♦♦♦
16-song collection drawn from his mid-'60s singles, as well as three unissued cuts. Simmons is a decent singer and about half the material is strong, but the real stars of the album are the Hi

session players, who lay down impeccable punchy, shuffling grooves. Besides "Haunted House," highlights include the rollicking "Ramblin' Man" and "Go on Shoes," which qualifies as one of the great hit-singles-that-never-was with its moody hooks and terrific soulful female backup vocals. — *Richie Unterberger*

Simon & Garfunkel
Group, Folk-Rock
Between Paul Simon's (b. Oct 13, 1941) warm lower tenor and Art Garfunkel's (b. Nov 5, 1941) sweet, airy choirboy upper tenor, Simon and Garfunkel's delicate harmonic interplay (coupled with Simon's brilliant song craftsmanship) earned them the distinction of being the most successful folk-pop duo of the '60s and early '70s. As early as 1955, the twosome were seriously working on music together and registering their originals at the Library of Congress. Under the moniker Tom & Jerry, they landed a deal (while in high school) on the Big label in 1957. Their first single, "Hey Schoolgirl," charted nationally, landing them a spot on *American Bandstand*.

They went to separate colleges in 1959 but continued to release singles as solo artists under various pseudonyms. In 1964, Simon traveled to England and became active in the folk scene. While there, he met up with the vacationing Garfunkel, and they became Simon & Garfunkel. Shortly thereafter, Tom Wilson signed them to Columbia.

Their first album, *Wednesday Morning 3 A.M.*, was a pretty straightforward folk effort, blending originals with song covers. It failed to make an impression on the marketplace. Without informing the duo, Wilson took a track called "Sounds of Silence" off the album, added electric guitars, drums, and bass, and remixed it as a single. It soared to the number one position for two weeks and boosted their debut. The album *Sounds of Silence*, featuring the electrified title track, also hit. It included another hit single, "I Am a Rock." By this time, Paul Simon's writing was being mentioned in the same breath as that of Dylan and Lennon/McCartney, but much of his best writing was yet to come.

Their next three albums, *Parsley, Sage, Rosemary and Thyme*, *Bookends*, and *Bridge Over Troubled Water*, and the soundtrack album from the movie *The Graduate* (number one for nine weeks) were huge artistic and commercial successes. The duo broke up during the recording of *Bridge Over Troubled Water*. Simon had become increasingly frustrated with Garfunkel's absence while he pursued a career in movie-acting.

Bridge Over Troubled Water, its number one hit title track, and Simon & Garfunkel cleaned up at the 1971 Grammy Awards. Other hits include "Mrs. Robinson," "The Boxer," "Cecilia," "Fakin' It," "Scarborough Fair/Canticle," "At the Zoo," "A Hazy Shade of Winter" (later a hit for the Bangles), "El Condor Pasa," and "My Little Town," recorded as a reunion single in 1975 and released on Simon's solo *Still Crazy After All These Years*. — *Rick Clark*

Wednesday Morning 3 A.M. / Oct. 1964 / Columbia ♦♦
This is something of a folk sampler, circa 1964. Only five of the 12 songs were written by Paul Simon, and they include the mournful "He Was My Brother," which Garfunkel, in his liner notes, accurately says is "cast in the Bob Dylan mold" and has "no subtlety." But "The Sounds Of Silence," here in its original acoustic version, is the first Paul Simon song in the mature sense. And the album also contains such early '60s folk standards as Ed McCurdy's "Last Night I Had The Strangest Dream" and Bob Gibson and Hamilton Camp's "You Can Tell The World," sung in S&G's trademark tenor harmonies. A promising beginning. — *William Ruhlmann*

The Sounds of Silence / Jan. 1966 / Columbia ♦♦♦
The sudden, if belated, success of the folk-rock version of "The Sounds Of Silence" as a single called for an immediate accompanying album, so Simon and Garfunkel, who had more or less disbanded after the commercial failure of *Wednesday Morning, 3 A.M.*, quickly reformed and recut many of the songs Simon had recorded in England for his *Paul Simon Songbook* solo album (issued only in the U.K. at the time). The album did not contain the followup hit to "The Sounds Of Silence," "Homeward Bound," but it did contain the followup to that, "I Am A Rock," as well as Simon's musical rewrite of Edward Arlington Robinson's poem "Richard Cory" and other songs that aspired to poetry with an earnestness that made up for their preciousness. Still, this was a rushed album (S&G would never rush again), and it shows. — *William Ruhlmann*

○ **Parsley, Sage, Rosemary & Thyme** / Sep. 1966 / Columbia ✦✦✦✦
A far more considered album than the rushed *Sounds Of Silence*, *PSR&T* features "Homeward Bound" and S&G's fourth hit single, "The Dangling Conversation" (their first not to be a big hit), plus a slew of memorable album tracks: "Scarborough Fair/Canticle," which became a single in the wake of its appearance in the film *The Graduate*; "The 59th Street Bridge Song (Feelin' Groovy)," which became a hit for Harpers Bizarre; and "For Emily, Whenever I May Find Her," a showcase for Garfunkel's heavenly voice, among other songs. —*William Ruhlmann*

○ **The Graduate** / Feb. 1968 / Columbia ✦✦✦✦
An okay release from the 1967 movie, featuring some of Simon & Garfunkel's tunes alternating with instrumentals by Dave Grusin. —*Bruce Eder*

○ **Bookends** / Mar. 1968 / Columbia ✦✦✦✦
A conceptual album about friendship and old age, *Bookends* was one of the best and most ambitious records of the 1960s. Album tracks like "America" and "Old Friends" have become S&G standards, and the LP also contains four hit singles: "Mrs. Robinson," "A Hazy Shade of Winter," "Fakin' It," and "At the Zoo" (the last two redone from their single versions). —*William Ruhlmann*

☆ **Bridge Over Troubled Water** / Feb. 1970 / Columbia ✦✦✦✦✦
The massive commercial success of *Bridge Over Troubled Water*— it topped the charts for 10 weeks, won the Grammy Award for Album of the Year, included four hit singles, and has sold more than five million copies in the U.S.—tends to exaggerate its significance in the Simon and Garfunkel catalog. Actually, it's a step down from the masterpiece of *Bookends*, containing some filler, such as the comic if slight "Baby Driver" and the pleasant if inessential live cover of the Everly Brothers' "Bye Bye Love"; it also lacks the previous album's musical and thematic unity. Still, one is admittedly splitting hairs when talking about an album that contains such classics as the title song and "The Boxer," as well as such notable tunes as "Cecilia," "El Condor Pasa," and "So Long, Frank Lloyd Wright." This is Simon and Garfunkel's most popular album because it legitimately spoke to its audience, and much of it continues to set standards in thoughtful pop music decades later. —*William Ruhlmann*

● **Greatest Hits** / Jun. 1972 / Columbia ✦✦✦✦
Nothing much more than what it says, although the live tracks are interesting. —*Bruce Eder*

☆ **Collected Works** / 1981 / Columbia ✦✦✦✦✦
This 3-CD set is the only way to get the original albums with the best sound that's ever likely to turn up. —*Bruce Eder*

○ **Concert in Central Park** / Feb. 1982 / Warner Brothers ✦✦✦✦
Simon and Garfunkel reunited on September 19, 1981, to perform a free concert in Central Park, New York City. This two-record set presents some of the duo's biggest hits in a live context and also allows listeners a chance to hear what many Simon solo numbers could sound like in S&G mode. —*William Ruhlmann*

Carly Simon

b. Jun. 25, 1945
Singer-Songwriter, Pop
Simon, who possesses an airy, somewhat unsteady alto, was one of the more popular female artists of the '70s, presenting a blend of singer/songwriter introspection and slick pop-smarts. She worked with her sister in a music group (The Simon Sisters) and experienced a false solo-artist start in 1966. Simon's career took a turn for the better with her self-titled debut. It produced a #10 hit in "That's the Way I've Always Heard It Should Be," and "Anticipation" (#13). The followup, *Hotcakes*, was practically a duet album with then-husband James Taylor (they split in 1982). With her third effort, *No Secrets*, Simon linked up with producer Richard Perry, resulting in a #1 album that included her politely snotty putdown hit, "You're So Vain."
Simon has continued to enjoy periodic chart success in recent years. Her hits include "Nobody Does It Better," "The Right Thing to Do," "Haven't Got Time for the Pain," "You Belong to Me," "Jesse," and "Coming Around Again." —*Rick Clark*

Carly Simon / 1971 / Elektra ✦✦
Anticipation / Nov. 1971 / Elektra ✦✦✦
Carly Simon's second album found her extending the gutsy persona she had established on her debut album, notably on the title track, "Legend In Your Own Time" (both of them hit singles), and "I've Got To Have You." The last especially suggested a frankly pas-

sionate person whose vulnerability was a source of strength, not weakness, a valuable feminist trait and one Simon would pursue in her later work. —*William Ruhlmann*

○ **No Secrets** / Dec. 1972 / Elektra ✦✦✦✦
Hotcakes / Jan. 1974 / Elektra ✦✦
A glowing, pregnant Carly Simon smiles out from the cover of *Hotcakes*, one of her biggest selling albums, which featured the gold single "Mockingbird," a duet with her husband James Taylor that effectively remade the old Inez and Charlie Foxx hit and bested it on the charts. The album also included another hit, "Haven't Got Time For The Pain," as well as "Misfit," in which a wife implores her carousing husband to come home, and "Think I'm Gonna Have A Baby," which celebrated the joys of same. With such tracks, *Hotcakes* was an autobiographical concept album that defined domestic bliss at a time when Simon's listeners also were catching their breath and turning inward. —*William Ruhlmann*

Playing Possum / 1975 / Elektra ✦✦✦
● **The Best of Carly Simon** / Nov. 1975 / Elektra ✦✦✦✦
Good collection from Simon's most popular period, including "Anticipation," "That's the Way I've Always Heard It Should Be," and "You're So Vain." —*Cub Koda*

Another Passenger / 1976 / Elektra ✦✦✦
Takin' It Easy / 1977 / Warner Brothers ✦✦
Boys in the Trees / Apr. 1978 / Elektra ✦✦✦
Spy / 1979 / Elektra ✦✦✦
Come Upstairs / 1980 / Warner Brothers ✦✦
Torch / 1981 / Warner Brothers ✦✦✦
Carly Simon slightly anticipated the trend toward contemporary pop singers turning to pop standards here, singing songs like "I Got It Bad And That Ain't Good" and "Body And Soul." The theme, of course, was romantic torment, and it was expressed no better than on the final track, a new song from Stephen Sondheim's then-upcoming musical *Merrily We Roll Along* called "Not A Day Goes By" that Simon delivered with heartbreaking conviction. —*William Ruhlmann*

Hello Big Man / 1983 / Warner Brothers ✦✦✦
Spoiled Girl / 1985 / Epic ✦✦
Leaving Warner Bros. after the relative commercial failure of *Hello, Big Man*, Carly Simon moved to the Epic label, which gave her the big-budget star treatment on the appropriately named *Spoiled Girl*. No less than eight producers labored over this, and they included such heavyweights as Don Was and Phil Ramone, although everyone from disco king Arthur Baker to the team of T-Bone Wolk and G.E. Smith, late of the Hall and Oates band, got a shot. Simon's sales continued to slide, with the album topping out at #88, and she and Epic parted company after only one release. —*William Ruhlmann*

Coming Around Again / Mar. 1987 / Arista ✦✦✦
After the debacle that was *Spoiled Girl*, Carly Simon moved to her fourth record label, Arista, and returned to soundtrack work. This time, she wrote "Coming Around Again" for *Heartburn*, and it hit #18 in early 1987, her biggest hit in more than six years. That set up Simon's comeback with this album, which became her biggest hit in a decade, producing two more chart singles, "Give Me All Night" (#61) and "All I Want Is You" (#54), and going platinum. Once again, a bevy of producers—nine this time—weighed in in an attempt to vary Simon's appeal. The big difference was that this time, Simon was willing to go to her strengths as a ballad singer rather than romping amid synthesized blips. Better to flirt with retro than disco, at least as far as Simon's audience is concerned. —*William Ruhlmann*

Greatest Hits Live / 1988 / Arista ✦✦✦
Have You Seen Me Lately / 1990 / Arista ✦✦✦
Have You Seen Me Lately? was Carly Simon's first studio album of original material in three and a half years. Simon has always written songs for her age group; here, it's the fortysomethings of the 1990s. "I've been doing a lot of thinking/About growing older and moving on," she sings, and in her world that entails "protein shakes," "twelve-step groups," and stays in clinics. Some relief is provided in the single "Better Not Tell Her" and "Fisherman's Song," on which Simon duets with Judy Collins. But you can't help thinking that the ongoing life story portrayed in Simon's songs has become somewhat limited. At the end, "We Just Got Here" provides the summer's-end metaphor for middle age, and we are left

with the impression that there's nothing ahead but cold weather. — *William Ruhlmann*

My Romance / Mar. 1990 / Arista ✦✦✦
On her second album of pop standards, Carly Simon was a little less interested in the lovelorn songs that had filled 1981's *Torch*, although she did soldier through "By Myself" and "When Your Lover Has Gone." For the most part, the theme was romantic, with classics like "My Funny Valentine" and "Bewitched" handled in Simon's sexy, plaintive style. Okay, she was no Peggy Lee, but she wasn't bad. — *William Ruhlmann*

This Is My Life / 1992 / Qwest ✦✦
Singing on soundtracks had been very good for Carly Simon, who scored four chart hits with movie themes between 1977 and 1989, so it's surprising she never did a full score until this, Nora Ephron's directorial debut about a single mother who becomes a standup comic. (Ephron had written the screenplay for *Heartburn*, which featured Simon's comeback hit, "Coming Around Again.") Simon contributed five light songs and some instrumentals in what for her was an unusually relaxed, playful style. In retrospect, maybe she wishes she'd waited and scored Ephron's second feature, the hit *Sleepless In Seattle*, the following year. ("Love Of My Life" hit #16 on the Adult Contemporary chart, but the album itself did not chart.) — *William Ruhlmann*

Carly Simon's Romulus Hunt: A Family Opera / 1993 / Angel ✦✦
Fitting into that category also occupied by *Paul McCartney's Liverpool Oratorio*, *Carly Simon's Romulus Hunt: A Family Opera* is a 46-minute musical about a 12-year-old upper-class boy living in New York City who tries to effect a reconciliation between his divorced parents. The music is pop-classical, and the singing is done by a cast of five. Simon certainly knows the material, and it gives her a chance to stretch musically, but it might better have been rendered as an afterschool TV-movie than as an operetta. (Simon herself appears only at the end, singing one of the songs as a bonus track.) — *William Ruhlmann*

Joe Simon

b. Sep. 2, 1943
Soul
His plaintive baritone equally conversant with R&B and country phrasing, Joe Simon married the two genres with startling success during the late '60s, adapting Nashville material to the soul sound and repeatedly coming up a winner. Simon began recording in the Bay Area, but a switch in recording sites (first to Muscle Shoals for Vee-Jay and then to Nashville, upon signing with deejay John Richbourg's Sound Stage 7 label in 1966) heightened his national appeal. With easy access to prime country-oriented material, Simon soon found his true calling, scoring major hits with "Nine Pound Steel," "(You Keep Me) Hangin' On," and the #1 R&B smash "The Chokin' Kind," penned by Music Row tunesmith Harlan Howard. Still dabbling in country covers after switching to the Spring imprint in 1970, Simon was even more successful when assigned to Philadelphia producers Kenny Gamble and Leon Huff, who produced the moody "Drowning in the Sea of Love" the next year. Simon tried his hand at disco in 1975 with the sizzling "Get Down, Get Down (Get on the Floor)" and "Music in My Bones," two of the most palatable artifacts of the era. Simon eventually retired from active performing to devote his life to the church. — *Bill Dahl*

Pure Soul / 1967 / Sound Stage 7 ✦✦✦
Joe Simon established himself as a poignant, folksy, yet urgent vocalist with his debut album on the Sound Stage label. He was then working with the great disc jockey John "R" Richbourg, who helped him find the right blend of soulful ardor and countrified narrative. While neither "Teenager's Prayer" nor "Nine Pound Steel" hit the charts, they laid the groundwork for Simon's monster hits that followed two years later. This album has long been deleted; look for it on collector's auction lists or in used record stores. — *Ron Wynn*

No Sad Songs / 1968 / Sound Stage 7 ✦✦✦
Joe Simon's second album predated his big soul hits, but contained superb vocals and some wonderful country-tinged numbers. His voice was as smooth as glass and had the perfect mix of downhome wit and intensity. He glided through his lyrics, never screaming or wailing, yet still turning ballads into expressive triumphs and caressing the groove while punctuating the lyrics on the uptempo numbers. — *Ron Wynn*

○ **Simon Sings** / 1969 / Sound Stage 7 ✦✦✦✦
Joe Simon was just a step away from being a star when he issued his third album in 1969. His voice was becoming deeper, his style and delivery more confident, and he was getting stronger material. The country/soul blend came together on this album, and he was now mixing sassy uptempo tunes with smoky ballads and starting to break beyond Dixie. — *Ron Wynn*

Better Than Ever / 1969 / Sound Stage 7 ✦✦✦
This followup to Joe Simon's big hit album *The Chokin' Kind* was his third issued that year. The overkill probably resulted in it not doing very well, and there was no song as brilliant as "The Chokin' Kind," which had topped the R&B charts and cracked the pop Top 20. But Simon did generate a pair of moderate R&B hits and kept the momentum building so much that he soon left Sound Stage for Spring. — *Ron Wynn*

● **Golden Classics** / Collectables ✦✦✦✦
Simon had good minor hits, most of which are here. — *Dan Heilman*

Paul Simon (Paul Frederick Simon)

b. Oct. 13, 1941, Newark, New Jersey
Singer-Songwriter, Pop/Rock
In a career dating back to the 1950s, Paul Simon has established himself among the best and most popular songwriters of the rock era. Growing up in Queens, NY, Simon befriended schoolmate Art Garfunkel, who had an angelic tenor voice, and the two teamed up as Tom and Jerry, taking the names of the cartoon characters. In the winter of 1957-58, they scored a chart hit with "Hey Schoolgirl"; both were 16 years old.

Simon continued to try to score hits in the late '50s and early '60s, reaching the charts briefly in 1962 in the group Tico and the Triumphs with "Motorcycle" and under the name Jerry Landis in 1963 with "The Lone Teen Ranger." He and Garfunkel teamed up again as a folk duo in Greenwich Village, signed to Columbia Records, and released *Wednesday Morning 3 A.M.* (October 1964). The album flopped initially, but Simon, who had been spending a lot of time in England, was picked up as a solo artist by CBS [UK] and recorded *The Paul Simon Songbook*, released only in Great Britain in the spring of 1965.

In the wake of the folk-rock trend prevalent that year, producer Tom Wilson took the acoustic track "The Sounds of Silence" from the *Wednesday Morning* album, overdubbed electric guitar, bass, and drums, and released the result as a single in October 1965, a full year after the album's release. It took off and hit #1, establishing Simon and Garfunkel.

For the next five years, they were one of the most successful acts in pop music. Simon wrote the songs, and the two harmonized on a series of hit singles and albums. They split up in 1970, after the release of their most popular album, *Bridge Over Troubled Water*.

Simon returned to solo work with *Paul Simon* (January 1972), which could not hope to match the success of *Bridge*, but which did sell a million copies and feature the reggae-tinged Top Ten single "Mother and Child Reunion." *There Goes Rhymin' Simon* (May 1973) was another million-seller, containing the hits "Kodachrome" and "Loves Me like a Rock." After a 1974 live album, Simon released *Still Crazy After All These Years* (October 1975), which topped the charts, won the Grammy for Album of the Year, and included the #1 hit "50 Ways to Leave Your Lover."

Simon took his time following this success, though he did release a greatest hits album featuring a new hit, "Slip Slidin' Away," and contributed to a remake of "What a Wonderful World" with Garfunkel and James Taylor. Moving to Warner Bros. Records, he wrote and starred in the film *One Trick Pony* (August 1980), the soundtrack of which contained the Top Ten hit "Late in the Evening."

Another three years passed before Simon returned with *Hearts & Bones* (October 1983), which did not match his usual level of commercial success. Simon experimented with songwriting styles and became interested in South African music, resulting in *Graceland* (August 1986), which became his biggest selling solo album and won him another Album of the Year Grammy. Four years later, he delivered *The Rhythm of the Saints* (October 1990), which did for Brazilian music what *Graceland* had done for South African music and was another multi-platinum seller. Simon played a free concert in Central Park in August 1991 (ten years after Simon and Garfunkel had done one) and released a live album from the show. In 1993, Warner Bros. released a boxed set retrospective on Simon's career, and he undertook a tour that featured Garfunkel on their old hits, as well as covering other aspects of his career. — *William Ruhlmann*

☆ **Paul Simon** / 1972 / Warner Brothers ✦✦✦✦✦
Backing away from the heavy production of the last Simon & Garfunkel album, Paul Simon's first solo outing is a quiet affair based around acoustic guitar. "Mother and Child Reunion," a successful experiment with reggae, is included, as is "Me and Julio Down by the Schoolyard"; the great Stephane Grappelli guests on "Hobo's Blues." Many of Simon's finest songs are found here. — *Stephen Thomas Erlewine*

☆ **There Goes Rhymin' Simon** / 1973 / Warner Brothers ✦✦✦✦✦
Simon listened to R&B when he was growing up, and he returns to those roots on *Rhymin' Simon*. At times, the results are true R&B and even gospel ("Loves Me like a Rock" was recorded with the Dixie Hummingbirds), but mostly there is a lot of beautiful, sophisticated pop shaded with blues ("St. Judy's Comet" and "Something So Right.") Not as fully realized as *Paul Simon*, but there is much rewarding listening to be found. — *Stephen Thomas Erlewine*

Live Rhymin' / 1974 / Warner Brothers ✦✦✦

☆ **Still Crazy After All These Years** / 1975 / Warner Brothers ✦✦✦✦✦
Replacing the guitar with the piano as the primary instrument, Simon produced a quiet, introspective Grammy-winning album centering around lost love. Simon reunites with Garfunkel on "My Little Town," a track that sounds nothing like old S&G songs. *Still Crazy* doesn't really resemble Simon's two previous albums; it is a serious, somber album with none of the light touches present on *Paul Simon* and *Rhymin' Simon*. — *Stephen Thomas Erlewine*

One Trick Pony [O.S.T.] / 1980 / Warner Brothers ✦✦✦
This is usually categorized as a regular Paul Simon album, although its songs were featured in the Simon-written-and-starring film of the same name. Featuring New York session aces like Steve Gadd, Richard Tee, Tony Levin, and Eric Gale, the music has a contemporary jazz feel, and typical of a Simon album there are some extraordinary lyrics. "Late in the Evening" was the hit, but that's only the beginning. — *William Ruhlmann*

○ **Hearts & Bones** / 1983 / Warner Brothers ✦✦✦✦
An understated set of introspective folk-rock that contains some of Simon's finest, most literate songs. — *Stephen Thomas Erlewine*

☆ **Graceland** / 1986 / Warner Brothers ✦✦✦✦✦
Graceland is immediately accessible because the music is exotic yet familiar. As Simon says in the liner notes, he was drawn to South African music because it sounded "like '50s rock & roll out of the Atlantic Records school of simple three-chord pop." Simon put his own melodies and lyrics to South African rhythms and chords, producing a remarkable hybrid. The songs are some of his best, recovering from a ten-year dry spell. Los Lobos guests on "All Around the World." *Graceland* is not only Simon's best album but an all-time classic rock & roll album. — *Stephen Thomas Erlewine*

★ **Negotiations & Love Songs 1971-1986** / 1988 / Warner Brothers ✦✦✦✦✦
A good sampler of Paul Simon's personal favorites and hits. Many of his frequent changes in style are captured here, as are the highlights of the *One Trick Pony* and *Hearts & Bones* albums. — *Stephen Thomas Erlewine*

○ **Rhythm of the Saints** / 1990 / Warner Brothers ✦✦✦✦
Simon moved from Africa to Brazil and produced an album that resembles *Graceland*, but is harder to grasp. The songs are more oblique than *Graceland's* and the music is harder to absorb in one listen. After a couple of repeat listenings, the album begins to take shape, and melodies emerge under the heavy percussion. It's necessary to put some time into this album, but the results are well worth it. — *Stephen Thomas Erlewine*

○ **Paul Simon's Concert in the Park, August 15, 1991** / 1992 / Warner Brothers ✦✦✦✦
Simon plays all the favorites from his African and Brazilian albums and recasts some old favorites in these settings. Sometimes the results are thought-provoking ("Bridge Over Troubled Water" and "Sound of Silence"), sometimes severely faulted ("Kodachrome" and "Cecilia"), but the album is immensely entertaining and listenable. — *Stephen Thomas Erlewine*

1964-1993 / 1993 / Warner Brothers ✦✦✦
Simon's box set contains a great deal of fine music, including all of his hits, as well as a smattering of rare and unreleased material. However, he has already released two other fine compilations, and *1964-1990* treads the same ground as those. It also draws too heavily on *Graceland* and *The Rhythm of the Saints*, devoting an entire disc to these two albums, while shortchanging his work with Simon & Garfunkel. Collectors will also be frustrated by the small amount of rarities, as well as the poorly executed packaging. There's no denying that the music here is great, but this box could have been much more than what it is. — *Stephen Thomas Erlewine*

Simple Minds

Group, Alternative Pop/Rock
Simple Minds was conceived in 1977 out of the remains of the Glasgow, Scotland, band Johnny & the Self-Abusers. Their initial albums were rather dissonant, moody, synth-heavy dance-music excursions that enjoyed increasing popularity in the British Isles, due to the band's incessant touring. The 1982 album *New Gold Dream (1981, '82, '83, '84)* (U.K. #3) spent a year on the British charts and produced three hit singles; the followup, *Sparkle in the Rain*, was a #1 hit in England. In 1984, lead singer Jim Kerr's marriage to Chrissie Hynde of the Pretenders became a pop-media event.
Nevertheless, it wasn't until the band recorded a non-original track, "Don't You Forget About Me" (#1), for the 1985 brat-pack film *The Breakfast Club* that the group began making a big impression stateside. During that time, Simple Minds played at the historic Live Aid benefit in Philadelphia. Their next album, *Once Upon a Time* (#10), featured a clean, radio-friendly production by Bob Clearmountain and Jimmy Iovine and generated a few Top 40 hits.
Subsequent efforts have included a fine live album and a couple of dramatically produced studio releases that continue the band's hopeful humanitarian themes. — *Rick Clark*

Life in a Day / 1979 / Virgin ✦✦
Real to Real Cacophony / 1980 / Virgin ✦✦
Empires and Dance / 1980 / Sport ✦✦
Sons and Fascination / Jan. 1981 / Virgin ✦✦✦
Sister Feelings Call / Feb. 1981 / Virgin ✦✦✦
Life in a Simple Day / 1982 / Virgin ✦✦
Celebration / 1982 / Virgin ✦✦✦

○ **New Gold Dream** / 1982 / A&M ✦✦✦✦
New Gold Dream was the first effort (after many spotty earlier releases) to exhibit a focused collection of strong songs. The material, overall, is a coolly elegant style of synth-rich dance-pop. Among the album's highlights are "Promised You a Miracle," "Glittering Prize," and the title song. — *Rick Clark*

○ **Sparkle in the Rain** / 1984 / A&M ✦✦✦✦
On *Sparkle in the Rain*, Simple Minds assembled the best songs of their career and brought in producer Steve Lillywhite (XTC, Psychedelic Furs, U2) to help articulate their vision. The result was the best album of their career, thus far. Lillywhite's sweeping cinematic soundscapes perfectly suited grand songs like "WaterFront," "Book of Brilliant Things," "Up on the Catwalk," "East of Easter," and a version of Lou Reed's "Street Hassle." "Kick Inside of Me" rocks harder than anything the band has ever done. Highly recommended! — *Rick Clark*

○ **Once upon a Time** / 1985 / A&M ✦✦✦✦
On the wings of the popular 1985 *Breakfast Club* soundtrack hit, Simple Minds enlisted in-demand producers Jimmy Iovine and Bob Clearmountain and released the ready-made-for-American-FM-radio *Once Upon a Time*. In spite of the fact that this album generated three hits with "Alive & Kicking" (number three), "Sanctify Yourself" (number 14), and "All the Things She Said" (number 28), Simple Minds had lost the inspirational edge they had attained on *Sparkle in the Rain*. — *Rick Clark*

Live in the City of Light / 1987 / A&M ✦✦✦
Simple Minds has a reputation as an excellent live unit, and this well-recorded 1986 set done in Paris is a testament to that fact. With the help of extra sidemen (background vocalists, computer programmer, and violinist) the band runs through a wide sampling of their best material. — *Rick Clark*

Street Fighting Years / 1989 / A&M ✦✦✦

Real Life / 1991 / A&M ✦✦

● **Glittering Prize** / 1993 / A&M ✦✦✦✦

Glittering Prize falls short of being a true anthology of Simple Minds, eliminating many key tracks (not even "Glittering Prize," the song the album is named after, is included) and giving too much weight to the band's later years (an inexplicable three tracks from 1991's *Real Life* are included). Still, all the mid-'80s hits are here, including "(Don't You) Forget About Me," making its first appearance on a Simple Minds album, which will be enough for most casual fans. —*Stephen Thomas Erlewine*

Good News From The Next World / 1995 / Virgin ✦✦✦

Appearing after the commercial failure of *The Real Life*, *Good News from the Next World* managed to stir up some attention from both album and alternative rock stations. However, the record quickly faded and it's easy to see why—apart from the slick "She's a River," there is no strong single material. It's well-produced and performed, yet Simple Minds' songs just miss the mark. —*Stephen Thomas Erlewine*

Simply Red

Group, Soul, Pop/Rock
Led by the vocalist Mick Hucknall, the English blue-eyed soul band Simply Red became international stars with their debut album, *Picture Book*. With the hit ballad "Holding Back the Years," Hucknall proved that he could sing soulfully without affectation and their cover of the Valentine Brothers' "Money's Too Tight to Mention" proved that they could do light-funk capably. With each album, their fan base has expanded, especially in the U.K.; their latest album, 1991's *Stars*, outsold 1991 albums from U2, Guns N' Roses, and Michael Jackson in Britain. —*Stephen Thomas Erlewine*

● **Picture Book** / 1985 / Elektra ✦✦✦✦

The band finds a steady R&B groove reminiscent of '60s Stax house band the MG's, and, as with the MG's, it's all in the service of a big-voiced soul singer, in this case a British redhead. Features the U.S. #1 "Holding Back the Years" and the U.K. Top 20 "Money's Too Tight (To Mention)." —*William Ruhlmann*

Men & Women / 1987 / Elektra ✦✦✦

After a monster debut, Simply Red's follow-up album simply didn't get the job done. It wasn't a half-hearted effort; Mick Hucknall's crackling vocals were just as exuberant, and the band's Stax/Volt-influenced lines were effectively played. The songs, however, were an uneven batch and lacked the kind of standout single Hucknall had enjoyed on the previous album with "Holding Back The Years." They did turn in an interesting version of "Ev'ry Time We Say Goodbye." —*Ron Wynn*

○ **A New Flame** / 1989 / Elektra ✦✦✦✦

Although Hucknall tries to resurrect soul in his own original songs, he's most successful at evoking the past, notably on Simply Red's second #1, a remake of the Harold Melvin & the Blue Notes classic "If You Don't Know Me by Now." —*William Ruhlmann*

○ **Stars** / 1991 / East West ✦✦✦✦

Although it didn't have a single as strong as "Holding Back the Years" or "If You Don't Know Me By Now," *Stars* was Simply Red's best album since its debut. It was smoother and more polished than their previous work, while Mick Hucknall was singing better than ever and his songwriting was improving. —*Stephen Thomas Erlewine*

Nancy Sinatra

Group, Pop, Pop/Rock
A pop/rock performer who leaned very heavily toward the "pop" side of that designation, Frank Sinatra's daughter Nancy enjoyed a brief run of superstardom between 1966 and 1968. Not nearly the vocalist her father is, the family name didn't hurt her advances in the business, nor did the fact that she recorded for Frank's label, Reprise. Her first few singles met with little success, and Nancy was on the verge of being dropped when she hooked up with producer Lee Hazlewood and arranger Billy Strange. They urged her to lower her voice and toughen her delivery, and crafted material emphasizing growling bass lines and "go-go" tempos. One of their first efforts, the 1966 single "These Boots Are Made for Walkin" topped the charts, inaugurating a series of hits over the next couple years, the biggest of which were "Sugar Town," "Lightning's Girl," "Love Eyes," and her number one hit duet with her father,

"Somethin' Stupid." No one could advance serious claims for Nancy as a significant artist, and her unabashedly pop output was certainly at odds with the innovations setting the worlds of rock and soul afire in the psychedelic era. But they were good fun, and her best singles are still good listening, capturing the most lightweight period charm of the top 40 of her time.

Nancy's singles were as notable for their distinctive arrangements and the odd, brooding compositions of Lee Hazlewood, who wrote most of her hits, as her own sex-kitten vocals. Specializing in oddly disquieting songs with a sort of modern Western theme, Hazlewood teamed up with Sinatra for a few duets which presented the chalk'n'cheese combination of Nancy's thin voice with Lee's gravelly, almost spoken delivery, which recalled an off-kilter Johnny Cash. The team actually managed a few hits, some of which, especially "Some Velvet Morning," rank as some of the most bizarre MOR Top 40 pop hits of all time. Nancy didn't enter the Top 40, with or without Hazlewood, after early 1968. Sundazed has embarked upon an extensive Nancy Sinatra reissue series of her original albums, though all but completists should be satisfied by her greatest hits compilations. —*Richie Unterberger*

○ **Boots** / 1966 / Reprise ✦✦✦✦

Unexceptional debut album, built around "These Boots Are Made For Walkin'" and covers of contemporary rock and pop hits, with a couple of other Lee Hazlewood songs. The CD reissue adds a few rare early single tracks (all penned by Hazlewood) as bonus cuts, as well as the mono single version of "Boots." —*Richie Unterberger*

How Does That Grab You? / 1966 / Reprise ✦✦✦

Sophomore effort sticks to her usual LP formula: a hit title track, a bunch of pop covers ("Bang Bang" is the best), and some unremarkable Lee Hazlewood songs, the exception being the classy Nancy & Lee duet "Sand." Four notable bonus tracks on the CD reissue from 45s: the fuzz-guitar-driven single "Lightning's Girl" (one of her very best songs), a cover of Buffy St. Marie's "Until It's Time For You To Go," the single "The Last Of The Secret Agent," and the breezy California pop duet with her father, "Feelin' Kinda Sunday." —*Richie Unterberger*

Nancy in London / 1966 / Reprise ✦✦✦

The change of locale for Nancy's third album didn't change her approach much: it's dominated by humdrum covers of contemporary pop and rock hits and pop standards, with some second-rank Lee Hazlewood country songs thrown in, though his compositions "Friday Child" and "Summer Wine" (the second of which is a Nancy/Lee duet) are strong, moody highlights. The four bonus tracks, taken from singles, outclass the original LP: "100 Years," "You Only Live Twice" (the single version), "Tony Rome," and her cringingly dated duet with her father, "Life's A Trippy Thing." —*Richie Unterberger*

Country, My Way / 1967 / Reprise ✦✦

Sugar / 1967 / Reprise ✦✦

Even major Nancy fans may find their patience taxed by this album, on which she concentrates on non-rock popular standards by the likes of Irving Berlin, complete with weak vaudevillian MOR arrangements. Highlights are the Hazlewood-penned Top Ten hit "Sugar Town," and the two CD bonus tracks, taken from singles: "Somethin' Stupid" and the dramatic, almost menacing "Love Eyes." —*Richie Unterberger*

● **The Hit Years** / 1986 / Rhino ✦✦✦✦

Contains all the essential tracks: every hit, including those with her father and with Hazlewood, and a bunch of interesting misses, such as the theme song to the James Bond film *You Only Live Twice*. Focuses mostly on material penned by Hazlewood, and has comprehensive liner notes. An Australian best-of on the Raven label, *Lightning's Girl*, has a few more songs, but this less expensive 18-track domestic compilation covers all the key bases. —*Richie Unterberger*

○ **Fairy Tales & Fantasies: Best of Nancy Sinatra and Lee Hazlewood** / 1989 / Rhino ✦✦✦✦

Basically a reissue of the 1968 album *Nancy and Lee*, with some bonus tracks. Has all of the duo's hits ("Summer Wine," "Jackson," "Sand," "Lady Bird," and "Some Velvet Morning"), which easily outclass the filler material. And those hits are about as inspired as middle-of-the-road pop gets, especially the eerie "Some Velvet Morning," one of the strangest songs ever to crack the Top 40. —*Richie Unterberger*

Siouxsie & the Banshees

Group, Punk, Alternative Pop/Rock, New Wave
One of the first U.K. punk bands inspired directly by the Sex Pis-

tols, Siouxsie and the Banshees fashioned their own dark, confrontational brand of rock, becoming one of the first goth bands. Led by the cold, detached vocals of singer Siouxsie Sioux, the band's music was abrasive but not fast; it was a wall of terror and darkness. On stage she frequently flirted with Nazi symbols, causing quite a controversy in Britain; despite the onstage imagery, the band's music was gathering quite a following in the U.K.

After their first few albums, the band began softening its harsh sound, wandering into pop territory; in 1983, the group had a U.K. hit with its sublime version of the Beatles' "Dear Prudence." Siouxise's voice had become warmer and more accessible, which helped the band become more commercially successful. All the while, the band has never lost their creative edge, exploring new territory with each new album. —*Stephen Thomas Erlewine*

○ **The Scream** / 1978 / Geffen ✦✦✦✦
By waiting until punk essentially had blown over to sign a contract, the Banshees had a clear field for their harsh rock attack, and plenty of time to prepare it. The result is this fierce debut, which fulfills the promise of punk and suggests (unlike most of its progenitors) that it has a future. —*William Ruhlmann*

○ **Join Hands** / 1979 / Geffen ✦✦✦✦

Kaleidoscope / 1980 / Geffen ✦✦✦

Juju / 1981 / Geffen ✦✦✦
They're shifting gradually toward a more straightforward rock sound, but the Banshees also add Middle Eastern touches here. Contains the British hits "Spellbound" and "Arabian Knights." —*William Ruhlmann*

● **Once upon a Time: The Singles** / 1981 / Geffen ✦✦✦✦
This compilation of U.K. singles (some appearing on an album for the first time) emphasizes the more pop sound of Siouxsie and the Banshees. Still not easy listening, though. —*William Ruhlmann*

Kiss in the Dream House / 1982 / Geffen ✦✦✦

Nocturne / 1983 / Geffen ✦✦✦

Hyaena / 1984 / Geffen ✦✦✦
Siouxsie and the Banshees's first album to benefit from a major-label push in the U.S. (and make the charts) finds them taking a more melodic, expressive approach and even covering the Beatles' "Dear Prudence." Old fans howled, but there were a lot of new fans. —*William Ruhlmann*

○ **Tinderbox** / 1986 / Geffen ✦✦✦✦

Through the Looking Glass / 1987 / Geffen ✦✦✦
Well-selected album of rock and pop cover songs, including everything from Sparks' "This Town Ain't Big Enough for Both of Us" to "Strange Fruit." —*William Ruhlmann*

Peep Show / 1988 / Geffen ✦✦✦

● **Twice upon a Time: The Singles** / Oct. 13, 1992 / Geffen ✦✦✦✦
A good collection of singles, *Twice upon a Time* picks up where *Once upon a Time* left off—1981 to 1993, their more mainstream period. The albums from this time span may be too ambitious for some but the singles shouldn't be missed. This is probably the best introduction to the band. —*Chris Woodstra*

The Sir Douglas Quintet

Group, Rock & Roll, Tex-Mex
Texas had always had its own brand of rock & roll—a little bit o' country, a little bit o' blues, with a heapin' helpin' o' hot sauce poured over the top. Doug Sahm was no stranger to the studio when he formed the Sir Douglas Quintet in 1964; he'd been at it since the age of six, and already possessed an encyclopedic knowledge and innate understanding of those local flavors when the band cut its first big hit, "She's About a Mover."

The ingredient that set the Quintet apart was Tex-Mex, that curious, joyous, irresistible, danceable, festive feast that married the jumpy Mexican *conjunto* to good ol' rock & roll. With Augie Meyers on the organ and a rhythm section that couldn't stop cookin', Sir Doug Sahm let it be known that good-time music was alive and kickin' in San Antone.

After the Quintet itself dissolved, Sahm cut numerous solo albums and collaborations, spreading the Tex-Mex influence. In the late '80s he and Meyers teamed up with two of their mentors, Freddy Fender and Flaco Jimenez, to form the Texas Tornados, keeping that high and happy sound alive. —*Jeff Tamarkin*

○ **Sir Doug's Recording Trip: The Mercury Years** / 1988 / Edsel ✦✦✦✦
An incredible 30-song sampling of his Quintet and solo years, it features most of the hits, some rare delicacies, and an educational set of notes by Ed Ward. (Import) —*John Floyd*

● **The Best of Doug Sahm & Sir Douglas Quintet** / 1990 / PolyGram ✦✦✦✦
This is not as thorough as *Sir Doug's Recording Trip*, but it's easier to find and gives you 22 essential tracks in sterling digital fidelity. —*John Floyd*

Sir Mix-A-Lot

Rap
Sir Mix-A-Lot put Seattle on the rap map in the late '80s with catchy, comedic dramas drenched in b-boy culture and punctuated by his whiny vocals.

Sir Mix-A-Lot vaulted into the spotlight and into controversy with the single "Baby Got Back." Not only was it an enormous pop and R&B hit, it triggered a backlash against what was widely viewed as both sexist and racist lyrics from Mix-A-Lot in his celebration of rear ends and putdown of women who lacked them. It helped make the *Mack Daddy* album one of '92's biggest. —*John Floyd*

Swass / 1988 / Def American ✦✦✦
Sir Mix-A-Lot's debut album fluctuated between heavy bass tracks reminiscent of 2 Live Crew and heavy metal/rap fusions, like a heavier version of Run-D.M.C. At this point, he hadn't perfected his goofy, almost satiric, take on gangsta rap, although some tracks pointed the way towards his finest album, 1992's *Mack Daddy*. —*Stephen Thomas Erlewine*

Seminar / Mar. 1988 / Def American ✦✦✦

● **Mack Daddy** / Apr. 1992 / Def American ✦✦✦✦
Sir Mix-A-Lot scored a huge sleeper hit with his ridiculous paean to large buttocks, "Baby Got Back," in the summer of 1992. For those who want it, the rest of *Mack Daddy* offers more of the same—skeletal raps that verge on the point of parody. Sir Mix-A-Lot can barely rap, and his lyrics are full of posturing tales that never have a dose of reality. But this is the very element that makes *Mack Daddy* fun, because Sir Mix-A-Lot tries so hard and sounds so silly. —*Stephen Thomas Erlewine*

Chief Booty Knocka / 1994 / Rhyme Cartel ✦✦✦

Sister Sledge

Group, Disco, Soul
Sisters Debra, Joan, Kim, and Kathie began recording as Sisters Sledge for Money Back in 1971. They also did numerous sessions before dropping the "s" from their first name. They collaborated with Chic for some seminal dance/soul hits in the late '70s and early '80s. Sister Sledge enjoyed two number one R&B hits and two other Top Ten singles from 1979 to 1981, as well as Top Ten pop hits. Both "He's the Greatest Dancer" and "We Are Family" were international smashes, with the Pittsburgh Pirates adopting "We Are Family" as their theme song during their 1979 championship season in 1979. "Got to Love Somebody" and "All American Girls" were also major hits. The group began producing its own singles in 1981, but ran into tough sledding in the wake of the anti-disco backlash. They began on Atco in 1974, and remained on Cotillion from 1976-1983. They moved to Atlantic in 1985, but were unable to regain their former glory. Kathy Sledge issued her own LP on Epic, *Heart*, in 1992. —*Ron Wynn*

Circle of Love / 1975 / Atlantic ✦✦✦

Together / 1977 / Cotillion ✦✦✦

○ **We Are Family** / 1979 / Cotillion ✦✦✦✦
The Sledge sisters floundered in search of a format for several years before Atlantic gave them, almost in desperation, to the Chic production team. This 1979 album ended eight years of frustration and was their greatest triumph. The title track became the theme song for the world champion Pittsburgh Pirates baseball team, while Nile Rodgers' splintering guitar and Bernard Edwards' steady bass, plus the duo's production genius, garnered two huge hits for Sister Sledge in "We Are Family" and "He's The Greatest Dancer." —*Ron Wynn*

○ **Got to Love Somebody Today** / 1980 / Cotillion ✦✦✦✦
A decline was inevitable after the platinum across-the-board success of *We Are Family*, but *Love Somebody Today* wasn't quite the dropoff many claimed at the time. Nile Rodgers and Bernard Ed-

wards again properly kept the emphasis on their harmonies, interaction and vocal flexibility, and provided them with more fine material. But this time around, only "Got To Love Somebody" managed to click. The anti-disco backlash was in full bloom, and fine singles like "Easy Street," "How To Love" and "Reach Your Peak" were completely ignored. R&B stations reacted in a lukewarm fashion as well, even though "Reach Your Peak" did prove a moderate R&B hit. —*Ron Wynn*

Love Somebody Today / 1980 / Cotillion ✦✦✦

All American Girls / 1981 / Cotillion ✦✦✦

Sister Sledge / 1981 / Cotillion ✦✦✦

The Sisters / 1982 / Cotillion ✦✦✦

Sister Sledge seized the production reins, but weren't able to equal Chic's sophistication or success. This album included a decent remake of Mary Wells' "My Guy," the original version of "All The Man That I Need" (later made a number one hit by Whitney Houston) and the curious "Il Macquillage Lady," but it seemed like a return to the unfocused, erratic music they had previously recorded. There was some fine vocal work on "Grandma" and "Jacki's Theme: There's No Stopping Us," but things had worsened for groups with a disco reputation, and there were few takers for this record. "My Guy" did crack the R&B Top 20. —*Ron Wynn*

Bet Cha Say That to All the Girls / 1983 / WEA ✦✦✦

● **The Best of Sister Sledge (1973-1985)** / 1992 / Rhino ✦✦✦✦

Containing seven of their eight Hot 100 hits plus a host of lesser-known tracks, *Best of Sister Sledge (1973-1985)* is the definitive Sister Sledge collection. —*AMG*

Sisters of Mercy

Group, Alternative Pop/Rock, Gothic
A Leeds outfit, headed by lyricist Andrew Eldritch, Sisters of Mercy started with pounding heavy metal in its 1982 debut EP and since then has moved steadily toward danceable pop-funk. —*David Szatmary*

First & Last & Always / 1985 / Elektra ✦✦✦

Sisters of Mercy's first full-length album didn't quite have the powerful musical vision of their early EPs, but its gloom was more focused, making it an impressive debut album. —*Stephen Thomas Erlewine*

○ **Floodland** / 1987 / Elektra ✦✦✦✦

Sisters of Mercy's second album was a monolithic slab of goth-rock, featuring a more ambitious and accomplished musical scope than the debut, along with better lyrics. —*Stephen Thomas Erlewine*

○ **Vision Thing** / 1990 / Elektra ✦✦✦✦

Guitar-based pop fueled by the bright-sounding sensibilities of ex-Generation X axeman Tony James. —*David Szatmary*

● **Some Girls Wander by Mistake** / 1992 / Elektra ✦✦✦✦

Collecting a number of their better singles, *Some Girls Wander by Mistake* offers a good introduction to the Sisters of Mercy. —*AMG*

Skid Row

Group, Hard Rock, Heavy Metal
Before alternative music crossed over into the mainstream, Skid Row was one of the top heavy metal bands of the '90s, pounding out a radio-friendly mix of Bon Jovi, Aerosmith, and Led Zeppelin. On the strength of the "18 and Life" and "I Remember You" singles, their 1989 debut album sold over three million copies. The 1991 follow-up, *Slave to the Grind*, sold a million copies and hit number one. Later that year, the band began a quick fall from the limelight, as Nirvana's success (who, ironically, were called Skid Row in an earlier incarnation) changed the rules of hard rock, making Skid Row seem irrelevant. In 1995, they released their third album, *Subhuman Race.* —*Stephen Thomas Erlewine*

Skid Row / 1989 / Atlantic ✦✦✦

With enough exposure, Skid Row became impossible to ignore. This is the beginning of a good band. —*John Book*

● **Slave to the Grind** / 1991 / Atlantic ✦✦✦✦

Skid Row's impressive second album has some great rockers, a nice ballad or two, and even a heavy venture into thrash. It was one of the best metal albums of 1991. —*John Book*

B-side Ourselves / 1992 / Atlantic ✦✦✦

○ **Subhuman Race** / 1995 / WEA Japan ✦✦✦✦

Skid Row waited out the grunge storm and returned in 1995 with *Subhuman Race*, their strongest and most vicious record to date. Abandoning most of the pop-metal posturing of their early hit albums, Skid Row strips back their music to the basics—roaring guitars and Sebastian Bach's shriek. It wasn't a hit on the size of *Slave to the Grind*, yet it made an impressive showing, climbing into the Top 40. —*Stephen Thomas Erlewine*

Skinny Puppy

Group, Industrial, Alternative Pop/Rock
Skinny Puppy was one of the pioneers of industrial music, cultivating a scalding mix of electronics, samples, found sounds, and beats. All of their albums are thunderously menacing experimentations with dance and synthesizers, creating a consistent body of dense, dark music that owes a debt to the nightmarish vision of Cabaret Voltaire and Throbbing Gristle. Skinny Puppy were primarily responsible for popularizing the cut-and-paste techniques of those '70s electronic forefathers during the late '80s; Ministry and Nine Inch Nails picked up much of their sonic terrorism from Skinny Puppy's early records. After industrial music had worked its way into the mainstream in the early '90s, Skinny Puppy landed their first major-label contract with American Records. —*Stephen Thomas Erlewine*

Bites / 1985 / Nettwerk ✦✦✦

Skinny Puppy's first album recalls the gloomy throb of Cabaret Voltaire, but with a more pronounced beat; their debut EP, *Remission*, is included on the CD version of *Bites.* —*Stephen Thomas Erlewine*

Mind: the Perpetual Intercourse / 1986 / Nettwerk ✦✦

Skinny Puppy doesn't deviate from its dark vision on their second album; in fact, the record doesn't sound all that much different than the first. —*Stephen Thomas Erlewine*

○ **Cleanse Fold & Manipulate** / 1987 / Nettwerk ✦✦✦✦

While it doesn't deviate from their previous lyrical territory, the music is more intense and scary; for the first time, Skinny Puppy has made an album that actually *sounds* frightening. —*Stephen Thomas Erlewine*

○ **Vivi Sect VI** / Jul. 1988 / Nettwerk ✦✦✦✦

Vivi SectVI is the first explicitly political Skinny Puppy album, which adds some depth to their standard throbbing, gloomy industrial dance-rock. —*Stephen Thomas Erlewine*

Rabies / 1989 / Nettwerk ✦✦✦

Despite the presence of Ministry's Al Jourgensen and his brutal guitar riffs, Skinny Puppy sounds as if they're at a loss for ideas on their fifth album. —*Stephen Thomas Erlewine*

● **12 Inch Anthology** / 1990 / Nettwerk ✦✦✦✦

Featuring both sides of four 12-inch singles from 1985-1989, *12-Inch Anthology* offers a good introduction to Skinny Puppy's psycho-terrorist dance music. —*Stephen Thomas Erlewine*

○ **Too Dark Park** / 1990 / Nettwerk ✦✦✦✦

Skinny Puppy's first album of the 1990s is a thicker, more layered and bass-heavy record than their previous work, which makes it one of the most interesting albums they have released. —*Stephen Thomas Erlewine*

Tormentor / 1992 / Nettwerk ✦✦✦

Last Rights / Mar. 16, 1992 / Nettwerk ✦✦✦

Chainsaw / Apr. 27, 1993 / Nettwerk ✦✦

Skyliners

Group, Doo-Wop
This Pittsburgh vocal group made a magnificent heartache ballad in 1959, "Since I Don't Have You." It remains among R&B's ultimate agonizing triumphs, and Chuck Jackson later did an equally gripping version. Jimmy Beaumont was the lead vocalist, with Janet Vogel, Wally Lester, Joe VerScharen, and Jackie Taylor. Beaumont, Taylor, and Lester had been in the Crescents, while Vogel and VerScharen were alumni of the El Rios. Their follow-up, "This I Swear," was a creditable effort that peaked at number 20 on the R&B charts, but few remember it. Oddly, "Since I Don't Have You" only reached number three on the R&B side and number 12 on the pop charts. But it's certainly one song for whom the numbers really don't come close to telling the story. The Skyliners had two

chart singles on Callico and then had one other song reach the R&B Top 40 in 1965, "The Loser," for Jubilee. —Ron Wynn

● **Skyliner's Greatest Hits** / Original Sound ✦✦✦✦
○ **Since I Don't Have You** / Ace ✦✦✦✦

The Skyliners were among the more dramatic, theatrical white doo-wop groups. Their hit "Since I Don't Have You" has been covered by numerous performers, and it's among the 21 singles featured on this Ace anthology covering numbers recorded for Calico and Laurie. Jimmy Beaumont's tremendous leads distinguished "I Swear," "It Happened Today," and the title track, among others. It's no surprise that such flamboyant performers as Patti Labelle and Chuck Jackson are big Skyliners fans. —Ron Wynn

Slade

Group, Hard Rock, Glam Rock
One of the most successful British bands of the early '70s, Slade made it to the top of the charts after several years on the road. The band formed in 1966 in Wolverhapton as the N'Betweens. After taking on former Animals bassist Chas Chandler as their manager, they changed their name to Ambrose Slade, then shortened it to Slade.

Many of their records were a variations of upfront lead vocals, fat, loud, distorted guitar chords, a basic foot-stomping beat, and anthemic choruses. The simplicity of it all was played up even further by the deliberate misspelling of words in the song titles. At the turn of the '70s, "Get Down and Get with It" cracked the U.K. Top 20 and there was no turning back. Their next dozen singles were U.K. Top Five hits, six of them reaching number one. Their success wasn't limited to the singles charts, either; three of their albums also topped the charts during the same period. Their holiday song, "Merry Xmas Everybody," has entered the U.K. charts seven times, as well.

Despite their British success Slade barely cracked the U.S. Hot 100. Even in England, the big hits stopped coming during the punk revolution in the late '70s. They enjoyed a brief revival in the early '80s when Quiet Riot covered "Cum on Feel the Noize" and took it to the top of the charts around the world. This revival even enabled Slade to chart in the American Top Forty with "Run Runaway" and "My Oh My." Slade recently celebrated its 25th anniversary and shows no sign of stopping. —Jim Powers

○ **Slayed** / 1972 / Polydor ✦✦✦✦
Slayed was Slade's best and most consistent original album, featuring "Mama Weer All Crazee Now." —Stephen Thomas Erlewine

● **Sladest** / 1973 / Reprise ✦✦✦✦
Sladest contains all of the British band's finest moments, including "Look Wot You Dun," "Mama Weer All Crazee Now," and "Cum on Feel the Noize." —Stephen Thomas Erlewine

○ **Keep Your Hands off My Power Supply** / 1984 / Epic ✦✦✦✦
An early-'80s album that managed to climb into the Top 40, thanks to the success of Quiet Riot's versions of "Cum On Feel the Noize" and "Mama Weer All Crazee Now." On *Keep Your Hands Off My Power Supply*, Slade shows that they are still the masters of loud, trashy hard rock. —Stephen Thomas Erlewine

Slave

Group, Soul, Funk, Disco
Arguably the hottest of the '70s Ohio funk bands, Slave had a great run in the late '70s and early '80s. Trumpeter Steve Washington formed the group in Dayton in 1975. Vocalist Floyd Miller teamed with Tom Lockett, Jr., Charles Bradley, Mark Adams, Mark Hicks, Danny Webster, Orion Wilhoite, and Tim Dozier. Vocalists Steve Arrington and Starleana Young came aboard in 1978, with Arrington ultimately becoming lead vocalist. Their first big hit was the thumping single "Slide" in 1977 for Cotillion, where they remained until 1984. Their best tracks were lyrically simple and at times silly, but the arrangements and rhythms were intense and hypnotic. Other Top Ten R&B hits were "Just a Touch of Love" in 1979, "Watching You" in 1980, and "Snap Shot" in 1981. Young, Washington, and Lockett departed to form Aurra in 1979. Arrington himself left in the early '80s. They added Charles C. Carter, Delbert Taylor, Sam Carter, Kevin Johnson, and Roger Parker as replacements and continued on, though much less successfully, into the late '80s. They moved to Atlantic for one LP in 1984, then switched to the Atlanta-based Ichiban in 1986 for singles and LPs that were just a shade of the former vibrant Slave sound. Their most recent release was *The Funk Strikes Back* in 1992. Rhino is-

sued *Stellar Funk: The Best of Slave*, a first-rate anthology of their finest cuts, in 1994. —Ron Wynn

● **Stellar Funk: Best of** / 1994 / Rhino ✦✦✦✦
Slave's music was straight, simple funk: prominent bass lines, catchy phrases and either comical or throwaway lyrics. This excellent 15-track anthology contains Slave's finest hits, each with a captivating, thudding bass riff: "Slide," "Just A Touch Of Love," and "Watching You," among others. There are also five Steve Arrington numbers, among them his best dance cut ("Weak At The Knees") and topical tune ("Feel So Real"). Although not as acclaimed as Parliament/Funkadelic or Earth, Wind and Fire, this CD shows that Slave deserves recognition for its ability to keep the funk with style and verve. —Ron Wynn

Slayer

Group, Thrash, Heavy Metal
Slayer formed in Los Angeles in 1982, featuring bassist/vocalist Tom Araya, guitarists Jeff Hanneman and Kerry King, and drummer Dave Lombardo. They got their start when one of their songs was featured on the *Metal Massacre III* compilation. Soon after that, they were signed to Metal Blade Records. In their early years, the band wore a great deal of eye makeup and took an over-the-top, often self-parodying approach to their lyrics, which addressed evil, death, Satan, graphic mutilation, and their corollaries. The band usually wore upside-down crosses and incorporated an inverted pentagram into its logo. Many in metal circles considered them a joke at the time, but they found a small following among metal listeners looking for something new, different, and extreme. *Hell Awaits*, their second album, was released to much excitement among their fans and showed strong improvement, but their sound was still somewhat murky. The band caught the attention of Def Jam owner and producer Rick Rubin, who at that time was known primarily for working with hip-hop artists. Rubin signed them to his label and took a raw, stripped-down approach to their third studio album. CBS refused to distribute the record due to what they perceived as advocacy of Satanism, giving the band wide publicity; Geffen eventually stepped in and took over. The record, *Reign In Blood*, was not only the band's finest moment, but perhaps the entire speed metal genre's finest moment, winning over legions of new fans and becoming an instant classic.

Reign established Slayer as the fastest and most graphically extreme band in metal, but the band didn't want themselves pigeonholed, so for their next album, *South of Heaven*, they slowed things down and attempted a more refined approach, which did not prove quite as popular. *Seasons In the Abyss* brought them back a bit, combining the approaches of their last two albums. After their 1991 live album, Lombardo left the band to form Grip Inc. with former Overkill guitarist Bobby Gustafson. Slayer regrouped, hiring ex-Forbidden drummer Paul Bostaph. 1994's *Divine Intervention* was released to glowing reviews and debuted in *Billboard*'s Top Ten.

Slayer's jarring, disturbing style is not only a very effective way of expressing their ideas, but it has also proven highly influential. The band is one of the major inspirations behind the burgeoning underground phenomenon of death metal, which takes Slayer-esque songwriting and subject matter to an even more extreme realm, both sonically and lyrically. Slayer is one of the few truly unique metal bands, and they continue to prove their worth, relevance, and originality today. —Steve Huey

Show No Mercy / 1984 / Metal Blade ✦✦
Slayer's debut came when the band wore make-up and were considered a joke in some circles. It was a big difference and a far cry from what they sound like now. —John Book

Hell Awaits / 1985 / Metal Blade ✦✦✦
Slayer's first relevant album is loosely tied together by the theme of eternal damnation. Some of the lyrics are pretty silly, and some of the songs could have been trimmed a bit, but it hints at the heights they would reach on their next release. It's also interesting to hear one of the genre's true innovators developing and honing their sound. —Steve Huey

★ **Reign in Blood** / 1986 / Def American ✦✦✦✦✦
Slayer's masterpiece opens and closes with two longer, now-standard tracks, "Angel of Death" and "Raining Blood." Sandwiched in between are eight short (all under three minutes), very fast bursts of aggression that change tempo or feel without warning, keeping the listener off balance and producing a very wild, disjointed, barely controlled effect. The short songs prevent the extreme

graphic violence and paranoia in the lyrics from descending into self-parody. This is simply Slayer's best music, and it proved hugely influential in the evolution of the death metal style. Along with Metallica's *Master of Puppets, Reign in Blood* is the pinnacle of thrash. — *Steve Huey*

South of Heaven / 1988 / Def American ✦✦
The follow-up to *Reign in Blood* was slower and more subdued, and Araya attempted more actual singing as the band tried to avoid backing themselves into a creative corner. This did not prove to be one of the band's more popular albums. — *Steve Huey*

Seasons in the Abyss / 1990 / Def American ✦✦✦
Slayer bounces back here, alternating between pounding speed and more mid-tempo grooves. Their music continues in a more refined direction, and it works better than on *South of Heaven*. The band doesn't turn to the supernatural quite as much for its subject matter, preferring to examine real topics like war, murder, and human weakness from the traditional dark, dramatic Slayer viewpoint, but their music is so effective that the mood is much the same. This is probably their most accessible album, but it doesn't compromise a bit. — *Steve Huey*

Decade of Aggression: Live / 1991 / Def American ✦✦✦
A double-length set, it has all of Slayer's great songs done in the only way the band should be experienced: in concert. This is the best-sounding live speed-metal album so far. — *John Book*

○ **Divine Intervention** / 1994 / American ✦✦✦✦
Slayer sounds revitalized on *Divine Intervention*, with a raw sound and a rhythmic spark provided by new drummer Paul Bostaph. They continue in a more political direction lyrically, and the vocals are better than ever. The band hasn't sounded this fierce, nor has the music been this visceral, since *Reign in Blood*. Slayer shows that they remain a vital and creative force, something that very few metal bands have been able to do in the post-Nirvana '90s. — *Steve Huey*

Percy Sledge

b. Nov. 25, 1941, Leighton, AL
Soul
"When a Man Loves a Woman" existed long before Michael Bolton ever came on the scene—it's hard to believe that anyone could be unaware of Percy Sledge's original version of the song. As the first Southern soul recording to top both the R&B and pop charts in 1966, the emotionally supercharged ballad was a groundbreaker, and Sledge's remarkably anguished performance ranks as an unrivaled masterpiece of the soul genre. Sledge often seems to teeter on the verge of tears on his best Atlantic label releases of the late '60s. A product of the musically fertile area around Muscle Shoals, AL, Sledge recorded "When a Man Loves a Woman" and the equally moving followups "It Tears Me Up," "Out of Left Field," and "Take Time to Know Her" with the same session aces that played on most Muscle Shoals classics of the period. By the turn of the decade, Sledge's well had run dry, although he's recorded off and on ever since. — *Bill Dahl*

○ **When a Man Loves a Woman** / 1966 / Collectables ✦✦✦✦
A country/soul masterpiece. The title track remains among the most beloved, anthemic explanations of love's impact and travails ever written or performed. Had Sledge never made another song, he would still deserve kudos just for that one. But he continued to score with more simple, heartfelt, unsophisticated stories about disappointment, pain, rejection, and perseverance. — *Ron Wynn*

The Percy Sledge Way / 1967 / Atlantic ✦✦✦
This late-'60s album contains hard-hitting, memorable country/soul testimonies from Percy Sledge, who had hit his stride at Atlantic. His narratives were perfectly paced, written with irony and insight, and sung with the ideal mixture of crunching soul and country wit and wisdom. Hopefully, Rhino will one day reissue some of soul's archival sessions like this one, for it needs full exposure. — *Ron Wynn*

Take Time to Know Her / 1968 / Collectables ✦✦✦
The title track was another smashing Sledge gem, while the remainder of the album continues his evocative country/soul tales of woe and heartache. Sledge's late-'60s Atlantic singles and albums were landmarks in the genre; they should have been major country events just as Ray Charles' earlier cuts, but were simply too rooted in Black nuance to get any shot with the unimaginative types running country radio (although to be fair, there were also some great country songs in the period that should have been

aired on soul stations). The songs were produced and arranged with the right amount of care and sensitivity, never intruding or crowding Sledge as his stories unfolded. — *Ron Wynn*

I'll Be Your Everything / 1974 / Capricorn ✦✦✦
Some wonderful country/soul from Percy Sledge, whose throaty, energized, wonderfully Southern delivery hadn't lost either its earthiness or its zeal, but was so regional that it was losing its appeal to the cosmopolitan, urban types gaining hegemony in black music circles. Sledge delivered several grainy, earnest country/soul weepers and wailers when he moved to Capricorn in the mid-'70s, but they didn't generate much attention anywhere beyond the South. — *Ron Wynn*

★ **It Tears Me Up** / 1992 / Rhino ✦✦✦✦✦
This stunning compilation from the vaults of Atlantic Records spotlights the voice that gave us the original version of "When a Man Loves a Woman." Lesser-known hits like "It Tears Me Up," "Take Time to Know Her," and "Warm and Tender Love" are equally wonderful, and all are included in this must-have package. Great liner notes by Dave Marsh. Soul music just doesn't get any more heart-wrenching than this. Absolutely essential! — *Christine Ohlman*

Sleeper

Group, Alternative Pop/Rock
Louise Wener (vocals, guitar); Jon Stewart (guitar); Andy Maclure (drums); Diid Osman (bass). Wener and Stewart met at while studying politics at school in Manchester, England. Relocating to London, the two recruited Osman and Maclure and began playing Wener's original songs. The group made its debut in 1993, which led to a series of positive reviews in the British music weeklies. By November of 1993, the group had released an independent single ("Alice in Vain"). In February 1994, the band released "Swallow," which charted in the Top 100; the following May, "Delicious" was released and it became a number one independent single. During May, Sleeper supported Blur on the London band's enormously successful *Parklife* tour. In February 1995, Sleeper released their debut album *Smart*, which entered the U.K. album chart at number five and the independent chart at number one; it would be certified a silver album in four months. *Smart* was released in the U.S. in March to positive reviews, yet it failed to duplicate the band's British commercial success. — *Stephen Thomas Erlewine*

● **Smart** / 1995 / Arista ✦✦✦✦
"Inbetweener" is an intoxicating single. Fuzz guitars, light harmonies, sing-song melodies and hooks keep piling up until the whole thing collapses in a heap after three minutes. Unfortunately, there's nothing that matches it on *Smart*, Sleeper's debut album. Occasionally, Louise Wener comes up with a memorable hook, melody or lyric, but never can quite pull them together into something as well-crafted (and sexy) as "Inbetweener." Still, the flashes of inspiration scattered across *Smart* prove Sleeper has potential—which they have already fulfilled once, with the single. — *Stephen Thomas Erlewine*

Slick Rick

b. London, England
Rap
Born in London and raised in the Bronx, Ricky Walters carved himself a niche with his debut album *The Great Adventures of Slick Rick*, with a sly, drawling delivery and detailed and inventive storybook raps. The onetime partner of Doug E. Fresh, Slick Rick eventually wound up in jail following a shooting incident, and has been charged with attempted murder. — *John Floyd & Ron Wynn*

★ **The Great Adventures of Slick Rick** / 1989 / Def Jam ✦✦✦✦✦
Superb slices and excellent rap technique on this fast-paced release. — *Ron Wynn*

○ **The Ruler's Back** / 1991 / Def Jam ✦✦✦✦
A fine followup from a troubled soul. — *Ron Wynn*

Behind Bars / 1994 / Def Jam ✦✦

Slint

Group, Alternative Pop/Rock
Although Slint was rather unknown while they were recording in the late-'80s, they influenced a number of American underground bands of the '90s with their rhythmic, experimental indie-metal. Based in Louisville, KY, Slint only released two albums, 1989's *Tweez* and 1991's *Spiderland*, before breaking up. — *John Bush*

● **Tweez** / 1989 / Plan 9/Caroline ♦♦♦♦
Tweez is a fine, if bizarre recording, often switching from bass-led rhythm to rhythm in the same song. The guitars are harsh, but not especially fast. Instead of singing, bits of dialogue, sound effects, and spoken lyrics are used. *—John Bush*
Spiderland / 1991 / Touch & Go ♦♦♦

Slits

Group, Punk, New Wave
Along with the Raincoats and Liliput, the Slits are one of the most significant female punk-rock bands of the late '70s. Not only did they bravely (or foolishly, you be the judge) leap into the fray with little, if any, musical ability (on their debut tour with the Clash, Mick Jones used to tune their guitars for them), but through sheer emotion and desire created some great music, especially when they began working with veteran reggae producer Dennis Bovell, setting the stage for a future generation of riot grrrls. The Slits formed in 1976 when 14-year-old Ari Upp (sometimes Arri Up) ran into her friend Palmolive at a Patti Smith gig in London. The latter suggested the former consider becoming the lead singer for a new all-girl punk band. Upp agreed on the spot, and the Slits, with borrowed equipment and knowledge of two, maybe three chords, were a reality. They made some crude recordings (so crude that they make early Mekons recordings sound like 64-track by comparison) that were never widely circulated, and it wasn't until they nabbed the opening spot on the Clash's "White Riot" tour of England in 1977 that the Slits became a part of the punk pantheon. Despite this sudden notoriety, little was recorded by the Slits in the early days, save for a couple of sessions of John Peel's BBC radio show. These recordings place the Slits firmly in the punk rock aesthetic of blaring guitars and braying vocals. But it's not generic-sounding rant: Ari's voice bounces along, alternately hiccuping and bellowing to the stiff rhythms; the songs are meditations on alienation, but there is a satiric, tongue-in-cheek quality to the songs instead of strident preachiness.
   It wasn't until 1979 that the Slits made their first proper record under the watchful, supportive eyes and ears of reggae vet Dennis Bovell. By the time *Cut* was released, the raging guitars were replaced by subtle reggae riddims, the band was now a trio (Palmolive had been replaced by new drummer Budgie, soon to join Siouxsie and the Banshees), and there was a stylistic suppleness that the Slits had heretofore never displayed. Ari's voice still warbled uncertain of the key, but for a band that had been playing their instruments for a little more than two years, this is a remarkably confident record. It was two years before a second record was released (*Return of the Giant Slits*), which was denser, darker and full of surprises. But the Slits, due primarily to their interest in incorporating other forms of ethnic music into their mix, were leaping beyond what was commonly accepted as punk rock, and as a result, were no longer seen as a punk band. I'm sure this didn't distress them in the least, as they were more interested in expanding the barriers of punk rock rather than simply adhering to "rules" that claimed all punk bands must bash out simplistic guitar rant. By the close of 1981, Arri Up was singing in Adrian Sherwood's dub/funk aggregation the New Age Steppers, and the Slits had become both legendary and somewhat notorious. Though much derided in their short existence, what the Slits achieved and what they meant to succeeding generations of young female rockers cannot be underestimated. *—John Dougan*

● **Cut** / 1979 / Antilles ♦♦♦♦
Almost as well known for its cover (the three Slits are half-naked and covered in mud) as it was for the music, *Cut* is an ebullient piece of post-punk mastery that finds the Slits' interest in Caribbean and African rhythms smoothly incorporated into their harsher, punk rock stylings. Ari Upp's wandering voice (a touch like Yoko Ono) might be initially offputting, but not so much so that it makes listening to the record difficult. Six tracks are revamped from earlier Peel sessions and sound better for the extra effort (especially "New Town" and "Love and Romance"). With its goofy charm, gleeful swing and sway, and subtle yet compelling libertarian feminism (get up and do it girls!), this is one of the best records of the era. *—John Dougan*

○ **Retrospective** / 1980 / Rough Trade ♦♦♦♦
Return of the Giant Slits / 1981 / CBS ♦♦♦
Never released in America, the Slits' second and final record found them pushing the envelope rhythmically. Although designed to be more commercial than *Cut*, it's actually less so, sounding more

like the innovative work a young Adrian Sherwood was doing with Creation Rebel. Fans of the early Slits, who were put off by the reggae of *Cut*, were no doubt further alienated by this record's comfortable use of Afro-pop tempos and style. Which was a shame, because this music was interesting, daring and exciting. *— John Dougan*

○ **The Peel Sessions** / 1989 / Dutch East India ♦♦♦♦
This seven-track disc contains all of the material recorded at two sessions for John Peel's BBC radio show. It's vintage early Slits, lots of crashing and bashing, but with a touch of the sophistication and Caribbean influence that was to follow about a year later on *Cut*. Not just for completists, this is a valuable addition to any serious collection of the music of the punk era, and an interesting document of a young band's growth. *—John Dougan*

P.F. Sloan

Singer-Songwriter, Folk-Rock
He was there at the dawn of surf music, he was crowned king of the West Coast protest folkies, and he created some of the great American pop records of the '60s, yet today, the name P. F. Sloan is scarcely remembered outside of a circle of collectors and other period enthusiasts. Teamed early with Steve Barri, Sloan had a lasting partner. The duo cashed in on the surf craze as the Fantastic Baggies, and Sloan has claimed to be involved with countless more surf productions. Sloan and Barri wrote and produced hits for the likes of the Turtles and Johnny Rivers, and may best be remembered for Barry McGuire's "Eve of Destruction." Sloan's own albums for Dunhill were based on the kind of material he had given McGuire, and despite being dismissed by the "serious" protest-folk community of the day, they stand as excellent on their own merits.
   Sloan's attempt to shift away from the West Coast folk-rock he largely created was reflected with the R&B-tinged album *Measure for Pleasure*, and following another album in the early '70s, he was gone. In spite of the occasional live gig and rumors of a comeback, it appears that P. F. Sloan will remain forever connected with his '60s work, his behind-the-scenes efforts overshadowing the fine music under his own name. *—Steve Aldrich*

● **Anthology** / 1993 / One Way ♦♦♦♦
A well-compiled 18-track anthology featuring Sloan's overlooked recording career. This is essential folk-rock in the singer/songwriter tradition. Included is his wonderful version of "Eve of Destruction," which was written by Sloan and popularized by Barry McGuire. *—Chris Woodstra*

Slowdive

Group, Alternative Pop/Rock
Comprised of Neil Halstead (guitar, vocals), Rachael Gowell (vocals, guitar), Christian Savill (guitar), Nick Chaplin (bass), and Simon Scott (drums), Slowdive formed in England in 1989. Slowdive fit into the trance-pop scene of the early '90s, combining ethereal vocals with highly processed and distorted guitar. Creation Records signed the band, releasing their debut album, *Just for a Day*, in 1991. Signed to SBK in the U.S., the band had a tumultuous relationship with their American label; most of the arguments were over marketing and promotion. The American release of the band's second album, *Souvlaki*, came six months later than its U.K. release, which became a major point of contention between the band and its label, SBK. The group parted with the label in 1994. *—Stephen Thomas Erlewine*

○ **Just for a Day** / 1991 / SBK ♦♦♦♦
● **Souvlaki** / 1994 / SBK ♦♦♦♦

Sly & the Family Stone

Group, Soul, Funk, R&B, Pop/Rock
Sylvester Stewart came charging out of the psychedelic environs of San Francisco in 1967 with a band—and a sound—that made good on the communal spirit most acid-scorched bands only talked about. The Family Stone was rock's first fully integrated group: men and women, Black and White, they refused to play the music-business game of racial and sexual segregation, mixing rock and R&B until, as critic Dave Marsh pointed out, "you couldn't find where one began and the other left off."
   Songs such as "Everyday People" explained Stone's desire to mix everything up, while "I Want to Take You Higher" and "Dance to the Music" made explicit the community of the Family Stone.

But Stone's optimism began to sour in the wake of Dr. Martin Luther King's assassination and the return of segregation, and his music took on a chilling tone. The dizzy glee of "Hot Fun in the Summertime" gave way to the scathing "Thank You (Falettinme Be Mice Elf Agin)" and *There's a Riot Goin' On.* Eventually, his career bogged down under a shroud of drug problems. But Sly Stone's stamp is as indelibly placed on pop music as James Brown's, and his influence can be heard and felt in the work of Kool and the Gang, Prince, George Clinton, and dozens of others. —*John Floyd*

Whole New Thing / 1967 / Epic ✦✦✦

Dance to the Music / 1968 / Epic ✦✦✦

Sly's second album reached the lower echelons of *Billboard*'s album charts due to the quintessential psychedelic soul single, "Dance to the Music." The rest of the album is uneven, early, and tentative, with the full funk being a little further around the bend. —*Rob Bowman*

○ **Life** / 1968 / Epic ✦✦✦✦

The Family Stone's third album was a step forward with a harder drum sound, sharper horn lines, and more focused writing. Despite these developments, *Life* failed to yield a hit single ("Plastic Jim," "Life," and "M'Lady" were all fine candidates). —*Rob Bowman*

☆ **Stand!** / 1969 / Epic ✦✦✦✦✦

The album on which Sly's integrationist vision paid big dividends. Four of the record's seven songs, including "I Want to Take You Higher" and "Everyday People," charted as singles. The group contained Blacks and Whites, men and women; voices and instruments careened off one another in one apocalyptic vision of community. At the time, such an album seemed to be the clarion call of a new day. Brilliant. —*Rob Bowman*

★ **Greatest Hits** / 1970 / Epic ✦✦✦✦✦

This greatest-hits package was released as a stopgap while Sly was taking two years to record *There's a Riot Goin' On.* It's what you would expect from a greatest-hits package, with the addition of two newly recorded monster-hit singles, "Hot Fun in the Summertime" and "Thank You (Falettinme Be Mice Elf Agin)." —*Rob Bowman*

☆ **There's a Riot Goin' On** / 1971 / Epic ✦✦✦✦✦

Sly gets darker and funkier. By *Riot*, Sly was a bona fide superstar. His personal behavior became more erratic, and his songwriting became more eclectic and adventurous. There is no precedent for such a record; songs were conceived from the rhythm up, and often left in sparse, naked, seemingly semi-finished form. Sly's earlier hit, "Thank You (Falettinme Be Mice Elf Agin)" is slowed down, turned inside out, and retitled "Thank You for Talkin' to Me Africa." The result is an extremely personal stab at exorcism that takes the listener through the new reality of Black and White America in the early '70s. Mesmerizing. The album's most accessible songs, "Family Affair" and "Runnin' Away," were R&B and pop hit singles, the former reaching the #1 spot on both charts. —*Rob Bowman*

☆ **Fresh** / 1973 / Epic ✦✦✦✦✦

Stripped down and funky, minus thumb-popping bass whiz Larry Graham (who had left to found Graham Central Station), Sly turned in a fine album. One Top Ten R&B hit resulted with "If You Want Me to Stay," while two other songs, "Frisky" and "If It Were Left up to Me," also received substantial airplay on Black radio. In the wake of Sly's politics on *Riot* and his increasingly erratic personal and concert behavior, most pop-radio programmers seemed to grow leery of the Family Stone. The first single, "If You Want Me to Stay," reached #12 pop, but it was to be the last Sly Stone record to receive any significant pop success. —*Rob Bowman*

Small Talk / 1974 / Epic ✦✦

A new bass player and drummer signaled a toned-down Family Stone sound. Partially in keeping with changes in much of popular music in the early '70s, and maybe the result of marriage and a child, Sly became more introspective, quieter, and calmer, even employing a string section on various cuts. A less exhilarating album than earlier efforts, there is still much of merit here, including the Top Ten R&B hit "Time for Livin'." —*Rob Bowman*

★ **Anthology** / 1981 / Epic ✦✦✦✦✦

This repeats some cuts from *Greatest Hits* but also includes highlights from *Riot* and *Fresh*. But you should hear those albums in their entirety. —*John Floyd*

The Small Faces

Group, British Invasion

The Small Faces were the best English band never to hit it big in America. On this side of the Atlantic, all anybody remembers them only for is their sole stateside hit, "Itchycoo Park"—but in England, the Small Faces were one of the most extraordinary and successful bands of the mid-'60s; their music remains some of the most valuable and enjoyable of the era.

Lead singer/guitarist Steve Marriott's formal background was on the stage; as a young teenager, he'd auditioned and won the part of the Artful Dodger in the Lionel Bart musical *Oliver!* Marriott was earning his living at a music shop when he made the acquaintance of Ronnie Lane (bass, backing vocals), who had formed a band called the Pioneers, which included drummer Kenney Jones. Lane invited Marriott to jam with the Pioneers at a show they were playing at a local club—the gig was a disaster, but out of that show the group decided to turn their talents toward American R&B. The band—with Marriott now installed permanently and Jimmy Winston recruited on organ—cast its lot with a faction of British youth known as the Mods, stylish posers who, among their other attributes, affected a dandified look and a fanatical love of American R&B. The quartet, now christened the Small Faces ("face" being a piece of Mod slang for a fashion leader), began making a name for themselves on stage, sparked by the group's no-holds-barred performance style.

The quartet was signed by manager Don Arden, and brought to Decca/London to record. The band's debut single, "What'cha Gonna Do About It," was released in August of 1965 and reached number 14 on the charts; a second single, "I've Got Mine," failed to chart when released in November. Soon after its recording, Winston exited the line-up; he was replaced by Ian McLagen (organ/guitar/vocals). The group returned to the charts in February of 1966 with "Sha-La-La-La-Lee," which rose to number three in England. Three months later, they were back at number ten with "Hey Girl," and heralded this new single release with their first album, *Small Faces.* "All or Nothing" marked their first chart-topping entry, and its follow-up, "My Mind's Eye," followed it nearly as high. On the surface, nothing could possibly have seemed wrong for the band. Keeping up the standard of songwriting and recording that they were maintaining was difficult, however, and they were increasingly unhappy with Arden. At the end of 1966, the band severed their ties with him and eventually moved under the wing of Rolling Stones manager/producer Andrew "Loog" Oldham. Oldham signed the group as clients; by the middle of the 1967 he had gotten them moved over to his new Immediate Records label.

With the shift in management and label, the group suddenly found themselves with a drastically reduced touring schedule and vastly increased time available in the studio. Their sound immediately became looser. They remained a top-flight R&B-driven band, but a much wider array of sounds and instruments began figuring in their music. Their first Immediate album, entitled *Small Faces* (known in the U.S.A as *There Are but Four Small Faces*), was issued in mid-1967, and was an instant hit. In August of the year, they released "Itchycoo Park," a lilting, lyrical idyll to the Summer of Love that captured the hearts of listeners on both sides of the Atlantic. The band had bigger aspirations than doing more hit singles, and set to work across five months during 1968 in at least four different studios recording what proved to be their magnum opus, *Ogden's Nut Gone Flake.* The group's fortunes didn't equal the artistic success of the album. In June of 1968, to announce the release of the album, Immediate took out an ad in the music trade papers that included a parody of the Lord's Prayer that managed to offend several million people before an apology from the band was issued. And Immediate, over the objections of Marriott, chose to release the song "Lazy Sunday"—which he'd recorded as a joke—as a single, and its rise to number two on the British charts did nothing to ease his unhappiness.

Already, the group was showing serious signs of strain. A tour of Australia ended with complaints from the authorities concerning the band's behavior, and there were reports of late arrivals (or no-shows) by the band at their English gigs. "The Universal," a single released in the summer of 1968, was to have been Marriott's most serious effort in that vein in over a year; it subsequently failed to crack the Top 20, and much of his interest in continuing with the band seemed to falter. The end came soon after, on New Year's Day, 1969, when Marriott suddenly left the stage while the band was jamming to "Lazy Sunday" during a show at the Alexandria Palace; he later called Peter Frampton, a guitarist from the Herd, and the two began mapping plans for a band of their own called Humble Pie.

The Small Faces did carry on into 1969, but it wasn't the same. With Marriott gone, they needed a replacement singer and lead guitarist, and found them in Rod Stewart and Ron Wood. They carried on under the name the Small Faces for one album, before dropping the "Small" and going on to greater glory as the Faces. During the mid-1970s the Small Faces reunited (without Ronnie Lane) for two albums, *Playmates* and *78 in the Shade*, that attracted a lot of press attention but nothing resembling the chart action of their earlier releases. Lane recorded with Pete Townshend, amongst others, before contracting multiple sclerosis, which ended his career as a musician (he later organized the A.R.M.S. benefit concerts to raise money for research into a cure for the disease). Jones subsequently joined the Who, replacing Keith Moon after the latter's sudden death in 1978, and did a couple of tours and a pair of albums with the band. Steve Marriott always seemed poised for a comeback, and in 1991 it looked as though he was going to finally pull it off—alas, he died in his sleep when fire swept his home in England, tragically just a couple of days after beginning work on a new album in America with his former bandmate Peter Frampton. *—Bruce Eder*

○ **Small Faces** / 1966 / PolyGram ✦✦✦✦
The group's debut album is a rip-roaring R&B showcase, built on the interplay of Steve Marriott's loud, mourning soul-shouting voice and the grinding sound of his guitar and Ian McLagan's organ. Especially not to be missed by anyone who likes the early Rolling Stones or the Who in their early R&B period. *—Bruce Eder*

From the Beginning / 1967 / PolyGram ✦✦✦
There's some overlap between this record and those that came before and after, owing to the band's exit from their Decca Records contract in the spring of 1967. The sound is still loud R&B, but there are new subtleties appearing that add some extra variety. *—Bruce Eder*

☆ **There Are But Four Small Faces** / 1968 / Sony ✦✦✦✦✦
The band's first album for Andrew "Loog" Oldham's Immediate label originally appeared in two different forms in England (where it was known as *Small Faces*) and America, and the two song lineups have been combined on an early-'90s American Sony Music reissue. The music here is much more fully developed and experimental than their preceding album, still largely R&B-based (apart from the delightfully trippy "Itchycoo Park," the band's sole American hit) but with lots of unusual sounds and recording techniques being attempted. *—Bruce Eder*

★ **Ogden's Nut Gone Flake** / 1968 / Sony ✦✦✦✦✦
The best album the Small Faces ever released, and one of the great records of the late '60s, a kind of Cockney *Sgt. Pepper*, with tough, grinding rock numbers, blues shouts, and psychedelia all mixing together into one brilliant whole. A vital addition to any record or CD collection, and also a controversial one at the time— a promotional ad taken out in the British music trades at the time managed to blaspheme several religions at once. Alas, Steve Marriott decided to call it quits with the group less than six months after this record was released. *—Bruce Eder*

Autumn Stone / 1969 / Immediate ✦✦✦
An excellent collection of most of the band's most important songs from both their later Decca and their entire Immediate history, rounded out with their final single, "The Universal," and five live tracks taken from a 1968 concert. A decent set of liner notes would've been nice, though. *—Bruce Eder*

Playmates / 1977 / Atlantic ✦
78 in the Shade / 1978 / Atlantic ✦✦
Playmates and *78 in the Shade* are a pair of mid-'70s reunion albums that did little to advance the group's reputation. The recording on *Playmates*, in particular, seems flat and muted, and while *78 in the Shade* comes off better, it still wasn't going to make anyone forget the band's early history or revive its fortunes, either. *—Bruce Eder*

★ **25 Greatest Hits** / 1992 / Repertoire ✦✦✦✦✦
Featuring all of their big British hits from "What'cha Gonna Do About It" to "The Universal," as well as worthy obscurities like "Donkey Rides a Penny a Glass," *25 Greatest Hits* is the best Small Faces compilation available, even if the tracks aren't presented in chronological order. *—Stephen Thomas Erlewine*

○ **All or Nothing** / CBS ✦✦✦✦
The best collection to date of odd outtakes, obscure B-sides, and other rarities, remastered for superior sound and reconfigured so that, among other advantages, the live tracks from *The Autumn Stone* are assembled together in sequence. Also contains lots of alternate takes, instrumental backing tracks etc. *—Bruce Eder*

Smashing Pumpkins

Group, Alternative Pop/Rock
Smashing Pumpkins played the indie rock game, although they didn't quite fit in with the rest of the crowd. Out of his affection for '70s stadium and progressive rock, guitarist/vocalist Billy Corgan fashioned a distinctive, layered sound for the band, dripping with distortion, thick hooks, and airy melodies. Unlike most alternative bands, Smashing Pumpkins don't try to disguise their pretentions or their roots; they are an album rock band, in the tradition of Queen and Black Sabbath. Where most alternative bands use guitar for sonic texture, they use it as a lead instrument in intricate compositions. Smashing Pumpkins rose to success through the alternative scene instead of AOR for two reasons. First, their music was too detailed, creative and different to fit easily into the conservative hard rock radio formats of the pre-Nirvana '90s. Secondly, Corgan's lyrics are definitely post-punk, celebrating self-proclaimed geeks and detailing depression and angst. Their mammoth guitars and fragility made them alternative superstars with their 1991 debut *Gish*. When they honed their riffs and Corgan tightened his songwriting for the follow-up, 1993's major-label debut *Siamese Dream,* the band crossed over into the mainstream. After all, most of their new fans didn't pay attention to the lyrics of "Cherub Rock" or "Today"—they just liked the way those guitars sounded. *—Stephen Thomas Erlewine*

○ **Gish** / 1991 / Caroline ✦✦✦✦
A fine debut album that follows a simple structural philosophy: fast songs good, slow songs not so good. Snazzy sound courtesy of hip independent producer Butch Vig. *—John Dougan*

Lull / 1992 / Caroline ✦✦✦

● **Siamese Dream** / 1993 / Virgin ✦✦✦✦
Dense with detail and texture, Smashing Pumpkins' breakthrough second album is a highly personal, ambitious record that unfolds after a few plays. *Siamese Dream* expands on all the promise of *Gish,* offering more pop melodies, heavy metal riffs, bombastic progressive instrumental sections, and punk angst. Apart from the succinct "Today," the music is so dense and insular that it requires some patience for it to make sense, but given some time, *Siamese Dream* becomes addictive. *—Stephen Thomas Erlewine*

Pisces Iscariot / 1994 / Capitol ✦✦✦
Some bands can pull off a thoroughly entertaining compilation of B-sides and outtakes; Smashing Pumpkins cannot. While there are some gems in the fourteen tracks—the introspective acoustic lament "Soothe" and the full-blown "Plume" and "La Dolly Vita," in particular—*Pisces Iscariot* lacks the focus which made *Siamese Dream* so impressive. Hardcore fans will find several tracks of interest, but the album will wear on more casual listeners. *—Stephen Thomas Erlewine*

Smith

Group, Pop/Rock
Basically a mainstream pop/rock band with hard rock and soul-influenced arrangements, Smith hit the Top Ten in 1969 with their drastically revised cover of the Shirelles' "Baby It's You." Featuring three lead singers and a B-3 Hammond organ, their strongest asset was their most frequent vocalist, Gayle McCormick, an accomplished female blue-eyed soul belter. Most of their material consisted of covers of popular rock and R&B tunes, and they broke up after a couple of albums, though the singles "What Am I Gonna Do" (co-written by Carole King) and "Take a Look Around" made the middle of the charts. McCormick had a couple small hits in 1971, and made a few albums in the early '70s as a soloist. *—Richie Unterberger*

● **A Group Called Smith** / 1969 / Varese Sarabande ✦✦✦✦
Their debut album, featuring "Baby It's You." The CD reissue adds five significant bonus tracks: the singles "Take A Look Around" and "What Am I Gonna Do," Gayle McCormick's solo singles "Gonna Be Alright Now" and "It's A Cryin' Shame," and Smith's version of "The Weight," which was included on the *Easy Rider* soundtrack. *—Richie Unterberger*

Huey Piano Smith

b. Jan. 26, 1934, New Orleans, LA
New Orleans R&B

At one time a madcap vocalist and underrated pianist, Huey "Piano" Smith was a star in New Orleans during the '50s. He sang with Earl King in the early '50s, then recorded with Guitar Slim from 1951 to 1954. He did several sessions and also led the Clowns, whose roster at one point included Bobby Marchan. Smith's biggest hit wasn't the song he's best known for, "Rocking Pneumonia and the Boogie Woogie Flu," but "Don't You Just Know It," which was his only Top Ten pop and R&B hit. It reached number four R&B and number nine pop in 1958, a year after "Rocking Pneumonia" peaked at number five R&B. Smith kept going until he became a Jehovah's Witness and left the music business. *—Ron Wynn*

● **Rock & Roll Revival** / Jan. 1991 / Ace ♦♦♦♦

A terrific sixteen-track collection of Huey "Piano" Smith & the Clowns' biggest hits and best material, including "Rocking Pneumonia" and "Don't You Just Know It," plus a couple of fine previously unreleased tracks. *—Stephen Thomas Erlewine*

Kendra Smith

Alternative Pop/Rock

Kendra Smith was one of the creative forces behind the Californian psychedelic band Opal in the mid-'80s. She left during the band's final tour and was replaced by Hope Sandoval (Opal then changed to Mazzy Tour after that tour). Smith then formed the Guild of Temporal Adventureers for one eponymous EP in 1992, and then remained silent for a number of years. In 1995 she released *Five Ways of Disappearing,* her solo debut, which features a number of different sounds and styles. *—Heather Phares*

Five Ways of Disappearing / 1995 / 4AD ♦♦♦

Five Ways of Disappearing marks Smith's return to recording, and the album reflects both her psychedelic background and the more ethnic/folky material she creates now. Songs like "Aurelia Zebulon" and "Temporarily Lucy" are heavy, droning pieces bordering on gothic, while "In Your Head" is a demure pop song, and "Maggots" is an odd tune with a nonsensical chorus of "maggots/do-do-do-do." Her deadpan vocal delivery adds another layer of individuality to an offbeat album by an offbeat artist. *—Heather Phares*

Patti Smith

b. Dec. 30, 1946
Alternative Pop/Rock, Punk

Patti Smith is a poet and rock singer who first gained notice when reading her poetry at gatherings in New York City in the early '70s. By 1974 Smith had edged toward music by reading with the backup of electric guitarist and rock critic Lenny Kaye, notably on her independent-label single, "Piss Factory." By 1975 Smith had organized a band that was playing in such clubs as the punk birthplace in New York, CBGB's, and she earned a contract with Arista Records. This resulted in the release of *Horses,* a critically acclaimed album that featured her songs, sometimes melded to dramatic readings, and such rock oldies as "Land of 1,000 Dances." *Radio Ethiopia* was both mainstream-rock-oriented and more experimental, depending on which track you played. With 1978's *Easter,* Smith was definitely moving in a more commercial direction, especially by pairing with Bruce Springsteen for the hit single "Because the Night." That marked the high point of Smith's rock career. *Wave* (1979) found her waving goodbye; she married ex-MC5 guitarist Fred "Sonic" Smith and retired from the music business. Her return came with the promising 1988 album *Dream of Life,* but she was not back to full-time duty. *—William Ruhlmann*

★ **Horses** / 1975 / Arista ♦♦♦♦♦

One of the more successful matings of poetry and rock, this landmark changed the role of women in rock and paved the way for rock without excess. *—Jeff Tamarkin*

○ **Radio Ethiopia** / 1976 / Arista ♦♦♦♦

Her disjointed second album takes the focus off of Smith's words and shifts it to her excellent band. Intelligent rock & roll, minus a bit of the edge. *—Jeff Tamarkin*

○ **Easter** / 1978 / Arista ♦♦♦♦

Although it contained the hit cover of Springsteen's "Because the Night," Smith's writing was weaker on this third album. The group burns though. *—Jeff Tamarkin*

Wave / 1979 / Arista ♦♦♦

The Todd Rundgren-produced final album by the PSG is unfocused and over-produced. Smith was smart to quit while she was ahead. *—Jeff Tamarkin*

Dream of Life / 1988 / Arista ♦♦♦

The long-awaited comeback of 1988 was certainly the work of an older, more settled artist. If Smith was still viable, there were few signs here. *—Jeff Tamarkin*

Teenage Perversity and Ships In The Night / Bootleg ♦♦♦

Patti Smith released some good albums, but any serious fan of hers will tell you that she performed most of her material better live. There are a number of fine Patti Smith bootlegs, but this one—taken from a January 1976 show at the Roxy in Los Angeles, with near-perfect fidelity—is both her best and her best-known. Besides incendiary versions of several songs from her first few LPs, it features covers of "Louie Louie," "My Generation" (with John Cale guesting), and the Velvet Underground's "We're Gonna Have a Good Time Together" and "Pale Blue Eyes," as well as entertaining between-song raps and even a brief cameo by Iggy Pop. It's no exaggeration to claim that this may be her best album, and one of the best '70s punk/new wave albums of all. *—Richie Unterberger*

Warren Smith

b. Feb. 7, 1933, **d.** Jan. 31, 1980
Rockabilly

For sheer, heartfelt vocalizing abilities, of all the folks who stood in front of the microphone at Sun studio, Warren Smith may have been the most talented. Equally adept at storming rockabilly and the most gut-wrenching of country ballads, Smith always sang it from the heart, without giving in to phony rasping or histrionics. Though typecast as strictly a rocker, Smith left Sun and achieved minor success in the '60s as a country singer, his first love. *—Cub Koda*

● **The Classic Recordings 1956-59** / 1992 / Bear Family ♦♦♦♦

Smith's entire output (31 tracks in all) for Sun Records. Includes the rockabilly classics "Rock & Roll Ruby," "Ubangi Stomp," and "Miss Froggie," as well as heartfelt country performances on "The Darkest Cloud," "I'd Rather Be Safe than Sorry," and "Goodbye Mr. Love." No Sun collection can really be considered complete without adding this one to the list. *—Cub Koda*

The Smithereens

Group, Rock & Roll

Pat DiNizio (vocals, guitar), Jim Babjak (guitar), Mike Mesaros (bass), and Dennis Diken (drums) make up the Smithereens, formed in New Jersey in 1980 when DiNizio answered an ad placed by the three others. The band plays in a '60s British Invasion rock & roll style, DiNizio's songs overtly evoking that era. The Smithereens gigged around the New York area and recorded a couple of EPs on small labels in the early '80s, then scored a record contract with the independent Enigma, which issued *Especially for You* in 1986. It stayed on the charts nearly a year. Its follow-up, *Green Thoughts* (1988), also showed staying power in the charts, producing the AOR radio hit "Only a Memory." The Smithereens reached the pop Top 40 with "A Girl Like You" from their third album *11* in 1989. A fourth album, *Blow Up,* stirred college and AOR radio interest for the track "Top of the Pops" in 1991, but it was less of a sales success. The group's fifth album, *A Date With The Smithereens* (1994), didn't gain much attention at either radio or retail. The band released a greatest hits collection the following year. *—William Ruhlmann*

Beauty & Sadness / 1983 / Enigma ♦♦♦

The Smithereens' second EP is an impressive collection of melodic guitar-driven power-pop, particularly the title cut. Fans of the band should seek this out, but the uninitiated will get a better picture of the band with *Especially for You* and *Green Thoughts. —Rick Clark*

○ **Especially for You** / 1986 / Enigma ♦♦♦♦

On *Especially for You,* Smithereens achieved a near-perfect blend of exuberant rockers and moody excursions. Don Dixon's production captured the band's exciting chemistry, while keeping lead singer Pat DiNizio up front in the mix, on this, their best album. "Behind the Wall of Sleep" and "Blood and Roses" were big college-music favorites, helping pave the way for greater success. Other highlights included "Strangers When We Meet," "Time and Time Again," "Groovy Tuesday," and "Alone at Midnight." *—Rick Clark*

Live / 1987 / Restless ✦✦✦
This CD is a great document of Smithereens's live power. Everyone plays impeccably, and the song selection is mint, with a version of "Beauty & Sadness" that surpasses the original and a knocked-out rendition of the Who-chestnut "The Seeker." To enhance the authenticity of the gig experience, the mix is loaded with the kind of fatiguingly brittle midrange that only a veteran live engineer could achieve. *—Rick Clark*

○ **Green Thoughts** / 1988 / Capitol ✦✦✦✦
The followup to *Especially for You* was another impressive batch of power-pop rockers. "Only a Memory" and "House We Used to Live In" were FM rock hits. Again, Dixon's production demonstrated his empathy for the band's sound. Other highlights included "Something New," "Drown in My Own Tears," and the title track. *—Rick Clark*

11 / 1990 / Capitol ✦✦✦
On *11*, the Smithereens employed alternative hard rock producer Ed Stasium (Cavedogs, Living Colour) to beef up their sound. The result was a thick guitar-riff-heavy sound. The approach helped "A Girl like You" become a big rock and MTV hit but, taken as a whole, *11* lacked the dynamics and natural soundstage that made their earlier work so fresh-sounding. "Yesterday Girl," "Baby Be Good," and "A Girl like You" are highlights, though. *—Rick Clark*

Blow Up / 1991 / Capitol ✦✦✦
An improvement over *11, Blow Up* displays Stasium's state-of-the-art power-rock production and a greater range of material. The soulful "Too Much Passion" was a hit, as was "Top of the Pops." *—Rick Clark*

Date with the Smithereens / 1994 / RCA ✦✦✦
Producer Don Dixon returns to the helm, creating an album that synthesizes the jangly melodic appeal of *Green Thoughts* with the finesse of *11*. It includes the single "Miles from Nowhere." *—Rick Clark*

● **Blown To Smithereens: The Best of the Smithereens** / 1995 / Capitol ✦✦✦✦
Collecting together all the hits and highlights from the Smithereens' Capitol albums, *Blown to Smithereens* contains all of their finest hard-rocking pop gems. *—Stephen Thomas Erlewine*

The Smiths

Group, Alternative Pop/Rock
At the beginning of the '80s, both the British pop and independent charts were filled with synth-pop, goth-rock, and lightweight new wave. In this climate, the Smiths' first single, "Hand in Glove," caused a quiet revolution. With their first album and singles, the Smiths led rock & roll into a new era, where songs were again of the utmost importance, guitars replaced synthesizers as the prominent instrument on the pop and indie charts, and where lyrics were unabashedly personal and poetic; in short, they helped post-punk become alternative rock. In their native England, the band were superstars; each of their albums hit the Top Ten. America never warmed to their distinctly British sensibility, yet they did earn a sizable cult following across the U.S.A. Ten years after the release of their first album, their influence is still substantial; from the Stone Roses to Suede, the Smiths were the root of nearly every significant development in British music since 1984.

At its core, the Smiths' music was pure guitar-based pop/rock, recalling hooks and textures from the '60s. While their music was rooted in British pop, it also borrowed significantly from the energy and independence of punk; it never sounded dated or derivative. Morrissey's yearning voice and literate lyrics complimented Johnny Marr's understated, textured guitar to the point where the two were inseparable. Marr had a skill for writing melodic hooks that sounded simple and direct, yet were a incredibly complex web of interweaving guitar lines. But Morrissey was the focal point of the band. Some critics accused him of being tuneless, yet he was a great vocalist, effortlessly conveying the exaggerated angst and self-depricating humor of his words with unusual, unexpected pitches and phrasing. Morrissey's introspective lyrics strongly connected with disaffected youth around the world, yet

they aren't adolescent; beneath his grandly dramatic vocals, there is genuine emotion, humor, melancholy, and compassion in Morrissey's writing.

The songwriting team of Morrissey and Marr was remarkably inventive and prolific; during their brief four-year career, the Smiths released four proper albums, several non-LP singles and B-sides, and two singles compilations. All of their material was remarkably consistent, proving the band's mastery of pop songwriting.

The Smiths broke up in early fall of 1987, just before the release of their fourth and final album, *Strangeways Here We Come*. Bassist Andy Rourke and drummer Mike Joyce supported Sinead O'Connor for a time; Joyce eventually joined the reunited Buzzcocks. Marr went on to work with the Pretenders, The The, and Electronic. Morrissey began a solo career that proved just as popular as the Smiths'. *—Stephen Thomas Erlewine*

☆ **The Smiths** / 1984 / Sire ✦✦✦✦✦
The Smiths make ear-pleasing, catchy pop-rock, and it seduces the listener into paying attention to Morrissey's dead-pan lyrics, which are deliberately self-pitying, sometimes caustic, and usually funny. "Reel around the Fountain" is a classic, and the album also contains the U.K. singles "Hand in Glove" and "What Difference Does It Make?" *—William Ruhlmann*

☆ **Hatful of Hollow** / 1984 / Sire ✦✦✦✦✦
A collection of singles, B-sides, and BBC radio sessions, *Hatful of Hollow* shows how rapidly the Smiths were evolving. Containing some of their best songs—"William, It Was Really Nothing," "How Soon Is Now?," "This Charming Man," "Hand in Glove," "Reel Around the Fountain," "Please, Please, Please, Let Me Get What I Want"—the album is a more exciting and effective record than their debut album. *—Stephen Thomas Erlewine*

Meat Is Murder / 1985 / Sire ✦✦✦
The Smiths' second album isn't a great leap forward, but it does contain some fine guitar-pop, including "The Headmaster Ritual," "Rusholme Ruffians," and "That Joke Isn't Funny Anymore." The American version included the pulsating "How Soon is Now?," which doesn't fit the mood of the rest of the album. *—Stephen Thomas Erlewine*

☆ **The Queen Is Dead** / 1986 / Sire ✦✦✦✦✦
The Queen is Dead is the Smiths' masterpiece, boasting an amazingly accomplished set of songs, including the surrealistic humor of the title track, the lilting "The Boy With the Thorn in His Side," the deceptively sunny pop of "Cemetry Gates," the nasty "Bigmouth Strikes Again," and the gorgeous "There Is a Light That Never Goes Out." Morrissey's lyrics have never been better and Marr's hooks are among his best. *—Stephen Thomas Erlewine*

World Won't Listen / 1987 / Rough Trade ✦✦✦

○ **Louder than Bombs** / 1987 / Sire ✦✦✦✦
The Smiths' second singles and B-sides collection is every bit as essential as the first, containing such brilliant songs as "Panic," "London," "You Just Haven't Earned it Yet, Baby," and "Is It Really So Strange." There's a bit of duplication with *Hatful of Hollow*, but the music on *Louder Than Bombs* was some of the most vital and timeless pop music of the 1980s. *—Stephen Thomas Erlewine*

○ **Strangeways Here We Come** / 1987 / Sire ✦✦✦✦
While there are some fine songs here, *Strangeways Here We Come* is ultimately a disappointing final effort from the Smiths. Nevertheless, the album's best songs—"Stop Me if You've Heard This One Before," "I Won't Share You," "Last Night I Dreamt That Somebody Loved Me," "Girlfriend in a Coma"—are among the best the band recorded. *—Stephen Thomas Erlewine*

Rank / 1988 / Sire ✦✦
A solid but unexceptional live album recorded on the *Queen is Dead* tour. *—Stephen Thomas Erlewine*

The Best, Vol. 1 / 1992 / Sire ✦✦
With or without its companion volume, this remains a less than excellent compilation. Even when viewed with *Volume 2*, these collections include odd selections at the expense of more obvious ones. The faithful will already have everything here. And neophyte fans would do better with *Louder than Bombs* along with *Queen* and the debut. *—Steve Aldrich*

The Best, Vol. 2 / Dec. 8, 1992 / Sire ✦✦
Best of—Vol. 2 fills in the gaps from the first volume, but like its predecessor, it lacks cohesion or a sense of what made the Smiths important. Many great songs are included, but, ultimately, it cheats the legacy of Britain's most important band of the '80s. *—AMG*

★ **Singles** / 1995 / Reprise ✦✦✦✦✦
The *Best of the Smiths* collections didn't work since they didn't have a sense of history and distorted the underlying sense of urgency that helped make the Smiths important. *Singles* simply collects all of the singles from one of the greatest singles bands since the Beatles. It's essential and influential guitar-pop, presented in a way that makes sense and is endlessly listenable —*Stephen Thomas Erlewine*

Smog

Group, Alternative Pop/Rock
One of the gloomiest bands since the demise of Joy Divison, Smog is the project of guitarist/vocalist/keyboardist Bill Callahan, who is occasionally joined by guitarist/vocalist Cynthia Dall and a host of drummers and cellists. From the first, Smog has been an unusual band, mixing grim subject matter and instrumentations with a punk/indie aesthetic. The intensely emotional and claustrophobic result is catalogued on the group's two full-length albums and the *Burning Kingdom* EP. While often difficult and probably not everyday listening, Smog is oddly dramatic and affecting. It won't cheer you up, but it will provoke a reaction. —*Heather Phares*

Julius Caesar / 1993 / Drag City ✦✦✦
The debut album from Bill Callahan, Cynthia Dall and company is rife with downbeat and occasionally poignant indie-pop that mixes clangy guitars with strings and synthesizers for a unique, evocative sound. One of the standout tracks is "Your Wedding," as bitter and complex a jealousy song as you're likely to hear. —*Heather Phares*

Burning Kingdom / 1994 / Drag City ✦✦✦
Four vignettes of concentrated sadness, *Burning Kingdom* has to be one of the darkest-sounding EPs released in recent memory. Particularly effective is the haunting "Reneé Died," which pits Dall's frail voice against brittle acoustic guitars. —*Heather Phares*

● **Wild Love** / 1995 / Drag City ✦✦✦✦
The group's second full-length album is slightly less melancholy than *Burning Kingdom*, and even manages some pitch-black humor in tracks like "Prince Alone in the Studio," "Be Hit" and "Sweet Smog Children." But some of the most poignant songs Callahan has written appear on *Wild Love*, including "Bathysphere," "The Candle," "Limited Capacity," and the luminous, empathetic "It's Rough." "Goldfish Bowl" is one of the catchiest numbers on *Wild Love*, which is Smog's finest work to date. —*Heather Phares*

The Smoke

Group, British Invasion, Psychedelic
More than any other band, the Smoke epitomized the groove of Swinging London. Their sound fell somewhere between mod and the Beatles—their instrumental attack was somewhat Who/Small Faces-like, yet they delighted in cheerful vocals and infectious harmonies and melodies. Only slightly popular on their home turf, and unknown in the U.S., their biggest success was in Germany (oddly enough, for such a British-sounding group). *It's Smoke Time*, their only album, was issued in Germany in 1967 and is one of the most cheerful records ever made, though not at all wimpy. "My Friend Jack," with its crushing reverb feedback, was a big hit in Germany, and on its way to becoming a hit in the U.K. when it was banned by British radio for supposed drug references. The Smoke issued several rare singles, some of them quite good, after the album before disbanding. —*Richie Unterberger*

● **It's Smoke Time** / 1994 / Repertoire ✦✦✦✦
Besides "My Friend Jack," other highlights of the group's only album (all but one of whose tracks were group originals) include the beautiful mid-tempo ballad "Waterfall" and the bee-humming guitars and lilting backup vocals on "You Can't Catch Me." The German CD reissue adds fourteen additional cuts, including non-LP singles, a single issued in 1965 by the Shots (an earlier version of the group), a single puzzlingly issued under the alias the Chords Five, and an interesting alternate take of "My Friend Jack." A lot of these tracks pale in comparison to the twelve from the original album, but "Have Some More Tea" is a great Who-ish number, and "Sydney Gill" is a good stab at a more progressive mood. —*Richie Unterberger*

Patti Smyth

Pop/Rock
After leaving Scandal in 1984, vocalist Patty Smyth waited three years before launching her solo career with the *Never Enough* album. Although it sold respectably, it didn't have any major hit singles. Smyth returned to the top of the charts in 1992 with "Sometimes Love Just Ain't Enough," a duet with Don Henley; the single hit number two and went gold. Its parent album, *Patty Smyth*, also went gold and featured two other minor hits, "No Mistakes" and "I Should Be Laughing." —*Stephen Thomas Erlewine*

Never Enough / 1987 / Columbia ✦✦✦

● **Patty Smyth** / 1992 / MCA ✦✦✦✦
Five years after her first solo album, *Never Enough*, Smyth decided "there's such a thing as too much love" and proceeded to detail lover's trials for an entire album. Despite production by Bruce Springsteen keyboardist Roy Bittan, this isn't as good as *Never Enough*, although "Sometimes Love Just Ain't Enough," a duet with Don Henley, got tons of radio play. —*Brian Mansfield*

The Sneakers

Group, Power Pop/Anglo-Pop
While the Sneakers never made much of an impact when they were together, the band marks the first appearance of several seminal figures of the alternative pop scene of the early '80s. Chris Stamey, Mitch Easter, and Will Rigby formed the core of the Sneakers, writing well-crafted, guitar-driven pop rockers; their self-titled debut EP was engineered by Don Dixon, who went on to be a successful producer, as well as a solo artist. After one excellent full-length album, the Sneakers broke up. Stamey and Rigby went on to form the dB's, one of the '80s best American guitar-pop bands; Easter led Let's Active, as well as becoming a record producer (including R.E.M.'s first two albums). However, the Sneakers are more than historical curiosity; although they didn't record very much, their album and EP contain some of the finest power-pop of the late '70s. —*Stephen Thomas Erlewine*

In the Red / 1978 / CAR ✦✦✦

● **Racket** / 1993 / East Side Digital ✦✦✦✦
This disc contains selections from the Sneakers' unfinished third record, *Wig Cleaner*, as well as all the original compositions from *In the Red* and the band's first release, *Carnivorous #1*. While all of the songs were written in the late '70s, some of the recordings were done as recently as 1992. Songs like "Some Kinda Fool" and "Story of a Girl" exude an effortless sophistication of chord structure and melody. Lovers of quirky guitar pop/rock (read: early dB's fans) should have this one. —*Rick Clark*

Snoop Doggy Dogg

Rap
Rap's reigning superstar, Snoop Doggy Dogg made his debut on Dr. Dre's *The Chronic*. His laconic, low-volume rap style struck a nerve with hip-hop audiences and his debut release, *Doggystyle*, became the first album ever by a new artist to make its initial entry onto the pop albums chart at number one. The album had sold over four million copies by the midpoint of 1994, and also generated plenty of controversy for its sexist and homophobic tendencies and explicit language. The record did shine the spotlight on some neglected acts and music from the '70s, notably the Dramatics, who appeared in one of Dogg's videos and backed him on one single. —*Ron Wynn*

○ **Doggystyle** / 1993 / Interscope ✦✦✦✦
Snoop Doggy Dogg's debut entered the charts at number one, and it has proven popular even though there's little departure musically or production-wise from Dr. Dre's release. *Doggystyle* features more of Dogg's part-drawl, part-spoken word narratives, but expresses a vision more paranoid than confident. Throughout the disc, Snoop has nightmares about being killed, and spends most of his time either defaming women or getting out of conflicts. The single "Who Am I (What's My Name)" uses nearly the same samples and bass lines as "Dre Day," as only Snoop's lean, almost casual sneers and rejoinders differentiate it from Dre's prior recording. He also throws a few darts at Eazy-E, but otherwise, this is prototype gangsta rap with Snoop's signature style as its major hook. —*Ron Wynn*

Phoebe Snow (Phoebe Laub)

b. Jul. 17, 1952, New York City, NY
Singer-Songwriter, Pop

This pop-jazz singer/songwriter with a broad, melismatic contralto voice broke through in 1975 with her debut album on Shelter, then made several albums for Columbia and Atlantic despite legal and personal difficulties that distracted her from her career. She returned to recording on Elektra in 1989 after an eight-year layoff and was also part of Donald Fagen's New York Rock and Soul Revue. — *William Ruhlmann*

Snowbird / 1974 / Camden ✦✦✦

● **Phoebe Snow** / Jul. 1974 / DCC ✦✦✦✦
A wondrous folk, pop, and jazz album of Snow's original songs and some well-chosen covers, all showcasing her one-of-a-kind voice. Includes the Top Five hit "Poetry Man." — *William Ruhlmann*

Second Childhood / Jan. 1976 / Columbia ✦✦✦
Although it lacked a hit single to match "Poetry Man," Phoebe Snow's second album was another folk-pop-jazz confection that effectively showcased her one-of-a-kind voice in musical settings featuring the cream of New York's session musicians, produced by Phil Ramone. It was a classy job on which Snow contributed seven originals and displayed her versatility on covers ranging from Motown to Gershwin. — *William Ruhlmann*

○ **It Looks Like Snow** / Feb. 1976 / Columbia ✦✦✦✦
The cover songs start to overwhelm the originals, but when Snow is able to bring such powerful interpretations to "Don't Let Me Down," "Shakey Ground," and "Teach Me Tonight," who could complain? — *William Ruhlmann*

Never Letting Go / Oct. 1977 / Columbia ✦✦✦
Phoebe Snow made it onto the soul chart with her version of Barbara Acklin's 1968 hit "Love Makes A Woman" (#87), which served as the lead-off track of her fourth album. But the record marked a fall-off in both her commercial success and her artistic accomplishment. The tasty studio musicians and Phil Ramone's pop-jazz production were still in place, and Snow remained a remarkable singer, but her synthesis of styles was beginning to seem not so much inspired as muddled. — *William Ruhlmann*

Against the Grain / Oct. 1978 / Columbia ✦✦✦
Phoebe Snow should have, could have had hits with her covers of Paul McCartney's "Every Night" and the Roches' "The Married Men," but by her fourth Columbia album and fifth release overall, the company seems to have been content to let her records find their audience without pushing them. (Actually, "Every Night" did hit #79 in the U.K.) Maybe they'd given up trying to figure out whether she was a folksinger, a pop singer, a soul singer, or a jazz singer, and forgot that she was a great singer. The decision to add Barry Beckett as co-producer with Phil Ramone helped add an R&B depth and fervor, but *Against The Grain* was just a more impassioned effort than its predecessor. That didn't keep Columbia from dropping Phoebe Snow when it didn't hit, though. — *William Ruhlmann*

● **The Best of Phoebe Snow** / 1981 / Columbia ✦✦✦✦

Rock Away / Mar. 1981 / Atlantic ✦✦
Phoebe Snow a rock singer? Well, she certainly had the pipes, and producers Greg Ladanyi and Richie Cannata surrounded her with Billy Joel's backup band for a standard New York rock sound. With Snow contributing only three original tunes, the song selection was odd—Rod Stewart's "Gasoline Alley," the Buckinghams/Cannonball Adderley hit "Mercy, Mercy, Mercy," Bob Dylan's "I Believe In You." *Rock Away* sold better than her last two albums and produced two chart singles, "Games" (#46) and "Mercy, Mercy, Mercy" (#52). But anyone who had heard her first two albums knew that this was not the whole story by a long shot. — *William Ruhlmann*

Something Real / Feb. 1989 / Elektra ✦✦✦
"This time when I reach out, it may be my last try," warns Phoebe Snow on the title track to her seventh album, which is her first in eight years. Perhaps with that in mind, it's a well-considered effort, and one that brought moderate success, including two Adult Contemporary chart hits in "If I Can Just Get Through The Night" (#13) and "Something Real" (#29). Snow takes a slightly more relaxed approach to the rock style of her last album, *Rock Away*. She sticks to contemporary songs for the most part (there's a dance music cover of the Emotions' "Best Of My Love"), and writes half of them herself. She tends to de-emphasize the more unusual aspects of her voice, although not so much that you'd confuse it with

anybody else's. The result is a sturdy, respectable set, although not one likely to launch a major comeback. — *William Ruhlmann*

Social Distortion
Group, Alternative Pop/Rock, Rock & Roll, Punk
Social Distortion was an early high mark in California punk. Actually, with their 1977-era power chords and an artistic scope that was comfortable enough to include Johnny Cash covers, this Fullerton, CA, band came on like a throwback to British punk groups like Stiff Little Fingers and the Vibrators. They were also able to move their chunky punk rock into the mainstream without cutting back on the energy, the power chords, or the nihilism. And that's something few West Coast hardcore bands can claim. —*John Floyd*

○ **Mommy's Little Monster** / 1983 / Time Bomb ✦✦✦✦
Their debut is full of wailing guitars, sharp lyrics, tugging melodies, and snarling vocals. —*John Floyd*

Prison Bound / 1988 / Time Bomb ✦✦✦
The release of this album brought acoustic guitars, ballads, and a cautious step toward the rock mainstream that makes their music of use for more than just hardcore nihilists. —*John Floyd*

○ **Social Distortion** / 1990 / Epic ✦✦✦✦
Their major-label debut repeated the winning formula of *Prison Bound*—Ramones meet the Blasters meet Johnny Thunders—but with better production. —*John Floyd*

● **Somewhere between Heaven and Hell** / 1991 / Epic ✦✦✦✦
Social Distortion wallows in rock & roll rebellion and fatalism. The combination of urgent lyrics and unbeatable riffs make this their best album. —*John Floyd*

Mainliner (Wreckage of the Past) / 1995 / Time Bomb ✦✦✦

The Soft Boys
Group, Alternative Pop/Rock, New Wave
While they were together, the Soft Boys recorded three discs of blissful post-punk weirdness, fueled by the winding guitar of Kimberly Rew and the warped vision of Robyn Hitchcock. Rew joined the band after an independent EP, in time for the recording of their full-length debut, *A Can of Bees*. But the focal point of the band was singer/guitarist Hitchcock, a bizarrely gifted pop songwriter with an affection for Syd Barrett and John Lennon. Hitchcock melded the psychedelic guitars of *Revolver*-era Beatles with the sheer dementia of Barrett, creating a stripped-down guitar rock unlike anything else in the post-punk world. And the Soft Boys were assuredly inspired by punk—both their raw sound and lyrical obsessions were outgrowths of the punk era. Their time together was brief—about three years—yet their music has inspired a cult of devoted fans. Hitchcock went on to a successful cult career as a singer/songwriter; Rew formed Katrina & the Waves, where he earned a surprising amount of pop success. —*Stephen Thomas Erlewine*

○ **A Can of Bees** / 1979 / Rykodisc ✦✦✦✦
The Soft Boys' debut album *A Can of Bees* was an uneven but impressive debut featuring a set of catchy, warped pop songs driven by the ringing guitar riffs of Kimberly Rew and Robyn Hitchcock. —*Stephen Thomas Erlewine*

★ **Underwater Moonlight** / 1980 / Rykodisc ✦✦✦✦✦
Wry, savage humor permeates this near-virtuoso album. Extraordinarily well played, especially the guitars. —*Bruce Eder*

○ **Invisible Hits** / 1983 / Rykodisc ✦✦✦✦
A collection of outtakes and singles recorded in 1978 and 1979 but released in 1983, *Invisible Hits* isn't an inferior collection to *A Can of Bees* and *Underwater Moonlight*. Instead, it illustrates the creativity and the distinctiveness of their guitar-pop and contains a couple of their classics, including "Have a Heart, Betty (I'm Not Fireproof)," "Let Me Put It Next to You," and "Blues in the Dark." —*Stephen Thomas Erlewine*

1976-81 / 1994 / Rykodisc ✦✦✦
Along with several classic album tracks, the double-disc collection *1976-81* is filled with rarities and live tracks, making it more appealing to the collector than the neophyte. —*Stephen Thomas Erlewine*

Soft Cell
Group, Dance-Pop, New Wave
Like the traditional synthesizer-driven dance-pop of the early '80s,

Soft Cell was detached from their material, yet they were not cold. Instead, the duo of vocalist Marc Almond and keyboardist David Ball was warm and human; they were joyfully sleazy, celebrating kinky sex and trashing pop standards. Their finest moment came with a single from their first album, *Non-Stop Erotic Cabaret*, in 1981. "Tainted Love" represents everything Soft Cell wanted to achieve and it was an enormous success, spending nearly a year on the *Billboard* singles charts. After that, the duo occasionally recaptured some of the spark of that single (their cover of "Where Did Our Love Go?," in particular) but more frequently slipped into self-parody; they broke up in 1984. —*Stephen Thomas Erlewine*

● **Memorabilia: Singles** / 1991 / Mercury ◆◆◆◆
Although it doesn't contain a couple of key tracks, including the 12-inch version of "Tainted Love/Where Did Our Love Go," *Memorabilia* is the best Soft Cell collection available. —*Stephen Thomas Erlewine*

Soft Machine

Group, Art-Rock/Progressive-Rock, Psychedelic
Soft Machine gave us over a decade's-worth of consistently challenging and highly creative music, even though the group that began the project was a vastly different one in both sound and make-up than the group that concluded at the end of the '70s. Emerging from England's Canterbury scene, the founding line-up mixed elements of free jazz and electronic composition into their already dizzy brand of psychedelic rock. The group experimented with horns, with saxophonist Elton Dean joining for a lengthy stay. It should be noted that Soft Machine's line-up changed constantly, from the outset on through their career. With the band's third album, vocals were phased out, and the group emphasized their jazzier side, relying heavily on Mike Ratledge's distinctive over-driven organ sound.

With the pattern now set for the rest of their run, Soft Machine delivered numerous albums of high quality British fusion music, and has been sorely underrated in their efforts in this vein. Eventually, even the long-serving Ratledge departed leaving the group essentially under the leadership of Karl Jenkins, until the project came to a halt at the end of the '70s. —*Steve Aldrich*

○ **The Soft Machine** / 1968 / One Way ◆◆◆◆
○ **Soft Machine, Vol. 2** / 1969 / Probe ◆◆◆◆
○ **Third** / 1970 / Columbia ◆◆◆◆
This album marks the beginning of their penchant for long, jazz-influenced pieces, and the end of the youthful, madcap era. —*Myles Boisen*

Fourth / 1971 / Columbia ◆◆◆
Fifth / 1972 / CBS ◆◆◆
○ **1 & 2** / 1973 / Probe ◆◆◆◆
Six / 1973 / CBS ◆◆◆
Soft Machine Seven / May 1974 / Columbia ◆◆
Bundles / 1975 / See For Miles ◆◆◆
Live at the Proms 1970 / 1988 / Reckless ◆◆◆
Initially recorded for the BBC in August 1970, this is a good document of the group in concert shortly after the release of *Third*, stripped down to the quartet of Wyatt, Ratledge, Hopper, and saxophonist Elton Dean. Most of the material comes from their second and third albums, and Wyatt, disappointingly, barely sings at all. These versions aren't much different from the ones found on the official releases, though they're perhaps a bit more spontaneous, so this is primarily recommended for hardcore fans. —*Richie Unterberger*

● **Vols. 1 & 2** / Sep. 1989 / Big Beat ◆◆◆◆
A combination of their first two studio albums onto one CD. Their first (originally titled *The Soft Machine*, from 1968), recorded with the trio of Wyatt, Ratledge, and Ayers, combines goofy humor, psychedelia, and some free jazz into an erratic but invigorating brew that was comparable to little else in the late-'60s rock world. Ayers had left to be replaced by Hugh Hopper for 1969's *Volume Two*, which took a definite spin toward jazz and increasingly surrealistic material, stringing together whimsical bits and pieces for side-long suites. Not as pop-oriented as their initial 1967 recordings or as jazz-oriented as their final albums with Wyatt, the material compiled here is perhaps the best representation of the Soft Machine's accomplishments. —*Richie Unterberger*

○ **Jet-Propelled Photograph** / Charly ◆◆◆◆
The latest available CD version of a title which has been repackaged and retitled several times over the last 20 years. Recorded in London in April 1967 and produced by the legendary Giorgio Gomelsky, these nine demos feature the original Soft Machine lineup of Robert Wyatt, Kevin Ayers, Mike Ratledge, and Daevid Allen. Although not intended for release, these rough but accomplished performances show the band at their most pop- and song-oriented. Not far removed from Syd Barrett-era Pink Floyd, the jazzy chord changes, unpredictable bursts of scat singing, glib free-association lyrics, ominous buzzing organ, and Robert Wyatt's soulful rasp convey the freewheeling abandon and giddy high spirits that characterized the best early British psychedelia. For similar but more elaborately produced relics from the Daevid Allen lineup, check for the three tracks on the hard-to-find triple LP *Triple Echo*. —*Richie Unterberger*

Sonic Youth

Group, Alternative Pop/Rock, Experimental
When Sonic Youth began as a downtown New York band in the early '80s, they rejected most traditional rock & roll formalities such as Western tuning and song structure. With screwdrivers randomly stuck into their guitar necks, the quartet created discordant, droning, mantralike songs, which were quietly forceful. As they matured, their material became more accessible and the songs more conventional, even as they retained their discordance. By the early 90s, Sonic Youth was approaching mainstream acceptance.

The band (Kim Gordon, bass and vocal; Thurston Moore, guitar and vocal; Lee Ranaldo, guitar; Steve Shelley, drums) had several releases before their sound crystallized. *Sonic Youth, Confusion Is Sex, Kill Your Idols*, and *Sonic Death* document a band learning to express their complex ideas. These releases are often coarse and brash, sometimes unlistenable, and frequently startling in their power.

The band's cult following continued to grow throughout the late '80s, culminating in a major-label contract with Geffen Records. The corporate machine helped them develop a still-larger following. After their Geffen debut, 1990's *Goo*, Sonic Youth rested for two years. Their past indicates that a pause to regroup is usually followed by a burst of new creativity.

The band re-emerged with *Dirty*, their most direct stab at traditional pop/rock songwriting. The album was more successful than any of their past efforts, making the band popular with MTV-weaned adolescents. Naturally, Sonic Youth responded with a change in direction. *Experimental Jet Set, Trash & No Star* (1994) was their calmest record, yet it was more abstract than either of their major-label releases; it had an instant alternative radio/MTV hit with "Bull in the Heather." After headlining the fifth Lollapalooza package tour in the summer of 1995, Sonic Youth released *Washing Machine*, their tenth album of original material, in the fall. —*Robert Gordon*

Sonic Youth / 1982 / SST ◆◆
Kill Your Idols / 1983 / Zensor ◆◆
Confusion Is Sex / 1983 / SST ◆◆
Out of all their early recordings, *Confusion Is Sex* is Sonic Youth's most listenable record, but that doesn't mean it's an easy listen, by any means. Dense with ideas and noisy guitars, the record only works in fits and spurts, but it reveals the band's potential, even if most of the record is exceedingly difficult and under-developed. —*Stephen Thomas Erlewine*

Sonic Death / 1984 / SST ◆◆
Bad Moon Rising / 1985 / DGC ◆◆◆
On *Bad Moon Rising*, the songs gained a focus so that moods and styles which formerly had spread scross several releases could be accomplished in one album. —*Robert Gordon*

○ **EVOL** / 1986 / SST ◆◆◆◆
EVOL ("love" spelled backwards) is composed of catchy rhythms and melodies, even some hooks; however, a menacing darkness remained, even dominated. Vocals were split pretty evenly between Gordon and Moore. *EVOL* remains a high point for the band, with provocative songs that force us, even after punk, to question what was commonplace in pop. Featured are "Green Light" and "Expressway to Yr Skull." —*Robert Gordon*

☆ **Sister** / 1987 / SST ◆◆◆◆◆
Sister found them largely embracing the rock aesthetic, though with little sacrifice to their own code. The album retains its menace and punkish attitude while totally rocking out. It's sort of the

other side of the *EVOL* coin. They achieve a similar end, but instead of using spacious and brooding songs, they play hard, succinct, and tight. The CD features the bonus track "Master Dik." — *Robert Gordon*

★ **Daydream Nation** / 1988 / DGC ✦✦✦✦✦

Daydream Nation is a double album that warrants its indulgences; if the songs run long, they're worth it. When "Total Trash" devolves into a furious jam, its cacophony is beautiful, surpassed only by the surprise return to structure. The appeal of the "Teenage Riot" single brought the band a greater audience, and, if it seems to compromise their stance, in the context of the album it makes perfect sense. —*Robert Gordon*

Goo / 1990 / DGC ✦✦✦

Though *Goo* is not a sellout, it didn't advance the band in the leaps their previous few albums had. Mostly it sounds like *Daydream Nation* rehashed. Included are "Tunic," "Dirty Boots," and "Kool Thing." —*Robert Gordon*

○ **Dirty** / 1992 / DGC ✦✦✦✦

Sonic Youth could never sell out, no matter how hard they tried. Their sound—a jarring barrage of distorted guitars and feedback—is entirely too singular and avant-garde to ever completely cross over. However, *Dirty* is the closest Sonic Youth has ever come to the mainstream, and it is their most accessible album to date. "100%" is nearly a pop single, complete with hooks and an identifiable song structure. But Sonic Youth hasn't lost their edge, as Kim Gordon's tracks in particular prove. —*Stephen Thomas Erlewine*

Experimental Jet Set, Trash & No Star / 1994 / DGC ✦✦

Opening with their first acoustic number ever, *Experimental Jet Set, Trash & No Star* is Sonic Youth's calmest record to date. While the band's sound is different, their ideas aren't—they're essentially repeating *Sister*. There are a couple of interesting tracks, but most of the album is surprisingly boring. —*Stephen Thomas Erlewine*

Made in USA / 1995 / Rhino ✦✦

A soundtrack to an obscure 1986 movie, *Made in USA* captures Sonic Youth trying to fit their expansive ideas into the brief space allotted to incidental film music. Keeping the atmospherics but scaling back the noise, the band manages to evoke different textures than their albums, textures that are drier and less overtly avant-garde. Nevertheless, *Made in USA* doesn't rank among their finest work but not because its on a smaller scale, but because it all sounds tossed-off; there's not much thought to any of this music. Even so, the disc is still quite listenable, which shows how good the band was in 1985 and 1986. —*Stephen Thomas Erlewine*

Screaming Fields of Sonic Love / 1995 / DGC ✦✦✦

Sonic Youth isn't really a singles band, nor a band that works best taken as individual songs, so the idea of a compilation seems a little half-hearted. And, *Screaming Fields of Sonic Love* is a bit haphazard. —*Stephen Thomas Erlewine*

The Sonics

Group, Rock & Roll, Garage Rock

A rock & roll band from Tacoma, WA, the Sonics' original members were Gerry Roslie (lead singer and piano/organ), Andy Parypa (guitar), Larry Parypa (bass), Bob Bennett (drums), and Rob Lind (saxophone). Forming in the wake of the early-'60s success of local favorites the Kingsmen and the Wailers (whose Etiquette label they recorded for), the Sonics combined the classic Northwest-area teen-band raunch with early English band grit (particularly influenced by the Kinks), relentless rhythmic drive, and unabashed '50s-style blues-shouting for a combination that still makes their brand of rock & roll perhaps the raunchiest ever captured on wax. Lead singer Gerry Roslie was no less than a White Little Richard, whose harrowing soul-screams were startling even to the Northwest teen audience, who liked their music powerful and driving with little regard to commercial subtleties. With hit after hit on the local charts (and influencing every local band that ever took the stage), the band inexplicably was never able to break out nationally, leaving their sound largely unbuilded for mass consumption. Breaking up in the late '60s (after one ill-fated album attempt to water down their style for national attention), the Sonics continue today to be revered by '60s collectors the world over for their unique brand of rock & roll raunch. —*Cub Koda*

Here Are the Sonics!!! / 1965 / Etiquette ✦✦✦

Debut album, featuring early local hits "The Witch" and "Psycho." —*Cub Koda*

The Sonics Boom / 1966 / Etiquette ✦✦✦

Second album, featuring unusual take on "Louie Louie." —*Cub Koda*

● **Here Are the Ultimate Sonics** / 1991 / Etiquette ✦✦✦✦

Combining all the tracks from their first two Etiquette albums, three tracks from the label's Christmas album, live tracks, and an alternate take of "The Witch," this compilation more than lives up to its title. The definitive overview. —*Cub Koda*

Sonny & Cher

Group, Folk-Rock, Pop/Rock

Sonny & Cher proved one of the magical musical combinations of the '60s, with their wisecracking repartee providing counterpoint to a series of adoring hit duets. Sonny Bono (b. Feb 16, 1935) started out at Los Angeles-based Specialty Records as a songwriter in the late '50s. While working sessions with legendary producer Phil Spector, Bono met and married background singer Cher (born Cherilyn Lapierre, May 20, 1946) and formed a duet with his new wife. Neither was blessed with an outstanding vocal range, but no matter—they went gold in 1965 with the pop chart-topper "I Got You Babe" on Atco and did well with "Baby Don't Go" on Reprise. At the same time, both enjoyed success separately—Sonny with "Laugh at Me" for Atco, Cher with "All I Really Want to Do" and "Bang Bang (My Baby Shot Me Down)" on Imperial. "The Beat Goes On" in 1967 and "All I Ever Need Is You" four years later presaged the pair's anointment as popular TV variety-hour hosts from 1971 to 1974 (the year they were divorced). Since then, Cher has gone on to mega-stardom on record and on the silver screen. Sonny, meanwhile, was elected mayor of Palm Springs, CA. —*Bill Dahl*

● **The Beat Goes On: The Best of Sonny & Cher** / 1975 / Atco ✦✦✦✦

They were the ultimate "hip luv" couple of the '60s and their many hits are still fun to listen to. "I Got You Babe," "Laugh at Me," and the title track are three of the 21 original recordings included on this definitive collection. —*Jeff Tamarkin*

The Sons of Champlin

Group, Rock & Roll

One of the last, and more obscure, bands to emerge from the late '60s San Francisco psychedelic scene. The Sons of Champlin were relatively unusual among Bay Area bands for favoring heavily soul-influenced material, and employing a prominent horn section. Their more introspective songs can recall the more subdued efforts of Quicksilver Messenger Service and Moby Grape, and the longer compositions boasted unusually complex song structures and tempo shifts. Revered by some collectors, their work hasn't aged as well as the best of their peers; the vocals weren't gritty enough to carry the R&B-based material, and the ambitious longer tracks were prone to some half-baked songwriting and meandering jamming. Their first three albums (issued on Capitol between 1969 and 1971) are considered their best, though they recorded some other LPs in the 1970s with shifting personnel. —*Richie Unterberger*

● **The Best of the Sons of Champlin** / Jun. 21, 1993 / Capitol ✦✦✦✦

14 of the most enduring cuts from 1969-71, leaning most heavily on their '69 debut, *Loosen Up Naturally*, and also including the 1970 single "Terry's Tune." —*Richie Unterberger*

The Sorrows

Group, British Invasion

One of the most overlooked bands of the British Invasion, the Sorrows offered a tough brand of R&B-infused rock that recalled the Pretty Things (though not as R&B-oriented) and the Kinks (though not as pop-oriented). Their biggest British hit, "Take a Heart," stopped just outside the U.K. Top 20; several other fine mid-'60s singles met with either slim or a total lack of success. With the rich, gritty vocals of Don Fardon, taut raunchy guitars, and good material (both self-penned and from outside writers), they rank as one of the better British bands of their era, and certainly among the very best never to achieve success of any kind in the U.S. After their sole LP (also titled "Take a Heart"), they issued a couple impressive singles with psychedelic and Dylanesque overtones, and had somehow relocated to Italy in the late '60s, where they played out their string with material in a much more progressive (and less distinctive) vein. Don Fardon had a Top 20 hit in America with a pre-Raiders version of "Indian Reservation" in 1968. —*Richie Unterberger*

● **Take a Heart** / 1965 / Repertoire ✦✦✦✦
A reissue of their mid-'60s album, with eight bonus tracks, including the fine non-LP singles by the original lineup and foreign-language versions of some tunes. One of the best obscure British Invasion records. —*Richie Unterberger*

In Italy / 1983 / Eva ✦✦✦
With an altered lineup, the Sorrows cut these tracks in a much more progressive vein in the late '60s, heavily influenced by Traffic, Family, and the Small Faces (five of the fourteen songs here are covers of compositions by those groups). Not nearly as impressive as their beat material. —*Richie Unterberger*

● **The Sorrows** / 1991 / Sequel ✦✦✦✦
The best reissue of the *Take A Heart* album (which has also been reissued in other configurations). Includes all the tracks from the LP, all the important non-LP singles, a couple unissued tracks, and Don Fardon's version of "Indian Reservation." —*Richie Unterberger*

Soul Asylum

Group, Alternative Pop/Rock, Rock & Roll
Initially, Soul Asylum didn't sound that much different from their Minneapolis peers Hüsker Dü and the Replacements, churning out fast, spirited punk rockers. Even at that stage, there were hints of musical diversity, from folk and country to straight-ahead pop, beneath the roar. As the band's career progressed, the songwriting of lead vocalist/guitarist Dave Pirner became sharper, relying on conventional, melodic song structure instead of aimless, raging sound; guitarist Dan Murphy's writing was equally as good. After they signed to A&M in 1988, Soul Asylum hit their artistic stride, releasing two excellent albums that suffered from poor promotion on the label's part; the label dropped the band after their *And the Horse They Rode On* album.

Soul Asylum's last chance for success was 1992's *Grave Dancers Union*, an album that was more accessible than their previous albums without compromising their artistic integrity. Amazingly, the band *did* hit the big time, thanks to the folkie ballad "Runaway Train." The band became superstars, touring the world for nearly two years and going platinum several times over; they even performed at the White House. For a band that seemed destined to the same fate as their long-gone Minneapolis contemporaries, their success was nothing short of a miracle. Soul Asylum's commercial success continued with *Let Your Dim Light Shine*, their 1995 followup to *Grave Dancers Union*. —*Stephen Thomas Erlewine*

Say What You Will / 1984 / Twin/Tone ✦✦✦
Produced by Hüsker Dü's Bob Mould, it's unsurprising that Soul Asylum's debut record shares the same tendencies as the Hüskers to loud, fast punk rock. Compared to the more structured songs he writes today, Dave Pirner was jumpy with nervous energy, and the songs reflect this frantic need to communicate and make some noise. Fans of post-stardom Soul Asylum might find this a bit too much to handle, but it remains expressive speed-rock that will leave you breathless. —*John Dougan*

While You Were Out / 1986 / Twin/Tone ✦✦✦
Producer and ex-Suicide Commando Chris Osgood was an excellent choice to produce this first attempt at a breakthrough record. And, despite a few songs simply sounding like retreads, this is a pretty snappy collection, with Pirner's songwriting showing a depth and nuance that had previously been lost amid the roaring. The LP closer, "Passing Sad Daydream," was even a country-tinged wallow that, despite being too long, was an indication that this band was developing a style that would allow them to make the transition out of speed-rock's obsession with, well, speed. —*John Dougan*

Made to Be Broken / 1986 / Twin/Tone ✦✦
If *Say What You Will's* inchoate, raunchy blur is a bit much, then album number two, again produced by Mould, straightens things out a bit and lets riffs emerge from the walls of distortion. The record's first single, "Tied to the Tracks," is a rip-snorting bull ride of volume and power, but then again, so is much of the record. Although they were derisively written off by some wags as Hüsker

Jr., that was a critical view offered by the short-sighted. They may have shared the same sound, but were very different bands. —*John Dougan*

Time's Incinerator / 1986 / Twin/Tone ✦✦✦
A cassette-only release, this is a collection of outtakes and live tracks covering the period from 1981-1986 when the band was metamorphosing from their former selves as Loud Fast Rules into Soul Asylum. Obviously, when you give your band a name like Loud Fast Rules, you're not going to be playing folk-rock, but despite the insistence on speed and volume, there are some surprises here, most notably a live cover of James Brown's "Hot Pants." An interesting document of a band growing up and becoming more comfortable with getting better, whether they wanted to or not. —*John Dougan*

○ **Clam Dip and Other Delights** / Jan. 1988 / Twin/Tone ✦✦✦✦
A great EP with a hysterical cover parody of Herb Alpert's sexy *Whipped Cream and Other Delights* album cover, this shows Soul Asylum growing up but not growing old. Starting with the huge thudding riff of "Just Plain Evil," this adds the triumphantly poppy "Chains" and the funky "Take it To the Root," which originally appeared on *Time's Incinerator*. Oddly, what was originally intended as a minor release turned out to be a major work in Soul Asylum's early career. —*John Dougan*

● **Hang Time** / Feb. 1988 / A&M ✦✦✦✦
More riff-heavy than usual, with considerable help from producer Lenny Kaye, *Hang Time* turned out to be the best of Soul Asylum's early records. The guitars of Pirner and Dan Murphy synchronize into a sonic wad of incredible power, while the songs (especially "Cartoon," "Some Time To Return," and "Beggars and Choosers") showed that Pirner had become a first rate songwriter. Clever without being glib, and heartfelt without resorting to cliches, Pirner was doing something that eluded many of his peers: dealing with the transition from youth to adulthood and all the inherent conflicts that arise during this time. They would become superstars later, but this record should have done the trick. —*John Dougan*

○ **And the Horse They Rode On** / 1990 / A&M ✦✦✦✦
Thanks to Steve Jordan's live production approach and some great material, *And the Horse They Rode On* is one of Soul Asylum's best efforts. Among this album's many highlights are "Veil of Tears" (a nice Stones riff), the spastic hyper-drive of "Spinnin'," the ugly funk of "Something out of Nothing," and the dynamic rocker "Nice Guys (Don't Get Paid)." —*Rick Clark*

Grave Dancers Union / May 1992 / Columbia ✦✦✦
Soul Asylum's first Columbia release, *Grave Dancers Union*, is a significant step down from *And the Horse They Rode On*. From the start of the album, it's clear that Dave Pirner has been somewhat lost with the band's lack of success. Soul Asylum frequently sounds like a band that has lost their footing, grabbing onto anything they can. Pirner currently writes big, rootsy ballads and Stones/Replacements-style rockers instead of the songs typical of their earlier, punky material. The addition of strings and the synths/horns on "The Sun Maid" sounds forced. Still, the crunching "99%" and wistful "Runaway Train" prove that Pirner can write a killer song when needed. —*Stephen Thomas Erlewine*

Let Your Dim Light Shine / 1995 / Columbia ✦✦
Following the same pattern and approach as *Grave Dancers Union*, *Let Your Dim Light Shine* firmly positions Soul Asylum as a mainstream rock & roll band. Gone are the breakneck punk rockers, replaced with searching, introspective ballads and socially conscious mid-tempo rockers. In itself, that wouldn't be a problem, but Dave Pirner has taken the weight of the world upon his shoulders, which becomes apparent from the lyrics. Pirner's lyrics are so overwrought that they not only approach self-parody, they go completely beyond it. Every lyric is weighted with such self-importance, making it easy to overlook the relative merits of the music, which isn't quite as impressive as their previous records. —*Stephen Thomas Erlewine*

Soul II Soul

Group, Soul, Urban, Dance-Pop
Led by producer/vocalist/songwriter/DJ Jazzie B, Soul II Soul were one of the most innovative dance/R&B outfits of the late '80s, creating a seductive, deep R&B that borrowed from Philly soul, disco, reggae and '80s hip-hop. Originally featuring Jazzie B, producer/arranger Nellee Hooper, and instrumentalist Philip "Dad-

dae" Harvey, the musical collective came together in the late '80s. The group had a residency at the Africa Centre in Covent Garden, which led to a record contract with 10, a subsidiary of Virgin. Two singles, "Fairplay" and "Feel Free," began to attract attention both in clubs and in the press.

Featuring the vocals of Caron Wheeler, Soul II Soul's third single "Keep on Movin'," reached the U.K. Top Five in March of 1989. Released in the summer of 1989, "Back to Life" also featured Wheeler and became another Top Ten hit. Soul II Soul released their debut album, *Club Classics Volume One*, shortly afterward. The album was released in America under the title *Keep on Movin';* both "Keep on Movin'" and "Get a Life" became substantial hits, propelling the album to double platinum status.

Wheeler left the group before the recording of the group's second album, *Vol. 2: 1990—A New Decade*. The album debuted at number one in the U.K., yet it caught the group in a holding pattern. Hooper soon left the collective, leaving Jazzie B. to soldier on alone. Hooper went on to work with several of the most influential and popular acts of the early '90s, including Massive Attack (*Blue Lines*), Bjork (*Debut* and *Post*), Madonna (*Bedtime Stories*), and U2 ("Hold Me, Thrill Me, Kiss Me, Kill Me"). In 1992, Soul II Soul released *Vol. 3: Just Right*, to both lukewarm reviews and sales. The group's fourth album of original material was scheduled for release in the fall of 1995. —*Stephen Thomas Erlewine*

● **Keep on Movin'** / 1988 / Virgin ✦✦✦✦
The group's debut (originally titled *Club Classics Vol. One* in Europe) contains their finest single, "Keep On Movin'," and "Back to Life" but is padded by stilted raps and plodding beat fodder. — *John Floyd*

○ **Vol. 2: 1990—a New Decade** / 1990 / Virgin ✦✦✦✦
A better album but a deceptive one: even the best songs here don't intoxicate as thoroughly as "Keep On Movin'," but within the context of the album, each plays a vital part. In other words, this is a genuine *album*, and not a pastiche of singles. —*John Floyd*

Vol. 3: Just Right / 1992 / Virgin ✦✦

The Soul Survivors

Group, Vocal
Soul Survivors' only giant hit, "Expressway to Your Heart," was one of the first notable productions by Philadelphia wizards Kenny Gamble and Leon Huff in 1967. Although they were White, the Soul Survivors adopted a convincing R&B sound for their early singles on Crimson. Gamble and Huff loaded "Expressway to Your Heart" with honking horns and other automotive sound effects, but the record's principal strength lay in its soulful vocals and pounding beat. After a less successful followup, "Explosion in Your Soul," the band faded but returned for one more hit in 1974. —*Bill Dahl*

● **When the Whistle Blows Anything Goes** / 1967 / Collectables ✦✦✦✦
The first band to help establish the Gamble-Huff combine. A great white soul ensemble. —*Ron Wynn*

Take Another Look / 1968 / Atco ✦✦✦
The Soul Survivors flamed out quite quickly, but their second album wasn't a bad bit of blue-eyed R&B. They could do effective hard-driving dance tunes or decent ballads, and while Gamble and Huff hadn't yet become legends, they provided workmanlike production and arrangements. What stopped the Soul Survivors was the fact that they were merely a good band, and in an era loaded with great ones, they couldn't generate enough "Expressway To Your Heart" gems to maintain audience interest. —*Ron Wynn*

The Soul Survivors / 1975 / T S O P ✦✦✦
Do not be fooled someday, if this pops up, into thinking that you'll be grabbing a lost treasure. By the mid-'70s, the bloom had long since come off the Soul Survivors' rose. They tried to regroup, signing with one-time mentors and producers Gamble and Huff's label. Only Richard and Charles Ingui from the original lineup were in this edition, and they simply didn't have the old magic. Even if they had, it's highly doubtful that '60s-style blue-eyed soul would have meant much in the mid-'70s. —*Ron Wynn*

Jimmy Soul

R&B
Soul, a former preacher born James McCleese, was a Gary "US" Bonds soundalike who shared the same producer (Frank Guida) and netted a 1962 hit with "If You Wanna Be Happy." —*John Floyd*

● **The Best of Jimmy Soul** / 1991 / Rhino ✦✦✦✦
A nice novelty and pop-soul singer who also was a pioneer in utilizing calypso/caribbean influences. —*Ron Wynn*

Soundgarden

Group, Alternative Pop/Rock, Heavy Metal
Soundgarden was responsible for making true, gutsy heavy metal hip in the American underground of the late '80s. Fueled by the primal, sub-Sabbath riffing of guitarist Kim Thayil and the shrieking wail of vocalist Chris Cornell, Soundgarden offers a revamped, post-punk take on heavy metal. While they never dispense with the traditions of metal—pummelling riffs, long solos, machismo—they add a significant amount of angst and irony. Their songs are always more intricate than the average Black Sabbath number, yet never as detailed as Led Zeppelin.

Soundgarden worked its way into the mainstream through a series of late '80s independent releases, culminating in a major-label deal with A&M; their first major label album, *Louder than Love*, was released in 1989. Before Nirvana exploded down the doors for alternative rockers in general and Seattle bands in particular in 1991, Soundgarden had earned a following that was larger than any other Seattle band; with songs like "Big Dumb Sex" and "Hands All Over" they appealed both to the riff-hungry heavy metal fans as well as the cool, detached alternative rock fans. But their real mainstream breakthrough didn't come until 1994, when the band released the critically-acclaimed *Superunknown*. The album expanded their primal metal into a variety of new musical territory without ever losing sight of the core of their music—their overpowering riffs. It established the band as one of the most popular rock bands of the early '90s, selling over three million copies. —*Stephen Thomas Erlewine*

○ **Ultramega OK** / 1989 / SST ✦✦✦✦
A noticeable improvement from their EPs, Soundgarden's first full-length release is an impressive mixture of slow Zeppelin/Sabbath-style riffs updated for a new generation with even more murkiness. Cornell's vocals can be irritatingly overblown, and the band can be unfocused (as on their cover of Howlin' Wolf's "Smokestack Lightning"), but the whole thing sounds fresh. —*Stephen Thomas Erlewine*

Louder Than Love / 1990 / A&M ✦✦✦
The first major-label release from Soundgarden is a step down from the independent *Ultramega OK*, as Thayil's guitar drowns in the murkiness of the production that Cornell tries to bellow through. It's uneven, but there are some staple Soundgarden songs that are among their best, including "Full on Kevin's Mom," "Hands All Over," "Ugly Truth," and the extraordinarily stupid "Big Dumb Sex." —*Stephen Thomas Erlewine*

Screaming Life / Fopp / 1990 / Sub Pop ✦✦✦
A reissue of two early (1987 and 1988) EPs, which capture the band in its formative stages. Worth any true fan's time. —*Stephen Thomas Erlewine*

○ **Badmotorfinger** / 1991 / A&M ✦✦✦✦
Soundgarden's most accessible and accomplished album captures the band stretching out and successfully experimenting. Unlike those on *Louder Than Love*, the songs have varied tempos and textures, along with memorable riffs. With Cornell singing better than he ever has on a Soundgarden album, the band delivered a set of songs that now stands as their signature statement. —*Stephen Thomas Erlewine*

● **Superunknown** / Mar. 8, 1994 / A&M ✦✦✦✦
Superunknown expands on the bottomless heavy metal of *Badmotorfinger* by adding touches of psychedelia and pop to Soundgarden's signature sludge. The result is the band's best album, full of powerful, expertly crafted hard rock that improves with repeated listens. —*Stephen Thomas Erlewine*

The Soup Dragons

Group, Alternative Pop/Rock, Dance-Pop
This Scottish quartet released its debut album in 1986. Initially heavily influenced by the Buzzcocks, by 1990 the band moved toward the dance-club sound. —*David Szatmary*

○ **Hang-Ten!** / 1987 / Sire ✦✦✦✦
Raw, fast, punkish pop, it's propelled by the twin guitars of Jim McCulloch and Sean Dickson, who also doubles as vocalist. —*David Szatmary*

This Is Our Art / 1988 / Sire ✦✦✦

● **Lovegod** / 1990 / Big Life ✦✦✦✦
Psychedelicized dance music, it includes the hit remake of the Rolling Stones' "I'm Free." —*David Szatmary*

Hotwired / 1992 / Big Life ✦✦✦
On the whole, *Hotwired* is stronger than the Soup Dragons' previous album, but it never deviates from their popular lightweight guitar dance-pop, exemplified by the catchy hit single "Divine Thing." —*Stephen Thomas Erlewine*

Pleasure / 1994 / PolyGram ✦✦
By the time of *Pleasure*, the Soup Dragons were reduced to guitarist/vocalist Sean Dickson and he crafted an album that ranged from their early punk-pop explosions to their later dance-pop hits, but none of the songs were catchy enough to make an impression. —*Stephen Thomas Erlewine*

Joe South

b. Feb. 28, 1940
Singer-Songwriter, Pop/Rock
By the time Joe South hit as a solo artist, he had become a veritable jack-of-all trades, being a country DJ and an in-demand session guitar player, providing electric guitar for Simon & Garfunkel's hit "Sounds of Silence." As a producer, he produced Billy Joe Royal, who scored with two South compositions, "Down in the Boondocks" (#9) and "I Knew You When" (#14). South also penned "Hush," a #52 hit for Royal and a #4 hit for the British band Deep Purple.

South signed to Capitol Records in 1968 and released his debut, *Introspect* (#117), with the single "Birds of a Feather." It didn't chart but became a #23 hit for the Raiders. The second single from that album, "Games People Play" (#12), was his first big solo hit, and it established South as a rather preachy straight-talking Southern artist. His followup singles were "Walk a Mile in My Shoes" (#12), "Don't It Make You Want to Go Home" (#41), and "Fool Me" (#78). In 1971 South had his greatest songwriting success when country singer Lynn Anderson landed a worldwide million-selling hit with "Rose Garden" (#3), which Elvis Presley and many other artists recorded as well. Except for a few relatively obscure mid-'70s solo albums, South dropped out and hasn't been heard from since. —*Rick Clark*

● **The Best of** / 1990 / Rhino ✦✦✦✦
This is an essential collection featuring South's brand of Southern-style pop idealism. Classic hits like "Games People Play," "Walk a Mile in My Shoes," "Don't It Make You Want to Go Home," and "Birds of a Feather," as well as notable South originals like "Down in the Boondocks," "Rose Garden," "I Knew You When," and "Hush" are here, too. Good liner notes and sound round out this package. —*Rick Clark*

John David Souther

b. 1946
Singer-Songwriter
This Detroit-born songwriter, singer, and guitarist is best known for the cover versions of his songs found on Linda Ronstadt albums and his hit co-compositions with members of the Eagles ("Best of My Love," "New Kid in Town," "Heartache Tonight"). Also a member of the Souther, Hillman, Furay Band in the mid-'70s. —*William Ruhlmann*

John David Souther / 1971 / Asylum ✦✦✦
It may be that the only thing that kept Souther from becoming a major star in the '70s was that his friends the Eagles beat him to the country-rock style demonstrated on this album, which features "The Fast One" and "Run like a Thief," both recorded by Linda Ronstadt. —*William Ruhlmann*

○ **Black Rose** / 1976 / Asylum ✦✦✦✦
Excellent album steeped in the Southern California country-rock sound of the '70s, with all the usual suspects (Danny Kortchmar, Waddy Wachtel, Kenny Edwards, and Russ Kunkel, and producer Peter Asher—all Ronstadt veterans—plus Glenn Frey and Don Henley from the Eagles) in place on such songs as "Faithless Love," "Simple Man, Simple Dream," and "Silver Blue." —*William Ruhlmann*

● **You're Only Lonely** / 1979 / Columbia ✦✦✦✦
Souther finally scored a hit single with the '50s-ish title track, and the album also includes such lovely ballads as "White Rhythm and Blues," as well as the solo version of the Souther, Hillman, Furay song "Trouble in Paradise." —*William Ruhlmann*

Southside Johnny & the Asbury Jukes

Group, Rock & Roll
A ragtag collection of Jersey-shore bar-band vets, they are led by harmonica-playing, late night-voiced "Southside" Johnny Lyon. The Jukes coalesced under the direction, production, and songwriting assistance of Miami Steve Van Zandt and Bruce Springsteen and churned out a string of superb albums that merged horn-driven R&B raveups with strong original material. Some seldom-heard Springsteen-written chestnuts show up on the Jukes' albums, including "The Fever," "Love on the Wrong Side of Town," "When You Dance," and the ravishing "Hearts of Stone." The group fell apart when guitarist Billy Rush left, but then re-formed for a stunning comeback album, *Better Days*. —*Kit Kiefer*

Live at the Bottom Line / 1976 / Epic ✦✦
This promotional live album was recorded at the Bottom Line club in New York City on October 16 and 17, 1976, four months after the release of Southside Johnny and the Asbury Jukes' debut album, *I Don't Want To Go Home*. Fellow Asbury Park graduate Bruce Springsteen had gotten a career boost by appearing at the 400-seat club in 1975, and Southside got considerable radio play from this limited edition, which featured songs from the album as well as some notable rock 'n' roll oldies. The Jukes were a bar band, and the Bottom Line is a bar. This is the next best thing to being there, and if you open a cool one and close your eyes, it's just about the same. —*William Ruhlmann*

○ **I Don't Want to Go Home** / 1976 / Epic ✦✦✦✦
The Jukes' debut is an R&B revivalist's delight, capped by splendid duets with Lee Dorsey ("How Come You Treat Me So Bad?") and Ronnie Spector ("You Mean So Much to Me"). —*Kit Kiefer*

○ **This Time It's for Real** / 1977 / Epic ✦✦✦✦
Southside Johnny's sophomore release was another strong collection of early-'60s R&B- and doo wop-influenced pop/rock. To underscore those elements, *This Time It's for Real* features guest appearances by the Drifters, the Coasters, and the Five Satins. Highlights include "Without Love," "Love on the Wrong Side of Town," and the title track. —*Rick Clark*

○ **Hearts of Stone** / 1978 / Epic ✦✦✦✦
This is the most successful merger of old R&B with modern songwriting and sensibilities in the Jukes' catalog. "Hearts of Stone" features more great Van Zandt originals ("Got to Be a Better Way Home," "This Time Baby's Gone for Good") and Springsteen's knockout title tune. —*Kit Kiefer*

○ **Havin' a Party with Southside Johnny** / 1979 / Epic ✦✦✦✦
The highlights of this New Jersey band's first few albums are included, plus a fine remake of Sam Cooke's "Having a Party." It's a great starting place for the uninitiated. —*Rick Clark*

The Jukes / 1979 / Mercury ✦✦✦
After none of the Jukes' first three records got higher than #85 in the charts, Epic Records dropped the band. The feeling was that Southside was too closely identified with Springsteen and Van Zandt, and needed to establish a separate identity. So, the band dumped its producer and songwriter and moved to Mercury Records for its fourth album, on which Jukes guitarist Billy Rush took over the songwriting. Given that, however, the result is not half bad. Southside and Rush collaborate on the excellent leadoff track, "All I Want Is Everything," and Rush contributes "I'm So Anxious," "Living In The Real World," and several other respectable numbers. The glory days were over, and the band really wouldn't make a big success on its own, but they remained workmen making the best of a bad situation. —*William Ruhlmann*

Love Is a Sacrifice / 1980 / Mercury ✦✦
The title track is the best of the Jukes' second album under the writing aegis of Billy Rush and Southside Johnny. It seems to have been determined that covers were out, so the band generates soul retreads in search of something that will catch fire with listeners. —*William Ruhlmann*

Reach up & Touch the Sky / 1981 / Mercury
Southside Johnny and the Asbury Jukes' first commercially released live album, a two-LP set, was recorded in June and July 1980 and allowed the band to mine its catalog for songs previously heard on the excellent Epic albums as well as re-opening the door on covers (there's a fine Sam Cooke medley). They may have been at an artistic impasse, but they were a fun band to see live. —*William Ruhlmann*

Reach up & Touch the Sky: Live / 1981 / Mercury ✦✦✦
○ **Trash It Up** / 1983 / Mirage ✦✦✦✦

For their first studio album in three years, the Jukes moved to their third record label, the Mirage subsidiary of Atlantic, dropped the "Asbury" from their name, and hired hot producer Nile Rodgers to give them a dance rock sheen like the one he'd given to David Bowie on *Let's Dance*. It didn't work. — *William Ruhlmann*

In the Heat / 1984 / Atco

Atlantic (Atco) let Southside Johnny and Billy Rush produce themselves after things didn't work out with Nile Rodgers and *Trash It Up*. They tried a few covers in addition to Rush's well-meant but not classic originals, including Smokey Robinson's "Don't Look Back" and Tom Waits' "New Coat of Paint." These gave diversity to the proceedings, but on the whole this still wasn't great Jukes. — *William Ruhlmann*

At Least We Got Shoes / 1986 / Atlantic

Billy Rush had decamped by the time the Jukes reconvened to record their third and final Atlantic album. Southside Johnny's originals were only okay, although the selection of covers—"Walk Away Renee" and "I Only Want To Be With You"—was stellar as usual. Still, this was something of a swan song for the band, who did not record again for five years. — *William Ruhlmann*

Slow Dance / Oct. 1988 / Cypress

This is a Southside Johnny "solo" album, although members of the Jukes, notably guitarist Bobby Bandiera, turn up here and there. But the attempt is to take Southside out of the bar band, R&B, horn-filled Jukes style and put him with contemporary synthesizer sounds and programmed drums. Still, he can't resist covering Smokey Robinson and Jerry Butler, and there's a collaboration with Bruce Springsteen on "Walking Through Midnight." It's a noble, but failed experiment. — *William Ruhlmann*

○ **Better Days** / Oct. 1991 / Impact ✦✦✦✦

A comeback album that by all rights shouldn't be this good, *Better Days* reunites Southside Johnny with his old cohorts Springsteen and Van Zandt, plus some special guests (Jon Bon Jovi, Flo and Eddie) for 11 bittersweet originals capped by the gorgeous soul ballad "It's Been a Long Time." — *Kit Kiefer*

● **The Best of Southside Johnny & the Asbury Jukes** / Aug. 11, 1992 / Columbia/Legacy ✦✦✦✦

Concentrating on the highlights from Southside Johnny & the Asbury Jukes' late-'70s albums, *Best of Southside Johnny* offers a good introduction to the hard R&B-influenced rock of the New Jersey band. — *Stephen Thomas Erlewine*

● **All I Want Is Everything** / 1993 / Rhino ✦✦✦✦

The companion to Epic's *Best Of* (52733), this 14-song compilation traces the Jukes' career through their stints on Mercury/Polygram, Mirage/Atlantic, and Impact/MCA. These were not their best years, but on each album they managed a few worthy cuts, and this set chooses the best of the period, making for a collection that nearly matches the Epic years. — *William Ruhlmann*

Spacemen 3

Group, Alternative Pop/Rock, Experimental
Spacemen 3 were psychedelic in the loosest sense of the word; their guitar explorations were colorfully mind-altering, but not in the sense of the acid rock of the '60s. Instead, the band developed its own minimalistic psychedelia, relying on heavily distorted guitars to clash and produce their own harmonic overtones; frequently, they would lead up to walls of distortion with over-amplified acoustic guitars and synths. Often the band would jam on one chord or play a series of songs all in the same tempo and key. After several albums in the late '80s, the band fell apart after in 1991; guitarist Jason Pierce made his side-project, Spiritualized, his full-time band. — *Stephen Thomas Erlewine*

Sound of Confusion / 1986 / Glass ✦✦
○ **Perfect Prescription** / 1987 / Genmark ✦✦✦✦

Spacy, with lots of guitar noise and simplistic drum thumping. — *John Dougan*

Performance / 1988 / Genius ✦✦✦

Ugly and noisy, in front of a tiny audience. — *John Dougan*

Playing with Fire / 1989 / Fire ✦✦✦
Taking Drugs to Make Music to Take Drugs To / 1990 / Father Yod Production ✦✦✦
● **Recurring** / 1991 / Dedicated ✦✦✦✦

Kind of danceable in an odd way. — *John Dougan*

Spandau Ballet

Group, New Wave, Dance-Pop, Pop
After recording two albums in the early '80s of new romantic synth-pop that resulted in only one great single ("To Cut a Long Story Short"), Spandau Ballet abruptly changed their style to a smooth, soul-influenced pop sound. The change in direction resulted in their biggest success, with the international hit "True" and its accompanying album. After another album in the same vein didn't sell, they changed their direction again, becoming an arena rock outfit; the new records failed miserably. By 1989, the band combined *all* of their previous incarnations into one faceless album. At that time, the acting careers of guitarist Gary Kemp and bassist Martin Kemp took off, earning a substantial amount of critical acclaim for their roles in the English gangster film *The Krays*. — *Stephen Thomas Erlewine*

● **The Singles Collection** / 1985 / Chrysalis ✦✦✦✦

Traces the group's development from the melodramatic, "new-romantic" dance-pop style of "To Cut a Long Story Short" to the lush ballad "True." Spandau Ballet always went in for big effects, but they became more subtle as they went along. — *William Ruhlmann*

Sparkletones

Group, Rockabilly
Five 16-year olds from Spartanburg, SC, the Sparkletones were one of the finest rockabilly acts ever to record. Mostly their style was fast and spirited, with a frenetic energy that made most of the competition (even Elvis) seem geriatric by comparison. Singer and guitarist Joe Bennett's "Black Slacks" remains their defining song, but everything they did was worthwhile. — *Bruce Eder*

○ **Black Slacks** / MCA ✦✦✦✦

This topflight collection does not contain everything, but the ten best songs this rockabilly quintet left behind are here. As fine as any Elvis collection of 1956. — *Bruce Eder*

Sparks

Group, Pop/Rock
An American pop/rock group led by two brothers, Ron (keyboards) and Russell Mael (vocals), with varying backup. They were especially popular in the mid-'70s in England, where the singles "This Town Ain't Big Enough for Both of Us," "Amateur Hour," and "Beat the Clock," and the albums *Kimono My House* and *Propaganda* all hit the Top Ten. — *William Ruhlmann*

Sparks / 1971 / Bearsville ✦✦✦
A Woofer in Tweeter's Clothing / 1972 / Bearsville ✦✦✦
○ **Kimono My House** / 1974 / Island ✦✦✦✦

Sparks specializes in keyboard-based pop songs with clever, ironic lyrics (by Ron Mael), sung in a near-falsetto by Russell Mael. Examples include "Here in Heaven" (in which a disappointed, dead Romeo sings to a still-living Juliet who "broke our little pact"), "Thank God It's Not Christmas," and the U.K. hits "This Town Ain't Big Enough for Both of Us" and "Amateur Hour." — *William Ruhlmann*

○ **Propaganda** / 1974 / Island ✦✦✦✦

More of Ron's wit ("Don't Leave Me Alone with Her," "Who Don't Like Kids") and Russell's operatic singing with catchy rock backings, though it's hard to get the jokes without the lyric sheet. — *William Ruhlmann*

Number One in Heaven / 1979 / Elektra ✦✦✦

After flirting with hard rock, Sparks turned to disco producer Giorgio Moroder and scored three U.K. hits, "Tryouts for the Human Race," "Beat the Clock," and "The No. 1 Song in Heaven," all in an aggressive electro-dance rock style. — *William Ruhlmann*

Angst in My Pants / 1982 / Atlantic ✦✦✦

Sparks turns to power-pop and scores their first U.S. singles chart entry with the hilarious "I Predict" on an album that also includes such novelties as "Eaten by the Monster of Love." — *William Ruhlmann*

Sparks in Outer Space / 1983 / Teldec ◆◆◆
"Cool Places," an uptempo duet with ex-Go-Go Jane Wiedlin (and #49 hit) paces this collection, perhaps Sparks's biggest U.S. seller. —*William Ruhlmann*

● **Profile: Ultimate Collection** / 1991 / Rhino ◆◆◆◆
A double-disc collection of Sparks' finest moments, *Profile* is the definitive anthology of the quirky '70s pop/rockers. —*AMG*

Spearhead

Group, Rap
Michael Franti released only one album as half of Disposable Heroes of Hiphoprisy, but it was praised for his insightful raps and Public Enemy-influenced beats. After disappearing for two years, Franti resurfaced in 1994 with Spearhead, a band more rooted in '70s funk. —*John Bush*

Home / 1994 / Capitol ◆◆◆
Franti shifts from political issues to social problems plaguing the black nation. The vibes are more positive than Franti's previous work and the backing is reminiscent of Arrested Development's roots 'n rap, but defiant rumblings do pop up. —*John Bush*

Special Ed

Rap
In 1989 this 16-year-old released a technically dazzling debut album that highlighted his rapid-fire delivery and the ace production of hip-hop mastermind Howie "Hitman" Tee. —*John Floyd*

Youngest in Charge / 1989 / Profile ◆◆◆
The debut from this hugely confident teenage rapper with a very adult, mature rapping style and boastful, though effective lyrics and themes. —*Ron Wynn*

● **Legal** / 1990 / Profile ◆◆◆◆
Release number two by Special Ed marks his turning 18 and has a more varied, less excessive, production approach. Ed also moves smoothly between topical and romantic material, as well as serious and satirical tones. —*Ron Wynn*

The Specials

Group, Ska-Revival
True innovators of the punk era, the Specials began the British ska-revival craze, combining the highly danceable ska and rocksteady beat with punk's energy and attitude, and taking on a more focused and informed political and social stance than their predecessors. The band was formed in Coventry in 1977 as the Coventry Automatics and later the Special A.K.A. by songwriter/keyboardist Jerry Dammers with Terry Hall (vocals), Lynval Golding (guitar, vocals), Neville Staples (vocals, percussion), Roddy Radiation (guitar), Sir Horace Gentleman (bass), and John Bradbury (drums). An opening slot for the Clash stirred up interest with the major labels, but Dammers instead opted to start his own 2-Tone label, named for its multi-racial agenda and after the two-tone tonic suits favored by the like-minded mods of the '60s. The Dammers-designed logos, based in '60s pop art with black and white checks, gave the label an instantly identifiable look. Dammers' eye for detail and authenticity also led to the band adopting '60s-period rude-boy outfits (porkpie hats, tonic and mohair suits, and loafers). The band released the "Gangsters" single which reached the U.K. top 10. Soon after, hordes of bands and fans followed in the same tradition and the movement was in full swing. Over the next several months, 2-Tone enjoyed hits by similar-sounding bands, such as Madness, the (English) Beat, and the Selecter. Late in 1979, the band released its self-titled debut album, produced by Elvis Costello. They followed with several 2-Tone package tours and a live EP, *Too Much Too Young* (confusingly credited to Special A.K.A.). The title track, a pro-contraception song, was banned by the BBC but reached the number one spot in the U.K. At this time, the band switched musical directions, releasing album number two, *More Specials*, with a new neo-lounge persona. Signs indicated that the movement was fading and 2-Tone began to experience financial troubles. The Specials released the timely "Ghost Town" single in 1981 amid race-related unemployment riots in Brixton and Liverpool. The single jumped to number one, but the band was falling apart. Hall, Staples and Golding left to form Fun Boy Three, leaving the band without its trademark vocal. Dammers held on, reverting back to the old name, Special A.K.A. and enlisting a new vocalist, Stan Campbell. After several years in the studio, they returned with *In the Studio* in 1984. The album

managed a few hits with "Racist Friend" and "Free Nelson Mandella" but the album stiffed. Dammers dissolved the unit, pursuing political causes such as Artists Against Apartheid. —*Chris Woodstra*

☆ **The Specials** / 1979 / 2 Tone/Chrysalis ◆◆◆◆◆
The Specials' self-titled debut sparked the Two-Tone movement in the late '70s. With well-chosen ska classics and Prince Buster-inspired originals, the band mixed political and social activism and blended punk's intensity with an infectious dance beat. This is essential listening. Produced by Elvis Costello. —*Chris Woodstra*

Live: Too Much Too Young [EP] / 1980 / Receiver ◆◆◆
Though the sound quality is less than perfect, this 1979 live EP perfectly captures the raw energy of the band in its prime. The title track was the band's first number one hit in the U.K. —*Chris Woodstra*

○ **More Specials** / 1980 / 2 Tone/Chrysalis ◆◆◆◆
Losing some of their ska roots, the band moves directionlessly into a neo-lounge act. Still in full force is the biting social commentary only in a slightly skewed environment. While somewhat of a disappointment after the brilliant debut, with time *More Specials* can be nearly as rewarding. —*Chris Woodstra*

In the Studio / 1984 / 2 Tone/Chrysalis ◆◆◆
When Hall, Staples, and Golding left to become Fun Boy Three, Jerry Dammers decided to continue with the addition of vocalist Stan Campbell. Nearly three years in the making, *In the Studio* lacks any hint of ska and Campbell's vocals, while good, lack the tension needed for the overtly political direction of the band. The highpoints, "Racist Friend" and the anthem "Free Nelson Mandela" can be found on the *Singles Collection* so only completists need to bother. —*Chris Woodstra*

★ **The Singles Collection** / 1991 / 2 Tone/Chrysalis ◆◆◆◆◆
All of the essential singles from their three albums are present on this 15-track collection. Not only the perfect starting point for the curious, the inclusion of B-sides and rarities, like an inspired cover of Dylan's "Maggie's Farm," makes this essential for fans. —*Chris Woodstra*

Coventry Automatics AKA The Specials: Dawning Of a New Era / 1994 / Receiver ◆◆
The first incarnation of the Specials, a six-piece band called the Automatics, recorded a batch of demos in London in 1978, hoping to obtain a major recording deal; *Dawning of a New Era* presents them for the first time. As is the case with most demos, these recordings have a limited audience but diehard fans will thrill to the early, rawer versions of their favorites along with songs that never made it to actual albums. —*Chris Woodstra*

Phil Spector

Rock & Roll, Pop/Rock
Strictly speaking, Phil Spector doesn't belong in this section—he's a musician, yes, but he very rarely released records under his name. However, as a producer—and, to a significant extent, songwriter, label owner, and session player—he's influenced the course of rock & roll more than all but a handful of performers. The "Wall of Sound" that he perfected in the early '60s opened unlimited possibilities for arrangements and sound construction in rock and pop, and his brilliant talents imprinted the discs that he produced with an artistic vision that was much more attributable to him than the talented performers with whom he worked.

Spector entered the record business in 1958 as songwriter, guitarist, and backup singer for the L.A. group the Teddy Bears, who landed a left-field number one with their first release, "To Know Him Is to Love Him." The Teddy Bears couldn't follow their hit up and soon disbanded, but Spector almost immediately moved to New York and became a songwriter and producer. After producing a few hits, he founded his own label, Philles, and ran off a series of brilliant smashes, primarily with girl groups the Crystals and the Ronettes.

To an extent that had never been imagined in rock & roll, Spector pumped his records full of orchestration—strings, horns, rattling percussion—that coalesced into teenage symphonies, never overwhelming the material or the passionate vocals. Often called a mad genius because of his eccentric and temperamental behavior, Spector's idiosyncrasies were almost always validated by the artistic and commercial results of his sessions, which combined dozens of instruments and innovative production techniques into end products which only he could combine into works of art. His influence was immense, not only in the dozens of imitation Wall of Sound productions (some very accurate and worthy, it must be added) that flooded the market between 1962 and 1965, but as an inspiration to Brian Wilson of the Beach Boys, Rolling Stones producer Andrew Loog Oldham, and others.

Spector was hip to the British Invasion before it had even reached the U.S., befriending the Beatles and Rolling Stones, but had nearly as much trouble as the rest of the industry in maintaining his success. Self-contained bands were writing more adventurous material and finding more adventurous sounds, and Spector's teen operas were becoming out of fashion, although he enjoyed a lot of success with blue-eyed soul duo the Righteous Brothers in the mid-'60s. After the failure of Ike & Tina Turner's 1966 single "River Deep, Mountain High"—which he always considered among his greatest achievements, blaming a vengeful U.S. music industry for its poor sales (although it was a big hit in Britain)—he retired to his L.A. mansion, marrying Ronnie Spector, lead singer of the Ronettes.

Spector re-emerged in the late '60s, and was hired by the Beatles to do post-production on their controversial *Let It Be* album; critics and Paul McCartney himself found his work faulty, although it must be pointed out that the material he was given to work with didn't rank among the Beatles' best work. He then produced George Harrison and John Lennon's first solo albums; though these were artistic triumphs, they were hardly Spector productions in the classic sense, owing much more of their success to the talents of the performers than the producer. For the past couple of decades, he's been active only sporadically, producing isolated albums by Dion, Leonard Cohen, and the Ramones. Today he's one of rock's most legendary recluses, rarely appearing in public, but his accomplishments cast a shadow over all performers and producers who aspire to create works of art in the studio. — *Richie Unterberger*

★ **Christmas Gift for You from Phil Spector** / 1963 / ABKCO ✦✦✦✦✦

Featuring Phil Spector's "Wall of Sound" in its prime and his early stable of artists, the Ronettes, Crystals, Darlene Love, and Bob B. Soxx & the Blue Jeans, this stands as inarguably the greatest Christmas record of all time. Spector believed he could produce a record for the holidays that would capture not only the essence of the Christmas spirit, but also be a pop masterpiece that would stand against any work these artists had already done. He succeeded on every level, with all four groups/singers recording some of their most memorable performances. This is the Christmas album by which all later holiday releases had to be judged, and it has inspired a host of imitators. (Note: This CD is available separately and as part of the highly recommended four-disc box set, *Phil Spector: Back to Mono [1958-1969]*.) —*Decibel Dennis MacDonald*

Early Productions 1958-1961 / 1983 / Rhino ✦✦✦

A sampling of Spector's earliest work, generally more pop-oriented, sappy, and far less distinguished than his early and mid-'60s classics. The Teddy Bears' "To Know Him Is To Love Him," Gene Pitney's "Every Breath I Take," the Paris Sisters' "I Love How You Love Me," and Curtis Lee's "Pretty Little Angel Eyes" are fine hits that reveal much of the talent that would fully blossom on his Philles singles. The other tracks, including rarities by the Ducanes, Kell Osborne, and Spector's Three, suffer from weak songwriting, and would be downright dispensable if not for their historical significance. —*Richie Unterberger*

☆ **Back to Mono (1958-1969)** / 1991 / ABKCO ✦✦✦✦✦

If you look hard enough, you can find decent one-album samplers of Phil Spector's greatest recordings, but this four-disc boxed set (three sets of singles and the entire *A Christmas Gift for You* on the fourth) is the jewel of Spector's legacy. Aside from his sporadic '70s productions, *Back to Mono* contains everything you'd ever want by rock's supreme romantic: early productions with Curtis Lee, Ben E. King, and Gene Pitney; the girl group effervescence of the Ronettes, the Crystals, and Darlene Love; the soul innovations of the Righteous Brothers and the Checkmates; and his notorious sessions with Ike and Tina Turner. Throughout the set, Spector's artistic vision (which has influenced dozens of producers and hundreds of performers) shines like the smile on a lover's lips. This is one of the greatest and most fully realized boxed sets ever issued. —*John Floyd*

BOOKS

✦✦✦✦ **He's A Rebel**, by Mark Ribowsky (E.P. Dutton, 1989). Comprehensive biography of Phil Spector, drawing upon interviews

with numerous producers, music biz associates, performers, songwriters, session musicians, friends, and lovers who knew him well in his heyday. As expected, there's a lot of sordid material about his personal life, some of which is quite scandalous and tumultuous. But the focus is largely upon the music, with a lot of behind-the-scene insights into how he shaped the Wall of Sound, at his peak and during his more erratic projects in the 1970s. Great stories about all the legends he's worked with, running from Darlene Love and the Righteous Brothers to John Lennon; includes complete discography. —*Richie Unterberger*

Benny Spellman

b. 1938
New Orleans R&B

New Orleans R&B vocalist. His deep bass voice booms through loud and clear on many early-'60s Allen Toussaint productions, but Benny Spellman enjoyed a major hit of his own in 1962, "Lipstick Traces (On a Cigarette)." Spellman spent some time with Huey "Piano" Smith and the Clowns before signing with Minit, where Toussaint utilized his deep pipes to full advantage as a backing vocalist behind Ernie K-Doe on "Mother-in-Law" and countless others. The Rolling Stones covered "Fortune Teller," the flip-side of this hit. Spellman recorded through much of the '60s, his "Word Game" turning up on Atlantic in 1965, before he took a day gig as a beer salesman. —*Bill Dahl*

○ **Fortune Teller** / 1988 / Collectables ✦✦✦✦

Infectious and influential early-'60s New Orleans R&B. Spellman's low-pitched vocals are perfectly produced by pianist Allen Toussaint. —*Bill Dahl*

Skip Spence

b. Apr. 18, 1946, Windsor, Canada
Singer-Songwriter, Psychedelic, Folk-Rock

Like a rough, more obscure American counterpart to Syd Barrett, Skip Spence was one of the late '60s' most colorful acid casualties. The original Jefferson Airplane drummer (although he was a guitarist who had never played drums before joining the group), Spence left after their first album to join Moby Grape. Like every member of that legendary band, he was a strong presence on their first album, playing guitar, singing, and writing "Omaha," one of the LP's best songs.

The group ran into rough times in 1968, and Spence had the roughest flipping out and (according to varying accounts) running amok in a record studio with a fire axe, ending up committed to New York's Bellevue Hospital. Upon his release, Spence cut an acid-charred classic, *Oar*, in 1969. Though released on a major label (Columbia), this was reportedly one of the lowest-selling items in its catalog, and is hence one of the most valued psychedelic collector items. Much rawer and more homespun than the early Grape records, it features Spence on all (mostly acoustic) guitars, percussion, and vocals.

With an overriding blues influence and doses of country, gospel, and acid freakout thrown in, this sounds something like Mississippi Fred McDowell imbued with the spirit of Haight-Ashbury 1967. It also featured great cryptic, punning lyrics and wonderful wraithlike vocals that range from a low Fred Neil with gravel hoarseness to a barely-there high wisp. Sadly, it was his only solo recording; more sadly, mental illness continues to prevent Spence from reaching a fully functional state to this day, although he periodically plays music, sometimes with former members of Grape. —*Richie Unterberger*

● **Oar** / 1969 / Sony ✦✦✦✦

The tight, charging S.F. rock of the Grape in no way prepares the listener for the spaced-out, rural ambience here. Drug-addled, yes, but also inspirational, warm, and haunting, like a charred but charming survivor of the Summer of Love. The CD reissue of this premier acid folk album adds a few previously unreleased loose jams. —*Richie Unterberger*

Jon Spencer

Alternative Pop/Rock

After a long and semi-successful tenure as leader of scuzz-rock heroes Pussy Galore, Jon Spencer took his anti-rock vision and hooked up with guitarist Judah Bauer and drummer Russell Simins to create the scuzz-blues trio the Jon Spencer Blues Explosion. Postmodern to the core, this is an ironic name; little of what this band plays resembles standard blues. There is, however, a blues feel to what they play, meaning that in many instances they appropriate aspects of the blues (very often cliches) and incorporate them into their anarchic, noisy sound. Not part of alternarock's commercial establishment, Spencer has also managed to sharply divide critics who tend to see him as either inspired showman or mendacious con man (frankly, he's both). He is, however, gaining popularity and critical respect, and, as of this writing, seems poised for greater success.

As with Royal Trux, the other band to emerge after the breakup of Pussy Galore, the Blues Explosion's earliest recordings are virtually incomprehensible (and impossible to find). The bass-less mix is awash in distorted guitars, precious little backbeat and howled vocals. In its favor is the music's exciting, improvisatory feel; also true is that it's frequently incoherent and careless and doesn't hold up well to repeated listenings. It was with the band's 1992 self-titled release that the band began to write semi-coherent songs; Spencer adopted an imitation blues vocal style, and the band riffed wildly and crashed around him in a bluesy sort of way. It was mostly fun, but it also seemed like a bit of a put-on, and more than a little smug.

The Blues Explosion's "breakthrough" came (as it did for Royal Trux) when they began to sound like a '70s rock band. With the release of *Extra Width* in 1993, Spencer and Co. actually got some air time on MTV's alternarock show *120 Minutes* with the video for the song "Afro." The most noticeable change was the new emphasis on tight songs, funky backbeats, and loads of catchy riffs and hooks. As for Spencer, he was now singing like a grade-Z Elvis impersonator, but in turn lost some of the condescending attitude. Live, the band was (and remains) quite a show, generating the kind of sweat and excitement that became anathema to many punk and post-punk bands. The most recent release, *Orange*, which is even more accessible than *Extra Width*, has netted the band even more fans, and it seems likely that Spencer may see his greatest commercial success with this admittedly odd group. Still, there is a compelling argument to be made that despite his hip credentials, Spencer is more style than substance. Love him or loathe him (and it's easy to do both), he's a force to be reckoned with. *—John Dougan*

The Jon Spencer Blues Explosion / Apr. 24, 1992 / Caroline ✦✦✦
Produced by underground rock's most notorious producer, Steve Albini, this is as close as you're going to get to the Blues Explosion's primal, industrial strength noise-rock. From the cacophonous start of "Write a Song," it's clear that this is not going to be your average blues album. Still, it's contagious in a demented kind of way, and the sloppiness, intentional crudeness, and semicoherence are punk rock to the core (the furious, psychobilly track "Rachel"). Not recommended as a place to start with Spencer, and definitely not recommended to those who think they're going to hear Muddy Waters songs. *—John Dougan*

○ **Extra Width** / 1993 / Matador ✦✦✦✦
Much more accessible than the aforementioned record, but in no way does its accessibility detract from the record's adventurousness. *Extra Width* is a crankin' piece of bluesoid ranting, with Spencer working up one hysterical performance after another. "Afro" is as funky as all get-out and sounds like an old Curtis Mayfield track. Similarly, "Soul Letter" is a hefty chunk of riff-muck, as is the noisy bliss of "Soul Typecast." The playing is energetic and unhinged, and Spencer drives the engine with his whoopin' and hollerin'. Plenty of noticeably '70s production techniques add to the atmosphere, contributing significantly to what may be Spencer's best record. *—John Dougan*

● **Orange** / 1994 / Matador ✦✦✦✦
By this juncture, you either love Spencer enough to listen to every record, or you've heard plenty and are decidedly uninterested. Still, *Orange* mines the same territory as *Extra Width*, and that may not be enough. At times, even during *Orange*'s best tracks ("Bell Bottoms"), the thin, retro-'70s worshipping sounds phoned-in and lacking in real emotional commitment. But, as with a lot of junk-rock, sometimes it can be appreciated for simply being junk, and that's fine. But I'm willing to bet that Spencer's core fans like the idea of the blues more than the reality. In other words, they don't mind the pose, nor do they mind the facade. In Jon Spencer's world, image is everything. *—John Dougan*

Spice 1

Group, Rap
Too $hort discovered rapper Spice 1, who'd been born in Texas be-

fore moving to California. His self-titled debut was as vivid and fatalistic a gangsta album as possible, and his hard-edged, angry and pessimistic rapping style and tone only added to the despair emanating from the disc. He followed it with an even more bitter and nihilistic release, *187 He Wrote* in 1993, complete with simulated gunfire. *—Ron Wynn*

Let It Be Known / 1988 / Triad ✦✦

Spice 1 / May 12, 1992 / Jive ✦✦✦
The sheer vulgarity, anger, coarseness, sexism and horror unveiled, celebrated and presented on Oakland rapper Spice 1's debut release can be frustrating and saddening. But more importantly, it should not be ignored. Spice 1 has done what "gangsta" rap's detractors should want; he's stripped away even the slightest veneer of glamour around the atmosphere of casual violence, sexual exploitation and drug selling he examines. His style, an appropriate mix of irony, disdain, acceptance and confusion, never succumbs to the situation or seeks to justify or downplay the sense of impending doom. *—Ron Wynn*

● **187 He Wrote** / Sep. 28, 1993 / Jive ✦✦✦✦
Spice 1 continues his bleak, stripped-down version of gangsta rap with *187 He Wrote*, an album that can be harrowing and appalling. Throughout the record, the spare, funky production keeps the music engaging, making the disturbing lyrics cut even deeper. *—Stephen Thomas Erlewine*

Amerikkka's Nightmare / 1995 / Jive ✦✦✦

Spiders

Group, R&B
A fine New Orleans vocal ensemble who started as a gospel group, The Spiders scored five Top Ten R&B hits for Imperial in 1954 and 1955. They were originally the Zion City Harmonizers in the '40s, and also did radio work as the Delta Southernaires in 1952 and 1953. Lead singer Hayward "Chuck" Carbo, Joe Maxon, Matthew West, Oliver Howard, and Leonard "Chick" Carbo got their first hit with "I Didn't Want to Do It" in 1954. It was also their biggest, peaking at number three. They continued the string until the end of 1955. The Carbo brothers departed in 1956, moving on to solo careers. *—Ron Wynn*

● **The Imperial Sessions** / 1993 / Bear Family ✦✦✦✦
All of the Spiders' best songs are collected on this extensive double-disc set. *—AMG*

Spin Doctors

Group, Rock & Roll, Pop/Rock
There were many pseudo-hippie, jam-oriented blues rockers in New York during the early '90s, but only the the Spin Doctors made it big. And they made it big because not only could they immerse themselves in a groove, but they also had concise pop skills. "Little Miss Can't Be Wrong" and "Two Princes" were cleverly written singles, full of clean, blues-inflected licks and ingratiating pop melodies. *Pocket Full of Kryptonite* had been around for nearly a year when MTV and radio began playing "Little Miss Can't Be Wrong," but once they started playing it, they couldn't stop. The Spin Doctors became an overnight sensation, selling millions of albums around the world.

Their second album, 1994's *Turn It Upside Down*, didn't sell very well when it was released, largely because the first single, "Cleopatra's Cat," was a failed experiment in funk. But the second single, "You Let Your Heart Go Too Fast," was in the vein of "Two Princes," and the album began to sell after the song was released. *—Stephen Thomas Erlewine*

Up for Grabs . . . Live / Jan. 1991 / Epic ✦✦✦
Although billed as a mere EP, this six-song live set recorded at New York City's Wetlands club in September 1990 runs 45 minutes, which used to be the length of a full-fledged album. Calling it an EP is a way of de-emphasizing its significance, since it is intended more as an introduction to the band than as the major statement implied by a debut album. Fair enough: *Up For Grabs* gives you the kinetic, groove-heavy approach of Spin Doctors, especially on the lead-off song, "Big Fat Funky Booty," and Christopher Barron proves to be a funny, crowd-pleasing frontman, but it's also obvious that not much money was spent producing this record. *—William Ruhlmann*

● Pocket Full of Kryptonite / Aug. 1991 / Epic ◆◆◆◆

This sleeper album took a while to catch on, but when it did, the Spin Doctors' slightly jazzy style of funky groove rock went multi-platinum. The first single, "Little Miss Can't Be Wrong," is a like-able, lightweight bit of pop that sounds like something Steve Miller could've done. "Two Princes" was another huge hit. Other highlights include "Jimmy Olsen's Blues," "What Time is It?" and "Forty or Fifty." —*Rick Clark*

Homebelly Groove: Live / Nov. 24, 1992 / Epic ◆◆◆

While the band was undergoing the endless tour in support of *Kryptonite*, Epic re-released a remixed version of their first EP, a live recording called *Up for Grabs*, and added several more tracks. The result is this disc, a good example of the band's concert chops. —*Rick Clark*

Turn it Upside Down / 1994 / Epic ◆◆◆

A weaker album than *Kryptonite*, *Turn It Upside Down* suffers from weaker material and lifeless production. Nevertheless, the first single, "Cleopatra's Cat" is an appealing slice of bop funk-rock. A few steps down there's "Big Fat Funky Booty," "Biscuit Head," and "You Let Your Heart Go Too Fast." —*Rick Clark*

The Spinners

Group, Soul

There were plenty of Philly-soul groups that were as good as the Spinners, but none of them were better. They never cut anything as searing as the O'Jays's "For the Love of Money;" Teddy Pender-grass brought more eroticism to the hits of the Blue Notes; and they never matched the breathy, helium croon of the Stylistics's Russell Tompkins. What the Spinners and producer Thom Bell did was consolidate the best elements of Philly-soul into a hit-making machine that could be as topical ("Ghetto Child"), romantic ("Could It Be I'm Falling in Love"), and blistering ("I'm Coming Home") as anything Gamble and Huff ever whipped up for Eddie LeVert and Teddy Pendergrass. And Spinners lead vocalist Philippe Wynne had a voice that damn near outflanked anyone for versatility and sheer gospel slow-burn; think of him as soul's an-swer to Claude Jeter, with the mental imbalance of James Carr.

The group didn't last as long as their slick-soul contemporaries: Wynne left the fold in 1977 and they never found a suitable re-placement. (Wynne died of a heart attack in 1984 while perform-ing in San Francisco.) Most of their work is still in print, and urban stations regularly program the hits from the Spinners's glory years. If you think pure soul singing died in the '60s (and some people do), a session with the Spinners should change your mind. —*John Floyd*

Party: My Pad After Surfin' / 1963 / Time ◆◆◆

Their debut for Tri-Phi put the Spinners on the R&B map quickly with the single "That's What Girls Are Made For." Of course, con-fusion quickly reigned when it turned out that Harvey Fuqua had sung the lead and wasn't even in the group. Chico Edwards re-placed George Dixon when the band was signed to Motown, but they wouldn't enjoy another huge hit until they left Motown for Atlantic. If you find this album, grab it immediately. It's been deleted forever. —*Ron Wynn*

The Second Time Around / 1970 / VIP ◆◆◆

The Spinners began making some soul noise in 1970, when Stevie Wonder produced a pair of hit singles for them. "It's A Shame" was their first Top 10 R&B song since 1965, and was the swan song for G.C. Cameron as lead vocalist. Phillipe Wynne stepped in and shortly after made everyone forget (who remembered) that Cameron was ever in the band. The follow-up tune, "We'll Have It Made," wasn't bad either. —*Ron Wynn*

○ Mighty Love / Jan. 1974 / Atlantic ◆◆◆◆

Phillippe Wynne's twisting, soulful, frequently captivating voice was at its finest on this 1974 album. The title track was a smash in edited single form, and the extended album version contains mar-velous Wynne ad-libs and exchanges nicely contrasted by the group's harmonizing. The album contains many other fine songs, like "Ain't No Price On Happiness" and "I'm Coming Home," and was their second Atlantic release. It equaled the gold-selling pace of its predecessor and cemented the Spinners' status as R&B stars. —*Ron Wynn*

New & Improved / Feb. 1974 / Atlantic ◆◆◆

Live / 1975 / Atlantic ◆◆

A nice concert album that did much better than anticipated. It fea-tured extended versions, concert ambience, and exuberant har-monies and treatments of familiar numbers. Like most live dates, it had its padding and filler, but as a portrait of an R&B institution doing its thing before the faithful, it was well worth the cost of a double album. —*Ron Wynn*

○ Pick of the Litter / 1975 / Atlantic ◆◆◆◆

The Spinners were rolling in the 1970s, and this proved to be their biggest album ever. It peaked in the pop Top 10 at number eight, and they racked up four consecutive R&B Top 10 singles, includ-ing the chart topper "They Just Can't Stop It (The Games People Play)." Phillippe Wynne sang with an amazing mix of class and fire, sophistication and earthiness, that hadn't been heard in soul cir-cles for years. Of course, this is now out of print. —*Ron Wynn*

Happiness Is Being with the Spinners / 1976 / Atlantic ◆◆◆

○ Spinners / 1977 / Atlantic ◆◆◆◆

A superb album, arguably their finest, though not their biggest, crossover work. The Spinners teamed with Thom Bell and made Motown look stupid with this album of glorious anthems. "I'll Be Around" and "Could It Be I'm Falling In Love" ended any discus-sions, mentions, or even thoughts of their former lead singer G.C. Cameron, as Phillippe Wynne was emerging as the king of im-maculate, sophisticated soul. They had three R&B chart toppers from this album and were now dominating the Motown acts they once idolized. —*Ron Wynn*

Yesterday Today & Tomorrow / 1977 / Atlantic ◆◆◆

○ The Best of the Spinners / 1978 / Atlantic ◆◆◆◆

The Spinners lost lead singer Philippe Wynne in 1977, as he left to join Parliament/Funkadelic. While they were getting replacement John Edwards acclimated, Atlantic issued this greatest-hits LP con-taining all the gems with Wynne as their lead singer. Until the At-lantic 2-CD set was issued, this was a definitive work, and it's still as complete a single album package as available. It includes "Could It Be I'm Falling In Love," "How Could I Let You Get Away," "Mighty Love," "Rubberman" and "One Of A Kind (Love Af-fair)," among others. —*Ron Wynn*

Detroit Spinners / 1978 / Atlantic ◆◆◆

Dancin' and Lovin' / 1979 / Rhino ◆◆◆

While soul purists recoiled in horror, the Spinners climbed off the ropes and soared back into the spotlight by recasting themselves as a modified dance/crossover band with soul/R&B influences. It worked in the short run, as their remake of the Four Seasons' "Working My Way Back To You," mixed with their own wailer, "Forgive Me Girl," made a nice sandwich at number two pop and number six R&B. It took nearly a year, but they were revived. While they wore the formula out with a similar followup, it gave them a fresh start and the necessary credibility to eventually re-turn to their customary sophisticated soul. —*Ron Wynn*

From Here to Eternally / 1979 / Atlantic ◆◆◆

The Spinners began the slow climb back to respectability with this album. Phillippe Wynne's second tenure had ended due to poor health (he eventually suffered a fatal heart attack), and they started a resurgence with a new lead singer, John Edwards. Ed-wards had been tearing up Southern soul clubs for years, but many wondered if he could adjust to being in a group rather than being the whole show. He quickly proved that he could, and the Spinners were on their way back. —*Ron Wynn*

Love Trippin' / 1980 / Atlantic ◆◆◆

Labor of Love / 1981 / Atlantic ◆◆◆

The Spinners began to slide again with this release, following two consecutive big albums. The problem was that they had estab-lished an identity that had crossover and pop types thinking they were just a cover band. When they returned to the ebullient soul ballads and uptempo tunes that had been their forte since the 1960s, the trendy types moved on to the next fashionable thing. Meanwhile, the R&B landscape was shifting, and they were caught in the move. They also went to the medley well one more time with "Yesterday Once More/Nothing Remains The Same." —*Ron Wynn*

Superstar Series, Vol. 9 / 1981 / Motown ◆◆◆

They weren't really superstars while at Motown, but this anthol-ogy does collect their best material. It shows that the Spinners had the potential to achieve at Motown what they did at Atlantic, but weren't given the horses until the end. G.C. Cameron never made much noise on his own, but on "It's a Shame," he achieved greatness. —*Ron Wynn*

Grand Slam / 1982 / Atlantic ✦✦✦
This wasn't quite a disaster, but it was too close for comfort. The confidence and renewed vigor that the Spinners had shown in the 1980s seemed shaken, although the lightweight ballads and uninspired uptempo material they received for this date may have had something to do with that. The album didn't flop as quickly as its predecessor, but it didn't last long on the charts either. —*Ron Wynn*

Cross Fire / 1984 / Atlantic ✦✦✦

Lovin' Feelings / 1985 / Mirage ✦✦✦
Nothing worked from start to finish on this mid-'80s number, both a commercial and artistic flop. John Edwards couldn't generate any energy or fire, while the usually splendid harmonies were both feeble and often flat, and the production, arrangements, and compositions weren't able to retain any interest. —*Ron Wynn*

Best of the Spinners / 1988 / Motown ✦✦✦
Yet another Motown collection (that makes at least three for a group that only had four hits from 1965 to 1971) of Spinners singles. It's not as extensive as the anthology, so if you only want hits, they're available. Otherwise, take your pick between it and the others. —*Ron Wynn*

Down to Buisness / 1989 / Volt ✦✦✦
The Spinners made a bid for renewed stardom on a soul independent when they signed with the revived Volt in 1989. Unfortunately, they also found out quickly that being on Volt didn't mean in the late '80s what it meant in the '60s and '70s. Despite a representative effort, with some excellent harmonizing and fine, soulful leads from John Edwards, they couldn't even get a nibble from urban contemporary radio. They're still working the nostalgia/oldies circuit, but this one was a shocker all around. —*Ron Wynn*

The Best of the Spinners / 1990 / Atlantic ✦✦✦
The genuine article—the finest singles from the Spinners' long run on Atlantic. If Rhino's exhaustive two-disc set doesn't interest you or costs too much, this is the best single-disc collection. It shows why the Spinners were the 1970s' best soul group for most of the decade, and why Phillippe Wynne should someday be recognized as a major vocalist. —*Ron Wynn*

Can't Shake This Feeling / 1990 / Atlantic ✦✦✦
The Spinners revival was waning when this album was released, and it didn't stop the downward slide. They had run out of entertaining medleys and uptempo tunes, and the ballads were uninspired as well. Not even the usually dynamic John Edwards could do much with this collection of half-hearted tracks, disjointed production, and leaden arrangements. —*Ron Wynn*

☆ **One of a Kind Love Affair** / 1991 / Atlantic ✦✦✦✦✦
Spanning from their first single, 1961's "That's What Girls Are Made For," to their last charting single more than twenty years later, *One of a Kind Love Affair—The Anthology* is the definitive Spinners collection. The bulk of the 2-CD compilation is the group's work with Thom Bell during the mid-'70s, easily the best work they ever recorded and arguably the finest Philly soul singles. All of the Spinners' major hits are here, as are excellent, informative liner notes (including complete personnel and discography). —*Stephen Thomas Erlewine*

★ **Very Best of** / 1993 / Rhino ✦✦✦✦✦
A nice, condensed version of Atlantic's excellent double-CD collection is perfect for those who don't want such a comprehensive Spinners compilation. —*AMG*

Motown Superstar Series / Motown ✦✦✦
A still somewhat definitive anthology, although it was blown out of the box by Rhino's comprehensive two-disc package. But if you don't want everything and aren't interested in the group's history and personnel, then this one will suffice. They made some nice songs at Motown, but weren't high enough on the privilege ladder or hit meter to get the deluxe treatmnt. —*Ron Wynn*

Spirit

Group, Art-Rock/Progressive-Rock, Psychedelic
Of all the unusual musical groups that graced the West Coast in the late '60s, Spirit (formed in 1967) was certainly one of the most peculiar, both visually and musically. At a time when psychedelic music was in its most dissonant and disorganized state, the band performed elegantly quirky music with a kind of disciplined restraint. Except for the band's biggest hit, "I Got a Line on You" (#25), from *The Family That Plays Together* (#22), Spirit never really was a rock band in the usual sense; rather they were an ensemble of musical iconoclasts who sometimes embraced rock's abandon. The unique sustain-drenched lead-work of Randy California (b. Randy Wolfe, Feb 20, 1951) and the forcefully melodic percussion playing of his stepfather Ed Cassidy (b. May 4, 1931) were readily identifiable signatures for Spirit's ambient fusion of jazz, rock, and folk.

After the band's third album, *Clear Spirit* (#55), it became apparent that their sales were slipping. They released "1984" (#69), which linked police brutality to a developing Orwellian nightmare in America. Not surprisingly, conservatives and radio tip-sheets gave the track the "Eight Miles High" treatment and had the song pulled for possible subversiveness.

In 1971, Neil Young-producer David Briggs worked with Spirit on their next and last album with the original lineup. *The 12 Dreams of Dr. Sardonicus* (#63) ultimately earned the band their greatest commercial success, with FM hits on "Nature's Way, "Mr. Skin," and "Animal Zoo." That year, bassist Mark Andes (b. Feb 19, 1948) and vocalist Jay Ferguson (b. May 10, 1947) left to form the marginally successful Jo Jo Gunne. Cassidy and California continue to tour and release periodic albums as Spirit. —*Rick Clark*

○ **Spirit** / 1968 / Epic ✦✦✦✦
This is a strong debut by this quartet, featuring "Fresh Garbage," "Elijah," "Mechanical World," and "Uncle Jack." (Import). —*Rick Clark*

○ **Clear** / 1969 / Edsel ✦✦✦✦
Previous to the recording of this album, Spirit had been working on music for a soundtrack for the movie *The Model Shop*. *Clear* reflected that effort with an odd blend of off-the-wall (occasionally goofy-sounding) rock-influenced songs and strangely sparse instrumentals (with titles like "Ice" and "Clear"). Highlights include "Dark Eyed Woman" (number 118), "Policeman's Ball," "Give a Life, Take a Life" and "New Dope in Town." (Import). —*Rick Clark*

○ **Family That Plays Together** / 1969 / Edsel ✦✦✦✦
Lou Adler's unusual production, coupled with Marty Paich's ethereal orchestrations, on songs like "Aren't You Glad?," "It Shall Be," "Poor Richard," and "Silky Sam," gave Spirit's music a quality of icy distance. The only other band that comes to mind who employed such otherworldly arrangements was Love, with their masterful *Forever Changes*. This is a wonderful album worth getting. (Import) —*Rick Clark*

○ **12 Dreams of Dr. Sardonicus** / 1970 / Epic ✦✦✦✦
One of Spirit's most successful albums, it contains "Nature's Way" (number 111), "Mr. Skin" (number 92), "Animal Zoo" (number 97), and "Nothin' to Hide." (Also available as a Mobile Fidelity Ultradisc) —*Rick Clark*

Feedback / 1972 / Epic ✦✦

The Best of Spirit / 1973 / Epic ✦✦✦

Spirit of '76 / 1975 / Mercury ✦✦

● **Time Circle** / 1991 / Epic ✦✦✦✦
A generous helping of practically everything Spirit accomplished in their years on Lou Adler's Ode Records and Epic Records, this collection is sonically satisfactory and there are generous, informative liner notes. —*Rick Clark*

Spiritualized

Group, Alternative Pop/Rock
The trance-rock band Spiritualized was started in 1989, when guitarist/vocalist Jason Pierce was still in the equally ethereal Spacemen 3. After releasing many singles and EPs, the band released its breakthrough album *Lazer Guided Melodies* in 1992; the record featured the lineup of Pierce, guitarist Mark Refoy, vocalist/keyboardist Kate Radley, bassist Willie Carruthers and percussionist Jon Mattock. In 1995, the group released *Pure Phase* with a streamlined roster: Pierce, Radley, and Sean Cook on bass. Both of these albums showcase the group's beautifully shimmering, droning sound. —*Heather Phares*

○ **Lazer Guided Melodies** / 1992 / Dedicated ✦✦✦✦

Split Enz

Group, New Wave
This New Zealand art-rock (and later synth-pop) band was formed

in 1972 by art student and guitarist Phil Judd and singer/keyboardist Tim Finn. Their stylistic influences include Roxy Music, Genesis, and the post-*Sgt. Pepper* Beatles. They were known for their wild costumes and haircuts as much as for their eccentric blend of British dancehall and rock music. After Phil Judd left the band in 1977, he was replaced by Tim's younger brother Neil, and the Finn brothers took the band in a more commercial direction. Pleasing melodic pop with some still-lingering offbeat impulses made their middle-period albums enjoyable. Neil's budding songwriting talent garnered attention with the pop hit "I Got You" from the 1979 *True Colours* album (also the world's first laser-etched LP, whose surface was covered with prismatic designs). He wrote several of the band's better-known hits like "One Step Ahead" and "History Never Repeats," but the band never received much chart success. Tim left for a solo career in 1983, and Neil carried on for one more album before disbanding the Enz and forming the trio Crowded House. *—Scott Bultman*

○ **Mental Notes [Mushroom]** / 1975 / Mushroom ✦✦✦✦

The first proper Enz album features the band at its eccentric best. *Mental Notes* is completely non-commercial art-rock filled with ambitious arrangements and slightly disturbing themes courtesy of the Phil Judd and Tim Finn songwriting partnership. Finn's bittersweet crooning perfectly compliments Judd's madman persona on tracks like "Stranger than Fiction." Although the album would be repackaged, renamed, and rerecorded in years to come, the band would never again produce anything like it. A favorite with the fans. *—Chris Woodstra*

Second Thoughts / 1976 / Mushroom ✦✦✦

After *Mental Notes* failed commercially, the band left for England to rework the tracks with Roxy Music's Phil Manzanera producing. *Second Thoughts* is an eccentric album filled with the theatrics that gained the band its early notoriety. Mainly new versions of old songs, the album adds some new tracks such as the brilliant "Late Last Night" and "Woman Who Loves You." Released in America and the U.K. as *Mental Notes* with a modified cover. *—Chris Woodstra*

Dizrhythmia / 1977 / Mushroom ✦✦✦

With Tim Finn's leadership and brother Neil replacing founding member Phil Judd, the band makes a move into the mainstream. While the eccentricity is still evident, the album shines with a melodic pop sensibility. Contains the classics "Bold as Brass," "Charlie," and "Crosswords." *—Chris Woodstra*

Frenzy [Australian] / 1978 / Mushroom ✦✦✦

Although often thought of as a transitional album, *Frenzy* shows the band in top form. Produced in England on a diminished budget, the album showcases pure pop with a hungry edge. "I See Red," added after the initial pressing, became a huge hit in Australia and New Zealand, allowing the band the financial freedom to follow up with the blockbuster *True Colours* in 1980. Stripped down of the earlier excesses, the album more than hints at greatness to come in the '80s. The album was reissued in the U.S. in 1981, dropping half of the tracks and adding songs from the legendary "Rootin' Tootin' Luton Tapes" recorded in 1978. *—Chris Woodstra*

○ **True Colours** / 1979 / A&M ✦✦✦✦

This New Zealand band's most cohesive pop statement was their most successful American release. On these clever pop songs with synthesizer textures, Neil Finn comes into his own as a writer in his brother's band. *—Scott Bultman*

○ **Beginning of the Ends** / 1979 / Mushroom ✦✦✦✦

A compilation of demos from 1972-1975. This Australian-only release shows the band in its eccentric formative years before a recording contract. Light acoustic arrangements of songs appearing on later albums coupled with long forgotten gems make this a favorite among die-hard fans. Not the most representative picture of the band, but an interesting one. *—Chris Woodstra*

Beginning of the Enz / 1980 / Chrysalis ✦✦

Not to be confused with the Australian *Beginning of the Ends*, this British release compiles early Enz tracks from 1975-1977. A nice introduction to the band's earlier work but the albums should really be heard in their entirety. The inclusion of the non-LP track "Another Great Divide" makes this essential for collectors/completists. *—Chris Woodstra*

Waiata / 1981 / A&M ✦✦✦

Also titled *Corroboree* (in Australia and New Zealand), this followup to the successful *True Colours* album offers more Neil Finn-penned gems like "One Step Ahead" and "History Never Repeats," although the music is less edgy, with more emphasis on pleasant synth pop. It includes three instrumentals: "Iris," "Ships," and "Albert of India." *—Scott Bultman*

○ **Time & Tide** / 1982 / A&M ✦✦✦✦

Time and Tide is the band's creative high point and most fully realized effort. Combining beautiful melodies with introverted, soul searching lyrics, the album gives listeners new insights into the band. Both Tim and Neil Finn reach new peaks in their songwriting. Includes the hits "Dirty Creature" and "Six Months in a Leaky Boat." *—Chris Woodstra*

Conflicting Emotions / 1983 / A&M ✦✦✦

Less focused than *Time and Tide*, *Conflicting Emotions* is still a high point for the band. With Tim Finn stepping back and Neil Finn playing a more dominant role in the songwriting, the album is both dark and beautiful. Neil Finn's strong sense of melody builds on heavy rhythms and direct playing to produce a solid, if not exceptional album. Highlights include "Message to My Girl" and "Bullet Brain and Cactus Head."

Note to collectors: The first pressing in New Zealand came with a bonus 12" single with two new songs: "Kia Kaha" and "Parasite." *—Chris Woodstra*

○ **Enz of an Era** / 1983 / Mushroom ✦✦✦✦

A solid collection of the singles from *Second Thoughts* (1976) to *Time and Tide* (1982). Although not all of the singles are present, all of the hits from that period are covered. *Enz of an Era* is most notable for inclusion of the rare "Another Great Divide" but it has been superceded by more current (and more easily found) collections. *—Chris Woodstra*

See Ya Round / 1984 / Mushroom ✦✦

With Tim Finn departing for a solo career, Neil Finn takes charge of the aging band for their final studio album. While not living up to the band's previous brilliance, songs such as "Years Go By," "One Mouth Is Fed" and an early version of "I Walk Away" are delightful Finn compositions. Side two features songs written by each of the remaining members. Released only in Australia, New Zealand and Canada. *—Chris Woodstra*

Living Enz / 1985 / Mushroom ✦✦✦

A double live album with tracks from the farewell *Enz with a Bang* tour and a few from the 1982 *Time and Tide* tour. Rather than just focusing on the hit singles, the album revives old album favorites with new live arrangements. Mainly a gift for the fans, this album is a showcase for the band at its crowd-pleasing best. *—Chris Woodstra*

● **History Never Repeats: The Best of Split Enz** / 1987 / A&M ✦✦✦✦

All the best songs from their American albums (A&M new wave period—1979-1983) are here, although many other great songs can be found on their import CDs. A good place to get acquainted with the band; the fans already have the albums. *—Scott Bultman*

1973-1979: Oddz & Enz / 1993 / Mushroom ✦✦✦

This Australian-only box set covers the band's more experimental beginnings (1973-1979). From the light acoustic demos of *Beginning of the Enz* and the art-rock of *Mental Notes*, to the edgy-pop of *Frenzy*, the listener gets a strong sense of the band's pre-popularity evolution. With over an hour of non-LP tracks on the bonus disc and improved sound quality, this is essential for fans. *—Chris Woodstra*

1980-1984: Rear Enz / 1993 / Mushroom ✦✦✦

This Australian-only box set covers the period of the band's peak in popularity (1980-1984). Beginning with *True Colours* and ending with their swansong, *See Ya Round*, it shows the band in perfect pop form. While this is too ambitious for the casual fan, the devoted will find this essential for considerably improved sound and the bonus disc of previously unreleased tracks. *—Chris Woodstra*

Anniversary / 1994 / Mushroom ✦✦

Recorded live during the band's 20th Anniversary tour of New Zealand in March 1993, *Anniversary* serves mainly as a souvenir for long-time fans. There are some interesting song choices, such as the never-before-released "Best Friend" and the rarely-heard first single, "Split Ends," but the band seems to lack the energy that the enthusiastic audience deserved. Fans will delight in this release but *Living Enz* is still a better representation of the band's live shows. —*Chris Woodstra*

Best Of Split Enz / 1994 / Chrysalis ✦✦✦
Chrysalis Records handled the band's non-Australia/New Zealand releases from 1976-1977—an extremely low point in terms of sales. Not surprisingly, *Best of Split Enz* focuses a little too heavily on this early period to truly give the casual listener a representative collection of the band. The big A&M hits ("I Got You," "One Step Ahead") are covered adequately but this was clearly an attempt to cash in on Crowded House's success in Europe the year before. —*Chris Woodstra*

Spongetones

Group, Power Pop/Anglo-Pop
One of the most underrated pop bands of the '80s, the Spongetones released several albums of effortlessly melodic, catchy guitar-pop that captured the feel of '60s British Invasion pop with remarkable accuracy and feeling. While they never received much critical or commercial attention, their music has aged much better than most power-pop from the era; the band continues to record and perform in the 90s. —*Chris Woodstra*

Beat Music / 1982 / Ripete ✦✦✦

Torn Apart / 1983 / Ripete ✦✦✦

Where-Ever Land / 1984 / Triapore ✦✦
Not their strongest effort, *Where-Ever Land* is nevertheless a fun exercise in Mersey-pop revival with a slightly harder, radio-ready gloss. —*Chris Woodstra*

● **Oh Yeah!** / 1991 / Black Vinyl ✦✦✦✦
The Spongetones return after a long absence with 1991's *Oh Yeah!* They effectively pick up where they left off in the '80s with their infectious Beatlesque power-pop. Easily their best songwriting and a good place to get acquainted with the band. —*Chris Woodstra*

○ **Beat & Torn** / 1994 / Black Vinyl ✦✦✦✦
Now combined on one CD, *Beat Music* and *Torn Apart* represent the band's earliest recordings and some of their finest. Southern power-pop at its best. —*Chris Woodstra*

Textural Drone Thing / 1995 / Black Vinyl ✦✦✦

Dusty Springfield (Mary O'Brien)

b. Apr. 16, 1939, London, England
Soul, Pop/Rock
Born Mary O'Brien before changing her name professionally, Dusty Springfield first emerged during the early '60s as one-third of the British folk-pop trio the Springfields, which also included her brother Tom. They had several hits, including "Island of Dreams" and "Silver Thread and Golden Needles," and the latter topped the U.S. charts a year before the Beatles first records.

In 1963, the Springfields split up, with Tom going off to produce the Seekers. Dusty made herself over vocally, evolving from a folk alto into a powerful White soul singer, capable of credibly covering Motown material (she dueted with Martha Reeves on television's *Ready, Steady, Go* without embarrassing herself at all) and belting out British pop numbers with seismic intensity. "I Only Want to Be with You," "Stay Awhile," "Wishin' and Hopin'," and "24 Hours from Tulsa" were just a few of her successes, and all were heavily played in either England or America. In 1969, Springfield recorded *Dusty in Memphis*, a landmark White soul album done at Stax studios, which received critical raves and is something of a legendary record.

Since the early '70s, Springfield has recorded and made infrequent appearances, but none of her work since the Memphis album has been taken up by the public. She remains a respected and much-loved figure from British rock's heyday, however, even 30 years on. —*Bruce Eder*

Dusty / 1964 / Philips ✦✦✦
Not quite as good as her first American LP, but a good mix of soul/R&B covers and orchestrated pop-rock in the manner of early Dionne Warwick. Standouts include the cover of Bacharach-David's "I Just Don't Know What To Do With Myself" (a British hit), "All Cried Out," and the epic ballad "Summer Is Over," which foreshadows the style she'd use on her later hit "You Don't Have To Say You Love Me." —*Richie Unterberger*

○ **Stay Awhile/I Only Want to Be With You** / 1964 / Philips ✦✦✦✦
Her most rock & roll-oriented album, and one of the finest solo rock albums of the mid-'60s. Besides the two hit title tracks, Dusty covers various American soul and pop tunes that usually rank at least equal to the originals, in some cases totally outclassing them. In particular, she improves upon "24 Hours From Tulsa," "Anyone Who Had A Heart," "You Don't Own Me," and "When The Lovelight Starts Shining Through His Eyes." The production is the most credible approximation of the Phil Spector wall of sound ever managed in the U.K., with full brass and strings, soulful female backup choruses, and pounding piano and drums. Also includes a first-rate Springfield original, "Somethin' Special." —*Richie Unterberger*

Oooooooweeee!!! / 1965 / Philips ✦✦✦
No hits here (though "Losing You" made the British Top 10), and a couple of pointless repeats from the first album. Still, it's another solid set of exuberant, soulful girl-group-style British Invasion pop. "Losing You," "Once Upon A Time," and "He's Got Something" remain some of her most unjustly overlooked performances. —*Richie Unterberger*

Ev'rything's Coming Up Dusty / 1965 / Beat Goes On ✦✦✦
Dusty started to lean in a somewhat less R&B and somewhat more pop direction on this album, with covers of "La Bamba" and Anthony Newley's "Who Can I Turn To?" Still, it has good interpretations of songs by Goffin/King, Jerry Ragovoy, Randy Newman, Bacharach-David, and the Zombies' Rod Argent, highlighted by "Oh No! Not My Baby" and Newman's "I've Been Wrong Before." —*Richie Unterberger*

○ **Golden Hits** / 1966 / Philips ✦✦✦✦
A fair representation of her mid-'60s hits, with major gaps. The imported CDs are preferable. —*Bruce Eder*

★ **Dusty in Memphis** / 1969 / Rhino ✦✦✦✦✦
A sultry, subtle, soulful classic, key in any collection. —*Bruce Eder*

○ **A Brand New Me** / 1970 / Rhino ✦✦✦✦
While it's not quite as uniformly excellent as *Dusty in Memphis*, *A Brand New Me* comes close to recapturing its predecessor's magic and is easily one of Springfield's best albums. —*Stephen Thomas Erlewine*

● **The Silver Collection** / Jan. 1988 / Philips ✦✦✦✦
Twenty-four songs, encompassing her British and American chart history for the '60s. Superb sound. —*Bruce Eder*

BOOKS

✦✦ **Dusty**, by Lucy O'Brien (Sidgwick & Jackson, UK, 1989). She may have been the finest British female rock singer of the '60s, but the raw material of the life and times of Dusty Springfield is a bit stretched to yield enough material for a book-length biography, even one that only weighs in at 177 pages (lengthy discography included). There's a fair number of archival quotes from Dusty, though these aren't on the whole terribly artistically insightful. Early producer Ivor Raymonde offers some interesting recollections, and the sessions that produced the cult classic *Dusty in Memphis* are recounted in detail. But the coverage of her post-1970 career, generally quite fallow both artistically and commercially, is lacking in exciting source material, and the author speculates a great deal on Springfield's ambiguous sexuality, though this is far from the most central or interesting aspect of her music or public life. Primarily for major Springfield fans. —*Richie Unterberger*

Rick Springfield

b. Aug. 23, 1949, Sydney, Australia
Power Pop/Anglo-Pop, Pop/Rock
Before he became a soap star, Rick Springfield was a rock star in his native Australia. After scoring several hits with his band Zoot in the early '70s, he went solo and tried to make the big time in America. Springfield released several power-pop albums to no success; he then decided to become a television actor, landing a role on *General Hospital*. While he was acting on the soap opera, he gained a strong following, which led him to revive his singing career in the early '80s. This time, his records were more successful—"Jessie's Girl," his first single since returning to music, hit number one. Several other Top Ten hits followed, before his career started to slip in the mid-'80s; despite his diminished sales, he continued recording and acting through the rest of the decade. —*Stephen Thomas Erlewine*

Beginnings / 1972 / Capitol ✦✦
"Come on Everybody" aside, this is a different side of Springfield of which fans of his work in the '80s may not be aware. This is the work of an artist trying to fit into the sensitive singer/songwriter mold. While not a bad record, it's most interesting for "Speak to the Sky," his first American hit, and as a clue to the roots of the work for which he is best known. —*Jim Worbois*

Comic Book Heroes / 1974 / Columbia ✦✦✦
Springfield grew considerably as a writer between his first record and *Comic Book Heroes*. Although he is still doing some sensitive singer/songwriter material, it no longer sounds as awkward. In fact, a couple tracks, like "Weep No More," are very memorable. On the other hand, "Misty Water Woman" sounds like an overly melodramatic attempt at being Elton John. Still, the good stuff makes it worth owning. —*Jim Worbois*

Mission Magic / 1974 / Wizard ✦✦

Wait for Night / 1976 / Chelsea ✦✦
While there is nothing that really jumps off *Wait for Night* that makes it stick in your mind, it is still quite a nice record. Of course, the addition of Elton John's rhythm section and Jimmy Haskell's string work contributes to the album's overall quality. —*Jim Worbois*

● **Working Class Dog** / 1981 / RCA ✦✦✦✦
Forget that Rick Springfield was a soap star for a moment and listen to his music, because he made some of the finest guitar-driven mainstream pop-rock of the early '80s. *Working Class Dog* is his finest moment, filled with expertly crafted pop songs, highlighted by the massive hit "Jessie's Girl." —*Stephen Thomas Erlewine*

○ **Success Hasn't Spoiled Me Yet** / 1982 / RCA ✦✦✦
Rick Springfield's follow-up to his commercial breakthrough *Working Class Dog* wasn't quite as consistent, but it contained a number of solid power-pop tracks, including "Calling All Girls," "What Kind of Fool Am I," "How Do You Talk to Girls," "The American Girl," and the Top Ten hit "Don't Talk to Strangers." —*Stephen Thomas Erlewine*

Living in Oz / 1983 / RCA ✦✦✦
Although the singles "Affair of the Heart" and "Human Touch" were Rick Springfield classics, the rest of *Living in Oz* contained too much filler to make it rank with *Working Class Dog* and *Success Hasn't Spoiled Me Yet* as one of his best albums. —*Stephen Thomas Erlewine*

Beautiful Feelings / 1984 / Mercury ✦✦

Hard to Hold / 1984 / RCA ✦✦
The soundtrack to Rick Springfield's movie features the powerful rocker "Love Somebody," but the rest of the album comprises filler instrumentals, lukewarm power-pop tracks from Springfield and bland tracks from Graham Parker, Nena Hendryx, and Peter Gabriel. —*Stephen Thomas Erlewine*

Tao / 1985 / RCA ✦✦✦

Rock of Life / 1988 / RCA ✦✦

○ **Greatest Hits** / 1989 / RCA ✦✦✦
A good collection, it includes Springfield's greatest hits. —*David Jehnzen*

Bruce Springsteen

b. Sep. 23, 1949, Freehold, NJ
Rock & Roll, Singer/Songwriter
When Bruce Springsteen finally broke through to national recognition in the fall of 1975, after a decade of trying, critics hailed him as the savior of rock & roll, the single artist who brought together all the exuberance of '50s rock and the thoughtfulness of '60s rock, molded into a '70s style. He rocked as hard as Jerry Lee Lewis, his lyrics were as complicated as Bob Dylan's, and his concerts were near-religious celebrations of all that was best in the music. One critic became so enamored that he quit reviewing to become Springsteen's manager.

But the hosannas, when piped through the publicity machine of a major record company, were perceived as hype by a significant part of the public as well as the mainstream media—Springsteen landed on the covers of *Time* and *Newsweek*, but both magazines were covering the phenomenon, not the music. Springsteen's album, *Born to Run*, became a hit, and he jumped to arena status as a live act, but as many people were turned off by the press campaign as turned on by the records and shows.

Two decades later, however, Springsteen remained an estab-

lished star who could look back on a career that had produced one of the best-selling albums of all time, sold-out stadium shows, Grammy Awards and an Oscar, and a group of imitators who constituted their own subgenre of popular music. If he no longer seemed divine, he remained popular enough for his *Greatest Hits* album to enter the charts at number one, and he had won over many of those skeptics from 1975.

Growing up in southern New Jersey, Springsteen turned to rock & roll as a teenager and played in a series of bands from the mid-'60s on, varying in style from garage rock to power trio blues-rock. By the early '70s, he was trying his hand at being a folkie singer/songwriter in Greenwich Village. But when he was signed to Columbia Records in 1972, he brought into the studio many of the New Jersey-based musicians with whom he'd played over the years.

The result was *Greetings from Asbury Park, NJ* (January 1973), which went unnoticed upon initial release, though Manfred Mann's Earth Band would turn its lead-off track, "Blinded by the Light," into a number one hit four years later. *The Wild, the Innocent and the E Street Shuffle* (1973) also failed to sell, despite some rave reviews. (Both albums have since gone platinum.)

The following year, Springsteen revised his backup group—dubbed "The E Street Band"—settling on a lineup that included saxophone player Clarence Clemons, second guitarist "Miami" Steve Van Zandt, organist Danny Federici, pianist Roy Bittan, bassist Gary Tallent, and drummer Max Weinberg. With this unit he barnstormed the country while working on his third and last chance with Columbia. By the time *Born to Run* (August 1975) was released, the critics and a significant cult audience were with him, and the title song became a Top 40 hit while the album reached the Top Ten.

What Springsteen needed to do in the wake of the hype, of course, was to play and record more to consolidate his position. He was prevented at least from the latter by a former manager, who kept him in court during the next couple of years. Meanwhile, the musical world changed. Part of the reason critics had welcomed Springsteen so enthusiastically in 1975 was that he seemed a return to basic rock & roll values in a world of soft rock, heavy metal, and art-rock.

By the time Springsteen returned with his fourth album, *Darkness on the Edge of Town* (May 1978), however, the punk/new wave movement had outflanked him, pushing him from the vanguard to the mainstream. Similar sounding heartland rockers such as Bob Seger had appeared, so that Springsteen sounded less like an innovator than a member of an established genre.

Nevertheless, he set about winning fans with an album that found the lost children of his early albums stuck in factory jobs, still longing for some escape. The album was a hit, though it did not match the success of *Born to Run*. Springsteen returned with the double album *The River* (October 1980), which topped the charts and featured his first Top Ten hit, "Hungry Heart."

Nobody was calling him a hype anymore, but Springsteen retreated from his expanding success, next recording the low-key album *Nebraska* (September 1982), a virtual demo tape-on-vinyl. (Springsteen did not tour to promote the album, and in the interim E Street Band guitarist Van Zandt amicably left the group for a solo career, to be replaced by Nils Lofgren.)

But then came *Born in the U.S.A.* (June 1984) and a two-year international tour. The album threw off seven hit singles and sold over ten million copies, putting Springsteen in the pop heavens with Michael Jackson and Prince. After touring for more than a year, he released a five-LP/three-CD concert album, *Live 1975-1985* (1986), which topped the charts.

Characteristically, Springsteen returned with a more introverted effort, *Tunnel of Love* (October 1987), which presaged his divorce from his first wife. (He married a second time to singer Patti Scialfa, who had joined the E Street Band.)

After another marathon tour, Springsteen gave the E Street Band notice in November 1989, breaking up a celebrated unit that had stayed together 15 years. In March 1992, he simultaneously released *Human Touch* and *Lucky Town*, and though the albums premiered near the top of the charts, they were less successful with fans than previous albums. In the fall, Springsteen taped an *MTV Unplugged* segment (though he plugged in after one song), and the performance was released as an album in Europe in 1993.

Springsteen continued to tour until July 1993. In the fall, he wrote and recorded "Streets of Philadelphia" for the soundtrack to the film *Philadelphia*, which concerned a lawyer dying of AIDS.

The song became a Top Ten hit in 1994, winning the Academy Award for Best Song and cleaning up in the Grammys the following year. At the same time, Springsteen had readied his *Greatest Hits* album (March 1995), reassembling the E Street Band to record a few new tracks. The album was an immediate best-seller. — *William Ruhlmann*

Greetings from Asbury Park NJ / Jan. 5, 1973 / Columbia ✦✦✦
The songs, laced with Dylanistic wordplay, are gorgeous street vignettes fused with romance, idealism, and a true sense of wonder. — *John Floyd*

☆ **The Wild, the Innocent and the E Street Shuffle** / 1973 / Columbia ✦✦✦✦✦
The Wild, the Innocent & the E Street Shuffle is a subtle masterpiece. The grooves are tougher, revealing the R&B heart that *Greetings from Asbury Park* stifled, and the songs are long enough to let him develop his characters and their situations. — *John Floyd*

☆ **Born to Run** / Aug. 25, 1975 / Columbia ✦✦✦✦✦
A bombastic masterpiece, his breakthrough is a testament not only to the sound of Phil Spector's '60s hits, but to the romanticism, the longing, and the determination of those hits. The title cut and "Thunder Road" are anthems that deserve that status. — *John Floyd*

○ **Darkness on the Edge of Town** / Jun. 2, 1978 / Columbia ✦✦✦✦
On this, the flip side of *Born to Run*, the idealism of those characters turns into stark terror once they hit adulthood. This is where Springsteen's reputation as a working-class mouthpiece is based, but there's much more here than that. — *John Floyd*

☆ **The River** / Oct. 10, 1980 / Columbia ✦✦✦✦✦
In many ways his best album, it balances the dashed dreams of *Darkness on the Edge of Town* with the hope of *Born to Run*, but it trades the Spectorian wallop for a taut, frat-rock sound that is alternately wiry, delicate, and full-blown. — *John Floyd*

☆ **Nebraska** / Sep. 20, 1982 / Columbia ✦✦✦✦✦
A set of acoustic demos, it offers ravaged tales of despair, defeat, and defiance. — *John Floyd*

★ **Born in the U.S.A.** / Jun. 4, 1984 / Columbia ✦✦✦✦✦
The album that pushed him into superstar status ironically examines the dirty underbelly of America in both political and domestic terms. The big, catchy, hard-slamming rock & roll that carries the lyrics only adds to the irony. — *John Floyd*

○ **Live 1975-1985** / 1986 / Columbia ✦✦✦✦
A career-defining three-disc live collection, it is among the three or four greatest boxed sets ever issued. — *John Floyd*

☆ **Tunnel of Love** / Oct. 1987 / Columbia ✦✦✦✦✦
A moody and dark inquiry, it asks why people fall in love, why they get married, why they lose faith in the people closest to them, and why they even bother. Required listening for anyone contemplating the altar. — *John Floyd*

Chimes of Freedom / 1988 / Columbia ✦✦
A four-song live EP from his 1988 tour, it includes a riveting version of Dylan's "Chimes of Freedom" and an acoustic rendering of "Born to Run." — *John Floyd*

Human Touch / Mar. 1992 / Columbia ✦✦
His first proper recording without the E Street Band, Springsteen continues the conversation started on *Tunnel of Love* through the pleading urgency of "Soul Driver" and the forthright admissions on "Real World." Musically, the set balances E Street retreads ("Roll of the Dice," "All or Nothin' at All") with taut soul grooves and slashing hard rock, emphasizing Springsteen's astonishing guitar playing. — *John Floyd*

Lucky Town / Mar. 1992 / Columbia ✦✦✦
Because they failed to repeat the massive success of *Born in the USA*, and because they eschewed the working-class posturing of his most famous work, many critics claimed *Human Touch* and *Lucky Town* offered proof that Springsteen had lost his creative foothold. Nothing could be further from the truth. Rather than letting a cast of desolate losers and struggling optimists do his talking, Springsteen forced *himself* to do it. They're both strikingly personal and confessional albums that analyze the difficulties of making commitments and the necessity of making those commitments. *Lucky Town*, recorded chiefly by Springsteen, with occasional assistance from keyboardist Roy Bittan, is the thematic antithesis of Dylan's *Blood on the Tracks*, an album devoted to the requisiteness of love and romance and how empty lives are without that love and romance. *Lucky Town* offers living proof

that Bruce Springsteen's grappling with domestic bliss and superstardom is just as enlightening as his struggle to attain them. — *John Floyd*

In Concert/MTV Plugged / 1993 / Columbia ✦✦✦
This is a limited-edition European release of most of Springsteen's *MTV Unplugged* concert, which he wound up doing electric. Fans will need to have this, not only because the performance is good but because there are two songs that aren't available anywhere else. — *AMG*

Greatest Hits / 1995 / Columbia ✦✦✦
Compiling a "Greatest Hits" of Bruce Springsteen should be an easy task, yet *Greatest Hits* manages to miss the mark. Nothing from his first two albums is included and the set includes such non-hits like "Atlantic City" and "The River" instead of hits like "Cover Me," "Tunnel of Love," and "Fade Away." In fact, a good portion of his hits are missing, as are important album tracks like "Backstreets," "Rosalita," and "Candy's Room," making this neither a straight hits collection nor a compilation of his best tracks. What's left is some of his biggest hits and best songs ("Born to Run," "Glory Days," "The River"), but not all of them, as well as four new tracks, the best of which is an outtake from the *Born in the U.S.A.* sessions ("Murder Inc.") Aside from "Murder Inc.," the new tracks follow the synth-laden adult contemporary direction Springsteen began pursuing with "Streets of Philadelphia," only without the lyricism or melody. So, it's a mixed bag, drawing an incomplete portrait of one of the prime rockers of the '70s and '80s. Casual fans would be better served by *Born in the U.S.A.*, which encompasses all of Springsteen's sides. — *Stephen Thomas Erlewine*

Squeeze

Group, New Wave, Pop/Rock
Squeeze is a British pop/rock quintet that serves as a forum for the songs of its lead singer Glenn Tilbrook (b. Aug 31, 1957) and his partner, guitarist Chris Difford. The duo formed Squeeze in 1974 with keyboardist Jools Holland (b. Jan 24, 1958), whose bubbly personality made him a natural frontman, bassist Harry Kakouli (replaced by John Bentley after the first album), and drummer Gilson Lavis (b. Jun 27, 1951). They reached the U.K. Top 20 in 1978 with the single "Take Me I'm Yours," but really broke through the following year, when their second album, *Cool for Cats*, produced two U.K. Top Ten hits in the title track and the Difford-sung "Up the Junction." *Argybargy*, their third album, was a moderate success in 1980 (and their first U.S. chart entry), but their next milestone came in 1981 with *East Side Story*, an album for which Holland was replaced by former Ace lead singer Paul Carrack (b.Apr 22, 1951), who sang lead on "Tempted," Squeeze's first U.S. chart single. The album, which hit the U.K. Top 20, also featured a #4 British hit, "Labelled with Love." As it turned out, Carrack left after the one album, replaced by Don Snow (b. Jan 13, 1957) for *Sweets for a Stranger*, after which Squeeze disbanded. They re-formed in 1985 with Tilbrook, Difford, Holland, and Lavis, plus Keith Wilkinson on bass, to release *Cosi Fan Tutti Frutti* and then, in 1987, *Babylon and On*, which featured "Hourglass," a Top 20 hit on both sides of the Atlantic. *Frank* came out in 1989, followed in 1990 with the live album *A Round and a Bout*, which finished Squeeze's contract with A&M. They then signed to Warner Bros. and released *Play* in 1991.

After the sluggish sales of *Play*, Warner dropped the band; they re-signed with A&M soon afterward. Gilson Lavis left the band before they recorded 1993's *Some Fantastic Place*, leaving only Difford and Tilbrook as the band's only original members. — *William Ruhlmann*

U.K. Squeeze / 1978 / A&M ✦✦
Their debut of rough-edged British pub rock appeared during the peak of the punk years. — *Scott Bultman*

○ **Cool for Cats** / 1979 / A&M ✦✦✦✦
The band's second album shows a great leap in songwriting skills. While an emphasis on English themes can leave most Americans bewildered, the catchy pop melodies crossed with a pub rock sensibility are simply irresistible. Highlights include "Cool for Cats" and "Up the Junction," a pure pop masterpiece. — *Chris Woodstra*

○ **Argybargy** / 1980 / A&M ✦✦✦✦
Upbeat, cleverly crafted pop/rock with decidedly British themes. Tilbrook's guitar work and Jools Holland's keyboards shine as Squeeze moves from being pub-rockers to critics' darlings. — *Scott Bultman*

○ **East Side Story** / 1981 / A&M ✦✦✦✦
Their U.S. breakthrough album featured the hit "Tempted," sung and written by Paul Carrack (of the '70s band Ace), who was Squeeze's keyboardist for this one album. This is the album that sparked the comparisons of Difford/Tilbrook to Lennon/McCartney. A broader pop style with classical overtones and a country influence courtesy of producers Elvis Costello and Dave Edmunds. —*Scott Bultman*

Sweets from a Stranger / 1982 / A&M ✦✦
Still riding high on the success of *East Side Story,* Squeeze continues to write perky, upbeat tunes, but with the blue-eyed soul influence of the quickly departed Paul Carrack, they begin their move away from their classic sound. The hit "Black Coffee in Bed" sounds amazingly like a Paul Carrack song, perhaps an attempt to duplicate the success of Carrack's "Tempted." —*Scott Bultman*

★ **Singles 45's & Under** / 1982 / A&M ✦✦✦✦✦
This consists of twelve early Squeeze singles and one non-album track ("Annie Get Your Gun"). This is classic Squeeze, the songs that made them. Includes "Tempted," "Black Coffee in Bed," and "Another Nail for My Heart." —*Scott Bultman*

Cosi Fan Tutti Frutti / 1985 / A&M ✦✦✦
After *Sweets from a Stranger* and the Difford/Tilbrook solo effort, this re-formed Squeeze (with Jools Holland returning on keyboards) makes a move in another direction, with a less-overt soul influence, and high pop-craft and experimentation. Laurie Latham's technicolor/cinerama production makes this their most glossy album. Keith Wilkinson takes over on bass. —*Scott Bultman*

Classics, Vol. 25 / 1987 / A&M ✦✦✦
This 19-cut sampler of their 1978-1987 work was the 25th CD in A&M's 25th anniversary reissue of the best material on the label. Six cuts overlap with the *Singles 45's & Under* package, but the other 13 tracks make this a worthwhile companion for those not up to buying the original albums. At 72+ minutes, this is a bargain. —*Scott Bultman*

Babylon and on / 1987 / A&M ✦✦
Yet another step back to their classic sound, this time rewarded with minor chart success. Squeeze regains their drive and perkiness, firing on all cylinders. —*Scott Bultman*

Frank / 1989 / A&M ✦✦
Along with the return of keyboardist Jools Holland, comes a return to the classic Squeeze sound. "If It's Love" and "She Doesn't Have to Shave" more than make up for the blandness of the previous album with their memorable hooks and irresistible melodies. —*Chris Woodstra*

A Round & A Bout (Live) / 1990 / IRS ✦✦
Recorded on 1990's *Frank* tour in England, this live album finds the band still having fun playing their nearly ten-year-old classics. A nice companion to their greatest hits. —*Chris Woodstra*

Play / 1991 / Reprise ✦✦✦
This unfortunately overlooked album finds the songwriting team of Difford and Tilbrook still in strong form through a 12-track song cycle. Now a four-piece band, there is less dependence on keyboards and a focus on more acoustic arrangements. A considerably more subdued mood but no less rewarding on repeated listening. —*Chris Woodstra*

Some Fantastic Place / Sep. 14, 1993 / A&M ✦✦✦
The band's tenth proper album reunites the core of Glen Tilbrook and Chris Difford with former member Paul Carrack and adds drummer Pete Thomas (Elvis Costello & the Attractions). Their classic sound is still there through the melodic power-pop of "Third Rail" to the blue-eyed soul of "Loving You Tonight" (nearly a rewrite of "Tempted"). Another in a series of commercial sleepers, but it's sure to delight those who give it a try. —*Chris Woodstra*

● **Greatest Hits** / 1994 / A&M ✦✦✦✦
A U.K.-only collection of the classic singles which covers more ground than *Singles 45's and Under* and certainly has a better song selection than *Classics, Greatest Hits* is the best hits package, though the import price is somewhat prohibitive. —*Chris Woodstra*

Billy Squier

b. May 12, 1950, Wellesley, MA
Hard Rock

Billy Squier was making pop-metal years before Bon Jovi came along. With his sharp, hard-rocking riffs and sweet, slick melodies, Squier became one of the biggest hard rock stars of the early '80s, earning two multi-platinum albums. But his fall from commercial prominence was just as quick as his rise; 1984's *Signs of Life* was his last album to sell over a million copies and even then he seemed slightly behind the times. Squier wasn't able to translate his AOR hits over to MTV, causing him to fall down the charts. However, he never lost his hard-core fans; he continued to tour and record successfully right into the '90s. —*Stephen Thomas Erlewine*

○ **Don't Say No** / 1981 / Capitol ✦✦✦✦
This is far and away the most consistent and solid work from this hard rock singer/songwriter and guitarist. This studio-polished debut plays like a greatest-hits album, including "In the Dark," "The Stroke," and "Lonely Is the Night." —*Donna DiChario*

○ **Emotions in Motion** / 1982 / Capitol ✦✦✦✦
● **16 Strokes** / 1995 / Capitol ✦✦✦✦
Billy Squier was an album rocker that never made a consistent album. He would come close, but there was always a fair amount of filler on his records. *16 Strokes* condenses his hit singles and album-oriented radio tracks to a manageable album, one that rarely sags. For most fans, this is all the Squier they'll need. —*Stephen Thomas Erlewine*

Chris Squire

b. Mar. 4, 1948, London, England
Art-Rock/Progressive-Rock
Bassist and a cofounder of Yes, with an original and very distinctive style on his instrument, Squire may have the greatest critical respect of any of his fellow Yes men. He hasn't pursued his solo career as aggressively as Steve Howe or Jon Anderson, but he does have a single album of his own to his credit. —*Bruce Eder*

○ **Fish out of Water** / 1975 / Arista ✦✦✦✦
Almost a lost Yes album, with more expressive lyrics than the band is known for. Tasteful orchestrations and guitar/bass playing by Squire which is superb much of the time, with (surprise!) an under-produced feel. (Import) —*Bruce Eder*

Squirrel Bait

Group, Alternative Pop/Rock, Thrash
Sadly defunct thrash-pop band from Louisville, Kentucky, Squirrel Bait (especially lead singer Peter Searcy) sounded a bit like the Replacements, only with the throttle *always* to the floor. As they got older, they tempered their assault, but they continued to make good records. —*John Dougan*

Squirrel Bait / 1985 / Homestead ✦✦✦
Unmitigated thrashing songs (yes, songs). —*Robert Gordon*

○ **Skag Heaven** / 1987 / Homestead ✦✦✦✦
Controlled thrash, it features a wondrous cover of Phil Ochs' "Tape from California." —*Robert Gordon*

● **Squirrel Bait/Skag Heaven** / Homestead ✦✦✦✦
All of their work on compact disc. Hüsker Dü/Replacements-inspired, you bet. But this is still great, if overlooked and too-soon-forgotten indie-pop. —*John Dougan*

SRC

Group, Hard Rock, Psychedelic
Along with the Stooges, MC5, and the Amboy Dukes, SRC were local heroes of the Michigan rock scene in the late '60s and early '70s, although in terms of national success, they were relegated to the second division populated by such bands as the Frost and the Rationals. Led by the Quackenbush brothers Gary and Glenn, the Ann Arbor group evolved out of the Fugitives, adding lead singer Scott Richardson from fellow garage band the Chosen Few. SRC recorded three erratic albums for Capitol that blended Motor City crunch with sustain-laden psychedelic guitar, pompous bursts of organ, spacy lyrics, and unexpectedly wispy, vulnerable vocals, throwing in some pretty ballads and harmonies to temper the hard rock excess. —*Richie Unterberger*

● **SRC** / 1968 / One Way ✦✦✦✦
Milestones / 1969 / One Way ✦✦✦
Traveller's Tale / 1970 / Capitol ✦✦✦
Lost Masters / 1972 / One Way ✦✦
● **The Revenge of the Quackenbush Brothers** / 1987 / Bam Caruso ✦✦✦✦

Good selection of key cuts from all three albums; "Daystar," "Marionette," and "Black Sheep" are first-rate hard psychedelia. One Way has reissued all of the original albums, as well as some unissued material, but this is the best and most judicious selection. Comes with detailed group history. —*Richie Unterberger*

Chris Stamey

Power Pop/Anglo-Pop, Experimental
Chris Stamey might not be a household name, but among the cult of melodic guitar pop/rock fans, he's a major player. Stamey played with seminal the North Carolina '70s pop band the Sneakers and was a founding member of the dB's. After the dB's fell apart, Chris Stamey recorded an album with his fellow dB Peter Holsapple; after that album, Stamey released his first solo record in 1991. —*Rick Clark*

Instant Excitement / 1984 / Coyote ✦✦✦
○ **It's Alright** / 1987 / A&M ✦✦✦✦
With the help of Alex Chilton, Richard Lloyd, Mitch Easter, Marshall Crenshaw, and others, Stamey presented a cohesive body of fine pop/rock songs, most notably "Cara Lee," "Incredible Happiness," "27 Years in a Single Day," and "The Seduction." —*Rick Clark*

● **Fireworks** / 1991 / Rhino ✦✦✦✦
Fireworks, the album that A&M allegedly rejected, surfaced on Rhino's new artist imprint RNA. While it is arguably his best solo album, the overly reverberant production and thin sounds steal the thunder from this album. Another problem comes in the lyric department. Stamey's earnest lyrics are often too arty, while failing to communicate any real enhancing art. Nevertheless, Stamey delivers some beautiful melodies and songs like "The Company of Light," "Something Came Over Me," "Glorious Delusion," and "On the Radio (For Ray Davies)" are wonderful listens. —*Rick Clark*

Wonderful Life / 1992 / East Side Digital ✦✦✦
This playful disc includes Stamey's 1982 solo effort, *It's a Wonderful Life* and 1984's *Instant Excitement*. Stamey experiments with percussion triggering other types of instrumental sounds—something he calls the Groovegate System. All in all this disc feels like an idea scrapbook more than a polished release. —*Rick Clark*

Robust Beauty / 1995 / East Side Digital ✦✦

The Standells

Group, Garage Rock
A '60s Los Angeles-based rock group. The Standells had the greasy garage-band sound down to perfection, and their pounding ode to Boston's "Dirty Water" was a huge hit in 1966. Prior to hitting national playlists, the band had recorded for MGM and Liberty and appeared in the 1964 movie *Get Yourself a College Girl*. Signed to Capitol's Tower subsidiary, drummer (former Mouseketeer) Dick Dodd's snarling vocal and pounding backbeat made "Dirty Water" (produced by Ed Cobb of the Four Preps, who were about as far opposed to the Standells' approach as could possibly be) their topseller. Three subsequent 1966-1967 Standells singles also charted, but the quartet fell apart before the end of the decade. —*Bill Dahl*

Dirty Water / 1966 / Sundazed ✦✦✦
Along with *Why Pick on Me*, this was the group's strongest album, although you're always better off with a greatest hits collection. "There Is a Storm Comin'" and "Pride and Devotion" are a couple of strong numbers that don't make it onto compilations, and "Rari," the moody B-side of "Dirty Water," is one of their best little-known tracks. The CD reissue takes off one cut (the easily found "Sometimes Good Guys Don't Wear White") and adds six bonus tracks of only mild interest, including a version of "Batman." Add points for finding a longer version of "Rari," though. —*Richie Unterberger*

Why Pick on Me / 1966 / Sundazed ✦✦✦
This pop-punk relic isn't bad, but as the best of these songs—"Why Pick on Me," "Sometimes Good Guys Don't Wear White," "Mainline"—have been issued on whatever best-of-Standells compilation you might pick up, its appeal is really limited to big fans. Of the

more obscure tracks, "Black Hearted Woman" is a decent slow, menacing number, "Mr. Nobody" a decent punky cut, and "The Girl and the Moon" one of their best pop-oriented compositions. This CD reissue adds five tracks that were previously unissued in the U.S., which are okay but nothing too special. —*Richie Unterberger*

Hot Ones / 1966 / Sundazed ✦✦
Having the Standells do an album of 1966 Top 40 covers—in 1966—was a boneheaded idea to begin with, and hardly worthy of revisitation. This CD reissue eliminates a couple of the ten songs (which are available on other Standells reissues on Sundazed), and adds seven rare tracks of mild interest, most of which were previously unissued, or previously unavailable in the U.S. These include the early 1965 cut "You Were the One," a vaguely Beatleish number; a couple of outtakes from their 1966 *Try It* album, including a reasonably nifty 11-minute instrumental jam, their unreleased version of "Misty Lane," which was done better by the Chocolate Watch Band; a rendition of the Graham Gouldman song "School Girl," and the awful, vaudevillian-flavored single they issued under the name the Sllednats. —*Richie Unterberger*

Try It / 1967 / Sundazed ✦✦
The Standells' final studio album is a mixed effort, despite the outstanding title track. The early Pink Floyd-like "All Fall Down," "Barracuda," and especially "Riot on Sunset Strip" are top-notch pop-punk, but the record is weighed down by some ill-chosen soul covers and some weak pop material. The CD reissue adds five rare but unremarkable bonus tracks, including outtakes and a non-LP single. —*Richie Unterberger*

● **The Best of the Standells** / 1984 / Rhino ✦✦✦✦
Most '60s punk bands could barely fill an album side with decent material. This 18-song compilation is a tribute to the vitality of the Standells' raunch-and-roll attack, including not only their one hit ("Dirty Water") but salacious essentials ranging from the swaggering "Sometimes Good Guys Don't Wear White" to the horny wail of "Barracuda." —*John Floyd*

Lisa Stansfield

b. 1965
Dance-Pop, Urban
English vocalist Lisa Stansfield was the lead singer of the group the Blue Zone, and featured on Coldcut's "People Hold On" in 1989. She zoomed into the spotlight with *Affection* in 1990. The album went platinum and earned her a number three pop and number one R&B single with "All Around the World." *Affection*, and its follow-up CD *Real Love*, were deeply influenced by the '70s disco sound of Barry White, from arrangements to mood and even Stansfield's own technique. —*Ron Wynn*

● **Affection** / 1989 / Arista ✦✦✦✦
Stansfield's voice serves this retro-disco material extremely well, best exemplified by the hits "All Around the World" and "You Can't Deny It." An impressive debut. —*Stephen Thomas Erlewine*
○ **Real Love** / 1991 / Arista ✦✦✦✦
Another strong effort from Stansfield. —*Stephen Thomas Erlewine*
So Natural / 1993 / Arista ✦✦✦

The Staple Singers

Group, Soul, Gospel
The Staples's story goes all the way back to Winona, MS, in 1915. It was then and there that patriarch Roebuck Staples entered the world. A contemporary and familiar of Charley Patton, Roebuck quickly became adept as a solo blues guitarist, entertaining at local dances and picnics. Gradually drawn to the church, by 1937 he was singing and playing guitar with a spiritual group based out of Drew, MS, the Golden Trumpets. Moving to Chicago four years later, he continued playing gospel music with the Windy City's Trumpet Jubilees. A decade later Pops Staples (as he had become known) presented two of his daughters, Cleotha and Mavis, and his one son, Pervis, in front of a church audience, and the Staple Singers were born.

The Staples recorded in an older, slightly archaic, deeply Southern spiritual style first for United and then for Vee-Jay. Pops and Mavis Staples shared lead vocal chores, with most records underpinned by Pops's heavily reverbed Mississippi cottonpatch guitar. In 1960 the Staples signed with Riverside, a label that specialized in jazz and folk. With Riverside and later Epic, the Staples attempted to move into the then-burgeoning White folk boom. Two Epic releases, "Why (Am I Treated So Bad)" and a cover of Stephen Stills's "For What It's Worth," briefly graced the pop charts in 1967.

In 1968 the Staples signed with Memphis-based Stax. The first two albums, *Soul Folk in Action* and *We'll Get Over*, were produced by Steve Cropper and backed by Booker T and the MGs. The Staples were now singing entirely contemporary "message" songs such as "Long Walk to D.C." and "When Will We Be Paid." In 1970 Pervis Staples left, and was replaced by sister Yvonne Staples. Even more significantly, Al Bell took over production chores. Bell took them down the road to Muscle Shoals, and things got decidedly funky.

Starting with "Heavy Makes You Happy (Sha-Na-Boom Boom)" and "I'll Take You There," the Staples counted 12 chart hits at Stax. When Stax encountered financial problems, Curtis Mayfield signed the Staples to his Curtom label and produced a number one hit in "Let's Do It Again." The Staples went on to continued chart success, albeit less spectacularly, with Warner, through 1979. One more album followed on 20th Century-Fox in 1981. After a three-year hiatus, they signed a two-album deal with Private I and hit the R&B charts five more times, once with an unlikely cover of Talking Heads' "Slippery People."

The Staple Singers found a new audience in 1994 when they teamed with Marty Stuart to perform "The Weight" on the *Rhythm, Country and Blues* LP for MCA. —*Rob Bowman*

○ **Uncloudy Day/Will The Circle Be Unbroken** / 1955-1960 / Vee-Jay ✦✦✦✦
The Staple Singers brilliantly fused gospel, folk, blues, and soul into a cohesive, commercially potent sound in the '50s and '60s. They perfected this approach during their tenure at Vee-Jay, the first label that allowed the twangy, expert guitar licks of Roebuck "Pop" Staples to be heard in the group's mix and fully presented their harmonies. This single disc contains two pivotal Staples albums: *Uncloudy Day* includes such gospel favorites as "I Know I Got Religion" and "Let Me Ride," while *Will the Circle Be Unbroken* offers the splendid title track, plus masterpieces like "Pray On" and "Come Up in Glory." —*Ron Wynn*

Great Day / 1963 / Milestone ✦✦✦
This two-album Fantasy reissue is an anthology of the material the Staples recorded for Riverside between 1960 and 1963. For Riverside, the Staples recorded mostly gospel but the shouting was toned down a bit. A few modern-day "message" songs make their way into their repertoire as well, including Bob Dylan's "Masters of War." Not quite as cataclysmic as their Vee-Jay material but still essential. —*Rob Bowman*

Make You Happy / 1964 / Epic ✦✦✦
From Riverside, the Staples moved on to Columbia subsidiary Epic in 1964. With Epic, they delved further into the secular realm, hitting the pop charts twice with Pops Staples's plaintive "Why Am (I Treated So Bad)?" and a cover of Stephen Stills's "For What It's Worth." Both are included on this two-disc anthology, as is a stunning side of live performance. Great stuff. —*Rob Bowman*

Freedom Highway / 1965 / CBS ✦✦✦
A reissue of their first great Riverside collection, with "Daddy" Roebuck and the legendary Mavis Staples as leads. The Staples once again mix a positive political message with a dash of religion. —*Kip Lornell*

Soul Folk in Action / 1968 / Stax ✦✦✦
The Staples' debut Stax release included covers of Otis Redding's "(Sittin' On) The Dock of the Bay" and the Band's "The Weight." Steve Cropper produced and the Stax songwriting staff concocted a number of socially concious lyrics, the most notable being "Long Walk to D.C." —*Rob Bowman*

○ **Pray on** / 1968 / Hob ✦✦✦✦
The Staple Singers recorded ten 78s over a four-year period for Chicago's Vee-Jay. These have been reissued countless times in various forms. The Charly CD is simply the most recent. For Vee-Jay the Staples recorded a number of Pops Staples originals as well as radical rearrangements of standards. Pops Staples and Mavis Staples shared the lead singing chores, with Pervis and Cleotha Staples moaning in the background. Superb gospel shouting. —*Rob Bowman*

We'll Get Over / 1970 / Stax ✦✦✦
Their second Stax release was similar to *Soul Folk in Action*. The album's highlight is Randall Stewart's "When Will We Be Paid?" —*Rob Bowman*

The Staple Swingers / 1971 / Stax ✦✦✦
The Staples' first album produced by Al Bell and recorded in Muscle Shoals hit the winning formula. Other changes saw Pervis Staples departing just before the album was recorded and being replaced by sister Yvonne Staples. Everything was now in place for the Staples' golden years. Three songs, "Heavy Makes You Happy," "Love Is Plentiful," and "You've Got to Earn It," all charted. —*Rob Bowman*

Be Altitude: Respect Yourself / 1972 / Stax ✦✦✦
The Staples' finest single album, containing three Top Ten R&B hits, "Respect Yourself," "I'll Take You There," and "This World." The first two also were pop Top 20s, "I'll Take You There" going all the way to #1. —*Rob Bowman*

Be What You Are / 1973 / Stax ✦✦✦
Continuing in the same vein, *Be What You Are* contained three chart hits, the title song, "If You're Ready (Come Go with Me)," and "Touch a Hand, Make a Friend." The Stax songwriters, combined with Mavis Staples's unbelievably seductive vocals, were on a roll. —*Rob Bowman*

City in the Sky / 1974 / Stax ✦✦✦
Stax was teetering on its last legs, but the label still managed to squeeze two final chart hits out of the Staple Singers in the title cut and "My Main Man." A cut below the previous three albums. —*Rob Bowman*

Best of the Staple Singers [Stax] / 1975 / Buddah ✦✦✦
Exactly what the title implies—seven monster soul hits plus three judiciously chosen album cuts. One chart hit, "Oh La De Dah," makes its only album appearance here. This disc is nearly too rich for one sitting. Early-'70s soul simply does not get better. —*Rob Bowman*

Let's Do It Again / 1975 / Curtom ✦✦✦
As Stax neared bankruptcy, the Staples signed with Curtis Mayfield's Curtom label for this soundtrack album. The title track was a #1 hit and "New Orleans" reached #70, returning the Staples to the upper echelons of the charts for the last time. —*Rob Bowman*

● **Chronicle** / 1979 / Stax ✦✦✦✦

Mavis Staples

b. 1940, Chicago, IL
Soul
Born in 1940 in Chicago, most of Mavis Staples's career has been as lead singer for the Staple Singers. She first recorded solo for Stax subsidiary Volt in 1969. Subsequent efforts included a Curtis Mayfield-produced soundtrack on Curtom, a disappointing nod to disco for Warner in 1979, a misguided stab at electro-pop with Holland-Dozier-Holland in 1984, and, most recently, an uneven album for Paisley Park. Staples has a rich contralto voice that has neither the range of Aretha Franklin nor the power of Patti LaBelle. Her otherworldly power comes instead from a masterful command of phrasing and a deep-seated sensuality expressed through timbre manipulation.

Both The Staple Singers and Mavis Staples found fresh audiences stemming from their participation on the CD *Rhythm, Country and Blues*. She also announced in April '94 that she had found a new recording home. —*Rob Bowman*

Mavis Staples / 1969 / Fantasy ✦✦✦
A powerhouse soul belter and wailer, Mavis Staples doesn't have to play second fiddle to anyone, including Aretha Franklin, when it comes to pure, house-rocking, testifying authority. She's seldom gotten a complete album of quality material, but on this 1969 debut, she took half-baked material and made it memorable. "I Have Learned To Do Without You" wasn't a classic, but her vocal made it mighty close. —*Ron Wynn*

○ **Only for the Lonely** / 1970 / Stax ✦✦✦✦
This 21-track anthology collects songs recorded in 1969 and issued on three albums. The roster includes a strong duet with Johnnie Taylor called "That's The Way Love Is" and her signature tune, "A House Is Not A Home." Steve Cropper produced and arranged 11 cuts, with Don Davis producing another eight. Staples's energy, delivery, timing and technique were consistently awesome. Unfortunately, only a few of these songs got much attention outside R&B circles, but their quality shows Staples's greatness as a soul vocalist. —*Ron Wynn*

All the Discomforts of Home / 1978 / Paisley Park ✦✦✦

Time Waits for No One / 1989 / Paisley Park ✦✦✦
Prince took a great interest in Mavis Staples after she provided him rousing background vocals and appeared in the 1990 film *Graffiti Bridge*. He signed her to his label and wrote and produced

some of the tracks on this disc. Unfortunately, it enjoyed little impact sales-wise, although Staples soared, shouted and roared with splendor. But her sound and approach were so soulful that it seemed out of place in the detached setting of urban radio. There were both fiery message tracks and blistering love songs, with Staples' assertive, tender and intense vocals. However, not even Prince's name could break the embargo on acts considered too old-school for modern audiences. —*Ron Wynn*

● **Don't Change Me Now** / 1990 / Ace ✦✦✦✦
Mavis Staples's solo career has been largely undistinguished. *Don't Change Me Now* pulls together most of her better efforts, being a composite of Staples's two Volt solo albums, *Mavis Staples* and *Only for the Lonely*, recorded for Stax subsidiary Volt in 1969 and 1970, respectively. Ace has added a number of originally unreleased tracks to this collection. The liner notes are well written and the sound is fine. —*Rob Bowman*

Edwin Starr

b. Jan. 21, 1942, Nashville, TN
Soul, Motown
One of the best soul-shouters to come from the Motown stable, Starr's style was closer to James Brown than to any of the other male Motown artists. Best known for his 1970 hit "War," he made a brief comeback during the disco craze, but he now tours Europe and plays the oldies circuit. Detroit vocalist Edwin Starr returned to the vocal wars in 1984 when he recorded a tribute album to Marvin Gaye for England's Streetwave label. He had relocated to Britain and moved to Warwickshire. Starr signed with Hippodrome and issued a pair of singles on that label in '85 and '86. He then recorded briefly for Virgin, being produced by the Stock/Aitken/Waterman trio, and then recorded for Motorcity in England and WEA in Germany. Starr also had some songs featured on the Walt Disney release *Mousersize*. —*Rick A. Bueche*

○ **Soulmaster** / 1968 / Motown ✦✦✦✦
Edwin Starr was never able to hit a groove while at Motown. He made some good and a few great tracks, but just couldn't get the steady stream of great material and hit records that made many others at Motown household names. This was arguably his best album; it included both Gordy and Ric Tic singles like "Agent Double-O-Soul." It shows that at times Starr could be as riveting and exciting as any male singer on the soul circuit; he was simply unable to consistently maintain that level. —*Ron Wynn*

Just We Two / 1969 / Motown ✦✦✦

○ **War & Peace** / 1970 / Motown ✦✦✦✦
Edwin Starr went from run-of-the-mill second-level act to hit-maker with this 1970 album, without question his finest. Norman Whitfield gave Starr the chance to cut a song that had been intended for the Temptations. They later did a version of "War," but Starr completely vaporized their rendition to the extent that most people today think he wrote it. Starr was now a celebrity and briefly in Motown's top echelon. The fact that everything else on the album is only fair to average didn't even matter in the scope of things. —*Ron Wynn*

Hell up in Harlem / 1970 / Motown ✦✦✦
Edwin Starr got both creative control and topical material on this soundtrack, turning in strong, confident vocals. Starr was so thrilled at getting room to express himself and call the shots that he soon bolted Motown and signed with 20th Century. Like many 1970s "blaxploitation" flicks, Starr's songs and music were superior to the film. —*Ron Wynn*

Involved / 1971 / Motown ✦✦✦
Although he didn't repeat the enormous successes of 1970, Starr continued to make his presence felt on the soul trail. But the album lacked any strong lead single, and almost dissipated the momentum Starr had built with his previous smash hits. —*Ron Wynn*

Edwin Starr / 1977 / GTO ✦✦
Edwin Starr marked time with this late-'70s release. He hadn't become acclimated to disco, and wasn't really getting first-rate soul and R&B songs either, so he tried to slip between the cracks and revamp himself into a modified supper-club and light soul vocalist. It wasn't fully successful, but wasn't a travesty either. He landed a low chart single, and the album had a few good ballads. It's now history, but at the time, it kept Starr afloat in a tenuous era for soul and R&B vocalists. —*Ron Wynn*

Clean / 1978 / 20th Century ✦✦✦
In the late '70s, Edwin Starr was adjusting to the disco era, like many other soul and R&B vocalists. He hadn't gotten fully comfortable with bustling dance tracks, but this album helped ease the transition. It laid the groundwork for Starr's next LP, in which he returned to prominence and found a way to accomodate the demands of the dance floor without sacrificing his own integrity. —*Ron Wynn*

● **Motown Superstar Series, Vol. 3** / 1980 / Motown ✦✦✦✦
Not every vocalist enjoyed consistent success on Motown. Edwin Starr, despite having a bombastic style and striking voice, only enjoyed a few hits during his Motown tenure. But they were definitive ones, notably "25 Miles" and the landmark "War." Although the Temptations also cut the single, Starr's shattering, angular version was unforgettable. Those and other lesser-known Starr tracks are included on this anthology. It's an interesting release showing that sometimes Starr didn't get first-rate material, and at other times, his own performances weren't that grabbing. —*Ron Wynn*

The Best of Edwin Starr / 1981 / 20th Century ✦✦✦
Starr's best Motown singles were jubilant, energetic, and emancipating in their power and vocal brilliance. He didn't make enough to justify a greatest hits collection or anthology, but if you don't have the singles and want to get them, as well as some decent follow-up singles and album cuts, this will be worth the purchase. —*Ron Wynn*

○ **25 Miles/War and Peace** / Motown ✦✦✦✦
Edwin Starr was never a great album artist, but he could sure pack a punch on the right single. Both of these albums are loaded with filler, but their title cuts are triumphant. Starr managed to obliterate the Temptations' version of "War," his greatest single ever. He was almost that good on "25 Miles," helped by a great arrangement darting in and out at the perfect times, allowing his booming voice to re-enter and punch the lyrics home. Those songs make this a good two-in-one CD, especially if you're a Starr fan. —*Ron Wynn*

Ringo Starr (Richard Starkey)

b. Jul. 7, 1940, Dingle, Liverpool
Pop/Rock
Ringo Starr, born Richard Starkey, was the drummer in the Beatles from 1962 to 1970 and thus one of the most famous musicians of the '60s. Though the least prominent member of the quartet, he distinguished himself as an occasional singer of good-natured material and as an actor. Upon the group's split, Starr went solo with two novelty projects: the first, an album called *Sentimental Journey*, found him covering pre-rock standards, and the second, *Beaucoups of Blues*, was a country music collection.

Starr then scored Top Ten hits with two nonalbum singles, "It Don't Come Easy" in 1971 and "Back off Boogaloo" in 1972. In 1973 he paired with producer Richard Perry and, with assistance from the three other ex-Beatles, made *Ringo*, which featured two #1 hits, "Photograph" and "You're Sixteen." "Oh My My," a Top Ten hit, was also included. Almost as successful was the 1974 follow-up, *Goodnight Vienna*, which featured the hits "Only You" and "No No Song."

Starr continued to release albums through 1981, though with diminishing success. His 1983 album *Old Wave* did not find a U.S. distributor. Starr was also suffering from the excesses of his lifestyle, but by the late '80s he had cleaned up, and in 1989 he toured with his "All-Starr Band." In 1992, he signed to Private Music and released a new studio album, *Time Takes Time.* —*William Ruhlmann*

Sentimental Journey / Apr. 24, 1970 / Capitol ✦✦✦
A trip down memory lane—Ringo does the '40s. —*Jeff Tamarkin*

○ **Beacoups of Blues** / Sep. 28, 1970 / Capitol ✦✦✦✦
More sentimental nostalgia while Ringo decided whether life after Beatles existed. —*Jeff Tamarkin*

● **Ringo** / Nov. 2, 1973 / Capitol ✦✦✦✦
One of the great Beatle solo albums, and the only one to feature a little help from all three ex-friends in the band. Starr's apex. The 1991 CD reissue of *Ringo* contains three bonus tracks, the hit single "It Don't Come Easy," the autobiographical B-side "Early 1970," and "Down and Out." —*Jeff Tamarkin*

Goodnight Vienna / Nov. 18, 1974 / Capitol ✦✦✦
Even with Johns Lennon and Elton, and a couple of bonafide hits, little here holds up. —*Jeff Tamarkin*

○ **Blast from Your Past** / Nov. 20, 1975 / Capitol ✦✦✦✦
A formidable collection, including a couple of the more venerable hits. —*Jeff Tamarkin*

Ringo's Rotogravure / Sep. 27, 1976 / Atlantic ✦✦✦
More guest Beatles and others, but not a single song stands out. —*Jeff Tamarkin*

Ringo the 4th / Sep. 26, 1977 / Atlantic ✦✦
The Beatles' clown ain't nothin' but a joke by this album. —*Jeff Tamarkin*

Bad Boy / Apr. 21, 1978 / Epic ✦✦
Bad album. —*Jeff Tamarkin*

Stop & Smell the Roses / Oct. 27, 1981 / Capitol ✦✦
Another all-Starr cast and another bust. *Stop and Smell the Roses* was reissued on CD with bonus tracks by Right Stuff/Capitol on September 6, 1994. —*Jeff Tamarkin*

Old Wave / Jun. 16, 1983 / Capitol ✦
Deemed so awful his U.S. label wouldn't release it. Wise choice. *Old Wave* finally was released in the U.S. on CD with bonus tracks by Right Stuff/Capitol on September 6, 1994. —*Jeff Tamarkin*

Starr Struck: Best of, Vol. 2 / 1989 / Rhino ✦✦✦
For Beatles loyalists only—leftovers and losers only. —*Jeff Tamarkin*

All-Starr Band / 1990 / Rykodisc ✦✦✦
"Soundtrack" from the 1989 tour, with contributions from not only Starr, but Joe Walsh, Billy Preston, and others. —*Jeff Tamarkin*

○ **Time Takes Time** / May 1992 / Private Music ✦✦✦✦
A sober, reflective Ringo Starr returns, after a near-decade's absence, with a solid set of songs that could have been the work of, well, a Beatle. —*Jeff Tamarkin*

Live From Montreux, Vol. 2 / 1994 / Rykodisc ✦✦

Starship

Group, Pop
After long-time band leader Paul Kantner left Jefferson Starship in 1984, the band dropped the first word in its name. At that point it consisted of singers Mickey Thomas and Grace Slick (b. Oct 30, 1939), guitarist Craig Chaquico (b. 1955), bassist Pete Sears, and drummer Donny Baldwin. This unit immediately scored with the #1 hits "We Built This City" and "Sara" and the million-selling album *Knee Deep in the Hoopla*. Sears had left by the time of the 1987 follow-up, *No Protection*, which featured the #1 "Nothing's Gonna Stop Us Now" and the Top Ten "It's Not Over ('Til It's Over)." Slick then departed, and the remaining trio recruited keyboard player Mark Moragan and bassist Brett Bloomfield for the 1989 album *Love among the Cannibals*, which featured the Top 20 hit "It's Not Enough." In 1991, when RCA released a Starship greatest-hits album, the one new track on the album had been recorded by Thomas and studio musicians, leading to doubt that Starship remained a functioning band. —*William Ruhlmann*

○ **Knee Deep in the Hoopla** / 1985 / Grunt ✦✦✦✦
Keyboard arrangements dominate here, along with Thomas's soaring vocals, with Grace Slick along mostly for counterpoint (though her showcase is the stirring "Rock Myself to Sleep") on the hits "We Built This City" and "Sara." —*William Ruhlmann*

No Protection / 1987 / Grunt ✦✦✦

Love among the Cannibals / 1989 / RCA ✦✦

● **Starship's Greatest Hits: Ten Years of Change** / 1991 / RCA ✦✦✦✦
The Mickey Thomas era, half of it is also the Paul Kantner era, the choices reflecting taste ("Stranger" and "Layin' It on the Line" are included) rather than strict chart rankings (hits like "Be My Lady" and "Tomorrow Doesn't Matter Tonight" are missing). —*William Ruhlmann*

Start

Group, Alternative Pop/Rock
This Lawrence, KS, band produced one of the finer overlooked new wave/power pop/indie albums of the early '80s, *Look Around*. Once described as a hybrid of the Doors and the Jam, their haunting keyboard-based minor melodies mesh with the straightforward rush of mod/power-pop to form a surprisingly successful hybrid. Start were distinguished from the many similar bands of the era by a sense of brooding poignancy, sounding in some respects like a more understated and vulnerable Elvis Costello. Little

known even in the underground, they broke up shortly after their sole LP, their only other studio effort being a rare three-song seven-inch. —*Richie Unterberger*

● **Look Around** / 1983 / Fresh Sounds ✦✦✦✦
"Lies," "Where I Want To Be," and the brooding post-apocalyptic report "My Town" highlight this eight-song mini-LP, which also has a little-known collaboration with Allen Ginsberg, "Little Fish/Big Fish." —*Richie Unterberger*

Status Quo

Group, Hard Rock, Psychedelic
During the late '60s, Status Quo was one of England's best psychedelic bands, creating an indisputable classic with their 1967 debut single, "Pictures of Matchstick Men." After a couple more psychedelic albums that weren't successful, the group was pegged as a has-been. However, Status Quo refashioned themselves as a heavy, hard-rocking boogie band in 1970. The change in direction proved to be a massive success; since the release of *Ma Kelly's Greasy Spoon* in 1970, they have been stars in England. In America, they've only managed one album in the lower reaches of *Billboard's* Top 200 chart in 1976. Status Quo continues to tour and record into the '90s and in England, they are almost considered legendary. —*Stephen Thomas Erlewine*

○ **Picturesque Matchstickable** / 1968 / Pye ✦✦✦✦

Status Quotation / 1969 / Marble Arch ✦✦✦

○ **Ma Kelly's Greasy Spoon** / 1970 / Castle ✦✦✦✦

● **Collection** / 1985 / Pickwick ✦✦✦✦
Featuring everything from their early psychedelic days to the years when they were the kings of simple, heavy guitar boogie, *Collection: Status Quo* is the definitive single-disc collection of this popular British band. —*Stephen Thomas Erlewine*

Steely Dan

Group, Pop/Rock
If most art-rock bands borrowed from the European folk and classical-music traditions for their attempts at heightened hybrids of rock, Steely Dan (formed in 1972) drew inspiration from American jazz, big band, and R&B artists like Charlie Parker, Stan Kenton, and Ray Charles, as well as Brill Building types, to arrive at their sophisticated rock mutations. To say that Steely Dan was a rock band made about as much sense as saying Gentle Giant was a rock band. True, they employed rock instrumentation and various production values, but rock & roll was clearly not the bottom line in their artistic vision. Built around Donald Fagen (b. Jan 10, 1948) and Walter Becker (b. Feb 20, 1950), Steely Dan was more a studio vehicle for their songwriting and arrangement concepts than a real live touring unit. In fact, as Steely Dan shed members, Becker and Fagen merely plugged the holes by incorporating more session sidemen, as opposed to maintaining a band.

Thematically, Becker and Fagen relished exploring the fetishes, twisted logic, and misadventures of society's losers and misfits, with a blackly humorous, cryptic lyric style. Sonically, Steely Dan's albums have earned them raves from practically ever corner of the audiophile world. Their 1973 debut, *Can't Buy a Thrill* (#17), presented a six-piece band (with a handful of sidemen), sounding like a sophisticated alternative to fellow ABC labelmates Three Dog Night on tracks like "Midnight Cruiser," "Kings," and "Dirty Work." That album produced Steely Dan's first two hits, "Do It Again" (#6) and "Reeling in the Years" (#11).

By the time of their fifth album, the 1977 platinum *Aja* (#3), Becker and Fagen had fine-tuned their spare grooves, quirky melodies, and mildly dissonant jazz chordal clusters into a peculiarly seamless pop sound that was embraced by practically every radio format outside of country music. Sophisticated hits like "FM (No Static at All)" (#22), "Deacon Blues" (#19), "Peg" (#11), and "Josie" (#26) were among the many songs that became required soundtracks for every fern bar in the country. Becker and Fagen disengaged Steely Dan indefinitely after the 1981 release *Gaucho* (#9), which included the classy title cut and hits "Hey Nineteen" (#10) and "Time out of Mind" (#22).

Since then Becker has produced other artists, like China Crisis, and Fagen released a successful solo album, *The Nightfly* (#11), which produced a hit with "I.G.Y. (What a Beautiful World)" (#26). Fagen has also recorded "Century's End" for the movie *Bright Lights, Big City*.

Becker produced Fagen's second solo album, 1993's *Ka-*

makiriad; the collaboration led to a Steely Dan reunion, which has resulted in two successful tours but no recordings to date. —*Rick Clark*

You Gotta Walk It Like You Talk It (Or You'll Lose That Beat) / 1971 / Visa ✦✦
This is an eight-track, 31-1/2 minute soundtrack to a low-budget 1970 film that features an embryonic version of Steely Dan—Donald Fagen on keyboards, Walter Becker on bass and guitar, and Denny Dias on guitar and percussion, plus John Discepolo on drums. There are only four actual songs, plus three instrumentals and a reprise of the title track. Yet the playing is suggestive of the sinuous sound that Becker and Fagen would cook up a couple of years hence in the Dan. Nevertheless, it should be sought out by the hard-core fans only; there are no gems here, only some baubles. —*William Ruhlmann*

Can't Buy a Thrill / 1972 / MCA ✦✦✦
The Steely Dan that appeared on this debut was basically a sophisticated perversion of the sound forged by fellow-ABC-label-mates Three Dog Night. Check out "Dirty Work," "Kings," and "Midnight Cruiser," and say that it isn't true. It's certainly one of the best debuts by any group to emerge from the '70s. *Can't Buy a Thrill* also produced two classic hits with the dirty Latin-influenced groove of "Do It Again" and the edgy shuffle "Reelin' in the Years." —*Rick Clark*

☆ **Countdown to Ecstasy** / 1973 / MCA ✦✦✦✦✦
Compared to their debut, *Countdown to Ecstasy* was a commercial failure (rocketing up and down the charts in three weeks) once it became apparent that this wasn't *Reelin' in the Years—Part II*. The melodies and arrangements were more subtle and the lyrics a little more impenetrable. Nevertheless, this is the album that initially hooked many hardcore Dan fans. "Show Biz Kids" and "My Old School" became moderate hits. Other standouts include the jazzy rocker "Bodhisattva" and "King of the World." —*Rick Clark*

☆ **Pretzel Logic** / 1974 / MCA ✦✦✦✦✦
On *Pretzel Logic* Steely Dan most successfully synthesized their love for jazz into their dense pop/rock sound. The grooves were funky ("Night by Night," "Monkey in Your Soul") and the arrangements sophisticated ("Parker's Band," "Through with Buzz"). "Rikki Don't Lose That Number," featuring an incredibly lyrical guitar solo by Jeff Baxter, became Dan's biggest hit at number four. The title track and "Any Major Dude Will Tell You" are more highlights. —*Rick Clark*

☆ **Katy Lied** / 1975 / MCA ✦✦✦✦
With its appealing melodies and oddball themes, this was a strong successor to *Pretzel Logic*. By this time, Steely Dan was Becker and Fagen, aided by an army of Los Angeles's "A"-list session stars—Hugh McCracken, Larry Carlton, Jeff Porcaro, Hal Blaine, Michael McDonald, and more. Sonically, *Katy Lied*'s super-clean mix pointed the way to the elegantly shrink-wrapped sound of their later work. Among the standout tracks are "Black Friday," "Daddy Don't Live in That New York City No More," "Chain Lightning," and "Throw Back the Little Ones," featuring an expressive closing piano improvization by Michael Omartian. —*Rick Clark*

The Royal Scam / 1976 / MCA ✦✦✦
With *The Royal Scam*, Steely Dan delivered a rather cluttered, abrasive-sounding collection of tracks, which were further undermined by weaker melodies. If fusion ever found a home in disco, "Kid Charlemagne" was it. Smugly humorous tracks like "Haitian Divorce," "Green Earrings," and the fetish sendup, "The Fez," are some of *Scam*'s highlights. —*Rick Clark*

○ **Aja** / 1977 / MCA ✦✦✦✦
During the late '70s, *Aja* became required soundtrack music for fern bars throughout the country whose owners desired an upscale ambience. This was due to precision-crafted jazz-fusion pop/rock tracks like "Deacon Blues," "Josie," "Peg," and the title track, which featured a wonderfully musical drum solo by Steve Gadd. —*Rick Clark*

Gaucho / 1980 / MCA ✦✦✦
Three years after *Aja*, Becker and Fagen returned with the obsessively streamlined *Gaucho*. This impeccably recorded set contained two fine hits, "Hey Nineteen" and "Time out of Mind." "Babylon Sisters" was another memorable highlight, while the title track sported one of the most entrancingly convoluted melodies of their career. However, "Glamour Profession," with its sophisticated disco feel, seemed tailor-made for the perpetual happy hour. —*Rick Clark*

○ **Gold** / 1982 / MCA ✦✦✦✦
Now expanded past its original length, this companion to *Decade* features newly remastered versions of tracks like "FM (No Static at All)," Donald Fagen's "Century's End," and previously unreleased live work. —*Rick Clark*

★ **A Decade of Steely Dan** / 1985 / MCA ✦✦✦✦✦
This collection features many of Dan's high spots, but it's hardly definitive. Nevertheless, this is the place to go if you are only budgeting for a single disc. —*Cub Koda*

Citizen Steely Dan / 1993 / MCA ✦✦✦
Collecting all of Steely Dan's albums in chronological order, plus all of their two or three B-sides and one demo in a four-CD box, *Citizen Steely Dan* is only worthwhile for the fan replacing their old records. The remastering on the box is exactly the same as the newly upgraded CDs, and everything but the demo is available on other discs. —*Stephen Thomas Erlewine*

Steppenwolf

Group, Hard Rock, Psychedelic
Led by John Kay (b. Joachim Krauledat, Apr 12, 1944), Steppenwolf's blazing biker anthem "Born to Be Wild" roared out of speakers everywhere in the fiery summer of 1968, John Kay's threatening rasp sounding a mesmerizing call to arms to the counterculture movement rapidly sprouting up nationwide. German immigrant Kay got his professional start in a bluesy Toronto band called Sparrow, recording for Columbia in 1966. After Sparrow disbanded, Kay relocated to the West Coast and formed Steppenwolf, named after the Herman Hesse novel. "Born to Be Wild," their third single on ABC-Dunhill, was immortalized on the soundtrack of Dennis Hopper's underground film classic *Easy Rider*. The song's reference to "heavy metal thunder" finally gave an assignable name to an emerging genre. Steppenwolf's second monster hit that year, the psychedelic "Magic Carpet Ride," and the followups "Rock Me," "Move Over," and "Hey Lawdy Mama" further established the band's credibility on the hard-rock circuit. By the early '70s, Steppenwolf ran out of steam and disbanded. Kay continued to record solo, as other members put together ersatz versions of the band for touring purposes. During the mid '80s Kay re-formed his own version of Steppenwolf, grinding out his hits (and some new songs) at oldies shows. Nevertheless, they'll be remembered for generations to come for creating one of the ultimate gas'n'go rock anthems of all time. —*Bill Dahl & Cub Koda*

Early Steppenwolf / 1969 / MCA ✦✦✦
Early live recordings made when the band was still called "Sparrow," working more out of a blues-band mold; features a surprisingly great version of Junior Wells's "Messin' with the Kid." —*Cub Koda*

● **16 Greatest Hits** / 1973 / MCA ✦✦✦✦
Just what the name implies; "Born to Be Wild," "Magic Carpet Ride," "The Pusher," and "Rock Me" are just some of the highlights. Everything you're going to want to hear in one neat little package. —*Cub Koda*

○ **Born to Be Wild: A Retrospective** / 1991 / MCA ✦✦✦✦
A double-disc collection of Steppenwolf's lengthy career, *Born To Be Wild: A Retrospective* includes more music than anyone but hardcore fans need, but the song selection and packaging are superb, making it essential for those devoted fans. —*Stephen Thomas Erlewine*

Stereolab

Group, Alternative Pop/Rock, Experimental
One of the most distinctive bands making music today, Stereolab formed when songwriter/guitarist/keyboardist Tim Gane dissolved his previous group McCarthy and met songwriter/vocalist Laetitia Sadier. Together, along with Mary Hanson (vocals, moog), Duncan Brown (bass), Andy Ramsay (drums) and Sean O'Hagan (keyboards) the band makes music that alternates between swirling and ethereal and harsh and atonal; the title of one of their songs, "John Cage Bubblegum," sums up their aesthetic. The mix of heavy, droning keyboards, Sadier's and Hanson's mellifluous vocals and the group's socialist leanings make for some cutting-edge space age bachelor pad music. —*Heather Phares*

Switched On / 1992 / Slumberland ✦✦✦
The Groop Played "Space Age Batchelor Pad Music" is a mini-album, comprised mainly of instrumentals, including two tracks consisting of nothing but rippling keyboards. —*Stephen Thomas Erlewine*

○ **Peng!** / 1992 / ✦✦✦✦
Peng! was essentially a refinement of *Switched On*, containing smoother songs and more flowing soundscapes, which display a greater melodic invention than most of the material on *Switched On*. —*Stephen Thomas Erlewine*

● **Transient Random-Noise Bursts with Announcements** / 1993 / Elektra ✦✦✦✦

Stereolab is about sound, not songs, and their major-label debut, *Transient Random Noise Bursts With Announcements*, has some of the best entrancing, ambient dance drones around. You won't notice that some tracks run over twenty minutes long, because the guitar-keyboard grooves are so hypnotizing and unique. —*Stephen Thomas Erlewine*

The Groop Played "Space Age Batchelor Pad Music" / 1993 / Too Pure/American ✦✦✦

○ **Mars Audiac Quintet** / 1994 / Elektra ✦✦✦✦
Without abandoning their trademark mesmerizing minimalistic aural explorations, Stereolab tightens up their songwriting on *Mars Audiac Quintet*, their second major-label album. While the record isn't as exciting as *Transient Random Noise Bursts*, it is nearly as impressive, especially since the band is able to boil their sound down to a genuine pop single, "Ping Pong." —*Stephen Thomas Erlewine*

○ **Music For the Amorphous Body Center** / Apr. 1995 / ✦✦✦✦
Recorded especially for an art exhibit, *Music for the Amorphous Body Center* expands on Stereolab's trademark guitar-and-organ drone by adding strings. With the subtle, lush strings as support, the group's easy listening and '60s pop inclinations become more pronounced, making the overlapping textures of "Pop Quiz" swirl magnificently. Such small adjustments make the EP quite wonderful; it proves that there are hidden variations in Stereolab's music that don't quite come to the forefront immediately. —*Stephen Thomas Erlewine*

Stetsasonic

Group, Rap
This Brooklyn-based rap group established a unique sound by using real instruments in addition to the twin-turntable techniques of Prince Paul and Wise. Prince Paul has become a formidable producer, working with the likes of 3rd Bass, De La Soul, and Queen Latifah, among others. —*John Floyd*

On Fire / 1986 / Tommy Boy ✦✦✦
There weren't many bands utilizing a hip-hop format in the mid-'80s, making Stetsasonic quite unique on the pop front in 1986. While their subject matter was invariably light and their raps now hopelessly tame and effete, they were ground-breaking at the time and retain a certain charm. —*Ron Wynn*

● **In Full Gear** / 1988 / Tommy Boy ✦✦✦✦
They're not "the world's only hip-hop band" anymore, but this seven-piece group (real drums even!) paved the way. Their second disc documents their innovative best, culminating in the anthemic "Talkin' All That Jazz." —*John Floyd*

Blood, Sweat & No Tears / 1991 / Tommy Boy ✦✦✦

Cat Stevens (Steve Georgiou)

b. Jul. 21, 1947, London
Singer-Songwriter
Cat Stevens (born Steve Georgiou in London) was the son of a Greek father and a Swedish mother. Stevens became interested in folk and rock & roll in his teens and scored his first U.K. hit, "I Love My Dog," before he turned 20. Stevens reached the singles charts four more times, getting to #2 with "Matthew and Son" and releasing the similarly titled Top Ten album before he contracted tuberculosis in 1968 and was forced to retire from music. He re-emerged with a new, mature style in 1970 with the album *Mona Bone Jakon* and hit the U.K. Top Ten with "Lady D'Arbanville." But it was his late 1970 follow-up, *Tea for the Tillerman*, that made him an international success. The album hit the Top Ten and went gold in the U.S., producing the hit "Wild World." *Teaser and the Firecat*, released in 1971, did even better, including the hits "Peace Train" and "Morning Has Broken." Stevens became so successful as an albums artist that, even though his next couple of albums did not generate big hit singles, they were still big sellers: *Catch*

Bull at Four (1972) went to #1 and *Foreigner* (1973) reached #3. Stevens's 1974 album *Buddha and the Chocolate Box*, which included the #10 hit "Oh Very Young," reached #2. Stevens's records were gradually less successful during the second half of the '70s. In 1979, he became a Muslim, adopted the name Yusef Islam, and retired from music. He was not heard from for another ten years, until he shocked admirers at the end of the '80s by supporting the death sentence ordered by the Ayatollah Khomeini against novelist Salman Rushdie for writing the book *The Satanic Verses*. Some "classic rock" radio stations discontinued playing him as a result, though his music remains popular. —*William Ruhlmann*

Matthew & Son / 1967 / Deram ✦✦✦
Released in the late winter of 1967, 19-year-old Cat Stevens's debut album, *Matthew & Son*, contained his breakthrough U.K. hits "I Love My Dog" (#28) and the title song (#2), and spawned a third, "I'm Gonna Get Me A Gun" (#6). (The Tremeloes took a cover of the album's "Here Comes My Baby" to U.K. #4.) While it is a precocious effort (Stevens wrote all the songs) and the material is undeniably catchy, it's also wildly overproduced, with gimmicky arrangements typical of the mid-'60s British pop sound around the time of *Sgt. Pepper*. This is especially noticeable, heard in the context of Stevens' later, less-produced, more meaningful efforts. —*William Ruhlmann*

New Masters / 1967 / Deram ✦✦
Cat Stevens's first career proved short-lived as this, his second album, failed to chart in the U.K. when it was released at the end of 1967. The album contained Stevens's fifth—and lowest—charting single, "Kitty" (#47), but in retrospect is best remembered for "The First Cut Is The Deepest," a #18 U.K. hit for P.P. Arnold prior to the album's release and since then a hit for Rod Stewart. —*William Ruhlmann*

World of Cat Stevens / 1970 / Decca ✦✦

Mona Bone Jakon / Jul. 1970 / A&M ✦✦✦
Mona Bone Jakon was Stevens's first effort for A&M Records, unveiling him as a sensitive singer/songwriter, with gentle tracks like "Trouble," "Katmandu," "Lady D'Arbanville," "Lily White," and "I Wish I Wish." Fans of *Teaser and the Firecat* or *Tea for the Tillerman* should check this one out. —*Rick Clark*

☆ **Tea for the Tillerman** / Nov. 1970 / A&M ✦✦✦✦✦
Tea for the Tillerman is like a musical collection of children's tales by Stevens. The delicacy of the arrangements, Paul Samwell-Smith's brilliant otherworldly production, and Stevens's entrancing melodies and images easily make this his best work. "Wild World" was a huge hit, but emotive tracks like "Father and Son," "Where Do the Children Play?," and the haunting "Into White" and "Sad Lisa" make this a must-own for fans of singer/songwriter pop. —*Rick Clark*

○ **Teaser & the Firecat** / Oct. 1971 / A&M ✦✦✦✦
The followup to *Tea for the Tillerman* was almost as impressive. Sonically, less energy was put into creating empty real soundscapes, with more emphasis on tighter song constructions and immediacy. The result paid off with three international hits, "Peace Train," "Moonshadow," and "Morning has Broken." Other highlights included "Tuesday's Dead," "The Wind," "Bitter Blue," and "Ruby Love." After *Tea for the Tillerman*, this is the one to get. —*Rick Clark*

Very Young & Early Songs / 1972 / Deram ✦✦

○ **Catch Bull at Four** / Oct. 1972 / A&M ✦✦✦✦
Catch Bull at Four was Stevens's commercial peak, holding the #1 spot for three weeks. Much of the reason for this was probably public anticipation that this would be as smoothly appealing as his previous two outings. With this album, Stevens's melodies became more ornate and his delivery became a little gruffer. Overall, it is one of his better albums with "Eighteenth Avenue," "Sitting," and "Can't Keep It In" as highlights. —*Rick Clark*

Foreigner / Aug. 1973 / A&M ✦✦

Buddha & the Chocolate Box / Apr. 1974 / A&M ✦✦✦
At the time of its release, this was heralded as Stevens' best effort since *Tea*....It wasn't. It did have a few good tunes, particularly "Oh Very Young" and "Ready," both hits. —*Rick Clark*

● **Greatest Hits** / Jun. 1975 / A&M ✦✦✦✦
This is the most popular best-of collection. It has his biggest hits and a couple of important album tracks. The CD version is just a straight reissue of the original LP release, therefore utilizing only about half of the time available on disc. —*Rick Clark*

Numbers / Nov. 1975 / A&M ✦✦✦

Izitso / May 1977 / A&M ✦✦

Back to Earth / 1978 / A&M ✦

Cat's Cradle / 1978 / London ✦✦

○ **Footsteps in the Dark: Greatest Hits, Vol. 2** / 1984 / A&M ✦✦✦✦
This is a spotty attempt to fill the holes left open from the first *Greatest Hits* collection. Key tracks from *Mona Bone Jakon* and *Harold & Maude* are here. Unfortunately, the remastering on this disc is less than desirable. —*Rick Clark*

○ **Classics, Vol. 24** / 1987 / A&M ✦✦✦✦
After several collections, there has yet to be a definitive representation of Stevens's work. Half of his Top 40 hits (like "Wild World," "Another Saturday Night," "Two Fine People," "The Hurt," and "Ready") are missing. On the plus side, some nice album cuts like "The Wind" and "18th Avenue" and highlights from the movie *Harold & Maude* are here. —*Rick Clark*

Al Stewart

b. Sep. 5, 1945
Singer-Songwriter, Folk-Rock
Al Stewart has made a career out of wistful pop odes obsessed with time and historical events, all delivered with a slightly cosmic twist. During the early and mid-'60s, Stewart embraced the English folk scene and released the albums *Bedsitter Images* and *Love Chronicles*, which featured the guitar work of then-future Led Zeppelinite Jimmy Page. Stewart made his first dent on the U.S. charts with *Past, Present & Future* (#133), an album inspired by the works of the ancient soothsayer Nostradamus. His followup, *Modern Times*, did even better, reaching #30, but it was the Alan Parsons-produced *Year of the Cat* (#5) that catapulted Stewart into brief stardom. The title track went #8 and "On the Border" rode to #42. Stewart changed labels to Clive Davis's Arista in 1978, releasing *Time Passages* (#10), also produced by Parsons. At #7, the title cut became the highest charting hit of Stewart's career. By this time, Stewart's sound possessed a sweeping airy quality brought on in part by his light voice and Parsons's cinematic production style. "Song on the Radio" (#29) and "Midnight Rocks" (#24) were Stewart's remaining hits. Stewart continues to play live and record. —*Rick Clark*

Bedsitter Images / 1967 / CBS ✦✦
Al Stewart's debut album was an intriguing but hesitant effort, filled with searching acoustic love songs laced with strings. —*Daevid Jehnzen*

Love Chronicles / 1969 / Epic ✦✦✦
It's notable for the 18-minute coming-of-age title cut, which caused a stir at the time for its use of the word "f*cking." Jimmy Page is featured on guitar. —*Rick Clark*

Zero She Flies / 1970 / CBS ✦✦✦
On his third album, *Zero She Flies*, Al Stewart continued in a familiar gentle, folk-based singer/songwriter vein. The album's key track was "Manuscript," one of Stewart's first historical songs. —*Daevid Jehnzen*

Orange / 1972 / Beat Goes On ✦✦✦
Orange was the last album Al Stewart recorded where the love songs were prominent, and it was one of his most lovely records. —*Daevid Jehnzen*

Past, Present & Future / 1973 / Arista ✦✦✦
On *Past, Present & Future*, Al Stewart began to reach his artistic fruition, as he crafted a lush, winding song cycle about the writings of Nostradamus, highlighted by the majestic "Nostradamus." —*Daevid Jehnzen*

○ **Modern Times** / 1975 / Rhino ✦✦✦✦
Stewart's airy (sometimes sentimental) obsessions with the passage of time take on a special resonance on this outing. Highlights include "Carol," "Apple Cider Re-Constitution," "Dark and Rolling Sea," and "The Modern Times." —*Rick Clark*

○ **Year of the Cat** / 1976 / Arista ✦✦✦✦
Stewart's calm delivery gives his songs a reserved, tasteful sense of understatement, especially on the title track, one of those "mysterious woman" songs, which captivated listeners and turned the album into a million-seller. —*William Ruhlmann*

○ **Time Passages** / 1978 / Arista ✦✦✦✦
A return to Stewart's historical themes lyrically, though it's still the overall smoothness of his music that connected with another million listeners. —*William Ruhlmann*

24 Carrots / 1980 / Razor & Tie ✦✦✦
One of his most underrated albums, *24 Carrots* features some of Al Stewart's finest songs about historical events, all set to a lush sonic backdrop. —*Daevid Jehnzen*

Live Indian Summer / 1981 / Arista ✦✦
Comprised of a professional but uninspiring live set and a handful of new studio tracks, *Live Indian Summer* is one of Al Stewart's lesser efforts. —*Daevid Jehnzen*

Russians & Americans / 1984 / Passport ✦✦
Out of all of Al Stewart's grandly ambitious albums, *Russians & Americans* is among the most problematic, since he takes an actual political position, which tends to hurt the flow of the music. —*Daevid Jehnzen*

● **The Best of Al Stewart** / 1988 / Arista ✦✦✦✦
All of Al Stewart's stateside hits are available here, as well as most of the best cuts from the hit albums *Year of the Cat* and *Time Passages*. Not a comprehensive overview of his career, it's still the best sampler available. —*Rick Clark*

Last Days of the Century / 1988 / Enigma ✦✦
Al Stewart was prevented from releasing new music for four years in the mid-'80s, and when he did return, it was with the muddled *Last Days of the Century*, which failed to capture the excitement of his earlier work. —*Daevid Jehnzen*

Rhymes in Rooms / 1992 / Mesa Blue Moon ✦✦✦
A pleasant unplugged set featuring most of Al Stewart's greatest hits, *Rhymes in Rooms* is a delight for devoted fans. —*Daevid Jehnzen*

Famous Last Words / 1993 / Mesa ✦✦✦

To Whom It May Concern / 1993 / EMI ✦✦✦

Between the Wars / 1995 / Mesa ✦✦

Billy Stewart

b. Mar. 24, 1937, Washington, DC, **d.** Jan. 17, 1970
Soul
Billy Stewart was one of the most distinctive vocal stylists of the '60s. His stuttering, word-doubling attack owed more to jazz scat singing than to the gospel influences of many of his peers. A jovial, rotund piano player who toured with Bo Diddley and, through him, gained entry to Chess Records, Stewart scored biggest in 1966 with a smash Top Ten version of George Gershwin and Dubose Heyward's "Summertime," an atypically (for Chess) big-band arrangement (featuring Earth, Wind & Fire's Maurice White on drums) with Stewart in a vocal tour de force, masterfully scatting around, stuttering through, and generally turning the melody inside out. It was not your typical '60s soul music, but Stewart's success opened the door for other jazz-influenced singers like Georgie Fame to gain a place on radio playlists of the day. Stewart died tragically at age 33 in a 1970 auto accident. —*Christine Ohlman*

○ **I Do Love You** / 1965 / Chess ✦✦✦✦
Billy Stewart's greatest album and song were both contained on this fine LP from the mid-'60s. "I Do Love You" was that rare anguished testimonial that never became vapid, sappy, or overly sentimental, and was compelling and captivating throughout Stewart's marvelous leads and the piercing harmonies. The album also contained other gems like "Fat Boy," "Reap What You Sow," and "Sitting In The Park." Maybe someday this album will be reissued intact, after Stewart's hits have finally been recycled to death. —*Ron Wynn*

○ **Unbelievable** / 1966 / Chess ✦✦✦✦
The second legitimate Billy Stewart album that wasn't a later rehash or repackaged collection. It was issued in 1966 and contained some magnificent numbers, among them the great "Summertime," "Foggy Day," "Moon River," and "Misty." Chess kept priming the pump after Stewart's tragic death, repeatedly putting these songs onto different anthologies and collections. They were sung with beauty, dignity, and passion, and should be heard in the manner they were released. —*Ron Wynn*

Teaches Old Standards New Tricks / 1967 / Chess ✦✦✦
This is merely a rehash of the same material featured on *Old Standards, New Tricks*, but Stewart's singing certainly makes it worthwhile. It's been long gone and probably isn't destined to return. —*Ron Wynn*

○ **Billy Stewart Remembered** / 1970 / Chess ✦✦✦✦
When Billy Stewart's car plunged into a river in 1970, soul music lost a legendary stylist. He didn't enjoy sustained commercial success, but possessed one of the genre's signature voices. Unfortunately, shortly after his death and ever since, his songs have been repeatedly savaged, recycled, repackaged, and reissued. This was the first of a series of collections, some good, some horrid. This has long since vanished, so it's almost irrelevant, but it was a decent compilation of his material. —*Ron Wynn*

His Greatest Hits / 1975 / Chess ✦✦✦
Yet another Stewart compilation. If you can't find any of the original albums (and you can't outside of a specialty store or collector's auction), then grab the MCA anthology. It's the best-mastered and most comprehensive, although even it could be improved. Either this or the '80s compilation *His Greatest Sides* will suffice for a hits package. —*Ron Wynn*

● **One More Time: The Chess Years** / 1990 / Chess ✦✦✦✦
Although a minor soul star of the '60s, Stewart possessed one of the most unique and sweetest styles. His hits "Summertime," "I Do Love You," and "Sitting in the Park" are classics of the era. —*Jeff Tamarkin*

The Greatest Sides / Chess ✦✦✦
Billy Stewart was a marvelous 1960s soul vocalist, whose stuttering, exploding delivery and majestic sound were beloved by soul junkies, but seldom broke through to the mainstream. This is a fine single-album set of some of Stewart's strongest material, including one of the better versions of "I Do Love You." It was issued when Sugar Hill owned Chess and has since been supplanted by the MCA Stewart anthology. But any Stewart is worth getting, so if you find it, jump on it right away. —*Ron Wynn*

○ **Old Standards, New Tricks** / Chess ✦✦✦✦
Billy Stewart sang more than pleading, anguished love ballads. He was a good crooner in the classic supper club/cabaret fashion, and that was the focus of this collection of jazz-based pop and pre-rock numbers done by Stewart at various points in the 1960s. The tour-de-force was "Summertime," a stuttering, rumbling improvisation with him stretching out in the middle and concluding with a flourish. This has been out-of-print for quite a while. —*Ron Wynn*

Dave Stewart & Spiritual Cowboys

b. Sep. 9, 1952
Pop/Rock

Dave Stewart was the musical mastermind of Eurythmics, but on his solo recordings with the Spiritual Cowboys, he made more atmospheric, guitar-based albums that became minor hits in the U.K. in the early '90s. Stewart also has written several soundtracks and produced many artists, including Bob Dylan and Mick Jagger. —*Stephen Thomas Erlewine*

Lily Was Here / 1989 / Anxious ✦✦✦
The soundtrack to a fairly unknown film, *Lily Was Here* was Dave Stewart's first solo effort. It's an atmospheric, subdued effort, highlighted by a revamped "Here Comes the Rain Again," with Annie Lennox on lead vocals, and a handful of tracks featuring saxophonist Candy Dulfer. —*Sara Sytsma*

● **Dave Stewart & Spiritual Cowboys** / 1990 / Arista ✦✦✦✦
Dave Stewart's first album with the Spiritual Cowboys is a fine collection of atmospheric pop/rock. —*AMG*

Honest / 1991 / Arista ✦✦✦
Dave Stewart's second album with the Spiritualized Cowboys expanded the musical ideas of their debut, although it was slightly less focused and pop-oriented than its predecessor. —*Sara Sytsma*

Greetings from the Gutter / 1995 / East West ✦✦✦
Greetings from the Gutter is Dave Stewart's first official solo album and it's his most mainstream album to date, featuring several concise pop songs, as well as a handful of more complex, involved pieces. —*Sara Sytsma*

Rod Stewart

b. Jan. 10, 1945, London, England
Rock & Roll, Pop/Rock

Rod Stewart may have began his career as a respected singer, yet he lost much of that respect as he got older. While he has recorded some terrible albums—and he would admit that freely—Stewart was once rock & roll's best interpretive singer, as well as an accomplished songwriter, creating a raw combination of folk, rock,

blues and country that sounded like no other folk-rock or country-rock. Instead of finding the folk in rock, he found how folk rocked like hell on its own. After he became successful, he began to lose the rootsier elements of his music, yet he remained a superb singer. Soon, Stewart abandoned the thought of blazing his own artistic path, choosing to follow pop trends.

Stewart began his musical career after spending some time as an apprentice with the Brentford Football Club, touring Europe with folksinger Wizz Jones in the early '60s; during this time he was deported from Spain for vagrancy. When he returned to England in 1963, he joined the Birmingham-based R&B group Jimmy Powell and the Five Dimensions, as a vocalist and harmonica player. The band toured the U.K. and recorded one single for Pye Records, which featured Stewart on blues harp. After moving back to London, he joined Long John Baldry's band, the Hoochie Coochie Men. The group recorded a single in 1964, "Good Morning Little Schoolgirl," which failed to chart and soon afterward the group evolved into Steampacket, featuring Stewart, Baldry, Brian Auger, Julie Driscoll, Mickey Waller, and Rick Brown.

During the summer of 1965, the group supported the Rolling Stones and the Walker Brothers on a U.K. tour, as well as recording an album that remained unreleased until 1970. That fall, Stewart appeared in a television documentary called *Rod the Mod*, which chronicled the life of a typical mod in London. Early in 1966, Steampacket disbanded and Stewart became a member of the blues-rock combo Shotgun Express; other members of the group included vocalist Beryl Marsden, guitarist Peter Green, keyboardist Peter Bardens, bassist Dave Ambrose, and drummer Mick Fleetwood. Shotgun Express released one single that Fall before splitting. Rod Stewart then joined the Jeff Beck Group at the end of 1966.

With the Jeff Beck Group, Rod Stewart began his climb to stardom. Stewart and the former Yardbird guitarist pioneered the heavy blues-rock team of a virtuoso guitarist and a dynamic, sexy lead vocalist which became the standard blueprint for heavy metal. *Truth*, the band's debut album, was released in the fall of 1968, becoming a hit in both America and Britain. The Jeff Beck Group toured both countries several times in 1968 and 1969, gaining a dedicated following. In the summer of 1969, they released their second album, *Beck-Ola*, which became another hit record in both the U.S. and U.K. However, the group fell apart in the fall.

After rejecting an offer to join the American rock group Cactus, Stewart and Jeff Beck Group bassist Ron Wood joined the Small Faces, replacing the departed vocalist/guitarist Steve Marriott. With Wood switching over to guitar, the group shortened their name to the Faces and recorded their debut album, *First Step*. During this time, Stewart had also signed a solo contract, releasing his first album, *An Old Raincoat Won't Let You Down* (re-titled *The Rod Stewart Album* for its American release), at the end of 1969; the record failed to chart in the U.K., yet it made it to number 139 on the U.S. charts. On the album, Stewart's folk roots meshed with his R&B and rock influences, creating a distinctive, stripped-down acoustic-based rock & roll that signalled he was a creative force in his own right.

The Faces released *First Step* in the spring of 1970. The album was a departure both from the R&B/pop direction of the Small Faces and the heavy blues of the Jeff Beck Group; instead, the group became a boisterous, boozy and sloppy Stones-inspired rock & roll band. The album fared better in the U.K. than it did in the U.S., yet the group built a devoted following on both continents with their wreckless, messy live shows. Stewart released his second solo album, *Gasoline Alley*, in the fall of 1970, supporting it with an American tour.

1971 proved to be the pivotal year in Stewart's career. At the beginning of the year, the Faces' released their second album, *Long Player*, which became a bigger hit than *First Step*, yet his third solo album, *Every Picture Tells a Story*, made Rod Stewart a household name, reaching number one in both America and Britain. "Reason to Believe" was the first single from the album, becoming a minor hit in both the countries, but when DJs began playing the B-side, "Maggie May," the single became a number one hit in both the U.K. and U.S. for five weeks in September. The Faces released their third album, *A Nod Is as Good as a Wink...To a Blind Horse*, a couple of months later. Thanks to the success of *Every Picture Tells a Story*, the album was a Top Ten hit in both countries; it also launched the single "Stay with Me," which became the band's only Top 40 hit in the U.S.

The following year, the Faces began a lengthy spring tour. During the tour, tensions grew within the band as Stewart's solo career increased in popularity. That summer, Stewart released his fourth solo album, *Never a Dull Moment*, which nearly equalled the success of *Every Picture Tells a Story*, peaking at number two in the U.S. and number one in the U.K. In the spring of 1973, the Faces released their final album, *Ooh La La*. Stewart expressed his disdain for the record in the press, yet it hit number one in the U.K. and number 21 in the U.S. After releasing the "Pool Hall Richard" single in the beginning of 1974, the band went on tour; it would prove to be their last. Stewart released *Smiler* in the fall of 1975. *Smiler* followed the same formula as his previous four albums—and it also became a hit—yet it showed signs that the formula was wearing thin. In March of 1975, he began a love affair with Swedish actress Britt Ekland; the romance, along with a bitter fight with U.K. tax collectors, prompted him to apply for U.S. citizenship. *Atlantic Crossing*, released in the summer of 1975, made the singer's relocation explicit—the cover was an illustration of Stewart literally crossing the Atlantic Ocean. Recorded with producer Tom Dowd and the Muscle Shoals rhythm section, the album removed much of the singer's folk roots and accentuated his pop appeal. At the end of the year, Stewart left the Faces and the band finally called it quits.

Recorded in Los Angeles with a group of studio musicians, 1976's *A Night on the Town* continued Stewart's move to slicker pop territory and proved quite successful, becoming his first platinum album; it featured the hit single "Tonight's the Night," which was number one in the U.S. for eight weeks. *Foot Loose and Fancy Free*, released the following year, followed the same artistic pattern as *A Night on the Town* while surpassing its commercial performance, selling over three million copies. Stewart incorporated some disco to his musical formula for 1978's *Blondes Have More Fun*. Supported by the number one single "Da Ya Think I'm Sexy?," the record became Stewart's first number one album since *Every Picture Tells a Story*, selling over four million records. By this time, Stewart was notorious for his jet-set lifestyle, particularly the series of actresses and models he dated.

With 1981's *Tonight I'm Yours*, Stewart began adding elements of new wave and synth-pop to his formula, resulting in another platinum album. Soon afterward, his career hit a slump—his next four albums sounded forced and he only scored three Top Ten hits between 1982 and 1988; out of those four albums, only 1983's *Camouflage* went gold. Stewart rebounded with 1988's *Out of Order*, recorded with Duran Duran's Andy Taylor and Chic's Bernard Edwards. His version of Tom Waits's "Downtown Train," taken from the 1989 four-disc box set *Storyteller*, became his biggest hit since "Da Ya Think I'm Sexy?" *Vagabond Heart* (1991) reflected a more mature and reflective Rod Stewart and continued his comeback streak. Stewart reunited with Ron Wood to record an *MTV Unplugged* concert in 1993; the accompanying album launched the Top Ten hit single, "Have I Told You Lately." *Unplugged* also returned Stewart to a more acoustic-based sound, reminiscent of his early '70s albums. On his 1995 album, *A Spanner in the Works*, the singer explored a more polished version of this sound, scoring another hit with Tom Petty's "Leave Virginia Alone." *—Stephen Thomas Erlewine*

○ **The Rod Stewart Album** / 1969 / Mercury ✦✦✦✦
This interesting, if spotty, hodgepodge of delicate folk ballads and blazing rave-ups is highlighted by "An Old Overcoat Won't Ever Let You Down." *—John Floyd*

☆ **Gasoline Alley** / 1970 / Mercury ✦✦✦✦✦
A full-blown folk outing, it conjures the despair and humor of Woody Guthrie and, on occasion, the wildcat appeal of rockabilly. *—John Floyd*

★ **Every Picture Tells a Story** / 1971 / Mercury ✦✦✦✦✦
Achieving the same variety as the debut, Stewart's title cut and "Maggie May," plus his covers of vintage Temptations, Arthur Crudup, and Tim Hardin material, flaunt the versatility and savvy of his vision. A grand statement by a major player. *—John Floyd*

☆ **Never a Dull Moment** / 1972 / Mercury ✦✦✦✦✦
This repeats the formula of *Every Picture Tells a Story*, but the originals, with the exception of the beautiful "Italian Girls," are just slightly below par. Still worthwhile though. *—John Floyd*

Smiler / 1974 / Mercury ✦✦
Rod Stewart's classic formula ran out of gas on *Smiler*, his fifth solo album. The failure of *Smiler* wasn't a matter of weak songs, nor was it a matter of Stewart being in poor voice. Instead, the al-

bum failed because everything, from the choice of songs to the production, sounded too pat and predictable. The predictability held "Sweet Little Rock 'N Roller" from truly rocking and it made the reworking of "(You Make Me Feel Like) A Natural Man" unbearably smug. Apart from the free-wheeling take on Elton John's "Let Me Be Your Car" and the inspired version of Dylan's "Girl from the North Country," *Smiler* is an utter waste of time. *— Stephen Thomas Erlewine*

○ **Atlantic Crossing** / 1975 / Warner Brothers ✦✦✦✦
Atlantic Crossing wasn't simply the moment when Rod Stewart left Britain for the greener pasture of America, it was the moment when he accepted his role as a full-fledged, jet-setting superstar. Stewart abandoned the formula of his first five solo records, as well as most of his folk-rock and hard rock undercurrents, trading them for a professionally-polished, rock and soul-inflected pop, courtesy of Muscle Shoals' musicians and producer Tom Dowd. The glossy production doesn't obscure or trivialize Stewart's talents—coming after the tired *Smiler*, the slickness actually accentuated his strength as an interpretive singer. "The fast half" suffers from a couple of weak tracks, but "Three Time Loser" and "Stone Cold Sober" catch fire, and "the slow half" is generally excellent, but Stewart's heart-wrenching rendition of Danny Whitten's "I Don't Want to Talk About It" ranks as one of his finest performances. *— Stephen Thomas Erlewine*

○ **A Night on the Town** / 1976 / Warner Brothers ✦✦✦✦
After bouncing back to life with *Atlantic Crossing*, Rod Stewart crafted his most self-consciously ambitious record with *A Night on the Town*. The centerpiece of the album, "The Killing of Georgie (Part I and II)," was a long, winding Dylan-esque tale of the murder of one of Stewart's gay friends and was one of his better songs of the mid-'70s. Even if "The Killing of Georgie" was the conscious artistic focal point of *A Night on the Town*, the true masterpiece of the album was an eloquent rendition of Cat Stevens's "The First Cut Is the Deepest." Apart from the flawed political platitudes of "Trade Winds," the rest of the album was filled with competent, professional pop/rock, highlighted by the number one hit "Tonight's the Night (Gonna Be Alright)," a ballad where the gallant Rod relieves a teenager of her virginity. And, again, the "Slow Half" was more convincing than the frequently perfunctory "Fast Half." *— Stephen Thomas Erlewine*

Foot Loose & Fancy Free / 1977 / Warner Brothers ✦✦
Following the same formula as *Atlantic Crossing* and *A Night on the Town*, but not explicitly breaking the record into fast and slow sides, *Foot Loose & Fancy Free* was a limp effort from an increasingly complacent Rod Stewart. With the exception of the dumb, sleazy "Hot Legs," none of the rockers are discernable from each other, and this time he doesn't have a strong set of ballads to save him. The affectionately sappy acoustic ballad "You're in My Heart" was the big hit, but Stewart sounds completely convincing only on "I Was Only Joking." Coming at the end of the album, the song seems like a justification for the uninspired, by-the-book record that preceded it. *— Stephen Thomas Erlewine*

Blondes Have More Fun / 1978 / Warner Brothers ✦✦✦
In its simplest terms, *Blondes Have More Fun* is Rod Stewart's disco album, filled with pulsating rhythms and slick, synthesized textures. It's also his trashiest, most disposable album, filled with cheap come-ons and bad double entendres. Of course, that makes *Blondes Have More Fun* one of his most enjoyable records, even if all the pleasures are guilty. With its swirling strings and nagging chorus, "Da Ya Think I'm Sexy?" was the reason the record hit number one and, two decades later, the song stands as one of the best rock-disco fusions. The rest of the record isn't as engaging, but he throws out a handful of winning tracks in the same mold, including "Ain't Love a Bitch," "Attractive Female Wanted," and the title track. *— Stephen Thomas Erlewine*

○ **Greatest Hits** / 1979 / Warner Brothers ✦✦✦✦
Even though it has a couple of flaws—particularly the appearance of "Maggie May," which doesn't quite fit in with the rest of the material —*Greatest Hits* is an enjoyable sampler of Rod Stewart's first four Warner albums, including most of the hits but not necessarily all of his greatest performances. *— Stephen Thomas Erlewine*

Foolish Behaviour / 1980 / Warner Brothers ✦✦

○ **Tonight I'm Yours** / 1981 / Warner Brothers ✦✦✦✦
This lacks the muscle of the early stuff but remains Stewart's last burst of creativity. This is the last time he sounds like he cares. *— John Floyd*

Absolutely Live / 1982 / Warner Brothers ✦
Rod Stewart followed the faux-disco trash of *Blondes Have More Fun* with *Foolish Behaviour*, which sanded out most of the character of the previous album. The result was a bland, but professional—even at their worst, Rod and his band are always professionals—collection, mainly comprised of dance-oriented, lightly synthesized pop/rock. The passionless "Passion" was the hit but the only worthwhile song was the gorgeous "Oh God, I Wish I Was Home Tonight," which has the clever wit and self-deprecating melancholy of his finest work. —*Stephen Thomas Erlewine*

Body Wishes / 1983 / Warner Brothers ✦
Two of the songs are first-rate synth-laden, disposable pop/rock filler—"Baby Jane" and "What Am I Gonna Do (I'm So in Love with You)"—but when those songs sound *substantial* next to dreck like "Ready Now" and "Sweet Surrender," it's clear that *Body Wishes* is one of Rod Stewart's worst efforts. —*Stephen Thomas Erlewine*

Camouflage / 1984 / Warner Brothers ✦✦
Camouflage is better than the disastrous *Body Wishes*, but that's only a relative term. Jeff Beck adds the occasional rock guitar flourish, but that doesn't save the faceless material. Again, the two singles—"Infatuation" and "Some Guys Have All the Luck"—are fine, ready-made pop hits, but they wear thin after a few plays, and they're the best things on the record. —*Stephen Thomas Erlewine*

Rod Stewart / 1986 / Warner Brothers ✦
Featuring a set of amazingly vapid material—led by the empty Top Ten hit "Love Touch"—and an embalmed, mechanical production, *Rod Stewart* is the wost album the singer recorded. After a series of faceless albums, it's not surprising that the record was uninspired; what was surprising was the utter lack of convincing pop-craft. The highlights of the album, "Love Touch" and "Every Beat of My Heart," were the singles but they lacked the well-constructed precision of "Some Guys Have All the Luck," "Infatuation," and "Baby Jane," which leaves *Rod Stewart* a soulless, and ultimately depressing, album. —*Stephen Thomas Erlewine*

Out of Order / 1988 / Warner Brothers ✦✦✦
With the support of the Power Station's guitarist Andy Taylor and drummer Bernard Edwards, Rod Stewart rebounds from his previous career nadir of "Love Touch" with *Out of Order*. Alternating between professional, driving rock & roll like "Lost in You" and ballads like "My Heart Can't Tell You No," *Out of Order* is a well-constructed set of mainstream pop/rock and his best album since *Tonight I'm Yours*, even if none of the songs rank among his best work. —*Stephen Thomas Erlewine*

○ **Storyteller: Complete Anthology** / 1989 / Warner Brothers ✦✦✦✦
This 4-disc set contains most of the essentials (but not enough material from the Faces) and all the late-'70s and '80s hits for those who care. It should've been better. —*John Floyd*

Downtown Train (Selections from the Storyteller Anthology) / Mar. 6, 1990 / Warner Brothers ✦✦✦
Downtown Train—Selections from Storyteller is a single-disc, condensed version of the *Storyteller* boxed set, concentrating on the highlights of Rod Stewart's '80s albums and adding the Faces' only hit "Stay With Me" for good measure. —*AMG*

○ **Vagabond Heart** / Mar. 26, 1991 / Warner Brothers ✦✦✦✦
Rod Stewart continued to regain his strength with *Vagabond Heart*, the follow-up to his comeback album, *Out of Order*. *Vagabond Heart* is a stronger, more diverse album than its predecessor, featuring a more consistent set of songs, including Robbie Robertson's "Broken Arrow" and the hit "Motown Song," as well as a convincing, impassioned performance by Stewart. —*Stephen Thomas Erlewine*

○ **The Mercury Anthology** / 1992 / Mercury ✦✦✦✦
A two-disc anthology of Rod Stewart's early Mercury recordings, which, in conjunction with the albums he recorded with the Faces, are inarguably his finest (nothing from the Faces records is included). Most of the highlights of his terrific first four albums are here—"Maggie May," "You Wear It Well," "Handbags and Gladrags," "Gasoline Alley"—as well as selections from the lukewarm *Smiler*, a live album recorded with the Faces, and a couple of rare B-sides. —*Stephen Thomas Erlewine*

Unplugged . . . and Seated / May 25, 1993 / Warner Brothers ✦✦✦
The inherent problem with Rod Stewart's *Unplugged* album is that it seems like a supremely calculated attempt to revive his career exactly as Eric Clapton did. Stewart returns to the acoustic rock & roll and folk that marked his greatest recordings; Ron Wood's supporting guitar is a nice bonus recalling the glory days. Naturally, *Unplugged* can't hope to match *Gasoline Alley* or *Every Picture Tells a Story*, but the amazing thing is how close it comes at times. He sounds fine, if a little bit ragged at first, but as the album progresses, his performances become more genuine and heartfelt, culminating in yet another sublime Tom Waits cover with "Tom Traubert's Blues (Waltzing Matilda)," as well as a hit single with Van Morrison's "Have I Told You Lately?" —*Stephen Thomas Erlewine*

Spanner In The Works / 1995 / Warner Brothers ✦✦✦
Following the success of *Unplugged…and Seated*, Rod Stewart had shrewdly repositioned himself as a mature, middle-aged man who still had a slight streak of his wilder days in him. Unsurprisingly, the music both recalled his past glories in instrumentation, yet the attack was different—the acoustics rocked, but it wasn't bracing; it was like a back-porch jam session. Stewart expanded that approach on *A Spanner in the Works*, his first album since *Unplugged*. The acoustics are still there, but they're strummed a little more gently and set in a bed of unobtrusive synths. More importantly, Stewart tackles his most ambitious and varied set of material since *A Night on the Town*. From the pop/rock of Tom Petty's "Leave Virginia Alone" and the reflective take on Dylan's "Sweetheart like You" through the R&B tribute of "Muddy, Sam and Otis" and the rocking "Delicious" to the British folk of "Purple Heather," the songs recall his classic early albums in ambition and musical diversity. *A Spanner in the Works* isn't quite as successful as *Gasoline Alley* or *Every Picture Tells a Story*—it's a content album, not a probing one, which is appropriate for a middle-aged singer—yet it is the most inspired and ambitious record Stewart has released in nearly 20 years. —*Stephen Thomas Erlewine*

Stiff Little Fingers

Group, Punk
A taut, explosive Belfast-based punk band, Stiff Little Fingers (named after a Vibrators song) had the dubious distinction of being referred to as "The Irish Clash." What must have seemed like a compliment at the time did little to help their career, only because it made comparisons between the two bands inevitable. Granted, there were many similarities: both bands debuted playing revved-up late-'70s punk rock, both were politically inclined, featured pissed-off lead singers, a love for reggae, and a near-palpable sense of isolation and desperation. But as we all know, the Clash offered complexity, panache, and a consistently breathtaking body of work. Stiff Little Fingers, on the other hand, were simply a very good punk rock band. With sandpaper-throated frontman Jake Burns leading the way, SLF did release an auspicious, if badly produced, debut album, *Inflammable Material*, that featured the band's two best songs, "Alternative Ulster" and "Suspect Device." Both were passionate, ferocious songs dealing with the harsh, deadly realities of growing up in the middle of two decades of Northern Ireland's violence. These songs thrust SLF into the limelight and got them loads of enthusiastic press, which led to a contract with the decidedly anti-punk Chrysalis label in 1980. After that, SLF released a handful of pretty good records (including a terrific live album, *Hanx*), but their unregenerate fast and loud punk style started to sound stale. In 1982, the band released their most non-punk record (*Now Then…*), which was greeted by general apathy. In a musical rut, dogged by the facile Clash comparisons, and with punk rock running out of steam, Burns pulled the plug on SLF.

Sadly, the band's breakup lasted only five years. After a string of forgettable solo singles and a stint as a BBC Radio producer, Burns, hoping to cash in on punk nostalgia, reformed SLF (with another aging punk rocker, ex-Jam bassist Bruce Foxton) in 1987 and released a bunch of lousy (mostly live) records for the rest of the decade. —*John Dougan*

● **Inflammable Materials** / 1979 / Restless ✦✦✦✦
With "Alternative Ulster" and "Suspect Device" leading the way, this is a compelling, raging record that derives most of its style from the Sex Pistols and simply cranks up the personal political issues a notch or two. There is a so-so version of Bob Marley's "Johnny Was" (call it the obligatory reggae cover), but that doesn't hamper the enjoyment, nor does it detract from the record's overwhelming power. Issued on CD by Restless Retro in 1990. —*John Dougan*

Hanx / 1980 / Restless ✦✦✦

The other SLF studio recordings all contain some fine songs, but are recommended only to hardcore fans. *Hanx*, however, is a live recording that brilliantly serves two purposes: first, as proof of what incendiary live shows SLF was capable of; second, as a greatest hits record. Unsurprisingly, the tempos hear are much faster than the studio recordings, but that simply adds to the excitement. Overlooked upon its release, *Hanx* is a raging, non-stop hunk of punk rock that sounds great even after all these years. Issued on CD by Restless Retro in 1990. —*John Dougan*

○ **Nobody's Hero** / Jan. 1980 / Restless ✦✦✦✦

Go for It / 1981 / Restless ✦✦✦

Now Then / 1982 / Chrysalis ✦✦✦

○ **All the Best A** / 1983 / One Way ✦✦✦✦

The best anthology of SLF available. A 30-track chronological overview that's as articulate an argument for SLF's greatness as anything else they released. A perfect way to hear their development from the early punk days to their more "mature" punk-pop period just prior to their breakup: Jake Burns goes from shouter to singer, hooks and riffs replace simple walls of distorted guitars, the reggae influence becomes stronger and is played with greater dexterity; all and all, you simply can't go wrong here. —*John Dougan*

See You up There! / 1989 / Caroline ✦✦✦

Harp / 1994 / ✦✦

Stephen Stills

b. Jan. 3, 1945

Singer-Songwriter, Pop/Rock

Singer/songwriter and multi-instrumentalist Stephen Stills first gained prominence with the legendary late-'60s group, Buffalo Springfield. Their first hit was the Stills-penned "For What It's Worth" (#7), inspired by Los Angeles police oppression of the youth community. Another Springfield classic written by Stills was "Bluebird" (#58), which featured his distinctive gutsy acoustic lead-guitar style and his mildly husky lower tenor voice. Stills left Buffalo Springfield in 1968 to form the distinctively harmonic Crosby, Stills & Nash. As a solo artist, Stills has produced several successful albums that mine a blend of acoustic/electric folk-rock with occasional gospelish undertones. He recorded two albums with his own group Manassas in 1972 and 1973.

His biggest hits were "Love the One You're With" (#14), "Sit Yourself Down" (#37), "Change Partners" (#43), "Marianne" (#42), and "It Doesn't Matter" (#61). —*Rick Clark*

● **Stephen Stills** / 1970 / Atlantic ✦✦✦✦

Stephen Stills's self-titled debut started out his solo career with much promise. The opening cut, "Love the One You're With" (number 14), was a huge hit. His warm, husky voice is used to great effect on most of these tracks, and the album features a cast of 1970 all-stars like Jimi Hendrix, Eric Clapton, David Crosby, Graham Nash, John Sebastian, and Rita Coolidge. Hendrix's lead contribution is occasionally buried by Stills's overbearing organ work, and Clapton's guitar tone is too thin and brittle, but the hit "Sit Yourself Down" (number 37), with its powerful piano introduction, is flawless in production and performance. —*Rick Clark*

Stephen Stills 2 / 1971 / Atlantic ✦✦✦

○ **Manassas** / 1972 / Atlantic ✦✦✦✦

After the uneven 1971 release *Stephen Stills 2*, Stills formed a band around him of some solid players (Chris Hillman, Joe Lala, Al Perkins, Fuzzy Samuels, Dallas Taylor, etc.) and called it Manassas. Their first of two albums was a self-titled double-record set. Many consider *Manassas* to be Stills's finest effort; it would have made a grand single album. Atlantic has managed to fit the whole thing on a single CD. —*Rick Clark*

Down the Road / 1973 / Atlantic ✦✦

Stills / 1975 / Columbia ✦✦

Illegal Stills / 1976 / Columbia ✦✦

○ **Long May You Run** / 1976 / Reprise ✦✦✦✦

○ **The Best of Stephen Stills** / 1977 / Atlantic ✦✦✦✦

This is a decent sampling of his solo work up to this point. It includes "Change Partners" from *Stephen Stills 2*, as well as main tracks from the debut. —*Rick Clark*

Thoroughfare Gap / 1978 / CBS ✦✦

Live / 1979 / Atlantic ✦✦

Right by You / 1984 / Atlantic ✦✦

Stills Alone / 1991 / Vision ✦✦✦

Sting (Gordon Sumner)

b. Oct. 2, 1951

Pop/Rock

Sting launched his musical career as the lead singer of the successful rock band the Police. After the Police split in 1984, the English singer/songwriter and bassist embarked upon a successful solo career. Sting's solo works focus less on achieving pop success, instead voicing his political views and concerns. His 1985 debut album, *Dream of the Blue Turtles*, is heavily jazz-influenced and boasts a number of jazz musicians, including Branford Marsalis. This album, while it contained lyrical references to turbulent Soviet-American relations and the British coal-miners strike, still managed to sell two million copies. The *Dream* tour resulted in a two-disc live album, *Bring on the Night*, which featured some new live renditions of Police songs. In 1987, Sting released a second solo album, *Nothing like the Sun...*, which was very politically based as well. One of the most powerful songs on the album is "They Dance Alone," an outright criticism of the regime of Chilean General Augusto Pinochet. The *Soul Cages*, released in 1991, deals with the deaths of Sting's mother and father and veers away from political issues. It was a more introspective work, although rather gloomy, dealing with the ideas of death and loss. In addition to his music, Sting has also appeared in a number of movies and plays, including *The Bride* and *The Threepenny Opera*. Sting has used his status as a well-known performer to lend assistance to many worthy organizations, including Band Aid, Live Aid, Special Olympics, Greenpeace, Amnesty International, and the Rainforest Foundation. Sting has made a significant contribution, not only to the music world but to the rest of the world as well. —*Iotis Erlewine*

○ **The Dream of the Blue Turtles** / 1985 / A&M ✦✦✦✦

Sting's early jazz experience was very evident on his solo debut album. Kenny Kirkland (piano), Omar Hakim (drums), Darryl Jones (bass), and Branford Marsalis (sax) contributed greatly to the jazz "feel" of the songs. This captures some of the energy and exuberance of the early Police, like *Regatta de Blanc*, but also maintains some of the somber, serious tone of *Synchronicity*. Sting's first album is his most impressive, boasting such songs as "Love Is the Seventh Wave," "Fortress Around Your Heart," "Children's Crusade," and "Moon over Bourbon Steet." —*Iotis Erlewine*

Bring on the Night / 1986 / A&M ✦✦✦

A terrific live-concert album, this contains songs dating back to Sting's years with the Police, as well as works from his first solo album, *Dream of the Blue Turtles*. In addition to performances of well-known songs, Sting performs the haunting "I Burn for You," a song written for the film *Brimstone and Treacle* (in which Sting had a role) but not included on any of Sting's own albums. This two-CD set features Branford Marsalis (sax), Omar Hakim (drums), Darryl Jones (bass), Kenny Kirkland (keyboards), and Janie Pendarvis and Dolette McDonald (vocals). —*Iotis Erlewine*

○ **Nothing like the Sun** / 1987 / A&M ✦✦✦✦

This album is more somber than *Dream of the Blue Turtles* and light on the jazz influences, focusing more on Brazilian and Hispanic rhythms. Not as lively and concise as *Dream* due to the heavy, political lyrics (on such songs as "They Dance Alone" and "Fragile"), this is a good album, nevertheless. Along with Sting's own songs, the album includes a cover of Hendrix's "Little Wing." This album includes guests Mark Knopfler, Eric Clapton, the Gil Evans Band, former Police bandmember Andy Summers (who plays on "Lazarus Heart"), and, once again, Branford Marsalis featured on sax. —*Iotis Erlewine*

Nada Como el Sol... / 1988 / A&M ✦✦

This album consists of five songs from *Nothing Like the Sun...* re-recorded in Spanish and Portuguese. This was a well-done project—the translations are good and Sting manages the Spanish and Portuguese pronunciations well. However, unless you are a huge fan, or enjoy hearing the songs sung in different languages, this is an album you'll want to pass over. —*Iotis Erlewine*

The Soul Cages / 1991 / A&M ✦✦✦

This long-awaited album followed the death of Sting's father, which may explain the melancholy, pained tone of these songs. The focus here is very much on death and dying, making the album a bit of a downer and hard to listen to in a single sitting. Although the material may not be as good overall as Sting's previous work, the song "All This Time" is definitely one of his best. —*Iotis Erlewine*

● **Ten Summoner's Tales** / Mar. 9, 1993 / A&M ◆◆◆◆
Ten Summoner's Tales is the most song-oriented, lighthearted collection Sting has delivered since his solo debut. Sting's songs remain densely literate, although the melodies aren't; they are devoid of the jazz pretensions of *Nothing Like the Sun* and the oppressive seriousness of *The Soul Cages*. When he doesn't get carried away by his own cleverness, Sting can deliver the goods with some terrific pop songs ("If I Ever Lose My Faith in You," "It's Probably Me," "Epilogue [Nothin' 'Bout Me]," and "Seven Days"). Those songs help make *Ten Summoner's Tales* one of his strongest solo releases. —*Stephen Thomas Erlewine*

Fields of Gold: Best of Sting 1984-1994 / 1994 / A&M ◆◆◆
This collection eliminates a lot of the more pretentiously "sophisticated" album tracks. The legion of Sting fans who consider the previous sentence heresy already own 12 out of 14 tracks; two new songs are included: "When We Dance" and "This Cowboy Song." —*Roch Parisien*

Stone Poneys

Group, Folk-Rock, Pop/Rock
Before becoming a solo act, Linda Ronstadt was the lead singer of the Stone Poneys, an L.A.-based trio with an acoustic, folkish sound and strong original material. The band's focal point and greatest asset was Ronstadt's clear, powerful vocals. Originally recording in a coffeehouse folk style not far removed from Peter, Paul & Mary, the group rocked up their sound slightly and scored a Top 20 hit with "Different Drum," written by Mike Nesmith of the Monkees, in 1967. —*Richie Unterberger*

● **Stone Poneys Featuring Linda Ronstadt** / 1967 / Capitol ◆◆◆◆
It doesn't have "Different Drum," but the first Stone Poneys album is their folkiest and best, dominated by close harmonies and strong original material by the group's guitarists, Bob Kimmel and Ken Edwards. —*Richie Unterberger*

Evergreen, Vol. 2 / 1967 / Capitol ◆◆◆
Evergreen, Vol. 2 wasn't as strong as their debut album, but it did contain their only hit, "Different Drum," as well as several other pleasant songs in a similar vein. —*Stephen Thomas Erlewine*

Stone Poneys & Friends, Vol. 3 / 1968 / Capitol ◆◆◆

The Stone Roses

Group, Alternative Pop/Rock
Meshing '60s-styled guitar pop with an understated '80s dance beat, the Stone Roses defined the Manchester scene of the late '80s and early '90s. With their self-titled 1989 debut, the group mastered the subtle art of catchy guitar hooks and sighing melodies, mainly supplied by guitarist John Squire; even when they stretch out into a jangly funk vein (as on "Fool's Gold" or "I Am the Resurrection"), their music never loses its direction. After the album became an English sensation, countless other groups in the same vein became popular, including the Charlatans (U.K.), Inspiral Carpets, and Happy Mondays. However, none of them had the strong songwriting of the Stone Roses; "I Wanna Be Adored," "She Bangs the Drums," and "Made of Stone" are smart, melodic pop songs that rank among the best of the '80s.

After their remarkable first album, they became embroiled in several severe lawsuits with their record companies; after a few years, the suits were settled and the band wound up on Geffen. The Stone Roses began working on their second album in 1992, with a projected release date of 1993, but it was quickly pulled from the release schedule. In 1993, the British music newspaper *New Musical Express* voted *The Stone Roses* as the best album of the '80s and placed it in the Top Ten albums of all time. The Stone Roses continued working on the followup throughout 1994; the album, titled *Second Coming*, finally appeared in December of 1994 (it was released in early 1995 in America), five years after the release of their debut. A harder-rocking album than *The Stone Roses, Second Coming* received mixed reviews and didn't match commercial expectations. It began a year of troubles and misfortunes for the Stone Roses. In the spring of 1995, Reni left the band, due to publishing disputes; he was replaced by Robbie Maddox. At the end of a short American tour—their first appearances in the U.S.—John Squire broke his collarbone in a bike accident, forcing

them to cancel a headlining spot at the British Glastonbury Festival, which would have been their first concert in the U.K. in five years. During this time, the group's popularity continued to slide, while their descendents—everyone from Blur to Oasis—dominated the charts and their fellow Madchaster musician, Happy Mondays' leader Shaun Ryder, made an unexpectedly triumphant comeback with his new band, Black Grape. The Stone Roses, however, were continually ridiculed in the press and their singles failed to become big hits. In August, the group finally performed their first U.K. concert in half a decade; again, the group received mixed reviews. —*Stephen Thomas Erlewine*

★ **The Stone Roses** / 1989 / Silvertone ◆◆◆◆◆
This vital debut defined late-'80s U.K. rock, while maintaining a strong link with psychedelic-tinged sounds. This reissue includes previously unreleased material. —*Steve Aldrich*

Turns into Stone / Oct. 27, 1992 / Silvertone ◆◆◆
Not a new Stone Roses album, it's another collection of European B-sides and selected songs from their debut album. If they don't already own the singles, hardcore fans will want to purchase this despite the heavy repetition of tracks; most listeners will be content with the debut. —*AMG*

Second Coming / Dec. 1994 / Geffen ◆◆◆
There's no denying that *Second Coming* is a bit of a letdown. None of the songs are quite as strong as the best on their debut, but there is plenty of good music on the band's much-delayed second record. The Stone Roses create a dense tapestry of interweaving guitars and pulsing bass grooves. Ian Brown growls a little more than before, but he isn't the center of the music; John Squire's endlessly colorful riffs are. It's clear that Squire has been listening to a bit of hard rock, particularly Led Zeppelin. While the songs occasionally take a back seat to the grooves, several tracks—"Ten Storey Love Song," "Begging You," "Tightrope," "How Do You Sleep," and "Love Spreads"—rank as true classics. It might not be the long-awaited masterpiece it was rumored to be, but *Second Coming* is a fine sophomore effort. —*Stephen Thomas Erlewine*

○ **Complete Stone Roses** / 1995 / ◆◆◆◆
The title's a bit of a misnomer. *The Complete Stone Roses* concentrates on the band's first album, compiling the A-and B-sides of the group's hits from "Elephant Stone" to "One Love." In addition to the familiar material, the disc includes rare, early singles like "So Young" and "Sally Cinnamon" for the first time on compact disc, giving their classic material some context. The loud guitars of "So Young" are clearly the work of a hesitant band, while "Sally Cinnamon" is the first indication of John Squire's gift for ringing, melodic guitar hooks. However, their inclusion—as well as the appearance of the B-sides, which lack the consistent brilliance of "I Wanna Be Adored," "She Bangs the Drums," "Elephant Stone," "Waterfall," etc.—make *The Complete Stone Roses* a flawed introduction to the band. Nevertheless, there's a fair amount of classic pop here and the rarities are necessary for dedicated fans. —*Stephen Thomas Erlewine*

Stone Temple Pilots

Group, Hard Rock, Alternative Pop/Rock
Stone Temple Pilots were able to make alternative rock into stadium rock; naturally, they became the most critically despised band of their era. Accused by many critics of being nothing more than rip-off artists, pilfering from Pearl Jam, Soundgarden, and Alice in Chains, the band nevertheless became major stars in 1993. And the influences of those bands *are* apparent in their music, but Stone Temple Pilots do manage to change things around a bit. STP are more concerned with tight song structure and riffs than punk rage. Their closest antecedents are not the Sex Pistols or Hüsker Dü; instead the band resembles arena rock acts from the '70s—it's popular hard rock that sounds good on the radio and in concert. No matter what the critics might say, Stone Temple Pilots have undeniably catchy riffs and production; there's a reason why over three million people bought their debut album, *Core*, and why their second album, *Purple*, shot to number one when it was released. —*Stephen Thomas Erlewine*

● **Core** / 1992 / Atlantic ◆◆◆◆
While the Stone Temple Pilots may not be sincere alternative rockers, they do know how to write a killer riff, which is why their debut album sold nearly as many copies as Pearl Jam. Admittedly, STP can sound like either Pearl Jam ("Plush"), Alice in Chains ("Sex Type Thing" and "Wicked Garden"), Soundgarden ("Dead & Bloated"), or even R.E.M. ("Creep"), depending on their mood, but

their hooks are undeniably catchy, making the songs much better than they have any right to be. In fact, Stone Temple Pilots appear to be the hard-rock arena act for the 1990s, and that's a compliment. —*Stephen Thomas Erlewine*

○ **Purple** / 1994 / Atlantic ◆◆◆◆
Stone Temple Pilots may have topped the charts with *Core*, yet it was with *Purple* that they established their across-the-boards popularity. Trimming back the excesses of their debut, *Purple* is a lean, throttling piece of post-alternative hard rock. STP doesn't rely simply on riffs, although there is a fair share of killer hooks; the band writes songs, where the melodies and chords intertwine, becoming inseparable. From the brooding ballad "The Big Empty" to the simple, pounding, fuzzy riffs of "Vasoline," the group has improved in every facet—their songs are stronger and their playing is more convincing and powerful. Best of all is "Interstate Love Song." Clocking in at under three minutes, the record became one of the biggest album rock hits ever, spending 15 weeks at the top of the charts, and deservedly so—with its carefully measured dynamics and memorable melody, it's a showcase for everything that's good about hard rock. —*Stephen Thomas Erlewine*

The Stooges
Group, Punk, Hard Rock
This Detroit rock & roll band was formed in 1967 as the Psychedelic Stooges with lead singer Iggy Pop (born James Newell Osterberg, 1947; original stage name was Iggy Stooge, the Iggy appelation coming from his drumming tenure with local teen band the Iguanas). The group also included Ron Asheton (guitar), Scott Asheton (drums), and Dave Alexander (bass). If local favorites the MC5 struck fear into the hearts of Motor City parents with their manifesto of sex, drugs, rock & roll, and politics, they looked normal in comparison to the stage antics of Iggy & the Stooges. Violent interaction with members of the audience (both verbal and physical), vomiting, and self-mutilation with beer bottles were some of the more predictable aspects of their live presentation, while the music itself was simplistic and angry one- to three-chord grunge-rock, with lyrics ranging from teenage disorientation to animal lust. Two excellent albums for Elektra followed (they were signed the same night as the MC5), but the drug lifestyle of the band caused its breakup in the early '70s. They re-formed with James Williamson on guitar and Asheton moving over to bass for the next album in 1973, but disbanded again a year later. Working with David Bowie, Iggy cut two good solo albums in the mid '70s, when bands like the Sex Pistols defined him as "The Godfather of Punk." He has kept recording and touring to his hardcore cult following up to the present time, with small acting roles in *The Color of Money* and *Cry Baby* as well. —*Cub Koda*

○ **The Stooges** / 1969 / Elektra ◆◆◆◆
Debut album; the true birth of punk rock. —*Cub Koda*

☆ **Fun House** / 1970 / Elektra ◆◆◆◆◆
Their second album, equally as great. —*Cub Koda*

★ **Raw Power** / 1973 / Columbia ◆◆◆◆◆
The title says it all. The blueprint for the Sex Pistols and the entire punk rock movement. —*Cub Koda*

○ **Metallic K O** / 1976 / Skydog ◆◆◆◆
The last Stooges live show; scary as hell. Bootleg import. Worth the search. —*Cub Koda*

○ **Kill City** / 1978 / Bomp! ◆◆◆◆

I Got a Right / 1987 / Revenge ◆◆◆

Rubber Legs / 1987 / Fan Club ◆◆◆

Stories
Group, Pop/Rock
After the demise of the Left Banke, classically trained keyboardist and songwriter Michael Brown (b.Apr 25, 1949) formed Stories in 1972 with singer Ian Lloyd. Their first two albums, *Stories* and (particularly) *About Us*, featured a brilliant collection of ultra-melodic pop/rock songs that were less baroque than those of Left Banke and (at times) harder-hitting than those of fellow pop/rockers like Badfinger.

Neither of these albums achieved any real success, and Stories would have (more than likely) sadly sunk without a trace had fate not intervened with the totally left-field hit (about an interracial encounter) titled "Brother Louie" (#1), written by Errol Brown of the British group Hot Chocolate. Their label, Kama Sutra, jammed the tune on *About Us*, and the album ended up charting at #29.

Brown left the group, and they released the spotty *Travelling Underground*, which produced the "Brother Louie"-carbon-copy "Mammy Blue" (#50) and "If It Feels Good, Do It" (#88). Stories broke up shortly thereafter. —*Rick Clark*

○ **Stories** / 1972 / Kama Sutra ◆◆◆◆

Travelling Underground / 1973 / Kama Sutra ◆◆◆

● **About Us** / 1973 / Pair ◆◆◆◆
The second Stories album melded ornate Anglo-pop with ever-so-slight art-pop tendencies. Loaded with great melodies and smart arrangements. Fans of Badfinger and Beatles-style pop/rock should love this outing. It was a commercial sleeper until the band's version of Hot Chocolate's "Brother Louie" became a number one hit. Unfortunately, the song didn't resemble anything else on the album. Highlights include "Darling," "Hey France," "Please Please," "What Comes After," and "Top of the City." This disc may be hard to find, since their reissue label has historically done little to promote reissue product. —*Rick Clark*

Walk Away from the Left Banke / See For Miles ◆◆◆

Stormtroopers of Death
Group, Thrash, Heavy Metal
Formed in 1985 when Anthrax was taking a break from recording sessions and touring. Guitarist Scott Ian and drummer Charlie Benante got their former bassist Danny Lilker, as well as their roadie Billy Milano, and decided to form S.O.D. A day before they were to enter the studio, Ian and Milano recorded a cruddy 59-song demo under the name of Crab Society North. It was very fast and was to become the groundwork for S.O.D.

For three days in early July they recorded the album. What made S.O.D. different from Anthrax was that S.O.D. was mixing punk, hardcore, and thrash, with a heavy emphasis on hardcore. The songs ranged from violent to racist and sexist, but it was the attitude given through the music that was a force to reckon with. As soon as 1986 began, S.O.D. was no more, but the band and *Speak English or Die*, the album they left behind, became a milestone for thrash metal. —*John Book*

● **Speak English or Die** / Dec. 1985 / Megaforce ◆◆◆◆
The album that made the crossbreed of punk rock and heavy metal official, it is essential and mandatory for students of thrash. —*John Book*

Live at Budokan / 1992 / Megaforce ◆◆◆

Izzy Stradlin
Rock & Roll
After leaving Guns N' Roses, guitarist Izzy Stradlin formed a band, the Ju Ju Hounds, that accentuated the Stones and Faces undertones that were always in his music. His 1992 debut is an underrated record, full of great songwriting and effortless rocking. —*Stephen Thomas Erlewine*

○ **Izzy Stradlin & the Ju Ju Hounds** / Oct. 13, 1992 / Geffen ◆◆◆◆
Izzy Stradlin was always the most gifted member of Guns N' Roses, able to put a modern spin on the classic rock of Chuck Berry, the Stones, and the Faces, as well as the New York Dolls and Sex Pistols. Axl may have had the angst and Slash may have had the chops, but Izzy had the smarts and the heart. On his debut album, the traditional elements that had always formed the backbone of Stradlin's music with Guns N' Roses comes to the forefront—it's Stones and Faces all the way, but it is done well. *Izzy Stradlin & the Ju Ju Hounds* is terrific only half of the time, which is good enough for a debut album. —*Stephen Thomas Erlewine*

Straitjacket Fits
Group, Alternative Pop/Rock
Auckland, New Zealand's Straitjacket Fits are cast in much the same mold as other bands on the Flying Nun label, playing hooky guitar pop with the usual mood of longing. However, the band distinguishes itself by injecting some guitar muscle every now and then and bringing more attitude than many of their contemporaries. The band is led by vocalists/guitarists Shayne Carter and Andrew Brough. —*Steve Huey*

● **Hail** / 1990 / Rough Trade ◆◆◆◆
Dissonant, dreamy, and hypnotic garage rock with an aggressive edge from this New Zealand band. Highlights include "She Speeds" and "All That That Brings." The import CD contains additional tracks. —*Scott Bultman*

Melt / 1991 / Arista ✦✦✦
Not as soaring as their first U.S. album, their musicianship and dark hypnotic energy make it worthwhile. — *Scott Bultman*
Blow / May 25, 1993 / Arista ✦✦

Strangeloves

Group, Rock & Roll
While the Strangeloves managed to produce one garage band classic, their story is probably more interesting than their actual music. Bob Feldman, Jerry Goldstein, and Richard Gottehrer were a trio of Brooklyn songwriter-producers who landed a number one girl group hit with the Angels' "My Boyfriend's Back." When the British Invasion crested in the mid-'60s, they decided to get in on the act by recording as a group, billing themselves as an Australian outfit to cash in on the mystique being attached to foreign groups.

"I Want Candy," with its crunching Bo Diddley beat, joyous chorus, and rambling lead guitar, was their great moment, reaching number 11 in 1965. Forced to put together a live act to support their disc, they made outrageous claims to hail from the nonexistent town of Armstrong, Australia, where they had made a fortune as sheepherders who had developed a cross-breed. They also made the Top 40 with a couple fairly gutsy follow-ups, "Cara-Lin" and "Night Time," both of which were built around crunching claps, stomps, and drums. Also recording an album and several non-hit singles, most of their material unashamedly plagiarized the Bo Diddley beats of "I Want Candy," with forgettable results. They withdrew from performing and recording to concentrate on writing and producing for the McCoys, although Strangeloves releases continued to appear until 1968. Goldstein went on to produce records for War in the 1970s, and Gottehrer produced efforts by Blondie, the Go-Go's, and others. — *Richie Unterberger*

● **I Want Candy: The Best Of The Strangeloves** / 1995 / Legacy/Epic ✦✦✦✦
20 tracks from the mid-'60s, including all the hits, a lot of stuff from their sole LP, non-hit singles, rare 45s they recorded for Swan (in 1964) and Sire (in 1968), and an item they put out under the pseudonym of the Beach-Nuts. But it's really not deserving of such thoughtful archiving; beyond "I Want Candy," "Cara-Lin," and "Night Time," only hardcore collectors will be interested. — *Richie Unterberger*

The Stranglers

Group, Rock & Roll, Punk
As were their contemporaries the Vibrators, the Stranglers were faux-punks; grimy, slightly arty rockers that found the notoriety surrounding punk bands too irresistible to ignore. So armed with short haircuts and reticent about revealing their true ages (drummer Jet Black was a certifiable old fart when the band formed in 1975), the Stranglers became stars of Brit punk's class of 1976-77, garnering headlines for their sexist posturing, drug use, occasional arrests, and oh yeah, their music too.

Truth be told, the Stranglers became a far less interesting band immediately after they stopped acting like a punk band. At least on the first two albums (*IV Rattus Norvegicus* and *No More Heroes*) there were plenty of taut, guitar-driven songs, rife with urban doom, gloom and paranoia. With the nasty vocals and slashing guitar of Hugh Cornwell setting the pace, bassist Jean-Jacques Burnel added his distorted grumbling to a mix that also featured Dave Greenfield's cheesy organ fills. Usually dressed in black, always unsmiling, and rude to their audiences (listen to Cornwell's between-song badinage on the LP *Live (X-Cert)*) the Stranglers worked very hard at being difficult and unlikable. They also made no bones about the fact that women were good for sex and little else, making their feeling clear on such transparently chauvinistic doggerel as "London Lady" and "Bring on the Nubiles."

Rock critics at the time were suspicious of the Stranglers' motives: although they ran in "proper" punk circles, and gigged at "proper" punk clubs, they always seemed slightly out-of-place musically with the London-based punk scene dominated by the Sex Pistols, the Damned, and Clash. The Stranglers offered no sense of outrage (despite being outrageous) or unpredictability, every move seemed calculated, as if it were an approximation of a punk aesthetic. Consequently, with each passing record, the Stranglers seemed more and more intent upon distancing themselves from the movement that had provided them their initial career momentum.

After 1978's *Black and White* failed to generate interest beyond their somewhat rabid fan base (more so in Europe than in America), A&M dropped them, but unlike many bands of the time that became trivia questions, the Stranglers soldiered on and focused their attention on their devoted Euro-fans, a wise move considering their records were no longer consistently released in America. In 1982, the band signed with Epic and began a lengthy relationship that lasted through the decade and into the '90s. The music, never really compelling in the first place, suffered greatly during this time. Prisoners of their own careerist impulses, the Stranglers turned to covering older rock classics in a desperate attempt to win American ears. Trying twice, first with the Kinks' "All Day and All of the Night" and then ? and the Mysterians "96 Tears," the Stranglers sounded as if flogging a dead horse was the best they could do. Gone also was their characteristic gritty and grimy sound replaced by a pop sheen that smelled of adult, new wave marketability (eventually Queen producer Roy Thomas Baker was brought in to help). There were plenty of mostly lousy solo records by everyone but Jet Black, and some fairly good compilations, but the saga of the Stranglers ends with them hanging around far too long. — *John Dougan*

Rattus Norvegicus / 1977 / A&M
○ **No More Heroes** / 1977 / A&M ✦✦✦✦
Rattus is hardly a punk rock classic but still is a pretty good chunk of art-punk. Hugh Cornwell's testosterone level is very high here and the macho preening gets a bit much, but it's still an enjoyable bit of noise that holds up better than I'm sure anyone would have guessed at the time. Still, it's odd to think of this as a part of the punk rock era, with the exception of the fast and sloppy production by Martin Rushent, and the short songs, there's not much that's overtly punk about it. *Heroes* on the other hand is faster, nastier and better. At this point the Stranglers were on top of their game and the ferocity and anger that suffuses these records would never be repeated. — *John Dougan*

Black & White / 1978 / A&M
Live (X Cert) / 1979 / IRS
Recorded at various gigs in 1977-78, *X Cert* is worthy if only to hear Hugh Cornwell bait and insult the audience (very punk!). Plus the band sounds pretty good, loads of aggression and volume add to the fun. Not essential but a very interesting snapshot of an era. — *John Dougan*

The Raven / 1979 / United Artists
Stranglers IV / 1980 / IRS
The Men in Black / 1981 / Liberty
La Folie / 1981 / Liberty
Feline / 1982 / Epic
Great Lost / 1983 / United Artists
Great Lost Continued / 1983 / United Artists
Aural Sculpture / 1984 / Epic
Off the Beaten Track / 1985 / Liberty
Dreamtime / 1987 / Epic
10 / 1990 / Epic
● **Greatest Hits 1977-1990** / 1990 / Epic ✦✦✦✦
Despite its rather cheeky title, this is a good place to sample the entire Stranglers output. From the squalor of the late-'70s material, to the smoothed out gloom pop of songs like "Skin Deep" and other mid- to late-'80s neo-Goth rock, this is a solid anthology that values substance over style and exhaustive track selection. Trust me, a well-edited Stranglers anthology is the only way to enjoy them, they recorded way too much dross to spend time searching out all of their plentiful, marginal records. — *John Dougan*
Season to Risk / Jun. 8, 1993 / VCY

Strawberry Alarm Clock

Group, Psychedelic
Strawberry Alarm Clock were a psychedelic bubblegum band of the mid-'60s, reaching the top of the charts with "Incense and Peppermints" at the height of the flower power era. Originally called the Sixpence, the Californian group consisted of Ed King (lead guitar), Lee Freeman (rhythm guitar), Gary Lovetro (bass), Mark Weitz (organ), and Randy Seol (drums). On the band's debut single, "Incense and Peppermints," lead vocals were sung by Greg Munford, a 16-year-old friend of the band. Before recording their full-length

debut album, the band added George Bunnell, who also played bass; more importantly, Bunnell became the group's main songwriter. In the summer of 1967, the Strawberry Alarm Clock contributed music to the film *Psych-Out*, as well as appearing in it. Gary Lovetro left the band before they recorded their second album, *Wake Up It's Tomorrow*, which also appeared in 1967. Between 1968's *The World in a Seashell* and 1969's *Good Morning Starshine* the band went through a number of lineup changes; as of *Good Morning Starshine* the band featured King on bass, Weitz, guitarist Jimmy Pitman, and drummer Gene Gunnels. By this time, the Strawberry Alarm Clock had lost much of its audience. They managed to keep performing until 1971, when the band finally broke up. Ed King went on to join Lynyrd Skynyrd; several of the former members of Strawberry Alarm Clock reunited in the '80s to perform on oldies tours. —*Stephen Thomas Erlewine*

● **Anthology** / 1993 / One Way ✦✦✦✦

The Strawbs

Group, Art-Rock/Progressive-Rock, Folk-Rock

One of the better British progressive bands of the early '70s, the Strawbs differed from their more successful compatriots—the Moody Blues, King Crimson, Pink Floyd—principally in that their sound originated in English folk music, rather than rock.

Founded in 1967 as a bluegrass-based trio called the Strawberry Hill Boys by singer/guitarist Dave Cousins, the group at that time consisted of Cousins, guitarist/singer Tony Hooper, and mandolin player Arthur Philips, who was replaced in 1968 by Ron Chesterman on bass. That same year, the group—now rechristened the Strawbs, and doing repertory well beyond the bounds of bluegrass music—briefly became a quartet with the temporary addition of Sandy Denny, who stayed long enough to record a relative handful of tracks (including the original version of her "Who Knows Where the Time Goes," which became a hit for Judy Collins) with the group on the Hallmark label before going off to join Fairport Convention.

In 1969, the Strawbs were signed to A&M Records, and cut their first album, the acoustic-textured *Strawbs*, that same year. For their second album, *Dragonfly*, recorded and released the following year, the group broadened their sound with the presence of a group of session musicians, including piano/organist Rick Wakeman. Soon after the release of this record, the group became a full-fledged band with the addition not only of Wakeman but also Richard Hudson and John Ford, both formerly of Elmer Gantry's Velvet Opera, on drums and bass, respectively. These changes, coupled with Cousins's increasing dexterity on electric guitar, gave the Strawbs a much more powerful sound that was showcased on their next album.

Just a Collection of Antiques and Curios (1970) was a bold move for a band just breaking itself before the public, recorded live at a concert at London's Queen Elizabeth Hall. In many ways, however, it was also a natural choice, showing off the quintet at its best, capable of doing credible versions of their early acoustic material but also jamming for long stretches on songs such as "Where Is that Dream of Your Youth," which gave Wakeman a major workout on the ivories and Hudson and Ford a chance to stretch out in the rhythm section. The album sold well, and was followed up the next year with *From the Witchwood*, a haunting collection of electric folk numbers that also addressed contemporary politics, especially the continuing strife in Northern Ireland. Wakeman's keyboard playing embellished much of the album to superb effect, and with surprising subtlety considering the flashiness of his subsequent work.

In 1971, however, he exited the Strawbs in order to join Yes, who were about a keyboard player with the departure of Tony Kaye, and Wakeman was replaced by Blue Weaver, formerly of the Immediate Records pop group the Amen Corner. *Grave New World* (1972) showed the band entering its strongest period, with Cousins' songwriting augmented by the new prowess of the composing team of Hudson and Ford, who wrote in a style completely different from (but perfectly compatible with) Cousins. This record, which managed to put a progressive rock slant on inspirational sources dating back hundreds of years (the cover was derived from an engraving by William Blake, which fit the music perfectly), became their best-selling album to date. Unfortunately, this release also heralded the exit of Tony Hooper, who was feeling out of place as an acoustic guitarist trapped within the group's heavily amplified surroundings. He was replaced by Dave Lambert, a much more aggressive, rock-oriented guitarist, and his addition

brought the group into its peak period. By this time, the group had acquired a cult following in the United States, where their albums from *Antiques and Curios* onward had all been issued.

Their 1973 album, *Bursting at the Seams*, seemed to say it all—every track was strong and memorable, resplendent in powerful guitar playing hooked around memorable riffs (acoustic as well as electric) and gorgeous synthesizer and Mellotron ornamentation. Two numbers off the album, "Lay Down" and "Part of the Union" (the former written by Cousins and the latter by Hudson and Ford), became Top Ten British hits, and one album track, "Down By the Sea," racked up substantial airplay on American FM radio. During this same period, Cousins recorded a solo album, *Two Weeks Last Summer*, that featured some of his more beautiful and introspective songs that the group had not recorded.

It was all too good to last, and it didn't. Blue Weaver left after one more tour, while Hudson and Ford—chafing at the ego problems resulting from their sudden rivalry with Cousins as songwriter—exited to form Hudson-Ford, also signed to A&M. The Strawbs regrouped in 1974 with *Hero and Heroine*, recorded with a new lineup consisting of Cousins, Lambert, John Hawken (formerly of the Nashville Teens) on keyboards, Chas Cronk (late of the original Renaissance) on bass, and ex-Stealers Wheel member Rod Coombes on drums. The new album was a critical and commercial failure in England, but proved popular in America, where the group's success over the previous two years had left them with a growing cult following. Their next two albums, *Ghosts* (1975) and *Nomadness* (1976), both did better in the United States than they did in England. None of this was enough to sustain the group, however, which continued to lose members and also left A&M Records. Two more albums of the Oyster label were poorly distributed and received, and one album for Arista, *Deadlines* (1978), was a failure, while a second record for the label was never released. By this time, the band was sandwiched between punk and disco, and unlike such rival progressive bands as the Moody Blues, who had a big enough following to ride out those twin storms on a wave of nostalgia, the Strawbs couldn't hold their audience well enough to sustain the interest of a major record label.

The group ceased to exist at the end of the 1970's, and Cousins embarked on some solo projects in association with guitarist Brian Willoughby that attracted the interest of die-hard fans but few others. That might have been the end of the group's history, if it hadn't been for an invitation to play the 1983 Cambridge Folk Festival. The Strawbs responded, in the guise of Cousins, Hooper, Hudson, Ford, Weaver, and Willoughby, and the response was so favorable that a tour was scheduled, which, in turn, led to their return to America in the mid-'80s. The group followed this up with two new studio albums released in Canada, and still plays whenever other commitments allow Cousins and company (with Rod Demick on bass and Chris Parren on keyboards) to get together. In 1993, they released their own retrospective concert album *Greatest Hits Live!*, which summed up many of the high points of their history. —*Bruce Eder*

○ **Sandy Denny & the Strawbs** / 1968 / Hannibal ✦✦✦✦
Acoustic folk and bluegrass. Mostly a showcase for Denny, plus a few clues to the group's future evolution. —*Bruce Eder*

Strawbs / 1969 / A&M ✦✦✦
Still an acoustic sound but with a much more expansive song structure and growing seriousness. (import)—*Bruce Eder*

Dragonfly / 1970 / A&M ✦✦✦
A transitional record, profound in some of its intent, but lacking muscle and excitement. (import) —*Bruce Eder*

Just a Collection of Antiques and Curios / 1970 / A&M ✦✦
A live recording from Queen Elizabeth Hall. The still-acoustic ensemble pulls their sound together in a series of long jams, but keyboardist Rick Wakeman's solo just doesn't fit. (Japanese import). —*Bruce Eder*

From the Witchwood / 1971 / A&M ✦✦✦

● **Grave New World** / 1972 / A&M ✦✦✦✦
Fulfillment! Singer/songwriter Dave Cousins finds a space somewhere between Bob Dylan and John Bunyan, Hudson and Ford come up with some superb hooks, and the electric sound is powerful and majestic. Powerful and sincere, if a little too serious and downbeat. (Japanese import) —*Bruce Eder*

○ **Bursting at the Seams** / 1973 / A&M ✦✦✦✦
A magnum opus: romantic, mystical, electrifying, and it rocks with a defiant smile. "Down by the Sea" is as fine a piece of progressive rock as was ever produced. (German import) —*Bruce Eder*

Strawbs by Choice / 1974 / A&M ✦✦✦

A concise retrospective of some of the better moments from the first four A&M albums. (Out-of-print import) —*Bruce Eder*

Hero & Heroine / 1974 / A&M ✦✦✦

The group's last great album, filled with mysticism and sexuality but lacking melodic subtlety. Loud, but with less richness of expression. (Canadian import) —*Bruce Eder*

Ghosts / 1975 / A&M ✦✦

Deteriorated sound and material, with beautiful and profound moments, but too much forgettable material around them. —*Bruce Eder*

Nomadness / 1976 / A&M ✦✦✦

○ **Deep Cuts** / 1976 / A&M ✦✦✦✦

Burning for You / 1977 / A&M ✦✦✦

Deadlines / 1978 / Arista ✦✦✦

Best of Strawbs / 1978 / A&M ✦✦✦

A double-album retrospective that misses the mark with too little of the best material from their best albums. Too much dross, and somehow flat-sounding. (Out of print) —*Bruce Eder*

● **A Choice Selection of Strawbs** / 1993 / A&M ✦✦✦✦

Very few of the U.K. group's albums have been released in CD format, and this comprehensive, 74-minute collection goes a long way to sating the resultant thirst. While there are elements of the Strawbs' mellotron-based sound that make *A Choice Selection* sound dated at times, the material survives better than many of the group's "progressive-minded" contemporaries. The Strawbs' roots went back to folk and bluegrass, and leader David Cousins never let instrumental virtuosity get in the way of a good song and well-turned lyric. —*Roch Parisien*

The Stray Cats

Group, Rockabilly

This U.S. rock trio consists of Brian Setzer (b. 1960), standup bass slapper Lee Rock (born Lee Drucher), and drummer Slim Jim Phantom (born James McDonnell). It was formed in 1979 in the midst of the punk/new wave scene, playing retro-rockabilly style. Emigrating to England shortly thereafter, they caught on quickly with a music scene that was always interested in the "next big thing," and their top-notch production by Dave Edmunds quickly moved them into the charts. Visual image and European success augered well for their return to the U.S. just in time to mine the early motherlode of MTV video-land. By the mid-'80s, after much success, the gimmick had worn off, and the band broke up by late 1984. They regrouped in the '90s after various solo projects had fizzled, with their style relatively unchanged. —*Cub Koda*

○ **Built for Speed** / 1982 / EMI America ✦✦✦✦

The best tracks from the Stray Cats' two U.K. albums, the best produced by Dave Edmunds, as the group updates rockabilly and Brian Setzer comes on like a rock star. Infectious. —*William Ruhlmann*

○ **Rant N' Rave with the Stray Cats** / 1983 / EMI America ✦✦✦✦

Rant N' Rave, the Stray Cats' second album, sounded identical to *Built for Speed,* and—thanks to the hits "(She's) Sexy + 17" and the ballad "I Won't Stand in Your Way"—it was equally as strong. —*Stephen Thomas Erlewine*

Rock Therapy / 1986 / EMI America ✦✦✦

Rock Therapy wasn't as consistently engaging as *Built for Speed* and *Rant N' Rave,* but it was a spirited, inspired effort that continued their trademark sound to a fine effect. —*Stephen Thomas Erlewine*

Blast Off / 1989 / EMI America ✦✦

Featuring a set of pleasant, but unexciting, songs, *Blast Off* indicated that the Stray Cats' revved-up rockabilly ran out of gas quickly. —*David Jehnzen*

● **The Best of Stray Cats: Rock This Town** / 1990 / EMI America ✦✦✦✦

Best of the Stray Cats—Rock This Town is a nice, solid compilation, featuring the title track, "Stray Cat Strut," and others. —*Cub Koda*

Choo Choo Hot Fish / 1992 / JRS ✦

Tear It Up / 1993 / Rre

Barbra Streisand

b. Apr. 24, 1942

Pop

Despite having to compete with rock singers during what is known as the "rock era," Barbra Streisand has turned out to be one of the most successful recording artists since WWII. As of the end of 1989, she had collected more platinum records than any other person, and her gold albums were exceeded only by Elvis Presley's. Streisand is also a successful actress and film director.

She got her start in New York City nightclubs and in musical comedy, appearing in *I Can Get It for You Wholesale* on Broadway when she was signed to CBS Records (now Sony Music). She went on to a starring role in *Funny Girl* (she would also star in the film version), by which time she had released her first album, *The Barbra Streisand Album.* During the mid-'60s, Streisand's albums were consistent sellers, though only her first single, "People," made the Top Ten. That meant she appealed primarily to adults and, as the '60s wore on, the music business became increasingly youth-oriented. In addition, Streisand turned more of her attention to Hollywood, resulting in a slight fall-off in her popularity as a singer.

She began to address this in the early '70s by singing more rock-oriented material, notably a Top Ten version of Laura Nyro's "Stoney End," but by the mid '70s she had found a niche as a singer of contemporary ballad material (for example, the theme song from her hit film *The Way We Were*). Streisand helped her own cause by co-writing the #1 hit "Evergreen" from her next film, *A Star Is Born,* and thereafter displayed a remarkable versatility that even found her at home in duets with disco diva Donna Summer and Bee Gee Barry Gibb. She was less active as a recording artist in the '80s, though in 1985 she scored an amazing success with *The Broadway Album,* probably her best-selling album ever. In 1991, she released a boxed-set retrospective, *Just for the Record…,* and in 1992 was thought to be close to re-signing a lucrative deal with Sony, covering both her musical and film activities. —*William Ruhlmann*

Pins and Needles [O.S.T.] / 1962 / Columbia

☆ **The Barbra Streisand Album** / 1962 / Columbia ✦✦✦✦✦

The birth of a legend, best exemplified by Streisand's slow ballad treatment of "Happy Days Are Here Again," which transforms it from a frothy celebration song into a far more complicated mixture of remorse and warmth. —*William Ruhlmann*

The Second Album / 1963 / Columbia

Funny Girl / 1964 / Columbia

People / 1964 / Columbia

The Third Album / May 1964 / Columbia

Color Me Barbra / 1966 / Columbia

☆ **Barbra's Christmas Album** / 1967 / Columbia ✦✦✦✦✦

This essential collection includes "Sleep in Heavenly Peace (Silent Night)" and "Jingle Bells." —*David A. Milberg*

Je M'appelle Barbra / 1967 / Columbia

A Happening in Central Park / 1968 / Columbia ✦✦✦

Streisand's personality is on full display here, and her singing is mesmerizing. —*William Ruhlmann*

What About Today? / 1969 / Columbia ✦✦✦

Streisand's first, tentative attempt to try out the work of contemporary songwriters. —*William Ruhlmann*

The Owl and the Pussycat / 1970 / Columbia ✦

The movie represented a comeback for Barbra Streisand after the big-budget disasters of *Hello, Dolly* and *On a Clear Day You Can See Forever.* But the soundtrack album is the lowest charting record of her career, perhaps because she doesn't sing! What she does do is talk—the album consists of dialogue from the movie, endless bickering between Streisand and George Segal, with background music by Blood, Sweat & Tears. —*William Ruhlmann*

★ **Greatest Hits** / 1970 / Columbia ✦✦✦✦✦

Barbra's best of the '60s. —*William Ruhlmann*

Stoney End / 1970 / Columbia

Emotion / 1970 / Columbia

○ **Barbra Joan Streisand** / 1971 / Columbia ✦✦✦✦

A confident Streisand takes on the songs of John Lennon and Carole King and even throws in an otherwise unheard tune by Steely Dan's Walter Becker and Donald Fagen. —*William Ruhlmann*

Live Concert at the Forum / 1971 / Columbia
Simply Streisand / 1972 / Columbia
Classical Barbra / 1974 / Columbia
Lazy Afternoon / 1975 / Columbia
Funny Lady / 1975 / Bay Cities ♦♦
Barbra Streisand is not known for singing standards, so the chief virtue of this soundtrack to the disappointing sequel to *Funny Girl* is hearing her singing songs like "Am I Blue." This is not a great virtue, however, especially when you also have to endure the singing of James Caan. — *William Ruhlmann*

Butterfly / 1975 / Columbia
Streisand Superman / 1977 / Columbia
☆ **Barbra Streisand's Greatest Hits, Vol. 2** / 1978 / Columbia ♦♦♦♦♦
The best of Barbra in the '70s. — *William Ruhlmann*

Songbird / 1978 / Columbia
Wet / 1979 / Columbia
The Main Event / Jun. 1979 / Columbia ♦♦
Barbra Streisand performs long, short, and ballad versions of the disco-ish title track, and the album is filled out by some rock 'n' roll oldies and more disco tracks. Upon release, this record (like the film) was at least timely, and both were successful. Neither has worn well, and today this is a very minor entry in the Streisand catalog. — *William Ruhlmann*

Guilty / 1980 / Columbia ♦♦♦
A chart-topping collaboration with Barry Gibb, featuring three Top Ten hits. — *William Ruhlmann*

The Way We Were / 1982 / Columbia
Memories / 1982 / Columbia
Yentl / 1983 / Columbia
The Legend of Barbra Streisand / 1983 / Columbia
☆ **The Broadway Album** / 1985 / Columbia ♦♦♦♦♦
Streisand's abandonment of Broadway was the worst thing that happened to the theater in the '60s. This album, including masterful versions of the work of Stephen Sondheim along with some older classics, is some small recompense. It is also the best work of a very great career. — *William Ruhlmann*

One Voice / 1986 / Columbia
Barbra Streisand . . . and Other Musical Instruments / 1988 / Columbia
○ **Greatest Hits . . . and More** / 1989 / Columbia ♦♦♦♦
This is really the third volume of Barbra's greatest hits, her best from the '80s. — *William Ruhlmann*

Prince of Tides / 1991 / Columbia
My Name Is Barbra 2 / 1991 / Columbia
Just for the Record . . . / Sep. 24, 1991 / Columbia
Highlights from "Just for the Record" / Jul. 30, 1992 / Columbia
Barbra: The Concert / 1994 / Sony
Back to Broadway / Columbia ♦♦♦

Barrett Strong

Soul, R&B, Motown
A pivotal figure in Motown's formative years, singer/composer Barrett Strong was a key associate and friend of Berry Gordy. It was his hit "Money (That's What I Want)" for Anna Records in 1960 that provided vital capital for Gordy to expand his operation. The song gave Strong his only major hit as a vocalist, reaching number two on the R&B charts and barely missing the pop Top 20. During the late '60s and early '70s, Strong collaborated with Norman Whitfield on some historic songs that included Marvin Gaye's "I Heard It Through the Grapevine" and "Too Busy Thinking About My Baby," the Temptations' "Papa Was a Rolling Stone" and "Ball of Confusion", Edwin Starr's "War," and "Take Me in Your Arms and Love Me" for Gladys Knight and the Pips, which he also co-wrote. Strong left Motown when they moved to Los Angeles in 1972, and he signed with Epic. After one failed single, Strong moved to Capitol, where he had the LP *Stronghold* released in 1975 and later *Live & Love* in 1976. Though it wasn't a hit, his song "Man up in the Sky" was a '70s soul gem. Johnny Bristol later re-recorded it. Strong continued into the '80s, recording "Rock It Easy" for an independent label and writing and arranging "You

Can Depend on Me," which was included on the Dells' *The Second Time* LP in 1988. — *Ron Wynn*

● **Stronghold** / 1975 / Capitol ♦♦♦♦
Live & Love / 1976 / Capitol ♦♦

Nolan Strong & the Diablos

Group, R&B
This early Detroit R&B vocal group formed in 1950, originally featuring Nolan Strong, Juan Guiterriec, Willie Hunter, Quentin Eubanks, and Bob "Chico" Edwards on guitar. Strong was blessed with a beautiful high tenor voice (and even higher falsetto) and writing and arranging skills far surpassing those of most doo-wop groups of the era. What makes his recordings (with and without the Diablos) so special is that we're hearing the Motown sound in its embryonic form. Nolan was the original Smokey Robinson, the original Michael Jackson, years before either of them stood before a microphone at Motown. Recording his entire career for the tiny independent Fortune (Detroit's first Black R&B label), Strong's influence on Smokey and the early Motown stable of talent was unmistakable. As late as the early '60s, Berry Gordy tried to buy Nolan's contract from Fortune and install him as head arranger and producer but to no avail. (The job went instead to Robinson.) Incredibly handsome with a strong stage presence, Strong came close to the big time on several occasions (when his "Mind Over Matter" started to break nationally, Gordy recruited the Temptations to cover it under the name the Pirates, the only time in the history of Motown that this was done), but his erratic temperament and lifestyle ensured that it was not to be. The genius of one of the greatest and yet most underappreciated artists in the history of pop music lives on in the 20-odd years of recordings Strong did in a tiny, crudely equipped studio situated in the back of a record shop. The original sound of the Motor City, indeed. — *Cub Koda*

● **Fortune of Hits, Vol. 1** / 1961 / Fortune ♦♦♦♦
All the early hits, and the perfect place to start. — *Cub Koda*
○ **Fortune of Hits, Vol. 2** / 1962 / Fortune ♦♦♦♦
Mind over Matter / 1963 / Fortune ♦♦♦
Early '60s. Very soulful. — *Cub Koda*
Daddy Rock / 1963 / Fortune ♦♦♦
A great batch of rare and unreleased sides. — *Cub Koda*

Joe Strummer

Rock & Roll, Alternative Pop/Rock
One of the most talented songwriters of his generation, Joe Strummer has seemed lost since disbanding the Clash after the wretched *Cut the Crap* in 1986. Strummer has done some respectable soundtrack work (*Walker, Straight to Hell,* five strong tracks for *Permanent Record,* and the theme song for *Sid & Nancy*). He acted impressively in Jim Jarmusch's *Mystery Train* and Alex Cox's *Straight to Hell,* collaborated with ex-partner Mick Jones, and released one solo album, 1989's *Earthquake Weather.* — *Stephen Thomas Erlewine*

● **Earthquake Weather** / 1989 / Epic ♦♦♦♦
Strummer's first solo album is a muddled hodgepodge of roots-rock and world explorations. His compositions are fine, but are often undercut by the limp kick of the band. — *Stephen Thomas Erlewine*

The Style Council

Group, Pop/Rock
Guitarist/vocalist Paul Weller broke up the Jam, the most popular British band of the early '80s, at the very height of their success in 1982 because he was dissatisfied with their musical direction. Weller wanted to incorporate more elements of soul, R&B, and jazz into his songwriting, which is something he felt his bandmates, with their roots in punk, were incapable of performing. In order to pursue this musical direction, he teamed up in 1983 with keyboardist Mick Talbot, a former member of the mod-revival band the Merton Parkas, a group that was heavily inspired by the Jam. Together, Weller and Talbot became the Style Council—other musicians were added according to what kind of music the duo were performing. With the Style Council, the underlying intellectual pretensions that ran throughout Weller's music came to the forefront. Although the music was rooted in American R&B, it was performed slickly—complete with layers of synthesizers and drum machines—and filtered through European styles and attitudes. Weller's lyrics were typically earnest, yet his leftist political lean-

ings became more pronounced. His scathing criticisms of racism, unemployment, Margaret Thatcher, and sexism sat uneasily beside his burgeoning obsession with high culture, as he wrote self-mockingly pompous liner notes under the name "The Cappuccino Kid" as well as a full-fledged classical piece on their last record. As his pretensions increased, the number of hits the Style Council had decreased; by the end of the decade, the group was barely able to crack the British Top 40 and Weller had turned from a hero into a has-been.

Released in March of 1983, the Style Council's first single "Speak like a Child" sounded like an outtake from the Jam's final album, *The Gift* and it became an immediate hit, reaching number four on the British charts. Three months later, the looser and funkier "The Money-Go-Round" peaked at number 11 on the charts, as the group had an EP, *Paris*, which appeared in August; the EP reached number three. Originally intended as the last Jam single, "Solid Bond in Your Heart" became another hit for the Style Council in November, peaking at number 11 on the British charts. Weller and Talbot named their recording studio, Solid Bond, after the single. Compiled from the first U.K. singles, the mini-album *Introducing the Style Council* was released in America, peaking at number 172.

The Style Council released their first full-length album, *Cafe Bleu*, in March of 1984; two months later, a resequenced version of the record, re-titled *My Ever Changing Moods*, was released in May. *Cafe Bleu* was Weller's most stylistically ambitious album to date, drawing from jazz, soul, rap, and pop. While it was musically all over the map, it was their most successful album, peaking at number five in the U.K. and number 56 in the U.S. *Groovin'*, an EP featuring two songs drawn from the album ("You're the Best Thing" and "Big Boss Groove") reached number five, while "My Ever Changing Moods" was their first U.S. hit, peaking at number 29. Following the number seven hit "Shout to the Top," Weller organized the Council Collective, a benefit for the U.K. coal miners strike, featuring Jimmy Ruffin and Junior. The collective recorded "Soul Deep," with all profits from the single going to Women Against the Pit Closures and the widow of taxi driver David Wilkie, who was killed in the strike.

In the summer of 1985, the Style Council had another U.K. Top Ten hit with "The Walls Come Tumbling Down." The single was taken from *Our Favourite Shop*, which reached number one on the U.K. charts; the record was released as *Internationalists* in the U.S. At the beginning of 1986, the group took part in the "Red Wedge" tour, which was a series of concerts featuring several left-wing acts that was designed to gather youth votes for the U.K. Labour Party. In February of 1986, Weller folded his record label Respond Records, which achieved only a small amount of success. "Have You Ever Had It Blue," taken from Julien Temple's film *Absolute Beginners*, became a number 14 U.K. hit single that spring. It was followed shortly afterward by the live album, *Home and Abroad*, which peaked at number eight. At the end of the year, Weller married Dee C. Lee, who had been a backup singer for the Style Council since 1984.

The Style Council had its last Top Ten single with "It Didn't Matter" in January of 1987. *Cost of Loving*, an album that featured a heavy emphasis on jazz-inspired soul, followed in February. Although it received unfavorable reviews, the record peaked at number two in the U.K.; in the U.S., it was a more modest success, reaching number 122. That spring, "Waiting" became the group's first single not to crack the British Top 40, signalling that their popularity was rapidly declining. The Style Council also released *JerUSAlem*, a 30-minute movie that satirized the music industry, to movie theaters that spring. "Wanted" was released that fall, yet it failed to make it past number 20.

Weller sold Solid Bond in April of 1988, just prior to the release of "Life at a Top People's Health Farm." The single was a relative disappointment, peaking at number 28. In July, the Style Council released their last album, *Confessions of a Pop Group*, which featured Weller's most spiteful and pessimistic lyrics, as well as his most self-important and pompous music—the second side of the record was entitled "The Piano Paintings," featuring several jazzy numbers and a ten-minute classical-styled, orchestral suite called "The Gardener of Eden." The record charted fairly well, reaching number 15 in the U.K., but it received terrible reviews. Taken from *Confessions*, "How She Threw It All Away" failed to reach the U.K. Top 40. The group released one more single, "Promised Land," in early 1989, yet it didn't make it past number 27 on the charts. That March, the Style Council released a compilation, *The Singular Ad-*

ventures of the Style Council, which reached number three on the charts; a remix of "Long Hot Summer" released that summer peaked at number 48. Later that year, Weller delivered a new Style Council album, which reflected his infatuation with house and club music, to the band's record label Polydor. Polydor rejected the album and dropped both the Style Council and Weller from the label. Paul Weller and Mick Talbot officially broke up the Style Council in 1990. In early 1991, Weller returned with the Paul Weller Movement, who released its first single in Japan only, because no other record label would sign him. However, within two years he would return to both critical and commercial favor with his first two solo albums, *Paul Weller* (1992) and *Wild Wood* (1993). *—Stephen Thomas Erlewine*

○ **Introducing the Style Council** / 1983 / Polydor ✦✦✦✦

A solid EP collection of the band's initial British singles, it includes the ersatz soul of "Long Hot Summer," the bubbling pop of "Speak like a Child," and "Money-Go-Round," a fine British-funk manifesto. *—John Floyd*

○ **My Ever Changing Moods** / 1984 / Geffen ✦✦✦✦

○ **Cafe Bleu** / 1984 / Polydor ✦✦✦✦

Style Council's first proper album *Cafe Bleu* was one of their better efforts, but it indicated the group's fatal flaw—a tendency to be too eclectic and overambitious. Amidst the lazy jazz instrumentals, many of them courtesy of Mick Talbot, Paul Weller inserted several solid soul-tinged pop songs, including "My Ever Changing Moods," "Headstart for Happiness," "You're the Best Thing," and "Here's One that Got Away." However, that doesn't excuse the rap experiment, "A Gospel." The album was later released with a slightly different running order as *My Ever Changing Moods* in the U.S.; the American edition included the U.K. hit "A Solid Bond in Your Heart." *—Stephen Thomas Erlewine*

○ **Internationalists** / 1985 / Geffen ✦✦✦✦

○ **Our Favourite Shop** / 1985 / Polydor ✦✦✦✦

Our Favourite Shop, the Style Council's second proper album, was still quite eclectic, but it didn't seem as schizophrenically diverse as *Cafe Bleu*. Weller had been able to incorporate his soul and jazz experiments into his songwriting, writing the fine "Walls Come Tumbling Down," "Come to Milton Keys," "Boy Who Cried Wolf," and "Down in the Seine," which were some of his best songs for the Style Council. The occasional misguided experiment remained—the stiff funk of "The Internationalists" and the self-righteous "The Stand Up Comic's Instructions" were particularly embarrassing—but the record was more cohesive and stronger than the debut. In America, the album was released without "Our Favourite Shop" and retitled *Internationalists*. *—Stephen Thomas Erlewine*

Home & Abroad / 1986 / Geffen ✦✦

Home & Abroad is a slick and earnest live set, but it's only of interest to die-hard Paul Weller fans. *—Stephen Thomas Erlewine*

Cost of Loving / 1987 / Polydor ✦✦

A full-fledged soul album, *The Cost of Loving* illustrated why Paul Weller's star was rapidly declining in the late '80s. Filled with bland, professional soul-pop, few of the songs have memorable melodies and the band tends to meander through the slick arrangements. Weller's lyrics were self-important and under-developed, with only the hit single "It Didn't Matter" making a lasting impression among the undistinguished songs that comprised the majority of the album. *—Stephen Thomas Erlewine*

Confessions of a Pop Group / 1988 / Polydor ✦

If *The Cost of Loving* was a thoroughly mediocre affair, *Confessions of a Pop Group* was flat-out bad, without a single like "It Didn't Matter" to redeem its indulgences. Throughout the album, Weller engages in some of his most pretentious and mean-spirited lyrics, but they are no match for the music he's written, which ranges from self-important jazz-pop fusions to an orchestral suite that finishes the album. The result was bad enough to leave him without a record contract in the U.K., where he was considered a god just eight years earlier. *—Stephen Thomas Erlewine*

● **The Singular Adventures of The Style Council** / 1989 / Polydor ✦✦✦✦

An adequate hits collection, it skims the cream from their otherwise disappointing albums and includes "You're the Best Thing," the closest they've ever come to a U.S. hit. *—John Floyd*

Here's Some That Got Away / Feb. 22, 1994 / Polydor ✦✦✦
Since the Style Council's albums were either inconsistent or down-right boring, the idea of a B-sides and rarities collection isn't exactly enticing. However, *Here's Some That Got Away* is surprisingly enjoyable, proving that Paul Weller was at his best when he wasn't trying to make serious, self-important music. —*Stephen Thomas Erlewine*

The Stylistics

Group, Soul
One of the sweetest soul groups hailing from Philly, with an incredible run of soul smashes from 1971 to 1975. The fragile falsetto of Russell Thompkins, Jr. (b. Mar 21, 1951) and sumptuous production of Thom Bell added up to serious long-term success for the Stylistics. The quintet debuted on the charts in 1971 with "You're a Big Girl Now" and proceeded to set the soul and pop markets ablaze with "You Are Everything," "Betcha by Golly Wow," "I'm Stone in Love with You," "Break Up to Make Up"—all ballads—and the untypical rocker "Rockin' Roll Baby" on Abco. Although they left the label in 1976, the hits rolled on for another decade, albeit not on so lofty a scale. —*Bill Dahl*

The Stylistics / 1971 / Avco Embassy ✦✦✦
The brilliant album that got everything started. Heads turned, people snapped to attention (women especially), and the "sweet" soul fraternity was turned on its head when this five-member group featuring the sugary, sweeping falsetto of Russell Tompkins, Jr. hit the scene with such singles as "Betcha By Golly Wow," "People Make The World Go Round," and "Stop, Look and Listen To Your Heart." His delivery, shimmering style, and brilliant pacing and control temporarily rendered almost every other "sweet" soul vocalist and group speechless; pretty soon, the Delfonics, Blue Magic, Moments, and others would fight back, but in 1972, everyone was playing catchup to the Stylistics. —*Ron Wynn*

○ **Round 2** / 1972 / Amherst ✦✦✦✦
The Russell Tompkins, Jr. legend began to grow in the early '70s with this superb album. His version of "You'll Never Get To Heaven If You Break My Heart" inspired fantasies from women that probably surpassed what Dionne Warwick generated in men, while "Break Up To Make Up" and "I'm Stone In Love With You" were instant anthems and are still among the great 1970s love ballads. —*Ron Wynn*

○ **Rock'n'Roll Baby** / 1973 / H&L ✦✦✦✦
○ **Love Hits** / 1974 / Amherst ✦✦✦✦
Another anthology, this one covering the beautiful love songs and romantic ballads that were the Stylistics' specialty. These are all magnificent, some of the finest sentimental soul that's ever been recorded. But it's also been issued before, and Amherst's mastering isn't anything to write home about, especially the way they tend to wash out Russell Tompkins, Jr.'s high notes. —*Ron Wynn*

Let's Put It All Together / 1974 / Avco Embassy ✦✦✦
Their finest album, the Stylistics climbed the "sweet" soul mountain in 1974. "You Make Me Feel Brand New" and the title cut were among the year's prime love/romance numbers, and Russell Tompkins, Jr. had nudged past Blue Magic's Ted Mills and the Delfonics' Hart brothers as the falsetto voice of choice among female fans. Their run on Avco, with Thom Bell at the production helm, was one of the greatest in modern soul annals. —*Ron Wynn*

Heavy / 1974 / Avco Embassy ✦✦✦
The magical union between the Stylistics and producer/writer Thom Bell ended with this album, but the legacy had included a string of fabulous hit singles and arguably the greatest "sweet" soul productions of all time. Russell Tompkins, Jr. was in his prime as a lead vocalist, and while this album didn't have any blockbusters like its predecessors, it still had plenty of exquisitely sung, nicely harmonized ballads and love tunes. —*Ron Wynn*

● **The Best of the Stylistics** / 1975 / Amherst ✦✦✦✦
Any of their collections are good, but this one features their biggest and best hits, including "I'm Stone in Love with You," "Rockin' Roll Baby," "Betcha by Golly Wow," and "You Make Me Feel Brand New." —*Cub Koda*

Thank You Baby / 1975 / Avco Embassy ✦✦✦
The group's decline began with this album, their next to last on Avco and their weakest to that point. Thom Bell's departure hastened the slump, for such songs as "Can't Give You Anything (But My Love)" and "Thank You Baby" lacked the lyrical insight, flow, and rhyme scheme that characterized their past triumphs. Russell

Tompkins, Jr., didn't seem as focused or effective, and the backing was feeble, as were the arrangements. —*Ron Wynn*

You Are Beautiful / 1975 / Avco Embassy ✦✦
The Stylistics' slump continued as they concluded the Avco years with this 1975 album. It was clear from the content of "Day the Clown Came to Town" and "Na-Na Is the Saddest Word" how much they missed Thom Bell. Russell Tompkins, Jr., was merely competent, and sometimes sounded dispirited, as did the remaining members behind him. The production, arrangements, and compositions ranged from routine to banal, and the entire affair was a sorry way for a great group to leave a label after several wonderful years. —*Ron Wynn*

○ **All-Time Classics** / 1976 / Amherst ✦✦✦✦
When the Stylistics switched to Amherst in the '80s, their glorious "sweet" soul hits were repackaged on a couple of collections. This was a singular set covering their finest '70s numbers; another package split them into a two-part release. It's slightly improved in sound quality over the 1975 *The Best of The Stylistics*, and hearing Russell Tompkins, Jr.'s quavering falsetto at any time is a treat. —*Ron Wynn*

○ **The Best of the Stylistics, Vol. 2** / 1976 / Amherst ✦✦✦✦
This was the second volume in a two-part collection that resulted in Amherst Records issuing the same music three times. The songs are wonderful, the tactic ethically dubious at best. There hasn't been anything fresh issued since Amherst obtained their masters, and they don't do all that great a job of remastering the hits. —*Ron Wynn*

○ **Wonder Woman** / 1978 / H&L ✦✦✦✦
The Stylistics' tenure on Mercury wasn't memorable. They couldn't find the right songs and couldn't get their albums or singles in the right hands, or aired on radio. This album actually had some nice tracks; the title cut was fine, and "First Impressions" made the charts. But the overall product was limp and the group didn't remain with Mercury very long. —*Ron Wynn*

In Fashion / 1978 / Mercury ✦✦✦
The Stylistics' late-'70s slump continued with this album. The up-tempo tunes were completely flat, while the ballads often had a good lead vocal from Russell Tompkins, Jr., and solid harmonizing behind him, but were sabotaged by third-rate lyrics or even worse production and arrangements. —*Ron Wynn*

Love Spell / 1979 / Mercury ✦✦✦
The Stylistics showed signs of life with this late-'70s effort. Their vocals were once more vigorous and assertive, while Russell Tompkins, Jr. reached back and began singing with the soaring force and might that had characterized their best songs. They still didn't have top-flight, or even good material, and the production and arrangements were again dreary. But at least the group didn't sound ready to call it a career. —*Ron Wynn*

Hurry up This Way Again / 1980 / Philadelphia International ✦✦✦
The Stylistics' last album to hit the pop charts, this eased them into the 1980s on somewhat solid ground. While the "sweet" sound was no longer a force in black music, they had regrouped with a deal on TSOP, and the title cut garnered them one final Top 20 R&B hit. It was the end of an era, as delicately sung, innocently written pop and "sweet" soul would soon be relegated to the graveyard of nostalgia. —*Ron Wynn*

○ **Closer Than Close** / 1981 / Philadelphia International ✦✦✦✦
A nice, though slightly disappointing album that saw the Stylistics fail to regain the chart momentum they had enjoyed in the 1970s, despite getting superior production and decent songs from the Gamble/Huff team. "Sweet" soul had pretty much run its course by the early '80s, and urban contemporary radio hadn't yet stratified to the degree where the group could have been marketed to no-rap outlets. But the vocals were above-average, and Russell Tompkins, Jr. had emerged from his late-'70s funk and was again singing with flair, expressiveness, and conviction. —*Ron Wynn*

1982 / 1982 / Philadelphia International ✦✦✦
The Stylistics didn't always get hits when they were with Gamble and Huff, but their albums sure sounded great. That was the case with *1982*. But the superb production and mastering aside, this was the least interesting, off-centered album the group did while at TSOP. There wasn't one song that charted, nor were there any that deserved to be hits, which was almost shocking considering the parties involved. —*Ron Wynn*

● **Very Best of the Stylistics** / 1983 / H&L ✦✦✦✦
This is one of many collections that gather their hit singles; "Make Up To Break Up," "You Are Everything," "Rock and Roll Baby" and many others are landmark numbers, even if thematic variety and stylistic diversity weren't Stylistics traits. —*Ron Wynn*

Some Things Never Change / 1985 / Streetwise ✦✦✦
The Stylistics got a little mileage from the title track, but this late-'80s album on Streetwise was a far cry from the glory years. The production was uneven, the sound muffled and muddy, and the arrangements undistinguished. Even Russell Tompkins, Jr.'s normally shimmering falsetto sounded meek and unconvincing, and the backgrounds were equally flat. Only completely uncritical completists would want this one. —*Ron Wynn*

Love Talk / 1991 / Amherst ✦✦✦
The Stylistics sounded much better than many thought was possible on this early-'90s release. It wasn't the heavenly material they did with Thom Bell, but it also wasn't hack work. Russell Tompkins, Jr. still managed to sound as though he were a young tenor, even if his falsetto cracked at times. What slowed the comeback, besides being on a label (Amherst) no one knew existed, was an absence of a killer single and the general reluctance of trendy urban radio programmers to even consider airing a single by from a group of 1970s icons. —*Ron Wynn*

Styx

Group, Hard Rock, Art-Rock/Progressive-Rock
Styx were one of the biggest art-rock bands of the late '70s, capable of producing monster hits with their stadium rock, power ballads, and concept albums. More than any other art-rock band, Styx was able to cross over into the pop charts, scoring hits with "Babe," "Lady," "Come Sail Away," "Too Much Time on My Hands," and "Don't Let It End." Never one for subtlety, their ballads featured sweeping, over-arranged guitars and keyboards while their rockers were long and detailed, with several different sections and gargantuan guitar solos. When MTV rolled around in the early '80s, the hits stopped coming; they broke up in 1984. Six years later, they reunited and released *Edge of the Century*; the record featured "Show Me the Way," which became popular as a Gulf War anthem. The band went on hiatus a couple of years after the album's release. —*Stephen Thomas Erlewine*

The Serpent Is Rising / 1973 / RCA ✦✦
Styx II / 1973 / RCA ✦✦✦
Styx's second album was a belated success, scoring a Top Ten hit with "Lady," two years after its release. In retrospect, it is easy to see why *Styx II* was ignored upon its release. Apart from "Lady" and "You Need Love," most of the album is bland. However, it's the best of the group's first three records. —*Stephen Thomas Erlewine*

Man of Miracles / 1974 / RCA ✦✦
Equinox benefitted from the belated success of *Styx II* and its single, "Lady," spending 50 weeks on the charts. The record was actually stronger than the earlier set, featuring a more consistent set of songs including the Top 40 hit "Lorelei." —*Stephen Thomas Erlewine*

Equinox / 1975 / A&M ✦✦✦
Crystal Ball / 1976 / A&M ✦✦✦
Crystal Ball wasn't as successful as *Equinox*, but it was a better album, showcasing Styx's increased skill for crafting simple, catchy pop hooks out of their bombastic sound. —*Daevid Jehnzen*

○ **The Grand Illusion** / 1977 / A&M ✦✦✦✦
With *The Grand Illusion*, Styx catapulted to Top Ten and multiplatinum status, thanks to the hit single, "Come Sail Away." Although the group's sound was still based in art-rock, the best moments on the record occur when they fit majestic pomp into the constraints of a pop song like "Fooling Yourself (The Angry Young Man)" or "Come Sail Away." —*Stephen Thomas Erlewine*

○ **Pieces of Eight** / 1978 / A&M ✦✦✦✦
Pieces of Eight continued Styx's winning streak, selling over three million copies over the years. Styx was savvy enough to make their art-rock appear like arena-rock, as the "Blue Collar Man (Long Nights)" single indicates, as well as the hit "Renegade." —*Stephen Thomas Erlewine*

○ **Cornerstone** / 1979 / A&M ✦✦✦✦
"Babe" became Styx's first number one single and its accompanying album, *Cornerstone*, saw the band expanding their pop accessibility without dispensing the art-rock traditions that made them famous. —*Stephen Thomas Erlewine*

○ **Paradise Theater** / 1980 / A&M ✦✦✦✦
Paradise Theater was Styx's masterpiece, filled with conceptually ambitious songs as well as concise pop singles, like the driving hard rocker "Too Much Time on My Hands" and the power ballad "The Best of Times." It perfectly encapsulates both Styx's progessive side and their catchy, hard rock leanings. —*Daevid Jehnzen*

Kilroy Was Here / 1983 / A&M ✦✦✦
An ambitious—and, to be frank, pretty silly—concept album about an Orwellian future controlled by a fascist dictator who has outlawed rock & roll and the rebellion led by an exiled rocker, *Kilroy Was Here* was a pretty odd way for the original lineup of Styx to end their recording career. Some of the album is quite listenable—the ballad "Don't Let It End" is powerful, while "Mr. Roboto" is an infectious pomp-rocker—but the album is hampered by a lack of memorable melodies. —*Stephen Thomas Erlewine*

Caught in the Act / 1984 / A&M ✦
A live set recorded during their 1983 tour, *Caught in the Act* is a lackluster record. —*Daevid Jehnzen*

● **Classics, Vol. 15** / 1987 / A&M ✦✦✦✦
This best-of collection amply covers this group's primary radio hits and key album cuts. Included are "Babe," "Best of Times," "Too Much Time on My Hands," "Mr. Roboto," "Don't Let it End," "Blue Collar Man (Long Nights)," "Come Sail Away," "Crystal Ball," and "Grand Illusion." —*Rick Clark*

Edge of the Century / 1990 / A&M ✦✦
Melodic hard pop and power ballads, obviously cut from the same cloth as Journey, but with a nod to modern metal. "I've Got a Lot to Learn About Love," the song that sounds the most like classic Journey, was an AOR hit. —*Brian Mansfield*

The Subdudes

Group, Rock & Roll
The Subdudes embrace New Orleans and Memphis soul and filter it through an earthy acoustic/electric style, with rich, heartfelt harmonies. The fact that the Subdudes lack a drummer makes them unique in an idiom traditionally built on a foundation of solid drumming. They compensate with a percussionist who manages to make a tambourine sound like a trap set. —*Rick Clark*

● **The Subdudes** / 1990 / East West ✦✦✦✦
Lovers of earthy soulful music, heavy in New Orleans spirit, should check out this impressive debut, produced by Don Gehman (John Mellencamp, Treat Her Right). "Need Somebody," "Any Cure," "Got You on His Mind," and a version of the Crescent City-standard "Big Chief" are among the highlights. —*Rick Clark*

Lucky / 1991 / East West ✦✦✦
This sophomore outing contains a nice version of Al Green's "Tired of Being Alone." Overall it's almost as consistent-sounding as their debut. —*Rick Clark*

Annunciation / Mar. 29, 1994 / High Street ✦✦

The Subterranean Dining Rooms

Group, Alternative Pop/Rock
One of the zaniest and most satisfying underground acts to emerge at the end of the 1980s, details are scarce on this Italian outfit. Judging from the numerous rotating personnel heard and listed on their two albums, they're a collective of sorts. Whoever they or their principal driving forces are, they're obviously besotted by the quirky, melodic folk-rock of British eccentrics like Syd Barrett and Nikki Sudden. Sung in accented English, they create the kind of hushed, melodic acoustic rock that fills the room in the wee hours. Little known even in the underground, and poorly distributed in the U.S., they deserve a wider audience. —*Richie Unterberger*

● **There's No Rock'n Roll Singer Without A Spanish Knife** / 1988 / Crazy Mannequin ✦✦✦✦
A nine-song mini-album of short, bittersweet tunes, strongly recalling their probable inspiration Syd Barrett on "I Don't Care." Mostly acoustic, with bursts of noise on the cover of the Velvet Underground's "European" and the psychedelic backwards/phased guitar piece that closes each side (in different versions). A fine, oddball effort that displays some of the best attributes of late-'60s/early-'70s folk and progressive rock without sounding retro. —*Richie Unterberger*

○ **Ghosts In The Sun** / 1989 / Crazy Mannequin ✦✦✦✦
A more diverse and elaborately produced effort than their debut, embellishing the minor-key acoustic guitar strumming with ominous piano, flamenco runs, and occasional backwards guitar. Al-

ternating between a high, wispy female singer and a rough-hewn male vocalist, they explore somber, ethereal territory here, as one could gather from titles like "Fog Thru The Night," "A Kiss In French Night," and "Ghosts In The Sun." More top-rank late-night music, a bit more heavy-hearted than the first LP, with hauntingly pretty melodies that rescue this material from gloom'n'doom fare. —*Richie Unterberger*

Suede

Group, Alternative Pop/Rock

Like many English bands that receive massive praise from the British press, Suede was dismissed as mere hype by most listeners before they had even released a record. However, this was one time that the press were right. Suede might not be entirely original, yet their sweaty, sensual mix of the decadent elegance of '70s glam rock and the tortured angst of the post-punk British rock of the '80s makes them one of the most exciting English guitar bands of the '90s. Bernard Butler's guitar combines the crunch of Mick Ronson with the innovative, intricate rhythms and textures of Johnny Marr; Bret Anderson's exaggerated accent can be grating to some ears, yet it fits the grandly theatrical ballads "So Young" and "Stay Together," as well as throttling rockers like "Metal Mickey" and "Animal Nitrate." Anderson's impressionistic lyrics can be a little precious, but the band's musical ability saves him from his pretensions. Suede's self-titled 1993 debut was a huge hit in England, but they only gained a small cult in America. As the band was recording their follow-up in 1994, an obscure American jazz-pop singer that called herself Suede forced the band to change their name to the London Suede in the U.S.; in the rest of the world, they've been able to retain their name.

Bernard Butler left the band prior to the release of their second album, *Dog Man Star;* he was replaced by Richard Oakes. —*Stephen Thomas Erlewine*

● **Suede** / Apr. 1993 / Nude/Columbia ✦✦✦✦

It's not often that an album can live up to its pre-release hype, but Suede's debut album is one of those rare occasions. A uniquely original amalgam of glam-rock and post-punk rock, *Suede* takes the snarling guitars of early-'70s rock and sets them to the angst of the Smiths. Although he is a fine singer, there is no doubt that Brett Anderson's grandly theatrical vocals are an acquired taste, but the strength of their material warrants such indulgences. It's been a while since a rock & roll band has captured adolescent sexual yearnings so well. —*Stephen Thomas Erlewine*

○ **Dog Man Star** / Oct. 1994 / Nude/Columbia ✦✦✦✦

Recorded as guitarist Bernard Butler's relationship with songwriting partner Brett Anderson was fraying, *Dog Man Star* is a sweeping, cinematic triumph of a second album. While some of the youthful energy of "The Drowners" and "Metal Mickey" remain (particularly on the crunching "This Hollywood Life"), most of *Dog Man Star* finds Suede creating grand, lush, seething soundscapes. Occasionally boosted by dramatic strings, the songs are the best Butler and Anderson have ever written; from the sleazy, muscular pulse of "We Are the Pigs" through the aching ballad "The Wild Ones" to the finale "Still Life," the entire album fulfills the potential of Suede's debut. —*Stephen Thomas Erlewine*

Sugar

Group, Alternative Pop/Rock

After two solo albums, ex-Hüsker Dü guitarist/vocalist Bob Mould formed Sugar, another punk-pop trio, with bassist David Barbe and drummer Malcolm Travis. Sugar recalls Mould's days with the seminal Hüsker Dü more than his solo albums, yet the band is not a carbon copy of *Flip Your Wig* or *New Day Rising.* Instead, Sugar's music is more streamlined and pop-oriented than Hüsker, without sacrificing Mould's trademark intensity—*Beaster* is one of the most uncompromising recordings he has ever released. Although their first two releases were dominated by Mould, he has insisted that Sugar is a group in all senses of the word and from the sound of the band, he's right—they interact brilliantly with each other, producing a cohesive sound that was missing from Mould's last solo album, *Black Sheets of Rain.*

After their difficult second record, *File Under: Easy Listening,* in 1994, Bob Mould began complaining that he felt limited by the group, claiming that lo-fi recordings by Sebadoh and Guided by Voices were more inspiring and immediate. Sugar was officially on hiatus during the summer of 1995. —*Stephen Thomas Erlewine*

● **Copper Blue** / 1992 / Rykodisc ✦✦✦✦

Featuring some of Mould's best songwriting, Sugar's debut album is a stunning piece of hook-laden punk-pop, highlighted by the '60s-style "If I Can't Change Your Mind," the loud, beautiful guitars of "Man on the Moon" and "Helpless," and the tongue-in-cheek Pixies tribute, "A Good Idea." —*Stephen Thomas Erlewine*

Beaster / 1993 / Rykodisc ✦✦✦

Recorded at the same time as *Copper Blue, Beaster* is a darker, more intense record than Sugar's debut, but it's never as black as Mould's *Black Sheets of Rain.* The fusion of pop melodies with a punk roar, which made *Copper Blue* so magnificent, is here, but the guitars are harsher and the loose crucifixion concept provides a downbeat atmosphere, provided you can hear the lyrics. Mould's vocals are mixed beneath all the other instruments, contributing to the claustrophobic, oppressive atmosphere. But *Beaster* is not nihilistic. In fact, Mould ends the EP optimistically, albeit cautiously, with the gorgeously circular organ-based "Walking Away." —*Stephen Thomas Erlewine*

○ **File Under: Easy Listening** / 1994 / Rykodisc ✦✦✦✦

Given Bob Mould's reputation for searing electric rock & roll, it may be easy to think that the title is ironic, and it is to a certain extent. But beneath the loud guitars lay the friendliest, most relaxed pop songs Mould has ever written. "Your Favorite Thing" and "Can't Help You Anymore" are two of Mould's most direct, pop-oriented songs, driven by instantly memorable melodies and hooks; they are also the most conventional songs on the record. The best moments come when Sugar push the boundaries a bit, whether it's on the country-rock of "Believe What You're Saying," the swirling "What You Want it To Be" and "Company Book," the searching ballad "Panama City Motel," or "Explode and Make Up," which bristles even at its most delicate moments. Mould throws in one classic spite-fueled rocker, "Granny Cool," but the record's finest moment is "Gee Angel," a powerhouse melodic scorcher. —*Stephen Thomas Erlewine*

Besides / 1995 / Rykodisc ✦✦✦

The strength of *Besides* is not only a measure of the quality of Bob Mould's songwriting, it's a measure of how good a band Sugar is. Collecting all of the B-sides and rare tracks left over from the group's three albums, *Besides* isn't filled with sub-par material. Frequently, Mould would leave fine songs off the album because it didn't fit the mood, such as the scorching rocker "Needle Hits E." That consistent quality means the record is a thoroughly engaging experience, even during live and alternate versions of "Explode and Make Up" and "If I Can't Change Your Mind." The first 25,000 copies included a bonus disc, featuring a complete Sugar concert; it's a typically mesmerizing, galvanizing show. —*Stephen Thomas Erlewine*

Sugarcubes

Group, Alternative Pop/Rock

To call them the greatest rock band from Iceland is like saying you know the greatest hockey player from Chile—it just doesn't mean much. Arty and pretentious, the Sugarcubes took the British pop press by storm with their artifice-laden pop in 1988. After a good first album, *Life's Too Good,* they tried to live up to their press clippings, releasing several flawed follow-up albums. Lead singer Bjork left the band in 1992 and the Sugarcubes disbanded; she began a more successful solo career the following year, releasing the international hit album, *Debut.* The Sugarcubes re-formed without Bjork in 1995. —*John Dougan*

● **Life's Too Good** / 1988 / Elektra ✦✦✦✦

With strong songs built around Bjork Gudmundsdottir's piercing, striking voice, this record lived up to all the advance hype. With songs like "Birthday" and "Motorcrash," this is the perfect introduction to the 'Cubes. —*John Dougan*

Here Today Tomorrow Next Week / 1989 / Elektra ✦✦✦

A slip from the first album, but not so much that it's without merit. —*John Dougan*

Stick Around for Joy / 1992 / Elektra ✦✦✦

While it's a bit better than their second record, the Sugarcubes' final album isn't as exciting as their debut, even if it shows more musical range. Too often, it slips into a self-conscious goofiness, and even Bjork's fine vocals can't save the music from its smirking, self-involved in-jokes. —*Stephen Thomas Erlewine*

The Sugarhill Gang

Group, Rap

The Sugarhill Gang—Master Gee (born Guy O'Brien, 1963), Wonder Mike (born Michael Wright, 1958), and Big Bank Hank (born Henry Jackson, 1958)—were the first group to record rap music, releasing the popular single "Rapper's Delight" in 1979. — *William Ruhlmann*

★ **Rapper's Delight: Hip Hop Remix** / 1980 / Sugar Hill ✦✦✦✦✦
The Sugarhill Gang's 1979 hit "Rapper's Delight" is arguably the first true rap song to gain widespread recognition and, as such, the progenitor of one of the major musical genres of the '80s. No wonder it doesn't sound dated yet. — *William Ruhlmann*

○ **The Sugarhill Gang** / 1980 / Sugar Hill ✦✦✦✦

8th Wonder / 1992 / Sugar Hill ✦✦✦
The Sugarhill Gang enjoyed its final moments in the spotlight with this 1982 LP. They scored two moderate hits with the title cut and "Apache," while continuing the old-school approach that initially gained mainstream attention and exposure for rap. — *Ron Wynn*

Suicidal Tendencies

Group, Hardcore, Heavy Metal

Suicidal Tendencies were formed in Venice, California as a punk/hardcore band and virtually came to define the phrase "skate-punk." Vocalist/bandleader Mike Muir has earned a reputation for addressing various political and personal topics with focused rage and thoughtfulness, and also for his keen sense of humor, which helps set the band apart from its competition. During the '80s, the group was frequently banned in the Los Angeles area, as their gigs often turned into out-of-control melees. Over the years, the band has mixed speed metal, more relaxed alternative rock, and touches of funk into its sound. Muir and bass virtuoso Robert Trujillo formed the metal/funk party band Infectious Grooves as a side project for Muir's non-political side. — *Steve Huey*

● **Suicidal Tendencies** / 1983 / Frontier ✦✦✦✦
The album that started it for this band, it's not heavy metal but hardcore punk. A lot of aggression, with some fun, it includes the classic song, "Institutionalized." — *John Book*

Join the Army / 1987 / Caroline ✦✦✦
The band incorporates a little more metal influences on this one and includes "Possessed to Skate." — *John Book*

○ **How Will I Laugh Tomorrow When I Can't Even Smile Today** / 1988 / Epic ✦✦✦✦
The band is a bit more metal oriented but still as aggressive as in their punk days. *How Will I Laugh Tomorrow When I Can't Even Smile Today* has lots of great songs, including "Trip to the Brain" and the title track. — *John Book*

Still Cyco After All These Years / 1989 / Epic ✦✦✦

Controlled by Hatred/Feel Like Shit . . . Deja Vu / 1989 / Epic ✦✦
An EP, it has a lot of good material. — *John Book*

Lights . . . Camera . . . Revolution! / 1990 / Epic ✦✦✦
Their strongest album since the debut has great songs like "Send Me Your Money" and "You Can't Bring Me Down." — *John Book*

The Art of Rebellion / Jun. 1992 / Epic ✦✦
On the group's earliest albums, vocalist Mike Muir specialized in intense, angst-ridden rants, harrowing but one-dimensional. He has since developed into a rock-solid vocalist, his voice a powerful and fluid instrument. Muir still delivers emotionally ferocious spoken-word segments on "Nobody Hears" and "I Wasn't Meant To Hear This," but the trademark is woven into good songs rather than being an end onto itself. A clenched fist in a velvet glove—or is it an open hand in chain mail?—whichever, *The Art Of Rebellion* packs a punch that should win over new devotees while maintaining the group's hardcore following. — *Roch Parisien*

Suicide

Group, Electronic, Punk, New Wave

Although they barely receive credit, Suicide (singer Alan Vega and keyboardist Martin Rev) is the sourcepoint for virtually every synth-pop duo that glutted the pop marketplace (especially in England) in the early '80s. Without the trailblazing Rev and Vega, there would have been no Soft Cell, Erasure, Bronski Beat, Yaz, you name 'em, and while many would tell you that that's nothing to crow about, the aforementioned synth-poppers merely appropriated Suicide's keyboards/singer look and none of Rev and Vega's extremely confrontational performance style and love of dissonance. The few who did (Throbbing Gristle, Cabaret Voltaire) were considered too extreme for most tastes.

Suicide had been a part of the performing arts scene in New York City's Lower East Side in the early/mid-'70s New York Dolls era. Their approach to music was simple: Rev would create minimalistic, spooky, hypnotic washes of dissonant keyboards and synthesizers, while Vega sang, ranted, and spat neo-Beat lyrics in a jumpy, disjointed fashion. Onstage, Vega became confrontational, often baiting the crowd into a riotous frenzy that occasionally led to full-blown violence, usually with the crowd attacking Vega. With their reputation as controversial performers solidified, what was lost was that Suicide recorded some amazingly seductive and terrifying music. A relationship with Cars mastermind Ric Ocasek proved successful, bringing their music to a wider audience and developing unlikely fans (Bruce Springsteen went on record as loving Suicide's Vietnam-vet saga "Frankie Teardrop"), but after numerous breakups and reconciliations, Rev and Vega settled for being more influential than commercially successful.

Ironically, the '90s proved to be a decade of vindication for Suicide with the rise of industrial dance music, Chicago's Wax Trax label, and the bands associated with it (Revolting Cocks, Ministry, 1000 Homo DJs, etc.). Although not a big part of the scene anymore, the profound influence of Suicide on a generation of younger bands is readily apparent. — *John Dougan*

● **Suicide** / 1977 / Restless ✦✦✦✦
Suicide's debut is extreme, noisy, confrontational, and everything you'd want them to be. A slap in the face of the guitar-oriented punk rock that was coming out of New York and England at this time, Rev and Vega prove they were ahead of their time, even if audiences hated them for it. What doesn't hurt this record is the presence of some of their best material, "Rocket USA" and the deathless "Frankie Teardrop." — *John Dougan*

24 Minutes over Brussels / 1978 / Bronze ✦✦

○ **Half Alive** / 1981 / ROIR ✦✦✦✦
Nasty live stuff. Singer Alan Vega is especially obnoxious. — *John Dougan*

Ghost Riders / 1986 / ROIR ✦✦✦
Originally a cassette-only release, this live recording at Walker Arts Center in Minneapolis marked Rev and Vega's 10th anniversary. And while not as deliberately offensive as some of their earlier live gigs (the impossible-to-locate *24 Minutes over Brussels*), this is a compelling, interesting document of their ever-evolving stage show. Not as transcendent as their debut album, but well worth the effort. Reissued on CD by the French Danceteria label in 1990. — *John Dougan*

The Way of Life / 1988 / Wax Trax! ✦✦✦

Donna Summer

b. Dec. 31, 1948, Boston

Disco, Pop

Born Donna Gaines, to a church-going family in the Mission Hill section of Boston, Summer took her name from Helmut Sommer, whom she married while living in Munich, Germany as a member of a travelling cast of *Hair*. Italian electro-pop arranger Giorgio Moroder met her, and in 1975 they recorded "Love to Love You Baby," a 16-minute, riff-driven update of Jane Birkin and Serge Gainsbourg's version of "Je t'aime . . . moi non plus." But Summer, as it turned out, had a sturdiness quite different from Birkin's short bursts of this and that, and a flair for kitschy show tunes and overproduced slickness, both of which ideally complemented the transparent impersonality of Moroder's electronic rhythms. She and Moroder created entire sub-genres of disco, and there was no stopping them until Summer stopped herself.

Beginning with 1980's *The Wanderer* (except for the title song) she began to sing exactly the kind of pop/rock material her daring impressionism had fought against. She tried to become a pop singer; and when, as in *She Works Hard for the Money*, she drew upon gospel styles, she was listened to. But during the '70s, she wasn't merely listened to, she was a leader. Today Summer tries to catch up, sadly, with a generation whose greatest aesthetic achievement was to catch up with her. — *Michael Freedberg*

○ **Love to Love You Baby** / Sep. 1975 / Casablanca ✦✦✦✦

"Love to Love You Baby"'s 16:50 of arousal and refill—ticklishly sensitive rhythm and fusion—threw disco into a tizzy overnight, but the tonally starved blues-of-isolation on the B-side isn't to be missed, either: the broken promises Summer bemoans in "Full of Emptiness"; "Need-A-Man Blues," with its unrequitedly sexy guitar rhythm as out of range of Summer's voice as she of satisfaction; the imaginary seaside hold-me in "Whispering Waves"; and "Pandora's Box," where Summer and guitar scream icily at one another as they turn their backs on each other's body music. Hunger without recourse; essential disco. —*Michael Freedberg*

Love Trilogy / Mar. 1976 / Casablanca ✦✦✦

Summer's quizzical "Try Me," "I Know," and "We Can Make It" wings her nervous little falsetto from risk to dare and from dare to mad hope, and her rhythm section gropes from testy touch beats to tightrope-walkers' guitar figures and safety-net harmonies. The second side substitutes dance with imaginary lovers for the debut album's love starvation blues. Don't dismiss its subtle mood poems the way fans of "Love to Love You" sped right past the B-side of Summer's debut; the flightier Summer plays a rhythm, the dicier her resolution. —*Michael Freedberg*

Four Seasons of Love / Oct. 1976 / Casablanca ✦✦✦

One's inclined to resist this package of self-conscious stardom concepts—the LP sports its own 1977 calendar featuring La Summer dressed up as winter, spring, summer, and Marilyn Monroe vamping on the subway grating (fall, I guess), and the four "seasonal" dancey suites promise more and say less than Summer's intimate touch-me's deliver without any hype. Fortunately the music has a mind of its own. The rhythms push and go poof as delicately as ever, the horn section mutes and jazzes the melody, the beats stop, run, and stop again when ever they damn please, and Summer falsettoes in private rapture as she smooches oohs and aahs onto the mix like lipstick traces. —*Michael Freedberg*

I Remember Yesterday / May 1977 / Casablanca ✦✦✦

Donna Summer continued her climb to superstardom with this late-'70s album, her first since the attention-grabbing *Love To Love You Baby* album in 1975 to crack the pop Top 20. The single "I Feel Love" was her second Top 10 R&B and pop hit, and paved the way for Summer to emerge shortly after as disco's reigning queen. —*Ron Wynn*

Once upon a Time / Nov. 1977 / Casablanca ✦✦✦

Summer and her liberators have created one audience and redefined another, and this record's four sides of dreamworlds without end sometimes manipulate each audience. The candy-girl music of "Fairy Tale High," "Queen for a Day," and "If You Got It, Flaunt It" explicitly recognizes her newly created gay audience, a daring acknowledgement coming from a mainstream pop star. As for her redefined audience of naive young things who live in the suburbs and dream of romance, adventure and sex while they search for identity, Summer works her music into a true-to-life Cinderella story staged as four acts of impatient pulse, delirious space noise, wish-upon-a-star voice monologues, and motion. —*Michael Freedberg*

Best of Donna Summer: Live & More / Sep. 1978 / Casablanca ✦✦

A fine collection of early Donna Summer material, plus a decent batch of unreleased studio cuts. It had good cover art and some fine concert versions of her best dance tunes. While Summer's live shows have always been iffy, especially if she's in a bad mood or having vocal problems, they wisely collected songs from her good nights. —*Ron Wynn*

Live & More / Sep. 1978 / Casablanca ✦✦

Live at the Universal Amphitheater, she sings her hits up to the time plus a medley of standards featuring "The Man I Love" and "I Got It Bad and That Ain't Good." Also included is one side of studio music with "Heaven Knows" and "MacArthur's Park." —*Bil Carpenter*

○ **Bad Girls** / May 1979 / Casablanca ✦✦✦✦

Summer defined "feminine" for an age in love with femininity and made the disco experience an adventure, even for those who had trouble learning how to fantasize. Now, on her third two-record set in two years, she has altered her outlook on femininity and changed her mind about the adventure. The disco queen becomes a streetwalker ready to sell her voice to any guy (read: producer) for a dime ("Bad Girls," "Hot Stuff") or anyone at all blindly searching for a lover they'll never find ("Sunset People"). —*Michael Freedberg*

★ **On the Radio (Greatest Hits)** / Oct. 1979 / Casablanca ✦✦✦✦✦

On the Radio—Greatest Hits I & II. If you want to be unadventurous and just go for the '70s hits, stop here; however, you will still be missing some of Summer's finest work. Besides, in order to cram all the hits into a two-record set, many of them were abridged, including the stunning guitar solo on "Hot Stuff." —*Bil Carpenter*

○ **Walk Away: The Best of Donna Summer (1977-1980)** / 1980 / Casablanca ✦✦✦✦

A collection of later Donna Summer material, including such song as "Winter Melody," "I Feel Love," and "Bad Girls." Although disco was beginning to peak, Summer was riding high, dominating the R&B and pop charts. In some ways, these songs were more varied than her pre-'77 cuts, because only "Love to Love You Baby," from her *Oasis* material, was a major hit. —*Ron Wynn*

○ **The Wanderer** / Oct. 1980 / Geffen ✦✦✦✦

This first post-Casablanca set has a hard-rock edge that shines best on the title cut, "Cold Love," and "Night Life." —*Bil Carpenter*

Donna Summer / Jul. 1982 / Geffen ✦✦✦

The follow-up to Donna Summer's first big Geffen album did reasonably well and proved to be the lull before the storm. "State of Independence" just missed being a hit, and "Woman In Me" cracked the pop and R&B Top 40, although it wasn't a smash. But the album mostly reaffirmed that Summer was back in stride and hadn't merely scored a fluke with her previous release. —*Ron Wynn*

○ **She Works Hard for the Money** / Jun. 1983 / Casablanca ✦✦✦✦

Summer's brassy, matter-of-fact mezzo does not play the sexy sanctified diva, and her musicians' crisp loud beats don't evoke rapture or delirium. Instead, she and her rhythm men live up to the title of "She Works Hard for the Money." Here's praise for a waitress's 12-hour workday that sums up Summer's own post-dance queen job status as well as disco fans' own spotlighted lives and maintains the pressure from the steel-and-synth riffs of "Stop, Look & Listen" to the impatient tenderness of "People, People." No one writes about love with as mesmeric a sense of wonder as Summer confesses in "Love Has a Mind of Its Own," "Unconditional Love," and "I Do Believe (I Fell in Love)." —*Michael Freedberg*

Cats without Claws / 1984 / Warner Brothers ✦✦

Although it's now widely perceived as a flop, in truth Donna Summer made the Top 40 with this album, and the song "There Goes My Baby" reached the Top 30 on both the R&B and pop charts, while "Supernatural Love" also made both surveys. But it wasn't as lofty a triumph as Summer had routinely enjoyed, and there were danger signs lurking in her relationship with Geffen. Still, as her 1980s output goes, this was far superior to the reviews it received and the reputation it carries. —*Ron Wynn*

The Summer Collection: Greatest Hits / 1985 / Casablanca ✦✦✦

Donna Summer's hit legacy has been ransacked almost as much as some of Motown's finest. This collection was issued in 1985, and since then, there have been dance/extended remix anthologies, other greatest hits packages, and Polygram's recent line, which is really the one to get if you want the whole Summer story. It is available on CD. —*Ron Wynn*

All Systems Go / 1987 / Geffen ✦✦

Donna Summer's return to glory and steadily building comeback lost precious ground with this album, a symptom of what went wrong with her Geffen albums. It wasn't aggressive rock, entertaining pop, or rhythmically exciting dance/disco. Instead, it was an indecisively sung, poorly produced collection of pop/rock clichés and superficial songs. It did contain one nice song in her cover of Brenda Russell's "Dinner with Gershwin," but she couldn't build from that number. —*Ron Wynn*

Another Place & Time / 1989 / Atlantic ✦✦

The last Donna Summer effort to make the charts was another album that was better than originally assessed. The single "This Time I Know It's for Real" was one of that year's finest and her best uptempo tune since "She Works Hard for the Money." If Atlantic had properly promoted the record, it might have been a bigger hit. As it was, it sold respectably, even with Summer in the midst of touring the country and ripping her old music for its sinful lyrics and orientation. —*Ron Wynn*

Mistaken Identity / 1991 / Atlantic ✦✦✦

Teamed with Keith Diamond, Summer returned in 1991 to aggressive dance music of her late '70s records on "Work That Magic," "Be My Fred Astaire," and "What Is It You Want?" Also included is the acoustic ballad "Heaven Is Just a Whisper Away" and the pop anthem "Let There Be Peace." —*Bil Carpenter*

● **The Donna Summer Anthology (Chronicles Series)** / Sep. 21, 1993 / Casablanca ✦✦✦✦
A double-disc set that collects all of Summer's biggest hits and finest moments, it's the definitive anthology. —*AMG*

Melody of Love / 1994 / Casablanca ✦✦

The Sundays

Group, Alternative Pop/Rock
A British alternative-pop band, the Sundays feature the airy vocal phrasing of Harriet Wheeler and the R.E.M.-meets-U2 ambient guitar jangle of David Gavurin. Their sound is simultaneously atmospheric and driving. —*Rick Clark*

● **Reading Writing & Arithmetic** / 1990 / DGC ✦✦✦✦
The Sundays' debut album built on the layered, ringing guitar hooks and unconventional pop melodies of the Smiths, adding more ethereal vocals and a stronger backbeat. As evidenced by the lilting, melancholy single "Here's Where the Story Ends," it was a winning combination, making *Reading, Writing and Arithmetic* a thoroughly engaging debut. —*Stephen Thomas Erlewine*

Blind / 1992 / DGC ✦✦✦
Featuring gentle, folk-based guitars and pop melodies, the Sundays' second album isn't much of a sonic departure from their first album. While it does have several fine numbers, it doesn't have as many outstanding songs as *Reading Writing & Arithmetic;* nevertheless, *Blind* will please most fans of the group. —*Stephen Thomas Erlewine*

Superchunk

Group, Alternative Pop/Rock
In the big-business world of '90s alternative rock, Superchunk remains a staunchly independent guitar rock band. When their record label, Matador, signed a major-label distribution deal, the band refused to be a part of the deal; with their next record, they switched labels to their privately owned Merge label. All the while, the band continues to gain more fans. Superchunk's stripped-down, speedy punk rock is proudly low-fidelity, yet their songs are well-written, packed with hooks and raw, energetic rocking. Although their singles and albums show little stylistic variation, they rock so hard the similiarity hardly matters. —*Stephen Thomas Erlewine*

○ **No Pocky for Kitty** / 1992 / Matador ✦✦✦✦
After a series of blistering singles, Superchunk released *No Pocky for Kitty,* which confirmed their status as one of the best and most diverse punk rock groups of the early '90s. —*Stephen Thomas Erlewine*

● **Tossing Seeds (singles 89-91)** / 1992 / Merge ✦✦✦✦
Featuring the classic '90s anti-anthem "Slack Motherfucker," *Tossing Seeds (singles 89-91)* is a superb collection of early non-LP singles by one of the best indie guitar bands of the early '90s. —*Stephen Thomas Erlewine*

○ **On The Mouth** / 1993 / Matador ✦✦✦✦
On the Mouth is one of Superchunk's best albums, not because it offers anything different from their previous work, but because the band's songwriting is at a peak, which make songs like "The Question Is How Fast" sound fresh and exciting, not empty exercises in punk nostalgia. —*Stephen Thomas Erlewine*

Foolish / Dec. 1993 / Merge ✦✦✦
Foolish may not be as consistent as *On the Mouth,* but it makes up for that with musical ambition and strong songwriting. —*Stephen Thomas Erlewine*

○ **Incidental Music** / ✦✦✦✦
Singles are the most effective forum for Superchunk's music, which makes *Incidental Music (singles 92-94)* one of their most consistent records. It might not have a single song as definitive as "Slack Motherfucker," but this collection of non-LP singles is filled with some of their finest moments. —*Stephen Thomas Erlewine*

Supergrass

Group, Alternative Pop/Rock
Like many other British bands of the '90s, Supergrass's musical roots lie in the infectiously catchy punk-pop of the Buzzcocks and the Jam, as well as the post-punk pop of Madness and the traditional British pop of the Kinks and Small Faces. Perhaps because of their age—two of the trio were still in their teens when they recorded their debut single—the band also brings in elements of decidedly un-hip groups like Elton John, as well as classic rockers like David Bowie, the Beatles and the Rolling Stones. With an exuberant, youthful enthusiasm, Supergrass tied all of their influences together in new surprising ways, where a Buzzcocks riff could slam into three-part harmonies out of "Crocodile Rock," or have a galloping music hall rhythm stutter like the best moments of the Who.

Consisting of guitarist/vocalist Gaz Coombes, bassist Mickey Quinn, and drummer Danny Goffey, Supergrass released their first single, the semi-autobiographical "Caught By the Fuzz," in the summer of 1994 on the indie label Backbeat; Parlophone signed the band and reissued the single in the fall of the year. "Caught by the Fuzz" generated a significant amount of buzz, including praise from Blur and Elastica. "Mansize Rooster," the group's second single, was released in the spring of 1995; it made it into the pop charts, as did "Lenny," which was released right before their debut album, *I Should Coco.*

Released in May, 1995, *I Should Coco* received glowing reviews in the U.K. press and debuted in the Top Ten. The band's popularity continued to grow, leading to the number two double-A-sided single, "Alright"/"Time." Staying in the top three for nearly a month, the single pushed the album to number one. *I Should Coco* was released in the U.S. three months later and a buzz began to build there, as "Caught by the Fuzz" began receiving MTV and radio play. —*Stephen Thomas Erlewine*

○ **I Should Coco** / 1995 / Parlophone ✦✦✦✦
The unbridled energy of the album shows that the band is young, yet what really illustrates the age of the band is how they borrow from their predecessors. Supergrass treat the Buzzcocks, the Beatles, Elton John, David Bowie, Blur, and Madness as if they were all the same thing—they don't make any distinction between what is cool and what isn't, they just throw everything together. —*Stephen Thomas Erlewine*

Supersister

Group, Art-Rock/Progressive-Rock
Holland's R.J. Stipps is one of rock's great unknown keyboardists and tunesmiths. From his early Zappaesque prog-pop ditties to full blown symphonic rock, his imagination ranged far and wide thematically. —*Archie Patterson*

○ **Pudding and Gisteren** / 1972 / Polydor ✦✦✦✦
Pudding & Gisteren, music composed and performed in conjunction with a ballet, was a masterful potpourri of classical, Eastern, pop and jazz influences. —*Archie Patterson*

Supersuckers

Group, Alternative Pop/Rock
Originally from Tucson, the Supersuckers moved to Seattle just before the grunge explosion of late 1991 and 1992. Though those underappreciative of the Supersuckers' Satan, Wild West, booze and heroin imagery may rely on the grunge moniker to pinpoint the group's sound, the Supersuckers are a true power-chord driven punk band, albeit with a penchant for heavy metal posturing.

After the departure of guitarist Ron Heathman in 1995, the Supersuckers recruited guitarist Rick Sims, from the recently disbanded Didjits, to record their third Sub Pop album, *The Sacrilicious Sounds of the Supersuckers.* —*Matt Carlson*

The Smoke of Hell / Sep. 4, 1992 / Sub Pop ✦✦✦
In the midst of the grunge revolution, the Supersuckers released this largely unnoticed album, *The Smoke of Hell,* which begins with a song that can not only be praised for its muscle but also for its psychic prediction—"Coattail Rider." The band perked things up a bit since their dreary early singles. Songs like "Luck," "Caliente," and "Hot Rod Rally" rapidly surge with electric power chord fury, while the band brings it down some for the blues ramble of "Hell City, Hell." —*Matt Carlson*

● **La Mano Cornuda** / 1994 / Sub Pop ✦✦✦✦
La Mano Cornuda, or the horns of the devil, is the Supersuckers' most ambitious record to date as the intense guitar chord explosion first heard on *The Smoke of Hell* is joined with a more aggressive lead guitar attack that almost verges on the Supersuckers' closet dream of heavy metal machismo. Every song on *La Mano Cornuda* (with the exception of the limp punk-pop slacker anthem "On the Couch") embraces an overpowering rock jock attitude that will either disgust you or leave you rolling on the floor. —*Matt Carlson*

Sacrilicious / 1995 / Sub Pop ✦✦✦
One would think that with the addition of one of punk rock's best guitarists, ex-Didjit Rick Sims, the Supersuckers would easily recover from the departure of Ron Heathman and maybe be the better for it. But, as *Sacrilicious* painfully illustrates, Heathman added much more bulk to the Supersuckers' sound than Sims provides here. While *Sacrilicious* offers less of the spirited blunt edge found on *La Mano Cornuda*, songs like the amphetamine-country stampede of "Born With A Tail" and the Bourbon St. blues shuffle of "Don't Turn Blue" thankfully expand the Supersuckers' musical vocabulary. Most, however, are unfortunately indistinct hard-rock songs, but give this new lineup time to evolve. —*Matt Carlson*

Songs All Sound the Same / Empty ✦✦
Though the songs don't all sound the same, the songs do have a subpar production level, and most suffer from limp, sloppy chord progressions. This singles collection, however, does show some punk promise on tracks like "Saddletramp" and "Sex & Outrage." Other songs teeter on the thin line that separates punk rock from heavy metal, as versions of the Dead Boys' "What Love Is…" and Nazareth's "Razzmanazz" suggest that the Supersuckers want to play rock utilizing the energy of punk while taking advantage of the glamour and excess of heavy metal. Another cover, Madonna's "Burnin' Up," doesn't suggest anything except complete inanity, but also happens to be the most memorable song on the record. —*Matt Carlson*

Supertramp

Group, Art-Rock/Progressive-Rock, Pop/Rock
Once upon a time in 1969, a young Dutch millionaire by the name of Stanley August Miesegaes gave his acquaintance, vocalist and keyboardist Roger Davies a "genuine opportunity" to form his own band; he could form the band of his dreams and Miesegaes would pay for it. After placing an ad in *Melody Maker,* Davies assembled Supertramp. Supertramp released two long-winded progressive rock albums before Miesegaes withdrew his support. With no money or fan base to speak of, the band was forced to redesign their sound. Coming up with a more pop-oriented form of progressive rock, the band had a hit with their third album, *Crime of the Century.* Throughout the decade, Supertramp had a number of best-selling albums, culminating in their 1979 masterpiece, *Breakfast in America. Breakfast in America* marked their first album that tipped the scale completely in the favor of pop songs; on the strength of the hit singles "Goodbye Stranger," "Logical Song," and "Take the Long Way Home" it sold over 18 million copies worldwide. After that album, Supertramp continued to develop a more R&B-flavored style; the change in direction was successful on 1982's *Famous Last Words,* but they soon ran out of hits. The band continued to record and tour into the '90s. —*Stephen Thomas Erlewine*

Supertramp / 1970 / A&M ✦✦
Supertramp's debut album was by and large an undistinguished progressive rock affair, filled with long, ponderous instrumental solos. —*Stephen Thomas Erlewine*

Indelibly Stamped / 1971 / A&M ✦✦
Indelibly Stamped, Supertramp's second album, was an improvement on their debut, although the group did have a tendency to indulge themselves in long-winded instrumental sections. —*Stephen Thomas Erlewine*

○ **Crime of the Century** / 1974 / A&M ✦✦✦✦
With *Crime of the Century,* Supertramp established themselves as one of the handful of progressive rock acts that could sell albums and have hit singles. Stripping away the longwinded excesses of their first two albums, *Crime of the Century* featured tighter, more melodic songs, as evidenced by the singles "Bloody Well Right" and "Dreamer." —*Stephen Thomas Erlewine*

Crisis? What Crisis? / 1975 / A&M ✦✦✦
Crisis? What Crisis? wasn't quite as fully developed as its predecessor, *Crime of the Century,* lacking any instant standouts like "Dreamer" or "Bloody Well Right." Nevertheless, it had a handful of fine songs which signalled that Supertramp was continuing to refine and expand their sound. —*Stephen Thomas Erlewine*

○ **Even in the Quietest Moments** / 1977 / A&M ✦✦✦
Like *Crisis? What Crisis?, Even in the Quietest Moments* is a jumbled affair, alternating between long, unfocused sections and relatively concise pop songs, like the hit "Give a Little Bit." —*Stephen Thomas Erlewine*

● **Breakfast in America** / 1979 / A&M ✦✦✦✦
With *Breakfast in America,* Supertramp had a genuine blockbuster hit, topping the charts for four weeks in the U.S. and selling millions of copies worldwide; by the 1990s, the album had sold over 18 million units across the world. Although their previous records had some popular success, they never even hinted at the massive sales of *Breakfast in America.* Then again, Supertramp's earlier records weren't as pop-oriented as *Breakfast.* The majority of the album consisted of tightly-written, catchy, well-constructed pop songs, like the hits "The Logical Song," "Take the Long Way Home," and "Goodbye Stranger." Supertramp still had a tendency to indulge themselves occasionally, but *Breakfast in America* had very few weak moments. It was clearly their high-water mark. —*Stephen Thomas Erlewine*

Paris / 1980 / A&M ✦✦
Recorded in the wake of the global success of *Breakfast in America, Paris* is a competent but ultimately unnecessary live album which fails to live up to the standards of their studio material. —*Stephen Thomas Erlewine*

…famous last words… / 1982 / A&M ✦✦✦
Even though *…famous last words…,* Supertramp's follow-up to *Breakfast in America,* was slicker and more pop-oriented than its predecessor, it wasn't quite as successful. Where the singles on *Breakfast* still had a progressive rock edge, most of *…famous last words…* was light, synthesized pop, with the shimmering "It's Raining Again" being the only song melodic enough to support the lush, layered sound. —*Stephen Thomas Erlewine*

Brother Where You Bound / 1985 / A&M ✦✦
On *Brother Where You Bound,* Supertramp appeared to be floundering in an attempt to keep their trademark sound current without losing their dedicated fan base. The band managed to score a hit with "Cannonball," but most of the album was too ponderous for pop success and too simple to qualify as good progressive rock. Not surprisingly, the group's lead vocalist, Roger Hodgson, left after the record's release. —*Stephen Thomas Erlewine*

Free as a Bird / 1987 / A&M ✦

● **Classics, Vol. 9** / 1987 / A&M ✦✦✦✦
This is a fairly good sampler of this band's bigger radio tracks as well as key album numbers. Included are "Bloody Well Right," "Ain't Nobody but Me," "The Logical Song," "Give a Little Bit," "It's Raining Again," "Goodbye Stranger," "Take the Long Way Home," and "Dreamer." Unfortunately, "Even in the Quietest Moments" is curiously omitted. —*AMG*

The Supremes

Group, Soul, Motown
The Supremes evolved from the Primettes to become the preeminent female group of their day, and Diana Ross emerged from the Supremes to become one of the all-time great pop divas. The Primettes were a local Detroit group that had recorded unsuccessfully for Lupine before they signed with Motown and changed their name to the Supremes—a name that seemed to create a self-fulfilling prophecy. After a few false starts, they broke through in 1964 with "Where Did Our Love Go?" From there, the roll call of hits is as familiar as Diana Ross's false eyelashes; they are part of the collective unconscious of anyone who lived through the '60s. The hits were the work of the production team of Holland-Dozier-Holland, which had been seconded from Martha & the Vandellas, a move that was later the font of considerable acrimony. Whether the hits were R&B or pop is a moot point. Certainly Diana Ross had pop aspirations aplenty, as her solo recordings showed, but it was a trend already evident on forlorn albums of standards that the Supremes cut at Motown. There is every indication that Motown-founder Berry Gordy saw Diana Ross (with whom he had a close personal relationship) and the Supremes as his ticket into legitimate show business.

Ross left in 1970, immediately after "Someday We'll Be Together," and although the Supremes soldiered on (even scoring another #1 R&B hit with "Stoned Love"), there is no doubt that to most people the Supremes will be forever associated with their former lead singer. —*Colin Escott*

○ **Where Did Our Love Go** / Aug. 1964 / Motown ✦✦✦✦
The group's second album, and the first to explode onto the charts. The suggestion that Diana Ross replace Florence Ballard as lead singer forever altered the course of Motown and popular music, and is still being felt to this day. The decision to put them in the

hands of Holland-Dozier-Holland was equally pivotal; they crafted the title track and started the group on its way to superstardom. This album has a charm and innocence sorely missing from their later LPs, when Ross was aware that she was a star. This was just three young women expressing what was in their hearts with no affectation, primness, or fluff. —*Ron Wynn*

A Little Bit of Liverpool / Oct. 1964 / Motown ✦✦✦

At the Copa / Nov. 1965 / Motown ✦✦✦
This live date has its charms. The between-song patter and ambience are dated but still appealing, while the performances are mostly entertaining, though uneven in quality. The group was never the most compelling concert attraction, but this album did a solid job of detailing everything good (and a bit pretentious) about the Supremes circa 1965. It's well worth the expense if you ever see it in a used record store. —*Ron Wynn*

○ **I Hear a Symphony** / Feb. 1966 / Motown ✦✦✦✦
The Supremes ruled the roost in 1966, topping the pop charts, dominating the R&B/soul surveys, and establishing themselves as the greatest women's vocal group of all time. They had had a brief slump with the single "Nothing But Heartaches," but were back on top with the title track, and destroyed any competition with four R&B and pop hits, half of them number one on both sides, plus two top 10 albums. Diana Ross had become the group's star, and her vocals indicated that she deserved that position. —*Ron Wynn*

○ **Supremes A-Go-Go** / Aug. 1966 / Motown ✦✦✦✦
A number one album, and the greatest dance-based release Motown ever issued. The Supremes were lapping the field at this point, getting superb material, production and arrangements, plus musical backing from pop's finest instrumentalists. "Love Is Like An Itching In My Heart" set the stage for another run of smash number one hits, and this was one of only two Supremes LPs that stayed on top for more than one week (the other was their first greatest hits album). —*Ron Wynn*

★ **Greatest Hits** / Aug. 1967 / Motown ✦✦✦✦✦
Although all of these 20 songs were credited to the Supremes when they were released between 1963 and 1967, this album marked the first LP on which the group was billed as "Diana Ross and the Supremes." However you credit it, this out-of-print double-LP contains the bulk of the best of the Supremes, no less than 10 #1 hits from "Where Did Our Love Go" to "The Happening," and thus some of the most popular music of the 1960s. Ross and the Supremes, together and separately, continued to score afterwards, but this was their peak. —*William Ruhlmann*

Greatest Hits, Vol. 3 / Dec. 1969 / Motown ✦✦✦
Greatest Hits, released in August 1967, was a double album, thus nominally constituting volumes 1 and 2 of the Supremes' hits, 1963-1967, and this 11-track album picked up the story, containing singles from 1967 to the end of 1969 and the end of Diana Ross's tenure with the group. Their sound and approach changed during this period, as they moved from the slinky Holland-Dozier-Holland songs to the more psychedelic ("Reflections") and grittier ("Love Child") styles of the late '60s. But the hits kept coming, up until the ironic "Someday We'll Be Together," released just as they split apart. —*William Ruhlmann*

Right on / May 1970 / Motown ✦✦✦
The best of the post-Diana Ross group features savvy Frank Wilson production. —*Rick A. Bueche*

The Magnificent 7 / Sep. 1970 / Motown ✦✦✦
Motown tried to recapture the success of their previous Temptations/Supremes pairing by putting the post-Diana Ross Supremes alongside the Four Tops. It proved an inspired idea; the album was not only one of the best that this Supremes lineup ever made, but it revitalized the Four Tops. Their version of "River Deep—Mountain High" shocked everyone by cracking the R&B Top 10 and pop Top 20 almost a year after it had been issued, and certainly helped make the ordinary followup tune "Nathan Jones" a hit. —*Ron Wynn*

★ **Anthology** / May 1974 / Motown ✦✦✦✦✦
A complete collection of their nonstop Motown hits, it's a must-have. —*Rick A. Bueche*

70's Greatest Hits & Rare Classics / Motown ✦✦✦
An interesting anthology, one of the few that don't merely recycle shopworn hits. This collection covers the Supremes in the post-Diana Ross era, with tracks that featured both the group and solo tracks from Jean Terrell and Scherrie Payne, plus the few hits they

had when Mary Wilson shared the leads with Terrell. It also contains some rare Supremes album tracks. Overall, it's more valuable than the umpteenth repackaged Diana Ross album. —*Ron Wynn*

BOOKS

✦✦✦ **Dreamgirl: My Life As A Supreme**, by Mary Wilson with Patricia Romanowski & Ahrgus Juilliard (St. Martin's Press, 1986). There have been a few Motown biographies in the last 15 years that have stripped the mystique from the label's glory days, and this is one of the better ones. There may be a bit too much showbiz gossip for some reader's tastes (though Wilson's tone is never bitter or vengeful), but there are a lot of inside stories about Motown and the Supremes: Diana Ross' relentless ambition, the decision to cast Ross as the Supremes' main voice for commercial considerations, the beginnings in Detroit's Brewster Projects, the early grueling Motown tours through the South, Flo Ballard's sad ouster from the group and subsequent decline, the disbanding of the original lineup as Ross planned her solo career. Without throwing up a great deal of dirt, it does lend a human dimension to Ross and Motown boss Berry Gordy, Jr., from one who was very much in the middle of things, although she virtually never sang lead on record. —*Richie Unterberger*

The Surfaris

Group, Surf
Glendora, CA surf group remembered for "Wipe Out," the number two 1963 hit that ranks as one of the great rock instrumentals, featuring a classic up-and-down guitar riff and a classic solo drum roll break, both of which were emulated by millions (the number is no exaggeration) of beginning rock & rollers. They recorded an astonishing number of albums (about half a dozen) and singles in the mid-'60s; the "Wipe Out" follow-up "Point Panic" was the only one to struggle up to the middle of the charts. The Surfaris were not extraordinary, but they were more talented than the typical one-shot surf group; drummer Ron Wilson was praised by session stickman extraordinaire Hal Blaine, and his uninhibited splashing style sounds like a direct ancestor to Keith Moon. He also took the lead vocals on the group's occasional passable Beach Boy imitations. —*Richie Unterberger*

● **Wipe Out! The Best of the Surfaris** / 1994 / Varese Sarabande ✦✦✦✦
Decent 18-track distillation of their 1962-65 work, including several album tracks and non-LP singles. "Wipe Out" is by far the best cut, of course, but the instrumentals, packed with reverbed guitars, honking saxes, and high-end drums aplenty, usually have an admirably sleek power. Two of the vocal surf tunes were co-written by Gary Usher, who also worked with the Beach Boys during this time. —*Richie Unterberger*

Screaming Lord Sutch

Rock & Roll
He couldn't properly be considered part of the British Invasion—he never had a hit in the U.S. or the U.K.—but Screaming Lord Sutch laid some unheralded groundwork for the phenomenon. With a rock'n'horror act based to a large degree on Screamin' Jay Hawkins, David "Lord" Sutch was one of the first genuine rock & roll longhairs, and his bands employed such sterling instrumentalists as Jimmy Page, Jeff Beck, Ritchie Blackmore, Nicky Hopkins, and Mitch Mitchell before they became famous. His early '60s singles—mostly over-the-top Halloween novelties or covers of early rock and R&B standards—aren't brilliant, but they are genuinely energetic and fun performances that rank among the few out-and-out raunchy rock & roll records waxed in Britain before the ascension of the Beatles. Twiddling the knobs on his first five singles was the legendarily eccentric Joe Meek, who embellished Sutch's modest talents with his usual grab bag of treated instruments, compression, and odd effects. While he holds a position of undeniable importance in the history of British rock, Sutch was not a talented singer or musician, and the records he made after the mid-'60s were pretty lame, despite the presence of some stars who remembered him fondly (and had even sometimes played in his band in the old days). A well-known public figure in Britain, he ran for Parliament several times in the '60s representing the "national teenage party," and founded the pirate radio station Radio Sutch in 1964. He published his autobiography in the early '90s. —*Richie Unterberger*

● **Story** / ✦✦✦✦
Except for one B-side, this has both sides of his first seven singles (released 1961-66), most produced by Joe Meek between 1961 and 1965, some featuring sterling guitar work by Mssrs. Page, Beck, and Blackmore. Divided into a "horror" and a "rock" side, this is fun if silly stuff; tracks like "She's Fallen in Love with the Monsterman," "Monster in Black Tights," and "Dracula's Daughter" are great for Halloween parties. No record label name is given for this reissue, but it's easy enough to locate through specialty mail-order outfits. —*Richie Unterberger*

Swamp Dogg

Group, Soul, R&B, Blues Rock
One of the great characters in rock and soul music is Jerry Williams, better known as the eccentric, idiosyncratic, and always entertaining Swamp Dogg (no relation to Snoop Doggy Dogg). A Virginia native, Williams invented his own legend by claiming that he had little proper schooling, only to wake up one day and find himself a musical genius (his words). Actually, Williams is very talented, and an early association with Jerry Wexler and Phil Walden led to him working for a number of years as a producer, engineer and occasional songwriter with Atlantic in the '60s. At decade's end, however, he decided that the time was right to unleash Swamp Dogg's singular view of the world on an unsuspecting public. The initial result was one of the most gloriously gonzo soul recordings of all time, *Total Destruction to Your Mind*. Along with living up to its title, it was a renegade chunk of not-quite-commercial music, with an unforgettable (though fuzzy) cover shot of the portly Dogg in his underwear. Although undeniably great, *Total Destruction to Your Mind* is one of the most obscure soul records ever made. That, however, has nothing to do with the music, which rocks in a way reminiscent of Solomon Burke or Wilson Pickett. It may have to do with Dogg's worldview, part libertarian politics, part Zappa-style critiques of commerciality and capitalism, and part horny male, the latter defining for better and worse his view of women. Although he spent years working in the industry, Dogg was simply not the standard-issue soul player. And that was good. Dogg has continued to make records, albeit infrequently, since 1969, some good, a few great, and most all extremely difficult to find. With contemporary soul (Boyz II Men, En Vogue, Mary J. Blige) sounding increasingly mannered and sterile, Dogg's yelling, screaming and general craziness are missed. Thankfully, he hasn't disappeared for good, although he only makes records when he feels like it. His last release, *Surfin' In Harlem*, came out in 1991. And as is often the case with quirky "legends," what he's up to at any given time is the source of wild speculation. He's allegedly been driving a cab, pitching songs and fighting over royalty checks, all to make ends meet. It would be wise to not count him out; just when you think this Dogg is down and out, he sneaks up and bites you. —*John Dougan*

● **Total Destruction to Your Mind** / 1970 / Canyon ✦✦✦✦
Easily on my Top Ten list of long-out-of-print records that deserve a CD reissue. The title track is a slam-bangin' chunk of rock and funk that's pushed by a great session band including guitarist Jesse Carr and drummer Johnny Sandlin, and is easily Dogg's finest moment on record. But the rest of this is great too, ranging from the consumer nightmare "Synthetic World" to the paternity blues of "Mama's Baby, Daddy's Maybe." Plus, Dogg is a great singer, and his dizzying range gets a workout on these songs. Good luck finding a copy. —*John Dougan*

Rat on / 1971 / Elektra ✦✦✦

○ **Cuffed, Collared and Tagged** / 1972 / Cream ✦✦✦✦
This U.K. import, part of a two-fer, features a great band with dynamite lyrics. —*Richard Pack*

○ **Gag a Maggot** / 1973 / Stonedogg ✦✦✦✦
Another great album title, another tiny label, another great record long forgotten. Not as consistently manic as *Destruction*, *Maggot* is as ferocious sounding and does have a good cover of Wilson Pickett's "In The Midnight Hour." Never one to let a love lyric go by without a sarcastic twist, Dogg's love song here is called "I Couldn't Pay For What I Got Last Night." —*John Dougan*

● **I'm Not Selling Out, I'm Buying In** / 1981 / Takoma ✦✦✦✦
After years of keeping a low profile, Dogg emerged from out of nowhere with this fine record. Instead of soulful hard soul, this record carries a rock & roll clout that keeps even its most banal moments ("Wine, Women and Rock 'n' Roll") from terminal te-

dium. Song title highlight: Dogg's duet with Esther Phillips, "The Love We Got Ain't Worth Two Dead Flies." Kind of says it all, doesn't it. —*John Dougan*

Billy Swan

b. May 12, 1942, Cape Giradeau, MS
Rock & Roll, Country-Rock
One of rock's more interesting fringe characters, Billy Swan had been in the music business for more than a decade before he landed a surprise number one neo-rockabilly hit in 1974 with "I Can Help." His composition "Lover Please" was a hit for Clyde McPhatter in the early '60s, and he spent the rest of the decade as a combination roadie, engineer's assistant, and songwriter, penning material for Conway Twitty, Waylon Jennings, and Mel Tillis. He played with Kris Kristofferson, Kinky Friedman, and Billy Joe Shaver in the '70s before the success of "I Can Help," whose swirling organ and classic '50s rockabilly arrangement anchored one of the best hit singles of the mid-'70s. Swan recorded a few albums as a solo act that were well received by critics, but he never hit the Top 40 again. Too eclectic to be characterized as a '50s revivalist, he actually mixed country, soul, and pop into his sound more frequently than out-and-out rockabilly. After a few years, Swan returned to Kristofferson's band, where he stayed until 1992. —*Richie Unterberger*

● **Billy Swan's Best** / 1993 / Red Baron ✦✦✦✦
Listeners expecting tuneful updated rockabilly along the lines of "I Can Help" (which leads off this collection) may be disappointed by this CD. There's nothing as instantly compelling as the big hit (only "Vanessa" approaches its energy), much of the material lies closer to country than rock, and there are a few tame covers of '50s oldies. Nonetheless, Swan ranks among the more interesting country-pop-rock hybrids, as you could guess from the song title "(You Just) Woman Handled My Mind," and his thin, wavering voice is oddly memorable. Most of the material on this best-of is written by Swan, with occasional assistance from notables Guy Clark, Buddy Emmons, and Kris Kristofferson. —*Richie Unterberger*

Bettye Swann

b. Oct. 24, 1944
Soul, R&B, Country, Gospel
Los Angeles soul vocalist. Scored a #1 R&B hit in 1967 with her lilting mid-tempo "Make Me Yours." Swann began recording for the Money label in 1964 and found herself on the charts the next year with "Don't Wait Too Long." After "Make Me Yours" made her some money on Money, she stopped off at Capitol long enough to enjoy a hit with "Don't Touch Me" in 1969 and then settled in at Atlantic, where she notched several soul hits during the early '70s (including "Victim of a Foolish Heart"). —*Bill Dahl*

Make Me Yours / 1967 / Collectables ✦✦✦
The Money label tracks (1964-1967) include her #1 R&B hit, "Make Me Yours." —*Richard Pack*

● **The Soul View Now** / 1968 / Capitol ✦✦✦✦
This is a gem of haunting deep-soul ballads. —*Richard Pack*

Don't You Ever Get Tired of Hurting Me / 1969 / Capitol ✦✦✦
Classic country-soul. —*Richard Pack*

Keith Sweat

Urban
Keith Sweat is a Harlem-born R&B singer/songwriter who released his debut album, *Make It Last Forever*, at the end of 1987. The album sold over three million copies, spawning the hits "I Want Her" (#1 R&B, #5 pop), "Something Just Ain't Right" (#3 R&B), "Make It Last Forever" (#2 R&B), and "Don't Stop Your Love" (#9 R&B). It was followed in June 1990 by *I'll Give All My Love to You*, another million-seller, that featured the hits "Make You Sweat" (#1 R&B, #14 pop), "Merry Go Round" (#2 R&B), "I'll Give All My Love to You" (#1 R&B, #7 pop), and "Your Love—Part 2" (#4 R&B). Sweat's third album was *Keep It Comin',* an R&B chart-topper at the end of 1991, whose title track was another #1 R&B hit. —*William Ruhlmann*

○ **Make It Last Forever** / 1988 / Elektra ✦✦✦✦
This set features "I Want Her" and several other equally danceable tracks. —*Bil Carpenter*

● **I'll Give All My Love to You** / 1990 / Vintertainment ✦✦✦✦
Keith Sweat represents a new generation of R&B love men who combine the ballad strength of singers like Luther Vandross with percussion-heavy dance music, called new jack swing, that an-

swers the needs of the current dance floor. His second album, with its four hit singles, is typical of his approach. —*William Ruhlmann*

Keep It Comin' / 1991 / Elektra ◆◆◆

Get Up on It / 1994 / Elektra ◆◆◆

Sweet

Group, Rock & Roll, Glam Rock
Mid-'70s English glam-rock pioneers, the Sweet churned out Who-like Chapmann- and Chinn-composed teen raunch that, by the '90s, approached neoclassic status. With their chirpy harmonies and fuzzy (but never too dangerous) guitars, the Sweet's commercial grunge became far more influential than anyone had predicted. —*John Dougan*

○ **Desolation Boulevard** / 1974 / Capitol ◆◆◆◆
This surprisingly solid hard rock record features "Ballroom Blitz." —*Dan Heilman*

● **The Best of Sweet** / Mar. 1, 1993 / Capitol ◆◆◆◆
Nobody played rock & roll trashier or dumber than Sweet, and their best moments shine on this terrific 16-track compilation. Every one of their hits were powered by an irresistibly stupid melody, big dumb guitars, and, on occasion, a whining synthesizer. It was glitter-rock for teens at its best, without the dark sensuality of T. Rex. Even today, Sweet's best songs—"Ballroom Blitz," "Little Willy," "Blockbuster," "Teenage Rampage," and the nearly-perfect "Fox on the Run"—still sound gloriously trashy. —*Stephen Thomas Erlewine*

Sweet Inspirations

Group, Soul
If you were cutting a soul, R&B, pop, rock, or girl group record in New York in the 1960s and needed female backup vocals, chances are you'd try to get the Sweet Inspirations first. The group found their way onto numerous recordings, including hits by the Drifters, Van Morrison, Wilson Pickett, Solomon Burke, Garnett Mimms, and most famously, Aretha Franklin (with whom they sometimes toured).

The group evolved from the '50s gospel group the Drinkard Singers. At various points, soul singers Doris Troy, Judy Clay, Dionne Warwick, and sister Dee Dee Warwick were members. By the time they began to record on their own in 1967, their leader was Cissy Houston (mother of Whitney), and the women were renamed the Sweet Inspirations.

As an Atlantic recording act, the group cut some fine sides that rank among the clearest illustrations of the close links between soul music and gospel harmony. Usually sticking to material by famed soul and pop songwriters, they had about half a dozen moderate R&B hits in the late '60s; the biggest, "Sweet Inspiration," was a Top 20 pop single. Houston left the group at the end of the '60s, and the Inspirations left Atlantic in the early '70s, sometimes working with Elvis Presley, and recording an album for Stax in 1973. —*Richie Unterberger*

● **Best of the Sweet Inspirations** / 1994 / Ichiban/Soul Classics ◆◆◆◆
Solid retrospective of their Atlantic years (1967-71), including all the hits and several misses. A lot of the songs were cut at Muscle Shoals, Memphis, or Atlantic Studios, and accordingly the arrangements have a deep soul flavor characteristic of Atlantic's late-'60s releases (although they worked briefly in Philadelphia in 1969 for a Gamble-Huff-flavored sound). Includes covers of songs by Isaac Hayes, Roebuck Staples, Dan Penn, and Gamble/Huff, all of which they make their own with lovely harmonies and imaginative interpretations. —*Richie Unterberger*

Sweet Thursday

Group, Folk-Rock
A short-lived minor-league supergroup of sorts, Sweet Thursday featured supersessionman Nicky Hopkins on keyboards and Jon Mark (of Bluesbreakers fame) on vocals and guitar. Their sole, self-titled album (from 1969) was extremely derivative of Bob Dylan's *Blonde on Blonde* period, with hoarse vocals, piano-organ arrangements, and weary, slightly abstract narratives and love songs. —*Richie Unterberger*

Sweet Thursday / 1969 / Tetragrammaton ◆◆◆
A fine, understated collection of late-'60s folk-rock with a slightly British slant. Jon Mark (who wrote half the songs) is the focus of the band, and several of his compositions are standouts—the symbol-laden "Dealer," the folky baroque love song "Jenny," the jazz-tinged, waltzing "Rescue Me." A subdued and stately effort that only succumbs to self-indulgence on the ten-minute "Gilbert Street," a blatant cop of Dylan's "Desolation Row." —*Richie Unterberger*

Matthew Sweet

Alternative Pop/Rock
For the most of the '80s, Matthew Sweet played guitar with Oh-OK and Lloyd Cole; he released his first solo album, *Inside*, in 1986. Both *Inside* and 1989's *Earth* showed promise, drawing equally from the jangly guitar pop of the Byrds and Big Star and the Southern pop of R.E.M. and the dB's. But it wasn't until *Girlfriend* that Sweet made came into his own artistically. Where his other albums were good, *Girlfriend* was exceptional, full of raging guitars (courtesy of Richard Lloyd and Robert Quine) and aching melodies; it expertly fused the Beatles, Big Star, and Neil Young into one distinctive, melodic style. The album was critically acclaimed, as well as relatively commercially successful; Sweet had a minor hit with the title track and he earned many fans. *Altered Beast*, released the following year, was sloppier yet it expanded his cult and helped him inch his way into the mainstream. —*Stephen Thomas Erlewine*

Inside / 1986 / Columbia ◆◆
Matthew Sweet's debut solo album was a tentative effort, featuring a handful of good songs, but it was weighed down by too many guest artists (everyone from Valerie Simpson and the Heartbreakers' Mike Campbell to Chris Stamey, Bernie Worrell, and Anton Fier) and a glossy, synth-heavy production. —*Stephen Thomas Erlewine*

Earth / 1989 / A&M ◆◆◆
Despite the presence of guitarists Richard Lloyd and Robert Quine, Matthew Sweet's second album, *Earth,* remains a spotty affair. Like *Inside* before it, *Earth* has an overly glossy production, as well as a set of songs that are, by and large, forgettable—in fact, the songs on the second album are even more undistinguished than the ones on the previous record. —*Stephen Thomas Erlewine*

● **Girlfriend** / 1991 / Zoo ◆◆◆◆
Matthew Sweet's third album is a remarkable artistic breakthrough. Grounded in the guitar-pop of the Beatles, Big Star, Byrds, R.E.M., and Neil Young, *Girlfriend* melds all of Sweet's influences into one majestic, wrenching sound that encompasses both the gentle country-rock of "Winona" and the winding guitars of the title track and "Divine Intervention." Sweet's music might have recognizable roots, but *Girlfriend* never sounds derivative; thanks to his exceptional songwriting, the album is a fresh, original interpretation of a classic sound. —*Stephen Thomas Erlewine*

○ **Altered Beast** / Feb. 1993 / Zoo ◆◆◆◆
Compared to the concise songwriting of *Girlfriend, Altered Beast* is all over the place, both emotionally and musically. Ranging from piercing guitar rave-ups ("Dinosaur Act") to gorgeous country-rock ("Time Capsule"), the album not only covers all sides of Sweet's musical personality, but pastes them together haphazardly. Consequently, it takes a bit of time for all of it to make sense, but after a few listens, it falls together, and its best moments equal *Girlfriend*. —*Stephen Thomas Erlewine*

Son of Altered Beast / Mar. 15, 1994 / Zoo ◆◆◆
Collecting several B-sides and outtakes, *Son of Altered Beast* is actually more consistent and enjoyable than the full-length *Altered Beast*. —*Stephen Thomas Erlewine*

100% Fun / 1995 / Zoo ◆◆◆
Clocking in at 45 minutes, Matthew Sweet's third record of guitar-dominated, hook-laden power-pop runs through its 12 songs at a classic speed, piling up songs that lovingly conform to the three-minute pop tradition. Richard Lloyd's gnarled guitars save Sweet's melodies and harmonies from being saccharine or sappy. Behind Sweet's bright hooks lies something darker—the self-loathing of "Sick of Myself" and the mental manipulation of "We're the Same" aren't evident from the sound of the record, which obliterates any hidden meanings with its chiming guitars and driving rhythms. It might not have the consistent barrage of great songs like *Girlfriend*, yet it tames the wilder impulses of *Altered Beast* into an al-

bum that rocks its worries away without ever getting rid of them. —*Stephen Thomas Erlewine*

Rachel Sweet

b. 1963, Akron, Ohio
New Wave, Pop/Rock
After a couple of failed singles as a teenage country singer, the diminutive Sweet plugged her big voice into the burgeoning punk movement after being signed to Stiff Records. Along with Lene Lovich, she was one of the early women recording for the label, with a succession of great records that garnered much critical acclaim but failed to catch on in the marketplace. She dropped out of sight for a few years, then came back working for director John Waters both on and off the screen (*Hairspray, Cry Baby*) and has recently turned up working on cable's Comedy Channel. —*Cub Koda*

● **Fool Around** / 1978 / Rhino ✦✦✦✦
A solid best-of collection showcasing Sweet's dazzling vocal capabilities. —*Cub Koda*

○ **Protect the Innocent** / 1980 / Rhino ✦✦✦✦
Sweet's second and most perfectly realized album features "Take Good Care of Me" and a slam-bang version of "Baby, Let's Play House." Out of print, but it's worth the search. —*Cub Koda*

And Then He Kissed Me / 1981 / Columbia/Legacy ✦✦✦

Blame It on Love / 1982 / Columbia ✦✦

Swell Maps

Group, Alternative Pop/Rock
Swell Maps was one of the most diverse bands of the immediate post-punk era. Although the band had formed in 1972, their first record didn't appear until 1979 and their eclectic, low-fidelity sound and aesthetic values tied them into the punk rock movement. Featuring brothers Nikki Sudden (guitar, vocals) and Epic Soundtracks (drums, vocals), as well as bassist Jowe Head, vocalist Richard Earl, and singer David Barrington, the band released two albums—*Trip to Marineville* (1979) and *Jane from Occupied Europe* (1980)—before splitting in 1980. —*Stephen Thomas Erlewine*

○ **Trip to Marineville** / 1979 / Mute ✦✦✦✦
Swell Maps' debut album was a scattershot affair, ranging from blistering three-chord punk to free-form noise experiments, that was intriguing, yet frequently incoherent. —*Stephen Thomas Erlewine*

○ **In "Jane from Occupied Europe"** / 1980 / Mute ✦✦✦✦
On their second album, Swell Maps displayed even more ambition and confidence than on their debut, which was a plus. Even though their music was still somewhat fragmented, *Jane from Occupied Europe* was more focused and compelling than their debut. —*Stephen Thomas Erlewine*

Whatever Happens Next / 1981 / Mute ✦✦
Featuring two albums of home-made demos, some of them dating back to the early '70s, *Whatever Happens Next* contains a fair number of fine songs, but the overall quality of the album is too inconsistent to make *Whatever Happens Next…* worthwhile for anyone besides dedicated fans. —*Stephen Thomas Erlewine*

○ **Train out of It** / 1987 / Mute ✦✦✦✦
Compiling a number of outtakes and singles, *Train Out of It* features more quality material than their similar rarities collection, *Whatever Happens Next…* —*Stephen Thomas Erlewine*

● **Collision Time Revisited** / 1989 / Mute ✦✦✦✦
A terrific compilation, which touches on all phases of their career without a lot of the dross. —*John Dougan*

Swervedriver

Group, Alternative Pop/Rock
Guitarists Adam Franklin and Jimmy Hartridge formed Swervedriver from the ashes of the Oxford group Shake Appeal. Continuing with their former group's Stooges-inspired drone rock, the band recorded their first record, *Raise*, for Creation Records in 1991. Two years later, the band released *Mezcal Head*, supported by the new rhythm section of Steven George (bass) and Jez (drums). —*Stephen Thomas Erlewine*

Raise / 1991 / A&M ✦✦✦
Set upon a British music scene that favored rhythm over melody, Swervedriver's debut is an oddity. Taking the Stooges' guitar skronk, the Velvet Underground's dreamy edge, the Beatles'

melodic pop, and Pink Floyd's psychedelic vibration, *Raise* flows through most of its nine songs soothingly. And the spots where the pace picks up and the music's edge is sharper highlight Swervedriver's lush tranquility. Sometimes it works as musical meditation; sometimes it dulls synapses. Then, in songs that incorporate the hard and the smooth, "Rave Down" and "Sci-Flyer," Swervedriver hits upon a perfect pop combination. —*Matt Carlson*

● **Mezcal Head** / Oct. 5, 1993 / A&M ✦✦✦✦
Powered by a rush of swirling guitars, Swervedriver's second album is a thoroughly intoxicating record, landing halfway between psychedelia and shoegazing, with enough hooks and riffs to ground the album in a punk reality and not spiral off into the netherworld. —*Stephen Thomas Erlewine*

Swingers

Group, New Wave
After leaving Split Enz, guitarist/singer/songwriter Phil Judd left behind his previous arty-pretensions in favor of a straight-forward punky three piece, with Dwayne "Bones" Hillman (bass) and Buster Stiggs (drums). The band, formed in 1978, received favorable reviews and a great deal of early exposure playing support slots for established Aussie bands (including Split Enz) through the late '70s. In 1980, Stiggs left and was replaced by Ian "Killjoy" Gilroy. *Practical Jokers* LP (released by Mushroom Records) became an instant hit in their homeland with the infectious "Counting the Beat" reaching the number one spot. Resequenced and edited, the album saw an American release under the title *Counting the Beat* in 1982 on Backstreet Records. The title track, "It Ain't What You Dance," and the newly added single, "One Good Reason (Gimme Love)," seemed to fit perfectly into the new wave and found a fair amount of exposure on the then-infant MTV. A major role in the cult film *Starstruck* had the band poised for a major breakthrough. Judd instead opted to dissolve the band in favor of a solo career. Hillman later found success as a member of Midnight Oil. Judd released one poorly received solo album and two more with ex-Split Enz bandmates as Schnell Fenster; he now divides his time between painting and composing music for films. —*Chris Woodstra*

● **Practical Jokers** / 1979 / Mushroom ✦✦✦✦
For *Practical Jokers*, his first post-Enz project, Judd left his arty leanings behind in favor of a tight blend of mid-'60s pop, punk and new wave, resulting in a fine collection of fractured, eccentric pop songs. With the exception of "Ayatollah," which instantly dates the album, it remains just as fresh and enjoyable 15 years after its release. The quirky "Counting the Beat" became a hit single in Australia/New Zealand. —*Chris Woodstra*

○ **Counting the Beat** / 1982 / Backstreet ✦✦✦✦
In an attempt to capitalize on U.S. interest in the band generated by their appearance in the cult film *Starstruck*, Backstreet Records resequenced the *Practical Jokers* album, adding "One Good Reason (Gimme Love)" from the film. Unfortunately, it failed to make much of an impact in the States and quickly disappeared. —*Chris Woodstra*

Swinging Blue Jeans

Group, British Invasion
Although they're only remembered today for their 1964 hit "Hippy Hippy Shake," the Swinging Blue Jeans were actually one of the strongest of the Liverpool bands from the '60s British Invasion. "Hippy Hippy Shake"—a cover of an obscure '50s rocker that was actually done much better by the Beatles on tapes of their BBC performances—was their only Top 30 entry in the U.S. But the band enjoyed some other major and minor hits in the U.K., including a top-notch Merseyization of Betty Everett's (and later Linda Ronstadt's) "You're No Good," which they took into the British Top Five in 1964. They also wrote some catchy and energetic, if slightly sappy, originals in the purest Merseybeat style. While it doesn't add up to an enduring legacy, there's a lot to be said for the naive energy of the best of their early tunes. —*Richie Unterberger*

The Best of the EMI Years / 1992 / EMI ✦✦✦
Weighing in at a hefty 34 tracks, this is the most exhaustive Swinging Blue Jeans anthology available. Do not mistake this, however, for the best collection of these cheery Liverpool British Invaders. That honor belongs to the American *Hippy Hippy Shake* collection, which is nearly as comprehensive (at 26 tracks) but much more well-chosen. All their U.K. hits—half a dozen, more or

less—are included here, as well as many B-sides, flop singles, and eight previously unreleased tracks (most of which bear the writing credits "unknown," even the relatively well-known Little Richard song "Ready Teddy"). At their best, the Blue Jeans were one of the better British Invasion pop-rockers, and they did manage a fair number of good tracks, but a great deal of the selections here are uneventful or downright difficult to bear in their dated quaintness, fallow MOR pop, or lame rehashing of '50s rock. The small bonus is that the version of their 1968 single "Now That You've Got Me (You Don't Seem To Want Me)," written by Clint Ballard (also responsible for "You're No Good" and other great '60s tunes), is, for some reason, much better than the one on *Hippy Hippy Shake*. That's hardly worth the fairly hefty price of this import—stick with the U.S. compilation. —*Richie Unterberger*

● **Hippy Hippy Shake: The Definitive Collection** / May 4, 1993 / Capitol ✦✦✦✦
All of their U.K. and U.S. hits are included on this compilation. Highlights are "You're No Good," "Hippy Hippy Shake," and their fine (pre-Who) cover of Johnny Kidd's "Shakin' All Over," though even for the Anglophile, about half of this CD is forgettable, especially the dreary post-1966 stuff. This anthology includes several non-LP/rare singles and unreleased songs. —*Richie Unterberger*

Sylvers

Group, Disco
Among the more popular family acts on the '70s R&B circuit, Memphis's Sylvers recorded for Pride, MGM, Capitol, Casablanca, and Geffen during their 13-year chart run. There were ten brothers and sisters in the family, and the group were viewed as a Southern version of the Jackson 5. Their 1972 Pride single "Fool's Paradise" got things going in the right direction, reaching number 14 on the R&B charts. They had three other Top Ten R&B hits in the '70s, but their biggest song was "Boogie Fever" in 1975. It perfectly captured the disco spirit and topped both the R&B and pop charts that year. "Hot Line" was another Top Ten on both lists in 1976, and their second biggest single. They scored another Top 20 R&B single on Casablanca in 1978, "Don't Stop, Get Off," but the charming qualities of their earlier material seemed more calculated. They couldn't recapture the spark during their mid-'80s period on Geffen. —*Ron Wynn*

● **Boogie Fever: The Best of the Sylvers** / 1995 / Razor & Tie ✦✦✦✦

Sylvester

Group, Funk, Disco
Sylvester was born Sylvester James and was raised by his grandmother, blues singer Julia Morgan. After a short-lived gospel career, he performed with the transvestite vocal group the Cockettes. His solo-career backing vocalists included Martha Wash, Izora Rhodes (both of whom went on to form Two Tons of Fun and the Weather Girls), and Jeanie Tracy, and his shows were often outrageous and won him a large following in San Francisco's gay community. He died of AIDS-related complications in 1988. —*Steve Huey*

○ **Living Proof** / Feb. 1979 / Fantasy ✦✦✦✦
This was the followup to the marvelous *Mighty Real* album, and Sylvester was at his roaring best. His voice was rich, joyous, and energetic throughout, and even the songs that were lyrically weak had great, celebratory arrangements. Sylvester never got better material or support than his years at Prestige; they were among the very best productions issued during the disco era. —*Ron Wynn*

All I Need / 1983 / Megatone ✦✦✦
Sylvester was on the downside of his career in the mid-'80s. He still had the glorious tones and booming voice, but was now floundering, with his high-energy brand of disco out of fashion. Sylvester tried to fashion a comeback by mixing in lightweight pop arrangements and production while singing his old fashion. The results were not encouraging, but that wasn't because the songs lacked style; they were just the wrong things for the time. —*Ron Wynn*

Call Me / 1984 / Megatone ✦✦
Sylvester peaked in the late '70s, was still making interesting music in the early '80s, and then began the slow and painful decline that ended in his death. This one wasn't ruined by his singing, which was still impressive, but by erratic production and compositions. Sylvester tried to be comic, soul man, tease, dance star, and

pop artist and was so torn between guises that he never established one on the album. —*Ron Wynn*

● **Original Hits** / 1989 / Fantasy ✦✦✦✦
Some of the same tunes as on the *Greatest Hits* album, plus newer urban soul. —*Bil Carpenter*

David Sylvian

Art-Rock/Progressive-Rock
An alternative-rock vocal stylist from the band Japan, Sylvian's solo efforts include work with progressive sidemen such as Robert Fripp (King Crimson), Bill Nelson (Be Bop Deluxe), and Holger Czukay (Can). He draws his style from '70s art-rock fixtures like Roxy Music and David Bowie, with a spark from the experimental electronic movement of the '80s. —*AMG*

Gone to Earth / 1986 / Virgin ✦✦✦
Sylvian is joined by guitarists Robert Fripp and Bill Nelson on this 68-minute CD, which features tracks of Sylvian's trademark vocals and instrumentals. These dreamy, atmospheric works have nice musical support from Steve Nye, Kenny Wheeler, and Mel Collins. —*Scott Bultman*

● **Secrets of the Beehive** / 1987 / Virgin ✦✦✦✦
A consistent mood is sustained throughout this one. Sylvian is joined by Ryuichi Sakamoto, David Torn, Mark Isham, ex-Japan drummer Steve Jansen, and others. It includes a vocal version of the Sylvian/Sakamoto cut "Forbidden Colours" from the *Merry Christmas, Mr. Lawrence* soundtrack. —*Scott Bultman*

○ **Plight & Premonition** / 1988 / Venture ✦✦✦✦
This is a collaboration between David Sylvian, frontman for Japan, and Holger Czukay, the bassist for Can. —*Michael P. Dawson*

Flux and Mutability / 1989 / Venture ✦✦✦
A followup to *Plight and Premonition*, it features Holger Czukay and consists of two lengthy, dreamlike pieces. —*Michael P. Dawson*

The System

Group, Soul, Dance-Pop, R&B
The System is a techno-funk duo from New York City featuring Mic Murphy and David Frank. They had a Top Ten hit in 1987 with "Don't Disturb This Groove," plus a couple of other minor chart hits. —*Steve Huey*

● **Sweat** / 1983 / Mirage ✦✦✦✦
Mic Murphy and David Frank created a new group mixing funk and technology in the early '80s. While the debut wasn't a huge pop hit, it made an immediate impact in the R&B community. The synthesized backbeat of "You Are In My System" rose up the charts and made Murphy and Frank the hot R&B production tandem of the day. The rest of *Sweat* wasn't quite as successful, but it had already launched them into stardom. —*Ron Wynn*

X-Periment / 1984 / Polydor ✦✦✦

Pleasure Seekers / 1985 / Mirage ✦✦✦
The team of Mic Murphy and David Frank hadn't cooled off when this '85 album was issued. Their artful synth-funk was being featured on numerous sessions by Howard Johnson, Angela Bofill, Chaka Kahn, and Pauli Carmen, among others, and they were also keeping some good songs for their sessions. One they didn't give another band was "This Is For You," which resulted in another R&B top 10 single. —*Ron Wynn*

○ **Don't Disturb This Groove** / 1987 / Atlantic ✦✦✦✦
The title cut was Mic Murphy and David Frank's greatest record, a catchy title, decent vocals, and outstanding rhythm track, making it both a club and radio staple throughout 1987. It was also a high water mark for their techno-funk; this was their last record to make such an impact. Techno-funk was being supplanted by hip-hop, dancehall, New Jack Swing, house and hip-house. But while it lasted, Murphy and Frank were on the R&B throne. —*Ron Wynn*

Rhythm & Romance / 1989 / Atlantic ✦✦
The final System album of the 1980s lacked the definitive grooves or celebratory energy of its hit predecessor. The Murphy/Frank team had written and/or produced so many hits that it seemed they'd never lose their touch, but just as suddenly, their techno-funk got lost in the transition as urban contemporary embraced hip-hop flavored productions, dancehall, and New Jack, while dance music splintered into various techno directions, and such things as hip-house were the rage. —*Ron Wynn*

T

The T-Bones

Group, British Invasion

One of the many British R&B groups fighting for attention in 1964 and 1965, the T-Bones (not to be confused with the American group that had an instrumental hit in 1965 with "No Matter What Shape") were reared in the shadow of the Yardbirds, sharing their manager (Giorgio Gomelsky), taking over their residency at London's famed Marquee club, and confounding collectors when a picture of the Yardbirds appeared on a French T-Bones EP. A decent, energetic act, they lacked the interpretative vision of the Yardbirds and other major British bands on the R&B scene, and, like so many of the era's groups, had virtually no songwriting acumen. Keith Emerson was briefly a member, and lead singer Gary Farr recorded some solo albums. Gomelsky licensed a lot of material by his former bands haphazardly all over the world, and the T-Bones were not spared, accounting for the availability of a lot of unissued material this extremely minor band recorded in the mid-'60s. —*Richie Unterberger*

T-Bones With Gary Farr / 1984 / Eva ✦✦✦

Enjoyably energetic but routine, second- to third-division first-wave British R&B on this compilation of 16 tracks from 1964 to 1965, virtually all covers of well-known tunes. The T-Bones nick the composition credits for three Bo Diddley tunes alone. A couple tracks find them trying a more commercial soul/pop style, including "Give All She's Got," a dead ringer for the early Moody Blues. Keith Emerson, incidentally, is not present on any of the songs. —*Richie Unterberger*

The Tages

Group, Rock & Roll

Without a doubt, the best Swedish band of the '60s, and one of the best '60s rock acts of any sort from a non-English-speaking country. Although the group's first recordings were pretty weak Merseybeat derivations, in the mid-'60s they developed a tough, mod-influenced sound which echoed the Who and the Kinks, and recorded quite a few good originals, making the Swedish Top Ten over a dozen times in all. More than any other Continental group, the Tages could have passed for a genuine British band, following the U.K. acts that served as their obvious inspirations into hard rock, baroque pop, and blue-eyed soul. Big throughout Scandinavia, the group actually made a determined effort to crack the English market in 1968, playing quite a few U.K. shows and releasing records there; they failed, and disbanded at the end of the year. The Tages evolved into Blond in the late '60s, a pop-oriented group which had an album released in the United States. —*Richie Unterberger*

● **1964-68!** / 1983 / EMI (Sweden) ✦✦✦✦

Definitive double-album anthology, including all of their hit singles and many other tracks. "The One for You," "Crazy 'Bout My Baby," "The Man You'll Be Looking For," and "Miss McBaren," especially, are accomplished mod rockers on par with some of the best material of the sort being produced in Britain in the mid-'60s. —*Richie Unterberger*

Talk Talk

Group, Techno-Pop/Dance, New Wave

Talk Talk began their career as a synth-pop new wave band, but as the years moved on, the group refashioned themselves as an art-rock outfit, recording albums that flirted with the ambient, tex-tural experimentations of Brian Eno. Formed in England in 1981, Talk Talk comprised Mark Hollis (vocals), Simon Brenner (keyboards), Paul Webb (bass), and Lee Harris (drums). They were quickly signed to EMI, Duran Duran's record label. Like Duran Duran, Talk Talk looked pretty and sounded slick, enabling them to fit in with the "new romantic" pop movement of the early '80s. After scoring a couple of hits—"Talk Talk" and "Today"—and touring with Duran Duran, the group took a year off to regroup. Hollis reorganized the lineup during the recording of the group's second album, 1984's *It's My Life*. While it was slightly more experimental than their previous album, it still followed pop structures. *The Colour of Spring*, released two years later, completed the group's transition to an art-rock group. Appearing in 1988, *Spirit of Eden* was Talk Talk's most experimental record, which proved to be a commercial disaster—it led to EMI dropping the band. Talk Talk then signed with Polydor Records, releasing *Laughing Stock* in 1991. —*Stephen Thomas Erlewine*

The Party's Over / 1982 / EMI America ✦✦✦

○ **It's My Life** / 1984 / EMI America ✦✦✦✦

The followup is more polished, less like Duran Duran and more like Roxy Music. It features the hit title track. —*Scott Bultman*

○ **The Colour of Spring** / 1986 / EMI America ✦✦✦✦

Talk Talk begins their move away from light pop into more adventurous ground. The results are hit-and-miss, but several good tracks like "Life's What You Make It" are worthwhile. —*Scott Bultman*

Spirit of Eden / 1988 / EMI America ✦✦✦

● **The Natural History: The Very Best of Talk Talk** / 1990 / EMI America ✦✦✦✦

Natural History is a collection of the best material from their first four albums, plus two live tracks. All their hits and highlights are here, like "It's My Life," "Such a Shame," and "Life's What You Make It." —*Scott Bultman*

History Revisited / 1991 / EMI America ✦✦✦

Laughing Stock / 1991 / Polydor ✦✦✦

This hauntingly beautiful dissonance is almost like free-form jazz. Not pop music, to be sure, but interesting atmospheric instrumentals. This is the culmination of the direction they were taking on their previous two albums. —*Scott Bultman*

Talking Heads

Group, New Wave, Pop/Rock

At the start of their career, Talking Heads were all nervous energy, detached emotion, and subdued minimalism. When they released their last album about twelve years later, the band had recorded everything from art-funk to polyrhythmic worldbeat explorations and simple, melodic guitar-pop. Between their first album in 1977 and their last in 1988, Talking Heads became one of the most critically acclaimed bands of the '80s, while managing to earn several pop hits. While some of their music can seem too self-consciously experimental, clever, and intellectual for its own good, at their best, Talking Heads represents everything good about art-school punks.

And they were literally art-school punks. Guitarist/vocalist David Byrne, drummer Chris Franz, and bassist Tina Weymouth met at the Rhode Island School of Design in the early '70s; they decided to move to New York in 1974 to concentrate on making music. The next year, the band won a spot opening for the Ramones at the seminal New York punk club, CBGB's. In 1976, keyboardist Jerry Harrison, a former member of Jonathan Richman's Modern Lovers, was added to the lineup. By 1977, the band had signed to Sire Records and released their first album, *Talking Heads '77.* It received a considerable amount of acclaim for its stripped-down rock & roll, particularly Byrne's geeky, overly intellectual lyrics and uncomfortable, jerky vocals.

For their next album, 1978's *More Songs About Buildings and Food,* the band worked with producer Brian Eno, recording a set of carefully constructed, arty pop songs, distinguished by extensive experimenting with combined acoustic and electronic instruments, as well as touches of surprisingly credible funk. On their next album, the Eno-produced *Fear of Music,* Talking Heads began to rely heavily on their rhythm section, adding flourishes of African-styled polyrhythms. This approach came to a full fruition with 1980's *Remain in Light,* which was again produced by Eno. Talking Heads added several sidemen, including a horn section, leaving them free to explore their dense amalgam of African percussion, funk bass and keyboards, pop songs, and electronics.

After a long tour, the band concentrated on solo projects for a couple of years. By the time of 1983's *Speaking in Tongues,* the band had severed their ties with Brian Eno; the result was an album that still relied on the rhythmic innovations of *Remain in Light,* except within a more rigid pop-song structure. After its release, Talking Heads embarked on another extensive tour, which would turn out to be their last; it's captured on the Jonathan Demme-directed concert film, *Stop Making Sense.* After releasing the straightforward pop album *Little Creatures* in 1985, Byrne directed his first movie, *True Stories* the following year; the band's next album featured songs from the film. Two years later, Talking Heads released *Naked,* which marked a return to their worldbeat explorations, although it sometimes suffered from Byrne's lyrical pretensions.

After its release, Talking Heads were put on "hiatus," Byrne pursued some solo projects, as did Harrison; Franz and Weymouth continued with their side project, the Tom Tom Club. In 1991, the band issued an announcement that they had broken up. *—Stephen Thomas Erlewine*

☆ **Talking Heads '77** / 1977 / Sire ♦♦♦♦♦
This edgy set of weird, funk-like rockers introduced David Byrne's skewed world outlook. "Pull Me Up" and "New Feeling" are the standouts. *—John Floyd*

☆ **More Songs about Buildings & Food** / 1978 / Sire ♦♦♦♦♦
Producer Brian Eno added muscle and flair to the group's arty funk-rock, making this a dense and beautiful set. *—John Floyd*

○ **Fear of Music** / 1979 / Sire ♦♦♦♦
A weird, dance-worthy album was made creepy by Byrne's paranoid vision and Eno's dense production. But "Life during Wartime" is one hell of a single. *—John Floyd*

☆ **Remain in Light** / 1980 / Sire ♦♦♦♦♦
Song structure shimmies out the window as Eno and the band flex their Afro-funk muscles. It works as both brain music and dance music. *—John Floyd*

The Name of This Band Is Talking Heads / 1982 / Sire ♦♦♦
This live double album traces the band's progression, culminating in two sides of scalding material from *Remain in Light. —John Floyd*

Speaking in Tongues / 1983 / Sire ♦♦♦
A pulsating mix of the heavy funk of *Remain in Light* and song structures that hark back to *More Songs About Buildings & Food.* It contains the hit "Burning Down the House" and the hypnotic "This Must Be the Place." *—John Floyd*

Stop Making Sense / 1984 / Sire ♦♦♦
Like *The Name of This Band Is Talking Heads,* the soundtrack to their concert film *Stop Making Sense* captures the group at the peak of their live powers. Even though it duplicates three numbers from the previous live album, the performances on *Stop Making Sense* are so energetic that the album never sounds like a retread. *—Stephen Thomas Erlewine*

○ **Little Creatures** / 1985 / Sire ♦♦♦♦
Musically, this is a return to spare production and simple melodies, but this is also Byrne's most coherent and mature set of songs. *—John Floyd*

True Stories / 1986 / Sire ♦♦
Featuring songs written for David Byrne's film of the same name, *True Stories* is even more pop-oriented than *Little Creatures,* full of simple, catchy melodies and guitar hooks. Unfortunately, Byrne

thinks pop should not only be simple, but simplistic; too often, his genuinely engaging songs are weighed down by his trite lyrics and condescending attitude. Fortunately, with their exceptional musical versatility, the rest of the band keeps the album from being a complete failure. *—Stephen Thomas Erlewine*

Naked / 1988 / Fly ♦♦
Another dense set of Third-World funk, this time with some help from genuine African musicians and lyrics that talk loudly but mostly say nothing. *—John Floyd*

● **Popular Favorites, 1984-1992: Sand in the Vaseline** / Oct. 13, 1992 / Sire ♦♦♦♦
Featuring material from every Talking Heads album except the live *The Name of This Band is Talking Heads, Sand in the Vaseline* is a terrific double-disc retrospective of the band's long and varied career. Featuring all of their hit singles and trademark songs ("Psycho Killer," "Take Me to the River," "Burning Down the House," "And She Was," "Once In a Lifetime," "Swamp," "Memories Can't Wait," "Crosseyed and Painless," "Road to Nowhere," "(Nothing But) Flowers," "Life During Wartime"), the set also includes five previously unreleased tracks. *—Stephen Thomas Erlewine*

Tall Dwarfs

Group, Alternative Pop/Rock
Formed in the early '80s by ex-Toy Love members Alex Bathgate and Chris Knox, the Tall Dwarfss were one of the most influential bands to emerge from New Zealand's independent scene of the '80s. Arguably the first low-fi band in indie-rock, the Tall Dwarfs' albums were made at home on a four-track tape recorder. While the group's songs were highly melodic, the fidelity of their recordings—as well as the fact they frequently employed non-conventional instruments—always twisted their most accessible material into something otherworldly.

The group's first record, the *Three Songs EP,* was released in 1981; two years later, the group released its first full-length album, *Canned Music.* Since they were all recorded with the same equipment, their recordings are more or less interchangeable; surprisingly, the quality of their material was remarkably high as well. The Tall Dwarfs stopped recording around 1988 when Chris Knox began a solo career. Even in New Zealand their original recordings are rare; *Hello Cruel World* collects the highlights of their career on one disc. *—Stephen Thomas Erlewine*

○ **Canned Music** / 1983 / Flying Nun ♦♦♦♦

That's the Short and Long of It / 1985 / Flying Nun ♦♦

Throw a Sickie / 1986 / Flying Nun ♦♦♦

● **Hello Cruel World** / 1987 / Positive ♦♦♦♦
The band's U.S. debut, *Hello Cruel World,* collects their legendary and most influential early recordings from 1981 to 1984—with selections from the ultra-rare *Three Songs* EP (1981), *Louis Loves His Daily Dip* EP (1982), *Canned Music* (1983), and *Slugbucket Hairybreath Monster* EP (1984). An excellent introduction to a truly unique and innovative band. *—Chris Woodstra*

Weeville / Homestead ♦♦♦

Tams

Group, Soul
A "beach" music favorite, Atlanta's Tams were among the more popular uptempo soul groups of the '60s, although they were never able to break Motown's pop stranglehold. Joseph Pope's gravelly voiced leads were their selling point. He was joined by his brother Charles, Robert Smith, Floyd Ashton, and Horace Key. They began on Swan in 1960, then landed their first hit with "Untie Me" for Arlen in 1962. It peaked at number 12 on the R&B charts (number 11 pop). They moved to ABC-Paramount the next year, where they remained until 1968. They scored their biggest hit in 1963 with "What Kind of Fool (Do You Think I Am)." But many soul fans regard 1968's "Be Young, Be Foolish, Be Happy" as their ultimate hit, although it only reached number 26 on the R&B charts. *—Ron Wynn*

● **18 Greatest Hits** / Onyx Classix ♦♦♦♦

Tangerine Dream

Group, Electronic, Art-Rock/Progressive-Rock, Experimental
Formed as a rock group in 1967 by Edgar Froese, Tangerine Dream is one of the most important entities to shape contempo-

rary instrumental music over the last 20 years. The turbulent '60s, Froese's association with surrealist painter Salvador Dali, and the arrival of the Moog synthesizer were just a few of the forces that helped to fuel this German electronic group through a barrage of constant change in style and personnel. Core members over the years have included Froese and Chris Franke as well as Peter Baumann, who went on to start the Private Music label. Curiously enough, the band's most recent addition is Jerome Froese, Edgar's son, whose enigmatic photos as a baby can be found in the artwork to TD's early albums. Over the past 25 years or so, the TD sound has moved from the droning nightmares of *Zeit*, to the mesmerizing sequencer-based masterpieces of *Rubycon* and *Ricochet* in the '70s, to the sparkling high-tech rock of the '80s. A cult phenomenon for decades, Tangerine Dream gained wider recognition when the group's highly evocative music attracted the interest of William Friedkin. This resulted in the score to the film *Sorcerer* and the beginning of a large number of soundtracks. (TD's music for the Tom Cruise scorcher, *Risky Business*, probably attracted the most attention.) In recent years, Tangerine Dream has moved toward shorter, song-based pieces that seem superficial and predictable compared to the group's pioneering work, yet Froese and company must be admired for TD's continuous output and place in electronic-music history. —*Linda Kohanov*

Zeit / 1972 / Relativity ✦✦✦
T.D.'s purest expression of "space music," this double album ebbs and flows effortlessly from one tone cluster to another. Almost classical in construction, the music is structured so as to evolve in sections as one theme literally melts into the next. Florian Fricke (of Popol Vuh) played the big moog on this album and the overall texture of the electronics is warm and shimmering. —*Archie Patterson*

Rubycon / 1975 / Virgin ✦✦✦
Classic, uncompromising Tangerine Dream, it is a must for any serious collector of electronic music. —*Linda Kohanov*

○ **Logos** / 1982 / Virgin ✦✦✦✦
This live recording captures the Dream at a high point that occurred midway through the band's career. Longer, more intricate pieces are present, yet the action takes place at a brisk pace, moving through many of the trademark TD motifs and soundscapes. The recording's studio quality and engrossing performances are clearly inspired. —*Linda Kohanov*

○ **Le Parc** / 1985 / Relativity ✦✦✦✦
A selection of different moods, all of a consistently high quality. Each track takes its name and inspiration from a different park in the world, like Central or Yellowstone, for example. —*Vladimir Bogdanov*

○ **Canyon Dreams** / 1987 / Miramar ✦✦✦✦
TD received its first Grammy nomination with this album. The music was originally composed for a scenic video on the Grand Canyon, released under the same title. The style is a rather ingenious combination of the group's progressive style and current commercial leanings, and, as such, is Tangerine Dream's finest album of recent years. —*Linda Kohanov*

Melrose / 1990 / Private Music ✦✦✦
Quite a contrast from *Logos*, this album is one of the better examples of the band's recent immersion in adult-alternative electronic pop. —*Linda Kohanov*

● **Tangents: 1973-83** / 1994 / Capitol ✦✦✦✦

Howard Tate
Soul
Tate was a Georgia-born, Philadelphia-raised soul singer whose early work was guided by organist Bill Doggett. During the mid '60s, Tate teamed up with producer/songwriter Jerry Ragovoy on the Verve label. His bluesy, plaintive falsetto and melismatic, gospel-influenced style were wedded to some fine Ragovoy/Shuman compositions. "Get It While You Can" was later a mega-hit for Janis Joplin; "Look at Granny Run Run" was covered by Ry Cooder. Tate went on to cut sides for Lloyd Price's NYC-based Turntable label. Sad to say, as of early 1992, the work of this fine singer is out of print. —*Christine Ohlman*

○ **Get It While You Can** / 1966 / Verve ✦✦✦✦
Fine Jerry Ragovoy production and soulful, wailing vocals from Tate. Includes original versions of "Get It While You Can" and "Look at Granny Run Run." —*Christine Ohlman*

Reaction / 1981 / Turntable ✦✦✦
A good album of vintage Southern soul, delivered with conviction and earnestness by Howard Tate. At his best, Tate's blend of gospel-tinged shouting and wailing and countrified inflections and delivery put him close to Percy Sledge. But he just wasn't able to get over the hump, mainly because he never had a full album's worth of consistently solid material, and also seldom recorded for labels with any foothold in the R&B/soul market. —*Ron Wynn*

● **Get It While You Can: Legendary Sessions** / 1995 / Mercury ✦✦✦✦

James Taylor
b. Mar. 12, 1948
Singer-Songwriter
When people use the term "singer/songwriter" (often with the word "sensitive"), in praise or in criticism, it's James Taylor that they're thinking of. Yet in a career now extending over a quarter-century, Taylor's biggest hits have come with his cover versions of other people's songs. Go figure. Taylor grew up in Massachusetts and North Carolina, forming the band the Flying Machine with guitarist Danny Kortchmar in 1967. He was signed as a solo artist by Apple in 1968 and released his debut album, *James Taylor*, in 1969. But it was his 1970 album, *Sweet Baby James*, with its understated autobiographical hit, "Fire and Rain," that was his commercial breakthrough. *Mud Slide Slim and the Blue Horizon* went to #2 in 1971 and contained the #1 single, "You've Got a Friend," written by Carole King. Taylor scored his next big hit with a remake of Marvin Gaye's "How Sweet It Is (To Be Loved by You)" in 1975, and hit again in 1977 with Jimmy Jones's "Handy Man." He has recorded with Simon & Garfunkel, his ex-wife Carly Simon, and J. D. Souther, and he continues to release gold-selling albums every few years. —*William Ruhlmann*

James Taylor And The Original Flying Machine / 1967 / Euphoria ✦✦

○ **James Taylor** / 1969 / Capitol ✦✦✦✦
A lovely debut album, beautifully produced by Peter Asher. It features Taylor's sometimes dour sentiments sung in his compelling but quiet voice. "Something in the Way She Moves," "Carolina in My Mind," and "Rainy Day Man." —*William Ruhlmann*

James Taylor and the Flying Machine / 1970 / Springboard ✦✦✦
James Taylor And The Flying Machine—1967, released in the wake of the commercial success of *Sweet Baby James*, contains early recordings of songs James Taylor and his partner, Danny Kortchmar, were playing in Greenwich Village clubs like the Night Owl in 1967, and which they would record for Taylor's debut solo album in 1968. The songs are good, of course, but this isn't a finished, full-fledged album; It has only seven tracks, and among them are two versions of "Knocking 'Round The Zoo," one with lead vocals by Taylor and the other by Kortchmar, and "Something's Wrong," presented only as an instrumental track. For completists only. —*William Ruhlmann*

☆ **Sweet Baby James** / Feb. 1970 / Warner Brothers ✦✦✦✦✦
The heart of James Taylor's appeal is that you can take him two ways. On the one hand, his music, including that warm voice, is soothing; its minor key melodies and restrained playing draw in the listener. On the other hand, his world view, especially on such songs as "Fire and Rain," reflects the pessimism and desperation of the '60s hangover that was the early '70s. Either way, this is impressive stuff. —*William Ruhlmann*

○ **Mud Slide Slim and the Blue Horizon** / Mar. 1971 / Warner Brothers ✦✦✦✦
The changeover here—and it's the big changeover in Taylor's work—is that he is trying to jettison the past ("Don't come to me with your sorrows anymore" is the album's opening line) and look to a hopeful future. That he doesn't quite succeed makes the album itself a success. You need a little darkness to make the light stand out. —*William Ruhlmann*

One Man Dog / Nov. 1972 / Warner Brothers ✦✦✦
A lot was riding on this album, James Taylor's follow-up to his two big hits, *Sweet Baby James* and *Mud Slide Slim and The Blue Horizon*; this was released 21 months after the latter, a long time between records in those days. And what a letdown. *One Man Dog* contained 18 tracks, some of them instrumentals, many of them running less than two minutes. A lot of it was sketchy and seemingly unfinished, and none of it had the impact of the best songs on the last two albums. *One Man Dog* spawned a Top 20 hit in

"Don't Let Me Be Lonely Tonight," and it made the Top Ten and went gold itself largely on the momentum of Taylor's career. But it disappointed fans, and in the 19 months it took him to record another album, Taylor was bypassed by the singer-songwriter movement. — *William Ruhlmann*

Walking Man / Jun. 1974 / Warner Brothers ✦✦✦
One Man Dog drastically lowered expectations for a new James Taylor album, and those expectations were almost met by *Walking Man*, a more considered effort than its predecessor that managed to be just as trivial but even less interesting. As a result, it became the worst-selling album of Taylor's career. Somehow, a songwriter who had seemed in 1970 to have as precise an idea of the national mood as Bob Dylan had had in 1965 now seemed to be a man without a country. Instead, *Walking Man*, which began with Taylor asking, "Who is this walking man?" and ended with him commenting, "It's really not so bad to be fading away," sounded like the statement of a songwriter who either had nothing to say or didn't know how to say it. — *William Ruhlmann*

Gorilla / May 1975 / Warner Brothers ✦✦✦
After a three-year slump, Taylor made *Gorilla*, a comeback album of sorts. Its slick blend of light reflective originals and *Big Chill*-style song covers set the tone for many of his subsequent releases. Highlights included a remake of Marvin Gaye's "How Sweet It Is (To Be Loved by You)" (number five), "Mexico" (number 49), the steamy "You Make It Easy," and "Sarah Maria," an ode to his daughter. All in all, *Gorilla* is one of Taylor's more enjoyable post-*Sweet Baby James* efforts. — *Rick Clark*

In the Pocket / Jun. 1976 / Warner Brothers ✦✦✦
James Taylor's seventh album and last new recording for Warner Bros. is notable for producing his biggest self-written hit in four years, "Shower The People" (#22 pop, #1 easy listening). Bobby Womack's "Woman's Gotta Have It" was the album's only cover, and elsewhere Taylor took on a surprisingly rough set of issues in his typically gentle style, including "A Junkie's Lament" and "Money Machine." There were also reflections on being a "Family Man" even if, due to his peripatetic touring life, "Daddy's All Gone." Guest stars included Art Garfunkel, who harmonized on "Captain Jim's Drunken Dream," and Stevie Wonder, who co-wrote and played harmonica on "Don't Be Sad 'Cause Your Sun Is Down." On the whole, a respectable effort for an artist who was evolving into more of a craftsman than a virtuoso. — *William Ruhlmann*

● **Greatest Hits** / Oct. 1976 / Warner Brothers ✦✦✦✦
Pretty great. Be warned, however, that the versions of "Something in the Way She Moves" and "Carolina in My Mind" are re-recordings. — *William Ruhlmann*

○ **JT** / Jun. 1977 / Columbia ✦✦✦✦
The bad news is that by the time he switched to Columbia, Taylor had made the transition to craftsmanlike pop music, abandoning the shadows of his earlier work. The good news is that the Columbia work *is* so well crafted, forcing you to acknowledge what a good singer Taylor is. If the songs are less thoughtful, they are no less appealing as music. This is the best of six Columbia studio albums so far, but they're all of a piece. Good, easy listening. — *William Ruhlmann*

○ **Flag** / May 1979 / Columbia ✦✦✦✦
James Taylor followed his double-platinum Columbia Records label debut *JT* with this hodgepodge of a record. There are pointless covers of the Beatles' "Day Tripper" and the Drifters' "Up On The Roof" (#7 Adult Contemporary, #28 Pop), a remake of Taylor's own "Rainy Day Man," songs written for the failed Broadway musical *Working*, and a few inconsequential new Taylor compositions. The usual brain trust (producer Peter Asher) and the usual backup team (Danny Kortchmar, Dan Grolnick, Leland Sklar, Russ Kunkel) were on board, but the cruise was a snooze. — *William Ruhlmann*

Dad Loves His Work / Mar. 1981 / Columbia ✦✦✦
James Taylor bounced back from the spotty *Flag* with this all-original album led by his collaboration with J.D. Souther on "Her Town Too" (#11 Pop, #5 Adult Contemporary), his biggest pop hit since "Handy Man" and biggest non-cover hit since his first, "Fire And Rain," in 1970. Also included were "Hard Times" (#72 Pop, #23 Adult Contemporary) and "Summer's Here" (#25 Adult Contemporary), not to mention the unusually impassioned "Stand And Fight." After simmering this long, there wasn't much hope Taylor would ever come to a boil, but that track indicated he could at least heat up now and then. — *William Ruhlmann*

That's Why I'm Here / Oct. 1985 / Columbia ✦✦✦
Taylor took four and a half years off from record-making in the early 1980s, returning with *That's Why I'm Here*, which suggested he had found his long-term niche with Baby Boomer fans now permanently tuned to soft-rock radio—this was Taylor's first record to spawn three Top Ten adult contemporary hits, with the title track, "Only One," and a cover of Buddy Holly's "Everyday." But those boomers just don't go to the record store as often as their children, and the album failed to go gold and was his lowest-charting effort since his debut. If, in the title song, he had reconciled himself to the notion that he was here to sing "Fire And Rain" at summer concerts, that also meant he was settling for a complacent position in which his new material was virtually irrelevant, and that being the case, why should people buy it? — *William Ruhlmann*

Never Die Young / Jan. 1988 / Columbia ✦✦
While his aging contemporaries took a variety of tacks to keep up with changing fashions, from adopting more synthesized, percussive production styles to assembling an orchestra and singing standards, James Taylor just kept playing a summer concert tour each year and periodically putting out another collection of similar-sounding songs. *Never Die Young* was unusual only in that there was no big oldies cover from the '50s or '60s—every song was written or co-written by Taylor—but otherwise it addressed the same audience in much the same terms as he always had. The title song and "Baby Boom Baby" (both Adult Contemporary hits) referred to the passage of time, and the rest floated on a sea of yuppie contentment. "I work hard to see that you remember my name," he sang, and that work seemed to consist of reminding his listeners why they had liked him in the first place. — *William Ruhlmann*

● **Classic Songs** / 1990 / CBS ✦✦✦✦
Classic Songs is the only compilation to feature the original versions of all of James Taylor's classics. Unfortunately, it's only available overseas, yet it remains the best collection of his work to date. — *Sara Sytsma*

New Moon Shine / Sep. 24, 1991 / Columbia ✦✦✦

Live / 1993 / Columbia ✦✦
The pleasant *Live* will suit the needs of those who want a collection of Taylor's best-known songs, although his performance is unremarkable. — *AMG*

Johnnie Taylor

b. May 5, 1938
Soul
Aptly dubbed the "Philosopher of Soul" by the Stax publicity department, Johnnie Taylor set the ladies' hearts aflutter during the early '70s with his tender brand of Memphis soul. Taylor wasn't always the sincere crooner he developed into. A Sam Cooke protégé who took over with the Soul Stirrers when Cooke went secular, and who retained a hint of his mentor's mellifluous delivery, Taylor took the same pop route via Cooke's SAR label in 1961. Once he got on the Stax label in 1966, the vocalist forged a sublime blues/soul synthesis with a series of absolutely gorgeous efforts. But there was nothing subtle about Taylor's first number one in 1968: "Who's Making Love" was an uncompromising treatise on cheating lovers, with storming brass and slashing guitar. The follow-ups "Take Care of Your Homework" and "Jody's Got Your Girl and Gone" pounded the same message home from different angles. As the decade turned, though, Taylor perceptibly mellowed, turning increasingly to ballads for inspiration—"I Believe in You (You Believe in Me)," "We're Getting Careless with Our Love." By the time he went platinum with the horribly repetitive "Disco Lady" in 1976, the rough edges that made his early work so absorbing were smoothed away, although his recent Malaco output sometimes manages to suggest Taylor's glory years. — *Bill Dahl*

● **Johnnie Taylor Chronicle** / 1977 / Stax ✦✦✦✦
The definitive Johnnie Taylor retrospective/anthology package. It contains every major Stax hit, some album cuts, and an extensive set of liner notes from Robert Palmer. While the soul hardcore had already purchased it in vinyl, anyone who missed it that time around should immediately rush and get the CD. If you love soul, you can't be without it. — *Ron Wynn*

T.C. Atlantic

Group, Psychedelic, Garage Rock
In the mid- and late '60s, T.C. Atlantic were one of the biggest

groups in Minneapolis, recording a few singles and a live LP that were little heard outside of the region. They did manage to cut one song, "Faces," that became deservedly revered by '60s collectors as one of the finest garage psychedelic 45s after it was reissued on *Pebbles Vol. 3*. Nothing else they did matched that single's magnificent snaky melody and guitars, though their live album (consisting entirely of covers) has a certain *je ne sais quoi* that distinguishes it as one of the best all-cover '60s garage LPs. —*Richie Unterberger*

T.C. Atlantic / 1984 / Eva ✦✦✦
A haphazard reissue, combining their live album with some rare studio singles. The live material, consisting almost entirely of soul and R&B covers, has an appealing brashness; the studio stuff is okay, presenting a much poppier, Zombies/Remains-styled group, with the exception of the lousy heavy/progressive number "Judgement Train." Major strikes against this compilation are the absences of "Faces" and the good 45 studio version of "Mona," both of which, oddly, show up on the Eva compilation *The Finest Hours Of U.S. '60s Punk*. —*Richie Unterberger*

Bram Tchaikovsky

Group, Rock & Roll, New Wave, Power Pop/Anglo-Pop
Bram Tchaikovsky (b. Peter Bramall) began playing in local pub-rock bands in Lincolnshire, England, in the late '60s. He joined the Motors in 1977 and was relegated to mere sideman status by the nucleus of the band, songwriters Andy McMaster and Nick Garvey. While waiting on pre-production work for the second Motors album, Tchaikovsky took the opportunity to do some recording of his own. The resulting single, "Sarah Smiles," drew enough interest for him to leave the Motors and form his own band. In addition to its leader, the band Bram Tchaikovsky consisted of Mike Broadbent (bass, keyboards) and Keith Boyce (drums). They signed to the new Radar label in 1978 along with Stiff expatriates Nick Lowe and Elvis Costello. The band showed a great deal of promise with their first album, *Strange Man, Changed Man*, fitting in nicely with the growing power-pop movement. The unforgettable "Girl of My Dreams," a true high point of the time, became a minor hit on both sides of the Atlantic. Tchaikovsky continued on through rapid personnel changes for two more albums, *The Russians Are Coming* (Released in the U.S. as *Pressure*) in 1980 and *Funland* in 1981. A considerable drop in sales prompted Tchaikovsky to dissolve the band and retire from the music business. —*Chris Woodstra*

● **Strange Man, Changed Man** / 1979 / Polydor ✦✦✦✦
Strange Man, Changed Man remains Bram Tchaikovsky's finest moment. Produced by his former Motors bandmate Nick Garvey on a shoestring buget, the resulting thin sound only serves to enhance the songs which owe as much to '60s pop as they do to pub/punk rock. The pure pop of "Girl of My Dreams" (a minor hit in the U.S.) perfectly encapsulates late-'70s Brit-pop. —*Chris Woodstra*

Pressure / 1980 / Polydor ✦✦✦
Pressure, released in the U.K. as *The Russians Are Coming*, is not quite as strong as the first album but still worthwhile. —*Chris Woodstra*

Funland / 1981 / Arista ✦✦
By the time of the difficult third album, constant personnel changes and general lack of inspiration on the part of the band's leader had taken its toll. The deceptively titled *Funland* is a lackluster effort that effectively ended the band's career. —*Chris Woodstra*

The Teardrop Explodes

Group, New Wave
This British new wave band was formed in 1978. Original members included Julian Cope (b. 1957), Mick Finkler, Paul Simpson and Gary Dwyer. Simpson was replaced by Big in Japan's Dave Balfe, whose keyboard work was an important part of the band's sound, highly reminiscent of U.S. '60s group, Love. The group disbanded in 1982. —*Cub Koda*

● **Kilimanjaro** / 1980 / Skyclad ✦✦✦✦
The Teardrop Explodes' debut album was a surprisingly accomplished set of lush, layered psychedelic pop, that creates a consistent, dream-like mood. The album was released in different editions in the U.K. and the U.S., but the essential qualities of the music remained the same in both versions. —*Stephen Thomas Erlewine*

Wilder / 1981 / Skyclad ✦✦✦
Although the individual songs on the Teardrop Explodes' second album, *Wilder*, were more concise than the ones on their debut, the record wasn't quite as focused or mesmerizing as the debut. Nevertheless, it features a number of fine, compelling moments. —*Stephen Thomas Erlewine*

○ **Everybody Wants to Shag the Teardrop Explodes** / 1990 / Fontana ✦✦✦✦
Released eight years after their dissolution, *Everybody Wants to Shag the Teardrop Explodes* reconstructs the band's aborted third album, gathering seven outtakes with the four-track *You Disappear from View* EP. Although it isn't as polished as their two official studio albums, *Everybody* is filled with adventurous music and is frequently more exciting than *Wilder*. —*Stephen Thomas Erlewine*

Piano / 1990 / Document ✦✦
Piano collects the Teardrop Explodes' early recordings, featuring three singles and three tracks recorded for compilations. The songs make it clear the band were still trying to figure out their musical direction, but *Piano* is fascinating listening for dedicated fans of the group. —*Stephen Thomas Erlewine*

Tears for Fears

Group, Pop/Rock
Childhood friends Curt Smith (b. Jun 24, 1961) and Roland Orzabal (b. Aug 22, 1961) first worked together in 1980 with the ska/pop quintet Graduate, which produced an oddball British single "Elvis Should Play Ska." After the demise of Graduate, the twosome began recording demos of some of Orzabal's morose synth-pop tunes, "Suffer the Children" and "Pale Shelter," which eventually become part of *The Hurting*, their debut release as Tears for Fears (the name was inspired by primal scream therapy psychologist Arthur Janov).

Their 1985 sophomore release, *Songs from the Big Chair*, became a worldwide success, containing several huge hits in "Shout" (#1), "Everybody Wants to Rule the World" (#1), "Head over Heels" (#3), and "Mother's Talk" (#27).

Perfectionism delayed their over-reaching third album, *The Seeds of Love*, by four years. One of the album's highlights was the addition of soulful American singer Oleta Adams, whom Orzabal and Smith discovered singing in a Kansas City hotel lounge. That album's hits included "Sowing the Seeds of Love," "Woman in Chains," and "Advice for the Young at Heart."

Before the recording of their fourth album, Smith and Orzabal had a falling out, leaving Orzabal as the only member of Tears for Fears; he released *Elemental* in 1993 to respectable sales. —*Rick Clark*

○ **The Hurting** / 1983 / Mercury ✦✦✦✦
Roland Orzabal and Curt Smith's debut featured the morose synth-pop hits "Pale Shelter" and "Mad World." —*Scott Bultman*

○ **Songs from the Big Chair** / 1985 / Mercury ✦✦✦✦
Their best album is a good mix of synthesizers and traditional instruments. It includes the hits "Shout," "Head over Heels," and "Everybody Wants to Rule the World." —*Kenneth M. Cassidy*

The Seeds of Love / 1989 / Fontana ✦✦✦
Their third album was an overreaching effort that (in spite of itself) produced a couple of gems, particularly "Sowing the Seeds of Love" and "Woman in Chains." Oleta Adams's soulful voice added life to the proceedings. —*Rick Clark*

● **Tears Fall Down (The Hits 1982-1992)** / 1992 / Fontana ✦✦✦✦
All of this duo's hits (plus some other key tracks) are included, from throughout their career. It's a perfect overview and (essentially) the only disc to have. This anthology includes "Pale Shelter," "Shout," "Everybody Wants to Rule the World," "Head over Heels", and "Sowing the Seeds of Love," among others. —*Rick Clark*

Elemental / Jun. 22, 1993 / Mercury ✦✦
On *Elemental*, Tears for Fears *is* Roland Orzabal, and he backs away from the cinematic production of *The Seeds of Love*, preferring a more direct and soulful style of pop music that appealed to both adult contemporary and adult alternative radio audiences. While some of the material was a little weak, the record was easily as good as its immediate predecessor. —*Stephen Thomas Erlewine*

Teenage Fanclub

Group, Alternative Pop/Rock

Although their music may not be particularly innovative, Teenage Fanclub are great synthesizers of pop music, tying together everything from the Beach Boys and Big Star to Sonic Youth, Neil Young and Madonna. On their earlier records, they leaned toward loud guitar pop, drenched in dissonance. Starting with 1991's *Bandwagonesque*, the band toned down the noise and reached deeper into their melodic gifts; the result was a brilliant homage to Big Star's chiming guitars and Neil Young's lazy melodies. The record earned them substantial critical praise—*Spin* named it the record of the year—as well as some critical scorn. While the album helped the band gain a cult following in America, it made them stars in England. Two years later, they delivered *Thirteen*, which showed the band incorporating their influences into their own signature sound instead of just paying homage to them. While it wasn't as big a success as *Bandwagonesque*, it showed that Teenage Fanclub hadn't lost their gift for loud, lush guitar pop. —*Stephen Thomas Erlewine*

Catholic Education / 1990 / Matador ✦✦✦
A grimy pop record that never loses its charm, even when it becomes nearly impenetrable. Filled to the brim with charm and ebullience (as well as a snotty attitude), this is a dazzling record. —*John Dougan*

● **Bandwagonesque** / 1991 / DGC ✦✦✦✦
Much cleaner than the debut, this is a slice of Big Star worship that never fails to deliver the goods. Although it gets bogged down in obviousness from time to time, Teenage Fanclub prove they are a fine pop band, loaded with ringing guitars and breathtaking choruses. —*John Dougan*

Thirteen / 1993 / DGC ✦✦✦
Opening with the snarling T. Rex-meets-Nirvana guitar of "Hang On," which soon melts away into a sea of gorgeous Beatlesque harmonies, *Thirteen* marks a shedding of the Big Star devotions that made *Bandwagonesque* so delicious, but that doesn't make it any less enjoyable. Instead of concentrating on one band, Teenage Fanclub pillages through all of the pages of pop history, producing a layered, infectious slice of guitar pop that only gets better with repeated listenings. —*Stephen Thomas Erlewine*

Deep Fried Fanclub / 1995 / Paperhouse/Fire ✦✦
An odds-and-sods collection of outtakes and B-sides, *Deep Fried Fanclub* is woefully short on memorable material, making it worthwhile only for the most devoted fans of the group. —*Stephen Thomas Erlewine*

○ **Grand Prix** / 1995 / DGC ✦✦✦✦
Grand Prix returns Teenage Fanclub to the more concise pop structures of *Bandwagonesque* while keeping much of the ambitious arrangements of *Thirteen*. Their writing has gotten tighter, with catchier, simpler hooks, making the record their most cohesive statement. —*Stephen Thomas Erlewine*

Television

Group, Punk, New Wave

Television were one of the most creative bands to emerge from New York's punk scene of the mid-'70s, creating an influential new guitar vocabulary. While guitarists Tom Verlaine and Richard Lloyd liked to jam, they didn't follow the accepted rock structures for improvisation—they removed the blues while retaining the raw energy of garage rock, adding complex, lyrical solo lines that recalled both jazz and rock. With its angular rhythms and fluid leads, Television's music always went in unconventional directions, laying the groundwork for many of the guitar-based post-punk pop groups of the late-'70s and '80s.

In the early '70s, Television began as the Neon Boys, a group featuring guitarist/vocalist Tom Verlaine, drummer Billy Ficca, and bassist Richard Hell. At the end of 1973, the group reunited under the name Television, adding rhythm guitarist Richard Lloyd. The following year, the band made its live debut at New York's Townhouse theater and began to build up an underground following. Soon, their fan base was large enough that Verlaine was able to persuade CBGB's to begin featuring live bands on a regular basis; the club would become an important venue for punk and new wave bands. That year, Verlaine played guitar on Patti Smith's first single, "Hey Joe"/"Piss Factory," as well as writing a book of poetry with the singer.

Television recorded a demo tape for Island Records with Brian

Eno in 1975, yet the label decided not to sign the band. Hell left the band after the recording of the demo tape, forming the Heartbreakers with former New York Doll guitarist Johnny Thunders; the following year, he began a solo career supported by the Voivods, releasing a debut album, *Blank Generation*, in 1977. Hell was replaced by ex-Blondie bassist Fred Smith and Television recorded "Little Johnny Jewel," releasing it on their own Ork record label. "Little Johnny Jewel" became an underground hit, attracting the attention of major record labels. In 1976, the band released a British EP on Stiff Records, which expanded their reputation. They signed with Elektra Records and began recording their debut album.

Marquee Moon, the group's first album, was released in early 1977 to great critical acclaim, yet it failed to attract a wide audience in America; in the U.K., it reached number 28 on the charts, launching the Top 40 singles "Prove It" and "Foxhole." Television supported Blondie on the group's 1977 tour, but the shows didn't increase the group's following significantly.

Television released its second album, *Adventure*, in the spring of 1978. While its American sales were better than those of *Marquee Moon*, the record didn't make the charts; in Britain, it became a Top Ten hit. Months later, the group suddenly broke up, largely due to tensions between the two guitarists. Smith rejoined Blondie, while Verlaine and Lloyd both pursued solo careers; Lloyd also played on John Doe's first solo album, as well as joining Matthew Sweet's supporting band with the 1991 album, *Girlfriend*.

Nearly fourteen years after their breakup, Television re-formed in late 1991, recording a new album for Capitol Records. The reunited band began their comeback with a performance at England's Glastonbury summer festival in 1992, releasing *Television* a couple months later. The album received good reviews, as did the tour that followed, yet the reunion was short-lived—the group disbanded again in early 1993. —*Stephen Thomas Erlewine*

★ **Marquee Moon** / 1977 / Elektra ✦✦✦✦✦
It's hard to overrate this one, which features whiplash guitars, thrusting rhythms, and Verlaine's piercing vocals on his best set of songs. —*John Floyd*

○ **Adventure** / 1978 / Elektra ✦✦✦✦
This is a subdued set in both sound and content, but the songs sport stronger melodies, and "Glory" anticipates R.E.M.'s sound. —*John Floyd*

Blow Up / 1982 / ROIR ✦✦✦
Crappy fidelity mars this live set, but Verlaine and Lloyd conjure some scarifying and beautiful six-string magic. —*John Floyd*

Television / Sep. 28, 1992 / Capitol ✦✦✦
It's been 13 years since New York avant-rockers Television split after releasing the seminal/influential *Marquee Moon* and its followup *Adventure*. Now that the rest of the music universe has caught up with the group's sparse but progressive sensibilities, the four original members have reunited for the new *Television*. Once again, guitarist and nerve center Tom Verlaine's dry, '50s-instrumental, murder-mystery style entwines masterfully with Richard Lloyd's more emotive, pealing riffs. The performances range from hypnotically atonal to ragingly cascading; the mood from paranoid to blissful. *Television*'s highlights include the blistering ecstasy of "Call Mr. Lee," and the trance and dance of "Shane, She Wrote This." —*Roch Parisien*

Temple of the Dog

Group, Hard Rock, Alternative Pop/Rock

Soundgarden's singer Chris Cornell and drummer Matt Cameron teamed with guitarist Stone Gossard and bassist Jeff Ament from Mother Love Bone to record this 1990 tribute to the deceased Mother Love Bone lead vocalist, Andrew Wood. Several tracks feature vocalist Eddie Vedder, who had joined Gossard and Ament to form Pearl Jam shortly before *Temple of the Dog* was recorded. —*Stephen Thomas Erlewine*

○ **Temple of the Dog** / Dec. 1990 / A&M ✦✦✦✦
While it doesn't sound all that different from either Soundgarden or Pearl Jam, *Temple of the Dog* does feature some of the finest music that members of either band have ever made. Chris Cornell displays a better grasp of melody and song structure than he ever had on any previous Soundgarden album, and Eddie Vedder shows signs of developing into a distinctive, original vocalist. But the real power of the album is in the guitars of Stone Gossard and the rhythm section of Jeff Ament and Matt Cameron; together,

they make the occasionally cliched tributes to the late Andrew Wood into a genuinely moving, heartfelt elegy for their departed friend. —*Stephen Thomas Erlewine*

The Temptations

Group, Soul, R&B, Motown

The early history of the Temptations parallels that of the Supremes. The Tempts started as the Primes, the Supremes as the Primettes. They joined Motown at roughly the same time and broke through at the same time. That the Temptations had a more thorough grounding in the R&B tradition, though, is a fact evident in their work. They employed the classic gospel-group formula: a light tenor against a gutbucket rasp, with flashes of falsetto for emphasis. The Temptations had the benefit of the writing and production skills of Norman Whitfield and Smokey Robinson, who crafted songs for them such as "The Way You Do the Things You Do" and "My Girl."

With a classic lineup that included David Ruffin and Eddie Kendricks, the Temptations were the hottest R&B group during the ten-year period between 1965 and 1975. Ruffin left in 1968, the year the group experimented with psychedelia ("Cloud Nine" and later "Psychedelic Shack"); Kendricks quit in 1971. Increasingly, they fell under the spell of Norman Whitfield's preoccupations and grandiose productions, although Whitfield rose to the occasion magnificently in 1972 with "Papa Was a Rolling Stone." It was the group's last #1 pop hit, and in 1976 the group left Motown for a brief stint with Atlantic before returning to the fold. They continue to record and score R&B hits, but most people associate them with their golden period. —*Colin Escott*

Meet the Temptations / Mar. 1964 / Motown ✦✦✦
The album that effectively introduced soul's greatest vocal group. It was quite tentative in retrospect, containing only one hit, "The Way You Do The Things You Do." But that glittering single, with Eddie Kendricks's feathery tenor floating out of the arrangement and smashing harmonies nicely punching home the theme, were an indication that lightning would soon strike. The label has thankfully reissued this on CD. —*Ron Wynn*

○ **Sing Smokey** / Feb. 1965 / Motown ✦✦✦✦
A fabulous album, the Temptations' first masterpiece and the LP that established them as soul's finest vocal group. Smokey Robinson's spectacular productions, lyrics, and arrangements were sung in majestic fashion by the David Ruffin/Eddie Kendricks vocal frontline, and what more need be said about immortal songs like "My Girl," "It's Growing" and "The Way You Do The Things You Do," a carryover from the first album? —*Ron Wynn*

○ **The Temptin' Temptations** / Nov. 1965 / Motown ✦✦✦✦
Any doubts that the Temptations would be the ruling vocal group of the soul era were forever erased with their third album. This contained many classics written and produced by Smokey Robinson, and such songs as "Don't Look Back," "Girl (Why You Wanna Make Me Blue)," "I'll Be In Trouble," and "My Baby" were seldom off the airwaves or turntables. There was also the incredible "Since I Lost My Baby," still perhaps their definitive heartache ballad. —*Ron Wynn*

○ **Gettin' Ready** / Jun. 1966 / Motown ✦✦✦✦
The marvelous title track alone, with Eddie Kendricks gliding into the stratosphere, made this an instant winner. There were several fine songs that weren't hits, such as "Not Now, I'll Tell You Later" and "I've Been Good To You," and there sure wasn't anything wrong with powerhouse cuts like "Ain't Too Proud To Beg." The Temptations would score four straight number one hits in the mid-'60s, each one an unforgettable classic. —*Ron Wynn*

○ **With a Lot o' Soul** / Jul. 1967 / Motown ✦✦✦✦
A fabulous album, and one that's thankfully available on CD. It contained scorching uptempo hits with David Ruffin in blazing, anthemic form on "(I Know) I'm Losing You" and "(Loneliness Made Me Realize) It's You That I Need." He and Kendricks brilliantly alternated leads on "You're My Everything." Sadly, Ruffin's push to get his name placed in front of the other Temptations would eventually result in him being booted from the band. —*Ron Wynn*

In a Mellow Mood / Jul. 1967 / Motown ✦✦✦
The Temptations moved into world of jazzy pre-rock pop and showed that great singers can handle anything. While many soul fans were surprised that they issued an album with versions of "Ol' Man River," "Somewhere" and "Taste Of Honey," they were

hooked once they heard it. This LP was another indication of how much Berry Gordy wanted to show mainstream audiences that Motown acts were versatile. —*Ron Wynn*

○ **The Temptations Wish It Would Rain** / 1968 / Motown ✦✦✦✦
Another in their impressive string of remarkable albums that began with their second in 1965, *The Temptations Sing Smokey*, and continued until *Hear To Tempt You* in 1977. The title cut was a David Ruffin triumph, among his best anguished/heartache numbers. Kendricks equaled his emotional brilliance without registering identical pain on "Please Return Your Love To Me." Yes, it's available on CD. —*Ron Wynn*

○ **I Wish It Would Rain** / Apr. 1968 / Motown ✦✦✦✦
This was perhaps David Ruffin's greatest collection of performances while in the Temptations, topped by his smashing, transcendent vocal on the title track. He was just as magnificent on "I Could Never Love Another (After Loving You)," while Eddie Kendricks didn't falter on "Please Return Your Love To Me." The Temptations were now superstars, and every single and album was an event. —*Ron Wynn*

○ **Cloud Nine** / Feb. 1969 / Motown ✦✦✦✦
The Temptations angered some individuals, surprised others, and generated a mini-controversy with this title cut, which would certainly trigger a firestorm today. While you could certainly argue that it's as much of an anti-drug song as an endorsement, the smoking lead, outstanding harmonies, and ahead-of-its-time production aren't arguable. They followed that a few months later with the equally arresting "Runaway Child, Running Wild" and rode out the storm. —*Ron Wynn*

Puzzle People / Sep. 1969 / Motown ✦✦✦
A sorely overlooked album, this late-'60s release included a pair of great commentary pieces, "Message From A Black Man" and "Don't Let The Joneses Get You Down." But the song that made the album was "I Can't Get Next To You," the greatest Dennis Edwards lead vocal in his Temptations tenure. Although Edwards always sang with passion and exuberance, he came close to surpassing David Ruffin's zeal and shattering brilliance on this track; he only equaled this performance one other time, and it wasn't with the Temptations, but on the classic single "Don't Look Any Further." —*Ron Wynn*

The Sky's the Limit / Apr. 1971 / Motown ✦✦✦
Eddie Kendricks said so long to the Temptations on this early-'70s album, with the glorious "Just My Imagination" being his swan song. The song that everyone missed was their lengthy, imaginative version of "Smiling Faces Sometimes," which wasn't a huge hit for them, but became a smash for the Undisputed Truth. Although they were successful with Damon Harris replacing Kendricks, things would never be the same. —*Ron Wynn*

○ **All Directions** / Jul. 1972 / Motown ✦✦✦✦
A monster album, the one that put them back in the spotlight and signaled that Norman Whitfield had saved the day. Damon Harris had replaced Eddie Kendricks, and there were many doubters convinced the band was finished. Instead, Whitfield revitalized them via the majestic single, "Papa Was A Rolling Stone." Despite its length, Whitfield's decision to open with an extensive, multi-layered musical suite and tease listeners was a master stroke. By the time Dennis Edwards's voice came rushing in, no one would dare turn it off. The single, as well as "Law Of The Land" and others, ended the funeral arrangements that had been prepared for the Temptations. —*Ron Wynn*

★ **Anthology** / Feb. 1973 / Motown ✦✦✦✦✦
The best hit collection available is exhausting! —*Rick A. Bueche*

Masterpiece / Feb. 1973 / Motown ✦✦✦
Norman Whitfield hit the motherlode with this 1973 epic, finally getting the right blend of elaborate production effects, ambitious compositions and convincing, energetic vocals from the Temptations. The title track ripped into the Top 10 on both the pop and R&B charts, while "Plastic Man" was a cutting indictment of hypocrisy and "Hey Girl (I Like Your Style)" was a brassy yet effective number blending arrogance, suggestiveness and vulnerability. —*Ron Wynn*

25th Anniversary / 1986 / Motown ✦✦✦
Motown celebrated the Temptations' 25th anniversary by issuing a retrospective/anthology album complete with an eight-page booklet that offered more details about the group's accomplishments than the three-record *Anthology* had years earlier. It was also interesting as to what songs they included ("Cloud Nine," "Don't

Look Back," "Papa Was A Rolling Stone," "Power," "My Girl" and "Since I Lost My Baby," among others) and excluded ("Girl Why You Wanna Make Me Blue," "Ball Of Confusion (That's What The World Is Today)," and "Way You Do The Things You Do"). They fleshed the set out with previously unreleased tracks, none of them surpassing prior Temptations hits. —*Ron Wynn*

Hum Along and Dance: More of the Best (1963-1974) / 1993 / Rhino ✦✦✦
This 18-track compilation contains Temptations B-sides, non-hit cuts and obscure sides recorded from 1963-1974. It includes such sumptuous ballads as "What Love Has Joined Together" and "Gonna Keep On Trying Till I Win Your Love," plus uptempo wailers and an occasional dud ("Stop The War Now"). The early tracks show the group evolving from its doo-wop roots into soul's premier group. While the cuts on this disc aren't the ones that made the Temptations popular music institutions, they're still a vital part of their legacy. —*Ron Wynn*

○ **Emperors Of Soul** / 1994 / Motown ✦✦✦✦
The Temptations were unquestionably one of Motown's greatest groups, recording a large number of classic singles. They were also one of the handful of Motown groups that were able to successfully make the transition from the '60s to the '70s, giving them a sizable amount of quality material from both decades. *Emperors of Soul*, a lavishly produced five-CD box set, draws from the Temptations' entire career, treating all aspects of it with equal respect. For the dedicated fan, the box set is a treasure—the sound is great and there are numerous rarities. However, for most listeners, it is simply too much music, featuring too many unfamiliar songs. —*Stephen Thomas Erlewine*

10cc

Group, Pop/Rock
Formed in 1972, 10CC mixed pop craftsmanship with art-rock affectations. The band members already had quite a professional pedigree: Graham Gouldman (b. May 10, 1945) had already penned hits for the Yardbirds ("For Your Love") and the Hollies ("Bus Stop"), among others. While working in the Mindbenders, Gouldman met Eric Stewart (b. Jan 20, 1945), as well as Kevin Godley (b. Oct 7, 1945) and Lol Creme (b. Sep 9, 1947), both graphic arts students who had signed with ex-Yardbirds manager Giorgio Gomelsky's Marmalade label under the moniker of Frabjoy and Runcible. While they were recording their first single, "I'm Beside Myself," they met Gouldman and Stewart, sidemen for the session.

The foursome produced a number of records under a variety of fake band names, scoring a worldwide two-million-selling hit, "Neanderthal Man" (#22), using the name Hotlegs. Brit-pop impresario Jonathon King heard the foursome's satirical '50s-style demos, "Donna" and "Waterfall," and signed them to his UK Records label, giving them the name 10CC along the way. "Donna" quickly became a huge English hit at number two. The bouncy "Rubber Bullets" went number one in the U.K. Subsequent albums became increasingly ambitious until the departure of Godley and Creme, who pursued an idiosyncratic duo career and a very successful venture into video direction. Stewart and Gouldman continued with 10CC until 1983. —*Rick Clark*

● **10 CC/Sheet Music** / 1973 / DCC ✦✦✦✦
This includes both of 10CC's first two albums on a single disc. The self-titled debut featured material that spoofed lightweight late-'50s/early-'60s pop, with songs like "Donna" (which became a number two U.K. hit) and "Johnny Don't Do It." "Rubber Bullets," off that album, became a #1 UK hit, reaching number 73 stateside. On *Sheet Music*, 10CC took a more sophisticated arty direction. With that album, they became favorites of college-radio programmers, who liked the band's clever pretensions. Highlights on *Sheet Music* include "Wall Street Shuffle" (number 103) and "The Worst Band in the World." Steve Hoffman mastered this CD for Dunhill, and the sound is quite good. Even though none of the band's major hits are here, this is probably the best starting place for the uninitiated. —*Rick Clark*

The Original Soundtrack / 1975 / Mercury ✦✦✦
There are some very nice *sounding* songs here. The atmospheric "I'm Not in Love" was a worldwide hit. "Brand New Day" and "Second Sitting for the Last Supper" are highlights, but extended pieces like "Une Nuit Á Paris" come off like art-pop for the terminally cute. —*Rick Clark*

How Dare You? / 1976 / Mercury ✦✦✦
"Lazy Days" and the title cut are nice, and fans of the band champion tracks like "I'm Mandy, Fly Me" (#60), "Art for Art's Sake," and "I Want to Rule the World" as evidence of 10CC's smarts, but the end result is a little too smug at times. In terms of production, 10CC's ultra-clean production sound is impressive. —*Rick Clark*

Deceptive Bends / 1977 / Mercury ✦✦✦
After *How Dare You*, Lol Creme and Kevin Godley left Eric Stewart and Graham Gouldman to their own devices. The result was *Deceptive Bends*, a poppier, at times McCartneyish album, which produced three hits: "People in Love" (number 40), "Good Morning Judge" (number 69), and the internationally successful "The Things We Do for Love," which hit number five. —*Rick Clark*

Bloody Tourists / 1978 / Mercury ✦✦

10,000 Maniacs

Group, Alternative Pop/Rock, Folk-Rock
10,000 Maniacs (named after the low-budget horror movie *2,000 Maniacs*) was formed in Jamestown, NY, in 1981 by singer Natalie Merchant and guitarist John Lombardo. Other members of the sextet were Robert Buck (guitar), Steven Gustafson (bass), Dennis Drew (keyboards), and Jerry Ausugstyniak (drums). The group gigged extensively and recorded independently before signing with Elektra and making *The Wishing Chair* in 1985. Co-founder Lombardo left the band in 1986, and they continued as a quintet, releasing the second album, *In My Tribe*, in 1987. This album broke into the charts, where it stayed 77 weeks, peaking at #37. *Blind Man's Zoo*, the 1989 follow-up, hit #13 and went gold.

After 1992's *Our Time in Eden* had finished its run on the charts, Natalie Merchant announced that she was leaving for a solo career. *MTV Unplugged* was released a few months after her departure. The remaining 10,000 Maniacs decided to continue performing, adding the folk-rock duo John & Mary. Merchant released her first solo album, *Tiger Lily*, in the summer of 1995. —*William Ruhlmann*

Human Conflict Number Five / 1982 / Mark ✦✦

Secrets of the I Ching / 1983 / Christian Burial Music ✦✦

The Wishing Chair / 1985 / Elektra ✦✦✦
Put simply, 10,000 Maniacs sound a lot like Fairport Convention with Sandy Denny, so it's appropriate that Fairport's original producer, Joe Boyd, was brought in to handle their major-label debut. The result is a gentle folk/rock record that highlights the haunting voice of Natalie Merchant. —*William Ruhlmann*

● **In My Tribe** / 1987 / Elektra ✦✦✦✦
With guest vocal by Michael Stipe of R.E.M., it includes "Like the Weather" and their remake of "Peace Train." The album was produced by Peter Asher. —*Kenneth M. Cassidy*

Blind Man's Zoo / 1989 / Elektra ✦✦✦
Natalie Merchant's lyrics have a subtle urgency on such tracks as "Eat for Two" and "Trouble Me," while the band contrives textured folk/rock backing and producer Peter Asher creates a well-articulated rock sound. —*William Ruhlmann*

Hope Chest: The Fredonia Recordings 1982-1983 / 1990 / Elektra ✦✦
This is a reissue of the band's first recordings. —*Kenneth M. Cassidy*

○ **Our Time in Eden** / Sep. 29, 1992 / Elektra ✦✦✦✦
On their last album, *Our Time In Eden*, 10,000 Maniacs experiment with their trademark sound without ever losing sight of the gentle, melodic folk-rock that has gained them legions of fans. They wind up with their best album since *In My Tribe*, highlighted by the rolling "These Are Days" and the horn-spiked "Candy Everybody Wants." —*Stephen Thomas Erlewine*

MTV Unplugged / 1993 / Elektra ✦✦
When it was recorded, nobody knew that *MTV Unplugged* would be 10,000 Maniacs' last album with Natalie Merchant. As it stands, it's a quiet, gentle way for her to bow out, offering no new revelations but several solid versions of the group's signature songs (mainly concentrating on *Our Time in Eden*) and a cover of Patti Smith's "Because the Night." It's nothing new, but for fans it's a graceful way to say goodbye. —*Stephen Thomas Erlewine*

Ten Years After

Group, Blues Rock
Ten Years After is a British blues-rock quartet consisting of Alvin

Lee (b. Dec 19, 1944), guitar and vocals; Chick Churchill (b. Jan 2, 1949), keyboards; Leo Lyons (b. Nov 30, 1944) bass; and Ric Lee (b. Oct 20, 1945), drums. The group was formed in 1967 and signed to Decca in England. Its first album was not a success, but its second, the live *Undead* (1968) containing "I'm Going Home," a six-minute blues workout by the fleet-fingered Alvin hit the charts on both sides of the Atlantic. *Stonedhenge* (1969) hit the U.K. Top Ten in early 1969. Ten Years After's U.S. breakthrough came as a result of its appearance at Woodstock, at which it played a nine-minute version of "I'm Going Home." Its next album, *Ssssh*, reached the U.S. Top 20, and *Cricklewood Green*, containing the hit single "Love Like a Man," reached #14. *Watt* completed the group's Decca contract, after which it signed with Columbia and moved in a more mainstream pop direction, typified by the gold-selling 1971 album *A Space in Time* and its Top 40 single "I'd Love to Change the World." Subsequent efforts in that direction were less successful, however, and Ten Years After split up after the release of *Positive Vibrations* in 1974. They reunited in 1988 for concerts in Europe and recorded their first new album in 15 years, *About Time*, in 1989. *— William Ruhlmann*

○ **Undead** / 1968 / Deram ✦✦✦✦
A live album from a group best experienced live, including some amazing guitar playing at phenomenal speeds from Alvin Lee. — *William Ruhlmann*

○ **Greatest Hits** / 1977 / Deram ✦✦✦✦
The group's 1968-1970 best, including the hit "Love like a Man" and the Woodstock version of "I'm Going Home." *— William Ruhlmann*

● **Essential** / 1991 / Chrysalis ✦✦✦✦
While it doesn't include all of their prime material, *Essential* features enough of their best songs to make it a fine introduction. — *AMG*

Tenpole Tudor

New Wave
Tenpole Tudor was one the strangest and silliest groups on Stiff Records, a label that was known for its odd-balls. Led by Eddie Tudor (born Edward Tudor-Pole), a former actor that could barely carry a tune, the group played a mixture of punk, roots-rock, pop and British dance-hall music, developing a thoroughly entertaining and ridiculous style. Tudor formed the band in 1974 with guitarist Bob Kingston, bassist Dick Crippen, and drummer Gary Long. Before recording the band's first album, Tudor appeared in the Sex Pistols' movie *The Great Rock 'N' Roll Swindle*, singing "Who Killed Bambi." After releasing a single on Korova records, the group joined the Stiff Roster, releasing "Three Bells in a Row." Tenpole Tudor released their debut album, *Eddie, Old Bob, Dick and Gary* in 1981; it sold well, launching two minor singles in addition to "Three Bells in a Row"—"Wunderbar" and "Swords of a Thousand Men." That same year, the group released their second album, *Let the Four Winds Blow*, which also performed well. The following year, Eddie Tudor broke up Tenpole Tudor; while he led a cajun-inspired version of Tenpole Tudor, the rest of the band became the Tudors. After the new incarnation of Tenpole Tudor failed, Tudor left Stiff Records and began performing in jazz and swing bands, as well as returning to acting; he has since concentrated on acting, although he has assembled new versions of Tenpole Tudor since. *— Stephen Thomas Erlewine*

● **Eddie, Old Bob, Dick & Gary** / 1981 / Stiff ✦✦✦✦
Let the Four Winds Blow / 1981 / Stiff ✦✦✦

Tammi Terrell

b. 1946, Philadelphia, PA, **d.** Mar. 16, 1970
Soul, Motown
Signed to Motown in the mid-'60s as a soloist, her greatest successes were duets with Marvin Gaye, including the original "Ain't No Mountain High Enough." Her solo successes were limited and her potential never fully realized, due to her illness and subsequent death from a brain tumor in 1970. *— Rick A. Bueche*

○ **Irresistible** / 1968 / Motown ✦✦✦✦
Tammi Terrell had a sexy, hypnotic voice and alluring sensibility that not only made her an ideal partner for Marvin Gaye, but could have resulted in substantial impact as a solo singer. This album includes her finest solo single, "I Can't Believe You Love Me," and some other interesting numbers, although Terrell never received any songs for herself that matched what she did with Gaye. *—Ron Wynn*

● **Greatest Hits** / 1970 / Motown ✦✦✦✦
This is actually a greatest hits LP for Marvin Gaye and Tammi Terrell, and there's little more that needs to be said about these numbers—the writing of Ashford and Simpson and the vocals of Gaye and Terrell were an epic collaboration. "Ain't No Mountain High Enough," "Ain't Nothing Like The Real Thing," "If This World Were Mine," and the list continues, classics each and every one. *—Ron Wynn*

Tesla

Group, Hard Rock, Heavy Metal
With their first album, *Mechanical Resonance*, Tesla quickly established themselves as one of the better hard rock/heavy metal bands of the late '80s. Although they weren't utterly original, the band was tight and showed an ability for crafting melodic, driving riffs. What made Tesla different from other metal bands with pop inclinations was the fact that their music was grounded in gritty, bluesy hard rock instead of slick, arena rock.

Although their debut climbed all the way to number 32 on the *Billboard* charts, their second album, 1989's *The Great Radio Controversy*, was an even greater success, scoring a Top Ten hit with the ballad "Love Song." Their follow-up album, *Five Man Acoustical Jam*, showed that the band didn't need overdriven amplifiers in order to play; it also showed that they had a fondness for sentimental hippie oldies, as their hit version of "Signs" proved. The record also turned out to be their biggest hit, reaching number 12 on the charts. While its follow-up, *Psychotic Supper*, wasn't as commercially successful, it captured Tesla branching into new musical territories; it proved that the band hadn't lost its creative spark. *—Stephen Thomas Erlewine*

○ **Mechanical Resonance** / 1986 / David Geffen Co. ✦✦✦✦
Tesla's debut is one of their stronger albums. *—John Book*

● **The Great Radio Controversy** / 1989 / David Geffen Co. ✦✦✦✦
More use of acoustic instruments make this a treat. It features the Top Ten hit "Love Song," as well as "The Way It Is" and "Heaven's Trail (No Way Out)." *—John Book*

Five Man Acoustical Jam / 1990 / David Geffen Co. ✦✦✦
With the advent of *MTV Unplugged*, it became popular for all types of groups to prove that they didn't have to rely on walls of amps and outboard gear to get their music across. *Five Man Acoustical Jam* was one of the most successful outings of that type, featuring versions of the Five Man Electrical Band's "Signs," Creedence's "Lodi," and a smattering of originals. *—Rick Clark*

Psychotic Supper / 1991 / David Geffen Co. ✦✦✦
This is one of the few heavy metal bands who can release albums with more than ten songs and still end up with quality product. *— John Book*

Bust a Nut / 1994 / Geffen ✦✦

Joe Tex (Joe Arrington, Jr)

b. Aug. 8, 1933, Rogers, TX, **d.** Aug. 13, 1982
Soul, Funk
Often pausing in the middle of a ballad for a brief but sincere secular sermon on the inherent value of true love or the hazards of cheating, Joe Tex was one of the Southern soul genre's most enduring performers—and one of its most versatile. With a stage surname reflecting his home state, Tex first entered a recording studio in 1955 for King, singing some potent R&B before trying his luck in New Orleans with Ace. Tex joined forces with Nashville producer Buddy Killen (who formed the Dial logo to market the singer's output) and finally scaled the pop playlists in 1965 with his smash "Hold What You've Got." The intense gospel-tinged ballad proved the prototypical Tex track, loaded with sound advice and downhome homilies.

That's not to say that Tex didn't record some hard-driving uptempo soul during the mid-'60s—"A Sweet Woman like You," "S.Y.S.L.J.F.M. (The Letter Song)," and "Show Me" all sizzle, while the hilarious "Skinny Legs and All," another major R&B and pop hit, accurately testifies to Tex's live charisma. With his microphone-stand acrobatics a longtime trademark, Tex's winning streak endured into the next decade with the grunting "I Gotcha," his biggest crossover success in 1972. He eked out another smash in the midst of disco fever with "Ain't Gonna Bump No More (With No Big Fat Woman)," his ebullient sense of humor still intact. Tex died in 1982. *—Bill Dahl*

● **I Believe I'm Gonna Make It** / 1988 / Rhino ✦✦✦✦
First-rate country/soul, sung with the just the right blend of
whimsy, worry, and relief. Joe Tex was routinely turning out excellent cuts throughout the mid-'60s, but it wasn't until his
novelty/disco tunes of the mid-'70s that he finally attained any
widespread recognition. Sadly, none of his great Dial albums are
currently in print. —*Ron Wynn*

that dog.
Group, Alternative Pop/Rock
That dog. are a quartet out of Los Angeles headed by guitarist/vo-
calist Anna Waronker, the daughter of Warner bigwig Lenny
Waronker. However, the group's material is surprisingly non-commercial and challenging, considering (or perhaps in spite of) family ties. That dog. mixes amateurish, riot grrrlish guitar stylings
with violins and three-part harmonies, and with dry, witty lyrics
that give lie to the group's seeming innocence. The group formed
in 1990 and released their self-titled debut in 1994, to some critical recognition but almost no sales. Their second album, *Totally
Crushed Out!* (1995), shows a vast improvement both in technique
and songwriting, while still keeping the quirkiness and charm
that made the group initially interesting. —*Heather Phares*

that dog. / 1994 / DGC ✦✦✦
The group's debut is uneven but exciting. The mix of sweet harmonies, crunchy guitars and scratchy violins makes it an entertaining listen, especially on songs like "Raina" and "Punk Rock
Girl." —*Heather Phares*

● **Totally Crushed Out!** / 1995 / DGC ✦✦✦✦
An appealing concept album about crushes and puppy love, *Totally Crushed Out!* is full of tight punk-pop and pretty ballads.
Tracks like "Ms. Wrong," "Silently" and "One Summer Night" capture the giddiness of first love with their three-part harmonies and
sweet melodies. *Totally Crushed Out!* is cute and clever without
being too cutesy or precious, and almost as memorable as a first
crush. —*Heather Phares*

That Petrol Emotion
Group, Alternative Pop/Rock
After the Undertones broke up, brothers Sean (formerly known as
John) and Damian O'Neill formed That Petrol Emotion. While they
were more politically oriented and noisier than the Undertones,
they managed to keep their former band's energetic, melodic kick.
With their first album, *Manic Pop Thrill*, That Petrol Emotion became critics' favorites, as well as earning a respectable following
in the U.K. Over the years, their music remained endlessly diverse,
incorporating elements of every style of independent guitar rock.
Occasionally, their albums would be wildly uncohesive because of
this, yet they managed to turn in several excellent songs on each
record. Sean left the band after their third album, *End of the Millennium Psychosis Blues*. The album showed signs that That
Petrol Emotion's exuberant diversity was beginning to wear thin;
their next albums proved that they were running out of things to
say. After eight years, That Petrol Emotion broke up in 1994. —
Stephen Thomas Erlewine

Manic Pop Thrill / 1986 / Demon ✦✦

● **Babble** / 1987 / Polydor ✦✦✦✦
On their second album, That Petrol Emotion's electrifying mix of
spiky guitar hooks, direct melodies, and righteous, socially conscious lyrics solidifies into a distinctive sound that's a little messy
but completely invigorating. Although they released several
records in the next seven years, the band were never able to replicate the sheer power and solid hooks of *Babble*. —*Stephen
Thomas Erlewine*

End of the Millennium Psychosis Blues / 1988 / Virgin ✦✦✦

Chemicrazy / 1990 / Virgin ✦✦✦

Fireproof / Feb. 15, 1994 / Rykodisc ✦✦

The The
Group, Alternative Pop/Rock
The The is essentially the solo project of Londoner Matt Johnson.
Johnson released a solo album, *Burning Blue Soul*, in the early
'80s which sketched out The The's sound—atmospheric, experimental songs that rely more on sound than song. With the first official The The album, 1983's *Soul Mining*, Johnson expanded his
sound somewhat, concentrating more on songwriting while retaining the hollow, haunting ambience of his sound. With 1986's

Infected, he began recording with studio musicians; this allowed
him to embellish his music with several different styles, particularly dance. On The The's next album, 1989's *Mind Bomb* former
Smiths guitarist Johnny Marr joined the band, which helped Johnson to present his music more clearly. With each release, The The
became more direct; 1993's *Dusk* was their most straightforward
album yet. Even though Johnson has strayed slightly from his
spare, experimental roots, he remains an ambitious artist that has
always satisfied and challenged his cult. —*Stephen Thomas Erlewine*

Uncertain Smile / 1982 / Maxi ✦✦

Soul Mining / 1983 / Epic ✦✦✦
On The The's first album, Matt Johnson crafted a pleasant but unengaging set of dance-pop just barely hinting at the experimentalism he would develop on later records like *Infected* or *Mind
Bomb*. —*Stephen Thomas Erlewine*

○ **Infected** / 1986 / Epic ✦✦✦✦
Infected is such a leap forward from *Soul Mining* that the album
hardly seems like the work of the same band. Instead of the light,
agreeable dance-pop of the previous album, *Infected* draws a
dense, dark sonic landscape that accurately conveys the alienation
and despair Matt Johnson sings about. —*Stephen Thomas Erlewine*

● **Mind Bomb** / 1989 / Epic ✦✦✦✦
With the addition of former Smiths guitarist Johnny Marr, the The
attempted their most ambitious album yet with *Mind Bomb*. Instead of the darkly polished dance-pop stylings of *Infected*, *Mind
Bomb* opens up the music to reveal a slow, winding textured
world of sound that celebrates its rough edges instead of hiding
them. It's serious, dance-influenced rock of the highest order. —
Stephen Thomas Erlewine

○ **Dusk** / Jan. 5, 1993 / Epic ✦✦✦✦
Sixth album *Dusk*—with its themes of desire, fall, redemption, and
death—creates both a familiar and dislocating atmosphere, like a
well-known film-noir plot for a movie produced on some other
planet. Several songs have echoed, phased vocals—as if they were
alien transmissions being randomly captured by this life-cycle
soundtrack. The mutant blues of "Dogs of Lust" is an especially effective example of this unsettling terrain. Even when Johnson gets
more conventional, there is no lack of depth. Dusk never looked so
convergingly bright—and dark—than on *Dusk*. —*Roch Parisien*

Hanky Panky / 1995 / 550 Music/Epic ✦✦✦
It is true that Matt Johnson offers some startlingly original interpretations of Hank Williams songs on *Hanky Panky*—he makes
them sound like The The songs. That doesn't necessarily mean
he's tapped into the essence of Williams's music, it means that he
is a gifted arranger. Most of the song pulse to an electronic beat
and the atmosphere is thick with forboding doom. Strangely
enough, it works better than several The The records, since Hank
Williams is a better songwriter than Matt Johnson. —*Stephen
Thomas Erlewine*

Thee Midniters
Group, Rock & Roll, Garage Rock
Indisputably the greatest Latino rock band of the '60s, Thee Midnighters took their inspiration from both the British Invasion
sound of the Rolling Stones and the more traditional R&B that
they were weaned on in their native Los Angeles. Hugely popular
in east Los Angeles, the group, featuring both guitars and horns,
had a local hit (and a small national one) with their storming version of "Land of a Thousand Dances" in 1965. Much of their repertoire featured driving, slightly punkish rock/R&B, yet lead singer
Willie Garcia also had a heartbreaking delivery on slow and
steamy ballads. In the manner of other local phenomenons like
the Rationals (from Detroit), they were equally talented at whipping up a storm with uptempo numbers and offering smoldering,
romantic soul tunes. After a few albums and an interesting detour
into social consciousness with the single "Chicano Power," the
group split in the early '70s, though their legacy is felt in later
popular Latino L.A. rock acts like Los Lobos. —*Richie Unterberger*

Unlimited / 1967 / Whittier ✦✦✦
Except for the greatest-hits compilation, this is the group's most interesting album, as eight of the twelve songs were group originals.
They favor a more straightforward blue-eyed soul approach than
they do on many of their singles over the course of this LP, which

also includes the unusually punky (for them) number "Never Knew I Had It So Bad." —*Richie Unterberger*

● **Best of Thee Midniters** / 1983 / Rhino ◆◆◆◆
An excellent compilation of 14 of their best songs, including "Land of a Thousand Dances" and "Chicano Power." They make a fair Latino Rolling Stones on "Empty Heart," "Everybody Needs Somebody," and "Whittier Blvd." (a thinly disguised reworking of the Stones' "2120 South Michigan Ave."); "That's All," "Dreaming Casually," and "Sad Girl" are exceptional slow R&B ballads; and "Jump, Jive and Harmonize" is a tough garage-punk original. —*Richie Unterberger*

Them

Group, British Invasion
Not strictly a British group, but packaged as part of the British Invasion, Them forged their hard-nosed R&B sound in Belfast, Ireland, moving to England in 1964 after landing a deal with Decca Records. The band's simmering sound was dominated by boiling organ riffs, lean guitars, and the tough vocals of lead singer Van Morrison, whose recordings with Them rank among the very best performances of the British Invasion. Morrison also wrote topnotch original material for the outfit, whose lineup changed numerous times over the course of their brief existence. As a hitmaking act, their résumé was brief—"Here Comes the Night" and "Baby Please Don't Go" were Top Ten hits in England, "Mystic Eyes" and "Here Comes the Night" made the Top 40 in the U.S.—but their influence was considerable, reaching bands like the Doors, who Them played with during a residency in Los Angeles just before Van Morrison quit the band in 1966. Their most influential song of all, the classic three-chord stormer "Gloria," was actually a B-side, although the Shadows of Knight had a hit in the U.S. with a faithful, tamer cover version.

Morrison has recalled his days with Them with some bitterness, noting that the heart of the original group was torn out by image-conscious record company politics, and that session men (including Jimmy Page, who played a scorching solo on "Baby Please Don't Go") often replaced members on recordings. That may be, but whether the records are faithful to the original Them sound or not, they were usually great—in addition to hits, Them released a couple fine albums and several flop singles that mixed fine Morrison compositions with hot R&B and soul covers, as well as a few songs written for them by producers like Bert Berns (who penned "Here Comes the Night"). After Morrison left the group, Them splintered into the Belfast Gypsies, who released a decent album that (except for the vocals) approximated Them's early records, and a psychedelic outfit that kept the name Them, releasing four fairly weak LPs with little resemblance to the tough sounds of their mid-'60s heyday.

Them's legacy is disgracefully underrepresented on CD; no major British Invasion act has been worse served by reissues in the digital age. Almost everything they recorded under Morrison's leadership is worth hearing, and a double CD compiling all several dozen of their songs from 1964 to 1966 would have little filler. For the time being, their output is scattered among some skimpy CD collections and various out-of-print LPs. —*Richie Unterberger*

Them Again / Apr. 1966 / Parrot ◆◆◆
Them's second album didn't contain any hits, although songs like "Could You Would You" and "I Can Only Give You Everything" aped their earlier hits, "Here Comes the Night" and "Gloria." It did contain some excellent Van Morrison originals and some well-played covers of songs like "Turn on Your Love Light" and "Hello Josephine," as well as a Morrison take on Bob Dylan's "It's All Over Now, Baby Blue." It was: Morrison left the band in June 1966, and this was Them's last regular album release with him, although there would be compilations and a couple of Morrison-less albums released on Tower Records. (That's right, there was a 1960s record label called Tower Records before there was a chain of record stores by that name.) —*William Ruhlmann*

Backtrackin' / 1974 / London ◆◆◆
This collection of ten tracks from all phases of their career is haphazard, but the material is mostly excellent. Highlights include their blistering raveup of "Baby Please Don't Go" with Jimmy Page on guitar, a Top Ten hit in Britain; the angry cover of Paul Simon's "Richard Cory," their breakneck version of Slim Harpo's "Don't Start Crying Now," which was their first single in 1964; the great obscure, bluesy Morrison-penned B-side, "All for Myself," and

the vicious cover of the R&B standard "Just a Little Bit." —*Richie Unterberger*

Story of Them / 1977 / London ◆◆◆
Another ragtag compilation of material that somehow hadn't found its way to an American album, this uneven but worthy collection is divided between R&B covers (Jimmy Reed's "Bright Lights, Big City" and Jimmy Witherspoon's "Times Gettin' Tougher Than Tough" are the best) and some good Morrison originals. Of those, the folk-tinged "Philosphy" and "Friday's Child" point to his more expressive solo work, and "The Story of Them" is a rambling, seven-and-a-half-minute autobiographical talking blues about the group's early days. —*Richie Unterberger*

● **Them Featuring Van Morrison [CD]** / 1987 / London ◆◆◆◆
Not to be confused with the identically titled Parrot Records release, which is an out-of-print 20-track double-LP set, this is a 13-track single CD set and a U.S. reissue of the Decca U.K. LP from 1982. It would have been less confusing if they had called it *Them's Greatest Hits*, since it is primarily a singles compilation. But then, only four of Them's singles were hits, either in the U.K. or the U.S.—"Baby, Please Don't Go," "Gloria," "Here Comes the Night," and "Mystic Eyes," all included here. Also featured are such non-charting singles as "Don't Start Crying Now," "One More Time," "(It Won't Hurt) Half As Much," and "Richard Cory." This is not the ideal Them compilation, but this is the one in print on CD and that contains Them's most familiar material, so it will stand as the pick among their releases unless PolyGram, which owns the catalog, decides to do the kind of thorough retrospective the group deserves. —*William Ruhlmann*

Therapy?

Group, Alternative Pop/Rock, Heavy Metal
With their buzzing guitars, tortured lyrics, and undeniable melodic gifts, Therapy? is one of the best post-modern heavy metal bands. Hailing from Belfast, Ireland, Therapy? combines the sonic rush of Hüsker Dü and the Buzzcocks with the straightforward riffing and sensibility of Black Sabbath. Guitarist Andy Cairns' soul-baring can be embarrassingly clichéd at times, yet the melodrama of the lyrics can be easily ignored when the band locks into their intense, tuneful grind. —*Stephen Thomas Erlewine*

Caucasian Psychosis / 1992 / Quarterstick ◆◆
○ **Nurse** / 1993 / A&M ◆◆◆◆
Therapy?'s debut album is a brutal fusion of heavy metal and hardcore punk with a surprising dose of straight melody. Their ability to write songs that are simultaneously abrasive and melodic separates them from such one-dimensional riff-mongers as Helmet. —*Stephen Thomas Erlewine*

Hats off to the Insane / Sep. 7, 1993 / A&M ◆◆◆
A stopgap EP finds Therapy? honing their melodic skills while keeping the aggressive guitar assault. Although its best moments are repeated on the full-length *Troublegum*, the rest of the EP is strong enough to satisfy fans. —*Stephen Thomas Erlewine*

● **Trouble Gum** / 1994 / A&M ◆◆◆◆
On their second album, Therapy? hit their stride, strengthening their considerable melodic gifts while sharpening their razor-sharp guitars. At times, Therapy?'s assault resembles a more straightforward Bob Mould or a more melodic Helmet. Unfortunately, the trite, angst-ridden lyrics sometimes undercut the power of their music, but when faced with the drilling guitars and irresistible hooks of "Screamager" and "Nowhere," such minor complaints are forgotten. —*Stephen Thomas Erlewine*

They Might Be Giants

Group, Alternative Pop/Rock
This Brooklyn-based duo, made up of John Flansburgh and John Linell, gives a new twist to pop music. Their lyrics (which are often funny and always offbeat) are accompanied by Flansburgh's guitar and Linell's accordion, giving their songs a unique sound. Full of puns, wisecracks, and thesaurus-dependent lyrics, TMBG's music is always entertaining. —*Iotis Erlewine*

○ **They Might Be Giants** / 1986 / Restless ◆◆◆◆
TMBG's debut album. The album includes a few good songs, such as "Don't Let's Start," "Put Your Hand Inside the Puppet Head," and "I Hope That I Get Old Before I Die." Overall, the album is too rough and tedious, featuring TMBG's trademark "under three-minute" songs. —*Iotis Erlewine*

● **Lincoln** / 1989 / Restless ✦✦✦✦
TMBG's most entertaining album lets you have fun with the songs without trying to ferret out any deeper meaning in the bizarre lyrics. Here, TMBG reaches a good balance between goofy lyrics and listenable music. The songs won't spark any deep intellectual conversations, but you might just enjoy yourself. —*Iotis Erlewine*

Flood / 1990 / Elektra ✦✦✦
Musically, this is their best album, but in their attempt to put meaning into their lyrics, they have lost sight of TMBG's most appealing quality—the fun. *Flood* features a cover of "Istanbul (Not Constantinople)," written by J. Kennedy and N. Simon. There are a few outstanding songs, such as "Birdhouse in Your Soul" and "Particle Man." —*Iotis Erlewine*

Miscellaneous T / 1991 / Bar/None ✦✦✦
This album is a collection of TMBG's B-sides that includes several previously unreleased songs. For die-hard fans only. —*Iotis Erlewine*

Apollo 18 / 1992 / Elektra ✦✦✦
TMBG goes off the deep end. The group got so into trying to be simultaneously bizarre and witty that the resulting album is almost unlistenable. For example, the album contains 20 tracks of six-second song clips. And I thought their two-minute songs were short! Unfortunately this once-entertaining group has crossed over the line from being silly but appealing, to being pretentious, self-important, and tedious. —*Iotis Erlewine*

John Henry / 1994 / Elektra ✦✦
They Might Be Giants recorded with a full band for the first time in their career on *John Henry*. Instead of relying on their quirky charm, the album is direct and obvious, lacking the infectious melodies and cleverly geeky lyrics that characterize the best of their work. —*Stephen Thomas Erlewine*

Thin Lizzy

Group, Hard Rock, Heavy Metal
Despite a huge hit single in the mid-'70s ("The Boys Are Back in Town") and becoming a popular act with hard rock/heavy metal fans, Thin Lizzy are still, in the pantheon of '70s rock bands, underappreciated. Formed in the late '60s by Irish singer/songwriter/bassist Phil Lynott, Lizzy, though not the first band to do so, combined romanticized working-class sentiments with their ferocious, twin-lead guitar attack. As the band's creative force, Lynott was a more insightful and intelligent writer than many of his ilk, preferring slice-of-life working-class dramas of love and hate influenced by Bob Dylan, Bruce Springsteen and virtually all of the Irish literary tradition. Also, as a black man, Lynott was an anomaly in the nearly all-white world of hard rock, and as such imbued much of his work with a sense of alienation; he was the outsider, the romantic guy from the other side of the tracks, a self-styled poet of the lovelorn and downtrodden. His sweeping vision and writerly impulses at times gave way to pretentious songs aspiring to cliched notions of literary significance, but Lynott's limitless charisma made even the most misguided moments worth hearing.
After a few early records that hinted at the band's potential, Lizzy released *Fighting* in 1975, and the band (Lynott, guitarists Brian Robertson and Scott Gorham, and drummer Brian Downey) had molded itself into a pretty tight recording and performing unit. Lynott's thick, soulful vocals were the perfect vehicle for his tightly written melodic lines. Gorham and Robertson generally played lead lines in harmonic tandem, while Downey (a great drummer who had equal amounts of power and style) drove the engine. Lizzy's big break came with their next album, *Jailbreak*, and the record's first single, "The Boys Are Back in Town." A paean to the joys of working-class guys letting loose, the song resembled similar odes to Bruce Springsteen, with the exception of the Who-like power chords in the chorus. With the support of radio and every frat boy in America, "Boys" became a huge hit, enough of a hit as to ensure record contracts and media attention for the next decade ("Boys" is now used in beer advertising).
Never the toast of critics (the majority writing in the '70s hated hard rock and heavy metal), Lizzy toured relentlessly, building an unassailable reputation as a terrific live band, despite the lead guitar spot becoming a revolving door (Eric Bell, Gary Moore, Brian Robertson, Snowy White, and John Sykes all stood next to Scott Gorham). The records came fast and furious, and despite attempts to repeat the formula that worked like a charm with "Boys," Lynott began writing more ambitious songs and wrapping them up in vaguely articulated concept albums. The large fan base the

band had built as a result of "Boys" turned into a smaller, yet still enthusiastic bunch of hard rockers. Adding insult to injury was the rise of punk rock, which Lynott vigorously supported, but made Lizzy look too traditional and too much like tired old rock stars.
By the mid-'80s, resembling the dinosaur that punk rock wanted to annihilate, Thin Lizzy called it a career. Lynott recorded solo records that more explicitly examined issues of class and race, published a now-out-of-print book of poetry, and sadly, became a victim of his longtime abuse of heroin, cocaine and alcohol, dying in 1986 at age 35. As the mega-popular alternative rock bands of the mid-'90s appropriate numerous musical messages from their '70s forebears, it's hoped that the work of Phil Lynott and Thin Lizzy will been seen for the influential rock & roll it is. —*John Dougan*

Thin Lizzy / 1971 / Deram ✦✦✦

Shades of a Blue Orphanage / 1972 / Deram ✦✦✦

Vagabonds of the Western World / 1973 / Deram ✦✦

Night Life / 1974 / Mercury ✦✦✦

Fighting / 1975 / Mercury ✦✦✦

○ **Jailbreak** / 1976 / Mercury ✦✦✦✦
Purely and simply a great rock and roll record. "Boys" is here in all its rabble-rousing glory, but better yet is the title track. Robertson and Gorham sound inspired, and Lynott's solid singing is made better by the sharp melodies he's written. Perhaps a greatest hits compilation is a better place for the uninitiated to start, but *Jailbreak* is a keeper. —*John Dougan*

Johnny the Fox / 1976 / Mercury ✦✦✦
Hot on the heels of *Jailbreak* came *Johnny the Fox*, which was a thematically linked group of songs that (fortunately) worked individually or as a concept record. The band sounds looser and funkier here (Lynott was sucker for a James Brown-style rhythmic kick), and that pays off big time. Not essential, but by no means a waste of time. —*John Dougan*

Bad Reputation / 1977 / Mercury ✦✦✦
Although this record had an obvious attempt at a hit single ("Dancing in the Moonlight"), it also had the relentlessly propulsive title track and a half-dozen or so great songs that showed a band hitting its stride, comfortable with its place in the world and not losing one bit of power. Lizzy's third great record in a row. —*John Dougan*

○ **Live & Dangerous** / 1978 / Warner Brothers ✦✦✦✦
Some prefer the 1983 set *Life* (and it's very good), but I like this (albeit studio-enhanced) live record, which has as strong a selection of Lizzy fare in one place as one is likely to find. Along with the live standards ("Boys," "Cowboy Song," "Jailbreak," and "Dancing in the Moonlight"), there are some great semi-obscurities (Bob Seger's "Rosalie" and the macho "The Rocker"). Loud, proud and chock full of dazzling guitar solos, this is a hard rock dream come true. Proof positive that in the arena rock sweepstakes, few bands were better onstage than Thin Lizzy. —*John Dougan*

Black Rose / 1979 / Warner Brothers ✦✦✦

Chinatown / 1980 / Warner Brothers ✦✦✦
The band enter the '80s in high fashion with a well-produced and performed album, featuring the hit "Killer on the Loose." Snowy White replaced Gary Moore for this release. —*John Book*

Renegade / 1981 / Warner Brothers ✦✦✦
After the release of *Renegade*, Thin Lizzy's popularity dwindled considerably, but this 1982 album did fare well among other releases by Judas Priest and the Scorpions. It features "Angel of Death," "Hollywood," and the popular title track. —*John Book*

● **Dedication: The Very Best of Thin Lizzy** / 1991 / Mercury ✦✦✦✦
A good, if somewhat brief look at all the high spots, featuring great guitar from fretmeisters Gary Moore, Eric Bell, John Sykes, and others. —*Cub Koda*

Things To Come

Group, Garage Rock
Emerging from the glut of Southern Californian rock groups in the mid-'60s, Things To Come formed in 1966. Their original lineup included lead singer Steve Runolfsson, drummer Russ Kunkel (who would go on to become a top sessionman), and bassist Bryan Garofalo (also a future sessionman, and a member of Glenn Frey's band since 1982). The group cut only three singles in their brief lifetime; Runolfsson was replaced after the first one.

Mining a bluesy, British Invasion-styled garage rock in the manner of countless other bands, most of their work remained unheard until a 1994 CD reissue. —*Richie Unterberger*

I Want Out / 1994 / Sundazed ✦✦✦
The liner notes of '60s garage reissues can tend to go overboard on the hyperbole, but the praise lavished upon this unknown outfit in this booklet really does exceed tasteful limits. This is hardly a band that was "in some ways...charting the same grounds as the Doors." Like many other groups in California and across the country, Things To Come played basic teen raunch with psychedelic touches. With their Farfisa organ, wheezing harmonica, and Steve Runolfsson's snarling vocals, their sound was rather slavishly imitative of the Stones and especially Them, with hints of Love and the Seeds creeping in now and then. Not only were Things To Come not nearly as good as the Stones, Them, Doors or Love, but they were not nearly as good as many other similar garage bands who also imitated the heavyweights listed above. This CD reissues both sides of the only single to feature the original lineup, as well as 16 previously unreleased demos from 1965-67. Most of the material is original, derivative, and rather weak, recycling the "Gloria" riff a number of times. The management-instigated firing of the sandpaper-voiced Runolfsson is presented as a tragedy that short-circuited the group's potential in the enclosed band history, but neither he nor his band had what it took to stand amongst their competition. —*Richie Unterberger*

Thinking Fellers Union Local #282

Group, Alternative Pop/Rock, Experimental
With such a longwinded moniker, it's almost a given that this group could be nothing but a bunch of pretentious art-school rejects. Fortunately, that's pretty far from the truth. Thinking Fellers Union Local #282 formed in 1987 in San Francisco and released their first album, *Wormed By Leonard*, on their own label Thwart a year later. In 1991, the group made the jump to the Matador label, where nearly all of their material has been released since, from 1991's critically acclaimed *Lovelyville* to 1994's *Strangers from the Universe*. Their sound is based on noodling on organs, electric banjos and mandolins, and heavy, fuzzed-out guitar blasts. A hybrid of art-rock and punk rock, Thinking Fellers Union Local #282 is worth joining. —*Heather Phares*

Wormed, By Leonard / 1988 / Thwart Productions ✦✦
The group's difficult-to-find, cassette-only debut album finds the group performing some of their most avante-garde, inaccessible lunacy. —*Heather Phares*

Tangle / 1989 / Thwart Productions ✦✦✦
Tangle, the group's second album, contains more melodic but no less bizarre material than their debut. Both these albums are released on the group's own aptly named Thwart Productions record label. —*Heather Phares*

○ **Lovelyville** / 1991 / Matador ✦✦✦✦
The group's first album for Matador is also one of their more accessible ones, with the group's penchant for willful eccentricity colliding with some hummable melodies. However, this release also contains plenty of what TFUL #282 fans lovingly call "Fellerfiller," i.e., noise-pieces that have no real beginning, or ending, or point for that matter. —*Heather Phares*

Mother of All Saints / 1992 / Matador ✦✦✦
Mother of All Saints is the Fellers' magnum opus. At 23 songs, it might be longer than most people's attention spans, but inside it lurks some of their finest moments, such as "Tell Me," "Hive," "Hummingbird in a Cube of Ice," and "Infection." True, there is plenty of "Feller-filler" on *Mother of All Saints* (an inspired piece called "Tuning Notes" attests to that) but the group's melodic sensibilities prevail on the actual songs on this album. —*Heather Phares*

● **Strangers of the Universe** / 1994 / Matador ✦✦✦✦
The group's most subdued and melodic album yet, *Strangers* is ironically the Feller's least strange album. It's also their most diverse; the goofy "My Pal the Tortoise" shares space with the genuinely disturbing "The Operation" and the genuinely catchy weirdo-pop of "Socket," and "The Piston and the Shaft," "Noble Experiment," "February," and "Cup of Dreams" explore the group's rare sentimental side, and the result is the group's most complete and listenable album. —*Heather Phares*

3rd Bass

Group, Rap
Along with the Beastie Boys, 3rd Bass stand as the rare white hip-hop act that's actually won respect and credibility among the rap hardcore. Pete Nice, one-time English major at Columbia whose radio program "Top of the Hip-hop" was unceremoniously cancelled by the purportedly progressive WKCR-FM, teamed with MC Serch to offer devastating put-downs of the hip-hop lifestyle and worldview. They have since disbanded, but their two albums were definitive, if at times uneven. —*Ron Wynn*

● **The Cactus Album** / 1989 / Def Jam ✦✦✦✦
With their first album, 3rd Bass turned in a surrealistically funky record of uproarious jokes, cutting social criticism, and eclectic music, drawing from Stax and Blood, Sweat and Tears. —*Stephen Thomas Erlewine*

Derelicts of Dialect / 1991 / Def Jam ✦✦✦
After countless false starts and an EP/remix filler, 3rd Bass finally issued their second album. It was an impressive statement, with a devastating attack on Vanilla Ice via the cut "Pop Goes the Weasel." —*Ron Wynn*

Thirteenth Floor Elevators

Group, Psychedelic, Garage Rock
Featuring the yelping vocals and visionary, occasionally demented lyrics of Roky Erickson, the 13th Floor Elevators were one of the original acid-rock bands. Formed in Texas in the mid-'60s, the Elevators started as a garage rock outfit, scoring their one and only modest national hit with "You're Gonna Miss Me." While Erickson's loopy persona, along with Tommy Hall's odd "jug" percussion, was the band's most distinguishing feature, several members of the group's original lineup contributed strong material to their albums. Although these inconsistent efforts sometimes wander off into a cloudy haze, they also include sturdy folk-rock tunes and driving psychedelic rockers. Trips to San Francisco established the group as up-and-coming underground favorites, but Erickson's drug problems led to the singer's commission to a state mental hospital in the late '60s, an ordeal from which he has never fully recovered. The band was really only at full power for a couple of albums, although all of their releases for the legendary International Artists label—produced by, of all people, Kenny Rogers's brother Leland—are revered among psychedelic collectors. Live recordings and outtakes of the Elevators continue to surface, though a cogent domestic compilation of the best of these erratic pioneers' work remains overdue. —*Richie Unterberger*

● **Thirteenth Floor Elevators** / 1966 / International Artists ✦✦✦✦
Their first album is their best, although their second (*Easter Everywhere*) also had some good material. Besides "You're Gonna Miss Me," it includes "Fire Engine," "Tried to Hide," "Roller Coaster," and Erickson's best composition, the gentle folk-rocker "Splash 1." —*Richie Unterberger*

Easter Everywhere / 1967 / Collectables ✦✦✦
Basically an extension of the sound of their first album, but more overtly trippy, with material that is not quite as strong. "She Lives (In a Time of Her Own)" is probably the best cut; the rustic folk mood on "Dust" and "I Had to Tell You" is a good change of pace. —*Richie Unterberger*

Bull of the Woods / 1968 / Decal ✦✦✦
Guitarist Stacy Sutherland wrote most of the songs on the band's final studio album, as Roky was largely absent due to drugs and problems with the law. Decent psychedelic rock—pretty straightahead and disciplined for the genre, actually—that doesn't match the inspired heights of their previous material. The closing "May the Circle Be Unbroken," with its wads and wads of reverb, may be the strangest thing the band ever cut. —*Richie Unterberger*

Fire in My Bones / 1985 / Texas Archive ✦✦✦
The best collection of previously unreleased Elevators. Side one has six songs from an early 1966 live Dallas TV broadcast, including "You're Gonna Miss Me" and "Fire Engine," as well as covers of hits by the Kinks, Them, and Chuck Berry. Side two has alternate versions of four songs from the first LP that are more uninhibited in spots than the official versions, as well as the previously unreleased song "Fire in My Bones" and a live jam. —*Richie Unterberger*

Elevator Tracks / 1987 / Texas Archive ✦✦✦
More unreleased tracks. Side one has a previously unreleased acetate of "I Don't Ever Want to Come Down," and six alternate takes of officially released tunes (circa 1966) that are pretty close

to the records, including "You're Gonna Miss Me," "Tried to Hide," and "Splash One." Side two is a fair-quality recording of a live summer 1966 gig in Houston, including covers of "Satisfaction," the Beatles' "I'm Down," and James Brown's "I Feel Good." Decent, but for completists. —*Richie Unterberger*

Original Sound of / 1988 / 13th Hour - ♦♦
The outtake barrel starts to run thin on yet another collection of unreleased material. Side one has different (not too different) studio versions of songs from the first LP, and Side two is a fair-quality tape of five songs from a club gig in Austin in 1966. —*Richie Unterberger*

● **Best of the 13th Floor Elevators** / 1994 / Eva ♦♦♦♦
Finally, a best-of compilation for one of the most popular cult psychedelic groups of all time. The 22 tracks draw most heavily upon the first LP, with choice bits from the second and third, as well as some material Roky Erickson cut with his pre-Elevators group the Spades. —*Richie Unterberger*

.38 Special

Group, Southern Rock
This hard-touring Jacksonville-based band (formed 1975) featured lead singer Donnie Van Zant, brother of Lynyrd Skynyrd's lead singer Ronnie Van Zant. .38 Special delivered a brand of Southern pop/rock that wasn't quite so hard-hitting as Skynyrd's, while showcasing an Allman Brothers-like lineup, with two lead guitarists and two drummers. They also charted more hits than either of those bands. Their most popular hits included "Caught up in You" (#10), "Hold on Loosely" (#27), "Back Where You Belong" (#20), "Like No Other Night" (#14), "Second Chance" (#6), "If I'd Been the One" (#19), and "Rockin' into the Night" (#43). —*Rick Clark*

Wild Eyed & Live / 1978 / A&M ♦♦♦
A live album featuring an even balance of hits and smokin' crowd pleasers. —*Cub Koda*

● **Flashback: Best of .38 Special** / 1987 / A&M ♦♦♦♦
An excellent retrospective, featuring all the hits. The last commercial flowering of Southern rock. —*Cub Koda*

This Mortal Coil

Group, Alternative Pop/Rock
This Mortal Coil is the brainchild of 4AD's president, Ivo Watts. It's not really a band, it's a way for Watts to explore different musical territory and cover his favorite artists, including Syd Barrett, Alex Chilton, Talking Heads, Tim Buckley, and Gene Clark. Over the years, the lineup has featured various stars from the record label's roster including Kim Deal, Tanya Donelly, Heidi Berry, and Robin Guthrie and Elizabeth Fraser from the Cocteau Twins. Like most 4AD bands, This Mortal Coil is atmospheric, sometimes dreamy, other times haunting. Watts has said that 1991's *Blood* is the last album the outfit will release. —*Stephen Thomas Erlewine*

It'll End in Tears / 1984 / 4AD ♦♦♦
This is a studio project by various artists from the 4AD stable. —*Michael P. Dawson*

○ **Filigree & Shadow** / 1986 / 4AD ♦♦♦♦
Ethereal, nostalgic, and wonderful. —*Michael P. Dawson*

● **Blood** / 1991 / 4AD ♦♦♦♦
It's notable for a cover of Syd Barrett's "Late Night." —*Michael P. Dawson*

1983-1991 / 1993 / 4AD ♦♦♦
All three of This Mortal Coil's albums packaged in an expensive slipcase, along with a disc of the original versions of the songs they covered. Fans of 4AD bands like Throwing Muses, the Cocteau Twins, and Dead Can Dance will thoroughly enjoy This Mortal Coil's lush, haunting music; some members of these bands play on various tracks on the box, including a standout duet between Kim Deal and Tanya Donelly on Chris Bell's "You and Your Sister." Although the packaging is beautiful, there are no liner notes. —*Stephen Thomas Erlewine*

Carla Thomas

b. Dec. 21, 1942, Memphis, TN
Soul
In the glorious decade and a half of sound that was Stax in the '60s and early '70s, Carla Thomas was the Queen of Memphis Soul. She was born in Memphis in 1942, and 18 years later she recorded a duet with her father Rufus Thomas, giving the fledgling

Satellite label its first taste of success with the regional hit "Cause I Love You." As her 18th birthday drew nigh, she cut her first solo single, the teen ballad "Gee Whiz (Look at His Eyes)." Written a few years earlier and rejected by Vee-Jay in Chicago, it gave Satellite its first national hit, breaking the Top Ten mark on both the R&B and pop charts. Shortly thereafter Satellite became Stax, and Carla proceeded to claw her way onto the national charts another 22 times with such immortal slices of soul as her answer song to Sam Cooke, "I'll Bring It on Home to You," as well as "Let Me Be Good to You," "B-A-B-Y," "Tramp" (with Otis Redding), and "I Like What You're Doing to Me." Carla released six solo albums and, with Otis Redding, one duet album on Stax between 1961 and 1971. —*Rob Bowman*

Gee Whiz / 1961 / Atlantic ♦♦♦
Carla Thomas's first album was typical fare for the R&B market of the time, combining two chart entries (the title song and "A Love of My Own") with covers of recent chart hits (the Drifters' "Fools Fall in Love" and "Dance with Me," the Five Satins' "To the Aisle"), standards ("The Masquerade Is Over"), and a handful of originals. This was the first album produced by the then-fledgling Stax label and the unique Stax sound was not yet manifest. —*Rob Bowman*

○ **Carla** / 1966 / Atlantic ♦♦♦♦
Paired with Stax writing whiz-kids Isaac Hayes and David Porter, Thomas had her greatest chart run, beginning with the hit "B-A-B-Y" and continuing with "Let Me Be Good to You." Both of those appear here, alongside evocative slabs of country-soul in covers of Hank Williams's "I'm So Lonesome I Could Cry" and Patsy Cline's "I Fall to Pieces." For good measure, Thomas also tries her hand at the blues with covers of Howlin' Wolf's "Little Red Rooster" and Jimmy Reed's "Baby What You Want Me to Do?" —*Rob Bowman*

○ **Comfort Me** / 1966 / Atlantic ♦♦♦♦
A collection of twelve tracks recorded over a year and a half, *Comfort Me* showcases Thomas in the midst of the developed Stax sound. Backed by Booker T. and the MG's and the Mar-Key horns, Thomas turns in fine covers of Baby Washington's "Move on Drifter," the Marvelettes' "Forever," the Shirelles' "Will You Love Me Tomorrow?," the Everly Brothers' "Let It Be Me," Jackie DeShannon's "What the World Needs Now," the Toys' "Lover's Concerto," and Barbara Mason's "Yes I'm Ready," coupled with a number of efforts by Thomas herself, Steve Cropper, and Eddie Floyd. The highlight is the Cropper-Floyd title cut, with utterly gorgeous backing by Gladys Knight and the Pips. —*Rob Bowman*

○ **The Queen Alone** / 1969 / Rhino ♦♦♦♦
The queen of Stax shines on tracks like "When Tomorrow Comes," "Unchanging Love," "Lie to Keep Me from Crying," and "Any Day Now" (the Chuck Jackson classic). This album was recorded in 1967, a year after her hit "B-A-B-Y"; the mood is funky, the singing self-assured. Fine Memphis soul music. —*Christine Ohlman*

Memphis Queen / 1975 / Stax ♦♦♦
Half recorded in Memphis with the usual stax crew and half recorded in New York with local session musicians (all overdubbed in Detroit), *Memphis Queen* finds Thomas and the Stax label in transition. Motown alumnus Don Davis handled production, draping many cuts in large, lush orchestral settings. "I Like What You're Doing (To Me)" was a Top Ten R&B hit, and three other tracks had brief chart runs. —*Rob Bowman*

○ **Chronicle: Their Greatest Stax Hits** / 1979 / Stax ♦♦♦♦
Rufus and Carla Thomas helped launch the Stax era, both individually and as a team. Thomas bought his daughter to Stax in the hopes of finding suitable material, and she soon had "Gee Whiz" soaring to the top. Had Carla chosen to tour extensively, she might have been a great star in Aretha Franklin's class; she sang with equal ferocity and power during this period. Rufus Thomas parlayed his dance/novelty tracks into international superstardom, but he was also a fine straight soul vocalist. This album splits its bill between the two, offering each a side to showcase their hits. —*Ron Wynn*

Hidden Gems / 1992 / Stax ♦♦♦
Twenty outtakes recorded for Stax between 1960 and 1968, a number of which are gems. In fact, it is really surprising just how good the unreleased Stax stuff was in the '60s. "Loneliness," "Sweet Sensation," and "It Ain't No Easy Thing" all could have been superb singles. —*Rob Bowman*

● **Gee Whiz: The Best of Carla Thomas** / 1994 / Rhino ♦♦♦♦
A sterling collection, it includes all of Carla Thomas's biggest hits and best material. —*AMG*

Irma Thomas

b. Feb. 18, 1941
Soul, New Orleans R&B

Radiating an outgoing joy that's inevitably at the heart of her infectious vocal delivery, Irma Thomas has no rivals as the Soul Queen of New Orleans. Working at a Crescent City nightery as a waitress in 1959, Thomas sat in one night with Tommy Ridgely's band and made such a favorable impression that the veteran bandleader hustled her into the studio shortly thereafter to wax her first hit for the Ron label, the driving "Don't Mess with My Man." She joined forces with producer Allen Toussaint to make some of her most moving outings for Minit Records during the early 60s, notably "It's Raining," "Ruler of My Heart," and "Cry On," before venturing to the West Coast, where she cut both her biggest seller, the lushly produced "Wish Someone Would Care," and her best-known song, the original "Time Is on My Side"—and she's still bitter enough about the Rolling Stones' cover stealing her thunder to discourage requests for the tune.

The highly adaptable chanteuse also made some sizzling soul at Rich Hall's Muscle Shoals studio for Chess in the summer of 1967 before cooling off for a while during the 70s. But she's back now, as radiant as ever—and for convincing proof, listen to her buoyant 1990 concert performance on Rounder, *Live! Simply the Best.* Now that's truth in packaging!

Irma Thomas finally fulfilled a lifelong ambition in 1994 by recording her first gospel release. *Walk Around Heaven* was as magnificently sung and emotionally convincing as any of her classic New Orleans soul cuts. —*Bill Dahl*

Ruler of Hearts / 1989 / Charly ✦✦✦

Sides from her early-'60s Minit sessions. The most New Orleans R&B-influenced of Thomas's early work, it includes "Cry On," "It's Raining," and "Ruler Of My Heart," as well as lesser-known but equally moving cuts like "Two Winters Long" and "It's Too Soon To Know." —*Richie Unterberger*

★ **Time Is on My Side (The Best of Irma Thomas), Vol. 1** / 1992 / EMI America ✦✦✦✦✦

Twenty-three sides representing the cream of Irma Thomas's brilliant Minit/Liberty years (1961-1966), when her reputation as "The Soul Queen of New Orleans" was built. Virtually all her best-known tunes are here—"Wish Someone Would Care," "Ruler of My Heart," "It's Raining," and "Time Is on My Side" (covered note-for-note by the Stones). Beautiful singing from one of the first ladies of soul music. Essential. —*Christine Ohlman*

Rufus Thomas

b. Mar. 26, 1917
Soul, R&B

The self-proclaimed "world's oldest teenager" has been a staple on the Memphis music scene since the '20s. He recorded the first hit for Sun Records ("Bear Cat," from 1953); was a celebrity DJ on Memphis's WDIA; and, with his daughter Carla, he gave Stax their first hit (1960's "Cause I Love You"). He recorded an album for Alligator in 1988 but his best work was done for Sun and Stax. His Sun material is available on several various-artist collections. —*John Floyd*

○ **Walking the Dog** / 1964 / Stax ✦✦✦✦

Thomas's first album on Stax contains many of his best early hits, including the title track and several other dance- and novelty-oriented gems. —*John Floyd*

May I Have Your Ticket Please / 1969 / Stax ✦✦✦

Rufus Thomas played it halfway between inspired lunacy and straight soul sanity, and was only partly successful here. Thomas hadn't yet found the formula for dance/novelty success, and didn't really have any strong singles on this release. His bluesy vocals were well done, but not enough to generate any action for the record. —*Ron Wynn*

Do the Funky Chicken / 1970 / Stax ✦✦✦

Rufus Thomas would storm the soul charts in 1970, scoring three hits, two of them in the Top 10. The title track and his number one smash "(Do The) Push and Pull" were identical—dance-based novelty tunes featuring Thomas' manic instructions and bluesy shouts backed by surging, horn-based soul and funk from the Stax band. It wasn't earth-shaking, just fun, brilliantly produced and arranged stuff. —*Ron Wynn*

Doing the Push and Pull Live at P.J.'s / 1971 / Stax ✦✦✦

One of only a couple of Rufus Thomas albums that actually cracked the pop charts, this featured live versions of "Do The Funky Chicken" and "(Do The) Push and Pull," plus warhorses like "The Preacher and the Bear" and "Night Time Is the Right Time." The label also stuck the recent number one hit "Walkin' The Dog" onto the album from its prior release, an unnecessary move and one that couldn't get it any more pop action than it enjoyed. —*Ron Wynn*

○ **Crown Prince of Dance** / 1973 / Stax ✦✦✦✦

The "world's oldest teenager" was springy, sassy, and jubilant when he cut this date in the mid-'70s. Thomas, whose career goes back to the days of the Rabbit Foot Minstrels, made some brilliant novelty cuts for Stax in the 1970s. He simply went into the studio and clowned, backed by the great Stax session pros. The results are comic gems, numbers that are purposefully lightweight and succeed without sounding sappy. —*Ron Wynn*

● **Chronicle** / 1986 / Stax ✦✦✦✦

Half of *Chronicle* features the greatest hits of Rufus Thomas's daughter, Carla, while the other half features the best of the man himself; it's a good introduction to the music of both artists. —*AMG*

The Thompson Twins

Group, Dance-Pop, Pop/Rock

This British trio, composed of Tom Bailey (b. Jan 18, 1956), Alannah Currie (b. Sep 28, 1957), and Joe Leeway (b. Nov 15, 1957), specialized in accessible early-MTV-style synth/dance-pop. Among their hits were "Hold Me Now" (#3), "Lay Your Hands on Me" (#6), "King for a Day" (#8), "Doctor! Doctor!" (#11), and "Lies" (#30). Baily and Currie renamed the band Babble in 1993. —*Rick Clark*

Side Kicks / 1983 / Arista ✦✦✦

● **Into the Gap** / 1984 / Arista ✦✦✦✦

Their American breakthrough album featured the hits "Doctor, Doctor" and "Hold Me Now." This is the best single album. —*Kenneth M. Cassidy*

○ **Here's to Future Days** / 1985 / Arista ✦✦✦✦

On their follow-up to the commercial breakthrough *Into the Gap*, the Thompson Twins attempt to toughen up their sound, but the results are only partially successful. In fact, the most infectious number, "Lay Your Hands on Me," sounds like it could have been an outtake from the previous album. —*Stephen Thomas Erlewine*

Close to the Bone / 1987 / Arista ✦✦

Greatest Mixes: Best of The Thompson Twins / 1988 / Arista ✦✦✦

A collection of their best on Arista, it was downhill once they switched record labels. —*Kenneth M. Cassidy*

Big Trash / Mar. 1989 / Red Eye ✦✦✦

Queer / Oct. 1991 / Warner Brothers ✦✦

Richard Thompson

b. Apr. 3, 1949
Singer-Songwriter, Folk-Rock

From his days in the Fairport Convention, through his albums recorded with his wife Linda, to his solo records of the past decade, Richard Thompson has remained a brilliantly gifted songwriter and guitarist. Since the beginning of his career, Thompson has been melding traditional British folk and Celtic music with rock & roll, creating a unique, innovative body of work. He has made a remarkably consistent body of work; every album features songs that are complexly detailed, full of forboding and regret. Even when he was in his early 20s, Thompson sounded like an old man scarred by lost love and hope. This consistency can make some of his lesser songs sound repetitious, but the overwhelming majority of his music is excellent; both his writing and his playing are distinctive and greatly rewarding.

Thompson's greatest work came during the '70s, when he recorded with his wife, Linda. Linda's clear, warm alto added another dimension to the fear and melancholy of Richard's lyrics. His own deep baritone voice was naturally filled with sadness, which only made his music more serious and sombre. Together, the duo provided a beautiful balance of light and darkness, recording six albums that were critically praised, but were commercial failures.

After performing together for ten years, the Thompsons' marriage fell apart in 1982, around the time their masterpiece *Shoot out the Lights* was released. The following year, both Richard and Linda pursued their own solo careers. Linda released her only solo album in 1985, but Richard's *Hand of Kindness* came out in 1983. Since that record, Thompson's stature as a songwriter has only grown, as fellow artists and critics alike rush to praise his talents. However, his albums have been slightly similar in sound, although each has featured several exceptional songs. Nevertheless, Thompson remains one of the finest songwriters of his generation, as well as one of the best guitarists in rock & roll. — *Stephen Thomas Erlewine*

○ **Henry the Human Fly** / 1972 / Hannibal ✦✦✦✦
Supposedly the worst-selling album in the history of Warner Bros. Records (now available through Hannibal), this was Richard Thompson's debut solo album after a couple of years of playing sessions that followed his departure from Fairport Convention in 1970. It's a dry run for his six duet albums with his wife Linda, who is credited here under her maiden name, Linda Peters, and features some terrific folk songs, notably "Nobody's Wedding." — *William Ruhlmann*

☆ **I Want to See the Bright Lights Tonight** / 1974 / Hannibal ✦✦✦✦✦
I Want to See the Bright Lights Tonight contains some of Richard Thompson's darkest songs and several beautiful vocal performances by Linda Thompson. "When I Get to the Border," "Calvary Cross," and "Withered and Died" define their early direction. — *John Floyd*

Hokey Pokey / 1974 / Hannibal ✦✦✦
Richard and Linda Thompson's second album (not released in the U.S. until 1983) was a somewhat lighter one than their debut, *I Want To See The Bright Lights Tonight*, from earlier in 1974, but with tracks like "The Sun Never Shines On The Poor," not much. "I'll Regret It All In The Morning" and especially "A Heart Needs A Home" were classics. — *William Ruhlmann*

○ **Pour Down Like Silver** / 1975 / Hannibal ✦✦✦✦
The third Richard and Linda Thompson album (and the first to be released in the U.S.) features "For Shame Of Doing Wrong," "Beat The Retreat," and "Dimming Of The Day/Dargai," all doomy Richard Thompson songs, the last with an extensive guitar coda. But there's also the rollicking "Jet Plane In A Rocking Chair." The couple appeared on the album cover in mufti, indicative of their dedication to the Sufi sect of Islam, which would consume their attention for the next few years, such that they didn't release another new album until 1978. — *William Ruhlmann*

Guitar, Vocal / 1976 / Hannibal ✦✦

Richard Thompson Live ! (More or Less) / 1976 / Island ✦✦
With Richard and Linda Thompson in temporary religious retirement, Island Records, their label at the time, issued differing compilation albums on each side of the Atlantic. In the U.S., there was this double record set, which consists of the Thompsons' debut album, *I Want To See The Bright Lights Tonight*, not previously released in America, and a second album compiling various outtakes and live performances by Fairport Convention, Richard solo, and Richard and Linda. This second disc was an abbreviation of the set Island issued in England, *Guitar, Vocal*. Subsequently, that album and *Bright Lights* were released in the U.S. on Hannibal, and this album, now redundant, went out of print. — *William Ruhlmann*

First Light / 1978 / Hannibal ✦✦✦
Richard and Linda Thompson returned to action with this, their fourth duo album, after three years away from music. It was not one of their best albums, although it did include the impressive "Don't Let A Thief Steal Into Your Heart" and the title track. — *William Ruhlmann*

Sunnyvista / 1979 / Hannibal ✦✦✦
Richard and Linda Thompson's fifth album was more of a pop record than previous releases (although Chrysalis, their label, didn't see fit to release it in the U.S. after *First Light* failed to sell, and it didn't appear domestically until it was picked up by Hannibal in 1983). Many Fairport Conventioneers guested, but the songwriting was not up to Richard Thompson's usual standard. — *William Ruhlmann*

Strict Tempo! / 1981 / Hannibal ✦✦

★ **Shoot out the Lights** / 1982 / Hannibal ✦✦✦✦✦
One of the most mesmerizing recordings ever committed to tape by a husband/wife team, *Shoot out the Lights* is the sound of a marriage falling apart—particularly Richard and Linda Thomp-

son's. Linda's beautifully world-weary alto and Richard's indignant quaver deliver some monumental performances on tracks like "The Wall of Death," "Don't Renege on Our Love," "Did She Jump or Was She Pushed?," "Walking on a Wire," and "Just the Motion." The title track features some incredible lead-guitar playing by Richard. It's indispensable for any comprehensive rock collection, particularly fans of folk-rock. — *Rick Clark*

○ **Hand of Kindness** / 1983 / Hannibal ✦✦✦✦
His first post-divorce release is an uncharacteristically bouncy set, shifting from 12-bar stompers to lilting folk ditties. — *John Floyd*

Small Town Romance / 1984 / Hannibal ✦✦✦
This is a live album taken from club appearances made by a solo, acoustic Richard Thompson in January and September 1982. It provides an opportunity to hear songs from throughout his career (plus previously unreleased ones) in a bare setting, and many are all the better for that. Nevertheless, Thompson has expressed antipathy for the album, and Hannibal has obediently let it go out of print. — *William Ruhlmann*

Across a Crowded Room / 1985 / Polydor ✦✦✦
A somewhat predictable set of bitter love songs is accompanied by radio-ready production and, unfortunately, not enough guitar. — *John Floyd*

Daring Adventures / Mar. 1986 / Polydor ✦✦✦
Richard Thompson's second Polydor album contained some terrific and varied songs, from the raucous "A Bone Through Her Nose" to the mournful "Missie How You Let Me Down" and "Al Bowlly's In Heaven." Good as it was, it didn't establish Thompson as a big seller, and Polydor dropped him. — *William Ruhlmann*

○ **Amnesia** / 1988 / Capitol ✦✦✦✦
Here Thompson has really redefined himself, taking the more pop sound of *Dangerous Adventures* further. Again produced by Mitchel Froom, this record smokes with the concert favorite "Turning of the Tide," "The Reckless Kind" and the bittersweet "Waltzing for Dreamers." — *Richard Meyer*

○ **Rumor and Sigh** / 1991 / Capitol ✦✦✦✦
Another creative triumph, it's not quite so lashing as *Amnesia*, but here's the source of many future Thompson classics. — *John Floyd*

○ **Watching the Dark** / May 11, 1993 / Hannibal ✦✦✦✦
A sprawling three-disc compilation tracing Richard Thompson's career from his beginnings with Fairport Convention, through his days with his ex-wife Linda, to his recent solo recordings, *Watching the Dark* is a treasure for longtime fans as well as those who want an introduction to his distinctive English folk-rock. Instead of being assembled chronologically, each disc contains three separate eras, which helps illustrate how consistently rich his music has been through the years. Nearly half of the tracks are rare or unreleased; instead of betraying Thompson's gifts, the song selection helps convey the breadth and scope of his talents. Although the material might be skewed towards hardcore fans, anyone unfamiliar with Thompson will realize why he is one of the most revered (and, unfortunately, unknown) songwriters and guitarists of his era by listening to *Watching the Dark*. — *AMG*

Mirror Blue / Feb. 8, 1994 / Capitol ✦✦
In many ways, *Mirror Blue* is Thompson's pop radio record, with shorter songs and a crisp, slick production. While that may put some fans off, the songs prove to be another set of rich, detailed stories; even the supposed toss-offs are bright, catchy, and memorable. In fact, the best moments of *Mirror Blue* equal the best of *Rumor and Sigh*—it's hard to equal the subtle power of "Mingus Eyes" or "Mascara Tears," and the closing song, "Taking My Business Elsewhere," is one of the best things he has ever written. — *Stephen Thomas Erlewine*

George Thorogood & the Destroyers

Group, Blues Rock
A Delaware-based blues band formed in 1973 and led by guitarist/singer George Thorogood, who brings a rough-voiced enthusiasm to the music of John Lee Hooker, Elmore James, and others. The group scored five gold albums in 1980-1988. — *William Ruhlmann*

○ **George Thorogood & the Destroyers** / 1978 / Rounder ✦✦✦✦
Contains Thorogood's crowd-pleasing rendition of John Lee Hooker's "One Bourbon, One Scotch, One Beer." Its basic approach—heavy on Thorogood's bluesy guitar playing—serves as the prototype for every Destroyers record that followed. — *William Ruhlmann*

Move It on Over / Jan. 1979 / Rounder ✦✦✦

In 1978, George Thorogood was just beginning to make some noise on the blues-rock circuit. This was his second album, and what's now almost a cliche then sounded fresh and vital. Thorogood's energy, rousing vocals and driving guitar playing came roaring through on inspired covers of Elmore James' "The Sky Is Crying," Bo Diddley's "Who Do You Love" and Chuck Berry's "It Wasn't Me." He even did a credible Piedmont blues on Brownie McGhee's "So Much Trouble." While Thorogood went on to make more commercially successful albums, the spirit and innocence in his early releases has seldom been duplicated. This Rounder CD reissue returns him to a simpler, and in some ways superior, period. —*Ron Wynn*

More George Thorogood and the Destroyers / 1980 / Rounder ✦✦

George Thorogood was honing his focus and getting the Destroyers concept down pat on this 1986 album. He hadn't yet become so established and comfortable that his rocking blues licks and vocals were more show business than intensity and energy. Thorogood's playing and singing on such tracks as "House of Blue Lights," "Night Time" and "I'm Wanted" was earnest enough to make the treatments convincing, and retain interest. While this wasn't quite as memorable as his earlier dates, George Thorogood still had the hunger that fueled his breakout sessions. —*Ron Wynn*

○ **Bad to the Bone** / 1982 / EMI America ✦✦✦

Though songs such as "Back to Wentzville" are credited to G. Thorogood, he'd be the first to admit that they are proudly derivative of Chuck Berry and his other mentors. The title track, another Thorogood copyright, has become ubiquitous in *Terminator 2* and the *Problem Child* movies and elsewhere, but it's still terrific. —*William Ruhlmann*

● **The Baddest of George Thorogood and the Destroyers** / 1992 / EMI America ✦✦✦

The aptly-titled *The Baddest of George Thorogood and the Destroyers* offers a dozen tracks that cleanse the church of rock'n'roll of all but its most basic elements: guitar, bass, drums, and a pile of Chuck Berry, Bo Diddley and Rolling Stone licks. Delaware's George Thorogood has never quite captured his wildman live presence in the studio, but having all his best material gathered on one disc—including "Bad to the Bone," "Move It on Over," and "One Bourbon, One Scotch, One Beer"—makes for a great party. Steve Morse's liner notes are brief but, like the songs, get right to the point... cut to the bone, you might say. —*Roch Parisien*

Haircut / 1993 / EMI America ✦✦

You wouldn't expect any changes from George Thorogood, whose pile-driving rocking-blues and boogie have maintained their appeal despite the emergence of numerous similar-sounding ensembles. Thorogood's rough-hewn singing and always tantalizing playing are on target through the usual mix of originals and covers (this time including Bo Diddley and Willie Dixon). Besides the bonus of major label engineering and production, Thorogood's work has never lost its edge because he avoids becoming indulgent or a parody, and continues to sound genuinely interested in and a fan of the tunes he's doing. —*Ron Wynn*

Three Dog Night

Group, Pop/Rock

At a time when rock elitists deemed Top 40 radio decidedly uncool, the slick multivocal blend of soulful pop/rock of Three Dog Night (formed 1968) made 21 trips to the charts from 1969 to 1975.

The centerpiece of Three Dog Night's sound was the band's trio of lead singers: Danny Hutton (b. Sep 10, 1946), Chuck Negron (b. Jun 8, 1942), and Cory Wells (b. Feb 5, 1944). Composed of seasoned players, the band displayed quite a bit of proficiency musically, even though their lurching, soulful dance rhythms occasionally sounded awkward.

Since the band lacked any real songwriting resource from within, they were smart enough to look outside for material and had the good taste to plug into some of the era's best songwriters. While Three Dog Night's versions of the material may not have been definitive, they opened the door to the mass market's awareness of talented writers like Steve Winwood, Harry Nilsson, Robbie Robertson, Randy Newman, Hoyt Axton, Neil Young, Laura Nyro, and many others. Elton John and Bernie Taupin had their

first stateside success with Three Dog Night's cover of "Lady Samantha." —*Rick Clark*

● **The Best of Three Dog Night** / 1983 / MCA ✦✦✦✦

This collection contains all of Three Dog Night's hits, plus a few key album tracks. Among the tracks included are "One" (number five), "Easy to Be Hard" (number four), "Eli's Coming" (number ten), "Mama Told Me Not to Come" (number one), "Joy to the World" (number one), "Black & White" (number one), "Shambala" (number three), "An Old-Fashioned Love Song" (number four), "Never Been to Spain" (number five), and "Celebrate" (number 15). —*Rick Clark*

Celebrate: The Three Dog Night Story, 1965-1975 / 1993 / MCA ✦✦✦

A comprehensive double-disc anthology, *Celebrate* is necessary for devoted fans of Three Dog Night, but most listeners will be content with *The Best of Three Dog Night*, which features all of the hits on a single disc. —*AMG*

Throbbing Gristle

Group, Industrial, Alternative Pop/Rock

This is the group that defined the industrial sound, forging their distinctively dark outlook with sonic experimentation and dance beats at the dawn of the punk age. Although Throbbing Gristle followed no formulas—producing many unpredictable albums and hundreds of live tapes in just a few years—the pop aspects of industrial dance music became an identifiable mainstream genre. Consequently, the group split up into two entities, with members Chris and Cosey following the dance trend, while Genesis P. Orridge took the underground route in Psychic TV. —*Myles Boisen*

2nd Annual Report / 1977 / Mute ✦✦✦

Actually their first album, it has singles and different live versions of two early pieces. —*Myles Boisen*

○ **20 Jazz Funk Greats** / 1979 / Mute ✦✦✦✦

This is as close as they got to the industrial-dance style of their many imitators; it's fairly accessible. —*Myles Boisen*

D.O.A. / 1979 / Mute ✦✦✦

A dark lyrical content dominates these 15 tracks. —*Myles Boisen*

Heathen Earth / 1979 / Mute ✦✦✦

Live in the studio, this combines the best of both harrowing worlds. —*Myles Boisen*

Mission of Dead Souls / 1981 / Mute ✦✦✦

Their final and perhaps most extreme musical assault was recorded live in San Francisco. —*Myles Boisen*

● **Greatest Hits** / 1984 / Mute ✦✦✦✦

Like the title says (with irony), it's an industrial primer with song sensibility. —*Myles Boisen*

CD 1 / 1986 / Resonance ✦✦✦

A very raw studio session. —*Myles Boisen*

Throwing Muses

Group, Alternative Pop/Rock

One of the quietly great college bands from the 1980s, Throwing Muses was formed in 1983 by guitarist/vocalist Kristin Hersh and her half-sister guitarist/vocalist Tanya Donelly (now of Belly) with a few friends from high school. In 1986 the group's debut album was put out by the prestigious British label 4AD; Throwing Muses were the first American band to be released on that label. Throwing Muses' angular, anguished, mercurial sound had much to do with Hersh's mental illness (she suffered from a form of bipolarity that caused her to hallucinate), especially on the early albums like *House Tornado*. 1991's *The Real Ramona* marked a break from the heaviness of the previous albums, with lots of shimmery pop gems penned both by Hersh and Donelly, who contributed at least one song an album throughout her stay in the band. Creative tensions between the two songwriters rose until Donelly left in 1992 to play with the Breeders and ultimately form Belly. That year Hersh reformed the Muses with drummer David Narcizo and released the band's fourth album, *Red Heaven*. After that, Hersh released a solo album and toured extensively, leaving fans to wonder about the status of the Muses. In 1995, however, Hersh and the rest of the Muses (Narcizo and bassist Bernard Georges) released *University*, one of the band's most cohesive and accessible efforts. Though Throwing Muses have had little commercial success throughout their career, they have released some of the most challenging and genuine music of recent years — and hopefully will continue to do so. —*Heather Phares*

○ **Throwing Muses** / 1986 / 4AD ◆◆◆◆
The band's eponymous first album is a startling, uncompromising collection of musings from Hersh and Donelly. Songs like "Hate My Way, " "Call Me" and "Vicky's Box" feature mercurial dynamic and meter shifts. Hersh's guitar playing and voice are particularly dramatic; both swing from delicate melodicism to shrill atonality, especially on "Rabbits Dying" and "Delicate Cutters." Tanya Donelly contributes an ethereally beautiful love song in "Green." While this is not the most accessible album in the Muses' repertoire, it is an emotionally powerful and genuine one. —*Heather Phares*

Chains Changed [EP] / 1987 / 4AD ◆◆◆
This four-song EP is difficult to find, but is nevertheless worth the search. It contains some of Hersh's finest songs, including the rockabilly-tinged "Cry Baby Cry," the tumultuous "Finished" and "Snailhead." *Chain's Changed* combines the group's fiery intensity and moodiness with the pop prowess the band gradually developed. —*Heather Phares*

The Fat Skier [EP] / 1988 / 4AD/Sire ◆◆◆
Like the *Chains Changed* EP, this release is hard to find on its own, but is included on the import version of *House Tornado.* Some of their most commanding music is included, like the mesmerizing "A Feeling" and Donelly's "Pools in Eyes." The punky "Garaux Des Larmes" and wrenching "A She Wolf After the War" make this a concise but accurate sample of the Muses' variety. — *Heather Phares*

House Tornado / 1988 / 4AD/Sire ◆◆◆
House Tornado is a more melodic take on Throwing Muses' challenging style, Hersh's vocals are commanding and varied, especially on "Colder" and "Saving Grace." But the Muses' pop side surfaces more on this album than on their previous work, particularly on tracks like "Juno," "Run Letter," and on Donelly's "Giant." Like their debut, this album is an acquired taste, but an ultimately rewarding one. —*Heather Phares*

Hunkpapa / 1990 / 4AD/Sire ◆◆
On the group's third full-length album and their second for Sire, Throwing Muses display a rare creative lull. Many of the songs are just not as powerful as their prior material, but the album is not a total loss. The wild, desolate "Bea" and explosive "Mania" are two of Hersh's finest songs, and Donelly's "Dragonhead" and "Angel" show her growing prowess as a songwriter. —*Heather Phares*

● **The Real Ramona** / 1991 / 4AD/Sire ◆◆◆◆
The Real Ramona is the Muses' finest pop moment. Hersh's material is some of her most melodic and accessible, yet it retains her unflinching honesty and emotional pull. "Counting Backwards," "Ellen West," "Hook in Her Head" and "Red Shoes" are both catchy and riveting works of songwriting. "Graffiti" and "Two-Step" are two of Hersh's most appealing pop snippets, and Donelly contributes two of the best songs she's ever written, the gleeful and giddy "Not Too Soon" and "Honeychain." Simply put, *The Real Ramona* is a great starting point for new Muses fans. —*Heather Phares*

Red Heaven / 1992 / 4AD/Sire ◆◆◆
The Muses' fourth album is their first as a trio, with Tanya Donelly exiting and original bassist Leslie Langston replacing Fred Abong. The material is more rock-oriented than on the Muses' lighter and more abstract material, especially on "Furious," "Firepile" and "Dio," on which Hersh duets with Bob Mould. "Summer St." is one of Hersh's most endearing songs, and tunes like "Carnival Wig" and "Earl" maintain her reputation as an inventive and thoughtful songwriter. —*Heather Phares*

○ **University** / 1995 / Sire/Reprise ◆◆◆◆
University, the group's most recent album, sees Hersh, drummer David Narcizo and new bassist Bernard Georges grow into writing and playing material for a trio. The result is some of the group's most buoyant punk-pop music, with "Bright Yellow Gun," "Start" and "Shimmer" being the chief examples. The delicate melodies of "That's All You Wanted" and "Crabtown" and the intensity of "Fever Few" show that Hersh has not lost her creative edge. Another good introduction to the Muses work, especially their post-Donelly material. —*Heather Phares*

Johnny Thunders

b. 1941, d. Apr. 23, 1991
Rock & Roll, Punk
Following footsteps of his idol Keith Richards, Johnny Thunders

(born John Anthony Genzale, Jr.) lived the ultimate rock & roll life, spending most of his days wasted and churning out tough, sloppy three-chord rock & roll. He made his greatest impact as a member of the New York Dolls, the proto-punk glam rockers of the early '70s. During the late '70s, he was a familiar figure on the New York punk scene, both with the Heartbreakers and as a solo artist. Thunders kept performing and recording until his death in 1991, turning out a series of records that inadvertently documented his descent into heroin addiction.

Under the name Johnny Volume, Genzale began performing in high school with Johnny and the Jaywalkers; after leaving that band, he joined Actress, which featured future Dolls Arthur Kane and Billy Murcia. Actress became the New York Dolls in 1971 and Genzale renamed himself Johnny Thunders. After recording two acclaimed but unsuccessful albums, the Dolls broke up. In 1975, Thunders and the group's drummer Jerry Nolan formed the Heart-breakers with former Television bassist Richard Hell and guitarist Walter Lure. Hell left the group shortly afterward to form the Voidoid and was replaced by Billy Rath. With Thunders leading the band, the Heartbreakers toured America and Britain, releasing one official album, *L.A.M.F.*, in 1977. The group relocated to the U.K., where their popularity was significantly greater, particularly among punk bands, than it was in the U.S. Thunders earned a reputation for incoherent, sloppy, drunken performances, as well as appearing on stage, unannounced, with other artists. After several months, the group returned to America, where they played a series of farewell gigs in New York.

Thunders went solo in 1978, recording *So Alone* with various rock and punk celebrities, including the Sex Pistols' Steve Jones and Paul Cook, Steve Marriott (Small Faces, Humble Pie), Peter Perrett (Only Ones), Paul Gray (Eddie and the Hot Rods, the Damned), and Thin Lizzy's Phil Lynott. After its release, Thunders and Sex Pistols bassist Sid Vicious played in the Living Dead for a short time. During the early '80s, Thunders re-formed the Heart-breakers for various tours; the group recorded their final album in 1984.

For most of the '80s, the only Johnny Thunders products available were haphazard compilations of live tracks and demos. In 1985, he released *Que Sera Sera*, a collection of new songs that showed he could still perform convincingly. Three years later, the guitarist recorded an album of rock and R&B covers with vocalist Patti Palladin, *Copy Cats*. Late in the decade, Thunders formed a group with ex-MC5 guitarist Wayne Kramer called Gang War; they released one album in 1990.

After years of abuse, Johnny Thunders was found dead in a New Orleans hotel room in April of 1991. While the autopsy didn't disclose the cause of death, most later reports claimed the guitarist died of a heroin overdose. Although it was a sad ending, it was appropriate—no other rock & roller ever lived as hard as Johnny Thunders. —*Stephen Thomas Erlewine*

● **So Alone** / 1978 / Real Music ◆◆◆◆
Thunders's first solo shot enlisted members of the Sex Pistols, the Hot Rods, and the Only Ones, featuring a variety of material that showcased both his mangy vocals and his strangling guitar attack. —*John Floyd*

New Too Much Junkie Business / 1983 / Combat ◆◆◆
The best of Thunders's live and outtake documents is for diehards only. —*John Floyd*

Que Sera, Sera / 1985 / Jungle ◆◆◆

Copycats / 1988 / Restless ◆◆◆

Gang War / 1990 / Zodiac-DeMilo ◆◆

'Til Tuesday

Group, Pop/Rock
Aimee Mann was the lead singer and bass player in the Boston-based 'Til Tuesday, which scored a Top Ten hit with "Voices Carry" and a gold-selling album of the same name in 1985. The rest of the group was Michael Hausmann, drums; Robert Holmes, guitar; and Joey Pesce, keyboards. The group recorded two more albums but broke up after *Everything's Different Now* in 1988. —*William Ruhlmann*

○ **Voices Carry** / 1985 / Epic ◆◆◆◆
'Til Tuesday showed a lot of promise with this debut album, which focused on Aimee Mann's emotive singing, notably on the title track. —*William Ruhlmann*

Welcome Home / 1986 / Epic ◆◆◆
Big Trash was a successful attempt to add a stronger rhythmic sensibility to the Thompson Twins' sound, but the album failed to produce any hit bigger than the number 28 "Sugar Daddy," although there were several other strong numbers on the record. —*Stephen Thomas Erlewine*

● **Everything's Different Now** / 1988 / Epic ◆◆◆◆
Til Tuesday's final album is their best record, showcasing Aimee Mann's emergence as a songwriter capable of impeccably crafted guitar-pop gems. —*Stephen Thomas Erlewine*

Johnny Tillotson
Pop/Rock, Teen Idol
A second-tier teen idol in the late '50s and early '60s, Tillotson was unusual for the genre in that he wrote a few of his hits, and displayed a strong inclination towards straight country material. His most well-remembered songs, though, were delivered with a not-so-great voice in a soft pop/rock manner that emphasized the pop half of the equation, and epitomized the blandness of the teen idol style. He had a dozen Top 40 hits, the biggest and best being "Poetry in Motion" (number two, 1960), the most countryish "It Keeps Right on a-Hurtin'" (number three, 1962). Tillotson moved into the lounge circuit after the British Invasion struck, though he managed a final Top 40 hit in 1965 with "Heartaches by the Number." —*Richie Unterberger*

● **Poetry in Motion: The Best of Johnny Tillotson** / 1995 / Varese Sarabande ◆◆◆◆
All of his biggest hits are on this 17-song compilation; all but one of the tracks were chart singles. Missing a couple of Top 40 hits that he cut for MGM in the mid-'60s, but everything else of note is here. —*Richie Unterberger*

Tim Dog
Rap
Bronx rapper Tim Dog (born Tim Blair) fired fresh shots in the long simmering hip-hop coastal warfare with his 1991 album *Penicillin on Wax*. His single "F—Compton" triggered answers and comebacks in West and East Coast circles, and helped his album become an underground sensation, though not a major hit. Tim Dog's alternately leering and fiery tone, his confrontational diatribes and cutting beats were even more vigorous on the follow-up *Do or Die* in 1993. —*Ron Wynn*

● **Penicillin on Wax** / Nov. 12, 1991 / Ruffhouse ◆◆◆◆
Driven by the furious "F—Compton," Tim Dog's debut album offered some of the hardest gangsta rap of 1991, as well as some of the worst; the best moments make *Penicillin on Wax* worthwhile. —*Stephen Thomas Erlewine*

Do or Die / 1993 / Ruffhouse ◆◆◆
Tim Dog fired more shots in the constant East vs. West Coast war. His second CD was just as defiant and disrespectful as his debut. Dog once more refused to moderate his chip-on-the-shoulder attitude, the results sometimes being mildly amusing and extremely offensive on other occasions. —*Ron Wynn*

Time
Group, Soul, Funk
From their origins as Prince's first pet project to their self-produced funk-rock oeuvre, the Time has been a fascinating and outrageous congregation. Vocalist Morris Day infused his cocky, swaggering personality into dance hits that would make Rufus Thomas envious, and, unlike most of the competition, the band managed to do something unique with Prince's genre-busting innovations. Time broke up in the late '80s, with Day going on to a somewhat disastrous solo career, Jesse Johnson crafting two dazzling solo albums, and Jimmy Jam and Terry Lewis becoming one of the most successful production teams this side of Gamble-Huff, working with everyone from Full Force and Janet Jackson to the S.O.S. Band and Human League. The group re-formed in 1990 and released the excellent *Pandemonium*. —*John Floyd*

The Time / 1981 / Warner Brothers ◆◆◆
These Prince proteges became stars in their own right in the early '80s. Their debut album had a smart combination of funk, rock, pop, and punk, with Morris Day the erstwhile lead singer and a cast also including Terry Lewis, Jimmy "Jam" Harris, Jesse Johnson, and Jellybean Johnson. Their early singles "Get It Up" and "Cool" were surly, suggestive, and just as energetic and electric as Prince's. —*Ron Wynn*

● **What Time Is It?** / 1982 / Warner Brothers ◆◆◆◆
After a tentative debut, the Time bounced back with one of 1982's best dance albums, full of hilarious stompers and braggadocio ballads. —*John Floyd*

○ **Ice Cream Castle** / 1984 / Warner Brothers ◆◆◆◆
Ice Cream Castle finds the band stepping out of Prince's purple shadow and discovering their own personality. The relentless "Jungle Love" is their best song. —*John Floyd*

Pandemonium / 1990 / Paisley Park ◆◆
Jam and Lewis bring their groundbreaking production techniques to a set that alternately demonstrates just how timeless the Time's boogie can be and just what the band members picked up during their sabbatical. —*John Floyd*

Tin Machine
Group, Hard Rock
To some ears, Tin Machine's sheets of guitar feedback and bash-ola drums may be overkill, but this quartet, fronted by pop chameleon David Bowie, takes aggressive, dissonant hard rock to bracing extremes, particularly on their exciting self-titled debut. —*Rick Clark*

● **Tin Machine** / 1989 / EMI America ◆◆◆◆
For fans of wildly dissonant hard rock, Tin Machine's debut effort (uneven as it is) is a gem. The band's chemistry, on tracks like "Heaven Is Here" (check the lead ride at the end), "I Can't Read," "Crack City," and "Baby Can Dance," is great. "Amazing" sports a nice descending guitar pattern and one of the album's more memorable melodies, but their version of Lennon's "Working Class Hero" rings hollow. Lyrically, most of this is Bowie at his most half-baked. —*Rick Clark*

Tin Machine II / 1991 / Victory ◆◆◆
On their second album, Tin Machine streamlined their approach somewhat, trading the occasional noisy guitar flourish for a cleaner, more conventional lead line. However, that doesn't mean the group has abandoned the plodding dissonance that distinguished their debut—they've just made it more accessible. And that doesn't mean they've written better songs. Nothing on *Tin Machine II* compares with the highlights of the debut—it sounds like a collection of outtakes. It's not surprising that David Bowie chose to resume his solo career after the release of this collection. —*Stephen Thomas Erlewine*

Oy Vey, Baby / 1991 / Victory ◆◆
Tin Machine's live album *Oy Vey, Baby* features a looser performance than normal by the band, but it's still not enough to rescue the batch of under-developed songs that form the backbone of the record. —*Stephen Thomas Erlewine*

Tindersticks
Group, Alternative Pop/Rock
Formed in early 1992, the British group Tindersticks' dark, difficult pop draws from gloomy romantics like Leonard Cohen, Ian Curtis, Nick Cave and Scott Walker. Their self-titled 1993 debut was named Album of the Year by *Melody Maker* and their untitled 1995 follow-up received equally glowing reviews. —*Stephen Thomas Erlewine*

○ **Tindersticks [debut]** / 1994 / Bar/None ◆◆◆◆
The Tindersticks' first album is a long, dense affair, filled with layered, melancholy songs and indiscernible vocals. —*Sara Sytsma*

● **Tindersticks [second album]** / 1995 / ◆◆◆◆
Adding strings to the mix has helped the Tindersticks fulfill their promises. The group's untitled second album is a darkly lush set of sad songs that gain a rich majesty through the intricate arrangements. —*Sara Sytsma*

TLC
Group, Hip Hop, Urban
Comprised of Tionne "T-Boz" Watkins, Rozonda "Chilli" Thomas," and Lisa "Left Eye" Lopes, the Atlanta, Georgia-based hip-hop trio TLC released their first album, *Ooooooooh…On the TLC Tip*, in early 1992 with immediate success. Masterminded by the successful R&B producer/singer Pebbles, the group had three consecutive Top Ten hits in 1992, including "Ain't 2 Proud 2 Beg," "What About Your Friends," and "Baby-Baby-Baby." Shortly before the release of their second album, Lopes was arrested for burning down the house of her boyfriend, Andre Rison, a member of the Atlanta Falcons. Lopes's arrest didn't affect the sales of their second album,

1994's *Crazysexycool*, which featured three number one singles and sold over four million copies. —*Stephen Thomas Erlewine*

Ooooooohhh . . . On the TLC Tip / 1992 / La Face ◆◆◆
TLC's debut album was a well-produced but inconsistent effort, with the three hit singles—"Ain't 2 Proud 2 Beg," "Baby-Baby-Baby," and "What About Your Friends"—being the catchiest and most memorable songs on the album. —*Sara Sytsma*

● **CrazySexyCool** / 1994 / La Face ◆◆◆◆
On their second album, TLC downplays their overt rap connections, recording a smooth, seductive collection of contemporary soul reminiscent of both Philly soul and Prince, powered by new jack and hip-hop beats. Lisa Lopes contributes the occasional rap, but the majority of *CrazySexyCool* belongs to Tionne Watkins and Rozonda Thomas. While they're not the most accomplished vocalists—they have a tendency to be just slightly off-key—the material they sing is consistently strong. As the cover of Prince's "If I Was Your Girlfriend" indicates, TLC favors erotic, mid-tempo funk. Yet the group removes any of the psychosexual complexities of Prince's material, leaving a batch of sexy material that just sounds good, especially the hit singles. Both "Creep" and "Red Light Special" have a deep groove that accentuates the slinky hooks, but it's "Waterfalls," with its gently insistent horns and guitar lines and instantly memorable chorus, that ranks as one of the classic R&B songs of the '90s. —*Stephen Thomas Erlewine*

Toad the Wet Sprocket

Group, Folk-Rock, Pop/Rock
Toad the Wet Sprocket's second-generation, R.E.M.-derived guitar-pop made them stars in 1992, with the gentle, highly melodic *Fear*. Although they released two albums before their commercial breakthrough, they hadn't yet developed a signature style; with *Fear* the band's songwriting improved and their sound developed into a graceful, folk-rock which incorporated the band's influences instead of mimicking them. Both radio and MTV played the singles "All I Want" and "Walk on the Ocean" constantly, making the album a hit. In 1994, the band released *Dulcinea*, which was a hit upon its release, thanks to the single, "Fall Down." —*Sara Sytsma*

Bread & Circus / 1989 / Columbia ◆◆◆
○ **Pale** / 1990 / Columbia ◆◆◆◆
Pale improved on the formula Toad the Wet Sprocket sketched out on their debut, *Bread and Circus*, since the band contributed a set of stronger songs with catchier melodies. —*Sara Sytsma*

● **Fear** / 1991 / Columbia ◆◆◆◆
Since their first release, *Bread and Circus*, Toad has grown dramatically as players and songcrafters. *Fear* is the pleasant result of these developments. It contains the Top 40/alternative hit single "All I Want"; the opening track, "Walk on the Ocean," is another highlight. —*Rick Clark*

Dulcinea / 1994 / Columbia ◆◆◆
Over two years in the making, *Dulcinea* builds upon the sound laid down in *Fear*. "Fall Down" was the first hit, while "Fly from Heaven" and "Inside" have the same potential for both alternative and mainstream pop/rock appeal. —*Rick Clark*

The Tokens

Group, Doo-Wop
This Brooklyn doo-wop group was originally known as the Linc-Tones when they formed in 1955 at Lincoln High School. Hank Medress, Neil Sedaka, Eddie Rabkin, and Cynthia Zolitin didn't have much impact in their early days recording for Melba. They later disbanded, but Medress re-formed the group in 1960 as the Tokens. Brothers Phil and Mitch Margo and Jay Siegel were now the members. They recorded for Warwick in 1960, then had their one glorious hit in 1962, "The Lion Sleeps Tonight." It was based on the South African Zulu song "Wimoweh," and reached number seven on the R&B chart while topping the pop surveys. The Tokens formed their own label in 1964, B.T. Puppy, but weren't able to keep the hits coming very long, although "The Lion Sleeps Tonight" remains a standard. —*Ron Wynn*

○ **Oldies Are Now** / 1993 / B.T. Puppy ◆◆◆◆
One of the few truly successful modern-day doo-wop albums, with a variety of material and top notch performances to commend it. The recuts of their early hits ("The Lion Sleeps Tonight," "I Hear Trumpets Blow," "Tonight I Fell in Love") sound wonderful, the

new material (the title track, "Merry Merry," "Just a Thought") works, and the group sings like angels. What more could you ask for? Highly recommended. —*Cub Koda*

● **Wimoweh: Best Of** / 1994 / RCA ◆◆◆◆

Tommy Tutone

Group, New Wave, Power Pop/Anglo-Pop, Pop/Rock
Tommy Tutone were an early-'80s power-pop band led by vocalist Tommy Heath and guitarist Jim Keller. The group's first single, 1980's "Angel Say No," scraped the bottom of the American Top 40, yet it was 1981's "867-5309/Jenny" that sent the group to the top of the charts. Peaking in early 1982, the single hit number four and went gold. Tommy Tutone was never able to duplicate that success and the band broke up after the release of their third album, 1983's *National Emotion*. —*Stephen Thomas Erlewine*

Tommy Tutone / 1980 / Columbia ◆◆◆
Main songwriters Jim Keller and Tom Heath show a rare talent for writing catchy hook and memorable melodies on this fine debut. Despite a considerable promotional push from Columbia and no shortage of quality material, this record lacked the extra something needed to distinguish it from the masses of similar sounding bands of the time. The single "Angel Say No" was a minor U.S. hit. —*Chris Woodstra*

● **Tommy Tutone 2** / 1981 / Columbia ◆◆◆◆
The band's breakthrough features the unforgettable "867-5309/Jenny" and its lesser follow-up, "Which Man Are You" along with a batch of similar sounding originals. *Tommy Tutone-2* is consistently fun, hard-driving, working-class power-pop that was unfortunately overshadowed by the smash hit single. —*Chris Woodstra*

National Emotion / 1983 / Columbia ◆◆
Nothing could follow up "867-5309/Jenny," and it seems the band realized that. *National Emotion* finds the band going through the motions, half-heartedly repeating the formula of *Tommy Tutone-2*, rocking harder in places but generally lacking inspiration. —*Chris Woodstra*

Tomorrow

Group, Psychedelic
In the early days of British psychedelia, three bands were consistently cited as first-generation figureheads of the London-based underground sound: Pink Floyd, the Soft Machine, and Tomorrow. Pink Floyd became superstars, and the Soft Machine, influential cult legends, but Tomorrow is mostly remembered (if at all) for featuring Steve Howe as their lead guitarist in his pre-Yes days. That's a pity, as Tomorrow were nearly the equal of the two more celebrated outfits. With the early Floyd and Softs, they shared a propensity for flower-power whimsy. Though they were less recklessly innovative and imaginative, their songwriting was accomplished, with adroit harmonies, psychedelic guitar work, and adventurous structures and tempo changes. They never succumbed to mindless indulgence or jamming; indeed, their tracks were rather short and tightly woven in comparison with most psychedelic bands. A couple singles (especially "My White Bicycle") were underground favorites, but the group only managed to record one album before breaking up in 1968. Lead singer Keith West, even before the breakup, had a number two British hit with "Excerpt from a Teenage Opera," which helped inspire Pete Townshend's *Tommy*. Drummer Twink joined the Pretty Things and, later, the Pink Fairies. —*Richie Unterberger*

● **Tomorrow** / 1968 / Decal ◆◆◆◆
Tomorrow's sole album was a solid effort, with quite a few first-rate tracks. "My White Bicycle" was one of the first songs to prominently feature backwards guitar phasing, "Real Life Permanent Dream" has engaging English harmonies and sitar riffs, "Revolution" is an infectious hippie anthem, and "Now Your Time Has Come" features intricate riffing from Steve Howe. "Hallucinations," with its irresistible melody, gentle harmonies, and affectingly trippy lyrics, was perhaps their best track. The more self-conscious English whimsy—populated by jolly little dwarfs, Auntie Mary's dress shop, colonels, and the like—is less successful, although the band's craftsmanship is strong enough to avoid embarrassment. The 1986 reissue of this album features detailed liner notes and the worthy B-side "Claremont Lake," though unfortunately West's sappy but influential "Excerpt From A Teenage Opera" was deleted. —*Richie Unterberger*

Tone-Loc

Rap

Tone-Loc (born Tony Smith) soared from obscurity into pop stardom in 1989 when his hoarse voice and unmistakable delivery made the song "Wild Thing" (using a sample from Van Halen's "Jamie's Cryin'") a massive hit. The song was co-written by Marvin Young, better known as Young MC, as was the second single smash "Funky Cold Medina." The album *Loc'ed After Dark* became the second rap release to top the pop charts.

Tone-Loc expanded his horizons into acting in 1992 and 1993, appearing a few times on the FOX sitcom *Roc*. He was also in the films *Posse* and *Ace Ventura: Pet Detective*. —*Ron Wynn*

● **Loc'ed After Dark** / 1989 / Delicious Vinyl ◆◆◆◆
An engaging debut, it contains both "Wild Thing" and "Funky Cold Medina." —*Dan Heilman*

Cool Hand Loc / 1992 / Delicious Vinyl ◆◆◆
Tone Loc's second album didn't generate the widespread pop appeal or quiet the rumblings and disdain he had earned from the hardcore audience for his double-platinum smash *Loc-ed After Dark*. In fact, things were so commercially uneventful that Loc began putting more energy into acting, securing television and film roles with relish. —*Ron Wynn*

All Through the Night / PolyGram ◆◆

Tony! Toni! Tone!

Group, Soul, Funk, Urban

Brothers Dwayne and Raphael Wiggins and cousin Timothy Christian have proven themselves durable guardians of the soul and funk tradition, while also infusing their music with enough contemporary devices to remain popular. This Oakland trio scored a number one R&B hit right out of the box in 1988 with "Little Walter," a song that generated some criticism from gospel audiences for its use of the melody from "Wade in the Water." But they've since been able to keep things going on their own, as their LPs, *The Revival* in 1990 and *Sons of Soul* in 1993, have also been enormously successful. —*Ron Wynn*

Who? / Jan. 1988 / Wing ◆◆◆
Dwayne and Raphael Wiggins, along with cousin Timothy Christian, made a quick and lasting impact with their 1988 debut album. The lead single, "Little Walter," used the melody from "Wade in the Water" and laid out in vivid detail the rise and fall of a comrade who lacked control and direction. It proved a huge R&B hit and got moderate pop attention, but it helped establish the trio and their creative mix of vintage soul and contemporary hip-hop and New Jack production. "Baby Doll" and "For the Love of You" also got sizable pop attention, and Tony! Toni! Tone! were on their way. —*Ron Wynn*

○ **The Revival** / 1990 / Wing ◆◆◆◆
The trio followed their fine debut album with an even more polished and better produced second effort. "Feels Good" was an uptempo, hook-laden hit, while "It Never Rains In Southern California" was a nicely sung, elegantly arranged and tightly performed ballad, and a sign that they were real craftsmen rather than trendy followers. "The Blues" expressed their love for vintage music, while "Whatever You Want" was another love tune that displayed genuine style and compositional depth. —*Ron Wynn*

● **Sons of Soul** / 1993 / PolyGram 3145 ◆◆◆◆
With their third album, Tony! Toni! Tone! received their greatest chart success, without compromising their music; it was still the finely crafted, highly eclectic and funky pop-soul that distinguished their first two albums, while the band's songwriting and playing had improved. The result was the band's most successful album yet, both commercially and successfully. —*Stephen Thomas Erlewine*

Too Short

Group, Rap

Oakland rapper Todd Shaw has become a huge star without getting any pop airplay or crossover support. He's mined the mack (pimp) routine effectively, turning out albums routinely loaded with plenty of X-rated sexual escapades and commentary or variations on a day in the life of a player/pimp. He did score one classic sociopolitical number, his take on "The Ghetto," and has also done a good anticensorship bit with Ice Cube on "Ain't Nothin' but a Word to Me."

Too $hort's eighth release *Get in Where You Fit In* had plenty of

pimping, explicit language and commentary on players. The unrepentant $hort maintained he had no plans to moderate his language to accommodate those who protested that his lyrics demeaned African-American women. He also established headquarters in Atlanta, building a studio and home there. —*Ron Wynn*

○ **Life Is . . . Too Short** / 1988 / Jive ◆◆◆◆
Essential, bawdy, and often offensive and troubling. —*Ron Wynn*

Born to Mack / 1989 / Jive ◆◆◆
A breakout release. —*Ron Wynn*

● **Short Dog's in the House** / 1990 / Jive ◆◆◆◆
A tremendous combination of outrage, anger, and morbid outlook. —*Ron Wynn*

Shorty the Pimp / Jul. 14, 1992 / Jive ◆◆◆

Get In Where You Fit In / 1993 / Jive ◆◆
Although he tries to cop part of the current P-Funk inspired gangsta rap, Too $hort sounds lost and dated on his latest album, the overlong, sample-reliant, grotesquely misogynist, and musically muddled *Get in Where You Fit In*. —*AMG*

○ **Greatest Hits, Vol. 1: The Player Years, 1983-1988** / 1993 / In-A-Minute ◆◆◆◆
If you've never read the collected works of Chester Himes or Iceberg Slim, simply run through this Too $hort anthology and you'll have the general idea. Although never an inventive rapper or clever composer of rhymes, Too $hort was smart enough to find his niche and stick to it. Most people who continually mined the pimp arena quickly become merely tedious; Too $hort became both tedious and profitable. —*Ron Wynn*

Cocktails / 1995 / Jive ◆◆

Tool

Group, Alternative Pop/Rock, Heavy Metal

When their first full-length album was released in 1993 (they released an EP a year earlier), Tool won lots of fans with their grinding, post-Jane's Addiction heavy metal. With their dark, angry lyrics and numbing guitar drilling, they appealed both to metalheads and alternative rock fans. When they landed an opening spot on Lollapalooza, their audience grew by leaps and bounds; the increased exposure helped their debut album, *Undertow*, go gold. —*Stephen Thomas Erlewine*

Opiate / 1992 / Zoo ◆◆◆
Tool's debut EP, *Opiate*, is as tough and brutal as *Undertow* and will more than satisfy fans of that album. —*AMG*

● **Undertow** / 1993 / Zoo ◆◆◆◆
With their angst-ridden hard rock, Tool appears to be something new, but the band falls right into metal's grand tradition of white male adolescent aggression. It's the angry, politically aware lyrics that qualifies this as "alternative rock," because their grinding, assaultive attack isn't that different from Helmet, or Iron Maiden and Black Sabbath, for that matter. Anyone who found "Sober" both rocking and disturbing will undoubtedly be thrilled with *Undertow*'s pulverizing consistency. —*Stephen Thomas Erlewine*

Tornadoes

Group, Surf Rock

The Tornadoes were one of California's earliest exponents of the surf instrumental sound that swept the nation in the early '60s. —*Cub Koda*

○ **Bustin' Surfboards** / 1963 / Sundazed ◆◆◆◆
The Tornadoes' biggest hit became the title track of this, their only album, which also includes acknowledged surf classics like "Shootin' Beavers" and "The Gremmie." The inclusion of three bonus tracks (including the previously unreleased "Charge of the Tornadoes") make this a must-own for fans of the surfin' sound. —*Cub Koda*

Tornados

Group, Rock & Roll

A fascinating footnote in '60s rock, the Tornados topped the charts in both Britain and the U.S. in 1962 with their instrumental classic "Telstar." Inspired by the American satellite, this haunting, otherworldly tune—with its inimitable piercing clavioline, harp-like glissandos, outer-space sound effects, and mysterious wordless chanting near the end—was probably Joe Meek's finest production. It was also the first British rock & roll record to top the charts in the U.S., beating the Beatles by a full year.

The Tornados were actually a group of British sessionmen that

Meek had been using on his independently produced recordings. Quite a few Meek-produced singles followed in the next few years, all employing piercing organ and mysterious percolating percussion, sounding like nothing so much as pre-psychedelic roller rink music. None of them came close to matching the majestic "Telstar"; in fact, they were usually pretty thin and gimmicky, although tracks like "Ridin' the Wind," "Love and Fury," and "Blue, Blue, Blue Beat" fascinate with their spectral, shimmering organs. The Tornados never entered the U.S. Top 40 again, though they had more Top 20 hits at home in 1963 with "Globetrotter," "Ice Cream Man," and "Robot." Bassist Heinz Burt departed in 1963 for brief stardom as a Meek-produced solo vocalist. *—Richie Unterberger*

Away from It All / 1963 / Castle ✦✦
The only album recorded by the original lineup. Even if your interest in the Tornados extends beyond "Telstar," you may find this effort a humdrum affair, with weak material that can't overcome their trademark outer space roller rink organ and Meek's usual, at times cliched bag-of-tricks production. Has no overlap with their greatest hits CD on Music Club, if that is a concern. *—Richie Unterberger*

● **Telstar: The Original Sixties Hits of the Tornados** / 1994 / Music Club ✦✦✦✦
All you could possibly want to hear: both sides of the nine singles they cut for Decca between 1962 and 1964, along with the small U.S. hit "Ridin' the Wind" and a cut from a soundtrack LP. A fun, if slight, document of one of the most distinctive instrumental rock groups of the early '60s, with thorough liner notes. *—Richie Unterberger*

Toto

Group, Pop/Rock
Formed in 1978, Toto immediately became favorites on FM rock and pop formats with their million-selling mainstream rocker "Hold the Line," followed by the mildly funky "Georgy Porgy." Their sound, honed from years of session work, had a steely precision that, while sounding impressive, seemed bloodless. Nevertheless, their fourth album, *Toto IV* (1983), became the biggest album of their career, earning six Grammy awards. During this time, Toto continued doing session work for many artists, in a sense defining much of the sound of radio during the mid-'80s. *—Rick Clark*

○ **Toto** / 1978 / Columbia ✦✦✦✦
Toto's self-titled debut established their slick, professional pop/rock sound with hits like the driving "Hold the Line" and the R&B-inflected "Georgy Porgy." *—David Jehnzen*

Hydra / 1979 / Columbia ✦✦✦
Although it followed the same formula as their debut, Toto's second album *Hydra* wasn't quite as big a success. That was probably due to the fact that while the songs on *Hydra* were well-produced, they weren't necessarily catchy. *—David Jehnzen*

Turn Back / 1981 / Columbia ✦✦✦

○ **Toto IV** / 1982 / Columbia ✦✦✦✦
This is the album that cleaned up at the 1982 Grammys. Most of *Toto IV* is a seamless collection of precision-crafted hard rockers and power ballads. The album contains five hits, the biggest being "Africa," "Rosanna," and "I Won't Hold You Back." *—Rick Clark*

Isolation / 1984 / Columbia ✦✦✦
While *Isolation* didn't have as many memorable songs as the blockbuster *Toto IV*, it was an effective continuation of the band's trademark sound, especially the hit "Stranger in Town." *—David Jehnzen*

Fahrenheit / 1986 / Columbia ✦✦

The Seventh One / 1988 / Columbia ✦✦

● **Past to Present 1977-1990** / 1990 / Columbia ✦✦✦✦
Past to Present 1977-90 is a complete set of the biggest songs from this group of Los Angeles session pros, including "Africa" (# 1), "Hold the Line" (number five), "Rosanna" (# 2), "I Won't Hold You Back" (# 10), "Stranger in Town" (# 30), "99" (# 26), "Make Believe" (# 30), and "Georgy Porgy" (# 48). *—Rick Clark*

Kingdom of Desire / May 11, 1993 / Combat ✦✦

Tourists

Group, New Wave, Pop/Rock
In a brief career lasting from 1979 to 1980, the Tourists recorded

three albums, *The Tourists*, *Reality Effect*, and *Luminous Basement*, all of which made the U.K. charts. They also scored five chart singles, two of which, "I Only Want to Be with You" and "So Good to Be Back Home Again," made the Top Ten. The band included singer Annie Lennox (b. Dec 25, 1954), keyboardist/guitarist Dave Stewart (b. Sep 9, 1952), vocalist/guitarist Pete Coombes (who wrote most of the songs), bassist Eddie Chin, and drummer Jim Toomey. After the split, Stewart and Lennox formed Eurythmics. *—William Ruhlmann*

● **Should Have Been Greatest Hits** / 1984 / Epic ✦✦✦✦
A best-of released in the wake of Eurythmics's success, and therefore emphasizing Stewart and Lennox's contributions over Coombes's. Nevertheless, it's a well-chosen selection and includes four of their five UK hits, among them their sole U.S. chart entry, a terrific remake of Dusty Springfield's "I Only Want to Be with You." *—William Ruhlmann*

Allen Toussaint

b. 1938
New Orleans R&B
His inherently funky piano work heavily influenced by his Crescent City forefathers—Professor Longhair, Huey "Piano" Smith, and Fats Domino—and with a heavy dose of Ray Charles, a young visionary named Allen Toussaint almost singlehandedly fashioned a fresh, vital New Orleans R&B sound for the early '60s. Earning a vaunted reputation as a session pianist, Toussaint debuted on vinyl in 1958 with an obscure RCA album whimsically billed as "A. Tousan." When Joe Banashak inaugurated his Minit label in 1960, Toussaint joined the firm as A&R man and quickly proved himself the ultimate behind-the-scenes wizard on the New Orleans scene. During the early to mid '60s, Toussaint tirelessly wrote, arranged, produced, and played on hits by Ernie K-Doe, Irma Thomas, Jessie Hill, Chris Kenner, Barbara George, Lee Dorsey, Benny Spellman, the Showmen, and many more, his rolling keyboards vital to the charm of virtually all of them.

After unleashing the Meters on the world, Toussaint finally began to step out as a front man in 1970, although his low-key vocals have never achieved quite the same level of success as his previous productions for others. His brilliant compositions have been covered by everyone from Herb Alpert & the Tijuana Brass to Robert Palmer and Bonnie Raitt. Allen Toussaint's stature as a New Orleans musical giant endures.

Allen Toussaint found a new audience in 1994 when he joined country legend Chet Atkins for an updated rendition of "Southern Nights" on the CD *Rhythm, Country and Blues. —Bill Dahl*

○ **The Wild Sound of New Orleans** / 1958 / RCA Victor ✦✦✦✦
His debut album, featuring a killer band, storming second-line instrumentals, and Toussaint's rolling 88s. *—Bill Dahl*

Toussaint / 1971 / Scepter ✦✦✦
New Orleans production and performing wizard Allen Toussaint launched his solo career with this early-'70s release. But for some strange reason, the same performer who's written and produced marvelous material for Irma Thomas, Lee Dorsey, Chocolate Milk, and General Johnson among others was never able to score the same success working as a lead act. There was nothing on this album even in the same arena as his classic R&B tunes, and throughout Toussaint's run of solo releases, only the song "Southern Nights," which Glen Campbell made a hit, could be even mentioned in the same sentence with Toussaint classics like "Ride Your Pony" or "It Will Stand." *—Ron Wynn*

Motion / Aug. 1978 / Reprise ✦✦✦
A nicely produced, competently performed, but disappointing album by New Orleans giant Allen Toussaint. He seemed unable to find a groove or a sound, dabbling in pop, light R&B, rock, and mild funk, but never coming close to duplicating prior magical productions or compositions. This was perhaps Toussaint's least impressive material, and was especially surprising in light of the artistic success of his prior Warner Bros. album *Homage. —Ron Wynn*

● **Allen Tousaint Collection** / 1991 / Reprise ✦✦✦✦
A representative cross-section of the legendary New Orleans piano man's solo output—uneven but interesting. *—Bill Dahl*

○ **The Complete "Tousan" Sessions** / 1992 / Bear Family ✦✦✦✦
A compilation of instrumentals from 1958 and 1959 featuring Toussaint at the top of his form, *The Complete "Tousan" Sessions* is a wonderful portrait of the seminal New Orleans pianist; it's also

the first time this material has ever been available on CD. — *Stephen Thomas Erlewine*

Tower of Power

Group, Soul, Funk

Studio-session work has never lent itself to wide recognition except among other musicians, yet when not on the road as Tower of Power, the individuals who make up the critically acclaimed West Coast horn section might as well go by another name: "Backup for the World." Individually and in various incarnations, members of Tower of Power (fronted by Emilio Castillo) have recorded as sidemen for Elton John, Santana, Bonnie Raitt, Huey Lewis, Little Feat, David Sanborn, Michelle Shocked, Paula Abdul, Aaron Neville, and Riot.

Tower of Power has had their share of personnel changes over the years, but the core group members (including Castillo on saxes and vocals, Stephen "Doc" Kupka on baritone sax, Greg Adams on trumpet and vocals, and Rocco Prestia on bass) have remained, giving the band a percussive horn-based sound that is not rooted in any one genre. —*Richard Skelly*

East Bay Grease / 1971 / Rhino ✦✦✦

The first Tower of Power album, when the band was only honing its concept and seeking a lead singer. On some songs, notably "Sparkling in the Sand," you can hear the group beginning to come together. They already had a fine horn section, and were only some good arrangements away from becoming one of the best pop and soul bands in the nation. The vocals were uneven, although Rick Stevens would later emerge as the prime vocalist. Despite its flaws, it's worth having because the diamond was being cut on these selections. It's recently been reissued on CD. —*Ron Wynn*

Bump City / Nov. 1971 / Warner Brothers ✦✦✦

The second Tower of Power LP, and the first that made any impact. The group went to Memphis, cut their first great single in "You're Still A Young Man," and learned firsthand about funk and soul. The production and arrangements were much improved over the debut album, as was the engineering and overall technical quality. Their lines were crisper, the unison and ensemble passages much sharper, and they were beginning to round into shape. —*Ron Wynn*

○ **Tower of Power** / 1973 / Warner Brothers ✦✦✦✦

The Tower of Power finally found their ideal lead singer on this album. Lenny Williams came aboard and gave them both the uptempo belter and convincing balladeer they had previously lacked. They landed their biggest single hit, "So Very Hard To Go," and also had two other top tunes in "What Is Hip" and "This Time It's Real." The arrangements and production were also excellent, and the horn section was at its explosive best. —*Ron Wynn*

○ **Urban Renewal** / 1974 / Warner Brothers ✦✦✦✦

A fine workout album, with surging horn funk and charts, punchy songs, excellent lead vocals from Lenny Williams, and only an occasional out-of-place tune. The Tower of Power were the finest West Coast funk/soul band of the early and mid-'70s, and organist/keyboardist Chester Thompson provided them with another strong instrumentalist in the rhythm section. —*Ron Wynn*

● **Back to Oakland** / May 1974 / Warner Brothers ✦✦✦✦

The Tower of Power followed their self-titled gold album with an even better album that didn't enjoy similar sales success. *Back To Oakland* had tougher, funkier and better produced cuts, stronger vocals from Lenny Williams, who was now more comfortable as their lead singer, and included an excellent ballad in "Time Will Tell," plus the rousing "Don't Change Horses (In The Middle of A Stream)." The Tower of Power horn section reaffirmed its reputation in both soul and pop circles, and the album included a powerhouse instrumental. —*Ron Wynn*

Ain't Nothin' Stoppin' Us Now / 1976 / Columbia ✦✦✦

Edward McGhee turned in mostly above-average performances on their first post-Lenny Williams release, but it was the beginning of the end. With funk losing its foothold among R&B audiences, they couldn't keep it together. McGhee was an energetic, exuberant vocalist who held his own on uptempo tunes like "You Ought To Be Havin' Fun" and the title song, but lacked Williams' range or tonal quality on ballads. The group always had a weakness for ponderous message cuts, and "Can't Stand To See The Slaughter" and "While We Went To The Moon" were well-intentioned but clumsy tracks. This was almost the Tower of Power's swan song. —*Ron Wynn*

Live & in Living Color / 1976 / Warner Brothers ✦✦✦

A good, if uneven, live portrait of the Tower of Power. This mid-'70s album came as they were preparing to leave Warner Bros. and also to get a new lead singer. But it serves as a concert greatest hits collection, with decent versions of "What Is Hip?," "You're Still A Young Man," and "Down To The Nightclub." —*Ron Wynn*

Pete Townshend

b. May 19, 1945

Rock & Roll

Pete Townshend was the guitarist and songwriter for the Who from 1964 to 1982. Best-known for his conceptual works, he wrote *Tommy* and *Quadrophenia* for the group. Townshend made his first, tentative solo album, *Who Came First*, in 1972. Dedicated to his guru, Meher Baba, the album continued themes pursued in the previous Who album, *Who's Next*, and contained material from an abortive conceptual work, *Lifehouse*. The album sold modestly. In 1976, Townshend made a duo album, *Rough Mix*, with Ronnie Lane, formerly the bassist in the Small Faces.

Townshend's first full-fledged solo effort, however, was *Empty Glass* (1980), which sold half a million copies, reached the Top Five, and featured the Top Ten hit "Let My Love Open the Door," as well as the minor hits "A Little Is Enough" and "Rough Boys." Townshend followed this in 1982 with *All the Best Cowboys Have Chinese Eyes*.

Following the demise of the Who, Townshend released *Scoop*, a two-disc collection of demos, in 1983 (a second volume appeared in 1987). In 1985 he returned to thematic efforts with the album *White City—A Novel*, which included the Top 30 single "Face the Face." In the same year, Townshend published a book of short stories, *Horse's Neck*. As part of the *White City* project, Townshend appeared in an accompanying film, for which he organized a band called Pete Townshend's Deep End. The unit played only a few gigs, but one was videotaped and recorded, resulting in the 1986 album *Pete Townshend's Deep End Live!* In 1989, Townshend released an album based on Ted Hughes's children's story, *The Iron Man*. The record featured guest vocals by John Lee Hooker and Nina Simone, as well as two tracks featuring the three surviving members of the Who. Simultaneous with the album's release, Townshend embarked on a reunion tour with the Who.

Although the reunion tour was successful, it didn't help *The Iron Man* at all. Four years later, Townshend delivered *Psychoderelict* to mixed reviews and lukewarm sales. By that time, he had successfully reinvented himself as a Broadway tunesmith—the Broadway production of *The Who's Tommy* had become a runaway hit, earning Townshend a Tony and prompting him to pursue more stage musicals. —*William Ruhlmann*

Who Came First / 1972 / Rykodisc ✦✦✦

Pete Townshend's first solo album was a homespun, charming forum for low-key, personal songs that weren't deemed suitable for the Who, as well as spiritual paeans (direct and indirect) to his spiritual guru Meher Baba. Who fans will be immediately attracted by the presence of a couple of songs from the aborted Who concept album *Lifehouse* (much of which ended up on *Who's Next*), "Pure & Easy" and "Let's See Action." The Who did eventually release their own versions of both those songs. But Townshend's own versions aren't the highlights of this record, which shows a folkier and gentler side to the Who's chief muse than his albums with the group. "Sheraton Gibson" is a neat tune about rock & roll road life, and "Time Is Passing" takes very subtle inspiration from Baba. Most of the rest of the album contains some of the most unusual pieces Townshend has released: his acoustic cover of Jim Reeves' "There's A Heartache Following Me" (recorded because it was one of Baba's favorite tunes), "Evolution" (which is actually pretty much a solo track by his buddy Ronnie Lane of the Faces), "Parvardigar" (adapted from Baba's Universal Prayer), and "Content" (a philosophical poem by Maud Kennedy that Townshend put to music). The 1993 reissue of this LP for compact disc fleshes out the program considerably with six previously unreleased tracks, including Townshend's demo of the Who single "The Seeker." The other bonus cuts are by no means filler; meditative and melancholy originals, they're just as strong as the tracks on the original release. —*Richie Unterberger*

Rough Mix / 1977 / Atco ✦✦✦

Pete Townshend and Ronnie Lane rock it up, with some good melodies thrown in. Tops among Townshend's non-Who projects. —*Bruce Eder*

★ **Empty Glass** / 1980 / Atco ✦✦✦✦✦
A bright, energetic rock album, tightly played and sung in a manner equalling the best Who albums. —*Bruce Eder*

All the Best Cowboys Have Chinese Eyes / 1982 / Atco ✦✦✦
Pete Townshend followed his pop breakthrough *Empty Glass* with *All the Best Cowboys Have Chinese Eyes*, his most ambitious and difficult album. Abandoning conventional pop structures, Townshend creates a long, twisting soundscapes with intricate, synth-based arrangements and dense poetry. For some, the self-conscious poetry and obtuse, winding melody lines are nearly impenetrable, but the album features some of his most intriguing and beautiful work, including the cascading "The Sea Refuses No River" and "Uniforms." —*Stephen Thomas Erlewine*

○ **Scoop** / 1983 / Atco ✦✦✦✦
Townshend's first batch of Who demos. Not viscerally exciting, but musically intriguing. —*Bruce Eder*

White City: A Novel / 1985 / Atco ✦✦✦
After the experimental *All the Best Cowboys Have Chinese Eyes*, Pete Townshend returned to a more traditional form of concept album with *White City*. Built around a loose narrative concerning urban despair, the album doesn't work very well conceptually, yet a handful of the individual songs are among his finest solo work, including the punchy "Face the Face" and the anthemic "Give Blood." —*Stephen Thomas Erlewine*

○ **Pete Townshend's Deep End Live!** / 1986 / Atco ✦✦✦✦
An energetic live album featuring a handful of R&B classics (including "Barefootin'"), a few Who chestnuts, and some of his best solo work, *Pete Townshend's Deep End Live!* is the tightest rock & roll record he released as a solo artist. —*Stephen Thomas Erlewine*

○ **Another Scoop** / 1987 / Atco ✦✦✦✦
The second batch of Who demos, with better songs than the first. Some surprises for the serious fan. —*Bruce Eder*

The Iron Man: A Musical / 1989 / Atlantic ✦✦
Pete Townshend adapted "The Iron Man," a children's fable written by the British poet Ted Hughes, for his sixth studio solo album, *Iron Man: A Musical*. Casting himself, Roger Daltrey, Nina Simone, and John Lee Hooker in leading roles, the album doesn't suffer from a lack of talent—it suffers from a lack of songs. Townshend has failed to come up with a set of compelling melodies for Hughes's poems and the arrangements are obvious and overblown, making *Iron Man* an overwrought, ambitious failure. —*Stephen Thomas Erlewine*

Psychoderelict / Jun. 15, 1993 / Atlantic ✦✦
In the past, Townshend has let his lyrics tell the story from within the music, and that has allowed much of his work to stand timeless both as individual songs and entire concept pieces. On *Psychoderelict*, songs and music fight the spoken word "drama" throughout. Some individual songs are interesting; many are forgettable. Townsend shoots for hip, self-deprecating irony in numbers like "Let's Get Pretentious" and "Outlive The Dinosaur," but the strategy is transparent. Throw in the added static of instrumentals passages paying tribute to Townsend's spiritual mentor Meher Baba, and the overall effect is disjointed and most unsatisfying. —*Roch Parisien*

Trader Horne

Group, Folk-Rock
One of the most interesting one-shots of the early '70s, this duo featured Irish multi-instrumentalist Jackie McAuley, who was responsible for some of those great organ lines on Them's early records, and Judy Dyble, who sang on Fairport Convention's first album before being replaced by Sandy Denny in 1968. Their sole LP, *Morning Way*, is nice if slightly precious British folk-rock with an Olde-English, fairytale air, and will appeal to fans of the early work of both Donovan and Fairport. —*Richie Unterberger*

● **Morning Way** / 1970 / Janus ✦✦✦✦
Jackie McAuley's original material dominates the group's only album (Judy Dyble also wrote or co-wrote a couple tunes), a nifty bit of British folk-rock with both traditional and pop influences. A British CD reissue adds a few bonus tracks. —*Richie Unterberger*

Traffic

Group, Art-Rock/Progressive-Rock, Psychedelic, Pop/Rock
Among all the bands to emerge from England in the '60s, Traffic is one of the few who have aged gracefully.

At the time of Traffic's inception in 1967, former Spencer Davis bandmate Stevie Winwood (b. May 12, 1948) was its most noted member, but with the release of their debut, *Mr. Fantasy*, it became clear that this was truly a band of four equally creative multi-instrumentalists. Their initial efforts fused an ecumenical range of musical genres through a fairly psychedelic sensibility, most of it among the best examples of that approach to late-'60s pop/rock. Guitarist and vocalist Dave Mason (b. May 10, 1947) penned some particularly strong material on those first Traffic albums, especially "Feelin' Alright," a song that was later popularized by Joe Cocker, Three Dog Night, and many others.

After many instances of quitting the band over creative differences (the remaining three were resistant to his obvious pop tendencies), Mason left for good after 1971's *Welcome to the Canteen* (#26), a live album. By then, he had already earned a gold album for his 1970 debut, *Alone Together* (#22).

After their second self-titled album, Traffic parted ways when Winwood joined the short-lived supergroup, Blind Faith. After Blind Faith's demise, Winwood began a solo effort, tentatively titled *Mad Shadows*. As the project developed, Winwood increasingly sought the input of Chris Wood and Jim Capaldi. The result was the funkier, earthier *John Barleycorn Must Die* (#5).

Traffic's studio follow-up, *The Low Spark of High Heeled Boys* (#7), incorporated a spacier improvisational sound. The title cut became an FM rock-radio standard. Several more albums followed, and the band parted ways in 1974.

Wood died on July 12, 1983, of liver failure. Capaldi and Dave Mason have experienced sporadically successful solo careers. Winwood, on the other hand, has had a long and profitable string of releases.

When Winwood's solo career began to sag in 1994, he reformed with Capaldi; Mason didn't participate, choosing to stay in Fleetwood Mac. While the album proved a commercial disappointment, the reunited Traffic tour was successful, although neither proved exciting. —*Rick Clark*

☆ **Mr. Fantasy** / Jan. 1967 / Island ✦✦✦✦✦
Produced by Jimmy Miller (Rolling Stones, Spooky Tooth, Blind Faith), *Mr. Fantasy* is sonically decked out in *Sgt. Pepper*-period psychedelic splendor. Although much music of the period sounds quite dated, *Mr. Fantasy* and the self-titled follow-up have aged gracefully. This is in no small part due to Dave Mason's refined pop sensibilities. Even though he occasionally gets lost in a sea of sitars ("Utterly Simple"), Mason gives the material much of the form and restraint that latter-period Traffic, at times, desperately needed. Even Winwood turns in some of the tightest pop-song constructions in his career, thanks to Jim Capaldi and Chris Wood's co-writing input. The band's almost whimsical approach to integrating its eclectic influences keeps the material sounding fresh too. Traffic's hodgepodge of psychedelia always sounds like the product of a band that really plays together rather than existing as a studio concoction. Check out "Coloured Rain" or the title cut for an example. —*Rick Clark*

★ **Traffic** / Feb. 1968 / Island ✦✦✦✦✦
It's songs like "Feelin' Alright," "Pearly Queen," "You Can All Join In," "Vagabond Virgin," and "40,000 Headmen" that make Traffic's self-titled second effort a classic. Although not quite as trippy as their debut, most of the sonic observations mentioned for *Mr. Fantasy* apply here. —*Rick Clark*

Last Exit / Jan. 1969 / Island ✦✦✦
This collection of leftover studio tracks and live recordings from their 1968 tour was thrown together after Winwood jumped ship to go play with Blind Faith. It's a little spotty, but "Shanghai Noodle Factory" and the funky "Medicated Goo" are among their best early recorded work. —*Rick Clark*

○ **John Barleycorn Must Die** / Jan. 1970 / Island ✦✦✦✦
Upon the demise of the short-lived supergroup Blind Faith, Stevie Winwood began work on a solo album entitled *Mad Shadows*. As the project developed, it evolved into a Traffic reunion of sorts, as Winwood brought in Wood and Capaldi. The result, *John Barleycorn Must Die*, became an instant success, with its lengthy funky, R&B, jazz, and folk explorations. The playing is top-notch throughout, with Wood blowing some inspired sax, Capaldi laying down his trademark fluid percussion grooves, and Winwood's Hammond B3 and piano work in peak form. "Glad," "Freedom Rider," "Empty Pages," and the title cut are the highlights. —*Rick Clark*

The Low Spark of High Heeled Boys / Jan. 1971 / Island ✦✦✦
Opening with the pastoral "Hidden Treasure," *Low Spark* flows effortlessly, almost lazily, to the last song, "Rainmaker." The band does shake things up a little with "Rock & Roll Stew" (number 93) and "Light Up or Leave Me Alone." The title cut, at over 12 minutes of spacey jamming, is one of Traffic's most well-known FM hits. —*Rick Clark*

Welcome to the Canteen / Feb. 1971 / Island ✦✦✦
This fine live effort revealed Traffic as a seven-man touring unit, a precursor to their upcoming studio directions. On board for this outing were percussionist Reebop Kwaku Baah, drummer Jim Gordon, bassist Rick Grech, and Dave Mason, who briefly rejoined Winwood, Capaldi, and Wood for the tour. A revamped version of the Spencer Davis classic "Gimmie Some Lovin' (Part One)" became a moderate hit (number 68). —*Rick Clark*

Traffic: on the Road / 1973 / Island ✦✦✦
This is another solid document of their live work. —*Rick Clark*

Shoot out at the Fantasy Factory / 1973 / Island ✦✦✦
The title cut has its moments, but the augmentation of Muscle Shoals studio heavies Barry Beckett, Roger Hawkins, and David Hood ultimately turned down most of the remaining sparks in search of the eternal groove. —*Rick Clark*

When the Eagle Flies / 1974 / Asylum ✦✦
○ **Smiling Phases** / 1991 / Island ✦✦✦✦
Island remastered the tracks included in this double-disc anthology, and the difference is remarkable. Except for a few curious omissions, this is absolutely essential. —*Rick Clark*

Far from Home / 1994 / Virgin ✦✦
Far from Home / May 3, 1994 / Virgin America, Inc. ✦✦
In terms of capturing the spirit of playful creativity found on Traffic's best early work, this polished 1994 reunion album is indeed *Far from Home*. Traffic lovers may be disappointed, but fans of Winwood's later solo work will probably like this. Essentially, it is an extension of the sound he's created for the last ten years, with more instrumental stretching out—a nod to the band esthetic of '70s-era Traffic. —*Rick Clark*

Perfumed Garden / Bootleg ✦✦✦
If you're looking for unreleased early Traffic, this is certainly the collection to get, with 15 BBC tracks from 1967-68 and six marginally different alternate studio takes from 1967. Contains different versions of most of the songs from their first two albums and early singles; sound quality is variable, but usually quite good, and never less than listenable. In the manner of many BBC sessions, the differences between the studio and live versions are slight, but interesting for serious fans. —*Richie Unterberger*

Tragically Hip

Group, Rock & Roll
Ontario band the Tragically Hip fuses a rough & tumble Stonesy ensemble guitar attack with more of a hard rock rhythm drive. Their lyrics at times mix Delta folk-blues imagery with distinctly Canadian themes. —*Rick Clark*

The Tragically Hip / 1987 / MCA ✦✦✦
This debut release revealed a band with a strong Canadian point of view, executing an edgy Heartland-rock sound. "Last American Exit" and "Small Town Bringdown" are two standout tracks. —*Rick Clark*

● **Up to Here** / 1989 / MCA ✦✦✦✦
Their first major stateside release has a very dry, in-your-face, and unadorned sound. Blues influences are more evident here, melodically and in the form of raw electric-slide work. Highlights include "Blow at High Dough," "New Orleans Is Sinking," "38 Years Old," and "When the Weight Comes Down." —*Rick Clark*

○ **Road Apples** / 1991 / MCA ✦✦✦✦
The Hip reunite with Don Smith, going down the river to Dan Lanois's studio in New Orleans for this batch. Smith continues to go for a lean, hard sound, this time with a few more embellishments. The melodies are a little stronger this time out. "The Luxury," "On the Verge," "Little Bones," and the acoustic "Fiddler's Green" are particularly strong. —*Rick Clark*

Fully Completely / 1993 / MCA ✦✦✦
This third full outing retains the group's tough, tuneful, accessible rock while instilling at the same time an uneasy, dangerous feeling that everything could overboil at any moment. The Hip specialize in locking into a groove that entwines razor sharp images

with free-association ravings in a taut whirlwind of instruments and vocals. You can sense the gleam in vocalist Gordon Downie's eyes shifting from rational and visionary to demented and out of control. *Fully Completely* reinforces 1992 as a year of excellent domestic releases that are distinctively Canadian with universal appeal. —*Roch Parisien*

Day for Night / 1995 / Atlantic ✦✦✦
Tragically Hip continue to refine their rough edges, turning in a competent set of arena rock with *Day for Night*. The occasional Townshend flourish keeps the record from sinking into its pretensions, though the lack of the grit that permeated their early albums is noticeable. —*Stephen Thomas Erlewine*

The Trammps

Group, Soul, Disco
Disco's most soulful vocal group began in the '60s as the Volcanos, and were also called the Moods. Gene Faith was the original lead vocalist, with Earl Young, Jimmy Ellis, guitarist Dennis Harris, keyboardist Ron Kersey, organist John Hart, bassist Stanley Wade, and drummer Michael Thomas. But by the time they'd gone through various identities and emerged as the Trammps in the mid-'70s, the lineup featured lead vocalist Ellis, Harold and Stanley Wade, Robert Upchurch, and Young. A snappy revival of Judy Garland's '40s tune "Zing Went the Strings of My Heart" was their first chart single, reaching number 17 on the R&B list in 1972. Despite their well-deserved reputation and boisterous, jubilant harmonies and sound, the Trammps were never huge commercial successes even during disco's heyday. Indeed, they had only three R&B Top Ten hits from 1972 through 1978, and such wonderful records as "Soul Bones," "Ninety-Nine and a Half," and "I Feel Like I've Been Livin' (On the Dark Side of the Moon)" stiffed on the charts though they were beloved by club audiences and R&B fans alike. Their only huge hit was "Disco Inferno" in 1977, which was a number nine R&B single in 1977 and was also featured in *Saturday Night Fever*. Yet it missed the pop Top Ten, peaking at number 11. But the Trammps' prowess can't be measured by chart popularity; Jimmy Ellis's booming, joyous vocals brilliantly championed the celebratory fervor and atmosphere that made disco both beloved and hated among music fans. —*Ron Wynn*

● **The Best of the Trammps** / 1978 / Atlantic ✦✦✦✦
A good collection of the band's best tracks, including the monolithic "Disco Inferno" and "Disco Party." —*Stephen Thomas Erlewine*

The Trashmen

Group, Rock & Roll, Surf, Garage Rock
A Minneapolis rock & roll band, they evolved from a group Jim Thaxter & the Travelers, recording one single under that name ("Sally Jo"/"Cyclone"). The group comprises Tony Andreason (lead guitar), Dan Winslow (guitar/ vocals), Bob Reed (bass), and Steve Wahrer (drums/vocals). Unfairly depicted as a novelty act, the Trashmen were in actuality a top-notch rock & roll combo, enormously popular on the teen-club circuit, playing primarily surf music to a landlocked Minnesota audience. Drummer Steve Wahrer combined two songs by the Rivingtons ("The Bird's the Word" and "Pa Pa Ooh Mow Mow"), added freakish vocal effects and a pounding rhythm to the mix, and, by early 1964, the group was in the Top Ten nationwide with "Surfin' Bird." Though the group continued to release great followup singles and an excellent album, their moment in the sun had come and gone; they disbanded by late 1967/early 1968. They re-formed in the mid '80s and continued to play locally until Wahrer's death. The Trashmen are revered by '60s collectors as one of the great American teen-band combos of all time, their lone hit exemplifying wild, unabashed rock & roll at its most demented, bare-bones-basic, lone-E-chord finest. —*Cub Koda*

○ **Surfin' Bird** / 1964 / Soma ✦✦✦✦
The only album released by the group during their lifetime actually outstrips most of the Southern California-based competition, due to the ferocious grit of the playing and a vaguely demented, go-for-broke recklessness. A good mix of instrumentals and vocals, though nothing else is on the level of the title cut; the CD reissue adds demos of "Surfin' Bird" and "Bird Dance Beat," and a couple rare singles. —*Richie Unterberger*

○ **The Great Lost Trashmen Album!** / 1991 / Sundazed ✦✦✦✦
Live Bird '65-'67 / Sundazed ✦✦✦
Storming unreleased live recordings. —*Cub Koda*

● **Best of the Trashmen** / Sundazed ✦✦✦✦
The original *Surfin' Bird* album, plus all the original Garrett singles from that period. The perfect primer set. —*Cub Koda*

The Traveling Wilburys

Group, Pop/Rock
Reversing the usual process by which groups break up and give way to solo careers, the Traveling Wilburys are a group made up of solo stars. The group was organized by former Beatle George Harrison (b. Feb 25, 1943), former Electric Light Orchestra leader Jeff Lynne (b. Dec 30, 1947), Bob Dylan (b. May 24, 1941), Tom Petty (b. Oct 20, 1953), and Roy Orbison (b. Apr 23, 1936—d. Dec 6, 1988), thus representing three generations of rock stars. In 1988, the five (who had known each other for years) came together to record a Harrison B-side single and ended up writing and recording an album on which they shared lead vocals. It turned out to be a way to transcend the high expectations made of any of them as individuals, and a delighted public sent the album to number three, with two singles, "Handle with Care" and "End of the Line," hitting the charts. Unfortunately, Orbison died of a heart attack only a few weeks after the album's release.

Two years later, the remaining quartet released a second album, inexplicably titled *Vol. 3*. It was another million-selling hit. —*William Ruhlmann*

● **The Traveling Wilburys** / 1988 / Wilbury ✦✦✦✦
The idea of Dylan, Orbison, Harrison, Lynne, Petty, and session drummer Jim Keltner getting together on a single album was pretty bizarre, inspiring curiosity and a little dread. Instead of trying to create something on a grand scale, these guys achieved much more by tossing together a refreshingly playful and unpretentious collection of homey pop/rock tunes. "Handle with Care" (number 45) and "End of the Line" (number 63) were the hits from this release. —*Rick Clark*

Traveling Wilburys, Vol. 3 / 1990 / Wilbury ✦✦✦
Skipping over *Volume 2*, the Wilburys managed a more unified and harder-rocking sound. Party rave-ups like "Wilbury Twist," and "She's My Baby" indicate that these guys seem to enjoy how their fabricated identities have allowed them to ditch their living-legends status and possibly become more themselves in the process. —*Rick Clark*

The Tremeloes

Group, British Invasion, Pop/Rock
Quartet most famous for being picked for a contract by England's Decca Records in early 1962 in place of the Beatles. They actually started long before the Beatles, but it wasn't until after the Liverpool quartet hit that they saw any success in England or America. Their biggest British success was a version of the Contours' "Do You Love Me," but the hottest number on their first album was a searing (by British standards) rendition of "I Want Candy," later popularized by the Strangeloves, whose Bo Diddley-based beat, Bob Porter and company handled with admirable style. Poole later faded into obscurity, while the Tremeloes achieved success on their own. —*Bruce Eder*

○ **Here Come the Tremeloes** / 1967 / CBS ✦✦✦✦
A pleasant, upbeat collection with a jovial mood, but nothing as impressive as their Brian Poole-era "I Want Candy." (Out of print.) —*Bruce Eder*

● **The Best of the Tremeloes** / 1992 / Rhino ✦✦✦✦
A generous twenty-track collection of the band's finest moments, it includes all of their US hits. —*AMG*

The Treniers

Group, R&B, Jump Blues
Featuring twin brothers Cliff and Claude Trenier, the Treniers helped link swing music to rock & roll with their brand of hot jump blues in the late '40s and early '50s. To the latter-day listener, their early '50s singles can sound closer to swing than rock; indeed, Cliff and Claude had once sung with the Jimmie Lunceford Orchestra. The group did anticipate some crucial elements of rock & roll, though, with their solid, thumping beats, their squealing saxophone solos, and their song titles, such as "Rocking on Sunday Night," "Rockin' Is Our Business," and "It Rocks! It Rolls! It Swings!" The Treniers' brand of swing-cum-R&B was undoubtedly an influence on Bill Haley, who saw them when both acts were playing summer shows at Wildwood, NJ. Their best work was

recorded for OKeh in the early '50s; by the middle of the decade, their sound was more R&B-oriented. Like many early R&B pioneers, they were unable to find success in the rock & roll era, though they appeared in a few of the first rock & roll films. —*Richie Unterberger*

● **They Rock! They Roll! They Swing!: The Best of the Treniers** / 1995 / Legacy/Epic ✦✦✦✦
This 20-track compilation has all of their key early- and mid-'50s Okeh singles (only one of which, "Go! Go! Go!," was actually an R&B hit), five previously unreleased songs, and their 1953 version of Bill Haley's "Rock-A-Beatin' Boogie," which must rank as one of the first (if not the very first) covers of a White rock song by a Black artist. —*Richie Unterberger*

T. Rex

Group, Glam Rock, Rock & Roll
Initially a British folk-rock combo called Tyrannosaurus Rex, T. Rex was the primary force in glam rock, thanks to the creative direction of guitarist/vocalist Marc Bolan (born Marc Feld, September 30, 1947— d. September 16, 1977). Bolan created a deliberately trashy form of rock & roll that was proud of its own disposability. T. Rex's music borrowed the underlying sexuality of early rock & roll, adding dirty, simple grooves and fat distorted guitars, as well as an overarching folkie/hippie spirituality that always came through the clearest on ballads. While most of his peers concentrated on making cohesive albums, Bolan kept the idea of a three-minute pop single alive in the early '70s. In Britain, he became a superstar, sparking a period of "T. Rextacy" among the pop audience with a series of Top Ten hits, including four number one singles. Over in America, Bolan only had one major hit—the Top Ten "Bang a Gong (Get It On)"—before disappearing from the charts in 1973. T. Rex's popularity in the U.K. didn't begin to waver until 1975, yet they retained a devoted following until Marc Bolan's death in 1977. Over the next two decades, Bolan has remained popular in the U.K. and the music of T. Rex has been remarkably influential on hard rock, punk, new wave, and alternative rock.

Following a career as a teenage model—which also included a feature article in *Town* magazine that profiled him as one of leaders of London's mod scene—Marc Bolan began performing music professionally in 1965, releasing his first single, "The Wizard," on Decca Records and appearing on *Ready Steady Go!* Bolan joined the psychedelic folk-rock combo John's Children in 1967, appearing on three unsuccessful singles before the group disbanded later that year. Following the breakup, he formed the folk duo Tyrannosaurus Rex with percussionist Steve Peregrine Took. The duo landed a record deal with a subsidiary of EMI in February 1968, recording their debut album with producer Tony Visconti. "Debora," the group's first single, peaked at number 34 in May of that year, setting the stage for the successful summer release of their debut album, *My People Were Fair and Had Sky in Their Hair, but Now They're Content to Wear Stars on Their Brow*, the album reached number 15 on the U.K. charts. The duo released their second album, *Prophets, Seers and Sages, the Angels of the Ages*, in November of 1968.

By this time, Tyrannosaurus Rex was building a sizable underground following, which helped Bolan's book of poetry, *The Warlock of Love*, enter the British best-seller charts. In the summer of 1969, the duo released their third album, *Unicorn*, as well as the single "King of the Rumbling Sprires," the first Tyrannosaurus Rex song to feature an electric guitar. Following an unsuccessful American tour that fall, Took left the band and was replaced by Mickey Finn. The new duo's first single did not chart, yet their first album, 1970's *A Beard of Stars*, reached number 21. *A Beard of Stars* picked up the electric experiments of "King of the Rumbling Spires," while remaining essentially folky in spirit.

The turning point in Bolan's career came in October of 1970, when he shortened the group's name to T. Rex and released "Ride a White Swan," a fuzz-drenched single driven by a rolling backbeat. "Ride a White Swan" became a major hit in the U.K., climbing all the way to number two. The band's next album, T. Rex, peaked at number 13 and stayed on the charts for six months. Encouraged by the results, Bolan expanded T. Rex to a full band, adding bassist Steve Currie and drummer Bill Fifield (who Bolan renamed Bill Legend, due to his membership in Mickey Jupp's group, Legend). The new lineup recorded "Hot Love," which spent six weeks at number one in early 1971. That summer, T. Rex released "Get It On" (retitled "Bang a Gong (Get It On)" in the U.S.), which became their second straight U.K. number one; the single would go on to be their biggest international hit, reaching number ten in the U.S. in 1972. *Electric Warrior*, the first album recorded by the full band, was released in the fall of 1971; it was number one for six weeks in Britain and cracked America's Top 40. "Jeepster," released as a single without Bolan's permission, reached number two on the charts.

By now, "T. Rextacy" was in full swing in England, as the band had captured the imaginations of both teenagers and the media with its sequined, heavily made-up look; the image of Marc Bolan in a top hat, feather boa, and platform shoes, performing "Get It On" on BBC television became as memorable as his music. At the beginning of 1972, T. Rex signed with EMI, setting up a distribution deal for Bolan's own T.Rex Wax Co. record label. "Telegram Sam," the group's first EMI single, became their third number one single. Following the success of "Telegram Sam," T. Rex played two sold-out concerts at Empire Pool in Wembley, London for crowds of 100,000; the shows were filmed by Ringo Starr for his documentary about the band, called *Born to Boogie*. After a reissued single of "Debora"/"One Inch Rock" hit number seven, the new single, "Metal Guru" became the band's fourth number one single, spending four weeks at the top of the chart. *The Slider*, released in the summer of 1972, shot to number four upon its release, allegedly selling 100,000 copies in four days; the album was also T. Rex's most successful American release, reaching number 17.

Appearing in the spring of 1973, *Tanx* was another Top Five hit for T. Rex; the singles "20th Century Boy" and "The Groover" soon followed it to the upper ranks of the charts. However, those singles would prove to be the band's last two Top Ten hits. In the summer of 1973, rhythm guitarist Jack Green joined the band, as did three backup vocalists, including the American soul singer Gloria Jones; Jones would soon become Bolan's girlfriend. In August, Bolan released "Blackjack" under the name Marc Bolan with Big Carrot, yet the single failed to chart. At the beginning of 1974, drummer Bill Legend left the group and was replaced by Davy Lutton, as Jones became the group's keyboardist.

In early 1974, the single "Teenage Dream" was the first record to be released under the name Marc Bolan and T. Rex. The following album, *Zinc Alloy and the Hidden Riders of Tomorrow*, was the last Bolan recorded with Tony Visconti. Throughout the year, T. Rex's popularity rapidly declined; "Teenage Dream" hit number 13 early in the year, but by the time "Zip Gun Boogie" was released in November, it could only reach number 41. Finn and Green left the group at the end of the year, while keyboardist Dino Dins joined. The decline of T. Rex's popularity was confirmed by the performance of 1975's *Bolan's Zip Gun*, which failed to even make the charts. Bolan took the rest of the year off, taking care of his new baby, Rolan, and recording a new album.

Released in the spring of 1976, *Futuristic Dragon* featured some disco experiments, yet it was more successful than *Zip Gun*, peaking at number 50 on the charts. Released in the summer of 1976, "I Love to Boogie," a disco-flavored three-chord thumper, became Bolan's last Top 20 hit. By this time, none of the original T. Rex members outside of Bolan remained in the group. For T. Rex's tour at the end of the year, the band was comprised entirely of session players; ironically, the opening act for that tour was the Damned, one of the first British punk bands.

Bolan released *Dandy in the Underworld* in the spring of 1977; it was a modest hit, peaking at number 26. While "The Soul of My Suit" reached number 42 on the charts, T. Rex's next two singles—"Dandy in the Underworld" and "Celebrate Summer"—failed to chart. Sensing it was time for a change of direction, Bolan began expanding his horizons in August. In addition to contributing a weekly column for *Record Mirror*, he hosted his own variety television show, called *Marc*. Featuring guest appearances by artists like David Bowie and Generation X, Marc helped restore Bolan's hip image. Signing with RCA Records, the guitarist formed a new band with bassist Herbie Flowers and drummer Tony Newman, yet he never was able to record with the group. While driving home from a London club, Gloria Jones lost control of her car, smashing into a tree. Marc Bolan, riding in the passenger's seat of the car, was killed instantly; he was two weeks away from his thirtieth birthday.

While T. Rex's music was intended to be disposable, it has proven surprisingly influential over the years. Hard rock and heavy metal bands borrowed the heavily made-up image, as well as the pounding insistence of their guitars. Punk bands may have

discarded the high heels, feather boas, and top hats that made T. Rex infamous, yet they adhered to the simple three-chord structures and pop aesthetics that made the band popular. This connection was made particularly clear when punk led to post-punk, and groups like Bauhaus began covering T. Rex. Throughout the '80s, traces of T. Rex's music could be found in groups as diverse as Def Leppard, the Pixies, Flaming Lips, and Power Station. Prince took "Cream," a "Bang a Gong" tribute, to the top of the charts in 1991; Oasis followed a similar path with their U.K. hit "Cigarettes and Alcohol" in 1994. T. Rex may have been scorned at the time—and Marc Bolan may have never intended that his music have a lasting impact—yet their records helped shape modern rock & roll. — *Stephen Thomas Erlewine*

My People Were Fair / 1968 / Regal Zonophone ✦✦

Prophet Seers & Sages / 1968 / Regal Zonophone ✦✦

Unicorn / 1969 / Blue Thumb ✦✦✦

Beard of Stars / 1970 / Regal Zonophone ✦✦✦

T Rex / 1970 / Fly ✦✦✦

T. Rex's self-titled first album was still heavily indebted to Marc Bolan's folk roots, even featuring a revamped version of "One Inch Rock," but it showed that hints of the trashy rock and pop synthesis that would come to a fruition on T. Rex's next album, *Electric Warrior*. —*Stephen Thomas Erlewine*

★ **Electric Warrior** / 1971 / Reprise ✦✦✦✦✦

Kicking off with the fat guitars of "Mambo Sun," *Electric Warrior* winds through all of Marc Bolan's obsessions, from sleazy teenage rock & roll to spacy mysticism. "Bang a Gong (Get It On)" was the well-deserved hit, full of lust and flamboyance, but it's by no means the only good thing here. With the trashy blues stomps of "Jeepster" and "Lean Woman Blues" sitting next to the space-age rock of "Monolith" and "Planet Queen," *Electric Warrior* has nothing but teenage kicks; it's glam rock at its absolute best. Without question, the definitive, classic T. Rex. —*Stephen Thomas Erlewine*

☆ **The Slider** / Jan. 1972 / Relativity ✦✦✦✦✦

Surprisingly, *The Slider* was T. Rex's highest-charting record, without the benefit of a hit single. Even without a hit, the record was a gas, powered by the killer riffs of "Baby Strange," "Buick Makane," and "Telegram Sam." *The Slider* offers nothing new—it's still the same trashy glam-rock that made *Electric Warrior* and *Tanx* sublime—but that's why it's special. No one else could get away with "Metal Guru," "Baby Boomerang," and "Chariot Choogle" without seeming like a fool. Bolan does it with style and grace, and with a wink. It's tremendous fun and the last great record he would ever make. —*Stephen Thomas Erlewine*

○ **Tanx** / Feb. 1973 / Relativity ✦✦✦✦

Although the songs are not quite as well-constructed as those on *Electric Warrior*, *Tanx* still finds Bolan and T. Rex in top form, storming through a set of songs that kick hard, like "Country Honey," swing, like "Mad Donna," and sigh, like "Brokenhearted Blues." It's prime T. Rex and a terrific record. —*Stephen Thomas Erlewine*

Zinc Alloy & the Hidden Riders / 1974 / Combat ✦✦

Coming after a series of well-constructed and best-selling albums, *Zinc Alloy and the Hidden Riders of Tomorrow* was a bit of a disappointment, with a good majority of the material seeming forced and incomplete, but the swaggering "Venus Loon" and "Teenage Dream" make up for the weaker moments. —*Stephen Thomas Erlewine*

Zip Gun / 1975 / EMI ✦✦

Bolan's *Zip Gun* was an improvement over the stilted, over-produced *Zinc Alloy*, featuring a relatively stripped-back production and a number of tight rockers, including "Light of Love" and "Token of My Love." —*Stephen Thomas Erlewine*

Futuristic Dragon / 1976 / Relativity ✦✦✦

Marc Bolan tried to make T. Rex's sound more contemporary on *Futuristic Dragon*, adding elements of disco and soul. Nevertheless, his simple, swaggering rock & roll was the dominant musical approach on the album, which featured his most consistent set of songs since *Tanx*. —*Stephen Thomas Erlewine*

Dandy in the Underworld / 1977 / Relativity ✦✦✦

Dandy in the Underworld abandoned the disco experiments of *Futuristic Dragon* for a more direct rock & roll approach that recalled the early T. Rex albums. The material wasn't quite as strong as *Tanx* or even *Zip Gun*, but there were a handful of stomping rockers that ranked with the best of his work. —*Stephen Thomas Erlewine*

20th Century Boy / 1985 / Relativity ✦✦✦
20th Century Boy is a solid compilation that features most of his hits, but not necessarily all of his best material. A serviceable introduction, but nothing more. —*Stephen Thomas Erlewine*

Essential Collection / 1991 / Relativity ✦✦
T. Rex is worthy of a great box set, but *The Essential Collection* isn't it. Bypassing all of Bolan's earlier folk work, the set has no cohesion—it's just a bunch of tracks piled together haphazardly. "Jeepster," not "Bang a Gong (Get It On)," is the only track from *Electric Warrior* to make the box, leaving their best record woefully underrepresented; the box concentrates on the spottier records from the mid-'70s. Ultimately, *The Essential Collection* does a disservice to T. Rex. —*Stephen Thomas Erlewine*

Rabbit Fighter (The Alternate Slider) / 1994 / Edsel ✦✦
When Edsel Records reissued the T. Rex catalog with bonus tracks in 1994, they also began releasing alternate versions of each of T. Rex's albums, compiled from alternate takes and demos of the finished records, as well as adding alternate versions of the B-sides. *Rabbit Fighter: The Alternate Slider* was the first in the series and it reveals the depths of Marc Bolan's musical vision, as all of the arrangements of the final album were already sketched out on the demo tapes. Casual fans might find *Rabbit Fighter* tedious, but it's a goldmine for dedicated followers. —*Stephen Thomas Erlewine*

○ **Definitive Tyrannosaurus Rex** / 1994 / Sequel ✦✦✦✦
Featuring over 20 tracks of prime Tyrannosaurus Rex material, *The Definitive Tyrannosaurus Rex* is indeed the definitive portrait of Marc Bolan's early years. —*Stephen Thomas Erlewine*

Unchained / 1995 / Demon ✦✦
As part of their T. Rex reissue series, Edsel Records began releasing a series of discs that compiled all of Marc Bolan's outtakes and demos on a year-by-year basis. *T. Rex Unchained: Unreleased Recordings* is certainly designed with the fan in mind—several of the songs are unfinished and the liner notes are lovingly detailed—but the discs prove that Bolan was holding back material that was the equal of what he released, so they may be of interest even to casual fans. —*Stephen Thomas Erlewine*

Left Hand Luke / 1995 / Demon ✦✦
Left Hand Luke: The Alternate Tanx is quite similar to *Rabbit Fighter* in its presentation and content, presenting a fascinating working version of *Tanx*. Again, the album is primarily of interest to dedicated fans, but it is a compelling listen. —*Stephen Thomas Erlewine*

A Tribe Called Quest

Group, Rap
The junior part of the Native Tongues—the prolific Afrocentric family from New York that also includes the Jungle Brothers and De La Soul—this foursome displayed intriguing subject variety on their debut, covering everything from social ills to the adventures of a shaggy dog and problems with lice. Their second effort, *The Low End Theory*, reflected through arrangements and sensibility the influence of an emerging jazz/rap stylistic coalition, and yielded a huge hit in "Scenario."

A Tribe Called Quest modified their jazz ties with *Midnight Marauders* in 1993. Though it still had an improvisational undergirding, the raps were tougher, the production tighter and the beats more unpredictable and varied. —*Ron Wynn*

People's Instinctive Travels and the Paths of Rhythm / 1990 / Jive ✦✦✦
People's Instinctive Travels and the Paths of Rhythm is a brilliant concept with jazzy edges and tense, biting narratives. It's a visionary release blending the improvisatory force of jazz with the technological wizardry and verbal inventiveness of hip-hop. —*Ron Wynn*

★ **The Low End Theory** / 1991 / Jive ✦✦✦✦✦
Excellent raps and production. —*Ron Wynn*

○ **Midnight Marauders** / 1993 / Jive ✦✦✦✦
Midnight Marauders was an intriguing and smartly paced collection that ranged from descriptive verbal essays on city life to confrontational taunts, comic expositions, denunciations, and even quasi-religious theorizing. While their celebrated hip-hop/jazz roots were often evident, the group also utilized fusion, urban contemporary, Afro-Latin and funk samples, while Q-Tip's rap style

could be cool and deadpan, reflective, analytical, satirical, or disgusted and angry. There was precious little "gangsta" posturing or sexist rhetoric, and such numbers as "Sucka Nigga," "God Lives Through," "Electric Relaxation" and "Award Tour" were cleverly delivered and brilliantly composed. —*Ron Wynn*

Tricky

Alternative Pop/Rock, Dance
An inventive, colorful musician, Tricky began recording with the seminal hip-hop/techno outfit Massive Attack in 1990. In 1992, he discovered vocalist Martine and started recording tracks with her, and formed the group Tricky. Their sound is both hard-hitting and surprisingly ethereal, mixing the chatting rap style of Tricky with Martine's smooth yet slightly abrasive singing. Trick samples Smashing Pumpkins, covers Public Enemy songs, and yet still remains entirely unique from the groups it is compared with, such as Massive Attack and Portishead. —*Heather Phares*

● **Maxinquaye** / 1995 / 4th & Broadway ✦✦✦✦
Though he hates the label of trip-hop, Tricky's debut album *Maxinquaye* is one of the finest that the genre has to offer. "Ponderosa," "Suffocated Love," and "Pumpkin" are disturbing and beautiful, with ominous background noises and Martine's soaring vocals, while tracks like the group's cover of "Black Steel" show off their harder side. A striking debut, Tricky's *Maxinquaye* is only the beginning for this innovative artist. —*Heather Phares*

The Troggs

Group, British Invasion
Remembered chiefly as proto-punkers who reached the top of the charts with the "caveman rock" of "Wild Thing" (1966), the Troggs were also adept at crafting power-pop and ballads. Hearkening back to a somewhat simpler, more basic British Invasion approach as psychedelia began to explode in the late '60s, the group also reached the Top Five with their flower-power ballad "Love Is All Around" in 1968. While more popular in their native England than the U.S., the band also fashioned memorable, insistently riffing hit singles like "With a Girl like You," "Night of the Long Grass," and the notoriously salacious "I Can't Control Myself" between 1966 and 1968. Paced by Reg Presley's lusting vocals, the group—which composed most of their own material—could crunch with the best of them, but were also capable of quite a bit more range and melodic invention than they've been given credit for. The hits dried up after 1968, but the group continued to work, record, and produce the odd memorable tracks well into the '70s. —*Richie Unterberger*

● **The Best of the Troggs** / 1988 / PolyGram ✦✦✦✦
"Wild Thing" is the hit, but there's lots of good, raunchy rock here. —*Dan Heilman*

○ **Archeology (1967-1977)** / 1992 / Fontana ✦✦✦✦
A double-CD, 52-track box set that proves there was a lot more to the Troggs than "Wild Thing" and "Love Is All Around." This archetypally primitive British Invasion quartet scored many hits in the U.K. that barely dented the charts in the U.S., like "With A Girl Like You," "Night Of The Long Grass," and the notoriously racy "I Can't Control Myself." They're all here, along with notable album cuts, B-sides, and worldwide post-1968 flops. Primitive they may have been, but the Troggs—who wrote most of their own material—did not lack a flair for hard pop hooks, and could display a surprising delicacy in their ballads. Several of their obscure singles and album tracks are equal in worth to their hits, like the gothic but pretty "Cousin Jane," and the witty light psychedelia of "Maybe the Madman" and "Purple Shades." Some of the '70s hard rockers and glammish novelties are unimpressive, and 52 songs are arguably excessive. But there are a fair number of obscure gems to be found on this well-annotated package. —*Richie Unterberger*

Athens Andover / 1992 / Rhino ✦✦✦
Most comeback albums never work; *Athens Andover* is the rare exception that does. Backed by members of R.E.M. and the dB's, the Troggs make some of their best pop ever, full of ringing guitars and chiming melodies. —*Stephen Thomas Erlewine*

Doris Troy

Soul, Pop
Surely one of the most talented one-hit wonders of the rock era, Doris Troy hit the Top Ten with "Just One Look" in 1963, but also

recorded many other fine pop-soul sides for Atlantic between 1963 and 1965. Unlike many soul performers of the time, Troy wrote most of her own material (under the pseudonym Payne), and had already written for other artists, and sung backup with Dionne and Dee Dee Warwick and Cissy Houston on New York soul records, before striking out on her own. More melodically ambitious and stylistically eclectic than many of her peers, her Atlantic sides blend elements of gospel, girl group, blues, and pop into a rich New York soul sound. Troy never reached the charts again after "Just One Look," but was more appreciated in England, where she toured occasionally, and where the Hollies covered her "What'cha Gonna Do About It" on their first album. Moving to Britain, she recorded an album for Apple in 1970 with assistance from George Harrison and Billy Preston. In the early '70s, she sang backup vocals for British rock groups, as well as recording a couple more albums. In the '80s, she starred in *Mama I Want to Sing*, a musical based on her life story. *—Richie Unterberger*

Doris Troy / 1970 / Capitol ♦♦♦
An all-star cast supported Troy on her lone Apple effort: George Harrison, Billy Preston, Peter Frampton, Stephen Stills, Klaus Voormann, Jackie Lomax, Eric Clapton, Leon Russell, and Delaney & Bonnie all contributed, and Harrison, Stills, Lomax, Preston, Voormann, and Ringo Starr pitched in on the songwriting, though Troy wrote or co-wrote most of the songs. Well-received by some critics, it really doesn't add up to the sum of its parts. Troy is in great voice, but much of the material is pedestrian, and the heavy rock/soul arrangements often have an over-beefy, early-'70s super-session feel. It works best when Troy puts the brakes on the hard rock to deliver emotional, slower soul tunes. The CD reissue adds five interesting cuts from non-LP singles and outtakes. *—Richie Unterberger*

● **Just One Look: The Best Of Doris Troy** / 1994 / Ichiban/Soul Classics ♦♦♦♦
This 21-track anthology of her 1963-65 Atlantic sides is as comprehensive as one could ask for. It includes all of her singles, her rare album, three cuts only issued on British singles, and her rare 1965 single for the Calla label, "I'll Do Anything (He Wants Me To Do)." Besides "Just One Look," there are quite a few other downright excellent lost gems here: "What'cha Gonna Do About It," the bluesy "Draw Me Closer," the driving "You'd Better Stop" (with a fierce guitar break that sounds like a young Jimmy Page), and the soulful wall of sound on "I'll Do Anything." "How My Heart Aches" is a special standout that ranks among the very finest wrenching, melancholy soul ever waxed. Much more than a collector's item, this proves Troy to be a genuinely overlooked major talent. *—Richie Unterberger*

Tsunami

Group, Alternative Pop/Rock
Tsunami are a punk-pop band from Arlington, Virginia. Guitarist/vocalist Jenny Toomey (also of Grenadine and Licorice) and Kristin Thomson (bass) run their own record label, Simple Machines, on which they release their own material and works from like-minded artists (such as Scrawl). Like many indie bands, Tsunami have appeared on a plethora of singles and EPs since their 1990 inception. They released their first full-length album, *Deep End*, in 1993 and followed it up with *The Heart's Tremelo* in 1994. A much-needed singles compilation was released in 1995. Their mix of politics, melodicism and heavy guitars make them a strong and respected voice in the alternative community. *—Heather Phares*

● **Deep End** / May 31, 1993 / SMA ♦♦♦♦

The Tubes

Group, Pop/Rock
The Tubes were fronted by vocalist Fee Waybill. Taking their cue from Frank Zappa's Mothers of Invention, the Tubes were one of the first to bring performance art (albeit with a satirical edge) to arena rock & roll. By the early '80s they had toned their image down to a more commercial, MTV-acceptable format. *—Cub Koda*

The Tubes / 1975 / A&M ♦♦♦
The debut album for the Tubes, featuring the anthem "White Punks on Dope." *—Cub Koda*

○ **Young & Rich** / 1976 / A&M ♦♦♦♦
Their breakthrough album and the best representation of the band's early days. *—Cub Koda*

What Do You Want from Life / 1978 / A&M ♦♦♦
A great live album, featuring a good sampling from their mind-boggling '70s stage act. *—Cub Koda*

● **The Best of the Tubes** / Nov. 9, 1992 / Capitol ♦♦♦♦
The Best of the Tubes is the best Tubes disc available, containing all of their hits and trademark songs. *—AMG*

Maureen Tucker

Alternative Pop/Rock
When the Velvet Underground was America's most admired avant-garde rock band, it was easy to imagine solo success for principal songwriter Lou Reed and enigmatic Welsh multi-instrumentalist John Cale, but no one could have predicted that some of the best solo recordings from a former member of this seminal band would come from drummer Maureen (Moe) Tucker. After the demise of the Velvets, Tucker lived in relative obscurity in Douglas, Georgia, raising her children and working for minimum wage at a Wal-Mart—salient points that form the thematic basis of her solo career. No longer strictly a drummer, Tucker switched to guitar, and with the help of a new generation of avant-rock players (Half Japanese's Jad and David Fair, Daniel Johnston, Sonic Youth) and longtime pals (Lou Reed) began recording terse, guitar-driven songs about single motherhood, working hard for minimum wage, and hating the corporatization of rock & roll. These were proud, no-bullshit, pissed-off songs that found a home on the wonderfully idiosyncratic indie label 50 Skidillion Watts, principally owned by Velvets fan Penn Jillette (of the comedy/magic duo Penn and Teller), who gave Tucker a regular outlet for her music. Occasionally, Tucker has had to return to the underpaying world of 9-5 to supplement her rock & roll income, but as she released more records, her popularity in alternative-rock circles has grown (especially in Europe) to the point where she can make a living as a full-time musician. Good news indeed! *—John Dougan*

● **Playin' Possum** / 1981 / Trash ♦♦♦♦
Moe is the whole show on her 1981 debut, singing and playing drums, guitars, bass, and a variety of other instruments. Consisting mostly of raw and primitive covers of rock & roll oldies by Bo Diddley, Little Richard, and Chuck Berry, she also throws in a version of "Heroin" and covers of Dylan's "I'll Be Your Baby Tonight" and Vivaldi's "Concerto In D Major," as well as the "original" "Ellas," which is a six-minute extrapolation of the basic Bo Diddley beat. This inspired lesson in rock & roll auteurism is probably her best effort. *—Richie Unterberger*

Moejadkatebarry / 1987 / 50 Skidillion Watts ♦♦♦

○ **Life in Exile after Abdication** / 1989 / 50 Skidillion Watts ♦♦♦♦
Fantastic. Wonderfully dry, witty and sarcastic songs about everyday life, *Life in Exile* features help from Lou Reed and Sonic Youth and terrific songs like the Andy Warhol eulogy "Andy" and a great cover of the Velvets' "Pale Blue Eyes." Best of all, though, is the working-class lament "Spam Again," which, more than most songs about stretching paychecks, connects with equal amounts of anger and humor. *—John Dougan*

○ **I Spent a Week There the Other Night** / 1991 / Young God ♦♦♦♦
With more help from her indie-rock bigshot pals (Don Fleming, Brian Ritchie), *Week* also featured the first (sort of) Velvet Underground reunion, with Cale, Reed and Sterling Morrison guesting on separate tracks. Covering "And Then He Kissed Me" was inspired, as is the inclusion of the accusatory (and appropriately titled) "Fired Up." From start to finish, it rocks like crazy. *—John Dougan*

The Turbans

Group, Doo-Wop
Decked out in their trademark headgear, the Turbans scorched the R&B charts in 1955 with "When You Dance." This teenage quartet from Philadelphia signed with Al Silver's Herald imprint. They debuted with the Latin-beat classic "When You Dance," with Al Banks's (b. Jul 26, 1937) high-flying falsetto prominent. "Sister Sookey" was a worthy upbeat followup for the group in early 1956 but failed to chart, as did three more fine 1956-1958 outings on Herald that met the same undeserved fate. The Turbans went on to record for Imperial and Roulette, with no tangible results. Banks later worked with one of the leading groups of Drifters populating the '70s lounge circuit before his death. *—Bill Dahl*

● **The Best of the Turbans** / 1985 / Collectables ♦♦♦♦
This features "When You Dance" and other mid-'50s doo-wop gems, with sax-led small-combo backing. A glimpse into a bygone era. *—Hank Davis*

Big Joe Turner (Joseph Vernon Turner)

b. May 18, 1911, Kansas City, MO, **d.** Nov. 24, 1985, Inglewood, CA

R&B, Jump Blues

Big Joe Turner enjoyed stardom in two related, but quite different eras. The Big Chill generation appreciates Turner for his contribution to rock & roll; those who know pre-rock history cherish his vocal contributions to the boogie-woogie and Kansas City jazz eras. He was among the greatest, most vociferous shouters ever, able to holler and roar above a striding big band, yet also fit his huge sound into situations with boogie-woogie players relying on timing and pace. Turner was tending bar and singing at age 14 in Kansas City. Known as the "singing bandleader," the youth attracted the attention of such bandleaders as Bennie Moten, Andy Kirk and Count Basie. He and pianist Pete Johnson became great friends and a popular touring act in the late '30s and the '40s. After his appearance with Johnson at the "Spirituals to Swing" Carnegie Hall concert in 1938, Turner made his first recordings, notably the spectacular "Roll 'Em Pete." Turner's huge voice half shouts, half sings, with the piece's tension superbly developed via his use of repeated phrases and Johnson's rumbling, churning riffs and accompaniment. Turner was an equally gifted slow blues and ballad stylist, and his work with pianists and bands reflected his fluidity, knowledge of inflections and ability to develop themes and embellish lyrics. He recorded with Joe Sullivan, Benny Carter and Art Tatum among others. But his early '50s R&B hits "Still in the Dark," "Chains of Love" and "Sweet Sixteen" were forerunners of a new era. "Honey Hush" and "Shake, Rattle and Roll" marked Joe Turner's move to the pop arena, even though cover versions of both songs did better sales wise than his originals. But after his rock success ebbed, Turner returned to the jazzy blues he'd always done; he made fine dates in the '70s with Count Basie, the Trumpet Kings, Cleanhead Eddie Vinson, and Jimmy Witherspoon. In 1983, two years before his death, Turner recorded with Roomful of Blues. —*Ron Wynn and John Floyd*

★ **Greatest Hits** / Apr. 19, 1951-Jan. 22, 1958 / Atlantic ◆◆◆◆◆
These are Turner's finest early-rock-era recordings, including his best and best-known) hits and some tasty obscurities. A must-have. —*John Floyd*

○ **Big, Bad & Blue: The Big Joe Turner Anthology** / 1994 / Rhino ◆◆◆◆
A comprehensive, three-CD collection, *Big, Bad & Blue* is the only truly definitive Joe Turner compilation available, complete with stunning audio and terrific liner notes; it stands as a testament to the lasting influence of this seminal jump blues/R&B shouter. New fans will want to stick with the single-disc *Greatest Hits*, because the sheer weight of *Big, Bad & Blue* is a little intimidating. —*Stephen Thomas Erlewine*

○ **Jumpin' with Joe: The Complete Aladdin & Imperial Recordings** / Jan. 11, 1994 / EMI America ◆◆◆◆
Big Joe Turner's remarkable recordings for Atlantic and Decca have been frequently reissued and evaluated. But his singles for other labels haven't gotten similar treatment, which makes this 18-cut single-disc anthology of Aladdin and Imperial material so welcome. These were recorded in the late '40s and early '50s and were closer to the Kansas City swing Turner had done earlier in his career; there was more emphasis on lyric interpretation, swing, and timing than sheer volume and volcanic, non-stop hollering. Although these songs aren't remembered as fondly as the landmark Atlantic numbers, they're just as important a part of Turner's legacy. —*Ron Wynn*

Tell Me Pretty Baby / Arhoolie ◆◆◆
Nice late-'40s compilation with Pete Johnson's Boogie 88s. —*Bill Dahl*

Ike Turner

Group, Soul, R&B

It is arguably true that Ike Turner would have never amounted to more than a footnote in rock history if he hadn't joined forces with Tina Turner in 1960. But as a solo artist, he's an important footnote. In 1951, he made a lasting contribution to the music by playing piano on Jackie Brenston's "Rocket 88," which is often cited as one of the very first rock & roll records. That session was one of the first blues/R&B/rock & roll dates produced in Sun Studios in Memphis; Turner learned guitar shortly afterwards, and backed up other R&B artists at Sun in the early '50s. Throughout the

decade, the guitarist and piano player was a prolific session player, contributing to records by blues legends Elmore James, Howlin' Wolf, and Otis Rush.

Ike also backed a host of obscure R&B artists in his early years, occasionally issuing discs under his name. Not much of a singer, both his own records and the ones he contributed to and/or produced often showcased his stinging, bluesy licks, and the best of his solo outings tended to be his instrumentals. He continued to put out the occasional solo session and work with other artists after he hooked up with Tina, sometimes under the name Ike Turner's Kings of Rhythm. His career has lurched along in obscurity since he broke up with Tina in the mid-'70s, though he remains active. —*Richie Unterberger*

● **I Like Ike! The Best of Ike Turner** / 1994 / Rhino ◆◆◆◆
Eighteen songs spotlighting Turner's work as a bandleader, guitarist, and solo artist from 1951 to 1972, concentrating heavily on his work in the 1950s and early '60s. Leading off with Jackie Brenston's classic "Rocket 88," it includes rare singles featuring Turner by Dennis Binder, the Sly Fox, Willie King, and others, along with rare Turner solo recordings, some under the pseudonym Icky Renrut, and a 1958 45 with Tina, then known as Annie Mae Bullock, on backing vocals. These singers are usually journeymen, frankly, and the material is rather standard-issue R&B; better are the instrumentals, which give Ike a chance to really strut his distinctive tone. —*Richie Unterberger*

○ **1958-1959** / Flyright ◆◆◆◆
Ever the hustler, Ike Turner found himself picking up some extra money on a road trip through Chicago recording for Cobra Records both as a bandleader and sideman. After contributing the sparkle to several Otis Rush classics (an alternate of one of them, "Keep on Loving Me Baby" is found here) and some early Buddy Guy sides, Turner also recorded a handful of sides, scant few of them seeing release until now. This CD collects them all up, including surviving alternate versions and is a delightful fly on the wall invite to a '50s Chicago blues session. —*Cub Koda*

Ike and Tina Turner

Group, Soul, R&B

There was a time when the Ike and Tina Turner Revue was one of the hottest, most durable, and potentially most explosive of all R&B ensembles. Fronted by Tina, with one of the rawest, most sensual and impossibly dynamic voices in Black music, the Ike and Tina Revue was an ensemble that dripped musical discipline while manifesting nearly unbearable tension, eventually giving way to wave upon wave of catharsis.

Their story is a long and convoluted one. Ike was born in 1931 in Clarksdale, MS; Tina was born Anna Mae Bullock in 1938 in Nutbush, TN. They met in 1959 in East St. Louis, where Ike's Kings of Rhythm were the reigning patriarchs of the local R&B scene. Up to that point, Ike had been a DJ on WROX in Clarksdale, a talent scout and producer for Modern Records (waxing sides for the likes of B. B. King, Rosco Gordon, Elmore James, and Junior Parker), and a recording artist, his Kings of Rhythm appearing in one guise or another on Chess, Modern, King, Cobra, Artistic, and Stevens. Their most famous record, *Rocket 88*, appeared under the moniker "Jackie Brenston with his Delta Cats" in 1951. It played an integral part in jump-starting the rock & roll revolution.

Once Tina joined the Kings of Rhythm, life changed for all concerned. They recorded a demo of "A Fool in Love" in late 1959; by the autumn of 1960 the record was a number two R&B hit on Sue Records. "I Idolize You," "It's Gonna Work Out Fine," "Poor Fool," and "Tra La La La La" all quickly followed, giving the Revue five Top Ten R&B hits in two and a half years. All told, from 1960 to 1975 Ike and Tina Turner placed 25 records on the R&B charts for nine separate record companies. Their most successful pop recording was a reworking of Creedence Clearwater Revival's "Proud Mary" in 1971. —*Rob Bowman*

○ **River Deep & Mountain High** / 1966 / A&M ◆◆◆◆
These sessions, recorded in 1966, were produced by Phil Spector. Spector's production chops and Tina's voice were a match made in heaven. Tina possesses one of the strongest voices ever committed to wax; Spector envelops it in the grandest version of his Wall of Sound that he ever conceived. Besides the title track, Spector cut the Turners redoing their first three chart hits, "A Fool in Love," "I Idolize You," and "It's Gonna Work Out Fine." Although it's a sacrilege to say so, these versions are better than the originals. Finally, Turner's performance of the obscure Holland-Dozier-Holland ditty

"A Love like Yours" bowls me over with every listen. —*Rob Bowman*

Workin' Together / 1970 / Liberty ✦✦✦
The most successful album ever issued by Ike and Tina Turner, this contains their best message song in the title selection, plus arguably their best-known song in their version of "Proud Mary" and a good cover of "Ooh Poo Pah Doo." Things went plunging downhill from here, as Tina Turner's autobiography vividly detailed years later. —*Ron Wynn*

○ **Nutbush City Limits** / 1973 / United Artists ✦✦✦✦
The album that marked the end of the Ike and Tina Turner alliance, although it wasn't their last album. But the turmoil that they were undergoing off stage would soon shatter their personal and professional union. They scored a major international hit with the title cut, and also told their life story, although it turned out that this tale was a fantasy. Here's one of the few Ike and Tina Turner albums that deserves to be back in print. —*Ron Wynn*

● **Proud Mary: The Best of Ike & Tina Turner** / Mar. 18, 1991 / EMI America ✦✦✦✦
Proud Mary—The Best of Ike and Tina Turner is a fine 23-track collection that looks at the Turners' career at the beginning and the end. Their early-'60s hits on Juggy Murray's Sue label are included, as are their early- and mid-'70s successes on Liberty and United Artists. The mid- and late-'60s recordings for Kent, Loma, Modern, Innis, Blue Thumb, and Minit are not here, unfortunately. Superior liner notes round out a fine package. —*Rob Bowman*

Tina Turner (Annie Mae Bullock)

b. Nov. 26, 1938, Nutbush, Tennessee
Soul, R&B, Pop/Rock
The woman who taught the world how to dance in high heels, Tina Turner has never been less than electrifying. Her full-throated rasp, full of low-note rumblings and soulful shrieks, is one of the most distinctive in any field of music, and her overtly sexual stage presence is nothing short of mesmerizing. The early part of her career, with then-husband Ike Turner, has been well documented (see entry for Ike and Tina Turner), but she really hit her stride and found a whole new audience with the coming of the MTV generation, her solo career bringing her the acclaim that had been long overdue. —*Cub Koda*

● **Private Dancer** / 1984 / Capitol ✦✦✦✦
The one that won her a pile of awards, and rightly so, because it's simply her finest solo album. Using a multitude of producers and cut in a variety of locations, *Private Dancer* still sounds amazingly unified. Includes the title cut, "What's Love Got to Do with It," "Let's Stay Together," "Better Be Good to Me," and a blistering Jeff Beck solo on "Steel Claw." —*Cub Koda*

Break Every Rule / 1986 / Capitol ✦✦✦
A moderately successful Tina Turner album, but far from the levels she'd reached with *Private Dancer*. Turner sounded more like a comfortable, posturing singer than the dynamic, take-no-stuff vocalist of that album. "Typical Male" was a good put-down tune, and "Two People" and "What You Get Is What You See" came close to recapturing *Private Dancer*'s haughty/sassy mood, but the album was more a restatement than another step forward. —*Ron Wynn*

Tina Live in Europe / 1988 / Capitol ✦✦
A "live" 2-fer of her hits from the '60s to present. —*Bil Carpenter*

Foreign Affair / Sep. 13, 1989 / Capitol ✦✦✦
Uptempo funk and blues-style rock/dance music. —*Bil Carpenter*

○ **Simply the Best** / 1991 / Capitol ✦✦✦✦
A solid greatest-hits collection culled from her solo Capitol albums. Includes "Typical Male," "Steamy Windows" (written and produced by Tony Joe White), "I Can't Stand the Rain," and a duet with Rod Stewart on "It Takes Two." —*Cub Koda*

What's Love Got to Do with It / Jun. 15, 1993 / Capitol ✦✦✦
This is the soundtrack for the Tina Turner film that got Angela Bassett and Lawrence Fishburne Oscar nominations. There's little here that you couldn't get elsewhere in better versions, but if you only want a hint of the music Tina Turner made in various contexts, with and without Ike, this would be a serviceable purchase. Otherwise, get the film and hear the music in the correct setting. —*Ron Wynn*

Collected Recordings—Sixties to Nineties / 1994 / Capitol ✦✦✦
Over the course of three discs, *Collected Recordings—Sixties to Nineties* runs through most of Tina Turner's biggest hits, both with and without Ike Turner. However, the third disc comprises nothing but obscurities, making the collection a bit too much for anyone but the most devoted fans. —*Stephen Thomas Erlewine*

The Turtles

Group, Folk-Rock, Pop/Rock
The Turtles were a pop/rock quintet 1963-69, with varying personnel, though always featuring lead singer Howard Kaylan (b. Jun 22, 1945) and backup/harmony singer Mark Volman (b. Apr 19, 1944). Other original members were guitarists Al Nichol (b. Mar 31, 1945) and Jim Tucker, and bassist Chuck Portz (b. Nov 8, 1945). They began life as a surf band called the Crossfires, but by the time of their debut album on White Whale Records, they'd become a folk-rock group singing Bob Dylan songs including their first hit, "It Ain't Me Babe." More characteristic of their style, however, was the sweet pop hit "You Baby" of 1966. The Turtles topped the charts with "Happy Together" in 1967 and scored several more romantic pop hits before they split up at the end of the '60s, after which Kaylan and Volman hooked up with Frank Zappa in the Mothers, then performed on their own as Flo and Eddie. Today, they continue to perform under that name and as the Turtles. —*William Ruhlmann*

○ **It Ain't Me Babe** / 1965 / Rhino ✦✦✦✦
The Turtles' first album presents them as a folk-rock group covering a lot of Dylan and P. F. Sloan material. They also found "It Was a Very Good Year" on a Kingston Trio album and cut it. Frank Sinatra heard their version and had one of his bigger hits with it, but their version is good too. —*William Ruhlmann*

You Baby / 1966 / Rhino ✦✦✦
On their second album, the Turtles stuck to the same brand of sunny, commercial folk-rock as their debut. It's pleasant fare, but hardly in the same league as the Byrds, Lovin' Spoonful, or the Mamas & the Papas, and the group's original material is spotty and sometimes awkward. The best cuts are the ones penned by the Barri/Sloan songwriting team, including the hits "You Baby" and "Can I Get to Know You Better." —*Richie Unterberger*

○ **Happy Together** / 1967 / Rhino ✦✦✦✦
The Turtles's best studio album includes the title hit, "She'd Rather Be with Me," "Guide for the Married Man," and then-unknown Warren Zevon's "Like the Seasons," among other songs. —*William Ruhlmann*

Wooden Head / 1970 / Rhino ✦✦✦
In 1970, both White Whale Records and the Turtles, their biggest act, were on the verge of ending. This assortment of unreleased odds and ends from their early years was hastily assembled as a posthumous collection, although several of the tracks hadn't been properly finished. Surprisingly, it survives as one of their stronger albums, focusing almost exclusively on their early pop-folk-rock sound; arguably, it's better than either of their first two official LPs, perhaps because they weren't able to sweeten the tracks with superfluous overdubs. Besides several strong originals, it features interesting compositions by P.F. Sloan, David Gates, and Peter & Gordon. The Rhino reissue adds the nice folk-rocker "Is It Any Wonder?" and the odd, mordant, psychedelic-tinged 1966 flop single "Grim Reaper Of Love" as bonus tracks. The album has also been issued as a German import by Repertoire, also with bonus tracks. —*Richie Unterberger*

● **20 Greatest Hits** / 1983 / Rhino ✦✦✦✦
A witty and underrated band, the Turtles compiled this fine set themselves. —*Dan Heilman*

Twenty Twenty

Group, Power Pop/Anglo-Pop
20/20 was formed in Tulsa, Oklahoma, by high school friends Steve Allen (guitar, vocals) and Ron Flynt (bass, vocals). They relocated to Los Angeles in 1977, adding Mike Gallo on drums, and began playing local clubs. Greg Shaw, the head of Bomp! Records, was impressed with their highly charged power-pop and signed them to his label in 1978. The resulting single, "Under the Freeway," created enough interest in the band to secure a deal with Portrait Records. They added keyboardist Chris Sylgali and recorded their first LP, *20/20.* "Cheri" from the album saw some minor regional success but the album was virtually ignored apart

from critical acclaim. The follow-up, *Look Out!* (1981), was equally strong but again failed. The band was dropped by Portrait in 1982 and effectively disbanded. They returned in 1983 with the independently released *Sex Trap*, but by this time, their sound was out of style and the band finally called it quits. A revived interest in the genre in the '90s inspired the band to reunite, contributing a few new songs to Big Deal's *Yellow Pills* compilations and recording a new album for the fall of 1995. —*Chris Woodstra*

● **20/20** / 1980 / Portrait ✦✦✦✦
Released during the initial power-pop craze of the late '70s, the band's self-titled debut quickly stood out among the masses with its consistent quality, strict adherance to the melodic three-minute form, and tight, driving rhythm. Though the sales didn't reflect the strength of the album, songs like "Cheri" and "Yellow Pills" are considered classics of the period, the latter becoming the title for the premier power-pop fanzine, still in existence today. —*Chris Woodstra*

○ **Look Out!** / 1981 / Portrait ✦✦✦✦
An equally strong follow-up, *Look Out!*, is a pure pop artifact with its teen anthems discussing the "nuclear boys in the nuclear world," obsessing over girls (the haunting "Girl like You"), and telling the tale of a bizarre alien love affair (the silly "Alien"). *Look Out!* and *20/20* have been reissued as a two-fer CD on Oglio in 1995—an essential part of any power-pop collection. —*Chris Woodstra*

Sex Trap / 1984 / Teldec ✦✦
The mid-'80s were not kind to "skinny tie" bands like 20/20. By 1984, Portrait had dropped the band, forcing them to go independent with *Sex Trap*. As the title indicates, they shifted to a raunchier, harder rocking band, with all of the gloss of the previous efforts removed. A sad misstep. —*Chris Woodstra*

The Twilights
Group, Pop/Rock
One of the better Australian groups of the '60s, the Twilights were not especially innovative, but played competent, harmony-driven British Invasion-styled rock, strongly recalling both the "beat" and pseudo-psychedelic era Hollies. Relying largely on the original material of guitarist Terry Britten, they recorded over a dozen singles, as well as a couple albums, between 1965 and 1968, chalking up a few large Australian hits. Like many Australian stars of the period, they traveled to England for a while in an attempt to crack the international market, managing to record a few tracks in London with renowned producer/engineer Norman Smith (who had worked with the Beatles, Pink Floyd, Pretty Things, and others). Like other Australian acts in the U.K., with the exception of the Bee Gees and Easybeats, they totally failed in this regard, returning to Australia for more sporadic success in the homeland before disbanding in early 1969. —*Richie Unterberger*

● **The Way They Played** / 1989 / Raven ✦✦✦✦
Over 20 tracks of their best material, drawing largely on their Australian singles, most of them self-penned. —*Richie Unterberger*

Dwight Twilley
b. Jun. 6, 1951
Power Pop/Anglo-Pop
Dwight Twilley fused rockabilly, mid-'60s Anglo-pop, and Byrdsy jangle into a distinctly reverberant sound. In 1976 Twilley and his partner Phil Seymour released the exceptional number 16 Anglo-rockabilly hit "I'm on Fire" on Denny Cordell's Shelter label. Unfortunately, Shelter's lack of organization delayed the release of Twilley's debut album, *Sincerely*, by over a year. In spite of glowing reviews concerning the album's rich melodicism and sparkling production, *Sincerely* sank without a trace.

After the follow-up, *Twilley Don't Mind*, Twilley jumped ship for Arista, releasing a self-titled album. In spite of some brilliant power-pop ("Alone in My Room," "It Takes a Lotta Love"), problems arose at the label, and Twilley jumped again to EMI, releasing *Scuba Divers*. It was on his next album that he scored his next hit, "Girls." —*Rick Clark*

● **Sincerely** / 1976 / DCC ✦✦✦✦
From the opening Anglo-pop/rock-meets-rockabilly blast of the Top 20 hit single "I'm on Fire," through breezy jangle-rock numbers like "You're So Warm," "Just like the Sun," and "England," to the dirge-like psychedelia of the title song, *Sincerely* is Twilley's finest album. It's a must-own for fans of guitar pop/rock. The CD includes four bonus tracks. —*Rick Clark*

Twilley Don't Mind / 1977 / DCC ✦✦✦
Twilley drops the ball slightly on this second album, in spite of good tracks like "Looking for the Magic," "Here She Come," "Sleeping," and the title cut. —*Rick Clark*

○ **Twilley** / 1979 / Arista ✦✦✦✦
This self-titled third album rivals Twilley's debut as best album with super tracks like "Alone in My Room," "It Takes a Lot of Love," "Darlin'," and "I Want to Make Love to You." As of this printing, this fine pop/rock album has yet to see a CD release. If you like Twilley's other albums, then this is worth the search. —*Rick Clark*

○ **Scuba Divers** / 1982 / EMI ✦✦✦✦
1982's *Scuba Divers* continues the band's fine pop tradition though the material is not quite up to the standards of its predecessors. —*AMG*

○ **Jungle** / 1984 / EMI ✦✦✦✦
Twilley makes an unexpected return to the charts with the Top 20 hit single "Girls"; an equally enjoyable album. —*AMG*

The Great Lost Twilley Album / Apr. 1993 / Shelter ✦✦✦
This collection of unreleased tracks from 1974 to 1980 will please fans. Good songs, but the uninitiated should go to the first or third albums. —*Rick Clark*

Twisted Sister
Group, Hard Rock, Heavy Metal
Long Island metal band featuring lead singer Dee Snider, with guitarists Jay French and Eddie Ojeda, bassist Mark "The Animal" Mendoza (formerly of the Dictators), and drummer A.J. Pero. Their original purpose was to be the antithesis of disco, creating a bizarre, outrageous look for themselves with frizzy hair and heavy makeup. Musically, they played simple, melodic metal with consciously provocative lyrics and oft-repeated choruses. The group got a major push from MTV in 1984, as their image attracted the attention of teenage boys throughout the country. Their adolescent anthems "We're Not Gonna Take It" and "I Wanna Rock" pushed *Stay Hungry*'s sales into the double-platinum range. This proved to be the peak of their success, and they disbanded in 1987 when their label decided they had run out of ideas. Snider then formed Desperado. —*Steve Huey*

Under the Blade / 1982 / Secret ✦✦
You Can't Stop Rock 'n' Roll / 1983 / Atlantic ✦✦✦

○ **Stay Hungry** / 1984 / Atlantic ✦✦✦✦
Hard-hitting aggressively progressive metal, this set includes "The Price," "I Wanna Rock," and "We're Not Gonna Take It." —*Bil Carpenter*

Come out & Play / 1985 / Atlantic ✦✦✦
Love Is for Suckers / 1987 / Atlantic ✦✦

● **Big Hits and Nasty Cuts: Best of Twisted Sister** / 1992 / Atlantic ✦✦✦✦
All of the highlights of Twisted Sister's long career are included on this collection. —*AMG*

2 Live Crew
Group, Rap
This Florida rap band was organized, supervised, and conceived by Luther Campbell, a promoter, record label owner, and rapper, as an updated version of oldtime X-rated party performers. Campbell's production consists of heavy doses of booming synthesized bass, scratching effects, samples, and explicit sex raps and leers. From their beginnings in 1986, the notoriety of Campbell and the group grew in direct proportion to the lewdness of the material. As their songs attained more national prominence, Campbell has become part of a national controversy involving censorship and lyrics. He's issued two solo records.

2 Live Crew hasn't found the going quite as smooth in the '90s. They've continued recording for Luke Records, but haven't scored as much success with such releases as *Move Somethin'* and *Sports Weekend*. Founder Luther Campbell issued both clean and dirty versions in an effort to defuse criticism, but 2 Live Crew's detractors have moved on to gangsta-rap and the group's most recent releases have been almost ignored. They resurfaced in 1994 as The New 2 Live Crew, releasing *Back at Your Ass for the Nine 4*. Campbell also announced plans to start a men's magazine in either 1994 or 1995.

Back at Your Ass for the Nine 4 did well briefly, peaking at number nine on the R&B chart. But their brand of X-rated humor seemed almost tame compared to the mix of explicit sex and violence available on more hardcore gangsta-rap sessions, while the Jamaican toasters like Shabba Ranks or the Mad Cobra outdistanced them in creative lewdness. —*Ron Wynn*

2 Live Crew Is What We Are / 1986 / Luke ✦✦✦
The record that launched the whole phenomenon. If the puerile language and vulgarity had been allowed to run its course without censorship attempts, this lunacy might have ended right here. The production does provide good examples of Miami "bass" music. —*Ron Wynn*

Move Somethin' / 1987 / Luke ✦✦✦
Luther Campbell hits on the ingenious idea of issuing clean and dirty versions simultaneously in an ill-fated attempt to take censorship heat off. The clean version lacks guts; the dirty version lacks taste. —*Ron Wynn*

○ **As Nasty As They Wanna Be** / 1989 / Luke ✦✦✦✦
Not only did it cause all the legal controversies, but *As Nasty as They Wanna Be* is the quintessential 2 Live Crew album, showing all of their tasteless, bass-driven glory. —*AMG*

Live in Concert / 1990 / Effect/Luke ✦
A two-record sprawling set that's as lowbrow as humanely possible; deplorable sexist diatribes and lewd comments galore. —*Ron Wynn*

Banned in the USA / 1990 / Atlantic ✦✦✦
This offers an interesting, if somewhat perverse version of Springsteen's "Born in the USA" as the title track and underlying theme. The rest is an erratic, meandering blend of X-rated sexual comments and quasi-political rhetoric. —*Ron Wynn*

Sports Weekend: As Nasty as They Wanna Be, Pt. 2 / 1991 / Luke ✦✦
● **Greatest Hits** / 1992 / Luke ✦✦✦✦
Full of the low-minded humor that made this Miami outfit notorious throughout the country, *Greatest Hits* does contain the best material 2 Live Crew ever recorded; it is all the 2 Live Crew most will ever need to hear. —*Stephen Thomas Erlewine*

2 Pac

Group, Rap
Rapper Tupac Amaru Shakur treatened to supplant Luther Campbell and Ice-T as the most demonized figure in hip-hop. The former Digital Underground member became a solo performer with *2Pacalypse Now*, then his status soared following a critically acclaimed performance in *Juice*. His follow-up album also earned a hit with "Keep Your Head Up." But Shakur generated much more negative publicity for several incidents, one of which earned him a criminal record. He was convicted of assault for attacking the Hughes brothers, who'd fired him from the film *Menace II Society*. He was also awaiting trials on other charges stemming for various incidents. This hadn't stopped his acting career; there were appearances in the films *Poetic Justice* with Janet Jackson and *Above the Rim*. —*Ron Wynn*

2Pacalypse Now / 1992 / Interscope ✦✦✦
Few expected former Digital Underground member Tupac Amaru Shakur to become hip-hop enemy number one when he made his solo debut with this 1992 album. Songs like "Crooked Ass Nigga" and "Tha' Lunatic" might have hinted that storm clouds were on the horizon, but there were also excellent advocacy numbers like "Words Of Wisdom" and "Young Black Male." This didn't make him a celebrity, but it put Tupac Shakur on the road to stardom. —*Ron Wynn*

● **Strictly 4 My N.I.G.G.A.Z.** / 1993 / Atlantic ✦✦✦✦
Tupac Shakur not only became a crossover acting and singing success with this release, but found himself on police blotters coast-to-coast and the designated demon of anti-rap forces nationwide. This disc yielded a couple of hits, with the fiery message track "Keep Your Head Up" particularly outstanding. Unfortunately, several ugly personal incidents, among them a public physical fight with film directors the Hughes brothers, allegations of violent attacks on an off-duty police officer, and sexual misconduct threaten to derail a promising multi-media career. —*Ron Wynn*

○ **Me Against the World** / 1995 / Interscope ✦✦✦✦
Released just after 2 Pac began serving a jail sentence for sexual assault, *Me Against the World* became a number one hit and it's fairly easy to see why—the record is impeccably produced, with rumbling, funky bass and rhythms that flow throughout the entire album. 2 Pac's rhymes are so considered and graceful that it's hard to believe the same man is imprisoned. —*David Jehnzen*

Type O Negative

Group, Heavy Metal
New York goth-metal quartet led by vocalist/bassist/songwriter Peter Steele and featuring guitarist Ken Hickey. Steele was formerly in the band Carnivore; his not-quite-serious treatment of subjects like depression, death, and evil has become the band's trademark. 1993's *Bloody Kisses*, with its mix of goth-rock, Beatlesque melodies, and dark humor, slowly won the band a cult following, in spite of Steele's frequent protests that Type O Negative has no talent whatsoever. For whatever reason, his songs seem to strike a chord anyway, and the album cracked Billboard's Top 200 well over a year after its release. In interviews, Steele predicted a complete sell-out on the band's next album, saying that he will write even more melodies so that the record will sell well and he can make money. —*Steve Huey*

Slow Deep and Hard / 1991 / Roadrunner ✦✦✦
Type O Negative's melodramatic goth-rock style encompasses long songs built on simple riffs, theatrical shouting vocals, churchy-sounding organ and vocal-harmony passages, and the odd mechanical noise. Vocalist Steele, who wrote all the songs, shows an obnoxious sense of humor, but directs it at himself and the band as much as everyone else he doesn't like. There are some very un-P.C. sentiments on several topics, chiefly breakups, which, although comically dramatic, are quite suitable for angry moping. —*Steve Huey*

The Origin of the Feces / 1992 / Roadrunner ✦✦
Recorded live at Brighton Beach on Halloween, neither the band nor the audience appreciated each other, and there are a couple of disruptions. Most of this material appeared on their first album as sections of longer songs. One exception is a rewrite of "Hey Joe" entitled "Hey Pete," which makes the singer into an ax murderer. Steele introduces his "vampire" vocal style here. —*Steve Huey*

● **Bloody Kisses** / 1993 / Roadrunner ✦✦✦✦
Peter Steele's dark, melodramatic songs address mostly heartbreak and loneliness, and there is still some smart-aleck ranting. But this time, much of the humor is delivered slyly and subtly. He sounds serious, but when one looks past his overkill, he's also satirizing his own emotional excesses, something rare in the alternative age. The long, repetitive songs are helped by the addition of more atmospheric synth and out-of-left-field Beatle-esque pop melodies, underlining the latter influence with Indian instruments on the closing track. Steele sings most of the album in his best vampire impression, which lends hilarious irony to a depressing cover of Seals & Crofts' "Summer Breeze." It's much more enjoyable than it has a right to be. —*Steve Huey*

U

U2

Group, Alternative Pop/Rock

In 1976, four Dublin schoolboys started the band that, under the name U2, would dominate rock music in the late '80s. Consisting of lead singer Bono (born Paul Hewson, May 10, 1960), guitarist the Edge (born David Evans, Aug 8, 1961), bassist Adam Clayton (b.Mar 13, 1960), and percussionist Larry Mullen, Jr. (b.Oct 31, 1961), U2 has helped to open up the doors for many other Irish bands.

U2 started out as a Dublin pub band and began earning recognition after the band won a talent contest sponsored by Guinness in 1979. This led to the Irish release of a three-track EP, *U2-3*, that topped the charts in Ireland and won them quite a following. They were signed by the Island label in 1980 and released their debut album, *Boy*, later that year. Unfortunately, *Boy* and the band's 1981 follow-up, *October*, did not gain much recognition outside of Ireland (where the band was playing sold-out concerts). It was not until the 1983 release of the critically acclaimed album, *War*, that U2 began to get a taste of success. *War* was the band's major breakthrough in the U.S., going platinum although the first two albums had never made it into the Top 40. *Under a Blood Red Sky*, a live concert album from the *War* tour, was released in 1983, followed by *The Unforgettable Fire* in 1984; both went platinum in the States as well.

With the release of *The Joshua Tree* (1987), U2 became one of the world's leading rock bands. Entering at number one on the U.K. charts, *The Joshua Tree* went platinum within 48 hours. The album also spent nine weeks at number one on the U.S. charts, and "With or Without You" became the band's first number one single in America, followed by "I Still Haven't Found What I'm Looking For." As the new rock sensation, U2 appeared on the covers of *Time, Musician*, and *Rolling Stone* and won two awards at the 1988 Grammy Awards, including Album of the Year. In 1988 the band went on to release a full-length concert film, *Rattle and Hum*, and an album of the same name.

Achtung Baby, released in late 1991, proved to be quite a departure from their previous work. Darker and more atmospheric than their other albums, it proved to be not only successful commercially and artistically, but it preserved their image of being on the cutting edge. After the release of *Achtung Baby*, U2 embarked on a major world tour, called *Zoo TV*, that featured state-of-the-art video images. During the tour, they recorded *Zooropa*, which was released in 1993; it was even more experimental and darker than their previous album. Naturally, it was a world-wide hit, even if it didn't have any hit singles as big as "One" or "Mysterious Ways."

U2 could arguably be called the greatest rock band of the '80s. Out of sheer determination (or cockiness), they have avoided the musical ruts that stardom can produce and have gone out of their way to experiment with new sounds and musical ideas. It is this musical growth and exploration that make U2 a great band. —*Iotis Erlewine*

○ **Boy** / 1980 / Island ✦✦✦✦

The inexperience of the band, not yet at its musical peak, is compensated for by its raw power. The songs on *Boy* are full of teen angst and rebellion, a result of the influence of punk bands like the Virgin Prunes. In spite of the roughness of this album, its simplicity and directness are very appealing. Including "I Will Follow" and "Out of Control," this album is a good example of U2's early work; so far, the band has been unable to match the sheer energy of *Boy*. —*Iotis Erlewine*

October / 1981 / Island ✦✦✦

U2's second album lost a lot of the fire and momentum that was in *Boy*. The band is better musically on this album, but it lacks spontaneity and seems a little too rehearsed. *October* incorporates Christian religious symbolism, apparent in songs like "Gloria" and "Rejoice." The album has some great songs (such as the minor U.K. hit "Gloria" and the melancholy "Tomorrow") but as a whole is a rather weak follow-up. —*Iotis Erlewine*

☆ **War** / 1983 / Island ✦✦✦✦✦

This album was a major turning point for U2—the band went from being a minor Irish band to being a world-renowned rock group. *War* retains some of the anger that is found on *Boy*, but it is more subtle and mature. This album features some of U2's best-known songs—"New Year's Day," "Sunday Bloody Sunday," "Seconds," and "Two Hearts Beat as One." In spite of all the protest, aggression, and outrage in these songs, the album ends with the optimistic "40," a song that sets the uplifting words of Psalm 40 to music. With such spectacular songs and emotion, *War* is a must for any fan of rock music. —*Iotis Erlewine*

Under a Blood Red Sky / 1983 / Island ✦✦✦

This is a great concert album from U2's *War* tour, most of which was recorded during their concert at the Red Rocks Festival in Colorado. The album includes "11 O'Clock Tick Tock" and "Party Girl" (which previously were available only as singles) and intense performances of "New Year's Day" and "Sunday Bloody Sunday." *Under a Blood Red Sky* captures some of the power and charisma that make U2 such a great live band. —*Iotis Erlewine*

The Unforgettable Fire / 1984 / Island ✦✦✦

After *War*, this was U2's second number one album in the U.K. (number 12 in the U.S.), and it features two of the band's better-known songs, "Pride" and "Bad." Ironically, even in spite of its relative success, this remains one of U2's "forgotten" albums. The quality of the songs may play a part in this—either the songs are outstanding or they are not even worth mentioning. It is this kind of inconsistency that causes this album to be so frequently overlooked. —*Iotis Erlewine*

Wide Awake in America / 1985 / Island ✦✦

This is a four-song EP that includes excellent live versions of "A Sort of a Homecoming" and "Bad," plus two largely forgettable songs, "Three Sunrises" and "Love Come Tumbling," that had previously only been released on singles. Unless you have to own the complete U2 collection, this album is not a necessity. —*Iotis Erlewine*

★ **The Joshua Tree** / 1987 / Island ✦✦✦✦✦

The Joshua Tree is the album that won the U.S. (and the rest of the world) over. Before this release, the band had met with considerable success but nothing like what was to follow *The Joshua Tree*. This album moved away from the loud anger of *War* and focused on a more subtle, refined sound. The wistful, searching quality of this album captures U2 at a transition, as the band attempts to rediscover themselves. Including such songs as "With or Without You," "I Still Haven't Found What I'm Looking For," "Where the Streets Have No Name," "In God's Country," and "Running to Stand Still," this album is among U2's best works. —*Iotis Erlewine*

Rattle & Hum / 1988 / Island ✦✦✦

U2's ego manifests itself. Billed as U2's "exploration of America," this album was a grave disappointment. There are, however, some excellent tracks, such as "When Love Comes to Town" (featuring B. B. King), "All I Want Is You," "Desire," and "Angel of Harlem." —*Iotis Erlewine*

☆ **Achtung Baby** / 1991 / Island ✦✦✦✦✦
This album was a big change in style for U2—it's the band's only album to date that you can dance to. On this album, the group drops some of the pretentiousness of the last few albums and stops taking itself so seriously, and the result is very impressive. Although some of the lyrics are downright laughable, *Achtung Baby* is more direct and honest than some of the previous, preachier albums. Promoted as U2's "dark, trashy" album, this is, as far as I'm concerned, the most sophisticated work the band has yet created. The songs on this album (like the powerful "One" and "Love Is Blindness") revolve around human emotion instead of politics. I highly recommend *Achtung Baby*—it may be a shock the first time you hear it, but the more you listen, the better it gets. —*Iotis Erlewine*

○ **Zooropa** / May 1993 / Island ✦✦✦✦
After their successful artistic renewal with 1991's *Achtung Baby*, U2 mounted a staggering world tour filled with glitz, empty slogans, mammoth TV screens, and stunning music. Originally intended as an EP, *Zooropa* was recorded in a short break in their European tour. Instead of sounding like a pure piece of product, *Zooropa* is a complex album that takes the sonic experimentations of *Achtung Baby* even further—listen to the grinding "Numb" for proof. Some of the songwriting isn't as fully developed as it could have been, but the album creates a terrifically claustrophobic atmosphere that comes to an incredible close with "The Wanderer," where Johnny Cash's lead vocal sounds completely natural among the ominous synthesizers. —*Stephen Thomas Erlewine*

UB40

Group, Reggae, Pop/Rock
Along with the 2-Tone groups that emerged during the late-'70s ska revival that dominated the British charts, UB40 managed to insinuate their own personality into the conservative genre of reggae. Mixing leftist politics with pop-based melodies, the band scored many hits in England, their first was "Red Red Wine," a song recorded by the band in 1984 but rereleased in 1988, that broke them in America.
After "Red Red Wine," the band began to hit the charts frequently with their smooth, reggae-tinged versions of classic oldies like "Way You Do the Things You Do" and "I Can't Help Falling in Love." In the process, the band became less politicized and lost the spark that had distinguished their early albums. —*John Floyd*

Signing Off / 1980 / Graduate ✦✦✦

Present Arms / 1981 / Virgin ✦✦✦

Present Arms in Dub / 1981 / Virgin ✦✦

Best of UB40 (1980-1983) / 1983 / A&M ✦✦✦
This U.S. compilation gathers the best of the early days of the UK's top White reggae band, displaying their love of dub and some of their best songs of the period, such as the caustic "One in Ten." —*William Ruhlmann*

Live / 1983 / Virgin ✦✦✦

More UB40 Music / 1983 / Graduate ✦✦✦
This two-LP set, released in Europe, showcases early UB40 in extended form, featuring the 12-inch versions of such songs as "I Think It's Going To Rain Today" and "The Earth Dies Screaming." —*William Ruhlmann*

● **Labour of Love** / Sep. 1983 / A&M ✦✦✦✦
Long stars in England, UB40 finally found Stateside success (and that belatedly) by recording an album of their favorite Jamaican cover tunes. One of these, "Red Red Wine," finally took off in the U.S. in 1988 and went to #1. —*William Ruhlmann*

○ **Geffery Morgan** / 1984 / A&M ✦✦✦✦
UB40 was faced with following up the surprisingly successful covers album *Labour Of Love* (which had topped the U.K. chart and become their U.S. chart debut) with this album of original material. Their own songs were good, but no match for what then seemed a one-of-a-kind collection. "If It Happens Again," which went to #9 in Britain, sounded like a song by the English Beat, while the second single, "Riddle Me" (#59), was a deeper reggae groove tune. It was a good set, but without a classic like "Red, Red Wine" suffered from a certain anonymity, especially in the U.S. —*William Ruhlmann*

Little Baggaridim / 1985 / A&M ✦✦✦
UB40 scored their first Top 30 hit in the U.S. with a cover of Sonny and Cher's "I Got You, Babe," set to a reggae beat and sung with the Pretenders' Chrissie Hynde, heard on this mini-album. —*William Ruhlmann*

Baggaridim / 1985 / DEP Int'l ✦✦✦

○ **Rat in the Kitchen** / 1986 / A&M ✦✦✦✦
In the U.K., UB40 were major stars, and this album was their sixth Top 10 hit, featuring the singles "Sing Your Own Song" (#5), "All I Want To Do" (#41), and "Rat In Me Kitchen" (#12). In the U.S., the group remained a developing act with a modest following, only able to score a hit by covering a previous hit like "I Got You, Babe." *Rat In The Kitchen* did nothing to change that, although it was, as usual, a tuneful collection of reggae. —*William Ruhlmann*

UB40 CCCP: Live in Moscow / 1987 / A&M ✦✦
It's hard to imagine what A&M had in mind releasing a live album by a group that hadn't really broken in the U.S. yet. Nevertheless, the record actually spent eight weeks in the charts, but it sold only to diehards, and although it's an appealing enough set, featuring covers like "Cherry Oh Baby" and "I Got You, Babe" (minus Chrissie Hynde) and such British hits as "If It Happens Again" and "Sing Our Song," it's hard to imagine it doing any better. —*William Ruhlmann*

○ **UB40** / 1988 / A&M ✦✦✦✦

Labour of Love II / 1989 / Virgin ✦✦
UB40 repeats their formula for even more success, with reggae versions of "Here I Am (Come and Take Me)" and "The Way You Do the Things You Do." —*William Ruhlmann*

Promises & Lies / 1993 / Virgin ✦✦
Carried by the hit "I Can't Help Falling in Love With You," *Promises and Lies* finishes UB40's transition from a reggae band to an adult-contemporary band that plays reggae-pop. Fans of the single will be satisfied by *Promises and Lies*, but older fans will find the whole affair rather dismaying. —*AMG*

UFO

Group, Hard Rock, Heavy Metal
During the '70s, UFO was one of the most popular heavy metal bands in the world, thanks in no small part to the blistering guitar work of Michael Schenker. After recording several best-selling albums, Schenker quit in 1978 to join the Scorpions. With his departure, UFO lost their personality; working through several lineup changes, they continued to record right into the '90s, churning out faceless arena rock. It was a far cry from when their metallic riffs were a sure thing for teenagers across the world. —*Stephen Thomas Erlewine*

● **Essential UFO** / 1992 / Chrysalis ✦✦✦✦
UFO's best tracks, compiled on one smartly assembled single-disc collection. —*Stephen Thomas Erlewine*

The Ugly Ducklings

Group, Garage Rock
Along with the Haunted, the Ugly Ducklings were probably the best Canadian rock group of the mid-'60s. Like the Haunted, they drew heavily from the Rolling Stones—as well as bits of the Kinks and Pretty Things—for their raunchy R&B/rock sound, but had the edge over the Haunted in that they wrote stronger original material. Scoring a national hit with "Nothin'," the Toronto band recorded an album in 1966 and a few singles in 1966 and 1967, perhaps gaining their greatest international exposure when their "Just in Case You're Wondering" made it onto one of the *Pebbles* compilations. —*Richie Unterberger*

● **Ugly Ducklings** / 1982 / Yorktown ✦✦✦✦
Half of their 1966 *Somewhere Outside* album, as well as a few non-LP singles and unreleased tracks; half original material, half covers of staples of the era like "My Little Red Book" and "I Ain't Gonna Eat Out My Heart Anymore." "Nothin'," "She Ain't No Use To Me," and "Just In Case You Wonder" are good original tunes, blending Kinks-Stones riffing with North American garage raunch. —*Richie Unterberger*

U.K. Subs

Group, Punk
Formed by R&B singer Charlie Harper in 1976, the London punk band U.K. may have tackled the occasional social or political topic, yet they were distinguished by their roaring, rocking three-chord ravers. In addition to Harper, the group featured guitarist Nicky Garratt, bassist Paul Slack, and drummer Pete Davies. The U.K. Subs released several singles in the late '70s, including "Stranglehold" and "Tomorrow's Girls," which managed to hit the British Top 40. As the '80s progressed, the band began to lose its audience as they incorporated heavy metal into the sound. Throughout their career the

band's lineup has been fluctuating, with Harper being the only constant in the group's career. The U.K. Subs continued recording right into the '90s, although their audience has decreased substantially. — *Stephen Thomas Erlewine*

● **Singles 1978-1982** / Progressive ◆◆◆◆

Tracey Ullman

New Wave, Pop/Rock
Before she became a famous TV comedienne, Tracy Ullman recorded two albums in the early '80s that effortlessly recalled the classic girl group sound of the '60s. Ullman covered everything from Doris Day ("Move over Darling") to Blondie ("(I'm Always Touched by Your) Presence, Dear"), finding the underlying connections between classic pop songs of all eras. *You Broke My Heart in 17 Places,* her debut album, was a hit in the U.K. and she even managed to have a Top Ten hit in America with a version of Kirsty MacColl's "They Don't Know." Although it had some fine numbers, the follow-up *You Caught Me Out* wasn't as successful, prompting Ullman to return to television. By the end of the '80s, her comedy show, *The Tracy Ullman Show,* was one of the most critically-acclaimed television shows in America; she hasn't recorded any music since. — *Stephen Thomas Erlewine*

○ **You Broke My Heart in 17 Places** / 1983 / Stiff ◆◆◆◆
Ullman's first album, recorded in the middle of the new wave and synth-pop movements, provided a refreshing break with its retro girl group sound. Includes her only U.S. hit, "They Don't Know" (written by Kirsty MacColl) as well as carefully chosen obscure oldies. One of the great lost classics. — *Chris Woodstra*

You Caught Me Out / 1984 / Repertoire ◆◆◆
The second album follows the same formula as the first—a well-chosen collection of covers from obscure oldies to contemporary favorites (Madness's "My Girl"—retitled here as "My Guy") and even another stab at a Kirsty MacColl song ("Terry")—all done in the classic '60s girl group sound. Though it failed to produce the smash hits of the debut, "My Guy" and "Sunglasses" were minor hits in the U.K., and the album is nearly as much fun. Repertoire has released a CD version with six bonus tracks. — *Chris Woodstra*

● **The Best of Tracey Ullman** / 1991 / Rhino ◆◆◆◆
This 20-track compilation provides an extensive look at the nearly forgotten singing career of this now famous actress. Combining the entire first LP, *You Broke My Heart in 17 Places,* the highlights from her second effort *You Caught Me Out,* and well chosen B-sides, it more than lives up to its name. Although this material was recorded in the early '80s, lovers of the classic '60s-girl-group sound will find these retro-gems a familiar delight. — *Chris Woodstra*

Ultravox

Group, New Wave, Pop/Rock
Ultravox (or Ultravox!—as it was called at first) had two separate identities and styles of music during its existence. Formed in London in 1974, it was originally intended as a platform for singer John Foxx (born Dennis Leigh) and included guitarist Stevie Shears, keyboardist and violinist Billy Currie, bassist Chris Cross, and drummer Warren Cann. With this lineup, the group recorded its debut album, *Ultravox!* (1977), produced by Brian Eno and Steve Lillywhite during the height of the punk/new wave movement. A second album, *Ha! Ha! Ha!* (1977), was released only in the U.K. A third, *Systems of Romance* (1978), marked the last appearance of Foxx, who went solo, and of guitarist Robin Simon, who had replaced Shears. The remaining trio enlisted singer/guitarist Midge Ure, formerly of the teenybop band ilk, and recorded *Vienna* (1980), which marked a sharp turn toward synthesizer pop and helped give birth to the British "new romantic" movement of the early '80s. The album was Ultravox's first to chart; the title track went to number two and "All Stood Still" reached the Top Ten. There followed a series of successful albums in the U.K.: *Rage in Eden* (1981), *Quartet* (1982), *Monument—The Soundtrack* (1983), *Lament* (1984), and *U-Vox* (1986). *The Collection* (1984) was a hits album. Of these, only *Quartet* made any significant inroads in the U.S. Ultravox split in mid-1987, when Ure decided to turn his full attention to his solo career. — *William Ruhlmann*

Ultravox / 1977 / Island ◆◆◆
John Foxx proves to have an odd, Bowie-influenced vision, here aided and abetted by Brian Eno (then a Bowie crony) and Steve Lillywhite. "My Sex" and "I Want to Be a Machine" are standouts. — *William Ruhlmann*

Ha Ha Ha / 1977 / Island ◆◆◆

Systems of Romance / 1978 / Island ◆◆◆

○ **Vienna** / 1980 / Chrysalis ◆◆◆◆
The new Ultravox, under Midge Ure, has a dreamy, ethereal sound heard at its best on its debut album, which features the title song, "All Stood Still," "Passing Strangers," and "Sleepwalk," all UK hits. — *William Ruhlmann*

Rage in Eden / 1981 / Chrysalis ◆◆◆

Quartet / 1982 / Chrysalis ◆◆◆

○ **Lament** / 1984 / Chrysalis ◆◆◆◆

● **The Collection** / 1984 / Chrysalis ◆◆◆◆
Ultravox's UK hit singles during the Midge Ure era. — *William Ruhlmann*

U-Vox / 1986 / Chrysalis ◆◆

Rare, Vol. 1 / 1994 / Chrysalis ◆◆
Compiles in chronological order 17 rare single B-side tracks which the British electro-pop group released between 1980 and 1983. For hardcore fans only. — *Roch Parisien*

● **Very Best of** / Chrysalis ◆◆◆◆

Uncle Tupelo

Group, Country-Rock, Alternative Pop/Rock
Uncle Tupelo's skillful updating of country and folk for the post-punk era made the band one of the best of the early '90s. Beginning with their first independent record in 1990, the band played direct, hardcore country, injecting it with the loud fervor of punk. Over the course of four albums, the overt punk elements of their music became less dominant, as the group's fascination with country came to the forefront. By the time of their major label debut in 1993, Uncle Tupelo had developed a familiar, yet distinct, sound that had traces of the Flying Burrito Brothers, Neil Young, and Hank Williams; their music was based in tradition, yet it didn't sound nostalgic—their conviction and passion made it sound vital and contemporary. Unfortunately, the band broke up the following year; the group's two songwriters—Jay Farrar and Jeff Tweedy—each had formed new bands by the end of the year. — *Stephen Thomas Erlewine*

No Depression / 1990 / Gasatanka ◆◆◆

○ **March 16-20, 1992** / 1992 / Gasatanka ◆◆◆◆
A remarkably accomplished set of contemporary country-rock. — *Stephen Thomas Erlewine*

● **Anodyne** / May 1993 / Sire ◆◆◆◆
Uncle Tupelo's other albums are impressive, but their final record, *Anodyne* is a brilliant reinterpretation of traditional country, folk, and country-rock. Filled with excellent songs, it sounds both contemporary and timeless. — *Stephen Thomas Erlewine*

Undertones

Group, Punk, New Wave
There are those who would disagree vehemently, but in my estimation the Undertones were Ireland's best rock band—ever. Roaring out of the Northern Ireland city of Derry in 1976, the Undertones fused speedy, loud Ramones-inspired walls of guitar racket with irresistible '60s pop hooks, with just a touch of mid-'70s glam rock for good measure. With the singular tenor vocals of frontman Feargal Sharkey making them instantaneously recognizable, Undertones songs tended to eschew punk vitriol for songs about teenage love, girls, snotty cousins, and summertime—life's simple joys (and pains). No more succinct a summation of their style, wit, and power can be found than on their out-of-print debut EP *Teenage Kicks,* released in 1978 on the Belfast indie label Good Vibrations. A record of startling ebullience, the songs (many of which showed up on their eponymous debut album) sound as exhilarating today as they did nearly 20 years ago. However, the Undertones did not go into creative stasis with their winning punk-pop and simply replicate a proven formula over and over. As they grew as musicians, so did their albums change, incorporating some of the Tamla/Motown soul music they loved as kids. As a live band, they were tremendous; just ask anyone who saw them opening for the Clash in the late '70s. Sadly, the Undertones' story ended far too quickly. Growing up meant too much change too fast, and by the time they released their mediocre fourth album, restlessness and "musical differences" were splitting them apart. Sharkey went off to a short-lived solo career, while the guitar-playing O'Neill brothers put together the politically charged That Petrol Emotion. In the late '80s, there were whispers of a reunion

which didn't occur, much to the relief of those who preferred the Undertones' legacy to remain unsullied. —*John Dougan*

★ **The Undertones** / 1979 / Rykodisc ✦✦✦✦✦
An absolutely essential purchase. One of the best albums of the punk era, or any era. Song after song is infused with a liberating joy and intensity that only a handful of rock records at the time equalled. A crucial record, the 'Tones' debut shows how influential '70s commercial pop was on the growing punk community, who embraced it and then tore it all to hell. A record that hasn't lost its luster after hundreds of plays and nearly two decades. Reissued on CD with seven bonus tracks by Rykodisc in 1994. —*John Dougan*

○ **Hypnotised** / 1980 / Rykodisc ✦✦✦✦
It's ridiculous to not encourage you to purchase the first three Undertones records, because they are such wonderful distillations of all that makes rock and roll great. *Hypnotised* picks up where the debut leaves off, but adds a slightly more sarcastic touch to some of the songs, especially the witty "My Perfect Cousin" and the goofy "More Songs About Chocolate and Girls" (a not-so-subtle parody of the title of Talking Heads' second LP *More Songs About Buildings and Food*). Reissued on CD with five bonus tracks by Rykodisc in 1994. —*John Dougan*

Positive Touch / 1981 / Rykodisc ✦✦✦
By this time, the Undertones had switched labels and recorded a challenging, slightly arty record that didn't sound much like their first two, and showed an amazing artistic development. There are musical elements not on the previous recordings (horns, Paul Carrack's keyboards); still, the band's creativity, intelligence and personality make this a tremendously rewarding record. Not where one unfamiliar with the 'Tones should start (get that guitar rush first), but once under their spell, *Positive Touch* will become almost as important as the first two. Reissued on CD with four bonus tracks by Rykodisc in 1994. —*John Dougan*

The Sins of Pride / 1983 / EMI ✦✦

All Wrapped Up / 1983 / Capitol ✦✦✦

○ **The Very Best of the Undertones** / 1994 / Rykodisc ✦✦✦✦
The Very Best Of The Undertones collects the cream of the catalogue. The group's earliest high-energy teenage anthems (themes of doubt, deceit, yearning, and infatuation) give way, over the course of 25 songs, to the sublime intimacy of "Wednesday Week" and "Julie Ocean," and then the sophisticated, Tamla/Motown layering of "Soul Seven." Group members discuss each track in the informative liner notes. Start here, fall in love, then go find the individual albums! —*Roch Parisien*

The United States Of America

Group, Psychedelic
Formed at the University of California at Los Angeles, the United States Of America released a self-titled album in 1968 that blended an avant-garde sensibility (leader/founder Joseph Byrd was a respected contemporary composer) with eerie, piercing instrumentation and coolly foreboding lyrics. Musically it's quite advanced for its era, with an eclectic array of then-futuristic electronic instruments augmenting the standard rock lineup. But what saves the music from coming off as too calculated are Dorothy Moskowitz's lovely vocals, which bring to mind a somewhat icier Grace Slick. The group dissolved quickly, breaking up after just one LP. Joe Byrd released a similar, less impressive album as the leader of Joe Byrd & the Field Hippies; Moskowitz briefly joined Country Joe & the Fish in the early '70s. —*Richie Unterberger*

○ **United States of America** / 1992 / Sony ✦✦✦✦
Originally released on Columbia in 1968, this is one of the legendary pure psychedelic space records. Some of the harder-rocking tunes have a funhouse recklessness that recall aspects of early Pink Floyd and the Velvet Underground at their freakiest; the sedate, exquisitely orchestrated ballads, especially "Cloud Song" and the wonderfully titled "Love Song for the Dead Che," are among the best relics of dreamy psychedelia. Occasionally things get too excessive and self-conscious, and the attempts at comedy are a bit flat, but otherwise this is a near classic. The CD reissue adds two previously unreleased outtakes. —*Richie Unterberger*

Univers Zero

Group, Art-Rock/Progressive-Rock, Experimental
Univers Zero was founded in Brussels, Belgium in 1974 by drummer Daniel Denis and guitarist Roger Trigaux. The music of Univers Zero has a dark, Gothic character. The band was a member of Rock

in Opposition, a cooperative movement of some of Europe's finest new-music bands, formed along political lines as much as musical direction. The group released *1313* and *Heresie* before Trigaux left in 1980 to form Present. Univers Zero added electric instruments to its acoustic sound, and enlisted keyboard player Andy Kirk. The group released *Ceux Du Dehors* in 1981. *UZED* was released in 1984, and *Heatwave* in 1987. The group disbanded after this release. All of Univers Zero's albums were subsequently reissued on CD by Cuneiform. —*Jim Dorsch*

1313 / 1977 / Cuneiform ✦✦✦
The Belgian group's debut is a dark, foreboding mixture of rock and chamber music. —*Michael P. Dawson*

Univers Zero / 1978 / Atem ✦✦
This was a revelation upon release and marked the start of what has become today the revival of Dark Ages depressionism in rock and electronic music. —*Archie Patterson*

Heresie / 1979 / Cuneiform ✦✦✦
This features a smaller lineup but a similarly tense and innovative sound. —*Michael P. Dawson*

● **Uzed** / 1984 / Cuneiform ✦✦✦✦
This stunning 1984 recording is at times akin to the best of King Crimson. —*Michael P. Dawson*

Heatwave / 1986 / Cuneiform ✦✦✦
The Belgian avant-rocker farewell boasts a more electronic sound than earlier albums. —*Michael P. Dawson*

The Unknowns

Group, New Wave
This unusual L.A. group blended stripped-down punk energy and gloomy contemporary lyrical settings with the reverb-heavy instrumental guitar sound of the Ventures and early surf groups, as well as a dash of rockabilly. After a disappointing EP on Sire (*Dream Sequence*), the group released a raw, self-titled album on the small indie Invasion in 1982 that ranks among the finest obscure new wave releases of the time with its strong songwriting, dripping wet production values, magnificent drumming, and crisp Mosrite guitar sound. Lead singer Bruce Joyner (who co-wrote most of the material with guitarist Mark Neill) has released several less impressive albums with backing groups the Plantations and the Tinglers. —*Richie Unterberger*

● **Unknowns** / 1982 / Invasion ✦✦✦✦
Driving surf-punk-rockabilly-influenced new wave with intelligence and good melodic hooks. Bruce Joyner's singing is urgent and foreboding, his lyrics filled with murky, somber imagery—sleazy sexual trysts, the conformity of modern man, the dangerous edge of contemporary urban life. —*Richie Unterberger*

Unrest

Group, Alternative Pop/Rock
Unrest formed in the early 1980s and was originally concieved as an artsy-hardcore act. In this incarnation, the Washington, D.C., group released many singles and seven inches, but did not gain their definitive, ultra-melodic and catchy sound until bassist/songwriter/vocalist Bridget Cross joined in 1990. In 1992 the band released their first full-length album, *Imperial f.f.r.r.* which featured the closely intertwined, harmonic playing of Cross and guitarist/songwriter/vocalist Mark Robinson. More singles and EPs followed, culminating in the release of 1993's more experimental *Perfect Teeth*. After a few more singles, the group broke up in early 1994, with Robinson and Cross forming the group Air Miami after the split. —*Heather Phares*

Malcolm X Park / 1988 / Caroline ✦✦

Kustom Karnal Blackxploitation / 1990 / Caroline ✦✦

○ **Imperial f.f.r.r.** / Jul. 14, 1992 / Number Six ✦✦✦✦
Imperial is Unrest's full-length debut. It fleshes out the pop promise of their early singles, and expands on their pop and experimental background as well. " I Do Believe You Are Blushing," "Cherry Cream On," "Suki," "Isabel" and "June" are still some of the band's best songs, mixing high-energy guitars and subjects like girls and death to infectious effect. A near-perfect album of indie-pop. —*Heather Phares*

○ **Isabel Bishop [EP]** / 1993 / 4AD/TeenBeat ✦✦✦✦
This mini-album is Unrest's debut on 4AD, a re-recorded, lusher "Isabel" starts off this small but great collection, which includes "Teenage Suicide," "Yes She Is My Skinhead Girl," and "I'd Like to Know." —*Heather Phares*

● **Perfect Teeth** / 1993 / 4AD/Warner Brothers ✦✦✦✦
The band's final and best album is both jangly and lush, and covers many styles of pop music, "Angel, I'll Walk You Home" is filled with pristine vocal harmonies, while "Cath Carroll" is flashy, thrashy punk-pop. "Light Brigade" is both wistful and triumphant. "Breather x.o.x.o" is majestically melancholy, and "West Coast Love Affair" is breezy and tongue-in-cheek. Unrest's experimental and pop leanings come together with terrific success on *Perfect Teeth*, making it a high point in the band's too-brief recording career. *—Heather Phares*

Fuck Pussy Galore and All Her Friends / 1994 / Matador ✦✦✦
This aptly-titled album is a collection of the group's B-sides. If anything, it shows just how important bassist Bridget Cross was in shaping the group's sound. While it's a welcome addition to the Unrest fan's collection, not much here is absolutely vital. *—Heather Phares*

Midge Ure

Pop/Rock
One of the key members of the new wave band Ultravox, guitarist/vocalist Midge Ure began his professional music career with Salvation, a Glasgow-based group that became the bubblegum band Slik in 1974. Upset in the change of direction, Ure left the band to join the Rich Kids, a punk-pop group led by former Sex Pistol bassist Glen Matlock. The Rich Kids only released one album, 1978's *Ghosts of Princes in Towers*, before breaking up later that same year. Ure spent a brief time with the Misfits (not the American hardcore band) before forming Visage with drummer Rusty Egan and vocalist Steve Strange; he left the group to replace Gary Moore in Thin Lizzy, who left in the middle of an American tour. After the tour was finished, he fulfilled an agreement to join Ultravox.

Once he joined the band in 1980, Ure helped make Ultravox a mainstream success; during this time he also worked as a producer, making records with Steve Harley and Modern Man. In 1982, Ure released a solo single, a cover of the Walker Brothers' hit "No Regrets;" it climbed into the U.K. Top Ten. Ure and Bob Geldof formed Band Aid, a special project to aid famine relief efforts in Ethiopia, in 1984. The two wrote the song "Do They Know It's Christmas?" and assembled an all-star band of British musicians to record the single; it sold millions of copies over the 1984 holiday season and prompted Geldof to organize the benefit concert Live Aid in 1985.

In 1985, Ultravox was put on hiatus and Ure began to pursue a full-time solo career. Recorded entirely by Ure, his 1985 solo debut *The Gift* launched the number one single "If I Was," as well as the minor hits "That Certain Smile" and "Call of the Wild." The following year, he recorded the final Ultravox album; in 1987, the band broke up and he began recording his second solo album. The resulting record, 1988's *Answers to Nothing*, was less successful than *The Gift* in the U.K., yet it charted in the U.S., which is something Ure's previous album failed to do. Three years later, Ure released his third album, *Pure*, while it didn't do any business in America, the album featured the Top 20 British hit "Cold, Cold Heart." *—Stephen Thomas Erlewine*

The Gift / 1985 / Chrysalis ✦✦✦
○ **Answers to Nothing** / 1988 / Chrysalis ✦✦✦✦
Pure / Sep. 24, 1991 / RCA ✦✦✦
● **If I Was: The Very Best of Midge Ure & Ultravox** / 1993 / Chrysalis ✦✦✦✦
All of Midge Ure and Ultravox's best tracks are here (including "Dear God," "Reap the Wild Wind," and Band Aid's "Do They Know It's Christmas?," which was co-written by Midge Ure), collected on one definitive 17-track CD. *—AMG*

Urge Overkill

Group, Alternative Pop/Rock, Rock & Roll
Unlike most alternative rock bands, Urge Overkill set out to be rock stars. They found an image—stylish, hip swingers with impeccable taste in fashion, music, and women—and made music that suited that persona. Picking up their Les Pauls and turning up their Marshall stacks, Urge Overkill made rock & roll that was full of instantly memorable choruses, guitar solos, loud and catchy guitars, and a powerful backbeat; in short, music that *rocked*. Of course, it took them a couple of albums before they got that good. Initially, they were another Steve Albini-produced, buzzing guitar band from Chicago. With their second album, *Americruiser*, they began to write actual songs. By 1991's *Supersonic Storybook* album, the band's

lineup was set in stone—Nash Kato on guitar and vocals, "Eddie" King Roeser on bass, guitar, and vocals, and drummer Blackie Onassis—and Urge released their first consistent album; it had stadium-sized riffs played with punkish aggression. Before they made the jump to the major labels, they released their most varied and diverse recording, the *Stull* EP. And with 1993's *Saturation*, Urge finally perfected the glamorous, powerful rock & roll that they always wanted to record. While it didn't make them the superstars they wanted to be, it sold well and had a minor hit with "Sister Havana." *—Stephen Thomas Erlewine*

Jesus Urge Superstar / 1989 / Touch & Go ✦✦
Americruiser / 1990 / Touch & Go ✦✦✦
Americruiser/Jesus Urge Superstar / 1990 / Touch & Go ✦✦✦
Urge's first two albums were recorded at a time when their visions eclipsed their talents—while there are a lot of good indie-guitar bluster here, there aren't that many memorable songs. With its flat Steve Albini production, *Jesus Urge Superstar* is the weaker of the records. *Americruiser*, with production courtesy of Butch Vig, not only has a fuller sound, but also some real songs. "Ticket to L.A." is a classic rocker, with a locomotive riff and great lyrics. It was a sign of things to come. (The CD also includes their gonzo cover of Jimmy Webb's "Wichitaw Lineman.") *—Stephen Thomas Erlewine*

○ **The Supersonic Storybook** / 1991 / Touch & Go ✦✦✦✦
With the addition of drummer Blackie Onassis, Urge Overkill shapes up into a killer rock & roll combo. It also doesn't hurt that the songs are the finest they have written to date. Although the production is a little flat, there's no denying the force of the best tracks. "The Candidate" boasts a huge, stadium-size riff, "The Kids Are Insane" is a frenzied, frenetic rocker, "Today Is Blackie's Birthday" is gleefully stupid, and the band is surprisingly sexy on the old soul song "Emmaline." Things bog down a bit on the second side, but Urge is starting to sound like the rock stars they always knew they were. *—Stephen Thomas Erlewine*

○ **Stull [EP]** / 1992 / Touch & Go ✦✦✦✦
It's not the full-throttle rock masterpiece that *Supersonic Storybook* suggested, but the *Stull* is almost as remarkable. Opening with a straight cover of Neil Diamond's "Girl, You'll Be a Woman Soon" (which fits Urge Overkill's image perfectly), the EP is an atmospheric guitar workout. While "Stitches" is a salute to their punk roots, the most impressive moments come during the stylish kiss-off to indie-rock "Goodbye to Guyville" and "Stull," with its sly, laidback groove. As the richness of *Stull* proves, Urge's vision was too large for the independents, and it was time to move on. *—Stephen Thomas Erlewine*

● **Saturation** / Jun. 8, 1993 / Geffen ✦✦✦✦
When they hit the major labels, Urge Overkill followed through on their promise with the blistering *Saturation*. It's stadium rock by clever post-punkers who are smart enough to not let their carefully crafted image interfere with the music. Every one of the twelve songs is a killer, from the outlandish menace of "Stalker" to the moving ballad "Back On Me," as well as the tongue-in-cheek "Woman 2 Woman" and the radio hit "Sister Havana." *—Stephen Thomas Erlewine*

Uriah Heep

Group, Hard Rock, Heavy Metal
Uriah Heep's by-the-books progressive heavy metal made the British band one of the most popular hard rock groups of the early '70s. Formed by vocalist David Byron and guitarist Mick Box in the late '60s, the group went through an astonishing number of members over the next two decades—nearly 30 different musicians passed through the band over the years. Byron and Box were members of the mid-'60s rock band called the Stalkers; once that band broke up, the duo formed another group called Spice. Spice would eventually turn into Uriah Heep in the late '60s, once Ken Hensley (guitar, keyboards, vocals) and bassist Paul Newton joined the pair. Former Spice drummer Alex Napier was the band's drummer for a brief time; he was quickly replaced by Nigel Olsson.

Uriah Heep released their debut album *Very 'eavy, Very 'umble* (called *Uriah Heep* in the U.S.) in 1970. After its release, Keith Baker became the group's drummer; he recorded *Salisbury*, the group's second album, before deciding he couldn't keep up with the band's extensive touring and was replaced by Ian Clarke. Featuring a 16-minute title track recorded with a 26-piece orchestra, *Salisbury* showcased the band's more progressive tendencies. Later that year, Ian Clarke was replaced by Lee Kerslake and Mark Clarke replaced

Newton; Mark Clarke quickly left the band and Gary Thain became the group's bassist. This lineup of Uriah Heep was its most stable and popular; beginning with 1972's *Demons and Wizards*, they released five albums between 1972 and 1975.

After 1975, the band's popularity began to slip. Byron left the band in 1977 and was replaced by John Lawton, yet the group's fortunes kept declining right into the early '80s. However, Uriah Heep soldiers on, continuing to release albums in the '90s. —*Stephen Thomas Erlewine*

Very 'umble Very 'eavy / 1970 / Mercury ✦✦✦
It may not have approached the musical complexity of their mid-'70s work, but Uriah Heep's debut album was a heavy, stomp-rock delight. —*Daevid Jehnzen*

Salisbury / 1971 / Mercury ✦✦✦
No, not the steak, but Uriah Heep does raise the stakes on their second album, *Salisbury*. Instead of relying on the throbbing boogie of *Very 'eavy, Very 'umble*, weaving a complex instrumental web imbedded with twisting, winding solos. The album achieves its summit with the epic, 16-minute title track, recorded with a lush, 26-piece orchestra. It exposes just how grand Uriah Heep's ambitions are. —*Daevid Jehnzen*

○ Look at Yourself / 1971 / Mercury ✦✦✦✦
Look at Yourself was the beginning of Uriah Heep's commercial fortunes, as it became the first of their albums to hit the U.K. charts. Musically, it compromised the boogie of their debut with the sweeping ambitions of *Salisbury*. —*Daevid Jehnzen*

○ Demons & Wizards / Jan. 1972 / Mercury ✦✦✦✦
As the fanciful title suggests, Uriah Heep began to delve deeper and deeper into mystical lyricism on their fourth album, which was supported by their spacy but earthy guitar rock. —*Daevid Jehnzen*

○ Magician's Birthday / Feb. 1972 / Mercury ✦✦✦✦
Magician's Birthday continued to expand the mystical concerns of *Demons & Wizards*, and it was nearly as successful, thanks to the group's knack for heavy guitars. —*Daevid Jehnzen*

Uriah Heep Live / 1973 / Mercury ✦✦
Uriah Heep may have been a popular concert attraction, but that didn't necessarily mean their concerts were always entertaining, as the dull *Uriah Heep Live* proves. —*Daevid Jehnzen*

○ Sweet Freedom / 1973 / Roadrunner ✦✦✦✦
Sweet Freedom continued Uriah Heep's mid-'70s winning streak. —*Daevid Jehnzen*

Wonderworld / 1974 / Roadrunner ✦✦✦
Wonderworld is indeed a wonderous world of heavy rock and spacy rock. Sadly, it was their last big hit album in the U.S. Sometimes, people just don't realize what they've got until it's gone. Fortunately, Uriah Heep stuck around for another 20 years to remind them of what they were missing. —*Daevid Jehnzen*

Return to Fantasy / 1975 / Castle ✦✦✦
Return to Fantasy? The lads never really *left* fantasy behind, but the intent is appreciated all the same. Fans hoped the record would be a *Return to Magic* with the addition of ex-Roxy Music John Wetton, but it was nothing more than another fine Uriah Heep album. And, sometimes, that's enough, but a little magic every once and a while would be nice, too. —*Daevid Jehnzen*

● The Best of Uriah Heep / 1976 / Mercury ✦✦✦✦
Collecting the best moments of their sometimes inconsistent albums, *Best of Uriah Heep* is an effective introduction to the band. —*Daevid Jehnzen*

High and Mighty / 1976 / Bronze ✦✦
Well, they better not be getting *High and Mighty* if this is the kind of lukewarm product they're going to be pawning off on fans. The beginning of the decline is right here, folks. —*Daevid Jehnzen*

Firefly / 1977 / Castle ✦✦
Featuring a new singer in John Lawton, Uriah Heep still couldn't pull themselves up by the bootstraps with *Firefly*. —*Daevid Jehnzen*

Innocent Victim / 1977 / Castle ✦
Innocent Victim? Well, I guess they're talking about their fans, since there's no way they were asking for this kind of faceless, plodding heavy rock. Again, I have to ask, *where is the magic?* —*Daevid Jehnzen*

Fallen Angel / 1978 / Castle ✦
Evidently the boys are speaking about themselves, since nothing illustrates Uriah Heep's fall from grace better than the bland boogie rock of *Fallen Angel*. —*Daevid Jehnzen*

Conquest / 1980 / Castle ✦✦
Wonderful / 1980 / Chrysalis ✦✦
○ Abominog / 1982 / Castle ✦✦✦✦
Head First / 1983 / Castle ✦✦✦
Equator / 1985 / Portrait ✦✦
Live in Moscow / 1988 / World Of Hurt ✦✦
Raging Silence / Feb. 1989 / Enigma ✦

Gary Usher
Surf, Pop/Rock
Gary Usher's importance in the history of California rock is considerable. He co-wrote several of the Beach Boys' early songs with Brian Wilson, including classics like "In My Room," and "409," and produced the Byrds' *Younger than Yesterday* and *Notorious Byrd Brothers* albums. He was also an occasional performer. —*Richie Unterberger*

○ Hot Rod U.S.A. / 1994 / Usher ✦✦✦✦
This quasi-legitimate release collects 30 tunes (mostly hot rod & surf) that Usher had a hand in as producer and/or performer between 1960 and 1965, most taken from rare collector 45s. While there are occasional touches of Buddy Holly, girl groups, or the Four Seasons, it sounds like nothing as much as a collection of Beach Boys/Jan & Dean outtakes from the early '60s. That's not to say, though, that they're on par with the average early Beach Boys albums; it's pretty innocuous (if not downright formulaic) stuff, and after a while you might start to wish it *was* the Beach Boys and not so relentlessly lightweight. Some of the better tracks are actually the ones on which he and/or his studio charges eschew the sub-Beach Boy approach altogether for raunchy, reverb-soaked surf instrumentals. This set includes some rare, virtually unknown cuts that Brian Wilson himself co-wrote, by the likes of the Super Stocks, the Timers, and Rachel & the Revolvers, but its appeal is really limited to surf/Beach Boy fanatics. —*Richie Unterberger*

King Uszniewicz & His Uszniewicztones
Group, Rock & Roll
A hilariously inept Detroit bowling-alley/lounge band fronted by Ernie "King" Uszniewicz (b.1945) from 1969 to 1979. The crudest tenor saxophonist in the history of rock & roll, King Uszniewicz (pronounced "you-snev-vitch") & the U-Tones had only one single, issued on a local label during the '70s. Dubbed by one critic as "the worst oldies band I ever heard in my life," they played with a bludgeoning energy, oblivious to the fact that they were woefully shy in the talent department. However, when the group's first album showed up on several college-radio playlists in 1989, they earned a minor cult following among both record collectors and young alternative-music fans. —*Stephen Thomas Erlewine*

Teenage Dance Party / Norton ✦✦✦
Their first album, featuring both sides of their original and lone 45 ("Surfin' School"/"Cry on My Shoulder") and insane versions of "Papa Ooh Mow Mow," "Little Latin Lupe Lu," and "This Should Go On Forever." Raw, crude, tuneless and wonderful. —*Stephen Thomas Erlewine*

● Twistin' and Bowlin' / Norton ✦✦✦✦
Subtitled "just when you thought it was safe to go back into the bowling alley," and more than living up to all that implies. Drunken, out-of-control versions of "Way Down Yonder in New Orleans," "Peppermint Twist," and Johnny Mathis's "Chances Are" are among the numerous highlights. Scary. —*Stephen Thomas Erlewine*

○ Doin' the Woo-Hoo / Norton ✦✦✦✦
More oldies-band mayhem. "At the Hop," "G.T.O.," "Love Letters in the Sand," the title cut, and King Uszniewicz's wife Arlene belting out "It's My Party" are just a few of the standout tracks. Extremely potent stuff. —*Stephen Thomas Erlewine*

U.T.F.O.
Group, Rap
Doctor Ice, the Kangol Kid, and the Educated Rapper (later joined by Mix-Master Ice) formed the Brooklyn group Untouchable Force Organization (U.T.F.O.) by dreaming up a tune about a gorgeous woman oblivious to their charms and appeals. "Roxanne, Roxanne" dominated the airwaves for much of 1984 and 1985, yielding eventually over 100 answer versions. Their first albums included the hit single plus "Roxanne Part 2" and "The Real Roxanne." The group's

popularity and influence waned as the Roxanne fad peaked, and subsequent releases had limited appeal. *—Ron Wynn*

● **UTFO** / 1985 / Elektra ✦✦✦✦
The Brooklyn production/performance combo UTFO shot to fame in the mid-'80s with their story about "Roxanne, Roxanne." It generated a flood of answer songs, started the careers of both Roxanne Shante and the Real Roxanne, and for a moment put UTFO in the thick of hip-hop and urban contemporary music. Unfortunately, they really weren't that gifted, as they showed on such singles as "Bite It," "Beats and Rhymes," and "Lisa Lips." They're now rightly regarded as novelty/one-hit wonders. *—Ron Wynn*

Skeezer Pleezer / 1986 / Elektra ✦✦✦
Reality began to set in for UTFO with their second album in 1986. They got a little buzz from the single "We Work Hard," but were essentially already in stylistic retreat as the gimmick tag they picked up for the success of "Roxanne, Roxanne" was proving difficult to shake. It didn't help that songs like "Bad Luck Barry" and "House Will Rock" didn't exactly inspire generations of aspiring rappers. *—Ron Wynn*

Lethal / 1987 / Select ✦✦
Everyone including Roxanne (The Real one and all stand-ins, substitutes and replacements) had forgotten by the time of album number four that UTFO had once had an underground smash with "Roxanne, Roxanne." Instead, audiences had tuned out the group's novelty/comic fare, microphone challenges, sexual posturing and anything else they tried. *—Ron Wynn*

Doin' It! / 1989 / Select ✦✦

Bag It & Bone It / 1990 / Jive ✦✦

Utopia

Group, Art-Rock/Progressive-Rock, Pop/Rock
Utopia is a rock quartet that theoretically features equal participation by its members, although singer and guitarist Todd Rundgren (b. Jun 22, 1948), who formed the band, is a recognized solo star and frequently dominates the group. The first two albums found them billed as Todd Rundgren's Utopia, a six-piece unit. But as of the third album, *Ra*, Utopia was a four-piece unit, including Rundgren, Roger Powell, John Wilcox, and Kasim Sulton, and that lineup was still in place as of 1986, which is the last time they released new material. *—William Ruhlmann*

Todd Rundgren's Utopia / Oct. 1974 / Bearsville ✦✦
After five solo albums released between 1970 and 1974, Todd Rundgren organized the band Utopia, although he also maintained a solo career. At this point, the group, a sextet featuring Kevin Ellman on percussion, Moogy Klingman and Ralph Schukett on keyboards, M. Frog Labat on synthesizers, and John Siegler on bass and cello, had little independent existence, as indicated by its billing, but later it would be a more equal unit. On this debut album, TR's U plays extended compositions—three of the four tracks run over 10 minutes each, with "The Ikon" clocking in over half an hour—in a hard rock/heavy metal/progressive rock mode with little of Rundgren's usual melodic appeal. *—William Ruhlmann*

RA / Feb. 1977 / Bearsville ✦✦
By the time of its third album, Utopia had become an independent band, without the possessive "Todd Rundgren's" attached to it, and it was stripped down to a quartet of Rundgren, Roger Powell (keyboards), Kasim Sulton (bass), and John ("Willie") Wilcox (drums). Rundgren shared writing and lead vocal chores with his band mates. Ironically, the result sounded more like Rundgren's solo work than Utopia's first two albums, mixing Bernard Herrmann movie music with the show music approach of "Magic Dragon Theatre" and a typically Rundgrenesque ballad style on "Eternal Love," which was written by Powell and Sulton and sung by Sulton. All of that was on side one, however, with side two largely given over to "Singring and the Glass Guitar," the kind of extended, progressive rock composition that must have helped inspire *This Is Spinal Tap.* *—William Ruhlmann*

Oops! Wrong Planet / Sep. 1977 / Bearsville ✦✦✦
Utopia's fourth album (and second to be released in 1977) found the quartet moving in a much more pop-rock direction, with Todd Rundgren especially contributing catchy songs like "Love in Action" and "Love Is the Answer." *—William Ruhlmann*

Back to the Bars / 1978 / Rhino ✦✦

Adventures in Utopia / Jan. 1980 / Bearsville ✦✦✦
At this point in Todd Rundgren's career, he seems to have juggled a schedule of alternating one year's solo work, during which he'd record two albums, with a year's work with Utopia, during which he'd also record two albums. Thus, in January, 1980, Utopia returned for the first of two albums, *Adventures in Utopia*. Having moved Utopia in more of a pop direction, Rundgren and company went even farther this time and were rewarded with two hit singles, "Set Me Free" (#27) and "The Very Last Time" (#76), while the album, reaching #32, was Utopia's highest-charting ever. Anyone who enjoyed the pop sound of Rundgren's early work would feel comfortable here. *—William Ruhlmann*

Deface the Music / Oct. 1980 / Bearsville ✦✦✦
On his solo album *Faithful*, Todd Rundgren had devoted a side of the LP to remaking elaborate studio recordings like the Beach Boys' "Good Vibrations" exactly. On Utopia's sixth album, it took a slightly different tack on the same notion, recording original songs in the style of the Beatles, as the Beatles had evolved from "I Want To Hold Your Hand" to their more psychedelic efforts. The result is not unlike Eric Idle's parody album *The Rutles. —William Ruhlmann*

Swing to the Right / Mar. 1982 / Bearsville ✦✦
After Todd Rundgren's 1981 solo year with *Healing*, Utopia returned to action with two 1982 albums, the first of which was this R&B-flavored effort, a far cry from the band's progressive rock beginnings, which even featured a cover of "For The Love Of Money." Maybe because things at Bearsville were winding down (this was the last Rundgren or Utopia album on the label), *Swing To The Right* missed cracking the Top 100 on the LP chart, but songs like "Lysistrata," a Rundgren pop tune based on the Greek anti-war play, showed the group was still in good form on occasion. *—William Ruhlmann*

Utopia / Sep. 1982 / Rhino ✦✦
For its second album of 1982, Utopia moved from the Bearsville subsidiary of Warner Bros. Records, a division of Warner Communications, to the Network subsidiary of Elektra/Asylum Records, another division of Warner Communications. Sounds like corporate shuffling, but it's the difference between being in print (the Bearsville recordings were reissued by Rhino in 1987) and being out of print. That's a shame, since this self-titled album-and-a-half (it was issued as two LPs; the second had Side Three pressed on both sides) is one of Utopia's better efforts, featuring their third and final hit single, "Feet Don't Fail Me Now" (#82), as well as the excellent "Hammer In My Heart" and "Princess Of The Universe," one of the group's best rockers, sung by drummer Willie Wilcox. *—William Ruhlmann*

POV / Jan. 1985 / Food For Thought ✦✦
Utopia's last album of new material, *POV* is not one of its more impressive efforts. Its best track is "Mated," a characteristically emotional Todd Rundgren ballad, but otherwise the songs don't live up to Utopia's usual standards. *—William Ruhlmann*

Trivia / Jun. 1986 / Passport ✦✦
Trivia is a compilation album of Utopia tracks from 1982-1986, including such favorites as "Hammer In My Heart," "Feet Don't Fail Me Now," "Princess Of The Universe," "Crybaby," and "Mated." It's a good selection, but it was superseded by the more complete *Anthology (1974-1985)* in 1989 and is, in any case, out of print. *—William Ruhlmann*

● **Anthology** / 1989 / Rhino ✦✦✦✦
Annotator Bud Scoppa calls this "the definitive Utopia album," which is fair enough. Utopia's ten albums tended to be uneven affairs, with the first three, *Todd Rundgren's Utopia, Another Live*, and *RA*, very much in a fusion/progressive style that could be somewhat opaque. *Deface The Music* was an overt pastiche of the Beatles, but the other six albums also bore the influence of pop's master group, as the four band members shared songwriting and lead vocal duties in a series of commercial-sounding ballads and rockers, only three of which became charting singles. *Anthology* rescues those tracks and several others from *Oblivion* (one of their ironic album titles) and even gives a taste of the band's early space-rock tendencies. A good companion to the Todd Rundgren *Anthology* released simultaneously by Rhino. *—William Ruhlmann*

Redux '92: Live in Japan / May 1992 / Rhino ✦✦

V

Steve Vai

Hard Rock, Fusion

Vai was a pupil of Joe Satriani as a teenager and studied at the Berklee School of Music before moving to Los Angeles at age 19. He was a huge fan of Frank Zappa's and joined Zappa's band after proving that he knew most of the repertoire and could transcribe orchestral pieces by ear. Zappa credited him on albums as the "stunt guitarist." He released the self-produced *Flex-able* in 1984, combining his Zappa and Satriani influences, and went on to play with Alcatrazz, David Lee Roth, and Whitesnake. Vai released his finest solo effort, the varied *Passion and Warfare*, in 1990. He then formed a backing group called VAI featuring vocalist Devin Townsend for *Sex & Religion* before recording the solo *Alien Love Secrets*. Vai is considered to be one of rock's top instrumentalists. —*Steve Huey*

○ **Flex-able** / 1984 / Akashic ♦♦♦♦
The self-released solo album from this former Zappa guitarist, featuring Zappa-influenced vocals, was recorded by Vai at home on an eight-track machine. The CD offers extra material from the *Flex-able* sessions originally released as a 10-inch EP. —*Paul Kohler*

● **Passion & Warfare** / Sep. 1990 / Relativity ♦♦♦♦
One of the most creative, musical, and mystical guitar albums ever made, it is a must-have. —*Paul Kohler*

Sex & Religion / Jul. 27, 1993 / Relativity ♦♦
Steve Vai formed a new straight-ahead heavy metal combo for the follow-up to his instrumental masterpiece, *Passion & Warfare*. In this context, the imaginative guitarist is saddled down by a pedestrian band and an overwrought vocalist, which limits Vai's ability to stretch out. Consequently, the record is the most predictable and conventional—not to mention boring—of Vai's usually remarkable career. —*Stephen Thomas Erlewine*

Alien Love Secrets / 1995 / Relativity ♦♦♦
After the disastrous full-band heavy metal project of *Sex & Religion*, Steve Vai returned to recording solo with *Alien Love Secrets*. It's a moodier, more atmospheric collection than his masterpiece *Passion and Warfare*, which makes it slightly revelatory. With the new sonic textures, the guitarist again demonstrates his fluid technique, which manages to never become completely mechanical. —*Stephen Thomas Erlewine*

Ritchie Valens

b. May 13, 1941, d. Feb. 3, 1959
Rock & Roll

A singer/guitarist of mixed Mexican-American and Native-American descent, Valens was the first Hispanic rocker of any consequence. During an effective career of barely a year (until his death in the same plane crash that killed Buddy Holly in 1959), Valens emerged with a basic high-energy rock sound that, at its most raucous, became an influence on performers up through the Kinks and Jonathan Richman. He delivered two classic songs, "Donna" and "La Bamba." —*Bruce Eder*

In Concert at Pacioma Jr. High / 1960 / Rhino ♦♦♦
A bizarre piece of work: a home-made tape of a high school concert. Possibly rock's earliest "official" live album, padded with narration and unfinished studio tracks. In shaky sound, but unique. —*Bruce Eder*

● **The Best of Ritchie Valens** / 1986 / Rhino ♦♦♦♦
The virtually complete recording legacy of an all-too-brief career. —*Bruce Eder*

The Ritchie Valens Story / Jun. 15, 1993 / Del Fi ♦♦
While this compilation features the official versions of Ritchie's three biggest songs ("La Bamba," "Donna," and "Come on, Let's Go"), the bulk of it is turned over to recently unearthed rehearsal takes and demos of his better-known sides. Not the place to start your Valens collection, but a real good place to go after you've absorbed the hits. —*Cub Koda*

Valentines

Group, Urban

While there are differing incarnations using the name Valentines, arguably the best was the one fronted by "Richie" Barrett and primarily backed by the Jimmy Wright Combo. They recorded for Rama from 1955 to 1957. There was one edition that recorded for King, Bethlehem, and United Artists in the early '60s; another known as Little Tom and the Valentines recorded for Mr. Big in 1961, and a female version cut a single for Ludix in 1962. Yet another Valentines ensemble recorded for Lee in 1963. —*Ron Wynn*

○ **The Best of the Valentines** / Collectables ♦♦♦♦
A good collection featuring the Valentines, a solid jump and ballad doo-wop aggregation who recorded in the 1950s and '60s for such labels as Old Town, Rama, King, Bethlelem, and United Artists. There were some Valentine albums on Murray Hill in the late '80s, but these are the better-known songs, although the group never really had any R&B or pop hits. —*Ron Wynn*

Frankie Valli & the Four Seasons (Francis Castelluccio)

Group, Pop/Rock

Frankie Valli, the lead singer of the Four Seasons, launched a solo career in 1965 after several years of chart-topping success, while still continuing with the group, which was re-billed as "Frankie Valli and the Four Seasons." He had actually begun as a solo, releasing the 1953 single "My Mother's Eyes" under the name Frankie Valley. His debut solo single was "(You're Gonna) Hurt Yourself" at the end of 1965, but his first solo success came with the gold-selling "Can't Take My Eyes Off You" (June 1967), which appeared on his first solo album, *Frankie Valli-Solo* (July 1967). This was followed by *Timeless* (1968). Valli discontinued solo work for half a dozen years, concentrating on the group. But he returned to solo recordings in the mid-'70s. His subsequent solo hits included the number one "My Eyes Adored You" (November 1974), "Swearin' to God" (May 1975), "Our Day Will Come" (October 1975), and the number one "Grease" (May 1978). —*William Ruhlmann*

○ **25th Anniversary** / 1987 / Rhino ♦♦♦♦
Frankie Valli and the Four Seasons scored hits from 1962 to 1978 under a variety of guises. Lead singer Valli started making solo records in 1965, and he had his own hits. They are all included in this long-overdue four-disc set, which runs from the Seasons' "Sherry" to Valli's "Grease." —*William Ruhlmann*

★ **Anthology** / 1989 / Rhino ♦♦♦♦♦
Over the course of twenty tracks, *Anthology* covers all of the Four Seasons' essential hits, as well as Valli's solo "Can't Take My Eyes off You"; it's the definitive collection. —*Stephen Thomas Erlewine*

Van Der Graaf Generator

Group, Art-Rock/Progressive-Rock
This art-rock group was principally centered around keyboardist, composer, and vocalist Peter Joseph Andrew Hammill (b. 1948). With floating personnel, which changed from record to record, and "sound paintings" that varied from heavy-handed to somber, Van Der Graaf Generator was cited by British punk bands as a seminal influence. Hammill continued to release solo albums in a similar vein throughout the '80s. — *Cub Koda*

Least We Can Do Is Wave / Feb. 1969 / Blue Plate ◆◆◆
On their ambitious second album, bandleader Peter Hammill was already writing enduring songs. — *Michael P. Dawson*

● **H to He, Who Am the Only One** / Jan. 1970 / Blue Plate ◆◆◆◆
A superb album, it includes the heavy metal-ish "Killer" and a guest appearance by guitarist Robert Fripp. — *Michael P. Dawson*

○ **Pawn Hearts** / 1971 / Blue Plate ◆◆◆◆
Lengthy prog-rock epics mix with Peter Hammill's intensely emotional lyrics. Robert Fripp guests on guitar. — *Michael P. Dawson*

Godbluff / 1975 / Blue Plate ◆◆◆
The start of a mid-'70s comeback, after a long hiatus, was stark, doomy and richly musical. — *Michael P. Dawson*

○ **World Record** / 1976 / Blue Plate ◆◆◆◆
The last album by the "classic" Van Der Graaf lineup was released in 1976. — *Michael P. Dawson*

○ **Still Life** / 1976 / Blue Plate ◆◆◆◆
The second and best of the mid-'70s comeback albums, it's highlighted by the incredible title track. — *Michael P. Dawson*

Quiet Zone / 1977 / Blue Plate ◆◆◆
This recording debuted a new VDGG lineup, with violin and bass taking the place of sax and organ—a somewhat rawer sound. — *Michael P. Dawson*

Vital Live / 1978 / Blue Plate ◆◆
The last Van Der Graaf releas was a 1978 live double-LP on a single CD. — *Michael P. Dawson*

Luther Vandross

b. 1951
Soul, Urban
In R&B music, Luther Vandross ranked with Prince, Stevie Wonder, and Michael Jackson as one of the most successful singer/songwriters and producers of the '80s. Amazingly, unlike those peers, Vandross for the most part did not cross over to widespread pop appeal, a situation that finally began to change at the end of the '80s and the start of the '90s. Born in New York City, Vandross has an elastic tenor that made him a natural for backup singing and commercial work in the '70s, when he became a top session vocalist. In 1975, Vandross worked with David Bowie on the latter's *Young Americans* album, even co-writing (with Bowie and John Lennon) the number one hit "Fame." In the second half of the '70s, he recorded under a variety of guises, cutting two albums for Cotillion under the name "Luther," recording with the session groups Roundtree and Change, and singing on hits by Chic.

In 1981, Vandross signed with Epic and released his debut album *Never Too Much*, which topped the R&B chart and sold a million copies. The title track was also an R&B number one single and reached the pop Top 40. Vandross went on to produce albums for Aretha Franklin and other female singers, while maintaining his own career through the '80s. His albums *Forever for Always for Love* (1982), *Busy Body* (1983), *The Night I Fell in Love* (1985), *Give Me the Reason* (1986), and *Any Love* (1988) were all million-sellers that spawned major R&B hits, but Vandross's pop success was spotty until 1989, when Epic released *The Best of Luther Vandross... The Best of Love*, a double-pocket greatest-hits album containing the new track "Here and Now," which became Vandross's first Top Ten pop hit. That proved his breakthrough, and Vandross's next album, *Power of Love* (1991), another million-seller, featured two pop hits, "Power of Love/Love Power" and "Don't Want to Be a Fool."

Things basically went smooth for Luther Vandross on the commercial front in the early '90s, though not so smoothly behind the scenes. He toured with Anita Baker in 1990 and En Vogue in 1993, and on both tours there were disputes that eventually went public. Vandross issued *Never Let Me Go* in 1993, and while it did well, it wasn't quite the commercial powerhouse of his past releases. — *William Ruhlmann*

○ **Never Too Much** / 1981 / Epic ◆◆◆◆
The auspicious debut, demonstrating Vandross's gorgeous vocal arrangements and his lush, romantic singing on the #1 R&B smash "Never Too Much" and the Top Ten "Don't You Know That?," plus the tour de force version of "A House Is Not a Home." — *William Ruhlmann*

Forever for Always for Love / 1982 / Epic ◆◆◆
Luther Vandross scored his first platinum album and cemented his status as the new heartthrob king of the 1980s with this fine second release. Strangely, his sublime version of "Since I Lost My Baby" wasn't issued as a single, but the combination hit "Bad Boy/Having A Party" was an R&B sensation and helped secure the album's crossover success. — *Ron Wynn*

Busy Body / 1983 / Epic ◆◆◆
An accurate title for a man who seemed to be producing all the divas in the business at this time, including Dionne Warwick, who turns up for a duet on "How Many More Times Can We Say Goodbye." It's one of three R&B Top Ten hits here, the others being "I'll Let You Slide" and the brilliant medley "Superstar/Until You Come Back to Me (That's What I'm Gonna Do)." — *William Ruhlmann*

○ **The Night I Fell in Love** / 1985 / Epic ◆◆◆◆
A wonderful version of Stevie Wonder's "Creepin'" almost gets lost on another hit-filled collection, which includes the Top Five R&B smashes "'Til My Baby Comes Home" and "It's Over Now." — *William Ruhlmann*

Give Me the Reason / 1986 / Epic ◆◆◆
Luther Vandross was riding high in the 1980s, dominating the R&B charts and slowly, but steadily, increasing his pop exposure. This was his fourth consecutive platinum smash and second straight double-platinum winner, but beyond that was a superbly sung, expressive triumph. "Stop To Love" and "Give Me The Reason" were beautifully produced, arranged, and performed numbers and huge R&B hits (the latter a chart topper), and deserved a better pop fate. — *Ron Wynn*

○ **Any Love** / 1988 / Epic ◆◆◆◆
There were some who felt that Vandross suffered a slight slump when this album only reached the platinum level after two consecutive double-platinum winners. But "Here And Now" was a huge smash, and by now the pop crowd was fully aware of Vandross' vocal charms and allure. "She Won't Talk To Me" was a bit on the posturing side, but still managed to do decently, while there were also fine album cuts like "I Wonder" and "Are You Gonna Love Me." — *Ron Wynn*

★ **The Best of Luther Vandross** / 1989 / Epic ◆◆◆◆◆
By the time this way-overdue double-record hits collection came out, Vandross had done many more R&B singles than could fit on it, so *The Best of Luther Vandross... The Best of Love* is inadequate to encompass him. It does, however, contain "Here and Now," which broke Vandross through to the pop Top Ten long after most people had given up hope that he'd ever cross over. — *William Ruhlmann*

Power of Love / 1991 / Epic ◆◆◆

Never Let Me Go / Jun. 1, 1993 / Epic ◆◆
Luther Vandross may have fallen a bit from his lofty perch among R&B stars, but it wasn't due to any dip in skills. This release contains more examples of his supple, fluid vocals, expert delivery, and sophisticated yet soulful style. Indeed, Vandross hasn't made many better overall albums from a strict singing standpoint; his voice is full and impressive in every register, and there's no sign of strain when he reaches to the top of an arrangement or extends notes and phrases. Perhaps there are signs of creative wear and tear; there's no real blockbuster single, and the final medley, which blends classics from the Spinners and Bee Gees, sounds thrown together. A retooling might be in order. — *Ron Wynn*

Songs / 1994 / Sony ◆◆
Luther Vandross could sing almost anything convincingly, which is one of the reasons *Songs* is so entertaining. A collection of personal favorites, *Songs* suffers from the common flaws of covers albums—it isn't consistent, it sounds slightly canned, and seems like a way to buy time between "real" albums. Nevertheless, Vandross is a truly fine singer, which is what makes *Songs* worthwhile. — *Stephen Thomas Erlewine*

Van Halen

Group, Hard Rock, Heavy Metal, Pop/Rock
Van Halen was one of the most popular American hard rock/heavy metal bands to emerge in the '70s, primarily distinguished by the fleet fingers of guitarist Eddie Van Halen. Actually, Eddie and his brother Alex, who played the drums, were born in the Netherlands, though they moved to California as children, as did bassist Michael Anthony and singer David Lee Roth. They formed the group in Pasadena in 1974 and worked their way up the Southern California club circuit, signing with Warner Brothers in 1977. Their debut album, *Van Halen,* released in 1978, went gold in three months, platinum in eight. Every album since has sold at least a million copies.

The group hit a popular peak in 1984 with *1984,* which sold four million copies in its first year of release, and its #1 single, "Jump," after which Roth left the band for a solo career. He was replaced by Sammy Hagar, and the success has continued, with four successive chart-topping albums to date. —*William Ruhlmann*

★ **Van Halen** / 1978 / Warner Brothers ✦✦✦✦✦
The prototype: Eddie Van Halen proves the hand is quicker than the ear, while David Lee Roth plays the role of outrageous frontman to perfection. Includes "You Really Got Me" and "Runnin' with the Devil." —*William Ruhlmann*

Van Halen II / 1979 / Warner Brothers ✦✦✦
Van Halen's second album sounded identical to their debut, yet it lacked the consistent songwriting of the first album. "Dance the Night Away" was a Top 20 hit and "Beautiful Girls" became one of their AOR staples, but most of the album sounded rushed and incomplete. —*Stephen Thomas Erlewine*

○ **Women & Children First** / 1980 / Warner Brothers ✦✦✦✦
Women and Children First expanded the musical range of Van Halen, as Eddie Van Halen increased his bag of tricks, flipping out bizarre noises and lightning-fast licks as mere asides. David Lee Roth used Eddie's aural jokes as a platform for lyrical jokes. In a whirlwind performance, Roth acted more like a comedian than a lead singer, and while that may be annoying on occasion, it certainly kept the record interesting. —*Stephen Thomas Erlewine*

Fair Warning / 1981 / Warner Brothers ✦✦✦
Perhaps as a reaction to David Lee Roth's unhinged performance on *Women & Children First, Fair Warning* was dominated by Eddie Van Halen, who has rarely played better than he has here, filling the record with imaginative sonic textures. However, sonic textures don't necessarily make for great songs, and that's the main problem with *Fair Warning.* Eddie's guitar has as much personality as Diamond Dave's strutting vocals, and given the right context could carry an album as effectively as Roth did with *Women & Children First,* but the songs do not provide a consistently strong support for his playing. Still, few guitarists match his power or his grace, and his performance is quite compelling. —*Stephen Thomas Erlewine*

Diver Down / 1982 / Warner Brothers ✦✦✦
Although it went platinum, *Fair Warning* didn't match the multi-platinum standards of Van Halen's first three records, so the group revamped their sound slightly for the follow-up, *Diver Down.* Adding the slightest hints of synthesizers and streamlining both the guitar indulgences of Eddie Van Halen and the vocal excesses of David Lee Roth, the album contained some of the group's most pop-oriented performances—and they were all in the guise of covers. "(Oh) Pretty Woman" and "Dancing in the Street" had the traditional mechanical Van Halen rhythmic pulse, as well as concise solos from Eddie and restrained vocals from Diamond Dave, which helped them become the hits they were designed to be. If they were off-set by more original material like "Hang 'Em High," the concessions would have been acceptable, but the rest of *Diver Down* is filled with covers, including "Big Bad Bill," "Where Have All the Good Times Gone," and a closing "Happy Trails." All of the songs are professionally performed, and the music features more ideas than most previous Van Halen albums, but the lack of strong original material makes *Diver Down* less of an accomplishment than it appears. —*Stephen Thomas Erlewine*

☆ **1984** / 1984 / Warner Brothers ✦✦✦✦✦
Adding synthesizers to the mix, Van Halen turned pop while retaining much of its hard-rock propulsion, resulting in a quantum leap in sales. Includes "Jump," "I'll Wait," "Panama," and "Hot for Teacher." —*William Ruhlmann*

5150 / 1986 / Warner Brothers ✦✦✦
Van Halen proves it can survive in the post-Roth era, as Eddie continues to burn up the fretboard and Sammy Hagar turns out to fit into the group's style just fine. Includes "Why Can't This Be Love," "Dreams," and "Love Walks In." —*William Ruhlmann*

○ **OU812** / 1988 / Warner Brothers ✦✦✦✦
Van Halen broke open the pop innovations of *5150* with *OU812,* their second album with Sammy Hagar. On *OU812,* Hagar's direct approach is fully incorporated into the group, as the band churns out straightahead heavy rockers like "Black and Blue" and pulsing power ballads like "Feels So Good." Under Eddie's direction, the group adds a couple of stylistic quirks—from the chicken-picking of "Finish What You Started" and the Hawaiian flourishes of "Cabo Wabo" to the driving, jazz-inflected metallic "Mine All Mine"—which make *OU812* one of the band's most intriguing and rewarding albums. —*Stephen Thomas Erlewine*

For Unlawful Carnal Knowledge / 1991 / Warner Brothers ✦✦✦
The smirking title indicates the true nature of *For Unlawful Carnal Knowledge,* Van Halen's third album with Sammy Hagar. Backing away from the diversity of *OU812,* the band turns in some of the most basic, straightforward rock & roll of their career. At times, *F.U.C.K.* recalls the sleek hard rock of Hagar's early-'80s albums, and it's undeniable that his limited vocal power had a great deal to do with the obvious nature of most of this music. While the band is still tight and professional—and Eddie's guitarwork remains impressive—the songwriting is, by and large, undistinguished, with the anthemic "Right Now" standing out as the most memorable song of the batch, mainly because of its incessant chorus. —*Stephen Thomas Erlewine*

Van Halen Live: Right Here, Right Now / 1993 / Warner Brothers ✦✦
Van Halen assembled its first live album, the two-CD *Live: Right Here Right Now,* from a collection of tapes dating from 1985, when Sammy Hagar replaced David Lee Roth, to the present. Only a few songs recall Roth's days, and too many songs from *For Unlawful Carnal Knowledge* are featured (10 of its 11). With the exception of the consistently impressive Eddie Van Halen, the album slows to a halt during the solo passages. Most of the time, the performances aren't all that different from the original studio recordings. Despite the moments of tedium, *Live: Right Here Right Now* deserves to be in any real Van Halen fan's collection; those who aren't devoted to the band would be advised to stick with the original albums. —*Stephen Thomas Erlewine*

Balance / 1995 / Warner Brothers ✦✦
Balance tries to open up the Van Hagar formula somewhat. Eddie Van Halen sincerely attempts to improve the group musically, by adding more subtle and assured ballads and more fearless rockers. No matter how hard he tries, he's weighed down by the most predictable rhythm section in all of rock & roll, which gives each number the same unvarying deadlocked pulse, completely obliterating the Eddie's increased musical sensitivity. Of course, he isn't helped by Hagar, either. Hagar also tries to follow the social conscience that served him so well on "Right Now," as the first single "(Don't Tell Me What) Love Can Do." Unfortunately, he can't help himself and slips back to the raucous partying of "Amsterdam"—you know, the place where they're allowed to smoke pot and stuff. —*Stephen Thomas Erlewine*

Vanilla Fudge

Group, Hard Rock, Psychedelic
Specializing in thundering psychedelia, Vanilla Fudge gave the Supremes hit "You Keep Me Hangin' On" an ultra-serious, somewhat indulgent arrangement and hit big in 1968. They were introduced to Atco by veteran producer Shadow Morton and fronted by keyboardist Mark Stein. "You Keep Me Hangin' On" was only a minor seller in 1967. Reissued a year later, it proved far more potent its second time around. Bassist Tim Bogert and drummer Carmine Appice later played with Jeff Beck and Rod Stewart. —*Bill Dahl*

● **Psychedelic Sundae: The Best of Vanilla Fudge** / 1993 / Rhino ✦✦✦✦
A generous compilation, *Psychedelic Sundae* includes the best of this heavy, progressive, psychedelic band from the late '60s. —*AMG*

Vanilla Ice

Rap
With his hit single "Ice Ice Baby" and its accompanying album, *To the Extreme,* Vanilla Ice became the second White rapper to top the charts. Unlike the Beastie Boys, he didn't have any street credibility, so the Miami-born rapper decided to invent some of his own, claming he had a seriously violent gangster past. Nevertheless, "Ice Ice Baby" became a number one hit late in 1990, thanks to the pulsating bass riff from David Bowie and Queen's "Under Pressure." *To the Extreme* also went to the top of the charts, spending 16 weeks at number one and selling over seven million copies. Ice began filming a feature film, *Cool as Ice,* in the spring of 1990, but by the time the film came out in the fall, his star had fallen dramatically; *To the Extreme* was at number one longer than the soundtrack to *Cool as Ice* was on the charts.

Sensing that his time had passed, Vanilla Ice took a couple years off, re-emerging in 1994 with *Mind Blowin.* Dispensing with the pop-rap formula of his debut, the rapper adopting the lazy, rolling funk of Cypress Hill, as well that trio's obsession with pot. The album was a commercial disaster, disappearing from sight immediately after its release. — *Stephen Thomas Erlewine*

● **To the Extreme** / 1990 / SBK ✦✦✦✦
On the strength of the incessantly catchy single "Ice Ice Baby," *To the Extreme* was an enormous success, holding the number one slot for 16 weeks and selling over seven million copies in America. Apart from that single and a cover of Wild Cherry's "Play That Funky Music," the album was unmemorable, with limp beats and tepid rhymes. — *Stephen Thomas Erlewine*

Cool As Ice [O.S.T.] / 1991 / SBK ✦✦

Extremely Live / Mar. 1991 / SBK ✦
Vanilla Ice's reputation had already been shredded by the time this live CD was issued. It really wouldn't have mattered that he had invented an identity (standard operating procedure on the hip-hop circuit) if he had the skills, but Vanilla Ice proved himself amazingly bad beyond even the most militant hip-hopper's dreams. Nobody expected stunning insights, compelling raps or brilliant rhymes, but they at least expected his live show to be funny. Instead, it was just sad. — *Ron Wynn*

Mind Blowin / 1994 / SBK ✦✦
Four years after *To the Extreme,* Vanilla Ice came back with a refashioned, modern sound, borrowing from the blunted Cypress Hill, the deep funk of Dr. Dre, the quick-tongued rapping of Das EFX—basically, anything that's been popular since his first album. While he spends an obscene amount of time dissing 3rd Bass, he counters all charges of being a sellout by stating that he has sold over 11 million records. There isn't a single moment that establishes a distinct musical identity, and the whole thing is rather embarrassing. Not surprisingly, the record dropped out of sight almost a month after its release. — *Stephen Thomas Erlewine*

Vapors

Group, New Wave, Power Pop/Anglo-Pop
Led by vocalist/guitarist Dave Fenton, the Vapors were a short-lived new wave guitar group that is best known for the spiky pop single "Turning Japanese." Fenton formed the first version of the Vapors in 1978, yet he was the only member to survive that lineup; in 1979, former Ellery Bops members Ed Bazalgette (lead guitar) and Howard Smith (drums) joined the band and bassist Steve Smith came aboard shortly afterward. One of the band's first concert was seen by the Jam's Bruce Foxton, who asked them to perform on his group's *Setting Sons* tour. Before long, the Vapors were managed by Foxton and John Weller, the manager of the Jam, as well as the father of the group's leader, Paul Weller.

The Vapors signed to United Artists, releasing their first single, "Prisoners," at the end of 1979; it failed to chart. "Turning Japanese," the band's second single, became a major hit, reaching number three on the U.K. charts in March of 1980. *New Clear Days,* the band's debut album, was released two months later, which didn't sell as well as the single. In 1981, the Vapors released the more ambitious *Magnets,* yet it received lukewarm reviews and poor sales; the group disbanded shortly after its release. — *Stephen Thomas Erlewine*

○ **New Clear Days** / 1980 / United Artists ✦✦✦✦
It's easy to dismiss this band as a one-hit wonder—surely the album has nothing quite as infectious as the single, "Turning Japanese." *New Clear Days* is, however, a fine example of punchy British

pop in the vein of the Jam that holds up better than most albums from the period. — *Chris Woodstra*

Magnets / 1981 / Liberty ✦✦✦
David Fenton was obviously growing tired of being written off as light-weight after "Turning Japanese" and responded with the more ambitious and mature *Magnets.* Here he explores the darker side of life, discussing the Kennedy assassination ("Magnets"), police harrassment ("Civic Hall") and even cult leader/mass murder Rev. Jim Jones ("Jimmy Jones," the failed single). Musically the band is more sophisticated, taking the occasional misstep in the arrangements by adding an annoying sythesizer in songs like "Spiders." Virtually ignored by both critics and the buying public, this is a strong follow-up that deserved a better fate. — *Chris Woodstra*

● **Anthology** / 1995 / One Way ✦✦✦✦
A somewhat misleading title, *Anthology* is a straight reissue of *New Clear Days* with four songs from *Magnets* tacked on to the end. Since the band only made two albums it would have been nice to release both as a two-fer—or at least add some rare tracks to the anthology. Minor complaints aside, this is probably all the Vapors most people will ever need. — *Chris Woodstra*

Vaselines

Group, Alternative Pop/Rock
Eugene Kelly and Frances McKee were bored with their town, so they decided to form a band; they were called the Vaselines. Adding Charles Kelly on drums and bassist James Seenan, the Scottish quartet began rehearsing in their basements; soon they began recording their rough, simple and highly melodic pop songs in studios in Glasgow and Edinburgh. They recorded about 20 raw, pure pop gems that were barely heard by anyone. The Vaselines would likely have faded away into obscurity if it wasn't for Nirvana, who recorded two of their songs (both appear on the *Incesticide* compilation); Kurt Cobain was very vocal about his admiration for the band and Eugene Kelly in particular. By this time, the Vaselines had broken up and Kelly had formed Captain America, which later became Eugenius; soon, Eugenius became a hip band in alternative circles and the Vaselines' music was reissued. — *Stephen Thomas Erlewine*

● **The Way of the Vaselines** / Jul. 31, 1992 / Sub Pop ✦✦✦✦
The Way of the Vaselines collects everything the Vaselines ever recorded; it's a rough gem of raw pop. — *Stephen Thomas Erlewine*

Jimmie Vaughan

Blues Rock
Jimmy Vaughan was lead guitarist for Austin, TX's Fabulous Thunderbirds and also recorded with brother Stevie Ray for the Vaughan Brothers' sole album. Unlike Stevie's thick Hendrix and Beck-influenced stylings, Jimmy's tone is leaner and cleaner. — *Rick Clark*

○ **Strange Pleasure** / Epic ✦✦✦✦
Vaughan's solid solo debut is loaded with good-time Austin roadhouse blues-influenced rock. Guest artists include Lou Ann Barton, Dr. John and Nile Rodgers. Lovers of a good earthy groove and fine economical guitar work should pick up on this. — *Rick Clark*

Stevie Ray Vaughan

b. Oct. 3, 1954, **d.** Aug. 27, 1990
Blues Rock
Stevie Ray Vaughan was the most impressive blues guitarist to appear in the '80s, which made his death in a helicopter crash at the start of the '90s all the more tragic. Vaughan grew up in Dallas, the younger brother of Jimmie Vaughan (co-founder of the Fabulous Thunderbirds). Stevie began playing in clubs at 12, and by 17 had dropped out of high school and moved to Austin. There followed years of struggling until April 23, 1982, when Vaughan and his group, Double Trouble, played a private audition for the Rolling Stones in New York. The gig led to an invitation to appear at the Montreux Jazz Festival, at which Vaughan was seen by David Bowie, who hired him to play guitar on his *Let's Dance* album, and Jackson Browne, who offered the free use of his recording studio. Vaughan took up that offer after being signed by legendary talent scout John Hammond to Epic, recording his debut album, *Texas Flood,* in the fall of 1982.

The release of the album led to a wave of recognition that included gold albums, Grammy awards, and other accolades over the next seven years. In 1987, Vaughan took time out to go through a rehabilitation program to overcome alcohol and drug addiction, and he wrote about the experience on his final studio album, *In Step* (1989). In the last year of his life, he embarked on a co-headlining tour with Jeff Beck and recorded a duo album with his brother. He had just finished a jam with Eric Clapton and Robert Cray at a show at Alpine Valley in East Troy, WI, when he was killed. In 1991 Epic released the posthumous *The Sky Is Crying*, assembled by Jimmie Vaughan. — *William Ruhlmann*

Texas Flood / 1983 / Epic ✦✦✦
A late-arriving star, Vaughan did not make his first album until the age of 28. By that time he had become a seasoned player, so this doesn't really sound like a debut album; rather, it sounds like a blues guitar master at the top of his form. Highlights include "Pride & Joy," "Love Struck Baby," "Lenny," and the hard blues title cut. — *William Ruhlmann*

○ **Couldn't Stand the Weather** / 1984 / Epic ✦✦✦✦
Vaughan does not ease up on this second set, even taking on Jimi Hendrix in a rendition of "Voodoo Chile (Slight Return)," and handling it beautifully. — *William Ruhlmann*

○ **Soul to Soul** / 1985 / Epic ✦✦✦✦
Soul to Soul shows that Vaughan is a great guitarist, but everybody already knew that. What makes this album different from his two previous efforts is the inspired backing of Double Trouble—who finally sound like they aren't intimdated by their leader—and Vaughan's considerably more soulful and assertive vocals. — *Stephen Thomas Erlewine*

Live Alive / 1986 / Epic ✦✦✦
Live Alive not only covers many of Vaughan's most popular album tracks, but it also showcases a version of Stevie Wonder's "Superstition." Other standout tracks include "Look at Little Sister," "Willie the Wimp," and "Cold Shot." — *Rick Clark*

★ **In Step** / 1989 / Epic ✦✦✦✦✦
Vaughan sounds just as fierce sober as he did before, and he is beginning to bloom as a songwriter, a fact most notable on the driving "The House Is Rockin'" and the confessional "Wall of Denial." — *William Ruhlmann*

Family Style / Jan. 1990 / Epic ✦✦✦
Jimmie and Stevie Ray Vaughan team up for this relaxed one-off, produced by Nile Rodgers. In spite of a couple of throwaway songs, "Hard to Be," and "Good Texan" showcase their lean Austin-style electric blues/roadhouse R&B to good effect. "Tick Tock" became a poignant hit, released just as Stevie Ray died in a helicopter crash. — *Rick Clark*

○ **The Sky Is Crying** / 1991 / Epic ✦✦✦✦
The posthumously released *The Sky Is Crying*, assembled out of tracks recorded between 1984 and 1989, is a lovingly assembled tribute to Vaughan's brilliance as a guitarist. Arguably this is Vaughan's finest album. The first-rate playing is unforced and natural in execution. On the songs, from his impeccable version of Hendrix's "Little Wing" to the hard blues shuffle of "Empty Arms," Vaughan's execution is unforced and his phrasing is relaxed. The release contains great liner notes and track information. Fans of hard blues-rock should check this one out. — *Rick Clark*

In the Beginning / Oct. 6, 1992 / Epic ✦✦✦
Although this is a very rough early concert from 1980, this album captures an energetic Stevie Ray Vaughan still developing his signature style, which makes it essential to fans. — *Stephen Thomas Erlewine*

Bobby Vee

Pop/Rock, Teen Idol
Bobby Vee enjoyed his greatest success in the early '60s, with five Top Ten singles, including the classic, "Take Good Care of My Baby." Vee's vocal style was similar to that of his hero, Buddy Holly. Ironically, Vee's break came when he filled in for Holly the day after his death in a plane crash. Like those of many of his contemporaries, his career went into a tailspin with the arrival of the British Invasion in 1964. He did score one more Top Ten single in 1967 with "Come Back When You Grow Up." — *Kenneth M. Cassidy*

Bobby Vee Meets the Crickets / 1962 / EMI America ✦✦✦
The reissue of this enjoyable album includes *ten* bonus tracks, including alternate takes, unreleased songs, and the "Buddy Holly Medley," a recent recording by Vee and the Crickets. — *Stephen Thomas Erlewine*

I Remember Buddy Holly / 1963 / EMI America ✦✦✦
Vee's fun tribute to Buddy Holly has been beefed up on its CD reissue. Ten bonus tracks have been included, and any songs that overlap with the *Meets the Crickets* album have been replaced with alternate versions. — *Stephen Thomas Erlewine*

● **Legendary Masters** / 1990 / EMI America ✦✦✦✦
The most complete collection of Vee's recordings includes "Take Good Care of My Baby," "Rubber Ball," and "The Night Has a Thousand Eyes." — *Kenneth M. Cassidy*

Suzanne Vega

b. Aug. 12, 1959, Santa Monica, CA
Singer-Songwriter
Vega was born in Santa Monica, CA, and moved to New York City at age two. She attended the High School of Performing Arts, then Barnard College. Vega was still at Barnard when she began attracting attention at Greenwich Village folk clubs and was featured on several issues of the songwriters' magazine/record album *The CooP* (later *The Fast Folk Musical Magazine*) in 1982. She was signed to A&M Records in 1984 and released her first album, *Suzanne Vega* in 1985. It was a critical success and a moderate seller. Vega's second album, *Solitude Standing*, featured "Luka," a song about child abuse that became a surprise hit single in 1987. The album itself went gold. Vega took three years to release the follow-up, *Days of Open Hand* (1990), which was a commercial disappointment, though a few months later a couple of British DJs, under the name D.N.A., put out a dance version of her a cappella song "Tom's Diner" from the album *Solitude Standing*, and it became a hit.

On her next album, 1992's *99.9 Degrees F.*, Vega experimented with the dance rhythms that made "Tom's Diner" a hit; although the result was interesting, it didn't give her any hits. Vega's fifth album was scheduled for release in the spring of 1996. — *William Ruhlmann*

○ **Suzanne Vega** / 1985 / A&M ✦✦✦✦
Vega's most consistent collection of songs spotlights her hushed, restrained singing style and the spare, precise backup produced by Lenny Kaye. But it's those songs—"Small Blue Thing," "Undertow," "Marlene on the Wall"—with their brittle imagery (things are always frozen, flat, or cracking) and restraint—that let you know there's a big new talent here. — *William Ruhlmann*

● **Solitude Standing** / 1987 / A&M ✦✦✦✦
A more uneven but still striking album, featuring "Tom's Diner" (in its pre-disco version) and the hit "Luka." — *William Ruhlmann*

Days of Open Hand / 1990 / A&M ✦✦
99.9 Degrees F. / Sep. 8, 1992 / A&M ✦✦✦
While this is not the techno album that Suzanne Vega was rumored to be making, *99.9 Degrees F.* does offer a significant departure from her previous contemporary folk albums. Vega uses more synthesizers and drum machines, often evoking a bizarre carnival-esque atmosphere on the album. Still, *99.9 Degrees F.* is a folk album at heart; every song is steeped in traditional song form, and Vega's writing is strong. Fans of Vega's previous work might be taken aback, but those willing to listen to the album will find that Vega has produced one of her strongest records yet. — *Stephen Thomas Erlewine*

Velvet Crush

Group, Country-Rock, Power Pop/Anglo-Pop
Formed in the late '80s, the power-pop trio Velvet Crush combines Beatlesque melodies with R.E.M. hooks and a loose, rocking attitude. *In the Presence Of*, their 1991 debut, didn't capture much of an audience outside of college radio; the 1994 follow-up, *Teenage Symphonies to God* also failed to break into the mainstream, yet it did increase their following slightly. — *Stephen Thomas Erlewine*

In the Presence Of / Oct. 18, 1991 / Ringers Lactate ✦✦✦
Velvet Crush's debut album had a couple of fine cuts, yet it was a rather unfocused effort, saved by the band's infectious energy. — *Sara Sytsma*

● **Teenage Symphonies to God** / 1994 / Epic ✦✦✦✦
Velvet Crush's second album is an old-fashioned pop record: 12 songs in 40 minutes, filled with ultra-melodic guitar hooks and simple, memorable melodies. While it's traditional in form, the music on *Teenage Symphonies to God* isn't retro. Velvet Crush manage to inject a real enthusiasm and freshness in the standard three-minute pop song, whether they're playing originals that

sound like forgotten classics ("Time Wraps Around You," "This Life is Killing Me," "My Blank Pages," "Hold Me Up") or forgotten classics themselves (Gene Clark's "Why Not Your Baby" and Matthew Sweet's "Something's Gotta Give"). With a crisp, warm production from Mitch Easter, *Teenage Symphonies to God* is one record that deserves to take its title from Brian Wilson. *—Stephen Thomas Erlewine*

The Velvet Underground

Group, Rock & Roll
The Velvet Underground was one of the few bands of consequence to emerge from New York City in the '60s. They played their first gig near the end of 1965, and shortly thereafter hooked up with pop artist Andy Warhol. Warhol in effect "sponsored" the band, allowing them to rehearse at his studio, known as the "Factory," and putting together a multimedia extravaganza featuring the Velvets, entitled *The Exploding Plastic Inevitable*. Warhol also grafted German chanteuse, model, actress, and would-be singer Nico onto the group's core: Lou Reed (vocals, guitar), John Cale (vocals, bass, viola), Sterling Morrison (guitar), and Maureen Tucker (drums).

Reed was the group's main songwriter. Via material such as "Heroin," "Sister Ray," "Candy Says," and "I'm Waiting for My Man," he chronicled a number of aspects of his community, as all folksingers have done. In Reed's case, the community was that of lower Manhattan: a mix of artists, junkies, homosexuals, and transvestites. Such being the case, the Velvets had problems even having radio ads for their first album. Their deliberate aesthetic of amateurish primitivism, raw, distorted production, drones, and feedback did not help win them radio play. On top of all this, their stage presence (wearing wraparound shades and black clothes, making deadpan stage announcements, and at all times projecting ennui) appeared to be closed and hostile, flying directly in the face of the then-prevailing ethos of "love, peace, happiness, and the dawning of a new age." It is one of the great ironies of rock that they sold very few albums while together (1967-1970), yet in the '80s and early '90s their influence was pervasive, manifesting itself in the work of groups as disparate as R.E.M. and the Jesus & Mary Chain. The joke has always been that they didn't sell a lot of albums, but everyone who bought one started a band. One of the results of this is that everything they issued is still in print.

All told, the Velvets released four studio albums, one a year from 1967 through 1970. Nico left after the first, Cale after the second. Doug Yule took Cale's place for the final two studio albums.

After Reed's departure in 1970, the Velvet Underground recorded one more album without any of the original members; the band fell apart quickly after its release. During the '70s, two live live albums were issued and in the '80s, Polygram released two albums of demos and outtakes.

After years of denying reunion rumors, the original Velvet Underground (Reed, Cale, Morrison, Tucker) reunited for a European concert tour in 1993. Although they planned to tour the U.S. and record an *MTV Unplugged* album, tensions between John Cale and Lou Reed escalated quickly and the band split again, only a few months after their European tour. Cale and Reed vowed never to work with each other again because, as Reed said, they "can't stand each other." *—Rob Bowman*

☆ **The Velvet Underground & Nico** / Jan. 1967 / Verve ◆◆◆◆◆
Nominally produced by Andy Warhol, *The Velvet Underground and Nico* is one of the most important and influential albums of all time. The only record the group recorded with Nico, the disc includes the seminal "Heroin," "I'm Waiting for the Man," and "Venus in Furs." As with the finest films and books, each song provides a window into a world that most will otherwise not have experienced. "Heroin" is probably the finest example of this, with the rush and subsequent down of the drug masterfully conveyed via Tucker's unorthodox drum style (simply involving padded beaters on a bass drum turned on its side), continuous changes in tempo, different musicians playing in different tempos at the same time, and Cale's shrieking viola-induced feedback at the end. In terms of sound the whole album is wide ranging, moving from the melodic beauty of "Femme Fatale" to the intense cacophony of "European Son." *—Rob Bowman*

☆ **White Light/White Heat** / 1967 / Verve ◆◆◆◆◆
By the time of *White Light/White Heat*, Nico had departed to embark upon a solo career. The Velvets, now also minus Warhol, concocted an extraordinarily abrasive, tension-filled album, full of mind-numbing feedback and incessant drones. The playing and

production on this album herald a punk aesthetic eight years ahead of the fact. Standout tracks include the sidelong improvisatory "Sister Ray" and the John Cale-narrated, Lou Reed-written "The Gift." *—Rob Bowman*

☆ **The Velvet Underground** / 1969 / Verve ◆◆◆◆◆
In an unexpected, abrupt departure from the ferocity of their first two albums, the Velvets' third album is a muted, folk-rockish, even warm affair. The impression is almost of a band deliberately turning down to create a restrained, haunting ambience, but it suffers not in the least for the loss of volume: "Pale Blue Eyes," "I'm Set Free," and "Candy Says" are some of Reed's greatest songs, "Some Kinda Love" will satisfy those looking for the requisite Velvet kinkiness, and "Beginning To See The Light" and "What Goes On" prove that the group can handle straightforward, charging rockers masterfully. *—Richie Unterberger*

☆ **Loaded** / 1970 / Warner Brothers ◆◆◆◆◆
Recorded in the summer of 1970 while the band was playing a summer-long residency at Max's Kansas City in New York. Feeling increasingly disaffected, Reed walked out after the last gig at Max's, never to return. The album was remixed and edited without him, much to his later chagrin. Whatever imperfections may have consequently occurred, *Loaded* remains an absolute must. The Velvets were now playing stripped-down rock & roll and Reed was writing such enduring classics as "Sweet Jane" and "Rock & Roll," as well as the underrated "New Age," "Train Round the Bend," and "Oh! Sweet Nuthin'." *—Rob Bowman*

Live at Max's Kansas City / 1972 / Cotillion ◆◆◆
Literally recorded the last night Lou Reed ever played with the Velvet Underground, at New York's Max's Kansas City, we have this album due to the foresight of Warhol acolyte and employee Brigid Polk, who happened to bring her cassette recorder to document that evening. The sound is a little one-dimensional, and you can hear Jim Carroll ask for Tylenol and others order drinks over the course of the record, but the recording is nonetheless fascinating. Brigid's tape was about an hour and a half long. Cotillion released just under half of it. The sound of the group is a little different, because Doug Yule's brother Billy was temporarily replacing drummer Maureen Tucker, since the latter was pregnant with her first child. *—Rob Bowman*

Squeeze / 1973 / Polydor ◆
After Lou Reed left the Velvet Underground, bassist Doug Yule took control of the group. Retaining the name "The Velvet Underground," Yule assembled several new lineups of the band and toured the U.S. By the time Yule's VU recorded their first album, the band featured Boston-based vocalist Willie Alexander and was playing a set of conventional pop/rock songs. *Squeeze*, the only album recorded with a bastardised version of the Velvet Underground, was released in 1973 to uniformly terrible reviews; Yule broke up the band shortly after its release. Over the years, *Squeeze* has not only become increasingly rare—after all, not many copies of the record were pressed—it has disappeared from the official Velvet Underground discography and Yule's attempt to prolong the band's career has virtually been forgotten. *—Stephen Thomas Erlewine*

☆ **1969: Velvet Underground Live** / 1974 / Mercury ◆◆◆◆◆
Originally a double album and released in two volumes with added songs on CD, *1969: Velvet Underground Live* is a stunning document of the Reed, Yule, Morrison, Tucker edition of the Velvets at their pinnacle. Recorded privately in Texas and San Francisco, the Velvets play extended, intensely driven, out-and-out versions of songs from their first three albums as well as then-unreleased material such as "Ocean," "Real Good Time Together," and "Sweet Bonnie Brown." *—Rob Bowman*

Etc. [Bootleg] / 1979 / Plastic Inevitable ◆◆◆
The impact of this bootleg has been blunted by the *VU* compilation, which presented the four key late-'60s outtakes here in vastly superior sound. At the time, though, it was a revelation for fans of their booming cult, and the remaining six tracks are intriguing listening, if you can track down a copy. There are four mid-'60s garage-rock tunes that Reed played, sang, and either wrote or co-wrote for shoddy exploitation labels as a member of the Primitives, the Roughnecks, and the Beachnuts; crude and more crassly pop than anything the Velvets attempted, they nonetheless betray clear hints of things to come. It also has a couple of sound collages from 1966 and 1967 with marginal Velvet participation that ended up on a rare album and flexi-disc; these are collectibles and nothing more. *—Richie Unterberger*

And So On [Bootleg] / 1982 / Plastic Inevitable ✦✦✦
The release of the long-expected Velvet Underground box set may render the contents of this bootleg nearly useless, and two of the tracks have already shown up in much-improved sound on *VU.* For the time being, it has some valuable unreleased material, including a couple of pretty, acoustic Lou Reed ballads, a ferocious 1967 live performance of the unreleased rocker "Guess I'm Falling In Love," and a 1966 John Cale avant-garde burst of noise that appeared on a little-known flexi-disc. —*Richie Unterberger*

☆ **Vu** / 1985 / Verve ✦✦✦✦✦
Composed principally of songs that would have appeared on the Velvets' unreleased fourth MGM album, this is only slightly less impressive than their first three LPs, striking a balance between the searing pre-punk of their first two efforts and the calm eloquence of the third. "Lisa Says," "Ocean," and "Stephanie Says" are some of Reed's greatest ballads; "I Can't Stand It" is one of the Velvets' toughest and best conventional hard rock songs. Some of the other tunes are slight (if engaging) in comparison with the Velvets' prime work. Many of the tracks were re-recorded by Reed on his early solo albums, and in every instance, the Velvets' versions are better. —*Richie Unterberger*

Another View / 1986 / Verve ✦✦✦
Polygram finally started to scrape the bottom of the barrel with this grab bag of outtakes from 1967 to 1969, most of which don't approach the magnificence of most of the Velvets' studio output. It's never less than interesting, though, and certainly worth perusal by Velvets fans. Especially noteworthy are a gloriously tough version of "We're Gonna Have A Good Time Together" (one of their best simple rock tunes), the grinding instrumental "Guess I'm Falling In Love," and an early version of "Rock And Roll." —*Richie Unterberger*

● **Best of the Velvet Underground** / 1989 / Verve ✦✦✦✦
The Best of the Velvet Underground: Words and Music of Lou Reed is a 15-track summary of the Velvets' career, borrowing heavily from the debut (six tracks) and featuring "Sweet Jane" and "Rock & Roll," licensed from Atlantic. —*William Ruhlmann*

Live MCMXCIII / 1993 / Warner Brothers ✦✦
The four original Velvets chose to put decades-old differences aside and reunite for a series of European concerts. Recorded at L'Olympia Theatre in Paris over three nights, *Live MCMXCIII* is available as either a two-disc set containing the whole show, or as an abridged single-disc set. There's a real cutting edge to this concert recording that screams rejuvenation. The dour Velvets are actually having fun. Vocals are right up front in the mix, not a consistent advantage, as Reed sometimes comes unglued here. In a daring move, Cale takes effective vocal turns on "All Tomorrow's Parties" and "Femme Fatale." But it's the often overlooked Tucker and Morrison who construct a flawless percussive and rhythmic backbone that give the event its real cohesion and structure. —*Roch Parisien*

What Goes On? / 1993 / Raven ✦✦✦
An Australian box set covering their enormously influential career, *What Goes On?* sums up the Velvet Underground quite nicely. Nearly all of their most famous songs are here ("The Gift" is missing), but its real strength is in its rarities. Hardcore fans will adore the radio commercials for the band, as well the original mono mixes from *The Velvet Underground & Nico* and the alternate, "closet mixes" of the third album. Because of these tracks, die-hard fans will need this box, but it will also serve as a perfect, if expensive, introduction for those unfamiliar with the band. —*Stephen Thomas Erlewine*

BOOK

✦✦✦ **Up-tight: The Velvet Underground Story**, by Victor Bockris & Gerard Malanga (Omnibus, 1983). It's kind of surprising that such a vastly influential group has only merited one biography, but this slim volume does a good job at capturing both the essential details of their history and the flavor of their musical and social circle. That's probably because most of the story is told by the characters themselves, in their own words: most of the text consists of extended quotes from the band and important associates, taken from both first-hand and previously published sources, with narrative links from the authors to establish continuity. The stories behind the Velvets' albums and performances, as well as the Andy Warhol Factory that they were an essential part of at the beginning of their career, are fascinating. And there are plenty of them: blow-by-blow ac-

counts of each album, the contributions and dismissals of John Cale and Nico, their confrontational performances, and the overall joy and struggle of swimming against the currents of both mainstream and underground '60s rock to explore bold territory. Some of these memories have been fleshed out in subsequent years, and some minor inaccuracies corrected (see especially the excellent Velvet Underground magazine *What Goes On*), but this remains a superb read, with lots of great vintage photos. —*Richie Unterberger*

Velvets

Group, R&B, Doo-Wop
A Texas-based R&B vocal group, discovered by Roy Orbison in 1960. The Velvets tasted fleeting pop success with their violin-enriched "Tonight (Could Be the Night)." Lead singer Virgil Johnson was an Odessa, TX, high school teacher, and he recruited four of his students to form the Velvets. Orbison brought the quintet to Nashville-based Monument, but in spite of well-crafted material from the Big O (who also cut "Lana" himself at Monument) and the presence of Nashville's finest session players, only the uptempo "Tonight (Could Be the Night)," penned by Johnson, and the spirited Orbison/Joe Melson tune "Laugh" graced the pop charts in 1961. —*Bill Dahl*

● **Tonight (Could Be the Night)** / Sony ✦✦✦✦
This Texas R&B vocal quintet shares Orbison's trademark musical approach, with soaring lead vocals by Virgil Johnson and sumptuous string-drenched arrangements. —*Bill Dahl*

The Ventures

Group, Surf Rock, Rock & Roll
From Tacoma, WA, the Ventures were formed in 1959, originally named the Versatones. The early lineup consisted of Don Wilson (b. 1937), rhythm guitar; Bob Bogle (b. 1937), lead guitar; Nokie Edwards (b. 1939), bass; and Howie Johnson, drums. They pressed a twangy, rocked-up version of Johnny Smith's "Walk Don't Run" on their own Blue Horizon label, which was later picked up by Dolton Records. It became a #2 hit in 1960. Bogle and Edwards switched instruments and Mel Taylor replaced Johnson on drums in 1963. More hit singles featuring their cleanly played but rockin' style followed, but the band wisely entered the album market early on, and it was there they found their true format placing 37 chart entries and more than 50 albums between 1960 and the mid '70s.

The Ventures are the biggest-selling instrumental group of all time, but their influence extends far beyond mere record sales. With their solid-body Fender guitars (later switching to Mosrite Ventures models) and matching suits, their album covers defined what a rock & roll combo should look like. Likewise, their sound was so popular that they released several successful instructional albums in the *Play with the Ventures* series that many later rock stars cut their teeth on. Because they played instrumentals, they were among the first American bands to break big in Japan (no language barrier), eventually honored as the first foreign members of that country's Conservatory of Music for selling over 40 million records. Edwards left and was replaced for a while by Jerry McGee, but he returned in 1972, restoring the early '60s lineup, which has endured to the present day. They continued to tour and record, sounding better than ever, their place in rock & roll guitar history assured. —*Cub Koda*

Ventures Play Telstar & the Lonely Bull / 1962 / Liberty ✦✦
A Top Ten album for the group in early 1963, it really doesn't hold up today. Like many of their LPs, it demonstrates their versatility on faithful covers of a number of contemporary hits, ranging from rock to soul to easy listening. In every case, you're better off with the original versions. The CD reissue combines this album and their 1963 LP *The Ventures in Space*. —*Richie Unterberger*

Ventures in Space / 1963 / Dolton ✦✦✦
Few listeners need to dig deeper than a greatest hits collection for the Ventures, but this early effort is an arguable exception. The group embellished their trademark sleek guitar instrumentals with creepy, then-futuristic production effects, sounding at times like a mix of surf music and the incidental music to *Star Trek*. The ghostly, theremin-like sounds on several tracks were actually produced by top session player Red Rhodes on steel guitar. The British instrumental group the Tornados (of "Telstar" fame) did this kind of stuff better, if you're looking for this kind of thing. The

CD reissue combines this album and the 1962 LP *The Ventures Play Telstar—The Lonely Bull and Others.* —*Richie Unterberger*

○ **The Ventures on Stage** / 1965 / Dolton ✦✦✦✦
Explosive live recordings from Japan, England, and the U.S., with a hot greatest-hits medley and a wild "Driving Guitars" being among the highlights. *The Ventures on Stage Around the World* is out of print but worth any search. —*Cub Koda*

★ **Walk, Don't Run: The Best of the Ventures** / 1990 / EMI America ✦✦✦✦✦
A perfect 29-track CD compilation, with great notes and superlative sound. All the hits, from "Walk Don't Run" to "Hawaii Five-O." Important album sides, plus interviews and radio spots. A perfect introduction. —*Cub Koda*

○ **Live In Japan '65** / 1995 / ✦✦✦✦
Originally released in Japan as a double album, this live set was unavailable in the U.S. until 1995. So cleanly recorded (the drums are especially crisp) that one is tempted to believe these tracks might have actually been laid down in the studios, it has a speedy, frenetic, well-executed edge that makes this worth checking out by Ventures fans. 78 minutes of material, including most of their big '60s hits, covers of then-contemporary surf and British Invasion tunes, and surprises like "The Pink Panther Theme" and a 10-minute version of Duke Ellington's "Caravan." —*Richie Unterberger*

Tom Verlaine

b. 1949, Wilmington, DE
Alternative Pop/Rock
Ex-Television leader recorded numerous albums following the band's breakup. The best of them hint at what that group could've done, had they stuck it out for a few more albums. —*John Floyd*

○ **Tom Verlaine** / 1979 / Elektra ✦✦✦✦
This, his solo debut, expands the musical vocabulary of Television, while elaborating on Verlaine's sometimes sketchy lyricism. —*John Floyd*

● **Dreamtime** / 1981 / Warner Brothers ✦✦✦✦
The closest he's come to crafting a solo masterpiece features dense guitar structures and his best set of songs since Television's *Marquee Moon* hit the racks. —*John Floyd*

Always / 1981 / Warner Brothers ✦✦✦

Words from the Front / 1982 / Warner Brothers ✦✦✦
The material is patchy enough to make this one worthwhile only for devotees, who will no doubt scarf up the angst-ridden title cut. Others will groove on the picture-pop-perfect "Postcards from Waterloo." —*John Floyd*

○ **Cover** / 1984 / Warner Brothers ✦✦✦✦
Dense, synth-heavy production notwithstanding, this 1984 set is a sharp and poignant set of desperate romantic gems. —*John Floyd*

Flash Light / 1987 / IRS ✦✦
The guitars are brought back up front, but most of the songs are half-baked. Diehards will dig it, nonetheless. —*John Floyd*

The Wonder / 1990 / Fontana ✦✦

Warm and Cool / 1992 / Rykodisc ✦✦✦
Warm and Cool serves as a primer of instrumental electric guitar stylings, from the '50s rumble of Link Wray, twang of Duanne Eddy and surf of The Ventures right up to contemporary, whitelight experimental feedback. These influences are filtered through Verlaine's moody grasp of urban paranoia. The overall feel of the 14 tracks is hypnotic, mysterious, and somewhat foreboding, like the soundtrack to a good film noir. —*Roch Parisien*

Verlaines

Group, Alternative Pop/Rock
New Zealand guitar-pop group the Verlaines released their first record in 1984. Led by singer/songwriter/guitarist Graeme Downes, the group has gone through several lineup changes throughout their career; by 1993, he was the only original member left in the group. —*Stephen Thomas Erlewine*

Hallelujah All the Way Home / 1985 / Positive ✦✦✦
Hallelujah All the Way Home finds the band looking for a style, somewhat aimlessly. Through epic-length complex compositions, the band sometimes loses its way, but in a few cases (such as "It Was Raining") a glimpse of potential is revealed. Not a great album, but a few very good songs. —*Chris Woodstra*

● **Bird Dog** / 1987 / Homestead ✦✦✦✦
The strongest of their early albums and probably the defining Verlaines work, *Bird Dog* is the band's first great album and serves as the blueprint for much of their later work with its ambitious arrangements, unorthodox song structures and a mood that rapidly shifts from manic to melancholy . —*Chris Woodstra*

○ **Juvenilia** / 1987 / Positive ✦✦✦✦
A collection of singles from the band's early career which provides an adequate introduction to the Verlaines's unique style. —*Chris Woodstra*

Some Disenchanted Evening / 1990 / Positive ✦✦✦
Some Disenchanted Evening returns with an approximation of its predecessor's brilliance. This time the band is more effective on the more traditional straightahead rock than on the experiments. While it's not as cohesive an effort, "Jesus What a Jerk" is probably their best pop song to date. —*Chris Woodstra*

Ready to Fly / Jul. 1991 / Slash ✦✦
Ready to Fly marked the band's major label debut and (predictably) an increased mainstream pop awareness—the album sounds sort of like Verlaines-lite. Though it lacks the punch of *Bird Dog*, it is not without good points—Graeme Downes's songwriting is nearly flawless, as usual. —*Chris Woodstra*

Way Out Where / 1993 / Slash ✦✦
Now the only original member remaining in the band, songwriter Graeme Downes seems to have lost interest in his pet project. The songs are craftsmanlike pop but uninspired. Its commercial failure made the band decide to call it quits. —*Chris Woodstra*

Veruca Salt

Group, Alternative Pop/Rock
Veruca Salt reshaped the jagged, abrasive punk-pop of the Pixies and Breeders into a more-accessible, riff-driven power-pop formula that also borrowed from hard pop-rockers like Cheap Trick. It was a successful formula, both musically and commercially, yet it didn't ensure them indie-rock credibility; in fact, they became one of the most harshly criticized bands of the post-Nirvana alternative rock era.

Led by guitarist/vocalist Louise Post and Nina Gordon, Veruca Salt released their debut single, "Seether"/"All Hail Me," in 1994 on a Chicago-based independent label, Minty Fresh. Produced by Brad Wood (Liz Phair), the record became a word-of-mouth sensation, working its way to alternative and college radio stations. While supporting Hole on their fall tour, Veruca Salt released their debut album, *American Thighs*, on Minty Fresh, yet they soon cut a deal with Geffen, who re-released the album. "Seether" became an MTV hit as well, and soon the single was an across-the-board success. However, the group received scathing criticism from magazines and fanzines, claiming the band was nothing but rip-off artists, using Minty Fresh as a way to gain credibility. Nevertheless, the group's popularity didn't suffer and *American Thighs* went gold, even though their next two singles—"Number One Blind" and "All Hail Me"—didn't attract half the attention of "Seether." —*Stephen Thomas Erlewine*

● **American Thighs** / 1994 / Minty Fresh ✦✦✦✦
With their thin, sing-song vocals and fuzzed-out guitars, Veruca Salt may sound like the Breeders and the Pixies, but lack either band's talent for inverting pop conventions or taste for the bizarre. What Veruca Salt has instead is a raw talent for simple, infectious pop songs; the result is a surprisingly fresh fusion of alternative pop and bubblegum. Louise Gordon and Nina Post try hard to inject meaning into the sweet, distorted rush of "Seether," but all that sticks is the infectious melody and crushing guitars. That also applies to the slower songs, from the enchanting lust of "Spiderman '79" to "Forsythia," which is too close to the Breeders' *Pod* for comfort. But musically, *American Thighs* is surprisingly satisfying; it's a pure pop album masquerading as the next big thing. —*Stephen Thomas Erlewine*

The Verve

Group, Alternative Pop/Rock
In the early '90s, Verve gained a strong following in the native England with their crushingly loud, guitar-soaked neo-psychedelic pop. In America, the band had to change their name to *the* Verve, in order to avoid a lawsuit with Verve Records. —*Stephen Thomas Erlewine*

● **A Storm in Heaven** / Jun. 1993 / Vernon Yard ✦✦✦✦
The Verve's debut album is a collection of cascading guitars and meandering melodies made memorable by the band's elliptical sense of songwriting. —*Stephen Thomas Erlewine*

No Come Down / May 17, 1994 / Vernon Yard ✦✦✦
No Come Down collects various singles, B-sides, and rarities; it's for devoted fans only. —*Stephen Thomas Erlewine*

○ **A Northern Soul** / 1995 / Vernon Yard ✦✦✦✦
At the Verve's first album arrived admist a torrent of good reviews and high commercial expectations, English guitar rock was just being revived with the glam-stop of Suede. By the time *A Northern Soul,* their second full-length album, was released, a lot had changed. Oasis and Blur had changed the scene of British guitar rock, bringing it away from the long, trance-inducing meditations of "My Bloody Valentine" and to a harder, more pop-oriented rock & roll. With *A Northern Soul,* the band tried to reign in their psychedelic flourishes, working with Oasis's producer Owen Morris, bringing a more distinctive pounding back beat no matter what they do, their songs drag on a little too long to capitalize on their sheer sonic power—instead of seeming epic, the songs just seem ponderous. —*Stephen Thomas Erlewine*

Vibrators

Group, Punk
One of the great myths in rock & roll is that only serious, dedicated musicians can make great records; a philosophical tract dictating that great rock & roll is not the province of bandwagon jumpers, poseurs, fakes and commercially-minded trend groupies. The reality is that great rock & roll can be made by anyone, even accidentally. Case in point, the Vibrators. If you saw a photograph of this "punk" band a few months before they signed a label deal with Columbia in 1976, you would have seen long hair, and bell-bottom trousers—they were bloody hippies! But, by the time they released their debut LP, *Pure Mania,* they had short hair, fake leopard skin pants, safety pins, cheap sunglasses, all the accoutrements a good born-again punk band needed. Did that make them inherently bad? Not really, a tad disingenuous perhaps, but no worse than a punk band (e.g., Generation X) that professed to being real punks all the while secretly harboring the desire of being as commercially viable as the dinosaur bands they purportedly loathed.

Although the existence of *Pure Mania* is a good illustration of accidental inspiration, it also proves that moments like this can happen once in a dross-filled career. Such was the case with the Vibrators who went on to record nearly a dozen records over a 15-year period, none of them worth mentioning. *Pure Mania,* on the other hand, remains as good now as it did when it was released. This is due to the fact that the band simply adapted a formula that eschewed the rage and fury of the Sex Pistols and Clash for the relative accessibility of the Ramones and the Damned. So, while the Pistols sang "No Future," *Pure Mania* is jumpstarted by a track called "Into the Future." Even the songs about emotional desolation ("No Heart") are more catchy than frightening or ominous. Sure, *Pure Mania* is a fake though and through, but hating it for that reason alone makes you the boring old fart. Besides, the speedy guitars, irresistible hooks and snappy songs are infectious. —*John Dougan*

○ **Pure Mania** / 1977 / Columbia ✦✦✦✦
Don't be fooled into thinking that, based on *Pure Mania,* the Vibrators released anything else of merit. They didn't. But this is a fine, funny fake of a record from the squalling "Into the Future…" to the softcore fantasy "Whips and Furs" to the tongue-in-cheek sexism of "I Need a Slave." Punky pop not punk rage. Not inspirational, but what did you expect from a bunch of poseurs? —*John Dougan*

● **The Power of Money: The Best of the Vibrators** / Dec. 1991 / Continuum ✦✦✦✦
By taking the best moments from the Vibrators' debut *Pure Mania,* as well as their inconsistent follow-ups, *Power of Money* winds up as a fine collection of their energetically melodic punk rock. —*Stephen Thomas Erlewine*

Village People

Group, Disco
Part clever concept, part exaggerated camp act, the Village People were worldwide sensations during disco's heyday and keep reviving like the phoenix. Producer Jacques Morali in 1977 assembled a group designed to attract gay audiences while parodying (some claimed exploiting) that same constituency's stereotypes. He landed a deal with Casablanca, then carefully recruited an appropriate cast of characters. These included go-go dancer Felipe Rose, who was dressed in Native American headdress when first spotted, Alexander Briley, Randy Jones, David Hodo, Glenn Hughes, and Victor Willis, the one group member with some genuine vocal skills. Songwriters Phil Hurtt and Peter Whitehead were tabbed to compose songs with gay underpinnings, and other roles and costumes were carefully selected; among them were a cowboy, biker, soldier, policeman, and construction worker complete with hard hat. The group clicked first in England with the single "San Francisco (You Got Me)" in 1977, then reaped stateside honors with "Macho Man" in 1978. "Y.M.C.A." and "In the Navy" were worldwide smashes, both peaking at number two on the pop charts. Neither song did as well on the R&B/soul side, with "In the Navy" doing best at number 30. Though a disco band rather than an R&B, soul, or funk unit, the Village People's ranks included at one time or another three solid singers in original lead vocalist Willis, his replacement Ray Simpson, and later Miles Jaye, who took Simpson's place. After two more successful singles, "Go West" and "Can't Stop the Music," the group's fortunes plummeted, in large part due to their participation in the ill-fated film also titled *Can't Stop the Music.* They tried a comeback with updated dance-rock material, but flopped. They've resurfaced in the '90s with more new cuts, though they haven't rekindled past success. Jaye became a major figure in Urban Contemporary circles in 1987, and continues recording and performing as a solo vocalist. —*Ron Wynn*

● **Greatest Hits** / 1988 / Rhino ✦✦✦✦
The best collection of their campy disco hits available. —*Stephen Thomas Erlewine*

○ **The Best of the Village People** / Mar. 22, 1994 / Casablanca ✦✦✦✦
Although it isn't as listenable as Rhino's collection, this disc does contain all of their hits, making it a good purchase. —*Stephen Thomas Erlewine*

Gene Vincent (Vincent Eugene Craddock)

b. 1935, **d.** Oct. 12, 1971
Rock & Roll
Though his chart hits were few, no one defined the initial greasy-haired, leather-jacketed, hot-rods 'n' babes spark of rock & roll more than Gene Vincent. Far more influential as a live performer, Vincent, with his backing group the Blue Caps, defined the lifestyle and visual prowess of the music, as well as touring with a wild-ass stage show that usually left a sea of destroyed equipment, hotel rooms, deflowered schoolgirls, and musical converts in their wake. Dogged by tax problems and the emerging teen-idol trend in pop music, he emigrated to the U.K. by the early '60s, where he found himself revered as a founding father of the music. Several bids for a chart comeback failed, and by the late '60s, alcoholism had reduced his once-energetic stage prowess to a bloated self-parody. But a quick spin of his '50s Capitol sides dispels all that: the rebellious spirit of rock & roll's first flowering lives on in the supercharged recordings of Gene Vincent & the Blue Caps. Be-Bop-A-Lula, indeed. —*Cub Koda*

○ **The Capitol Years 1956-63** / 1987 / Charly ✦✦✦✦
While Vincent recorded a fair number of overlooked gems during his prime, he also cut a greater number of uninspired tracks. This lavishly packaged and exhaustively annotated ten-album set inadvertently charts the rapidly plummeting quality of his recordings, even as it unearths worthy obscurities. It does manage to gather all of his classic 1956 sessions with guitarist Cliff Gallup in the same place, but Gene's subsequent efforts could have easily been boiled down to a supplementary disc or two. —*Richie Unterberger*

★ **Capitol Collectors Series** / 1990 / Capitol ✦✦✦✦✦
Breathless, unintelligible, and spirited rockabilly at its non-Sun best, this 21-track compilation covers Vincent's Capitol recordings (including "Be-Bop-A-Lula," "Race with the Devil," and "Lotta Lovin'") in admirable form. —*Hank Davis & Stephen Thomas Erlewine*

○ **Gene Vincent Box Set** / 1994 / EMI ✦✦✦✦
Six CDs containing the complete Capitol and EMI-Columbia recordings by Vincent, from 1956 through 1964. The 151 tracks may seem excessive, but the sound glitters, and since most of the post-1962 material was never issued in the United States, this stuff

could be revelatory to serious fans. And the booklet is filled with detailed notes, sessionographies, and great photos. —*Bruce Eder*

BOOK

✦✦✦ The Day The World Turned Blue: A Biography Of Gene Vincent, by Britt Hagarty (Blandford Press, 1984). In both the best and worst senses, Vincent was an archetype for the rock & roll lifestyle. A dynamic performer who risked life and (literally) limb for the music, he was also plagued by health problems (mostly associated with his bum leg), alcoholism, and increasing mental instability, contributing to his early death in his mid-30s. This is a good bio, one of the best of the early rock & roll stars, in fact. Vincent's commercial and artistic peak was brief, and his decline excruciatingly long, although he remained an extremely popular performer in Europe for most of his life. Hagarty follows the whole trail without romanticizing it, drawing upon memories from many members of Gene's backing bands, fellow musicians, ex-wives, and other associates. It covers the early hits, the frequent bouts of pain and temper, the death of his close friend Eddie Cochran in 1960 in a car accident in which Gene himself narrowly escaped death, and the prolonged dissipation of his final decade. —*Richie Unterberger*

Violent Femmes

Group, Alternative Pop/Rock

With their geeky, nervous folk-pop, the Violent Femmes became one of the '80s' biggest cult bands. The new wave group features Gordon Gano (vocals, guitar, songwriter), Brian Ritchie (bass), and Victor DeLorenzo (drums). The Femmes formed in the early '80s in Milwaukee, WI. In 1982, they released their self-titled debut, which has approached neo-classic status in some circles. Their following albums weren't as popular or consistent, yet each one has a few good songs. —*Michael Anne Erlewine*

★ **Violent Femmes** / 1983 / Slash ✦✦✦✦✦
One of the leading albums in alternative rock. On their first album (by far their best) the Violent Femmes began their professional career with a style that proves both entertaining and distinctive. Includes "Blister in the Sun," "Add It Up," and "Gone Daddy Gone." —*Meredith Erlewine*

Hallowed Ground / 1985 / Slash ✦✦✦
Though mistaken for a parody when it was released, *Hallowed Ground* features Gordon Gano's serious Christian convictions. The teenage angst is pushed aside on this more mature effort based, for the most part, in traditional American folk—of course, it's slightly skewed. —*Chris Woodstra*

○ **Blind Leading the Naked** / 1986 / Slash ✦✦✦✦
A more mainstream effort courtesy of producer Jerry Harrison (Talking Heads). Gano returns to his troubled teen persona and the band rocks harder than on the previous two releases. A nice cover of the T-Rex classic "Children of the Revolution" and the yearning "I Held Her in My Arms," complete with a horn section. —*Chris Woodstra*

3 / 1989 / Slash ✦✦
The fourth album finds the band in somewhat of a rut creatively. Fans of the band's early days will appreciate the slightly stripped-back acoustic production but without much energy, the album falls flat in most places. Only the single, "Nightmares" and the confessional "See My Ships" leave any lasting impression. —*Chris Woodstra*

○ **Debacle: The First Decade** / 1991 / Slash ✦✦✦✦
This album is a compilation of all of their best recordings. Even though it contains a variety of the Femmes' changes in style, it doesn't live up to the standards of their first release. Still, enough highlights are covered to make this album the only other Violent Femmes album you'll need. —*Meredith Erlewine*

Why Do Birds Sing? / 1991 / Reprise ✦✦✦
After a several year absence, the Femmes make a comeback of sorts with the charming *Why Do Birds Sing?* Returning to their street-busking roots, the band plays stripped-back acoustic songs as a three piece. Though they can't fight the fact that they have grown up, the songs show that they can still have fun. —*Chris Woodstra*

○ **Add It Up (1981-1993)** / 1993 / Warner Brothers ✦✦✦✦
Although it isn't as comprehensive as it seems, *Add It Up* is a good collection of most of the Violent Femmes' best tracks. —*AMG*

New Times / 1994 / Elektra ✦✦

The Vogues

Group, Pop, Pop/Rock

This Pittsburgh vocal group from the '60s was formed in 1960 and produced a series of wholesome lite-garage-pop hits, with "You're the One" (#4), "Five O'Clock World" (#4), "Magic Town" (#21) and "The Land of Milk and Honey" (#29), before transforming into a viable alternative for fans of the Lettermen with their hits "Turn Around, Look at Me" (#7) and "My Special Angel" (#7). —*Rick Clark*

● **Greatest Hits** / 1988 / Rhino ✦✦✦✦
An essential overview of this Pennsylvania group, it contains all of the above-mentioned hits. —*Rick Clark*

W

The Wailers [U.S.A.]

Group, Rock & Roll, Garage Rock

The historical importance of the Wailers is undeniable. They were one of the very first, if not the first, of the American garage bands. Backing Rockin' Robin Roberts, they revamped an obscure R&B song called "Louie Louie" into a 1961 local hit (included here) that served as the prototype for the countless subsequent versions of the most popular garage song of the '60s. And their stomping, hard-nosed R&B/rock fusion inspired the Sonics, who took the Wailers' raunch to unimaginable extremes. While they anticipated the British Invasion bands with their brash, self-contained sound, their inability to write first-rate original material, as well as their rather outdated sax and organ-driven frat rock, put them in a distinctly lower echelon. As the decade progressed, the group did absorb mild folk-rock and psychedelic influences without great effect, either commercially or on their sound itself. *—Richie Unterberger*

● **Fabulous Wailers, The Boys From Tacoma: Anthology 1961-1969** / 1993 / Etiquette ◆◆◆◆

A 27-song anthology drawn from their many singles and albums. Whether backing other singers, playing instrumentals, or performing their own material, the group rarely escaped the classic three-chord progression. What must have been a revelation in the teen ballrooms of the early '60s is a rather flat and repetitious listening experience. This is a fun compilation, but it should not be mistaken for a work of major significance. *—Richie Unterberger*

The Waitresses

Group, New Wave

The Waitresses existed for the purpose of performing the witty, often female-oriented songs of guitarist Chris Butler, who had previously led a series of new wave bands in Cleveland. The personnel of the band as of its 1982 debut album, *Wasn't Tomorrow Wonderful,* was, in addition to Butler, singer Patty Donahue, backup singer Ariel Warner, reed player Mars Williams, bassist David Horstra, drummer Billy Ficca (a once and future member of Television), and keyboardist Dan Klayman. The group recorded two albums and a mini-LP in the early '80s, stirring critical acclaim and international interest before both Donahue and Butler left. Ficca fronted the band for a while, then they broke up. *—William Ruhlmann*

○ **Wasn't Tomorrow Wonderful?** / 1982 / Polydor ◆◆◆

"No Guilt," in which Donahue's matter-of-fact voice details what a spurned lover has found out since the breakup ("I learned the reason for a three-pronged outlet"), and "I Know What Boys Like" are the standouts among these clever songs, but the whole album has an attitude that won't quit. *—William Ruhlmann*

Bruiseology / 1983 / Polydor ◆◆

● **The Best of the Waitresses** / 1990 / Polydor ◆◆◆◆

This is a fine collection of the Waitresses' best tracks and biggest hits. *—AMG*

Tom Waits

b. Dec. 7, 1949, Pomona, CA

Rock & Roll, Singer-Songwriter, Alternative Pop/Rock

Singer/songwriter and actor Tom Waits has garnered considerable critical acclaim and a cult following during a 20-year singing career (he has also built up quite a resumé as a film actor since the late '70s), and his songs have been successfully covered by such mainstream artists as the Eagles and Rod Stewart, though he himself has never scored a notable commercial hit. Born in Pomona,

CA, Waits was heavily influenced by the Beat writers of the '50s and, by the early '70s, had developed a performing persona as a heavy-drinking, heavy-smoking street poet. He signed to Elektra/Asylum and released his debut album, *Closing Time,* a relatively conventional singer/songwriter album of the day, in 1973. One of its songs, "Ol' 55," turned up on an Eagles album. Waits followed it with *Heart of a Saturday Night,* which found him celebrating the same street life found in Bruce Springsteen's early albums. (Springsteen later recorded Waits's song "Jersey Girl.") *Nighthawks at the Diner,* a double live album, represented a peak in this material. On his albums after the mid-'70s, Waits's voice, already a raspy one, seemed to drop an octave, and his songs became less melodic. In the early '80s he switched to the Island label, and on albums such as *Swordfishtrombones,* his music became more experimental. He wrote and starred in a stage presentation called *Frank's Wild Years* in the mid-'80s, and it was transferred to film under the title *Big Time.* *—William Ruhlmann*

● **Closing Time** / 1973 / Asylum ◆◆◆◆

The bluesy cocktail-jazz accompaniment underscores Waits's boozy, sentimental tales of life after hours. But songs like "Ol' 55" and "Martha" transcend the somewhat hackneyed form to be genuinely touching. *—William Ruhlmann*

○ **Small Change** / 1973 / Asylum ◆◆◆◆

On *Small Change,* Waits alternates between playing the sleazoid barker with "Step Right Up" and the sentimental bum on tracks like "Tom Traubert's Blues" and "I Wish I Was in New Orleans." This might not be one of Waits's best efforts, but fans of his drunken croak of a voice will find this enjoyable. Like many of his recordings from his Asylum period, *Small Change* was recorded live to two-track and produced by Bones Howe. Sonically, these albums are quite impressive. *—Rick Clark*

The Heart of Saturday Night / 1974 / Asylum ◆◆◆

The touchstone here isn't so much Charles Bukowski as it is Hoagy Carmichael, even if, in Waits's interpretation, it's a "bloodshot moon in that burgundy sky." *—William Ruhlmann*

○ **Nighthawks at the Diner** / 1975 / Asylum ◆◆◆◆

There are those who consider this two-record live set the culmination of Waits's nightlife persona, and others who worry that it's a comedy act in which the singer veers into self-parody. It's one of those tough questions, like, how drunk is *too* drunk? *—William Ruhlmann*

Foreign Affairs / 1977 / Asylum ◆◆◆

Foreign Affairs continues Waits's immersion into orchestrated street short stories with tracks like "Burma-Shave," "A Sight for Sore Eyes," and "Muriel." Bette Midler duets with Waits on "I Never Talk to Strangers." *—Rick Clark*

Blue Valentine / 1978 / Asylum ◆◆◆

With this effort, Waits continues the bum-fronting-an-orchestra approach he started on *Small Change.* Particularly striking is his interpretation of *West Side Story's* "Somewhere." Other highlights include the bittersweet sentimentality of "Christmas Card from a Hooker in Minneapolis," the bluesy "$29.00," and "Romeo Is Bleeding." *—Rick Clark*

Heartattack and Vine / 1980 / Asylum ◆◆◆

☆ **Swordfishtrombones** / 1983 / Island ◆◆◆◆◆

On *Swordfishtrombones,* Waits (by now with a voice even deeper and more gravelly than ever) dropped Hoagy Carmichael as his chief influence and adopted Kurt Weill and Bertolt Brecht. Employing odd percussive instruments and horns, he turned to this imaginative, impressionistic approach, which is also followed on subsequent albums. — *William Ruhlmann*

○ **Anthology of Tom Waits** / 1985 / Asylum ✦✦✦✦
Anthology collects most of the key tracks from Waits's Asylum years, except for *Nighthawks at the Diner*. — *Rick Clark*

★ **Rain Dogs** / 1985 / Island ✦✦✦✦✦
From the New York streets to the Orient ("Singapore") and back, Waits continues his colorful survey, alternately challenging the listener (especially in Marc Ribot's guitar playing) and returning to the melodic style of the past ("Downtown Train"). Keith Richards guests on gritty "Big Black Mariah," while "Time" is one of his best ballads. — *William Ruhlmann*

○ **Frank's Wild Years** / 1987 / Island ✦✦✦✦
Frank's Wild Years continued Waits's weird blend of theatrical melodies and unusual production, which he began on *Swordfishtrombones*. "Rainville" and "Hang on St. Christopher" are highlights. Not as strong as *Rain Dogs*, this is still one of his better albums from this period. — *Rick Clark*

Big Time / 1988 / Island ✦✦✦
This is the soundtrack to Waits's in-concert film *Big Time*. It covers tracks from *Frank's Wild Years* and *Rain Dogs*, plus two new tracks, "Falling Down" and "Strange Weather." His careening version of "Big Black Mariah," with its dissonant guitar and roller-rink organ, is even ruder than the original version. — *Rick Clark*

○ **The Early Years** / 1991 / Rhino ✦✦✦✦
A collection of early demos and recordings that is fascinating for devoted fans. — *Stephen Thomas Erlewine*

Night on Earth / 1992 / Island ✦✦

☆ **Bone Machine** / 1992 / Island ✦✦✦✦✦
A set of dark, stripped-down songs, *Bone Machine* is a bleak, melancholy song cycle of decay and despair. It's also his best album, full of wonderfully evocative songs and haunting, primitive sounds. — *Stephen Thomas Erlewine*

○ **The Early Years, Vol. 2** / 1993 / Rhino ✦✦✦✦
A collection of early demos, it was recorded before Waits received a record contract. Essential for fans, but most listeners will want to stick with the original albums. — *AMG*

The Black Rider / Feb. 1993 / Island ✦✦
Written with William S. Burroughs and Robert Wilson, Tom Waits' version of their operetta is an intriguing mess that tends to be too scattered to be truly effective. — *Stephen Thomas Erlewine*

Rick Wakeman

Art-Rock/Progressive-Rock
Born in Perivale, Middlesex, England on May 18, 1949, Rick Wakeman's interest in music manifested itself very early, and from the age of seven on he studied classical piano. At the age of 14, he joined a local band, Atlantic Blues, the same year he left school to enroll in the Royal College of Music. He had his eye on a career as a concert pianist, but his skills and the demand for them got the better of him, and Wakeman was dismissed from the college after it became clear that he preferred playing in clubs to studying classical piano technique.

By his late teens, he was an established session man, playing on records by such diverse acts as Black Sabbath, Brotherhood of Man, and Edison Lighthouse, and had expanded his instrumental range from the piano to encompass the organ, the Mellotron, and the synthesizer. At the end of the 1960s, his name also began appearing on the credits of albums by such artists as Al Stewart and David Bowie, and one set of session gigs with a folk-cum-rock band called the Strawbs led to his joining the group in 1970.

Wakeman got his first solo spot on an album on their concert recording, *Just a Collection of Antiques and Curios*, done live at London's Queen Elizabeth Hall, which presented him in an early, relatively low-wattage version of the kind of solo set he would later do with Yes. Wakeman's ability to stretch out at the keyboards was relatively limited within the context of the Strawbs' folk-based music, which was focused on the vocals and lyrics of its founder/leader Dave Cousins and the songwriting team of drummer Richard Hudson and bassist John Ford.

After two albums with the Strawbs, Wakeman made the jump into a much more ambitious instrumental setting, and to international stardom, when he joined Yes, a post-psychedelic hard rock band, known already for its loud and distinctive instrumental sound, that had attracted considerable attention with their first

three albums. Their original keyboard player, Tony Kaye, had left at the outset of recording their fourth album, to be called *Fragile*, and Wakeman's arrival played a key role in the final shape of the record. The diversity of sound from all of the members—each of whom had a distinctive technique on his instrument—suited Wakeman perfectly, and his technique at the ivories rose to the occasion. He created a fierce, swirling sound on an array of synthesizers, Mellotrons, electric and acoustic pianos, such as had never been heard before on a rock record.

The album not only gave him ample room for keyboard flourishes, but it seemed as though Wakeman's sound was everywhere on the record, his Mellotron providing an almost orchestra-scale continuity in front of which the other members—most notably guitarist Steve Howe and bassist Chris Squire—turned in their distinctive solos. But *Fragile* only featured a handful (albeit three of them very long) of numbers by the group proper, the rest of its length filled up with relatively modest solo outings by Wakeman, Howe, Squire, and drummer Bill Bruford. As was later revealed, the reason for the solo numbers was the band's need to release the album in a hurry, to pay for the huge number of keyboard instruments needed by Wakeman to complete the record. *Fragile* was a hit, driven by the chart success of the single "Roundabout," and Wakeman was suddenly elevated to star status, both as a member of the band, and as a rival to Keith Emerson, the progressive rock keyboard virtuoso who'd had virtually sole domination of that field for four years, first as a member of the Nice and then as part of progressive rock's first power trio, Emerson, Lake & Palmer.

The group's next album, *Close to the Edge*, consisting of three extended numbers, only expanded his audience and his appeal, for his instruments were heard almost continually on the record, both in prominent solos and as accompaniment to the rest of the band, whose popularity continued to soar. A film made during the accompanying tour, *Yessongs*, gave more time to Wakeman's performance than to any of the other band members. During the making of *Close to the Edge* in 1972, Wakeman also recorded his first solo album, an instrumental work entitled *The Six Wives of Henry VIII*, which consisted of his musical interpretations of the lives and personalities of the said six royal spouses. Released early in 1973 on A&M Records (to which he'd been signed as a solo act, since his days with the Strawbs), it performed respectably if not spectacularly on the charts. On the subsequent *Close to the Edge* tour, Wakeman's solo spots were frequently based on highlights from the album.

All was not well within Yes, as the 1974 release of their next studio album, *Tales from Topographic Oceans*, showed. Expanded from one to two LPs, this collection of four extended songs seemed to stretch the format of *Close to the Edge* to the breaking point. Public reception of the album was mixed, and the critics were merciless in their attacks upon the seeming excesses of the record. The album's extended tracks were built up from Jon Anderson's philosophical and religious musings (one 18-minute track had its roots in a footnote that Anderson had seen in a religious text), and the related ramblings of guitarist Steve Howe and bassist Chris Squire—Wakeman went along, and played superbly, albeit in somewhat less flamboyant form than his previous outings with the group, and then exited before the subsequent tour. His replacement, Patrick Moraz, lasted for two albums. Meanwhile, Wakeman's new solo album, *Journey to the Center of the Earth*, adapted from the writings of Jules Verne, and featuring a rock band, narrator (David Hemmings), and full orchestral and choral accompaniment, was released to tremendous public response in both America and England, where it topped the long-player charts.

The critics had long since begun to tire of progressive rock's pretentions and ambitions, but it seemed as though, for the public, Wakeman could do no wrong. His next album, *The Myths and Legends of King Arthur and the Knights of the Round Table* (1975), was given a grand-scale premiere at Wembley's Empire Pool, which generated a huge amount of excitement, although it also cost Wakeman a fortune to stage the event on ice. During this same period, Wakeman began working on film scores with the music for Ken Russell's *Lisztomania*, which was a modest hit.

In 1977, Wakeman returned to Yes, with which he has continued recording and touring (even joining his predecessor, Tony Kaye, in a ten-man lineup of past and present members in the early 1990's). His solo career continued on A&M into the end of the 1970's, with *Criminal Record* and *Rhapsodies*, which were modestly successful. Wakeman's biggest media splash during this period, however, came through his alleged role in getting the Sex Pistols dropped by

A&M Records soon after being signed—an understandably ardent opponent of punk rock, he supposedly (according to some accounts) helped push the band out the door, and given the rock press's indifference to his progressive music at the time, this supposed incident became some of the biggest coverage that he received.

None of this bothered his fans, which rapidly expanded to encompass those he picked up through his work with lyricist Tim Rice on a musical adaptation of George Orwell's *1984,* and his burgeoning film work, which included the music to movies about the 1976 Winter Olympics and the 1982 soccer World Cup competition. Additionally, he became a regular on Britain's Channel 4. Wakeman's audience and reputation survived the 1980's better than almost any progressive rock star of his era, as he continued releasing albums on his own label.

The rise to popularity of the compact disc format enhanced the impact of his music, whose myriad electronic textures are well suited to digital recording, and in addition to his new albums, and standard CD reissues of his old albums, his classic vintage albums such as *Journey to the Center of the Earth* have also appeared in gold-plated audiophile CD reissues. He was also a beneficiary of the substantial continued popularity of Yes, with which he has remained associated into the 1990's.

Essentially a light classic virtuoso with a rock background—sort of a rock music version of classical pianist Earl Wild—Wakeman's music at its best combines the strongest Romantic traditions of Franz Liszt in the 19th century and John Williams (the Boston Pops/soundtrack guy, not the classical guitarist) in the 20th century. He was only a recipient of critical goodwill for a short time early in his career, but his popularity and work seem impervious to the resentments of the rock press. —*Bruce Eder*

● **The Six Wives of Henry the VIII** / 1973 / A&M ✦✦✦✦

Wakeman's first solo album is also his least pretentious work and, in many respects, his most effective. Essentially a selection of six electronic tone paintings done on a multitude of synthesizers, Mellotrons, and other keyboard instruments, all of the material here is beautifully melodic and excitingly played and arranged, based on the lives and perceived personalities of Henry VIII's six spouses. Some of the music comes off as trite 19th-century Romantic meanderings, but the running times are held in check, and besides, that seems to be exactly what Wakeman was aiming for. —*Bruce Eder*

○ **Journey to the Center of the Earth** / Jan. 1974 / A&M ✦✦✦✦

Wakeman's chart-topping album (in England) paints a broader musical canvas than its predecessor, with orchestra, chorus, narrator, and rock band surrounding his dozen or so swirling keyboard instruments. The mass of sounds is nowhere near as neat or concise as Wakeman's first album, but it evidently satisfied people looking for a post-psychedelic thrill as well as the more majestic side of progressive rock, and in its own pretentious way, is very effective. —*Bruce Eder*

Lisztomania / 1975 / A&M ✦✦

The soundtrack to Ken Russell's movie provided Wakeman with a canvas upon which to work his magic (or do his damage—it depends upon one's attitude) upon the music of Franz Liszt and, to a lesser degree, Richard Wagner. Actually, much of what is here is more substantial than the material on *Journey or Myths and Legends,* which can be attributed largely to the composers' contributions. —*Bruce Eder*

Myths and Legends of King Arthur & the Knights of the Round Table / 1975 / A&M ✦✦

Just as ambitious as *Journey to the Center of the Earth,* this album treads little new ground. Essentially more of the same, with a little less freshness this time out since it is the second album of its kind. —*Bruce Eder*

No Earthly Connection / 1976 / A&M ✦✦

○ **Rick Wakeman's Criminal Record** / 1977 / A&M ✦✦✦✦

White Rock / 1977 / A&M ✦✦✦

○ **Best Known Works** / 1978 / A&M ✦✦✦✦

○ **Rhapsodies** / 1979 / A&M ✦✦✦✦

1984 / 1981 / Charisma ✦✦

The Burning / 1982 / Varese Sarabande ✦✦✦

Rock & Roll Prophet / 1982 / Moon ✦✦

Country Airs / 1986 / Gopaco ✦✦

Family Album / 1987 / Combat ✦✦

Cost of Living / 1987 / Virgin ✦✦✦

A Suite of Gods / 1988 / Relativity ✦✦

Zodiaque / 1988 / Relativity ✦✦✦

Walker Brothers

Group, British Invasion, Pop/Rock

They weren't British, they weren't brothers, and their real names weren't Walker, but Californians Scott Engel, John Maus, and Gary Leeds were briefly huge stars in England (and small ones in their native land) at the peak of the British Invasion. Engel and Maus were playing together in Hollywood when drummer Leeds suggested they form a trio and try to make it in England. And they did—with surprising swiftness, they hit the top of the British charts with "Make It Easy on Yourself" in 1965. "The Sun Ain't Gonna Shine Any More" repeated the feat the following year, and the group also had U.K. hits with "My Ship Is Coming In," "(Baby) You Don't Have to Tell Me," "Another Tear Falls," and others. For a few months they experienced frenzied adulation almost on the level of the Beatles and Stones, though in the U.S. (where they rarely performed), only "Make It Easy on Yourself" and "The Sun Ain't Gonna Shine Any More" entered the Top 20.

While the Walkers looked the part of British Invaders with their shaggy moptops, in fact they were far more pop than rock. Nor did they play on most of their records. With producer Johnny Franz and veteran British arrangers like Ivor Raymonde (who also worked with Dusty Springfield) and Reg Guest, they favored orchestrated ballads that were a studied attempt to emulate the success of another brother act who weren't really brothers—the Righteous Brothers. Not as soulful as the Righteous Brothers, lead singer Scott Walker's deep croon wasn't chopped liver by any means, although it betrayed strong debts to non-rock vocalists like Tony Bennett and Frank Sinatra. While their biggest hits were covers of songs by American pop songwriting teams like Bacharach-David and Mann-Weill, Scott (and occasionally John Walker) could write strong brooding originals in a more personal, less overblown style when given the chance.

In the intensely competitive days of 1967, the Walkers' brand of pop suddenly became passé, and the group disbanded in the face of diminishing success and Scott's increasingly fruitful solo career. Scott ran off a series of Top Ten British solo albums in the late '60s, which have attracted a sizable cult with their idiosyncratic marriage of Scott's brooding, insular songs and ornate orchestral arrangements. Gary Walker released a few singles, and an album, with his group the Rain in a much harder rocking guitar-oriented format. The Walkers reunited for a while in the mid-'70s, which produced a final British hit ("No Regrets") but disappointing music. Much of the Walkers' story is retold in the biography *Scott Walker: A Deep Shade of Blue,* published only in Britain. —*Richie Unterberger*

Introducing the Walker Brothers / 1965 / Smash ✦✦✦

Their debut album was an erratic affair; they hit their trademark balladeering groove with the hits "Make It Easy On Yourself" and "My Ship Is Comin' In," but sound stiff on uptempo R&B numbers like "Land of 1,000 Dances" and "Dancing in the Street." It does include some interesting tracks which haven't been reissued, most notably the obscure early Randy Newman composition "I Don't Want to Hear It Any More" and the Scott Engel original "You're All Around Me," both of which are the kind of pop/rock ballads which were the Walkers' strongest suit. —*Richie Unterberger*

No Regrets / 1975 / GTO ✦✦✦

The Walker Brothers reunited in 1975 to record *No Regrets,* a collection of well-produced pop, soul, and folk covers. Although both Scott Walker and John Maus are in fine voice, the majority of the album is overly slick and fails to make much of an impression. Nevertheless, the title track is a masterpiece, featuring an achingly gorgeous vocal from Scott that ranks among the band's finest performances. —*Stephen Thomas Erlewine*

Nite Flights / 1978 / GTO ✦✦✦

Nite Flights was another mixed effort by the reunited Walker Brothers, but it had a side of original Scott Walker compositions that were his best in years, particularly the haunting "The Electrician," which attracted praise from Brian Eno and David Bowie and reinvigorated Scott's solo career. —*Stephen Thomas Erlewine*

● **After The Lights Go Out: The Best Of 1965-1967** / 1990 / Fontana ✦✦✦✦
20 of their best songs, including all of their hit singles. On original compositions like "Mrs. Murphy," "Archangel," "Orpheus," and "Deadlier Than The Male," Scott Walker unveils the disturbed visions that would characterize his solo work, and John Walker's "Saddest Night In The World" and "I Can't Let It Happen To You" display a solid writing talent that he was sadly unable to develop into a solo career of his own. —*Richie Unterberger*

● **Anthology** / 1995 / One Way ✦✦✦✦
Although it contains the Walker Brothers' big hits from the '60s, *Anthology* is basically a resequenced version of the group's first album, adding a couple of bonus tracks. Nevertheless, it's a serviceable introduction to the group. —*Stephen Thomas Erlewine*

Junior Walker & the All-Stars

b. 1942, Blytheville, Arkansas
Soul, Motown
Of all the great musicians who played on scores of Motown records, none of them got label credit, much less a chance to bask in the spotlight. The lone exception was Junior Walker (born Audrey Dewalt), whose tenor sax wailings were made up of equal parts Illinois Jacquet high-note shrieks, Coleman Hawkins growls, and pure Midwest soul. Never much of a vocalist, Walker nonetheless sliced hits with his rough-grained chops, though the sax solos remained the definite focal point. Highly influential on the Tom Scott/David Sanborn crowd, Walker should be close to the top of any list of rock & roll's great tenor saxophonists. —*Cub Koda*

○ **Shotgun** / 1965 / Motown ✦✦✦✦
All the early hits are here, including "Cleo's Mood," "Shake & Fingerpop," and "Road Runner"—along with King Curtis and Maceo Parker the soul sax man—and probably the most influential. —*George Bedard*

○ **Roadrunner** / 1966 / Motown ✦✦✦✦
This collection is a good mix of instrumentals and covers of Motown hits by other artists. —*George Bedard*

Home Cookin' / 1969 / Motown ✦✦✦
Solid, mostly uptempo album, featuring some of his biggest late-'60s hits: "What Does It Take (To Win Your Love)," "Come See About Me," and "Hip City." Among the other tracks, the bittersweet instrumental "Sweet Soul" is a highlight. As with many Motown albums, the most noteworthy tracks are featured on best-of compilations. —*Richie Unterberger*

● **Greatest Hits** / 1982 / Motown ✦✦✦✦
All the hits, including "Shotgun," "What Does It Take to Win Your Love," and "Roadrunner." The definitive package. —*Cub Koda*

○ **Nothing But Soul: The Singles** / 1994 / Motown ✦✦✦✦
This 40-song double CD includes virtually every Walker track of significance, and then some. Walker is a great player and hits a great groove, but that groove can get tiring over the course of several dozen tracks, especially the similar-sounding early instrumental cuts. Also, the post-'60s selections that take up much of disc two are hampered by material that is inferior to the best output of his '60s heyday. Excellent package and liner notes, but most listeners should be satisfied with the single-disc *Greatest Hits*, leaving this one for the collectors and specialists. —*Richie Unterberger*

Scott Walker (Noel Scott Engel)

b. Jan. 9, 1944, Hamilton, OH
Pop/Rock, Experimental
One of the most enigmatic figures in rock history, Scott Walker was known as Scotty Engel when he cut obscure, flop records in the late '50s and early '60s in the teen idol vein. He then hooked up with John Maus and Gary Leeds to form the Walker Brothers. They weren't named Walker, they weren't brothers, and they weren't English, but they nevertheless became a part of the British Invasion after moving to the U.K. in 1965. They enjoyed a couple years of massive success there (and a couple hits in the U.S.) in a Righteous Brothers vein. As their full-throated lead singer and principal songwriter, Scott was the dominant artistic force in the group, which split in 1967.

While remaining virtually unknown in his homeland, Scott launched a hugely successful solo career in Britain with a unique blend of orchestrated, almost MOR arrangements with idiosyncratic and morose lyrics. At the height of psychedelia, Walker openly looked to crooners like Sinatra, Jack Jones, and Tony Ben-

nett for inspiration, and to Jacques Brel for much of his material. None of those balladeers, however, would have sung about the oddball subjects—prostitutes, transvestites, suicidal brooders, plagues, and Joseph Stalin—that populated Walker's songs. His first four albums hit the Top Ten in the U.K.—his second, in fact, reached number one in 1968, in the midst of the hippie era. By the time of 1969's *Scott 4*, the singer was writing all of his material. Although this was perhaps his finest album, it was a commercial disappointment, and unfortunately discouraged him from relying entirely upon his own material on subsequent releases.

The 1970s were a frustrating period for Walker, pocked with increasingly sporadic releases and a largely unsuccessful reunion with his "brothers" in the middle of the decade. His work on the Walkers' final album in 1978 prompted admiration from David Bowie and Brian Eno. After a long period of hibernation, he emerged with an album in 1984, *Climate of Hunter*, which drew critical raves for a minimalistic, trance-like ambience that showed him keeping abreast of cutting-edge '80s rock trends. This notoriously reclusive figure, who has rarely been interviewed or even seen in public since his days of stardom, emerged from hibernation in 1995 with a new album, *Tilt*. He was a substantial, if largely overlooked, influence upon the vocal style of David Bowie and Bryan Ferry. A biography, *Scott Walker: A Deep Shade of Blue*, was published by Virgin in the U.K. in 1994. —*Richie Unterberger*

○ **Scott** / 1967 / Fontana ✦✦✦✦
Scott Walker's success as a teen idol singer of Spectorish ballads with the Walker Brothers in no way prepared listeners for the mordant, despairing lyrics of his solo debut. To compound the surprise, he does his best to imitate the vocal girth of Tony Bennett and Frank Sinatra on this mix of original tunes and covers, which also features sweeping, bloated orchestral arrangements. It was hardly rock, and pop of a most oddball sort, but it found a surprisingly large audience—in Britain, anyway, where it reached the Top Three in 1967. Poke behind the velvet curtain of the languid MOR arrangements, and one finds a surprisingly literate existentialist at the helm of these proceedings. His lyrical nuances were probably lost on his audience of predominately teenage girls, though they've earned him a small cult audience that endures to this day. Besides presenting three of his own compositions, Walker covers tunes by Weill/Mann, Tim Hardin, and Andre & Dory Previn on this album, as well as three songs by his favorite writer, Jacques Brel. Highlights include his exquisitely anguished rendition of Brel's classic "Amsterdam" and his dramatic cover of the early-'60s Timi Yuro pop ballad "The Big Hurt." —*Richie Unterberger*

○ **Scott 2** / 1968 / Philips ✦✦✦✦
Although Walker's second album was his biggest commercial success, actually reaching #1 in Britain, it was not his greatest artistic triumph. His taste remains eclectic, encompassing Bacharach/David, Tim Hardin, and of course his main man Jacques Brel (who is covered three times on this album). And his own songwriting efforts hold their own in this esteemed company. "The Girls From the Streets" and "Plastic Palace People" show an uncommonly ambitious lyricist cloaked behind the over-the-top, schmaltzy orchestral arrangements, one more interested in examining the seamy underside of glamour and romance than celebrating its glitter. The Brel tune "Next" must have lifted a few teenage mums' eyebrows with its not-so-hidden hints of homosexuality and abuse. Another Brel tune, "The Girl And The Dogs," is less controversial, but hardly less nasty in its jaded view of romance. Some of the material is not nearly as memorable, however, and the over-the-top show ballad production can get overbearing. The album included his first Top 20 U.K. hit, "Jackie." —*Richie Unterberger*

Scott 3 / 1969 / Philips ✦✦✦
Scott Walker's final British Top Ten album was the first to be dominated by his own songwriting. Ten of the thirteen tunes on this 1969 LP are originals; the remaining three, naturally, were written by one of his chief inspirations, Jacques Brel. There are some interesting moments here. "Big Louise" talks about a hefty prostitute with shocking explicitness for a pop star album of the era. "Copenhagen" (like much of Walker's '60s work) foreshadows David Bowie. "No Last Tango" is a particularly vicious Brel song. "30 Century Man" is an uncommonly folkish and focused tune for Walker. "We Came Through" is an oddball cavalry charge featuring one of his occasional forays into Ennio Morricone spaghetti-Western-like production. The tension between Walker's dense, foreboding lyrics and orchestral production is unusual, to say the least. But too often, it's too difficult to penetrate Walker's insights through Wally Scott's

string-drenched production. It shrouds the lyrics in a fog that's often too syrupy to justify the effort needed to fight through it. — *Richie Unterberger*

○ **Scott 4** / 1969 / Philips ✦✦✦✦
Walker dropped out of the British Top Ten with his fourth album, but the result was probably his finest '60s LP. While the tension between the bloated production and his introspective, ambitious lyrics remains, much of the over-the-top bombast of the orchestral arrangements has been reined in, leaving a relatively stripped-down approach that complements his songs rather than smothering them. This is the first Walker album to feature entirely original material, and his songwriting is more lucid and cutting. Several of the tracks stand among his finest. "The Seventh Seal," based upon the classic film by Ingmar Bergman, features remarkably ambitious (and relatively successful) lyrics set against a haunting Ennio Morricone-style arrangement. "The Old Man's Back Again" also echoes Morricone, and tackles no less ambitious a lyrical palette; "dedicated to the neo-Stalinist regime," the "old man" of this song was supposedly Josef Stalin. "Hero Of The War" is also one of Walker's better vignettes, serenading his war hero with a cryptic mix of tribute and irony. Other songs show engaging folk, country, and soul influences that were largely buried on his previous solo albums. — *Richie Unterberger*

The Moviegoer / 1972 / Philips ✦✦

Stretch / 1973 / CBS ✦✦

We Had It All / 1974 / CBS ✦✦

Sings Jacques Brel / 1981 / Philips ✦✦✦

Climate of Hunter / 1984 / Virgin ✦✦

● **Boy Child: Best of 1967-1970** / 1992 / Fontana ✦✦✦✦
This collection of "Scott's best self-composed songs" features 20 Walker originals from his 1967-70 heyday. While he covered some interesting material on his albums during this period, paying tribute to Jacques Brel with special devotion and frequency, his original compositions are his most enduring achievements. Besides such highlights as "Big Louise," "We Came Through," "The Seventh Seal," "Plastic Palace People," and "The Old Man's Back Again," it includes half a dozen songs that were not included on the four other solo albums that Fontana UK has reissued on CD. Some of those cuts are very strong, especially "The Rope And The Colt," a dramatic Western ballad with an arrangement that would do Ennio Morricone proud; the positively eloquent despair of the ennui-ridden "Time Operator"; and "The Plague," a representative sampling of Walker's taste for the disquieting and bizarre. This is a recommended starting point for those interested in checking out this singularly strange '60s phenomenon, who was a relatively unacknowledged and undetected, but nonetheless substantial, influence on David Bowie and other fashionably decadent British singers. — *Richie Unterberger*

○ **No Regrets: Best of Scott Walker & Walker Brothers** / 1992 / Fontana ✦✦✦✦
Including both of the Walker Brothers' big hits ("The Sun Ain't Gonna Shine Any More," "Make It Easy On Yourself") and material from Scott Walker's solo albums, *No Regrets: The Best of the Walker Brothers* is the best introduction to Walker's more pop-oriented music. — *Stephen Thomas Erlewine*

Tilt / 1995 / Fontana ✦✦
Tilt, Scott Walker's first album in eleven years, is a dense, impenetrable record, bleak in its outlook and approach. Walker has dispensed with conventional pop songwriting—actually, he's dispensed with pop altogether. *Tilt* is nearly operatic, with long, twisting melody lines, no verses and no choruses. Lyrically, the record is just as inaccessible, with obscure literary references and winding, oblique prose. There's no escaping that the record is some sort of an accomplishment—very few pop musicians have ever attempted a record of this scope, one that is free-form in structure but with carefully considered arrangements. Nevertheless, it's hard to like the album because very little of it ever sinks in, and it's hard to appreciate it because it takes its pretentions so seriously. It's arguably the most inaccessible, difficult album ever recorded. — *Stephen Thomas Erlewine*

BOOK

✦✦✦ **Scott Walker: A Deep Shade Of Blue**, by Mike Watkinson & Pete Anderson (Virgin, UK, 1994). There are many intriguing aspects of the Scott Walker story: an American who was a huge

star in England, but virtually unknown at home; a '60s pop star who disdained the rock of the era, preferring crooners and ballad singers; a star ill at ease with his success, dabbling in socialism and visits to monasteries; a recluse who's virtually vanished from public view. The authors have assembled a detailed account of his life, drawing heavily from vintage press clips, and recent first-hand interviews with other members of the Walker Brothers and key figures like engineer Peter Olliff. Yet it's not as fascinating as one might think, partially because the authors are prone to wildly overestimating the quality and influence of Walker's work; he is an extremely interesting cult artist, but not one of the very top performers and songwriters of his era. The latter part of the book can be dull, as Walker has rarely worked since the early '70s; his reclusion does not lend itself to fascinating stories, as those related by the authors in their fine biography of Syd Barrett. Walker is not a mad genius, but someone who hasn't felt compelled to work and push himself as a public figure since his salad days, and in-depth reporting of his sundry activities during the past two decades can be tiresome. — *Richie Unterberger*

Joe Walsh

b. 1947
Rock & Roll
After coming to national fame as the leader of the James Gang, Walsh's skewed humor and bluesy guitar chops have forged a nice solo career for him. Walsh's solo debut *Barnstorm* displayed him as not only an innovative guitarist but a competent keyboardist and a songwriter with much scope. Walsh's second solo effort, *The Smoker You Drink, the Player You Get*, perfectly suited the tastes of FM-rock programmers and firmly established his career. "Rocky Mountain Way" and "Meadows" are hits off that album. Walsh also produced some outside projects, including Dan Fogelberg's first hit album, *Souvenirs*.

The Eagles enlisted Walsh as a replacement for Bernie Leadon in December of 1975. Their next studio album, *Hotel California*, heavily featured Walsh's playing, particularly on "Life in the Fast Lane" and "Hotel California." Walsh played on their live album and *The Long Run*, the band's swan song.

All along, Walsh has continued his solo efforts, scoring big in 1978 with *But Seriously Folks...*, an album that brings his goofy humor to the forefront, with the hit "Life's Been Good." "All Night Long," a track from the *Urban Cowboy* soundtrack, continued Walsh's string of success. During the '80s, Walsh has had sporadic success.

In addition to Dan Fogelberg, Walsh has produced other atists, including Spirit's Jay Ferguson, and Ringo Starr (working as bandleader on Starr's late-'80s/early-'90s tours). In 1994, Walsh joined the reunited Eagles for their *Hell Freezes Over* tour. — *Cub Koda and Rick Clark*

○ **Barnstorm** / 1972 / Mobile Fidelity ✦✦✦✦
Even though he had developed quite a rep as the lead guitarist for the James Gang, Joe Walsh's debut (under the band moniker Barnstorm) was an impressive showcase for his songwriting and arranging. Produced by Bill Szymczyk, *Barnstorm* exudes a thick, textured sound. Some of Walsh's most distinctive guitar sounds are found here. Sonically, *Barnstorm* is shown to fine effect on this Mobile Fidelity reissue. (Currently, there isn't a regular domestic disc available.) Highlights include "Here We Go," "Mother Says," and "Turn to Stone." — *Rick Clark*

○ **The Smoker You Drink, the Player You Get** / 1973 / MCA ✦✦✦✦
On Walsh's second outing, he fused the dynamics and textures of *Barnstorm*, mixed in a few well-crafted tunes, perfect for FM radio, and scored his highest charting album. *Smoker's* centerpiece was the plodding "Rocky Mountain Way," a perfect vehicle for his soaring slidework and squirrelly tenor strangle. "Meadows" was also a substantial FM hit. Other highlights are "Days Gone By" and "Happy Ways." — *Rick Clark*

So What / 1975 / MCA ✦✦✦

You Can't Argue with a Sick Mind / 1976 / MCA ✦✦

● **The Best of Joe Walsh** / 1978 / MCA ✦✦✦✦
Featuring the biggest James Gang hits and early solo hits. — *Cub Koda*

○ **But Seriously Folks** / 1978 / Asylum ✦✦✦✦
This is his biggest solo success, featuring the hit "Life's Been Good." — *Cub Koda*

There Goes the Neighborhood / 1981 / Asylum ✦✦✦
You Bought It: You Name It / 1983 / Warner Brothers ✦✦
The Confessor / 1985 / Full Moon ✦✦
Got Any Gum? / 1987 / Full Moon ✦✦
Ordinary Average Guy / Jan. 1991 / Epic ✦✦✦
Songs for a Dying Planet / May 1992 / Epic ✦✦
Future to This Life / 1995 / Pyramid/Rhino ✦✦
● **Look What I Did!: The Joe Walsh Anthology** / 1995 / MCA ✦✦✦✦
A double-disc set that draws from all of the phases of Joe Walsh's career, with the notable exception of the Eagles, *Look What I Did!* features almost every worthwhile song the guitarist ever recorded, even though it does contain pure dreck like "I.L.B.T.s," which is also known as "I Love Big Tits." —*David Jehnzen*

Travis Wammack

b. 1946
Rock & Roll
A guitarist, singer, and young instrumental genius from Memphis who cut his first record at the tender age of twelve, Travis Wammack is one of the great unheralded guitarists of rock & roll. A contemporary of Lonnie Mack, Wammack was simply the fastest guitar player in a town bursting at the seams with great guitarists. By the time he was 17, he appeared on the national charts with "Scratchy," a speed-burner instrumental featuring incredible distortion and dazzling technique. Several incredible singles followed, but none charted. By the late '60s, Wammack had moved into session work at the FAME Studios in Muscle Shoals, AL, playing on countless hits. He continues recording and touring to the present day (recently working as musical director for Little Richard), his hot and speedy guitar chops intact. —*Cub Koda*
○ **That Scratchy Guitar from Memphis** / 1987 / Bear Family ✦✦✦✦
Wammack's best instrumental and vocal sides, 1964-1967. Simply incredible. —*Cub Koda*

Wang Chung

Group, Dance-Pop, Pop/Rock
The London-based new wave group Wang Chung had a handful of hits in the mid-'80s, achieving their greatest popularity in the U.S. Originally called Huang Chung, the band consisted of vocalist/guitarist Jack Hues, bassist Nick Feldman, and drummer Darren Costin. The band recorded four tracks for 101 Records in the late '70s, all of which appeared on a pair of compilation albums. Huang Chung released their first single, "Isn't It About Time We Were on Television?," in 1980; the record led to a contract with Arista Records. The group released their first album, *Huang Chung*, in 1982. By the time they recorded 1984's *Points on a Curve*, the band had changed their name to Wang Chung. "Dance Hall Days" was a small hit in Britain, yet the band hit the Top 40 twice in America—"Don't Let Go" made it to number 36, while "Dance Hall Days" reached number 16. From this point on, Wang Chung ignored the U.K. market, choosing to concentrate on the U.S. "To Live and Die in L.A.," the theme song from William Friedken's thriller, just missed making the Top 40 in 1985. That same year, Wang Chung switched from Geffen Records to A&M and Costin left the band. Hues and Feldman continued as a duo and released *Mosaic* in 1986. The album was their biggest hit, launching the number two hit "Everybody Have Fun Tonight" and the Top Ten "Let's Go!"
Wang Chung returned in 1989 with *The Warmer Side of Cool*, which spent a mere six weeks on the charts, spawning the minor hit, "Praying to a New God." After the relative disappointment of the album, the group quietly stopped touring and recording. —*Stephen Thomas Erlewine*

Huang Chung / 1982 / Arista ✦✦
● **Points on the Curve** / 1984 / Geffen ✦✦✦✦
Wang Chung's second album became a moderate hit thanks to the hit singles "Dance Hall Days" and "Don't Let Go." While there was some pleasant new wave-influenced pop/rock on the rest of the album, none of the songs matched the inspired pop craft of the hits. —*Stephen Thomas Erlewine*

To Live and Die in L.A. / 1985 / Geffen ✦✦✦
Wang Chung provided the score for William Friedken's thriller *To Live and Die in L.A.*, contributing a set of atmospheric, moody synth-pop, highlighted by the hit single "To Live and Die in L.A." —*Stephen Thomas Erlewine*

Mosaic / 1986 / Geffen ✦✦✦
The incessantly catchy pop-funk number "Everybody Have Fun Tonight" illustrates the change in musical direction Wang Chung undertook on *Mosaic*. Backing away from the synth-laced pop/rock that characterized their earlier albums, the duo concentrated on dance-pop. Apart from the singles "Everybody Have Fun Tonight," "Let's Go!," and "Hypnotize Me," the band had trouble coming up with well-constructed pop songs, making *Mosaic* a checkered affair. —*Stephen Thomas Erlewine*

The Warmer Side of Cool / 1989 / Geffen ✦✦
With *The Warmer Side of Cool*, Wang Chung continued the dance-pop direction of *Mosaic*, yet they failed to come up with enough memorable material to produce a successful follow-up. —*Stephen Thomas Erlewine*

War

Group, Soul, Funk, Pop/Rock
Freewheeling War mixed rock, jazz, and soul influences into a spicy stew throughout the '70s, resulting in a series of R&B and pop hits sporting funky melodies and politically aware messages. Born in Long Beach in 1969, the large combo initially served as rocker Eric Burdon's group, backing the ex-Animal on his 1970 million-seller "Spill the Wine." Bidding Burdon adieu, the band signed with United Artists in 1971 and enjoyed its first smash the next year with "Slippin' into Darkness." Tapping into a sizzling, horn-fueled rock/soul synthesis, "The World Is a Ghetto," "The Cisco Kid," and "Why Can't We Be Friends?" all went gold during the mid-'70s. Despite numerous personnel and label changes, War remained eminent throughout the '80s.
In the early '90s, War experienced a revival, partially due to the fact that all of their albums were reissued. But the group was also acknowledged as a primary influence on contemporary R&B and hip-hop. War released a new album in 1994 to capitalize on their new-found popularity. —*Bill Dahl*

Eric Burdon Declares War / 1970 / Rhino ✦✦✦
The debut effort by Eric Burdon & War was an erratic effort that hinted at more potential than it actually delivered. Three of the five tunes are meandering blues-jazz-psychedelic jams, two of which, "Tobacco Road" and "Blues For Memphis Slim," chug along for nearly 15 minutes. These showcase the then-unknown War's funky fusion and Burdon's still-impressive vocals, but suffer from a lack of focus and substance. "Spill The Wine," on the other hand, is inarguably the greatest moment of the Burdon-fronted lineup. Not only was this goofy funk shaggy-dog story one of the most truly inspired off-the-wall hit singles of all time, it was War's first smash—and Eric Burdon's last. The odd closing track, a short piece of avant-garde sentimentality called "You're No Stranger," was deleted from rereleases of this album for years due to legal complications, but was restored for its CD reissue. —*Richie Unterberger*

○ **The Black-Man's Burdon** / 1970 / Rhino ✦✦✦✦
Burdon's second and final album with War was a double set that could have benefited from quite a bit of judicious editing. Composed mostly of sprawling psychedelic funk jams, it does find War mapping out much of the jazz/Latin/soul grooves that, cut down to much more economical song structures, would shortly bring them success on their own. Highlights include the soulful vamps "Pretty Colors" and "They Can't Take Away Our Music"; the 13-minute "Paint It Black" medley is the height of their eccentricity; and not one, but two covers of "Nights In White Satin" are absurd low points. —*Richie Unterberger*

War / Jan. 1971 / Rhino ✦✦
War laid the groundwork for future developments on their debut album without Eric Burdon. The intriguing "Sun Oh Son," with its nice vocal arrangement, and "Lonely Feeling" were close-but-no-cigar singles. Still, they did what they had to do: establish an identity without Burdon and begin to blend their diverse elements. —*Ron Wynn*

○ **All Day Music** / Feb. 1971 / Rhino ✦✦✦✦
A great War album, the first where all their influences meshed. They blended gospel-tinged soul, funk, Afro-Latin, and light jazz, with enthusiastic group vocals and interplay, plus just the right amount of instrumental support and occasional solos by Lee Oskar on harmonica, Lonnie Jordan on keyboards, and Charles Miller on saxophones and flute. It also contained the fantastic "Slippin' Into Darkness," one of their best-arranged and performed numbers. —*Ron Wynn*

The World Is a Ghetto / 1972 / Rhino ✦✦✦✦

War hit its peak with this 1972 album, the only one they ever released that topped the pop charts. The title track was a triumphant blend of great exchanges and unison vocals, plus concise and spirited musical contributions all around. It also contained the delightful "Cisco Kid" and elaborate "City, Country, City," plus the curious "Beetles in the Bog." Harmonica player Lee Oskar and percussionist Papa Dee Allen were at their best, as were keyboardist Lonnie Jordan and saxophonist/flutist Charles Miller. —*Ron Wynn*

Deliver the Word / 1973 / Rhino ✦✦✦

War began to slide a bit from their early-'70s peak with this release. The best selection, "Gypsy Man," had to be edited for radio, and thus Lee Oskar's roaring harmonica wasn't heard by anyone who didn't purchase the album. "Me and Baby Brother" was another of their mock-humorous hits, but overall, this wasn't nearly as sharp or effective an album as the ones they had been making. —*Ron Wynn*

War Live / 1973 / Rhino ✦✦

Live albums are usually throwaways issued to fill the gap between sessions, or to keep an act's name in public for a label they've left. But War was at its peak when this live date was issued, although they were having a few internal problems. It served its purpose, giving its fans concert versions of "All Day Music," "Cisco Kid," and "Slipping Into Darkness," while the new track "Ballero" even became a hit." —*Ron Wynn*

○ **Why Can't We Be Friends** / 1975 / Rhino ✦✦✦✦

War returned with a vengeance and new material in the mid-'70s, as the title hit was both a pop and R&B top 10 smash and "Low Rider" did even better, topping the soul surveys and peaking at number seven pop. More importantly, they were once more a carefree, loose, jamming band. Unfortunately, it was the last definitive War album, as ego and production battles would soon undermine their success. —*Ron Wynn*

★ **Greatest Hits** / 1976 / United Artists ✦✦✦✦✦

If you can find this collection (only available on vinyl), get it. *Greatest Hits* truly lives up to the title, with tracks like "Summer," "All Day Music," "Slippin' into Darkness," "The World Is a Ghetto," and more. —*Rick Clark*

Love Is All Around / 1976 / ABC ✦✦✦

When War debuted as Eric Burdon's backing band in the late '60s, they were on ABC-Paramount. The group was still hot in 1976, and ABC reissued vault material from their early days in a deceptive package trying to coast on the band's hitmaker status. The album deservedly flopped, and ABC's clumsy attempt failed. —*Ron Wynn*

Platinum Jazz / 1977 / MCA ✦✦

War became a superstar funk unit in the '70s by seamlessly fusing several elements: R&B vocals, Afro-Latin rhythms, rock theatrics, and even occasional jazz strains. This 12-track reissue presents instrumentals featured on War albums, songs that were generally longer than their hit singles and didn't get much attention in original issue. They show that while the band members weren't great soloists, they had an energy and improvisational elan that kept their extended jams from dragging. —*Ron Wynn*

Galaxy / 1977 / Rhino ✦✦✦

War had been on cruise control for over two years due to internal and record company troubles when they resurfaced in the late '70s on MCA. This album was a pleasant surprise, even though it had more disco production than their funk fans wanted. But they got a hit out of the title track, and the better tracks retained the old War grit and eclectic fire. —*Ron Wynn*

Youngblood / 1978 / United Artists ✦✦

War got decent mileage from the soundtrack for this B-movie, which premiered near the end of the first blaxploitation era. They ended with two R&B hits, and while they were perturbed that United Artists, the label they had left, reaped the benefits, it at least kept them active and in the R&B hunt. —*Ron Wynn*

Music Band 2 / 1979 / MCA ✦✦

The four *Music Band* albums covered a painful period for War fans. They seemed past their prime and had resorted to issuing half-hearted remakes of old hits, while trying to find a new way to restate their classic funk/soul/Afro-Latin formula. This second in the series contained a sad remake of "The World Is A Ghetto," while only "Don't Take It Away" was reminiscent of their glorious legacy. —*Ron Wynn*

Music Band / 1979 / MCA ✦✦

The first of the four *Music Band* releases was the best, and it wasn't anything to get excited about. They had lost their focus, the harmonies and arrangements were routine at best, and the interplay and instrumental exchanges sounded wooden. "Good, Good Feeling" was a barely acceptable number, far from a great War tune, and things went downhill from there. —*Ron Wynn*

Music Band Live / 1980 / MCA ✦

This was really a desultory affair, a live version of the group singing material that wasn't that strong in the studio. It was a totally forgettable affair from beginning to end, perhaps their worst album as a band. —*Ron Wynn*

○ **Best of War** / 1982 / MCA ✦✦✦✦

This second greatest hits collection contained a couple of new tracks as a kicker, but was otherwise just a re-release of the previous anthology issued 11 years earlier. It was the last War album to make the pop charts, and it served as a reminder that the group funk era in black pop was truly over. —*Ron Wynn*

Outlaw / 1982 / RCA ✦✦✦

The final War hit single, and the last album they issued that made any noise. When they moved to RCA, fans hoped that War could return to previous levels, and it seemed as if they were on their way with this album. The song "You've Got The Power" had all the bite, energy, and production magic of their vintage classics, while the other tracks were decent enough to make the album their best since the late '70s. Unfortunately, it proved to be a last gasp rather than a resurgence. —*Ron Wynn*

Life (Is So Strange) / 1983 / RCA ✦✦

War kept battling in the mid-'80s, switching labels and trying different producers in an attempt to maintain their viability. This was the second of two albums they recorded for RCA, and they were unable to sustain the comeback begun with the previous album. The title track was a moderate success, but by now they sounded weary and uninspired. The same was true for their production, arrangements, and compositions, as well as past strengths like group interplay, musical support, and solos. —*Ron Wynn*

★ **The Best of War & More** / 1991 / Rhino/Avenue ✦✦✦✦✦

It's not a perfect compilation by any means—there's no "The World is a Ghetto" and a bad remix of "Low Rider," for starters—but *Best of War & More* is the only compilation available from this influential band, so it's the pick by default. But search for that original vinyl, because it was definitive. —*Stephen Thomas Erlewine*

● **Anthology** / 1994 / Rhino/Avenue ✦✦✦✦

War / 1994 / Rhino/Avenue ✦✦

Billy Ward

R&B

The ultra-strict disciplinarian and bandleader of a seminal R&B group, Billy Ward ruled over the Dominoes in a tight-fisted manner. He attempted to regulate everything from onstage harmonies to offstage lifestyles. The group's ranks at one time included Clyde McPhatter and Jackie Wilson, but Ward's insistence on dictatorial control resulted in both of them soon bolting for solo status. The group remained active until the early '60s and scored ten Top Ten R&B hits and two colossal number one singles during its heyday from 1951 to 1957. "Sixty Minute Man" in 1951 was the ultimate innuendo hit, while "Have Mercy Baby" was a landmark uptempo stomper. Each topped the R&B charts for more than two months. All their hits were on either Federal or King, except for their final one, a cover of "Star Dust" in 1957 for Liberty that reached number five R&B and number 12 pop. —*Ron Wynn*

The Dominoes Featuring Clyde Mcphatter / 1958 / King ✦✦✦

The first album for King collects a dozen of their best sides, including "The Bells" and "Have Mercy Baby." —*Cub Koda*

★ **Sixty Minute Men: The Best of Billy Ward & His Dominoes** / 1993 / Rhino ✦✦✦✦✦

Billy Ward was neither a flamboyant vocalist nor a great instrumentalist; his success came directly from his ability to spot and nurture talent. Unfortunately, Ward was also a taskmaster and couldn't hold onto singers very long after discovering and recruiting them for his groups. But for a short period in the 1950s, Ward and the Dominoes ruled R&B by featuring two of its premier vocalists, Clyde McPhatter and Jackie Wilson. Neither stayed long, but were in the band enough time to make some seminal hits, included in this 20-cut anthology. Ironically, the song the group is remembered for the most featured bass vocalist Bill Brown doing the lead on the title track. —*Ron Wynn*

Jennifer Warnes

b. Seattle, WA
Country-Rock, Pop
Over the last 25 years, Jennifer Warnes has enjoyed a widely varied career, including performing the lead female role in the Los Angeles production of *Hair*, appearing as a regular on the '60s hit show *The Smothers Brothers Comedy Hour*, scoring hits as a country pop/rock singer ("Right Time of the Night," "I Know a Heartache When I See One," winning a Grammy for her duet with Joe Cocker on their version of "Up Where We Belong" from the movie *An Officer and a Gentleman*, and garnering critical acclaim for her solo interpretations of Leonard Cohen's songs on the album *Famous Blue Raincoat*. In 1987 Warnes was featured on Roy Orbison's TV special, and she also landed a hit duet with former Righteous Brother Bill Medley on "(I've Had) the Time of My Life" from the film *Dirty Dancing*. —*Rick Clark*

I Can Remember / 1968 / Parrot ♦♦
See Me / 1968 / Parrot ♦♦
Jennifer / 1972 / Reprise ♦♦♦
Jennifer Warnes / 1977 / Arista ♦♦♦
Shot through the Heart / 1979 / Arista ♦♦♦
○ **The Best of Jennifer Warnes** / 1982 / Arista ♦♦♦♦
This collection covers Warnes's earlier hits, like "Right Time of the Night" (number six), "I Know a Heartache When I See One" (number 19), "When the Feeling Comes Around" (number 45), and "Could It Be Love" (number 47). The omission of her chart-topping duets with Bill Medley ("The Time of My Life") and Joe Cocker ("Up Where We Belong") as well as key *Famous Blue Raincoat* tracks keeps this from being definitive. —*Rick Clark*

● **Famous Blue Raincoat** / 1987 / Private Music ♦♦♦♦
Leonard Cohen's material never received a more elegant treatment than the one Jennifer Warnes gave him on *Famous Blue Raincoat*. Warnes is supported by an impressive cast of sidemen, including Stevie Ray Vaughan. The quality of this recording is first-rate. Among the many great songs found here is a powerful version of "Joan of Arc." "Song of Bernadette," "Coming Back to You," and "Came So Far for Beauty" are other highlights. —*Rick Clark*

The Hunter / Jun. 9, 1992 / Private Music ♦♦♦
It took Jennifer Warnes five years to construct a followup to *Famous Blue Raincoat*, and she still wasn't able to come up with a unifying concept as simple and workable as recording a set of songs by Leonard Cohen. She did find some excellent covers, including Todd Rundgren's "Pretending To Care" and the Waterboys' "The Whole Of The Moon," that may have been new to her listeners, and got a song from Donald Fagen ("Big Noise, New York"). She also did some of her own writing and got participation from Cohen on "Way Down Deep." All of which is to say that there are some worthy selections on *The Hunter*, but on the whole the record doesn't match its illustrious predecessor. —*William Ruhlmann*

Warrant

Group, Hard Rock, Pop/Rock, Heavy Metal
With a pair of double-platinum albums, Warrant were one of the most popular pop-metal bands of the late '80s. Formed in Los Angeles in the mid-'80s, the group featured vocalist Jani Lane, guitarist Erik Turner, guitarist Joey Allen, bassist Jerry Dixon, and drummer Steven Sweet. They released *Dirty Rotten Filthy Stinking Rich* late in 1988; by the middle of 1989, it had climbed into the Top Ten and launched the hit singles "Down Boys" and "Sometimes She Cries." Released in the summer of 1990, *Cherry Pie* was an even bigger success, climbing into the Top Ten and featuring the Top Ten hits "I Saw Red," "Cherry Pie," and "Heaven," which reached number two. Warrant had some trouble continuing their multi-platinum success during the alternative explosion of 1992, although their third album, *Dog Eat Dog*, did go gold. —*Stephen Thomas Erlewine*

○ **Dirty Rotten Filthy Stinking Rich** / 1989 / Columbia ♦♦♦♦
Warrant's debut album was filled with bright, catchy heavy metal like "Down Boys," but the band's true strength was their power ballads, as the number two hit "Heaven" and the Top 20 "Sometimes She Cries" proves. —*Stephen Thomas Erlewine*

● **Cherry Pie** / 1990 / Columbia ♦♦♦♦
Cherry Pie, Warrant's second album, was a tighter, more consistent effort than their debut that managed to incorporate some blues into their pop-metal formula. Not only could they rock harder this time around, as the sleazy title track indicates, their ballads were better written, with "I Saw Red" standing as one of their finest moments. —*Stephen Thomas Erlewine*

Dog Eat Dog / Apr. 1992 / Columbia ♦♦♦
As a reaction to the grunge that had wiped pop-metal off the charts, Warrant spat out the tough *Dog Eat Dog*. While the majority of the record is more aggressive and powerful than their first two albums, the songwriting isn't as solid, suffering from a lack of memorable hooks. —*Stephen Thomas Erlewine*

Dee Dee Warwick

Soul, R&B
The much lesser-known sister of Dionne, Dee Dee emerged from similar gospel roots and backup session work. Her '60s recordings, while much less successful than Dionne's, were good New York pop-soul with a more pronounced R&B influence than her sister's. A compilation of her best sides is overdue. —*Richie Unterberger*

● **I Want to Be with You** / 1967 / Mercury ♦♦♦♦
Not too easy to find, but a strong album that features the original versions of "I'm Gonna Make You Love Me" (which would reach number two as a duet between the Supremes and the Temptations), "Gotta Get a Hold of Myself" (covered by the Zombies), and the Latin-tinged "House of Gold," which sounds like a super-soulful cover of a Jay & the Americans tune. —*Richie Unterberger*

○ **Foolish Fool** / 1969 / Mercury ♦♦♦♦
Turnin' Around / 1970 / Atco ♦♦♦

Dionne Warwick

b. Dec. 12, 1940
Soul, Pop
The magically melodic voice of Dionne Warwick and the sophisticated pop compositions of Burt Bacharach and Hal David were the proverbial match made in heaven. Warwick proved the prolific songwriting team's favorite interpreter, scaling the pop and soul charts time and again with her soaring renditions of their memorable songs.
   Warwick hailed from a musical brood with a strong gospel heritage, and her sister Dee Dee scored a few hits of her own. Dionne's sultry pipes stood out, even on the highly competitive background vocal scene in New York, and she got a chance to step out front in 1963, hitting big on Scepter with the uptown soul classic "Don't Make Me Over."
   Under the expert tutelage of Bacharach and David, who doubled as her producers, Warwick's sound soon became smoother and more accessible to pop programming—a formula that resulted in the massive acceptance of her "Walk On By," "I Say a Little Prayer," "This Girl's in Love with You," and a slew of others.
   Strangely, Warwick never made it to the top of the pop charts until she broke away from her mentors, traveling to Philadelphia to record the R&B-oriented "Then Came You" with the Spinners in 1974. As elegant and tasteful as ever, Dionne Warwick's breathy vocals still haven't gone out of style—she's managed to remain contemporary while never jeopardizing her appeal. —*Bill Dahl*

Anyone Who Had a Heart / 1964 / Scepter ♦♦♦
Dionne Warwick was in her most vulnerable-sounding, pop/soul best on this mid-'60s album. The title cut was among her first smash hits and would reappear on later albums. She found in the Bacharach/David writing team the lyricists and composers that would give her magical hits throughout the 1960s. —*Ron Wynn*

Make Way For / 1964 / Scepter ♦♦♦
Dionne Warwick's first LP to make the pop charts introduced her soulful, yet elegant and restrained style to mainstream audiences in 1964. The 23-year-old singer hadn't begun getting the definitive tunes from Burt Bacharach and Hal David that would make her a 1960s icon, and there was an innocence and awkwardness in "Get Rid Of Him" and "I Smiled Yesterday" that the songwriting duo later exploited to perfection. —*Ron Wynn*

○ **The Sensitive Sound of Dionne Warwick** / 1965 / Scepter ♦♦♦♦
Things were just beginning to explode for Dionne Warwick in the mid-'60s. This album shows her sound maturing, the Bacharach/David team beginning to write the patented anguished laments and sophisticated soul tunes that were her forte, and War-

wick gradually weaning the gospel out of her voice and smoothing out her delivery. While she actually didn't fare that well commercially, you can hear the groundwork being laid on such songs as "Who Can I Turn To" and "You Can Have Him." —*Ron Wynn*

Dionne Warwick in Paris / 1966 / Scepter ♦♦♦
Outside of a brilliant live version of "House Is Not A Home," this album was more politely sung than most of what Dionne Warwick turned in regularly throughout the 1960s. It was a nice departure and did reasonably well, but wasn't a showcase or definitive concert album. It's long gone now, but might be worth it if you come across it in an auction. —*Ron Wynn*

○ **Here I Am** / 1966 / Scepter ♦♦♦♦
Dionne Warwick was beginning to establish consistent greatness during the mid-'60s, and this was her first really successful LP. It included "Are You There With Another Girl" and "Here I Am," and put Warwick squarely on her way to superstardom. It's now long out of print. —*Ron Wynn*

Here Where There Is Love / 1967 / Scepter ♦♦♦
Dionne Warwick was the epitome of a singles artist during her years at Scepter. The biggest albums she ever had were compilations, mainly because her albums were always stuffed with filler around classic singles. That was certainly the case here, with "I Just Don't Know What To Do With Myself" and "Trains and Boats and Planes" sandwiched by "As Long As He Needs Me" and "Go With Love." —*Ron Wynn*

On Stage and in the Movies / 1967 / Scepter ♦♦♦
A nice collection of show tunes and movie songs, one of her best non-greatest hits or anthology albums. Warwick's brand of sophisticated, soft pop/soul translated well to the stage and film song arena, even if she didn't always get quality numbers. But these songs were expertly chosen and brilliantly performed. —*Ron Wynn*

The Valley of the Dolls / 1968 / Scepter ♦♦♦
The biggest hit album of her career, even though it was far from her greatest music. Warwick stayed on the charts for almost a year with his release. The theme song just missed topping the charts, while "Do You Know The Way To San Jose" rivals "Promises, Promises" and "I Say A Little Prayer" as Warwick's best uptempo number. —*Ron Wynn*

○ **The Windows of the World** / 1968 / Scepter ♦♦♦♦
This proved both one of Warwick's strongest albums and a solid commercial LP as well. It included such hits as "I Say A Little Prayer" and "(There's) Always Something There To Remind Me," and had some fine album cuts as well. The title track had the kind of haunting refrain and anguished lyrics that became a Warwick specialty. —*Ron Wynn*

Promises, Promises / 1969 / Scepter ♦♦♦
Dionne Warwick was still rolling along in the late '60s, as the Bacharach/David axis hadn't yet disintegrated. While the material was getting safer and more pop-centered, it retained its lyrical quality and production sheen. Both the title song and "This Girl's In Love With You," the distaff version of the Herb Alpert hit, were superbly crafted and wonderfully sung. Warwick hadn't yet encountered the demons that would make the early '70s such a turbulent time. —*Ron Wynn*

Soulful / 1969 / Scepter ♦♦
Dionne Warwick maintained her position with this release, one of three that Scepter issued during the year. She only had one hit, a good cover of the Righteous Brothers' "You've Lost That Lovin' Feelin'," although it was far inferior to the original. The other songs ranged from mellow to mediocre, but Warwick was so well-established that it didn't really hurt her that much. —*Ron Wynn*

I'll Never Fall in Love Again / 1970 / Scepter ♦♦♦
While Herb Alpert had a number one hit with his version of the title track, Dionne Warwick captured the real contradictory flavor and irony in the theme. It was one of her last albums for Scepter, and her relationship with the Bacharach/Davis team had soured. But she turned in some good album cuts for a change, and such songs as "Let Me Go To Him" and "Paper Mache" were nice followup numbers. —*Ron Wynn*

Dionne / 1979 / Warner Brothers ♦♦
Dionne Warwick's career was revived when she teamed with Barry Manilow on this 1979 LP. Manilow's production of such heavily orchestrated numbers as "I Know I'll Never Love This Way Again" put Warwick back in the spotlight, as she once again sounded confident and compelling. It was the first platinum album of her career, and also her first album in 10 years to crack the Top 10 on the pop album chart. Warwick scored another hit with "Deja Vu" and was back on track. —*Ron Wynn*

Heartbreaker / Feb. 1982 / Arista ♦♦♦
Barry Gibb took his shot at producing Dionne Warwick and had quite a bit of success with this early-'80s album. While the title track sounded awkward and forced, it cracked the Top 10. Warwick was squarely back in the mainstream, and although she wasn't making transcendent hits, she was making creditable ones. —*Ron Wynn*

Friends / 1985 / Arista ♦♦
The huge chart topper "That's What Friends Are For" ensured that this would be a big hit album for Dionne Warwick. The song has become a signature piece, even though it's not as compelling as "Walk On By," and Warwick's vocal isn't as gripping as that of either Gladys Knight or Stevie Wonder (or even Elton John). But it was the perfect tune for the times and made everything else on the LP insignificant (which it was anyhow). —*Ron Wynn*

Greatest Hits 79-90 / 1989 / Arista ♦♦♦
This collection gathered the great hits from Dionne Warwick's rebirth on Arista. Barry Manilow wisely recast her doing sophisticated pop, moving her into adult contemporary love ballads and away from straight soul and R&B. It was an inspired move, and returned her to the top of the charts frequently in the late '70s and '80s. But while the songs were good, the collection didn't fare so well on the charts. —*Ron Wynn*

★ **The Dionne Warwick Collection: Her All-time Greatest Hits** / 1989 / Rhino ♦♦♦♦♦
The finest collection of Warwick material compiled by anyone, this excellent set gathered every Warwick gem and smartly remastered them. It's a definitive CD, containing several landmark releases featuring the collaborative compositions of Burt Bacharach and Hal David. These songs underscored Warwick's ability to embody her pop tunes with a soulful, but also light and innocent, quality. It also has excellent liner notes and intelligent sequencing. This is by far the set to get if you want a comprehensive presentation of Warwick's pop/soul greatness. —*Ron Wynn*

○ **Hidden Gems: Best of Dionne Warwick, Vol. 2** / 1992 / Rhino ♦♦♦♦
A fine collection of rarities and forgotten singles from Warwick's heyday with Bacharach/David; it's a good supplement to Rhino's *Dionne Warwick Collection*. —*Stephen Thomas Erlewine*

Was (Not Was)

Group, Soul, Pop/Rock
Was (Not Was) plays contemporary R&B dance music, with lyrics that range from the satiric to the bizarre. The group is led by Detroit-natives David Weiss (David Was), who plays flute and writes those lyrics, and Don Fagenson (Don Was), who plays bass and writes music, but the group is fronted by singers Harry Bowens and Sweet Pea Atkinson. Was (Not Was) first gained notice for a dance single called "Wheel Me Out" in 1980. Their first album, *Was (Not Was)* (1981), did not reach the charts, but its follow-up, *Born to Laugh at Tornados* (1983), did. Then little was heard from the group for five years. They returned in 1988 with *What Up, Dog?*, which featured the #16 hit "Spy in the House of Love" and the number seven hit "Walk the Dinosaur." (During this period, Don Was had become a prominent record producer, handling the board for Bonnie Raitt's Grammy-winning *Nick of Time*, among many other mainstream pop records.) The fourth Was (Not Was) album, *Are You Okay?*, appeared in 1990.
Are You Okay? wasn't as commercially successful as the previous *What Up, Dog?* After the album's release, Don Was continued to pursue his production career, which began to increase tensions between him and David. In 1993, Was (Not Was) officially parted ways. —*William Ruhlmann*

Was (Not Was) / 1981 / Island ♦♦

Born to Laugh at Tornados / 1983 / Geffen ♦♦♦
The Was brothers provide a strange bunch of songs with irresistible dance beats, plus an array of guest singers that is, well, unusual to say the least: Mitch Ryder, Doug Fieger (of the Knack), Ozzy Osbourne, and, on the ballad "Zaz Turned Blue," Mel Tormé. —*William Ruhlmann*

● **What Up, Dog?** / 1988 / Chrysalis ♦♦♦♦
The guests are fewer (though Frank Sinatra, Jr., sings one song), but the oddities go on, with "11 MPH," a review of the JFK assassination, and "Dad I'm in Jail," a proud rant by David Was. Also in-

cluded: the hits "Spy in the House of Love" and "Walk the Dinosaur." — *William Ruhlmann*

Are You Okay? / 1990 / Chrysalis ✦✦✦
The "hit" is a remake of "Papa Was a Rollin' Stone," but the album
is more memorable for typically oddball tunes like "I Blew Up the
United States" and "Elvis' Rolls Royce," which features a droll vocal
by Leonard Cohen. — *William Ruhlmann*

The Washington D.C.'s
Group, British Invasion
A relatively faceless British Invasion band who never came close to
a hit on either side of the Atlantic, the Washington D.C.s' height of
exposure occurred when their material was used to fill out an exploitative reissue of pre-"Glad All Over" Dave Clark Five singles.
One of the countless British bands slogging around on support bills
and German clubs, their early material was typical Merseyish covers of early American rock tunes. They recorded a couple of decent
British pop/rock singles in 1966 and 1967, "32nd Floor" and "Seek
and Find," the latter of which was produced by ex-Yardbird Paul
Samwell Smith, and featured John Paul Jones on bass. — *Richie Unterberger*

Dave Clark Five/The Washington D.C.s / 1993 / Repertoire ✦✦✦
This oddly titled reissue includes everything recorded by the D.C.s:
their entire 1966 LP, their four non-LP singles, and a couple previously unreleased outtakes. Besides the 17 Washington D.C.s tracks,
this CD reissue includes six sides from rare early-'60s singles cut
by the Dave Clark Five before their rise to fame. For British Invasion completists only. — *Richie Unterberger*

Baby Washington
b. Nov. 13, 1940, South Carolina
Soul, R&B
Her sultry delivery earned Justine "Baby" Washington R&B chart
bows in four different decades, most notably on the delectable uptown soul classic "That's How Heartaches Are Made" for Sue
Records in 1963. Born in South Carolina but raised in Harlem,
Washington was a member of the Hearts in 1956 before tallying
her first R&B hit in 1959 with "The Time" for Neptune. Billed occasionally as Jeanette or Justine Washington, she scaled the soul
charts into the mid-'70s with hits still hot from the '60s, such as her
nugget "Only Those in Love." — *Bill Dahl*

That's How Heartaches Are Made / 1963 / Collectables ✦✦✦
Jeanette "Baby" Washington cut her finest songs for Sue in the
early '60s. Although few made the charts, all were delivered with
conviction, sung in an earnest and riveting manner, and produced
with minimal gimmicks. While the title track is perhaps her best
cut, this album thankfully covers many lesser-known tracks and
avoids the singles that have frequently popped up on numerous anthologies. "Careless Hands" and "Standing on the Pier" are superior
to material that did get airplay; even the always troublesome Collectables sound quality can't override the importance of this release. — *Ron Wynn*

● **The Best of Baby Washington** / 1987 / Collectables ✦✦✦✦
Jeanne "Baby" Washington could sound like a hard-edged, no-nonsense wailer one moment and a wounded sparrow the next. She
never enjoyed any pop attention, but equaled Dionne Warwick and
Maxine Brown among female light soul singers. This collection
covers her late-'50s and early-'60s songs for Neptune and Sue, including "The Bells," "The Time" and "That's How Heartaches Are
Made." — *Ron Wynn*

The Waterboys
Group, Alternative Pop/Rock, Folk-Rock
A critically acclaimed folk-rock band led by Scottish singer/song-
writer and guitarist Mike Scott. The group's first recording was a
five-track mini-album, *The Waterboys*, released in 1984, at which
time the only other regular band member was sax player Anthony
Thistlewaite. By the time their second album, *A Pagan Place*, was
released, they had added keyboard player Karl Wallinger. They first
gained extensive recognition for their third album, *This Is the Sea*
(1985), which got to number 37 in the U.K. charts and included the
number 26 single "The Whole of the Moon." Wallinger then left to
form World Party and Scott spent more than three years preparing
Fisherman's Blues, which, when it appeared in late 1988, showed a
distinct turn toward Irish folk music. It was followed two years
later by *Room to Roam*.

Scott backed away from Irish folk on 1993's *Dream Harder*,
which featured a more straightforward, epic rock that recalled their
earlier albums. — *William Ruhlmann*

○ **The Waterboys** / 1983 / Ensign ✦✦✦✦
A Pagan Place / 1984 / Chrysalis ✦✦✦
○ **This Is the Sea** / 1985 / Chrysalis ✦✦✦✦
Mike Scott combines the forcefulness of rock with the earnestness
of folk and adds a mystical poetic soul to this brilliant album,
which also features notable musical contributions from saxophon-
ist Anthony Thistlewaite and keyboardist Karl Wallinger. —
William Ruhlmann

○ **Fisherman's Blues** / 1988 / Ensign ✦✦✦✦
The Waterboys turn into a neo-traditional Irish folk band, complete
with mandolins and fiddles, and Mike Scott's poetic muse just gets
better. — *William Ruhlmann*

Room to Roam / 1990 / Ensign ✦✦✦
● **The Best of the Waterboys (1981—1990)** / 1991 / Ensign ✦✦✦✦
Sums up the story so far, tracing the band's evolution from rock to
folk, the constant sensibility of Mike Scott remaining intact. —
William Ruhlmann

Dream Harder / May 25, 1993 / Geffen ✦✦
After two albums of neo-traditional Irish music, Mike Scott brings
the Waterboys back to the big rock sound of earlier albums like
This is the Sea. Coming after the commercial success of *Fishermen's Blues* and *Room to Roam*, *Dream Harder* is a bit of a disappointment. Its best material doesn't carry the same weight as compositions from *Blues*—compare the simple beauty of *Fishermen's
Blues'* "Has Anyone Hear Seen Hank" to *Dream Harder*'s
overblown "The Return of Jimi Hendrix." Scott can still bang out
some good songs, but on *Dream Harder* there aren't as many as on
previous efforts. — *Stephen Thomas Erlewine*

The Secret Life Of The Waterboys 81-85 / 1994 / Chrysalis ✦✦

Crystal Waters
Urban, Dance
A New Jersey vocalist who majored in computer science at
Howard, Crystal Waters had one of 1991's surprise left-field hits
with "Gypsy Woman (She's Homeless)." The song had both a potent
message and wonderful vocal that smartly mixed anger, irony, and
humor. None of Waters's other songs were quite that inspired, but
her debut LP, *Surprise*, got her in the hunt. — *Ron Wynn*

○ **Surprise** / 1991 / Mercury ✦✦✦✦
House star of 1991; made smashing debut. — *Ron Wynn*

● **Storyteller** / 1994 / Mercury ✦✦✦✦
Crystal Waters's most recent release demonstrates the flexibility
and insights that characterized her surprising hit debut. Her tone
and voice are light and supple, and she seldom sounds intense or
animated during a song, even on a number where the lyrics would
seem to require a more heated approach. But she can stun, alert
and inform with her range and subject matter. "Storyteller" and
"Daddy Do" aren't frilly numbers; the former describes a relationship gone sour in literate, emotionally compelling terms, while the
latter is a hard-hitting attack on wife abuse. Waters scores lots of
points through delivery and inflection, and her CD is much more
than a dance/disco diva's outpourings. — *Ron Wynn*

Roger Waters
b. Sep. 6, 1944
Art-Rock/Progressive-Rock
Roger Waters was the bassist for Pink Floyd from 1965 to 1983. Waters assumed an increasingly dominant position in the band, writing all lyrics in addition to some of the music as of *The Dark Side
of the Moon* (1973) and singing most of the lead vocals on *The Wall*
(1979). Waters issued his debut solo album, *The Pros and Cons of
Hitch-Hiking*, in 1984. In the mid-'80s, he engaged in a protracted
legal battle, arguing that the other members of Pink Floyd could
not continue using the name without him in the band; he lost. In
1987, Waters released his second album, *Radio K.A.O.S.*, and in
1990 he staged a concert version of *The Wall* in Berlin. In 1992 he
released his third album, *Amused to Death*. — *William Ruhlmann*

Music from "The Body" / 1970 / Restless ✦✦✦
This soundtrack album, credited to Ron Geesin and Roger Waters,
contains various sound effects and musical fragments, plus a few
folkish songs on which Waters accompanies himself on acoustic
guitar and sings. The result is a precursor to some of Waters's and

Pink Floyd's later work ("Breathe," for example, is suggestive of *The Dark Side Of The Moon*), but in an embryonic form. — *William Ruhlmann*

○ **The Pros & Cons of Hitch-Hiking** / 1984 / Columbia ✦✦✦✦
The loose framing device of this album is a series of daydreams experienced while waking up. Eric Clapton contributes guitar, but he can't provide enough musical interest to sustain Roger Waters's lyric-heavy ruminations. — *William Ruhlmann*

○ **Radio K.A.O.S.** / 1987 / Columbia ✦✦✦✦
There's more story than can be effectively told on this concept album dealing with radio, computers, and the threat of nuclear war, but many of the songs are up to Waters's Pink Floyd standard, and some rock out more than his former band ever did. — *William Ruhlmann*

The Wall in Berlin 1990 / 1990 / Mercury ✦✦✦
This is a gala two-disc live rendition of the Pink Floyd concept album, employing a raft of guest stars including Van Morrison, Sinéad O'Connor, Joni Mitchell, the Scorpions, and others. — *William Ruhlmann*

● **Amused to Death** / Sep. 1, 1992 / Columbia ✦✦✦✦
Yet another installment in Waters's lectures about the horrors of war and man's inhumanity to man, *Amused to Death* is helped considerably by the presence of Jeff Beck, who contributes some brilliant, free-form guitar to the meandering songs. Waters himself is in fine form, spitting out bitter, sarcastic lyrics over his slow, grandiose instrumental backdrops. While he could have fleshed out the melodies a little bit more, his execution is what matters, and his performance on *Amused to Death* is the liveliest of any of his solo records. — *Stephen Thomas Erlewine*

Jody Watley

b. Jan. 30, 1959, Chicago, IL.
Dance-Pop, Urban
Jody Watley got her start as a dancer on the TV show *Soul Train*. From 1977 to 1984, she was a singer in the group Shalamar. Her debut solo album, *Jody Watley* (1987), sold a million copies and produced three Top Ten hits—"Looking for a New Love," "Don't You Want Me," and "Some Kind of Lover." As a result of its success, Watley won the Grammy Award for Best New Artist of 1987. Her second album, *Larger than Life* (1989), went gold and contained the number two pop hit "Real Love" as well as the Top Tens "Friends" and "Everything." *You Wanna Dance with Me?*, released at the end of that year, contained dance remixes of her hits. Watley's third album, *Affairs of the Heart*, was released at the end of 1991. — *William Ruhlmann*

● **Jody Watley** / 1987 / MCA ✦✦✦✦
State-of-the-art R&B/dance-pop, by a singer who was a veteran of the genre long before cutting her debut album. — *William Ruhlmann*

○ **Larger than Life** / 1989 / MCA ✦✦✦✦
The former Shalamar member and goddaughter of Jackie Wilson followed her hit debut album with a solid second entry, although it was much more uptempo and dance-dominated. Watley secured a huge pop and R&B hit with "Real Love," and "Friends" was a New Jack Swing number with rap contributions from Whodini. "Everything" was another Top Ten pop and R&B success. While the thinness of Watley's vocals and the preponderance of predictable beats seemed to indicate that trouble lay ahead, she happily took the gold record certification for the album. — *Ron Wynn*

You Wanna Dance with Me? / 1990 / MCA ✦✦
One of the more depressing and tiresome trends that emerged in the 1980s and has continued into the 1990s is the remix album. While labels sweat out down periods between releases, they often issue discs containing remixes of previous songs by hit acts. This one presented "fresh" versions of Jody Watley smashes "Don't You Want Me," "Friends," "Most of All," "I'm Looking For A New Love," "Real Love" and "Still A Thrill." These provided no insights, imaginative arrangements or surprising twists, and didn't even elicit much response on the dance circuit, since they had already heard club remixes when the songs were originally hits. — *Ron Wynn*

Affairs of the Heart / 1991 / MCA ✦✦✦

Mike Watt

Alternative Pop/Rock
Former Minutemen and fIREHOSE bassist Mike Watt struck out on

his own solo career in 1995, with the critically-acclaimed *Ball-Hog or Tugboat?* — *Stephen Thomas Erlewine*

● **Ball-Hog or Tugboat?** / 1995 / Columbia ✦✦✦✦
For his first solo album, Mike Watt assembled a different band for each track, creating a veritable who's-who of post-punk and alternative rock—Eddie Vedder, Dave Grohl, Thurston Moore, J. Mascis, Frank Black, Evan Dando, Dave Pirner, Henry Rollins, Flea, Lee Ranaldo, Mike D, and Pat Smear all appear, among others. Predictably, the sound is somewhat schizophrenic, but no more so than the average Minutemen album. *Ball-Hog or Tugboat?* is more polished than anything the Minutemen released, yet looser than fIRE-HOSE, filled with jazz-inflected breaks and sheer sonic freak-outs, but dominated by a surprisingly large number of pop songs. On the power-pop rush of "Piss-Bottle Man," Dando sings with more emotion than on most Lemonheads records, and "Chinese Fire Drill" shows an effective folky side to Watt's music. And Watt's own vocals on "Big Train" are as big-hearted, sly and funny as the album itself. — *Stephen Thomas Erlewine*

The Weather Girls

Group, Soul, R&B
The Weather Girls, Martha Wash and Izora Rhodes, started out in the gospel group NOW (News of the World) before becoming backup singers with Sylvester in the '70s. They formed the duo Two Tons of Fun, later changing their name to the Weather Girls and recording in the early '80s. Wash later went on to do session singing and was the uncredited lead vocalist on "You're My One and Only (True Love)" by Seduction, "Everybody Everybody" by Black Box, and "Gonna Make You Sweat (Everybody Dance Now)" by C&C Music Factory. Wash, who is overweight, was invariably replaced in the songs' videos by lip-syncing models, and was forced to resort to legal action to get a proper share of the royalties for her work. — *Steve Huey*

○ **Success** / 1983 / Columbia ✦✦✦✦
It was fun while it lasted for Martha Wash and Izora Rhodes, better known as Two Tons of Fun. The single "It's Raining Men" was one of the better left-field hits of 1982, and it helped make their debut album a mild success, although it lacked either a suitable followup single or consistently strong material. It also failed to show how strong the women's voices were or exploit their gospel roots. — *Ron Wynn*

Big Girls Don't Cry / 1985 / Columbia ✦✦✦
The final Columbia vehicle for Martha Wash and Izora Redman-Armstead; things had soured for the duo with the label. They began as a novelty act, but were truly a gospel-tinged soul unit who could also score with the dance crowd. They never really were allowed to showcase their real personalities or styles, and by the time this album was issued, they were doing formula pop/soul and dance filler. — *Ron Wynn*

● **Weather Girls** / 1988 / Columbia ✦✦✦✦
The third and final Weather Girls album was a disappointment, as it was evident that the major labels weren't willing to take the duo of Martha Wash and Izora Rhodes seriously enough to get them capable producers and find them suitable material. Instead, they struggled through another collection of cliches, weak tracks, and uninspired production and arrangements. The former backup singers for Sylvester never got as a lead act the kind of label support their late ex-boss received at Fantasy. — *Ron Wynn*

Jimmy Webb

Singer-Songwriter, Pop/Rock
Even if you never have heard a Jimmy Webb album, you have at least heard his songs. During the late '60s and early '70s, Webb was writing a series of hits for the Fifth Dimension, Glen Campbell, Richard Harris, and Cher, including "Wichita Lineman" and "By the Time I Get to Phoenix;" both songs have become pop standards. His first hit was the Fifth Dimension's "Up, Up and Away," which was eventually used in TWA television commercials.

After having many different artists record his songs successfully, Webb officially launched a solo career in 1970; a collection of his demos had been released against his will in 1968. Although his debut album, *Words and Music*, earned mixed reviews, it helped him gain a sizable cult following. While he recorded a series of overlooked albums in the '70s, other artists continued to record his songs, including Art Garfunkel, Judy Collins, Joe Cocker, and Lowell George. During the '80s, he concentrated on scoring films and television shows, releasing only one album. In 1993, he returned to the studio to record his first album since 1982; produced by Linda Rondstadt, *Suspending Disbelief* earned good reviews, but poor sales, which seems to be Webb's curse. Even though he has never had success with his own recordings, Jimmy Webb remains one of the best-loved and most-recorded songwriters of his generation. —*Stephen Thomas Erlewine*

Jim Webb Sings Jim Webb / 1968 / Epic ♦♦
Released without Webb's approval, this collection of early songwriting demos has him singing his own songs which became hits for others. Though his delivery lacks the confidence the songs deserve, fans will find this of interest. —*Chris Woodstra*

Words & Music / Feb. 1970 / Reprise ♦♦♦
Words and Music marked Webb's official debut as a singer of his own songs. Though the second side's experiments (a suite in three movements and a song cycle/medley linking "Let It Be Me," "Never My Love," and "I Wanna Be Free") are a little too ambitious for comfort, side one features the concise, well-crafted pop (such as "P.F. Sloan" and "Love Song") that would feature heavily on later releases. —*Chris Woodstra*

And So On / 1971 / Reprise ♦♦♦
Webb's second album stripped down the excesses of its predecessor for a more consistently enjoyable set, featuring the haunting "Met Her on a Plane" (later covered by Ian Matthews) as well as the equally powerful "If Ships Were Made to Sail," "One Lady" and "All My Love's Laughter." —*Chris Woodstra*

Letters / 1972 / Reprise ♦♦♦

Lands End / 1974 / Asylum ♦♦♦

○ **El Mirage** / 1977 / Atlantic ♦♦♦♦
Produced by George Martin, *El Mirage* is one of Webb's strongest albums. As always, the songs are perfectly constructed but this time sung with more confidence than ever before. Highlights include "If You See Me Getting Smaller" and "Christian No." —*Chris Woodstra*

Angel Heart / 1982 / Sony ♦♦
Even though Webb delivers another solid batch of songs on this 1982 album, the MOR-schlock arrangements are far too over-the-top, making this the weakest of his catalog. —*Chris Woodstra*

Suspending Disbelief / 1993 / Elektra ♦♦♦
After a several year absence, Webb returns with one of his most polished efforts to date. His hook-filled melodies are instantly endearing, while he sings a love song to his sports car and remembers a meeting with Elvis. His voice, never one his strong points in the past, has aged particularly well. —*Chris Woodstra*

● **Archive** / 1993 / WEA ♦♦♦♦
Archive is an excellent 20-track (U.K. import only) overview of Webb's criminally overlooked career as a performer from 1970 to 1977, his most productive period. While he is best remebered as the composer of hits for others, this collection offers proof that he was equally adept at interpreting his own songs—often times bringing more emotion to them. —*Chris Woodstra*

The Wedding Present

Group, Alternative Pop/Rock
Leeds native David Gedge is the only original member remaining in the Wedding Present. During 1992, the band released a single for each month of the year; most went Top 20 in England, and the first six (plus B-sides) are collected on *Hit Parade, Vol. 1*. In 1994, the band released *Watusi*. —*John Bush*

○ **Bizarro** / 1989 / RCA ♦♦♦♦
Suprisingly listenable frenetic rock. —*Robert Gordon*

Seamonsters / 1991 / First Warning ♦♦♦
Steve Albini's production gives *Seamonsters* a noisy, discordant feel in some spots, but David Gedge's delightful songwriting lies just under the surface. He manipulates his limited vocal range into a rich, wistful voice just about to crack. The Wedding Present work best on this album when Gedge's plaintive love songs explode into a distorted fury, as on "Dalliance," and "Suck." —*John Bush*

● **The Hit Parade, Part 1** / 1992 / First Warning ♦♦♦♦
Britain's The Wedding Present has hit on an interesting marketing ploy in its home country: the group has been releasing one limited edition single for each month of 1992. *Hit Parade 1*, a 12-track compilation of the first six, presents a rather unrelenting onslaught of fuzzy guitars and dour, aggressive vocals. The effect can be riveting or disconcerting, depending on your mood. —*Roch Parisien*

○ **Watusi** / 1994 / PolyGram ♦♦♦♦
A year and a half after *Hit Parade*, the band released their Island debut. On *Watusi*, the noisy rhythms of *Seamonsters* are gone. Steve Fisk's production gives the LP a more varied musical feel; he lends his piano and organ skills over the crackling and popping of a turntable on the beautiful "Spangle." The first track, "So Long, Baby," begins as a normal, uptempo number, but then completely changes rhythm and melody for the chorus, a surprising and enjoyable move. "Yeah Yeah Yeah Yeah Yeah" is a high-powered, infectious sing-along. Although *Seamonsters* has more beautiful songs, *Watusi*'s diversity gives it an added edge. —*John Bush*

Ween

Group, Alternative Pop/Rock
Since 1990, Ween have been making records that consume pop culture whole and smirkingly spit it back out. The duo of Dean and Gene Ween (born Mickey Melchiondo and Aaron Freeman) make records that read like parodies but sound like pop albums. Essentially, they are two spoiled, over-educated suburban college kids, screwing around with a four-track cassette recorder in their parents' basement; they sing in funny voices, speed up the tape, make noises with their instruments, slow down the tape, and write some incredibly enjoyable, subversive pop songs. It's like what They Might Be Giants would sound like if they relied on smart-ass humor instead of hooks and melodies. —*Stephen Thomas Erlewine*

GodWeenSatan: The Oneness / 1990 / Twin/Tone ♦♦♦
A crank phone call of epic proportions, this 20-plus song strong debut is filled with plenty of inanity, insanity, and obscenity. Stylistically, the group veers off in all directions. The helium-laced pop of "Don't Laugh, I Love You," the stomp of "Old Queen Cole" and the delicate ballad "Squelch the Little Weasel" make this a crazy, unfocused collection of gross fun. —*Heather Phares*

The Pod / 1991 / Shimmy Disc ♦♦♦
The Pod continues the wackiness and effrontery that the Ween brothers started on *GodWeenSatan*. However, the tone of the album is more sluggish and off-kilter, perhaps from the severe case of mononucleosis the group had when they recorded this. "Dr. Rock" and "Pollo Asado" are two standouts on this bizarre and somewhat inaccessible album. —*Heather Phares*

○ **Pure Guava** / 1992 / Elektra ♦♦♦♦
The band's third album finds them moving in a more pop direction. Tunes like "Push the Little Daisies," "Springtheme" and "Don't Get Too Close to My Fantasy," though certainly bizarre, are catchy and fun to listen to. However, the Ween boys don't forget to be disgusting, as song titles like "Reggaejunkiejew" and "Flies on my Dick" subtly hint. —*Heather Phares*

● **Chocolate & Cheese** / 1994 / Elektra ♦♦♦♦
Chocolate and Cheese is the group's fourth and most accomplished album yet, focusing their gonzo sensibilities into a collection of hummable tunes. "Take Me Away" and "Tear for Eddie" are clever parodies of classic rock, while "Roses Are Free" and "Freedom of '76" pay homage to Prince and '70s soul respectively. The touching Mexican ballad "Buenos Tardes Amigo" and the downright creepy "Spinal Meningitis Got Me Down" show that Ween's smirks are still firmly on their faces, even if they are creating increasingly memorable tunes. *Chocolate and Cheese* is a good beginning point for novices to the crazy world of Dean and Gene Ween. —*Heather Phares*

Weezer

Group, Alternative Pop/Rock
Led by guitarist/vocalist/songwriter Rivers Cuomo, Weezer mixed the off-kilter punk-pop of the Pixies with a new wave pop sensibility and arena rock beat, becoming one of the surprise success stories of 1994. Cuomo was still in college when their self-titled debut record came out in the summer of 1994. Produced by Ric Ocasek, the record shot to popularity once MTV began playing the incessant "Undone (The Sweater Song)" heavily. The band followed through with another hit single, "Buddy Holly," at the end of the year. In the spring of 1995, the album had gone platinum; the band's third single, "Say It Ain't So," became their third straight modern rock hit in the summer of 1995. —*Stephen Thomas Erlewine*

● **Weezer** / 1994 / Geffen ♦♦♦♦
Falling between the warped pop of the Pixies and the straightahead thump of arena rock, Weezer's debut album offers embarrassingly pleasurable pop thrills. Weezer is unabashedly pop. Songs like

"Buddy Holly," "Undone—The Sweater Song," "In the Garage," "The World Has Turned and Left Me Here," and "Surf Wax America" are filled with strong, simple guitar hooks and relentlessly catchy melodies. What makes the band so enjoyable is their charming geekiness; instead of singing about despair, they sing about love, which is kind of refreshing in the gloom-drenched world of '90s guitar-pop. —*Stephen Thomas Erlewine*

Bob Weir

b. Oct. 6, 1947
Rock & Roll
Bob Weir is a guitarist and vocalist in the Grateful Dead. He was a founding member of the group in 1965 and has been with it throughout its history. Weir began making records under his own name and in other configurations in 1972 and has released solo albums as well as leading Kingfish and Bobby and the Midnites. Most recently Weir has toured in a duo with bassist Rob Wasserman, and they are said to be making an album together, perhaps under the name *Scaring the Children*. —*William Ruhlmann*

● Ace / 1972 / Grateful Dead ◆◆◆◆
Weir's debut solo album is really a Grateful Dead album in disguise and, at that, not a bad followup to the group's *American Beauty* album. While Weir handles lead vocals, the rest of the band is on the album, and the selections, including "Greatest Story Ever Told," "Playing in the Band," "One More Saturday Night," and "Cassidy," have entered the Dead's concert repertoire and the list of Dead Head favorites. —*William Ruhlmann*

Heaven Help the Fool / 1978 / Arista ◆◆◆
A slickly produced pop-rock album, but one that demonstrates the range of Weir's abilities. —*William Ruhlmann*

○ Bobby & the Midnites / 1981 / Arista ◆◆◆◆
Weir gets jazzy with drummer Billy Cobham and others. —*Jeff Tamarkin*

Paul Weller

Pop/Rock
After disbanding the Style Council, former Jam leader Paul Weller went solo, making a series of soul-inspired pop/rock records. While his self-titled 1992 debut a return to form, it was the following year's *Wildwood* (not released in the U.S. until 1994) that showed he was still a vital songwriter and artist. Like the rest of Weller's work, the album was a hit in nearly every country except the United States. —*Stephen Thomas Erlewine*

○ Paul Weller / 1992 / London ◆◆◆◆
Weller's voice has matured into a deep, soulful, resonant instrument, in keeping with his new inward-looking material. He's obviously come to terms with being an effective chronicler of his own feelings rather than being the spokesperson of a generation. His ease with this role makes *Paul Weller* a comfortable—if not groundbreaking—listening experience all around. —*Roch Parisien*

● Wildwood / 1993 / PolyGram ◆◆◆◆
Paul Weller signalled that the songwriter had returned to form, but *Wildwood* is the album that reestablished him as a British superstar. And for good reason, too. Expanding the tight, stripped-down soul and R&B-inflected pop of his debut, Weller adds a relaxed, laidback approach that recalls the better moments of Traffic. Throughout the record, Weller's songwriting is concise and soulful, giving the musicians a solid foundations for their instrumental excursions, which never become boring and indulgent. —*Stephen Thomas Erlewine*

Live Wood / 1994 / Go! Discs ◆◆◆
Weller's career was revitalized with *Wildwood*, which sparked an equally successful world tour captured on the energetic *Live Wood*. The songs remain just as impressive, but what makes the live record worthwhile is the wonderful interplay of the band. They frequently launch into tight jams that never seem bloated, which is the mark of a good live album. —*Stephen Thomas Erlewine*

Stanley Road / 1995 / Go! Discs ◆◆◆
In many ways, *Stanley Road* is *Wildwood—Part Two*, a continuation of the laidback, soul-inflected rock that dominated his previous albums. Named after the street where he grew up, *Stanley Road* could be seen as a return to Paul Weller's roots, yet his roots are in the Who and the Kinks, not in Traffic. (At this point, the sound of the Jam matters little in what his music sounds like.) Weller's music has always had R&B roots—the major difference with both *Wildwood* and *Stanley Road* is how much he and his band stretch

out. *Stanley Road* in particular features more jamming than any of his previous work. That doesn't mean he has neglected his songwriting—a handful of Weller classics are scattered throughout the album. Unfortunately, too much of it is spent on drawn-out grooves that are self-conscious about their own authenticity. Still, he has the good sense to revive Dr. John's "I Walk on Gilded Splinters" and invite his disciple Noel Gallagher (Oasis) along to jam. —*Stephen Thomas Erlewine*

Mary Wells

b. May 13, 1943, Detroit, MI, **d.** Jul. 26, 1992
Soul, Motown
Time and legions of other soul superstars have obscured the fact that for a brief moment, Mary Wells was Motown's biggest star. She came to the attention of Berry Gordy as a 17-year-old, hawking a song she'd written for Jackie Wilson; that song, "Bye Bye Baby," became her first Motown hit in 1961. The full-throated approach of that single was quickly toned down in favor of a pop-soul sound. Few other soul singers managed to be as shy and sexy at the same time as Wells (Barbara Lewis is the only other that springs to mind), and the soft-voiced singer found a perfect match with the emerging Motown production team, especially Smokey Robinson. Smokey wrote and produced her biggest Motown hits—"Two Lovers," "You Beat Me to the Punch," and "The One Who Really Loves You" all made the Top Ten in the early '60s, and "My Guy" hit the number one spot in mid-1964, at the very height of Beatlemania.

Mary turned 21 years old as "My Guy" was rising to the top of the charts, and left Motown almost immediately afterwards for a reported advance of several hundred thousand dollars from 20th Century Fox. The circumstances remain cloudy thirty years later, but Wells and her husband-manager felt Motown wasn't coming through with enough money for its new superstar; she was also lured by the prospect of movie roles through 20th Century Fox (which never materialized). It's been rumored that Wells was being groomed for the sort of plans that were subsequently lavished upon Diana Ross; more nefariously, it's also been rumored that Motown quietly discouraged radio stations from playing Wells's subsequent releases. What is certain is that Wells never remotely approached the success of her Motown years, entering the pop Top 40 only once (although she had some R&B hits). Motown, for its part, took care throughout the rest of the '60s not to lose its big stars to larger labels.

Wells's departure from Motown was so dramatic and unsuccessful that it's tended to overshadow the quality of her later work, which has almost always been dismissed as trivial by critics. True, it didn't match the quality of her Motown recordings—Smokey Robinson could not be replaced. But her '60s singles for 20th Century Fox (whom she ended up leaving after only a year), Atco, and Jubilee were solid pop-soul on which her vocal talents remained undiminished. She wrote and produced a lot of her late '60s and early '70s sessions with her second husband, guitarist Cecil Womack (brother of Bobby), and these found her exploring a somewhat earthier groove than her more widely known pop efforts. She had trouble landing recording deals in the '70s and '80s, and succumbed to throat cancer in 1992. —*Richie Unterberger*

Bye, Bye Baby, I Don't Want to Take a Chance / 1961 / Motown ◆◆◆
Mary Wells wasn't yet a polished vocalist when she first signed with Motown in the early '60s, and she later became the first performer to score a number one single and Top 10 pop hit for the label. But that didn't happen with these songs, although they have an edge, toughness and spark that weren't always evident in the slicker hits that Wells made. —*Ron Wynn*

The One Who Really Loves You / Jun. 1962 / Motown ◆◆◆
Fairly solid effort, with most of the songs penned by Motown mainstays like Smokey Robinson, Berry Gordy, and Mickey Stevenson. Includes the Top 10 hits "The One Who Really Loves You" and "You Beat Me To The Punch," as well as one of the few Wells originals she recorded while at Motown, "Drifting Love." But considering that seven of the ten songs appear on *Looking Back*, only Wells collectors need to pick this up. —*Richie Unterberger*

Live on Stage / Sep. 1963 / Motown ◆◆◆
A fine, but unfortunately deleted, album featuring Mary Wells in concert during her peak years. She was a shouting, triumphant vocalist in the early '60s, one whose delivery and manner were alter-

nately seductive, defiant, and vulnerable. Motown should get this back into print immediately. —*Ron Wynn*

○ **Greatest Hits** / Apr. 15, 1964 / Motown ✦✦✦✦
Since Mary Wells left Motown in 1964, this 12-song compilation, released at the time, contains all her successful singles for the label, from "Bye Bye Baby" to "My Guy," with the exception of "I Don't Want To Take A Chance." As such, it is just about all the Mary Wells anyone reasonably needs. —*William Ruhlmann*

○ **My Guy** / Jun. 1964 / Motown ✦✦✦✦
On this album, Smokey Robinson demonstrated his ability to craft and hone great material for female acts, something he would later repeat with the Marvelettes. Besides the title track, which became Motown's first Top Ten and #1 pop hit, there were other strong tunes, such as "He's the One I Love" and "At Last," that weren't hits but certainly should have been. —*Ron Wynn*

Mary Wells / 1965 / 20th Century ✦✦✦
Mary Wells's first non-Motown outing made a little noise, but it was clear that she wouldn't be getting the kind of songwriting, production, supporting performances, or instrumental backup she had previously received. —*Ron Wynn*

In and out of Love / 1981 / EPK ✦✦
What happened to Mary Wells was one of Motown's greatest disgraces. She was way past her prime on this early-'80s album, and was also hampered by poor material and unimaginative production. Someone who had made such marvelous music for Motown in its formative years shouldn't even have been working at that point, and certainly shouldn't have suffered the humiliation of churning out unrepresentative material to earn a living. —*Ron Wynn*

○ **Compact Command Performances** / 1985 / Motown ✦✦✦✦
The recent two-disc Mary Wells collection eclipses the value of this set, which was previously perhaps the definitive Wells anthology. It contains just what you'd expect: "My Guy" and "You Beat Me To The Punch," plus hits with Marvin Gaye and other representative cuts. It was decently remastered as well. —*Ron Wynn*

Keeping My Mind on Love / 1990 / Quality ✦✦✦
Mary Wells battled valiantly in the late '80s against the throat cancer that finally killed her in 1992. She clearly was singing strictly on emotion, desire, and willpower throughout this session, which was recorded in 1987 and issued in 1990 by Ian Levine. It should be regarded more as a final testament rather than judged, since Wells was in no shape to even be singing at that point. Levine deserves thanks for giving her one last shot, and any fan hearing it will be saddened that she's no longer around. —*Ron Wynn*

○ **Complete Jubilee Sessions** / 1993 / Sequel ✦✦✦✦
More proof that Wells still had what it took after leaving Motown. This 26-song collection assembles everything she recorded for the Jubilee label in the late '60s and early '70s: her 1968 LP *Servin' Up Some Soul*, a couple non-LP B-sides, and the entirety of a scrapped follow-up album (although some of the songs from that unreleased LP appeared on singles, seven were unreleased before this reissue). This is Wells's gutsiest period, with the majority of the material penned by her and husband Cecil Womack, who provides some excellent bluesy guitar licks. Wells is in top voice on both the fairly strong originals and a variety of well-done covers. The earlier *Servin' Up Some Soul* sessions have the edge over the later, slicker tracks, but almost all of it is well worth hearing. —*Richie Unterberger*

★ **Looking Back 1961-1964** / Sep. 7, 1993 / Motown ✦✦✦✦✦
This two-CD, 43-track box set is the most comprehensive retrospective of Motown's biggest female star before Diana Ross. Although her first hit, "Bye Bye Baby," presented Wells as a blues belter, she quickly settled into a sly and sassy groove. Subsequent hits like "You Beat Me To The Punch," "Two Lovers," and "My Guy" (all included here) made the most of her shy, seductive voice by teaming her with some great songs and production by Smokey Robinson. Though many of these tunes were relegated to B-sides, album tracks, or even the can (11 were previously unreleased), the material—written by Motown stalwarts like Berry Gordy, Holland-Dozier-Holland, and Mickey Stevenson when Smokey was unavailable—is not far below the hits in quality. This is as much a testimony to Motown's overflow of prolific talent as Wells, but doesn't detract from the consistency of this set, which includes her duets with Marvin Gaye (as well as a previously unreleased duet with Smokey Robinson). Includes a comprehensive essay in the photo-packed booklet, although the mysterious absence of the excellent "Was It Worth It" is a notable loss. —*Richie Unterberger*

Ain't It the Truth: The Best of Mary Wells 1964-1982 / 1994 / Varese Sarabande ✦✦✦
It doesn't have anything from her 1965-67 years with Atco (those tracks are compiled on a separate collection), but otherwise this does a good job of assembling the highlights of her post-Motown career. The focus is on her handful of minor mid-'60s hits for 20th Century Fox (which were conscious or half-conscious attempts to emulate her Motown sound) and her grittier 1968-70 recordings for Jubilee (which she co-wrote and co-produced with guitarist and husband/producer Cecil Womack). A couple of unimpressive tracks from her 1981 Epic album round out the collection; Wells is in fine form throughout. —*Richie Unterberger*

Dear Lover: The Atco Sessions / 1995 / Ichiban/Soul Classics ✦✦✦
In his autobiography, Jerry Wexler characterized Wells's tenure with Atlantic from 1965-67 as a failure for all parties concerned, but he's being too harsh. Commercially, it was certainly a fallow period; only the title track (a Top Ten R&B hit) paid off. But actually, her Atco singles were solid mid-'60s soul, usually recorded in Chicago and bearing the influence of that city's noted soul producer, Carl Davis (who produced some of these tracks). This collection includes both sides of all four of her Atco singles, five covers from her sole Atco LP, and a couple of decent previously unreleased tracks. —*Richie Unterberger*

Fred Wesley

Soul, Funk, R&B
Wesley has played with Count Basie's orchestra. During the '60s and '70s, he was a pivotal member of James Brown's bands, serving at times as musical director. His slippery riffs and pungent, precise solos, contrasting with those of saxophonist Maceo Parker, gave Brown's R&B, soul, and funk tunes their instrumental punch. He later left Brown and spent several years playing with George Clinton's various Parliament/Funkadelic projects, even recording a couple of albums as a spin-off group, The Horny Horns. He recently cut an album as a leader on Antilles, working with many young-lion types, who remember his music with Brown and are interested in finding common ground between improvisatory and funk/R&B territory. —*Ron Wynn*

A Blow for Me, a Toot to You / 1977 / Atlantic ✦✦✦

● **New Friends** / 1991 / Antilles ✦✦✦✦
All-star lineup doing soul-jazz, funk, and blues. Has been highly popular, despite dubious value. —*Ron Wynn*

The J.B. Horns / 1991 / Mesa Blue Moon ✦✦

○ **Comme Ci Comme Ca** / 1991 / Antilles ✦✦✦✦
This trombonist shines in a jazz context with an eight-piece. Hugh Ragin on trumpet, Karl Denson and Maceo Parker on sax, and the Peter Madsen Trio are featured on this album of two standards, two pop-styled tunes, and originals played with punch. The title track is especially right-on. —*Michael G. Nastos*

The West Coast Pop Art Experimental Band

Group, Psychedelic
If a band could ever be called the "average" psychedelic group, the West Coast Pop Art Experimental Band fit the bill. This somewhat mysterious collection of L.A. players issued several albums in the late '60s that plugged into the era's standard folk-rock, freakouts, and trippy lyrics without establishing a solid identity of their own. But, because the currents they were riding were themselves so inspired, "average" in this case doesn't necessarily mean bad. In fact, they cut a fair number of pretty strong tracks, moving without rhyme or reason from straightforward Byrds and Kinks cops to zany orchestrated self-absorbed psychedelic pop to self-conscious exercises in hippy outrageousness (including, of all things, a cover of the Mothers' "Help I'm a Rock"). Though their legacy reeks of determined trendiness, the best of their output holds up reasonably well. —*Richie Unterberger*

● **Transparent Day** / 1986 / Edsel ✦✦✦✦
Well-chosen collection of 16 tracks from their first two albums. "Transparent Day" is a ringing folk-rocker, the throbbing "I Won't Hurt You" a soundtrack to the beginning of an acid trip; "Shifting Sands" and the string-laden "Will You Walk With Me" are tremulous tunes with an odd undercurrent of fear and uncertainty. Other highlights are the early Kinks copy "If You Want This Love" and the P.F. Sloan cover "Here's Where You Belong." —*Richie Unterberger*

Paul Westerberg

Rock & Roll, Alternative Pop/Rock

After disbanding the Replacements in 1991, singer/songwriter Paul Westerberg resurfaced the following year with two songs on the *Singles* soundtrack. A year later, he began his solo career in earnest with *14 Songs*, a loose effort that recalled a cross between the driving pop/rock of *Pleased to Meet Me* and the weary, acoustic ballads of *All Shook Down*. —*Stephen Thomas Erlewine*

● **14 Songs** / Jun. 15, 1993 / Sire ✦✦✦✦
Westerberg's first solo album since the breakup of the Replacements is a strong yet incoherent collection of songs from one of the most influential songwriters of the 1980s. Falling somewhere between the sound of *All Shook Down* and the songwriting of *Tim*, *14 Songs* is a more mature effort from Westerberg, sounding like the optimistic brother of the last Replacements album. It's not as raw as *Let it Be* or *Tim* or as consistent as *Pleased to Meet Me*, but it is a solid collection of expertly crafted rock and pop songs. —*Stephen Thomas Erlewine*

Wham!

Group, Dance-Pop, Pop/Rock

Wham! was a U.K. pop-dance duo formed in 1981 by George Michael (born Yorgos Panayiotou, Jun 26, 1963) and Andrew Ridgeley (b. Jun 25, 1963). Combining light soul music with slow, romantic ballads, they first hit the U.K. charts in the fall of 1982 with "Young Guns (Go for It)." It hit number three, the first of ten U.K. Top Ten hits for the duo. The first Wham! album, *Fantastic,* topped the U.K. charts in 1983. The group broke through in the U.S. the following year with "Wake Me Up Before You Go-Go," the first of three straight number one hits. The second of those chart-toppers was "Careless Whisper," billed as "featuring George Michael," the first sign that Michael, who sang lead and wrote the songs, was emerging as a solo entity. Nevertheless, Wham! continued through 1986, finishing their career at Wembley Stadium in England, after which Michael went on to a successful solo career. —*William Ruhlmann*

Fantastic! / 1983 / Columbia ✦✦
● **Make It Big** / 1984 / Columbia ✦✦✦✦
George Michael demonstrates a thorough knowledge of danceable pop, from the 60s-ish "Wake Me up Before You Go-Go" to the tearjerking ballad "Careless Whisper." Also includes "Everything She Wants" and "Freedom." —*William Ruhlmann*

Music from the Edge of Heaven / 1986 / Columbia ✦✦✦
More of a hodgepodge of tracks than a coherent album, this still includes the Top Ten hits "I'm Your Man," "A Different Corner," and "The Edge of Heaven." —*William Ruhlmann*

Caron Wheeler

Soul, Dance-Pop, Urban

An excellent vocalist in either dance or Urban Contemporary settings, Caron Wheeler first gained fame singing with Soul II Soul. She initially sang in such reggae bands as Brown Sugar and Afrodiziak before doing sessions with Phil Collins, Erasure, and Elvis Costello. Her leads on the songs "Keep on Movin'" and "Back to Life" were featured on Soul II Soul's smash LP, *Keep on Movin',* in 1989. The album sold two million copies and "Back to Life" was a Top Ten pop and R&B hit. Wheeler left in 1990, and her solo debut was *UK Blak* on EMI. Her most recent release was *Beach of the War Goddess* in 1993. —*Ron Wynn*

U.K. Blak / May 1990 / EMI America ✦✦✦
● **Beach of the War Goddess** / 1993 / Capitol ✦✦✦✦
Caron Wheeler's second venture outside the Soul II Soul enterprise proves far more rewarding than her debut. She's gotten better production, material, and arrangements, and also sings with more confidence and assertiveness on both dance tracks and ballads; her voice has more strength and the album is better sequenced and designed. Her cover of "The Wind Cries Mary," which includes Hendrix vocal and guitar samples, works because she doesn't try to overwhelm it but also is not obscured by Hendrix, while the Yoruba chants on the title cut are a nice twist. —*Ron Wynn*

The Whispers

Group, Soul, R&B, Urban

The Whispers are a veteran R&B quintet with an impressive 23-year legacy of R&B hits. Formed in Los Angeles by twins Walter

and Wallace Scott, Nicholas Caldwell, Marcus Hutson, and Gordy Harmon (who left in 1973), the Whispers turned up on the Dore label in 1964 with "I Was Born When You Kissed Me." In 1969, the quintet climbed the soul charts for the first time with "The Time Has Come" on Soul Clock, and they cracked the R&B Top Ten the next year with "Seems Like I Gotta Do Wrong." They've remained hitmakers ever since for the labels Janus, Soul Train, and Solar, with smashes like the solid gold chart-topper "And the Beat Goes On" in 1980 and another number one urban-contemporary hit, "Rock Steady," in 1987.

After being their backbone and selling point since the group's inception, twin lead vocalists Walter and Wallace Scott departed for solo careers in 1993. —*Bill Dahl*

● **The Best of the Whispers** / 1982 / Solar ✦✦✦✦
This isn't a completely accurate title, as the collection doesn't contain their Dore or Janus material. Instead, it focuses on their best-known cuts from the Solar years, when they became an R&B power. The twin leads of Walter and Wallace Scott, plus their polished productions and smoother sound made them quite popular in the 1970s, and such singles as "It's A Love Thing," "Lady," and "Make It with You" were included. —*Ron Wynn*

Just Gets Better with Time / 1987 / Solar ✦✦✦
A reissue of their landmark release. —*Ron Wynn*

○ **More of the Night** / Jul. 23, 1990 / Capitol ✦✦✦✦
A highly representative session. —*Ron Wynn*

● **30th Anniversary** / 1994 / ✦✦✦✦

Ian Whitcomb

British Invasion

An odd footnote of the British Invasion, English singer and pianist Ian Whitcomb formed his R&B group, Bluesville, in Dublin, Ireland, never had a hit in the U.K., and wasn't all that wild about rock & roll in the first place, preferring traditional forms of blues, ragtime, and Tin Pan Alley. But "You Turn Me On"—a tongue-in-cheek three-chord knockoff at the end of a session, with exaggerated falsetto vocals and an unforgettable orgasmic vocal hook—hit number eight in America in 1965, and Whitcomb was briefly a star. The bluesy follow-up, "N-N-Nervous," was a small hit, and that was the end of Whitcomb's hitmaking days. Not much of a rock & roll singer, Whitcomb quickly turned to vaudevillian, British music hall-styled material on his subsequent releases (which continue to this day), with meager commercial (and artistic) results. A dedicated archivist, Whitcomb's book *After the Ball* is a thorough history of pre-rock popular music forms, the most entertaining part being his autobiographical account of his fleeting rock & roll stardom. —*Richie Unterberger*

● **Best of Ian Whitcomb** / 1985 / Rhino ✦✦✦✦
15 songs from 1965-67, including "You Turn Me On," the small hits "This Sporting Life" and "N-N-Nervous," and the protest song "Too Many Cars On The Road." The rockers are okay, but the post-1965 vaudevillian tunes that compose the bulk of this compilation are lame indeed, sounding almost unbearably quaint and stilted nearly 30 years later. Session players supporting Ian on these tracks (most recorded in Hollywood) include James Burton, Delaney Bramlett, Gerry Roslie of the Sonics, and Mitch Mitchell. Includes exhaustive liner notes by Whitcomb himself. —*Richie Unterberger*

White Zombie

Group, Hard Rock, Alternative Pop/Rock, Heavy Metal

All garish colors and trashy noise, White Zombie brought some sleazy fun back to heavy metal, celebrating the sheer schlock of cheap sex and bad horror movies. Although they gathered a cult following with a series of independent albums in the late '80s, it wasn't until their video for "Thunder Kiss '65" was aired on MTV's *Beavis & Butt-head* in 1993 that the band crossed over to a large audience. And they were the rare metal band that could appeal to jaded, post-modern hipsters; with their campy lyrics and theatrics, it was clear that the band didn't take themselves seriously. —*Stephen Thomas Erlewine*

Psycho-head Blowout / 1986 / Silent Explosion ✦✦
○ **Soul Crusher** / 1987 / Caroline ✦✦✦✦
Make Them Die Slowly / 1989 / Caroline ✦✦✦
● **La Sexorcisto: Devil Music, Vol. 1** / 1992 / Geffen ✦✦✦✦
White Zombie carves out a unique identity for itself in the grunge/thrash genre with this one. The prerequisite loud guitars and shouting vocalist are here, but this album shows an obsession with '60s trash culture, particularly fast cars and grade-B horror

movies. The subject matter of Rob Zombie's lyrics, along with frequent movie samples, help this group stand out from their more generic, disaffected brethren. —*Steve Huey*

Astro Creep: 2000 / 1995 / Geffen ✦✦✦
Following the belated surprise success of *La Sexorcisto, Astro-Creep: 2000—Songs of Love, Destruction and Other Synthetic Delusions of the Electric Head* carried the weight of high expectations, something that White Zombie was never familiar with before. Unsurprisingly, White Zombie plays it safe on *Astro-Creep*, never straying from their white-trash-on-acid metal. While it's undeniably campy, the band genuinely loves the trash they sing about, so they fit right into the tradition of tongue-in-cheek heavy metal bands from Alice Cooper to Kiss. Where those bands relied on songcraft beneath their schtick, White Zombie relies on a full-throttle roar. Borrowing such techniques as distorted vocals and drilling riffs from pseudo-industrial metal like Ministry, the band beefs up their basic sound, making it powerful enough to disguise the lack of solid song structures and memorable riffs. Sonically, *Astro Creep* delivers the initial goods, yet it never develops into trash as substantial as "Thunder Kiss '65." —*Stephen Thomas Erlewine*

Barry White

b. Sep. 12, 1944
Soul, Disco, Urban
Barry White has been involved in the popular music industry since age 11, when he played piano on Jesse Belvin's hit single "Goodnight My Love." He recorded with the Upfronts for Lumntone in 1960, then as a lead vocalist for Atlantic in 1964 and for Downey and Veep in 1965 under the name of Barry Lee. He was an A&R man for Mustang/Bronco Records in 1966 and 1967. White formed the female trio Love Unlimited in 1969, and also became leader of the 40-piece Love Unlimited orchestra. His solo career was revitalized in the early '70s as his formidable, deep, captivating bass, coupled with pseudo-sophisticated strings and elaborate productions, helped him rack up five number one hits and seven other Top Ten R&B hits from 1973 until 1978 for 20th Century Records. He also scored five Top Ten pop singles and one number one in that same stretch. "I'm Gonna Love You a Little More Baby" started the string in 1973, and his final Top Ten R&B single was "Your Sweetness Is My Weakness," which peaked at number two in 1978. White continued recording for United Gold, 20th Century again, United Gold, and A&M. He scored a mild comeback by being one of the featured vocalists on Quincy Jones's single "The Garden" in 1989 and continues recording for A&M in the '90s. *The Icon Is Love* (1994) marked White's return as a potent commercial force. —*Ron Wynn*

○ **Greatest Hits, Vol. 1** / 1975 / Casablanca ✦✦✦✦
Before a definitive multi-disc boxed set was issued in the 1990s, there were two single-album volumes of Barry White hits released by Casablanca in the 1970s. The first edition was the best, with sweeping versions of such disco classics as "Can't Get Enough of Your Love, Babe" and "You're the First, The Last, My Everything." White's productions and arrangements were never as intricate as they seemed, but his booming baritone and romantic dialogue sounded convincing when underscored by the lush backgrounds. If you only want a little Barry White, this is the album to grab. —*Ron Wynn*

○ **Greatest Hits, Vol. 2** / 1981 / Casablanca ✦✦✦✦
This second set of Barry White hits isn't quite as impressive or essential as its predecessor. White's arrangements and compositions grew stale as the 1970s wore on, and he recycled the romantic dialogue and exploited the robust baritone until he became a caricature of himself. Put this one in the "for fans only" category. —*Ron Wynn*

○ **Just for You** / 1992 / Casablanca ✦✦✦✦
A three-disc box set containing more music than anyone but the most devoted fan could want. —*Stephen Thomas Erlewine*

○ **The Icon Is Love** / 1994 / A&M/Perspective ✦✦✦✦
Barry White scored his biggest hit since the 1970s with *The Icon Is Love*, and it's easy to see why. Not only has his voice not lost an ounce of its seductive power with age, but his music is frequently better-written and produced than most contemporary R&B. As a result, *The Icon Is Love* is not only a remarkable comeback, it's one of the best albums of his career. —*Stephen Thomas Erlewine*

★ **All Time Greatest Hits** / 1995 / Mercury ✦✦✦✦✦
Condensing the best moments from the two *Greatest Hits* collections onto one disc, *All Time Greatest Hits* is the deep-voiced disco crooner's one essential album. —*Stephen Thomas Erlewine*

Whitesnake

Group, Hard Rock, Heavy Metal
After recording two solo albums, former Deep Purple vocalist David Coverdale formed Whitesnake around 1977. In the glut of hard rock and heavy metal bands of the late '70s, their first albums got somewhat lost in the shuffle, although they were fairly popular in Europe in Japan. During 1982, Coverdale took some time off, so he could take care of his sick daughter. When he re-emerged with a new version of Whitesnake in 1984, the band sounded revitalized and energetic. *Slide It In* may have relied on Led Zeppelin and Deep Purple's old tricks, but the band had a knack for writing hooks; the record became their first platinum album. Three years later, Whitesnake released an eponymous album which was even better. Portions of the album were blatantly derivative—"Still of the Night" was a dead ringer for early Zeppelin—but the group could write powerful, heavy rockers like "Here I Go Again" that were driven as much by melody as riffs, as well as hit power ballads like "Is This Love." *Whitesnake* was an enormous international success, selling over six million copies in the U.S. alone.

Before they recorded their follow-up, 1989's *Slip of the Tongue*, Coverdale again assembled a completely new version of the band, featuring guitar virtuoso Steve Vai. Although the record went platinum, it was a considerable disappointment after the across-the-boards success of *Whitesnake*. Coverdale put Whitesnake on hiatus after that album. In 1993, he released a collaboration with former Led Zeppelin guitarist Jimmy Page that was surprisingly lackluster. The following year, Whitesnake released a greatest hits album and it seemed likely that Coverdale was going to form a new version of the band. —*Stephen Thomas Erlewine*

Snakebite / Jan. 1978 / David Geffen Co. ✦✦
Trouble / Feb. 1978 / David Geffen Co. ✦✦
Love Hunter / 1979 / David Geffen Co. ✦✦✦
○ **Ready & Willing** / 1980 / United Artists ✦✦✦✦
Live in the Heart of the City / 1980 / David Geffen Co. ✦✦✦
Come An' Get It / 1981 / David Geffen Co. ✦✦✦
Saints & Sinners / 1982 / David Geffen Co. ✦✦
○ **Slide It In** / 1984 / David Geffen Co. ✦✦✦✦
With its combination of stadium-sized hard-rock riffing and solid commercial melodies, *Slide It In* laid the groundwork for the blockbuster follow-up *Whitesnake*. Nevertheless, the album is rawer and cruder than their subsequent pop hit and is more representative of the band's metal roots. —*Stephen Thomas Erlewine*

○ **Whitesnake** / 1987 / David Geffen Co. ✦✦✦✦
After slugging it out in the British hard rock market for almost ten years, Whitesnake achieved platinum success with this highly crafted mainstream AOR. It includes the #1 "Here I Go Again," "Is This Love?" (#2), and the Led Zeppelin rip "Still of the Night." —*AMG*

Slip of the Tongue / Feb. 1989 / David Geffen Co. ✦✦✦
A replica of the mega-hit *Whitesnake, Slip of the Tongue* wasn't as successful because the band's songs weren't as catchy and the riffs weren't as powerful. Not even the presence of guitar superhero Steve Vai could add excitement to the band's bland, futile attempt at keeping its pop audience. —*Stephen Thomas Erlewine*

● **Whitesnake's Greatest Hits** / 1994 / Geffen ✦✦✦✦
All of the best moments from Whitesnake's late-'80s glory days collected on one disc. —*Stephen Thomas Erlewine*

Chris Whitley

Blues Rock, Singer-Songwriter
Chris Whitley writes and sings provocatively dark folky blues-pop. His debut featured an appropriately haunting production job by Daniel Lanois (U2, Bob Dylan). —*Rick Clark*

● **Living with the Law** / Dec. 5, 1991 / Columbia ✦✦✦✦
A stirring and classy debut of well-crafted blues, which was released to a flurry of critical praise. Whitley combines dreamy storytelling with commanding electric guitar work—all with the touch of a journeyman's blues. —*Donna DiChario*

Din of Ecstasy / 1995 / Work ✦✦
On his second album, Whitley abandons the atmospheric acoustic blues-rock of his debut for a hard-hitting, grungy guitar attack. Appropriately, the songs are all about losers and hard times—it's a dark, bleak album, twisting through its songs with a grim determination. The problem is, it doesn't always work. Whitley's lyrics are

still rooted in the folk-blues storytelling tradition, while his music follows the rules of contemporary hard rock, complete with start-stop dynamics and thick layers of distortion. However, he can't write riffs that equal the best of Nirvana, Pearl Jam, and Soundgarden, nor does he have melodies to rival theirs. His music works best a lyrical level and the musical approach on *Din of Ecstasy* obscures his lyrics, making the record a muddled affair. —*Stephen Thomas Erlewine*

The Who

Group, British Invasion, Hard Rock

Founded in the early '60s by Pete Townshend, John Entwistle, and Roger Daltrey (with Keith Moon coming along slightly later), the Who were originally a fairly conventional R&B-based outfit, with Townshend and Daltrey sharing guitar chores, Entwistle on bass, and Doug Sanden (later replaced by Keith Moon) on drums. Early on, however, they fell under the influence of Johnny Kidd & the Pirates, a British band that pioneered a lean, muscular sound built around a single guitar and a rhythm section of bass and drums (most British bands of the period also featured a rhythm guitar very prominently) behind a lone singer. Kidd had hit originally with "Shakin' All Over," a number that the Who would adopt into their repertoire. Daltrey gave up the guitar to concentrate on singing, Townshend turned his rhythm guitar into a lead instrument, and the band emerged with a powerful, sweaty brand of R&B, all very Memphis-influenced ("Green Onions" was long part of their stage act) and louder than anything that London audiences were used to. They quickly became favorites of the R&B-loving mods, and by 1964 were ready to cut their first single, a quickie rewrite of "Got Love If You Want It" entitled "I'm the Face" ("face" being a key part of mod slang) under the temporary name the High Numbers.

It was around this time that Pete Townshend discovered two key talents. As a songwriter, Townshend showed a remarkable capacity for writing anthem-like songs, which, if not exactly Top 40 material, were certainly memorable to their core audience and just different enough to get airplay. "My Generation" was the first and most important of these, and while his songwriting would broaden in coming years to embrace longer thematic canvases (including the so-called rock opera), it was songs like "My Generation," "The Magic Bus," and the epic-length "Won't Get Fooled Again" that would make the most lasting impact on rock & roll. Townsend's other major talent was in the area of destruction—by accident one night, he shattered the neck of his guitar during a performance, and the crowd seemed to appreciate it. Gradually guitar smashing became a trademark of the band's sets, an effective but extremely expensive publicity vehicle.

Meanwhile, Roger Daltrey emerged as one of the most powerful singers of his generation, a soul-shouter whose voice could be heard even above Townshend's ringing power-chords and Keith Moon's flamboyant drumming. They built their reputations gradually in the U.S. during the mid '60s, emerging as one of the better acts at the Monterey Pop Festival (alongside Jimi Hendrix), but it was their rock opera, *Tommy*, that finally transformed the group into a major international rock act.

Tommy's pretensions aside, the passions and seemingly allegorical search for truth behind the story of the deaf, dumb, and blind boy seemed to strike a chord with an entire generation of teenagers and college students who were searching for something different and more genuine in their own lives—the opera's clear rejection of drugs (which echoed Townshend's own philosophy) was conveniently ignored, and the sky seemed to be the limit for the band for the ten years after *Tommy*'s release.

A live album followed, reminding audiences of the group's R&B roots, and after a false start on a film project, in 1971 the Who released *Who's Next*, which was probably their strongest individual album. Very little that they did afterward was quite as successful artistically as this brilliant compendium of religious musings, idealism at high volume, and revolutionary anthems, but it didn't matter. *Quadrophenia* was too vague a subject for Americans who were unfamiliar with its mod-culture roots, *Who by Numbers* seemed slight after the records that had preceded it; and *Who Are You* showed a certain softening of the edges, but the audiences kept buying albums and, even more important, kept going to concerts. Then in 1978, shortly after the release of *Who Are You*, Keith Moon died, and that was pretty much it for the Who. Their work became softer and less urgent (a process that might have been hastened also by Pete Townshend's progressive hearing loss), and

while the audiences still bought tickets, their music no longer seemed very important. What little musical capital the group still possessed in the late '80s was squandered on one-too-many farewell tours. —*Bruce Eder*

○ **The Sings My Generation** / 1966 / MCA ✦✦✦✦
The group's debut album is more R&B-oriented than their subsequent records, but it's honest and direct. Includes covers of James Brown material amid the Beatlesque originals such as "The Kids Are Alright." —*Bruce Eder*

○ **A Quick One (Happy Jack)** / 1966 / MCA ✦✦✦✦
The group's second album is a transitional work, containing a rudimentary rock opera ("A Quick One") and a bizarre collection of originals by Roger Daltrey and Keith Moon as well as the expected Pete Townshend and John Entwistle. The flashes of brilliance make up for the defects in the writing, and Entwistle's "Boris the Spider" and "Whiskey Man" are among the best songs he has ever written. The 1995 CD reissue adds ten bonus tracks: some 1966-67 B-sides, their U.K.-only 1966 *Ready Steady Who!* EP, an acoustic version of "Happy Jack," and a previously unreleased cover of the Everly Brothers' "Man with the Money." —*Bruce Eder*

☆ **The Who Sell Out** / 1967 / MCA ✦✦✦✦✦
Arguably rock's first important concept album and infinitely more effective and humorous than *Tommy* or *Quadrophenia*, this is a full-length tribute to Britain's pirate radio stations, complete with commercials by the band. "I Can See for Miles" was the hit off of the record, but the material ranges from the ethereal "Sunrise" to the proto-*Tommy* mini-opera "Rael." Funny as well as scintillating. The 1995 CD reissue has over half a dozen interesting outtakes from the time of the sessions, as well as unused commercials, the B-side "Someone's Coming," and an alternate version of "Mary Anne with the Shaky Hand." —*Bruce Eder*

Magic Bus / 1968 / MCA ✦✦✦
A second-rate collection of leftover tracks surrounding the Bo Diddley-based title song, *Magic Bus* is better than much of what else was coming out of England at the time but difficult to accept in this presentation. —*Bruce Eder*

○ **Tommy** / 1969 / MCA ✦✦✦✦
The original rock opera. The material hasn't worn well as a conceptual creation, but the individual songs still have an energy that is refreshing. Keith Moon's nasty sense of humor stands out. —*Bruce Eder*

☆ **Live at Leeds** / 1970 / MCA ✦✦✦✦✦
A loud, raunchy concert showcase for the group, with surprisingly little material from *Tommy*. The group's R&B roots are showcased here far better than on their post-*My Generation* studio albums, and the only problem for some listeners is the lack of the sophisticated studio sound they'd developed on previous releases. The 1995 CD reissue doubles the length of the original LP, with plenty of additional material from the same performance, including versions of some more of their early singles and unexpected items like "Tattoo" and the R&B standard "Fortune Teller." —*Bruce Eder*

★ **Meaty, Beaty, Big & Bouncy** / 1971 / MCA ✦✦✦✦✦
The first halfway-decent retrospective on the group, covering their American singles as of 1972, including "I Can See for Miles," "My Generation," "The Magic Bus," "The Seeker," and a lot of other material that subsequently became staples of FM radio. —*Bruce Eder*

★ **Who's Next** / 1971 / MCA ✦✦✦✦✦
The group's magnum opus, a rich, expressive, loud piece of hard rock that summed up the first six years of the band's history. "Won't Get Fooled Again" became a major radio anthem and "Behind Blue Eyes" unexpectedly became a favorite Pete Townshend number as well. Roger Daltrey never sang better, and John Entwistle's bass achieved new heights of prominence, while Keith Moon turned in an explosive performance on drums. —*Bruce Eder*

○ **Quadrophenia** / 1973 / MCA ✦✦✦✦
The group's second rock opera wasn't nearly the success that *Tommy* had been, but it proved more fertile in other media—"Love Reign o'er Me" was a moderate success as a single but precious little else seemed to register with the public. Ironically, this is a finely produced album, with a sound that is both hard and lush, and Roger Daltrey seemed to achieve a larger-than-life performance as the embattled mod Jimmy. (Mobile Fidelity's gold-disc reissue includes a beautiful, lavishly produced booklet reproducing the photos and liners from the original LP release in addition to improved sonics.) —*Bruce Eder*

Odds & Sods / 1974 / MCA ✦✦✦

Odds is right—a collection of outtakes and mistakes from the first eight years of the group's history, all of it listenable and half of it indispensable. "Long Live Rock" (which later turned up on the *Quadrophenia* soundtrack album) was the best song, but most of the rest is worth a listen. —*Bruce Eder*

The Who By Numbers / 1975 / MCA ✦✦✦

The Who By Numbers functions as Pete Townshend's confessional singer/songwriter album, as he chronicles his problems with alcohol ("However Much I Booze"), women ("Dreaming from the Waist" and "They Are All in Love"), and life in general. However, his introspective musings are rendered ineffective by Roger Daltrey's bluster and the cloying, lightweight filler of "Squeeze Box." In addition, Townshend's songs tend to be under-developed, relying on verbosity instead of melodicism, with only the simple power of "Slip Kid," the grace of "Blue Red and Gray," and John Entwistle's heavy rocker "Success Story" making much of an impact. —*Stephen Thomas Erlewine*

Who Are You / 1978 / MCA ✦✦✦

The final worthwhile album by the band, a somewhat arch collection of pretentious rock anthems and failed concepts surrounding a powerful title track whose video clip marked Keith Moon's final public appearance with the band. —*Bruce Eder*

○ **The Kids Are Alright** / 1979 / MCA ✦✦✦✦

Soundtrack to a dazzling video portrait of the band, better in many ways than any of the hits collections out of the group for the surprises and odd takes that it contains. —*Bruce Eder*

Quadrophenia [O.S.T.] / 1979 / MCA ✦✦✦

Face Dances / 1981 / MCA ✦✦✦

Without Keith Moon, the Who may have lacked the restless firepower that distinguished their earlier albums, but *Face Dances* had some of Pete Townshend's best, most incisive compositions since *Quadrophenia*. "Don't Let Go the Coat" was one of his better odes to the Meher Baba, "You Better You Bet" was a driving rocker, as was the rueful "Cache Cache," while "How Can You Do It Alone" was a solid ballad. While Townshend's songs were graceful and introspective, Roger Daltrey delivered them without any subtlety, rendering their power impotent. —*Stephen Thomas Erlewine*

Hooligans / 1982 / MCA ✦✦✦

Surprisingly unimpressive collection of hits and major songs, because of its redundancy—there were too many hits collections out previously, and the sound is amazingly flat. —*Bruce Eder*

It's Hard / 1982 / MCA ✦✦

Driven by Pete Townshend's arching musical ambitions, *It's Hard* was an undistinguished final effort from the Who. Featuring layers of synthesizers and long-winded, twisting song structures, the album featured few memorable melodies and little energy, with only the anthemic "Athena" and the terse "Eminence Front" making a lasting impression. —*Stephen Thomas Erlewine*

Greatest Hits / 1983 / MCA ✦✦✦

One of too many similar packages. Okay, but nothing more. —*Bruce Eder*

Who's Last / 1984 / MCA ✦✦

A double-disc document of the Who's 1982 farewell tour, *Who's Last* is a tepid and utterly forgettable album. —*Stephen Thomas Erlewine*

Who's Missing / 1985 / MCA ✦✦✦

A collection of loose ends from the group's early years, mostly B-sides and some R&B covers. —*Bruce Eder*

Two's Missing / 1987 / MCA ✦✦✦

A follow-up to *Who's Missing*, with more obscure B-sides, little-known R&B covers, and other relics of the band's early history, of which the best part is their soulful rendition of "Anytime You Want Me." —*Bruce Eder*

● **Who's Better Who's Best** / Nov. 14, 1988 / MCA ✦✦✦✦

This unexpectedly entertaining video anthology covers their whole history. It's superior to the accompanying album. —*Bruce Eder*

Join Together / 1990 / MCA ✦✦

Join Together is a double-disc document of the Who's 1989 reunion tour. One disc is an entire performance of *Tommy*, the other a selection of their greatest hits. Both are professionally performed crowd-pleasers and neither disc provides any compelling listening. —*Stephen Thomas Erlewine*

Thirty Years of Maximum R&B / 1994 / MCA ✦✦✦

One of the more overblown recent box sets, this four-CD collection does include all of their big hits and the lion's share of their key album tracks. Previously unreleased rarities include some interesting selections (the '60s outtakes "Early Morning Cold Taxi" and "Melancholia"), but these bits and pieces, which include some live versions, commercials, Keith Moon sketches, and the like, are mostly inessential. The post-Keith Moon cuts that bring us up to the present are out of the league of the body of the Who's work. As most of the Who's '60s and '70s albums are very strong, cohesive works in and of themselves, this can't be recommended as either a starting point or a necessary addition. —*Richie Unterberger*

Maximum BBC / Bootleg ✦✦✦

A most worthwhile find for the serious Who fan, comprising 27 tracks that the group recorded for the BBC between 1965 and 1970, the accent falling heavily on the 1965-67 period. Decent though not pristine sound and good performances, which usually don't deviate a great deal from the record, but are occasionally substantially different: Entwistle's bass, in particular, comes through much more strongly on some of the 1966-67 material. It also includes some unusual covers that never made their way onto official releases: "Just You And Me" (James Brown), "Man With Money" (the Everly Brothers), and "Dancing In The Streets." The 1970 version of "Shakin' All Over" may be the best take of this concert staple ever taped by the band. —*Richie Unterberger*

Live at the Fillmore East, 4/5/68 / Bootleg ✦✦✦

Recorded during their early 1968 American tour, this was considered as an official release, but rejected by the group. The only really satisfactory quality live Who tape from the '60s that has surfaced, it has good performances and an interesting song selection, including quite a few numbers that weren't included on Who releases of the time: "Little Billy," "Fortune Teller," and Eddie Cochran's "My Way" (here credited as "Easy Goin' Guy"). There's also a much heavier and elongated version of "Relax" (which unfortunately cuts off in the instrumental break), as well as standbys like "Can't Explain," "Happy Jack," and "Shakin' All Over." It's recommended for those who want the firepower of *Live at Leeds* without as much of the heavy guitar bombast. —*Richie Unterberger*

Tommy Demos / Bootleg ✦✦✦

Superb quality demos for the famous rock opera, including working versions of almost all of the songs that ended up on the album. Townshend takes lead vocals on a lot of these, which are, more often than not, extremely similar in arrangement and delivery to the versions that ended up on the finished product; one assumes that most of these may be Pete's own recordings, on which he played most or all of the instruments. It's low on extraordinary revelations, but it's an interesting document of the creative process for this hugely influential album. —*Richie Unterberger*

BOOK

✦✦✦✦ **Before I Get Old**, by Dave Marsh (St. Martin's, 1983). By far the most exhaustive biography of the Who—indeed, at 500+ pages, one of the most exhaustive biographies of any rock group. Voluminously researched, with first-hand interviews with band members and many of their associates, this is exhaustively detailed, passionately critical, and essential reading for fans of the band. The only mild criticisms to offer are Marsh's occasional propensity for long-winded editorializing, and (not the author's fault) the inevitable decline of interest in the subject matter after the death of Keith Moon. —*Richie Unterberger*

Whodini

Group, Rap, Funk

The influential Brooklyn, NY, rap group Whodini was one of the better groups to merge straight R&B with pop-fueled hip-hop. Whodini started recording in 1983 and broke up in 1988, scoring hits with "Magic's Wand" and "Freaks Come out at Night." —*John Floyd*

Whodini / 1983 / Jive ✦✦✦

More singers than straight rappers, Jali Hutchins and Ecstasty made a successful conversion to hip-hop, scoring two hits on their debut with "Rap Attack" and "The Haunted House of Funk," a reworking of "The Monster Mash." —*Ron Wynn*

○ **Escape** / 1984 / Jive ✦✦✦✦

Their best release, containing "Friends," "Freaks Come out at Night," and "Big Mouth." Memorable tunes and state-of-the-art (for that time) production. —*Ron Wynn*

Back in Black / 1986 / Jive ✦✦✦
Signs of stagnation and decay are evident, though the cut "Funky Beat" forestalled the decline for a short while. —*Ron Wynn*

Open Sesame / 1987 / Jive ✦✦
Mille Jackson made a wonderful guest appearance on "Be Yourself," but not only was the handwriting on the wall, it was soon readable by everyone. —*Ron Wynn*

★ **Greatest Hits** / 1990 / Jive ✦✦✦✦✦
A worthwhile compilation that shows what all the fuss was about regarding this unit in the early '80s. —*Ron Wynn*

Bag-A-Trix / 1991 / MCA ✦✦

Widespread Panic

Group, Rock & Roll
Since their formation in 1986, Athens, GA's Widespread Panic has become a extremely popular touring unit, primarily due to their style of extended Allmans-meets-Grateful Dead jam-oriented material. —*Rick Clark*

● **Space Wrangler** / Feb. 4, 1988 / Capricorn ✦✦✦✦
Widespread's debut album, *Space Wrangler,* is regarded by many of their fans as their finest work. It's understandable, thanks to strong material like "Travelin' Light," "Coconut," "Driving Song," "Chilly Water" and the title cut—the album's musical centerpiece. —*Rick Clark*

○ **Widespread Panic** / Mar. 1991 / Capricorn ✦✦✦✦
The band's Capricorn debut is another strong collection of songs and extended instrumental work-outs. Includes "Walkin' (For Your Love)," "Mercy," "Send Your Mind," "Makes Sense to Me," and "Barstools and Dreamers." —*Rick Clark*

Everyday / 1993 / Capricorn ✦✦✦
Not as strong or fresh sounding as the previous two albums, there are, however, enough good tunes here to hold the interest of anyone checking out this band. —*Rick Clark*

Ain't Life Grand / 1994 / Capricorn ✦✦✦

Wigwam

Group, Art-Rock/Progressive-Rock
During their initial period, Wigwam was perhaps the world's most intellectual "pop" band. The dual keyboards, Jukka Gustavson's organ and Jim Pembroke's piano, coupled with satiric and sharply conceptual lyrics, gave the music both heart and soul. —*Archie Patterson*

● **Being** / 1974 / Love ✦✦✦✦
Being was their masterpiece, a rock opera of progressive ideology and pop music. Imagine John Lennon, collaborating with Stevie Wonder, circa *Songs in the Key of Life*-era. —*Archie Patterson*

Wilco

Group, Country-Rock, Alternative Pop/Rock
After the acclaimed country-rock outfit Uncle Tupelo broke up in 1994, guitarist Jeff Tweedy and drummer formed Wilco. Adding several additional sidemen, the duo expanded their Gram Parsons and Neil Young influenced rock. The band released their debut album, *A.M.,* in the spring of 1995. —*Stephen Thomas Erlewine*

● **A.M.** / 1995 / Sire/Reprise ✦✦✦✦
Not surprisingly, Wilco's debut album, *A.M.,* isn't a great departure from Uncle Tupelo. Wilco's music rocks in a more conventional way than Uncle Tupelo, rolling along with a loping beat that swings more than it rocks. "Casino Queen" is a shambling, bluesy honky-tonk number that's boozier than anything Tupelo recorded, which is indicative of the major difference between the bands. Wilco wears its heart on its sleeve, writing songs that fit into the conventions of country-rock, not ones that rework the rules. "Box Full of Letters" doesn't deviate from the standard mid-tempo country-rock number, yet it's done so well, it doesn't matter. Still, the opener, "I Must Be High"—a clever love song that subtly tweaks both lyrical and musical cliches, as well as featuring a killer melody—casts a shadow over *A.M.,* offering the knowledge that Wilco can subvert the genre without losing its accessibility. In its light, all the very good songs that follow seem somewhat disappointing. —*Stephen Thomas Erlewine*

Wilde Flowers

Group, British Invasion, Psychedelic
The Wilde Flowers never released a record during their existence, but their influence exceeds that of many groups with lengthy discographies. The band served as the wellspring of the so-called "Canterbury sound": future Soft Machine members Robert Wyatt, Kevin Ayers, and Hugh Hopper all played with the Wilde Flowers before the Softs were founded, and Pye Hastings, David Sinclair, Richard Sinclair, and Richard Coughlan played in the group at various points before forming Caravan. The musicians who wandered through the Wilde Flowers (which went through several lineups between 1963 and 1969) came from a far more intellectual, jazz-oriented, and artistic background than was the norm for pop musicians in the mid-'60s. Thus, although the group played "beat" fare much like thousands of other British combos in their formative days, when they began to write their own material, it betrayed the bemused whimsy—replete with odd jazzy flourishes, droll obtuse lyrics, and adventurous chord changes—that would come to characterize the Canterbury bands, and prove influential on the development of psychedelia and progressive rock. At long last, a wealth of Wilde Flowers demos and unreleased recordings was released in 1994. —*Richie Unterberger*

● **Tales of Canterbury: The Wilde Flowers Story** / 1994 / Voiceprint ✦✦✦✦
Twenty-two tracks, recorded between 1965 and 1969 by various aggregations of the band. Some of the fidelity is primitive, and the performances are much more tentative and less virtuosic than what the musicians would tender on their Soft Machine and Caravan records. But the songs are playful and melodic, pushing the boundaries of the British Invasion pop they began with towards something more idiosyncratic and adventurous. Several of the songs, like "Memories" (three versions, considerably different from each other, are included here), ended up in the Soft Machine's early repertoire. Indeed, it's a shame that the Softs didn't record more of them; the chief flaw of these tracks is that the arrangements and instrumental proficiency are underdeveloped, and the Soft Machine could have transformed them into prime stuff. A few of the cuts were recorded in late 1969, and could have easily slotted in on the Wyatt-era Soft Machine albums. Wyatt and Hugh Hopper appear on most of the 22 tracks; to a lesser extent, Kevin Ayers, Pye Hastings, and even Mike Ratledge also pop up. Comes with an excellent booklet of photos and an extensive history by Wilde Flowers guitarist Brian Hopper, brother of Hugh. —*Richie Unterberger*

Kim Wilde

New Wave
The daughter of '50s British pop singer Marty Wilde, Kim Wilde had several pop hits during the '80s. Initially, her synth-driven pop fit in with the new wave movement, but as the decade progressed, it became clear that her strength was mainstream pop.

In 1980, Kim Wilde signed with producer Mickie Most's Rak Records, releasing her first single, "Kids in America" early in 1981. "Kids in America" climbed to number two on the British charts that spring, while her second single, "Chequered Love" made it into the Top Ten; her self-titled debut album performed as well as her singles. The following year, "Kids in America" became a Top 40 hit in America, while *Select* kept her in the British charts. However, Wilde wasn't able to keep her momentum going and it wasn't until late 1986 that she had another hit with a dance cover of the Supremes' "You Keep Me Hangin' On," which charted in the Top Ten on both sides of the Atlantic. Wilde never had another hit in America, yet she was back in the charts in the summer of 1987 with "Another Step (Closer to You)," a duet with Junior Giscombe. After the single's success, she began changing her image, becoming sexier. The approach didn't entirely pay off, though she had a handful of hit singles from her 1988 album, *Close,* including "You Came," "Never Trust a Stranger" and "Four Letter Word." Wilde has continued to record in the '90s, scoring the occasional hit, either in the dance or adult contemporary field. —*Stephen Thomas Erlewine*

● **The Singles Collection 1981-1993** / 1993 / MCA ✦✦✦✦
A 16-track collection featuring all of her greatest hits, *The Singles Collection 1981-1993* is not only an effective introduction to Kim Wilde's music, it's the finest moment of her career. —*Stephen Thomas Erlewine*

Webb Wilder

Group, Roots-Rock
The Webb Wilder character was created for a short film about a backwoods private detective who fell out of the '50s and happened to also be a musician. As a group, Webb Wilder combined the surf guitar of the Ventures with the rock roots of Duane Eddy, drawing

on the feel of both country music and film noir. Though sometimes bordering on the gimmicky, they are quite humorous and play serious music. *It Came from Nashville* featured a cover of Steve Earle's "Devil's Right Hand," appropriate because, like Earle, Wilder rocked too hard to be country but kept a twang that might put off mainstream rock fans. Their next two albums didn't necessarily forge new ground but refined their sound somewhat, making their R&B influence more apparent. In concert, Wilder often gives stream-of-consciousness recitations that touch on motor homes, voodoo, television, and other somewhat kitschy subjects; usually they're funny enough to work. But if Webb Wilder intends to expand his audience, he will have to grow musically and steer away from too much camp. He has made another, longer film, indicating a potential career in that medium. —*Robert Gordon*

Hybrid Vigor / 1989 / Island ✦✦✦

○ **Doo Dad** / 1991 / Zoo ✦✦✦✦

Living in a swamp would be a much more attractive proposition if Webb Wilder was your next door neighbor. Rather than an icky bog, Wilder's musical bayou is populated by hoodoo witches, crazed landlords, Russian satellites, strange dreams and self-effacing humor. The Mississippi-raised Wilder and band start from a basic blues style fused to rootsy rock, then shish-kebab the result with a skewered view of mundane existence. Echoes of '50s instrumental rock, British Invasion, garage grunge and psychedelia all surface throughout the album. *Doo Dad* doesn't quite hit the emotional depth of the group's previous *Hybrid Vigor* release, but Wilder sure knows how to ladle out the Southern hospitality. —*Roch Parisien*

● **It Came from Nashville** / 1993 / Landslide ✦✦✦✦

Rock & roll at its heart, with gimmicks on its shoulder. Lots of fun. —*Robert Gordon*

Town & Country / 1995 / Watermelon ✦✦

Andre Williams

b. 1936
R&B

Singer, songwriter, arranger, producer and one of the mightiest talents to emerge from Detroit's pre-Motown era, Andre Williams started recording in 1957 for the tiny Fortune label, with his group, the Five Dollars (aka the Don Juans), and as a solo artist. Employing his stop-time "wavy gravy" beat and hitting the charts with oddball spoken-word numbers like "Bacon Fat," "The Greasy Chicken," and "Jail Bait," Williams was the original rapper before there was ever a name for it. Moving to Chicago in the early '60s, he wrote "Shake a Tail Feather" for the 5 Du-Tones and "Twine Time" for Alvin Cash, produced albums for Bobby Blue Bland, and scored national hits of his own for Chess with "Cadillac Jack," "Girdle Up," and "Humpin', Bumpin' & Thumpin'." He continues to record and produce other artists sporadically, still keeping abreast of the times, still "Mr. Rhythm," the original rappin' man. —*Cub Koda*

Directly from the Streets / SDE ✦✦✦

● **Jail Bait** / Fortune ✦✦✦✦

Deniece Williams

b. Jun. 3, 1950, Gary, IN
Soul, Gospel, Pop

As a child, Deniece Williams sang in a gospel choir, making her first records when she was a teenager in the late '60s. Williams decided to become a nurse, yet she was drawn away from the profession when she got an offer to become a member of Stevie Wonder's backing vocal group, Wonderlove. After recording four albums with Wonder, she left to begin a solo career. Released in 1976, her debut record *This Is Niecy* featured the U.K. number one hit "Free." While the song hit number 25 in the U.S., it wasn't until 1978 that she had a number one hit in America—"Too Much Too Little Too Late," taken from her duet album with Johnny Mathis, *That's What Friends Are For*. Even though the record was a success, Williams was unable to provide a follow-up that matched its popularity until 1982's Thom Bell-produced "It's Gonna Take a Miracle." Two years later, Williams experienced her greatest success with the number one hit, "Let's Hear It for the Boy," taken from the *Footloose* soundtrack. Again, she was unable to record a single that matched the popularity of her previous record and in 1988 she returned to gospel music with the *So Glad I Know* album. Since then, she has recorded both sacred and secular albums. —*Stephen Thomas Erlewine*

● **This Is Niecy** / 1976 / Columbia ✦✦✦✦

After singing in Stevie Wonder's backup band Wonderlove from 1972 to 1975, Deniece Williams made her solo debut and enjoyed an immediate impact. Her lilting, rising voice and upper-register range, which she nicely exploited on "Free," sounded daring and refreshing in 1976. Williams also had several other solid secondary tunes, like "Because You Love Me Baby" and "If You Don't Believe." She smartly blended inspirational fervor and quasi-sophistication, including a couple of pop gospel tunes. This record holds up much better than most of her other albums. —*Ron Wynn*

Song Bird / 1977 / Columbia ✦✦✦

That's What Friends Are for / 1978 / Columbia ✦✦✦

Johnny Mathis and Deniece Williams made a fine team on this collection of sentimental love songs and light pop ballads. They had had previous success on the title track, which had been included on her first release, so they opted for a full session. They had a moderate hit with a cover of "You're All I Need To Get By," and they also reworked Stevie Wonder's "Until You Come Back To Me (That's What I'm Going To Do)." It peaked at number 19 on the pop chart and actually proved Williams's most consistent album from a sales standpoint. —*Ron Wynn*

When Love Comes Calling / 1979 / Columbia ✦✦✦

○ **My Melody** / 1981 / Columbia ✦✦✦✦

○ **Niecy** / 1982 / Columbia ✦✦✦✦

I'm So Proud / 1983 / Columbia ✦✦✦

○ **Let's Hear It for the Boy** / 1984 / Columbia ✦✦✦✦

Williams's pop breakthrough features the title song and several other good pop/rockers. —*All-Music-Guide*

So Glad I Know / 1988 / Sparrow ✦✦

Deniece Williams raised some eyebrows when she decided to begin splitting her focus between urban contemporary and contemporary gospel. The results have thus been quite mixed, and this first gospel venture not only wasn't a major success, but didn't even get widespread exposure in the gospel ranks. It was likewise ignored by pop and R&B audiences. The vocals were competent, the production dull and the material surprisingly timid. —*Ron Wynn*

As Good As It Gets / 1988 / Columbia ✦✦

Special Love / 1989 / MCA ✦✦

Larry Williams

b. May 10, 1935, New Orleans, LA, **d.** Jan. 7, 1980
R&B, Rock & Roll

Specialty groomed Williams to reinforce their rock & roll credentials after they lost Little Richard to religion in the late '50s. Williams recorded a few standards ("Bad Boy," "Dizzy, Miss Lizzy," "She Said Yeah"), which were covered by the Beatles and the Rolling Stones during their formative years. —*John Floyd*

○ **Here's Larry Williams** / 1959 / Specialty ✦✦✦✦

Hocus Pocus / 1986 / Specialty ✦✦✦

Unreleased Larry Williams / 1986 / Specialty ✦✦✦

This deeper look into the obscure and alternate takes of Williams's work is mostly for collectors. —*Hank Davis*

★ **Bad Boy** / 1989 / Specialty ✦✦✦✦✦

Vintage (1957-1958) rock from this Little Richard soundalike, it features backing from hot New Orleans and Los Angeles sidemen. This is an excellent 23-track collection with informative notes. —*Hank Davis*

Lucinda Williams

b. Louisiana
Folk, Singer-Songwriter, Folk-Rock

Born in Louisiana, Lucinda Williams recorded two albums for Folkways at the turn of the '80s, then spent a long time in the wilderness before cutting *Lucinda Williams* for Rough Trade in 1988, an album that was widely hailed for its passionate singing and eclectic music but not widely heard due to the limited resources of the record company (which has since gone bankrupt). Look for her new work on American. —*William Ruhlmann*

Ramblin' / Mar. 1978 / Smithsonian/Folkways ✦✦

Happy Woman Blues / 1980 / Smithsonian/Folkways ✦✦✦

○ **Lucinda Williams** / 1988 / Rough Trade ✦✦✦✦

One of the most exciting recording artists to emerge in the second half of the 80s, Williams combined a recklessly passionate lyrical style with an exuberant, energetic performing approach to achieve this stunning result—an infectious album full of compelling songs like "Passionate Kisses" and "I Just Wanted to See You So Bad." Watch for her in the near future; meanwhile, try to find this album. —*William Ruhlmann*

Passionate Kisses / 1989 / Chameleon ✦✦✦

● **Sweet Old World** / 1992 / Chameleon ✦✦✦✦

Is it country, folk, pop, or blues? Take your pick on Lucinda Williams' *Sweet Old World.* Her literate songs—stemming from a country story-telling tradition—deal with the ravages of abuse on "He Never Got Enough Love," coming to grips with a loved one's suicide on the title track, and finding salvation amid the crumbling urban landscape on "Sidewalks Of The City." The highlight is "Hot Blood," in which glass-shattering warbles and razor-sharp slide-guitar combine to send chills down the spine. File under Great Roots Music. —*Roch Parisien*

Maurice Williams & the Zodiacs

Group, Doo-Wop

After recording one single for Excello as the Marigolds ("Little Darlin'," later covered by the Diamonds), Maurice Williams rechristened his group and scored a huge hit in 1960 with "Stay," which contains one of the greatest falsettos in the pantheon of soul. Later hits included "May I" and "Come Along." —*John Floyd*

● **Best of Maurice & the Zodiacs** / 1989 / Relic ✦✦✦✦

Not much thought went into this set, but it'll do. —*Dan Heilman*

Vanessa Williams

b. Mar. 18, 1963
Dance-Pop, Urban

When Vanessa Williams lost her Miss America crown in 1984, it seemed like her career was over. Actually, the truth was quite different. Four years later, she re-emerged as an urban R&B vocalist with *The Right Stuff,* which featured the Top Ten hit "Dreamin'." Her next album was an even bigger success, thanks to the smash hit "Saving the Best for Last"; it confirmed her status as one of urban R&B's most popular vocalists. —*Stephen Thomas Erlewine*

○ **The Right Stuff** / Feb. 1988 / Wing ✦✦✦✦

The disc is evenly divided between dance floor fodder and AOR fluff, and it ain't half bad. Despite the fact that Williams works with six producers and eight songwriters, the disc has a consistent feel, and while Vanessa doesn't have a voice suited to belting out raunchy R&B, she's smart enough to stay within her limitations and let her personality take up the slack. —*J. Poet*

● **The Comfort Zone** / 1991 / Wing ✦✦✦✦

Former Miss America Vanessa Williams retained the momentum from her hit debut release *The Right Stuff* with this prototype urban contemporary album. She used different producers, arrangers and songwriters on almost every track, nicely balanced the menu between dance-oriented uptempo numbers, like the title track and "Running Back To You," with syrupy but extremely popular ballads like "Save The Best For Last" and "Just For Tonight." While far from being soulful, Williams's voice had enough earnestness and conviction to make the love songs seem sincere and not be buried in the mix on the rhythm cuts. —*Ron Wynn*

Sweetest Days / 1995 / Wing ✦✦✦

Victoria Williams

Singer-Songwriter, Folk-Rock

During the late '80s and early '90s, singer/songwriter Victoria Williams recorded two critically acclaimed albums, featuring her distinctive, lyrical songwriting. Occasionally, her thin voice can be a little shrill, yet her music is consistently complex, drawing from folk, pop, gospel, and country. At times, Williams's lyrics can be slightly cloying, but more often, she writes rich, detailed, narratives.

After the release of 1990's *Swing the Statue!,* Williams was diagnosed as being ill with multiple sclerosis. She had no money or insurance to pay for her expensive hospital bills. Her dire situation led to a bunch of her musician friends assembling a relief fund for her; the fund led to the 1993 tribute album *Sweet Relief,* which featured fourteen artists covering her songs. The proceeds were donated to Williams, as well as the Sweet Relief Musicians Trust Fund, designed to help musicians who, like Victoria Williams, have no money for health insurance. After the album was a success, her two records were reissued by Geffen. During this time, Williams went into remission. She released her third album, *Loose,* in 1994. —*Stephen Thomas Erlewine*

Happy Come Home / 1987 / David Geffen Co. ✦✦✦

● **Swing the Statue** / 1990 / Rough Trade ✦✦✦✦

Victoria Williams' second album was her most accomplished set of folk-rock, featuring the remarkable "Summer of Drugs." —*Stephen Thomas Erlewine*

○ **Loose** / 1994 / Atlantic ✦✦✦✦

Victoria Williams's first album since the well-publicized tribute album *Sweet Relief* ranks as one of her finest, even if the production is much more pop-oriented than her two other records. —*Stephen Thomas Erlewine*

Chuck Willis

b. Jan. 31, 1928, Atlanta, GA, **d.** Apr. 10, 1958
R&B

Chuck Willis was one of the greatest R&B songwriters and vocalists, from his early-'50s stint with Okeh up to his work with Atlantic. His best songs, "It's Too Late," "I Feel So Bad," and "What Am I Livin' For"—focused on romantic pain and suffering, but he also produced one of rock's finest statements of longevity: "Hang Up My Rock and Roll Shoes." Willis died of peritonitis in 1958. —*John Floyd*

○ **My Story** / 1980 / Columbia ✦✦✦✦

These are the best Okeh recordings by this brilliant R&B songwriter and vocalist, best known for his later work in the '50s on Atlantic. Great liner notes by Peter Guralnick. —*John Floyd*

○ **Let's Jump Tonight! The Best of Chuck Willis 1951-56** / 1994 / Epic/Legacy ✦✦✦✦

Before his brief turn as a rock & roll star with Atlantic, Willis cut a lot of material for Okeh in much more of an R&B/jump blues vein. This 26-cut collection includes all of his early and mid-'50s R&B hits—"My Story," "Goin' To The River," "Don't Deceive Me," "You're Still My Baby," and his most famous number from this period, "I Feel So Bad" (revived by Elvis Presley, among others). The influence of Joe Turner, Charles Brown, early Lloyd Price, and similar performers is strongly felt; Willis could shout competently, but was much better on the emotional R&B ballads. Not as strong or distinctive as his Atlantic material, this includes several cuts that were previously unreleased or previously unavailable in the U.S. —*Richie Unterberger*

Wilson Phillips

Group, Pop

A female vocal trio consisting of Carnie and Wendy Wilson (daughters of Beach Boy Brian Wilson) and Chynna Phillips (daughter of John and Michelle Phillips of the Mamas & the Papas). They broke through to enormous pop success with their debut album, which sold four million copies. The follow-up, *Shadows and Light,* got off to a fast start in the spring of 1992. Although the album was successful, selling over a million copies, it didn't have the staying power of their debut. Wilson Phillips broke up the following year. —*William Ruhlmann*

● **Wilson Phillips** / 1990 / Capitol ✦✦✦✦

A pleasant, harmony-filled pop-rock album, featuring hits such as "Hold On," "Release Me," and "You're in Love." —*William Ruhlmann*

Shadows & Light / Jun. 2, 1992 / SBK ✦✦✦

While it contains a couple of strong tracks, most notably the single "Give It Up," none of the songs on Wilson Phillips's second album are as appealing as "Hold On" or "The Dream Is Still Alive," and the entire record sounds like a forced attempt to replicate the multi-platinum success of their debut. —*Stephen Thomas Erlewine*

Brian Wilson

b. Jun. 20, 1942
Pop/Rock

Brian Wilson is arguably the greatest American composer of popular music in the rock era. Born and raised in Hawthorne, CA, Wilson formed the Beach Boys, with his two younger brothers, cousin Mike Love, and school friend Alan Jardine, and they became the most successful American rock band in history by performing his songs, which initially combined the rock urgency of Chuck Berry with the harmonies of the Four Freshmen. Wilson's musical imagination expanded during the '60s to the point of such remarkable works as "Good Vibrations," a chart-topping Beach Boys single of 1966. Wilson retreated from his dominance of the Beach Boys after 1967, as their popularity declined. He made sporadic contributions to their records, returning briefly as a songwriter and producer in the mid-'70s. Wilson issued a debut solo album in 1988, but his second one, *Sweet Insanity,* was rejected by Sire Records. Wilson was said to be preparing his next album. *—William Ruhlmann*

● **Brian Wilson** / 1988 / Sire ◆◆◆◆
Any suggestion that Wilson's talents had waned was erased by this solo masterpiece, which found his sense of composition and arrangement—especially the gorgeous harmonies—intact, and even growing. *—William Ruhlmann*

Dennis Wilson

b. Dec. 4, 1944, **d.** Dec. 28, 1983
Pop/Rock
Dennis Wilson was the drummer in the Beach Boys. Like the other members of the group, he took a more active role in writing and producing the band's material after his older brother Brian ceased to dominate the group in 1967. Dennis cut a well-received solo album in 1977. He died of drowning. *—William Ruhlmann*

○ **Pacific Ocean Blue** / 1977 / Caribou ◆◆◆◆
This elaborately produced album demonstrates many of the qualities of the Beach Boys' music, especially the vocal harmonies, but also demonstrates an individual vision. It's a shame there wasn't more after this. *—William Ruhlmann*

Jackie Wilson

b. Jun. 9, 1934, Detroit, MI, **d.** Jan. 21, 1984
Soul, R&B
In terms of range, vocal gymnastics, and showmanship—not to mention the ability to simply belt out a song—nobody could match Jackie Wilson. Graduating from Billy Ward's Dominoes, he signed with the Brunswick label and began his career performing songs co-written by fellow Detroiter Berry Gordy, later the founder of Motown. These included "To Be Loved," "Lonely Teardrops," and "Reet Petite." Wilson trod the line between R&B and pop, often favoring the latter where he could use his astonishing range to good effect. His records were frequently characterized by a surfeit of brass and *Tonight Show* arrangements. Fans contend that Jackie Wilson was incapable of making a bad record, but his output remains a mixed bag to most ears. The best is among the most thrilling music to emerge from the late '50s and early '60s.

Wilson's career entered the doldrums as the British invaded, and it took a new producer, Carl Davis, to revitalize him. Davis produced the timeless soul classics "Whispers" (1966) and "Higher and Higher" (1967), and Wilson was still charting on a regular—if somewhat lowly—basis when he collapsed onstage in 1975. He lived in a coma for another eight-and-a-half years. *—Colin Escott*

○ **Mr. Excitement** / 1992 / Rhino ◆◆◆◆
A three-CD box from the experts of reissue at Rhino, *Mr. Excitement* takes Wilson's career from his first sides with Billy Ward and the Dominoes in 1956 through his final recordings in the early '70s. The former Detroit boxer hit either the R&B or pop chart over 50 times, making him the 26th most successful R&B artist, in chart terms at least. Every one of those recordings is contained in this set, including such classics as "Reet Petite," "Lonely Teardrops," and "(Your Love Keeps Lifting Me) Higher and Higher." Wilson had an explosive falsetto and a downright weird sense of phrasing that made him utterly unique. Some of his productions were a little overwrought but even in the most extreme cases, that voice was a gift from God. Seminal. *—Rob Bowman*

★ **Very Best of Jackie Wilson** / 1993 / Ace ◆◆◆◆◆
A terrific single-disc collection of Jackie Wilson's biggest hits and finest moments. *—Stephen Thomas Erlewine*

Wimple Winch

Group, British Invasion, Psychedelic
Despite the silly name and their near-total lack of commercial success, Wimple Winch were an interesting British '60s group, weaving soul, intricate harmonies, and unusual whimsical lyrics into their original material. Starting out as Just Four Men, the Liverpool-area outfit were initially just one of the dozens of Mersey groups riding the Beatles' coattails, although they cut a couple of fair singles. Changing their name to Wimple Winch, they released three much more progressive singles that were popular locally, including the explosive raver "Save My Soul" and the dramatic story-song "Rumble on Mersey Square South." Arguably the most creative group to work from Liverpool after the Merseybeat boom

dried up, they broke up in the late '60s, leaving a wealth of unreleased material. Much of that material, as well as their rare singles, eventually appeared on compilations of British Invasion and British psychedelic rarities in the 1980s. *—Richie Unterberger*

The Wimple Story 1963-1968 / 1992 / Bam Caruso ◆◆◆
The definitive document, including all the Just Four Men and Wimple Winch singles, as well as a wealth of unreleased music recorded by both incarnations of the band—28 songs and 78 minutes in all. Despite the group's meager legacy, the material (almost all self-penned) is generally quite strong. The psychedelic-era songs in particular are intriguing blends of crunching mod pop, psychedelia, and soul, with unexpected tempo shifts, superb harmonies, strong melodies, and unusual lyrics, although they sometimes get a little airy-fairy. *—Richie Unterberger*

Jesse Winchester

b. May 17, 1944, Shreveport
Folk, Singer-Songwriter
The country/folk singer/songwriter Jesse Winchester first gained notice for his debut album, *Jesse Winchester* (1970), produced by the Band's Robbie Robertson. It featured such songs as "The Brand New Tennessee Waltz" and "Yankee Lady," which were covered by a wide range of performers. The subtext of his appeal, however (and of songs like "Yankee Lady"), was that Winchester was an American living in Canada to avoid the draft. Born in Shreveport, LA, he had grown up in Memphis and attended Williams College, from which he graduated in 1966. While studying in Germany in 1967, he received his draft notice and moved to Montreal. Winchester's second album, *Third Down 110 to Go,* was released in 1972 and got into the charts briefly, but he was hindered by his inability to play in the U.S. In 1973, Winchester became a Canadian citizen. He released more records, but it wasn't until 1977, when President Jimmy Carter instituted an amnesty for draft resisters, that Winchester was able to appear in the U.S. His appearances made his next album, *Nothing but a Breeze,* his biggest seller yet. *A Touch on the Rainy Side* (1978) was a more moderate success, while *Talk Memphis* (1981) featured the Top 40 hit "Say What." This was his last album for seven years, until the independent Sugar Hill label issued *Humour Me* (1988). Winchester continues to tour. *—William Ruhlmann*

○ **Jesse Winchester** / 1970 / Rhino ◆◆◆◆
Robbie Robertson and Levon Helm lend a Bandlike sound to these tracks, which, while not typical of Winchester's later work, nevertheless have a pleasing rock feel. Some of Winchester's best songs are here, and the album made him a legend. *—William Ruhlmann*

○ **Third Down, 110 to Go** / 1972 / Bearsville ◆◆◆◆
Winchester's best album is full of songs about following your desires and taking risks against high odds, though they're sung and played buoyantly: "If we're treading on thin ice," Winchester sings, "then we might as well dance." *—William Ruhlmann*

Learn to Love It / 1974 / Bearsville ◆◆◆

Live at the Bijou Cafe / 1975 / Bearsville ◆◆

Let the Rough Side Drag / 1976 / Bearsville ◆◆◆
A well-produced country-rock album with more songs offering sage advice, from the title track to "Damned If You Do" and "Blow On, Chilly Wind." *—William Ruhlmann*

Nothing But a Breeze / 1977 / Bearsville ◆◆◆

A Touch on the Rainy Side / 1978 / Bearsville ◆◆◆

Talk Memphis / 1981 / Bearsville ◆◆◆

Humour Me / 1988 / Sugar Hill ◆◆

● **The Best of Jesse Winchester** / 1988 / Rhino ◆◆◆◆
Not a perfect selection but good enough to give a reasonable representation of Winchester's Bearsville years, 1970-1981. Includes this transplanted Southerner's haunting "Mississippi You're on My Mind," as well as "The Brand New Tennessee Waltz," "Bowling Green," "Biloxi," and "Talk Memphis." *—William Ruhlmann*

Winger

Group, Hard Rock, Heavy Metal
A former member of Alice Cooper's band, bassist Kip Winger formed his own group in 1986; in addition to vocalist/bassist Winger, the group featured guitarist Reb Beach, bassist Paul Taylor, and drummer Rod Morgenstein, formerly of the Dixie Dregs. Taking its name from its leader, Winger specialized in the stylish pop-metal that sent Bon Jovi and Poison to the top of the charts. The

band's eponymous debut sold over a million copies on the strength of the rocker "Seventeen" and the ballad "Headed for a Heartbreak." Winger's second album, 1990's *In the Heart of the Young*, was equally successful, selling over a million copies and featuring the hit power-ballad "Miles Away." However, the band didn't outlast the post-alternative pop-metal backlash and the group faded away after the release of its 1993 album, *Pull.* —*Stephen Thomas Erlewine*

● **Winger** / 1988 / Atlantic ✦✦✦✦
Well-written heavy metal with good hooks and lyrics, it was a best-selling debut. —*John Book*

In the Heart of the Young / 1990 / Atlantic ✦✦✦
The songwriting from bassist/vocalist Kip Winger matures with this second release. —*John Book*

Pull / May 18, 1993 / Atlantic ✦✦

Winter Hours

Group, Folk, Alternative Pop/Rock
An '80s/'90s quintet strongly influenced by early Buffalo Springfield, early Dylan, and the Gene Clark-era Byrds, Winter Hours had a refreshingly aggressive, high-energy approach. They specialized in what might best be called loud folk-rock with a vengeance. Articulate, creative, and talented, they didn't stand a chance in the '80s. —*Bruce Eder*

● **Winter Hours** / 1985 / Chrysalis ✦✦✦✦
Self-titled album resounds with echoes of Neil Young, Pete Townshend, and Phil Ochs, haunting melodies, and dazzling guitar by Mike Carlucci. A must-own for anyone who ever cared about any of those influences. —*Bruce Eder*

○ **Wait Till Tomorrow Comes** / 1986 / Line ✦✦✦✦
Compilation of two early EPs and some singles. It lacks the punch of Chrysalis's release but is a very tuneful and engaging record, with some pleasing rough edges. —*Bruce Eder*

Leaving Time / 1989 / Link ✦✦✦

Edgar Winter

b. Dec. 28, 1946, Beaumont, TX
Rock & Roll
Johnny's younger brother. Multi-instrumentalist and possessor of a vocal range of about a zillion octaves, Edgar has zipped through so many styles he's simply not worth pinning down. If you like unhinged blues-rock and R&B, you'll like the early part of his career. If you like commercial hard rock, there are songs like the mega-hit "Frankenstein." Whatever you fancy, chances are Edgar's recorded it. —*John Dougan*

Entrance / Nov. 1970 / Epic ✦✦✦

○ **White Trash** / 1971 / Epic ✦✦✦✦
A full R&B outfit with horns. Texas raunch. Only the ballad sounds dated. —*Robert Gordon*

Roadwork / 1972 / Epic ✦✦✦

○ **They Only Come out at Night** / 1972 / Epic ✦✦✦✦
The commercial hits were "Free Ride" and "Frankenstein." —*Robert Gordon*

Shock Treatment / 1974 / Epic ✦✦

● **Collection** / 1986 / Rhino ✦✦✦✦

Johnny Winter

b. Feb. 23, 1944
Blues Rock
Blues guitarist Winter became a major star in the late '60s and early '70s. Since that time he's confirmed his reputation in the blues by working with Muddy Waters and continuing to play in the style, despite musical fashion. Born in Leland, MS, Winter formed his first band at 14 with his brother Edgar in Beaumont, TX, and spent his youth in recording studios cutting regional singles and in bars playing the blues. His discovery on a national level came via an article in *Rolling Stone* in 1968, which led to a management contract with New York club owner Steve Paul and a record deal with Columbia. His debut album (there are numerous albums of juvenilia), *Johnny Winter*, reached the charts in 1969. Starting out with a trio, Winter later formed a band with former members of the McCoys, including second guitarist Rick Derringer. It was called Johnny Winter And. He achieved a sales peak in 1971 with the gold-selling *Live/Johnny Winter And.* He returned in 1973 with *Still Alive and*

Well, his highest-charting album. His albums became more overtly blues-oriented in the late '70s and he also produced several albums for Muddy Waters. In the '80s he switched to the blues label Alligator for three albums, and has since recorded for the labels MCA and Virgin. —*William Ruhlmann*

○ **Johnny Winter** / 1969 / Columbia ✦✦✦✦
Winter's stunning debut features his fiery blues playing in both electric and acoustic settings, with backup that includes Willie Dixon. —*William Ruhlmann*

● **Second Winter** / 1969 / Columbia ✦✦✦✦
Winter leans more toward mainstream rock & roll, though the guitar playing remains fierce. Originally a *three*-sided LP, this now makes a long CD. —*William Ruhlmann*

○ **Johnny Winter and . . .** / 1970 / Columbia ✦✦✦✦
Winter puts together a new band and takes on the assistance of Rick Derringer, who coproduces and provides such great songs as "Rock and Roll, Hoochie Koo." —*William Ruhlmann*

Johnny Winter and . . . Live / 1971 / Columbia ✦✦✦
Winter and his new band turn out hard-rock versions of "Jumpin' Jack Flash," "Johnny B. Goode," and other rock & roll favorites. —*William Ruhlmann*

Still Alive and Well / 1973 / Columbia ✦✦✦

Saints & Sinners / 1974 / Columbia ✦✦✦

John Dawson Winter III / 1974 / Blue Sky ✦✦✦

Captured Live! / 1976 / Blue Sky ✦✦✦

○ **Nothin' but the Blues** / 1977 / Blue Sky ✦✦✦✦
After a long period making rock records, Winter fronts the Muddy Waters band (with Waters singing) on this Chicago blues workout. He sounds happier than ever before. —*William Ruhlmann*

○ **Guitar Slinger** / 1984 / Alligator ✦✦✦✦
The first of three blues albums recorded after a four-year studio hiatus finds Winter as fleet-fingered as before and sounding more vocally involved than in some of the later Columbia material. —*William Ruhlmann*

Serious Business / 1985 / Alligator ✦✦

Third Degree / 1986 / Alligator ✦✦✦

The Winter of '88 / 1988 / Voyager ✦✦

○ **Birds Can't Row Boats** / 1988 / Relix ✦✦✦✦
Aside from "Ice Cube" (a 1959 instrumental), these tracks date from 1965-68. Many are previously unissued or only available on rare 45s. Those accustomed to his more famous recordings are in for a jolt, as this shows Johnny in several unexpected settings: grinding Texas psych-punk, the British Invasion-cum-folk-rock garage single "Gone for Bad," an Everly Brothers cover, a *Highway 61*-era Dylan imitation, and even a shit-kickin' C&W tune. There are also some straight, predominantly acoustic blues numbers. —*Richie Unterberger*

○ **Let Me In** / 1991 / Point Blank ✦✦✦✦

Scorchin' Blues / Jun. 16, 1992 / Epic ✦✦
Johnny Winter has remained a vital roots-music force for 30 years because no matter how high his rock star has risen (notably in the early to mid-'70s), he has never lost his passion for the blues nor forgotten his debt to its originators. *Scorchin' Blues* marries tracks from Winter's early Columbia albums—including the classic National steel-driven "Dallas" from his 1969 debut—with material from his return-to-roots Blue Sky period in the late '70s. The aggressive playing and raunchy vocals will appeal to both blues and rock fans, and Ben Sandmel crams an authoritative biography into seven pages, complete with interesting Winter quotes. The one downside: a miserly ten tracks spread over only 45 minutes of playing time. —*Roch Parisien*

Hey, Where's Your Brother? / Jul. 1992 / Point Blank ✦✦✦
On the classic, 1972 live album *Roadwork,* Edgar Winter immortalized the words, when introducing brother Johnny: "Everybody asks me . . . where's your brother?" It's a question that fans have besieged both Winters with for over two decades, and now Johnny gets a chance to return the tribute with his latest. Edgar does in fact guest on the sessions, blowing sax and tinkling keys on a few tracks, and dueting with big bro on a superb, seasonal rendition of "Please Come Home for Christmas." —*Roch Parisien*

Steve Winwood

b. May 12, 1948
Pop/Rock

Singer/songwriter, keyboardist, and guitarist Steve Winwood was a well-known musician long before he finally embarked on a solo career in the second half of the '70s. Born in Birmingham, England, Winwood joined the Spencer Davis Group with his older brother Muff when he was only 15 years old. His was the soulful, Ray Charles-like voice on such hits as "Gimme Some Lovin'" and "I'm a Man," songs he also co-wrote. In 1967 he formed Traffic, which he led, with time off for the supergroup Blind Faith in 1969, until 1974. Winwood finally released his first solo album in 1977 and, in 1981 had his first million-seller with his second album, *Arc of a Diver*. *Talking Back to the Night* (1982) was not as much of a success, and Winwood spent four years preparing *Back in the High Life* (1986), which sold three million copies. *Roll with It* (1988) went to number one, but *Refugees of the Heart* (1990) was not up to his usual standard.

After the relative failure of *Refugees of the Heart*, Winwood and Jim Capaldi re-formed Traffic in 1994; although their record and tour were well-received, the reunion wasn't as successful as expected. —*William Ruhlmann*

Winwood / 1971 / United Artists ♦♦♦
A two-disc compilation of Winwood's group activities, 1966-1970, including work with the Spencer Davis Group, Powerhouse, Traffic, and Blind Faith. —*William Ruhlmann*

Steve Winwood / Jun. 1977 / Island ♦♦♦
Rock fans had been waiting for a Steve Winwood solo album for more than a decade, as he made his way through such bands as the Spencer Davis Group and Traffic. When Winwood finally delivered with this LP, just about everybody was disappointed. Traffic had finally petered out three years before, but Winwood, using such former members as Jim Capaldi and Reebop Kwaku Baah, failed to project a strong individual identity outside the group. That great voice was singing the songs, that talented guitarist/keyboardist was playing them, and that excellent songwriter had composed them, but nothing here was memorable, and the long-awaited debut proved a bust. —*William Ruhlmann*

○ **Arc of a Diver** / Jan. 1981 / Island ♦♦♦♦
Utterly unencumbered by the baggage of his long years in the music business, Winwood reinvents himself as a completely contemporary artist on this outstanding album, leading off with his best solo song, "While You See a Chance." Winwood also plays all the instruments. —*William Ruhlmann*

Talking Back to the Night / Aug. 1982 / Island ♦♦♦
Okay, so after missing with his first solo album, Steve Winwood had hit the jackpot with his second, *Arc of a Diver*, finally fulfilling his enormous promise. What did he do next? He returned to the record racks only a year and a half later with this retread, which attempted to turn the "While You See a Chance" sound into a formula and to a large extent succeeded, unfortunately. "Valerie" (number 70 U.S., number 51 U.K.), the lead-off track, had that same keyboard sound and tempo, and Winwood kept it up for much of the rest of the record, including the album's biggest U.S. single, "Still in the Game" (number 47). Fans were dismayed, and *Talking Back to the Night* had an even lower chart peak than *Steve Winwood*. —*William Ruhlmann*

● **Back in the High Life** / Jun. 1986 / Island ♦♦♦♦
Turning to involved percussion tracks and horns, Winwood turns another musical corner on this sophisticated album, which contains echoes of everything from gospel to Caribbean music. Contains the number one hit "Higher Love." —*William Ruhlmann*

○ **Chronicles** / Nov. 1987 / Island ♦♦♦♦
This isn't an adequate compilation of the years 1977-1986, but it does manage to gather some of the better songs of the period. —*William Ruhlmann*

Roll with It / Jun. 1988 / Virgin ♦♦♦
Winwood manages to reintroduce some of the R&B elements of the Spencer Davis Group and some of the psychedelic effects of early Traffic here, though this is also an effective followup to the directions indicated on *Back in the High Life*. Contains the number one title track and "Don't You Know What the Night Can Do?" —*William Ruhlmann*

Refugees of the Heart / Nov. 1990 / Virgin ♦♦♦
The key to Steve Winwood's solo career is inconsistency; *Refugees Of The Heart* was a letdown. The distinction between a great Winwood album and one that's only okay is dangerously small—it has more to do with performance than composition—and on *Refugees of the Heart*, as on *Talking Back to the Night*, Winwood was unable

to invest Will Jennings's pedestrian lyrics with the soulful feeling of which he's capable. The album's standout is a collaboration with ex-Traffic partner Jim Capaldi, "One and Only Man," which topped *Billboard*'s Album Rock Tracks chart. Perhaps noting this exception, Winwood next teamed with Capaldi in a 1994 reunion of Traffic. —*William Ruhlmann*

○ **The Finer Things** / 1995 / Island ♦♦♦♦
Steve Winwood has led a long and varied career, recording everything from straight R&B and jazz-flavored rock to folk and pop. Over the course of four discs, *The Finer Things* chronicles the entirety of his career, beginning with the Spencer Davis Group, through Traffic and Blind Faith, right until his successful solo career. It includes all of the hits and many of his finest album tracks, yet the overall approach is rather exhausting—the rarities are rarely illuminating, they're just there for the sake of being there. Nevertheless, it is a worthwhile purchase for anyone wanting a comprehensive picture of Winwood in all of his various guises. —*Stephen Thomas Erlewine*

BOOK

♦♦♦ **Steve Winwood: Roll With It**, by Chris Welch with Steve Winwood (Perigee, 1990). Winwood was undeniably one of the most talented rock musicians to emerge during the 1960s, but he wasn't the most colorful figure. Thus this bio is not packed with saucy revelations, but is rather a decent, if workmanlike, survey of his musical career, with plenty of first-hand memories from Steve. Welch, one of the first British rock journalists to write about the music with serious intelligence and passion, was already quite familiar with his subject, having interviewed Winwood and seen him perform in various guises since his days with the Spencer Davis Group. Weighted toward his early groups (the Spencer Davis is covered the most heavily, though Traffic gets quite a bit of ink as well), it also includes anecdotes from important colleagues such as Spencer Davis, Muff Winwood, and Jim Capaldi. —*Richie Unterberger*

The Wipers

Group, Punk, Alternative Pop/Rock
By bridging the gap between hard rock and punk, the Wipers managed to create a surprisingly influential style of post-punk. Led by guitarist Greg Sage, the band melded the furious rage and independent punk ethic with a fondness for loud, long guitar workouts. Sage was one of the few immediate post-punk guitarists that played by the conventional rules of a guitar hero, including several long guitar solos, without losing his indie edge.

The Wipers formed in Portland, OR, in the late '70s; the group released their first album in 1979. Two years later, the band delivered the *Youth of America* EP, which featured a slightly different lineup than the debut. The group recorded five more albums during the '80s (Sage also released a solo record, *Straight Ahead*, in 1985), before breaking up in 1988. While they never gained much more than a cult audience while they were recording, the Wipers managed to influence a number of musicians, including Nirvana's Kurt Cobain and J. Mascis of Dinosaur Jr. Consequently, the band was arguably better known in the early '90s than in the early '80s, when they were active. —*Stephen Thomas Erlewine*

Is This Real / 1979 / Sub Pop ♦♦♦

○ **Youth of America** / 1981 / Restless ♦♦♦♦
First EP. Set the stage for *Over the Edge*. —*John Dougan*

● **Over the Edge** / 1983 / Restless ♦♦♦♦
By far their best. Aggressive and direct, this burns! —*John Dougan*

The Wipers / 1985 / Enigma ♦♦

Land of the Lost / 1986 / Restless ♦♦♦

Follow Blind / 1987 / Restless ♦♦

The Circle / 1988 / Restless ♦♦♦

● **The Best of the Wipers** / 1990 / Restless ♦♦♦♦

Wire

Group, Punk, Alternative Pop/Rock
Wire's brief, fractured songs and minimalistic sound made the band the artiest of all punk bands, as well as one of the most influential. Unlike most other punk bands, their stripped-down approach was not an attempt to get back to rock's roots; it was cutting the music to its raw nerve, so nothing extraneous was left. On their 1977 debut, *Pink Flag*, Wire managed to tear through 21 songs in under 40 minutes. Although they never managed to match that al-

bum's accomplishment, they recorded two other excellent albums before breaking up in late 1979.

Wire was quiet for several years. They returned to recording in 1986 with the *Snakedrill* EP, quickly following it with 1987's full-length *The Ideal Copy*. Amazingly, Wire's capabilities were still intact; the only concession the group made was adding synthesizers to their music, which they managed to work in quite well. However, after *The Ideal Copy*, the band began to slip, as they were attempting to incorporate synths and samplers to a greater degree; their experimental tendencies began to overshadow their musical sense. Eventually, the band shortened their name to Wir; their first release in this new incarnation was 1991's *The First Letter.* — *Stephen Thomas Erlewine*

Pink Flag / 1977 / Restless ♦♦♦♦♦

Wire's debut effort, *Pink Flag*, was one of the strongest releases of the late-'70s British punk scene, mixing the aggressive punch of the Sex Pistols with the humor and brevity of the Ramones. *Pink Flag* packed 21 tracks into the space of 37 minutes; twelve of the tracks were under a minute and a half. ("Field Day for the Sundays" clocked in at just 28 seconds.) Somehow none of these tracks felt short; Wire merely made their point and moved on to the next idea. — *Rick Clark*

Chairs Missing / 1978 / Restless ♦♦♦♦

In *Chair's Missing*, Wire stretched out into longer pieces and artier production. Not as impressive as *Pink Flag*, the album does contain some standout tracks with "Outdoor Miner," "French Film Blurred," "I Am the Fly," and "Question of Degree." — *Rick Clark*

154 / 1979 / Restless ♦♦♦♦

154 integrated more keyboards and slowed the pace down a bit, but Wire didn't lose any of the eccentric edge. They just kept getting stranger. If *Ummagumma*-period Pink Floyd, early King Crimson, and the Moody Blues at their musically most cosmic, were filtered through the punk movement, you'd get an idea what a peculiar album *154* is. Call it psychedelic punk. Among the highlights are "Two People in a Room," "The 15th," "Map Ref. 41ø N 93ø W," "The Other Window," "Single K.O.," and "40 Versions." — *Rick Clark*

Document & Eyewitness / 1981 / Mute ♦♦

Snakedrill / 1986 / Enigma ♦♦♦

The Ideal Copy / 1987 / Enigma ♦♦♦

A Bell Is a Cup . . . Until It Is Struck / 1988 / Enigma ♦♦♦

It's Beginning to & Back Again / 1989 / Enigma ♦♦♦

On Returning (1977-1979) / 1989 / Restless ♦♦♦♦

This magnificent 31-song overview collects highlights from *Pink Flag*, and many of the best songs from the two followups, plus some interesting rarities. — *John Floyd*

Manscape / 1990 / Restless ♦♦

The First Letter / 1991 / Mute ♦♦

A List / 1993 / Elektra ♦♦

Bill Withers

b. Jul. 4, 1938, Slab Fork, WV
Soul, Urban

It was a chance 1970 meeting with the legendary Booker T. Jones (of Stax's Booker T. & the MG's) that opened the door for Bill Withers into the world of pop success. At the time of their meeting, Withers was working in a factory that built toilet seats for jet airplanes. Jones, impressed with Withers's demos, helped secure a deal with Sussex Records. Withers's Jones-produced debut, *Just As I Am*, was a classic of folky acoustic-guitar-driven soul, complemented by Withers's earthy vocal delivery and largely autobiographical tales. His next few albums capitalized on that sound, but as the late '70s came around, Withers gravitated toward a sophisticated urban R&B sound, sometimes collaborating with groups like the Crusaders. — *Rick Clark*

Greatest Hits / 1981 / Columbia ♦♦♦♦

A good sampler of Withers's hits, plus a few key album tracks, it covers his transition from funky acoustic-guitar-rooted soul to smooth urban pop. Included are "Use Me," "Lean on Me," "Just the Two of Us," "Ain't No Sunshine," and "Who Is He and What Is He to You?" Now if only Withers's early albums, like *Still Bill*, would see the light of day on CD . . . — *Rick Clark*

Lean on Me: The Best of Bill Withers / 1994 / ♦♦♦♦

18 tracks, from the early '70s to the mid-'80s, including his early Top Ten singles, but also minor hits like "Grandma's Hands," "Kissing My Love," and "Lovely Day." Those who admire songs like

"Lean on Me" and "Ain't No Sunshine" are advised to approach this best-of with caution; from the mid-'70s onward, Withers forsook his folky singer-songwriter soul for more anonymous, slick MOR soul and urban contemporary. His early sound was far more distinctive, and his early-'70s Sussex albums are recommended alternatives to this compilation. — *Richie Unterberger*

Peter Wolf

b. Mar. 7, 1946
Rock & Roll, Pop/Rock

Peter Wolf was the lead singer of the J. Geils Band from 1967 to 1983. After splitting from the band, he released three solo albums in 1984-1990, with varying success. — *William Ruhlmann*

Lights Out / 1984 / EMI America ♦♦♦♦

On his own, Wolf achieves a more contemporary pop sound than that of the bluesy J. Geils Band and scores three chart hits: "Lights Out" (#12), "I Need You Tonight" (#36), and "Oo-Ee-Diddley-Bop!" (#61). — *William Ruhlmann*

Come As You Are / 1987 / EMI America ♦♦♦♦

Wolf gets back in the Top 15 with the title track, but the best song is the leadoff, an R&B raveup ironically called, "Can't Get Started." — *William Ruhlmann*

Up to No Good / 1990 / MCA ♦♦♦

Womack & Womack

Group, Soul, R&B

Cecil Womack (b. 1947) and his wife Linda (b. 1952) had a long history before the release of their first duo album in 1983. Cecil was one of the gospel-singing Womack brothers who became the Valentinos and toured with Sam Cooke in the early '60s; Linda was Cooke's daughter. Both Womacks were successful songwriters for such performers as Teddy Pendergrass, Wilson Pickett, and Aretha Franklin prior to hooking up as a performing team. The focus is on songwriting in their collaboration; they began with *Love Wars*, which featured the Top 40 R&B hit "Baby I'm Scared of You." *Radio M.U.S.I.C. Man* (1985) contains unfinished Sam Cooke songs completed by the duo. It was followed by *Conscience* in 1988 and *Family Spirit* in 1991. — *William Ruhlmann*

Love Wars / 1983 / Elektra ♦♦♦♦

Womack and Womack are steeped in the early-'60s style of Cecil's Valentinos and Linda's father, Sam Cooke, but they have updated the style. Nevertheless, this is contemporary soul likely to be embraced by fans of Cooke, Otis Redding, and others of the genre. — *William Ruhlmann*

Radio M.U.S.I.C. Man / 1985 / Elektra ♦♦♦

Nice interaction and captivating lyrics. — *Ron Wynn*

Conscience / Jun. 13, 1988 / Island ♦♦♦

This album didn't get airplay or a push, but it didn't lack quality. — *Ron Wynn*

Family Spirit / 1991 / RCA ♦♦♦

A good, although not great, session. — *Ron Wynn*

Transformation to the House of Zekkariyas / May 25, 1993 / Warner Brothers ♦♦

Bobby Womack

b. Mar. 4, 1944
Soul, R&B

Few careers in American popular music have been as consistently productive and influential as that of singer/songwriter and guitarist Bobby Womack. Sam Cooke, for whom Womack played guitar, financed his first recordings in the early '60s. With his brothers as the Valentinos, he cut two R&B classics, "It's All Over Now" (later a hit for the Stones) and "Lookin' for a Love" (a mega-hit for J. Geils). The Valentinos' combination of shouting lead vocals and blues/gospel harmonies predated late-'60s soul music.

Womack knew and championed Jimi Hendrix early on, befriending him during a 1962 soul package tour. Womack's lean, groundbreaking guitar work, so similar in flavor to that of his contemporary Curtis Mayfield, influenced Hendrix. Later, Hendrix would return the favor by popularizing the wah-wah—an effect Womack would use to chilling effect on Sly Stone's *There's a Riot Goin' On* album and its smash single, "Family Affair" (he doubled here on bass). That's also Womack's guitar on Wilson Pickett's "Funky Broadway" and on Aretha Franklin's *Lady Soul* album.

In fact, Womack himself was one of the legendary "wild" soul men, friend and partying companion of Wilson Pickett, for whom he wrote "Midnight Mover" and "I'm in Love." He even scored a movie, *Across 110th Street*, which came out at the same time as the landmark blaxploitation film *Shaft*.

Womack's singing career resumed in the '70s; James Taylor covered his number one R&B hit, "Woman's Got to Have It." He made a stunning 1981 comeback with the number one R&B album *The Poet* and reunited with old Memphis studio friends and producer Chips Moman on 1986's *Womagic*.

Bobby Womack's career is far from over. Look for more greatness from this soulful, innovative musician and singer. P.S.: He belongs in the Rock & Roll Hall of Fame! —*Christine Ohlman*

○ **Greatest Hits** / 1974 / Liberty ✦✦✦✦
Includes his great remake of the Valentinos hit "Lookin' for a Love," as well as his other chart hits—"That's the Way I Fell About Cha," "Harry Hippy," and "Nobody Wants You When You're Down and Out." —*Christine Ohlman*

The Poet / 1981 / Beverly Glen ✦✦✦

Poet 2 / 1984 / Beverly Glen ✦✦✦

○ **Lookin' for a Love Again** / Jan. 1993 / Razor & Tie ✦✦✦✦
This is a strong collection of Bobby Womack's influential R&B songs. —*AMG*

● **Midnight Mover** / Feb. 1993 / EMI ✦✦✦✦
Spanning the length of his influential career, *Midnight Mover* features two discs of one of the major figures of contemporary soul and R&B, covering all of his hits and best moments. It is essential for any R&B collection. —*AMG*

Wonder Stuff

Group, Alternative Pop/Rock
When the Wonder Stuff released their first album, *The Eight Legged Groove Machine*, in 1988, the British press wrote scores of articles about the band, mainly because of the arrogant self-confidence of their leader, vocalist/guitarist Miles Hunt. Hunt's brash public image was the Wonder Stuff personified—mean, self-satisfied, self-serving, and scathingly witty. Accordingly, their colorful mixture of pop melodies, loud guitars, sneering lyrics, and touches of dance music was sometimes brilliant and sometimes banal. Between 1988 and 1993, the band kept incorporating more stylistic flourishes to their basic, punk and new wave-inspired pop/rock. The band were instant stars in England; America never warmed to their music. After trying to gain a worldwide audience for five years, the band broke up in 1994. —*Stephen Thomas Erlewine*

○ **The Eight Legged Groove Machine** / 1988 / Polydor ✦✦✦✦
A brash, scattershot debut driven by the band's sheer arrogance as much as their catchy, but erratic, guitar hooks. —*Stephen Thomas Erlewine*

Hup! / 1989 / Polydor ✦✦✦
The Wonder Stuff's second album isn't as snotty as their first, but it's more ambitious, adding bits of folk, psychedelia, and art-rock to their self-involved punk-pop. Unfortunately, they didn't bring as many hooks and melodies this time around, leaving *Hup!* an admirable but failed experimentation. —*Stephen Thomas Erlewine*

○ **Never Loved Elvis** / 1991 / Polydor ✦✦✦✦
The Wonder Stuff's carefully constructed melodies, endless ambition, spiky guitars, and self-confidence combined into a consistently engaging sound on their third album. —*Stephen Thomas Erlewine*

Construction for the Modern Idiot / Oct. 5, 1993 / Polydor ✦✦
With *Construction for the Modern Idiot*, the Wonder Stuff rebounds from a somewhat lackluster streak of records with an album of brash guitar pop rivaling its earlier releases. —*Stephen Thomas Erlewine*

● **If The Beatles Had Read Hunter . . . The Singles** / 1994 / Polydor/PolyGram ✦✦✦✦
The Wonder Stuff's albums were wildly incoherent, which makes this British collection of their U.K. hit singles not only their most consistent album, but also their most entertaining. —*Stephen Thomas Erlewine*

Stevie Wonder (Steveland Morris)

b. May 13, 1950, Saginaw, MI
Soul, Motown, Pop/Rock
When Stevie Wonder began recording in 1963, he was only thirteen years old. Even then, his talent was evident, although there was no sign of how deep it was. After all, the music was the work of a startlingly gifted child; it was all exuberant flash, with few complexi-

ties. Soon, Wonder would go far beyond the infectious energy of "Fingertips (Part 2)." In two years, he became one of Motown's finest artists, recording a series of brilliant singles for a solid nine years, the overwhelming majority of which he wrote himself. During this time, his albums were like other Motown albums—a combination of killer singles and pleasant filler, only Wonder was allowed to record the occasional number that reflected his increasing social consciousness, like his hit version of Bob Dylan's "Blowin' in the Wind." By the end of the '60s, he was not only hitting the charts with his own records, but writing material for many other Motown artists, including the Spinners' "It's a Shame" and co-writing "The Tears of a Clown" with Smokey Robinson.

With his creativity growing by leaps and bounds, Wonder soon felt limited by Motown's strict production and publishing contracts. When his record contract expired in 1971, Wonder recorded two full albums by himself and used them as a bargaining tool during contract negotiations with Motown. The record label gave him total artistic control of his albums, as well as the rights to his own songs. Soon afterwards, the two albums—*Where I'm Coming From* and *Music of My Mind*—were released.

Music of My Mind, especially, helped usher in a new era of soul/R&B. Along with Sly Stone and Marvin Gaye, Wonder was responsible for making soul and R&B albums not just collections of singles, but cohesive artistic statments, where artists could extend their music beyond the confines of a three-minute hit single. With his next two albums, *Talking Book* and *Innervisions*, Wonder's music became richly complex and inventive; in addition to his musical innovations, Wonder's lyrics addressed social and racial issues as eloquently and incisively as any other pop songwriter. Wonder sustained his creative peak through 1974's *Fulfillingness' First Finale* and 1976's *Songs in the Key of Life*.

Three years later, he released the ambitious and bewildering *Journey Through the Secret Life of Plants*, which received terrible reviews upon its release. Wonder released the more straightforward *Hotter than July* in 1980; the album received substantially better reviews and became his first platinum album. However, he wasn't able to sustain that momentum for the rest of the decade. Although his records sold well and he scored the occasional hit—including the smash hit ballad "I Just Called to Say I Love You"—his albums weren't as focused as they were a decade earlier. By the '90s, he was still an immensely respected musician, but his music was no longer on the cutting edge. —*Stephen Thomas Erlewine*

The Jazz Soul of Little Stevie Wonder / Sep. 1962 / Motown ✦✦✦
More than any single LP, this album showed how much pure talent Stevie Wonder possessed. He was a gifted drummer, fantastic chromatic harmonica player, engaging vocalist and exceptional composer. All these skills were highlighted throughout this record, and Wonder's youthful, exuberant voice had a maturity suggesting that greatness was around the corner. —*Ron Wynn*

○ **A Tribute to Uncle Ray** / Oct. 1962 / Motown ✦✦✦✦
"Little Stevie Wonder, Tamla's 11 year old musical genius, is blind, a similarity he shares with a famed musician and vocalist of today," shamelessly announce the liner notes of this album. Unfortunately, Wonder at 11 does not share much of Ray Charles's vocal abilities, even when he is singing Charles's songs (others are "originals in the style of his idol") and, since he doesn't play on the record, there's no similarity there either. Today, listening to a child emote his way through songs like "Drown In My Own Tears" is a curiosity at best, and the album is only for hard-core Wonder fanatics. —*William Ruhlmann*

The 12 Year Old Genius / May 31, 1963 / Motown ✦✦✦
Recorded live, this includes the full seven-minute version of his #1 hit "Fingertips." The rest of the album shows him as a young prodigy fixated on Ray Charles; indeed, the final three songs are covers of the early Charles tunes "Hallelujah I Love Her So," "Drown In My Own Tears," and "Don't You Know." A couple jams and a cover of "(I'm Afraid) The Masquerade Is Over" fill out this seven-song LP. —*Richie Unterberger*

With a Song in My Heart / Dec. 28, 1963 / Motown ✦✦✦
Having tried to turn Little Stevie Wonder into Big Ray Charles, then broken him through with "Fingertips—Pt. 2," Motown now gave us Steve Wonder, Lounge Lizard. At least, that's what you'd think listening to this string-filled crooning session, in which the 13-year-old earnestly makes his way through the likes of Johnny Mercer's "Dream," "Get Happy," "Without A Song," and other superclub standards. Berry Gordy's wish for all his artists may have been to play the Copacabana, but this one was far below the legal

drinking age, and, although Wonder brought his usual willingness to the project, it was years beyond his abilities. —*William Ruhlmann*

○ **Up-Tight (Everything's Alright)** / May 4, 1966 / Motown ✦✦✦✦
Stevie Wonder began demonstrating his production skills and compositional acumen on his first of two albums in 1966. Although still just a teenager, Wonder was already anxious to do more than simply grind out love tunes. He covered Bob Dylan's "Blowin' In The Wind" and also contributed "Pretty Little Angel" alongside the monster hits "Nothin's Too Good For My Baby" and the title song. It was also a signal Wonder had moved beyond simply paying homage to Ray Charles and now wanted to establish his own musical identity. —*Ron Wynn*

Down to Earth / Nov. 16, 1966 / Motown ✦✦✦
Stevie Wonder's third album signaled more artistic growth, but was the first of his career that didn't make much commercial headway. It didn't contain a single big hit, something that wouldn't happen again to Wonder for many, many years. There were moments of uncertainty and awkwardness on such songs as "Angel Baby (Don't You Ever Leave Me)" and "Lonesome Road." Wonder was laying the groundwork for numerous classics that routinely came throughout the 1970s and '80s; his voice was losing its cuteness and beginning to gain the richness and edge that punctuated many of his future albums. —*Ron Wynn*

I Was Made to Love Her / Aug. 29, 1967 / Motown ✦✦✦
This album was rushed out to capitalize on the success of the title song, which was Wonder's biggest pop hit since "Fingertips—Pt. 2" and would not be bettered until "Superstition" in 1972. Other than the hit, it's all filler, but not uninteresting for that. There are several contributions from the Wonder team at Motown, covers of other Motown hits, and stabs at sounding like Ray Charles, James Brown, and Otis Redding. At 17, Wonder was becoming both a remarkable mimic and an original talent on his own. —*William Ruhlmann*

○ **Greatest Hits** / Mar. 1968 / Motown ✦✦✦✦
When it was released, Stevie Wonder's first hits collection, a 12-track disc tracing his work from 1963 to 1967, served a common function of compilations: it gathered together stray, disparate pieces, from "Fingertips—Pt. 2" to "I Was Made to Love Her," and focused attention on the artist. Wonder had a spotty singles record: five Top Ten hits, but only two of them in succession, over the four and a half years, but *Greatest Hits* made him seem like a consistent hitmaker with an astounding range, from those early harmonica instrumentals to soulful wailers like "Uptight (Everything's Alright)" and even oddball ballads like "A Place in the Sun." By now this set has long since been eclipsed, notably by the *Looking Back* album, but as a demonstration of Wonder's early promise, it is notable. —*William Ruhlmann*

Eivets Rednow . . . Alfie / Nov. 20, 1968 / Motown ✦✦✦
By 1968, Motown had Wonder pegged as a soul-pop shouter, so his harmonica instrumental of "Alfie," the movie theme that had been a Top 15 hit for Dionne Warwick in 1967, was released under another name—his own spelled backwards—and on a different record label. This album, issued after that single made number 66 on the pop chart, consists of more harmonica instrumentals, everything from "A House Is Not A Home" to "Grazing in the Grass," and is enough to convince you that Wonder, who, after all, broke through playing harmonica, is a tuneful player of the instrument, more a Larry Adler than a Bob Dylan. Nevertheless, this is a minor item in the Wonder catalog. —*William Ruhlmann*

For Once in My Life / Dec. 6, 1968 / Motown ✦✦✦
Rather than rushing out an album in the spring of 1968, when "Shoo-Be-Doo-Be-Doo-Da-Day" (#9 Pop, #1 R&B) hit, Motown waited, through the modest summer success of "You Met Your Match" (#35 Pop, #2 R&B) until "For Once in My Life" (#2 Pop and R&B) became Wonder's next mammoth single, to release an album. As a result, this LP contained all three hits, making it one of Wonder's more consistent albums of the '60s, even with filler like "Sunny" and "God Bless the Child." The real find, however, is the driving "I Don't Know Why," which, when placed on the B-side of Wonder's next single, "My Cherie Amour," became a hit on its own, going #39 Pop, #16 R&B. —*William Ruhlmann*

My Cherie Amour / Aug. 29, 1969 / Motown ✦✦✦
Notable for containing Wonder's then most recent Top 10 hit, the title track, and its followup, "Yester-Me, Yester-You, Yesterday," this album otherwise contains contemporary filler like "Light My Fire,"

plus a peculiar arrangement of "Hello, Young Lovers" from *The King And I* that makes it sound like "For Once In My Life." —*William Ruhlmann*

Signed, Sealed & Delivered / Aug. 7, 1970 / Motown ✦✦✦
Stevie Wonder was beginning to rebel against the Motown hit factory mentality in the early '70s. While he certainly hadn't lost his commercial touch, Wonder was anxious to address social concerns, experiment with electronics and not be restricted by radio and marketplace considerations. Still, he gave the label another definitive smash with the title track, while sneaking in a cover of the Beatles' "We Can Work It Out" and penning more intriguing tunes like "I Can't Let My Heaven Walk Away" and "Never Had A Dream Come True." —*Ron Wynn*

○ **Where I'm Coming From** / Apr. 12, 1971 / Motown ✦✦✦✦
Released one month before Stevie Wonder's 21st birthday, *Where I'm Coming From* is really his first adult album, and although it was not a massive hit, it anticipated the musical approach of his commercial breakthrough, *Talking Book*, by a year and a half. The lovely "Never Dreamed You'd Leave In Summer," as the B-side to a cover of the Beatles' "We Can Work It Out," has become a Wonder standard, and the album's real hit, "If You Really Love Me" (#8 pop, #4 R&B), marked the first rewards of his alliance with then-wife Syreeta Wright. Elsewhere, Wonder, who produced and composed all the tracks, introduced the funky keyboard style that would take him through the next few years, as well as the social concerns that would absorb him later on. This album was a shot across the bow, fair warning that a major, nearly mature talent had arrived. —*William Ruhlmann*

Greatest Hits, Vol. 2 / Oct. 1971 / Motown ✦✦✦
Stevie Wonder's second hits collection, gathering together his singles from 1968 to 1971, traces his development into a virtuoso talent, from upbeat Motown numbers like "For Once In My Life" to the emergence of Wonder's own style in songs like "Never Dreamed You'd Leave In Summer" and "If You Really Love Me." Along the way, he demonstrates an amazingly broad pop sensibility that allows him to handle soul, pop/rock, and ballads, all with equal ease. And, of course, the remarkable thing is that this set was obselete the day it came out, summing up of what turned out to be only the first phase of Wonder's remarkable career. This LP has been superseded by the *Looking Back* compilation. —*William Ruhlmann*

○ **Music of My Mind** / Mar. 1972 / Motown ✦✦✦✦
When Wonder turned 21 he renegotiated his Motown contract; the key issue was control. Stevie Wonder had a vision that veered far away from that of the Motown hit-making machine. Influenced by the work of Isaac Hayes in 1969 and 1970 and labelmate Marvin Gaye in 1971, Wonder was no longer content with putting out albums that were a collection of two or three hit singles plus filler; he wanted to record full-length albums that had an integrity unto themselves. *Music of My Mind* was the first such effort. Wonder produced, wrote the songs, and played the majority of the instruments. At the time it was a revelation. Compared with Wonder's subsequent efforts, it pales just slightly. —*Rob Bowman*

☆ **Talking Book** / Nov. 1972 / Motown ✦✦✦✦✦
Talking Book is the album that crystallized Wonder as the self-contained singer/songwriter. "Superstition" and "You Are the Sunshine of My Life" were both #1 singles. The rest of the album maintains an equally torrid level. —*Rob Bowman*

☆ **Innervisions** / Aug. 1973 / Motown ✦✦✦✦✦
For my money, Stevie Wonder's finest moment. Three massive hits, "Higher Ground," "Living for the City," and "Don't You Worry 'Bout a Thing," were drawn from the album. "Golden Lady" and "He's Misstra Know-It-All" could have been equally successful. From the titles alone, one can see that Wonder had developed a social conscience and, as many other singer/songwriters of the time were doing, he politicized his music. Intelligent lyrics that one can boogie to—what more could one want from popular music? —*Rob Bowman*

○ **Fulfillingness' First Finale** / Jul. 1974 / Motown ✦✦✦✦
Two funky, clarinet-dominated singles, "Boogie on, Reggae Woman" and "You Haven't Done Nothin'," are the high points of this record. Much of the rest of the album is centered around the electric piano, a sound ubiquitous in Black music in the early '70s. Wonder occasionally gets a little syrupy on the non-hit material, al-

though his phrasing is so fine that one tends to be forgiving. —*Rob Bowman*

○ **Songs in the Key of Life** / Sep. 1976 / Motown ✦✦✦✦
Wonder the auteur began to get out of hand with this sprawling double album plus four-song-EP set. Much is maudlin, cloying, and pretentious; yet great songs, such as "Sir Duke," rear their heads at various junctures throughout the set. —*Rob Bowman*

★ **Looking Back** / Dec. 1977 / Motown ✦✦✦✦✦
Between 1963 and the end of 1971, Little Stevie Wonder placed 25 songs on *Billboard*'s charts. Twenty-four of those, including such radio staples as "Fingertips—Pt. 2," "Uptight (Everything's Alright)," "I Was Made to Love Her," "For Once in My Life," "My Cherie Amour," and "Signed, Sealed, Delivered, I'm Yours" appear on *Looking Back*. Wonder's recordings in the '60s stand apart from most Motown acts partially because he was paired with producers and writers who very rarely worked with the Temptations, Supremes, et al. In the beginning Wonder was often produced by Clarence Paul and/or William Stevenson; during the golden years Henry Cosby was usually manning the controls. Then in 1970 Wonder started producing himself, beginning with "Signed, Sealed, Delivered." Most of Wonder's singles were written by Wonder himself in tandem with a variety of others, or by Ron Miller. The hits alternated between stomping barnburners and mid-tempo, understated ballads. —*Rob Bowman*

Journey Through the Secret Life of Plants / Oct. 1979 / Motown ✦✦✦
Perhaps the most curious album in Stevie Wonder's career, this was ostensibly a soundtrack for a film few people saw (if indeed it was ever released). These were mostly instrumentals, plus a few oddball vocals, but most observers didn't know what to make of it at the time. Wonder was so hot that the record peaked at number four on the pop albums chart, despite the lack of any real singles and confounding almost everyone who heard it. "Outside My Window" was the lone tune to scrape the middle regions of the pop charts, while the R&B community ignored the entire album. —*Ron Wynn*

○ **Hotter Than July** / Sep. 1980 / Motown ✦✦✦✦
Hotter Than July was Wonder's real follow-up to *Songs In The Key Of Life*, even if it took him the then-unconscionably long four years to release it. Wonder had been perhaps the most accomplished and successful pop artist of the years 1972-1977, but his absence had cooled him off commercially, and this album demonstrated that, artistically, he was also past his peak. Individual moments suggested his earlier triumphs, and Wonder remained a remarkably facile singer/player/composer, but he had lost his ability to amaze his listeners. The album's biggest single was "Master Blaster (Jammin')" (#5 pop, #1 R&B), an adequate but unremarkable reggae number, but the standout track was "Happy Birthday," the theme song for the ultimately successful campaign to make Dr. Martin Luther King, Jr.'s birthday a national holiday. —*William Ruhlmann*

★ **Original Musiquarium I** / May 1982 / Motown ✦✦✦✦✦
Most of Wonder's chart hits from 1972 through 1982 (although why "You Haven't Done Nothin'" is not here I will never know) are included on *Stevie Wonder's Original Musiquarium I*, plus three newly written and recorded tunes. Simply put, some of the finest Black music made in the '70s. Essential. —*Rob Bowman*

The Woman in Red / Aug. 1984 / Motown ✦✦✦
Stevie Wonder's career in the 1980s was a source of frustration to the fans he had earned in the '60s and '70s. In 1982, there were a few new songs on a greatest hits album and a duet with Paul McCartney. Then came this soundtrack to a Gene Wilder comedy that was simultaneously most of a pop vocal album than most soundtracks and yet less than a full-fledged Wonder record. The gold-selling #1 hit that resulted was the sappy "I Just Called To Say I Love You," a formulaic TV commercial-in-the-making. "Love Light In Flight" also hit, and the album featured Dionne Warwick on two duets and one solo. This was a pleasant record, but slight, and after four years, Wonder fans wanted more than that. —*William Ruhlmann*

In Square Circle / 1985 / Motown ✦✦✦
Although it went platinum, nothing stands as better evidence of how cyclical the pop experience is than the response to *In Square Circle*. Wonder actually wrote some superb songs, and several, like "Overjoyed" and "I Love You Too Much," were superior to the hit single "Part-Time Lover." But that one zoomed to the top spot and became the album's definitive tune in the minds of many. —*Ron Wynn*

Characters / Nov. 1987 / Motown ✦✦✦
Wonder shocked fans by taking only two years to release his next new non-soundtrack studio album, *Characters*. Unfortunately, it had long since become clear that Wonder was willing to settle for good pop music without challenging himself to make great pop music. And by now, a big chunk of his formerly mass audience had gotten the message: this was Wonder's first new album to miss the pop Top Five in 15 years. (The Black music audience, however, responded far more favorably, as the album topped the R&B charts for seven weeks.) The biggest single was the "Superstition"-like dance track "Skeletons" (#19 Pop, #1 R&B), and Wonder also charted with the pretty "You Will Know" and an uptempo duet with Michael Jackson, "Get It." —*William Ruhlmann*

Jungle Fever / May 28, 1991 / Motown ✦✦✦
Despite all of the hype surrounding it, the soundtrack to *Jungle Fever* is Stevie Wonder's best work in years. Although it can't compare to Wonder's glory days, *Jungle Fever* is a considerable improvement from his bland late-'80s albums. Wonder still borders on saccharine in his ballads, although even the sappiest of them ("These Three Words") is never as sickening as "I Just Called To Say I Love You." While the keyboard funk of "Chemical Love," "Gotta Have You" and "Queen in the Black" doesn't sound new, it does sound alive, which is better than Wonder has sounded in years. —*Stephen Thomas Erlewine*

Conversation Peace / 1995 / Motown ✦✦✦
Stevie Wonder's albums have not caught the public's attention since the mid-'80s and *Conversation Peace* did not change that, although it wasn't for lack of trying. Wonder's gift for melody is still in place and he incorporates understated hip-hop rhythms into his music well, yet he isn't able to make music that fits into the rigid playlists of '90s urban contemporary radio. —*Stephen Thomas Erlewine*

BOOK

✦✦✦ **Stevie Wonder**, by John Swenson (Harper & Row, 1986). The inner life of Stevie Wonder, as is the case with many Motown stars, has remained fairly mysterious to the public. This large-format paperback is short on revelations about his psyche and personal relationships, but does a pretty good job at documenting his music, through both detailed criticism and much commentary (both firsthand and from other sources) by Wonder himself. Every one of his Motown singles and albums through the mid-'80s is discussed in depth, from his days as a pre-teen prodigy through his evolution into a visionary singer-songwriter and master of studio technology in the 1970s. As with many pop/rock giants, Wonder is driven by the tension between his urge to experiment and be accessible to as many people as possible, and between his desire for social change and his need for love and romantic relationships. This straightforward bio documents this well, by looking at the music and the circumstances of its production rather than speculating on its motivations.—*Richie Unterberger*

Brenton Wood

b. Jun. 26, 1941, Shreveport, LA
Soul
Wood's quirky rhythmic sense and happy-go-lucky vocal delivery clicked with R&B and pop audiences in 1967, when "The Oogum Boogum Song" and "Gimme Little Sign" both proved potent hits. Born in Shreveport, LA, Wood moved west to San Pedro and found inspiration in the mellifluous styles of Sam Cooke and Jesse Belvin. He formed a vocal group called the Quotations while attending college, before signing with Double Shot Records and hooking up with producers Joe Hooven and Hal Winn. After making it three hits in a row with "Baby You Got It," Wood only notched a couple more minor chart items for the label in 1968. —*Bill Dahl*

○ **The Best of Brenton Wood** / 1986 / Rhino ✦✦✦✦
The best are included with much of the rest. —*Dan Heilman*

● **Brenton Wood's 18 Best** / Original Sound ✦✦✦✦

Ron Wood

b. Jun. 1, 1947
Rock & Roll
U.K. guitarist Ron Wood has spent most of his career in groups—the Creation, the Jeff Beck Group, Faces, and, since 1976, the Rolling Stones—but he's found time to make a variety of non-group albums, including duet albums with Ronnie Lane and with Bo Diddley, and even a few solo albums that serve as assemblages of his friends. —*William Ruhlmann*

○ **I've Got My Own Album to Do** / 1974 / Warner Brothers ✦✦✦✦
For his first album, Ron Wood enlisted Keith Richards and the Faces' pianist Ian McLagan as support and turned in a loose, good-humored album that catches fire on the swaggering "Take a Look at the Guy," the earnest cover of "If You Gotta Make a Fool of Somebody," and the grinding R&B workout "Crotch Music." — *Stephen Thomas Erlewine*

○ **Now Look** / 1975 / Warner Brothers ✦✦✦✦
Now Look, Ron Wood's second solo album, was a tighter affair than his debut, yet it lost none of its predecessor's off-the-cuff charm, thanks to convincing, ragged covers of Ann Peeble's "I Can't Stand the Rain" and "I Got Lost When I Found You," which was written by the album's producer, Bobby Womack. — *Stephen Thomas Erlewine*

Mahoney's Last Stand / 1976 / Atco ✦✦✦

● **Gimme Some Neck** / 1979 / Columbia ✦✦✦✦
Wood leads a pickup band that includes, on various cuts, fellow Rolling Stones Charlie Watts, Mick Jagger, and Keith Richards, plus Mick Fleetwood, Dave Mason, and other notables. The highlight is a then-unreleased Bob Dylan song called "Seven Days," where the rough-voiced Wood sounds uncannily like Mr. D himself. — *William Ruhlmann*

1234 / 1981 / CBS ✦✦

Slide on This / Sep. 1992 / Continuum ✦✦✦
Ron Wood's first solo album in over ten years is a relaxed, rocking, star-studded affair, including appearances by Charlie Watts, Hothouse Flowers, Joe Elliott from Def Leppard, and the Edge. Nothing here is earth-shaking, but the quality of "Knock Yer Teeth Out," "Show Me," and a cover of the Parliaments' "Testify" makes *Slide on This* Wood's best solo album. — *AMG*

Slide on Live / 1994 / Continuum ✦✦
A document of an energetic live show, *Live at the Ritz* is an enjoyable but inconsequential record. — *Stephen Thomas Erlewine*

Roy Wood

Rock & Roll, Art-Rock/Progressive-Rock
Roy Wood, born Ulysses Adrian Wood in Birmingham, England, has long been regarded as one of the most important, if eccentric, rock musicians to have come out of that city, which also spawned the Moody Blues. As leader/cofounder of both the Move and the Electric Light Orchestra, Wood has been an influence on two decades of rock music.

Wood took up the guitar in his early teens and was a member of local bands such as the Falcons and the Lawmen. The first "successful" band of which he was a member was Gerry Levene and the Avengers, which actually got to record a single, and whose membership included future Moody Blues drummer Graeme Edge. They broke up in mid-1964, and Wood joined Mike Sheridan and the Nightriders, who recorded his song "Make Them Understand." During this period, Wood attended the Moseley College of Art, from which he was expelled in 1964. That same year, he organized The Move, with Bev Bevan, formerly of Moody Blues founding member Denny Laine's band Denny and the Diplomats, on drums, Carl Wayne on lead vocals, Ace Kefford on bass, and Trevor Burton on guitar. The band was fortunate enough to land Tony Secunda as their manager, and later a residency at London's Marquee Club, where they began to build an enthusiastic following, especially for such antics as smashing TV tubes on the stage.

The Move started out heavily influenced by Wood as composer and leader, and became more so as they went along, with the guitarist contributing most of the songs and eventually many of the vocals as well. Their single "Night of Fear," a Wood adaptation of a melody derived from Tchaikovsky's *1812 Overture*, rose to number two on the English charts in early 1967 and anticipated the foundation of the Electric Light Orchestra. Eight more singles followed, all composed by Wood, and from "Fire Brigade" onward he also handled the lead vocals. The group evolved over the ensuing three years, down to a quartet and with the addition of Jeff Lynne, formerly of the Birmingham-based band the Idle Race, and passed through psychedelic, progressive, and heavy metal phases, through albums such as *Shazam*, *Message from the Country*, and *Looking On*, and were popular in England but virtually unknown in America. Their sound embraced everything from old time rock & roll, including Duane Eddy and even some doo-wop influences, but also displayed Beatles-style harmonies and lyrical complexity.

By 1971, Wood had developed ideas and ambitions that were too wide to be embraced by any one band, and proposed the formation of an offshoot of the Move—now effectively reduced to himself, Lynne, and Bev Bevan—called the Electric Light Orchestra. Augmented with pianist Bill Hunt and cellist Hugh McDowell, their first album, Electric Light Orchestra, was released on the Harvest label in England (and United Artists in the United States) to strong critical approval and decent sales—indeed, the new band seemed to attract more serious attention than the Move had been getting. Originally the Electric Light Orchestra and the Move were to have existed side-by-side, but the ELO supplanted the Move, and the latter ceased to exist.

Wood exited soon after, leaving the ELO in the hands of Lynne and Bevan, while Wood went off to form Wizzard with ex-Move guitarist Rick Price, Bill Hunt on the piano, harpsichord, and French horn, Hugh McDowell on the electric cello, Nick Pentelow and Mike Burney on saxes, and Keith Smart on the drums.

Wizzard's first single, "Ballpark Incident," combined the Move's hard rock & roll sound with a texture reminiscent of Phil Spector's "wall of sound" productions from the mid-'60s, and rose to number six on the British charts. In April of 1973, Wizzard reached number one with "See My Baby Jive," and repeated this feat in August of the same year with "Angel Fingers." Unfortunately, the band's first album, *Wizzard's Brew*, didn't fare nearly as well, being a highly experimental body of work, of which "You Can Dance the Rock 'N Roll" was the most accessible track. The group's fortunes, even as a singles band, faltered after this, partly because of Wood's decision to continue recording and releasing records under his own name in addition to his work with Wizzard. His Phil Spector-ish "I Wish I Could Be Christmas Everyday" reached number four in England in 1973, and "Forever"—a tribute to Brian Wilson and the Beach Boys—made it to number eight the same year, while "Goin' Down the Road" only made it up to number 13, and "Oh What a Shame" only reached that level. The Wizzard albums *See My Baby Jive* and *Eddie & the Falcons* were both critical and commercial failures, and the unsuccessful release of the latter led to the demise of the group. Meanwhile, Wood's own solo albums, *Boulders* (1970) and *Mustard* (1975) were considered too idiosyncratic to achieve major followings.

Wood's biggest problem is the sheer range of the music that he is capable of making, which is as likely to include oboe and cello accompaniment as rock & roll saxophone in the same song. One of the hardest rockers, and most enthusiastic rock & rollers in his generation of British rock stars, his music has always also displayed a Beatlesque lushness. This makes much of his work sound like what that band might've accomplished had they turned back to their rock & roll roots for the *Magical Mystery Tour* and subsequent projects (one could easily see Wood doing a psychedelic-style cover of "Back in the USSR").

Certainly even after his exit, the Electric Light Orchestra continued to use the start he gave them until the mid-'70s, even covering his Move-era standard "Do Ya." *The Roy Wood Story* (Harvest), released in 1976, summed up his career with EMI Records, and performed well as a best-of. His subsequent records, *On the Road* (1979) and *Starting Up* (1987) failed to achieve anything like the success of his early-'70s work, and since then Wood has become one of the more elusive active musicians of his generation, although he has continued to record into the 1990's. — *Bruce Eder*

○ **Boulders** / 1973 / United Artists ✦✦✦✦
Wood's solo albums are a mixed lot, mostly thanks to the sheer diversity of sound that he's comfortable dealing with. *Boulders* is his best solo work to date, a strangely offbeat, hard-rocking yet progressive, lush yet minimalist-sounding work that encompasses all of Wood's influences, from Duane Eddy to the Beatles to classical music's late-19th-century Romanticism. — *Bruce Eder*

Wizzards Brew / 1973 / United Artists ✦✦✦

See My Baby Jive / 1974 / Harvest ✦✦

Eddie & the Falcons (Wizzard) / 1974 / United Artists ✦✦✦

Mustard / 1975 / United Artists ✦✦✦

On the Road Again / 1979 / Warner Brothers ✦✦

Starting Up / 1994 / Griffin ✦✦

● **The Roy Wood Years 1971-73 You Can Dance The Rock 'N Roll** / EMI/Harvest ✦✦✦✦
The finest compilation of Wood's work to date, drawing on his closing years with the Move, his sole album with ELO, the biggest hits of Wizzard, and Wood's official solo albums and singles. — *Bruce Eder*

Woodentops

Group, Alternative Pop/Rock
Taking punk's D.I.Y. ideals and applying it to stripped-down acoustic pop, the Woodentops achieved a great deal of critical success in the short time they were together. Formed in the early '80s in Northhampton, England, the group consisted of Rolo McGinty (vocals, guitar), Frank de Freitas (bass), Simon Mawby (guitar), Benny Staples (drums), and Alice Thompson (keyboards). The band released their debut single "Plenty" on Food Records; the record led to a contract with Rough Trade. Throughout 1985, the Woodentops released a series of singles, all written by McGinty, that began to attract an audience in the U.K. The group released their acclaimed debut album, *Giant*, in 1986. The following year, the band began experimenting with their sound, adding tougher guitars and electronics. These changes were particularly evident in their live show, as shown by their 1987 live recording, *Hypno-Beat*. Featuring the contributions of professional studio musicians Bernie Worrell and Doug Wimbish among others, 1988's *Wooden Foot Cops on the Highway* continued the group's experimentations with rhythmic and sonic textures.

While the band managed to keep creative, they weren't able to gain much of an audience anywhere outside Japan. In 1991 and 1992, they toured the world without ever becoming any bigger than a cult band. Soon after, the Woodentops broke up. *—Stephen Thomas Erlewine*

○ **Well Well Well: The Unabridged Singles Collection** / 1986 / Upside ✦✦✦✦

● **Giant** / 1986 / Columbia ✦✦✦✦

Hypno-Beat / 1987 / Upside ✦✦

Wooden Foot Cops on the Highway / 1988 / Columbia ✦✦

World Party

Group, Pop/Rock
Basically, World Party *is* singer/songwriter and multi-instrumentalist Karl Wallinger. Formerly of the popular British band the Waterboys, Wallinger's albums are fascinating, unapologetic exercises in pop self-referentialism. At times Wallinger's retro-'60s obsessions and his vocal blend of Dylan and Jagger (less distinctive than either), coupled with his occasional forays into funk, make him sound like Prince fixated on classic rock. All in all, Wallinger manages to make the effect flow seamlessly. *—Rick Clark*

○ **Private Revolution** / 1986 / Ensign ✦✦✦✦
This debut album from World Party is a solid release, even if it is a bit heavy on the synthesized sounds (what can you expect from a one-man band?). Wallinger's insightful songs deal primarily with the responsibility of the individual to recognize and cope with the problems of the world. Features mainly original songs like "Private Revolution," "World Party," and "It's All Mine," as well as a cover of Dylan's "All I Really Want to Do," which remains surprisingly true to the original version. *—Iotis Erlewine*

● **Goodbye Jumbo** / 1990 / Ensign ✦✦✦✦
This excellent follow-up album from World Party is much tighter than the debut. Dealing with issues from the environment ("Take It Up," "Put the Message in the Box") to relationship woes ("And I Fell Back Alone"), these tracks manage to maintain a hopeful, positive mood without becoming trivial. In these songs, Wallinger has developed his own distinct style. A great album, worth checking out just for the uptempo groove of "Way Down Now." *—Iotis Erlewine*

Bang! / 1993 / Capitol ✦✦✦
On his previous releases, Wallinger has displayed a social conscience, but never has it taken prominence like it does on *Bang!*, World Party's third album. *Bang!* does contain some glorious music that equals his masterpiece *Goodbye Jumbo*, but the album slows down when he tries to say too much (as in the quasi-operatic "And God Said"). Even then, Wallinger's preaching doesn't obliterate the considerable pleasures of the music. Wallinger has often been accused of recycling the Beatles, but the truth is that he can combine the Beatles, Beach Boys, Sly Stone, Dylan, and Prince into a musical style that is distinctive and unique yet familiar. *Bang!*, for all of its shortcomings, is as strong an album as any Wallinger has released. *—Stephen Thomas Erlewine*

Link Wray

b. 1930
Rock & Roll

Up until Link Wray's groundbreaking instrumental "Rumble" (1958), White guitarists in the main either took the jazz route or tried their best to emulate some form of the Chet Atkins/Merle Travis style. Link changed all that. With the pioneering use of distortion, tremolo, and feedback, plus an unabashed attack that owed much to soul-blues, Wray created a style that was years ahead of its time. Creating one great instrumental after another on primarily chordal themes (making him the godfather of the now-common power chord), his music contained the groundbreaking roots of heavy metal, ten years before it came into being. A seminal influence on Pete Townshend, Jeff Beck, and others, Wray continues to record sporadically, sounding wilder and crazier than ever, giving the lie to the cliché of being "too old to rock & roll." *—Cub Koda*

Link Wray & the Wraymen / 1960 / Edsel ✦✦✦
Sides from the '50s and early '60s; some of his best. *—Cub Koda*

○ **The Original Rumble** / Nov. 1989 / Ace ✦✦✦✦
A good cross-section of Link's best. *—Cub Koda*

○ **Walkin' with Link** / Apr. 1992 / Epic ✦✦✦✦
An excellent 20-track compendium of Wray's tenure with Columbia-Epic back in the late '50s and early '60s. Nasty, searing, guitar instrumentals like "Ramble," "Rawhide," "Comanche," and "Radar" make this an indispensable part of any Link collection. *—Cub Koda*

★ **Rumble! Best of** / 1993 / Rhino ✦✦✦✦✦
Finally, a multi-label Link Wray collection spanning his lengthy career is available. Starting, appropriately enough, with "Rumble," *Rumble! The Best of Link Wray* illustrates through its 20 tracks (15 on cassette) that Wray was indeed one of the pioneering guitarists of rock & roll, expanding the sonic possibilites of the instrument with a variety of effects. All of the tracks feature some truly warped, genius-caliber fretboard work from Wray, and a few also feature his equally demented vocals. *Rumble! The Best of Link Wray* is the definitive Wray collection. *—Stephen Thomas Erlewine*

○ **Mr. Guitar** / 1995 / Norton ✦✦✦✦
While Link cut some great records in the late '50s and early '60s, he really reached his peak during his stay with the Swan label in the early and mid-'60s. This double-CD, 63-song set documents this period with as much thoroughness as anyone is likely to attempt, including great singles like "Jack The Ripper," "Mr. Guitar," "Ace Of Spades," and "The Fat Back," where Link let loose with his dirtiest and most groundbreaking fuzz tones. Including quite a few rarities and tracks that were never previously released in the U.S., as well as a good number of vocal performances (which were never Wray's forte), this is perhaps too exhaustive for the average fan. A single-disc distillation of his best Swan sides would be absolutely killer, but this is still one of the greatest collections of instrumental rock out there, despite its unevenness. *—Richie Unterberger*

○ **Missing Links, Vols. 1-3** / Ace ✦✦✦✦
A brilliant three-volume set of rare recordings. *—Cub Koda*

Wreckless Eric

Group, Rock & Roll, New Wave
Wreckless Eric's music wasn't much more than simple, basic rock & roll played with an energetic abandon, but at his best, he made pop singles that were immediately gripping and surprisingly timeless. During the late '70s, he recorded several minor punk/new wave classics on Stiff Records, including "Whole Wide World" and "Semaphore Signals," which sound fresh and exciting a decade and a half after they were recorded. Those two songs, benefited from the brilliant pop sense of Nick Lowe, who produced the single and provided instrumental support for Eric's snarling vocals. After Lowe left Stiff, Wreckless Eric was left without a strong producer and bandleader, making his music much more inconsistent, yet still highly enjoyable. During the '80s, his sound was polished up slightly, which removed much of the crackling energy of his early records. Now, he lives in France and continues to tour and record, playing for a small cult of fans in Europe. *—Stephen Thomas Erlewine*

Wreckless Eric / 1978 / Stiff ✦✦✦
A wonderful collection of sloppy, snarling rock & roll that nearly makes good on the promise of "Whole Wide World." *—Stephen Thomas Erlewine*

Wonderful World of Wreckless Eric / 1978 / Stiff ✦✦✦
Wreckless Eric's second album is a tighter, more pop-oriented collection that still has a vital, ragged edge. *—Stephen Thomas Erlewine*

● **The Whole Wide World** / 1979 / Stiff ✦✦✦✦
Taking the best moments from Wreckless Eric's first two exciting but spotty albums, *Whole Wide World* contains everything you need to know about this forgotten but charming punk/new wave rocker. —*Stephen Thomas Erlewine*

○ **Big Smash** / 1980 / Stiff ✦✦✦✦

○ **Le Beat Group Electrique** / 1989 / New Rose ✦✦✦✦
This overlooked comeback effort was an unheralded triumph for Eric, on which he fronted a guitar-bass-drums trio (he also plays his usual cheesy organ) on a stripped-down set of strong songs with a live production feel. With his strangled, yearning vocals, basic melodic hooks, and songs about messed-up relationships, Wreckless recalls the work of Lou Reed and Syd Barrett's better solo work, as he makes his confusion a cause for infectious celebration instead of gloomy moping. —*Richie Unterberger*

Donovan of Trash / 1991 / Sympathy For The Record Industry ✦✦✦

Wrecks-N-Effect

Group, Rap
Wrecks-N-Effect earned a huge crossover smash with the single "Rump Shaker" off their 1992 album *Hard or Smooth*. The accompanying video with its array of shapely women following the directions of the lead singer generated nearly as much heat as Sir Mix-A-Lot's "Baby Got Back." It also helped the group secure a platinum certification, something it hardly seemed they'd earn from their Motown debut *Wrecks-N-Effect* in 1990. Markell Riley, brother of super producer Teddy Riley, was part of the rap ensemble along with Aquil Davidson and Brandon Mitchell; Mitchell was killed in a 1990 shooting. —*Ron Wynn*

● **Wrecks-N-Effect** / 1991 / Atlantic ✦✦✦✦
A striking mix of go-go funk and new jack swing is highlighted by "New Jack Swing," an anthem for the new beat. Produced by Teddy Riley, who created that new beat with Guy. —*John Floyd*

○ **Hard or Smooth** / 1992 / MCA ✦✦✦✦
Although nothing else on *Hard or Smooth* compares to the monster groove of "Rump Shaker," the rest of the album offers enough beats to satisfy most fans of the hit singles. —*AMG*

Betty Wright

b. Dec. 21, 1953, Miami, FL
Soul
A consistently strong presence on the Miami music scene throughout the '70s and '80s, Betty Wright was just 15 when she cut the Top 40 "Girls Can't Do What the Guys Do." A child gospel star who switched to R&B at age 13, she put the Miami scene on the map in 1971 with the #6 hit "Clean Up Woman," notable for its prominent guitar riff and Wright's swaggering lead vocal. She won a Grammy in 1974 for "Where Is the Love?" (not to be confused with the Roberta Flack/Donny Hathaway tune of the same name). She collaborated with Stevie Wonder in 1981 on the Epic hit "What Are You Gonna Do with It?" Betty continues to live and work in the Miami area. —*Christine Ohlman*

● **The Best of Betty Wright** / 1992 / Rhino ✦✦✦✦
An excellent collection, covering the years between 1968 and 1978; it's twenty tracks of Betty Wright at her best. —*Stephen Thomas Erlewine*

Charles Wright

Soul, Funk
Charles Wright headed one of the late '60s and early '70s great funk groups, the Watts 103rd Street Band. Wright, who was born in Clarksdale, MS, was a singer, pianist, guitarist, and leader of the eight-member band, recruited from Watts in Los Angeles. They were originally known as the Soul Runners. Bill Cosby helped get the band off the ground by giving them appearances at his gigs. They began recording for Keyman in 1967, then moved to Warner Bros. in 1969. While "Do Your Thing" and "Till You Get Enough" were Top 20 R&B hits, their finest selection was "Express Yourself," a song that expressed the urge for freedom as adroitly as the Isley Brothers' "It's Your Thing" had in the '60s. It has also been among the most sampled funk tracks for hip-hop and rap groups. "Your Love (Means Everything to Me)" was their final R&B hit in 1971, peaking at number nine R&B and number 12 pop. The group's best ballad, "Love Land," did better pop-wise than among R&B fans, many of whom saw it as a bit soft. They continued recording for

Dunhill in 1973 before disbanding. Drummer James Gadson and guitarist Al McKay, who later joined Earth, Wind and Fire, were among the instrumental corps of the Watts 103rd Street Rhythm Band. —*Ron Wynn*

● **Express Yourself: The Best Of** / 1993 / Warner Brothers ✦✦✦✦
A definitive, 16-track collection of Charles Wright's best material. —*Stephen Thomas Erlewine*

O.V. Wright

b. Oct. 9, 1939, **d.** Nov. 16, 1980
Soul
A truly incendiary deep-soul performer. O. V. Wright's melismatic vocals and Willie Mitchell's vaunted Hi Rhythm Section combined to make classic Memphis soul during the early 70s. Overton Vertis Wright learned his trade on the gospel circuit with the Sunset Travelers before going secular in 1964 with the passionate ballad "That's How Strong My Love Is" for Goldwax in Memphis. Otis Redding liked the song so much that he covered it, killing any chance of Wright's version hitting. Since Wright was already under contract to Houston-based Peacock as a gospel act, owner Don Robey demanded his return, and from then on, Wright appeared on Robey's Backbeat subsidiary. Wright's sanctified sound oozes sweet soul on the spine-chilling "You're Gonna Make Me Cry," a 1965 smash, but it took Memphis producer Willie Mitchell to wring the best consistently from Wright. Utilizing Mitchell's surging house rhythm section, Wright's early-70s Backbeat singles "Ace of Spades," "A Nickel and a Nail," and "I Can't Take It" rank among the very best Southern soul of their era. No disco bandwagon for O. V. Wright—he kept right on pouring out his emotions through the 70s, convincing his faithful that he'd "I'd Rather Be (Blind, Crippled & Crazy)," that he was "Into Something (Can't Shake Loose)." Unfortunately, he apparently was—drugs have often been cited as causing Wright's downfall; the soul great died at only 41 years of age in 1980. —*Bill Dahl*

● **The Soul of O. V. Wright** / 1992 / MCA ✦✦✦✦
O.V. Wright epitomized gospel-based soul singing. He screamed, roared, belted, hollered, and wailed, proclaiming his need for love. His songs were simple; they were often anguished remembrances of lost loves or pleas that this time things might be different. Occasionally, he did an uptempo dance or novelty number, but Wright was at his best on slow burners. This collection of 1960s and '70s material for Don Robey's Back Beat label includes evocative ballads, lightweight but enjoyable numbers, and songs which returned him to his gospel days. While several foreign anthologies spotlighting Wright have been issued, this 18-track CD stands as the most complete domestic reissue package currently available. —*Ron Wynn*

Wu-Tang Clan

Group, Rap
When the Wu-Tang Clan appeared in 1993, the release of their debut album *Enter the 36 Chambers* sent shock waves throughout the hip-hop community. With their sparse, dark funk and bracingly violent martial arts imagery, the group immediately attracted a following. However, the band self-destructed within a year of their record's release, with rappers Method Man and Ol' Dirty Bastard going onto solo success in their own right. —*Stephen Thomas Erlewine*

○ **Enter the Wu-Tang (36 Chambers)** / Nov. 1993 / Loud ✦✦✦✦

Robert Wyatt

Art-Rock/Progressive-Rock
An enduring figure who came to prominence in the early days of the English art-rock scene, Robert Wyatt has produced a significant body of work, both as the original drummer for art-rockers the Soft Machine and as a radical political singer/songwriter. Born in Bristol, England, Wyatt came to the Soft Machine during the exciting slightly post-psychedelic Canterbury scene of the mid-'60s that produced bands like Gong and Pink Floyd. Unlike many of the art-rock bands that would come later (Jethro Tull, Yes, King Crimson), Soft Machine eschewed bloated theatrical excess, preferring a standard rock format that interpolated jazz riffing, extended soloing, and some forays into experimental noise. Wyatt, then Soft Machine's drummer, left the band during its initial wave of popularity for a solo career that was built less around his abilities as a percussionist and more around his frail tenor voice, capable of breaking your heart with its falsetto range.

It was not long after his first solo release, *End of an Ear*, that Wyatt fell from an open window during a party, fracturing his back and permanently paralyzing him from the waist down. After months of painful recuperation, Wyatt re-emerged with the harrowing *Rock Bottom* (1974) and the bizarre *Ruth is Stranger Than Richard* (1975), the former dealing explicitly with his post-accident life, the latter a series of surreal fables. And while the music on these records is trance-like and experimental, Wyatt shockingly recorded a straight version of the Monkees "I'm a Believer" in 1974 that became a big British hit. Controversy ensued when the BBC's long-running weekly pop music program *Top of the Pops* refused to allow Wyatt to perform the song in his wheelchair. After a significant protest played out in the music trade papers, Wyatt did perform.

Despite his success, Wyatt remained quiet for much of the rest of the decade, breaking his silence during the punk era with a handful of singles recorded for the great English indie label Rough Trade. Again, going against audience expectations, he recorded a beautiful version of Chic's "At Last I Am Free," which signalled the start of a full-fledged career renaissance that included numerous albums and artists such as Elvis Costello writing songs for him. His albums were lush, at times almost meditative, and Wyatt's voice— clear, emotionally charged and always on the verge of breaking— brought great depth and soul to songs that, if recorded by a lesser artist, would have sounded terse and tired.

Always on the political left, Wyatt's radicalism increased exponentially during Margaret Thatcher's years as Prime Minister, as he maintained an unwavering support of Communism even as *glasnost* was nigh. The resulting music he recorded during this period reflects his strong, bordering on strident political beliefs. Lately, Wyatt has comfortably worked in and out of the music business. He records when he feels like it, paints, writes, devotes time to political work and continues to show no interest in the machinations of the music industry. But, despite his occasionally strident political posture, he has recorded some stunning music, full of wonder, possibility and pure emotion, that remains undiscovered by many. *—John Dougan*

○ **Rock Bottom** / 1974 / Blue Plate ◆◆◆◆
A progressive rock-era masterpiece, it features brilliantly simple songs, poems, and textures, with all-star support. *—Myles Boisen*

○ **Ruth Is Stranger Than Richard** / 1975 / Blue Plate ◆◆◆◆
Another enduring collaboration with Brian Eno, Fred Frith, and other '70s luminaries, it's on a par with *Rock Bottom*. *—Myles Boisen*

○ **Nothing Can Stop Us Now** / 1981 / Mesa Blue Moon ◆◆◆◆

● **Rock Bottom/Ruth Is Stranger** / 1981 / Virgin ◆◆◆◆
The CD era makes these two hard-to-find recordings available on one disc. Of the two, *Rock Bottom* is the most intense, and perhaps the most odd—the songs are repetitive, meditative and spacy in a way that anticipates the ambient music of Brian Eno and the more contemporary Orb and Moby. Two different versions of the same song show up here ("Little Red Riding Hood Hit the Road"), but that's not a criticism as much as a statement of fact. The backing musicians are a classy bunch of veteran English avant-garde, artrock types (Hugh Hopper, Richard Sinclair, Fred Frith) who play with great skill and style. The music tends to be melancholy, but is not self-pitying or lachrymose. This is prime Wyatt in the early part of his post-accident career. That they are both on one disc makes for rewarding, if difficult, listening. *—John Dougan*

○ **Old Rottenhat** / 1985 / Gramavision ◆◆◆◆

Peel Sessions / 1987 / Dutch East India ◆◆◆
This appearance on John Peel's BBC Radio show promoted Robert's

then current single "I'm a Believer" and his *Rock Bottom* album. The versions on this disc are minimal compared to the original album versions; they consist of Wyatt's vocal and piano over an organ drone. The clever "Soup Song" definitely benefits from this treatment. *—Jim Powers*

○ **Compilation** / 1990 / Gramavision ◆◆◆◆
Somewhat erroneously titled, this is not a collection of Wyatt's work but rather 1981's *Nothing Can Stop Us Now* and 1985's *Old Rottenhat* on one CD. A bit strident politically and a tad cynical, these are, however, wonderful records built upon righteous indignation that is never cruel or simplistic. As with much of Wyatt's work, these recordings are emotionally complex, somewhat ambiguous, and always rewarding. *—John Dougan*

Dondestan / 1991 / Rhino ◆◆◆

○ **Mid-Eighties** / 1993 / Gramavision ◆◆◆◆

Floatsam Jetsam / 1994 / Rough Trade ◆◆◆
Not for the neophytes, this is a spectacular collection of unreleased oddities that span the years 1968-1990. Included are Wyatt's work with Jimi Hendrix (Soft Machine toured America as Hendrix's opening act in 1968) and his work with veteran avantgardists Lol Coxhill and Dagmar Krause. Nothing here matches Wyatt's most important work, but for those so inclined, this is a unique opportunity to explore some of the hidden nooks and crannies of an always-interesting artist's career. Caveat emptor: as with *Going Back a Bit*, this is an expensive English import. *— John Dougan*

● **Going Back a Bit: A Little History of Robert Wyatt** / 1994 / Virgin ◆◆◆◆
A wonderfully compiled 28-track, two-CD set that includes some of Wyatt's work with Soft Machine and his short-lived band of radical politicos Matching Mole (who, frankly, are not very interesting). Also, this generous set includes some outtakes and unreleased material. As for a basic overview of Wyatt's career that's doesn't skimp on the strong stuff and provides a sense of chronology, you can't do much better. The lone drawback is that the set is only available as a pricy English import. But if you've got the time and money, it's well worth the investment. *—John Dougan*

BOOK

◆◆◆◆ **Wrong Movements: A Robert Wyatt History**, by Michael King (SAF, UK, 1994). Robert Wyatt is that real rarity in the world of rock: a performer who's managed to combine the personal with the political, and who has kept abreast of changing cutting-edge underground rock styles for decades, displaying a penchant for artistic growth and relevance that has eluded almost every other rock musician of note who first came to prominence in the '60s. This isn't so much a biography as an extremely well-done scrapbook, arranged chronologically, weaving quotes from Wyatt and his many professional associates around many photos, press clippings, and listings documenting all of his known performances and recordings. Following Wyatt from his Canterbury beginnings with the Wilde Flowers through his progressive rock days with the Soft Machine and Matching Mole, past the 1973 accident that left him paralyzed from the waist down (and slowed his artistic motivation not in the least), right up through his solo recordings from the mid-'70s through the present, it also has a thorough discography. Wyatt comes off as a figure of rare intelligence, humor, and humility for a rock musician, offering many interesting insights both musical and political. *—Richie Unterberger*

X

X

Group, Punk, Alternative Pop/Rock

X was a Los Angeles-based punk rock band of the '80s. It was an outstanding critical success, especially in its first years of record making, but it never broke through to the kind of record sales necessary to sustain a band on a national level. X was formed in the winter of 1977-1978 by singer and bassist John Doe (b. Feb 24, 1954), guitarist Billy Zoom (b. Feb 20, late 1940s), singer Exene Cervenka (b. Feb 1, 1956), and D. J. Bonebrake (b. Dec 8, 1955).

Over the next couple of years, they rose to the top of a punk rock scene that had begun to emerge just as the ones in New York and London were fading away. The group signed to the local Slash label and released their debut album, *Los Angeles* (produced by Ray Manzarek of the Doors), in 1980. The album, with its driving rock, led by Zoom's Chuck Berry-influenced guitar, and the co-lead vocals of Cervenka and Doe on a series of poetic, socially conscious lyrics, was a critical success and sold well for an album on a small label. *Wild Gift* (1981) did even better, even reaching the national charts. Inevitably, X then signed to a major label, Elektra, and went from being a big fish in a small pond to the opposite. Their third album, *Under the Big Black Sun* (1982), was well received, but *More Fun in the New World* (1983) and *Ain't Love Grand* (1985) failed to expand their audience or to excite critics the way earlier records had done. Billy Zoom left X in late 1985 and was replaced by former Blasters guitarist Dave Alvin, who had played with Cervenka and Doe in a country-rock spin-off band, the Knitters. Tony Gilkyson, formerly of Lone Justice, was added as a second guitarist in March 1986. This quintet recorded *See How We Are* (1987) (though Alvin had quit for a solo career before it was released); it was considered a critical comeback but its sales were unimpressive. X released a double live album in 1988, then announced a hiatus. Both Cervenka and Doe have made solo albums during the next five years.

X reunited in 1993, releasing the *Hey Zeus!* album and touring the country; although the album received respectable reviews, it didn't sell very many copies. — *William Ruhlmann*

○ **Los Angeles** / 1980 / Slash ♦♦♦♦

Although classified as punk because of their simple hard rock sound and caustic lyrics ("The World's a Mess; It's in My Kiss"), X always had more of a rockabilly edge, courtesy of former Gene Vincent guitarist Billy Zoom, and were always funnier than the punk label implies, which may be why they were a cut above their competition. — *William Ruhlmann*

○ **Wild Gift** / 1981 / Slash ♦♦♦♦

As with many groups, X had more good songs in their repertoire than could fit on their debut, and their second album presents the rest. Appropriately, the two albums have been packaged together on a single CD. — *William Ruhlmann*

○ **Under the Big Black Sun** / 1982 / Elektra ♦♦♦♦

Unlike many groups, X responded to the pressure to write a new body of material after their initial burst of songs, by coming up with the goods, especially "The Hungry Wolf" and "Riding with Mary." — *William Ruhlmann*

○ **More Fun in the New World** / 1983 / Elektra ♦♦♦♦

More Fun in the New World is essentially a continuation of the sound X began to fashion on *Under the Big Black Sun*. While the musical direction of the album isn't as focused as its predecessor, the songwriting is just as accomplished, featuring highlights like "The New World," "Breathless," and "I Must Not Think Bad Thoughts." — *Stephen Thomas Erlewine*

Ain't Love Grand! / 1985 / Elektra ♦♦

X's final album with Billy Zoom suffered from a slick, hard rock production that tended to dampen the terse, nervous energy of the band. The storming "Burning House of Love" manages to break free of the constraints of the production, but most of the record is chained to a conventional hard rock sound that doesn't fit the band's style. — *Stephen Thomas Erlewine*

○ **See How We Are** / 1987 / Elektra ♦♦♦♦

X had moved toward becoming more of a mainstream hard-rock act by the time of their last studio album and, given how good the song "4th of July" is, it's a shame its writer, Dave Alvin, didn't stay with the band long enough to contribute more. — *William Ruhlmann*

Live at the Whiskey a Go-Go / 1988 / Elektra ♦♦♦

A ferocious live set featuring six new songs and 18 classic X tracks, *Live at the Whiskey A Go-Go on the Fabulous Sunset Strip* is seething with energy and eclipses their previous two albums in terms of sheer power. After showing signs of life with this set, the band called it quits shortly after its release; they reunited three years later. — *Stephen Thomas Erlewine*

★ **Los Angeles/Wild Gift** / Sep. 20, 1988 / Slash ♦♦♦♦♦

Hey Zeus! / Jun. 8, 1993 / Big Life ♦♦

Hey Zeus! isn't an embarrassing reunion effort, but it isn't particularly engaging, which is partially due to the overly-slick production, but it's also because the quality of the songs is decidedly uneven. — *Stephen Thomas Erlewine*

Unclogged / 1995 / ♦♦♦

Unclogged is comprised of acoustic versions of many of X's classic songs. The new setting reveals the quality of John Doe and Exene Cervenka's songwriting and the eerie power of their harmonies, as well as the depth of Doe's country and rock & roll roots. — *Stephen Thomas Erlewine*

X-Ray Spex

Group, Punk

One of the great English punk bands of the late '70s, there is only one thing wrong with the careers of X-Ray Spex and lead singer Poly Styrene—they didn't record enough music. Formed in 1976 by school friends Marion Elliot (Styrene) and Susan Whitby (saxophonist Lora Logic), X-Ray Spex exploded onto the punk scene with one of the era's great singles, the feminist punk rallying cry "Oh Bondage, Up Yours." With Logic's sax stating the melody semitunefully and Jak Airport's guitar laying down a wash of distorted chords, Poly's vocal, especially on the chorus, is a marvel. Along with the early Sex Pistols and Clash singles, this was one of punk rock's great moments.

So, too, was X-Ray Spex's debut LP *Germ Free Adolescents*, which was great in spite of "Oh Bondage" not being on it (a situation that would be rectified with the 1993 CD reissue). Lora Logic was gone (to form Essential Logic), but her replacement Rudi Thompson played in as rudimentary a fashion, but stayed in tune a little more. The songs were guitar-driven punk-pop that combined outrage and aggression with a sense of alienation and disenfranchisement about rampant commerciality and an increasingly sterile and artificial world. Poly's songs were more likely to be about drowning in a sea of corporate-designed consumer fantasies than straight-out attacks against the government. This didn't mean the songs were any less political; they simply attacked the zeitgeist from a different vantage point.

Tragically, there was no second X-Ray Spex record. But there was Poly Styrene's only full-length solo record, *Translucence*. Abandoning completely the loud guitars of X-Ray Spex, *Translucence* is quiet and jazzy in a way that anticipates the work of Ben Watt and Tracey Thorn in *Everything But the Girl*. It's a bit of a shock coming after *Germ Free Adolescents*, but it's a beautiful album, and her singing, though not as exciting and unhinged, is frequently stunning. Consistent with her career up to this point, Poly Styrene dropped out of music entirely shortly after the release of *Translucence* and joined a London-based Hare Krishna sect. She emerged from "retirement" in 1986 with a wonderful EP titled *Gods and Goddesses*. Although rumored to be preparing another LP, she's been pretty quiet for the last decade. *—John Dougan*

● **Germ Free Adolescents** / 1978 / Blue Plate ✦✦✦✦
The CD adds "Oh Bondage, Up Yours," making this one of the five best punk records made. The excitement here is contagious, the songs smart and captivating, the playing energetic if occasionally sloppy. In other words, brilliant. Buy it today. *—John Dougan*

Live at the Roxy Club / 1991 / Receiver ✦✦

XTC

Group, Alternative Pop/Rock, New Wave
XTC was one of the smartest—and catchiest—British pop bands to emerge from the punk and new wave explosion of the late '70s. From the tense, jerky riffs of their early singles to the lushly arranged, meticulous pop of their later albums, XTC's music has always been driven by the hook-laden songwriting of guitarist Andy Partridge and bassist Colin Moulding. While popular success has eluded them in both Britain and America, the group has developed a devoted cult following in both countries, that remains loyal nearly 20 years after their first records.

Partridge, Moulding, and drummer Terry Chambers formed the first version of the band around 1976, calling themselves Star Park. As punk rock took off in 1977, the group changed their name to Helium Kidz and added former King Crimson keyboardist Barry Andrews. After being turned down by CBS Records, the band changed their name to XTC and secured a record contract with Virgin; they released their first EP, *3-D*, in October of 1977. *White Music*, the band's first full-length album, was recorded in a week and released by the end of the year. Critics praised the angular yet melodic pop, and the album reached number 38 in the U.K. charts. However, none of the singles released from the album charted (including "This Is Pop"), nor did "Are You Receiving Me?," the teaser single for their second album, *Go 2* (1978).

After returning from a brief U.S. tour, Andrews quit the band; he would eventually form the League of Gentlemen with Robert Fripp, as well as pursue a solo career. Guitarist David Gregory was added to the lineup after Andrews's departure and the group recorded their first charting single, "Life Begins at the Hop." XTC released their third album, the calmer, more pop-oriented *Drums and Wires*, that summer; the record climbed to number 37 on the charts, thanks to the hit single "Making Plans for Nigel." While *Drums and Wires* began to climb the U.S. charts, Partridge released his first solo album early in 1980; outside of the band's devoted fans, the record appeared without much fanfare.

XTC continued to smooth out their edges on 1980's *Black Sea*, bringing in elements of mid-'60s Beatles and Kinks to their guitar-driven pop; thanks to the singles "Generals and Majors" and "Towers of London," the album was the group's most successful American album, peaking at number 41 while reaching number 16 on the British charts. Released the following year, *English Settlement* featured more complex arrangements, as well as more intellectual lyrics, particularly from Andy Partridge. Nevertheless, the album was XTC's biggest success in the U.K., reaching number five on the album charts and launching the Top Ten single, "Senses Working Overtime."

While on tour in March of 1982, Partridge collapsed while on stage, suffering from exhaustion. Less than a month later, he collapsed again with a stomach ulcer. The band cancelled the tour shortly after his second collapse, prompting Chambers to leave the group. In November, Partridge announced that XTC would never play live again, concentrating on recording instead; he also blamed his collapses on intense stage fright. As the band completed their new album, a compilation called *Waxworks—Some Singles (1977-1982)* was released at the end of the year. *Mummer*, the first album the studio-bound XTC recorded, appeared in the summer of 1983; former Glitter Band member Pete

Phipps recorded the drum tracks for the record. XTC refused to tour for the record, which caused some tension between the band and Virgin, and was presumably the reason why "Love on a Farmboy's Wages" didn't make it past number 50 on the charts. Recording under the name the Three Wise Men, the group released the holiday single "Thanks for Christmas" at the end of the year.

Released in the fall of 1984, *The Big Express* essentially followed the same pattern as *Mummer*, yet it charted higher in the U.K. XTC released a psychedelic parody album, *25 O'Clock*, under the name the Dukes of Stratosphear in 1985. After a difficult recording session with producer Todd Rundgren, the pastoral *Skylarking* appeared in the fall of 1986. Upon its release the album was hailed as a masterwork by critics, even though the band were claiming they were unsatisfied with the production. *Skylarking* was a bigger hit in the U.S. than it was in the U.K., spending over six months on the charts and peaking at number 70.

XTC recorded another Dukes of Stratosphear album, *Psonic Psunspot*, in 1987; the two Stratosphear albums were collected on one disc the following year. *Oranges and Lemons* (1989) reworked the psychedelia of the Stratosphear side-project, leaving out much of the loopy humor and replacing it with a Ray Davies-inspired nostalgia. The album was a minor hit in both Britain and America, reaching number 28 and number 44, respectively; "Mayor of Simpleton" became XTC's only charting U.S. single, reaching number 72 while peaking at number 46 on the British charts. Three years later, the group released *Nonsuch*, an album that recalled both *Pet Sounds* and *Revolver*. Like every XTC record, its critical acclaim was greater than its sales—the album dropped out of the British charts after two weeks. In America, *Nonsuch* was more successful, reaching number 97 and staying on the charts for 11 weeks.

XTC's lack of commercial success isn't because their music isn't accessible—their bright, occasionally melancholy, melodies flow with more grace than most bands—it has more to do with the group constantly being out of step with the times. However, the band has left behind a remarkably rich and varied series of albums that make a convincing argument that XTC is the great lost pop band. *—Stephen Thomas Erlewine*

White Music / Jan. 1978 / Geffen ✦✦✦
XTC's first full album shows the band going full throttle in true punk spirit. More dissonant than their latter period, the young band shines with directionless energy and a good sense of humor. Highlights include the catchy singles, "This Is Pop" and "Radios in Motion" as well as a jumpy version of "All Along the Watchtower." Their first release, *3D EP*, has been appended to the CD version. *—Chris Woodstra*

Go 2 / Feb. 1978 / Geffen ✦✦
The band's second album, *Go 2*, continues in the same high energy vein as *White Music* with slightly less memorable results. *—Chris Woodstra*

○ **Drums & Wires** / 1979 / Geffen ✦✦✦✦
By the release of the Steve Lillywhite-produced *Drums and Wires*, XTC had developed a unique sound that integrated (and plundered) late-'70s new wave, '60s-style pop, and psychedelia. The album produced XTC's first big British hit, "Making Plans for Nigel" (number 17 UK). *—Rick Clark*

○ **Black Sea** / 1980 / Geffen ✦✦✦✦
On *Black Sea*, again produced by Steve Lillywhite, XTC turned influences (like the Beatles and Beach Boys) inside out with agitated rhythms and mildly dissonant instrumental voicings. *Black Sea* generated four moderate British hit singles. One of them, "Towers of London," features a marvelously twisted Badfinger-style guitar hook set against a wonderfully gallumping bass line. "Respectable Street" is another standout on this, one of their best albums. *—Rick Clark*

○ **Waxworks: Some Singles 1977-1982** / 1982 / Geffen ✦✦✦✦
This is a smartly assembled collection of the band's better early tracks. *—Rick Clark*

○ **English Settlement** / 1982 / Geffen ✦✦✦✦
English Settlement, a double-album set, heightened XTC's stateside visibility with the track "Senses Working Overtime." Unfortunately, the album lacked the consistency of *Black Sea*, primarily because of the flat-sounding production, which seemed to steal the impact of the music. *—Rick Clark*

Beeswax: Some B-Sides 1977-1982 / 1982 / Virgin ✦✦✦
A nice companion to *Waxworks, Beeswax* does a fine job of collecting the B-sides to the singles up to 1982. While these songs were often as engaging as the A-sides, their addition to the CDs as bonus tracks now makes this collection redundant. —*Chris Woodstra*

Mummer / 1983 / Geffen ✦✦✦
With a couple of exceptions, *Mummer* is a relaxed, somewhat flat-sounding affair. Andy Partridge still manages to get a little venom out with the acidic "Funk Pop 'a Roll." Other highlights are Colin Moulding's "Love on a Farmboy's Wages" (number 50 U.K.), "Wonderland," and "Great Fire." —*Rick Clark*

The Big Express / 1984 / Geffen ✦✦✦
Following up the relatively somnolent *Mummer, The Big Express* was a return to the playful upbeat pop/rock of some of XTC's previous works. "The Everyday Story of a Small Town" is a highlight, as well as "All You Pretty Girls." —*Rick Clark*

● **Compact XTC: The Singles 1978-85** / 1985 / Virgin ✦✦✦✦
Taking the *Waxworks* collection one step further, this 18-track disc collects all of the pre-*Skylarking* singles. A nice place for beginners to start. —*Chris Woodstra*

★ **Skylarking** / 1986 / Geffen ✦✦✦✦✦
With *Skylarking,* XTC addressed coming-of-age issues like marriage ("Big Day"), supporting a family ("Earn Enough for Us"), and the existence of a loving God ("Dear God"), while clothing them with performances that suggested XTC hadn't lost the capacity for childlike wonder. Todd Rundgren's production of *Skylarking* is one of his best, bathing the album in a pleasantly trippy soundstage. Other highlights include "The Meeting Place" and "Grass." —*Rick Clark*

○ **Oranges & Lemons** / 1989 / Geffen ✦✦✦✦
Compared to their best work, *Oranges & Lemons* is a little uneven—a case of a double album that would have made a great single release if XTC had pared it down. *Oranges & Lemons* did produce two big alternative pop/rock hits, "The Mayor of Simpleton" and "King for a Day." Other highlights include the optimistic "The Loving" and "Pink Thing." —*Rick Clark*

Explode Together (The Dub Experiments '78-'80) / 1990 / Virgin ✦✦
Between 1978 and 1980, Andy Partridge experimented with the power of the studio—the results were the puzzling releases of *Go+* (an EP of dub remixes of the *Go 2* album) and *Take Away/Lure of the Salvage* (an electronic collage based on the *Drums and Wires* album and credited under the name Mr. Partridge). *Explode Together* combines the two unusual projects. This is purely experimental music for the curious completists only. —*Chris Woodstra*

Rag 'N' Bone Buffet / 1990 / Geffen ✦✦✦
This is a collection of B-sides, live performances, and alternative versions culled from throughout their career. Among the oddities contained here is a cleaned-up-for-radio version of "Respectable Street," from *Black Sea*. Among the live recordings are "Another Satellite," taken from a BBC broadcast, and a great version of "Scissor Man," originally on *Drums and Wires*. Also included are various solo recordings by bandmates Andy Partridge and Colin Moulding.

All in all, *Rag 'N' Bone Buffet* is a desirable item for any XTC fan looking to round out their collection of this band's work. —*Rick Clark*

○ **Nonsuch** / Oct. 1992 / Geffen ✦✦✦✦
Nonsuch, produced by Gus Dudgeon (Elton John, Bowie), trims the excesses found on *Oranges and Lemons* and recalls the pastoral refinement of *Skylarking* and the rocky edge found on *The Big Express*. Andy Partridge's "The Ballad of Peter Pumpkinhead," "The Disappointed," and "Crocodile" are highlights, as are Colin Moulding's "Books Are Burning" and "Bungalow." It's one of their better albums. —*Rick Clark*

Drums And Wireless: BBC Live / 1994 / Virgin ✦✦✦
Drums and Wireless does a good job of collecting the bulk of the band's BBC appearances from 1977 to 1989—many of which have previously been available only on inferior bootlegs. While many band's BBC sessions differ only slightly from the studio recordings, XTC was able to stretch out on their sessions for significantly different interpretations. This is a necessary addition to any fan's collection. —*Chris Woodstra*

Xymox

Group, Alternative Pop/Rock
Amsterdam's Xymox started out as the Clan of Xymox, playing gloomy, Gothic Euro-dance music. Their name comes from the word "zymotic," meaning "of fermentation." They shortened their name to Xymox and took a new direction in 1989, playing more upbeat, commercially-oriented pop. The group, which includes Ronny Moerings, Pieter Nooten, Frank Weyzig, and Anke Wolbert, has been criticized as lacking much distinction from its peers. —*Steve Huey*

○ **Clan of Xymox** / 1985 / Combat ✦✦✦✦
● **Twist of Shadows** / 1989 / Wing ✦✦✦✦
Phoenix / 1991 / Wing ✦✦✦
Metamorphosis / 1993 / Jrs ✦✦✦
Headclouds / 1994 / Off Beat ✦✦

Y

Yachts

Group, Rock & Roll, New Wave, Power Pop/Anglo-Pop
Power-pop/new wave group, the Yachts, was formed in 1978 by Liverpool art-schoolmates Henry Priestman (vocals, keyboards), Martin Watson (guitar, vocals), Martin Dempsey (bass, vocals), Bob Bellis (drums, vocals) and J.J. Campbell (vocals). They signed to Stiff Records after a supporting spot for Elvis Costello in 1977, releasing the endlessly catchy "Suffice to Say" single (produced by Will Birch) before following Costello to Radar Records. They released two power-pop classics, *Yachts* (1979) and *Yachts Without Radar* (1980), before disbanding in the early '80s when power-pop fell from favor. —*Chris Woodstra*

● **Yachts** / 1979 / Radar ✦✦✦
On the Yachts' self-titled debut (also known as *S.O.S* due to the misleading cover art), the former art-school students couldn't completely leave behind their arty pretentions, but power-pop eventually prevails. Frontman Henry Priestman's tacky organ flourishes surprisingly complement the typical power-pop arrangements. Includes "Suffice to Say," the striking debut single, as well as the infectious "Yachting Type" and "Look Back in Love." —*Chris Woodstra*

Yachts Without Radar / 1980 / Radar ✦✦
The second album, titled to reflect their parting of ways with their British label (Radar), is a mediocre follow-up and the band's parting shot. —*Chris Woodstra*

The Yardbirds

Group, Blues Rock, British Invasion, Psychedelic
Formed in 1963, the Yardbirds are one of the most influential groups in the history of rock & roll. (The term "Yardbird" came from the designation given to hobos in a Jack Kerouac novel.) During the course of their career, the Yardbirds featured three of rock's greatest guitarists: Eric Clapton, Jeff Beck, and Jimmy Page. During their early period with Clapton, they pursued a highly charged style of electric blues, highlighted best on *Five Live Yardbirds*. Clapton split when he sensed the band was getting too pop with the release of their first single, "For Your Love."

Jeff Beck brought on phase two of the band's development with a highly experimental style that pioneered the application of feedback, fuzz, and unusual melodic scales. It was here that the Yardbirds achieved their creative peak, with songs like "I'm a Man," "Heart Full of Soul," "Evil Hearted You," "Lost Woman," and the masterly "Shapes of Things."

Around the time Beck began unraveling at the seams, Jimmy Page came on board. For a very brief time, the Yardbirds had a dream twin-lead guitar lineup, best chronicled on the hits "Happenings Ten Years Time Ago" and "Stroll On," from the movie *Blow Up*.

After Beck left, Page hung on for a little over a year, recording the rather lightweight album *Little Games*. Shortly afterwards, the band fell apart, when Page formed Led Zeppelin. Lead singer Keith Relf helped form the art-rock group Renaissance and bassist Paul Samwell-Smith went on to a successful production career for artists like Cat Stevens and Carly Simon. Even though the Yardbirds weren't among the most commercially successful bands of the '60s British Invasion, their profound impact on rock laid the groundwork for hard blues-based rock and heavy metal.

Of particular note to those seeking out the best-sounding Yardbirds discs: none of their CD reissues utilize the original first-generation masters. EMI England has them but won't license them out, due to an unpaid studio bill dating back from the mid-'60s. On the other hand, the Edsel import of *Roger the Engineer* sounds impeccable. The reason: the band owns the original masters. —*Rick Clark*

○ **Five Live Yardbirds** / Dec. 1964 / Rhino ✦✦✦✦
Recorded live at London's Marquee Club, *Five Live Yardbirds* is the best document of Eric Clapton's work with the band. Tracks like "Too Much Monkey Business," "Got Love If You Want It," and "Smokestack Lightning" were good representations of the Yardbirds's "rave-ups," which were open-ended improvisations that helped lay the groundwork for groups like Cream and the Jimi Hendrix Experience. —*Rick Clark*

○ **Roger the Engineer** / 1966 / Edsel ✦✦✦✦
Roger the Engineer is a classic Yardbirds studio album, thanks to tracks like "Lost Woman," "Over Under Sideways Down," "What Do You Want?," "Psycho Daisies," and "Ever Since the World Began." Not available in the States, this British import (on Edsel) is the best-sounding Yardbirds CD by a long shot and a must-own for fans of this band. —*Rick Clark*

With Sonny Boy Williamson / 1966 / Mercury ✦✦
★ **Greatest Hits, Vol. 1: 1964-1966** / 1986 / Rhino ✦✦✦✦✦
Sonically, these tracks fail to match the brilliance and warmth of the original vinyl pressings, but *Greatest Hits* has more punch. "For Your Love" is an exception, with the record version sounding extremely compressed. Of the various Yardbird collections that exist, this is still the most intelligently chosen, even though it lacks key tracks from *Roger the Engineer*. —*Rick Clark*

On Air / 1991 / Band Of Joy ✦✦✦
Like most of the major British Invasion bands, the Yardbirds recorded many sessions for the BBC during their heyday. *On Air* contains 27 of these, recorded between 1965 and 1968; 21 of them feature Jeff Beck, the rest Jimmy Page (Eric Clapton is not featured on any). The BBC sessions offered listeners the opportunity to hear groups in a relatively live setting with relatively good sound quality, and that's basically what you get here. Most of their major hits—"For Your Love," "Heart Full of Soul," "Shapes of Things," "Over Under Sideways Down," "Still I'm Sad"—are included. By and large, these versions don't differ enormously from the studio cuts, with slightly different arrangements and guitar solos. One could argue, of course, that with a band so responsible for pushing rock guitar to the stratosphere, different guitar solos are a tasty discovery. And they are interesting, but they don't outdo the stellar studio renditions. Of most interest, if not highest quality, are a few covers never waxed by the group on their official releases: "Dust My Blues," "The Sun Is Shining," Garnett Mimms' "My Baby," and Dylan's "Most Likely You'll Go Your Way." On cuts like "I'm Not Talking" and "Too Much Monkey Business," Beck's pyrotechnics are truly breathtaking. But generally this release is more for Yardbirds fans than novices. —*Richie Unterberger*

○ **Vol. 1: Smokestack Lightning** / 1991 / Sony ✦✦✦✦
This double-disc set focuses on tracks from *For Your Love* and *Having a Rave-Up with the Yardbirds*. Included are live tracks recorded at the Crawdaddy Club while touring with Sonny Boy Williamson. Most of these tracks on *Smokestack Lightning* (as well as *Blues, Backtracks*) were mastered off of safety tapes, as opposed to the original masters, since EMI England has possession

of them. Considering that EMI won't release the masters to anyone, this is a respectable sound—though not as good as the first vinyl pressings. —*Rick Clark*

○ **Vol. 2: Blues, Backtrack's and Shapes of Things** / 1991 / Sony ✦✦✦✦
Another double-disc set, this covers some later hits (including the classic future-rock of "Shapes of Things"), *Roger the Engineer* outtakes, and various other oddities. The sound on some of the outtakes is pretty respectable, considering some of them were taken from the original acetates. —*Rick Clark*

The Yardbirds Little Games Sessions & More / 1992 / EMI America ✦✦✦
This digitally remastered 39-track, double-disc set covers Jimmy Page's tenure with the Yardbirds. This period didn't contain the band's best work, mainly because Mickie Most's poppish production reined in the band's experimental strengths. Nevertheless, tracks like "Little Games," "Puzzles," "Smile on Me," "Drinking Muddy Water," and a wonderful acoustic version of Jimmy Page's "White Summer" make this a good overview of the Yardbird's final stretch as a band. This set includes extensive liner notes and discography—a real treat for fans. —*Rick Clark*

Yaz

Group, Dance-Pop, Techno-Pop/Dance, New Wave
Yaz was the American name taken by Yazoo, a British duo made up of former Depeche Mode synthesizer player Vince Clarke and singer Alison Moyet (b.Jun 18, 1961). The two stayed together only about a year and a half (1982-1983), but that was long enough to score four British hit singles and two top-selling albums. Moyet then went solo and Clarke eventually formed another successful duo, Erasure. —*William Ruhlmann*

○ **Upstairs at Eric's** / 1982 / Sire ✦✦✦✦
Yaz's music is spare, striking electronic backup contrasted with full-throated, emotional singing, but one shouldn't discount some remarkable songwriting, especially the hits "Don't Go," "Only You," and "Situation." —*William Ruhlmann*

● **You & Me Both** / 1983 / Sire ✦✦✦✦
Perhaps a more consistent collection overall than the first album, this one demonstrates that the duo was anything but played out. While both have gone on to successful careers, you can't help regretting that this is the end of Yaz. —*William Ruhlmann*

Yello

Group, Art-Rock/Progressive-Rock
This group from Switzerland is a picture of professionalism, although none of the members are trained musicians. Boris Blank, Dieter Meier, and Carlos Peron do not go overboard trying to be innovative and original, but that is certainly the outcome. They have created a distinctive and bright listening style, unusual and very simplistic, not based on traditional harmony or pretensions. Their rich, unique sound and strong emphasis on modern synthesizer technology make this group one of the most significant in contemporary music history. —*Valdimir Bogdanov*

○ **Stella** / 1985 / Mercury ✦✦✦✦
This is one of their disco-oriented albums. Includes "Desire" and "Sometimes." —*Vladimir Bogdanov*

One Second / 1987 / Mercury ✦✦✦
This album offers a great variety of styles, effects, textures, and rhythms. Includes the songs "The Rhythm Divine" and "The Secret Fazida." —*Vladimir Bogdanov*

○ **Flag** / 1988 / Mercury ✦✦✦✦
This is Yello's most dynamic album, with excellent composition. Picking highlights would be difficult, since the songs segue, and the album just begs to be listened to as a whole. —*Vladimir Bogdanov*

● **Essential** / Smash ✦✦✦✦
This good compilation will satisfy fans of their infamous "Oh Yeah." —*AMG*

Yes

Group, Art-Rock/Progressive-Rock, Pop/Rock
Yes is, without a doubt, the definitive English progressive-rock band, purveyors of cosmic lyrics, virtuoso playing, and vast musical tapestries topped off with heart-stoppingly gorgeous melodies

and sealed with a rock & roll kick. Yes was formed in London in 1968 by singer Jon Anderson and bassist Chris Squire, both owners of high, clear tenor voices that blend seamlessly in the band's trademark harmonies. The history of Yes is one of constant changes in personnel, but the group's most celebrated lineup came about when founding members Anderson, Squire, and drummer Bill Bruford, plus guitarist Steve Howe (who had enlisted in 1970), were joined in 1971 by keyboard whiz Rick Wakeman. Thus constituted, the band cut its signature tune, "Roundabout" (from the fourth Yes album, *Fragile*), not to mention the sumptuously symphonic magnum opus *Close to the Edge*. A further series of comings and goings led to a disastrous 1980 lineup (documented on "Drama") in which Squire was the only remaining original member. After a three-year hiatus, a revamped Yes (Anderson, Squire, original keyboardist Tony Kaye, long-time drummer Alan White, and South African guitarist Trevor Rabin) emerged in 1983 with a streamlined, commercialized sound, topping the charts with the danceable "Owner of a Lonely Heart." Anderson split in 1988, teaming up with some old cohorts as Anderson Bruford Wakeman Howe—essentially a rival version of Yes! The two bands joined forces in 1991 as an eight-man "mega-Yes," combining their separately recorded efforts on *Union.* —*Michael P. Dawson*

Yes / Oct. 15, 1969 / Atlantic ✦✦✦
Early pop/folk-rock. Their first, and it should be taken as such. —*Bruce Eder*

Time and a Word / Nov. 2, 1970 / Atlantic ✦✦✦
A more ambitious second album, in search of a style. —*Bruce Eder*

○ **The Yes Album** / Mar. 19, 1971 / Atlantic ✦✦✦✦
This is the album that first gave shape to the established Yes sound, built around science-fiction concepts, folk melodies, and soaring organ, guitar, and vocal showpieces. "Your Move" actually got some airplay as a single, and "Starship Troopers" became a much-loved part of the band's set. —*Bruce Eder*

★ **Fragile** / Jan. 4, 1972 / Atlantic ✦✦✦✦✦
The breakthrough album for the band, in which the science-fiction and fantasy elements of the songs became dominant and the addition of Rick Wakeman on organ added a larger-than-life element to the group's sound. Ironically, the album was a patchwork job, hastily assembled to help cover the cost of Wakeman's expanded array of instruments, but the short form of "Roundabout" clicked on AM radio, album buyers liked the long version, plus the rest of the material they found, and the band was made. —*Bruce Eder*

☆ **Close to the Edge** / Sep. 13, 1972 / Atlantic ✦✦✦✦✦
The group's sound broke more boundaries here, as side-long suites allowed Jon Anderson even more opportunity for vocal acrobatics and Wakeman an even bigger canvas on which to paint his electronic-synthesizer swirls and organ arpeggios. The poetry also had a peculiarly hypnotic quality, which overcame its relatively obscure passages. —*Bruce Eder*

Yessongs / May 4, 1973 / Atlantic ✦✦✦
The best live album to emerge from the entire art-rock scene, a compendium of blazing performances covering the previous three studio albums by the group and the accompanying solo career of Rick Wakeman. Some of the performances are superior to their studio originals, although "And You and I" is something of a disappointment next to the version on *Close to the Edge.* —*Bruce Eder*

Tales from Topographic Oceans / Jan. 9, 1974 / Atlantic ✦
This was where the Yes spell began to break, partly due to the excesses inherent in a double album containing one long song per side. Jon Anderson's fascination with Eastern religions swelled to mammoth proportions here, and while individual parts of this album are gorgeous and fascinating, the piece as a whole proved overwhelming to many critics. —*AMG*

Relayer / Dec. 5, 1974 / Atlantic ✦✦

Yesterdays / Feb. 27, 1975 / Atlantic ✦✦✦
A slightly disappointing compendium of odd early tracks. For true fanatics. Supplanted, in part, by *Yesyears.* —*Bruce Eder*

Going for the One / Jul. 7, 1977 / Atlantic ✦✦✦

Tormato / Sep. 20, 1978 / Atlantic ✦✦

Drama / Aug. 18, 1980 / Atlantic ✦✦✦

Yesshows / Nov. 24, 1980 / Arista ✦✦✦
A double album chronicling the late-'70s repertoire of the group, less interesting than *Yessongs* but probably the best compendium of this material that is likely to emerge. —*Bruce Eder*

○ **Classic Yes** / Nov. 30, 1981 / Atlantic ✦✦✦✦

○ **90125** / Nov. 7, 1983 / Atlantic ✦✦✦✦
A ridiculously successful "comeback" album with a slightly different membership. For completists. —*Bruce Eder*

Big Generator / Sep. 17, 1987 / Atlantic ✦✦
The four-years-in-the-making follow-up to Yes's comeback album, *90125*, *Big Generator* was also a million-selling hit, although not as successful as its predecessor, probably because the singles "Love Will Find a Way" (#30) and "Rhythm of Love" (#40) couldn't match "Owner of a Lonely Heart" from the previous LP, even if they were favorites on AOR radio at the time. Actually, it was the title track that was a carbon-copy of "Owner," so maybe that was the problem. More likely, though, "Owner" was a one-shot (courtesy of producer Trevor Horn), and as Yes asserted itself more here, they reverted more to their old style, making for some confusion. Nevertheless, this album was the group's last major hit. —*William Ruhlmann*

Union / 1991 / Arista ✦✦
The various Yes members settled their differences by putting together a mega-version of the band, featuring eight members from various eras, and recorded this compromise effort, on which they attempted to recapture the early '70s sound of Yes. AOR radio was willing, and the single "Lift Me Up" topped Billboard's Album Rock Tracks chart for six weeks, with two other cuts also making the list. But the single limped to #86 on the Hot 100, and although the album shot to #15 and went gold, this was a serious fall-off from previous sales, appropriate to an album that was one of those (increasingly frequent) corporate attempts to clone a band's old style. —*William Ruhlmann*

○ **Yesyears** / 1991 / Atlantic ✦✦✦✦
This four-CD set is sonically so far superior to the individual CDs by the group that on this basis alone it is worth owning. Unfortunately, there are important songs that didn't get the remastering treatment, and they are missed. —*Bruce Eder*

● **The Very Best of Yes** / 1993 / Atlantic ✦✦✦✦
The very best of Yes is hard to stick on merely one disc; this set includes tracks from each era of the band. Not essential, it's still a decent sampler. —*Rick Clark*

Talk / 1994 / Victory ✦✦
The tenth lineup of Yes features Jon Anderson, Trevor Rabin, Tony Kaye, Chris Squire, and Alan White. *Talk* makes some effort to get away from the group's indulgent art-rock pretensions, at least to the extent of using a spare, spacious production full of closely miked drums and sharp guitars. (No wonder, since guitarist Trevor Rabin produced the record.) Rabin and Anderson are the main composers, and they fail to come up with really distinctive songs, which may help explain why this album had a lower chart peak than any new Yes album since 1972 and a shorter chart run than any Yes album except the compilation album *Classic Yes*. In other words, a disaster. —*William Ruhlmann*

Yo La Tengo

Group, Alternative Pop/Rock
Those who claim that rock critics are little more than frustrated musicians have evidently spent little time listening to former critic Ira Kaplan's great band Yo La Tengo. Coming out of the Hoboken, NJ scene (sourcepoint: the very hip club Maxwell's) in the mid-'80s, Yo La Tengo (Spanish for "I've got it"; Kaplan took the expression in honor of a Latin ballplayer for his beloved New York Mets) is an extreme band in the sense that they ran the gamut from harsh, coruscating walls of feedback to supple, endearing folk-derived pop. But, despite the disparate nature of the two genres, Kaplan and his creative partner and wife Georgia Hubley make the two work seamlessly, and by doing so have created a large and excellent body of work that stands in stark contrast to the careerists and manipulators that glut the "alternative" landscape. As a former critic and compulsive record collector, Kaplan's influence on the band is one that prides eclecticism and unpredictability over career moves that would firmly ensconce Yo La Tengo in the profitable alternative rock sweepstakes. Because they are slippery and somewhat undefinable (which is a big part of their charm), Yo La Tengo will probably never be MTV's next-big-thing, nor will they have Soundgarden-like sales figures. And, if pressed, I bet Kaplan and Hubley wouldn't care all that much. Instead, they soldier on, recording great music for those whose taste for pop music runs the gamut from the Velvet Underground and

Sonic Youth to the Holy Modal Rounders and NRBQ. —*John Dougan*

○ **Ride the Tiger** / 1986 / Coyote/Twintone ✦✦✦✦
A fine debut that shows off this band's smarts and style. Not as aggressive in the noise department as some later releases, this is still a confident and assured record. As usual, Kaplan comes up with a cool, if fairly obscure cover or two (here it's Ray Davies's "Big Sky") as well as loading up the record with some fine originals. The presence of ex-Mission of Burma bassist Clint Conley as producer adds a touch of professionalism that doesn't detract from the album's cheery and insistent low-fi charm. —*John Dougan*

○ **New Wave Hot Dogs** / 1987 / Coyote/Twintone ✦✦✦✦
With heavy guitar and solid songs, they know that we know that they know it's too calculated, but it sounds good anyway. —*Robert Gordon*

○ **President Yo La Tengo/New Wave Hot Dogs** / 1989 / Twin/Tone ✦✦✦✦
Two records now available as a single CD, these really show off Yo La Tengo's ability to create musical extremes. *New Wave Hot Dogs* has the firm pop sense and strong songwriting of the debut, but *President Yo La Tengo* offers up a little more free-form skronk in the ten-minute live version of "The Evil That Men Do," a gloriously squalling, over-the-top crash and bash session which proves how liberating and fun sonic dissonance can be. Just in case you don't like that sort of thing, "Evil" also shows up as a straightahead folk-rock track. This is a great collection of material that, as well as anything else they have recorded, gets to the heart of what makes this band tick. —*John Dougan*

○ **President Yo La Tengo** / 1989 / Twin/Tone ✦✦✦✦
Features the 40-minute jam they've always wanted to do. —*Robert Gordon*

○ **Fakebook** / 1990 / Bar/None ✦✦✦✦
Recommending *Fakebook* as the best place to begin a relationship with Yo La Tengo is slightly disingenuous, mainly because Yo La Tengo has never made another record like it, and perhaps never will. So, as completely wonderful as this record is (and believe me, it is), it's an accurate representation of one side of Yo La Tengo, and assuming that everything sounds like *Fakebook* might be disappointing. A collection of cover songs that lean towards the idiosyncratic (e.g., Peter Stampfel, Daniel Johnston, Jad Fair), *Fakebook* is warm, low-key and lovely, with heartfelt singing and playing that never flags after hundreds of replays. It's impossible to imagine playing this record and not smiling and singing along. A big bonus is a great version of the Flamin' Groovies "You Tore Me Down." —*John Dougan*

May I Sing with Me / 1992 / Alias ✦✦✦
With song titles like "Mushroom Cloud of Hiss" and "Five-Cornered Drone (Crispy Duck)," *May I* is classic Yo La Tengo merging pop and noise in an awesome aural display. Songs start with Kaplan's repetitive (and very simple) chord changes, as Hubley and (at this juncture) regular bassist James McNew add layer after layer of supportive sound. During the noisier tracks (especially the aforementioned "Mushroom Cloud of Hiss"), the song explodes in paroxysms of feedback and drops the rhythmic pulse altogether, eventually returning the backbeat after a few minutes of white noise. That may not be everybody's cup of tea, but for those who like this adventurousness and recklessness, it's a lot of fun. —*John Dougan*

Upside Down / Apr. 1992 / Alias ✦✦✦

● **Painful** / 1993 / Matador ✦✦✦✦
Yo La Tengo has released several fine albums before, but only *Painful* encapsulates their folky guitar experimentalism perfectly. Alternating between dreamy Velvet Underground-style ballads and raving, Sonic Youth guitar squalls, *Painful* also finds the group improving their songwriting skills immeasurably. Before, they relied on soundscapes; now, the sound fleshes out their songs, from the trance-like "Nowhere Near" to the dense "From A Motel 6" and the two versions of "Big Day Coming," which cover both ends of the spectrum. A subtly addicting album. —*Stephen Thomas Erlewine*

Electr-O-Pura / 1995 / Matador ✦✦✦

Yo-Yo

Group, Rap
Yolanda Whitaker has been among the most sophisticated and un-

predictable female rappers around. She doesn't take an overtly feminist tack but urges young women to show sexual restraint and use their minds as well as their bodies. She's released two records as a leader.

Yo Yo came out less embracing and more confrontational on *You Better Ask Somebody,* her 1993 album. There was little compromise in her rapping, or the record's mood. Where before she'd sometimes seemed conciliatory, this time she was stark and combative, particularly in her demands for respect. *—Ron Wynn*

▸ **Make Way for the Motherlode** / 1991 / East West ◆◆◆◆
Intelligent, forceful, and affirmative rap from a woman whose cadence, tone, and delivery are as hard as any man on either coast and anywhere in-between. *—Ron Wynn*

▸ **Black Pearl [uncensored]** / 1992 / East West ◆◆◆◆
Yo-Yo's positive (but not simplistic or naive) messages regarding female sexuality, self-esteem and achievement were grounded in hard raps and thudding beats on this album, still her most complete and effective production. Unfortunately, it seemed that only cutesy material like "You Can't Play With My Yo-Yo" from her first release could get the widespread support and attention necessary for a hit. *—Ron Wynn*

The You Know Who Group

Group, Pop/Rock
Most likely an exploitative joke, but a fairly good one, the You Know Who Group were a calculated attempt to capitalize on the British Invasion by emulating the Mersey sound with anonymous studio players who purported to be a bonafide British group (and who were pictured with masks on the sleeve of their album). Masterminded by producer and arranger Bob Gallo, the group, if they could be called that, actually managed a small hit with "Roses Are Red, My Love." With their exaggerated fake British accents, moderately catchy, minor-chord heavy songs, and wheezing harmonica, they sounded like a low-rent Beau Brummels—an ironic twist, as the Beau Brummels were the first American group to successfully emulate the British Invasion sound. *—Richie Unterberger*

The You Know Who Group / 1965 / International Allied ◆◆◆
An instant collector's item, it's hard to determine just how comic these guys were in their intentions, with gratuitous "yeahs" and "woos" punctuating these hurriedly written and recorded imitations of the lowest common denominators of the British Invasion sound. Don't approach this hard-to-find album with serious expectations of first-class pop-rock; as a period curiosity, though, it has undeniable charm, and it comes off a lot better than many American productions that were trying to copy the British Invasion sound without a tongue in their cheek. *—Richie Unterberger*

Young M.C.

Group, Rap, Singer-Songwriter
Although his good looks and pop appeal would suggest he's beaten LL Cool J to the crossover punch, MC (Marvin) Young has pumped his own personality into some of rap's greatest across-the-board hits. "Bust a Move" and "Principal's Office," among others, hit harder than the similar work of Jazzy Jeff and the Fresh Prince, and the jokes last longer than the ones you'll find in the Fat Boys catalog. He also wrote Tone-Loc's smash single, "Funky Cold Medina" and co-wrote "Wild Thing."

Despite his enormous pop success, Young M.C. tried for a more hardcore effect on *What's the Flavor.* The results were mixed, but the general reaction was he was much better doing light material than trying to sound hard. *—John Floyd*

Brainstorm / 1989 / Capitol ◆◆◆
While *Brainstorm* was not a bad record, it didn't capture the energetic spark of his debut; consequently, the album wasn't the across-the-boards smash of *Stone Cold Rhymin',* even though it sounded quite similar. *—Stephen Thomas Erlewine*

● **Stone Cold Rhymin'** / 1989 / Delicious Vinyl ◆◆◆◆
Young MC's first album was a major hit, featuring pop-rap crossover classics like "Bust a Move" and "Principal's Office." With his friendly, clever rhyming and a warm, funky production dominating the album, *Stone Cold Rhymin'* was not only Young MC's most popular album, but also his best. *—Stephen Thomas Erlewine*

What's the Flavor? / 1993 / Capitol ◆◆◆
On his third album, Young MC was trying to recapture his audience, adding elements of jazz-rap—thanks to the production of A Tribe Called Quest's Ali Shaheed—to his pop-oriented style. While

it didn't rocket him back to the top of the charts, the results were agreeable and likeable, with only a couple of embarrassing tracks. *—Stephen Thomas Erlewine*

Neil Young

b. Nov. 12, 1945, Toronto, Canada
Rock & Roll, Country-Rock, Singer-Songwriter, Hard Rock, Folk-Rock
With the exception only of Bob Dylan, Neil Young is the most acclaimed and accomplished singer/songwriter of his generation. Born in Toronto, Young learned to play ukelele and then guitar in his teens, and played in a variety of groups. He moved to Los Angeles with his friend, bassist Bruce Palmer, and hooked up with Stephen Stills, Richie Furay, and Dewey Martin to form Buffalo Springfield in 1966. After the Springfield split in 1968, Young went solo, releasing his first album, *Neil Young,* an acoustic effort with strings, in January 1969. Characteristically, Young followed it only four months later with the hard rock *Everybody Knows This Is Nowhere,* backed by the electric three-piece band Crazy Horse; it became his first gold-selling album. Young joined Crosby, Stills & Nash in June 1969, and combined solo and group careers until the band split the following summer. His third solo album, *After the Gold Rush* (August 1970), reached the Top Ten and included his first Top 40 hit, "Only Love Can Break Your Heart." But Young's commercial peak came early in 1972, when he released the number one, three-million-selling album *Harvest,* which contained the chart-topping gold single "Heart of Gold."

Instead of following up such success, Young worked on the documentary film *Journey through the Past* (and its accompanying soundtrack album) for the rest of the year, then launched a concert tour in early 1973, by which time Crazy Horse's guitarist Danny Whitten had died of a heroin overdose. The tour was a ragged affair chronicled on the live album *Time Fades Away.* After it, Young recorded (but did not release) *Tonight's the Night,* which memorialized Whitten and Bruce Berry, a Young roadie who had also overdosed.

Young's first new studio album in 18 months, *On the Beach,* was released in the summer of 1974. Much of it was acoustic, and it expressed dire sentiments. He finally put out *Tonight's the Night* in the summer of 1975, and the hard-rocking *Zuma* the following autumn. In the spring of 1976, Young toured with Stephen Stills, and the two recorded the duo album *Long May You Run.* Young's next solo album was 1977's *American Stars 'n' Bars,* made up of studio tracks dating back three years. In the fall of 1977, he released *Decade,* a three-album (later two-CD) career retrospective. 1978 saw the release of *Comes a Time,* Young's most country-folk-oriented album since *Harvest,* and his first since *Harvest* to reach the Top Ten. In 1979 Young launched a tour with Crazy Horse under the banner *Rust Never Sleeps,* including a critically acclaimed album of the same name and, eventually, a tour film and a live album called *Live Rust.*

Young spent the better part of the '80s veering from one musical style to another, as his commercial fortunes declined. He turned to electronic music on *Trans,* to rockabilly on *Everybody's Rockin',* to country on *Old Ways,* and to horn-backed R&B on *This Note's for You.* In 1989, however, Young returned to his more familiar folk and rock styles for *Freedom,* and was rewarded with critical hosannas and his first gold album in a decade. The hard-rocking *Ragged Glory* was even more rapturously received, topping the *Village Voice* critic's poll for Best Album of 1990. In late 1991, Young issued a double live album, *Weld,* as well as *Arc,* an album of instrumental guitar feedback. He was said to be working on a boxed-set retrospective follow-up to *Decade.*

In 1992, Young was being hailed as "the Godfather of Grunge," as dozens of new rock & roll bands from Pearl Jam to the Jayhawks were claiming him as an influence. Naturally, Young backed away from the hard, overdriven rock of *Weld* and *Ragged Glory,* releasing the quiet *Harvest Moon,* the sequel to his country-rock landmark, *Harvest.* In 1993, he released a live album (*Unplugged*) while he worked on his long-awaited box set; also released another album recorded with Crazy Horse, *Sleeps With Angels,* in late summer of 1994. The following summer Young released *Mirror Ball,* which was recorded with Pearl Jam. *—William Ruhlmann*

Neil Young / Jan. 1969 / Reprise ◆◆◆
Neil Young's debut solo album, after three records with Buffalo Springfield, found him in a quiet mood, his songs frequently backed only by acoustic guitar and strings arranged by Jack

Nitzsche. There were instrumentals and a long, Dylanish ballad called "The Last Trip to Tulsa," while the most memorable song was "The Loner." Young failed to attract an audience with this approach—*Neil Young* was his only solo album to miss the charts—and he immediately turned around and produced a rock album, *Everybody Knows This Is Nowhere*, which appeared within months and established him as a solo star. — *William Ruhlmann*

☆ **Everybody Knows This Is Nowhere** / May 1969 / Reprise ✦✦✦✦✦
Young's breakthrough album is also the first one to feature the backup of Crazy Horse for a seminal rock session that produced the Young favorites "Cinnamon Girl," "Down by the River," and "Cowgirl in the Sand." — *William Ruhlmann*

☆ **After the Gold Rush** / Aug. 1970 / Reprise ✦✦✦✦✦
The years have only been kind to what sounded like Young's best album when it was released. It's a mixture of his folkie ("Tell Me Why"), country ("Oh, Lonesome Me"), and hard-rocking ("Southern Man") selves, and there's also that mystical title track, which remains Neil Young's definitive statement of purpose. — *William Ruhlmann*

○ **Harvest** / Feb. 1972 / Reprise ✦✦✦✦
Uneven, yes, perhaps due to the overambitiousness of the orchestral pieces, but this album, Young's biggest seller, still contains "Heart of Gold," the rocker "Alabama," and such telling ballads as "Old Man." — *William Ruhlmann*

Journey through the Past / Nov. 1972 / Reprise ✦✦
Neil Young's unexpected followup to the million-selling *Harvest* was this two-LP soundtrack to his rarely seen film. It contains performances by Buffalo Springfield and Crosby, Stills, Nash and Young, plus Young himself, all previously familiar, except for one minor new Young song, "Soldier." — *William Ruhlmann*

Time Fades Away / Oct. 1973 / Reprise ✦✦✦
The beginning of Young's mid-'70s descent into decadence, this is part of a trilogy including *Tonight's the Night* and *On the Beach* that explores drug addiction, desperation, and determination, and the subject matter isn't only expressed in the lyrics, it's in the roughly played music and the strained vocals. The most gripping music of Young's career. — *William Ruhlmann*

☆ **On the Beach** / Jul. 1974 / Reprise ✦✦✦✦✦
Part three of the doom trilogy was actually the second to be released, as Young began to dig himself out of the depression of the previous year, noting that "Sooner or later, it all gets real" but also fearing that he's "just pissing in the wind." — *William Ruhlmann*

☆ **Tonight's the Night** / Jun. 1975 / Reprise ✦✦✦✦✦
This belatedly released masterpiece (part two of the trilogy) is one of the scariest records ever released. It names names and spares no one in its depiction of the ravages of the druggy life of rock & roll. Least of all spared is the author, who often sounds like he's about to nod out himself. Probably the best album Neil Young will ever make, and not listed as his pick only because it's not the place to start. — *William Ruhlmann*

○ **Zuma** / Nov. 1975 / Reprise ✦✦✦✦
"Don't cry no tears around me," Young declares, trying for the second album in a row (after *On the Beach*) to put the past behind him and take on new topics and directions. And so he does, though by calling on other aspects of his past. Crazy Horse is back, with Frank Sampedro replacing Danny Whitten, and Young even includes "Through My Sails," a track from an abortive Crosby, Stills, Nash and Young session. But the highlight is "Cortez the Killer," Young's best guitar workout since *Everybody Knows This is Nowhere*. — *William Ruhlmann*

Long May You Run / Aug. 1976 / Reprise ✦✦
This is not a Neil Young solo album. It is credited to "The Stills-Young Band," a short-lived joint venture between Young and his longtime compatriot Stephen Stills. It tends to get lumped in with Young's records, however, because only his compositions (notably the title track) are worth mentioning on it. Young's decision to pull out of the touring part of this project may have been capricious, but it was artistically valid on the evidence of this tepid collection. — *William Ruhlmann*

American Stars & Bars / Jun. 1977 / Reprise ✦✦✦
Neil Young's first solo album in 19 months (which is a long time for him) is a patchwork effort drawn from sessions held between November 1974 and April 1977. Side 1 is in the country-rock style of *Harvest*, while Side 2 is more varied. Despite the scattered feel,

there are a few excellent songs, notably "Like A Hurricane," which went on to become one of Young's standards. — *William Ruhlmann*

★ **Decade** / Oct. 1977 / Reprise ✦✦✦✦✦
A 3-LP/2-CD retrospective with material dating back to Buffalo Springfield (some of it unreleased) and including such previously non-LP gems as "Sugar Mountain." As a best-of, it's idiosyncratic, but as a rarities album, it's invaluable. — *William Ruhlmann*

○ **Comes a Time** / Oct. 1978 / Reprise ✦✦✦✦
From the reflective opener "Goin' Back," to the airy remake of Ian & Sylvia's "Four Strong Winds," *Comes a Time* is Young's most delicately (and oddly) atmospheric album. The album's dreamy country-folk music frames Young's homey discourses on "Peace of Mind," the "Field of Opportunity," and the "Human Highway." The collective effect is a lulling optimism, even when his mind at times seems to be bangin' on one cylinder—merely dishing out alien-sounding toss-offs clothed in plain-speak. Overall, *Comes a Time* is a strangely entrancing high point in Young's willfully erratic career. — *Rick Clark*

☆ **Rust Never Sleeps** / Jun. 1979 / Reprise ✦✦✦✦✦
Like the album that followed it, *Live Rust*, this is a live album. The difference is that this is a single disc containing all-new material. The songs are among Young's best ever, "My My, Hey Hey (Out of the Blue)," "Thrasher," and "Powderfinger," among them. — *William Ruhlmann*

○ **Live Rust** / Nov. 1979 / Reprise ✦✦✦✦
This two-record set is a live album culled from Neil Young's 1979 tour with Crazy Horse and a de facto soundtrack album to his concert movie, *Rust Never Sleeps*. Its 16 songs chronicle his career from early efforts like "Sugar Mountain" and "The Loner" to recent compositions heard on the *Rust Never Sleeps* album from five months before (with which there is some overlap). — *William Ruhlmann*

Hawks & Doves / Nov. 1980 / Reprise ✦✦✦
Neil Young hit a commercial peak with *Harvest* in 1972 and a critical peak with *Rust Never Sleeps* in 1979. Most of the 1980s, when he was frequently distracted by personal problems, were problematic on both scores, starting with this album, a patchwork effort from various sessions in the manner of *American Stars 'N Bars*, but without any really strong material. Subsequent efforts, however, would prove it one of his better efforts of the decade. — *William Ruhlmann*

Re-ac-tor / Nov. 1981 / Reprise ✦✦
The news that Neil Young is recording with Crazy Horse usually means that fans are in for a superior, rocking effort. Not this time. Young could have written the songs in an afternoon (one consists of the repeated lines, "Got mashed potato / Ain't got no t-bone") and recorded them that night. Raggedness is what one looks for in a Neil Young/Crazy Horse release, but not toss-offs. This is mere product. — *William Ruhlmann*

Trans / Jan. 1983 / Geffen ✦✦
After two disappointing albums, Neil Young turned weird. Employing synthesizers to distort his voice, he made an album that succeeded in sounding not much like a Neil Young album. Actually, songs like "Sample And Hold" and "Like An Inca" were good, but the new techno version of the Buffalo Springfield oldie "Mr. Soul" tested the patience of fans. (This was Young's debut on Geffen Records, which later would sue him for making uncommercial albums like this one.) — *William Ruhlmann*

Everybody's Rockin' / Aug. 1983 / Geffen ✦✦
From the future to the past: Having made the most of synthesizers on *Trans*, Neil Young went retro on *Everybody's Rockin'*, constructing a neo-rockabilly album to be credited to "Neil And The Shocking Pinks." If the skimpy album, which combined oldies like "Betty Lou's Got A New Pair Of Shoes" with comparable Young originals like "Kinda Fonda Wanda," had been marketed as an EP instead of a full-fledged album, it might have been more acceptable. As it was, it was an expensive joke. — *William Ruhlmann*

Old Ways / Aug. 1985 / Geffen ✦✦✦
Having confused and alienated his fans by going techno (*Trans*), then retro (*Everybody's Rockin'*), then given interviews in which he endorsed President Ronald Reagan for re-election, Young returned to the apparently familiar with this countryish collection. But this was no country-rock fusion like *Harvest*; this was hardcore country, on which Young duetted with Waylon Jennings and Willie Nelson. It was, in fact, too country for country radio, which

refused to play it, as did rock radio, resulting in Young's lowest chart placing since his debut album. — *William Ruhlmann*

Landing on Water / Jul. 1986 / Geffen ♦♦

It was some relief to fans that Neil Young finally turned back to conventional guitar rock for the first time in five years on this album, but the relief was shortlived if only because, like *Hawks & Doves* and *Re-ac-tor*, this proved to be a mediocre collection of songs and suggested, in a way that the genre exercises with which he'd been occupying himself did not, that he was artistically exhausted. — *William Ruhlmann*

Life / Jul. 1987 / Geffen ♦♦♦

Neil Young made his first album with Crazy Horse since 1981's *Re-ac-tor* on *Life*, and although nobody seems to have noticed at the time, he was starting to come back from the wilderness. Songs like "Mideast Vacation" had the insight and humor one associated with Young's offbeat masterpieces, and if this on the whole was not one of his strongest efforts, it was encouraging. By now, however, he was in legal trouble with Geffen, and this, his last album for the label, got scant attention. — *William Ruhlmann*

This Note's for You / Apr. 1988 / Reprise ♦♦♦

This Note's for You was another installment in Neil Young's '80s tour of genres, recorded with a ten-piece, horn-driven blues band. In terms of style, it was merely another genre exercise, but the songs on the album were his strongest in several years, particularly the haunting "Coupe Deville," and began his late '80s return to form. — *Stephen Thomas Erlewine*

Eldorado / 1989 / Reprise ♦♦♦

When this five-song, 25-minute EP was released in Japan in 1989, it served notice that Neil Young was capable of writing powerful songs and playing fierce rock 'n' roll again, a fact confirmed by the subsequent release of the *Freedom* album. Three of the songs on *Eldorado* turned up on that record ("Don't Cry" in a different version), but "Cocaine Eyes" and "Heavy Love" did not, making this disc a necessary purchase for Young completists. — *William Ruhlmann*

○ **Freedom** / Oct. 1989 / Reprise ♦♦♦♦

"Rockin' in the Free World" represents a renewal of Young's commitment to his artistic vision and to his audience, and, as with all his best work, it recognizes the worst while it hopes for the best. A stunning return to form for an artist who seemed to have wandered too far from his original promise ever to find his way back. — *William Ruhlmann*

☆ **Ragged Glory** / Sep. 1990 / Reprise ♦♦♦♦♦

Young is reunited with Crazy Horse for an album of noisy guitar rock that sounds perfect when played right after *Everybody Knows This Is Nowhere*, and that's a high recommendation. — *William Ruhlmann*

○ **Weld** / Oct. 1991 / Reprise ♦♦♦♦

With the double-disc *Weld*, Neil Young closes the door on his return to overamplified guitar grunge. Recorded at various tour stops during the Gulf War in 1991, *Weld* is full of anger, patriotism, optimism, and confusion, perfectly capturing the atmosphere of the time. Although there is a heavy political undertow on *Weld*, the main reason to listen to it is that it rocks like a demon. Neil Young has never released such a towering monument of noise before, and the sheer rage and volume of *Weld* are overpowering. Live albums are rarely this good or this relevant. (Note: The first editions of *Weld* featured *Arc*, a 35-minute aural collage of feedback recorded throughout the tour. Although the premise sounds frightening, *Arc* is a surprisingly accessible, enjoyable listen. It was later issued separately as an EP.) — *Stephen Thomas Erlewine*

Arc / Oct. 1991 / Reprise ♦♦

Harvest Moon / Nov. 3, 1992 / Reprise ♦♦♦

After 20 years, Neil Young finally decided to release the sequel to *Harvest*, his most commercially successful album. *Harvest Moon* is a better album, lacking the orchestral bombast that stifled some of the songs on the first album and boasting a stronger overall selection of songs. *Harvest Moon* manages to be sentimental without being sappy, wistful without being nostalgic. The lovely "Unknown Legend," "From Hank To Hendrix" and the beautiful "Harvest Moon" are among Young's best songs. Only the overlong (11 minutes) and oversimplified "Natural Beauty" hurts a beautiful album that proudly displays scars, heartaches, and love. — *Stephen Thomas Erlewine*

Lucky Thirteen / 1993 / Geffen ♦♦♦

Lucky Thirteen compiles 13 tracks from his years on the Geffen label. It would be difficult to argue with the fact that 1982 to 1988 was not Young's most consistent period. Apart from compiling the best material from most of these releases (nothing from *Rockin'.*), what makes *Lucky Thirteen* valuable is that Young himself scoured the vaults for interesting outtakes and live tracks from the period. — *Roch Parisien*

○ **Unplugged** / Jun. 15, 1993 / Reprise ♦♦♦♦

Like Paul McCartney's, Neil Young's *Unplugged* seems to be an attempt to thwart bootleggers by releasing the material before they get a chance. Young's album doesn't offer any revelations—it's just a solid, thoroughly enjoyable concert. Acoustic performances of "Mr. Soul," "World On a String," "Like a Hurricane," and especially the synthesized "Transformer Man" are essential for the serious Young collector. Fans of *Harvest, After the Gold Rush, Comes A Time*, and *Harvest Moon* will find that *this* is the live Neil Young they need in their collection; hardcore fans will realize that this is the acoustic equivalent of the stunning *Weld*. — *Stephen Thomas Erlewine*

○ **Sleeps with Angels** / Aug. 16, 1994 / Reprise ♦♦♦♦

Reportedly spurred by the death of Kurt Cobain (who quoted Young's line, "It's better to burn out than to fade away," in his suicide note), Young turns in an unusually low-key, elegiac effort, its songs worrying about depression, lack of communication, and drive-by shootings, its music (despite the presence of Crazy Horse) slow and meditative (except for the funny change-of-pace rocker "Piece Of Crap"). The result is not as gloomy as *Tonight's The Night* (in which Young seemed past the point of caring and even managed a certain gallows humor), but extremely mournful, with only glimmers of hope. — *William Ruhlmann*

Mirror Ball / 1995 / Reprise ♦♦♦

Knocked out in about two weeks, Neil Young's collaboration with Pearl Jam is considerably different than *Sleeps with Angels*; the record sounds like a spiritual rebirth after its bleaker predecessor. Playing with the Seattle band has reinvigorated Young. In fact, it has reinvigorated him so much that he hasn't spent much time on the songs, preferring to let the music carry the record. Pearl Jam's grooves are more elastic than Crazy Horse, yet new drummer Jack Irons reigns in the group's tendency to meander. As does Young himself, who dominates the proceedings with his jerky, wailing guitar. A couple of stray, minute-long organ-and-voice fragments from the *Sleeps with Angels* album punctuate the second side, yet the album isn't contemplative—it barrels ahead. — *Stephen Thomas Erlewine*

Paul Young

b. Jan. 17, 1956
Pop/Rock

A soulful U.K. interpretive singer who gained fame in his native country in 1983 with a cover of Marvin Gaye's "Wherever I Lay My Hat (That's My Home)" and in the U.S. with Daryl Hall's "Everytime You Go Away" in 1985. Young found less success writing his own songs, then returned to the U.S. Top Ten with a cover of the Chi-Lites's "Oh Girl" in 1990. In 1992, he left Columbia and moved to MCA. — *William Ruhlmann*

○ **No Parlez** / 1983 / Columbia ♦♦♦♦

Paul Young's debut album was a strong set of soulful covers of forgotten classics ("Love of the Common People," "Wherever I Lay My Hat (That's My Home)") and contemporary classics ("Love Will Tear Us Apart"), as well as the occasional made-to-order original, like the hit "Come Back and Stay." — *Stephen Thomas Erlewine*

○ **The Secret of Association** / 1985 / Columbia ♦♦♦♦

The Secret of Association continued the formula of *No Parlez* to a fine effect and, thanks to a number one version of Hall & Oates' "Everytime You Go Away" that bettered the original, it was a bigger hit. — *Stephen Thomas Erlewine*

Between Two Fires / 1986 / Columbia ♦♦

Paul Young's third album, *Between Two Fires*, suffered from a lack of strong material and an overly slick production, with only the minor hit single "Some People" to recommend it. — *Stephen Thomas Erlewine*

Other Voices / 1990 / Columbia ♦♦♦

Other Voices marked a comeback from the tepid *Between Two Fires*, featuring a set of lush, soulful covers (the Top Ten hit "Oh Girl") and several harder rocking numbers, including a cover of Free's "A Little Bit of Love." — *Stephen Thomas Erlewine*

● **From Time to Time: The Singles Collection** / 1991 / Columbia ♦♦♦♦
All Young's UK and US hits, among them "Everytime You Go Away," "Come Back and Stay," "I'm Gonna Tear Your Playhouse Down," "Love of the Common People," "Wherever I Lay My Hat (That's My Home)," and "Oh Girl." — *William Ruhlmann*

The Youngbloods

Group, Folk-Rock

The Youngbloods, formed in 1965, were led by singer/songwriter Jesse Colin Young (born Perry Miller, Nov 11, 1944). They incorporated bluegrass, folk, country, rock, and bits of psychedelia into their music. Their biggest hit was an up-with-people-style folk-rock anthem called "Get Together," which charted twice (#62 in 1967, #5 in 1969). Other hits included the jug band-influenced "Grizzly Bear" (#52); "Darkness, Darkness" (#86), a dramatic rocker that Mott the Hoople later recorded; and the gentle, acoustic "Sunlight." — *Rick Clark*

○ **The Youngbloods** / 1967 / Edsel ♦♦♦♦
The New York quartet come off as a mini-Lovin' Spoonful on their engaging debut, with a deeper touch of melancholy and more prominent electric keyboards. As with the Spoonful, they would have been better off leaving the blues alone, but the rest of the material is good, highlighted by "Get Together" and the achingly tuneful "All Over The World (La-La)." — *Richie Unterberger*

Earth Music / 1967 / Edsel ♦♦♦
Similar but a bit inferior to their debut, with the same division between accomplished folk-rock, good-timey ragtime-influenced romps, and pedestrian blues-rock. Includes one of the best versions of Tim Hardin's oft-covered standard "Reason to Believe." — *Richie Unterberger*

○ **Elephant Mountain** / 1969 / RCA ♦♦♦♦
By the time they made this album, the group had relocated to Northern California from New York and guitarist Jerry Corbitt had departed, leaving the songwriting chores almost exclusively in the hands of Jesse Colin Young. The mellower, more psychedelic sound reflected the group's new surroundings, and despite some weak moments, it remains their strongest and most cohesive LP. Young's acoustic love song "Sunlight" is his best original composition, and the Youngbloods' best track besides "Get To-gether"; "Darkness, Darkness" and "Smug" are also outstanding. — *Richie Unterberger*

● **The Best of the Youngbloods** / 1970 / RCA ♦♦♦♦
It's a bit short at ten songs, but this collection offers a nice overview of this '60s band's growth from good-time ragtimers to laidback jammers. — *Jeff Tamarkin*

○ **This Is the Youngbloods** / 1972 / RCA ♦♦♦♦
This out-of-print double-album collection is still the most comprehensive. — *Jeff Tamarkin*

Timi Yuro

Pop, Pop/Rock

Known as "the little girl with the big voice," Timi Yuro's booming, resonant vocals were sometimes mistaken for being black, being a man's, or both. Her voice was indeed mammoth, and her delivery astonishingly mature, on her debut single, "Hurt." This 1961 version of the pop standard reached number four, and was followed by a brief period of stardom in the early '60s. Too pop in orientation to be called a rock singer, too conscious of rock and soul trends to be pigeonholed into what was then called the "adult" market, Yuro's undoubted talents never fully jibed with her material. While there was soul in her voice, it was of the Dinah Washington or Nancy Wilson sort, with perhaps more of a bent for straight pop than pop/rock. Over the course of the few years following "Hurt," she actually found her greatest success on the easy listening charts, but also dabbled in girl group pop, R&B, Gene Pitney-like ballads, and Patsy Cline-like country. She scored several minor hits during this time, the biggest of which was the most soulful, "What's a Matter Baby (Is It Hurting You)"; reaching number 12 in the U.S., it was covered by the Small Faces a few years later as the B-side of their first single. Continuing to record throughout the '60s and into the '70s, she experienced little success after leaving the Liberty label in 1964. — *Richie Unterberger*

● **The Best of Timi Yuro: Hurt** / 1992 / EMI America ♦♦♦♦
Twenty-five-song compilation of her Liberty work, all but one dating from her commercial and artistic peak in 1961-64. Includes all of her chart singles, and some of her more memorable LP tracks, as well as an informative history by Dawn Eden. A jumpy document of an impressive talent whose material was not always up to her skills, with early-'60s orchestral arrangements ranging from effective to dated. — *Richie Unterberger*

Z

Zakary Thaks

Group, Garage Rock

One of the best garage bands of the '60s, and one of the best teenage rock groups of all time, Zakary Thaks released a half-dozen regionally distributed singles in 1966 and 1967; some were hits in their hometown of Corpus Christi, TX, but none were heard elsewhere until they achieved renown among '60s collectors. Heavily indebted (as were so many bands) to R&B-influenced British heavyweights like the Stones, Kinks, and Yardbirds, the group added a thick dollop of Texas raunch with their fuzzy, distorted guitars and hell-bent energy. Most importantly, they were first-rate songwriters, with the breakneck "Bad Girl" (later compiled on *Pebbles Vol. 2*), "Won't Come Back," the smoking "Face to Face," "Can't You Hear Your Daddy's Footsteps," and the folk-rock/Mersey hybrid "Please" ranking among the top echelon of American '60s garage rock. Their 1967 singles found the group moving into psychedelic territory; some songs betrayed a Moby Grape influence, and some good melodic numbers were diluted by poppy arrangements that recalled the Buckinghams and Grass Roots. Lead singer Chris Gerniottis, only 15 when Zakary Thaks began making records, joined another interesting Corpus Christi garage-psychedelic group, the Liberty Bell. —*Richie Unterberger*

● **Texas Band** / 1980 / Moxie ✦✦✦✦

Both sides of all six of their singles, marred only by some subpar sound quality (the tracks were mastered from rare singles). —*Richie Unterberger*

Texas Reverberations / 1982 / Texas Archive ✦✦✦

Side One has a couple of alternate takes (an instrumental version of "Daddy's Footsteps," a longer cut of "Face To Face") and some songs by the Liberty Bell. Side Two is a subpar fidelity live recording (though the performances are rabble-rousing) of cover versions the band performed in a promotional film. For collectors only. —*Richie Unterberger*

J-Beck Story 2 / 1984 / Eva ✦✦✦

All 12 of their officially released songs, plus a couple rarities. Remastered from tape, this would displace *Texas Band* as the definitive Zakary Thaks collection, except that the remixes have actually diluted the punch of several of the tracks. —*Richie Unterberger*

Robin Zander

Group, Pop/Rock

Singer/guitarist Robin Zander (b. January 23, 1952) is best known as the lead singer for Cheap Trick, who were one of the most successful rock bands of the '70s. During the early '90s, the band's commercial fortunes had declined, giving Zander the time to cut his own solo album in 1993. *Robin Zander* featured contributions from band members Rick Nielsen and Tom Petersson, as well as Heartbreaker Mike Campbell, Stevie Nicks, Dave Stewart, and Dr. John. —*Stephen Thomas Erlewine*

Robin Zander / Jul. 6, 1993 / Interscope ✦✦✦

Cheap Trick's lead singer's first solo album is a fine collection of mainstream rock in the vein of Tom Petty, not a return to the power-pop of Cheap Trick's early albums. —*AMG*

Frank Zappa (Francis Vincent Zappa)

Group, Rock & Roll, Hard Rock, Fusion, Art-Rock/Progressive-Rock, Experimental

Frank Zappa was one of the most accomplished composers of the rock era; his music combines an understanding of and apprecia-tion for such contemporary classical figures as Stravinsky, Stockhausen, and Varese with an affection for late-'50s doo-wop rock & roll and a facility for the guitar-heavy rock that dominated pop in the '70s. But Zappa was also a satirist whose reserves of scorn seemed bottomless and whose wicked sense of humor and absurdity have delighted his numerous fans, even when his lyrics crossed over the broadest bounds of taste. Finally, Zappa was perhaps the most prolific record-maker of his time, turning out massive amounts of music on his own Barking Pumpkin label and through distribution deals with Rykodisc and Rhino after long, unhappy associations with industry giants like Warner Brothers and the now-defunct MGM.

Zappa became interested in music early and pursued his studies in school, up through a six-month stint at Chaffey College in Alta Loma, CA. He scored a couple of low-budget films and used the money to buy a low-budget recording studio. In 1964, he joined a local band called the Soul Giants, which, over the course of the next two years, evolved into the Mothers, who played songs written by Zappa. The band was signed to the Verve division of MGM by producer Tom Wilson in 1966 and recorded its first album, a two-LP set called *Freak Out!*, which introduced Zappa's interests in both serious music and pop as well as his scathing wit. (Verve insisted on adding "of Invention" to the band's name.)

Subsequent albums extended the musical and lyrical themes of the debut, and they came frequently. Three albums, for example, hit the charts in 1968: *We're Only in It for the Money,* a Mothers album that made fun of hippies and *Sgt. Pepper, Lumpy Gravy,* a Zappa solo album recorded with an orchestra; and *Cruising with Ruben & the Jets,* on which the Mothers played neo-doo wop. Toward the end of the '60s, Zappa expanded the Mothers lineup, turning more toward instrumental jazz-rock, much of which displayed his technically accomplished guitar playing. But by the end of the decade, he had broken up the band.

In 1970, however, Zappa reassembled a new edition of the Mothers, featuring former Turtles lead singers Mark Volman and Howard Kaylan as frontmen. The lineup moved the group more in the direction of X-rated comedy, notably on the album *Fillmore East June 1971,* but it was short-lived: during a performance at the Rainbow Theatre in London, Zappa was pushed from the stage by a demented fan and seriously injured.

While he recovered, Zappa released several albums, then he reformed the Mothers with himself as lead singer and made pop/rock albums, such as *Over-nite Sensation,* which were among his best-selling records ever. By the end of the '70s, Zappa was recording on his own labels, distributed in some cases by the majors, and he had attracted a consistent cult following for both his humor and his complex music. (Zappa's band, in fact, became a training ground for high-quality rock musicians, much as Miles Davis's was for jazz players.)

In the '80s, Zappa gained the rights to his old albums and began to reissue them, at first on his own and then through the pioneering Rykodisc CD label. He wrote his autobiography and embarked on a world tour in 1988. That was the end of his live performing, except for such isolated appearances as one in Czechoslovakia at the invitation of its post-Communist president, Zappa fan Vaclav Havel.

In late 1991, it was confirmed that Zappa was seriously ill with cancer. Nevertheless, his schedule of album releases continued to be rapid.

Zappa died in December of 1993. —*William Ruhlmann*

○ **Freak Out** / Jul. 1966 / Rykodisc ✦✦✦✦
Once an LP, now an hour-long CD, but still featuring the Mothers' opening salvo to the world, playing what is often melodic '60s pop/rock with doo-wop influences. But the lyrics in songs like "Who Are the Brain Police?" and "Trouble Every Day" mark composer Frank Zappa as having a social conscience and a wickedly satiric sense of humor. — *William Ruhlmann*

○ **Absolutely Free** / May 26, 1967 / Rykodisc ✦✦✦✦
The satire gets even sharper on such songs as "Plastic People" and "Status Back Baby," while the references are often only local to the band's Los Angeles environs (and, increasingly, part of a private, absurdist language), and the music gets increasingly complicated. — *William Ruhlmann*

★ **We're Only in It for the Money** / Jan. 1968 / Verve ✦✦✦✦✦
A simultaneous condemnation of the straights and the hippies, its songs segue as on *Sgt. Pepper* and, with verbal asides included, a sound collage that was the original Mothers' highest-charting album. (Note: Recommendation is for the original LP release, and not the CD reissue—which, available on one disc with *Lumpy Gravy*, has re-recorded rhythm tracks.) — *William Ruhlmann*

○ **Lumpy Gravy** / Mar. 1968 / Verve ✦✦✦✦
Initially commissioned by Capitol Records when the Mothers of Invention were signed to Verve, *Lumpy Gravy* was Frank Zappa's first solo album, one on which be continued his tape experiments and employed an orchestra along with members of the Mothers. Snatches of conversation and sound collages make up the bulk of it, so that it is the most exploratory (but not the most accomplished) album Zappa made in the 1960s. (Reissued by Rykodisc in 1986 on a single CD with *We're Only In It For The Money*.) — *William Ruhlmann*

Cruising with Ruben and the Jets / Oct. 1968 / Rykodisc ✦✦✦
The music of Frank Zappa and the Mothers of Invention always retained roots in soul and doo wop, even at its most satirical. On this, the Mothers' fourth album (and their final release for Verve, now available as a Rykodisc CD reissue), they tried playing it straight, making an affectionate genre album for the low-riding Los Angeles pachucos, although the result is still tongue-in-cheek, as the cover blurb, "Is this the Mothers of Invention recording under a different name in a last ditch attempt to get their cruddy music on the radio?," makes clear. When Zappa prepared the album for reissue in the 1980s, he rerecorded the rhythm tracks, which mars the original. It is this version that is the only one currently available, however. — *William Ruhlmann*

○ **Uncle Meat** / Apr. 1969 / Rykodisc ✦✦✦✦
A sprawling, largely instrumental soundtrack to a movie that was never finished, including everything from the pop tune "The Air" to the extended "King Kong," complete with variations. — *William Ruhlmann*

○ **Burnt Weenie Sandwich** / Jun. 1969 / Barking Pumpkin ✦✦✦✦
Burnt Weenie Sandwich was the first of two albums by Frank Zappa and the "original" Mothers of Invention (1965-1969) compiled by Zappa from live and studio recordings after he disbanded the group. (The second was *Weasels Ripped My Flesh.*) It is bookended by doo-wop songs in the style of *Cruising With Ruben & The Jets*, and in between are extended instrumental passages with solos by pianists Ian Underwood and Don Preston and violinist Sugar Cane Harris. — *William Ruhlmann*

○ **Hot Rats** / Oct. 10, 1969 / Rykodisc ✦✦✦✦
Zappa disbanded the original Mothers group in 1969 and cut this solo album, most of which consists of well-organized jazz-rock instrumentals such as "Peaches En Regalia," one of his most appealing compositions. Captain Beefheart provides a guest vocal on "Willie the Pimp," which also features violin by Jean-Luc Ponty. — *William Ruhlmann*

The Mothers of Invention / 1970 / MGM ✦✦✦
Part of MGM's "Golden Archive Series," this compilation album presents 10 tracks from the Mothers of Invention albums *Freak Out!, Absolutely Free*, and *We're Only In It For The Money*. It is out of print and unlikely to be reissued. — *William Ruhlmann*

○ **Weasels Ripped My Flesh** / Aug. 1970 / Rykodisc ✦✦✦✦
An album of live material recorded from 1967 to 1969 and featuring an expanded lineup with horn section. Highlights include Sugar Cane Harris's violin work on Little Richard's "Directly from My Heart to You" and Zappa's vocal on "My Guitar Wants to Kill Your Mama." — *William Ruhlmann*

Chunga's Revenge / Oct. 23, 1970 / Rykodisc ✦✦✦
Live at Fillmore East / 1971 / Bizarre ✦✦
Fillmore East: June 1971 / Aug. 1971 / Rykodisc ✦✦✦
A new Mothers lineup led by ex-Turtles singers Mark Volman and Howard Kaylan makes for a virtual comedy act based on the theme of life on the road. Very funny, and some of the playing is amazing too. — *William Ruhlmann*

200 Motels / Oct. 1971 / United Artists ✦✦
The soundtrack to Zappa's crazed movie is full of great music and is great fun. — *Cub Koda*

○ **The Grand Wazoo** / 1972 / Rykodisc ✦✦✦✦
Just Another Band from L.A. / Apr. 1972 / Rykodisc ✦✦
Waka/Jawaka / Jul. 5, 1972 / Rykodisc ✦✦✦
Recorded by Frank Zappa in the spring of 1972 while he recuperated from the injuries he sustained when he was pushed off the stage of the Rainbow on Dec. 10, 1971, *Waka/Jawaka* was intended as a followup to his "solo" album, *Hot Rats*. It found him turning away from the comic vocal approach of the Howard Kaylan/Mark Volman edition of the Mothers and more toward a horn-filled, jazz-fusion approach, notably on the title track and "Big Swifty." — *William Ruhlmann*

○ **Grand Wazoo** / Nov. 1972 / Rykodisc ✦✦✦✦
Frank Zappa continued to experiment with an expanded musical unit on this largely instrumental album, which took a big band approach, prominently featuring reeds and horns. — *William Ruhlmann*

○ **Over-Nite Sensation** / Sep. 1973 / Barking Pumpkin ✦✦✦✦
This is actually Zappa's first new studio album of vocal music in three years, and it finds him with another edition of Mothers (from this point, Mothers group albums and Zappa solo albums become indistinguishable), this time taking the lead vocals himself and writing a new set of catchy, satiric rock-pop songs like "Camarillo Brillo" and "Montana." — *William Ruhlmann*

○ **Apostrophe** / Mar. 1974 / Barking Pumpkin ✦✦✦✦
Zappa's only gold-selling Top Ten album, featuring the satiric "Don't Eat the Yellow Snow," along with other parodic songs in the same style as *Over-Nite Sensation*. — *William Ruhlmann*

Roxy & Elsewhere / Sep. 10, 1974 / Barking Pumpkin ✦✦✦
One Size Fits All / Jun. 25, 1975 / Rykodisc ✦✦✦
The first Mothers of Invention studio album since the group's biggest hit, *Over-Nite Sensation* (although the Zappa solo album *Apostrophe'* and the live group album *Roxy & Elsewhere* came in between), *One Size Fits All* found Frank Zappa retreating from the frontman position he took on the previous album, sharing lead vocals with keyboard player George Duke, reed man Napoleon Murphy Brock, and guitarist Johnny "Guitar" Watson. The lyrics are the usual mix of scorn, absurdity, humor, and local references ("San Ber'dino") and the music leans toward heavy metal and fusion, although with the usual Zappa signature elements of sudden rhythmic changes and short, startling passages, many of them provided by vibes player Ruth Underwood. The album's standout is the stately "Sofa No. 2," which is sung in German. — *William Ruhlmann*

Bongo Fury / Oct. 2, 1975 / Rykodisc ✦✦✦
A live album recorded with Captain Beefheart on lead vocals, which combines Zappa's provocative songs with Beefheart's peculiar perspective. Contains the should-have-been-a-hit "Carolina Hard-Core Ecstasy." — *William Ruhlmann*

Zoot Allures / Oct. 29, 1976 / Rykodisc ✦✦✦
Zappa in New York / Mar. 3, 1978 / Barking Pumpkin ✦✦✦
This album was recorded in December 1976 at the Palladium in New York and originally intended for release in 1977. It was held up due to arguments between Frank Zappa and his then-record label, Warner Bros. When the two-LP set finally appeared in March 1978, Warner had deleted "Punky's Whips," a song about drummer Terry Bozzio's attraction to Punky Meadows of Angel. When Zappa reacquired the album and released it as a double-CD in 1991, he restored "Punky's Whips" and added four bonus tracks. The Zappa band, which includes bassist Patrick O'Hearn, percussionist Ruth Underwood, and keyboard player Eddie Jobson, along with a horn section including the two Brecker brothers, was one of the band-

leader's most accomplished, which it had to be to play songs like "Black Page," even in the "easy" version presented here. Zappa also was at the height of his comic stagecraft, notably on songs like "Titties & Beer," which essentially is a comedy routine between Zappa and Bozzio, and "The Illinois Enema Bandit," which features TV announcer Don Pardo. — *William Ruhlmann*

Studio Tan / Sep. 15, 1978 / Barking Pumpkin ✦✦
The material on this album originally was intended to be part of a four-record set called *Lather*, prepared for release in 1977. Then Frank Zappa got into a disagreement with his record company, Warner Bros., and *Lather* was split up into several different releases as part of a contractual agreement. The results were dumped on the market during 1978 and 1979, while Zappa moved on to his own record label. *Studio Tan* contains four selections: a 20-minute recitative called "The Adventures Of Greggery Peccary" in the imaginative, comic style of "Billy The Mountain" (who makes an appearance in the narrative), an orchestral instrumental, a pop tune called "Lemme Take You To The Beach," and a rock instrumental. All are typical Zappa, but none are particularly memorable. — *William Ruhlmann*

Sleep Dirt / Jan. 19, 1979 / Barking Pumpkin ✦✦✦
The material on this album originally was intended to be part of a four-record set called *Lather*, prepared for release in 1977. Then Frank Zappa got into a disagreement with his record company, Warner Bros., and *Lather* was split up into several different releases as part of a contractual agreement. The results were dumped on the market during 1978 and 1979, while Zappa moved on to his own record label. *Sleep Dirt* consists of miscellaneous tracks recorded between 1974 and 1976, including "Flambay," "Spider Of Destiny," and "Time Is Money," songs that apparently were part of an unissued Zappa musical/rock opera from 1972 called *Hunchentoot*. They are sung by soparano Thana Harris. It's impossible to say what the entire work would have been like, but this album is little more than musical fragments. — *William Ruhlmann*

Sheik Yerbouti / Mar. 3, 1979 / Rykodisc ✦✦✦

Orchestral Favorites / May 4, 1979 / Barking Pumpkin ✦✦✦
The material on this album originally was intended to be part of a four-record set called *Lather*, prepared for release in 1977. Then Frank Zappa got into a disagreement with his record company, Warner Bros., and *Lather* was split up into several different releases as part of a contractual agreement. The results were dumped on the market during 1978 and 1979, while Zappa moved on to his own record label. *Orchestral Favorites* consists of material recorded on September 17 and 18, 1975, with a 37-piece orchestra and includes such familiar Zappa themes as "Duke Of Prunes" (from *Absolutely Free*) and "Strictly Genteel" (from *200 Motels*); "Bogus Pomp" also consisted largely of *200 Motels* music. The themes are melodic and often majestic, with various startling juxtapositions and changes. This was the first release of Zappa orchestral material since *Lumpy Gravy* and a precursor of things to come. — *William Ruhlmann*

Joe's Garage: Act 1 / Sep. 17, 1979 / Zappa ✦✦
Free from his Warner Bros. Records contract, Frank Zappa was able to issue new albums as frequently as he liked, which would turn out to be very frequently. Six months after the release of the two-record set *Sheik Yerbouti*, he was ready with the first LP in a three-record set, a cautionary concept piece about the adventures of a musician named Joe. In *Act I*, Zappa continued his fascination with road stories, ethnic stereotypes ("Catholic Girls"), and bathroom activities ("Why Does It Hurt When I Pee?"). But although his concern with government censorship would see a later flowering in his battles with the Parents Music Resource Center (PMRC), here he wasn't able to use it to fulfill a satisfying dramatic function. (The complete *Joe's Garage* was released as a double-CD on Rykodisc RCD 10060/10061-on June 17, 1987.) — *William Ruhlmann*

Joe's Garage: Acts 2 & 3 / Nov. 19, 1979 / Rykodisc ✦✦✦
Two months after the release of *Act I*, Frank Zappa completed *Joe's Garage* with this two-LP set, meaning that, counting the two contractual albums *Sleep Dirt* and *Orchestral Favorites*, he released seven LPs' worth of new material in 1979. Maybe that's why *Joe's Garage* seems so thin and thrown together, musically and dramatically, especially on its second and third discs. (The complete *Joe's Garage* was released as a double-CD on Rykodisc RCD 10060/10061 on June 17, 1987.) — *William Ruhlmann*

○ **Return of the Son of Shut up 'n Play** / May 11, 1981 / Barking Pumpkin ✦✦✦✦
This is the third of three albums of guitar solos by Frank Zappa released simultaneously by his mail order record company, Barking Pumpkin, and subsequently released to retail by Rykodisc on September 1, 1986, as part of a two-CD set called *Shut Up 'N Play Yer Guitar*. The tracks were recorded, mostly in concert, in 1979 and 1980, and they demonstrate Zappa's mastery of the electric guitar, establishing him as the peer of the other guitar heroes of his generation. — *William Ruhlmann*

Tinsel Town Rebellion / May 17, 1981 / Rykodisc ✦✦✦
From the mid-70s on, Frank Zappa's music divided ever more extremely into complex instrumental passages and broadly satiric songs, which stopped sounding clever and started seeming smutty and sophomoric. There are elements of these excesses on this live double album, but for the most part the appeal of the music and the fine performances overcome objections. There are also remakes of such old favorites as "Brown Shoes Don't Make It." — *William Ruhlmann*

○ **You Are What You Is** / Sep. 1981 / Rykodisc ✦✦✦✦
1981 proved to be another prolific year for Frank Zappa, as, counting his three LPs of guitar solos and his two-LP set *Tinsel Town Rebellion*, along with this two-LP set, he released seven LPs' worth of material during the year, just as he had in 1979. The sarcasm was running heavy on this studio album, with Zappa taking off especially on the beauty/fashion industry in songs like "I'm A Beautiful Guy," "Beauty Knows No Pain," and "Charlie's Enormous Mouth" (the last based on a then-current TV commercial for perfume). Elsewhere, Zappa skewered punk ("Mudd Club"), the hesitant ("The Meek Shall Inherit Nothing"), the stupid ("Dumb All Over"), the religious ("Heavenly Bank Account"), and the depressed ("Suicide Chump") for good measure. — *William Ruhlmann*

Ship Arriving Too Late to Save a Drowning Witch / May 1982 / FZ/Rykodisc ✦✦✦
Ship Arriving Too Late To Save a Drowning Witch features the novelty hit "Valley Girl," with vocals by Zappa's daughter, Moon. (Steve Vai is featured on the appropriately credited "impossible guitar.") — *William Ruhlmann*

Man from Utopia / Mar. 1983 / Barking Pumpkin ✦✦
A rock album featuring one of Zappa's more accomplished bands (Steve Vai plays guitar, Vinnie Colaiuta drums on two tracks), *The Man From Utopia* presents Frank Zappa's standard mixture of bawdy and comic lyrical interests ("Sex," "The Dangerous Kitchen") with complicated musical passages, notably on the instrumentals "Tink Walks Amok," "Moggio," and "We Are Not Alone." Several songs were presented in a jazz vocalese style that was hard to take, but the version of the old hit "Mary Lou" was entertaining. The CD version, released in 1993, differs from the 1983 LP in some respects. The tracks have been edited differently ("Cocaine Decisions" is almost a minute longer on the CD, "Moggio" is 40 seconds shorter), they have been resequenced, and there is one added track, "Luigi & The Wise Guys." — *William Ruhlmann*

Baby Snakes / Mar. 1983 / Barking Pumpkin ✦✦
This soundtrack to the 1979 movie *Baby Snakes* was belatedly released by Frank Zappa's mail-order record company, Barking Pumpkin, as a picture disc LP. It consists of live recordings made in October 1976, the same kind of material that turned up on the 1978 album *Zappa In New York*, such as "Titties 'N' Beer" and "Punky's Whips," as well as such concert favorites as "Dinah Moe Humm." — *William Ruhlmann*

Zappa, Vol. 1 / Jun. 9, 1983 / Barking Pumpkin ✦✦✦
This LP contains the first set of recordings to be released from a session held in January 1983 at which some of Frank Zappa's orchestral works were recorded by the London Symphony Orchestra, conducted by Kent Nagano. The pieces are "Sad Jane," "Pedro's Dowry (large orchestra version)," "Envelopes," and "Mo 'N Herb's Vacation," in three movements. Although Zappa himself has criticized these recordings, they represent the best rendition so far of his orchestral ambitions, more accomplished than *Lumpy Gravy* or *Orchestral Favorites*. The music is moody and ponderous, slow with sudden dramatic passages, in the manner of Stravinsky, and exhibits little of Zappa's usual melodic invention and humor. (In 1986, Rykodisc released a CD version of the sessions under the title *London Symphony Orchestra* (RCD 10022) that deleted "Sad Jane" and "Pedro's Dowry" and added the 24 1/2-minute "Bogus Pomp.") — *William Ruhlmann*

Boulez Conducts Zappa/The Perfect Stranger / Aug. 23, 1984 / EMI America ✦✦✦
Having recorded some works with a large orchestra in January 1983, in January 1984, Frank Zappa arranged for some of his chamber works to be performed by Pierre Boulez's Ensemble InterContemporain, a 16-piece group. "The Perfect Stranger," "Naval Aviation In Art?," and "Dupree's Paradise" were given this treatment, and the four remaining tracks are the product of Zappa's music synthesizer, the Synclavier. As usual, Zappa's "serious" works are rhythmically interesting and make for challenging listening. Originally released on LP on the classical Angel/EMI label, this album was reissued on CD on Zappa's Barking Pumpkin label in 1992, at which time he resequenced it. — *William Ruhlmann*

Them or Us / Oct. 1984 / Rykodisc ✦✦✦
A caution against the dangers of traveling "In France," a tribute to "Sharleena," a cover of the Allman Brothers Band's "Whipping Post," the double-LP set *Them Or Us* (subsequently reissued on a single CD) found Frank Zappa repeating himself with his usual scorn and formidable musicianship, but not breaking any new ground. — *William Ruhlmann*

Thing-Fish / Nov. 1984 / Rykodisc ✦✦✦
A three-record box set (subsequently reissued as a double-CD), *Thing-Fish* purported to be the cast album for an unproduced Broadway show, but was in fact a savage satire on theater and several other things that could not have been produced theatrically. Ike Willis's "Amos 'n' Andy" patois had long since passed into the objectionable by this point, and the composer's preoccupation with sexual and excretory functions had become extreme. This was something of a culmination of Zappa's tendencies over the last decade, and their most complete expression. Certainly, he retreated from such works in the future, in fact releasing relatively little new material in the last nine years of his life. — *William Ruhlmann*

Francesco Zappa / Nov. 1984 / Barking Pumpkin ✦✦
This is chamber music written by an 18th century Italian composer who may or may not have been an ancestor of Frank Zappa. The younger Zappa discovered the music at the music library at the University of California at Berkeley and programmed it into his Synclavier. The result is pleasant-enough European classical music with an electronic twinge—in the same catagory as *Switched-On Bach.* — *William Ruhlmann*

○ **Old Masters Box 1 [ABCDE + New]** / Apr. 19, 1985 / Barking Pumpkin ✦✦✦✦
This is a seven-LP box set that contains Frank Zappa and the Mothers of Invention's first five albums—*Freak Out!, Absolutely Free, We're Only In It For The Money, Lumpy Gravy,* and *Cruising With Ruben & The Jets*—originally released between 1966 and 1968, plus a "Mystery Disc" of previously unreleased material from the era and earlier. Note that *Money* and *Ruben* have rerecorded rhythm tracks. — *William Ruhlmann*

Meets the Mothers of Prevention [US Vers] / Nov. 1985 / Rykodisc ✦✦✦

Does Humor Belong in Music ? / 1986 / EMI ✦✦✦
This is a Europe-only album that was released without Frank Zappa's permission and subsequently withdrawn. It is the accompaniment to a 1985 home video, although only some of the songs are the same. It is a live album drawn from Zappa's 1984 tour, featuring a cross-section of Zappa's work, from the early "Trouble Every Day" to more recent material. — *William Ruhlmann*

○ **Shut up 'n Play Yer Guitar** / Sep. 1, 1986 / Rykodisc ✦✦✦✦
This is the first of three albums of guitar solos by Frank Zappa released simultaneously by his mail order record company, Barking Pumpkin, and subsequently released to retail by Rykodisc on September, 1, 1986, as part of a two-CD set, also called *Shut Up 'N Play Yer Guitar.* The tracks were recorded, mostly in concert, in 1979 and 1980, and they demonstrate Zappa's mastery of the electric guitar, establishing him as the peer of the other guitar heroes of his generation. — *William Ruhlmann*

○ **Shut 'n Play Yer Guitar Some More** / Sep. 1, 1986 / Barking Pumpkin ✦✦✦✦
This is the second of three albums of guitar solos by Frank Zappa released simultaneously by his mail order record company, Barking Pumpkin, and subsequently released to retail by Rykodisc on September 1, 1986, as part of a two-CD set called *Shut Up 'N Play Yer Guitar.* This one features "Variations On The Carlos Santana

Secret Chord Progression," which should be useful to guitar students everywhere. — *William Ruhlmann*

○ **Jazz from Hell** / Nov. 15, 1986 / Rykodisc ✦✦✦✦
This is an album of jazz-rock-oriented instrumental music that, with the exception of the track "St. Etienne," was recorded on the Synclavier music synthesizer. As an expression of Frank Zappa's more popular music styles, it ranks in execution with such albums as *Hot Rats.* It is the winner of a Grammy Award for Best Rock Instrumental Performance (Orchestra Group or Soloist). — *William Ruhlmann*

London Symphony Orchestra 2 / 1987 / Rykodisc ✦✦✦
This is a CD reissue of *Zappa Volume I* with the addition of the 24 1/2-minute "Bogus Pomp" and the deletion of "Pedro's Dowry" and "Envelopes." Common to both LP and CD are "Sad Jane" and "Mo 'N Herb's Vacation." These are orchestral works by Frank Zappa, played by the London Symphony Orchestra, conducted by Kent Nagano. Although Zappa himself has criticized these recordings, they represent the best rendition so far of his orchestral ambitions, more accomplished than *Lumpy Gravy* or *Orchestral Favorites.* The music is moody and ponderous, slow with sudden dramatic passages, in the manner of Stravinsky, and exhibits little of Zappa's usual melodic invention and humor. — *William Ruhlmann*

○ **You Can't Do That on Stage (Sampler)** / 1988 / Zappa ✦✦✦✦

○ **Guitar** / Apr. 1988 / Rykodisc ✦✦✦✦
Frank Zappa's followup to *Shut Up 'N Play Yer Guitar,* this double-CD (there is also a double-LP on Barking Pumpkin with fewer tracks) again excerpts Zappa's guitar solos from live performances, recorded between 1979 and 1984. Guitar aficionados will have another field day. (Release date is for the LP; the CD was released on May 23, 1988.) — *William Ruhlmann*

● **You Can't Do That on Stage Anymore, Vol. 1** / May 16, 1988 / Rykodisc ✦✦✦✦
This two-LP set provides a curtain-raiser on the massive *You Can't Do That On Stage Anymore* series and is typical of the approach of the series in that it jumps from one time and band and location to another, leading off, for example, with a version of "Plastic People" recorded by the Mothers of Invention in 1969 and moving immediately to a version of "The Torture Never Stops" by Frank Zappa's band in 1977. Some of Zappa's more entertaining numbers are here, such as "Montana," "King Kong" (a short version from 1982), and "Cosmic Debris," but, as with most of the series, the jumping around gives the album an unfocused feel. — *William Ruhlmann*

○ **You Can't Do That on Stage Anymore, Vol. 2** / Oct. 1988 / Rykodisc ✦✦✦✦
Unlike the other volumes in Frank Zappa's giant reissue series of concert recordings, *Volume 2* chronicles a single performance, "The Helsinki Concert," which occurred on September 22, 1974. At the time, Zappa was leading a relatively small band consisting of himself on guitar and vocals, Napoleon Murphy Brock on sax and vocals, George Duke on keyboard and vocals, Ruth Underwood on percussion, Tom Fowler on bass, and Chester Thompson on drums. "The repertoire is basically the same as the *Roxy* album," Zappa writes in the liner notes, referring to *Roxy & Elsewhere,* which is true, although the 20 tracks include material from earlier (such as "The Idiot Bastard Son") and later, as well as some unreleased material. As Zappa suggests, the band, which had been on the road a year, is tight, and this is a strong, coherent live performance. — *William Ruhlmann*

● **Broadway the Hardway** / Oct. 1988 / Rykodisc ✦✦✦✦
A live album culled from Zappa's final world tour of 1988. It features his comments on Elvis Presley ("Elvis Has Just Left the Building"), televangelists ("Jesus Thinks You're a Jerk"), and other objects of political scorn. — *William Ruhlmann*

○ **You Can't Do That on Stage Anymore, Vol. 3** / 1989 / Rykodisc ✦✦✦✦
On the third volume of his live reissue series, after devoting *Volume 2* to a single concert, Frank Zappa returned to his policy of mixing times, bands, and repertoire from throughout his career from one track to the next. The first disc, however, is drawn entirely from Zappa's 1984 tour, which gives it more musical coherence than the second disc, which ranges from 1971 to 1984. Many familiar tunes are featured, notably a 24 1/2-minute version of "King Kong" that is edited from performances in 1982 and 1971, and there are several previously unreleased compositions. — *William Ruhlmann*

Frank Zappa Meets the Mothers of Prevention / May 1990 / Rykodisc ◆◆◆
This album mixes the usual Frank Zappa satire with excerpts from Zappa's testimony before Congress in opposition to censorship and to the Parents Music Resource Center (PMRC). The album was issued in three different forms. The U.S. LP version (Barking Pumpkin ST 74203) contains seven tracks. The European LP version (EMI EMC 3507), released in February 1986, eliminated the 12-minute track "Porn Wars" on the grounds that it "would not have been interesting to listeners outside the U.S.," as a sleeve note explained, and substituted three new tracks, "I Don't Even Care," "One Man—One Vote," and "H.R. 2911." The U.S. CD version (Rykodisc RCD 10023), released September 1, 1986, added "I Don't Even Care" and "One Man—One Vote" to the U.S. LP track listing. —*William Ruhlmann*

Tis the Season to Be Jelly / 1991 / Rhino ◆◆◆
Recorded live in Sweden in 1967, this spotlights the humor of the early Mothers on a parody medley of doo-wop and early rock & roll that is both reverent and sardonic. "King Kong" and "It Can't Happen Here," on the other hand, show them equally interested in contemporary avant-garde compositions. —*Richie Unterberger*

Rare Beefheart/Vintage Zappa / 1991 / Pop Almanac ◆◆◆
Frank's half of this disc has six rare sides that he had a hand in for the Del-Fi label during the early '60s. These crude but adventurous productions clearly point toward the Mothers with their skilled R&B and doo-wop chops that walk the line between affection and parody, and inventive montage of sound effects on the bizarre Dracula novelty single "Dear Jeepers"/"Letter From Jeepers." Disappointingly, it isn't taken from the master tapes, but the singles themselves, although the surface noise is minor. Five rarities from fellow Southern California mad genius Captain Beefheart (alternate takes from his *Strictly Personal* album) fill out the disc; these are also available on a more complete CD of *Strictly Personal* outtakes on the British Sequel label, and it's too bad they couldn't have just fit everything from that collection, as there's plenty of room. —*Richie Unterberger*

Trick or Treat / 1991 / Rhino ◆◆◆
Divided between interesting late-'60s studio outtakes and a 1968 show at London's Royal Festival Hall. The outtakes include both satirical songs and guitar workouts, while the concert finds the band looking forward to the *Uncle Meat* era, with the focus on jazzy and mostly instrumental material. —*Richie Unterberger*

○ **The Best Band You Never Heard in Your Life** / Apr. 1991 / Barking Pumpkin ◆◆◆◆
This is the second album that Frank Zappa culled from live performances on his final 1988 world tour, the first being *Broadway The Hard Way*. That release contained newly written material; this one, in contrast, contains, as Zappa puts it in his liner notes, "big-band arrangements of concert favorites and obscure album cuts, along with deranged versions of cover tunes and a few premiere recordings." In practice, that means you have the opportunity to hear Zappa treatments of such surprising songs as "Ring Of Fire," "I Left My Heart In San Francisco," "Bolero," "Purple Haze," and "Stairway To Heaven." In other words, even for an idiosyncratic artist, this is an idiosyncratic album. (The title derives from Zappa's note that the band "self-destructed" before most of the U.S. could hear it play.) —*William Ruhlmann*

Make a Jazz Noise Here / Jun. 1991 / Barking Pumpkin ◆◆◆
This is the third album Frank Zappa culled from his final 1988 world tour. The first, *Broadway The Hard Way*, featured new material, and the second, *The Best Band You Never Heard In Your Life*, offered many unusual cover songs. This album displays the band's musical acuity on various demanding Zappa compositions, such as "The Black Page (new age version)" and even includes snatches of Stravinsky and Bartok. —*William Ruhlmann*

○ **You Can't Do That on Stage Anymore, Vol. 4** / Jun. 21, 1991 / Rykodisc ◆◆◆◆
The fourth volume in Frank Zappa's series of CD compilations of live material is typical in that it features recordings made between 1969 and 1988, including such familiar songs as "My Guitar Wants To Kill Your Mama," "Willie The Pimp," and "Disco Boy." There is, however, an unusually large complement of previously unreleased songs here, including a cover of "Take Me Out To The Ball Game," and the first performance of "The Torture Never Stops," running more than nine minutes, is a highlight. —*William Ruhlmann*

Beat the Boots! [Box] / Jul. 7, 1991 / Rhino ◆◆◆
Frank Zappa frequently has been the victim of bootleggers, and with this release he turns the tables on his tormentors. This boxed eight-cassette set (also available as separate CDs) presents a series of bootlegs as they appeared, without any improvement. Nevertheless, the sound is often surprisingly good, and especially the recordings by the original Mothers (*The Ark*, RHI 70538, for instance) will be of interest to Zappaphiles. (A second version of *Beat the Boots!*, available only as a boxed set, appeared in 1992.) —*William Ruhlmann*

○ **You Can't Do That on Stage Anymore, Vol. 5** / 1992 / Rykodisc ◆◆◆◆
One of Frank Zappa's avowed purposes in compiling his series of archival live recordings under the *You Can't Do That On Stage Anymore* rubric was to demonstrate to fans that, despite what they thought, his bands after the original Mothers of Invention were an improvement over that legendary outfit. On *Volume 5*, however, he seems to have dropped this effort, devoting the first disc to '60s material. And what do you know? It proves him wrong, at least on an emotional level. Maybe the Mothers weren't great technical musicians and maybe these tapes aren't as high-tech as later ones, but the first disc here is more fun than the rest of the series combined. Disc Two is given over to a 1982 European concert tour distinguished by Zappa's threat in Geneva to end the concert if anyone else threw something. Can you guess what happened then? —*William Ruhlmann*

Beat the Boots #2 / Jun. 16, 1992 / Rhino ◆◆◆
Frank Zappa followed the release of the first *Beat The Boots!* box set—his own collection of unretouched bootleg albums—with this second set, which contained seven more albums. While the first box set was cassette-only (plus a small run of LPs), with each album also available individually on CD, this box came in a CD version, again with the different albums separately released. Although there are individual selections that might be of interest to more general Zappa fans, the box is, practically by definition, a collector's item. Note, however, that if you buy the box rather than the individual discs, you get a beret and an extensive scrapbook-like booklet containing news reports and interviews spanning Zappa's career. —*William Ruhlmann*

Playground Psychotics / Oct. 1992 / Capitol ◆◆◆
This archival release returns us to the 1971 edition of the Mothers, fronted by singers Mark Volman and Howard Kaylan, as they travel the road, rehearse, and perform the elaborate comic stories of life on the road that distinguished this lineup of the band. Also included is Frank Zappa's version of the *Fillmore East* recordings with John Lennon and Yoko Ono previously issued by them on the *Sometime In New York City* album in 1972. —*William Ruhlmann*

○ **You Can't Do That on Stage Anymore, Vol. 6** / Oct. 23, 1992 / Rykodisc ◆◆◆◆
Frank Zappa ended his series of albums of previously unreleased concert recordings with this volume, which features one disc given over to "songs dealing generally with the topic of sex (safe and otherwise)," as Zappa puts it in the liner notes. Actually, with songs like "Alien Orifice," "Crew Slut," and "Take Your Clothes Off When You Dance," the same theme pervades Disc Two, also. —*William Ruhlmann*

● **Zappa: The Yellow Shark** / 1993 / Barking Pumpkin ◆◆◆◆
Released only a month before Frank Zappa's death, *The Yellow Shark* is an album of orchestral treatments of Zappa's compositions done by the 25-piece Ensemble Modern orchestra, conducted by Peter Rundel. It features vintage material like "Dog Breath Variations" as well as more recent work, played with more sensitivity and verve than previous orchestras have brought to Zappa's music. Hence, the "pick" notation should alert fans who want to hear the orchestral Zappa—this is the best executed and most varied of the albums Zappa devoted to his "serious" music. —*William Ruhlmann*

Ahead of Their Time / Mar. 23, 1993 / Capitol ◆◆◆
This album contains a previously unreleased live concert by the Mothers of Invention recorded October 28, 1968, at the Royal Festival Hall in London. It finds the band still playing some of its familiar repertoire ("Help, I'm A Rock," "Sleeping In A Jar," "Let's Make The Water Turn Black") from its early albums, but also looking forward to the more ambitious *Uncle Meat*, which would be released the following spring ("King Kong"). Members of the BBC Symphony Orchestra accompany the Mothers on some of Frank

Zappa's early orchestral efforts. This is a recording from a key point in the Mothers' history. —*William Ruhlmann*

Civilization Phaze III / 1995 / Barking Pumpkin ✦✦✦

BOOK

✦✦✦ **The Real Frank Zappa Book**, by Frank Zappa with Peter Occhoigrosso (Poseidon, 1989). Whether you're interested in his music or not, Zappa ranked as one of the most articulate, and funniest, contemporary musicians and social critics of any sort. This is not a conventional "been there, done that" autobiography, though there are plenty of personal memories, ranging from his days as a youth obsessed with R&B and contemporary composition, through his tours with the Mothers and debates with the PMRC. It's more of a platform for Frank to espouse his entertainingly insightful, if sometimes didactic and eccentric, opinions about a wealth of subjects, musical or otherwise: recording and performing with bands and orchestras; the narrow-minded behavior of authorities within the record business and the court of law; marriage and family; the vapidity of much popular songwriting; the military-industrial complex; and, of course, censorship. Some more detailed memories of his records and songs, particularly his great early albums, would have been welcome; no Zappa book satisfactorily covers his work in the 1960s, which still ranks as his best, though Frank would probably contest that evaluation. But it's usually a thought-provoking and funny volume. —*Richie Unterberger*

Warren Zevon

b. Jan. 24, 1947, Chicago, IL
Singer-Songwriter
How did a guy with such a wickedly black sense of humor and a love for tough rock & roll get to be a '70s Los Angeles songwriting pro? By tempering that dark streak with some evocative and personal ballads, which surveyed the trappings of the Los Angeles lifestyle. Even at his worst, Zevon was always better than the Eagles, and with less sexism to boot. —*John Floyd*

○ **Warren Zevon** / 1976 / Asylum ✦✦✦✦
A beautiful and ambitious debut, it paints a gloomy and cryptic portrait of Hollywood's casualties through gripping songs like "Carmelita," "I'll Sleep When I'm Dead," and "Mohammed's Radio." —*John Floyd*

○ **Excitable Boy** / 1978 / Asylum ✦✦✦✦
A disappointing followup, Zevon's sensitivity is sacrificed for mere weirdness. Nevertheless, there's some fine music here. —*John Floyd*

Bad Luck Streak in Dancing School / 1980 / Asylum ✦✦
Warren Zevon's third album *Bad Luck Streak in Dancing School* was a step down from his first two records. Zevon's material either reworks his earlier songs or are flawed attempts to expand his sound, leaving the record a stylistic mess. —*Stephen Thomas Erlewine*

Stand in the Fire / 1981 / Asylum ✦✦✦
This live set rocks harder than his studio discs and also works as a career overview. —*John Floyd*

The Envoy / 1982 / Asylum ✦✦✦
On *The Envoy*, Warren Zevon's reflective side came to the forefront, as he created a set of songs that were more carefully crafted and subtle than his previous work, particularly the wistful "Looking for the Next Best Thing," but also had time for grinding rockers like "Ain't That Pretty at All." —*Stephen Thomas Erlewine*

● **A Quiet Normal Life: The Best of Warren Zevon** / 1986 / Asylum ✦✦✦✦
This is an adequate but skimpy best-of. —*John Floyd*

○ **Sentimental Hygiene** / 1987 / Virgin ✦✦✦✦
Warren Zevon returned in 1987 with his first new album in five years, *Sentimental Hygiene*. Featuring musical support by R.E.M., Zevon's songs take on a tough but melodic edge and the songs comprise his most consistent and impressive set since *Excitable Boy*. —*Stephen Thomas Erlewine*

Transverse City / 1989 / Virgin ✦✦✦
Zevon's attempt to integrate the influence of Stravinsky makes this album a complex, dense but still absorbing blast of jagged rock. —*John Floyd*

Mr. Bad Example / 1991 / Giant ✦✦
For Zevon, this is a rather tranquil set of soul searchers, but there's still some trenchant humor here. —*John Floyd*

Learning to Flinch / 1993 / Warner Brothers ✦✦✦
Warren Zevon recorded the acoustic *Learning to Flinch* at various venues all over the world. All of his best-known songs are here, in riveting rough acoustic forms. Longtime Zevon fans will find this essential and it may win him a few new ones too. —*AMG*

Mutineer / 1995 / Giant ✦✦
Recorded at home, the spare instrumentation of *Mutineer* doesn't work in favor of the album. Instead, it emphasizes the pretentious nature of many of the songs, along with their lack of melody, as the dirge-like "Something Bad Happened to a Clown" indicates. —*Stephen Thomas Erlewine*

Zombies

Group, British Invasion
Aside from the Beatles and perhaps the Beach Boys, no mid-'60s rock group wrote melodies as gorgeous as the Zombies. Dominated by Colin Blunstone's breathy vocals, choral backup harmonies, and Rod Argent's shining jazz- and classical-influenced organ and piano, the band sounded utterly unique for their era. Indeed, their material—penned by either Argent or guitarist Chris White, with unexpected shifts from major to minor keys—was perhaps too adventurous for the singles market. After scoring two quick hits with "She's Not There" and "Tell Her No" (which were actually much more popular in the U.S. than the U.K.) in late 1964 and early 1965, the Zombies released a string of equally fine, intricately arranged singles that flopped commercially. "Remember When I Loved Her," "I Want You Back Again," "Indication," "She's Coming Home," "Whenever You're Ready," "Gotta Get a Hold of Myself," "I Must Move," "Remember You," "Just out of Reach," "How We Were Before"—all are lost classics, some relegated to B-sides, that went virtually unheard.

The Zombies had already decided to pack up in 1967 when they recorded their only cohesive full-length platter, *Odyssey and Oracle* (their first album was largely pasted together from singles and covers). A near-masterpiece of pop-psychedelia, it showed the band reaching new levels of sophistication in composition and performance, and was one of the first albums to prominently feature the Mellotron. The group had been defunct for some time when one of the tracks, the great "Time of the Season," took off in early 1969 to become their biggest hit. Resisting temptations to reform, Rod Argent went in a harder rock direction as the leader of Argent, and Colin Blunstone had some success (more in Britain than America) as a solo vocalist. Much more influential than their commercial success would indicate, echoes of the Zombies' innovations can be heard in the Doors, the Byrds, the Left Banke, the Kinks, and many others. —*Richie Unterberger*

○ **Odessey & Oracle** / 1968 / Rhino ✦✦✦✦
A psychedelic effort whose best song, "Time of the Season" became a monster hit with a sultry, soulful sound not replicated elsewhere on the album. —*Bruce Eder*

Time of the Zombies / 1973 / Epic ✦✦✦
This double LP, containing the entire *Odyssey And Oracle* and another disc of hits and outtakes, is not recommended as an overall sampler; there are other compilations that do a much better job. Zombie collectors, though, will be interested in finding this; Side Two contains eight songs that have rarely been available anywhere else, comprised mostly of late-'60s outtakes and a rare single, some of which may have been recorded in the post-Zombies, pre-Argent days without Blunstone. This material doesn't rank among their best (though Dusty Springfield did cover "If It Don't Work Out" in the mid-'60s), but the piano-dominated "I'll Call You Mine" would have been easily strong enough to fit into *Odyssey And Oracle*. —*Richie Unterberger*

Live on the BBC / 1985 / Rhino ✦✦✦
While this compilation of 14 BBC airshots has barely different versions of their self-penned singles "Tell Her No," "Just Out Of Reach," and "Whenever You're Ready," it concentrates on their covers of a surprisingly wide array of soul and R&B standards that the group never released on record. Unlike, say, the Stones, the Zombies were much more noted for their compositional prowess than their original interpretations of American rock and soul; the group's tasteful, melodic restraint could make them sound tame and out of their depth when they tackled chestnuts like "I've Got My Mojo Working" on their first LP. But the covers here, empha-

sizing the band's harmonies and Rod Argent's keyboards, are reasonably well done. Includes songs originally performed by the Isley Brothers, Aretha Franklin, Gene Vincent, the Supremes, Curtis Mayfield, and others, some of them quite obscure even in their original incarnations. Excellent sound rounds off an album that gives some unexpected insight into the Zombies' influences. — *Richie Unterberger*

Best & the Rest of the Zombies / 1986 / Back-Trac ✦✦✦
This half-baked compilation, with only eight songs, is noteworthy only in that it includes three previously unreleased songs, two of which were actually recorded by Rod Argent and Chris White in the late '60s without Colin Blunstone. One of those, "Girl Help Me," is a really fine ballad, and the mid-'60s outtake "I'll Keep Trying" is a decent, characteristic uptempo number. — *Richie Unterberger*

★ **Singles A's & B's** / 1990 / See For Miles ✦✦✦✦✦
While "She's Not There" and "Tell Her No" are the only well-remembered mid-'60s Zombies singles, they recorded quite a few great non-hit 45s as well during this period. This outstanding collection (now available on CD) features all 22 of the sides they released on singles between 1964-67, and shows the group to be among the most superbly inventive pop-rock composers of their era, exploring moody minor-key melodies more than anyone before or since. Colin Blunstone's delicate, neurotic vocals and Rod Argent's biting electric keyboards pace the band on this set, which features the two big hits and such great lost classics as "Remember When I Loved Her," "I Want You Back Again," "I Must Move," "Indication," and "Gotta Get a Hold of Myself." Essential British Invasion music. — *Richie Unterberger*

● **Greatest Hits** / DCC ✦✦✦✦
The early sides. All well-chosen Brit-beat with a strong R&B influence. — *Bruce Eder*

ZZ Top

Group, Rock & Roll, Blues Rock
American blues-rock trio from Texas consists of Billy Gibbons (guitar), Dusty Hill (bass), and Frank Beard (drums). They were formed in 1970 in and around Houston from rival bands, the Moving Sidewalks (Gibbons) and the American Blues (Hill and Beard). Their first two albums reflected the strong blues roots and Texas humor of the band. The third album (*Tres Hombres*) gained them national attention with hit "La Grange," a signature riff tune to this day. Their success continued unabated throughout the '70s, culminating with the year-and-a-half-long Worldwide Texas Tour. Exhausted from the overwhelming work load, they took a three-year break, then switched labels and returned to form with *Deguello* and *El Loco,* both harbingers of what was to come. By their next album *Eliminator* and its worldwide smash follow-up *Afterburner,* they had successfully harnessed the potential of synthesizers to their patented grunge-groove, giving their material a more contemporary edge while retaining their patented Texas style. Now sporting long beards, golf hats, and boiler suits, they met the emerging video age head-on, reducing their "message" to simple iconography. Becoming even more popular in the long run, they moved with the times while simultaneously bucking every trend that crossed their path. As genuine roots musicians, they have few peers; Gibbons is one of America's finest blues guitarists working in the arena of rock idiom, while Hill and Beard provide the ultimate rhythm section support. The only rock & roll group that's out there with its original members still aboard after 20-plus years, ZZ Top's music is always instantly recognizable, eminently powerful, profoundly soulful, and 100% American in derivation. — *Cub Koda*

ZZ Top's First Album / 1970 / Warner Brothers ✦✦✦
This Texas trio's debut was a gritty exercise in bare-boned blues boogie. Tracks like "Brown Sugar," "Neighbor Neighbor," and "Shakin' Your Tree" helped establish them as a regionally successful act in the South. — *Rick Clark*

Rio Grande Mud / 1972 / Warner Brothers ✦✦✦
Rio Grande Mud possessed a beefier sound than its predecessor. The "Brown Sugar"-style "Francene" became their first hit at number 69. Other highlights included "Chevrolet" and "Just Got Paid." — *Rick Clark*

○ **Tres Hombres** / 1973 / Warner Brothers ✦✦✦✦
Constant touring and favorable radio exposure made *Tres Hombres* ZZ's first hit album, thanks in no small part to "La Grange" (number 41), an ode to a whorehouse. By this album, Billy Gib-

bons had practically perfected his distinctively dirty electric-guitar sound. His riffs and chordal voicings were also more memorable. Highlights included "Beer Drinkers & Hell Raisers," "Precious & Grace," and the two-some "Waitin' for the Bus," and "Jesus Just Left Chicago." — *Rick Clark*

Fandango / 1975 / Warner Brothers ✦✦✦
Fandango is a half-studio/half-live effort. The concert side is a fairly straightahead, no-nonsense affair, which includes a version of "Jailhouse Rock." The studio side featured their first Top 40 hit, "Tush" (number 20). The hyper-boogie of "Heard It on the X" was another popular track off of this release. — *Rick Clark*

Takin' Texas to the People / 1976 / London ✦✦

Tejas / 1976 / Warner Brothers ✦✦

★ **The Best of ZZ Top** / 1977 / Warner Brothers ✦✦✦✦✦
The sound may be a little muddy, but this anthology is still the best representation of ZZ's early work. It contains classic rude, riff-heavy blues rockers like "Just Got Paid," "Jesus Just Left Chicago," "Heard It on the X," "Tush," and "La Grange." — *Rick Clark*

○ **Deguello** / 1979 / Warner Brothers ✦✦✦✦
Deguello was ZZ's best album from their pre-robotic blues-rock period—the last reminder of what a tough ensemble this trio could be. It was the first time they infused their lunkhead approach to fast cars, kinky girls, and partying with some bizarre humor. Their version of Sam & Dave's "I Thank You" (number 34) became their first Top 40 hit in five years. Other highlights included the oddball "Manic Mechanic," a rip-roaring version of Elmore James's "Dust My Broom," the funky boogie of "Cheap Sunglasses," and "Fool for Your Stockings," a down-and-dirty fetish blues. — *Rick Clark*

El Loco / 1981 / Warner Brothers ✦✦✦
Not as strong as *Deguello, El Loco* vacillates between half-baked ballads ("Leila") and novelty rockers ("Party on the Patio," "Groovy Little Hippie Pad," "Heaven, Hell or Houston"). "Pearl Necklace," with its not-too-subtle sexual double-entendre and Police-inspired groove, was a big AOR hit. — *Rick Clark*

● **Eliminator** / 1983 / Warner Brothers ✦✦✦✦
Hardcore fans might have cried "sellout," but ZZ's introduction of a streamlined synth-heavy sound (and three slickly produced T&A videos) turned this trio from potential blues-rock has-beens to multi-platinum purveyors of space boogie. Most of this album became a staple on album rock radio, with "Gimme All Your Lovin'" (number 37), "Sharp Dressed Man" (number 56), and "Legs" (number 8) becoming the primary hits. — *Rick Clark*

Afterburner / 1985 / Warner Brothers ✦✦✦
Basically a carbon-copy of *Eliminator, Afterburner* continued ZZ's winning streak, which includes four hit singles: "Sleeping Bag" (#8), "Stages" (#21), "Rough Boy" (#22), and "Velcro Fly" (#35). — *Rick Clark*

Six Pack / 1987 / Warner Brothers ✦✦
The idea of compiling albums one through five, plus their seventh effort, onto a three-disc set seemed like a good one. After all, there's a load of great playing on these discs. Unfortunately, the first five albums were hastily remixed from the original multi-tracks. The sound might have more definition and punch, but the effort to update the drum sounds with triggered samples, re-amped guitars, and cold digital reverbs gave some of the music a stiff, clinical quality. Why a band that touts the power of an organic genre like the blues would so insensitively plunder the recordings they made when they really were a real live band, makes one wonder if the sequencers had finally gone to their brains. That ZZ's management and Warner allowed such a half-baked job on the market seems to support that assertion. — *Rick Clark*

Recycler / 1990 / Warner Brothers ✦✦✦
ZZ seemed to be running low on good material as they cranked up the Fairlights for a third go-round. "My Head's in Mississippi," however, is a fine rocker, which synthesized the gritty virtues of their earlier sound with the hi-tech gloss of their later work. *Recycler* also includes "Doubleback," their hit from the movie *Back to the Future—Part III.* — *Rick Clark*

Greatest Hits / 1992 / Warner Brothers ✦✦✦
An 18-song compilation, it features the greatest hits of ZZ Top's MTV era, including "Gimme All Your Lovin'," "Sharp Dressed Man," "Tush," "Pearl Necklace," "Cheap Sunglasses," "Sleeping Bag," "Rough Boy," and a remixed version of "Legs." It's a good, fun collection that should have been sequenced better and, unfortunately, omits a few good songs. — *AMG*

Antenna / 1994 / RCA ✦✦✦

Like precious few bands from the '70s whose best work is mummified daily thanks to classic rock radio, ZZ Top just keeps rolling on into the next decade. There"s much to love here, from the downright nasty stomp of "Fuzzbox Voodoo," the powerhouse slow blues of "Cover Your Rig," the bass pumping looniness of "Girl in a T-Shirt," to the slow grind of "Breakaway." While Billy Gibbon's guitar tones on this album are highly reminiscent of *Tres Hombres* (an early high-water mark for the band), the high production sheen from their '80s albums remains intact. But Gibbons hasn"t played with this much over-the-top abandon since thei rpre-beard 'n' babes days, and that's

what separates this album from the three that came before it. – Cub Koda

One Foot In The Blues / 1994 / Warner Brothers ✦✦

Before they sweated their image down to beards, babes and hot rods, ZZ Top were a down 'n' dirty blues-rock trio with a bonafide hot guitar player in Billy Gibbons. On this 14-track offering Warners goes back through the back ZZ catalog and cobbles together an interesting collection of the Texas trio's bluesier sides that originally appeared on their earliest albums. Highlights include "Brown Sugar," "A Fool for Your Stockings," "My Head's in Mississippi," "Apologies to Pearly" and Gibbons's storming stringwork on "Bar-B-Q." —*Cub Koda*

VARIOUS ARTISTS

○ **20 Hard to Find Classics, Vol. 2** / Motown ♦♦♦♦
This second volume contains some not-so-rare tracks that remain ageless. —*Rick A. Bueche*

○ **20 Hard-To-Find Motown Classics, Vol. 1** / Motown ♦♦♦♦
This is a good collection of superb but overlooked Motown singles. —*AMG*

○ **25 #1 Hits in 25 Years** / 1983 / Motown ♦♦♦♦
This is an excellent collection of the company's gems. —*Rick A. Bueche*

★ **25 Hard to Find Motown Classics, Vol. 3** / 1986 / Motown ♦♦♦♦♦
Included are the best of the *Hard to Find* series. —*Rick A. Bueche*

○ **7 Inch Wonders of the World** / SST ♦♦♦♦
The best of SST's singles from the early '80s. —*John Dougan*

70's Greatest Rock Hits, Vol. 1—Hard N' Heavy / 1991 / Priority ♦♦♦
Priority has released fifteen volumes of '70s hits, loosely arranged around such themes as *Southern Comfort, High Times,* and *Kickin' Back.* While the discs aren't definitive, they nevertheless offer a good portrait of their particular theme. Each disc features the original hit version; the remastering is fine, but the liner notes are nonexistent. Despite its flaws, *'70s Greatest Rock Hits* is one of the best budget-line series available—each disc presents the original version of popular singles in one hit-filled, ten-track disc. —*Stephen Thomas Erlewine*

The 80's Greatest Rock Hits, Vol. 1: Passion & Power / Priority ♦♦♦
Like Priority's corresponding *'70s Greatest Rock Hits* series, *'80s Greatest Rock Hits* arranges several hit singles according to loose themes like *Arena Rock* and *The Agony & the Ecstasy.* Each disc contains the original hit version in good fidelity; like other Priority releases, this also lacks liner notes. However, the discs are enjoyable and several discs feature songs that are hard to find on other releases. Priority later began their *Rock of the '80s* series, which covered the same ground in a more haphazard, yet more enjoyable, manner. —*Stephen Thomas Erlewine*

○ **Ace Story, Vol. 1** / ACE ♦♦♦♦
With five separate volumes, *The Ace Story* is the most comprehensive portrait of the seminal New Orleans R&B record label. Over the course of the series, each of the label's hits are featured, including "Sea Cruise," "Rockin' Pneumonia," "Pop Eye," among others, as well as many lesser-known gems. During the late '50s and early '60s, Ace's roster featured such R&B giants as Huey "Piano" Smith, Eddie Bo, Joe Tex, Lightnin' Hopkins, Charles Brown, Amos Milburn, and Earl King; each artist is featured on at least one disc of *The Ace Story,* along with several acts that didn't have hits, but recorded some outstanding tracks. Start with the first volume, then proceed to the other discs; every one is filled with timeless R&B. —*Stephen Thomas Erlewine*

Acid Jazz: Collection 1 / Scotti Brothers ♦♦♦
Scotti Brothers has issued three separate volumes of acid jazz, a popular dance genre of the late '80s and early '90s that combines elements of jazz, hip-hop, funk, and R&B. Like most dance music, it is primarily a singles medium, so compilations serve the music well; none of the featured songs were pop hits, yet almost every track has something to recommend it, whether it's the beat, vocals, or instrumentals. While some major names of the genre are missing from the three discs, any volume of *Acid Jazz—Collection* is a

good place to be introduced to the music. —*Stephen Thomas Erlewine*

Acid Rock / 198? / Rhino ♦♦♦
Switching to a decidedly heavier mode, this comp includes hits by Love, the Byrds, Steppenwolf, Iron Butterfly, the Chambers Brothers, Vanilla Fudge, and the Strawberry Alarm Clock, as well as worthy lighter, slightly obscure offerings by the Grass Roots, the Monkees, and the Young Rascals. —*Richie Unterberger*

● **Acid Visions: Best of Texas Punk/Psychedelic, Vol. 1** / Collectables ♦♦♦♦
One of the very best '60s garage compilations, a high compliment given the thousands of competitors, and the very best Texas '60s garage anthology. With the possible exception of California, Texas was home to more fine obscure garage records than any other state, and these 14 cuts are among the finest. Roy Head delivers a fine Johnny Winter tune, "Easy Lovin' Girl," and Winter himself sings a prime slice of folk-rock-acid-punk, "Birds Can't Row Boats" (this version, incidentally, is much better than the one found on the early Winter compilation of the same name). The other names are totally obscure, and some of the tracks weren't even released until the 1980s. But the Things and the Bad Roads come through with fine pop-punk numbers, and A-440's "Torture," Satori's "Time Machine," and the Pandas' "Walk" have been belatedly recognized as some of the best garage psychedelia ever, combining sharp melodic hooks and songwriting with out-and-out dementia. —*Richie Unterberger*

☆ **Atlantic R&B—1947-1974** / 1991 / Atlantic ♦♦♦♦♦
Along with Specialty, Aladdin, Chess, Sun, and a few other labels, Atlantic paved the way for rock & roll. Started by Ahmet Ertegun and Herb Abramson in 1947, Atlantic brought meticulous recording techniques—usually reserved only for jazz sessions—to R&B. They assembled a revolving cast of crack studio musicians. This seven-disc set (eight CDs on the boxed set) is a perfect collection of all the best singles from Atlantic Records. —*John Floyd*

○ **Atlantic Sisters of Soul** / 1992 / Rhino ♦♦♦♦
A fine collection of lesser-known female soul artists on Atlantic, including artists that aren't normally associated with the label, like Mary Wells and the Pointer Sisters. All of the songs were recorded in the late '60s and early '70s, and only three of the disc's 23 tracks scratched the R&B Top 20, although most the tracks were good enough to be hits. While the songs may not be familiar, their sweet sound is, making the disc a worthwhile purchase for fans of early-'70s soul. —*Stephen Thomas Erlewine*

○ **Atlantic Soul Classics** / Warner Brothers ♦♦♦♦
This was the first CD collection of Atlantic's greatest '60s soul burners. You can now find most of these on better collections, but this still isn't a bad place to start your education. —*John Floyd*

Back to the Streets / 1993 / Shanachie ♦♦♦
Every facet of Don Covay's arsenal is covered on this 16-cut tribute album loaded with rock celebrity types, but proves to be much more than an empty, posturing session. Surprises include Barrence Whitfield's rousing "Pony Time," with a fine guitar solo from Milton Reder, Billy Squier's animated "See Saw," Nona Hendryx's wistful "We Can't Make It No More" and Bobby Womack's marvelous "Checkin' Out." Even less than stalwart efforts, like Ron Wood's "Chain of Fools" and Robert Cray's "He Don't Know," are listenable, and when the duo of Arlene Smith and Johnny Colla make "Letter Full of Tears" poignant, it is the ultimate testimony to Don Covay's greatness. —*Ron Wynn*

☆ **Beach Classics: All Original Recordings** / 1987 / Dcc ✦✦✦✦✦
A terrific 20-song collection of surf hits from the early '60s, including the classics "Miserlou," "California Sun," and "Surfin' Bird," as well as many forgotten gems. Not only is the song selection first-rate, but the sound is as good as it could be, considering that the original master tapes were probably not well-preserved. — *Stephen Thomas Erlewine*

○ **Beachbeat Shaggin'** / Dcc ✦✦✦✦
This is a good overview of light '60s soul nuggets known on the Atlantic coast as beach music. —*John Floyd*

The Beavis & Butt-Head Experience / 1993 / Geffen ✦✦✦
Based on the popular and conterversial MTV show, *The Beavis & Butt-Head Experience* is a collection of hard-rock bands that... don't suck. Although the humor sketches wear thin after only one play, the music doesn't; some of the songs—especially Jackyl's—are subpar, but Nirvana, Primus, White Zombie, and Beavis & Butt-Head's "Come to Butt-Head" make the disc worthwhile. —*Stephen Thomas Erlewine*

● **Best of Ace Records, Vol. 2: R&B Hits** / 1993 / SCB ✦✦✦✦
Scotti Brothers' two volumes of highlights from Ace Records' roster are the best available sampler of the label's late-'50s/early-'60s R&B and pop hits, featuring such stars as Huey "Piano" Smith, Frankie Ford, Joe Tex, and Jimmy Clanton. Both volumes have detailed liner notes and great songs; both are essential for comprehensive rock and R&B collections. —*Stephen Thomas Erlewine*

Best of Buddah / 1953 / Pair ✦✦
This single-disc Cliff Notes-style version of Buddah's hit catalog is a decent sampler for the uninitiated. The sound quality lacks some clarity. Brief liner notes are included. —*Rick Clark*

Best of Candlelite Records, Vol. 1 / 1993 / Juke Box Treasures ✦✦✦
This is the original installment in this landmark series, collecting 28 obscure doo wop tracks that were originally issued on Wayne Stierle's Candlelite label. The original "Why Don't You Write Me" by The Feathers is here, along with Jesse Belvin sitting in with them on "Love Song." The crude and crazed "Jeannie" by The Thrashers also makes its first CD appearance, along with the teenage bop of "Come on Baby" by The Five Discs and the dreamy teen sentimentality of "Lost Lover" by The Cameos and "Romance in the Spring" by The Five Roses. An excellent compilation covering the super-obscure side of the genre, and great listening every note of the way.— Cub Koda

☆ **The Best of Chess R&B, Vol. 1** / Chess ✦✦✦✦✦
This Chess R&B anthology came out initially in a pair of double album sets. Then it was reissued on two CDs, with each disc covering one of the albums, although they left some tracks off each volume due to programming restrictions. This covers the first double album and includes cuts from the Moonglows, some early Miracles, Etta James, Sugar Pie Desanto, Jan Bradley, Billy Stewart, and Little Milton. —*Ron Wynn*

☆ **The Best of Chess R&B, Vol. 2** / Chess ✦✦✦✦✦
The second Chess CD covers the second double album and features later R&B cuts from Billy Stewart, Mitty Collier, the Dells, Jackie Ross, Etta James, the Ramsey Lewis Trio, and the Radiants. The stylistic lines are blurred a bit here, since some of these artists were also featured on the *Best of Chess* soul anthology that had been previously issued. —*Ron Wynn*

☆ **Best of Chess Rhythm & Blues** / Chess ✦✦✦✦✦
A good various-artists collection from the great Chicago R&B label, it includes Fontella Bass's "Rescue Me," Billy Stewart's "Summertime," Jan Bradley's "Mama Didn't Lie," and an early Smokey Robinson & the Miracles effort, "Bad Girl." —*Dan Heilman*

☆ **The Best of Chess Rock & Roll** / Chess ✦✦✦✦✦
Over two separate volumes, *Best of Chess Rock & Roll* gives a good portrait of the seminal record label's massive contributions to rock & roll. Not only are landmarks like Chuck Berry's "Johnny B. Goode" and Bo Diddley's "Bo Diddley" covered, cult favorites like the Moonglows and the Students are also featured. With "Johnny B. Goode," "Maybelline," "Who Do You Love," "Ain't Got No Home," "Rocket 88," and "Susie Q" all on the first volume, it is one of the most essential single-disc rock collections ever assembled; the second volume is nearly as important, with "Book of Love," "High Heel Sneakers," "No Particular Place to Go," "Ten Commandments of Love," and "Road Runner" among the featured tracks. —*Stephen Thomas Erlewine*

○ **The Best of Chess Rock & Roll, Vol. 1** / Chess ✦✦✦✦
Two-volume set featuring landmark recordings by Bo Diddley, Chuck Berry, Dale Hawkins and others. —*Cub Koda*

○ **The Best of Chess Vocal Groups** / Chess ✦✦✦✦
Rounding out the trilogy of Chess sampler albums, this one features "Long Lonely Nights" by Lee Andrews & the Hearts, the highly influential "Every Day of the Week" by the Students, and the Southern soul of the Knight Brothers "Temptation 'Bout to Get Me." —*Cub Koda*

○ **The Best of Chess Vocal Groups, Vol. 1** / Chess ✦✦✦✦
Classic doo wop from the Moonglows, the Flamingos, etc. —*Cub Koda*

○ **The Best of Chess Vocal Groups, Vol. 2** / Chess ✦✦✦✦
Companion volume to the above, no less intense, with a nod toward rare material. —*Cub Koda*

☆ **Best of Doo Wop Ballads** / 1989 / Rhino ✦✦✦✦✦
The other part of this doo wop hits collection, novices would do well to start right here. —*John Floyd*

☆ **Best of Doo Wop Uptempo** / 1989 / Rhino ✦✦✦✦✦
Rhino's *Best of Doo Wop* compilations are a glorious pair of discs that salute the finest doo wop hits. Most collectors already have this stuff, but novices would do well to start right here. —*John Floyd*

☆ **Best of Excello Records, Vol. 1** / 1991 / Rhino ✦✦✦✦✦
The Nashville-based Excello label specialized in obscure blues, R&B, and rock & roll from the '50s and early '60s. This first volume of *Sound of the Swamp (The Best of Excello Records)* covers the best from Crowley, LA, producer Jay Miller's blues, rockabilly, and swamp-pop sides. —*John Floyd*

☆ **Best of Excello Records, Vol. 2** / 1991 / Rhino ✦✦✦✦✦
The second volume of *The Best of Excello Records* isn't as consistent as the first, but nevertheless there is some fine material here. —*AMG*

☆ **The Best of House Music** / 1988 / Profile ✦✦✦✦✦
Use this as an introduction into the frenetic world of house music. —*Ron Wynn*

○ **Best of House Music, Vol. 2** / 1988 / Profile ✦✦✦✦
Gotta Have House—the journey continues... —*Ron Wynn*

○ **Best of House Music, Vol. 3: All Night Long** / 1988 / Profile ✦✦✦✦
The culmination of the trip. —*Ron Wynn*

○ **The Best of Metal Blade, Vol. 1** / 1988 / Metal Blade ✦✦✦✦
The first best-of package from Metal Blade contains very early tracks from Bitch, Celtic Frost, Fates Warning, Hallow's Eve, Hirax, Lizzy Borden, Metal Church, Slayer, Trouble, and Voivod. —*John Book*

○ **The Best of Metal Blade, Vol. 2** / 1988 / Capitol ✦✦✦✦
A sampler of music from the excellent Metal Blade label, considered to be music for the "headbanging connoisseur." —*John Book*

★ **The Best of New Orleans Rhythm & Blues, Vol. 1** / 1988 / Rhino ✦✦✦✦✦
Some of the greatest music ever, period—the Meters, Clarence Henry, Lloyd Price, etc. Endless groovin'. —*Jeff Tamarkin*

☆ **The Best of New Orleans Rhythm & Blues, Vol. 2** / 1988 / Rhino ✦✦✦✦✦
More funky gumbo, from Smiley Lewis, Irma Thomas, Earl King, and others who know how to have a good time. —*Jeff Tamarkin*

☆ **Best of Nuggets** / Rhino ✦✦✦✦✦
Punk and garage rock from the '60s, raw and essential. Probably the best compilation ever done on the genre, featuring classics by the Seeds, the Syndicate of Sound, the Count Five, the Chocolate Watchband, and others. Part of a continuing series. —*Cub Koda*

○ **Best of Ric Records, Vol. 1: Carnival Time** / Rounder ✦✦✦✦
One of two great '50s-vintage collections of music from the New Orleans Ric and Ron records, there's no hits here, but plenty to keep you rocking. —*John Floyd*

○ **Best of Ron Records, Vol. 1: We Got a Party** / Rounder ✦✦✦✦
This is the second half of a collection of '50s vintage music on the New Orleans-based Ric and Ron records labels, including some rare Professor Longhair sides. —*John Floyd*

○ **The Best of Sue Records** / Collectables ✦✦✦✦
Find out why Sue Records was one of New Orleans's greatest and most revered R&B/soul labels, and the early home to such artists as Aaron Neville and Ike & Tina Turner. —*John Floyd*

○ **The Best of Techno, Vol. 1** / 1991 / Profile ✦✦✦✦
Techno is a rapidly expanding and changing genre, so any collection can't possibly capture the full diversity of the music. Still, Priority's three discs of *Best of Techno* does a fair job in conveying part of the music's excitement and stylistic variety; it's strictly for novices, and any volume serves as an adequate introduction to techno. —*Stephen Thomas Erlewine*

Best of a Cappella / 1965 / Relic ✦✦✦
Relic, the nation's premier doowop reissue label, celebrates its past with this 20-track retrospective reissue of their first album from 1965. They spotlighted East Coast vocal groups, most of them new and unknown at the time. The fact that they stayed that way does not detract from the set's significance. These numbers are sung with simplicity and at times with an almost painful innocence and the natural exuberance that comes from a labor of love. The absence of supporting (or masking) technology ensures that you hear everything, including mistakes, flat notes, superb and awful harmonies, great leads and not-so-great voices. While not everything qualifies as even good, it is all compelling. —*Ron Wynn*

Beyond The Beach / 1995 / Upstart/Denon ✦✦✦
Beyond The Beach is a 19-track compilation of contemporary surf and instrumental combos. Rocket fueled with twangy guitars drenched in reverb (with the occasional fuzz-charged tip of the hat to Link Wray), the music collected here takes the instrumental form straight into the '90s. Highlights include Teisco Del Rey's "Twango" (with guest appearance by Duane Eddy's saxman, the late Steve Douglas), Finnish group Laika & the Cosmonauts' "Global Village," The Goldentones' "Outbound," and Paul Johnson (of The Bel-Airs) cranking out "Tsunami." —*Cub Koda*

Beyond The Wall Of Sound / ✦✦✦
Like its sister compilation *Lookin' For Boys*, this is the finest anthology of obscure girl-group singles. *Lookin' For Boys* has the edge for its slightly stronger track selection, but this features several cuts that are almost as great as the best classics of the genre, especially the rarities like Diane Renay ("Watch Out Sally"), Shelley Fabares ("He Don't Love Me"), and Shirley Matthews ("Big Town Boy"). —*Richie Unterberger*

○ **The Big Itch** / Mr. Mannicotti ✦✦✦✦
Insane compilation of extremely raw, crude, and obscure rock and roll tracks. Side 1 is all "Pa Pa Ooh Mow Mow" and "Surfin' Bird"-related tunes, while Side 2 charts territory into the awesomely arcane, featuring the title track and offerings by King Uszniewicz and Trez Trezo. Not for the faint of heart. —*Cub Koda*

○ **Billboard Top Dance Hits: 1976** / 1992 / Rhino ✦✦✦✦
Covering the disco years in detail, Rhino's five-volume *Billboard Top Dance Hits* series is a worthwhile budget retrospective. It isn't as complete or definitive as the label's *Disco Years* series, but it features several tracks that didn't make that series, as well as songs that aren't easily available on other compilations, making it necessary for disco fans. Ten of the top dance hits for each year from 1976 to 1980 are featured on each disc, including such hits as "You Should Be Dancing," "Love Hangover," "Ring My Bell," "You Make Me Feel (Mighty Real)," "Funkytown," "Got to Give It Up," and "Call Me" in their original single form. Unlike the other *Billboard* series, *Top Dance Hits* actually has liner notes about the songs, not trivia about a particular year. —*Stephen Thomas Erlewine*

☆ **Billboard Top Hits: 1975** / 1991 / Rhino ✦✦✦✦✦
Rhino ended its *Billboard Top Rock & Roll Hits* series with the 1974 volume, replacing it with the *Billboard Top Hits* series beginning with the year 1975. It has the same faults and attributes as the *Rock & Roll* series; the only difference is the fact that it merges R&B with the pop singles. Since the late '70s were filled with cheerfully disposable pop singles, each volume differs greatly in quality; the 1978 and 1979 discs are the most consistent, with several soft-rock and disco hits on each album. Rhino's *Have A Nice Day* and *Disco Years* series cover this era in greater detail, with more hits and novelty items on both series; however, these are concise, fun snapshots of a particularly embarrassing and enjoyable moment in pop history. —*Stephen Thomas Erlewine*

☆ **Billboard Top Hits: 1980** / 1992 / Rhino ✦✦✦✦✦
When Rhino's *Billboard Top Hits* series hit the 1980s, the collection began to lose a little steam. From 1980 through 1985, the discs are representative of the pop mainstream, although there were the usual major artists missing. Still, the discs contained plenty of one-hit wonders and classic singles like "Bette Davis Eyes," "Jessie's Girl," "Down Under," "Maneater," and "Centerfold," with the highest concentration of good singles on the 1983 volume. As the series approached the end of the decade, the problem of licensing reared its ugly head; not only were major artists like Madonna, Prince, Phil Collins, and Guns N' Roses unavailable, but smaller artists like Rick Astley, Roxette, Poison, and Michael Damien also don't appear. Although there are a couple of enjoyable period pieces, like Donny Osmond's "Soldier of Love," the bulk of the tracks can't cover the absence of "Never Gonna Give You Up," "Every Rose Has Its Thorn," and "The Look." Perhaps these should have waited a couple of years. —*Stephen Thomas Erlewine*

☆ **Billboard Top R&B Hits: 1955** / 1989 / Rhino ✦✦✦✦✦
Despite its faults, Rhino's *Billboard Top R&B Hits* is one of the finest retrospectives of R&B from 1955 to 1974 ever assembled. The song selection was sometimes puzzling, the liner notes nonexistent, and each disc only had ten tracks, frequently lasting under half an hour. However, the 20-disc series featured most of the major artists and singles of each individual year, as well as providing a rough sketch of the evolution from R&B to soul to disco. For beginners, such an affordable introduction was invaluable; for collectors, the brevity may have been frustrating, but they couldn't argue with the fidelity or the fact that many of these songs were appearing on disc for the first time. Legends like Clyde McPhatter, Little Richard, Jackie Wilson, James Brown, Ben E. King, Brook Benton, Marvin Gaye, Temptations, Supremes, Aretha Franklin, Smokey Robinson, Isley Brothers, Sly Stone, and Curtis Mayfield are featured. The series is currently out of print, but can still be found in cut-out bins. —*Stephen Thomas Erlewine*

☆ **Billboard Top Rock & Roll Hits: 1955** / 1988 / Rhino ✦✦✦✦✦
Despite its many faults, Rhino's *Billboard Top Rock & Roll Hits* is as good an introduction to consistently diverse music as possible. It's marred by a confusing song selection, poor liner notes, and brevity, as well as the omission of several important pop, rock, and album-rock artists. However, the series isn't attempting to be comprehensive. Instead, it offers a view of the popular mainstream for each year from 1955 to 1974 at an affordable price. With Elvis, Chuck Berry, Fats Domino, Jerry Lee Lewis, the Everly Brothers, Buddy Holly, and Carl Perkins on the initial '50s volumes, the discs are essential. As the series moves into the '60s, the discs remain remarkably consistent, featuring several Phil Spector hits, the Beach Boys, Dion, and the Kingsmen. It's only in the mid-'60s that the series begins to represent only radio hits, instead of portraying what was really happening during the era. Nevertheless, the 20 discs remain enjoyable listening. —*Stephen Thomas Erlewine*

○ **Black Rock Coalition: History of Our Future** / 1990 / Rykodisc ✦✦✦✦
Black Rock Coalition—History of Our Future is a fantastic collection of Black rock & roll from the organization formed by Living Colour's Vernon Reid. Diversity is the game here, with cuts by Blackasaurus Mex, Michael Hill's Bluesland, and Shock Council, mixing up funk, metal, and hip-hop as though they'd never heard of segregated radio playlists. —*John Floyd*

Black on White: R&B Covers of Rock / May 18, 1993 / Rhino ✦✦✦
Black On White collects a bunch of R&B covers of pop hits, including Run-D.M.C.'s "Walk This Way," Wilson Pickett's "Hey Jude," and Aretha Franklin's "Satisfaction." Although it sounds like a cheap gimmick, the results are surprisingly good and thoroughly listenable, with no embarrassing tracks; in fact, the best material is positively transcendent. —*Stephen Thomas Erlewine*

○ **Blackbox: Wax Trax! Records: The First 13 Years** / 1994 / Wax Trax!/TVT ✦✦✦✦
Wax Trax is the defining industrial music label; *Blackbox* is the definitive statement on their accomplishment. More than any other label, they defined the corrosive guitars, synths, distorted vocals and jackhammer beats that came to define industrial. Ministry, KMFDM, and Trent Reznor all recorded for them. *Blackbox* gathers nearly every worthwhile song to emerge from the Chicago label, including many rare singles, and provides an excellent introduction and summary of the most cutting-edge dance music of the 1980s and '90s. —*Stephen Thomas Erlewine*

Born Bad, Vol. 1 / Born Bad ✦✦✦
A five-disc series of supremely rare, trashy rockabilly and '60s garage punk, *Born Bad* showcases some of the wildest and most bizarre records ever recorded. A couple of artists and songs are fa-

miliar, most notably Little Willie John, Dale Hawkins, Wanda Jackson, Tommy James & the Shondells, and Charlie Feathers, but the bulk of the series is devoted to "Chop Suey Rock," "Bop Pills," and "Hot Lips Baby," which are what great rock & roll is made of. The first volume is the best starting place, but don't miss volume 4, which includes the *Mad Magazine* flexi-disc "It's A Gas." —*Stephen Thomas Erlewine*

Born to Choose / 1993 / Rykodisc ✦✦✦

A benefit album for abortion rights, *Born to Choose* features an almost standard cast of alternative musicians (including R.E.M., Natalie Merchant, Matthew Sweet, Bob Mould, and Soundgarden) supporting the most overtly political of all recent tribute collections. *Born to Choose* would be meaningless if the music was weak. Even though it is the standard mix of outtakes, B-sides, and live tracks, the music is worth the price, with R.E.M. & Natalie Merchant's "Photograph," Pavement's "Greenlander," and Sweet's "She Said, She Said" being the major highlights. —*Stephen Thomas Erlewine*

○ **Brace Yourself!: a Tribute to Otis Blackwell** / 1993 / Shanachie ✦✦✦✦

Most tribute albums fail because the interpretations are too diverse to make the album consistent. *Brace Yourself: A Tribute to Otis Blackwell* sidesteps that problem by having the artists record with a house band well-versed in the material of the legendary rock & roll/R&B songwriter. Thankfully, the approach works; none of the artists turn in a bad performance, and the disc rocks (albeit rather gently) from start to finish. But then again, it wasn't that hard to make a good album when the artists included Dave Edmunds, Graham Parker, Chrissie Hynde, Frank Black, the Smithereens, and Kris Kristofferson. —*Stephen Thomas Erlewine*

○ **The Bridge: A Tribute to Neil Young** / 1989 / Caroline ✦✦✦✦

In theory, *The Bridge: A Tribute to Neil Young* was a perfect concept, since most alternative bands of the late '80s owed the singer/songwriter a heavy debt. In practice, it wasn't entirely satisfying. Some groups, like Bongwater's collage of "Mr. Soul," made their interpretations self-consciously distinctive, while others, like Soul Asylum and Loop, played it close to the original. But the best moments came when a band played the song like it was their own. Listen to Sonic Youth's rampaging "Computer Age," Dinosaur Jr.'s faithful "Lotta Love," or the Pixies' gorgeous take on "Winterlong" for proof. —*Stephen Thomas Erlewine*

○ **Brief History of Ambient, Vol. 1** / Feb. 22, 1994 / Virgin ✦✦✦✦

Although it seemed to arrive out of nowhere in the early '90s, ambient music actually has a long and varied history, leading back to Brian Eno and Kraftwerk's electronic experiments in the 1970s right up to Aphex Twin's textural techno soundscapes. As an introduction and history lesson, the two-disc *A Brief History of Ambient Music* can't be beat; it shows that the latest techno trend has roots that most fans wouldn't even realize existed. —*Stephen Thomas Erlewine*

○ **Brill Building Sound** / 1993 / Era ✦✦✦✦

Although Phil Spector's songs weren't available due to licensing restrictions, the four-CD box set *The Brill Building Sound* remains an important and entertaining collection, featuring many of the songs that made the Brill Building a pop music institution in the early '60s. —*Stephen Thomas Erlewine*

★ **The British Invasion: History of British Rock, Vols. 1-9** / Jan. 21, 1992 / Rhino ✦✦✦✦✦

Imagine nine CDs (available separately or in a box) of those classic AM radio hits of the '60s, all of them from England, most of them as fresh-sounding and exciting as they were more than two decades ago. Now imagine that these nine CDs are devoid of Beatles (except for one early track), Stones, Who, early Animals, Dave Clark Five, and Herman's Hermits (all due to licensing problems), but that you won't miss them, and you'll get an idea of just how much quality pop/rock & roll came out of the UK in those several years. Included are the Kinks, Zombies, Hollies, Small Faces, Yardbirds, Manfred Mann, Them, Donovan, Peter and Gordon, Bee Gees, Cream, and much more. —*Jeff Tamarkin*

British R & B Explosion: '62–'68, Vol. 1 / See For Miles ✦✦✦

There really isn't any thread tying this 20-track compilation together, other than the fact that all of them originally appeared on Decca Records. It does offer the British Invasion collector a convenient way to gather up some loose ends, including rare early sin-

gles by Rod Stewart and Joe Cocker, three Graham Bond rarities that only appeared on an EP and a compilation, obscure 45s by cult artists Graham Gouldman, Duffy Power, and Zoot Money, and garage-cum-R&B cuts by Blues By Five, the Fairies, and others. The problem is, most of it's fairly humdrum: the really good selections (by the Fairies and Them) are easily available elsewhere, and much of the rest is pedestrian, even strained, British R&B. The top find is Tony Knight's "I Feel So Blue," which is not exactly R&B, but sounds like a Joe Meek production with its hyperventilating tempo and brilliant nervous guitar line. —*Richie Unterberger*

● **Bubblegum Classics Vol. 1 & 2** / 1995 / Varese Vintage ✦✦✦✦

Although they're missing a few key tracks (notably the Archies' hits and Kasenetz-Katz's "Quick Joey Small"), these are the best collections of late-'60s and early-'70s bubblegum hits ever assembled, including most of the major hits and a fair number of enticing rarities. In their favor, they encompass not just the most infantile, pre-teen smashes of the genre (1910 Fruitgum Co., Tommmy Roe, Bobby Sherman), but also quite a few cuts that could just as easily be classified as enjoyable, highly polished mainstream pop/rock (the Monkees, Tommy James, the Cuff Links, Keith, the Five Americans, the Flying Machine). Running at 20 tracks each, they're maybe a bit much all at once, but they're the best overview of a significant chapter in rock history. —*Richie Unterberger*

○ **Buddah Box** / 1993 / Essex ✦✦✦✦

During the '60s and '70s, Buddah Records enjoyed the role as America's most successful purveyor of Top 40 bubblegum and one-hit wonders. Along the way, they also signed a few significantly successful artists. They are all represented here on this three-disc, 45-track box set, which features hit tracks by the Lovin' Spoonful, Curtis Mayfield, Stories, Gladys Knight & the Pips, Bill Withers, Melanie, Ohio Express, 1910 Fruitgum Company, Edwin Hawkins Singers, Steve Goodman, Sha Na Na and many more. —*Rick Clark*

Buddy Holly Sound / 1988 / Rock & Country ✦✦✦

An intriguing compilation of 16 Buddy Holly soundalike singles, circa 1959-1963. With the exception of Tommy Roe's #1 hit (and "Peggy Sue" ripoff) "Sheila," these are all taken from excruciatingly rare 45s on tiny labels. Of course, this is not a substitute for listening to Buddy himself, but in the spirit of digging the Knickerbockers' superb Beatle knockoff "Lies," this is a nifty sampling of the best Holly imitations, from such never-weres as Bobby Jamesons, Marty Evans, Royce Clark, and Ray Ruff. Not only that, you get several different attempted angles on cornering the Holly sound: rockabilly raveups, sweet orchestrated ballads, easygoing three-chord guitar tunes. Sometimes the similarity is close enough to tell exactly what song they have in mind to evoke, be it "Peggy Sue" (used more than once), "Everyday," or something else. As sub-Buddy Holly attempts go, this anthology is much more successful—and much more enjoyable listening—than the efforts during the same era by the Holly-less Crickets. Besides Roe (who has two obscure cuts in addition to "Sheila"), other names to watch for here are Bobby Fuller, with both sides of his first locally pressed 45 (different than the versions on his *Tapes* reissue), and one David Box, who was briefly the lead singer for the Crickets after Holly died. —*Richie Unterberger*

Can't Stop Dancin' / 197z / K-Tel ✦✦✦

K-Tel hits a homer with the dance-oriented segment of its 1970s soul reissue lineup. While B.T. Express's "Express" and Brass Construction's "Moving" are easily obtainable, they are also seminal disco/funk numbers; so are "Fire" by the Ohio Players and "Get Down Tonight" by K.C. and the Sunshine Band. The Gary Toms Empire cut is a nice touch not usually included on '70s samplers. Only Kool and the Gang's "Jungle Boogie," Parliament's "Tear The Roof Off The Sucker (Give Up The Funk)" and Wild Cherry's "Play That Funky Music" qualify as possibly worthy of exclusion. —*Ron Wynn*

○ **Carnival Time: The Best of Ric Records, Vol. 1** / Rounder ✦✦✦✦

Stomping, romping good time numbers are the menu on this 14-track anthology issued in 1988. Such artists as Joe Jones, Al Johnson, Johnny Adams and Edgar Blanchard were hit acts in New Orleans at the time, but made raw music intended for only for the R&B faithful. While an occasional number like Adams' "I Won't Cry" or Jones' "You Talk Too Much" got a little pop attention, most, like Blanchard's hot "Let's Get It" and Tommy Ridgley's "She's Got What It Takes," didn't move anyone who didn't already have the soul spirit, and that's what made them great. —*Ron Wynn*

○ **Casablanca Records Story** / 1994 / Casablanca/Mercury ◆◆◆◆

Even though it includes four discs, *The Casablanca Records Story* ignores the record label's biggest success, Kiss. But that doesn't matter; Kiss didn't fit into the rest of the label's roster. Driven by the massive success of Donna Summer, Casablanca was arguably the definitive disco label in the late '70s, scoring a string of hit singles that have become classics of the era. Featuring four discs of original single versions and 12-inch mixes, *The Casablanca Records Story* features most of the best music the label released, even though it probably could have been more effectively compiled on two or three discs. Nevertheless, there is plenty of fine, even seminal, music here, which makes it essential for serious disco collectors. —*Stephen Thomas Erlewine*

○ **Chartbusters: The Best of Beserkley, 1975-1978** / Rhino ◆◆◆◆

Beserkley never scored any chart hits, but they were one of the best American independent record labels of the late '70s and early '80s, featuring such cult favorites as Jonathan Richman and Greg Kihn. *Best of the Beserkley Years* gathers up some the label's stripped-down rock & roll, offering a good picture of their music. —*Stephen Thomas Erlewine*

Cheatin': From A Man's Point Of View / 1995 / Ichiban/Soul Classics ◆◆◆

The companion volume to Ichiban's *Cheatin': From A Woman's Point Of View* offers similar anti-Valentine's Day messages from a variety of soul performers, most recorded between the mid-'60s and mid-'70s. The woman's volume is perhaps more interesting because it assembles more obscurities, but this is another generally worthy collection of non-cliched soul hits by the Impressions, Little Milton, Johnnie Taylor, Clarence Carter, Luther Ingram, Billy Paul, Don Covay, William Bell, and Z.Z. Hill. Most of them were much bigger R&B sellers than pop ones, and some don't appear on many anthologies. —*Richie Unterberger*

Cheatin': From A Woman's Point Of View / 1995 / Ichiban/Soul Classics ◆◆◆

Nifty collection of soul tunes which, just as the title says, deal with cheatin' lovers. Most of these date from the late '60s and early '70s, and while one of these was a Top Ten pop hit (Betty Wright's "Clean Up Woman"), the majority were much bigger on the R&B charts. These include little-anthologized Top Ten R&B hits by Dee Dee Warwick, the Soul Children, and Barbara Mason. There are also pretty well-known soul classics by Laura Lee ("Dirty Man") and Ann Peebles ("Part Time Love"), one of Gladys Knight's more obscure Motown hits ("I Don't Want To Do Wrong"), and little-heard numbers by Irma Thomas, the Emotions, and Margie Joseph. Shirley Murdock and Millie Jackson offer tracks from the past decade, in contrast to the rest of the set. On the whole, this functions as an excuse to pick up some decent, off-the-beaten-path soul. —*Richie Unterberger*

☆ **Chess Rhythm & Roll** / 1994 / Chess ◆◆◆◆◆

A four-disc set chronicling the more rockin' sides in this landmark label's catalog. Here we have the landmark early recordings by Chuck Berry, Bo Diddley, The Moonglows, The Flamingos, marvelous one-shot artists like The Monotones ("Book Of Love"), Dale Hawkins ("Susie-Q"), The Sensations ("Let Me In"), as well as seminal soul sides from Etta James, Billy Stewart and Tommy Tucker's original "High Heel Sneakers." Essential doesn't even begin to describe this box; music from a landmark label that changed the world. —*Cub Koda*

○ **Chunks** / 1981 / SST ◆◆◆◆

Another worthwhile compilation of SST's enigmatic roster of artists. —*John Dougan*

Classic Rock Box: Wnew-Fm 25th Anniversary Box / 1992 / PolyGram ◆◆◆

One of the more confusing box sets, *Classic Rock Box* collects a slew of FM album-rock standards in one hulking black box. No rarities are included—it would defeat the intent of the box. Listening to this box is exactly like listening to the radio for four hours straight; in that regard, the *Classic Rock Box* fills its purpose perfectly. —*Stephen Thomas Erlewine*

○ **Club Columbia: A Collection of Classic Dance Mixes** / 1990 / Columbia ◆◆◆◆

Club Columbia—A Collection of Classic Dance Mixes contains extended versions of disco hits; SOS Band, Shalamar, and others. —*Ron Wynn*

Colpix Dimension Story / 1994 / Rhino ◆◆◆

In the first half of the 1960s, Colpix and Dimension were record label offshoots of Columbia Pictures; Colpix tended toward teen idols, while Dimension was mainly an outlet for the compositions of the Gerry Goffin/Carole King songwriting team. This 40-song double CD includes all the major hits on the labels by the Marcels, James Darren, Shelley Fabares, Paul Petersen, Little Eva, the Cookies, and Carole King herself, as well as quite a few rarities. Although the compilers have done a thorough job, the jumble of disparate styles—sappy teen-idol pop, rhythm and blues, girl groups, soul, even a garage band—makes for tough end-to-end listening. Several of the sides by Darren and Petersen are unbearably cloying; the ones by Fabares, Teddy Randazzo, and Sandy Stewart are barely any better. The hits by Little Eva and the Cookies, on the other hand, are great dynamic girl-group performances. And some of the rarities are pretty cool—Carole King's odd, almost folk-rockish flop single "He's A Bad Boy," Earl-Jean's original version of "I'm Into Something Good" (covered for a hit by Herman's Hermits), the Girlfriends' "My One And Only, Jimmy Boy" (the best Wall of Sound girl-group record not produced by Phil Spector), the little-anthologized Top 10 soul hit "Hey Girl" by Freddie Scott, rare sides by Lou Christie and Duane Eddy, a silly Beatle parody by Sonny Curtis, and extremely rare (if not terribly good) singles by David Jones and Michael Nesmith before they joined the Monkees. —*Richie Unterberger*

☆ **The Complete Stax-Volt Singles 1959-1968** / 1991 / Atlantic ◆◆◆◆◆

This 244-track, nine-disc boxed set includes *all* of the 45 rpm A-sides ever released (as well as a few choice B-sides) on these legendary Memphis labels, during and preceding their association with Atlantic Records. Even though Stax/Volt continued to release more strong sides after 1968, with Isaac Hayes ("Shaft") and the Staple Singers, many consider that their classic sound is the one represented here. The consistently great songs and performances found on this collection, by artists like Otis Redding, Carla Thomas, Sam & Dave, Booker T. & the MG's, Eddie Floyd and many more, are a testament to Stax/Volt's vision. The tracks (remastered from the original mono masters on specially modified equipment) sound amazingly warm and full. Included is a booklet with extensively detailed liner notes and a generous selection of photos. For anyone who has the change to part with for a boxed set of this size, this is absolutely essential, provided you are a serious lover of gritty soul music. —*Rick Clark*

○ **The Complete Stax-Volt Soul Singles, Vol. 2, 1968-1971** / 1993 / Stax ◆◆◆◆

Massive nine-CD deluxe box set containing all 216 singles released by the seminal soul label. During their first four years after leaving Atlantic's distribution wing, Stax had some of the biggest soul hits (and stars) of the day, and they're all here, with deluxe packaging and superb sound. This is a perfect companion to the Atlantic Stax box set. —*Cub Koda*

Concussion! / Mr. Mannicotti ◆◆◆

A rock-solid compilation of 18 stompin' instrumentals from the golden age of guitar combos, 1958-1965. No hits, no big names (unless you count Punk Carson & the Chucklers), just great raw rockin'. —*Cub Koda*

Conmemorativo: A Tribute to Gram Parsons / 1993 / Rhino ◆◆◆

Conmemortivo is a scattered, yet enjoyable, tribute to Gram Parsons, the legendary father of country-rock. As with most tribute records, the results are a mixed bag; some bands play the songs as straight rock without any trace of country, but the best moments capture the spirit, if not the exact sound, of Parsons' originals. Bob Mould and Vic Chesnutt's mournful rendition of "Hickory Wind" is a particular highlight. —*Stephen Thomas Erlewine*

Cracks in the Sidewalk / 1971 / SST ◆◆◆

Great compilation of early-'80s California hardcore punk. —*John Dougan*

○ **Creole Kings of New Orleans** / 1992 / Specialty ◆◆◆◆

Creole Kings of New Orleans is a splendid 26-track sampler of Specialty Records' numerous R&B legends, including Professor Longhair, Percy Mayfield, Lloyd Price, Joe Liggins, and Guitar

Slim. Although only a couple of big hits are included, the material is consistently strong, making the disc an excellent purchase. — *Stephen Thomas Erlewine*

Crystalize Your Mind / 1994 / Big Beat ✦✦

Big Beat's *Nuggets Of The Golden State* series is a disappointing collection of unreleased, vaguely psychedelic '60s garage rock from the San Francisco area, much of it (the entirety of this CD) from the archives of the Golden State Recorders studio. This volume is the least impressive of the lot, combining unreleased material with rare singles on the MTA, Tower, and Uptown labels. There are occasional good moments—the fruity psych-pop of the Love Exchange, the primitive psychedelia of the Vejtables—but they're drowned by the generic material of no-names like the Living Children, the Poor Souls, the Rear Exit, and the Transatlantic Train. The psychedelic influences that make themselves heard are clumsy and grating, and judged as garage rock, it's considerably below average. —*Richie Unterberger*

★ **D.I.Y.: Anarchy in the Uk: Uk Punk I (1976-77)** / Jan. 19, 1993 / Rhino ✦✦✦✦✦

With the exception of the Clash, who could not be included because of licensing obstacles, this 19-song collection includes all of the major originators of British punk music. The Sex Pistols are here, of course, with somewhat rawer demo versions of "Anarchy In The U.K." and "God Save The Queen" that have previously appeared on various quasi-legitimate albums. Otherwise, you get the major singles from a posse of leading bands of the movement, including the Damned, the Saints, the Jam, and the Buzzcocks. Cult acts of nearly equal importance, like X-Ray Spex, the Adverts, the Only Ones, Generation X, and Wire also weigh in with trailblazing singles like "Orgasm Addict" and "One Chord Wonders." Major punk fans and collectors won't find anything here that they don't already have. But for those who didn't pick up everything the first time around, or weren't around the first time around, it's an ideal an introduction as can be imagined to a sound that totally realigned rock with its emphasis on brittle guitars, amphetamine rhythms, and socially charged songwriting. The booklet includes a lengthy, informative essay by Jon Savage, author of the British punk history *England's Dreaming*. —*Richie Unterberger*

★ **D.I.Y.: Blank Generation: The New York Scene (1975-78)** / 1993 / Rhino ✦✦✦✦✦

Disc #5—*Blank Generation*—is actually where the story begins. It was the mid-70s rumblings of Patti Smith and the Ramones emanating from NYC's famed C.B.G.B.'s club that served as the catalyst for what followed. The Ramones debut album, released in May 1976, lit a match to the dry tinder of England's alienated youth and set the pace for the Sex Pistols and the Damned, who—in turn—are captured in all their primitive glory on *Disc #1*. —*Roch Parisien*

★ **D.I.Y.: Come out and Play: American Power Pop** ... / 1993 / Rhino ✦✦✦✦✦

Come Out and Play, the first of two discs of American power-pop in the *D.I.Y.* series, is a terrific 19-track collection of heavyweights such as Cheap Trick, Flamin' Groovies, Chris Stamey, and Chris Bell, as well as more obscure bands like Fotomaker, Pezband, and the Diodes. It's essential for fans of power-pop or anyone who loves a good melody. —*Stephen Thomas Erlewine*

○ **D.I.Y.: Mass. Ave.: the Boston Scene (1979-83)** / 1993 / Rhino ✦✦✦✦

Out of all of the volumes in the *D.I.Y.* series, *Mass. Ave—The Boston Scene (1975-1983)* is probably the weakest, but by no means does that mean it's worthless; it does chronicle its scene very well, but Boston's punk/new-wave scene was not as strong as New York's or Los Angeles'. The CD is full of wonderful moments, including Mission of Burma, the Lyres, a demo from the Cars, Willie Alexander, and Human Sexual Response among its 19 tracks. It's definitely worth purchasing for punk and new-wave aficionados. —*Stephen Thomas Erlewine*

○ **D.I.Y.: Shake It up: Americam Power Pop 2** ... / 1993 / Rhino ✦✦✦✦

Shake It Up!, *D.I.Y.*'s second volume of American power-pop, is slightly less consistent than the first, but it's still full of wonderful music, making it just as essential as the first volume. Includes the Shoes, Chris Stamey and the DB's, Pearl Harbor & the Explosions, the Plimsouls, and the Romantics' infectious "What I Like About You." —*Stephen Thomas Erlewine*

☆ **D.I.Y.: Starry Eyes: Uk Pop, Vol. 2** / 1993 / Rhino ✦✦✦✦✦

★ **D.I.Y.: Teenage Kicks: Uk Pop (1976-79)** / Jan. 19, 1993 / Rhino ✦✦✦✦✦

Discs #3 (*Teenage Kicks*) and [its companion volume] #4 (*Starry Eyes*) capture the evolution from the early Stiff Records sound of Nick Lowe and Wreckless Eric, to hard, crystalline gems from Ireland's the Undertones and the comic-book hyberbole of Scotland's the Rezillos. Many performers charted in England, but went virtually ignored in North America. Early tracks from longer-lived names like XTC, Squeeze, and Joe Jackson are also included. Back in New York City, *Blank Generation* offers period essentials from Television, Richard Hell & the Voidoids, the Dictators, Blondie, Dead Boys, and the Heartbreakers, in addition to Smith and the Ramones. —*Roch Parisien*

☆ **D.I.Y.: The Modern World: Uk Punk 2 (1077-78)** / 1993 / Rhino ✦✦✦✦✦

Disc #2—This Is The Modern World—chronicles the splintering of the initial punk wave into different factions and styles: Mod-inspired workouts from The Jam, working-class anthems by 999 and Sham 69, the progressive tendencies of Magazine and The Fall, emerging psychedelia from The Soft Boys, and powerful politics from Ireland's Stiff Little Fingers.

Concurrently (and in a symbiotic relationship with) the new punk sounds, British pub-rock was evolving into tight, frenetic and witty pop that would soon be called New Wave. —*Roch Parisien*

○ **D.I.Y.: We're Desperate: the L.A. Scene (1976-79)** / 1993 / Rhino ✦✦✦✦

Twenty-one tracks of raw Los Angeles punk form *We're Desperate—The L.A. Scene (1976-79)*, another solid installment in Rhino's *D.I.Y.* punk/new-wave series. Although it isn't a front-to-back blowout like the New York volume, *We're Desperate* is a disc all punk and new-wave fans will want to add to their collection, considering that the original versionS of all of the singles have been included. The CDs feature such bands as the Germs, the Dickies, the Weirdos, the Plugz, the Zippers, the Motels, and X, Los Angeles' quintessential punk band. —*Stephen Thomas Erlewine*

○ **Dance Craze** / 1983 / Two Tone ✦✦✦✦

Finally available on CD, this classic collection compiles live tracks from the English Beat, the Specials, Bad Manners, and other '80s ska-revival bands. — *Scott Bultman*

☆ **Dangerhouse, Vol. 1** / 1991 / Frontier ✦✦✦✦✦

An essential punk compilation, it consists of bands from the late '70s, many of which have influenced a lot of other groups. Some of the bands on the album include X, the Eyes (featuring Go-Go's guitarist Charlotte Caffey), the Weirdos, the Avengers, Rhino 39, and Black Randy & the Metrosquad. Many of the songs here are expensive to get on the original albums, making this a cost-effective collection. —*John Book*

○ **Deadicated: a Tribute to the Grateful Dead** / 1991 / Arista ✦✦✦✦

This tribute record features everyone from Elvis Costello to Midnight Oil to Dr. John doin' the Dead. An attempt to showcase the Dead's songwriting. The rigid arrangements could have used more imagination, but the interpretations are mostly agreeable. —*Jeff Tamarkin*

Desperate Rock 'n' roll, Vol. 1 / 1992 / Flame ✦✦✦

Dynamite single-disc compilation culled from earlier vinyl volumes of this series featuring some of the wildest and most obscure rockabilly records of all time. —*Cub Koda*

★ **The Disco Years, Vol. 1: Turn the Beat Around** / 1990 / Rhino ✦✦✦✦✦

A comprehensive series featuring many of the greatest disco songs ever recorded, Rhino's five-volume *Disco Years* set accurately chronicles *the* pop music sensation of the mid-'70s. The first two volumes are the places to start; the other three are necessary for devoted disco fans and pop music historians. —*Stephen Thomas Erlewine*

Donovan: Island of Circles / Nettwerk ✦✦✦

While Donovan was (type) cast as the mystical, hippy druid to Bob Dylan's rural-rooted, visionary shaman, the British entry deserves this tribute disc painstakingly assembled by Vancouver's Nettwerk Productions.

Sixteen performers from four countries and a dizzying range of musical backgrounds (Irish reggae to B.C. sludge-rock) all converge on *Island Of Circles*. Although these alternative-music tribute recordings are usually inconsistent, what unifies this project is that most participants—rather than just smashing out a cover as a lark—show a genuine affection (if not reverence) for their subject. Britain-based Brix Smith redeems herself with a passionate, angelic rendition of Hurdy Gurdy Man, easily besting Sarah McLachlan's competent Wear Your Love Like Heaven in the disc's solo female vocal stakes. —*Roch Parisien*

★ **Doo Wop Box** / 1994 / Rhino ✦✦✦✦✦
Rhino's four-disc collection *The Doo Wop Box* may not contain every classic doo-wop single ever recorded, but it comes damn close. Featuring a hundred tracks, superb sound, and amazingly detailed liner notes, the set is one of the best various-artist box sets ever assembled; although these four discs will be all the doo-wop some listeners will ever need, hopefully the set will make most listeners want to investigate the genre even further. — *Stephen Thomas Erlewine*

○ **Doo Wop: 4 Funky Flashes from the 50s** / Specialty ✦✦✦✦
A good batch from the Specialty vaults, released in 1991; jump and vocal groups. —*Ron Wynn*

○ **Doo-Wop Jive, Vol. 1** / 1993 / Juke Box Treaures ✦✦✦
Another solid collection in this series with the emphasis on 'jump' recordings from the era. The Penguins, The Spaniels, and The Medallions are the big names here, but lovers of the genre will be equally at home with the more obscure artists collected here. — *Cub Koda*

○ **Doo-Wop from Dolphin's of Hollywood, Vol. 1** / 1992 / Specialty ✦✦✦✦
This mid-'50s Los Angeles doo wop was produced by John Dolphin. Groups include the Turbans, the Voices, the Gassers, Bobby Relf, the Turks, Gaynell Hodge and the Blue-Aires, Bobby Byrd, and the Jaguars. —*AMG*

○ **Doo-Wop from Dolphin's of Hollywood, Vol. 2** / Specialty ✦✦✦✦
More mid-'50s Los Angeles doo wop appear here. Groups include the Hollywood Arist-O-Kats, the Turks, the Hollywood Flames, Grady Chapman and the Suedes, the Sunrisers, and others. — *AMG*

○ **Dope Guns & Fucking in the Streets, Vols. 1-3** / 1989 / Amphetamine Reptile ✦✦✦✦
Released in 1989, this is alienated, second-generation, post-hardcore guitar rant. —*John Dougan*

Down & Dirty: Immediate Blues Story, Vol. 3 / CBS ✦✦✦
Eric Clapton and Jimmy Page are the big names on this anthology, but the real value lies in songs by the late Jo Ann Kelly, who sounds utterly authentic. —*Bruce Eder*

Dream Babies / 1985 / ✦✦✦
One of the few major-label girl-group compilations ever released is a disappointment. The tracks by the Exciters and the Honeys are better heard within the context of their own compilations; the previously unreleased songs by the post-Phil Spector version of the Crystals are less than enthralling, and several of the others are simply uninspired. Highlights are Cher's pre-fame 1964 single "Dream Baby" and Alder Ray's "Cause I Love Him," both of which rank among the best obscure Spector-style girl-group productions. There's also a single by Merry Clayton, later to reach fame as the backup singer on the Rolling Stones' "Gimme Shelter"; she did "It's In His Kiss" before Betty Everett had a hit with it, but Everett's version is much better. —*Richie Unterberger*

Dusty & Forgotten / 1993 / Flyright ✦✦✦
An interesting 25-track compilation of unknowns, unissued and alternative takes from Gotham Records' vocal group harmony vaults. While none of the groups here qualify for name status, the sound is there on every track, and that's what ultimately counts. — *Cub Koda*

Early San Francisco / 1985 / Rhino ✦✦✦
A fine collection of pre-Summer of Love rarities from the mid-'60s. Besides hits by the Beau Brummels and We Five, it features rarities by the Vejtables, the Great Society (featuring a pre-Jefferson Airplane Grace Slick), and Country Joe & the Fish. —*Richie Unterberger*

Electric Sugar Cube Flashbacks, Vols. 1-4 / ✦✦✦
In comparison to U.S. bands, obscure British groups of the mid- and late '60s have been ill-served by compilations; there are dozens of Pebbles volumes, and hundreds of American garage rock compilations in the same vein, but comparatively few for their British counterparts. There are, however, some in the *Elec-*

tric Sugar Cube Flashbacks series is probably the best of them, spotlighting rare early British R&B, "beat," and psychedelic recordings from impossibly rare 45s, many of which were never released in the States. The British bands tended to be somewhat more accomplished, tuneful, and imaginative in their lyrics and arrangements than their American counterparts; those looking for obscure music in the classic British '60s R&B/rock and power-pop style should check these out, with the awareness that they're generally more crudely performed, written, and produced than the material by the British Invasion giants we know and love. As is the case with all AIP series, the volumes tend to get worse as the series progresses; Volume One, if you can find it, is by far the best. —*Richie Unterberger*

○ **Elpee's Worth of Productions** / 1992 / Rhino ✦✦✦✦
Essentially a scrapbook of Rundgren's productions with artists like Patti Smith, Meatloaf, New York Dolls, Grand Funk Railroad, Pursuit of Happiness, XTC, and more. The diversity of artists makes a nice case for Rundgren's wide range of taste, but many of the selections seem odd choices, considering that better material existed on those albums. —*Rick Clark*

○ **Elvis Mania** / Live Gold ✦✦✦✦
A two-CD, 52-track compilation featuring all manner of Elvis tribute records. While covering a 22 year span of these recorded cult items, the transfer to the digital medium on some of these discs leaves quite a bit to be desired. For the diehard Elvis fan who thought they had everything. —*Cub Koda*

English Freakbeat, Vol. 5 / 1993 / Aip ✦✦✦
The English Freakbeat series is devoted to unearthing obscure, non-hit treasures of the British Invasion that are known only to obsessive collectors. Truth be told, many of those treasures were obscure for a reason, which makes these anthologies wildly uneven listening, but there are some gems to be found here. The highlights of this 21-song volume include a surprisingly pleasant slice of punk-pop from ex-Beatle drummer Pete Best, "The Way I Feel." Thane Russal's "I Need You" is a first-rate Them imitation, Geoff Goddard's "Sky Man" is a truly inspired piece of Joe Meek-produced lunacy about benign space aliens, and the Greenbeats' Merseyish "You Must Be The One" is undoubtedly the most obscure song that Mick Jagger and Keith Richard wrote in the '60s (no, the Rolling Stones never did get around to recording it). That gives you the flavor of the manic variety on hand here. Some of the cuts are shamelessly derivative early British R&B, and others are simply not as striking as the gushing liner notes would have you believe. The CD also includes some extremely obscure productions by Shel Talmy and Joe Meek, as well as an obscure composition by Jackie DeShannon, that in no way approximates the greatness of their famous work. —*Richie Unterberger*

English Freakbeat, Vol. 5 / 1993 / Voxx ✦✦✦
The English Freakbeat series is devoted to unearthing obscure, non-hit treasures of the British Invasion that are known only to obsessive collectors. Truth be told, many of those treasures were obscure for a reason, which makes these anthologies wildly uneven listening, but there are some gems to be found here. The highlights of this 21-song volume include a surprisingly pleasant slice of punk-pop from ex-Beatle drummer Pete Best, "The Way I Feel." Thane Russal's "I Need You" is a first-rate Them imitation, Geoff Goddard's "Sky Man" is a truly inspired piece of Joe Meek-produced lunacy about benign space aliens, and the Greenbeats' Merseyish "You Must Be The One" is undoubtedly the most obscure song that Mick Jagger and Keith Richard wrote in the '60s (no, the Rolling Stones never did get around to recording it). That gives you the flavor of the manic variety on hand here. Some of the cuts are shamelessly derivative early British R&B, and others are simply not as striking as the gushing liner notes would have you believe. The CD also includes some extremely obscure productions by Shel Talmy and Joe Meek, as well as an obscure composition by Jackie DeShannon, that in no way approximates the greatness of their famous work. —*Richie Unterberger*

○ **Faster & Louder: Hardcore Punk, Vol. 1** / 1993 / Rhino ✦✦✦✦
○ **Faster & Louder: Hardcore Punk, Vol. 2** / 1993 / Rhino ✦✦✦✦
Considered unimaginably over-the-top and atonal at the time, the early sounds of hardcore punk don't sound nearly as noisy fifteen years later. Dare we say, they even sound a bit poppy and tightly conceived in comparison with the uncompromisingly bleak, rushed, and amelodic sounds of today's underground hardcore groups. That's not to take away from the undeniable influence and

power of first-generation hardcore. *Faster & Louder: Hardcore Punk, Vol. 2* does a good job of assembling some of the most enduring and accessible moments of the genre's genesis. This 17-song compilation includes the first singles by Husker Du and X, who went on to transcend hardcore's limitations pretty rapidly. It also includes seminal tracks by Agent Orange and Wire, as well as influential bands with smaller cults like the Wipers, the Dils, and Zero Boys, down to nearly forgotten acts (Dys, Stranglehold). The bleakest and most vicious strand of early hardcore is represented by Fear, the Germs, and the Subhumans. Not a bad package for those who want to sample the genre's highlights and limit its representation in their collection to this fairly small and manageable dose. —*Richie Unterberger*

Fillmore: The Last Days / 1972 / Columbia/Legacy ✦✦✦
In the summer of 1971, Bill Graham closed the two halls that had redefined the way live rock music was heard. In San Francisco, the Fillmore Auditorium, and later the Fillmore West, had been home to virtually every major performing band of the era, a neighborhood meeting place and dance palace rolled into one. It was the place to see the Dead, the Airplane, Santana, and any visiting musical act with any hipness quotient at all. This 2-CD package features some of the recordings from the final week of shows at the fabled Fillmore West. Not all of the bands are remembered today (Lamb, anyone?) but with hot entries from Quicksilver Messenger Service, Tower of Power, Hot Tuna, Boz Scaggs, the Dead, Santana, etc., it's a tribute both to a time and place and to the inestimable contributions of the late Graham. The sound quality is lacking by today's standards, but the free 'n' easy Fillmore atmosphere comes through. —*Jeff Tamarkin*

Flight To Lowland's Paradise: The Netherlands, Part 1 & 2 / Moxie ✦✦✦
Pebbles Vol. 15: The Netherlands remains the best compilation of mid-'60s Dutch beat/punk, but these two anthologies, issued in the U.S. in the mid-'80s, are nearly on the same level. Each volume has 16 tracks demonstrating the uniquely brooding Dutch take on British Invasion R&B and mod, with songs by both well-known acts on the scene (the Outsiders, Les Baroques, the Motions, Cuby & the Blizzards) and total unknowns. Good stuff, not mere rare novelties. —*Richie Unterberger*

Folk Rock / 198? / Rhino ✦✦✦
One of the weakest offerings in the series, with oft-anthologized hits by the Byrds, Turtles, Scott McKenzie, and Barry McGuire. The non-hit cuts tend toward the lightest, poppiest facets of folk-rock. An exception is the powerful acoustic, original version of "Dazed And Confused" by Jake Holmes, which was transformed into heavy metal by Led Zeppelin. —*Richie Unterberger*

☆ **Footstompin' Oldies** / Garland ✦✦✦✦✦
This fine collection of early rock and soul hits is expertly remastered by Steve Hoffman. It includes the Rocky Fellers hit "Killer Joe" and 15 other cuts you should own. —*John Floyd*

☆ **Frat Rock** / 1991 / Rhino ✦✦✦✦✦
Rhino's *Frat Rock* series is an excellent overview of '60s rock & roll and R&B party anthems like the Kingsmen's "Louie Louie," "Double Shot of My Baby's Love" (Swinging Medallions), "La La La La La" (Blendells), "Shout" (Isley Brothers), "Do You Love Me?" (The Contours), and "Mony Mony" (Tommy James & the Shondells). —*John Floyd*

Freak Beat Phantoms / 1989 / Bam Caruso ✦✦✦
If you only want one album of very obscure mid-'60s British rock, you're best advised to track this down. "Freak beat" is the compilers' term for the brand of British rock that was produced circa 1965-67, when the initial impetus of the Merseybeat and R&B bands gave way to wilder mod, power-pop, and early psychedelic sounds. None of these groups "made it" to any degree, but the tuneful crunch (often embellished with distorted guitars) of acts like the Buzz, the Game, Southern Sound, and Fleur De Lys will appeal to anyone who digs the sounds of vintage Who, Yardbirds, and Pretty Things. —*Richie Unterberger*

○ **Funky Stuff: The Best of Funk Essentials** / May 18, 1993 / Mercury ✦✦✦✦
This terrific compilation of the highlights of Mercury's *Funk Essentials* series (which includes individual titles by Parliament, the Bar-Kays, Cameo, and Con Funk Shun), also includes songs from artists that don't have their own CDs. It's essential for anyone curious about the funk. —*AMG*

○ **Get Down Tonight: Best of T.K. Records** / 1990 / Rhino ✦✦✦✦
A fine collection of the best tracks from the seminal '70s disco label, including tracks by KC & the Sunshine Band, George McCrae, Gwen McCrae, Betty Wright, Latimore, and Little Beaver. —*Stephen Thomas Erlewine*

○ **Get Hot or Go Home: Vintage Rca Rockabilly '56-'59—Vols. I & II** / CMF ✦✦✦✦
This two-fer contains an extensive set of recordings from some of the top legends in rockabilly, artists like Milton Allen, Roy Orbison, Janis Martin, Homer & Jethro, Joe Clay, Martha Carson, Pee Wee King, and many more. The informative booklet includes photos and a discography. —*AMG*

Get with the Beat: Mar-Vel' Masters / 1989 / Rykodisc ✦✦✦
Based near Chicago, the Mar Vel' label recorded lots of regional roots music during the 1950s and early '60s. Although they recorded some R&B and rockabilly, this compilation of 27 cuts by 19 artists—none of whom achieved any national fame whatsoever—leans toward hillbilly, country boogie, and country swing. Though these rarities have their merits, they aren't nearly as good as the classic material by stars mining the same territory. —*Richie Unterberger*

Girls In The Garage, Vols. 1-6 / Romulan ✦✦✦
Even more than most rock & roll styles, garage rock is thought of as a primarily male terrain, especially given the macho posturing adopted by most of its proponents. *Girls In The Garage* proves that there were also quite a few female groups mining similar territory in the mid-'60s. The compilers have gone far and wide to assemble dozens of doggoned rare singles to fill out these anthologies, and if they don't exactly place among the very top rank of the hundreds of '60s garage rock collections, there's a fair amount of rare stuff to be found here. There simply weren't a lot of females with guitars forming their own groups in the '60s, and so a lot of this material isn't "garage" in the classic sense; a fair amount is raw girl group-style stuff, novelties, or classic garage bands that happened to feature a female singer. Which isn't a drawback, as the collections have more variety than you'll find on your average garage comp. Good liner notes too, although Romulan seems to have resorted to filling out the volumes with some unmemorable, even inept tracks due to the scarcity of source material to choose from. —*Richie Unterberger*

Global Dance Experience, II / 1994 / SBK ✦✦✦
This second SBK dance anthology improves on its predecessor by spotlighting revived veterans (Boy George, Lulu, Tina Turner) and emerging stars (Alison Limerick, K-klass, Aly-us), plus acts already enjoying significant pop attention (Lisa Stansfield, Jon Secada). The 11 tracks are featured as club versions, with Stansfield's 1970s disco and Philly soul influences nicely highlighted, alongside Secada's Miami Afro-Latin and soul touches and Lulu's Stax/Muscle Shoals references. This will register most strongly with R&B/soul and urban fans who also enjoy dance, while the techno/trance crew won't find it so interesting. —*Ron Wynn*

○ **Go Go Posse** / 1988 / Heads Up ✦✦✦✦
A vital collection depicting the mid- and late-70s premier Black sound. —*Ron Wynn*

The Golden Age of Black Music: 1977-1988 / 1988 / Atlantic ✦✦✦
A three-volume anthology full of established, easy-to-find soul/pop hits. —*Ron Wynn*

○ **Golden Groups** / 1993 / Specialty ✦✦✦✦
Originally compiled and issued on Relic Records as part of their superlative label-by-label Golden Groups series, this boasts the addition of eight bonus tracks and improved remastering quality. Featuring such wild West Coast gems as The Pentagons' "Silly Dilly," Tony Allen's "Night Owl," not to mention early recordings by Clydie King and Darlene Love (as part of her first group, The Echoes), this makes a wonderful companion volume to *Hardcore Doo Wop: In the Hallway—Under the Streetlamp*. —*Cub Koda*

Good Things Are Happening / 1994 / Big Beat ✦✦✦
27-song anthology of material recorded at the Golden State Recorders studio in San Francisco in the mid-'60s, almost all of it by Bay Area-based bands. None of these garage groups made it big, though the Vejtables had a small hit with "I Still Love You" (not included here), and the Mourning Reign's "Satisfaction Guaranteed" is one of the most esteemed rarities in garage collector circles. Well over half the tracks are previously unreleased and betray a strong British Invasion influence, often sounding very sub-Beau

Brummels. Which may be too charitable; the material is weak and derivative (the E-Types' pop-rock is the shining exception), and the Vejtables' cuts are much worse than the earlier folk-rock they recorded for the Beau Brummels' Autumn label. The sound and packaging are excellent, but this is really a way below average garage-pop collection. —*Richie Unterberger*

☆ **Grandson of Frat Rock** / 1991 / Rhino ✦✦✦✦✦
Rhino's *Frat Rock* series is an excellent overview of '60s rock & roll and R&B party anthems like the Kingsmen's "Louie Louie," "Double Shot of My Baby's Love" (Swinging Medallions), "La La La La La" (Blendells), "Shout" (Isley Brothers), "Do You Love Me?" (The Contours), and "Mony Mony" (Tommy James & the Shondells). —*John Floyd*

○ **Groove 'n' Grind: 50's & 60's Dance Hits** / Rhino ✦✦✦✦
An 18-cut assemblage of '60s rock, soul, and R&B/dance tunes, it's essential for strollers, peppermint twisters, hully-gulliers, monkey-timers, and cool-jerks. —*John Floyd*

○ **Guitar Player Presents Rock: the 50s, Vol. 1** / 1991 / Rhino ✦✦✦✦
Nice collection of tracks featuring dazzling guitar work and classic sides from Chuck Berry, Bo Diddley, Les Paul, James Burton, Carl Perkins, and 12 others. —*Cub Koda*

○ **Guitar Player Presents Rock: the 50s, Vol. 2** / 1991 / Rhino ✦✦✦✦
Companion volume to the above, with dynamite tracks from Ike Turner, Joe Maphis, Ritchie Valens, Scotty Moore, Duane Eddy, Larry Collins, and 12 more. —*Cub Koda*

○ **Guitar Player Presents Rock: the 60s, Vol. 1** / 1991 / Rhino ✦✦✦✦
Excellent 18-track CD featuring dazzling guitar work by the Ventures, Steve Cropper, Dave Edmunds, the Byrds, Chet Atkins, Lonnie Mack, and others, showing the breadth of '60s guitar work. —*Cub Koda*

○ **Guitar Player Presents Rock: the 60s, Vol. 2** / 1991 / Rhino ✦✦✦✦
Companion volume to the above, featuring tracks by Jeff Beck, the Fendermen, Travis Wammack, Roy Buchanan, Eric Clapton, and other guitar giants of the '60s. —*Cub Koda*

○ **Guitar Player Presents Rock: the 70s, Vol. 1** / 1991 / Rhino ✦✦✦✦
Showcasing a selected sampling of the lesser-heralded guitarists of the era, this 18-track CD features selections by Rick Derringer, Brownsville Station's Cub Koda, the Outlaws, Ted Nugent, James Gang, and others. A nice selection with excellent sound. —*Dan Heilman*

○ **Guitar Player Presents: Legends of Guitar—Surf, Vol. 1** / 1991 / Rhino ✦✦✦✦
Guitar was always the driving force in surf rock, which means this edition of the *Legends of Guitar* series serves as a good introduction to the sub-genre in general. —*AMG*

○ **Hard-To-Find Motown Classics, Vol. 1** / 1986 / Motown ✦✦✦✦
Included are rare classics from the label's more obscure artists, like the Elgins, Rare Earth, and others. —*Rick A. Bueche*

★ **Hardcore Doo-Wop: In the Hallway-Under The Street Lamp** / 1993 / Specialty ✦✦✦✦✦
This compact disc collects 25 doo wop collector's classics from a variety of small West Coast R&B labels who dabbled in the genre. The California version of the streetcorner vocal group phenomena had stronger leanings toward bluesier harmonies and vocal performances bordering on madness. As best exemplified here by groups like Arthur Lee Maye & the Crowns and Byron "Slick" Gipson & the Sliders, the West Coast doo wop movement definitely had a sound all its own. —*Cub Koda*

○ **Harlem Shuffle: 60s Soul Classics** / Charly ✦✦✦✦
A perfect selection (and disc order) of lesser-known but essential soul hits, including the Barbara Lewis hits "Hello Stranger," "Make Me Your Baby," and "Baby I'm Yours," plus "Oogum Boogum Song" and "Gimme Little Sign" by Brenton Wood, and "Get on up and Get Away" by the Esquires. 21 classic sides in all, every one a delight. An import but worth the trouble to find. —*Michael Erlewine*

☆ **The Hi Records Story** / Hi ✦✦✦✦✦
This is a marvelous tribute to Willie Mitchell's Hi label, which, like Stax, revolutionized Memphis soul. A 24-song disc features the best of the two American volumes and a few different cuts. (British import) —*John Floyd*

Highs In The Mid-'60s, Vols. 1-23 / ✦✦✦
A spinoff of the Pebbles series, *Highs In The Mid-'60s* assembles yet more rare garage rock recordings, the difference being that each volume focuses upon a city or region such as Los Angeles, Texas, or Michigan. This does provide a public service of sorts by assembling and reissuing hordes of rare singles that would be impossible for any one individual to acquire on his or her own. It must be pointed out, though, that Pebbles itself plundered a lot of the prime garage material, and the quality on these supplementary volumes is very patchy. This shouldn't come as that much of a surprise when they include entire LPs devoted to mid-'60s garage-rock recordings from Colorado, two volumes to Wisconsin, or several volumes to L.A.; there just wasn't an infinite supply of great regional bands to go around, and much of the material is annoyingly generic if taken at once, starting to melt into one big sneer and fuzz riff. As is usually the case in these series, the earlier volumes tend to be better. —*Richie Unterberger*

History of British Blues / Sire ✦✦✦
The second LP of this double album gets bogged down in lumbering boogie, but otherwise this is a good sampler of British '60s blues-rock. Includes rare cuts by Spencer Davis, the Yardbirds, Graham Bond, Cyril Davies, and Alexis Korner, and off-the-beaten tracks by John Mayall, the Downliners Sect, Fleetwood Mac, Chicken Shack, and Christine Perfect (the future Christine McVie). —*Richie Unterberger*

○ **History of Hi Records R&B, Vol. 1: Beginnings** / 1988 / MCA ✦✦✦✦
A terrific two-volume tribute to Willie Mitchell's Hi label, it features a hodgepodge of rockabilly and soul from such artists as Mitchell and Ace Cannon. —*John Floyd*

○ **History of Hi Records R&B, Vol. 2: Glory Years** / 1988 / MCA ✦✦✦✦
Great 70s soul from Al Green, Ann Peebles, and associates. —*Ron Wynn*

☆ **History of New Orleans R&B, Vol. 1** / Rhino ✦✦✦✦✦
Simply the best sounding and most enjoyable series (two discs/three cassettes) of the bouncy, piano-driven sound that could only come from a goodtime town like New Orleans. Lots of star power—Art Neville, Lee Dorsey, Irma Thomas, Frankie Ford, Shirley & Lee, Lloyd Price, Guitar Slim. Earl King, and many more. —*Myles Boisen*

Hitsville Usa, Vol. 2: the Motown Singles Collection (1972-1992) / Oct. 19, 1993 / Motown ✦✦✦
Where the first *Hitsville* box suffered from not featuring enough material, the sequel suffers from having too many tracks. During the 1970s, the label lost its distinctive sound, although the hits continued to come for a number of years. Unfortunately, as the years progress, the hits become fewer and less distinctive—they follow the trends, instead of setting them. Perhaps this could have been a successful 2-CD set, but at four discs, there aren't enough gems to justify the hefty price ticket. —*Stephen Thomas Erlewine*

☆ **Hitsville Usa: The Motown Singles . . .** / 1992 / Motown ✦✦✦✦✦
A terrific four-disc box set that features many of Motown's greatest hits in superb sound. While nearly every song is a gem, this is one of the few box sets that isn't comprehensive enough. If anything, it could have used another disc to fit in some more material, particularly more songs by the Supremes. Nevertheless, what is here is transcendent. —*Stephen Thomas Erlewine*

I Live for the Sun / 1986 / EMI America ✦✦✦
Patchy compilation of early and mid-'60s surf music from the EMI catalog. The cuts by Jan & Dean and the Beach Boys are great, but hardly obscure, and a lot of the rest is so-so, the instrumental cuts towering over the cheesy vocal numbers. Two fine tunes, though, that are rarely reissued: the Sunrays, a deliberate Beach Boys clone managed by the Wilsons' father Murry, had a hit with their infectious harmonies on "I Live For The Sun," and the Ventures' "The Cruel Sea" is starkly and magnificently powerful. What's most interesting is how many of these acts featured musicians and producers that would play a role in interesting mid- and late-'60s California rock recordings, including Gary Usher, P.F. Sloan, Richie Polodor, and future Blue Cheer guitarist Randy Holden. —*Richie Unterberger*

○ **I'm Your Fan (Tribute to Leonard Cohen)** / 1991 / Atlantic ✦✦✦
An incoherent tribute to Leonard Cohen, *I'm Your Fan* contains some fine versions of some of his best songs, but too often these renditions are half-hearted. Of particular interest are R.E.M.'s "First

We'll Take Manhattan" and the Pixies' "I Can't Forget." —*Stephen Thomas Erlewine*

○ **The Immediate Singles Collection, Vol. 1** / 1991 / Sony ✦✦✦✦
Interesting 20-song compilation of very British tunes by Small Faces, the Nice, and others, with an American or two thrown in. —*Jeff Tamarkin*

The Immediate Singles Collection, Vol. 2 / 1991 / Sony ✦✦✦
For collectors of obscure '60s British rock only—includes Humble Pie, P.P. Arnold, Amen Corner, and more. —*Jeff Tamarkin*

The Immediate Singles Collection, Vol. 3 / 1991 / Sony Music Special Products ✦✦✦
Not much here to recommend to those who don't get excited about minor psychedelia. —*Jeff Tamarkin*

○ **In Yo' Face! (The History of Funk), Vol. 1** / 1993 / Rhino ✦✦✦✦
Funk fans eagerly anticipated Rhino's five-part series, thinking that they would get something equivalent to the label's wonderful 1970s soul line. While the final results are good, things are not quite as rosy as earlier reports indicated. The most disappointing thing was the decision to settle for single versions of tracks rather than extended ones. This was how the songs sounded on radio, but the results are truncated versions of "Sex Machine" and "Keep On Truckin'," rather than the glorious full cuts with complete musical interludes. Otherwise, most song choices are great, especially the JB's, Funkadelic, and Lyn Collins. —*Ron Wynn*

○ **In Yo' Face! (The History of Funk), Vol. 2** / Rhino ✦✦✦✦
Volume two of Rhino's funk series offers 15 more mostly strong cuts, although it is disappointing to hear edited versions of great anthems. The marvelous trumpet solo and additional chorus from the O'Jays' "For The Love of Money" has been trimmed, and although they don't tell you, only part of B.T. Express' "Do It ('Til You're Satisfied)" is included. There's still plenty of wonderful funk, including classics by Sly & the Family Stone, James Brown, Kool & The Gang, Rufus, Parliament, AWB, and the Temptations. —*Ron Wynn*

○ **In Yo' Face! (The History of Funk), Vol. 3** / Rhino ✦✦✦✦
By the third volume of Rhino's generally solid funk series, it has become apparent who did and did not permit their songs to be licensed. Once more there are songs from James Brown, Sly & the Family Stone, Parliament, Funkadelic, the O'Jays, and AWB, and it's great that George McRae's delightful "I Get Lifted" made the cut, as well as Graham Central Station's "The Jam." Cameo's "Funk Funk" reveals how close to Parliament they were early in their career, while the Brothers Johnson, Kool and the Gang in their great pre-J.T. Taylor phase, and one-hit wonders Wild Cherry complete the disc. —*Ron Wynn*

○ **In Yo' Face! (The History of Funk), Vol. 4** / 1993 / Rhino ✦✦✦✦
Familiar names comprise the bulk of the final volume in Rhino's funk series. There are more tracks by James Brown, Sly & the Family Stone and AWB, plus numbers from repeat entries the Isley Brothers, Earth, Wind & Fire, Kool & the Gang and Graham Central Station. But new acts offer prototype funk on some smoking numbers such as Slave's "Slide," the Bar-Kays' "Shake Your Rump To The Funk," Brick's "Dazz" and George Duke's "Reach For It." Bootsy's "The Pinocchio Theory" was a classic, and the same is true for Marvin Gaye's "Got To Give It Up, Part 1." Only Brass Construction's "L-O-V-E-U" falls below the standard. —*Ron Wynn*

○ **In Yo' Face! (The History of Funk), Vol. 5** / Rhino ✦✦✦✦
Another solid installment in the *In Yo' Face* series, the fifth volume contains essential tracks from Parliament, Con Funk Shun, Rick James, Zapp, and Cameo. —*AMG*

○ **In Yo' Face! (The Roots of Funk), Vol. 1/ 2** / 1994 / Rhino ✦✦✦✦

○ **Juke Box: R&B** / 1993 / Virgin ✦✦✦✦
A fine collection of '50s R&B, it features solid but frequently uncelebrated tracks by classic artists like B.B. King, Elmore James, Ike & Tina Turner, Etta James, and Lowell Fulsom. —*AMG*

☆ **Just Can't Get Enough: New Wave Hits of the 80s 1-15** / 1994 / Rhino ✦✦✦✦✦
Rhino's first five volumes of their fifteen-disc new wave retrospective are filled with classic tracks from the early '80s, from "Love Will Tear Us Apart" to "867-5309/Jenny." Each disc is loosely chronological and contains a number of obscurities and novelties along with the hits. For sound and content, this is likely to be the best series of new wave hits ever to be released. Start with the fifth volume, which contains "I Want Candy," "Someday, Someway," "The Kids in America," "Love Plus One," "Valley Girl," and other

gems; then work your way through the rest of the discs. —*Stephen Thomas Erlewine*

○ **Kill Rock Stars** / 1991 / KK ✦✦✦✦
Excellent modern-day punk rock collection of various cutting edge artists, including Nirvana and riot grrrls Bikini Kill. Alternative-rock fans will find much to savor here. (The band [not the singer] Courtney Love's acoustic "Don't Mix the Colors" is particularly noteworthy. —*Stephen Thomas Erlewine*

Kiss 'n' Tell / 1993 / ACE ✦✦✦
Compilation of 30 rare girl-group tunes, almost all from the early and mid-'60s, though a couple from the late '60s sneak in. Truth to tell, this is an inoffensive but hardly inspiring compilation of a genre that produced innumerable great records, both famous and obscure. The two famous cuts—Claudine Clark's "Party Lights" and the Donays' "Devil In His Heart" (covered by the Beatles on their second album)—are readily available elsewhere, in better company. Otherwise, there are rare, flop singles, as well as some unissued tracks, by the likes of Earline & Her Girlfriends, Lorraine & The Delights, and the Martin Sisters that simply don't stack up to the cream of the crop. The rare tracks by the Shirelles are pretty good (though already issued on other Ace compilations), Maxine Brown's "Little Girl Lost" is one of the most girl group-oriented singles by a singer who really belongs more in the soul category, and the tracks by Nella Dodds and Dean & Jean good examples of girl groups' sultriest side. Candy & The Kisses' are good too, although they're more in a Motown vein than a classic girl-group style. The Chiffons are represented by a couple fairly weak covers and a 1969 tune that barely resembles their girl group origins at all. Annette Funicello weighs in with one of her more standard pop-rock efforts, the unexceptional 1965 single "Better Be Ready." In sum, a pretty erratic compilation with good and unremarkable moments, the balance tilting toward the unremarkable. If you're looking for compilations of interesting non-hit girl-group songs, there are much better (if harder to find) ones about, including *Lookin' For Boys* and *Beyond The Wall Of Sound* (both on Roxy) and *Ultimate Girl Groups* (on Goldmine). —*Richie Unterberger*

○ **Live Stiffs** / Edsel ✦✦✦✦
Recorded on the first "Live Stiffs" tour in the late '70s, this record contains some fine performances by Elvis Costello, Nick Lowe, and Graham Parker. —*AMG*

○ **Living In Oblivion, Vol. 1** / 1993 / Capitol ✦✦✦✦
A somewhat haphazardly assembled retrospective of '80s pop, *Living in Oblivion* contains not only classic new wave cuts, but also features several MTV hits from the mid-'80s and radio hits from the end of the decade. While there are some great songs on every volume, each disc is wildly inconsistent; only the first disc is somewhat coherent. Nevertheless, *Living in Oblivion* captures the fractured mainstream of the decade quite well and manages to include some classic pop songs along the way. —*Stephen Thomas Erlewine*

Lonely As an Eyesore / 4AD ✦✦✦
Rare tracks from the 4AD label include songs by the Cocteau Twins, Throwing Muses, Dead Can Dance, and This Mortal Coil. —*Michael P. Dawson*

○ **Lookin' For Boys** / 198? / ✦✦✦✦
Quite simply, this is the best compilation of little-known early- to mid-'60s girl-group singles ever assembled, and proof that quite a few songs never get to be hits for reasons that having nothing to do with their quality. A couple of these (the Girlfriends' "Jimmy Boy" and Earl-Jean's original version of "I'm Into Something Good") were small hits, but by and large these were flops. What's amazing is how meticulously produced and tuneful they were; in 1963, the industry was dazzled by Phil Spector's success, and employed quite a few producers and performers that emulated the master very well. Great melodies, harmonies, and Wall-of-Sound Jr. production on most of these, and noted songwriter Ellie Greenwich's dramatic "You Don't Know" is one of the finest obscure mid-'60s rock & roll singles of any genre. —*Richie Unterberger*

○ **Max Weinberg Presents: Let There Be Drums, Vol. 1-3** / Rhino ✦✦✦✦
Weinberg was the drummer for Bruce Springsteen's E Street Band for many years, and assembled this series as a retrospective of some of the greatest drum playing to be heard on rock & roll records. Sometimes that means actually drummers with solos, like Sandy Nelson, Preston Epps, and Cozy Cole; sometimes that means hits that feature classic brief drum solos, like the Ventures'

"Walk, Don't Run" and the Surfaris' "Wipe Out." Most often, though, it means classic hits that owe a lot of their strength to the rhythm, from Little Richard to the Edgar Winter Group. Volume One covers the '50s, Volume Two the '60s, Volume Three the '70s; Weinberg provides extensive liner notes throughout, illuminating the many types of drum styles heard on these early rockabilly, soul, British Invasion, progressive rock, funk, and even folk-rock records. For those who don't pay special attention to the drums, it's more of a collection of great vintage rock classics with an assortment of great beats. —*Richie Unterberger*

Mega Hits Dance Classics, Vols. 1-14 / Priority ✦✦✦
This is a spotty but exhaustive series of '70s and '80s disco hits. The packaging is awful, with horrid graphics and no liner notes, but there are some rarities to be found on some of the sets. Every volume contains at least one treasure. —*John Floyd*

○ **Mercury Rhythm & Blues: 1946-1962** / 1990 / PolyGram ✦✦✦✦
Though it leaned more toward pop-flavored R&B like the Platters, Mercury had some fertile years. This set catches them well. —*Dan Heilman*

○ **Metal Age: The Roots of Metal** / 1992 / Rhino ✦✦✦✦
Actually, *Roots of Metal* comes closer to representing the heyday of heavy metal. From Status Quo to Motorhead, all kinds of '70s arena hard rock and metal are covered; over the course of the disc, it becomes clear that metal does *not* all sound the same—there's quite a difference between the thuggish Wishbone Ash, the melodic Cheap Trick, snarling Runaways, and the bloated blues of Beck, Bogert and Appice. Some of it holds up surprisingly well and some of it is embarrassing, but there's no question that it captures its era particularly well. —*Stephen Thomas Erlewine*

★ **Monster Summer Hits: Wild Surf** / Jul. 22, 1991 / Capitol ✦✦✦✦✦
The two-album *Monster Summer Hits* (the above album, *Drag City*, and this one, *Wild Surf*) is surf and hot rod material culled from the Capitol archives. There's lots of obvious cuts by the Beach Boys, Jan and Dean, and the Ventures, but plenty of rare stuff to keep you interested, with great sound quality too. —*John Floyd*

○ **Monterey International Pop Festival Box Set** / Jun. 1967 / Rhino ✦✦✦✦
A sumptuous, four-CD box set with all the deluxe trimmings celebrating the grandaddy of all outdoor rock concerts. With legendary performances by Otis Redding, the Who, Jimi Hendrix, Janis Joplin, the Byrds, and Paul Butterfield all taken from the mobile-unit multi-track masters (not to mention an album-sized booklet that'll knock your eyes out), this box evokes a sound and an era the way few (if any) retrospectives of like material ever do. Important music from a turning point in rock's history. —*Cub Koda*

Motown's Brightest Stars / 1986 / Motown ✦✦✦
On these unreleased tracks, the quality is not as good as *From the Vaults*, Motown 1978. —*Rick A. Bueche*

Movin' on up: Songs from the Civil Rights Struggle / Feb. 8, 1994 / The Right Stuff ✦✦✦
The civil rights movement of the 1960s found some of its greatest artistic expression through the giants of soul music. The compilation *Movin' On Up* includes thirteen of the era's most enduring statements of African-American pride. While this has a few Top Ten singles, it also brings to light several strong cuts by superstars like Otis Redding, Stevie Wonder, Curtis Mayfield, James Brown, and Nina Simone that are not nearly as well known as their biggest hits. Among the most interesting finds here are Redding's interpretation of Sam Cooke's heartbreaking ballad "A Change Is Gonna Come," Stevie Wonder's unexpected cover of Bob Dylan's "Blowin' In The Wind," James Brown's seven-minute declaration of black pride, "I Don't Want Nobody To Give Me Nothing (Open Up The Door, I'll Get It Myself)," Nina Simone's explicitly angry "Mississippi Goddam," and Donny Hathaway's gospelish version of Simone's composition "To Be Young, Gifted & Black." Detailed liner notes by R&B writer David Nathan clarify the connections between the music and the times. —*Richie Unterberger*

○ **The Muscle Shoals Sound** / Rhino ✦✦✦✦
In a series of nondescript studios in tiny towns tucked in the corner of northwest Alabama, a small band of musicians, singers, and producers sculpted a sound that revolutionized rhythm and blues in the 1960s. Dubbed the "Muscle Shoals Sound" after one of those towns, this region gave birth to the grittiest and funkiest Southern soul music of the era. The 18-song compilation *The Muscle Shoals Sound* presents a cross-section of some of the most influential grooves laid down in these studios during its golden

decade (1962-1972). Besides hits by soul giants like Otis Redding, Aretha Franklin, and Wilson Pickett, it includes influential sides by lesser stars like Percy Sledge ("When A Man Loves A Woman"), Etta James ("Tell Mama"), Arthur Conley ("Sweet Soul Music"), and Clarence Carter ("Patches"). It also includes the very first hit cut in the region, Arthur Alexander's "You Better Move On." Behind the scenes, songwriters and musicians like Spooner Oldham, Dan Penn, and Duane Allman were equally important in crafting a style distinguished by rock-solid rhythms and passionate performances. With thorough liner notes about the songs, performers, and musicians, this is a fine introduction to the "deep soul" music that was envied by such heavyweights as the Rolling Stones. —*Richie Unterberger*

○ **New Orleans Ladies: Rhythm & Blues from the . . .** / 1988 / Rounder ✦✦✦✦
With the exception of Irma Thomas, this anthology covers female vocalists whose contributions to New Orleans R&B were overlooked or devalued. Both Martha Nelson (Carter) and Leona Buckles were excellent uptempo, dance-oriented vocalists who had no trouble maintaining their vocal authority and clout over driving arrangements, and could also handle steamy ballads or confessional material. Buckles' "I'm Waiting (To Give You My Love)" and "Baby We're Through" were exuberantly sung. The Thomas tracks include her outstanding "Don't Mess With My Man" and three other lesser-known early-'60s numbers that weren't smashes, but displayed the majestic voice and dramatic delivery that ultimately became a dominant part of New Orleans soul. These aren't throwaway numbers, despite their obscurity. —*Ron Wynn*

○ **New Wave of British Heavy Metal** / 1990 / Metal Blade ✦✦✦✦
Many of today's thrash bands, like Metallica and Anthrax, were heavily influenced by British '80s bands, including Samson, Iron Maiden, Def Leppard, and Diamond Head. In the '70s these bands offered something different from metal/hard rock, appealing to kids looking for a change. —*John Book*

New York Beat: Hottest Club / 1979 / Priority ✦✦✦
A good collection of extended cuts and dance productions by acts that were among the hottest house and disco/dance performers in New York City clubs at the time. No crossover attractions, but ideal for hardcore club/dance fanatics or those seeking some idea of the ever-changing dance world. —*Ron Wynn*

○ **New York Thrash** / ROIR ✦✦✦✦
A classic collection of many hardcore bands from New York, who influenced a lot of metal bands to incorporate punk into their sound. It features music from Bad Brains, Beastie Boys, Adrenalin O.D., Nihilistics, and False Prophets. —*John Book*

○ **Nipper's #1 Hits: 1956-1986** / RCA ✦✦✦✦
A good cross-section of RCA's pop hits, featuring everyone from Perry Como to Elvis and beyond. An interesting chronicle of pop music in general. —*Cub Koda*

○ **No Alternative** / 1993 / Arista ✦✦✦✦
A mixture of B-sides, outtakes, live tracks, and newly recorded songs, *No Alternative* is the most successful benefit album of 1993, both commercially and artistically. Exceptional songs from Nirvana, Bob Mould, Urge Overkill, Smashing Pumpkins, American Music Club, and Pavement enhance fine outtakes from Buffalo Tom and Matthew Sweet, strengthen Uncle Tupelo and Soul Asylum's strong covers, and make the weak live tracks from the Beastie Boys, Sonic Youth, and the Breeders tolerable. However, nothing can save the Goo Goo Dolls' atrocious pop-metal take on the Rolling Stones' "Bitch." Still, that's only one song out of 19, making *No Alternative* a worthy purchase. —*Stephen Thomas Erlewine*

Northwest / 198? / Rhino ✦✦✦
The Northwest was renowned for some of the rawest, most R&B-grounded garage bands of the '60s. While the region wasn't as studded with riches as Texas and California, this comp has strong cuts by the Sonics and national hits by the Kingsmen and Paul Revere & the Raiders, as well as decent folk-rock psychedelia by the Daily Flash. —*Richie Unterberger*

Nuggets, Vol. 10: Folk Rock / 198? / Rhino ✦✦
One of the weakest offerings in the series, with oft-anthologized hits by the Byrds, Turtles, Scott McKenzie, and Barry McGuire. The non-hit cuts tend toward the lightest, poppiest facets of folk-rock. An exception is the powerful acoustic, original version of "Dazed And Confused" by Jake Holmes, which was transformed into heavy metal by Led Zeppelin. —*Richie Unterberger*

Nuggets, Vol. 11: Pop, Pt. 4 / 198? / Rhino ◆◆◆
Solid collection of slightly psychedelic-influenced, progressive '60s pop. Fine hits by the Left Banke, Fever Tree, and the Grass Roots, neat tracks by the Blues Project, Lee Michaels, and Gene Clark, worthy obscurities by the Magicians, Montage (a Left Banke spin-off), the Critters, and Keith. —*Richie Unterberger*

Nuggets, Vol. 12: Punk, Pt. 3 / 198? / Rhino ◆◆◆
Decent offering of strong cuts by some of the most esteemed regional garage bands of the '60s. The hits by the Hombres, the Syndicate of Sound, and Paul Revere are actually outdone by the tracks from Mouse & the Traps, the Remains, the Unrelated Segments, Kenny & the Kasuals, and the Lollipop Shoppe. Includes the hit "Shape of Things To Come," performed by Max Frost & the Troopers in the psychedelic exploitation film *Wild In The Streets*. —*Richie Unterberger*

☆ **Nuggets, Vol. 1: the Hits** / 1986 / Rhino ◆◆◆◆◆
A straightforward collection of garage-punk chart successes, including "Psychotic Reaction," "Dirty Water," "Nobody but Me," and "I Had Too Much to Dream Last Night." —*Bruce Eder*

☆ **Nuggets, Vol. 2** / 1987 / Rhino ◆◆◆◆◆
A top-notch collection of some of rock's spacier singles, B-sides, and odd tracks. —*Bruce Eder*

○ **Nuggets, Vol. 3: Psychedelic** / Rhino ◆◆◆◆
A good assembly of spaced-out works. —*Bruce Eder*

Nuggets, Vol. 4: Pop, Pt. 2 / 1984 / Rhino ◆◆◆
Most of the acts here take their cues from the lightest aspects of the Beatles. More often than not, the results are pretty infectious. Highlights include the E-Types, the Royal Guardsmen, and the Palace Guard, which featured future Merry-Go-Round leader Emmitt Rhodes. —*Richie Unterberger*

Nuggets, Vol. 5: Pop, Pt. 3 / 1985 / Rhino ◆◆◆
A little sappier than the previous "pop" installments of this series. Highlighted by obscure, minor hit singles by the Strawberry Alarm Clock, the Knickerbockers, the Association, and the Lovin' Spoonful. —*Richie Unterberger*

○ **Nuggets, Vol. 6: Punk, Pt. 2** / 1985 / Rhino ◆◆◆◆
Includes a lot of the greatest regional garage hits of the mid-'60s: the Brogues, We The People, the Unrelated Segments, the Chocolate Watch Band, and Mouse & the Traps all weigh in with strong cuts. Also includes worthy obscurities by Captain Beefheart ("Diddy Wah Diddy") and minor but exciting hits by the Shadows of Knight ("Oh Yeah") and the Electric Prunes (the psychedelic classic "Get Me To The World On Time"). —*Richie Unterberger*

○ **Nuggets, Vol. 7: Early San Francisco** / 1985 / Rhino ◆◆◆◆
A fine collection of pre-Summer of Love rarities from the mid-'60s. Besides hits by the Beau Brummels and We Five, it features rarities by the Vejtables, the Great Society (featuring a pre-Jefferson Airplane Grace Slick), and Country Joe & the Fish. —*Richie Unterberger*

Nuggets, Vol. 8: the Northwest / 198? / Rhino ◆◆◆
The Northwest was renowned for some of the rawest, most R&B-grounded garage bands of the '60s. While the region wasn't as studded with riches as Texas and California, this comp has strong cuts by the Sonics and national hits by the Kingsmen and Paul Revere & the Raiders, as well as decent folk-rock psychedelia by the Daily Flash. —*Richie Unterberger*

Nuggets, Vol. 9: Acid Rock / 198? / Rhino ◆◆◆
Switching to a decidedly heavier mode, this comp includes hits by Love, the Byrds, Steppenwolf, Iron Butterfly, the Chambers Brothers, Vanilla Fudge, and the Strawberry Alarm Clock, as well as worthy lighter, slightly obscure offerings by the Grass Roots, the Monkees, and the Young Rascals. —*Richie Unterberger*

○ **Oh Yeah! the Best of Dunwich Records** / 1992 / Sundazed ◆◆◆
Dunwich Records was to '60s garage bands what Sun was to rockabilly. This CD features a generous sampling of the best of Chicago's teen scene of that period. Great sound and liner info too. —*Cub Koda*

○ **The Okeh Rhythm & Blues** / Apr. 1, 1993 / Columbia ◆◆◆◆
A fine three-disc box, it features most of the greatest hits from the seminal R&B label. —*AMG*

Oldies But Goodies, Vol. 1 / Original Sound ◆◆◆
Oldies But Goodies was the first rock & roll anthology, setting the standards for various artists anthologies when it was originally issued in the early '60s. Over the years, the series has held up well

in many respects; although there isn't a unifying theme to any of the albums, the music is first-rate, full of popular singles that form the basis of oldies radio stations. However, when the series made its transition to compact disc in 1987, it wasn't nearly as successful. Taken on their own terms, the fidelity of these fourteen discs is quite bad, with muffled, distorted sound on almost every song; compared to CD reissues by other labels, the discs sound positively atrocious. If bad sound doesn't stand in your way, there's plenty of good music to be found on these CDs; the original records remain fine items. —*Stephen Thomas Erlewine*

○ **One Hit Wonders: The 60s, Vol. 1** / Rhino ◆◆◆◆
So what if Barry & the Tamerlanes and Jimmy Soul never had another hit? The dozen tracks here by them and others like them will hold up long after a bigger star's music has faded. —*Jeff Tamarkin*

● **One Hit Wonders: The 60s, Vol. 2** / Rhino ◆◆◆◆
This stuff is too much fun! The Hombres, Soul Survivors, and more are a sure thing every time. —*Jeff Tamarkin*

○ **Pebbles, Vols. 1-28** / ◆◆◆◆
In the early '70s, the *Nuggets* compilation reawakened listeners to the sounds of mid-'60s garage rock. As much of a revelation as that double album was at the time, it only focused on the tip of the iceberg of garage rock. Behind those forgotten hits and semihits lurked hundreds, if not thousands, of regional hits and flops from the same era, most even rawer and cruder. In the late '70s, the Pebbles compilations came along to fill in the gap and then some. Each volume gathered 15-20 obscure 45s—originally issued on tiny labels, and remastered right from the excruciatingly rare original vinyl—of prime mid-'60s garage rock. Sometimes a track by a relatively well-known performer would show up, but by and large these acts were unknown to anyone but collectors and those who happened to have lived in the areas where the bands played. More than any other factor, these compilations were responsible for the resurgence of interest in garage rock, which remains high among collectors to this day. The lyrical attitudes of the bands immortalized on *Pebbles* by and large have to do with cheating girls, adolescent rebellion, and high times. At times downright juvenile and sexist, the lyrics aren't the main attraction so much as the sound and stance, which anticipates the outrage of punk rock, but tempers it with tough British Invasion-inspired melodies, harmonies, and hooks, as well as fuzz-toned guitars, Farfisa organs, and wildly manic songwriting and performances. There are a lot of great unknown songs on *Pebbles*, way too many to cite in a brief review, from all over North America, most from 1965-67. There are also a fair number of generic tunes that have little to recommend beyond an excess of energy, which can make listening to an entire volume at once as much a challenge as a joy. Listeners approaching this series for the first time should search for the first ten volumes; after this initial burst, the well ran increasingly dry, and the later volumes can be a chore. Most of the individual installments don't have themes, but those looking for a concentration of certain items should check out Volume 3 (psychedelia) and Volume 6 (British R&B/mod); Volume 4, devoted to surf, is actually the weakest of the early volumes. Of special interest among the later volumes are installments devoted to obscurities from the European continent. More wide-ranging in style than the typical volume covering U.S. garage, these include albums devoted to '60s rarities from Holland, Sweden, Denmark, and Switzerland; though wildly uneven, they contain some surprisingly strong material. —*Richie Unterberger*

☆ **Phat Trax, Vols. 1-5** / 1994 / Rhino ◆◆◆◆◆
Rhino's five-volume chronicle of '70s and '80s funk eclipses their *In Yo' Face* series simply by including more rarities and 12-inch mixes than its predecessor. The grooves on this series laid the groundwork for much of the hip-hop and R&B of the '80s and '90s, which makes it essential listening. —*Stephen Thomas Erlewine*

★ **Phil Spector: Back to MONO (1958-1969)** / 1991 / ABKCO ◆◆◆◆◆

Philly Classics (1973-1977) / 1988 / Philadelphia International ◆◆◆
A decent sampler of '70s soul hits from the Philadelphia International label, it could've been better. —*John Floyd*

○ **Pimps, Players & Private Eyes** / Jan. 14, 1992 / Sire ◆◆◆◆
This entertaining collection of early-'70s funk and soul features classic cuts by Isaac Hayes and Curtis Mayfield. —*AMG*

Raging Harlem Hit Parade / 1992 / Relic ✦✦✦
An eclectic mix of '50s and '60s blues nuggets from the vaults of Fire, Fury, and other minor labels, it includes hits by Lightnin' Hopkins, Buster Brown, King Curtis, and Wilbert Harrison. —*John Floyd*

Rare Soul: Beach Music Classics, Vol. 1 / 1992 / Rhino ✦✦✦
A fine collection of '60s soul, it includes excellent tracks from Barbara Lewis and Archie Bell & the Drells. —*AMG*

Rare Soul: Beach Music Classics, Vol. 2 / 1992 / Rhino ✦✦✦
The second volume of *Rare Soul* is just as enjoyable as the first, featuring tracks by the Clovers, Mary Wells, and Sam & Dave. —*AMG*

Rare Soul: Beach Music Classics, Vol. 3 / 1992 / Rhino ✦✦✦
The final volume of *Rare Soul* is arguably the best, featuring dynamite songs by Ruth Brown and Willie Tee. —*AMG*

○ **Rarest Rockabilly & Hillbilly Boogie: The Best . . .** / ACE ✦✦✦✦
This is actually two earlier vinyl compilations on one compact disc, 28 tracks in all, hence the overlong title. The first compilation features artists incredibly obscure, playing music with a delightful, home-spun crudity to all of it that's home grown rock 'n 'roll in a most embryonic stage. The second features more name-brand artists, the majority of them from the Starday catalog, and offers classic '50s sides from Sonny Fisher, Sleepy LaBeef, and a very young George Jones. —*Cub Koda*

Rave New World / Jun. 15, 1993 / Rhino ✦✦✦
A compilation of ten new recordings from some of rave's biggest names (including Mark Picchiotti, Dave Sears, and Bleu), *Rave New World* is a good introduction to all of the different styles of one of the largest underground movements in the '90s. —*AMG*

○ **Rebel Rousers: Southern Rock Classics** / Jan. 24, 1992 / Special Music ✦✦✦✦
An audio tour of some of the genre's best moments, featuring seminal tracks by Lynyrd Skynyrd, The Allman Brothers Band, The Outlaws, The Marshall Tucker Band, and .38 Special. Interesting to compare these sides with the early-'90s vogue in country music. —*Cub Koda*

○ **Red Bird Story** / 1991 / Charly ✦✦✦✦
Red Bird was a great label in the mid-'60s, releasing some excellent soul/pop hybrids and some of the greatest girl group records of all time, especially those by the Shangri-Las and the Dixie Cups. This 4-CD, 96-track compilation is a frustratingly mixed attempt to enshrine its legacy. There are lots of great sides here: all the Shangri-Las and Dixie Cups hits, many of their rarities, one-shots by the Ad Libs, Jelly Beans, Butterflies, and Tradewinds, and cool rarities by Bessie Banks, Dee Dee Warwick, Evie Sands, Ellie Greenwich, the Soul Brothers, Cathy Saint, Linda Jones, and Andy Kim. But the programming is unnervingly jumpy and haphazard, the liner notes surprisingly fuzzy (no information whatsoever is given about many of the lesser-known artists), and, in the absence of master tapes, some of the cuts were obviously taken from records. And for all its length, it's not even a complete collection of Red Bird's output; some songs that were excluded had even surfaced on previous Charly vinyl anthologies. There's still a lot of great music here, but the execution could have been a lot better. —*Richie Unterberger*

○ **Red Hot & Blue** / 1990 / Chrysalis ✦✦✦✦
These new recordings of Cole Porter songs (released in 1990) benefit AIDS research. Artists include U2, the Neville Brothers, Fine Young Cannibals, K. D. Lang, and Annie Lennox. The songs, recorded in a wide variety of styles, reaffirm what a great, timeless writer Porter was. —*Kenneth M. Cassidy*

Red Hot & Dance / Jun. 30, 1992 / Columbia ✦✦✦
This compilation to raise money for AIDS research features George Michael, Madonna, Seal, PM Dawn, Lisa Stansfield, Young Disciples, Sabrina Johnston, Crystal Waters, Sly & The Family Stone, EMF, and Tomandandy. —*AMG*

○ **Reservoir Dogs** / 1992 / MCA ✦✦✦✦
Only five songs here were featured prominently in Quentin Tarantino's rousing crime film ("Little Green Bag," "Hooked On a Feeling," "I Gotcha," "Stuck In the Middle With You," and "Coconut"), but they include Steven Wright's introductions from the film (separately indexed, thankfully), as well as Tarantino's infamous interpretation of the meaning of Madonna's "Like a Virgin" and Harvey Keitel's monologue on how to rob a jewelry store. In total, that's about fifteen to twenty minutes of material. Padding out the rest of the disc are three new songs—"Fool for Love" is very good,

"Harvest Moon" passable, and "Magic Carpet Ride" is abominable. After this, the disc has passed the half hour mark by two minutes. The amount of music you'll actually want to listen to makes it even shorter, but it is a soundtrack you'll want to return to. —*Stephen Thomas Erlewine*

○ **Risque Rhythm: Nasty 50s R&B** / 1991 / Rhino ✦✦✦✦
Would-be censors and PMRC fans take note: NWA and Guns N' Roses ain't got nothin' on the Dominoes or Dinah Washington. Double-entendre R&B at its most suggestively raw. —*Jeff Tamarkin*

○ **Rock Instrumental Classics, Vol. 3** / 1971 / Rhino ✦✦✦✦
Rhino's third rock instrumentals volume covers the '70s, a period that found disco, funk, and fusion joining the formula alongside one-shot concept works and the usual novelty numbers. The 18 cuts include stomping club/funk from B.T. Express and Brass Construction, King Curtis' updated honking sax cover of Led Zeppelin's "Whole Lotta Love," very stylized material from the Electric Light Orchestra and Deodato, and memorable outings by Billy Preston, Edgar Winter and AWB. Gary Glitter, Edgar Winter, the Chakachas, Rhinoceros, and Van McCoy offer lighter pop variations, and "Sun Goddess" was a musically adventurous excursion into fusion by Earth, Wind and Fire. —*Ron Wynn*

☆ **Rock Instrumental Classics, Vol. 4** / 1962 / Rhino ✦✦✦✦✦
While the material on volume four of Rhino's rock instrumentals set chronologically preceded what was on the third volume, no soul, R&B or even soul-jazz and funk fan should mind these 18 genuine classics, including two superb numbers from Booker T. and the MGs, seminal tracks by the Mar-Keys, Bar-Kays and Cannonball Adderley, and great Latin tunes from Ray Barretto and Mongo Santamaria. There's absolutely no fluff, and the presence on CD of rare cuts like the Young Holt Trio's "Wack Wack" and Alvin Cash & The Crawlers' "Twine Time" is most welcome. —*Ron Wynn*

☆ **Rock Instrumental Classics, Vol. 5** / 1961 / Rhino ✦✦✦✦✦
Rhino closes its five-volume rock instrumentals series with an 18-track outing devoted to surf guitar. This fast-paced, prickly and frequently exciting form may not be among the most diversified structurally, but if does offer some surging playing from its practitioners. They rang from founding father Dick Dale to its most popular bands, the Surfaris, Belairs, Ventures and Chantays. While not particularly a hardcore surf collection, this disc certainly outlines its virtues, and the tunes were long enough to display guitar proficiency, but short enough to prevent self-indulgence and repetition. —*Ron Wynn*

☆ **Rock Instrumental Classics, Vol. 1** / 1994 / Rhino ✦✦✦✦✦
Rhino begins yet another concept line with 18 tasty instrumentals from the rock era. It's the first of a five-volume set devoted to this genre, and they certainly picked the right era to launch it. From Duane Eddy's shuddering guitar riffs and Link Wray's rumbling licks to Lee Allen's honking sax lines and bleating phrases, Dave "Baby" Cortez's distorted organ and Ernie Fields' swing/boogie, this anthology shows how early rock and roll emerged through the union of seemingly disparate musical elements. Besides big band jazz and shouting blues, there were also bits of rockabilly, pop, novelty tunes and country, reworked and presented in short, captivating ditties. —*Ron Wynn*

☆ **Rock Instrumental Classics, Vol. 2** / Rhino ✦✦✦✦✦
The second release in Rhino's rock instrumentals series moves into the 1960s, again presenting a wide array of material. There's jazz-tinged fare by pianist Ray Bryant, roadhouse blues/boogie from Lonnie Mack, the Ventures' signature surf tune "Walk Don't Run" and another Duane Eddy floor-shaker, "Because They're Young." This collection also shows that the novelty and silly tunes weren't quite as inspired in the 1960s; neither the Fireballs' "Bulldog" or the T-Bones' "No Matter What Shape (Your Stomach's In)" will ever make anyone forget the Coasters. There are several interesting gimmick and period-piece oddities, from Mason Williams' "Classical Gas" to Jorgen Ingmann's "Apache" and "(Ghost) Riders In The Sky" by the Ramroads. It's shorter than the first volume, and has a bit more fluff, but is still quite valuable. —*Ron Wynn*

★ **Rock This Town: Rockabilly Hits, Vol. 1** / 1991 / Rhino ✦✦✦✦
This devastating '50s rockabilly anthology expertly cuts across label and stylistic restraints. —*Bill Dahl*

☆ **Rock This Town: Rockabilly Hits, Vol. 2** / 1991 / Rhino ✦✦✦✦✦
The second volume of this anthology is just as satisfying through the first ten tracks, when it suddenly veers toward contemporary interpreters. —*Bill Dahl*

Rock and Roll: The Early Days / RCA ◆◆◆
Paltry but powerful collection of a dozen classics by Elvis, Haley, Waters, Berry, and more. —*Jeff Tamarkin*

Rock of the 80's / Priority ◆◆◆
Like Priority's *'70s Greatest Rock Hits* series, the fifteen-volume *Rock of the '80s* offers a haphazard, yet enjoyable, presentation of hit singles and one-hit wonders from each year of the decade. While the '70s discs are loosely arranged according to theme, the '80s discs just feature ten songs, regardless of when they were released or what they are about. Nevertheless, the series features a nice cross-section of songs and the sound is good, even if there are no liner notes. Despite its flaws, the series remains a good sampler of '80s pop hits. —*Stephen Thomas Erlewine*

○ **Rock, Baby, Rock It!** / Rhino ◆◆◆◆
The best and worst '50s rock & roll movie ever made. It was shot on location in Dallas, TX, on a shoestring budget utilizing local rockabilly talent. No plot, no big-name musical talent, and crappy acting abounds throughout, but this film perfectly encapsulates the driving spirit of rock & roll's earliest days. —*Cub Koda*

○ **Rockabilly Stars, Vol. 1** / 1981 / Columbia ◆◆◆◆
Featured are 24 cuts from Carl Perkins, Johnny Cash, Marty Robbins, Charlie Rich, the Collins Kids, and others. —*AMG*

○ **Rockabilly Stars, Vol. 2** / Columbia ◆◆◆◆
This second album contains 24 more tracks by Carl Perkins, Sid King & the Five Strings, and others. —*AMG*

○ **Rockabilly in Memphis: 1954-1968** / 1954-1968 / Smithsonian ◆◆◆◆
Many superb rockabilly acts never got their day in the sun, and the genre has not received the documentation it merits. This 18-cut anthology goes a long way towards straightening out this problem; it includes cuts from such neglected performers as Ray Harris, Sonny Burgess, Carl Mann, Malcolm Yelvington and Ray Smith. Robert Gordon's notes detail exactly how the intersection of Southern black and white cultures resulted in rockabilly, a genuine hybrid that shared characteristics of both. While such selections as Johnny Cash's "I Walk The Line" and Roy Orbison's "Ooby Dooby" have been reissued to death, hearing them one more time is not much to ask for the chance to get Carl McVoy's version of "You Are My Sunshine." —*Ron Wynn*

☆ **Rockin' Again at the I's 2** / 1990 / ACE ◆◆◆◆◆
Easily the highest-quality multiartist compilation of pre-Beatles British rock, although not the most comprehensive. The material features artists ranging from Bertice Reading to Janice Peters and styles ranging from R&B and rockabilly to proto-punk. All of it is high grade, even if little of it saw huge chart action. (Import) —*Bruce Eder*

○ **Rockin' in the Farmhouse: Original Rockabilly and Chicken Bop, Vol. 2** / 1992 / Sundazed ◆◆◆◆
Rockin' in the Farmhouse—Original Rockabilly and Chicken Bop—Vol. 2 is an excellent 20-track compilation featuring the best of the Roulette label's rarest rockabilly tracks. Highlights include Don "Red" Roberts's "Only One," Jimmy Isle's "Goin' Wild," Jimmy Lloyd's "Rocket in My Pocket," and five chaotic unissued tracks by the Rock-A-Teens. —*Cub Koda*

☆ **Roots of British Rock** / Sire ◆◆◆◆◆
Easily the most comprehensive rock collection ever assembled and all the more amazing, since it is a US release. From Tommy Steele in 1956 to the Tornadoes in 1962, there are few major stones left unturned on this jewel of a two-record set. An honest look at what was popular in Britain before the Beatles. A vital addition to any oldies collection. —*Bruce Eder*

○ **Rumble** / Relic ◆◆◆◆
This excellent New York doo-wop anthology features mid-'50s work by the Channels, the Bop Chords, the Love Notes, and the Continentals with great sound quality from the original master tapes. —*Bill Dahl*

○ **Rutles Highway Revisited** / 1990 / Shimmy Disc ◆◆◆◆
Of the hundreds of tribute albums that have been assembled since the mid-'80s, this had one of the most clever concepts: perform a "tribute" to a band that never existed. The Rutles, Eric Idle's spot-on television parody of the Beatles, were never a bonafide unit, but they did record some fine satires for the film's soundtrack, composed by Rutle and ex-Bonzo Dog Band honcho Neil Innes. What we have here are 20 alternative acts of the '90s covering all of the Rutles' songs. Better than most tributes, it still falls prey to

the genre's chief pitfalls: compared to the original, it's forced, stiff, and lacking. The best interpretations tend to be the most straightforward, like Syd Straw and Marc Ribot's acoustic "I Must Be In Love"; Shonen Knife's "Goose Step Mama," with its high-pitched vocals and jerky tempos, would have fit easily onto one of their actual albums. Alternative rock collectors may want to pick this up for the otherwise unavailable tracks by Galaxie 500, King Missile, Jellyfish, and Daniel Johnston; there are also some half-famous stalwarts of the indie scene like Das Damen, Unrest, and Peter Stampfel, as well as total obscurities like the Tinklers and Paleface. —*Richie Unterberger*

○ **San Francisco Nights** / 1991 / Rhino ◆◆◆◆
Probably the most interesting and accessible collection of its kind ever to come from America, more substantial than many European collections. Featuring the obvious and the weird, including the Beau Brummels, the Charlatans, the Vegetables, and the Mystery Trend. —*Bruce Eder*

☆ **The Scepter Records Story** / May 26, 1992 / Capricorn ◆◆◆◆◆
During the '50s and early '60s, NYC-based Scepter Records and its subsidiary Wand were part of a group of independents whose artists churned out hit after hit, defining the sound of the day and shaping the sound of the future. The Shirelles, Dionne Warwick, and the Isley Brothers all got their start there; if you love tough, pre-soul-era records like "Will You Still Love Me Tomorrow," "Twist and Shout," and "Walk on By," then this is for you. The label's roster also included singers Chuck Jackson, Maxine Brown, and Tommy Hunt; instrumentalist King Curtis; proto-pop/country artists B. J. Thomas and Ronnie Milsap; and punksters Kingsmen. That's right—"Louie Louie" is here, along with lots of other truly great music. Even though the three discs could have been condensed to a killer two, this box gets high marks. —*Christine Ohlman*

● **Searchin' For Shakes: Swedish Beat 1965-1968** / 1984 / Amigo ◆◆◆◆
One of the very best compilations of '60s rock from a non-English-speaking country, with excellent fidelity (usually not the case with these productions). With their barely accented English vocals and the heavy mod rock flavor (with a pinch of Merseybeat thrown in), a bunch of these Swedish bands could pass for overlooked British Invasion groups. The Who's brand of auto-destruct guitar noise seemed to hit home particularly hard in Sweden, and the cuts by the Steampacket II, Lee Kings, Tages, Namelosers, and Boot-jacks will appeal to anyone who reveres the early Who and Creation. Other highlights include the Mascots, whose track is one of the best early Merseybeat imitations to be found anywhere, and the Lea Riders, whose "Dom Kellar Dos Mods" (previously issued on a *Pebbles* volume) is one of the prime demented psychedelic obscurities of all time. —*Richie Unterberger*

Sedated in the Eighties / Nov. 16, 1993 / The Right Stuff ◆◆◆
This collection contains a number of the songs that launched MTV—the stuff that frats partied and puked to at college beer busts throughout the '80s. You know the Ramones' "I Wanna Be Sedated," the Romantics' "What I Like About You," Modern English's "I Melt with You," Smithereens' "Behind a Wall of Sleep" and, well you get the picture. —*Rick Clark*

Shut Down '66 / Ernie Douglas ◆◆◆
Subtitled *The World's Only '60s Punk Record*, this compilation features 18 garage band rockers from the wimpier, "My Baby Shot Me Down" side of the equation. Plenty of 12-string guitars, Farfisa organ, and teenage angst—great fun all. —*Cub Koda*

Slash Early Sessions / Warner Brothers ◆◆◆
This is a decent overview of '80s cuts from the West Coast label that brought you Los Lobos, the Blasters, X, and the Gun Club. —*John Floyd*

Smack My Crack / 1987 / Giorno Poetry Systems ◆◆◆
John Giorno continues to explore the connection between contemporary poetry and the more extreme forms of rock music, including selections by the Butthole Surfers, the Swans, and Nick Cave, along with more typical contributors such as William S. Burroughs and Tom Waits. —*William Ruhlmann*

○ **Songs By Richard Thompson** / 1994 / Capitol ◆◆◆◆
One of the better tribute albums of 1994, *Beat the Retreat* manages to capture not only the dark grace of Richard Thompson, but also his spirit. R.E.M.'s faithful reading of "Wall of Death" is full of beautiful melancholy, while Bob Mould's galloping take on "Turning of the Tide" pays homage to Thompson's breathtaking instru-

mental skills simply by making the song his own. Most of *Beat the Retreat* works in the same way. The artists' love for the material never shadows their appreciation for Thompson's individuality. Hence, the songs are never replications of the original versions; they are interpretations, which is much more effective. —*Stephen Thomas Erlewine*

Songs of Protest / 1991 / Rhino ✦✦✦
Of course there are too many noteworthy songs of protest to fit onto one collection, even (or especially) if you're limiting youself to the '60s, as Rhino does on this compilation. Still, it does a good job of mixing monster hits by Barry McGuire, Sonny Bono, Dion, the Kingston Trio, the Temptations, and Edwin Starr with more obscure cuts. Country Joe's "I-Feel-Like-I'm-Fixin'-To-Die Rag" is here, as well as Sonny Bono's self-pitying "Laugh At Me," the pre-electric Donovan's cover of Buffy Saint-Marie's "Universal Soldier," and Manfred Mann's fine, overlooked cover of Dylan's "With God On Our Side." The most hard-to-find songs span the opposite ends of the spectrum. "It's Good News Week," a 1966 hit for the Jonathan King-led group Hedgehoppers Anonymous, is a lightweight catalog of social ills that retains considerable period charm. Far more earnest is Phil Ochs' "I Ain't Marchin' Anymore," represented here by the non-LP, electric folk-rock version released as a single in 1966. Although it made no commercial impact, it holds up to the best protest anthems of the era, both musically and lyrically. —*Richie Unterberger*

☆ **Soul Hits of the 70s: Didn't It Blow Your Mind, Vol. 1** / 1991 / Rhino ✦✦✦✦✦
This 15-volume set was released in 1991 and is a veritable Comstock Lode of overlooked hits from an era most rock fans have yet to discover. By offering the best recordings by the likes of the O'-Jays, the Blue Notes, the Chi-Lites, and many others, *Soul Hits* gives the listener a feel for just how vital Black pop and disco was in an era when rock was starting to sag. But the inclusion of dozens of forgotten one-shot hits makes each volume a history lesson in the continued innovation and sheer joy of R&B, proving that Blacks didn't stop making great music after Muddy Waters and Sly Stone bit the dust. —*John Floyd*

○ **Soul Shots, Vol. 10: More Sweet Soul** / 1988 / Rhino ✦✦✦✦
At least as good, and perhaps better than, the original "Sweet Soul" volume. This has classic hits by Tyrone Davis, Major Lance, James Carr, the Impressions, and the Dells, as well as lesser-known selections by the O'Jays and Eddie Floyd, and hard-to-find items by the likes of the Radiants, Tony Clarke, Bobby Moore, and the Poets. The Showmen's "39-21-46," featuring future Chairmen of the Board lead singer General Johnson, is one of early soul's most genuinely eccentric moments. —*Richie Unterberger*

○ **Soul Shots, Vol. 11: More Ballads** / 1988 / Rhino ✦✦✦✦
For the soul fan looking to dig a little deeper than established classics, this is probably more exciting than the previous ballad collection in this series. McKinley Mitchell, Spyder Turner, Betty Harris, Jimmy Holiday—they're all names known primarily to collectors, and they're all represented here. So are stars like the Impressions, Chuck Jackson, the Dells, and O.V. Wright, but the tracks are not among the famous hits. Especially interesting are the original versions of "Get It While You Can" (by Howard Tate), later covered by Janis Joplin, and "You Can Make It If You Try" (by Gene Allison), covered by the Rolling Stones on their first album. Other highlights are Jay Wiggins' "Sad Girl," one of the most haunting soul ballads ever, and Gloria Walker's "Talking About My Baby," one of the most deliciously bitchy and spiteful female soul performances, despite the fact that it rips off Etta James' "I'd Rather Go Blind." —*Richie Unterberger*

○ **Soul Shots, Vol. 1: We Got More Soul (Dance Party)** / 1987 / Rhino ✦✦✦✦
The 11-volume *Soul Shots* series, originally issued on vinyl in the late '80s, are the best general overview compilations of soul music. They've since been condensed into a four-CD series which reprises some of the highlights from the records and adds some new tracks. As many of the songs from the original 11-volume set didn't make it onto the CDs, the vinyl editions, which are still easy to find, are still recommended, and even necessary, for the soul connoisseur. Volume One, with the focus on raucous uptempo numbers, has a characteristic mix of stars (James Brown, Jackie Wilson) with important minor figures (Jackie Lee, J.J. Jackson, Dyke & the Blazers, Robert Parker). With thorough liner notes, these compilations are great ways to catch up on a lot of the best one- and two-shot artists of the soul era. —*Richie Unterberger*

○ **Soul Shots, Vol. 2: the "In" Crowd** / 1987 / Rhino ✦✦✦✦
"Sweet soul" is not slow ballads, but light-hearted, pop-oriented soul, with the accent on pleasant (often high) vocal arrangements. Not as critically respected as dance soul, deep soul, Motown, or some other subgenres, there were nonetheless many fine cuts recorded in this style during soul's heyday. This compilation has a lot of good ones, including Brenton Wood's "Gimme Little Sign," Deon Jackson's "Love Makes The World Go Round," the Esquires' "Get On Up," the Larks' "The Jerk," Bobby Hebb's "Sunny," and several other lesser-known cuts. —*Richie Unterberger*

○ **Soul Shots, Vol. 3: Soul Twist (Soul Instrumentals)** / 1987 / Rhino ✦✦✦✦
More than other mid- and late-'60s pop styles, soul lent itself well to instrumentals, both party tunes and slower romantic stuff. This volume has big hits by most of the major soul instrumental stars (Booker T. & the MG's, the Mar-Keys, King Curtis, the Bar-Kays, Young-Holt Unlimited, Ramsey Lewis, Hugh Masekela), as well as one-shots like Cliff Nobles ("The Horse") and cuts by Alvin Cash and the Viscounts that rarely get played on oldies radio. —*Richie Unterberger*

○ **Soul Shots, Vol. 4: Tell Mama (Screamin' Soul Sisters)** / 1987 / Rhino ✦✦✦✦
One of the best volumes of the series, assembling some of soul's most emotional and expressive female performers. Running from Motown imitations to novelties to pop-soul to raw deep soul to blues-soul, it has outstanding cuts by Etta James, Koko Taylor, Maxine Brown, Fontella Bass, Barbara George, Gloria Jones, and Shirley Ellis. Lorraine Ellison, Linda Jones, and Patti Drew are names only known to serious soul fans, but their tracks are just as fine as the ones by more famous names, and the two selections by Aretha Franklin are among her more obscure ("Lee Cross," from her Columbia era, and the 1968 B-side "You Send Me"). —*Richie Unterberger*

○ **Soul Shots, Vol. 5: La-La Means I Love You** / 1987 / Rhino ✦✦✦✦
Another good mixture of stars and one-shots, different regions, and different styles. This has cuts by the Impressions, James Carr, Lou Rawls, and Aaron Neville, Philly soul by the Delfonics and Eddie Holman, girl-group soul by Barbara Mason, blue-eyed soul by Thee Midniters, New York soul by Garnett Mimms, and eccentric soul by Billy Stewart. All cuts are first-rate slow-tempo smoochers. —*Richie Unterberger*

○ **Soul Shots, Vol. 6: Blue-Eyed Soul** / 1988 / Rhino ✦✦✦✦
There weren't a great deal of white performers who sang and wrote soul with authentic conviction—most knew better than to try—but there were a few who not only pulled it off, but did it well, sometimes even crossing over into the black audience. This LP has many of the more notable blue-eyed soul performers: the Rascals, Tony Joe White, Roy Head, Bill Deal, the Soul Survivors—as well as interesting obscurities in the style by the likes of Bob Kuban and Dean Parrish, and cuts in a blue-eyed soul vein by performers not strictly associated with the style, like P.J. Proby, Billy Joe Royal, Lonnie Mack, and Wayne Cochran. It's missing major blue-eyed soulsters like the Righteous Brothers, John Fred, and the Box Tops, but those performers have good anthologies of their own. —*Richie Unterberger*

○ **Soul Shots, Vol. 7: Urban Blues** / 1988 / Rhino ✦✦✦✦
Another interesting subgenre that doesn't get a lot of critical attention: city blues bearing heavy soul influences. Every one of the performers on this compilation was a blues or soul performer of significance. B.B. King, Junior Wells, Albert King, Buddy Guy, and Otis Rush are bluesmen represented by some of their most soul-soaked cuts; Little Junior Parker, Bobby Bland, Little Milton, and Lowell Fulsom worked the territory between soul, R&B, and blues; Tommy Tucker and Little Johnny Taylor were R&B singers who had hits with heavy blues influences, rounding out the several perspectives of this anthology. —*Richie Unterberger*

○ **Soul Shots, Vol. 8: Sweet Soul Sisters** / 1988 / Rhino ✦✦✦✦
They may be sweet in that they sing about love and have a lot of pop appeal, but the female soul singers on this anthology are measurably earthier and heavier than the male "sweet" soul singers spotlighted on Volume Two of this series. Jan Bradley, the Jewels, and Betty Everett fall close to the girl group sound; the Sweet Inspirations, led by Cissy Houston (mother of Whitney), take it to the most gospel-flavored extreme. Barbara Acklin and Brenda & the Tabulations are among the better-known minor female soul stars;

there are also obscure singers like Jackie Ross, Patti Drew, and the Flirtations, whose hit "Nothing But A Heartache" was one of the best soul one-shots of the '60s. For many listeners, the highlight will be Gloria Jones' original version of "Tainted Love," emasculated into a synth-pop hit much later by Soft Cell. Jones' rendition isn't exactly sweet soul, but a storming dance number that ranks as one of the great hits-that-never-were of the '60s. —*Richie Unterberger*

○ **Soul Shots, Vol. 9: More Dance Party** / 1988 / Rhino ✦✦✦✦
As *Soul Shots* volumes go, this is populated with more obscure performers/songs than usual, enhancing its appeal for collectors without decreasing in accessibility whatsoever. Etta James, Ike & Tina Turner, and Johnnie Taylor are stars, of course; there are also thrilling one-shots by the Capitols ("Cool Jerk"), the Parliaments ("I Wanna Testify," with a lineup including George Clinton), and the Marvelows ("I Do"). Jamo Thomas' "I Spy (For The FBI)" is one of soul's finer novelties, and the compilation also includes the rare original versions of the standards "Shake A Tail Feather" (by the Five Du-Tones) and "Mustang Sally" (by Sir Mack Rice). —*Richie Unterberger*

○ **Soul Train: Hall of Fame, 20th Anniversary** / 1994 / Rhino ✦✦✦✦
Soul Train, the longest-running weekly syndicated program in television, gave black artists and dancers a forum when there was no interest from the major networks. This fine three-disc boxed set celebrates the show's two decades and serves as a good overview for how contemporary black pop has changed during its run. The opening disc is by far the most diverse; during the mid-'70s, there was still room for Southern soul and blues, stylish pop, funk and vocal groups. The second disc mirrors the turn toward more sophisticated production, a less soulful sound and the coming of disco. The final CD begins with light soul and pop-tinged fare, then slides into rap, hip-hop and New Jack swing. Most of these songs are available elsewhere, but this collection gives listeners a consistently entertaining tour. Rhino deserves bonus points for using all original versions throughout. —*Ron Wynn*

○ **The Specialty Story** / 1994 / Specialty ✦✦✦✦
Label-owner Art Rupe was a savvy business man who knew the black jukebox industry and what made it tick when he started his Specialty label in the late-'40s. This sumptuous five-disc box set contains a bevy of highlights from this seminal R&B/rock & roll label. Over the years, Rupe recorded a little bit of everything; early big band jump (the Liggins brothers), down-home blues and zydeco (Guitar Slim, Frankie Lee Sims, Clifton Chenier), gospel (early Sam Cooke and the Soul Stirrers) and doo wop (The Pentagons, Jesse Belvin). But with the discovery of the label's biggest star, Little Richard, in 1955, here is where the real story of rock & roll begins. A box set that no lover of the real thing can be without.—*Cub Koda*

Spy Music, Vol. 1 / 1994 / Rhino ✦✦✦
A rather slight, but well done, concept for a compilation: '60s "spy" music, either inspired by spy films, or used as themes for the spy flicks themselves. Besides the original versions of some monster hits ("Secret Agent Man," "Peter Gunn," "Goldfinger," "Mission Impossible"), you get some nifty soul rarities by Edwin Starr, Smokey Robinson, and Rex Garvin, as well as the novelty "99" by Barbara Feldon, who played the character of the same name in the *Get Smart* series. —*Richie Unterberger*

☆ **The Stiff Records Box Set** / 1992 / Rhino ✦✦✦✦✦
Stiff Records was the first independent record label in England, partially responsible for starting the punk and new wave revolution of the late '70s. Under the guidance of house producer Nick Lowe, Stiff turned out an enormous number of seminal punk and new wave singles in their first years, including classic tracks by the Damned, Elvis Costello, Graham Parker, the Adverts, Ian Dury, and Lowe himself. But what really gave the label its wild, original flavor were minor artists like Ian Dury, Wreckless Eric, Tenpole Tudor, the Yachts, Lene Lovich, Rachel Sweet, and Mickey Jupp, who turned out a series of raw pop gems that were everything good rock & roll singles should be—catchy, energetic, and memorable. Over 100 of Stiff's finest tracks are collected on this wonderful four-disc box set. While most of these songs weren't hits, they are classic rock & roll. The first three discs are excellent; the fourth disc contains some bright moments, but by that time, their artists were pretty much spent. However, the box remains one of the most compulsively listenable sets ever assembled, providing the definitive retrospective of arguably the most important and influ-

ential British record label of the late '70s. —*Stephen Thomas Erlewine*

○ **Sub-Pop-200** / 1988 / Sub Pop ✦✦✦✦
A fine overview of the Seattle grunge-rock scene. —*John Dougan*

The Sullivan Years: Born to Be Wild—Rock / 1991 / Tee Vee Toons ✦✦✦
The Airplane, the Vanilla Fudge, Jams, and others bring classic rock to the masses in the '60s in this 1991 release. —*Jeff Tamarkin*

○ **The Sullivan Years: British Invasion** / 1990 / Tee Vee Toons ✦✦✦✦
Probably the best of TVT's Sullivan series. Sullivan can actually take a good deal of the credit for breaking the British Invasion in the United States, featuring most of the top bands on his show in the mid-'60s. This compilation has 16 songs from 1964-66 broadcasts by the Searchers, the Animals, Billy J. Kramer, Peter & Gordon, Gerry & the Pacemakers, Herman's Hermits, and Freddie & the Dreamers. Occasionally it's obvious that they're singing to a backing track, but most of the performances are totally live and make for a pleasant listen, though they don't match or redefine the studio versions; the Animals come off the best. Presumably, material by the Beatles, Rolling Stones, and the Dave Clark Five—all of whom played on the show several times—was unavailable for licensing. —*Richie Unterberger*

Sullivan Years: Happy Together / 1991 / Tee Vee Toons ✦✦✦
'60s hitmakers including the Turtles, the Lovin' Spoonful, and the Grass Roots, live (sometimes fake-live, though) on the legendary TV show. —*Jeff Tamarkin*

Sullivan Years: Mod Sound / 1990 / Tee Vee Toons ✦✦✦
This is not so much the "mod" sound of the '60s as the "pop" sound, featuring many of the day's top mainstream pop-rockers: the Mamas & the Papas, Dusty Springfield, Petula Clark, Lulu, Jackie DeShannon, the Seekers, the 5th Dimension, and the Friends of Distinction. Female singers figure prominently on almost all of the tracks, and it's certainly a pleasant enough collection, most of the performances featuring noticeably thinner orchestral arrangements than the hit versions. But it's a souvenir more than anything; you're better off with the originals in every case. —*Richie Unterberger*

The Sullivan Years: Rhythm & Blues Revue / 1993 / TVT ✦✦✦
Ed Sullivan wasn't exactly a champion of R&B, but his show was open to R&B performers at a time when black entertainers in general had a hard time getting prime-time exposure. This compilation draws almost exclusively from the 1950s, although B.B. King does end the set with a performance of his 1970 hit "The Thrill Is Gone." It also features, in blurry fidelity, cuts by Jackie Wilson, Louis Jordan, the Platters, LaVern Baker, and Brook Benton, sometimes with inappropriately square accompaniment by the show's orchestra. The highlight is Bo Diddley's 1955 rendition of his self-titled debut single; one can only imagine the audience reaction to the fierce rock & roller at a time when Elvis Presley had yet to achieve national success. —*Richie Unterberger*

The Sullivan Years: Rock 'n' Roll Pioneers 1955-1959 / 1993 / TVT ✦✦✦
Live TV spots by Buddy Holly, Bill Haley, Fats Domino, Chubby Checker, Lloyd Price, Gene Vincent, Frankie Lymon, Jerry Lee Lewis, Jimmie Rodgers, Joe Bennett, and the Champs on this compilation. Like the rest of the Sullivan series, it's essentially a collector's item; the performances are spirited, deviate little from the records except that the arrangements are usually thinner, and are exceedingly short (over half the cuts clock in at under two minutes). The Buddy Holly songs are the most valuable, especially considering that barely any live recordings of him survive. The Jerry Lee Lewis medley, incidentally, is from 1969, not the '50s. —*Richie Unterberger*

Summer & Sun / 1989 / Rhino ✦✦✦
An entertaining roundup of summer-oriented hits from the '50s, '60s, and '70s. —*Dan Heilman*

Summer of Love / 1987 / Rhino ✦✦✦
This double album focuses on the sunniest, poppiest aspects of psychedelia. Actually, a lot of this is closer to pure pop than acid, but it has good hits in that vein by Donovan, the Troggs, the Mamas & the Papas, and the Young Rascals. At the rawer end of the spectrum are the Electric Prunes, Strawberry Alarm Clock, and the Byrds; Petula Clark, the 5th Dimension, and the Cowsills, on the other hand, were only as hippie-ish as they needed to be to get in the Top 40 in 1967. —*Richie Unterberger*

Sun City / 1985 / Razor & Tie ✦✦✦
Sun City was certainly the most political of all of the charity rock albums of the 1980s. Little Steven organized a number of artists for this protest against apartheid, including such heavyweights as Miles Davis, Bob Dylan, Peter Gabriel, Jimmy Cliff, Bruce Springsteen, Jackson Browne, Run-D.M.C., and Lou Reed. Thankfully, the result was extremely listenable as well as fiercely political; it's one of the few charity or protest albums that stands up to repeated listenings, thanks to the extended instrumental workouts. Arguably the finest moment on the record is one that was added at the last minute—a spare, stripped-down version of U2's "Silver and Gold" by Bono, Keith Richards, and Ron Wood. —*Stephen Thomas Erlewine*

★ **The Sun Records Story** / 1986 / Rhino ✦✦✦✦✦
Landmark '50s recordings from Memphis by Presley, Cash, Orbison, Jerry Lee Lewis, Carl Perkins, and others. —*Hank Davis*

○ **Sun Records: the Rockabilly Years** / Charly ✦✦✦✦
Gigantic 12-record import, 52-page book anthology of Sun's landmark contribution to the genre it virtually founded. Many classic sides by the better-known artists and even more great unissued sides by unknown rockers like Jimmy Wages and Tommy Blake, among others. Beyond classic. —*Cub Koda*

☆ **Sun Rockabilly: Classic Recordings** / Rounder ✦✦✦✦✦
As the title suggests, this is Memphis rockabilly at its best, featuring Carl Perkins, Warren Smith, Billy Riley, and a stellar cast of musical pioneers. —*Hank Davis*

☆ **Sun Story** / 1994 / Rhino ✦✦✦✦✦
There have been a lot of Sun compilations over the years; this three-CD, 74-song compilation strikes the medium ground between abridged single-disc highlights and overkill ten-album box sets. What this means is that you get virtually all the key sides of this vastly influential blues, country, and rockabilly label, including the biggest Sun hits cut by Elvis, Carl Perkins, Jerry Lee Lewis, Johnny Cash, Charlie Rich, and Roy Orbison. There's also a lot of the pioneering electric blues cut by label head Sam Phillips before he made rockabilly Sun's focus, including sides by Howlin' Wolf, B.B. King, Rufus Thomas, Junior Parker, and James Cotton. Then there are the interesting small hits and flops by minor rockabilly figures like Warren Smith, Billy Lee Riley, Malcolm Yelvington, Onie Wheeler, and Carl Mann. There aren't any previously unreleased songs, so the Sun specialist most likely already has everything here; it's a better buy for the avid, knowledgeable fan who isn't a completist. —*Richie Unterberger*

☆ **Super Hits of the '70s: Have a Nice Day, Vol. 1** / Jan. 1990 / Rhino ✦✦✦✦✦
Rhino's ridiculously large (over twenty discs) series of the schlockiest pop hits of the '70s provides the definitive portrait of that decade's musical mainstream. Each of the volume contains at least two pop classics, but the most consistent volumes are 2, 5, and 14. —*Stephen Thomas Erlewine*

○ **Surf & Drag, Vol. 1** / 1989 / Sundazed ✦✦✦✦
All the great surf and hot-rod sides from the Challenge label. Features Gary Usher, the Four Speeds, the Knickerbockers, Jan and Dean, the Royal Coachmen, Donna Loren, and the Rhythm Rockers. Powerful genre material—this is as good as it gets. —*Cub Koda*

Surf & Drag, Vol. 2 / 1993 / Sundazed ✦✦✦
Featuring more rare tracks from the second tier of surf and hot-rod performers, this volume is no less potent than the first. Highlights include the original version of "She Rides with Me" by Paul Petersen, "Bustin' Surfboards" by The Tornadoes, and "GeeTO Tiger" by The Tigers. —*Cub Koda*

○ **Surf Legends & Rumors '61-'64** / 1989 / Garland ✦✦✦✦
A superb assortment of rare surf instrumentals from 1961-1964, it doesn't have many hits but included are plenty of previously unreleased gems. —*John Floyd*

○ **Sweet Relief: Benefit for Victoria Williams** / Jul. 6, 1993 / Choas ✦✦✦✦
The shear breath and diversity of artists gathered for this benefit project is a tribute to the affection with which Victoria Williams is held by her peers. It conveniently also makes for heady listening for any fan of contemporary music. The hard brittle edges of Soul Asylum ("Summer Of Drugs") and Buffalo Tom ("Merry Go Round") stand shoulder to shoulder with the country-folk of Lucinda Williams ("Main Road") and Maria McKee (an inspired and rivetting "Opelousas—Sweet Relief"). Sweet Relief offers a unique

opportunity to introduce yourself to an enduring songwriter while savouring some of the day's most intriguing musicians. How sweet it is! —*Roch Parisien*

○ **Tamla Special #1** / 1962 / Motown ✦✦✦✦
Includes extremely rare tracks from some obscure early Motown artists. —*Rick A. Bueche*

○ **Taste of Doo-Wop, Vol. 1** / 1993 / Vee-Jay ✦✦✦✦
No R&B label had more prolific doo-wop talent than Vee-Jay, which turned the fertile Chicago area into a goldmine in the '50s and early '60s. This 25-cut anthology contains a healthy sample and thankfully focuses on acts like the 5 Echoes, Orchids, Magnificents, and Rhythm Aces, fine ensembles that didn't score the huge hits of their contemporaries but made several solid records nonetheless. There are also acts that became bigger on other labels, like Sonny Til and his Orioles, the Pips (later Gladys Knight and the Pips), and a funky unreleased version of "The Twist," by the Midnighters (Hank Ballard and company). —*Ron Wynn*

○ **Taste of Doo-Wop, Vol. 2** / 1993 / Vee-Jay ✦✦✦✦
The second Vee-Jay various artists anthology showcasing diverse doo-wop hits takes the same formula as its predecessor, featuring strong songs by more obscure acts rather than huge hits from established greats. The Kool Gents (a group that once included Dee Clark), the Prodigals, the Hi-Liters, and the El Dorados, plus set one holdovers the Magnificents, 5 Echoes, and Impressions are on hand providing 25 more examples of marvelous harmony singing, jump cuts, and swooning romantic ballads. —*Ron Wynn*

○ **Teenage Riot!** / Atomic Passion ✦✦✦✦
Insanely great rock & roll compilation centered around juveniledelinquent themes and featuring promo drop-ins from teen-gang movies and anti-rock & roll sermons. Gene Maltais's "Gang War" is not to be missed. —*Cub Koda*

○ **Ten Years of Collectors Records** / White Label ✦✦✦✦
Highlights culled from a decade of issuing great rockabilly comps. The Lonesome Drifters hit "Eager Boy" and Charles Dean's "Train Whistle Boogie" and "Parking in the Dark" are just some of the highlights. —*Cub Koda*

○ **Texas Kat Music** / Gulf Coast ✦✦✦✦
A 15-track collection of rockabilly and rock & roll from the Texasbased Felco label. Cuts by Billy Taylor ("Wombie Zombie"), Irwin Russ ("Crazy Alligator"), and the Twisters (the awesome "Bandstand Rocket") are featured. —*Cub Koda*

Texas Music, Vol. 3: Garage Bands & Psychedelia / 1994 / Rhino ✦✦✦
Texas arguably produced the most manic and raunchiest garage rock of any state during the 1960s. While seasoned collectors will find little on this 18-song compilation that they don't already have, it's a decent intro to some of the Lone Star State's shining moments. Long renowned as a melting pot of sounds, Texas groups often flavored their records with R&B, blues, and Tex-Mex, which means that in addition to classic garage sides by the Bobby Fuller Four, the Thirteenth Floor Elevators, Kenny & the Kasuals, and Mouse & the Traps, you get blues-rock (Steve Miller, Johnny Winter), blue-eyed soul (Roy Head's "Treat Her Right"), Tex-Mex-flavored rock (Sam the Sham & the Pharoahs and the Sir Douglas Quintet), and the all-out weirdness of the Legendary Stardust Cowboy ("Paralyzed"). There are also garage singles by the Chessmen, Scotty McKay, and Nobody's Children that were quite rare in their day, though they've appeared on easy-to-find garage compilations. The real find is the Ron-Dels' (featuring Delbert McClinton) "If You Really Want Me To, I'll Go," a country-flavored beat ballad strongly reminiscent of the Beatles' similar material from 1964 and 1965. —*Richie Unterberger*

○ **That'll Flat Git It!, Vol. 2: Rockabilly From . . .** / 1992 / Bear Family ✦✦✦✦
This is a sterling collection of obscure rockabilly from the vaults of Decca Records. Both hardcore and casual rockabilly fans will find much to treasure in this wonderful package. —*AMG*

○ **That'll Flat Git It!, Vol. 3: Rockabilly From . . .** / 1992 / Bear Family ✦✦✦✦
More raw rockabilly and country bop, this time from the vaults of Capitol Records. While the label had Gene Vincent and Esquerita, a quick listen to these will reveal rockabilly sounds with the accent on 'billy. Skeets McDonald's "You Oughta See Grandma Rock" goes a long way toward defining the compilation's strengths, and Tommy Sands, long thought of as a teen idol singing pop mush, stokes the fires here with "The Worryin' Kind"

and "Playin' the Field." While Ferlin Husky masquerading as Simon Crum on "Bop Cat Bop," the Rio Rockers' "Mexicali Baby" and Bobby Lee Trammell's "You Mostest Girl" show the length and breadth of the genre, perhaps the most fascinating earful of all is the Louvin Brothers testing the waters of rockabilly with "Red Hen Hop" and "Cash on the Barrelhead." (Import) —*Cub Koda*

○ **The Unavailable 16 & The Original Nitty Gritty** / 1962 / Vee-Jay ✦✦✦✦
Pair of early '60s albums from the Vee-Jay vaults. The first 16 numbers are old doo-wop tunes by such groups as the Quintones, El Dorados, and single vocalists Harold Dorman and Tony Bellis. There's a good ratio of hits to flops, notably the Moonglows' "Secret Love" and "Angel Baby" by Rosie & the Originals, plus fine performances from the Dells, Spaniels, Impressions, and Magnificents. The other album has a mixed bag of pop, doo-wop, R&B, and even blues from a diverse artist list ranging from Roscoe Gordon and Harold Burrage to Pee Wee Crayton, Eddie Taylor, Jerry Butler, and Joe Buckner. —*Ron Wynn*

☆ **There's a Riot Goin'** / 1991 / Rhino ✦✦✦✦✦
Sure, you can spend a lot of dough buying CD reissues of all the bands Leiber and Stoller wrote songs for. And while that would give you a great record collection (especially of Drifters and Coasters material), you might want to start with this indispensable 18-track collection. All the big hits are here, as are the songs that show off Leiber and Stoller's melodramatic way with a song ("I Who Have Nothing") and their deft comic touch ("Charlie Brown"). The essence of Leiber and Stoller's genius is here, and I'm willing to wager you'll recognize nearly every one of these songs as soon as they start. Memory can be a wonderful thing. —*John Dougan*

○ **This Are Two Tone** / 1983 / Chrysalis ✦✦✦✦
Here's the best of the neo-ska label of the early '80s, featuring the Specials, English Beat, and others. —*Dan Heilman*

This is Merseybeat / 1989 / Edsel ✦✦✦
At the outset of Beatlemania in July 1963, the tiny U.K. Oriole label went to Liverpool with a mobile sound unit to record unsigned local beat groups for a pair of compilation LPs (combined onto this reissue). Only a couple of them (the Nomads, who soon became the Mojos, and the Merseybeats) achieved any British hits. A full 24 of these 28 tunes are covers of U.S. R&B/rock/pop standards. In comparison to the originals they sound pale—the vocals are often especially twee—and the four originals are derivative and unexceptional, a bit cloddish even. This comp illustrates that the Beatles were more a unique product of the Mersey sound than a representative one. —*Richie Unterberger*

☆ **Top of the Stax: Twenty Greatest Hits, Vol. 2** / 1934-1956 / Stax ✦✦✦✦✦
Memphis Soul 101. *Top of the Stax* is the history of Stax in two concise volumes, tracing the music from the early hits of the Mar-Keys, Otis Redding, and Sam & Dave up to the major hits of the '70s. —*John Floyd*

○ **Treasure Chest of Musty Dusties, Vol. 1** / 196z / Fortune ✦✦✦✦
Twelve-song compilation (originally issued in the early '60s) featuring the best-known sides of the lesser-known Fortune Records vocal groups. Some of the best of Detroit's pre-Motown R&B era is presented here, the Swans' "Wedding Bells" being a particular highlight. —*Cub Koda*

○ **Treasure Chest of Musty Dusties, Vol. 2** / 196z / Fortune ✦✦✦✦
Companion volume to the above (and no less essential), featuring more great Detroit doo wop and R&B sounds from the pre-Motown era. Heavy emphasis on unissued tracks, bringing to light several gems that make this compilation live up to its title. —*Cub Koda*

○ **Tribute to Kurt Weill: Lost in the Stars** / A&M ✦✦✦✦
Eclectic updates of Kurt Weill's distinctive German theater music, with help from Sting, Marianne Faithfull, John Zorn, Lou Reed, Carla Bley, Tom Waits, Charlie Haden, and more. —*Myles Boisen*

☆ **The Two Tone Compilation: Checkered Past** / Nov. 16, 1993 / Chrysalis ✦✦✦✦✦
An essential double-disc set, it provides all the greatest tracks from the seminal ska-revival record label, including classic singles by the Specials and the English Beat. —*AMG*

○ **Ugly Things, Vols. 1-3** / ✦✦✦✦
U.S. and U.K. audiences were totally unaware at the time, but Australia was home to a thriving garage-punk scene in the mid-'60s. The scope and output of these groups was limited by the country's population, which was only about 15 million or somewhat less, af-

ter all. But there was a surprisingly large number of fine singles, some of which measured up to the manic, over-the-top R&B-derived energy of anything coming from Texas, California, or London. Volume 1 is by far the best of the series, and indeed, one of the best '60s garage compilations ever, filled with good hooks, screams, and crunching riffs. Volumes 2 and 3 aren't nearly as good, peppered with undistinguished covers and unmemorable tracks, although some excellent ones do surface, including some from neighboring New Zealand; the best of these two LPs should have been combined into one. Raven has put out a best-of compilation CD from the Ugly Things series that draws from all of the volumes and adds some other cuts. —*Richie Unterberger*

Ultimate Girl Groups / ✦✦✦
One of the best compilations of obscure girl-group singles from the mid-'60s. And we are talking obscure; Diane Renay is the only artist on this 27-track compilation who had a hit of any sort. These actually fall much closer to girl-group soul than girl-group pop/rock, the influence of Motown being particularly prevalent. These aren't meant as criticisms; these are mostly infectious, well-produced tracks, some of which, like Judy Hughes's "Fine, Fine, Fine," could have been big hits. —*Richie Unterberger*

Uptown MTV Unplugged / 1993 / MCA/Uptown ✦✦✦
New Jack vocals are the main course on this latest entry in the unplugged sweepstakes, a collection featuring artists from MCA's Uptown label. Jodeci, Mary J. Blige, Father M.C., Christopher Williams, and Heavy D and the Boyz are the participants, with Jodeci and Williams sounding energetic and animated, if at times a bit overwrought. Blige, whom one might expect to dominate the proceedings, comes across more understated than expected, while Heavy D. turns in his customary mix of humor and hip-hop insolence, and Father M.C. does something that's in between balladry, rapping, and comedy. —*Ron Wynn*

○ **The Vee-Jay Story: 1953-1993** / 1993 / Vee-Jay ✦✦✦✦
This definitive three-disc retrospective documents this seminal R&B and blues record label. —*AMG*

Vol. 2 / Mr. Mannicotti ✦✦✦
More nutzo offerings on this memorial album for Joe E. Ross, which features Ross (of *Car 54 Where Are You?* fame) doing "Ooh-Ooh," Archie Pier's "Tamales & Rock 'n' Roll," and the best/worst version of "Heartbreak Hotel" you'll ever hear. —*Cub Koda*

Vol. 2 / Flame ✦✦✦
Storming compilation of extremely rare early rock & roll sides. The master tapes are history, but the music and the energy contained here more than make up for the lack of fidelity. —*Cub Koda*

Vol. 3 / Mr. Mannicotti ✦✦✦
The third offering in an ongoing series, this time featuring the cast of *McHale's Navy* doing "Pa Pa Ooh Mow Mow," Terry Tene's "Curse of the Hearse," Jerry Coulston's "Cave Man Hop," and T. Valentine's "Hello Lucille, Are You a Lesbian?" as some of the crazed highlights. As insane as the first two volumes and then some. —*Cub Koda*

Walkin' Thru The Sleepy City / 1982 / ✦✦✦
It's never been too easy to find, but this Japanese compilation will intrigue Rolling Stones fans, as it collects 13 singles from the mid-'60s that Mick Jagger and Keith Richards wrote for other artists, rather in the manner of John Lennon and Paul McCartney writing for Peter & Gordon or Billy J. Kramer. About half of the material would eventually turn up on the Stones' releases (sometimes not until the bottom-of-the-barrel mid-'70s compilation *Metamorphosis*); they never released their own versions of the rest. Rather surprisingly, the songs are quite mediocre, lightweight Merseybeat/Beatles-style concoctions. When Jagger and Richards began writing for themselves, it took them a good year or so to lock into a fierce R&B/rock groove, and most of these compositions—some of them quite dreary, actually—date from the era when they were struggling to find their own identity and vocabulary. The most famous tracks, Marianne Faithfull's "As Tears Go By" and "Sister Morphine" and Lulu's "Surprise, Surprise," are easily available elsewhere. The obscurities by George Bean, Adrienne Porter, the Mighty Avengers, Bobby Jameson, the Mighty Avengers, Thee, and Vashti are of historical interest only, and the LP doesn't include the relatively decent songs they penned for Gene Pitney ("That Girl Belongs To Yesterday") and the Toggery Five ("I'd Much Rather Be Out With The Boys"). —*Richie Unterberger*

○ **Wax 'Em Down** / Revell ◆◆◆◆
Cool compilation of rare surf tunes, not too hard to find despite appearing on a tiny reissue label. Divided about equally between instrumentals and vocals; the instrumentals, usually featuring magnificent reverb-soaked guitar lines, certainly have the edge. Only a couple of recognizable names here: the Original Surfaris' "Surfari" is the B-side of their well-known "Bombora," and Sandy Nelson's "Casbah" is a great lost treasure, with searing guitar by well-known session player and producer Richie Polodor. Also includes a first-rate surf novelty in Frank Sinatra, Jr.'s "Beach Girls & The Monster" (included in both vocal and instrumental versions). —*Richie Unterberger*

○ **We Got a Party: Best of Ron Records, Vol. 1** / 1988 / Rounder ◆◆◆◆
There's something for R&B, blues and soul fans of all persuasions on this anthology spotlighting various New Orleans artists who recorded for the Ron label in the late '50s and early '60s. There were celebrities, like pianist Professor Longhair and the sultry soul queen Irma Thomas, country/rockabilly singers like Warren Lee, novelty specialist Chris Kenner and shouters such as Bobby Mitchell. The 14 tracks on the CD are all good; most are wonderful, even if most of the singers never attained any recognition outside Crescent City R&B circles. —*Ron Wynn*

A Week or Two In the Real World / 1995 / Real World/Virgin ◆◆◆
Gathering choice tracks from Peter Gabriel's Real World recording weeks of 1991 and 1992, it focuses less on collaborative efforts than *Arcane*. There are hits and misses among the 16 tracks, all of a subjective nature depending on the listener's perspective. The disc plays it safe from a Western perspective on several tracks— Van Morrison's joint venture with The Holmes Brothers falls into this category, as does the conventional soul/R&B of Carole Rawley, Simon Emmerson and Raw Stylus. Peak moments come from Laplander Mari Boine's astounding circular breathing, traditional joik song style, Ashkhabad's soundtrack to some Middle Eastern desert convoy, and the heavily percussive Toto La Momposina Y Sus Tambores. —*Roch Parisien*

○ **West Coast Doo-Wop** / ACE ◆◆◆◆
Nice collection of vocal group sides from the vaults of Modern Records. Arthur Lee Maye & the Crowns' "Loop-De-Loop-De-Loop" and "Oochie Pachie" are among the numerous highlights. —*Cub Koda*

West End Story / 1981 / West End ◆◆◆
While disco was no longer commercially in vogue in the early '80s, there were outstanding songs being recorded and performed. This first CD in a four-disc line begins with a dance classic, the slithering, loping "Heartbeat," sung by Taana Gardner with an ideal mix of suggestiveness, longing and reserve. Other highlights include Raw Silk's "Do It To The Music" and B.T.'s hot, sensual, yet also foreboding "You Can't Have Your Cake and Eat It Too." All songs are in their original disco length and mode. —*Ron Wynn*

West End Story, Vol. 2 / 1978 / West End ◆◆◆
The second volume in West End's anthology/reissue line reaches back to the end of the 1970s for some great soul-disco in Bettye Lavette's sassy "Doin' The Best That I Can" and another definitive Taana Gardner number, "Work That Body." There's also Loose Joints' great bit of comic innuendo "Is It All Over My Face," and even more sexually aggressive fare from Stone, "Girl I Like The Way You Move." Barbara Mason's "Another Man" was considered hilarious in 1983, but would undoubtedly be considered controversial at best and homophobic at worst in today's climate. There's also representative material from Billy Nichols and Raw Silk. —*Ron Wynn*

What's Shakin' / 1966 / Elektra ◆◆◆
An odd, erratic, but interesting anthology of rare performances recorded by Elektra in the mid-'60s, when it was just getting its feet wet with rock. Leading the way are the Paul Butterfield Blues Band, whose five tracks are very much in the style of their first LP; the Butterfield original "Lovin' Cup" is about as good as anything

he ever did. Eric Clapton & the Powerhouse are a most interesting aggregation, also featuring Stevie Winwood, Paul Jones, Jack Bruce, and Spencer Davis Group drummer Pete York; their three tracks include early versions of "Steppin' Out" and "Crossroads," which Clapton would record with the Bluesbreakers and Cream, respectively. The Lovin' Spoonful's four tracks date from before reaching stardom with the Kama Sutra label; here they concentrate on blues and early rock & roll-style songs, which frankly don't measure up to their folk-rock. Rare tracks by Tom Rush and Al Kooper (who reworked his contribution, "Can't Keep From Crying Sometimes," with the Blues Project) round out the set. —*Richie Unterberger*

Where the Pyramid Meets The Eye: A Tribute to Roky Erickson / Oct. 30, 1990 / Sire ◆◆◆
Wherein Warner Brothers guys like R.E.M., Jesus and Mary Chain, ZZ Top, and Doug Sahm pay homage to Texas weirdo Erickson, who's best known for his work with the '60s punk group the 13th Floor Elevators. Not great but you'll find a few nice surprises. —*John Floyd*

○ **Wild Men Ride Wild Guitars** / 1991 / Sundazed ◆◆◆◆
Great rockabilly/hillbilly-boogie compilation of tracks from the vaults of Challenge Records. Highlights include Big Al Downing's "Down on the Farm," and Charlie Ryan's "Hot Rod Rocket." —*Cub Koda*

Wild Things: Wild Kiwi Garage 1966-1969 / 1991 / ◆◆◆
New Zealand, a tiny country with a population less than the metropolitan San Francisco Bay Area, nevertheless had a fairly prolific and interesting garage/beat scene in the mid-'60s. This collects 16 singles that, with one or two exceptions, were obscure even in the land of their release. Like the bands from neighboring Australia, the Kiwis compensated for their isolation with crude mania, and this has some ferocious sub-Stones pounders from the likes of the La De Da's, Chants R&B, and the Bluestars. An above-average garage collection, well worth checking out by '60s aficionados. —*Richie Unterberger*

Woodstock / Aug. 1970 / Cotillion ◆◆◆
The wrong notes are jarring and the recording flaws seem obvious, but the energy and enthusiasm compensate. —*Bruce Eder*

Woodstock '94 / 1994 / A&M ◆
It's easy to pick on the second Woodstock festival, and much of the criticism is deserved. *Woodstock '94* collects one track from 27 of the artists that performed at the festival, which might sound fine in theory, but fails miserably in practice, mainly because the tracks included are generally terrible. Because of contractual agreements, the album is comprised of also-rans, obscurities and only a couple of hits. For instance, Nine Inch Nails shine on "Happiness in Slavery," but who needs to hear Blind Melon's "Soup?" Most of the two discs are filled with "Soup," which makes sorting out the gems particularly tedious. As a concert memento, *Woodstock '94* captures the schizophrenia of the show, but it's never enjoyable listening. —*Stephen Thomas Erlewine*

Wrinkles / 1989 / MCA/Chess ◆◆◆
Ten obscure blues, R&B, and rock instrumentals from the Chess label, spanning 1952-63. The Jody Williams track is a scorcher that stands up to Mickey Baker and Otis Rush's best work. Also includes rarities by Chuck Berry, Bo Diddley, Otis Spann, and Little Walter. A ragtag comp, but a good one. —*Richie Unterberger*

○ **Yellow Pills Vol. 2** / 1994 / Big Deal ◆◆◆◆
○ **Yellow Pills, Vol. 1** / 1994 / Big Deal ◆◆◆◆
A dynamic power-pop collection featuring new and old tracks by some of the leading groups of the last ten years, including Dwight Twilley, the Shoes, the Rubinoos, and Tommy Keene. The music on *Yellow Pills* is strong enough to convert casual fans into hardcore power-pop fanatics. —*Stephen Thomas Erlewine*

○ **Yesterday's Heroes: '70s Teen Idols** / Rhino ◆◆◆◆
A fun collection of the lightweight pin-up stars of the '70s. *Yesterday's Heroes: '70s Teen Idols* is the perfect compliment to Rhino's *Have a Nice Day* series. It's some serious fun. —*AMG*

ROCK STYLES

The 50-year history of rock & roll has seen the music evolve through literally dozens of major styles and sub genres, both mainstream and underground, Black and White, American and British. It seems impossible at times to identify such diverse performers as Chuck Berry, De La Soul, the Beatles, the Smiths, Aretha Franklin, and Liz Phair as part of the same tradition. But the more one studies the history of rock, and, more importantly, the more one listens to and enjoys music from different styles and eras, the more it becomes evident how deep the connections are from generation to generation, and how much fine music of the past remains to be discovered or rediscovered.

With this section of the *All Music Guide to Rock*, we hope to provide contexts for fuller appreciation of the reviews and biographies that form the main body of this volume. The first and biggest part of this section presents essays on several dozen of the most crucial styles and trends of the rock era, arranged in roughly chronological order from the roots of rock & roll to the present. Besides providing a succinct history of each style's birth, growth, influence, and key performers, we've also listed some of each genre's most important and influential recordings (most of which are given full-length reviews in the main text of the book). Producers, songwriters, labels, and technological developments have had a substantial impact on many of these styles, and you'll often find their roles discussed as well. Some of these essays are accompanied by music maps that graphically illustrate the development of a certain style, and the links between their key performers.

These profiles should not be taken as definitive assessments of all of rock's major historical movements. We haven't been able to cover every important aspect of the music, and our own tastes and biases are inevitably reflected when we try to pare down the contributions of hundreds of major musicians into a couple of pages. And because of the boundaries we were obliged to draw, some of the greatest rockers and most renowned albums of all time that did not happen to fit comfortably into our categories are not discussed at length in these profiles. Those omitted often rank among our personal favorites, including Bo Diddley, the Everly Brothers, Roy Orbison, the Velvet Underground, the Band, and quite a few others. No slight is intended, and you should be able to find informative bios and reviews of their most crucial work in the preceding section.

Likewise, the lists of recommended recordings should not be taken as definitive best-of groupings, but as both suggested starting points for those discovering certain sounds, and building blocks for those who want to refresh or expand their knowledge. Keeping in mind that both novices and scholars will be taking these plunges, we've included a few tasty surprises and unheralded works among the tried-and-true classics that even aficionados of these genres might have overlooked. You should be able to find reviews and bios of many of your favorites that didn't make these lists in our regular review section as well.

Rock was not born and did not evolve in isolation. More than most musical categories, arguably, it is a hybrid of rich and diverse popular music traditions, and continues to be heavily influenced by performers and styles that could not be defined as rock, and indeed are sometimes way beyond that music's parameters. The second part of this section contains basic overviews of several (by no means all) of the outside genres that have played a key role in rock's mutations, and which continue to do so.

These overviews illustrate some of the key connections between other styles of music and rock, and how each has influenced the other. You'll also find a list of some of the most fundamental classics of each genre, with brief capsule reviews of these recordings, as many are not included in the previous section. The lists of recommended recordings are intended to provide useful starting points for rock listeners looking to expand their horizons, from which they can continue in as much depth as they wish. The hope is not so much to get readers listening to every type of music they can get their hands on as to give something of a window to the many outside currents that have helped shape rock itself. For those who wish to delve into these styles further, the ever-growing series of *All Music Guide* books and on-line services provide in-depth coverage, and there are many other excellent reference books, some of which are reviewed in the third part of this section.

The third part of this section includes sketches of some miscellaneous and often underappreciated influences on rock music, such as producers, session musicians, and independent labels. You'll also find some features on formats, resources, and references that are crucial to getting the most out of what you hear, including bootlegs, fanzines, reissues, box sets, reference books, magazines, and mail-order resources. As comprehensive as we've tried to make *The All Music Guide to Rock*, the point can't be made too strongly that the greatest education you'll receive will come from your own firsthand investigation. Many of the reference books we review cover, often in considerable depth, styles and performers we have missed entirely, and everyone's encouraged to make use of as many of these as they can.

And we hope you apply the same spirit of inquiry to whatever you may learn from the following pages. Rock writing can sometimes bog down in classifications and ratings. Our lists, essays, and critical assessments aren't intended to provide the final word on what's best and most significant, but rather to offer one of many maps to the immense and always surprising jungle of rock music. We're always discovering new and old artists, overlooked connections, and sounds that move us as we've never been moved before. The search is often frustrating, sometimes borders on detective work, but wouldn't mean as much if it was clearly mapped out before us. For, as you're about to read in the first essay, nobody planned rock & roll, anymore than anyone planned a jungle, and the map is still being drawn.

– Richie Unterberger

The Birth of Rock & Roll

For those of us born too late to experience the birth of rock & roll firsthand, an unlikely parallel might be drawn to the Internet. It has been written that no one planned the Internet; it just happened. And the same could be said of rock & roll. No one planned rock & roll, and it overtook the musical culture of America and then the world, with a sudden impact that revolutionized popular music as surely as the Internet is revolutionizing telecommunications.

It has often been said that rock & roll was the result of cross-breeding between rhythm and blues and country & western music. That's a large part of the equation, of course, but hardly the entire picture. Gospel music, swing jazz, jump blues combos, country swing bands, Tin Pan Alley publishers – they were just some of the other key building blocks of the music.

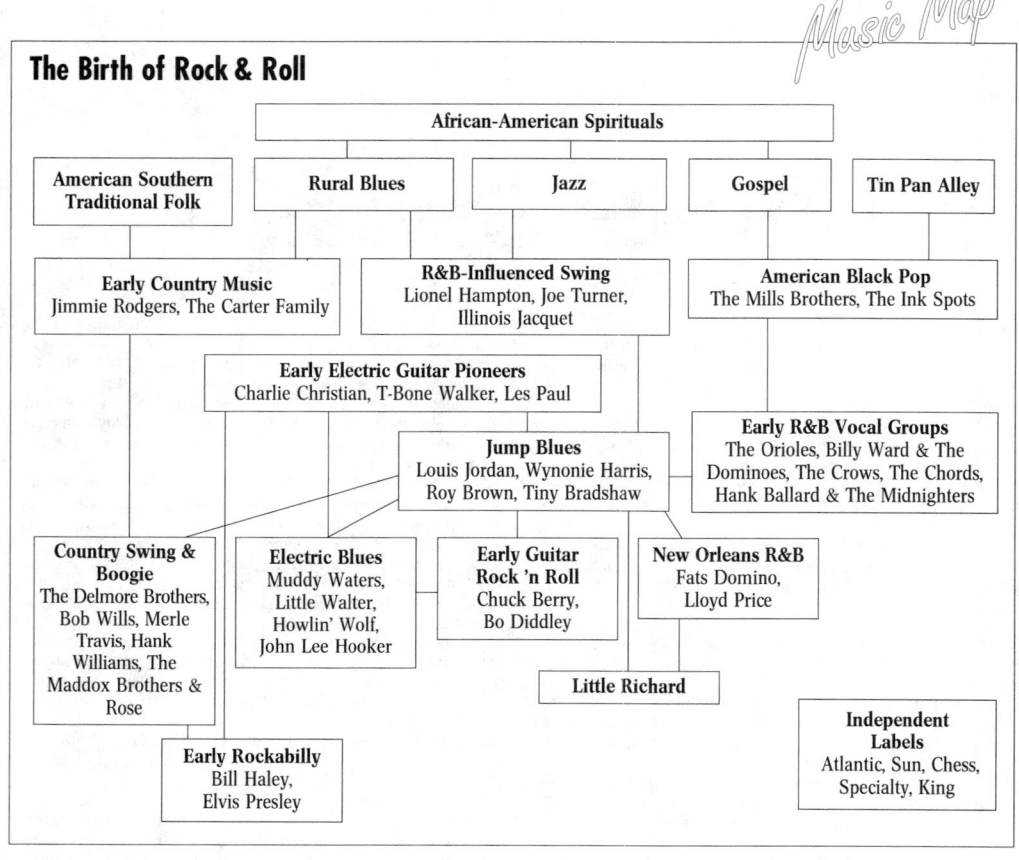

Music Map

The Birth of Rock & Roll

African-American Spirituals

American Southern Traditional Folk — **Rural Blues** — **Jazz** — **Gospel** — **Tin Pan Alley**

Early Country Music
Jimmie Rodgers, The Carter Family

R&B-Influenced Swing
Lionel Hampton, Joe Turner, Illinois Jacquet

American Black Pop
The Mills Brothers, The Ink Spots

Early Electric Guitar Pioneers
Charlie Christian, T-Bone Walker, Les Paul

Jump Blues
Louis Jordan, Wynonie Harris, Roy Brown, Tiny Bradshaw

Early R&B Vocal Groups
The Orioles, Billy Ward & The Dominoes, The Crows, The Chords, Hank Ballard & The Midnighters

Country Swing & Boogie
The Delmore Brothers, Bob Wills, Merle Travis, Hank Williams, The Maddox Brothers & Rose

Electric Blues
Muddy Waters, Little Walter, Howlin' Wolf, John Lee Hooker

Early Guitar Rock 'n Roll
Chuck Berry, Bo Diddley

New Orleans R&B
Fats Domino, Lloyd Price

Little Richard

Independent Labels
Atlantic, Sun, Chess, Specialty, King

Early Rockabilly
Bill Haley, Elvis Presley

Few would dispute that rock & roll owes much of its origins to the musical traditions of America's African-American population. From Africa, Blacks brought strong oral musical traditions which, modified in the United States under incredibly harsh conditions, eventually became the backbone of blues music. As segregated as American society has been, there still has been constant personal interchange and cultural exchange between races throughout the nation's history. The White southern population of the United States had its own musical conventions: Anglo-Saxon folk songs, Appalachian music, and religious music for the church. African Americans absorbed these influences from Whites in their use of stringed instruments and harmonies. The development of jazz around the turn of the 20th century introduced larger bands and stronger rhythmic elements.

Technological developments accelerated the growth of popular music. The phonograph record enabled artists to reach and influence an exponentially larger audience of listeners and fellow musicians. Huge numbers of Blacks from the South migrated to urban communities, where music and dancing took place in considerably more crowded and hectic environments. In order to be heard in these venues, musicians eventually had no choice but to use electronic amplification and, eventually, electric instruments.

As early as the 1930s, strong intimations of rock & roll could be found in the rhythmic, increasingly riff-driven swing jazz music, as well as blues-influenced country recordings of the Delmore Brothers, Bob Wills, Jimmie Rodgers, the Maddox Brothers, and others. Charlie Christian pioneered the use of the electric guitar in the early 1940s, at the same time as jazz musicians like Lionel Hampton were putting out riff-heavy hits like "Flyin' Home." As the '40s progressed, jazz musicians like Illinois

Jacquet, Big Joe Turner, Louis Jordan, Jay McShann, and others were upping the R&B quotient with honking saxes, "shouter" vocals, and pounding boogie-woogie piano.

Big bands became increasingly less economically viable after World War II, and smaller combos became more in vogue. They still had to play just as loudly as ever, though, and riffs, electric guitars, "shouting" R&B vocals, and prominent beats were usually the ticket. So it was that jump blues came into style, paced by Louis Jordan and singers like Wynonie Harris, Tiny Bradshaw, and Roy Brown.

While jump blues was an early precursor, the '50s brought other changes precipitating the birth of rock & roll. The Delmore Brothers recorded frenetic country-boogie that anticipated the spirit of rockabilly. Vocal groups like the Orioles took the smooth popular stylings of Black harmony ensembles like the Mills Brothers and the Ink Spots and added a more pronounced R&B and gospel feel. Delta musicians like Muddy Waters amplified their guitars and added rhythm sections, creating a fullbodied electric blues band sound in Chicago, Memphis, and other urban centers. Fats Domino, Lloyd Price, and others pioneered the keyboard-and-horn-driven grooves of New Orleans R&B. Les Paul took electric guitar wattage to new heights with his innovative multitrack recordings.

There were also major rumblings in the music industry and American society itself. Independent companies like Atlantic, King, Sun, Specialty, Chess, and numerous others recorded R&B and hillbilly music, catering to audiences that the major labels deemed too specialized and uncouth to service. Young White listeners began tuning in to radio stations that played music for these supposed minority tastes. And the increasingly affluent economy meant that these young listeners had more time and money than ever to spend on records.

These disparate strands began to collide and merge as the '50s progressed. There are a great number of opinions as to what could be called the first "rock & roll" record; indeed, an entire book (the fine *What Was the First Rock'n'Roll Record?*) has been written on the subject. Certainly, early sides by Jackie Brenston ("Rocket 88"), Bill Haley, Lloyd Price, Hank Ballard, Fats Domino, and others have strong claims. Whatever it was, and whenever it became a style, by 1954 there were several records in the Top 30 that couldn't, from a latter-day vantage point, be called anything but rock & roll: Bill Haley's primitive rockabilly ("Shake, Rattle, and Roll"), the joyous doo wop of the Crows and the Chords ("Gee" and "Sh-Boom"), the saucy R&B of Hank Ballard ("Work with Me Annie"). The music needed a name, and several theories have been advanced as to how the term "rock & roll" came about. Influential Cleveland and New York DJ Alan Freed's claim to have originated the phrase is probably the most widely circulated, though rocking and rolling had long been a euphemism, especially in the Black community, for dancing, partying, and more private pleasures.

In 1955, Bill Haley's "Rock Around the Clock" became the first #1 rock & roll hit; Little Richard and Chuck Berry had their first national smashes that year with "Tutti Frutti" and "Maybellene," songs which put electric guitar leads, honking saxes, whooping vocals, and lyrics about cars and girls to the forefront in a glorious package. In early 1956, Elvis Presley's #1 hit "Heartbreak Hotel" ended any doubt (or hope by the more conservative factions of the music business) that rock & roll would fade.

An emerging regional sensation, Elvis pioneered rockabilly on his legendary recordings for Sun records in 1954 and 1955 by marrying the feel of the blues and country boogie with his hard-driving rhythms and frenetic vocals. His jump to a major label – and assimilation of slightly more pop-oriented values into his recordings, which didn't diminish his genius in the slightest (at least at first) – made rock & roll an international phenomenon. His massive success, and the success of the countless rock & rollers who followed, was the end of the line in the evolution of the forces that gave birth to rock music – and the beginning, of course, of much more.

15 Essential Recordings

The Delmore Brothers, *The Best of the Delmore Brothers* (Starday). Country boogie with a reckless feel, close harmonies, and pounding backbeat, separated from rockabilly only by the level of electric instruments and a rhythm section. This collection of their late 1940s sides contains much of their most raucous work.

Bill Haley & His Comets, *Rock the Joint!* (Schoolkids'). A collection of his early 1950s singles, prior to his breakthrough to mass success with "Shake, Rattle, and Roll" and "Rock Around the Clock." The earliest White rock & roll ever recorded, combining country swing, electric guitars, saxophones, and R&B rhythms to create something different altogether.

Louis Jordan, *The Best of Louis Jordan* (MCA). A crucial bridge from swing jazz to jump blues, and a major influence upon Chuck Berry.

The Maddox Brothers & Rose, *Vol. 1* (Arhoolie). Another hillbilly band that anticipated elements of rockabilly with their rumbling boogie and slap-back bass. This has 27 of their songs from 1946-51.

Various Artists, *Hillbilly Music Vol. 1...Thank God!* (Capitol). A double album of rowdy hillbilly music from the late '40s to the mid-'50s, featuring such country giants as Tennessee Ernie Ford, Merle Travis, Buck Owens, and the Louvin Brothers. No other compilation illustrates the White country roots of rock & roll as well.

Various Artists, *Atlantic R&B: 1947-1952* (Atlantic). The Atlantic label was arguably the greatest and most influential record company specializing in rhythm & blues in rock & roll's formative years. This is the first volume of a seven-part series, also available as part of a box set.

Various Artists, *Atlantic R&B: 1952-1955* (Atlantic). More classic performances from the early Atlantic roster, edging closer to rock & roll from its more blues- and R&B-based beginnings.

Various Artists, *Blues Masters Volume 5: Jump Blues Classics* (Rhino). The best jump blues compilation, with classics by Big Jay McNeely, Wynonie Harris, Tiny Bradshaw, Big Joe Turner, and others. A second volume in the *Blues Masters* series (*More Jump Blues Classics*) is of equally high quality.

Various Artists, *Blues Masters Volume 6: Blues Originals*

(Rhino). Many of these songs helped form the backbone of the rock repertoire. Often popularized by White performers such as Elvis Presley and the Rolling Stones, here is where you'll find the original versions of classics like "That's All Right", "Back Door Man", and "Love in Vain".

Various Artists, *A History of New Orleans Rhythm and Blues Vol. 1* (Rhino). The first part of this three-volume series features key performances from the early and mid-1950s by artists who laid the foundations for the New Orleans sound, such as Lloyd Price and Guitar Slim.

Billy Ward, *Sixty Minute Men: The Best of Billy Ward & His Dominoes* (Rhino). One of the first great Black harmony groups of rhythm & blues, featuring lead vocals by two singers who would go on to become early rock & roll stars in their own right, Clyde McPhatter and Jackie Wilson.

Muddy Waters, *The Best of Muddy Waters* (Chess). The cream of the prolific output of the man who did more than any other performer to shape the course of modern electric blues, one of the primary currents feeding into the rock of both the past and present.

Various Artists, *A Sun Blues Collection* (Rhino). Excellent single-disc survey of the electrified country blues that the Sun label specialized in before moving to rockabilly, with great early and mid-'50s sides by Rufus Thomas, B.B. King, James Cotton, and others.

Various Artists, *A Sun Country Collection* (Rhino). The other side of the Sun equation has the country roots of the Southern rockabilly sound, with country hillbilly-verging-on-rockabilly by Johnny Cash, Carl Perkins, Jerry Lee Lewis, Warren Smith, Charlie Feathers, and more obscure performers.

Elvis Presley, *The Complete Sun Sessions* (RCA). The full-fledged birth of rockabilly on Elvis' legendary 1954-55 recordings, which in the eyes of some critics have never been surpassed in the entire history of rock & roll.

Books

What Was the First Rock'n'Roll Record?, by Jim Dawson & Steve Propes (Faber & Faber, 1992)

Unsung Heroes of Rock'n'Roll, by Nick Tosches (Charles Scribner's Sons, 1984)

The Sound of the City, by Charlie Gillett (Pantheon, 1983)

– *Richie Unterberger*

Early Rhythm and Blues

When rhythm and blues began in the mid-'40s, it didn't even have a name. When the term caught on, though, it caught on in a big way. Right up until the present day, R&B is the term used to refer to the entire world of Black popular music – rather than rap, soul, or urban contemporary – if only by specialized audiences and music industry insiders, not general fans.

In its earliest form, rhythm and blues was one of the most important precursors of rock & roll, if not *the* most important. Early rock & roll is basically R&B blended with country and western and pop influences. R&B wasn't only a crucial bridge between blues and rock & roll, but between blues and soul, R&B's longest-lived and most important offshoot.

The blues, of course, was a big part of rhythm and blues, but jazz was nearly as important. The earliest rhythm & blues artists emerged from the big-band and swing-jazz era. Before World War II, jazz, much more so than today, was a dance-oriented music, often featuring vocalists. Around World War II, many major jazz players began developing bebop and cool jazz, a decidedly less danceable (though equally worthy) style; economic factors, as well as the draft and wartime restrictions on travel, made big bands less viable. Audiences, especially the rapidly growing metropolitan African-American communities, still wanted dance music. The musicians accommodated them by playing louder, more electric instruments, and accentuating riffs, boogies, and vocals.

The first popular style of rhythm and blues is often referred to as "jump" blues. From jazz, jump blues took its horn-driven line-up and swing rhythms; from blues, it took its general riffs and chord structures. Cab Calloway was perhaps the chief precursor of the style, but in jump blues, the vocals were harsher, the rhythms faster. The instrumentation was different, too; the pianos pounded harder, and, the saxes didn't just blow, they honked and squealed.

The most important and popular jump blues star was Louis Jordan, whose records, unusually for the era, enjoyed success with both Black and White audiences; he was a particularly big influence on Chuck Berry. Many of the early jump blues performers emerged from Los Angeles, where a large Black community had been growing during the Depression and the war; most other big cities had jump blues stars of their own by the end of the 1940s. Independent labels such as L.A.'s Specialty and Alladin jump-started their success with the jump blues sound, filling a demand that the majors were basically unaware of. Joe Liggins, Tiny Bradshaw (the original performer of "The Train Kept A-Rollin'"), Amos Milburn, Camille Howard – all are largely forgotten except by record collectors, but all had huge R&B successes in the jump blues style, and ranked among the most popular Black musicians of their time.

Jump blues itself came in several different styles. There were the vocalists that came to be known as the "shouters," adding energy, soul, and gospel to the more restrained brand of big-band singing. Big Joe Turner, who got his start with Kansas City jazz bands, was the most legendary link between the eras, shifting R&B with ease, and even scoring some early rock & roll hits. Wynonie Harris, Roy Brown, Roy Milton, and Nappy Brown were a few of the most popular "shouters" of the late '40s and early '50s, although they aren't nearly as well remembered as Turner. There were also showmen, usually saxophonists, whose appeal was primarily instrumental: Big Jay McNeely, Illinois Jacquet, and Joe Houston, with strong roots in jazz, drove dance crowds crazy with their acrobatic honking. And there were smoother, more urbane singers, like Charles Brown, Percy Mayfield, and Cecil Gant, who were as adept at ballads as uptempo material.

By the time the '50s started, "race" music, as it was known within the industry, had been renamed the more appropriate "rhythm and blues" by Billboard magazine staff-member Jerry Wexler. As an A&R man at Atlantic Records, Wexler helped shape jump blues into something with more appeal to pop listeners and teenagers. The recordings by early Atlantic stars like Ruth Brown, LaVern Baker, the first incarnation of the Drifters, and Chuck Willis (who actually began at the Okeh label) retained a strong jump blues flavor, but their rhythms, riffs, and lyrics point more clearly toward rock & roll. Indeed, Baker and Willis managed to enjoy some success in the early rock & roll era with material that was tailored toward a younger audience. As rock & roll began to emerge in the early and mid-'50s, several distinct branches of R&B had developed that would each exert a large influence on popular music in its own right: doo wop groups, electric blues, and New Orleans rhythm and blues. All of these subgenres would prove to have a greater and more lasting impact on rock & roll than the earlier, jazzier forms of R&B.

Still, there were quite a few performers who survived through the 1950s, and sometimes thrived, recording music that could not be called anything but R&B. Ike Turner, Ivory Joe Hunter, Faye Adams, Wynona Carr, Big Mama Thornton, Big Maybelle – none of these were straight blues artists, but their music wasn't rock & roll either. Blues singers like Bobby "Blue" Bland, Junior Parker, and Little Milton bridged electric blues and soul, but they couldn't be pigeonholed as straight rock & roll singers. Occasionally R&B performers like Johnny Otis, Screamin' Jay Hawkins, and Wilbert Harrison crossed over to the rock & roll audience with their most hook-savvy songs; Harrison's "Kansas City" is largely jump blues with a shuffle beat, at least until it gets to the searing electric guitar break.

Several 1950s singers began as more or less straight R&B performers, but added an earthier, more pronounced gospel and church influence than had ever been heard before. Today, we recognize the greatest of these vocalists – Ray Charles, James Brown, Jackie Wilson, Little Willie John, Johnny Ace, Jessie Belvin, and Clyde McPhatter – as the forefathers of soul. Some of them, like Charles and Brown, would indeed become soul superstars in the '60s. Others, like McPhatter and John, were unable to make the transition, due to a combination of an inability to grow with the times and personal problems that proved insurmountable. R&B, though it has changed greatly since its birth, remains a crucial part of rock, soul, and rap.

For all of its monumental significance, and the vast critical acclaim it has belatedly received, early R&B recordings can be tough for the neophyte to swallow in large lumps. The R&B performers and labels of the '40s and '50s were concerned with entertaining, not establishing diverse artistic oeuvres, and the similar chord patterns and arrangements can be wearing on a compact disc as opposed to a juke box or dance floor, which is where the songs were often played in their heyday. Those investigating the genre in-depth for the first time are advised to start with some var-

ious artist samplers, and move on from there according to their degree of interest.

15 Recommended Recordings:

Various Artists, *Blues Masters, Volume 5: Jump Blues Classics* (Rhino). The best jump blues introduction, with key cuts by Joe Turner, Wynonie Harris, Roy Brown, Tiny Bradshaw, Jay McNeely, Big Mama Thornton, Ruth Brown, and others.

Various Artists, *Blues Masters, Volume 14: More Jump Blues* (Rhino). On the same level as *Jump Blues Classics*, with tracks by Louis Jordan, LaVern Baker, Big Maybelle, Faye Adams, and more.

Big Joe Turner, *Big, Bad & Blue: The Big Joe Turner Anthology* (Rhino). As mammoth as the man himself, this three-disc set encompasses several decades, reflecting R&B's evolution from the days of big-band jazz through rock & roll. Too extensive for the casual fan; as alternatives, there are other Turner anthologies that focus on specific phases of his career.

Louis Jordan, *The Best of Louis Jordan* (MCA). Jordan recorded a great deal of material in the 1940s and 1950s, and no collection satisfactorily encompasses all of his classics; this one is the best.

Various Artists, *Atlantic Rhythm & Blues Vol. 1-4* (Atlantic). The most important label in the development of modern R&B, this is part of a seven-volume series that goes up to 1974. There's a whole box set of them if you want to go whole hog, but the first four cover 1947-1962, before R&B had been fully renamed rock and soul.

Various Artists, *Specialty Story* (Specialty). At five discs, this is too much for non-specialists, if you'll pardon the pun. But it does offer a comprehensive survey of one of the most important early R&B and rock & roll labels, with tracks by such greats as Joe Liggins, Percy Mayfield, Roy Milton, and Lloyd Price, up through early rock stars like Little Richard and Larry Williams.

Ruth Brown, *Miss Rhythm* (Rhino). The singer on whom much of Atlantic's early fortune was built, this double disc contains her most popular 1950s sides.

LaVern Baker, *Soul on Fire: The Best of LaVern Baker* (Rhino). One of the most important singers to lead the transition from R&B to rock & roll.

The Drifters, *Let the Boogie-Woogie Roll: Greatest Hits (1953-1958)* (Atlantic). The first lineup of the Drifters, featuring Clyde McPhatter, could be called a doo wop group as well, but it also had strong early R&B/jump blues influences.

Ike Turner, *I Like Ike: The Best of Ike Turner* (Rhino). Before joining Tina, Ike was an important talent scout, sideman, and bandleader. This collection of odds'n'ends is mostly from the 1950s, and often walks the edge between R&B and electric blues.

Ray Charles, *Birth of Soul* (Rhino). Aptly titled three-disc box of Charles's work for Atlantic in the 1950s.

Johnny Otis, *The Capitol Years* (Capitol). An enormously popular figure in R&B as a bandleader, musician, and talent scout, Otis crossed over to success in the rock market in the late '50s by adding a Bo Diddley beat. Although Otis himself preferred straight R&B, this collection of late-'50s sides is his best.

Little Willie John, *Fever: The Best of Little Willie John* (Rhino). One of R&B's most versatile vocalists, and a huge influence on James Brown.

Clyde McPhatter, *Deep Sea Ball: The Best of Clyde McPhatter* (Rhino). His biggest hits for Atlantic in the late '50s, after he left the Drifters.

James Brown, *Roots of a Revolution* (PolyGram). A double-CD retrospective of 1956-1964 recordings, bringing us from hardcore R&B to the verge of the birth of funk.

– Richie Unterberger

New Orleans R&B

When it comes down to naming which American cities contributed most to the birth of rock & roll, it really only comes down to two: Memphis and New Orleans. New Orleans, of course, already occupies a rarefied place in the legacy of American popular music for its crucial role in the birth of jazz music. Its contribution to rock & roll was nearly equal in stature, supplying the music with many of its bedrock rhythms, as well as much of its playful humor. Its population, a vibrant mix of Creole, Cajun, Black, and White cultures, cultivated precisely the kind of melting pot of music that led to the early styles of rock & roll.

The early New Orleans sound was characterized by boogie piano, honking saxes, and relaxed, unfettered performances.

Pianist Professor Longhair embodies the true sound of New Orleans for some listeners, but this sound wasn't established as a major commercial force until the emergence of Fats Domino. His 1950 single "The Fat Man" is one of the dozens of performances routinely cited as one of the first rock & roll records. It took a while for Fats to cross over to the pop audience, but once he did, starting with 1955's "Ain't That a Shame," he became one of the most popular early rock & roll performers, rolling off hit after hit for the next half-dozen years.

Another Crescent City candidate for the title of first rock & roll record was Lloyd Price's "Lawdy Miss Clawdy," a 1952 #1 R&B hit. Price's late-'50s hits had a much more commercial sound, but his early work was much rawer, and influenced his label, the L.A.-based Specialty Records, to move its focus from jump blues to rock & roll. Their biggest star was Little Richard, a Georgia native who didn't find his groove until he started recording in New Orleans, reeling off a batch of hugely influential hit singles in the mid-'50s that helped define early rock & roll with their wooly vocals, pounding piano, and shrieking horns.

The chief behind-the-scenes architect of the New Orleans sound was Dave Bartholomew, a trumpeter, songwriter, and producer who graced many early classic New Orleans R&B/rock sessions, not the least of which were those of Fats Domino (whose hits Bartholomew co-wrote). Session players like drummer Earl Palmer and saxophonists Alvin "Red" Tyler and Lee Allen also played on numerous sessions, and were instrumental in putting the stamp on the early New Orleans sound.

Little Richard and Fats Domino were the only superstars to emerge from the city's rock & roll scene in the 1950s, but there were also many artists with only one or two national hits that recorded a wealth of fine material (much of which gave them sizable regional hits). Shirley & Lee ("Let the Good Times Roll"), Huey "Piano" Smith ("Rocking Pneumonia & the Boogie-Woogie Flu"), and Clarence "Frogman" Henry ("Ain't Got No Home") all recorded classics which remain at the heart of the rock & roll repertoire. Most of the music was recorded by Blacks, but Bobby Charles ("See You Later Alligator") and Frankie Ford ("Sea Cruise") proved that Whites could also rock convincingly in the New Orleans style.

In the early '60s, the New Orleans sound altered slightly, reflecting trends in the still-young soul scene. Pianist, songwriter, and producer Allen Toussaint inherited Dave Bartholomew's crown as the city's chief rock & roll visionary. Again, while there were no stars of the magnitude of Fats Domino or Little Richard, there were many classic hits and non-hits by the likes of Ernie K-Doe ("Mother-In-Law"), Chris Kenner ("I Like It Like That"), the Showmen ("It Will Stand"), Barbara George ("I Know"), and Benny Spellman ("Fortune Teller").

Some of the New Orleans performers emerging during this period have enjoyed long-term success, though they never became superstars. Irma Thomas may be the finest female New Orleans R&B singer of all time, not to mention one of the finest soul-R&B singers of any kind; in addition to her classic early New Orleans ballads, she also recorded great pop/rock sides in L.A. and "deep soul" tracks with the Muscle Shoals rhythm section. Lee Dorsey had charming novelty-tinged hits with "Ya Ya," "Working in a Coal Mine," and "Ride Your Pony." Clarence "Frogman" Henry roared back into the charts in the early '60s with several singles in a sort of updated Fats Domino style. The Dixie Cups ran off several great girl group singles in the mid-'60s, one of which, "Iko Iko," was a variation on a traditional Mardi Gras Indian chant. Barbara Lynn recorded many early soul singles, although only one, "You'll Lose a Good Thing," was a big national smash.

After the mid-'60s, national New Orleans R&B hits were relatively rare, although the city continued to house a lively music scene. The most influential latter-day Crescent City performers were the Meters, who mixed New Orleans rhythms with funk; Dr. John, a session player with extensive roots in the New Orleans scene dating back to the late '50s, who created a sort of mystic voodoo-tinged updating of the vintage New Orleans sound; and the Neville Brothers, a prodigiously talented family that had been releasing fine R&B and soul records, together and separately, since the mid-'50s.

The New Orleans sound may not be a big commercial presence nowadays – the Neville Brothers are the only big touring act, and they've never delivered the classic record that critics expect expected. But the city carries on its traditions with little help from the rest of the nation, and many R&B musicians continue to base themselves in New Orleans and play to a regional audience. The city also continues to feature dozens of its R&B, blues, and rock performers in the massive New Orleans Jazz Festival, which attracts huge crowds from around the world every year.

Music Map

New Orleans R&B

Jazz	Boogie Woogie R&B	Blues

Professor Longhair

Early New Orleans R&B Fats Domino, Lloyd Price, Little Richard, Dave Bartholomew	**White New Orleans R&B** Bobby Charles, Frankie Ford

Mid-To-Late '50s New Orleans R&B
Huey "Piano" Smith, Clarence "Frogman" Henry, Shirley & Lee

'60s New Orleans R&B
Allen Toussaint, Irma Thomas, Lee Dorsey, Barbara Lynn, Ernie K-Doe

Funk and Rock-Influenced New Orleans R&B
The Neville Brothers, Dr. John, The Meters

12 Essential Recordings

Various Artists, *A History of New Orleans Rhythm & Blues Vol. 1-3* (Rhino)
Fats Domino, *My Blue Heaven: Best of Fats Domino* (EMI)
Little Richard, *18 Greatest Hits* (Rhino)
Lee Dorsey, *Holy Cow!: Best of Lee Dorsey* (Arista)
Dr. John, *Anthology* (Rhino)
Irma Thomas, *Time Is on My Side (The Best of Irma Thomas), Vol. 1* (EMI)
Lloyd Price, *Lawdy!* (Specialty)
The Neville Brothers, *Treacherous – A History of the Neville Brothers (1955-1985)* (Rhino)
The Meters, *Funkify Your Life: The Meters Anthology* (Rhino)
Professor Longhair, *Fess: Professor Longhair Anthology* (Rhino)
Dave Bartholomew, *Spirit of New Orleans* (EMI)
Huey "Piano" Smith, *Rock & Roll Revival* (Ace, UK)
– *Richie Unterberger*

Doo Wop

"Doo wop" – the words bring smiles to the faces of most knowledgeable rock listeners. In some cases, they're smirks of derision, from those who feel that the form exemplifies rock & roll at its most innocuous, silliest, and embarrassingly quaint. From those who grew up during the '50s, however, it's more likely a smile of pleasure from someone who treasures the exquisite vocal harmonies and mourns the loss of the utter lack of pretension and guile that characterized great doo wop recordings.

Love it or hate it, doo wop is a major part of rock & roll's lexicon. The rhythm and blues ballads and uptempo numbers of doo wop are characterized by those harmonies, of course, but also by

Music Map

Doo Wop

Gospel	Early Black Pop Vocal Groups The Mills Brothers, The Ink Spots

Early R&B Vocal Groups
The Orioles, The Ravens, The Clovers

Early Doo Wop Groups
The Crows, The Penguins, The El-Dorados, The Turbans

Doo Wop Stars
The Platters, The Coasters, The Moonglows,
Frankie Lymon & The Teenagers, The Flamingos

Italian-American Doo Wop Dion & The Belmonts, The Mystics	Early '60s Doo Wop The Marcels, Shep & The Limelites	Early Soul and Girl Groups The Miracles, The Impressions, The Shirelles

'60s Doo Wop-Influenced Acts
Dion, The 4 Seasons, The Beach Boys, Jan & Dean

the nonsense syllables that often formed the backbone of the backup vocals. "Doo wop" was just one of those common phrases; "bop-bop," "dip-dip," "bomp-a-bomp-bomp-bomp, buh-dang-a-dang-dang," "wah wah, shoop shoop," "dooby dooby doo," and "yip-yip-yip-yip-yip-yip-yip-yip" were just a few of the others. Usually they were love songs, but often they were outrageous comic novelty tunes as well. This was early rock & roll at its most sentimental and humorous.

Doo wop – like all great African-American music – has much of its roots in the harmonies and emotive phrasing of gospel. Its more pop-oriented side came from such popular American Black vocal groups as the Ink Spots and the Mills Brothers. Adding a rhythm and blues flavor to this blueprint, as well as a strong "church" feel, the Orioles had a #1 R&B hit in 1948 with "It's Too Soon to Know," which is often cited as the first doo wop (and sometimes, even the first rock & roll) record.

Several groups followed in the Orioles' style over the next few years, including the Ravens, the Cardinals, and the Larks (many of the early doo wop acts named themselves after birds). The Clovers drew more explicitly from rhythm and blues, and the snappier rhythms and saucier lyrics of jump blues infiltrated the form in recordings by the Dominoes (featuring Clyde McPhatter) and Hank Ballard and the Midnighters.

By 1954, singles by the Crows ("Gee"), Dominoes, Orioles, and Hank Ballard had crossed over from the R&B market to become bonafide pop chart hits. Numerous urban vocal groups sprang up – a lot of them probably did start on the street corner, as legend would have it – and numerous record companies rushed to get a piece of the action. As rock & roll gained momentum, doo wop become brassier, with more honking sax solos, outrageous stuttering vocal interplay, and more explicitly teenage and young adult themes.

There were probably over a thousand groups that eventually cut a doo wop record over the next decade, leading to a vociferous collector community that probably ranks as the most devoted of its kind in rock & roll. A great many of the records originated in New York, though Los Angeles and Philadelphia were also

active centers, and scattered doo wop acts were active, in the studio and otherwise, across the country.

Most of the doo wop groups, if they made it onto the charts at all, were one- or two-shot acts, quickly fading into obscurity after failing to secure follow-ups. The Penguins, the Five Satins, the Monotones, the El Dorados, the Dell Vikings, the Silhouettes – these are just a few of those glorious names, though in some cases they recorded some non-hit efforts that were nearly as fine as their smashes.

There were also a few groups that managed to maintain a presence on the R&B and pop charts for a few years running, sometimes with numerous personnel changes. The Clovers, the Flamingos, Little Anthony & the Imperials, and the Moonglows were a few of the best. With the Teenagers, Frankie Lymon pioneered a brand of pre-teen soul that was rightfully pinpointed as an influence on Michael Jackson when the Jackson 5 emerged many years later. Before Clyde McPhatter left to become a solo act, the first incarnation of the Drifters was one of the most popular R&B acts of the mid-'50s.

At the top of the pyramid were a couple of groups that ranked among the most popular early rock & rollers. The Platters were one of the most pop-oriented of all of the doo wop groups, and appealed to the adult audience more than almost any of the early major rock & roll acts. The Coasters were among the wittiest rock groups of any era, courtesy of Jerry Lieber and Mike Stoller, who penned and produced many classic songs for the singers, including "Searchin'," "Young Blood," "Yakety Yak," and "Poison Ivy."

As the '50s progressed, more and more White performers sang doo wop, sometimes in integrated ensembles (such as the Dell Vikings and the Impalas), sometimes as all-White groups (the Mystics, Dion & the Belmonts). Often Italian-American in origin, by the time the '60s began, these White singers were a major part of the form, which was becoming less of a commercial force. But before doo wop vanished from the charts altogether, it underwent a revival of sorts in the early '60s, which saw huge doo wop hits by the likes of the Marcels, the Capris, Maurice Williams, and Shep & the Limelites. By the time of the British Invasion, though, there was barely a ripple of pure doo wop to be found on the charts.

Doo wop did not vanish so much as become permanently absorbed into rock and soul. Early soul giants like the Miracles and the Impressions owed huge debts to doo wop; indeed, their early records pretty much *are* doo wop. A lot of doo wop could be heard in the girl groups of the early '60s. Many hits by the Four Seasons and Dion were doo wop in construction, if not always in production. In vocal surf music, there's no doubt that doo wop was a prime influence on the ensemble singing of the Beach Boys and Jan & Dean. You can also hear it in the early records by the Beatles and several other British Invasion groups, as well as many of Frank Zappa's satirical efforts. And right on up to Boyz II Men, soul music has built upon the harmonies and vocal arrangements of doo wop music.

12 Essential Recordings

Various Artists, *The Doo Wop Box* (Rhino)
Billy Ward & the Dominoes, *Sixty Minute Men: The Best of Billy Ward & His Dominoes* (Rhino)
Hank Ballard & the Midnighters, *Sexy Ways: The Best of Hank Ballard & the Midnighters* (Rhino)
The Drifters, *Let the Boogie Woogie Roll – Greatest Hits (1953- 1958)* (Atlantic)
The Platters, *Magic Touch: An Anthology* (Mercury)
Frankie Lymon & the Teenagers, *Best of Frankie Lymon & the Teenagers* (Rhino)
Dion & the Belmonts, *Everything You Always Wanted to Hear by Dion & the Belmonts* (Laurie)
The Coasters, *50 Coastin' Classics* (Rhino)
The Clovers, *Down in the Alley: The Best of the Clovers* (Atlantic)
The Moonglows, *Blue Velvet: The Ultimate Collection* (Chess)
Various Artists, *The Best of Doo Wop Uptempo Vol. 1-2* (Rhino)
Various Artists, *The Best of Doo Wop Ballads Vol. 1-2* (Rhino)

BOOKS

Doo Wop: The Forgotten Third of Rock 'N Roll, by Dr. Anthony Gribin & Dr. Matthew Shiff (Krause Publications, 1992)
They All Sang on the Corner, by Phillip Groia (Phillie Dee Enterprises, 1983)

– *Richie Unterberger*

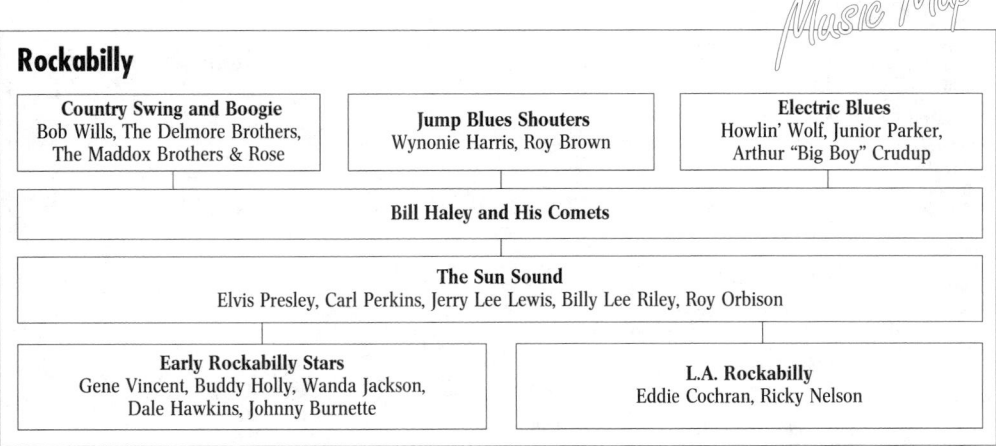

Music Map

Rockabilly

Country Swing and Boogie	Jump Blues Shouters	Electric Blues
Bob Wills, The Delmore Brothers, The Maddox Brothers & Rose	Wynonie Harris, Roy Brown	Howlin' Wolf, Junior Parker, Arthur "Big Boy" Crudup

Bill Haley and His Comets

The Sun Sound
Elvis Presley, Carl Perkins, Jerry Lee Lewis, Billy Lee Riley, Roy Orbison

Early Rockabilly Stars	L.A. Rockabilly
Gene Vincent, Buddy Holly, Wanda Jackson, Dale Hawkins, Johnny Burnette	Eddie Cochran, Ricky Nelson

Rockabilly

If rock & roll can be called the child of rhythm and blues and country & western music, no style is a purer blend than rockabilly. The first form of rock & roll performed by White musicians, its duration of mass popularity was brief, but the best of it remains among the most exciting and frenetic rock & roll ever waxed.

Even in the segregated American South of the early 20th century, Blacks and Whites often had cause to interact with each other on a daily basis. The interaction carried over to music, and White hillbilly country performers have reflected the influence of the blues and other African-American music since they began recording, as a listen to Jimmie Rodgers will attest. Just as blues became jazzier, faster, and more electric throughout the 1940s and early '50s, so did country, through swing bands like Bob Wills and the Maddox Brothers. The Delmore Brothers, starting as a more traditional hillbilly harmony act, anticipated much of rockabilly's mania when they added a thumping country boogie beat to the equation on their finest recordings in the late '40s. Nearly forgotten performers like Arthur Smith and Hardrock Gunter laid down country boogie sides that brought the guitar to the forefront.

Considering that most rockabilly musicians of importance came from the South, it's ironic that the first records that could be termed as honest-to-god rockabilly were issued by a Northerner, Bill Haley. The Philadelphian had been pursuing a hillbilly career with generally dismal results until 1951, when he covered Jackie Brenston's "Rocket 88" (which is often cited as one of the very first rock & roll records). Although they aren't nearly as well known as his huge rock & roll hits like "Rock Around the Clock," the sides he cut for the small Essex label between 1951 and 1954 are groundbreaking early rockabilly; the 1952 single "Rock the Joint," in fact, is almost identical in melody and arrangement to "Rock Around the Clock." Haley was no Elvis vocally, and the steel guitars and jump beats of his Comets betrayed lingering influences of hillbilly and swing music. But he was undoubtedly the first to bring together R&B and C&W with such force, although nobody knew quite what to call the music at the time.

There were certainly numerous musicians in the South experimenting with primitive rockabilly-like sounds by mid-1954. Sam Phillips and his Memphis record label, Sun Records, were chiefly responsible for honing the sound and capturing it on vinyl.

Often quoted as having said that Phillips could make a fortune with a White singer who sounded Black (though he has denied saying this in such explicit terms), found the perfect vehicle for doing so with Elvis Presley, who recorded five singles for Sun between mid-1954 and the end of 1955. Supported by guitarist Scotty Moore and bassist Bill Black, this was rockabilly, if not rock & roll, at its best and purest; as great as his subsequent achievements when critical consensus this handful of 45s ranks as Elvis's finest work. Presley didn't set off a mass wave of imitators right away; he was primarily a regional sensation until his contract was bought by RCA. Sam Phillips used the money from

the sale to develop his own formidable stable of rockabilly performers. Carl Perkins's "Blue Suede Shoes" almost beat Elvis's "Heartbreak Hotel" to the top of the charts, and although Perkins was never able to duplicate Elvis's success, Sun generated a wealth of great rockabilly hits and misses over the next few years by Jerry Lee Lewis, Billy Lee Riley, Sonny Burgess, Carl Mann, and Roy Orbison. The Sun Sound – echo-chamber vocals, crisp electric guitar leads, and slap-back bass – became the standard of rockabilly excellence, often imitated, never recaptured.

Presleymania overran the country in 1956, setting off a wave of rockabilly recordings, nationally and (more often) regionally distributed, that was similar in some respects to the garage band explosion of a decade later. Hundreds of performers found their way into studios in Tennessee, Texas, California, and other locales, embracing the new sound with a hepped-up enthusiasm that often bordered on mania. The singles were usually crudely recorded and extremely basic and derivative, their not inconsiderable saving grace being their infectious energy.

While the Sun Sound was the pinnacle of rockabilly, several performers became legends outside of Sam Phillips's studio. Gene Vincent's 1956 sides, featuring his breathy vocals and the speed-of-light guitar of Cliff Gallup from Vincent's backing band the Blue Caps, were usually brilliant. Eddie Cochran brought a sophisticated brand of teenage rebellion to his rockabilly hits, which helped pioneer the use of overdubbed guitars and vocals. Ricky Nelson recorded first-class rockabilly pop in Hollywood with the help of ace guitarist James Burton. Johnny Burnette and his trio recorded some of the raunchiest Elvis-derived rock & roll of the time, including the first rock version of "The Train Kept A-Rollin'." Dale Hawkins cut a crackling classic with "Suzy Q," and Wanda Jackson's raspy rockabilly sides rank as the finest rock & roll recorded by a female singer in the 1950s.

Rockabilly began to fade as a commercial force around 1958, not just because of fickle popular taste, but because of the rapid evolution of rock & roll itself. One of the greatest rockabilly singers, Buddy Holly, displayed a facility for melodic invention that branched into all forms of pop/rock, and had a far-reaching influence on all of pop that extended to the British Invasion. Along with the Everly Brothers and Ricky Nelson, he began gravitating toward a more gentle, melodic sound that was less structurally limited, if not as energetic, as pure rockabilly. Elvis himself was moving toward more straightforward rock material, and then toward pop after his hitch in the Army.

Those performers that stuck with the basic rockabilly sound faced diminishing returns. Some, like Gene Vincent, simply vanished from the charts, although they maintained loyal audiences, especially overseas. Roy Orbison, never comfortable as a rockabilly singer in the first place, reinvented himself as a masterful crooner of pop/rock ballads. Jerry Lee Lewis's career was crippled by scandal. Eventually he would find success in the country & western mainstream, a path followed by many other singers who had achieved limited success with rockabilly.

Rockabilly never returned to the charts in a significant way after the '50s, though several acts have scored big hits in the style, such as Billy Swan and the Stray Cats. A huge influence on the early Beatles, Creedence Clearwater Revival, and others, rockabilly was instrumental in establishing the focus of rock & roll on the electric guitar-bass-drums combination, with a simple joy and force that has helped inspire generations of musicians.

12 Essential Recordings

Elvis Presley, *King of Rock'n'Roll: Complete '50s Masters* (RCA)
Buddy Holly, *Buddy Holly Collection* (MCA)
Gene Vincent, *Capitol Collectors Series* (Capitol)
Carl Perkins, *Original Sun Greatest Hits* (Rhino)
Jerry Lee Lewis, *18 Original Sun Greatest Hits* (Rhino)
Johnny Burnette, *Tear It Up* (Solid Smoke)
Eddie Cochran, *Legendary Masters* (EMI)
Ricky Nelson, *Legendary Masters* (EMI)
Wanda Jackson, *Rockin' with Wanda* (Capitol)
The Collins Kids, *Introducing Larry and Laurie* (Epic)
Bill Haley and His Comets, *Rock the Joint!* (School kids')
Various Artists, *Rock This Town Vol. 1 & 2* (Rhino)

BOOKS

Good Rockin' Tonight: Sun Records and the Birth of Rock'n'Roll, by Colin Escott with Martin Hawkins (St. Martin's, 1991)
Last Train to Memphis, by Peter Guralnick (Little, Brown & Co., 1994)
Elvis: The Illustrated Record, by Roy Carr & Mick Farren (Harmony, 1982)
Remembering Buddy: The Definitive Biography of Buddy Holly, by John Goldrosen and John Beecher (Penguin, 1987)
The Day the World Turned Blue: A Biography of Gene Vincent, by Britt Hagarty (Blandford Press, U.K., 1984)
Ricky Nelson: Idol for a Generation, by Joel Selvin (Contemporary, 1990)

– Richie Unterberger

Teen Idols

For many avid rock historians, the teen idols – who were firmly entrenched on the top of the charts between the death of Buddy Holly and the rise of the Beatles – represented the greatest threat to rock's survival. Wimpy, overwhelmingly bland and safe, their connection to rock & roll was often tenuous, and their commercial ascendancy has even been discussed as a conspiracy by the music business and sundry other moral authorities to rob rock & roll of its vitality.

In retrospect, that seems fairly unlikely, though there's no doubt that the more conservative elements of the entertainment industry and the status quo as a whole felt more comfortable with these performers. Owing as much or more to traditional Tin Pan Alley and middle-of-the-road values than pure rock & roll, their massive success nonetheless didn't come close to stamping out the forces that gave birth to the explosive soul, surf, and British Invasion sounds that reclaimed the airwaves after only a few years.

"Teen idols" were by no means a phenomenon that began with the rock & roll era; bobbysoxers had been pining to the sound of mainstream pop crooners for a good decade or more before Elvis hit the scene. As far as rock was concerned, the original teen idol was Pat Boone, whose first hits were bowdlerized versions of classic rockers by Little Richard and Fats Domino. As Greg Shaw wittily pointed out in *The Rolling Stone Illustrated History of Rock'n'Roll,* Boone "began as a safe alternative to Elvis, and is still a safe alternative to just about everything."

The first two teen idols to achieve mass success after Boone could hardly have defined the polar extremes of the genre better. There was Paul Anka, whose early hits were mainstream ballads with mild rock & roll trimmings, who exemplified the style at its most operatic and melodramatic. Then there was Ricky Nelson, whose success was virtually guaranteed by his popular weekly TV series, and whose rockabilly records were better than they had any right to be.

The Philadelphia teen idols of the late '50s – Bobby Rydell, Frankie Avalon, and Fabian – patterned themselves after Anka much more than Nelson. Recorded on the local Cameo-Parkway, Chancellor, and Swan labels, they were launched into national success with regular appearances on *American Bandstand,* hosted

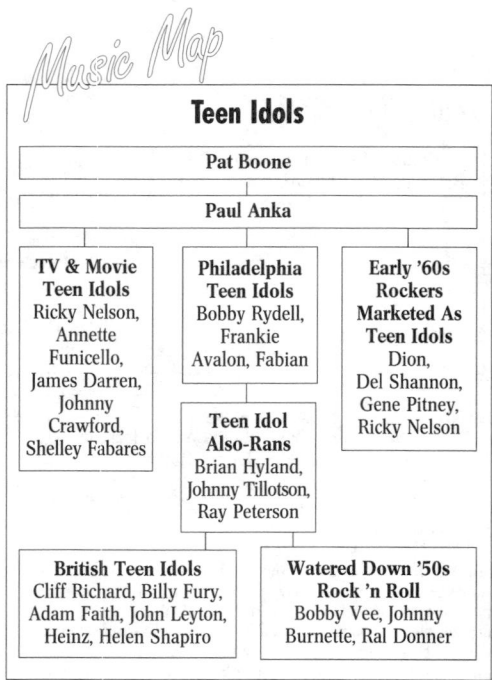

Music Map

Teen Idols

Pat Boone

Paul Anka

TV & Movie Teen Idols	Philadelphia Teen Idols	Early '60s Rockers Marketed As Teen Idols
Ricky Nelson, Annette Funicello, James Darren, Johnny Crawford, Shelley Fabares	Bobby Rydell, Frankie Avalon, Fabian	Dion, Del Shannon, Gene Pitney, Ricky Nelson

Teen Idol Also-Rans
Brian Hyland, Johnny Tillotson, Ray Peterson

British Teen Idols	Watered Down '50s Rock 'n Roll
Cliff Richard, Billy Fury, Adam Faith, John Leyton, Heinz, Helen Shapiro	Bobby Vee, Johnny Burnette, Ral Donner

by Dick Clark, who sometimes held financial interests in the record companies of the singers he pushed in this manner. Rydell, at least, could sing; few would contest that Avalon and Fabian were promoted more for their appearance than their limited vocal abilities, and both would move into movies and television work after their initial musical success.

It worked the other way around as well, of course; established teenage television stars with meager vocal abilities were hustled into recording studios to capitalize on their screen images. Ex-Mouseketeer Annette Funicello became one of the first big female teen idols in this fashion, and Ed "Kookie" Byrnes, Connie Stevens, Johnny Crawford, James Darren, and Shelley Fabares also joined the hit parade after becoming established TV performers. Artistically, this was the weakest wing of the teen idol genre; unsuited for singing in the first place, their material often sank to the level of drivel, with a few unexpected choice items thrown in, usually from Brill Building songwriters.

A great many teen idol singers had one or two big hits in this era without establishing a long recording career. Mark Dinning ("Teen Angel") and Ray Peterson ("Tell Laura I Love Her") capitalized on the short-lived vogue for teen death melodrama; Troy Shondell, Johnny Tillotson, Brian Hyland, and even a young Tony Orlando were merely some of the more successful of the legions of young faces who were packaged for the young, middle-class, White, predominantly teenage audience in this era.

Then there were the singers who happened to be packaged as teen idols, but who were probably good enough to have succeeded anyway. Dion, Gene Pitney, and Del Shannon, as well as Ricky Nelson, all fall in this category; their music sometimes contained the melodramatic hallmarks of the teen idol style, but they were genuine pop/rock innovators each and every one, and have too often been dismissed as superfluous by listeners more concerned with these performers' images than their actual accomplishments.

And there were also teen idols whose music was obviously a watered-down version of early rock & roll forms. Bobby Vee was a transparent Buddy Holly clone, though much softer; Ral Donner was the most accurate Elvis Presley soundalike, though he took after Elvis's pop/rock ballads rather than the King's rockers; and Johnny Burnette had a brief career as a mainstream teen idol after moderate success as one of the best early rockabilly singers.

Finally, there was an entire wing of British teen idols, although they had virtually no success in the States. Cliff Richard was by far

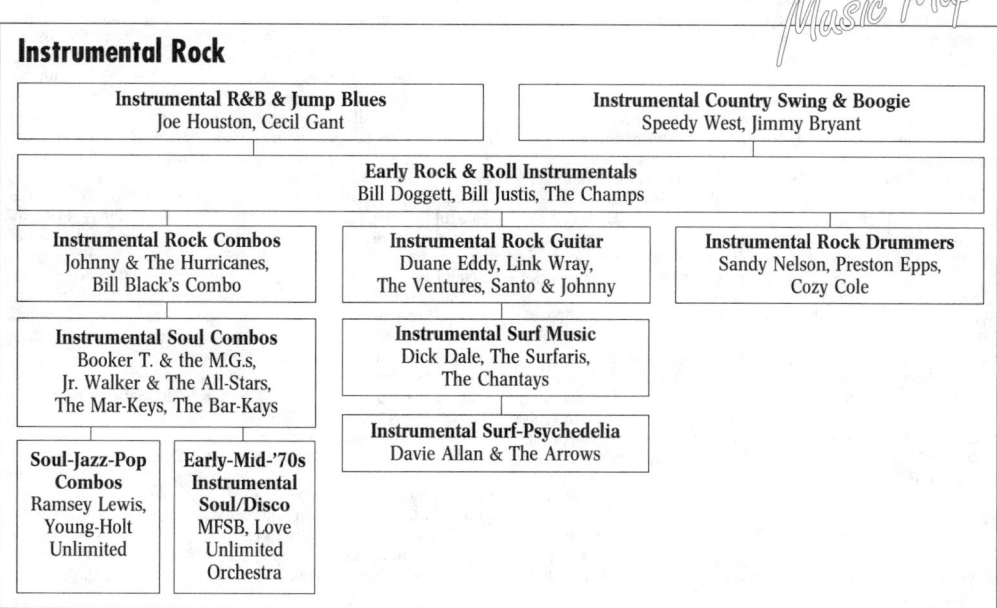

Instrumental Rock

Instrumental R&B & Jump Blues
Joe Houston, Cecil Gant

Instrumental Country Swing & Boogie
Speedy West, Jimmy Bryant

Early Rock & Roll Instrumentals
Bill Doggett, Bill Justis, The Champs

Instrumental Rock Combos
Johnny & The Hurricanes,
Bill Black's Combo

Instrumental Rock Guitar
Duane Eddy, Link Wray,
The Ventures, Santo & Johnny

Instrumental Rock Drummers
Sandy Nelson, Preston Epps,
Cozy Cole

Instrumental Soul Combos
Booker T. & the M.G.s,
Jr. Walker & The All-Stars,
The Mar-Keys, The Bar-Kays

Instrumental Surf Music
Dick Dale, The Surfaris,
The Chantays

Instrumental Surf-Psychedelia
Davie Allan & The Arrows

Soul-Jazz-Pop Combos
Ramsey Lewis,
Young-Holt
Unlimited

Early-Mid-'70s Instrumental Soul/Disco
MFSB, Love
Unlimited
Orchestra

---

the biggest, followed by a stable of singers with unlikely movie-star names, most managed by British impresario Larry Parnes. Billy Fury was the best of them; Adam Faith, John Leyton, Heinz, Helen Shapiro, and others were also big in their homeland before they largely sank into irrelevance after the rise of the Beatles in 1963.

The teen idol style was already on the wane before the Beatles landed in America in early 1964; Motown and other forms of soul music were on the rise, girl groups were big, surf sounds were at their crest. The manufacturing of face and image over content and ability that characterized the teen idol era has repeated itself, to a smaller extent, ever since, though one may call them the preteen idols now. Bobby Sherman and David Cassidy, the Bay City Rollers, Tiffany, Debbie Gibson, Milli Vanilli, New Kids on the Block – all strongly echoed the teen idol era, and sold millions of records despite the wrath of rock critics the world over, as other teen idols will do in the future.

10 Essential Recordings

Various Artists, *Teen Idols* (Rhino)
Dion, *24 Golden Greats* (Arista)
Gene Pitney, *Anthology 1961-1968* (Rhino)
Del Shannon, *Greatest Hits* (Rhino)
Pat Boone, *Greatest Hits* (MCA)
Paul Anka, *30th Anniversary Collection* (Rhino)
Ricky Nelson, *The Best of Rick Nelson Vol. 1 & 2* (EMI)
Annette Funicello, *Annette: A Musical Reunion with America's Girl Next Door* (Disney)
Bobby Vee, *Legendary Masters* (EMI)
Ral Donner, *She's Everything* (Murray Hill)

– *Richie Unterberger*

Instrumental Rock

Except for a brief period at the end of the '50s and the early '60s, instrumental rock hasn't been a major commercial force. There have always been instrumental rock hits, of course, and the best instrumental rockers have acted as key inspirations to many of the best rock & roll musicians.

Even before rock & roll became the nation's dominant popular music in the mid-'50s, instrumentals were common in the R&B, jump blues, and country boogie that ranked as rock's chief ancestors. Raunchy R&B saxophonist Joe Houston and lightning-fast

country boogie steel guitarist Speedy West were just two of the primarily instrumental musicians who were key influences on first generation rock & rollers. In 1956, organist Bill Doggett's "Honky Tonk" became the first massive instrumental hit of the rock era, although it was more notable for the sax riffs of Clifford Scott than the playing of bandleader Doggett.

The earliest rock & roll instrumental hits, such as the Champs' "Tequila," featured the sax as the lead instrument, but in 1958 Duane Eddy was responsible for changing the emphasis of instrumental rock to the guitar. With his distinctively low, twanging leads (augmented by Steve Douglas's superb saxophone), Eddy was one of the most popular singles artists of his era. His material can sound somewhat repetitious and dated these days, but he was a major influence on the next generation of rock guitarists, from George Harrison on down.

The Ventures were perhaps even more influential, offering a sleek sound with dual lead guitars and crisp drumming. A key building block of instrumental surf music, the group inspired countless nascent guitarists and were extremely popular, especially overseas, where the English language wasn't as key a component of rock music.

Link Wray, although nowhere near as successful as Eddy or the Ventures, may have been the most innovative guitarist of the era. On his 1958 hit "Rumble" and numerous excellent non-hit follow-ups, he pioneered guitar fuzz and distortion on vicious rockers. He was cited as an influence by Pete Townshend, who with several other British guitarists would take Wray's sound a few steps further in the distortion and feedback-riddled guitar leads of British Invasion and psychedelic rock.

In southern California, Dick Dale developed a reverb-heavy sound with his Fender Telecaster that became known as "surf music." Though relatively few surf instrumentals were big national hits (the Surfaris' "Wipe Out" and the Chantays' "Pipeline" were the biggest), the surf scene was huge in California, and of course a big influence on the Beach Boys, who (along with Jan & Dean) developed a vocal surf sound that became an important part of early- and mid-'60s rock & roll.

The years 1958-1963 were also riddled with many exciting hits, big and small, by performers who were never heard from again, or only managed to run off two or three big tunes. Besides guitarists like Santo & Johnny and Lonnie Mack, drummers (Sandy Nelson, Preston Epps, Cozy Cole), organists (Dave "Baby" Cortez), saxophone-driven combos (Johnny & the Hurricanes), and even bass players (ex-Elvis Presley sideman Bill Black) got in on the act with memorable hit tunes.

Instrumental rock was already decreasing in popularity when the British Invasion overran the States, making vocalists a near-necessity. In the years between the initial rock & roll explosion and the Beatles, however, instrumental performers were responsible for some of the most thrilling and gutsy rock & roll available. A key force in the preservation of rock's most exciting elements, instrumental rock was also hugely popular at a local level, and many musicians who wet their chops in instrumental combos went on to join, or develop into, important '60s rock groups. In any case, mid- and late-'60s rock groups never neglected instrumental rock entirely – Paul Butterfield's "East West," the Rolling Stones' "2120 South Michigan Avenue," the Who's "Underture," Quicksilver Messenger Service's "Gold and Silver," the Yardbirds' "Jeff's Boogie," Pink Floyd's "Interstellar Overdrive," and Country Joe & the Fish's "Section 43" are only a few of the great hard rock and psychedelic instrumentals of the era.

While the British Invasion is often thought of as sounding a death knell for instrumental rock, instrumentals remained a key strand of soul music for the next decade. The most popular and influential instrumental soul combo was Booker T. & the MGs. In addition to backing most of the greatest performances on the Stax/Volt label, the Memphis group also ran off a long string of marvelously taut instrumental hits of their own. The Mar-Keys and the Bar-Kays were also popular instrumental exponents of the Memphis soul sound. Saxophonist Junior Walker took Motown to its grittiest extremes on his instrumentals (though he often used vocals as well).

There was also no shortage of one-shot soul instrumental hits. Cliff Nobles ("The Horse"), jazzman Hugh Masekela ("Grazing in the Grass"), Billy Preston ("Outa-Space"), Love Unlimited Orchestra ("Love's Theme"), MFSB ("TSOP"), and the Average White Band ("Pick up the Pieces") all had mammoth pop hits with soul instrumentals, although these groups by and large didn't limit their material to instrumentals exclusively. Ramsey Lewis developed a breed of soul-jazz-pop in the mid-'60s, as did his ex-sidemen Young-Holt Unlimited, who hit the Top Ten when they added a lot of straight funk and came up with "Soulful Strut."

While rock and soul instrumentals haven't been nearly as prevalent in the 1980s and '90s as they were in earlier decades, instrumentals will always be a presence in the music, as surprise hit singles and a testament to the power of guitars, saxophones, drums, and other instruments to move listeners without the benefit of vocals.

12 Most Important Albums

Various Artists, *Rock Instrumental Classics, Vol. 1: The '50s* (Rhino)

Various Artists, *Rock Instrumental Classics, Vol. 2: The '60s* (Rhino)

Various Artists, *Rock Instrumental Classics, Vol. 3: The '70s* (Rhino)

Various Artists, *Rock Instrumental Classics, Vol. 4: Soul* (Rhino)

Various Artists, *Rock Instrumental Classics, Vol. 5: Surf* (Rhino)

Duane Eddy, *Twang Thang: The Anthology* (Rhino)

Link Wray, *Rumble! The Best of Link Wray* (Rhino)

The Ventures, *Walk, Don't Run: The Best of the Ventures* (EMI)

Booker T. & the M.G.s, *The Very Best of Booker T. & the M.G.s* (Rhino)

Booker T. & the M.G.s, *Best of Booker T. & the M.G.s* (Fantasy)

Dick Dale, *King of Surf Guitar: Best of Dick Dale* (Rhino)

Various Artists, *Guitar Player Presents Legends of Guitar, Surf: Vol. 1* (Rhino)

– Richie Unterberger

British Rock before the Beatles

For virtually everyone outside the British Isles – and for many who were born and raised there – the story of British rock begins with the Beatles. Britain did have rock & roll performers in the late '50s and early '60s, but they were really no more than a footnote to the real thing, which shook the U.K. in 1963 as the Beat Boom, and the world in 1964 as the British Invasion. This little-known early scene has its interest, though, and even its gems, though they're few and far between.

When rock & roll became an international phenomenon in the

mid-'50s, Britain, it would seem, was more equipped to emulate the music on its home shores than almost any other country outside North America. After all, the primary barrier to singing rock & roll is linguistic, and as the second-largest English-speaking nation in the world, Great Britain at least didn't have that obstacle to worry about. But the indigenous music of the U.K., with the possible exception of British Isles folk, had little parallel with the stew of blues, country, gospel, and Tin Pan Alley pop that gave birth to rock & roll in the States. It took a long time for the country's performers to come to grips with these influences, and master a vocabulary that would enable British rock to hold its own in the international marketplace.

British rock & rollers sprang up almost immediately in the wake of Bill Haley and Elvis Presley; Wee Willie Harris is usually credited as the first, and Tommy Steele was the most successful of the very first batch. The earliest British rock & roll records were, it could be said, hardly rock & roll at all; often they were cover versions of American rock hits that framed the songs in much more conventional and saccharine pop arrangements. In this respect, the British music industry was reacting along similar lines as some American labels, who responded to rock & roll's ascendancy by whitewashing R&B hits with sterile pop covers, or developed teen idols whose music was only marginally connected to the real thing.

A more important British development was the emergence of skiffle, principally popularized by Lonnie Donegan, who had first come to prominence as a traditional jazz and blues performer in Chris Barber's band. Skiffle's appeal, in the manner of garage and punk music right to the present day, was that it didn't take a great deal of technical proficiency to perform: you needed a few chords on guitar and banjo, a washboard for percussion, and a repertoire of a few folk songs. Donegan was a hugely successful singer in the late '50s in Britain (his "Rock Island Line" was also a big hit in the States), and many of the skiffle groups he inspired, such as the Quarrymen (soon to become the Beatles), would become key players in the British Invasion. Another Chris Barber-sideman, Alexis Korner, would become mentor to such blues and R&B-based rock groups as the Rolling Stones, Kinks, Yardbirds, and others, though his contributions really fall beyond the scope of pre-Beatle British rock.

In the meantime, however, the teenagers in these skiffle bands had to suffer through bland pop/rock, or a vapid facsimile of such, on their own hit parade. The most popular of the early British rock singers was Cliff Richard, a sort of mini-Elvis who actually managed some respectable rock & roll on his earliest singles in the late '50s, especially on his debut hit, "Move It." He was backed by the Shadows, a tight unit that scored many instrumental hits on their own, emphasizing spare, precise (one might even say clean-cut) riffs.

Cliff Richard and the Shadows are remembered fondly by many in British rock circles, and Shadows guitarist Hank Marvin is cited as an influence by many British guitar heroes. But listening to that band's peak output several decades later, one suspects that this may be more due to nostalgia than the quality of their music; the overwhelming majority of their repertoire consists of watered-down derivations of American pop, pop/rock, and instrumental rock. Shadows bassist Jet Harris, however, sometimes in collaboration with Shadows drummer Tony Meehan, did have some nifty, growling instrumental hits just before the Beatles broke.

There were quite a few British teen idols in the late '50s and early '60s, usually with fanciful show-business names such as Johnny Gentle, Marty Wilde, Vince Eager, Adam Faith, and Duffy Power (the last of whom, surprisingly, turned out to be a decent cult blues-rock performer in the '60s). Like their American cousins, they were innocent and harmless to the point of dopiness. The best of them, Billy Fury, managed to cut some fair, and self-penned, approximations of American rockabilly on his 1960 LP *Sound of Fury* with the help of guitarist Joe Brown (who would have some hits of his own in the early '60s). Fury was also an inspiration to Malcolm McLaren when he was casting about to form the Sex Pistols, but again, one suspects nostalgia as an ingredient for this latter-day respect; Fury was a competent singer, but he too went heavy on the drippy ballads for the hit parade, and as a rockabilly singer, he would have been an also-ran in the States.

Amidst all the dross, there were some genuinely fierce British rockers in these dark days. Tony Sheridan, though he never got a chance to adequately showcase his talents on record, was of course an inspiration to the early Beatles, who backed him on several

German recordings. Vince Taylor managed a couple respectable Gene Vincent-type numbers, most notably "Brand New Cadillac."

The best by far, though, and indeed the best pre-Beatle British rockers by a wide margin, were Johnny Kidd & the Pirates. Their late-'50s and early-'60s singles were tough, rockabilly-influenced performances that came off as a cross between Jerry Lee Lewis and Gene Vincent. Kidd was also an underappreciated factor in establishing the dominance of guitar in '60s British rock; several of his songs featured superbly menacing riffs from session players like Joe Moretti that were quite advanced for their time, especially the one from "Shakin' All Over". This last was perhaps the only true pre-Beatle classic of British rock, and the only one which became a rock standard (in versions by the Who, Guess Who, and others). Kidd, alas, was already in a decline phase when the Beat Boom hit, and died in a car crash in 1966.

Besides the Pirates, the hardest rocking British band of the early '60s was Screaming Lord Sutch and the Savages. Sutch, a colorful figure who wore long hair years before it was fashionable, shamelessly emulated Screamin' Jay Hawkins, and ran for Parliament advocating such causes as the right of teenagers to vote and pirate radio, wasn't much of a singer. But his band did play real rock & roll of the hard-driving sort, at a time when that was rarely done in the British Isles, and his early-'60s singles (most recorded after the Beatles had debuted), though hardly classics, had a sense of hard-driving reckless fun that anticipated the spirit of the British Invasion. His bands also provided early schooling for such mainstays of British rock as Nicky Hopkins and Ritchie Blackmore (who also recorded some sides as a teenager in the early '60s as part of the instrumental group the Outlaws).

Sutch and the Outlaws were both produced by Joe Meek, who was the very first British producer to establish his own production company for leasing masters to labels, ensuring control over his product. A legendary eccentric obsessed with the occult and UFOs, Meek imprinted his recordings with as distinctive a sound as any other producer. Compression, sped-up vocals, otherwordly organs, howling wind, and ghostly choruses combined into a sort of space-age sound that was quite futuristic for its time, and is best heard on the Tornados' instrumental "Telstar," which topped the charts on both sides of the Atlantic over a year before the Beatles broke in America.

Had Meek worked with more talented acts and better material, there would be no question of his important stature. As it was, he usually favored simpering teen idols, anonymous instrumental groups, and cringingly dippy material, though he almost always added adventurous production that made the records stand out in the vapid early-'60s British scene. He did manage some tough-rocking sides with the Outlaws, Heinz, Tornadoes, and especially Screaming Lord Sutch, and sustained his success into the early British Invasion with the Honeycombs. As a producer he was ahead of his time, but his taste in material was rendered hopelessly passé by the Beat Boom, and he died in sordid circumstances (a combination murder-suicide) in early 1967.

The weakness of pre-Beatle rock is reflected in the near-total lack of cover versions of early British rock tunes by British Invasion bands. Though most of those groups' early repertoires were dominated by rock & roll covers, they rarely looked to their own countrymen. *The Complete Beatles Chronicle*, for example, documents the hundreds of songs the group was known to have performed onstage before 1963; only about ten odds and ends by British performers appear, by singers like Lonnie Donegan and Joe Brown.

What was happening, really, was that it was necessary for an entirely new generation of musicians, one which had grown up listening and playing rock & roll, to emerge to really play the music properly. The Beatles, and hundreds of other beat combos, looked to the U.S. for inspiration, not their own land. And when they had mastered their instruments, performance, and songwriting enough to offer quality material on record, the result turned the British music industry on its head literally within months. The old guard hung on for a few more hits; in some cases, such as Cliff Richard's, they maintained a reasonable degree of popularity.

In the U.S., pre-Beatle British pop hits only crossed over very occasionally. When they did make it into the American hit parade, they tended to be rather quaint pop novelty items, such as Laurie London's "He's Got the Whole World in His Hands," the Caravelles' "You Don't Have to Be a Baby to Cry," and Frank Ifield's "I Remember You" ("Telstar," though real instrumental rock, was also a novelty). Early British rock never meant a thing

British Rock Before the Beatles

First British Rock Singers
Wee Willie Harris, Tommy Steele, Cliff Richard

British Teen Idols
Billy Fury, John Leyton, Adam Faith, Helen Shapiro

Early '60s British Instrumental Groups	**Early '60s British Rockers**
The Shadows, The Tornados, The Outlaws	Vince Taylor, Johnny Kidd & The Pirates, Screaming Lord Sutch

Joe Meek Productions
John Leyton, The Tornados, The Outlaws, Screaming Lord Sutch, Mike Berry

in the States, and that's why the Beatles and other British groups couldn't get a foothold in the U.S. in 1963; the industry had no reason to expect anything that they couldn't find, cheaper and better, in their own backyard. With "I Want to Hold Your Hand" in early 1964, that all changed – for which we can all be thankful, on both sides of the Atlantic.

10 Essential Recordings

Lonnie Donegan, *Collection* (Castle, UK)
Cliff Richard, *20 Rock'n'Roll Hits* (EMI, UK)
Various Artists, *Roots of British Rock* (Sire)
Billy Fury, *Sound of Fury Plus 10* (PolyGram)
Jet Harris & Tony Meehan, *Diamonds & Other Gems* (Deram, UK)
Johnny Kidd & the Pirates, *Complete Johnny Kidd* (EMI, UK)
Screaming Lord Sutch, *Story* (no label)
The Tornados, *Telstar: The Original Sixties Hits of the Tornados* (Music Club, UK)
The Shadows, *20 Golden Greats* (EMI, UK)
The Outlaws, *Ride Again (The Singles As & Bs)* (See for Miles, UK)

– *Richie Unterberger*

The Brill Building Sound

Rock & roll is usually thought of as a hybrid of several types of American roots music – the blues, country and western, R&B, gospel, and others. The influence of mainstream American popular songwriting, embodied by the conglomerate of professional composers and publishers dubbed Tin Pan Alley, on rock's early development is sometimes overlooked. While rock & roll was to a significant degree a reaction against the overly professional, sentimental, and sterile conventions of pre-rock American pop, the best of Tin Pan Alley's melodic and lyrical hallmarks were incorporated into rock & roll to raise the music to new levels of sophistication.

The songwriters most crucial to this process congregated in the early '60s in a New York block known as the Brill Building. Home to leading music industry publishers, it also bred a stable of young songwriters who were just as steeped in rock & roll and rhythm and blues as Tin Pan Alley, if not more so. Several of the most prominent worked for Aldon Music, a publishing firm headed by Al Nevins and Don Kirshner, the same Don Kirshner who would later mastermind the Monkees' hits and act as a legendarily bland master of ceremonies for network TV rock specials.

Many pop/rock songwriters worked in the Brill Building in the early '60s, but several teams carved a legendary legacy, including Gerry Goffin & Carole King, Barry Mann & Cynthia Weil, Jerry Leiber & Mike Stoller, Jeff Barry & Ellie Greenwich, and Doc Pomus & Mort Shuman. Responsible for literally pages worth of

Brill Building

Tin Pan Alley	Early Rock & Roll and R&B

Top Brill Building Songwriters

Pop–Rock Songwriters
Gerry Goffin-Carole King, Barry Mann-Cynthia Weil,
Jeff Barry-Ellie Greenwich, Phil Spector

R&B/Soul–Oriented Songwriters
Jerry Leiber-Mike Stoller, Doc Pomus-Mort Shuman,
Bert Berns, Van McCoy

Pop-Oriented Songwriters
Neil Sedaka-Howard Greenfield,
Burt Bacharach-Hal David

L.A.-Based Pop-Rock Songwriters
Jackie De Shannon, Randy Newman,
David Gates, Nilsson

hits in the late '50s and first half of the '60s, they matched Tin Pan Alley's highest standards of inventive melodies and lyrics, but they were clearly different from their predecessors. The rock & roll market demanded tunes targeted at teenagers, with earthier concerns than the classics of the '30s and '40s. For many of these songwriters, the task hardly required an adjustment; they were barely out of (or even still in) their teens, and they were going through the pangs of young love and the search for identity themselves. For good measure, Goffin-King, Mann-Weil, and Barry-Greenwich were married to each other, infusing their work with a passion that was actually grounded in their real-life romances.

Brill Building compositions were placed all over the pop/rock map, but had their greatest impact and success with girl groups. It was a heavenly match: girl groups sang about young love with forlorn and passionate innocence, and were largely based near New York City, but very few were songwriters, and they needed suitable material; young Brill Building songwriters wrote about young love with forlorn and passionate innocence, and were largely based near New York City, but needed suitable performers. Most of the classic hits by the Ronettes, Chiffons, Shangri-Las, Dixie Cups, and Little Eva originated at the Brill Building, as well as a few classic one-shots and misses.

Other prime outlets for Brill Building material were teen idols like Connie Francis, Bobby Vee, James Darren, and Neil Sedaka (the last of whom was one of the most successful Brill Building songwriters himself, often in collaboration with Howard Greenfield). These tended to be the most lightweight Brill Building confections, at times even approaching disposable, as a listen to a James Darren greatest hits compilation confirms. Uneven quality couldn't be helped; the songwriters were under tremendous pressure to deliver tunes in a near-assembly-line fashion, and couldn't be expected to come up with "Will You Love Me Tomorrow" or "On Broadway" every time out.

Leiber-Stoller and Pomus-Shuman, however, usually wrote for pop-flavored R&B and early soul acts. Leiber-Stoller wrote (and produced) most of the Coasters' classic comic vignettes, and Pomus-Shuman penned several of the Drifters' hits. Both teams also wrote some of the greatest Elvis Presley songs of the late '50s and early '60s; Goffin-King and Mann-Weil, for their part, would supply songs for the Drifters and Phil Spector's great productions with the best blue-eyed soul act of the '60s, the Righteous Brothers.

Other notable Brill Building mainstays included Phil Spector, a great songwriter and even greater producer; Bert Berns, who

also wore both songwriting and production hats, though he worked in more of a pop-soul vein; and Bacharach-David, who probably owed the most to Tin Pan Alley classic traditions, although that didn't prevent them from writing some great pop/rock songs for the Shirelles, Dionne Warwick, and others. And for every Goffin-King, it must be remembered, there were dozens of much less successful hopefuls scuffling around the edges of the Brill Building crowd, including future folk-rock stars Paul Simon and Jim McGuinn, and future disco king of the "hustle," Van McCoy.

Though Phil Spector is by far the most legendary producer with Brill Building associations, most of the great Brill Building songwriters were also great producers, although they weren't always credited on the label. Several of them were also great performers, and it has been said that the demos they cut were often as good or better than the versions recorded by the performers to whom they were given. Barry Mann, Carole King, and Jeff Barry & Ellie Greenwich (the latter pair as the Raindrops) actually had some hit records on their own, though they much preferred to run things behind the scenes.

There were also quite a few Los Angeles-based songwriters who, though not at the actual Brill Building, operated in an almost identical fashion. David Gates, Jackie De Shannon, Randy Newman, and Nilsson were some of the best; eventually, all of them would become singing-songwriting stars in their own right.

The British Invasion turned the focus of rock & roll on to performers that wrote their own material, and while that didn't spell the end of the success of the great Brill Building songwriters, it meant some adjustments were in order. Girl group records were still hugely successful in 1964, the first year of the British Invasion, but it was soon obvious that their time was coming to an end. The irony was that John Lennon and Paul McCartney owed a great deal to the Brill Building, openly declaring Goffin and King as their greatest songwriting influences, and covering Brill Building classics by the Shirelles, Cookies, and Isley Brothers. Manfred Mann ("Do Wah Diddy Diddy"), Herman's Hermits ("I'm into Something Good"), and other British Invasion groups also took Brill Building covers into the top of the charts.

Occasionally Brill Building songwriters actually managed to supply fresh material to British Invasion groups, as Mann-Weil did with the Animals, and Bert Berns did with Them and Lulu. But inevitably, the proliferation of self-contained rock groups, not to mention soul singers who wrote their own material, meant less of a need for professional tunesmiths. And the fact was, both the world and the songwriters were changing as fast as everything else was in the '60s; the composers wanted to express more mature concerns, and much of the rock audience had progressed beyond adolescent love affairs.

The principal architects of the Brill Building coped with these changes in varying fashions. Some became jingle writers; some (Ellie Greenwich) eventually wrote musicals; some (Jeff Barry) wrote and produced bubblegum for the Archies; some (Phil Spector) retired; some (Bacharach-David) moved from pop/rock to MOR pop. The most resourceful became singer/songwriter stars themselves; not only the aforementioned L.A. composers, but also Carole King, who became a superstar as a solo act. The legacy of the Brill Building was enormous, setting a standard for pop/rock songwriting that has been emulated ever since, by everyone from the Beatles on down.

10 Essential Albums

Various Artists, *Brill Building Sound* (Era)
Phil Spector, *Back to Mono* (ABKCO)
The Drifters, *All-Time Greatest Hits & More: 1959-1965* (Atlantic)
The Coasters, *50 Coastin' Classics* (Rhino)
Various Artists, *The Colpix-Dimension Story* (Rhino)
The Shangri-Las, *Golden Hits of the Shangri-Las* (Polygram)
Neil Sedaka, *All-Time Greatest Hits* (RCA)
Various Artists, *The Red Bird Story* (Charly, UK)
Various Artists, *The Best of the Girl Groups, Vol. 1* (Rhino)
Various Artists, *The Best of the Girl Groups, Vol. 2* (Rhino)
– *Richie Unterberger*

Girl Groups

The story of the "girl group" sound – which reached its commercial and artistic peak in the early and mid-'60s – is not just the

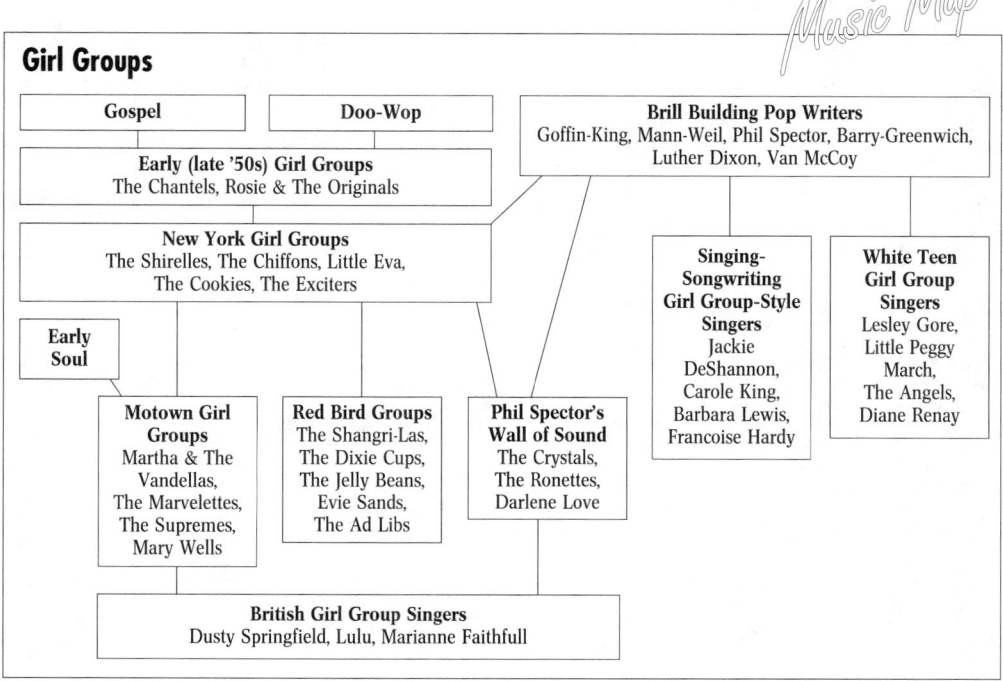

Girl Groups

Music Map

- **Gospel**
- **Doo-Wop**
- **Brill Building Pop Writers**
  Goffin-King, Mann-Weil, Phil Spector, Barry-Greenwich, Luther Dixon, Van McCoy

Early (late '50s) Girl Groups
The Chantels, Rosie & The Originals

New York Girl Groups
The Shirelles, The Chiffons, Little Eva, The Cookies, The Exciters

Singing-Songwriting Girl Group-Style Singers
Jackie DeShannon, Carole King, Barbara Lewis, Francoise Hardy

White Teen Girl Group Singers
Lesley Gore, Little Peggy March, The Angels, Diane Renay

Early Soul

Motown Girl Groups
Martha & The Vandellas, The Marvelettes, The Supremes, Mary Wells

Red Bird Groups
The Shangri-Las, The Dixie Cups, The Jelly Beans, Evie Sands, The Ad Libs

Phil Spector's Wall of Sound
The Crystals, The Ronettes, Darlene Love

British Girl Group Singers
Dusty Springfield, Lulu, Marianne Faithfull

story of the performers. More than any other style in rock & roll, it was the product of more or less equal partnerships between the singer/performers, songwriters, and producers. The result was one of the most vital links between the birth of rock & roll and the British Invasion, the arrival of which gradually eroded the presence of girl groups on the charts even as it acknowledged enormous debts to the genre.

Girl groups were more polished than the early rock & roll pioneers, more innocent than the soul music that was originating at the same time, and as firmly planted in Tin Pan Alley as rhythm and blues. While it wasn't the rawest or most artistically expressive pop music, few forms of rock were as affecting, romantic, and tuneful. Girl groups also provided the forums and mouthpieces for some of pop/rock's most talented songwriting teams, as well as laid the foundation for groundbreaking orchestral production that lent an increased sophistication to rock & roll.

The Chantels, led by the heart-wrenching vocals of Arlene Smith, are generally acknowledged as the first girl group. Their Top 20 hit "Maybe" (1958) had obvious roots in gospel and doo wop, but also displayed yearning, innocent, and vulnerable qualities not apparent in the more suave male doo wop outfits.

It was the Shirelles, however, who really established girl groups as a major force with their #1 hit, "Will You Love Me Tomorrow?," in 1960. Significantly, that hit also featured many of the classic girl group trademarks – sweeping orchestral strings, full background harmonies, and a lead vocal that projected soul, warmth, hope, and uncertainty. The Shirelles scored a half-dozen Top 20 singles in the next couple of years (along with several memorable smaller hits), and ranked as the most successful female vocal group of the era.

The song was written by the songwriting team of Gerry Goffin and Carole King, which went on to write many girl group classics in the next few years, and was one of the hottest songwriting teams of the "Brill Building" sound. Named after a complex of music publishing offices on Broadway in New York, the Brill Building also gave birth to the partnerships of Jeff Barry and Ellie Greenwich, and Barry Mann and Cynthia Weil. These teams were responsible for the lion's share of the best girl group recordings, investing rock & roll with the best melodic and lyrical qualities of classic pop, while retaining a feel for the rhythm and blues roots

of the performers. Less celebrated writers like Luther Dixon (who wrote several songs for the Shirelles) and a pre-disco Van McCoy also contributed classics to the genre.

It took Phil Spector to take the girl group sound to its pinnacle. The producer set material from the cream of the Brill Building crop (as well as his own original compositions) to grandly majestic, orchestral arrangements that achieved an unheard-of density without sacrificing any of the music's passion and melody. The Crystals, the Ronettes, and Darlene Love (who sang uncredited vocals on some of the Crystals' biggest smashes) were the most talented pilots of Spector's grandiose "Wall of Sound" productions, most of which were released on his own label, Philles.

While the Shirelles and Phil Spector's acts were the most prominent girl groups in the years preceding the British Invasion, the sound was emulated by several one- or two-shot groups, and less-celebrated producers, with great success. The Chiffons, Claudine Clark, the Cookies, the Jaynetts, Little Eva, and the Exciters all contributed timeless classics. And there were dozens – if not hundreds – of worthy singles in the style that, for one reason or another, didn't become blockbusters, although they had most or all of the essential elements.

Most of the great girl groups were African-American, with clear affinities for R&B and doo wop, but the most innocent qualities of the sound (and occasionally the most soulful ones) were projected in many records by White teen girl singers as well. Lesley Gore was the most renowned of these performers, who also included the Angels, the Raindrops (with Ellie Greenwich on lead vocals), and one-shot artists like Diane Renay and the Murmaids.

While the arrival of the Beatles in 1964 is often thought of as the beginning of the end for the girl groups, girl group records were actually as successful as ever during that year. The rise of the Red Bird label, featuring the Dixie Cups and the Shangri-Las (who both scored #1 hits in 1964), did much to boost the style's commercial fortunes.

Although financial problems caused the Red Bird label to fold within a few years of its founding, the years 1964 and 1965 saw the label shine brightly indeed, and songwriters like Jeff Barry, Barry Mann, Ellie Greenwich, Jerry Lieber, and Mike Stoller oversaw most of its output from the producer's booth. Producer and songwriter Shadow Morton – almost as idiosyncratic a talent as Phil

Spector – created some of the greatest girl group records with the Shangri-Las. These tough-talking but tender-hearted Queens Teens records may have made the sassiest and most heart-wrenching girl group mini-operas of all.

Although the burgeoning Motown empire wasn't strongly rooted in the girl group sound, 1964 saw the release of breakthrough discs by Mary Wells, the Supremes, and Martha & the Vandellas that were largely indebted to the style. Relying heavily on the production and songwriting talents of Smokey Robinson and Berry Gordy, Jr. (among others), the Motown sound was nonetheless grittier and bluesier than the New York school, and its personas (on record and in performance) more distinctive.

There's no doubt that girl groups were among the British Invasion's chief influences. John Lennon stated that he and Paul McCartney hoped to duplicate the success of Goffin and King with their songwriting partnership, and the Beatles' early albums included covers of hits by the Shirelles, the Cookies, and the Marvelettes. Manfred Mann, despite its R&B roots, scored its biggest U.S. hits with covers of songs by the Exciters ("Do Wah Diddy Diddy") and the Shirelles ("Sha La La"), and several other British groups, ranging from Herman's Hermits and the Searchers to the Mindbenders, also made it big with girl group covers.

However, the most successful British groups – the Beatles first and foremost among them – were those that relied primarily upon their own material. And it was this shift in emphasis toward self-contained rock groups that played their own instruments that spelled the end of the girl groups as a major force, although singers like Jackie DeShannon, Dusty Springfield, Lulu, Evie Sands, Barbara Lewis, and others continued to produce classic recordings (and sometimes score major hits) in the girl group vein throughout the '60s.

The girl group sound, though, never really went away. You can hear it in many female vocal groups, self-contained and otherwise, through the present day. In the case of some soul groups (such as the Pointer Sisters) or new wave bands (the Bangles, Blondie, and the Go-Go's), the influence is worn quite cheerfully on the sleeve.

More subtly, its echoes are heard in all rock that relies upon orchestral production, harmonies, and/or crafty, melodic compositions to send its message.

12 Essential Albums

The Shirelles, *The World's Greatest Girl Group* (Tomato/Rhino)
The Shangri-Las, *Golden Hits of the Shangri-Las* (PolyGram)
The Ronettes, *Best of the Ronettes* (ABKCO)
The Crystals, *Best of the Crystals* (ABKCO)
The Chiffons, *Best of the Chiffons* (Laurie)
The Supremes, *Anthology* (Motown)
Martha & the Vandellas, *Live Wire! The Singles 1962-1972* (Motown)
Mary Wells, *Looking Back 1961-1964* (Motown)
Lesley Gore, *Anthology* (Rhino)
The Marvelettes, *Deliver: The Singles 1961-1971* (Rhino)
Various Artists, *The Best of the Girl Groups, Vol. 1 & 2* (Rhino)
The Exciters, *Tell Him* (EMI)

BOOKS

Girl Groups: The Story of a Sound, by Alan Betrock (Delilah, 1982)
Will You Still Love Me Tomorrow? Girl Groups from the 50s On..., by Charlotte Greig (Virago, U.K. 1989)

                                         – *Richie Unterberger*

Surf Music

In terms of commercial impact, surf music was a short-lived phenomenon. The vast majority of popular surf recordings were waxed between 1961 and 1965; even then, their success was often confined to an isolated region (more often than not, southern California). Yet surf music's influence upon the sound of the rock & roll guitar is incalculable. Felt by hundreds of artists, it continues to surface, in a much modified form, to this very day.

From the late 1950s, when the initial explosion of rock & roll was winding down, to the British Invasion, instrumental rock was responsible for keeping alive the raunchiest and wildest aspects of the music more than any other style. It was also responsible for keeping the electric guitar at the forefront of the music, and surf music was certainly the most guitar-oriented style of instrumen-

tal rock & roll, though splashing drums and honking saxes were also prime features of the sound.

Southern California-guitarist Dick Dale is roundly acknowledged as the father of surf music. In the late '50s, he developed its trademark reverb sound. Whether intentionally or otherwise, the "wet," full echo of surf guitars evoked the rides and waves of surfing, which in the early '60s was still an emerging teenage sport that was little known outside of southern California and Hawaii. Ironically, Jimi Hendrix, who intoned "you'll never hear surf music again" on "Third Stone from the Sun" from his debut album, is said to have been influenced by Dale, who like Hendrix played his guitar left-handed and upside-down.

"For most surf instrumentals," wrote surf music authority John Blair in his liner notes to *Guitar Player Magazine Presents Legends of Guitar: Surf, Vol. 1,* "a small electronic device called a reverberation unit, or 'reverb' for short, was used to create the distinctive 'surf' guitar sound. Although several companies had reverbs on the market, the one made by the Fender Musical Instrument Company (introduced in the summer of 1961) was the popular choice of most surf bands...

"[Dick Dale] used Fender amplifiers and even had the company customize a special left-handed (he played upside-down and left-handed) gold metalflake Stratocaster guitar, which he still plays. In fact, Dale's close association with Fender enabled him to 'roadtest' new equipment for the company. The powerful Dual Showman amplifier, introduced in late 1962, was developed with Dale's help."

On vinyl, the surf craze kicked off with Dale's late-1961 single, "Let's Go Trippin'." Although it was only a regional hit, its influence was tremendous, and within months, dozens of bands – virtually all of them based in southern California – were playing surf music. Hundreds would record surf singles and albums before the fad started to fade in the mid-'60s. Although they were not Californian, and would certainly not identify themselves as a surf group, the dark, reverberant guitars of the Ventures – then reaching the peak of their massive popularity – were also formidable influences on these groups.

On a national level, the impact of instrumental surf bands was notable, but much slighter. The Chantays ("Pipeline") and the Surfaris ("Wipe Out") scored huge national hits, but few others dented the Top 40, let alone the Top Ten. The Pyramids' early-1964 single "Penetration" was the last big national instrumental surf hit.

While most surf groups were based in southern California, the genre was not strictly isolated to the region. The Astronauts (from Colorado) and the Trashmen (from Minneapolis) were the most successful of the not inconsiderable number of landlocked bands who played surf music, or at least made a few stabs at it. The Trashmen, indeed, went to the Top Five with "Surfin' Bird" in early 1964; only the Beatles, then hitting the U.S. with full force, kept them from the top spot. One of the very best instrumental surf groups, the Atlantics, were not even from the U.S., but from Australia, where they scored some massive hits in 1963 and 1964.

Surf music would achieve its most lasting influence not with instrumentals, but with vocal groups, in particular the Beach Boys. There's no doubting that Dick Dale was a profound influence on the Hawthorne, CA, group, who covered Dale's "Let's Go Trippin'" on their second album, *Surfin' U.S.A.* They recorded a few other surf instrumentals on their first few albums as well, but from the beginning, they were primarily a vocal group, heavily influenced by Chuck Berry, the Four Freshmen, doo wop, and other styles. They were the first group, however, to successfully sing about the surf music phenomenon, adding complex harmonies and clever lyrics to the driving guitars and chugging rhythms. In their wake, some groups like the aforementioned Astronauts and Trashmen tried to play the field with both instrumental and vocal numbers.

Other California vocal acts were quick to jump on the bandwagon, but besides the Beach Boys, only Jan & Dean (who were occasionally beneficiaries of songs and harmonies by Beach Boy leader Brian Wilson) were a significant success, commercially or artistically. Jan & Dean had been a modestly successful duo for years before latching onto the surf fad, and – like the Beach Boys – they would soon adapt the surf sound to hot rod lyrics emphasizing cars and drag racing. Acts like Ronny & the Daytonas ("G.T.O.") and the Rip Chords ("Hey Little Cobra") hit the Top Ten with one-shot hits in the same style, but were out of their depth when they tried to mine it for memorable follow-ups.

Indeed, after 1963, the Beach Boys – still remembered by many

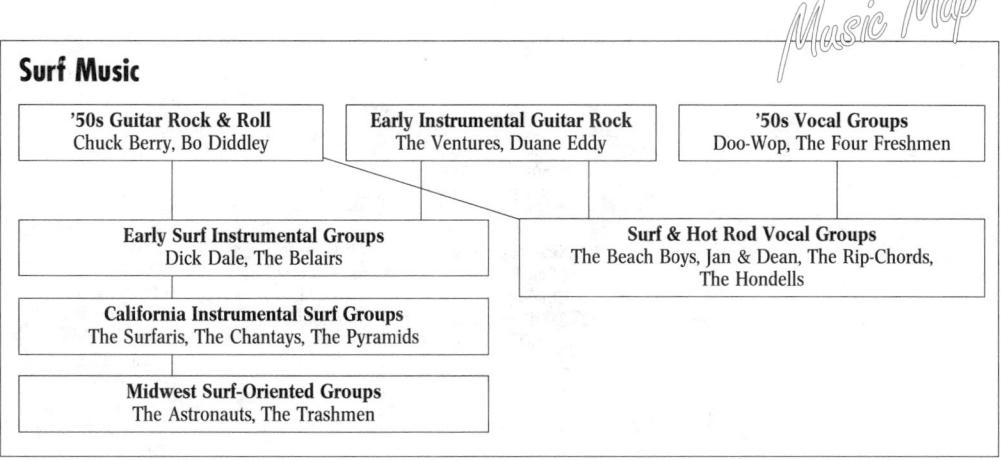

Surf Music

'50s Guitar Rock & Roll	Early Instrumental Guitar Rock	'50s Vocal Groups
Chuck Berry, Bo Diddley	The Ventures, Duane Eddy	Doo-Wop, The Four Freshmen

Early Surf Instrumental Groups	Surf & Hot Rod Vocal Groups
Dick Dale, The Belairs	The Beach Boys, Jan & Dean, The Rip-Chords, The Hondells

California Instrumental Surf Groups
The Surfaris, The Chantays, The Pyramids

Midwest Surf-Oriented Groups
The Astronauts, The Trashmen

listeners primarily as a surf group – left the subject behind for good. They soon broadened their scope leagues beyond hot rods and girls to create challenging, personal pop/rock on a competitive level with the British Invasion groups that sounded the death knell for surf music at the beginning of 1964. Even Jan & Dean's hits were not solely limited to surf and hot rod tunes, though their career came to a skidding halt when Jan Berry was severely injured in a car crash in 1966 on Sunset Boulevard.

The Beach Boys' harmonies, however, left their stamp on countless other groups. The Who's Keith Moon was a huge surf music fan, and the manic splashing of his drum kit owes something to the bashing rumble of surf ensembles; the Who's own harmonies owed surprisingly large debts to the Beach Boys. The lineups of several obscure surf groups included members who went on to fame in surprisingly different contexts. The Crossfires, for example, evolved into the Turtles, and the Jesters, led by Jim Messina, also featured Glenn Frey of the Eagles.

Three decades later, few groups play surf music, although Dick Dale made a surprisingly strong comeback on record and as a national touring act in the early '90s. Echoes of the style, however, live on whenever you heard a reverbed guitar or sweet, high vocal harmonies in a rock & roll song.

12 Essential Recordings

The Beach Boys, *Good Vibrations* (Capitol)
The Beach Boys, *Surfin' U.S.A.* (Capitol)
The Beach Boys, *Surfer Girl* (Capitol)
Jan & Dean, *The Legendary Master Series* (EMI)
Dick Dale, *King of the Surf Guitar: The Best of Dick Dale* (Rhino)
The Astronauts, *Surf Party* (RCA)
The Trashmen, *Best of the Trashmen* (Sundazed)
Various Artists, *Guitar Player Presents Legends of Guitar – Surf, Vol. 1* (Rhino)
Various Artists, *The History of Surf Music, Vol. 1* (Rhino)
Various Artists, *Surfin' Hits* (Rhino)
The Atlantics, *The CBS Singles Collection 1963-1965* (Canetoad, Australia)
The Surfaris, *Wipe Out! The Best of the Surfaris* (Varese Sarabande)

BOOK

The Beach Boys, by David Leaf (Courage, 1985)
– Richie Unterberger

Soul

More than almost any other genre of the rock era, soul is a wide-ranging and immensely diverse style. Peaking in the 1960s, it helped define the African-American experience in America with a passion, pride, and optimism rare in any art form.

Broadly speaking, soul was the combination of rhythm & blues, gospel, and pop. The gospel ingredient was most evident in the supremely emotional, pleading and jubilant vocals and harmonies. Rock-solid rhythm sections, punchy horn arrangements, and tight instrumental and vocal ensemble work were also frequent hallmarks of the classic soul sound.

The forefathers of soul were veterans of 1950s rhythm & blues. Ray Charles was perhaps the first to merge gospel, pop, and rhythm and blues in a style that we recognize as a direct ancestor of soul with his 1954 hit "I Got a Woman." Other important pioneers were Jackie Wilson, Sam Cooke, and James Brown. They came from somewhat different backgrounds – Wilson from the R&B vocal group tradition, Cooke from straight gospel as the lead singer of the Soul Stirrers, Brown from the "chitlin" circuit – but they shared an appetite for constantly modernizing their sound with both pop crossover material and R&B-based work that put their emotions at the fore with an arresting grit, naked emotion, and increasingly mature lyrical concerns.

As R&B grew into soul in the early '60s, the arrangements became more intricate, as did the harmonies (though they were often rooted in doo wop, as is obvious from listening to the early work of the Miracles and the Impressions). Romance was usually the subject, but it often was a more complex, adult, and bittersweet form of love than the adolescent fare of much early rock & roll and R&B. Songwriter/performer/producers like Smokey Robinson and Curtis Mayfield put a greater personal stamp on their product than was customary in the 1950s. The session players at labels like Stax/Volt and Motown, though sometimes uncredited on the releases, set a level of instrumental discipline and virtuosity that remains a benchmark of musical excellence in contemporary popular music. Starting with the Drifters, strings were often used to tastefully embellish the material without detracting from the performers' gutsy power.

There were literally hundreds of soul performers who created bodies of work that endure several decades later. In many cases, the artists themselves grew enormously over the course of their career, and cannot be conveniently pigeonholed into a certain subgenre or peak output – Marvin Gaye, Aretha Franklin, Curtis Mayfield, and Stevie Wonder are only a few of those. There were certain regional styles that developed, although soul was such a nationwide, overlapping phenomenon that these too cannot be categorized too narrowly, and great acts like the Isley Brothers couldn't be conveniently pigeonholed into any certain school.

By far the most successful style of soul was the kind that came to be identified with Motown Records in Detroit. Emphasizing melodic hooks, bright, clear production, and possessing an extraordinary roster of talented vocalists, Motown was the most successful independent label of its era, crossing over to the pop charts for literally hundreds of Top 20 hits during the 1960s. Instrumental in bringing the sounds of Black America into mainstream American life, Motown has been disdained by some latter-

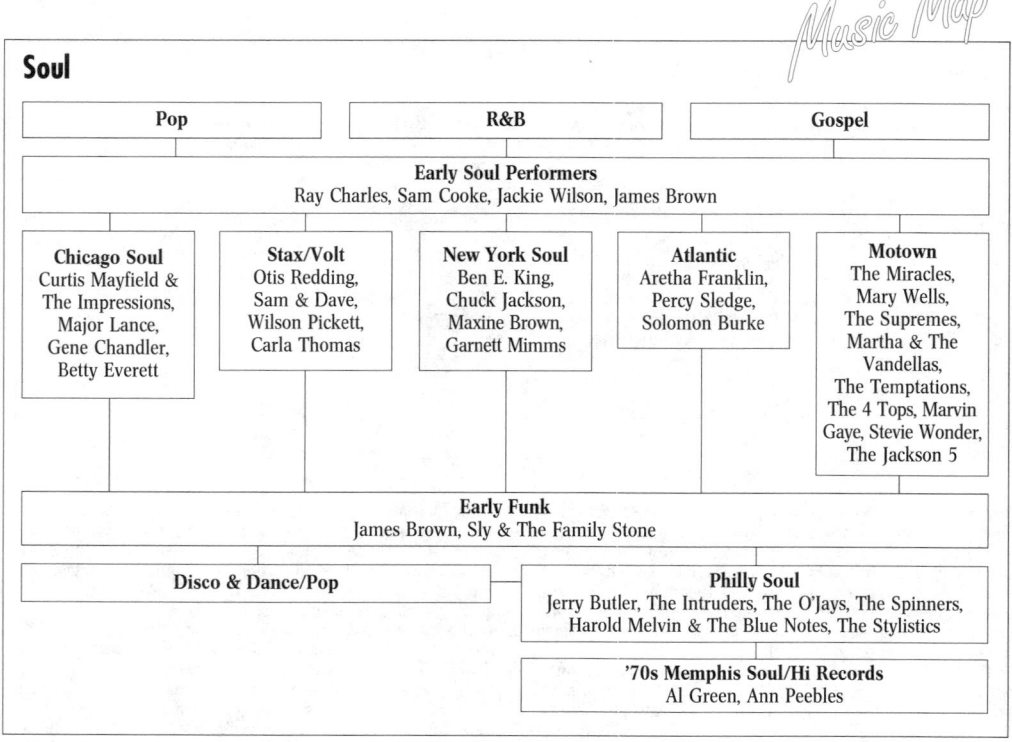

Soul

Pop	R&B	Gospel

Early Soul Performers
Ray Charles, Sam Cooke, Jackie Wilson, James Brown

Chicago Soul Curtis Mayfield & The Impressions, Major Lance, Gene Chandler, Betty Everett	**Stax/Volt** Otis Redding, Sam & Dave, Wilson Pickett, Carla Thomas	**New York Soul** Ben E. King, Chuck Jackson, Maxine Brown, Garnett Mimms	**Atlantic** Aretha Franklin, Percy Sledge, Solomon Burke	**Motown** The Miracles, Mary Wells, The Supremes, Martha & The Vandellas, The Temptations, The 4 Tops, Marvin Gaye, Stevie Wonder, The Jackson 5

Early Funk
James Brown, Sly & The Family Stone

Disco & Dance/Pop	**Philly Soul** Jerry Butler, The Intruders, The O'Jays, The Spinners, Harold Melvin & The Blue Notes, The Stylistics

'70s Memphis Soul/Hi Records
Al Green, Ann Peebles

day critics for a formulaic approach, and for appealing to Whites, teenagers, and pop listeners more than other kinds of down-home soul music. These are really fairly ridiculous assertions. Motown was if anything more popular with Black audiences than White ones, and its legendary performers – Smokey Robinson, the Temptations, Martha & the Vandellas, Marvin Gaye, Stevie Wonder, the Supremes, Mary Wells, the Four Tops, the Jackson Five, and many others – released an astonishingly large and diverse body of classic work in the 1960s and beyond.

Motown's most serious rival for soul supremacy was the Stax/Volt label, based in Memphis. With Booker T. & the MGs (stars in their own right) usually providing the backing, these records offered a funkier, rootsier brand of soul, with generally rawer vocals and a heavier reliance on horn riffs. Otis Redding, Wilson Pickett, Carla Thomas, and Sam & Dave were the biggest stars to emerge from the Stax/Volt label, which was absorbed into Atlantic in the late '60s. Atlantic Records itself was one of the most influential soul labels, with gritty soul sensations like Solomon Burke and Percy Sledge. A great deal of soul with a similar down-home southern sensibility also emerged from the legendary studios in Muscle Shoals, Alabama; Muscle Shoals players backed Aretha Franklin on many of her greatest sides.

In Chicago, performers like the Impressions, Jerry Butler, Betty Everett, Major Lance, and Gene Chandler established their own distinctive regional sound, prominently featuring blaring horns and smooth harmonic interplay. New York had a somewhat more pop-oriented, "uptown" sound, typified by Chuck Jackson and Maxine Brown, although as always there were rootsier exceptions like Garnett Mimms, and artists who combined the best of both worlds, like Ben E. King (both as lead singer of the Drifters and as a solo artist). Philadelphia soul records leaned toward doo wop-like group harmonies, eventually evolving into a serious rival of Motown's production machines with the ascendance of Gamble & Huff and Thom Bell.

By the late '60s, soul was changing with the times. Motown-producer Norman Whitfield expanded the label's lyrical scope into psychedelia and social consciousness with songs like the

Temptations' "Cloud Nine." James Brown pioneered funk music with incredible churning rhythms backing increasingly assertive statements of Black pride. Sly & the Family Stone merged hippie concerns and funk on a string of hit singles and albums. In the early '70s, Motown veterans Marvin Gaye and Stevie Wonder broke free of the label's hit-oriented production process to issue vastly influential, album-length statements. The Philadelphia sound, string-drenched and impeccably produced and harmonized, took soul to another level of slickness. In Memphis, Al Green established himself as an heir to Otis Redding with Hi Records and the Memphis Horns.

Soul diminished as a commercial presence in the mid-'70s, as funk and disco began to put more emphasis on danceable rhythms rather than songwriting and singing. Al Green, seen by some fans as the standardbearer of the classic soul sound, turned to gospel; the once-thriving Stax/Volt empire collapsed in a confusing mess. Much Black soul music became increasingly middle-of-the-road, leading to the new genre of urban contemporary music. Soul is still very much alive, of course, in the harmonies and production that continue to inform contemporary African-American popular music, whether in funk, disco, dance-pop, or rap. The "classic" soul style lives on in different ways – old stars continue to release and record new material for a specialized audience, and veteran performers like Tina Turner and Patti LaBelle have achieved new levels of superstardom with their updated brand of contemporary soul.

15 Essential Recordings

Various Artists, *Soul Shots* series (Rhino)
Various Artists, *The Complete Stax-Volt Singles 1959-1968* (Atlantic)
James Brown, *Star Time* (PolyGram)
Otis Redding, *Otis! The Definitive Otis Redding* (Rhino)
Aretha Franklin, *Queen of Soul: The Atlantic Recordings* (Rhino)
Curtis Mayfield & the Impressions, *Anthology 1961-1977* (MCA)

Music Map

```
┌─────────────────────────────────────────────────────────────────────────────────────────┐
│  Motown                                                                                    │
│                                                                                            │
│   ┌──────────────────────┐    ┌──────────────────────┐    ┌──────────────────────┐        │
│   │        Gospel         │    │         R&B          │    │         Pop          │        │
│   └──────────────────────┘    └──────────────────────┘    └──────────────────────┘        │
│                                                                                            │
│   ┌──────────────────────────────────────────────────────────────────────────────┐        │
│   │                          Early Motown Stars                                     │        │
│   │          The Miracles, The Marvelettes, Mary Wells, The Contours               │        │
│   └──────────────────────────────────────────────────────────────────────────────┘        │
│                                                                                            │
│  ┌───────────────────────┐  ┌──────────────────────┐  ┌─────────────────────────┐          │
│  │ Motown Star Female    │  │  Motown Solo Stars    │  │ Motown Star Male Groups  │          │
│  │      Groups           │  │ Marvin Gaye, Stevie   │  │ The Temptations, The 4   │          │
│  │   The Supremes,       │  │ Wonder, Edwin Starr,  │  │ Tops, The Jackson 5      │          │
│  │ Martha Reeves & The   │  │   Brenda Holloway     │  │                          │          │
│  │ Vandellas, Gladys     │  │                       │  │                          │          │
│  │ Knight & The Pips     │  │                       │  │                          │          │
│  └───────────────────────┘  └──────────────────────┘  └─────────────────────────┘          │
│                                                                                            │
│   ┌──────────────────────────────────────────────────────────────────────────────┐        │
│   │              Motown Producers, Songwriters, and Musicians                      │        │
│   │  Berry Gordy, Jr., Mickey Stevenson, Holland-Dozier-Holland, Norman Whitfield, │        │
│   │                  James Jamerson, Benny Benjamin                                 │        │
│   └──────────────────────────────────────────────────────────────────────────────┘        │
└─────────────────────────────────────────────────────────────────────────────────────────┘
```

Sam Cooke, *Man & His Music* (RCA)
Ray Charles, *Birth of Soul* (Rhino)
Ben E. King, *Anthology* (Rhino)
Sly & the Family Stone, *Anthology* (Epic)
Al Green, *Al Green's Greatest Hits* (Hi)
The Isley Brothers, *Story, Vol. 1* (Rhino)
Wilson Pickett, *A Man and a Half: The Best of Wilson Pickett* (Rhino)
Jackie Wilson, *Mr. Excitement* (Rhino)
Solomon Burke, *Home in Your Heart* (Rhino)

BOOKS

The Blackwell Guide to Soul Recordings, edited by Robert Pruter (Blackwell, 1993)
Where Did Our Love Go? The Rise and Fall of the Motown Sound, by Nelson George (St. Martin's Press, 1985)
Sweet Soul Music, by Peter Guralnick (Harper & Row, 1986)
Nowhere to Run: The Story of Soul Music, by Gerry Hirshey (Times Books, 1984)

– *Richie Unterberger*

Motown

Many labels have left their mark on rock & roll – Sun, Atlantic, Chess, Stax/Volt, Stiff, and lots of others left a permanent imprint on the music's legacy by honing distinctive styles and attitudes. Only one label, however, is immediately identified as a genre of its own. And not just by scholars and record collectors – Motown, to anyone who's listened to popular music since 1960, is not just a label in the middle of a record, but a *sound* that ranks among the most distinctive in rock history.

In its heyday, the Detroit label was home to the most commercially successful synthesis of R&B and pop ever produced. Motown developed many superstars, but performers were only part of the story. Equally important were the songwriters, including such masters as Smokey Robinson and the Holland-Dozier-Holland team; producers (who often doubled as songwriters); the (often uncredited) backing musicians, like bassist James Jamerson and drummer Benny Benjamin, who gave the music its rock-solid foundation; and the vision of owner Berry Gordy, Jr. You could almost always identify a Motown Record: instantly hummable melodies, pulsing bass lines, punchy tambourines and handclaps, rousing horns and violins, and vocals that evoked a gospel flavor with the call-and-response lines between the lead and backup singers.

The Motown empire, which eventually grew into the biggest Black-owned business in America, was a success story as unlikely as those of Elvis or the Beatles. A former boxer and failed jazz record-store owner, Gordy was a struggling hustler on the edges of the R&B music business in the late '50s, writing some hits for Jackie Wilson. In 1959, he borrowed money from his family to start an independent production company. After leasing hits by Marv Johnson and Barrett Strong to other labels, Gordy formed his own labels. The releases would appear both on Motown and other imprints like Tamla, Gordy, and Soul.

Motown quickly established itself in the early '60s with hits by the Miracles, the Marvelettes, and Mary Wells. It was Gordy's increasingly refined and systematic production techniques, however, that would ensure that the label continued to succeed and grow. The Motown sound has often been compared to an assembly line, drawing upon the influence of Detroit's automobile plants, with performers, songwriters, producers, and musicians embellishing a basic tried-and-true blueprint. If it were indeed true that Motown's formula was nothing more than an assembly line, it most likely would have exhausted itself quickly. Gordy, and Motown's, genius was that it was able to spin almost infinite variations on its hugely appealing recipes, while still retaining an instantly recognizable sound, endearing itself to millions of listeners through both innovation and familiarity.

Motown releases might have shared many general similarities, but in time its superstars would develop strong identities of their own. The Miracles, paced by Smokey Robinson (who wrote many of Motown's best songs, both for the Miracles and other artists), handled both romantic ballads and uptempo dance tunes; the Temptations were the most polished soul group of their day; the Four Tops were gritty and emotional; Mary Wells and the Marvelettes recorded the most soulful girl group singles around; child prodigy Stevie Wonder developed into a magnificently gifted songwriter and instrumentalist; Martha Reeves & the Vandellas were Motown at its most feverish and gospel-influenced; Diana Ross & the Supremes were, aside from the Beatles, the most successful pop group of the '60s; Marvin Gaye, along with Stevie Wonder, would prove to be the most eclectic and innovative singer/songwriter on the Motown roster, not even reaching his maturity as an artist (like Wonder) until the 1970s; Junior Walker cut the label's earthiest, most party-oriented R&B.

These were the superstars; there were other fine performers who recorded a notable body of work for Motown in the 1960s, including Gladys Knight, Brenda Holloway, Edwin Starr, Kim Weston, Tammi Terrell, and the Contours. The label's roster was so deep, in fact, that some illustrious artists were neglected; the Spinners didn't do much of anything until they left Motown in the early '70s, the Isley Brothers had only one big hit during their several years there (perhaps because of their inability to truly adapt to the Motown formula), and early-'60s soul star Chuck Jackson had only minimal success after moving to Motown.

Even the stars sometimes expressed dissatisfaction about how they were promoted and directed by Motown, but they most likely knew that their success was at least equally attributable to the label as to their own talents. The point was underscored by Mary Wells's surprise decision to leave Motown in 1964 just after her #1 hit, "My Guy." Lured away by a big contract and the promise of a movie career, Wells never had another big hit; without the estimable Motown team, she was just another soul singer.

The loss of Wells was covered by the burgeoning careers of other Motown stars, but Gordy faced a much more serious problem in late 1967, when the songwriting and production team of Brian Holland, Lamont Dozier, and Eddie Holland demanded an accounting of their royalties. After initiating a suit against

Motown, the trio left the label to establish a company of their own. For a few years, Motown's fortunes were unaffected; it launched the Jackson 5 as superstars, and producers such as Norman Whitfield infused Motown with contemporary funk, psychedelia, and social commentary on tracks like the Temptations' "Cloud Nine," "Psychedelic Shack," and "Ball of Confusion."

Motown's golden age truly ended, however, in 1971, when the company moved from Detroit to Los Angeles. Around this time, the careers of some of Motown's mainstays, such as Martha Reeves and the Marvelettes, had petered out; Diana Ross had already left the Supremes. Marvin Gaye and Stevie Wonder recorded some stupendous album-length statements in the 1970s that showed their full gifts as songwriters and performers for the first time, as well as expanding their lyrical concerns beyond the romantic themes that Motown had largely stuck to. But Motown no longer bred scads of stars, or honed a distinctive sound; it was simply a soul/R&B record label, albeit a very big and successful one.

When people talk about the Motown sound, they're referring to those 1960s and early '70s recordings. The most successful label of its day, and the most successful independent label of all time (it's now part of MCA), it was the most influential factor in establishing African-American music as an integral part of mainstream U.S. culture.

15 Essential Recordings

Smokey Robinson & the Miracles, *Anthology*
Mary Wells, *Looking Back 1961-1964*
Martha Reeves & the Vandellas, *Live Wire! The Singles 1962-1972*
The Marvelettes, *Marvelettes' Greatest Hits*
Marvin Gaye, *Anthology*
Stevie Wonder, *Looking Back*
The Supremes, *Anthology*
The Temptations, *Emperors of Soul*
The Four Tops, *Anthology*
The Jackson 5, *Anthology*
Junior Walker, *Greatest Hits*
Gladys Knight & the Pips, *Anthology*
Brenda Holloway, *Greatest Hits & Rare Classics*
Edwin Starr, *Motown Superstar Series Vol. 3*
Various Artists, *Hitsville USA: The Motown Singles Collection 1959-1971*

BOOK

Where Did Our Love Go?: The Rise and Fall of the Motown Sound, by Nelson George (St. Martin's, 1985)
– Richie Unterberger

The British Invasion

Of all the movements that have shaken the world of rock & roll in the last 40 years, the British Invasion ranks among the most exciting and important. Only the music's actual birth as a popular phenomenon with the rise of Elvis Presley is comparable; the punk/new wave explosion of the mid-'70s, while equally unexpected and revolutionary, lacked the British Invasion's across-the-board impact on mainstream popular music and culture.

The British Invasion has sometimes been unfairly disparaged as a bunch of White guitar groups re-selling second-hand, vintage American rock & roll and R&B to a public that had forgotten it, or had never been exposed to it in the first place. While it's true that early American rock and soul were the performers' chief inspirations, the best of the groups broke immense ground as performers, songwriters, and stylists, introducing many of the attitudes and innovations that are taken for granted as part and parcel of rock music today.

The British Invasion had its roots in the country's skiffle craze of the mid-'50s, sparked by Lonnie Donegan. Innumerable British teenagers were inspired to form groups based on the simple (and cheap) instrumentation of guitars and washboards. The watered-down folk and blues sound of skiffle can sound unbearably stilted today, but many of those teenage musicians quickly graduated to electric guitars and drums as the focus of their interest shifted to classic early American rock & roll.

There *was* a homegrown British rock & roll scene in the late '50s and early '60s, but it was overpopulated by pale imitations of American rock, clean-cut instrumentals, and teen idols who offered little more than slightly reworked MOR ballad fare. Tours by American rock & rollers were uncommon, and rock & roll itself was only played on the radio a few hours per week. Which meant that young British musicians and listeners devoted to rock & roll had no alternative but to create a grassroots scene themselves.

While Liverpool was by far the biggest breeding ground for the "beat boom," with hundreds of bands in action by the early '60s, groups were sprouting up all over the British Isles – in Manchester, London, Belfast, and elsewhere. While early pioneers of rock were dying, retiring, facing scandal, or falling into commercial disfavor in the United States, these British musicians maintained a fanatical devotion to their idols' music. Chuck Berry and Buddy Holly were arguably the most influential heroes to this generation of musicians, but the British also revered a wide range of other great American performers, including the Everly Brothers, Elvis, Gene Vincent, girl groups, the early Motown acts, and many more.

A listen to the Beatles' early recordings leaves no doubt about their adulation for, and mastery of, the styles of their heroes, but they added a lot more themselves. They were pioneers in so many areas: writing most of their material at a time when that was rarely done; devising melodies and harmonies that were more inventive than any others that had been used in rock & roll; writing and performing as a self-contained group with distinctive individual talents and personalities, rather than as a star with anonymous backing musicians; and embodying the spirit of rebellious youth with their energetic performances, humor, and nonconformist attitudes. They, and the best of their fellow British groups, did this with a giddy exuberance that has rarely been matched in the history of rock & roll.

The impact of Beatlemania – which blanketed Britain in 1963, and the United States the following year – can not be overestimated, not only in terms of commercial success (as in the oft-quoted statistic of the Beatles claiming the top five singles in the U.S. one week in early 1964), but in how it changed rock & roll itself. Sometimes unfairly criticized as a "safe" alternative to the moodier and blacker Rolling Stones, the Beatles displayed an enormous versatility that refutes such categorizations. They could rock as hard as anyone when that suited them, but more important, they were pop's greatest eclectics, constantly evolving and experimenting in their successful quest to create the most diverse and innovative body of work ever produced by a rock group.

The first flush of "beat" bands, as they were called initially, to overtake Britain and (slightly later) the United States were often from Liverpool, and tended to emulate the Beatles' lightest, most innocuous characteristics. Dubbed "Merseybeat," guitars and harmonies were to the fore, as were bouncy, irresistible melodies (sometimes actual Lennon-McCartney compositions that the Beatles had rejected for their own recordings). Cute and clean-cut, the recordings of Gerry & the Pacemakers, Billy J. Kramer, Freddie & the Dreamers, and Herman's Hermits have fared poorly in jaded latter-day rock critiques for their lightweight, at times insipid content. But this shouldn't obscure the glittering harmonies and chiming guitars of the Searchers, the Hollies, and Peter and Gordon, who were probably the best bands that followed the mold of the Beatles' most pop-oriented recordings.

The Beatles' greatest challenge came from the London-based R&B scene, through groups who drew from American electric bluesmen like Muddy Waters and Chess Records rockers like Bo Diddley. Schooled by such early British bluesmen as Alexis Korner and Cyril Davies, the Rolling Stones, the Yardbirds, Manfred Mann, the Kinks, the Pretty Things, the Who, and non-London acts like the Animals, the Spencer Davis Group, and Them took the bulk of their early repertoires from obscure blues and R&B recordings, investing them with accelerated tempos and a reckless guitar-based approach. As personalities, they took the Beatles' anti-Establishment stance further, rebelling against society more openly and wearing their hair even longer.

The difference between these R&B cultists and the Beatles is not nearly as great as it has sometimes been portrayed. The Beatles and the R&B groups often covered the same songs, not just by Chuck Berry, but by many others; the Beatles and the Stones – and for that matter, Freddie & the Dreamers – recorded the early Motown tune "Money"; the Stones' first big British hit was a cover of Lennon-McCartney's "I Wanna Be Your Man," their second was a cover of a Buddy Holly song. Manfred Mann covered obscure girl group tunes for their biggest hits, and the Kinks would draw upon British

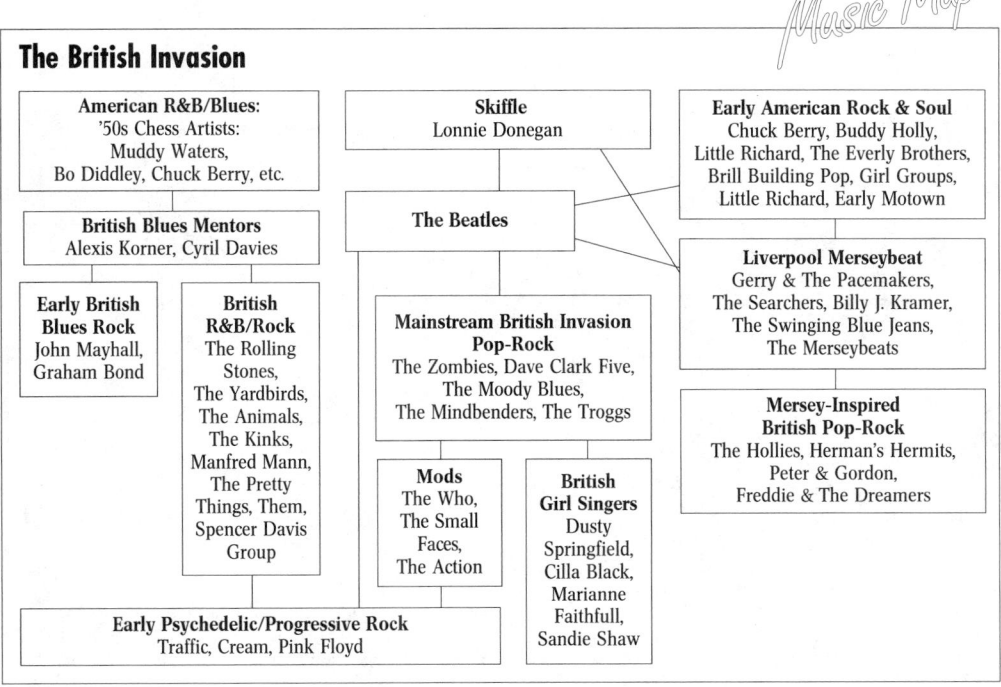

The British Invasion

American R&B/Blues:
'50s Chess Artists:
Muddy Waters,
Bo Diddley, Chuck Berry, etc.

Skiffle
Lonnie Donegan

Early American Rock & Soul
Chuck Berry, Buddy Holly,
Little Richard, The Everly Brothers,
Brill Building Pop, Girl Groups,
Little Richard, Early Motown

British Blues Mentors
Alexis Korner, Cyril Davies

The Beatles

Liverpool Merseybeat
Gerry & The Pacemakers,
The Searchers, Billy J. Kramer,
The Swinging Blue Jeans,
The Merseybeats

**Early British
Blues Rock**
John Mayhall,
Graham Bond

**British
R&B/Rock**
The Rolling
Stones,
The Yardbirds,
The Animals,
The Kinks,
Manfred Mann,
The Pretty
Things, Them,
Spencer Davis
Group

**Mainstream British Invasion
Pop-Rock**
The Zombies, Dave Clark Five,
The Moody Blues,
The Mindbenders, The Troggs

**Mersey-Inspired
British Pop-Rock**
The Hollies, Herman's Hermits,
Peter & Gordon,
Freddie & The Dreamers

Mods
The Who,
The Small
Faces,
The Action

**British
Girl Singers**
Dusty
Springfield,
Cilla Black,
Marianne
Faithfull,
Sandie Shaw

Early Psychedelic/Progressive Rock
Traffic, Cream, Pink Floyd

---

music hall traditions for their most creative work. All the groups from this earthier faction would come to pen their own material, often placing a premium upon melodic invention and harmonies.

Sometimes overlooked in this battle of supposed opposites were the groups that favored neither the R&B nor the dippy pop approach, instead focusing their efforts on masterful straightforward rock. The Zombies were probably second only to the Beatles in their breathtakingly adventurous melodies, the Dave Clark Five pounded out tuneful rockers with glorious abandon, and the first incarnation of the Moody Blues sang haunting pop/rock tunes that borrowed from R&B, soul, and the Brill Building.

In 1964 and 1965, the army of British Invaders seemed endless, but in the face of a volatile rock scene, it became clear that only the bands that could both write their own material and evolve stylistically would survive. The Beatles, Stones, Who, and Kinks were the only British bands to maintain a high standard of work throughout the '60s, expanding their songwriting talents and instrumental resources at a dizzying pace. Bands like the Yardbirds and Zombies briefly exhibited similar resources for pioneering psychedelia and experimentation before folding due to internal and external pressures. Groups like Gerry & The Pacemakers, the Dave Clark Five, and the Searchers fell off the map commercially due to their inability to write top-notch material or evolve with the times. And a few, like the Hollies and Manfred Mann, survived by incorporating enough progressive elements into their brand of pop/rock to remain hip (and commercially successful).

While a few first-rate bands like the mod Small Faces and the crude Troggs emerged in 1966, that year saw the impetus of the original British Invasion start to fade. A second generation of bands sprung up that took progressive experimentation, cohesive albums, and self-contained songwriting as a given. Some (Traffic, Cream) featured veterans of the first wave of the invasion; others (Pink Floyd) owed little to the movement at all.

In reality, though, the British Invasion has never stopped. Artists from the British Isles continue to invade the American, and indeed the international, audience at a rapid pace, if not nearly as phenomenal a rate as the heady days of 1964 and 1965. Folk-rock, garage-rock, and psychedelia grew directly out of the innovations

of the best British Invasion groups. And rock & roll owes much of its climate of artistic freedom and individual expression – not to mention its harmonies, melodies, and guitar-based ensemble sound – to the ground broken by the Beatles and their followers.

15 Essential Recordings

The Beatles, all of their albums, though *The Beatles 1962-66* (Capitol) has their biggest early hits.
The Rolling Stones, *The Singles Collection* (ABKCO)
The Who, *Meaty, Beaty, Big and Bouncy* (MCA)
The Kinks, *Greatest Hits* (Rhino)
The Yardbirds, *Greatest Hits, Vol. 1* (Rhino)
The Animals, *The Complete Animals* (EMI, UK)
The Zombies, *Singles As & Bs* (See For Miles, UK)
Manfred Mann, *The Manfred Mann Collection* (EMI)
The Dave Clark Five, *The History of the Dave Clark Five* (Hollywood)
The Hollies, *30th Anniversary Collection* (EMI)
Them, *Them Featuring Van Morrison* (Parrot)
Various Artists, *The British Invasion Vol. 1-9* (Rhino)
The Pretty Things, *Get A Buzz: The Best of the Fontana Years* (Fontana)
The Small Faces, *The Small Faces* (PolyGram)
The Spencer Davis Group, *The Best of the Spencer Davis Group* (Rhino)

BOOKS

The British Invasion, by Nicholas Schaffner (McGraw Hill)

Videos

A Hard Day's Night (also available as a CD-ROM from Voyager)
The Compleat Beatles

– *Richie Unterberger*

Folk Rock

In the early '60s, any suggestion that the folk and rock & roll

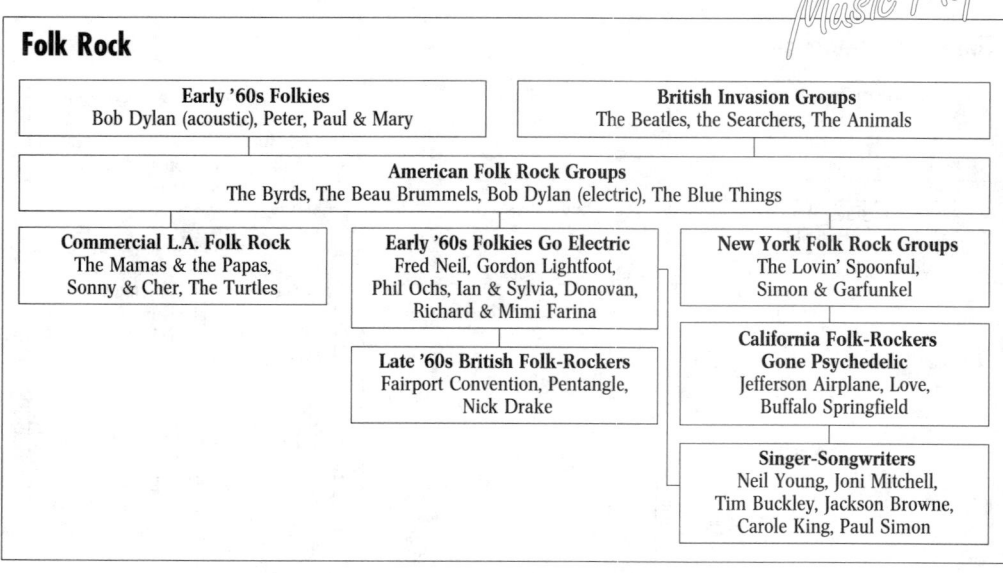

Folk Rock

Early '60s Folkies	British Invasion Groups
Bob Dylan (acoustic), Peter, Paul & Mary	The Beatles, the Searchers, The Animals

American Folk Rock Groups
The Byrds, The Beau Brummels, Bob Dylan (electric), The Blue Things

Commercial L.A. Folk Rock
The Mamas & the Papas,
Sonny & Cher, The Turtles

Early '60s Folkies Go Electric
Fred Neil, Gordon Lightfoot,
Phil Ochs, Ian & Sylvia, Donovan,
Richard & Mimi Farina

New York Folk Rock Groups
The Lovin' Spoonful,
Simon & Garfunkel

Late '60s British Folk-Rockers
Fairport Convention, Pentangle,
Nick Drake

**California Folk-Rockers
Gone Psychedelic**
Jefferson Airplane, Love,
Buffalo Springfield

Singer-Songwriters
Neil Young, Joni Mitchell,
Tim Buckley, Jackson Browne,
Carole King, Paul Simon

worlds would intertwine to create a hybrid called folk-rock would have been met with utter disbelief from both camps. The folk community prided itself on its purity, which meant acoustic instruments and songs of substance; they regarded rock & roll as vulgar and commercial. Rock & rollers, for the most part, were utterly ignorant of folk traditions, and unconcerned with broadening their lyrical content beyond tried-and-true themes of romance and youthful partying. Yet within a few years, folk and rock not only combined into a new form of popular music, but one which became hugely successful and influential.

By 1964, Bob Dylan had already done much to revolutionize contemporary folk music by singing about topical issues and (after a couple years) abstract personal and romantic concerns in a poetic and uniquely expressive fashion. Dylan harbored a secret admiration for the Beatles and other major British Invasion bands, a fascination which was mutual. It was only a matter of time before each started to influence the other.

The roots of folk-rock can be detected in a few pre-1965 recordings by the Searchers and Jackie DeShannon (who helped introduce the ringing, circular 12-string guitar riffs that became one of the music's major trademarks), as well as the Beau Brummels, the Animals' superb bluesy interpretation of the traditional folk standard "The House of the Rising Sun," and the Beatles' own "I'm a Loser." It took the Byrds, however, to really kick the movement into gear with their electric version of Dylan's "Mr. Tambourine Man," which topped the charts in mid-1965.

The first and best folk-rock band, the Byrds was comprised of ex-folkies who had only picked up their electric instruments a year or so before they became superstars. But they were, if anything, influenced more by the Beatles than Dylan; as they were once quoted (albeit tongue in cheek), they based their sound on "21% Beatles, 11% Zombies, 8% Dillards, 18% Dylan, 14% Pete Seeger, 16% Searchers, and 12% trial and error/ignorance/accident/originality." Leader Roger McGuinn's chiming 12-string guitar set the sonic standard for the new genre, as did the group's beautiful choral harmonies and superb interpretations of songs by Dylan and Seeger, traditional folk ballads, and their own first-rate original material.

Dylan himself moved into folk-rock around the same time as the Byrds on his *Bringing It All Back Home* album, divided into electric and acoustic sides. The subsequent *Highway 61 Revisited* and *Blonde on Blonde* were full-bore electric rock records, marrying Dylan's intense, at times surrealistic poetry to a tough beat, provided by soon-to-be-stars in their own right like Mike Bloomfield, Al Kooper, and the Band. His conversion to rock &

roll outraged much of his original constituency, which was more than offset by his legions of new fans; indeed, all three of his albums from 1965 and 1966 made the Top Ten, as did the singles "Like a Rolling Stone," "Positively 4th Street," and "Rainy Day Women #12 & 35."

The success of the Byrds and Dylan ignited a firestorm of emulators and imitators. The Lovin' Spoonful, from Dylan's own stomping ground of Greenwich Village, were the era's greatest exponents of good-time folk-rock; the Mamas & the Papas, led by ex-folkie John Phillips, were at the head of a slickly produced L.A. variation of the sound; Sonny & Cher, the most commercial of the bunch, latched on to a few of folk-rock's most saleable attributes on their first batch of smashes, and went on to highly successful careers in pop's mainstream. Donovan, one of the most talented mid-'60s folkies to follow in Dylan's footsteps, went not only electric, but psychedelic. Producers added 12-string guitars and a rhythm section to an old track by Simon & Garfunkel; after "Sounds of Silence" became a #1 hit, the duo became one of the most successful folk-rock acts of all. Obscure regional groups like the Leaves (from L.A.) and the Blue Things (from Kansas) recorded some wonderful folk-rock singles and even albums that were in the same class as the hits by the top folk-rock stars.

The "rock" in folk-rock was always more prominent than the "folk"; all of the above acts had a highly commercial sense of melody, grafting guitar patterns and somewhat more personal, topical lyrical concerns from folk music into their own superb pop/rock creations. Performers approaching the hybrid from the folk side were less frequent and less commercially successful, but singer/songwriters like Fred Neil, Phil Ochs, Gordon Lightfoot, Ian & Sylvia, Richard & Mimi Farina, and others proved willing and able to electrify their sound with positive commercial and artistic results.

Folk-rock was not only a tremendous success on the charts in 1965 and 1966, but tremendously influential in expanding the sonic and lyrical vistas of rock as a whole. The Beatles were already addressing more personal concerns on the mid-1965 tunes "Help" and "You've Got to Hide Your Love Away"; *Rubber Soul*, issued at the end of the year, was one of folk-rock's greatest triumphs. Many of the early psychedelic bands from San Francisco were comprised of renegade folkies, and while groups like the Jefferson Airplane and the Beatles themselves would move beyond folk-rock to psychedelia fairly quickly, there's no doubt that folk-rock whetted their appetites for lyrical and instrumental experimentation and innovation.

While folk-rock's commercial heyday was in 1965 and 1966, in truth it has been a strong presence in rock ever since, fading only as a marketing term for a sound that was initially perceived by the industry as a fad, not a permanent addition to the rock & roll lexicon. In 1967, L.A. bands Buffalo Springfield and Love would release classic recordings that drew upon folk-rock as their core, adding elements of eclecticism and psychedelia. In the late '60s, British groups like Fairport Convention and Pentangle achieved perhaps the purest folk-rock blend, with nearly equal balances between the electric and the acoustic, and between modern compositions and traditional numbers. The singer/songwriter movement of the late '60s and early '70s was not as prone to electric guitars and group ensembles, perhaps, but also took folk-rock as its chief inspiration. The harmonies, ringing guitars, and chord patterns of classic folk-rock live on in countless contemporary acts, ranging from bands like R.E.M. to singers like Tracy Chapman.

15 Essential Recordings:

The Byrds, *Mr. Tambourine Man* (Columbia)
The Byrds, *Greatest Hits* (Columbia)
Bob Dylan, *Blonde on Blonde* (Columbia)
Bob Dylan, *Highway 61 Revisited* (Columbia)
The Lovin' Spoonful, *Anthology* (Rhino)
The Beatles, *Rubber Soul* (Capitol)
Donovan, *Troubadour: The Definitive Collection 1964-1976* (Epic)
Simon & Garfunkel, *Collected Works* (Columbia)
Buffalo Springfield, *Buffalo Springfield* (1973 double-LP compilation) (Atco)
Love, *Forever Changes* (Elektra)
The Mamas & The Papas, *Creeque Alley* (MCA)
The Blue Things, *Story Vol. 1-3* (Cicadelic)
The Beau Brummels, *Best of the Beau Brummels* (Rhino)
Richard & Mimi Farina, *The Best of Richard & Mimi Farina* (Vanguard)
The Leaves, *1966* (Panda)

BOOK

Timeless Flight: The Definitive Biography of the Byrds, by Johnny Rogan (Square One, U.K., 1990)

– Richie Unterberger

Garage Rock

For those who prize adolescent, primitive energy as one of rock & roll's best features, the garage rock bands of the '60s rank at or near the top of the rock & roll pyramid. Ignored or even scorned by critics in its heyday, garage rock proved an influential inspiration for the punk rock explosion of the '70s, and experienced a renaissance of sorts in the '80s, among the rock underground and collector community if nowhere else.

Largely a North American phenomenon, the garage band movement began in the wake of the British Invasion in 1964. There were already plenty of young, White rock groups throughout the U.S., but they were usually found playing instrumental (sometimes surf) rock or heavily R&B-influenced "frat rock," and were largely unconcerned with writing their own songs or making individualistic, rebellious statements. The Beatles, Rolling Stones, Kinks, Animals, and others changed that overnight. Caught off-guard by this unexpected onslaught, teenage groups put the focus on loud electric guitars and grew their hair long in attempts to emulate their heroes.

What emerged was a distinctly cruder and more adolescent variation on the British Invasion sound (which itself had been largely inspired by American rock and R&B in the first place). It is not accurate to say that the garage groups matched the talents of their British idols, or of American outfits like the Byrds; they were usually considerably younger and less sophisticated, and lacked the songwriting skills or instrumental finesse of the era's major groups. By way of compensation, perhaps, they placed a premium on sheer outrageousness: over-the-top vocal screams and sneers fought it out with loud guitars that almost always had a fuzztone attached. Garage bands were so named after the habitual practice space of the musicians, who were overwhelmingly White, suburban, and teenaged. While scattered 1964 recordings by groups like the Gestures and the Barbarians served as early blueprints for the sound, it didn't blanket the country properly until 1965, when virtually every major city (and many minor ones) became home to dozens of new guitar groups hungering for

a piece of the action – which meant parties, girls and, of course, records.

These records were usually pressed on tiny local labels, and usually only heard within a 50-100 mile radius (if they were heard on local radio at all). Occasionally they were picked up for nationwide distribution by a larger company; more occasionally still, they became bonafide national hits. The Shadows of Knight, the Count Five, the 13th Floor Elevators, the Standells, the Seeds, ? & the Mysterians, and the Gentrys were among the lucky few who hit this jackpot, although their time in the spotlight was brief.

An enormous amount of records were released by garage bands in the '60s, particularly between 1965 and 1967. California and Texas were probably home to more of these bands per capita than any other state, but the number of groups that recorded, let alone played, was staggering. Detroit, Boston, Chicago, Minneapolis, Seattle, Pittsburgh, Cleveland, Phoenix; they were all home to large local scenes supporting several dozens of bands, much in the manner of today's alternative rock and punk communities.

There are a great many generic garage band recordings: fuzzy variations of the "Satisfaction" or "You Really Got Me" riffs, inept guitar solos, cheesy organ riffs, simplistic lyrics about cheating girlfriends; and there are also many great garage band records by bands that combined their energy with sharp songwriting skills, compelling hooks, or sheer unpredictable mania.

The Texas bands favored galloping rhythms with bigger-than-life fuzztones; the California bands often copped folk-rock and psychedelic licks from their own local heroes; Midwest groups sometimes drew upon trends in soul music; New England groups were more prone to use Zombies-like keyboards and melodies; Cleveland acts showed a strong affinity for Merseybeat and British power-pop. But the bands from these far-flung territories had a lot more in common than not; all of them kept abreast of the latest trends in British rock, folk-rock, and psychedelic music.

A number of factors conspired to slow the momentum of the garage phenomenon around 1967 and 1968. Facing college, lack of national success and, worst of all, the military draft, many of the bands simply didn't stay together for very long. Increasingly homogenous national radio airplay and distribution meant less of a chance for regional labels to succeed or get their records played, and hence less opportunities for local talent to enter the studio. And the fact was, a lot of the garage bands were outgrowing the pop/rock of the first wave of the British Invasion, and moving – as their inspirations were – toward more progressive and psychedelic sounds, with lyrics that, for better or worse, addressed more mature concerns than picking up girls and adolescent rebellion.

Almost immediately forgotten by rock historians, garage music began its comeback when future Patti Smith Group guitarist Lenny Kaye compiled the original *Nuggets* album in 1972. This double set featured the most popular garage band recordings by the likes of the Standells, Seeds, Chocolate Watch Band, and others; Kaye helped coin the term "punk rock" in his liner notes, in reference to bands such as these that celebrated rock & roll at its most primal and unself conscious. Adding a measure of contemporary lyrical content and attitude, bands like the Sex Pistols would embellish this prototype and give birth to modern punk rock a few years later.

The *Pebbles* series of the late '70s took the *Nuggets* approach several steps further, unearthing even rarer and rawer garage band recordings from across the nation. Eventually numbering dozens of volumes, *Pebbles* in turn kicked off a deluge of '60s garage band reissues and compilations; often great, sometimes awful, these numbered in the hundreds by the late '80s. Contemporary groups like the Fuzztones, the Pandoras, Thee Fourgiven, and dozens of others played garage revival music in the 1980s, though in truth they never approached the authentic qualities of the best of the '60s garage bands, and never made a significant impact on either the mainstream or underground rock scenes.

The reissues introduced young and old listeners to scores of fine bands, ironically giving them their greatest international exposure decades after they broke up. Some, like the Remains or the Music Machine, were arguably too talented and innovative to be lumped in with the garage crowd in the first place. Others, like Zakary Thaks, the Chocolate Watch Band, and the Rising Storm, personified teenage rock & roll at its most enjoyable. All of the above-mentioned groups – and quite a few others – were nearly as good as the more accomplished and more famous British and

Music Map

Garage Rock

Instrumental and Surf Groups	British Invasion Groups	Frat Rock Groups
The Ventures, Dick Dale, The Trashmen, The Astronauts	The Beatles, The Rolling Stones, The Animals, The Kinks, The Yardbirds	The Kingsmen, the Rivieras

Early Garage Bands
The Gestures, the Barbarians, the Chartbusters

British Pop-Rock Influenced Garage Bands	Raunchy R&B-Influenced Garage Bands
The Remains, New Colony Six	The Chocolate Watchband, The Standells, The Shadows of Knight, The Count Five

Garage Psychedelia
The Music Machine, The Electric Prunes, The Seeds, The 13th Floor Elevators

---

American hitmaking bands of the era, and deserve belated recognition as first-rate '60s rock & rollers.

13 Essential Records

Various Artists, *Nuggets Vol. 1-12* (Rhino)
Various Artists, *Pebbles Vol. 1-10* (AIP)
The New Colony Six, *At the River's Edge* (Sundazed)
The Chocolate Watch Band, *Best of the Chocolate Watch Band* (Rhino)
The Standells, *Best of the Standells* (Rhino)
Zakary Thaks, *Texas Band* (Moxie)
The Music Machine, *Best of the Music Machine* (Rhino)
The Rising Storm, *Calm Before* (Arf Arf)
The Remains, *The Remains* (Epic)
We the People, *Declaration of Independence* (Eva, France)
The Shadows of Knight, *Dark Sides: The Best of the Shadows of Knight* (Rhino)
The Mystic Tide, *Solid Sound* (Distortions)
The Lemon Drops, *Crystal Pure* (Cicadelic)

– Richie Unterberger

Stax/Volt and Southern Soul

Aside from Motown, the Memphis-based Stax label (along with its Volt subsidiary) was the most successful and influential soul record company of the '60s. The comparison shouldn't be taken too far: Motown was far more successful than Stax/Volt, which didn't cross over into the pop market nearly as heavily as its Detroit-based competition. In its salad days, the Stax/Volt sound was nearly as identifiable as Motown, and embodied many of the most distinguishing traits of southern soul, or "deep" soul, as it's sometimes called.

Stax was founded in the early '60s by Jim Stewart and his sister Estelle Axton, shortly after they'd taken teenaged Carla Thomas (daughter of R&B-legend Rufus Thomas) into the Top Ten on the Satellite label with the early soul ballad "Gee Whiz." In the Thomases, Stax already had a couple of first-class R&B/soul singers who would score consistent hits into the early '70s. The next Top Ten hit on Stax, the Mar-Keys' instrumental "Last Night," was a breakthrough on a couple of levels. The combination of sleek horn lines, sharp guitar licks, and organ was a blueprint for the Stax soul sound; equally important, some of the Mar-Keys' members eventually formed the nucleus of Booker T. & the MGs, which virtually became Stax's house band for the next decade.

The MGs also ran off a series of instrumental hits that made them stars in their own right. On these, you can hear the sound of Memphis soul stripped down to its essence: the bluesy, surgeon-sharp leads and chords of guitarist Steve Cropper, the choked organ of Booker T. Jones, and the super-tight rhythm section of Duck Dunn and the late Al Jackson. When they played ses-

sions, they were often augmented by the Memphis Horns, whose similarly spare but beefy riffs also came to characterize the Stax/Volt sound. In contrast to the brilliant assembly-line precision of the Motown factory, the Memphis studios created a looser and funkier groove, a reflection of the more casual atmosphere of both the control room and the region itself.

The instrumental backing was just one key part of the Stax/Volt-Memphis equation. The material, penned by such greats as David Porter and Isaac Hayes, had much more of a country influence than most '60s soul. Mind you, you'd never mistake it for Grand Ole Opry fodder, but the melodies, chord changes, and plaintive, emotive tone of much of the material betrayed the melting pot of Black and White southern influences, even in a society as segregated as the American South was in the 1960s. Memphis had been an important blues center for decades, and that influence was also apparent in both the material and the arrangements (with bluesman Albert King, Stax/Volt would successfully merge blues and soul). And the vocals betrayed a strong gospel feel – not that gospel wasn't strongly felt in the soul being produced everywhere else in the United States as well.

Stax/Volt releases were hugely successful on the R&B and soul charts, but not nearly as big with White pop audiences, though the label had plenty of Top 40 entries throughout the '60s. Several possible explanations could be offered for this: the Stax/Volt sound was certainly grittier, slower, and more R&B-based than the most successful pop-soul of the period; Stax/Volt performers were certainly heroes to many White rock musicians, from the Rolling Stones on down; and a 1967 tour of Europe by the Stax/Volt Revue (documented on several recordings) was a huge success, enabling the musicians to realize for the first time just how much of an impact they were making internationally.

The sessionmen and songwriters were crucial cogs in the Stax/Volt machine, but as with Motown, one shouldn't overlook the fact that the singers were the most important factor. Carla Thomas, Rufus Thomas, as well as names which are revered nowadays mostly by hardcore soul fans, such as Johnnie Taylor, Eddie Floyd, and William Bell, all made the songs their own (and often wrote the songs as well). The most popular Stax/Volt acts of the mid-'60s were Sam & Dave, who brought the gospel elements of Memphis soul to the forefront, and Otis Redding, one of the most revered vocalists in rock and soul history. Redding, already a soul superstar, seemed poised for a breakthrough to wide pop stardom after a hugely successful appearance at the Monterey Pop Festival in 1967. It happened, but only after Redding's death, in the wake of which "Dock of the Bay" – a classic which pointed to new introspective and personal directions for both Redding and Stax/Volt – went to number one in early 1968.

Redding's death notwithstanding, Stax/Volt seemed poised to enter an era of great prosperity in the late '60s, but the empire became unraveled in a series of mammoth mishaps which ranks among the most tragic stories in the rock business. In 1968, Stax/Volt ended its partnership with Atlantic, opting for bigger corporate distribution. Atlantic, which had arranged for Wilson Pickett to record a clutch of mid-'60s classics at Stax's studios that were Stax/Volt recordings in all but name, took the Redding and Sam & Dave catalogs with them.

Stax, frustrated by the economics of leasing studio facilities to outside labels and performers, had already restricted itself to in-house projects in 1966. Atlantic's Jerry Wexler responded by approximating the Stax sound (extremely successfully, from both aesthetic and commercial viewpoints) at other southern studios, including Fame and Muscle Shoals in Alabama, and Criteria in Miami. Mid- and late-'60s classics by Atlantic artists such as Percy Sledge, Arthur Conley, Aretha Franklin, and others may not be Stax/Volt recordings, but sonically they would certainly fit comfortably into the label's vision.

Stax continued to score hits well into the 1970s with a vast roster, including several of their most dependable '60s performers, and new additions such as the Staple Singers and Isaac Hayes. With the dissolution of Booker T. & the MGs, the Stax sound grew more diffuse, though it retained much of its earthy identity. But in the mid-'70s, Stax ran into a quagmire of financial troubles that are too labyrinthine to detail in less than a few pages. In early 1976, the label was shut down by order of a federal bankruptcy judge.

Stax/Volt, incidentally, didn't have a monopoly on Memphis soul. The small Goldwax label issued releases in the '60s that are coveted by deep soul collectors, particularly those by James Carr, esteemed by some cultists as one of the greatest soul vocalists ever. As noted above, the sound of Stax/Volt was successfully emulated and recreated at other studios. And in the early '70s, Hi Records, featuring the Hi Rhythm Section and, often, musicians who had played at Stax/Volt (such as the Memphis Horns), established itself as a major source of the era's best funky soul. Al Green was the label's only superstar, but other Hi performers like Ann Peebles and Syl Johnson enjoyed a lot of success with the soul audience with recordings that are usually judged superior to the ones issued by Stax/Volt in the early '70s.

When Stax/Volt shut its doors, though, it was a major blow to the city's music scene, eliminating a prime source of work and inspiration for many of the city's brightest talents (some of whom had moved on to other music centers anyway). Arguably, it's a blow from which the region has yet to recover; since the advent of Sun Records, Memphis had been a central location for much of rock, R&B, and soul's finest moments, but today it's somewhat of a musical ghost town in terms of local production. The Stax/Volt story is exhaustively detailed in the liner notes of the three Stax/Volt box sets, and journalist Rob Bowman is currently working on a book about the label.

12 Essential Recordings

Various Artists, *The Complete Stax/Volt Soul Singles Vol. 1 1959-1968* (Atlantic)
Various Artists, *The Complete Stax/Volt Soul Singles Vol. 2 1968-1971* (Stax)
Various Artists, *The Complete Stax/Volt Soul Singles Vol. 3 1972-1975* (Stax)
Booker T. & the MGs, *The Very Best of Booker T. & the MGs* (Rhino)
Carla Thomas, *Gee Whiz: The Best of Carla Thomas* (Rhino)
Otis Redding, *Otis! The Definitive Otis Redding* (Rhino)
Wilson Pickett, *The Exciting Wilson Pickett* (Atlantic)
Sam & Dave, *Sweat 'N' Soul* (Rhino/Atlantic)
Johnnie Taylor, *Chronicle* (Stax)
James Carr, *Essential James Carr* (Razor & Tie)
Al Green, *Greatest Hits* (Hi)
Various Artists, *Hi Times: The Hi Records R&B Years* (The Right Stuff)

– *Richie Unterberger*

Blue-Eyed Soul

"Can White men sing the blues?" That's been a point of contention in the worlds of rock and soul since White musicians began singing music with heavy debts to rhythm and blues. White attempts to sing African-American-derived music have often been embarrassing (if sometimes touching in their naiveté). But at the same time, some Whites have crossed into the world of R&B and soul with a natural ease that proves that music, like all good

Stax/Volt-Memphis Soul

Early Stax/Volt Stars
Carla Thomas, Rufus Thomas, Booker T. & The MGs

Stars of Stax/ Volt's Prime
Otis Redding, Sam & Dave, Albert King, Eddie Floyd, Johnnie Taylor, William Bell

'60s Stars Inspired By Stax/Volt	**'70s Stax/Volt Stars**	**Goldwax**
Wilson Pickett, Percy Sledge, Arthur Conley, Aretha Franklin	Isaac Hayes, The Staple Singers, The Bar-Kays	James Car

Hi Records
Al Green, Ann Peebles, Syl Johnson

things in life, is color-blind. During soul music's heyday, a handful of Whites handled the challenge with confidence, giving rise to the relatively small but important subgenre of soul music called blue-eyed soul.

The roots of blue-eyed soul could probably be traced back as far as Elvis Presley's legendary Sun singles, on which he masterfully interpreted a handful of blues and R&B classics. It can also be detected in the many Italian-American doo wop singers during that music's last phase, as well as early '60s acts like Dion and the Four Seasons, who borrowed heavily from R&B phrasing and harmonies.

The first of the classic blue-eyed soul acts, and one which was instrumental to defining the genre, was the Righteous Brothers. Hailing from Orange County, CA, of all places, Bill Medley and Bobby Hatfield looked very White, but sounded Black. After teaming up with Phil Spector in the mid-'60s, they reeled off a brief string of huge hits that were as soaked with gospel feeling as any African-American soul, but the group was unable to maintain their artistic or commercial momentum after their association with Spector ended.

The most successful blue-eyed soul group of the '60s was the Rascals. Young veterans of New York's Italian-American rock & roll scene, they flavored their strong (and mostly original) material with horns, harmonies, and a touch of British Invasion energy. Although they worked within the self-contained rock band format, playing their own instruments and writing their own songs, their sound owed as much, if not more, to soul as '60s rock trends. They were also one of the relatively few blue-eyed soul acts to successfully change with the times, writing increasingly reflective and sophisticated material, culminating with the rabble-rousing anthem "People Got to Be Free" in 1968.

Blue-eyed soul acts tended to spring up around regions with active soul scenes. Detroit's biggest contribution to the genre was Mitch Ryder and the Detroit Wheels, who served up some of the sweatiest soul-rock hybrids ever waxed. Motown couldn't help but influence a lot of the city's White rock and garage bands, and the Motor City sound is reflected in the fine regional Michigan rock hits of the time by the Rationals and Bob Seger.

White southern performers also absorbed the inflections of deep soul into their own earthy sounds. John Fred and Tony Joe White displayed the influence of New Orleans and Louisiana R&B and soul in their brand of swamp pop; Bill Deal and the Rhondels played a kind of soul frat-rock that drew from the "beach music" cult of the Carolinas; Roy Head drew upon the melting pot of Texas blues and R&B for one of the mid-'60s best one-shot hits, "Treat Her Right." In Memphis, Dan Penn, a White Alabaman who helped write many great deep soul records, produced hits by the

Music Map

Blue-Eyed Soul

R&B	Early Soul

Blue-Eyed Soul Forerunners
Dion, The 4 Seasons

Blue-Eyed Soul Stars
The Righteous Brothers, The Rascals

Detroit Blue-Eyed Soul Mitch Ryder, The Rationals	**Southern Blue-Eyed Soul** The Boxtops, John Fred, Roy Head, Tony Joe White, Bill Deal & The Rhondels	**British Blue-Eyed Soul** Georgie Fame, Dusty Springfield

Blue-Eyed Soul of the '70s
Hall & Oates, The Average White Band,
Robert Palmer, Boz Scaggs

Box Tops; teenage lead singer Alex Chilton's vocals were so unnaturally gravelly that many listeners were convinced he was Black. In Los Angeles, there were several Latin soul-rock-R&B acts, the best of which was Thee Midniters (although the group also played convincing Rolling Stones-styled garage rock).

The line between R&B-influenced rock & roll and blue-eyed soul is a thin one that was skirted by many of the British Invasion's finest performers. Certainly Eric Burdon (of the Animals), Stevie Winwood (of the Spencer Davis Group and Traffic), and Van Morrison were extremely soulful singers, even if their material and the sound of their backing groups were more rock-oriented than classic soul grooves. Georgie Fame probably fit the classic blue-eyed soul mold more than any other British Invasion performer, although he also owed quite a bit to Mose Allison's brand of jazz. Dusty Springfield was the best female blue-eyed soul singer of the '60s, though she also sang girl group, rock, and pop ballad material; at the end of the '60s, she traveled to Stax studios in Memphis to cut *Dusty in Memphis*, considered by many listeners to be one of the finest White soul albums of all time.

It's worth pointing out that many classic soul records of the '60s by Black performers featured White musicians. Booker T. & the MGs, an integrated ensemble featuring the economic, biting licks of White guitarist Steve Cropper, played on most of the great Stax/Volt soul hits of the '60s, as well as cutting a lot of instrumental soul smashes on their own. Stax/Volt's strongest rival in the field of deep southern soul was the Muscle Shoals Studio in Alabama, which also featured White musicians on many of their sessions, backing soul greats from Aretha Franklin on down. Duane Allman may be mostly known for helping to found southern rock with the Allman Brothers, but he also played guitar on sessions by Franklin, Wilson Pickett, Clarence Carter, and King Curtis.

The heyday of blue-eyed soul, like soul music itself, was in the 1960s; after that decade, it was a more scattered presence, although acts like Hall & Oates, the Average White Band, Boz Scaggs, Robert Palmer, David Bowie (in one of his many phases), the latter-day Bee Gees, and Billy Swan all carried the blue-eyed soul torch to large degrees. Contemporary acts like Michael Bolton and George Michael have also been labeled as blue-eyed soul, although their material owes more to classic MOR pop than the original pioneers of the style.

10 Essential Albums

Various Artists, *Soul Shots Vol. 6: Blue-Eyed Soul* (Rhino)

The Righteous Brothers, *Anthology 1962-74* (Rhino)
The Rascals, *Anthology (1965-1972)* (Rhino)
Mitch Ryder, *Rev-Up: The Best of Mitch Ryder & the Detroit Wheels* (Rhino)
The Box Tops, *Ultimate Box Tops* (Warner Brothers)
Dusty Springfield, *Dusty in Memphis* (Rhino)
John Fred & the Playboys, *The History of John Fred & the Playboys* (Paula)
Tony Joe White, *The Best of Tony Joe White* (Warner)
Georgie Fame, *20 Beat Classics* (RSO)
Thee Midniters, *The Best of Thee Midniters* (Rhino)
– *Richie Unterberger*

Psychedelic Rock

Psychedelia represented rock & roll at its most breathtakingly adventurous and innovative – and sometimes, at its most foolish. While the most self-conscious experiments of the mid- and late '60s have dated badly, the best psychedelic rock had an exhilarating recklessness that has been difficult to recapture in the ensuing decades.

Psychedelic music was fed by many sources. The desire to replicate a drug-altered state in sound is its most sensational feature. But the musicians who pioneered psychedelia were equally driven by a hunger to expand rock's boundaries and enhance its eclecticism by incorporating influences from Middle Eastern music and improvisational jazz. This went hand-in-hand with exploring the frontiers of amplified sound and instrumental textures (primarily on the electric guitar), as well as lyrics that addressed the burning social and psychological issues of the day.

Trying to pin down the first psychedelic record is nearly as elusive as trying to name the first rock & roll record. Far fetched claims have been advanced for songs ranging from the Tornados' futuristic 1962 #1 instrumental "Telstar" to the Dave Clark Five's massively reverb-laden "Any Way You Want It." In 1964, the Beatles introduced guitar feedback on "I Feel Fine"; a year later, they introduced the sitar to rock on "Norwegian Wood." But two groups from different sides of the Atlantic with somewhat similar names, the Yardbirds and the Byrds, were really the most responsible for sounding the psychedelic siren.

With their ominous minor key melodies, hyperactive instrumental breaks (called "rave-ups"), unpredictable tempo changes, and use of Gregorian chants (most notably on the single "Still I'm Sad"), the Yardbirds helped define the manic eclecticism that would characterize early psychedelic rock. Jeff Beck's fuzzy, distorted guitar sustain laid the blueprint for psychedelic guitar.

Their early '66 hit "Shapes of Things" was arguably the first out-and-out psychedelic rock song, with its blistering feedback breaks, veering tempos, and stream-of-consciousness lyrics that owed nothing to traditional romantic themes. The Yardbirds' psychedelic peak was brief, but subsequent 1966 recordings – "Over Under Sideways Down" and "Happenings Ten Years Time Ago" especially – found them approximating speed-of-light trips, drug-induced or otherwise, with nervy but taut daring.

Just a couple months after "Shapes of Things," the Byrds flew into uncharted territory with "Eight Miles High." While the group always claimed that the title referred to an airplane flight, the impressionistic lyrics were taken by many to reflect the psychedelic drug experience, while the furious guitar and bass breaks illustrated the group's assimilation of John Coltrane's free jazz and Ravi Shankar's Indian music. The single's B-side ("Why") and many of the songs on their 1966 album *Fifth Dimension* crashed through similar sonic frontiers. Although the Byrds would trade in their spacesuits for cowboy threads in just a couple of years, they continued to produce exciting psychedelic-influenced music through the end of 1967.

Ideas traveled fast in the crucible of 1966 rock, and within a few months many of the era's top bands were flashing psychedelic colors on their recordings. The Beatles' 1966 single "Rain" used backwards guitars and vocals, and their *Revolver* album was by far their most eclectic pre-'67 work, imbued with churning, distorted guitars, coy references to drug trips, and even quotes from Timothy Leary's version of the *Tibetan Book of the Dead*. The Rolling Stones used the sitar – perhaps to its greatest effect in a rock & roll song – on "Paint It Black," and constructed a dense morass of psychedelic sound and lyrics on "Have You Seen Your Mother, Baby, Standing in the Shadow?" Donovan forsook his

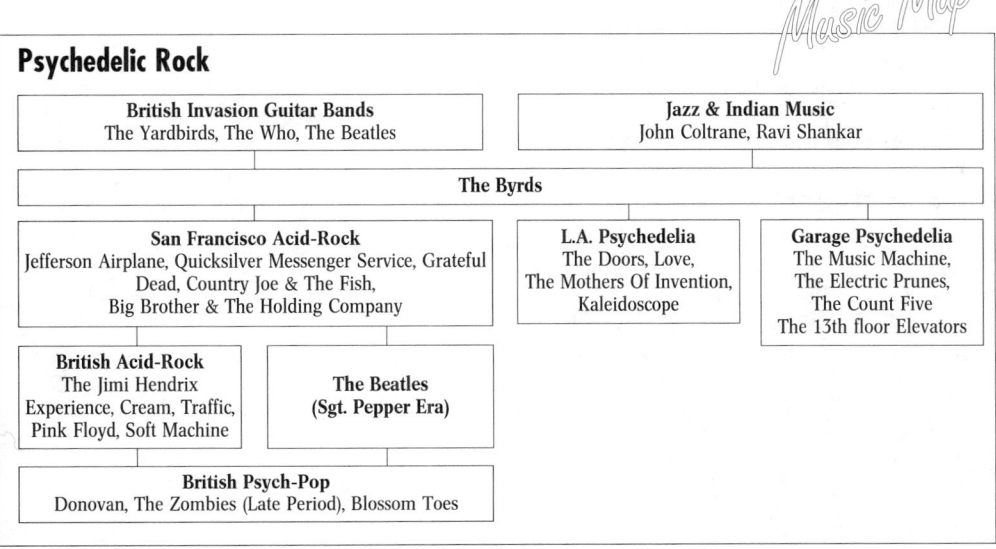

Psychedelic Rock

British Invasion Guitar Bands	Jazz & Indian Music
The Yardbirds, The Who, The Beatles	John Coltrane, Ravi Shankar

The Byrds

San Francisco Acid-Rock	L.A. Psychedelia	Garage Psychedelia
Jefferson Airplane, Quicksilver Messenger Service, Grateful Dead, Country Joe & The Fish, Big Brother & The Holding Company	The Doors, Love, The Mothers Of Invention, Kaleidoscope	The Music Machine, The Electric Prunes, The Count Five The 13th floor Elevators

British Acid-Rock	The Beatles
The Jimi Hendrix Experience, Cream, Traffic, Pink Floyd, Soft Machine	(Sgt. Pepper Era)

British Psych-Pop
Donovan, The Zombies (Late Period), Blossom Toes

---

acoustic guitar for storybook wanderings in densely orchestrated musical arrangements that drew from both Indian sitars and fog-bound British moors. Garage bands, already attuned to distorted guitars via their attempts to emulate the fuzz riffs on Stones classics like "Satisfaction," went the extra nine yards into all-out freakouts on cuts like the Magic Mushrooms' "It's-A-Happening."

In the United States, psychedelic music took root most firmly in California, particularly San Francisco, where an increasingly large bohemian community had been living the psychedelic lifestyle for a year or two before it infiltrated rock & roll. In 1965 and 1966, disaffected folk musicians formed the Grateful Dead, the Jefferson Airplane, the Charlatans, the Great Society, Country Joe & the Fish, Big Brother & the Holding Company, Quicksilver Messenger Service, and many other less famous combos with equally (for the time) outrageous names. It took them a while to get a handle on their electric instruments, as some of their tentative and awkward pre-'67 recordings can attest to. But after honing their chops on the fertile Haight-Ashbury scene, these bands introduced a whole new spacy element into the psychedelic brew with their searing guitars and euphoric melodies.

The British strain of psychedelia tended to be more whimsical and fairytale-ish than the West Coast brand of acid-rock. Ethereal organs and mellotrons often set the tone of the generally more symphonic arrangements; the lyrics, occasionally wry to the point of surrealism, were often populated with eccentric British character types, or took a storybook, child's perspective. The Beatles, brilliant, early '67 "Strawberry Fields"/"Penny Lane" single was the apex of this genre, and newly emerging bands like Pink Floyd and Traffic, as well as less successful but equally intriguing underground acts like the Soft Machine and Tomorrow, also mined this field with great success.

1967's "Summer of Love" was the pinnacle of psychedelic music. The Beatles released their definitive psychedelic statement, *Sgt. Pepper*, the San Francisco groups made an international impact via the Monterey Pop Festival; Pink Floyd, the Jefferson Airplane, and Traffic issued their best psychedelic albums. Jimi Hendrix and Cream became international superstars with guitar-based acid-rock that had its roots in the Yardbirds' innovations. The Doors' first album explored the dark and mysterious crannies of psychedelia with an impact that neither they nor anyone else would match. Even the Rolling Stones joined the psychedelic bandwagon, with an underappreciated LP, *Their Satanic Majesties Request*, that was accused by many of being an ersatz *Sgt. Pepper* despite including several first-rate songs.

Psychedelic music was a strong presence in rock & roll throughout the rest of the '60s, but there's no doubt that the genre

began to become tired and self-indulgent as the decade approached its end. Following the lead, perhaps, of Bob Dylan's calm and simple *John Wesley Harding*, the Beatles, Byrds, and Rolling Stones all released albums in 1968 with a decidedly earthy and back-to-basics tone (although they didn't eschew progressive experiments altogether). Cream, Traffic, and the original Jimi Hendrix Experience broke up; Pink Floyd's leader, Syd Barrett, became the era's first acid casualty after their brilliant debut album; the Doors peaked early and couldn't repeat the fluid consistency of their own debut, despite releasing several worthy attempts. Pre-heavy metal groups like Iron Butterfly and Blue Cheer emulated the roar of psychedelic guitar growl without paying any heed to the style's more subtle attractions. And quite a few groups presented psychedelic clichés – long guitar solos, florid lyrics, effects-happy production – without saying much of anything original.

Many of the trimmings of psychedelic rock would form the backbone of progressive rock and heavy metal, which devoted themselves to the most extreme ends of the genre – ambitious, neo-classical epics on the one hand, mind-melting guitar distortion on the other. While groups ranging from Echo & the Bunnymen to Sonic Youth have (usually erroneously) been termed neo-psychedelic at one time or another, psychedelia has retreated from the front of rock's collective consciousness since about 1970 or so.

In its time, however, the psychedelic sound fueled some of the '60s finest moments, influencing most of the top rock acts to some degree. While groups like the Who, the Beach Boys, Love, and Buffalo Springfield could not exactly be called "psychedelic," some of their finest recordings – "I Can See for Miles," "Good Vibrations," Love's *Forever Changes* LP, Buffalo Springfield's "Expecting to Fly" and "Broken Arrow" – betray a strong psychedelic influence, and could not have been made without the inspiration of their more overtly trippy peers. And the intricate arrangements and heavily amplified/distorted guitars of psychedelic productions broke ground that has been utilized routinely in rock recordings from the late '60s to the present day.

15 Essential Albums

The Beatles, *Sgt. Pepper's Lonely Hearts Club Band* (Capitol)
The Beatles, *Magical Mystery Tour* (Capitol)
The Yardbirds, *Roger the Engineer* (Edsel)
The Byrds, *Fifth Dimension* (Columbia)
The Doors, *The Doors* (Elektra)
The Jefferson Airplane, *Jefferson Airplane Loves You* (RCA)

Pink Floyd, *Piper at the Gates of Dawn* (Capitol)
The Jimi Hendrix Experience, *Are You Experienced?* (Reprise)
The Great Society, *Collector's Item* (Columbia)
The Mothers of Invention, *We're Only in It for the Money* (Rykodisc)
The Rolling Stones, *Their Satanic Majesties Request* (ABKCO)
Donovan, *Sunshine Superman* (Epic)
Cream, *Disraeli Gears* (Polydor)
Traffic, *Mr. Fantasy* (Island)
The Misunderstood, *Before the Dream Faded* (Cherry Red)
– Richie Unterberger

The San Francisco Sound

Since the mid-'60s, the San Francisco Bay Area has produced numerous influential and important groups, both mainstream and underground, popular and obscure. When people talk about "The San Francisco Sound," however, they're usually referring to the psychedelic acid rock played by many of the area's bands in the late '60s. Innovative, indulgent, both innocent and ambitious, these groups spread their bohemian, drug-charged messages of peace, love, and musical freedom throughout the world, and retain a vociferous cult following to this day.

In rock & roll's early days, the Bay Area produced some notable rock & roll and R&B singers, such as Bobby Freeman and Jimmy McCracklin, but it was far from a hotbed of either talent or record production. The first self-contained rock group of note to emerge from the city – and indeed, the first American band of note to successfully emulate the sounds of the British Invasion – were the Beau Brummels, who also helped lay the groundwork for folk-rock with their first-rate songwriting and melodic harmonies.

Usually disdained as a teenybopper group of sorts by the underground rock community that emerged a year or two later, the Beau Brummels in fact could rightfully claim to be the true forefathers of the San Francisco scene. Their minor-key melodies, acoustic/electric guitar blends, and soaring harmonies in particular were adopted as key elements by many of the bands that followed in their wake. Other, more commercial folk-rock acts from the Bay Area, such as the Vejtables and the We Five, also recorded underrated prototypes of the early San Francisco sound, especially in the blend of male and female harmonies, as in the case of the two aforementioned artists.

What made these bands unhip in the eyes of the underground was not so much their sound as their attitude and approach; they had commercial images and aimed for hit singles. In the city's youth culture, particularly in the neighborhood of Haight-Ashbury, a self-consciously bohemian community was emerging, concerned not so much with achieving conventional success as artistic expression, experimental drug use, and the overall exploration of alternatives to "straight" society. The Charlatans are usually credited as the first group to reflect the attitudes of this nascent counterculture.

The Charlatans were much more important as social figures than musical innovators. They helped set the nonconformist standard with their attire and loose attitudes, but musically they offered rather unexceptional material heavy on folk, blues, and jugband influences and were unable to land a record deal until way past their prime. The scene was developing fast, though, and within a matter of months several important groups emerged that placed a far greater primacy on the sustain-laden electric guitars, soaring harmonies, distortion and feedback, Indian and jazz influences, and stoned romantic whimsy that came to characterize the best San Francisco psychedelic rock. The ingredients varied, but overall it could be said that the bands strove to create, often in a drug-influenced fashion, the musical equivalent of the changes that were expanding their social and personal horizons.

The Jefferson Airplane, featuring a staggering array of vocal and instrumental talent and exceptionally strong folk-rock-derived material, were the best of these groups, and the first to become national stars with their 1967 Top Five album *Surrealistic Pillow*, which contained the hits "Somebody to Love" and "White Rabbit." Both were sung by Grace Slick, who had actually left underrated psychedelic pioneers the Great Society to join the Airplane in 1966. Though not as tight instrumentally as the Airplane, the Great Society featured equally innovative material that made effective, often thrilling use of raga-like guitar lines and improvisations. Grace Slick sung both "White Rabbit" and "Somebody to Love" with the group before jumping ship for the Airplane; the

Music Map

The San Francisco Sound

| San Francisco Folk Rock |
| The Beau Brummels, The Vejtables, We Five |

| Early San Francisco Psychedelic Bands |
| The Great Society, The Mystery Trend, The Charlatans |

| San Francisco Acid Rock Stars |
| The Jefferson Airplane, Big Brother & The Holding Company, Quicksilver Messenger Service, Country Joe & The Fish, The Grateful Dead, Moby Grape, The Steve Miller Band |

Late '60s San Francisco Psychedelia	Non-Acid Rock '60s San Francisco-Area Rock Superstars
Santana, Mad River It's A Beautiful Day, Lee Michaels	Sly & The Family Stone, Creedence Clearwater Revival

Society immediately disbanded, though their legacy is preserved on a couple posthumous albums of live material.

In 1966, several groups following the Airplane model began to achieve considerable popularity on the local circuit. The only one to rise to a comparable level of international fame (and then only briefly) was Big Brother and the Holding Company, who would have most likely been also-rans in the psychedelic sweepstakes if not for the addition of Janis Joplin as their lead vocalist. Their (more particularly, Joplin's) electrifying appearance at the Monterey Pop Festival in 1967 vaulted them to stardom almost overnight, but they had trouble both getting along and penning first-rate material, and Joplin left the group to go solo shortly after *Cheap Thrills* topped the charts in 1968.

The Monterey Pop Festival acted as a general lightning rod in drawing attention to the exploding San Francisco scene, which peaked in the summer of 1967, known as "The Summer of Love." Several of the bands performing at the festival had already commanded huge local followings before committing their work to vinyl. The Grateful Dead and Quicksilver Messenger Service specialized in both blues-rock and improvised jams; both featured virtuoso instrumentalists (particularly lead guitarists Jerry Garcia of the Dead and John Cippolina of Quicksilver), but neither had consistently first-rate material or vocalists. They, and several other San Francisco groups, found it nearly impossible to duplicate their live magic on record, and their late-'60s albums can sound kind of pale and tame in comparison to the glowing memories of their live performances.

A few other major groups of the era took much tighter approaches to their songwriting and recording, without forsaking the loose and joyful ambience that ranked as the San Francisco sound's most ingratiating trait. Country Joe & the Fish wrote both sharp political satire and druggy anthems, although they exhausted their supply of first-rate original material after their fine 1967 debut. Moby Grape was probably the tightest act of the era, at least initially, with three guitarists and five competent songwriters; their debut was an acclaimed collection of fiery straightahead rock with heavy blues and country influences, but they lost their momentum almost immediately after severe internal disputes and external pressures. The Steve Miller Band, initially the most blues-oriented of the area's acts, made its mark with psychedelic-tinged, bluesy late-'60s rock.

In addition to all of these internationally acclaimed bands were several acts that tapped into the San Francisco vibe with erratic, at times enthralling, results. It's a Beautiful Day, Mother Earth, and Lee Michaels (the last of whom is not always strictly identified with the scene) made worthwhile recordings; other decent acts such as the Other Half, Mad River, the Mystery Trend, and

Frumious Bandersnatch are nowadays known only to record collectors and those who saw them in their heyday. Sly & the Family Stone and Creedence Clearwater Revival were both superstars, and both plugged into the progressive elements of the San Francisco sound to some extent, but they were never really considered a big part of it; Sly & the Family Stone drew upon soul as much as psychedelia, and Creedence played rock in a much more classic and economic tradition. And there were many obscure bands who played the city's live circuit, or released a record or two of sloppy loud guitars, half-baked psychedelic songwriting, and boring jams, and are deservedly forgotten.

The golden glow of the San Francisco sound began to rapidly dissipate in the late '60s, principally due to the mundane reasons that erode many important rock genres. Some of the era's best groups, such as the Airplane, Moby Grape, Quicksilver, and Big Brother, suffered important personnel losses, ran short of inspiration and top-flight material, and eventually broke up. Haight-Ashbury, originally a haven for youths seeking alternatives to corrupt mainstream society, suffered heavily from some of the same ills as the larger community, such as excessive drug use, crime, and poverty. The bohemian musicians that had emerged from such communities to become stars no longer lived in the neighborhood, and fresh talent didn't emerge to replenish them. The city's live circuit of psychedelic concerts, spearheaded by Chet Helms and Bill Graham, also dried up, fundamentally changing the intimate performer-audience relationships that helped make the scene special.

Santana, which combined psychedelic rock with Afro-Latin influences, was the last superstar group to emerge from the San Francisco psychedelic community. By the early '70s, it was basically over, though of course a few of the genre's pioneers – such as Santana, the Grateful Dead, and Steve Miller – enjoyed long, successful, and increasingly mainstream careers. The San Francisco sound was a vital cog in the best psychedelic rock, and, along with the best British Invasion and folk-rock groups, was crucial in establishing rock as a vehicle for literate, self-consciously adventurous expression that drew from all manner of musical and social influences.

12 Essential Recordings

Various Artists, *Nuggets Vol. 7: Early San Francisco* (Rhino)
The Beau Brummels, *Best of the Beau Brummels* (Rhino)
The Charlatans, *Alabama Bound* (Eva, France)
The Jefferson Airplane, *Jefferson Airplane Loves You* (RCA)
The Great Society, *Collector's Item* (Columbia)
Janis Joplin, *Janis* (Columbia/Legacy) (box set, includes recordings with Big Brother & the Holding Company)
Country Joe & the Fish, *Electric Music for the Mind and Body* (Vanguard)
Moby Grape, *Vintage: Very Best* (CBS)
Quicksilver Messenger Service, *Quicksilver Messenger Service* (Capitol)
The Grateful Dead, *Live/Dead* (Warner Brothers)
The Steve Miller Band, *Children of the Future* (Capitol)
Santana, *Santana* (Columbia)

BOOKS

Summer of Love, by Joel Selvin (Dutton, 1994)
San Francisco Nights, by Gene Sculatti & Davin Seay (St. Martin's, 1985)
The Haight-Ashbury, by Charles Perry (Rolling Stone Press, 1984)
Grace Slick: The Biography, by Barbara Rowes (Doubleday, 1980)
Pearl: The Obsessions and Passions of Janis Joplin, by Ellis Amburn (Warner Books, 1992)

– Richie Unterberger

Blues Rock

The blues and rock & roll are often divided by the thinnest of margins. Blues, more than any other musical style, influenced the birth of rock & roll, and the amplified electric blues of Chicago, Memphis, and other cities during the 1950s was separated from the new music only by its more traditional chord patterns, cruder production values, and narrower market. The term "blues-rock" came into being only around the mid-'60s, when White musicians infused electric blues with somewhat louder guitars and flashy

images that helped the music make inroads into the White rock audience.

Many of the early blues rockers were British musicians who had been schooled by Alexis Korner. Helping to organize the first overseas tours by many major American bluesmen, Korner – as well as his former boss Chris Barber, and his early collaborator Cyril Davies – was more responsible than any other musician for introducing the blues to Britain. More important, he acted as a mentor to many younger musicians who would form the R&B-oriented wing of the British Invasion, including Jack Bruce, members of Manfred Mann, Eric Clapton, and, most significantly, the Rolling Stones, whose lead vocalist, Mick Jagger, sang with Korner before the Stones were firmly established.

The Rolling Stones featured a wealth of stone cold blues in their early repertoire. They and other British groups like the Yardbirds and Animals brought a faster and brasher flavor to traditional numbers. They quickly branched out from 12-bar blues to R&B, soul, and finally, original material of a much more innovative and rock-oriented nature, without ever losing sight of their blues roots.

Several British acts, however, were more steadfast in their devotion to traditional blues, sacrificing commercial success for purism. These included the early Graham Bond Organisation (which featured future Cream members Jack Bruce and Ginger Baker) and, more significantly, John Mayall's Bluesbreakers. In early 1965, Mayall's group provided a refuge for Eric Clapton, who left the Yardbirds on the eve of international success in protest of their forays into pop/rock. His sole album with Mayall, *Bluesbreakers with Eric Clapton* (1966), was an unexpected Top Ten hit in the U.K. Clapton's lightning fast and fluid leads were vastly influential, both on fellow musicians and in introducing tough electric blues to a wide audience.

While Clapton would rapidly depart the Bluesbreakers to form Cream (which took blues-rock to more amplified and psychedelic levels), Mayall continued to be Britain's foremost exponent of blues-rock, as a bandleader of innumerable Bluesbreakers lineups. Many musicians of note were schooled by Mayall, the most prominent being Clapton's successors, Peter Green and future Rolling Stone Mick Taylor. Like Clapton, Green left Mayall after just one album, forming the first incarnation of Fleetwood Mac with a couple members of Mayall's rhythm section, John McVie and Mick Fleetwood. Under Green's helm, Fleetwood Mac was the finest British blues-rock act of the late '60s. They invested electric Chicago blues with zest and humor, but their own material – featuring Green's icy guitar tone, rich vocals, and personal, often somber lyrics – was more impressive, and extremely successful in Britain, where they racked up several hit albums and singles.

As a bandleader of rotating lineups featuring budding guitar geniuses, Chicago harmonica player Paul Butterfield was Mayall's American counterpart; the two even recorded a rare EP together in the late '60s. The Paul Butterfield Blues Band's first pair of albums featured the sterling guitar duo of Mike Bloomfield and Elvin Bishop, as well as bonafide African-American Chicago bluesmen in the rhythm section. Willing to tackle soul, jazz, and even psychedelic jams in addition to Chicago blues, they were the first American blues-rock band, and perhaps the best.

While blues-rock was less of a commercial or artistic force in the U.S. than the U.K., several other American blues-rockers of note emerged in the '60s. Canned Heat was probably the most successful, reaching the Top 20 with "On the Road Again" and an electric update of an obscure rural blues number, "Going up the Country." Steve Miller played mostly blues, with Barry Goldberg and as the leader of his own band, in his early days before tuning into the psychedelic ethos of his adopted base of San Francisco. Captain Beefheart was briefly a White counterpart to Howlin' Wolf before heading off on a furious avant-garde tangent.

In New York, Bob Dylan used Mike Bloomfield on much of his *Highway 61 Revisited* album, and teamed with the Butterfield Band for his enormously controversial electric appearance at the 1965 Newport Folk Festival. John Hammond recorded blues-rock in the mid-'60s with future members of the Band, and Dion cut some overlooked blues-rock sides after being exposed to classic blues by Hammond's father, the legendary Columbia A&R man John Hammond, Sr. The Blues Project, led by Al Kooper, often reworked blues songs with rock arrangements, although their vision was too eclectic to be pigeonholed as blues-rock, also encompassing folk-rock, pop/rock, and psychedelia.

The influence of the first generation of blues-rockers is evident

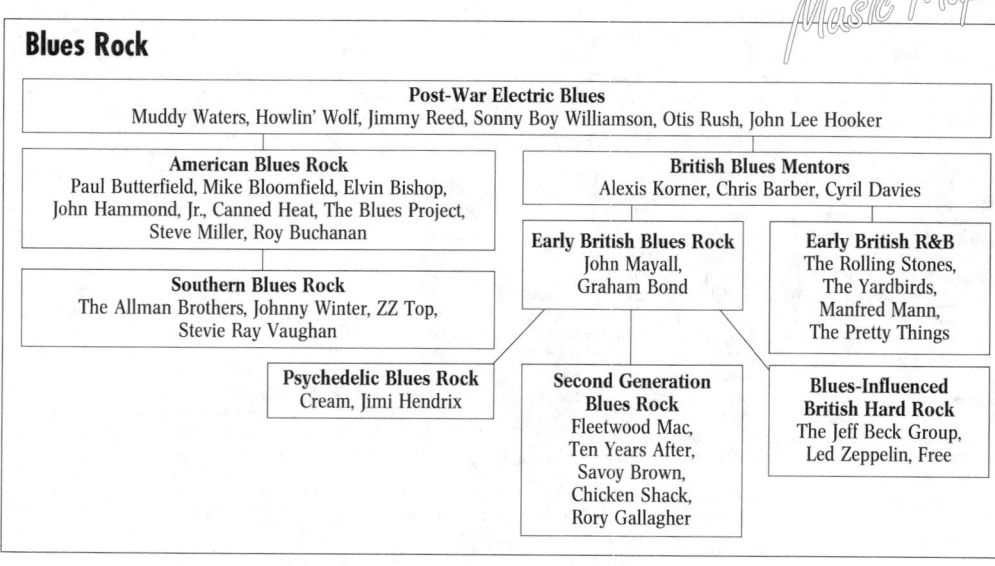

Blues Rock

Post-War Electric Blues
Muddy Waters, Howlin' Wolf, Jimmy Reed, Sonny Boy Williamson, Otis Rush, John Lee Hooker

American Blues Rock
Paul Butterfield, Mike Bloomfield, Elvin Bishop, John Hammond, Jr., Canned Heat, The Blues Project, Steve Miller, Roy Buchanan

British Blues Mentors
Alexis Korner, Chris Barber, Cyril Davies

Early British Blues Rock
John Mayall, Graham Bond

Early British R&B
The Rolling Stones, The Yardbirds, Manfred Mann, The Pretty Things

Southern Blues Rock
The Allman Brothers, Johnny Winter, ZZ Top, Stevie Ray Vaughan

Psychedelic Blues Rock
Cream, Jimi Hendrix

Second Generation Blues Rock
Fleetwood Mac, Ten Years After, Savoy Brown, Chicken Shack, Rory Gallagher

Blues-Influenced British Hard Rock
The Jeff Beck Group, Led Zeppelin, Free

---

in the early recordings of Jimi Hendrix, and indeed Jimi always had a strong element of the blues in his material.

Albert King and B.B. King couldn't exactly be called blues-rockers, but their late '60s material betrays contemporary influences from the worlds of rock and soul that found them leaning more in that direction. Early hard rock bands like Led Zeppelin, Free, and the Jeff Beck Group played a great deal of blues, though not enough for purists to consider them actual blues acts.

The blues-rock form became more pedestrian and boogie-oriented as the '60s came to a close. From Britain, Ten Years After, Savoy Brown, the Climax Blues Band, Rory Gallagher, Chicken Shack, Juicy Lucy, and Foghat all achieved some success. In the U.S., blues-rock was the cornerstone of the Allman Brothers' innovative early '70s recordings (which in turn spawned the blues-influenced school of southern rock), and Johnny Winter had success with a much more traditional approach.

While blues-rock hasn't been a major commercial force since the late '60s, the style has spawned some hugely successful acts, like ZZ Top and Foghat, as well as influencing all hard rock since the late '60s to some degree. The success of Stevie Ray Vaughan in the 1980s, and groups like Blues Traveler and Spin Doctors in the 1990s, shows that its audience is far from dead. And it is a cliché, but it is often true, that many White listeners would be unaware of Black blues performers if they hadn't been led to them through the work of White blues-rock bands.

12 Essential Recordings

John Mayall, *Bluesbreakers with Eric Clapton* (PolyGram)
John Mayall, *London Blues (1964-1969)* (PolyGram)
The Paul Butterfield Blues Band, *East-West* (Elektra)
Fleetwood Mac, *Black Magic Woman* (Epic)
Fleetwood Mac, *Then Play On* (Reprise)
Jimi Hendrix, *Blues* (MCA)
The Graham Bond Organisation, *The Sound of '65* (Edsel)
Canned Heat, *Best of Canned Heat* (EMI)
Cream, *Fresh Cream* (Polydor)
John Hammond, Jr., *So Many Roads* (Vanguard)
The Allman Brothers, *At Fillmore East* (Polydor)
Duffy Power, *Little Boy Blue* (Demon/Edsel)

Book

Blues – The British Connection, by Bob Brunning (Blandford Press, 1986)

– Richie Unterberger

Country Rock

Country-rock is one of the hardest rock & roll styles to map and define. Country music, of course, was integral to the birth of rock & roll, and has continued to exert a huge influence on rock until the present. You can find innumerable examples of rock & roll performers that are saturated with country, from Elvis Presley to Elvis Costello. As a label and as a movement, however, country-rock is primarily identified with a school of bands in the late '60s and early '70s that brought the modern and irreverent qualities of rock to the more traditional musical values of country music.

There are many antecedents to country-rock; the close harmonies and acoustic guitars on much of the Everly Brothers' material foreshadows much of it. In the mid-'60s, Del Shannon recorded an entire album of Hank Williams tunes, George Jones and Gene Pitney teamed up for an LP of duets, and the trashy British R&B/punk band the Downliners Sect recorded a bizarre straight country album that was unnoticed commercially and unsuccessful artistically. Several of the '60s, top groups dallied successfully with countrified rock & roll at times, such as the Beatles (especially around the *Beatles for Sale* period, on tracks like "I Don't Want to Spoil the Party"), the early Byrds ("Satisfied Mind," "Mr. Spaceman," "Time Between"), and Buffalo Springfield ("Go and Say Goodbye," "Kind Woman"); all of these bands placed a premium on close harmonies, and could incorporate country signatures into their sound with natural ease when the spirit moved them.

The term "country-rock" actually began to get used around 1968, when most of the major rock acts were retreating from their psychedelic experiments into a "back to basics" approach. Bob Dylan, who had never embraced psychedelia in the first place, led the way with his *John Wesley Harding* album. Dylan had recorded in Nashville before, but this early 1968 effort was far more basic in instrumentation and far more country in tone. In 1969, he would largely eschew his inscrutable wordplay for basic homilies on *Nashville Skyline*, as well as recording an entire unreleased LP with one of his chief mentors, Johnny Cash.

The true god of country-rock, though, was guitarist and singer Gram Parsons. As the leader of the International Submarine Band, he recorded an album in 1967, *Safe at Home*, that prominently used pedal steel guitar. The LP is seen by some scholars as the first true country-rock record, although it was little noticed upon its release. Shortly afterwards, Parsons joined the Byrds, and was almost single-handedly responsible for altering the band's focus from folk-rock to country-rock. Byrds leader Roger McGuinn had

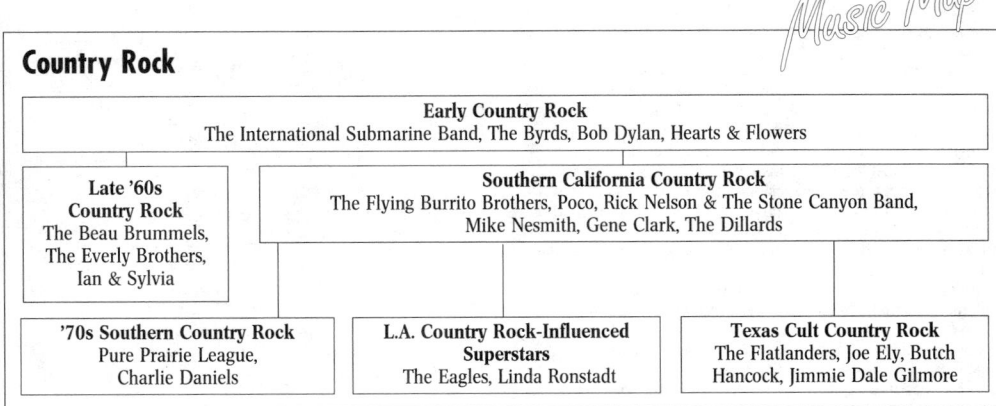

Music Map

Country Rock

Early Country Rock
The International Submarine Band, The Byrds, Bob Dylan, Hearts & Flowers

Late '60s Country Rock
The Beau Brummels, The Everly Brothers, Ian & Sylvia

Southern California Country Rock
The Flying Burrito Brothers, Poco, Rick Nelson & The Stone Canyon Band, Mike Nesmith, Gene Clark, The Dillards

'70s Southern Country Rock
Pure Prairie League, Charlie Daniels

L.A. Country Rock-Influenced Superstars
The Eagles, Linda Ronstadt

Texas Cult Country Rock
The Flatlanders, Joe Ely, Butch Hancock, Jimmie Dale Gilmore

been entertaining the idea of an ambitious double album with heavy use of electronics, but the project was scuppered in favor of *Sweetheart of the Rodeo*. The 1968 release is almost universally hailed as one of the first and best country-rock efforts.

The Byrds' country-rock era was short; Parsons left the band after less than a year. Longtime Byrds bassist Chris Hillman left the group around the same time, and quickly teamed with Parsons to form the nucleus of the Flying Burrito Brothers. Parsons only stayed with the band for a couple albums, but these works, also prominently featuring Sneeky Pete Kleinow on pedal steel, are the purest and most influential country-rock hybrids, and among the few major country-rock recordings that are not closer to rock than country.

Country music may have sprung from the southern states, but country-rock primarily flourished in southern California. Other country-rock acts of note in the late '60s included the little-known Hearts & Flowers, who actually surfaced before 1968, but were classified as folk-rock at the time, and Poco, featuring former Buffalo Springfield members Richie Furay and Jim Messina. In northern California, in the early '70s, the New Riders of the Purple Sage established themselves as a more countrified and laidback cousin of the Grateful Dead.

Some veteran acts primarily associated with other forms of rock and folk became country-rockers for a time in the late '60s. Folk-rock pioneers the Beau Brummels went to Nashville to record *Bradley's Barn* at the legendary studio of the same name; the Everly Brothers' *Roots* was their most critically acclaimed '60s work; Ian & Sylvia moved from contemporary folk to country as a duo and leaders of the band Great Speckled Bird; Rick Nelson had an artistic renaissance while fronting the Stone Canyon Band, which featured future Eagle Randy Meisner. Former Byrd Gene Clark recorded country-rock on his own and as part of Dillard & Clark. The Dillards themselves, primarily known as a bluegrass act before the late'60s, had already served as important figures in folk-rock by helping teach the Byrds harmony vocals, and employing Dewey Martin on drums before he left to join Buffalo Springfield. On 1968's *Wheatstraw Suite*, they became one of the few noted country-rock performers to move into the style from country rather than rock.

Country-rock wasn't big commercially, and may have made its greatest impact on other performers. The Band, the Grateful Dead, Creedence Clearwater Revival, and George Harrison, for instance, could not be called country-rock performers by any means, but all recorded some impressive country-rock material on their late-'60s and early-'70s albums. Gram Parsons was a big influence on the Rolling Stones around this time, and on Keith Richards in particular, though it should be pointed out that the Stones had fused country and rock as far back as 1966 on "High and Dry." Still, their *Let It Bleed* and *Sticky Fingers* albums had quite a few country licks, most famously on "Wild Horses" (which was covered by the Flying Burrito Brothers before the Stones released their own version).

Country-rock hasn't gotten much attention as a movement

since the early '70s. Commercially, it found its greatest success in the mid-'70s on hits by the Eagles (featuring ex-members of the Burritos, Poco, and the Stone Canyon Band) and Linda Ronstadt, both of whom absorbed country-rock into their brands of soft rock and pop. Southern bands like Pure Prairie League and Charlie Daniels had some success with more southern-fried sounds, and southern rock bands like the Allman Brothers, the Ozark Mountain Daredevils, and Lynyrd Skynyrd recorded some country-influenced material, although their focus remained blues-rock and hard rock. In the 1980s and 1990s, it could be argued that Nashville has been a lot more successful in borrowing from rock than the other way around.

Country-rock arguably never recovered from the death of Gram Parsons in 1973, but it's remained alive and kicking, if hardly omnipresent. Elvis Costello made an all-out country album, albeit a commercial flop, in 1981 with *Almost Blue*; country music informs much of Neil Young's work, in whatever decade he's working in; alternative rockers like the Meat Puppets and the Jayhawks have leaned heavily on country-rock at times. Texas eccentrics Joe Ely, Butch Hancock, and Jimmie Dale Gilmore (all of whom have played with each other at some point) have formed a sort of extended family for their brand of maverick country-rock. Once in a while a country-rock band will get a big push, like Lone Justice, but the hybrid seems to resist huge commercial success.

12 Essential Albums

The Byrds *Sweetheart of the Rodeo* (Columbia)
The Flying Burrito Brothers, *Farther Along: The Best of the Flying Burrito Brothers* (A&M)
The International Submarine Band, *Safe at Home* (Rhino)
Hearts & Flowers, *Now Is the Time* (Bam Caruso, UK)
The Beau Brummels, *Bradley's Barn* (Edsel, UK)
Poco, *Pickin' up the Pieces* (Epic)
The Everly Brothers, *Roots* (Warner)
The Dillards, *Wheatstraw Suite* (Elektra)
Bob Dylan, *John Wesley Harding* (Columbia)
Various Artists, *Hillbilly Fever Vol. 5* (Rhino)
The Flatlanders, *More a Legend than a Band* (Rounder)
Neil Young, *Harvest Moon* (Reprise)

Books

Gram Parsons: A Music Biography, by Sid Griffin (Sierra, 1985)
Hickory Wind: The Gram Parsons Story, by Ben Fong-Torres
— *Richie Unterberger*

Bubblegum

Considering bubblegum's fairly meager legacy – a few dozen hits in the late 1960s and early 1970s – it inspired a lot of heated discussion and revisionism. It arose at a time when the listener demographic for rock was expanding rapidly; originally marketed almost exclusively to teenagers, those teenagers were now growing up, leaving their teens, and continuing to buy and play rock & roll. At the same time, the purchasing power of *pre*-teens was growing. Too young in most cases to appreciate the subtleties of *Tommy* or "Cloud Nine," they needed a simple form of rock & roll to identify with, and bubblegum was created to satisfy their desires.

While 1967 was a year that saw rock and soul shake with paroxysms of change, it also saw million-selling singles by the Monkees, who starred in a show whose audience was composed more of small kids than any other type of viewer. It also saw hits by singers like Tommy James, whose sharp but catchy pop/rock was probably vastly more popular with pre-teens than post-adolescents. Although the Monkees' and Tommy James's best work holds up today as outstanding pop/rock, at the time it pointed the way for even more simple and naive music. And although the Monkees eventually played their own instruments on their records, industry insiders were well aware that their early hits were crafted by studio musicians, and knew that bonafide self-contained groups weren't strictly necessary to create smash records.

Most of the early bubblegum records were manufactured at Buddah Records by the production team of Jerry Kasenetz and Jeff Katz. Emphasizing repetitive, throbbing bass lines, simple singalong lyrics, cheesy organs, and insinuatingly (some would say obnoxiously) catchy melodies, their hit singles by the Ohio Express and the 1910 Fruitgum Co. were played by sessionmen – the "groups" didn't exist outside of the studio. Dubbed "bubblegum" for its childish qualities, mass production values, and instant disposability, it was celebrated as such in the minor 1969 hit single "Bubble Gum Music," released by the unforgettable Rock & Roll Dubble Bubble Trading Card Co. of Philadelphia 19141.

It didn't take long for the Archies, masterminded by brilliant Brill Building tunesmith and producer Jeff Barry, to establish themselves as the most successful bubblegum group. "Jingle Jangle" and particularly the number one hit "Sugar Sugar" were unavoidable if you were within earshot of a radio in 1969; the latter song's qualities were recognized by Wilson Pickett, who made the tune his own in a soul cover version. Another studio-only group, the Archies' records were tied in to a cartoon series based on the famous comic strip, with Archie, Jughead, and the gang playing the songs on the program.

The cross-promotion value of the Monkees' and the Archies' television programs was duplicated by the Partridge Family, the Banana Splits, and to some degree by Bobby Sherman, a pre-teen idol. The Partridge Family itself was picking up a fumble by the Cowsills, a clean-cut pop/rock family act that the Partridges were loosely based upon (although the Cowsills' arrangements were somewhat more sophisticated than the bubblegum norm). When the Partridges peaked, they in turn were supplanted by the Osmonds, a bubblegum version of the Jackson 5 (who, naturally, also had their own TV cartoon series around this time). The Partridges and Osmonds even inspired briefly successful imitators, the DeFranco Family.

In bubblegum's prime, there were also several huge one-shot hits by "artists" destined never to be heard from again. The Cuff Links, "Tracy," from 1969, featured the same singer who took the lead for the Archies. Daddy Dewdrop ("Chick-A-Boom"), the Pipkins ("Gimme Dat Ding"), and Crazy Elephant ("Gimme Gimme Good Lovin'") were some of the others whose tunes continued to echo in the brain long after their equally silly monikers had faded from memory. A few pop/rock veterans got some mileage out of bubblegum, like Tommy Roe, who cut bubblegum hits with "Dizzy" and "Jam up Jelly Tight"; the Troggs even recorded a bubblegum single, "Hip Hip Hooray," modeled after the Ohio Express.

Bubblegum was savaged by the rock press, which was outraged that simple clap-trap like "Yummy Yummy Yummy" – records by groups that didn't even exist outside of the studio – could sell millions of copies while sensitive, literate progressive rockers and singer/songwriters struggled to be heard. After bubblegum faded and punk emerged in the late '70s, some critics took a revisionist stance, hailing bubblegum for its innovative production techniques and for boiling pop/rock down to its irreducible essence. It's often been pointed out that one of the first songs the Talking Heads performed was the 1910 Fruitgum Co.'s "1-2-3 Red Light," and the simple throbbing rhythm and lyrics of numbers like "Psycho Killer" have a distant relation to bubblegum, although no one's going to confuse *Talking Heads 77* with music aimed at pre-teens.

Bubblegum's influence continues to pervade all music aimed at

---

Bubblegum Music

Bubblegum Forerunners
The Monkees, Tommy James, Tommy Roe

Kasenetz-Katz Productions
The Ohio Express, The 1910 Fruitgum Co.

TV Bubblegum Stars
The Archies, The Banana Splits

Pre-Teen Idols
The Partridge Family, The Osmonds,
Bobby Sherman, The De Franco Family

---

the record-buying public's youngest segment, which doesn't care who wrote the songs or even played on the records. Bubblegum was hardly one of the high points of rock history, but even the most serious-minded listeners are probably fooling themselves if they can't admit to the ingratiating catchiness of hits like "Tracy" and "Sugar, Sugar."

5 Essential Recordings

Various Artists, *The Best of the Ohio Express & Other Bubblegum Smashes* (Rhino)
Various Artists, *The Best of the 1910 Fruitgum Company & Other Bubblegum Smashes* (Rhino)
Various Artists, *Bubblegum Classics Vol. 1 & 2* (Varese Sarabande)
The Archies, *The Archies' Greatest Hits* (Kirschner)
Tommy Roe, *Greatest Hits* (MCA)

– Richie Unterberger

Singer-Songwriters

The definition of a rock singer/songwriter is elusive. Chuck Berry, the Beatles, Marvin Gaye, Patti Smith, Elvis Costello, Paul Westerberg, Liz Phair – are they not all singers and songwriters of the first degree? Of course they are, but none of them fit the label of a singer/songwriter that has been applied since the form's heyday in the late '60s and early '70s. Generally speaking, singer/songwriters put the emphasis on their material, rather than their vocal delivery, stylistic signatures, or musical backing (although those factors are certainly important). Both the compositions and the arrangements are written primarily as solo vehicles, rather than with full rock & roll bands in mind. Singer/songwriters almost exclusively play guitar and piano; quite a few play both. More than most rock styles, singer/songwriter records draw from folk and acoustic music. There is a higher percentage of women using the singer/songwriter format than you'll find in almost any other form of rock. The material tends toward the introspective, sensitive, romantic, and confessional, though it is not as wholly self-absorbed as some critics claim. Singer-songwriters are not singles-oriented artists (though there have been quite a few massive singer/songwriter hit singles), but craft albums as complete, flowing statements.

The golden age of singer/songwriters was in many respects a blend of American contemporary folk and professional pop/rock songcraft. In the early '60s, Bob Dylan was more responsible than any other songwriter for pioneering personal expression and idiosyncratic lyrics; when he moved from acoustic folk arrangements to folk-rock, many of his peers followed. In the mid- and late '60s, Fred Neil, Tim Hardin, Phil Ochs, and Gordon Lightfoot were some of the more notable folkies who followed Dylan into singer/songwriter territory.

There was also a school of songwriters who came to the singer/songwriting camp from the opposite direction of pop/rock. Composers like Randy Newman, Jackie De Shannon, Nilsson, and

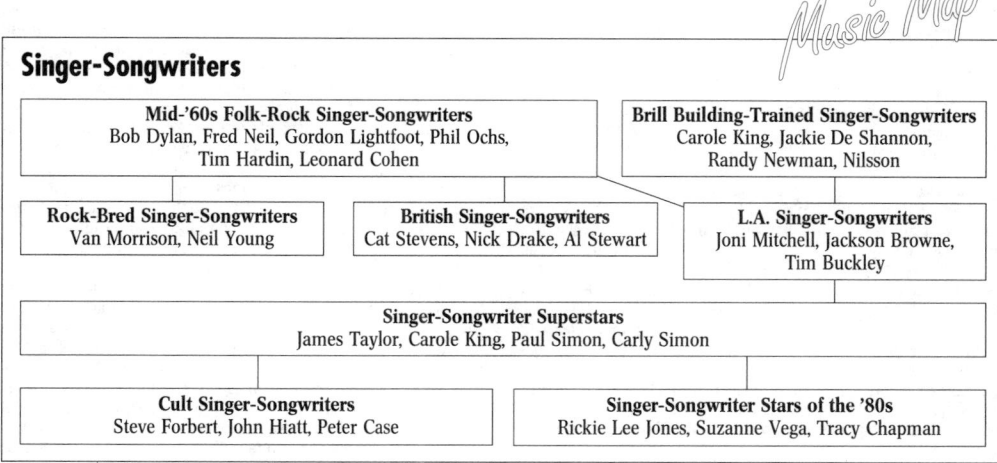

Singer-Songwriters

Mid-'60s Folk-Rock Singer-Songwriters
Bob Dylan, Fred Neil, Gordon Lightfoot, Phil Ochs, Tim Hardin, Leonard Cohen

Brill Building-Trained Singer-Songwriters
Carole King, Jackie De Shannon, Randy Newman, Nilsson

Rock-Bred Singer-Songwriters
Van Morrison, Neil Young

British Singer-Songwriters
Cat Stevens, Nick Drake, Al Stewart

L.A. Singer-Songwriters
Joni Mitchell, Jackson Browne, Tim Buckley

Singer-Songwriter Superstars
James Taylor, Carole King, Paul Simon, Carly Simon

Cult Singer-Songwriters
Steve Forbert, John Hiatt, Peter Case

Singer-Songwriter Stars of the '80s
Rickie Lee Jones, Suzanne Vega, Tracy Chapman

Carole King began their professional careers primarily as songwriters supplying material for pop acts, not as performers in their own right. De Shannon – an extremely underrated pioneer of the singer/songwriter genre – was the first of these to become a recording star on her own. By the late '60s, many others had stepped out from behind the scenes to begin singing their own songs, even if their voices and images didn't conform to normal commercial music business standards of what was marketable.

Not all came from one wing or the other, of course. Leonard Cohen was already an established poet when he ventured into the musical arena with material that ranks among the most literary rock ever committed to vinyl. Laura Nyro, one of the first critically acclaimed singer/songwriters, drew upon soul and Tin Pan Alley. Neil Young and Van Morrison were seasoned rock & roll performers as members of influential '60s bands, although Young's work has been too eclectic and, at times, fiercely rocking for him to be classified as a singer/songwriter in the classic mold. Paul Simon, as many have pointed out, drew equally from pop and folk traditions, and was a veteran folk-rock star as half of Simon & Garfunkel before moving into more personal territory as a solo act.

Singer/songwriters were overwhelmingly White, middle-class, and well-educated; unsurprisingly, perhaps, many were based in southern California or the Northeast, particularly Los Angeles or New York City. Los Angeles was always a chief wellspring of folk-rock, and in the late '60s, many talented singer/songwriters emerged that helped define the sound's folk-pop, laidback milieu. The best of these, Joni Mitchell, actually (like Neil Young) hailed from Canada, but was based in L.A. by the time she began recording. Mitchell's acoustic guitar- and piano-based sound, along with her intimate vocals and largely romantic themes, was a prototype of sorts for the singer/songwriter genre, although she moved on to experiment with jazz in both her vocals and arrangements after reaching superstardom in the mid-'70s.

Other important southern California singer/songwriters were Randy Newman, who infused the form with humor and (occasionally bitter) satire, and Jackson Browne, whose even-tempoed, easygoing ruminations have defined, for better or worse, the mellow L.A. rock sound in the minds of many listeners. A more eclectic singer/songwriter from the region was Tim Buckley, who dovetailed with psychedelia, jazz, soul, and just plain strange vocal experimentation within the singer/songwriter format.

As far as bringing singer/songwriters to Middle America, no performer was more influential than Carole King, who had already enjoyed a long career dating back to the early '60s as one of America's most successful songwriters. Her 1971 album *Tapestry* remains one of the best-selling recordings of all time. James Taylor, perhaps, was King's closest counterpart; his cover version of King's "You've Got a Friend" (from *Tapestry*) made it to number one, and his 1970 album *Sweet Baby James* epitomized the calming soft rock trends of the early '70s.

Singer/songwriters weren't as big a deal in Britain, but several did emerge that put their own spins on the form. Al Stewart took a more narrative, fanciful, and third-person approach; Nick Drake delved into dark and ambiguous themes that the stars found uncomfortable, or were unwilling to explore. Cat Stevens, the most successful British singer/songwriter of the '70s, was also the most similar in sound and content to his American counterparts.

Singer/songwriters – like almost everything else, but even more so – were a target of early punk and new wave performers, who disdained what they viewed as the genre's self-satisfied, complacent hippie homilies. The style, however, had already crested by the time punk arrived. The huge stars remained popular, sometimes at the same plateau (Paul Simon), more often at steady but diminishing levels. New crops of talent, however, did not arrive; there were occasional waves from performers like Rickie Lee Jones, and critical cults for artists like Steve Forbert, Peter Case, and John Hiatt, whose sheafs of good press never translated into major record sales.

Suzanne Vega and Tracy Chapman were by far the biggest singer/songwriter stars to emerge after 1980, and others, like Shawn Colvin, Joe Henry, and Luka Bloom, continue to make their mark, although usually more with the critics than the masses. And the influence of the singer/songwriter is strongly felt in dozens, if not hundreds, of artists not strictly identified with the style, ranging from Stevie Wonder and Bruce Springsteen to Mary-Chapin Carpenter and Bob Mould.

12 Essential Albums

Joni Mitchell, *Clouds* (Reprise)
Carole King, *Tapestry* (Epic)
Tim Buckley, *Goodbye & Hello* (Elektra)
Paul Simon, *Negotiations & Love Songs 1971-1986* (Warner Brothers)
Leonard Cohen, *Songs of Leonard Cohen* (CBS)
Nick Drake, *Fruit Tree* (Rykodisc)
James Taylor, *Sweet Baby James* (Warner Brothers)
Jackson Browne, *Late for the Sky* (Asylum)
Randy Newman, *12 Songs* (Reprise)
Neil Young, *After the Gold Rush* (Reprise)
Suzanne Vega, *Suzanne Vega* (A&M)
Tracy Chapman, *Tracy Chapman* (Elektra)

– *Richie Unterberger*

Progressive Rock

Devotees of progressive rock have to fend off more vilification than fans of almost any other rock genre. Pure-bred rock & rollers scorn it for lacking rock's earthier and poppier elements; scholars of classical and serious music find it too simple and undemanding to merit attention; latter-day punks and new wavers targeted it as the embodiment of the self-satisfied dinosaur that the music business had become (in the days when John Lydon joined the Sex Pistols he wore a T-shirt emblazened with the logo "I hate Pink Floyd"). Nonetheless, progressive rock was one of the defining styles of '70s rock, and responsible for some of rock's most ambitious – and pretentious – efforts.

Progressive rock came in many shapes and sizes, but it can be loosely defined as music that attempted to combine rock and psychedelia with classical, symphonic, and literary elements. Most of the groups placed instrumental virtuosity at a premium, used keyboards more than the typical rock group, and used synthesizers a lot more than the typical rock group. Electric guitars were also important, sometimes battling it out with the keyboards, sometimes taking off for lofty, lengthy solos of their own. Lyrically, prog-rockers didn't neglect love songs entirely, but were usually more concerned with weighty philosophical matters, often influenced by psychedelic drugs, science fiction, and fantasy, sometimes on an epic scale. Virtually all of the major prog-rock groups were British in origin, although some came from the European continent as well.

Progressive rock – sometimes called "art-rock" – originated in the British psychedelic scene of the late '60s. The Moody Blues was the first group to combine rock with classical symphonic music on its 1967 album *Days of Future Passed*. On subsequent albums, they dispensed with the actual orchestra and used synthesizers and sophisticated studio techniques to create symphonies by themselves. Few groups have endured as much frenzied adulation and vituperative criticism as the Moodies; undeniably pretentious, they were also one of progressive rock's most infectiously melodic acts.

Also massively popular was Pink Floyd, who turned increasingly serious-minded after the departure of their original leader, Syd Barrett, in early 1968. Many thought the band was dead with the loss of Barrett, their original songwriter, guitarist, and singer, whose inimitable sense of whimsy made the group's 1967 debut, *Piper at the Gates of Dawn*, one of the greatest psychedelic rock albums. The Floyd surprised their critics by getting bigger and bigger, with increasingly lengthy and spacious experimental epics whose electronic eeriness defined early "head music" for many listeners. While their big international breakthrough was 1973's *Dark Side of the Moon*, which remains one of the best-selling albums of all time, their earlier output contained some of their most original work, and the group never entirely lost sight of their pop and blues roots.

Other key British bands of the late '60s were the Soft Machine, who incorporated jazz and Dadaism into their psychedelic hard rock; Procol Harum, who used multi-layered keyboards, melodies with strong echoes of classical music, and the consciously literary lyrics of Keith Reid; the Nice, who featured Keith Emerson's virtuosic, classical-inspired keyboards and flamboyant showmanship; the Pretty Things, whose rock opera *S.F. Sorrow* predated the Who's *Tommy* by about a year; and Jethro Tull, whose early mixes of blues-rock and Rahsaan Roland Kirk soon metamorphosed into inscrutable album-length epic poems with strong hints of traditional English folk music.

For many aficionados, the first true progressive rock band was King Crimson, whose 1969 debut was a groundbreaking synthesis of stately virtuosity, fierce guitars and Mellotrons. Although some critics would be loathe to concur, early reviewers often compared King Crimson's first lineup to the similarly melodic and Mellotron-laden excursions of the early Moody Blues. With guitarist Robert Fripp at the helm, the group endured several rapid changes of personnel and quickly became a less song-oriented outfit, with increasing emphasis on flights of instrumental virtuosity and dense, challenging material with strong jazz and avant-garde influences.

Even as early as 1970, there were striking subdivisions within the progressive rock school. Several of the most critically respected bands clustered around the banner of the Canterbury sound; spearheaded by the Soft Machine, these also included Caravan, Hatfield & the North, and Soft Machine-offshoots like Matching Mole, Gong, and the solo work of ex-Softs Robert Wyatt and Kevin Ayers. Lighter in tone than the most commercially successful exponents of the genre, they also frequently exhibited a sense of humor that the superstars were not exactly prone to display.

While these bands may have gotten critical accolades, it was up to Emerson, Lake & Palmer, Yes, Pink Floyd, Jethro Tull, and

Genesis to move serious units. While Pink Floyd used fairly economic licks on their epics, the other stars tended to brandish flashy instrumental passages by guitar and keyboard heroes like Steve Howe, Rick Wakeman, and Keith Emerson. All their considerable bombast couldn't mask the firm grasp of songwriting hooks and tasty instrumental riffs that the masses found most palatable.

When they deigned to examine art-rock, critics reserved a lot of their enthusiasm for Roxy Music, whose ironic pop was flavored with unnerving synthesizer blasts from Brian Eno. After a short time with Roxy, Eno split for a solo career and recorded increasingly abstract, and increasingly instrumental, rock-flavored compositions that rank among the most well-respected art-rock and avant-rock recordings of all time, although Eno would largely forsake rock by the late '70s for contemporary composition (he continues to work with many rock performers as a producer).

Progressive rock also had a branch that was primarily instrumental. Unsurprisingly, many of these acts came from the European continent, and used the instrumental format as a way to circumvent their limited grasp of English, the lingua franca of popular music. Germany's Kraftwerk had a surprise Top Ten album in the mid-'70s with *Autobahn*; their foreboding, electronic textures, as well as those of fellow German bands like Can, Amon Duul, Faust, and Tangerine Dream, gave rise to the school of "Kraut rock" (dubbed as such by England's Virgin Records, who marketed the bands to an international audience). These bands had a considerable influence on new wave acts several years later. Holland's Focus, featuring guitar wizard Jan Akkerman, Greece's Aphrodite's Child, featuring a young Vangelis, and Italy's P.F.M. also made international inroads. And in the U.K., Mike Oldfield (who had played guitar with Kevin Ayers) had a huge international hit with the instrumental suite "Tubular Bells."

Progressive rock's influence declined after the mid-'70s; the punk/new wave and disco explosions were factors, but more important, a lot of the bands broke up, moved toward more pop-oriented fare, or simply played themselves out. The British Harvest and Virgin labels, instrumental in exposing the music to a wide audience, either wound down their activities (Harvest) or moved on to the larger pop/rock market (Virgin). Groups like Electric Light Orchestra, Boston, Foreigner, Journey, Asia, Kansas, and Supertramp became massively successful by incorporating progressive rock's flashiest attributes into their brands of mainstream pop/rock.

With a more modified symphonic lens, bands like the Moody Blues and Pink Floyd remain superstar concert attractions and big record sellers whenever they reassemble to work in the studio or hit the road, and scattered modern bands like Marillion pursue the original prog-rock ideal. From the other side of the spectrum, performers like Fred Frith, Henry Kaiser, Robert Fripp, Material, and Public Image Limited took progressive rock further into avant-garde territory than it ever dared to go during its heyday. And there's no doubt that the loftier excursions of performers like the Who, Led Zeppelin, the Mothers of Invention, Peter Gabriel, and David Bowie owe not a little to the better values of progressive rock.

12 Essential Albums

Pink Floyd, *Dark Side of the Moon* (Capitol)
Procol Harum, *Procol Harum* (Deram)
The Moody Blues, *Days of Future Passed* (Polydor)
Yes, *Fragile* (Atlantic)
Eno, *Here Come the Warm Jets* (EG)
The Soft Machine, *Volumes 1 & 2* (Big Beat, UK)
Caravan, *Canterbury Tales* (Polydor)
Mike Oldfield, *Tubular Bells* (Virgin)
King Crimson, *Frame by Frame* (Caroline)
Kraftwerk, *Autobahn* (Warner Brothers)
The Pretty Things, *S.F. Sorrow* (Edsel)
Jethro Tull, *20 Years of Jethro Tull: Highlights* (Chrysalis)
                   – *Richie Unterberger*

Heavy Metal

Heavy metal is the bastard son of rock & roll. For years, critics tried to ignore its existence, as parents attempted to prevent their children from listening to it. Nevertheless, heavy metal emerged in the early '70s as arguably the most commercially successful form of rock & roll. In the next 25 years, heavy metal has gone in and out of fashion, adapting itself to the times but always remaining near the top of the charts in some form.

At its core, heavy metal is an adolescent experience. Teenagers

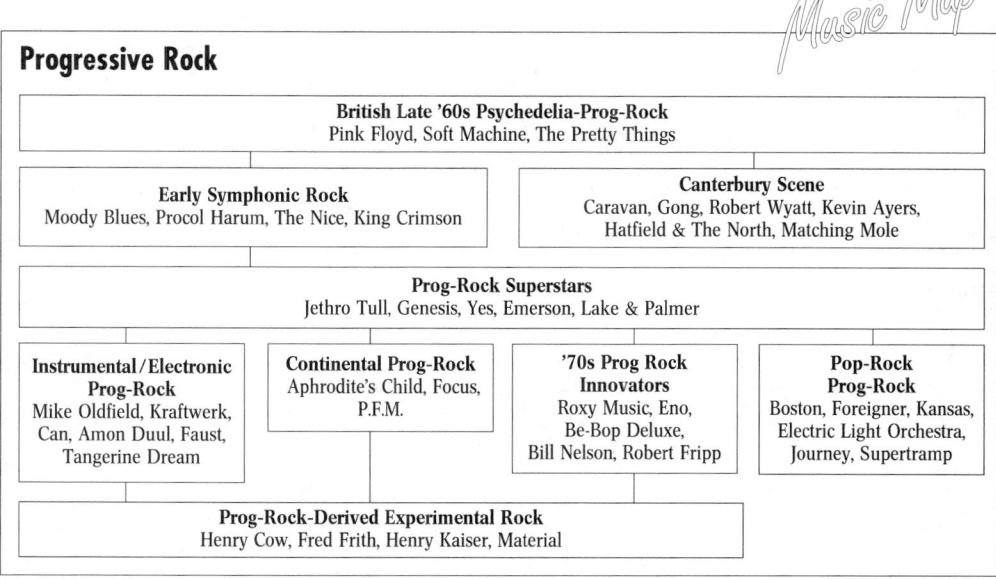

– primarily white males – form its core audience, buying the records, wearing the bands' T-shirts, and going to the shows. Because of the number of adolescent fans, some critics dismiss heavy metal as simplistic, primal pounding. Certainly, a fair share of metal is nothing but three-chord riffing, yet most metal bands place a premium on technical skill. From Led Zeppelin's Jimmy Page to Eddie Van Halen to Metallica's Kirk Hammett and Soundgarden's Kim Thayil, metal guitarists have always been innovators in technique, speed, and skill. In every subgenre of heavy metal, the guitar is the center of the music. The songs are assembled around the riff, with the guitar solo taking prominence. By and large, heavy metal is rock & roll with all of the roll stripped out – the blues remains, but it doesn't swing. All of the rhythms are fairly rigid, almost military in origin. Bombast is the key – from the drums to the guitars, it's about being as loud as possible.

Most trends in rock & roll last a finite amount of time. Like psychedelia, many listeners expected metal to fade after its initial glory days of the early '70s. And it did fade slightly for a couple of years in the late '70s, but it came back in a newer, tougher form. In each decade, heavy metal always finds its specific audience. In the '70s it was either mystical or boogie-oriented. In the '80s, it was pseudo-glam bubblegum in the mainstream and brutal, fast doom-mongers in the underground. In the '90s, the doom-mongers reigned supreme, as the lines between heavy metal and punk became indistinguishable.

Heavy metal's roots can be traced to the British Invasion, particularly the two-chord opening of the Kinks' "You Really Got Me." "You Really Got Me" didn't swing, it pounded, laying the groundwork for the simplistic hard rock of AC/DC and the scores of boogie bands of the mid-'70s. For all their sheer firepower, the Kinks didn't revel in the pompous, improvisational instrumental sections that defined metal, as much as the catchy, simplistic riffs. It wasn't until Cream that rock & roll had a band that pushed the boundaries of blues-based rock. Cream attempted to make rock an improvisational art such as jazz. While their records could often be surprisingly pop, the band stretched all rock conventions in concert, spending over ten minutes on one song and letting each instrument improvise. More importantly, they were deafeningly loud. Soon after Cream's debut, Jimi Hendrix appeared and he pushed those boundaries even further, bringing a new sonic vocabulary to rock with distortion and feedback. Although they were nowhere near as accomplished as Cream or Hendrix, Blue Cheer pushed the volume up as far as it could go. The result wasn't much more than volume, yet its primal roar earned the group the distinction of being labeled the first heavy metal band.

The group that wrote the blueprint for the conventional four-piece heavy metal band was the Jeff Beck Group. Keeping the power trio format of Cream and Hendrix, the Jeff Beck Group added a charismatic frontman to the lineup in the person of Rod Stewart. The interplay between the guitarist and the singer became enormously influential, and most heavy metal bands followed the pattern in the following years.

Shortly after the Jeff Beck Group's first album, Led Zeppelin was formed. The Jeff Beck Group may have provided the template, but Led Zeppelin was the definitive heavy metal band. Like the Jeff Beck Group, Led Zeppelin performed blues standards at a crushing volume and featured long trade-offs between vocalist Robert Plant and guitarist Jimmy Page. The band was also made up of superior musicians, as well as songwriters and arrangers, leading the music into a territory that was blues-based but couldn't reasonably be called blues-rock. Zeppelin also brought in touches of British folk, country music, rockabilly and rock & roll to the mix, as well as a lyrical fascination with the occult and medieval imagery that traded time with their sexually oriented songs.

For much of the early '70s, fantastical imagery dominated heavy metal, both through Led Zeppelin and their closest competitors, Black Sabbath. In contrast to the meticulously arranged and surprisingly subtle shifting dynamics of Zeppelin, Sabbath just flailed away at their guitars, creating an impenetrably slow and heavy sludge. Sabbath never sang about sex – they sang of "Warpigs" and "Iron Men." However, their slow beat, gargantuan guitars, and Ozzy Osbourne's wail made them seem grittier and more down to earth. In turn, they would influence nearly as many bands as Led Zeppelin, many of whom forgot about what Sabbath sang about and concentrated on the grimy, dirty riffs.

While Zeppelin and Sabbath ruled the theaters and arenas of America and Britain, they had some competition from the thick boogie of Foghat and Grand Funk Railroad, who attracted legions of fans with their simple, by-the-books heavy blues-rock. However, Foghat and Grand Funk never had the lasting influence of Alice Cooper. With a stage show designed to shock – filled with fake blood and decapitations – and music to match, Alice Cooper created a grandly theatrical form of heavy metal that also was quite pop-conscious. Not only could the group grind out teenage anthems like "School's Out" and "I'm Eighteen," they wrote songs like "No More Mr. Nice Guy" which essentially was a pop song dressed up with loud guitars. Led by the heavily made-up Vincent Furnier (who eventually adopted the name Alice Cooper as his own), the group's flamboyant stage shows and melodic metal set the stage for the pop-metal of the '80s.

Although neither band could officially be termed heavy metal, the New York Dolls and T. Rex had an impact in the metal world. T. Rex's influence wouldn't be felt until the '80s, when a number of bands, particularly Def Leppard, adopted the group's sleek, simple riffs and pretty look. The New York Dolls, however, had immediate impact. Dressing in drag and playing a hard, raunchy variation of the Rolling Stones' swagger, the Dolls never sold many records, but bands such as Aerosmith and Kiss built on their trashy retro-chic look and the group's sleazy hard rock. Aerosmith was tamer than the Dolls, never indulging in the group's stylistic excesses, but they made the basic blues-rock of the Stones and the Dolls heavier without losing any of the bluesy swing. Lead vocalist Stephen Tyler was a flamboyant frontman, halfway between Mick Jagger and David Johansen, with a penchant for crude double entendres. Aerosmith's heavy blues-rock didn't quite fit in with the lunkheaded thud of Foghat, and it was much grittier than the mystical visions of Zeppelin and Sabbath. For a while, it took the band some time to find an audience, but the proto-power ballad of "Dream On" and the lean *Toys in the Attic* broke the band into the big-time.

Kiss, on the other hand, was all about pure theatrics. Every member of the band was disguised in heavy makeup and ridiculous costumes and was never seen without their makeup, Their stage show was more theatrical than Alice Cooper's, complete with elaborate light shows, dry ice, and fake blood. Accordingly, their music also expanded on Alice Cooper's blueprint, making the heavy guitars heavier and the melodies poppier. For the latter part of the decade, Kiss was among the most popular heavy metal bands in America.

Queen arrived at roughly the same time as Aerosmith and Kiss, although their music could hardly have been more different. Taking their direction from Led Zeppelin's most majestic moments, Queen created a meticulous, multi-layered sound that featured dozens of guitar and vocal overdubs. The band provided a bridge between progressive rock and heavy metal by adopting the pretensions of prog-rock with the melodic sensibilities and loud guitars of metal. Queen was also the most eclectic heavy metal band since Led Zeppelin, adding elements of pop, English music-hall, folk, opera, rockabilly, and, eventually, disco and new wave. That off-kilter musical sensibility was part of the reason the group's music was influential over the years, with bands as diverse as Metallica and Smashing Pumpkins claiming Queen as an inspiration.

AC/DC was the last of the important heavy metal bands to emerge in the mid-'70s, and they were completely different than the orchestrated bombast of Queen. Crude and vulgar, both lyrically and musically, AC/DC were rock hooligans of the highest order; in their own words, they rode the "Highway to Hell." Angus Young's rhythm guitar stripped the riffs down to their barest essentials, while Bon Scott's piercing shriek was positively primal in its power. The rhythm section pounded away, and they had a sense of groove missing from most metal bands of their era. But nothing could take away from the all-mighty riff, which was the one important thing in AC/DC's music. With their minimalistic power and working-class image, it could be argued that AC/DC were proto-punks, stripping rock & roll to its core. But neither AC/DC nor any punk rocker would agree.

In the late '70s, heavy metal began to fall out of favor, as disco and punk captured the imaginations of mainstream audiences and critics, respectively. Van Halen helped reverse that trend. Releasing their first album in 1978, the group carried out the metal prototype of a lead singer/lead guitarist interplay to ludicrous extremes. Lead vocalist David Lee Roth treated his frontman role as vaudevillian performance art, while lead guitarist Eddie Van Halen spat out a series of amazingly fast leads. Van Halen's guitar pyrotechnics – which included popularizing the two-handed tapping technique, allowing for guitar licks that sounded faster and more complicated than they actually were – didn't simply expand the boundaries of the instrument, they wrote a whole new book. Throughout the next two decades, most guitarists copied and developed Van Halen's techniques, making his style a familiar part of the musical language. Guitarists from Kirk Hammett through Toto's Steve Lukather to Bon Jovi's Richie Sambora helped incorporate Van Halen's style into speed-metal, pop, and pop-metal.

Van Halen quickly became multi-platinum superstars, capable selling out arenas. As soon as they entered that status, a new batch of heavy metal bands emerged from the British underground.

Dubbed the New Wave of British Heavy Metal, the bands took Sabbath's heaviness, made it leaner and tougher, and dressed it in leather. At first, their lyrical concerns were just as drenched in mysticism as Sabbath, but the groups began singing about death, depression, sex, and life in more realistic terms, at a faster, relentless speed. Judas Priest and Iron Maiden were the leaders of the movement, yet bands like Diamond Head were equally influential on the emerging ranks of speed-metal bands like Metallica and Anthrax. But more than any other band, Motörhead helped create speed-metal – and, in the process, break down the doors between punk and metal. Motörhead took their cues from punk and the Ramones in particular, making their music harder, faster, louder. All of Motörhead's music sounds the same, but that doesn't dilute the impact of its rampaging riffs and Lemmy's bark.

In the early '80s, America developed its own underground metal scene, which expanded on the bleak, hard heavy metal of the New Wave of British Heavy Metal, while adding a greater reliance on technical proficiency, and intricate, multi-layered compositions. The band that would bring that movement to popularity was Metallica, a Californian band that emphasized exceptionally tight, fast playing and stark lyrical imagery. *Kill 'Em All*, their 1982 debut, articulated their bleak, percussive vision and caused an instant underground sensation.

However, the group didn't begin to earn mainstream attention until the middle of the decade, when they released their masterpiece, *Master of Puppets*, in 1986. In the meantime, a slicker, more pop-oriented variation of heavy metal began to dominate the pop charts in the early '80s, after new wave began to fade away. AC/DC had their commercial breakthrough in 1980, but that turned out to be a fluke, as no other band followed them to the top of the charts. Quiet Riot's version of Slade's "Cum on Feel the Noize" was a hit in 1983, but what really broke metal into the mainstream was Def Leppard's *Pyromania*.

The rise of pop-metal had a great deal to do with the emergence of MTV. Pop-metal bands tended to be better-looking than the gritty heavy metal bands of the '70s, which made MTV more receptive to their videos. After Def Leppard's success with "Photograph" and *Pyromania*, legions of pop-metal bands began filtering into MTV and the mainstream. Van Halen had a major hit in 1984 with the aptly titled *1984*, and Mötley Crüe had a Top Ten hit with the sleazy glam-metal of *Theatre of Pain* in 1985, but it wasn't until Bon Jovi's breakthrough in 1986 that pop-metal became a genuine commercial force.

Like most pop-metal bands – who critics derisively tagged "hair bands" because of their stylized, blow-dried appearance – Bon Jovi emphasized the pop melodies in their music, using loud guitar riffs and solos as an embellishment, not as the primary force. They had slick rockers like "You Give Love a Bad Name" and power ballads like "Wanted: Dead or Alive." A veritable flood of bands followed Bon Jovi through the door, including newer bands like Poison and revamped veteran rockers like Whitesnake. Mötley Crüe managed to straddle the line between pop-metal and sleazy, Los Angeles glam-metal, becoming one of the most popular rock & roll bands of the latter half of the decade. Pop-metal had a prominent place on the pop charts all the way into 1991, when post-punk alternative rock made a commercial breakthrough with Nirvana's *Nevermind*.

As pop-metal ruled the charts, a dirtier, harder brand of metal came to the forefront, as well. In 1988, the Los Angeles band Guns N' Roses had a hit single with "Sweet Child O' Mine." The band's album had been out for a year, but it immediately began selling following the hit single, eventually hitting number one. Guns N' Roses updated the raunchy hard rock of Aerosmith with a nihilistic, punk-rock fervor, opening the doors for mass commercial acceptance of such speed-metal bands as Metallica, Megadeth, Anthrax, and Slayer. Before, most metal bands were relegated to MTV's Saturday night ghetto, *Headbanger's Ball,* which provided an excellent forum for both new and established bands. Metallica immediately reaped the benefits of the more accommodating airwaves, earning a Grammy nomination and critical acclaim in mainstream publications.

While pop-metal, Guns N' Roses and their offspring, and speed-metal bands became hot chart items, a handful of bands in the alternative underground were sketching out a brazen fusion of punk and heavy metal, led by the sludgy, heavy riffs of Soundgarden and the pompous art-rock and metal of Jane's Addiction. Both bands received heavy college airplay and positive critical response, earning a small but dedicated following that continued to grow throughout the end of the decade. Jane's Addiction, in particular, became a powerful force in breaking down the barriers between album-rock radio and alternative rock before Nirvana's *Nevermind* in 1991. Not only did the group's second album, 1990's *Ritual De Lo Habitual*, receive prominent MTV airplay, their lead vocalist, Perry Farrell, organized the group's farewell tour, Lollapalooza, as a traveling festival designed to feature alternative bands, most of whom had metal leanings like Jane's themselves – Living Colour, Nine Inch Nails, Ice-T's Body Count, and the Rollins Band.

Throughout 1991, metal bands like Skid Row Mötley Crüe dominated the charts, but it was Metallica's commercial breakthrough, *Metallica*, that signaled the tastes of the mainstream audience were beginning to change. Guns N' Roses delivered their long-awaited second album, *Use Your Illusion I & II*, in the fall of 1991, but they were soon eclipsed by Nirvana's *Nevermind*, as were all of the pop-metal bands that were ruling the singles charts. *Nevermind* not only ushered in alternative rock as a major commercial force, it re-wrote the book for metal bands, forcing all the previous pop-metal groups to toughen up their charts. Most of these efforts were unsuccessful, since there were legions of bands ready to claim the heavy metal audience.

Nirvana was adopted by certain portions of the metal audience, yet they were never really heavy metal. However, their fellow Seattle bands, Alice in Chains and Soundgarden, were decidedly heavy metal and they became genuine arena-rock stars in the early '90s. Alice in Chains fell in between Sabbath and Van Halen, turning out a grinding, heavy rock that was determinedly grim and bleak. Soundgarden recaptured the majestic heaviness of Led Zeppelin and Black Sabbath with 1991's *Badmotorfinger* and 1994's staggering *Superunknown*, which became their commercial breakthrough. More than any other metal band since Metallica, Soundgarden captured the imaginations of both the critics and the audience, establishing themselves as a major force in the '90s. Quasi-metal bands like Smashing Pumpkins had their roots in '70s metal groups like Sabbath and Queen and were quite popular, yet their musical approach and attitude connected them with alternative audiences, not metal. No matter how loud they played, they sounded soft.

While alternative metal had become mainstream, a new underground of heavy metal bands had developed. Inspired by the fast, grim visions of Metallica and Slayer, as well as cult bands like the Accused and Napalm Death, these legions of bands were dubbed death-metal, black-metal, and grindcore, according to the minute variations in their sound. Outsiders could not distinguish between Emperor and Brutal Truth, but there were differences in their music nevertheless. Black-metal, which became the most popular term for the trend, was a defiantly underground phenomenon, with most mainstream publications ignoring it completely; it wasn't allowed any airtime on MTV, since the network cancelled its long-running heavy metal program, *Headbanger's Ball*. Nevertheless, the black-metal cult grew quite large by the middle of the decade, large enough to make Slayer's 1994 album debut at number one.

As the rock & roll of the '90s has proven, heavy metal has become part of rock & roll's heritage, working its way into several different forms of pop music. Nevertheless, there's always a metal underground, filled with unrespected and unsavory groups, ready to take over. In addition to the black-metal cult, many of the pop-metal bands of the '80s have retreated to the club circuit, which may mean that they are sowing the seeds of a future comeback. In either case, it's clear that heavy metal will never go away.

21 Essential Albums:

Led Zeppelin, *Led Zeppelin II* (Swan Song)
Led Zeppelin, *Led Zeppelin IV* (Swan Song)
Black Sabbath, *Paranoid*(Warner Bros.)
Black Sabbath, *Masters of Reality* (Warner Bros.)
Deep Purple, *Machine Head* (Warner Bros.)
Aerosmith, *Toys in the Attic* (Columbia)
Alice Cooper, *Greatest Hits* (Warner Bros.)
Queen, *Sheer Heart Attack* (Hollywood)
AC/DC, *Highway to Hell* (Atco)
AC/DC, *Back in Black* (Atco)
Motörhead, *The Best of Motörhead* (Roadrunner)
Judas Priest, *British Steel* (Columbia)
Van Halen, *Van Halen* (Warner Bros.)
Def Leppard, *Pyromania* (Mercury)
Metallica, *Kill 'Em All* (Elektra)

Metallica, *Master of Puppets* (Elektra)
Slayer, *Reign in Blood* (Def American)
Guns N' Roses, *Appetite for Destruction* (Geffen)
Mötley Crüe, *Decade of Decadence* (Elektra)
Jane's Addiction, *Ritual De Lo Habitual* (Warner Bros.)
Soundgarden, *Superunknown* (A&M)

– Stephen Thomas Erlewine

Jazz Rock

More than most such subgenres, jazz-rock is a hybrid that has resisted true alchemy. The impulse to blend the basic drive of rock with the improvisational verve and rhythmic complexity of jazz is a challenge that has been taken up by many. It has only been successfully accomplished by a few, and the results are often more weighted toward either rock or jazz than a true fusion of the styles.

Half a century ago, rock and jazz were much more closely intertwined than they are today. In the big-band and swing era, jazz was a much more dance-oriented music; early R&B and jump blues acts that helped lay the foundation for rock & roll drew much of their boogies, riffs, and rhythms (as well as instrumentalists) from jazz. Artists like Joe Turner and Jay McShann could have been classified as either jazz or R&B, but as rock & roll grew into a full-grown giant and jazz evolved toward bebop, the styles took substantially divergent paths.

Jazz's influence on rock & roll during the '50s and '60s wasn't negligible. Lots of R&B and soul bands, including those of Little Richard, Ray Charles, and James Brown, featured musicians from jazz backgrounds. Respected jazz musicians like Barney Kessel played on many rock & roll sessions to help pay the rent, and drummer Cozy Cole crossed over to the rock & roll market with his instrumental smash "Topsy." In the mid-'60s, the Byrds openly credited John Coltrane as an influence on early psychedelic landmarks like "Eight Miles High," and used South African jazz trumpeter Hugh Masekela as a prominent sessionman on a couple of their singles. Notable '60s groups like the Doors, Zombies, Blues Project, Paul Butterfield, Manfred Mann, Traffic, and Santana clearly displayed important secondary jazz influences. Jazz was also an important element in Van Morrison's late-'60s album *Astral Weeks*, which featured the rhythm section of noted jazz players Richard Davis on bass and Connie Kay of the Modern Jazz Quartet on drums.

Not to be overlooked, either, is '60s soul-jazz, a form which attracts little critical attention today, but was quite popular in its day – indeed, it might have been *the* most popular form of jazz with urban, African-American audiences. Using organs, vocals, and R&B riffs with greater frequency than other jazz musicians, the most popular performers in this subgenre would include Jimmy Smith, Jimmy McGriff, Big John Patton, and Jack McDuff. Ramsey Lewis and the spinoff combo Young-Holt Trio (later to become Young-Holt Unlimited) had a more pop-oriented take on soul jazz that led to substantial Top 40 success.

"Jazz-rock" as a self-conscious label, however, didn't evolve until the late '60s. The first acts to be widely identified as jazz-rock bands (and, to this day, the most successful) weren't so much jazz-rockers as R&B-oriented White rock bands with jazzy horn sections. The Electric Flag, featuring Mike Bloomfield, Buddy Miles, and Nick Gravenites, was the first of these; Blood, Sweat & Tears and Chicago became huge stars, although the MOR nature of their hits led some critics to dub them as "wedding band" or "barmitzvah" soul.

A more ambitious, although extremely obscure, jazz-rock record that predates any of the bands in the above paragraph was the sole album by the New York-based Free Spirits, featuring the young Larry Coryell on guitar. This interesting but erratic effort came much closer to truly striking a midpoint between rock song forms and jazz instrumentation, although the songs remained in the neighborhood of three minutes, and the vocals were fairly weak. Concentrating more on the jazz and instrumental side of things, Coryell became one of the leading early jazz-rock and fusion performers as the leader of Eleventh House and as a solo artist.

Several British '60s bands featured players that emerged from a jazz background, most notably the Graham Bond Organization. Besides the leader, they featured Jack Bruce and Ginger Baker in their pre-Cream days, and, for a time, guitarist John McLaughlin, although they quickly gravitated toward the R&B and blues

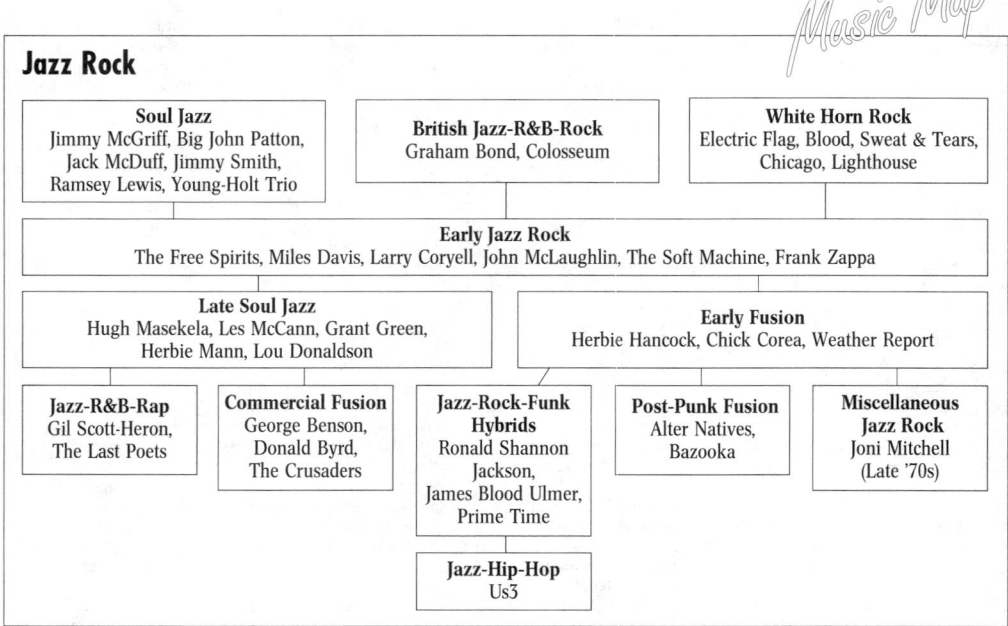

Music Map

Jazz Rock

Soul Jazz Jimmy McGriff, Big John Patton, Jack McDuff, Jimmy Smith, Ramsey Lewis, Young-Holt Trio	**British Jazz-R&B-Rock** Graham Bond, Colosseum	**White Horn Rock** Electric Flag, Blood, Sweat & Tears, Chicago, Lighthouse

Early Jazz Rock
The Free Spirits, Miles Davis, Larry Coryell, John McLaughlin, The Soft Machine, Frank Zappa

Late Soul Jazz
Hugh Masekela, Les McCann, Grant Green,
Herbie Mann, Lou Donaldson

Early Fusion
Herbie Hancock, Chick Corea, Weather Report

Jazz-R&B-Rap Gil Scott-Heron, The Last Poets	**Commercial Fusion** George Benson, Donald Byrd, The Crusaders	**Jazz-Rock-Funk Hybrids** Ronald Shannon Jackson, James Blood Ulmer, Prime Time	**Post-Punk Fusion** Alter Natives, Bazooka	**Miscellaneous Jazz Rock** Joni Mitchell (Late '70s)

Jazz-Hip-Hop
Us3

sounds of the day. Bruce and Baker have occasionally recorded respectable jazz albums right up to the present, and Bond-John Mayall spinoff-band Colosseum was probably the best jazz-oriented act to emerge from the British R&B-blues scene. The most successful British jazz-rock band of all, and indeed the one act that could be termed to have truly fused the two styles more than any other, was the Soft Machine. Starting as an underground psychedelic group (and a very good one), their late-'60s and early-'70s albums turned toward an increasingly improvisational and instrumental sound, retaining rock elements in Mike Ratledge's buzzing organ and Robert Wyatt's brilliant drumming and soulful vocals.

For most critics, though, the true peak of jazz-rock was reached by Miles Davis on his early-'70s recordings. Impressed by Jimi Hendrix and other late-'60s rock musicians, Davis brought electric guitars and keyboards into his band, culminating in the landmark 1970 LP *Bitches Brew,* roundly acclaimed as one of the most influential jazz recordings of all time. That record featured guitarist John McLaughlin, who would immediately become a leading jazz-rock figure himself, on his own, with Davis, with the Mahavishnu Orchestra, and in collaborations with ex-Davis drummer Tony Williams and Carlos Santana.

Other jazz musicians took the cue from Davis, always a leader and innovator, and added electric instruments and rock-influenced rhythms to their sound. Herbie Hancock, Chick Corea, and Weather Report were the best of these groups, although it's fair to say that, even more than Davis, they were really "rock-influenced jazz," not "jazz-rock." The compositions were usually instrumental, the melodic themes and improvisations clearly from the jazz tradition; the rock influence was felt in the electric instruments and the forceful funk of the arrangements.

Not unsurprisingly, jazz-rock quickly turned in a more commercial, watered-down direction that resulted in the style known as "fusion." As work became harder to find in the struggling jazz scene of the late '60s, notable jazzmen like Lou Donaldson, Herbie Mann, Les McCann, Hugh Masekela, and Grant Green were turning in a jazz-soul direction as a means to both broaden their horizons and to survive. Many jazz players, usually for brief periods, brought electric instruments and funk rhythms into their arrangements during the 1970s, resulting by and large in unimpressive, at times embarrassing, results. Guitarist George Benson and trumpeter Donald Byrd, to name two of the most obvious

examples, found much greater commercial success as pop-fusioneers than with their more critically respected straight jazz efforts of the '60s.

Jazz-rock hasn't been a big critical or commercial deal since the mid-'70s, but occasional innovators have produced interesting efforts along the lines of the best jazz-rock pioneers. Frank Zappa couldn't properly be considered a jazz-rock musician, but several of his '70s recordings, most notably *Hot Rats,* rank among the most ambitious blends of rock and jazz principles. Guitarist James Blood Ulmer and drummer Ronald Shannon Jackson (whose band, the Decoding Society, featured future Living Colour guitarist Vernon Reid) were both students of the Ornette Coleman school of harmolodics. The best of their records have melded jazz improvisation, funk rhythms, and visceral electric drive. Coleman himself drew on jazz-rock innovations with his Prime Time band. Streetwise jazz poets Gil-Scott Heron and the Last Poets helped lay the foundation for rap music. Defunkt merged jazz and funk rhythms without, at least at the beginning, pandering to watered-down commercial fusion interests. And, most unpredictably, folk-rock star Joni Mitchell delved heavily into jazz improvisation in the late '70s with the help of sidemen Jaco Pastorius and Pat Metheny, and put lyrics to Charles Mingus's last compositions (at his request) on the 1979 album, *Mingus.*

The jazz-rock fusion continues to tempt musicians intermittently in the '90s. Several bands on the alternative rock label SST, most notably Alter Natives and Bazooka, played what was essentially improvisational jazz with fierce electric guitar-driven arrangements. The downtown New York avant-rock-whatchama-callit scene is too eclectic to be figured easily into the jazz-rock equation, but many of its performers are clearly strongly influenced by both worlds.

Under the pseudonym Buckshot LeFonque, leading contemporary jazz musician Branford Marsalis took a stab at jazz-funk-R&B-soul-hip-hop. British act Us3 grafted hip-hop samples onto classic Blue Note jazz recordings, sparking some occasionally inspired jazz-hip-hop crossover recordings in the jazz community itself.

15 Recommended Recordings

Various Artists, *Blue Funk: The History of the Hammond Organ* (Blue Note). More quality soul-jazz was recorded on the

Blue Note label than any other, and this compilation includes tracks by most of the biggest stars of the genre: Jimmy Smith, Jimmy McGriff, Jack McDuff, Grant Green, Big John Patton, Lou Donaldson.

The Free Spirits, *Out of Sight, Out of Sound* (ABC). Pretty hard to find these days, this stakes a strong claim as the first jazz-rock record.

The Electric Flag, *A Long Time Comin'* (Columbia). The best of the records by late-'60s White rock groups to be classified as "jazz-rock."

Miles Davis, *Bitches Brew* (Columbia). Still the most influential and respected jazz-rock recording.

The Soft Machine, *3rd* (Columbia). Their most successful pure jazz-rock outing, although their earlier, more psychedelic rock-flavored albums weren't too shabby either.

John McLaughlin, *Devotion* (Restless). It's really a matter of taste as to which early-'70s McLaughlin album stands as his best, but rock listeners might find this one of the more approachable ones, as it uses Jimi Hendrix's Band of Gypsies rhythm section.

Frank Zappa, *Hot Rats* (Rykodisc). One of his most jazz-rock-oriented recordings, this largely instrumental 1970 effort features some of his best guitar playing.

Herbie Hancock, *Head Hunters* (Columbia). The album that broke fusion as a commercial force, though those looking for something a bit more adventurous in the jazz-rock vein might try the early-'70s LPs he released just prior to this effort.

Gil-Scott Heron, *The Revolution Will Not Be Televised* (Flying Dutchman). The leading jazz-R&B-rock poet.

Miles Davis, *Pangaea* (Columbia). Arguably the most recklessly electric of Davis's fusion sessions, featuring the guitar pyrotechnics of Pete Cosey. Those looking for something slightly less experimental should try *Agharta*, recorded on the same day.

Joni Mitchell, *Mingus* (Asylum). The central recording of Mitchell's jazz-rock phase, a period which inspired much debate among both fans and critics.

James Blood Ulmer, *Are You Glad to Be in America?* (Artists House). None of Ulmer's records could exactly be termed accessible, but this strikes the best balance between funk-R&B grooves and harmolodics.

Ronald Shannon Jackson, *Decode Yourself* (Island). None of Jackson's albums particularly stands out as his most influential; this 1985 Bill Laswell-produced session is one of the more accessible.

Bazooka, *Blowhole* (SST). A group that, like others on the SST label, pursues the elusive goal of wedding Ornette Coleman to post-punk attitude and eclecticism.

Various Artists, *Stolen Moments: Red, Hot & Cool* (GRP). The best jazz-hip-hop compilation, featuring some of the top talents from both worlds.

– Richie Unterberger

Southern Rock

While the South, more than any other American region, was responsible for breeding rock & roll, it lacked a readily identifiable White rock band sound after the decline of rockabilly. Southern rock groups were hardly unknown in the 1960s: John Fred & the Playboys, the Boxtops, and Bill Deal & the Rondels rank among the most talented blue-eyed soul performers, and there were occasional bands following the British Invasion and folk-rock trends, such as the underappreciated Gants. Soul music, of course, thrived in Memphis, New Orleans, and other southern regions throughout the '60s, and white session musicians (especially the white half of Booker T. & the MGs) contributed mightily to the sounds crafted at Stax/Volt Records and the Muscle Shoals and Fame studios.

But southern rock, as an identifiable style, didn't come into its own until about 1970. Like many subgenres of rock & roll, southern rock peaked very early in its development. Its story is more tragic than most, perhaps, because it fell from grace not so much from the usual reasons of flagging inspiration and rampant imitation, but from sudden tragedies that tore the heart out of its two flagship groups.

Southern rock proper began with the Allman Brothers, who had already made some recordings in California as the Hourglass; lead guitarist Duane Allman was a respected session player, contributing to records by Aretha Franklin, Boz Scaggs, and (after the Allmans were established) Eric Clapton. The Allman Brothers established the blueprint for southern rock in their heavy debts to roots music forms: the blues was foremost, as were boogie, soul,

and hints of country. They weren't at all like either the early rockabilly performers or the contemporary soul musicians, however, in that the guitar-dominated thrust of their arrangements were clearly inspired by the leading hard rock and psychedelic bands of the day, such as Cream and Jimi Hendrix.

While the Allmans were to some degree responsible for some of southern rock's lesser attributes – the endless jams, the repetitive boogie riffs – they executed these with more polish than any of their descendants, and at their best demonstrated a real facility for combining muscular rock with improvisation. Anchored by Gregg Allman's soulful vocals and the twin lead guitars of Duane Allman and Dickey Betts, the group became stars after the release of the double LP *Live at the Fillmore East*, still one of the most popular live rock recordings of all time. Duane Allman was killed in a motorcycle accident in late 1971, shortly after the release of *Fillmore East*, and bassist Berry Oakley died in eerily similar circumstances a year later. The band has continued to record to the present day, at times with great commercial success, but has never approached the artistic height of their original lineup. In the wake of the Allmans' success, several other southern bands arose to mine the same territory of rootsy boogies and guitar-driven stomp, usually with considerably less subtlety. The most successful, both critically and commercially, was Lynyrd Skynyrd. Attracting important and influential fans in Al Kooper (who produced their debut) and Pete Townshend (who had the group open for the Who during a tour in the early '70s), Lynyrd Skynyrd boasted three lead guitarists. As songwriters and performers, they helped establish the good ol' boy (or, as some would put it less kindly, redneck) image of southern rock, and helped define '70s guitar rock with "Freebird," which vies with "Stairway to Heaven" as the most overplayed classic rock song of all time. At the same time, they could show uncommon lyrical subtlety for the genre, as well as economic hook-savvy smarts. They were one of America's most popular bands by 1977, when lead singer Ronnie Van Zandt and guitarist Steve Gaines died in a plane crash. Subsequent recordings by the group, as well as the spinoff Rossington-Collins Band, didn't measure up to those by the Zandt-fronted lineup.

While no other southern rock bands of the '70s approached the Allmans or Lynyrd Skynyrd in popularity or influence, quite a few of them were big. The Charlie Daniels Band and the Outlaws were the most country-influenced; the Dixie Dregs and Sea Level (both of whom recorded for the Allmans' label, Capricorn) were the jazziest; Wet Willie was the most R&B and gospel-influenced; the Ozark Mountain Daredevils and the Atlanta Rhythm Section, briefly stars, were the most pop-influenced. American blues-rock performers with southern roots like Johnny Winter, Edgar Winter, ZZ Top, and Elvin Bishop were sometimes lumped in the southern rock school, although they were really on the edge of the style both geographically and stylistically.

The bar-band boogie hallmarks of southern rock always go over big live, and several fairly generic bands rose to a level of considerable popularity without offering anything particularly valuable, and, at their worst, perpetuating the worst "redneck rock" stereotypes of brawling, good-time southern boys. Included in this category would be .38 Special and Molly Hatchet. The Marshall Tucker Band, originators of a seemingly endless stream of competently indistinguishable southern rock albums, epitomized the common denominator of the genre.

As a big commercial force, southern rock didn't last into the 1980s. Many notable alternative rock bands, such as R.E.M. and the B-52s, came from the south, but their allegiance was to punk, pop, and new wave, not the blues, country, soul, and hard rock of the '70s southern rock groups. The Georgia Satellites and the Black Crowes had big chart albums in the '80s and '90s, though their hard rock was less identifiably southern than their '70s ancestors.

Like most rock styles, southern rock will continue to command a significant audience that occasionally results in artists that break out nationally. The mid-'90s success of Widespread Panic and the Dave Matthews Band proved its current viability, though these groups do not so much develop the southern rock tradition as keep it alive.

12 Recommended Recordings

The Allman Brothers Band, *Beginnings* (Polydor)
The Allman Brothers Band, *The Allman Brothers, Live at the Fillmore East* (Polydor)

Music Map

Southern Rock

Founders
The Allman Brothers Band

Southern Country Rock	Descendants	Jazzy Southern Rock	Pop-Influenced Southern Rock
Charlie Daniels, The Outlaws	Lynyrd Skynyrd, Wet Willie, Ozark Mountain Daredevils	Sea Level, Dixie Dregs	Atlanta Rhythm Section

Southern Bar Band Rock
Marshall Tucker Band,
.38 Special, Molly Hatchet

Contemporary Southern Rock
The Georgia Satellites,
The Black Crowes,
The Dave Matthews Band,
Widespread Panic

Lynyrd Skynyrd, *Gold & Platinum* (MCA)
Various Artists, *Rebel Rousers: Southern Rock Classics* (Rhino)
The Ozark Mountain Daredevils, *The Best* (A&M)
The Dixie Dregs, *The Best of the Dixie Dregs* (Grand Slamm)
The Charlie Daniels Band, *A Decade of Hits* (Epic)
The Atlanta Rhythm Section, *A Rock and Roll Alternative* (Polydor)
Sea Level, *Sea Level* (Capricorn)
Wet Willie, *The Best of Wet Willie* (Polydor)
The Georgia Satellites, *The Georgia Satellites* (Elektra)
The Black Crowes, *Shake Your Money Maker* (Def American)

– Richie Unterberger

Funk

Bridging the classic soul era and the dawn of disco, funk was R&B at its most rhythmic, earthy, and (occasionally) wild and experimental. Not as hugely successful with the masses as soul or disco, it has proven to be about as influential, strongly affecting not just all post-1970 R&B, but also contemporary rap and alternative rock music.

What exactly puts the "unk" into "funk" can be hard to pigeonhole, but there are some basic traits which distinguish it from mainstream soul and rock music. The emphasis, above all, is on the rhythm, and on the bass and drums of the rhythm section. The accent is often placed on the downbeat, or the first and third beats of 4/4 patterns. The function of the guitar becomes more rhythmic than melodic, often employing what has been called "scratch" or even "chicken scratch" staccato bursts of percussive strings; the horns also take a stronger rhythmic role than in traditional soul music, used for percussive riffing and punctuation as well as taking solos or providing harmonic support.

The rhythms, though, are often anything but simple, building upon each other and playing in counterpoint to build a polyrhythmic drive. Both the lead and backup singers often do their part to add to the excitement with chants, grunts, and screams. The lyrics have at times been quite sophisticated and socially conscious, but more often are principally concerned, like the music itself, with stream-of-consciousness grooves, built around slogans and exhortations to dance and party. Adding to the ferment are unpredictable influences from psychedelic and hard guitar rock, Latin music, doo wop, and other elements of the melting pot of American rock, soul, and pop.

Few would dispute that James Brown is not only the Godfather of Soul, but the Godfather of Funk as well. The ignition of the funk explosion can be boiled down to his landmark mid-'60s sin-

gles "Out of Sight" and especially "Papa's Got a Brand New Bag," the first smashes to incorporate the syncopated horns, stream-of-consciousness lyrics, and staccato guitars that would become funk trademarks. Although it would be a few years before the music began to be called funk, in the last half of the '60s Brown would continue to lay the funk prototype with workouts like "Cold Sweat" and "There Was a Time" that grew increasingly polyrhythmic, jazzy, and improvisational, pushing the melody to the background in favor of the churning beat and Brown's inimitable screams and groans.

The word "funk" itself began to enter the R&B/soul vocabulary with Dyke & the Blazers' R&B dance hit "Funky Broadway." Several theories and explanations of the origins of the actual word "funk" have been offered, the most likely consensus being that, like rock & roll and jazz, it was a euphemism for sexual activity, though "funk" often stood for smelly, gritty, or earthy stuff within the African-American community. By the end of the 1960s, it had come to stand for the greasiest and earthiest variant of soul music.

Although James Brown's early-'70s work was not nearly as commercially successful with the pop audience as the recordings of his 1965-69 peak (though they remained huge R&B sellers), with time they have come to be viewed as nearly as important and influential. These discs found him getting deeper and deeper into the polyrhythmic funk groove, with increasingly basic workouts that in time came to resemble one continuous (if often compelling) performance. His backup band of the era, the JBs, are now recognized as some of funk's greatest musicians, particularly guitarist Jimmy Nolen and horn-players Fred Wesley, Pee Wee Ellis, Maceo Parker, and Clair Pinckney; they also cut many underappreciated instrumental funk workouts on their own.

Another influential Brown sideman, although he was only with the band for a couple of years, was bassist Bootsy Collins, who was instrumental in boosting the importance of the bass in the funk mix. After leaving Brown in the early '70s, Bootsy teamed up with George Clinton to become a vital cog in what many funk fans regard as the finest exponents of the genre, Parliament-Funkadelic. Clinton was a veteran R&B/soul performer who changed gears radically around 1970, constructing elaborate funk heavily influenced by the acid rock of Jimi Hendrix, as well as touches of jazz and psychedelia. Almost anything went with Clinton and his troops, including extended spacy jams, inscrutable self-mythologizing, and unfathomable concept opuses about spaceships and funk itself, though the bands never lost their slightly absurd sense of humor.

The Parliament-Funkadelic family tree is among the most

Music Map

Funk

| **Funk Originators** |
| James Brown, Dyke & The Blazers, Charles Wright & The Watts 103rd Street Band |

Space & Acid Funk	**Early & Mid-'70s Funk Stars**	**Instrumental Funk**	**Funk Influenced Soul Superstars**	**Jazz-Funk Fusion**
Sly & The Family Stone, Parliament, Funkadelic, Bootsy Collins, George Clinton	War, Isaac Hayes, The Isley Brothers, Tower Of Power, Graham Central Station, Ohio Players, Kool & The Gang, Earth, Wind & Fire	The JBs, The Meters	Curtis Mayfield, Stevie Wonder, Marvin Gaye, Wilson Pickett, The Temptations	Herbie Hancock, Donald Byrd, Freddie Hubbard, Lonnie Smith

| **Latter-Day Funk-Soul** |
| Rick James, Cameo, The Gap Band, The Commodores |

twisted and difficult to follow in rock history, with a revolving door of musicians who often played in both Parliament and Funkadelic (for tangled contractual reasons, Clinton led similar groups recording under both names, sometimes simultaneously). It grew more complex when Bootsy Collins became a solo star in his own right with a similar (perhaps even more excessive) cosmic vision, as a solo act and leader of Bootsy's Rubber Band. Both Clinton and Collins remain active and influential musicians to this day, as both individual artists and collaborators with other heavyweights.

Although they are usually categorized as a soul act rather than a funk one, Sly & the Family Stone also did a great deal to cross-fertilize soul and psychedelia to come up with some of the most adventurous funk of the early '70s. Larry Graham's distinctive finger-popping bass sound has become perhaps *the* single most identifying characteristic associated with funk, and Sly Stone's commentaries on racial injustice and people power rank as some of the genre's most sophisticated lyrics. While their early, more soul- and pop-flavored work of the late '60s is equally important, their 1971 album *There's a Riot Goin' On* is their deepest foray into hardcore funk, and remains one of the few funk LPs that hits as deep with its words as its grooves.

The late '60s and early '70s saw several other less important but interesting groups make their mark in the funk parade. Dyke & the Blazers and the Watts 103rd St. Rhythm Band (most famous for "Express Yourself") were among the style's earliest practitioners. After an apprenticeship with Eric Burdon, War stormed the charts in the early and mid-'70s with a series of hits that incorporated Latin rhythms, loose, jazzy grooves, and vague social pontifications. The Meters took the sound of New Orleans R&B, already a bedrock of much post-1950 R&B, soul, and rock, into the funk era, largely on instrumentals (at least at first). Isaac Hayes took endless bubbling funk monologues onto both album and single charts, as his "Shaft" took the wah-wah guitar signatures often found in funk to their limit.

There were also quite a few funk classics in the early '70s committed to vinyl by performers who are really best categorized as soul musicians, but were deeply influenced by the funk groove. These years certainly saw some of the best work of soul giants Curtis Mayfield, Stevie Wonder, Wilson Pickett, and Marvin Gaye, all of whom drew heavily upon the expanded lyrical and musical grooves opened up by funk. The Isley Brothers, always among soul's most eclectic stars, came close to being an out-and-out funk band after beefing up their guitars and arrangements under the

influence of Jimi Hendrix and Sly Stone. Even more traditional soul vocal groups like the Temptations and O'Jays delved quite heavily into funk for a time to come up with some of their most memorable hits.

Opinions differ on the matter, but it could be argued that the early '70s saw funk at its peak. The music remained extremely popular through the mid-'70s, though, with less sophisticated acts that either concentrated on the dance-and-party element (Kool & the Gang, the Ohio Players, Graham Central Station) or the slicker, more soul- and harmony-influenced variants (Earth, Wind & Fire, Tower of Power). As for the original innovators, James Brown had seemingly run out of fresh ideas by the middle of the decade, accused even by his backup musicians of not only repeating himself but copying his imitators. Sly Stone fell victim to well-documented substance abuse and financial problems, and the Parliament-Funkadelic clan, while continuing to churn out music at the top of their game, were just too eccentric to truly catch on with the masses.

Disco, although it owed a great deal to funk in its dance rhythms, overran its ancestor in popularity in the mid- and late '70s. Some pop- and dance-oriented acts that owed a considerable debt to funk did enjoy great success in the late '70s and '80s, though, including Rick James, Cameo, the Gap Band, and the Commodores. The influence of funk was also felt in the jazz world with the advent of fusion, particularly in the work of Herbie Hancock, Donald Byrd, Freddie Hubbard, and Lonnie Smith.

If anything, funk has undergone a bit of a renaissance in the 1990s. Bootsy Collins and George Clinton are both venerated pioneers who continue to record critically respected albums and draw huge crowds on the club circuit, although they don't chart like they did at their peak. Funk was a big element in the mix of the '80s biggest African-American superstars, Michael Jackson and Prince, and funk classics are sampled constantly (some would say excessively) by contemporary rappers. And even some of the biggest White alternative rock acts, such as the Red Hot Chili Peppers, Faith No More, and Primus, draw heavily on funk's rhythms and in-your-face attitudes, if not delivering as much soul as its original progenitors.

15 Recommended Recordings

Various Artists, *In Yo' Face! The Roots of Funk, Vol. 1/2* (Rhino) [Note: this is volume one-half, or the "prequel" to the *In Yo' Face* History of Funk Series listed below]

Various Artists, *In Yo' Face! The History of Funk, Vol. 1-5* (Rhino)
James Brown, *Love Power Peace: Live at the Olympia Paris 1971* (PolyGram)
Various Artists, *James Brown's Funky People Parts 1 & 2* (PolyGram)
The J.B.s, *Funky Good Time* (PolyGram)
Dyke & the Blazers, *Dyke's Greatest Hits* (Original Sound)
Charles Wright & the Watts 103rd Street Band, *Express Yourself: The Best Of* (Warner Brothers)
Sly & the Family Stone, *There's a Riot Goin' On* (Epic)
Parliament, *Tear the Roof Off* (Casablanca)
Funkadelic, *Music for Your Mother* (Westbound)
Bootsy Collins, *Back in the Day: The Best Of* (Warners)
War, *Anthology (1970-1994)* (Rhino)
The Meters, *Funkify Your Life: The Meters Anthology* (Rhino)
Curtis Mayfield, *Superfly* (Curtom)

– Richie Unterberger

Philadelphia Soul

The last major movement of the classic soul era to make a wide impact, Philadelphia soul represented the style at its sweetest, and soul production at its most sophisticated. Its severest critics would contend that much of the genre was overly slick, the most lightweight of which helped set the ground for the more mechanized elements of disco and urban contemporary. Others would praise the music for almost exactly the same reasons, seeing the Philly sound as soul at its most romantic, ushering in an era of elaborate instrumental and vocal arrangements that continue to play a large part in Black pop music today.

The hallmarks of Philadelphia soul – the lush, buoyant strings and horns, the smooth group harmonies with a touch of street corner a cappella, the insistent danceable rhythms and smoldering ballads – were often the handiwork of an extremely small clique of producers. Most of the classic Philly soul recordings of the late '60s and first half of the '70s were devised by the producers Kenny Gamble and Leon Huff (who worked as a team), as well as producer Thom Bell (who sometimes arranged material for Gamble-Huff). Their extremely prolific output, maintaining enough diversity to ensure continuing public interest while stamping each record with distinctive Philly soul qualities, was reminiscent in some respects of Motown's production line during their 1960s glory days. Gamble & Huff, like Motown, also used a house band of sorts, a core group of musicians that contributed mightily to establishing a sound that could be identified with their records.

None of this could have been accomplished without first-rate singers, both soloists and groups, and the Philly soul stars, like those of Motown, were distinctive talents in their own right. They did differ from their counterparts in that while Motown's stars were largely tapped from their Detroit base, the Philadelphia performers were often (though not by any means always) transplants. Indeed, after the Philly sound had become a major industry force, established soul stars like Wilson Pickett, Dionne Warwick, and Lou Rawls would travel to the city specifically to record with top producers. There was generally less grit involved in the Philadelphia studios, and though it's a matter of conjecture whether the performer's role was more or less limited than it was at Motown or other soul centers, there's no doubt that production was just as important, if not more, as material or performance.

Gamble and Huff were young veterans of the Philly music scene who began scoring their first big national hits in the late '60s with smooth vocal groups like the Intruders and Delfonics, and more raucous, dance-oriented records with Archie Bell & the Drells. It was a long-running association with Jerry Butler, already a star with many popular Chicago soul recordings under his belt, that really got them on a roll. The team rode high through the mid-'70s with hits by the aforementioned acts and Joe Simon, Harold Melvin & the Blue Notes (featuring Teddy Pendergrass), and above all the O'Jays, who may have done more than any other act to define the Philadelphia soul sound.

Thom Bell oversaw a smaller roster, and generally pursued a smoother (though only slightly smoother) sound. His big acts were the Stylistics, whose creamy harmonies sailed on top of the frothiest Philly soul hits, and the Spinners, who found massive success in Philadelphia studios after years of recording as also-rans for Motown and other labels.

While Gamble-Huff and Bell dominated the Philly scene, they didn't produce every last hit of the era by any means. In particu-

lar, Bunny Sigler helped produce some successes for Gamble-Huff's Philadelphia International label, and Peter DeAngelis (who cut his teeth with, of all people, Frankie Avalon and Fabian) arranged and produced Philly soul records for Eddie Holman that both recalled and stood up to the best that Gamble-Huff were churning out at the same time.

Philadelphia soul hits occasionally boasted strong, socially aware lyrics, especially on some of the O'Jays' hottest sellers; "Back Stabbers" in particular is often cited as one of the hardest-hitting reflections of urban street life in soul music. By and large, though, they focused on the joys and sorrows of romance, instead of political themes. That didn't affect commercial sales in the least, but did perhaps limit their impact upon the world of rock at a time when the pressure for lyrical significance was high. David Bowie, always looking for something new to sink his teeth into, brought a lot of Philadelphia soul into his work in the mid-'70s when he unpredictably terminated his arty glam rock phase and traveled to Sigma Sound Studios, where many classic Philly soul hits were recorded, to cut some of his most commercially (though not critically) successful work.

With a rhythmic and elaborate production line already in place, the Philadelphia sound was more equipped than any other soul scene to face the disco era. Indeed, the mid-'70s saw many of the biggest early disco hits emerge from Philadelphia, including recordings which found stalwarts like the O'Jays adapting to the new trend, and new disco acts like the Trammps. Not as critically esteemed as the earlier Philadelphia soul productions, they were nonetheless extremely successful in the marketplace.

But the Philadelphia sound, as practiced by Gamble-Huff and their brethren, had spent most of its power as a major artistic force by the end of the '70s, much as Motown lost most of its impetus after the '60s. Unlike Motown, though, the Philadelphia producers didn't maintain a respectable sales profile, largely dropping from sight after the early 1980s. Philadelphia soul lingers, however, in almost all urban contemporary soul and R&B, both by veterans like Patti LaBelle and newcomers like Boyz II Men.

10 Recommended Recordings

The Delfonics, *Best of the Delfonics* (Arista)
The Intruders, *Super Hits* (Philadelphia International)
Archie Bell & The Drells, *The Best Of* (Rhino)
Jerry Butler, *Iceman: The Mercury Years* (PolyGram)
The O'Jays, *The O'Jays in Philadelphia* (Philadelphia International)
Eddie Holman, *I Love You* (Varese Sarabande)
The Stylistics, *Best of the Stylistics* (Amherst)
The O'Jays, *Greatest Hits* (Philadelphia International)
The Spinners, *One of a Kind Love Affair – The Anthology* (Atlantic)
Harold Melvin & the Blue Notes, *Collector's Item* (Philadelphia International)

– Richie Unterberger

Pub Rock

Defiantly unpretentious and unfazed by the zeitgeist, pub rock, despite being a short-lived permutation of British rock, was in essence a roots-rock retrenchment that flew in the face of the British glam/glitter rock of the early and mid-'70s. Many of pub rock's proponents came from a mixture of mid-'60s British R&B, hippie folk-blues, and country backgrounds, and this conflation of similar styles led to some wonderfully spirited rock & roll that, somewhat unintentionally, turned into a subtle rebellion by musicians against the machinations of the pop music industry. Pub rock never caught on in a big way; in fact some critics assert its heyday was only between 1971-74. Nonetheless, there were plenty of excellent pub rock bands, and many musicians who cut their teeth during this time went on to join some of the seminal English bands of the late '70s.

Although it shares many common elements with American roots-rock, pub rock is distinctly British; the result of a small but supportive community-based scene that was focused in pubs around London. The scene coalesced around a former London jazz club, the Tally Ho, and soon spread to dozens of other pubs in the city keen to book rock bands. With glitter/glam rock dominating the British charts, pub rock musicians, fans, and the pub owners who booked them regarded this music as a way to reject the egregious trappings of pop superstardom for something that was more honest, direct, and communal.

Ironically, the band that gets the credit for jumpstarting pub rock is an obscure American R&B band, Eggs over Easy, which gigged at the Tally Ho in 1972. Despite this jarring piece of history, it should be known that the English musicians inspired by the Eggs had been playing in mid-to-late-'60s blues, folk, and R&B bands such as the Action and Kippington Lodge (the latter featuring Brinsley Schwarz and Nick Lowe). British rock critic Pete Frame, who has written definitively about pub rock, notes three periods in the genre's development roughly spanning the years 1972-1975: first was the early Tally Ho period featuring bands such as Bees Make Honey (their moniker a tribute to Eggs over Easy), Brinsley Schwarz, and Ducks Deluxe; the second wave of bands included Kilburn and the High Roads (featuring Ian Dury), Chilli Willi and the Red Hot Peppers, and Ace; the third and final bunch of pub rockers were led by the Winkies, Sniff and the Tears, and the great Dr. Feelgood.

Of the aforementioned bands, the one perhaps most familiar to American audiences is Brinsley Schwarz. Named after their great lead guitarist, they, more than any other band, defined all that was good about pub rock. And, unlike many of their ilk (up until Dr. Feelgood), they had the longest and most successful recording career and managed to get many of their LPs released in America. Despite a storied public-relations disaster wherein the band was flown to the Fillmore East for a showcase gig and subsequently was slammed by American rock critics (effectively ending stateside interest in pub rock), Brinsley Schwarz set up a two-gigs-a-week residency at the Tally Ho, providing the inspiration for literally every pub rock band that came in their wake. Brinsley Schwarz broke up in 1975, bassist Nick Lowe went on to a solo career, as did guitarist Ian Gomm, while Schwarz and keyboardist Bob Andrews joined forces with ex-Ducks Deluxe guitarist Martin Belmont to form Graham Parker's phenomenal backing band, the Rumour.

Lowe's success and the rise of Graham Parker and the Rumour are a small indication of the kind of influence pub rock had on the next generation of British rock & rollers. After Kilburn and the High Roads, Ian Dury embarked on a wonderful, if inconsistent, solo career; Elvis Costello's earliest musical days were with pub rockers Flip City and he found future Attractions drummer Pete Thomas as a crucial link to early pub rock; Clash frontman Joe Strummer made his first records in a late-period pub rock band, the 101ers; even enigmatic avant-gardists the Residents had significant musical contributions made to their records by pub rock vet, the late Phil "Snakefinger" Lithman, another ex-member of Chilli Willi. And lest one think that pub rock had no impact on the American Top Ten, remember that the song "How Long" by pub rock veterans Ace, featuring vocalist/keyboardist Paul Carrack reached number three in 1975.

Pete Frame argues (and he's right) that after the breakup of Brinsley Schwarz and Ducks Deluxe in 1975, pub rock was, for all intents and purposes, over. However, a wild, high-energy blues/R&B band from Canvey Island in Essex named Dr. Feelgood was the most vital band of the late pub rock era and served as a crucial link to early punk rock. Fronted by the late great Lee Brilleaux (who succumbed to cancer in 1994), and the inspired guitar playing of Wilko Johnson, the Feelgoods released their first LP, *Down by the Jetty* (recorded in mono), in 1975 and released four great LPs before Johnson's departure in 1977. The band soldiered on until Brilleaux's death (at the end Brilleaux was the lone original member), and made some good records, but lacked the panache that Wilko supplied.

What's important to note is that the members of Feelgood lent the necessary cash for pub rock-fan Dave Robinson to start his great independent label Stiff and give artists like Nick Lowe, Elvis Costello, Ian Dury, Wreckless Eric, the Damned, and Dave Edmunds a place to record.

In many ways, pub rock, because of its insularity, smallness, and disinterest in becoming an international pop phenomenon, was destined to last only a short while. And although it remains somewhat of a mystery to many American ears, the music that resulted from this scene retains its vigorous, incorruptable spirit. It was the music of the moment, played by musicians who cared more about sincerity and less about fame.

8 Essential Recordings

Ace, *Five a Side* (Anchor)
Bees Make Honey, *Music Every Night* (EMI)
Brinsley Schwarz, *Brinsley Schwarz* and *Silver Pistol* (Capitol/Edsel)

Chilli Willi and the Red Hot Peppers, *Bongos over Balham* (Mooncrest)
Ducks Deluxe, *Don't Mind Rockin' Tonight* (RCA)
Dr. Feelgood, *Malpractice* and *Stupidity* (Columbia/Liberty)
The 101ers, *Elgin Avenue Breakdown* (Andalucia)
The Winkies, *The Winkies* (Chrysalis)

– John Dougan

Punk Rock

English critic Jon Savage noted that history is made by those who say "No," and in 1976 there was no louder "No" than that of punk rock. Dismissed by the shortsighted as crude anti-musicality, punk dared to place itself in direct confrontation to the then-ruling rock hegemony: generally thirty-something pop stars content to reinvent and regurgitate clichés in a sort of stylistic stasis, a dire situation exacerbated by the tightly controlled mid-to-late-'70s FM programming style known as AOR (album-oriented rock) which was glutted with a seemingly endless array of not-so-hard-rock and not-quite-so-heavy-metal bands that sounded as if they'd been created by record-label marketing departments.

From the start, punk angrily stood in direct contrast to the zeitgeist. Still, as with all rock genres and subgenres, it was hardly an organic movement. Its antecedents included the noisy primitivism of the Velvet Underground, the mega-loud working-class anger of the Who, the high-energy guitar spuzz of the MC5 and the Stooges, and the androgyny of the New York Dolls (with a few dollops of Bowie and early Roxy Music for good measure). Of course as punk developed (Note: The first known use of "punk rock" as a genre identifier goes back to the early '70s, *Creem* magazine, and critics Dave Marsh and Lester Bangs), it metamorphosed into numerous subgenres that championed a host of influences as disparate as reggae, mid-'60s bubblegum, early psychedelic rock, art-rock, free jazz, and musique concrète. Literally anything fit the equation: it was just a matter of attitude and presentation.

In a purely historical sense, punk's timeline is 1975-1978, and even that's somewhat generous. But with its supernova long since faded and its style coopted by greedy major labels who turned it into the more sanitized "new wave," punk's impact is still being felt in the '90s. It almost singlehandedly revived the independent record-label network and helped start a legitimate network of underground journals and a new style of music criticism. Most importantly, it imbued a younger generation with the belief that they too could become part of the great rock & roll whatsis, thereby planting the seeds for the future development of many successful U.S. and U.K. regional alternative rock scenes (e.g., Los Angeles; Minneapolis; Seattle; Athens, GA; Manchester, England). It's hard to imagine bands like the Replacements, Nirvana, or even R.E.M. existing without the contributions of the Sex Pistols, Clash, the Ramones, and the Buzzcocks.

These days, the term "punk" seems almost quaint. And the story of punk and its pervasive influence is only now being told. But as with rap and current heavy metal (two genres that share punk's attitude), punk always seemed to be about the unencumbered joy of self-expression: total, unequivocal and often unedited. If you listen to a handful of the records listed below, you'll soon hear that, even today, punk never seems too far from the pop zeitgeist, a range of influence far greater than its originators had in mind.

BOOKS

Punk Diary, by George Dimarc (St. Martin's, 1994)

– John Dougan

British Punk

Taking cues from some American bands, as well as the English mini-phenomenon known as "pub rock," English punk transmogrified into an entirely different beast, one that also valued stripped-down, primal guitar rock and a DIY (do it yourself) attitude, but which openly embraced multiculturalism (e.g., ska and reggae), politics (a dysfunctional late-'70s government), and radical philosophy (e.g., the French Situationists). With the galvanic Sex Pistols leading the way, English rock would never be the same, as the sybaritic excesses of the post-hippie era were replaced by angry kids yelling "no future" and referring to successful rock stars as "boring old farts."

Punk took Great Britain – both its entertainment industry and its general citizenry – by surprise. In the mid-'70s, the massive tornado of the British Invasion was a fading memory whose survivors sat atop the charts with pale echoes of their best work. Disco and soft pop/rock were the trends of the day, as they were in the U.S. The nation's economy was flailing, and more and more teenagers left school to go straight on the dole (a British equivalent of welfare), with little hope for financial success or social stimulation in the near future.

Malcolm McLaren, who with his wife Vivienne Westwood ran a boutique that catered to an ever-changing clientele seeking alternative fashions, was on the lookout for a band of loutish post-adolescents to use as a platform for his loosely held anarchist and Situationist ideas. He harbored aspirations to take over the New York Dolls' management, but when that band splintered, he looked to the even scruffier, younger musicians that frequented his store. In late 1975, the Sex Pistols began to perform, with McLaren as their manager.

An "alternative" scene did exist in Britain on a small level, as "pub rock." In truth, bands like Dr. Feelgood, Eggs over Easy, Ducks Deluxe, and even the acclaimed Brinsley Schwarz sound pretty tame and unrevolutionary in comparison to punk. What they shared with punk was a disdain for contemporary pop and progressive rock trends, and a love for basic, stripped-down, guitar-oriented music. Besides supplying punk with some of its early figureheads, such as the principal movers of Stiff Records and Joe Strummer (who left his pub rock band the 101ers to join the Clash), the pub rock performance circuit provided crucial live venues for punk acts when the music was struggling to get off the ground.

Throughout 1976, the Sex Pistols built up a fierce underground reputation with their incendiary live shows (which were often as not, violence-ridden, chaotic affairs). In late 1976, their debut single "Anarchy in the U.K.," established punk's modus operandi: scabrous guitars, hyperkinetic rhythms, and inflammatory, venomous lyrics, with crude energy overall.

The Pistols endured a complicated tangle of personnel, management, and label problems in 1977 that kept them from releasing a full-length album for about a year (although a couple more key singles appeared in the meantime). Other groups were already following their blueprint, however, and stepped into the breach that Johnny Rotten had opened. The most famous members of what has come to be called "The Class of '77" include the Damned; the Clash, who infused punk with revolutionary politics and reggae rhythms; the Jam, post-mods who modeled themselves after the early Who; and the Buzzcocks, whose nervous, accelerated rhythms didn't hide a keen grasp of pop hooks.

As with all momentous musical movements, these figureheads (they would have disdained the label "stars" at the time) were the tip of an explosion that saw many minor but important groups adding their voices to the clamor, as well as interesting one- and two-shots leaping into the volcano. Generation X, the Adverts, the Vibrators, and the Saints (from Australia) recorded important early punk records; X-Ray Spex did a lot to smash rock stereotypes by featuring a half-black teenage female with braces as their lead singer. Groups like Chelsea, Eater, Johnny Moped, and Slaughter & the Dogs are esteemed by collectors for the one or two memorable songs they had in them.

Today, early British punk records still sound exciting, but are hardly the epitome of nihilistic shock. At the time, however, they could not have caused more of a sensation, inspiring equal measures of fervent praise and outright hostility. The tempo was FAST (although hardcore made it go even faster), the guitars and vocals slashing and LOUD, and the lyrics – a lot of which, though by no means all, being negative in nature – addressed politics, sex, depression, and society with a frank realism that had rarely been heard in pop music, and never as part of a broad-based movement. The performers were not seasoned virtuosos, valuing inspiration and attitude above professionalism. Some listeners viewed the results as unbearably crude; others welcomed them as a necessary shot of fresh air to blast rock & roll out of its complacency.

Punk never took hold in the U.S. as it did in Britain, although those who were converted took up the music with a passion that equaled their U.K. counterparts. The Sex Pistols found this out the hard way, with John Lydon (né Rotten) leaving the group in early 1978 after the last show of a brief, legendarily chaotic tour of the States, where their album stopped just short of the Top 100.

British punk did not so much die out as mutate and diversify,

Music Map

British Punk

Pub Rock	Early '70s American Proto-Punk

1st Generation British Punk
The Sex Pistols, The Clash, The Jam, The Damned, Generation X, The Buzzcocks

Second Generation British Punk
The Adverts, The Undertones, X-Ray Spex, The Vibrators

Early British New Wave Elvis Costello, Nick Lowe, Tom Robinson	**Arty British Punk/ New Wave** Wire, Joy Division, The Fall, Magazine, Siouxsie & The Banshees

as any vital musical style needs to do in order to survive. As liberating as the first wave of punk was, it was impossible to perform an endless loop of hyper-fast, bile-filled anthems, as the musicians' ambitions broadened and their skills improved. The Jam remained huge stars in their homeland through the early '80s. Like the Clash, who became stars in the U.S. at long last after 1979's London Calling, they refined their sound and incorporated R&B, soul, and pop into their compositions without compromising their integrity. While original British punkers like Generation X and Sham 69 played themselves out almost immediately, others went into arty minimalism (Wire, the Fall), post-psychedelia (the Soft Boys), pop-punk (the Undertones, from Northern Ireland), or new wave (Siouxsie & the Banshees).

A fertile, more techno-oriented scene developed in the Buzzcocks' home territory of Manchester, spearheaded by Joy Division and other acts on Factory Records. And pub rock veterans like Nick Lowe, Elvis Costello, and Tom Robinson tapped into punk's energy to create new wave, which by 1980 had become the new label for a modified, tamed, but innovative offspring of the original punk explosion.

12 Essential Recordings

The Sex Pistols, *Never Mind the Bollocks* (Warner Brothers)
Various Artists, *Anarchy in the UK – UK Punk I (1976-77)* (Rhino)
Various Artists, *The Modern World – UK Punk II (1977-78)* (Rhino)
The Clash, *The Clash* (Epic)
The Jam, *Snap!* (Polydor)
The Buzzcocks, *Singles Going Steady* (IRS)
The Adverts, *Crossing the Sea with the Adverts* (Link Classics, UK)
X-Ray Spex, *Germ-Free Adolescents* (EMI)
The Vibrators, *Power of Money: The Best of the Vibrators* (Continuum)
The Undertones, *The Undertones* (Rykodisc)
Generation X, *Generation X* (Chrysalis)
The Damned, *Damned Damned Damned* (Frontier)

BOOK

England's Dreaming: Sex Pistols and Punk Rock, by Jon Savage (St. Martin's, 1991)

– *Richie Unterberger & John Dougan*

American Punk

American punk rock was actively brewing years before the U.K. scene. The trade-off, perhaps, was that it was less explosive, less of a broad-based movement, less confrontational, and less concerned with disowning time-honored rock & roll traditions. Still, it was not only a crucial source of inspiration for Britain's more volatile brand of punk, but a more diverse (though diffuse) movement whose effects were just as influential and long-reaching.

Some have argued that the true source of American punk rock lies in the incredibly active garage rock scene of the mid-'60s, and indeed the term "punk rock" was originally coined by critics like Dave Marsh, Lester Bangs, and future Patti Smith Group guitarist Lenny Kaye to refer to these bands. In the late '60s, Detroit groups the MC5 and the Stooges played amphetamined rock driven by fuzzed-out guitars and outraged (and outrageous) lyrics that sound all but indistinguishable from early punk records.

An equally important, artier strand of raw rock & roll minimalism was pioneered in New York in the late '60s by the Velvet Underground. Not all of their work foreshadowed punk, but even their songs that didn't feature street-life vignettes and overamped guitars (and there were plenty of both, especially on their early albums) had a no-frills, unembellished attitude that acted as the standard for the many groups, in New York and elsewhere, that looked to them for inspiration.

Two American acts blazed lonely trails in the early '70s that midwifed the birth of punk. In Boston, the Modern Lovers, led by Jonathan Richman, added youthful naiveté to the Velvets' glorious primitivism. Their early '70s recordings rank among the most joyous and affecting proto-punk/new wave efforts, although, tragically, the original and best lineup of the band released nothing during their lifetime. The New York Dolls affected a trashy, early Rolling Stones glam rock image that attracted raves from local critics, but made little national impact, although Malcolm McLaren's brief association with the band in their dying days gave him many ideas to pass on to the Sex Pistols.

The American punk scene coalesced around New York City's Lower East Side, specifically at Hilly Kristal's Bowery club, CBGB's. By late 1975/early 1976, bands such as the Patti Smith Group, the Ramones, Talking Heads, Blondie, Television, and the Heartbreakers (featuring former New York Doll Johnny Thunders) had pretty much made this dive their home, and complacent old American rock now faced a significant challenge.

Suddenly there was a scene that offered cultural solidarity, if little in the way of stylistic unanimity: the fast, loud, minimalism of the Ramones was offset by Patti Smith's poetic incantations, Television's spiraling guitar duels, Blondie's sexy neo-Spector pop, the egghead pop of the Talking Heads, and the fierce synthesizer minimalism of Suicide. What connected these bands was a sense of purpose and community; they were angry outsiders who insisted that the only way to change rock & roll was to dismantle it and rebuild it, thereby reclaiming it. That didn't mean they weren't cognizant of rock's best traditions: "Hey Joe," "Surfin' Bird," "1-2-3 Red Light," and old songs by the 13th Floor Elevators, Al Green, and Randy & the Rainbows were featured prominently in the early repertoires of several of the bands listed above.

At the outset, these bands were more influential than popular on a national level, though Patti Smith did fairly well, and Blondie and the Talking Heads would eventually break through to superstardom. In fact, Television was far more popular in the U.K., where their second album even made the Top Ten. The Ramones were also more popular there, and extremely influential; indeed, their "1-2-3-4!" brand of accelerated rock & roll made them one of the only early CBGB's bands to fit most listeners' basic conceptions of punk rock. It's been claimed that Malcolm McLaren took the prototype safety pin and torn T-shirt punk look from Richard Hell, who helped ignite the scene with Tom Verlaine in the original Television lineup before fronting the Voidoids.

Outside of New York, the U.S. lacked a strong punk scene. With innovative but impossibly uncommercial groups like the Electric Eels, as well as more accessible acts like Rocket from the Tombs and Mirrors, Cleveland had an active proto-punk scene that lacked the exposure, either in a renowned club or on national record labels, necessary to spread its influence. Devo (not actually from Cleveland, but from the Ohio town of Akron) and Pere Ubu eventually broke through to widespread recognition with a style of new wave that was bleaker and more mechanized than most anything happening in New York. Many Boston bands would appear by the late '70s, on the whole more identified with power-pop than punk.

In 1977, active punk scenes quickly sprung up in California, particularly in Los Angeles, which owed considerably more to the influence of early British punk – just making its inroads in the

Music Map

American Punk

'60s Proto-Punk Groups The Velvet Underground, The Stooges, The MC5	
Early '70s Proto-Punk Groups The Modern Lovers, The New York Dolls	
CBGB's Groups The Patti Smith Group, The Ramones, Television, Blondie, Richard Hell & The Voidoids, Talking Heads, The Heartbreakers	**Ohio Groups** Pere Ubu, Devo
California Punk The Avengers, X, The Dils, The Germs	**New York No-Wave** Suicide, Lydia Lunch, James Chance, Glenn Branca

States via import records – than the New York bands. Generally, these groups played a harder, nastier, more jaded type of punk. Not as commercial as either the London or New York punk acts – not that any of the California bands would have cared – the Dils, the Germs, the Avengers, and the Dickies laid the foundation for thrash/hardcore. X, very much a part of the early L.A. scene, would be one of the few to break out into any sort of large-scale success, by which time they'd tempered and diversified their original sound.

Isolated pockets of punk activity took hold in quite a few U.S. cities, mainly ones with large, youthful, artistic-leaning populations, such as Seattle and Austin. But the fact of the matter is, punk never seized the collective consciousness in the States, partly because of industry resistance to the music, and at least partly because many (perhaps most) rock listeners didn't like it. Nonetheless, American punk bands were a bedrock of much of the music of the 1980s and 1990s: the Athens, GA, new wave scene; alternative rock; the "no-wave" of New York avant-rockers ranging from Lydia Lunch and James Chance to Glenn Branca and Sonic Youth; hardcore; grunge – all of these developments derived key inspiration from the original punk bands.

12 Essential U.S. Punk Recordings

The Modern Lovers, *Modern Lovers* (Bomp)
The Patti Smith Group, *Horses* (Arista)
The Ramones, *All the Stuff & More, Vol. 1* (Warner Brothers)
Television, *Marquee Moon* (Elektra)
Blondie, *Blondie* (Chrysalis)
The Talking Heads, *Talking Heads '77* (Sire)
Various Artists, *Blank Generation – The New York Scene* (Rhino)
Various Artists, *We're Desperate – The L.A. Scene* (Rhino)
Richard Hell & the Voidoids, *Blank Generation* (Sire)
The Avengers, *Avengers* (CD Presents)
Suicide, *Suicide* (Restless)
Pere Ubu, *Terminal Tower* (Twintone)

Book

From the Velvets to the Voidoids, by Clinton Heylin (Penguin, 1993)

– Richie Unterberger & John Dougan

New Wave

Of the many thorny issues inherent in writing about rock & roll, none is more perplexing and alienating than the use of genre identifiers to corral disparate groups of musicians into one simple category. While it makes it easier for the general public to develop some idea of the kind of music a band plays, unless it's a description that eliminates all possibility of being misconstrued (e.g., fans of folk music are not likely to check out a heavy metal band), there is simply too much grey area and too many bands that can fit under one classification. In addition rock journalists (myself included) lazily overuse the terminology as if it had real meaning.

Which brings us to "new wave." What is it? Well, essentially it's all post-punk era music (circa 1979) that journalists, record-label A&R people, disc jockeys, and assorted music-biz folk didn't want to call punk rock. Despite punk's grassroots success here and abroad, to describe a band as "punk" still doomed it commercially. Why? Mainly because punk rock was relegated outsider status; it was music that was considered too harsh, radical and alienating to speak to larger, more traditional rock and pop audiences. Hence the term "new wave" (whose cultural origins go back to its use as a description of avant-garde French filmmaking in the late '50s) was substituted to indicate bands that were progressive, different, but not necessarily threatening, nor devoid of commercial potential. A yin/yang concept in the truest sense, new wave yielded many fine bands and great records. However, there were just as many posers and fakers who were deemed "new wave" by industry types who believed that reasonable facsimiles would sell as well as the real thing. In some instances, they were right.

In America the punk/new wave dichotomy began almost from the moment punk rock became part of the language. In the Bowery scene at CBGB's, bands like the Ramones and Richard Hell and the Voidoids were "punk," but Blondie and Talking Heads were "new wave." Similarly, in burgeoning underground music scenes across America new wave could describe bands as far afield as the Cars, the Motels, the Go Go's, Pere Ubu, Jonathan Richman, the B-52s, REM, Devo, X, the Blasters, the Residents, and dozens more, good, bad and indifferent, who took their musical cues from punk rock, yet seemed less overtly anti-social and more marketable. This explains why nearly all of the aforementioned bands eventually landed contracts with major labels, who saw a greater profit potential in new wave than in punk; primarily because in the disparate, amorphous world of new wave, there was no one formula for success.

Despite being lumped into the same category, there were significant differences between the wan, solipsistic, radio-friendly pop fodder offered up by the Motels and the brilliant, bizarre, challenging, art-punk of Pere Ubu. Also, some of the performers dubbed "new wave" had in fact been around since before the days of punk rock (e.g., Richman and the Residents) or were just plain weird fringe bands that had zero commercial appeal (e.g., bands that made up the New York "no wave" scene). What was becoming clear was that new wave as a genre identifier tried to cover too much ground and as a result became an almost meaningless term. Power-pop bands were new wave, but so were art-punks; roots-rock revisionists like the Blasters were new wave, but so was the kitschy dance-rock of the B-52s. This democratization and stylistic interdependence was exciting, but ultimately it was confusing, and rock music fans just wanted good rock music, regardless of what subgenre it was assigned.

Across the pond, in England, new wave began by conflating punk's aggression with the anti-pop-star attitude of pub rock and, early on, produced some of rock's best singer/songwriters. Elvis Costello, Graham Parker and Nick Lowe (although Lowe had been around the block a time or two) created rock that was bristling with venom and sarcasm, and was mostly free of the narcissistic self-indulgence of the American singer/songwriters of the early '70s.

Along with this decidedly working-class resentment, English new wave, like its American counterpart, seemed to encompass anything and everything. There was the speedy, trash-pop of the Rezillos, who were sort of a Scottish B-52s; the dread-filled doom and gloom of Joy Division (who became the dance-rock New Order after the death of Ian Curtis); the agit-prop noise-rock of the Pop Group; the calculated, melodic pop-punk of the Police; the dissonant, politically oriented left-wing ranting of the Mekons and the Gang of Four; the feminist-inspired reggae-funk of the Slits (who spanned both the punk and new wave eras); the retro-psychedelia of the Cure and later bands such as Happy Mondays, Inspiral Carpets; and the dour, tuneful, self-aggrandizing rock of the Smiths.

There were also mini-revivals associated with British new wave

such as the neo-Mod movement, which produced no worthwhile music and was thankfully short-lived, and the ska revival, which produced great bands like the Specials, Selecter and (for the first couple of LPs) Madness.

Today, what was once new wave is now alternative rock; a term that also suffers from diminished meaning as its use increases. These days, what is new wave is more a retrenchment to music of the early days of punk rock that was considered uncommercial in the late '70s. Ironically this buzzsaw guitar sound has now fueled the mega-platinum success of bands like Green Day and the Offspring. Yet, no matter what the time period, sweeping, indefinable terms will always be used by critics and scenesters to grapple with the question, "How can you lump a lot of likeminded bands who don't play the same kind of music into one category?" Great new wave bands both past and present would have existed no matter what they were called, however, and so much good music has been associated with new wave that it is an important part of contemporary rock history.

20 Essential Records

Pere Ubu, *The Modern Dance* (Blank)
X, *Los Angeles/Wild Gift* (Slash/Warner Bros.)
B-52s, *The B-52s* (Warner Bros.)
Devo, *Are We Not Men? We Are Devo!* (Warner Bros.)
Residents, *Meet the Residents* (Ralph)
Talking Heads, *Popular Favorites: 1984-1992 Sand in the Vaseline* (Sire)
The Modern Lovers, *Modern Lovers* (Rhino)
Blondie, *Best of Blondie* (Chrysalis)
Rezillos, *Can't Stand the Rezillos: The Almost Complete Rezillos* (Sire)
The Smiths, *The Singles* (Sire)
Elvis Costello, *My Aim Is True* and *This Year's Model* (Rykodisc)
Graham Parker, *Howlin' Wind* and *Heat Treatment* (Mercury)
XTC, *Waxworks-Some Singles 1977-1982* (Geffen)
Joy Division, *Unknown Pleasures* (Qwest)
The Cure, *Standing on a Beach: The Singles* (Elektra)
The Slits, *Cut* (Antilles)
The Blasters, *Blasters Collection* (Slash)
New Order, *Movement* (Factory)

– John Dougan

Power-Pop

While there is nothing inherently wrong with power-pop, it's often seen as a post-punk major-label marketing scam, helped along by greedy do-anything-to-make-it musicians who were willing to trade in their spiky haircuts and alienation for skinny ties and sunny dispositions. As true as this is, it represents only a fraction of what can accurately be described as power-pop. While it's very easy (and tempting) to dismiss this subgenre as egregious, market-driven dross, the fact remains that power-pop, even at its sleaziest and most manipulative, has a longer history than many people realize, producing some terrific bands and equally terrific music.

The musical sourcepoint for nearly all power-pop is the Beatles. Virtually all stylistic appropriations begin with them: distinctive harmony singing, strong melodic lines, unforgettable guitar riffs, lyrics about boys and girls in love; they created the model that other power-poppers copied for the next couple of decades. Other profound influences include the Who, the Kinks, and the Move, bands whose aggressive melodies and loud distorted guitars put the "power" in power-pop. Actually, in order to be complete, it's safe to say that an authoritative genealogical tree of power-pop influences would include virtually all of the bands of the British Invasion and Mod era. Which brings up a subtle, yet essential facet of nearly all (era notwithstanding) American power-pop bands — they seem, vaguely, British. That is, they sing with a slight English lilt to their voices, are likely to cover songs by British bands and, as was the case with many British mod bands, dress up rather than down. Even the most prominent American power-pop influence, the jangly folk-rock of the mid-'60s Byrds, had a British tinge to it a la the Searchers and the Hollies.

American power-pop's first heyday (ironically, before it was called power-pop) was the early '70s. Few American bands encapsulated the commercial popularity and influential cult status of early power-pop better than the Raspberries and Big Star. Both recorded great records, and while Big Star's entire recorded output (thanks mainly to the talents of Alex Chilton) remains inarguably the best of the bunch, both bands approached their craft with a similar intent: to write smart, punchy, hook-filled songs. For the Raspberries, a Cleveland-based band built around the Brit-rock obsessions of vocalist Eric Carmen and guitarist Wally Bryson, it was a string of huge hits like "Go All the Way," "Tonight" and the autobiographical "Overnight Sensation (Hit Record)" that made them one of the best commercial rock bands of the early '70s. Granted, their songs were hardly deep, but as heartfelt evocations of romantic teen angst and the naiveté of young love, they remain unbeatable. Memphis-natives Big Star, on the other hand, did record deep, emotionally complex songs on three amazing records (#1 Record, Radio City and Sister Lovers) that went unheard in their day but contained the best songs of American power-pop ("Ballad of El Goodo," "Mod Lang," and the stunning "September Gurls"). Rediscovered by a later generation of pop-loving rockers (most notably the Replacements' Paul Westerberg), Big Star, though never touching the commercial success enjoyed by the Raspberries, became significantly more influential and revered.

By the mid-to-late-'70s, power-pop's lifeline continued with fluke hits like Dwight Twilley's 1975 Top 20 smash "I'm on Fire." Twilley, a native of Tulsa, OK, along with partner Phil Seymour, recorded a wonderful debut record, Sincerely, that along with containing the aforementioned hit, is an excellent example of ebullient, tuneful, rockabilly-tinged power-pop. Around the same time, Cheap Trick, a hard rock/pop quartet from Rockford, IL, capitalized on the strong vocals and good looks of lead singer Robin Zander, and the bizarre antics and the surreal lyrical narratives of guitarist Rick Neilsen, recording some of the finest pop/rock of the time. After three undeniably great records, the worldwide success of a so-so live album signalled the beginning of the end as Cheap Trick began living up to its name, their greatness reduced to formula.

Power-pop, however, was not solely the province of American bands who wanted to sound British; there was a British power-pop "invasion" of sorts in the '70s. Badfinger was the most blatantly Beatles-influenced (they even recorded for the Beatles' Apple label and had Paul McCartney as a producer), but they produced some excellent, occasionally thrilling songs such as "No Matter What," "Baby Blue," and "Day After Day," all three Top 20 hits in 1970-71. Loaded with lush guitars, instantly recognizable melodies and two fine singers in Pete Ham and Joey Molland (a fellow Liverpudlian who bears a strong resemblance to McCartney), Badfinger was the model of a great power-pop band. Sadly, guitarist and songwriter Pete Ham committed suicide in 1975, effectively ending the band's career.

By the mid-'70s English power-pop was essentially the music of glam rock: stiff, boot-stomping rhythms that sounded like football (i.e. soccer) chants. Glam rock cranked up the guitars while sweetening the melodies, thereby making loud, bubblegum rock fodder perfect for radio. With artists such as Gary Glitter, the Sweet, Slade, and Suzi Quatro (an American who found great success in England) leading the way, glam rock produced a handful of good songs, one great band (Slade) and the obsequious marketing of negligibly talented teen idols (e.g. Bay City Rollers) that would become common practice in the early-'80s power-pop sweepstakes.

Power-pop's nadir was reached, ironically, during an amazingly fertile period in its history. In the wake of Cheap Trick, excellent Midwestern power-pop bands like the Pezband and the Shoes (both from Illinois) made great records. On the West Coast, Jack Lee, Peter Case and Paul Collins formed the punk-pop Nerves; in Boston, the Real Kids released their debut LP; in Athens, GA, R.E.M. released the Chronic Town EP, a gem of Byrdsian power-pop; and in New York, Chris Stamey and Peter Holsapple formed the dB's and released two of the smartest and most ambitious power-pop records ever made. Even in England, former pub rocker Will Birch of the Kursaal Flyers formed the Records, a snazzy little combo that released a couple of fine records and an unforgettable single, "Starry Eyes."

However, power-pop of the late-'70s/early-'80s is also remembered for the slavish imitators and skinny-tie-wearing no-talents, writing second-generation Raspberries ripoffs, pouting and posing on destined-for-the-cut-out-bin album covers that major labels vomited at an alarming rate. They were faceless hacks like the Cretones, Fotomaker (sadly with ex-Raspberry Wally Bryson), the Producers, Sue Saad and the Next, the Romantics (who had two hit singles and are mostly remembered for their song "What I Like About You" which was used in beer ads), Tattoo, the Tourists (with future-Eurythmics Dave Stewart and Annie Lennox!), the

Jags, the Sinceros, the Yachts, Yipes!, and countless other bandwagon jumpers.

But, the sine qua non of power-pop condescension and sleaze was without a doubt, the Knack. Fueled by their malodorous 1979 #1 hit single, "My Sharona," the Knack singlehandedly gave power-pop its bad name. Unctuous to the nth degree, obvious in their Beatle fakery, the Knack were less a band and more a marketing-department creation (who laughed all the way to the bank), were a trivia question by the mid-'80s, had the audacity to regroup in the early '90s (mainly because Knack leader Doug Feiger is a boyhood friend of hotshot producer Don Was), and recorded another lousy record, which didn't sell.

Although most people are loathe to use the term these days, power-pop still exists. Alternarock bands like the Posies, Belly, Throwing Muses, Elastica, Echobelly, Urge Overkill and the Gin Blossoms are not too far removed from the power-pop days of yore. There are flashes of it in Nirvana, and even in retro-punk bands such as the Offspring and Green Day. Inevitably, there are also bands like Material Issue and Jellyfish, who are merely the next generation of Cretones and Jags, fobbing off style and mechanical reproduction as substance. Ultimately power-pop is much better than the term implies, and it seems as though it's not willing to go away anytime soon. Which is fine, just as long as skinny ties never make a comeback.

20 Essential Records

Rhino's DIY American and English Power Pop Anthologies
Badfinger, Straight Up (Capitol)
Big Star, #1 Record and Radio City (Stax)
Cheap Trick, In Color (Epic)
The dB's, Stands for Decibels and Repercussion (IRS)
Flamin' Groovies, Shake Some Action (Sire)
Go-Go's, Go-Go's Greatest (IRS)
Nick Lowe, Pure Pop for Now People (Columbia)
Pezband, 30 Seconds over Shaumburg (PVC)
Raspberries, The Raspberries' Best (featuring Eric Carmen) (Capitol)
The Real Kids, The Real Kids (Norton)
The Records, The Records (Virgin)
Scruffs, Wanna Meet the Scruffs? (Powerplay)
Shoes, Black Vinyl Shoes (Black Vinyl)
Slade, Best of Slade (Polydor)
Sweet, Best of Sweet (Capitol)
Dwight Twilley Band, Sincerely (DDC)

– John Dougan

Hardcore & Thrash

Few rock listeners have noncommital, or even mixed, opinions about hardcore and thrash. The substantial majority will not only never develop a fondness for the music, but will always view it with active dislike; quite a few figuratively cover their ears and run as fast as they can in the opposite direction. On the other hand, its "core" audience, if you will, is one of the most fiercely loyal and zealous subcultures in all of rock & roll. The hardcore scene, love it or hate it, has exerted a substantial influence on rock & roll, one that is felt in today's Top 40 more than it was in its early-'80s heyday.

Hardcore, to use what by now has become a cliché, was harder, louder, and faster than its direct ancestor, early punk music. As shocking an assault as first-generation punk was on the heart of the rock industry, hardcore turned on the heat and tightened the screws. Lots of listeners already found the Ramones, Buzzcocks, the Clash, and other early punk giants impossibly fast, loud, and abrasive. Hardcore took the Ramones' trademark "1-2-3-4!" kick-off countdown and sped up the tempos as fast as humanly possible, sticking largely to monochrome guitars, bass, and drums, and favoring half-shouted lyrics venting the most inflammatory sentiments the singers and songwriters could devise.

Hardcore's roots could be traced to the early American reaction to the supernova of 1977 British punk. In a similiar manner to garage bands reacting to the British Invasion in the mid-'60s, American groups came up with an even cruder and rawer variation. A great many of these bands were based in California, particularly southern California and the San Francisco Bay Area. Outfits like the Avengers, Dils, and Germs played a more jaded and nastier version of British punk. Very shortly afterwards, other bands (who were often peers of the aforementioned acts) went the last nine yards into

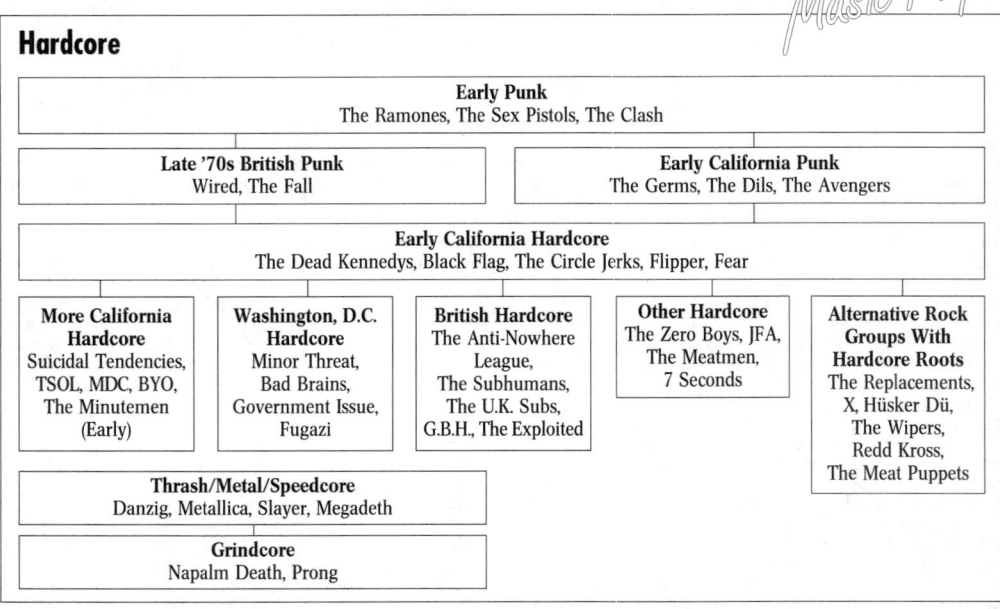

Music Map

Hardcore

| **Early Punk** |
| The Ramones, The Sex Pistols, The Clash |

| **Late '70s British Punk** | **Early California Punk** |
| Wired, The Fall | The Germs, The Dils, The Avengers |

| **Early California Hardcore** |
| The Dead Kennedys, Black Flag, The Circle Jerks, Flipper, Fear |

| **More California Hardcore** | **Washington, D.C. Hardcore** | **British Hardcore** | **Other Hardcore** | **Alternative Rock Groups With Hardcore Roots** |
| Suicidal Tendencies, TSOL, MDC, BYO, The Minutemen (Early) | Minor Threat, Bad Brains, Government Issue, Fugazi | The Anti-Nowhere League, The Subhumans, The U.K. Subs, G.B.H., The Exploited | The Zero Boys, JFA, The Meatmen, 7 Seconds | The Replacements, X, Hüsker Dü, The Wipers, Redd Kross, The Meat Puppets |

| **Thrash/Metal/Speedcore** |
| Danzig, Metallica, Slayer, Megadeth |

| **Grindcore** |
| Napalm Death, Prong |

hardcore, although the line between "straight ahead" punk and hardcore/thrash could often be (and often still is) thin.

The giants of early hardcore were mostly Californians: the Dead Kennedys, Black Flag, Flipper, the Circle Jerks. Just as almost every city or university town had its punk scene, so they soon had their hardcore bands. Washington, D.C., home of Minor Threat, the Bad Brains, and many other groups, was arguably the biggest hotspot outside of the Golden State, but there were many groups in cities like Vancouver and Boston, to cite just the tip of the iceberg. British hardcore bands were not unknown – early records by Wire and the Fall were certainly hardcore keystones with their melodically minimal, percussive structures, and groups like the Anti-Nowhere League, the Subhumans, G.B.H., the Exploited, and the U.K. Subs had big international followings. Indeed, there were scads of hardcore bands all over the globe, but North America was always the chief breeding ground.

Melody, it's fair to say, wasn't uppermost in the minds of most thrashers. Not infrequently, it wasn't a consideration at all. Energy and, much more often than not, outrage were paramount. As in rap music, the lyrics and the message took precedence, though hardcore never matched the textural and sonic variety of rap. The lyrics were often more pointedly sociopolitical than anything else around, and often pointed fingers: at the government, institutions, teachers, employers, and authority figures of every kind. There was always sexism, racism, the arms race, yuppies, and conformists of all kinds to share the blame as well. A lot of hardcore bands lacked a sense of humor, not surprisingly, but a lot of them could also be quite funny. The Dead Kennedys, Black Flag, Suicidal Tendencies, and many other groups managed the difficult feat of lambasting their targets with considerable humor, and songs such as "TV Party" (Black Flag) and "Institutionalized" (Suicidal Tendencies) provoked some honest-to-god belly laughs, and not exclusively from punks.

What is striking when listening to early hardcore is how melodic and poppy it can sound in comparison to later recordings in the genre, although it seemed unimaginably fast and devoid of melody at the time. Hardcore, more than the typical rock genre, didn't require much in the way of traditional instrumental and songwriting skills; virtually all hardcore records were released on small independent labels, often by the bands themselves. Given these low hurdles, the scene was soon crowded with generic bands. Some of the slightly-later-than-first-generation hardcore outfits garnered substantial followings: TSOL, the Wipers, MDC

(which stood for Millions of Dead Cops, Multi-Death Corporation, Millions of Damn Christians, and other such phrases during various points in their existence), JFA (an acronym for Jodie Foster's Army), and Redd Kross (barely in their teens when they became nationally known) were some of the most famous. Each month (at its peak, each week) saw cheapo albums, singles, and tapes unleashed on the marketplace, many poorly recorded and songs virtually indistinguishable from track to track; any back issue of the international flagship punk zine, *Maximum Rock'n'Roll*, yields dozens of tiny reviews of bands from all over the place that are virtually forgotten, or were not even known at the time.

Hardcore, even more than most subcultures, was a sea of contradictions. It placed a premium on non-conformism, but a great deal of the music adhered to extremely cliched conventions (the number of hardcore songs starting with a blast of guitar distortion, a shouted "1, 2, 1-2-3-4," followed by a dog-pulls-the-tablecloth-off-the-kitchen-during-dinner blur of chords, must number in the thousands). Its politics were generally well to the left of center (sometimes openly proclaiming anarchy), yet its fashions and sometimes even music were picked up by some Fascist and neo-Nazi youth. It placed great value on the message of the lyrics, which were often shouted so throatily as to be indecipherable. The music was played violently, confrontationally; the lyrics often preached tolerance, unity, and peace. Laudably, it championed racial and sexual equality; its performers and audience were usually White and male. It preached against apathy, and advocated social change, but often reduced larger society to cartoon stereotypes, and was defiantly inaccessible and uncommercial, ensuring that the vast majority of rock listeners (let alone the population) would never hear the music. And when performers with roots in the thrash community did attract a larger audience, they were invariably accused of selling out.

While it may be true that such performers were attracted by the prospects of commercial success, the more difficult truth to swallow was that they also felt constrained by the melodic, lyrical, and stylistic limits of hardcore, which are more severe than most any other subgenre of rock. The Replacements, X, the Meat Puppets, and Hüsker Dü all started out as more or less hardcore acts; none broadened their success beyond a cult level until they broadened the scope of their music (and, it must be pointed out, all eventually betrayed the original punk/hardcore ideal by signing with major labels). All of these groups helped lay the foundation for "alternative rock," though none achieved the multi-platinum success of Green Day and Nirvana, groups that likely listened to hardcore quite devotedly at some point in their youth. In the mid-'90s, early hardcore "stars" like Henry Rollins (of Black Flag), Bob Mould (of Hüsker Dü), and Mike Watt (of the Minutemen, so-named for the brevity of their songs, and later of FIREHOSE) are genuine rock stars; they don't play hardcore anymore, but their music shows debts to the form, and they've rarely if ever compromised their product in exchange for sales. There are even rare cases of also-ran hardcore bands that radically changed their game plan and hit the commercial jackpot; the Beastie Boys are the main example of this.

Unexpectedly, hardcore and thrash also had a substantial influence on some of the '80s and '90s biggest metal bands, which combined the guitar octane of metal with a degree of the faster tempos and lyrical consciousness of hardcore. Metallica, Slayer, Danzig (whose lead singer, Glenn Danzig, started out in the late '70s with punk/hardcore band the Misfits), and Megadeth have all done this to a large degree; the hybrid is sometimes called "thrash-metal," "death-metal" (actually not often an accurate designation), or "speedcore," among other terms. Prong, Napalm Death, and others mixed punky nihilism with grinding metal to come up with "grindcore." Groups like Helmet have achieved critical acclaim with artsy punk-metal blends that, like bleached hair, show hardcore roots if you listen hard enough. On the fairly rare occasions that hardcore stars (like Suicidal Tendencies) or groups with hardcorish leanings (like Social Distortion) were signed to major labels, they probed, or were urged into, a more hard rock, metalish direction.

When the hardcore community is noticed by the outside world, unfortunately, the consequences can be severe. No one knows this more than Dead Kennedys lead singer Jello Biafra, who also helps run the Alternative Tentacles label. In association with a poster included in a Dead Kennedys album, he and others were prosecuted by the Los Angeles City Attorney's office for distributing material harmful to minors. He was eventually acquitted, but the long and exhausting legal defense led to the break up of the Dead Kennedys. Hardcore records are all but ignored by the media (even most of the alternative publications), but hardcore has retained a significant audience in the last decade, linked by a tight (some would say insular) network of zines, skateboarder cliques, and tiny performance spaces. Some acts, like 7 Seconds, the deliberately offensive Meatmen, and the long-gone BYO, were huge within the hardcore community while passing virtually unnoticed by the larger rock world. Very occasionally, bands like Fugazi (led by Ian MacKaye, formerly with "straight-edge" pioneers Minor Threat) achieve wide acclaim in the rock underground by broadening the hardcore base of their sound without alienating the hardcore base of their fans. *Maximum Rock'n'Roll*, the monthly punk journal, continues to review hardcore recordings by the boatload, and espouses a fervently radical sociopolitical view that some feel to be unhealthily rigid. When Jello Biafra had his leg mangled by slam-dancing thugs (who accused him of being a sell-out rock star as they stomped on him) at a Berkeley, CA, punk club with strong ties to the magazine in 1994, it was not so much the end of an era as a reflection of the long, strange road this most uncommercial breed of rock music has taken, and the contradictions it continues to embody.

12 Recommended Recordings

Various Artists, *Faster & Louder: Hardcore Punk, Vol. 1* (Rhino)
Various Artists, *Faster & Louder: Hardcore Punk, Vol. 2* (Rhino)
The Dead Kennedys, *Fresh Fruit for Rotting Vegetables* (IRS)
Black Flag, *The First Four Years* (SST)
The Wipers, *Over the Edge* (Restless)
Bad Brains, *Rock for Light* (Caroline)
Hüsker Dü, *Metal Circus* (SST)
The Replacements, *Sorry Ma, Forgot to Take out the Trash* (Twin/Tone)
The Minutemen, *Double Nickels on the Dime* (SST)
Minor Threat, *Complete* (Dischord)
Suicidal Tendencies, *Suicidal Tendencies* (Frontier)
Fugazi, *Repeater* (Dischord)

– Richie Unterberger

Australian Rock

In 1975, most Americans' relationship with Australian rock consisted of maybe being able to sing the Easybeats' (who weren't native Australians) "Friday on My Mind." A geographically isolated continent, Australia's impact on the global rock & roll market seemed tangential at best; touring was difficult, most people carelessly lumped you in with English bands, and there was a strong feeling that no matter how good you might be, your career was limited to the Western Hemisphere.

In fact, rock & roll has been produced in Australia since the music made its first international impact in the mid-'50s. In 1957, Gene Vincent, Eddie Cochran, and Little Richard became the first rock & roll stars to tour the continent (in fact, it was during this tour that Richard declared his intention to renounce rock & roll for the ministry). Australia had its homegrown rockers in the late '50s and early '60s, like Johnny Rebb, who were unknown elsewhere in the world, and remain little-heard to this day even among rabid collectors and historians. The best of the pre-Beatle groups were the Atlantics, and recorded quite a few storming surf records that match the best instrumental surf music issued in southern California around the same time.

Beatlemania had as great an impact in Australia as in the U.K. or U.S., and after the Beatles swept through Australasia on a mid-1964 tour, many British Invasion-inspired combos sprung up throughout the country. One of the first, and the most famous by far, were the Easybeats, who created a mini-Beatlemania of their own (dubbed "Easyfever") on their home turf. Actually composed of musicians who had emigrated from Britain and Holland to Australia during their childhood or teens, the Easybeats boasted prolific writers in guitarists George Young and Harry Vanda. Much of their output during their mid-'60s prime bears a great deal of similarity to the Kinks, Small Faces, and of course the Beatles, with a bouncier, more pop-oriented feel. After moving to Britain in 1966, they had an international smash with "Friday on My Mind," as well as some lesser U.K. hits, and dabbled in increasingly sophisticated studio concoctions before packing it up at the end of the decade. They ultimately do not measure up to the level of greatness of the best British Invasion bands, but were indisputably the most original and influential Australian group of their time.

Australia was still something of a backwater in the '60s – major American and British groups didn't tour there often, sophisticated equipment and studios were hard to come by, and albums were a rarity, reserved for big stars like the Easybeats. Lacking first hand exposure to their idols, or easy access to an international audience, Australian groups had to generate their own scene, much in the manner of regional garage groups in the United States. As with the garage bands, the result was often a rawer, less professional variation of the British Invasion sound.

At their best, the Australian garage groups were a match for the best American ones, compensating for their lack of virtuosity with an overdose of outrage. They're represented on a variety of compilations, which (as with American garage comps) mix gems with tedious genre exercises and unimaginative covers, although *Ugly Things Vol. 1* is recognized as one of the very best '60s garage anthologies from anywhere. Albums and compilations by some of the better and more prolific groups, like the Loved Ones, the Twilights, and the super-raw Missing Links, are spotty, but worth checking out for '60s collectors. The best '60s Australian group bar the Easybeats were the Masters Apprentices, who issued some terrific power-pop-garage singles in their early years, and evolved with the times through psychedelia and progressive rock, attaining some modest recognition in the U.K. after moving there for a time in the early '70s. Reissues of work by all of the bands mentioned in this paragraph, as well as *Ugly Things* and various other compilations, are available on the Raven label, the company primarily responsible for bringing some measure of belated acclaim to '60s Australian rock. (The Strangeloves, though billed as Australian when they hit with "I Want Candy" in 1965, were not the genuine article; they were in fact New York session musicians/songwriters, using the fake nationality as an attention-grabbing gimmick.)

The most successful Australian rock act of the '60s are not often classified as Australian. The Bee Gees were composed of three brothers who had emigrated from Britain as children; in 1967, they moved to England and successfully invaded the British and American markets as lightweight Beatle emulators, becoming even bigger in the 1970s as they moved into disco. They'd been stars in Australia for some time before 1967, though. Their underappreciated 1964-66 work, though rarely heard, reveals them to be among the best British Invasion-wannabes from anywhere in the globe, often recalling the Hollies' best mid-'60s recordings.

Australian rock, like much rock from outside of North America or the British Isles, was extremely derivative and imitative of American and British trends, and the late '60s and early '70s produced many Australian clones of psychedelia, soul, progressive, glam, and other rock trends, almost without exception unworthy of close scrutiny. And Australian bands never rated more than a footnote until ex-Easybeats Harry Vanda and George Young decided to record the band started by George's younger brothers Angus and Malcolm. Ridiculed from the start by critics, and passionately loved by their fans, AC/DC went on to become (and continue to be) a hugely popular heavy metal band. Driven by Angus Young's spastic, mega-loud guitar playing and exhausting stage antics (while dressed up in a schoolboy's uniform), and Bon Scott's screeching tenor voice (Scott died in 1980, his spot filled by Scottish shrieker Brian Johnson), AC/DC stripped away all artifice, laying down a thudding, insistent, riff-driven feral assault that was as catchy as it was simple. In many ways AC/DC's no-frills faster-and-louder approach to rock & roll anticipated what was to be a defining element of the early punk rock scene.

AC/DC, despite a "punky," anti-authoritarian attitude, were never truly a punk band (nor for that matter were they really Australian: Malcolm and Angus, like older brother George, were born in Scotland). They were more precisely the most successful practitioners of Australia's popular working class hard rock/heavy metal scene, which included such influential but lesser known bands as the Angels (known later as Angel City) and Rose Tattoo. And while the aggressive attitude of these bands made a significant impact on young Australian punks-to-be, another important ingredient precipitating this genesis came in the early '70s when Ann Arbor, MI-native Deniz Tek immigrated to Sydney. A guitarist and fan of the hyped up, loud and direct, proto-punk motor sound of the Stooges and MC5, Tek joined forces with blond, gruff-voiced Aussie native Rob Younger and formed the seminal (and arguably first) Australian punk band, Radio Birdman. In 1976, Radio Birdman released a scorching EP, *Burn My Eye*, following it up with a terrific steeped-in-the-Stooges debut LP, *Radios Appear* (the title taken from a Blue Oyster Cult song). But despite beating everyone else in getting a record out, and providing the critical impetus that influenced other bands, Radio Birdman were not the center of media attention (especially in the English rock press) for the then nascent Aussie punk movement. That recognition went to a quartet from Brisbane called the Saints.

Co-led by Ed Kuepper and Chris Bailey, the Saints' debut, *(I'm) Stranded*, was every inch a classic late '70s punk rock record: Bailey's snarling, petulant vocals; the speedy, superdistorted guitars; the (mostly) brief songs; and one of the punk era's best tunes (one that could only be written by an Aussie band) about alienation, "(I'm) Stranded." Because they were the first of their ilk to get to England, the U.K. pop press enthusiastically dubbed them the Aussie punk band to be reckoned with, thereby cementing their reputation and causing "(I'm) Stranded" to be a hit single. The Saints became the band that (almost) singlehandedly informed the rest of the world that there was a thriving and interesting alternative rock and roll scene in Australia. Unlike Radio Birdman, who were finished by 1981 (Tek did, however, live out a dream by forming the short-lived New Race with ex-Stooges guitarist Ron Asheton and ex-MC5 drummer Dennis Thompson), the Saints (despite Kuepper's departure in 1978 to form the arty, psychedelic Laughing Clowns) continued to record into the '90s as Bailey took them from raw, blitzspeed punk into more deliberate, tuneful, and far less confrontational pop/rock.

As Australia's largest city, Sydney was the putative focal point of the burgeoning Aussie punk scene. However, many interesting, innovative bands were popping up all over the continent. Especially in Melbourne, a city with a rock tradition that went back to the mid-'60s and the much loved Loved Ones. Its large student population formed the sympathetic core audience for a more arty, avant-garde brand of punk that was less interested in fast guitars, and more interested in free-form musical and literary explorations. Seminal Melbourne underground musicians such as Ollie Olson in his bands Whirlywind and No created a churning din of sound, punctuated by vituperative lyrical broadsides, culminating in extreme performances that sometimes included self-inflicted violence and bloodshed. Still, with much of the student community supporting this sound, Melbourne was soon producing bands unlike anywhere else on the continent. (For an interesting fictional account of the early days of the Melbourne scene see the 1987 film *Dogs in Space*, which surprisingly features a fine performance by INXS lead singer Michael Hutchence.)

Few bands from the Melbourne scene were more interesting, and exhibited more promise, than did the Boys Next Door. Led by the doomy baritone voice and poetically inclined pen of Jim Morrison acolyte Nick Cave and the twisted, noisy, gnarled guitar playing of Rowland S. Howard, the Boys released *Door Door* in 1979 and almost immediately became one of Melbourne's most influential punk bands. However, Melbourne wasn't big enough, or close enough to international audiences for the Boys. By 1980, they had changed their name to the Birthday Party, moved to London, and went on to become one of the post-punk era's most enduring and copied bands. Cave, after going solo in 1984, has had more success than that of the Birthday Party and the Boys combined. With and without his backing band the Bad Seeds, Cave has pursued the darker impulses of rock & roll, incorporating Delta blues and country music into his cauldron of musical ideas. As of this writing, Cave (with the Bad Seeds) has been a featured act on the Lollapalooza tour, published a novel, become a dad, and kicked a long-standing heroin addiction. He's now at the peak of his popularity, with a career that spans well over a decade and dozens of recordings.

By the early '80s, the punk-inspired deluge of bands had given Australia more musical recognition than ever before. New bands, influenced by Anglo and American punk rock, Radio Birdman, the Saints, and the Melbourne scene, sprang up everywhere, embracing punk's DIY ethos while replicating and reinventing rock & roll. From the remote western city of Perth came the Kim Salmon-led Scientists; '60s psychedelic garage rock was reinterpreted by the Lime Spiders; hook-filled pure pop was the calling card of the Hoodoo Gurus; and a melancholic take on Beatles-inspired pop was offered up by Marty-Willson Piper, Steve Kilbey, and Peter Koppes in the popular Church. There were art-punks Feedtime (who sounded like Flipper); the Melbourne-influenced King Snake Roost and Hunters and Collectors; the commercial hard rock of the Divinyls (great first record, everything else is worthless); the criminally overlooked Died Pretty; the over-amped pop of the Screaming Tribesmen; the extremely popular, but negligibly interesting, dance-rock of INXS (featuring Michael Hutchence); Rob Younger's post-Birdman outfit, the New Christs; hardcore punks the Cosmic Psychos and the delicately named Hard Ons; Brisbane's brilliant the Go-Betweens, featuring Grant McLennan and Robert Forster; and two very important Sydney-based bands: the Celibate Rifles and Midnight Oil.

Midnight Oil began as a punk-influenced band big with Sydney's sizable surfing community. Led by the imposing figure of surfer/lawyer Peter Garrett, the Oils, as they were affectionately dubbed by fans, began recording in 1978, but it wasn't until five years later, when they released *10, 9, 8, 7, 6, 5, 4, 3, 2, 1*, that (thanks to its huge success in Australia) they established a toehold in the international rock marketplace. Early Oils music is loud, technically adept, and very aggressive, indicative of their fondness for punk. Also it was the kind of assertive, boisterous rock that went down well with the surfer crowds they played to in Sydney-area bars. By the time they recorded *10, 9, 8*... the Oils' music was becoming more polished and pop-oriented, but not so much so that it sacrificed the guitar-driven mania from whence they sprang. Longtime advocates for the environment and aboriginal land rights, and with the articulate Garrett acting as band spokesman, it wasn't long before Midnight Oil became the biggest Aussie rock act since AC/DC. Much of it was due to the enormous success of the single and video "Beds Are Burning" (from the 1987 album *Diesel and Dust*) and ferocious live shows. Although their recent efforts have not yielded a hit single the magnitude of "Beds Are Burning," the Oils have developed a devoted fan base, and continue to make solid, if much less aggressive, records that consistently sell in the millions.

The stripped-down, loud and fast, Ramones-inspired rock of the Celibate Rifles deserves special mention, for this Sydney-based band proved to be the best Australian rock band to emerge from the Radio Birdman/Saints era. With droll, deadpan lead vocals supplied by Damien Lovelock, the core of the Rifles was built around the rampaging guitars of Kent Steedman and Dave Morris. And while they valued power, speed, and volume, they weren't shy about tastefully adding horns, acoustic instruments, and slowing down the tempo. Perhaps too extreme and enigmatic to make a big splash in America, the Rifles did develop a solid, supportive fan base in indie rock circles. However, they toured America sporadically, and as the '80s ended they seemed content to spend much of their time in Australia. Since they released their first EP in 1982, the Rifles' output has been frequently stunning, proving them to be the best Australian rock band you've never heard. Aussie rock music is more diverse than the hard rock and punk-influenced rock that dominates American and British rock. Unfortunately, there are plenty of standard issue types like gruff-voiced Bob Seger wannabe Jimmy Barnes; hugely popular teenage soap star ("Neighbors") turned sexpot dance-pop singer Kylie Minogue; so-so hard rockers Cold Chisel; worthless, radio/MTV panderers like '80s popular one-shots Men at Work. Far more interesting are recent performers such as blues guitarist Dave Hole and aboriginal singer/songwriter Archie Roach, who have recorded exciting, very different-sounding records than what emanates from both the Aussie mainstream and alternative rock communities.

The success of Archie Roach and the band Yothu Yindi (whose influences include mid-'80s aboriginal rock bands such as Goanna and the Warumpi Band) has created a new focus on music made by Australia's aboriginal population, resulting in other established, yet heretofore unknown, Australian performers finding more acceptance (and more fans) in the global pop community, and on previously monochromatic Aussie pop music radio. Artists such as Ruby Hunter, Kev Carmody (the Australian Bob Dylan), and Blek Bela Mujik send a clear signal that there is much more to contemporary Australian rock & roll than simply White boys flailing away at guitars.

As more and more bands receive international acclaim, the Aussie music scene has been accorded more respect and, as a result, is more vigilantly watched by label executives for marketable bands. So, the next generation of Aussie bands, populated by up-and-comers like Silverchair, Spiderbait, the Mark of Cain, and the Joy of Noise, will have a much larger ready-made audience than did their predecessors. Even an old-timer like Deniz Tek has returned to the fray, teaming up with Celibate Rifle Kent Steedman in a part-time project that recaptures the high energy Detroit rock sound that played such a pivotal role in the development of punk and post-punk Australian rock. Despite being on the other side of the planet, the truth is, since the late '70s, rock & roll has helped bring Australia a lot closer to the rest of the world and made it a lot more influential than anyone would have guessed.

20 Essential Recordings

The Easybeats, *Absolute Anthology* (EMI, Australia)
Various Artists, *Ugly Things Vol. 1* (Raven, Australia)
The Bee Gees, *The Early Years Vol. 1 & 2* (Excelsior)
The Masters Apprentices, *Hands of Time 1965-72* (Raven, Australia)
AC/DC, *Back in Black* (Atlantic)
Radio Birdman, *Radios Appear* (Sire)
The Saints, *(I'm) Stranded* (Sire)
Midnight Oil, *10, 9, 8, 7, 6, 5, 4, 3, 2, 1* (Columbia)
The Celibate Rifles, *Roman Beach Party* (What Goes On)
The Celibate Rifles, *Blind Ear* (EMI-True Tone, Australia)
Feedtime, *Shovel* (Aberrant/Rough Trade)
The Go-Betweens, *1978-1990* (Beggars Banquet/Capitol)
Divinyls, *Desperate* (Chrysalis)
Archie Roach, *Charcoal Lane* (Hightone)
Yothu Yindi, *Freedom* (Hollywood)
Birthday Party, *Hits* (Warner Brothers)
Nick Cave & the Bad Seeds *The First Born Is Dead* (Mute)
Died Pretty, *Free Dirt* (What Goes On)
The Hoodoo Gurus, *Stoneage Romeos* (A&M)
The Scientists, *Weird Love* (Big Time)

Film

Dogs in Space (1987)

– John Dougan & Richie Unterberger

Rap

The most popular and influential form of African-American pop music of the 1980s and 1990s, rap is also one of the most controversial styles of the rock era. And not just among the guardians of cultural taste and purity that have always been counted among rock & roll's chief enemies – Black, White, rock, and soul audiences continue to fiercely debate the musical and social merits of rap, whose most radical innovations subverted many of the musical and cultural tenets upon which rock was built.

Antecedents of rap are easy to find in rock and other kinds of music. Music is often used to tell a story, often with spoken rhymes over instruments and rhythms. Talking blues, spoken passages of sanctified prose in gospel, and numerous hits that call out slogans and rhymes, from Bo Diddley's "Say Man" to Shirley Ellis's "The Name Game" to Jerry Reed's "When You're Hot, You're Hot" – you can find pre-raps in material by performers as diverse as Lou Reed, the Shangri-Las, and the Jimmy Castor Bunch, if you want to stretch it.

More direct paths leading to rap, though, can be found in a few of the trends of the late '60s and '70s. In R&B, funk and disco stripped down soul down to its most basic rhythms, foregoing much of the instrumentation and vocals habitually used as embellishments. James Brown in particular is often cited as a forefather in his use of stream-of-consciousness raps over elemental funk backup, and he (and some other funk giants) have been sampled by modern-day rappers on innumerable occasions.

Two much more overlooked influences originated from outside of the R&B and rock mainstream. The Last Poets, Gil Scott-Heron, and Jayne Cortez set highly politicized tales of African-American and urban life against percussive jazz tracks in the early '70s. In reggae, the use of DJs, or "toasters," to rap over basic instrumental backing tracks when they took their mobile sound systems to dances, became widespread. New York City, particularly Brooklyn and (more importantly in terms of rap's birth) the Bronx, was home to a large Jamaican community. Jamaican DJs (DJ Kool Herc has been credited as the first) mixed sounds from several turntables, a device which would become one of rap's trademarks.

Although mixing from large sound systems began to be employed at New York house parties in the 1970s, it didn't really emerge as a recorded sound until the Sugarhill Gang's "Rapper's Delight" in 1979. While many critics and listeners shrugged the song aside as a fluke novelty hit, the early rap sound – usually composed of slangy, boastful spoken rhymes over basic bass and percussion grooves – continued to spread in the early '80s, due in large part to the efforts of the Sugarhill label itself. Grandmaster Flash's hard-hitting 1982 single, "The Message," really stands as rap's watershed mark, with its massive impact belied by its relatively modest peak on the pop charts. No longer could rap be ignored as a frivolous micro-genre; here was straight-up social comment, reporting from the front lines of the ghetto with more immediacy than almost any newspaper or television broadcast.

From its inception, rap endured a lot of hostility from listeners – many, but not all, White – who found the music too harsh, monotonous, and lacking in traditional melodic values. However, millions of others – often, though not always, young African-Americans from underprivileged inner-city backgrounds – found an immediate connection with the style. Here was poetry of the street, directly reflecting and addressing the day-to-day reality of the ghetto in a confrontational fashion not found in any other music or media. What's more, you could dance to it, rhyme to it, bring it most anywhere on increasingly ubiquitous portable cassette players (dubbed "ghetto blasters"), and, in the best rock & roll tradition, form your own band without much in the way of formal training.

The basic workouts of early rappers like Kurtis Blow and the Fat Boys (eventually referred to as "old school" rap) can sound a bit tame today, although the productions of veterans like Afrika Bambaataa and Keith LeBlanc have lost none of their luster. Many were still expecting the music to peter out before Run-D.M.C. came along. Rap was, and to a large degree still is, a singles-oriented medium, but these Queens men proved that rappers could maintain interest and diversity over the course of entire full-length albums. Combining hard beats and innovative production with strong material that emphasized positive social activism without ignoring the cruel realities of urban life, they found as much favor with the critics as the street. Among the first rap groups to climb the pop charts in a big way, they also were among the first to make big inroads into the White and Middle American audiences when they teamed up with Aerosmith's Stephen Tyler and Joe Perry for the hit single "Walk This Way."

The mid- and late '80s saw rap continuing to explode in popularity, with the ascendancy of superstars like LL Cool J and Hammer (the latter of whom is often accused of providing a safe rap-pop alternative). Although most early rap productions originated in New York City and its environs, the music took hold as a national phenomenon, with strong scenes developing in other East Coast cities like Philadelphia, as well as West Coast strongholds in Los Angeles and Oakland. Production techniques became increasingly sophisticated; electronics, stop-on-a-dime editing, and – most importantly – sampling from previously recorded sources

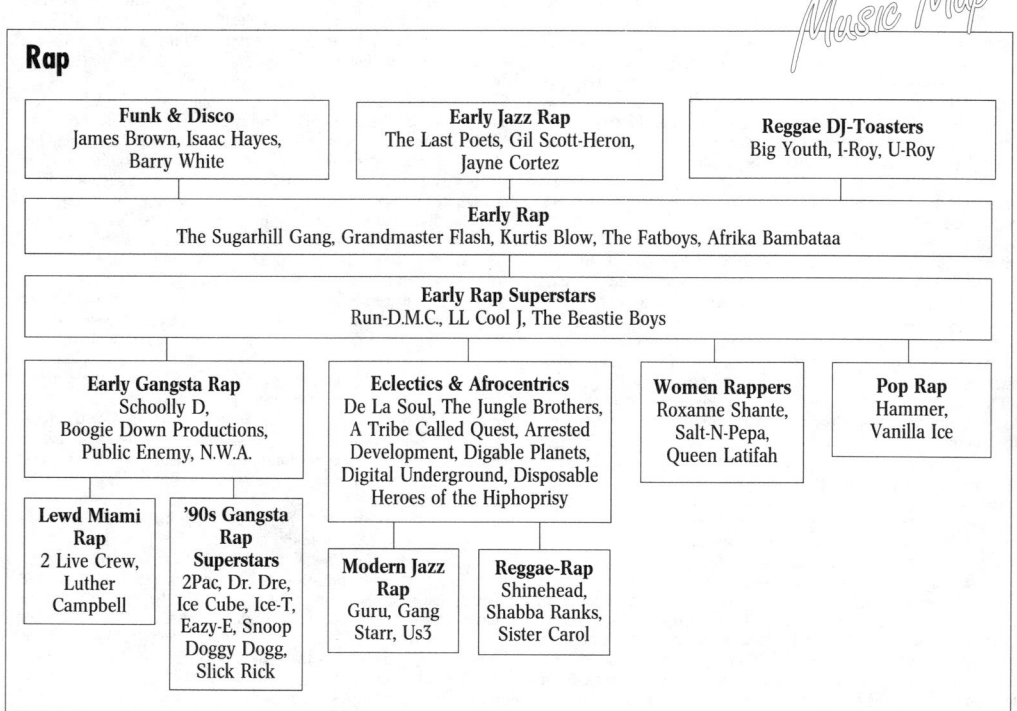

became prominent (although turntable mixing, along with the "scratching" produced by wiggling records back and forth, continued to be a strong ingredient). The increased emphasis on electronic beats led to the popularization of the term "hip-hop," a designation which is by now used more or less interchangeably with rap. The Beastie Boys, obnoxious White ex-punks from New York, brought rap further into the Middle American mainstream with their vastly popular hybrids of hip-hop, hard rock, and in-your-face braggadocio.

While rap had always forthrightly dealt with urban struggle, the late '80s saw the emergence of a more militant strain of the music. Sometimes dubbed "gangsta-rap," the hotbed of this school was found in the disadvantaged neighborhoods of South Central Los Angeles, although performers like Philadelphia's Schoolly D proved that the genre was not specific to the area. Boogie Down Productions laid down a prototype that was taken to more extreme measures by N.W.A. (Niggaz with Attitude), who reported on the crime, sex, and violence of the ghetto with an explicit verve that some viewed as verging on celebration rather than journalism. Enormously controversial, and enormously popular with record buyers, several N.W.A. members went on to stardom as solo acts, including Ice Cube, Eazy-E, and Dr. Dre. Other boys from their 'hood also made their mark with inflammatory works, such as Ice-T and Snoop Doggy Dogg.

The most popular and controversial of the militant rappers, the New York-based Public Enemy, were perhaps the most political as well. Their brand of activism, like that of Malcolm X's two decades earlier, made a lot of people, including liberals, pretty uncomfortable, with its emphasis upon black nationalism and careless anti-Semitic, homophobic, and sexist references.

Groups such as Public Enemy ignited an ongoing debate in the media. Activist-oriented critics and audiences found a lot to praise in their music: powerful articulations against social and racial injustice, uncompromising portraits of realities that the mainstream media shies away from, exhortations to the disadvantaged to empower themselves, and the sometimes overlooked fact that rap generated most of the few massive-selling independent releas-

es produced outside of the corporate major-label machine. At the same time, they could not let the xenophobic tendencies of these acts pass unnoticed, or ignore the frequent quasi-celebration in much rap music of misogyny, drugs, and violence, and the status to be gained in the urban community by the practice thereof. Many rap and rock & roll fans were also concerned parents, torn almost against their will between wanting to support the struggle against race and class oppression, and wanting to protect their children against possible identification with the violence- and obscenity-riddled content of the records themselves. Passionate advocates of civil liberties and free speech wondered, sometimes aloud, whether rappers were taking those privileges too far.

It's a conundrum that remains unresolved as of this writing in 1995. The apolitical, over-the-top explicit sexual boasting of 2 Live Crew and the several acts propagated by the group's mastermind and label entrepreneur, Luther Campbell, seemed too comically overdrawn to really inspire serious controversy. Some government authorities felt otherwise, subjecting the Miami-based Campbell to serious legal pressure and harassment. First Amendment champions found themselves in the awkward position of defending his and other rappers' rights to spew content that they found morally reprehensible. Newly emerging gangsta rappers like Snoop Doggy Dogg, Slick Rick, and 2Pac not only take the violent subject matter of their lyrics to new extremes (and to the top of the charts), but have been accused of enacting their scenarios in real life, landing in jail for manslaughter or fighting similarly grave charges.

These performers often unrepentantly contend they are only reporting things as they happen in the 'hood, a culture that not only shoots people, but is being shot *at*. Many critics find their line between art and reality too thin, and are loathe to see them spreading their gospel from the top of the charts (2Pac's 1995 album "Me Against the World" debuted at number one even as he was serving a prison sentence), or serving as role models for international youth.

Gangsta rap may have gotten a lot of the headlines in recent years, but the field of rap as a whole remains diverse, and not as dominated by the shoot-'em-out minidramas of gangsta rap as many would have you believe. De La Soul took rap and hip-hop production to new heights with their 1989 debut *Three Feet High & Rising*, an almost psychedelic melange of sampling and editing of a wildly eclectic pool of sources that would do Frank Zappa proud. Their humorous and cheerful vibe inspired a mini-school of "Afrocentric" acts, the most notable of which were the Jungle Brothers and A Tribe Called Quest. Arrested Development, Digable Planets, and Digital Underground also pursued playful, heavily jazz- and funk-oriented paths to immense success and high critical praise. Rap is a highly macho (some would say sexist) environment, but some female performers arose to provide a much-needed counterpoint, from various perspectives: the saucy (the various Roxannes), the pop (Salt-N-Pepa), and the feminist (Queen Latifah).

It is a measure of rap's huge influence that the style has infiltrated mainstream soul and rock as well. Producer Teddy Riley gave urban-contemporary performers like Bobby Brown a vaguely hip edge with his brand of "New Jack Swing"; White alternative rockers like G. Love, Bobby Sichran, and most notably Beck devised a strange hybrid of rap, blues, and rock. Vanilla Ice proved that whitebread pop-rap could top the charts, though he was unable to sustain his success.

More than most genres, rap/hip-hop has become a culture with its own subgenres and buzzwords, which can seem almost impenetrable to the novice. "Dope" and "fresh" beats, "old school," "new school," East Coast and West Coast tips, B-boys and flygirls, Miami bass, phat bass, G-style funk – all are terms thrown around in rap magazines, differentiated by small gradations which can seem almost trivial to the outsider. Despite this proliferation of schools of production and performance, many rap records can appear virtually indistinguishable from each other to the novice listener. And there's no getting around the fact that a lot of them are – the market is saturated with repetitive beats and monotonously uncompromising slices of urban street life, to the point that they've lost a lot of both their musical novelty and shock value.

Rap music has lost none of its momentum – or its capacity to inspire outrage in society as a whole – as we head into the last half of the 1990s. Scenes continue to proliferate, not just on the coasts, but in Atlanta, Houston, and such unlikely locales as Paris (home of leading French rapper MC Solaar). It may appeal more to inner-city adolescents than anyone else, but gangsta rap may be bigger than anything else in R&B music commercially, and there are more multi-platinum rap/hip-hop acts than you can shake a stick at, far too many than could be specifically cited in this brief essay. Shinehead, Shabba Ranks, and less-heralded performers like Sister Carol have fused reggae and rap. And the jazz and rap worlds are being brought closer together than ever through the efforts of Gang Starr and their leader Guru, Us3, and the landmark *Stolen Moments: Red, Hot + Cool* compilation, which united many of the top names in hip-hop and jazz.

21 Essential Albums

Various Artists, *Street Jams–Hip-Hop from the Top, Vol. 1-4* (Rhino)
Various Artists, *Street Jams–Electric Funk, Vol. 1-4* (Rhino)
Various Artists, *Hip-Hop Greats–Classic Raps* (Rhino)
Afrika Bambaataa, *Planet Rock* (Tommy Boy)
Run-D.M.C., *Together Forever: Greatest Hits* (Profile)
LL Cool J, *Radio* (Def Jam)
The Beastie Boys, *Licensed to Ill* (Def Jam)
Public Enemy, *It Takes a Nation of Millions to Hold Us Back* (Def Jam)
Boogie Down Productions, *Criminal Minded* (Sugar Hill Rap)
N.W.A., *Straight Outta Compton* (Priority)
De La Soul, *Three Feet High & Rising* (Tommy Boy)
Queen Latifah, *All Hail the Queen* (Tommy Boy)
Shinehead, *Unity* (Elektra)
Digable Planets, *Reachin': A New Refutation...* (Pendulum)
Various Artists, *Stolen Moments: Red, Hot + Cool* (GRP)
Ice-T, *O.G. Original Gangster* (Priority)
Salt-N-Pepa, *Blacks' Magic* (London)
Digital Underground, *Sex Packets* (Tommy Boy)
Arrested Development, *Three Years, Five Months & Two Days in the Life Of...* (Chrysalis)
Guru, *Jazzmatazz, Vol. 1* (Chrysalis)
Dr. Dre, *The Chronic* (Priority)

– Jimmy James

American Alternative Rock

Like new wave before it, "alternative" is basically a meaningless term. Punk, heavy metal, funk, rap, pop, rock & roll, singer/songwriter – everything fits under the term. Essentially, "alternative" is a catch-all for post-punk bands that appeared as new wave began to die out in 1983-84, and runs all the way into 1995, when alternative pop/rock is the mainstream. Although there's nothing alternative about Live and Silverchair, their inspiration by R.E.M. and Nirvana was decidedly part of an underground, anti-mainstream rock & roll movement. But what really distinguishes alternative pop/rock is how it reprocesses and reworks rock history, bringing together diverse strands into a whole. Alternative followed somewhat different paths in America and Britain; although the two countries have had bands that were big on both continents, like R.E.M., certain phenomena like Pearl Jam or the Stone Roses haven't translated particularly well. In addition, entire subgenres are isolated to either the U.S. or the U.K. (funk-metal, for instance, has never been very popular in Britain).

Alternative pop/rock has its basic roots in punk, new wave and hardcore; it does recall other genres, particularly '60s pop and heavy metal, but the entire subculture first emerged from the punk movement. To over-simplify things, the first American alternative bands were R.E.M. and Hüsker Dü. Both bands formed in the early '80s or late '70s, releasing records on small independent labels before moving to bigger indies and then the majors. In their wake, thousands of bands followed, both musically and ideologically. Hüsker Dü broke up without achieving any mainstream success, while R.E.M. soldiered on into the '90s, becoming one of the most popular rock & roll bands in the world.

For most of the '80s, alternative rock remained the province of small clubs, independent labels, fanzines, and college radio, with the occasional song breaking into MTV and Top 40, or the occasional album receiving critical praise in mainstream publications like *Rolling Stone*. However, the commercial appeal of most alternative bands was nearly nonexistent. Instead, the bands built underground followings by touring constantly and releasing a low-budget album every year. New bands would form in their wake and soon there was a sizable underground circuit in America, with different parts of the country having different scenes.

R.E.M. immediately had the most impact, both commercially and musically. *Murmur*, the band's 1983 debut album, received enormous critical praise, helping the album chart in the Top 40. Legions of jangling imitators followed, and the group's success helped other southern guitar-pop bands like the dB's and Let's Active get exposure. Also, they helped kick off a group of bands dubbed "The Paisley Underground" that drew from the Velvet Underground and '60s psychedelia. R.E.M. toured non-stop throughout the decade, releasing a record each year and slowly expanding their following, setting the stage for their Top Ten breakthrough in 1987 with *Document* and "The One I Love." By that time, the group's ringing, chiming guitars and Michael Stipe's mumbling vocals had become commonplace on college radio.

While R.E.M.'s success provided a blueprint for many bands of the late '80s and '90s, Hüsker Dü,'s music had an equally large impact. Starting as a blistering hardcore band, the trio soon moved away from the confines of their subgenre. Without abandoning the loud guitars and furious tempos of hardcore, Hüsker Dü created a music that was both abrasive and melodic, filled with shards of noise and catchy hooks. *Zen Arcade*, a double album released in 1984, was their creative breakthrough, filled with concise pop and noisy, winding instrumental stretches. The group's last album, 1987's *Warehouse: Songs and Stories*, had a more polished sound than their earlier records, but it provided a template for the shiny punk-pop production of Nirvana's seminal *Nevermind*. Hüsker Dü was signed to SST Records, the label founded by Black Flag leader Greg Ginn in the early '80s. SST was the most influential American independent label of the '80s, not only featuring Black Flag and Hüsker Dü but also Sonic Youth, the Minutemen, the Meat Puppets, and Dinosaur Jr., among others. While they didn't necessarily pave the way for Sonic Youth – the New York band was already recording when Hüsker came to prominence – Hüsker Dü's albums prepared both critics and audiences for the all-out noise experiments of the group. Sonic Youth was more self-consciously arty than either R.E.M. or Hüsker Dü, with their lyrics sounding like performance-art poetry and their songs essentially being long, winding dissonant soundscapes. Hüsker Dü were also the leaders of the loose Minneapolis scene, which also included the Replacements and Soul Asylum, who both initially sounded a great deal like the Hüskers. However, the Replacements wound up providing a link between punk and traditional Stones/Faces rock & roll, as well as narrowing the gap between R.E.M.'s pop and Hüsker Dü's noise. At that point in time, Hüsker Dü had broken up, R.E.M. had made a commercial breakthrough, the Minutemen were crippled by the death of D. Boon and Sonic Youth were inactive between 1988 and 1990, as they were preparing to move to a major label. Consequently, several different subgenres that had thrived underneath the reign of the SST bands and R.E.M. came to the forefront. In addition to the loud, sloppy punky rock & roll of the Replacements and Soul Asylum, quirky alternative pop and noisy industrial rock dominated the late '80s American alternative scene.

Much of the alternative guitar-pop of the late '80s had its roots in the awkward, jangly music of the Feelies and the nervous, geeky folk-rock of the Violent Femmes, who both released their debut albums in the early '80s. The Feelies never sold many records at the time, yet their chiming guitar riffs helped pave the way for R.E.M. Unlike R.E.M., the Feelies' melodies and lyrics were twitchy and uptight, quite similar to the songs that Gordon Gano wrote for the Violent Femmes' self-titled debut. Both of the bands began a trend of geeky guitar-pop groups that emphasized their strangeness and bizarre humor. Since they were actively recording and touring at the time quirky guitar-pop became prominent, the Violent Femmes and the Feelies were part of the movement as well as being its forefathers. However, there were many other bands, from the jokey duo They Might Be Giants to the warped eclecticism of Camper Van Beethoven, that kept the music alive on the college charts. A number of off-kilter British guitar-pop bands fit into this trend as well, finding a larger following on American college radio stations than in their homeland. Robyn Hitchcock, the leader of the Soft Boys (who were an acknowledged influence on R.E.M.), was one of the British pop musicians who was warmly welcomed in the U.S. By this point in their career, XTC had a larger fan base in America than they had in Britain, which meant that their intelligent, meticulously crafted pop was prominently featured on American college radio.

In direct contrast to the good-natured, quirky pop of the Violent Femmes and XTC stood the legions of industrial and post-hardcore noise bands. While many industrial bands had their roots in European electronic groups, both the industrial and post-hardcore bands owed a great debt to Chicago's Big Black. Led by guitarist Steve Albini, Big Black created bleak, scathing, noisy soundscapes with two guitars, a bass, and a drum machine. The group's thin, tinny guitar roar became part of indie-rock musical vocabulary, as did its shards of white noise. Their records, particularly 1986's *Atomizer*, prepared alternative audiences and college radio audiences for the jarring guitar grind of the Butthole Surfers, Scratch Acid and its offspring, the Jesus Lizard, and countless bands that appropriated the same noise as their own. Most of these bands were also produced by Steve Albini, who continued to be a prominent figure in underground rock into the '90s.

Big Black's records also paved the way for industrial groups that spliced together noisy guitars, dense samples, and relentless drum-machine driven beats. European bands like Front 242, Einstürzende Neubauten, and KMFDM were pioneers in the music and gained a significant amount of American college airplay, but it was Chicago's Ministry that popularized the genre. Originally a synth-pop band in the early '80s, the group, led by guitarist/keyboardist Al Jourgensen, changed direction in the mid-'80s, incorporating elements of dance, heavy metal, electronic music and hiphop. Ministry's artistic breakthrough, and the record that helped establish industrial music as a staple of alternative rock, was 1988's *The Land of Rape and Honey*. As the years progressed, Ministry began leaning toward heavy metal, helping to make industrial techniques part of mainstream rock. Just as important was Cleveland's Nine Inch Nails, led by Trent Reznor. Nine Inch Nails were more pop-oriented than any other industrial band, which meant they were the ones that brought the music to a wider audience. But by the time that their 1989 debut, *Pretty Hate Machine*, became popular in 1991, industrial music had become passé in most alternative circles.

What had replaced industrial rock as a favored source of noise were revamped versions of Stooges-style punk and heavy metal. After the rise of industrial and quirky guitar pop, the spiky punk-pop of the Pixies and heavy grandeur of Jane's Addiction were the two most popular bands in alternative rock. The Pixies returned a sense of punk brevity to alternative music, as well as working raw

noise into pop song structures that were deliberately off-center. Their fractured, stripped-down punk-pop provided a blueprint for groups as diverse as Nirvana, Pavement, Weezer, and Radiohead, who all appropriated portions of the Pixies' music into their rock & roll. Although the Pixies were stars in most of Europe, they never achieved commercial success in America. Jane's Addiction were among the first to break down the walls between alternative and AOR radio, which, given their affection for ponderous heavy metal, wasn't surprising. Perry Farrell's lyrics may have had the performance-art shock of Sonic Youth, but the band's music was heavy metal in the vein of Led Zeppelin. Similarly, Seattle's Soundgarden reworked Zeppelin/Black Sabbath heavy metal territory, yet they injected a raw, punkish intensity to the familiar sludge. Both Jane's Addiction and Soundgarden received positive reviews in mainstream publications like *Rolling Stone*, earning them a sizable cult following.

Soundgarden was the first of the Seattle bands to earn widespread acclaim in America. In England, Mudhoney was the first Seattle band to earn positive reviews. Mudhoney's Stooges-soaked fuzz-toned 1988 single "Touch Me, I'm Sick," received a significant amount of acclaim in Britain, and the band earned a cult following in the U.K. by constant touring. To varying degrees, the success of Soundgarden, Mudhoney, the Pixies, and Jane's Addiction, as well as R.E.M., set the stage for Nirvana's breakthrough in late 1991.

Nirvana was the turning point for alternative rock as a commercially viable genre. Other bands had hits before them – particularly R.E.M. and Jane's Addiction – but Nirvana broke down the doors forever with their brand of punk-pop, which took equally from the Pixies, Sonic Youth, Soundgarden, and the Beatles. Following the number one success of *Nevermind* – which symbolically knocked Michael Jackson's *Dangerous* off the top of the charts – bands that had been on the fringe became multi-platinum stars, including the funk-metal of the Red Hot Chili Peppers and Primus, the industrial rock of Ministry and Nine Inch Nails, and the revamped arena-rock of Pearl Jam.

Although Nirvana's success did help send scores of bands, from Pearl Jam and Stone Temple Pilots to Green Day and the Offspring, to the top of the charts, it didn't eliminate the underground – it just gave it more exposure. Initially, this resulted in a flood of Seattle bands achieving considerable commercial success, including Pearl Jam, Alice in Chains, and Offspring. Nirvana's breakthrough also popularized so-called "Generation X" and "slacker" culture. Slackers came in many forms, but no band embodied the aesthetic quite as well as the Beastie Boys. Initially a hardcore band, the Beasties turned to rap in the early '80s, recording *Licensed to Ill*, one of hip-hop's major commercial breakthroughs. In 1989, the group released *Paul's Boutique*, a dense collage of pop and literary references that virtually defined the multi-culturalism and junk culture aesthetic that dominated much of the popular alternative rock of the '90s. However, *Paul's Boutique* was a commercial failure. When the Beastie Boys released *Check Your Head* in 1992, they had returned to playing their instruments and created a record that fused punk culture with hip-hop culture.

While the Beastie Boys presented another commercially successful alternative to heavy alternative rock, a number of female rockers began to gain attention both in the rock press and, occasionally, on MTV. During the '80s, women had prominent roles in important bands like Sonic Youth (bassist Kim Gordon) and the Pixies (bassist Kim Deal). In the late '80s, a number of new female singer/songwriters emerged, particularly Michelle Shocked, Tracy Chapman, Sinéad O'Connor, and Kristin Hersh of the Throwing Muses. While Shocked and Chapman were essentially folkies, O'Connor and Hersh bent the rules of rock & roll. O'Connor experimented with folk, punk, dance, and art-rock, creating a creative amalgam of styles that paid off with her 1990 commercial breakthrough, *I Do Not Want What I Haven't Got* Under the direction of Kristin Hersh – and occasionally her step-sister, Tanya Donnelly – Throwing Muses created a bracing music that had unpredictable lyrical and song structures placed the band somewhere between punk, pop and folk.

The late '80s female singer/songwriters prepared the rock media for the onslaught of the early '90s, as well as directly influencing several musicians. In particular, the songs on Liz Phair's 1993 debut *Exile in Guyville* recall music that was made in the late '80s, but her music included elements of rock & roll, power-pop, Joni Mitchell-styled folk-rock, and lo-fi alternative rock. There were other singer/songwriters similar to Phair, particularly the blues-punk of England's P.J. Harvey, but most of the female rock & roll acts of the early '90s were punk rock bands, with the occasional fusion of punk and heavy metal which recalled the music of Nirvana and Soundgarden. L7, Babes In Toyland, and Hole fit into this category, but there were underground bands like Bikini Kill and Bratmobile that sketched out an amateurish and politically confrontational form of punk labeled riot grrrl. There were also guitar-pop acts like Belly and the Juliana Hatfield which were decidedly sunnier than their counterparts, butt bands like the Breeders, led by Kim Deal, straddled the line between arty punk and pop without surrendering to either side.

Because of a media-created desire to lump all of these acts under the banner of "women in rock," most of these bands received a fair amount of press, but only a handful – Belly, Breeders, Hole, and Liz Phair – sold many records. After the initial onslaught of Nirvana, Pearl Jam, Soundgarden, Smashing Pumpkins, and Red Hot Chili Peppers, the groups that sold the most records were neo-punk rockers Green Day and the Offspring. Although it didn't sound much different than their two previous indie releases, Green Day's third album, *Dookie*, and the singles, "Long View" and "Basketcase," sent the group to the top of the charts in the summer of 1994; by the summer of 1995, *Dookie* had sold over eight million copies. Green Day's music essentially was revamped power-pop with hints of the Clash and the Jam, but the band's success led to the multi-platinum breakthrough of the metallic punk band the Offspring, who adopted the look of a punk group and the attack of a metal band. In their wake, Green Day and the Offspring focused attention on the hundreds of punk bands that played on the West Coast, particularly Rancid and Pennywise.

For all their ties with independent rock & roll and the underground, Green Day and the Offspring had little to do with alternative music by the time they broke into the mainstream. After Nirvana's breakthrough, the American underground divided into several factions that were all united by their desire to remain underground. There were neo-punk bands like North Carolina's Superchunk, which developed devoted followings but never had any desire to break beyond the level of an indie-rock band. There were arty, minimalist pop bands like Unrest, which were knowingly clever, post-modern and ironic, but made melodic catchy songs that were never destined to break out of their cult following because the band never intended them for anything larger than a cult audience. There were handfuls of country-rockers like Uncle Tupelo that imploded before they could reach any success. Most important to the '90s American underground were the group of pop-rockers that were lumped under the "lo-fi" label, named after the poor sound of the band's generally homemade recordings. Beck helped popularize the subgenre with his debut album, *Mellow Gold*. However, *Mellow Gold* was not strictly a lo-fi record – it was too well-produced to fit that label. Nevertheless, Beck acted like a scavenger, much like the Beastie Boys, taking bits and pieces from different musical genres, recording songs that alternately recalled hip-hop, folk, garage-rock, and psychedelia. Beck's other records, the noisy *Stereopathetic Soul Manure* and the folky *One Foot in the Grave*, were genuine lo-fi records, but the success of *Mellow Gold* helped draw attention to the leaders of the movement, Sebadoh and Pavement. Both bands had earned a significant amount of critical acclaim, as well as sizable cult followings, before Beck, but his success began a trend in the rock press to lump all of the bands together.

If any band embodies everything that is good and bad about lo-fi, it is Sebadoh. Led by former Dinosaur Jr. member Lou Barlow, Sebadoh isn't so much a band as it is a collective, with each individual member turning in their own songs. Barlow became the figurehead for the lo-fi movement, as he released an amazing amount of recordings in the early '90s under Sebadoh's name, Sentridoh, the Folk Implosion, and his own name. Essentially, Barlow is a post-punk singer/songwriter, writing fairly conventional pop songs that are distinguished by his recording techniques and the occasional burst of pop noise. Nevertheless, the aesthetic is as important as the songs for many lo-fi fans, and Lou Barlow's work provides plenty of good songs and bad songs, all characterized by the thin recording techniques.

The one band that transcends the label of lo-fi is Pavement. What was important about Pavement's music was not the aesthetics, but the concepts. The group reassembled a variety of different rock & roll genres – from noise-rock to country-rock, hitting on power-pop, folk-rock, rock & roll, soul, etc. along the way

– into a fractured, but tuneful, kaleidoscope of pop music. Unlike Beck's eclecticism, Pavement's songs – mainly written by guitarist/vocalist Stephen Malkmus – not only recontextualize familiar rock genres, they frequently subvert conventional pop structures. Pavement's three albums and numerous singles have earned them a sizable cult following as well as a wealth of critical praise, in effect, establishing the band as a leader of the post-Nirvana American alternative underground. Currently, they don't seem poised for a commercial breakthrough, but many observers felt that way about R.E.M. in 1985.

24 Recommended Albums:

The Feelies, *Crazy Rhythms* (A&M)
Violent Femmes, *Violent Femmes* (Slash)
R.E.M., *Murmur* (IRS)
Replacements, *Let It Be* (Twin/Tone)
Hüsker Dü, *New Day Rising* (SST)
Big Black, *The Rich Man's Eight-Track* (Touch & Go)
Throwing Muses, *Throwing Muses* (4AD)
Dinosaur Jr., *You're Living All Over Me* (SST)
R.E.M., *Document* (IRS)
10,000 Maniacs, *In My Tribe* (Elektra)
Ministry, *The Land of Rape and Honey* (Sire)
Sonic Youth, *Daydream Nation* (DGC)
Michelle Shocked, *Short Sharp Shocked* (Mercury)
Jane's Addiction, *Nothing's Shocking* (Warner Bros.)
Soundgarden, *Louder than Love* (A&M)
Mudhoney, *Superfuzz Bigmuff* (Sub Pop)
Pixies, *Doolittle* (4AD/Elektra)
Nine Inch Nails, *Pretty Hate Machine* (TVT)
Nirvana, *Nevermind* (DGC)
Pearl Jam, *Ten* (Epic)
Liz Phair, *Exile in Guyville* (Matador)
Pavement, *Slanted & Enchanted* (Matador)
Beastie Boys, *Check Your Head* (Capitol)
Beck, *Mellow Gold* (DGC)

– Stephen Thomas Erlewine

British Alternative Rock

Two things separate British alternative rock from its American counterpart. By and large, it's considerably more pop-oriented. Of course, there are some exceptions, particularly goth-rock and shoegazing, but most of the bands concentrate on singles as well as albums. Secondly, it acknowledges dance and club culture freely, with pop/rock groups frequently experimenting with dance rhythms and textures. Both of these factors are part of the reason why very few British alternative bands were successful in America between 1984-1995. The other major factor is a tendency to write about specifically British concerns. From the Smiths to Blur, the lyrics of many British groups are dense with British references. However, 1994 and 1995 showed that the success of American alternative rock had begun to break down the barriers in the U.S. for British bands, as Blur had a Top 60 hit, Oasis had a gold album, and Elastica had two charting hits, as well as a prime spot on Lollapalooza.

Like R.E.M. in the U.S., the Smiths functioned as the turning point between new wave and alternative rock. Hailing from Manchester, the group's layered guitar-pop recalled the Beatles and the Kinks, as well as various girl groups and less-celebrated '60s pop groups. Johnny Marr's innovative, ringing guitar riffs were offset by the literate, self-deprecating and viciously intelligent lyrics of Morrissey. In addition to his distinctive, clever lyrics, Morrissey's voice was unusual, alternating between mild crooning and abrupt yelps, particularly on the band's earlier records. Although the Smiths had only two Top Ten hits, the band's influence loomed large over the next decade, as various bands appropriated Marr's riffs and neo-'60s look. Morrissey's lyrical preoccupations became familiar as well, particularly his tales about English life. The Smiths' lifespan was quite short – their first album was released in 1984, their last in 1987 – but no other British band since the Sex Pistols had as large of a musical impact as the Manchester quartet.

For the latter half of the '80s, British alternative pop/rock was dominated by the goth rock of the Cure, the dance-rock of New Order, and the noisy, neo-psychedelia of the Jesus and Mary Chain. The Cure had formed during the heyday of punk rock, yet their cult began to expand in 1983 and 1984, after which they had a series of best-selling albums and singles. Driven by slow tempos, droning guitars and keyboards, and Robert Smith's self-absorbed, morbid lyrics, the Cure appealed to some of the Smiths' audience, yet they were decidedly gloomier and less pop-oriented. Bands that copied the music of the Cure and Joy Division were quite popular in the late '80s, particularly Sisters of Mercy and Mission (UK).

Joy Division was arguably more important to goth rock than the Cure, but after the band's lead vocalist, Ian Curtis, committed suicide in 1980, the group moved in a different direction under the name New Order. Instead of relying on rock rhythms, New Order experimented with dance, disco, and club beats, creating a fusion between rock and dance which proved to be commercially successful and musically influential. Although not many bands immediately imitated the sound of the band, it laid the groundwork for the Manchester scene of the early '90s.

Although they used a drum machine on their earliest recordings, the Jesus and Mary Chain were as far away from the dance textures of New Order as possible. Instead, the band unearthed the droning noise of the Velvet Underground, adding more distortion, tighter song structure, and floating harmonies. The Jesus and Mary Chain, along with the gargantuan guitar roar of America's Pixies and Sonic Youth, instigated a flood of bands in the '90s that relied on shatteringly loud guitars and ethereal, Beach Boys-derived harmonies.

During this time, a number of British acts found greater success in America than they did at home. While artists like the Cure and the Smiths were popular in both countries, certain musicians were virtually ignored in the U.K. but thrived on American college radio. Foremost among these groups was XTC. Although the group had hits when they first appeared at the height of punk and new wave, they failed to have more than one hit between 1984 and 1989. Nevertheless, the band's late-'80s albums of lush, psychedelic pop found a home in the American alternative scene, particularly 1987's *Skylarking*. Like XTC, Robyn Hitchcock was a new wave survivor, although his former group the Soft Boys were never anywhere near as popular as XTC. However, the Soft Boys' tough, ringing guitar-pop had an influence on many alternative bands of the '80s, particularly R.E.M. Once Hitchcock went solo, he gained a cult following in his native England and America, but had considerably more success in the U.S., thanks to support from college radio. His 1988 major-label debut, *Globe of Frogs*, marked the peak of his popularity, spending 15 weeks on the American charts. In addition to the off-center pop of XTC and Robyn Hitchcock, there were guitar bands that refined the jangling, multi-layered pop of the Smiths, making it smoother, more laid-back and sophisticated. These bands, particularly the Housemartins, managed to sustain popularity on the British charts as well as American college radio. However, the most significant British band of the late '80s and early '90s was the Stone Roses. Like their fellow Mancunians the Smiths, the Stone Roses specialized in an updated version of '60s guitar-pop. Unlike the Smiths, the Stone Roses were in debt to neo-psychedelic guitar-pop and experimented with club textures, particularly on the singles "Fool's Gold" and "One Love." But the key to the band's success was guitarist John Squire, who crafted songs that sounded like forgotten classics but were driven by an urgent energy and cocksure arrogance.

The success of the Stone Roses opened the gates for a flood of bands that reworked the same territory, like the Charlatans and Inspiral Carpets. Of these bands, the Happy Mondays – who were also based in Manchester, giving way to the nickname "Madchester" for the entire pseudo-psychedelic dance scene – were the most noteworthy. Where the Stone Roses only flirted with dance music, the Happy Mondays immersed themselves in it, particularly the funky rhythms and psychedelic drugs like Ecstasy. Shaun Ryder, the band's lead vocalist, wrote lyrics that were cryptically surreal and melodies that appropriated hooks from other pop songs (the Mondays' "Kinky Afro" had the same melody as Labelle's "Lady Marmalade").

At the beginning of the '90s, it appeared as if the Stone Roses and Happy Mondays would be the leading figures in British pop music for the next few years. However, the Madchester scene quickly collapsed. The Stone Roses became embroiled in a debilitating lawsuit with their record company which took two years to resolve; after the case was settled, they took another three years to deliver a follow-up album, ruining any chances of world domination. The Happy Mondays ran out of steam quickly, mainly due to

Ryder's drug addictions. Within a year, British alternative rock was robbed of its two most popular bands, leaving the legions of the Jesus and Mary Chain imitators to come to the forefront. Well, initially they were imitators of the Jesus and Mary Chain. However, by the time the so-called "shoegazers" – a term coined by the British music press for their tendency to do nothing but stare at the floor during concerts – came to popularity in 1991, they were mining the territory My Bloody Valentine established in the late '80s.

My Bloody Valentine formed before the Jesus and Mary Chain, but their records didn't gain attention until 1987, when they released a series of EPs, culminating in 1988's album *Isn't Anything*. MBV's music was louder and more ethereal than JMC's records, creating shimmering soundscapes constructed from dissonance and distortion and detached vocals. Soon, the band's influence eclipsed that of the Jesus and Mary Chain, with numerous bands forming in its wake, including Ride, Lush and the Boo Radleys. Out of all the shoegazing records released in 1991, My Bloody Valentine's *Loveless* was the one that defined the entire scene.

Apart from shoegazing, the other major British musical development of 1991 was the release of Primal Scream's third album, *Screamadelica*. Compared to *Screamadelica* the dance-oriented music of the Happy Mondays was positively tentative. Primal Scream employed a number of dance and techno producers, particularly Andrew Weatherall, to help them create their album. The group's basic compositions were clearly rock songs – the single "Movin' on Up" recalled both the Rolling Stones and Stephen Stills's "Love the One You're With" – but the producers took the songs into new territory with the inclusion of dance-club production techniques. The result was one of the most critically acclaimed albums of the year, as well as a commercial hit. More importantly, *Screamadelica* helped open the doors for techno and club music to be discussed seriously in the British music press, which helped the careers of such techno and ambient musicians as the Orb and the Aphex Twin, as well as dance-oriented bands like Massive Attack, Portishead, and Tricky.

However, neither Primal Scream nor the legions of shoegazers provided as much good copy as the Stone Roses and Happy Mondays, which is crucial for an industry with weekly music newspapers. For all of 1991 and most of 1992, the two trends dominated British alternative rock, as well as the presence of American groups like Nirvana and Pearl Jam. The arrival of Suede in late 1992 kick-started a revival of British guitar-pop that reached fruition two years later. Under the leadership of vocalist Brett Anderson and guitarist Bernard Butler, Suede created a pop-savvy fusion of glam-rock and the Smiths' guitar-pop. The band was praised by the music weeklies as the "Best Band in Britain" before their first single was even released, and Morrissey began covering "My Insatiable One" in concert, setting the stage for enormous expectations. By and large, Suede fulfilled the expectations, as they had a series of hit singles that all charted higher than the first, and their 1993 self-titled debut became the fastest-selling record in British history. The band single-handedly knocked the shoegazers off the front cover of *Melody Maker* and *NME*, setting the stage for British alternative rock's breakthrough into the mainstream in 1994.

Suede may have become British stars in 1993, but they couldn't find a niche in America. During 1994, the band's star began to fade, as Butler left the group before the completion of their second album. That alone wouldn't have been enough to dim their stardom, but the band had created a monster with their debut album that soon outgrew the band itself. Over the course of 1994, no less than three bands emerged as massively popular artists, both commercially and critically.

Of these bands, Blur was the first and most successful. Blur had originally emerged during the height of shoegazing in 1991 with *Leisure*, a record that combined strands of shoegazing with the Madchester craze. Initially, they were popular, but they quickly fell out of favor. The group returned in 1993 with *Modern Life Is Rubbish*, a record that recalled the glory days of British pop, featuring elements of the Kinks, Small Faces, the Jam, and Madness. It was a moderate success, but its performance did nothing to indicate the magnitude of Blur's 1994 breakthrough with *Parklife*. Although it was as fiercely British as its predecessor, *Parklife* was more focused and featured stronger songs, several of which added elements of '80s synth-pop and new wave. "Girls and Boys," the album's opening dance-pop number, entered the charts at number five upon its release in the spring of 1994, opening the doors for British alternative rock which became the dominating musical force in the country for a year. By the end of the year, *Parklife* had gone triple platinum in the U.K., establishing Blur as arguably the most popular band in the country.

As *Parklife* was beginning to take off in the spring of 1994, a new Manchester-based quintet called Oasis began receiving overwhelming positive reviews in the weeklies. By the end of the summer, Oasis had a genuine hit with "Live Forever," and their debut album, *Definitely Maybe*, had unseated *Suede* as the fastest-selling debut album in U.K. history.

Oasis quickly became as popular as Blur, scoring a #1 single in the spring of 1995 with "Some Might Say", by summer 1995, *Definitely Maybe* had gone triple platinum. In addition to Oasis and Blur, a flood of independent and alternative bands began ruling the British pop charts. The spiky new wave revivalism of Elastica, the elegantly wasted synth-pop of Pulp, the youthful exuberance of Supergrass, the streamlined Smiths guitar-pop of Gene, the Boo Radleys, and Shaun Ryder's new band, Black Grape, all enjoyed Top Ten hits on the pop charts, including several number ones. It was the equivalent of Nirvana's American breakthrough, as nearly every one of Britain's most popular bands had its roots in the alternative pop/rock scene of the past decade.

16 Essential Records:

The Smiths, *Singles* (Sire)
The Smiths, *The Queen Is Dead* (Sire)
The Cure, *Staring at the Sea* (Elektra)
The Jesus and Mary Chain, *Psychocandy* (Def American)
New Order, *Substance* (Quest)
XTC, *Skylarking* (Geffen)
Robyn Hitchcock, *Globe of Frogs* (A&M)
The Housemartins, *London 0 Hull 4* (Go! Discs)
The Stone Roses, *The Stone Roses* (Silvertone)
The La's, *The La's* (London)
Happy Mondays, *Pills, Thrills, N' Bellyaches* (Elektra)
My Bloody Valentine, *Loveless* (Sire)
Primal Scream, *Screamadelica* (Sire)
Suede, *Suede* (Nude/Columbia)
Blur, *Parklife* (Capitol)
Oasis, *Definitely Maybe* (Epic)

– by Stephen Thomas Erlewine

New Zealand Rock

New Zealand's influence upon the international rock & roll scene has been limited by its size and isolation. The total population of the nation's two islands is about three million; considerably less than, for instance, the population of the San Francisco Bay Area. The country didn't even have a recording studio until 1948, and as recently as 1989, it took only 7500 units of sales to quality for a gold record. Yet its very size and isolation have also helped foster a brand of rock that may have been too idiosyncratic to flourish elsewhere.

The very first New Zealand rock & roll record was cut way back in August 1955, when John Cooper recorded a version of "Rock Around the Clock." Like its much larger neighbor Australia, New Zealand had plenty of homegrown Kiwi rock & roll in the late '50s and '60s, especially after the British Invasion sparked the formation of self-contained guitar bands. Some of this was fairly good: Ray Columbus & the Invaders (British Invasion-styled pop) and the La-De-Das (British Invasion-styled R&B/rock) were about the best, and the best of the handful of outrageous New Zealand garage bands can be heard on the compilation *Wild Things*, which holds its own with most international '60s garage reissues.

The great majority of New Zealand rock and pop, however, was extremely, at times slavishly, derivative of British and American rock trends. To a large degree, this was also characteristic of Australian rock, but the best '60s Australian rock had a more distinctive flavor, and occasionally bands met with international success. Few listeners outside the Antipodes heard New Zealand rock until the moderate success of Split Enz, beginning in the mid-'70s.

At various times characterized as art-rock, new wave, or comedy-rock, Split Enz attracted the attention of Roxy Music guitarist Phil Manzanera, who produced one of their early albums. Big

stars at home, they also made splashes, in progressively smaller order, in Australia, the U.K., and the U.S. Outside of New Zealand and Australia, they remain very much a cult item, despite their frequent pop/rock focus; listeners tend to either find them intriguingly offbeat, or gimmicky performers who epitomized some of new wave's sillier aspects. In the mid-'80s, Split Enz mainstay Neil Finn (eventually joined by his brother Tim) led Crowded House to international success with tuneful, just-left-of-mainstream pop/rock.

To this day, there continue to be a good many mainstream New Zealand rockers who are popular, or even stars, in their native country. Almost without exception, they are lesser variations on mainstream rock trends originating in the U.K. or U.S. There are several bands featuring blends of rock and the music of the indigenous Maori people of the islands, but this music is rarely distributed internationally, and often leans more toward the tame pop/rock side of things than ethnic roots. Of much more interest to the inquisitive rock fan are the many alternative Kiwi bands, which emerged from a scene that really didn't get going until the late '70s and early '80s.

If there could be said to be a founding father of New Zealand alternative rock, the title would probably be awarded to Chris Knox. A singer in one of the country's first punk bands, the Enemy, he subsequently fronted the energetic new wave group Toy Love, probably the first alternative rock group of its sort to gain a lot of success in the islands. He subsequently teamed with Alec Bathgate to form half of Tall Dwarfs, which has produced quite a few albums of determinedly individual, eccentric, and funkily recorded punk- and new wave-influenced rock that set the tone for the New Zealand underground of the 1980s. Knox has also recorded some similar albums on his own, and remains quite active in the scene to this day.

Tall Dwarfs was one of the first bands to record for the Flying Nun label, the company which has become almost synonymous with New Zealand underground/alternative rock. The small Kiwi punk scene of the late '70s had given birth to a few independent labels (Ripper and Propeller were the best known); those releases have rarely been heard overseas, and then usually on obscure compilations. Flying Nun, begun in 1981 by record-store manager Roger Shepherd, almost immediately placed a couple of singles on the country's charts, and acted as a magnet for the best non-mainstream Kiwi rock talent. By the late '80s, it seemed as though virtually every alternative Kiwi rock act of note was affiliated with the company.

Although Flying Nun become home to a fairly diverse roster of artists, there are certain attributes which could be broadly applied to their sound, and by association the New Zealand alternative scene as a whole. The bands were very much of the D.I.Y. generation spawned by punk and new wave, but placed a high premium on tuneful melodies and a sprinkling of pop hooks. They eschewed in-your-face booming hi-tech production, usually sticking to classic guitar-organ-bass-drums lineups. At the same time, however, they weren't averse to embellishing their products with all manner of odd production touches, often in the four-track manner pioneered by the Tall Dwarfs. Without being slavishly reverent, their music betrayed a strong influence of '60s psychedelia, as well as the jangle-pop of the Byrds; the ghost of Syd Barrett's brilliant pop-psychedelia fusions is particularly strong, hovering over many if not most of the NZ groups.

An equally important factor in the warm reception granted New Zealand bands by alternative rock fans worldwide was the innocence, naiveté, and humility of the music. New Zealand is a modern society, but it is the most isolated of the English-speaking territories; overseas records, books, and films take months and years to arrive in the islands, if they become available there at all. In its low-key lifestyle, it's closer to the America of the 1950s than the 1990s.

This relative lack of overwhelming outside influence, as well as the tight-knit camaraderie of a scene which remains a minority taste on its home turf, accounts to some degree for the originality of the Flying Nun product, right down to the artful, colorful, at times seemingly hand-drawn sleeves.

One could be forgiven for viewing the Flying Nun label as a sort of extended family of New Zealand rock groups; the groups tend to change personnel quite frequently, often joining or rejoining each other's bands, or forming spinoffs of their own. The label is based in New Zealand's largest city, Auckland, yet many of the musicians hail from the relatively small south island town of Dunedin, as well as its bigger south island neighbor Christchurch. Considering the rather limited population pool, Flying Nun cultivated an impressively lengthy roster of bands that made an international impression of sorts in the 1980s the Chills, the Bats, the Clean, the Jean-Paul Sartre Experience, the Verlaines, Straightjacket Fits, and Bailter Space, on down to more cultish acts like Able Tasmans, Headless Chickens, and the Cake Kitchen.

On an international level, the most successful of these bands were the Chills, which had gone through a dozen or so lineups under the leadership of Martin Phillipps, and the Bats, whose guitar-dominated sound fit in most readily with the music favored by college radio in the late '80s. The Verlaines, the Jean-Paul Sartre Experience, and Straightjacket Fits also landed overseas licensing deals; Homestead, Rough Trade, and Communion were the prime outlets for NZ product in the U.S. Since the mid-'80s, appreciation for the Flying Nun sound has grown steadily overseas, especially in the United States. Granted these fans tend to cluster in big cities and university towns; San Francisco has a particularly large clique of Flying Nun aficionados, as does Los Angeles, New York, and Chicago. Judging by the large amounts of ink devoted to Flying Nun bands in underground rock publications and fanzines, one would assume they were stars.

They're not, actually, outside of the fairly small community of listeners who read these publications. Mainstream audiences have not so much disliked these groups as never heard them, although a couple (most notably the Chills) had major-label deals. The bands at least gathered enough of a following to enable them to tour the U.S., although in most cases these tours were limited to the East and West Coasts.

Lest one be tempted to think that Flying Nun remains the first and last word in New Zealand indie rock, other Kiwi indies such as Xpressway and IND have also released a few albums that have achieved international recognition; the excruciating noise-rock of the Dead C and the Syd Barrettisms of Alastair Galbraith being two of the more widely known examples. Flying Nun remains as active as ever in the mid-'90s, even though its roster seems increasingly static, the new acts often composed of spinoffs of groups that first recorded with the label in the 1980s. In judging the health of the New Zealand indie scene, one runs up against the isolation problem in reverse: it can take years for bands to get heard overseas, if they get heard at all. The islands retain considerable pride, though, in schooling a brand of alternative rock that rarely bows to commercial pressures from the mainstream or the underground, while remaining accessible to all who manage to find it.

12 Essential Recordings

Various Artists, *Wild Things* (Flying Nun)
Split Enz, *History Never Repeats: The Best of Split Enz* (A&M)
Toy Love, *Toy Love* (WEA, New Zealand)
Various Artists, *Tuatara* (Flying Nun)
The Tall Dwarfs, *Hello Cruel World* (Homestead)
The Chills, *Kaleidoscope World* (Homestead)
The Clean, *Compilation* (Homestead)
The Bats, *The Law of Things* (Communion)
The Jean-Paul Sartre Experience, *Love Songs* (Communion)
The Verlaines, *Juvenilia* (Homestead)
Straightjacket Fits, *Hail* (Flying Nun)
Alastair Galbraith, *Seely Girn* (Feel Good All Over)

BOOK:

Stranded in Paradise: New Zealand Rock'n'Roll 1955-1988, by John Dix (Paradise Publications, New Zealand, 1988)
– *by Richie Unterberger*

Lo-Fi

Over the last several decades, there's been a more or less ongoing clique of staunch traditionalists who insist that hi-tech, glossy production values are taking the soul and spontaneity out of rock & roll music. As rock heads into the 21st century – in an age where such technology-dependent musics as techno, ambient, and rap are gaining an unstoppable momentum, and multi-track recordings and "punch-in" vocals are standard practice – it's ironic that one of the most influential trends of alternative rock in the '90s has deliberately cast itself in opposition to studio sophistication. Called "lo-fi" artists, more by the rock underground than by them-

selves, they see simple, even primitive recording quality as an advantage, not a hindrance.

If you're so inclined, you can trace lo-fi right back to the beginning of rock & roll, when thousands of rockabilly and doo wop artists recorded in primitive circumstances, lending their records a unique naiveté that is impossible to recreate today. The garage bands of the mid-'60s, of course, often recorded in facilities as primitive as the ones they rehearsed in, a quality which was duplicated in the '70s by many of the early punk bands.

The difference between these earlier rock & rollers and today's lo-fi artists is that, in all probability, virtually all of the earlier records sounded primitive due to financial limitations rather than conscious decision. If these rockabilly, garage, and even punks had been asked at the time whether they would like to be recording in more sophisticated facilities, with greater time and budgets at their disposal, the vast majority of them would have likely said yes without a second thought. While today's lo-fi artists are often limited by budgetary constraints as well, the defining difference is that they are by and large making a conscious choice to aim for the spontaneity and distinctive distorted, grainy sonic qualities that can arise from recording quickly on simple, even outdated, equipment.

Again, this approach isn't unique to the '90s, and in fact has pretty deep roots. On their second album, *White Light/White Heat*, the Velvet Underground deliberately turned their amps to 11 and gleefully watched the needles go into the red, ignoring the engineer's pleas to turn down the volume to eliminate distortion. The Beatles deliberately created distortion on tracks like "Revolution"; the Rolling Stones recorded some of "Jumping Jack Flash"'s guitars on cassette to get the right amount of dirt into the sound.

But lo-fi, as the label's applied in 1995, really has its roots in the do-it-yourself ethic that arose from the punk movement in the late '70s. One of its basic (if not always observed) tenets was that anybody could form a band, record their music, and issue it on their own label. By the early '80s, this was taken a step further by some independent artists, who realized that they need not even enter a studio to record their own music, or even "release" it through traditional vinyl means, instead recording at home, dubbing their own cassettes, and selling/trading those at gigs or through the mail. The fuzzy sound, distorted guitars, simple instrumentation, and occasional mistakes were not viewed as flaws, but as actual enhancements, increasing the most intimate and personal quality of the performances, and the truest representation of the artists' visions. Many alternative acts of the '80s were lo-fi in this classic sense, although the label hadn't been created at the time. Page through any issue of alternative/underground publications such as *Op, Option*, or *Forced Exposure*, and there will be plenty of them, on vinyl, cassette, and eventually, compact disc. The K label, run by Calvin Johnson of Beat Happening, is (in retrospect) the most famous and influential repository of the lo-fi aesthetic. But there were innumerable others following the same path, most (but not all) rock-based, although they didn't achieve even a modicum of mainstream recognition: Jandek, Kath Bloom, Walls of Genius, Linda Smith, and Loren Mazzacane are but a few of the better under-appreciated trailblazers of the genre. Content as well as attitude was needed to make this stuff work, as the music of the unspeakably, deliberately awful Happy Flowers – along with literally thousands of cassette tapes – could attest to.

At the beginning of the 1990s, several alternative rock acts using the lo-fi aesthetic began to rise to levels of attention previously reserved for R.E.M. clones and British gloom-mongers. Chief among these were Sebadoh, formed by Dinosaur, Jr. castoff Lou Barlow; Pavement, a California band that seemed to positively pride itself on non-promotion and an elusive image; and Guided by Voices, an Ohio band that had been releasing its own albums for a good half-dozen years before suddenly getting "discovered" by listeners extending beyond its circle of friends.

Most likely, these bands achieved a level of recognition unattained by previous lo-fi pioneers because of the relatively pop-oriented base of their material. Guided by Voices, for instance, likes nothing more than to be compared to a lost power-pop British Invasion band; Pavement is frequently compared to Lou Reed. Don't be under the illusion, though, that listening to these guys is like putting on a Big Star or Go-Betweens record: there are frequent side trips into experimentalism, free-form song structures, and even downright noise. There's also no doubt of their love for lo-fi textures. Certainly the sound could be "cleaned up" by utilizing moderately more expensive, state-of-the-art studios and equipment, but they realize that deliberate distortion and muffled textures, used purposefully, have desirable aesthetic qualities that would be smothered by more state-of-the-art methods.

The rise of lo-fi brought belated appreciation to some of the progenitors of the genre. The New York noise group Pussy Galore was one of the root bands of lo-fi, especially with its almost legendary (if seldom heard) song-by-song cassette rendition of the Rolling Stones' *Exile on Main Street*. It gave birth to two more accessible, traditionally rock-oriented acts which draw on the lo-fi aesthetic to some degree, the Jon Spencer Blues Explosion and Royal Trux (the latter of which boasted that it never spent more than $1000 on recording an album until it hooked up with a major label). In New Zealand, Chris Knox, a pivotal figure in that country's punk/new wave scene, recorded intriguing alternative pop both on his own and with his partner Alec Bathgate in Tall Dwarfs, often hastily working on four-track equipment. Many other Kiwi alternative bands, associated with Flying Nun and other labels, prefer to work in similar no-frills fashions; Alastair Galbraith even told *Option* that he intentionally leaves clicks in place when he puts overdubs onto his four-track recordings.

Beat Happening, meanwhile, continues to work today, and Calvin Johnson is still busy organizing and promoting artists working with the lo-fi modus operandi for K records and cassettes with artists like Lois. He also provides an outlet for the less commercial recordings of Beck, who took lo-fi (in a cleaned-up fashion) to the Top 20 with his debut, *Mellow Gold*; his more acoustic-oriented, less-polished efforts can be found on his K release, *One Foot in the Grave*.

The mid-'90s also saw an enormous amount of critical attention lavished upon Jack Logan, discovered in his mid-30s almost by accident after making over 500 home recordings with friends in his small Georgia home. Several dozen of these were culled for a double-CD debut release which made many national critics' Best of 1994 lists, although it didn't sell more than a few thousand copies. Also hailed by national publications were Palace Brothers, a floating ensemble built around Will Oldham, linking lo-fi to acoustic folk traditions. Palace Brothers are far darker than the relatively cheery and pop-based ruminations of Logan, but are positively jolly when juxtaposed with the more obscure Smog, a nom de plume for various projects of the reclusive Bill Callahan, who builds depressing but compelling, gripping soundscapes of the demons troubling his inner psyche. In this respect Smog, Palace Brothers, Beck, and other lo-fi hounds owe an oft-unacknowledged debt to Skip Spence, the brilliant but demented ex-Moby Grape guitarist. Spence's 1969 solo album, *Oar,* anticipated much of the

lo-fi aesthetic with its minimal, goofy, and hushed, tormented ambience, constructed primarily as a one-man acoustical band.

One of the greatest lo-fi recordings was never released to the general public. Before gaining instant fame with her 1993 debut *Exile in Guyville*, Liz Phair recorded lo-fi tapes of much of the material that ended up on the record (along with songs she recorded for her second album and ones she never released), using only multi-tracked tapes of her voice and guitar, for limited circulation (primarily to friends and acquaintances). Literally thousands of unauthorized copies of the tapes, dubbed *Girlysound*, have made the rounds with Phair fans, many of whom rank the songs among her best and most unaffected performances, despite the hissy fidelity. Phair is in some important respects a lo-fi anomaly; her two official albums are too elaborately produced to be classified as lo-fi, and *Girlysound* could be categorized with the many excellent bootlegs by famous artists which happen to have primitive sound quality, such as the Beatles' acoustic *White Album* demos. But unlike most of those superstar bootlegs, *Girlysound* has a deliberately minimalist and naked D.I.Y. outlook that could only have been produced in the age of lo-fi.

Lo-fi may have a much higher profile than ever as we go to press, but the vast majority of the music is still unheard even by much of the underground. And not only by groups that have generated a modest buzz, such as Superchunk, the Grifters, the Silver Jews, and Portastatic, or the multitudinous and incestuous side projects of many of the top lo-fi bands. The fountain of lo-fi remains the bedrooms and basements of home recording artists, where those who prize feeling over polish pour their hearts out in a format that works in direct opposition to the unwritten rules of today's music studios, equipment manufacturers, and record labels.

12 Essential Recordings

Beat Happening, *Dreamy* (Sub Pop)
Pavement, *Westing (By Musket & Sextant)* (Drag City)
Sebadoh, *Smash Your Head on the Punk Rock* (Sub Pop)
Beck, *One Foot in the Grave* (K)
Guided By Voices, *Bee Thousand* (Matador)
Liz Phair, *Girlysound* (bootleg tape)
Alastair Galbraith, *Seely Girn* (Feel Good All Over)
The Tall Dwarfs, *Hello Cruel World* (Homestead)
Smog, *Burning Kingdom* (Drag City)
Jack Logan, *Bulk* (Medium Cool)
Lois, *Strumpet* (K)
Palace Brothers, *Palace Brothers* (Drag City)

– by Richie Unterberger

NON-ROCK STYLES THAT INFLUENCED ROCK

Acoustic Blues

The blues is only one of the foundations of rock & roll music, but it may be the sturdiest and most central. Even in its earliest forms, it pointed toward rock & roll in its reliance upon guitar, piano, and percussion, its raw energy, and its classic chord patterns. Embellished with instruments, fuller arrangements, and electricity, it provided the building blocks for jazz, R&B, and electric blues, from which it was just a few more steps to rock music. Rock itself has always looked back to the blues, both electric and acoustic, for inspiration and regeneration.

The history of the blues is a long, complicated, and often fascinating one, which is beyond the scope of this brief overview, in which we'll just note its roots in African chants and rhythms, plantation work songs and field hollers, gospel, ragtime, and minstrel music. Largely a southern-based music, the blues had been around for decades, if not centuries, before it began to be widely recorded in the 1920s.

Even then, there were several distinct types of blues music.

The most popular kind was the music sung by the early female blues vocalists, who were closely tied to jazz and even pop/vaudeville. Mamie Smith, Ma Rainey, Bessie Smith, and Victoria Spivey were stars with a wide audience, and enjoyed great popularity in the cities. Not enormously influential on the course of R&B and rock, these vocalists were nonetheless greatly admired by Janis Joplin and Tracy Nelson (who recorded an entire album of Ma Rainey and Bessie Smith songs in her folkie days), and they in turn influenced numerous rock performers who had never heard the originals.

After its resurgence in the 1960s, the early blues acquired a romantic image as a musical reflection of suffering and hard times that was unrivaled in its authenticity. It comes as a surprise to some modern listeners to find that there were plenty of early blues performers that didn't conform to that stereotype. There were blues singers with strong shades of ragtime, vaudeville, and gospel in their music. Many were entertainers, able to perform hard-bitten tales of toil when the spirit moved them, but also able to sing all types of music ranging from country to pop when their audience required it. There were also quite a few jug bands, several in Memphis alone, that frequently used fiddles, banjos, kazoos, and other instruments that hardly fit the blues stereotype.

Unquestionably, however, it was the southern solo guitarists of the first generation of recorded bluesmen that cast the greatest shadow over rock, and held the greatest mystique for listeners that weren't around (or, usually, even born) when the blues first became available on record. Many of them came from the Mississippi Delta, such as Son House, Charley Patton, Bukka White, Fred McDowell, Skip James, Robert Johnson, and these, especially Robert Johnson, have all acquired mythic stature. There were also blues legends active throughout the rest of the South, especially Texas (Blind Lemon Jefferson), Atlanta (Blind Willie McTell), and Memphis (Furry Lewis, Memphis Minnie), and the southeastern performers (Blind Blake and Blind Boy Fuller) came to be referred to as the Piedmont School.

Not all major blues artists were guitarists – there were also quite a few pianists in the barrelhouse and boogie styles, such as Peetie Wheatstraw, Cow Cow Davenport, and a host of incredibly obscure names that usually only turn up on import compilations. But the guitarists, understandably, were the source of greatest influence and fascination for subsequent generations of rock & rollers. The guitar, after all, is rock's premier instrument, and quite a few of the picking styles, riffs, and even songs can be traced directly back to rural blues. Rockers past and present have been equally enamored with its raw vocals and personal lyrics as a direct expression of their joys and struggles.

Numerous examples could be made of old blues songs that have taken on new lives as rock hits. A particularly colorful example is "Matchbox," originally performed by Blind Lemon Jefferson. The song, which may well have been traditional in origin, was spruced up into rockabilly in the mid-'50s by Carl Perkins (who claimed the writing credits); ten years later, it was transformed yet again into full-bore rock & roll by the Beatles, who learned the song from the Perkins version, and may not have even been aware that Jefferson recorded it in the 1920s.

Acoustic blues records were quite popular with Black listeners when they first appeared, but the Depression prevented many from affording records at all. Hence many blues performers rarely recorded, or never got to record at all, during much of the 1930s and 1940s. When the blues became popular again, it was a new kind of blues, played with electric guitars and drums, in cities like Chicago and Memphis. A lot of these performers, such as Muddy Waters, Elmore James, and Johnny Shines, had moved to the city from the Delta, where they had already perfected their craft as acoustic performers. They electrified as a matter of professional survival, and updated the classical rural guitar blues sound as much as they changed it – you can hear strong echoes of the Delta in everything they did, down to the 12-bar structure that was established as the classic blues form.

Many of the original country blues performers were forgotten until the blues revival of the early 1960s. Not everyone went to the same lengths as guitarist John Fahey, who located Bukka White by writing a letter to "Bukka White, Old Blues Singer, c/o General Delivery, Aberdeen, Mississippi" (a town mentioned in one of his songs), but many blues singers, unknown and obscure even in their hometowns, were rediscovered and coaxed out of retirement by White enthusiasts. They found an entire new audience, mostly young and collegiate, waiting for them, and were often, as White was, able to tour and record internationally to considerable acclaim in their remaining years. Singers like Mississippi John Hurt, Skip James, and Fred McDowell may have reached more listeners by touring the folk circuit in the '60s than they did during their prime.

The rediscovery and reappreciation of these early blues legends saw some major rock bands, who had already plundered electric blues for much of their inspiration, going back even further to the earlier acoustic blues. The Rolling Stones were the most successful; their late '60s and early '70s albums often tap into the Delta spirit without sounding like a slavish imitation or bad parody, both on original material like "Salt of the Earth" and covers of classics by Robert Wilkins, Robert Johnson, and Fred McDowell. McDowell himself toured with Bonnie Raitt, who has openly credited the bluesman as a major influence. Canned Heat updated a Henry Thomas panpipe number, "Bull Doze Blues," into the Top 20 single "Going up the Country." The Allman Brothers revived Blind Willie McTell's "Statesboro Blues." Cream recorded exciting electric versions of Skip James's "I'm So Glad" and Robert Johnson's "Crossroads." So it continues until today: Nirvana's posthumous *Unplugged* release included a version of Leadbelly's "Where Did You Sleep Last Night?"

Acoustic blues will always be an element of rock & roll,

although not nearly as much as electric blues, both as an influence and as a source of cover material. Acoustic blues itself isn't recorded or performed much these days; it is the modern age, after all, and the great majority of blues performers are working in the electric format both out of choice and necessity. The surprise success of Robert Johnson's 1990 box set, which sold several hundred thousand copies in these days of synthesizers and 64-track production, proves that acoustic blues will always strike listeners with its power and passion, no matter what the era.

Despite its indisputed importance, the unseasoned listener is urged to ease her or his way into the classic blues repertoire. The primitive sound (in which the guitar and vocals sometimes appear to be in the process of being fried on the skillet), the limited melodic variation, and the harsh execution can disappoint those led by enthusiastic critics to expect an instantly transforming experience. Rather than jump into the legacy of legendarily challenging legends like Robert Pete Williams, it might be best to start with more accessible collections, such as the ones listed below.

15 Recommended Recordings

Various Artists, *Blues Masters, Vol. 10: Blues Roots* (Rhino). Just what it says, focusing on forms like prison songs, work songs, and native African music.

Various Artists, *Blues Masters, Vol. 11: Classic Blues Women* (Rhino). The early female blues stars: Bessie Smith, Mamie Smith, Sippie Wallace, Billie Holiday, Ma Rainey.

Various Artists, *Roots of Robert Johnson* (Yazoo). An interesting concept: the performances that can be seen, with hindsight, to have influenced Johnson, by fellow Mississippi Delta bluesmen like Skip James, Charley Patton, Son House, and Lonnie Johnson.

Various Artists, *Slide Guitar – Bottles Knives & Steel, Vol. 1 & 2* (CBS). The slide guitar is many people's favorite feature of early blues, and these collections have cuts by major practitioners like Bukka White, Tampa Red, Blind Willie Johnson, and Leadbelly.

Skip James, *The Complete Early Recordings* (Yazoo). The most thorough collection of his 1930s sides, including the original version of "I'm So Glad."

Mississippi John Hurt, *1928 Sessions* (Yazoo). One of the finest fingerpicking early blues guitarists. For those who find remastered 78s tough listening, the Vanguard albums he recorded in the 1960s following his rediscovery are a recommended alternative.

Blind Willie McTell, *The Definitive Blind Willie McTell* (Columbia). Double disc of 1929-33 material by the versatile performer, an innovator of 12-string guitar playing.

Leadbelly, *King of the 12-String Guitar* (CBS). Through his popularization of "Goodnight, Irene," "Midnight Special," and others, Leadbelly's influence was also felt in the folk and pop worlds.

Memphis Minnie, *Hoodoo Lady (1933-37)* (CBS). Singer-guitarist roundly considered to be the greatest pre-World War II blueswoman.

Robert Johnson, *The Complete Recordings* (CBS). More may have been written and analyzed about this set of tracks than those found on any other blues collection.

Bukka White, *The Complete Bukka White* (Columbia). One of the most hard-bitten and starkly personal blues singers, these 1937 and 1940 sessions are considered to be his best work.

Muddy Waters, *The Complete Plantation Recordings* (MCA). Recorded for the Library of Congress in the early 1940s, when Muddy lived in Mississippi, and had yet to plug in an electric guitar. A fascinating link between the old and new guard, even if no one could have been aware at the time.

Mississippi Fred McDowell, *Mississippi Delta Blues* (Arhoolie). Although he was born shortly after 1900, this bottleneck slide guitarist wasn't discovered and recorded until 1959; these mid-'60s recordings are considered among his best.

J.B. Lenoir, *Down in Mississippi* (L&R, Germany). A second-division electric Chicago bluesman who recorded for Chess and other labels, Lenoir made a couple little-known European albums in the mid-'60s shortly before his death. These found him expanding the acoustic blues traditions in interesting ways, writing topical songs about contemporary issues like segregation and Vietnam, and using African-derived percussive rhythms. This is recommended above the similar *Alabama Blues* for its greater accessibility.

Ted Hawkins, *Happy Hour* (Rounder). A street performer on the Venice Beach boardwalk in Los Angeles for many years, Hawkins was one of the few acoustic blues musicians to achieve

widespread recognition in the 1980s and 1990s, though his material and vocals actually owed as much to soul and R&B as straight blues. Hawkins released his first major label album at the age of 58, shortly before his death in 1995; this 1987 effort uses sparer instrumentation.

Books

Deep Blues, by Robert Palmer (Viking Press, 1981)
The Blackwell Guide to Blues Records, edited by Paul Oliver Blackwell, 1989)
The Story of the Blues, by Paul Oliver (Chilton, 1970)
                      – *Richie Unterberger*

Gospel

Gospel music has rarely been a significant presence in the commercial mainstream, and indeed its fervent religious content will most likely always limit it to a specialized audience. Rock and pop fans often find pure gospel rough going, both due to its intensely spiritual focus and its melodic and compositional strictures. Yet even for those rock fans who never develop a passion for the form, it's worth appreciation as one of rock's and soul's bedrock influences.

There are strong gospel traditions, reaching back through several centuries, in both the Black and White populations of America. The Black tradition, a combination of indigenous African music with Western religious influences, found its expression in both "work songs" and the church, one of the few places where the Black community could openly express itself in the days of segregation. When Black gospel traditions began to mix with the music of the secular world, the combinations that resulted were pivotal in the birth of R&B and soul.

The groaning, moaning, pleading, and supplicating qualities of gospel are easy to hear in the vocals of jump blues artists like Percy Mayfield, Roy Brown, and Wynona Carr, as well as early soul pioneers like Ray Charles, James Brown, Clyde McPhatter, and Little Willie John, even if they may be singing about raucous and romantic joys. Likewise, the harmonies and call-and-response interplay of the classic doo wop groups, from the Orioles through the early work of the Impressions, were refined in the chapel as well as on the street corner.

The connection between gospel and soul, however, is often far more direct. A few of soul's greatest singers, including Wilson Pickett and Little Johnny Taylor, got their starts in gospel quartets. Taylor had been in the Soul Stirrers, also the breeding ground for Sam Cooke, the most famous singer to cross over to pop after establishing himself as a gospel star. Gospel fans were outraged when Cooke abandoned the circuit for pop stardom in the late '50s, but pop and rock fans were enriched immeasurably, as Cooke's work until his death in 1964 was immensely important in paving the road for modern soul music.

Notable female soul and pop singers who began as gospel vocalists include Dionne Warwick and Whitney Houston, whose mother, Cissy, directed the Sweet Inspirations, who sang backup vocals on some of Aretha Franklin's early hits. Franklin herself was the daughter of noted preacher and gospel singer C.L. Franklin, and recorded some gospel as a teenager. When she reached superstardom with a burst of soul smashes in 1967, listeners were responding to a voice letting loose the unbridled passion of gospel on contemporary pop-R&B. Franklin's vision is really too wide to be categorized as a gospel offshoot, but she has always remained cognizant of her roots, occasionally immersing herself in them, as on her acclaimed 1972 live album, *Amazing Grace*.

Other notable gospel-soul crossovers include the Chambers Brothers, who were one of the few Black groups to become favorites with the psychedelic crowd; the Edwin Hawkins Singers, who landed a surprise Top Five hit in 1969 with "Oh Happy Day"; and the Staple Singers, whose Memphis soul-gospel approach yielded some of the most inspirational hits of the early '70s. Also from Memphis is Al Green, the most famous singer to travel in the reverse direction, abandoning pop superstardom for gospel. The music world was shocked when Green embraced gospel in the late '70s after a reign of five years or so as soul's most popular performer, and though he's largely a memory for the masses, he's been very active in the studio and as a performer in the gospel world.

In the world of White rock & roll, gospel has been a less prominent but nevertheless important influence. The church was a focal point of White southern rural culture, and often offered the easiest place to sing and play music, as it did in the early African-American community. Most of the first White rock & rollers were southern, and they were also schooled in gospel harmonies and spiritual standards. Many early country acts, like the Carter Family, Bill Monroe, and Tennessee Ernie Ford, took a large part of their repertoire from gospel. The close harmonies of acts like the Delmore Brothers often derived from, and were sometimes actually used on, sacred songs, in turn influencing early rock & rollers who didn't actually perform gospel, the Everly Brothers being the most famous example.

Many early rockabilly stars may have been set on raising hell onstage and in the studio, but gospel was a big part of their background, even in the most unlikely cases – Jerry Lee Lewis, for instance, is Jimmy Swaggart's cousin, and can be heard debating spiritual matters with Sam Phillips on a famous outtake from Sun Studios. When Lewis, Elvis Presley, Carl Perkins, and others gathered in the same studio in 1956 for the famous Million Dollar Quartet session, they jammed on the songs they all shared and knew by heart – many of which, to the surprise of some latter-day listeners, were gospel tunes. Elvis counted gospel groups like the Statesmen and the Blackwood Brothers among his biggest influences, and employed a gospel group, the Jordanaires, to harmonize and sing backing vocals on most of his biggest hits. He also recorded a good deal of straight gospel himself, from 1957 on through to the 1970s.

Rock stars without direct gospel influences have occasionally called on gospel singers to record appropriate embellishments to particular recordings; Paul Simon was never one to let a good ethnic flavor pass unnoticed, and his use of the Dixie Hummingbirds on the 1973 hit "Loves Me Like a Rock" is one of the most famous examples. Occasionally, rockers have embraced religion long after establishing themselves as secular pop stars, recording gospel-influenced albums that have by and large not been well received, Bob Dylan being the most famous of these. Dylan was outraged at his audience for, as he saw it, dismissing his music because of its religious values; this may have been partly true, but his fans were also turning a cold shoulder to the records because spiritual music was not his strongest suit, and because they didn't enjoy being hammered over the head with a message, fundamentalist or otherwise. When Violent Femmes leader Gordon Gano recorded a gospel album with his side group the Mercy Seat, the reaction was not so much hostility as indifference, partly because Gano wasn't nearly as mythological a figure as Dylan.

In contemporary music, gospel usually isn't a visible factor, not because its influence is negligible, but because it has permeated the rock and soul mainstream so deeply that it's become permanently absorbed into its structure. It continues to permeate urban contemporary R&B in the smooth harmonies and lead vocals, even if the singers are no longer as directly steeped in the church as they were in the 1950s and 1960s. And there are still instances of singers moving from spiritual music to secular pop/rock, as Amy Grant has done on a superstar level, and singer/songwriter Sam Phillips has done as a cult alternative rock favorite.

12 Recommended Recordings

Various Artists, *Jubilation Vol. 1-3* (Rhino). Anthologies of classic gospel. The first two volumes cover Black artists like the Soul Stirrers, the Swan Silvertones, Aretha Franklin, Mahalia Jackson, the Staple Singers, and the Five Blind Boys; the third focuses on white country gospel, with sides by the Carter Family, the Louvin Brothers, Kitty Wells, George Jones and Tammy Wynette, Bill Monroe, Johnny Cash, and Hank Williams.

The Soul Stirrers, *The Gospel Soul of Sam Cooke, Vol. 2* (Specialty). An entire disc of Cooke's sides with the gospel group during the first half of the 1950s. Other Soul Stirrers discs, if you want to go further, include performances by Johnnie Taylor and other noteworthy singers who took the leads when Cooke wasn't in the group.

Various Artists, *Something Got a Hold of Me* (RCA). Classic country gospel by the Carter Family, Bill Monroe, the Blue Sky Boys, Uncle Dave Macon, and other less celebrated acts.

Elvis Presley, *The Million Dollar Quartet* (RCA). Actually Elvis, Carl Perkins, and Jerry Lee Lewis, plus a few other musicians (Johnny Cash was present for the photo but not for the recording, apparently), jamming on rock, R&B, and not a little gospel. The double-CD *Amazing Grace* is the most wide-ranging compilation of Presley's gospel recordings, but will have considerably less appeal for the rock fan.

Mahalia Jackson, *Gospels, Spirituals & Hymns* (CBS). Often rated as the best gospel singer of all.

Various Artists, *Sam Cooke's SAR Records Story 1959-1965* (ABKCO). Cooke acted as label owner and frequent producer and songwriter for SAR, recording gospel, soul, and combinations of the two by performers like the Womack Brothers, Johnnie Taylor, and the Valentinos.

The Chambers Brothers, *Greatest Hits* (Columbia). An erratic group whose funk and psychedelic excesses never hid their gospel roots.

The Staple Singers, *Greatest Hits* (Fantasy). A compilation of early-'60s material that gives listeners a sampling of their gospel roots tempered by contemporary influences. No Staple Singers collection surveys their entire career, which stretches across several decades; try Vee Jay compilations for their earliest and purest gospel material, and *The Best of the Staple Singers* (on Stax) for their soul hits.

Aretha Franklin, *Amazing Grace* (Atlantic). Her 1972 gospel album, also featuring James Cleveland and the Southern California Community Choir.

The Dixie Hummingbirds, *Live* (MCA). A 75-minute live set from the mid-'70s.

Al Green, *The Belle Album* (Hi). His last album (from 1977) before his conversion to full-time gospel, catching him bridging secular soul music with personal spiritual concerns.

Sweet Honey in the Rock, *Live at Carnegie Hall* (Flying Fish). Not purely a gospel group, though heavily gospel-influenced, this all-woman African-American a cappella group is proof that music can both draw on gospel traditions and comment on contemporary political, social, and personal concerns. Active since the mid-'70s, with various lineups under the leadership of Bernice Reagon, this is a 1988 concert recording.

– Richie Unterberger

Electric Blues

Of all the many forms of music that contributed to the birth of rock & roll, electric blues has arguably exerted the most fundamental and durable influence. It's not just that electric blues helped establish the prototype of the basic rock lineup – electric guitars and a rhythm section – and that much early rock & roll, from both America and Great Britain, was an embellishment of electric blues with somewhat different rhythms and song construction. It's also that electric blues, in sound, spirit, and execution, is separated from rock & roll by only the thinnest of boundaries. It's rare indeed to find a rock & roll fan who doesn't have the same visceral response to electric blues, even though the music isn't nearly as dominant a presence in the media and the marketplace.

The blues started to become electrified shortly before World War II, as a direct result of major shifts in the lives of millions of African Americans. The large Black migration from rural areas to urban factories, in search of better employment opportunities and living conditions, resulted in a swelling of the Black communities in America's inner cities. A great many of these Blacks came from the South, settling in metropolises like Chicago, St. Louis, Detroit, and Los Angeles. They brought their musical tastes with them, but rural blues had to be adapted to city life to survive. The pace of urban life was faster, the performance venues larger and more lively. To cut through the noise of the crowds, electric instruments and drums were a necessity.

It's unclear exactly who the first electric blues guitarist was, but most likely bluesmen began to try amplified instruments in the late '30s; there have even been rumors that Robert Johnson was playing electric guitar with a band shortly before his death in 1938. Early electric jazz guitar pioneers Eddie Durham and, especially, Charlie Christian mapped out the single-string solo style that early electric blues guitarists would build upon. Guitarist T-Bone Walker, a Texan who relocated to Los Angeles, is almost universally credited as the first electric blues master. Starting around 1940, he combined electric blues with elements of R&B and jazz, enjoying a prolific career that stretched over several decades.

What most people think of as the classic electric blues sound, however, developed in Chicago shortly after World War II. Many of the great Chicago blues musicians had relocated from the Mississippi Delta, long a fountain of great blues performers, and indeed many of the new arrivals had already perfected their craft on acoustic instruments. A brasher, faster electric style was required for professional survival in the Windy City. By the 1950s, Chicago electric blues was thriving, in a small combo format established by bandleaders like Muddy Waters.

Waters was not the first notable electric blues musician in Chicago; John Lee Williamson (the first "Sonny Boy" Williamson), Johnny Shines, and a few others had already used amplification by the time he arrived in the city in 1943. Waters himself was already a blues performer of some note, recording acoustic sessions for the Library of Congress in the early '40s at the Mississippi plantation where he worked. He knew he needed to adapt, though, and assembled a powerhouse band that would, at various points, feature performers who were stars in their own right, including Little Walter, Jimmy Rogers, Otis Spann, Junior Wells, and James Cotton. Driven by compelling riffs on guitar and harmonica, a forceful rhythm section, and strong original material that derived from and updated the classic Delta blues Waters had already mastered, his band was the prototype for Chicago electric blues.

Waters recorded for Chess Records, which quickly became the city's most successful blues and R&B label, with a roster including Little Walter, Howlin' Wolf, Sonny Boy Williamson, and Jimmy Rogers, as well as (for brief periods) Elmore James, John Lee Hooker, Otis Rush, and many interesting minor performers. The Chess sound, spare, clear, and reverberant, did a lot in its own right to refine and solidify the music without sacrificing its raw power. A lot of the credit for Chess's success belongs to arranger, bassist, songwriter, and occasional performer Willie Dixon, who perhaps wrote more classic blues songs than any other songwriter.

A lot of classic Chicago blues from this era was recorded on other labels by greats like Rush, James, Billy Boy Arnold, and Jimmy Reed. And while Chicago had by far the greatest concentration of talent, the blues became electrified in similar patterns in other cities. Memphis had Howlin' Wolf before he moved to Chicago, as well as B.B. King, Ike Turner, and Junior Parker; before he moved into rockabilly, Sam Phillips of Sun Records was often responsible for recording the best Memphis blues musicians. Detroit had John Lee Hooker, the king of boogie; Guitar Slim and Slim Harpo recorded swamp blues in Louisiana; and there were strong scenes in Houston, St. Louis, and California.

Blues didn't only adapt the classic 12-bar, three-chord pattern when it became electrified, it also combined with jazz, pop, and gospel to feed into rhythm and blues, in the form of jump blues "shouters" like Big Joe Turner, Tiny Bradshaw, Ruth Brown, and Jimmy Witherspoon. R&B, of course, eventually fed into rock & roll, and early soul pioneers like Ray Charles, James Brown, and Little Willie John were strongly influenced by the blues. Bobby "Blue" Bland was the most prominent vocalist who borrowed in fairly equal measure from blues, R&B, and soul. Guitarists like Chuck Berry and Bo Diddley took the electric blues foundation and pioneered rock & roll by adding R&B, jump blues, and pop elements. Ironically (more so considering that Berry and Diddley actually recorded for Chess), rock & roll had cut deeply into the blues audience by the end of the 1950s, and electric blues, a huge commercial success on the R&B charts in the early and mid-'50s, was relegated to a small corner of the record-buying public once again.

Electric blues still thrived in the local clubs, and came roaring back into public consciousness again in the mid-'60s, as British Invasion bands like the Rolling Stones and Yardbirds popularized electric blues classics for a mass audience, and folk festivals and European tours introduced living legends like Waters to White listeners who would never have come across the music otherwise. Some of the best electric blues dates from this decade, when some greats leavened their sound with contemporary R&B and soul influences without removing their blues foundations. Junior Wells, Magic Sam, Buddy Guy, and Albert King recorded their best work in this era; B.B. King even crossed over to the pop charts, a feat that has remained rare for electric blues of all kinds.

It's the Chicago sound of the 1950s that remains the electric blues form with the most influence on rock. Jazzed up with faster tempos and more flexible melodies, it was a primary foundation for a great deal of early rockabilly and rock & roll. Many British bands, and a few American ones, built their early chops by covering classics from this time, and built their original material around blues riffs (see separate essay on blues-rock). Hundreds of classic songs from this era, by Dixon, Waters, James, Reed, and many others, remain at the heart of the rock & roll repertoire.

Blues has not been a significant commercial presence in the past couple of decades, but continues to thrive, albeit fitfully, on a local level, and via a worldwide network of enthusiasts, festivals, and independent labels. A lot of the Chicago legends are very much alive and active, joined by younger masters like Son Seals and Robert Cray, the latter of whom proved that blues could still sell to the masses on his albums of the late '80s and '90s. Electric blues is a huge and diverse field, with literally hundreds of noteworthy performers. The list below is not meant to be a definitive distillation of the cream of the crop – there are entire books devoted to that purpose – but some top-notch ports of entry.

20 Recommended Albums

Various Artists, *Blues Masters, Vol. 1-15* (Rhino). The most comprehensive introductory history to all forms of electric and acoustic blues, including special volumes for Memphis, Texas, Chicago, urban, and jump blues. *Volume 6, Blues Originals*, illustrates the connection between blues and rock most vividly, with original versions of blues classics made popular by rock performers.

T-Bone Walker, *The Complete Imperial Recordings* (EMI America). A double CD of early-'50s sides; wider-ranging, but more expensive and hard-to-find, is the six-CD set *The Complete T-Bone Walker Recordings*.

Muddy Waters, *The Best of Muddy Waters* (Chess). The best single-CD collection; to dip deeper into his huge repertoire, try the three-CD *Chess Box*.

Little Walter, *The Essential Little Walter* (MCA). Double CD of the greatest and most influential blues harmonica player of all time.

Howlin' Wolf, *Howlin' Wolf/Moanin' in the Moonlight* (MCA). This combination of Wolf's first and second albums on one CD is chock full of blues classics that would later became rock & roll staples, including "Little Red Rooster," "Wang Wang Doodle," "Spoonful," and "Back Door Man." Those with a deeper interest and bigger budget should go for the three-CD *Chess Box*.

Elmore James, *The Sky Is Crying* (Rhino). The best single-disc CD of the best blues slide guitarist. This prolific artist has several good compilations available; this is the most wide-ranging, and hence a recommended starting point.

John Lee Hooker, *The Ultimate Collection (1948-90)* (Rhino). The singer whose low, booming voice and stomping rhythms defined electric blues boogie has recorded a staggering quantity of material; this double disc is not so much the best as the most wide-ranging.

Jimmy Reed, *Speak the Lyrics to Me, Mama Reed* (Vee Jay). 25 tracks on a single disc of the singer whose lazy, shuffling blues-R&B yielded several blues-rock classics, including "Big Boss Man," "Baby What You Want Me to Do?," and "Bright Lights, Big City."

Sonny Boy Williamson, *Essential Sonny Boy Williamson* (MCA). Probably the least famous and striking of the four Chess blues superstars (Waters, Little Walter, and Howlin' Wolf were the others), but an outstanding harmonica player and songwriter.

Various Artists, *A Sun Blues Collection* (Rhino). Important early and mid-'50s Memphis blues sides by Howling Wolf, Rufus Thomas, Little Milton, James Cotton, Junior Parker, B.B. King, and others.

Otis Rush, *Cobra Recordings, 1956-58* (Flyright). Minor-key blues with a gospel moan and chilling, stinging guitar runs.

Slim Harpo, *The Best of Slim Harpo* (Rhino). The best swamp-bluesman, influential on the Rolling Stones, Kinks, and Yardbirds, including his top 40 hits "Baby, Scratch My Back" and "Rainin' in My Heart," as well as the original versions of "I'm a King Bee," "Got Love If You Want It."

B.B. King, *Live at the Regal* (MCA). This 1965 album is almost universally regarded as the best live blues recording. The four-CD box set *King of the Blues* is the most comprehensive anthology of this major blues legend.

Bobby "Blue" Bland, *I Pity the Fool* (MCA). Double-CD compilation of the most respected performer to bridge blues with soul and R&B.

Junior Wells, *Hoodoo Man Blues* (Delmark). One of the greatest blues albums, enlivened by soul, R&B, and Latin influences, this enthralling 1965 session also features Buddy Guy on guitar.

Magic Sam, *West Side Soul* (Delmark). The best album by a bluesman who was just reaching his peak when he died at the end of the 1960s.

Koko Taylor, *What It Takes – The Chess Years* (Chess). The best of the early sides by the premier modern female blues singer.

Albert King, *Ultimate Collection* (Rhino). Double CD of the great soul-influenced bluesman, a big influence on Eric Clapton, among others.

Son Seals, *The Son Seals Blues Band* (Alligator). A fiery guitarist, Seals is the most respected Chicago bluesman to achieve national recognition after the 1960s.

Robert Cray, *Strong Persuader* (Mercury). The 1986 album that brought blues back to the commercial spotlight, adding modern rock influences to the classic electric blues prototype.

Books

Deep Blues, by Robert Palmer (Viking Press, 1981)
I Am the Blues, by Willie Dixon with Don Snowden (Da Capo, 1989)
The Blackwell Guide to Blues Records, edited by Paul Oliver (Blackwell, 1989)

– *Richie Unterberger*

American Folk

American folk music, like most everything else American, is not so much an indigenous sound as it is a melting pot of traditional forms and songs from Europe (especially the British Isles) and Africa, honed in the U.S., especially in the South, since the 17th century. Usually (but not exclusively) played on acoustic string instruments, the folk repertoire was passed down from generation to generation, influencing the birth of rock & roll less directly than blues, country, gospel, and jazz, although it was part of the collective consciousness of all American musicians. Folk's revival after World War II, culminating in an all-out boom in the early '60s, was safeguarded from commercial corruption by zealous traditionalists, who insisted on reverent interpretation and acoustic instruments. For a while, that is; by the mid-'60s, it would alter the course of rock and pop in ways that no one foresaw just a few short years earlier.

In the early days of the record business, traditional folk music was a small corner of the market indeed. Certainly the early acoustic blues musicians, and country stars such as Jimmie Rodgers and the Carter Family, owed a great deal to folk music, although they weren't classified and marketed as such. The folk that was recorded was often being preserved for historical, scholarly purposes (as with the extensive Library of Congress catalog), or commercialized almost beyond recognition, or geared toward extremely specialized audiences (as with early Yiddish and Klezmer recordings directed toward the Jewish immigrant community).

Woody Guthrie, more than any other performer, was responsible for linking traditional American folk forms to concerns of the present day. Although he often drew upon classic folk melodies, he was the first major folksinger to develop an extensive repertoire of original material that drew upon his personal experiences and commented directly on contemporary life and social conditions. Contemporaries like Cisco Houston and Oscar Brand also followed this model, but Guthrie, who recorded hundreds of sides in the 1940s and early 1950s, was by far the most influential, on both slightly younger performers like Pete Seeger and Jack Elliott, and singers of the next generation, especially Bob Dylan.

In the late 1940s, the Weavers, a harmonizing folk group featuring Pete Seeger, brought folk to the masses. Although hugely successful – their 1950 #1 hit "Goodnight Irene" topped the charts for 13 weeks – their left-leaning politics did not escape the attention of certain government authorities in the Communist-fearing early '50s, and their career was prematurely snuffed by blacklists. In the latter half of the decade, the Weavers resumed activity and, along with other veteran performers and newly emerging interpreters of traditional material like Joan Baez, Dave Van Ronk, and Judy Collins, spearheaded a folk revival.

The folk music that was actually on the charts, however, was usually a highly commercial, watered-down variant of traditional sounds and material. The Kingston Trio, Harry Belafonte, the Rooftop Singers, and the Limeliters were the most popular of these, and they deserve some credit for at least making many Americans aware of folk music in the first place, although they should in no way be taken as its most authentic ambassadors. Other performers, like Bob Gibson and more particularly Peter, Paul & Mary, combined commercial appeal with more passion and material that ran closer to the motherlode of traditional folk.

Small independent labels, chiefly Elektra, Vanguard, and Folkways, did their part to record the era's most earnest interpreters. The audience for these more "authentic" sounds was usually found on campuses and cities with large intellectual, politically progressive populations, like Boston, Berkeley, and New York, where the scene was centered in Greenwich Village. Large festivals, like the ones staged at Newport, were important showcases for the era's best talent. And so the music might have stayed for some time – a popular, if minority, taste, nurtured by a large alternative community – if not for a new generation of performers intent on combining folk with contemporary musical and social influences.

Chief among these was Bob Dylan, who was inspired to become a folk performer after becoming enamored of Woody Guthrie. Dylan assimilated a wide variety of American traditional folk music as well as anyone of his time, as he demonstrated on his debut album (consisting mostly of folk standards) and the astonishingly extensive repertoire of traditional material that he ran through, and to a large extent continues to run through, in live performances and on oodles of bootlegs. His second LP, *Freewheelin' Bob Dylan* (1962), was his true groundbreaker, consisting mostly of original material that commented specifically on contemporary political issues and the feelings of his generation.

Dylan was initially embraced as a savior by the folk community, who howled in dismay when he quickly moved away from protest material to personal, romantic tunes and surrealistic poems. The howls became battle cries when, with the British Invasion in full swing, he embraced electric instruments and rock & roll, creating the hybrid folk-rock along with the Byrds and others. The old guard crucified Bob as a sellout, but virtually all of his contemporaries – Phil Ochs, Fred Neil, Tim Hardin, Judy Collins, Joan Baez, Gordon Lightfoot, Ian & Sylvia, Buffy Sainte-Marie – followed suit, sooner rather than later. And it wasn't done just to make money and keep pace with the times; to a man and to a woman, every contemporary folk performer knew that original material (or, at least, covers of contemporary songwriters) and electric instruments paved the way for wider expression and, hence, greater art, unfettered by the now outdated demands for purism in the folk community.

All of the performers mentioned in the above paragraph retained a great deal of folk's strength in their folk-rock; the primacy of guitars, the earnest passion and commitment, the incorporation of time-honored American traditional forms. Some more than others; Phil Ochs, for instance, inherited Dylan's mantle as the day's premier protest singer, and while he recorded a lot of non-political material, he never wholly abandoned his left-leaning political consciousness. The folk-rock movement is covered in detail in a separate essay, but it's important to point out that many of the '60s' leading folk-rock and psychedelic musicians were ex-folkies, led back to the rock & roll of their youth by the Beatles and Dylan. The Byrds, the Jefferson Airplane, the Buffalo Springfield, the Grateful Dead, and many others were populated by ex-folk musicians who would have probably remained obscure, and never reached their exceptional artistic heights, if they hadn't realized that the social consciousness of folk could be expressed with far more vitality in rock arrangements.

The interplay between folk and rock has never been nearly as intense as it was in the mid-'60s, probably because the attributes of folk music were absorbed into rock's framework so quickly and deeply. The singer/songwriter movement of the late '60s and early '70s owes a lot to folk music – indeed, some of its most popular practitioners started out as acoustic folkies. But no one would mistake singer/songwriter albums for traditional American folk; the accent was on individual expression and original material, and the arrangements, if somewhat softer than much other rock, did not eschew electric instruments and rhythm sections, although acoustic guitars, harmonicas, and pianos were often prominent in the mix.

While you might hear, say, Nirvana covering a Leadbelly song, or John Cougar Mellencamp and Bruce Springsteen paying lip service to Woody Guthrie, and all manner of bands showing up with acoustic instruments on MTV's *Unplugged* show, the influence of traditional folk on today's rock is pretty small. The "anti-folk" scene of the late 1980s, an attempt by New York musicians to provide an acoustic-based heir of sorts to the hootenannies of the '50s and '60s, had minimal impact; the Washington Squares, attempting to mimic the "beatnik folk" of Peter, Paul & Mary, were a failure on all counts.

Many fine performers of the last of couple decades have been labeled as folk because their arrangements are largely acoustic, but they really belong more in the singer/songwriter camp than traditional music; their category is often more a function of the audiences they play for, or the fact that acoustic guitars are at the forefront of their arrangements. Hence you might find Kate Wolf,

Lucinda Williams, Tish Hinojosa, Mary McCaslin, Peter Stampfel, the McGarrigle Sisters, Townes Van Zandt, and Bill Morrissey in folk sections, although they sing original, at times compelling material about the here and now, and are often not adverse to using some electric instruments. Indeed, the music of the above performers is not terribly dissimilar to artists commonly marketed as rock and pop musicians, such as Joni Mitchell.

Some performers who are in many respects troubadours in the folk tradition, like Michelle Shocked or Phranc, are marketed as rock because that is where their audience is perceived to be; the Eleventh Dream Day offshoot Freakwater was marketed to alternative/indie rock listeners more because of their pedigree than their music, which hearkens in spirit back to the Carter Family. Nanci Griffith has been increasingly directed toward a country market, although she's as much a contemporary folk singer/songwriter as anything else, and has attracted such decided rock fans as Paul Westerberg.

Such separation of performers into folk or non-folk categories approaches arbitrariness at times, which is unfortunate. Contemporary folk continues to produce interesting performers and songwriters that share rock's impulse to reflect and affect the times we live in, although it will often be necessary to check out the folk circuit and the specialized programming of non-commercial and college radio stations to find them.

15 Recommended Albums

Various Artists, *The Sounds of the South* (Atlantic). A four-CD box set of field recordings made by premier folklorist Alan Lomax in 1959, this captures the wide variety of American southern folk traditions, White and Black, in about as authentic a context as modern times allow, including Black gospel, White spirituals, Appalachian music, rural blues, and traditional children's songs.

Woody Guthrie, *The Greatest Songs of Woody Guthrie* (Vanguard). Guthrie has many discs available; this 23-song collection has his most famous performances, and is thus the best starting point, though *Dust Bowl Ballads* was the album that specifically inspired Bob Dylan more than any other.

The Weavers, *Weavers at Carnegie Hall* (Vanguard). Their 1955 comeback concert from their McCarthy-imposed hiatus, unfettered by the orchestration that appears on some of their hits.

Various Artists, *Troubadours of the Folk Era, Vol. 1-3* (Rhino). Encompassing Woody Guthrie, Pete Seeger, the Weavers, and the Kingston Trio up through '60s singer/songwriters like Tim Hardin, Richard Farina, Fred Neil, and Buffy Sainte-Marie, this is the best delineation of folk's evolution from traditional to modern forms.

Peter, Paul & Mary, *Peter, Paul & Mary* (Warner Brothers). Sounds dated now, but this was the act with the soaring harmonies that was responsible for popularizing folk in the early '60s more than any other, and the first to bring Dylan to the attention of mass audience via their covers of "Blowin' in the Wind" and other songs.

Dave Van Ronk, *Inside Dave Van Ronk* (Fantasy). A CD repackage of two early '60s albums by this gruff and knowing acoustic interpreter of traditional blues and folk, whose impassioned delivery was a big influence on Dylan, among others.

Bob Dylan, *Freewheelin' Bob Dylan* (Columbia). Plenty of Bob Dylan albums have a strong folk influence, but this was the one which established his territory as a contemporary songwriter and performer.

Ian & Sylvia, *Greatest Hits* (Vanguard). This Canadian duo played a large, if somewhat unheralded, role in updating traditional folk and paving the way for folk-rock by being among the first to cover material by Dylan and Gordon Lightfoot, among the first to use bass on their recordings, and writing strong material of their own, like "You Were on My Mind." Their wide repertoire of original and traditional material, as well as their blend of male and female harmonies, was an overlooked influence on the Jefferson Airplane, the Mamas & the Papas, and Fairport Convention.

Judy Collins, *#3* (Elektra). Another overlooked link from folk to folk-rock, this 1963 album mixed standards with covers of material by Dylan, Bob Gibson, Pete Seeger, and Shel Silverstein. Future Byrd Jim McGuinn contributed arrangements, second guitar, and banjo, and may have gotten the idea to revamp Seeger's "Turn! Turn! Turn!" (which was a #1 hit for the Byrds in 1966) from Collins, who recorded a fine version on this LP.

John Fahey, *Return of the Repressed* (Rhino). A master of the acoustic guitar, Fahey twisted blues and folk with an adventurous spirit and irreverence that anticipated the innovations of psychedelic rock. This is a double CD of selections from his huge catalog, spanning the late 1950s to the mid-1980s.

Phil Ochs, *Chords of Fame* (A&M). Double-LP compilation of the best acoustic and electric work by the finest topical songwriter of the '60s, at ease in both folk and rock settings.

The Holy Modal Rounders, *The Moray Eels Eat the Holy Modal Rounders* (Elektra). Greenwich village folkies Peter Stampfel and Steve Weber were determined to take acoustic traditional music to its most bizarre limits, and were a chief inspiration for the Fugs (on whose albums the Rounders sometimes played). This late '60s album is perhaps the ultimate psychedelic folk fusion, and while not for everybody (certainly not for traditionalists), is a humorous and vibrant example of the '60s folk scene at its most wacked-out.

Mary McCaslin, *The Best of Mary McCaslin* (Rounder). Not a household name by any means, McCaslin was one of several outstanding folk-based contemporary singer/songwriters to emerge during the '70s, along with Kate Wolf, the McGarrigle Sisters, and several others. This album was selected because she is arguably the most accessible of these to rock listeners, and because she has recorded some of the best Beatle covers with folk arrangements.

Nanci Griffith, *The Last of the True Believers* (Philo). Perhaps the most widely known songwriter of recent years with clear roots in traditional American folk music, her major label albums have been more country-oriented than this 1986 recording, her last before signing with MCA.

Freakwater, *Dancing Underwater* (Amoeba). Featuring Eleventh Dream Day drummer/singer Janet Bean (who primarily plays guitar with Freakwater), this acoustic side project, with Appalachian overtones and close country harmonies, is proof that post-punk alternative rockers can draw upon American folk traditions with conviction. This CD includes both the 1991 album *Dancing Underwater* and their starker, self-titled 1989 debut.

Books

Bringing It All Back Home, by Robbie Wolliver (Pantheon, 1986)
Dylan, by Anthony Scaduto (Grosset & Dunlap, 1971)
Death of a Rebel: A Biography of Phil Ochs, by Marc Eliot (Franklin Watts, 1989)

– *Richie Unterberger*

British Isles Folk

Since the British began to colonize North America, the indigenous folk music of the British Isles has been a notable factor in American folk music, informing the development of Appalachian and southern folk sounds and thus, by extension, country and rock. Rock wouldn't really feel the direct influence of British folk until the mid-'60s, though, and then primarily on its native soil, although hybrids of British folk and contemporary rock enjoy a strong cult following in the U.S.

In the early '60s, Britain had a traditional folk scene that was comparable to the United States in its strength, though it was smaller. Both communities were increasingly strait-jacketed by an overly insular and reverent attitude that demanded traditional instrumentation and interpretation – demands that seemed increasingly stultifying as music became more turbulent and amplified. The emergence of Bob Dylan, a performer who wrote his own songs and directly commented on the here and now, was welcomed as much in the U.K. as the U.S.; he toured Britain several times in the early and mid-'60s, and even his acoustic albums were Top Ten sellers.

Dylan himself had been influenced by British Isles folk, as he was by most kinds of folk music; indeed, top Irish traditional band the Clancy Brothers were pals of Dylan's in his Greenwich Village days. Dylan had also learned some tunes from British guitarist Martin Carthy (he adapted one of them for "Girl from the North Country"), a seminal figure in the British folk heritage and still very much a figurehead of the British folk scene.

It wasn't long before Britain had produced an answer of sorts to Bob Dylan in Donovan, who made his mark (and even had a few hits) with acoustic material in 1965 before moving into pop-psychedelia. The Scottish singer has been unfairly disparaged by those who remember him primarily as a blissed-out hippie that couldn't match the sophistication of Dylan; his early work was quite bound in British folk, and his earliest albums are littered with old British folk songs made relevant to the day's young generation with lively interpretations.

The earliest records of British folkies of the era like Shirley Collins and Martin Carthy hardly sound groundbreaking several decades later, but they were important in how they opened up the British folk repertoire to imaginative interpretations instead of ossifications. Carthy's influence indirectly extended to the masses when Paul Simon moved to Britain for about a year in the mid-'60s, before Simon & Garfunkel had taken off. Carthy taught Simon "Scarborough Fair," which became one of S&G's most popular early tracks.

Simon learned another of his popular early album tracks, "Anji," from guitarist Davy Graham. Though he wasn't much of a vocalist, Graham was vastly influential in synthesizing and extending various traditional folk styles into something new and progressive, though still acoustic, blending blues, folk, jazz, and Middle Eastern music. A more widely heralded British guitarist was Bert Jansch, also a talented songwriter and singer, whose early recordings were reminiscent of the early efforts of fellow Scotsman Donovan. Jansch left an imprint on the rock world as well through his impact on the styles of Neil Young and Jimmy Page, both of whom have cited Jansch as an important influence.

Jansch began recording as a solo artist, but soon teamed up with guitarist John Renbourn to form Pentangle. While Pentangle used almost exclusively acoustic instrumentation, they performed, wrote, and interpreted with an energy and flexible imagination that was unquestionably derived, at least in part, from rock, making them one of Britain's greatest folk-rock hybrids. Though they peaked early, it's no exaggeration to note that the talented ensemble was a Beatles of sorts in how its members' different but complementary talents expanded British folk into uncharted horizons, drawing from jazz, blues, and classical as well as rock.

The British folk community was certainly aware of psychedelia, and though you wouldn't find its performers using mellotrons and backwards tapes, the influence was reflected in the community's willingness to expand its boundaries and incorporate more adventurous lyrics, arrangements (sometimes electric), and instruments. The most psychedelic-oriented of the British folk acts was the Incredible String Band, a duo of colorful Scotsmen who acted as psychedelic minstrels of sorts with their whimsical songs and unpredictable combinations of sounds, though they remained largely acoustic-based.

For many listeners, the foremost exponent of British folk-rock was Fairport Convention. Starting out as a straight folk-rock ensemble, the group began to veer toward more and more traditional material without altering its forceful electric guitars and rhythm section. Their 1969 album *Liege and Lief* was perhaps the ultimate fusion between electric rock instrumentation and traditional British folk. Equally important, the group acted as the springboard for an astounding range of spin-offs that came to dominate the British folk-rock scene, including Fotheringay, Steeleye Span, the Albion Band, and the solo careers of Richard Thompson, Sandy Denny, and Ian Matthews.

The early half of the 1970s was probably the golden age of British folk-rock. Fairport Convention and its spin-offs, as well as groups like Lindisfarne and the Strawbs, not only continued to electrify British folk fundamentals, but were actually quite commercially successful in the U.K., landing several albums in the Top Ten. Their repertoire varied from heavily traditional to mostly self-penned, sharing a general commitment to, as a member of Steeleye Span once put it, "put traditional music back into current musical language – to make folk music less esoteric." And this wasn't a scene limited to the young upstarts; veterans Shirley Collins and Martin Carthy showed up for a time in the Albion Band and Steeleye Span. Nick Drake and the solo recordings of Richard Thompson owe more to the singer/songwriter tradition than traditional British Isles fare, but their work did reflect its influence, Thompson's much more so than Drake's.

These bands never made it big in the States, although several achieved enough underground acclaim and FM radio exposure to tour there. By the late '70s, they were no longer stars at home, but the musicians, whether they stuck with their bands or headed to other projects, maintained a fairly solid audience.

The British folk-rock scene never died as an artistic force, reviving in the 1980s under the banner of "rogue folk." Due to the efforts of Britain's *Folk Roots* magazine and others, appreciation of acoustic and roots music began to rise in the U.K. In the mid-'80s, a couple of bonafide stars emerged: the Pogues infused Irish

traditional folk with punk energy, and Billy Bragg delivered articulate political and social commentary using (on his early records, at least) little more than a guitar. Bragg's guitar was electric, though, and his rough-hewn attitudes and vocals marked him as a clear product of the post-punk revolution, though he was also a folk troubadour in the best sense of that tradition.

There were other acclaimed "rogue folk" performers that combined folk traditions with modern (often electric) instruments and attitudes, most of whom (unlike Bragg or the Pogues) remain virtually unknown in the States. Scottish guitarist Dick Gaughan sang both traditional material and contemporary political fare, and songwriter Leon Rosselson has been compared to Phil Ochs. The Oyster Band drew from traditional material and contemporary political commentary in their rock-influenced modern folk dance music. In the United States, a society somewhat more removed in everyday life from acoustic musical traditions than Britain or Ireland, these artists will probably never achieve much more than college and community radio exposure. American bands that actually follow the British folk-rock mold are quite rare; Boiled in Lead, from Minneapolis, is the only one to attain even a modest level of recognition.

On the commercial airwaves, however, you can hear the strains – usually indirect, sometimes fairly evident – of Irish traditional music in that country's most successful rock stars, like Van Morrison, Sinéad O'Connor, and U2. The Levellers, stars in the U.K. and thus far a flop stateside, derive much of their influence from British traditional music. And performers from British folk-rock's most successful phase, such as Richard Thompson and June Tabor, continue to record and tour to considerable acclaim in their middle age.

15 Recommended Recordings

Donovan, *Spotlight on Donovan* (Pye, UK). Donovan's early mid-'60s acoustic recordings are frustratingly scattered and haphazardly reissued; this double-LP import is the best collection, though it's getting harder to find.

Davy Graham, *Folk Blues and All Points in Between* (See For Miles, UK). A reissue of the eclectic guitarist's groundbreaking 1965 album, with additional bonus cuts from the best of his late '60s recordings.

Bert Jansch, *Bert Jansch/Jack Orion* (Demon/Transatlantic, UK). His first and third albums, from the mid-'60s, combined onto a double CD, demonstrate his facility with both original and traditional material.

The Incredible String Band, *The Hangman's Beautiful Daughter* (Rykodisc). This 1967 album was the ISB's most acclaimed effort. Those looking for a wide-ranging sampler should try to find the two-record Relics compilation.

The Pentangle, *Sweet Child* (Reprise). This late-'60s double set, a mixture of studio and live material, is only given the nod because of its length and variety; their self-titled debut and *Basket of Light* are equally worthy.

Fairport Convention, *Liege and Lief* (Hannibal). Not their best album – their previous, more rock-oriented efforts, *What We Did on Our Holidays* and *Unhalfbricking*, were better – but in terms of rock and British folk fusion, this was their most influential. Or, for a compilation with greater breadth, try to find *Chronicles*.

Sandy Denny, *Who Knows Where the Time Goes* (Hannibal). Three-CD box set of Britain's finest folk-rock singer, featuring both solo tracks and performances with Fairport Convention, the Strawbs, and Fotheringay.

Richard Thompson, *Watching the Dark* (Hannibal). Another three-CD compilation, including solo work and cuts with Fairport and his ex-wife Linda.

Steeleye Span, *Spanning the Years* (Chrysalis). Getting harder to find, but this double CD is the widest-spanning collection of a prolific group that changed personnel quite a few times.

Clannad, *Clannad* (Polydor). Most of this famous Irish group's releases have leaned towards either the traditional or pop; on this overlooked 1973 debut, they came off as a sort of Irish Pentangle. It's been issued on different labels, depending upon which country has a copy available.

Billy Bragg, *Back to Basics* (Elektra). A compilation of his first two albums, as well as an early EP. Bragg subsequently added fuller rock arrangements without diluting his integrity, but these initial tracks – many only featuring him and his electric guitar – are the recordings most closely tied to British folk sounds.

The Pogues, *Rum, Sodomy & the Lash* (MCA). Their second album, produced by Elvis Costello, blends punk and Irish folk without compromising either form, and includes their best-known tune, a cover of Ewan MacColl's "Dirty Old Town."

The Oyster Band, *From Little Rock to Leipzig* (Rykodisc). With quite a few albums to their credit, it's hard to single out one as the best starting point. This live outing was chosen because it includes versions of material from several of their releases.

The Chieftains, *Long Black Veil* (RCA). The foremost Irish traditional folk band performs folk, pop, and country & western with the Rolling Stones, Sting, Ry Cooder, Marianne Faithfull, Sinead O'Connor, Tom Jones, Mick Jagger, and Van Morrison. In 1988, Morrison recorded an entire album of traditional Irish songs with the Chieftains, *Irish Heartbeat* (Mercury).

June Tabor, *Against the Stream* (Green Linnet). Britain's most acclaimed contemporary folk singer interprets traditional tunes and songs by Richard Thompson and her big fan, Elvis Costello, on this elegantly subdued and moody 1994 record, demonstrating the continued flexibility of modern British folk.

– Richie Unterberger

Reggae

No form of popular music from the third world has made as much of an international impact as reggae. It has borrowed from rock & roll, and rock in turn has borrowed from it, but it remains a minority, specialty taste for much of the rock audience. That's nothing for reggae proponents to be ashamed of; that the tiny island of Jamaica has produced a wealth of musicians that affected the course of international rock and pop music is astounding.

Reggae had its beginnings in the late '50s, when Jamaican popular musicians combined their indigenous folk music with jazz, African and Caribbean rhythms, and New Orleans rhythm & blues to come up with a music of their own: ska. An oft-repeated folk legend has it that the frenetic, offbeat rhythm was created when islanders listened to New Orleans R&B stations on their transistor radios; the static garbled the rhythms so much that the musicians bastardized the sound into something else altogether when they tried to imitate it. Most likely that's a fanciful tale, but there's no doubt that R&B, particularly the New Orleans variety, was a dominant influence on early ska, and that the ska rhythm never quite locked into an accurate reproduction of its inspiration.

Ska was a relentlessly joyous and upbeat music, finding great popularity not only in Jamaica, but in Britain, which had a large West Indian population. Lots of ska records were imported and licensed for release in Britain, and some British-based musicians recorded their own ska. One of these productions, Mille Small's "My Boy Lollipop," became a huge hit in both the U.K. and the U.S. in 1964, bringing ska to an international audience, and remaining – incredibly – one of the very best-selling Jamaican discs ever. This single was produced by White Jamaican expatriate Chris Blackwell, whose label, Island, licensed and produced many ska singles in the '60s, and would be instrumental in exposing reggae to a worldwide audience over the next few decades.

By around 1966, the hyper rhythms of ska began to give way to the slower, loping beats of rocksteady. Dreamy and ideal for romantic dancing, harmonies (which had often been a prominent ingredient of ska) came to the forefront, and the squeaky, jazzy horns that characterized ska were muted and pushed down in the mix. It's obvious from the passionate vocals on classic rocksteady that Jamaican performers of this era were heavily attuned to American soul, as heavy echoes of Motown, Memphis, and harmonizing R&B groups are obvious in the recordings.

Reggae, as much Jamaican popular music came to be known at the end of the 1960s, embellished the bedrock rhythms of ska and rocksteady with political and social lyrics, often influenced by Rastafarianism, racial pride, and the turbulent Jamaican political climate. The rhythms ebbed and flowed with the hypnotic, jerky pulse that has become reggae's most identifiable trademark, and the bass and choppy rhythm tracks became not just prominent, but dominant. For many fans, this is reggae's golden age; several of its greatest legends emerged or cut their prime work during this period, including Toots & the Maytals, Burning Spear, and above all the Wailers. The Wailers' Bob Marley would become reggae's towering figure, revered in many Third World countries with a zeal on par with American and British fanaticism for the Beatles; fellow-Wailers Peter Tosh and Bunny Wailer also established influential solo careers.

The influence of reggae was felt in rock almost immediately,

but usually surfaced only as a tangential reference in some stars' isolated songs. The early Beatles song "I Call Your Name," for instance, has a ska break; a few years later, the Beatles would appropriate the reggae rhythm for "Ob-La-Di, Ob-La-Da." Jamaican singer Jackie Edwards wrote a couple of ska-flavored rock-soul hits for the Spencer Davis Group, "Keep on Running" and "Somebody Help Me"; Paul Simon, never one to let a good ethnic sound pass unnoticed, put a reggae beat behind one of his first solo hits, "Mother and Child Reunion." Paul McCartney went full-tilt into reggae on his early solo track "C Moon," and Eric Clapton had a #1 hit with his cover of Bob Marley's "I Shot the Sheriff." Stevie Wonder sometimes flirted with reggae rhythms, as on his hit "Boogie on Reggae Woman." But aside from Johnny Nash, a Texan soul singer who actually did some recording in Jamaica and landed big hits with reggae-soul concoctions like "Hold Me Tight," "I Can See Clearly Now," and Marley's "Stir It Up," hardly any rock or soul performers made reggae an integral component of their work.

Occasionally reggae performers would cross over to the rock and pop audience, as with Jimmy Cliff's "Wonderful World, Beautiful People," and Desmond Dekker's "The Israelites," but international reggae hits remained a rare phenomenon. When artists like the Wailers began to get wide international distribution in the early and mid-'70s (usually on Island), the music garnered a sizable cult following on both sides of the Atlantic, primarily with White audiences. Reggae's greatest attributes – its spare power, its outspoken (sometimes militant) commentary on politics, class strife, and religion, its idiosyncratic production flourishes – may also have been what kept it from gaining anything close to the commercial foothold enjoyed by rock and soul.

Reggae itself continued to evolve, not always in accordance with the preferences of its overseas audience. The operators of mobile "sound systems" in Jamaica had often embellished their presentations with voiceovers, and this was eventually practiced in the studio as the art of DJing or toasting, wherein the artist chanted, rhymed, and expounded over a musical backing track. There was also dub music, which erased vocals and stripped tracks to their bones of bass and rhythm, over which all manner of strange and wonderful echo, reverb, and miscellaneous sound effects were overlaid to create spacy and pulsating instrumentals.

Toward the end of the 1970s, reggae's influence made itself felt on a couple of the era's rock and R&B trends. Punk and new wave performers were often big reggae fans, particularly in Britain; the West Indian population was much larger there than in the U.S., and punks felt a kinship with their struggles as an oppressed minority. The Clash sometimes used reggae rhythms and production touches, even enlisting top dub reggae artist Lee Perry to produce some tracks, and punk bands like the Slits incorporated reggae signatures into their music. Top new wave bands Blondie, and more particularly the Police, built some of their hits around watered-down reggae flourishes. British reggae group Steel Pulse built its following by playing punk venues, and Bob Marley himself encouraged the alliance with a British single, "Punky Reggae Party." The Ruts (who evolved into Ruts D.C.) blended reggae and punk in the late '70s and early '80s, a fusion which the Bad Brains would also attempt throughout the 1980s. In the early '80s, producer Adrian Sherwood used early punk musicians like the Slits, Public Image Ltd., the Raincoats, and the Pop Group to enhance his edgy, hard-to-classify excursions into dub reggae with the New Age Steppers.

At the tail end of the decade, Britain experienced an all-out ska revival. Bands like the Specials, Madness, the Selecter, and the English Beat enjoyed huge popularity at home – and cult popularity in the U.S. – with their hybrid of ska and new wave. Sometimes called the Two-Tone sound (in honor of the label on which many of the bands appeared), this brand of ska-cum-rock is still kicking today, albeit on a much smaller level.

In the United States around this time, young African-Americans – by and large in New York, home to a very large Jamaican community – began to build upon the DJs and toasters to come up with their own stream-of-consciousness poems. The connection between reggae and rap has never gotten a lot of attention, but there's no doubt that reggae contributed to the genesis of what became the most flamboyant African-American music of the 1980s and '90s. Of course, the backing tracks of American rap are usually harsher and starker than reggae, and with isolated exceptions like Shinehead, few have tried to bridge the styles, perhaps because reggae never had an appreciable audience among African Americans.

With the death of Bob Marley in 1981, followed by the murder of Peter Tosh in 1987, many listeners felt that the golden age of reggae has gone forever. It continues to thrive in Jamaica, where more records are released per capita than any other country in the world. DJ and toasting has produced the spinoff dancehall, which has a more electronic-driven rhythm and, sometimes, risque or "slack" vocals and lyrics. Reggae itself continues to exert a tangential influence on rock and pop – many stars from the Rolling Stones down have occasionally appropriated reggae rhythms, top Jamaican rhythm section Sly & Robbie guest on albums by major figures like Bob Dylan, and reggae-pop hybrids like UB40 and Aswad have even had chart success with pop-conscious adaptations of reggae sounds.

15 Recommended Albums

Various Artists, *Tougher than Tough: The Story of Jamaican Music* (Mango). This four-disc box set documents the evolution of reggae from its beginnings to the present, from ska and rocksteady up through dub and dancehall. Of course no box set can cover the music definitively, and this one doesn't claim to, but it's the best retrospective of reggae as a whole, including tracks by most of its major performers.

Various Artists, *Scandal Ska* (Mango). Because it was a soundtrack tie-in to a movie about the 1963 British Profumo scandal, this superb anthology was pretty much ignored by critics. It's probably the best introductory ska sampler, though, with early-'60s sides by Jimmy Cliff, Bob Marley, Desmond Dekker, Laurel Aitken, Ernest Ranglin, Roland Alphonso, and others.

Alton & Hortense Ellis, *Alton & Hortense* (Heartbeat). There are more wide-ranging rocksteady anthologies available, but this collection of late-'60s sides, featuring solo performances by one of Jamaica's premier vocalists (Alton) and his much less famous but similarly talented sister (Hortense), is enchanting romantic music that makes clear the influence of American '60s soul on reggae.

Johnny Nash, *The Reggae Collection* (Epic/Legacy). 20-track collection spanning the late '60s to the mid-'70s, focusing on the reggae-inspired work of the first (and, still, one of the few) musicians to fuse rock and soul with reggae for commercial success. Includes the big hits and several less famous songs.

Bob Marley, *Legend* (Tuff Gong). 14 of his most famous tracks. If you want to dig deeper after this, there are many albums to choose from; the Wailers' *Burnin'* and *Catch a Fire* are the most celebrated single LPs, and the four-CD box *Songs of Freedom* is the most extensive career retrospective.

Various Artists, *The Harder They Come* (Island). This cult film deserved a lot of credit for introducing worldwide audiences to reggae, both via its gritty picture of Jamaican culture and its top-notch soundtrack, which featured music by Jimmy Cliff (who starred in the film as well), the Maytals, the Melodians, Desmond Dekker, and others.

Toots & the Maytals, *Funky Kingston* (Mango). The most acclaimed album by Toots Hibbert, widely acknowledged as reggae's most soulful singer.

Lee Perry, *The Greatest* (Mango). Vintage productions by dub's top exponent, featuring the Heptones, Junior Murvin, Max Romeo, Prince Jazzbo, and Perry himself. Those wishing to go deeper should look for *The Upsetter Compact Set*; actually issued under the name of Perry's studio band, the Upsetters, this is a three-CD package of some of his best work.

Burning Spear, *Marcus Garvey* (Mango). The mid-'70s record that brought them to international attention remains one of reggae's most powerful album-length statements.

Various Artists, *The Best of Punky Reggae* (Rhino). 17-track anthology illustrates the cross-fertilization of punk and reggae, with tracks by Patti Smith, Graham Parker, Devo, Pere Ubu, Blondie, Steel Pulse, the Specials, Selecter, the English Beat, UB40, Madness, Keith Levene, and others. Missing influential cuts by the Clash and Bob Marley, presumably because of licensing hurdles.

Various Artists, *Two Tone Compilation: A Checkered Past* (Chrysalis). Double CD of the best tracks from the premier British ska revival label, including hits by the Specials, the English Beat, Madness, the Selecter, and various spinoffs.

Various Artists, *Inna Reggae Style* (EMI). Not one of the greatest reggae albums of all time, it's included on this list because it illustrates connections between rock and reggae with covers of rock and soul songs by reggae performers like Peter Tosh, the Heptones, and Toots & the Maytals, reggae cuts by rock acts like Blondie and Boy George, pop-reggae hybrids by Aswad, the

English Beat, and Third World, and a duet between Peter Tosh and Mick Jagger.

Shinehead, *Unity* (Elektra). The 1988 debut by one of the few performers to successfully bridge reggae with rap.

Divination, *Ambient Dub Vol. 1 & 2.* Bassist Bill Laswell is the heaviest contributor to these explorations by top experimental rock musicians into dub music, twisting it into more sinister and electronic forms.

Various Artists, *Mash up the Place – The Best of Reggae Dancehall* (Rhino). There are a lot of reggae dancehall compilations; Rhino gets the nod because, typically, it provides the most cohesive and informative packaging. Includes tracks by Shabba Ranks, Ninja Man, Macka B, and others.

– Richie Unterberger

World Beat

What "world beat" is depends to some degree on whom you're asking for a definition, but in general it could be said to refer to contemporary music produced from outside of mainstream American and European rock and pop forms, often incorporating rock, pop, and modern technology into indigenous traditional music. It could be argued that world beat has been around as long as rock & roll, or even much longer, but it wasn't until the beginning of the 1980s that world music began to exert a significant influence on Western rock culture.

Western pop has never been closed to music from other climes; many Latin artists enjoyed significant success in the United States from the time hit parades first began to be published. In the early days of rock, Jamaican calypso singer Harry Belafonte was hugely popular; slightly later, South African vocalist Miriam Makeba enjoyed similar success, and bossa nova performers like Astrud Gilberto had big international hits. If you're determined to locate specific traces of world music in rock & roll, you can find them: calypso (Mickey & Sylvia), Latin dance rhythms (the Drifters), Mexican music (Ritchie Valens, early surf instrumentals), Middle Eastern wailing (Gene Pitney's "Mecca").

More direct influences from other shores began to filter into the music in the mid-'60s, around the time that rock started to take itself seriously as an art form. Indian music, particularly the kind associated with the sitar, made a strong impact on the Beatles' mid-'60s recordings, especially George Harrison's compositions. The Byrds, Donovan, the Rolling Stones, and several San Francisco psychedelic groups also made memorable use of the sitar and/or Indian-inspired ragas and melodic lines. With his appearance at the Monterey Pop Festival in 1967, Ravi Shankar became one of the first world musicians to gain a large chunk of the rock audience. In other realms, Simon & Garfunkel, 20 years before it would become fashionable, openly acknowledged the influence of Bulgarian traditional vocals. The Rolling Stones' Brian Jones became fascinated by Moroccan music, recording an album of trance music in the country, and some of the rhythms filtered onto the Stones' controversial *Their Satanic Majesties Request.* Of all the '60s bands, the Californian psychedelic-folk-rock group Kaleidoscope were the most proficient at blending Middle Eastern influences into their sound frequently and successfully; their extended jams "Taxim" and "Seven-Ate Sweet" are among the most exciting fusions of Middle Eastern melody and rock energy ever recorded.

Still, throughout the '60s and '70s, most of the rock audience remained unaware of world beat, and most rock performers were immune to its influence. This was not because of willful ignorance, but because the music was simply unavailable to most people. The Nonesuch label released a lot of fine ethnic music recordings, and the explosion of reggae's popularity increased a lot of people's general awareness of music from the third world, but very few contemporary world music albums were widely distributed in the U.S. (European consumers had somewhat better access to it, especially in Paris, with its large African population).

The conditions did not hold in reverse: the West didn't hear much world music, but the rest of the world heard a lot of Western rock and soul. It had a great impact on musicians from Africa, Brazil, Asia, and other regions, who in turn were not so much inspired to imitate it as borrow from it. What this usually meant was electrifying the instrumentation, adding danceable rhythms, and performing material that addressed a wide range of contemporary concerns (though romance, as in the West, would always be a big topic). Traditional material, melodies, and instruments remained vital ingredients, to varying degrees.

African performers were the first "world beat" acts to attract attention, at first largely in the rock press and alternative/underground community. Cameroon's Manu Dibango paved the way with "Soul Makossa," a fluke hit from the early '70s that was also one of the first disco smashes. Fela, from Nigeria, also made a stir with his incendiary brand of funk, and King Sunny Ade catapulted African pop to a new level of recognition with his bubbling, irrepressible highlife. Of course, lumping all of these stars together into a genre is about as appropriate as lumping together the Rolling Stones, the Steve Miller Band, and James Brown; Africa is a huge continent, with an infinite assortment of distinct regional styles. These African stars, however, opened Western ears to a flood of contemporary African pop performers that remains unabated in the mid-'90s; Youssou N'Dour, Ali Farka Toure, Alpha Blondy, Baaba Maal, Angelique Kidjo, and Thomas Mapfumo are just a few of the better-known ones.

South African performers in particular received a good deal of attention after adding much of the flavor to Paul Simon's 1985 megasmash *Graceland*. Simon was criticized in some quarters for diluting African music, not to mention defying a United Nations decree against recording in South Africa, but there's no question that it opened a lot of ears to previously unheard music by groups like Ladysmith Black Mambazo, which provided a lot of the album's backup vocals. The South African compilation *The Indestructible Beat of Soweto* made a lot of rock critics' best-of lists, and adventurous listeners were incited to seek out further recordings by other groups from the country, such as Mahlathini and the Mahotella Queens.

Another brand of world music to make an unexpected splash with rock audiences in the 1980s was traditional Bulgarian vocal music, as performed by the Bulgarian State Radio and Television Choir, operating under the nom de plume Le Mystere Des Voix Bulgares. Touring Europe and North America to great acclaim, their albums actually landed in the Top 200. A left-field hit of even bigger dimensions was scored in 1994 by the Benedictine Monks of Santo Domingo, whose collection of Gregorian chants went all the way to the Top 20. Less exotic, perhaps, but probably hardly any less expected, was the huge success of Spain's Gipsy Kings, who updated flamenco music into more modern hybrids.

These are just the most successful imports, of course. Zouk, the Israeli pop of Ofra Haza, soca, the Brazilian pop of Gilberto Gil and Caetano Veloso, Astor Piazolla's tangos, Nusreh Ali Fateh Khan, Tuvan throat singers, Indian/Anglo bhangra beat, and lots of other music, way too numerous to summarize here – all have made big inroads into the Western audience, usually with listeners schooled in rock backgrounds. Large independent companies like Shanachie, Globestyle, and Rykodisc did a great deal to distribute the music in the U.S. and U.K.; major labels had subsidiaries that specialized in world beat releases, such as Mango.

Despite the exceptions listed in the above paragraph, the music did not assume a commercial presence equal to rock, rap, or soul. Foreign language lyrics and non-Western pop structures and rhythms are, and may remain, a large barrier to making world music as successful with the masses as it is with the critics, although it now enjoys one of the largest and most rapidly expanding specialty markets in the industry. A reflection of listeners' increasing tendencies to embrace a more eclectic, multicultural assortment of music, the popularity of world music is also an underrated factor in heightening the prospects for global cooperation and world peace as we prepare to enter the environmental, technological, and sociopolitical chaos of the 21st century.

World music hasn't exerted a deep influence on contemporary rock & roll, though it's become much more common to hear African rhythms or find guest appearances by noted musicians from the third world on rock albums. Occasionally, though, rock stars have borrowed from world music quite heavily – Simon, of course, but also David Byrne, Grateful Dead percussionist Mickey Hart, Dead Can Dance, and Peter Gabriel, who tirelessly champions the real thing via the WOMAD organization and the extensive roster of world music performers on his Real World label. Much in the manner that British Invasion bands were accused of ripping off Black blues and soul artists for a lot of their ideas, these performers are sometimes snubbed for presenting world music in a much more profitable, pop-ready package. A humorous Drew Friedman cartoon a few years ago aptly satirized the situation by presenting Paul Simon and David Byrne, tape recorders in hand, bumping into each other in the deepest depths of the jun-

gle, each searching for suitable ethnic rhythms to plagiarize before the other found them.

Like those old British bands, though, Simon and Byrne are indirectly leading many listeners to the source; and like those old British bands, they aren't exactly making a big secret of their influences. These sources, like old blues records, are more widely available today than ever before. Putting together a list of 15 recommended world music recordings is about as impossible a task as summarizing the Bible in a two-hour movie; the records below should not be treated as an encapsulation of the best world music, but some suggested highlights, illustrations of links between world beat and rock, and starting points to an infinite body of work.

15 Recommended Recordings

Various Artists, *Africa Dances* (Original Music). One of the first widely available compilations of African dance music, this compilation, encompassing several regions and spanning the 1950s to the 1970s, displays the roots of today's African pop, as well as being highly enjoyable in its own right.

Joseph Spence, *Happy All the Time* (Carthage). 1964 album by the Bahamian guitarist whose percussive playing and mirthful vocals defied classification, and influenced adventurous rock-oriented guitarists like Ry Cooder and Henry Kaiser.

Hamza El Din, *Music of Nubia* (Vanguard). A Sudanese lute player who was one of the first African musicians to attract wide attention in the West, eventually sharing the stage with the Grateful Dead. This is his 1964 debut.

Kaleidoscope, *Rampe Rampe* (Edsel, UK). The most Middle Eastern-oriented material of the '60s psychedelic band, including their mesmerizing jams "Taxim" and "Seven-Ate Sweet."

Fela Anikulapo Kuti, *Zombie* (Mercury). The father of Afrobeat has dozens of albums; this 1977 recording is one of his most cohesive and most readily available.

The Talking Heads, *Remain in Light* (Sire). With assistance from producer Eno, David Byrne's group recorded one of the first popular rock albums to incorporate Afrobeat rhythms. Byrne delved heavily into Latin and South American music in his solo career, particularly on *Rei Momo*.

King Sunny Ade, *Juju Music* (Mango). The 1982 album that made Ade an international figure.

Various Artists, *The Indestructible Beat of Soweto* (Shanachie). The 1986 compilation of South African music, featuring Ladysmith Black Mambazo, Mahlathini, and others, remains one of the most popular world beat releases of all time.

Paul Simon, *Graceland* (Warner Brothers). Whether you love it or not, the most popular album ever released to make extensive use of African rhythms.

Le Mystere Des Voix Bulgares, *Le Mystere Des Voix Bulgares* (Nonesuch). There are several volumes of this ensemble by now, all consistently beautiful and otherworldly in their polyphonic, multilayered vocals.

The Gipsy Kings, *Gipsy Kings* (Elektra). The 1988 album that broke them in the U.S. market, recommended above subsequent efforts that have tried to broaden their appeal with slicker technology.

Sheila Chandra, *Silk 1983-1990* (Shanachie). As the lead singer of Monsoon and a solo artist, Chandra has been the most successful performer to blend Indian and Western pop/rock music. This was chosen because it draws from several recordings; her approach can vary from dance-pop to traditional to avant-garde. Those seeking the latter should check out her most recent release, 1994's *The Zen Kiss*.

Aisha Kandisha's Jarring Effects, *El Buya* (Barraka El Farnatshi). By far the least well-known album on this list, this Moroccan production from the early '90s is recommended because of its sensational mix of traditional Moroccan music with electronic tweaking, turntable DJing, and dub-like reverb. One of the relatively few African albums that uses modern technology to move indigenous music into new territory without compromising the beauty of the original article in the least.

Dead Can Dance, *Into the Labyrinth* (4AD). Originally affiliated with the gloomy British alternative rock school championed by the 4AD label, they've broadened their approach considerably in the 1990s, incorporating Gregorian chants, European medieval music, and the like so heavily at times that they don't sound like a rock or pop group at all.

Ali Farka Toure & Ry Cooder, *Talking Timbuktu* (Hannibal). From Senegal, Toure is often referred to as the John Lee Hooker of Africa because of his pounding, insistent strumming and vocal phrasing. Although Ry Cooder is co-billed, this is actually much more Toure's show, as the guitarists sympathetically complement each other on a set of material that, from the sound of it, was guided much more by the African than the American.

Books

The Rough Guide to World Music (Rough Guides, 1994)
The Virgin Directory to World Music, by Philip Sweeney (Henry Holt, 1992)

– Richie Unterberger

Comedy & Rock

Overblown progressive rock epics aside, rock & roll has always displayed a vivid sense of humor. The humor is usually more subtle than overt, felt in the exuberant vocals and performances, and the celebration of the moment. Often it's quite overt, as in Chuck Berry and Bo Diddley's narratives about everyday life, the Coasters' jibes about detectives, movies, and teenage gangs, Jan & Dean's goofy little old ladies drag racing in southern California, the Beatles' obscure B-side lounge lizard cutup "You Know My Name," the Who's fake radio jingles on *The Who Sell Out,* De La Soul's surreal whimsy, and scads of novelty songs from the '50s to the present. Those novelty songs are compiled on many anthologies (there are quite a few collections on the Rhino label alone), as well as broadcast on the widely syndicated radio show of Dr. Demento (also known as Barry Hansen, one of the leading doo wop experts and rock & roll record collectors alive).

There are relatively few rock acts, however, that base a lengthy and artistically valid career on comedy and satire. It's hard to make good rock & roll music; it's hard to be really, really funny; it's harder still to do both at the same time. The most difficult feat of all, perhaps, is making rock & roll comedy records that stand up to repeated listenings without sounding dated or wearing thin, or that even stand up to more than three or four playings before the joke wears off.

Before rock musicians attempted ambitious, self-consciously satirical works, their trail had been blazed to some extent by non-rock performers of earlier eras. Spike Jones, a brilliant multi-instrumentalist bandleader who lovingly deconstructed and deflated all forms of popular music, is almost universally acknowledged as the most important of these figures. Also influential were Lord Buckley, a jazz beatnik of sorts whose free association ramblings on history were very popular with '60s rock stars when they were coming of age, and Stan Freberg, who, it must be pointed out, displayed considerable animosity toward rock & roll in some of his parodies.

The first band to capably combine social satire with rock were the Fugs, formed by Lower East Side New York beat poets Ed Sanders and Tuli Kupferberg. Even more impressively, they managed to take a left-wing perspective and avoid sounding self-important or smug when taking on the CIA, the military-industrial complex, and censorship. Their sexually explicit lyrics were taboo-breaking, but, as Sanders himself admits today, largely juvenile and immature (though it's difficult to resist laughing when they sing cheerily off-key odes to slum goddesses from the Lower East Side). But by and large, their '60s albums, especially their initial pair on the avant-garde ESP label, are still quite ticklish, even if some of the specific issues they were protesting are not in the news anymore (though in a larger sense, the social injustices they were pointing out remain very much a part of contemporary life). On their early recordings, the Fugs were aided by New York folkies Peter Stampfel and Steve Weber, who went on to make a shambles of folk conventions as the Holy Modal Rounders. Most of their recordings are *too* uneven to hold up well, but the best, *The Moray Eels Eat the Holy Modal Rounders,* was the most bizarrely deluded take on psychedelic folk.

The Mothers of Invention, led by Frank Zappa, were also concerned with social satire, with important differences. Unlike the core members of the Fugs, they were accomplished, serious musicians; the issues they satirized tended to be general social conventions, not specific sociopolitical issues; and they simultaneously paid homage to and ripped apart rock & roll genres like love songs and doo wop. Their late-'60s albums on Verve are perhaps *the* most successful rock satires ever recorded, losing little or none of their humorous bite when heard in the 1990s; *We're Only in It*

for the Money, a vicious send-up of the psychedelic counterculture, is the best album-length concept comedy album of sorts ever produced. While Zappa's early work remains his funniest, he continued to satirize all manner of sacred cows throughout the rest of his life, in addition to pursuing serious contemporary composition (sometimes doing both at once).

British comedy-rock tended, unsurprisingly, to be droller and subtler, though no less eccentric. The godfather of this genre, Peter Sellers, wasn't a musician exactly, but did record some great musical satires, taking his Shakespearean reading of "A Hard Day's Night" into the British Top 20 in 1965, and even making appearances on tracks by the Hollies and Steeleye Span. Many of his recordings in the '50s and '60s were produced by George Martin, and indeed Martin's association with Sellers helped the Beatles to hit it off with the producer from their very first audition for EMI. The Beatles were great admirers of Sellers and the *Goon Show* radio shows he did with Spike Milligan, and you can hear traces of that humor in their recordings. The Sellers records also required Martin to develop an expertise with sound effects and unusual production methods that served the Beatles well when their recordings became more sophisticated in the late '60s. The Beatles' Christmas records, available only to members of their fan club, were usually sketches that were obviously inspired by the *Goon Show* comic tradition.

The influence of Sellers, the *Goon Show,* and all manner of British music hall and vaudevillian traditions can be heard in a lot of British rock, dating from the Kinks and Syd Barrett to Robyn Hitchcock and XTC (who recorded an entire psychedelic homage/parody as their alter ego, the Dukes of Stratosphear). The best British comic band, by a long stretch, was the Bonzo Dog Band. Sometimes compared to the Mothers of Invention, their humor was much gentler, if no less side-splitting, and owed more to vaudevillian traditional jazz and surrealism (their original moniker was Bonzo Dog Da Da Band, named after the surrealist Dadaist art movement).

The Bonzos were undoubtedly an influence on Monty Python, and even worked with Pythonites Michael Palin and Terry Jones on a children's TV series shortly before the Pythons premiered their classic show in 1969. Monty Python were themselves sometimes referred to as the Beatles of comedy as they had a similar blend of diverse talents and towered over everything else in their field. The Beatles were all fans of Monty Python (who frequently used musical jokes, rock and otherwise, in their sketches), and in 1978, Python member Eric Idle returned the favor by producing one of the two greatest satirical rock documentaries of all time, *The Rutles* (modeled, obviously, on the Beatle legend). The made-for-TV special starred ex-Bonzo Dog member Neil Innes (in the John Lennon role) who also wrote all the brilliant Beatle parodies used on the soundtrack, which itself is perhaps the greatest rock parody ever waxed. All this in turn was a great influence on the other great fake rockumentary, *This Is Spinal Tap,* although the soundtrack to that theatrical release doesn't sound as well on its own as *The Rutles* (although it works brilliantly within the context of the film itself).

There's no parallel in the United States for such a reciprocal relationship between huge rock and comedy stars. One comedy troupe that did plug into a late-'60s countercultural vibe was the Firesign Theatre, which was also quite likely well aware of Zappa's brilliant montages. As has been pointed out elsewhere, the Firesign Theatre was among the few comedy troupes to use the recorded album as their primary vehicle. Their LPs used sound effects and funhouse segues from sketch to sketch with great skill, and their surrealistic (but often quite pointed) observations of contemporary life found a large audience in the rock underground (as did their less subtle peers at the *National Lampoon,* who nonetheless released a brilliant John Lennon parody on one of their albums).

It's all a matter of taste, of course, but one can argue that there haven't been the kind of outstanding symbiotic relationships between rock and comedy in the '80s and '90s as there were in the '60s and '70s. Some of the more notable rock comedians, or comic rockers, depending on how you look at it, would include Mojo Nixon, whose satires on Elvis, MTV VJs, and the like seem to provoke either wild applause or loathing; the Dead Milkmen, the smarmily juvenile disgust punk/new wave smartasses; Gwar, an over-the-top fake metal band whose satire works far better in performance than on record; the Tubes, whose theatrical rock already sounds quite dated, but was quite popular at times; Half

Japanese, loony avant-punks that the general rock listener will find infuriatingly irritating; and King Missile (and spin-off Dogbowl), whose wistful but truly demented musings continue the Lower East Side tradition established by the Fugs, minus much of the sociopolitical outrage.

As far as recent rock musicians carrying the banner raised by the Fugs and Zappa long ago, you could turn to Eugene Chadbourne, the experimental guitarist who also skewers all sorts of social institutions from a clever and learned left-wing perspective; he releases too many recordings for his own good, but the best of his work is incisive. The most popular comedy-rock outfit as we go to press is Ween, sometimes compared to Zappa for their accomplished satires of all sorts of social types and most genres of rock music. They can be pretty juvenile at times, but then so could Zappa.

12 Recommended Recordings:

Spike Jones, *Musical Depreciation Revue: The Spike Jones Anthology* (Rhino). There are several worthwhile Jones albums available; as usual, Rhino's double-CD package wins because of its extensive liner notes and the breadth of its coverage.

Lord Buckley, *The Best of Lord Buckley* (Elektra). Not too easy to find, and not as funny as some reviews may lead you to believe, but it was bold for its day, and influential.

Peter Sellers, *A Celebration of Sellers* (EMI). Four-CD box set heavy on the '50s and '60s recordings produced by George Martin, including several Beatles satires.

The Fugs, *Second Album* (Fantasy). Their funniest and most melodic by a wide margin, it includes the classics "Dirty Old Man," "Frenzy," "Kill for Peace," and "Doin' All Right."

The Mothers of Invention, *We're only in It for the Money* (Rykodisc). The funniest rock satire ever, period.

The Bonzo Dog Band, *The Best of the Bonzo Dog Band* (Rhino). Their first few albums work very well as individual pieces too.

The Beatles, *The Beatles' Christmas Album* (Apple). A compilation of all their fan-club records, mailed only to members in 1971, but widely available as a bootleg ever since. No serious music on these, but a lot of chat and sketches, which grew increasingly elaborate and surrealistic as the '60s progressed.

The Holy Modal Rounders, *The Moray Eels Eat the Holy Modal Rounders* (Elektra). One of the weirdest records of the '60s, which is saying a lot.

Monty Python, *The Instant Monty Python CD Collection* (Virgin). Six CDs, containing eight albums, and still lacking a few of their records. The sketches, of course, work better on film, but the Pythons also devised and recorded a fair amount of material exclusively for record.

The Firesign Theatre, *Don't Crush That Dwarf, Hand Me the Pliers* (Columbia). One of the greatest comedy albums ever, constructed as a marathon late-night flip between TV channels.

The Rutles, *The Rutles* (Rhino). Neil Innes brilliantly parodied all stages of the Beatles' career in song. Get the CD reissue, which has, we kid you not, six bonus tracks heard on the film, but not included on the original LP.

Ween, *Chocolate and Cheese* (Elektra). The most accessible album by the hottest contemporary comedy-rock outfit.

– Richie Unterberger

Spoken Word and Poetry

Many rock performers were attracted to rock music in the first place because it provided a means of unconventional artistic expression. It's no surprise, then, that a lot of rock & rollers were similarly fascinated with literature. Just as rock & roll provided an outlet for ideas and emotions that ran against the status quo, so have many authors. When rock & roll lyrics became more self-consciously literary, beginning in the mid-'60s, the influence of many writers and poets was also felt in the music itself. Authors from Homer to Rimbaud have been cited as influences by various songwriters, and it would take at least an entire separate volume to completely examine such threads. As far as exchange between contemporary writers and rock musicians, that can probably be traced to the beat era.

The '50s beats were not rock & roll fans – indeed, their music of choice was jazz, sometimes folk – but their writing evinced a sense of rebellion, waywardness, and personal freedom that appealed to a lot of teenagers and young adults who would

become second-generation rock & rollers. Jack Kerouac and Allen Ginsberg were probably the most influential of these beats, both for their writing and personal charisma.

Kerouac, ironically, disavowed the hippie generation, but Ginsberg evolved with the times, and established personal relationships with several notable performers, such as Marianne Faithfull and, especially, Bob Dylan. Dylan was influenced by a lot of musicians and writers, and it's safe to say that Ginsberg (who appears in the Dylan documentaries *Don't Look Back* and *Renaldo and Clara*) was one of the figures who triggered Bob's more ambitious bursts of lyrical free association. Moreover, Ginsberg has made guest appearances on a number of rock records, ranging from the extremely obscure early-'80s alternative rock band Start to the Clash, as well as making musical recordings of his own.

Another writer intimate with many of the beats, although he usually is not himself classified as a beat author, is William Burroughs. There may be no other non-musical artist who has made his or her presence felt in rock music as much as this ancient, and as of 1995, still-active legend. His novels of the 1950s and 1960s prefigured the birth of the counterculture, and his 1965 album (featuring readings of passages from his books) circulated among heavyweights like the Beatles and Rolling Stones. His "cut-up" writing and audio techniques influenced the Soft Machine (who took their name from one of his books, and whose original guitarist, David Allen, actually worked on cut-ups with Burroughs in the early '60s) and David Bowie (who wrote some material using the cut-up technique). Burroughs even inadvertently coined the term heavy metal, as the phrase was lifted from the author and first used in rock by Steppenwolf in their hard rock hit "Born to Be Wild." He's made cameo appearances on recordings by the Soft Machine, Blondie, Ministry, Tom Waits, Kurt Cobain, and others. In the 1990s, producer Hal Willner constructed an album (with some musical arrangements) around Burroughs's readings, as he did around the same time for Allen Ginsberg.

Many notable rock performers had been published writers, or became published writers, including John Lennon, Dylan, Jim Morrison, and Patti Smith. Both Morrison and Smith (on whom Morrison himself was an influence) sometimes included extended spoken-word passages on their actual recordings; Smith's pieces of this sort rank among her most acclaimed work, though Morrison's were generally less well-received. Richard Farina, who formed a fine if not widely heralded folk-rock duo with his wife Mimi (Joan Baez's sister), wrote a novel, *Been Down So Long That It Looks Like Up to Me,* that became a counterculture favorite. The Fugs, older than the typical rock group of the mid-'60s, had their roots in New York's Lower East Side beat scene. Group-mainstays Ed Sanders and Tuli Kupferberg were respected, published poets (and still are), and even set a couple William Blake poems to music on their first album. Leonard Cohen, in a reversal of form, was a poet of international stature before making the first of several esteemed folk-rock albums in the '60s.

It took several Black performers in the 1970s, however, to achieve a truly memorable fusion of music and spoken word on record. The Last Poets, Gil-Scott Heron, and more obscure performers such as Jayne Cortez voiced the sociopolitical concerns of African Americans, sometimes in a quite militant fashion, against inspired R&B-inflected jazz rhythms. Linton Kwesi Johnson and other "dub poets" such as Mutabaruka, did the same for Jamaican minorities, using the hypnotic throb of reggae as their backbeat. None of these were "rock" performers per se, but their work would prove vastly influential, as they paved the way for the major African-American popular music of the '80s, rap. (A genre that owes a great deal, to say the least, to spoken word, rap is covered in a separate essay.)

Like Patti Smith, many punk and post-punk performers were poets and authors; some may well have turned out to be writers under different circumstances. John Doe and Exene Cervenka, the (now former) husband-and-wife duo who formed the core of X, met at an alternative writers workshop in Los Angeles. Henry Rollins, the Black Flag singer who has now broadened his audience as the leader of his own band, has published several volumes of his own prose. Jello Biafra, after the Dead Kennedys broke up, became a combination comedian/social commentator/anti-censorship spokesperson, traveling the spoken word/lecture circuit several times since the late '80s. Cervenka, Rollins, and Biafra have all released spoken-word albums on their own.

It's safe to say, though, that none of these spoken-word albums will attain the legendary status of the musical ventures of X, Black Flag, or the Dead Kennedys. For one thing, the plain spoken word doesn't lend itself nearly as well to record as music does; or, to phrase it differently, it lends itself better to the printed page, or performance, than tape in most cases.

Another problem is that, unlike Burroughs or Ginsberg, these are musicians, not authors/readers, first. A compelling singer may have a flat spoken delivery; Rollins and Biafra may sound amusing and insightful in print, but can deliver harangues in a fashion that crosses the line from rap to rant when they commit their prose to record. For this reason, compilations of spoken-word performances by musicians (as in the *Giorno Poetry* series), and/or minimal atmospheric musical backing of spoken word pieces, can work better by ensuring more sonic variety and interest.

Popular music, to a great extent, is the poetry of our age, and as long as rock & roll thrives, spoken word will have a presence in the music. Spoken-word performance will rarely be a priority of the major labels, and even more rarely be heard on commercial radio, but small companies such as New Alliance and Rhino's Word Beat subsidiary (which plans to release spoken-word material by Robyn Hitchcock) will continue to provide outlets for it.

10 Recommended Recordings

Jack Kerouac, *The Jack Kerouac Collection* (Rhino). Three-CD set features some musical backing by Steve Allen and jazzmen Al Cohn and Zoot Sims.

Allen Ginsberg, *Holy Soul Jelly Roll: Poems and Songs 1949-1993* (Rhino). Four-CD box covers his career from the '50s to the present, including the epic poem "Howl," collaborations with the Clash and Dylan, and the famous new wave single "Bird Brain."

William Burroughs, *Call Me Burroughs* (Rhino). Originally issued in 1965, this cult album had a wide share of international hipster admirers. Those who prefer some musical variety to spice Burroughs's legendary news announcer style can try the 1990 effort *Dead City Radio*, produced by Hal Willner.

The Last Poets, *The Last Poets* (Douglas). A lot of this prefigures rap.

Gil Scott-Heron, *The Revolution Will Not Be Televised* (Flying Dutchman). Scott-Heron shares a lot with the Last Poets besides the title track, though his phrasing is jazzier. He's remained active in the two decades since this 1974 album.

Linton Kwesi Johnson, *Forces of Victory* (Mango). This 1979 album is usually cited as his best.

Various Artists, *Better an Old Demon than a New God* (Giorno Poetry Systems). The Giorno Poetry Systems albums are, to say the least, uneven. Bound to be collector items in the future, they do mix spoken-word performances with tracks by a few leading punk and new wave musicians (who are frequently the speakers as well). This mid-'80s volume has cuts by William Burroughs, Psychic TV, Lydia Lunch, David Johansen, Richard Hell, and Arto Lindsay.

Various Artists, *Neighborhood Rhythms* (Freeway/Rhino). The spoken-word/poetry scene had a fair amount of influence on the L.A. alternative rock community. Not too easy to find these days, this 1984 double album has lots of spoken-word tracks, including performances by Dave Alvin and Exene Cervenka, and is produced more imaginatively than most such sets.

Jello Biafra, *No More Cocoons* (Alternative Tentacles). From 1987, the first of several spoken word releases by the former Dead Kennedys lead singer.

Hakim Bey, *T.A.Z.* (Axiom). One of the most imaginative recent spoken-word projects pits author Bey's readings against trance/world/dub/avant-rock musical backing by Bill Laswell and friends.
             – Richie Unterberger

The Avant-Garde and Contemporary Composition

Until the mid-1960s, the avant-garde and contemporary composition had virtually no influence upon rock & roll, or indeed upon any sort of pop music. The beginning of their relationship with rock & roll had much to do with changes both in rock itself, and in the kinds of musicians who were making it. The original rock & rollers, whether White or Black, were usually from lower-income backgrounds. Very few of them went to college; many did not finish high school. They may have been committed to the music they were making creatively and spiritually, but they large-

ly viewed their work as entertainment, not art. This is not to say they were any less intelligent or innovative than succeeding generations, but that they formed their music in an age of different expectations.

As it became clear that rock & roll was going to stick around, more and more musicians from educated middle-class backgrounds began to pick up instruments. In their schools and universities, they may have been studying more "respectable" music, but unlike students of previous generations, they had grown up with rock & roll, which created a passion that no discouragement from higher echelons could erase.

Many key figures of the British Invasion – including John Lennon, Keith Richards, Pete Townshend, and members of numerous other groups – were art school students before turning professional musicians. They had no less of a feel for pure rock & roll than anyone else, but their background had exposed them to bohemian enclaves and intellectual currents of thought in both art and music. The best of the British Invasion groups were instrumental in turning rock & roll into a more consciously artistic statement that was open to cutting-edge ideas from the art, fashion, literary, and of course non-rock musical worlds.

The Velvet Underground was the first rock band to incorporate many ideas from the musical avant-garde. The pivotal man in establishing this connection was original Velvets bassist/violist/organist John Cale, a Welshman who had studied with experimental composer Cornelius Cardew, and came to the United States under a Leonard Bernstein scholarship to study modern composition with Iannis Xenakis at Tanglewood, MA. Cale actually got a photo spread in the *New York Times* in 1963 after participating in an 18-hour rendition of Erik Satie's "Vexation" with John Cage. Moving to New York, he was a member of the Dream Syndicate with minimalism pioneer La Monte Young, and other musicians who would play with members of the Velvets before the group had properly formed.

Cale brought the droning textures of Young's work to the Velvet Underground. While Lou Reed was always the group's principal songwriter and visionary, cuts from their first two albums, such as "Black Angel's Death Song," "European Son," "All Tomorrow's Parties," and "Venus in Furs," owe much of their sonic palette to Cale's viola and keyboards. Feedback-ridden freakouts like "I Heard Her Call My Name" and "Sister Ray" also owe much of their adventurous structure and recklessly abrasive arrangements to ideas from the New York-based avant-garde community. The Velvets also took considerable inspiration for their modern multimedia assault from their first manager, Andy Warhol.

When Cale left the band in 1968, the Velvets became a far more conventional-sounding outfit (though their later work was also hugely important in setting the scene for punk/new wave). In their solo careers, the ex-Velvets continue to be among the most avant-garde-influenced musicians. Cale has collaborated with minimalist Terry Riley, constructed performance art pieces of sorts with Bob Neuwirth and Lou Reed and produced gothic, harmonium-drenched avant-rock albums for original sometime Velvet-vocalist Nico. Although Reed's solo career has run an extremely erratic course that finds him working conventional rock territory more often than not, he has never entirely forsaken his avant-garde roots with the Velvets. His 1975 double album, *Metal Machine Music*, consisting entirely of blistering electronic musique concrète guaranteed to clear the room under any circumstances, ranks as one of the most avant-garde (and uncommercial) records ever released by a rock performer, though opinion remains divided as to whether it was a serious artistic statement, a mean-spirited joke, or a contract-breaker.

Around the same time as the Velvets began recording, Frank Zappa and the Mothers of Invention were exploring elements of contemporary composition in their early albums. Zappa claimed Edgard Varèse as his principal hero (he is even said to have turned on Chicago, the pop-jazz-rock group, to the composer), and his side-long "Help I'm a Rock" (from the Mothers' debut LP, *Freak Out*) was certainly the most avant-garde piece that had been committed to a rock record at that point. Zappa's interest in contemporary composition remained constant throughout his career, although it was satirical rock that usually brought in the bacon for him; 1967's *Lumpy Gravy* was the first of several serious orchestral works that he released before his death in 1993.

Many psychedelic groups were aware of avant-garde music, although they only used it to pepper their rock compositions, not diving into its rigors nearly as whole-hog as Zappa did. The Beatles, for instance, proclaimed their admiration for Stockhausen, and the Grateful Dead's Phil Lesh was well-versed in electronic and "serious" music before joining the band. Sometimes groups would put bonafide avant-garde sound collages on their albums, as with "Revolution 9" (the Beatles), "What's Become of the Baby" (the Dead), and "A Small Package of Value Will Come to You, Shortly" (the Jefferson Airplane). These were neither extremely well-received by rock listeners and critics, nor especially admired by "serious" musicians, and such efforts were generally viewed as side indulgences. There were rare examples of musicians from the avant-garde community trying their hand at rock; the still-obscure United States of America, led by composer Joseph Byrd and featuring innovative electronic instrumentation, were the best of these.

With the dawn of art-rock, some musicians became more, well, serious in their appropriation of serious music. Spooky Tooth collaborated with composer Pierre Henry, and Pink Floyd's Roger Waters collaborated with composer Ron Geesin for the soundtrack of *The Body*. Geesin would in turn embellish Floyd's *Atom Heart Mother* with orchestral arrangements, and most of the group's late '60s and '70s albums showed considerable familiarity, if not expertise, with elements of electronic composition. Indeed, the Floyd took much of their early inspiration from the British avant-garde ensemble AMM, who (like the early Floyd) were managed by Peter Jenner; Syd Barrett picked up the trick of sliding ball bearings up and down his guitar from them. Brian Eno, after leaving Roxy Music, pioneered ambient music on his '70s solo albums; today he is recognized as a legitimate major contemporary composer (though he continues to work with many rock groups as a producer). And European art-rock groups like Tangerine Dream, Can, and Faust took many of their cues from electronic and experimental music.

Punk often proclaimed its contempt of "serious" rock, but it was hardly bereft of avant-garde influences. It's now a well-known fact that Yoko Ono's caterwauling screams – so ridiculed when she married John Lennon in the late '60s – influenced early new wave singers like the B-52's and Lene Lovich. The Residents' grim sound collages prefigured and reflected punk in its determination to destroy and deconstruct established icons of rock music. The multilayered minimalism of the electric guitar armies directed by Rhys Chatham and Glenn Branca was vastly influential on Sonic Youth (whose guitarist, Thurston Moore, played in one of Branca's early ensembles). New York no-wavers like Lydia Lunch, Suicide, and DNA also displayed a lot of primal avant-garde angst, carrying over to confrontational performances which bore the influences of the city's performance artists. Performance art and pop would indeed meet halfway with the success of Laurie Anderson in the 1980s.

Almost inevitably, the avant-garde itself began to reflect the influences of rock. Composers like Branca, Chatham, Paul Dresher, John Oswald, and others don't play rock, but they grew up with it, and the energy of rock informs what they are doing. Serious ensembles like the Kronos Quartet challenged the academic community with their willingness to interpret the works of Jimi Hendrix as well as Webern and other dead composers. Esteemed ambient composer Harold Budd collaborated not only with Eno, but also with moody British alternative rock group the Cocteau Twins.

In New York especially, but in many other communities, musicians are determined to explore the avant-garde with electric instruments; they think of themselves as "rock" musicians sometimes (or, like guitarist Elliott Sharp, either rock or avant-garde depending on whom they're playing with), but they're not interested in constructing their music in accessible, melodically conventional pop forms. John Zorn is probably the best known of these performers, determined to blend the avant-garde with rock

and other kinds of popular music, but never in a fashion that will be embraced by the *Billboard* chart listings.

In the 1990s, the influence of the avant-garde is strongly felt in the emerging ambient/techno scene, with its frequent use of dense electronics, found sound, and strategically placed silence. As the 21st century approaches, it's likely that the interchange between rock and the avant-garde will become more frequent, as younger generations of musicians are increasingly unconcerned with distinctions between genres, and increasingly determined to blur them.

13 Recommended Avant-Garde Recordings

La Monte Young, *The Well-Tuned Piano* (Gramavision). Young, a legendary perfectionist, rarely records; this is his most widely available piece. Neophytes are advised to listen to a copy before buying unheard; comprising five CDs, it's a steeply priced introduction.

Frank Zappa, *Lumpy Gravy* (Verve). From 1967, his first orchestral work.

John Cale & Terry Riley, *Church of Anthrax* (Columbia). Actually, not the highlight of either men's careers; Riley's *In C* and *Rainbow in Curved Air* were his most acclaimed works, and indeed some of the most acclaimed avant-garde works of the '60s.

Roger Waters & Ron Geesin, *Music from the Body* (Harvest). Not so much a collaboration as a complementation, as Waters and Geesin recorded their contributions separately.

Yoko Ono, *Walking on Thin Ice* (Rykodisc). Single-disc compilation focuses on some of her most accessible work; for the blood-curdling epics, go for the 6-CD *Onobox*, which will tax the patience of all but the hardiest fans.

Lou Reed, *Metal Machine Music* (RCA). The considerable controversy surrounding this album (described by the *Rolling Stone Album Guide* as a "gigantic 'fuck you' disguised as a groundbreaking experiment") tends to obscure the fact that this is not an uninterrupted burst of amplifier noise, but a genuine composition with different movements and modulations, though none are more accessible for that.

The Residents, *The Residents Present the Third Reich & Roll* (Ralph). Still their most (in)famous work, devoted to side-long medleys of unrecognizable maulings of '60s rock classics.

Brian Eno, *Another Green World* (EG). Caught halfway between rock and avant-garde, this album has Eno begining to de-emphasize vocals and pop melodies to concentrate on textures and the use of the recording studio as an instrument.

Various Artists, *No New York* (Antilles). The skronk of avant-garde noise-rock, caught in its birth pangs on this 1978 no-wave compilation.

Glenn Branca, *The Ascension* (99). Masses of guitars on one of the most electric contemporary compositional works.

Laurie Anderson, *Big Science* (Warner Bros.). The 1982 album that exposed Anderson to the pop world, although she had already been an established performance artist (and occasional recording artist) for some time. Includes the novelty hit "O Superman."

Harold Budd, Elizabeth Fraser, Robin Guthrie, & Simon Raymonde, *The Moon and the Melodies* (4AD). The ambient composer's collaboration with the Cocteau Twins. The result is, perhaps, overly polite, with neither party exhibiting work that scaled higher or even different heights than their previous output.

John Zorn, *Naked City* (Nonesuch/Elektra). Zorn actually owes at least as much to jazz as to rock, but he's one of the most popular, if not *the* most popular, downtown New York avant-garder with the alternative rock audience.

– Richie Unterberger

OTHER ESSAYS, RESOURCES, AND REFERENCES

Producers

Since rock began, the role of the producer in rock & roll has both changed a great deal and remained the same in many of its most essential aspects. Production duties vary from artist to artist and record to record, but generally speaking, the producer takes varying degrees of responsibility for shaping the sound of what we hear when discs get into our hands. Arguably, who producers are and what they do matter a lot more to critics and industry types than the average consumer, who is mostly concerned with the sound and image of the artists themselves. But producers have played key roles in rock & roll, at times stamping their records with artistic visions comparable to those of the performers.

A common stereotype of the producer, reinforced by some dramatized situations in movies, is that of someone sitting behind a mammoth console, surrounded by reels of tape and equipment, divided from the band only by a thin glass partition. He twiddles knobs, raises and lowers faders, shouts very specific instructions about the performance, and guides the musicians through take after take. Some producers did and do get involved on such an intensely physical level, but in reality their roles are much more diverse, and with increased specialization, much of the hands-on knob-twiddling and microphone placement are handled by engineers and studio technicians, not producers. And, unfortunately, the producer is still, in 1995, almost always a "he"; more than almost any other realm in rock & roll, it remains an almost exclusively male domain.

When rock & roll was born, the term "producer" was not used in the industry as much as the designation "artist and repertoire" staff member, usually shortened to A&R. A&R men were responsible for matching artists on a label's roster with material; in rock's early days, that sometimes meant songs that were actually written by the artists, but more often meant tunes from outside sources. Matching artists with material, or at least selecting among and suggesting material, from both internal and external sources, often remains one of the producer's principal activities. A&R staff are generally not found in the studio these days, instead concentrating their efforts on scouting for talent and helping sign artists to labels.

Broadly speaking, production was less sophisticated and much more of a "live" affair in the 1950s. Nor were most artists expected to have a long career, and producers were generally more concerned with finding hit songs and building effective arrangements for them than with building a distinctive sound to complement the artists themselves. There were, of course, many distinct production sounds and innovations during the era: Sam Phillips's "slap-back" echo techniques at Sun Studios did much to define rockabilly, Norman Petty helped craft Buddy Holly's greatest records at a small studio in New Mexico, and Fred Foster of Monument pioneered orchestral pop/rock with Roy Orbison.

It was Phil Spector, though, who was the first to fully realize the potential for rock production. Utilizing multi-track recording techniques, echo chambers, and scads of session musicians on both traditional rock instruments and full horn and string sections, he created symphonic rock & roll. Also a noteworthy musician and songwriter, Spector, more than any other rock producer before or since, was not just a technician or arranger, but an artist; while his classic singles were performed by the Ronettes, Crystals, Righteous Brothers, and others, they were above all his own work. He was also among the first to establish himself as an independent producer (and record-label owner), not beholden to label

superiors when pursuing his muse; British producer Joe Meek blazed a similar trail in Britain, though his material was not nearly in the same league as Spector's.

The soul music of the 1960s was distinguished by production styles specific to certain labels and regions. The most famous of these styles were the "assembly-line" techniques of Motown Records, the "deep soul" attributed to the Stax/Volt label, and (in the '70s) the lush, string-laden Philly soul sound. Heavily reliant upon the talents of the performers and ace session players, these and other schools of soul had trademark sounds that were both instantly identifiable yet varied and inspired enough to avoid formulaic repetition. They remain benchmark references for contemporary musicians.

The British Invasion gave rise to self-contained groups, both in the U.K. and the U.S., who demanded a much greater voice in their material and, subsequently, production. Buddy Holly had already began to control his own sessions before his premature death; Brian Wilson of the Beach Boys assumed virtual control of his group's production very early on in their career (though that often meant recording the Beach Boys' records with session musicians while the rest of the band was on tour). The Beatles, greatly aided by George Martin, were relentless in expanding the horizons of rock production at Abbey Road Studios through both new kinds of instruments and experimental production techniques. Other British producers like Shel Talmy (actually an American expatriate) maximized the impact of new groups like the Kinks and the Who by helping to craft a more powerful guitar sound than had previously been thought possible on rock records.

The role of the producer himself thus changed to a degree which is still felt in the industry. He did not so much delegate and direct sessions as work with the musicians to help realize their artistic visions and hopefully achieve commercial success. This no longer meant standing behind the board or developing certain kinds of reverb or instrumental balances, which was often the territory of the engineers (some of whom, like Shel Talmy's frequent assistant Glyn Johns, were stars in their own right, eventually assuming the producer's chair). It meant reviewing the material and suggesting modifications for the purpose of achieving the best *recorded* sound, not the best *live* sound, and helping to translate the musicians' more ambitious notions via outside horn and string players.

In certain cases, the most well-known being George Martin with the Beatles, the producer acts as a fifth or sixth member of the band, actually playing instruments on the recording, either to flesh out the arrangements or handle instruments that the band members aren't able to play with the same degree of proficiency. Or sometimes, the producer applies the dictum "less is more," and realizes that his greatest contribution is to stay out of the way and let the musicians be themselves. Occasionally, the producer is not so much the producer in the musical sense as in the financial sense of many movie producers. Andy Warhol, for instance, made minimal musical contributions to the Velvet Underground's classic first album; he is, however, listed as producer, for the very important reason that he financed the sessions, as well as pretty much carried the band economically during their early days.

In the modern rock era, to a much greater degree than many listeners realize, the producer is not so much a technician or creative force as a moderator, and a settler of arguments. Decisions about which material to use when more than one bandmember is a songwriter; decisions about whether to use session musicians when a bandmember can't cut it; asking/instructing musicians to put more work into a song before it is deemed complete and ready for recording; kicking out friends, groupies, drug pushers, and other hangers-on who slow down sessions; drawing the line when experimentation is draining the allotted budget; determining the sound balance when none of the individual musicians are willing to sacrifice their self-interest – it often comes down to the producer to break the stalemate.

These can be thankless tasks, and rock musicians are more often than not grudging in their praise of producers. Often their criticisms are justified; just as often, their talents and accompanying egos make it difficult to accept that creative collaboration and restraint is often necessary. In reading rock biographies, one often comes across comments of the sort, "If we had the chance to record it again our way, it would come out so much better. The producer didn't grasp what we were trying to accomplish/was unsympathetic to our ideas/rushed us through the sessions."

What's unspoken here is that if most musicians were allowed to carry on as they wished, the results would often be half-baked and less satisfactory to both the musicians and their audience. It's a difficult task, translating sounds that others hear in their heads, and while some producers do botch the job, in many cases they are arriving at the best possible realization of the musicians' ideas with the available talent, material, and equipment. Of course that hasn't stopped many musicians from taking over production duties, or even production and engineering duties, themselves. Sometimes the results are self-indulgent messes, but performers like Prince, Stevie Wonder, the Rolling Stones, and quite a few others have proved quite able at handling these tasks, sometimes down to the smallest detail. We're not going to name any names here, but some artists credit themselves as producers or co-producers when their contribution is relatively minimal, such as helping to select material, approve final mixes or finance the sessions.

In the late '60s and '70s, recording budgets ballooned as artists became more perfectionistic, and signed recording contracts granting them specific artistic freedom. Better home-stereo equipment made better technology a concern, and more attention than ever was lavished upon overdubs, multi-track recording, and mixes. Many charged that the soul of the music was being driven out of recorded performance, and the punk/new wave explosion was partly a reaction against this. Many of the seminal punk recordings had a spontaneous, raw, live feel generated by quick, low-budget sessions, but most of the early punk and new wave artists that established career longevity came to appreciate the value of thoughtful, even elaborate production as their music became more diverse. And even the Sex Pistols' *Never Mind the Bollocks* was subject to all sorts of remixing and re-recording until it was finally released after months of sessions, which John Lydon still bitches about to this day.

Some music trends of the 1980s and 1990s have seen the role of the producer further redefined. Rap music demands facility with sampling and stop-on-a-dime editing techniques; rap and dance music have brought the roles of the engineer, mixer, and remixer to new levels, as specific sonic textures are created for certain radio and club formats, and the production is sometimes considered to be of equal or greater importance than the performer or the material. Dub music, in reggae and reggae-rock crossover productions, places far greater importance upon sound manipulation and reverb than performance or material. Ambient/techno/rave productions can be much more dependent upon manipulation and arrangement of source materials, beats, and samples with synthesizers and other highly sophisticated electronic equipment than anything else.

All of these developments have lead to familiar charges that elaborate production techniques are driving the humanity out of contemporary music, though all of the above genres rank among the fastest-growing styles of rock & roll as the 20th century draws to a close. Those looking for producers who establish their distinctive imprint on the course of rock music with more conventional producer-musician relationships can continue to find many examples, such as "New Jack Swing" king Teddy Riley, or Bill Laswell, whose production credit seemingly attaches itself to every other experimental rock record; also Steve Albini, Butch Vig, and Brendan O'Brien who have all have been instrumental in establishing the grunge and post-punk sound which finally met with mass success in the early '90s.

– Richie Unterberger

Session Musicians

If one were to write the hidden history of rock & roll, session musicians would have many of the most prominent roles. Often uncredited in the 1950s and 1960s, there are hundreds of musicians who are not stars in their own right, but have done much to shape the course of rock music. Even today, when most session musicians are routinely credited on album jackets, they enjoy far less recognition than the performers they back in the studio. Session musicians, of course, have been used since music began to be recorded for commercial purposes early in the 20th century, and were a feature of pop music long before rock & roll emerged. When rock & roll began to take shape in the late '40s and early '50s, session musicians were already a big part of the game in the studio. A lot of rock & roll singers, regardless of the era, don't play instruments, and while they were sometimes big enough to support touring bands of their own, they didn't always use these bands in the studio. Singers that were just starting out didn't have bands of their own, and were usually provided with accompaniment from whatever musicians the label could provide. Then as now, a lot of rock & roll musicians who played their own instruments onstage did not, for various reasons, always play their instruments on records.

The session musicians on early rock & roll records would have rarely identified themselves as rock & roll musicians; some would have found the term insulting, but more to the point, the term rock & roll itself hardly existed, and most professional musicians were schooled in different genres of music. In the large urban centers, quite a few of them were jazz musicians making money on the side; guitarists, saxophonists, bassists, and drummers were in demand for both jazz and rock purposes. Also, jazz and rock were both much closer in their evolutionary paths to their blues and R&B roots than they are today, and it wasn't as difficult to switch modes by the day, sometimes by the hour, as it might appear. Other early rock session musicians were conversant with straight pop or even classical; those that recorded for regional independent labels were often from country and blues backgrounds.

It was only decades later, when rock scholarship had grown to a sufficient level, that many of these session players received some measure of public recognition, usually confined to serious fans. While space precludes the listing of every musician who played a great riff or solo, a few of the more notable ones include guitarist Mickey Baker, who played on tons of R&B and rock sessions for Atlantic in addition to gaining stardom as half of Mickey & Sylvia; guitarist James Burton, responsible for the brilliant rockabilly licks on Ricky Nelson's classic singles; guitarist Scotty Moore, who did the same for Elvis Presley's best work; drummer Earl Palmer and saxophonists Lee Allen and Alvin Tyler, responsible for much of what we recognize as the classic New Orleans R&B sound; Willie Dixon, who played bass on many of the great '50s Chess blues and rock & roll sides; and even Chet Atkins, who though mostly identified with country, lent his guitar to some of the Everly Brothers' great early material.

Under the guidance of Phil Spector, Brian Wilson, and others, rock production became more sophisticated in the early and mid-'60s. In New York and Los Angeles, session musicians were an important component in the realization of the complex, multi-tracked sound that such producers were after. Some of these musicians became stars in their own right, within the industry: saxophonist Steve Douglas, bassist Carole Kaye, guitarist Glen Campbell (before stardom as a solo act), and drummer Hal Blaine. These performers were both virtuosos and extremely adaptable to many kinds of material, and their flair for rock & roll did much to establish Los Angeles in particular as a recording center for rock music. Not to be neglected are the backup vocalists for many '60s rock artists, some of whom had a soulfulness on par with the star attractions, especially Darlene Love (who sang uncredited lead vocals on some of the Crystals' hits) and the Sweet Inspirations. Love and the Sweet Inspirations recorded some fine sides on their own, but were never accorded a level of stardom on par with the respect they achieved within the industry.

Session players were extremely important in establishing the success of the day's most popular soul labels, Motown and Stax/Volt. Motown favored an assembly-line approach which gave its records an instantly identifiable appeal, and its musicians, particularly bassist James Jamerson, were worshiped by millions who never knew their names, as they were seldom credited on releases (Berry Gordy, Jr., has pointed out, with some validity, that hardly any labels printed credits in the '60s, and that it wasn't a conscious policy of Motown to keep its hidden assets undiscovered, but simply the status quo of the era). Stax/Volt's most frequent sessionmen, Booker T. & the MGs, were not only not secrets, but stars in their own right. Other Memphis-area session musicians were frequently sought after, such as the Memphis Horns, the Hi Rhythm Section, and the many musicians who worked in nearby Muscle Shoals, AL, in the Fame Studios. James Brown's pioneering funk bands featured numerous talented musicians, such as Bootsy Collins, Maceo Parker, and Fred Wesley, who are only now starting to get recognition as individual innovators in their own right.

In pre-British Invasion England, session work for rock records was carried out, as it was in the worst American rock & roll records, by bored, middle-aged musicians more conversant with MOR pop. This changed with the Beatles and the British Invasion, as a whole generation of musicians came of age that had grown up with rock & roll, and came by the music naturally. Session musicians continued to be used on many British record dates, and several future guitar heroes, including Jeff Beck, John McLaughlin, and Ritchie Blackmore, gained much of their early recording experience playing for others.

Before joining the Yardbirds, Jimmy Page was probably *the* most active rock & roll session player in all of Britain, gracing countless sides, including major hits by Them, the Who, and the Kinks. Other musicians, like drummer Bobby Graham, future Led Zeppelin bassist John Paul Jones (who worked with such pop acts as Herman's Hermits and Lulu), and piano player Nicky Hopkins were guests on numerous records, ranging in Hopkins's case from the Stones to the Who to the Beatles to the Kinks (Ray Davies has been said to have written the Kinks' "Session Man" about him). And there's the strange case of Ian Stewart, a brilliant keyboard player who was officially kicked out of the Rolling Stones by management just before the group began recording, but continued to play with them on many of their records and tours, functioning in effect as their sixth member.

The rise of the self-contained rock group was a double-edged sword in some cases. For the bandmembers, there was the increased prestige and creative freedom that came with playing their own instruments and writing their own material. What the public didn't realize was that many self-contained groups still relied on session players to some extent, leading to some well-publicized controversies when it was revealed that some groups didn't play everything on their records. It has been belatedly discovered, for instance, that many of the Beach Boys' greatest records were recorded by Brian Wilson and session musicians while the group was out on tour. The Byrds recorded their breakthrough single "Mr. Tambourine Man" with mostly sessionmen, although, contrary to some published accounts, the rest of their classic '60s records featured the group as principal players. Much of the scorn dumped upon the Monkees was generated by the revelation that they didn't play on their early records (though they made no secret of this when confronted with the fact).

While rock groups continued to use session players, they were wary of relying upon them for the bulk of their recorded parts. This hadn't been an issue for most top groups, but they began turning increasingly to friends from other groups, not just professionals assigned to them by labels and/or producers. This was to some degree indicative of the increased self-consciousness and self-sufficiency of the late-'60s rock scene, and while the "heavy friends" syndrome lent itself to some self-indulgent jams, it also produced numerous instances of inspired collaborations which were sparked by the musicians' obvious camaraderie and mutual respect, qualities that would have been absent in many cases if hired hands had been used. Duane Allman's duets with Eric Clapton on Derek and the Dominos' "Layla" is one frequently cited example of such a rapport. (Allman himself was a session player of note before the Allman Brothers became big, contributing notable parts to records by Wilson Pickett, Aretha Franklin, and others.)

There were still many solo performers in rock, and many of them couldn't afford to support their own bands, or were not inclined to carry bands to begin with. Many of these were singer/songwriters who had begun as solo acoustic acts, and particularly in the early days of folk-rock, giants like Dylan (who used such illustrious musicians as Mike Bloomfield, Al Kooper, the Band, and country harmonica player Charlie McCoy as sidemen in the '60s) were heavily reliant upon session players to effect

their transition to electric music. When singer/songwriters became huge in the early '70s, much of their sound was crafted by session musicians, particularly in Los Angeles, leading to a general homogeneity of sound within the southern Californian rock community as a whole. Such professionalism was attacked by the early punk/new wave groups, yet many of them also used session musicians to improve their material in the studio.

There have been tons of session players in rock in the last couple of decades, yet in comparison to rock & roll's early days, there are relatively few musicians content to make their living, and their artistic impression, primarily from sessions. This is a reflection of two factors. First, musicians are much more likely to tap members of other groups, or fellow musicians who may be "between" groups or solo acts, rather than professionals who do not choose to record under their own name or affiliate themselves with ongoing recording and touring acts. Second, instrumentalists themselves are generally much more interested in becoming a member of a group or a solo act than going it alone as a session player. Session players are credited on most album sleeves these days, it's true, but the level of public recognition remains much lower than artists that work under their own name. Equally important, playing sessions affords much less chance for the songwriting and creativity that have become de rigueur for most rock musicians since the mid-'60s.

If you're looking for musicians who make a good living primarily as session players, you'll find a lot more of them in MOR rock, or urban contemporary R&B, than most other rock genres. For that matter, you'll find much more of them in Nashville, playing country music, than playing rock music altogether. There do remain respected musicians primarily identified as session players within the rock world, such as drummers Kenny Aronoff and Michael Blair; rhythm section Sly and Robbie (whose bread-and-butter gig remains reggae, as they seemingly appear on every other record released in Jamaica); guitarists Marc Ribot and Robert Quine; rap label Sugar Hill's house band Keith LeBlanc (drums), Doug Wimbish (bass), and Skip McDonald (guitar; they're also members of the groups Tackhead and Little Axe); keyboardist Benmont Tench (also a member of Tom Petty's band); and bassist Bill Laswell (also a prolific producer and recording artist).

– Richie Unterberger

Independent Labels

The story of rock & roll is not just one of musicians, songwriters, and producers. For many listeners, labels are nothing more than a name in the middle of an album or on the spine of a CD; "major" and "indie" are distinctions that concern serious fans, journalists, and industry insiders. Rock's ascension as the most popular music of the last half of the 20th century, however, owes much to the pioneering efforts of independent labels, which continue to act as a source of innovation, both on their own and as an influence on "majors," labels run or distributed by major corporations. When rock & roll had its first birth pangs just after World War II, the record industry was dominated by a half dozen major labels – Capitol, MGM, Decca, Mercury, Columbia, and RCA. By and large they played it safe in the popular music field, leaving the more specialized tastes of the R&B and country & western audiences to smaller, regional companies. Somewhat condescendingly referred to as "race" and "hillbilly" music, the majors felt these markets were too small and crude to cater to, and their A&R departments developed little in the way of such talent for their rosters.

This left the field open for smaller enterpreneurs, who faced a much tougher battle in recording their acts, promoting them, and getting them airplay. On the other hand, they were less constrained by established formulas, and able to record more creative and uninhibited performers, satisfying the increasingly hungry demand for raucous R&B and C&W sounds. Charlie Gillett's history of rock & roll, *The Sound of the City*, views the birth of rock & roll primarily as a phenomenon of independent labels developing and marketing music that the majors were ignoring, and does an excellent job of detailing the many influential independent early rock and R&B labels and their rise to commercial success.

It would be a mistake to cast these independent labels as champions of the artistic vanguard, fighting corporate monoliths. Many independent executives treated their artists shoddily, signing them to exploitative contracts, withholding royalties, and casting them aside when they fell from commercial grace. While visionaries such as Sun Records' Sam Phillips and Atlantic's Jerry Wexler were probably motivated as much or more by love of music as profit, many were hustlers seeking a piece of the action by finding whatever niche market they could. Lacking the powerful distribution networks of the majors, all of them were compelled to do things the hard way, driving from town to town to push their latest singles, chatting up and giving gifts to influential DJs in exchange for airplay.

Stations that gave the new sounds such airplay become increasingly plentiful after 1950, and by the mid-'50s the music which was just starting to be called "rock & roll" was becoming an important part of the popular music market. The great majority of the early rock & roll records were released on independent labels, many of which have assumed legendary status in the decades since. Sun, Atlantic, Specialty, Chess, Imperial, Modern, VeeJay, King, Duke/Peacock – all boasted rosters of incredible talent that left permanent imprints on rock & roll. And there were dozens of other independent labels of note, some of which only released one or two hits, some of which released only regional hits, but many of which recorded lasting contributions to rock history.

The majors responded defensively at first, either ignoring rock & roll almost entirely (as Columbia did) or recording watered-down "cover" versions for the pop market. Innovators like Bill Haley and Elvis Presley were signed to major labels and launched to superstardom after establishing themselves on independent labels. The majors vs. indies battle wasn't black-and-white by any means – early greats Gene Vincent and Buddy Holly were signed by majors without any track record, and went on to record some of the very best rock & roll of the 1950s.

By the end of the 1950s, independents were responsible for about twice as many Top Ten singles as majors, and about three times as many Top Ten rock singles. In the 1960s, major labels didn't so much fight back against indies as adapt to the rock era, starting to focus their energies on developing rock talent rather than more middle-of-the-road sounds. Indies were still a major force in rock & roll; labels like Kama Sutra, Red Bird, Philles, Stax/Volt, and many others developed outstanding rosters, and Motown became the most successful independent label of all time, establishing a commercial presence that rivaled the majors – with the R&B and soul performers that would have been considered a mere "race" market 10-15 years earlier.

In Britain, at the time the Beatles and others claimed a large part of the international pop market, the situation was much more restrictive. Virtually every artist recorded for one of four major companies: EMI, Decca, Pye, and Philips. However, these labels had huge and varied rosters that were somewhat more adventurous than their U.S. counterparts. In the mid-'60s, several British independents began to make their presence known by recording some of the era's most innovative rock. Encompassing artists like the Small Faces, the Who, Cream, Traffic, Jimi Hendrix, and (in the late '60s) the Beatles, labels like Immediate, Reaction, Track, Island (which began primarily as a ska and bluebeat concern), and the Beatles' Apple unleashed determinedly progressive sounds, although it's important to note that all of those labels benefited from distribution deals with majors. In the U.S. there were also companies that fostered self-consciously progressive rosters, especially Elektra, which hit it big with the Doors and recorded several other influential folk-rock and psychedelic acts.

The 1970s were a time of conglomeration, in which the majors expanded their power by establishing distribution deals with some of the most successful independents. Plenty of independent R&B and Black pop continued to chart, but that genre was increasingly becoming the province of the majors. Mid- and late-'70s punk and new wave bands were often thwarted by industry resistance, which gave birth to the D.I.Y. (do-it-yourself) ethic in both Britain and the U.S. Realizing that majors weren't going to sign and promote them, or would try to refine their sound, bands put out their own records, formed their own labels, or signed with indies, trading commercial success for artistic freedom. Labels like Britain's Stiff were instrumental in shaping new wave music, though Stiff, like some others, was not averse to major-label distribution to achieve wider exposure.

In the 1980s, the indie ethic became more sociopolitical and divisive. Many performers, critics, label owners, and fans took a virulent anti-major-label stance, seeing major labels as a malignant, homogenizing force that threatened to destroy creativity and hinder artistic expression. The independent/alternative rock network of hundreds of labels, fanzines, and college/community radio stations allowed artists to record and release music that was not only outside of the commercial mainstream, but often actively opposed to it. Labels like SST, Alternative Tentacles, Touch & Go, Sub Pop, and 4AD developed identifiable sounds and styles that constituted artistic visions in and of themselves. Others, like Slash, tried to play it both ways, arranging for distribution deals with majors. The majors tapped into the growing alternative rock market by cutting distribution deals with successful indies, or treating indie labels as farm teams, signing the most successful prospects (bands) after they'd honed their sounds in the minor leagues (which were usually clubs and college radio stations).

Rap was another form of music which encountered some industry resistance, giving rise to many independent rap labels. By and large they weren't as suspicious of mainstream acceptance, and many of the most successful indie records of the '80s were rap discs by superstars like Run-D.M.C. and Salt-N-Pepa. Actually, these were among the very few 100% indie productions to become hits; the majors were now composed of six mega-conglomerates, which in the mid-'90s were Sony, CEMA, BMG, PGD, WEA, and UNI (the initials may change according to corporate sales and reorganizations in the future). It's difficult to ascertain an exact figure, but an educated guess would estimate that these labels are responsible for about 90% of the sales in today's market.

The push-and-pull between major and indie labels continues unabated in the mid-'90s. When indie rock superstars like Hüsker Dü leaped to major labels in the mid-'80s, the sales figures were modest. The multi-million-selling success of Nirvana, however, paved the way for grunge music and a wholesale infiltration of the charts by scabrous alternative rockers like Pearl Jam, Nine Inch Nails, Green Day, Liz Phair, and Beck that wouldn't have stood a chance of denting the Top 100 just ten years ago. It's an explosion that wouldn't have been possible without the efforts of independent labels, which were the first to record and develop most of these acts.

Indie labels, however, shouldn't be viewed merely as a proving ground for the stars of tomorrow. It's the music that matters, and independent labels continue to house some of the best talent in rock and pop, as well as cultivate some of its most innovative sounds and trends by offering a climate that isn't as obsessed with charts and commercial success. The non-rock music that continues to influence rock – folk, blues, jazz, reggae, world beat, the avant-garde – is also usually found on small labels. All indies continue to fight the same obstacles of limited distribution, budgets, and exposure as they did 50 years ago, but they will continue to exert a major influence as long as rock & roll is around.

Books

The Sound of the City, by Charlie Gillett (Pantheon, 1970)

Making Tracks: The Story of Atlantic Records, by Charlie Gillett (Souvenir Press, 1974)

Good Rockin' Tonight: Sun Records and the Birth of Rock'n'Roll, by Colin Escott with Martin Hawkins (St. Martin's, 1991)

– *Richie Unterberger*

Bootlegs

Music bootlegs – illegally reproduced and distributed recordings – have been with us about as long as sound reproduction itself. Few issues in the music industry inspire as much heated debate. A constant irritant to many record companies and musicians, they are a source of pleasure – albeit a bit of a guilty pleasure – to countless fans. Despite periodic efforts by the industry to crack down on manufacturers and retailers of unauthorized recordings, bootlegging continues to persist and make an impact upon a large audience, much as independent labels continue to proliferate even as corporate companies seek to consolidate their domination of the music industry.

There are several kinds of bootlegs. There are pirates, which reissue official material (usually rare and out-of-print) without official permission. There are counterfeits, which duplicate the content (and often sleeve and label) of a record as it appeared in its original release. The most influential and commonly discussed bootlegs collect totally unreleased performances – live concerts, studio outtakes, demos, and radio broadcasts.

Bootlegging was hardly unknown in jazz, classical, and other collector recordings before it began to infiltrate the rock audience. A live recording of the Beatles performing "Some Other Guy," a staple of their early sets that they never officially cut in the studio, made the rounds in Liverpool as early as 1963. That same year, the first unauthorized live recording of the Rolling Stones was pressed, giving hardcore fans a memento of their heroes before their rapid ascent to international fame.

It was a late-'60s Bob Dylan bootleg, however, that really got the scene rolling. Titled *The Great White Wonder*, this collection of *Basement Tapes*-era demos and other odds and ends, packaged in a plain white sleeve, was manna from heaven for Dylan acolytes desperate for any word of his continued existence. And here was a clutch of unreleased, more or less realized studio performances, available for just a bit more than the standard price of an LP. Similarly popular bootlegs of the Beatles' early 1969 *Get Back* sessions and a show from the Rolling Stones' 1969 U.S. tour (*Liver Than You'll Ever Be*) quickly followed. Soon there were live and (considerably less frequently) unreleased studio recordings by most of the major bands (and many minor ones) for purchase on the underground market.

Bootleg product ebbs and flows according to periodic crackdowns by the law and the record industry, but basically it's been uninterrupted. At collector conventions, specialty shops, London flea markets, and the streets of New York, illicit recordings spanning several decades continue to swap hands. Search hard enough for those Liz Phair demos, that Patti Smith broadcast, or last week's Elvis Costello show, and you'll find it, though it may involve considerable expense and mileage. Realizing they were unable to stop the massive circulation of live tapes among "Deadheads," the Grateful Dead more or less condoned the taping and trading of their live performances.

Occasionally, a bootleg album slips through this underground web to make an impact upon the mass audience. Such was the case with Prince's unreleased *Black Album* in the late 1980s. Outselling a great deal of its legitimately released competition, it attracted attention and reviews in the mainstream press, and even some airplay on commercial radio stations.

Aesthetically, the most frequent complaint against bootlegs is that they sound terrible. And quite a few of them do, especially the older live ones. But bootleg technology has improved enormously over the last decade. Many boots – perhaps even the majority by now – boast excellent pressings, duplication from first-generation sound board and master tapes, and artwork/packaging that is better than the real thing.

Many labels and performers claim to be hurt financially and artistically by bootlegs, arguing that they are not being compensated for the sale of their property; that boots are a violation of their sacrosanct artistic wishes; and that unauthorized material damages their artistic reputation. Fans counter that consumers of bootlegs almost invariably own all of the artists' official releases anyway; that many bootlegs expose valuable work to a relatively wide audience and cast new light upon an artist's ouevre; and that any damage, financial or otherwise, suffered by the artist is compensated for by the free publicity illicit material generates. From corporate boardrooms to on-line bulletin boards, variations of the above debate rage. And the audience for bootlegs continues to grow.

Whatever one's position, it is undeniable that bootleggers have been responsible for bringing many great performances to light. No appraisal of Bob Dylan is complete without listening to his legendary 1966 Albert Hall concert with the Band; no picture of the Beatles complete without hearing their BBC tapes, during which they performed 35 covers (and one original!) never released on their official albums; and no assessment of the Beach Boys made without hearing their legendary unreleased *Smile* album. Indeed, as of mid-1995, several collections of highly touted unreleased material that have circulated as bootlegs for many years have actually gained official release. In late 1994, a double CD of the best Beatle BBC sessions finally appeared on Capitol, and Prince's *Black Album* came out. Strong rumors of the imminent appearance of *Smile*, Dylan's Albert Hall concert, several CDs of unreleased Beatle music, and other top-rank archival music indicate that lots of other collections of similar material will be made available to the general public in the near future. The list will continue to expand as long as there is a serious interest in musicians and their art.

– Richie Unterberger

Fanzines

Major record labels and the established music press sometimes leave precious little room for innovative ideas and idiosyncratic talents. And just as musicians can choose to work outside the system by recording for independent labels, or even their own labels, music fans have their own do-it-yourself alternatives for reading about, writing about, or publishing their favorite sounds in fanzines.

The term "fanzine" originated among avid science-fiction fans in the 1950s, who would spread news and opinions about their fave works in tiny magazines (or 'zines), which were usually mimeographed and distributed through the mail to other acolytes. These days, fanzines – music and otherwise – are often distributed in stores, and sometimes mushroom into "real" magazines, but remain forums for opinions and information that are impossible to get from the usual sources.

Neither its readers nor its publishers ever thought of it as such, but an argument could be made for citing *Mersey Beat* as the first music fanzine. The tabloid was founded by Bill Harry, an art school chum of John Lennon's and a sci-fi zine reader, in 1961 to fill a void in Liverpool. The burgeoning "beat" music scene had become an explosion numbering several hundred groups and several thousand avid fans, but was virtually uncovered in the region's newspapers, let alone on vinyl or radio.

Launched with 50 pounds and a staff of two (Harry and his girlfriend) to cover the area's groups and music news, *Mersey Beat* was a smash success in its brief heyday (1961-64). John Lennon and Paul McCartney themselves contributed writing to the paper, which – with its comprehensive gigs and entertainment coverage – was something of a forerunner of the "alternative weeklies" of today. Brian Epstein, owner of Liverpool's largest record shop, contributed a regular column for a while in 1961, and it has been theorized that he first found out about the Beatles by reading the publication, though he always claimed otherwise.

In the United States, the first rock & roll fanzine of note was founded by Greg Shaw. Like Harry, Shaw was active in the sci-fi fanzine community, corresponding with future KISS member Gene Simmons, among others. In the mid-'60s, the teenaged Shaw got the idea to create a rock fanzine. Launched in 1966 in San Francisco's Haight-Ashbury as the Summer of Love was just beginning to bloom, *Mojo Navigator* made the rounds of local record stores, head shops, and other grass-roots channels as a xeroxed paper. Greil Marcus and future *Rolling Stone* publisher Jann Wenner were among those who helped at the zine's collating parties. An excerpt from an early issue, an interview with the then-unsigned and barely known Big Brother & the Holding Company, was reprinted on the insert to the live album *Cheaper Thrills* (recorded in 1966, issued in 1984).

Shaw's next fanzine venture, *Bomp*, would prove considerably more far-reaching and influential. Based in southern California, it was the first zine to feature the unrestrained rantings of cult critics like Richard Meltzer and Lester Bangs. Equally important, it was one of the first rock magazines, if not the first, to cover music of both the past and present, the '60s in particular being Shaw's abiding fascination. From its beginnings as a mimeographed periodical, *Bomp* evolved into a regularly published magazine with a circulation of 30,000 before it folded in 1979.

It was the birth of punk in the mid-'70s, though, that really gave rise to a widespread music fanzine culture. Just as musicians were resorting to pressing their own records and promoting their own gigs to make their presence known, frustrated writers (who were often musicians as well) published their own reviews, features, and diatribes in the absence of any coverage of punk and new wave in slick magazines and newspapers. In keeping with the tone of early punk rock, the writing itself was often far more scathing, not to say scatological, than anything the glossier periodicals would have printed, music-related or not.

Like many punk groups of the time, many of the early zines were short-lived, lasting only an issue or two. Even these productions were viewed as a triumph by the underground, inasmuch as, like groups who said all they could say in a single or two before they broke up or lost inspiration, writers and publishers were sending a message that they could write about what they wanted in the way they wanted – at least, until the money or inspiration ran out. These efforts weren't always short-lived by any means; zines like *Search and Destroy* ran for some time, and the less explicitly punk-oriented and vitriolic *New York Rocker* made it through 52 issues.

Just as the punk scene itself started to fragment and diversify, so did fanzines, moving from the slash'n'burn style of the mid-'70s to somewhat more professional and readable formats, and a wider scope of subjects, encompassing non-punk rock, '50s and '60s music, individual groups/performers, or even non-rock. Fanzines devoted to blues, reggae, rockabilly, folk, the Velvet Underground, or nursing home residents reviewing records of all kinds (the famous *Duplex Planet*, still active in a modified format) were all fair game.

The '80s saw the fanzine field further diversify and stratify. Some were clearly intended for a local audience or mail distribution to friends, printed in quantities of a few hundred or even less. Productions like *The Offense Newsletter* and *Conflict* were just as uncompromising in their reflection of the authors' tastes, but stirred enough interest to attract national distribution. And, at times, these had an actual influence on the larger community: Tim Anstett's *Offense Newsletter* was probably the single most important factor in attracting American attention to the British alternative rock label 4AD, and *Conflict* publisher Gerard Cosloy went on to be the A&R honcho of the influential indie rock labels Homestead and (as of 1995) Matador.

Then there were the bigger, slicker, and more comprehensive zines that became, well, real magazines, and may never have been true zines in the first place, although the grass-roots nature of their coverage and the sensibilities of their audience would not have been possible without the groundwork laid by smaller and less compromising publications. *Op*, which began as a supplement to a program guide of a college radio station in Olympia, Washington, evolved in stages into *Option* magazine; despite its far larger size and glossier appearance, it remains focused on alternative and independent music. *Dirty Linen* began as a Fairport Convention fanzine, and is now the leading folk and world music magazine in the U.S. In Britain, *Southern Rag* traveled a similar road when it evolved from its zine-like beginnings into *Folk Roots*, the leading folk and roots music magazine in the world. *Trouser Press*, one of the very few nationally distributed publications to cover underground rock upon its inception in the mid-'70s, folded in 1984, but gave birth to the regularly published *Trouser Press Record Guide*, the most definitive guidebook to punk and new wave records available.

Then there are the fanzines which manage to be huge, in-depth, painstakingly designed, and totally uncompromising in their championship of the individual tastes of the authors. *Forced Exposure*, dominated by the writing and record collections of editor/publishers Jimmy Johnson and Byron Coley, has defined the most acerbic aspects of the rock underground since the mid-'80s; *Kicks*, run by Billy Miller and Miriam Linna, displays a similar exhaustive devotion to early rockabilly, R&B, surf, and garage rock acts. The specialized tastes (not to mention pointed jabs at anyone who doesn't like what they like) of such zines will prevent them from ever reaching a large readership or even publishing regularly (though they're not especially interested in doing so anyway), but ensures them a far more devoted audience than most publications of any sort, above-ground or underground.

Delving into the vast and unpredictable world of fanzines is often as easy as stopping into a few of the hippest record stores in large U.S. or U.K. cities. Those who don't have the resources to check those out should try reading reviews in *Factsheet Five* (which covers fanzines of all types) or contacting See Hear (59 E. 7th St., NYC 10003), a store which mail-orders a large selection of music zines, magazines, and books.

– *Richie Unterberger*

Reissues

Whatever your taste or specialty – doo wop, electric blues, British Invasion, girl group, garage bands, punk, soul, funk, psychedelic – as a record collector, you're in a much better position in 1995 to track down your favorite records than you were even three years ago. Actually, you're in a much better position to track them down than you were when they were actually released, whether they came out in 1985 or 1955. The reissue explosion of the 1980s and 1990s has made records from more different eras more widely available than at any other time in history, and the selection increases daily.

The history of the rock reissue actually goes back nearly as far as rock itself. "Oldies" rock & roll radio formats came into being

in the early '60s, and Original Sound's extensive reissue compilation series, eventually numbering over a dozen volumes, helped keep many of rock & roll's earliest and greatest hits relatively accessible. This was a time when little thought was given to preserving rock's heritage – the music hadn't even been around that long to begin with – and while it may have been easier to buy rare obscurities for a nickel apiece in thrift stores and warehouses, it was much more difficult to find music more than a few years old unless it was recorded by big stars.

The 1970s saw the emergence of the first companies dedicated to thoughtful, intelligent compilations of vintage rock & roll. Sire was predominantly a contemporary rock label, handling several influential punk and new wave artists, but it also found time for a series of archival releases of such great acts as the Small Faces, the Troggs, Fleetwood Mac, Del Shannon, and Duane Eddy, as well as issuing the original *Nuggets* compilation. In the U.K., Charly became the first of many European labels to plunder rock's history with a fanatical zealousness that, ironically, exceeded anything found in the music's American birthplace. The label scored a major coup by licensing the Sun Records catalog, and expanded its focus to most kinds of rock & roll, soul, and R&B music of the '50s and '60s.

Several other British labels followed suit in the 1980s, plundering the vaults of American labels that, again ironically, weren't able to license their material for U.S. release. The biggest of these were Ace (with several subsidiaries, such as Big Beat), and Demon/Edsel, Elvis Costello's British label. Both companies, as well as Charly, are still around and thriving – joined by others like See for Miles, Sequel, and Beat Goes On – assembling compilations of vintage rock & roll, soul, R&B, British Invasion, and psychedelia whose appeal is probably limited to several thousand buyers worldwide in most cases.

Some authorities have pointed to these reissues, as well as similar compilations of vintage American music from Germany, France, Japan, and even Australia, as proof that great American music is more appreciated overseas than in its birthplace, where the trend-conscious and mindless masses are willfully ignorant of their own heritage. It makes for a nice romantic myth, but a more likely explanation is that American companies are more reluctant to reissue obscure, vintage material for small, specialized audiences.

The U.S. is home to one of the world's leading reissue labels, Rhino, which has expanded from its humble beginnings issuing novelty records to a catalog of several hundred titles, including many vintage Atlantic releases. The label claims that if your collection consisted of nothing but Rhino releases, you'd still have a damned good collection, and for once, the hype is no empty boast. Through its compilations and single-artist collections, Rhino has repackaged truckloads of classic rock & roll of all types from the last 50 years. It tends not to delve into as obscure artists and vaults as its European counterparts, but even so, it still makes room for compilations of acts like the Shadows of Knight and the New Colony Six that were hardly superstars, as well as assembling little-known work by superstars like David Bowie and Roy Orbison, and previously unreleased material by Tim Buckley and Phil Ochs.

The advent of the CD format in the late '80s set off further reissues, for reasons not entirely connected to the industry's belated recognition of its massive heritage. Major labels realized that many listeners – most of them, Baby Boomers – were interested in "upgrading" their scratchy vinyl records with CD versions. They also realized that many consumers were interested in buying albums and compilations of artists whose work had lingered out-of-print for quite some time.

Thus they began reissuing their own back catalog, in addition to licensing it, eventually creating entire subsidiaries like Legacy, the Right Stuff, and Polydor Chronicles for that purpose. Relative to new artists, the production, royalty, and promotion costs on reissues were minimal. Many of these reissues added the further enticements of additional bonus tracks (sometimes unreleased, sometimes from rare non-LP singles), remastering and remixing, and scholarly liner notes. For artists with wide appeal, these factors were often combined into box sets (see separate essay).

U.S. box sets were often fairly selective in their presentation, and the real fanatics continued to go overseas for boxes that were zealously – sometimes indiscriminately – completist. The champion in this department has to be Germany's Bear Family, which has issued box sets of artists like the Browns, Johnny & Jack, Wanda Jackson, and Lefty Frizzell that would be considered impossibly uncommercial in the States. As a whole, Bear Family has been a treasure trove of compilations for American roots music of the '40s, '50s, and (sometimes) '60s, encompassing not just R&B and rockabilly, but country & western, blues, and even an entire box set of music associated with the *Bonanza* TV program, all with exquisitely detailed liner notes. Other overseas companies of note include Germany's Repertoire, with an especially deep '60s catalog, which often adds more bonus tracks than were on the original albums in the first place. Australia's Raven has been crucial in making that country's '60s rock available internationally, and it also packages obscure but worthy British and American rock from the same era, as well as sometimes delving into the '50s and '70s.

It's still true that many U.S. collectors have to go overseas for a good portion, maybe even the majority, of their reissue purchases. There are, however, several companies of note besides Rhino that operate in the United States, including Sundazed (specializing in '60s music of all types), One Way, and Collectables (the most R&B-oriented of the trio). All of these reissue material by "cult" artists that Rhino and the majors may pass on because of their relatively limited audiences.

Finding reissues – which by now number in the thousands, produced by hundreds of companies – doesn't require a secret password, but it does require more work and diligence than driving down to the mini-mall. Collectors are advised to check out *Goldmine* magazine for the best mail-order sources of records that are impossible to find in local stores. Midnight Records (catalog available from P.O. Box 390, Old Chelsea Station, New York, NY 10113-0390) is the most comprehensive of these, although you should check out a few to find what you want and find out what's available on an ongoing basis.

– Richie Unterberger

The Box Set

Walk past a big record store during the Christmas rush, and you're apt to spy Annette Funicello, Barry Manilow, Janis Joplin, and Led Zeppelin under the same tree. An all-star benefit, perhaps, in which the legends have agreed to return from the dead and set aside their stylistic differences for the sake of some good cause or another? Hardly. It's a phenomenon made possible by the rise of the box set. Literally hundreds of artists have now been anthologized in these lavish packages, which now encompass a smorgasbord of musical eras and styles that was unimaginable a decade ago.

According to *Pulse!* magazine, over 150 boxed set retrospectives were released in the U.S. and abroad in 1993. (The figure went down slightly in 1994.) If you were to buy all of them at once, that would set you back about $6500. No one's maniacal enough to go to that extreme, but listeners who go beyond the day's current charts to collect their music have more multi-disc options than ever before.

The box set has been a feature of the music industry for almost as long as records have been manufactured. Before the introduction of the long-playing record in the late 1940s, several 78 rpm discs were occasionally packaged together in boxes, sometimes in accordion-style binders. Material by superstars like Paul Robeson, Duke Ellington, and Benny Goodman was released in this fashion, although the limitations of the 78 required a good deal more disc rotation than multiple CD collections do in the digital age.

With the LP format, it was possible to release several hours of music within a box at once. The boxed set rapidly became widespread in classical releases, but was used much less often to package jazz or pop music. It was virtually never used to house rock & roll music.

After landmark albums like Dylan's *Blonde on Blonde*, the Mothers of Invention's *Freak Out*, and the Beatles' *White Album* made double LPs acceptable in rock, boxes began to appear – although very rarely – to package multi-disc productions. George Harrison's *All Things Must Pass* and *The Concert for Bangladesh* were a couple of the best-selling examples, but they remained rare events. Eventually, box set collections appeared in small quantities by artists with devoted fan bases like the Beatles, Brian Eno, and Bill Nelson.

The introduction of the compact disc, along with the increasing

spending power of Baby Boomers eager to assemble collected works of classic rock and soul musicians, began to spur the production of rock box sets in the mid-1980s. In 1986, Bob Dylan's five-LP *Biograph* set became the first rock retrospective of such size to reach the Top 40 album charts. More importantly, its mix of classic hits, key album cuts, rarities, and previously unreleased material, as well as a lavish booklet, became a model of sorts for the hundreds of rock and pop retrospectives that would follow. Later that year, a five-album box set of live Bruce Springsteen material went to number one. Multi-album live boxes didn't sprout in its aftermath; hardly anyone, after all, has as fanatical a following as Springsteen. What it did prove was that fans were willing to pay for such big, lavish packages in much greater force than most people expected.

Within a few years, the box set as concept had picked up a lot of momentum. Most major rock artists – including Elvis Presley, the Rolling Stones, the Who, Pink Floyd, Aerosmith, Aretha Franklin, Otis Redding, and the Beach Boys – have received the box set treatment. In some cases, such as Elvis's, there are a few box sets, each devoted to different periods of his career. If your favorite famous artist doesn't have a box set yet, wait a while. It may take a few months or a few years, but odds are that one or several will certainly appear.

The impetus for box set production came from both consumers and the industry. Some music journalists may rant and rave about the ignorance of the great majority of the record-buying public, but the fact is that, on the whole, today's rock & roll buyers are probably more conscious of musical history than ever before, and more willing to revisit past favorites and explore vintage releases that they never became familiar with in the first place. From an industry viewpoint, the CD format has enabled labels to present mammoth quantities of material in a more, well, compact form than was possible with the 12-inch LP.

More cynically, the CD format has generated extensive back catalog reissues because it enables the industry to re-sell albums to consumers that they already have in their collection, but may wish to "upgrade" from analog to digital. In comparison with new artists, such back catalog releases require a minimum of fuss in terms of artist development, production, and promotion.

Collectors approach box set reissues with a mixture of joy and resentment. Often billed as "remixed" or "digitally remastered from the original tapes" (although the actual sonic differences may be extremely slight or even nonexistent), some listeners welcome the chance to replace their surface-noise-infested vinyl with fresh packages that will not deteriorate over time. Just as often, it seems, some killjoy or other determines that the remastered and remixed versions are actually distinctly inferior to their analog counterparts, sometimes radically so.

For listeners who aren't audiophiles, the issue of value-for-money remains. Who is the typical box set – with its mixture of hits, rarities, and album cuts – really satisfying? The casual fan will be more likely to pick up a greatest hits collection, or one or two LPs, and leave it at that. It's very rare that a box set will feature every last cut by an artist, so it's seldom that it acts as the definitive collection in and of itself.

Listeners who are serious fans of an artist, but not unduly concerned with fancy packaging or remastering, find themselves caught in the middle. Enticed by rare and unreleased cuts that appear on almost every one of these sets – but rarely make up the majority of the content – they often find themselves paying quite a few dollars for the five to 15 cuts from a multi-disc box that they really want, and repurchasing quite a bit of music that they already have in their collection, and had no intention of buying again. And it's rare that a record company will accommodate these discerning listeners by issuing a separate collection that only contains the sought-after rarities.

For the truly comprehensive box sets, listeners often need to look to Europe, where reissue labels are truly fanatical about their music. Germany's Bear Family is particularly legendary for its almost humorously exhaustive retrospectives, such as its five-CD Lesley Gore compilation, its four-CD Marvin Rainwater set, and its eight-CD Lonnie Donegan project. These can be just as exhausting as exhaustive – do you *really* want to hear that Gene Vincent alternate take, or over 200 Fats Domino songs?

An essential part of record collecting as the 20th century ends, the box sets offer a mixed blessing – access to more rock music than ever before, but at a higher price.

– Richie Unterberger

Cassette Culture

The punk and new wave explosion of the late '70s is remembered, among other things, for having brought the do-it-yourself ethic into popular music. The formation of numerous independent labels, distribution networks, fanzines, studios, and whatnot were unified not so much by musical style as a determination to do things their way, without concessions to corporate or commercial demands. One application of the DIY ethic that was relatively unheralded, then and now, was the proliferation of independently recorded music distributed by cassette. Perhaps the purest expression of the DIY ethic, its impact upon the commercial scene has been almost nonexistent, even as the number of cassette-only releases has multiplied many times over the last 15 years.

The cassette tape itself is a relatively new technology, only becoming a commonplace household item in the 1970s. It was introduced by the recording industry as a step up from bulky reel-to-reel tapes in portability (if not sound quality), and from the clunky eight-track tapes in both portability *and* sound quality. In the marketplace, it's been an unqualified success, accounting for more sales than any other format (that statistic can vary according to the source you read). Many listeners turned improved technology to their advantage taping their friends' records or by taping music off the radio, actions that continue to get the industry up in arms and threatening sales taxes, although the actual impact of such home taping on overall sales is probably pretty slight.

Cassettes, of course, could be used to tape lots of other things besides official releases, including privately performed music. As many channels as the DIY ethic had opened for independent and self-released vinyl (compact discs weren't around then), it didn't necessarily open the door for any old musician who wanted to record and distribute his or her music. Independent labels still need to be fairly selective about who they sign, and the costs of pressing discs on your own label can be fairly high for those on a tight budget. Releasing music on cassette, though there is a slight drop in sonic quality in comparison to vinyl or compact disc, became an increasingly popular alternative for musicians who were unable to land a record contract, were determined to do things exactly their way without the involvement of third parties, or who simply wanted to record their own work as an avocation.

The range of cassette-only releases is, to say the least, extremely diverse. There are probably more rock (especially underground rock), experimental, and electronic cassettes than any other, but all types are represented, including traditional folk, world music, jazz, reggae, and what have you. The sound quality can vary from state-of-the-art to absolutely excruciating, challenging the negative standards of the worst bootlegs.

The purposes of these cassettes are similarly varied. Some are only meant for circulation to friends and family; some are intended to be taken as legitimate releases and judged on the same level as commercially available CDs; some are basically demo tapes, sent to stir up interest from record companies or clubs; some are out-and-out self-indulgent wanking, of no possible interest to anyone other than the perpetrators. Musicians without record deals often have a stock of professionally recorded cassettes of their work to sell at their gigs, or even on the street if they perform there.

A genuine network of musicians and listeners attuned to the cassette-only format didn't begin to evolve until the early '80s, when cassette-only releases received increasing attention in fanzines and national publications, especially the defunct *Op*. Cassette culture continues to get a reasonable amount of attention in underground publications to this day, although there's no central magazine or clearinghouse dealing with the sub genre; *Option* printed many cassette reviews in its early years, shrinking its coverage of the medium steadily until now it only reviews such releases rarely. Radio stations (though almost exclusively college and non-commercial ones) also give cassette releases much more exposure than they did 10 or 15 years ago, occasionally devoting entire program slots to such items.

Just as a glass can be viewed as half empty or half full, there are two valid ways of looking at cassette-only releases. From the most positive viewpoint, no recording medium is as unencumbered by commercial expectations, or as conducive to total artistic freedom. This applies right down to the sleeves, which are often hand-printed or hand-designed. For the increasingly large numbers of musicians who have home studios, or at least enough home studio equipment to record music with some semblance of professional quality, it's the easiest way to record and distribute their music.

Some would argue that the DIY ethic, wonderful in principle, allows many unformed, imitative, repetitious, and downright embarrassing musical ventures to be expressed through the cassette medium. Just as cassettes enable quality artists to record their music free of commercial pressures, they also enable those without any appreciable talent to record their mediocre, or downright excruciating, music for posterity. Without any professional standards to adhere to, the sound quality on many cassettes is awful, at times absolutely unlistenable. There are even some top-flight cassette artists who abuse the lack of quality-control in the medium by flooding the market with dozens of releases, some of them half-baked live performances or studio experiments.

Those aiming to take a gander at the world of cassettes should be aware that it's not only a haven for musicians who don't have a home on conventional record labels, but for entire genres of music that gain CD release very infrequently. Thus there is a high percentage of tape-only releases in the noise/industrial/experimental category, as well as other fairly esoteric genres like natural sounds and spoken word. That's not to say that the best of these aren't quality work, but that the medium as a whole leans considerably further to the avant-garde end of the spectrum than the larger music community.

Very few artists make significant profits through their cassette-only releases; the great majority are available solely through the mail, usually from the musicians themselves, who are often quite amenable to simply trading for other tapes. There are a few artists in cassetteland who have established a reputation, albeit a cult one,for the large volume and high quality of their tapes. R. Stevie Moore, who has made his own tapes since the 1970s (as well as occasional vinyl), is one of the most famous, purveying a sort of avant-garde pop/rock. Underground rock guitarist Eugene Chadbourne, though he's released many "real" albums, has released many more cassettes, often sold on the road at gigs. Experimental musicians Amy Denio and John Oswald, among others, released cassettes before attaining a higher level of visibility within the "new music" community.

Cassette culture's influence upon alternative rock is slight but tangible. The grand majority of rock bands choosing cassettes as their medium will never be heard by the larger audience, although there are occasional examples of well-known, or somewhat-known, bands like Throwing Muses, Sebadoh, or Pianosaurus that released their own cassettes before landing record deals. Liz Phair's *Girlysound* tapes introduced much of the material that later became famous on her first two albums in intimate, low-fi versions, although these were largely intended for friends rather than a general audience. They were instrumental in landing her record deal, however, and are now among the most popular "unreleased" tapes ever recorded by a major artist. The British band Cleaners from Venus was usually content to release its delightfully eccentric British pop, which held its own with XTC and Robyn Hitchcock, via cassette only. Calvin Johnson's K label introduced notable alternative rock acts like Lois and Johnson's own band, Beat Happening, on cassette releases; the first American Shonen Knife release was on a K cassette (although the music had appeared on vinyl in Japan). Artists like Linda Smith and Jeff Kelly issued high-quality music on cassette that was inferior to "officially" released alternative rock only in its channels of distribution. And occasionally, talented performers who found themselves without a record contract for no apparent reason released their own cassettes to fill the gap, as Penelope Houston did in the early '90s.

Most rap music is played and bought on cassette, and the cassette – in the form of special mixes, self-produced and distributed releases, or (more nefariously) bootlegs – is a big part of rap/hip-hop culture, particularly in New York City, where one can pick up cassette compilations and mixes of hot sounds literally on the street. Oakland rapper Too Short began his climb to platinum success with a self-distributed cassette that sold in the thousands before he hooked up with a record label.

There are also a few cassette labels that have carved an identity for themselves as repositories of high quality, non-mainstream music, differing only from similar record companies in their choice of format. Some of the most prominent of these include ROIR, with an extensive catalog of cassette-only releases by big-name alternative rock artists (with occasional detours into other music) such as Television, Richard Hell, and Nico; Tellus, one of the leading experimental/new music labels of any sort; and Global Village and Music of the World, both specializing in world music. Several of these labels have switched to the compact disc format, upgrading some or all of their back catalog in the wake of the CD revolution.

Finally, it's worth remembering that the cassette remains the primary means of musical distribution, by far, in the Third World. In many of these countries, copyright laws are lax, nonexistent, or unenforced, and pirate tapes are common items in markets and stores, ranging from local musicians to international superstars like the Beatles, Bob Marley, Dire Straits, and Marvin Gaye. Much of the music from these countries is only available in the cassette format, as it's by far the cheapest medium for populations with much lower per-capita incomes than the U.S. or Europe, and a great deal of fine world music is only available on cassette, and only within the performers' native territories.

Book

Cassette Mythos, edited by Robin James (Autonomedia, 1992)
— *Richie Unterberger*

Reference Books

♦♦♦ Behind the Hits: Inside Stories of Classic Pop and Rock and Roll *by Bob Shannon & John Javna* (Warner Books, 1986) Not highbrow stuff, but a pretty fun collection of little-known stories about hit rock records from the '50s to the '80s, weighted considerably toward the '60s and '50s. Grouped by categories like accidental hits, covers, "firsts", novelty tunes, songs inspired by real characters, and classics that came to life in freak studio circumstances, covering over a couple hundred songs. And they choose classics, generally, although occasionally one has cause to wonder whether anyone's interested in the genesis of Toto's "Rosanna" or Henry Gross's "Shannon." Well researched, with lots of fascinating and funny stories from the artists, session musicians, songwriters, DJs, and producers – *Richie Unterberger*

♦♦ The Billboard Book of Top 40 Hits *by Joel Whitburn* (Billboard, 1992). One should avoid the temptation to view this as a gospel of pop and rock history, given all the dubious chart measurement standards and payola scandals that have gone down in the rock era. Nevertheless, this fat listing of every single to make the Billboard Top 40 charts from 1955 to mid-1991 is a useful reference work, tracking the most widely used standard of sales and popularity – the charts published in *Billboard* magazine. Every listing includes the single's peak position, date of entry, and weeks on the chart, along with the label and catalog number. Arranged by artist, every song title is indexed in the back. The personnel listings, birthdates, and other trivia that accompany many of the entries can be useful, but be aware that they contain a surprising number of errors. – Richie Unterberger

♦♦ The Blackwell Guide To Blues Records *edited by Paul Oliver* (Blackwell, 1989) The most comprehensive reference book of its sort, not to say that it's even close to perfect, but there's really not much competition. The Blackwell layout is daunting for the novice: lots of essays of varying quality on regional styles, tons of song listings, and many fine capsule reviews of albums, ranging from famous to very, very obscure. Divided into chapters covering both regions (such as postwar Chicago) and styles (piano blues, "downhome postwar blues"), it also covers subgenres like rhythm and blues and soul blues that some purists would have regarded as too diluted and commercial to include. It's not the kind of thing you can read in a few sittings, but if you have reasonable patience, there's a lot of valuable information here, and the authors are good at pinpointing the best anthologies and starting points. – *Richie Unterberger*

♦♦ The Blackwell Guide to Soul Recordings *edited by Robert Pruter* (Blackwell, 1993) As books, the Blackwell Guides aren't the greatest; the essays sometimes cover such wide territory that they lose readers who aren't familiar with the subject, the writing can be dry, and the interspersion of reviews, essays, and discographical data is a bit of a jumble. Still, this is the best survey of soul recordings, divided by region, covering the music from its '50s R&B beginnings through "funk and later trends," as the last chapter is titled. In addition to all the expected big names, there are reviews of quite a few performers known primarily to the soul collector community, such as McKinley Mitchell, Lorraine Ellison, Shorty Long, Howard Tate, and Betty Harris. The book might benefit from focusing more on the concise reviews, which are usually quite good, but in any case this has info on a lot of performers that aren't reviewed in the more famous record guides. Inevitably, it misses a lot of reissues from the last two or three years that have been generated from the compact disc explosion. – *Richie Unterberger*

♦♦♦ Blues: The British Connection *by Bob Brunning* (Blanford Press, 1986) Brunning is not only an authority on British blues-rock, he was there: he played bass in the first lineup of Fleetwood Mac before John McVie joined, and went on to play with Savoy Brown and other blues-rock groups. This is a good survey of British blues-rock from the days of Alexis Korner through the 1980s, concentrating mostly on the 1960s, when the form was in its heyday. There are chapters devoted to all the major groups: the Yardbirds, John Mayall, Pretty Things, Spencer Davis, Manfred Mann, Graham Bond, Fleetwood Mac, Groundhogs, Ten Years After, Chicken Shack, Rory Gallagher, producer Mike Vernon. A lot of them are spiced by first hand recollections from band members; the ones missing these are considerably weaker. The sections on minor figures like Dave Kelly, Savoy Brown, and the Blues Band hold considerably less interest than the ones on the more important musicians, but it does give a pretty complete picture of the scene. –*Richie Unterberger*

♦♦♦♦ Bootleg: The Secret History of the Other Recording Industry *by Clinton Heylin* (St. Martin's, 1995) The inner machinations of the rock bootleg industry, responsible for literally thousands of important recordings that have never surfaced via official music business channels, have remained shadowy and murky even to many bootleg enthusiasts. This book doesn't solve all of the mysteries, but it's an often fascinating document of the growth of bootlegs since the late '60s, when unreleased recordings by Dylan, the Beatles, and the Stones gave them a jump start. Heylin talks to many of the principal bootleggers of the past and present (going on the record, necessarily, anonymously). This sheds valuable light on how the industry grew – the often farcical circumstances under which bootlegs were clandestinely manufactured and distributed, about absorbing anecdotes behind the acquisition of rare studio tapes, the mechanics of unauthorized live taping, the vehement attempts by the international record industry to eliminate bootlegs from public access. There are also discussions of the musical content of dozens of the most crucial bootlegs, investigations of music industry claims that they are financially harmful and artistically inferior, and evaluations of the importance of material archived on bootleg and the public's right to hear it. The lengthy passages detailing copyrights and legalities may be too dry for the music-oriented reader, and I would have preferred more extensive comments about the music itself (though there's a fair amount of that). But it's a valuable window into a previously hush-hush topic, and even those opposed to bootlegs will find much to think about in Heylin's persuasive arguments that unauthorized recordings represent no threat to the above-ground industry or artists' livelihood (the average bootleg title sells well under 5000 units), and have brought to light recordings of immense importance. – *Richie Unterberger*

♦♦♦ Bringing It All Back Home *by Robbie Woliver* (Pantheon, 1986) Ostensibly built around the New York club Folk City, this is really a story of the music scene of Greenwich Village, which has been crucial to the folk, folk-rock, and singer/songwriter scenes since the early '60s. Most of the book is oral history, with Woliver providing brief narrative links. Dozens of interviewees get space to tell stories, and the list covers just about everybody who was anybody who was based in New York (and some who weren't) and participated in the scene: Dylan, Roger McGuinn, Joan Baez, Judy Collins, Arlo Guthrie, John Sebastian, Dave Van Ronk, Peter Stampfel, Mary Travers, Lenny Kaye, Steve Forbert, Pete Seeger, and Suzanne Vega, among many others, on down to fairly obscure, if influential, figures like Carolyn Hester, Jean Ritchie, and Buzzy Linhart. The book loses a bit of continuity in the last sections, as the scene expanded to include punk and new wave acts like Patti Smith, Talking Heads, the Ramones, the Violent Femmes, and so forth who couldn't be considered part of the folk and folk-rock lineage. But it still contains a great deal of lore that will interest almost any folk and rock fan. An identical version of the book was issued by St. Martin's under the title *Hoot!: A 25-Year History of the Greenwich Village Music Scene. – Richie Unterberger*

✦✦✦✦✦ The British Invasion *by Nicholas Schaffner* (McGraw-Hill, 1982) By far the best account of the '60s musical movement that, more than virtually any other, changed the face of rock music. A combination reference work and general interest account, with the accent on the general interest, Schaffner devotes entire chapters to the Beatles, Rolling Stones, Who, Pink Floyd, Kinks, T. Rex, and David Bowie, adding an overview of the punk/new wave explosion. These performers have been written about at great length elsewhere, to be sure, but Schaffner uncovers a great deal of obscure information and quotes from old reviews while telling their stories in an entertaining and critically acute fashion. There are also brief but info-packed one- and two-page sketches of 100 of the most notable British rockers, from 1964 to 1980. It includes a wealth of photos and chart information as well.. – *Richie Unterberger*

✦✦ Call Up the Groups!, *by Alan Clayson* (Blandford Press, 1985) Dedicated to "The Golden Age of British Beat 1962-67," this is a 200-page collection of profiles of virtually every U.K. group to land a British or American hit during the British Invasion, as well as a few who didn't. As a reference book, it has shortcomings. Clayson's writing is erratic, both in quality and depth. Many entries stick to dry, bare-bones facts without offering insightful description or critiques of the performers' music; others have some colorful commentary about their stage presence or behavior without really conveying a sense of what they sounded like, or assessing their significance to the British rock scene. And there are no essays covering the development of the British Invasion as a whole, or putting its various sub genres and styles into some kind of context. Stick with Nicholas Schaffner's *The British Invasion* for the best document of the movement, but those who want to dig deeper will find a lot of details on more obscure acts (although the coverage could be a lot better), as well as a wealth of photos. – *Richie Unterberger*

✦✦✦✦ Christgau's Record Guide: Rock Albums of the '70s *by Robert Christgau* (Da Capo Press, 1990) As the longtime rock critic for the *Village Voice*, Christgau is one of the most famous American rock journalists. In a monthly column, he offers paragraph-long reviews of most significant releases, assigning each of them a grade, from A to E. This is a book-length compilation, almost 500 pages worth, of such reviews from the '70s, refurbished a bit from their original publication. Very few people feel neutral about Christgau; the blunt viciousness of some of his putdowns is bound to make all of his readers angry at some point or another, and the academic obtuseness of some of his evaluations can be infuriating. As a reference book, though, this is pretty valuable, covering just about every release of major significance from the decade, and quite a few of minor significance. You will often disagree with him, but he almost always knows what he's talking about, and most of the pithy reviews convey the essential characteristics of the disc, even if you find his "grade" incorrect. Covers all kinds of rock and soul, and a fair number of reggae, jazz, and other sundry non-rock releases as well. – *Richie Unterberger*

✦✦✦✦ Christgau's Record Guide: The '80s *by Robert Christgau* (Pantheon, 1990) 500 more pages, in exactly the same format as his compilation of '70s reviews, this time covering the following decade. All of the comments for his '70s volume apply here, though it seems as though there's a higher percentage of frustratingly obtuse reviews. Again, covers all kinds of aboveground and underground rock and soul, as well as plenty of world music, reggae, country, and other kinds of non-rock. The most significant gap is the absence of quite a few indie alternative rock records; as Christgau himself notes in his opening essays, the '80s were categorized by fragmentation and increasing diversity, and he drew the line at absorbing and reviewing a lot of records he might have found time for in previous years. For those, we'll have to look in *The Trouser Press Record Guide* and *Option*. Includes extensive introductory remarks about '80s rock. – *Richie Unterberger*

✦✦✦✦ Country on Compact Disc *by the Country Music Foundation, edited by Paul Kingsbury* (1993, Grove Press) There's a major shortage of good critical reference works on country records – country of all kinds, encompassing traditional sounds, bluegrass, and Nashville. This is by far the best, strongly resem-

bling the *Rolling Stone Album Guide* in format, with its one-to-five star rating system and combination career/discography overviews. The writing's very good – a rarity in country journalism – and very catholic in taste, viewing Jimmie Rodgers and Garth Brooks as part of the same spectrum, in the manner that rock critics can view Elvis Presley and Madonna as part of the same phenomenon. Some might find their assessments of the current Nashville crop too generous, but in treating the so-called "Hats" with seriousness, they are according them respectful evaluations that are merited by the fact that much of mainstream America listens to such music more than anything else. The chief flaw is the limited scope of the volume – as the title implies, only albums which have been issued on compact disc are reviewed, which makes the guide extremely strong on records of the late '80s and early '90s, but omits quite a few vintage albums that hadn't come out on CD by 1993. – *Richie Unterberger*

✦✦✦✦ Deep Blues *by Robert Palmer* (Viking Press, 1981). Renowned critic, and sometime musician, Palmer traces the evolution of a major (perhaps THE major) strain of blues, from rural Mississippi Delta acoustic forms through its move to the cities, particularly Chicago, where it became amplified and provided a bedrock foundation for rock & roll. There are more comprehensive, scholarly analyses of the blues available, but this is the most readable and accessible by a wide margin, with plenty of first hand recollections from Muddy Waters, Robert Lockwood, Jr., Sam Phillips, and others. – *Richie Unterberger*

✦✦✦✦✦ England's Dreaming *by Jon Savage* (Faber & Faber, 1991) A mammoth, absorbing history of the birth of British punk, focusing primarily on the Sex Pistols, but including lots of coverage of early pioneers such as the Clash and the Buzzcocks, as well as the accompanying birth of a punk subculture as reflected through fanzines and the music's audience. Packed with great stories about the group's unlikely birth and success, peppered with succinct social analysis and recollections from a lot of those who were there at the time. Even if you don't care for punk, this is fascinating reading, exploring the birth of a movement that upset the industry, and the public at large, to an almost unimaginable extent. Sometimes the focus rambles, and sometimes the sociopolitical analysis gets a trifle too weighty, but these are minor quibbles. Includes a huge discography, with critical commentary, on almost every early punk record of note. – *Richie Unterberger*

✦✦✦✦ Feel Like Going Home, *by Peter Guralnick* (Vintage, 1971) Guralnick is one of America's premier writers and critics of roots music, and this collection of his early essays is an important work, offering sensitive and in-depth portraits of a gaggle of major early rock and blues stars: Jerry Lee Lewis, Howlin' Wolf, Charlie Rich, Muddy Waters, Skip James, Johnny Shines, Charlie Rich, and the owners of Sun and Chess Records. Guralnick spent a lot of time with each of his subjects, often observing them at home or on stage; in some cases, he was apparently the first journalist to treat the musician as a serious artist. Perhaps as a result, he landed some poignant and personal material, the kind that publicists have learned to shield from serious but inquisitive writers. Guralnick does tend to romanticize his heroes as artists who have never received their just due, but this is one of the best books of its kind. – *Richie Unterberger*

✦✦✦✦✦ From the Velvets to the Voidoids: A Pre-punk History for a Post-Punk World *by Clinton Heylin* (Penguin, 1993) The definitive history of early American punk and new wave, focusing mostly upon the New York scene clustered around CBGB's, as well as some Cleveland artists (the groups that sprang up in the wake of the early punk explosion in California and other areas are not covered). Alternating between Heylin's text and dozens of fascinating quotes and recollections from key players like Patti Smith, Tom Verlaine, and David Johansen, this has lots of little-heard stories of punk's evolution in the early and mid-'70s. Patti Smith, Television, Blondie, the Ramones, the New York Dolls, the Talking Heads, Suicide, Richard Hell, and Pere Ubu are all covered exhaustively, and the early chapters document such important pre-punk pioneers as the Velvet Underground, the MC5, the Stooges, and the Modern Lovers. A large critical discography covers both released material and bootlegs. Combined with Jon Savage's British punk history, *England's Dreaming*, it's the best document of early punk to date. – *Richie Unterberger*

✦✦ Fortunate Son: The Best of Dave Marsh *by Dave Marsh* (Random House, 1985) Probably America's most famous rock critic, Dave Marsh has often ranked among the nation's best, though his reputation has suffered in the past decade or so due to his idolatry of Bruce Springsteen, the hectoring tone of his publication, *Rock'n'Roll Confidential,* and his inability to fully come to grips with alternative rock and other recent trends. This anthology covers roughly 15 years of his writing, and doesn't dig beyond the mainstream too much. That's not a flaw; there are dozens of interesting, at times insightful, pieces here on many of the most worthy rock icons, including Marvin Gaye, Muddy Waters, Elvis Presley, Sly & the Family Stone, and the Rolling Stones, in addition to essays on general developments in soul, disco, and punk, as well as probes into film, books, and aspects of the rock business. Sometimes his opinions are didactic, and he's as much bewildered by punk and post-early '70s underground rock as excited by it. But this collection is worth reading, highlighted perhaps by passionate musings on heroes from his Detroit hometown (Mitch Ryder, Bob Seger, Iggy Pop, the MC5). – *Richie Unterberger*

✦✦✦✦✦ Girl Groups: The Story of a Sound *by Alan Betrock* (Delilah, 1982) Definitive and entertaining history of the early '60s girl groups, covering all of the keystones of the style: the singers, the producers, and the songwriters. It has in-depth histories of all of the major girl group performers: the Chantels, the Shirelles, the Shangri-Las, Lesley Gore, Mary Wells, Martha & the Vandellas, the Supremes, the Ronettes, the Crystals, the Chiffons, the Dixie Cups, the Angels, and more. But it's not a reference book: it's written as a story, with large sections on the Brill Building songwriters who wrote many girl group classics, Phil Spector, and the Red Bird label (home of several of the best girl groups). With first-hand memories from many of the principal singers and songwriters, lots of photos, and penetrating commentary about the reasons for the style's vast success and swift downfall in the mid-'60s, this is one of the best rock & roll books. –*Richie Unterberger*

✦✦✦✦✦ Good Rockin' Tonight: Sun Records and the Birth of Rock 'n' Roll *by Colin Escott with Martin Hawkins* (St. Martin's Press, 1991) Excellent history of what was, in the final estimation, the label most responsible for launching rock & roll, although the contributions of other indies like Atlantic were also immensely important. Includes chapters on all the major Sun stars: Elvis, Johnny Cash, Carl Perkins, Jerry Lee Lewis, and Roy Orbison. Of equal interest, though, are the descriptions of owner/producer Sam Phillips's slap-echo studio sound and distinctive artistic vision, which also encompassed a wealth of blues and country music. Besides first- and second-hand interviews with the most famous characters in the Sun story, you also hear from more obscure performers and sidemen, and get profiles of relatively unheralded artists like Warren Smith and Junior Parker. Fascinating stuff, this is an updated version of a history first published around 1980, and includes a good deal of new information and many great photos. – *Richie Unterberger*

✦✦ The Haight-Ashbury, *by Charles Perry* (Rolling Stone Press, 1984) Not a rock book, this is nonetheless recommended reading for anyone interested in late-'60s rock in general, and in San Francisco psychedelic rock in particular. The interplay between counterculture and music was more fervid in San Francisco's Haight-Ashbury in the mid- and late '60s than almost any other scene. Perry was there, and he chronicles the period with absorbing detail, covering the psychedelic drug culture, the community organizations, the local press, the live performance spaces, the clashes between youth and authority, and the music. – *Richie Unterberger*

✦✦ The History of Scottish Rock and Pop: All That Ever Mattered *by Brian Hogg* (Guinness Publishing, UK, 1993) Like Ireland, Scotland, a tiny country (a little over five million people), has made impressive contributions to rock history way out of proportion to its actual size. The problem in assembling a history of Scottish rock for this volume, a companion to a BBC television series, is that it (like Irish rock, for that matter) lacks strong unifying stylistic elements. Lulu, Alex Harvey, the Bay City Rollers, Donovan, the Average White Band, the Incredible String Band, Gerry Rafferty, Simple Minds, the Jesus & Mary Chain, Primal Scream, Teenage Fanclub – yes, all have made an international impact, but they haven't exactly sprung from similar musical schools. And while most rock fans will be interested in the histories of a few of these performers, very few will be interested in all of them, which makes this quite a jumpy read, no matter what your taste. The 400 pages contain a lot of information, much of it quite obscure, and as such, it's a reasonably valuable reference, but general readers are advised to go for the chapters or sections covering performers they're interested in, and not feel guilty about skipping chunks altogether. – *Richie Unterberger*

✦✦✦ Hollywood Rock *by Marshall Crenshaw* (Harper Perennial, 1994) "A guide to rock'n'roll in the movies," this falls second to the best reference book to rock films, *Rock on Film,* despite covering movies through 1993 (*Rock on Film* only got to the beginning of the 1980s). The reviews are longer, but the writing isn't quite as good, and it fails to mention some interesting items entirely that made it into *Rock on Film.* There aren't any separate essays to put the whole rock film genre into context, and more importantly, the reviewers often demonstrate a weakness for schlock, giving too many four- and five-star ratings to silly beach and exploitation films, as fun as those might be if you're in a certain mood. Still, a very useful guide to have around, including about 300 reviews, and brief capsule descriptions of a few hundred more. – *Richie Unterberger*

✦✦✦✦ Incredibly Strange Music, Volume 1 & 2 (RE/SEARCH, 1993 & 1994). For all the tens of thousands of albums covered by current reference books music recordings, there are tens of thousands of others that never get covered. These are the kind of albums and singles that populate thrift shops, garage sales, and attics: exotica, novelty, soundtracks, unknown regional 45s of all styles. These fat volumes consist primarily of fascinating interviews with major record collectors, talking about their weirdest obscure albums. And these are plenty weird, ranging from inept musical excursions by celebrities to a choir of ex-drug addicts to fusions of psychedelia and muzak. Several of these collectors are musical celebrities in their own right, such as Jello Biafra, the Cramps, and *Kicks* magazine publishers Billy Miller and Miriam Linna; there are also interviews with cult artists like exotica king Martin Denny, spoken word master Ken Nordine, and Robert Moog. Judging from the compilation of music that Caroline put out to accompany the first volume, a lot of this stuff might not be as mindbendingly strange and exciting as it seems from the descriptions. Still, for anyone interested in record collecting or musical/pop culture of all sorts, this is real edge-of-the-chair reading, with hundreds of great reproductions of some of the strangest album sleeves you'll ever see. –*Richie Unterberger*

✦✦ The L.A. Musical History Tour *by Art Fein* (Faber & Faber, 1991) "A guide to the rock and roll landmarks of Los Angeles," this has photos and entertaining capsule descriptions of over 200 local homes, studios, clubs, record stores, hotels, restaurants, album cover sites, gravestones, and other locations that made their mark on rock & roll history. Fein's a witty and knowledgeable writer, as interested in Eddie Cochran's gravestone or the canyon where the Rolling Stones were photographed for the High Tide sleeve as world-famous images like the Capitol Records Tower and the Whisky-A-Go-Go. Full of interesting trivia, this is a frivolous project, yes, but a highly enjoyable one. –*Richie Unterberger*

✦✦✦✦ Lost Highway, *by Peter Guralnick* (Vintage, 1979) Like his previous *Feel Like Going Home,* these are more first-rate, extremely human portrayals of major American roots musicians, going much heavier on the Country & Western this time around (though blues and early rock musicians are also included). Many musicians of the first echelon and a few more obscure noteworthies are included in this gallery of portraits, including Ernest Tubb, Hank Snow, Rufus Thomas, Bobby Bland, Scotty Moore, Charlie Feathers, Mickey Gilley, Waylon Jennings, Merle Haggard, James Talley, Joe Turner, Howlin' Wolf, and Otis Spann. – *Richie Unterberger*

✦✦✦ Louie, Louie, *by Dave Marsh* (Hyperion, 1993). An unusual idea for a rock book, done well. "Louie Louie" is the quintessential garage rock tune, and has been covered by more artists than almost any other rock & roll song. Marsh traces its genesis through the decades, from the original 1956 version by unsung L.A. R&B singer Richard Berry (who himself based it on a riff from an obscure cha cha number). A regional hit that was pretty much left for dead, it was revived a few years later by several Northwest bands, culminating in the unlikely number two national hit by the Kingsmen in 1963. Its classic three-chord riff came to ensure its place as a rock & roll standard, after overcoming a ludicrous FBI investigation into the supposed lewdness of its lyrics. Eventually it inspired "Louie Louie" radio marathons, and campaigns to adopt it as the official Washington State song. Marsh follows the trail all the way (the description of the early-'60s Northwest rock & roll scene, a forerunner of garage rock and punk, is especially interesting), ending with the rights to the composition finally getting restored to its rightful owner, Richard Berry. Some of Marsh's recent work has been heavy-handed, but this study, if it can be called that, combines an appropriate sense of humor and affection with its scholarly detail.

♦♦♦ Making Tracks by Charlie Gillett (1974, Souvenir Press) Gillett is the author of the first comprehensive (and still one of the most acclaimed) rock & roll histories, The Sound of the City. This is his history of Atlantic Records, the most successful independent to survive from rock & roll's earliest days. More a history of the music than the business, anyone who's interested in early R&B and rock will find a lot of absorbing reading here. Gillett interviewed Atlantic principals Ahmet Ertegun and (to a significantly greater degree) Jerry Wexler extensively, yielding a lot of firsthand recollections about the early careers of such important artists as Ruth Brown, Clyde McPhatter, Joe Turner, Ray Charles, Solomon Burke, Otis Redding, and Aretha Franklin. Important ancillary figures like Jesse Stone, songwriters Jerry Leiber and Mike Stoller, and Rick Hall of Fame Studios in Muscle Shoals, AL, also get a chance to speak. Gillett is principally an R&B and soul man, so Atlantic's ventures into pop, White rock, and British rock are covered in considerably less depth, although they aren't neglected. —Richie Unterberger

♦♦ Music Man by Dorothy Wade & Justine Picardie (1990, W.W. Norton) Atlantic Records chief Ahmet Ertegun may have been a more conscientious guy, and more knowledgeable musical authority, than most of the other figureheads of independent companies that helped launch rock & roll. He still had to play the music business game to survive and thrive, especially in the early days, when that meant courting favor with disc jockeys or wangling complicated and tense deals to ensure the company's success. Knowledge of this underbelly of intrigue behind rock & roll is valuable, if fairly depressing in its low premium upon ethics. The book details the machinations behind a big record label fairly well at times, but suffers from two problems. First, it can't decide whether to be a specific history of Ertegun/Atlantic or of rock & roll wheeling and dealing as a whole, veering off into tangents about such avaracious early rock businessmen as Morris Levy and Alan Freed, and throwing in bits of history about other independent labels and scandalous behavior in the music industry. Second, little sense of Ertegun/Atlantic's specific vision, which saw them launch or sustain the careers of such giants as Ray Charles, Aretha Franklin, Led Zeppelin, Crosby, Stills & Nash, and the Rolling Stones, emerges. For that tale, as well as a much more focused read, seek out Charlie Gillett's Making Tracks, a fine history of Atlantic from a more musical perspective. —Richie Unterberger

♦♦ Off The Record: An Oral History Of Popular Music by Joe Smith, edited by Mitchell Fink (1988, Warner Books) As a DJ, and more especially as a high-ranking executive for Warner Brothers, Elektra/Asylum, and Capitol, Joe Smith has been an important figure in the music business. Over the course of four decades or so, he's met most of the major players, and this 430-page volume has oral histories from over 200 of them; musicians mostly, but also important producers, songwriters, and industry moguls. Breadth is not the problem here; the majority of the major rock legends are present, from Dylan and members of the Beatles and Stones down. Each history, though, runs only a page or two, so this could hardly be considered an in-depth or satisfying work, though plenty of interesting morsels and trivia emerge in these brief overviews. —Richie Unterberger

♦♦♦♦♦ The Penguin Guide To Jazz On CD, LP & Cassette by Richard Cook & Brian Morton (1994, Penguin) One of the most impressive musical reference books of any sort, this has 1,400 pages of informed, detailed criticism of several thousands of jazz

albums of every stripe. The authors really know their stuff, and rate each record on a scale from one to four stars. Some minor reservations: the listings, as mammoth as they are, include only albums that are in print, excluding quite a few noteworthy, even classic, works; the writing can be a bit obtuse; and the entries usually plunge right into reviews of specific albums, without supplying thumbnail biographical data or a summary/perspective of the artists' significance and their overall contribution to jazz. It's still an essential reference work, one which no jazz fan should be without. —Richie Unterberger

♦♦♦ Pete Frame's Rock Family Trees, by Pete Frame (1979, Quick Fox) If your collection is big enough, chances are you've got some Pete Frame family trees residing in your liner notes. Rock fanatic and graphic artist Frame specializes in family trees detailing a band's evolution, through the years and different lineups; he'll often group several bands of a particular region or style together to illustrate the incestuous trades and comings-and-goings. Alongside the "trees," in tiny print, is commentary not only explaining who played what and when, and why people came and left, but also featuring some fascinating trivia and critical comments. This volume gathers together a few dozen of his best trees, encompassing many of the major bands of the '60s and '70s, and is both a fun read and a valuable resource work. A second volume documents the trees of less interesting artists, and is much less essential; both volumes were recently combined into one book and reissued. —Richie Unterberger

♦♦♦ Punk Diary 1970-1979 by George Gimarc (1994, St. Martin's) Not a personal diary, but a comprehensive diary of notable record releases, live shows, band personnel changes, and other noteworthy developments in early punk rock, concentrating of course much more heavily on 1976-79 than 1970-75, arranged by exact date. This is somewhat more developed than an assemblage of raw data, but somewhat less than a work of prose. Gimarc condenses the events into matter-of-fact sentences and paragraphs, drawing heavily from quotes and articles that appeared at the time in magazines like NME, peppering the entries with reproductions of record sleeves and promotional posters. It's only recommended to serious punk fans, but those will find it a valuable reference work, if a bit on the dry side. —Richie Unterberger

♦♦♦ Rythm Oil by Stanley Booth (1991, Pantheon) He hasn't written prolifically, and he hasn't written much about music that was performed after the early '70s, but Memphis writer Booth is one of the best chroniclers of blues, soul, and rock that draws upon those influences. This collection of essays, often drawn from first-person experiences with the musicians at recording sessions, concerts, and their homes, includes good pieces on Otis Redding, Furry Lewis, B.B. King, Elvis, Janis Joplin, Al Green, James Brown, and little-known but widely respected Memphis jazz pianist Phineas Newborn. An adept critic, Booth's special skill is drawing upon the cultural ambience of the music – often Memphis, almost always the American South – to give a deeper understanding of how their environment, professional and personal, informs their art. —Richie Unterberger

♦♦ Rock Around The Bloc by Timothy W. Ryback (1990, Oxford University Press) Ever since rock began, it's been received with vociferous enthusiasm in Eastern Europe and the former Soviet Union, and, until the recent thaw of the cold war, met with equally zealous official oppression. This is an extremely thorough, if a bit dry, history of the music in the region. As a basic informational source, it's a useful volume, drawing upon hundreds of sources to present events and developments that were rarely reported in the West. The rare concerts behind the Iron Curtain by Western performers, ranging from the Rolling Stones to Uriah Heep, almost always provoked a brouhaha of sorts (even those by such relatively mild acts as the Nitty Gritty Dirt Band), and these are detailed as well. Readable despite its somewhat academic treatment, it gives us a lot of the what, but not enough of the how and why. Lots of musicians and listeners went to considerable risk to hear and play rock in the Eastern Bloc; in the late '50s, rock & roll records were pirated onto the emulsion of discarded X-ray plates, and Czechoslavakia's Plastic People were imprisoned for playing their music. But the actual Eastern Bloc rock community doesn't tell its story here, and the music that Eastern Bloc performers created is not analyzed in great critical depth (although many of them never got to record). —*Richie Unterberger*

✦✦✦ Rock'n'roll Road Trip by *A.M. Nolan* (1992, Pharos) Subtitled "the ultimate guide to the sites, the shrines and the legends across America," and lives up to its billing. This has the addresses and succinct, informative capsule descriptions of clubs and concert halls (many still active), birthplaces, studios, record stores, gravesites, album cover landmarks, and various other sites of interest to devoted rock fans throughout America. Including lots of photos, the book's strength is that it's not a mere collection of listings. Nolan also tells the stories behind the places, and what makes their history interesting, which makes for good reading even if you don't do a lot of traveling. —*Richie Unterberger*

✦✦✦✦ Rock On Film by *David Ehrenstein & Bill Reed* (1982, Delilah) It only goes up to the beginning of the 1980s, but this is the best book about, well, rock on film. A combination reference book/critical study, it lists nearly 500 films – documentaries, festivals, fiction films starring rock musicians in prominent roles, fiction films in which rock music is a central or vital ingredient, films which feature memorable cameo musical performances by notable rock musicians, films for which major rock musicians provided the soundtrack, and more. Each entry is accompanied by a pithy capsule summary/critique. The listings are preceded by 100 pages of good critical essays about various subgenres like the rockumentary, the Beatles on film, beach movies, and rock soundtracks. —Richie Unterberger

✦✦✦✦ Rolling Stone Album Guide edited by *Anthony DeCurtis & James Henke with Holly George-Warren* (Straight Arrow, 1992). There's a lot to criticize about this 800+ page reference work, if you're so inclined. Many worthwhile performers are not listed, particularly alternative and independent rock artists; the reviewers are sometimes brief to a fault; they are often churlish, even brutally nasty, in their assessment of some acts that do not measure up to current standards of hipness. The fact remains, though, that this is the best overall guide to rock recordings available. The writing is informed and passionate, if occasionally smug; virtually all artists of truly major significance are included; the discographies are pretty thorough, with a handy (if unavoidably inconsistent) rating system ranging from one to five stars. Incidentally, this is the third edition of the book, completely revised from the original 1979 volume, which was edited by Dave Marsh. That redcovered edition, called *The Rolling Stone Record Guide*, is well worth picking up if you find it used; the reviews are entirely different, and the entries cover quite a few artists and out-of-print albums that didn't make it into the current revision. The second edition (identifiable by its blue cover), from the mid-1980s, is dispensable. —*Richie Unterberger*

✦✦✦✦✦ The Rolling Stone Illustrated History Of Rock & Roll by *Anthony DeCurtis & James Henke with Holly George-Warren* (Straight Arrow, 1992). Still the best general history of rock music, comprising about 100 succinct essays on rock's most important performers and most important genres. Many of the best rock journalists contribute to this volume, including Greil Marcus, Dave Marsh, Peter Guralnick, Robert Palmer, Robert Christgau, Lester Bangs, and Greg Shaw. It is packed with both critical insight and historical detail, with excellent discographies and many wonderful photos. Only two flaws to consider: unavoidably, a lot of interesting performers were omitted (you'd need several volumes of this size to satisfactorily cover every worthwhile rock musician). More seriously, the coverage is heavily weighted towards, and much stronger on, pre-1980 rock; it really seems to run out of steam, in both breadth and quality, when it approaches the modern era. Hold on to the original mid-'70s edition as well, if you still have it; many photos were reproduced in larger formats in that volume, and some essays that appeared in the initial version have been excised or revised for no good reason. —*Richie Unterberger*

✦✦✦✦ The Rolling Stone Interviews, Vol. 1 (1971, Straight Arrow) *Rolling Stone* was the first American publication to treat rock & roll musicians as cultural and artistic figures of major significance. The musicians were thankful to have a forum to express their views and opinions with seriousness, and in its early years, the magazine ran many fascinating, extremely lengthy (by

1990s standards) interviews with most of the period's leading rockers. Their first interview anthology, long out of print but easy to find as a cheap used paperback, was the best, containing almost 500 pages of Q & A's with John Lennon, Eric Clapton, Jim Morrison, Grace Slick, Mick Jagger, Phil Spector, John Fogerty, Bob Dylan, Pete Townshend, Chuck Berry, Little Richard, David Crosby, Frank Zappa, and others. —*Richie Unterberger*

✦✦✦✦✦ The Rough Guide To World Music (1994, Rough Guides) Easily the best reference book currently available for world music, which in the editors' terms covers everything except western classical music and Anglo-American rock, soul, rap, jazz, and country. That leaves 700 pages covering traditional and popular sounds from all continents, from Celtic folk to Indonesian pop to soukous and zouk to reggae and gamelan to flamenco and Indian film music. The chapters are divided into lengthy scene overviews, with sidebars covering musical terms, notable festivals, and portraits of/interviews with important performers like Youssou N'Dour, Baaba Maal, Ruben Blades, Caetano Veloso, and many others. The variety of focus, skilled, passionate writing, and plenty of photos make this a much more enjoyable experience than the typical reference work. It's not a discography or compendium of record reviews, if that's what you're looking for, although there are numerous brief capsule descriptions of the most essential recordings of each region/country/genre. —*Richie Unterberger*

✦✦✦ San Francisco Nights: The Psychedelic Music Trip 1965-1968 by *Gene Sculatti & Davin Seay* (1985, St. Martin's) Not as comprehensive as Joel Selvin's more recent *Summer of Love*, and more anecdotal in approach, but a more enjoyable read, overall. Selvin's book was written as a recreation of events; Sculatti and Seay take a lot of first-hand memories and quotes from such key figures as Quicksilver Messenger Service's John Cipollina and Big Brother's Peter Albin. Focuses very much on the birth of the scene and its early days, with attention paid to the biggest groups like the Airplane and Dead, but a fair amount is also told of the Mystery Trend and the Charlatans as well. Also a lot of history of the early psychedelic concert circuit, with plenty of photos and concert posters from the scene's halcyon days. —*Richie Unterberger*

✦✦✦✦✦ The Sound Of The City, by *Charlie Gillett* (1970, Pantheon) Originating as a university thesis, this was the first attempt to write a comprehensive history of rock & roll, dealing with the form primarily in musical terms, not celebrity or popular culture ones. It's still one of the best, although the coverage only extends into the early '70s. Gillett's scholarship, though quite readable, is intensely detailed, accurately describing the cross-fertilization of vocal, instrumental, and production styles from the mid-'40s through the next several decades. He views the struggle of independent labels, as well as the struggle of major labels to come to terms with rock's popularity, as one of the most important undercurrents of rock; hence the performers are often discussed in terms of their labels and producers, as well as their regions or styles. Gillett's tastes run towards R&B and roots-rock, and singles rather than album-length statements; some readers may be taken aback by his bluntly clinical, not-wholly-enthusiastic assessments of the Beatles, Jimi Hendrix, Elvis Presley, and other major rock deities. And the focus, concerned with what's in the grooves rather than personality and attitude, may strike some as too detached and analytical. Gillett covered an enormous amount of ground with this volume, though, intelligently and objectively, and this remains an important foundation of rock scholarship. The Pantheon revised edition adds a little material to the 1970 printing, basically just extending the coverage a year or two into the 1970s. —*Richie Unterberger*

✦✦ Starmakers And Svengalis, by *Johnny Rogan* (1988, Queen Anne Press, UK) Rogan is one of Britain's most dedicated rock scribes, penning lengthy histories of the Byrds, the Smiths, the Kinks, and Neil Young, among others. This collection of profiles of Britain's most famous rock and pop managers, never issued in the States, deserves points for broaching unusual subject matter, but doesn't stand up as well as his other bios. Not through much fault of Rogan's: he does his usual thorough research and firsthand interviews, profiling the most famous (Brian Epstein, Andrew Oldham, Malcolm McLaren) along with names that are less familiar to Americans (Don Arden, Reg Calvert, early Bowie mentor Kenneth Pitt). Concentrating more on the business/professional side of things than the artistic one, the subjects of these profiles are, to put it simply, generally, less interesting than musicians, and it's debatable how many readers are concerned with reading about someone like Gordon Mills (whose prize clients were Tom Jones, Engelbert Humperdinck, and Gilbert O'Sullivan). There are anecdotes concerning most major, and many minor, British acts of the '60s and '70s (not as many, or as interesting, as you might expect). The chapters on Larry Parnes and Reg Calvert provide glimpses into the little-documented world of pre-Beatles British rock and pop, but by the end of the book, one has tired of reading about the ego battles and business headaches that afflict, in similar fashions, most successful rock acts. —*Richie Unterberger*

♦♦♦ **Stranded** *edited by Greil Marcus* (1979, Alfred A. Knopf) Marcus' question: If you were stranded on a desert island, what record would you take with you? He asked 20 writers, including such noted rock critics as Dave Marsh, Robert Christgau, Jim Miller, Simon Frith, Nick Tosches, Ellen Willis, Lester Bangs, Ed Ward, and John Rockwell, to produce chapter-length essays on their choice. How much you enjoy the result depends to a large degree on what chapter you're on, and how much you like the album in question, as the picks covered a fairly wide range of critics' pets (Jackson Browne, Van Morrison, the Ramones, the New York Dolls, the Kinks, the Rolling Stones, the Velvet Underground, Captain Beefheart), with some surprises (the Ronettes, Little Willie John, Huey "Piano" Smith, the 5 Royales). Interesting, but generally overwrought, at times taxing; it could also be fairly asked exactly how many people are really interested in reading ten-to-twenty-page exegeses of the Eagles' *Desperado* and Linda Ronstadt's *Living in the U.S.A.* Marcus' 45-page discography of his personal faves, with pithy critical comments, is the best section of the book. Published in 1979, so no records from the '80s or '90s are covered. —*Richie Unterberger*

♦♦♦ **Stranded In Paradise: New Zealand Rock'n'roll 1955-1988** *by John Dix* (1988, Paradise Publications, New Zealand) Not too easy to hunt down by any means, but this 354-page history of Kiwi rock is not only the definitive word on the subject, but one of the best volumes ever devoted to a pretty obscure sub-branch of rock music. Rock & roll was present in New Zealand from 1955, when Johnny Cooper recorded a cover of "Rock Around the Clock," and the country produced its share of rockabilly singers, British Invasion-type acts, psychedelia, and blue-eyed soulsters. Here are the detailed stories of local heroes like rockabilly wildman Johnny Devlin, garage/R&B band the La-De-Das, mod/beat rockers Ray Columbus & the Invaders, and many others. The story continues through the '70s success of Split Enz (the first N.Z. band to attract significant international attention), the punk/new wave scene, the reggae and Maori-influenced Polynesian rock, and the rise of the Flying Nun label, one of the most respected alternative rock companies in the world. Along the way there are plenty of interesting (and some not so interesting) stories of little-known performers, both mainstream and underground, who never made the slightest impression outside of the country. Dix also places the music in context with the times and the industry, covering rock journalism, rock festivals, radio, and record companies as well. A great deal of New Zealand rock, particularly in its early days, was extremely derivative of British and American forms, and if there's a fault to this volume, it's that a lot of the acts fall into this category, and really don't merit in-depth discussion. Still, serious rock fanatics should pick this up if they can find it; it's crammed with well-written anecdotes and facts and fine photos, and gorgeously designed. —*Richie Unterberger*

♦♦♦ **Summer Of Love** *by Joel Selvin* (1994, Dutton) Not necessarily the best, but the most wide-ranging and comprehensive history of the San Francisco psychedelic rock scene in the late '60s. Selvin constructs the book as interweaving stories of the principal bands of the area: the Jefferson Airplane, Big Brother/Janis Joplin, and the Grateful Dead especially, and also Quicksilver Messenger Service, Country Joe & the Fish, Moby Grape, Santana, the Charlatans, and Hot Tuna. Other important bands like the Great Society, Steve Miller, and Creedence Clearwater Revival are covered in less depth; minor ones like It's a Beautiful Day, Sons of Champlin, and Cold Blood are only touched upon, and the Beau Brummels, the first San Francisco band of note, are barely men-

tioned. The straight musical coverage is spiced with lots of anecdotes about the general acid-soaked Haight-Ashbury milieu and the city's live concert scene, sparked by Chet Helms and dominated by promoter Bill Graham. Some more material on the less famous artists might have been nice, but as it is this covers the most essential players fairly well, from the mid-'60s birth pangs of the Charlatans in the Haight-Ashbury to the general dissolution of the golden era in the early '70s. —*Richie Unterberger*

♦♦♦♦♦ **Sweet Soul Music,** *by Peter Guralnick* (1986, Harper & Row) What "deep soul" actually means is a matter of varying opinions, but whatever it is, this is the best history of it, covering the evolution of much Southern-based soul (along with a few northern performers with clear ties to the style) in the 1960s. Besides entire chapters on such giants as James Brown, Otis Redding, Aretha Franklin, and Solomon Burke, there's a wealth of material - much gleaned from first-hand interviews - with the dozens of songwriters, label executives, session players, producers, and minor performers that made the music happen. Lots of coverage of the Stax/Volt/Atlantic axis and the Muscle Shoals studio in particular, and anecdote upon anecdote from such legendary behind-the-scenes figures as songwriter Dan Penn. Guralnick also takes a wider perspective than an in-depth musical account, illustrating how the music could not have reached the heights it did without collaboration between Blacks and Whites - a symbiosis which was still highly fraught with tension in the American South of the 1960s. If there's a major fault to be found, it's that the breadth of focus, as wide as it is, is fairly arbitrary - what, for example, makes Ray Charles worthy of inclusion, but not Curtis Mayfield? - *Richie Unterberger*

♦♦ **'Til The Cows Come Home: Rock'n'roll Nebraska** *by Bart Becker* (1985, Real Gone) Granted the audience for this - an actual history of rock & roll in Nebraska from the early '50s through the mid-'80s - will be small. Also granted that Nebraska is not one of the leading hotbeds of rock & roll, though it, like almost every state of the union, has spawned some notable performers, and many also-rans. This is a pretty neat project, though, well-written and laid out, with great pictures and expert commentary. And it's not a dry archival guide: there are detailed rundowns on some pretty interesting performers, like early woman rockabilly singer Sparkle Moore, definitive one-shot wonders Zager & Evans ("In the Year 2525"), R&B/jazzman Preston Love, and local garage bands like the Rumbles and the Coachmen. Including introductory history, alphabetical entries for performer bios, and discography, the serious rock fan will actually find this worth searching for. —*Richie Unterberger*

♦♦♦♦ **The Trouser Press Record Guide** *edited by Ira A. Robbins* (Collier, 1991). A necessary supplement to the more mainstream *Rolling Stone* guides, this 750-page volume focuses almost entirely on post-1975 punk, new wave, and alternative rock (a little rap, reggae, and other odds and ends slip in). Reviewing about 2,500 artists and almost 10,000 records, it covers a great many indies and imports. The writing could be better; the assessments are sometimes lacking in precise descriptive detail, and the evaluations are on the whole too nondescript and generous. Nonetheless, it's easily the best (and one of the few) reference works of its kind. It has gone through four editions, and unless the fifth is on the way soon, the latest one, published in 1991, has started to date substantially. —*Richie Unterberger*

♦♦♦ **Unsung Heroes Of Rock'n'roll** *by Nick Tosches* (1984, Charles Scribner's Sons) Brief profiles of 25 pioneers of rock & roll, mostly from the decade before rock & roll was widely known (1945-55). Some are extremely famous (Nat King Cole, Louis Jordan, Big Joe Turner, Bill Haley), but most are known these days to collectors (Stick McGhee, Cecil Gant, Skeets McDonald, Hardrock Gunter); most are early R&B performers, a few are hillbilly C&W singers. Tosches' style is not for everybody, emphasizing lewd and suggestive angles that some may find offensive. He is also of the unequivocal conviction that rock & roll peaked, in essence, before it really started, and his biases can be irritating. Still, this is a handy primer that illustrates how deep rock & roll's roots lie in the most energetic R&B and C&W of the late '40s and early '50s, although the mid-'50s are commonly thought of as the music's true starting point. The lengthy final section includes a chronology of the development of rock & roll from 1945 to 1955, and discographies for all of the performers profiled. —*Richie Unterberger*

♦♦♦ **The Virgin Directory Of World Music** *by Philip Sweeney* (1991, Owl) Much less lively and more outdated than *The Rough Guide to World Music*, but still worth picking up as a decent world music reference book. This has useful overviews of the regional music of a little over 100 countries, covering general stylistic developments and key performers, and listing (but not reviewing) the most essential recordings at the end of each chapter. Each section has an introductory essay by a notable world music personality; these include Manu Dibango, Peter Gabriel, British DJ Andy Kershaw, and Gilberto Gil. —*Richie Unterberger*

♦♦♦♦♦ **What Was The First Rock'n'roll Record?** *by Jim Dawson & Steve Propers* (1992, Faber & Faber) Everyone can agree that rock & roll came into being sometime in the decade after World War II, but its exact origins can be hard to pinpoint. This is an absolutely fascinating study of 50 key records which pointed the way for rock & roll, or popularized it, between 1944 and 1956. It doesn't so much answer the question posed by the title as illustrate how many divergent strands of music were involved in rock's conception, and what a fascinating and exciting process it was. Major singles by Louis Jordan, John Lee Hooker, Fats Domino, Muddy Waters, Bill Haley, and Elvis are discussed in depth, as are ones by much more obscure artists such as Hardrock Gunter, Big Boy Crudup, Stick McGhee, Jackie Brenston, and Arkie Shibley. Besides explaining the significance of each record with detailed musical analysis, the authors tracked down key artists, session musicians, and producers for their comments, unearthing a wealth of compelling anecdotes. Essential for anyone interested in rock's birth. —*Richie Unterberger*

♦♦♦ **Where Are You Now, Bo Diddley?** *by Edward Kiersh* (1986, Doubleday) In the 1980s, Kiersh tracked down over 40 rock & roll legends from the past, primarily from the 1960s, although a few from the '50s and '70s appear as well. Each one gets a few pages to reminisce about their ups and downs – the ups, unsurprisingly, were considerably briefer in duration than the downs. Equally unsurprisingly, it's somewhat suffused with nostalgia – a lot of these people are has-beens, even if they were great for a time, and many display a mystification at the changing and fickle music business trends that effectively put them out to the pasture after a year or ten of outrageous success. And it seems like quite a few interviewees claim that, at one point, there was no one bigger than they except the Beatles. If such occasional sentiments don't bother you, it's still a pretty fun read, covering the gamut of rock & roll, from James Brown and Dave Clark to Donovan and Fabian, from Tommy James and Robbie Robertson to the Fugs and Janis Ian, although one sometimes wishes the more interesting subjects had more than ten or so pages to tell their stories. —*Richie Unterberger*

♦♦♦♦♦ **Where Did Our Love Go?** *by Nelson George* (1985, St. Martin's) Absolutely the best, by a wide margin, of the several histories of Motown Records. One of the leading authorities on R&B music, and one of the finest contemporary music journalists, George rightfully focuses on Motown's golden decade, the '60s, though some attention is given to its far less fascinating (though commercially successful) phase after its move from Detroit to L.A. The history of Motown, for all its greatness, was shrouded with a sort of mystery and vagueness. George discusses all the big stars, but he views the company as a team effort of performers, songwriters, producers, session players, and label boss Berry Gordy, Jr., that concocted something far greater than the sum of the parts. In his determination to examine all cogs of the machine, he uncovers a great deal of previously untold stories and unheralded figures that do not diminish the company's achievements, or the beauty and clarity of its artistic vision, in the least. Combining a wealth of information with acute critical passion, this is necessary reading for the serious rock fan. —*Richie Unterberger*

♦♦♦ **The Wicked Ways Of Malcolm McLaren** *by Craig Bromberg* (1989, Harper & Row) If you're primarily concerned with learning about the Sex Pistols, that story has been better told elsewhere, particularly in Jon Savage's *England's Dreaming*. This is a pretty worthwhile complement, though, written straightforwardly, exhaustively researched, and drawing upon material from

dozens of McLaren's associates, including Steve Jones and Glen Matlock. Besides plenty of interesting stories about the Pistols' early days, there's coverage of the other notable, if not always terribly important, acts he had a hand in, including the New York Dolls, Bow Bow Bow, and (before they became stars) Boy George and Adam Ant. McLaren comes off as a con man, albeit one who has anticipated and helped midwife some notable musical trends, more concerned with his own ego and commercial fortunes than the anti-establishment statements he often purports to be making, and whose principal talent is obtaining advances for ideas which are usually not finished or realized. —*Richie Unterberger*

♦♦♦ **Will You Still Love Me Tomorrow?: Girl Groups From The '50s On** *by Charlotte Greig* (1989, Virago) For Greig, "girl groups" are not specifically identified with the early and mid-'60s, in the common use of the term within rock criticism. There's a lot of coverage of the classic "girl group" sound within this volume, but it's just one section of the book, which covers groups of female singers working within the pop/rock/R&B mainstream from the '50s through the '80s. For those looking for straight historical coverage, there are a lot of first-hand interviews with major performers like the Shirelles, the Supremes, Ellie Greenwich, Sister Sledge, and Salt 'n Pepa. The main thrust of the book, though, is social criticism: Greig analyzes the lyrics and attitudes (which, much more often than not, are concerned with romance) quite seriously, without investing them with unwarranted significance. This doesn't come at the expense of readability, and the post-1970 material in particular covers quite a few artists, along the lines of Honey Cone, the Three Degrees, the Emotions, the Pointer Sisters, and Vanity 6, with considerably more depth and seriousness than they're accorded elsewhere. Those interested in a more musical account of the classic girl group sound are directed toward Alan Betrock's fine *Girl Groups*, but this is worthy further reading for a more wide-ranging and scholarly viewpoint. —*Richie Unterberger*

Catalogs

CD International • This is the most complete catalog of CDs in print we have yet seen. A recent edition has 73,116 album titles on 120,827 discs (popular music only). For each title, the label and number are given for that release (if available) in the U.S., U.K., Germany, Japan, and Canada. This is the catalog of choice among the music pros, and the only one that lets you see what is available in other countries at a glance. The format is 8 1/2 x 11; 650 pages. For more information, write to CDI Publishing Corp., P.O. Box 22014, Milwaukie, OR 97222 — *JME*

CD International (American Guide) • CD International offers an additional volume that contains only American CDs – some 21,369 discs. Similar format to the above and about 300 pages long. For many of these discs, individual track listings and playing times (track by track) are included. CDI Publishing Corporation can be reached at P.O. Box 22014 Milwaukie, OR 97222. — *JME*

Record Roundup • This is the grandfather of companies offering music by mail with reviews. Started in 1979 as an offshoot of Rounder Records, *Record Roundup* issues a 70-page newsletter free of charge several times a year. Each issue is chock-full of reviews and comments about the quality of the recordings offered. P.O. Box 154, North Cambridge, MA 02140; (617) 661-6308 (customer service) or (800) 44-DISCS (credit card orders). — *Michael Erlewine*

Roots & Rhythm • (Down Home Music) If Record Roundup started it all, then the *Roots & Rhythm* catalog (begun in 1978) has perfected the art of catalog/album reviews. Originally called *Down Home Music*, and affiliated with the Arhoolie record label, *Roots & Rhythm* reads more like a magazine of reviews than a catalog. Each issue is filled with expert opinion, comment, and reviews on the latest in domestic and imported releases. The latest catalog, between 60 and 100 pages, is free. In addition to providing information on domestic labels, *Roots & Rhythm* stocks and reviews a great number of imported albums that are available nowhere else. Certainly this company deserves some sort of award for the groundbreaking work they have done and the example they have set for catalogs with music reviews. *Roots & Rhythm* can be reached at 6921 Stockton Ave., El Cerrito, CA 94530; (510) 525-1494. — *Michael Erlewine*

SKR Classical • If you don't have a good classical record/CD shop in your town, you may be interested in SKR Classical mail-order. Here is a well-stocked classical store that is staffed by some of the most knowledgeable and approachable staff that I have yet met. Not only do they have comparative listening down pat, but they are experienced in mail-order. I often use them myself. — *Michael Erlewine*

    SKR Classical
    539 E. Liberty Street
    Ann Arbor, MI 48104
    (800) 272-4506

Schoolkid's Records • Not everyone has a well-stocked record store in their town. For those who do not, here is a record store that has not only a great stock but also a very knowledgeable staff that can talk to you about the music you are interested in. They are experienced in mail-order, have the best stuff always in stock, and can get anything else for you in a short time. I have shopped with them for many years. — *Michael Erlewine*

    Schoolkid's Records
    523 E. Liberty Street
    Ann Arbor, MI 48104
    (800) 445-2361

J&R Music World • An established catalog of both audio equipment and recorded music, all discounted. You can get a free catalog via their 800 number. — *AMG*

    J&R Music World
    59-50 Queens-Midtown Expressway
    Maspeth, NY 11378-9896
    (800) 221-8180
    FAX (718) 497-1791

Bose Express Music • This is one of the larger and better-known of the mail-order companies. They carry all kinds of music and offer a 300-page catalog (70,000 CDs and cassettes) and a year's subscription to their monthly newsletter for $6. Each newsletter offers about 1000 CDs on special sale. They carry no vinyl but do offer a variety of accessories (CD racks, tapes, etc.). If a title is not in stock, Bose will find that CD you are looking for and ship it to you. Visa, M/C, AmEx. — *Michael Erlewine*

    Bose Express Music
    The Mountain
    Framingham, MA 01701
    (800) 451-BOSE
    FAX (508) 875 0604

Music Master • This is the largest music service company in Great Britain, similar to Phonlog (Trade Service, Inc.) in the U.S. They offer a variety of publications that may interest some of our readers:

    Music Master
    Unit 4
    Durham Road
    Boreham Wood
    Herts WD6 1LW
    England
    (081) 953-5433
    FAX (081) 207-5814

Music Master Subscription Package: Includes a large and exhaustive listing of over 200,000 recordings. Monthly supplements.

Magazines and Newsletters

Goldmine Magazine • Published since 1974, *Goldmine* is just that – a goldmine of discographical information, extended articles, and great album reviews. Nowhere else will you find in-depth articles on individual artists and groups of this length and breadth. And almost every article is accompanied by a complete discography. *Goldmine* is geared to the record collector. In fact, a good part of each issue is filled with the ads of collectors.

Reading through these is an experience in itself. Those of us who don't collect may have little idea of the amount of activity in out-of-print and hard-to-find albums. Thanks to these folks, it is possible to find almost any hard-to-find album.

Goldmine has some of the best writers in the business, and almost every major freelance writer has written for them at one time or another. It is a tabloid-size magazine of about 170 pages published bi-weekly! There is a lot of information here. If you have never browsed through a copy, you have an experience in store for you. It's an eye-opener. Write to them and mention the *All Music Guide* and you will receive a free sample issue. 700 E. State St., Iola, WI 54990; (715)445-2214 — *JME*

Discoveries Magazine • Like *Goldmine*, this is a tabloid-size magazine (published monthly) devoted to record collectors and record collecting. And also like *Goldmine*, it is filled with articles (and discographies) on artists and groups that will interest non-collectors. The two magazines differ somewhat in the music and forms they try to cover. *Goldmine* is geared to rock & roll, blues, and R&B, both on vinyl and CDs, while *Discoveries* is oriented more toward vinyl, focusing on earlier rock and even some traditional popular music. In addition, *Discoveries* encourages readers to communicate with each other about various music trivia and record questions through their mail-box. Write to them, mention the *All Music Guide*, and receive a free sample issue. P.O. Box 255, Port Townsend, WA 98368;/ (206) 385-1200. — *JME*

Both Sides Now Newsletter • This is the quarterly newsletter from which *Both Sides Now* is assembled. It covers both CDs and vinyl and includes interviews with the people who put together oldies reissue packages, previously unpublished discographies, and all kinds of information. Write to Both Sides Now, Box 384, Fairfax Station, VA 22039. (*Both Sides Now* is also a book.) — *JME*

Forced Exposure • While its sporadic publishing schedule qualifies this underground rock journal as a fanzine, its 100+ page length and professional layout are of magazine quality. Principally edited and written by famed critics and gargantuan record collectors Jimmy Johnson and Byron Coley, this is rock journalism at its most uncompromising: the authors write about what they like and little else, enthuse wildly and denigrate viciously, and aren't apologetic in the least. Each issue includes massive interviews with underground rock heroes, fiction and essays by underground rock musicians and other noted counterculture authors, and a huge review section which includes many imports, bootlegs, reissues, and obscurities that you're not going to read about anywhere else. (Box 9102, Waltham, MA 02254) —*Richie Unterberger*

Ugly Things • Issued approximately once a year, this is essential for '60s specialists, especially British Invasion and garage rock enthusiasts. Contains fascinating, minutely detailed interviews with both legends and obscure collector cult figures of the time, ranging from the Pretty Things and the Monks to the Music Machine, the Leaves, Tomorrow, the Downliners Sect, and many others. Well written and laid out, with a large review section (principally for reissues). (405 W. Washington St. #237, San Diego, CA 92103) – *Richie Unterberger*

Wired • Not a music magazine, although it has a tiny review section, and occasionally features stories about musicians making use of technology in cutting-edge fashions. This is by far the most comprehensive and readable general interest magazine about "the information superhighway" and the accompanying technological developments. Every issue has news about CD-ROM, online, and other sorts of technologies that may change the way music is listened to and distributed in the near future. (520 3rd St., 4th Floor, San Francisco, CA 94107) — *Richie Unterberger*

Alternative Press • The writing and production quality aren't up to the level of *Option*, but this monthly offers comprehensive coverage of the alternative rock scene, focusing almost wholly on the bands to be found on college radio stations. Given over almost entirely to features, interviews, and reviews, it's a barometer of sorts as to what's getting played and listened to by the alternative rock crowd. Not as slick or imaginative as some of the competition, but there's a lot of info here. It's stuck to a regular publishing schedule for a long time (a rare feat in the alternative rock world), and it's steadily improved over the years. (P.O. Box 17136, N. Hollywood, CA 91615-9817) — *Richie Unterberger*

Country Music • Country may be the most popular music in the land bar rock, but the quality of journalistic coverage and criticism given to the music is surprisingly poor. *Country Music* is, by a wide margin, the best national publication devoted to the style. In fact, it is the only country magazine worth recommending, and the only one to offer intelligent, knowledgeable criticism. Adhering mostly to the standard feature/ interview/ review format, it covers the entire spectrum of country: the Nashville superstars, of course, get a bigger chunk than anyone else, but there's also a goodly amount of space for more rootsy and acoustic-based performers, independent label releases, vintage reissues, and hillbilly. Includes regular contributions from nationally renowned writers like Rich Kienzle and John Morthland. (329 Riverside Ave., Westport, CT 06880) — *Richie Unterberger*

Dirty Linen • The leading American magazine devoted to "folk, electric folk, traditional and world music," by a long shot. This bi-monthly has plenty of features, oodles of CD, tape, video, concert, and book reviews, roundups of neglected genres and old recordings, listings of new releases, and lots of miscellaneous news. Also offers tour information via several online services. Not as glossy, well-written, or wide-ranging as *Folk Roots*, but almost as informative, complementing that British magazine's coverage well. (P.O. Box 66600, Baltimore, MD 21239-6600) — *Richie Unterberger*

ICE • Steeply priced ($3.95 for 20-page issues), but this newsletter is extremely useful for the hard-bitten record collector, as well as for those involved in the music industry at almost any level. Includes the most comprehensive schedule of upcoming releases, both new and reissues; lots of news about in-the-works projects and reissue packages; items about hard-to-find imports; a column devoted to complaints about inadequate CD remastering, track selection, or packaging, featuring responses from the labels themselves; and listings (with brief comments) of CD bootlegs. Most interesting are the feature stories about major reissues, box sets, or new releases, which often highlight in-depth, inside scoops from the label, compilers, or artists themselves. Mostly rock-oriented, with some coverage of jazz, country, blues, and other genres. (P.O. Box 3043, Santa Monica, CA 90408). — *Richie Unterberger*

Living Blues • Absolutely the best blues publication available, and in fact one of the best specialized music magazines of any kind. Features huge, definitive interviews with major and minor blues performers, a big review section that covers almost every blues release available (lots of imports included), news, obituaries, and miscellaneous other features. It's upgraded its production values recently without sacrificing the depth and integrity of the content. Well-written and accessible to the general reader, not just a scholarly publication for blues fanatics. (Center for the Study of Southern Culture, The University of Mississippi, University, MS 38677-9836) — *Richie Unterberger*

Musician • Perhaps the most intelligent and well-written mainstream U.S. music publication, with the emphasis on long (but not exhausting) features and interviews. Leans a bit toward the classic rock side of the coin, or new performers in the classic rock mold, but there's reasonable coverage of alternative rock, as well as some jazz and other music (hip-hop and Black pop gets a pretty thin slice). Also a fair amount of technology info, including equipment reviews and details of specific musicians' instruments, along with comments about them from the artists themselves. —*Richie Unterberger*

New Musical Express • This weekly tabloid remains the most widely read and circulated British music publication. Resolutely trendy, *NME* is so eager to find and hype The Next Big Thing that there's a certain breathless tone to the coverage, with fickle, mercurial critical evaluations that can run from gushing praise to merciless putdowns within a matter of weeks. Americans may find the prose difficult to follow at times, occasionally approaching impenetrability. They may also be surprised at the intense importance attached to musicians' opinions on all sorts of matters

not strictly musical, including politics, sex, personal relationships, and other bands. That said, it's the best source for keeping up with the volatile U.K. music scene, including scads of reviews, and many profiles of upcoming bands (or even stars) months and years before they become known, or release records, on U.S. shores. (P.O. Box 272, Oakfield House, Perrymount Rd, Haywards Heath, West Sussex RH16 3ZA, England) — *Richie Unterberger*

Option • The production values have gotten steadily slicker in the decade since this bi-monthly started, and the coverage of widely known, major label acts has expanded, with a corresponding (but slighter) decrease in the articles about total unknowns. Still, it's the leading international publication devoted to coverage of alternative and indie music of all kinds, and there's still plenty of space for way-underground acts in both the features and reviews sections. Reviews about 200 releases, mostly independent, in every issue, and contains columns devoted to alternative music industry trends and developments, other media, and miscellaneous news. — *Richie Unterberger*

Q • This glossy British monthly is probably the best general interest rock and pop music publication. The review section of each issue covers literally hundreds of new releases, including a lot of British imports and reissues. In-depth features on major performers covering the entire rock and pop spectrum, departments for up-and-coming bands and gossip, book and movie reviews, cool "where are they now?" reports, and eyewitness recollections of major moments in rock history. The writing is much more straightforward and accessible to Yankee readers than the more whimsical and personality-oriented British rock weeklies. Expensive, but worth it, and widely distributed in the U.S. (Tower Publishing Services Ltd., Tower House, Lathkill St., Sovereign Park, Market Harborough LE16 9EF, U.K.) — *Richie Unterberger*

Rap Pages • Not as good or as in-depth as *The Source*, but worth reading by rap fans. Nothing remarkable about the format, but has its share of reviews, articles, and interviews. (LFP Inc., 9171 Wilshire Blvd., Suite 300, Beverly Hills, CA 90210) — *Richie Unterberger*

Rolling Stone • Still the most widely circulated music-oriented publication in the United States. At this point, it's pretty widely disdained by the alternative community for moving squarely into the mainstream of the marketplace. As one staff member admitted in a book about the magazine, it has become a tracker of American taste, rather than a pacesetter of American taste. There are still plenty of well-written features about both established and emerging performers, and a small review section with in-depth evaluations of noteworthy new releases. It has given more space to alternative rock of late, though that may be as much of a reflection of that style's radically increased commercial presence as a conscious decision. — *Richie Unterberger*

The Source • "The magazine of hip-hop music, culture & politics" has experienced some well-circulated internal conflicts of late, but remains the most in-depth rap magazine. The writing is erratic, and those who are not immersed in this aspect of African-American culture will find the lingo that peppers much of the writing occasionally difficult to understand impenetrable at times. But it gets the interviews with a lot of performers who are hard to read about elsewhere, not shying away from controversial gangsta rappers, and includes departments for record reviews, radio, film/TV, and gossip. (P.O. Box 586, Mt. Morris, IL 61054) — *Richie Unterberger*

Spin • Launched as the principal competitor to *Rolling Stone* in the mid-'80s, *Spin* is clearly here to stay, after some wobbly crises in it's early days. Covers alternative rock much more aggressively than its rival, ranging from the very popular to the absolutely unknown, and everything in between, though pieces on historical figures and classic rock are seldom presented. Considering its high profile as the second largest music publication in the United States, the writing and focus remain surprisingly erratic. Much more personality-oriented (both in terms of the acts it covers and the writers themselves) than the other big rock magazine in New York, which leads to both liveliness and self-indulgence. Also includes a fair amount of coverage of politics and popular culture. — *Richie Unterberger*

Urb • Devoted mostly to dance music, usually of Black origin, but not always. Covers hip-hop, acid house, acid jazz, club music, some soul, reggae, and rock. Consisting mostly of reviews, features, and interviews, it's distinguished from the somewhat overlapping coverage of *The Source* and *Rap Pages* by a wider scope, more readable format, higher production values, and better writing. (1680 N. Vine, Suite 1012, Los Angeles., CA 90028) — *Richie Unterberger*

Vibe • Certainly the slickest and biggest magazine devoted to African-American music, this monthly covers Black pop of all sorts – urban contemporary, soul, hip-hop, dance, and more. Usually fairly mainstream in its coverage, but there are plenty of deviations into emerging and more obscure acts, as well as some White rock releases that have heavy debts to R&B, funk, and hip-hop. Also includes coverage of African-American popular culture. — *Richie Unterberger*

Mojo • Fat, glossy general interest British monthly rock magazine with much more of a historical perspective than most. Coverage is about equally divided between current acts and artists from the past, with a bit (not much) of a bias toward "classic rock" performers. The in-depth interviews, historical surveys, and eyewitness recollections of all sorts of interesting star and cult rock icons of the past are often fascinating, and usually considerably more well-written and less oriented toward collector details than those that appear in *Goldmine*. Also includes record and book reviews, news bits, and other interesting columns. (Tower House, Sovereign Park, Lathkill St., Market Harborough, Leics. LE 16 9EF, U.K.) — *Richie Unterberger*

C-Bub Productions • Specializing in back issues of music magazines from the past 35 yuears, C-Bub provides collectors and researchers with information on the values of magazines and rock memorabilia, provides sources for buying and selling and resources for magazines and articles from rare and long out-of-print music magazines. If you"re looking for the *Rolling Stone* with John Lennon on the cover or the first time Nirvana appeared on the cover of *Circus* magazine, C-Bub can help you. For a free list contact C-Bub with the artists or groups you are interested in.. (C-Bub Productions, P.O. Box 83812-MG, Portland, OR 97283-0812 (503) 735-0934 Fax: (503) 735-9876.

Mail Order

For those millions of us unlucky enough to reside in places outside the realm of superstores (in other words, most folks), trying to find even the lastest hyped major label jazz item in a mall store, standard retail outlet or neighborhood mom-and-pop one-stop can be disastrous. Assuming the clerk even knows what you're talking about "Duke who?", you've got a better chance of striking oil in the back yard than you do of finding much jazz.

Thus, you're inevitably forced to the option of mail order. Granted, there are many disadvantages to this. For one, unless you're a preferred customer, by the time you find out about sales, most of the prime items are gone. Frequently you send the money in for six titles and two weeks later get four, with either a refund check or an inquiry asking if you want to back order. Plus, nothing's preferable to walking into a store, browsing, winnowing down a pile of potential buys and finally walking out with records (discs/tapes) in hand. Anyway, here are a few places that we've personally dealt with over the years without problems. This means they have reasonable shipping rates, will actually send you what you order, the product arrives in playable shape, and they issue catalogs in a timely manner.

By no means are these the only options available: such magazines as *Goldmine, Record Collector* and *Discoveries* are full of ads for stores that deal in jazz mail order; there are also many collectors nationwide who regularly hold auctions and set sales. But, if you have never ventured into the wild world of mail order, here are some good places to start. The following is just a selection of some of the longest-lived and most extensive mail-order outfits specializing in rock recordings (and often, those of rock-related genres). Note that this listing just covers a few of the many useful companies of this sort; listeners should also check the advertisements in collector-oriented magazines, especially *Goldmine*, the leader in that field. Most mail-order operations will send you their catalog for a small fee, or for free.

Midnight Records • The world's largest mail-order company specializing in independent and reissued rock CDs and LPs. Astonishing depth of selection, with thousands of imports from all over the world in addition to domestic titles. Especially strong in '50s and '60s rock and independent alternative rock, but also good in vintage soul, blues, some '50s pop. They also have a long list of out-of-print rarities. P.O. Box 390, New York, NY 10113-390; (212)675-2768.

Wayside Music • The most extensive selection of avant garde/experimental/progressive rock music by mail. P.O. Box 8427, Silver Spring, MD 20907-8427.

Metro Music • A similar focus as Midnight, on '60s reissues and new independent rock, lots of imports. Not as deep a selection as Midnight, but always offers some stuff no one else has, and has a large list of out-of-print LPs and 45s. P.O. Box 10004, Silver Spring, MD 20904-0004; (301)622-2473.

Eurock • Archie Patterson, a journalist for more than 20 years, started Eurock Ltd. in 1973 to promote and distribute electronic and progressive music from around the world. He's written about some of today's name artists, before they broke into the mainstream and continues today exploring the far corners of the globe for adventurous new music. Eurock, P.O. Box 13718, Portland, OR 97213; (503)281-0247.

INDEX

Also available from Miller Freeman Books

All Music Guide

The Best CDs, Albums & Tapes
Second Edition
Edited by Michael Erlewine, with Chris Woodstra and Vladimir Bogdanov
This completely updated guide leads readers to the topnotch recordings of 6,000-plus artists and groups. From rock to rap, classical to country, and everything in between, more than 23,000 recordings in 22 categories are reviewed and rated by 150 top music critics.

"Broad coverage, knowledgeable comments, and low cost make it a valuable resource." —*Booklist*

1,417pp, ISBN 0-87930-331-X, $26.95

All Music Guide to Jazz

The Best CDs, Albums & Tapes
Edited by Ron Wynn, with Michael Erlewine & Vladimir Bogdanov
This is the most comprehensive, easy-to-use guide to jazz, compiled by some of the best music critics in the nation. These critics have selected 9,000 of the the best recordings, produced by more than 1,150 artists and groups. Special features include music maps, label histories, producers, venues, and jazz styles and terms.

"A marvelously produced 750-page volume, which fans of any jazz era will find indispensable." —*San Francisco Examiner*

751 pages, ISBN 0-87930-308-5, $22.95.

Available at bookstores and music stores everywhere, or for more information please contact:
   Miller Freeman Books
   600 Harrison Street
   San Francisco, CA 94107
   Phone 415-905-2281
   Fax 415-905-2239
   E-mail: mfbooks@mfi.com
   World Wide Web: http://www.mfi.com/mf-books/

Related Products
   Miller Freeman publishes many other books for musicians, popular music enthusiasts, fans, and instrument collectors. For a complete list of books, please contact the address above. Coming in spring 1996: *The All Music Guide to World Music.*

   Miller Freeman also publishes *Guitar Player, Bass Player,* and *Keyboard* magazines, available at newstands everywhere. For subscription information, please call 415-905-2200.

   For information on other ALL MUSIC GUIDE products and resources, please refer to page *v* at the beginning of this book.